Presented to

_____

By

_____

On

_____

_____

THE
LAYMAN'S
PARALLEL
BIBLE

THE
LAYMAN'S
PARALLEL
BIBLE

King James Version

New International Version

Living Bible

New Revised Standard Version

ZONDERVAN PUBLISHING HOUSE
GRAND RAPIDS, MI

The Layman's Parallel Bible

Printed in the United States of America
98 97 96 95 94 93 92 91
8 7 6 5 4 3 2 1

AG/H

Contents

PUBLISHER'S PREFACE

ix

King James Version

The Epistle Dedicatory, xi

New International Version

Preface xii

Living Bible

Preface, xv

New Revised Standard Version

Preface, xvi

THE OLD TESTAMENT

THE NEW TESTAMENT

Publisher's Preface

O UT OF the multiplicity of modern language translations of the Scriptures published in recent years has come one of the most rewarding methods of Bible study. Bible students have discovered that by comparing translations they can gain new insights into Scriptural truth, and a new awareness of the relevancy of the Word of God to contemporary life. *The New Layman's Parallel Bible* offers the Bible student three of the most helpful modern translations—*The Living Bible, New International Version,* and the *New Revised Standard Version* —in parallel columns alongside the classic *King James Version* for comparison and amplification.

The King James Version has been, for centuries, the most loved and used translation of the Scriptures, and its ministry of blessing seems destined to continue for many years to come. Its majestic style and rich cadence give it an enduring quality that will live on in our contemporary world. It remains a standard of excellence in Bible translation.

The New International Version is a scholarly translation that accurately expresses the original Bible texts in clear and contemporary English while remaining faithful to the thoughts of the Biblical writers. Its readability,

accuracy, and beauty of style make it the most popular modern translation available.

The Living Bible is a paraphrase rather than a translation. A paraphrase does not attempt to translate word by word, but rather, thought by thought. A good paraphrase is a careful restatement of the Biblical author's thoughts (examples of paraphrasing may be found in the Bible itself, where New Testament writers rephrase a quotation from the Old Testament). In this sense, a paraphrase can communicate more vividly than a word translation, since it provides, in contemporary conversational style, the gist of what the author would have said if he had spoken to us today.

The New Revised Standard Version is, basically, a revision commissioned for the purpose of maintaining the standard of the Tyndale-King James tradition based on present knowledge of the Hebrew and Greek texts, as well as the current English word meanings.

The New Layman's Parallel Bible is an indispensible study tool, a work you will want to use both in the study and in the discussion group. It will be an invaluable aid as you compare these translations in public reading and in the exposition of the Scriptures.

THE PUBLISHERS

King James Version

TO THE MOST HIGH AND MIGHTY PRINCE

JAMES

BY THE GRACE OF GOD

KING OF GREAT BRITAIN, FRANCE, AND IRELAND

DEFENDER OF THE FAITH, &c.

The Translators of the Bible wish Grace, Mercy, and Peace through JESUS CHRIST our Lord

Great and manifold were the blessings, most dread Sovereign, which Almighty God, the Father of all mercies, bestowed upon us the people of *England,* when first he sent Your Majesty's Royal Person to rule and reign over us. For whereas it was the expectation of many, who wished not well unto our *Sion,* that upon the setting of that bright *Occidental Star,* Queen *Elizabeth* of most happy memory, some thick and palpable clouds of darkness would so have overshadowed this Land, that men should have been in doubt which way they were to walk; and that it should hardly be known, who was to direct the unsettled State; the appearance of Your Majesty, as of the *Sun* in his strength, instantly dispelled those supposed and surmised mists, and gave unto all that were well affected exceeding cause of comfort; especially when we beheld the Government established in Your Highness, and Your hopeful Seed, by an undoubted Title, and this also accompanied with peace and tranquility at home and abroad.

But among all our joys, there was no one that more filled our hearts, than the blessed continuance of the preaching of God's sacred Word among us; which is that inestimable treasure, which excelleth all the riches of the earth; because the fruit thereof extendeth itself, not only to the time spent in this transitory world, but directeth and disposeth men unto that eternal happiness which is above in heaven.

Then not to suffer this to fall to the ground, but rather to take it up, and to continue it in that state, wherein the famous Predecessor of Your Highness did leave it: nay, to go forward with the confidence and resolution of a Man in maintaining the truth of Christ, and propagating it far and near, is that which hath so bound and firmly knit the hearts of all Your Majesty's loyal and religious people unto You, that Your very name is precious among them: their eye doth behold You with comfort, and they bless You in their hearts, as that sanctified Person who, under God, is the immediate Author of their true happiness. And this their contentment doth not diminish or decay, but every day increaseth and taketh strength, when they observe, that the zeal of Your Majesty toward the house of God doth not slack or go backward, but is more and more kindled, manifesting itself abroad in the farthest parts of *Christiandom,* by writing in defence of the Truth, (which hath given such a blow unto that man of sin, as will not be healed,) and every day at home, by religious and learned discourse, by frequenting the house of God, by hearing the Word preached, by cherishing the Teachers thereof, by caring for the Church, as a most tender and loving nursing Father.

There are infinite arguments of this right Christian and religious affection in Your Majesty; but none is more forcible to declare it to others than the vehement and perpetuated desire of accomplishing and publishing of this work, which now with all humility we present unto Your Majesty. For when Your Highness had once out of deep judgment apprehended how convenient it was, that out of the Original Sacred Tongues, together with comparing of the labours, both in our own, and other foreign Languages, of many worthy men who went before us, there should be one more exact Translation of the holy Scriptures into the *English Tongue;* Your Majesty did never desist to urge and to excite those to whom it was commended, that the work might be hastened, and that the business might be expedited in so decent a manner, as a matter of such importance might justly require.

And now at last, by the mercy of God, and the continuance of our labours, it being brought unto such a conclusion, as that we have great hopes that the Church of *England* shall reap good fruit thereby; we hold it our duty to offer it to Your Majesty, not only as to our King and Sovereign, but as to the principal Mover and Author of the work: humbly craving of Your most Sacred Majesty, that since things of this quality have ever been subject to the censures of illmeaning and discontented persons, it may receive approbation and patronage from so learned and judicious a Prince as Your Highness is, whose allowance and acceptance of our labours shall more honour and encourage us, than all the calumniations and hard interpretations of other men shall dismay us. So that if, on the one side, we shall be traduced by Popish Persons at home or abroad, who therefore will malign us, because we are poor instruments to make God's holy Truth to be yet more and more known unto the people, whom they desire still to keep in ignorance and darkness; or if, on the other side, we shall be maligned by selfconceited Brethren, who run their own ways, and give liking unto nothing, but what is framed by themselves, and hammered on their anvil; we may rest secure, supported within by the truth and innocency of a good conscience, having walked the ways of simplicity and integrity, as before the Lord; and sustained without by powerful protection of Your Majesty's grace and favour, which will ever give countenance to honest and Christian endeavours against bitter censures and uncharitable imputations.

The Lord of heaven and earth bless Your Majesty with many and happy days, that, as his heavenly hand hath enriched Your Highness with many singular and extraordinary graces, so You may be the wonder of the world in this latter age for happiness and true felicity, to the honour of that great GOD, and the good of his Church, through Jesus Christ our Lord and only Saviour.

New International Version

TRANSLATOR'S PREFACE

The New International Version is a completely new translation of the Holy Bible made by over a hundred scholars working directly from the best available Hebrew, Aramaic and Greek texts. It had its beginning in 1965 when, after several years of exploratory study by committees from the Christian Reformed Church and the National Association of Evangelicals, a group of scholars met at Palos Heights, Illinois, and concurred in the need for a new translation of the Bible in contemporary English. This group, though not made up of official church representatives, was transdenominational. Its conclusion was endorsed by a large number of leaders from many denominations who met in Chicago in 1966.

Responsibility for the new version was delegated by the Palos Heights group to a self-governing body of fifteen, the Committee on Bible Translation, composed for the most part of biblical scholars from colleges, universities and seminaries. In 1967 the New York Bible Society (now the International Bible Society) generously undertook the financial sponsorship of the project—a sponsorship that made it possible to enlist the help of many distinguished scholars. The fact that participants from the United States, Great Britain, Canada, Australia and New Zealand worked together gave the project its international scope. That they were from many denominations—including Anglican, Assemblies of God, Baptist, Brethren, Christian Reformed, Church of Christ, Evangelical Free, Lutheran, Mennonite, Methodist, Nazarene, Presbyterian, Wesleyan and other churches—helped to safeguard the translation from sectarian bias.

How it was made helps to give the New International Version its distinctiveness. The translation of each book was assigned to a team of scholars. Next, one of the Intermediate Editorial Committees revised the initial translation, with constant reference to the Hebrew, Aramaic or Greek. Their work then went to one of the General Editorial Committees, which checked it in detail and made another thorough revision. This revision in turn was carefully reviewed by the Committee on Bible Translation, which made further changes and then released the final version for publication. In this way the entire Bible underwent three revisions, during each of which the translation was examined for its faithfulness to the original languages and for its English style.

All this involved many thousands of hours of research and discussion regarding the meaning of the texts and the precise way of putting them into English. It may well be that no other translation has been made by a more thorough process of review and revision from committee to committee than this one.

From the beginning of the project, the Committee on Bible Translation held to certain goals for the New International Version: that it would be an accurate translation and one that would have clarity and literary quality and so prove suitable for public and private reading, teaching, preaching, memorizing and liturgical use. The Committee also sought to preserve some measure of continuity with the long tradition of translating the Scriptures into English.

In working toward these goals, the translators were united in their commitment to the authority and infallibility of the Bible as God's Word in written form. They believe that it contains the divine answer to the deepest needs of humanity, that it sheds unique light on our path in a dark world, and that it sets forth the way to our eternal well-being.

The first concern of the translators has been the accuracy of the translation and its fidelity to the thought of the biblical writers. They have weighed the significance of the lexical and grammatical details of the Hebrew, Aramaic and Greek texts. At the same time, they have striven for more than a word-for-word translation. Because thought patterns and syntax differ from language to language, faithful communication of the meaning of the writers of the Bible demands frequent modifications in sentence structure and constant regard for the contextual meanings of words.

A sensitive feeling for style does not always accompany scholarship. Accordingly the Committee on Bible Translation submitted the developing version to a number of stylistic consultants. Two of them read every book of both Old and New Testaments twice—once before and once after the last major revision—and made invaluable suggestions. Samples of the translation were tested for clarity and ease of reading by various kinds of people—young and old, highly educated and less well educated, ministers and laymen.

Concern for clear and natural English—that the New International Version should be idiomatic but not idiosyncratic, contemporary but not dated—motivated the translators and consultants. At the same time, they tried to reflect the differing styles of the biblical writers. In view of the international use of English, the translators sought to avoid obvious Americanisms on the one hand and obvious Anglicisms on the other. A British edition reflects the comparatively few differences of significant idiom and of spelling.

As for the traditional pronouns "thou," "thee" and "thine" in reference to the Deity, the translators judged that to use these archaisms (along with the old verb forms such as "doest," "wouldest" and "hadst") would violate accuracy in translation. Neither Hebrew, Aramaic nor Greek uses special pronouns for the persons of the Godhead. A present-day translation is not enhanced by forms that in the time of the King James Version were used in everyday speech, whether referring to God or man.

For the Old Testament the standard Hebrew text, the Masoretic Text as published in the latest editions of *Biblia Hebraica*, was used throughout. The Dead Sea Scrolls contain material bearing on an earlier stage of the Hebrew text. They were consulted, as were the Samaritan Pentateuch and the ancient scribal traditions relating to textual changes. Sometimes a variant Hebrew reading in the margin of the Masoretic Text was followed instead of the text itself. Such instances, being variants within the Masoretic tradition, are not specified by footnotes. In rare cases, words in the consonantal text were divided differently from the way they appear in the Masoretic Text. Footnotes indicate this. The translators also consulted the more important early versions—the Septuagint; Aquila, Symmachus and Theodotion; the Vulgate; the Syriac Peshitta; the Targums; and for the Psalms the *Juxta Hebraica* of Jerome. Readings from these versions were occasionally followed where the Masoretic Text seemed doubtful and where accepted principles of textual criticism showed that one or more of these textual witnesses appeared to provide the correct reading. Such instances are footnoted. Sometimes vowel letters and vowel signs did not, in the judgment of the translators, represent the correct vowels for the original consonantal text. Accordingly some words were read with a different set of vowels. These instances are usually not indicated by footnotes.

The Greek text used in translating the New Testament was an eclectic one. No other piece of ancient literature has such an abundance of manuscript witnesses as does the New Testament. Where existing manuscripts differ, the translators made their choice of readings according to accepted principles of New Testament textual criticism. Footnotes call attention to places where there was uncertainty about what the original text was. The best current printed texts of the Greek New Testament were used.

There is a sense in which the work of translation is never wholly finished. This applies to all great literature and uniquely so to the Bible. In 1973 the New Testament in the

New International Version was published. Since then, suggestions for corrections and revisions have been received from various sources. The Committee on Bible Translation carefully considered the suggestions and adopted a number of them. These were incorporated in the first printing of the entire Bible in 1978. Additional revisions were made by the Committee on Bible Translation in 1983 and appear in printings after that date.

As in other ancient documents, the precise meaning of the biblical texts is sometimes uncertain. This is more often the case with the Hebrew and Aramaic texts than with the Greek text. Although archaeological and linguistic discoveries in this century aid in understanding difficult passages, some uncertainties remain. The more significant of these have been called to the reader's attention in the footnotes.

In regard to the divine name *YHWH*, commonly referred to as the *Tetragrammaton*, the translators adopted the device used in most English versions of rendering that name as "LORD" in capital letters to distinguish it from *Adonai*, another Hebrew word rendered "Lord," for which small letters are used. Wherever the two names stand together in the Old Testament as a compound name of God, they are rendered "Sovereign LORD."

Because for most readers today the phrases "the LORD of hosts" and "God of hosts" have little meaning, this version renders them "the LORD Almighty" and "God Almighty." These renderings convey the sense of the Hebrew, namely, "he who is sovereign over all the 'hosts' (powers) in heaven and on earth, especially over the 'hosts' (armies) of Israel." For readers unacquainted with Hebrew this does not make clear the distinction between *Sabaoth* ("hosts" or "Almighty") and *Shaddai* (which can also be translated "Almighty"), but the latter occurs infrequently and is always footnoted. When *Adonai* and *YHWH Sabaoth* occur together, they are rendered "the Lord, the LORD Almighty."

As for other proper nouns, the familiar spellings of the King James Version are generally retained. Names traditionally spelled with "ch," except where it is final, are usually spelled in this translation with "k" or "c," since the biblical languages do not have the sound that "ch" frequently indicates in English—for example, in *chant*. For well-known names such as Zechariah, however, the traditional spelling has been retained. Variation in the spelling of names in the original languages has usually not been indicated. Where a person or place has two or more different names in the Hebrew, Aramaic or Greek texts, the more familiar one has generally been used, with footnotes where needed.

To achieve clarity the translators sometimes supplied words not in the original texts but required by the context. If there was uncertainty about such material, it is enclosed in brackets. Also for the sake of clarity or style, nouns, including some proper nouns, are sometimes substituted for pronouns, and vice versa. And though the Hebrew writers often shifted back and forth between first, second and third personal pronouns without change of antecedent, this translation often makes them uniform, in accordance with English style and without the use of footnotes.

Poetical passages are printed as poetry, that is, with indentation of lines with separate stanzas. These are generally designed to reflect the structure of Hebrew poetry. This poetry is normally characterized by parallelism in balanced lines. Most of the poetry in the Bible is in the Old Testament, and scholars differ regarding the scansion of Hebrew lines. The translators determined the stanza divisions for the most part by analysis of the subject matter. The stanzas therefore serve as poetic paragraphs.

As an aid to the reader, italicized sectional headings are inserted in most of the books. They are not to be regarded as part of the NIV text, are not for oral reading, and are not intended to dictate the interpretation of the sections they head.

The footnotes in this version are of several kinds, most of which need no explanation. Those giving alternative translations begin with "Or" and generally introduce the alternative with the last word preceding it in the text, except when it is a single-word alternative; in poetry quoted in a footnote a slant mark indicates a line division. Footnotes introduced by "Or" do not have uniform significance. In some cases two possible translations were considered to have about equal validity. In other cases, though the translators were convinced that the translation in the text was correct, they judged that another interpretation was possible and of sufficient importance to be represented in a footnote.

In the New Testament, footnotes that refer to uncertainty regarding the original text are introduced by "Some manuscripts" or similar expressions. In the Old Testament, evidence for the reading chosen is given first and evidence for the alternative is added after a semicolon (for example: Septuagint; Hebrew *father*). In such notes the term "Hebrew" refers to the Masoretic Text.

It should be noted that minerals, flora and fauna, architectural details, articles of clothing and jewelry, musical instruments and other articles cannot always be identified with precision. Also measures of capacity in the biblical period are particularly uncertain (see the table of weights and measures following the text).

Like all translations of the Bible, made as they are by imperfect man, this one undoubtedly falls short of its goals. Yet we are grateful to God for the extent to which he has enabled us to realize these goals and for the strength he has given us and our colleagues to complete our task. We offer this version of the Bible to him in whose name and for whose glory it has been made. We pray that it will lead many into a better understanding of the Holy Scriptures and a fuller knowledge of Jesus Christ the incarnate Word, of whom the Scriptures so faithfully testify.

The Committee on Bible Translation
June 1978
(Revised August 1983)
Names of the translators and editors may be secured from the International Bible Society, translation sponsors of the New International Version,
P .O. Box 62970, Colorado Springs, Colorado, 80962-2970 U.S.A.

Living Bible

PREFACE

In this wonderful day of many new translations and revisions we can greet another new one with either dread or joy! Dread that "people will become confused" or joy that some will understand more perfectly what the Bible is talking about. We choose the way of joy! For each new presentation of God's Word will find its circle, large or small, of those to whom it will minister strength and blessing.

This book, though arriving late on the current translation scene, has been under way for many years. It has undergone several major manuscript revisions and has been under the careful scrutiny of a team of Greek and Hebrew experts to check content, and of English critics for style. Their many suggestions have been largely followed, though none of those consulted feels entirely satisfied with the present result. This is therefore a tentative edition. Further suggestions as to both renderings and style will be gladly considered as future printings are called for.

A word should be said here about paraphrases. What are they? To paraphrase is to say something in different words than the author used. It is a restatement of an author's thoughts, using different words than he did. This book is a paraphrase of the Old and New Testaments. Its purpose is to say as exactly as possible what the writers of the Scriptures meant, and to say it simply, expanding where necessary for a clear understanding by the modern reader.

The Bible writers often used idioms and patterns of thought that are hard for us to follow today. Frequently the thought sequence is fast-moving, leaving gaps for the reader to understand and fill in, or the thought jumps ahead or backs up to something said before (as one would do in conversation) without clearly stating the antecedent reference. Some-times the result for us, with our present-day stress on careful sentence construction and sequential logic, is that we are left far behind.

Then too, the writers often have compressed enormous thoughts into single technical words that are full of meaning, but need expansion and amplification if we are to be sure of understanding what the author meant to include in such words as "justification," "righteousness," "redemption," "baptism for the dead," "elect," and "saints." Such amplification is permitted in a paraphrase but exceeds the responsibilities of a strict translation.

There are dangers in paraphrases, as well as values. For whenever the author's exact words are not translated from the original languages, there is a possibility that the translator, however honest, may be giving the English reader something that the original writer did not mean to say. This is because a paraphrase is guided not only by the translator's skill in simplifying but also by the clarity of his understanding of what the author meant and by his theology. For when the Greek or Hebrew is not clear, then the theology of the translator is his guide, along with his sense of logic, unless perchance the translation is allowed to stand without any clear meaning at all. The theological lodestar in this book has been a rigid evangelical position.

If this paraphrase helps to simplify the deep and often complex thoughts of the Word of God, and if it makes the Bible easier to understand and follow, deepening the Christian lives of its readers and making it easier for them to follow their Lord, then the book has achieved its goal.

Adapted from the preface to the first edition of
Living Letters

New Revised Standard Version

TRANSLATOR'S PREFACE

This preface is addressed to you by the Committee of translators, who wish to explain, as briefly as possible, the origin and character of our work. The publication of our revision is yet another step in the long, continual process of making the Bible available in the form of the English language that is most widely current in our day. To summarize in a single sentence: the New Revised Standard Version of the Bible is an authorized revision of the Revised Standard Version, published in 1952, which was a revision of the American Standard Version, published in 1901, which, in turn, embodied earlier revisions of the King James Version, published in 1611.

In the course of time, the King James Version came to be regarded as "the Authorized Version." With good reason it has been termed "the noblest monument of English prose," and it has entered, as no other book has, into the making of the personal character and the public institutions of the English-speaking peoples. We owe to it an incalculable debt.

Yet the King James Version has serious defects. By the middle of the nineteenth century, the development of biblical studies and the discovery of many biblical manuscripts more ancient than those on which the King James Version was based made it apparent that these defects were so many as to call for revision. The task was begun, by authority of the Church of England, in 1870. The (British) Revised Version of the Bible was published in 1881–1885; and the American Standard Version, its variant embodying the preferences of the American scholars associated with the work, was published, as was mentioned above, in 1901. In 1928 the copyright of the latter was acquired by the International Council of Religious Education and thus passed into the ownership of the churches of the United States and Canada that were associated in this Council through their boards of education and publication.

The Council appointed a committee of scholars to have charge of the text of the American Standard Version and to undertake inquiry concerning the need for further revision. After studying the questions whether or not revision should be undertaken, and if so, what its nature and extent should be, in 1937 the Council authorized a revision. The scholars who served as members of the Committee worked in two sections, one dealing with the Old Testament and one with the New Testament. In 1946 the Revised Standard Version of the New Testament was published. The publication of the Revised Standard Version of the Bible, containing the Old and New Testaments, took place on September 30, 1952. A translation of the Apocryphal/Deuterocanonical Books of the Old Testament followed in 1957. In 1977 this collection was issued in an expanded edition, containing three additional texts received by Eastern Orthodox communions (3 and 4Maccabees and Psalm 151). Thereafter the Revised Standard Version gained the distinction of being officially authorized for use by all major Christian churches: Protestant, Anglican, Roman Catholic, and Eastern Orthodox.

The Revised Standard Version Bible Committee is a continuing body, comprising about thirty members, both men and women. Ecumenical in representation, it includes scholars affiliated with various Protestant denominations, as well as several Roman Catholic members, an Eastern Orthodox member, and a Jewish member who serves in the Old Testament section. For a period of time the Committee included several members from Canada and from England.

Because no translation of the Bible is perfect or is acceptable to all groups of readers, and because discoveries of older manuscripts and further investigation of linguistic features of the text continue to become available, renderings of the Bible have proliferated. During the years following the publication of the Revised Standard Version, twenty-six other English translations and revisions of the Bible were produced by committees and by individual scholars—not to mention twenty-five other translations and revisions of the New Testament alone. One of the latter was the second edition of the RSV New Testament, issued in 1971, twenty-five years after its initial publication.

Following the publication of the RSV Old Testament in 1952, significant advances were made in the discovery and interpretation of documents in Semitic languages related to Hebrew. In addition to the information that had become available in the late 1940s from the Dead Sea texts of Isaiah and Habakkuk, subsequent acquisitions from the same area brought to light many other early copies of all the books of the Hebrew Scriptures (except Esther), though most of these copies are fragmentary. During the same period early Greek manuscript copies of books of the New Testament also became available.

In order to take these discoveries into account, along with recent studies of documents in Semitic languages related to Hebrew, in 1974 the Policies Committee of the Revised Standard Version, which is a standing committee of the National Council of the Churches of Christ in the U.S.A., authorized the preparation of a revision of the entire RSV Bible.

For the Old Testament the Committee has made use of the *Biblia Hebraica Stuttgartensia* (1977; ed. sec. emendata, 1983). This is an edition of the Hebrew and Aramaic text as current early in the Christian era and fixed by Jewish scholars (the "Masoretes") of the sixth to the ninth centuries. The vowel signs, which were added by the Masoretes, are accepted in the main, but where a more probable and convincing reading can be obtained by assuming different vowels, this has been done. No notes are given in such cases, because the vowel points are less ancient and reliable than the consonants. When an alternative reading given by the Masoretes is translated in a footnote, this is identified by the words "Another reading is."

Departures from the consonantal text of the best manuscripts have been made only where it seems clear that errors in copying had been made before the text was standardized. Most of the corrections adopted are based on the ancient versions (translations into Greek, Aramaic, Syriac, and Latin), which were made prior to the time of the work of the Masoretes and which therefore may reflect earlier forms of the Hebrew text. In such instances a footnote specifies the version or versions from which the correction has been derived and also gives a translation of the Masoretic Text. Where it was deemed appropriate to do so, information is supplied in footnotes from subsidiary Jewish traditions concerning other textual readings (the *Tiqqune Sopherim*, "emendations of the scribes"). These are identified in the footnotes as "Ancient Heb tradition."

Occasionally it is evident that the text has suffered in transmission and that none of the versions provides a satisfactory restoration. Here we can only follow the best judgment of competent scholars as to the most probable reconstruction of the original text. Such reconstructions are indicated in footnotes by the abbreviation Cn ("Correction"), and a translation of the Masoretic Text is added.

For the New Testament the Committee has based its work on the most recent edition of *The Greek New Testament*, prepared by an interconfessional and international committee and published by the United Bible Societies (1966; 3rd ed. corrected, 1983; information concerning changes to be introduced into the critical apparatus of the forthcoming 4th edition was available to the Committee). As in that edition, double brackets are used to enclose a few passages that are generally regarded to be later additions to the text, but which we have retained because of their evident antiquity and their importance in the textual tradition. Only in very rare instances have we replaced the text or the punctuation of the Bible Societies' edition by an alternative that seemed to us to be superior. Here and there in the footnotes the phrase, "Other ancient authorities read," identifies alternative readings preserved by Greek manuscripts and early versions. In both Testaments, alternative renderings of the text are indicated by the word "Or."

As for the style of English adopted for the present revision, among the mandates given to the Committee in 1980 by the Division of Education and Ministry of the National Council of Churches of Christ (which now holds the copyright of the RSV Bible) was the directive to continue in the tradition of the King James Bible, but to introduce such changes as are warranted on the basis of accuracy, clarity, euphony, and current English usage. Within the constraints set by the original texts and by the mandates of the Division, the Committee has followed the maxim, "As literal as possible, as free as necessary." As a consequence, the New Revised Standard Version (NRSV) remains essentially a literal translation. Paraphrastic renderings have been adopted only sparingly, and then chiefly to compensate for a deficiency in the English language—the lack of a common gender third person singular pronoun.

During the almost half a century since the publication of the RSV, many in the churches have become sensitive to the danger of linguistic sexism arising from the inherent bias of the English language towards the masculine gender, a bias that in the case of the Bible has often restricted or obscured the meaning of the original text. The mandates from the Division specified that, in references to men and women, masculine-oriented language should be eliminated as far as this can be done without altering passages that reflect the historical situation of ancient patriarchal culture. As can be appreciated, more than once the Committee found that the several mandates stood in tension and even in conflict. The various concerns had to be balanced case by case in order to provide a faithful and acceptable rendering without using contrived English. Only very occasionally has the pronoun "he" or "him" been retained in passages where the reference may have been to a woman as well as to a man; for example, in several legal texts in Leviticus and Deuteronomy. In such instances of formal, legal language, the options of either putting the passage in the plural or of introducing additional nouns to avoid masculine pronouns in English seemed to the Committee to obscure the historic structure and literary character of the original. In the vast majority of cases, however, inclusiveness has been attained by simple rephrasing or by introducing plural forms when this does not distort the meaning of the passage. Of course, in narrative and in parable no attempt was made to generalize the sex of individual persons.

Another aspect of style will be detected by readers who compare the more stately English rendering of the Old Testament with the less formal rendering adopted for the New Testament. For example, the traditional distinction between *shall* and *will* in English has been retained in the Old Testament as appropriate in rendering a document that embodies what may be termed the classic form of Hebrew, while in the New Testament the abandonment of such distinctions in the usage of the future tense in English reflects the more colloquial nature of the koine Greek used by most New Testament authors except when they are quoting the Old Testament.

Careful readers will notice that here and there in the Old Testament the word Lord (or in certain cases God) is printed in capital letters. This represents the traditional manner in English versions of rendering the Divine Name, the "Tetragrammaton" (see the notes on Exodus 3.14, 15), following the precedent of the ancient Greek and Latin translators and the long established practice in the reading of the Hebrew Scriptures in the synagogue. While it is almost if not quite certain that the Name was originally pronounced "Yahweh," this pronunciation was not indicated when the Masoretes added vowel sounds to the consonantal Hebrew text. To the four consonants YHWH of the Name, which had come to be regarded as too sacred to be pronounced, they attached vowel signs indicating that in its place should be read the Hebrew word *Adonai* meaning "Lord" (or *Elohim* meaning "God"). Ancient Greek translators employed the word *Kyrios* ("Lord") for the Name. The Vulgate likewise used the Latin word *Dominus* ("Lord"). The form "Jehovah" is of late medieval origin; it is a combination of the consonants of the Divine Name and the vowels attached to it by the Masoretes but belonging to an entirely different word. Although the American Standard Version (1901) had used "Jehovah" to render the Tetragrammaton (the sound of Y being represented by J and the sound of W by V, as in Latin), for two reasons the Committees that produced the RSV and the NRSV returned to the more familiar usage of the King James Version. (1) The word "Jehovah" does not accurately represent any form of the Name ever used in Hebrew. (2) The use of any proper name for the one and only God, as though there were other gods from whom the true God had to be distinguished, began to be discontinued in Judaism before the Christian era and is inappropriate for the universal faith of the Christian Church.

It will be seen that in the Psalms and in other prayers addressed to God the archaic second person singular pronouns (*thee, thou, thine*) and verb forms (*art, hast, hadst*) are no longer used. Although some readers may regret this change, it should be pointed out that in the original languages neither the Old Testament nor the New makes any linguistic distinction between addressing a human being and addressing the Deity. Furthermore, in the tradition of the King James Version one will not expect to find the use of capital letters for pronouns that refer to the Deity—such capitalization is an unnecessary innovation that has only recently been introduced into a few English translations of the Bible. Finally, we have left to the discretion of the licensed publishers such matters as section headings, cross-references, and clues to the pronunciation of proper names.

This new version seeks to preserve all that is best in the English Bible as it has been known and used through the years. It is intended for use in public reading and congregational worship, as well as in private study, instruction, and meditation. We have resisted the temptation to introduce terms and phrases that merely reflect current moods, and have tried to put the message of the Scriptures in simple, enduring words and expressions that are worthy to stand in the great tradition of the King James Bible and its predecessors.

In traditional Judaism and Christianity, the Bible has been more than a historical document to be preserved or a classic of literature to be cherished and admired; it is recognized as the unique record of God's dealings with people over the ages. The Old Testament sets forth the call of a special people to enter into covenant relation with the God of justice and steadfast love and to bring God's law to the nations. The New Testament records the life and work of Jesus Christ, the one in whom "the Word became flesh," as well as describes the rise and spread of the early Christian Church. The Bible carries its full message, not to those who regard it simply as a noble literary heritage of the past or who wish to use it to enhance political purposes and advance otherwise desirable goals, but to all persons and communities who read it so that they may discern and understand what God is saying to them. That message must not be disguised in phrases that are no longer clear, or hidden under words that have changed or lost their meaning; it must be presented in language that is direct and plain and meaningful to people today. It is the hope and prayer of the translators that this version of the Bible may continue to hold a large place in congregational life and to speak to all readers, young and old alike, helping them to understand and believe and respond to its message.

For the Committee,

Bruce Metzger

The Old Testament

THE FIRST BOOK OF MOSES, CALLED

Genesis

Genesis

1 IN THE beginning God created the heaven and the earth.
2And the earth was without form, and void; and darkness *was* upon the face of the deep. And the spirit of God moved upon the face of the waters.
3And God said, Let there be light: and there was light.
4And God saw the light, that *it was* good: and God divided the light from the darkness.
5And God called the light Day, and the darkness he called Night. And the evening and the morning were the first day.
6¶ And God said, Let there be a firmament in the midst of the waters, and let it divide the waters from the waters.
7And God made the firmament, and divided the waters which *were* under the firmament from the waters which *were* above the firmament: and it was so.
8And God called the firmament Heaven. And the evening and the morning were the second day.
9¶ And God said, Let the waters under the heaven be gathered together unto one place, and let the dry *land* appear: and it was so.
10And God called the dry *land* Earth; and the gathering together of the waters called he Seas: and God saw that *it was* good.
11And God said, Let the earth bring forth grass, the herb yielding seed, *and* the fruit tree yielding fruit after his kind, whose seed *is* in itself, upon the earth: and it was so.
12And the earth brought forth grass, *and* herb yielding seed after his kind, and the tree yielding fruit, whose seed *was* in itself, after his kind: and God saw that *it was* good.
13And the evening and the morning were the third day.
14¶ And God said, Let there be lights in the firmament of the heaven to divide the day from the night; and let them be for signs, and for seasons, and for days, and years:
15And let them be for lights in the firmament of the heaven to give light upon the earth: and it was so.
16And God made two great lights; the greater light to rule the day, and the lesser light to rule the night: *he made* the stars also.
17And God set them in the firmament of the heaven to give light upon the earth,
18And to rule over the day and over the night, and to divide the light from the darkness: and God saw that *it was* good.
19And the evening and the morning were the fourth day.
20And God said, Let the waters bring forth abundantly the moving creature that hath life, and fowl *that* may fly above the earth in the open firmament of heaven.

The Beginning

1 IN THE beginning God created the heavens and the earth. 2Now the earth wasª formless and empty, darkness was over the surface of the deep, and the Spirit of God was hovering over the waters.
3And God said, "Let there be light," and there was light. 4God saw that the light was good, and he separated the light from the darkness. 5God called the light "day," and the darkness he called "night." And there was evening, and there was morning—the first day.
6And God said, "Let there be an expanse between the waters to separate water from water." 7So God made the expanse and separated the water under the expanse from the water above it. And it was so. 8God called the expanse "sky." And there was evening, and there was morning—the second day.
9And God said, "Let the water under the sky be gathered to one place, and let dry ground appear." And it was so. 10God called the dry ground "land," and the gathered waters he called "seas." And God saw that it was good.
11Then God said, "Let the land produce vegetation: seed-bearing plants and trees on the land that bear fruit with seed in it, according to their various kinds." And it was so. 12The land produced vegetation: plants bearing seed according to their kinds and trees bearing fruit with seed in it according to their kinds. And God saw that it was good. 13And there was evening, and there was morning—the third day.
14And God said, "Let there be lights in the expanse of the sky to separate the day from the night, and let them serve as signs to mark seasons and days and years, 15and let them be lights in the expanse of the sky to give light on the earth." And it was so. 16God made two great lights—the greater light to govern the day and the lesser light to govern the night. He also made the stars. 17God set them in the expanse of the sky to give light on the earth, 18to govern the day and the night, and to separate light from darkness. And God saw that it was good. 19And there was evening, and there was morning—the fourth day.
20And God said, "Let the water teem with living creatures, and let birds fly above the earth across the expanse of the sky." 21So God created the

ª 2 Or possibly *became*

Genesis

Genesis

1 WHEN GOD began creating[b] the heavens and the earth, 2the earth was a shapeless, chaotic mass, with the Spirit of God brooding over the dark vapors.[c] 3Then God said, "Let there be light." And light appeared. 4, 5And God was pleased with it, and divided the light from the darkness. He called the light "daytime," and the darkness "nighttime." Together they formed the first day.[d]

6And God said, "Let the vapors separate[e] to form the sky above and the oceans below." 7, 8So God made the sky, dividing the vapor above from the water below. This all happened on the second day.[f]

9, 10Then God said, "Let the water beneath the sky be gathered into oceans so that the dry land will emerge." And so it was. Then God named the dry land "earth," and the water "seas." And God was pleased. 11, 12And he said, "Let the earth burst forth with every sort of grass and seed-bearing plant, and fruit trees with seeds inside the fruit, so that these seeds will produce the kinds of plants and fruits they came from." And so it was, and God was pleased. 13This all occurred on the third day.[g]

14, 15Then God said, "Let bright lights appear in the sky to give light to the earth and to identify the day and the night; they shall bring about the seasons on the earth, and mark the days and years." And so it was. 16For God had made two huge lights, the sun and moon, to shine down upon the earth—the larger one, the sun, to preside over the day and the smaller one, the moon, to preside through the night; he had also made the stars. 17And God set them in the sky to light the earth, 18and to preside over the day and night, and to divide the light from darkness. And God was pleased. 19This all happened on the fourth day.[h]

20Then God said, "Let the waters teem with fish and other life, and let the skies be filled with birds of every kind." 21, 22So God created great sea animals, and every

Six Days of Creation and the Sabbath

1 IN THE beginning when God created[i] the heavens and the earth, 2the earth was a formless void and darkness covered the face of the deep, while a wind from God[j] swept over the face of the waters. 3Then God said, "Let there be light"; and there was light. 4And God saw that the light was good; and God separated the light from the darkness. 5God called the light Day, and the darkness he called Night. And there was evening and there was morning, the first day.

6 And God said, "Let there be a dome in the midst of the waters, and let it separate the waters from the waters." 7So God made the dome and separated the waters that were under the dome from the waters that were above the dome. And it was so. 8God called the dome Sky. And there was evening and there was morning, the second day.

9 And God said, "Let the waters under the sky be gathered together into one place, and let the dry land appear." And it was so. 10God called the dry land Earth, and the waters that were gathered together he called Seas. And God saw that it was good. 11Then God said, "Let the earth put forth vegetation: plants yielding seed, and fruit trees of every kind on earth that bear fruit with the seed in it." And it was so. 12The earth brought forth vegetation: plants yielding seed of every kind, and trees of every kind bearing fruit with the seed in it. And God saw that it was good. 13And there was evening and there was morning, the third day.

14 And God said, "Let there be lights in the dome of the sky to separate the day from the night; and let them be for signs and for seasons and for days and years, 15and let them be lights in the dome of the sky to give light upon the earth." And it was so. 16God made the two great lights—the greater light to rule the day and the lesser light to rule the night—and the stars. 17God set them in the dome of the sky to give light upon the earth, 18to rule over the day and over the night, and to separate the light from the darkness. And God saw that it was good. 19And there was evening and there was morning, the fourth day.

20 And God said, "Let the waters bring forth swarms of living creatures, and let birds fly above the earth across the dome of the sky." 21So God created the

---

[b] *1:1 When God began creating,* or, "In the beginning God created . . ." [c] *1:2 The earth was,* or, "The earth became . . ." a shapeless, chaotic mass, or, "shapeless and void." *over the dark vapors,* or, "over the cloud of darkness," or, "over the darkness and waters," or even, "over the dark gaseous mass." There is no "right" way to translate these words. [d] *1:4, 5 Together they formed the first day,* literally, "And there was evening and there was morning, one day (or, 'period of time')." [e] *1:6 Let the vapors separate,* literally, "Let there be a dome to divide the waters." [f] *1:7, 8 This all happened on the second day,* literally, "There was evening and there was morning, a second day (or, 'period of time')." [g] *1:13 This all occurred on the third day,* literally, "And there was evening and there was morning, a third day (or, 'period of time')." [h] *1:19 This all happened on the fourth day,* literally, "And there was evening and there was morning, a fourth day (or, 'period of time')."

[i] Or *when God began to create* or *In the beginning God created* [j] Or *while the spirit of God* or *while a mighty wind*

King James

21And God created great whales, and every living creature that moveth, which the waters brought forth abundantly, after their kind, and every winged fowl after his kind: and God saw that *it was* good.

22And God blessed them, saying, Be fruitful, and multiply, and fill the waters in the seas, and let fowl multiply in the earth.

23And the evening and the morning were the fifth day.

24¶ And God said, Let the earth bring forth the living creature after his kind, cattle, and creeping thing, and beast of the earth after his kind: and it was so.

25And God made the beast of the earth after his kind, and cattle after their kind, and every thing that creepeth upon the earth after his kind: and God saw that *it was* good.

26¶ And God said, Let us make man in our image, after our likeness: and let them have dominion over the fish of the sea, and over the fowl of the air, and over the cattle, and over all the earth, and over every creeping thing that creepeth upon the earth.

27So God created man in his *own* image, in the image of God created he him; male and female created he them.

28And God blessed them, and God said unto them, Be fruitful, and multiply, and replenish the earth, and subdue it: and have dominion over the fish of the sea, and over the fowl of the air, and over every living thing that moveth upon the earth.

29¶ And God said, Behold, I have given you every herb bearing seed, which *is* upon the face of all the earth, and every tree, in the which *is* the fruit of a tree yielding seed; to you it shall be for meat.

30And to every beast of the earth, and to every fowl of the air, and to every thing that creepeth upon the earth, wherein *there is* life, *I have given* every green herb for meat: and it was so.

31And God saw every thing that he had made, and, behold, *it was* very good. And the evening and the morning were the sixth day.

2 THUS THE heavens and the earth were finished, and all the host of them.

2And on the seventh day God ended his work which he had made; and he rested on the seventh day from all his work which he had made.

3And God blessed the seventh day, and sanctified it: because that in it he had rested from all his work which God created and made.

4¶ These *are* the generations of the heavens and of the earth when they were created, in the day that the LORD God made the earth and the heavens,

5And every plant of the field before it was in the earth, and every herb of the field before it grew: for the LORD God had not caused it to rain upon the earth, and *there was* not a man to till the ground.

6But there went up a mist from the earth, and watered the whole face of the ground.

7And the LORD God formed man *of* the dust of the ground, and breathed into his nostrils the breath of life; and man became a living soul.

8¶ And the LORD God planted a garden eastward in Eden; and there he put the man whom he had formed.

New International

great creatures of the sea and every living and moving thing with which the water teems, according to their kinds, and every winged bird according to its kind. And God saw that it was good. 22God blessed them and said, "Be fruitful and increase in number and fill the water in the seas, and let the birds increase on the earth." 23And there was evening, and there was morning—the fifth day.

24And God said, "Let the land produce living creatures according to their kinds: livestock, creatures that move along the ground, and wild animals, each according to its kind." And it was so. 25God made the wild animals according to their kinds, the livestock according to their kinds, and all the creatures that move along the ground according to their kinds. And God saw that it was good.

26Then God said, "Let us make man in our image, in our likeness, and let them rule over the fish of the sea and the birds of the air, over the livestock, over all the earth,a and over all the creatures that move along the ground."

27So God created man in his own image,
    in the image of God he created him;
    male and female he created them.

28God blessed them and said to them, "Be fruitful and increase in number; fill the earth and subdue it. Rule over the fish of the sea and the birds of the air and over every living creature that moves on the ground."

29Then God said, "I give you every seed-bearing plant on the face of the whole earth and every tree that has fruit with seed in it. They will be yours for food. 30And to all the beasts of the earth and all the birds of the air and all the creatures that move on the ground—everything that has the breath of life in it—I give every green plant for food." And it was so.

31God saw all that he had made, and it was very good. And there was evening, and there was morning—the sixth day.

2 THUS THE heavens and the earth were completed in all their vast array.

2By the seventh day God had finished the work he had been doing; so on the seventh day he restedb from all his work. 3And God blessed the seventh day and made it holy, because on it he rested from all the work of creating that he had done.

Adam and Eve

4This is the account of the heavens and the earth when they were created.

When the LORD God made the earth and the heavens— 5and no shrub of the field had yet appeared on the earthc and no plant of the field had yet sprung up, for the LORD God had not sent rain on the earthc and there was no man to work the ground, 6but streamsd came up from the earth and watered the whole surface of the ground— 7the LORD God formed the mane from the dust of the ground and breathed into his nostrils the breath of life, and the man became a living being.

8Now the LORD God had planted a garden in the east, in Eden; and there he put the man he had formed. 9And

---

a 26 Hebrew; Syriac *all the wild animals*   b 2 Or *ceased*; also in verse 3
c 5 Or *land*; also in verse 6   d 6 Or *mist*   e 7 The Hebrew for *man* (*adam*)
sounds like and may be related to the Hebrew for *ground* (*adamah*); it is
also the name *Adam* (see Gen. 2:20).

Living Bible

sort of fish and every kind of bird. And God looked at them with pleasure, and blessed them all. "Multiply and stock the oceans," he told them, and to the birds he said, "Let your numbers increase. Fill the earth!" 23That ended the fifth day.f

24And God said, "Let the earth bring forth every kind of animal—cattle and reptiles and wildlife of every kind." And so it was. 25God made all sorts of wild animals and cattle and reptiles. And God was pleased with what he had done.

26Then God said, "Let us make a mang—someone like ourselves,h to be the master of all life upon the earth and in the skies and in the seas."

27So God made man like his Maker.

Like God did God make man;

Man and maid did he make them.

28And God blessed them and told them, "Multiply and fill the earth and subdue it; you are masters of the fish and birds and all the animals. 29And look! I have given you the seed-bearing plants throughout the earth, and all the fruit trees for your food. 30And I've given all the grass and plants to the animals and birds for their food." 31Then God looked over all that he had made, and it was excellent in every way. This ended the sixth day.i

2 NOW AT last the heavens and earth were successfully completed, with all that they contained. 2So on the seventh day, having finished his task, God ceased from this work he had been doing, 3and God blessed the seventh day and declared it holy, because it was the day when he ceased this work of creation.

4Here is a summary of the events in the creation of the heavens and earth when the Lord God made them. 5There were no plants or grain sprouting up across the earth at first, for the Lord God hadn't sent any rain; nor was there anyone to farm the soil. 6(However, water welled up from the ground at certain places and flowed across the land.)

7The time came when the Lord God formed a man's body from the dust of the groundj and breathed into it the breath of life. And man became a living person. 8Then the Lord God planted a garden in Eden, to the east, and placed in the garden the man he had formed.

New Revised Standard

great sea monsters and every living creature that moves, of every kind, with which the waters swarm, and every winged bird of every kind. And God saw that it was good. 22God blessed them, saying, "Be fruitful and multiply and fill the waters in the seas, and let birds multiply on the earth." 23And there was evening and there was morning, the fifth day.

24 And God said, "Let the earth bring forth living creatures of every kind: cattle and creeping things and wild animals of the earth of every kind." And it was so. 25God made the wild animals of the earth of every kind, and the cattle of every kind, and everything that creeps upon the ground of every kind. And God saw that it was good.

26 Then God said, "Let us make humankindk in our image, according to our likeness; and let them have dominion over the fish of the sea, and over the birds of the air, and over the cattle, and over all the wild animals of the earth,l and over every creeping thing that creeps upon the earth."

27 So God created humankindk in his image,

      in the image of God he created them;m

      male and female he created them.

28God blessed them, and God said to them, "Be fruitful and multiply, and fill the earth and subdue it; and have dominion over the fish of the sea and over the birds of the air and over every living thing that moves upon the earth." 29God said, "See, I have given you every plant yielding seed that is upon the face of all the earth, and every tree with seed in its fruit; you shall have them for food. 30And to every beast of the earth, and to every bird of the air, and to everything that creeps on the earth, everything that has the breath of life, I have given every green plant for food." And it was so. 31God saw everything that he had made, and indeed, it was very good. And there was evening and there was morning, the sixth day.

2 THUS THE heavens and the earth were finished, and all their multitude. 2And on the seventh day God finished the work that he had done, and he rested on the seventh day from all the work that he had done. 3So God blessed the seventh day and hallowed it, because on it God rested from all the work that he had done in creation.

4 These are the generations of the heavens and the earth when they were created.

Another Account of the Creation

In the day that the LORD God made the earth and the heavens, 5when no plant of the field was yet in the earth and no herb of the field had yet sprung up—for the LORD God had not caused it to rain upon the earth, and there was no one to till the ground; 6but a stream would rise from the earth, and water the whole face of the ground—7then the LORD God formed man from the dust of the ground,n and breathed into his nostrils the breath of life; and the man became a living being. 8And the LORD God planted a garden in Eden, in the east; and there he put the man whom he had formed. 9Out of the ground the

---

f 1:23 That ended the fifth day, literally, "And there was evening and there was morning, a fifth day (or, 'period of time')."   g 1:26 a man, literally, "men."   h 1:26 someone like ourselves, literally, "Let us make man in our image, in our likeness."   i 1:31 This ended the sixth day, literally, "And there was evening and there was morning, a sixth day (or, 'period of time')."   j 2:7 from the dust of the ground, or, "from a lump of soil," or, "from clods in the soil," or, "from a clod of clay."

k Heb adam   l Syr: Heb and over all the earth   m Heb him   n Or formed a man (Heb adam) of dust from the ground (Heb adamah)

King James

New International

9And out of the ground made the LORD God to grow every tree that is pleasant to the sight, and good for food; the tree of life also in the midst of the garden, and the tree of knowledge of good and evil.

10And a river went out of Eden to water the garden; and from thence it was parted, and became into four heads.

11The name of the first *is* Pison: that *is* it which compasseth the whole land of Havilah, where *there is* gold;

12And the gold of that land *is* good: there *is* bdellium and the onyx stone.

13And the name of the second river *is* Gihon: the same *is* it that compasseth the whole land of Ethiopia.

14And the name of the third river *is* Hiddekel: that *is* it which goeth toward the east of Assyria. And the fourth river *is* Euphrates.

15And the LORD God took the man, and put him into the garden of Eden to dress it and to keep it.

16And the LORD God commanded the man, saying, Of every tree of the garden thou mayest freely eat:

17But of the tree of the knowledge of good and evil, thou shalt not eat of it: for in the day that thou eatest thereof thou shalt surely die.

18¶ And the LORD God said, *It is* not good that the man should be alone; I will make him an help meet for him.

19And out of the ground the LORD God formed every beast of the field, and every fowl of the air; and brought *them* unto Adam to see what he would call them: and whatsoever Adam called every living creature, that *was* the name thereof.

20And Adam gave names to all cattle, and to the fowl of the air, and to every beast of the field; but for Adam there was not found an help meet for him.

21And the LORD God caused a deep sleep to fall upon Adam, and he slept: and he took one of his ribs, and closed up the flesh instead thereof;

22And the rib, which the LORD God had taken from man, made he a woman, and brought her unto the man.

23And Adam said, This *is* now bone of my bones, and flesh of my flesh: she shall be called Woman, because she was taken out of Man.

24Therefore shall a man leave his father and his mother, and shall cleave unto his wife: and they shall be one flesh.

25And they were both naked, the man and his wife, and were not ashamed.

3 NOW THE serpent was more subtle than any beast of the field which the LORD God had made. And he said unto the woman, Yea, hath God said, Ye shall not eat of every tree of the garden?

2And the woman said unto the serpent, We may eat of the fruit of the trees of the garden:

3But of the fruit of the tree which *is* in the midst of the garden, God hath said, Ye shall not eat of it, neither shall ye touch it, lest ye die.

4And the serpent said unto the woman, Ye shall not surely die:

5For God doth know that in the day ye eat thereof, then your eyes shall be opened, and ye shall be as gods, knowing good and evil.

6And when the woman saw that the tree *was* good for food, and that it *was* pleasant to the eyes, and a tree to be desired to make *one* wise, she took of the fruit thereof, and did eat, and gave also unto her husband with her; and he did eat.

7And the eyes of them both were opened, and they knew that they *were* naked; and they sewed fig leaves together, and made themselves aprons.

the LORD God made all kinds of trees grow out of the ground—trees that were pleasing to the eye and good for food. In the middle of the garden were the tree of life and the tree of the knowledge of good and evil.

10A river watering the garden flowed from Eden; from there it was separated into four headwaters. 11The name of the first is the Pishon; it winds through the entire land of Havilah, where there is gold. 12(The gold of that land is good; aromatic resina and onyx are also there.) 13The name of the second river is the Gihon; it winds through the entire land of Cush.b 14The name of the third river is the Tigris; it runs along the east side of Asshur. And the fourth river is the Euphrates.

15The LORD God took the man and put him in the Garden of Eden to work it and take care of it. 16And the LORD God commanded the man, "You are free to eat from any tree in the garden; 17but you must not eat from the tree of the knowledge of good and evil, for when you eat of it you will surely die."

18The LORD God said, "It is not good for the man to be alone. I will make a helper suitable for him."

19Now the LORD God had formed out of the ground all the beasts of the field and all the birds of the air. He brought them to the man to see what he would name them; and whatever the man called each living creature, that was its name. 20So the man gave names to all the livestock, the birds of the air and all the beasts of the field.

But for Adamc no suitable helper was found. 21So the LORD God caused the man to fall into a deep sleep; and while he was sleeping, he took one of the man's ribsd and closed up the place with flesh. 22Then the LORD God made a woman from the ribe he had taken out of the man, and he brought her to the man.

23The man said,

"This is now bone of my bones
    and flesh of my flesh;
she shall be called 'woman,'f
    for she was taken out of man."

24For this reason a man will leave his father and mother and be united to his wife, and they will become one flesh.

25The man and his wife were both naked, and they felt no shame.

The Fall of Man

3 NOW THE serpent was more crafty than any of the wild animals the LORD God had made. He said to the woman, "Did God really say, 'You must not eat from any tree in the garden'?"

2The woman said to the serpent, "We may eat fruit from the trees in the garden, 3but God did say, 'You must not eat fruit from the tree that is in the middle of the garden, and you must not touch it, or you will die.'"

4"You will not surely die," the serpent said to the woman. 5"For God knows that when you eat of it your eyes will be opened, and you will be like God, knowing good and evil."

6When the woman saw that the fruit of the tree was good for food and pleasing to the eye, and also desirable for gaining wisdom, she took some and ate it. She also gave some to her husband, who was with her, and he ate it. 7Then the eyes of both of them were opened, and they realized they were naked; so they sewed fig leaves together and made coverings for themselves.

---

a 12 Or good; pearls   b 13 Possibly southeast Mesopotamia   c 20 Or the man   d 21 Or took part of the man's side   e 22 Or part   f 23 The Hebrew for woman sounds like the Hebrew for man.

Living Bible

9The Lord God planted all sorts of beautiful trees there in the garden, trees producing the choicest of fruit. At the center of the garden he placed the Tree of Life, and also the Tree of Conscience, giving knowledge of Good and Bad. 10A river from the land of Eden flowed through the garden to water it; afterwards the river divided into four branches. 11, 12One of these was named the Pishon; it winds across the entire length of the land of Havilah,g where nuggets of pure gold are found, also beautiful bdellium and even lapis lazuli. 13The second branch is called the Gihon, crossing the entire length of the land of Cush. 14The third branch is the Tigris, which flows to the east of the city of Asher. And the fourth is the Euphrates.

15The Lord God placed the man in the Garden of Eden as its gardener, to tend and care for it. 16, 17But the Lord God gave the man this warning: "You may eat any fruit in the garden except fruit from the Tree of Conscience— for its fruit will open your eyes to make you aware of right and wrong, good and bad. If you eat its fruit, you will be doomed to die."

18And the Lord God said, "It isn't good for man to be alone; I will make a companion for him, a helper suited to his needs." 19, 20So the Lord God formed from the soil every kind of animal and bird, and brought them to the man to see what he would call them; and whatever he called them, that was their name. But still there was no proper helper for the man. 21Then the Lord God caused the man to fall into a deep sleep, and took one of his ribs and closed up the place from which he had removed it, 22and made the rib into a woman, and brought her to the man.

23"This is it!" Adam exclaimed. "She is part of my own bone and flesh! Her name is 'woman' because she was taken out of a man." 24This explains why a man leaves his father and mother and is joined to his wife in such a way that the two become one person.h 25Now although the man and his wife were both naked, neither of them was embarrassed or ashamed.

3 THE SERPENT was the craftiest of all the creatures the Lord God had made. So the serpent came to the woman. "Really?" he asked. "None of the fruit in the garden? God says you mustn't eat any of it?"

2, 3"Of course we may eat it," the woman told him. "It's only the fruit from the tree at the center of the garden that we are not to eat. God says we mustn't eat it or even touch it, or we will die."

4"That's a lie!" the serpent hissed. "You'll not die! 5God knows very well that the instant you eat it you will become like him, for your eyes will be opened—you will be able to distinguish good from evil!"

6The woman was convinced. How lovely and fresh looking it was! And it would make her so wise! So she ate some of the fruit and gave some to her husband, and he ate it too. 7And as they ate it, suddenly they became aware of their nakedness, and were embarrassed. So they strung fig leaves together to cover themselves around the hips.

New Revised Standard

LORD God made to grow every tree that is pleasant to the sight and good for food, the tree of life also in the midst of the garden, and the tree of the knowledge of good and evil.

10 A river flows out of Eden to water the garden, and from there it divides and becomes four branches. 11 The name of the first is Pishon; it is the one that flows around the whole land of Havilah, where there is gold; 12 and the gold of that land is good; bdellium and onyx stone are there. 13 The name of the second river is Gihon; it is the one that flows around the whole land of Cush. 14 The name of the third river is Tigris, which flows east of Assyria. And the fourth river is the Euphrates.

15 The LORD God took the man and put him in the garden of Eden to till it and keep it. 16 And the LORD God commanded the man, "You may freely eat of every tree of the garden; 17 but of the tree of the knowledge of good and evil you shall not eat, for in the day that you eat of it you shall die."

18 Then the LORD God said, "It is not good that the man should be alone; I will make him a helper as his partner." 19 So out of the ground the LORD God formed every animal of the field and every bird of the air, and brought them to the man to see what he would call them; and whatever the man called every living creature, that was its name. 20 The man gave names to all cattle, and to the birds of the air, and to every animal of the field; but for the mani there was not found a helper as his partner. 21 So the LORD God caused a deep sleep to fall upon the man, and he slept; then he took one of his ribs and closed up its place with flesh. 22 And the rib that the LORD God had taken from the man he made into a woman and brought her to the man. 23 Then the man said,

"This at last is bone of my bones
    and flesh of my flesh;
this one shall be called Woman,j
    for out of Mank this one was taken."
24 Therefore a man leaves his father and his mother and clings to his wife, and they become one flesh. 25 And the man and his wife were both naked, and were not ashamed.

The First Sin and Its Punishment

3 NOW THE serpent was more crafty than any other wild animal that the LORD God had made. He said to the woman, "Did God say, 'You shall not eat from any tree in the garden'?" 2 The woman said to the serpent, "We may eat of the fruit of the trees in the garden; 3 but God said, 'You shall not eat of the fruit of the tree that is in the middle of the garden, nor shall you touch it, or you shall die.' " 4 But the serpent said to the woman, "You will not die; 5 for God knows that when you eat of it your eyes will be opened, and you will be like God,l knowing good and evil." 6 So when the woman saw that the tree was good for food, and that it was a delight to the eyes, and that the tree was to be desired to make one wise, she took of its fruit and ate; and she also gave some to her husband, who was with her, and he ate. 7 Then the eyes of both were opened, and they knew that they were naked; and they sewed fig leaves together and made loincloths for themselves.

King James

8And they heard the voice of the LORD God walking in the garden in the cool of the day: and Adam and his wife hid themselves from the presence of the LORD God amongst the trees of the garden.

9And the LORD God called unto Adam, and said unto him, Where *art* thou?

10And he said, I heard thy voice in the garden, and I was afraid, because I *was* naked; and I hid myself.

11And he said, Who told thee that thou *wast* naked? Hast thou eaten of the tree, whereof I commanded thee that thou shouldest not eat?

12And the man said, The woman whom thou gavest *to be* with me, she gave me of the tree, and I did eat.

13And the LORD God said unto the woman, What *is* this *that* thou hast done? And the woman said, The serpent beguiled me, and I did eat.

14And the LORD God said unto the serpent, Because thou hast done this, thou *art* cursed above all cattle, and above every beast of the field; upon thy belly shalt thou go, and dust shalt thou eat all the days of thy life:

15And I will put enmity between thee and the woman, and between thy seed and her seed; it shall bruise thy head, and thou shalt bruise his heel.

16Unto the woman he said, I will greatly multiply thy sorrow and thy conception; in sorrow thou shalt bring forth children; and thy desire *shall be* to thy husband, and he shall rule over thee.

17And unto Adam he said, Because thou hast hearkened unto the voice of thy wife, and hast eaten of the tree, of which I commanded thee, saying, Thou shalt not eat of it: cursed *is* the ground for thy sake; in sorrow shalt thou eat *of* it all the days of thy life;

18Thorns also and thistles shall it bring forth to thee; and thou shalt eat the herb of the field;

19In the sweat of thy face shalt thou eat bread, till thou return unto the ground; for out of it wast thou taken: for dust thou *art*, and unto dust shalt thou return.

20And Adam called his wife's name Eve; because she was the mother of all living.

21Unto Adam also and to his wife did the LORD God make coats of skins, and clothed them.

22¶ And the LORD God said, Behold, the man is become as one of us, to know good and evil: and now, lest he put forth his hand, and take also of the tree of life, and eat, and live for ever:

23Therefore the LORD God sent him forth from the garden of Eden, to till the ground from whence he was taken.

24So he drove out the man; and he placed at the east of the garden of Eden Cherubims, and a flaming sword which turned every way, to keep the way of the tree of life.

New International

8Then the man and his wife heard the sound of the LORD God as he was walking in the garden in the cool of the day, and they hid from the LORD God among the trees of the garden. 9But the LORD God called to the man, "Where are you?"

10He answered, "I heard you in the garden, and I was afraid because I was naked; so I hid."

11And he said, "Who told you that you were naked? Have you eaten from the tree that I commanded you not to eat from?"

12The man said, "The woman you put here with me—she gave me some fruit from the tree, and I ate it."

13Then the LORD God said to the woman, "What is this you have done?"

The woman said, "The serpent deceived me, and I ate."

14So the LORD God said to the serpent, "Because you have done this,

> "Cursed are you above all the livestock
>   and all the wild animals!
> You will crawl on your belly
>   and you will eat dust
>   all the days of your life.
> 15And I will put enmity
>   between you and the woman,
>   and between your offspringa and hers;
> he will crushb your head,
>   and you will strike his heel."

16To the woman he said,

> "I will greatly increase your pains in
>   childbearing;
> with pain you will give birth to children.
> Your desire will be for your husband,
>   and he will rule over you."

17To Adam he said, "Because you listened to your wife and ate from the tree about which I commanded you, 'You must not eat of it,'

> "Cursed is the ground because of you;
>   through painful toil you will eat of it
>   all the days of your life.
> 18It will produce thorns and thistles for you,
>   and you will eat the plants of the field.
> 19By the sweat of your brow
>   you will eat your food
> until you return to the ground,
>   since from it you were taken;
> for dust you are
>   and to dust you will return."

20Adamc named his wife Eve,d because she would become the mother of all the living.

21The LORD God made garments of skin for Adam and his wife and clothed them. 22And the LORD God said, "The man has now become like one of us, knowing good and evil. He must not be allowed to reach out his hand and take also from the tree of life and eat, and live forever." 23So the LORD God banished him from the Garden of Eden to work the ground from which he had been taken. 24After he drove the man out, he placed on the east sidee of the Garden of Eden cherubim and a flaming sword flashing back and forth to guard the way to the tree of life.

a 15 Or *seed*   b 15 Or *strike*   c 20 Or *The man*   d 20 *Eve* probably means *living*.   e 24 Or *placed in front*

Living Bible

8That evening they heard the sound of the Lord God walking in the garden; and they hid themselves among the trees. 9The Lord God called to Adam, "Why are you hiding?"f

10And Adam replied, "I heard you coming and didn't want you to see me naked. So I hid."

11"Who told you you were naked?" the Lord God asked. "Have you eaten fruit from the tree I warned you about?"

12"Yes," Adam admitted, "but it was the woman you gave me who brought me some, and I ate it."

13Then the Lord God asked the woman, "How could you do such a thing?"

"The serpent tricked me," she replied.

14So the Lord God said to the serpent, "This is your punishment: You are singled out from among all the domestic and wild animals of the whole earth—to be cursed. You shall grovel in the dust as long as you live, crawling along on your belly. 15From now on you and the woman will be enemies, as will your offspring and hers. You will strike his heel, but he will crush your head."

16Then God said to the woman, "You shall bear children in intense pain and suffering; yet even so, you shall welcome your husband's affections, and he shall be your master."

17And to Adam, God said, "Because you listened to your wife and ate the fruit when I told you not to, I have placed a curse upon the soil. All your life you will struggle to extract a living from it. 18It will grow thorns and thistles for you, and you shall eat its grasses. 19All your life you will sweat to master it, until your dying day. Then you will return to the ground from which you came. For you were made from the ground, and to the ground you will return."

20The man named his wife Eve (meaningg "The life-giving one"), for he said, "She shall become the mother of all mankind"; 21and the Lord God clothed Adam and his wife with garments made from skins of animals.

22Then the Lord said, "Now that the man has become as we are, knowing good from bad, what if he eats the fruit of the Tree of Life and lives forever?" 23So the Lord God banished him forever from the Garden of Eden, and sent him out to farm the ground from which he had been taken. 24Thus God expelled him, and placed mighty angels at the east of the Garden of Eden, with a flaming sword to guard the entrance to the Tree of Life.

New Revised Standard

8 They heard the sound of the LORD God walking in the garden at the time of the evening breeze, and the man and his wife hid themselves from the presence of the LORD God among the trees of the garden. 9But the LORD God called to the man, and said to him, "Where are you?" 10He said, "I heard the sound of you in the garden, and I was afraid, because I was naked; and I hid myself." 11He said, "Who told you that you were naked? Have you eaten from the tree of which I commanded you not to eat?" 12The man said, "The woman whom you gave to be with me, she gave me fruit from the tree, and I ate." 13Then the LORD God said to the woman, "What is this that you have done?" The woman said, "The serpent tricked me, and I ate." 14The LORD God said to the serpent,

"Because you have done this,
    cursed are you among all animals
    and among all wild creatures;
upon your belly you shall go,
    and dust you shall eat
    all the days of your life.
15 I will put enmity between you and the
        woman,
    and between your offspring and hers;
he will strike your head,
    and you will strike his heel."

16To the woman he said,

"I will greatly increase your pangs in
        childbearing;
    in pain you shall bring forth children,
yet your desire shall be for your husband,
    and he shall rule over you."

17And to the manh he said,

"Because you have listened to the voice of
        your wife,
    and have eaten of the tree
about which I commanded you,
    'You shall not eat of it,'
cursed is the ground because of you;
    in toil you shall eat of it all the days of
        your life;
18 thorns and thistles it shall bring forth for you;
    and you shall eat the plants of the field.
19 By the sweat of your face
    you shall eat bread
until you return to the ground,
    for out of it you were taken;
you are dust,
    and to dust you shall return."

20 The man named his wife Eve,i because she was the mother of all living. 21And the LORD God made garments of skins for the manj and for his wife, and clothed them.

22 Then the LORD God said, "See, the man has become like one of us, knowing good and evil; and now, he might reach out his hand and take also from the tree of life, and eat, and live forever"— 23therefore the LORD God sent him forth from the garden of Eden, to till the ground from which he was taken. 24He drove out the man; and at the east of the garden of Eden he placed the cherubim, and a sword flaming and turning to guard the way to the tree of life.

---

f 3:9 Why are you hiding?, or, "Where are you?" g 3:20 Eve (meaning "The life-giving one"). Many Hebrew names are based on puns. In this instance the Hebrew word for Eve sounds similar to a Hebrew word that means "life-giving."

h Or to Adam   i In Heb Eve resembles the word for living   j Or for Adam

King James

4 AND ADAM knew Eve his wife; and she conceived, and bare Cain, and said, I have gotten a man from the LORD.

2And she again bare his brother Abel. And Abel was a keeper of sheep, but Cain was a tiller of the ground.

3And in process of time it came to pass, that Cain brought of the fruit of the ground an offering unto the LORD.

4And Abel, he also brought of the firstlings of his flock and of the fat thereof. And the LORD had respect unto Abel and to his offering:

5But unto Cain and to his offering he had not respect. And Cain was very wroth, and his countenance fell.

6And the LORD said unto Cain, Why art thou wroth? and why is thy countenance fallen?

7If thou doest well, shalt thou not be accepted? and if thou doest not well, sin lieth at the door. And unto thee *shall be* his desire, and thou shalt rule over him.

8And Cain talked with Abel his brother: and it came to pass, when they were in the field, that Cain rose up against Abel his brother, and slew him.

9¶ And the LORD said unto Cain, Where *is* Abel thy brother? And he said, I know not: *Am* I my brother's keeper?

10And he said, What hast thou done? the voice of thy brother's blood crieth unto me from the ground.

11And now *art* thou cursed from the earth, which hath opened her mouth to receive thy brother's blood from thy hand;

12When thou tillest the ground, it shall not henceforth yield unto thee her strength; a fugitive and a vagabond shalt thou be in the earth.

13And Cain said unto the LORD, My punishment *is* greater than I can bear.

14Behold, thou hast driven me out this day from the face of the earth; and from thy face shall I be hid; and I shall be a fugitive and a vagabond in the earth; and it shall come to pass, *that* every one that findeth me shall slay me.

15And the LORD said unto him, Therefore whosoever slayeth Cain, vengeance shall be taken on him sevenfold. And the LORD set a mark upon Cain, lest any finding him should kill him.

16¶ And Cain went out from the presence of the LORD, and dwelt in the land of Nod, on the east of Eden.

17And Cain knew his wife; and she conceived, and bare Enoch: and he builded a city, and called the name of the city, after the name of his son, Enoch.

18And unto Enoch was born Irad: and Irad begat Mehujael: and Mehujael begat Methusael: and Methusael begat Lamech.

19¶ And Lamech took unto him two wives: the name of the one *was* Adah, and the name of the other Zillah.

20And Adah bare Jabal: he was the father of such as dwell in tents, and *of such as have* cattle.

21And his brother's name *was* Jubal: he was the father of all such as handle the harp and organ.

22And Zillah, she also bare Tubal-cain, an instructor of every artificer in brass and iron: and the sister of Tubal-cain *was* Naamah.

23And Lamech said unto his wives, Adah and Zillah, Hear my voice; ye wives of Lamech, hearken unto my speech: for I have slain a man to my wounding, and a young man to my hurt.

24If Cain shall be avenged sevenfold, truly Lamech seventy and sevenfold.

25¶ And Adam knew his wife again; and she bare a son, and called his name Seth: For God, *said she,* hath appointed me another seed instead of Abel, whom Cain slew.

New International

Cain and Abel

4 ADAMa LAY with his wife Eve, and she became pregnant and gave birth to Cain.b She said, "With the help of the LORD I have brought forthc a man." 2Later she gave birth to his brother Abel.

Now Abel kept flocks, and Cain worked the soil. 3In the course of time Cain brought some of the fruits of the soil as an offering to the LORD. 4But Abel brought fat portions from some of the firstborn of his flock. The LORD looked with favor on Abel and his offering, 5but on Cain and his offering he did not look with favor. So Cain was very angry, and his face was downcast.

6Then the LORD said to Cain, "Why are you angry? Why is your face downcast? 7If you do what is right, will you not be accepted? But if you do not do what is right, sin is crouching at your door; it desires to have you, but you must master it."

8Now Cain said to his brother Abel, "Let's go out to the field."d And while they were in the field, Cain attacked his brother Abel and killed him.

9Then the LORD said to Cain, "Where is your brother Abel?"

"I don't know," he replied. "Am I my brother's keeper?"

10The LORD said, "What have you done? Listen! Your brother's blood cries out to me from the ground. 11Now you are under a curse and driven from the ground, which opened its mouth to receive your brother's blood from your hand. 12When you work the ground, it will no longer yield its crops for you. You will be a restless wanderer on the earth."

13Cain said to the LORD, "My punishment is more than I can bear. 14Today you are driving me from the land, and I will be hidden from your presence; I will be a restless wanderer on the earth, and whoever finds me will kill me."

15But the LORD said to him, "Not so;e if anyone kills Cain, he will suffer vengeance seven times over." Then the LORD put a mark on Cain so that no one who found him would kill him. 16So Cain went out from the LORD's presence and lived in the land of Nod,f east of Eden.

17Cain lay with his wife, and she became pregnant and gave birth to Enoch. Cain was then building a city, and he named it after his son Enoch. 18To Enoch was born Irad, and Irad was the father of Mehujael, and Mehujael was the father of Methushael, and Methushael was the father of Lamech.

19Lamech married two women, one named Adah and the other Zillah. 20Adah gave birth to Jabal; he was the father of those who live in tents and raise livestock. 21His brother's name was Jubal; he was the father of all who play the harp and flute. 22Zillah also had a son, Tubal-Cain, who forged all kinds of tools out ofg bronze and iron. Tubal-Cain's sister was Naamah.

23Lamech said to his wives,

"Adah and Zillah, listen to me;
     wives of Lamech, hear my words.
I have killedh a man for wounding me,
     a young man for injuring me.
24If Cain is avenged seven times,
     then Lamech seventy-seven times."

25Adam lay with his wife again, and she gave birth to a son and named him Seth,i saying, "God has granted me another child in place of Abel, since Cain killed him." 26Seth also had a son, and he named him Enosh.

---

a *1* Or *The man*   b *1 Cain* sounds like the Hebrew for *brought forth* or *acquired.*   c *1* Or *have acquired*   d *8* Samaritan Pentateuch, Septuagint, Vulgate and Syriac; Masoretic Text does not have *"Let's go out to the field."*   e *15* Septuagint, Vulgate and Syriac; Hebrew *Very well*   f *16 Nod* means *wandering* (see verses 12 and 14).   g *22* Or *who instructed all who work in*   h *23* Or *I will kill*   i *25 Seth* probably means *granted.*

Living Bible

4 THEN ADAM had sexual intercourse with Eve his wife, and she conceived and gave birth to a son, Cain (meaning "I have created"). For, as she said, "With God's help, I have created a man!" 2Her next child was his brother, Abel.

Abel became a shepherd, while Cain was a farmer. 3At harvest time Cain brought the Lord a gift of his farm produce, 4and Abel brought the fatty cuts of meat from his best lambs, and presented them to the Lord. And the Lord accepted Abel's offering, 5but not Cain's. This made Cain both dejected and very angry, and his face grew dark with fury.

6"Why are you angry?" the Lord asked him. "Why is your face so dark with rage? 7It can be bright with joy if you will do what you should! But if you refuse to obey, watch out. Sin is waiting to attack you, longing to destroy you. But you can conquer it!"

8One day Cain suggested to his brother, "Let's go out into the fields." And while they were together there, Cain attacked and killed his brother.

9But afterwards the Lord asked Cain, "Where is your brother? Where is Abel?"

"How should I know?" Cain retorted. "Am I supposed to keep track of him wherever he goes?"

10But the Lord said, "Your brother's blood calls to me from the ground. What have you done? 11You are hereby banished from this ground which you have defiled with your brother's blood. 12No longer will it yield crops for you, even if you toil on it forever! From now on you will be a fugitive and a tramp upon the earth, wandering from place to place."

13Cain replied to the Lord, "My punishment is greater than I can bear. 14For you have banished me from my farm and from you, and made me a fugitive and a tramp; and everyone who sees me will try to kill me."

15The Lord replied, "They won't kill you, for I will give seven times your punishment to anyone who does." Then the Lord put an identifying mark on Cain as a warning not to kill him. 16So Cain went out from the presence of the Lord and settled in the land of Nod, east of Eden.

17Then Cain's wife conceived and presented him with a baby son named Enoch; so when Cain founded a city, he named it Enoch, after his son.

18Enoch was the fatherj of Irad;
Irad was the father of Mehujael;
Mehujael was the father of Methusael;
Methusael was the father of Lamech;

19Lamech married two wives—Adah and Zillah. 20To Adah was born a baby named Jabal. He became the first of the cattlemen and those living in tents. 21His brother's name was Jubal, the first musician—the inventork of the harp and flute. 22To Lamech's other wife, Zillah, was born Tubal-cain. He opened the first foundryl forging instruments of bronze and iron.

23One day Lamech said to Adah and Zillah, "Listen to me, my wives. I have killed a youth who attacked and wounded me. 24If anyone who kills Cain will be punished seven times, anyone taking revenge against me for killing that youth should be punished seventy-seven times!"

25Later on Eve gave birth to another son and named him Seth (meaning "Granted"); for, as Eve put it, "God has granted me another son for the one Cain killed."

New Revised Standard

Cain Murders Abel

4 NOW THE man knew his wife Eve, and she conceived and bore Cain, saying, "I have producedm a man with the help of the LORD." 2Next she bore his brother Abel. Now Abel was a keeper of sheep, and Cain a tiller of the ground. 3In the course of time Cain brought to the LORD an offering of the fruit of the ground, 4and Abel for his part brought of the firstlings of his flock, their fat portions. And the LORD had regard for Abel and his offering, 5but for Cain and his offering he had no regard. So Cain was very angry, and his countenance fell. 6The LORD said to Cain, "Why are you angry, and why has your countenance fallen? 7If you do well, will you not be accepted? And if you do not do well, sin is lurking at the door; its desire is for you, but you must master it."

8 Cain said to his brother Abel, "Let us go out to the field."n And when they were in the field, Cain rose up against his brother Abel, and killed him. 9Then the LORD said to Cain, "Where is your brother Abel?" He said, "I do not know; am I my brother's keeper?" 10And the LORD said, "What have you done? Listen; your brother's blood is crying out to me from the ground! 11And now you are cursed from the ground, which has opened its mouth to receive your brother's blood from your hand. 12When you till the ground, it will no longer yield to you its strength; you will be a fugitive and a wanderer on the earth." 13Cain said to the LORD, "My punishment is greater than I can bear! 14Today you have driven me away from the soil, and I shall be hidden from your face; I shall be a fugitive and a wanderer on the earth, and anyone who meets me may kill me." 15Then the LORD said to him, "Not so!o Whoever kills Cain will suffer a sevenfold vengeance." And the LORD put a mark on Cain, so that no one who came upon him would kill him. 16Then Cain went away from the presence of the LORD, and settled in the land of Nod,p east of Eden.

Beginnings of Civilization

17 Cain knew his wife, and she conceived and bore Enoch; and he built a city, and named it Enoch after his son Enoch. 18To Enoch was born Irad; and Irad was the father of Mehujael, and Mehujael the father of Methushael, and Methushael the father of Lamech. 19Lamech took two wives; the name of the one was Adah, and the name of the other Zillah. 20Adah bore Jabal; he was the ancestor of those who live in tents and have livestock. 21His brother's name was Jubal; he was the ancestor of all those who play the lyre and pipe. 22Zillah bore Tubal-cain, who made all kinds of bronze and iron tools. The sister of Tubal-cain was Naamah.

23 Lamech said to his wives:
"Adah and Zillah, hear my voice;
    you wives of Lamech, listen to what I say:
I have killed a man for wounding me,
    a young man for striking me.
24 If Cain is avenged sevenfold,
    truly Lamech seventy-sevenfold."

25 Adam knew his wife again, and she bore a son and named him Seth, for she said, "God has appointedq for me another child instead of Abel, because Cain killed him." 26To Seth also a son was born, and he named him

---

j 4:18 or, "the ancestor of," and so also in the remainder of the verse.
k 4:21 the inventor of, literally, "He was the father of all such as handle the harp and pipe." l 4:22 He opened the first foundry, literally, "He was the father of all metal workers in bronze and iron."

m The verb in Heb resembles the word for Cain   n Sam Gk Syr Compare Vg: MT lacks Let us go out to the field   o Gk Syr Vg: Heb Therefore   p That is Wandering   q The verb in Heb resembles the word for Seth

King James

26And to Seth, to him also there was born a son; and he called his name Enos: then began men to call upon the name of the LORD.

5 THIS *IS* the book of the generations of Adam. In the day that God created man, in the likeness of God made he him;
2Male and female created he them; and blessed them, and called their name Adam, in the day when they were created.
3¶ And Adam lived an hundred and thirty years, and begat *a son* in his own likeness, after his image; and called his name Seth:
4And the days of Adam after he had begotten Seth were eight hundred years: and he begat sons and daughters:
5And all the days that Adam lived were nine hundred and thirty years: and he died.
6And Seth lived an hundred and five years, and begat Enos:
7And Seth lived after he begat Enos eight hundred and seven years, and begat sons and daughters:
8And all the days of Seth were nine hundred and twelve years: and he died.
9¶ And Enos lived ninety years, and begat Cainan:
10And Enos lived after he begat Cainan eight hundred and fifteen years, and begat sons and daughters:
11And all the days of Enos were nine hundred and five years: and he died.
12¶ And Cainan lived seventy years, and begat Mahalaleel:
13And Cainan lived after he begat Mahalaleel eight hundred and forty years, and begat sons and daughters:
14And all the days of Cainan were nine hundred and ten years: and he died.
15¶ And Mahalaleel lived sixty and five years, and begat Jared:
16And Mahalaleel lived after he begat Jared eight hundred and thirty years, and begat sons and daughters:
17And all the days of Mahalaleel were eight hundred ninety and five years: and he died.
18¶ And Jared lived an hundred sixty and two years, and he begat Enoch:
19And Jared lived after he begat Enoch eight hundred years, and begat sons and daughters:
20And all the days of Jared were nine hundred sixty and two years: and he died.
21¶ And Enoch lived sixty and five years, and begat Methuselah:
22And Enoch walked with God after he begat Methuselah three hundred years, and begat sons and daughters:
23And all the days of Enoch were three hundred sixty and five years:
24And Enoch walked with God: and he *was* not; for God took him.
25And Methuselah lived an hundred eighty and seven years, and begat Lamech:
26And Methuselah lived after he begat Lamech seven hundred eighty and two years, and begat sons and daughters:
27And all the days of Methuselah were nine hundred sixty and nine years: and he died.
28¶ And Lamech lived an hundred eighty and two years, and begat a son:

New International

At that time men began to call on[a] the name of the LORD.

From Adam to Noah

5 THIS IS the written account of Adam's line.

When God created man, he made him in the likeness of God. 2He created them male and female and blessed them. And when they were created, he called them "man.[b]"
3When Adam had lived 130 years, he had a son in his own likeness, in his own image; and he named him Seth. 4After Seth was born, Adam lived 800 years and had other sons and daughters. 5Altogether, Adam lived 930 years, and then he died.
6When Seth had lived 105 years, he became the father[c] of Enosh. 7And after he became the father of Enosh, Seth lived 807 years and had other sons and daughters. 8Altogether, Seth lived 912 years, and then he died.
9When Enosh had lived 90 years, he became the father of Kenan. 10And after he became the father of Kenan, Enosh lived 815 years and had other sons and daughters. 11Altogether, Enosh lived 905 years, and then he died.
12When Kenan had lived 70 years, he became the father of Mahalalel. 13And after he became the father of Mahalalel, Kenan lived 840 years and had other sons and daughters. 14Altogether, Kenan lived 910 years, and then he died.
15When Mahalalel had lived 65 years, he became the father of Jared. 16And after he became the father of Jared, Mahalalel lived 830 years and had other sons and daughters. 17Altogether, Mahalalel lived 895 years, and then he died.
18When Jared had lived 162 years, he became the father of Enoch. 19And after he became the father of Enoch, Jared lived 800 years and had other sons and daughters. 20Altogether, Jared lived 962 years, and then he died.
21When Enoch had lived 65 years, he became the father of Methuselah. 22And after he became the father of Methuselah, Enoch walked with God 300 years and had other sons and daughters. 23Altogether, Enoch lived 365 years. 24Enoch walked with God; then he was no more, because God took him away.
25When Methuselah had lived 187 years, he became the father of Lamech. 26And after he became the father of Lamech, Methuselah lived 782 years and had other sons and daughters. 27Altogether, Methuselah lived 969 years, and then he died.
28When Lamech had lived 182 years, he had a son.

a 26 Or *to proclaim*   b 2 Hebrew *adam*   c 6 *Father* may mean *ancestor*; also in verses 7-26.

Living Bible

26When Seth grew up, he had a son and named him Enosh. It was during his lifetime that men first began to call themselves "the Lord's people."d

5 HERE IS a list of somee of the descendants of Adam—the man who was like God from the day of his creation. 2God created man and woman and blessed them, and called them Man from the start. 3, 4, 5Adam: Adam was 130 years old when his sonf Seth was born, the very image of his father in every way.g After Seth was born,h Adam lived another 800 years, producing sons and daughters, and died at the age of 930. 6, 7, 8Seth: Seth was 105 years old when his son Enosh was born. Afterwards he lived another 807 years, producing sons and daughters, and died at the age of 912. 9, 10, 11Enosh: Enosh was ninety years old when his son Kenan was born. Afterwards he lived another 815 years, producing sons and daughters, and died at the age of 905. 12, 13, 14Kenan: Kenan was seventy years old when his son Mahalalel was born. Afterwards he lived another 840 years, producing sons and daughters, and died at the age of 910. 15, 16, 17Mahalalel: Mahalalel was sixty-five years old when his son Jared was born. Afterwards he lived 830 years, producing sons and daughters, and died at the age of 895. 18, 19, 20Jared: Jared was 162 years old when his son Enoch was born. Afterwards he lived another 800 years, producing sons and daughters, and died at the age of 962. 21–24Enoch: Enoch was sixty-five years old when his son Methuselah was born. Afterwards he lived another 300 years in fellowship with God, and produced sons and daughters; then, when he was 365, and in constant touch with God, he disappeared, for God took him! 25, 26, 27Methuselah: Methuselah was 187 years old when his son Lamech was born; afterwards he lived another 782 years, producing sons and daughters, and died at the age of 969. 28–31Lamech: Lamech was 182 years old

New Revised Standard

Enosh. At that time people began to invoke the name of the LORD.

Adam's Descendants to Noah and His Sons

5 THIS IS the list of the descendants of Adam. When God created humankind,i he made themi in the likeness of God. 2Male and female he created them, and he blessed them and named them "Humankind"i when they were created.

3 When Adam had lived one hundred thirty years, he became the father of a son in his likeness, according to his image, and named him Seth. 4The days of Adam after he became the father of Seth were eight hundred years; and he had other sons and daughters. 5Thus all the days that Adam lived were nine hundred thirty years; and he died.

6 When Seth had lived one hundred five years, he became the father of Enosh. 7Seth lived after the birth of Enosh eight hundred seven years, and had other sons and daughters. 8Thus all the days of Seth were nine hundred twelve years; and he died.

9 When Enosh had lived ninety years, he became the father of Kenan. 10Enosh lived after the birth of Kenan eight hundred fifteen years, and had other sons and daughters. 11Thus all the days of Enosh were nine hundred five years; and he died.

12 When Kenan had lived seventy years, he became the father of Mahalalel. 13Kenan lived after the birth of Mahalalel eight hundred and forty years, and had other sons and daughters. 14Thus all the days of Kenan were nine hundred and ten years; and he died.

15 When Mahalalel had lived sixty-five years, he became the father of Jared. 16Mahalalel lived after the birth of Jared eight hundred thirty years, and had other sons and daughters. 17Thus all the days of Mahalalel were eight hundred ninety-five years; and he died.

18 When Jared had lived one hundred sixty-two years he became the father of Enoch. 19Jared lived after the birth of Enoch eight hundred years, and had other sons and daughters. 20Thus all the days of Jared were nine hundred sixty-two years; and he died.

21 When Enoch had lived sixty-five years, he became the father of Methuselah. 22Enoch walked with God after the birth of Methuselah three hundred years, and had other sons and daughters. 23Thus all the days of Enoch were three hundred sixty-five years. 24Enoch walked with God; then he was no more, because God took him.

25 When Methuselah had lived one hundred eighty-seven years, he became the father of Lamech. 26Methuselah lived after the birth of Lamech seven hundred eighty-two years, and had other sons and daughters. 27Thus all the days of Methuselah were nine hundred sixty-nine years; and he died.

28 When Lamech had lived one hundred eighty-two years, he became the father of a son; 29he named him

---

d 4:26 men first began to call themselves "the Lord's people," literally, "This man was the first to invoke the name of Jehovah."   e 5:1 Here is a list of some of the descendants of Adam, literally, "This is the roll of Adam's descendants." the man who was like God, literally, "in the likeness of God." f 5:3-5 when his son, or, by Hebrew usage, "When his son, the ancestor (of Seth) was born." So also in verses 6, 9, 15, 18, 21, 25, 28, 32. g 5:3-5 the very image of his father in every way, literally, "In his own likeness, after his image."   h 5:3-5 After Seth was born, or, by Hebrew usage, "After this ancestor of Seth was born."

i Heb adam   j Heb him

King James

29And he called his name Noah, saying, This *same* shall comfort us concerning our work and toil of our hands, because of the ground which the LORD hath cursed.

30And Lamech lived after he begat Noah five hundred ninety and five years, and begat sons and daughters:

31And all the days of Lamech were seven hundred seventy and seven years: and he died.

32And Noah was five hundred years old: and Noah begat Shem, Ham, and Japheth.

6 AND IT came to pass, when men began to multiply on the face of the earth, and daughters were born unto them,

2That the sons of God saw the daughters of men that they *were* fair; and they took them wives of all which they chose.

3And the LORD said, My spirit shall not always strive with man, for that he also *is* flesh: yet his days shall be an hundred and twenty years.

4There were giants in the earth in those days; and also after that, when the sons of God came in unto the daughters of men, and they bare *children* to them, the same *became* mighty men which *were* of old, men of renown.

5¶ And GOD saw that the wickedness of man *was* great in the earth, and *that* every imagination of the thoughts of his heart *was* only evil continually.

6And it repented the LORD that he had made man on the earth, and it grieved him at his heart.

7And the LORD said, I will destroy man whom I have created from the face of the earth; both man, and beast, and the creeping thing, and the fowls of the air; for it repenteth me that I have made them.

8But Noah found grace in the eyes of the LORD.

9¶ These *are* the generations of Noah: Noah was a just man *and* perfect in his generations, *and* Noah walked with God.

10And Noah begat three sons, Shem, Ham, and Japheth.

11The earth also was corrupt before God, and the earth was filled with violence.

12And God looked upon the earth, and, behold, it was corrupt; for all flesh had corrupted his way upon the earth.

13And God said unto Noah, The end of all flesh is come before me; for the earth is filled with violence through them; and, behold, I will destroy them with the earth.

14¶ Make thee an ark of gopher wood; rooms shalt thou make in the ark, and shalt pitch it within and without with pitch.

15And this *is the fashion* which thou shalt make it *of*: The length of the ark *shall be* three hundred cubits, the breadth of it fifty cubits, and the height of it thirty cubits.

16A window shalt thou make to the ark, and in a cubit shalt thou finish it above; and the door of the ark shalt thou set in the side thereof; *with* lower, second, and third *stories* shalt thou make it.

17And, behold, I, even I, do bring a flood of waters upon the earth, to destroy all flesh, wherein *is* the breath of life, from under heaven; *and* every thing that *is* in the earth shall die.

18But with thee will I establish my covenant; and thou shalt come into the ark, thou, and thy sons, and thy wife, and thy sons' wives with thee.

New International

29He named him Noah[a] and said, "He will comfort us in the labor and painful toil of our hands caused by the ground the LORD has cursed." 30After Noah was born, Lamech lived 595 years and had other sons and daughters. 31Altogether, Lamech lived 777 years, and then he died.

32After Noah was 500 years old, he became the father of Shem, Ham and Japheth.

The Flood

6 WHEN MEN began to increase in number on the earth and daughters were born to them, 2the sons of God saw that the daughters of men were beautiful, and they married any of them they chose. 3Then the LORD said, "My Spirit will not contend with[b] man forever, for he is mortal[c]; his days will be a hundred and twenty years."

4The Nephilim were on the earth in those days—and also afterward—when the sons of God went to the daughters of men and had children by them. They were the heroes of old, men of renown.

5The LORD saw how great man's wickedness on the earth had become, and that every inclination of the thoughts of his heart was only evil all the time. 6The LORD was grieved that he had made man on the earth, and his heart was filled with pain. 7So the LORD said, "I will wipe mankind, whom I have created, from the face of the earth—men and animals, and creatures that move along the ground, and birds of the air—for I am grieved that I have made them." 8But Noah found favor in the eyes of the LORD.

9This is the account of Noah.

Noah was a righteous man, blameless among the people of his time, and he walked with God. 10Noah had three sons: Shem, Ham and Japheth.

11Now the earth was corrupt in God's sight and was full of violence. 12God saw how corrupt the earth had become, for all the people on earth had corrupted their ways. 13So God said to Noah, "I am going to put an end to all people, for the earth is filled with violence because of them. I am surely going to destroy both them and the earth. 14So make yourself an ark of cypress[d] wood; make rooms in it and coat it with pitch inside and out. 15This is how you are to build it: The ark is to be 450 feet long, 75 feet wide and 45 feet high.[e] 16Make a roof for it and finish[f] the ark to within 18 inches[g] of the top. Put a door in the side of the ark and make lower, middle and upper decks. 17I am going to bring floodwaters on the earth to destroy all life under the heavens, every creature that has the breath of life in it. Everything on earth will perish. 18But I will establish my covenant with you, and you will enter the ark—you and your sons and your wife and your sons' wives with you. 19You are to

---

a *29 Noah* sounds like the Hebrew for *comfort*.   b *3 Or My spirit will not remain in*   c *3 Or corrupt*   d *14 The meaning of the Hebrew for this word is uncertain.*   e *15 Hebrew 300 cubits long, 50 cubits wide and 30 cubits high (about 140 meters long, 23 meters wide and 13.5 meters high)*   f *16 Or Make an opening for light by finishing*   g *16 Hebrew a cubit (about 0.5 meter)*

Living Bible

when his son Noah was born. Lamech named him Noah (meaning "Relief") because he said, "He will bring us relief from the hard work of farming this ground which God has cursed." Afterwards Lamech lived 595 years, producing sons and daughters, and died at the age of 777. 32*Noah:* Noah was 500 years old and had three sons, Shem, Ham, and Japheth.

6 NOW A population explosion took place upon the earth. It was at this time that beings from the spirit worldh looked upon the beautiful earth women and took any they desired to be their wives. 3Then Jehovah said, "My Spirit must not forever be disgraced in man, wholly evil as he is. I will give him 120 years to mend his ways."

4In those days, and even afterwards, when the evil beings from the spirit world were sexually involved with human women, their children became giants, of whom so many legends are told. 5When the Lord God saw the extent of human wickedness, and that the trend and direction of men's lives were only towards evil, 6he was sorry he had made them. It broke his heart.

7And he said, "I will blot out from the face of the earth all mankind that I created. Yes, and the animals too, and the reptiles and the birds. For I am sorry I made them."

8But Noah was a pleasure to the Lord. Here is the story of Noah: 9, 10He was the only truly righteous man living on the earth at that time. He tried always to conduct his affairs according to God's will. And he had three sons—Shem, Ham, and Japheth.

11Meanwhile, the crime rate was rising rapidly across the earth, and, as seen by God, the world was rotten to the core.

12, 13As God observed how bad it was, and saw that all mankind was vicious and depraved, he said to Noah, "I have decided to destroy all mankind; for the earth is filled with crime because of man. Yes, I will destroy mankind from the earth. 14Make a boat from resinous wood, sealing it with tar; and construct decks and stalls throughout the ship. 15Make it 450 feet long, 75 feet wide, and 45 feet high. 16Construct a skylight all the way around the ship, eighteen inches below the roof; and make three decks inside the boat—a bottom, middle, and upper deck—and put a door in the side.

17"Look! I am going to cover the earth with a flood and destroy every living being—everything in which there is the breath of life. All will die. 18But I promise to keep you safe in the ship, with your wife and your sons and their wives. 19, 20Bring a pair of every ani-

New Revised Standard

Noah, saying, "Out of the ground that the LORD has cursed this one shall bring us relief from our work and from the toil of our hands." 30Lamech lived after the birth of Noah five hundred ninety-five years, and had other sons and daughters. 31Thus all the days of Lamech were seven hundred seventy-seven years; and he died.

32 After Noah was five hundred years old, Noah became the father of Shem, Ham, and Japheth.

The Wickedness of Humankind

6 WHEN PEOPLE began to multiply on the face of the ground, and daughters were born to them, 2the sons of God saw that they were fair; and they took wives for themselves of all that they chose. 3Then the LORD said, "My spirit shall not abidei in mortals forever, for they are flesh; their days shall be one hundred twenty years." 4The Nephilim were on the earth in those days—and also afterward—when the sons of God went in to the daughters of humans, who bore children to them. These were the heroes that were of old, warriors of renown.

5 The LORD saw that the wickedness of humankind was great in the earth, and that every inclination of the thoughts of their hearts was only evil continually. 6And the LORD was sorry that he had made humankind on the earth, and it grieved him to his heart. 7So the LORD said, "I will blot out from the earth the human beings I have created—people together with animals and creeping things and birds of the air, for I am sorry that I have made them." 8But Noah found favor in the sight of the LORD.

Noah Pleases God

9 These are the descendants of Noah. Noah was a righteous man, blameless in his generation; Noah walked with God. 10And Noah had three sons, Shem, Ham, and Japheth.

11 Now the earth was corrupt in God's sight, and the earth was filled with violence. 12And God saw that the earth was corrupt; for all flesh had corrupted its ways upon the earth. 13And God said to Noah, "I have determined to make an end of all flesh, for the earth is filled with violence because of them; now I am going to destroy them along with the earth. 14Make yourself an ark of cypressi wood; make rooms in the ark, and cover it inside and out with pitch. 15This is how you are to make it: the length of the ark three hundred cubits, its width fifty cubits, and its height thirty cubits. 16Make a roofi for the ark, and finish it to a cubit above; and put the door of the ark in its side; make it with lower, second, and third decks. 17For my part, I am going to bring a flood of waters on the earth, to destroy from under heaven all flesh in which is the breath of life; everything that is on the earth shall die. 18But I will establish my covenant with you; and you shall come into the ark, you, your sons, your wife, and your sons' wives with you. 19And

---

h *6:1, 2 beings from the spirit world,* literally, "sons of God," used here in the sense of his created, supernatural beings, but no longer godly in character (vs 3). Some commentators believe that the expression "sons of God" refers to the "godly line" of Seth, and "daughters of men" to women from the line of Cain.

i Meaning of Heb uncertain   j Or *window*

King James

19And of every living thing of all flesh, two of every *sort* shalt thou bring into the ark, to keep *them* alive with thee; they shall be male and female.

20Of fowls after their kind, and of cattle after their kind, of every creeping thing of the earth after his kind, two of every *sort* shall come unto thee, to keep *them* alive.

21And take thou unto thee of all food that is eaten, and thou shalt gather *it* to thee; and it shall be for food for thee, and for them.

22Thus did Noah; according to all that God commanded him, so did he.

7 AND THE LORD said unto Noah, Come thou and all thy house into the ark; for thee have I seen righteous before me in this generation.

2Of every clean beast thou shalt take to thee by sevens, the male and his female: and of beasts that *are* not clean by two, the male and his female.

3Of fowls also of the air by sevens, the male and the female; to keep seed alive upon the face of all the earth.

4For yet seven days, and I will cause it to rain upon the earth forty days and forty nights; and every living substance that I have made will I destroy from off the face of the earth.

5And Noah did according unto all that the LORD commanded him.

6And Noah *was* six hundred years old when the flood of waters was upon the earth.

7¶ And Noah went in, and his sons, and his wife, and his sons' wives with him, into the ark, because of the waters of the flood.

8Of clean beasts, and of beasts that *are* not clean, and of fowls, and of every thing that creepeth upon the earth,

9There went in two and two unto Noah into the ark, the male and the female, as God had commanded Noah.

10And it came to pass after seven days, that the waters of the flood were upon the earth.

11¶ In the six hundredth year of Noah's life, in the second month, the seventeenth day of the month, the same day were all the fountains of the great deep broken up, and the windows of heaven were opened.

12And the rain was upon the earth forty days and forty nights.

13In the selfsame day entered Noah, and Shem, and Ham, and Japheth, the sons of Noah, and Noah's wife, and the three wives of his sons with them, into the ark;

14They, and every beast after his kind, and all the cattle after their kind, and every creeping thing that creepeth upon the earth after his kind, and every fowl after his kind, every bird of every sort.

15And they went in unto Noah into the ark, two and two of all flesh, wherein *is* the breath of life.

16And they that went in, went in male and female of all flesh, as God had commanded him: and the LORD shut him in.

17And the flood was forty days upon the earth; and the waters increased, and bare up the ark, and it was lift up above the earth.

18And the waters prevailed, and were increased greatly upon the earth; and the ark went upon the face of the waters.

19And the waters prevailed exceedingly upon the earth; and all the high hills, that *were* under the whole heaven, were covered.

20Fifteen cubits upward did the waters prevail; and the mountains were covered.

21And all flesh died that moved upon the earth, both of fowl, and of cattle, and of beast, and of every creeping thing that creepeth upon the earth, and every man:

22All in whose nostrils *was* the breath of life, of all that *was* in the dry *land*, died.

New International

bring into the ark two of all living creatures, male and female, to keep them alive with you. 20Two of every kind of bird, of every kind of animal and of every kind of creature that moves along the ground will come to you to be kept alive. 21You are to take every kind of food that is to be eaten and store it away as food for you and for them."

22Noah did everything just as God commanded him.

7 THE LORD then said to Noah, "Go into the ark, you and your whole family, because I have found you righteous in this generation. 2Take with you sevena of every kind of clean animal, a male and its mate, and two of every kind of unclean animal, a male and its mate, 3and also seven of every kind of bird, male and female, to keep their various kinds alive throughout the earth. 4Seven days from now I will send rain on the earth for forty days and forty nights, and I will wipe from the face of the earth every living creature I have made."

5And Noah did all that the LORD commanded him.

6Noah was six hundred years old when the floodwaters came on the earth. 7And Noah and his sons and his wife and his sons' wives entered the ark to escape the waters of the flood. 8Pairs of clean and unclean animals, of birds and of all creatures that move along the ground, 9male and female, came to Noah and entered the ark, as God had commanded Noah. 10And after the seven days the floodwaters came on the earth.

11In the six hundredth year of Noah's life, on the seventeenth day of the second month—on that day all the springs of the great deep burst forth, and the floodgates of the heavens were opened. 12And rain fell on the earth forty days and forty nights.

13On that ve.y day Noah and his sons, Shem, Ham and Japheth, together with his wife and the wives of his three sons, entered the ark. 14They had with them every wild animal according to its kind, all livestock according to their kinds, every creature that moves along the ground according to its kind and every bird according to its kind, everything with wings. 15Pairs of all creatures that have the breath of life in them came to Noah and entered the ark. 16The animals going in were male and female of every living thing, as God had commanded Noah. Then the LORD shut him in.

17For forty days the flood kept coming on the earth, and as the waters increased they lifted the ark high above the earth. 18The waters rose and increased greatly on the earth, and the ark floated on the surface of the water. 19They rose greatly on the earth, and all the high mountains under the entire heavens were covered. 20The waters rose and covered the mountains to a depth of more than twenty feet.b,c 21Every living thing that moved on the earth perished—birds, livestock, wild animals, all the creatures that swarm over the earth, and all mankind. 22Everything on dry land that had the breath of life in its nostrils died. 23Every living thing on the face of the earth

a 2 Or *seven pairs; also in verse 3*   b 20 Hebrew *fifteen cubits* (about 6.9 meters)   c 20 Or *rose more than twenty feet, and the mountains were covered*

Living Bible

mal—a male and a female—into the boat with you, to keep them alive through the flood. Bring in a pair of each kind of bird and animal and reptile. 21Store away in the boat all the food that they and you will need." 22And Noah did everything as God commanded him.

7 FINALLY THE day came when the Lord said to Noah, "Go into the boat with all your family, for among all the people of the earth, I consider you alone to be righteous. 2Bring in the animals, too—a pair of each, except those kinds I have chosen for eating and for sacrifice: take seven pairs of each of them, 3and seven pairsd of every kind of bird. Thus there will be every kind of life reproducing again after the flood has ended. 4One week from today I will begin forty days and nights of rain; and all the animals and birds and reptiles I have made will die."

5So Noah did everything the Lord commanded him. 6He was 600 years old when the flood came. 7He boarded the boat with his wife and sons and their wives, to escape the flood. 8, 9With him were all the various kinds of animals—those for eating and sacrifice, and those that were not, and the birds and reptiles. They came into the boat in pairs, male and female, just as God commanded Noah.

10, 11, 12One week later, when Noah was 600 years, two months, and seventeen days old, the rain came down in mighty torrents from the sky, and the subterranean waters burst forth upon the earth for forty days and nights. 13But Noah had gone into the boat that very day with his wife and his sons, Shem, Ham, and Japheth, and their wives. 14, 15With them in the boat were pairs of every kind of animal—domestic and wild—and reptiles and birds of every sort. 16Two by two they came, male and female, just as God had commanded. Then the Lord Gode closed the door and shut them in.

17For forty days the roaring floods prevailed, covering the ground and lifting the boat high above the earth. 18As the water rose higher and higher above the ground, the boat floated safely upon it; 19until finally the water covered all the high mountains under the whole heaven, 20standing twenty-two feet and more above the highest peaks. 21And all living things upon the earth perished—birds, domestic and wild animals, and reptiles and all mankind— 22everything that breathed and lived upon dry land. 23All existence on the earth was blotted out—

New Revised Standard

of every living thing, of all flesh, you shall bring two of every kind into the ark, to keep them alive with you; they shall be male and female. 20Of the birds according to their kinds, and of the animals according to their kinds, of every creeping thing of the ground according to its kind, two of every kind shall come in to you, to keep them alive. 21 Also take with you every kind of food that is eaten, and store it up; and it shall serve as food for you and for them." 22Noah did this; he did all that God commanded him.

The Great Flood

7 THEN THE Lord said to Noah, "Go into the ark, you and all your household, for I have seen that you alone are righteous before me in this generation. 2Take with you seven pairs of all clean animals, the male and its mate; and a pair of the animals that are not clean, the male and its mate; 3and seven pairs of the birds of the air also, male and female, to keep their kind alive on the face of all the earth. 4For in seven days I will send rain on the earth for forty days and forty nights; and every living thing that I have made I will blot out from the face of the ground." 5And Noah did all that the Lord had commanded him.

6 Noah was six hundred years old when the flood of waters came on the earth. 7And Noah with his sons and his wife and his sons' wives went into the ark to escape the waters of the flood. 8Of clean animals, and of animals that are not clean, and of birds, and of everything that creeps on the ground, 9two and two, male and female, went into the ark with Noah, as God had commanded Noah. 10 And after seven days the waters of the flood came on the earth.

11 In the six hundredth year of Noah's life, in the second month, on the seventeenth day of the month, on that day all the fountains of the great deep burst forth, and the windows of the heavens were opened. 12The rain fell on the earth forty days and forty nights. 13On the very same day Noah with his sons, Shem and Ham and Japheth, and Noah's wife and the three wives of his sons entered the ark, 14they and every wild animal of every kind, and all domestic animals of every kind, and every creeping thing that creeps on the earth, and every bird of every kind—every bird, every winged creature. 15They went into the ark with Noah, two and two of all flesh in which there was the breath of life. 16And those that entered, male and female of all flesh, went in as God had commanded him; and the Lord shut him in.

17 The flood continued forty days on the earth; and the waters increased, and bore up the ark, and it rose high above the earth. 18The waters swelled and increased greatly on the earth; and the ark floated on the face of the waters. 19The waters swelled so mightily on the earth that all the high mountains under the whole heaven were covered; 20the waters swelled above the mountains, covering them fifteen cubits deep. 21And all flesh died that moved on the earth, birds, domestic animals, wild animals, all swarming creatures that swarm on the earth, and all human beings; 22everything on dry land in whose nostrils was the breath of life died. 23He

---

d 7:3 seven pairs, literally, "the male and female."   e 7:16 the Lord God, literally, "Jehovah."

King James

23And every living substance was destroyed which was upon the face of the ground, both man, and cattle, and the creeping things, and the fowl of the heaven; and they were destroyed from the earth: and Noah only remained *alive*, and they that *were* with him in the ark.

24And the waters prevailed upon the earth an hundred and fifty days.

8 AND GOD remembered Noah, and every living thing, and all the cattle that *was* with him in the ark: and God made a wind to pass over the earth, and the waters assuaged;

2The fountains also of the deep and the windows of heaven were stopped, and the rain from heaven was restrained;

3And the waters returned from off the earth continually: and after the end of the hundred and fifty days the waters were abated.

4And the ark rested in the seventh month, on the seventeenth day of the month, upon the mountains of Ararat.

5And the waters decreased continually until the tenth month: in the tenth *month*, on the first *day* of the month, were the tops of the mountains seen.

6¶ And it came to pass at the end of forty days, that Noah opened the window of the ark which he had made:

7And he sent forth a raven, which went forth to and fro, until the waters were dried up from off the earth.

8Also he sent forth a dove from him, to see if the waters were abated from off the face of the ground;

9But the dove found no rest for the sole of her foot, and she returned unto him into the ark, for the waters *were* on the face of the whole earth: then he put forth his hand, and took her, and pulled her in unto him into the ark.

10And he stayed yet other seven days; and again he sent forth the dove out of the ark;

11And the dove came in to him in the evening; and, lo, in her mouth *was* an olive leaf plucked off: so Noah knew that the waters were abated from off the earth.

12And he stayed yet other seven days; and sent forth the dove; which returned not again unto him any more.

13¶ And it came to pass in the six hundredth and first year, in the first *month*, the first *day* of the month, the waters were dried up from off the earth: and Noah removed the covering of the ark, and looked, and, behold, the face of the ground was dry.

14And in the second month, on the seven and twentieth day of the month, was the earth dried.

15¶ And God spake unto Noah, saying,

16Go forth of the ark, thou, and thy wife, and thy sons, and thy sons' wives with thee.

17Bring forth with thee every living thing that *is* with thee, of all flesh, *both* of fowl, and of cattle, and of every creeping thing that creepeth upon the earth; that they may breed abundantly in the earth, and be fruitful, and multiply upon the earth.

18And Noah went forth, and his sons, and his wife, and his sons' wives with him:

19Every beast, every creeping thing, and every fowl, *and* whatsoever creepeth upon the earth, after their kinds, went forth out of the ark.

20¶ And Noah builded an altar unto the LORD; and took of every clean beast, and of every clean fowl, and offered burnt offerings on the altar.

21And the LORD smelled a sweet savour; and the LORD said in his heart, I will not again curse the ground any more for man's sake; for the imagination of man's heart *is* evil from his youth; neither will I again smite any more every thing living, as I have done.

New International

was wiped out; men and animals and the creatures that move along the ground and the birds of the air were wiped from the earth. Only Noah was left, and those with him in the ark.

24The waters flooded the earth for a hundred and fifty days.

8 BUT GOD remembered Noah and all the wild animals and the livestock that were with him in the ark, and he sent a wind over the earth, and the waters receded. 2Now the springs of the deep and the floodgates of the heavens had been closed, and the rain had stopped falling from the sky. 3The water receded steadily from the earth. At the end of the hundred and fifty days the water had gone down, 4and on the seventeenth day of the seventh month the ark came to rest on the mountains of Ararat. 5The waters continued to recede until the tenth month, and on the first day of the tenth month the tops of the mountains became visible.

6After forty days Noah opened the window he had made in the ark 7and sent out a raven, and it kept flying back and forth until the water had dried up from the earth. 8Then he sent out a dove to see if the water had receded from the surface of the ground. 9But the dove could find no place to set its feet because there was water over all the surface of the earth; so it returned to Noah in the ark. He reached out his hand and took the dove and brought it back to himself in the ark. 10He waited seven more days and again sent out the dove from the ark. 11When the dove returned to him in the evening, there in its beak was a freshly plucked olive leaf! Then Noah knew that the water had receded from the earth. 12He waited seven more days and sent the dove out again, but this time it did not return to him.

13By the first day of the first month of Noah's six hundred and first year, the water had dried up from the earth. Noah then removed the covering from the ark and saw that the surface of the ground was dry. 14By the twenty-seventh day of the second month the earth was completely dry.

15Then God said to Noah, 16"Come out of the ark, you and your wife and your sons and their wives. 17Bring out every kind of living creature that is with you—the birds, the animals, and all the creatures that move along the ground—so they can multiply on the earth and be fruitful and increase in number upon it."

18So Noah came out, together with his sons and his wife and his sons' wives. 19All the animals and all the creatures that move along the ground and all the birds—everything that moves on the earth—came out of the ark, one kind after another.

20Then Noah built an altar to the LORD and, taking some of all the clean animals and clean birds, he sacrificed burnt offerings on it. 21The LORD smelled the pleasing aroma and said in his heart: "Never again will I curse the ground because of man, even thougha every inclination of his heart is evil from childhood. And never again will I destroy all living creatures, as I have done.

Living Bible

man and animals alike, and reptiles and birds. God destroyed them all, leaving only Noah alive, and those with him in the boat. 24And the water covered the earth 150 days.

8 GOD DIDN'T forget about Noah and all the animals in the boat! He sent a wind to blow across the waters, and the floods began to disappear, 2for the subterranean water sources ceased their gushing, and the torrential rains subsided. 3, 4So the flood gradually receded until, 150 days after it began, the boat came to rest upon the mountains of Ararat. 5Three months later,b as the waters continued to go down, other mountain peaks appeared.

6After another forty days, Noah opened a porthole 7and released a raven that flew back and forthc until the earth was dry. 8Meanwhile he sent out a dove to see if it could find dry ground, 9but the dove found no place to light, and returned to Noah, for the water was still too high. So Noah held out his hand and drew the dove back into the boat.

10Seven days later Noah released the dove again, 11and this time, towards evening, the bird returned to him with an olive leaf in her beak. So Noah knew that the water was almost gone. 12A week later he released the dove again, and this time she didn't come back.

13Twenty-nine days after that,d Noah opened the door to look, and the water was gone. 14Eight more weeks went by. Then at last the earth was dry. 15, 16Then God told Noah, "You may all go out. 17Release all the animals, birds, and reptiles, so that they will breed abundantly and reproduce in great numbers." 18, 19So the boat was soon empty. Noah, his wife, and his sons and their wives all disembarked, along with all the animals, reptiles, and birds—all left the ark in pairs and groups.

20Then Noah built an altar and sacrificed on it some of the animals and birds God had designatede for that purpose. 21And Jehovah was pleased withf the sacrifice and said to himself, "I will never do it again—I will never again curse the earth, destroying all living things, even though man's bent is always toward evil from his earliest youth, and even though he does such wicked things. 22As long as the earth remains, there will be

New Revised Standard

blotted out every living thing that was on the face of the ground, human beings and animals and creeping things and birds of the air; they were blotted out from the earth. Only Noah was left, and those that were with him in the ark. 24And the waters swelled on the earth for one hundred fifty days.

The Flood Subsides

8 BUT GOD remembered Noah and all the wild animals and all the domestic animals that were with him in the ark. And God made a wind blow over the earth, and the waters subsided; 2the fountains of the deep and the windows of the heavens were closed, the rain from the heavens was restrained, 3and the waters gradually receded from the earth. At the end of one hundred fifty days the waters had abated; 4and in the seventh month, on the seventeenth day of the month, the ark came to rest on the mountains of Ararat. 5The waters continued to abate until the tenth month; in the tenth month, on the first day of the month, the tops of the mountains appeared.

6 At the end of forty days Noah opened the window of the ark that he had made 7and sent out the raven; and it went to and fro until the waters were dried up from the earth. 8Then he sent out the dove from him, to see if the waters had subsided from the face of the ground; 9but the dove found no place to set its foot, and it returned to him to the ark, for the waters were still on the face of the whole earth. So he put out his hand and took it and brought it into the ark with him. 10He waited another seven days, and again he sent out the dove from the ark; 11and the dove came back to him in the evening, and there in its beak was a freshly plucked olive leaf; so Noah knew that the waters had subsided from the earth. 12Then he waited another seven days, and sent out the dove; and it did not return to him any more.

13 In the six hundred first year, in the first month, the first day of the month, the waters were dried up from the earth; and Noah removed the covering of the ark, and looked, and saw that the face of the ground was drying. 14In the second month, on the twenty-seventh day of the month, the earth was dry. 15Then God said to Noah, 16"Go out of the ark, you and your wife, and your sons and your sons' wives with you. 17Bring out with you every living thing that is with you of all flesh—birds and animals and every creeping thing that creeps on the earth—so that they may abound on the earth, and be fruitful and multiply on the earth." 18So Noah went out with his sons and his wife and his sons' wives. 19And every animal, every creeping thing, and every bird, everything that moves on the earth, went out of the ark by families.

God's Promise to Noah

20 Then Noah built an altar to the LORD, and took of every clean animal and of every clean bird, and offered burnt offerings on the altar. 21And when the LORD smelled the pleasing odor, the LORD said in his heart, "I will never again curse the ground because of humankind, for the inclination of the human heart is evil from youth; nor will I ever again destroy every living creature as I have done.

---

b 8:5 *three months later*, literally, "on the first day of the tenth month."
c 8:7 *a raven that flew back and forth.* Apparently lighting from time to time upon carcasses of dead animals floating on the water. The dove which Noah next dispatched would not alight on such floating carrion, and was thus a good indication of the water level.   d 8:13 *Twenty-nine days after that,* literally, "in the 601st year, in the first month, the first day of the month."
e 8:20 *some of the animals and birds God had designated,* literally, "Clean," i.e., ritually approved by God.   f 8:21 *Jehovah was pleased with the sacrifice,* literally, "and Jehovah smelled the delicious odor and said . . ."

King James

22While the earth remaineth, seedtime and harvest, and cold and heat, and summer and winter, and day and night shall not cease.

9 AND GOD blessed Noah and his sons, and said unto them, Be fruitful, and multiply, and replenish the earth.

2And the fear of you and the dread of you shall be upon every beast of the earth, and upon every fowl of the air, upon all that moveth *upon* the earth, and upon all the fishes of the sea; into your hand are they delivered.

3Every moving thing that liveth shall be meat for you; even as the green herb have I given you all things.

4But flesh with the life thereof, *which is* the blood thereof, shall ye not eat.

5And surely your blood of your lives will I require; at the hand of every beast will I require it, and at the hand of man; at the hand of every man's brother will I require the life of man.

6Whoso sheddeth man's blood, by man shall his blood be shed: for in the image of God made he man.

7And you, be ye fruitful, and multiply; bring forth abundantly in the earth, and multiply therein.

8¶ And God spake unto Noah, and to his sons with him, saying,

9And I, behold, I establish my covenant with you, and with your seed after you;

10And with every living creature that *is* with you, of the fowl, of the cattle, and of every beast of the earth with you; from all that go out of the ark, to every beast of the earth.

11And I will establish my covenant with you; neither shall all flesh be cut off any more by the waters of a flood; neither shall there any more be a flood to destroy the earth.

12And God said, This *is* the token of the covenant which I make between me and you and every living creature that *is* with you, for perpetual generations:

13I do set my bow in the cloud, and it shall be for a token of a covenant between me and the earth.

14And it shall come to pass, when I bring a cloud over the earth, that the bow shall be seen in the cloud:

15And I will remember my covenant, which *is* between me and you and every living creature of all flesh; and the waters shall no more become a flood to destroy all flesh.

16And the bow shall be in the cloud; and I will look upon it, that I may remember the everlasting covenant between God and every living creature of all flesh that *is* upon the earth.

17And God said unto Noah, This *is* the token of the covenant, which I have established between me and all flesh that *is* upon the earth.

18¶ And the sons of Noah, that went forth of the ark, were Shem, and Ham, and Japheth: and Ham *is* the father of Canaan.

19These *are* the three sons of Noah: and of them was the whole earth overspread.

20And Noah began *to be* an husbandman, and he planted a vineyard:

21And he drank of the wine, and was drunken; and he was uncovered within his tent.

22And Ham, the father of Canaan, saw the nakedness of his father, and told his two brethren without.

23And Shem and Japheth took a garment, and laid *it* upon both their shoulders, and went backward, and covered the nakedness of their father; and their faces *were* backward, and they saw not their father's nakedness.

New International

22"As long as the earth endures,
　　seedtime and harvest,
　　cold and heat,
　　summer and winter,
　　day and night
　　will never cease."

God's Covenant With Noah

9 THEN GOD blessed Noah and his sons, saying to them, "Be fruitful and increase in number and fill the earth. 2The fear and dread of you will fall upon all the beasts of the earth and all the birds of the air, upon every creature that moves along the ground, and upon all the fish of the sea; they are given into your hands. 3Everything that lives and moves will be food for you. Just as I gave you the green plants, I now give you everything.

4"But you must not eat meat that has its lifeblood still in it. 5And for your lifeblood I will surely demand an accounting. I will demand an accounting from every animal. And from each man, too, I will demand an accounting for the life of his fellow man.

6"Whoever sheds the blood of man,
　　by man shall his blood be shed;
　　for in the image of God
　　has God made man.

7As for you, be fruitful and increase in number; multiply on the earth and increase upon it."

8Then God said to Noah and to his sons with him: 9"I now establish my covenant with you and with your descendants after you 10and with every living creature that was with you—the birds, the livestock and all the wild animals, all those that came out of the ark with you—every living creature on earth. 11I establish my covenant with you: Never again will all life be cut off by the waters of a flood; never again will there be a flood to destroy the earth."

12And God said, "This is the sign of the covenant I am making between me and you and every living creature with you, a covenant for all generations to come: 13I have set my rainbow in the clouds, and it will be the sign of the covenant between me and the earth. 14Whenever I bring clouds over the earth and the rainbow appears in the clouds, 15I will remember my covenant between me and you and all living creatures of every kind. Never again will the waters become a flood to destroy all life. 16Whenever the rainbow appears in the clouds, I will see it and remember the everlasting covenant between God and all living creatures of every kind on the earth."

17So God said to Noah, "This is the sign of the covenant I have established between me and all life on the earth."

The Sons of Noah

18The sons of Noah who came out of the ark were Shem, Ham and Japheth. (Ham was the father of Canaan.) 19These were the three sons of Noah, and from them came the people who were scattered over the earth.

20Noah, a man of the soil, proceededa to plant a vineyard. 21When he drank some of its wine, he became drunk and lay uncovered inside his tent. 22Ham, the father of Canaan, saw his father's nakedness and told his two brothers outside. 23But Shem and Japheth took a garment and laid it across their shoulders; then they walked in backward and covered their father's nakedness. Their faces were turned the other way so that they would not see their father's nakedness.

a *20 Or soil, was the first*

Living Bible

springtime and harvest, cold and heat, winter and summer, day and night."

9 GOD BLESSED Noah and his sons and told them to have many children and to repopulate the earth. 2, 3"All wild animals and birds and fish will be afraid of you," God told him; "for I have placed them in your power, and they are yours to use for food, in addition to grain and vegetables. 4But never eat animals unless their life-blood has been drained off. 5, 6And murder is forbidden. Man-killing animals must die, and any man who murders shall be killed; for to kill a man is to kill one made like God. 7Yes, have many children and repopulate the earth and subdue it."

8Then God told Noah and his sons, 9, 10, 11"I solemnly promise you and your childrenb and the animals you brought with you—all these birds and cattle and wild animals—that I will never again send another flood to destroy the earth. 12And I seal this promise with this sign: 13I have placed my rainbow in the clouds as a sign of my promise until the end of time, to you and to all the earth. 14When I send clouds over the earth, the rainbow will be seen in the clouds, 15and I will remember my promise to you and to every being, that never again will the floods come and destroy all life. 16, 17For I will see the rainbow in the cloud and remember my eternal promise to every living being on the earth."

18The names of Noah's three sons were Shem, Ham, and Japheth. (Ham is the ancestor of the Canaanites.)c 19From these three sons of Noah came all the nations of the earth.

20, 21Noah became a farmer and planted a vineyard, and he made wine. One day as he was drunk and lay naked in his tent, 22Ham, the father of Canaan, saw his father's nakedness and went outside and told his two brothers. 23Then Shem and Japheth took a robe and held it over their shoulders and, walking backwards into the tent, let it fall across their father to cover his nakedness as they looked the other way. 24, 25When Noah awoke

New Revised Standard

22 As long as the earth endures,
   seedtime and harvest, cold and heat,
   summer and winter, day and night,
      shall not cease."

The Covenant with Noah

9 GOD BLESSED Noah and his sons, and said to them, "Be fruitful and multiply, and fill the earth. 2The fear and dread of you shall rest on every animal of the earth, and on every bird of the air, on everything that creeps on the ground, and on all the fish of the sea; into your hand they are delivered. 3Every moving thing that lives shall be food for you; and just as I gave you the green plants, I give you everything. 4Only, you shall not eat flesh with its life, that is, its blood. 5For your own lifeblood I will surely require a reckoning: from every animal I will require it and from human beings, each one for the blood of another, I will require a reckoning for human life.

6 Whoever sheds the blood of a human,
      by a human shall that person's blood be
         shed;
   for in his own image
         God made humankind.

7And you, be fruitful and multiply, abound on the earth and multiply in it."

8 Then God said to Noah and to his sons with him, 9"As for me, I am establishing my covenant with you and your descendants after you, 10and with every living creature that is with you, the birds, the domestic animals, and every animal of the earth with you, as many as came out of the ark.d 11I establish my covenant with you, that never again shall all flesh be cut off by the waters of a flood, and never again shall there be a flood to destroy the earth." 12God said, "This is the sign of the covenant that I make between me and you and every living creature that is with you, for all future generations: 13I have set my bow in the clouds, and it shall be a sign of the covenant between me and the earth. 14When I bring clouds over the earth and the bow is seen in the clouds, 15I will remember my covenant that is between me and you and every living creature of all flesh; and the waters shall never again become a flood to destroy all flesh. 16When the bow is in the clouds, I will see it and remember the everlasting covenant between God and every living creature of all flesh that is on the earth." 17God said to Noah, "This is the sign of the covenant that I have established between me and all flesh that is on the earth."

Noah and His Sons

18 The sons of Noah who went out of the ark were Shem, Ham, and Japheth. Ham was the father of Canaan. 19These three were the sons of Noah; and from these the whole earth was peopled.

20 Noah, a man of the soil, was the first to plant a vineyard. 21He drank some of the wine and became drunk, and he lay uncovered in his tent. 22And Ham, the father of Canaan, saw the nakedness of his father, and told his two brothers outside. 23Then Shem and Japheth took a garment, laid it on both their shoulders, and walked backward and covered the nakedness of their father; their faces were turned away, and they did not see their father's nakedness. 24When Noah awoke from his

b 9:9-11 *promise you and your children*, literally, "your seed."   c *9:18 Ham is the ancestor of the Canaanites*. Ham was not the ancestor of the Negro, as was once erroneously supposed.

d Gk: Heb adds *every animal of the earth*

King James

24And Noah awoke from his wine, and knew what his younger son had done unto him.

25And he said, Cursed be Canaan; a servant of servants shall he be unto his brethren.

26And he said, Blessed be the LORD God of Shem; and Canaan shall be his servant.

27God shall enlarge Japheth, and he shall dwell in the tents of Shem; and Canaan shall be his servant.

28¶ And Noah lived after the flood three hundred and fifty years.

29And all the days of Noah were nine hundred and fifty years: and he died.

10 NOW THESE are the generations of the sons of Noah, Shem, Ham, and Japheth: and unto them were sons born after the flood.

2The sons of Japheth; Gomer, and Magog, and Madai, and Javan, and Tubal, and Meshech, and Tiras.

3And the sons of Gomer; Ashkenaz, and Riphath, and Togarmah.

4And the sons of Javan; Elishah, and Tarshish, Kittim, and Dodanim.

5By these were the isles of the Gentiles divided in their lands; every one after his tongue, after their families, in their nations.

6¶ And the sons of Ham; Cush, and Mizraim, and Phut, and Canaan.

7And the sons of Cush; Seba, and Havilah, and Sabtah, and Raamah, and Sabtecha: and the sons of Raamah; Sheba, and Dedan.

8And Cush begat Nimrod: he began to be a mighty one in the earth.

9He was a mighty hunter before the LORD: wherefore it is said, Even as Nimrod the mighty hunter before the LORD.

10And the beginning of his kingdom was Babel, and Erech, and Accad, and Calneh, in the land of Shinar.

11Out of that land went forth Asshur, and builded Nineveh, and the city Rehoboth, and Calah,

12And Resen between Nineveh and Calah: the same is a great city.

13And Mizraim begat Ludim, and Anamim, and Lehabim, and Naphtuhim,

14And Pathrusim, and Casluhim, (out of whom came Philistim,) and Caphtorim.

15¶ And Canaan begat Sidon his firstborn, and Heth,

16And the Jebusite, and the Amorite, and the Girgasite,

17And the Hivite, and the Arkite, and the Sinite,

18And the Arvadite, and the Zemarite, and the Hamathite: and afterward were the families of the Canaanites spread abroad.

19And the border of the Canaanites was from Sidon, as thou comest to Gerar, unto Gaza; as thou goest, unto Sodom, and Gomorrah, and Admah, and Zeboim, even unto Lasha.

New International

24When Noah awoke from his wine and found out what his youngest son had done to him, 25he said,

"Cursed be Canaan!
   The lowest of slaves
   will he be to his brothers."

26He also said,

"Blessed be the LORD, the God of Shem!
   May Canaan be the slave of Shem.[a]
27May God extend the territory of Japheth[b];
   may Japheth live in the tents of Shem,
   and may Canaan be his[c] slave."

28After the flood Noah lived 350 years. 29Altogether, Noah lived 950 years, and then he died.

The Table of Nations

10 THIS IS the account of Shem, Ham and Japheth, Noah's sons, who themselves had sons after the flood.

The Japhethites

2The sons[d] of Japheth:
   Gomer, Magog, Madai, Javan, Tubal, Meshech and Tiras.
3The sons of Gomer:
   Ashkenaz, Riphath and Togarmah.
4The sons of Javan:
   Elishah, Tarshish, the Kittim and the Rodanim.[e] 5(From these the maritime peoples spread out into their territories by their clans within their nations, each with its own language.)

The Hamites

6The sons of Ham:
   Cush, Mizraim,[f] Put and Canaan.
7The sons of Cush:
   Seba, Havilah, Sabtah, Raamah and Sabteca.
   The sons of Raamah:
   Sheba and Dedan.

8Cush was the father[g] of Nimrod, who grew to be a mighty warrior on the earth. 9He was a mighty hunter before the LORD; that is why it is said, "Like Nimrod, a mighty hunter before the LORD." 10The first centers of his kingdom were Babylon, Erech, Akkad and Calneh, in[h] Shinar.[i] 11From that land he went to Assyria, where he built Nineveh, Rehoboth Ir,[j] Calah 12and Resen, which is between Nineveh and Calah; that is the great city.

13Mizraim was the father of
   the Ludites, Anamites, Lehabites, Naphtuhites, 14Pathrusites, Casluhites (from whom the Philistines came) and Caphtorites.
15Canaan was the father of
   Sidon his firstborn,[k] and of the Hittites, 16Jebusites, Amorites, Girgashites, 17Hivites, Arkites, Sinites, 18Arvadites, Zemarites and Hamathites.

Later the Canaanite clans scattered 19and the borders of Canaan reached from Sidon toward Gerar as far as Gaza, and then toward Sodom, Gomorrah, Admah and Zeboiim, as far as Lasha.

a 26 Or be his slave   b 27 Japheth sounds like the Hebrew for extend. c 27 Or their   d 2 Sons may mean descendants or successors or nations; also in verses 3, 4, 6, 7, 20-23, 29 and 31.   e 4 Some manuscripts of the Masoretic Text and Samaritan Pentateuch (see also Septuagint and 1 Chron. 1:7); most manuscripts of the Masoretic Text Dodanim   f 6 That is, Egypt; also in verse 13   g 8 Father may mean ancestor or predecessor or founder; also in verses 13, 15, 24 and 26.   h 10 Or Erech and Akkad—all of them in   i 10 That is, Babylonia   j 11 Or Nineveh with its city squares k 15 Or of the Sidonians, the foremost

Living Bible

from his drunken stupor, and learned what had happened and what Ham, his younger son, had done, he cursed Ham's descendants:[1]

"A curse upon the Canaanites," he swore.
"May they be the lowest of slaves
To the descendants of Shem and Japheth."
26, 27 Then he said,
"God bless Shem,
And may Canaan be his slave.[m]
God bless Japheth,
And let him share the prosperity of Shem,
And let Canaan be his slave."[m]
28 Noah lived another 350 years after the flood, 29 and was 950 years old at his death.

10 THESE ARE the families of Shem, Ham, and Japheth, who were the three sons of Noah; for sons were born to them after the flood.
2 The sons[n] of Japheth were: Gomer, Magog, Madai, Javan, Tubal, Meshech, Tiras.
3 The sons of Gomer:
Ashkenaz, Riphath, Togarmah.
4 The sons of Javan:
Elishah, Tarshish, Kittim, Dodanim.
5 Their descendants became the maritime nations in various lands, each with a separate language. 6 The sons of Ham were: Cush, Mizraim, Put, Canaan.
7 The sons of Cush were: Seba, Havilah, Sabtah, Raamah, Sabteca.
The sons of Raamah were: Sheba, Dedan.
8 One of the descendants[o] of Cush was Nimrod, who became the first of the kings. 9 He was a mighty hunter, blessed of God,[p] and his name became proverbial. People would speak of someone as being "like Nimrod—a mighty hunter, blessed of God."[p] 10 The heart of his empire included Babel, Erech, Accad, and Calneh in the land of Shinar. 11, 12 From there he extended his reign to Assyria. He built Nineveh, Rehoboth-Ir, Calah, and Resen (which is located between Nineveh and Calah), the main city of the empire.
13, 14 Mizraim was the ancestor[q] of the people inhabiting these areas:
Ludim, Anamim, Lehabim, Naphtuhim, Pathrusim, Casluhim (from whom came the Philistines), and Caphtorim.
15-19 Canaan's oldest son was Sidon, and he was also the father of Heth; from Canaan descended these nations:
Jebusites, Amorites, Girgashites, Hivites, Arkites, Sinites, Arvadites, Zemarites, Hamathites.
Eventually the descendants of Canaan spread from Sidon all the way to Gerar, in the Gaza strip; and to Sodom, Gomorrah, Admah, and Zeboiim, near Lasha.

New Revised Standard

wine and knew what his youngest son had done to him, 25 he said,
"Cursed be Canaan;
lowest of slaves shall he be to his brothers."
26 He also said,
"Blessed by the LORD my God be Shem;
and let Canaan be his slave.
27 May God make space for[r] Japheth,
and let him live in the tents of Shem;
and let Canaan be his slave."
28 After the flood Noah lived three hundred fifty years. 29 All the days of Noah were nine hundred fifty years; and he died.

Nations Descended from Noah

10 THESE ARE the descendants of Noah's sons, Shem, Ham, and Japheth; children were born to them after the flood.
2 The descendants of Japheth: Gomer, Magog, Madai, Javan, Tubal, Meshech, and Tiras. 3 The descendants of Gomer: Ashkenaz, Riphath, and Togarmah. 4 The descendants of Javan: Elishah, Tarshish, Kittim, and Rodanim.[s] 5 From these the coastland peoples spread. These are the descendants of Japheth[t] in their lands, with their own language, by their families, in their nations.
6 The descendants of Ham: Cush, Egypt, Put, and Canaan. 7 The descendants of Cush: Seba, Havilah, Sabtah, Raamah, and Sabteca. The descendants of Raamah: Sheba and Dedan. 8 Cush became the father of Nimrod; he was the first on earth to become a mighty warrior. 9 He was a mighty hunter before the LORD; therefore it is said, "Like Nimrod a mighty hunter before the LORD." 10 The beginning of his kingdom was Babel, Erech, and Accad, all of them in the land of Shinar. 11 From that land he went into Assyria, and built Nineveh, Rehoboth-ir, Calah, and 12 Resen between Nineveh and Calah; that is the great city. 13 Egypt became the father of Ludim, Anamim, Lehabim, Naphtuhim, 14 Pathrusim, Casluhim, and Caphtorim, from which the Philistines come.[u]
15 Canaan became the father of Sidon his firstborn, and Heth, 16 and the Jebusites, the Amorites, the Girgashites, 17 the Hivites, the Arkites, the Sinites, 18 the Arvadites, the Zemarites, and the Hamathites. Afterward the families of the Canaanites spread abroad. 19 And the territory of the Canaanites extended from Sidon, in the direction of Gerar, as far as Gaza, and in the direction of Sodom, Gomorrah, Admah, and Zeboiim, as far as Lasha. 20 These are the descendants of Ham, by their

---

[1] 9:24, 25 he cursed Ham's descendants, literally, "cursed be Canaan." The Canaanites were Ham's descendants.   [m] 9:26, 27 God bless Shem, and may Canaan be his slave, or, "Blessed be Jehovah, the God of Shem . . . and may the Canaanites be Shem's slaves."   [n] 10:2 The sons, or, "descendants."   [o] 10:8 One of the descendants, or, "the son of Cush."   [p] 10:9 a mighty hunter, blessed of God, or, "a mighty hunter against the Lord."   [q] 10:13, 14 ancestor, or, "father."

[r] Heb yapht, a play on Japheth   [s] Heb Mss Sam Gk See 1 Chr 1.7: MT Dodanim   [t] Compare verses 20, 31. Heb lacks These are the descendants of Japheth   [u] Cn: Heb Casluhim, from which the Philistines come, and Caphtorim

King James

20These *are* the sons of Ham, after their families, after their tongues, in their countries, *and* in their nations.

21¶ Unto Shem also, the father of all the children of Eber, the brother of Japheth the elder, even to him were *children* born.

22The children of Shem; Elam, and Asshur, and Arphaxad, and Lud, and Aram.

23And the children of Aram; Uz, and Hul, and Gether, and Mash.

24And Arphaxad begat Salah; and Salah begat Eber.

25And unto Eber were born two sons: the name of one *was* Peleg; for in his days was the earth divided; and his brother's name *was* Joktan.

26And Joktan begat Almodad, and Sheleph, and Hazarmaveth, and Jerah,

27And Hadoram, and Uzal, and Diklah,

28And Obal, and Abimael, and Sheba,

29And Ophir, and Havilah, and Jobab: all these *were* the sons of Joktan.

30And their dwelling was from Mesha, as thou goest unto Sephar a mount of the east.

31These *are* the sons of Shem, after their families, after their tongues, in their lands, after their nations.

32These *are* the families of the sons of Noah, after their generations, in their nations: and by these were the nations divided in the earth after the flood.

11 AND THE whole earth was of one language, and of one speech.

2And it came to pass, as they journeyed from the east, that they found a plain in the land of Shinar; and they dwelt there.

3And they said one to another, Go to, let us make brick, and burn them thoroughly. And they had brick for stone, and slime had they for mortar.

4And they said, Go to, let us build us a city and a tower, whose top *may reach* unto heaven; and let us make us a name, lest we be scattered abroad upon the face of the whole earth.

5And the LORD came down to see the city and the tower, which the children of men builded.

6And the LORD said, Behold, the people *is* one, and they have all one language; and this they begin to do: and now nothing will be restrained from them, which they have imagined to do.

7Go to, let us go down, and there confound their language, that they may not understand one another's speech.

8So the LORD scattered them abroad from thence upon the face of all the earth: and they left off to build the city.

9Therefore is the name of it called Babel; because the LORD did there confound the language of all the earth: and from thence did the LORD scatter them abroad upon the face of all the earth.

10¶ These *are* the generations of Shem: Shem *was* an hundred years old, and begat Arphaxad two years after the flood:

11And Shem lived after he begat Arphaxad five hundred years, and begat sons and daughters.

New International

20These are the sons of Ham by their clans and languages, in their territories and nations.

The Semites

21Sons were also born to Shem, whose older brother wasa Japheth; Shem was the ancestor of all the sons of Eber.

22The sons of Shem:
Elam, Asshur, Arphaxad, Lud and Aram.

23The sons of Aram:
Uz, Hul, Gether and Meshech.b

24Arphaxad was the father ofc Shelah,
and Shelah the father of Eber.

25Two sons were born to Eber:
One was named Peleg,d because in his time the earth was divided; his brother was named Joktan.

26Joktan was the father of
Almodad, Sheleph, Hazarmaveth, Jerah, 27Hadoram, Uzal, Diklah, 28Obal, Abimael, Sheba, 29Ophir, Havilah and Jobab. All these were sons of Joktan.

30The region where they lived stretched from Mesha toward Sephar, in the eastern hill country.

31These are the sons of Shem by their clans and languages, in their territories and nations.

32These are the clans of Noah's sons, according to their lines of descent, within their nations. From these the nations spread out over the earth after the flood.

The Tower of Babel

11 NOW THE whole world had one language and a common speech. 2As men moved eastward,e they found a plain in Shinarf and settled there.

3They said to each other, "Come, let's make bricks and bake them thoroughly." They used brick instead of stone, and tar for mortar. 4Then they said, "Come, let us build ourselves a city, with a tower that reaches to the heavens, so that we may make a name for ourselves and not be scattered over the face of the whole earth."

5But the LORD came down to see the city and the tower that the men were building. 6The LORD said, "If as one people speaking the same language they have begun to do this, then nothing they plan to do will be impossible for them. 7Come, let us go down and confuse their language so they will not understand each other."

8So the LORD scattered them from there over all the earth, and they stopped building the city. 9That is why it was called Babelg—because there the LORD confused the language of the whole world. From there the LORD scattered them over the face of the whole earth.

From Shem to Abram

10This is the account of Shem.

Two years after the flood, when Shem was 100 years old, he became the fatherh of Arphaxad. 11And after he became the father of Arphaxad, Shem lived 500 years and had other sons and daughters.

---

a *21* Or *Shem, the older brother of*   b *23* See Septuagint and 1 Chron. 1:17; Hebrew *Mash*   c *24* Hebrew; Septuagint *father of Cainan, and Cainan was the father of*   d *25 Peleg* means *division.*   e *2* Or *from the east;* or *in the east*   f *2* That is, Babylonia   g *9* That is, Babylon; *Babel* sounds like the Hebrew for *confused.*   h *10 Father* may mean *ancestor;* also in verses 11-25.

Living Bible

20These, then, were the descendants of Ham, spread abroad in many lands and nations, with many languages. 21Eber descended from Shem, the oldest brother of Japheth. 22Here is a list of Shem's other descendants:
Elam, Asshur, Arpachshad, Lud, Aram.
23Aram's sons[i] were:
Uz, Hul, Gether, Mash.
24Arpachshad's son was Shelah, and Shelah's son was Eber.
25Two sons were born to Eber:
Peleg (meaning "Division," for during his lifetime the people of the world were separated and dispersed), and Joktan (Peleg's brother).
26-30Joktan was the father[j] of Almodad, Sheleph, Hazarmaveth, Jerah, Hadoram, Uzal, Diklah, Obal, Abima-el, Sheba, Ophir, Havi-lah, Jobab.
These descendants of Joktan lived all the way from Mesha to the eastern hills of Sephar.
31These, then, were the descendants of Shem, classified according to their political groupings, languages, and geographical locations.
32All of the men listed above descended from Noah, through many generations, living in the various nations that developed after the flood.

11 AT THAT time all mankind spoke a single language. 2As the population grew and spread eastward, a plain was discovered in the land of Babylon,[k] and was soon thickly populated.[l] 3, 4The people who lived there began to talk about building a great city, with a temple-tower reaching to the skies—a proud, eternal monument to themselves.
"This will weld us together," they said, "and keep us from scattering all over the world." So they made great piles of hardburned brick, and collected bitumen to use as mortar.
5But when God came down to see the city and the tower mankind was making, 6he said, "Look! If they are able to accomplish all this when they have just *begun* to exploit their linguistic and political unity, just think of what they will do later! Nothing will be unattainable for them![m] 7Come, let us go down and give them different languages, so that they won't understand each other's words!"
8So, in that way, God scattered them all over the earth; and that ended the building of the city. 9That is why the city was called Babel (meaning "confusion"), because it was there that Jehovah confused them by giving them many languages, thus widely scattering them across the face of the earth.
10, 11Shem's line of descendants included Arpachshad, born two years after the flood when Shem was 100 years old; after that he lived another 500 years, and had many sons and daughters.

New Revised Standard

families, their languages, their lands, and their nations.
21 To Shem also, the father of all the children of Eber, the elder brother of Japheth, children were born. 22The descendants of Shem: Elam, Asshur, Arpachshad, Lud, and Aram. 23The descendants of Aram: Uz, Hul, Gether, and Mash. 24Arpachshad became the father of Shelah; and Shelah became the father of Eber. 25To Eber were born two sons: the name of the one was Peleg,[n] for in his days the earth was divided, and his brother's name was Joktan. 26Joktan became the father of Almodad, Sheleph, Hazarmaveth, Jerah, 27Hadoram, Uzal, Diklah, 28Obal, Abimael, Sheba, 29Ophir, Havilah, and Jobab; all these were the descendants of Joktan. 30The territory in which they lived extended from Mesha in the direction of Sephar, the hill country of the east. 31These are the descendants of Shem, by their families, their languages, their lands, and their nations.
32 These are the families of Noah's sons, according to their genealogies, in their nations; and from these the nations spread abroad on the earth after the flood.

The Tower of Babel

11 NOW THE whole earth had one language and the same words. 2And as they migrated from the east,[o] they came upon a plain in the land of Shinar and settled there. 3And they said to one another, "Come, let us make bricks, and burn them thoroughly." And they had brick for stone, and bitumen for mortar. 4Then they said, "Come, let us build ourselves a city, and a tower with its top in the heavens, and let us make a name for ourselves; otherwise we shall be scattered abroad upon the face of the whole earth." 5The LORD came down to see the city and the tower, which mortals had built. 6And the LORD said, "Look, they are one people, and they have all one language; and this is only the beginning of what they will do; nothing that they propose to do will now be impossible for them. 7Come, let us go down, and confuse their language there, so that they will not understand one another's speech." 8So the LORD scattered them abroad from there over the face of all the earth, and they left off building the city. 9Therefore it was called Babel, because there the LORD confused[p] the language of all the earth; and from there the LORD scattered them abroad over the face of all the earth.

Descendants of Shem

10 These are the descendants of Shem. When Shem was one hundred years old, he became the father of Arpachshad two years after the flood; 11and Shem lived after the birth of Arpachshad five hundred years, and had other sons and daughters.

---

i 10:23 *sons*, or, "descendants." j 10:26-30 *father*, or "ancestor." k 11:2 *the land of Babylon*, literally, "the land of Shinar," located at the mouth of the Persian Gulf. l 11:2 *and was soon thickly populated*, literally, "and they settled there." m 11:6 Language is the basis on which science feeds upon itself and grows. This was the beginning of an explosion of knowledge, nipped in the bud because of wrong motives and wrong use of the knowledge gained. Similarity with today's world is significant.

n That is *Division*   o Or *migrated eastward*   p Heb *balal*, meaning *to confuse*

King James

12And Arphaxad lived five and thirty years, and begat Salah:

13And Arphaxad lived after he begat Salah four hundred and three years, and begat sons and daughters.

14And Salah lived thirty years, and begat Eber:

15And Salah lived after he begat Eber four hundred and three years, and begat sons and daughters.

16And Eber lived four and thirty years, and begat Peleg:

17And Eber lived after he begat Peleg four hundred and thirty years, and begat sons and daughters.

18And Peleg lived thirty years, and begat Reu:

19And Peleg lived after he begat Reu two hundred and nine years, and begat sons and daughters.

20And Reu lived two and thirty years, and begat Serug:

21And Reu lived after he begat Serug two hundred and seven years, and begat sons and daughters.

22And Serug lived thirty years, and begat Nahor:

23And Serug lived after he begat Nahor two hundred years, and begat sons and daughters.

24And Nahor lived nine and twenty years, and begat Terah:

25And Nahor lived after he begat Terah an hundred and nineteen years, and begat sons and daughters.

26And Terah lived seventy years, and begat Abram, Nahor, and Haran.

27¶ Now these *are* the generations of Terah: Terah begat Abram, Nahor, and Haran; and Haran begat Lot.

28And Haran died before his father Terah in the land of his nativity, in Ur of the Chaldees.

29And Abram and Nahor took them wives: the name of Abram's wife *was* Sarai; and the name of Nahor's wife, Milcah, the daughter of Haran, the father of Milcah, and the father of Iscah.

30But Sarai was barren; she *had* no child.

31And Terah took Abram his son, and Lot the son of Haran his son's son, and Sarai his daughter-in-law, his son Abram's wife; and they went forth with them from Ur of the Chaldees, to go into the land of Canaan; and they came unto Haran, and dwelt there.

32And the days of Terah were two hundred and five years: and Terah died in Haran.

12 NOW THE LORD had said unto Abram, Get thee out of thy country, and from thy kindred, and from thy father's house, unto a land that I will show thee:

2And I will make of thee a great nation, and I will bless thee, and make thy name great; and thou shalt be a blessing:

3And I will bless them that bless thee, and curse him that curseth thee: and in thee shall all families of the earth be blessed.

4So Abram departed, as the LORD had spoken unto him; and Lot went with him: and Abram *was* seventy and five years old when he departed out of Haran.

5And Abram took Sarai his wife, and Lot his brother's son, and all their substance that they had gathered, and the souls that they had gotten in Haran; and they went forth to go into the land of Canaan; and into the land of Canaan they came.

New International

12When Arphaxad had lived 35 years, he became the father of Shelah. 13And after he became the father of Shelah, Arphaxad lived 403 years and had other sons and daughters.a

14When Shelah had lived 30 years, he became the father of Eber. 15And after he became the father of Eber, Shelah lived 403 years and had other sons and daughters.

16When Eber had lived 34 years, he became the father of Peleg. 17And after he became the father of Peleg, Eber lived 430 years and had other sons and daughters.

18When Peleg had lived 30 years, he became the father of Reu. 19And after he became the father of Reu, Peleg lived 209 years and had other sons and daughters.

20When Reu had lived 32 years, he became the father of Serug. 21And after he became the father of Serug, Reu lived 207 years and had other sons and daughters.

22When Serug had lived 30 years, he became the father of Nahor. 23And after he became the father of Nahor, Serug lived 200 years and had other sons and daughters.

24When Nahor had lived 29 years, he became the father of Terah. 25And after he became the father of Terah, Nahor lived 119 years and had other sons and daughters.

26After Terah had lived 70 years, he became the father of Abram, Nahor and Haran.

27This is the account of Terah.

Terah became the father of Abram, Nahor and Haran. And Haran became the father of Lot. 28While his father Terah was still alive, Haran died in Ur of the Chaldeans, in the land of his birth. 29Abram and Nahor both married. The name of Abram's wife was Sarai, and the name of Nahor's wife was Milcah; she was the daughter of Haran, the father of both Milcah and Iscah. 30Now Sarai was barren; she had no children.

31Terah took his son Abram, his grandson Lot son of Haran, and his daughter-in-law Sarai, the wife of his son Abram, and together they set out from Ur of the Chaldeans to go to Canaan. But when they came to Haran, they settled there.

32Terah lived 205 years, and he died in Haran.

The Call of Abram

12 THE LORD had said to Abram, "Leave your country, your people and your father's household and go to the land I will show you.

2"I will make you into a great nation
and I will bless you;
I will make your name great,
and you will be a blessing.
3I will bless those who bless you,
and whoever curses you I will curse;
and all peoples on earth
will be blessed through you."

4So Abram left, as the LORD had told him; and Lot went with him. Abram was seventy-five years old when he set out from Haran. 5He took his wife Sarai, his nephew Lot, all the possessions they had accumulated and the people they had acquired in Haran, and they set out for the land of Canaan, and they arrived there.

---

a *12,13 Hebrew; Septuagint (see also Luke 3:35, 36 and note at Gen. 10:24) 35 years, he became the father of Cainan. 13And after he became the father of Cainan, Arphaxad lived 430 years and had other sons and daughters, and then he died. When Cainan had lived 130 years, he became the father of Shelah. And after he became the father of Shelah, Cainan lived 330 years and had other sons and daughters*

Living Bible

12, 13When Arpachshad was thirty-five years old, his son[b] Shelah was born, and after that he lived another 403 years, and had many sons and daughters.

14, 15Shelah was thirty years old when his son Eber was born, living 403 years after that, and had many sons and daughters.

16, 17Eber was thirty-four years old when his son Peleg was born. He lived another 430 years afterwards, and had many sons and daughters.

18, 19Peleg was thirty years old when his son Reu was born. He lived another 209 years afterwards, and had many sons and daughters.

20, 21Reu was thirty-two years old when Serug was born. He lived 207 years after that, with many sons and daughters.

22, 23Serug was thirty years old when his son Nahor was born. He lived 200 years afterwards, with many sons and daughters.

24, 25Nahor was twenty-nine years old at the birth of his son Terah. He lived 119 years afterwards, and had sons and daughters.

26By the time Terah was seventy years old, he had three sons, Abram, Nahor, and Haran.

27And Haran had a son named Lot. 28But Haran died young, in the land where he was born (in Ur of the Chaldeans), and was survived by his father.

29Meanwhile, Abram married his half-sister[c] Sarai, while his brother Nahor married their orphaned niece Milcah,[d] who was the daughter of their brother Haran; and she had a sister named Iscah. 30But Sarai was barren; she had no children. 31Then Terah took his son Abram, his grandson Lot (his son Haran's child), and his daughter-in-law Sarai, and left Ur of the Chaldeans to go to the land of Canaan; but they stopped instead at the city of Haran and settled there. 32And there Terah died at the age of 205.[e]

12 GOD HAD told Abram, "Leave your own country behind you, and your own people, and go to the land I will guide you to. 2If you do, I will cause you to become the father of a great nation; I will bless you and make your name famous, and you will be a blessing to many others.[f] 3I will bless those who bless you and curse those who curse you; and the entire world will be blessed because of you."[g]

4So Abram departed as the Lord had instructed him, and Lot went too; Abram was seventy-five years old at that time. 5He took his wife Sarai, his nephew Lot, and all his wealth—the cattle and slaves he had gotten in Haran—and finally arrived in Canaan. 6Traveling

---

b 11:12, 13 his son, or, by Hebrew usage, "there was born to him the ancestor of Shelah, and after that . . ." So also throughout the remainder of the chapter. c 11:29 half-sister, implied. (See 20:12.) d 11:29 orphaned niece Milcah, implied. e 11:32 age of 205, implied. The Samaritan Pentateuch says that Terah died when he was 145 years old, so that his death occurred in the year of Abraham's departure from Haran. This is more consistent with 11:26 and 12:4. See also Acts 7:4. f 12:2 you will be a blessing to many others, or, "I will make your name so famous that it will be used to pronounce blessings on others." g 12:3 the entire world will be blessed because of you, or, "the nations will bless themselves because of you."

New Revised Standard

12 When Arpachshad had lived thirty-five years, he became the father of Shelah; 13and Arpachshad lived after the birth of Shelah four hundred three years, and had other sons and daughters.

14 When Shelah had lived thirty years, he became the father of Eber; 15and Shelah lived after the birth of Eber four hundred three years, and had other sons and daughters.

16 When Eber had lived thirty-four years, he became the father of Peleg; 17and Eber lived after the birth of Peleg four hundred thirty years, and had other sons and daughters.

18 When Peleg had lived thirty years, he became the father of Reu; 19and Peleg lived after the birth of Reu two hundred nine years, and had other sons and daughters.

20 When Reu had lived thirty-two years, he became the father of Serug; 21and Reu lived after the birth of Serug two hundred seven years, and had other sons and daughters.

22 When Serug had lived thirty years, he became the father of Nahor; 23and Serug lived after the birth of Nahor two hundred years, and had other sons and daughters.

24 When Nahor had lived twenty-nine years, he became the father of Terah; 25and Nahor lived after the birth of Terah one hundred nineteen years, and had other sons and daughters.

26 When Terah had lived seventy years, he became the father of Abram, Nahor, and Haran.

Descendants of Terah

27 Now these are the descendants of Terah. Terah was the father of Abram, Nahor, and Haran; and Haran was the father of Lot. 28Haran died before his father Terah in the land of his birth, in Ur of the Chaldeans. 29Abram and Nahor took wives; the name of Abram's wife was Sarai, and the name of Nahor's wife was Milcah. She was the daughter of Haran the father of Milcah and Iscah. 30Now Sarai was barren; she had no child.

31 Terah took his son Abram and his grandson Lot son of Haran, and his daughter-in-law Sarai, his son Abram's wife, and they went out together from Ur of the Chaldeans to go into the land of Canaan; but when they came to Haran, they settled there. 32The days of Terah were two hundred five years; and Terah died in Haran.

The Call of Abram

12 NOW THE LORD said to Abram, "Go from your country and your kindred and your father's house to the land that I will show you. 2I will make of you a great nation, and I will bless you, and make your name great, so that you will be a blessing. 3I will bless those who bless you, and the one who curses you I will curse; and in you all the families of the earth shall be blessed."[h]

4 So Abram went, as the LORD had told him; and Lot went with him. Abram was seventy-five years old when he departed from Haran. 5Abram took his wife Sarai and his brother's son Lot, and all the possessions that they had gathered, and the persons whom they had acquired in Haran; and they set forth to go to the land of Canaan. When they had come to the land of Canaan, 6Abram

---

h Or by you all the families of the earth shall bless themselves

King James

6¶ And Abram passed through the land unto the place of Sichem, unto the plain of Moreh. And the Canaanite *was* then in the land.

7And the LORD appeared unto Abram, and said, Unto thy seed will I give this land: and there builded he an altar unto the LORD, who appeared unto him.

8And he removed from thence unto a mountain on the east of Beth-el, and pitched his tent, *having* Beth-el on the west, and Hai on the east: and there he builded an altar unto the LORD, and called upon the name of the LORD.

9And Abram journeyed, going on still toward the south.

10¶ And there was a famine in the land: and Abram went down into Egypt to sojourn there; for the famine *was* grievous in the land.

11And it came to pass, when he was come near to enter into Egypt, that he said unto Sarai his wife, Behold now, I know that thou *art* a fair woman to look upon:

12Therefore it shall come to pass, when the Egyptians shall see thee, that they shall say, This *is* his wife: and they will kill me, but they will save thee alive.

13Say, I pray thee, thou *art* my sister: that it may be well with me for thy sake; and my soul shall live because of thee.

14¶ And it came to pass, that, when Abram was come into Egypt, the Egyptians beheld the woman that she *was* very fair.

15The princes also of Pharaoh saw her, and commended her before Pharaoh: and the woman was taken into Pharaoh's house.

16And he entreated Abram well for her sake: and he had sheep, and oxen, and he asses, and menservants, and maidservants, and she asses, and camels.

17And the LORD plagued Pharaoh and his house with great plagues because of Sarai Abram's wife.

18And Pharaoh called Abram, and said, What *is* this *that* thou hast done unto me? why didst thou not tell me that she *was* thy wife?

19Why saidst thou, She *is* my sister? so I might have taken her to me to wife: now therefore behold thy wife, take *her*, and go thy way.

20And Pharaoh commanded *his* men concerning him: and they sent him away, and his wife, and all that he had.

13 AND ABRAM went up out of Egypt, he, and his wife, and all that he had, and Lot with him, into the south.

2And Abram *was* very rich in cattle, in silver, and in gold.

3And he went on his journeys from the south even to Beth-el, unto the place where his tent had been at the beginning, between Beth-el and Hai;

4Unto the place of the altar, which he had made there at the first: and there Abram called on the name of the LORD.

5¶ And Lot also, which went with Abram, had flocks, and herds, and tents.

6And the land was not able to bear them, that they might dwell together: for their substance was great, so that they could not dwell together.

7And there was a strife between the herdmen of Abram's cattle and the herdmen of Lot's cattle: and the Canaanite and the Perizzite dwelled then in the land.

8And Abram said unto Lot, Let there be no strife, I pray thee, between me and thee, and between my herdmen and thy herdmen; for we *be* brethren.

New International

6Abram traveled through the land as far as the site of the great tree of Moreh at Shechem. At that time the Canaanites were in the land. 7The LORD appeared to Abram and said, "To your offspring[a] I will give this land." So he built an altar there to the LORD, who had appeared to him.

8From there he went on toward the hills east of Bethel and pitched his tent, with Bethel on the west and Ai on the east. There he built an altar to the LORD and called on the name of the LORD. 9Then Abram set out and continued toward the Negev.

Abram in Egypt

10Now there was a famine in the land, and Abram went down to Egypt to live there for a while because the famine was severe. 11As he was about to enter Egypt, he said to his wife Sarai, "I know what a beautiful woman you are. 12When the Egyptians see you, they will say, 'This is his wife.' Then they will kill me but will let you live. 13Say you are my sister, so that I will be treated well for your sake and my life will be spared because of you."

14When Abram came to Egypt, the Egyptians saw that she was a very beautiful woman. 15And when Pharaoh's officials saw her, they praised her to Pharaoh, and she was taken into his palace. 16He treated Abram well for her sake, and Abram acquired sheep and cattle, male and female donkeys, menservants and maidservants, and camels.

17But the LORD inflicted serious diseases on Pharaoh and his household because of Abram's wife Sarai. 18So Pharaoh summoned Abram. "What have you done to me?" he said. "Why didn't you tell me she was your wife? 19Why did you say, 'She is my sister,' so that I took her to be my wife? Now then, here is your wife. Take her and go!" 20Then Pharaoh gave orders about Abram to his men, and they sent him on his way, with his wife and everything he had.

Abram and Lot Separate

13 SO ABRAM went up from Egypt to the Negev, with his wife and everything he had, and Lot went with him. 2Abram had become very wealthy in livestock and in silver and gold.

3From the Negev he went from place to place until he came to Bethel, to the place between Bethel and Ai where his tent had been earlier 4and where he had first built an altar. There Abram called on the name of the LORD.

5Now Lot, who was moving about with Abram, also had flocks and herds and tents. 6But the land could not support them while they stayed together, for their possessions were so great that they were not able to stay together. 7And quarreling arose between Abram's herdsmen and the herdsmen of Lot. The Canaanites and Perizzites were also living in the land at that time.

8So Abram said to Lot, "Let's not have any quarreling between you and me, or between your herdsmen and mine, for we are brothers. 9Is not the whole land before

Living Bible

with them Lot—Abram's nephew[h] who lived in Sodom—and all he owned. 13One of the men who escaped came and told Abram the Hebrew, who was camping among the oaks belonging to Mamre the Amorite (brother of Eshcol and Aner, Abram's allies).

14When Abram learned that Lot had been captured, he called together the men born into his household, 318 of them in all, and chased after the retiring army as far as Dan. 15He divided his men and attacked during the night from several directions, and pursued the fleeing army to Hobah, north of Damascus, 16and recovered everything—the loot that had been taken, his relative Lot, and all of Lot's possessions, including the women and other captives.

17As Abram returned from his strike against Ched-or-laomer and the other kings at the Valley of Shaveh (later called King's Valley), the king of Sodom came out to meet him, 18and Melchizedek, the king of Salem (Jerusalem), who was a priest of the God of Highest Heaven, brought him bread and wine. 19, 20Then Melchizedek blessed Abram with this blessing:

"The blessing of the supreme God, Creator of heaven and earth, be upon you, Abram; and blessed be God, who has delivered your enemies over to you."

Then Abram gave Melchizedek a tenth of all the loot.

21The king of Sodom told him, "Just give me back my people who were captured; keep for yourself the booty stolen from my city."

22But Abram replied, "I have solemnly promised Jehovah, the supreme God, Creator of heaven and earth, 23that I will not take so much as a single thread from you, lest you say, 'Abram is rich because of what I gave him!' 24All I'll accept is what these young men of mine have eaten; but give a share of the loot to Aner, Eshcol, and Mamre, my allies."

15 AFTERWARDS JEHOVAH spoke to Abram in a vision, and this is what he told him: "Don't be fearful, Abram, for I will defend you. And I will give you great blessings."

2, 3But Abram replied, "O Lord Jehovah, what good are all your blessings when I have no son? For without a son, some other member of my household[i] will inherit all my wealth."

4Then Jehovah told him, "No, no one else will be your heir, for you will have a son to inherit everything you own."

5Then God brought Abram outside beneath the nighttime sky and told him, "Look up into the heavens and count the stars if you can. Your descendants will be like that—too many to count!" 6And Abram believed God; then God considered him righteous on account of his faith.

7And he told him, "I am Jehovah who brought you out of the city of Ur of the Chaldeans, to give you this land."

8But Abram replied, "O Lord Jehovah, how can I be sure that you will give it to me?" 9Then Jehovah told him to take a three-year-old heifer, a three-year-old female goat, a three-year-old ram, a turtledove and a young pigeon, 10and to slay them and to cut them apart down

New Revised Standard

who lived in Sodom, and his goods, and departed.

13 Then one who had escaped came and told Abram the Hebrew, who was living by the oaks[j] of Mamre the Amorite, brother of Eshcol and of Aner; these were allies of Abram. 14When Abram heard that his nephew had been taken captive, he led forth his trained men, born in his house, three hundred eighteen of them, and went in pursuit as far as Dan. 15He divided his forces against them by night, he and his servants, and routed them and pursued them to Hobah, north of Damascus. 16Then he brought back all the goods, and also brought back his nephew Lot with his goods, and the women and the people.

Abram Blessed by Melchizedek

17 After his return from the defeat of Chedorlaomer and the kings who were with him, the king of Sodom went out to meet him at the Valley of Shaveh (that is, the King's Valley). 18And King Melchizedek of Salem brought out bread and wine; he was priest of God Most High.[k] 19He blessed him and said,

"Blessed be Abram by God Most High,[k]
    maker of heaven and earth;
20 and blessed be God Most High,[k]
    who has delivered your enemies into your
        hand!"

And Abram gave him one tenth of everything. 21Then the king of Sodom said to Abram, "Give me the persons, but take the goods for yourself." 22But Abram said to the king of Sodom, "I have sworn to the LORD, God Most High,[k] maker of heaven and earth, 23that I would not take a thread or a sandal-thong or anything that is yours, so that you might not say, 'I have made Abram rich.' 24I will take nothing but what the young men have eaten, and the share of the men who went with me—Aner, Eshcol, and Mamre. Let them take their share."

God's Covenant with Abram

15 AFTER THESE things the word of the LORD came to Abram in a vision, "Do not be afraid, Abram, I am your shield; your reward shall be very great." 2But Abram said, "O Lord GOD, what will you give me, for I continue childless, and the heir of my house is Eliezer of Damascus?"[l] 3And Abram said, "You have given me no offspring, and so a slave born in my house is to be my heir." 4But the word of the LORD came to him, "This man shall not be your heir; no one but your very own issue shall be your heir." 5He brought him outside and said, "Look toward heaven and count the stars, if you are able to count them." Then he said to him, "So shall your descendants be." 6And he believed the LORD; and the LORD[m] reckoned it to him as righteousness.

7 Then he said to him, "I am the LORD who brought you from Ur of the Chaldeans, to give you this land to possess." 8But he said, "O Lord GOD, how am I to know that I shall possess it?" 9He said to him, "Bring me a heifer three years old, a female goat three years old, a ram three years old, a turtledove, and a young pigeon."

---

h 14:12 *Abram's nephew,* literally, "Abram's brother's son."
i 15:2, 3 *some other member of my household* was Eliezer of Damascus.

j Or *terebinths*   k Heb *El Elyon*   l Meaning of Heb uncertain   m Heb *he*

King James

10And he took unto him all these, and divided them in the midst, and laid each piece one against another: but the birds divided he not.

11And when the fowls came down upon the carcases, Abram drove them away.

12And when the sun was going down, a deep sleep fell upon Abram; and, lo, an horror of great darkness fell upon him.

13And he said unto Abram, Know of a surety that thy seed shall be a stranger in a land *that is* not theirs, and shall serve them; and they shall afflict them four hundred years;

14And also that nation, whom they shall serve, will I judge: and afterward shall they come out with great substance.

15And thou shalt go to thy fathers in peace; thou shalt be buried in a good old age.

16But in the fourth generation they shall come hither again: for the iniquity of the Amorites *is* not yet full.

17And it came to pass, that, when the sun went down, and it was dark, behold a smoking furnace, and a burning lamp that passed between those pieces.

18In the same day the LORD made a covenant with Abram, saying, Unto thy seed have I given this land, from the river of Egypt unto the great river, the river Euphrates:

19The Kenites, and the Kenizzites, and the Kadmonites,

20And the Hittites, and the Perizzites, and the Rephaims,

21And the Amorites, and the Canaanites, and the Girgashites, and the Jebusites.

16 NOW SARAI Abram's wife bare him no children: and she had an handmaid, an Egyptian, whose name *was* Hagar.

2And Sarai said unto Abram, Behold now, the LORD hath restrained me from bearing: I pray thee, go in unto my maid; it may be that I may obtain children by her. And Abram hearkened to the voice of Sarai.

3And Sarai Abram's wife took Hagar her maid the Egyptian, after Abram had dwelt ten years in the land of Canaan, and gave her to her husband Abram to be his wife.

4¶ And he went in unto Hagar, and she conceived: and when she saw that she had conceived, her mistress was despised in her eyes.

5And Sarai said unto Abram, My wrong *be* upon thee: I have given my maid into thy bosom; and when she saw that she had conceived, I was despised in her eyes: the LORD judge between me and thee.

6But Abram said unto Sarai, Behold, thy maid *is* in thy hand; do to her as it pleaseth thee. And when Sarai dealt hardly with her, she fled from her face.

7¶ And the angel of the LORD found her by a fountain of water in the wilderness, by the fountain in the way to Shur.

8And he said, Hagar, Sarai's maid, whence camest thou? and whither wilt thou go? And she said, I flee from the face of my mistress Sarai.

9And the angel of the LORD said unto her, Return to thy mistress, and submit thyself under her hands.

10And the angel of the LORD said unto her, I will multiply thy seed exceedingly, that it shall not be numbered for multitude.

New International

10Abram brought all these to him, cut them in two and arranged the halves opposite each other; the birds, however, he did not cut in half. 11Then birds of prey came down on the carcasses, but Abram drove them away.

12As the sun was setting, Abram fell into a deep sleep, and a thick and dreadful darkness came over him. 13Then the LORD said to him, "Know for certain that your descendants will be strangers in a country not their own, and they will be enslaved and mistreated four hundred years. 14But I will punish the nation they serve as slaves, and afterward they will come out with great possessions. 15You, however, will go to your fathers in peace and be buried at a good old age. 16In the fourth generation your descendants will come back here, for the sin of the Amorites has not yet reached its full measure."

17When the sun had set and darkness had fallen, a smoking firepot with a blazing torch appeared and passed between the pieces. 18On that day the LORD made a covenant with Abram and said, "To your descendants I give this land, from the river[a] of Egypt to the great river, the Euphrates— 19the land of the Kenites, Kenizzites, Kadmonites, 20Hittites, Perizzites, Rephaites, 21Amorites, Canaanites, Girgashites and Jebusites."

Hagar and Ishmael

16 NOW SARAI, Abram's wife, had borne him no children. But she had an Egyptian maidservant named Hagar; 2so she said to Abram, "The LORD has kept me from having children. Go, sleep with my maidservant; perhaps I can build a family through her."

Abram agreed to what Sarai said. 3So after Abram had been living in Canaan ten years, Sarai his wife took her Egyptian maidservant Hagar and gave her to her husband to be his wife. 4He slept with Hagar, and she conceived.

When she knew she was pregnant, she began to despise her mistress. 5Then Sarai said to Abram, "You are responsible for the wrong I am suffering. I put my servant in your arms, and now that she knows she is pregnant, she despises me. May the LORD judge between you and me."

6"Your servant is in your hands," Abram said. "Do with her whatever you think best." Then Sarai mistreated Hagar; so she fled from her.

7The angel of the LORD found Hagar near a spring in the desert; it was the spring that is beside the road to Shur. 8And he said, "Hagar, servant of Sarai, where have you come from, and where are you going?"

"I'm running away from my mistress Sarai," she answered.

9Then the angel of the LORD told her, "Go back to your mistress and submit to her." 10The angel added, "I will so increase your descendants that they will be too numerous to count."

Living Bible

the middle, and to separate the halves, but not to divide the birds. 11And when the vultures came down upon the carcasses, Abram shooed them away.

12That evening as the sun was going down, a deep sleep fell upon Abram, and a vision of terrible foreboding, darkness, and horror.

13Then Jehovah told Abram, "Your descendants will be oppressed as slaves in a foreign land for 400 years. 14But I will punish the nation that enslaves them, and at the end they will come away with great wealth. 15(But you will die in peace, at a ripe old age.) 16After four generations they will return here to this land; for the wickedness of the Amorite nations living here nowb will not be ready for punishment until then."

17As the sun went down and it was dark, Abram saw a smoking fire-pot and a flaming torch that passed between the halves of the carcasses. 18So that day Jehovah made this covenant with Abram: "I have given this land to your descendants from the Wadi-el-Arishc to the Euphrates River. 19, 20, 21And I give to them these nations: Kenites, Kenizzites, Kadmonites, Hittites, Perizzites, Rephaim, Amorites, Canaanites, Girgashites, Jebusites."

16 BUT SARAI and Abram had no children. So Sarai took her maid, an Egyptian girl named Hagar, 2, 3and gave her to Abram to be his second wife. "Since the Lord has given me no children," Sarai said, "you may sleep with my servant girl, and her children shall be mine."

And Abram agreed. (This took place ten years after Abram had first arrived in the land of Canaan.) 4So he slept with Hagar, and she conceived; and when she realized she was pregnant, she became very proud and arrogant toward her mistress Sarai.

5Then Sarai said to Abram, "It's all your fault. For now this servant girl of mine despises me, though I myself gave her the privilege of being your wife. May the Lord judge you for doing this to me!"d

6"You have my permission to punish the girl as you see fit," Abram replied. So Sarai beat her and she ran away.

7The Angel of the Lord found her beside a desert spring along the road to Shur.

8The Angel: "Hagar, Sarai's maid, where have you come from, and where are you going?"

Hagar: "I am running away from my mistress."

9-12The Angel: "Return to your mistress and act as you should, for I will make you into a great nation. Yes, you are pregnant and your baby will be a son, and you are to name him Ishmael ('God hears'), because God has heard your woes. This son of yours will be a wild one—free and untamed as a wild ass!

New Revised Standard

10He brought him all these and cut them in two, laying each half over against the other; but he did not cut the birds in two. 11And when birds of prey came down on the carcasses, Abram drove them away.

12 As the sun was going down, a deep sleep fell upon Abram, and a deep and terrifying darkness descended upon him. 13Then the LORDe said to Abram, "Know this for certain, that your offspring shall be aliens in a land that is not theirs, and shall be slaves there, and they shall be oppressed for four hundred years; 14but I will bring judgment on the nation that they serve, and afterward they shall come out with great possessions. 15As for yourself, you shall go to your ancestors in peace; you shall be buried in a good old age. 16And they shall come back here in the fourth generation; for the iniquity of the Amorites is not yet complete."

17 When the sun had gone down and it was dark, a smoking fire pot and a flaming torch passed between these pieces. 18On that day the LORD made a covenant with Abram, saying, "To your descendants I give this land, from the river of Egypt to the great river, the river Euphrates, 19the land of the Kenites, the Kenizzites, the Kadmonites, 20the Hittites, the Perizzites, the Rephaim, 21the Amorites, the Canaanites, the Girgashites, and the Jebusites."

The Birth of Ishmael

16 NOW SARAI, Abram's wife, bore him no children. She had an Egyptian slave-girl whose name was Hagar, 2and Sarai said to Abram, "You see that the LORD has prevented me from bearing children; go in to my slave-girl; it may be that I shall obtain children by her." And Abram listened to the voice of Sarai. 3So, after Abram had lived ten years in the land of Canaan, Sarai, Abram's wife, took Hagar the Egyptian, her slave-girl, and gave her to her husband Abram as a wife. 4He went in to Hagar, and she conceived; and when she saw that she had conceived, she looked with contempt on her mistress. 5Then Sarai said to Abram, "May the wrong done to me be on you! I gave my slave-girl to your embrace, and when she saw that she had conceived, she looked on me with contempt. May the LORD judge between you and me!" 6But Abram said to Sarai, "Your slave-girl is in your power; do to her as you please." Then Sarai dealt harshly with her, and she ran away from her.

7 The angel of the LORD found her by a spring of water in the wilderness, the spring on the way to Shur. 8And he said, "Hagar, slave-girl of Sarai, where have you come from and where are you going?" She said, "I am running away from my mistress Sarai." 9The angel of the LORD said to her, "Return to your mistress, and submit to her." 10The angel of the LORD also said to her, "I will so greatly multiply your offspring that they can-

---

b 15:16 Amorite nations living here now, implied.   c 15:18 Wadi-el-Arish, literally, "River of Egypt," at the southern border of Judah.   d 16:5 May the Lord judge you for doing this to me, literally, "Let the Lord judge between me and you."

e Heb he

King James

11And the angel of the LORD said unto her, Behold, thou *art* with child, and shalt bear a son, and shalt call his name Ishmael; because the LORD hath heard thy affliction.

12And he will be a wild man; his hand *will be* against every man, and every man's hand against him; and he shall dwell in the presence of all his brethren.

13And she called the name of the LORD that spake unto her, Thou God seest me: for she said, Have I also here looked after him that seeth me?

14Wherefore the well was called Beer-lahai-roi; behold, *it is* between Kadesh and Bered.

15¶ And Hagar bare Abram a son: and Abram called his son's name, which Hagar bare, Ishmael.

16And Abram *was* fourscore and six years old, when Hagar bare Ishmael to Abram.

17 AND WHEN Abram was ninety years old and nine, the LORD appeared to Abram, and said unto him, I *am* the Almighty God; walk before me, and be thou perfect.

2And I will make my covenant between me and thee, and will multiply thee exceedingly.

3And Abram fell on his face: and God talked with him, saying,

4As for me, behold, my covenant *is* with thee, and thou shalt be a father of many nations.

5Neither shall thy name any more be called Abram, but thy name shall be Abraham; for a father of many nations have I made thee.

6And I will make thee exceeding fruitful, and I will make nations of thee, and kings shall come out of thee.

7And I will establish my covenant between me and thee and thy seed after thee in their generations for an everlasting covenant, to be a God unto thee, and to thy seed after thee.

8And I will give unto thee, and to thy seed after thee, the land wherein thou art a stranger, all the land of Canaan, for an everlasting possession; and I will be their God.

9¶ And God said unto Abraham, Thou shalt keep my covenant therefore, thou, and thy seed after thee in their generations.

10This *is* my covenant, which ye shall keep, between me and you and thy seed after thee; Every man child among you shall be circumcised.

11And ye shall circumcise the flesh of your foreskin; and it shall be a token of the covenant betwixt me and you.

12And he that is eight days old shall be circumcised among you, every man child in your generations, he that is born in the house, or bought with money of any stranger, which *is* not of thy seed.

13He that is born in thy house, and he that is bought with thy money, must needs be circumcised: and my covenant shall be in your flesh for an everlasting covenant.

14And the uncircumcised man child whose flesh of his foreskin is not circumcised, that soul shall be cut off from his people; he hath broken my covenant.

15¶ And God said unto Abraham, As for Sarai thy wife, thou shalt not call her name Sarai, but Sarah *shall* her name *be*.

New International

11The angel of the LORD also said to her:

"You are now with child
  and you will have a son.
You shall name him Ishmael,[a]
  for the LORD has heard of your misery.
12He will be a wild donkey of a man;
  his hand will be against everyone
  and everyone's hand against him,
and he will live in hostility
  toward[b] all his brothers."

13She gave this name to the LORD who spoke to her: "You are the God who sees me," for she said, "I have now seen[c] the One who sees me." 14That is why the well was called Beer Lahai Roi[d]; it is still there, between Kadesh and Bered.

15So Hagar bore Abram a son, and Abram gave the name Ishmael to the son she had borne. 16Abram was eighty-six years old when Hagar bore him Ishmael.

The Covenant of Circumcision

17 WHEN ABRAM was ninety-nine years old, the LORD appeared to him and said, "I am God Almighty[e]; walk before me and be blameless. 2I will confirm my covenant between me and you and will greatly increase your numbers."

3Abram fell facedown, and God said to him, 4"As for me, this is my covenant with you: You will be the father of many nations. 5No longer will you be called Abram[f]; your name will be Abraham,[g] for I have made you a father of many nations. 6I will make you very fruitful; I will make nations of you, and kings will come from you. 7I will establish my covenant as an everlasting covenant between me and you and your descendants after you for the generations to come, to be your God and the God of your descendants after you. 8The whole land of Canaan, where you are now an alien, I will give as an everlasting possession to you and your descendants after you; and I will be their God."

9Then God said to Abraham, "As for you, you must keep my covenant, you and your descendants after you for the generations to come. 10This is my covenant with you and your descendants after you, the covenant you are to keep: Every male among you shall be circumcised. 11You are to undergo circumcision, and it will be the sign of the covenant between me and you. 12For the generations to come every male among you who is eight days old must be circumcised, including those born in your household or bought with money from a foreigner—those who are not your offspring. 13Whether born in your household or bought with your money, they must be circumcised. My covenant in your flesh is to be an everlasting covenant. 14Any uncircumcised male, who has not been circumcised in the flesh, will be cut off from his people; he has broken my covenant."

15God also said to Abraham, "As for Sarai your wife, you are no longer to call her Sarai; her name will be Sarah. 16I will bless her and will surely give you a son

a 11 *Ishmael* means *God hears*.   b 12 Or *live to the east / of*   c 13 Or *seen the back of*   d 14 *Beer Lahai Roi* means *well of the Living One who sees me*.   e 1 Hebrew *El-Shaddai*   f 5 *Abram* means *exalted father*.   g 5 *Abraham* means *father of many*.

Living Bible

He will be against everyone, and everyone will feel the same towards him. But he will live near the rest of his kin."

13Thereafterh Hagar spoke of Jehovah—for it was he who appeared to her—as "the God who looked upon me," for she thought, "I saw God and lived to tell it."

14Later that well was named "The Well of the Living One Who Sees Me." It lies between Kadesh and Bered.

15So Hagar gave Abram a son, and Abram named him Ishmael. 16(Abram was eighty-six years old at this time.)

17 WHEN ABRAM was ninety-nine years old, God appeared to him and told him, "I am the Almighty; obey me and live as you should. 2, 3, 4I will prepare a contract between us, guaranteeing to make you into a mighty nation. In fact you shall be the father of not only one nation, but a multitude of nations!" Abram fell face downward in the dust as God talked with him.

5"What's more," God told him, "I am changing your name. It is no longer 'Abram' ('Exalted Father'), but 'Abraham' ('Father of Nations')—for that is what you will be. I have declared it. 6I will give you millions of descendants who will form many nations! Kings shall be among your descendants! 7, 8And I will continue this agreement between us, generation after generation, forever, for it shall be between me and your children as well. It is a contract that I shall be your God and the God of your posterity. And I will give all this land of Canaan to you and them, forever. And I will be your God.

9, 10"Your part of the contract," God told him, "is to obey its terms. You personally and all your posterity have this continual responsibility: that every male among you shall be circumcised; 11the foreskin of his penis shall be cut off. This will be the proof that you and they accept this covenant. 12Every male shall be circumcised on the eighth day after birth. This applies to every foreign-born slave as well as to everyone born in your household. This is a permanent part of this contract, and it applies to all your posterity. 13All must be circumcised. Your bodies will thus be marked as participants in my everlasting covenant. 14Anyone who refuses these terms shall be cut off from his people; for he has violated my contract."

15Then God added, "Regarding Sarai your wife—her name is no longer 'Sarai' but 'Sarah' ('Princess'). 16And

New Revised Standard

not be counted for multitude." 11And the angel of the LORD said to her,

"Now you have conceived and shall bear a
son;
you shall call him Ishmael,i
for the LORD has given heed to your
affliction.
12 He shall be a wild ass of a man,
with his hand against everyone,
and everyone's hand against him;
and he shall live at odds with all his kin."

13So she named the LORD who spoke to her, "You are El-roi";j for she said, "Have I really seen God and remained alive after seeing him?"k 14Therefore the well was called Beer-lahai-roi;l it lies between Kadesh and Bered.

15 Hagar bore Abram a son; and Abram named his son, whom Hagar bore, Ishmael. 16Abram was eighty-six years old when Hagar bore himm Ishmael.

The Sign of the Covenant

17 WHEN ABRAM was ninety-nine years old, the LORD appeared to Abram, and said to him, "I am God Almighty;n walk before me, and be blameless. 2And I will make my covenant between me and you, and will make you exceedingly numerous." 3Then Abram fell on his face; and God said to him, 4"As for me, this is my covenant with you: You shall be the ancestor of a multitude of nations. 5No longer shall your name be Abram,o but your name shall be Abraham;p for I have made you the ancestor of a multitude of nations. 6I will make you exceedingly fruitful; and I will make nations of you, and kings shall come from you. 7I will establish my covenant between me and you, and your offspring after you throughout their generations, for an everlasting covenant, to be God to you and to your offspringq after you. 8And I will give to you, and to your offspring after you, the land where you are now an alien, all the land of Canaan, for a perpetual holding; and I will be their God."

9 God said to Abraham, "As for you, you shall keep my covenant, you and your offspring after you throughout their generations. 10This is my covenant, which you shall keep, between me and you and your offspring after you: Every male among you shall be circumcised. 11You shall circumcise the flesh of your foreskins, and it shall be a sign of the covenant between me and you. 12Throughout your generations every male among you shall be circumcised when he is eight days old, including the slave born in your house and the one bought with your money from any foreigner who is not of your offspring. 13Both the slave born in your house and the one bought with your money must be circumcised. So shall my covenant be in your flesh an everlasting covenant. 14Any uncircumcised male who is not circumcised in the flesh of his foreskin shall be cut off from his people; he has broken my covenant."

15 God said to Abraham, "As for Sarai your wife, you shall not call her Sarai, but Sarah shall be her name.

i That is God hears   j Perhaps God of seeing or God who sees   k Meaning of Heb uncertain   l That is the Well of the Living One who sees me   m Heb Abram   n Traditional rendering of Heb El Shaddai   o That is exalted ancestor   p Here taken to mean ancestor of a multitude   q Heb seed

h 16:13 Thereafter, implied.

King James

16And I will bless her, and give thee a son also of her: yea, I will bless her, and she shall be *a mother* of nations; kings of people shall be of her.

17Then Abraham fell upon his face, and laughed, and said in his heart, Shall *a child* be born unto him that is an hundred years old? and shall Sarah, that is ninety years old, bear?

18And Abraham said unto God, O that Ishmael might live before thee!

19And God said, Sarah thy wife shall bear thee a son indeed; and thou shalt call his name Isaac: and I will establish my covenant with him for an everlasting covenant, *and* with his seed after him.

20And as for Ishmael, I have heard thee: Behold, I have blessed him, and will make him fruitful, and will multiply him exceedingly; twelve princes shall he beget, and I will make him a great nation.

21But my covenant will I establish with Isaac, which Sarah shall bear unto thee at this set time in the next year.

22And he left off talking with him, and God went up from Abraham.

23¶ And Abraham took Ishmael his son, and all that were born in his house, and all that were bought with his money, every male among the men of Abraham's house; and circumcised the flesh of their foreskin in the selfsame day, as God had said unto him.

24And Abraham *was* ninety years old and nine, when he was circumcised in the flesh of his foreskin.

25And Ishmael his son *was* thirteen years old, when he was circumcised in the flesh of his foreskin.

26In the selfsame day was Abraham circumcised, and Ishmael his son.

27And all the men of his house, born in the house, and bought with money of the stranger, were circumcised with him.

18 AND THE LORD appeared unto him in the plains of Mamre: and he sat in the tent door in the heat of the day;

2And he lift up his eyes and looked, and, lo, three men stood by him: and when he saw *them*, he ran to meet them from the tent door, and bowed himself toward the ground,

3And said, My Lord, if now I have found favour in thy sight, pass not away, I pray thee, from thy servant:

4Let a little water, I pray you, be fetched, and wash your feet, and rest yourselves under the tree:

5And I will fetch a morsel of bread, and comfort ye your hearts; after that ye shall pass on: for therefore are ye come to your servant. And they said, So do, as thou hast said.

6And Abraham hastened into the tent unto Sarah, and said, Make ready quickly three measures of fine meal, knead *it*, and make cakes upon the hearth.

7And Abraham ran unto the herd, and fetched a calf tender and good, and gave *it* unto a young man; and he hasted to dress it.

8And he took butter, and milk, and the calf which he had dressed, and set *it* before them; and he stood by them under the tree, and they did eat.

9¶ And they said unto him, Where *is* Sarah thy wife? And he said, Behold, in the tent.

10And he said, I will certainly return unto thee according to the time of life; and, lo, Sarah thy wife shall have a son. And Sarah heard *it* in the tent door, which *was* behind him.

11Now Abraham and Sarah *were* old *and* well stricken in age; *and* it ceased to be with Sarah after the manner of women.

New International

by her. I will bless her so that she will be the mother of nations; kings of peoples will come from her."

17Abraham fell facedown; he laughed and said to himself, "Will a son be born to a man a hundred years old? Will Sarah bear a child at the age of ninety?" 18And Abraham said to God, "If only Ishmael might live under your blessing!"

19Then God said, "Yes, but your wife Sarah will bear you a son, and you will call him Isaac.[a] I will establish my covenant with him as an everlasting covenant for his descendants after him. 20And as for Ishmael, I have heard you: I will surely bless him; I will make him fruitful and will greatly increase his numbers. He will be the father of twelve rulers, and I will make him into a great nation. 21But my covenant I will establish with Isaac, whom Sarah will bear to you by this time next year." 22When he had finished speaking with Abraham, God went up from him.

23On that very day Abraham took his son Ishmael and all those born in his household or bought with his money, every male in his household, and circumcised them, as God told him. 24Abraham was ninety-nine years old when he was circumcised, 25and his son Ishmael was thirteen; 26Abraham and his son Ishmael were both circumcised on that same day. 27And every male in Abraham's household, including those born in his household or bought from a foreigner, was circumcised with him.

The Three Visitors

18 THE LORD appeared to Abraham near the great trees of Mamre while he was sitting at the entrance to his tent in the heat of the day. 2Abraham looked up and saw three men standing nearby. When he saw them, he hurried from the entrance of his tent to meet them and bowed low to the ground.

3He said, "If I have found favor in your eyes, my lord,[b] do not pass your servant by. 4Let a little water be brought, and then you may all wash your feet and rest under this tree. 5Let me get you something to eat, so you can be refreshed and then go on your way—now that you have come to your servant."

"Very well," they answered, "do as you say."

6So Abraham hurried into the tent to Sarah. "Quick," he said, "get three seahs[c] of fine flour and knead it and bake some bread."

7Then he ran to the herd and selected a choice, tender calf and gave it to a servant, who hurried to prepare it. 8He then brought some curds and milk and the calf that had been prepared, and set these before them. While they ate, he stood near them under a tree.

9"Where is your wife Sarah?" they asked him.

"There, in the tent," he said.

10Then the LORD[d] said, "I will surely return to you about this time next year, and Sarah your wife will have a son."

Now Sarah was listening at the entrance to the tent, which was behind him. 11Abraham and Sarah were already old and well advanced in years, and Sarah was past the age of childbearing. 12So Sarah laughed to her-

---

a *19 Isaac means he laughs.*   b *3 Or O Lord*   c *6 That is, probably about 20 quarts (about 22 liters)*   d *10 Hebrew Then he*

Living Bible

I will bless her and give you a son from her! Yes, I will bless her richly, and make her the mother of nations! Many kings shall be among your posterity."

17Then Abraham threw himself down in worship before the Lord, but inside he was laughing in disbelief!c "Me, be a father?" he said in amusement. "Me—100 years old? And Sarah, to have a baby at 90?"

18And Abraham said to God, "Yes, do bless Ishmael!"

19"No," God replied, "that isn't what I said. *Sarah* shall bear you a son; and you are to name him Isaac ('Laughter'), and I will sign my covenant with him forever, and with his descendants. 20As for Ishmael, all right, I will bless him also, just as you have asked me to. I will cause him to multiply and become a great nation. Twelve princes shall be among his posterity. 21But my contract is with Isaac, who will be born to you and Sarah next year at about this time."

22That ended the conversation and God left. 23Then, that very day, Abraham took Ishmael his son and every other male—born in his household or bought from outside—and cut off their foreskins, just as God had told him to. 24–27Abraham was ninety-nine years old at that time, and Ishmael was thirteen. Both were circumcised the same day, along with all the other men and boys of the household, whether born there or bought as slaves.

18 THE LORD appeared again to Abraham while he was living in the oak grove at Mamre. This is the way it happened: One hot summer afternoon as he was sitting in the opening of his tent, 2he suddenly noticed three men coming toward him. He sprang up and ran to meet them and welcomed them.

3, 4"Sirs," he said, "please don't go any further. Stop awhile and rest here in the shade of this tree while I get water to refresh your feet, 5and a bite to eat to strengthen you. Do stay awhile before continuing your journey."

"All right," they said, "do as you have said."

6Then Abraham ran back to the tent and said to Sarah, "Quick! Mix up some pancakes!f Use your best flour, and make enough for the three of them!" 7Then he ran out to the herd and selected a fat calf and told a servant to hurry and butcher it. 8Soon, taking them cheese and milk and the roast veal, he set it before the men and stood beneath the trees beside them as they ate.

9"Where is Sarah, your wife?" they asked him.

"In the tent," Abraham replied.

10Then the Lord said, "Next yearg I will give you and Sarah a son!" (Sarah was listening from the tent door behind him.) 11Now Abraham and Sarah were both very old, and Sarah was long since past the time when she could have a baby.

New Revised Standard

16I will bless her, and moreover I will give you a son by her. I will bless her, and she shall give rise to nations; kings of peoples shall come from her." 17Then Abraham fell on his face and laughed, and said to himself, "Can a child be born to a man who is a hundred years old? Can Sarah, who is ninety years old, bear a child?" 18And Abraham said to God, "O that Ishmael might live in your sight!" 19God said, "No, but your wife Sarah shall bear you a son, and you shall name him Isaac.h I will establish my covenant with him as an everlasting covenant for his offspring after him. 20As for Ishmael, I have heard you; I will bless him and make him fruitful and exceedingly numerous; he shall be the father of twelve princes, and I will make him a great nation. 21But my covenant I will establish with Isaac, whom Sarah shall bear to you at this season next year." 22And when he had finished talking with him, God went up from Abraham.

23 Then Abraham took his son Ishmael and all the slaves born in his house or bought with his money, every male among the men of Abraham's house, and he circumcised the flesh of their foreskins that very day, as God had said to him. 24Abraham was ninety-nine years old when he was circumcised in the flesh of his foreskin. 25And his son Ishmael was thirteen years old when he was circumcised in the flesh of his foreskin. 26That very day Abraham and his son Ishmael were circumcised; 27and all the men of his house, slaves born in the house and those bought with money from a foreigner, were circumcised with him.

A Son Promised to Abraham and Sarah

18 THE LORD appeared to Abrahami by the oaksj of Mamre, as he sat at the entrance of his tent in the heat of the day. 2He looked up and saw three men standing near him. When he saw them, he ran from the tent entrance to meet them, and bowed down to the ground. 3He said, "My lord, if I find favor with you, do not pass by your servant. 4Let a little water be brought, and wash your feet, and rest yourselves under the tree. 5Let me bring a little bread, that you may refresh yourselves, and after that you may pass on—since you have come to your servant." So they said, "Do as you have said." 6And Abraham hastened into the tent to Sarah, and said, "Make ready quickly three measuresk of choice flour, knead it, and make cakes." 7Abraham ran to the herd, and took a calf, tender and good, and gave it to the servant, who hastened to prepare it. 8Then he took curds and milk and the calf that he had prepared, and set it before them; and he stood by them under the tree while they ate.

9 They said to him, "Where is your wife Sarah?" And he said, "There, in the tent." 10Then one said, "I will surely return to you in due season, and your wife Sarah shall have a son." And Sarah was listening at the tent entrance behind him. 11Now Abraham and Sarah were old, advanced in age; it had ceased to be with Sarah after the manner of women. 12So Sarah laughed to her-

c 17:17 *inside he was laughing in disbelief,* implied.   f 18:6 *pancakes,* probably some sort of *tortilla.*   g 18:10 *next year,* literally, "when life would be due."

h That is *he laughs*   i Heb *him*   j Or *terebinths*   k Heb *seahs*

King James

12Therefore Sarah laughed within herself, saying, After I am waxed old shall I have pleasure, my lord being old also?

13And the LORD said unto Abraham, Wherefore did Sarah laugh, saying, Shall I of a surety bear a child, which am old?

14Is any thing too hard for the LORD? At the time appointed I will return unto thee, according to the time of life, and Sarah shall have a son.

15Then Sarah denied, saying, I laughed not; for she was afraid. And he said, Nay; but thou didst laugh.

16¶ And the men rose up from thence, and looked toward Sodom: and Abraham went with them to bring them on the way.

17And the LORD said, Shall I hide from Abraham that thing which I do;

18Seeing that Abraham shall surely become a great and mighty nation, and all the nations of the earth shall be blessed in him?

19For I know him, that he will command his children and his household after him, and they shall keep the way of the LORD, to do justice and judgment; that the LORD may bring upon Abraham that which he hath spoken of him.

20And the LORD said, Because the cry of Sodom and Gomorrah is great, and because their sin is very grievous;

21I will go down now, and see whether they have done altogether according to the cry of it, which is come unto me; and if not, I will know.

22And the men turned their faces from thence, and went toward Sodom: but Abraham stood yet before the LORD.

23¶ And Abraham drew near, and said, Wilt thou also destroy the righteous with the wicked?

24Peradventure there be fifty righteous within the city: wilt thou also destroy and not spare the place for the fifty righteous that *are* therein?

25That be far from thee to do after this manner, to slay the righteous with the wicked: and that the righteous should be as the wicked, that be far from thee: Shall not the Judge of all the earth do right?

26And the LORD said, If I find in Sodom fifty righteous within the city, then I will spare all the place for their sakes.

27And Abraham answered and said, Behold now, I have taken upon me to speak unto the Lord, which *am but* dust and ashes:

28Peradventure there shall lack five of the fifty righteous: wilt thou destroy all the city for *lack of* five? And he said, If I find there forty and five, I will not destroy *it*.

29And he spake unto him yet again, and said, Peradventure there shall be forty found there. And he said, I will not do *it* for forty's sake.

30And he said *unto him,* Oh let not the Lord be angry, and I will speak: Peradventure there shall thirty be found there. And he said, I will not do *it,* if I find thirty there.

31And he said, Behold now, I have taken upon me to speak unto the Lord: Peradventure there shall be twenty found there. And he said, I will not destroy *it* for twenty's sake.

32And he said, Oh let not the Lord be angry, and I will speak yet but this once: Peradventure ten shall be found there. And he said, I will not destroy *it* for ten's sake.

33And the LORD went his way, as soon as he had left communing with Abraham: and Abraham returned unto his place.

New International

self as she thought, "After I am worn out and my mastera is old, will I now have this pleasure?"

13Then the LORD said to Abraham, "Why did Sarah laugh and say, 'Will I really have a child, now that I am old?' 14Is anything too hard for the LORD? I will return to you at the appointed time next year and Sarah will have a son."

15Sarah was afraid, so she lied and said, "I did not laugh."

But he said, "Yes, you did laugh."

Abraham Pleads for Sodom

16When the men got up to leave, they looked down toward Sodom, and Abraham walked along with them to see them on their way. 17Then the LORD said, "Shall I hide from Abraham what I am about to do? 18Abraham will surely become a great and powerful nation, and all nations on earth will be blessed through him. 19For I have chosen him, so that he will direct his children and his household after him to keep the way of the LORD by doing what is right and just, so that the LORD will bring about for Abraham what he has promised him."

20Then the LORD said, "The outcry against Sodom and Gomorrah is so great and their sin so grievous 21that I will go down and see if what they have done is as bad as the outcry that has reached me. If not, I will know."

22The men turned away and went toward Sodom, but Abraham remained standing before the LORD.b 23Then Abraham approached him and said: "Will you sweep away the righteous with the wicked? 24What if there are fifty righteous people in the city? Will you really sweep it away and not sparec the place for the sake of the fifty righteous people in it? 25Far be it from you to do such a thing—to kill the righteous with the wicked, treating the righteous and the wicked alike. Far be it from you! Will not the Judged of all the earth do right?"

26The LORD said, "If I find fifty righteous people in the city of Sodom, I will spare the whole place for their sake."

27Then Abraham spoke up again: "Now that I have been so bold as to speak to the Lord, though I am nothing but dust and ashes, 28what if the number of the righteous is five less than fifty? Will you destroy the whole city because of five people?"

"If I find forty-five there," he said, "I will not destroy it."

29Once again he spoke to him, "What if only forty are found there?"

He said, "For the sake of forty, I will not do it."

30Then he said, "May the Lord not be angry, but let me speak. What if only thirty can be found there?"

He answered, "I will not do it if I find thirty there."

31Abraham said, "Now that I have been so bold as to speak to the Lord, what if only twenty can be found there?"

He said, "For the sake of twenty, I will not destroy it."

32Then he said, "May the Lord not be angry, but let me speak just once more. What if only ten can be found there?"

He answered, "For the sake of ten, I will not destroy it."

33When the LORD had finished speaking with Abraham, he left, and Abraham returned home.

Living Bible

12So Sarah laughed silently. "A woman my age have a baby?" she scoffed to herself. "And with a husband as old as mine?"

13Then God said to Abraham, "Why did Sarah laugh? Why did she say 'Can an old woman like me have a baby?' 14Is anything too hard for God? Next year, just as I told you, I will certainly see to it that Sarah has a son."

15But Sarah denied it. "I didn't laugh," she lied, for she was afraid.

16Then the men stood up from their meal and started on toward Sodom; and Abraham went with them part of the way.

17"Should I hide my plan from Abraham?" God asked. 18"For Abraham shall become a mighty nation, and he will be a source of blessing for all the nations of the earth. 19And I have picked him out to have godly descendants and a godly household—men who are just and good—so that I can do for him all I have promised."

20So the Lord told Abraham, "I have heard that the people of Sodom and Gomorrah are utterly evil, and that everything they do is wicked. 21I am going down to see whether these reports are true or not. Then I will know."

22, 23So the other two went on toward Sodom, but the Lord remained with Abraham a while. Then Abraham approached him and said, "Will you kill good and bad alike? 24Suppose you find fifty godly people there within the city—will you destroy it, and not spare it for their sakes? 25That wouldn't be right! Surely you wouldn't do such a thing, to kill the godly with the wicked! Why, you would be treating godly and wicked exactly the same! Surely you wouldn't do that! Should not the Judge of all the earth be fair?"

26And God replied, "If I find fifty godly people there, I will spare the entire city for their sake."

27Then Abraham spoke again. "Since I have begun, let me go on and speak further to the Lord, though I am but dust and ashes. 28*Suppose there are only forty-five?* Will you destroy the city for lack of five?"

And God said, "I will not destroy it if I find forty-five."

29Then Abraham went further with his request. *"Suppose there are only forty?"*

And God replied, "I won't destroy it if there are forty."

30"Please don't be angry," Abraham pleaded. "Let me speak: *suppose only thirty are found there?"*

And God replied, "I won't do it if there are thirty there."

31Then Abraham said, "Since I have dared to speak to God, let me continue—*Suppose there are only twenty?"*

And God said, "Then I won't destroy it for the sake of the twenty."

32Finally, Abraham said, "Oh, let not the Lord be angry; I will speak but this once more! *Suppose only ten are found?"*

And God said, "Then, for the sake of the ten, I won't destroy it."

33And the Lord went on his way when he had finished his conversation with Abraham. And Abraham returned to his tent.

New Revised Standard

self, saying, "After I have grown old, and my husband is old, shall I have pleasure?" 13The Lord said to Abraham, "Why did Sarah laugh, and say, 'Shall I indeed bear a child, now that I am old?' 14Is anything too wonderful for the Lord? At the set time I will return to you, in due season, and Sarah shall have a son." 15But Sarah denied, saying, "I did not laugh"; for she was afraid. He said, "Oh yes, you did laugh."

Judgment Pronounced on Sodom

16 Then the men set out from there, and they looked toward Sodom; and Abraham went with them to set them on their way. 17The Lord said, "Shall I hide from Abraham what I am about to do, 18seeing that Abraham shall become a great and mighty nation, and all the nations of the earth shall be blessed in him?e 19No, for I have chosenf him, that he may charge his children and his household after him to keep the way of the Lord by doing righteousness and justice; so that the Lord may bring about for Abraham what he has promised him." 20Then the Lord said, "How great is the outcry against Sodom and Gomorrah and how very grave their sin! 21I must go down and see whether they have done altogether according to the outcry that has come to me; and if not, I will know."

22 So the men turned from there, and went toward Sodom, while Abraham remained standing before the Lord.g 23Then Abraham came near and said, "Will you indeed sweep away the righteous with the wicked? 24Suppose there are fifty righteous within the city; will you then sweep away the place and not forgive it for the fifty righteous who are in it? 25Far be it from you to do such a thing, to slay the righteous with the wicked, so that the righteous fare as the wicked! Far be that from you! Shall not the Judge of all the earth do what is just?" 26And the Lord said, "If I find at Sodom fifty righteous in the city, I will forgive the whole place for their sake." 27Abraham answered, "Let me take it upon myself to speak to the Lord, I who am but dust and ashes. 28Suppose five of the fifty righteous are lacking? Will you destroy the whole city for lack of five?" And he said, "I will not destroy it if I find forty-five there." 29Again he spoke to him, "Suppose forty are found there." He answered, "For the sake of forty I will not do it." 30Then he said, "Oh do not let the Lord be angry if I speak. Suppose thirty are found there." He answered, "I will not do it, if I find thirty there." 31He said, "Let me take it upon myself to speak to the Lord. Suppose twenty are found there." He answered, "For the sake of twenty I will not destroy it." 32Then he said, "Oh do not let the Lord be angry if I speak just once more. Suppose ten are found there." He answered, "For the sake of ten I will not destroy it." 33And the Lord went his way, when he had finished speaking to Abraham; and Abraham returned to his place.

---

e Or *and all the nations of the earth shall bless themselves by him*   f Heb *known*   g Another ancient tradition reads *while the Lord remained standing before Abraham*

King James

19 AND THERE came two angels to Sodom at even; and Lot sat in the gate of Sodom: and Lot seeing *them* rose up to meet them; and he bowed himself with his face toward the ground;

2And he said, Behold now, my lords, turn in, I pray you, into your servant's house, and tarry all night, and wash your feet, and ye shall rise up early, and go on your ways. And they said, Nay; but we will abide in the street all night.

3And he pressed upon them greatly; and they turned in unto him, and entered into his house; and he made them a feast, and did bake unleavened bread, and they did eat.

4¶ But before they lay down, the men of the city, *even* the men of Sodom, compassed the house round, both old and young, all the people from every quarter:

5And they called unto Lot, and said unto him, Where *are* the men which came in to thee this night? bring them out unto us, that we may know them.

6And Lot went out at the door unto them, and shut the door after him,

7And said, I pray you, brethren, do not so wickedly.

8Behold now, I have two daughters which have not known man; let me, I pray you, bring them out unto you, and do ye to them as *is* good in your eyes: only unto these men do nothing; for therefore came they under the shadow of my roof.

9And they said, Stand back. And they said *again,* This one *fellow* came in to sojourn, and he will needs be a judge: now will we deal worse with thee, than with them. And they pressed sore upon the man, *even* Lot, and came near to break the door.

10But the men put forth their hand, and pulled Lot into the house to them, and shut to the door.

11And they smote the men that *were* at the door of the house with blindness, both small and great: so that they wearied themselves to find the door.

12¶ And the men said unto Lot, Hast thou here any besides? son-in-law, and thy sons, and thy daughters, and whatsoever thou hast in the city, bring *them* out of this place:

13For we will destroy this place, because the cry of them is waxen great before the face of the LORD; and the LORD hath sent us to destroy it.

14And Lot went out, and spake unto his sons in law, which married his daughters, and said, Up, get you out of this place; for the LORD will destroy this city. But he seemed as one that mocked unto his sons in law.

15¶ And when the morning arose, then the angels hastened Lot, saying, Arise, take thy wife, and thy two daughters, which are here; lest thou be consumed in the iniquity of the city.

16And while he lingered, the men laid hold upon his hand, and upon the hand of his wife, and upon the hand of his two daughters; the LORD being merciful unto him: and they brought him forth, and set him without the city.

17¶ And it came to pass, when they had brought them forth abroad, that he said, Escape for thy life; look not behind thee, neither stay thou in all the plain; escape to the mountain, lest thou be consumed.

18And Lot said unto them, Oh, not so, my Lord:

19Behold now, thy servant hath found grace in thy sight, and thou hast magnified thy mercy, which thou hast shown unto me in saving my life; and I cannot escape to the mountain, lest some evil take me, and I die:

20Behold now, this city *is* near to flee unto, and it *is* a little one: Oh, let me escape thither, (*is* it not a little one?) and my soul shall live.

21And he said unto him, See, I have accepted thee concerning this thing also, that I will not overthrow this city, for the which thou hast spoken.

New International

Sodom and Gomorrah Destroyed

19 THE TWO angels arrived at Sodom in the evening, and Lot was sitting in the gateway of the city. When he saw them, he got up to meet them and bowed down with his face to the ground. 2"My lords," he said, "please turn aside to your servant's house. You can wash your feet and spend the night and then go on your way early in the morning."

"No," they answered, "we will spend the night in the square."

3But he insisted so strongly that they did go with him and entered his house. He prepared a meal for them, baking bread without yeast, and they ate. 4Before they had gone to bed, all the men from every part of the city of Sodom—both young and old—surrounded the house. 5They called to Lot, "Where are the men who came to you tonight? Bring them out to us so that we can have sex with them."

6Lot went outside to meet them and shut the door behind him 7and said, "No, my friends. Don't do this wicked thing. 8Look, I have two daughters who have never slept with a man. Let me bring them out to you, and you can do what you like with them. But don't do anything to these men, for they have come under the protection of my roof."

9"Get out of our way," they replied. And they said, "This fellow came here as an alien, and now he wants to play the judge! We'll treat you worse than them." They kept bringing pressure on Lot and moved forward to break down the door.

10But the men inside reached out and pulled Lot back into the house and shut the door. 11Then they struck the men who were at the door of the house, young and old, with blindness so that they could not find the door.

12The two men said to Lot, "Do you have anyone else here—sons-in-law, sons or daughters, or anyone else in the city who belongs to you? Get them out of here, 13because we are going to destroy this place. The outcry to the LORD against its people is so great that he has sent us to destroy it."

14So Lot went out and spoke to his sons-in-law, who were pledged to marry[a] his daughters. He said, "Hurry and get out of this place, because the LORD is about to destroy the city!" But his sons-in-law thought he was joking.

15With the coming of dawn, the angels urged Lot, saying, "Hurry! Take your wife and your two daughters who are here, or you will be swept away when the city is punished."

16When he hesitated, the men grasped his hand and the hands of his wife and of his two daughters and led them safely out of the city, for the LORD was merciful to them. 17As soon as they had brought them out, one of them said, "Flee for your lives! Don't look back, and don't stop anywhere in the plain! Flee to the mountains or you will be swept away!"

18But Lot said to them, "No, my lords,[b] please! 19Your[c] servant has found favor in your[c] eyes, and you[c] have shown great kindness to me in sparing my life. But I can't flee to the mountains; this disaster will overtake me, and I'll die. 20Look, here is a town near enough to run to, and it is small. Let me flee to it—it is very small, isn't it? Then my life will be spared."

21He said to him, "Very well, I will grant this request too; I will not overthrow the town you speak of. 22But

---

a 14 Or *were married to*   b 18 Or *No, Lord*; or *No, my lord*   c 19 The Hebrew is singular.

Living Bible

19 THAT EVENING the two angels came to the entrance of the city of Sodom, and Lot was sitting there as they arrived. When he saw them he stood up to meet them, and welcomed them.

2"Sirs," he said, "come to my home as my guests for the night; you can get up as early as you like and be on your way again."

"Oh, no thanks," they said, "we'll just stretch out here along the street."

3But he was very urgent, until at last they went home with him, and he set a great feast before them, complete with freshly baked unleavened bread. After the meal, 4as they were preparing to retire for the night, the men of the city—yes, Sodomites, young and old from all over the city—surrounded the house 5and shouted to Lot, "Bring out those men to us so we can rape them."

6Lot stepped outside to talk to them, shutting the door behind him. 7"Please, fellows," he begged, "don't do such a wicked thing. 8Look—I have two virgin daughters, and I'll surrender them to you to do with as you wish. But leave these men alone, for they are under my protection."

9"Stand back," they yelled. "Who do you think you are? We let this fellow settle among us and now he tries to tell us what to do! We'll deal with you far worse than with those other men." And they lunged at Lot and began breaking down the door.

10But the two men reached out and pulled Lot in and bolted the door, 11and temporarily blinded the men of Sodom so that they couldn't find the door.

12"What relatives do you have here in the city?" the men asked. "Get them out of this place—sons-in-law, sons, daughters, or anyone else. 13For we will destroy the city completely. The stench of the place has reached to heaven and God has sent us to destroy it."

14So Lot rushed out to tell his daughters' fiancés, "Quick, get out of the city, for the Lord is going to destroy it." But the young men looked at him as though he had lost his senses.

15At dawn the next morning the angels became urgent. "Hurry," they said to Lot, "take your wife and your two daughters who are here and get out while you can, or you will be caught in the destruction of the city."

16When Lot still hesitated, the angels seized his hand and the hands of his wife and two daughters and rushed them to safety, outside the city, for the Lord was merciful.

17"Flee for your lives," the angels told him. *"And don't look back.* Escape to the mountains. Don't stay down here on the plain or you will die."

18, 19, 20"Oh no, sirs, please," Lot begged, "since you've been so kind to me and saved my life, and you've granted me such mercy, let me flee to that little village over there instead of into the mountains, for I fear disaster in the mountain. See, the village is close by and it is just a small one. Please, please, let me go there instead. Don't you see how small it is? And my life will be saved."

21"All right," the angel said, "I accept your proposition and won't destroy that little city. 22But hurry! For

New Revised Standard

The Depravity of Sodom

19 THE TWO angels came to Sodom in the evening, and Lot was sitting in the gateway of Sodom. When Lot saw them, he rose to meet them, and bowed down with his face to the ground. 2He said, "Please, my lords, turn aside to your servant's house and spend the night, and wash your feet; then you can rise early and go on your way." They said, "No; we will spend the night in the square." 3But he urged them strongly; so they turned aside to him and entered his house; and he made them a feast, and baked unleavened bread, and they ate. 4But before they lay down, the men of the city, the men of Sodom, both young and old, all the people to the last man, surrounded the house; 5and they called to Lot, "Where are the men who came to you tonight? Bring them out to us, so that we may know them." 6Lot went out of the door to the men, shut the door after him, 7and said, "I beg you, my brothers, do not act so wickedly. 8Look, I have two daughters who have not known a man; let me bring them out to you, and do to them as you please; only do nothing to these men, for they have come under the shelter of my roof." 9But they replied, "Stand back!" And they said, "This fellow came here as an alien, and he would play the judge! Now we will deal worse with you than with them." Then they pressed hard against the man Lot, and came near the door to break it down. 10But the men inside reached out their hands and brought Lot into the house with them, and shut the door. 11And they struck with blindness the men who were at the door of the house, both small and great, so that they were unable to find the door.

Sodom and Gomorrah Destroyed

12 Then the men said to Lot, "Have you anyone else here? Sons-in-law, sons, daughters, or anyone you have in the city—bring them out of the place. 13For we are about to destroy this place, because the outcry against its people has become great before the LORD, and the LORD has sent us to destroy it." 14So Lot went out and said to his sons-in-law, who were to marry his daughters, "Up, get out of this place; for the LORD is about to destroy the city." But he seemed to his sons-in-law to be jesting.

15 When morning dawned, the angels urged Lot, saying, "Get up, take your wife and your two daughters who are here, or else you will be consumed in the punishment of the city." 16But he lingered; so the men seized him and his wife and his two daughters by the hand, the LORD being merciful to him, and they brought him out and left him outside the city. 17When they had brought them outside, theyd said, "Flee for your life; do not look back or stop anywhere in the Plain; flee to the hills, or else you will be consumed." 18And Lot said to them, "Oh, no, my lords; 19your servant has found favor with you, and you have shown me great kindness in saving my life; but I cannot flee to the hills, for fear the disaster will overtake me and I die. 20Look, that city is near enough to flee to, and it is a little one. Let me escape there—is it not a little one?—and my life will be saved!" 21He said to him, "Very well, I grant you this favor too, and will not overthrow the city of which you have spoken. 22Hurry, escape there, for I can do nothing

King James

22Haste thee, escape thither; for I cannot do any thing till thou be come thither. Therefore the name of the city was called Zoar.

23¶ The sun was risen upon the earth when Lot entered into Zoar.

24Then the LORD rained upon Sodom and upon Gomorrah brimstone and fire from the LORD out of heaven;

25And he overthrew those cities, and all the plain, and all the inhabitants of the cities, and that which grew upon the ground.

26¶ But his wife looked back from behind him, and she became a pillar of salt.

27¶ And Abraham gat up early in the morning to the place where he stood before the LORD:

28And he looked toward Sodom and Gomorrah, and toward all the land of the plain, and beheld, and, lo, the smoke of the country went up as the smoke of a furnace.

29¶ And it came to pass, when God destroyed the cities of the plain, that God remembered Abraham, and sent Lot out of the midst of the overthrow, when he overthrew the cities in the which Lot dwelt.

30¶ And Lot went up out of Zoar, and dwelt in the mountain, and his two daughters with him; for he feared to dwell in Zoar: and he dwelt in a cave, he and his two daughters.

31And the firstborn said unto the younger, Our father *is* old, and *there is* not a man in the earth to come in unto us after the manner of all the earth:

32Come, let us make our father drink wine, and we will lie with him, that we may preserve seed of our father.

33And they made their father drink wine that night: and the firstborn went in, and lay with her father; and he perceived not when she lay down, nor when she arose.

34And it came to pass on the morrow, that the firstborn said unto the younger, Behold, I lay yesternight with my father: let us make him drink wine this night also; and go thou in, *and* lie with him, that we may preserve seed of our father.

35And they made their father drink wine that night also: and the younger arose, and lay with him; and he perceived not when she lay down, nor when she arose.

36Thus were both the daughters of Lot with child by their father.

37And the firstborn bare a son, and called his name Moab: the same *is* the father of the Moabites unto this day.

38And the younger, she also bare a son, and called his name Ben-ammi: the same *is* the father of the children of Ammon unto this day.

20 AND ABRAHAM journeyed from thence toward the south country, and dwelled between Kadesh and Shur, and sojourned in Gerar.

2And Abraham said of Sarah his wife, She *is* my sister: and Abimelech king of Gerar sent, and took Sarah.

3But God came to Abimelech in a dream by night, and said to him, Behold, thou *art but* a dead man, for the woman which thou hast taken; for she *is* a man's wife.

4But Abimelech had not come near her: and he said, Lord, wilt thou slay also a righteous nation?

5Said he not unto me, She *is* my sister? and she, even she herself said, He *is* my brother: in the integrity of my heart and innocency of my hands have I done this.

New International

flee there quickly, because I cannot do anything until you reach it." (That is why the town was called Zoar.a)

23By the time Lot reached Zoar, the sun had risen over the land. 24Then the LORD rained down burning sulfur on Sodom and Gomorrah—from the LORD out of the heavens. 25Thus he overthrew those cities and the entire plain, including all those living in the cities—and also the vegetation in the land. 26But Lot's wife looked back, and she became a pillar of salt.

27Early the next morning Abraham got up and returned to the place where he had stood before the LORD. 28He looked down toward Sodom and Gomorrah, toward all the land of the plain, and he saw dense smoke rising from the land, like smoke from a furnace.

29So when God destroyed the cities of the plain, he remembered Abraham, and he brought Lot out of the catastrophe that overthrew the cities where Lot had lived.

Lot and His Daughters

30Lot and his two daughters left Zoar and settled in the mountains, for he was afraid to stay in Zoar. He and his two daughters lived in a cave. 31One day the older daughter said to the younger, "Our father is old, and there is no man around here to lie with us, as is the custom all over the earth. 32Let's get our father to drink wine and then lie with him and preserve our family line through our father."

33That night they got their father to drink wine, and the older daughter went in and lay with him. He was not aware of it when she lay down or when she got up.

34The next day the older daughter said to the younger, "Last night I lay with my father. Let's get him to drink wine again tonight, and you go in and lie with him so we can preserve our family line through our father." 35So they got their father to drink wine that night also, and the younger daughter went and lay with him. Again he was not aware of it when she lay down or when she got up.

36So both of Lot's daughters became pregnant by their father. 37The older daughter had a son, and she named him Moabb; he is the father of the Moabites of today. 38The younger daughter also had a son, and she named him Ben-Ammic; he is the father of the Ammonites of today.

Abraham and Abimelech

20 NOW ABRAHAM moved on from there into the region of the Negev and lived between Kadesh and Shur. For a while he stayed in Gerar, 2and there Abraham said of his wife Sarah, "She is my sister." Then Abimelech king of Gerar sent for Sarah and took her.

3But God came to Abimelech in a dream one night and said to him, "You are as good as dead because of the woman you have taken; she is a married woman."

4Now Abimelech had not gone near her, so he said, "Lord, will you destroy an innocent nation? 5Did he not say to me, 'She is my sister,' and didn't she also say, 'He is my brother'? I have done this with a clear conscience and clean hands."

---

a 22 *Zoar* means *small.*   b 37 *Moab* sounds like the Hebrew for *from father*.
c 38 *Ben-Ammi* means *son of my people*.

Living Bible

I can do nothing until you are there." (From that time on that village was named Zoar, meaning "Little City.") 23The sun was rising as Lot reached the village. 24Then the Lord rained down fire and flaming tar from heaven upon Sodom and Gomorrah, 25and utterly destroyed them, along with the other cities and villages of the plain, eliminating all life—people, plants, and animals alike. 26But Lot's wife looked back as she was following along behind him, and became a pillar of salt.

27That morning Abraham was up early and hurried out to the place where he had stood before the Lord. 28He looked out across the plain to Sodom and Gomorrah and saw columns of smoke and fumes, as from a furnace, rising from the cities there. 29So God heeded Abraham's plea and kept Lot safe, removing him from the maelstrom of death that engulfed the cities.

30Afterwards Lot left Zoar, fearful of the people there, and went to live in a cave in the mountains with his two daughters. 31One day the older girl said to her sister, "There isn't a man anywhere in this entire area that our father would let us marry. And our father will soon be too old for having children. 32Come, let's fill him with wine and then we will sleep with him, so that our clan will not come to an end." 33So they got him drunk that night, and the older girl went in and had sexual intercourse with her father; but he was unaware of her lying down or getting up again.

34The next morning she said to her younger sister, "I slept with my father last night. Let's fill him with wine again tonight, and you go in and lie with him, so that our family line will continue." 35So they got him drunk again that night, and the younger girl went in and lay with him, and, as before, he didn't know that anyone was there. 36And so it was that both girls became pregnant from their father. 37The older girl's baby was named Moab; he became the ancestor of the nation of the Moabites. 38The name of the younger girl's baby was Benammi; he became the ancestor of the nation of the Ammonites.

New Revised Standard

until you arrive there." Therefore the city was called Zoar.d 23The sun had risen on the earth when Lot came to Zoar.

24 Then the LORD rained on Sodom and Gomorrah sulfur and fire from the LORD out of heaven; 25and he overthrew those cities, and all the Plain, and all the inhabitants of the cities, and what grew on the ground. 26But Lot's wife, behind him, looked back, and she became a pillar of salt.

27 Abraham went early in the morning to the place where he had stood before the LORD; 28and he looked down toward Sodom and Gomorrah and toward all the land of the Plain and saw the smoke of the land going up like the smoke of a furnace.

29 So it was that, when God destroyed the cities of the Plain, God remembered Abraham, and sent Lot out of the midst of the overthrow, when he overthrew the cities in which Lot had settled.

The Shameful Origin of Moab and Ammon

30 Now Lot went up out of Zoar and settled in the hills with his two daughters, for he was afraid to stay in Zoar; so he lived in a cave with his two daughters. 31And the firstborn said to the younger, "Our father is old, and there is not a man on earth to come in to us after the manner of all the world. 32Come, let us make our father drink wine, and we will lie with him, so that we may preserve offspring through our father." 33So they made their father drink wine that night; and the firstborn went in, and lay with her father; he did not know when she lay down or when she rose. 34On the next day, the firstborn said to the younger, "Look, I lay last night with my father; let us make him drink wine tonight also; then you go in and lie with him, so that we may preserve offspring through our father." 35So they made their father drink wine that night also; and the younger rose, and lay with him; and he did not know when she lay down or when she rose. 36Thus both the daughters of Lot became pregnant by their father. 37The firstborn bore a son, and named him Moab; he is the ancestor of the Moabites to this day. 38The younger also bore a son and named him Ben-ammi; he is the ancestor of the Ammonites to this day.

20 NOW ABRAHAM moved south to the Negeb, and settled between Kadesh and Shur. One day, when visiting the city of Gerar, 2he declared that Sarah was his sister! Then King Abimelech sent for her, and had her brought to him at his palace.

3But that night God came to him in a dream and told him, "You are a dead man, for that woman you took is married."

4But Abimelech hadn't slept with her yet, so he said, "Lord, will you slay an innocent man? 5He told me, 'She is my sister,' and she herself said, 'Yes, he is my brother.' I hadn't the slightest intention of doing anything wrong."

Abraham and Sarah at Gerar

20 FROM THERE Abraham journeyed toward the region of the Negeb, and settled between Kadesh and Shur. While residing in Gerar as an alien, 2Abraham said of his wife Sarah, "She is my sister." And King Abimelech of Gerar sent and took Sarah. 3But God came to Abimelech in a dream by night, and said to him, "You are about to die because of the woman whom you have taken; for she is a married woman." 4Now Abimelech had not approached her; so he said, "Lord, will you destroy an innocent people? 5Did he not himself say to me, 'She is my sister'? And she herself said, 'He is my brother.' I did this in the integrity of my heart and the innocence of my hands." 6Then God said

d That is Little

King James

6And God said unto him in a dream, Yea, I know that thou didst this in the integrity of thy heart; for I also withheld thee from sinning against me: therefore suffered I thee not to touch her.

7Now therefore restore the man *his* wife; for he *is* a prophet, and he shall pray for thee, and thou shalt live: and if thou restore *her* not, know thou that thou shalt surely die, thou, and all that *are* thine.

8Therefore Abimelech rose early in the morning, and called all his servants, and told all these things in their ears: and the men were sore afraid.

9Then Abimelech called Abraham, and said unto him, What hast thou done unto us? and what have I offended thee, that thou hast brought on me and on my kingdom a great sin? thou hast done deeds unto me that ought not to be done.

10And Abimelech said unto Abraham, What sawest thou, that thou hast done this thing?

11And Abraham said, Because I thought, Surely the fear of God *is* not in this place; and they will slay me for my wife's sake.

12And yet indeed *she is* my sister; she *is* the daughter of my father, but not the daughter of my mother; and she became my wife.

13And it came to pass, when God caused me to wander from my father's house, that I said unto her, This *is* thy kindness which thou shalt show unto me; at every place whither we shall come, say of me, He *is* my brother.

14And Abimelech took sheep, and oxen, and menservants, and womenservants, and gave *them* unto Abraham, and restored him Sarah his wife.

15And Abimelech said, Behold, my land *is* before thee: dwell where it pleaseth thee.

16And unto Sarah he said, Behold, I have given thy brother a thousand *pieces* of silver: behold, he *is* to thee a covering of the eyes, unto all that *are* with thee, and with all *other*: thus she was reproved.

17¶ So Abraham prayed unto God: and God healed Abimelech, and his wife, and his maidservants; and they bare *children*.

18For the LORD had fast closed up all the wombs of the house of Abimelech, because of Sarah Abraham's wife.

21 AND THE LORD visited Sarah as he had said, and the LORD did unto Sarah as he had spoken.

2For Sarah conceived, and bare Abraham a son in his old age, at the set time of which God had spoken to him.

3And Abraham called the name of his son that was born unto him, whom Sarah bare to him, Isaac.

4And Abraham circumcised his son Isaac being eight days old, as God had commanded him.

5And Abraham was an hundred years old, when his son Isaac was born unto him.

6¶ And Sarah said, God hath made me to laugh, *so that* all that hear will laugh with me.

7And she said, Who would have said unto Abraham, that Sarah should have given children suck? for I have born *him* a son in his old age.

8And the child grew, and was weaned: and Abraham made a great feast the *same* day that Isaac was weaned.

9¶ And Sarah saw the son of Hagar the Egyptian, which she had born unto Abraham, mocking.

10Wherefore she said unto Abraham, Cast out this bondwoman and her son: for the son of this bondwoman shall not be heir with my son, *even* with Isaac.

New International

6Then God said to him in the dream, "Yes, I know you did this with a clear conscience, and so I have kept you from sinning against me. That is why I did not let you touch her. 7Now return the man's wife, for he is a prophet, and he will pray for you and you will live. But if you do not return her, you may be sure that you and all yours will die."

8Early the next morning Abimelech summoned all his officials, and when he told them all that had happened, they were very much afraid. 9Then Abimelech called Abraham in and said, "What have you done to us? How have I wronged you that you have brought such great guilt upon me and my kingdom? You have done things to me that should not be done." 10And Abimelech asked Abraham, "What was your reason for doing this?"

11Abraham replied, "I said to myself, 'There is surely no fear of God in this place, and they will kill me because of my wife.' 12Besides, she really is my sister, the daughter of my father though not of my mother; and she became my wife. 13And when God had me wander from my father's household, I said to her, 'This is how you can show your love to me: Everywhere we go, say of me, "He is my brother."'"

14Then Abimelech brought sheep and cattle and male and female slaves and gave them to Abraham, and he returned Sarah his wife to him. 15And Abimelech said, "My land is before you; live wherever you like."

16To Sarah he said, "I am giving your brother a thousand shekels[a] of silver. This is to cover the offense against you before all who are with you; you are completely vindicated."

17Then Abraham prayed to God, and God healed Abimelech, his wife and his slave girls so they could have children again, 18for the LORD had closed up every womb in Abimelech's household because of Abraham's wife Sarah.

The Birth of Isaac

21 NOW THE LORD was gracious to Sarah as he had said, and the LORD did for Sarah what he had promised. 2Sarah became pregnant and bore a son to Abraham in his old age, at the very time God had promised him. 3Abraham gave the name Isaac[b] to the son Sarah bore him. 4When his son Isaac was eight days old, Abraham circumcised him, as God commanded him. 5Abraham was a hundred years old when his son Isaac was born to him.

6Sarah said, "God has brought me laughter, and everyone who hears about this will laugh with me." 7And she added, "Who would have said to Abraham that Sarah would nurse children? Yet I have borne him a son in his old age."

Hagar and Ishmael Sent Away

8The child grew and was weaned, and on the day Isaac was weaned Abraham held a great feast. 9But Sarah saw that the son whom Hagar the Egyptian had borne to Abraham was mocking, 10and she said to Abraham, "Get rid of that slave woman and her son, for that slave woman's son will never share in the inheritance with my son Isaac."

---

[a] *16* That is, about 25 pounds (about 11.5 kilograms)   [b] *3 Isaac* means *he laughs*.

Living Bible

6"Yes, I know," the Lord replied. "That is why I held you back from sinning against me; that is why I didn't let you touch her. 7Now restore her to her husband, and he will pray for you (for he is a prophet) and you shall live. But if you don't return her to him, you are doomed to death along with all your household."

8The king was up early the next morning, and hastily called a meeting of all the palace personnel and told them what had happened. And great fear swept through the crowd.

9, 10Then the king called for Abraham. "What is this you've done to us?" he demanded. "What have I done that deserves treatment like this, to make me and my kingdom guilty of this great sin? Who would suspect that you would do a thing like this to me? Whatever made you think of this vile deed?"

11, 12"Well," Abraham said, "I figured this to be a godless place. 'They will want my wife and will kill me to get her,' I thought. And besides, she *is* my sister—or at least a half-sister (we both have the same father)—and I married her. 13And when God sent me traveling far from my childhood home, I told her, 'Have the kindness to mention, wherever we come, that you are my sister.' "

14Then King Abimelech took sheep and oxen and servants—both men and women—and gave them to Abraham, and returned Sarah his wife to him.

15"Look my kingdom over, and choose the place where you want to live," the king told him. 16Then he turned to Sarah. "Look," he said, "I am giving your 'brother' a thousand silver pieces as damages for what I did, to compensate for any embarrassment and to settle any claim against me regarding this matter. Now justice has been done."

17Then Abraham prayed, asking God to cure the king and queen and the other women of the household, so that they could have children; 18for God had stricken all the women with barrenness to punish Abimelech for taking Abraham's wife.

21 THEN GOD did as he had promised, and Sarah became pregnant and gave Abraham a baby son in his old age, at the time God had said; 3and Abraham named him Isaac (meaning "Laughter!"). 4, 5Eight days after he was born, Abraham circumcised him, as God required. (Abraham was 100 years old at that time.)

6And Sarah declared, "God has brought me laughter! All who hear about this shall rejoice with me. 7For who would have dreamed that I would ever have a baby? Yet I have given Abraham a child in his old age!"

8Time went by and the child grew and was weaned; and Abraham gave a party to celebrate the happy occasion. 9But when Sarah noticed Ishmael—the son of Abraham and the Egyptian girl Hagar—teasingᶜ Isaac, 10she turned upon Abraham and demanded, "Get rid of that slave girl and her son. He is not going to share your property with my son. I won't have it."

New Revised Standard

to him in the dream, "Yes, I know that you did this in the integrity of your heart; furthermore it was I who kept you from sinning against me. Therefore I did not let you touch her. 7Now then, return the man's wife; for he is a prophet, and he will pray for you and you shall live. But if you do not restore her, know that you shall surely die, you and all that are yours."

8 So Abimelech rose early in the morning, and called all his servants and told them all these things; and the men were very much afraid. 9Then Abimelech called Abraham, and said to him, "What have you done to us? How have I sinned against you, that you have brought such great guilt on me and my kingdom? You have done things to me that ought not to be done." 10And Abimelech said to Abraham, "What were you thinking of, that you did this thing?" 11Abraham said, "I did it because I thought, There is no fear of God at all in this place, and they will kill me because of my wife. 12Besides, she is indeed my sister, the daughter of my father but not the daughter of my mother; and she became my wife. 13And when God caused me to wander from my father's house, I said to her, 'This is the kindness you must do me: at every place to which we come, say of me, He is my brother.' " 14Then Abimelech took sheep and oxen, and male and female slaves, and gave them to Abraham, and restored his wife Sarah to him. 15Abimelech said, "My land is before you; settle where it pleases you." 16To Sarah he said, "Look, I have given your brother a thousand pieces of silver; it is your exoneration before all who are with you; you are completely vindicated." 17Then Abraham prayed to God; and God healed Abimelech, and also healed his wife and female slaves so that they bore children. 18For the LORD had closed fast all the wombs of the house of Abimelech because of Sarah, Abraham's wife.

The Birth of Isaac

21 THE LORD dealt with Sarah as he had said, and the LORD did for Sarah as he had promised. 2Sarah conceived and bore Abraham a son in his old age, at the time of which God had spoken to him. 3Abraham gave the name Isaac to his son whom Sarah bore him. 4And Abraham circumcised his son Isaac when he was eight days old, as God had commanded him. 5Abraham was a hundred years old when his son Isaac was born to him. 6Now Sarah said, "God has brought laughter for me; everyone who hears will laugh with me." 7And she said, "Who would ever have said to Abraham that Sarah would nurse children? Yet I have borne him a son in his old age."

Hagar and Ishmael Sent Away

8 The child grew, and was weaned; and Abraham made a great feast on the day that Isaac was weaned. 9But Sarah saw the son of Hagar the Egyptian, whom she had borne to Abraham, playing with her son Isaac.ᵈ 10So she said to Abraham, "Cast out this slave woman with her son; for the son of this slave woman shall not inherit along with my son Isaac." 11The matter was very

---

ᶜ 21:9 *teasing*, or "mocking," whether in innocent fun or otherwise is not clear in the text.

ᵈ Gk Vg: Heb lacks *with her son Isaac*

King James

11And the thing was very grievous in Abraham's sight because of his son.

12¶ And God said unto Abraham, Let it not be grievous in thy sight because of the lad, and because of thy bondwoman; in all that Sarah hath said unto thee, hearken unto her voice; for in Isaac shall thy seed be called.

13And also of the son of the bondwoman will I make a nation, because he *is* thy seed.

14And Abraham rose up early in the morning, and took bread, and a bottle of water, and gave *it* unto Hagar, putting *it* on her shoulder, and the child, and sent her away: and she departed, and wandered in the wilderness of Beer-sheba.

15And the water was spent in the bottle, and she cast the child under one of the shrubs.

16And she went, and sat her down over against *him* a good way off, as it were a bowshot: for she said, Let me not see the death of the child. And she sat over against *him,* and lift up her voice, and wept.

17And God heard the voice of the lad; and the angel of God called to Hagar out of heaven, and said unto her, What aileth thee, Hagar? fear not; for God hath heard the voice of the lad where he *is.*

18Arise, lift up the lad, and hold him in thine hand; for I will make him a great nation.

19And God opened her eyes, and she saw a well of water; and she went, and filled the bottle with water, and gave the lad drink.

20And God was with the lad; and he grew, and dwelt in the wilderness, and became an archer.

21And he dwelt in the wilderness of Paran: and his mother took him a wife out of the land of Egypt.

22¶ And it came to pass at that time, that Abimelech and Phichol the chief captain of his host spake unto Abraham, saying, God *is* with thee in all that thou doest:

23Now therefore swear unto me here by God that thou wilt not deal falsely with me, nor with my son, nor with my son's son: *but* according to the kindness that I have done unto thee, thou shalt do unto me, and to the land wherein thou hast sojourned.

24And Abraham said, I will swear.

25And Abraham reproved Abimelech because of a well of water, which Abimelech's servants had violently taken away.

26And Abimelech said, I wot not who hath done this thing: neither didst thou tell me, neither yet heard I *of it,* but today.

27And Abraham took sheep and oxen, and gave them unto Abimelech; and both of them made a covenant.

28And Abraham set seven ewe lambs of the flock by themselves.

29And Abimelech said unto Abraham, What *mean* these seven ewe lambs which thou hast set by themselves?

30And he said, For *these* seven ewe lambs shalt thou take of my hand, that they may be a witness unto me, that I have digged this well.

31Wherefore he called that place Beer-sheba; because there they sware both of them.

32Thus they made a covenant at Beer-sheba: then Abimelech rose up, and Phichol the chief captain of his host, and they returned into the land of the Philistines.

33¶ And *Abraham* planted a grove in Beer-sheba, and called there on the name of the LORD, the everlasting God.

34And Abraham sojourned in the Philistines' land many days.

New International

11The matter distressed Abraham greatly because it concerned his son. 12But God said to him, "Do not be so distressed about the boy and your maidservant. Listen to whatever Sarah tells you, because it is through Isaac that your offspringa will be reckoned. 13I will make the son of the maidservant into a nation also, because he is your offspring."

14Early the next morning Abraham took some food and a skin of water and gave them to Hagar. He set them on her shoulders and then sent her off with the boy. She went on her way and wandered in the desert of Beersheba.

15When the water in the skin was gone, she put the boy under one of the bushes. 16Then she went off and sat down nearby, about a bowshot away, for she thought, "I cannot watch the boy die." And as she sat there nearby, sheb began to sob.

17God heard the boy crying, and the angel of God called to Hagar from heaven and said to her, "What is the matter, Hagar? Do not be afraid; God has heard the boy crying as he lies there. 18Lift the boy up and take him by the hand, for I will make him into a great nation."

19Then God opened her eyes and she saw a well of water. So she went and filled the skin with water and gave the boy a drink.

20God was with the boy as he grew up. He lived in the desert and became an archer. 21While he was living in the Desert of Paran, his mother got a wife for him from Egypt.

The Treaty at Beersheba

22At that time Abimelech and Phicol the commander of his forces said to Abraham, "God is with you in everything you do. 23Now swear to me here before God that you will not deal falsely with me or my children or my descendants. Show to me and the country where you are living as an alien the same kindness I have shown to you."

24Abraham said, "I swear it."

25Then Abraham complained to Abimelech about a well of water that Abimelech's servants had seized. 26But Abimelech said, "I don't know who has done this. You did not tell me, and I heard about it only today."

27So Abraham brought sheep and cattle and gave them to Abimelech, and the two men made a treaty. 28Abraham set apart seven ewe lambs from the flock, 29and Abimelech asked Abraham, "What is the meaning of these seven ewe lambs you have set apart by themselves?"

30He replied, "Accept these seven lambs from my hand as a witness that I dug this well."

31So that place was called Beersheba,c because the two men swore an oath there.

32After the treaty had been made at Beersheba, Abimelech and Phicol the commander of his forces returned to the land of the Philistines. 33Abraham planted a tamarisk tree in Beersheba, and there he called upon the name of the LORD, the Eternal God. 34And Abraham stayed in the land of the Philistines for a long time.

---

a *12 Or* seed   b *16 Hebrew; Septuagint* the child   c *31 Beersheba* can mean *well of seven* or *well of the oath.*

Living Bible

11This upset Abraham very much, for after all, Ishmael too was his son.

12But God told Abraham, "Don't be upset over the boy or your slave-girl wife; do as Sarah says, for Isaac is the son through whom my promise will be fulfilled. 13And I will make a nation of the descendants of the slave-girl's son, too, because he also is yours."

14So Abraham got up early the next morning, prepared food for the journey, and strapped a canteen of water to Hagar's shoulders and sent her away with their son. She walked out into the wilderness of Beersheba, wandering aimlessly.

15When the water was gone she left the youth in the shade of a bush 16and went off and sat down a hundred yards or so away. "I don't want to watch him die," she said, and burst into tears, sobbing wildly.

17Then God heard the boy crying, and the Angel of God called to Hagar from the sky, "Hagar, what's wrong? Don't be afraid! For God has heard the lad's cries as he is lying there. 18Go and get him and comfort him, for I will make a great nation from his descendants."

19Then God opened her eyes and she saw a well; so she refilled the canteen and gave the lad a drink. 20, 21And God blessed the boy and he grew up in the wilderness of Paran, and became an expert archer. And his mother arranged a marriage for him with a girl from Egypt.

22About this time King Abimelech, and Phicol, commander of his troops, came to Abraham and said to him, "It is evident that God helps you in everything you do; 23swear to me by God's name that you won't defraud me or my son or my grandson, but that you will be on friendly terms with my country, as I have been toward you."

24Abraham replied, "All right, I swear to it!" 25Then Abraham complained to the king about a well the king's servants had taken violently away from Abraham's servants.

26"This is the first I've heard of it," the king exclaimed, "and I have no idea who is responsible. Why didn't you tell me before?"

27Then Abraham gave sheep and oxen to the king, as sacrifices to seal their pact.

28, 29But when he took seven ewe lambs and set them off by themselves, the king inquired, "Why are you doing that?"

30And Abraham replied, "They are my gift to you as a public confirmation that this well is mine."

31So from that time on the well was called Beer-sheba ("Well of the Oath"), because that was the place where they made their covenant. 32Then King Abimelech, and Phicol, commander of his army, returned home again. 33And Abraham planted a tamarisk tree beside the well, and prayed there to the Lord, calling upon the Eternal God. 34And Abraham lived in the Philistine country for a long time.

New Revised Standard

distressing to Abraham on account of his son. 12But God said to Abraham, "Do not be distressed because of the boy and because of your slave woman; whatever Sarah says to you, do as she tells you, for it is through Isaac that offspring shall be named for you. 13As for the son of the slave woman, I will make a nation of him also, because he is your offspring." 14So Abraham rose early in the morning, and took bread and a skin of water, and gave it to Hagar, putting it on her shoulder, along with the child, and sent her away. And she departed, and wandered about in the wilderness of Beer-sheba.

15 When the water in the skin was gone, she cast the child under one of the bushes. 16Then she went and sat down opposite him a good way off, about the distance of a bowshot; for she said, "Do not let me look on the death of the child." And as she sat opposite him, she lifted up her voice and wept. 17And God heard the voice of the boy; and the angel of God called to Hagar from heaven, and said to her, "What troubles you, Hagar? Do not be afraid; for God has heard the voice of the boy where he is. 18Come, lift up the boy and hold him fast with your hand, for I will make a great nation of him." 19Then God opened her eyes and she saw a well of water. She went, and filled the skin with water, and gave the boy a drink.

20 God was with the boy, and he grew up; he lived in the wilderness, and became an expert with the bow. 21He lived in the wilderness of Paran; and his mother got a wife for him from the land of Egypt.

Abraham and Abimelech Make a Covenant

22 At that time Abimelech, with Phicol the commander of his army, said to Abraham, "God is with you in all that you do; 23now therefore swear to me here by God that you will not deal falsely with me or with my offspring or with my posterity, but as I have dealt loyally with you, you will deal with me and with the land where you have resided as an alien." 24And Abraham said, "I swear it."

25 When Abraham complained to Abimelech about a well of water that Abimelech's servants had seized, 26Abimelech said, "I do not know who has done this; you did not tell me, and I have not heard of it until today." 27So Abraham took sheep and oxen and gave them to Abimelech, and the two men made a covenant. 28Abraham set apart seven ewe lambs of the flock. 29And Abimelech said to Abraham, "What is the meaning of these seven ewe lambs that you have set apart?" 30He said, "These seven ewe lambs you shall accept from my hand, in order that you may be a witness for me that I dug this well." 31Therefore that place was called Beer-sheba;d because there both of them swore an oath. 32When they had made a covenant at Beer-sheba, Abimelech, with Phicol the commander of his army, left and returned to the land of the Philistines. 33Abrahame planted a tamarisk tree in Beer-sheba, and called there on the name of the Lord, the Everlasting God.f 34And Abraham resided as an alien many days in the land of the Philistines.

d That is Well of seven or Well of the oath   e Heb He   f Or the Lord, El Olam

King James

22 AND IT came to pass after these things, that God did tempt Abraham, and said unto him, Abraham: and he said, Behold, *here* I *am*.

2And he said, Take now thy son, thine only *son* Isaac, whom thou lovest, and get thee into the land of Moriah; and offer him there for a burnt offering upon one of the mountains which I will tell thee of.

3¶ And Abraham rose up early in the morning, and saddled his ass, and took two of his young men with him, and Isaac his son, and clave the wood for the burnt offering, and rose up, and went unto the place of which God had told him.

4Then on the third day Abraham lifted up his eyes, and saw the place afar off.

5And Abraham said unto his young men, Abide ye here with the ass; and I and the lad will go yonder and worship, and come again to you.

6And Abraham took the wood of the burnt offering, and laid *it* upon Isaac his son; and he took the fire in his hand, and a knife; and they went both of them together.

7And Isaac spake unto Abraham his father, and said, My father: and he said, Here *am* I, my son. And he said, Behold the fire and the wood: but where *is* the lamb for a burnt offering?

8And Abraham said, My son, God will provide himself a lamb for a burnt offering: so they went both of them together.

9And they came to the place which God had told him of; and Abraham built an altar there, and laid the wood in order, and bound Isaac his son, and laid him on the altar upon the wood.

10And Abraham stretched forth his hand, and took the knife to slay his son.

11And the angel of the LORD called unto him out of heaven, and said, Abraham, Abraham: and he said, Here *am* I.

12And he said, Lay not thine hand upon the lad, neither do thou any thing unto him: for now I know that thou fearest God, seeing thou hast not withheld thy son, thine only *son* from me.

13And Abraham lifted up his eyes, and looked, and behold behind *him* a ram caught in a thicket by his horns: and Abraham went and took the ram, and offered him up for a burnt offering in the stead of his son.

14And Abraham called the name of that place Jehovah-jireh: as it is said *to* this day, In the mount of the LORD it shall be seen.

15¶ And the angel of the LORD called unto Abraham out of heaven the second time,

16And said, By myself have I sworn, saith the LORD, for because thou hast done this thing, and hast not withheld thy son, thine only *son:*

17That in blessing I will bless thee, and in multiplying I will multiply thy seed as the stars of the heaven, and as the sand which *is* upon the sea shore; and thy seed shall possess the gate of his enemies;

18And in thy seed shall all the nations of the earth be blessed; because thou hast obeyed my voice.

19So Abraham returned unto his young men, and they rose up and went together to Beer-sheba; and Abraham dwelt at Beer-sheba.

20¶ And it came to pass after these things, that it was told Abraham, saying, Behold, Milcah, she hath also born children unto thy brother Nahor;

21Huz his firstborn, and Buz his brother, and Kemuel the father of Aram,

22And Chesed, and Hazo, and Pildash, and Jidlaph, and Bethuel.

23And Bethuel begat Rebekah: these eight Milcah did bear to Nahor, Abraham's brother.

24And his concubine, whose name *was* Reumah, she bare also Tebah, and Gaham, and Thahash, and Maachah.

New International

Abraham Tested

22 SOME TIME later God tested Abraham. He said to him, "Abraham!"

"Here I am," he replied.

2Then God said, "Take your son, your only son, Isaac, whom you love, and go to the region of Moriah. Sacrifice him there as a burnt offering on one of the mountains I will tell you about."

3Early the next morning Abraham got up and saddled his donkey. He took with him two of his servants and his son Isaac. When he had cut enough wood for the burnt offering, he set out for the place God had told him about. 4On the third day Abraham looked up and saw the place in the distance. 5He said to his servants, "Stay here with the donkey while I and the boy go over there. We will worship and then we will come back to you."

6Abraham took the wood for the burnt offering and placed it on his son Isaac, and he himself carried the fire and the knife. As the two of them went on together, 7Isaac spoke up and said to his father Abraham, "Father?"

"Yes, my son?" Abraham replied.

"The fire and wood are here," Isaac said, "but where is the lamb for the burnt offering?"

8Abraham answered, "God himself will provide the lamb for the burnt offering, my son." And the two of them went on together.

9When they reached the place God had told him about, Abraham built an altar there and arranged the wood on it. He bound his son Isaac and laid him on the altar, on top of the wood. 10Then he reached out his hand and took the knife to slay his son. 11But the angel of the LORD called out to him from heaven, "Abraham! Abraham!"

"Here I am," he replied.

12"Do not lay a hand on the boy," he said. "Do not do anything to him. Now I know that you fear God, because you have not withheld from me your son, your only son."

13Abraham looked up and there in a thicket he saw a ram[a] caught by its horns. He went over and took the ram and sacrificed it as a burnt offering instead of his son. 14So Abraham called that place The LORD Will Provide. And to this day it is said, "On the mountain of the LORD it will be provided."

15The angel of the LORD called to Abraham from heaven a second time 16and said, "I swear by myself, declares the LORD, that because you have done this and have not withheld your son, your only son, 17I will surely bless you and make your descendants as numerous as the stars in the sky and as the sand on the seashore. Your descendants will take possession of the cities of their enemies, 18and through your offspring[b] all nations on earth will be blessed, because you have obeyed me."

19Then Abraham returned to his servants, and they set off together for Beersheba. And Abraham stayed in Beersheba.

Nahor's Sons

20Some time later Abraham was told, "Milcah is also a mother; she has borne sons to your brother Nahor: 21Uz the firstborn, Buz his brother, Kemuel (the father of Aram), 22Kesed, Hazo, Pildash, Jidlaph and Bethuel." 23Bethuel became the father of Rebekah. Milcah bore these eight sons to Abraham's brother Nahor. 24His concubine, whose name was Reumah, also had sons: Tebah, Gaham, Tahash and Maacah.

---

a 13 Many manuscripts of the Masoretic Text, Samaritan Pentateuch, Septuagint and Syriac; most manuscripts of the Masoretic Text *a ram behind him.*   b 18 Or *seed*

Living Bible

22 LATER ON, God tested Abraham's [faith and obedience[c]].

"Abraham!" God called.

"Yes, Lord?" he replied.

2"Take with you your only son—yes, Isaac whom you love so much—and go to the land of Moriah and sacrifice him there as a burnt offering upon one of the mountains which I'll point out to you!"

3The next morning Abraham got up early, chopped wood for a fire upon the altar, saddled his donkey, and took with him his son Isaac and two young men who were his servants, and started off to the place where God had told him to go. 4On the third day of the journey Abraham saw the place in the distance.

5"Stay here with the donkey," Abraham told the young men, "and the lad and I will travel yonder and worship, and then come right back."

6Abraham placed the wood for the burnt offering upon Isaac's shoulders, while he himself carried the knife and the flint for striking a fire. So the two of them went on together.

7"Father," Isaac asked, "we have the wood and the flint to make the fire, but where is the lamb for the sacrifice?"

8"God will see to it, my son," Abraham replied. And they went on.

9When they arrived at the place where God had told Abraham to go, he built an altar and placed the wood in order, ready for the fire, and then tied Isaac and laid him on the altar over the wood. 10And Abraham took the knife and lifted it up to plunge it into his son, to slay him.

11At that moment the Angel of God shouted to him from heaven, "Abraham! Abraham!"

"Yes, Lord!" he answered.

12"Lay down the knife; don't hurt the lad in any way," the Angel said, "for I know that God is first in your life—you have not withheld even your beloved son from me."

13Then Abraham noticed a ram caught by its horns in a bush. So he took the ram and sacrificed it, instead of his son, as a burnt offering on the altar. 14Abraham named the place "Jehovah provides"—and it still goes by that name to this day.

15Then the Angel of God called again to Abraham from heaven. 16"I, the Lord, have sworn by myself that because you have obeyed me and have not withheld even your beloved son from me, 17I will bless you with incredible blessings and multiply your descendants into countless thousands and millions, like the stars above you in the sky, and like the sands along the seashore. They will conquer their enemies, 18and your offspring[d] will be a blessing to all the nations of the earth—all because you have obeyed me."

19So they returned to his young men, and traveled home again to Beer-sheba. 20–23After this, a message arrived that Milcah, the wife of Abraham's brother Nahor, had borne him eight sons. Their names were:

Uz, the oldest, Buz, the next oldest, Kemuel (father of Aram), Chesed, Hazo, Pildash, Jidlaph, Bethuel (father of Rebekah).

24He also had four other children from his concubine, Reumah:

Tebah, Gaham, Tahash, Maacah.

New Revised Standard

The Command to Sacrifice Isaac

22 AFTER THESE things God tested Abraham. He said to him, "Abraham!" And he said, "Here I am." 2He said, "Take your son, your only son Isaac, whom you love, and go to the land of Moriah, and offer him there as a burnt offering on one of the mountains that I shall show you." 3So Abraham rose early in the morning, saddled his donkey, and took two of his young men with him, and his son Isaac; he cut the wood for the burnt offering, and set out and went to the place in the distance that God had shown him. 4On the third day Abraham looked up and saw the place far away. 5Then Abraham said to his young men, "Stay here with the donkey; the boy and I will go over there; we will worship, and then we will come back to you." 6Abraham took the wood of the burnt offering and laid it on his son Isaac, and he himself carried the fire and the knife. So the two of them walked on together. 7Isaac said to his father Abraham, "Father!" And he said, "Here I am, my son." He said, "The fire and the wood are here, but where is the lamb for a burnt offering?" 8Abraham said, "God himself will provide the lamb for a burnt offering, my son." So the two of them walked on together.

9 When they came to the place that God had shown him, Abraham built an altar there and laid the wood in order. He bound his son Isaac, and laid him on the altar, on top of the wood. 10Then Abraham reached out his hand and took the knife to kill[e] his son. 11But the angel of the LORD called to him from heaven, and said, "Abraham, Abraham!" And he said, "Here I am." 12He said, "Do not lay your hand on the boy or do anything to him; for now I know that you fear God, since you have not withheld your son, your only son, from me." 13And Abraham looked up and saw a ram, caught in a thicket by its horns. Abraham went and took the ram and offered it up as a burnt offering instead of his son. 14So Abraham called that place "The LORD will provide";[f] as it is said to this day, "On the mount of the LORD it shall be provided."[g]

15 The angel of the LORD called to Abraham a second time from heaven, 16and said, "By myself I have sworn, says the LORD: Because you have done this, and have not withheld your son, your only son, 17I will indeed bless you, and I will make your offspring as numerous as the stars of heaven and as the sand that is on the seashore. And your offspring shall possess the gate of their enemies, 18and by your offspring shall all the nations of the earth gain blessing for themselves, because you have obeyed my voice." 19So Abraham returned to his young men, and they arose and went together to Beer-sheba; and Abraham lived at Beer-sheba.

The Children of Nahor

20 Now after these things it was told Abraham, "Milcah also has borne children, to your brother Nahor: 21Uz the firstborn, Buz his brother, Kemuel the father of Aram, 22Chesed, Hazo, Pildash, Jidlaph, and Bethuel." 23Bethuel became the father of Rebekah. These eight Milcah bore to Nahor, Abraham's brother. 24Moreover, his concubine, whose name was Reumah, bore Tebah, Gaham, Tahash, and Maacah.

---

c 22:1 *faith and obedience*, implied.   d 22:18 *your offspring*, or, "your seed."

e Or *to slaughter*   f Or *will see*; Heb traditionally transliterated *Jehovah Jireh*   g Or *he shall be seen*

King James

23 AND SARAH was an hundred and seven and twenty years old: *these were* the years of the life of Sarah.

2And Sarah died in Kirjath-arba; the same *is* Hebron in the land of Canaan: and Abraham came to mourn for Sarah, and to weep for her.

3¶ And Abraham stood up from before his dead, and spake unto the sons of Heth, saying,

4I *am* a stranger and a sojourner with you: give me a possession of a buryingplace with you, that I may bury my dead out of my sight.

5And the children of Heth answered Abraham, saying unto him,

6Hear us, my lord: thou *art* a mighty prince among us: in the choice of our sepulchres bury thy dead; none of us shall withhold from thee his sepulchre, but that thou mayest bury thy dead.

7And Abraham stood up, and bowed himself to the people of the land, *even* to the children of Heth.

8And he communed with them, saying, If it be your mind that I should bury my dead out of my sight; hear me, and entreat for me to Ephron the son of Zohar,

9That he may give me the cave of Machpelah, which he hath, which *is* in the end of his field; for as much money as it is worth he shall give it me for a possession of a buryingplace amongst you.

10And Ephron dwelt among the children of Heth: and Ephron the Hittite answered Abraham in the audience of the children of Heth, *even* of all that went in at the gate of his city, saying,

11Nay, my lord, hear me: the field give I thee, and the cave that *is* therein, I give it thee; in the presence of the sons of my people give I it thee: bury thy dead.

12And Abraham bowed down himself before the people of the land.

13And he spake unto Ephron in the audience of the people of the land, saying, But if thou *wilt give it,* I pray thee, hear me: I will give thee money for the field; take *it* of me, and I will bury my dead there.

14And Ephron answered Abraham, saying unto him,

15My lord, hearken unto me: the land *is worth* four hundred shekels of silver; what *is* that betwixt me and thee? bury therefore thy dead.

16And Abraham hearkened unto Ephron; and Abraham weighed to Ephron the silver, which he had named in the audience of the sons of Heth, four hundred shekels of silver, current *money* with the merchant.

17¶ And the field of Ephron, which *was* in Machpelah, which *was* before Mamre, the field, and the cave which *was* therein, and all the trees that *were* in the field, that *were* in all the borders round about, were made sure

18Unto Abraham for a possession in the presence of the children of Heth, before all that went in at the gate of his city.

19And after this, Abraham buried Sarah his wife in the cave of the field of Machpelah before Mamre: the same *is* Hebron in the land of Canaan.

20And the field, and the cave that *is* therein, were made sure unto Abraham for a possession of a buryingplace by the sons of Heth.

24 AND ABRAHAM was old, *and* well stricken in age: and the LORD had blessed Abraham in all things.

2And Abraham said unto his eldest servant of his house, that ruled over all that he had, Put, I pray thee, thy hand under my thigh:

New International

The Death of Sarah

23 SARAH LIVED to be a hundred and twenty-seven years old. 2She died at Kiriath Arba (that is, Hebron) in the land of Canaan, and Abraham went to mourn for Sarah and to weep over her.

3Then Abraham rose from beside his dead wife and spoke to the Hittites.[a] He said, 4"I am an alien and a stranger among you. Sell me some property for a burial site here so I can bury my dead."

5The Hittites replied to Abraham, 6"Sir, listen to us. You are a mighty prince among us. Bury your dead in the choicest of our tombs. None of us will refuse you his tomb for burying your dead."

7Then Abraham rose and bowed down before the people of the land, the Hittites. 8He said to them, "If you are willing to let me bury my dead, then listen to me and intercede with Ephron son of Zohar on my behalf 9so he will sell me the cave of Machpelah, which belongs to him and is at the end of his field. Ask him to sell it to me for the full price as a burial site among you."

10Ephron the Hittite was sitting among his people and he replied to Abraham in the hearing of all the Hittites who had come to the gate of his city. 11"No, my lord," he said. "Listen to me; I give[b] you the field, and I give[b] you the cave that is in it. I give[b] it to you in the presence of my people. Bury your dead."

12Again Abraham bowed down before the people of the land 13and he said to Ephron in their hearing, "Listen to me, if you will. I will pay the price of the field. Accept it from me so I can bury my dead there."

14Ephron answered Abraham, 15"Listen to me, my lord; the land is worth four hundred shekels[c] of silver, but what is that between me and you? Bury your dead."

16Abraham agreed to Ephron's terms and weighed out for him the price he had named in the hearing of the Hittites: four hundred shekels of silver, according to the weight current among the merchants.

17So Ephron's field in Machpelah near Mamre—both the field and the cave in it, and all the trees within the borders of the field—was deeded 18to Abraham as his property in the presence of all the Hittites who had come to the gate of the city. 19Afterward Abraham buried his wife Sarah in the cave in the field of Machpelah near Mamre (which is at Hebron) in the land of Canaan. 20So the field and the cave in it were deeded to Abraham by the Hittites as a burial site.

Isaac and Rebekah

24 ABRAHAM WAS now old and well advanced in years, and the LORD had blessed him in every way. 2He said to the chief[d] servant in his household, the one in charge of all that he had, "Put your hand under my thigh. 3I want you to swear by the LORD, the God

---

a 3 Or *the sons of Heth*; also in verses 5, 7, 10, 16, 18 and 20　　b 11 Or *sell*　　c 15 That is, about 10 pounds (about 4.5 kilograms)　　d 2 Or *oldest*

Living Bible

23 WHEN SARAH was 127 years old, she died in Hebron in the land of Canaan; there Abraham mourned and wept for her. ³Then, standing beside her body, he said to the men of Heth:

⁴"Here I am, a visitor in a foreign land, with no place to bury my wife. Please sell me a piece of ground for this purpose."

⁵, ⁶"Certainly," the men replied, "for you are an honored prince of God among us; it will be a privilege to have you choose the finest of our sepulchres, so that you can bury her there."

⁷Then Abraham bowed low before them and said, ⁸"Since this is your feeling in the matter, be so kind as to ask Ephron, Zohar's son, ⁹to sell me the cave of Mach-pelah, down at the end of his field. I will of course pay the full price for it, whatever is publicly agreed upon, and it will become a permanent cemetery for my family."

¹⁰Ephron was sitting there among the others, and now he spoke up, answering Abraham as the others listened, speaking publicly before all the citizens of the town: ¹¹"Sir," he said to Abraham, "please listen to me. I will give you the cave and the field without any charge. Here in the presence of my people, I give it to you free. Go and bury your dead."

¹²Abraham bowed again to the men of Heth, ¹³and replied to Ephron, as all listened: "No, let me buy it from you. Let me pay the full price of the field, and then I will bury my dead."

¹⁴, ¹⁵"Well, the land is worth 400 pieces of silver," Ephron said, "but what is that between friends? Go ahead and bury your dead."

¹⁶So Abraham paid Ephron the price he had suggested—400 pieces of silver, as publicly agreed. ¹⁷, ¹⁸This is the land he bought: Ephron's field at Mach-pelah, near Mamre, and the cave at the end of the field, and all the trees in the field. They became his permanent possession, by agreement in the presence of the men of Heth at the city gate. ¹⁹, ²⁰So Abraham buried Sarah there, in the field and cave deeded to him by the men of Heth as a burial plot.

24 ABRAHAM WAS now a very old man, and God blessed him in every way. ²One day Abraham said to his household administrator, who was his oldest servant,

New Revised Standard

Sarah's Death and Burial

23 SARAH LIVED one hundred twenty-seven years; this was the length of Sarah's life. ² And Sarah died at Kiriath-arba (that is, Hebron) in the land of Canaan; and Abraham went in to mourn for Sarah and to weep for her. ³ Abraham rose up from beside his dead, and said to the Hittites, ⁴"I am a stranger and an alien residing among you; give me property among you for a burying place, so that I may bury my dead out of my sight." ⁵ The Hittites answered Abraham, ⁶"Hear us, my lord; you are a mighty prince among us. Bury your dead in the choicest of our burial places; none of us will withhold from you any burial ground for burying your dead." ⁷ Abraham rose and bowed to the Hittites, the people of the land. ⁸ He said to them, "If you are willing that I should bury my dead out of my sight, hear me, and entreat for me Ephron son of Zohar, ⁹ so that he may give me the cave of Machpelah, which he owns; it is at the end of his field. For the full price let him give it to me in your presence as a possession for a burying place." ¹⁰ Now Ephron was sitting among the Hittites; and Ephron the Hittite answered Abraham in the hearing of the Hittites, of all who went in at the gate of his city, ¹¹ "No, my lord, hear me; I give you the field, and I give you the cave that is in it; in the presence of my people I give it to you; bury your dead." ¹² Then Abraham bowed down before the people of the land. ¹³ He said to Ephron in the hearing of the people of the land, "If you only will listen to me! I will give the price of the field; accept it from me, so that I may bury my dead there." ¹⁴ Ephron answered Abraham, ¹⁵ "My lord, listen to me; a piece of land worth four hundred shekels of silver— what is that between you and me? Bury your dead." ¹⁶ Abraham agreed with Ephron; and Abraham weighed out for Ephron the silver that he had named in the hearing of the Hittites, four hundred shekels of silver, according to the weights current among the merchants.

17 So the field of Ephron in Machpelah, which was to the east of Mamre, the field with the cave that was in it and all the trees that were in the field, throughout its whole area, passed ¹⁸to Abraham as a possession in the presence of the Hittites, in the presence of all who went in at the gate of his city. ¹⁹After this, Abraham buried Sarah his wife in the cave of the field of Machpelah facing Mamre (that is, Hebron) in the land of Canaan. ²⁰The field and the cave that is in it passed from the Hittites into Abraham's possession as a burying place.

The Marriage of Isaac and Rebekah

24 NOW ABRAHAM was old, well advanced in years; and the LORD had blessed Abraham in all things. ²Abraham said to his servant, the oldest of his house, who had charge of all that he had, "Put your hand under my thigh ³and I will make you swear by the LORD,

King James

3And I will make thee swear by the LORD, the God of heaven, and the God of the earth, that thou shalt not take a wife unto my son of the daughters of the Canaanites, among whom I dwell:

4But thou shalt go unto my country, and to my kindred, and take a wife unto my son Isaac.

5And the servant said unto him, Peradventure the woman will not be willing to follow me unto this land: must I needs bring thy son again unto the land from whence thou camest?

6And Abraham said unto him, Beware thou that thou bring not my son thither again.

7¶ The LORD God of heaven, which took me from my father's house, and from the land of my kindred, and which spake unto me, and that sware unto me, saying, Unto thy seed will I give this land; he shall send his angel before thee, and thou shalt take a wife unto my son from thence.

8And if the woman will not be willing to follow thee, then thou shalt be clear from this my oath: only bring not my son thither again.

9And the servant put his hand under the thigh of Abraham his master, and sware to him concerning that matter.

10¶ And the servant took ten camels of the camels of his master, and departed; for all the goods of his master *were* in his hand: and he arose, and went to Mesopotamia, unto the city of Nahor.

11And he made his camels to kneel down without the city by a well of water at the time of the evening, *even* the time that women go out to draw *water*.

12And he said, O LORD God of my master Abraham, I pray thee, send me good speed this day, and show kindness unto my master Abraham.

13Behold, I stand *here* by the well of water; and the daughters of the men of the city come out to draw water:

14And let it come to pass, that the damsel to whom I shall say, Let down thy pitcher, I pray thee, that I may drink; and she shall say, Drink, and I will give thy camels drink also: *let the same be* she *that* thou hast appointed for thy servant Isaac; and thereby shall I know that thou hast shown kindness unto my master.

15¶ And it came to pass, before he had done speaking, that, behold, Rebekah came out, who was born to Bethuel, son of Milcah, the wife of Nahor, Abraham's brother, with her pitcher upon her shoulder.

16And the damsel *was* very fair to look upon, a virgin, neither had any man known her: and she went down to the well, and filled her pitcher, and came up.

17And the servant ran to meet her, and said, Let me, I pray thee, drink a little water of thy pitcher.

18And she said, Drink, my lord: and she hasted, and let down her pitcher upon her hand, and gave him drink.

19And when she had done giving him drink, she said, I will draw *water* for thy camels also, until they have done drinking.

20And she hasted, and emptied her pitcher into the trough, and ran again unto the well to draw *water,* and drew for all his camels.

21And the man wondering at her held his peace, to wit whether the LORD had made his journey prosperous or not.

22And it came to pass, as the camels had done drinking, that the man took a golden earring of half a shekel weight, and two bracelets for her hands of ten *shekels* weight of gold;

23And said, Whose daughter *art* thou? tell me, I pray thee: is there room *in* thy father's house for us to lodge in?

24And she said unto him, I *am* the daughter of Bethuel the son of Milcah, which she bare unto Nahor.

25She said moreover unto him, We have both straw and provender enough, and room to lodge in.

26And the man bowed down his head, and worshipped the LORD.

New International

of heaven and the God of earth, that you will not get a wife for my son from the daughters of the Canaanites, among whom I am living, 4but will go to my country and my own relatives and get a wife for my son Isaac."

5The servant asked him, "What if the woman is unwilling to come back with me to this land? Shall I then take your son back to the country you came from?"

6"Make sure that you do not take my son back there," Abraham said. 7"The LORD, the God of heaven, who brought me out of my father's household and my native land and who spoke to me and promised me on oath, saying, 'To your offspring[a] I will give this land'—he will send his angel before you so that you can get a wife for my son from there. 8If the woman is unwilling to come back with you, then you will be released from this oath of mine. Only do not take my son back there." 9So the servant put his hand under the thigh of his master Abraham and swore an oath to him concerning this matter.

10Then the servant took ten of his master's camels and left, taking with him all kinds of good things from his master. He set out for Aram Naharaim[b] and made his way to the town of Nahor. 11He had the camels kneel down near the well outside the town; it was toward evening, the time the women go out to draw water.

12Then he prayed, "O LORD, God of my master Abraham, give me success today, and show kindness to my master Abraham. 13See, I am standing beside this spring, and the daughters of the townspeople are coming out to draw water. 14May it be that when I say to a girl, 'Please let down your jar that I may have a drink,' and she says, 'Drink, and I'll water your camels too'—let her be the one you have chosen for your servant Isaac. By this I will know that you have shown kindness to my master."

15Before he had finished praying, Rebekah came out with her jar on her shoulder. She was the daughter of Bethuel son of Milcah, who was the wife of Abraham's brother Nahor. 16The girl was very beautiful, a virgin; no man had ever lain with her. She went down to the spring, filled her jar and came up again.

17The servant hurried to meet her and said, "Please give me a little water from your jar."

18"Drink, my lord," she said, and quickly lowered the jar to her hands and gave him a drink.

19After she had given him a drink, she said, "I'll draw water for your camels too, until they have finished drinking." 20So she quickly emptied her jar into the trough, ran back to the well to draw more water, and drew enough for all his camels. 21Without saying a word, the man watched her closely to learn whether or not the LORD had made his journey successful.

22When the camels had finished drinking, the man took out a gold nose ring weighing a beka[c] and two gold bracelets weighing ten shekels.[d] 23Then he asked, "Whose daughter are you? Please tell me, is there room in your father's house for us to spend the night?"

24She answered him, "I am the daughter of Bethuel, the son that Milcah bore to Nahor." 25And she added, "We have plenty of straw and fodder, as well as room for you to spend the night."

26Then the man bowed down and worshiped the LORD, 27saying, "Praise be to the LORD, the God of my

---

a 7 Or *seed*   b 10 That is, Northwest Mesopotamia   c 22 That is, about 1/5 ounce (about 5.5 grams)   d 22 That is, about 4 ounces (about 110 grams)

Living Bible

3"Swear by Jehovah, the God of heaven and earth, that you will not let my son marry one of these local girls, these Canaanites. 4Go instead to my homeland, to my relatives, and find a wife for him there."

5"But suppose I can't find a girl who will come so far from home?" the servant asked. "Then shall I take Isaac there, to live among your relatives?"

6"No!" Abraham warned. "Be careful that you don't do that under any circumstance. 7For the Lord God of heaven told me to leave that land and my people, and promised to give me and my children this land. He will send his angel on ahead of you, and he will see to it that you find a girl from there to be my son's wife. 8But if you don't succeed, then you are free from this oath; but under no circumstances are you to take my son there."

9So the servant vowede to follow Abraham's instructions.

10He took with him ten of Abraham's camels loaded with samples of the best of everything his master owned, and journeyed to Iraq, to Nahor's village. 11There he made the camels kneel down outside the town, beside a spring. It was evening, and the women of the village were coming to draw water.

12"O Jehovah, the God of my master," he prayed, "show kindness to my master Abraham and help me to accomplish the purpose of my journey. 13See, here I am, standing beside this spring, and the girls of the village are coming out to draw water. 14This is my request: When I ask one of them for a drink and she says, 'Yes, certainly, and I will water your camels too!'—let her be the one you have appointed as Isaac's wife. That is how I will know."

15, 16As he was still speaking to the Lord about this, a beautiful young girl named Rebekah arrived with a water jug on her shoulder and filled it at the spring. (Her father was Bethuel the son of Nahor and his wife Milcah.)f 17Running over to her, the servant asked her for a drink.

18"Certainly, sir," she said, and quickly lowered the jug for him to drink. 19Then she said, "I'll draw water for your camels, too, until they have enough!"

20So she emptied the jug into the watering trough and ran down to the spring again and kept carrying water to the camels until they had enough. 21The servant said no more, but watched her carefully to see if she would finish the job,g so that he would know whether she was the one. 22Then at last, when the camels had finished drinking, he produced a quarter-ounce gold earringh and two five-ounce gold bracelets for her wrists.

23"Whose daughter are you, miss?" he asked. "Would your father have any room to put us up for the night?"

24"My father is Bethuel," she replied. "My grandparents are Milcah and Nahor. 25Yes, we have plenty of straw and food for the camels, and a guest room."

26The man stood there a moment with head bowed, worshiping Jehovah. 27"Thank you, Lord God of my

New Revised Standard

the God of heaven and earth, that you will not get a wife for my son from the daughters of the Canaanites, among whom I live, 4but will go to my country and to my kindred and get a wife for my son Isaac." 5The servant said to him, "Perhaps the woman may not be willing to follow me to this land; must I then take your son back to the land from which you came?" 6Abraham said to him, "See to it that you do not take my son back there. 7The Lord, the God of heaven, who took me from my father's house and from the land of my birth, and who spoke to me and swore to me, 'To your offspring I will give this land,' he will send his angel before you, and you shall take a wife for my son from there. 8But if the woman is not willing to follow you, then you will be free from this oath of mine; only you must not take my son back there." 9So the servant put his hand under the thigh of Abraham his master and swore to him concerning this matter.

10 Then the servant took ten of his master's camels and departed, taking all kinds of choice gifts from his master; and he set out and went to Aram-naharaim, to the city of Nahor. 11He made the camels kneel down outside the city by the well of water; it was toward evening, the time when women go out to draw water. 12And he said, "O Lord, God of my master Abraham, please grant me success today and show steadfast love to my master Abraham. 13I am standing here by the spring of water, and the daughters of the townspeople are coming out to draw water. 14Let the girl to whom I shall say, 'Please offer your jar that I may drink,' and who shall say, 'Drink, and I will water your camels'— let her be the one whom you have appointed for your servant Isaac. By this I shall know that you have shown steadfast love to my master."

15 Before he had finished speaking, there was Rebekah, who was born to Bethuel son of Milcah, the wife of Nahor, Abraham's brother, coming out with her water jar on her shoulder. 16The girl was very fair to look upon, a virgin, whom no man had known. She went down to the spring, filled her jar, and came up. 17Then the servant ran to meet her and said, "Please let me sip a little water from your jar." 18"Drink, my lord," she said, and quickly lowered her jar upon her hand and gave him a drink. 19When she had finished giving him a drink, she said, "I will draw for your camels also, until they have finished drinking." 20So she quickly emptied her jar into the trough and ran again to the well to draw, and she drew for all his camels. 21The man gazed at her in silence to learn whether or not the Lord had made his journey successful.

22 When the camels had finished drinking, the man took a gold nose-ring weighing a half shekel, and two bracelets for her arms weighing ten gold shekels, 23and said, "Tell me whose daughter you are. Is there room in your father's house for us to spend the night?" 24She said to him, "I am the daughter of Bethuel son of Milcah, whom she bore to Nahor." 25She added, "We have plenty of straw and fodder and a place to spend the night." 26The man bowed his head and worshiped the Lord

---

e 24:9 So the servant vowed, literally, "put his hand under the thigh of Abraham his master and swore to him that . . ."   f 24:15, 16 a beautiful young girl, literally, "a virgin." the son of Nahor, Abraham's brother.   g 24:21 to see if she would finish the job, implied.   h 24:22 gold earring, literally, "nose-ring."

King James

27And he said, Blessed *be* the LORD God of my master Abraham, who hath not left destitute my master of his mercy and his truth: I *being* in the way, the LORD led me to the house of my master's brethren.

28And the damsel ran, and told *them of* her mother's house these things.

29¶ And Rebekah had a brother, and his name *was* Laban: and Laban ran out unto the man, unto the well.

30And it came to pass, when he saw the earring and bracelets upon his sister's hands, and when he heard the words of Rebekah his sister, saying, Thus spake the man unto me; that he came unto the man; and, behold, he stood by the camels at the well.

31And he said, Come in, thou blessed of the LORD; wherefore standest thou without? for I have prepared the house, and room for the camels.

32¶ And the man came into the house: and he ungirded his camels, and gave straw and provender for the camels, and water to wash his feet, and the men's feet that *were* with him.

33And there was set *meat* before him to eat: but he said, I will not eat, until I have told mine errand. And he said, Speak on.

34And he said, I *am* Abraham's servant.

35And the LORD hath blessed my master greatly; and he is become great: and he hath given him flocks, and herds, and silver, and gold, and menservants, and maidservants, and camels, and asses.

36And Sarah my master's wife bare a son to my master when she was old: and unto him hath he given all that he hath.

37And my master made me swear, saying, Thou shalt not take a wife to my son of the daughters of the Canaanites, in whose land I dwell:

38But thou shalt go unto my father's house, and to my kindred, and take a wife unto my son.

39And I said unto my master, Peradventure the woman will not follow me.

40And he said unto me, The LORD, before whom I walk, will send his angel with thee, and prosper thy way; and thou shalt take a wife for my son of my kindred, and of my father's house:

41Then shalt thou be clear from *this* my oath, when thou comest to my kindred; and if they give not thee *one*, thou shalt be clear from my oath.

42And I came this day unto the well, and said, O LORD God of my master Abraham, if now thou do prosper my way which I go:

43Behold, I stand by the well of water; and it shall come to pass, that when the virgin cometh forth to draw *water*, and I say to her, Give me, I pray thee, a little water of thy pitcher to drink;

44And she say to me, Both drink thou, and I will also draw for thy camels: *let* the same *be* the woman whom the LORD hath appointed out for my master's son.

45And before I had done speaking in mine heart, behold, Rebekah came forth with her pitcher on her shoulder; and she went down unto the well, and drew *water:* and I said unto her, Let me drink, I pray thee.

46And she made haste, and let down her pitcher from her *shoulder*, and said, Drink, and I will give thy camels drink also: so I drank, and she made the camels drink also.

47And I asked her, and said, Whose daughter *art* thou? And she said, The daughter of Bethuel, Nahor's son, whom Milcah bare unto him: and I put the earring upon her face, and the bracelets upon her hands.

48And I bowed down my head, and worshipped the LORD, and blessed the LORD God of my master Abraham, which had led me in the right way to take my master's brother's daughter unto his son.

49And now if ye will deal kindly and truly with my master, tell me: and if not, tell me; that I may turn to the right hand, or to the left.

New International

master Abraham, who has not abandoned his kindness and faithfulness to my master. As for me, the LORD has led me on the journey to the house of my master's relatives."

28The girl ran and told her mother's household about these things. 29Now Rebekah had a brother named Laban, and he hurried out to the man at the spring. 30As soon as he had seen the nose ring, and the bracelets on his sister's arms, and had heard Rebekah tell what the man said to her, he went out to the man and found him standing by the camels near the spring. 31"Come, you who are blessed by the LORD," he said. "Why are you standing out here? I have prepared the house and a place for the camels."

32So the man went to the house, and the camels were unloaded. Straw and fodder were brought for the camels, and water for him and his men to wash their feet. 33Then food was set before him, but he said, "I will not eat until I have told you what I have to say."

"Then tell us," Laban said.

34So he said, "I am Abraham's servant. 35The LORD has blessed my master abundantly, and he has become wealthy. He has given him sheep and cattle, silver and gold, menservants and maidservants, and camels and donkeys. 36My master's wife Sarah has borne him a son in her[a] old age, and he has given him everything he owns. 37And my master made me swear an oath, and said, 'You must not get a wife for my son from the daughters of the Canaanites, in whose land I live, 38but go to my father's family and to my own clan, and get a wife for my son.'

39"Then I asked my master, 'What if the woman will not come back with me?'

40"He replied, 'The LORD, before whom I have walked, will send his angel with you and make your journey a success, so that you can get a wife for my son from my own clan and from my father's family. 41Then, when you go to my clan, you will be released from my oath even if they refuse to give her to you—you will be released from my oath.'

42"When I came to the spring today, I said, 'O LORD, God of my master Abraham, if you will, please grant success to the journey on which I have come. 43See, I am standing beside this spring; if a maiden comes out to draw water and I say to her, "Please let me drink a little water from your jar," 44and if she says to me, "Drink, and I'll draw water for your camels too," let her be the one the LORD has chosen for my master's son.'

45"Before I finished praying in my heart, Rebekah came out, with her jar on her shoulder. She went down to the spring and drew water, and I said to her, 'Please give me a drink.'

46"She quickly lowered her jar from her shoulder and said, 'Drink, and I'll water your camels too.' So I drank, and she watered the camels also.

47"I asked her, 'Whose daughter are you?'

"She said, 'The daughter of Bethuel son of Nahor, whom Milcah bore to him.'

"Then I put the ring in her nose and the bracelets on her arms, 48and I bowed down and worshiped the LORD. I praised the LORD, the God of my master Abraham, who had led me on the right road to get the granddaughter of my master's brother for his son. 49Now if you will show kindness and faithfulness to my master, tell me; and if not, tell me, so I may know which way to turn."

a 36 Or his

Living Bible

master Abraham," he prayed; "thank you for being so kind and true to him, and for leading me straight to the family of my master's relatives."

28The girl ran home to tell her folks,b 29, 30and when her brother Laban saw the ring, and the bracelets on his sister's wrists, and heard her story, he rushed out to the spring where the man was still standing beside his camels, and said to him, 31"Come and stay with us, friend;c why stand here outside the city when we have a room all ready for you, and a place prepared for the camels!"

32So the man went home with Laban, and Laban gave him straw to bed down the camels, and feed for them, and water for the camel drivers to wash their feet. 33Then supper was served. But the old man said, "I don't want to eat until I have told you why I am here."

"All right," Laban said, "tell us your errand."

34"I am Abraham's servant," he explained. 35"And Jehovah has overwhelmed my master with blessings so that he is a great man among the people of his land. God has given him flocks of sheep and herds of cattle, and a fortune in silver and gold, and many slaves and camels and donkeys.

36"Now when Sarah, my master's wife, was very old, she gave birth to my master's son, and my master has given him everything he owns. 37And my master made me promise not to let Isaac marry one of the local girls,d 38but to come to his relatives here in this far-off land, to his brother's family,e and to bring back a girl from here to marry his son. 39'But suppose I can't find a girl who will come?' I asked him. 40'She will,' he told me—'for my Lord, in whose presence I have walked, will send his angel with you and make your mission successful. Yes, find a girl from among my relatives, from my brother's family. 41You are under oath to go and ask. If they won't send anyone, then you are freed from your promise.'

42"Well, this afternoon when I came to the spring I prayed this prayer: 'O Jehovah, the God of my master Abraham, if you are planning to make my mission a success, please guide me in this way: 43Here I am, standing beside this spring. I will say to some girl who comes out to draw water, "Please give me a drink of water!" 44And she will reply, "Certainly! And I'll water your camels too!" Let that girl be the one you have selected to be the wife of my master's son.'

45"Well, while I was still speaking these words, Rebekah was coming along with her water jug upon her shoulder; and she went down to the spring and drew water and filled the jug. I said to her, 'Please give me a drink.' 46She quickly lifted the jug down from her shoulder so that I could drink, and told me, 'Certainly, sir, and I will water your camels too!' So she did! 47Then I asked her, 'Whose family are you from?' And she told me, 'Nahor's. My father is Bethuel, the son of Nahor and his wife Milcah.' So I gave her the ring and the bracelets. 48Then I bowed my head and worshiped and blessed Jehovah, the God of my master Abraham, because he had led me along just the right path to find a girl from the family of my master's brother.f 49So tell me, yes or no. Will you or won't you be kind to my master and do what is right? When you tell me, then I'll know what my next step should be, whether to move this way or that."

New Revised Standard

27and said, "Blessed be the LORD, the God of my master Abraham, who has not forsaken his steadfast love and his faithfulness toward my master. As for me, the LORD has led me on the way to the house of my master's kin."

28 Then the girl ran and told her mother's household about these things. 29Rebekah had a brother whose name was Laban; and Laban ran out to the man, to the spring. 30As soon as he had seen the nose-ring, and the bracelets on his sister's arms, and when he heard the words of his sister Rebekah, "Thus the man spoke to me," he went to the man; and there he was, standing by the camels at the spring. 31He said, "Come in, O blessed of the LORD. Why do you stand outside when I have prepared the house and a place for the camels?" 32So the man came into the house; and Laban unloaded the camels, and gave him straw and fodder for the camels, and water to wash his feet and the feet of the men who were with him. 33Then food was set before him to eat; but he said, "I will not eat until I have told my errand." He said, "Speak on."

34 So he said, "I am Abraham's servant. 35The LORD has greatly blessed my master, and he has become wealthy; he has given him flocks and herds, silver and gold, male and female slaves, camels and donkeys. 36And Sarah my master's wife bore a son to my master when she was old; and he has given him all that he has. 37My master made me swear, saying, 'You shall not take a wife for my son from the daughters of the Canaanites, in whose land I live; 38but you shall go to my father's house, to my kindred, and get a wife for my son.' 39I said to my master, 'Perhaps the woman will not follow me.' 40But he said to me, 'The LORD, before whom I walk, will send his angel with you and make your way successful. You shall get a wife for my son from my kindred, from my father's house. 41Then you will be free from my oath, when you come to my kindred; even if they will not give her to you, you will be free from my oath.'

42 "I came today to the spring, and said, 'O LORD, the God of my master Abraham, if now you will only make successful the way I am going! 43I am standing here by the spring of water; let the young woman who comes out to draw, to whom I shall say, "Please give me a little water from your jar to drink," 44and who will say to me, "Drink, and I will draw for your camels also"— let her be the woman whom the LORD has appointed for my master's son.'

45 "Before I had finished speaking in my heart, there was Rebekah coming out with her water jar on her shoulder; and she went down to the spring, and drew. I said to her, 'Please let me drink.' 46She quickly let down her jar from her shoulder, and said, 'Drink, and I will also water your camels.' So I drank, and she also watered the camels. 47Then I asked her, 'Whose daughter are you?' She said, 'The daughter of Bethuel, Nahor's son, whom Milcah bore to him.' So I put the ring on her nose, and the bracelets on her arms. 48Then I bowed my head and worshiped the LORD, and blessed the LORD, the God of my master Abraham, who had led me by the right way to obtain the daughter of my master's kinsman for his son. 49Now then, if you will deal loyally and truly with my master, tell me; and if not, tell me, so that I may turn either to the right hand or to the left."

---

b 24:28 the girl ran home to tell her folks. Doubtless to tell them that a messenger had arrived from her great-uncle. c 24:31 friend, literally, "blessed of Jehovah." d 24:37 local girls, literally, "daughters of the Canaanites." e 24:38 to his brother's family, literally, "go into my father's house." f 24:48 a girl from the family of my master's brother, literally, "my master's brother's daughter."

King James

50Then Laban and Bethuel answered and said, The thing proceedeth from the LORD: we cannot speak unto thee bad or good.

51Behold, Rebekah *is* before thee, take *her,* and go, and let her be thy master's son's wife, as the LORD hath spoken.

52And it came to pass, that, when Abraham's servant heard their words, he worshipped the LORD, *bowing himself* to the earth.

53And the servant brought forth jewels of silver, and jewels of gold, and raiment, and gave *them* to Rebekah: he gave also to her brother and to her mother precious things.

54And they did eat and drink, he and the men that *were* with him, and tarried all night; and they rose up in the morning, and he said, Send me away unto my master.

55And her brother and her mother said, Let the damsel abide with us *a few* days, at the least ten; after that she shall go.

56And he said unto them, Hinder me not, seeing the LORD hath prospered my way; send me away that I may go to my master.

57And they said, We will call the damsel, and inquire at her mouth.

58And they called Rebekah, and said unto her, Wilt thou go with this man? And she said, I will go.

59And they sent away Rebekah their sister, and her nurse, and Abraham's servant, and his men.

60And they blessed Rebekah, and said unto her, Thou *art* our sister, be thou *the mother* of thousands of millions, and let thy seed possess the gate of those which hate them.

61¶ And Rebekah arose, and her damsels, and they rode upon the camels, and followed the man: and the servant took Rebekah, and went his way.

62And Isaac came from the way of the well Lahai-roi; for he dwelt in the south country.

63And Isaac went out to meditate in the field at the eventide: and he lifted up his eyes, and saw, and, behold, the camels *were* coming.

64And Rebekah lifted up her eyes, and when she saw Isaac, she lighted off the camel.

65For she *had* said unto the servant, What man *is* this that walketh in the field to meet us? And the servant *had* said, It *is* my master: therefore she took a veil, and covered herself.

66And the servant told Isaac all things that he had done.

67And Isaac brought her into his mother Sarah's tent, and took Rebekah, and she became his wife; and he loved her: and Isaac was comforted after his mother's *death.*

25 THEN AGAIN Abraham took a wife, and her name *was* Keturah.

2And she bare him Zimran, and Jokshan, and Medan, and Midian, and Ishbak, and Shuah.

3And Jokshan begat Sheba, and Dedan. And the sons of Dedan were Asshurim, and Letushim, and Leummim.

4And the sons of Midian; Ephah, and Epher, and Hanoch, and Abidah, and Eldaah. All these *were* the children of Keturah.

5¶ And Abraham gave all that he had unto Isaac.

6But unto the sons of the concubines, which Abraham had, Abraham gave gifts, and sent them away from Isaac his son, while he yet lived, eastward, unto the east country.

New International

50Laban and Bethuel answered, "This is from the LORD; we can say nothing to you one way or the other. 51Here is Rebekah; take her and go, and let her become the wife of your master's son, as the LORD has directed."

52When Abraham's servant heard what they said, he bowed down to the ground before the LORD. 53Then the servant brought out gold and silver jewelry and articles of clothing and gave them to Rebekah; he also gave costly gifts to her brother and to her mother. 54Then he and the men who were with him ate and drank and spent the night there.

When they got up the next morning, he said, "Send me on my way to my master."

55But her brother and her mother replied, "Let the girl remain with us ten days or so; then youa may go."

56But he said to them, "Do not detain me, now that the LORD has granted success to my journey. Send me on my way so I may go to my master."

57Then they said, "Let's call the girl and ask her about it." 58So they called Rebekah and asked her, "Will you go with this man?"

"I will go," she said.

59So they sent their sister Rebekah on her way, along with her nurse and Abraham's servant and his men. 60And they blessed Rebekah and said to her,

"Our sister, may you increase
    to thousands upon thousands;
may your offspring possess
    the gates of their enemies."

61Then Rebekah and her maids got ready and mounted their camels and went back with the man. So the servant took Rebekah and left.

62Now Isaac had come from Beer Lahai Roi, for he was living in the Negev. 63He went out to the field one evening to meditate,b and as he looked up, he saw camels approaching. 64Rebekah also looked up and saw Isaac. She got down from her camel 65and asked the servant, "Who is that man in the field coming to meet us?"

"He is my master," the servant answered. So she took her veil and covered herself.

66Then the servant told Isaac all he had done. 67Isaac brought her into the tent of his mother Sarah, and he married Rebekah. So she became his wife, and he loved her; and Isaac was comforted after his mother's death.

The Death of Abraham

25 ABRAHAM TOOKc another wife, whose name was Keturah. 2She bore him Zimran, Jokshan, Medan, Midian, Ishbak and Shuah. 3Jokshan was the father of Sheba and Dedan; the descendants of Dedan were the Asshurites, the Letushites and the Leummites. 4The sons of Midian were Ephah, Epher, Hanoch, Abida and Eldaah. All these were descendants of Keturah.

5Abraham left everything he owned to Isaac. 6But while he was still living, he gave gifts to the sons of his concubines and sent them away from his son Isaac to the land of the east.

a 55 Or *she*   b 63 The meaning of the Hebrew for this word is uncertain.
c 1 Or *had taken*

Living Bible

⁵⁰Then Laban and Bethuel replied, "The Lord has obviously brought you here, so what can we say? ⁵¹Take her and go! Yes, let her be the wife of your master's son, as Jehovah has directed."

⁵²At this reply, Abraham's servant fell to his knees before Jehovah. ⁵³Then he brought out jewels set in solid gold and silver for Rebekah, and lovely clothing; and he gave many valuable presents to her mother and brother. ⁵⁴Then they had supper, and the servant and the men with him stayed there overnight. But early the next morning he said, "Send me back to my master!"

⁵⁵"But we want Rebekah here at least another ten days or so!" her mother and brother exclaimed. "Then she can go."

⁵⁶But he pleaded, "Don't hinder my return; the Lord has made my mission successful, and I want to report back to my master."

⁵⁷"Well," they said, "we'll call the girl and ask her what she thinks."

⁵⁸So they called Rebekah. "Are you willing to go with this man?" they asked her.

And she replied, "Yes, I will go."

⁵⁹So they told her good-bye, sending along the woman who had been her childhood nurse, ⁶⁰and blessed her with this blessing as they parted:

"Our sister,
May you become
The mother of many millions!
May your descendants
Overcome all your enemies."

⁶¹So Rebekah and her servant girls mounted the camels and went with him.

⁶²Meanwhile, Isaac, whose home was in the Negeb, had returned to Beer-lahai-roi. ⁶³One evening as he was taking a walk out in the fields, meditating, he looked up and saw the camels coming. ⁶⁴Rebekah noticed him and quickly dismounted.

⁶⁵"Who is that man walking through the fields to meet us?" she asked the servant.

And he replied, "It is my master's son!"ᵈ So she covered her face with her veil. ⁶⁶Then the servant told Isaac the whole story.

⁶⁷And Isaac brought Rebekah into his mother's tent, and she became his wife. He loved her very much, and she was a special comfort to him after the loss of his mother.

25 NOW ABRAHAM married again. Keturah was his new wife, and she bore him several children: Zimran, Jokshan, Medan, Midian, Ishbak, Shuah. ³Jokshan's two sons were Sheba and Dedan. Dedan's sons were Asshurim, Letushim, and Leummim. ⁴Midian's sons were Ephah, Epher, Hanoch, Abida, and Eldaah.ᵉ

⁵Abraham deeded everything he owned to Isaac; ⁶however, he gave gifts to the sons of his concubines and sent them off into the east, away from Isaac.

New Revised Standard

50 Then Laban and Bethuel answered, "The thing comes from the LORD; we cannot speak to you anything bad or good. ⁵¹Look, Rebekah is before you, take her and go, and let her be the wife of your master's son, as the LORD has spoken."

52 When Abraham's servant heard their words, he bowed himself to the ground before the LORD. ⁵³And the servant brought out jewelry of silver and of gold, and garments, and gave them to Rebekah; he also gave to her brother and to her mother costly ornaments. ⁵⁴Then he and the men who were with him ate and drank, and they spent the night there. When they rose in the morning, he said, "Send me back to my master." ⁵⁵Her brother and her mother said, "Let the girl remain with us a while, at least ten days; after that she may go." ⁵⁶But he said to them, "Do not delay me, since the LORD has made my journey successful; let me go that I may go to my master." ⁵⁷They said, "We will call the girl, and ask her." ⁵⁸And they called Rebekah, and said to her, "Will you go with this man?" She said, "I will." ⁵⁹So they sent away their sister Rebekah and her nurse along with Abraham's servant and his men. ⁶⁰And they blessed Rebekah and said to her,

"May you, our sister, become
  thousands of myriads;
may your offspring gain possession
  of the gates of their foes."

⁶¹Then Rebekah and her maids rose up, mounted the camels, and followed the man; thus the servant took Rebekah, and went his way.

62 Now Isaac had come fromᶠ Beer-lahai-roi, and was settled in the Negeb. ⁶³Isaac went out in the evening to walkᵍ in the field; and looking up, he saw camels coming. ⁶⁴And Rebekah looked up, and when she saw Isaac, she slipped quickly from the camel, ⁶⁵and said to the servant, "Who is the man over there, walking in the field to meet us?" The servant said, "It is my master." So she took her veil and covered herself. ⁶⁶And the servant told Isaac all the things that he had done. ⁶⁷Then Isaac brought her into his mother Sarah's tent. He took Rebekah, and she became his wife; and he loved her. So Isaac was comforted after his mother's death.

Abraham Marries Keturah

25 ABRAHAM TOOK another wife, whose name was Keturah. ²She bore him Zimran, Jokshan, Medan, Midian, Ishbak, and Shuah. ³Jokshan was the father of Sheba and Dedan. The sons of Dedan were Asshurim, Letushim, and Leummim. ⁴The sons of Midian were Ephah, Epher, Hanoch, Abida, and Eldaah. All these were the children of Keturah. ⁵Abraham gave all he had to Isaac. ⁶But to the sons of his concubines Abraham gave gifts, while he was still living, and he sent them away from his son Isaac, eastward to the east country.

ᵈ 24:65 *It is my master's son,* literally, "It is my master."   ᵉ *25:4 and Eldaah.* The text adds, "all these were the children of Keturah."

ᶠ Syr Tg: Heb *from coming to*   ᵍ Meaning of Heb word is uncertain

King James

7And these *are* the days of the years of Abraham's life which he lived, an hundred threescore and fifteen years.

8Then Abraham gave up the ghost, and died in a good old age, an old man, and full *of years;* and was gathered to his people.

9And his sons Isaac and Ishmael buried him in the cave of Machpelah, in the field of Ephron the son of Zohar the Hittite, which *is* before Mamre;

10The field which Abraham purchased of the sons of Heth: there was Abraham buried, and Sarah his wife.

11¶ And it came to pass after the death of Abraham, that God blessed his son Isaac; and Isaac dwelt by the well Lahai-roi.

12¶ Now these *are* the generations of Ishmael, Abraham's son, whom Hagar the Egyptian, Sarah's handmaid, bare unto Abraham:

13And these *are* the names of the sons of Ishmael, by their names, according to their generations: the firstborn of Ishmael, Nebajoth; and Kedar, and Adbeel, and Mibsam,

14And Mishma, and Dumah, and Massa,

15Hadar, and Tema, Jetur, Naphish, and Kedemah:

16These *are* the sons of Ishmael, and these *are* their names, by their towns, and by their castles; twelve princes according to their nations.

17And these *are* the years of the life of Ishmael, an hundred and thirty and seven years: and he gave up the ghost and died; and was gathered unto his people.

18And they dwelt from Havilah unto Shur, that *is* before Egypt, as thou goest toward Assyria: *and* he died in the presence of all his brethren.

19¶ And these *are* the generations of Isaac, Abraham's son: Abraham begat Isaac:

20And Isaac was forty years old when he took Rebekah to wife, the daughter of Bethuel the Syrian of Padan-aram, the sister to Laban the Syrian.

21And Isaac entreated the LORD for his wife, because she *was* barren: and the LORD was entreated of him, and Rebekah his wife conceived.

22And the children struggled together within her; and she said, If *it be* so, why *am* I thus? And she went to inquire of the LORD.

23And the LORD said unto her, Two nations *are* in thy womb, and two manner of people shall be separated from thy bowels; and *the one* people shall be stronger than *the other* people; and the elder shall serve the younger.

24¶ And when her days to be delivered were fulfilled, behold, *there were* twins in her womb.

25And the first came out red, all over like an hairy garment; and they called his name Esau.

26And after that came his brother out, and his hand took hold on Esau's heel; and his name was called Jacob: and Isaac *was* threescore years old when she bare them.

27And the boys grew: and Esau was a cunning hunter, a man of the field; and Jacob *was* a plain man, dwelling in tents.

28And Isaac loved Esau, because he did eat of *his* venison: but Rebekah loved Jacob.

29¶ And Jacob sod pottage: and Esau came from the field, and he *was* faint:

30And Esau said to Jacob, Feed me, I pray thee, with that same red *pottage;* for I *am* faint: therefore was his name called Edom.

31And Jacob said, Sell me this day thy birthright.

32And Esau said, Behold, I *am* at the point to die: and what profit shall this birthright do to me?

33And Jacob said, Swear to me this day; and he sware unto him: and he sold his birthright unto Jacob.

34Then Jacob gave Esau bread and pottage of lentiles; and he did eat and drink, and rose up, and went his way: thus Esau despised *his* birthright.

New International

7Altogether, Abraham lived a hundred and seventy-five years. 8Then Abraham breathed his last and died at a good old age, an old man and full of years; and he was gathered to his people. 9His sons Isaac and Ishmael buried him in the cave of Machpelah near Mamre, in the field of Ephron son of Zohar the Hittite, 10the field Abraham had bought from the Hittites.a There Abraham was buried with his wife Sarah. 11After Abraham's death, God blessed his son Isaac, who then lived near Beer Lahai Roi.

Ishmael's Sons

12This is the account of Abraham's son Ishmael, whom Sarah's maidservant, Hagar the Egyptian, bore to Abraham.

13These are the names of the sons of Ishmael, listed in the order of their birth: Nebaioth the firstborn of Ishmael, Kedar, Adbeel, Mibsam, 14Mishma, Dumah, Massa, 15Hadad, Tema, Jetur, Naphish and Kedemah. 16These were the sons of Ishmael, and these are the names of the twelve tribal rulers according to their settlements and camps. 17Altogether, Ishmael lived a hundred and thirty-seven years. He breathed his last and died, and he was gathered to his people. 18His descendants settled in the area from Havilah to Shur, near the border of Egypt, as you go toward Asshur. And they lived in hostility towardb all their brothers.

Jacob and Esau

19This is the account of Abraham's son Isaac.

Abraham became the father of Isaac, 20and Isaac was forty years old when he married Rebekah daughter of Bethuel the Aramean from Paddan Aramc and sister of Laban the Aramean.

21Isaac prayed to the LORD on behalf of his wife, because she was barren. The LORD answered his prayer, and his wife Rebekah became pregnant. 22The babies jostled each other within her, and she said, "Why is this happening to me?" So she went to inquire of the LORD.

23The LORD said to her,

> "Two nations are in your womb,
>   and two peoples from within you will be
>   separated;
> one people will be stronger than the other,
>   and the older will serve the younger."

24When the time came for her to give birth, there were twin boys in her womb. 25The first to come out was red, and his whole body was like a hairy garment; so they named him Esau.d 26After this, his brother came out, with his hand grasping Esau's heel; so he was named Jacob.e Isaac was sixty years old when Rebekah gave birth to them.

27The boys grew up, and Esau became a skillful hunter, a man of the open country, while Jacob was a quiet man, staying among the tents. 28Isaac, who had a taste for wild game, loved Esau, but Rebekah loved Jacob.

29Once when Jacob was cooking some stew, Esau came in from the open country, famished. 30He said to Jacob, "Quick, let me have some of that red stew! I'm famished!" (That is why he was also called Edom.f)

31Jacob replied, "First sell me your birthright."

32"Look, I am about to die," Esau said. "What good is the birthright to me?"

33But Jacob said, "Swear to me first." So he swore an oath to him, selling his birthright to Jacob.

34Then Jacob gave Esau some bread and some lentil stew. He ate and drank, and then got up and left.

So Esau despised his birthright.

a 10 Or *the sons of Heth*   b 18 Or *lived to the east of*   c 20 That is, Northwest Mesopotamia   d 25 *Esau* may mean *hairy*; he was also called Edom, which means *red*.   e 26 *Jacob* means *he grasps the heel* (figuratively, *he deceives*).   f 30 *Edom* means *red*.

Living Bible

7, 8Then Abraham died, at the ripe old age of 175, 9, 10and his sons Isaac and Ishmael buried him in the cave of Mach-pelah near Mamre, in the field Abraham had purchased from Ephron the son of Zohar, the Heth-ite, where Sarah, Abraham's wife was buried.

11After Abraham's death, God poured out rich bless-ings upon Isaac. (Isaac had now moved south to Beer-lahai-roi in the Negeb.)

12-15Here is a list, in the order of their births, of the descendants of Ishmael, who was the son of Abraham and Hagar the Egyptian, Sarah's slave girl:

Nebaioth, Kedar, Abdeel, Mibsam, Mishma, Du-mah, Massa, Hadad, Tema, Jetur, Naphish, Kede-mah.

16These twelve sons of his became the founders of twelve tribes that bore their names. 17Ishmael finally died at the age of 137, and joined his ancestors.g 18These descendants of Ishmael were scattered across the country from Havilah to Shur (which is a little way to the northeast of the Egyptian border in the direction of Assyria). And they were constantly at war with one another.

19This is the story of Isaac's children: 20Isaac was forty years old when he married Rebekah, the daughter of Bethuel the Aramean from Paddam-aram. Rebekah was the sister of Laban. 21Isaac pleaded with Jehovah to give Rebekah a child, for even after many years of mar-riageh she had no children. Then at last she became pregnant. 22And it seemed as though children were fighting each other inside her!

"I can't endure this," she exclaimed. So she asked the Lord about it.

23And he told her, "The sons in your womb shall become two rival nations. One will be stronger than the other; and the older shall be a servant of the younger!"

24And sure enough, she had twins. 25The first was born so covered with reddish hair that one would think he was wearing a fur coat! So they called him "Esau."i 26Then the other twin was born with his hand on Esau's heel! So they called him Jacob (meaning "Grabber"). Isaac was sixty years old when the twins were born.

27As the boys grew, Esau became a skillful hunter, while Jacob was a quiet sort who liked to stay at home. 28Isaac's favorite was Esau, because of the venison he brought home, and Rebekah's favorite was Jacob.

29One day Jacob was cooking stew when Esau arrived home exhausted from the hunt.

30Esau: "Boy, am I starved! Give me a bite of that red stuff there!" (From this came his nickname "Edom," which means "Red Stuff.")

31Jacob: "All right, trade me your birthright for it!"

32Esau: "When a man is dying of starvation, what good is his birthright?"

33Jacob: "Well then, vow to God that it is mine!"

And Esau vowed, thereby selling all his eldest-son rights to his younger brother. 34Then Jacob gave Esau bread, peas, and stew; so he ate and drank and went on about his business, indifferent to the loss of the rights he had thrown away.j

New Revised Standard

The Death of Abraham

7 This is the length of Abraham's life, one hundred seventy-five years. 8Abraham breathed his last and died in a good old age, an old man and full of years, and was gathered to his people. 9His sons Isaac and Ishmael buried him in the cave of Machpelah, in the field of Ephron son of Zohar the Hittite, east of Mamre, 10the field that Abraham purchased from the Hittites. There Abraham was buried, with his wife Sarah. 11After the death of Abraham God blessed his son Isaac. And Isaac settled at Beer-lahai-roi.

Ishmael's Descendants

12 These are the descendants of Ishmael, Abra-ham's son, whom Hagar the Egyptian, Sarah's slave-girl, bore to Abraham. 13These are the names of the sons of Ishmael, named in the order of their birth: Nebaioth, the firstborn of Ishmael; and Kedar, Adbeel, Mibsam, 14Mishma, Dumah, Massa, 15Hadad, Tema, Jetur, Na-phish, and Kedemah. 16These are the sons of Ishmael and these are their names, by their villages and by their encampments, twelve princes according to their tribes. 17(This is the length of the life of Ishmael, one hundred thirty-seven years; he breathed his last and died, and was gathered to his people.) 18They settled from Havilah to Shur, which is opposite Egypt in the direction of Assyr-ia; he settled downk alongside ofl all his people.

The Birth and Youth of Esau and Jacob

19 These are the descendants of Isaac, Abraham's son: Abraham was the father of Isaac, 20and Isaac was forty years old when he married Rebekah, daughter of Bethuel the Aramean of Paddan-aram, sister of Laban the Aramean. 21Isaac prayed to the LORD for his wife, because she was barren; and the LORD granted his prayer, and his wife Rebekah conceived. 22The children struggled together within her; and she said, "If it is to be this way, why do I live?"m So she went to inquire of the LORD. 23And the LORD said to her,

"Two nations are in your womb,
    and two peoples born of you shall be
        divided;
the one shall be stronger than the other,
    the elder shall serve the younger."

24When her time to give birth was at hand, there were twins in her womb. 25The first came out red, all his body like a hairy mantle; so they named him Esau. 26After-ward his brother came out, with his hand gripping Esau's heel; so he was named Jacob.n Isaac was sixty years old when she bore them.

27 When the boys grew up, Esau was a skillful hunt-er, a man of the field, while Jacob was a quiet man, living in tents. 28Isaac loved Esau, because he was fond of game; but Rebekah loved Jacob.

Esau Sells His Birthright

29 Once when Jacob was cooking a stew, Esau came in from the field, and he was famished. 30Esau said to Jacob, "Let me eat some of that red stuff, for I am famished!" (Therefore he was called Edom.o) 31Ja-cob said, "First sell me your birthright." 32Esau said, "I am about to die; of what use is a birthright to me?" 33Jacob said, "Swear to me first."p So he swore to him, and sold his birthright to Jacob. 34Then Jacob gave Esau bread and lentil stew, and he ate and drank, and rose and went his way. Thus Esau despised his birthright.

---

g 25:17 joined his ancestors, literally, "and was gathered to his people."
h 25:21 even after many years of marriage, implied in vss 20 and 26.
i 25:25 which sounds a little like the Hebrew word for "hair."
j 25:34 indifferent to the loss of the rights he had thrown away, literally, "thus did Esau consider his birthright to be of no value."

k Heb he fell l Or down in opposition to m Syr: Meaning of Heb uncertain
n That is He takes by the heel or He supplants o That is Red p Heb today

King James

26 AND THERE was a famine in the land, beside the first famine that was in the days of Abraham. And Isaac went unto Abimelech king of the Philistines unto Gerar.

2And the LORD appeared unto him, and said, Go not down into Egypt; dwell in the land which I shall tell thee of:

3Sojourn in this land, and I will be with thee, and will bless thee; for unto thee, and unto thy seed, I will give all these countries, and I will perform the oath which I sware unto Abraham thy father;

4And I will make thy seed to multiply as the stars of heaven, and will give unto thy seed all these countries; and in thy seed shall all the nations of the earth be blessed;

5Because that Abraham obeyed my voice, and kept my charge, my commandments, my statutes, and my laws.

6¶ And Isaac dwelt in Gerar:

7And the men of the place asked *him* of his wife; and he said, She *is* my sister: for he feared to say, *She is* my wife; lest, *said he,* the men of the place should kill me for Rebekah; because she *was* fair to look upon.

8And it came to pass, when he had been there a long time, that Abimelech king of the Philistines looked out at a window, and saw, and, behold, Isaac *was* sporting with Rebekah his wife.

9And Abimelech called Isaac, and said, Behold, of a surety she *is* thy wife: and how saidst thou, She *is* my sister? And Isaac said unto him, Because I said, Lest I die for her.

10And Abimelech said, What *is* this thou hast done unto us? one of the people might lightly have lain with thy wife, and thou shouldest have brought guiltiness upon us.

11And Abimelech charged all *his* people, saying, He that toucheth this man or his wife shall surely be put to death.

12Then Isaac sowed in that land, and received in the same year an hundredfold: and the LORD blessed him.

13And the man waxed great, and went forward, and grew until he became very great:

14For he had possession of flocks, and possession of herds, and great store of servants: and the Philistines envied him.

15For all the wells which his father's servants had digged in the days of Abraham his father, the Philistines had stopped them, and filled them with earth.

16And Abimelech said unto Isaac, Go from us; for thou art much mightier than we.

17¶ And Isaac departed thence, and pitched his tent in the valley of Gerar, and dwelt there.

18And Isaac digged again the wells of water, which they had digged in the days of Abraham his father; for the Philistines had stopped them after the death of Abraham: and he called their names after the names by which his father had called them.

19And Isaac's servants digged in the valley, and found there a well of springing water.

20And the herdmen of Gerar did strive with Isaac's herdmen, saying, The water *is* ours: and he called the name of the well Esek; because they strove with him.

21And they digged another well, and strove for that also: and he called the name of it Sitnah.

22And he removed from thence, and digged another well; and for that they strove not: and he called the name of it Rehoboth; and he said, For now the LORD hath made room for us, and we shall be fruitful in the land.

23And he went up from thence to Beer-sheba.

24And the LORD appeared unto him the same night, and said, I *am* the God of Abraham thy father: fear not, for I *am* with thee, and will bless thee, and multiply thy seed for my servant Abraham's sake.

New International

Isaac and Abimelech

26 NOW THERE was a famine in the land—besides the earlier famine of Abraham's time—and Isaac went to Abimelech king of the Philistines in Gerar. 2The LORD appeared to Isaac and said, "Do not go down to Egypt; live in the land where I tell you to live. 3Stay in this land for a while, and I will be with you and will bless you. For to you and your descendants I will give all these lands and will confirm the oath I swore to your father Abraham. 4I will make your descendants as numerous as the stars in the sky and will give them all these lands, and through your offspringa all nations on earth will be blessed, 5because Abraham obeyed me and kept my requirements, my commands, my decrees and my laws." 6So Isaac stayed in Gerar.

7When the men of that place asked him about his wife, he said, "She is my sister," because he was afraid to say, "She is my wife." He thought, "The men of this place might kill me on account of Rebekah, because she is beautiful."

8When Isaac had been there a long time, Abimelech king of the Philistines looked down from a window and saw Isaac caressing his wife Rebekah. 9So Abimelech summoned Isaac and said, "She is really your wife! Why did you say, 'She is my sister'?"

Isaac answered him, "Because I thought I might lose my life on account of her."

10Then Abimelech said, "What is this you have done to us? One of the men might well have slept with your wife, and you would have brought guilt upon us."

11So Abimelech gave orders to all the people: "Anyone who molests this man or his wife shall surely be put to death."

12Isaac planted crops in that land and the same year reaped a hundredfold, because the LORD blessed him. 13The man became rich, and his wealth continued to grow until he became very wealthy. 14He had so many flocks and herds and servants that the Philistines envied him. 15So all the wells that his father's servants had dug in the time of his father Abraham, the Philistines stopped up, filling them with earth.

16Then Abimelech said to Isaac, "Move away from us; you have become too powerful for us."

17So Isaac moved away from there and encamped in the Valley of Gerar and settled there. 18Isaac reopened the wells that had been dug in the time of his father Abraham, which the Philistines had stopped up after Abraham died, and he gave them the same names his father had given them.

19Isaac's servants dug in the valley and discovered a well of fresh water there. 20But the herdsmen of Gerar quarreled with Isaac's herdsmen and said, "The water is ours!" So he named the well Esek,b because they disputed with him. 21Then they dug another well, but they quarreled over that one also; so he named it Sitnah.c 22He moved on from there and dug another well, and no one quarreled over it. He named it Rehoboth,d saying, "Now the LORD has given us room and we will flourish in the land."

23From there he went up to Beersheba. 24That night the LORD appeared to him and said, "I am the God of your father Abraham. Do not be afraid, for I am with you; I will bless you and will increase the number of your descendants for the sake of my servant Abraham."

a 4 Or *seed*   b 20 Esek means *dispute.*   c 21 Sitnah means *opposition.*
d 22 Rehoboth means *room.*

Living Bible

26 NOW A severe famine overshadowed the land, as had happened before, in Abraham's time, and so Isaac moved to the city of Gerar where Abimelech, king of the Philistines, lived.

2Jehovah appeared to him there and told him, "Don't go to Egypt. 3Do as I say and stay here in this land. If you do, I will be with you and bless you, and I will give all this land to you and to your descendants, just as I promised Abraham your father. 4And I will cause your descendants to become as numerous as the stars! And I will give them all of these lands; and they shall be a blessing to all the nations of the earth. 5I will do this because Abraham obeyed my commandments and laws."

6So Isaac stayed in Gerar. 7And when the men there asked him about Rebekah, he said, "She is my sister!" For he feared for his life if he told them she was his wife; he was afraid they would kill him to get her, for she was very attractive. 8But sometime later, King Abimelech, king of the Philistines, looked out of a window and saw Isaac and Rebekah making love.

9Abimelech called for Isaac and exclaimed, "She is your wife! Why did you say she is your sister?"

"Because I was afraid I would be murdered," Isaac replied. "I thought someone would kill me to get her from me."

10"How could you treat us this way?" Abimelech exclaimed. "Someone might carelessly have raped her, and we would be doomed." 11Then Abimelech made a public proclamation: "Anyone harming this man or his wife shall die."

12That year Isaac's crops were tremendous—100 times the grain he sowed. For Jehovah blessed him. 13He was soon a man of great wealth, and became richer and richer. 14He had large flocks of sheep and goats, great herds of cattle, and many servants. And the Philistines became jealous of him. 15So they filled up his wells with earth—all those dug by the servants of his father Abraham.

16And King Abimelech asked Isaac to leave the country. "Go somewhere else," he said, "for you have become too rich and powerful for us."

17So Isaac moved to Gerar Valley and lived there instead. 18And Isaac redug the wells of his father Abraham, the ones the Philistines had filled after his father's death, and gave them the same names they had had before, when his father had named them. 19His shepherds also dug a new well in Gerar Valley, and found a gushing underground spring.

20Then the local shepherds came and claimed it. "This is our land and our well," they said, and argued over it with Isaac's herdsmen. So he named the well, "The Well of Argument!"e 21Isaac's men then dug another well, but again there was a fight over it. So he called it, "The Well of Anger."f 22Abandoning that one, he dug again, and the local residents finally left him alone. So he called it, "The Well of Room Enough for Us at Last!"g "For now at last," he said, "the Lord has made room for us and we shall thrive."

23When he went to Beer-sheba, 24Jehovah appeared to him on the night of his arrival. "I am the God of Abraham your father," he said. "Fear not, for I am with you and will bless you, and will give you so many descendants that they will become a great nation—because of my promise to Abraham, who obeyed me." 25Then

New Revised Standard

Isaac and Abimelech

26 NOW THERE was a famine in the land, besides the former famine that had occurred in the days of Abraham. And Isaac went to Gerar, to King Abimelech of the Philistines. 2The LORD appeared to Isaach and said, "Do not go down to Egypt; settle in the land that I shall show you. 3Reside in this land as an alien, and I will be with you, and will bless you; for to you and to your descendants I will give all these lands, and I will fulfill the oath that I swore to your father Abraham. 4I will make your offspring as numerous as the stars of heaven, and will give to your offspring all these lands; and all the nations of the earth shall gain blessing for themselves through your offspring, 5because Abraham obeyed my voice and kept my charge, my commandments, my statutes, and my laws."

6 So Isaac settled in Gerar. 7When the men of the place asked him about his wife, he said, "She is my sister"; for he was afraid to say, "My wife," thinking, "or else the men of the place might kill me for the sake of Rebekah, because she is attractive in appearance." 8When Isaac had been there a long time, King Abimelech of the Philistines looked out of a window and saw him fondling his wife Rebekah. 9So Abimelech called for Isaac, and said, "So she is your wife! Why then did you say, 'She is my sister'?" Isaac said to him, "Because I thought I might die because of her." 10Abimelech said, "What is this you have done to us? One of the people might easily have lain with your wife, and you would have brought guilt upon us." 11So Abimelech warned all the people, saying, "Whoever touches this man or his wife shall be put to death."

12 Isaac sowed seed in that land, and in the same year reaped a hundredfold. The LORD blessed him, 13and the man became rich; he prospered more and more until he became very wealthy. 14He had possessions of flocks and herds, and a great household, so that the Philistines envied him. 15(Now the Philistines had stopped up and filled with earth all the wells that his father's servants had dug in the days of his father Abraham.) 16And Abimelech said to Isaac, "Go away from us; you have become too powerful for us."

17 So Isaac departed from there and camped in the valley of Gerar and settled there. 18Isaac dug again the wells of water that had been dug in the days of his father Abraham; for the Philistines had stopped them up after the death of Abraham; and he gave them the names that his father had given them. 19But when Isaac's servants dug in the valley and found there a well of spring water, 20the herders of Gerar quarreled with Isaac's herders, saying, "The water is ours." So he called the well Esek,i because they contended with him. 21Then they dug another well, and they quarreled over that one also; so he called it Sitnah.j 22He moved from there and dug another well, and they did not quarrel over it; so he called it Rehoboth,k saying, "Now the LORD has made room for us, and we shall be fruitful in the land."

23 From there he went up to Beer-sheba. 24And that very night the LORD appeared to him and said, "I am the God of your father Abraham; do not be afraid, for I am with you and will bless you and make your offspring numerous for my servant Abraham's sake." 25So he

e 26:20 The Well of Argument, i.e., Ezek.   f 26:21 The Well of Anger, i.e., Sitnah.   g 26:22 The Well of Room Enough for Us at Last, i.e., Rehoboth.

h Heb him   i That is Contention   j That is Enmity   k That is Broad places or Room

King James

25And he builded an altar there, and called upon the name of the LORD, and pitched his tent there: and there Isaac's servants digged a well.

26¶ Then Abimelech went to him from Gerar, and Ahuzzath one of his friends, and Phichol the chief captain of his army.

27And Isaac said unto them, Wherefore come ye to me, seeing ye hate me, and have sent me away from you?

28And they said, We saw certainly that the LORD was with thee: and we said, Let there be now an oath betwixt us, *even* betwixt us and thee, and let us make a covenant with thee;

29That thou wilt do us no hurt, as we have not touched thee, and as we have done unto thee nothing but good, and have sent thee away in peace: thou *art* now the blessed of the LORD.

30And he made them a feast, and they did eat and drink.

31And they rose up betimes in the morning, and sware one to another: and Isaac sent them away, and they departed from him in peace.

32And it came to pass the same day, that Isaac's servants came, and told him concerning the well which they had digged, and said unto him, We have found water.

33And he called it Shebah: therefore the name of the city *is* Beer-sheba unto this day.

34¶ And Esau was forty years old when he took to wife Judith the daughter of Beeri the Hittite, and Bashemath the daughter of Elon the Hittite:

35Which were a grief of mind unto Isaac and to Rebekah.

27 AND IT came to pass, that when Isaac was old, and his eyes were dim, so that he could not see, he called Esau his eldest son, and said unto him, My son: and he said unto him, Behold, *here am* I.

2And he said, Behold now, I am old, I know not the day of my death:

3Now therefore take, I pray thee, thy weapons, thy quiver and thy bow, and go out to the field, and take me *some* venison;

4And make me savoury meat, such as I love, and bring *it* to me, that I may eat; that my soul may bless thee before I die.

5And Rebekah heard when Isaac spake to Esau his son. And Esau went to the field to hunt *for* venison, *and* to bring *it*.

6¶ And Rebekah spake unto Jacob her son, saying, Behold, I heard thy father speak unto Esau thy brother, saying,

7Bring me venison, and make me savoury meat, that I may eat, and bless thee before the LORD before my death.

8Now therefore, my son, obey my voice according to that which I command thee.

9Go now to the flock, and fetch me from thence two good kids of the goats; and I will make them savoury meat for thy father, such as he loveth:

10And thou shalt bring *it* to thy father, that he may eat, and that he may bless thee before his death.

11And Jacob said to Rebekah his mother, Behold, Esau my brother *is* a hairy man, and I *am* a smooth man:

12My father peradventure will feel me, and I shall seem to him as a deceiver; and I shall bring a curse upon me, and not a blessing.

13And his mother said unto him, Upon me *be* thy curse, my son: only obey my voice, and go fetch me *them*.

14And he went, and fetched, and brought *them* to his mother: and his mother made savoury meat, such as his father loved.

New International

25Isaac built an altar there and called on the name of the LORD. There he pitched his tent, and there his servants dug a well.

26Meanwhile, Abimelech had come to him from Gerar, with Ahuzzath his personal adviser and Phicol the commander of his forces. 27Isaac asked them, "Why have you come to me, since you were hostile to me and sent me away?"

28They answered, "We saw clearly that the LORD was with you; so we said, 'There ought to be a sworn agreement between us'—between us and you. Let us make a treaty with you 29that you will do us no harm, just as we did not molest you but always treated you well and sent you away in peace. And now you are blessed by the LORD."

30Isaac then made a feast for them, and they ate and drank. 31Early the next morning the men swore an oath to each other. Then Isaac sent them on their way, and they left him in peace.

32That day Isaac's servants came and told him about the well they had dug. They said, "We've found water!" 33He called it Shibah,[a] and to this day the name of the town has been Beersheba.[b]

34When Esau was forty years old, he married Judith daughter of Beeri the Hittite, and also Basemath daughter of Elon the Hittite. 35They were a source of grief to Isaac and Rebekah.

Jacob Gets Isaac's Blessing

27 WHEN ISAAC was old and his eyes were so weak that he could no longer see, he called for Esau his older son and said to him, "My son."

"Here I am," he answered.

2Isaac said, "I am now an old man and don't know the day of my death. 3Now then, get your weapons—your quiver and bow—and go out to the open country to hunt some wild game for me. 4Prepare me the kind of tasty food I like and bring it to me to eat, so that I may give you my blessing before I die."

5Now Rebekah was listening as Isaac spoke to his son Esau. When Esau left for the open country to hunt game and bring it back, 6Rebekah said to her son Jacob, "Look, I overheard your father say to your brother Esau, 7'Bring me some game and prepare me some tasty food to eat, so that I may give you my blessing in the presence of the LORD before I die.' 8Now, my son, listen carefully and do what I tell you: 9Go out to the flock and bring me two choice young goats, so I can prepare some tasty food for your father, just the way he likes it. 10Then take it to your father to eat, so that he may give you his blessing before he dies."

11Jacob said to Rebekah his mother, "But my brother Esau is a hairy man, and I'm a man with smooth skin. 12What if my father touches me? I would appear to be tricking him and would bring down a curse on myself rather than a blessing."

13His mother said to him, "My son, let the curse fall on me. Just do what I say; go and get them for me."

14So he went and got them and brought them to his mother, and she prepared some tasty food, just the way his father liked it. 15Then Rebekah took the best clothes

---

a 33 *Shibah* can mean *oath* or *seven*.   b 33 *Beersheba* can mean *well of the oath* or *well of seven.*

Living Bible

Isaac built an altar and worshiped Jehovah; and he settled there, and his servants dug a well.

26One day Isaac had visitors from Gerar. King Abimelech arrived with his advisor, Ahuzzath, and also Phicol, his army commander.

27"Why have you come?" Isaac asked them. "This is obviously no friendly visit, since you kicked me out in a most uncivil way."

28"Well," they said, "we can plainly see that Jehovah is blessing you. We've decided to ask for a treaty between us. 29Promise that you will not harm us, just as we have not harmed you, and in fact, have done only good to you and have sent you away in peace; we bless you in the name of the Lord."

30So Isaac prepared a great feast for them, and they ate and drank in preparation for the treaty ceremonies. 31In the morning, as soon as they were up, they each took solemn oaths to seal a non-aggression pact. Then Isaac sent them happily home again.

32That very same day Isaac's servants came to tell him, "We have found water"—in the well they had been digging. 33So he named the well, "The Well of the Oath," and the city that grew up there was named "Oath,"c and is called that to this day.

34Esau, at the age of forty, married a girl named Judith, daughter of Be-eri the Hethite; and he also married Basemath, daughter of Elon the Hethite. 35But Isaac and Rebekah were bitter about his marrying them.

27 ONE DAY, in Isaac's old age when he was almost blind, he called for Esau his oldest son. *Isaac:* "My son?"

Esau: "Yes, father?"

2, 3, 4*Isaac:* "I am an old man now, and expect every day to be my last. Take your bow and arrows out into the fields and get me some venison, and prepare it just the way I like it—savory and good—and bring it here for me to eat, and I will give you the blessings that belongd to you, my first-born son, before I die."

5But Rebekah overheard the conversation. So when Esau left for the field to hunt for the venison, 6, 7she called her son Jacob and told him what his father had said to his brother.

8, 9, 10*Rebekah:* "Now do exactly as I tell you. Go out to the flocks and bring me two young goats, and I'll prepare your father's favorite dish from them. Then take it to your father, and after he has enjoyed it he will bless *you* before his death, instead of Esau!"e

11, 12*Jacob:* "But mother! He won't be fooled that easily.f Think how hairy Esau is, and how smooth my skin is! What if my father feels me? He'll think I'm making a fool of him, and curse me instead of blessing me!"

13*Rebekah:* "Let his curses be on me, dear son. Just do what I tell you. Go out and get the goats."

14So Jacob followed his mother's instructions, bringing the dressed kids, which she prepared in his father's favorite way. 15Then she took Esau's best clothes—they

New Revised Standard

built an altar there, called on the name of the LORD, and pitched his tent there. And there Isaac's servants dug a well.

26 Then Abimelech went to him from Gerar, with Ahuzzath his adviser and Phicol the commander of his army. 27Isaac said to them, "Why have you come to me, seeing that you hate me and have sent me away from you?" 28They said, "We see plainly that the LORD has been with you; so we say, let there be an oath between you and us, and let us make a covenant with you 29so that you will do us no harm, just as we have not touched you and have done to you nothing but good and have sent you away in peace. You are now the blessed of the LORD." 30So he made them a feast, and they ate and drank. 31In the morning they rose early and exchanged oaths; and Isaac set them on their way, and they departed from him in peace. 32That same day Isaac's servants came and told him about the well that they had dug, and said to him, "We have found water!" 33He called it Shibah;g therefore the name of the city is Beer-shebah to this day.

Esau's Hittite Wives

34 When Esau was forty years old, he married Judith daughter of Beeri the Hittite, and Basemath daughter of Elon the Hittite; 35and they made life bitter for Isaac and Rebekah.

Isaac Blesses Jacob

27 WHEN ISAAC was old and his eyes were dim so that he could not see, he called his elder son Esau and said to him, "My son"; and he answered, "Here I am." 2He said, "See, I am old; I do not know the day of my death. 3Now then, take your weapons, your quiver and your bow, and go out to the field, and hunt game for me. 4Then prepare for me savory food, such as I like, and bring it to me to eat, so that I may bless you before I die."

5 Now Rebekah was listening when Isaac spoke to his son Esau. So when Esau went to the field to hunt for game and bring it, 6Rebekah said to her son Jacob, "I heard your father say to your brother Esau, 7'Bring me game, and prepare for me savory food to eat, that I may bless you before the LORD before I die.' 8Now therefore, my son, obey my word as I command you. 9Go to the flock, and get me two choice kids, so that I may prepare from them savory food for your father, such as he likes; 10and you shall take it to your father to eat, so that he may bless you before he dies." 11But Jacob said to his mother Rebekah, "Look, my brother Esau is a hairy man, and I am a man of smooth skin. 12Perhaps my father will feel me, and I shall seem to be mocking him, and bring a curse on myself and not a blessing." 13His mother said to him, "Let your curse be on me, my son; only obey my word, and go, get them for me." 14So he went and got them and brought them to his mother; and his mother prepared savory food, such as his father loved. 15Then Rebekah took the best garments of her

---

c *26:33 The Well of the Oath,* i.e., *Shibah. Oath,* i.e., *Beer-sheba.*
d *27:2-4 that belong to you, my first-born son,* implied.   e *27:8-10 instead of Esau,* implied.   f *27:11, 12 He won't be fooled that easily,* implied.

g A word resembling the word for *oath*   h That is *Well of the oath* or *Well of seven*

King James

¹⁵And Rebekah took goodly raiment of her eldest son Esau, which *were* with her in the house, and put them upon Jacob her younger son:

¹⁶And she put the skins of the kids of the goats upon his hands, and upon the smooth of his neck:

¹⁷And she gave the savoury meat and the bread, which she had prepared, into the hand of her son Jacob.

¹⁸¶ And he came unto his father, and said, My father: and he said, Here *am* I; who *art* thou, my son?

¹⁹And Jacob said unto his father, I *am* Esau thy firstborn; I have done according as thou badest me: arise, I pray thee, sit and eat of my venison, that thy soul may bless me.

²⁰And Isaac said unto his son, How *is it* that thou hast found *it* so quickly, my son? And he said, Because the LORD thy God brought *it* to me.

²¹And Isaac said unto Jacob, Come near, I pray thee, that I may feel thee, my son, whether thou *be* my very son Esau or not.

²²And Jacob went near unto Isaac his father; and he felt him, and said, The voice *is* Jacob's voice, but the hands *are* the hands of Esau.

²³And he discerned him not, because his hands were hairy, as his brother Esau's hands: so he blessed him.

²⁴And he said, *Art* thou my very son Esau? And he said, I *am*.

²⁵And he said, Bring *it* near to me, and I will eat of my son's venison, that my soul may bless thee. And he brought *it* near to him, and he did eat: and he brought him wine, and he drank.

²⁶And his father Isaac said unto him, Come near now, and kiss me, my son.

²⁷And he came near, and kissed him: and he smelled the smell of his raiment, and blessed him, and said, See, the smell of my son *is* as the smell of a field which the LORD hath blessed:

²⁸Therefore God give thee of the dew of heaven, and the fatness of the earth, and plenty of corn and wine:

²⁹Let people serve thee, and nations bow down to thee: be lord over thy brethren, and let thy mother's sons bow down to thee: cursed *be* every one that curseth thee, and blessed *be* he that blesseth thee.

³⁰¶ And it came to pass, as soon as Isaac had made an end of blessing Jacob, and Jacob was yet scarce gone out from the presence of Isaac his father, that Esau his brother came in from his hunting.

³¹And he also had made savoury meat, and brought it unto his father, and said unto his father, Let my father arise, and eat of his son's venison, that thy soul may bless me.

³²And Isaac his father said unto him, Who *art* thou? And he said, I *am* thy son, thy firstborn Esau.

³³And Isaac trembled very exceedingly, and said, Who? where *is* he that hath taken venison, and brought *it* me, and I have eaten of all before thou camest, and have blessed him? yea, *and* he shall be blessed.

³⁴And when Esau heard the words of his father, he cried with a great and exceeding bitter cry, and said unto his father, Bless me, *even* me also, O my father.

³⁵And he said, Thy brother came with subtlety, and hath taken away thy blessing.

³⁶And he said, Is not he rightly named Jacob? for he hath supplanted me these two times: he took away my birthright; and, behold, now he hath taken away my blessing. And he said, Hast thou not reserved a blessing for me?

³⁷And Isaac answered and said unto Esau, Behold, I have made him thy lord, and all his brethren have I given to him for servants; and with corn and wine have I sustained him: and what shall I do now unto thee, my son?

New International

of Esau her older son, which she had in the house, and put them on her younger son Jacob. ¹⁶She also covered his hands and the smooth part of his neck with the goatskins. ¹⁷Then she handed to her son Jacob the tasty food and the bread she had made.

¹⁸He went to his father and said, "My father."

"Yes, my son," he answered. "Who is it?"

¹⁹Jacob said to his father, "I am Esau your firstborn. I have done as you told me. Please sit up and eat some of my game so that you may give me your blessing."

²⁰Isaac asked his son, "How did you find it so quickly, my son?"

"The LORD your God gave me success," he replied.

²¹Then Isaac said to Jacob, "Come near so I can touch you, my son, to know whether you really are my son Esau or not."

²²Jacob went close to his father Isaac, who touched him and said, "The voice is the voice of Jacob, but the hands are the hands of Esau." ²³He did not recognize him, for his hands were hairy like those of his brother Esau; so he blessed him. ²⁴"Are you really my son Esau?" he asked.

"I am," he replied.

²⁵Then he said, "My son, bring me some of your game to eat, so that I may give you my blessing."

Jacob brought it to him and he ate; and he brought some wine and he drank. ²⁶Then his father Isaac said to him, "Come here, my son, and kiss me."

²⁷So he went to him and kissed him. When Isaac caught the smell of his clothes, he blessed him and said,

> "Ah, the smell of my son
>   is like the smell of a field
>   that the LORD has blessed.
> ²⁸May God give you of heaven's dew
>   and of earth's richness—
>   an abundance of grain and new wine.
> ²⁹May nations serve you
>   and peoples bow down to you.
> Be lord over your brothers,
>   and may the sons of your mother bow down
>   to you.
> May those who curse you be cursed
>   and those who bless you be blessed."

³⁰After Isaac finished blessing him and Jacob had scarcely left his father's presence, his brother Esau came in from hunting. ³¹He too prepared some tasty food and brought it to his father. Then he said to him, "My father, sit up and eat some of my game, so that you may give me your blessing."

³²His father Isaac asked him, "Who are you?"

"I am your son," he answered, "your firstborn, Esau."

³³Isaac trembled violently and said, "Who was it, then, that hunted game and brought it to me? I ate it just before you came and I blessed him—and indeed he will be blessed!"

³⁴When Esau heard his father's words, he burst out with a loud and bitter cry and said to his father, "Bless me—me too, my father!"

³⁵But he said, "Your brother came deceitfully and took your blessing."

³⁶Esau said, "Isn't he rightly named Jacob^a? He has deceived me these two times: He took my birthright, and now he's taken my blessing!" Then he asked, "Haven't you reserved any blessing for me?"

³⁷Isaac answered Esau, "I have made him lord over you and have made all his relatives his servants, and I have sustained him with grain and new wine. So what can I possibly do for you, my son?"

---

^a *36 Jacob* means *he grasps the heel* (figuratively, *he deceives*).

Living Bible

were there in the house—and instructed Jacob to put them on. 16And she made him a pair of gloves from the hairy skin of the young goats, and fastened a strip of the hide around his neck; 17then she gave him the meat, with its rich aroma, and some fresh-baked bread.

18Jacob carried the platter of food into the room where his father was lying.

Jacob: "Father?"

Isaac: "Yes? Who is it, my son—Esau or Jacob?"

19*Jacob:* "It's Esau, your oldest son. I've done as you told me to. Here is the delicious venison you wanted. Sit up and eat it, so that you will bless me with all your heart!"

20*Isaac:* "How were you able to find it so quickly, my son?"

Jacob: "Because Jehovah your God put it in my path!"

21*Isaac:* "Come over here. I want to feel you, and be sure it really is Esau!"

22(Jacob goes over to his father. He feels him!)

Isaac: (to himself) "The voice is Jacob's, but the hands are Esau's!"

23(The ruse convinces Isaac and he gives Jacob his blessings):

24*Isaac:* "Are you really Esau?"

Jacob: "Yes, of course."

25*Isaac:* "Then bring me the venison, and I will eat it and bless you with all my heart."

(Jacob takes it over to him and Isaac eats; he also drinks the wine Jacob brings him.)

26*Isaac:* "Come here and kiss me, my son!"

(Jacob goes over and kisses him on the cheek. Isaac sniffs his clothes, and finally seems convinced.)

27, 28, 29*Isaac:* "The smell of my son is the good smell of the earth and fields that Jehovah has blessed. May God always give you plenty of rain for your crops, and good harvests and grapes. May many nations be your slaves. Be the master of your brothers. May all your relatives bow low before you. Cursed are all who curse you, and blessed are all who bless you."

30(As soon as Isaac has blessed Jacob, and almost before Jacob leaves the room, Esau arrives, coming in from his hunting. 31He also has prepared his father's favorite dish and brings it to him.)

Esau: "Here I am, father, with the venison. Sit up and eat it so that you can give me your finest blessings!"

32*Isaac:* "Who is it?"

Esau: "Why, it's me, of course! Esau, your oldest son!"

33(Isaac begins to tremble noticeably.)

Isaac: "Then who is it who was just here with venison, and I have already eaten it and blessed him with irrevocable blessing?"

34(Esau begins to sob with deep and bitter sobs.)

Esau: "O my father, bless me, bless me too!"

35*Isaac:* "Your brother was here and tricked me and has carried away your blessing."

36*Esau:* (bitterly) "No wonder they call him 'The Cheater.'b For he took my birthright, and now he has stolen my blessing. Oh, haven't you saved even one blessing for me?"

37*Isaac:* "I have made him your master, and have given him yourself and all of his relatives as his servants. I have guaranteed him abundance of grain and wine—what is there left to give?"

New Revised Standard

elder son Esau, which were with her in the house, and put them on her younger son Jacob; 16and she put the skins of the kids on his hands and on the smooth part of his neck. 17Then she handed the savory food, and the bread that she had prepared, to her son Jacob.

18 So he went in to his father, and said, "My father"; and he said, "Here I am; who are you, my son?" 19Jacob said to his father, "I am Esau your firstborn. I have done as you told me; now sit up and eat of my game, so that you may bless me." 20But Isaac said to his son, "How is it that you have found it so quickly, my son?" He answered, "Because the LORD your God granted me success." 21Then Isaac said to Jacob, "Come near, that I may feel you, my son, to know whether you are really my son Esau or not." 22So Jacob went up to his father Isaac, who felt him and said, "The voice is Jacob's voice, but the hands are the hands of Esau." 23He did not recognize him, because his hands were hairy like his brother Esau's hands; so he blessed him. 24He said, "Are you really my son Esau?" He answered, "I am." 25Then he said, "Bring it to me, that I may eat of my son's game and bless you." So he brought it to him, and he ate; and he brought him wine, and he drank. 26Then his father Isaac said to him, "Come near and kiss me, my son." 27So he came near and kissed him; and he smelled the smell of his garments, and blessed him, and said,

> "Ah, the smell of my son
> is like the smell of a field that the LORD has
>   blessed.
> 28 May God give you of the dew of heaven,
>   and of the fatness of the earth,
>   and plenty of grain and wine.
> 29 Let peoples serve you,
>   and nations bow down to you.
> Be lord over your brothers,
>   and may your mother's sons bow down to
>   you.
> Cursed be everyone who curses you,
>   and blessed be everyone who blesses you!"

Esau's Lost Blessing

30 As soon as Isaac had finished blessing Jacob, when Jacob had scarcely gone out from the presence of his father Isaac, his brother Esau came in from his hunting. 31He also prepared savory food, and brought it to his father. And he said to his father, "Let my father sit up and eat of his son's game, so that you may bless me." 32His father Isaac said to him, "Who are you?" He answered, "I am your firstborn son, Esau." 33Then Isaac trembled violently, and said, "Who was it then that hunted game and brought it to me, and I ate it allc before you came, and I have blessed him?—yes, and blessed he shall be!" 34When Esau heard his father's words, he cried out with an exceedingly great and bitter cry, and said to his father, "Bless me, me also, father!" 35But he said, "Your brother came deceitfully, and he has taken away your blessing." 36Esau said, "Is he not rightly named Jacob?d For he has supplanted me these two times. He took away my birthright; and look, now he has taken away my blessing." Then he said, "Have you not reserved a blessing for me?" 37Isaac answered Esau, "I have already made him your lord, and I have given him all his brothers as servants, and with grain and wine I have sustained him. What then can I do for you, my son?" 38Esau said to his father, "Have you only one

---

b 27:36 *The Cheater.* "Jacob" means "Cheater."

c Cn: Heb *of all*   d That is *He supplants* or *He takes by the heel*

King James

38And Esau said unto his father, Hast thou but one blessing, my father? bless me, *even* me also, O my father. And Esau lifted up his voice, and wept.

39And Isaac his father answered and said unto him, Behold, thy dwelling shall be the fatness of the earth, and of the dew of heaven from above;

40And by thy sword shalt thou live, and shalt serve thy brother; and it shall come to pass when thou shalt have the dominion, that thou shalt break his yoke from off thy neck.

41¶ And Esau hated Jacob because of the blessing wherewith his father blessed him: and Esau said in his heart, The days of mourning for my father are at hand; then will I slay my brother Jacob.

42And these words of Esau her elder son were told to Rebekah: and she sent and called Jacob her younger son, and said unto him, Behold, thy brother Esau, as touching thee, doth comfort himself, *purposing* to kill thee.

43Now therefore, my son, obey my voice; and arise, flee thou to Laban my brother to Haran;

44And tarry with him a few days, until thy brother's fury turn away;

45Until thy brother's anger turn away from thee, and he forget *that* which thou hast done to him: then I will send, and fetch thee from thence: why should I be deprived also of you both in one day?

46And Rebekah said to Isaac, I am weary of my life because of the daughters of Heth: if Jacob take a wife of the daughters of Heth, such as these *which are* of the daughters of the land, what good shall my life do me?

28 AND ISAAC called Jacob, and blessed him, and charged him, and said unto him, Thou shalt not take a wife of the daughters of Canaan.

2Arise, go to Padan-aram, to the house of Bethuel thy mother's father; and take thee a wife from thence of the daughters of Laban thy mother's brother.

3And God Almighty bless thee, and make thee fruitful, and multiply thee, that thou mayest be a multitude of people;

4And give thee the blessing of Abraham, to thee, and to thy seed with thee; that thou mayest inherit the land wherein thou art a stranger, which God gave unto Abraham.

5And Isaac sent away Jacob: and he went to Padanaram unto Laban, son of Bethuel the Syrian, the brother of Rebekah, Jacob's and Esau's mother.

6¶ When Esau saw that Isaac had blessed Jacob, and sent him away to Padan-aram, to take him a wife from thence; and that as he blessed him he gave him a charge, saying, Thou shalt not take a wife of the daughters of Canaan;

7And that Jacob obeyed his father and his mother, and was gone to Padan-aram;

8And Esau seeing that the daughters of Canaan pleased not Isaac his father;

9Then went Esau unto Ishmael, and took unto the wives which he had Mahalath the daughter of Ishmael Abraham's son, the sister of Nebajoth, to be his wife.

10¶ And Jacob went out from Beer-sheba, and went toward Haran.

11And he lighted upon a certain place, and tarried there all night, because the sun was set; and he took of the stones of that place, and put *them for* his pillows, and lay down in that place to sleep.

12And he dreamed, and behold a ladder set up on the earth, and the top of it reached to heaven: and behold the angels of God ascending and descending on it.

New International

38Esau said to his father, "Do you have only one blessing, my father? Bless me too, my father!" Then Esau wept aloud.

39His father Isaac answered him,

"Your dwelling will be
   away from the earth's richness,
   away from the dew of heaven above.
40You will live by the sword
   and you will serve your brother.
But when you grow restless,
   you will throw his yoke
   from off your neck."

Jacob Flees to Laban

41Esau held a grudge against Jacob because of the blessing his father had given him. He said to himself, "The days of mourning for my father are near; then I will kill my brother Jacob."

42When Rebekah was told what her older son Esau had said, she sent for her younger son Jacob and said to him, "Your brother Esau is consoling himself with the thought of killing you. 43Now then, my son, do what I say: Flee at once to my brother Laban in Haran. 44Stay with him for a while until your brother's fury subsides. 45When your brother is no longer angry with you and forgets what you did to him, I'll send word for you to come back from there. Why should I lose both of you in one day?"

46Then Rebekah said to Isaac, "I'm disgusted with living because of these Hittite women. If Jacob takes a wife from among the women of this land, from Hittite women like these, my life will not be worth living."

28 SO ISAAC called for Jacob and blesseda him and commanded him: "Do not marry a Canaanite woman. 2Go at once to Paddan Aram,b to the house of your mother's father Bethuel. Take a wife for yourself there, from among the daughters of Laban, your mother's brother. 3May God Almightyc bless you and make you fruitful and increase your numbers until you become a community of peoples. 4May he give you and your descendants the blessing given to Abraham, so that you may take possession of the land where you now live as an alien, the land God gave to Abraham." 5Then Isaac sent Jacob on his way, and he went to Paddan Aram, to Laban son of Bethuel the Aramean, the brother of Rebekah, who was the mother of Jacob and Esau.

6Now Esau learned that Isaac had blessed Jacob and had sent him to Paddan Aram to take a wife from there, and that when he blessed him he commanded him, "Do not marry a Canaanite woman," 7and that Jacob had obeyed his father and mother and had gone to Paddan Aram. 8Esau then realized how displeasing the Canaanite women were to his father Isaac; 9so he went to Ishmael and married Mahalath, the sister of Nebaioth and daughter of Ishmael son of Abraham, in addition to the wives he already had.

Jacob's Dream at Bethel

10Jacob left Beersheba and set out for Haran. 11When he reached a certain place, he stopped for the night because the sun had set. Taking one of the stones there, he put it under his head and lay down to sleep. 12He had a dream in which he saw a stairwayd resting on the earth, with its top reaching to heaven, and the angels of God were ascending and descending on it. 13There

a *1* Or *greeted*   b *2* That is, Northwest Mesopotamia; also in verses 5, 6 and 7   c *3* Hebrew *El-Shaddai*   d *12* Or *ladder*

Living Bible

38*Esau:* "Not one blessing left for me? O my father, bless me too."

(Isaac says nothing[e] as Esau weeps.)

39, 40*Isaac:* "Yours will be no life of ease and luxury, but you shall hew your way with your sword. For a time you will serve your brother, but you will finally shake loose from him and be free."

41So Esau hated Jacob because of what he had done to him. He said to himself, "My father will soon be gone, and then I will kill Jacob." 42But someone got wind of what he was planning, and reported it to Rebekah. She sent for Jacob and told him that his life was being threatened by Esau.

43"This is what to do," she said. "Flee to your Uncle Laban in Haran. 44Stay there with him awhile until your brother's fury is spent, 45and he forgets what you have done. Then I will send for you. For why should I be bereaved of both of you in one day?"

46Then Rebekah said to Isaac, "I'm sick and tired of these local girls. I'd rather die than see Jacob marry one of them."

28 SO ISAAC called for Jacob and blessed him and said to him, "Don't marry one of these Canaanite girls. 2Instead, go at once to Paddan-aram, to the house of your grandfather Bethuel, and marry one of your cousins—your Uncle[f] Laban's daughters. 3God Almighty bless you and give you many children; may you become a great nation of many tribes! 4May God pass on to you and to your descendants the mighty blessings promised to Abraham. May you own this land where we now are foreigners, for God has given it to Abraham."

5So Isaac sent Jacob away, and he went to Paddan-aram to visit his Uncle Laban, his mother's brother—the son of Bethuel the Aramean. 6, 7, 8Esau realized that his father despised the local girls, and that his father and mother had sent Jacob to Paddan-aram, with his father's blessing, to get a wife from there, and that they had strictly warned him against marrying a Canaanite girl, and that Jacob had agreed and had left for Paddan-aram. 9So Esau went to his Uncle Ishmael's family and married another wife from there, besides the wives he already had. Her name was Mahalath, the sister of Nebaioth, and daughter of Ishmael, Abraham's son.

10So Jacob left Beer-sheba and journeyed toward Haran. 11That night, when he stopped to camp at sundown, he found a rock for a headrest and lay down to sleep, 12and dreamed that a staircase[g] reached from earth to heaven, and he saw the angels of God going up and down upon it.

New Revised Standard

blessing, father? Bless me, me also, father!" And Esau lifted up his voice and wept.

39 Then his father Isaac answered him:
"See, away from[h] the fatness of the earth
shall your home be,
and away from[i] the dew of heaven on high.
40 By your sword you shall live,
and you shall serve your brother;
but when you break loose,[j]
you shall break his yoke from your neck."

Jacob Escapes Esau's Fury

41 Now Esau hated Jacob because of the blessing with which his father had blessed him, and Esau said to himself, "The days of mourning for my father are approaching; then I will kill my brother Jacob." 42But the words of her elder son Esau were told to Rebekah; so she sent and called her younger son Jacob and said to him, "Your brother Esau is consoling himself by planning to kill you. 43Now therefore, my son, obey my voice; flee at once to my brother Laban in Haran, 44and stay with him a while, until your brother's fury turns away—45until your brother's anger against you turns away, and he forgets what you have done to him; then I will send, and bring you back from there. Why should I lose both of you in one day?"

46 Then Rebekah said to Isaac, "I am weary of my life because of the Hittite women. If Jacob marries one of the Hittite women such as these, one of the women of the land, what good will my life be to me?"

28 THEN ISAAC called Jacob and blessed him, and charged him, "You shall not marry one of the Canaanite women. 2Go at once to Paddan-aram to the house of Bethuel, your mother's father; and take as wife from there one of the daughters of Laban, your mother's brother. 3May God Almighty[k] bless you and make you fruitful and numerous, that you may become a company of peoples. 4May he give to you the blessing of Abraham, to you and to your offspring with you, so that you may take possession of the land where you now live as an alien—land that God gave to Abraham." 5Thus Isaac sent Jacob away; and he went to Paddan-aram, to Laban son of Bethuel the Aramean, the brother of Rebekah, Jacob's and Esau's mother.

Esau Marries Ishmael's Daughter

6 Now Esau saw that Isaac had blessed Jacob and sent him away to Paddan-aram to take a wife from there, and that as he blessed him he charged him, "You shall not marry one of the Canaanite women," 7and that Jacob had obeyed his father and his mother and gone to Paddan-aram. 8So when Esau saw that the Canaanite women did not please his father Isaac, 9Esau went to Ishmael and took Mahalath daughter of Abraham's son Ishmael, and sister of Nebaioth, to be his wife in addition to the wives he had.

Jacob's Dream at Bethel

10 Jacob left Beer-sheba and went toward Haran. 11He came to a certain place and stayed there for the night, because the sun had set. Taking one of the stones of the place, he put it under his head and lay down in that place. 12And he dreamed that there was a ladder[l] set up on the earth, the top of it reaching to heaven; and the angels of God were ascending and descending on it.

---

e 27:38 *Isaac says nothing.* This appears in some versions, not in others. f 28:2 *your grandfather,* literally, "your mother's father." *your Uncle Laban,* literally, "your mother's brother." g 28:12 *a staircase,* literally, "ladder."

h Or *See, of* i Or *and of* j Meaning of Heb uncertain k Traditional rendering of Heb *El Shaddai* l Or *stairway* or *ramp*

King James

13And, behold, the LORD stood above it, and said, I *am* the LORD God of Abraham thy father, and the God of Isaac: the land whereon thou liest, to thee will I give it, and to thy seed;

14And thy seed shall be as the dust of the earth, and thou shalt spread abroad to the west, and to the east, and to the north, and to the south: and in thee and in thy seed shall all the families of the earth be blessed.

15And, behold, I *am* with thee, and will keep thee in all *places* whither thou goest, and will bring thee again into this land; for I will not leave thee, until I have done *that* which I have spoken to thee of.

16¶ And Jacob awaked out of his sleep, and he said, Surely the LORD is in this place; and I knew *it* not.

17And he was afraid, and said, How dreadful *is* this place! this *is* none other but the house of God, and this *is* the gate of heaven.

18And Jacob rose up early in the morning, and took the stone that he had put *for* his pillows, and set it up *for* a pillar, and poured oil upon the top of it.

19And he called the name of that place Beth-el: but the name of that city *was called* Luz at the first.

20And Jacob vowed a vow, saying, If God will be with me, and will keep me in this way that I go, and will give me bread to eat, and raiment to put on,

21So that I come again to my father's house in peace; then shall the LORD be my God:

22And this stone, which I have set *for* a pillar, shall be God's house: and of all that thou shalt give me I will surely give the tenth unto thee.

29 THEN JACOB went on his journey, and came into the land of the people of the east.

2And he looked, and behold a well in the field, and, lo, there *were* three flocks of sheep lying by it; for out of that well they watered the flocks: and a great stone *was* upon the well's mouth.

3And thither were all the flocks gathered: and they rolled the stone from the well's mouth, and watered the sheep, and put the stone again upon the well's mouth in his place.

4And Jacob said unto them, My brethren, whence *be* ye? And they said, Of Haran *are* we.

5And he said unto them, Know ye Laban the son of Nahor? And they said, We know *him*.

6And he said unto them, *Is* he well? And they said, *He is* well: and, behold, Rachel his daughter cometh with the sheep.

7And he said, Lo, *it is* yet high day, neither *is it* time that the cattle should be gathered together: water ye the sheep, and go *and* feed *them*.

8And they said, We cannot, until all the flocks be gathered together, and *till* they roll the stone from the well's mouth; then we water the sheep.

9¶ And while he yet spake with them, Rachel came with her father's sheep: for she kept them.

10And it came to pass, when Jacob saw Rachel the daughter of Laban his mother's brother, and the sheep of Laban his mother's brother, that Jacob went near, and rolled the stone from the well's mouth, and watered the flock of Laban his mother's brother.

11And Jacob kissed Rachel, and lifted up his voice, and wept.

12And Jacob told Rachel that he *was* her father's brother, and that he *was* Rebekah's son: and she ran and told her father.

13And it came to pass, when Laban heard the tidings of Jacob his sister's son, that he ran to meet him, and embraced him, and kissed him, and brought him to his house. And he told Laban all these things.

New International

above ita stood the LORD, and he said: "I am the LORD, the God of your father Abraham and the God of Isaac. I will give you and your descendants the land on which you are lying. 14Your descendants will be like the dust of the earth, and you will spread out to the west and to the east, to the north and to the south. All peoples on earth will be blessed through you and your offspring. 15I am with you and will watch over you wherever you go, and I will bring you back to this land. I will not leave you until I have done what I have promised you."

16When Jacob awoke from his sleep, he thought, "Surely the LORD is in this place, and I was not aware of it." 17He was afraid and said, "How awesome is this place! This is none other than the house of God; this is the gate of heaven."

18Early the next morning Jacob took the stone he had placed under his head and set it up as a pillar and poured oil on top of it. 19He called that place Bethel,b though the city used to be called Luz.

20Then Jacob made a vow, saying, "If God will be with me and will watch over me on this journey I am taking and will give me food to eat and clothes to wear 21so that I return safely to my father's house, then the LORDc will be my God 22andd this stone that I have set up as a pillar will be God's house, and of all that you give me I will give you a tenth."

Jacob Arrives in Paddan Aram

29 THEN JACOB continued on his journey and came to the land of the eastern peoples. 2There he saw a well in the field, with three flocks of sheep lying near it because the flocks were watered from that well. The stone over the mouth of the well was large. 3When all the flocks were gathered there, the shepherds would roll the stone away from the well's mouth and water the sheep. Then they would return the stone to its place over the mouth of the well.

4Jacob asked the shepherds, "My brothers, where are you from?"

"We're from Haran," they replied.

5He said to them, "Do you know Laban, Nahor's grandson?"

"Yes, we know him," they answered.

6Then Jacob asked them, "Is he well?"

"Yes, he is," they said, "and here comes his daughter Rachel with the sheep."

7"Look," he said, "the sun is still high; it is not time for the flocks to be gathered. Water the sheep and take them back to pasture."

8"We can't," they replied, "until all the flocks are gathered and the stone has been rolled away from the mouth of the well. Then we will water the sheep."

9While he was still talking with them, Rachel came with her father's sheep, for she was a shepherdess. 10When Jacob saw Rachel daughter of Laban, his mother's brother, and Laban's sheep, he went over and rolled the stone away from the mouth of the well and watered his uncle's sheep. 11Then Jacob kissed Rachel and began to weep aloud. 12He had told Rachel that he was a relative of her father and a son of Rebekah. So she ran and told her father.

13As soon as Laban heard the news about Jacob, his sister's son, he hurried to meet him. He embraced him and kissed him and brought him to his home, and there

a *13* Or *There beside him*   b *19* *Bethel* means *house of God.*   c *20,21* Or *Since God . . . father's house, the LORD*   d *21,22* Or *house, and the LORD will be my God.* 22*then*

Living Bible

13At the top of the stairs stood the Lord. "I am Jehovah," he said, "the God of Abraham, and of your father Isaac. The ground you are lying on is yours! I will give it to you and to your descendants. 14For you will have descendants as many as dust! They will cover the land from east to west and from north to south; and all the nations of the earth will be blessed through you and your descendants. 15What's more, I am with you, and will protect you wherever you go, and will bring you back safely to this land; I will be with you constantly until I have finished giving you all I am promising."

16, 17Then Jacob woke up. "God lives here!" he exclaimed in terror. "I've stumbled into his home! This is the awesome entrance to heaven!" 18The next morning he got up very early and set his stone headrest upright as a memorial pillar, and poured olive oil over it. 19He named the place Bethel ("House of God"), though the previous name of the nearest village was Luz.e

20And Jacob vowed this vow to God: "If God will help and protect me on this journey and give me food and clothes, 21and will bring me back safely to my father, then I will choose Jehovah as my God! 22And this memorial pillar shall become a place for worship; and I will give you back a tenth of everything you give me!"

29 JACOB TRAVELED on, finally arriving in the land of the East. 2He saw in the distance three flocks of sheep lying beside a well in an open field, waiting to be watered. But a heavy stone covered the mouth of the well. 3(The custom was that the stone was not removed until all the flocks were there. After watering them, the stone was rolled back over the mouth of the well again.) 4Jacob went over to the shepherds and asked them where they lived.

"At Haran," they said.

5"Do you know a fellow there named Laban, the son of Nahor?"

"We sure do."

6"How is he?"

"He's well and prosperous. Look, there comes his daughter Rachel with the sheep."

7"Why don't you water the flocks so they can get back to grazing?" Jacob asked. "They'll be hungry if you stop so early in the day!"

8"We don't roll away the stone and begin the watering until all the flocks and shepherds are here," they replied.

9As this conversation was going on, Rachel arrived with her father's sheep, for she was a shepherdess. 10And because she was his cousin—the daughter of his mother's brother—and because the sheep were his uncle's, Jacob went over to the well and rolled away the stone and watered his uncle's flock. 11Then Jacob kissed Rachel and started crying! 12, 13He explained about being her cousin on her father's side, and that he was her Aunt Rebekah's son. She quickly ran and told her father, Laban, and as soon as he heard of Jacob's arrival, he rushed out to meet him and greeted him warmly and brought him home. Then Jacob told him his story.

New Revised Standard

13And the LORD stood beside himf and said, "I am the LORD, the God of Abraham your father and the God of Isaac; the land on which you lie I will give to you and to your offspring; 14and your offspring shall be like the dust of the earth, and you shall spread abroad to the west and to the east and to the north and to the south; and all the families of the earth shall be blessedg in you and in your offspring. 15Know that I am with you and will keep you wherever you go, and will bring you back to this land; for I will not leave you until I have done what I have promised you." 16Then Jacob woke from his sleep and said, "Surely the LORD is in this place—and I did not know it!" 17And he was afraid, and said, "How awesome is this place! This is none other than the house of God, and this is the gate of heaven."

18 So Jacob rose early in the morning, and he took the stone that he had put under his head and set it up for a pillar and poured oil on the top of it. 19He called that place Bethel;h but the name of the city was Luz at the first. 20Then Jacob made a vow, saying, "If God will be with me, and will keep me in this way that I go, and will give me bread to eat and clothing to wear, 21so that I come again to my father's house in peace, then the LORD shall be my God, 22and this stone, which I have set up for a pillar, shall be God's house; and of all that you give me I will surely give one tenth to you."

Jacob Meets Rachel

29 THEN JACOB went on his journey, and came to the land of the people of the east. 2As he looked, he saw a well in the field and three flocks of sheep lying there beside it; for out of that well the flocks were watered. The stone on the well's mouth was large, 3and when all the flocks were gathered there, the shepherds would roll the stone from the mouth of the well, and water the sheep, and put the stone back in its place on the mouth of the well.

4 Jacob said to them, "My brothers, where do you come from?" They said, "We are from Haran." 5He said to them, "Do you know Laban son of Nahor?" They said, "We do." 6He said to them, "Is it well with him?" "Yes," they replied, "and here is his daughter Rachel, coming with the sheep." 7He said, "Look, it is still broad daylight; it is not time for the animals to be gathered together. Water the sheep, and go, pasture them." 8But they said, "We cannot until all the flocks are gathered together, and the stone is rolled from the mouth of the well; then we water the sheep."

9 While he was still speaking with them, Rachel came with her father's sheep; for she kept them. 10Now when Jacob saw Rachel, the daughter of his mother's brother Laban, and the sheep of his mother's brother Laban, Jacob went up and rolled the stone from the well's mouth, and watered the flock of his mother's brother Laban. 11Then Jacob kissed Rachel, and wept aloud. 12And Jacob told Rachel that he was her father's kinsman, and that he was Rebekah's son; and she ran and told her father.

13 When Laban heard the news about his sister's son Jacob, he ran to meet him; he embraced him and kissed him, and brought him to his house. Jacobi told

---

e 28:19 of the nearest village, literally, "of the city."

f Or stood above it   g Or shall bless themselves   h That is House of God
i Heb He

King James

14And Laban said to him, Surely thou *art* my bone and my flesh. And he abode with him the space of a month.

15¶ And Laban said unto Jacob, Because thou *art* my brother, shouldest thou therefore serve me for nought? tell me, what *shall* thy wages *be?*

16And Laban had two daughters: the name of the elder *was* Leah, and the name of the younger *was* Rachel.

17Leah *was* tender eyed; but Rachel was beautiful and wellfavoured.

18And Jacob loved Rachel; and said, I will serve thee seven years for Rachel thy younger daughter.

19And Laban said, *It is* better that I give her to thee, than that I should give her to another man: abide with me.

20And Jacob served seven years for Rachel; and they seemed unto him *but* a few days, for the love he had to her.

21¶ And Jacob said unto Laban, Give *me* my wife, for my days are fulfilled, that I may go in unto her.

22And Laban gathered together all the men of the place, and made a feast.

23And it came to pass in the evening, that he took Leah his daughter, and brought her to him; and he went in unto her.

24And Laban gave unto his daughter Leah Zilpah his maid *for* an handmaid.

25And it came to pass, that in the morning, behold, it *was* Leah: and he said to Laban, What *is* this thou hast done unto me? did not I serve with thee for Rachel? wherefore then hast thou beguiled me?

26And Laban said, It must not be so done in our country, to give the younger before the firstborn.

27Fulfil her week, and we will give thee this also for the service which thou shalt serve with me yet seven other years.

28And Jacob did so, and fulfilled her week: and he gave him Rachel his daughter to wife also.

29And Laban gave to Rachel his daughter Bilhah his handmaid to be her maid.

30And he went in also unto Rachel, and he loved also Rachel more than Leah, and served with him yet seven other years.

31¶ And when the LORD saw that Leah *was* hated, he opened her womb: but Rachel *was* barren.

32And Leah conceived, and bare a son, and she called his name Reuben: for she said, Surely the LORD hath looked upon my affliction; now therefore my husband will love me.

33And she conceived again, and bare a son; and said, Because the LORD hath heard that I *was* hated, he hath therefore given me this *son* also: and she called his name Simeon.

34And she conceived again, and bare a son; and said, Now this time will my husband be joined unto me, because I have born him three sons: therefore was his name called Levi.

35And she conceived again, and bare a son: and she said, Now will I praise the LORD: therefore she called his name Judah; and left bearing.

30 AND WHEN Rachel saw that she bare Jacob no children, Rachel envied her sister; and said unto Jacob, Give me children, or else I die.

New International

Jacob told him all these things. 14Then Laban said to him, "You are my own flesh and blood."

Jacob Marries Leah and Rachel

After Jacob had stayed with him for a whole month, 15Laban said to him, "Just because you are a relative of mine, should you work for me for nothing? Tell me what your wages should be."

16Now Laban had two daughters; the name of the older was Leah, and the name of the younger was Rachel. 17Leah had weaka eyes, but Rachel was lovely in form, and beautiful. 18Jacob was in love with Rachel and said, "I'll work for you seven years in return for your younger daughter Rachel."

19Laban said, "It's better that I give her to you than to some other man. Stay here with me." 20So Jacob served seven years to get Rachel, but they seemed like only a few days to him because of his love for her.

21Then Jacob said to Laban, "Give me my wife. My time is completed, and I want to lie with her."

22So Laban brought together all the people of the place and gave a feast. 23But when evening came, he took his daughter Leah and gave her to Jacob, and Jacob lay with her. 24And Laban gave his servant girl Zilpah to his daughter as her maidservant.

25When morning came, there was Leah! So Jacob said to Laban, "What is this you have done to me? I served you for Rachel, didn't I? Why have you deceived me?"

26Laban replied, "It is not our custom here to give the younger daughter in marriage before the older one. 27Finish this daughter's bridal week; then we will give you the younger one also, in return for another seven years of work."

28And Jacob did so. He finished the week with Leah, and then Laban gave him his daughter Rachel to be his wife. 29Laban gave his servant girl Bilhah to his daughter Rachel as her maidservant. 30Jacob lay with Rachel also, and he loved Rachel more than Leah. And he worked for Laban another seven years.

Jacob's Children

31When the LORD saw that Leah was not loved, he opened her womb, but Rachel was barren. 32Leah became pregnant and gave birth to a son. She named him Reuben,b for she said, "It is because the LORD has seen my misery. Surely my husband will love me now."

33She conceived again, and when she gave birth to a son she said, "Because the LORD heard that I am not loved, he gave me this one too." So she named him Simeon.c

34Again she conceived, and when she gave birth to a son she said, "Now at last my husband will become attached to me, because I have borne him three sons." So he was named Levi.d

35She conceived again, and when she gave birth to a son she said, "This time I will praise the LORD." So she named him Judah.e Then she stopped having children.

30 WHEN RACHEL saw that she was not bearing Jacob any children, she became jealous of her sister. So she said to Jacob, "Give me children, or I'll die!"

---

a *17 Or delicate*   b *32 Reuben sounds like the Hebrew for he has seen my misery; the name means see, a son.*   c *33 Simeon probably means one who hears.*   d *34 Levi sounds like and may be derived from the Hebrew for attached.*   e *35 Judah sounds like and may be derived from the Hebrew for praise.*

Living Bible

14"Just think, my very own flesh and blood," Laban exclaimed.

After Jacob had been there about a month, 15Laban said to him one day, "Just because we are relatives is no reason for you to work for me without pay. How much do you want?" 16Now Laban had two daughters, Leah, the older, and her younger sister, Rachel. 17Leah had lovely eyes, but Rachel was shapely, and in every way a beauty. 18Well, Jacob was in love with Rachel. So he told her father, "I'll work for you seven years if you'll give me Rachel as my wife."

19"Agreed!" Laban replied. "I'd rather give her to you than to someone outside the family."

20So Jacob spent the next seven years working to pay for Rachel. But they seemed to him but a few days, he was so much in love. 21Finally the time came for him to marry her.

"I have fulfilled my contract," Jacob said to Laban. "Now give me my wife, so that I can sleep with her."

22So Laban invited all the men of the settlement to celebrate with Jacob at a big party. 23Afterwards, that night, when it was dark, Laban took Leah to Jacob, and he slept with her. 24(And Laban gave to Leah a servant girl, Zilpah, to be her maid.) 25But in the morning—it was Leah!

"What sort of trick is this?" Jacob raged at Laban. "I worked for seven years for Rachel. What do you mean by this trickery?"

26"It's not our custom to marry off a younger daughter ahead of her sister," Laban replied smoothly.f 27"Wait until the bridal week is over and you can have Rachel too—if you promise to work for me another seven years!"

28So Jacob agreed to work seven more years. Then Laban gave him Rachel, too. 29And Laban gave to Rachel a servant girl, Bilhah, to be her maid.) 30So Jacob slept with Rachel, too, and he loved her more than Leah, and stayed and worked the additional seven years.

31But because Jacob was slighting Leah, Jehovah let her have a child, while Rachel was barren. 32So Leah became pregnant and had a son, Reuben (meaning "God has noticed my trouble"), for she said, "Jehovah has noticed my trouble—now my husband will love me." 33She soon became pregnant again and had another son and named him Simeon (meaning "Jehovah heard"), for she said, "Jehovah heard that I was unloved, and so he has given me another son." 34Again she became pregnant and had a son, and named him Levi (meaning "Attachment") for she said, "Surely now my husband will feel affection for me, since I have given him three sons!" 35Once again she was pregnant and had a son and named him Judah (meaning "Praise"), for she said, "Now I will praise Jehovah!" And then she stopped having children.

30 RACHEL, REALIZING she was barren, became envious of her sister. "Give me children or I'll die," she exclaimed to Jacob.

New Revised Standard

Laban all these things, 14and Laban said to him, "Surely you are my bone and my flesh!" And he stayed with him a month.

Jacob Marries Laban's Daughters

15 Then Laban said to Jacob, "Because you are my kinsman, should you therefore serve me for nothing? Tell me, what shall your wages be?" 16Now Laban had two daughters; the name of the elder was Leah, and the name of the younger was Rachel. 17Leah's eyes were lovely,g and Rachel was graceful and beautiful. 18Jacob loved Rachel; so he said, "I will serve you seven years for your younger daughter Rachel." 19Laban said, "It is better that I give her to you than that I should give her to any other man; stay with me." 20So Jacob served seven years for Rachel, and they seemed to him but a few days because of the love he had for her.

21 Then Jacob said to Laban, "Give me my wife that I may go in to her, for my time is completed." 22So Laban gathered together all the people of the place, and made a feast. 23But in the evening he took his daughter Leah and brought her to Jacob; and he went in to her. 24(Laban gave his maid Zilpah to his daughter Leah to be her maid.) 25When morning came, it was Leah! And Jacob said to Laban, "What is this you have done to me? Did I not serve with you for Rachel? Why then have you deceived me?" 26Laban said, "This is not done in our country—giving the younger before the firstborn. 27Complete the week of this one, and we will give you the other also in return for serving me another seven years." 28Jacob did so, and completed her week; then Laban gave him his daughter Rachel as a wife. 29(Laban gave his maid Bilhah to his daughter Rachel to be her maid.) 30So Jacob went in to Rachel also, and he loved Rachel more than Leah. He served Labanh for another seven years.

31 When the LORD saw that Leah was unloved, he opened her womb; but Rachel was barren. 32Leah conceived and bore a son, and she named him Reuben;i for she said, "Because the LORD has looked on my affliction; surely now my husband will love me." 33She conceived again and bore a son, and said, "Because the LORD has heardj that I am hated, he has given me this son also"; and she named him Simeon. 34Again she conceived and bore a son, and said, "Now this time my husband will be joinedk to me, because I have borne him three sons"; therefore he was named Levi. 35She conceived again and bore a son, and said, "This time I will praisel the LORD"; therefore she named him Judah; then she ceased bearing.

30 WHEN RACHEL saw that she bore Jacob no children, she envied her sister; and she said to Jacob, "Give me children, or I shall die!" 2Jacob be-

---

f 29:26 Laban replied smoothly, implied from context.

g Meaning of Heb uncertain h Heb him i That is See, a son j Heb shama
k Heb lawah l Heb hodah

King James

2And Jacob's anger was kindled against Rachel: and he said, *Am* I in God's stead, who hath withheld from thee the fruit of the womb?

3And she said, Behold my maid Bilhah, go in unto her; and she shall bear upon my knees, that I may also have children by her.

4And she gave him Bilhah her handmaid to wife: and Jacob went in unto her.

5And Bilhah conceived, and bare Jacob a son.

6And Rachel said, God hath judged me, and hath also heard my voice, and hath given me a son: therefore called she his name Dan.

7And Bilhah Rachel's maid conceived again, and bare Jacob a second son.

8And Rachel said, With great wrestlings have I wrestled with my sister, and I have prevailed: and she called his name Naphtali.

9When Leah saw that she had left bearing, she took Zilpah her maid, and gave her Jacob to wife.

10And Zilpah Leah's maid bare Jacob a son.

11And Leah said, A troop cometh: and she called his name Gad.

12And Zilpah Leah's maid bare Jacob a second son.

13And Leah said, Happy am I, for the daughters will call me blessed: and she called his name Asher.

14¶ And Reuben went in the days of wheat harvest, and found mandrakes in the field, and brought them unto his mother Leah. Then Rachel said to Leah, Give me, I pray thee, of thy son's mandrakes.

15And she said unto her, *Is it* a small matter that thou hast taken my husband? and wouldest thou take away my son's mandrakes also? And Rachel said, Therefore he shall lie with thee to night for thy son's mandrakes.

16And Jacob came out of the field in the evening, and Leah went out to meet him, and said, Thou must come in unto me; for surely I have hired thee with my son's mandrakes. And he lay with her that night.

17And God hearkened unto Leah, and she conceived, and bare Jacob the fifth son.

18And Leah said, God hath given me my hire, because I have given my maiden to my husband: and she called his name Issachar.

19And Leah conceived again, and bare Jacob the sixth son.

20And Leah said, God hath endued me *with* a good dowry; now will my husband dwell with me, because I have born him six sons: and she called his name Zebulun.

21And afterwards she bare a daughter, and called her name Dinah.

22¶ And God remembered Rachel, and God hearkened to her, and opened her womb.

23And she conceived, and bare a son; and said, God hath taken away my reproach:

24And she called his name Joseph; and said, The LORD shall add to me another son.

25¶ And it came to pass, when Rachel had born Joseph, that Jacob said unto Laban, Send me away, that I may go unto mine own place, and to my country.

26Give *me* my wives and my children, for whom I have served thee, and let me go: for thou knowest my service which I have done thee.

27And Laban said unto him, I pray thee, if I have found favour in thine eyes, *tarry: for* I have learned by experience that the LORD hath blessed me for thy sake.

28And he said, Appoint me thy wages, and I will give *it.*

29And he said unto him, Thou knowest how I have served thee, and how thy cattle was with me.

New International

2Jacob became angry with her and said, "Am I in the place of God, who has kept you from having children?"

3Then she said, "Here is Bilhah, my maidservant. Sleep with her so that she can bear children for me and that through her I too can build a family."

4So she gave him her servant Bilhah as a wife. Jacob slept with her, 5and she became pregnant and bore him a son. 6Then Rachel said, "God has vindicated me; he has listened to my plea and given me a son." Because of this she named him Dan.a

7Rachel's servant Bilhah conceived again and bore Jacob a second son. 8Then Rachel said, "I have had a great struggle with my sister, and I have won." So she named him Naphtali.b

9When Leah saw that she had stopped having children, she took her maidservant Zilpah and gave her to Jacob as a wife. 10Leah's servant Zilpah bore Jacob a son. 11Then Leah said, "What good fortune!"c So she named him Gad.d

12Leah's servant Zilpah bore Jacob a second son. 13Then Leah said, "How happy I am! The women will call me happy." So she named him Asher.e

14During wheat harvest, Reuben went out into the fields and found some mandrake plants, which he brought to his mother Leah. Rachel said to Leah, "Please give me some of your son's mandrakes."

15But she said to her, "Wasn't it enough that you took away my husband? Will you take my son's mandrakes too?"

"Very well," Rachel said, "he can sleep with you tonight in return for your son's mandrakes."

16So when Jacob came in from the fields that evening, Leah went out to meet him. "You must sleep with me," she said. "I have hired you with my son's mandrakes." So he slept with her that night.

17God listened to Leah, and she became pregnant and bore Jacob a fifth son. 18Then Leah said, "God has rewarded me for giving my maidservant to my husband." So she named him Issachar.f

19Leah conceived again and bore Jacob a sixth son. 20Then Leah said, "God has presented me with a precious gift. This time my husband will treat me with honor, because I have borne him six sons." So she named him Zebulun.g

21Some time later she gave birth to a daughter and named her Dinah.

22Then God remembered Rachel; he listened to her and opened her womb. 23She became pregnant and gave birth to a son and said, "God has taken away my disgrace." 24She named him Joseph,h and said, "May the LORD add to me another son."

Jacob's Flocks Increase

25After Rachel gave birth to Joseph, Jacob said to Laban, "Send me on my way so I can go back to my own homeland. 26Give me my wives and children, for whom I have served you, and I will be on my way. You know how much work I've done for you."

27But Laban said to him, "If I have found favor in your eyes, please stay. I have learned by divination thati the LORD has blessed me because of you." 28He added, "Name your wages, and I will pay them."

29Jacob said to him, "You know how I have worked for you and how your livestock has fared under my care.

---

a 6 *Dan* here means *he has vindicated.*   b 8 *Naphtali* means *my struggle.*
c 11 Or *"A troop is coming!"*   d 11 *Gad* can mean *good fortune* or *a troop.*
e 13 *Asher* means *happy.*   f 18 *Issachar* sounds like the Hebrew for *reward.*
g 20 *Zebulun* probably means *honor.*   h 24 *Joseph* means *may he add.*
i 27 Or possibly *have become rich and*

Living Bible

2Jacob flew into a rage. "Am I God?" he flared. "He is the one who is responsible for your barrenness."

3Then Rachel told him, "Sleep with my servant-girl Bilhah, and her children will be mine." 4So she gave him Bilhah to be his wife, and he slept with her, 5and she became pregnant and presented him with a son. 6Rachel named him Dan (meaningj "Justice"), for she said, "God has given me justice, and heard my plea and given me a son." 7Then Bilhah, Rachel's servant-girl, became pregnant again and gave Jacob a second son. 8Rachel named him Naphtali (meaning "Wrestling"), for she said, "I am in a fierce contest with my sister and I am winning!"

9Meanwhile, when Leah realized that she wasn't getting pregnant anymore, she gave her servant-girl Zilpah to Jacob, to be his wife, 10and soon Zilpah presented him with a son. 11Leah named him Gad (meaning "My luck has turned!").

12Then Zilpah produced a second son, 13and Leah named him Asher (meaning "Happy"), for she said, "What joy is mine! The other women will think me blessed indeed!"

14One day during the wheat harvest, Reuben found some mandrakesk growing in a field and brought them to his mother Leah. Rachel begged Leah to give some of them to her.

15But Leah angrily replied, "Wasn't it enough to steal my husband? And now will you steal my son's mandrakes too?"

Rachel said sadly, "He will sleep with you tonight because of the mandrakes."

16That evening as Jacob was coming home from the fields, Leah went out to meet him. "You must sleep with me tonight!" she said; "for I am hiring you with some mandrakes my son has found!" So he did. 17And God answered her prayers and she became pregnant again, and gave birth to her fifth son. 18She named him Issachar (meaning "Wages"), for she said, "God has repaid me for giving my slave-girl to my husband." 19Then once again she became pregnant, with a sixth son. 20She named him Zebulun (meaning "Gifts"), for she said, "God has given me good gifts for my husband. Now he will honor me, for I have given him six sons." 21Afterwards she gave birth to a daughter and named her Dinah.

22Then God remembered about Rachel's plight, and answered her prayers by giving her a child. 23, 24For she became pregnant and gave birth to a son. "God has removed the dark slur against my name," she said. And she named him Joseph (meaning "May I also have another!"), for she said, "May Jehovah give me another son."

25Soon after the birth of Joseph to Rachel, Jacob said to Laban, "I want to go back home. 26Let me take my wives and children—for I earned them from you—and be gone, for you know how fully I have paid for them with my service to you."

27"Please don't leave me," Laban replied, "for a fortune-teller that I consultedl told me that the many blessings I've been enjoying are all because of your being here. 28How much of a raise do you need to get you to stay? Whatever it is, I'll pay it."

29Jacob replied, "You know how faithfully I've served you through these many years, and how your flocks and herds have grown. 30For it was little indeed

j 30:6 Dan (meaning "Justice"). The meaning is not of the actual Hebrew name, but of a Hebrew word sounding like the name. The name given is a Hebrew pun. An example in English might be, "Because of the large hospital bill the child was named 'Bill.'" k 30:14 Mandrakes were a leafy plant eaten by peasant women who supposed this would aid them in becoming pregnant. l 30:27 a fortune-teller that I consulted, literally, "I have learned by divination."

New Revised Standard

came very angry with Rachel and said, "Am I in the place of God, who has withheld from you the fruit of the womb?" 3Then she said, "Here is my maid Bilhah; go in to her, that she may bear upon my knees and that I too may have children through her." 4So she gave him her maid Bilhah as a wife; and Jacob went in to her. 5And Bilhah conceived and bore Jacob a son. 6Then Rachel said, "God has judged me, and has also heard my voice and given me a son"; therefore she named him Dan.m 7Rachel's maid Bilhah conceived again and bore Jacob a second son. 8Then Rachel said, "With mighty wrestlings I have wrestledn with my sister, and have prevailed"; so she named him Naphtali.

9 When Leah saw that she had ceased bearing children, she took her maid Zilpah and gave her to Jacob as a wife. 10Then Leah's maid Zilpah bore Jacob a son. 11And Leah said, "Good fortune!" so she named him Gad.o 12Leah's maid Zilpah bore Jacob a second son. 13And Leah said, "Happy am I! For the women will call me happy"; so she named him Asher.p

14 In the days of wheat harvest Reuben went and found mandrakes in the field, and brought them to his mother Leah. Then Rachel said to Leah, "Please give me some of your son's mandrakes." 15But she said to her, "Is it a small matter that you have taken away my husband? Would you take away my son's mandrakes also?" Rachel said, "Then he may lie with you tonight for your son's mandrakes." 16When Jacob came from the field in the evening, Leah went out to meet him, and said, "You must come in to me; for I have hired you with my son's mandrakes." So he lay with her that night. 17And God heeded Leah, and she conceived and bore Jacob a fifth son. 18Leah said, "God has given me my hireq because I gave my maid to my husband"; so she named him Issachar. 19And Leah conceived again, and she bore Jacob a sixth son. 20Then Leah said, "God has endowed me with a good dowry; now my husband will honorr me, because I have borne him six sons"; so she named him Zebulun. 21Afterwards she bore a daughter, and named her Dinah.

22 Then God remembered Rachel, and God heeded her and opened her womb. 23She conceived and bore a son, and said, "God has taken away my reproach"; 24and she named him Joseph,s saying, "May the LORD add to me another son!"

Jacob Prospers at Laban's Expense

25 When Rachel had borne Joseph, Jacob said to Laban, "Send me away, that I may go to my own home and country. 26Give me my wives and my children for whom I have served you, and let me go; for you know very well the service I have given you." 27But Laban said to him, "If you will allow me to say so, I have learned by divination that the LORD has blessed me because of you; 28name your wages, and I will give it." 29Jacob said to him, "You yourself know how I have served you, and how your cattle have fared with me.

m That is He judged n Heb niphtal o That is Fortune p That is Happy q Heb sakar r Heb zabal s That is He adds

King James

30For *it was* little which thou hadst before I *came,* and it is *now* increased unto a multitude; and the LORD hath blessed thee since my coming: and now when shall I provide for mine own house also?

31And he said, What shall I give thee? And Jacob said, Thou shalt not give me any thing: if thou wilt do this thing for me, I will again feed *and* keep thy flock.

32I will pass through all thy flock today, removing from thence all the speckled and spotted cattle, and all the brown cattle among the sheep, and the spotted and speckled among the goats: and *of such* shall be my hire.

33So shall my righteousness answer for me in time to come, when it shall come for my hire before thy face: every one that *is* not speckled and spotted among the goats, and brown among the sheep, that shall be counted stolen with me.

34And Laban said, Behold, I would it might be according to thy word.

35And he removed that day the he goats that were ringstraked and spotted, and all the she goats that were speckled and spotted, *and* every one that had *some* white in it, and all the brown among the sheep, and gave *them* into the hand of his sons.

36And he set three days' journey betwixt himself and Jacob: and Jacob fed the rest of Laban's flocks.

37¶ And Jacob took him rods of green poplar, and of the hazel and chestnut tree; and pilled white strakes in them, and made the white appear which *was* in the rods.

38And he set the rods which he had pilled before the flocks in the gutters in the watering troughs when the flocks came to drink, that they should conceive when they came to drink.

39And the flocks conceived before the rods, and brought forth cattle ringstraked, speckled, and spotted.

40And Jacob did separate the lambs, and set the faces of the flocks toward the ringstraked, and all the brown in the flock of Laban; and he put his own flocks by themselves, and put them not unto Laban's cattle.

41And it came to pass, whensoever the stronger cattle did conceive, that Jacob laid the rods before the eyes of the cattle in the gutters, that they might conceive among the rods.

42But when the cattle were feeble, he put *them* not in: so the feebler were Laban's, and the stronger Jacob's.

43And the man increased exceedingly, and had much cattle, and maidservants, and menservants, and camels, and asses.

31 AND HE heard the words of Laban's sons, saying, Jacob hath taken away all that *was* our father's; and of *that* which *was* our father's hath he gotten all this glory.

2And Jacob beheld the countenance of Laban, and, behold, it *was* not toward him as before.

3And the LORD said unto Jacob, Return unto the land of thy fathers, and to thy kindred; and I will be with thee.

4And Jacob sent and called Rachel and Leah to the field unto his flock,

5And said unto them, I see your father's countenance, that it *is* not toward me as before; but the God of my father hath been with me.

6And ye know that with all my power I have served your father.

7And your father hath deceived me, and changed my wages ten times; but God suffered him not to hurt me.

8If he said thus, The speckled shall be thy wages; then all the cattle bare speckled: and if he said thus, The ringstraked shall be thy hire; then bare all the cattle ringstraked.

9Thus God hath taken away the cattle of your father, and given *them* to me.

New International

30The little you had before I came has increased greatly, and the LORD has blessed you wherever I have been. But now, when may I do something for my own household?"

31"What shall I give you?" he asked.

"Don't give me anything," Jacob replied. "But if you will do this one thing for me, I will go on tending your flocks and watching over them: 32Let me go through all your flocks today and remove from them every speckled or spotted sheep, every dark-colored lamb and every spotted or speckled goat. They will be my wages. 33And my honesty will testify for me in the future, whenever you check on the wages you have paid me. Any goat in my possession that is not speckled or spotted, or any lamb that is not dark-colored, will be considered stolen."

34"Agreed," said Laban. "Let it be as you have said." 35That same day he removed all the male goats that were streaked or spotted, and all the speckled or spotted female goats (all that had white on them) and all the dark-colored lambs, and he placed them in the care of his sons. 36Then he put a three-day journey between himself and Jacob, while Jacob continued to tend the rest of Laban's flocks.

37Jacob, however, took fresh-cut branches from poplar, almond and plane trees and made white stripes on them by peeling the bark and exposing the white inner wood of the branches. 38Then he placed the peeled branches in all the watering troughs, so that they would be directly in front of the flocks when they came to drink. When the flocks were in heat and came to drink, 39they mated in front of the branches. And they bore young that were streaked or speckled or spotted. 40Jacob set apart the young of the flock by themselves, but made the rest face the streaked and dark-colored animals that belonged to Laban. Thus he made separate flocks for himself and did not put them with Laban's animals. 41Whenever the stronger females were in heat, Jacob would place the branches in the troughs in front of the animals so they would mate near the branches, 42but if the animals were weak, he would not place them there. So the weak animals went to Laban and the strong ones to Jacob. 43In this way the man grew exceedingly prosperous and came to own large flocks, and maidservants and menservants, and camels and donkeys.

Jacob Flees From Laban

31 JACOB HEARD that Laban's sons were saying, "Jacob has taken everything our father owned and has gained all this wealth from what belonged to our father." 2And Jacob noticed that Laban's attitude toward him was not what it had been.

3Then the LORD said to Jacob, "Go back to the land of your fathers and to your relatives, and I will be with you."

4So Jacob sent word to Rachel and Leah to come out to the fields where his flocks were. 5He said to them, "I see that your father's attitude toward me is not what it was before, but the God of my father has been with me. 6You know that I've worked for your father with all my strength, 7yet your father has cheated me by changing my wages ten times. However, God has not allowed him to harm me. 8If he said, 'The speckled ones will be your wages,' then all the flocks gave birth to speckled young; and if he said, 'The streaked ones will be your wages,' then all the flocks bore streaked young. 9So God has taken away your father's livestock and has given them to me.

Living Bible

you had before I came, and your wealth has increased enormously; Jehovah has blessed you from everything I do! But now, what about me? When should I provide for my own family?"

31, 32"What wages do you want?" Laban asked again.

Jacob replied, "If you will do one thing, I'll go back to work for you. Let me go out among your flocks today and remove all the goats that are speckled or spotted, and all the black sheep. Give them to me as my wages. 33Then if you ever find any white goats or sheep in my flock, you will know that I have stolen them from you!"

34"All right!" Laban replied. "It shall be as you have said!"

35, 36So that very day Laban went out and formed a flock for Jacob of all the male goats that were ringed and spotted, and the females that were speckled and spotted with any white patches, and all of the black sheep. He gave them to Jacob's sons to take them three days' distance, and Jacob stayed and cared for Laban's flock. 37Then Jacob took fresh shoots from poplar, almond, and sycamore trees, and peeled white streaks in them, 38and placed these rods beside the watering troughs so that Laban's flocks would see them when they came to drink; for that is when they mated. 39, 40So the flocks mated before the white-streaked rods, and their offspring were streaked and spotted, and Jacob added them to his flock. Then he divided out the ewes from Laban's flock and segregated them from the rams, and let them mate only with Jacob's black rams. Thus he built his flocks from Laban's. 41Moreover, he watched for the stronger animals to mate, and placed the peeled branches before them, 42but didn't with the feebler ones. So the less healthy lambs were Laban's and the stronger ones were Jacob's! 43As a result, Jacob's flocks increased rapidly and he became very wealthy, with many servants, camels, and donkeys.

31 BUT JACOB learned that Laban's sons were grumbling, "He owes everything he owns to our father. All his wealth is at our father's expense." 2Soon Jacob noticed a considerable cooling in Laban's attitude towards him.

3Jehovah now spoke to Jacob and told him, "Return to the land of your fathers, and to your relatives there; and I will be with you."

4So one day Jacob sent for Rachel and Leah to come out to the field where he was with the flocks, 5to talk things over with them.

"Your father has turned against me," he told them, "and now the God of my fathers has come and spoken to me. 6You know how hard I've worked for your father, 7but he has been completely unscrupulous and has broken his wage contract with me again and again and again. But God has not permitted him to do me any harm! 8For if he said the speckled animals would be mine, then all the flock produced speckled; and when he changed and said I could have the streaked ones, then all the lambs were streaked! 9In this way God has made me wealthy at your father's expense.

New Revised Standard

30For you had little before I came, and it has increased abundantly; and the LORD has blessed you wherever I turned. But now when shall I provide for my own household also?" 31He said, "What shall I give you?" Jacob said, "You shall not give me anything; if you will do this for me, I will again feed your flock and keep it: 32let me pass through all your flock today, removing from it every speckled and spotted sheep and every black lamb, and the spotted and speckled among the goats; and such shall be my wages. 33So my honesty will answer for me later, when you come to look into my wages with you. Every one that is not speckled and spotted among the goats and black among the lambs, if found with me, shall be counted stolen." 34Laban said, "Good! Let it be as you have said." 35But that day Laban removed the male goats that were striped and spotted, and all the female goats that were speckled and spotted, every one that had white on it, and every lamb that was black, and put them in charge of his sons; 36and he set a distance of three days' journey between himself and Jacob, while Jacob was pasturing the rest of Laban's flock.

37 Then Jacob took fresh rods of poplar and almond and plane, and peeled white streaks in them, exposing the white of the rods. 38He set the rods that he had peeled in front of the flocks in the troughs, that is, the watering places, where the flocks came to drink. And since they bred when they came to drink, 39the flocks bred in front of the rods, and so the flocks produced young that were striped, speckled, and spotted. 40Jacob separated the lambs, and set the faces of the flocks toward the striped and the completely black animals in the flock of Laban; and he put his own droves apart, and did not put them with Laban's flock. 41Whenever the stronger of the flock were breeding, Jacob laid the rods in the troughs before the eyes of the flock, that they might breed among the rods, 42but for the feebler of the flock he did not lay them there; so the feebler were Laban's, and the stronger Jacob's. 43Thus the man grew exceedingly rich, and had large flocks, and male and female slaves, and camels and donkeys.

Jacob Flees with Family and Flocks

31 NOW JACOB heard that the sons of Laban were saying, "Jacob has taken all that was our father's; he has gained all this wealth from what belonged to our father." 2And Jacob saw that Laban did not regard him as favorably as he did before. 3Then the LORD said to Jacob, "Return to the land of your ancestors and to your kindred, and I will be with you." 4So Jacob sent and called Rachel and Leah into the field where his flock was, 5and said to them, "I see that your father does not regard me as favorably as he did before. But the God of my father has been with me. 6You know that I have served your father with all my strength; 7yet your father has cheated me and changed my wages ten times, but God did not permit him to harm me. 8If he said, 'The speckled shall be your wages,' then all the flock bore speckled; and if he said, 'The striped shall be your wages,' then all the flock bore striped. 9Thus God has taken away the livestock of your father, and given them to me.

King James

10And it came to pass at the time that the cattle conceived, that I lifted up mine eyes, and saw in a dream, and, behold, the rams which leaped upon the cattle *were* ringstraked, speckled, and grisled.

11And the angel of God spake unto me in a dream, *saying,* Jacob: And I said, Here *am* I.

12And he said, Lift up now thine eyes, and see, all the rams which leap upon the cattle *are* ringstraked, speckled, and grisled: for I have seen all that Laban doeth unto thee.

13I *am* the God of Beth-el, where thou anointedst the pillar, *and* where thou vowedst a vow unto me: now arise, get thee out from this land, and return unto the land of thy kindred.

14And Rachel and Leah answered and said unto him, *Is there* yet any portion or inheritance for us in our father's house?

15Are we not counted of him strangers? for he hath sold us, and hath quite devoured also our money.

16For all the riches which God hath taken from our father, that *is* ours, and our children's: now then, whatsoever God hath said unto thee, do.

17¶ Then Jacob rose up, and set his sons and his wives upon camels;

18And he carried away all his cattle, and all his goods which he had gotten, the cattle of his getting, which he had gotten in Padan-aram, for to go to Isaac his father in the land of Canaan.

19And Laban went to shear his sheep: and Rachel had stolen the images that *were* her father's.

20And Jacob stole away unawares to Laban the Syrian, in that he told him not that he fled.

21So he fled with all that he had; and he rose up, and passed over the river, and set his face *toward* the mount Gilead.

22And it was told Laban on the third day that Jacob was fled.

23And he took his brethren with him, and pursued after him seven days' journey; and they overtook him in the mount Gilead.

24And God came to Laban the Syrian in a dream by night, and said unto him, Take heed that thou speak not to Jacob either good or bad.

25¶ Then Laban overtook Jacob. Now Jacob had pitched his tent in the mount: and Laban with his brethren pitched in the mount of Gilead.

26And Laban said to Jacob, What hast thou done, that thou hast stolen away unawares to me, and carried away my daughters, as captives *taken* with the sword?

27Wherefore didst thou flee away secretly, and steal away from me; and didst not tell me, that I might have sent thee away with mirth, and with songs, with tabret, and with harp?

28And hast not suffered me to kiss my sons and my daughters? thou hast now done foolishly in *so* doing.

29It is in the power of my hand to do you hurt: but the God of your father spake unto me yesternight, saying, Take thou heed that thou speak not to Jacob either good or bad.

30And now, *though* thou wouldest needs be gone, because thou sore longedst after thy father's house, *yet* wherefore hast thou stolen my gods?

31And Jacob answered and said to Laban, Because I was afraid: for I said, Peradventure thou wouldest take by force thy daughters from me.

32With whomsoever thou findest thy gods, let him not live: before our brethren discern thou what *is* thine with me, and take *it* to thee. For Jacob knew not that Rachel had stolen them.

33And Laban went into Jacob's tent, and into Leah's tent, and into the two maidservants' tents; but he found *them* not. Then went he out of Leah's tent, and entered into Rachel's tent.

New International

10"In breeding season I once had a dream in which I looked up and saw that the male goats mating with the flock were streaked, speckled or spotted. 11The angel of God said to me in the dream, 'Jacob.' I answered, 'Here I am.' 12And he said, 'Look up and see that all the male goats mating with the flock are streaked, speckled or spotted, for I have seen all that Laban has been doing to you. 13I am the God of Bethel, where you anointed a pillar and where you made a vow to me. Now leave this land at once and go back to your native land.' "

14Then Rachel and Leah replied, "Do we still have any share in the inheritance of our father's estate? 15Does he not regard us as foreigners? Not only has he sold us, but he has used up what was paid for us. 16Surely all the wealth that God took away from our father belongs to us and our children. So do whatever God has told you."

17Then Jacob put his children and his wives on camels, 18and he drove all his livestock ahead of him, along with all the goods he had accumulated in Paddan Aram,a to go to his father Isaac in the land of Canaan.

19When Laban had gone to shear his sheep, Rachel stole her father's household gods. 20Moreover, Jacob deceived Laban the Aramean by not telling him he was running away. 21So he fled with all he had, and crossing the River,b he headed for the hill country of Gilead.

Laban Pursues Jacob

22On the third day Laban was told that Jacob had fled. 23Taking his relatives with him, he pursued Jacob for seven days and caught up with him in the hill country of Gilead. 24Then God came to Laban the Aramean in a dream at night and said to him, "Be careful not to say anything to Jacob, either good or bad."

25Jacob had pitched his tent in the hill country of Gilead when Laban overtook him, and Laban and his relatives camped there too. 26Then Laban said to Jacob, "What have you done? You've deceived me, and you've carried off my daughters like captives in war. 27Why did you run off secretly and deceive me? Why didn't you tell me, so I could send you away with joy and singing to the music of tambourines and harps? 28You didn't even let me kiss my grandchildren and my daughters goodby. You have done a foolish thing. 29I have the power to harm you; but last night the God of your father said to me, 'Be careful not to say anything to Jacob, either good or bad.' 30Now you have gone off because you longed to return to your father's house. But why did you steal my gods?"

31Jacob answered Laban, "I was afraid, because I thought you would take your daughters away from me by force. 32But if you find anyone who has your gods, he shall not live. In the presence of our relatives, see for yourself whether there is anything of yours here with me; and if so, take it." Now Jacob did not know that Rachel had stolen the gods.

33So Laban went into Jacob's tent and into Leah's tent and into the tent of the two maidservants, but he found nothing. After he came out of Leah's tent, he entered Rachel's tent. 34Now Rachel had taken the household

---

a *18* That is, Northwest Mesopotamia   b *21* That is, the Euphrates

Living Bible

10"And at the mating season, I had a dream, and saw that the he-goats mating with the flock were streaked, speckled, and mottled. 11Then, in my dream, the Angel of God called to me 12and told me that I should mate the white[c] female goats with streaked, speckled, and mottled male goats. 'For I have seen all that Laban has done to you,' the Angel said. 13'I am the God you met at Bethel,' he continued, 'the place where you anointed the pillar and made a vow to serve me. Now leave this country and return to the land of your birth.' "

14Rachel and Leah replied, "That's fine with us! There's nothing for us here—none of our father's wealth will come to us anyway! 15He has reduced our rights to those of foreign women; he sold us, and what he received for us has disappeared. 16The riches God has given you from our father were legally ours and our children's to begin with! So go ahead and do whatever God has told you to."

17-20So one day while Laban was out shearing sheep, Jacob set his wives and sons on camels, and fled without telling Laban his intentions. He drove the flocks before him—Jacob's flocks he had gotten there at Paddan-aram—and took everything he owned and started out to return to his father Isaac in the land of Canaan. 21So he fled with all of his possessions (and Rachel stole her father's household gods and took them with her) and crossed the Euphrates River and headed for the territory of Gilead.

22Laban didn't learn of their flight for three days. 23Then, taking several men with him, he set out in hot pursuit and caught up with them seven days later, at Mount Gilead. 24That night God appeared to Laban in a dream.

"Watch out what you say to Jacob," he was told. "Don't give him your blessing and don't curse him." 25Laban finally caught up with Jacob as he was camped at the top of a ridge; Laban, meanwhile, camped below him in the mountains.

26"What do you mean by sneaking off like this?" Laban demanded. "Are my daughters prisoners, captured in a battle, that you have rushed them away like this? 27Why didn't you give me a chance to have a farewell party, with singing and orchestra and harp? 28Why didn't you let me kiss my grandchildren and tell them good-bye? This is a strange way to act. 29I could crush you, but the God of your father appeared to me last night and told me, 'Be careful not to be too hard on Jacob!' 30But see here—though you feel you must go, and long so intensely for your childhood home—why have you stolen my idols?"

31"I sneaked away because I was afraid," Jacob answered. "I said to myself, 'He'll take his daughters from me by force.' 32But as for your household idols, a curse upon anyone who took them. Let him die! If you find a single thing we've stolen from you, I swear before all these men, I'll give it back without question." For Jacob didn't know that Rachel had taken them.

33Laban went first into Jacob's tent to search there, then into Leah's, and then searched the two tents of the concubines, but didn't find them. Finally he went into Rachel's tent. 34Rachel, remember, was the one who

New Revised Standard

10 During the mating of the flock I once had a dream in which I looked up and saw that the male goats that leaped upon the flock were striped, speckled, and mottled. 11 Then the angel of God said to me in the dream, 'Jacob,' and I said, 'Here I am!' 12 And he said, 'Look up and see that all the goats that leap on the flock are striped, speckled, and mottled; for I have seen all that Laban is doing to you. 13 I am the God of Bethel,[d] where you anointed a pillar and made a vow to me. Now leave this land at once and return to the land of your birth.' "

14 Then Rachel and Leah answered him, "Is there any portion or inheritance left to us in our father's house? 15 Are we not regarded by him as foreigners? For he has sold us, and he has been using up the money given for us. 16 All the property that God has taken away from our father belongs to us and to our children; now then, do whatever God has said to you."

17 So Jacob arose, and set his children and his wives on camels; 18 and he drove away all his livestock, all the property that he had gained, the livestock in his possession that he had acquired in Paddan-aram, to go to his father Isaac in the land of Canaan.

19 Now Laban had gone to shear his sheep, and Rachel stole her father's household gods. 20 And Jacob deceived Laban the Aramean, in that he did not tell him that he intended to flee. 21 So he fled with all that he had; starting out he crossed the Euphrates,[e] and set his face toward the hill country of Gilead.

Laban Overtakes Jacob

22 On the third day Laban was told that Jacob had fled. 23 So he took his kinsfolk with him and pursued him for seven days until he caught up with him in the hill country of Gilead. 24 But God came to Laban the Aramean in a dream by night, and said to him, "Take heed that you say not a word to Jacob, either good or bad."

25 Laban overtook Jacob. Now Jacob had pitched his tent in the hill country, and Laban with his kinsfolk camped in the hill country of Gilead. 26 Laban said to Jacob, "What have you done? You have deceived me, and carried away my daughters like captives of the sword. 27 Why did you flee secretly and deceive me and not tell me? I would have sent you away with mirth and songs, with tambourine and lyre. 28 And why did you not permit me to kiss my sons and my daughters farewell? What you have done is foolish. 29 It is in my power to do you harm; but the God of your father spoke to me last night, saying, 'Take heed that you speak to Jacob neither good nor bad.' 30 Even though you had to go because you longed greatly for your father's house, why did you steal my gods?" 31 Jacob answered Laban, "Because I was afraid, for I thought that you would take your daughters from me by force. 32 But anyone with whom you find your gods shall not live. In the presence of our kinsfolk, point out what I have that is yours, and take it." Now Jacob did not know that Rachel had stolen the gods.[f]

33 So Laban went into Jacob's tent, and into Leah's tent, and into the tent of the two maids, but he did not find them. And he went out of Leah's tent, and entered Rachel's. 34 Now Rachel had taken the household gods

---

[c] 31:12 *and told me that I should mate the white female goats with streaked, speckled, and mottled male goats,* implied. Literally, "notice that all the mating males are speckled, streaked, and mottled."

[d] Cn: Meaning of Heb uncertain   [e] Heb *the river*   [f] Heb *them*

King James

34Now Rachel had taken the images, and put them in the camel's furniture, and sat upon them. And Laban searched all the tent, but found *them* not.

35And she said to her father, Let it not displease my lord that I cannot rise up before thee; for the custom of women *is* upon me. And he searched, but found not the images.

36¶ And Jacob was wroth, and chode with Laban: and Jacob answered and said to Laban, What *is* my trespass? what *is* my sin, that thou hast so hotly pursued after me?

37Whereas thou hast searched all my stuff, what hast thou found of all thy household stuff? set *it* here before my brethren and thy brethren, that they may judge betwixt us both.

38This twenty years *have* I *been* with thee; thy ewes and thy she goats have not cast their young, and the rams of thy flock have I not eaten.

39That which was torn *of beasts* I brought not unto thee; I bare the loss of it; of my hand didst thou require it, *whether* stolen by day, or stolen by night.

40*Thus* I was; in the day the drought consumed me, and the frost by night; and my sleep departed from mine eyes.

41Thus have I been twenty years in thy house; I served thee fourteen years for thy two daughters, and six years for thy cattle: and thou hast changed my wages ten times.

42Except the God of my father, the God of Abraham, and the fear of Isaac, had been with me, surely thou hadst sent me away now empty. God hath seen mine affliction and the labour of my hands, and rebuked *thee* yesternight.

43¶ And Laban answered and said unto Jacob, *These* daughters *are* my daughters, and *these* children *are* my children, and *these* cattle *are* my cattle, and all that thou seest *is* mine: and what can I do this day unto these my daughters, or unto their children which they have born?

44Now therefore come thou, let us make a covenant, I and thou; and let it be for a witness between me and thee.

45And Jacob took a stone, and set it up *for* a pillar.

46And Jacob said unto his brethren, Gather stones; and they took stones, and made an heap: and they did eat there upon the heap.

47And Laban called it Jegar-sahadutha: but Jacob called it Galeed.

48And Laban said, This heap *is* a witness between me and thee this day. Therefore was the name of it called Galeed;

49And Mizpah; for he said, The LORD watch between me and thee, when we are absent one from another.

50If thou shalt afflict my daughters, or if thou shalt take *other* wives beside my daughters, no man *is* with us; see, God *is* witness betwixt me and thee.

51And Laban said to Jacob, Behold this heap, and behold *this* pillar, which I have cast betwixt me and thee;

52This heap *be* witness, and *this* pillar *be* witness, that I will not pass over this heap to thee, and that thou shalt not pass over this heap and this pillar unto me, for harm.

53The God of Abraham, and the God of Nahor, the God of their father, judge betwixt us. And Jacob sware by the fear of his father Isaac.

54Then Jacob offered sacrifice upon the mount, and called his brethren to eat bread: and they did eat bread, and tarried all night in the mount.

55And early in the morning Laban rose up, and kissed his sons and his daughters, and blessed them: and Laban departed, and returned unto his place.

New International

gods and put them inside her camel's saddle and was sitting on them. Laban searched through everything in the tent but found nothing.

35Rachel said to her father, "Don't be angry, my lord, that I cannot stand up in your presence; I'm having my period." So he searched but could not find the household gods.

36Jacob was angry and took Laban to task. "What is my crime?" he asked Laban. "What sin have I committed that you hunt me down? 37Now that you have searched through all my goods, what have you found that belongs to your household? Put it here in front of your relatives and mine, and let them judge between the two of us.

38"I have been with you for twenty years now. Your sheep and goats have not miscarried, nor have I eaten rams from your flocks. 39I did not bring you animals torn by wild beasts; I bore the loss myself. And you demanded payment from me for whatever was stolen by day or night. 40This was my situation: The heat consumed me in the daytime and the cold at night, and sleep fled from my eyes. 41It was like this for the twenty years I was in your household. I worked for you fourteen years for your two daughters and six years for your flocks, and you changed my wages ten times. 42If the God of my father, the God of Abraham and the Fear of Isaac, had not been with me, you would surely have sent me away empty-handed. But God has seen my hardship and the toil of my hands, and last night he rebuked you."

43Laban answered Jacob, "The women are my daughters, the children are my children, and the flocks are my flocks. All you see is mine. Yet what can I do today about these daughters of mine, or about the children they have borne? 44Come now, let's make a covenant, you and I, and let it serve as a witness between us."

45So Jacob took a stone and set it up as a pillar. 46He said to his relatives, "Gather some stones." So they took stones and piled them in a heap, and they ate there by the heap. 47Laban called it Jegar Sahadutha,a and Jacob called it Galeed.b

48Laban said, "This heap is a witness between you and me today." That is why it was called Galeed. 49It was also called Mizpah,c because he said, "May the LORD keep watch between you and me when we are away from each other. 50If you mistreat my daughters or if you take any wives besides my daughters, even though no one is with us, remember that God is a witness between you and me."

51Laban also said to Jacob, "Here is this heap, and here is this pillar I have set up between you and me. 52This heap is a witness, and this pillar is a witness, that I will not go past this heap to your side to harm you and that you will not go past this heap and pillar to my side to harm me. 53May the God of Abraham and the God of Nahor, the God of their father, judge between us."

So Jacob took an oath in the name of the Fear of his father Isaac. 54He offered a sacrifice there in the hill country and invited his relatives to a meal. After they had eaten, they spent the night there.

55Early the next morning Laban kissed his grandchildren and his daughters and blessed them. Then he left and returned home.

a 47 The Aramaic *Jegar Sahadutha* means *witness heap.*   b 47 The Hebrew *Galeed* means *witness heap.*   c 49 Mizpah means *watchtower.*

Living Bible

had stolen the idols; she had stuffed them into her camel saddle and now was sitting on them! So although Laban searched the tents thoroughly, he didn't find them.

35"Forgive my not getting up, father," Rachel explained, "but I'm having my monthly period."d So Laban didn't find them.

36, 37Now Jacob got mad. "What did you find?" he demanded of Laban. "What is my crime? You have come rushing after me as though you were chasing a criminal and have searched through everything. Now put everything I stole out here in front of us, before your men and mine, for all to see and to decide whose it is! 38Twenty years I've been with you, and all that time I cared for your ewes and goats so that they produced healthy offspring, and I never touched one ram of yours for food. 39If any were attacked and killed by wild animals, did I show them to you and ask you to reduce the count of your flock? No, I took the loss. You made me pay for every animal stolen from the flocks, whether I could help it or not.e 40I worked for you through the scorching heat of the day, and through the cold and sleepless nights. 41Yes, twenty years—fourteen of them earning your two daughters, and six years to get the flock! And you have reduced my wages ten times! 42In fact, except for the grace of God—the God of my grandfather Abraham, even the glorious God of Isaac, my father—you would have sent me off without a penny to my name. But God has seen your cruelty and my hard work, and that is why he appeared to you last night."

43Laban replied, "These women are my daughters, and these children are mine, and these flocks and all that you have—all are mine. So how could I harm my own daughters and grandchildren? 44Come now and we will sign a peace pact, you and I, and will live by its terms."

45So Jacob took a stone and set it up as a monument, 46and told his men to gather stones and make a heap, and Jacob and Laban ate together beside the pile of rocks. 47, 48They named it "The Witness Pile"—"Jegar-sahadutha," in Laban's language, and "Galeed" in Jacob's.

"This pile of stones will stand as a witness against us [if either of us trespasses across this linef]," Laban said. 49So it was also called "The Watchtower" (Mizpah). For Laban said, "May the Lord see to it that we keep this bargain when we are out of each other's sight. 50And if you are harsh to my daughters, or take other wives, I won't know, but God will see it. 51, 52This heap," Laban continued, "stands between us as a witness of our vows that I will not cross this line to attack you and you will not cross it to attack me. 53I call upon the God of Abraham and Nahor, and of their father, to destroy either one of us who does."

So Jacob took oath before the mighty God of his father Isaac, to respect the boundary line. 54Then Jacob presented a sacrifice to God there at the top of the mountain, and invited his companions to a feast, and afterwards spent the night with them on the mountain. 55Laban was up early the next morning and kissed his daughters and grandchildren, and blessed them, and returned home.

New Revised Standard

and put them in the camel's saddle, and sat on them. Laban felt all about in the tent, but did not find them. 35And she said to her father, "Let not my lord be angry that I cannot rise before you, for the way of women is upon me." So he searched, but did not find the household gods.

36 Then Jacob became angry, and upbraided Laban. Jacob said to Laban, "What is my offense? What is my sin, that you have hotly pursued me? 37Although you have felt about through all my goods, what have you found of all your household goods? Set it here before my kinsfolk and your kinsfolk, so that they may decide between us two. 38These twenty years I have been with you; your ewes and your female goats have not miscarried, and I have not eaten the rams of your flocks. 39That which was torn by wild beasts I did not bring to you; I bore the loss of it myself; of my hand you required it, whether stolen by day or stolen by night. 40It was like this with me: by day the heat consumed me, and the cold by night, and my sleep fled from my eyes. 41These twenty years I have been in your house; I served you fourteen years for your two daughters, and six years for your flock, and you have changed my wages ten times. 42If the God of my father, the God of Abraham and the Fear of Isaac, had not been on my side, surely now you would have sent me away empty-handed. God saw my affliction and the labor of my hands, and rebuked you last night."

Laban and Jacob Make a Covenant

43 Then Laban answered and said to Jacob, "The daughters are my daughters, the children are my children, the flocks are my flocks, and all that you see is mine. But what can I do today about these daughters of mine, or about their children whom they have borne? 44Come now, let us make a covenant, you and I; and let it be a witness between you and me." 45So Jacob took a stone, and set it up as a pillar. 46And Jacob said to his kinsfolk, "Gather stones," and they took stones, and made a heap; and they ate there by the heap. 47Laban called it Jegar-sahadutha:h but Jacob called it Galeed.i 48Laban said, "This heap is a witness between you and me today." Therefore he called it Galeed, 49and the pillarj Mizpah,k for he said, "The LORD watch between you and me, when we are absent one from the other. 50If you ill-treat my daughters, or if you take wives in addition to my daughters, though no one else is with us, remember that God is witness between you and me."

51 Then Laban said to Jacob, "See this heap and see the pillar, which I have set between you and me. 52This heap is a witness, and the pillar is a witness, that I will not pass beyond this heap to you, and you will not pass beyond this heap and this pillar to me, for harm. 53May the God of Abraham and the God of Nahor"—the God of their father—"judge between us." So Jacob swore by the Fear of his father Isaac, 54and Jacob offered a sacrifice on the height and called his kinsfolk to eat bread; and they ate bread and tarried all night in the hill country.

55l Early in the morning Laban rose up, and kissed his grandchildren and his daughters and blessed them; then he departed and returned home.

---

d 31:35 *but I'm having my monthly period,* implied. Literally, "The manner of women is upon me." She was pregnant with Benjamin, but was falsely claiming her menstrual period, which, under the later Mosaic law, caused ceremonial defilement of all that she sat upon. See Lev 15.   e *31:39 whether I could help it or not,* literally, "stolen by day or by night."   f *31:47, 48 if either of us trespasses across this line,* implied.

g Meaning of Heb uncertain   h In Aramaic *The heap of witn.*   *The heap of witness*   j Compare Sam: MT lacks *the pi.*   *Watchpost*   l Ch 32.1 in Heb

King James

32 AND JACOB went on his way, and the angels of God met him.

2And when Jacob saw them, he said, This *is* God's host: and he called the name of that place Mahanaim.

3And Jacob sent messengers before him to Esau his brother unto the land of Seir, the country of Edom.

4And he commanded them, saying, Thus shall ye speak unto my lord Esau; Thy servant Jacob saith thus, I have sojourned with Laban, and stayed there until now:

5And I have oxen, and asses, flocks, and menservants, and womenservants: and I have sent to tell my lord, that I may find grace in thy sight.

6¶ And the messengers returned to Jacob, saying, We came to thy brother Esau, and also he cometh to meet thee, and four hundred men with him.

7Then Jacob was greatly afraid and distressed: and he divided the people that *was* with him, and the flocks, and herds, and the camels, into two bands;

8And said, If Esau come to the one company, and smite it, then the other company which is left shall escape.

9¶ And Jacob said, O God of my father Abraham, and God of my father Isaac, the LORD which saidst unto me, Return unto thy country, and to thy kindred, and I will deal well with thee:

10I am not worthy of the least of all the mercies, and of all the truth, which thou hast shown unto thy servant; for with my staff I passed over this Jordan; and now I am become two bands.

11Deliver me, I pray thee, from the hand of my brother, from the hand of Esau: for I fear him, lest he will come and smite me, *and* the mother with the children.

12And thou saidst, I will surely do thee good, and make thy seed as the sand of the sea, which cannot be numbered for multitude.

13¶ And he lodged there that same night; and took of that which came to his hand a present for Esau his brother;

14Two hundred she goats, and twenty he goats, two hundred ewes, and twenty rams,

15Thirty milch camels with their colts, forty kine, and ten bulls, twenty she asses, and ten foals.

16And he delivered *them* into the hand of his servants, every drove by themselves; and said unto his servants, Pass over before me, and put a space betwixt drove and drove.

17And he commanded the foremost, saying, When Esau my brother meeteth thee, and asketh thee, saying, Whose *art* thou? and whither goest thou? and whose *are* these before thee?

18Then thou shalt say, *They be* thy servant Jacob's; it *is* a present sent unto my lord Esau: and, behold, also he *is* behind us.

19And so commanded he the second, and the third, and all that followed the droves, saying, On this manner shall ye speak unto Esau, when ye find him.

20And say ye moreover, Behold, thy servant Jacob *is* behind us. For he said, I will appease him with the present that goeth before me, and afterward I will see his face; peradventure he will accept of me.

21So went the present over before him: and himself lodged that night in the company.

22And he rose up that night, and took his two wives, and his two womenservants, and his eleven sons, and passed over the ford Jabbok.

23And he took them, and sent them over the brook, and sent over that he had.

24¶ And Jacob was left alone; and there wrestled a man with him until the breaking of the day.

25And when he saw that he prevailed not against him, he touched the hollow of his thigh; and the hollow of Iacob's thigh was out of joint, as he wrestled with him.

New International

Jacob Prepares to Meet Esau

32 JACOB ALSO went on his way, and the angels of God met him. 2When Jacob saw them, he said, "This is the camp of God!" So he named that place Mahanaim.[a]

3Jacob sent messengers ahead of him to his brothe Esau in the land of Seir, the country of Edom. 4He instructed them: "This is what you are to say to my master Esau: 'Your servant Jacob says, I have been staying with Laban and have remained there till now. 5I have cattle and donkeys, sheep and goats, menservants and maidservants. Now I am sending this message to my lord, that I may find favor in your eyes.' "

6When the messengers returned to Jacob, they said, "We went to your brother Esau, and now he is coming to meet you, and four hundred men are with him."

7In great fear and distress Jacob divided the people who were with him into two groups,[b] and the flocks and herds and camels as well. 8He thought, "If Esau comes and attacks one group,[c] the group[c] that is left may escape."

9Then Jacob prayed, "O God of my father Abraham, God of my father Isaac, O LORD, who said to me, 'Go back to your country and your relatives, and I will make you prosper,' 10I am unworthy of all the kindness and faithfulness you have shown your servant. I had only my staff when I crossed this Jordan, but now I have become two groups. 11Save me, I pray, from the hand of my brother Esau, for I am afraid he will come and attack me, and also the mothers with their children. 12But you have said, 'I will surely make you prosper and will make your descendants like the sand of the sea, which cannot be counted.' "

13He spent the night there, and from what he had with him he selected a gift for his brother Esau: 14two hundred female goats and twenty male goats, two hundred ewes and twenty rams, 15thirty female camels with their young, forty cows and ten bulls, and twenty female donkeys and ten male donkeys. 16He put them in the care of his servants, each herd by itself, and said to his servants, "Go ahead of me, and keep some space between the herds."

17He instructed the one in the lead: "When my brother Esau meets you and asks, 'To whom do you belong, and where are you going, and who owns all these animals in front of you?' 18then you are to say, 'They belong to your servant Jacob. They are a gift sent to my lord Esau, and he is coming behind us.' "

19He also instructed the second, the third and all the others who followed the herds: "You are to say the same thing to Esau when you meet him. 20And be sure to say, 'Your servant Jacob is coming behind us.' " For he thought, "I will pacify him with these gifts I am sending on ahead; later, when I see him, perhaps he will receive me." 21So Jacob's gifts went on ahead of him, but he himself spent the night in the camp.

Jacob Wrestles With God

22That night Jacob got up and took his two wives, his two maidservants and his eleven sons and crossed the ford of the Jabbok. 23After he had sent them across the stream, he sent over all his possessions. 24So Jacob was left alone, and a man wrestled with him till daybreak. 25When the man saw that he could not overpower him, he touched the socket of Jacob's hip so that his hip was wrenched as he wrestled with the man. 26Then the man said, "Let me go, for it is daybreak."

---

[a] 2 *Mahanaim* means *two camps*.   [b] 7 Or *camps*; also in verse 10   [c] 8 Or *camp*

Living Bible

32 SO JACOB and his household started on again. And the angels of God came to meet him. When he saw them he exclaimed, "God lives here!" So he named the place "God's territory!"d

3Jacob now sent messengers to his brother Esau in Edom, in the land of Seir, 4with this message: "Hello from Jacob! I have been living with Uncle Laban until recently, 5and now I own oxen, donkeys, sheep, goats, and many servants, both men and women. I have sent these messengers to inform you of my coming, hoping that you will be friendly to us."

6The messengers returned with the news that Esau was on the way to meet Jacob—with an army of 400 men! 7Jacob was frantic with fear. He divided his household, along with the flocks and herds and camels, into two groups, 8for he said, "If Esau attacks one group, perhaps the other can escape."

9Then Jacob prayed, "O God of Abraham my grandfather, and of my father Isaac—O Jehovah who told me to return to the land of my relatives, and said that you would do me good— 10I am not worthy of the least of all your lovingkindnesses shown me again and again just as you promised me. For when I left homee I owned nothing except a walking stick! And now I am two armies! 11O Lord, please deliver me from destruction at the hand of my brother Esau, for I am frightened—terribly afraid that he is coming to kill me and these mothers and my children. 12But you promised to do me good, and to multiply my descendants until they become as the sands along the shores—too many to count."

13, 14, 15Jacob stayed where he was for the night, and prepared a present for his brother Esau:
    200 female goats,
    20 male goats,
    200 ewes,
    20 rams,
    30 milk camels, with their colts,
    40 cows,
    10 bulls,
    20 female donkeys,
    10 male donkeys.

16He instructed his servants to drive them on ahead, each group of animals by itself, separated by a distance between. 17He told the men driving the first group that when they met Esau and he asked, "Where are you going? Whose servants are you? Whose animals are these?"— 18they should reply: "These belong to your servant Jacob. They are a present for his master Esau! He is coming right behind us!"

19Jacob gave the same instructions to each driver, with the same message. 20Jacob's strategy was to appease Esau with the presents before meeting him face to face! "Perhaps," Jacob hoped, "he will be friendly to us." 21So the presents were sent on ahead, and Jacob spent that night in the camp.

22, 23, 24But during the night he got up and wakenedf his two wives and his two concubines and eleven sons, and sent them across the Jordan River at the Jabbok ford with all his possessions, then returned again to the camp and was there alone; and a Man wrestled with him until dawn. 25And when the Man saw that he couldn't win the match, he struck Jacob's hip, and knocked it out of joint at the socket.

New Revised Standard

32 JACOB WENT on his way and the angels of God met him; 2and when Jacob saw them he said, "This is God's camp!" So he called that place Mahanaim.g

Jacob Sends Presents to Appease Esau

3 Jacob sent messengers before him to his brother Esau in the land of Seir, the country of Edom, 4instructing them, "Thus you shall say to my lord Esau: Thus says your servant Jacob, 'I have lived with Laban as an alien, and stayed until now; 5and I have oxen, donkeys, flocks, male and female slaves; and I have sent to tell my lord, in order that I may find favor in your sight.'"

6 The messengers returned to Jacob, saying, "We came to your brother Esau, and he is coming to meet you, and four hundred men are with him." 7Then Jacob was greatly afraid and distressed; and he divided the people that were with him, and the flocks and herds and camels, into two companies, 8thinking, "If Esau comes to the one company and destroys it, then the company that is left will escape."

9 And Jacob said, "O God of my father Abraham and God of my father Isaac, O LORD who said to me, 'Return to your country and to your kindred, and I will do you good,' 10I am not worthy of the least of all the steadfast love and all the faithfulness that you have shown to your servant, for with only my staff I crossed this Jordan; and now I have become two companies. 11Deliver me, please, from the hand of my brother, from the hand of Esau, for I am afraid of him; he may come and kill us all, the mothers with the children. 12Yet you have said, 'I will surely do you good, and make your offspring as the sand of the sea, which cannot be counted because of their number.'"

13 So he spent that night there, and from what he had with him he took a present for his brother Esau, 14two hundred female goats and twenty male goats, two hundred ewes and twenty rams, 15thirty milch camels and their colts, forty cows and ten bulls, twenty female donkeys and ten male donkeys. 16These he delivered into the hand of his servants, every drove by itself, and said to his servants, "Pass on ahead of me, and put a space between drove and drove." 17He instructed the foremost, "When Esau my brother meets you, and asks you, 'To whom do you belong? Where are you going? And whose are these ahead of you?' 18then you shall say, 'They belong to your servant Jacob; they are a present sent to my lord Esau; and moreover he is behind us.'" 19He likewise instructed the second and the third and all who followed the droves, "You shall say the same thing to Esau when you meet him, 20and you shall say, 'Moreover your servant Jacob is behind us.'" For he thought, "I may appease him with the present that goes ahead of me, and afterwards I shall see his face; perhaps he will accept me." 21So the present passed on ahead of him; and he himself spent that night in the camp.

Jacob Wrestles at Peniel

22 The same night he got up and took his two wives, his two maids, and his eleven children, and crossed the ford of the Jabbok. 23He took them and sent them across the stream, and likewise everything that he had. 24Jacob was left alone; and a man wrestled with him until daybreak. 25When the man saw that he did not prevail against Jacob, he struck him on the hip socket; and Jacob's hip was put out of joint as he wrestled with him.

---

d 32:1, 2 So Jacob and his household, implied. God's territory, literally, "Two encampments."   e 32:10 left home, literally, "passed over this Jordan."
f 32:22, 23, 24 and wakened, implied.

g Here taken to mean Two camps

King James

26And he said, Let me go, for the day breaketh. And he said, I will not let thee go, except thou bless me.

27And he said unto him, What *is* thy name? And he said, Jacob.

28And he said, Thy name shall be called no more Jacob, but Israel: for as a prince hast thou power with God and with men, and hast prevailed.

29And Jacob asked *him,* and said, Tell *me,* I pray thee, thy name. And he said, Wherefore *is* it *that* thou dost ask after my name? And he blessed him there.

30And Jacob called the name of the place Peniel: for I have seen God face to face, and my life is preserved.

31And as he passed over Penuel the sun rose upon him, and he halted upon his thigh.

32Therefore the children of Israel eat not *of* the sinew which shrank, which *is* upon the hollow of the thigh, unto this day: because he touched the hollow of Jacob's thigh in the sinew that shrank.

33 AND JACOB lifted up his eyes, and looked, and, behold, Esau came, and with him four hundred men. And he divided the children unto Leah, and unto Rachel, and unto the two handmaids.

2And he put the handmaids and their children foremost, and Leah and her children after, and Rachel and Joseph hindermost.

3And he passed over before them, and bowed himself to the ground seven times, until he came near to his brother.

4And Esau ran to meet him, and embraced him, and fell on his neck, and kissed him: and they wept.

5And he lifted up his eyes, and saw the women and the children; and said, Who *are* those with thee? And he said, The children which God hath graciously given thy servant.

6Then the handmaidens came near, they and their children, and they bowed themselves.

7And Leah also with her children came near, and bowed themselves: and after came Joseph near and Rachel, and they bowed themselves.

8And he said, What *meanest* thou by all this drove which I met? And he said, *These are* to find grace in the sight of my lord.

9And Esau said, I have enough, my brother; keep that thou hast unto thyself.

10And Jacob said, Nay, I pray thee, if now I have found grace in thy sight, then receive my present at my hand: for therefore I have seen thy face, as though I had seen the face of God, and thou wast pleased with me.

11Take, I pray thee, my blessing that is brought to thee; because God hath dealt graciously with me, and because I have enough. And he urged him, and he took *it.*

12And he said, Let us take our journey, and let us go, and I will go before thee.

13And he said unto him, My lord knoweth that the children *are* tender, and the flocks and herds with young *are* with me: and if men should overdrive them one day, all the flock will die.

14Let my lord, I pray thee, pass over before his servant: and I will lead on softly, according as the cattle that goeth before me and the children be able to endure, until I come unto my lord unto Seir.

15And Esau said, Let me now leave with thee *some* of the folk that *are* with me. And he said, What needeth it? let me find grace in the sight of my lord.

16¶ So Esau returned that day on his way unto Seir.

17And Jacob journeyed to Succoth, and built him an house, and made booths for his cattle: therefore the name of the place is called Succoth.

New International

But Jacob replied, "I will not let you go unless you bless me."

27The man asked him, "What is your name?"

"Jacob," he answered.

28Then the man said, "Your name will no longer be Jacob, but Israel,[a] because you have struggled with God and with men and have overcome."

29Jacob said, "Please tell me your name."

But he replied, "Why do you ask my name?" Then he blessed him there.

30So Jacob called the place Peniel,[b] saying, "It is because I saw God face to face, and yet my life was spared."

31The sun rose above him as he passed Peniel,[c] and he was limping because of his hip. 32Therefore to this day the Israelites do not eat the tendon attached to the socket of the hip, because the socket of Jacob's hip was touched near the tendon.

Jacob Meets Esau

33 JACOB LOOKED up and there was Esau, coming with his four hundred men; so he divided the children among Leah, Rachel and the two maidservants. 2He put the maidservants and their children in front, Leah and her children next, and Rachel and Joseph in the rear. 3He himself went on ahead and bowed down to the ground seven times as he approached his brother.

4But Esau ran to meet Jacob and embraced him; he threw his arms around his neck and kissed him. And they wept. 5Then Esau looked up and saw the women and children. "Who are these with you?" he asked.

Jacob answered, "They are the children God has graciously given your servant."

6Then the maidservants and their children approached and bowed down. 7Next, Leah and her children came and bowed down. Last of all came Joseph and Rachel, and they too bowed down.

8Esau asked, "What do you mean by all these droves I met?"

"To find favor in your eyes, my lord," he said.

9But Esau said, "I already have plenty, my brother. Keep what you have for yourself."

10"No, please!" said Jacob. "If I have found favor in your eyes, accept this gift from me. For to see your face is like seeing the face of God, now that you have received me favorably. 11Please accept the present that was brought to you, for God has been gracious to me and I have all I need." And because Jacob insisted, Esau accepted it.

12Then Esau said, "Let us be on our way; I'll accompany you."

13But Jacob said to him, "My lord knows that the children are tender and that I must care for the ewes and cows that are nursing their young. If they are driven hard just one day, all the animals will die. 14So let my lord go on ahead of his servant, while I move along slowly at the pace of the droves before me and that of the children, until I come to my lord in Seir."

15Esau said, "Then let me leave some of my men with you."

"But why do that?" Jacob asked. "Just let me find favor in the eyes of my lord."

16So that day Esau started on his way back to Seir. 17Jacob, however, went to Succoth, where he built a place for himself and made shelters for his livestock. That is why the place is called Succoth.[d]

---

[a] 28 Israel means he struggles with God.   [b] 30 Peniel means face of God.
[c] 31 Hebrew Penuel, a variant of Peniel   [d] 17 Succoth means shelters.

Living Bible

26Then the Man said, "Let me go, for it is dawn." But Jacob panted, "I will not let you go until you bless me."

27"What is your name?" the Man asked.

"Jacob," was the reply.

28"It isn't anymore!" the Man told him. "It is Israel— one who has power with God. Because you have been strong with God, you shall prevail with men."

29"What is your name?" Jacob asked him.

"No, you mustn't ask," the Man told him. And he blessed him there.

30Jacob named the place "Peniel" ("The Face of God"), for he said, "I have seen God face to face, and yet my life is spared." 31The sun rose as he started on, and he was limping because of his hip. 32(That is why even today the people of Israel don't eat meat from near the hip, in memory of what happened that night.)

33 THEN, FAR in the distance, Jacob saw Esau coming with his 400 men. 2Jacob now arranged his family into a column, with his two concubines and their children at the head, Leah and her children next, and Rachel and Joseph last. 3Then Jacob went on ahead. As he approached his brother he bowed low seven times before him. 4And then Esau ran to meet him and embraced him affectionately and kissed him; and both of them were in tears!

5Then Esau looked at the women and children and asked, "Who are these people with you?"

"My children," Jacob replied. 6Then the concubines came forward with their children, and bowed low before him. 7Next came Leah with her children, and bowed, and finally Rachel and Joseph came and made their bows.

8"And what were all the flocks and herds I met as I came?" Esau asked.

And Jacob replied, "They are my gifts, to curry your favor!"

9"Brother, I have plenty," Esau laughed. "Keep what you have."

10"No, but please accept them," Jacob said, "for what a relief it is to see your friendly smile! I was as frightened of you as though approaching God!e 11Please take my gifts. For God has been very generous to me and I have enough." So Jacob insisted, and finally Esau accepted them.

12"Well, let's be going," Esau said. "My men and I will stay with you and lead the way."

13But Jacob replied, "As you can see,f some of the children are small, and the flocks and herds have their young, and if they are driven too hard, they will die. 14So you go on ahead of us and we'll follow at our own pace and meet you at Seir."

15"Well," Esau said, "at least let me leave you some of my men to assist you and be your guides."

"No," Jacob insisted, "we'll get along just fine. Please do as I suggest."

16So Esau started back to Seir that same day. 17Meanwhile Jacob and his household went as far as Succoth. There he built himself a camp, with pens for his flocks and herds. (That is why the place is called Succoth, meaning "huts.") 18Then they arrived safely at She-

New Revised Standard

26Then he said, "Let me go, for the day is breaking." But Jacob said, "I will not let you go, unless you bless me." 27So he said to him, "What is your name?" And he said, "Jacob." 28Then the mang said, "You shall no longer be called Jacob, but Israel,h for you have striven with God and with humans,i and have prevailed." 29Then Jacob asked him, "Please tell me your name." But he said, "Why is it that you ask my name?" And there he blessed him. 30So Jacob called the place Peniel,j saying, "For I have seen God face to face, and yet my life is preserved." 31The sun rose upon him as he passed Penuel, limping because of his hip. 32Therefore to this day the Israelites do not eat the thigh muscle that is on the hip socket, because he struck Jacob on the hip socket at the thigh muscle.

Jacob and Esau Meet

33 NOW JACOB looked up and saw Esau coming, and four hundred men with him. So he divided the children among Leah and Rachel and the two maids. 2He put the maids with their children in front, then Leah with her children, and Rachel and Joseph last of all. 3He himself went on ahead of them, bowing himself to the ground seven times, until he came near his brother.

4 But Esau ran to meet him, and embraced him, and fell on his neck and kissed him, and they wept. 5When Esau looked up and saw the women and children, he said, "Who are these with you?" Jacob said, "The children whom God has graciously given your servant." 6Then the maids drew near, they and their children, and bowed down; 7Leah likewise and her children drew near and bowed down; and finally Joseph and Rachel drew near, and they bowed down. 8Esau said, "What do you mean by all this company that I met?" Jacob answered, "To find favor with my lord." 9But Esau said, "I have enough, my brother; keep what you have for yourself." 10Jacob said, "No, please; if I find favor with you, then accept my present from my hand; for truly to see your face is like seeing the face of God—since you have received me with such favor. 11Please accept my gift that is brought to you, because God has dealt graciously with me, and because I have everything I want." So he urged him, and he took it.

12 Then Esau said, "Let us journey on our way, and I will go alongside you." 13But Jacob said to him, "My lord knows that the children are frail and that the flocks and herds, which are nursing, are a care to me; and if they are overdriven for one day, all the flocks will die. 14Let my lord pass on ahead of his servant, and I will lead on slowly, according to the pace of the cattle that are before me and according to the pace of the children, until I come to my lord in Seir."

15 So Esau said, "Let me leave with you some of the people who are with me." But he said, "Why should my lord be so kind to me?" 16So Esau returned that day on his way to Seir. 17But Jacob journeyed to Succoth,k and built himself a house, and made booths for his cattle; therefore the place is called Succoth.

---

e 33:10 I was as frightened of you as though approaching God, literally, "forasmuch as I have seen your face as one sees the face of God."   f 33:13 as you can see, implied.

g Heb he   h That is The one who strives with God or God st. with divine and human beings   j That is The face of God   k That .

King James

18¶ And Jacob came to Shalem, a city of Shechem, which *is* in the land of Canaan, when he came from Padan-aram; and pitched his tent before the city.

19And he bought a parcel of a field, where he had spread his tent, at the hand of the children of Hamor, Shechem's father, for an hundred pieces of money.

20And he erected there an altar, and called it El-elohe-Israel.

34 AND DINAH the daughter of Leah, which she bare unto Jacob, went out to see the daughters of the land.

2And when Shechem the son of Hamor the Hivite, prince of the country, saw her, he took her, and lay with her, and defiled her.

3And his soul clave unto Dinah the daughter of Jacob, and he loved the damsel, and spake kindly unto the damsel.

4And Shechem spake unto his father Hamor, saying, Get me this damsel to wife.

5And Jacob heard that he had defiled Dinah his daughter: now his sons were with his cattle in the field: and Jacob held his peace until they were come.

6¶ And Hamor the father of Shechem went out unto Jacob to commune with him.

7And the sons of Jacob came out of the field when they heard *it:* and the men were grieved, and they were very wroth, because he had wrought folly in Israel in lying with Jacob's daughter; which thing ought not to be done.

8And Hamor communed with them, saying, The soul of my son Shechem longeth for your daughter: I pray you give her him to wife.

9And make ye marriages with us, *and* give your daughters unto us, and take our daughters unto you.

10And ye shall dwell with us: and the land shall be before you; dwell and trade ye therein, and get you possessions therein.

11And Shechem said unto her father and unto her brethren, Let me find grace in your eyes, and what ye shall say unto me I will give.

12Ask me never so much dowry and gift, and I will give according as ye shall say unto me: but give me the damsel to wife.

13And the sons of Jacob answered Shechem and Hamor his father deceitfully, and said, because he had defiled Dinah their sister:

14And they said unto them, We cannot do this thing, to give our sister to one that is uncircumcised; for that *were* a reproach unto us:

15But in this will we consent unto you: If ye will be as we *be*, that every male of you be circumcised;

16Then will we give our daughters unto you, and we will take your daughters to us, and we will dwell with you, and we will become one people.

17But if ye will not hearken unto us, to be circumcised; then will we take our daughter, and we will be gone.

18And their words pleased Hamor, and Shechem Hamor's son.

19And the young man deferred not to do the thing, because he had delight in Jacob's daughter: and he *was* more honourable than all the house of his father.

20¶ And Hamor and Shechem his son came unto the gate of their city, and communed with the men of their city, saying,

21These men *are* peaceable with us; therefore let them dwell in the land, and trade therein; for the land, behold, *it is* large enough for them; let us take their daughters to us for wives, and let us give them our daughters.

New International

18After Jacob came from Paddan Aram,[a] he arrived safely at the[b] city of Shechem in Canaan and camped within sight of the city. 19For a hundred pieces of silver,[c] he bought from the sons of Hamor, the father of Shechem, the plot of ground where he pitched his tent. 20There he set up an altar and called it El Elohe Israel.[d]

Dinah and the Shechemites

34 NOW DINAH, the daughter Leah had borne to Jacob, went out to visit the women of the land. 2When Shechem son of Hamor the Hivite, the ruler of that area, saw her, he took her and violated her. 3His heart was drawn to Dinah daughter of Jacob, and he loved the girl and spoke tenderly to her. 4And Shechem said to his father Hamor, "Get me this girl as my wife."

5When Jacob heard that his daughter Dinah had been defiled, his sons were in the fields with his livestock; so he kept quiet about it until they came home.

6Then Shechem's father Hamor went out to talk with Jacob. 7Now Jacob's sons had come in from the fields as soon as they heard what had happened. They were filled with grief and fury, because Shechem had done a disgraceful thing in[e] Israel by lying with Jacob's daughter—a thing that should not be done.

8But Hamor said to them, "My son Shechem has his heart set on your daughter. Please give her to him as his wife. 9Intermarry with us; give us your daughters and take our daughters for yourselves. 10You can settle among us; the land is open to you. Live in it, trade[f] in it, and acquire property in it."

11Then Shechem said to Dinah's father and brothers, "Let me find favor in your eyes, and I will give you whatever you ask. 12Make the price for the bride and the gift I am to bring as great as you like, and I'll pay whatever you ask me. Only give me the girl as my wife."

13Because their sister Dinah had been defiled, Jacob's sons replied deceitfully as they spoke to Shechem and his father Hamor. 14They said to them, "We can't do such a thing; we can't give our sister to a man who is not circumcised. That would be a disgrace to us. 15We will give our consent to you on one condition only: that you become like us by circumcising all your males. 16Then we will give you our daughters and take your daughters for ourselves. We'll settle among you and become one people with you. 17But if you will not agree to be circumcised, we'll take our sister and go."

18Their proposal seemed good to Hamor and his son Shechem. 19The young man, who was the most honored of all his father's household, lost no time in doing what they said, because he was delighted with Jacob's daughter. 20So Hamor and his son Shechem went to the gate of their city to speak to their fellow townsmen. 21"These men are friendly toward us," they said. "Let them live in our land and trade in it; the land has plenty of room for them. We can marry their daughters and they can marry ours. 22But the men will consent to live with us

a *18* That is, Northwest Mesopotamia   b *18* Or *arrived at Shalem, a*
c *19* Hebrew *hundred kesitahs*; a kesitah was a unit of money of unknown weight and value.   d *20* El Elohe Israel can mean *God, the God of Israel* or *mighty is the God of Israel.*   e *7* Or *against*   f *10* Or *move about freely*; also in verse 21   g *17* Hebrew *daughter*

Living Bible

chem, in Canaan, and camped outside the city. 19(He
bought the land he camped on from the family of Hamor,
Shechem's father, for 100 pieces of silver. 20And there
he erected an altar and called it "El-Elohe-Israel," "The
Altar to the God of Israel.")

34 ONE DAY Dinah, Leah's daughter, went out to
visit some of the neighborhood girls, 2but when
Shechem, son of King Hamor the Hivite, saw her, he
took her and raped her. 3He fell deeply in love with her,
and tried to win her affection.

4Then he spoke to his father about it. "Get this girl
for me," he demanded. "I want to marry her."

5Word soon reached Jacob of what had happened, but
his sons were out in the fields herding cattle, so he did
nothing until their return. 6, 7Meanwhile King Hamor,
Shechem's father, went to talk with Jacob, arriving just
as Jacob's sons came in from the fields, too shocked and
angry to overlook the insult, for it was an outrage against
all of them.

8Hamor told Jacob, "My son Shechem is truly in love
with your daughter, and longs for her to be his wife.
Please let him marry her. 9, 10Moreover, we invite you
folks to live here among us and to let your daughters
marry our sons, and we will give our daughters as wives
for your young men. And you shall live among us
wherever you wish and carry on your business among
us and become rich!"

11Then Shechem addressed Dinah's father and brothers. "Please be kind to me and let me have her as my
wife," he begged. "I will give whatever you require.
12No matter what dowry or gift you demand, I will pay
it—only give me the girl as my wife."

13Her brothers then lied to Shechem and Hamor, acting dishonorably because of what Shechem had done to
their sister. 14They said, "We couldn't possibly. For you
are not circumcised. It would be a disgrace for her to
marry such a man. 15I'll tell you what we'll do—if every
man of you will be circumcised, 16then we will intermarry with you and live here and unite with you to become
one people. 17Otherwise we will take her and be on our
way."

18, 19Hamor and Shechem gladly agreed, and lost no
time in acting upon this request, for Shechem was very
much in love with Dinah, and could, he felt sure, sell
the idea to the other men of the city—for he was highly
respected and very popular. 20So Hamor and Shechem
appeared before the city councilh and presented their
request.

21"Those men are our friends," they said. "Let's invite them to live here among us and ply their trade. For
the land is large enough to hold them, and we can intermarry with them. 22But they will only consider staying

New Revised Standard

Jacob Reaches Shechem

18 Jacob came safely to the city of Shechem, which
is in the land of Canaan, on his way from Paddan-aram;
and he camped before the city. 19And from the sons of
Hamor, Shechem's father, he bought for one hundred
pieces of moneyi the plot of land on which he had
pitched his tent. 20There he erected an altar and called
it El-Elohe-Israel.j

The Rape of Dinah

34 NOW DINAH the daughter of Leah, whom she
had borne to Jacob, went out to visit the women
of the region. 2When Shechem son of Hamor the Hivite,
prince of the region, saw her, he seized her and lay with
her by force. 3And his soul was drawn to Dinah daughter
of Jacob; he loved the girl, and spoke tenderly to her.
4So Shechem spoke to his father Hamor, saying, "Get
me this girl to be my wife."

5 Now Jacob heard that Shechemk had defiled his
daughter Dinah; but his sons were with his cattle in the
field, so Jacob held his peace until they came. 6And
Hamor the father of Shechem went out to Jacob to speak
with him, 7just as the sons of Jacob came in from the
field. When they heard of it, the men were indignant and
very angry, because he had committed an outrage in
Israel by lying with Jacob's daughter, for such a thing
ought not to be done.

8 But Hamor spoke with them, saying, "The heart
of my son Shechem longs for your daughter; please give
her to him in marriage. 9Make marriages with us; give
your daughters to us, and take our daughters for yourselves. 10You shall live with us; and the land shall be
open to you; live and trade in it, and get property in it."
11Shechem also said to her father and to her brothers,
"Let me find favor with you, and whatever you say to
me I will give. 12Put the marriage present and gift as
high as you like, and I will give whatever you ask me;
only give me the girl to be my wife."

13 The sons of Jacob answered Shechem and his
father Hamor deceitfully, because he had defiled their
sister Dinah. 14They said to them, "We cannot do this
thing, to give our sister to one who is uncircumcised, for
that would be a disgrace to us. 15Only on this condition
will we consent to you: that you will become as we are
and every male among you be circumcised. 16Then we
will give our daughters to you, and we will take your
daughters for ourselves, and we will live among you and
become one people. 17But if you will not listen to us and
be circumcised, then we will take our daughter and be
gone."

18 Their words pleased Hamor and Hamor's son
Shechem. 19And the young man did not delay to do the
thing, because he was delighted with Jacob's daughter.
Now he was the most honored of all his family. 20So
Hamor and his son Shechem came to the gate of their
city and spoke to the men of their city, saying, 21"These
people are friendly with us; let them live in the land and
trade in it, for the land is large enough for them; let us
take their daughters in marriage, and let us give them our
daughters. 22Only on this condition will they agree to

---

h 34:20 appeared before the city council, literally, "came into the gate of
their city."

i Heb one hundred qesitah   j That is God, the God of Israel   k Heb he

King James

22Only herein will the men consent unto us for to dwell with us, to be one people, if every male among us be circumcised, as they *are* circumcised. 23*Shall* not their cattle and their substance and every beast of theirs *be* ours? only let us consent unto them, and they will dwell with us. 24And unto Hamor and unto Shechem his son hearkened all that went out of the gate of his city; and every male was circumcised, all that went out of the gate of his city. 25¶ And it came to pass on the third day, when they were sore, that two of the sons of Jacob, Simeon and Levi, Dinah's brethren, took each man his sword, and came upon the city boldly, and slew all the males. 26And they slew Hamor and Shechem his son with the edge of the sword, and took Dinah out of Shechem's house, and went out. 27The sons of Jacob came upon the slain, and spoiled the city, because they had defiled their sister. 28They took their sheep, and their oxen, and their asses, and that which *was* in the city, and that which *was* in the field, 29And all their wealth, and all their little ones, and their wives took they captive, and spoiled even all that *was* in the house. 30And Jacob said to Simeon and Levi, Ye have troubled me to make me to stink among the inhabitants of the land, among the Canaanites and the Perizzites: and I *being* few in number, they shall gather themselves together against me, and slay me; and I shall be destroyed, I and my house. 31And they said, Should he deal with our sister as with an harlot?

35 AND GOD said unto Jacob, Arise, go up to Beth-el, and dwell there: and make there an altar unto God, that appeared unto thee when thou fleddest from the face of Esau thy brother. 2Then Jacob said unto his household, and to all that *were* with him, Put away the strange gods that *are* among you, and be clean, and change your garments: 3And let us arise, and go up to Beth-el; and I will make there an altar unto God, who answered me in the day of my distress, and was with me in the way which I went. 4And they gave unto Jacob all the strange gods which *were* in their hand, and *all their* earrings which *were* in their ears; and Jacob hid them under the oak which *was* by Shechem. 5And they journeyed: and the terror of God was upon the cities that *were* round about them, and they did not pursue after the sons of Jacob. 6¶ So Jacob came to Luz, which *is* in the land of Canaan, that *is*, Beth-el, he and all the people that *were* with him. 7And he built there an altar, and called the place El-beth-el: because there God appeared unto him, when he fled from the face of his brother. 8But Deborah Rebekah's nurse died, and she was buried beneath Beth-el under an oak: and the name of it was called Allon-bachuth. 9¶ And God appeared unto Jacob again, when he came out of Padan-aram, and blessed him. 10And God said unto him, Thy name *is* Jacob: thy name shall not be called any more Jacob, but Israel shall be thy name: and he called his name Israel. 11And God said unto him, I *am* God Almighty: be fruitful and multiply; a nation and a company of nations shall be of thee, and kings shall come out of thy loins;

New International

as one people only on the condition that our males be circumcised, as they themselves are. 23Won't their livestock, their property and all their other animals become ours? So let us give our consent to them, and they will settle among us." 24All the men who went out of the city gate agreed with Hamor and his son Shechem, and every male in the city was circumcised. 25Three days later, while all of them were still in pain, two of Jacob's sons, Simeon and Levi, Dinah's brothers, took their swords and attacked the unsuspecting city, killing every male. 26They put Hamor and his son Shechem to the sword and took Dinah from Shechem's house and left. 27The sons of Jacob came upon the dead bodies and looted the city where[a] their sister had been defiled. 28They seized their flocks and herds and donkeys and everything else of theirs in the city and out in the fields. 29They carried off all their wealth and all their women and children, taking as plunder everything in the houses.

30Then Jacob said to Simeon and Levi, "You have brought trouble on me by making me a stench to the Canaanites and Perizzites, the people living in this land. We are few in number, and if they join forces against me and attack me, I and my household will be destroyed." 31But they replied, "Should he have treated our sister like a prostitute?"

Jacob Returns to Bethel

35 THEN GOD said to Jacob, "Go up to Bethel and settle there, and build an altar there to God, who appeared to you when you were fleeing from your brother Esau." 2So Jacob said to his household and to all who were with him, "Get rid of the foreign gods you have with you, and purify yourselves and change your clothes. 3Then come, let us go up to Bethel, where I will build an altar to God, who answered me in the day of my distress and who has been with me wherever I have gone." 4So they gave Jacob all the foreign gods they had and the rings in their ears, and Jacob buried them under the oak at Shechem. 5Then they set out, and the terror of God fell upon the towns all around them so that no one pursued them. 6Jacob and all the people with him came to Luz (that is, Bethel) in the land of Canaan. 7There he built an altar, and he called the place El Bethel,[b] because it was there that God revealed himself to him when he was fleeing from his brother. 8Now Deborah, Rebekah's nurse, died and was buried under the oak below Bethel. So it was named Allon Bacuth.[c] 9After Jacob returned from Paddan Aram,[d] God appeared to him again and blessed him. 10God said to him, "Your name is Jacob,[e] but you will no longer be called Jacob; your name will be Israel.[f]" So he named him Israel. 11And God said to him, "I am God Almighty[g]; be fruitful and increase in number. A nation and a community of nations will come from you, and kings will come from your body. 12The land I gave to Abraham and Isaac

---

[a] 27 Or *because*   [b] 7 *El Bethel* means *God of Bethel.*   [c] 8 *Allon Bacuth* means *oak of weeping.*   [d] 9 That is, Northwest Mesopotamia; also in verse 26   [e] 10 *Jacob* means *he grasps the heel* (figuratively, *he deceives*).   [f] 10 *Israel* means *he struggles with God.*   [g] 11 Hebrew *El-Shaddai*

Living Bible

here on one condition—that every one of us men be circumcised, the same as they are. 23But if we do this, then all they have will become ours and the land will be enriched. Come on, let's agree to this so that they will settle here among us.

24So all the men agreed, and all were circumcised. 25But three days later, when their wounds were sore and sensitive to every move they made, two of Dinah's brothers, Simeon and Levi, took their swords, entered the city without opposition, and slaughtered every man there, 26including Hamor and Shechem. They rescued Dinah from Shechem's house and returned to their camp again. 27Then all of Jacob's sons went over and plundered the city because their sister had been dishonored there. 28They confiscated all the flocks and herds and donkeys—everything they could lay their hands on, both inside the city and outside in the fields, 29and took all the women and children, and wealth of every kind.

30Then Jacob said to Levi and Simeon, "You have made me stink among all the people of this land—all the Canaanites and Perizzites. We are so few that they will come and crush us, and we will all be killed."

31"Should he treat our sister like a prostitute?" they retorted.

35 "MOVE ON to Bethel now, and settle there," God said to Jacob, "and build an altar to me to worship me—the God who appeared to you when you fled from your brother Esau."

2So Jacob instructed all those in his household to destroy the idols they had brought with them, and to wash themselves and to put on fresh clothing. 3"For we are going to Bethel," he told them, "and I will build an altar there to the God who answered my prayers in the day of my distress, and was with me on my journey."

4So they gave Jacob all their idols and their earrings, and he buried them beneath the oak tree near Shechem. 5Then they started on again. And the terror of God was upon all the cities they journeyed through, so that they were not attacked. 6Finally they arrived at Luz (also called Bethel), in Canaan. 7And Jacob erected an altar there and named it "The altar to the God who met me here at Bethel"h because it was there at Bethel that God appeared to him when he was fleeing from Esau.

8Soon after thisi Rebekah's old nurse Deborah died and was buried beneath the oak tree in the valley below Bethel. And ever after it was called "The Oak of Weeping."

9Upon Jacob's arrival at Bethel, en route from Paddan-aram, God appeared to him once again and blessed him. 10And God said to him, "You shall no longer be called Jacob ('Grabber'), but Israel ('One who prevails with God'). 11I am God Almighty," the Lord said to him, "and I will cause you to be fertile and to multiply and to become a great nation, yes, many nations; many kings shall be among your descendants. 12And I will

New Revised Standard

live among us, to become one people: that every male among us be circumcised as they are circumcised. 23Will not their livestock, their property, and all their animals be ours? Only let us agree with them, and they will live among us." 24And all who went out of the city gate heeded Hamor and his son Shechem; and every male was circumcised, all who went out of the gate of his city.

Dinah's Brothers Avenge Their Sister

25 On the third day, when they were still in pain, two of the sons of Jacob, Simeon and Levi, Dinah's brothers, took their swords and came against the city unawares, and killed all the males. 26They killed Hamor and his son Shechem with the sword, and took Dinah out of Shechem's house, and went away. 27And the other sons of Jacob came upon the slain, and plundered the city, because their sister had been defiled. 28They took their flocks and their herds, their donkeys, and whatever was in the city and in the field. 29All their wealth, all their little ones and their wives, all that was in the houses, they captured and made their prey. 30Then Jacob said to Simeon and Levi, "You have brought trouble on me by making me odious to the inhabitants of the land, the Canaanites and the Perizzites; my numbers are few, and if they gather themselves against me and attack me, I shall be destroyed, both I and my household." 31But they said, "Should our sister be treated like a whore?"

Jacob Returns to Bethel

35 GOD SAID to Jacob, "Arise, go up to Bethel, and settle there. Make an altar there to the God who appeared to you when you fled from your brother Esau." 2So Jacob said to his household and to all who were with him, "Put away the foreign gods that are among you, and purify yourselves, and change your clothes; 3then come, let us go up to Bethel, that I may make an altar there to the God who answered me in the day of my distress and has been with me wherever I have gone." 4So they gave to Jacob all the foreign gods that they had, and the rings that were in their ears; and Jacob hid them under the oak that was near Shechem.

5 As they journeyed, a terror from God fell upon the cities all around them, so that no one pursued them. 6Jacob came to Luz (that is, Bethel), which is in the land of Canaan, he and all the people who were with him, 7and there he built an altar and called the place El-bethel,j because it was there that God had revealed himself to him when he fled from his brother. 8And Deborah, Rebekah's nurse, died, and she was buried under an oak below Bethel. So it was called Allon-bacuth.k

9 God appeared to Jacob again when he came from Paddan-aram, and he blessed him. 10God said to him, "Your name is Jacob; no longer shall you be called Jacob, but Israel shall be your name." So he was called Israel. 11God said to him, "I am God Almighty:l be fruitful and multiply; a nation and a company of nations shall come from you, and kings shall spring from you."

---

h 35:7 the God who met me here at Bethel, literally, "The God of Bethel."
i 35:8 Soon after this, implied.

j That is God of Bethel   k That is Oak of weeping   l Traditional rendering of Heb El Shaddai

King James

12And the land which I gave Abraham and Isaac, to thee I will give it, and to thy seed after thee will I give the land.

13And God went up from him in the place where he talked with him.

14And Jacob set up a pillar in the place where he talked with him, *even* a pillar of stone: and he poured a drink offering thereon, and he poured oil thereon.

15And Jacob called the name of the place where God spake with him, Beth-el.

16¶ And they journeyed from Beth-el; and there was but a little way to come to Ephrath: and Rachel travailed, and she had hard labour.

17And it came to pass, when she was in hard labour, that the midwife said unto her, Fear not; thou shalt have this son also.

18And it came to pass, as her soul was in departing, (for she died) that she called his name Ben-oni: but his father called him Benjamin.

19And Rachel died, and was buried in the way to Ephrath, which *is* Beth-lehem.

20And Jacob set a pillar upon her grave: that *is* the pillar of Rachel's grave unto this day.

21¶ And Israel journeyed, and spread his tent beyond the tower of Edar.

22And it came to pass, when Israel dwelt in that land, that Reuben went and lay with Bilhah his father's concubine: and Israel heard *it*. Now the sons of Jacob were twelve:

23The sons of Leah; Reuben, Jacob's firstborn, and Simeon, and Levi, and Judah, and Issachar, and Zebulun:

24The sons of Rachel; Joseph, and Benjamin.

25And the sons of Bilhah, Rachel's handmaid; Dan, and Naphtali:

26And the sons of Zilpah, Leah's handmaid; Gad, and Asher: these *are* the sons of Jacob, which were born to him in Padan-aram.

27¶ And Jacob came unto Isaac his father unto Mamre, unto the city of Arbah, which *is* Hebron, where Abraham and Isaac sojourned.

28And the days of Isaac were an hundred and fourscore years.

29And Isaac gave up the ghost, and died, and was gathered unto his people, *being* old and full of days: and his sons Esau and Jacob buried him.

36 NOW THESE *are* the generations of Esau, who *is* Edom.

2Esau took his wives of the daughters of Canaan; Adah the daughter of Elon the Hittite, and Aholibamah the daughter of Anah the daughter of Zibeon the Hivite;

3And Bashemath Ishmael's daughter, sister of Nebajoth.

4And Adah bare to Esau Eliphaz; and Bashemath bare Reuel;

5And Aholibamah bare Jeush, and Jaalam, and Korah: these *are* the sons of Esau, which were born unto him in the land of Canaan.

6And Esau took his wives, and his sons, and his daughters, and all the persons of his house, and his cattle, and all his beasts, and all his substance, which he had got in the land of Canaan; and went into the country from the face of his brother Jacob.

7For their riches were more than that they might dwell together; and the land wherein they were strangers could not bear them because of their cattle.

8Thus dwelt Esau in mount Seir: Esau *is* Edom.

9¶ And these *are* the generations of Esau the father of the Edomites in mount Seir:

New International

I also give to you, and I will give this land to your descendants after you." 13Then God went up from him at the place where he had talked with him.

14Jacob set up a stone pillar at the place where God had talked with him, and he poured out a drink offering on it; he also poured oil on it. 15Jacob called the place where God had talked with him Bethel.[a]

The Deaths of Rachel and Isaac

16Then they moved on from Bethel. While they were still some distance from Ephrath, Rachel began to give birth and had great difficulty. 17And as she was having great difficulty in childbirth, the midwife said to her, "Don't be afraid, for you have another son." 18As she breathed her last—for she was dying—she named her son Ben-Oni.[b] But his father named him Benjamin.[c]

19So Rachel died and was buried on the way to Ephrath (that is, Bethlehem). 20Over her tomb Jacob set up a pillar, and to this day that pillar marks Rachel's tomb.

21Israel moved on again and pitched his tent beyond Migdal Eder. 22While Israel was living in that region, Reuben went in and slept with his father's concubine Bilhah, and Israel heard of it.

Jacob had twelve sons:

23The sons of Leah:
   Reuben the firstborn of Jacob,
   Simeon, Levi, Judah, Issachar and Zebulun.

24The sons of Rachel:
   Joseph and Benjamin.

25The sons of Rachel's maidservant Bilhah:
   Dan and Naphtali.

26The sons of Leah's maidservant Zilpah:
   Gad and Asher.

These were the sons of Jacob, who were born to him in Paddan Aram.

27Jacob came home to his father Isaac in Mamre, near Kiriath Arba (that is, Hebron), where Abraham and Isaac had stayed. 28Isaac lived a hundred and eighty years. 29Then he breathed his last and died and was gathered to his people, old and full of years. And his sons Esau and Jacob buried him.

Esau's Descendants

36 THIS IS the account of Esau (that is, Edom).

2Esau took his wives from the women of Canaan: Adah daughter of Elon the Hittite, and Oholibamah daughter of Anah and granddaughter of Zibeon the Hivite— 3also Basemath daughter of Ishmael and sister of Nebaioth.

4Adah bore Eliphaz to Esau, Basemath bore Reuel, 5and Oholibamah bore Jeush, Jalam and Korah. These were the sons of Esau, who were born to him in Canaan.

6Esau took his wives and sons and daughters and all the members of his household, as well as his livestock and all his other animals and all the goods he had acquired in Canaan, and moved to a land some distance from his brother Jacob. 7Their possessions were too great for them to remain together; the land where they were staying could not support them both because of their livestock. 8So Esau (that is, Edom) settled in the hill country of Seir.

9This is the account of Esau the father of the Edomites in the hill country of Seir.

---

[a] 15 Bethel means *house of God*.   [b] 18 Ben-Oni means *son of my trouble*.
[c] 18 Benjamin means *son of my right hand*.

Living Bible

pass on to you the land I gave to Abraham and Isaac. Yes, I will give it to you and to your descendants."

13, 14Afterwards Jacob built a stone pillar at the place where God had appeared to him; and he poured wine over it as an offering to God, and then anointed the pillar with olive oil. 15Jacob named the spot Bethel ("House of God"), because God had spoken to him there.

16Leaving Bethel, he and his household traveled on toward Ephrath (Bethlehem). But Rachel's pains of childbirth began while they were still a long way away. 17After a very hard delivery, the midwife finally exclaimed, "Wonderful—another boy!" 18And with Rachel's last breath (for she died) she named him "Ben-oni" ("Son of my sorrow"); but his father called him "Benjamin" ("Son of my right hand").

19So Rachel died, and was buried near the road to Ephrath (also called Bethlehem). 20And Jacob set up a monument of stones upon her grave, and it is there to this day.

21Then Israel journeyed on and camped beyond the Tower of Eder. 22It was while he was there that Reuben slept with Bilhah, his father's concubine, and someone told Israel about it.

Here are the names of the twelve sons of Jacob:
23The sons of Leah:
   Reuben, Jacob's oldest child,
   Simeon, Levi, Judah, Issachar, Zebulun.
24The sons of Rachel:
   Joseph, Benjamin.
25The sons of Bilhah, Rachel's servant-girl:
   Dan, Naphtali.
26The sons of Zilpah, Leah's servant-girl:
   Gad, Asher.
All these were born to him at Paddan-aram.

27So Jacob came at last to Isaac his father at Mamre in Kiriath-arba (now called Hebron), where Abraham too had lived. 28, 29Isaac died soon afterwards, at the ripe old age of 180. And his sons Esau and Jacob buried him.

36 HERE IS a list of the descendants of Esau (also called Edom): 2, 3Esau married three local girls from Canaan:
   Adah (daughter of Elon the Hethite),
   Oholibamah (daughter of Anah and granddaughter of Zibeon the Hivite),
   Basemath (his cousind—she was a daughter of Ishmael—the sister of Nebaioth).
4Esau and Adah had a son named Eliphaz. Esau and Basemath had a son named Reuel.
5Esau and Oholibamah had sons named Jeush, Jalam, and Korah. All these sons were born to Esau in the land of Canaan.
6, 7, 8Then Esau took his wives, children, household servants, cattle and flocks—all the wealth he had gained in the land of Canaan—and moved away from his brother Jacob to Mount Seir. (For there was not land enough to support them both because of all their cattle.)
9Here are the names of Esau's descendants, the Edomites, born to him in Mount Seir:

New Revised Standard

12The land that I gave to Abraham and Isaac I will give to you, and I will give the land to your offspring after you." 13Then God went up from him at the place where he had spoken with him. 14Jacob set up a pillar in the place where he had spoken with him, a pillar of stone; and he poured out a drink offering on it, and poured oil on it. 15So Jacob called the place where God had spoken with him Bethel.

The Birth of Benjamin and the Death of Rachel

16 Then they journeyed from Bethel; and when they were still some distance from Ephrath, Rachel was in childbirth, and she had hard labor. 17When she was in her hard labor, the midwife said to her, "Do not be afraid; for now you will have another son." 18As her soul was departing (for she died), she named him Ben-oni;e but his father called him Benjamin.f 19So Rachel died, and she was buried on the way to Ephrath (that is, Bethlehem), 20and Jacob set up a pillar at her grave; it is the pillar of Rachel's tomb, which is there to this day. 21Israel journeyed on, and pitched his tent beyond the tower of Eder.

22 While Israel lived in that land, Reuben went and lay with Bilhah his father's concubine; and Israel heard of it.

Now the sons of Jacob were twelve. 23The sons of Leah: Reuben (Jacob's firstborn), Simeon, Levi, Judah, Issachar, and Zebulun. 24The sons of Rachel: Joseph and Benjamin. 25The sons of Bilhah, Rachel's maid: Dan and Naphtali. 26The sons of Zilpah, Leah's maid: Gad and Asher. These were the sons of Jacob who were born to him in Paddan-aram.

The Death of Isaac

27 Jacob came to his father Isaac at Mamre, or Kiriath-arba (that is, Hebron), where Abraham and Isaac had resided as aliens. 28Now the days of Isaac were one hundred eighty years. 29And Isaac breathed his last; he died and was gathered to his people, old and full of days; and his sons Esau and Jacob buried him.

Esau's Descendants

36 THESE ARE the descendants of Esau (that is, Edom). 2Esau took his wives from the Canaanites: Adah daughter of Elon the Hittite, Oholibamah daughter of Anah son of Zibeon the Hivite, 3and Basemath, Ishmael's daughter, sister of Nebaioth. 4Adah bore Eliphaz to Esau; Basemath bore Reuel; 5and Oholibamah bore Jeush, Jalam, and Korah. These are the sons of Esau who were born to him in the land of Canaan.

6 Then Esau took his wives, his sons, his daughters, and all the members of his household, his cattle, all his livestock, and all the property he had acquired in the land of Canaan; and he moved to a land some distance from his brother Jacob. 7For their possessions were too great for them to live together; the land where they were staying could not support them because of their livestock. 8So Esau settled in the hill country of Seir; Esau is Edom.

9 These are the descendants of Esau, ancestor of the Edomites, in the hill country of Seir. 10These are the

---

d 36:2, 3 Basemath (his cousin . . .), implied. Literally, Basemath "the daughter of Ishmael."

e That is Son of my sorrow   f That is Son of the right hand or Son of the South   g Sam Gk Syr: Heb daughter

King James

¹⁰These *are* the names of Esau's sons; Eliphaz the son of Adah the wife of Esau, Reuel the son of Bashemath the wife of Esau.

¹¹And the sons of Eliphaz were Teman, Omar, Zepho, and Gatam, and Kenaz.

¹²And Timna was concubine to Eliphaz Esau's son; and she bare to Eliphaz Amalek: these *were* the sons of Adah Esau's wife.

¹³And these *are* the sons of Reuel; Nahath, and Zerah, Shammah, and Mizzah: these were the sons of Bashemath Esau's wife.

¹⁴¶ And these were the sons of Aholibamah, the daughter of Anah the daughter of Zibeon, Esau's wife: and she bare to Esau Jeush, and Jaalam, and Korah.

¹⁵¶ These *were* dukes of the sons of Esau: the sons of Eliphaz the firstborn *son* of Esau; duke Teman, duke Omar, duke Zepho, duke Kenaz,

¹⁶Duke Korah, duke Gatam, *and* duke Amalek: these *are* the dukes *that came* of Eliphaz in the land of Edom; these *were* the sons of Adah.

¹⁷¶ And these *are* the sons of Reuel Esau's son; duke Nahath, duke Zerah, duke Shammah, duke Mizzah: these *are* the dukes *that came* of Reuel in the land of Edom; these *are* the sons of Bashemath Esau's wife.

¹⁸¶ And these are the sons of Aholibamah Esau's wife; duke Jeush, duke Jaalam, duke Korah: these *were* the dukes *that came* of Aholibamah the daughter of Anah, Esau's wife.

¹⁹These *are* the sons of Esau, who *is* Edom, and these *are* their dukes.

²⁰¶ These *are* the sons of Seir the Horite, who inhabited the land; Lotan, and Shobal, and Zibeon, and Anah,

²¹And Dishon, and Ezer, and Dishan: these *are* the dukes of the Horites, the children of Seir in the land of Edom.

²²And the children of Lotan were Hori and Hemam; and Lotan's sister *was* Timna.

²³And the children of Shobal *were* these; Alvan, and Manahath, and Ebal, Shepho, and Onam.

²⁴And these *are* the children of Zibeon; both Ajah, and Anah: this *was that* Anah that found the mules in the wilderness, as he fed the asses of Zibeon his father.

²⁵And the children of Anah *were* these; Dishon, and Aholibamah the daughter of Anah.

²⁶And these *are* the children of Dishon; Hemdan, and Eshban, and Ithran, and Cheran.

²⁷The children of Ezer *are* these; Bilhan, and Zaavan, and Akan.

²⁸The children of Dishan *are* these; Uz, and Aran.

²⁹These *are* the dukes *that came* of the Horites; duke Lotan, duke Shobal, duke Zibeon, duke Anah,

³⁰Duke Dishon, duke Ezer, duke Dishan: these *are* the dukes *that came* of Hori, among their dukes in the land of Seir.

³¹¶ And these *are* the kings that reigned in the land of Edom, before there reigned any king over the children of Israel.

³²And Bela the son of Beor reigned in Edom: and the name of his city *was* Dinhabah.

³³And Bela died, and Jobab the son of Zerah of Bozrah reigned in his stead.

³⁴And Jobab died, and Husham of the land of Temani reigned in his stead.

New International

¹⁰These are the names of Esau's sons:

Eliphaz, the son of Esau's wife Adah, and Reuel, the son of Esau's wife Basemath.

¹¹The sons of Eliphaz:

Teman, Omar, Zepho, Gatam and Kenaz.

¹²Esau's son Eliphaz also had a concubine named Timna, who bore him Amalek. These were grandsons of Esau's wife Adah.

¹³The sons of Reuel:

Nahath, Zerah, Shammah and Mizzah. These were grandsons of Esau's wife Basemath.

¹⁴The sons of Esau's wife Oholibamah daughter of Anah and granddaughter of Zibeon, whom she bore to Esau:

Jeush, Jalam and Korah.

¹⁵These were the chiefs among Esau's descendants:

The sons of Eliphaz the firstborn of Esau:

Chiefs Teman, Omar, Zepho, Kenaz, ¹⁶Korah,[a] Gatam and Amalek. These were the chiefs descended from Eliphaz in Edom; they were grandsons of Adah.

¹⁷The sons of Esau's son Reuel:

Chiefs Nahath, Zerah, Shammah and Mizzah. These were the chiefs descended from Reuel in Edom; they were grandsons of Esau's wife Basemath.

¹⁸The sons of Esau's wife Oholibamah:

Chiefs Jeush, Jalam and Korah. These were the chiefs descended from Esau's wife Oholibamah daughter of Anah.

¹⁹These were the sons of Esau (that is, Edom), and these were their chiefs.

²⁰These were the sons of Seir the Horite, who were living in the region:

Lotan, Shobal, Zibeon, Anah, ²¹Dishon, Ezer and Dishan. These sons of Seir in Edom were Horite chiefs.

²²The sons of Lotan:

Hori and Homam.[b] Timna was Lotan's sister.

²³The sons of Shobal:

Alvan, Manahath, Ebal, Shepho and Onam.

²⁴The sons of Zibeon:

Aiah and Anah. This is the Anah who discovered the hot springs[c] in the desert while he was grazing the donkeys of his father Zibeon.

²⁵The children of Anah:

Dishon and Oholibamah daughter of Anah.

²⁶The sons of Dishon[d]:

Hemdan, Eshban, Ithran and Keran.

²⁷The sons of Ezer:

Bilhan, Zaavan and Akan.

²⁸The sons of Dishan:

Uz and Aran.

²⁹These were the Horite chiefs:

Lotan, Shobal, Zibeon, Anah, ³⁰Dishon, Ezer and Dishan. These were the Horite chiefs, according to their divisions, in the land of Seir.

The Rulers of Edom

³¹These were the kings who reigned in Edom before any Israelite king reigned[e]:

³²Bela son of Beor became king of Edom. His city was named Dinhabah.

³³When Bela died, Jobab son of Zerah from Bozrah succeeded him as king.

³⁴When Jobab died, Husham from the land of the Temanites succeeded him as king.

ᵃ *16* Masoretic Text; Samaritan Pentateuch (see also Gen. 36:11 and 1 Chron. 1:36) does not have *Korah*.   ᵇ *22* Hebrew *Hemam*, a variant of *Homam* (see 1 Chron. 1:39)   ᶜ *24* Vulgate; Syriac *discovered water*; the meaning of the Hebrew for this word is uncertain.   ᵈ *26* Hebrew *Dishan*, a variant of *Dishon*   ᵉ *31* Or *before an Israelite king reigned over them*

Living Bible

10, 11, 12Descended from his wife Adah, born to her son Eliphaz were:

Teman, Omar, Zepho, Gatam, Kenaz, Amalek (born to Timna, Eliphaz' concubine).

13, 14fEsau also had grandchildren from his wife Basemath. Born to her son Reuel were:

Nahath, Zerah, Shammah, Mizzah.

15, 16Esau's grandchildreng became the heads of clans, as listed here:

The clan of Teman,
The clan of Omar,
The clan of Zepho,
The clan of Kenaz,
The clan of Korah,
The clan of Gatam,
The clan of Amalek.

The above clans were the descendants of Eliphaz, the oldest son of Esau and Adah.

17The following clans were the descendants of Reuel, born to Esau and his wife Basemath while they lived in Canaan:

The clan of Nahath,
The clan of Zerah,
The clan of Shammah,
The clan of Mizzah.

18, 19And these are the clans named after the sons of Esau and his wife Oholibamah (daughter of Anah):

The clan of Jeush,
The clan of Jalam,
The clan of Korah.

20, 21These are the names of the tribes that descended from Seir, the Horite—one of the native families of the land of Seir:

The tribe of Lotan,
The tribe of Shobal,
The tribe of Zibeon,
The tribe of Anah,
The tribe of Dishon,
The tribe of Ezer,
The tribe of Dishan.

22The children of Lotan (the son of Seir) were Hori and Heman. (Lotan had a sister, Timna.)

23The children of Shobal: Alvan, Manahath, Ebal, Shepho, Onam. 24The children of Zibeon:

Aiah,

Anah. (This is the boy who discovered a hot springs in the wasteland while he was grazing his father's donkeys.)

25The children of Anah:

Dishon, Oholibamah.

26The children of Dishon:

Hemdan, Eshban,
Ithran, Cheran.

27The children of Ezer:

Bilhan, Zaavan, Akan.

28, 29, 30h The children of Dishan:

Uz, Aran.

31-39These are the names of the kings of Edom (before Israel had her first king):

King Bela (son of Beor), from Dinhabah in Edom.

Succeededi by: King Jobab (son of Zerah), from the city of Bozrah.

Succeeded by: King Husham, from the land of the Temanites.

Succeeded by: King Hadad (son of Bedad), the leader of the forces that defeated the army of Midian when it invaded Moab. His city was Avith.

New Revised Standard

names of Esau's sons: Eliphaz son of Adah the wife of Esau; Reuel, the son of Esau's wife Basemath. 11The sons of Eliphaz were Teman, Omar, Zepho, Gatam, and Kenaz. 12(Timna was a concubine of Eliphaz, Esau's son; she bore Amalek to Eliphaz.) These were the sons of Adah, Esau's wife. 13These were the sons of Reuel: Nahath, Zerah, Shammah, and Mizzah. These were the sons of Esau's wife, Basemath. 14These were the sons of Esau's wife Oholibamah, daughter of Anah soni of Zibeon: she bore to Esau Jeush, Jalam, and Korah.

Clans and Kings of Edom

15 These are the clansk of the sons of Esau. The sons of Eliphaz the firstborn of Esau: the clansk Teman, Omar, Zepho, Kenaz, 16Korah, Gatam, and Amalek; these are the clansk of Eliphaz in the land of Edom; they are the sons of Adah. 17These are the sons of Esau's son Reuel: the clansk Nahath, Zerah, Shammah, and Mizzah; these are the clansk of Reuel in the land of Edom; they are the sons of Esau's wife Basemath. 18These are the sons of Esau's wife Oholibamah: the clansk Jeush, Jalam, and Korah; these are the clansk born of Esau's wife Oholibamah, the daughter of Anah. 19These are the sons of Esau (that is, Edom), and these are their clans.k

20 These are the sons of Seir the Horite, the inhabitants of the land: Lotan, Shobal, Zibeon, Anah, 21Dishon, Ezer, and Dishan; these are the clansk of the Horites, the sons of Seir in the land of Edom. 22The sons of Lotan were Hori and Heman; and Lotan's sister was Timna. 23These are the sons of Shobal: Alvan, Manahath, Ebal, Shepho, and Onam. 24These are the sons of Zibeon: Aiah and Anah; he is the Anah who found the springsl in the wilderness, as he pastured the donkeys of his father Zibeon. 25These are the children of Anah: Dishon and Oholibamah daughter of Anah. 26These are the sons of Dishon: Hemdan, Eshban, Ithran, and Cheran. 27These are the sons of Ezer: Bilhan, Zaavan, and Akan. 28These are the sons of Dishan: Uz and Aran. 29These are the clansk of the Horites: the clansk Lotan, Shobal, Zibeon, Anah, 30Dishon, Ezer, and Dishan; these are the clansk of the Horites, clan by clanm in the land of Seir.

31 These are the kings who reigned in the land of Edom, before any king reigned over the Israelites. 32Bela son of Beor reigned in Edom, the name of his city being Dinhabah. 33Bela died, and Jobab son of Zerah of Bozrah succeeded him as king. 34Jobab died, and Husham of the land of the Temanites succeeded him as king. 35Husham died, and Hadad son of Bedad, who

King James

35And Husham died, and Hadad the son of Bedad, who smote Midian in the field of Moab, reigned in his stead: and the name of his city was Avith.

36And Hadad died, and Samlah of Masrekah reigned in his stead.

37And Samlah died, and Saul of Rehoboth by the river reigned in his stead.

38And Saul died, and Baal-hanan the son of Achbor reigned in his stead.

39And Baal-hanan the son of Achbor died, and Hadar reigned in his stead: and the name of his city was Pau; and his wife's name was Mehetabel, the daughter of Matred, the daughter of Mezahab.

40And these are the names of the dukes that came of Esau, according to their families, after their places, by their names; duke Timnah, duke Alvah, duke Jetheth,

41Duke Aholibamah, duke Elah, duke Pinon,

42Duke Kenaz, duke Teman, duke Mibzar,

43Duke Magdiel, duke Iram: these be the dukes of Edom, according to their habitations in the land of their possession: he is Esau the father of the Edomites.

37 AND JACOB dwelt in the land wherein his father was a stranger, in the land of Canaan.

2These are the generations of Jacob. Joseph, being seventeen years old, was feeding the flock with his brethren; and the lad was with the sons of Bilhah, and with the sons of Zilpah, his father's wives: and Joseph brought unto his father their evil report.

3Now Israel loved Joseph more than all his children, because he was the son of his old age: and he made him a coat of many colours.

4And when his brethren saw that their father loved him more than all his brethren, they hated him, and could not speak peaceably unto him.

5¶ And Joseph dreamed a dream, and he told it to his brethren: and they hated him yet the more.

6And he said unto them, Hear, I pray you, this dream which I have dreamed:

7For, behold, we were binding sheaves in the field, and, lo, my sheaf arose, and also stood upright; and, behold, your sheaves stood round about, and made obeisance to my sheaf.

8And his brethren said to him, Shalt thou indeed reign over us? or shalt thou indeed have dominion over us? And they hated him yet the more for his dreams, and for his words.

9¶ And he dreamed yet another dream, and told it his brethren, and said, Behold, I have dreamed a dream more; and, behold, the sun and the moon and the eleven stars made obeisance to me.

10And he told it to his father, and to his brethren: and his father rebuked him, and said unto him, What is this dream that thou hast dreamed? Shall I and thy mother and thy brethren indeed come to bow down ourselves to thee to the earth?

11And his brethren envied him; but his father observed the saying.

12¶ And his brethren went to feed their father's flock in Shechem.

New International

35When Husham died, Hadad son of Bedad, who defeated Midian in the country of Moab, succeeded him as king. His city was named Avith.

36When Hadad died, Samlah from Masrekah succeeded him as king.

37When Samlah died, Shaul from Rehoboth on the river[a] succeeded him as king.

38When Shaul died, Baal-Hanan son of Acbor succeeded him as king.

39When Baal-Hanan son of Acbor died, Hadad[b] succeeded him as king. His city was named Pau, and his wife's name was Mehetabel daughter of Matred, the daughter of Me-Zahab.

40These were the chiefs descended from Esau, by name, according to their clans and regions:

Timna, Alvah, Jetheth, 41Oholibamah, Elah, Pinon, 42Kenaz, Teman, Mibzar, 43Magdiel and Iram. These were the chiefs of Edom, according to their settlements in the land they occupied.

This was Esau the father of the Edomites.

Joseph's Dreams

37 JACOB LIVED in the land where his father had stayed, the land of Canaan.

2This is the account of Jacob.

Joseph, a young man of seventeen, was tending the flocks with his brothers, the sons of Bilhah and the sons of Zilpah, his father's wives, and he brought their father a bad report about them.

3Now Israel loved Joseph more than any of his other sons, because he had been born to him in his old age; and he made a richly ornamented[c] robe for him. 4When his brothers saw that their father loved him more than any of them, they hated him and could not speak a kind word to him.

5Joseph had a dream, and when he told it to his brothers, they hated him all the more. 6He said to them, "Listen to this dream I had: 7We were binding sheaves of grain out in the field when suddenly my sheaf rose and stood upright, while your sheaves gathered around mine and bowed down to it."

8His brothers said to him, "Do you intend to reign over us? Will you actually rule us?" And they hated him all the more because of his dream and what he had said.

9Then he had another dream, and he told it to his brothers. "Listen," he said, "I had another dream, and this time the sun and moon and eleven stars were bowing down to me."

10When he told his father as well as his brothers, his father rebuked him and said, "What is this dream you had? Will your mother and I and your brothers actually come and bow down to the ground before you?" 11His brothers were jealous of him, but his father kept the matter in mind.

Joseph Sold by His Brothers

12Now his brothers had gone to graze their father's flocks near Shechem, 13and Israel said to Joseph, "As

---

a 37 Possibly the Euphrates   b 39 Many manuscripts of the Masoretic Text, Samaritan Pentateuch and Syriac (see also 1 Chron. 1:50); most manuscripts of the Masoretic Text *Hadar*   c 3 The meaning of the Hebrew for *richly ornamented* is uncertain; also in verses 23 and 32.

Living Bible

Succeeded by: King Samlah, from Masrekah.

Succeeded by: King Shaul, from Rehoboth-by-the-River.

Succeeded by: King Baal-hanan (son of Achbor).

Succeeded by: King Hadad, from the city of Pau. King Hadad's wife was Mehetabel, daughter of Matred and granddaughter of Mezahab.

40-43Here are the names of the sub-tribes of Esau, living in the localities named after themselves:

The clan of Timna,
The clan of Alvah,
The clan of Jetheth,
The clan of Oholibamah,
The clan of Elah,
The clan of Pinon,
The clan of Kenaz,
The clan of Teman,
The clan of Mibzar,
The clan of Magdiel,
The clan of Iram.

These, then, are the names of the subtribes of Edom, each giving its name to the area it occupied. (All were Edomites, descendants of Esau.)

37 SO JACOB settled again in the land of Canaan, where his father had lived.

2Jacob's son Joseph was now seventeen years old. His job, along with his half-brothers, the sons of his father's wives Bilhah and Zilpah, was to shepherd his father's flocks. But Joseph reported to his father some of the bad things they were doing. 3Now as it happened, Israel loved Joseph more than any of his other children, because Joseph was born to him in his old age. So one day Jacob gave him a special gift—a brightly-colored coat.d 4His brothers of course noticed their father's partiality, and consequently hated Joseph; they couldn't say a kind word to him. 5One night Joseph had a dream and promptly reported the details to his brothers, causing even deeper hatred.

6"Listen to this," he proudly announced. 7"We were out in the field binding sheaves, and my sheaf stood up, and your sheaves all gathered around it and bowed low before it!"

8"So you want to be our king, do you?" his brothers derided. And they hated him both for the dream and for his cocky attitude.

9Then he had another dream and told it to his brothers. "Listen to my latest dream," he boasted. "The sun, moon, and eleven stars bowed low before me!" 10This time he told his father as well as his brothers; but his father rebuked him. "What is this?" he asked. "Shall I indeed, and your mother and brothers come and bow before you?" 11His brothers were fit to be tied concerning this affair, but his father gave it quite a bit of thought and wondered what it all meant.

12One day Joseph's brothers took their father's flocks to Shechem to graze them there. 13, 14A few days later

New Revised Standard

defeated Midian in the country of Moab, succeeded him as king, the name of his city being Avith. 36Hadad died, and Samlah of Masrekah succeeded him as king. 37Samlah died, and Shaul of Rehoboth on the Euphrates succeeded him as king. 38Shaul died, and Baal-hanan son of Achbor succeeded him as king. 39Baal-hanan son of Achbor died, and Hadar succeeded him as king, the name of his city being Pau; his wife's name was Mehetabel, the daughter of Matred, daughter of Me-zahab.

40 These are the names of the clanse of Esau, according to their families and their localities by their names: the clanse Timna, Alvah, Jetheth, 41Oholibamah, Elah, Pinon, 42Kenaz, Teman, Mibzar, 43Magdiel, and Iram; these are the clanse of Edom (that is, Esau, the father of Edom), according to their settlements in the land that they held.

Joseph Dreams of Greatness

37 JACOB SETTLED in the land where his father had lived as an alien, the land of Canaan. 2This is the story of the family of Jacob.

Joseph, being seventeen years old, was shepherding the flock with his brothers; he was a helper to the sons of Bilhah and Zilpah, his father's wives; and Joseph brought a bad report of them to their father. 3Now Israel loved Joseph more than any other of his children, because he was the son of his old age; and he had made him a long robe with sleeves.f 4But when his brothers saw that their father loved him more than all his brothers, they hated him, and could not speak peaceably to him.

5 Once Joseph had a dream, and when he told it to his brothers, they hated him even more. 6He said to them, "Listen to this dream that I dreamed. 7There we were, binding sheaves in the field. Suddenly my sheaf rose and stood upright; then your sheaves gathered around it, and bowed down to my sheaf." 8His brothers said to him, "Are you indeed to reign over us? Are you indeed to have dominion over us?" So they hated him even more because of his dreams and his words.

9 He had another dream, and told it to his brothers, saying, "Look, I have had another dream: the sun, the moon, and eleven stars were bowing down to me." 10But when he told it to his father and to his brothers, his father rebuked him, and said to him, "What kind of dream is this that you have had? Shall we indeed come, I and your mother and your brothers, and bow to the ground before you?" 11So his brothers were jealous of him, but his father kept the matter in mind.

Joseph Is Sold by His Brothers

12 Now his brothers went to pasture their father's flock near Shechem. 13And Israel said to Joseph, "Are

---

d 37:3 a brightly colored coat, more literally, "an ornamented tunic," or "long-sleeved tunic."

e Or chiefs   f Traditional rendering (compare Gk): a coat of many colors; Meaning of Heb uncertain

King James

13And Israel said unto Joseph, Do not thy brethren feed *the flock* in Shechem? come, and I will send thee unto them. And he said to him, Here *am I*.

14And he said to him, Go, I pray thee, see whether it be well with thy brethren, and well with the flocks; and bring me word again. So he sent him out of the vale of Hebron, and he came to Shechem.

15¶ And a certain man found him, and, behold, *he was* wandering in the field: and the man asked him, saying, What seekest thou?

16And he said, I seek my brethren: tell me, I pray thee, where they feed *their flocks*.

17And the man said, They are departed hence; for I heard them say, Let us go to Dothan. And Joseph went after his brethren, and found them in Dothan.

18And when they saw him afar off, even before he came near unto them, they conspired against him to slay him.

19And they said one to another, Behold, this dreamer cometh.

20Come now therefore, and let us slay him, and cast him into some pit, and we will say, Some evil beast hath devoured him: and we shall see what will become of his dreams.

21And Reuben heard *it*, and he delivered him out of their hands; and said, Let us not kill him.

22And Reuben said unto them, Shed no blood, *but* cast him into this pit that *is* in the wilderness, and lay no hand upon him; that he might rid him out of their hands, to deliver him to his father again.

23¶ And it came to pass, when Joseph was come unto his brethren, that they stripped Joseph out of his coat, *his* coat of *many* colours that *was* on him;

24And they took him, and cast him into a pit: and the pit *was* empty, *there was* no water in it.

25And they sat down to eat bread: and they lifted up their eyes and looked, and, behold, a company of Ishmeelites came from Gilead with their camels bearing spicery and balm and myrrh, going to carry *it* down to Egypt.

26And Judah said unto his brethren, What profit *is it* if we slay our brother, and conceal his blood?

27Come, and let us sell him to the Ishmeelites, and let not our hand be upon him; for he *is* our brother *and* our flesh. And his brethren were content.

28Then there passed by Midianites merchantmen; and they drew and lifted up Joseph out of the pit, and sold Joseph to the Ishmeelites for twenty *pieces* of silver: and they brought Joseph into Egypt.

29¶ And Reuben returned unto the pit; and, behold, Joseph *was* not in the pit; and he rent his clothes.

30And he returned unto his brethren, and said, The child *is* not; and I, whither shall I go?

31And they took Joseph's coat, and killed a kid of the goats, and dipped the coat in the blood;

32And they sent the coat of *many* colours, and they brought *it* to their father; and said, This have we found: know now whether it *be* thy son's coat or no.

33And he knew it, and said, It is my son's coat; an evil beast hath devoured him; Joseph is without doubt rent in pieces.

34And Jacob rent his clothes, and put sackcloth upon his loins, and mourned for his son many days.

35And all his sons and all his daughters rose up to comfort him; but he refused to be comforted; and he said, For I will go down into the grave unto my son mourning. Thus his father wept for him.

36And the Midianites sold him into Egypt unto Potiphar, an officer of Pharaoh's, *and* captain of the guard.

New International

you know, your brothers are grazing the flocks near Shechem. Come, I am going to send you to them."

"Very well," he replied.

14So he said to him, "Go and see if all is well with your brothers and with the flocks, and bring word back to me." Then he sent him off from the Valley of Hebron.

When Joseph arrived at Shechem, 15a man found him wandering around in the fields and asked him, "What are you looking for?"

16He replied, "I'm looking for my brothers. Can you tell me where they are grazing their flocks?"

17"They have moved on from here," the man answered. "I heard them say, 'Let's go to Dothan.'"

So Joseph went after his brothers and found them near Dothan. 18But they saw him in the distance, and before he reached them, they plotted to kill him.

19"Here comes that dreamer!" they said to each other. 20"Come now, let's kill him and throw him into one of these cisterns and say that a ferocious animal devoured him. Then we'll see what comes of his dreams."

21When Reuben heard this, he tried to rescue him from their hands. "Let's not take his life," he said. 22"Don't shed any blood. Throw him into this cistern here in the desert, but don't lay a hand on him." Reuben said this to rescue him from them and take him back to his father.

23So when Joseph came to his brothers, they stripped him of his robe—the richly ornamented robe he was wearing— 24and they took him and threw him into the cistern. Now the cistern was empty; there was no water in it.

25As they sat down to eat their meal, they looked up and saw a caravan of Ishmaelites coming from Gilead. Their camels were loaded with spices, balm and myrrh, and they were on their way to take them down to Egypt.

26Judah said to his brothers, "What will we gain if we kill our brother and cover up his blood? 27Come, let's sell him to the Ishmaelites and not lay our hands on him; after all, he is our brother, our own flesh and blood." His brothers agreed.

28So when the Midianite merchants came by, his brothers pulled Joseph up out of the cistern and sold him for twenty shekelsa of silver to the Ishmaelites, who took him to Egypt.

29When Reuben returned to the cistern and saw that Joseph was not there, he tore his clothes. 30He went back to his brothers and said, "The boy isn't there! Where can I turn now?"

31Then they got Joseph's robe, slaughtered a goat and dipped the robe in the blood. 32They took the ornamented robe back to their father and said, "We found this. Examine it to see whether it is your son's robe."

33He recognized it and said, "It is my son's robe! Some ferocious animal has devoured him. Joseph has surely been torn to pieces."

34Then Jacob tore his clothes, put on sackcloth and mourned for his son many days. 35All his sons and daughters came to comfort him, but he refused to be comforted. "No," he said, "in mourning will I go down to the graveb to my son." So his father wept for him.

36Meanwhile, the Midianitesc sold Joseph in Egypt to Potiphar, one of Pharaoh's officials, the captain of the guard.

---

a *28* That is, about 8 ounces (about 0.2 kilogram)   b *35* Hebrew *Sheol*
c *36* Samaritan Pentateuch, Septuagint, Vulgate and Syriac (see also verse 28); Masoretic Text *Medanites*

Living Bible

Israel called for Joseph, and told him, "Your brothers are over in Shechem grazing the flocks. Go and see how they are getting along, and how it is with the flocks, and bring me word."

"Very good," Joseph replied. So he traveled to Shechem from his home at Hebron Valley. 15A man noticed him wandering in the fields.

"Who are you looking for?" he asked.

16"For my brothers and their flocks," Joseph replied. "Have you seen them?"

17"Yes," the man told him, "they are no longer here. I heard your brothers say they were going to Dothan." So Joseph followed them to Dothan and found them there. 18But when they saw him coming, recognizing him in the distance, they decided to kill him!

19, 20"Here comes that master-dreamer," they exclaimed. "Come on, let's kill him and toss him into a well and tell father that a wild animal has eaten him. Then we'll see what will become of all his dreams!"

21, 22But Reuben hoped to spare Joseph's life. "Let's not kill him," he said; "we'll shed no blood—let's throw him alive into this well here; that way he'll die without our touching him!" (Reuben was planning to get him out later and return him to his father.) 23So when Joseph got there, they pulled off his brightly-colored robe, 24and threw him into an empty well—there was no water in it. 25Then they sat down for supper. Suddenly they noticed a string of camels coming towards them in the distance, probably Ishmaelite traders who were taking gum, spices, and herbs from Gilead to Egypt.

26, 27"Look there," Judah said to the others. "Here come some Ishmaelites. Let's sell Joseph to them! Why kill him and have a guilty conscience? Let's not be responsible for his death, for, after all, he is our brother!" And his brothers agreed. 28So when the tradersd came by, his brothers pulled Joseph out of the well and sold him to them for twenty pieces of silver, and they took him along to Egypt. 29Some time later, Reuben (who was away when the traders came by)e returned to get Joseph out of the well. When Joseph wasn't there, he ripped at his clothes in anguish and frustration.

30"The child is gone; and I, where shall I go now?" he wept to his brothers. 31Then the brothers killed a goat and spattered its blood on Joseph's coat, 32and took the coat to their father and asked him to identify it.

"We found this in the field," they told him. "Is it Joseph's coat or not?" 33Their father recognized it at once.

"Yes," he sobbed, "it is my son's coat. A wild animal has eaten him. Joseph is without doubt torn in pieces."

34Then Israel tore his garments and put on sackcloth and mourned for his son in deepest mourning for many weeks. 35His family all tried to comfort him, but it was no use.

"I will die in mourning for my son," he would say, and then break down and cry.

36Meanwhile, in Egypt, the traders sold Joseph to Potiphar, an officer of the Pharaoh—the king of Egypt. Potiphar was captain of the palace guard, the chief executioner.

New Revised Standard

not your brothers pasturing the flock at Shechem? Come, I will send you to them." He answered, "Here I am." 14So he said to him, "Go now, see if it is well with your brothers and with the flock; and bring word back to me." So he sent him from the valley of Hebron.

He came to Shechem, 15and a man found him wandering in the fields; the man asked him, "What are you seeking?" 16"I am seeking my brothers," he said; "tell me, please, where they are pasturing the flock." 17The man said, "They have gone away, for I heard them say, 'Let us go to Dothan.'" So Joseph went after his brothers, and found them at Dothan. 18They saw him from a distance, and before he came near to them, they conspired to kill him. 19They said to one another, "Here comes this dreamer. 20Come now, let us kill him and throw him into one of the pits; then we shall say that a wild animal has devoured him, and we shall see what will become of his dreams." 21But when Reuben heard it, he delivered him out of their hands, saying, "Let us not take his life." 22Reuben said to them, "Shed no blood; throw him into this pit here in the wilderness, but lay no hand on him"—that he might rescue him out of their hand and restore him to his father. 23So when Joseph came to his brothers, they stripped him of his robe, the long robe with sleevesf that he wore; 24and they took him and threw him into a pit. The pit was empty; there was no water in it.

25 Then they sat down to eat; and looking up they saw a caravan of Ishmaelites coming from Gilead, with their camels carrying gum, balm, and resin, on their way to carry it down to Egypt. 26Then Judah said to his brothers, "What profit is it if we kill our brother and conceal his blood? 27Come, let us sell him to the Ishmaelites, and not lay our hands on him, for he is our brother, our own flesh." And his brothers agreed. 28When some Midianite traders passed by, they drew Joseph up, lifting him out of the pit, and sold him to the Ishmaelites for twenty pieces of silver. And they took Joseph to Egypt.

29 When Reuben returned to the pit and saw that Joseph was not in the pit, he tore his clothes. 30He returned to his brothers, and said, "The boy is gone; and I, where can I turn?" 31Then they took Joseph's robe, slaughtered a goat, and dipped the robe in the blood. 32They had the long robe with sleevesf taken to their father, and they said, "This we have found; see now whether it is your son's robe or not." 33He recognized it, and said, "It is my son's robe! A wild animal has devoured him; Joseph is without doubt torn to pieces." 34Then Jacob tore his garments, and put sackcloth on his loins, and mourned for his son many days. 35All his sons and all his daughters sought to comfort him; but he refused to be comforted, and said, "No, I shall go down to Sheol to my son, mourning." Thus his father bewailed him. 36Meanwhile the Midianites had sold him in Egypt to Potiphar, one of Pharaoh's officials, the captain of the guard.

---

d 37:28 traders, literally, "Midianites." e 37:29 who was away when the traders came by, implied.　　f See note on 37.3

King James

38 AND IT came to pass at that time, that Judah went down from his brethren, and turned in to a certain Adullamite, whose name *was* Hirah.

2And Judah saw there a daughter of a certain Canaanite, whose name *was* Shuah; and he took her, and went in unto her.

3And she conceived, and bare a son; and he called his name Er.

4And she conceived again, and bare a son; and she called his name Onan.

5And she yet again conceived, and bare a son; and called his name Shelah: and he was at Chezib, when she bare him.

6And Judah took a wife for Er his firstborn, whose name *was* Tamar.

7And Er, Judah's firstborn, was wicked in the sight of the LORD; and the LORD slew him.

8And Judah said unto Onan, Go in unto thy brother's wife, and marry her, and raise up seed to thy brother.

9And Onan knew that the seed should not be his; and it came to pass, when he went in unto his brother's wife, that he spilled *it* on the ground, lest that he should give seed to his brother.

10And the thing which he did displeased the LORD: wherefore he slew him also.

11Then said Judah to Tamar his daughter-in-law, Remain a widow at thy father's house, till Shelah my son be grown: for he said, Lest peradventure he die also, as his brethren *did*. And Tamar went and dwelt in her father's house.

12¶ And in process of time the daughter of Shuah Judah's wife died; and Judah was comforted, and went up unto his sheepshearers to Timnath, he and his friend Hirah the Adullamite.

13And it was told Tamar, saying, Behold thy father-in-law goeth up to Timnath to shear his sheep.

14And she put her widow's garments off from her, and covered her with a veil, and wrapped herself, and sat in an open place, which *is* by the way to Timnath; for she saw that Shelah was grown, and she was not given unto him to wife.

15When Judah saw her, he thought her *to be* an harlot; because she had covered her face.

16And he turned unto her by the way, and said, Go to, I pray thee, let me come in unto thee; (for he knew not that she *was* his daughter-in-law.) And she said, What wilt thou give me, that thou mayest come in unto me?

17And he said, I will send *thee* a kid from the flock. And she said, Wilt thou give *me* a pledge, till thou send *it?*

18And he said, What pledge shall I give thee? And she said, Thy signet, and thy bracelets, and thy staff that *is* in thine hand. And he gave *it* her, and came in unto her, and she conceived by him.

19And she arose, and went away, and laid by her veil from her, and put on the garments of her widowhood.

20And Judah sent the kid by the hand of his friend the Adullamite, to receive *his* pledge from the woman's hand: but he found her not.

21Then he asked the men of that place, saying, Where *is* the harlot, that *was* openly by the way side? And they said, There was no harlot in this *place.*

22And he returned to Judah, and said, I cannot find her; and also the men of the place said, *that* there was no harlot in this *place.*

23And Judah said, Let her take *it* to her, lest we be shamed: behold, I sent this kid, and thou hast not found her.

New International

Judah and Tamar

38 AT THAT time, Judah left his brothers and went down to stay with a man of Adullam named Hirah. 2There Judah met the daughter of a Canaanite man named Shua. He married her and lay with her; 3she became pregnant and gave birth to a son, who was named Er. 4She conceived again and gave birth to a son and named him Onan. 5She gave birth to still another son and named him Shelah. It was at Kezib that she gave birth to him.

6Judah got a wife for Er, his firstborn, and her name was Tamar. 7But Er, Judah's firstborn, was wicked in the LORD's sight; so the LORD put him to death.

8Then Judah said to Onan, "Lie with your brother's wife and fulfill your duty to her as a brother-in-law to produce offspring for your brother." 9But Onan knew that the offspring would not be his; so whenever he lay with his brother's wife, he spilled his semen on the ground to keep from producing offspring for his brother. 10What he did was wicked in the LORD's sight; so he put him to death also.

11Judah then said to his daughter-in-law Tamar, "Live as a widow in your father's house until my son Shelah grows up." For he thought, "He may die too, just like his brothers." So Tamar went to live in her father's house.

12After a long time Judah's wife, the daughter of Shua, died. When Judah had recovered from his grief, he went up to Timnah, to the men who were shearing his sheep, and his friend Hirah the Adullamite went with him.

13When Tamar was told, "Your father-in-law is on his way to Timnah to shear his sheep," 14she took off her widow's clothes, covered herself with a veil to disguise herself, and then sat down at the entrance to Enaim, which is on the road to Timnah. For she saw that, though Shelah had now grown up, she had not been given to him as his wife.

15When Judah saw her, he thought she was a prostitute, for she had covered her face. 16Not realizing that she was his daughter-in-law, he went over to her by the roadside and said, "Come now, let me sleep with you."

"And what will you give me to sleep with you?" she asked.

17"I'll send you a young goat from my flock," he said.

"Will you give me something as a pledge until you send it?" she asked.

18He said, "What pledge should I give you?"

"Your seal and its cord, and the staff in your hand," she answered. So he gave them to her and slept with her, and she became pregnant by him. 19After she left, she took off her veil and put on her widow's clothes again.

20Meanwhile Judah sent the young goat by his friend the Adullamite in order to get his pledge back from the woman, but he did not find her. 21He asked the men who lived there, "Where is the shrine prostitute who was beside the road at Enaim?"

"There hasn't been any shrine prostitute here," they said.

22So he went back to Judah and said, "I didn't find her. Besides, the men who lived there said, 'There hasn't been any shrine prostitute here.' "

23Then Judah said, "Let her keep what she has, or we will become a laughingstock. After all, I did send her this young goat, but you didn't find her."

Living Bible

38 ABOUT THIS time, Judah left home and moved to Adullam and lived there with a man named Hirah. 2There he met and married a Canaanite girl—the daughter of Shua. 3, 4, 5They lived at Chezib and had three sons, Er, Onan, and Shelah. These names were given to them by their mother, except for Er, who was named by his father.

6When his oldest son Er grew up, Judah arranged for him to marry a girl named Tamar. 7But Er was a wicked man, and so the Lord killed him.

8Then Judah said to Er's brother, Onan, "You must marry Tamar, as our law requires of a dead man's brother; so that her sons from you will be your brother's heirs."

9But Onan was not willing to have a child who would not be counted as his own, and so, although he married her,a whenever he went in to sleep with her, he spilled the sperm on the bedb to prevent her from having a baby which would be his brother's. 10So far as the Lord was concerned, it was very wrong of him [to deny a child to his deceased brother], so he killed him, too. 11Then Judah told Tamar, his daughter-in-law, not to marry again at that time, but to return to her childhood home and to her parents, and to remain a widow there until his youngest son Shelah was old enough to marry her. (But he didn't really intend for Shelah to do this, for fear God would kill him, too, just as he had his two brothers.) So Tamar went home to her parents.

12In the process of time Judah's wife died. After the time of mourning was over, Judah and his friend Hirah, the Adullamite, went to Timnah to supervise the shearing of his sheep. 13When someone told Tamar that her father-in-law had left for the sheep-shearing at Timnah, 14and realizing by now that she was not going to be permitted to marry Shelah, though he was fully grown, she laid aside her widow's clothing and covered herself with a veil to disguise herself, and sat beside the road at the entrance to the village of Enaim, which is on the way to Timnah. 15Judah noticed her as he went by and thought she was a prostitute, since her face was veiled. 16So he stopped and propositioned her to sleep with him, not realizing of course that she was his own daughter-in-law.

"How much will you pay me?" she asked.

17"I'll send you a young goat from my flock," he promised.

"What pledge will you give me, so that I can be sure you will send it?" she asked.

18"Well, what do you want?" he inquired.

"Your identification seal and your walking stick," she replied. So he gave them to her and she let him come and sleep with her; and she became pregnant as a result. 19Afterwards she resumed wearing her widow's clothing as usual. 20Judah asked his friend Hirah the Adullamite to take the young goat back to her, and to pick up the pledges he had given her, but Hirah couldn't find her!

21So he asked around of the men of the city, "Where does the prostitute live who was soliciting out beside the road at the entrance of the village?"

"But we've never had a public prostitute here," they replied. 22So he returned to Judah and told him he couldn't find her anywhere, and what the men of the place had told him.

23"Then let her keep them!" Judah exclaimed. "We tried our best. We'd be the laughingstock of the town to go back again."

New Revised Standard

Judah and Tamar

38 IT HAPPENED at that time that Judah went down from his brothers and settled near a certain Adullamite whose name was Hirah. 2There Judah saw the daughter of a certain Canaanite whose name was Shua; he married her and went in to her. 3She conceived and bore a son; and he named him Er. 4Again she conceived and bore a son whom she named Onan. 5Yet again she bore a son, and she named him Shelah. Shec was in Chezib when she bore him. 6Judah took a wife for Er his firstborn; her name was Tamar. 7But Er, Judah's firstborn, was wicked in the sight of the Lord, and the Lord put him to death. 8Then Judah said to Onan, "Go in to your brother's wife and perform the duty of a brother-in-law to her; raise up offspring for your brother." 9But since Onan knew that the offspring would not be his, he spilled his semen on the ground whenever he went in to his brother's wife, so that he would not give offspring to his brother. 10What he did was displeasing in the sight of the Lord, and he put him to death also. 11Then Judah said to his daughter-in-law Tamar, "Remain a widow in your father's house until my son Shelah grows up"—for he feared that he too would die, like his brothers. So Tamar went to live in her father's house.

12 In course of time the wife of Judah, Shua's daughter, died; when Judah's time of mourning was over,d he went up to Timnah to his sheepshearers, he and his friend Hirah the Adullamite. 13When Tamar was told, "Your father-in-law is going up to Timnah to shear his sheep," 14she put off her widow's garments, put on a veil, wrapped herself up, and sat down at the entrance to Enaim, which is on the road to Timnah. She saw that Shelah was grown up, yet she had not been given to him in marriage. 15When Judah saw her, he thought her to be a prostitute, for she had covered her face. 16He went over to her at the road side, and said, "Come, let me come in to you," for he did not know that she was his daughter-in-law. She said, "What will you give me, that you may come in to me?" 17He answered, "I will send you a kid from the flock." And she said, "Only if you give me a pledge, until you send it." 18He said, "What pledge shall I give you?" She replied, "Your signet and your cord, and the staff that is in your hand." So he gave them to her, and went in to her, and she conceived by him. 19Then she got up and went away, and taking off her veil she put on the garments of her widowhood.

20 When Judah sent the kid by his friend the Adullamite, to recover the pledge from the woman, he could not find her. 21He asked the townspeople, "Where is the temple prostitute who was at Enaim by the wayside?" But they said, "No prostitute has been here." 22So he returned to Judah, and said, "I have not found her; moreover the townspeople said, 'No prostitute has been here.' " 23Judah replied, "Let her keep the things as her own, otherwise we will be laughed at; you see, I sent this kid, and you could not find her."

---

a 38:9 *although he married her,* implied.　　b 38:9 *he spilled the sperm on the bed,* literally, "spilled it on the ground."

c Gk: Heb *He*　　d Heb *when Judah was comforted*

King James

24¶ And it came to pass about three months after, that it was told Judah, saying, Tamar thy daughter-in-law hath played the harlot; and also, behold, she *is* with child by whoredom. And Judah said, Bring her forth, and let her be burnt.

25When she *was* brought forth, she sent to her father-in-law, saying, By the man, whose these *are, am* I with child: and she said, Discern, I pray thee, whose *are* these, the signet, and bracelets, and staff.

26And Judah acknowledged *them,* and said, She hath been more righteous than I; because that I gave her not to Shelah my son. And he knew her again no more.

27¶ And it came to pass in the time of her travail, that, behold, twins *were* in her womb.

28And it came to pass, when she travailed, that *the one* put out *his* hand: and the midwife took and bound upon his hand a scarlet thread, saying, This came out first.

29And it came to pass, as he drew back his hand, that, behold, his brother came out: and she said, How hast thou broken forth? *this* breach *be* upon thee: therefore his name was called Pharez.

30And afterward came out his brother, that had the scarlet thread upon his hand: and his name was called Zerah.

39 AND JOSEPH was brought down to Egypt; and Potiphar, an officer of Pharaoh, captain of the guard, an Egyptian, bought him of the hands of the Ishmeelites, which had brought him down thither.

2And the LORD was with Joseph, and he was a prosperous man; and he was in the house of his master the Egyptian.

3And his master saw that the LORD *was* with him, and that the LORD made all that he did to prosper in his hand.

4And Joseph found grace in his sight, and he served him: and he made him overseer over his house, and all *that* he had he put into his hand.

5And it came to pass from the time *that* he had made him overseer in his house, and over all that he had, that the LORD blessed the Egyptian's house for Joseph's sake; and the blessing of the LORD was upon all that he had in the house, and in the field.

6And he left all that he had in Joseph's hand; and he knew not aught he had, save the bread which he did eat. And Joseph was *a* goodly *person,* and wellfavoured.

7¶ And it came to pass after these things, that his master's wife cast her eyes upon Joseph; and she said, Lie with me.

8But he refused, and said unto his master's wife, Behold, my master wotteth not what *is* with me in the house, and he hath committed all that he hath to my hand;

9*There is* none greater in this house than I; neither hath he kept back any thing from me but thee, because thou *art* his wife: how then can I do this great wickedness, and sin against God?

10And it came to pass, as she spake to Joseph day by day, that he hearkened not unto her, to lie by her, *or* to be with her.

11And it came to pass about this time, that *Joseph* went into the house to do his business; and *there was* none of the men of the house there within.

12And she caught him by his garment, saying, Lie with me: and he left his garment in her hand, and fled, and got him out.

13And it came to pass, when she saw that he had left his garment in her hand, and was fled forth,

New International

24About three months later Judah was told, "Your daughter-in-law Tamar is guilty of prostitution, and as a result she is now pregnant."

Judah said, "Bring her out and have her burned to death!"

25As she was being brought out, she sent a message to her father-in-law. "I am pregnant by the man who owns these," she said. And she added, "See if you recognize whose seal and cord and staff these are."

26Judah recognized them and said, "She is more righteous than I, since I wouldn't give her to my son Shelah." And he did not sleep with her again.

27When the time came for her to give birth, there were twin boys in her womb. 28As she was giving birth, one of them put out his hand; so the midwife took a scarlet thread and tied it on his wrist and said, "This one came out first." 29But when he drew back his hand, his brother came out, and she said, "So this is how you have broken out!" And he was named Perez.[a] 30Then his brother, who had the scarlet thread on his wrist, came out and he was given the name Zerah.[b]

Joseph and Potiphar's Wife

39 NOW JOSEPH had been taken down to Egypt. Potiphar, an Egyptian who was one of Pharaoh's officials, the captain of the guard, bought him from the Ishmaelites who had taken him there.

2The LORD was with Joseph and he prospered, and he lived in the house of his Egyptian master. 3When his master saw that the LORD was with him and that the LORD gave him success in everything he did, 4Joseph found favor in his eyes and became his attendant. Potiphar put him in charge of his household, and he entrusted to his care everything he owned. 5From the time he put him in charge of his household and of all that he owned, the LORD blessed the household of the Egyptian because of Joseph. The blessing of the LORD was on everything Potiphar had, both in the house and in the field. 6So he left in Joseph's care everything he had; with Joseph in charge, he did not concern himself with anything except the food he ate.

Now Joseph was well-built and handsome, 7and after a while his master's wife took notice of Joseph and said, "Come to bed with me!"

8But he refused. "With me in charge," he told her, "my master does not concern himself with anything in the house; everything he owns he has entrusted to my care. 9No one is greater in this house than I am. My master has withheld nothing from me except you, because you are his wife. How then could I do such a wicked thing and sin against God?" 10And though she spoke to Joseph day after day, he refused to go to bed with her or even be with her.

11One day he went into the house to attend to his duties, and none of the household servants was inside. 12She caught him by his cloak and said, "Come to bed with me!" But he left his cloak in her hand and ran out of the house.

13When she saw that he had left his cloak in her hand and had run out of the house, 14she called her household

Living Bible

24About three months later word reached Judah that Tamar, his daughter-in-law, was pregnant, obviously as a result of prostitution.

"Bring her out and burn her," Judah shouted.

25But as they were taking her out to kill her she sent this message to her father-in-law: "The man who owns this identification seal and walking stick is the father of my child. Do you recognize them?"

26Judah admitted that they were his and said, "She is more in the right than I am, because I refused to keep my promise to give her to my son Shelah." But he did not marry her.

27In due season the time of her delivery arrived and she had twin sons. 28As they were being born, the midwife tied a scarlet thread around the wrist of the child who appeared first, 29but he drew back his hand and the other baby was actually the first to be born. "Where did *you* come from!" she exclaimed. And ever after he was called Perez (meaning "Bursting Out"). 30Then, soon afterwards, the baby with the scarlet thread on his wrist was born, and he was named Zerah.

39 WHEN JOSEPH arrived in Egypt as a captive of the Ishmaelite traders, he was purchased from them by Potiphar, a member of the personal staff of Pharaoh, the king of Egypt. Now this man Potiphar was the captain of the king's bodyguard and his chief executioner. 2The Lord greatly blessed Joseph there in the home of his master, so that everything he did succeeded. 3Potiphar noticed this and realized that the Lord was with Joseph in a very special way. 4So Joseph naturally became quite a favorite with him. Soon he was put in charge of the administration of Potiphar's household, and all of his business affairs. 5At once the Lord began blessing Potiphar for Joseph's sake. All his household affairs began to run smoothly, his crops flourished and his flocks multiplied. 6So Potiphar gave Joseph the complete administrative responsibility over everything he owned. He hadn't a worry in the world with Joseph there, except to decide what he wanted to eat! Joseph, by the way, was a very handsome young man.

7One day at about this time Potiphar's wife began making eyes at Joseph, and suggested that he come and sleep with her.

8Joseph refused. "Look," he told her, "my master trusts me with everything in the entire household; 9he himself has no more authority here than I have! He has held back nothing from me except you yourself because you are his wife. How can I do such a wicked thing as this? It would be a great sin against God."

10But she kept on with her suggestions day after day, even though he refused to listen, and kept out of her way as much as possible. 11Then one day as he was in the house going about his work—as it happened, no one else was around at the time— 12she came and grabbed him by the sleeve,c demanding, "Sleep with me." He tore himself away, but as he did, his jacket slipped off and she was left holding it as he fled from the house. 13When she saw that she had his jacket, and that he had fled, 14, 15she began screaming; and when the other men

New Revised Standard

24 About three months later Judah was told, "Your daughter-in-law Tamar has played the whore; moreover she is pregnant as a result of whoredom." And Judah said, "Bring her out, and let her be burned." 25As she was being brought out, she sent word to her father-in-law, "It was the owner of these who made me pregnant." And she said, "Take note, please, whose these are, the signet and the cord and the staff." 26Then Judah acknowledged them and said, "She is more in the right than I, since I did not give her to my son Shelah." And he did not lie with her again.

27 When the time of her delivery came, there were twins in her womb. 28While she was in labor, one put out a hand; and the midwife took and bound on his hand a crimson thread, saying, "This one came out first." 29But just then he drew back his hand, and out came his brother; and she said, "What a breach you have made for yourself!" Therefore he was named Perez.d 30Afterward his brother came out with the crimson thread on his hand; and he was named Zerah.e

Joseph and Potiphar's Wife

39 NOW JOSEPH was taken down to Egypt, and Potiphar, an officer of Pharaoh, the captain of the guard, an Egyptian, bought him from the Ishmaelites who had brought him down there. 2The LORD was with Joseph, and he became a successful man; he was in the house of his Egyptian master. 3His master saw that the LORD was with him, and that the LORD caused all that he did to prosper in his hands. 4So Joseph found favor in his sight and attended him; he made him overseer of his house and put him in charge of all that he had. 5From the time that he made him overseer in his house and over all that he had, the LORD blessed the Egyptian's house for Joseph's sake; the blessing of the LORD was on all that he had, in house and field. 6So he left all that he had in Joseph's charge; and, with him there, he had no concern for anything but the food that he ate.

Now Joseph was handsome and good-looking. 7And after a time his master's wife cast her eyes on Joseph and said, "Lie with me." 8But he refused and said to his master's wife, "Look, with me here, my master has no concern about anything in the house, and he has put everything that he has in my hand. 9He is not greater in this house than I am, nor has he kept back anything from me except yourself, because you are his wife. How then could I do this great wickedness, and sin against God?" 10And although she spoke to Joseph day after day, he would not consent to lie beside her or to be with her. 11One day, however, when he went into the house to do his work, and while no one else was in the house, 12she caught hold of his garment, saying, "Lie with me!" But he left his garment in her hand, and fled and ran outside. 13When she saw that he had left his garment in her hand and had fled outside, 14she called out to the members of

---

c 39:12 *sleeve*. The Hebrew word is not specific.

d That is *A breach*　e That is *Brightness*; perhaps alluding to the crimson thread

King James

14That she called unto the men of her house, and spake unto them, saying, See, he hath brought in an Hebrew unto us to mock us; he came in unto me to lie with me, and I cried with a loud voice:

15And it came to pass, when he heard that I lifted up my voice and cried, that he left his garment with me, and fled, and got him out.

16And she laid up his garment by her, until his lord came home.

17And she spake unto him according to these words, saying, The Hebrew servant, which thou hast brought unto us, came in unto me to mock me:

18And it came to pass, as I lifted up my voice and cried, that he left his garment with me, and fled out.

19And it came to pass, when his master heard the words of his wife, which she spake unto him, saying, After this manner did thy servant to me; that his wrath was kindled.

20And Joseph's master took him, and put him into the prison, a place where the king's prisoners were bound: and he was there in the prison.

21¶ But the LORD was with Joseph, and showed him mercy, and gave him favour in the sight of the keeper of the prison.

22And the keeper of the prison committed to Joseph's hand all the prisoners that were in the prison; and whatsoever they did there, he was the doer of it.

23The keeper of the prison looked not to any thing that was under his hand; because the LORD was with him, and that which he did, the LORD made it to prosper.

40 AND IT came to pass after these things, that the butler of the king of Egypt and his baker had offended their lord the king of Egypt.

2And Pharaoh was wroth against two of his officers, against the chief of the butlers, and against the chief of the bakers.

3And he put them in ward in the house of the captain of the guard, into the prison, the place where Joseph was bound.

4And the captain of the guard charged Joseph with them, and he served them: and they continued a season in ward.

5¶ And they dreamed a dream both of them, each man his dream in one night, each man according to the interpretation of his dream, the butler and the baker of the king of Egypt, which were bound in the prison.

6And Joseph came in unto them in the morning, and looked upon them, and, behold, they were sad.

7And he asked Pharaoh's officers that were with him in the ward of his lord's house, saying, Wherefore look ye so sadly today?

8And they said unto him, We have dreamed a dream, and there is no interpreter of it. And Joseph said unto them, Do not interpretations belong to God? tell me them, I pray you.

9And the chief butler told his dream to Joseph, and said to him, In my dream, behold, a vine was before me;

10And in the vine were three branches: and it was as though it budded, and her blossoms shot forth; and the clusters thereof brought forth ripe grapes:

11And Pharaoh's cup was in my hand: and I took the grapes, and pressed them into Pharaoh's cup, and I gave the cup into Pharaoh's hand.

12And Joseph said unto him, This is the interpretation of it: The three branches are three days:

13Yet within three days shall Pharaoh lift up thine head, and restore thee unto thy place: and thou shalt deliver Pharaoh's cup into his hand, after the former manner when thou wast his butler.

New International

servants. "Look," she said to them, "this Hebrew has been brought to us to make sport of us! He came in here to sleep with me, but I screamed. 15When he heard me scream for help, he left his cloak beside me and ran out of the house."

16She kept his cloak beside her until his master came home. 17Then she told him this story: "That Hebrew slave you brought us came to me to make sport of me. 18But as soon as I screamed for help, he left his cloak beside me and ran out of the house."

19When his master heard the story his wife told him, saying, "This is how your slave treated me," he burned with anger. 20Joseph's master took him and put him in prison, the place where the king's prisoners were confined.

But while Joseph was there in the prison, 21the LORD was with him; he showed him kindness and granted him favor in the eyes of the prison warden. 22So the warden put Joseph in charge of all those held in the prison, and he was made responsible for all that was done there. 23The warden paid no attention to anything under Joseph's care, because the LORD was with Joseph and gave him success in whatever he did.

The Cupbearer and the Baker

40 SOME TIME later, the cupbearer and the baker of the king of Egypt offended their master, the king of Egypt. 2Pharaoh was angry with his two officials, the chief cupbearer and the chief baker, 3and put them in custody in the house of the captain of the guard, in the same prison where Joseph was confined. 4The captain of the guard assigned them to Joseph, and he attended them.

After they had been in custody for some time, 5each of the two men—the cupbearer and the baker of the king of Egypt, who were being held in prison—had a dream the same night, and each dream had a meaning of its own.

6When Joseph came to them the next morning, he saw that they were dejected. 7So he asked Pharaoh's officials who were in custody with him in his master's house, "Why are your faces so sad today?"

8"We both had dreams," they answered, "but there is no one to interpret them."

Then Joseph said to them, "Do not interpretations belong to God? Tell me your dreams."

9So the chief cupbearer told Joseph his dream. He said to him, "In my dream I saw a vine in front of me, 10and on the vine were three branches. As soon as it budded, it blossomed, and its clusters ripened into grapes. 11Pharaoh's cup was in my hand, and I took the grapes, squeezed them into Pharaoh's cup and put the cup in his hand."

12"This is what it means," Joseph said to him. "The three branches are three days. 13Within three days Pharaoh will lift up your head and restore you to your position, and you will put Pharaoh's cup in his hand, just as you used to do when you were his cupbearer. 14But when

Living Bible

around the place came running in to see what had happened, she was crying hysterically. "My husband had to bring in this Hebrew slave to insult us!" she sobbed. "He tried to rape me, but when I screamed, he ran, and forgot to take his jacket."

16She kept the jacket, and when her husband came home that night, 17she told him her story.

"That Hebrew slave you've had around here tried to rape me, 18and I was only saved by my screams. He fled, leaving his jacket behind!"

19Well, when her husband heard his wife's story, he was furious. 20He threw Joseph into prison, where the king's prisoners were kept in chains. 21But the Lord was with Joseph there, too, and was kind to him by granting him favor with the chief jailer. 22In fact, the jailer soon handed over the entire prison administration to Joseph, so that all the other prisoners were responsible to him. 23The chief jailer had no more worries after that, for Joseph took care of everything, and the Lord was with him so that everything ran smoothly and well.

40 SOME TIME later it so happened that the king of Egypt became angry with both his chief baker and his chief butler, so he jailed them both in the prison where Joseph was, in the castle of Potiphar, the captain of the guard, who was the chief executioner. 4They remained under arrest there for quite some time, and Potiphar assigned Joseph to wait on them. 5One night each of them had a dream. 6The next morning Joseph noticed that they looked dejected and sad.

7"What in the world is the matter?" he asked.

8And they replied, "We both had dreams last night, but there is no one here to tell us what they mean."

"Interpreting dreams is God's business," Joseph replied. "Tell me what you saw."

9, 10The butler told his dream first. "In my dream," he said, "I saw a vine with three branches that began to bud and blossom, and soon there were clusters of ripe grapes. 11I was holding Pharaoh's wine cup in my hand, so I took the grapes and squeezed the juice into it, and gave it to him to drink."

12"I know what the dream means," Joseph said. "The three branches mean three days! 13Within three days Pharaoh is going to take you out of prison and give you back your job again as his chief butler. 14And please

New Revised Standard

her household and said to them, "See, my husbanda has brought among us a Hebrew to insult us! He came in to me to lie with me, and I cried out with a loud voice; 15and when he heard me raise my voice and cry out, he left his garment beside me, and fled outside." 16Then she kept his garment by her until his master came home, 17and she told him the same story, saying, "The Hebrew servant, whom you have brought among us, came in to me to insult me; 18but as soon as I raised my voice and cried out, he left his garment beside me, and fled outside."

19 When his master heard the words that his wife spoke to him, saying, "This is the way your servant treated me," he became enraged. 20And Joseph's master took him and put him into the prison, the place where the king's prisoners were confined; he remained there in prison. 21But the LORD was with Joseph and showed him steadfast love; he gave him favor in the sight of the chief jailer. 22The chief jailer committed to Joseph's care all the prisoners who were in the prison, and whatever was done there, he was the one who did it. 23The chief jailer paid no heed to anything that was in Joseph's care, because the LORD was with him; and whatever he did, the LORD made it prosper.

The Dreams of Two Prisoners

40 SOME TIME after this, the cupbearer of the king of Egypt and his baker offended their lord the king of Egypt. 2Pharaoh was angry with his two officers, the chief cupbearer and the chief baker, 3and he put them in custody in the house of the captain of the guard, in the prison where Joseph was confined. 4The captain of the guard charged Joseph with them, and he waited on them; and they continued for some time in custody. 5One night they both dreamed—the cupbearer and the baker of the king of Egypt, who were confined in the prison—each his own dream, and each dream with its own meaning. 6When Joseph came to them in the morning, he saw that they were troubled. 7So he asked Pharaoh's officers, who were with him in custody in his master's house, "Why are your faces downcast today?" 8They said to him, "We have had dreams, and there is no one to interpret them." And Joseph said to them, "Do not interpretations belong to God? Please tell them to me."

9 So the chief cupbearer told his dream to Joseph, and said to him, "In my dream there was a vine before me, 10and on the vine there were three branches. As soon as it budded, its blossoms came out and the clusters ripened into grapes. 11Pharaoh's cup was in my hand; and I took the grapes and pressed them into Pharaoh's cup, and placed the cup in Pharaoh's hand." 12Then Joseph said to him, "This is its interpretation: the three branches are three days; 13within three days Pharaoh will lift up your head and restore you to your office; and you shall place Pharaoh's cup in his hand, just as you used to do when you were his cupbearer. 14But remem-

---

a Heb *he*

King James

14But think on me when it shall be well with thee, and show kindness, I pray thee, unto me, and make mention of me unto Pharaoh, and bring me out of this house:

15For indeed I was stolen away out of the land of the Hebrews: and here also have I done nothing that they should put me into the dungeon.

16When the chief baker saw that the interpretation was good, he said unto Joseph, I also *was* in my dream, and, behold, *I had* three white baskets on my head:

17And in the uppermost basket *there was* of all manner of bakemeats for Pharaoh; and the birds did eat them out of the basket upon my head.

18And Joseph answered and said, This *is* the interpretation thereof: The three baskets *are* three days:

19Yet within three days shall Pharaoh lift up thy head from off thee, and shall hang thee on a tree; and the birds shall eat thy flesh from off thee.

20¶ And it came to pass the third day, *which was* Pharaoh's birthday, that he made a feast unto all his servants: and he lifted up the head of the chief butler and of the chief baker among his servants.

21And he restored the chief butler unto his butlership again; and he gave the cup into Pharaoh's hand:

22But he hanged the chief baker: as Joseph had interpreted to them.

23Yet did not the chief butler remember Joseph, but forgat him.

41 AND IT came to pass at the end of two full years, that Pharaoh dreamed: and, behold, he stood by the river.

2And, behold, there came up out of the river seven wellfavoured kine and fatfleshed; and they fed in a meadow.

3And, behold, seven other kine came up after them out of the river, ill favoured and leanfleshed; and stood by the *other* kine upon the brink of the river.

4And the ill favoured and leanfleshed kine did eat up the seven wellfavoured and fat kine. So Pharaoh awoke.

5And he slept and dreamed the second time: and, behold, seven ears of corn came up upon one stalk, rank and good.

6And, behold, seven thin ears and blasted with the east wind sprung up after them.

7And the seven thin ears devoured the seven rank and full ears. And Pharaoh awoke, and, behold, *it was* a dream.

8And it came to pass in the morning that his spirit was troubled; and he sent and called for all the magicians of Egypt, and all the wise men thereof: and Pharaoh told them his dream; but *there was* none that could interpret them unto Pharaoh.

9¶ Then spake the chief butler unto Pharaoh, saying, I do remember my faults this day:

10Pharaoh was wroth with his servants, and put me in ward in the captain of the guard's house, *both* me and the chief baker:

11And we dreamed a dream in one night, I and he; we dreamed each man according to the interpretation of his dream.

12And *there was* there with us a young man, an Hebrew, servant to the captain of the guard; and we told him, and he interpreted to us our dreams; to each man according to his dream he did interpret.

13And it came to pass, as he interpreted to us, so it was; me he restored unto mine office, and him he hanged.

14¶ Then Pharaoh sent and called Joseph, and they brought him hastily out of the dungeon: and he shaved *himself*, and changed his raiment, and came in unto Pharaoh.

New International

all goes well with you, remember me and show me kindness; mention me to Pharaoh and get me out of this prison. 15For I was forcibly carried off from the land of the Hebrews, and even here I have done nothing to deserve being put in a dungeon."

16When the chief baker saw that Joseph had given a favorable interpretation, he said to Joseph, "I too had a dream: On my head were three baskets of bread.[a] 17In the top basket were all kinds of baked goods for Pharaoh, but the birds were eating them out of the basket on my head."

18"This is what it means," Joseph said. "The three baskets are three days. 19Within three days Pharaoh will lift off your head and hang you on a tree.[b] And the birds will eat away your flesh."

20Now the third day was Pharaoh's birthday, and he gave a feast for all his officials. He lifted up the heads of the chief cupbearer and the chief baker in the presence of his officials: 21He restored the chief cupbearer to his position, so that he once again put the cup into Pharaoh's hand, 22but he hanged[c] the chief baker, just as Joseph had said to them in his interpretation.

23The chief cupbearer, however, did not remember Joseph; he forgot him.

Pharaoh's Dreams

41 WHEN TWO full years had passed, Pharaoh had a dream: He was standing by the Nile, 2when out of the river there came up seven cows, sleek and fat, and they grazed among the reeds. 3After them, seven other cows, ugly and gaunt, came up out of the Nile and stood beside those on the riverbank. 4And the cows that were ugly and gaunt ate up the seven sleek, fat cows. Then Pharaoh woke up.

5He fell asleep again and had a second dream: Seven heads of grain, healthy and good, were growing on a single stalk. 6After them, seven other heads of grain sprouted—thin and scorched by the east wind. 7The thin heads of grain swallowed up the seven healthy, full heads. Then Pharaoh woke up; it had been a dream.

8In the morning his mind was troubled, so he sent for all the magicians and wise men of Egypt. Pharaoh told them his dreams, but no one could interpret them for him.

9Then the chief cupbearer said to Pharaoh, "Today I am reminded of my shortcomings. 10Pharaoh was once angry with his servants, and he imprisoned me and the chief baker in the house of the captain of the guard. 11Each of us had a dream the same night, and each dream had a meaning of its own. 12Now a young Hebrew was there with us, a servant of the captain of the guard. We told him our dreams, and he interpreted them for us, giving each man the interpretation of his dream. 13And things turned out exactly as he interpreted them to us: I was restored to my position, and the other man was hanged.[c]"

14So Pharaoh sent for Joseph, and he was quickly brought from the dungeon. When he had shaved and changed his clothes, he came before Pharaoh.

---

a 16 Or *three wicker baskets*   b 19 Or *and impale you on a pole*
c 22,13 Or *impaled*

Living Bible

have some pity on me when you are back in his favor, and mention me to Pharaoh, and ask him to let me out of here. 15For I was kidnapped from my homeland among the Hebrews, and now this—here I am in jail when I did nothing to deserve it."

16When the chief baker saw that the first dream had such a good meaning, he told his dream to Joseph, too.

"In my dream," he said, "there were three baskets of pastries on my head. 17In the top basket were all kinds of bakery goods for Pharaoh, but the birds came and ate them."

18, 19"The three baskets mean three days," Joseph told him. "Three days from now Pharaoh will take off your head and impale your body on a pole, and the birds will come and pick off your flesh!"

20Pharaoh's birthday came three days later, and he held a party for all of his officials and household staff. He sent for his chief butler and chief baker, and they were brought to him from the prison. 21Then he restored the chief butler to his former position; 22but he sentenced the chief baker to be impaled, just as Joseph had predicted. 23Pharaoh's wine taster, however, promptly forgot all about Joseph, never giving him a thought.

41 ONE NIGHT two years later, Pharaoh dreamed that he was standing on the bank of the Nile River, 2when suddenly, seven sleek, fat cows came up out of the river and began grazing in the grass. 3Then seven other cows came up from the river, but they were very skinny and all their ribs stood out. They went over and stood beside the fat cows. 4Then the skinny cows ate the fat ones! At which point, Pharaoh woke up!

5Soon he fell asleep again and had a second dream. This time he saw seven heads of grain on one stalk, with every kernel well formed and plump. 6Then, suddenly, seven more heads appeared on the stalk, but these were shriveled and withered by the east wind. 7And these thin heads swallowed up the seven plump, well-formed heads! Then Pharaoh woke up again and realized it was all a dream. 8Next morning, as he thought about it, he became very concerned as to what the dreams might mean; he called for all the magicians and sages of Egypt and told them about it, but not one of them could suggest what his dreams meant. 9Then the king's wine taster spoke up. "Today I remember my sin!" he said. 10"Some time ago when you were angry with a couple of us and put me and the chief baker in jail in the castle of the captain of the guard, 11the chief baker and I each had a dream one night. 12We told the dreams to a young Hebrew fellow there who was a slave of the captain of the guard, and he told us what our dreams meant. 13And everything happened just as he said: I was restored to my position of wine taster, and the chief baker was executed, and impaled on a pole."

14Pharaoh sent at once for Joseph. He was brought hastily from the dungeon, and after a quick shave and change of clothes, came in before Pharaoh.

New Revised Standard

ber me when it is well with you; please do me the kindness to make mention of me to Pharaoh, and so get me out of this place. 15For in fact I was stolen out of the land of the Hebrews; and here also I have done nothing that they should have put me into the dungeon."

16 When the chief baker saw that the interpretation was favorable, he said to Joseph, "I also had a dream: there were three cake baskets on my head, 17and in the uppermost basket there were all sorts of baked food for Pharaoh, but the birds were eating it out of the basket on my head." 18And Joseph answered, "This is its interpretation: the three baskets are three days; 19within three days Pharaoh will lift up your head—from you!—and hang you on a pole; and the birds will eat the flesh from you."

20 On the third day, which was Pharaoh's birthday, he made a feast for all his servants, and lifted up the head of the chief cupbearer and the head of the chief baker among his servants. 21He restored the chief cupbearer to his cupbearing, and he placed the cup in Pharaoh's hand; 22but the chief baker he hanged, just as Joseph had interpreted to them. 23 Yet the chief cupbearer did not remember Joseph, but forgot him.

Joseph Interprets Pharaoh's Dream

41 AFTER TWO whole years, Pharaoh dreamed that he was standing by the Nile, 2and there came up out of the Nile seven sleek and fat cows, and they grazed in the reed grass. 3Then seven other cows, ugly and thin, came up out of the Nile after them, and stood by the other cows on the bank of the Nile. 4The ugly and thin cows ate up the seven sleek and fat cows. And Pharaoh awoke. 5Then he fell asleep and dreamed a second time; seven ears of grain, plump and good, were growing on one stalk. 6Then seven ears, thin and blighted by the east wind, sprouted after them. 7The thin ears swallowed up the seven plump and full ears. Pharaoh awoke, and it was a dream. 8In the morning his spirit was troubled; so he sent and called for all the magicians of Egypt and all its wise men. Pharaoh told them his dreams, but there was no one who could interpret them to Pharaoh.

9 Then the chief cupbearer said to Pharaoh, "I remember my faults today. 10Once Pharaoh was angry with his servants, and put me and the chief baker in custody in the house of the captain of the guard. 11We dreamed on the same night, he and I, each having a dream with its own meaning. 12A young Hebrew was there with us, a servant of the captain of the guard. When we told him, he interpreted our dreams to us, giving an interpretation to each according to his dream. 13As he interpreted to us, so it turned out; I was restored to my office, and the baker was hanged."

14 Then Pharaoh sent for Joseph, and he was hurriedly brought out of the dungeon. When he had shaved himself and changed his clothes, he came in before Pharaoh. 15And Pharaoh said to Joseph, "I have had a dream,

King James

15And Pharaoh said unto Joseph, I have dreamed a dream, and *there is* none that can interpret it: and I have heard say of thee, *that* thou canst understand a dream to interpret it.

16And Joseph answered Pharaoh, saying, *It is* not in me: God shall give Pharaoh an answer of peace.

17And Pharaoh said unto Joseph, In my dream, behold, I stood upon the bank of the river:

18And, behold, there came up out of the river seven kine, fatfleshed and wellfavoured; and they fed in a meadow:

19And, behold, seven other kine came up after them, poor and very ill favoured and leanfleshed, such as I never saw in all the land of Egypt for badness:

20And the lean and the ill favoured kine did eat up the first seven fat kine:

21And when they had eaten them up, it could not be known that they had eaten them; but they *were* still ill favoured, as at the beginning. So I awoke.

22And I saw in my dream, and, behold, seven ears came up in one stalk, full and good:

23And, behold, seven ears, withered, thin, *and* blasted with the east wind, sprung up after them:

24And the thin ears devoured the seven good ears: and I told *this* unto the magicians; but *there was* none that could declare *it* to me.

25¶ And Joseph said unto Pharaoh, The dream of Pharaoh *is* one: God hath shown Pharaoh what he *is* about to do.

26The seven good kine *are* seven years; and the seven good ears *are* seven years: the dream *is* one.

27And the seven thin and ill favoured kine that came up after them *are* seven years; and the seven empty ears blasted with the east wind shall be seven years of famine.

28This *is* the thing which I have spoken unto Pharaoh: What God *is* about to do he showeth unto Pharaoh.

29Behold, there come seven years of great plenty throughout all the land of Egypt:

30And there shall arise after them seven years of famine; and all the plenty shall be forgotten in the land of Egypt; and the famine shall consume the land;

31And the plenty shall not be known in the land by reason of that famine following; for it *shall be* very grievous.

32And for that the dream was doubled unto Pharaoh twice; *it is* because the thing *is* established by God, and God will shortly bring it to pass.

33Now therefore let Pharaoh look out a man discreet and wise, and set him over the land of Egypt.

34Let Pharaoh do *this,* and let him appoint officers over the land, and take up the fifth part of the land of Egypt in the seven plenteous years.

35And let them gather all the food of those good years that come, and lay up corn under the hand of Pharaoh, and let them keep food in the cities.

36And that food shall be for store to the land against the seven years of famine, which shall be in the land of Egypt; that the land perish not through the famine.

37¶ And the thing was good in the eyes of Pharaoh, and in the eyes of all his servants.

38And Pharaoh said unto his servants, Can we find *such a one* as this *is,* a man in whom the spirit of God *is?*

39And Pharaoh said unto Joseph, Forasmuch as God hath shown thee all this, *there is* none so discreet and wise as thou *art:*

40Thou shalt be over my house, and according unto thy word shall all my people be ruled: only in the throne will I be greater than thou.

41And Pharaoh said unto Joseph, See, I have set thee over all the land of Egypt.

42And Pharaoh took off his ring from his hand, and put it upon Joseph's hand, and arrayed him in vestures of fine linen, and put a gold chain about his neck;

New International

15Pharaoh said to Joseph, "I had a dream, and no one can interpret it. But I have heard it said of you that when you hear a dream you can interpret it."

16"I cannot do it," Joseph replied to Pharaoh, "but God will give Pharaoh the answer he desires."

17Then Pharaoh said to Joseph, "In my dream I was standing on the bank of the Nile, 18when out of the river there came up seven cows, fat and sleek, and they grazed among the reeds. 19After them, seven other cows came up—scrawny and very ugly and lean. I had never seen such ugly cows in all the land of Egypt. 20The lean, ugly cows ate up the seven fat cows that came up first. 21But even after they ate them, no one could tell that they had done so; they looked just as ugly as before. Then I woke up.

22"In my dreams I also saw seven heads of grain, full and good, growing on a single stalk. 23After them, seven other heads sprouted—withered and thin and scorched by the east wind. 24The thin heads of grain swallowed up the seven good heads. I told this to the magicians, but none could explain it to me."

25Then Joseph said to Pharaoh, "The dreams of Pharaoh are one and the same. God has revealed to Pharaoh what he is about to do. 26The seven good cows are seven years, and the seven good heads of grain are seven years; it is one and the same dream. 27The seven lean, ugly cows that came up afterward are seven years, and so are the seven worthless heads of grain scorched by the east wind: They are seven years of famine.

28"It is just as I said to Pharaoh: God has shown Pharaoh what he is about to do. 29Seven years of great abundance are coming throughout the land of Egypt, 30but seven years of famine will follow them. Then all the abundance in Egypt will be forgotten, and the famine will ravage the land. 31The abundance in the land will not be remembered, because the famine that follows it will be so severe. 32The reason the dream was given to Pharaoh in two forms is that the matter has been firmly decided by God, and God will do it soon.

33"And now let Pharaoh look for a discerning and wise man and put him in charge of the land of Egypt. 34Let Pharaoh appoint commissioners over the land to take a fifth of the harvest of Egypt during the seven years of abundance. 35They should collect all the food of these good years that are coming and store up the grain under the authority of Pharaoh, to be kept in the cities for food. 36This food should be held in reserve for the country, to be used during the seven years of famine that will come upon Egypt, so that the country may not be ruined by the famine."

37The plan seemed good to Pharaoh and to all his officials. 38So Pharaoh asked them, "Can we find anyone like this man, one in whom is the spirit of God[a]?"

39Then Pharaoh said to Joseph, "Since God has made all this known to you, there is no one so discerning and wise as you. 40You shall be in charge of my palace, and all my people are to submit to your orders. Only with respect to the throne will I be greater than you."

Joseph in Charge of Egypt

41So Pharaoh said to Joseph, "I hereby put you in charge of the whole land of Egypt." 42Then Pharaoh took his signet ring from his finger and put it on Joseph's finger. He dressed him in robes of fine linen and put a gold chain around his neck. 43He had him ride in a

---

a 38 Or *of the gods*

Living Bible

15"I had a dream last night," Pharaoh told him, "and none of these men can tell me what it means. But I have heard that you can interpret dreams, and that is why I have called for you."

16"I can't do it by myself," Joseph replied, "but God will tell you what it means!"

17So Pharaoh told him the dream. "I was standing upon the bank of the Nile River," he said, 18"when suddenly, seven fat, healthy-looking cows came up out of the river and began grazing along the river bank. 19But then seven other cows came up from the river, very skinny and bony—in fact, I've never seen such poor-looking specimens in all the land of Egypt. 20And these skinny cattle ate up the seven fat ones that had come out first, 21and afterwards they were still as skinny as before! Then I woke up.

22"A little later I had another dream. This time there were seven heads of grain on one stalk, and all seven heads were plump and full. 23Then, out of the same stalk, came seven withered, thin heads. 24And the thin heads swallowed up the fat ones! I told all this to my magicians, but not one of them could tell me the meaning."

25"Both dreams mean the same thing," Joseph told Pharaoh. "God was telling you what he is going to do here in the land of Egypt. 26The seven fat cows (and also the seven fat, well-formed heads of grain) mean that there are seven years of prosperity ahead. 27The seven skinny cows (and also the seven thin and withered heads of grain) indicate that there will be seven years of famine following the seven years of prosperity.

28"So God has showed you what he is about to do: 29The next seven years will be a period of great prosperity throughout all the land of Egypt; 30but afterwards there will be seven years of famine so great that all the prosperity will be forgotten and wiped out; famine will consume the land. 31The famine will be so terrible that even the memory of the good years will be erased. 32The double dream gives double impact, showing that what I have told you is certainly going to happen, for God has decreed it, and it is going to happen soon. 33My suggestion is that you find the wisest man in Egypt and put him in charge of administering a nation-wide farm program. 34, 35Let Pharaoh divide Egypt into five administrative districts,b and let the officials of these districts gather into the royal storehouses all the excess crops of the next seven years, 36so that there will be enough to eat when the seven years of famine come. Otherwise, disaster will surely strike."

37Joseph's suggestions were well received by Pharaoh and his assistants. 38As they discussed who should be appointed for the job, Pharaoh said, "Who could do it better than Joseph? For he is a man who is obviously filled with the Spirit of God." 39Turning to Joseph, Pharaoh said to him, "Since God has revealed the meaning of the dreams to you, you are the wisest man in the country! 40I am hereby appointing you to be in charge of this entire project. What you say goes, throughout all the land of Egypt. I alone will outrank you."

41, 42Then Pharaoh placed his own signet ring on Joseph's finger as a token of his authority, and dressed him in beautiful clothing and placed the royal gold chain about his neck and declared, "See, I have placed you in charge of all the land of Egypt."

New Revised Standard

and there is no one who can interpret it. I have heard it said of you that when you hear a dream you can interpret it." 16Joseph answered Pharaoh, "It is not I; God will give Pharaoh a favorable answer." 17Then Pharaoh said to Joseph, "In my dream I was standing on the banks of the Nile; 18and seven cows, fat and sleek, came up out of the Nile and fed in the reed grass. 19Then seven other cows came up after them, poor, very ugly, and thin. Never had I seen such ugly ones in all the land of Egypt. 20The thin and ugly cows ate up the first seven fat cows, 21but when they had eaten them no one would have known that they had done so, for they were still as ugly as before. Then I awoke. 22I fell asleep a second timec and I saw in my dream seven ears of grain, full and good, growing on one stalk, 23and seven ears, withered, thin, and blighted by the east wind, sprouting after them; 24and the thin ears swallowed up the seven good ears. But when I told it to the magicians, there was no one who could explain it to me."

25 Then Joseph said to Pharaoh, "Pharaoh's dreams are one and the same; God has revealed to Pharaoh what he is about to do. 26The seven good cows are seven years, and the seven good ears are seven years; the dreams are one. 27The seven lean and ugly cows that came up after them are seven years, as are the seven empty ears blighted by the east wind. They are seven years of famine. 28It is as I told Pharaoh; God has shown to Pharaoh what he is about to do. 29There will come seven years of great plenty throughout all the land of Egypt. 30After them there will arise seven years of famine, and all the plenty will be forgotten in the land of Egypt; the famine will consume the land. 31The plenty will no longer be known in the land because of the famine that will follow, for it will be very grievous. 32And the doubling of Pharaoh's dream means that the thing is fixed by God, and God will shortly bring it about. 33Now therefore let Pharaoh select a man who is discerning and wise, and set him over the land of Egypt. 34Let Pharaoh proceed to appoint overseers over the land, and take one-fifth of the produce of the land of Egypt during the seven plenteous years. 35Let them gather all the food of these good years that are coming, and lay up grain under the authority of Pharaoh for food in the cities, and let them keep it. 36That food shall be a reserve for the land against the seven years of famine that are to befall the land of Egypt, so that the land may not perish through the famine."

Joseph's Rise to Power

37 The proposal pleased Pharaoh and all his servants. 38Pharaoh said to his servants, "Can we find anyone else like this—one in whom is the spirit of God?" 39So Pharaoh said to Joseph, "Since God has shown you all this, there is no one so discerning and wise as you. 40You shall be over my house, and all my people shall order themselves as you command; only with regard to the throne will I be greater than you." 41And Pharaoh said to Joseph, "See, I have set you over all the land of Egypt." 42Removing his signet ring from his hand, Pharaoh put it on Joseph's hand; he arrayed him in garments of fine linen, and put a gold chain around his neck. 43He had him ride in the chariot of his second-in-

---

b 41:34, 35 Let Pharaoh divide Egypt into five administrative districts, or, "Let Pharaoh appoint officials to collect a fifth of all the crops . . . ."

c Gk Syr Vg: Heb lacks I fell asleep a second time

King James

43And he made him to ride in the second chariot which he had; and they cried before him, Bow the knee: and he made him *ruler* over all the land of Egypt.

44And Pharaoh said unto Joseph, I *am* Pharaoh, and without thee shall no man lift up his hand or foot in all the land of Egypt.

45And Pharaoh called Joseph's name Zaphnath-paaneah; and he gave him to wife Asenath the daughter of Poti-pherah priest of On. And Joseph went out over *all* the land of Egypt.

46¶ And Joseph *was* thirty years old when he stood before Pharaoh king of Egypt. And Joseph went out from the presence of Pharaoh, and went throughout all the land of Egypt.

47And in the seven plenteous years the earth brought forth by handfuls.

48And he gathered up all the food of the seven years, which were in the land of Egypt, and laid up the food in the cities: the food of the field, which *was* round about every city, laid he up in the same.

49And Joseph gathered corn as the sand of the sea, very much, until he left numbering; for *it was* without number.

50And unto Joseph were born two sons before the years of famine came, which Asenath the daughter of Poti-pherah priest of On bare unto him.

51And Joseph called the name of the firstborn Manasseh: For God, *said he,* hath made me forget all my toil, and all my father's house.

52And the name of the second called he Ephraim: For God hath caused me to be fruitful in the land of my affliction.

53¶ And the seven years of plenteousness, that was in the land of Egypt, were ended.

54And the seven years of dearth began to come, according as Joseph had said: and the dearth was in all lands; but in all the land of Egypt there was bread.

55And when all the land of Egypt was famished, the people cried to Pharaoh for bread: and Pharaoh said unto all the Egyptians, Go unto Joseph; what he saith to you, do.

56And the famine was over all the face of the earth: and Joseph opened all the storehouses, and sold unto the Egyptians; and the famine waxed sore in the land of Egypt.

57And all countries came into Egypt to Joseph for to buy *corn;* because that the famine was *so* sore in all lands.

42 NOW WHEN Jacob saw that there was corn in Egypt, Jacob said unto his sons, Why do ye look one upon another?

2And he said, Behold, I have heard that there is corn in Egypt: get you down thither, and buy for us from thence; that we may live, and not die.

3¶ And Joseph's ten brethren went down to buy corn in Egypt.

4But Benjamin, Joseph's brother, Jacob sent not with his brethren; for he said, Lest peradventure mischief befall him.

5And the sons of Israel came to buy *corn* among those that came: for the famine was in the land of Canaan.

6And Joseph *was* the governor over the land, *and he it was* that sold to all the people of the land: and Joseph's brethren came, and bowed down themselves before him *with* their faces to the earth.

New International

chariot as his second-in-command,[a] and men shouted before him, "Make way[b]!" Thus he put him in charge of the whole land of Egypt.

44Then Pharaoh said to Joseph, "I am Pharaoh, but without your word no one will lift hand or foot in all Egypt." 45Pharaoh gave Joseph the name Zaphenath-Paneah and gave him Asenath daughter of Potiphera, priest of On,[c] to be his wife. And Joseph went throughout the land of Egypt.

46Joseph was thirty years old when he entered the service of Pharaoh king of Egypt. And Joseph went out from Pharaoh's presence and traveled throughout Egypt. 47During the seven years of abundance the land produced plentifully. 48Joseph collected all the food produced in those seven years of abundance in Egypt and stored it in the cities. In each city he put the food grown in the fields surrounding it. 49Joseph stored up huge quantities of grain, like the sand of the sea; it was so much that he stopped keeping records because it was beyond measure.

50Before the years of famine came, two sons were born to Joseph by Asenath daughter of Potiphera, priest of On. 51Joseph named his firstborn Manasseh[d] and said, "It is because God has made me forget all my trouble and all my father's household." 52The second son he named Ephraim[e] and said, "It is because God has made me fruitful in the land of my suffering."

53The seven years of abundance in Egypt came to an end, 54and the seven years of famine began, just as Joseph had said. There was famine in all the other lands, but in the whole land of Egypt there was food. 55When all Egypt began to feel the famine, the people cried to Pharaoh for food. Then Pharaoh told all the Egyptians, "Go to Joseph and do what he tells you."

56When the famine had spread over the whole country, Joseph opened the storehouses and sold grain to the Egyptians, for the famine was severe throughout Egypt. 57And all the countries came to Egypt to buy grain from Joseph, because the famine was severe in all the world.

Joseph's Brothers Go to Egypt

42 WHEN JACOB learned that there was grain in Egypt, he said to his sons, "Why do you just keep looking at each other?" 2He continued, "I have heard that there is grain in Egypt. Go down there and buy some for us, so that we may live and not die."

3Then ten of Joseph's brothers went down to buy grain from Egypt. 4But Jacob did not send Benjamin, Joseph's brother, with the others, because he was afraid that harm might come to him. 5So Israel's sons were among those who went to buy grain, for the famine was in the land of Canaan also.

6Now Joseph was the governor of the land, the one who sold grain to all its people. So when Joseph's brothers arrived, they bowed down to him with their faces to the ground. 7As soon as Joseph saw his brothers, he

---

a 43 Or *in the chariot of his second-in-command;* or *in his second chariot*
b 43 Or *Bow down*   c 45 That is, Heliopolis; also in verse 50
d 51 *Manasseh* sounds like and may be derived from the Hebrew for *forget.*
e 52 *Ephraim* sounds like the Hebrew for *twice fruitful.*

Living Bible

43Pharaoh also gave Joseph the chariot of his second-in-command, and wherever he went the shout arose, "Kneel down!" 44And Pharaoh declared to Joseph, "I, the king of Egypt, swear that you shall have complete charge over all the land of Egypt."

45Pharaoh gave him a name meaning "He has the god-like power of life and death!" And he gave him a wife, a girl named Asenath, daughter of Potiphera, priest of Heliopolis.f So Joseph became famous throughout the land of Egypt. 46He was thirty years old as he entered the service of the king. Joseph went out from the presence of Pharaoh, and began traveling all across the land.

47And sure enough, for the next seven years there were bumper crops everywhere. 48During those years, Joseph requisitioned for the government a portion of all the crops grown throughout Egypt, storing them in near-by cities. 49After seven years of this, the granaries were full to overflowing, and there was so much that no one kept track of the amount.

50During this time before the arrival of the first of the famine years, two sons were born to Joseph by Asenath, the daughter of Potiphera, priest of the sun god Re of Heliopolis. 51Joseph named his oldest son Manasseh (meaning "Made to Forget"—what he meant was that God had made up to him for all the anguish of his youth, and for the loss of his father's home). 52The second boy was named Ephraim (meaning "Fruitful"—"For God has made me fruitful in this land of my slavery," he said). 53So at last the seven years of plenty came to an end. 54Then the seven years of famine began, just as Joseph had predicted. There were crop failures in all the surrounding countries too, but in Egypt there was plenty of grain in the storehouses. 55The people began to starve. They pleaded with Pharaoh for food, and he sent them to Joseph. "Do whatever he tells you to," he in-structed them.

56, 57So now, with severe famine all over the world, Joseph opened up the storehouses and sold grain to the Egyptians and to those from other lands who came to Egypt to buy grain from Joseph.

42 WHEN JACOB heard that there was grain available in Egypt he said to his sons, "Why are you standing around looking at one another? 2I have heard that there is grain available in Egypt. Go down and buy some for us before we all starve to death."

3So Joseph's ten olderg brothers went down to Egypt to buy grain. 4However, Jacob wouldn't let Joseph's younger brother Benjamin go with them, for fear some harm might happen to him [as it had to his brother Josephh]. 5So it was that Israel's sons arrived in Egypt along with many others from many lands to buy food, for the famine was as severe in Canaan as it was every-where else.

6Since Joseph was governor of all Egypt, and in charge of the sale of the grain, it was to him that his brothers came, and bowed low before him, with their

---

New Revised Standard

command; and they cried out in front of him, "Bow the knee!"i Thus he set him over all the land of Egypt. 44Moreover Pharaoh said to Joseph, "I am Pharaoh, and without your consent no one shall lift up hand or foot in all the land of Egypt." 45Pharaoh gave Joseph the name Zaphenath-paneah; and he gave him Asenath daughter of Potiphera, priest of On, as his wife. Thus Joseph gained authority over the land of Egypt.

46 Joseph was thirty years old when he entered the service of Pharaoh king of Egypt. And Joseph went out from the presence of Pharaoh, and went through all the land of Egypt. 47During the seven plenteous years the earth produced abundantly. 48He gathered up all the food of the seven years when there was plentyi in the land of Egypt, and stored up food in the cities; he stored up in every city the food from the fields around it. 49So Joseph stored up grain in such abundance—like the sand of the sea—that he stopped measuring it; it was beyond measure.

50 Before the years of famine came, Joseph had two sons, whom Asenath daughter of Potiphera, priest of On, bore to him. 51Joseph named the firstborn Manasseh,k "For," he said, "God has made me forget all my hardship and all my father's house." 52The second he named Ephraim,l "For God has made me fruitful in the land of my misfortunes."

53 The seven years of plenty that prevailed in the land of Egypt came to an end; 54and the seven years of famine began to come, just as Joseph had said. There was famine in every country, but throughout the land of Egypt there was bread. 55When all the land of Egypt was famished, the people cried to Pharaoh for bread. Phar-aoh said to all the Egyptians, "Go to Joseph; what he says to you, do." 56And since the famine had spread over all the land, Joseph opened all the storehouses,m and sold to the Egyptians, for the famine was severe in the land of Egypt. 57Moreover, all the world came to Joseph in Egypt to buy grain, because the famine be-came severe throughout the world.

Joseph's Brothers Go to Egypt

42 WHEN JACOB learned that there was grain in Egypt, he said to his sons, "Why do you keep looking at one another? 2I have heard," he said, "that there is grain in Egypt; go down and buy grain for us there, that we may live and not die." 3So ten of Joseph's brothers went down to buy grain in Egypt. 4But Jacob did not send Joseph's brother Benjamin with his broth-ers, for he feared that harm might come to him. 5Thus the sons of Israel were among the other people who came to buy grain, for the famine had reached the land of Canaan.

6 Now Joseph was governor over the land; it was he who sold to all the people of the land. And Joseph's brothers came and bowed themselves before him with their faces to the ground. 7When Joseph saw his broth-

---

f 41:45 He has the god-like power of life and death, or, "God (or Pharaoh) says, 'He is living.' " he gave him a wife, a . . . daughter of Potiphera, priest of Heliopolis. Joseph married into a family of high nobility, for his father-in-law was a major priest and politician of that time. g 42:3 ten older, implied. h 42:4 [as it had to his brother Joseph], implied.

i Abrek, apparently an Egyptian word similar in sound to the Hebrew word meaning to kneel j Sam Gk: MT the seven years that were k That is Making to forget l From a Hebrew word meaning to be fruitful m Gk Vg Compare Syr: Heb opened all that was in (or, among) them

King James

7And Joseph saw his brethren, and he knew them, but made himself strange unto them, and spake roughly unto them; and he said unto them, Whence come ye? And they said, From the land of Canaan to buy food.

8And Joseph knew his brethren, but they knew not him.

9And Joseph remembered the dreams which he dreamed of them, and said unto them, Ye *are* spies; to see the nakedness of the land ye are come.

10And they said unto him, Nay, my lord, but to buy food are thy servants come.

11We *are* all one man's sons; we *are* true *men,* thy servants are no spies.

12And he said unto them, Nay, but to see the nakedness of the land ye are come.

13And they said, Thy servants *are* twelve brethren, the sons of one man in the land of Canaan; and, behold, the youngest *is* this day with our father, and one *is* not.

14And Joseph said unto them, That *is it* that I spake unto you, saying, Ye *are* spies:

15Hereby ye shall be proved: By the life of Pharaoh ye shall not go forth hence, except your youngest brother come hither.

16Send one of you, and let him fetch your brother, and ye shall be kept in prison, that your words may be proved, whether *there be any* truth in you: or else by the life of Pharaoh surely ye *are* spies.

17And he put them all together into ward three days.

18And Joseph said unto them the third day, This do, and live; *for* I fear God:

19If ye *be* true *men,* let one of your brethren be bound in the house of your prison: go ye, carry corn for the famine of your houses:

20But bring your youngest brother unto me; so shall your words be verified, and ye shall not die. And they did so.

21¶ And they said one to another, We *are* verily guilty concerning our brother, in that we saw the anguish of his soul, when he besought us, and we would not hear; therefore is this distress come upon us.

22And Reuben answered them, saying, Spake I not unto you, saying, Do not sin against the child; and ye would not hear? therefore, behold, also his blood is required.

23And they knew not that Joseph understood *them;* for he spake unto them by an interpreter.

24And he turned himself about from them, and wept; and returned to them again, and communed with them, and took from them Simeon, and bound him before their eyes.

25¶ Then Joseph commanded to fill their sacks with corn, and to restore every man's money into his sack, and to give them provision for the way: and thus did he unto them.

26And they laded their asses with the corn, and departed thence.

27And as one of them opened his sack to give his ass provender in the inn, he espied his money; for, behold, it *was* in his sack's mouth.

28And he said unto his brethren, My money is restored; and, lo, *it is* even in my sack: and their heart failed *them,* and they were afraid, saying one to another, What *is* this *that* God hath done unto us?

29¶ And they came unto Jacob their father unto the land of Canaan, and told him all that befell unto them; saying,

30The man, *who is* the lord of the land, spake roughly to us, and took us for spies of the country.

31And we said unto him, We *are* true *men;* we are no spies:

32We *be* twelve brethren, sons of our father; one *is* not, and the youngest *is* this day with our father in the land of Canaan.

New International

recognized them, but he pretended to be a stranger and spoke harshly to them. "Where do you come from?" he asked.

"From the land of Canaan," they replied, "to buy food."

8Although Joseph recognized his brothers, they did not recognize him. 9Then he remembered his dreams about them and said to them, "You are spies! You have come to see where our land is unprotected."

10"No, my lord," they answered. "Your servants have come to buy food. 11We are all the sons of one man. Your servants are honest men, not spies."

12"No!" he said to them. "You have come to see where our land is unprotected."

13But they replied, "Your servants were twelve brothers, the sons of one man, who lives in the land of Canaan. The youngest is now with our father, and one is no more."

14Joseph said to them, "It is just as I told you: You are spies! 15And this is how you will be tested: As surely as Pharaoh lives, you will not leave this place unless your youngest brother comes here. 16Send one of your number to get your brother; the rest of you will be kept in prison, so that your words may be tested to see if you are telling the truth. If you are not, then as surely as Pharaoh lives, you are spies!" 17And he put them all in custody for three days.

18On the third day, Joseph said to them, "Do this and you will live, for I fear God: 19If you are honest men, let one of your brothers stay here in prison, while the rest of you go and take grain back for your starving households. 20But you must bring your youngest brother to me, so that your words may be verified and that you may not die." This they proceeded to do.

21They said to one another, "Surely we are being punished because of our brother. We saw how distressed he was when he pleaded with us for his life, but we would not listen; that's why this distress has come upon us."

22Reuben replied, "Didn't I tell you not to sin against the boy? But you wouldn't listen! Now we must give an accounting for his blood." 23They did not realize that Joseph could understand them, since he was using an interpreter.

24He turned away from them and began to weep, but then turned back and spoke to them again. He had Simeon taken from them and bound before their eyes.

25Joseph gave orders to fill their bags with grain, to put each man's silver back in his sack, and to give them provisions for their journey. After this was done for them, 26they loaded their grain on their donkeys and left.

27At the place where they stopped for the night one of them opened his sack to get feed for his donkey, and he saw his silver in the mouth of his sack. 28"My silver has been returned," he said to his brothers. "Here it is in my sack."

Their hearts sank and they turned to each other trembling and said, "What is this that God has done to us?"

29When they came to their father Jacob in the land of Canaan, they told him all that had happened to them. They said, 30"The man who is lord over the land spoke harshly to us and treated us as though we were spying on the land. 31But we said to him, 'We are honest men; we are not spies. 32We were twelve brothers, sons of one father. One is no more, and the youngest is now with our father in Canaan.'

Living Bible

faces to the earth. 7Joseph recognized them instantly, but pretended he didn't.

"Where are you from?" he demanded roughly.

"From the land of Canaan," they replied. "We have come to buy grain."

8, 9Then Joseph remembered the dreams of long ago! But he said to them, "You are spies. You have come to see how destitute the famine has made our land."

10"No, no," they exclaimed. "We have come to buy food. 11We are all brothers and honest men, sir! We are not spies!"

12"Yes, you are," he insisted. "You have come to see how weak we are."

13"Sir," they said, "there are twelve of us brothers, and our father is in the land of Canaan. Our youngest brother is there with our father, and one of our brothers is dead."

14"So?" Joseph asked. "What does that prove?a You are spies. 15This is the way I will test your story: I swear by the life of Pharaoh that you are not going to leave Egypt until this youngest brother comes here. 16One of you go and get your brother! I'll keep the rest of you here, bound in prison. Then we'll find out whether your story is true or not. If it turns out that you don't have a younger brother, then I'll know you are spies."

17So he threw them all into jail for three days.

18The third day Joseph said to them, "I am a God-fearing man and I'm going to give you an opportunity to prove yourselves. 19I'm going to take a chance that you are honorable;b only one of you shall remain in chains in jail, and the rest of you may go on home with grain for your families; 20but bring your youngest brother back to me. In this way I will know whether you are telling me the truth; and if you are, I will spare you." To this they agreed.

21Speaking among themselves, they said, "This has all happened because of what we did to Joseph long ago. We saw his terror and anguish and heard his pleadings, but we wouldn't listen."

22"Didn't I tell you not to do it?" Reuben asked. "But you wouldn't listen. And now we are going to die because we murdered him."

23Of course they didn't know that Joseph understood them as he was standing there, for he had been speaking to them through an interpreter. 24Now he left the room and found a place where he could weep. Returning, he selected Simeon from among them and had him bound before their eyes. 25Joseph then ordered his servants to fill the men's sacks with grain, but also gave secret instructions to put each brother's payment at the top of his sack! He also gave them provisions for their journey. 26So they loaded up their donkeys with the grain and started for home. 27But when they stopped for the night and one of them opened his sack to get some grain to feed the donkeys, there was his money in the mouth of the sack!

28"Look," he exclaimed to his brothers, "my money is here in my sack." They were filled with terror. Trembling, they exclaimed to each other. "What is this that God has done to us?" 29So they came to their father Jacob in the land of Canaan and told him all that had happened.

30"The king's chief assistant spoke very roughly to us," they told him, "and took us for spies. 31'No, no,' we said, 'we are honest men, not spies. 32We are twelve brothers, sons of one father; one is dead, and the youngest is with our father in the land of Canaan.' 33Then the

New Revised Standard

ers, he recognized them, but he treated them like strangers and spoke harshly to them. "Where do you come from?" he said. They said, "From the land of Canaan, to buy food." 8Although Joseph had recognized his brothers, they did not recognize him. 9Joseph also remembered the dreams that he had dreamed about them. He said to them, "You are spies; you have come to see the nakedness of the land!" 10They said to him, "No, my lord; your servants have come to buy food. 11We are all sons of one man; we are honest men; your servants have never been spies." 12But he said to them, "No, you have come to see the nakedness of the land!" 13They said, "We, your servants, are twelve brothers, the sons of a certain man in the land of Canaan; the youngest, however, is now with our father, and one is no more." 14But Joseph said to them, "It is just as I have said to you; you are spies! 15Here is how you shall be tested: as Pharaoh lives, you shall not leave this place unless your youngest brother comes here! 16Let one of you go and bring your brother, while the rest of you remain in prison, in order that your words may be tested, whether there is truth in you; or else, as Pharaoh lives, surely you are spies." 17And he put them all together in prison for three days.

18 On the third day Joseph said to them, "Do this and you will live, for I fear God: 19if you are honest men, let one of your brothers stay here where you are imprisoned. The rest of you shall go and carry grain for the famine of your households, 20and bring your youngest brother to me. Thus your words will be verified, and you shall not die." And they agreed to do so. 21They said to one another, "Alas, we are paying the penalty for what we did to our brother; we saw his anguish when he pleaded with us, but we would not listen. That is why this anguish has come upon us." 22Then Reuben answered them, "Did I not tell you not to wrong the boy? But you would not listen. So now there comes a reckoning for his blood." 23They did not know that Joseph understood them, since he spoke with them through an interpreter. 24He turned away from them and wept; then he returned and spoke to them. And he picked out Simeon and had him bound before their eyes. 25Joseph then gave orders to fill their bags with grain, to return every man's money to his sack, and to give them provisions for their journey. This was done for them.

Joseph's Brothers Return to Canaan

26 They loaded their donkeys with their grain, and departed. 27When one of them opened his sack to give his donkey fodder at the lodging place, he saw his money at the top of the sack. 28He said to his brothers, "My money has been put back; here it is in my sack!" At this they lost heart and turned trembling to one another, saying, "What is this that God has done to us?"

29 When they came to their father Jacob in the land of Canaan, they told him all that had happened to them, saying, 30"The man, the lord of the land, spoke harshly to us, and charged us with spying on the land. 31But we said to him, 'We are honest men, we are not spies. 32We are twelve brothers, sons of our father; one is no more, and the youngest is now with our father in the land of Canaan.' 33Then the man, the lord of the land, said to

---

a 42:14 *What does that prove?* Literally, "It is as I said: you are spies."
b 42:19 *I'm going to take a chance that you are honorable,* literally, "If you are forthright men."

King James

33And the man, the lord of the country, said unto us, Hereby shall I know that ye *are* true *men;* leave one of your brethren *here* with me, and take *food for* the famine of your households, and be gone:

34And bring your youngest brother unto me: then shall I know that ye *are* no spies, but *that* ye *are* true *men: so* will I deliver you your brother, and ye shall traffic in the land.

35¶ And it came to pass as they emptied their sacks, that, behold, every man's bundle of money *was* in his sack: and when *both* they and their father saw the bundles of money, they were afraid.

36And Jacob their father said unto them, Me have ye bereaved *of my children:* Joseph *is* not, and Simeon *is* not, and ye will take Benjamin *away:* all these things are against me.

37And Reuben spake unto his father, saying, Slay my two sons, if I bring him not to thee: deliver him into my hand, and I will bring him to thee again.

38And he said, My son shall not go down with you; for his brother is dead, and he is left alone: if mischief befall him by the way in the which ye go, then shall ye bring down my gray hairs with sorrow to the grave.

43 AND THE famine *was* sore in the land.
    2And it came to pass, when they had eaten up the corn which they had brought out of Egypt, their father said unto them, Go again, buy us a little food.

3And Judah spake unto him, saying, The man did solemnly protest unto us, saying, Ye shall not see my face, except your brother *be* with you.

4If thou wilt send our brother with us, we will go down and buy thee food:

5But if thou wilt not send *him,* we will not go down: for the man said unto us, Ye shall not see my face, except your brother *be* with you.

6And Israel said, Wherefore dealt ye *so* ill with me, *as* to tell the man whether ye had yet a brother?

7And they said, The man asked us straitly of our state, and of our kindred, saying, *Is* your father yet alive? have ye *another* brother? and we told him according to the tenor of these words: could we certainly know that he would say, Bring your brother down?

8And Judah said unto Israel his father, Send the lad with me, and we will arise and go; that we may live, and not die, both we, and thou, *and* also our little ones.

9I will be surety for him; of my hand shalt thou require him: if I bring him not unto thee, and set him before thee, then let me bear the blame for ever:

10For except we had lingered, surely now we had returned this second time.

11And their father Israel said unto them, If *it must be* so now, do this; take of the best fruits in the land in your vessels, and carry down the man a present, a little balm, and a little honey, spices, and myrrh, nuts, and almonds:

12And take double money in your hand; and the money that was brought again in the mouth of your sacks, carry *it* again in your hand; peradventure it *was* an oversight:

13Take also your brother, and arise, go again unto the man:

14And God Almighty give you mercy before the man, that he may send away your other brother, and Benjamin. If I be bereaved *of my children,* I am bereaved.

15¶ And the men took that present, and they took double money in their hand, and Benjamin; and rose up, and went down to Egypt, and stood before Joseph.

16And when Joseph saw Benjamin with them, he said to the ruler of his house, Bring *these* men home, and slay, and make ready; for *these* men shall dine with me at noon.

New International

33"Then the man who is lord over the land said to us, 'This is how I will know whether you are honest men: Leave one of your brothers here with me, and take food for your starving households and go. 34But bring your youngest brother to me so I will know that you are not spies but honest men. Then I will give your brother back to you, and you can trade[a] in the land.' "

35As they were emptying their sacks, there in each man's sack was his pouch of silver! When they and their father saw the money pouches, they were frightened. 36Their father Jacob said to them, "You have deprived me of my children. Joseph is no more and Simeon is no more, and now you want to take Benjamin. Everything is against me!"

37Then Reuben said to his father, "You may put both of my sons to death if I do not bring him back to you. Entrust him to my care, and I will bring him back."

38But Jacob said, "My son will not go down there with you; his brother is dead and he is the only one left. If harm comes to him on the journey you are taking, you will bring my gray head down to the grave[b] in sorrow."

The Second Journey to Egypt

43 NOW THE famine was still severe in the land.
    2So when they had eaten all the grain they had brought from Egypt, their father said to them, "Go back and buy us a little more food."

3But Judah said to him, "The man warned us solemnly, 'You will not see my face again unless your brother is with you.' 4If you will send our brother along with us, we will go down and buy food for you. 5But if you will not send him, we will not go down, because the man said to us, 'You will not see my face again unless your brother is with you.' "

6Israel asked, "Why did you bring this trouble on me by telling the man you had another brother?"

7They replied, "The man questioned us closely about ourselves and our family. 'Is your father still living?' he asked us. 'Do you have another brother?' We simply answered his questions. How were we to know he would say, 'Bring your brother down here'?"

8Then Judah said to Israel his father, "Send the boy along with me and we will go at once, so that we and you and our children may live and not die. 9I myself will guarantee his safety; you can hold me personally responsible for him. If I do not bring him back to you and set him here before you, I will bear the blame before you all my life. 10As it is, if we had not delayed, we could have gone and returned twice."

11Then their father Israel said to them, "If it must be, then do this: Put some of the best products of the land in your bags and take them down to the man as a gift—a little balm and a little honey, some spices and myrrh, some pistachio nuts and almonds. 12Take double the amount of silver with you, for you must return the silver that was put back into the mouths of your sacks. Perhaps it was a mistake. 13Take your brother also and go back to the man at once. 14And may God Almighty[c] grant you mercy before the man so that he will let your other brother and Benjamin come back with you. As for me, if I am bereaved, I am bereaved."

15So the men took the gifts and double the amount of silver, and Benjamin also. They hurried down to Egypt and presented themselves to Joseph. 16When Joseph saw Benjamin with them, he said to the steward of his house, "Take these men to my house, slaughter an animal and prepare dinner; they are to eat with me at noon."

---

a *34 Or move about freely*   b *38 Hebrew Sheol*   c *14 Hebrew El-Shaddai*

Living Bible

man told us, 'This is the way I will find out if you are what you claim to be. Leave one of your brothers here with me and take grain for your families and go on home, 34but bring your youngest brother back to me. Then I shall know whether you are spies or honest men; if you prove to be what you say, then I will give you back your brother and you can come as often as you like to purchase grain.' "

35As they emptied out the sacks, there at the top of each was the money paid for the grain! Terror gripped them, as it did their father.

36Then Jacob exclaimed, "You have bereaved me of my children—Joseph didn't come back, Simeon is gone, and now you want to take Benjamin too! Everything has been against me."

37Then Reuben said to his father, "Kill my two sons if I don't bring Benjamin back to you. I'll be responsible for him."

38But Jacob replied, "My son shall not go down with you, for his brother Joseph is dead and he alone is left of his mother's children. If anything should happen to him, I would die."

43 BUT THERE was no relief from the terrible famine throughout the land. 2When the grain they had brought from Egypt was almost gone, their father said to them, "Go again and buy us a little food." 3,4,5But Judah told him, "The man wasn't fooling one bit when he said, 'Don't ever come back again unless your brother is with you.' We cannot go unless you let Benjamin go with us."

6"Why did you ever tell him you had another brother?" Israel moaned. "Why did you have to treat me like that?"

7"But the man specifically asked us about our family," they told him. "He wanted to know whether our father was still living and he asked us if we had another brother, so we told him. How could we know that he was going to say, 'Bring me your brother'?"

8Judah said to his father, "Send the lad with me and we will be on our way; otherwise we will all die of starvation—and not only we, but you and all our little ones. 9I guarantee his safety. If I don't bring him back to you, then let me bear the blame forever. 10For we could have gone and returned by this time if you had let him come."

11So their father Israel finally said to them, "If it can't be avoided, then at least do this. Load your donkeys with the best products of the land. Take them to the man as gifts—balm, honey, spices, myrrh, pistachio nuts, and almonds. 12Take double money so that you can pay back what was in the mouths of your sacks, as it was probably someone's mistake, 13and take your brother and go. 14May God Almighty give you mercy before the man, so that he will release Simeon and return Benjamin. And if I must bear the anguish of their deaths, then so be it."

15So they took the gifts and double money and went to Egypt, and stood before Joseph. 16When Joseph saw that Benjamin was with them he said to the manager of his household, "These men will eat with me this noon. Take them home and prepare a big feast." 17So the man

New Revised Standard

us, 'By this I shall know that you are honest men: leave one of your brothers with me, take grain for the famine of your households, and go your way. 34Bring your youngest brother to me, and I shall know that you are not spies but honest men. Then I will release your brother to you, and you may trade in the land.' "

35 As they were emptying their sacks, there in each one's sack was his bag of money. When they and their father saw their bundles of money, they were dismayed. 36And their father Jacob said to them, "I am the one you have bereaved of children: Joseph is no more, and Simeon is no more, and now you would take Benjamin. All this has happened to me!" 37Then Reuben said to his father, "You may kill my two sons if I do not bring him back to you. Put him in my hands, and I will bring him back to you." 38But he said, "My son shall not go down with you, for his brother is dead, and he alone is left. If harm should come to him on the journey that you are to make, you would bring down my gray hairs with sorrow to Sheol."

The Brothers Come Again, Bringing Benjamin

43 NOW THE famine was severe in the land. 2And when they had eaten up the grain that they had brought from Egypt, their father said to them, "Go again, buy us a little more food." 3But Judah said to him, "The man solemnly warned us, saying, 'You shall not see my face unless your brother is with you.' 4If you will send our brother with us, we will go down and buy you food; 5but if you will not send him, we will not go down, for the man said to us, 'You shall not see my face, unless your brother is with you.' " 6Israel said, "Why did you treat me so badly as to tell the man that you had another brother?" 7They replied, "The man questioned us carefully about ourselves and our kindred, saying, 'Is your father still alive? Have you another brother?' What we told him was in answer to these questions. Could we in any way know that he would say, 'Bring your brother down'?" 8Then Judah said to his father Israel, "Send the boy with me, and let us be on our way, so that we may live and not die—you and we and also our little ones. 9I myself will be surety for him; you can hold me accountable for him. If I do not bring him back to you and set him before you, then let me bear the blame forever. 10If we had not delayed, we would now have returned twice."

11 Then their father Israel said to them, "If it must be so, then do this: take some of the choice fruits of the land in your bags, and carry them down as a present to the man—a little balm and a little honey, gum, resin, pistachio nuts, and almonds. 12Take double the money with you. Carry back with you the money that was returned in the top of your sacks; perhaps it was an oversight. 13Take your brother also, and be on your way again to the man; 14may God Almightyd grant you mercy before the man, so that he may send back your other brother and Benjamin. As for me, if I am bereaved of my children, I am bereaved." 15So the men took the present, and they took double the money with them, as well as Benjamin. Then they went on their way down to Egypt, and stood before Joseph.

16 When Joseph saw Benjamin with them, he said to the steward of his house, "Bring the men into the house, and slaughter an animal and make ready, for the men are to dine with me at noon." 17The man did as

---

d Traditional rendering of Heb El Shaddai

King James

17And the man did as Joseph bade; and the man brought the men into Joseph's house.

18And the men were afraid, because they were brought into Joseph's house; and they said, Because of the money that was returned in our sacks at the first time are we brought in; that he may seek occasion against us, and fall upon us, and take us for bondmen, and our asses.

19And they came near to the steward of Joseph's house, and they communed with him at the door of the house,

20And said, O sir, we came indeed down at the first time to buy food:

21And it came to pass, when we came to the inn, that we opened our sacks, and, behold, *every* man's money *was* in the mouth of his sack, our money in full weight: and we have brought it again in our hand.

22And other money have we brought down in our hands to buy food: we cannot tell who put our money in our sacks.

23And he said, Peace *be* to you, fear not: your God, and the God of your father, hath given you treasure in your sacks: I had your money. And he brought Simeon out unto them.

24And the man brought the men into Joseph's house, and gave *them* water, and they washed their feet; and he gave their asses provender.

25And they made ready the present against Joseph came at noon: for they heard that they should eat bread there.

26¶ And when Joseph came home, they brought him the present which *was* in their hand into the house, and bowed themselves to him to the earth.

27And he asked them of *their* welfare, and said, *Is* your father well, the old man of whom ye spake? *Is* he yet alive?

28And they answered, Thy servant our father *is* in good health, he *is* yet alive. And they bowed down their heads, and made obeisance.

29And he lifted up his eyes, and saw his brother Benjamin, his mother's son, and said, *Is* this your younger brother, of whom ye spake unto me? And he said, God be gracious unto thee, my son.

30And Joseph made haste; for his bowels did yearn upon his brother: and he sought *where* to weep; and he entered into *his* chamber, and wept there.

31And he washed his face, and went out, and refrained himself, and said, Set on bread.

32And they set on for him by himself, and for them by themselves, and for the Egyptians, which did eat with him, by themselves: because the Egyptians might not eat bread with the Hebrews; for that *is* an abomination unto the Egyptians.

33And they sat before him, the firstborn according to his birthright, and the youngest according to his youth: and the men marvelled one at another.

34And he took *and sent* messes unto them from before him: but Benjamin's mess was five times so much as any of theirs. And they drank, and were merry with him.

44 AND HE commanded the steward of his house, saying, Fill the men's sacks *with* food, as much as they can carry, and put every man's money in his sack's mouth.

2And put my cup, the silver cup, in the sack's mouth of the youngest, and his corn money. And he did according to the word that Joseph had spoken.

New International

17The man did as Joseph told him and took the men to Joseph's house. 18Now the men were frightened when they were taken to his house. They thought, "We were brought here because of the silver that was put back into our sacks the first time. He wants to attack us and overpower us and seize us as slaves and take our donkeys."

19So they went up to Joseph's steward and spoke to him at the entrance to the house. 20"Please, sir," they said, "we came down here the first time to buy food. 21But at the place where we stopped for the night we opened our sacks and each of us found his silver—the exact weight—in the mouth of his sack. So we have brought it back with us. 22We have also brought additional silver with us to buy food. We don't know who put our silver in our sacks."

23"It's all right," he said. "Don't be afraid. Your God, the God of your father, has given you treasure in your sacks; I received your silver." Then he brought Simeon out to them.

24The steward took the men into Joseph's house, gave them water to wash their feet and provided fodder for their donkeys. 25They prepared their gifts for Joseph's arrival at noon, because they had heard that they were to eat there.

26When Joseph came home, they presented to him the gifts they had brought into the house, and they bowed down before him to the ground. 27He asked them how they were, and then he said, "How is your aged father you told me about? Is he still living?"

28They replied, "Your servant our father is still alive and well." And they bowed low to pay him honor.

29As he looked about and saw his brother Benjamin, his own mother's son, he asked, "Is this your youngest brother, the one you told me about?" And he said, "God be gracious to you, my son." 30Deeply moved at the sight of his brother, Joseph hurried out and looked for a place to weep. He went into his private room and wept there.

31After he had washed his face, he came out and, controlling himself, said, "Serve the food."

32They served him by himself, the brothers by themselves, and the Egyptians who ate with him by themselves, because Egyptians could not eat with Hebrews, for that is detestable to Egyptians. 33The men had been seated before him in the order of their ages, from the firstborn to the youngest; and they looked at each other in astonishment. 34When portions were served to them from Joseph's table, Benjamin's portion was five times as much as anyone else's. So they feasted and drank freely with him.

A Silver Cup in a Sack

44 NOW JOSEPH gave these instructions to the steward of his house: "Fill the men's sacks with as much food as they can carry, and put each man's silver in the mouth of his sack. 2Then put my cup, the silver one, in the mouth of the youngest one's sack, along with the silver for his grain." And he did as Joseph said.

Living Bible

did as he was told and took them to Joseph's palace. [18]They were badly frightened when they saw where they were being taken.

"It's because of the money returned to us in our sacks," they said. "He wants to pretend we stole it and seize us as slaves, with our donkeys."

[19]As they arrived at the entrance to the palace, they went over to Joseph's household manager, [20]and said to him, "O sir, after our first trip to Egypt to buy food, [21]as we were returning home, we stopped for the night and opened our sacks, and the money was there that we had paid for the grain. Here it is; we have brought it back again, [22]along with additional money to buy more grain. We have no idea how the money got into our sacks."

[23]"Don't worry about it," the household manager told them; "your God, even the God of your fathers, must have put it there, for we collected your money all right."

Then he released Simeon and brought him out to them. [24]They were then conducted into the palace and given water to refresh their feet; and their donkeys were fed. [25]Then they got their presents ready for Joseph's arrival at noon, for they were told that they would be eating there. [26]When Joseph came home they gave him their presents, bowing low before him.

[27]He asked how they had been getting along. "And how is your father—the old man you spoke about? Is he still alive?"

[28]"Yes," they replied. "He is alive and well." Then again they bowed before him.

[29]Looking at his brother[a] Benjamin, he asked, "Is this your youngest brother, the one you told me about? How are you, my son? God be gracious to you." [30]Then Joseph made a hasty exit, for he was overcome with love for his brother and had to go out and cry. Going into his bedroom, he wept there. [31]Then he washed his face and came out, keeping himself under control. "Let's eat," he said.

[32]Joseph ate by himself, his brothers were served at a separate table, and the Egyptians at still another; for Egyptians despise Hebrews and never eat with them. [33]He told each of them where to sit, and seated them in the order of their ages, from the oldest to the youngest, much to their amazement! [34]Their food was served to them from his own table. He gave the largest serving to Benjamin—five times as much as to any of the others! They had a wonderful time bantering back and forth, and the wine flowed freely!

44 WHEN HIS brothers were ready to leave,[b] Joseph ordered his household manager to fill each of their sacks with as much grain as they could carry—and to put into the mouth of each man's sack the money he had paid! [2]He was also told to put Joseph's own silver cup at the top of Benjamin's sack, along with the grain money. So the household manager did as he was told.

New Revised Standard

Joseph said, and brought the men to Joseph's house. [18]Now the men were afraid because they were brought to Joseph's house, and they said, "It is because of the money, replaced in our sacks the first time, that we have been brought in, so that he may have an opportunity to fall upon us, to make slaves of us and take our donkeys." [19]So they went up to the steward of Joseph's house and spoke with him at the entrance to the house. [20]They said, "Oh, my lord, we came down the first time to buy food; [21]and when we came to the lodging place we opened our sacks, and there was each one's money in the top of his sack, our money in full weight. So we have brought it back with us. [22]Moreover we have brought down with us additional money to buy food. We do not know who put our money in our sacks." [23]He replied, "Rest assured, do not be afraid; your God and the God of your father must have put treasure in your sacks for you; I received your money." Then he brought Simeon out to them. [24]When the steward[c] had brought the men into Joseph's house, and given them water, and they had washed their feet, and when he had given their donkeys fodder, [25]they made the present ready for Joseph's coming at noon, for they had heard that they would dine there.

[26] When Joseph came home, they brought him the present that they had carried into the house, and bowed to the ground before him. [27]He inquired about their welfare, and said, "Is your father well, the old man of whom you spoke? Is he still alive?" [28]They said, "Your servant our father is well; he is still alive." And they bowed their heads and did obeisance. [29]Then he looked up and saw his brother Benjamin, his mother's son, and said, "Is this your youngest brother, of whom you spoke to me? God be gracious to you, my son!" [30]With that, Joseph hurried out, because he was overcome with affection for his brother, and he was about to weep. So he went into a private room and wept there. [31]Then he washed his face and came out; and controlling himself he said, "Serve the meal." [32]They served him by himself, and them by themselves, and the Egyptians who ate with him by themselves, because the Egyptians could not eat with the Hebrews, for that is an abomination to the Egyptians. [33]When they were seated before him, the firstborn according to his birthright and the youngest according to his youth, the men looked at one another in amazement. [34]Portions were taken to them from Joseph's table, but Benjamin's portion was five times as much as any of theirs. So they drank and were merry with him.

Joseph Detains Benjamin

44 THEN HE commanded the steward of his house, "Fill the men's sacks with food, as much as they can carry, and put each man's money in the top of his sack. [2]Put my cup, the silver cup, in the top of the sack of the youngest, with his money for the grain." And he did as Joseph told him. [3]As soon as the morning

---

[a] 43:29 Looking at his brother Benjamin, literally, "his brother Benjamin, his mother's son." [b] 44:1 When his brothers were ready to leave, implied.   [c] Heb the man

King James

³As soon as the morning was light, the men were sent away, they and their asses.

⁴And when they were gone out of the city, and not yet far off, Joseph said unto his steward, Up, follow after the men; and when thou dost overtake them, say unto them, Wherefore have ye rewarded evil for good?

⁵Is not this it in which my lord drinketh, and whereby indeed he divineth? ye have done evil in so doing.

⁶¶ And he overtook them, and he spake unto them these same words.

⁷And they said unto him, Wherefore saith my lord these words? God forbid that thy servants should do according to this thing:

⁸Behold, the money, which we found in our sacks' mouths, we brought again unto thee out of the land of Canaan: how then should we steal out of thy lord's house silver or gold?

⁹With whomsoever of thy servants it be found, both let him die, and we also will be my lord's bondmen.

¹⁰And he said, Now also let it be according unto your words: he with whom it is found shall be my servant; and ye shall be blameless.

¹¹Then they speedily took down every man his sack to the ground, and opened every man his sack.

¹²And he searched, and began at the eldest, and left at the youngest: and the cup was found in Benjamin's sack.

¹³Then they rent their clothes, and laded every man his ass, and returned to the city.

¹⁴¶ And Judah and his brethren came to Joseph's house; for he was yet there: and they fell before him on the ground.

¹⁵And Joseph said unto them, What deed is this that ye have done? wot ye not that such a man as I can certainly divine?

¹⁶And Judah said, What shall we say unto my lord? what shall we speak? or how shall we clear ourselves? God hath found out the iniquity of thy servants: behold, we are my lord's servants, both we, and he also with whom the cup is found.

¹⁷And he said, God forbid that I should do so: but the man in whose hand the cup is found, he shall be my servant; and as for you, get you up in peace unto your father.

¹⁸¶ Then Judah came near unto him, and said, Oh my lord, let thy servant, I pray thee, speak a word in my lord's ears, and let not thine anger burn against thy servant: for thou art even as Pharaoh.

¹⁹My lord asked his servants, saying, Have ye a father, or a brother?

²⁰And we said unto my lord, We have a father, an old man, and a child of his old age, a little one; and his brother is dead, and he alone is left of his mother, and his father loveth him.

²¹And thou saidst unto thy servants, Bring him down unto me, that I may set mine eyes upon him.

²²And we said unto my lord, The lad cannot leave his father: for if he should leave his father, his father would die.

²³And thou saidst unto thy servants, Except your youngest brother come down with you, ye shall see my face no more.

²⁴And it came to pass when we came up unto thy servant my father, we told him the words of my lord.

²⁵And our father said, Go again, and buy us a little food.

²⁶And we said, We cannot go down: if our youngest brother be with us, then will we go down: for we may not see the man's face, except our youngest brother be with us.

²⁷And thy servant my father said unto us, Ye know that my wife bare me two sons:

²⁸And the one went out from me, and I said, Surely he is torn in pieces; and I saw him not since:

New International

³As morning dawned, the men were sent on their way with their donkeys. ⁴They had not gone far from the city when Joseph said to his steward, "Go after those men at once, and when you catch up with them, say to them, 'Why have you repaid good with evil? ⁵Isn't this the cup my master drinks from and also uses for divination? This is a wicked thing you have done.' "

⁶When he caught up with them, he repeated these words to them. ⁷But they said to him, "Why does my lord say such things? Far be it from your servants to do anything like that! ⁸We even brought back to you from the land of Canaan the silver we found inside the mouths of our sacks. So why would we steal silver or gold from your master's house? ⁹If any of your servants is found to have it, he will die; and the rest of us will become my lord's slaves."

¹⁰"Very well, then," he said, "let it be as you say. Whoever is found to have it will become my slave; the rest of you will be free from blame."

¹¹Each of them quickly lowered his sack to the ground and opened it. ¹²Then the steward proceeded to search, beginning with the oldest and ending with the youngest. And the cup was found in Benjamin's sack. ¹³At this, they tore their clothes. Then they all loaded their donkeys and returned to the city.

¹⁴Joseph was still in the house when Judah and his brothers came in, and they threw themselves to the ground before him. ¹⁵Joseph said to them, "What is this you have done? Don't you know that a man like me can find things out by divination?"

¹⁶"What can we say to my lord?" Judah replied. "What can we say? How can we prove our innocence? God has uncovered your servants' guilt. We are now my lord's slaves—we ourselves and the one who was found to have the cup."

¹⁷But Joseph said, "Far be it from me to do such a thing! Only the man who was found to have the cup will become my slave. The rest of you, go back to your father in peace."

¹⁸Then Judah went up to him and said: "Please, my lord, let your servant speak a word to my lord. Do not be angry with your servant, though you are equal to Pharaoh himself. ¹⁹My lord asked his servants, 'Do you have a father or a brother?' ²⁰And we answered, 'We have an aged father, and there is a young son born to him in his old age. His brother is dead, and he is the only one of his mother's sons left, and his father loves him.'

²¹"Then you said to your servants, 'Bring him down to me so I can see him for myself.' ²²And we said to my lord, 'The boy cannot leave his father; if he leaves him, his father will die.' ²³But you told your servants, 'Unless your youngest brother comes down with you, you will not see my face again.' ²⁴When we went back to your servant my father, we told him what my lord had said.

²⁵"Then our father said, 'Go back and buy a little more food.' ²⁶But we said, 'We cannot go down. Only if our youngest brother is with us will we go. We cannot see the man's face unless our youngest brother is with us.'

²⁷"Your servant my father said to us, 'You know that my wife bore me two sons. ²⁸One of them went away from me, and I said, "He has surely been torn to pieces." And I have not seen him since. ²⁹If you take this one

Living Bible

3The brothers were up at dawn and on their way with their loaded donkeys.

4But when they were barely out of the city, Joseph said to his household manager, "Chase after them and stop them and ask them why they are acting like this when their benefactor has been so kind to them? 5Ask them, 'What do you mean by stealing my lord's personal silver drinking cup, which he uses for fortune telling? What a wicked thing you have done!' " 6So he caught up with them and spoke to them along the lines he had been instructed.

7"What in the world are you talking about?" they demanded. "What kind of people do you think we are, that you accuse us of such a terrible thing as that? 8Didn't we bring back the money we found in the mouth of our sacks? Why would we steal silver or gold from your master's house? 9If you find his cup with any one of us, let that one die. And all the rest of us will be slaves forever to your master."

10"Fair enough," the man replied, "except that only the one who stole it will be a slave, and the rest of you can go free."

11They quickly took down their sacks from the backs of their donkeys and opened them. 12He began searching the oldest brother's sack, going on down the line to the youngest. And the cup was found in Benjamin's! 13They ripped their clothing in despair, loaded the donkeys again, and returned to the city. 14Joseph was still home when Judah and his brothers arrived, and they fell to the ground before him.

15"What were you trying to do?" Joseph demanded. "Didn't you know such a man as I would know who stole it?"

16And Judah said, "Oh, what shall we say to my lord? How can we plead? How can we prove our innocence? God is punishing us for our sins. Sir, we have all returned to be your slaves, both we and he in whose sack the cup was found."

17"No," Joseph said. "Only the man who stole the cup, he shall be my slave. The rest of you can go on home to your father."

18Then Judah stepped forward and said, "O sir, let me say just this one word to you. Be patient with me for a moment, for I know you can doom me in an instant, as though you were Pharaoh himself.

19"Sir, you asked us if we had a father or a brother, 20and we said, 'Yes, we have a father, an old man, and a child of his old age, a little one. And his brother is dead, and he alone is left of his mother's children, and his father loves him very much.' 21And you said to us, 'Bring him here so that I can see him.' 22But we said to you, 'Sir, the lad cannot leave his father, for his father would die.' 23But you told us, 'Don't come back here unless your youngest brother is with you.' 24So we returned to our father and told him what you had said. 25And when he said, 'Go back again and buy us a little food,' 26we replied, 'We can't, unless you let our youngest brother go with us. Only then may we come.' 27"Then my father said to us, 'You know that my wife had two sons, 28and that one of them went away and never returned—doubtless torn to pieces by some wild animal; I have never seen him since. 29And if you take

New Revised Standard

was light, the men were sent away with their donkeys. 4When they had gone only a short distance from the city, Joseph said to his steward, "Go, follow after the men; and when you overtake them, say to them, 'Why have you returned evil for good? Why have you stolen my silver cup?a 5Is it not from this that my lord drinks? Does he not indeed use it for divination? You have done wrong in doing this.' "

6 When he overtook them, he repeated these words to them. 7They said to him, "Why does my lord speak such words as these? Far be it from your servants that they should do such a thing! 8Look, the money that we found at the top of our sacks, we brought back to you from the land of Canaan; why then would we steal silver or gold from your lord's house? 9Should it be found with any one of your servants, let him die; moreover the rest of us will become my lord's slaves." 10He said, "Even so; in accordance with your words, let it be: he with whom it is found shall become my slave, but the rest of you shall go free." 11Then each one quickly lowered his sack to the ground, and each opened his sack. 12He searched, beginning with the eldest and ending with the youngest; and the cup was found in Benjamin's sack. 13At this they tore their clothes. Then each one loaded his donkey, and they returned to the city.

14 Judah and his brothers came to Joseph's house while he was still there; and they fell to the ground before him. 15Joseph said to them, "What deed is this that you have done? Do you not know that one such as I can practice divination?" 16And Judah said, "What can we say to my lord? What can we speak? How can we clear ourselves? God has found out the guilt of your servants; here we are then, my lord's slaves, both we and also the one in whose possession the cup has been found." 17But he said, "Far be it from me that I should do so! Only the one in whose possession the cup was found shall be my slave; but as for you, go up in peace to your father."

Judah Pleads for Benjamin's Release

18 Then Judah stepped up to him and said, "O my lord, let your servant please speak a word in my lord's ears, and do not be angry with your servant; for you are like Pharaoh himself. 19My lord asked his servants, saying, 'Have you a father or a brother?' 20And we said to my lord, 'We have a father, an old man, and a young brother, the child of his old age. His brother is dead; he alone is left of his mother's children, and his father loves him.' 21Then you said to your servants, 'Bring him down to me, so that I may set my eyes on him.' 22We said to my lord, 'The boy cannot leave his father, for if he should leave his father, his father would die.' 23Then you said to your servants, 'Unless your youngest brother comes down with you, you shall see my face no more.' 24When we went back to your servant my father we told him the words of my lord. 25And when our father said, 'Go again, buy us a little food,' 26we said, 'We cannot go down. Only if our youngest brother goes with us, will we go down; for we cannot see the man's face unless our youngest brother is with us.' 27Then your servant my father said to us, 'You know that my wife bore me two sons; 28one left me, and I said, Surely he has been torn to pieces; and I have never seen him since. 29If you take

---

a Gk Compare Vg: Heb lacks *Why have you stolen my silver cup?*

King James

29And if ye take this also from me, and mischief befall him, ye shall bring down my gray hairs with sorrow to the grave.

30Now therefore when I come to thy servant my father, and the lad *be* not with us; seeing that his life is bound up in the lad's life;

31It shall come to pass, when he seeth that the lad *is* not *with us*, that he will die: and thy servants shall bring down the gray hairs of thy servant our father with sorrow to the grave.

32For thy servant became surety for the lad unto my father, saying, If I bring him not unto thee, then I shall bear the blame to my father for ever.

33Now therefore, I pray thee, let thy servant abide instead of the lad a bondman to my lord; and let the lad go up with his brethren.

34For how shall I go up to my father, and the lad *be* not with me? lest peradventure I see the evil that shall come on my father.

45 THEN JOSEPH could not refrain himself before all them that stood by him; and he cried, Cause every man to go out from me. And there stood no man with him, while Joseph made himself known unto his brethren.

2And he wept aloud: and the Egyptians and the house of Pharaoh heard.

3And Joseph said unto his brethren, I *am* Joseph; doth my father yet live? And his brethren could not answer him; for they were troubled at his presence.

4And Joseph said unto his brethren, Come near to me, I pray you. And they came near. And he said, I *am* Joseph your brother, whom ye sold into Egypt.

5Now therefore be not grieved, nor angry with yourselves, that ye sold me hither: for God did send me before you to preserve life.

6For these two years *hath* the famine *been* in the land: and yet *there are* five years, in the which *there shall* neither *be* earing nor harvest.

7And God sent me before you to preserve you a posterity in the earth, and to save your lives by a great deliverance.

8So now *it was* not you *that* sent me hither, but God: and he hath made me a father to Pharaoh, and lord of all his house, and a ruler throughout all the land of Egypt.

9Haste ye, and go up to my father, and say unto him, Thus saith my son Joseph, God hath made me lord of all Egypt: come down unto me, tarry not:

10And thou shalt dwell in the land of Goshen, and thou shalt be near unto me, thou, and thy children, and thy children's children, and thy flocks, and thy herds, and all that thou hast:

11And there will I nourish thee; for yet *there are* five years of famine; lest thou, and thy household, and all that thou hast, come to poverty.

12And, behold, your eyes see, and the eyes of my brother Benjamin, that *it is* my mouth that speaketh unto you.

13And ye shall tell my father of all my glory in Egypt, and of all that ye have seen; and ye shall haste and bring down my father hither.

14And he fell upon his brother Benjamin's neck, and wept; and Benjamin wept upon his neck.

15Moreover he kissed all his brethren, and wept upon them: and after that his brethren talked with him.

16¶ And the fame thereof was heard in Pharaoh's house, saying, Joseph's brethren are come: and it pleased Pharaoh well, and his servants.

17And Pharaoh said unto Joseph, Say unto thy brethren, This do ye; lade your beasts, and go, get you unto the land of Canaan;

New International

from me too and harm comes to him, you will bring my gray head down to the grave[a] in misery.'

30"So now, if the boy is not with us when I go back to your servant my father and if my father, whose life is closely bound up with the boy's life, 31sees that the boy isn't there, he will die. Your servants will bring the gray head of our father down to the grave in sorrow. 32Your servant guaranteed the boy's safety to my father. I said, 'If I do not bring him back to you, I will bear the blame before you, my father, all my life!'

33"Now then, please let your servant remain here as my lord's slave in place of the boy, and let the boy return with his brothers. 34How can I go back to my father if the boy is not with me? No! Do not let me see the misery that would come upon my father."

Joseph Makes Himself Known

45 THEN JOSEPH could no longer control himself before all his attendants, and he cried out, "Have everyone leave my presence!" So there was no one with Joseph when he made himself known to his brothers. 2And he wept so loudly that the Egyptians heard him, and Pharaoh's household heard about it.

3Joseph said to his brothers, "I am Joseph! Is my father still living?" But his brothers were not able to answer him, because they were terrified at his presence.

4Then Joseph said to his brothers, "Come close to me." When they had done so, he said, "I am your brother Joseph, the one you sold into Egypt! 5And now, do not be distressed and do not be angry with yourselves for selling me here, because it was to save lives that God sent me ahead of you. 6For two years now there has been famine in the land, and for the next five years there will not be plowing and reaping. 7But God sent me ahead of you to preserve for you a remnant on earth and to save your lives by a great deliverance.[b]

8"So then, it was not you who sent me here, but God. He made me father to Pharaoh, lord of his entire household and ruler of all Egypt. 9Now hurry back to my father and say to him, 'This is what your son Joseph says: God has made me lord of all Egypt. Come down to me; don't delay. 10You shall live in the region of Goshen and be near me—you, your children and grandchildren, your flocks and herds, and all you have. 11I will provide for you there, because five years of famine are still to come. Otherwise you and your household and all who belong to you will become destitute.'

12"You can see for yourselves, and so can my brother Benjamin, that it is really I who am speaking to you. 13Tell my father about all the honor accorded me in Egypt and about everything you have seen. And bring my father down here quickly."

14Then he threw his arms around his brother Benjamin and wept, and Benjamin embraced him, weeping. 15And he kissed all his brothers and wept over them. Afterward his brothers talked with him.

16When the news reached Pharaoh's palace that Joseph's brothers had come, Pharaoh and all his officials were pleased. 17Pharaoh said to Joseph, "Tell your brothers, 'Do this: Load your animals and return to the land of Canaan, 18and bring your father and your fami-

---

a 29 Hebrew *Sheol*; also in verse 31   b 7 Or *save you as a great band of survivors*

Living Bible

away his brother from me also, and any harm bef...ls him, I shall die with sorrow.' 30And now, sir, if I go back to my father and the lad is not with us—seeing that our father's life is bound up in the lad's life— 31when he sees that the boy is not with us, our father will die; and we will be responsible for bringing down his gray hairs with sorrow to the grave. 32Sir, I pledged my father that I would take care of the lad. I told him, 'If I don't bring him back to you, I shall bear the blame forever.' 33Please sir, let me stay here as a slave instead of the lad, and let the lad return with his brothers. 34For how shall I return to my father if the lad is not with me? I cannot bear to see what this would do to him."

45 JOSEPH COULD stand it no longer. "Out, all of you," he cried out to his attendants, and he was left alone with his brothers. 2Then he wept aloud. His sobs could be heard throughout the palace, and the news was quickly carried to Pharaoh's palace.

3"I am Joseph!" he said to his brothers. "Is my father still alive?" But his brothers couldn't say a word, they were so stunned with surprise.

4"Come over here," he said. So they came closer. And he said again, "I am Joseph, your brother whom you sold into Egypt! 5But don't be angry with yourselves that you did this to me, for God did it! He sent me here ahead of you to preserve your lives. 6These two years of famine will grow to seven, during which there will be neither plowing nor harvest. 7God has sent me here to keep you and your families alive, so that you will become a great nation. 8Yes, it was God who sent me here, not you! And he has made me a counselor to Pharaoh, and manager of this entire nation, ruler of all the land of Egypt.

9"Hurry, return to my father and tell him, 'Your son Joseph says, "God has made me chief of all the land of Egypt. Come down to me right away! 10You shall live in the land of Goshen so that you can be near me with all your children, your grandchildren, your flocks and herds, and all that you have. 11, 12I will take care of you there" ' (you men are witnesses of my promise, and my brother Benjamin has heard me say it) ' "for there are still five years of famine ahead of us. Otherwise you will come to utter poverty along with all your household." ' 13Tell our father about all my power here in Egypt, and how everyone obeys me. And bring him to me quickly."

14Then, weeping with joy, he embraced Benjamin and Benjamin began weeping too. 15And he did the same with each of his brothers, who finally found their tongues! 16The news soon reached Pharaoh—"Joseph's brothers have come"; and Pharaoh was very happy to hear it, as were his officials.

17Then Pharaoh said to Joseph, "Tell your brothers to load their pack animals and return quickly to their homes in Canaan, 18and to bring your father and all of your

New Revised Standard

this one also from me, and harm comes to him, you will bring down my gray hairs in sorrow to Sheol.' 30Now therefore, when I come to your servant my father and the boy is not with us, then, as his life is bound up in the boy's life, 31when he sees that the boy is not with us, he will die; and your servants will bring down the gray hairs of your servant our father with sorrow to Sheol. 32For your servant became surety for the boy to my father, saying, 'If I do not bring him back to you, then I will bear the blame in the sight of my father all my life.' 33Now therefore, please let your servant remain as a slave to my lord in place of the boy; and let the boy go back with his brothers. 34For how can I go back to my father if the boy is not with me? I fear to see the suffering that would come upon my father."

Joseph Reveals Himself to His Brothers

45 THEN JOSEPH could no longer control himself before all those who stood by him, and he cried out, "Send everyone away from me." So no one stayed with him when Joseph made himself known to his brothers. 2And he wept so loudly that the Egyptians heard it, and the household of Pharaoh heard it. 3Joseph said to his brothers, "I am Joseph. Is my father still alive?" But his brothers could not answer him, so dismayed were they at his presence.

4 Then Joseph said to his brothers, "Come closer to me." And they came closer. He said, "I am your brother, Joseph, whom you sold into Egypt. 5And now do not be distressed, or angry with yourselves, because you sold me here; for God sent me before you to preserve life. 6For the famine has been in the land these two years; and there are five more years in which there will be neither plowing nor harvest. 7God sent me before you to preserve for you a remnant on earth, and to keep alive for you many survivors. 8So it was not you who sent me here, but God; he has made me a father to Pharaoh, and lord of all his house and ruler over all the land of Egypt. 9Hurry and go up to my father and say to him, 'Thus says your son Joseph, God has made me lord of all Egypt; come down to me, do not delay. 10You shall settle in the land of Goshen, and you shall be near me, you and your children and your children's children, as well as your flocks, your herds, and all that you have. 11I will provide for you there—since there are five more years of famine to come—so that you and your household, and all that you have, will not come to poverty.' 12And now your eyes and the eyes of my brother Benjamin see that it is my own mouth that speaks to you. 13You must tell my father how greatly I am honored in Egypt, and all that you have seen. Hurry and bring my father down here." 14Then he fell upon his brother Benjamin's neck and wept, while Benjamin wept upon his neck. 15And he kissed all his brothers and wept upon them; and after that his brothers talked with him.

16 When the report was heard in Pharaoh's house, "Joseph's brothers have come," Pharaoh and his servants were pleased. 17Pharaoh said to Joseph, "Say to your brothers, 'Do this: load your animals and go back to the land of Canaan. 18Take your father and your

King James

18And take your father and your households, and come unto me: and I will give you the good of the land of Egypt, and ye shall eat the fat of the land.

19Now thou art commanded, this do ye; take you wagons out of the land of Egypt for your little ones, and for your wives, and bring your father, and come.

20Also regard not your stuff; for the good of all the land of Egypt *is* yours.

21And the children of Israel did so: and Joseph gave them wagons, according to the commandment of Pharaoh, and gave them provision for the way.

22To all of them he gave each man changes of raiment; but to Benjamin he gave three hundred *pieces* of silver, and five changes of raiment.

23And to his father he sent after this *manner;* ten asses laden with the good things of Egypt, and ten she asses laden with corn and bread and meat for his father by the way.

24So he sent his brethren away, and they departed: and he said unto them, See that ye fall not out by the way.

25¶ And they went up out of Egypt, and came into the land of Canaan unto Jacob their father,

26And told him, saying, Joseph *is* yet alive, and he *is* governor over all the land of Egypt. And Jacob's heart fainted, for he believed them not.

27And they told him all the words of Joseph, which he had said unto them: and when he saw the wagons which Joseph had sent to carry him, the spirit of Jacob their father revived:

28And Israel said, *It is* enough; Joseph my son *is* yet alive: I will go and see him before I die.

46 AND ISRAEL took his journey with all that he had, and came to Beer-sheba, and offered sacrifices unto the God of his father Isaac.

2And God spake unto Israel in the visions of the night, and said, Jacob, Jacob. And he said, Here *am* I.

3And he said, I *am* God, the God of thy father: fear not to go down into Egypt; for I will there make of thee a great nation:

4I will go down with thee into Egypt; and I will also surely bring thee up *again:* and Joseph shall put his hand upon thine eyes.

5And Jacob rose up from Beer-sheba: and the sons of Israel carried Jacob their father, and their little ones, and their wives, in the wagons which Pharaoh had sent to carry him.

6And they took their cattle, and their goods, which they had gotten in the land of Canaan, and came into Egypt, Jacob, and all his seed with him:

7His sons, and his sons' sons with him, his daughters, and his sons' daughters, and all his seed brought he with him into Egypt.

8¶ And these *are* the names of the children of Israel, which came into Egypt, Jacob and his sons: Reuben, Jacob's firstborn.

9And the sons of Reuben; Hanoch, and Phallu, and Hezron, and Carmi.

10¶ And the sons of Simeon; Jemuel, and Jamin, and Ohad, and Jachin, and Zohar, and Shaul the son of a Canaanitish woman.

11¶ And the sons of Levi; Gershon, Kohath, and Merari.

12¶ And the sons of Judah; Er, and Onan, and Shelah, and Pharez, and Zerah: but Er and Onan died in the land of Canaan. And the sons of Pharez were Hezron and Hamul.

New International

lies back to me. I will give you the best of the land of Egypt and you can enjoy the fat of the land.'

19"You are also directed to tell them, 'Do this: Take some carts from Egypt for your children and your wives, and get your father and come. 20Never mind about your belongings, because the best of all Egypt will be yours.' "

21So the sons of Israel did this. Joseph gave them carts, as Pharaoh had commanded, and he also gave them provisions for their journey. 22To each of them he gave new clothing, but to Benjamin he gave three hundred shekels[a] of silver and five sets of clothes. 23And this is what he sent to his father: ten donkeys loaded with the best things of Egypt, and ten female donkeys loaded with grain and bread and other provisions for his journey. 24Then he sent his brothers away, and as they were leaving he said to them, "Don't quarrel on the way!"

25So they went up out of Egypt and came to their father Jacob in the land of Canaan. 26They told him, "Joseph is still alive! In fact, he is ruler of all Egypt." Jacob was stunned; he did not believe them. 27But when they told him everything Joseph had said to them, and when he saw the carts Joseph had sent to carry him back, the spirit of their father Jacob revived. 28And Israel said, "I'm convinced! My son Joseph is still alive. I will go and see him before I die."

Jacob Goes to Egypt

46 SO ISRAEL set out with all that was his, and when he reached Beersheba, he offered sacrifices to the God of his father Isaac.

2And God spoke to Israel in a vision at night and said, "Jacob! Jacob!"

"Here I am," he replied.

3"I am God, the God of your father," he said. "Do not be afraid to go down to Egypt, for I will make you into a great nation there. 4I will go down to Egypt with you, and I will surely bring you back again. And Joseph's own hand will close your eyes."

5Then Jacob left Beersheba, and Israel's sons took their father Jacob and their children and their wives in the carts that Pharaoh had sent to transport him. 6They also took with them their livestock and the possessions they had acquired in Canaan, and Jacob and all his offspring went to Egypt. 7He took with him to Egypt his sons and grandsons and his daughters and granddaughters—all his offspring.

8These are the names of the sons of Israel (Jacob and his descendants) who went to Egypt:

Reuben the firstborn of Jacob.
9The sons of Reuben:
Hanoch, Pallu, Hezron and Carmi.
10The sons of Simeon:
Jemuel, Jamin, Ohad, Jakin, Zohar and Shaul the son of a Canaanite woman.
11The sons of Levi:
Gershon, Kohath and Merari.
12The sons of Judah:
Er, Onan, Shelah, Perez and Zerah (but Er and Onan had died in the land of Canaan).
The sons of Perez:
Hezron and Hamul.

---

[a] 22 That is, about 7 1/2 pounds (about 3.5 kilograms)

Living Bible

families and come here to Egypt to live. Tell them, 'Pharaoh will assign to you the very best territory in the land of Egypt. You shall live off the fat of the land!' 19And tell your brothers to take wagons from Egypt to carry their wives and little ones, and to bring your father here. 20Don't worry about your property, for the best of all the land of Egypt is yours."

21So Joseph gave them wagons, as Pharaoh had commanded, and provisions for the journey, 22and he gave each of them new clothes—but to Benjamin he gave five changes of clothes and three hundred pieces of silver! 23He sent his father ten donkey-loads of the good things of Egypt, and ten donkeys loaded with grain and all kinds of other food, to eat on his journey. 24So he sent his brothers off.

"Don't quarrel along the way!" was his parting shot! 25And leaving, they returned to the land of Canaan, to Jacob their father.

26"Joseph is alive," they shouted to him. "And he is ruler over all the land of Egypt!" But Jacob's heart was like a stone; he couldn't take it in. 27But when they had given him Joseph's messages, and when he saw the wagons filled with food that Joseph had sent him, his spirit revived.

28And he said, "It must be true! Joseph my son is alive! I will go and see him before I die."

46 SO ISRAEL set out with all his possessions, and came to Beer-sheba, and offered sacrifices there to the God of his father Isaac. 2During the night God spoke to him in a vision.

"Jacob! Jacob!" he called.

"Yes?" Jacob answered.

3, 4"I am God," the voice replied, "the God of your father. Don't be afraid to go down to Egypt, for I will see to it that you become a great nation there. And I will go down with you into Egypt and I will bring your descendants back again; but you shall die in Egypt with Joseph at your side."

5So Jacob left Beer-sheba, and his sons brought him to Egypt, along with their little ones and their wives, in the wagons Pharaoh had provided for them. 6They brought their livestock too, and all their belongings accumulated in the land of Canaan, and came to Egypt—Jacob and all his children, 7sons and daughters, grandsons and granddaughters—all his loved ones. 8–14Here are the names of his sons and grandchildren who went with him into Egypt:

Reuben, his oldest son;

Reuben's sons: Hanoch, Pallu, Hezron, and Carmi.

Simeon and his sons: Jemuel, Jamin, Ohad, Jachin, Zohar, and Shaul (Shaul's mother was a girl from Canaan).

Levi and his sons: Gershon, Kohath, Merari.

Judah and his sons: Er, Onan, Shelah, Perez, Zerah (however, Er and Onan died while still in Canaan, before Israel went to Egypt).

The sons of Perez were Hezron and Hamul.

New Revised Standard

households and come to me, so that I may give you the best of the land of Egypt, and you may enjoy the fat of the land.' 19You are further charged to say, 'Do this: take wagons from the land of Egypt for your little ones and for your wives, and bring your father, and come. 20Give no thought to your possessions, for the best of all the land of Egypt is yours.'"

21 The sons of Israel did so. Joseph gave them wagons according to the instruction of Pharaoh, and he gave them provisions for the journey. 22To each one of them he gave a set of garments; but to Benjamin he gave three hundred pieces of silver and five sets of garments. 23To his father he sent the following: ten donkeys loaded with the good things of Egypt, and ten female donkeys loaded with grain, bread, and provision for his father on the journey. 24Then he sent his brothers on their way, and as they were leaving he said to them, "Do not quarrelb along the way."

25 So they went up out of Egypt and came to their father Jacob in the land of Canaan. 26And they told him, "Joseph is still alive! He is even ruler over all the land of Egypt." He was stunned; he could not believe them. 27But when they told him all the words of Joseph that he had said to them, and when he saw the wagons that Joseph had sent to carry him, the spirit of their father Jacob revived. 28Israel said, "Enough! My son Joseph is still alive. I must go and see him before I die."

Jacob Brings His Whole Family to Egypt

46 WHEN ISRAEL set out on his journey with all that he had and came to Beer-sheba, he offered sacrifices to the God of his father Isaac. 2God spoke to Israel in visions of the night, and said, "Jacob, Jacob." And he said, "Here I am." 3Then he said, "I am God,c the God of your father; do not be afraid to go down to Egypt, for I will make of you a great nation there. 4I myself will go down with you to Egypt, and I will also bring you up again; and Joseph's own hand shall close your eyes."

5 Then Jacob set out from Beer-sheba; and the sons of Israel carried their father Jacob, their little ones, and their wives, in the wagons that Pharaoh had sent to carry him. 6They also took their livestock and the goods that they had acquired in the land of Canaan, and they came into Egypt, Jacob and all his offspring with him, 7his sons, and his sons' sons with him, his daughters, and his sons' daughters; all his offspring he brought with him into Egypt.

8 Now these are the names of the Israelites, Jacob and his offspring, who came to Egypt. Reuben, Jacob's firstborn, 9and the children of Reuben: Hanoch, Pallu, Hezron, and Carmi. 10The children of Simeon: Jemuel, Jamin, Ohad, Jachin, Zohar, and Shaul,d the son of a Canaanite woman. 11The children of Levi: Gershon, Kohath, and Merari. 12The children of Judah: Er, Onan, Shelah, Perez, and Zerah (but Er and Onan died in the land of Canaan); and the children of Perez were Hezron and Hamul. 13The children of Issachar: Tola, Puvah,

b Or be agitated   c Heb the God   d Or Saul

King James

13¶ And the sons of Issachar; Tola, and Phuvah, and Job, and Shimron.

14¶ And the sons of Zebulun; Sered, and Elon, and Jahleel.

15These *be* the sons of Leah, which she bare unto Jacob in Padan-aram, with his daughter Dinah: all the souls of his sons and his daughters *were* thirty and three.

16¶ And the sons of Gad; Ziphion, and Haggi, Shuni, and Ezbon, Eri, and Arodi, and Areli.

17¶ And the sons of Asher; Jimnah, and Ishuah, and Isui, and Beriah, and Serah their sister: and the sons of Beriah; Heber, and Malchiel.

18These *are* the sons of Zilpah, whom Laban gave to Leah his daughter, and these she bare unto Jacob, *even* sixteen souls.

19The sons of Rachel Jacob's wife; Joseph, and Benjamin.

20¶ And unto Joseph in the land of Egypt were born Manasseh and Ephraim, which Asenath the daughter of Poti-pherah priest of On bare unto him.

21¶ And the sons of Benjamin *were* Belah, and Becher, and Ashbel, Gera, and Naaman, Ehi, and Rosh, Muppim, and Huppim, and Ard.

22These *are* the sons of Rachel, which were born to Jacob: all the souls *were* fourteen.

23¶ And the sons of Dan; Hushim.

24¶ And the sons of Naphtali; Jahzeel, and Guni, and Jezer, and Shillem.

25These *are* the sons of Bilhah, which Laban gave unto Rachel his daughter, and she bare these unto Jacob: all the souls *were* seven.

26All the souls that came with Jacob into Egypt, which came out of his loins, besides Jacob's sons' wives, all the souls *were* threescore and six;

27And the sons of Joseph, which were born him in Egypt, *were* two souls: all the souls of the house of Jacob, which came into Egypt, *were* threescore and ten.

28¶ And he sent Judah before him unto Joseph, to direct his face unto Goshen; and they came into the land of Goshen.

29And Joseph made ready his chariot, and went up to meet Israel his father, to Goshen, and presented himself unto him; and he fell on his neck, and wept on his neck a good while.

30And Israel said unto Joseph, Now let me die, since I have seen thy face, because thou *art* yet alive.

31And Joseph said unto his brethren, and unto his father's house, I will go up, and show Pharaoh, and say unto him, My brethren, and my father's house, which *were* in the land of Canaan, are come unto me;

32And the men *are* shepherds, for their trade hath been to feed cattle; and they have brought their flocks, and their herds, and all that they have.

33And it shall come to pass, when Pharaoh shall call you, and shall say, What *is* your occupation?

34That ye shall say, Thy servants' trade hath been about cattle from our youth even until now, both we, *and* also our fathers: that ye may dwell in the land of Goshen; for every shepherd *is* an abomination unto the Egyptians.

New International

13The sons of Issachar:
  Tola, Puah,[a] Jashub[b] and Shimron.
14The sons of Zebulun:
  Sered, Elon and Jahleel.
15These were the sons Leah bore to Jacob in Paddan Aram,[c] besides his daughter Dinah. These sons and daughters of his were thirty-three in all.

16The sons of Gad:
  Zephon,[d] Haggi, Shuni, Ezbon, Eri, Arodi and Areli.
17The sons of Asher:
  Imnah, Ishvah, Ishvi and Beriah.
  Their sister was Serah.
  The sons of Beriah:
    Heber and Malkiel.
18These were the children born to Jacob by Zilpah, whom Laban had given to his daughter Leah—sixteen in all.

19The sons of Jacob's wife Rachel:
  Joseph and Benjamin. 20In Egypt, Manasseh and Ephraim were born to Joseph by Asenath daughter of Potiphera, priest of On.[e]
21The sons of Benjamin:
  Bela, Beker, Ashbel, Gera, Naaman, Ehi, Rosh, Muppim, Huppim and Ard.
22These were the sons of Rachel who were born to Jacob—fourteen in all.

23The son of Dan:
  Hushim.
24The sons of Naphtali:
  Jahziel, Guni, Jezer and Shillem.
25These were the sons born to Jacob by Bilhah, whom Laban had given to his daughter Rachel—seven in all.

26All those who went to Egypt with Jacob—those who were his direct descendants, not counting his sons' wives—numbered sixty-six persons. 27With the two sons[f] who had been born to Joseph in Egypt, the members of Jacob's family, which went to Egypt, were seventy[g] in all.

28Now Jacob sent Judah ahead of him to Joseph to get directions to Goshen. When they arrived in the region of Goshen, 29Joseph had his chariot made ready and went to Goshen to meet his father Israel. As soon as Joseph appeared before him, he threw his arms around his father[h] and wept for a long time.

30Israel said to Joseph, "Now I am ready to die, since I have seen for myself that you are still alive."

31Then Joseph said to his brothers and to his father's household, "I will go up and speak to Pharaoh and will say to him, 'My brothers and my father's household, who were living in the land of Canaan, have come to me. 32The men are shepherds; they tend livestock, and they have brought along their flocks and herds and everything they own.' 33When Pharaoh calls you in and asks, 'What is your occupation?' 34you should answer, 'Your servants have tended livestock from our boyhood on, just as our fathers did.' Then you will be allowed to settle in the region of Goshen, for all shepherds are detestable to the Egyptians."

---

a *13* Samaritan Pentateuch and Syriac (see also 1 Chron. 7:1); Masoretic Text *Puvah*   b *13* Samaritan Pentateuch and some Septuagint manuscripts (see also Num. 26:24 and 1 Chron. 7:1); Masoretic Text *Iob*   c *15* That is, Northwest Mesopotamia   d *16* Samaritan Pentateuch and Septuagint (see also Num. 26:15); Masoretic Text *Ziphion*   e *20* That is, Heliopolis   f *27* Hebrew; Septuagint *the nine children*   g *27* Hebrew (see also Exodus 1:5 and footnote); Septuagint (see also Acts 7:14) *seventy-five*   h *29* Hebrew *around him*

Living Bible

Issachar and his sons: Tola, Puvah, Iob, Shimron.
Zebulun and his sons: Sered, Elon, Jahleel.

15So these descendants of Jacob and Leah, not including their daughter Dinah, born to Jacob in Paddan-aram, were thirty-three in all.

16, 17Also accompanying him were:
Gad and his sons: Ziphion, Haggi, Shuni,
Ezbon, Eri, Arodi, and Areli.
Asher and his sons: Imnah, Ishvah, Ishvi,
Beriah, and a sister, Serah.
Beriah's sons were Heber and Malchiel.

18These sixteen persons were the sons of Jacob and Zilpah, the slave-girl given to Leah by her father, Laban.

19-22Also in the total of Jacob's household were these fourteen sons and descendants of Jacob and Rachel:
Joseph and Benjamin;
Joseph's sons, born in the land of Egypt, were Manasseh and Ephraim (their mother was Asenath, the daughter of Potiphera, priest of Heliopolis);
Benjamin's sons: Bela, Becher, Ashbel, Gera, Naaman, Ehi, Rosh, Muppim, Huppim, and Ard.

23, 24, 25Also in the group were these seven sons and descendants of Jacob and Bilhah, the slave-girl given to Rachel by her father, Laban:
Dan and his son: Hushim.
Naphtali and his sons: Jahzeel, Guni, Jezer, and Shillem.

26So the total number of those going to Egypt, of his own descendants, not counting the wives of Jacob's sons, was sixty-six. 27With Joseph and his two sons included, this total of Jacob's household there in Egypt totaled seventy.

28Jacob sent Judah on ahead to tell Joseph that they were on the way, and would soon arrive in Goshen—which they did. 29Joseph jumped into his chariot and journeyed to Goshen to meet his father and they fell into each other's arms and wept a long while.

30Then Israel said to Joseph, "Now let me die, for I have seen you again and know you are alive."

31And Joseph said to his brothers and to all their households, "I'll go and tell Pharaoh that you are here, and that you have come from the land of Canaan to join me. 32And I will tell him, 'These men are shepherds. They have brought with them their flocks and herds and everything they own.' 33So when Pharaoh calls you and asks you about your occupation, 34tell him, 'We have been shepherds from our youth, as our fathers have been for many generations.' When you tell him this, he will let you live here in the land of Goshen." For shepherds were despised and hated in other parts of Egypt.

New Revised Standard

Jashub,i and Shimron. 14The children of Zebulun: Sered, Elon, and Jahleel 15(these are the sons of Leah, whom she bore to Jacob in Paddan-aram, together with his daughter Dinah; in all his sons and his daughters numbered thirty-three). 16The children of Gad: Ziphion, Haggi, Shuni, Ezbon, Eri, Arodi, and Areli. 17The children of Asher: Imnah, Ishvah, Ishvi, Beriah, and their sister Serah. The children of Beriah: Heber and Malchiel 18(these are the children of Zilpah, whom Laban gave to his daughter Leah; and these she bore to Jacob—sixteen persons). 19The children of Jacob's wife Rachel: Joseph and Benjamin. 20To Joseph in the land of Egypt were born Manasseh and Ephraim, whom Asenath daughter of Potiphera, priest of On, bore to him. 21The children of Benjamin: Bela, Becher, Ashbel, Gera, Naaman, Ehi, Rosh, Muppim, Huppim, and Ard 22(these are the children of Rachel, who were born to Jacob—fourteen persons in all). 23The children of Dan: Hashum.j 24The children of Naphtali: Jahzeel, Guni, Jezer, and Shillem 25(these are the children of Bilhah, whom Laban gave to his daughter Rachel, and these she bore to Jacob—seven persons in all). 26All the persons belonging to Jacob who came into Egypt, who were his own offspring, not including the wives of his sons, were sixty-six persons in all. 27The children of Joseph, who were born to him in Egypt, were two; all the persons of the house of Jacob who came into Egypt were seventy.

Jacob Settles in Goshen

28 Israelk sent Judah ahead to Joseph to lead the way before him into Goshen. When they came to the land of Goshen, 29Joseph made ready his chariot and went up to meet his father Israel in Goshen. He presented himself to him, fell on his neck, and wept on his neck a good while. 30Israel said to Joseph, "I can die now, having seen for myself that you are still alive." 31Joseph said to his brothers and to his father's household, "I will go up and tell Pharaoh, and will say to him, 'My brothers and my father's household, who were in the land of Canaan, have come to me. 32The men are shepherds, for they have been keepers of livestock; and they have brought their flocks, and their herds, and all that they have.' 33When Pharaoh calls you, and says, 'What is your occupation?' 34you shall say, 'Your servants have been keepers of livestock from our youth even until now, both we and our ancestors'—in order that you may settle in the land of Goshen, because all shepherds are abhorrent to the Egyptians."

i Compare Sam Gk Num 26.24 1 Chr 7.1: MT Iob   j Gk: Heb Hushim   k Heb He

King James

47 THEN JOSEPH came and told Pharaoh, and said, My father and my brethren, and their flocks, and their herds, and all that they have, are come out of the land of Canaan; and, behold, they *are* in the land of Goshen.

2And he took some of his brethren, *even* five men, and presented them unto Pharaoh.

3And Pharaoh said unto his brethren, What *is* your occupation? And they said unto Pharaoh, Thy servants *are* shepherds, both we, *and* also our fathers.

4They said moreover unto Pharaoh, For to sojourn in the land are we come; for thy servants have no pasture for their flocks; for the famine *is* sore in the land of Canaan: now therefore, we pray thee, let thy servants dwell in the land of Goshen.

5And Pharaoh spake unto Joseph, saying, Thy father and thy brethren are come unto thee:

6The land of Egypt *is* before thee; in the best of the land make thy father and brethren to dwell; in the land of Goshen let them dwell: and if thou knowest *any* men of activity among them, then make them rulers over my cattle.

7And Joseph brought in Jacob his father, and set him before Pharaoh: and Jacob blessed Pharaoh.

8And Pharaoh said unto Jacob, How old *art* thou?

9And Jacob said unto Pharaoh, The days of the years of my pilgrimage *are* an hundred and thirty years: few and evil have the days of the years of my life been, and have not attained unto the days of the years of the life of my fathers in the days of their pilgrimage.

10And Jacob blessed Pharaoh, and went out from before Pharaoh.

11¶ And Joseph placed his father and his brethren, and gave them a possession in the land of Egypt, in the best of the land, in the land of Rameses, as Pharaoh had commanded.

12And Joseph nourished his father, and his brethren, and all his father's household, with bread, according to *their* families.

13¶ And *there was* no bread in all the land; for the famine *was* very sore, so that the land of Egypt and *all* the land of Canaan fainted by reason of the famine.

14And Joseph gathered up all the money that was found in the land of Egypt, and in the land of Canaan, for the corn which they bought: and Joseph brought the money into Pharaoh's house.

15And when money failed in the land of Egypt, and in the land of Canaan, all the Egyptians came unto Joseph, and said, Give us bread: for why should we die in thy presence? for the money faileth.

16And Joseph said, Give your cattle; and I will give you for your cattle, if money fail.

17And they brought their cattle unto Joseph: and Joseph gave them bread *in exchange* for horses, and for the flocks, and for the cattle of the herds, and for the asses: and he fed them with bread for all their cattle for that year.

18When that year was ended, they came unto him the second year, and said unto him, We will not hide *it* from my lord, how that our money is spent; my lord also hath our herds of cattle; there is not aught left in the sight of my lord, but our bodies, and our lands:

19Wherefore shall we die before thine eyes, both we and our land? buy us and our land for bread, and we and our land will be servants unto Pharaoh: and give *us* seed, that we may live, and not die, that the land be not desolate.

20And Joseph bought all the land of Egypt for Pharaoh; for the Egyptians sold every man his field, because the famine prevailed over them: so the land became Pharaoh's.

21And as for the people, he removed them to cities from *one* end of the borders of Egypt even to the *other* end thereof.

New International

47 JOSEPH WENT and told Pharaoh, "My father and brothers, with their flocks and herds and everything they own, have come from the land of Canaan and are now in Goshen." 2He chose five of his brothers and presented them before Pharaoh.

3Pharaoh asked the brothers, "What is your occupation?"

"Your servants are shepherds," they replied to Pharaoh, "just as our fathers were." 4They also said to him, "We have come to live here awhile, because the famine is severe in Canaan and your servants' flocks have no pasture. So now, please let your servants settle in Goshen."

5Pharaoh said to Joseph, "Your father and your brothers have come to you, 6and the land of Egypt is before you; settle your father and your brothers in the best part of the land. Let them live in Goshen. And if you know of any among them with special ability, put them in charge of my own livestock."

7Then Joseph brought his father Jacob in and presented him before Pharaoh. After Jacob blessed[a] Pharaoh, 8Pharaoh asked him, "How old are you?"

9And Jacob said to Pharaoh, "The years of my pilgrimage are a hundred and thirty. My years have been few and difficult, and they do not equal the years of the pilgrimage of my fathers." 10Then Jacob blessed[b] Pharaoh and went out from his presence.

11So Joseph settled his father and his brothers in Egypt and gave them property in the best part of the land, the district of Rameses, as Pharaoh directed. 12Joseph also provided his father and his brothers and all his father's household with food, according to the number of their children.

Joseph and the Famine

13There was no food, however, in the whole region because the famine was severe; both Egypt and Canaan wasted away because of the famine. 14Joseph collected all the money that was to be found in Egypt and Canaan in payment for the grain they were buying, and he brought it to Pharaoh's palace. 15When the money of the people of Egypt and Canaan was gone, all Egypt came to Joseph and said, "Give us food. Why should we die before your eyes? Our money is used up."

16"Then bring your livestock," said Joseph. "I will sell you food in exchange for your livestock, since your money is gone." 17So they brought their livestock to Joseph, and he gave them food in exchange for their horses, their sheep and goats, their cattle and donkeys. And he brought them through that year with food in exchange for all their livestock.

18When that year was over, they came to him the following year and said, "We cannot hide from our lord the fact that since our money is gone and our livestock belongs to you, there is nothing left for our lord except our bodies and our land. 19Why should we perish before your eyes—we and our land as well? Buy us and our land in exchange for food, and we with our land will be in bondage to Pharaoh. Give us seed so that we may live and not die, and that the land may not become desolate."

20So Joseph bought all the land in Egypt for Pharaoh. The Egyptians, one and all, sold their fields, because the famine was too severe for them. The land became Pharaoh's, 21and Joseph reduced the people to servitude,[c] from one end of Egypt to the other. 22However, he did

---

[a] 7 Or *greeted*　[b] 10 Or *said farewell to*　[c] 21 Samaritan Pentateuch and Septuagint (see also Vulgate); Masoretic Text *and he moved the people into the cities*

Living Bible

47 UPON THEIR arrival, Joseph went in to see Pharaoh.

"My father and my brothers are here from Canaan," he reported, "with all their flocks and herds and possessions. They wish to settle in the land of Goshen."

2He took five of his brothers with him, and presented them to Pharaoh.

3Pharaoh asked them, "What is your occupation?"

And they replied, "We are shepherds like our ancestors. 4We have come to live here in Egypt, for there is no pasture for our flocks in Canaan—the famine is very bitter there. We request permission to live in the land of Goshen."

5, 6And Pharaoh said to Joseph, "Choose anywhere you like for them to live. Give them the best land of Egypt. The land of Goshen will be fine. And if any of them are capable, put them in charge of my flocks, too."

7Then Joseph brought his father Jacob to Pharaoh. And Jacob blessed Pharaoh.

8"How old are you?" Pharaoh asked him.

9Jacob replied, "I have lived 130 long, hard years, and I am not nearly as old as many of my ancestors."

10Then Jacob blessed Pharaoh again before he left.

11So Joseph assigned the best land of Egypt—the land of Rameses—to his father and brothers, just as Pharaoh had commanded. 12And Joseph furnished food to them in accordance with the number of their dependents.

13The famine became worse and worse, so that all the land of Egypt and Canaan were starving. 14Joseph collected all the money in Egypt and Canaan in exchange for grain, and he brought the money to Pharaoh's treasure-houses. 15When the people were out of money, they came to Joseph crying again for food.

"Our money is gone," they said, "but give us bread; for why should we die?"

16"Well then," Joseph replied, "give me your livestock. I will trade you food in exchange."

17So they brought their cattle to Joseph in exchange for food. Soon all the horses, flocks, herds, and donkeys of Egypt were in Pharaoh's possession.

18The next year they came again and said, "Our money is gone, and our cattle are yours, and there is nothing left but our bodies and land. 19Why should we die? Buy us and our land and we will be serfs to Pharaoh. We will trade ourselves for food, then we will live, and the land won't be abandoned."

20So Joseph bought all the land of Egypt for Pharaoh; all the Egyptians sold him their fields because the famine was so severe. And the land became Pharaoh's. 21Thus all the people of Egypt became Pharaoh's serfs. 22The

New Revised Standard

47 SO JOSEPH went and told Pharaoh, "My father and my brothers, with their flocks and herds and all that they possess, have come from the land of Canaan; they are now in the land of Goshen." 2From among his brothers he took five men and presented them to Pharaoh. 3Pharaoh said to his brothers, "What is your occupation?" And they said to Pharaoh, "Your servants are shepherds, as our ancestors were." 4They said to Pharaoh, "We have come to reside as aliens in the land; for there is no pasture for your servants' flocks since the famine is severe in the land of Canaan. Now, we ask you, let your servants settle in the land of Goshen." 5Then Pharaoh said to Joseph, "Your father and your brothers have come to you. 6The land of Egypt is before you; settle your father and your brothers in the best part of the land; let them live in the land of Goshen; and if you know that there are capable men among them, put them in charge of my livestock."

7 Then Joseph brought in his father Jacob, and presented him before Pharaoh, and Jacob blessed Pharaoh. 8Pharaoh said to Jacob, "How many are the years of your life?" 9Jacob said to Pharaoh, "The years of my earthly sojourn are one hundred thirty; few and hard have been the years of my life. They do not compare with the years of the life of my ancestors during their long sojourn." 10Then Jacob blessed Pharaoh, and went out from the presence of Pharaoh. 11Joseph settled his father and his brothers, and granted them a holding in the land of Egypt, in the best part of the land, in the land of Rameses, as Pharaoh had instructed. 12And Joseph provided his father, his brothers, and all his father's household with food, according to the number of their dependents.

The Famine in Egypt

13 Now there was no food in all the land, for the famine was very severe. The land of Egypt and the land of Canaan languished because of the famine. 14Joseph collected all the money to be found in the land of Egypt and in the land of Canaan, in exchange for the grain that they bought; and Joseph brought the money into Pharaoh's house. 15When the money from the land of Egypt and from the land of Canaan was spent, all the Egyptians came to Joseph, and said, "Give us food! Why should we die before your eyes? For our money is gone." 16And Joseph answered, "Give me your livestock, and I will give you food in exchange for your livestock, if your money is gone." 17So they brought their livestock to Joseph; and Joseph gave them food in exchange for the horses, the flocks, the herds, and the donkeys. That year he supplied them with food in exchange for all their livestock. 18When that year was ended, they came to him the following year, and said to him, "We can not hide from my lord that our money is all spent; and the herds of cattle are my lord's. There is nothing left in the sight of my lord but our bodies and our lands. 19Shall we die before your eyes, both we and our land? Buy us and our land in exchange for food. We with our land will become slaves to Pharaoh; just give us seed, so that we may live and not die, and that the land may not become desolate."

20 So Joseph bought all the land of Egypt for Pharaoh. All the Egyptians sold their fields, because the famine was severe upon them; and the land became Pharaoh's. 21As for the people, he made slaves of them*d* from one end of Egypt to the other. 22Only the land of

---

d Sam Gk Compare Vg: MT He removed them to the cities

King James

22Only the land of the priests bought he not; for the priests had a portion *assigned them* of Pharaoh, and did eat their portion which Pharaoh gave them: wherefore they sold not their lands.

23Then Joseph said unto the people, Behold, I have bought you this day and your land for Pharaoh: lo, *here is* seed for you, and ye shall sow the land.

24And it shall come to pass in the increase, that ye shall give the fifth *part* unto Pharaoh, and four parts shall be your own, for seed of the field, and for your food, and for them of your households, and for food for your little ones.

25And they said, Thou hast saved our lives: let us find grace in the sight of my lord, and we will be Pharaoh's servants.

26And Joseph made it a law over the land of Egypt unto this day, *that* Pharaoh should have the fifth *part;* except the land of the priests only, *which* became not Pharaoh's.

27¶ And Israel dwelt in the land of Egypt, in the country of Goshen; and they had possessions therein, and grew, and multiplied exceedingly.

28And Jacob lived in the land of Egypt seventeen years: so the whole age of Jacob was an hundred forty and seven years.

29And the time drew nigh that Israel must die: and he called his son Joseph, and said unto him, If now I have found grace in thy sight, put, I pray thee, thy hand under my thigh, and deal kindly and truly with me; bury me not, I pray thee, in Egypt:

30But I will lie with my fathers, and thou shalt carry me out of Egypt, and bury me in their buryingplace. And he said, I will do as thou hast said.

31And he said, Swear unto me. And he sware unto him. And Israel bowed himself upon the bed's head.

48 AND IT came to pass after these things, that *one* told Joseph, Behold, thy father *is* sick: and he took with him his two sons, Manasseh and Ephraim.

2And *one* told Jacob, and said, Behold, thy son Joseph cometh unto thee: and Israel strengthened himself, and sat upon the bed.

3And Jacob said unto Joseph, God Almighty appeared unto me at Luz in the land of Canaan, and blessed me,

4And said unto me, Behold, I will make thee fruitful, and multiply thee, and I will make of thee a multitude of people; and will give this land to thy seed after thee *for* an everlasting possession.

5¶ And now thy two sons, Ephraim and Manasseh, which were born unto thee in the land of Egypt before I came unto thee into Egypt, *are* mine; as Reuben and Simeon, they shall be mine.

6And thy issue, which thou begettest after them, shall be thine, *and* shall be called after the name of their brethren in their inheritance.

7And as for me, when I came from Padan, Rachel died by me in the land of Canaan in the way, when yet *there was* but a little way to come unto Ephrath: and I buried her there in the way of Ephrath; the same *is* Bethlehem.

8And Israel beheld Joseph's sons, and said, Who *are* these?

9And Joseph said unto his father, They *are* my sons, whom God hath given me in this *place.* And he said, Bring them, I pray thee, unto me, and I will bless them.

10Now the eyes of Israel were dim for age, *so that* he could not see. And he brought them near unto him; and he kissed them, and embraced them.

New International

not buy the land of the priests, because they received a regular allotment from Pharaoh and had food enough from the allotment Pharaoh gave them. That is why they did not sell their land.

23Joseph said to the people, "Now that I have bought you and your land today for Pharaoh, here is seed for you so you can plant the ground. 24But when the crop comes in, give a fifth of it to Pharaoh. The other four-fifths you may keep as seed for the fields and as food for yourselves and your households and your children."

25"You have saved our lives," they said. "May we find favor in the eyes of our lord; we will be in bondage to Pharaoh."

26So Joseph established it as a law concerning land in Egypt—still in force today—that a fifth of the produce belongs to Pharaoh. It was only the land of the priests that did not become Pharaoh's.

27Now the Israelites settled in Egypt in the region of Goshen. They acquired property there and were fruitful and increased greatly in number.

28Jacob lived in Egypt seventeen years, and the years of his life were a hundred and forty-seven. 29When the time drew near for Israel to die, he called for his son Joseph and said to him, "If I have found favor in your eyes, put your hand under my thigh and promise that you will show me kindness and faithfulness. Do not bury me in Egypt, 30but when I rest with my fathers, carry me out of Egypt and bury me where they are buried."

"I will do as you say," he said.

31"Swear to me," he said. Then Joseph swore to him, and Israel worshiped as he leaned on the top of his staff.[a]

Manasseh and Ephraim

48 SOME TIME later Joseph was told, "Your father is ill." So he took his two sons Manasseh and Ephraim along with him. 2When Jacob was told, "Your son Joseph has come to you," Israel rallied his strength and sat up on the bed.

3Jacob said to Joseph, "God Almighty[b] appeared to me at Luz in the land of Canaan, and there he blessed me 4and said to me, 'I am going to make you fruitful and will increase your numbers. I will make you a community of peoples, and I will give this land as an everlasting possession to your descendants after you.'

5"Now then, your two sons born to you in Egypt before I came to you here will be reckoned as mine; Ephraim and Manasseh will be mine, just as Reuben and Simeon are mine. 6Any children born to you after them will be yours; in the territory they inherit they will be reckoned under the names of their brothers. 7As I was returning from Paddan,[c] to my sorrow Rachel died in the land of Canaan while we were still on the way, a little distance from Ephrath. So I buried her there beside the road to Ephrath" (that is, Bethlehem).

8When Israel saw the sons of Joseph, he asked, "Who are these?"

9"They are the sons God has given me here," Joseph said to his father.

Then Israel said, "Bring them to me so I may bless them."

10Now Israel's eyes were failing because of old age, and he could hardly see. So Joseph brought his sons close to him, and his father kissed them and embraced them.

---

[a] *31 Or Israel bowed down at the head of his bed*   [b] *3* Hebrew *El-Shaddai*
[c] *7* That is, Northwest Mesopotamia

Living Bible

only land he didn't buy was that belonging to the priests, for they were assigned food from Pharaoh and didn't need to sell. ²³Then Joseph said to the people, "See, I have bought you and your land for Pharaoh. Here is grain. Go and sow the land. ²⁴And when you harvest it, a fifth of everything you get belongs to Pharaoh. Keep four parts for yourselves to be used for next year's seed, and as food for yourselves and for your households and little ones."

²⁵"You have saved our lives," they said. "We will gladly be the serfs of Pharaoh."

²⁶So Joseph made it a law throughout the land of Egypt—and it is still the law—that Pharaoh should have as his tax twenty percent of all the crops except those produced on the land owned by the temples.

²⁷So Israel lived in the land of Goshen in Egypt, and soon the people of Israel began to prosper, and there was a veritable population explosion among them. ²⁸Jacob lived seventeen years after his arrival, so that he was 147 years old at the time of his death. ²⁹As the time drew near for him to die, he called for his son Joseph and said to him, "Swear to me most solemnly that you will honor this, my last request: do not bury me in Egypt. ³⁰But when I am dead, take me out of Egypt and bury me beside my ancestors." And Joseph promised. ³¹"Swear that you will do it," Jacob insisted. And Joseph did. Soon afterwards Jacob took to his bed.

48 ONE DAY not long after this, word came to Joseph that his father was failing rapidly. So, taking with him his two sons, Manasseh and Ephraim, he went to visit him. ²When Jacob heard that Joseph had arrived, he gathered his strength and sat up in the bed to greet him, ³and said to him, "God Almighty appeared to me at Luz in the land of Canaan and blessed me, ⁴and said to me, 'I will make you a great nation and I will give this land of Canaan to you and to your children's children, for an everlasting possession.' ⁵And now, as to these two sons of yours, Ephraim and Manasseh, born here in the land of Egypt before I arrived, I am adopting them as my own, and they will inherit from me just as Reuben and Simeon will. ⁶But any other children born to you shall be your own, and shall inherit Ephraim's and Manasseh's portion from you. ⁷For your mother Rachel died after only two childrenᵈ when I came from Paddan-aram, as we were just a short distance from Ephrath, and I buried her beside the road to Bethlehem." ⁸Then Israel looked over at the two boys. "Are these the ones?" he asked.

⁹"Yes," Joseph told him, "these are my sons whom God has given me here in Egypt."

And Israel said, "Bring them over to me and I will bless them."

¹⁰Israel was half blind with age, so that he could hardly see. So Joseph brought the boys close to him and he kissed and embraced them.

New Revised Standard

the priests he did not buy; for the priests had a fixed allowance from Pharaoh, and lived on the allowance that Pharaoh gave them; therefore they did not sell their land. ²³Then Joseph said to the people, "Now that I have this day bought you and your land for Pharaoh, here is seed for you; sow the land. ²⁴And at the harvests you shall give one-fifth to Pharaoh, and four-fifths shall be your own, as seed for the field and as food for yourselves and your households, and as food for your little ones." ²⁵They said, "You have saved our lives; may it please my lord, we will be slaves to Pharaoh." ²⁶So Joseph made it a statute concerning the land of Egypt, and it stands to this day, that Pharaoh should have the fifth. The land of the priests alone did not become Pharaoh's.

The Last Days of Jacob

27 Thus Israel settled in the land of Egypt, in the region of Goshen; and they gained possessions in it, and were fruitful and multiplied exceedingly. ²⁸Jacob lived in the land of Egypt seventeen years; so the days of Jacob, the years of his life, were one hundred forty-seven years.

29 When the time of Israel's death drew near, he called his son Joseph and said to him, "If I have found favor with you, put your hand under my thigh and promise to deal loyally and truly with me. Do not bury me in Egypt. ³⁰When I lie down with my ancestors, carry me out of Egypt and bury me in their burial place." He answered, "I will do as you have said." ³¹And he said, "Swear to me"; and he swore to him. Then Israel bowed himself on the head of his bed.

Jacob Blesses Joseph's Sons

48 AFTER THIS Joseph was told, "Your father is ill." So he took with him his two sons, Manasseh and Ephraim. ²When Jacob was told, "Your son Joseph has come to you," heᵉ summoned his strength and sat up in bed. ³And Jacob said to Joseph, "God Almightyᶠ appeared to me at Luz in the land of Canaan, and he blessed me, ⁴and said to me, 'I am going to make you fruitful and increase your numbers; I will make of you a company of peoples, and will give this land to your offspring after you for a perpetual holding.' ⁵Therefore your two sons, who were born to you in the land of Egypt before I came to you in Egypt, are now mine; Ephraim and Manasseh shall be mine, just as Reuben and Simeon are. ⁶As for the offspring born to you after them, they shall be yours. They shall be recorded under the names of their brothers with regard to their inheritance. ⁷For when I came from Paddan, Rachel, alas, died in the land of Canaan on the way, while there was still some distance to go to Ephrath; and I buried her there on the way to Ephrath" (that is, Bethlehem).

8 When Israel saw Joseph's sons, he said, "Who are these?" ⁹Joseph said to his father, "They are my sons, whom God has given me here." And he said, "Bring them to me, please, that I may bless them." ¹⁰Now the eyes of Israel were dim with age, and he could not see well. So Joseph brought them near him; and he kissed them and embraced them. ¹¹Israel said to Joseph, "I did

ᵈ 48:7 *after only two children*, implied.   ᵉ Heb *Israel*   ᶠ Traditional rendering of Heb *El Shaddai*

King James

11And Israel said unto Joseph, I had not thought to see thy face: and, lo, God hath shown me also thy seed.

12And Joseph brought them out from between his knees, and he bowed himself with his face to the earth.

13And Joseph took them both, Ephraim in his right hand toward Israel's left hand, and Manasseh in his left hand toward Israel's right hand, and brought *them* near unto him.

14And Israel stretched out his right hand, and laid *it* upon Ephraim's head, who *was* the younger, and his left hand upon Manasseh's head, guiding his hands wittingly; for Manasseh *was* the firstborn.

15¶ And he blessed Joseph, and said, God, before whom my fathers Abraham and Isaac did walk, the God which fed me all my life long unto this day,

16The Angel which redeemed me from all evil, bless the lads; and let my name be named on them, and the name of my fathers Abraham and Isaac; and let them grow into a multitude in the midst of the earth.

17And when Joseph saw that his father laid his right hand upon the head of Ephraim, it displeased him: and he held up his father's hand, to remove it from Ephraim's head unto Manasseh's head.

18And Joseph said unto his father, Not so, my father: for this *is* the firstborn; put thy right hand upon his head.

19And his father refused, and said, I know *it*, my son, I know *it*: he also shall become a people, and he also shall be great: but truly his younger brother shall be greater than he, and his seed shall become a multitude of nations.

20And he blessed them that day, saying, In thee shall Israel bless, saying, God make thee as Ephraim and as Manasseh: and he set Ephraim before Manasseh.

21And Israel said unto Joseph, Behold, I die: but God shall be with you, and bring you again unto the land of your fathers.

22Moreover I have given to thee one portion above thy brethren, which I took out of the hand of the Amorite with my sword and with my bow.

49 AND JACOB called unto his sons, and said, Gather yourselves together, that I may tell you *that* which shall befall you in the last days.

2Gather yourselves together, and hear, ye sons of Jacob; and hearken unto Israel your father.

3¶ Reuben, thou *art* my firstborn, my might, and the beginning of my strength, the excellency of dignity, and the excellency of power:

4Unstable as water, thou shalt not excel; because thou wentest up to thy father's bed; then defiledst thou *it:* he went up to my couch.

5¶ Simeon and Levi *are* brethren; instruments of cruelty *are in* their habitations.

6O my soul, come not thou into their secret; unto their assembly, mine honour, be not thou united: for in their anger they slew a man, and in their selfwill they digged down a wall.

New International

11Israel said to Joseph, "I never expected to see your face again, and now God has allowed me to see your children too."

12Then Joseph removed them from Israel's knees and bowed down with his face to the ground. 13And Joseph took both of them, Ephraim on his right toward Israel's left hand and Manasseh on his left toward Israel's right hand, and brought them close to him. 14But Israel reached out his right hand and put it on Ephraim's head, though he was the younger, and crossing his arms, he put his left hand on Manasseh's head, even though Manasseh was the firstborn.

15Then he blessed Joseph and said,

"May the God before whom my fathers
    Abraham and Isaac walked,
the God who has been my shepherd
    all my life to this day,
16the Angel who has delivered me from all harm
    —may he bless these boys.
May they be called by my name
    and the names of my fathers Abraham and
        Isaac,
and may they increase greatly
    upon the earth."

17When Joseph saw his father placing his right hand on Ephraim's head he was displeased; so he took hold of his father's hand to move it from Ephraim's head to Manasseh's head. 18Joseph said to him, "No, my father, this one is the firstborn; put your right hand on his head."

19But his father refused and said, "I know, my son, I know. He too will become a people, and he too will become great. Nevertheless, his younger brother will be greater than he, and his descendants will become a group of nations." 20He blessed them that day and said,

"In your[a] name will Israel pronounce this
        blessing:
    'May God make you like Ephraim and
        Manasseh.' "

So he put Ephraim ahead of Manasseh.

21Then Israel said to Joseph, "I am about to die, but God will be with you[b] and take you[b] back to the land of your[b] fathers. 22And to you, as one who is over your brothers, I give the ridge of land[c] I took from the Amorites with my sword and my bow."

Jacob Blesses His Sons

49 THEN JACOB called for his sons and said: "Gather around so I can tell you what will happen to you in days to come.

2"Assemble and listen, sons of Jacob;
    listen to your father Israel.

3"Reuben, you are my firstborn,
    my might, the first sign of my strength,
    excelling in honor, excelling in power.
4Turbulent as the waters, you will no longer
        excel,
    for you went up onto your father's bed,
        onto my couch and defiled it.

5"Simeon and Levi are brothers—
    their swords[d] are weapons of violence.
6Let me not enter their council,
    let me not join their assembly,
for they have killed men in their anger
    and hamstrung oxen as they pleased.

a 20 The Hebrew is singular.   b 21 The Hebrew is plural.   c 22 Or *And to you I give one portion more than to your brothers—the portion*   d 5 The meaning of the Hebrew for this word is uncertain.

Living Bible

11And Israel said to Joseph, "I never thought that I would see you again, but now God has let me see your children too."

12, 13Joseph took the boys by the hand, bowed deeply to him, and led the boys to their grandfather's knees—Ephraim at Israel's left hand and Manasseh at his right. 14But Israel crossed his arms as he stretched them out to lay his hands upon the boys' heads, so that his right hand was upon the head of Ephraim, the younger boy, and his left hand was upon the head of Manasseh, the older. He did this purposely.

15Then he blessed Joseph with this blessing: "May God, the God of my fathers Abraham and Isaac, the God who has shepherded me all my life, wonderfully bless these boys. 16He is the Angel who has kept me from all harm. May these boys be an honor to my name and to the names of my fathers Abraham and Isaac; and may they become a mighty nation."

17But Joseph was upset and displeased when he saw that his father had laid his right hand on Ephraim's head; so he lifted it to place it on Manasseh's head instead. 18"No, father," he said. "You've got your right hand on the wrong head! This one over here is the older. Put your right hand on him!"

19But his father refused. "I know what I'm doing, my son," he said. "Manasseh too shall become a great nation, but his younger brother shall become even greater."

20So Jacob blessed the boys that day with this blessing: "May the people of Israel bless each other by saying, 'God make you as prosperous as Ephraim and Manasseh.' " (Note that he put Ephraim before Manasseh.) 21Then Israel said to Joseph, "I am about to die, but God will be with you and will bring you again to Canaan, the land of your fathers. 22And I have given the choice land of Shekem to you instead of to your brothers, as your portion of that land which I took from the Amorites with my sword and with my bow."

49 THEN JACOB called together all his sons and said, "Gather around me and I will tell you what is going to happen to you in the days to come. 2Listen to me, O sons of Jacob; listen to Israel your father.

3"Reuben, you are my oldest son, the child of my vigorous youth. You are the head of the list in rank and in honor. 4But you are unruly as the wild waves of the sea, and you shall be first no longer. I am demoting you, for you slept with one of my wives and thus dishonored me.

5"Simeon and Levi are two of a kind. They are men of violence and injustice. 6O my soul, stay away from them. May I never be a party to their wicked plans. For in their anger they murdered a man, and maimed oxen just for fun. 7Cursed be their anger, for it is fierce and

New Revised Standard

not expect to see your face; and here God has let me see your children also." 12Then Joseph removed them from his father's knees,e and he bowed himself with his face to the earth. 13Joseph took them both, Ephraim in his right hand toward Israel's left, and Manasseh in his left hand toward Israel's right, and brought them near him. 14But Israel stretched out his right hand and laid it on the head of Ephraim, who was the younger, and his left hand on the head of Manasseh, crossing his hands, for Manasseh was the firstborn. 15He blessed Joseph, and said,

"The God before whom my ancestors
      Abraham and Isaac walked,
the God who has been my shepherd all my
      life to this day,
16   the angel who has redeemed me from all
      harm, bless the boys;
and in them let my name be perpetuated, and
      the name of my ancestors Abraham and
      Isaac;
and let them grow into a multitude on the
      earth."

17   When Joseph saw that his father laid his right hand on the head of Ephraim, it displeased him; so he took his father's hand, to remove it from Ephraim's head to Manasseh's head. 18Joseph said to his father, "Not so, my father! Since this one is the firstborn, put your right hand on his head." 19But his father refused, and said, "I know, my son, I know; he also shall become a people, and he also shall be great. Nevertheless his younger brother shall be greater than he, and his offspring shall become a multitude of nations." 20So he blessed them that day, saying,

"By youf Israel will invoke blessings, saying,
   'God make youf like Ephraim and like
      Manasseh.' "

So he put Ephraim ahead of Manasseh. 21Then Israel said to Joseph, "I am about to die, but God will be with you and will bring you again to the land of your ancestors. 22I now give to you one portiong more than to your brothers, the portiong that I took from the hand of the Amorites with my sword and with my bow."

Jacob's Last Words to His Sons

49 THEN JACOB called his sons, and said: "Gather around, that I may tell you what will happen to you in days to come.
2   Assemble and hear, O sons of Jacob;
      listen to Israel your father.

3   Reuben, you are my firstborn,
      my might and the first fruits of my vigor,
      excelling in rank and excelling in power.
4   Unstable as water, you shall no longer excel
      because you went up onto your father's bed;
      then you defiled it—youh went up onto my
         couch!

5   Simeon and Levi are brothers;
      weapons of violence are their swords.
6   May I never come into their council;
      may I not be joined to their company—
      for in their anger they killed men,
      and at their whim they hamstrung oxen.

e Heb from his knees   f you here is singular in Heb   g Or mountain slope
(Heb shekem, a play on the name of the town and district of Shechem)   h Gk
Syr Tg: Heb he

King James

7Cursed *be* their anger, for *it was* fierce; and their wrath, for it was cruel: I will divide them in Jacob, and scatter them in Israel.

8¶ Judah, thou *art he* whom thy brethren shall praise: thy hand *shall be* in the neck of thine enemies; thy father's children shall bow down before thee.

9Judah *is* a lion's whelp: from the prey, my son, thou art gone up: he stooped down, he couched as a lion, and as an old lion; who shall rouse him up?

10The sceptre shall not depart from Judah, nor a lawgiver from between his feet, until Shiloh come; and unto him *shall* the gathering of the people *be*.

11Binding his foal unto the vine, and his ass's colt unto the choice vine; he washed his garments in wine, and his clothes in the blood of grapes:

12His eyes *shall be* red with wine, and his teeth white with milk.

13¶ Zebulun shall dwell at the haven of the sea; and he *shall be* for an haven of ships; and his border *shall be* unto Zidon.

14¶ Issachar *is* a strong ass couching down between two burdens:

15And he saw that rest *was* good, and the land that *it was* pleasant; and bowed his shoulder to bear, and became a servant unto tribute.

16¶ Dan shall judge his people, as one of the tribes of Israel.

17Dan shall be a serpent by the way, an adder in the path, that biteth the horse heels, so that his rider shall fall backward.

18I have waited for thy salvation, O LORD.

19¶ Gad, a troop shall overcome him: but he shall overcome at the last.

20¶ Out of Asher his bread *shall be* fat, and he shall yield royal dainties.

21¶ Naphtali *is* a hind let loose: he giveth goodly words.

22¶ Joseph *is* a fruitful bough, *even* a fruitful bough by a well; *whose* branches run over the wall:

23The archers have sorely grieved him, and shot *at him*, and hated him:

24But his bow abode in strength, and the arms of his hands were made strong by the hands of the mighty *God* of Jacob; (from thence *is* the shepherd, the stone of Israel:)

25*Even* by the God of thy father, who shall help thee; and by the Almighty, who shall bless thee with blessings of heaven above, blessings of the deep that lieth under, blessings of the breasts, and of the womb:

New International

7Cursed be their anger, so fierce,
   and their fury, so cruel!
I will scatter them in Jacob
   and disperse them in Israel.

8"Judah,[a] your brothers will praise you;
   your hand will be on the neck of your
     enemies;
   your father's sons will bow down to you.
9You are a lion's cub, O Judah;
   you return from the prey, my son.
Like a lion he crouches and lies down,
   like a lioness—who dares to rouse him?
10The scepter will not depart from Judah,
   nor the ruler's staff from between his feet,
until he comes to whom it belongs[b]
   and the obedience of the nations is his.
11He will tether his donkey to a vine,
   his colt to the choicest branch;
he will wash his garments in wine,
   his robes in the blood of grapes.
12His eyes will be darker than wine,
   his teeth whiter than milk.[c]

13"Zebulun will live by the seashore
   and become a haven for ships;
   his border will extend toward Sidon.

14"Issachar is a rawboned[d] donkey
   lying down between two saddlebags.[e]
15When he sees how good is his resting place
   and how pleasant is his land,
he will bend his shoulder to the burden
   and submit to forced labor.

16"Dan[f] will provide justice for his people
   as one of the tribes of Israel.
17Dan will be a serpent by the roadside,
   a viper along the path,
that bites the horse's heels
   so that its rider tumbles backward.

18"I look for your deliverance, O LORD.

19"Gad[g] will be attacked by a band of raiders,
   but he will attack them at their heels.

20"Asher's food will be rich;
   he will provide delicacies fit for a king.

21"Naphtali is a doe set free
   that bears beautiful fawns.[h]

22"Joseph is a fruitful vine,
   a fruitful vine near a spring,
   whose branches climb over a wall.[i]
23With bitterness archers attacked him;
   they shot at him with hostility.
24But his bow remained steady,
   his strong arms stayed[j] limber,
because of the hand of the Mighty One of
    Jacob,
because of the Shepherd, the Rock of Israel,
25because of your father's God, who helps you,
   because of the Almighty,[k] who blesses you
with blessings of the heavens above,
   blessings of the deep that lies below,
   blessings of the breast and womb.

a 8 *Judah* sounds like and may be derived from the Hebrew for *praise*.
b 10 Or *until Shiloh comes;* or *until he comes to whom tribute belongs*
c 12 Or *will be dull from wine, / his teeth white from milk*   d 14 Or *strong*
e 14 Or *campfires*   f 16 *Dan* here means *he provides justice.*   g 19 *Gad* can mean *attack* and *band of raiders.*   h 21 Or *free; / he utters beautiful words*   i 22 Or *Joseph is a wild colt, / a wild colt near a spring, / a wild donkey on a terraced hill*   j 23,24 Or *archers will attack . . . will shoot . . . will remain . . . will stay*   k 25 Hebrew *Shaddai*

Living Bible

cruel. Therefore, I will scatter their descendants throughout Israel.[1]

8"Judah, your brothers shall praise you. You shall destroy your enemies. Your father's sons shall bow before you. 9Judah is a young lion that has finished eating its prey. He has settled down as a lion—who will dare to rouse him? 10The scepter shall not depart from Judah until Shiloh[m] comes, whom all people shall obey. 11He has chained his steed to the choicest vine, and washed his clothes in wine.[n] 12His eyes are darker than wine and his teeth are whiter than milk.

13"Zebulun shall dwell on the shores of the sea and shall be a harbor for ships, with his borders extending to Sidon.

14"Issachar is a strong beast of burden resting among the saddle bags. 15When he saw how good the countryside was, how pleasant the land, he willingly bent his shoulder to the task and served his masters with vigor.

16"Dan shall govern his people like any other tribe in Israel. 17He shall be a serpent in the path that bites the horses' heels, so that the rider falls off. 18I trust in your salvation, Lord.

19"A marauding band shall stamp upon Gad, but he shall rob and pursue them!

20"Asher shall produce rich foods, fit for kings!

21"Naphtali is a deer let loose, producing lovely fawns.

22"Joseph is a fruitful tree beside a fountain. His branches shade the wall. 23He has been severely injured by those who shot at him and persecuted him, 24but their weapons were shattered by the Mighty One of Jacob, the Shepherd, the Rock of Israel. 25May the God of your fathers, the Almighty, bless you with blessings of heaven above and of the earth beneath—blessings of the breasts and of the womb, 26blessings of the grain and

New Revised Standard

7   Cursed be their anger, for it is fierce,
        and their wrath, for it is cruel!
    I will divide them in Jacob,
        and scatter them in Israel.

8   Judah, your brothers shall praise you;
        your hand shall be on the neck of your
        enemies;
        your father's sons shall bow down before
        you.
9   Judah is a lion's whelp;
        from the prey, my son, you have gone up.
    He crouches down, he stretches out like a
        lion,
        like a lioness—who dares rouse him up?
10 The scepter shall not depart from Judah,
        nor the ruler's staff from between his feet,
    until tribute comes to him;[o]
        and the obedience of the peoples is his.
11 Binding his foal to the vine
        and his donkey's colt to the choice vine,
    he washes his garments in wine
        and his robe in the blood of grapes;
12 his eyes are darker than wine,
        and his teeth whiter than milk.

13 Zebulun shall settle at the shore of the sea;
        he shall be a haven for ships,
        and his border shall be at Sidon.

14 Issachar is a strong donkey,
        lying down between the sheepfolds;
15 he saw that a resting place was good,
        and that the land was pleasant;
    so he bowed his shoulder to the burden,
        and became a slave at forced labor.

16 Dan shall judge his people
        as one of the tribes of Israel.
17 Dan shall be a snake by the roadside,
        a viper along the path,
    that bites the horse's heels
        so that its rider falls backward.

18 I wait for your salvation, O LORD.

19 Gad shall be raided by raiders,
        but he shall raid at their heels.

20 Asher's[p] food shall be rich,
        and he shall provide royal delicacies.

21 Naphtali is a doe let loose
        that bears lovely fawns.[q]

22 Joseph is a fruitful bough,
        a fruitful bough by a spring;
        his branches run over the wall.[r]
23 The archers fiercely attacked him;
        they shot at him and pressed him hard.
24 Yet his bow remained taut,
        and his arms[s] were made agile
    by the hands of the Mighty One of Jacob,
        by the name of the Shepherd, the Rock of
        Israel,
25 by the God of your father, who will help you,
        by the Almighty[t] who will bless you
        with blessings of heaven above,
    blessings of the deep that lies beneath,
        blessings of the breasts and of the womb.

---

[1] *49:7 I will scatter their descendants throughout Israel.* That is, the tribes of Simeon and Levi were not given land holdings, as were their brother-tribes. [m] *49:10 until Shiloh comes* means also "he to whom it belongs." [n] *49:11 washed his clothes in wine.* Showing wealth and extravagance.

[o] Or *until Shiloh comes* or *until he comes to Shiloh* or (with Syr) *until he comes to whom it belongs* [p] Gk Vg Syr: Heb *From Asher* [q] Or *that gives beautiful words* [r] Meaning of Heb uncertain [s] Heb *the arms of his hands* [t] Traditional rendering of Heb *Shaddai*

King James

26The blessings of thy father have prevailed above the blessings of my progenitors unto the utmost bound of the everlasting hills: they shall be on the head of Joseph, and on the crown of the head of him that was separate from his brethren.

27¶ Benjamin shall ravin *as* a wolf: in the morning he shall devour the prey, and at night he shall divide the spoil.

28¶ All these *are* the twelve tribes of Israel: and this *is it* that their father spake unto them, and blessed them; every one according to his blessing he blessed them.

29And he charged them, and said unto them, I am to be gathered unto my people: bury me with my fathers in the cave that *is* in the field of Ephron the Hittite,

30In the cave that *is* in the field of Machpelah, which *is* before Mamre, in the land of Canaan, which Abraham bought with the field of Ephron the Hittite for a possession of a buryingplace.

31There they buried Abraham and Sarah his wife; there they buried Isaac and Rebekah his wife; and there I buried Leah.

32The purchase of the field and of the cave that *is* therein *was* from the children of Heth.

33And when Jacob had made an end of commanding his sons, he gathered up his feet into the bed, and yielded up the ghost, and was gathered unto his people.

50 AND JOSEPH fell upon his father's face, and wept upon him, and kissed him.

2And Joseph commanded his servants the physicians to embalm his father: and the physicians embalmed Israel.

3And forty days were fulfilled for him; for so are fulfilled the days of those which are embalmed: and the Egyptians mourned for him threescore and ten days.

4And when the days of his mourning were past, Joseph spake unto the house of Pharaoh, saying, If now I have found grace in your eyes, speak, I pray you, in the ears of Pharaoh, saying,

5My father made me swear, saying, Lo, I die: in my grave which I have digged for me in the land of Canaan, there shalt thou bury me. Now therefore let me go up, I pray thee, and bury my father, and I will come again.

6And Pharaoh said, Go up, and bury thy father, according as he made thee swear.

7¶ And Joseph went up to bury his father: and with him went up all the servants of Pharaoh, the elders of his house, and all the elders of the land of Egypt,

8And all the house of Joseph, and his brethren, and his father's house: only their little ones, and their flocks, and their herds, they left in the land of Goshen.

9And there went up with him both chariots and horsemen: and it was a very great company.

10And they came to the threshingfloor of Atad, which *is* beyond Jordan, and there they mourned with a great and very sore lamentation: and he made a mourning for his father seven days.

11And when the inhabitants of the land, the Canaanites, saw the mourning in the floor of Atad, they said, This *is* a grievous mourning to the Egyptians: wherefore the name of it was called Abel-mizraim, which *is* beyond Jordan.

12And his sons did unto him according as he commanded them:

13For his sons carried him into the land of Canaan, and buried him in the cave of the field of Machpelah, which Abraham bought with the field for a possession of a buryingplace of Ephron the Hittite, before Mamre.

New International

26Your father's blessings are greater
    than the blessings of the ancient mountains,
    thana the bounty of the age-old hills.
Let all these rest on the head of Joseph,
    on the brow of the prince amongb his
    brothers.

27"Benjamin is a ravenous wolf;
    in the morning he devours the prey,
    in the evening he divides the plunder."

28All these are the twelve tribes of Israel, and this is what their father said to them when he blessed them, giving each the blessing appropriate to him.

The Death of Jacob

29Then he gave them these instructions: "I am about to be gathered to my people. Bury me with my fathers in the cave in the field of Ephron the Hittite, 30the cave in the field of Machpelah, near Mamre in Canaan, which Abraham bought as a burial place from Ephron the Hittite, along with the field. 31There Abraham and his wife Sarah were buried, there Isaac and his wife Rebekah were buried, and there I buried Leah. 32The field and the cave in it were bought from the Hittites.c"

33When Jacob had finished giving instructions to his sons, he drew his feet up into the bed, breathed his last and was gathered to his people.

50 JOSEPH THREW himself upon his father and wept over him and kissed him. 2Then Joseph directed the physicians in his service to embalm his father Israel. So the physicians embalmed him, 3taking a full forty days, for that was the time required for embalming. And the Egyptians mourned for him seventy days.

4When the days of mourning had passed, Joseph said to Pharaoh's court, "If I have found favor in your eyes, speak to Pharaoh for me. Tell him, 5'My father made me swear an oath and said, "I am about to die; bury me in the tomb I dug for myself in the land of Canaan." Now let me go up and bury my father; then I will return.' "

6Pharaoh said, "Go up and bury your father, as he made you swear to do."

7So Joseph went up to bury his father. All Pharaoh's officials accompanied him—the dignitaries of his court and all the dignitaries of Egypt— 8besides all the members of Joseph's household and his brothers and those belonging to his father's household. Only their children and their flocks and herds were left in Goshen. 9Chariots and horsemend also went up with him. It was a very large company.

10When they reached the threshing floor of Atad, near the Jordan, they lamented loudly and bitterly; and there Joseph observed a seven-day period of mourning for his father. 11When the Canaanites who lived there saw the mourning at the threshing floor of Atad, they said, "The Egyptians are holding a solemn ceremony of mourning." That is why that place near the Jordan is called Abel Mizraim.e

12So Jacob's sons did as he had commanded them: 13They carried him to the land of Canaan and buried him in the cave in the field of Machpelah, near Mamre, which Abraham had bought as a burial place from Ephron the Hittite, along with the field. 14After burying

---

a 26 Or *of my progenitors, / as great as*   b 26 Or *the one separated from*   c 32 Or *the sons of Heth*   d 9 Or *charioteers*   e 11 *Abel Mizraim* means *mourning of the Egyptians.*

Living Bible

flowers, blessings reaching to the utmost bounds of the everlasting hills. These shall be the blessings upon the head of Joseph who was exiled from his brothers.

27"Benjamin is a wolf that prowls. He devours his enemies in the morning, and in the evening divides the loot."

28So these are the blessings that Israel their father blessed his twelve sons with.

29, 30Then he told them, "Soon I will die. You must bury me with my fathers in the land of Canaan, in the cave in the field of Mach-pelah, facing Mamre—the field Abraham bought from Ephron the Hethite for a burial ground. 31There they buried Abraham and Sarah his wife; there they buried Isaac and Rebekah his wife; and there I buried Leah. 32It is the cave which my grandfather Abraham purchased from the sons of Heth." 33Then, when Jacob had finished his prophecies to his sons, he lay back in the bed, breathed his last, and died.

50 JOSEPH THREW himself upon his father's body and wept over him and kissed him. 2Afterwards he commanded his morticians to embalm the body. 3The embalming process required forty days, with a period of national mourning of seventy days. 4Then, when at last the mourning was over, Joseph approached Pharaoh's staff and requested them to speak to Pharaoh on his behalf.

5"Tell his majesty," he requested them, "that Joseph's father made Joseph swear to take his body back to the land of Canaan, to bury him there. Ask his majesty to permit me to go and bury my father; assure him that I will return promptly."

6Pharaoh agreed. "Go and bury your father, as you promised," he said.

7So Joseph went, and a great number of Pharaoh's counselors and assistants—all the senior officers of the land, 8as well as all of Joseph's people—his brothers and their families. But they left their little children and flocks and herds in the land of Goshen. 9So a very great number of chariots, cavalry, and people accompanied Joseph.

10When they arrived at Atad[f] (meaning "Threshing Place of Brambles"), beyond the Jordan River, they held a very great and solemn funeral service, with a seven-day period of lamentation for Joseph's father. 11The local residents, the Canaanites, renamed the place Abel-mizraim (meaning "Egyptian Mourners") for they said, "It is a place of very deep mourning by these Egyptians." 12, 13So his sons did as Israel commanded them, and carried his body into the land of Canaan and buried it there in the cave of Mach-pelah—the cave Abraham had bought in the field of Ephron the Hethite, close to Mamre.

New Revised Standard

26 The blessings of your father
   are stronger than the blessings of the eternal
      mountains,
   the bounties of the everlasting hills;
   may they be on the head of Joseph,
   on the brow of him who was set apart from
      his brothers.

27 Benjamin is a ravenous wolf,
   in the morning devouring the prey,
   and at evening dividing the spoil."

28 All these are the twelve tribes of Israel, and this is what their father said to them when he blessed them, blessing each one of them with a suitable blessing.

Jacob's Death and Burial

29 Then he charged them, saying to them, "I am about to be gathered to my people. Bury me with my ancestors—in the cave in the field of Ephron the Hittite, 30in the cave in the field at Machpelah, near Mamre, in the land of Canaan, in the field that Abraham bought from Ephron the Hittite as a burial site. 31There Abraham and his wife Sarah were buried; there Isaac and his wife Rebekah were buried; and there I buried Leah— 32the field and the cave that is in it were purchased from the Hittites." 33When Jacob ended his charge to his sons, he drew up his feet into the bed, breathed his last, and was gathered to his people.

50 THEN JOSEPH threw himself on his father's face and wept over him and kissed him. 2Joseph commanded the physicians in his service to embalm his father. So the physicians embalmed Israel; 3they spent forty days in doing this, for that is the time required for embalming. And the Egyptians wept for him seventy days.

4 When the days of weeping for him were past, Joseph addressed the household of Pharaoh, "If now I have found favor with you, please speak to Pharaoh as follows: 5My father made me swear an oath; he said, 'I am about to die. In the tomb that I hewed out for myself in the land of Canaan, there you shall bury me.' Now therefore let me go up, so that I may bury my father; then I will return." 6Pharaoh answered, "Go up, and bury your father, as he made you swear to do."

7 So Joseph went up to bury his father. With him went up all the servants of Pharaoh, the elders of his household, and all the elders of the land of Egypt, 8as well as all the household of Joseph, his brothers, and his father's household. Only their children, their flocks, and their herds were left in the land of Goshen. 9Both chariots and charioteers went up with him. It was a very great company. 10When they came to the threshing floor of Atad, which is beyond the Jordan, they held there a very great and sorrowful lamentation; and he observed a time of mourning for his father seven days. 11When the Canaanite inhabitants of the land saw the mourning on the threshing floor of Atad, they said, "This is a grievous mourning on the part of the Egyptians." Therefore the place was named Abel-mizraim;[h] it is beyond the Jordan. 12Thus his sons did for him as he had instructed them. 13They carried him to the land of Canaan and buried him in the cave of the field at Machpelah, the field near Mamre, which Abraham bought as a burial site from Ephron the Hittite. 14After he had buried his

---

f 50:10 *Atad*. Located just west of the Jordan River, near Jericho.

g Cn Compare Gk: Heb *of my progenitors to the boundaries*   h That is *mourning* (or *meadow*) *of Egypt*

King James

14¶ And Joseph returned into Egypt, he, and his brethren, and all that went up with him to bury his father, after he had buried his father.

15¶ And when Joseph's brethren saw that their father was dead, they said, Joseph will peradventure hate us, and will certainly requite us all the evil which we did unto him.

16And they sent a messenger unto Joseph, saying, Thy father did command before he died, saying,

17So shall ye say unto Joseph, Forgive, I pray thee now, the trespass of thy brethren, and their sin; for they did unto thee evil: and now, we pray thee, forgive the trespass of the servants of the God of thy father. And Joseph wept when they spake unto him.

18And his brethren also went and fell down before his face; and they said, Behold, we *be* thy servants.

19And Joseph said unto them, Fear not: for *am* I in the place of God?

20But as for you, ye thought evil against me; *but* God meant it unto good, to bring to pass, as *it is* this day, to save much people alive.

21Now therefore fear ye not: I will nourish you, and your little ones. And he comforted them, and spake kindly unto them.

22¶ And Joseph dwelt in Egypt, he, and his father's house: and Joseph lived an hundred and ten years.

23And Joseph saw Ephraim's children of the third *generation:* the children also of Machir the son of Manasseh were brought up upon Joseph's knees.

24And Joseph said unto his brethren, I die: and God will surely visit you, and bring you out of this land unto the land which he sware to Abraham, to Isaac, and to Jacob.

25And Joseph took an oath of the children of Israel, saying, God will surely visit you, and ye shall carry up my bones from hence.

26So Joseph died, *being* an hundred and ten years old: and they embalmed him, and he was put in a coffin in Egypt.

New International

his father, Joseph returned to Egypt, together with his brothers and all the others who had gone with him to bury his father.

Joseph Reassures His Brothers

15When Joseph's brothers saw that their father was dead, they said, "What if Joseph holds a grudge against us and pays us back for all the wrongs we did to him?" 16So they sent word to Joseph, saying, "Your father left these instructions before he died: 17'This is what you are to say to Joseph: I ask you to forgive your brothers the sins and the wrongs they committed in treating you so badly.' Now please forgive the sins of the servants of the God of your father." When their message came to him, Joseph wept.

18His brothers then came and threw themselves down before him. "We are your slaves," they said.

19But Joseph said to them, "Don't be afraid. Am I in the place of God? 20You intended to harm me, but God intended it for good to accomplish what is now being done, the saving of many lives. 21So then, don't be afraid. I will provide for you and your children." And he reassured them and spoke kindly to them.

The Death of Joseph

22Joseph stayed in Egypt, along with all his father's family. He lived a hundred and ten years 23and saw the third generation of Ephraim's children. Also the children of Makir son of Manasseh were placed at birth on Joseph's knees.[a]

24Then Joseph said to his brothers, "I am about to die. But God will surely come to your aid and take you up out of this land to the land he promised on oath to Abraham, Isaac and Jacob." 25And Joseph made the sons of Israel swear an oath and said, "God will surely come to your aid, and then you must carry my bones up from this place."

26So Joseph died at the age of a hundred and ten. And after they embalmed him, he was placed in a coffin in Egypt.

---

a 23 That is, were counted as his

Living Bible

[14]Then Joseph returned to Egypt with his brothers and all who had accompanied him to the funeral of his father. [15]But now that their father was dead, Joseph's brothers were frightened.

"Now Joseph will pay us back for all the evil we did to him," they said. [16], [17]So they sent him this message: "Before he died, your father instructed us to tell you to forgive us for the great evil we did to you. We servants of the God of your father beg you to forgive us." When Joseph read the message, he broke down and cried.

[18]Then his brothers came and fell down before him and said, "We are your slaves."

[19]But Joseph told them, "Don't be afraid of me. Am I God, to judge and punish you? [20]As far as I am concerned, God turned into good what you meant for evil, for he brought me to this high position I have today so that I could save the lives of many people. [21]No, don't be afraid. Indeed, I myself will take care of you and your families." And he spoke very kindly to them, reassuring them.

[22]So Joseph and his brothers and their families continued to live in Egypt. Joseph was 110 years old when he died. [23]He lived to see the birth of his son Ephraim's children, and the children of Machir, Manasseh's son, who played at his feet.

[24]"Soon I will die," Joseph told his brothers, "but God will surely come and get you, and bring you out of this land of Egypt and take you back to the land he promised to the descendants of Abraham, Isaac and Jacob." [25]Then Joseph made his brothers promise with an oath that they would take his body back with them when they returned to Canaan. [26]So Joseph died at the age of 110, and they embalmed him, and his body was placed in a coffin in Egypt.

New Revised Standard

father, Joseph returned to Egypt with his brothers and all who had gone up with him to bury his father.

Joseph Forgives His Brothers

15 Realizing that their father was dead, Joseph's brothers said, "What if Joseph still bears a grudge against us and pays us back in full for all the wrong that we did to him?" [16]So they approached[b] Joseph, saying, "Your father gave this instruction before he died, [17]'Say to Joseph: I beg you, forgive the crime of your brothers and the wrong they did in harming you.' Now therefore please forgive the crime of the servants of the God of your father." Joseph wept when they spoke to him. [18]Then his brothers also wept,[c] fell down before him, and said, "We are here as your slaves." [19]But Joseph said to them, "Do not be afraid! Am I in the place of God? [20]Even though you intended to do harm to me, God intended it for good, in order to preserve a numerous people, as he is doing today. [21]So have no fear; I myself will provide for you and your little ones." In this way he reassured them, speaking kindly to them.

Joseph's Last Days and Death

22 So Joseph remained in Egypt, he and his father's household; and Joseph lived one hundred ten years. [23]Joseph saw Ephraim's children of the third generation; the children of Machir son of Manasseh were also born on Joseph's knees. [24]Then Joseph said to his brothers, "I am about to die; but God will surely come to you, and bring you up out of this land to the land that he swore to Abraham, to Isaac, and to Jacob." [25]So Joseph made the Israelites swear, saying, "When God comes to you, you shall carry up my bones from here." [26]And Joseph died, being one hundred ten years old; he was embalmed and placed in a coffin in Egypt.

---

[b] Gk Syr: Heb *they commanded*   [c] Cn: Heb *also came*

THE SECOND BOOK OF MOSES, CALLED

Exodus

Exodus

1 NOW THESE *are* the names of the children of Israel, which came into Egypt; every man and his household came with Jacob.

2Reuben, Simeon, Levi, and Judah,

3Issachar, Zebulun, and Benjamin,

4Dan, and Naphtali, Gad, and Asher.

5And all the souls that came out of the loins of Jacob were seventy souls: for Joseph was in Egypt *already*.

6And Joseph died, and all his brethren, and all that generation.

7¶ And the children of Israel were fruitful, and increased abundantly, and multiplied, and waxed exceeding mighty; and the land was filled with them.

8Now there arose up a new king over Egypt, which knew not Joseph.

9And he said unto his people, Behold, the people of the children of Israel *are* more and mightier than we:

10Come on, let us deal wisely with them; lest they multiply, and it come to pass, that, when there falleth out any war, they join also unto our enemies, and fight against us, and *so* get them up out of the land.

11Therefore they did set over them taskmasters to afflict them with their burdens. And they built for Pharaoh treasure cities, Pithom and Raamses.

12But the more they afflicted them, the more they multiplied and grew. And they were grieved because of the children of Israel.

13And the Egyptians made the children of Israel to serve with rigour:

14And they made their lives bitter with hard bondage, in mortar, and in brick, and in all manner of service in the field: all their service, wherein they made them serve, *was* with rigour.

15¶ And the king of Egypt spake to the Hebrew midwives, of which the name of the one *was* Shiphrah, and the name of the other Puah:

16And he said, When ye do the office of a midwife to the Hebrew women, and see *them* upon the stools; if it *be* a son, then ye shall kill him: but if it *be* a daughter, then she shall live.

17But the midwives feared God, and did not as the king of Egypt commanded them, but saved the men children alive.

18And the king of Egypt called for the midwives, and said unto them, Why have ye done this thing, and have saved the men children alive?

19And the midwives said unto Pharaoh, Because the Hebrew women *are* not as the Egyptian women; for they *are* lively, and are delivered ere the midwives come in unto them.

20Therefore God dealt well with the midwives: and the people multiplied, and waxed very mighty.

21And it came to pass, because the midwives feared God, that he made them houses.

22And Pharaoh charged all his people, saying, Every son that is born ye shall cast into the river, and every daughter ye shall save alive.

The Israelites Oppressed

1 THESE ARE the names of the sons of Israel who went to Egypt with Jacob, each with his family: 2Reuben, Simeon, Levi and Judah; 3Issachar, Zebulun and Benjamin; 4Dan and Naphtali; Gad and Asher. 5The descendants of Jacob numbered seventya in all; Joseph was already in Egypt.

6Now Joseph and all his brothers and all that generation died, 7but the Israelites were fruitful and multiplied greatly and became exceedingly numerous, so that the land was filled with them.

8Then a new king, who did not know about Joseph, came to power in Egypt. 9"Look," he said to his people, "the Israelites have become much too numerous for us. 10Come, we must deal shrewdly with them or they will become even more numerous and, if war breaks out, will join our enemies, fight against us and leave the country."

11So they put slave masters over them to oppress them with forced labor, and they built Pithom and Rameses as store cities for Pharaoh. 12But the more they were oppressed, the more they multiplied and spread; so the Egyptians came to dread the Israelites 13and worked them ruthlessly. 14They made their lives bitter with hard labor in brick and mortar and with all kinds of work in the fields; in all their hard labor the Egyptians used them ruthlessly.

15The king of Egypt said to the Hebrew midwives, whose names were Shiphrah and Puah, 16"When you help the Hebrew women in childbirth and observe them on the delivery stool, if it is a boy, kill him; but if it is a girl, let her live." 17The midwives, however, feared God and did not do what the king of Egypt had told them to do; they let the boys live. 18Then the king of Egypt summoned the midwives and asked them, "Why have you done this? Why have you let the boys live?"

19The midwives answered Pharaoh, "Hebrew women are not like Egyptian women; they are vigorous and give birth before the midwives arrive."

20So God was kind to the midwives and the people increased and became even more numerous. 21And because the midwives feared God, he gave them families of their own.

22Then Pharaoh gave this order to all his people: "Every boy that is bornb you must throw into the Nile, but let every girl live."

a 5 Masoretic Text (see also Gen. 46:27); Dead Sea Scrolls and Septuagint (see also Acts 7:14 and note at Gen. 46:27) *seventy-five*   b 22 Masoretic Text; Samaritan Pentateuch, Septuagint and Targums *born to the Hebrews*

Exodus

Exodus

Living Bible

1 THIS IS the list of the sons of Jacob who accompanied him to Egypt, with their families:
Reuben, Simeon, Levi, Judah, Issachar, Zebulun, Benjamin, Dan, Naphtali, Gad, Asher.
5So the total number who went with him was seventy (for Joseph was already there). 6In due season Joseph and each of his brothers died, ending that generation. 7Meanwhile, their descendants were very fertile, increasing rapidly in numbers; there was a veritable population explosion so that they soon became a large nation, and they filled the land of Goshen.

8Then, eventually,c a new king came to the throne of Egypt who felt no obligation to the descendants of Joseph.d

9He told his people, "These Israelis are becoming dangerous to us because there are so many of them. 10Let's figure out a way to put an end to this. If we don't, and war breaks out, they will join our enemies and fight against us and escape out of the country."

11So the Egyptians made slaves of them and put brutal taskmasters over them to wear them down under heavy burdens while building the cities of Pithom and Raamses as supply centers for the king. 12But the more the Egyptians mistreated and oppressed them, the more the Israelis seemed to multiply! The Egyptians became alarmed, 13, 14and made the Hebrew slavery more bitter still, forcing them to toil long and hard in the fields and to carry heavy loads of mortar and brick.

15, 16Then Pharaoh, the king of Egypt, instructed the Hebrew midwives (their names were Shiphrah and Puah) to kill all Hebrew boys as soon as they were born, but to let the girls live. 17But the midwives feared God and didn't obey the king—they let the boys live too.

18The king summoned them before him and demanded, "Why have you disobeyed my command and let the baby boys live?"

19"Sir," they told him, "the Hebrew women have their babies so quickly that we can't get there in time! They are not slow like the Egyptian women!"

20And God blessed the midwives [because they were God-fearing womene]. So the people of Israel continued to multiply and to become a mighty nation. 21And because the midwives revered God, he gave them children of their own. 22Then Pharaoh commanded all of his people to throw the newborn Hebrew boys into the Nile River. But the girls, he said, could live.

New Revised Standard

1 THESE ARE the names of the sons of Israel who came to Egypt with Jacob, each with his household: 2Reuben, Simeon, Levi, and Judah, 3Issachar, Zebulun, and Benjamin, 4Dan and Naphtali, Gad and Asher. 5The total number of people born to Jacob was seventy. Joseph was already in Egypt. 6Then Joseph died, and all his brothers, and that whole generation. 7But the Israelites were fruitful and prolific; they multiplied and grew exceedingly strong, so that the land was filled with them.

The Israelites Are Oppressed

8 Now a new king arose over Egypt, who did not know Joseph. 9He said to his people, "Look, the Israelite people are more numerous and more powerful than we. 10Come, let us deal shrewdly with them, or they will increase and, in the event of war, join our enemies and fight against us and escape from the land." 11Therefore they set taskmasters over them to oppress them with forced labor. They built supply cities, Pithom and Rameses, for Pharaoh. 12But the more they were oppressed, the more they multiplied and spread, so that the Egyptians came to dread the Israelites. 13The Egyptians became ruthless in imposing tasks on the Israelites, 14and made their lives bitter with hard service in mortar and brick and in every kind of field labor. They were ruthless in all the tasks that they imposed on them.

15 The king of Egypt said to the Hebrew midwives, one of whom was named Shiphrah and the other Puah, 16"When you act as midwives to the Hebrew women, and see them on the birthstool, if it is a boy, kill him; but if it is a girl, she shall live." 17But the midwives feared God; they did not do as the king of Egypt commanded them, but they let the boys live. 18So the king of Egypt summoned the midwives and said to them, "Why have you done this, and allowed the boys to live?" 19The midwives said to Pharaoh, "Because the Hebrew women are not like the Egyptian women; for they are vigorous and give birth before the midwife comes to them." 20So God dealt well with the midwives; and the people multiplied and became very strong. 21And because the midwives feared God, he gave them families. 22Then Pharaoh commanded all his people, "Every boy that is born to the Hebrewsf you shall throw into the Nile, but you shall let every girl live."

---

c 1:8 *eventually, a new king came*, implied. This incident occurred about four hundred years after Joseph's death.   d 1:8 *who felt no obligation to the descendants of Joseph*, literally, "who did not know Joseph."   e 1:20 *because they were God-fearing women*, implied from vs 21.

f Sam Gk Tg: Heb lacks *to the Hebrews*

King James

2 AND THERE went a man of the house of Levi,
and took *to wife* a daughter of Levi.

2And the woman conceived, and bare a son: and
when she saw him that he *was a* goodly *child,* she hid
him three months.

3And when she could not longer hide him, she took
for him an ark of bulrushes, and daubed it with slime and
with pitch, and put the child therein; and she laid *it* in
the flags by the river's brink.

4And his sister stood afar off, to wit what would be
done to him.

5¶ And the daughter of Pharaoh came down to wash
herself at the river; and her maidens walked along by the
river's side; and when she saw the ark among the flags,
she sent her maid to fetch it.

6And when she had opened *it,* she saw the child: and,
behold, the babe wept. And she had compassion on him,
and said, This *is one* of the Hebrews' children.

7Then said his sister to Pharaoh's daughter, Shall I go
and call to thee a nurse of the Hebrew women, that she
may nurse the child for thee?

8And Pharaoh's daughter said to her, Go. And the
maid went and called the child's mother.

9And Pharaoh's daughter said unto her, Take this
child away, and nurse it for me, and I will give *thee* thy
wages. And the woman took the child, and nursed it.

10And the child grew, and she brought him unto Pharaoh's daughter, and he became her son. And she called
his name Moses: and she said, Because I drew him out
of the water.

11¶ And it came to pass in those days, when Moses
was grown, that he went out unto his brethren, and
looked on their burdens: and he spied an Egyptian smiting an Hebrew, one of his brethren.

12And he looked this way and that way, and when he
saw that *there was* no man, he slew the Egyptian, and
hid him in the sand.

13And when he went out the second day, behold, two
men of the Hebrews strove together: and he said to him
that did the wrong, Wherefore smitest thou thy fellow?

14And he said, Who made thee a prince and a judge
over us? intendest thou to kill me, as thou killedst the
Egyptian? And Moses feared, and said, Surely this thing
is known.

15Now when Pharaoh heard this thing, he sought to
slay Moses. But Moses fled from the face of Pharaoh,
and dwelt in the land of Midian: and he sat down by a
well.

16Now the priest of Midian had seven daughters: and
they came and drew *water,* and filled the troughs to
water their father's flock.

17And the shepherds came and drove them away: but
Moses stood up and helped them, and watered their
flock.

18And when they came to Reuel their father, he said,
How *is it that* ye are come so soon today?

19And they said, An Egyptian delivered us out of the
hand of the shepherds, and also drew *water* enough for
us, and watered the flock.

20And he said unto his daughters, And where *is* he?
why *is it that* ye have left the man? call him, that he may
eat bread.

21And Moses was content to dwell with the man: and
he gave Moses Zipporah his daughter.

22And she bare *him* a son, and he called his name
Gershom: for he said, I have been a stranger in a strange
land.

23¶ And it came to pass in process of time, that the
king of Egypt died: and the children of Israel sighed by
reason of the bondage, and they cried, and their cry
came up unto God by reason of the bondage.

New International

The Birth of Moses

2 NOW A man of the house of Levi married a Levite
woman, 2and she became pregnant and gave birth
to a son. When she saw that he was a fine child, she hid
him for three months. 3But when she could hide him no
longer, she got a papyrus basket for him and coated it
with tar and pitch. Then she placed the child in it and
put it among the reeds along the bank of the Nile. 4His
sister stood at a distance to see what would happen to
him.

5Then Pharaoh's daughter went down to the Nile to
bathe, and her attendants were walking along the river
bank. She saw the basket among the reeds and sent her
slave girl to get it. 6She opened it and saw the baby. He
was crying, and she felt sorry for him. "This is one of
the Hebrew babies," she said.

7Then his sister asked Pharaoh's daughter, "Shall I go
and get one of the Hebrew women to nurse the baby for
you?"

8"Yes, go," she answered. And the girl went and got
the baby's mother. 9Pharaoh's daughter said to her,
"Take this baby and nurse him for me, and I will pay
you." So the woman took the baby and nursed him.
10When the child grew older, she took him to Pharaoh's
daughter and he became her son. She named him Moses,a saying, "I drew him out of the water."

Moses Flees to Midian

11One day, after Moses had grown up, he went out
to where his own people were and watched them at their
hard labor. He saw an Egyptian beating a Hebrew, one
of his own people. 12Glancing this way and that and
seeing no one, he killed the Egyptian and hid him in the
sand. 13The next day he went out and saw two Hebrews
fighting. He asked the one in the wrong, "Why are you
hitting your fellow Hebrew?"

14The man said, "Who made you ruler and judge over
us? Are you thinking of killing me as you killed the
Egyptian?" Then Moses was afraid and thought, "What
I did must have become known."

15When Pharaoh heard of this, he tried to kill Moses,
but Moses fled from Pharaoh and went to live in Midian,
where he sat down by a well. 16Now a priest of Midian
had seven daughters, and they came to draw water and
fill the troughs to water their father's flock. 17Some
shepherds came along and drove them away, but Moses
got up and came to their rescue and watered their flock.

18When the girls returned to Reuel their father, he
asked them, "Why have you returned so early today?"

19They answered, "An Egyptian rescued us from the
shepherds. He even drew water for us and watered the
flock."

20"And where is he?" he asked his daughters. "Why
did you leave him? Invite him to have something to eat."

21Moses agreed to stay with the man, who gave his
daughter Zipporah to Moses in marriage. 22Zipporah
gave birth to a son, and Moses named him Gershom,b
saying, "I have become an alien in a foreign land."

23During that long period, the king of Egypt died.
The Israelites groaned in their slavery and cried out, and
their cry for help because of their slavery went up to
God. 24God heard their groaning and he remembered his

---

a *10 Moses* sounds like the Hebrew for *draw out.*   b *22 Gershom* sounds
like the Hebrew for *an alien there.*

Living Bible

2 THERE WERE at this time a Hebrew fellow and girl of the tribe of Levi who married and had a family, and a baby son was born to them. When the baby's mother saw that he was an unusually beautiful baby, she hid him at home for three months. 3Then, when she could no longer hide him, she made a little boat from papyrus reeds, waterproofed it with tar, put the baby in it, and laid it among the reeds along the river's edge. 4The baby's sister watched from a distance to see what would happen to him.

5Well, this is what happened: A princess, one of Pharaoh's daughters, came down to bathe in the river, and as she and her maids were walking along the river bank, she spied the little boat among the reeds and sent one of the maids to bring it to her. 6When she opened it, there was a baby! And he was crying. This touched her heart. "He must be one of the Hebrew children!" she said.

7Then the baby's sister approached the princess and asked her, "Shall I go and find one of the Hebrew women to nurse the baby for you?"

8"Yes, do!" the princess replied. So the little girl rushed home and called her mother!

9"Take this child home and nurse him for me," the princess instructed the baby's mother, "and I will pay you well!" So she took him home and nursed him.

10Later, when he was older, she brought him back to the princess and he became her son. She named him Moses (meaningc "to draw out") because she had drawn him out of the water.

11One day, many years laterd when Moses had grown up and become a man, he went out to visit his fellow Hebrews and saw the terrible conditions they were under. During his visit he saw an Egyptian knock a Hebrew to the ground—one of his own Hebrew brothers! 12Moses looked this way and that to be sure no one was watching, then killed the Egyptian and hid his body in the sand.

13The next day as he was out visiting among the Hebrews again, he saw two of them fighting. "What are you doing, hitting your own Hebrew brother like that?" he said to the one in the wrong.

14"And who are you?" the man demanded. "I suppose you think you are *our* prince and judge! And do you plan to kill me as you did that Egyptian yesterday?" When Moses realized that his deed was known, he was frightened. 15And sure enough, when Pharaoh heard about it he ordered Moses arrested and executed. But Moses ran away into the land of Midian. As he was sitting there beside a well, 16seven girls who were daughters of the priest of Midian came to draw water and fill the water troughs for their father's flocks. 17But the shepherds chased the girls away. Moses then came to their aid and rescued them from the shepherds and watered their flocks.

18When they returned to their father Reuel he asked, "How did you get the flocks watered so quickly today?"

19"An Egyptian defended us against the shepherds," they told him; "he drew water for us and watered the flocks."

20"Well, where is he?" their father demanded. "Did you just leave him there? Invite him home for supper."

21Moses eventually decided to accept Reuel's invitation to live with them, and Reuel gave him one of the girls, Zipporah, as his wife. 22They had a baby named Gershom (meaning "foreigner"), for he said, "I am a stranger in a foreign land."

23Several years later the king of Egypt died. The Israelis were groaning beneath their burdens, in deep trouble because of their slavery, and weeping bitterly before the Lord. He heard their cries from heaven, 24and re-

New Revised Standard

Birth and Youth of Moses

2 NOW A man from the house of Levi went and married a Levite woman. 2The woman conceived and bore a son; and when she saw that he was a fine baby, she hid him three months. 3When she could hide him no longer she got a papyrus basket for him, and plastered it with bitumen and pitch; she put the child in it and placed it among the reeds on the bank of the river. 4His sister stood at a distance, to see what would happen to him.

5 The daughter of Pharaoh came down to bathe at the river, while her attendants walked beside the river. She saw the basket among the reeds and sent her maid to bring it. 6When she opened it, she saw the child. He was crying, and she took pity on him, "This must be one of the Hebrews' children," she said. 7Then his sister said to Pharaoh's daughter, "Shall I go and get you a nurse from the Hebrew women to nurse the child for you?" 8Pharaoh's daughter said to her, "Yes." So the girl went and called the child's mother. 9Pharaoh's daughter said to her, "Take this child and nurse it for me, and I will give you your wages." So the woman took the child and nursed it. 10When the child grew up, she brought him to Pharaoh's daughter, and she took him as her son. She named him Moses,e "because," she said, "I drew him outf of the water."

Moses Flees to Midian

11 One day, after Moses had grown up, he went out to his people and saw their forced labor. He saw an Egyptian beating a Hebrew, one of his kinsfolk. 12He looked this way and that, and seeing no one he killed the Egyptian and hid him in the sand. 13When he went out the next day, he saw two Hebrews fighting; and he said to the one who was in the wrong, "Why do you strike your fellow Hebrew?" 14He answered, "Who made you a ruler and judge over us? Do you mean to kill me as you killed the Egyptian?" Then Moses was afraid and thought, "Surely the thing is known." 15When Pharaoh heard of it, he sought to kill Moses.

But Moses fled from Pharaoh. He settled in the land of Midian, and sat down by a well. 16The priest of Midian had seven daughters. They came to draw water, and filled the troughs to water their father's flock. 17But some shepherds came and drove them away. Moses got up and came to their defense and watered their flock. 18When they returned to their father Reuel, he said, "How is it that you have come back so soon today?" 19They said, "An Egyptian helped us against the shepherds; he even drew water for us and watered the flock." 20He said to his daughters, "Where is he? Why did you leave the man? Invite him to break bread." 21Moses agreed to stay with the man, and he gave Moses his daughter Zipporah in marriage. 22She bore a son, and he named him Gershom; for he said, "I have been an alieng residing in a foreign land."

23 After a long time the king of Egypt died. The Israelites groaned under their slavery, and cried out. Out of the slavery their cry for help rose up to God. 24God

---

c 2:10 The name *Moses* sounds like another Hebrew word meaning "to draw out." d 2:11 *many years later*, implied.

e Heb *Mosheh*   f Heb *mashah*   g Heb *ger*

King James

24And God heard their groaning, and God remembered his covenant with Abraham, with Isaac, and with Jacob.

25And God looked upon the children of Israel, and God had respect unto *them*.

3 NOW MOSES kept the flock of Jethro his father-in-law, the priest of Midian: and he led the flock to the backside of the desert, and came to the mountain of God, *even* to Horeb.

2And the angel of the LORD appeared unto him in a flame of fire out of the midst of a bush: and he looked, and, behold, the bush burned with fire, and the bush *was* not consumed.

3And Moses said, I will now turn aside, and see this great sight, why the bush is not burnt.

4And when the LORD saw that he turned aside to see, God called unto him out of the midst of the bush, and said, Moses, Moses. And he said, Here *am* I.

5And he said, Draw not nigh hither: put off thy shoes from off thy feet, for the place whereon thou standest *is* holy ground.

6Moreover he said, I *am* the God of thy father, the God of Abraham, the God of Isaac, and the God of Jacob. And Moses hid his face; for he was afraid to look upon God.

7¶ And the LORD said, I have surely seen the affliction of my people which *are* in Egypt, and have heard their cry by reason of their taskmasters; for I know their sorrows;

8And I am come down to deliver them out of the hand of the Egyptians, and to bring them up out of that land unto a good land and a large, unto a land flowing with milk and honey; unto the place of the Canaanites, and the Hittites, and the Amorites, and the Perizzites, and the Hivites, and the Jebusites.

9Now therefore, behold, the cry of the children of Israel is come unto me: and I have also seen the oppression wherewith the Egyptians oppress them.

10Come now therefore, and I will send thee unto Pharaoh, that thou mayest bring forth my people the children of Israel out of Egypt.

11¶ And Moses said unto God, Who *am* I, that I should go unto Pharaoh, and that I should bring forth the children of Israel out of Egypt?

12And he said, Certainly I will be with thee; and this *shall be* a token unto thee, that I have sent thee: When thou hast brought forth the people out of Egypt, ye shall serve God upon this mountain.

13And Moses said unto God, Behold, *when* I come unto the children of Israel, and shall say unto them, The God of your fathers hath sent me unto you; and they shall say to me, What *is* his name? what shall I say unto them?

14And God said unto Moses, I AM THAT I AM: and he said, Thus shalt thou say unto the children of Israel, I AM hath sent me unto you.

15And God said moreover unto Moses, Thus shalt thou say unto the children of Israel, The LORD God of your fathers, the God of Abraham, the God of Isaac, and the God of Jacob, hath sent me unto you: this *is* my name for ever, and this *is* my memorial unto all generations.

16Go, and gather the elders of Israel together, and say unto them, The LORD God of your fathers, the God of Abraham, of Isaac, and of Jacob, appeared unto me, saying, I have surely visited you, and *seen* that which is done to you in Egypt:

17And I have said, I will bring you up out of the affliction of Egypt unto the land of the Canaanites, and the Hittites, and the Amorites, and the Perizzites, and the Hivites, and the Jebusites, unto a land flowing with milk and honey.

New International

covenant with Abraham, with Isaac and with Jacob. 25So God looked on the Israelites and was concerned about them.

Moses and the Burning Bush

3 NOW MOSES was tending the flock of Jethro his father-in-law, the priest of Midian, and he led the flock to the far side of the desert and came to Horeb, the mountain of God. 2There the angel of the LORD appeared to him in flames of fire from within a bush. Moses saw that though the bush was on fire it did not burn up. 3So Moses thought, "I will go over and see this strange sight—why the bush does not burn up."

4When the LORD saw that he had gone over to look, God called to him from within the bush, "Moses! Moses!"

And Moses said, "Here I am."

5"Do not come any closer," God said. "Take off your sandals, for the place where you are standing is holy ground." 6Then he said, "I am the God of your father, the God of Abraham, the God of Isaac and the God of Jacob." At this, Moses hid his face, because he was afraid to look at God.

7The LORD said, "I have indeed seen the misery of my people in Egypt. I have heard them crying out because of their slave drivers, and I am concerned about their suffering. 8So I have come down to rescue them from the hand of the Egyptians and to bring them up out of that land into a good and spacious land, a land flowing with milk and honey—the home of the Canaanites, Hittites, Amorites, Perizzites, Hivites and Jebusites. 9And now the cry of the Israelites has reached me, and I have seen the way the Egyptians are oppressing them. 10So now, go. I am sending you to Pharaoh to bring my people the Israelites out of Egypt."

11But Moses said to God, "Who am I, that I should go to Pharaoh and bring the Israelites out of Egypt?"

12And God said, "I will be with you. And this will be the sign to you that it is I who have sent you: When you have brought the people out of Egypt, youa will worship God on this mountain."

13Moses said to God, "Suppose I go to the Israelites and say to them, 'The God of your fathers has sent me to you,' and they ask me, 'What is his name?' Then what shall I tell them?"

14God said to Moses, "I AM WHO I AM.b This is what you are to say to the Israelites: 'I AM has sent me to you.'"

15God also said to Moses, "Say to the Israelites, 'The LORD,c the God of your fathers—the God of Abraham, the God of Isaac and the God of Jacob—has sent me to you.' This is my name forever, the name by which I am to be remembered from generation to generation.

16"Go, assemble the elders of Israel and say to them, 'The LORD, the God of your fathers—the God of Abraham, Isaac and Jacob—appeared to me and said: I have watched over you and have seen what has been done to you in Egypt. 17And I have promised to bring you up out of your misery in Egypt into the land of the Canaanites, Hittites, Amorites, Perizzites, Hivites and Jebusites—a land flowing with milk and honey.'

---

a 12 The Hebrew is plural.   b 14 Or I WILL BE WHAT I WILL BE   c 15 The Hebrew for LORD sounds like and may be derived from the Hebrew for I AM in verse 14.

Living Bible

membered his promise to Abraham, Isaac, and Jacob [to bring their descendants back into the land of Canaan[d]. 25Looking down upon them, he knew that the time had come for their rescue.[e]

3 ONE DAY as Moses was tending the flock of his father-in-law Jethro,[f] the priest of Midian, out at the edge of the desert near Horeb, the mountain of God, 2suddenly the Angel of Jehovah appeared to him as a flame of fire in a bush. When Moses saw that the bush was on fire and that it didn't burn up, 3, 4he went over to investigate. Then God called out to him,

"Moses! Moses!"

"Who is it?" Moses asked.

5"Don't come any closer," God told him. "Take off your shoes, for you are standing on holy ground. 6I am the God of your fathers—the God of Abraham, Isaac, and Jacob." (Moses covered his face with his hands, for he was afraid to look at God.)

7Then the Lord told him, "I have seen the deep sorrows of my people in Egypt, and have heard their pleas for freedom from their harsh taskmasters. 8I have come to deliver them from the Egyptians and to take them out of Egypt into a good land, a large land, a land 'flowing with milk and honey'—the land where the Canaanites, Hittites, Amorites, Perizzites, Hivites, and Jebusites live. 9Yes, the wail of the people of Israel has risen to me in heaven, and I have seen the heavy tasks the Egyptians have oppressed them with. 10Now I am going to send you to Pharaoh, to demand that he let you lead my people out of Egypt."

11"But I'm not the person for a job like that!" Moses exclaimed.

12Then God told him, "I will certainly be with you, and this is the proof that I am the one who is sending you: When you have led the people out of Egypt, you shall worship God here upon this mountain!"

13But Moses asked, "If I go to the people of Israel and tell them that their fathers' God has sent me, they will ask, 'Which God are you talking about?' What shall I tell them?"

14" 'The Sovereign God,' "[g] was the reply. "Just say, 'I Am has sent me!' 15Yes, tell them, 'Jehovah,[h] the God of your ancestors Abraham, Isaac, and Jacob, has sent me to you.' (This is my eternal name, to be used throughout all generations.)

16"Call together all the elders of Israel," God instructed him, "and tell them about Jehovah appearing to you here in this burning bush and that he said to you, 'I have visited my people, and have seen what is happening to them there in Egypt. 17I promise to rescue them from the drudgery and humiliation they are undergoing, and to take them to the land now occupied by the Canaanites, Hittites, Amorites, Perizzites, Hivites, and Jebusites, a land "flowing with milk and honey." ' 18The elders of

New Revised Standard

heard their groaning, and God remembered his covenant with Abraham, Isaac, and Jacob. 25God looked upon the Israelites, and God took notice of them.

Moses at the Burning Bush

3 MOSES WAS keeping the flock of his father-in-law Jethro, the priest of Midian; he led his flock beyond the wilderness, and came to Horeb, the mountain of God. 2There the angel of the LORD appeared to him in a flame of fire out of a bush; he looked, and the bush was blazing, yet it was not consumed. 3Then Moses said, "I must turn aside and look at this great sight, and see why the bush is not burned up." 4When the LORD saw that he had turned aside to see, God called to him out of the bush, "Moses, Moses!" And he said, "Here I am." 5Then he said, "Come no closer! Remove the sandals from your feet, for the place on which you are standing is holy ground." 6He said further, "I am the God of your father, the God of Abraham, the God of Isaac, and the God of Jacob." And Moses hid his face, for he was afraid to look at God.

7 Then the LORD said, "I have observed the misery of my people who are in Egypt; I have heard their cry on account of their taskmasters. Indeed, I know their sufferings, 8and I have come down to deliver them from the Egyptians, and to bring them up out of that land to a good and broad land, a land flowing with milk and honey, to the country of the Canaanites, the Hittites, the Amorites, the Perizzites, the Hivites, and the Jebusites. 9The cry of the Israelites has now come to me; I have also seen how the Egyptians oppress them. 10So come, I will send you to Pharaoh to bring my people, the Israelites, out of Egypt." 11But Moses said to God, "Who am I that I should go to Pharaoh, and bring the Israelites out of Egypt?" 12He said, "I will be with you; and this shall be the sign for you that it is I who sent you: when you have brought the people out of Egypt, you shall worship God on this mountain."

The Divine Name Revealed

13 But Moses said to God, "If I come to the Israelites and say to them, 'The God of your ancestors has sent me to you,' and they ask me, 'What is his name?' what shall I say to them?" 14God said to Moses, "I AM WHO I AM."[i] He said further, "Thus you shall say to the Israelites, 'I AM has sent me to you.' " 15God also said to Moses, "Thus you shall say to the Israelites, 'The LORD,[j] the God of your ancestors, the God of Abraham, the God of Isaac, and the God of Jacob, has sent me to you':

This is my name forever,
   and this my title for all generations.

16Go and assemble the elders of Israel, and say to them, 'The LORD, the God of your ancestors, the God of Abraham, of Isaac, and of Jacob, has appeared to me, saying: I have given heed to you and to what has been done to you in Egypt. 17I declare that I will bring you up out of the misery of Egypt, to the land of the Canaanites, the Hittites, the Amorites, the Perizzites, the Hivites, and the Jebusites, a land flowing with milk and honey.'

---

d 2:24 to bring their descendants back into the land of Canaan, implied. e 2:25 knew that the time had come for their rescue, literally, "knew their condition." f 3:1 his father-in-law Jethro. Moses' father-in-law goes under two names in these chapters, Jethro and Reuel. g 3:14 the Sovereign God, or, "the Living God." Literally, "I am what I am," or "I will be what I will be." h 3:15 Jehovah. Properly the name should be pronounced "Yahweh," as it is spelled in many modern versions. In this paraphrase "Yahweh" is translated either "Jehovah" or "Lord."

i Or I AM WHAT I AM or I WILL BE WHAT I WILL BE   j The word "LORD" when spelled with capital letters stands for the divine name, YHWH, which is here connected with the verb hayah, "to be"

King James

18And they shall hearken to thy voice: and thou shalt come, thou and the elders of Israel, unto the king of Egypt, and ye shall say unto him, The LORD God of the Hebrews hath met with us: and now let us go, we beseech thee, three days' journey into the wilderness, that we may sacrifice to the LORD our God.

19¶ And I am sure that the king of Egypt will not let you go, no, not by a mighty hand.

20And I will stretch out my hand, and smite Egypt with all my wonders which I will do in the midst thereof: and after that he will let you go.

21And I will give this people favour in the sight of the Egyptians: and it shall come to pass, that, when ye go, ye shall not go empty:

22But every woman shall borrow of her neighbour, and of her that sojourneth in her house, jewels of silver, and jewels of gold, and raiment: and ye shall put *them* upon your sons, and upon your daughters; and ye shall spoil the Egyptians.

4 AND MOSES answered and said, But, behold, they will not believe me, nor hearken unto my voice: for they will say, The LORD hath not appeared unto thee.

2And the LORD said unto him, What *is* that in thine hand? And he said, A rod.

3And he said, Cast it on the ground. And he cast it on the ground, and it became a serpent; and Moses fled from before it.

4And the LORD said unto Moses, Put forth thine hand, and take it by the tail. And he put forth his hand, and caught it, and it became a rod in his hand:

5That they may believe that the LORD God of their fathers, the God of Abraham, the God of Isaac, and the God of Jacob, hath appeared unto thee.

6¶ And the LORD said furthermore unto him, Put now thine hand into thy bosom. And he put his hand into his bosom: and when he took it out, behold, his hand *was* leprous as snow.

7And he said, Put thine hand into thy bosom again. And he put his hand into his bosom again; and plucked it out of his bosom, and, behold, it was turned again as his *other* flesh.

8And it shall come to pass, if they will not believe thee, neither hearken to the voice of the first sign, that they will believe the voice of the latter sign.

9And it shall come to pass, if they will not believe also these two signs, neither hearken unto thy voice, that thou shalt take of the water of the river, and pour *it* upon the dry *land:* and the water which thou takest out of the river shall become blood upon the dry *land.*

10¶ And Moses said unto the LORD, O my Lord, I *am* not eloquent, neither heretofore, nor since thou hast spoken unto thy servant: but I *am* slow of speech, and of a slow tongue.

11And the LORD said unto him, Who hath made man's mouth? or who maketh the dumb, or deaf, or the seeing, or the blind? have not I the LORD?

12Now therefore go, and I will be with thy mouth, and teach thee what thou shalt say.

13And he said, O my Lord, send, I pray thee, by the hand *of him whom* thou wilt send.

14And the anger of the LORD was kindled against Moses, and he said, *Is* not Aaron the Levite thy brother? I know that he can speak well. And also, behold, he cometh forth to meet thee: and when he seeth thee, he will be glad in his heart.

15And thou shalt speak unto him, and put words in his mouth: and I will be with thy mouth, and with his mouth, and will teach you what ye shall do.

New International

18"The elders of Israel will listen to you. Then you and the elders are to go to the king of Egypt and say to him, 'The LORD, the God of the Hebrews, has met with us. Let us take a three-day journey into the desert to offer sacrifices to the LORD our God.' 19But I know that the king of Egypt will not let you go unless a mighty hand compels him. 20So I will stretch out my hand and strike the Egyptians with all the wonders that I will perform among them. After that, he will let you go.

21"And I will make the Egyptians favorably disposed toward this people, so that when you leave you will not go empty-handed. 22Every woman is to ask her neighbor and any woman living in her house for articles of silver and gold and for clothing, which you will put on your sons and daughters. And so you will plunder the Egyptians."

Signs for Moses

4 MOSES ANSWERED, "What if they do not believe me or listen to me and say, 'The LORD did not appear to you'?"

2Then the LORD said to him, "What is that in your hand?"

"A staff," he replied.

3The LORD said, "Throw it on the ground."

Moses threw it on the ground and it became a snake, and he ran from it. 4Then the LORD said to him, "Reach out your hand and take it by the tail." So Moses reached out and took hold of the snake and it turned back into a staff in his hand. 5"This," said the LORD, "is so that they may believe that the LORD, the God of their fathers—the God of Abraham, the God of Isaac and the God of Jacob—has appeared to you."

6Then the LORD said, "Put your hand inside your cloak." So Moses put his hand into his cloak, and when he took it out, it was leprous,a like snow.

7"Now put it back into your cloak," he said. So Moses put his hand back into his cloak, and when he took it out, it was restored, like the rest of his flesh.

8Then the LORD said, "If they do not believe you or pay attention to the first miraculous sign, they may believe the second. 9But if they do not believe these two signs or listen to you, take some water from the Nile and pour it on the dry ground. The water you take from the river will become blood on the ground."

10Moses said to the LORD, "O Lord, I have never been eloquent, neither in the past nor since you have spoken to your servant. I am slow of speech and tongue."

11The LORD said to him, "Who gave man his mouth? Who makes him deaf or mute? Who gives him sight or makes him blind? Is it not I, the LORD? 12Now go; I will help you speak and will teach you what to say."

13But Moses said, "O Lord, please send someone else to do it."

14Then the LORD's anger burned against Moses and he said, "What about your brother, Aaron the Levite? I know he can speak well. He is already on his way to meet you, and his heart will be glad when he sees you. 15You shall speak to him and put words in his mouth; I will help both of you speak and will teach you what to do. 16He will speak to the people for you, and it will

---

a 6 The Hebrew word was used for various diseases affecting the skin—not necessarily leprosy.

Living Bible

the people of Israel will accept your message. They must go with you to the king of Egypt and tell him, 'Jehovah, the God of the Hebrews, has met with us and instructed us to go three days' journey into the desert to sacrifice to him. Give us your permission.'

19"But I know that the king of Egypt will not let you go except under heavy pressure. 20So I will give him all the pressure he needs! I will destroy Egypt with my miracles, and then at last he will let you go. 21And I will see to it that the Egyptians load you down with gifts when you leave, so that you will by no means go out empty-handed! 22Every woman will ask for jewels, silver, gold, and the finest of clothes from her Egyptian master's wife and neighbors. You will clothe your sons and daughters with the best of Egypt!"

4 BUT MOSES said, "They won't believe me! They won't do what *I* tell them to. They'll say, 'Jehovah never appeared to you!'"

2"What do you have there in your hand?" the Lord asked him.

And he replied, "A shepherd's rod."

3"Throw it down on the ground," the Lord told him. So he threw it down—and it became a serpent, and Moses ran from it!

4Then the Lord told him, "Grab it by the tail!" He did, and it became a rod in his hand again!

5"Do that and they will believe you!" the Lord told him. "Then they will realize that Jehovah, the God of their ancestors Abraham, Isaac, and Jacob, has really appeared to you. 6Now reach your hand inside your robe, next to your chest." And when he did, and took it out again, it was white with leprosy! 7"Now put it in again," Jehovah said. And when he did, and took it out again, it was normal, just as before! 8"If they don't believe the first miracle, they will the second," the Lord said, 9"and if they don't accept you after these two signs, then take water from the Nile River and pour it upon the dry land, and it will turn to blood."

10But Moses pleaded, "O Lord, I'm just not a good speaker. I never have been, and I'm not now, even after you have spoken to me, for I have a speech impediment."b

11"Who makes mouths?" Jehovah asked him. "Isn't it I, the Lord? Who makes a man so that he can speak or not speak, see or not see, hear or not hear? 12Now go ahead and do as I tell you, for I will help you to speak well, and I will tell you what to say."

13But Moses said, "Lord, please! Send someone else."

14Then the Lord became angry. "All right," he said, "your brother Aaronc is a good speaker. And he is coming here to look for you, and will be very happy when he finds you. 15So I will tell you what to tell him, and I will help both of you to speak well, and I will tell you what to do. 16He will be your spokesman to the people.

New Revised Standard

18They will listen to your voice; and you and the elders of Israel shall go to the king of Egypt and say to him, 'The LORD, the God of the Hebrews, has met with us; let us now go a three days' journey into the wilderness, so that we may sacrifice to the LORD our God.' 19I know, however, that the king of Egypt will not let you go unless compelled by a mighty hand.d 20So I will stretch out my hand and strike Egypt with all my wonders that I will perform in it; after that he will let you go. 21I will bring this people into such favor with the Egyptians that, when you go, you will not go empty-handed; 22each woman shall ask her neighbor and any woman living in the neighbor's house for jewelry of silver and of gold, and clothing, and you shall put them on your sons and on your daughters; and so you shall plunder the Egyptians."

Moses' Miraculous Power

4 THEN MOSES answered, "But suppose they do not believe me or listen to me, but say, 'The LORD did not appear to you.'" 2The LORD said to him, "What is that in your hand?" He said, "A staff." 3And he said, "Throw it on the ground." So he threw the staff on the ground, and it became a snake; and Moses drew back from it. 4Then the LORD said to Moses, "Reach out your hand, and seize it by the tail"—so he reached out his hand and grasped it, and it became a staff in his hand— 5"so that they may believe that the LORD, the God of their ancestors, the God of Abraham, the God of Isaac, and the God of Jacob, has appeared to you."

6 Again, the LORD said to him, "Put your hand inside your cloak." He put his hand into his cloak; and when he took it out, his hand was leprous,e as white as snow. 7Then God said, "Put your hand back into your cloak"—so he put his hand back into his cloak, and when he took it out, it was restored like the rest of his body— 8"If they will not believe you or heed the first sign, they may believe the second sign. 9If they will not believe even these two signs or heed you, you shall take some water from the Nile and pour it on the dry ground; and the water that you shall take from the Nile will become blood on the dry ground."

10 But Moses said to the LORD, "O my Lord, I have never been eloquent, neither in the past nor even now that you have spoken to your servant; but I am slow of speech and slow of tongue." 11Then the LORD said to him, "Who gives speech to mortals? Who makes them mute or deaf, seeing or blind? Is it not I, the LORD? 12Now go, and I will be with your mouth and teach you what you are to speak." 13But he said, "O my Lord, please send someone else." 14Then the anger of the LORD was kindled against Moses and he said, "What of your brother Aaron, the Levite? I know that he can speak fluently; even now he is coming out to meet you, and when he sees you his heart will be glad. 15You shall speak to him and put the words in his mouth; and I will be with your mouth and with his mouth, and will teach you what you shall do. 16He indeed shall speak for you

---

b *4:10 I have a speech impediment*, literally, "my speech is slow and halting."
c *4:14 your brother Aaron*, literally, "your brother the Levite."

d Gk Vg: Heb *no, not by a mighty hand*   e A term for several skin diseases; precise meaning uncertain

King James

16And he shall be thy spokesman unto the people: and he shall be, *even* he shall be to thee instead of a mouth, and thou shalt be to him instead of God.

17And thou shalt take this rod in thine hand, wherewith thou shalt do signs.

18¶ And Moses went and returned to Jethro his father-in-law, and said unto him, Let me go, I pray thee, and return unto my brethren which *are* in Egypt, and see whether they be yet alive. And Jethro said to Moses, Go in peace.

19And the LORD said unto Moses in Midian, Go, return into Egypt: for all the men are dead which sought thy life.

20And Moses took his wife and his sons, and set them upon an ass, and he returned to the land of Egypt: and Moses took the rod of God in his hand.

21And the LORD said unto Moses, When thou goest to return into Egypt, see that thou do all those wonders before Pharaoh, which I have put in thine hand: but I will harden his heart, that he shall not let the people go.

22And thou shalt say unto Pharaoh, Thus saith the LORD, Israel *is* my son, *even* my firstborn:

23And I say unto thee, Let my son go, that he may serve me: and if thou refuse to let him go, behold, I will slay thy son, *even* thy firstborn.

24¶ And it came to pass by the way in the inn, that the LORD met him, and sought to kill him.

25Then Zipporah took a sharp stone, and cut off the foreskin of her son, and cast *it* at his feet, and said, Surely a bloody husband *art* thou to me.

26So he let him go: then she said, A bloody husband *thou art*, because of the circumcision.

27¶ And the LORD said to Aaron, Go into the wilderness to meet Moses. And he went, and met him in the mount of God, and kissed him.

28And Moses told Aaron all the words of the LORD who had sent him, and all the signs which he had commanded him.

29¶ And Moses and Aaron went and gathered together all the elders of the children of Israel:

30And Aaron spake all the words which the LORD had spoken unto Moses, and did the signs in the sight of the people.

31And the people believed: and when they heard that the LORD had visited the children of Israel, and that he had looked upon their affliction, then they bowed their heads and worshipped.

5 AND AFTERWARD Moses and Aaron went in, and told Pharaoh, Thus saith the LORD God of Israel, Let my people go, that they may hold a feast unto me in the wilderness.

2And Pharaoh said, Who *is* the LORD, that I should obey his voice to let Israel go? I know not the LORD, neither will I let Israel go.

3And they said, The God of the Hebrews hath met with us: let us go, we pray thee, three days' journey into the desert, and sacrifice unto the LORD our God; lest he fall upon us with pestilence, or with the sword.

4And the king of Egypt said unto them, Wherefore do ye, Moses and Aaron, let the people from their works? get you unto your burdens.

5And Pharaoh said, Behold, the people of the land now *are* many, and ye make them rest from their burdens.

6And Pharaoh commanded the same day the taskmasters of the people, and their officers, saying,

New International

be as if he were your mouth and as if you were God to him. 17But take this staff in your hand so you can perform miraculous signs with it."

Moses Returns to Egypt

18Then Moses went back to Jethro his father-in-law and said to him, "Let me go back to my own people in Egypt to see if any of them are still alive."

Jethro said, "Go, and I wish you well."

19Now the LORD had said to Moses in Midian, "Go back to Egypt, for all the men who wanted to kill you are dead." 20So Moses took his wife and sons, put them on a donkey and started back to Egypt. And he took the staff of God in his hand.

21The LORD said to Moses, "When you return to Egypt, see that you perform before Pharaoh all the wonders I have given you the power to do. But I will harden his heart so that he will not let the people go. 22Then say to Pharaoh, 'This is what the LORD says: Israel is my firstborn son, 23and I told you, "Let my son go, so he may worship me." But you refused to let him go; so I will kill your firstborn son.' "

24At a lodging place on the way, the LORD met Moses,[a] and was about to kill him. 25But Zipporah took a flint knife, cut off her son's foreskin and touched Moses',[b] feet with it.[b] "Surely you are a bridegroom of blood to me," she said. 26So the LORD let him alone. (At that time she said "bridegroom of blood," referring to circumcision.)

27The LORD said to Aaron, "Go into the desert to meet Moses." So he met Moses at the mountain of God and kissed him. 28Then Moses told Aaron everything the LORD had sent him to say, and also about all the miraculous signs he had commanded him to perform.

29Moses and Aaron brought together all the elders of the Israelites, 30and Aaron told them everything the LORD had said to Moses. He also performed the signs before the people, 31and they believed. And when they heard that the LORD was concerned about them and had seen their misery, they bowed down and worshiped.

Bricks Without Straw

5 AFTERWARD MOSES and Aaron went to Pharaoh and said, "This is what the LORD, the God of Israel, says: 'Let my people go, so that they may hold a festival to me in the desert.' "

2Pharaoh said, "Who is the LORD, that I should obey him and let Israel go? I do not know the LORD and I will not let Israel go."

3Then they said, "The God of the Hebrews has met with us. Now let us take a three-day journey into the desert to offer sacrifices to the LORD our God, or he may strike us with plagues or with the sword."

4But the king of Egypt said, "Moses and Aaron, why are you taking the people away from their labor? Get back to your work!" 5Then Pharaoh said, "Look, the people of the land are now numerous, and you are stopping them from working."

6That same day Pharaoh gave this order to the slave drivers and foremen in charge of the people: 7"You are

---

[a] 24 Or *Moses' son*; Hebrew *him*   [b] 25 Or *and drew near Moses', feet*

Living Bible

And you will be as God to him, telling him what to say. ¹⁷And be sure to take your rod along so that you can perform the miracles I have shown you."

¹⁸Moses returned home and talked it over with Jethro, his father-in-law. "With your permission," Moses said, "I will go back to Egypt and visit my relatives. I don't even know whether they are still alive."

"Go with my blessing," Jethro replied.

¹⁹Before Moses left Midian, Jehovah said to him, "Don't be afraid to return to Egypt, for all those who wanted to kill you are dead."

²⁰So Moses took his wife and sons and put them on a donkey, and returned to the land of Egypt, holding tightly to the "rod of God"!

²¹Jehovah told him, "When you arrive back in Egypt you are to go to Pharaoh and do the miracles I have shown you, but I will make him stubborn so that he will not let the people go. ²²Then you are to tell him, 'Jehovah says, "Israel is my eldest son, ²³and I have commanded you to let him go away and worship me, but you have refused: and now see, I will slay your eldest son." '"

²⁴As Moses and his family were traveling along and had stopped for the night, Jehovah appeared to Moses and threatened to kill him. ²⁵, ²⁶Then Zipporah his wife took a flint knife and cut off the foreskin of her young son's penis, and threw it against Moses' feet, remarking disgustedly, "What a blood-smeared husband you've turned out to be!"

Then God let him alone.

²⁷Now Jehovah said to Aaron, "Go into the wilderness to meet Moses." So Aaron traveled to Mount Horeb, the mountain of God, and met Moses there, and they greeted each other warmly. ²⁸Moses told Aaron what God had said they must do, and what they were to say, and told him about the miracles they must do before Pharaoh.

²⁹So Moses and Aaron returned to Egypt and summoned the elders of the people of Israel to a council meeting. ³⁰Aaron told them what Jehovah had said to Moses, and Moses performed the miracles as they watched. ³¹Then the elders believed that God had sent them, and when they heard that Jehovah had visited them and had seen their sorrows, and had decided to rescue them, they all rejoiced and bowed their heads and worshiped.

5 AFTER THIS presentation to the elders, Moses and Aaron went to see Pharaoh. They told him, "We bring you a message from Jehovah, the God of Israel. He says, 'Let my people go, for they must make a holy pilgrimage out into the wilderness, for a religious feast, to worship me there.' "

²"Is that so?" retorted Pharaoh. "And who is Jehovah, that I should listen to him, and let Israel go? I don't know Jehovah and I will not let Israel go."

³But Aaron and Moses persisted. "The God of the Hebrews has met with us," they declared. "We must take a three days' trip into the wilderness and sacrifice there to Jehovah our God; if we don't obey him, we face death by plague or sword."

⁴, ⁵"Who do you think you are," Pharaoh shouted, "distracting the people from their work? Get back to your jobs!" ⁶That same day Pharaoh sent this order to the taskmasters and officers he had set over the people of Israel: ⁷, ⁸"Don't give the people any more straw for

New Revised Standard

to the people; he shall serve as a mouth for you, and you shall serve as God for him. ¹⁷Take in your hand this staff, with which you shall perform the signs."

Moses Returns to Egypt

18 Moses went back to his father-in-law Jethro and said to him, "Please let me go back to my kindred in Egypt and see whether they are still living." And Jethro said to Moses, "Go in peace." ¹⁹The LORD said to Moses in Midian, "Go back to Egypt; for all those who were seeking your life are dead." ²⁰So Moses took his wife and his sons, put them on a donkey, and went back to the land of Egypt; and Moses carried the staff of God in his hand.

21 And the LORD said to Moses, "When you go back to Egypt, see that you perform before Pharaoh all the wonders that I have put in your power; but I will harden his heart, so that he will not let the people go. ²²Then you shall say to Pharaoh, 'Thus says the LORD: Israel is my firstborn son. ²³I said to you, "Let my son go that he may worship me." But you refused to let him go; now I will kill your firstborn son.' "

24 On the way, at a place where they spent the night, the LORD met him and tried to kill him. ²⁵But Zipporah took a flint and cut off her son's foreskin, and touched Moses'ᶜ feet with it, and said, "Truly you are a bridegroom of blood to me!" ²⁶So he let him alone. It was then she said, "A bridegroom of blood by circumcision."

27 The LORD said to Aaron, "Go into the wilderness to meet Moses." So he went; and he met him at the mountain of God and kissed him. ²⁸Moses told Aaron all the words of the LORD with which he had sent him, and all the signs with which he had charged him. ²⁹Then Moses and Aaron went and assembled all the elders of the Israelites. ³⁰Aaron spoke all the words that the LORD had spoken to Moses, and performed the signs in the sight of the people. ³¹The people believed; and when they heard that the LORD had given heed to the Israelites and that he had seen their misery, they bowed down and worshiped.

Bricks without Straw

5 AFTERWARD MOSES and Aaron went to Pharaoh and said, "Thus says the LORD, the God of Israel, 'Let my people go, so that they may celebrate a festival to me in the wilderness.' " ²But Pharaoh said, "Who is the LORD, that I should heed him and let Israel go? I do not know the LORD, and I will not let Israel go." ³Then they said, "The God of the Hebrews has revealed himself to us; let us go a three days' journey into the wilderness to sacrifice to the LORD our God, or he will fall upon us with pestilence or sword." ⁴But the king of Egypt said to them, "Moses and Aaron, why are you taking the people away from their work? Get to your labors!" ⁵Pharaoh continued, "Now they are more numerous than the people of the landᵈ and yet you want them to stop working!" ⁶That same day Pharaoh commanded the taskmasters of the people, as well as their supervisors, ⁷"You shall no longer give the people straw

King James

7Ye shall no more give the people straw to make brick, as heretofore: let them go and gather straw for themselves.

8And the tale of the bricks, which they did make heretofore, ye shall lay upon them; ye shall not diminish *aught* thereof: for they *be* idle; therefore they cry, saying, Let us go *and* sacrifice to our God.

9Let there more work be laid upon the men, that they may labour therein; and let them not regard vain words.

10¶ And the taskmasters of the people went out, and their officers, and they spake to the people, saying, Thus saith Pharaoh, I will not give you straw.

11Go ye, get you straw where ye can find it: yet not aught of your work shall be diminished.

12So the people were scattered abroad throughout all the land of Egypt to gather stubble instead of straw.

13And the taskmasters hasted *them,* saying, Fulfil your works, *your* daily tasks, as when there was straw.

14And the officers of the children of Israel, which Pharaoh's taskmasters had set over them, were beaten, *and* demanded, Wherefore have ye not fulfilled your task in making brick both yesterday and today, as heretofore?

15¶ Then the officers of the children of Israel came and cried unto Pharaoh, saying, Wherefore dealest thou thus with thy servants?

16There is no straw given unto thy servants, and they say to us, Make brick: and, behold, thy servants *are* beaten; but the fault *is* in thine own people.

17But he said, Ye *are* idle, *ye are* idle: therefore ye say, Let us go *and* do sacrifice to the LORD.

18Go therefore now, *and* work; for there shall no straw be given you, yet shall ye deliver the tale of bricks.

19And the officers of the children of Israel did see *that* they *were* in evil *case,* after it was said, Ye shall not minish *aught* from your bricks of your daily task.

20¶ And they met Moses and Aaron, who stood in the way, as they came forth from Pharaoh:

21And they said unto them, The LORD look upon you, and judge; because ye have made our savour to be abhorred in the eyes of Pharaoh, and in the eyes of his servants, to put a sword in their hand to slay us.

22And Moses returned unto the LORD, and said, Lord, wherefore hast thou *so* evil entreated this people? why *is* it *that* thou hast sent me?

23For since I came to Pharaoh to speak in thy name, he hath done evil to this people; neither hast thou delivered thy people at all.

6   THEN THE LORD said unto Moses, Now shalt thou see what I will do to Pharaoh: for with a strong hand shall he let them go, and with a strong hand shall he drive them out of his land.

2And God spake unto Moses, and said unto him, I *am* the LORD:

3And I appeared unto Abraham, unto Isaac, and unto Jacob, by *the name of* God Almighty, but by my name JEHOVAH was I not known to them.

4And I have also established my covenant with them, to give them the land of Canaan, the land of their pilgrimage, wherein they were strangers.

5And I have also heard the groaning of the children of Israel, whom the Egyptians keep in bondage; and I have remembered my covenant.

6Wherefore say unto the children of Israel, I *am* the LORD, and I will bring you out from under the burdens of the Egyptians, and I will rid you out of their bondage, and I will redeem you with a stretched out arm, and with great judgments:

New International

no longer to supply the people with straw for making bricks; let them go and gather their own straw. 8But require them to make the same number of bricks as before; don't reduce the quota. They are lazy; that is why they are crying out, 'Let us go and sacrifice to our God.' 9Make the work harder for the men so that they keep working and pay no attention to lies."

10Then the slave drivers and the foremen went out and said to the people, "This is what Pharaoh says: 'I will not give you any more straw. 11Go and get your own straw wherever you can find it, but your work will not be reduced at all.' " 12So the people scattered all over Egypt to gather stubble to use for straw. 13The slave drivers kept pressing them, saying, "Complete the work required of you for each day, just as when you had straw." 14The Israelite foremen appointed by Pharaoh's slave drivers were beaten and were asked, "Why didn't you meet your quota of bricks yesterday or today, as before?"

15Then the Israelite foremen went and appealed to Pharaoh: "Why have you treated your servants this way? 16Your servants are given no straw, yet we are told, 'Make bricks!' Your servants are being beaten, but the fault is with your own people."

17Pharaoh said, "Lazy, that's what you are—lazy! That is why you keep saying, 'Let us go and sacrifice to the LORD.' 18Now get to work. You will not be given any straw, yet you must produce your full quota of bricks."

19The Israelite foremen realized they were in trouble when they were told, "You are not to reduce the number of bricks required of you for each day." 20When they left Pharaoh, they found Moses and Aaron waiting to meet them, 21and they said, "May the LORD look upon you and judge you! You have made us a stench to Pharaoh and his officials and have put a sword in their hand to kill us."

God Promises Deliverance

22Moses returned to the LORD and said, "O Lord, why have you brought trouble upon this people? Is this why you sent me? 23Ever since I went to Pharaoh to speak in your name, he has brought trouble upon this people, and you have not rescued your people at all."

6   THEN THE LORD said to Moses, "Now you will see what I will do to Pharaoh: Because of my mighty hand he will let them go; because of my mighty hand he will drive them out of his country."

2God also said to Moses, "I am the LORD. 3I appeared to Abraham, to Isaac and to Jacob as God Almighty,[a] but by my name the LORD[b] I did not make myself known to them.[c] 4I also established my covenant with them to give them the land of Canaan, where they lived as aliens. 5Moreover, I have heard the groaning of the Israelites, whom the Egyptians are enslaving, and I have remembered my covenant.

6"Therefore, say to the Israelites: 'I am the LORD, and I will bring you out from under the yoke of the Egyptians. I will free you from being slaves to them, and I will redeem you with an outstretched arm and with mighty acts of judgment. 7I will take you as my own

---

a *3* Hebrew *El-Shaddai*   b *3* See note at Exodus 3:15.   c *3* Or *Almighty, and by my name the LORD did I not let myself be known to them?*

Living Bible

making bricks! However, don't reduce their production quotas by a single brick, for they obviously don't have enough to do or else they wouldn't be talking about going out into the wilderness and sacrificing to their God. 9Load them with work and make them sweat; that will teach them to listen to Moses' and Aaron's lies!"

10, 11So the taskmasters and officers informed the people: "Pharaoh has given orders to furnish you with no more straw. Go and find it wherever you can; but you must produce just as many bricks as before!" 12So the people scattered everywhere to gather straw.

13The taskmasters were brutal. "Fulfill your daily quota just as before," they kept demanding. 14Then they whipped the Israeli work-crew bosses. "Why haven't you fulfilled your quotas either yesterday or today?" they roared.

15These foremen went to Pharaoh and pleaded with him. "Don't treat us like this," they begged. 16"We are given no straw and told to make as many bricks as before, and we are beaten for something that isn't our fault—it is the fault of your taskmasters for making such unreasonable demands."

17But Pharaoh replied, "You don't have enough work, or else you wouldn't be saying, 'Let us go and sacrifice to Jehovah.' 18Get back to work. No straw will be given you, and you must deliver the regular quota of bricks."

19Then the foremen saw that they were indeed in a bad situation. 20When they met Moses and Aaron waiting for them outside the palace, as they came out from their meeting with Pharaoh, 21they swore at them. "May God judge you for making us stink before Pharaoh and his people," they said, "and for giving them an excuse to kill us."

22Then Moses went back to the Lord. "Lord," he protested, "how can you mistreat your own people like this? Why did you ever send me, if you were going to do this to them? 23Ever since I gave Pharaoh your message, he has only been more and more brutal to them, and you have not delivered them at all!"

6 "NOW YOU will see what I shall do to Pharaoh," the Lord told Moses. "For he must be forced to let my people go; he will not only let them go, but will *drive them out of his land!* 2, 3I am Jehovah, the Almighty God who appeared to Abraham, Isaac, and Jacob—though I did not reveal my name, Jehovah, to them. 4And I entered into a solemn covenant with them; under its terms I promised to give them and their descendants the land of Canaan where they were living. 5And now I have heard the groanings of the people of Israel, in slavery now to the Egyptians, and I remember my promise.

6"Therefore tell the descendants of Israel that I will use my mighty power and perform great miracles to deliver them from slavery, and make them free. 7And I

New Revised Standard

to make bricks, as before; let them go and gather straw for themselves. 8But you shall require of them the same quantity of bricks as they have made previously; do not diminish it, for they are lazy; that is why they cry, 'Let us go and offer sacrifice to our God.' 9Let heavier work be laid on them; then they will labor at it and pay no attention to deceptive words."

10 So the taskmasters and the supervisors of the people went out and said to the people, "Thus says Pharaoh, 'I will not give you straw. 11Go and get straw yourselves, wherever you can find it; but your work will not be lessened in the least.' " 12So the people scattered throughout the land of Egypt, to gather stubble for straw. 13The taskmasters were urgent, saying, "Complete your work, the same daily assignment as when you were given straw." 14And the supervisors of the Israelites, whom Pharaoh's taskmasters had set over them, were beaten, and were asked, "Why did you not finish the required quantity of bricks yesterday and today, as you did before?"

15 Then the Israelite supervisors came to Pharaoh and cried, "Why do you treat your servants like this? 16No straw is given to your servants, yet they say to us, 'Make bricks!' Look how your servants are beaten! You are unjust to your own people."d 17He said, "You are lazy, lazy; that is why you say, 'Let us go and sacrifice to the LORD.' 18Go now, and work; for no straw shall be given you, but you shall still deliver the same number of bricks." 19The Israelite supervisors saw that they were in trouble when they were told, "You shall not lessen your daily number of bricks." 20As they left Pharaoh, they came upon Moses and Aaron who were waiting to meet them. 21They said to them, "The LORD look upon you and judge! You have brought us into bad odor with Pharaoh and his officials, and have put a sword in their hand to kill us."

22 Then Moses turned again to the LORD and said, "O LORD, why have you mistreated this people? Why did you ever send me? 23Since I first came to Pharaoh to speak in your name, he has mistreated this people, and you have done nothing at all to deliver your people."

Israel's Deliverance Assured

6 THEN THE LORD said to Moses, "Now you shall see what I will do to Pharaoh: Indeed, by a mighty hand he will let them go; by a mighty hand he will drive them out of his land."

2 God also spoke to Moses and said to him: "I am the LORD. 3I appeared to Abraham, Isaac, and Jacob as God Almighty,e but by my name 'The LORD'f I did not make myself known to them. 4I also established my covenant with them, to give them the land of Canaan, the land in which they resided as aliens. 5I have also heard the groaning of the Israelites whom the Egyptians are holding as slaves, and I have remembered my covenant. 6Say therefore to the Israelites, 'I am the LORD, and I will free you from the burdens of the Egyptians and deliver you from slavery to them. I will redeem you with an outstretched arm and with mighty acts of judgment.

d Gk Compare Syr Vg: Heb *beaten, and the sin of your people*   e Traditional rendering of Heb *El Shaddai*   f Heb *YHWH*; see note at 3.15

King James

7And I will take you to me for a people, and I will be to you a God: and ye shall know that I *am* the LORD your God, which bringeth you out from under the burdens of the Egyptians.

8And I will bring you in unto the land, concerning the which I did swear to give it to Abraham, to Isaac, and to Jacob; and I will give it you for an heritage: I *am* the LORD.

9¶ And Moses spake so unto the children of Israel: but they hearkened not unto Moses for anguish of spirit, and for cruel bondage.

10And the LORD spake unto Moses, saying,

11Go in, speak unto Pharaoh king of Egypt, that he let the children of Israel go out of his land.

12And Moses spake before the LORD, saying, Behold, the children of Israel have not hearkened unto me; how then shall Pharaoh hear me, who *am* of uncircumcised lips?

13And the LORD spake unto Moses and unto Aaron, and gave them a charge unto the children of Israel, and unto Pharaoh king of Egypt, to bring the children of Israel out of the land of Egypt.

14¶ These *be* the heads of their fathers' houses: The sons of Reuben the firstborn of Israel; Hanoch, and Pallu, Hezron, and Carmi: these *be* the families of Reuben.

15And the sons of Simeon; Jemuel, and Jamin, and Ohad, and Jachin, and Zohar, and Shaul the son of a Canaanitish woman: these *are* the families of Simeon.

16¶ And these *are* the names of the sons of Levi according to their generations; Gershon, and Kohath, and Merari: and the years of the life of Levi *were* an hundred thirty and seven years.

17The sons of Gershon; Libni, and Shimi, according to their families.

18And the sons of Kohath; Amram, and Izhar, and Hebron, and Uzziel: and the years of the life of Kohath *were* an hundred thirty and three years.

19And the sons of Merari; Mahali and Mushi: these *are* the families of Levi according to their generations.

20And Amram took him Jochebed his father's sister to wife; and she bare him Aaron and Moses: and the years of the life of Amram *were* an hundred and thirty and seven years.

21¶ And the sons of Izhar; Korah, and Nepheg, and Zichri.

22And the sons of Uzziel; Mishael, and Elzaphan, and Zithri.

23And Aaron took him Elisheba, daughter of Amminadab, sister of Naashon, to wife; and she bare him Nadab, and Abihu, Eleazar, and Ithamar.

24And the sons of Korah; Assir, and Elkanah, and Abiasaph: these *are* the families of the Korhites.

25And Eleazar Aaron's son took him *one* of the daughters of Putiel to wife; and she bare him Phinehas: these *are* the heads of the fathers of the Levites according to their families.

26These *are* that Aaron and Moses, to whom the LORD said, Bring out the children of Israel from the land of Egypt according to their armies.

27These *are* they which spake to Pharaoh king of Egypt, to bring out the children of Israel from Egypt: these *are* that Moses and Aaron.

28¶ And it came to pass on the day *when* the LORD spake unto Moses in the land of Egypt,

29That the LORD spake unto Moses, saying, I *am* the LORD: speak thou unto Pharaoh king of Egypt all that I say unto thee.

30And Moses said before the LORD, Behold, I *am* of uncircumcised lips, and how shall Pharaoh hearken unto me?

New International

people, and I will be your God. Then you will know that I am the LORD your God, who brought you out from under the yoke of the Egyptians. 8And I will bring you to the land I swore with uplifted hand to give to Abraham, to Isaac and to Jacob. I will give it to you as a possession. I am the LORD.' "

9Moses reported this to the Israelites, but they did not listen to him because of their discouragement and cruel bondage.

10Then the LORD said to Moses, 11"Go, tell Pharaoh king of Egypt to let the Israelites go out of his country."

12But Moses said to the LORD, "If the Israelites will not listen to me, why would Pharaoh listen to me, since I speak with faltering lips[a]?"

Family Record of Moses and Aaron

13Now the LORD spoke to Moses and Aaron about the Israelites and Pharaoh king of Egypt, and he commanded them to bring the Israelites out of Egypt.

14These were the heads of their families[b]:

The sons of Reuben the firstborn son of Israel were Hanoch and Pallu, Hezron and Carmi. These were the clans of Reuben.

15The sons of Simeon were Jemuel, Jamin, Ohad, Jakin, Zohar and Shaul the son of a Canaanite woman. These were the clans of Simeon.

16These were the names of the sons of Levi according to their records: Gershon, Kohath and Merari. Levi lived 137 years.

17The sons of Gershon, by clans, were Libni and Shimei.

18The sons of Kohath were Amram, Izhar, Hebron and Uzziel. Kohath lived 133 years.

19The sons of Merari were Mahli and Mushi. These were the clans of Levi according to their records.

20Amram married his father's sister Jochebed, who bore him Aaron and Moses. Amram lived 137 years.

21The sons of Izhar were Korah, Nepheg and Zicri.

22The sons of Uzziel were Mishael, Elzaphan and Sithri.

23Aaron married Elisheba, daughter of Amminadab and sister of Nahshon, and she bore him Nadab and Abihu, Eleazar and Ithamar.

24The sons of Korah were Assir, Elkanah and Abiasaph. These were the Korahite clans.

25Eleazar son of Aaron married one of the daughters of Putiel, and she bore him Phinehas.

These were the heads of the Levite families, clan by clan.

26It was this same Aaron and Moses to whom the LORD said, "Bring the Israelites out of Egypt by their divisions." 27They were the ones who spoke to Pharaoh king of Egypt about bringing the Israelites out of Egypt. It was the same Moses and Aaron.

Aaron to Speak for Moses

28Now when the LORD spoke to Moses in Egypt, 29he said to him, "I am the LORD. Tell Pharaoh king of Egypt everything I tell you."

30But Moses said to the LORD, "Since I speak with faltering lips, why would Pharaoh listen to me?"

---

a 12 Hebrew *I am uncircumcised of lips;* also in verse 30   b 14 The Hebrew for *families* here and in verse 25 refers to units larger than clans.

Living Bible

will accept them as my people and be their God. And they shall know that I am Jehovah their God who has rescued them from the Egyptians. 8, 9I will bring them into the land I promised to give to Abraham, Isaac, and Jacob. It shall belong to my people."

So Moses told the people what God had said, but they wouldn't listen any more because they were too dispirited after the tragic consequence of what he had said before.c

10Now the Lord spoke to Moses again and told him, 11"Go back again to Pharaoh and tell him that he *must* let the people of Israel go."

12"But look," Moses objected, "my own people won't even listen to me any more; how can I expect Pharaoh to? I'm no orator!"

13Then the Lord ordered Moses and Aaron to return to the people of Israel and to Pharaoh, king of Egypt, demanding that the people be permitted to leave.

14These are the names of the heads of the clans of the various tribes of Israel:

The sons of Reuben, Israel's oldest son:
Hanoch, Pallu, Hezron, Carmi.

15The heads of the clans of the tribe of Simeon:
Jemuel, Jamin, Ohad, Jachin, Zohar, Shaul (whose mother was a Canaanite).

16These are the names of the heads of the clans of the tribe of Levi, in the order of their ages:d
Gershon, Kohath, Merari. (Levi lived 137 years.)

17The sons of Gershon were:
Libni, Shime-i, (and their clans).

18The sons of Kohath:
Amram, Izhar, Hebron, Uzziel.
(Kohath lived 133 years.)

19The sons of Merari:
Mahli, Mushi.

The above are the families of the Levites, listed according to their ages.

20And Amrame married Jochebed, his father's sister; and Aaron and Moses were their sons.
Amram lived to the age of 137.

21The sons of Izhar:
Korah, Nepheg, Zichri.

22The sons of Uzziel:
Misha-el, Elzaphan, Sithri.

23Aaron married Elisheba, the daughter of Amminadab and sister of Nahshon. Their children were:
Nadab, Abihu, Eleazar, Ithamar.

24The sons of Korah:
Assir, Elkanah, Abiasaph.
These are the families within the clan of Korah.

25Aaron's son Eleazar married one of the daughters of Puti-el, and Phinehas was one of his children. These are all the names of the heads of the clans of the Levites, and the families within the clans.

26Aaron and Moses, included in that list, are the same Aaron and Moses to whom Jehovah said, "Lead all the people of Israel out of the land of Egypt," 27and who went to Pharaoh to ask permission to lead the people from the land, 28, 29and to whom the Lord said, "I am Jehovah. Go in and give Pharaoh the message I have given you."

30This is that Moses who argued with the Lord, "I can't do it; I'm no speaker—why should Pharaoh listen to *me?*"

New Revised Standard

7I will take you as my people, and I will be your God. You shall know that I am the LORD your God, who has freed you from the burdens of the Egyptians. 8I will bring you into the land that I swore to give to Abraham, Isaac, and Jacob; I will give it to you for a possession. I am the LORD.' " 9Moses told this to the Israelites; but they would not listen to Moses, because of their broken spirit and their cruel slavery.

10 Then the LORD spoke to Moses, 11"Go and tell Pharaoh king of Egypt to let the Israelites go out of his land." 12But Moses spoke to the LORD, "The Israelites have not listened to me; how then shall Pharaoh listen to me, poor speaker that I am?"f 13Thus the LORD spoke to Moses and Aaron, and gave them orders regarding the Israelites and Pharaoh king of Egypt, charging them to free the Israelites from the land of Egypt.

The Genealogy of Moses and Aaron

14 The following are the heads of their ancestral houses: the sons of Reuben, the firstborn of Israel: Hanoch, Pallu, Hezron, and Carmi; these are the families of Reuben. 15The sons of Simeon: Jemuel, Jamin, Ohad, Jachin, Zohar, and Shaul,g the son of a Canaanite woman; these are the families of Simeon. 16The following are the names of the sons of Levi according to their genealogies: Gershon,h Kohath, and Merari, and the length of Levi's life was one hundred thirty-seven years. 17The sons of Gershon:h Libni and Shimei, by their families. 18The sons of Kohath: Amram, Izhar, Hebron, and Uzziel, and the length of Kohath's life was one hundred thirty-three years. 19The sons of Merari: Mahli and Mushi. These are the families of the Levites according to their genealogies. 20Amram married Jochebed his father's sister and she bore him Aaron and Moses, and the length of Amram's life was one hundred thirty-seven years. 21The sons of Izhar: Korah, Nepheg, and Zichri. 22The sons of Uzziel: Mishael, Elzaphan, and Sithri. 23Aaron married Elisheba, daughter of Amminadab and sister of Nahshon, and she bore him Nadab, Abihu, Eleazar, and Ithamar. 24The sons of Korah: Assir, Elkanah, and Abiasaph; these are the families of the Korahites. 25Aaron's son Eleazar married one of the daughters of Putiel, and she bore him Phinehas. These are the heads of the ancestral houses of the Levites by their families.

26 It was this same Aaron and Moses to whom the LORD said, "Bring the Israelites out of the land of Egypt, company by company." 27It was they who spoke to Pharaoh king of Egypt to bring the Israelites out of Egypt, the same Moses and Aaron.

Moses and Aaron Obey God's Commands

28 On the day when the LORD spoke to Moses in the land of Egypt, 29he said to him, "I am the LORD; tell Pharaoh king of Egypt all that I am speaking to you." 30But Moses said in the LORD's presence, "Since I am a poor speaker,i why would Pharaoh listen to me?"

---

c 6:8, 9 because they were too dispirited after the tragic consequence of what he had said before, literally, "because of their broken spirit and the cruel bondage."   d 6:16 in the order of their ages, literally, "according to their generations." So also in verse 19.   e 6:20 Amram. See verse 18.

f Heb me? I am uncircumcised of lips   g Or Saul   h Also spelled Gershom; see 2.22   i Heb am uncircumcised of lips; see 6.12

King James

7 AND THE LORD said unto Moses, See, I have made thee a god to Pharaoh: and Aaron thy brother shall be thy prophet.

2Thou shalt speak all that I command thee: and Aaron thy brother shall speak unto Pharaoh, that he send the children of Israel out of his land.

3And I will harden Pharaoh's heart, and multiply my signs and my wonders in the land of Egypt.

4But Pharaoh shall not hearken unto you, that I may lay my hand upon Egypt, and bring forth mine armies, *and* my people the children of Israel, out of the land of Egypt by great judgments.

5And the Egyptians shall know that I *am* the LORD, when I stretch forth mine hand upon Egypt, and bring out the children of Israel from among them.

6And Moses and Aaron did as the LORD commanded them, so did they.

7And Moses *was* fourscore years old, and Aaron fourscore and three years old, when they spake unto Pharaoh.

8¶ And the LORD spake unto Moses and unto Aaron, saying,

9When Pharaoh shall speak unto you, saying, Show a miracle for you: then thou shalt say unto Aaron, Take thy rod, and cast *it* before Pharaoh, *and* it shall become a serpent.

10¶ And Moses and Aaron went in unto Pharaoh, and they did so as the LORD had commanded: and Aaron cast down his rod before Pharaoh, and before his servants, and it became a serpent.

11Then Pharaoh also called the wise men and the sorcerers: now the magicians of Egypt, they also did in like manner with their enchantments.

12For they cast down every man his rod, and they became serpents: but Aaron's rod swallowed up their rods.

13And he hardened Pharaoh's heart, that he hearkened not unto them; as the LORD had said.

14¶ And the LORD said unto Moses, Pharaoh's heart *is* hardened, he refuseth to let the people go.

15Get thee unto Pharaoh in the morning; lo, he goeth out unto the water; and thou shalt stand by the river's brink against he come; and the rod which was turned to a serpent shalt thou take in thine hand.

16And thou shalt say unto him, The LORD God of the Hebrews hath sent me unto thee, saying, Let my people go, that they may serve me in the wilderness: and, behold, hitherto thou wouldest not hear.

17Thus saith the LORD, In this thou shalt know that I *am* the LORD: behold, I will smite with the rod that *is* in mine hand upon the waters which *are* in the river, and they shall be turned to blood.

18And the fish that *is* in the river shall die, and the river shall stink; and the Egyptians shall loathe to drink of the water of the river.

19¶ And the LORD spake unto Moses, Say unto Aaron, Take thy rod, and stretch out thine hand upon the waters of Egypt, upon their streams, upon their rivers, and upon their ponds, and upon all their pools of water, that they may become blood; and *that* there may be blood throughout all the land of Egypt, both in *vessels of* wood, and in *vessels of* stone.

20And Moses and Aaron did so, as the LORD commanded; and he lifted up the rod, and smote the waters that *were* in the river, in the sight of Pharaoh, and in the sight of his servants; and all the waters that *were* in the river were turned to blood.

21And the fish that *was* in the river died; and the river stank, and the Egyptians could not drink of the water of the river; and there was blood throughout all the land of Egypt.

22And the magicians of Egypt did so with their enchantments: and Pharaoh's heart was hardened, neither did he hearken unto them; as the LORD had said.

New International

7 THEN THE LORD said to Moses, "See, I have made you like God to Pharaoh, and your brother Aaron will be your prophet. 2You are to say everything I command you, and your brother Aaron is to tell Pharaoh to let the Israelites go out of his country. 3But I will harden Pharaoh's heart, and though I multiply my miraculous signs and wonders in Egypt, 4he will not listen to you. Then I will lay my hand on Egypt and with mighty acts of judgment I will bring out my divisions, my people the Israelites. 5And the Egyptians will know that I am the LORD when I stretch out my hand against Egypt and bring the Israelites out of it."

6Moses and Aaron did just as the LORD commanded them. 7Moses was eighty years old and Aaron eighty-three when they spoke to Pharaoh.

Aaron's Staff Becomes a Snake

8The LORD said to Moses and Aaron, 9"When Pharaoh says to you, 'Perform a miracle,' then say to Aaron, 'Take your staff and throw it down before Pharaoh,' and it will become a snake."

10So Moses and Aaron went to Pharaoh and did just as the LORD commanded. Aaron threw his staff down in front of Pharaoh and his officials, and it became a snake. 11Pharaoh then summoned wise men and sorcerers, and the Egyptian magicians also did the same things by their secret arts: 12Each one threw down his staff and it became a snake. But Aaron's staff swallowed up their staffs. 13Yet Pharaoh's heart became hard and he would not listen to them, just as the LORD had said.

The Plague of Blood

14Then the LORD said to Moses, "Pharaoh's heart is unyielding; he refuses to let the people go. 15Go to Pharaoh in the morning as he goes out to the water. Wait on the bank of the Nile to meet him, and take in your hand the staff that was changed into a snake. 16Then say to him, 'The LORD, the God of the Hebrews, has sent me to say to you: Let my people go, so that they may worship me in the desert. But until now you have not listened. 17This is what the LORD says: By this you will know that I am the LORD: With the staff that is in my hand I will strike the water of the Nile, and it will be changed into blood. 18The fish in the Nile will die, and the river will stink; the Egyptians will not be able to drink its water.' "

19The LORD said to Moses, "Tell Aaron, 'Take your staff and stretch out your hand over the waters of Egypt—over the streams and canals, over the ponds and all the reservoirs'—and they will turn to blood. Blood will be everywhere in Egypt, even in the wooden buckets and stone jars."

20Moses and Aaron did just as the LORD had commanded. He raised his staff in the presence of Pharaoh and his officials and struck the water of the Nile, and all the water was changed into blood. 21The fish in the Nile died, and the river smelled so bad that the Egyptians could not drink its water. Blood was everywhere in Egypt.

22But the Egyptian magicians did the same things by their secret arts, and Pharaoh's heart became hard; he would not listen to Moses and Aaron, just as the LORD had said. 23Instead, he turned and went into his palace,

Living Bible

7 THEN THE Lord said to Moses, "See, I have appointed you as my ambassador to Pharaoh, and your brother Aaron shall be your spokesman. ²Tell Aaron everything I say to you, and he will announce it to Pharaoh, demanding that the people of Israel be allowed to leave Egypt. ³But I will cause Pharaoh to stubbornly refuse, and I will multiply my miracles in the land of Egypt. ⁴Yet even then Pharaoh won't listen to you; so I will crush Egypt with a final major disaster and then lead my people out. ⁵The Egyptians will find out that I am indeed God when I show them my power and force them to let my people go."

⁶So Moses and Aaron did as the Lord commanded them. ⁷Moses was eighty years old and Aaron eighty-three at this time of their confrontation with Pharaoh.

⁸Then the Lord said to Moses and Aaron, ⁹"Pharaoh will demand that you show him a miracle to prove that God has sent you; when he does, Aaron is to throw down his rod, and it will become a serpent."

¹⁰So Moses and Aaron went in to see Pharaoh, and performed the miracle, as Jehovah had instructed them—Aaron threw down his rod before Pharaoh and his court, and it became a serpent. ¹¹Then Pharaoh called in his sorcerers—the magicians of Egypt—and they were able to do the same thing with their magical arts! ¹²Their rods became serpents, too! But Aaron's serpent swallowed their serpents! ¹³Pharaoh's heart was still hard and stubborn, and he wouldn't listen, just as the Lord had predicted. ¹⁴The Lord pointed this out to Moses, that Pharaoh's heart had been unmoved, and that he would continue to refuse to let the people go.

¹⁵"Nevertheless," the Lord said, "go back to Pharaoh in the morning, to be there as he goes down to the river. Stand beside the river bank and meet him there, holding in your hand the rod that turned into a serpent. ¹⁶Say to him, 'Jehovah, the God of the Hebrews, has sent me back to demand that you let his people go to worship him in the wilderness. You wouldn't listen before, ¹⁷and now the Lord says this: "You are going to find out that I am God. For I have instructed Moses to hit the water of the Nile with his rod, and the river will turn to blood! ¹⁸The fish will die and the river will stink, so that the Egyptians will be unwilling to drink it." ' "

¹⁹Then the Lord instructed Moses: "Tell Aaron to point his rod toward the waters of Egypt: all its rivers, canals, marshes, and reservoirs, and even the water stored in bowls and pots in the homes will turn to blood."

²⁰So Moses and Aaron did as the Lord commanded them. As Pharaoh and all of his officials watched, Aaron hit the surface of the Nile with the rod, and the river turned to blood. ²¹The fish died and the water became so foul that the Egyptians couldn't drink it; and there was blood throughout the land of Egypt. ²²But then the magicians of Egypt used their secret arts and they, too, turned water into blood; so Pharaoh's heart remained hard and stubborn, and he wouldn't listen to Moses and Aaron, just as the Lord had predicted, ²³and he returned to his

New Revised Standard

7 THE LORD said to Moses, "See, I have made you like God to Pharaoh, and your brother Aaron shall be your prophet. ²You shall speak all that I command you, and your brother Aaron shall tell Pharaoh to let the Israelites go out of his land. ³But I will harden Pharaoh's heart, and I will multiply my signs and wonders in the land of Egypt. ⁴When Pharaoh does not listen to you, I will lay my hand upon Egypt and bring my people the Israelites, company by company, out of the land of Egypt by great acts of judgment. ⁵The Egyptians shall know that I am the LORD, when I stretch out my hand against Egypt and bring the Israelites out from among them." ⁶Moses and Aaron did so; they did just as the LORD commanded them. ⁷Moses was eighty years old and Aaron eighty-three when they spoke to Pharaoh.

Aaron's Miraculous Rod

⁸ The LORD said to Moses and Aaron, ⁹"When Pharaoh says to you, 'Perform a wonder,' then you shall say to Aaron, 'Take your staff and throw it down before Pharaoh, and it will become a snake.' " ¹⁰So Moses and Aaron went to Pharaoh and did as the LORD had commanded; Aaron threw down his staff before Pharaoh and his officials, and it became a snake. ¹¹Then Pharaoh summoned the wise men and the sorcerers; and they also, the magicians of Egypt, did the same by their secret arts. ¹²Each one threw down his staff, and they became snakes; but Aaron's staff swallowed up theirs. ¹³Still Pharaoh's heart was hardened, and he would not listen to them, as the LORD had said.

The First Plague: Water Turned to Blood

¹⁴ Then the LORD said to Moses, "Pharaoh's heart is hardened; he refuses to let the people go. ¹⁵Go to Pharaoh in the morning, as he is going out to the water; stand by at the river bank to meet him, and take in your hand the staff that was turned into a snake. ¹⁶Say to him, 'The LORD, the God of the Hebrews, sent me to you to say, "Let my people go, so that they may worship me in the wilderness." But until now you have not listened.' ¹⁷Thus says the LORD, "By this you shall know that I am the LORD." See, with the staff that is in my hand I will strike the water that is in the Nile, and it shall be turned to blood. ¹⁸The fish in the river shall die, the river itself shall stink, and the Egyptians shall be unable to drink water from the Nile.' " ¹⁹The LORD said to Moses, "Say to Aaron, 'Take your staff and stretch out your hand over the waters of Egypt—over its rivers, its canals, and its ponds, and all its pools of water—so that they may become blood; and there shall be blood throughout the whole land of Egypt, even in vessels of wood and in vessels of stone.' "

²⁰ Moses and Aaron did just as the LORD commanded. In the sight of Pharaoh and of his officials, Moses lifted up the staff and struck the water in the river, and all the water in the river was turned into blood, ²¹and the fish in the river died. The river stank so that the Egyptians could not drink its water, and there was blood throughout the whole land of Egypt. ²²But the magicians of Egypt did the same by their secret arts; so Pharaoh's heart remained hardened, and he would not listen to them; as the LORD had said. ²³Pharaoh turned and went

King James

23And Pharaoh turned and went into his house, neither did he set his heart to this also.

24And all the Egyptians digged round about the river for water to drink; for they could not drink of the water of the river.

25And seven days were fulfilled, after that the LORD had smitten the river.

8 AND THE LORD spake unto Moses, Go unto Pharaoh, and say unto him, Thus saith the LORD, Let my people go, that they may serve me.

2And if thou refuse to let *them* go, behold, I will smite all thy borders with frogs:

3And the river shall bring forth frogs abundantly, which shall go up and come into thine house, and into thy bedchamber, and upon thy bed, and into the house of thy servants, and upon thy people, and into thine ovens, and into thy kneadingtroughs:

4And the frogs shall come up both on thee, and upon thy people, and upon all thy servants.

5¶ And the LORD spake unto Moses, Say unto Aaron, Stretch forth thine hand with thy rod over the streams, over the rivers, and over the ponds, and cause frogs to come up upon the land of Egypt.

6And Aaron stretched out his hand over the waters of Egypt; and the frogs came up, and covered the land of Egypt.

7And the magicians did so with their enchantments, and brought up frogs upon the land of Egypt.

8¶ Then Pharaoh called for Moses and Aaron, and said, Entreat the LORD, that he may take away the frogs from me, and from my people; and I will let the people go, that they may do sacrifice unto the LORD.

9And Moses said unto Pharaoh, Glory over me: when shall I entreat for thee, and for thy servants, and for thy people, to destroy the frogs from thee and thy houses, *that* they may remain in the river only?

10And he said, Tomorrow. And he said, *Be it* according to thy word: that thou mayest know that *there is* none like the LORD our God.

11And the frogs shall depart from thee, and from thy houses, and from thy servants, and from thy people; they shall remain in the river only.

12And Moses and Aaron went out from Pharaoh: and Moses cried unto the LORD because of the frogs which he had brought against Pharaoh.

13And the LORD did according to the word of Moses; and the frogs died out of the houses, out of the villages, and out of the fields.

14And they gathered them together upon heaps: and the land stank.

15But when Pharaoh saw that there was respite, he hardened his heart, and hearkened not unto them; as the LORD had said.

16¶ And the LORD said unto Moses, Say unto Aaron, Stretch out thy rod, and smite the dust of the land, that it may become lice throughout all the land of Egypt.

17And they did so; for Aaron stretched out his hand with his rod, and smote the dust of the earth, and it became lice in man, and in beast; all the dust of the land became lice throughout all the land of Egypt.

18And the magicians did so with their enchantments to bring forth lice, but they could not: so there were lice upon man, and upon beast.

19Then the magicians said unto Pharaoh, This *is* the finger of God: and Pharaoh's heart was hardened, and he hearkened not unto them; as the LORD had said.

20¶ And the LORD said unto Moses, Rise up early in the morning, and stand before Pharaoh; lo, he cometh forth to the water; and say unto him, Thus saith the LORD, Let my people go, that they may serve me.

New International

and did not take even this to heart. 24And all the Egyptians dug along the Nile to get drinking water, because they could not drink the water of the river.

The Plague of Frogs

25Seven days passed after the LORD struck the Nile.

8 THEN THE LORD said to Moses, "Go to Pharaoh and say to him, 'This is what the LORD says: Let my people go, so that they may worship me. 2If you refuse to let them go, I will plague your whole country with frogs. 3The Nile will teem with frogs. They will come up into your palace and your bedroom and onto your bed, into the houses of your officials and on your people, and into your ovens and kneading troughs. 4The frogs will go up on you and your people and all your officials.' "

5Then the LORD said to Moses, "Tell Aaron, 'Stretch out your hand with your staff over the streams and canals and ponds, and make frogs come up on the land of Egypt.' "

6So Aaron stretched out his hand over the waters of Egypt, and the frogs came up and covered the land. 7But the magicians did the same things by their secret arts; they also made frogs come up on the land of Egypt.

8Pharaoh summoned Moses and Aaron and said, "Pray to the LORD to take the frogs away from me and my people, and I will let your people go to offer sacrifices to the LORD."

9Moses said to Pharaoh, "I leave to you the honor of setting the time for me to pray for you and your officials and your people that you and your houses may be rid of the frogs, except for those that remain in the Nile."

10"Tomorrow," Pharaoh said.

Moses replied, "It will be as you say, so that you may know there is no one like the LORD our God. 11The frogs will leave you and your houses, your officials and your people; they will remain only in the Nile."

12After Moses and Aaron left Pharaoh, Moses cried out to the LORD about the frogs he had brought on Pharaoh. 13And the LORD did what Moses asked. The frogs died in the houses, in the courtyards and in the fields. 14They were piled into heaps, and the land reeked of them. 15But when Pharaoh saw that there was relief, he hardened his heart and would not listen to Moses and Aaron, just as the LORD had said.

The Plague of Gnats

16Then the LORD said to Moses, "Tell Aaron, 'Stretch out your staff and strike the dust of the ground,' and throughout the land of Egypt the dust will become gnats." 17They did this, and when Aaron stretched out his hand with the staff and struck the dust of the ground, gnats came upon men and animals. All the dust throughout the land of Egypt became gnats. 18But when the magicians tried to produce gnats by their secret arts, they could not. And the gnats were on men and animals.

19The magicians said to Pharaoh, "This is the finger of God." But Pharaoh's heart was hard and he would not listen, just as the LORD had said.

The Plague of Flies

20Then the LORD said to Moses, "Get up early in the morning and confront Pharaoh as he goes to the water and say to him, 'This is what the LORD says: Let my people go, so that they may worship me. 21If you do not

Living Bible

palace, unimpressed. 24Then the Egyptians dug wells along the river bank to get drinking water, for they couldn't drink from the river.

25A week went by.

8 THEN THE Lord said to Moses, "Go in again to Pharaoh and tell him, 'Jehovah says, "Let my people go and worship me. 2If you refuse, I will send vast hordes of frogs across your land from one border to the other. 3, 4The Nile River will swarm with them, and they will come out into your houses, even into your bedrooms and right into your beds! Every home in Egypt will be filled with them. They will fill your ovens and your kneading bowls; you and your people will be immersed in them!" ' "

5Then the Lord said to Moses, "Instruct Aaron to point the rod toward all the rivers, streams, and pools of Egypt, so that there will be frogs in every corner of the land." 6Aaron did, and frogs covered the nation. 7But the magicians did the same with their secret arts, and they, too, caused frogs to come up upon the land.

8Then Pharaoh summoned Moses and Aaron and begged, "Plead with God to take the frogs away, and I will let the people go and sacrifice to him."

9"Be so kind as to tell me when you want them to go," Moses said, "and I will pray that the frogs will die at the time you specify, everywhere except in the river."

10"Do it tomorrow," Pharaoh said.

"All right," Moses replied, "it shall be as you have said; then you will know that there is no one like the Lord our God. 11All the frogs will be destroyed, except those in the river."

12So Moses and Aaron went out from the presence of Pharaoh, and Moses pleaded with the Lord concerning the frogs he had sent. 13And the Lord did as Moses promised—dead frogs covered the countryside and filled the nation's homes. 14They were piled into great heaps, making a terrible stench throughout the land. 15But when Pharaoh saw that the frogs were gone, he hardened his heart and refused to let the people go, just as the Lord had predicted.

16Then the Lord said to Moses, "Tell Aaron to strike the dust with his rod, and it will become lice, throughout all the land of Egypt." 17So Moses and Aaron did as God commanded, and suddenly lice infested the entire nation, covering the Egyptians and their animals. 18Then the magicians tried to do the same thing with their secret arts, but this time they failed.

19"This is the finger of God," they exclaimed to Pharaoh. But Pharaoh's heart was hard and stubborn, and he wouldn't listen to them, just as the Lord had predicted.

20Next the Lord told Moses, "Get up early in the morning and meet Pharaoh as he comes out to the river to bathe, and say to him, 'Jehovah says, "Let my people go and worship me. 21If you refuse I will send swarms

New Revised Standard

into his house, and he did not take even this to heart. 24And all the Egyptians had to dig along the Nile for water to drink, for they could not drink the water of the river.

25 Seven days passed after the LORD had struck the Nile.

The Second Plague: Frogs

8a THEN THE LORD said to Moses, "Go to Pharaoh and say to him, 'Thus says the LORD: Let my people go, so that they may worship me. 2If you refuse to let them go, I will plague your whole country with frogs. 3The river shall swarm with frogs; they shall come up into your palace, into your bedchamber and your bed, and into the houses of your officials and of your people,b and into your ovens and your kneading bowls. 4The frogs shall come up on you and on your people and on all your officials.' " 5cAnd the LORD said to Moses, "Say to Aaron, 'Stretch out your hand with your staff over the rivers, the canals, and the pools, and make frogs come up on the land of Egypt.' " 6So Aaron stretched out his hand over the waters of Egypt; and the frogs came up and covered the land of Egypt. 7But the magicians did the same by their secret arts, and brought frogs up on the land of Egypt.

8 Then Pharaoh called Moses and Aaron, and said, "Pray to the LORD to take away the frogs from me and my people, and I will let the people go to sacrifice to the LORD." 9Moses said to Pharaoh, "Kindly tell me when I am to pray for you and for your officials and for your people, that the frogs may be removed from you and your houses and be left only in the Nile." 10And he said, "Tomorrow." Moses said, "As you say! So that you may know that there is no one like the LORD our God, 11the frogs shall leave you and your houses and your officials and your people; they shall be left only in the Nile." 12Then Moses and Aaron went out from Pharaoh; and Moses cried out to the LORD concerning the frogs that he had brought upon Pharaoh.d 13And the LORD did as Moses requested: the frogs died in the houses, the courtyards, and the fields. 14And they gathered them together in heaps, and the land stank. 15But when Pharaoh saw that there was a respite, he hardened his heart, and would not listen to them, just as the LORD had said.

The Third Plague: Gnats

16 Then the LORD said to Moses, "Say to Aaron, 'Stretch out your staff and strike the dust of the earth, so that it may become gnats throughout the whole land of Egypt.' " 17And they did so; Aaron stretched out his hand with his staff and struck the dust of the earth, and gnats came on humans and animals alike; all the dust of the earth turned into gnats throughout the whole land of Egypt. 18The magicians tried to produce gnats by their secret arts, but they could not. There were gnats on both humans and animals. 19And the magicians said to Pharaoh, "This is the finger of God!" But Pharaoh's heart was hardened, and he would not listen to them, just as the LORD had said.

The Fourth Plague: Flies

20 Then the LORD said to Moses, "Rise early in the morning and present yourself before Pharaoh, as he goes out to the water, and say to him, 'Thus says the LORD: Let my people go, so that they may worship me. 21For

a Ch 7.26 in Heb   b Gk: Heb *upon your people*   c Ch 8.1 in Heb
d Or *frogs, as he had agreed with Pharaoh*

King James

21Else, if thou wilt not let my people go, behold, I will send swarms *of flies* upon thee, and upon thy servants, and upon thy people, and into thy houses: and the houses of the Egyptians shall be full of swarms *of flies,* and also the ground whereon they *are.*

22And I will sever in that day the land of Goshen, in which my people dwell, that no swarms *of flies* shall be there; to the end thou mayest know that I *am* the LORD in the midst of the earth.

23And I will put a division between my people and thy people: tomorrow shall this sign be.

24And the LORD did so; and there came a grievous swarm *of flies* into the house of Pharaoh, and *into* his servants' houses, and into all the land of Egypt: the land was corrupted by reason of the swarm *of flies.*

25¶ And Pharaoh called for Moses and for Aaron, and said, Go ye, sacrifice to your God in the land.

26And Moses said, It is not meet so to do; for we shall sacrifice the abomination of the Egyptians to the LORD our God: lo, shall we sacrifice the abomination of the Egyptians before their eyes, and will they not stone us?

27We will go three days' journey into the wilderness, and sacrifice to the LORD our God, as he shall command us.

28And Pharaoh said, I will let you go, that ye may sacrifice to the LORD your God in the wilderness; only ye shall not go very far away: entreat for me.

29And Moses said, Behold, I go out from thee, and I will entreat the LORD that the swarms *of flies* may depart from Pharaoh, from his servants, and from his people, tomorrow: but let not Pharaoh deal deceitfully any more in not letting the people go to sacrifice to the LORD.

30And Moses went out from Pharaoh, and entreated the LORD.

31And the LORD did according to the word of Moses; and he removed the swarms *of flies* from Pharaoh, from his servants, and from his people; there remained not one.

32And Pharaoh hardened his heart at this time also, neither would he let the people go.

9 THEN THE LORD said unto Moses, Go in unto Pharaoh, and tell him, Thus saith the LORD God of the Hebrews, Let my people go, that they may serve me.

2For if thou refuse to let *them* go, and wilt hold them still,

3Behold, the hand of the LORD is upon thy cattle which *is* in the field, upon the horses, upon the asses, upon the camels, upon the oxen, and upon the sheep: *there shall be* a very grievous murrain.

4And the LORD shall sever between the cattle of Israel and the cattle of Egypt: and there shall nothing die of all *that is* the children's of Israel.

5And the LORD appointed a set time, saying, Tomorrow the LORD shall do this thing in the land.

6And the LORD did that thing on the morrow, and all the cattle of Egypt died: but of the cattle of the children of Israel died not one.

7And Pharaoh sent, and, behold, there was not one of the cattle of the Israelites dead. And the heart of Pharaoh was hardened, and he did not let the people go.

8¶ And the LORD said unto Moses and unto Aaron, Take to you handfuls of ashes of the furnace, and let Moses sprinkle it toward the heaven in the sight of Pharaoh.

9And it shall become small dust in all the land of Egypt, and shall be a boil breaking forth *with* blains upon man, and upon beast, throughout all the land of Egypt.

New International

let my people go, I will send swarms of flies on you and your officials, on your people and into your houses. The houses of the Egyptians will be full of flies, and even the ground where they are.

22" 'But on that day I will deal differently with the land of Goshen, where my people live; no swarms of flies will be there, so that you will know that I, the LORD, am in this land. 23I will make a distinctiona between my people and your people. This miraculous sign will occur tomorrow.' "

24And the LORD did this. Dense swarms of flies poured into Pharaoh's palace and into the houses of his officials, and throughout Egypt the land was ruined by the flies.

25Then Pharaoh summoned Moses and Aaron and said, "Go, sacrifice to your God here in the land."

26But Moses said, "That would not be right. The sacrifices we offer the LORD our God would be detestable to the Egyptians. And if we offer sacrifices that are detestable in their eyes, will they not stone us? 27We must take a three-day journey into the desert to offer sacrifices to the LORD our God, as he commands us."

28Pharaoh said, "I will let you go to offer sacrifices to the LORD your God in the desert, but you must not go very far. Now pray for me."

29Moses answered, "As soon as I leave you, I will pray to the LORD, and tomorrow the flies will leave Pharaoh and his officials and his people. Only be sure that Pharaoh does not act deceitfully again by not letting the people go to offer sacrifices to the LORD."

30Then Moses left Pharaoh and prayed to the LORD, 31and the LORD did what Moses asked: The flies left Pharaoh and his officials and his people; not a fly remained. 32But this time also Pharaoh hardened his heart and would not let the people go.

The Plague on Livestock

9 THEN THE LORD said to Moses, "Go to Pharaoh and say to him, 'This is what the LORD, the God of the Hebrews, says: "Let my people go, so that they may worship me." 2If you refuse to let them go and continue to hold them back, 3the hand of the LORD will bring a terrible plague on your livestock in the field—on your horses and donkeys and camels and on your cattle and sheep and goats. 4But the LORD will make a distinction between the livestock of Israel and that of Egypt, so that no animal belonging to the Israelites will die.' "

5The LORD set a time and said, "Tomorrow the LORD will do this in the land." 6And the next day the LORD did it: All the livestock of the Egyptians died, but not one animal belonging to the Israelites died. 7Pharaoh sent men to investigate and found that not even one of the animals of the Israelites had died. Yet his heart was unyielding and he would not let the people go.

The Plague of Boils

8Then the LORD said to Moses and Aaron, "Take handfuls of soot from a furnace and have Moses toss it into the air in the presence of Pharaoh. 9It will become fine dust over the whole land of Egypt, and festering boils will break out on men and animals throughout the land."

a 23 Septuagint and Vulgate; Hebrew *will put a deliverance*

Living Bible

of flies throughout Egypt. Your homes will be filled with them and the ground will be covered with them. 22But it will be very different in the land of Goshen where the Israelis live. No flies will be there; thus you will know that I am the Lord God of all the earth, 23for I will make a distinction between your people and my people. All this will happen tomorrow." ' "

24And Jehovah did as he had said, so that there were terrible swarms of flies in Pharaoh's palace and in every home in Egypt.

25Pharaoh hastily summoned Moses and Aaron and said, "All right, go ahead and sacrifice to your God, but do it here in the land. Don't go out into the wilderness."

26But Moses replied, "That won't do! Our sacrifices to God are hated by the Egyptians, and if we do this right here before their eyes, they will kill us. 27We must take a three-day trip into the wilderness and sacrifice there to Jehovah our God, as he commanded us."

28"All right, go ahead," Pharaoh replied, "but don't go too far away. Now, hurry and plead with God for me."

29"Yes," Moses said, "I will ask him to cause the swarms of flies to disappear. But I am warning you that you must never again lie to us by promising to let the people go and then changing your mind."

30So Moses went out from Pharaoh and asked the Lord to get rid of the flies. 31, 32And the Lord did as Moses asked and caused the swarms to disappear, so that not one remained. But Pharaoh hardened his heart again and did not let the people go!

9 "GO BACK to Pharaoh," the Lord commanded Moses, "and tell him, 'Jehovah, the God of the Hebrews, demands that you let his people go to sacrifice to him. 2If you refuse, 3the power of God will send a deadly plague to destroy your cattle, horses, donkeys, camels, flocks, and herds. 4But the plague will affect only the cattle of Egypt; none of the Israeli herds and flocks will even be touched!' "

5The Lord announced that the plague would begin the very next day, 6and it did. The next morning all the cattle of the Egyptians began dying, but not one of the Israeli herds was even sick. 7Pharaoh sent to see whether it was true that none of the Israeli cattle were dead, yet when he found out that it was so, even then his mind remained unchanged and he refused to let the people go.

8Then Jehovah said to Moses and Aaron, "Take ashes from the kiln. Moses, toss it into the sky as Pharaoh watches. 9It will spread like fine dust over all the land of Egypt and cause boils to break out upon people and animals alike, throughout the land."

New Revised Standard

if you will not let my people go, I will send swarms of flies on you, your officials, and your people, and into your houses; and the houses of the Egyptians shall be filled with swarms of flies; so also the land where they live. 22But on that day I will set apart the land of Goshen, where my people live, so that no swarms of flies shall be there, that you may know that I the LORD am in this land. 23Thus I will make a distinction[b] between my people and your people. This sign shall appear tomorrow.' " 24The LORD did so, and great swarms of flies came into the house of Pharaoh and into his officials' houses; in all of Egypt the land was ruined because of the flies.

25 Then Pharaoh summoned Moses and Aaron, and said, "Go, sacrifice to your God within the land." 26But Moses said, "It would not be right to do so; for the sacrifices that we offer to the LORD our God are offensive to the Egyptians. If we offer in the sight of the Egyptians sacrifices that are offensive to them, will they not stone us? 27We must go a three days' journey into the wilderness and sacrifice to the LORD our God as he commands us." 28So Pharaoh said, "I will let you go to sacrifice to the LORD your God in the wilderness, provided you do not go very far away. Pray for me." 29Then Moses said, "As soon as I leave you, I will pray to the LORD that the swarms of flies may depart tomorrow from Pharaoh, from his officials, and from his people; only do not let Pharaoh again deal falsely by not letting the people go to sacrifice to the LORD."

30 So Moses went out from Pharaoh and prayed to the LORD. 31And the LORD did as Moses asked: he removed the swarms of flies from Pharaoh, from his officials, and from his people; not one remained. 32But Pharaoh hardened his heart this time also, and would not let the people go.

The Fifth Plague: Livestock Diseased

9 THEN THE LORD said to Moses, "Go to Pharaoh, and say to him, 'Thus says the LORD, the God of the Hebrews: Let my people go, so that they may worship me. 2For if you refuse to let them go and still hold them, 3the hand of the LORD will strike with a deadly pestilence your livestock in the field: the horses, the donkeys, the camels, the herds, and the flocks. 4But the LORD will make a distinction between the livestock of Israel and the livestock of Egypt, so that nothing shall die of all that belongs to the Israelites.' " 5The LORD set a time, saying, "Tomorrow the LORD will do this thing in the land." 6And on the next day the LORD did so; all the livestock of the Egyptians died, but of the livestock of the Israelites not one died. 7Pharaoh inquired and found that not one of the livestock of the Israelites was dead. But the heart of Pharaoh was hardened, and he would not let the people go.

The Sixth Plague: Boils

8 Then the LORD said to Moses and Aaron, "Take handfuls of soot from the kiln, and let Moses throw it in the air in the sight of Pharaoh. 9It shall become fine dust all over the land of Egypt, and shall cause festering boils on humans and animals throughout the whole land of Egypt." 10So they took soot from the kiln, and stood

b Gk Vg: Heb will set redemption

King James

10And they took ashes of the furnace, and stood before Pharaoh; and Moses sprinkled it up toward heaven; and it became a boil breaking forth *with* blains upon man, and upon beast.

11And the magicians could not stand before Moses because of the boils; for the boil was upon the magicians, and upon all the Egyptians.

12And the LORD hardened the heart of Pharaoh, and he hearkened not unto them; as the LORD had spoken unto Moses.

13¶ And the LORD said unto Moses, Rise up early in the morning, and stand before Pharaoh, and say unto him, Thus saith the LORD God of the Hebrews, Let my people go, that they may serve me.

14For I will at this time send all my plagues upon thine heart, and upon thy servants, and upon thy people; that thou mayest know that *there is* none like me in all the earth.

15For now I will stretch out my hand, that I may smite thee and thy people with pestilence; and thou shalt be cut off from the earth.

16And in very deed for this *cause* have I raised thee up, for to show *in* thee my power; and that my name may be declared throughout all the earth.

17As yet exaltest thou thyself against my people, that thou wilt not let them go?

18Behold, tomorrow about this time I will cause it to rain a very grievous hail, such as hath not been in Egypt since the foundation thereof even until now.

19Send therefore now, *and* gather thy cattle, and all that thou hast in the field; *for upon* every man and beast which shall be found in the field, and shall not be brought home, the hail shall come down upon them, and they shall die.

20He that feared the word of the LORD among the servants of Pharaoh made his servants and his cattle flee into the houses:

21And he that regarded not the word of the LORD left his servants and his cattle in the field.

22¶ And the LORD said unto Moses, Stretch forth thine hand toward heaven, that there may be hail in all the land of Egypt, upon man, and upon beast, and upon every herb of the field, throughout the land of Egypt.

23And Moses stretched forth his rod toward heaven: and the LORD sent thunder and hail, and the fire ran along upon the ground; and the LORD rained hail upon the land of Egypt.

24So there was hail, and fire mingled with the hail, very grievous, such as there was none like it in all the land of Egypt since it became a nation.

25And the hail smote throughout all the land of Egypt all that *was* in the field, both man and beast; and the hail smote every herb of the field, and brake every tree of the field.

26Only in the land of Goshen, where the children of Israel *were*, was there no hail.

27¶ And Pharaoh sent, and called for Moses and Aaron, and said unto them, I have sinned this time: the LORD *is* righteous, and I and my people *are* wicked.

28Entreat the LORD (for *it is* enough) that there be no *more* mighty thunderings and hail; and I will let you go, and ye shall stay no longer.

29And Moses said unto him, As soon as I am gone out of the city, I will spread abroad my hands unto the LORD; *and* the thunder shall cease, neither shall there be any more hail; that thou mayest know how that the earth *is* the LORD's.

30But as for thee and thy servants, I know that ye will not yet fear the LORD God.

31And the flax and the barley was smitten: for the barley *was* in the ear, and the flax *was* bolled.

32But the wheat and the rie were not smitten: for they *were* not grown up.

New International

10So they took soot from a furnace and stood before Pharaoh. Moses tossed it into the air, and festering boils broke out on men and animals. 11The magicians could not stand before Moses because of the boils that were on them and on all the Egyptians. 12But the LORD hardened Pharaoh's heart and he would not listen to Moses and Aaron, just as the LORD had said to Moses.

The Plague of Hail

13Then the LORD said to Moses, "Get up early in the morning, confront Pharaoh and say to him, 'This is what the LORD, the God of the Hebrews, says: Let my people go, so that they may worship me, 14or this time I will send the full force of my plagues against you and against your officials and your people, so you may know that there is no one like me in all the earth. 15For by now I could have stretched out my hand and struck you and your people with a plague that would have wiped you off the earth. 16But I have raised you upa for this very purpose, that I might show you my power and that my name might be proclaimed in all the earth. 17You still set yourself against my people and will not let them go. 18Therefore, at this time tomorrow I will send the worst hailstorm that has ever fallen on Egypt, from the day it was founded till now. 19Give an order now to bring your livestock and everything you have in the field to a place of shelter, because the hail will fall on every man and animal that has not been brought in and is still out in the field, and they will die.'"

20Those officials of Pharaoh who feared the word of the LORD hurried to bring their slaves and their livestock inside. 21But those who ignored the word of the LORD left their slaves and livestock in the field.

22Then the LORD said to Moses, "Stretch out your hand toward the sky so that hail will fall all over Egypt—on men and animals and on everything growing in the fields of Egypt." 23When Moses stretched out his staff toward the sky, the LORD sent thunder and hail, and lightning flashed down to the ground. So the LORD rained hail on the land of Egypt; 24hail fell and lightning flashed back and forth. It was the worst storm in all the land of Egypt since it had become a nation. 25Throughout Egypt hail struck everything in the fields—both men and animals; it beat down everything growing in the fields and stripped every tree. 26The only place it did not hail was the land of Goshen, where the Israelites were.

27Then Pharaoh summoned Moses and Aaron. "This time I have sinned," he said to them. "The LORD is in the right, and I and my people are in the wrong. 28Pray to the LORD, for we have had enough thunder and hail. I will let you go; you don't have to stay any longer."

29Moses replied, "When I have gone out of the city, I will spread out my hands in prayer to the LORD. The thunder will stop and there will be no more hail, so you may know that the earth is the LORD's. 30But I know that you and your officials still do not fear the LORD God."

31(The flax and barley were destroyed, since the barley had headed and the flax was in bloom. 32The wheat and spelt, however, were not destroyed, because they ripen later.)

a 16 Or *have spared you*

Living Bible

10So they took ashes from the kiln and went to Pharaoh; as he watched, Moses tossed it toward the sky, and it became boils that broke out on men and animals alike throughout all Egypt. 11And the magicians couldn't stand before Moses because of the boils, for the boils appeared upon them too. 12But Jehovah hardened Pharaoh in his stubbornness, so that he refused to listen, just as the Lord had predicted to Moses.

13Then the Lord said to Moses, "Get up early in the morning and stand before Pharaoh and tell him, 'Jehovah the God of the Hebrews says, "Let my people go to worship me. 14This time I am going to send a plague that will really speak to you and to your servants and to all the Egyptian people, and prove to you there is no other God in all the earth. 15I could have killed you all by now, 16but I didn't, for I wanted to demonstrate my power to you and to all the earth. 17So you still think you are so great, do you, and defy my power, and refuse to let my people go? 18Well, tomorrow about this time I will send a hailstorm across the nation such as there has never been since Egypt was founded! 19Quick! Bring in your cattle from the fields, for every man and animal left out in the fields will die beneath the hail!" ' "

20Some of the Egyptians, terrified by this threat, brought their cattle and slaves in from the fields; 21but those who had no regard for the word of Jehovah left them out in the storm.

22Then Jehovah said to Moses, "Point your hand toward heaven and cause the hail to fall throughout all Egypt, upon the people, animals, and trees."

23So Moses held out his hand, and the Lord sent thunder and hail and lightning. 24It was terrible beyond description. Never in all the history of Egypt had there been a storm like that. 25All Egypt lay in ruins. Everything left in the fields, men and animals alike, was killed, and the trees were shattered and the crops were destroyed. 26The only spot in all Egypt without hail that day was the land of Goshen where the people of Israel lived.

27Then Pharaoh sent for Moses and Aaron. "I finally see my fault," he confessed. "Jehovah is right, and I and my people have been wrong all along. 28Beg God to end this terrifying thunder and hail, and I will let you go at once."

29"All right," Moses replied, "as soon as I have left the city I will spread out my hands to the Lord, and the thunder and hail will stop. This will prove to you that the earth is controlled by Jehovah. 30But as for you and your officials, I know that even yet you will not obey him." 31All the flax and barley were knocked down and destroyed (for the barley was ripe, and the flax was in bloom), 32but the wheat and the emmer were not destroyed, for they were not yet out of the ground.

New Revised Standard

before Pharaoh, and Moses threw it in the air, and it caused festering boils on humans and animals. 11The magicians could not stand before Moses because of the boils, for the boils afflicted the magicians as well as all the Egyptians. 12But the LORD hardened the heart of Pharaoh, and he would not listen to them, just as the LORD had spoken to Moses.

The Seventh Plague: Thunder and Hail

13 Then the LORD said to Moses, "Rise up early in the morning and present yourself before Pharaoh, and say to him, 'Thus says the LORD, the God of the Hebrews: Let my people go, so that they may worship me. 14For this time I will send all my plagues upon you yourself, and upon your officials, and upon your people, so that you may know that there is no one like me in all the earth. 15For by now I could have stretched out my hand and struck you and your people with pestilence, and you would have been cut off from the earth. 16But this is why I have let you live: to show you my power, and to make my name resound through all the earth. 17You are still exalting yourself against my people, and will not let them go. 18Tomorrow at this time I will cause the heaviest hail to fall that has ever fallen in Egypt from the day it was founded until now. 19Send, therefore, and have your livestock and everything that you have in the open field brought to a secure place; every human or animal that is in the open field and is not brought under shelter will die when the hail comes down upon them.' " 20Those officials of Pharaoh who feared the word of the LORD hurried their slaves and livestock off to a secure place. 21Those who did not regard the word of the LORD left their slaves and livestock in the open field.

22 The LORD said to Moses, "Stretch out your hand toward heaven so that hail may fall on the whole land of Egypt, on humans and animals and all the plants of the field in the land of Egypt." 23Then Moses stretched out his staff toward heaven, and the LORD sent thunder and hail, and fire came down on the earth. And the LORD rained hail on the land of Egypt; 24there was hail with fire flashing continually in the midst of it, such heavy hail as had never fallen in all the land of Egypt since it became a nation. 25The hail struck down everything that was in the open field throughout all the land of Egypt, both human and animal; the hail also struck down all the plants of the field, and shattered every tree in the field. 26Only in the land of Goshen, where the Israelites were, there was no hail.

27 Then Pharaoh summoned Moses and Aaron, and said to them, "This time I have sinned; the LORD is in the right, and I and my people are in the wrong. 28Pray to the LORD! Enough of God's thunder and hail! I will let you go; you need stay no longer." 29Moses said to him, "As soon as I have gone out of the city, I will stretch out my hands to the LORD; the thunder will cease, and there will be no more hail, so that you may know that the earth is the LORD's. 30But as for you and your officials, I know that you do not yet fear the LORD God." 31(Now the flax and the barley were ruined, for the barley was in the ear and the flax was in bud. 32But the wheat and the spelt were not ruined, for they are late in coming up.) 33So Moses left Pharaoh, went out of the

King James

33And Moses went out of the city from Pharaoh, and spread abroad his hands unto the LORD: and the thunders and hail ceased, and the rain was not poured upon the earth.

34And when Pharaoh saw that the rain and the hail and the thunders were ceased, he sinned yet more, and hardened his heart, he and his servants.

35And the heart of Pharaoh was hardened, neither would he let the children of Israel go; as the LORD had spoken by Moses.

10 AND THE LORD said unto Moses, Go in unto Pharaoh: for I have hardened his heart, and the heart of his servants, that I might show these my signs before him:

2And that thou mayest tell in the ears of thy son, and of thy son's son, what things I have wrought in Egypt, and my signs which I have done among them; that ye may know how that I am the LORD.

3And Moses and Aaron came in unto Pharaoh, and said unto him, Thus saith the LORD God of the Hebrews, How long wilt thou refuse to humble thyself before me? let my people go, that they may serve me.

4Else, if thou refuse to let my people go, behold, tomorrow will I bring the locusts into thy coast:

5And they shall cover the face of the earth, that one cannot be able to see the earth: and they shall eat the residue of that which is escaped, which remaineth unto you from the hail, and shall eat every tree which groweth for you out of the field:

6And they shall fill thy houses, and the houses of all thy servants, and the houses of all the Egyptians; which neither thy fathers, nor thy fathers' fathers have seen, since the day that they were upon the earth unto this day. And he turned himself, and went out from Pharaoh.

7And Pharaoh's servants said unto him, How long shall this man be a snare unto us? let the men go, that they may serve the LORD their God: knowest thou not yet that Egypt is destroyed?

8And Moses and Aaron were brought again unto Pharaoh: and he said unto them, Go, serve the LORD your God: but who are they that shall go?

9And Moses said, We will go with our young and with our old, with our sons and with our daughters, with our flocks and with our herds will we go; for we must hold a feast unto the LORD.

10And he said unto them, Let the LORD be so with you, as I will let you go, and your little ones: look to it; for evil is before you.

11Not so: go now ye that are men, and serve the LORD; for that ye did desire. And they were driven out from Pharaoh's presence.

12¶ And the LORD said unto Moses, Stretch out thine hand over the land of Egypt for the locusts, that they may come up upon the land of Egypt, and eat every herb of the land, even all that the hail hath left.

13And Moses stretched forth his rod over the land of Egypt, and the LORD brought an east wind upon the land all that day, and all that night; and when it was morning, the east wind brought the locusts.

14And the locusts went up over all the land of Egypt, and rested in all the coasts of Egypt: very grievous were they; before them there were no such locusts as they, neither after them shall be such.

15For they covered the face of the whole earth, so that the land was darkened; and they did eat every herb of the land, and all the fruit of the trees which the hail had left: and there remained not any green thing in the trees, or in the herbs of the field, through all the land of Egypt.

16¶ Then Pharaoh called for Moses and Aaron in haste; and he said, I have sinned against the LORD your God, and against you.

New International

33Then Moses left Pharaoh and went out of the city. He spread out his hands toward the LORD; the thunder and hail stopped, and the rain no longer poured down on the land. 34When Pharaoh saw that the rain and hail and thunder had stopped, he sinned again: He and his officials hardened their hearts. 35So Pharaoh's heart was hard and he would not let the Israelites go, just as the LORD had said through Moses.

The Plague of Locusts

10 THEN THE LORD said to Moses, "Go to Pharaoh, for I have hardened his heart and the hearts of his officials so that I may perform these miraculous signs of mine among them 2that you may tell your children and grandchildren how I dealt harshly with the Egyptians and how I performed my signs among them, and that you may know that I am the LORD."

3So Moses and Aaron went to Pharaoh and said to him, "This is what the LORD, the God of the Hebrews, says: 'How long will you refuse to humble yourself before me? Let my people go, so that they may worship me. 4If you refuse to let them go, I will bring locusts into your country tomorrow. 5They will cover the face of the ground so that it cannot be seen. They will devour what little you have left after the hail, including every tree that is growing in your fields. 6They will fill your houses and those of all your officials and all the Egyptians—something neither your fathers nor your forefathers have ever seen from the day they settled in this land till now.'" Then Moses turned and left Pharaoh.

7Pharaoh's officials said to him, "How long will this man be a snare to us? Let the people go, so that they may worship the LORD their God. Do you not yet realize that Egypt is ruined?"

8Then Moses and Aaron were brought back to Pharaoh. "Go, worship the LORD your God," he said. "But just who will be going?"

9Moses answered, "We will go with our young and old, with our sons and daughters, and with our flocks and herds, because we are to celebrate a festival to the LORD."

10Pharaoh said, "The LORD be with you—if I let you go, along with your women and children! Clearly you are bent on evil.a 11No! Have only the men go; and worship the LORD, since that's what you have been asking for." Then Moses and Aaron were driven out of Pharaoh's presence.

12And the LORD said to Moses, "Stretch out your hand over Egypt so that locusts will swarm over the land and devour everything growing in the fields, everything left by the hail."

13So Moses stretched out his staff over Egypt, and the LORD made an east wind blow across the land all that day and all that night. By morning the wind had brought the locusts; 14they invaded all Egypt and settled down in every area of the country in great numbers. Never before had there been such a plague of locusts, nor will there ever be again. 15They covered all the ground until it was black. They devoured all that was left after the hail—everything growing in the fields and the fruit on the trees. Nothing green remained on tree or plant in all the land of Egypt.

16Pharaoh quickly summoned Moses and Aaron and said, "I have sinned against the LORD your God and against you. 17Now forgive my sin once more and pray

a 10 Or Be careful, trouble is in store for you!

Living Bible

33So Moses left Pharaoh and went out of the city and lifted his hands to heaven to the Lord, and the thunder and hail stopped, and the rain ceased pouring down. 34When Pharaoh saw this, he and his officials sinned yet more by their stubborn refusal to do what they had promised; 35so Pharaoh refused to let the people leave, just as the Lord had predicted to Moses.

10 THEN THE Lord said to Moses, "Go back again and make your demand upon Pharaoh; but I have hardened him and his officials, so that I can do more miracles demonstrating my power. 2What stories you can tell your children and grandchildren about the incredible things I am doing in Egypt! Tell them what fools I made of the Egyptians, and how I proved to you that I am Jehovah."

3So Moses and Aaron requested another audience with Pharaoh and told him: "Jehovah, the God of the Hebrews, asks, 'How long will you refuse to submit to me? Let my people go so they can worship me. 4, 5If you refuse, tomorrow I will cover the entire nation with a thick layer of locusts so that you won't even be able to see the ground, and they will finish destroying everything that escaped the hail. 6They will fill your palace, and the homes of your officials, and all the houses of Egypt. Never in the history of Egypt has there been a plague like this will be!' " Then Moses stalked out.

7The court officials now came to Pharaoh and asked him, "Are you going to destroy us completely? Don't you know even yet that all Egypt lies in ruins? Let the men go and serve Jehovah their God!"

8So Moses and Aaron were brought back to Pharaoh. "All right, go and serve Jehovah your God!" he said. "But just who is it you want to go?"

9"We will go with our sons and daughters, flocks and herds," Moses replied. "We will take everything with us; for we must all join in the holy pilgrimage."

10"In the name of God I will not let you take your little ones!" Pharaoh retorted. "I can see your plot! 11Never! You that are men, go and serve Jehovah, for that is what you asked for." And they were driven out from Pharaoh's presence.

12Then the Lord said to Moses, "Hold out your hand over the land of Egypt to bring locusts—they will cover the land and eat everything the hail has left."

13So Moses lifted his rod and Jehovah caused an east wind to blow all that day and night; and when it was morning, the east wind had brought the locusts. 14And the locusts covered the land of Egypt from border to border; it was the worst locust plague in all Egyptian history; and there will never again be another like it. 15For the locusts covered the face of the earth and blotted out the sun so that the land was darkened; and they ate every bit of vegetation the hail had left; there remained not one green thing—not a tree, not a plant throughout all the land of Egypt.

16Then Pharaoh sent an urgent call for Moses and Aaron and said to them, "I confess my sin against Jehovah your God, and against you. 17Forgive my sin only

New Revised Standard

city, and stretched out his hands to the LORD; then the thunder and the hail ceased, and the rain no longer poured down on the earth. 34But when Pharaoh saw that the rain and the hail and the thunder had ceased, he sinned once more and hardened his heart, he and his officials. 35So the heart of Pharaoh was hardened, and he would not let the Israelites go, just as the LORD had spoken through Moses.

The Eighth Plague: Locusts

10 THEN THE LORD said to Moses, "Go to Pharaoh; for I have hardened his heart and the heart of his officials, in order that I may show these signs of mine among them, 2and that you may tell your children and grandchildren how I have made fools of the Egyptians and what signs I have done among them—so that you may know that I am the LORD."

3 So Moses and Aaron went to Pharaoh, and said to him, "Thus says the LORD, the God of the Hebrews, 'How long will you refuse to humble yourself before me? Let my people go, so that they may worship me. 4For if you refuse to let my people go, tomorrow I will bring locusts into your country. 5They shall cover the surface of the land, so that no one will be able to see the land. They shall devour the last remnant left you after the hail, and they shall devour every tree of yours that grows in the field. 6They shall fill your houses, and the houses of all your officials and of all the Egyptians—something that neither your parents nor your grandparents have seen, from the day they came on earth to this day.' " Then he turned and went out from Pharaoh.

7 Pharaoh's officials said to him, "How long shall this fellow be a snare to us? Let the people go, so that they may worship the LORD their God; do you not yet understand that Egypt is ruined?" 8So Moses and Aaron were brought back to Pharaoh, and he said to them, "Go, worship the LORD your God! But which ones are to go?" 9Moses said, "We will go with our young and our old; we will go with our sons and daughters and with our flocks and herds, because we have the LORD's festival to celebrate." 10He said to them, "The LORD indeed will be with you, if ever I let your little ones go with you! Plainly, you have some evil purpose in mind. 11No, never! Your men may go and worship the LORD, for that is what you are asking." And they were driven out from Pharaoh's presence.

12 Then the LORD said to Moses, "Stretch out your hand over the land of Egypt, so that the locusts may come upon it and eat every plant in the land, all that the hail has left." 13So Moses stretched out his staff over the land of Egypt, and the LORD brought an east wind upon the land all that day and all that night; when morning came, the east wind had brought the locusts. 14The locusts came upon all the land of Egypt and settled on the whole country of Egypt, such a dense swarm of locusts as had never been before, nor ever shall be again. 15They covered the surface of the whole land, so that the land was black; and they ate all the plants in the land and all the fruit of the trees that the hail had left; nothing green was left, no tree, no plant in the field, in all the land of Egypt. 16Pharaoh hurriedly summoned Moses and Aaron and said, "I have sinned against the LORD your God, and against you. 17Do forgive my sin just this

King James

17Now therefore forgive, I pray thee, my sin only this once, and entreat the LORD your God, that he may take away from me this death only.

18And he went out from Pharaoh, and entreated the LORD.

19And the LORD turned a mighty strong west wind, which took away the locusts, and cast them into the Red sea; there remained not one locust in all the coasts of Egypt.

20But the LORD hardened Pharaoh's heart, so that he would not let the children of Israel go.

21¶ And the LORD said unto Moses, Stretch out thine hand toward heaven, that there may be darkness over the land of Egypt, even darkness *which* may be felt.

22And Moses stretched forth his hand toward heaven; and there was a thick darkness in all the land of Egypt three days:

23They saw not one another, neither rose any from his place for three days: but all the children of Israel had light in their dwellings.

24¶ And Pharaoh called unto Moses, and said, Go ye, serve the LORD; only let your flocks and your herds be stayed: let your little ones also go with you.

25And Moses said, Thou must give us also sacrifices and burnt offerings, that we may sacrifice unto the LORD our God.

26Our cattle also shall go with us; there shall not an hoof be left behind; for thereof must we take to serve the LORD our God; and we know not with what we must serve the LORD, until we come thither.

27¶ But the LORD hardened Pharaoh's heart, and he would not let them go.

28And Pharaoh said unto him, Get thee from me, take heed to thyself, see my face no more; for in *that* day thou seest my face thou shalt die.

29And Moses said, Thou hast spoken well, I will see thy face again no more.

11 AND THE LORD said unto Moses, Yet will I bring one plague *more* upon Pharaoh, and upon Egypt; afterwards he will let you go hence: when he shall let *you* go, he shall surely thrust you out hence altogether.

2Speak now in the ears of the people, and let every man borrow of his neighbour, and every woman of her neighbour, jewels of silver, and jewels of gold.

3And the LORD gave the people favour in the sight of the Egyptians. Moreover the man Moses *was* very great in the land of Egypt, in the sight of Pharaoh's servants, and in the sight of the people.

4And Moses said, Thus saith the LORD, About midnight will I go out into the midst of Egypt:

5And all the firstborn in the land of Egypt shall die, from the firstborn of Pharaoh that sitteth upon his throne, even unto the firstborn of the maidservant that *is* behind the mill; and all the firstborn of beasts.

6And there shall be a great cry throughout all the land of Egypt, such as there was none like it, nor shall be like it any more.

7But against any of the children of Israel shall not a dog move his tongue, against man or beast: that ye may know how that the LORD doth put a difference between the Egyptians and Israel.

8And all these thy servants shall come down unto me, and bow down themselves unto me, saying, Get thee out, and all the people that follow thee: and after that I will go out. And he went out from Pharaoh in a great anger.

9And the LORD said unto Moses, Pharaoh shall not hearken unto you; that my wonders may be multiplied in the land of Egypt.

New International

to the LORD your God to take this deadly plague away from me."

18Moses then left Pharaoh and prayed to the LORD. 19And the LORD changed the wind to a very strong west wind, which caught up the locusts and carried them into the Red Sea.a Not a locust was left anywhere in Egypt. 20But the LORD hardened Pharaoh's heart, and he would not let the Israelites go.

The Plague of Darkness

21Then the LORD said to Moses, "Stretch out your hand toward the sky so that darkness will spread over Egypt—darkness that can be felt." 22So Moses stretched out his hand toward the sky, and total darkness covered all Egypt for three days. 23No one could see anyone else or leave his place for three days. Yet all the Israelites had light in the places where they lived.

24Then Pharaoh summoned Moses and said, "Go, worship the LORD. Even your women and children may go with you; only leave your flocks and herds behind."

25But Moses said, "You must allow us to have sacrifices and burnt offerings to present to the LORD our God. 26Our livestock too must go with us; not a hoof is to be left behind. We have to use some of them in worshiping the LORD our God, and until we get there we will not know what we are to use to worship the LORD."

27But the LORD hardened Pharaoh's heart, and he was not willing to let them go. 28Pharaoh said to Moses, "Get out of my sight! Make sure you do not appear before me again! The day you see my face you will die."

29"Just as you say," Moses replied, "I will never appear before you again."

The Plague on the Firstborn

11 NOW THE LORD had said to Moses, "I will bring one more plague on Pharaoh and on Egypt. After that, he will let you go from here, and when he does, he will drive you out completely. 2Tell the people that men and women alike are to ask their neighbors for articles of silver and gold." 3(The LORD made the Egyptians favorably disposed toward the people, and Moses himself was highly regarded in Egypt by Pharaoh's officials and by the people.)

4So Moses said, "This is what the LORD says: 'About midnight I will go throughout Egypt. 5Every firstborn son in Egypt will die, from the firstborn son of Pharaoh, who sits on the throne, to the firstborn son of the slave girl, who is at her hand mill, and all the firstborn of the cattle as well. 6There will be loud wailing throughout Egypt—worse than there has ever been or ever will be again. 7But among the Israelites not a dog will bark at any man or animal.' Then you will know that the LORD makes a distinction between Egypt and Israel. 8All these officials of yours will come to me, bowing down before me and saying, 'Go, you and all the people who follow you!' After that I will leave." Then Moses, hot with anger, left Pharaoh.

9The LORD had said to Moses, "Pharaoh will refuse to listen to you—so that my wonders may be multiplied in Egypt." 10Moses and Aaron performed all these won-

---

a 19 Hebrew *Yam Suph*; that is, Sea of Reeds

Living Bible

this once, and beg Jehovah your God to take away this deadly plague. I solemnly promise that I will let you go as soon as the locusts are gone."

18So Moses went out from Pharaoh and entreated the Lord, 19and he sent a very strong west wind that blew the locusts out into the Red Sea, so that there remained not one locust in all the land of Egypt! 20But the Lord hardened Pharaoh's heart and he did not let the people go.

21Then Jehovah said to Moses, "Lift your hands to heaven, and darkness without a ray of light will descend upon the land of Egypt." 22So Moses did, and there was thick darkness over all the land for three days. 23During all that time the people scarcely moved—but all the people of Israel had light as usual.

24Then Pharaoh called for Moses and said, "Go and worship Jehovah—but let your flocks and herds stay here; you can even take your children with you."

25"No," Moses said, "we must take our flocks and herds for sacrifices and burnt offerings to Jehovah our God. 26Not a hoof shall be left behind; for we must have sacrifices for the Lord our God, and we do not know what he will choose until we get there."

27So the Lord hardened Pharaoh's heart and he would not let them go.

28"Get out of here and don't let me ever see you again," Pharaoh shouted at Moses. "The day you do, you shall die."

29"Very well," Moses replied. "I will never see you again."

11 THEN THE Lord said to Moses, "I will send just one more disaster on Pharaoh and his land, and after that he will let you go; in fact, he will be so anxious to get rid of you that he will practically throw you out of the country. 2Tell all the men and women of Israel to ask their Egyptian neighbors for gold and silver jewelry."

3(For God caused the Egyptians to be very favorable to the people of Israel, and Moses was a very great man in the land of Egypt and was revered by Pharaoh's officials and the Egyptian people alike.)

4Now Moses announced to Pharaoh,b "Jehovah says, 'About midnight I will pass through Egypt. 5And all the oldest sons shall die in every family in Egypt, from the oldest child of Pharaoh, heir to his throne, to the oldest child of his lowliest slave; and even the firstborn of the animals. 6The wail of death will resound throughout the entire land of Egypt; never before has there been such anguish, and it will never be again.

7" 'But not a dog shall move his tongue against any of the people of Israel, nor shall any of their animals die. Then you will know that Jehovah makes a distinction between Egyptians and Israelis.' 8All these officials of yours will come running to me, bowing low and begging, 'Please leave at once, and take all your people with you.' Only then will I go!" Then, red-faced with anger, Moses stomped from the palace.c

9The Lord had told Moses, "Pharaoh won't listen, and this will give me the opportunity of doing mighty miracles to demonstrate my power." 10So, although Mo-

New Revised Standard

once, and pray to the LORD your God that at the least he remove this deadly thing from me." 18So he went out from Pharaoh and prayed to the LORD. 19The LORD changed the wind into a very strong west wind, which lifted the locusts and drove them into the Red Sea;d not a single locust was left in all the country of Egypt. 20But the LORD hardened Pharaoh's heart, and he would not let the Israelites go.

The Ninth Plague: Darkness

21 Then the LORD said to Moses, "Stretch out your hand toward heaven so that there may be darkness over the land of Egypt, a darkness that can be felt." 22So Moses stretched out his hand toward heaven, and there was dense darkness in all the land of Egypt for three days. 23People could not see one another, and for three days they could not move from where they were; but all the Israelites had light where they lived. 24Then Pharaoh summoned Moses, and said, "Go, worship the LORD. Only your flocks and your herds shall remain behind. Even your children may go with you." 25But Moses said, "You must also let us have sacrifices and burnt offerings to sacrifice to the LORD our God. 26Our livestock also must go with us; not a hoof shall be left behind, for we must choose some of them for the worship of the LORD our God, and we will not know what to use to worship the LORD until we arrive there." 27But the LORD hardened Pharaoh's heart, and he was unwilling to let them go. 28Then Pharaoh said to him, "Get away from me! Take care that you do not see my face again, for on the day you see my face you shall die." 29Moses said, "Just as you say! I will never see your face again."

Warning of the Final Plague

11 THE LORD said to Moses, "I will bring one more plague upon Pharaoh and upon Egypt; afterwards he will let you go from here; indeed, when he lets you go, he will drive you away. 2Tell the people that every man is to ask his neighbor and every woman is to ask her neighbor for objects of silver and gold." 3The LORD gave the people favor in the sight of the Egyptians. Moreover, Moses himself was a man of great importance in the land of Egypt, in the sight of Pharaoh's officials and in the sight of the people.

4 Moses said, "Thus says the LORD: About midnight I will go out through Egypt. 5Every firstborn in the land of Egypt shall die, from the firstborn of Pharaoh who sits on his throne to the firstborn of the female slave who is behind the handmill, and all the firstborn of the livestock. 6Then there will be a loud cry throughout the whole land of Egypt, such as has never been or will ever be again. 7But not a dog shall growl at any of the Israelites—not at people, not at animals—so that you may know that the LORD makes a distinction between Egypt and Israel. 8Then all these officials of yours shall come down to me, and bow low to me, saying, 'Leave us, you and all the people who follow you.' After that I will leave." And in hot anger he left Pharaoh.

9 The LORD said to Moses, "Pharaoh will not listen to you, in order that my wonders may be multiplied in the land of Egypt." 10Moses and Aaron performed all

---

b 11:4 to Pharaoh, implied.   c 11:8 Moses stomped from the palace, literally, "he went out from Pharaoh."

d Or Sea of Reeds

King James

10And Moses and Aaron did all these wonders before Pharaoh: and the LORD hardened Pharaoh's heart, so that he would not let the children of Israel go out of his land.

12 AND THE LORD spake unto Moses and Aaron in the land of Egypt, saying,
2This month *shall be* unto you the beginning of months: it *shall be* the first month of the year to you.
3¶ Speak ye unto all the congregation of Israel, saying, In the tenth *day* of this month they shall take to them every man a lamb, according to the house of *their* fathers, a lamb for an house:
4And if the household be too little for the lamb, let him and his neighbour next unto his house take *it* according to the number of the souls; every man according to his eating shall make your count for the lamb.
5Your lamb shall be without blemish, a male of the first year: ye shall take *it* out from the sheep, or from the goats:
6And ye shall keep it up until the fourteenth day of the same month: and the whole assembly of the congregation of Israel shall kill it in the evening.
7And they shall take of the blood, and strike *it* on the two side posts and on the upper door post of the houses, wherein they shall eat it.
8And they shall eat the flesh in that night, roast with fire, and unleavened bread; *and* with bitter *herbs* they shall eat it.
9Eat not of it raw, nor sodden at all with water, but roast *with* fire; his head with his legs, and with the purtenance thereof.
10And ye shall let nothing of it remain until the morning; and that which remaineth of it until the morning ye shall burn with fire.
11¶ And thus shall ye eat it; *with* your loins girded, your shoes on your feet, and your staff in your hand; and ye shall eat it in haste: it *is* the LORD'S passover.
12For I will pass through the land of Egypt this night, and will smite all the firstborn in the land of Egypt, both man and beast; and against all the gods of Egypt I will execute judgment: I *am* the LORD.
13And the blood shall be to you for a token upon the houses where ye *are:* and when I see the blood, I will pass over you, and the plague shall not be upon you to destroy *you,* when I smite the land of Egypt.
14And this day shall be unto you for a memorial; and ye shall keep it a feast to the LORD throughout your generations; ye shall keep it a feast by an ordinance for ever.
15Seven days shall ye eat unleavened bread; even the first day ye shall put away leaven out of your houses: for whosoever eateth leavened bread from the first day until the seventh day, that soul shall be cut off from Israel.
16And in the first day *there shall be* an holy convocation, and in the seventh day there shall be an holy convocation to you; no manner of work shall be done in them, save *that* which every man must eat, that only may be done of you.
17And ye shall observe *the feast of* unleavened bread; for in this selfsame day have I brought your armies out of the land of Egypt: therefore shall ye observe this day in your generations by an ordinance for ever.
18¶ In the first *month,* on the fourteenth day of the month at even, ye shall eat unleavened bread, until the one and twentieth day of the month at even.
19Seven days shall there be no leaven found in your houses: for whosoever eateth that which is leavened, even that soul shall be cut off from the congregation of Israel, whether he be a stranger, or born in the land.
20Ye shall eat nothing leavened; in all your habitations shall ye eat unleavened bread.

New International

ders before Pharaoh, but the LORD hardened Pharaoh's heart, and he would not let the Israelites go out of his country.

The Passover

12 THE LORD said to Moses and Aaron in Egypt, 2"This month is to be for you the first month, the first month of your year. 3Tell the whole community of Israel that on the tenth day of this month each man is to take a lamb[a] for his family, one for each household. 4If any household is too small for a whole lamb, they must share one with their nearest neighbor, having taken into account the number of people there are. You are to determine the amount of lamb needed in accordance with what each person will eat. 5The animals you choose must be year-old males without defect, and you may take them from the sheep or the goats. 6Take care of them until the fourteenth day of the month, when all the people of the community of Israel must slaughter them at twilight. 7Then they are to take some of the blood and put it on the sides and tops of the doorframes of the houses where they eat the lambs. 8That same night they are to eat the meat roasted over the fire, along with bitter herbs, and bread made without yeast. 9Do not eat the meat raw or cooked in water, but roast it over the fire—head, legs and inner parts. 10Do not leave any of it till morning; if some is left till morning, you must burn it. 11This is how you are to eat it: with your cloak tucked into your belt, your sandals on your feet and your staff in your hand. Eat it in haste; it is the LORD's Passover.

12"On that same night I will pass through Egypt and strike down every firstborn—both men and animals—and I will bring judgment on all the gods of Egypt. I am the LORD. 13The blood will be a sign for you on the houses where you are; and when I see the blood, I will pass over you. No destructive plague will touch you when I strike Egypt.

14"This is a day you are to commemorate; for the generations to come you shall celebrate it as a festival to the LORD—a lasting ordinance. 15For seven days you are to eat bread made without yeast. On the first day remove the yeast from your houses, for whoever eats anything with yeast in it from the first day through the seventh must be cut off from Israel. 16On the first day hold a sacred assembly, and another one on the seventh day. Do no work at all on these days, except to prepare food for everyone to eat—that is all you may do.

17"Celebrate the Feast of Unleavened Bread, because it was on this very day that I brought your divisions out of Egypt. Celebrate this day as a lasting ordinance for the generations to come. 18In the first month you are to eat bread made without yeast, from the evening of the fourteenth day until the evening of the twenty-first day. 19For seven days no yeast is to be found in your houses. And whoever eats anything with yeast in it must be cut off from the community of Israel, whether he is an alien or native-born. 20Eat nothing made with yeast. Wherever you live, you must eat unleavened bread."

---

a 3 The Hebrew word can mean *lamb* or *kid;* also in verse 4.

Living Bible

ses and Aaron did these miracles right before Pharaoh's eyes, the Lord hardened his heart so that he wouldn't let the people leave the land.

12 THEN THE Lord said to Moses and Aaron, 2"From now on, this month will be the first and most important of the entire year. 3, 4Annually, on the tenth day of this month (announce this to all the people of Israel) each family shall get a lamb[b] (or, if a family is small, let it share the lamb with another small family in the neighborhood; whether to share in this way depends on the size of the families). 5This animal shall be a year-old male, either a sheep or a goat, without any defects.

6"On the evening of the fourteenth day of this month, all these lambs shall be killed, 7and their blood shall be placed on the two side-frames of the door of every home and on the panel above the door. Use the blood of the lamb eaten in that home. 8Everyone shall eat roast lamb that night, with unleavened bread and bitter herbs. 9The meat must not be eaten raw or boiled, but roasted, including the head, legs, heart, and liver.[c] 10Don't eat any of it the next day; if all is not eaten that night, burn what is left.

11"Eat it with your traveling clothes on, prepared for a long journey, wearing your walking shoes and carrying your walking sticks in your hands; eat it hurriedly. This observance shall be called the Lord's Passover. 12For I will pass through the land of Egypt tonight and kill all the oldest sons and firstborn male animals in all the land of Egypt, and execute judgment upon all the gods of Egypt—for I am Jehovah. 13The blood you have placed on the doorposts will be proof that you obey me, and when I see the blood I will pass over you and I will not destroy your firstborn children when I smite the land of Egypt.

14"You shall celebrate this event each year (this is a permanent law) to remind you of this fatal night. 15The celebration shall last seven days. For that entire period you are to eat only bread made without yeast. Anyone who disobeys this rule at any time during the seven days of the celebration shall be excommunicated from Israel. 16On the first day of the celebration, and again on the seventh day, there will be special religious services for the entire congregation, and no work of any kind may be done on those days except the preparation of food.

17"This annual 'Celebration with Unleavened Bread' will cause you always to remember today as the day when I brought you out of the land of Egypt; so it is a law that you must celebrate this day annually, generation after generation. 18Only bread without yeast may be eaten from the evening of the fourteenth day of the month until the evening of the twenty-first day of the month. 19For these seven days there must be no trace of yeast in your homes; during that time anyone who eats anything that has yeast in it shall be excommunicated from the congregation of Israel. These same rules apply to foreigners who are living among you just as much as to those born in the land. 20Again I repeat, during those days you must not eat anything made with yeast; serve only yeastless bread."

New Revised Standard

these wonders before Pharaoh; but the LORD hardened Pharaoh's heart, and he did not let the people of Israel go out of his land.

The First Passover Instituted

12 THE LORD said to Moses and Aaron in the land of Egypt: 2This month shall mark for you the beginning of months; it shall be the first month of the year for you. 3Tell the whole congregation of Israel that on the tenth of this month they are to take a lamb for each family, a lamb for each household. 4If a household is too small for a whole lamb, it shall join its closest neighbor in obtaining one; the lamb shall be divided in proportion to the number of people who eat of it. 5Your lamb shall be without blemish, a year-old male; you may take it from the sheep or from the goats. 6You shall keep it until the fourteenth day of this month; then the whole assembled congregation of Israel shall slaughter it at twilight. 7They shall take some of the blood and put it on the two doorposts and the lintel of the houses in which they eat it. 8They shall eat the lamb that same night; they shall eat it roasted over the fire with unleavened bread and bitter herbs. 9Do not eat any of it raw or boiled in water, but roasted over the fire, with its head, legs, and inner organs. 10You shall let none of it remain until the morning; anything that remains until the morning you shall burn. 11This is how you shall eat it: your loins girded, your sandals on your feet, and your staff in your hand; and you shall eat it hurriedly. It is the passover of the LORD. 12For I will pass through the land of Egypt that night, and I will strike down every firstborn in the land of Egypt, both human beings and animals; on all the gods of Egypt I will execute judgments: I am the LORD. 13The blood shall be a sign for you on the houses where you live: when I see the blood, I will pass over you, and no plague shall destroy you when I strike the land of Egypt.

14 This day shall be a day of remembrance for you. You shall celebrate it as a festival to the LORD; throughout your generations you shall observe it as a perpetual ordinance. 15Seven days you shall eat unleavened bread; on the first day you shall remove leaven from your houses, for whoever eats leavened bread from the first day until the seventh day shall be cut off from Israel. 16On the first day you shall hold a solemn assembly, and on the seventh day a solemn assembly; no work shall be done on those days; only what everyone must eat, that alone may be prepared by you. 17You shall observe the festival of unleavened bread, for on this very day I brought your companies out of the land of Egypt: you shall observe this day throughout your generations as a perpetual ordinance. 18In the first month, from the evening of the fourteenth day until the evening of the twenty-first day, you shall eat unleavened bread. 19For seven days no leaven shall be found in your houses; for whoever eats what is leavened shall be cut off from the congregation of Israel, whether an alien or a native of the land. 20You shall eat nothing leavened; in all your settlements you shall eat unleavened bread.

---

[b] 12:3, 4 The Hebrew word here translated "lamb" can also mean "kid"—a baby goat.   [c] 12:9 liver, literally, 'inner parts."

King James

21¶ Then Moses called for all the elders of Israel, and said unto them, Draw out and take you a lamb according to your families, and kill the passover.

22And ye shall take a bunch of hyssop, and dip *it* in the blood that *is* in the basin, and strike the lintel and the two side posts with the blood that *is* in the basin; and none of you shall go out at the door of his house until the morning.

23For the LORD will pass through to smite the Egyptians; and when he seeth the blood upon the lintel, and on the two side posts, the LORD will pass over the door, and will not suffer the destroyer to come in unto your houses to smite *you*.

24And ye shall observe this thing for an ordinance to thee and to thy sons for ever.

25And it shall come to pass, when ye be come to the land which the LORD will give you, according as he hath promised, that ye shall keep this service.

26And it shall come to pass, when your children shall say unto you, What mean ye by this service?

27That ye shall say, It *is* the sacrifice of the LORD's passover, who passed over the houses of the children of Israel in Egypt, when he smote the Egyptians, and delivered our houses. And the people bowed the head and worshipped.

28And the children of Israel went away, and did as the LORD had commanded Moses and Aaron, so did they.

29¶ And it came to pass, that at midnight the LORD smote all the firstborn in the land of Egypt, from the firstborn of Pharaoh that sat on his throne unto the firstborn of the captive that *was* in the dungeon; and all the firstborn of cattle.

30And Pharaoh rose up in the night, he, and all his servants, and all the Egyptians; and there was a great cry in Egypt; for *there was* not a house where *there was* not one dead.

31¶ And he called for Moses and Aaron by night, and said, Rise up, *and* get you forth from among my people, both ye and the children of Israel; and go, serve the LORD, as ye have said.

32Also take your flocks and your herds, as ye have said, and be gone; and bless me also.

33And the Egyptians were urgent upon the people, that they might send them out of the land in haste; for they said, We *be* all dead *men*.

34And the people took their dough before it was leavened, their kneadingtroughs being bound up in their clothes upon their shoulders.

35And the children of Israel did according to the word of Moses; and they borrowed of the Egyptians jewels of silver, and jewels of gold, and raiment:

36And the LORD gave the people favour in the sight of the Egyptians, so that they lent unto them *such things as they required*. And they spoiled the Egyptians.

37¶ And the children of Israel journeyed from Rameses to Succoth, about six hundred thousand on foot *that were* men, beside children.

38And a mixed multitude went up also with them; and flocks, and herds, *even* very much cattle.

39And they baked unleavened cakes of the dough which they brought forth out of Egypt, for it was not leavened; because they were thrust out of Egypt, and could not tarry, neither had they prepared for themselves any victual.

40¶ Now the sojourning of the children of Israel, who dwelt in Egypt, *was* four hundred and thirty years.

41And it came to pass at the end of the four hundred and thirty years, even the selfsame day it came to pass, that all the hosts of the LORD went out from the land of Egypt.

42It *is* a night to be much observed unto the LORD for bringing them out from the land of Egypt: this *is* that night of the LORD to be observed of all the children of Israel in their generations.

New International

21Then Moses summoned all the elders of Israel and said to them, "Go at once and select the animals for your families and slaughter the Passover lamb. 22Take a bunch of hyssop, dip it into the blood in the basin and put some of the blood on the top and on both sides of the doorframe. Not one of you shall go out the door of his house until morning. 23When the LORD goes through the land to strike down the Egyptians, he will see the blood on the top and sides of the doorframe and will pass over that doorway, and he will not permit the destroyer to enter your houses and strike you down.

24"Obey these instructions as a lasting ordinance for you and your descendants. 25When you enter the land that the LORD will give you as he promised, observe this ceremony. 26And when your children ask you, 'What does this ceremony mean to you?' 27then tell them, 'It is the Passover sacrifice to the LORD, who passed over the houses of the Israelites in Egypt and spared our homes when he struck down the Egyptians.' " Then the people bowed down and worshiped. 28The Israelites did just what the LORD commanded Moses and Aaron.

29At midnight the LORD struck down all the firstborn in Egypt, from the firstborn of Pharaoh, who sat on the throne, to the firstborn of the prisoner, who was in the dungeon, and the firstborn of all the livestock as well. 30Pharaoh and all his officials and all the Egyptians got up during the night, and there was loud wailing in Egypt, for there was not a house without someone dead.

The Exodus

31During the night Pharaoh summoned Moses and Aaron and said, "Up! Leave my people, you and the Israelites! Go, worship the LORD as you have requested. 32Take your flocks and herds, as you have said, and go. And also bless me."

33The Egyptians urged the people to hurry and leave the country. "For otherwise," they said, "we will all die!" 34So the people took their dough before the yeast was added, and carried it on their shoulders in kneading troughs wrapped in clothing. 35The Israelites did as Moses instructed and asked the Egyptians for articles of silver and gold and for clothing. 36The LORD had made the Egyptians favorably disposed toward the people, and they gave them what they asked for; so they plundered the Egyptians.

37The Israelites journeyed from Rameses to Succoth. There were about six hundred thousand men on foot, besides women and children. 38Many other people went up with them, as well as large droves of livestock, both flocks and herds. 39With the dough they had brought from Egypt, they baked cakes of unleavened bread. The dough was without yeast because they had been driven out of Egypt and did not have time to prepare food for themselves.

40Now the length of time the Israelite people lived in Egypt[a] was 430 years. 41At the end of the 430 years, to the very day, all the LORD's divisions left Egypt. 42Because the LORD kept vigil that night to bring them out of Egypt, on this night all the Israelites are to keep vigil to honor the LORD for the generations to come.

---

a 40 Masoretic Text; Samaritan Pentateuch and Septuagint *Egypt and Canaan*

Living Bible

21Then Moses called for all the elders of Israel and said to them, "Go and get lambs from your flocks, a lamb for one or more families depending upon the number of persons in the families, and kill the lamb so that God will pass over you and not destroy you. 22Drain the lamb's blood into a basin, and then take a cluster of hyssop branches and dip them into the lamb's blood, and strike the hyssop against the lintel above the door and against the two side panels, so that there will be blood upon them, and none of you shall go outside all night.

23"For Jehovah will pass through the land and kill the Egyptians; but when he sees the blood upon the panel at the top of the door and on the two side pieces, he will pass over[b] that home and not permit the Destroyer to enter and kill your firstborn. 24And remember, this is a permanent law for you and your posterity. 25And when you come into the land that the Lord will give you, just as he promised, and when you are celebrating the Passover, 26and your children ask, 'What does all this mean? What is this ceremony about?' 27you will reply, 'It is the celebration of Jehovah's passing over us, for he passed over the homes of the people of Israel, though he killed the Egyptians; he passed over our houses and did not come in to destroy us.' " And all the people bowed their heads and worshiped.

28So the people of Israel did as Moses and Aaron had commanded. 29And that night, at midnight, Jehovah killed the firstborn sons in the land of Egypt, from Pharaoh's oldest son to the oldest son of the captive in the dungeon; also all the firstborn of the cattle. 30Then Pharaoh and his officials and all the people of Egypt got up in the night; and there was bitter crying throughout all the land of Egypt, for there was not a house where there was not one dead.

31And Pharaoh summoned Moses and Aaron during the night and said, "Leave us; please go away, all of you; go and serve Jehovah as you said. 32Take your flocks and herds and be gone; and oh, give me a blessing[c] as you go." 33And the Egyptians were urgent upon the people of Israel, to get them out of the land as quickly as possible. For they said, "We are as good as dead."

34The Israelis took with them their bread dough without yeast, and bound their kneading troughs into their spare clothes, and carried them on their shoulders. 35And the people of Israel did as Moses said and asked the Egyptians for silver and gold jewelry, and for clothing. 36And the Lord gave the Israelis favor with the Egyptians, so that they gave them whatever they wanted. And the Egyptians were practically stripped of everything they owned!

37That night the people of Israel left Rameses and started for Succoth; there were six hundred thousand of them, besides all the women and children, going on foot. 38People of various sorts[d] went with them; and there were flocks and herds—a vast exodus of cattle. 39When they stopped to eat, they baked bread from the yeastless dough they had brought along. It was yeastless because the people were pushed out of Egypt and didn't have time to wait for bread to rise to take with them on the trip.

40, 41The sons of Jacob and their descendants had lived in Egypt 430 years, and it was on the last day of the 430th year that all of Jehovah's people left the land. 42This night was selected by the Lord to bring his people out from the land of Egypt; so the same night was selected as the date of the annual celebration of God's deliverance.

New Revised Standard

21 Then Moses called all the elders of Israel and said to them, "Go, select lambs for your families, and slaughter the passover lamb. 22Take a bunch of hyssop, dip it in the blood that is in the basin, and touch the lintel and the two doorposts with the blood in the basin. None of you shall go outside the door of your house until morning. 23For the LORD will pass through to strike down the Egyptians; when he sees the blood on the lintel and on the two doorposts, the LORD will pass over that door and will not allow the destroyer to enter your houses to strike you down. 24You shall observe this rite as a perpetual ordinance for you and your children. 25When you come to the land that the LORD will give you, as he has promised, you shall keep this observance. 26And when your children ask you, 'What do you mean by this observance?' 27you shall say, 'It is the passover sacrifice to the LORD, for he passed over the houses of the Israelites in Egypt, when he struck down the Egyptians but spared our houses.' " And the people bowed down and worshiped.

28 The Israelites went and did just as the LORD had commanded Moses and Aaron.

The Tenth Plague: Death of the Firstborn

29 At midnight the LORD struck down all the firstborn in the land of Egypt, from the firstborn of Pharaoh who sat on his throne to the firstborn of the prisoner who was in the dungeon, and all the firstborn of the livestock. 30Pharaoh arose in the night, he and all his officials and all the Egyptians; and there was a loud cry in Egypt, for there was not a house without someone dead. 31Then he summoned Moses and Aaron in the night, and said, "Rise up, go away from my people, both you and the Israelites! Go, worship the LORD, as you said. 32Take your flocks and your herds, as you said, and be gone. And bring a blessing on me too!"

The Exodus: From Rameses to Succoth

33 The Egyptians urged the people to hasten their departure from the land, for they said, "We shall all be dead." 34So the people took their dough before it was leavened, with their kneading bowls wrapped up in their cloaks on their shoulders. 35The Israelites had done as Moses told them; they had asked the Egyptians for jewelry of silver and gold, and for clothing, 36and the LORD had given the people favor in the sight of the Egyptians, so that they let them have what they asked. And so they plundered the Egyptians.

37 The Israelites journeyed from Rameses to Succoth, about six hundred thousand men on foot, besides children. 38A mixed crowd also went up with them, and livestock in great numbers, both flocks and herds. 39They baked unleavened cakes of the dough that they had brought out of Egypt; it was not leavened, because they were driven out of Egypt and could not wait, nor had they prepared any provisions for themselves.

40 The time that the Israelites had lived in Egypt was four hundred thirty years. 41At the end of four hundred thirty years, on that very day, all the companies of the LORD went out from the land of Egypt. 42That was for the LORD a night of vigil, to bring them out of the land of Egypt. That same night is a vigil to be kept for the LORD by all the Israelites throughout their generations.

---

[b] 12:23 he will pass over. . . . or, "He will pause at the door of that home and not permit the Destroyer to enter. . . ."   [c] 12:32 give me a blessing as you go, literally, "say farewell to me forever."   [d] 12:38 People of various sorts, literally, "a mixed multitude." The meaning is not clear.

King James

43¶ And the LORD said unto Moses and Aaron, This *is* the ordinance of the passover: There shall no stranger eat thereof:

44But every man's servant that is bought for money, when thou hast circumcised him, then shall he eat thereof.

45A foreigner and an hired servant shall not eat thereof.

46In one house shall it be eaten; thou shalt not carry forth aught of the flesh abroad out of the house; neither shall ye break a bone thereof.

47All the congregation of Israel shall keep it.

48And when a stranger shall sojourn with thee, and will keep the passover to the LORD, let all his males be circumcised, and then let him come near and keep it; and he shall be as one that is born in the land: for no uncircumcised person shall eat thereof.

49One law shall be to him that is homeborn, and unto the stranger that sojourneth among you.

50Thus did all the children of Israel; as the LORD commanded Moses and Aaron, so did they.

51And it came to pass the selfsame day, *that* the LORD did bring the children of Israel out of the land of Egypt by their armies.

13 AND THE LORD spake unto Moses, saying, 2Sanctify unto me all the firstborn, whatsoever openeth the womb among the children of Israel, *both* of man and of beast: it *is* mine.

3¶ And Moses said unto the people, Remember this day, in which ye came out from Egypt, out of the house of bondage; for by strength of hand the LORD brought you out from this *place:* there shall no leavened bread be eaten.

4This day came ye out in the month Abib.

5¶ And it shall be when the LORD shall bring thee into the land of the Canaanites, and the Hittites, and the Amorites, and the Hivites, and the Jebusites, which he sware unto thy fathers to give thee, a land flowing with milk and honey, that thou shalt keep this service in this month.

6Seven days thou shalt eat unleavened bread, and in the seventh day *shall be* a feast to the LORD.

7Unleavened bread shall be eaten seven days; and there shall no leavened bread be seen with thee, neither shall there be leaven seen with thee in all thy quarters.

8¶ And thou shalt show thy son in that day, saying, *This is done* because of that *which* the LORD did unto me when I came forth out of Egypt.

9And it shall be for a sign unto thee upon thine hand, and for a memorial between thine eyes, that the LORD's law may be in thy mouth: for with a strong hand hath the LORD brought thee out of Egypt.

10Thou shalt therefore keep this ordinance in his season from year to year.

11¶ And it shall be when the LORD shall bring thee into the land of the Canaanites, as he sware unto thee and to thy fathers, and shall give it thee,

12That thou shalt set apart unto the LORD all that openeth the matrix, and every firstling that cometh of a beast which thou hast; the males *shall be* the LORD's.

13And every firstling of an ass thou shalt redeem with a lamb; and if thou wilt not redeem it, then thou shalt break his neck: and all the firstborn of man among thy children shalt thou redeem.

14¶ And it shall be when thy son asketh thee in time to come, saying, What *is* this? that thou shalt say unto him, By strength of hand the LORD brought us out from Egypt, from the house of bondage:

New International

Passover Restrictions

43The LORD said to Moses and Aaron, "These are the regulations for the Passover:

"No foreigner is to eat of it. 44Any slave you have bought may eat of it after you have circumcised him, 45but a temporary resident and a hired worker may not eat of it.

46"It must be eaten inside one house; take none of the meat outside the house. Do not break any of the bones. 47The whole community of Israel must celebrate it.

48"An alien living among you who wants to celebrate the LORD's Passover must have all the males in his household circumcised; then he may take part like one born in the land. No uncircumcised male may eat of it. 49The same law applies to the native-born and to the alien living among you."

50All the Israelites did just what the LORD had commanded Moses and Aaron. 51And on that very day the LORD brought the Israelites out of Egypt by their divisions.

Consecration of the Firstborn

13 THE LORD said to Moses, 2"Consecrate to me every firstborn male. The first offspring of every womb among the Israelites belongs to me, whether man or animal."

3Then Moses said to the people, "Commemorate this day, the day you came out of Egypt, out of the land of slavery, because the LORD brought you out of it with a mighty hand. Eat nothing containing yeast. 4Today, in the month of Abib, you are leaving. 5When the LORD brings you into the land of the Canaanites, Amorites, Hivites and Jebusites—the land he swore to your forefathers to give you, a land flowing with milk and honey—you are to observe this ceremony in this month: 6For seven days eat bread made without yeast and on the seventh day hold a festival to the LORD. 7Eat unleavened bread during those seven days; nothing with yeast in it is to be seen among you, nor shall any yeast be seen anywhere within your borders. 8On that day tell your son, 'I do this because of what the LORD did for me when I came out of Egypt.' 9This observance will be for you like a sign on your hand and a reminder on your forehead that the law of the LORD is to be on your lips. For the LORD brought you out of Egypt with his mighty hand. 10You must keep this ordinance at the appointed time year after year.

11"After the LORD brings you into the land of the Canaanites and gives it to you, as he promised on oath to you and your forefathers, 12you are to give over to the LORD the first offspring of every womb. All the firstborn males of your livestock belong to the LORD. 13Redeem with a lamb every firstborn donkey, but if you do not redeem it, break its neck. Redeem every firstborn among your sons.

14"In days to come, when your son asks you, 'What does this mean?' say to him, 'With a mighty hand the LORD brought us out of Egypt, out of the land of slavery.

Living Bible

43Then Jehovah said to Moses and Aaron, "These are the rules concerning the observance of the Passover. No foreigners shall eat the lamb, 44but any slave who has been purchased may eat it if he has been circumcised. 45A hired servant or a visiting foreigner may not eat of it. 46You shall, all of you who eat each lamb, eat it together in one house, and not carry it outside; and you shall not break any of its bones. 47All the congregation of Israel shall observe this memorial at the same time.

48"As to foreigners, if they are living with you and want to observe the Passover with you, let all the males be circumcised, and then they may come and celebrate with you—then they shall be just as though they had been born among you; but no uncircumcised person shall ever eat the lamb. 49The same law applies to those born in Israel and to foreigners living among you."

50So the people of Israel followed all of Jehovah's instructions to Moses and Aaron. 51That very day the Lord brought out the people of Israel from the land of Egypt, wave after wave of them crossing the border.a

13 THE LORD instructed Moses, "Dedicate to me all of the firstborn sonsb of Israel, and every firstborn male animal; they are mine!"

3Then Moses said to the people, "This is a day to remember forever—the day of leaving Egypt and your slavery; for the Lord has brought you out with mighty miracles. Now remember, during the annual celebration of this event you are to use no yeast; don't even have any in your homes. 4, 5Celebrate this day of your exodus, at the end of Marchc each year, when Jehovah brings you into the land of the Canaanites, Hittites, Amorites, Hivites, and Jebusites—the land he promised your fathers, a land 'flowing with milk and honey.' 6, 7For seven days you shall eat only bread without yeast, and there must be no yeast in your homes, or anywhere within the borders of your land! Then, on the seventh day, a great feast to the Lord shall be held.

8"During those celebration days each year you must explain to your children why you are celebrating—it is a celebration of what the Lord did for you when you left Egypt. 9This annual memorial week will brand you as his own unique people, just as though he had branded his mark of ownership upon your hands or your forehead.

10"So celebrate the event annually in late March.d 11And remember, when the Lord brings you into the land he promised to your ancestors long ago, where the Canaanites are now living, 12all firstborn sons and firstborn male animals belong to the Lord, and you shall give them to him. 13A firstborn donkey may be purchased back from the Lord in exchange for a lamb or baby goat; but if you decide not to trade, the donkey shall be killed. However, you *must* buy back your firstborn sons.

14"And in the future, when your children ask you, 'What is this all about?' you shall tell them, 'With mighty miracles Jehovah brought us out of Egypt from our slavery. 15Pharaoh wouldn't let us go, so Jehovah

New Revised Standard

Directions for the Passover

43 The LORD said to Moses and Aaron: This is the ordinance for the passover: no foreigner shall eat of it, 44but any slave who has been purchased may eat of it after he has been circumcised; 45no bound or hired servant may eat of it. 46It shall be eaten in one house; you shall not take any of the animal outside the house, and you shall not break any of its bones. 47The whole congregation of Israel shall celebrate it. 48If an alien who resides with you wants to celebrate the passover to the LORD, all his males shall be circumcised; then he may draw near to celebrate it; he shall be regarded as a native of the land. But no uncircumcised person shall eat of it; 49there shall be one law for the native and for the alien who resides among you.

50 All the Israelites did just as the LORD had commanded Moses and Aaron. 51That very day the LORD brought the Israelites out of the land of Egypt, company by company.

13 THE LORD said to Moses: 2Consecrate to me all the firstborn; whatever is the first to open the womb among the Israelites, of human beings and animals, is mine.

The Festival of Unleavened Bread

3 Moses said to the people, "Remember this day on which you came out of Egypt, out of the house of slavery, because the LORD brought you out from there by strength of hand; no leavened bread shall be eaten. 4Today, in the month of Abib, you are going out. 5When the LORD brings you into the land of the Canaanites, the Hittites, the Amorites, the Hivites, and the Jebusites, which he swore to your ancestors to give you, a land flowing with milk and honey, you shall keep this observance in this month. 6Seven days you shall eat unleavened bread, and on the seventh day there shall be a festival to the LORD. 7Unleavened bread shall be eaten for seven days; no leavened bread shall be seen in your possession, and no leaven shall be seen among you in all your territory. 8You shall tell your child on that day, 'It is because of what the LORD did for me when I came out of Egypt.' 9It shall serve for you as a sign on your hand and as a reminder on your forehead, so that the teaching of the LORD may be on your lips; for with a strong hand the LORD brought you out of Egypt. 10You shall keep this ordinance at its proper time from year to year.

The Consecration of the Firstborn

11 "When the LORD has brought you into the land of the Canaanites, as he swore to you and your ancestors, and has given it to you, 12you shall set apart to the LORD all that first opens the womb. All the firstborn of your livestock that are males shall be the LORD's. 13But every firstborn donkey you shall redeem with a sheep; if you do not redeem it, you must break its neck. Every firstborn male among your children you shall redeem. 14When in the future your child asks you, 'What does this mean?' you shall answer, 'By strength of hand the LORD brought us out of Egypt, from the house of slavery. 15When Pharaoh stubbornly refused to let us go, the

a 12:51 *wave after wave of them crossing the border,* or, ". . . from the land of Egypt, all of the communities of them."   b 13:1, 2 *all of the firstborn sons,* literally, "all the firstborn."   c 13:4, 5 *the end of March,* literally, "at the appointed time each year."   d 13:10 *in late March,* literally, "in its season from year to year."

King James

15And it came to pass, when Pharaoh would hardly let us go, that the LORD slew all the firstborn in the land of Egypt, both the firstborn of man, and the firstborn of beast: therefore I sacrifice to the LORD all that openeth the matrix, being males; but all the firstborn of my children I redeem.

16And it shall be for a token upon thine hand, and for frontlets between thine eyes: for by strength of hand the LORD brought us forth out of Egypt.

17¶ And it came to pass, when Pharaoh had let the people go, that God led them not *through* the way of the land of the Philistines, although that *was* near; for God said, Lest peradventure the people repent when they see war, and they return to Egypt:

18But God led the people about, *through* the way of the wilderness of the Red sea: and the children of Israel went up harnessed out of the land of Egypt.

19And Moses took the bones of Joseph with him: for he had straitly sworn the children of Israel, saying, God will surely visit you; and ye shall carry up my bones away hence with you.

20¶ And they took their journey from Succoth, and encamped in Etham, in the edge of the wilderness.

21And the LORD went before them by day in a pillar of a cloud, to lead them the way; and by night in a pillar of fire, to give them light; to go by day and night:

22He took not away the pillar of the cloud by day, nor the pillar of fire by night, *from* before the people.

14 AND THE LORD spake unto Moses, saying, 2Speak unto the children of Israel, that they turn and encamp before Pi-hahiroth, between Migdol and the sea, over against Baal-zephon: before it shall ye encamp by the sea.

3For Pharaoh will say of the children of Israel, They *are* entangled in the land, the wilderness hath shut them in.

4And I will harden Pharaoh's heart, that he shall follow after them; and I will be honoured upon Pharaoh, and upon all his host; that the Egyptians may know that I *am* the LORD. And they did so.

5¶ And it was told the king of Egypt that the people fled: and the heart of Pharaoh and of his servants was turned against the people, and they said, Why have we done this, that we have let Israel go from serving us?

6And he made ready his chariot, and took his people with him:

7And he took six hundred chosen chariots, and all the chariots of Egypt, and captains over every one of them.

8And the LORD hardened the heart of Pharaoh king of Egypt, and he pursued after the children of Israel: and the children of Israel went out with an high hand.

9But the Egyptians pursued after them, all the horses *and* chariots of Pharaoh, and his horsemen, and his army, and overtook them encamping by the sea, beside Pi-hahiroth, before Baal-zephon.

10¶ And when Pharaoh drew nigh, the children of Israel lifted up their eyes, and, behold, the Egyptians marched after them; and they were sore afraid: and the children of Israel cried out unto the LORD.

11And they said unto Moses, Because *there were* no graves in Egypt, hast thou taken us away to die in the wilderness? wherefore hast thou dealt thus with us, to carry us forth out of Egypt?

12*Is* not this the word that we did tell thee in Egypt, saying, Let us alone, that we may serve the Egyptians? For *it had been* better for us to serve the Egyptians, than that we should die in the wilderness.

13¶ And Moses said unto the people, Fear ye not, stand still, and see the salvation of the LORD, which he will show to you today: for the Egyptians whom ye have seen today, ye shall see them again no more for ever.

New International

15When Pharaoh stubbornly refused to let us go, the LORD killed every firstborn in Egypt, both man and animal. This is why I sacrifice to the LORD the first male offspring of every womb and redeem each of my firstborn sons.' 16And it will be like a sign on your hand and a symbol on your forehead that the LORD brought us out of Egypt with his mighty hand."

Crossing the Sea

17When Pharaoh let the people go, God did not lead them on the road through the Philistine country, though that was shorter. For God said, "If they face war, they might change their minds and return to Egypt." 18So God led the people around by the desert road toward the Red Sea.a The Israelites went up out of Egypt armed for battle.

19Moses took the bones of Joseph with him because Joseph had made the sons of Israel swear an oath. He had said, "God will surely come to your aid, and then you must carry my bones up with you from this place."b

20After leaving Succoth they camped at Etham on the edge of the desert. 21By day the LORD went ahead of them in a pillar of cloud to guide them on their way and by night in a pillar of fire to give them light, so that they could travel by day or night. 22Neither the pillar of cloud by day nor the pillar of fire by night left its place in front of the people.

14 THEN THE LORD said to Moses, 2"Tell the Israelites to turn back and encamp near Pi Hahiroth, between Migdol and the sea. They are to encamp by the sea, directly opposite Baal Zephon. 3Pharaoh will think, 'The Israelites are wandering around the land in confusion, hemmed in by the desert.' 4And I will harden Pharaoh's heart, and he will pursue them. But I will gain glory for myself through Pharaoh and all his army, and the Egyptians will know that I am the LORD." So the Israelites did this.

5When the king of Egypt was told that the people had fled, Pharaoh and his officials changed their minds about them and said, "What have we done? We have let the Israelites go and have lost their services!" 6So he had his chariot made ready and took his army with him. 7He took six hundred of the best chariots, along with all the other chariots of Egypt, with officers over all of them. 8The LORD hardened the heart of Pharaoh king of Egypt, so that he pursued the Israelites, who were marching out boldly. 9The Egyptians—all Pharaoh's horses and chariots, horsemenc and troops—pursued the Israelites and overtook them as they camped by the sea near Pi Hahiroth, opposite Baal Zephon.

10As Pharaoh approached, the Israelites looked up, and there were the Egyptians, marching after them. They were terrified and cried out to the LORD. 11They said to Moses, "Was it because there were no graves in Egypt that you brought us to the desert to die? What have you done to us by bringing us out of Egypt? 12Didn't we say to you in Egypt, 'Leave us alone; let us serve the Egyptians'? It would have been better for us to serve the Egyptians than to die in the desert!"

13Moses answered the people, "Do not be afraid. Stand firm and you will see the deliverance the LORD will bring you today. The Egyptians you see today you

---

a *18* Hebrew *Yam Suph;* that is, Sea of Reeds   b *19* See Gen. 50:25.
c *9* Or *charioteers;* also in verses 17, 18, 23, 26 and 28

Living Bible

killed all the firstborn males throughout the land of Egypt, both of men and animals; that is why we now give all the firstborn males to the Lord—except that all the eldest sons are always bought back.' 16Again I say, this celebration shall identify you as God's people, just as much as if his brand of ownership were placed upon your foreheads. It is a reminder that the Lord brought us out of Egypt with great power."

17, 18So at last Pharaoh let the people go.

God did not lead them through the land of the Philistines, although that was the most direct route from Egypt to the Promised Land. The reason was that God felt the people might become discouraged by having to fight their way through, even though they had left Egypt armed; he thought they might return to Egypt. Instead, God led them along a route through the Red Sea wilderness.

19Moses took the bones of Joseph with them, for Joseph had made the sons of Israel vow before God that they would take his bones with them when God led them out of Egypt—as he was sure God would.

20Leaving Succoth, they camped in Etham at the edge of the wilderness. 21The Lord guided them by a pillar of cloud during the daytime, and by a pillar of fire at night. So they could travel either by day or night. 22The cloud and fire were never out of sight.

14 JEHOVAH NOW instructed Moses, 2"Tell the people to turn toward Piha-hiroth between Migdol and the sea, opposite Baal-zephon, and to camp there along the shore. 3For Pharaoh will think, 'Those Israelites are trapped now, between the desert and the sea!' 4And once again I will harden Pharaoh's heart and he will chase after you. I have planned this to gain great honor and glory over Pharaoh and all his armies, and the Egyptians shall know that I am the Lord."

So they camped where they were told.

5When word reached the king of Egypt that the Israelis were not planning to return to Egypt after three days, but to keep on going, Pharaoh and his staff became bold again. "What is this we have done, letting all these slaves get away?" they asked. 6So Pharaoh led the chase in his chariot, 7followed by the pick of Egypt's chariot corps—600 chariots in all—and other chariots driven by Egyptian officers. 8He pursued the people of Israel, for they had taken much of the wealth of Egypt with them. 9Pharaoh's entire cavalry—horses, chariots, and charioteers—was used in the chase; and the Egyptian army overtook the people of Israel as they were camped beside the shore near Piha-hiroth, across from Baal-zephon.

10As the Egyptian army approached, the people of Israel saw them far in the distance, speeding after them, and they were terribly frightened, and cried out to the Lord to help them.

11And they turned against Moses, whining, "Have you brought us out here to die in the desert because there were not enough graves for us in Egypt? Why did you make us leave Egypt? 12Isn't this what we told you, while we were slaves, to leave us alone? We said it would be better to be slaves to the Egyptians than dead in the wilderness."

13But Moses told the people, "Don't be afraid. Just stand where you are and watch, and you will see the wonderful way the Lord will rescue you today. The Egyptians you are looking at—you will never see them

New Revised Standard

Lord killed all the firstborn in the land of Egypt, from human firstborn to the firstborn of animals. Therefore I sacrifice to the Lord every male that first opens the womb, but every firstborn of my sons I redeem.' 16It shall serve as a sign on your hand and as an emblemd on your forehead that by strength of hand the Lord brought us out of Egypt."

The Pillars of Cloud and Fire

17 When Pharaoh let the people go, God did not lead them by way of the land of the Philistines, although that was nearer; for God thought, "If the people face war, they may change their minds and return to Egypt." 18So God led the people by the roundabout way of the wilderness toward the Red Sea.e The Israelites went up out of the land of Egypt prepared for battle. 19And Moses took with him the bones of Joseph who had required a solemn oath of the Israelites, saying, "God will surely take notice of you, and then you must carry my bones with you from here." 20They set out from Succoth, and camped at Etham, on the edge of the wilderness. 21The Lord went in front of them in a pillar of cloud by day, to lead them along the way, and in a pillar of fire by night, to give them light, so that they might travel by day and by night. 22Neither the pillar of cloud by day nor the pillar of fire by night left its place in front of the people.

Crossing the Red Sea

14 THEN THE Lord said to Moses: 2Tell the Israelites to turn back and camp in front of Pi-hahiroth, between Migdol and the sea, in front of Baal-zephon; you shall camp opposite it, by the sea. 3Pharaoh will say of the Israelites, 'They are wandering aimlessly in the land; the wilderness has closed in on them.' 4I will harden Pharaoh's heart, and he will pursue them, so that I will gain glory for myself over Pharaoh and all his army; and the Egyptians shall know that I am the Lord. And they did so.

5 When the king of Egypt was told that the people had fled, the minds of Pharaoh and his officials were changed toward the people, and they said, "What have we done, letting Israel leave our service?" 6So he had his chariot made ready, and took his army with him; 7he took six hundred picked chariots and all the other chariots of Egypt with officers over all of them. 8The Lord hardened the heart of Pharaoh king of Egypt and he pursued the Israelites, who were going out boldly. 9The Egyptians pursued them, all Pharaoh's horses and chariots, his chariot drivers and his army; they overtook them camped by the sea, by Pi-hahiroth, in front of Baal-zephon.

10 As Pharaoh drew near, the Israelites looked back, and there were the Egyptians advancing on them. In great fear the Israelites cried out to the Lord. 11They said to Moses, "Was it because there were no graves in Egypt that you have taken us away to die in the wilderness? What have you done to us, bringing us out of Egypt? 12Is this not the very thing we told you in Egypt, 'Let us alone and let us serve the Egyptians'? For it would have been better for us to serve the Egyptians than to die in the wilderness." 13But Moses said to the people, "Do not be afraid, stand firm, and see the deliverance that the Lord will accomplish for you today; for the Egyptians whom you see today you shall never see

d Or as a frontlet; Meaning of Heb uncertain   e Or Sea of Reeds

King James

¹⁴The LORD shall fight for you, and ye shall hold your peace.

¹⁵¶ And the LORD said unto Moses, Wherefore criest thou unto me? speak unto the children of Israel, that they go forward:

¹⁶But lift thou up thy rod, and stretch out thine hand over the sea, and divide it: and the children of Israel shall go on dry *ground* through the midst of the sea.

¹⁷And I, behold, I will harden the hearts of the Egyptians, and they shall follow them: and I will get me honour upon Pharaoh, and upon all his host, upon his chariots, and upon his horsemen.

¹⁸And the Egyptians shall know that I *am* the LORD, when I have gotten me honour upon Pharaoh, upon his chariots, and upon his horsemen.

¹⁹¶ And the angel of God, which went before the camp of Israel, removed and went behind them; and the pillar of the cloud went from before their face, and stood behind them:

²⁰And it came between the camp of the Egyptians and the camp of Israel; and it was a cloud and darkness *to them*, but it gave light by night *to these:* so that the one came not near the other all the night.

²¹And Moses stretched out his hand over the sea; and the LORD caused the sea to go *back* by a strong east wind all that night, and made the sea dry *land*, and the waters were divided.

²²And the children of Israel went into the midst of the sea upon the dry *ground:* and the waters *were* a wall unto them on their right hand, and on their left.

²³¶ And the Egyptians pursued, and went in after them to the midst of the sea, *even* all Pharaoh's horses, his chariots, and his horsemen.

²⁴And it came to pass, that in the morning watch the LORD looked unto the host of the Egyptians through the pillar of fire and of the cloud, and troubled the host of the Egyptians,

²⁵And took off their chariot wheels, that they drave them heavily: so that the Egyptians said, Let us flee from the face of Israel; for the LORD fighteth for them against the Egyptians.

²⁶¶ And the LORD said unto Moses, Stretch out thine hand over the sea, that the waters may come again upon the Egyptians, upon their chariots, and upon their horsemen.

²⁷And Moses stretched forth his hand over the sea, and the sea returned to his strength when the morning appeared; and the Egyptians fled against it; and the LORD overthrew the Egyptians in the midst of the sea.

²⁸And the waters returned, and covered the chariots, and the horsemen, *and* all the host of Pharaoh that came into the sea after them; there remained not so much as one of them.

²⁹But the children of Israel walked upon dry *land* in the midst of the sea; and the waters *were* a wall unto them on their right hand, and on their left.

³⁰Thus the LORD saved Israel that day out of the hand of the Egyptians; and Israel saw the Egyptians dead upon the sea shore.

³¹And Israel saw that great work which the LORD did upon the Egyptians: and the people feared the LORD, and believed the LORD, and his servant Moses.

New International

will never see again. ¹⁴The LORD will fight for you; you need only to be still."

¹⁵Then the LORD said to Moses, "Why are you crying out to me? Tell the Israelites to move on. ¹⁶Raise your staff and stretch out your hand over the sea to divide the water so that the Israelites can go through the sea on dry ground. ¹⁷I will harden the hearts of the Egyptians so that they will go in after them. And I will gain glory through Pharaoh and all his army, through his chariots and his horsemen. ¹⁸The Egyptians will know that I am the LORD when I gain glory through Pharaoh, his chariots and his horsemen."

¹⁹Then the angel of God, who had been traveling in front of Israel's army, withdrew and went behind them. The pillar of cloud also moved from in front and stood behind them, ²⁰coming between the armies of Egypt and Israel. Throughout the night the cloud brought darkness to the one side and light to the other side; so neither went near the other all night long.

²¹Then Moses stretched out his hand over the sea, and all that night the LORD drove the sea back with a strong east wind and turned it into dry land. The waters were divided, ²²and the Israelites went through the sea on dry ground, with a wall of water on their right and on their left.

²³The Egyptians pursued them, and all Pharaoh's horses and chariots and horsemen followed them into the sea. ²⁴During the last watch of the night the LORD looked down from the pillar of fire and cloud at the Egyptian army and threw it into confusion. ²⁵He made the wheels of their chariots come off^a so that they had difficulty driving. And the Egyptians said, "Let's get away from the Israelites! The LORD is fighting for them against Egypt."

²⁶Then the LORD said to Moses, "Stretch out your hand over the sea so that the waters may flow back over the Egyptians and their chariots and horsemen." ²⁷Moses stretched out his hand over the sea, and at daybreak the sea went back to its place. The Egyptians were fleeing toward^b it, and the LORD swept them into the sea. ²⁸The water flowed back and covered the chariots and horsemen—the entire army of Pharaoh that had followed the Israelites into the sea. Not one of them survived.

²⁹But the Israelites went through the sea on dry ground, with a wall of water on their right and on their left. ³⁰That day the LORD saved Israel from the hands of the Egyptians, and Israel saw the Egyptians lying dead on the shore. ³¹And when the Israelites saw the great power the LORD displayed against the Egyptians, the people feared the LORD and put their trust in him and in Moses his servant.

^a 25 Or *He jammed the wheels of their chariots* (see Samaritan Pentateuch, Septuagint and Syriac)　^b 27 Or *from*

Living Bible

again. [14]The Lord will fight for you, and you won't need to lift a finger!"[c]

[15]Then the Lord said to Moses, "Quit praying and get the people moving! Forward, march! [16]Use your rod—hold it out over the water, and the sea will open up a path before you, and all the people of Israel shall walk through on dry ground! [17]I will harden the hearts of the Egyptians and they will go in after you and you will see the honor I will get in defeating Pharaoh and all his armies, chariots, and horsemen. [18]And all Egypt shall know that I am Jehovah."

[19]Then the Angel of God, who was leading the people of Israel, moved the cloud around behind them, [20]and it stood between the people of Israel and the Egyptians. And that night, as it changed to a pillar of fire, it gave darkness to the Egyptians but light to the people of Israel! So the Egyptians couldn't find the Israelis!

[21]Meanwhile, Moses stretched his rod over the sea, and the Lord opened up a path through the sea, with walls of water on each side; and a strong east wind blew all that night, drying the sea bottom. [22]So the people of Israel walked through the sea on dry ground! The Egyptians followed them between the walls of water along the bottom of the sea—all of Pharaoh's horses, chariots, and horsemen. [24]But in the early morning Jehovah looked down from the cloud of fire upon the array of the Egyptians, and began to harass them. [25]Their chariot wheels began coming off, so that their chariots scraped along the dry ground. "Let's get out of here," the Egyptians yelled. "Jehovah is fighting for them and against us."

[26]When all the Israelites were on the other side,[d] the Lord said to Moses, "Stretch out your hand again over the sea, so that the waters will come back over the Egyptians and their chariots and horsemen." [27]Moses did, and the sea returned to normal beneath the morning light. The Egyptians tried to flee, but the Lord drowned them in the sea. [28]The water covered the path and the chariots and horsemen. And of all the army of Pharaoh that chased after Israel through the sea, not one remained alive.

[29]The people of Israel had walked through on dry land, and the waters had been walled up on either side of them. [30]Thus Jehovah saved Israel that day from the Egyptians; and the people of Israel saw the Egyptians dead, washed up on the seashore. [31]When the people of Israel saw the mighty miracle the Lord had done for them against the Egyptians, they were afraid and revered the Lord, and believed in him and in his servant Moses.

New Revised Standard

again. [14]The LORD will fight for you, and you have only to keep still."

[15] Then the LORD said to Moses, "Why do you cry out to me? Tell the Israelites to go forward. [16]But you lift up your staff, and stretch out your hand over the sea and divide it, that the Israelites may go into the sea on dry ground. [17]Then I will harden the hearts of the Egyptians so that they will go in after them; and so I will gain glory for myself over Pharaoh and all his army, his chariots, and his chariot drivers. [18]And the Egyptians shall know that I am the LORD, when I have gained glory for myself over Pharaoh, his chariots, and his chariot drivers."

[19] The angel of God who was going before the Israelite army moved and went behind them; and the pillar of cloud moved from in front of them and took its place behind them. [20]It came between the army of Egypt and the army of Israel. And so the cloud was there with the darkness, and it lit up the night; one did not come near the other all night.

[21] Then Moses stretched out his hand over the sea. The LORD drove the sea back by a strong east wind all night, and turned the sea into dry land; and the waters were divided. [22]The Israelites went into the sea on dry ground, the waters forming a wall for them on their right and on their left. [23]The Egyptians pursued, and went into the sea after them, all of Pharaoh's horses, chariots, and chariot drivers. [24]At the morning watch the LORD in the pillar of fire and cloud looked down upon the Egyptian army, and threw the Egyptian army into panic. [25]He clogged[e] their chariot wheels so that they turned with difficulty. The Egyptians said, "Let us flee from the Israelites, for the LORD is fighting for them against Egypt."

The Pursuers Drowned

[26] Then the LORD said to Moses, "Stretch out your hand over the sea, so that the water may come back upon the Egyptians, upon their chariots and chariot drivers." [27]So Moses stretched out his hand over the sea, and at dawn the sea returned to its normal depth. As the Egyptians fled before it, the LORD tossed the Egyptians into the sea. [28]The waters returned and covered the chariots and the chariot drivers, the entire army of Pharaoh that had followed them into the sea; not one of them remained. [29]But the Israelites walked on dry ground through the sea, the waters forming a wall for them on their right and on their left.

[30] Thus the LORD saved Israel that day from the Egyptians; and Israel saw the Egyptians dead on the seashore. [31]Israel saw the great work that the LORD did against the Egyptians. So the people feared the LORD and believed in the LORD and in his servant Moses.

---

[c] *14:14 you won't need to lift a finger,* or, "you will be speechless with amazement." [d] *14:26 When all the Israelites were on the other side,* implied.

[e] Sam Gk Syr: MT *removed*

King James

15 THEN SANG Moses and the children of Israel this song unto the LORD, and spake, saying, I will sing unto the LORD, for he hath triumphed gloriously: the horse and his rider hath he thrown into the sea.

2The LORD *is* my strength and song, and he is become my salvation: he *is* my God, and I will prepare him an habitation; my father's God, and I will exalt him.

3The LORD *is* a man of war: the LORD *is* his name.

4Pharaoh's chariots and his host hath he cast into the sea: his chosen captains also are drowned in the Red sea.

5The depths have covered them: they sank into the bottom as a stone.

6Thy right hand, O LORD, is become glorious in power: thy right hand, O LORD, hath dashed in pieces the enemy.

7And in the greatness of thine excellency thou hast overthrown them that rose up against thee: thou sentest forth thy wrath, *which* consumed them as stubble.

8And with the blast of thy nostrils the waters were gathered together, the floods stood upright as an heap, *and* the depths were congealed in the heart of the sea.

9The enemy said, I will pursue, I will overtake, I will divide the spoil; my lust shall be satisfied upon them; I will draw my sword, my hand shall destroy them.

10Thou didst blow with thy wind, the sea covered them: they sank as lead in the mighty waters.

11Who *is* like unto thee, O LORD, among the gods? who *is* like thee, glorious in holiness, fearful *in* praises, doing wonders?

12Thou stretchedst out thy right hand, the earth swallowed them.

13Thou in thy mercy hast led forth the people *which* thou hast redeemed: thou hast guided *them* in thy strength unto thy holy habitation.

14The people shall hear, *and* be afraid: sorrow shall take hold on the inhabitants of Palestina.

15Then the dukes of Edom shall be amazed; the mighty men of Moab, trembling shall take hold upon them; all the inhabitants of Canaan shall melt away.

16Fear and dread shall fall upon them; by the greatness of thine arm they shall be *as* still as a stone; till thy people pass over, O LORD, till the people pass over, *which* thou hast purchased.

New International

The Song of Moses and Miriam

15 THEN MOSES and the Israelites sang this song to the LORD:

"I will sing to the LORD,
  for he is highly exalted.
The horse and its rider
  he has hurled into the sea.
2The LORD is my strength and my song;
  he has become my salvation.
He is my God, and I will praise him,
  my father's God, and I will exalt him.
3The LORD is a warrior;
  the LORD is his name.
4Pharaoh's chariots and his army
  he has hurled into the sea.
The best of Pharaoh's officers
  are drowned in the Red Sea.ᵃ
5The deep waters have covered them;
  they sank to the depths like a stone.

6"Your right hand, O LORD,
  was majestic in power.
Your right hand, O LORD,
  shattered the enemy.
7In the greatness of your majesty
  you threw down those who opposed you.
You unleashed your burning anger;
  it consumed them like stubble.
8By the blast of your nostrils
  the waters piled up.
The surging waters stood firm like a wall;
  the deep waters congealed in the heart of the
    sea.

9"The enemy boasted,
  'I will pursue, I will overtake them.
I will divide the spoils;
  I will gorge myself on them.
I will draw my sword
  and my hand will destroy them.'
10But you blew with your breath,
  and the sea covered them.
They sank like lead
  in the mighty waters.

11"Who among the gods is like you, O LORD?
  Who is like you—
    majestic in holiness,
    awesome in glory,
    working wonders?
12You stretched out your right hand
  and the earth swallowed them.

13"In your unfailing love you will lead
  the people you have redeemed.
In your strength you will guide them
  to your holy dwelling.
14The nations will hear and tremble;
  anguish will grip the people of Philistia.
15The chiefs of Edom will be terrified,
  the leaders of Moab will be seized with
    trembling,
  the peopleᵇ of Canaan will melt away;
16 terror and dread will fall upon them.
By the power of your arm
  they will be as still as a stone—
until your people pass by, O LORD,
  until the people you boughtᶜ pass by.

ᵃ *4* Hebrew *Yam Suph;* that is, Sea of Reeds; also in verse 22   ᵇ *15* Or *rulers*
ᶜ *16* Or *created*

Living Bible

15 THEN MOSES and the people of Israel sang this song to the Lord:

I will sing to the Lord, for he has triumphed gloriously;
He has thrown both horse and rider into the sea.
²The Lord is my strength, my song, and my salvation.
He is my God, and I will praise him.
He is my father's God—I will exalt him.
³The Lord is a warrior—
Yes, Jehovah is his name.
⁴He has overthrown Pharaoh's chariots and armies,
Drowning them in the sea.
The famous Egyptian captains are dead beneath the waves.
⁵The water covers them.
They went down into the depths like a stone.
⁶Your right hand, O Lord, is glorious in power;
It dashes the enemy to pieces.
⁷In the greatness of your majesty
You overthrew all those who rose against you.
You sent forth your anger, and it consumed them as fire consumes straw.
⁸At the blast of your breath
The waters divided!
They stood as solid walls to hold the seas apart.
⁹The enemy said, "I will chase after them,
Catch up with them, destroy them.
I will cut them apart with my sword
And divide the captured booty."
¹⁰But God blew with his wind, and the sea covered them.
They sank as lead in the mighty waters.
¹¹Who else is like the Lord among the gods?
Who is glorious in holiness like him?
Who is so awesome in splendor,
A wonder-working God?
¹²You reached out your hand and the earth swallowed them.
¹³You have led the people you redeemed.
But in your lovingkindness
You have guided them wonderfully
To your holy land.
¹⁴The nations heard what happened, and they trembled.
Fear has gripped the people of Philistia.
¹⁵The leaders of Edom are appalled,
The mighty men of Moab tremble;
All the people of Canaan melt with fear.
¹⁶Terror and dread have overcome them.
O Lord, because of your great power they won't attack us!
Your people whom you purchased
Will pass by them in safety.

New Revised Standard

The Song of Moses

15 THEN MOSES and the Israelites sang this song to the Lord:

"I will sing to the Lord, for he has triumphed gloriously;
horse and rider he has thrown into the sea.
2 The Lord is my strength and my might,[d]
and he has become my salvation;
this is my God, and I will praise him,
my father's God, and I will exalt him.
3 The Lord is a warrior;
the Lord is his name.

4 "Pharaoh's chariots and his army he cast into the sea;
his picked officers were sunk in the Red Sea.[e]
5 The floods covered them;
they went down into the depths like a stone.
6 Your right hand, O Lord, glorious in power—
your right hand, O Lord, shattered the enemy.
7 In the greatness of your majesty you overthrew your adversaries;
you sent out your fury, it consumed them like stubble.
8 At the blast of your nostrils the waters piled up,
the floods stood up in a heap;
the deeps congealed in the heart of the sea.
9 The enemy said, 'I will pursue, I will overtake,
I will divide the spoil, my desire shall have its fill of them.
I will draw my sword, my hand shall destroy them.'
10 You blew with your wind, the sea covered them;
they sank like lead in the mighty waters.

11 "Who is like you, O Lord, among the gods?
Who is like you, majestic in holiness,
awesome in splendor, doing wonders?
12 You stretched out your right hand,
the earth swallowed them.

13 "In your steadfast love you led the people whom you redeemed;
you guided them by your strength to your holy abode.
14 The peoples heard, they trembled;
pangs seized the inhabitants of Philistia.
15 Then the chiefs of Edom were dismayed;
trembling seized the leaders of Moab;
all the inhabitants of Canaan melted away.
16 Terror and dread fell upon them;
by the might of your arm, they became still as a stone
until your people, O Lord, passed by,
until the people whom you acquired passed by.

---

d Or *song*   e Or *Sea of Reeds*

King James

17Thou shalt bring them in, and plant them in the mountain of thine inheritance, *in* the place, O LORD, *which* thou hast made for thee to dwell in, *in* the Sanctuary, O LORD, *which* thy hands have established.

18The LORD shall reign for ever and ever.

19For the horse of Pharaoh went in with his chariots and with his horsemen into the sea, and the LORD brought again the waters of the sea upon them; but the children of Israel went on dry *land* in the midst of the sea.

20¶ And Miriam the prophetess, the sister of Aaron, took a timbrel in her hand; and all the women went out after her with timbrels and with dances.

21And Miriam answered them, Sing ye to the LORD, for he hath triumphed gloriously; the horse and his rider hath he thrown into the sea.

22So Moses brought Israel from the Red sea, and they went out into the wilderness of Shur; and they went three days in the wilderness, and found no water.

23¶ And when they came to Marah, they could not drink of the waters of Marah, for they *were* bitter: therefore the name of it was called Marah.

24And the people murmured against Moses, saying, What shall we drink?

25And he cried unto the LORD; and the LORD showed him a tree, *which* when he had cast into the waters, the waters were made sweet: there he made for them a statute and an ordinance, and there he proved them,

26And said, If thou wilt diligently hearken to the voice of the LORD thy God, and wilt do that which is right in his sight, and wilt give ear to his commandments, and keep all his statutes, I will put none of these diseases upon thee, which I have brought upon the Egyptians: for I *am* the LORD that healeth thee.

27¶ And they came to Elim, where *were* twelve wells of water, and threescore and ten palm trees: and they encamped there by the waters.

16 AND THEY took their journey from Elim, and all the congregation of the children of Israel came unto the wilderness of Sin, which *is* between Elim and Sinai, on the fifteenth day of the second month after their departing out of the land of Egypt.

2And the whole congregation of the children of Israel murmured against Moses and Aaron in the wilderness:

3And the children of Israel said unto them, Would to God we had died by the hand of the LORD in the land of Egypt, when we sat by the flesh pots, *and* when we did eat bread to the full; for ye have brought us forth into this wilderness, to kill this whole assembly with hunger.

4¶ Then said the LORD unto Moses, Behold, I will rain bread from heaven for you; and the people shall go out and gather a certain rate every day, that I may prove them, whether they will walk in my law, or no.

5And it shall come to pass, that on the sixth day they shall prepare *that* which they bring in; and it shall be twice as much as they gather daily.

6And Moses and Aaron said unto all the children of Israel, At even, then ye shall know that the LORD hath brought you out from the land of Egypt:

New International

17You will bring them in and plant them
  on the mountain of your inheritance—
  the place, O LORD, you made for your
    dwelling,
  the sanctuary, O Lord, your hands
    established.
18The LORD will reign
  for ever and ever."

19When Pharaoh's horses, chariots and horsemen[a] went into the sea, the LORD brought the waters of the sea back over them, but the Israelites walked through the sea on dry ground. 20Then Miriam the prophetess, Aaron's sister, took a tambourine in her hand, and all the women followed her, with tambourines and dancing. 21Miriam sang to them:

  "Sing to the LORD,
    for he is highly exalted.
  The horse and its rider
    he has hurled into the sea."

The Waters of Marah and Elim

22Then Moses led Israel from the Red Sea and they went into the Desert of Shur. For three days they traveled in the desert without finding water. 23When they came to Marah, they could not drink its water because it was bitter. (That is why the place is called Marah.[b]) 24So the people grumbled against Moses, saying, "What are we to drink?"

25Then Moses cried out to the LORD, and the LORD showed him a piece of wood. He threw it into the water, and the water became sweet.

There the LORD made a decree and a law for them, and there he tested them. 26He said, "If you listen carefully to the voice of the LORD your God and do what is right in his eyes, if you pay attention to his commands and keep all his decrees, I will not bring on you any of the diseases I brought on the Egyptians, for I am the LORD, who heals you."

27Then they came to Elim, where there were twelve springs and seventy palm trees, and they camped there near the water.

Manna and Quail

16 THE WHOLE Israelite community set out from Elim and came to the Desert of Sin, which is between Elim and Sinai, on the fifteenth day of the second month after they had come out of Egypt. 2In the desert the whole community grumbled against Moses and Aaron. 3The Israelites said to them, "If only we had died by the LORD's hand in Egypt! There we sat around pots of meat and ate all the food we wanted, but you have brought us out into this desert to starve this entire assembly to death."

4Then the LORD said to Moses, "I will rain down bread from heaven for you. The people are to go out each day and gather enough for that day. In this way I will test them and see whether they will follow my instructions. 5On the sixth day they are to prepare what they bring in, and that is to be twice as much as they gather on the other days."

6So Moses and Aaron said to all the Israelites, "In the evening you will know that it was the LORD who brought you out of Egypt, 7and in the morning you will see the

a 19 Or *charioteers*   b 23 *Marah* means *bitter*.

Living Bible

17You will bring them in and plant them on your
  mountain,
Your own homeland, Lord—
The sanctuary you made for them to live in.
18Jehovah shall reign forever and forever.
19The horses of Pharaoh, his horsemen, and his chariots
Tried to follow through the sea;
But the Lord let down the walls of water on them
While the people of Israel walked through on dry
  land.
20Then Miriam the prophetess, the sister of Aaron,
took a tambourine and led the women in dances.
21And Miriam sang this song:
Sing to the Lord, for he has triumphed gloriously.
The horse and rider have been drowned in the sea.
22Then Moses led the people of Israel on from the Red
Sea, and they moved out into the wilderness of Shur and
were there three days without water. 23Arriving at Marah, they couldn't drink the water because it was bitter
(that is why the place was called Marah, meaning "bitter").
  24Then the people turned against Moses. "Must we
die of thirst?" they demanded.
  25Moses pleaded with the Lord to help them, and the
Lord showed him a tree to throw into the water, and the
water became sweet.
  It was there at Marah that the Lord laid before them
the following conditions, to test their commitment to
him: 26"If you will listen to the voice of the Lord your
God, and obey it, and do what is right, then I will not
make you suffer the diseases I sent on the Egyptians, for
I am the Lord who heals you." 27And they came to Elim
where there were twelve springs and seventy palm trees;
and they camped there beside the springs.

16 NOW THEY left Elim and journeyed on into
the Sihn Wilderness, between Elim and Mt. Sinai, arriving there on the fifteenth day of the second
month after leaving Egypt. 2There too, the people spoke
bitterly against Moses and Aaron.
  3"Oh, that we were back in Egypt," they moaned,
"and that the Lord had killed us there! For there we had
plenty to eat. But now you have brought us into this
wilderness to kill us with starvation."
  4Then the Lord said to Moses, "Look, I'm going to
rain down food from heaven for them. Everyone can go
out each day and gather as much food as he needs. And
I will test them in this, to see whether they will follow
my instructions or not. 5Tell them to gather twice as
much as usual on the sixth day of each week."
  6Then Moses and Aaron called a meeting of all the
people of Israel and told them, "This evening you will
realize that it was the Lord who brought you out of the
land of Egypt. 7, 8, 9In the morning you will see more

New Revised Standard

17 You brought them in and planted them on the
        mountain of your own possession,
      the place, O LORD, that you made your
        abode,
      the sanctuary, O LORD, that your hands
        have established.
18   The LORD will reign forever and ever."
  19 When the horses of Pharaoh with his chariots and
his chariot drivers went into the sea, the LORD brought
back the waters of the sea upon them; but the Israelites
walked through the sea on dry ground.

The Song of Miriam

  20 Then the prophet Miriam, Aaron's sister, took a
tambourine in her hand; and all the women went out after
her with tambourines and with dancing. 21And Miriam
sang to them:
      "Sing to the LORD, for he has triumphed
        gloriously;
      horse and rider he has thrown into the sea."

Bitter Water Made Sweet

  22 Then Moses ordered Israel to set out from the
Red Sea,c and they went into the wilderness of Shur.
They went three days in the wilderness and found no
water. 23When they came to Marah, they could not drink
the water of Marah because it was bitter. That is why it
was called Marah.d 24And the people complained
against Moses, saying, "What shall we drink?" 25He
cried out to the LORD; and the LORD showed him a piece
of wood;e he threw it into the water, and the water
became sweet.
  There the LORDf made for them a statute and an
ordinance and there he put them to the test. 26He said,
"If you will listen carefully to the voice of the LORD your
God, and do what is right in his sight, and give heed to
his commandments and keep all his statutes, I will not
bring upon you any of the diseases that I brought upon
the Egyptians; for I am the LORD who heals you."
  27 Then they came to Elim, where there were
twelve springs of water and seventy palm trees; and they
camped there by the water.

Bread from Heaven

16 THE WHOLE congregation of the Israelites set
out from Elim; and Israel came to the wilderness of Sin, which is between Elim and Sinai, on the
fifteenth day of the second month after they had departed
from the land of Egypt. 2The whole congregation of the
Israelites complained against Moses and Aaron in the
wilderness. 3The Israelites said to them, "If only we had
died by the hand of the LORD in the land of Egypt, when
we sat by the fleshpots and ate our fill of bread; for you
have brought us out into this wilderness to kill this whole
assembly with hunger."
  4 Then the LORD said to Moses, "I am going to rain
bread from heaven for you, and each day the people shall
go out and gather enough for that day. In that way I will
test them, whether they will follow my instruction or
not. 5On the sixth day, when they prepare what they
bring in, it will be twice as much as they gather on other
days." 6So Moses and Aaron said to all the Israelites,
"In the evening you shall know that it was the LORD who
brought you out of the land of Egypt, 7and in the morn-

---

c Or Sea of Reeds   d That is Bitterness   e Or a tree   f Heb he

King James

7And in the morning, then ye shall see the glory of the LORD; for that he heareth your murmurings against the LORD: and what *are* we, that ye murmur against us?

8And Moses said, *This shall be,* when the LORD shall give you in the evening flesh to eat, and in the morning bread to the full; for that the LORD heareth your murmurings which ye murmur against him: and what *are* we? your murmurings *are* not against us, but against the LORD.

9¶ And Moses spake unto Aaron, Say unto all the congregation of the children of Israel, Come near before the LORD: for he hath heard your murmurings.

10And it came to pass, as Aaron spake unto the whole congregation of the children of Israel, that they looked toward the wilderness, and, behold, the glory of the LORD appeared in the cloud.

11¶ And the LORD spake unto Moses, saying,

12I have heard the murmurings of the children of Israel: speak unto them, saying, At even ye shall eat flesh, and in the morning ye shall be filled with bread; and ye shall know that I *am* the LORD your God.

13And it came to pass, that at even the quails came up, and covered the camp: and in the morning the dew lay round about the host.

14And when the dew that lay was gone up, behold, upon the face of the wilderness *there lay* a small round thing, *as* small as the hoar frost on the ground.

15And when the children of Israel saw *it,* they said one to another, It *is* manna: for they wist not what it *was.* And Moses said unto them, This *is* the bread which the LORD hath given you to eat.

16¶ This *is* the thing which the LORD hath commanded, Gather of it every man according to his eating, an omer for every man, *according to* the number of your persons; take ye every man for *them* which *are* in his tents.

17And the children of Israel did so, and gathered, some more, some less.

18And when they did mete *it* with an omer, he that gathered much had nothing over, and he that gathered little had no lack; they gathered every man according to his eating.

19And Moses said, Let no man leave of it till the morning.

20Notwithstanding they hearkened not unto Moses; but some of them left of it until the morning, and it bred worms, and stank: and Moses was wroth with them.

21And they gathered it every morning, every man according to his eating: and when the sun waxed hot, it melted.

22¶ And it came to pass, *that* on the sixth day they gathered twice as much bread, two omers for one *man:* and all the rulers of the congregation came and told Moses.

23And he said unto them, This *is that* which the LORD hath said, Tomorrow *is* the rest of the holy sabbath unto the LORD: bake *that* which ye will bake *today,* and seethe that ye will seethe; and that which remaineth over lay up for you to be kept until the morning.

24And they laid it up till the morning, as Moses bade: and it did not stink, neither was there any worm therein.

25And Moses said, Eat that today; for today *is* a sabbath unto the LORD: today ye shall not find it in the field.

26Six days ye shall gather it; but on the seventh day, *which is* the sabbath, in it there shall be none.

27¶ And it came to pass, *that* there went out *some* of the people on the seventh day for to gather, and they found none.

28And the LORD said unto Moses, How long refuse ye to keep my commandments and my laws?

29See, for that the LORD hath given you the sabbath, therefore he giveth you on the sixth day the bread of two days; abide ye every man in his place, let no man go out of his place on the seventh day.

30So the people rested on the seventh day.

New International

glory of the LORD, because he has heard your grumbling against him. Who are we, that you should grumble against us?" 8Moses also said, "You will know that it was the LORD when he gives you meat to eat in the evening and all the bread you want in the morning, because he has heard your grumbling against him. Who are we? You are not grumbling against us, but against the LORD."

9Then Moses told Aaron, "Say to the entire Israelite community, 'Come before the LORD, for he has heard your grumbling.' "

10While Aaron was speaking to the whole Israelite community, they looked toward the desert, and there was the glory of the LORD appearing in the cloud.

11The LORD said to Moses, 12"I have heard the grumbling of the Israelites. Tell them, 'At twilight you will eat meat, and in the morning you will be filled with bread. Then you will know that I am the LORD your God.' "

13That evening quail came and covered the camp, and in the morning there was a layer of dew around the camp. 14When the dew was gone, thin flakes like frost on the ground appeared on the desert floor. 15When the Israelites saw it, they said to each other, "What is it?" For they did not know what it was.

Moses said to them, "It is the bread the LORD has given you to eat. 16This is what the LORD has commanded: 'Each one is to gather as much as he needs. Take an omer[a] for each person you have in your tent.' "

17The Israelites did as they were told; some gathered much, some little. 18And when they measured it by the omer, he who gathered much did not have too much, and he who gathered little did not have too little. Each one gathered as much as he needed.

19Then Moses said to them, "No one is to keep any of it until morning."

20However, some of them paid no attention to Moses; they kept part of it until morning, but it was full of maggots and began to smell. So Moses was angry with them.

21Each morning everyone gathered as much as he needed, and when the sun grew hot, it melted away. 22On the sixth day, they gathered twice as much—two omers[b] for each person—and the leaders of the community came and reported this to Moses. 23He said to them, "This is what the LORD commanded: 'Tomorrow is to be a day of rest, a holy Sabbath to the LORD. So bake what you want to bake and boil what you want to boil. Save whatever is left and keep it until morning.' "

24So they saved it until morning, as Moses commanded, and it did not stink or get maggots in it. 25"Eat it today," Moses said, "because today is a Sabbath to the LORD. You will not find any of it on the ground today. 26Six days you are to gather it, but on the seventh day, the Sabbath, there will not be any."

27Nevertheless, some of the people went out on the seventh day to gather it, but they found none. 28Then the LORD said to Moses, "How long will you[c] refuse to keep my commands and my instructions? 29Bear in mind that the LORD has given you the Sabbath; that is why on the sixth day he gives you bread for two days. Everyone is to stay where he is on the seventh day; no one is to go out." 30So the people rested on the seventh day.

---

a *16* That is, probably about 2 quarts (about 2 liters); also in verses 18, 32, 33 and 36   b *22* That is, probably about 4 quarts (about 4.5 liters)   c *28* The Hebrew is plural.

Living Bible

of his glory; for he has heard your complaints against him (for you aren't really complaining against *us*—who are *we?*). The Lord will give you meat to eat in the evening, and bread in the morning. Come now before Jehovah, and hear his reply to your complaints."

10So Aaron called them together and suddenly, out toward the wilderness, from within the guiding cloud, there appeared the awesome glory of Jehovah.

11, 12And Jehovah said to Moses, "I have heard their complaints. Tell them, 'In the evening you will have meat and in the morning you will be stuffed with bread, and you shall know that I am Jehovah your God.' "

13That evening vast numbers of quail arrived and covered the camp, and in the morning the desert all around the camp was wet with dew; 14and when the dew disappeared later in the morning it left thin white flakes that covered the ground like frost. 15When the people of Israel saw it they asked each other, "What is it?"

And Moses told them, "It is the food Jehovah has given you. 16Jehovah has said for everyone to gather as much as is needed for his household—about two quartsd for each person."

17So the people of Israel went out and gathered it— some getting more and some less before it melted on the ground, 18and there was just enough for everyone. Those who gathered more had nothing left over and those who gathered little had no lack! Each home had just enough.

19And Moses told them, "Don't leave it overnight."

20But of course some of them wouldn't listen, and left it until morning; and when they looked, it was full of maggots and had a terrible odor; and Moses was very angry with them. 21So they gathered the food morning by morning, each home according to its need; and when the sun became hot upon the ground, the food melted and disappeared. 22On the sixth day there was twice as much as usual on the ground—four quarts instead of two; the leaders of the people came and asked Moses why this had happened.

23And he told them, "Because the Lord has appointed tomorrow as a day of seriousness and rest, a holy Sabbath to the Lord when we must refrain from doing our daily tasks. So cook as much as you want to today, and keep what is left for tomorrow."

24And the next morning the food was wholesome and good, without maggots or odor. 25Moses said, "This is your food for today, for today is the Sabbath to Jehovah and there will be no food on the ground today. 26Gather the food for six days, but the seventh is a Sabbath, and there will be none there for you on that day."

27But some of the people went out anyway to gather food, even though it was the Sabbath, but there wasn't any.

28, 29"How long will these people refuse to obey?" the Lord asked Moses. "Don't they realize that I am giving them twice as much on the sixth day, so that there will be enough for two days? For the Lord has given you the seventh day as a day of Sabbath rest; stay in your tents and don't go out to pick up food from the ground that day." 30So the people rested on the seventh day.

New Revised Standard

ing you shall see the glory of the LORD, because he has heard your complaining against the LORD. For what are we, that you complain against us?" 8And Moses said, "When the LORD gives you meat to eat in the evening and your fill of bread in the morning, because the LORD has heard the complaining that you utter against him— what are we? Your complaining is not against us but against the LORD."

9 Then Moses said to Aaron, "Say to the whole congregation of the Israelites, 'Draw near to the LORD, for he has heard your complaining.' " 10And as Aaron spoke to the whole congregation of the Israelites, they looked toward the wilderness, and the glory of the LORD appeared in the cloud. 11The LORD spoke to Moses and said, 12"I have heard the complaining of the Israelites; say to them, 'At twilight you shall eat meat, and in the morning you shall have your fill of bread; then you shall know that I am the LORD your God.' "

13 In the evening quails came up and covered the camp; and in the morning there was a layer of dew around the camp. 14When the layer of dew lifted, there on the surface of the wilderness was a fine flaky substance, as fine as frost on the ground. 15When the Israelites saw it, they said to one another, "What is it?"e For they did not know what it was. Moses said to them, "It is the bread that the LORD has given you to eat. 16This is what the LORD has commanded: 'Gather as much of it as each of you needs, an omer to a person according to the number of persons, all providing for those in their own tents.' " 17The Israelites did so, some gathering more, some less. 18But when they measured it with an omer, those who gathered much had nothing over, and those who gathered little had no shortage; they gathered as much as each of them needed. 19And Moses said to them, "Let no one leave any of it over until morning." 20But they did not listen to Moses; some left part of it until morning, and it bred worms and became foul. And Moses was angry with them. 21Morning by morning they gathered it, as much as each needed; but when the sun grew hot, it melted.

22 On the sixth day they gathered twice as much food, two omers apiece. When all the leaders of the congregation came and told Moses, 23he said to them, "This is what the LORD has commanded: 'Tomorrow is a day of solemn rest, a holy sabbath to the LORD; bake what you want to bake and boil what you want to boil, and all that is left over put aside to be kept until morning.' " 24So they put it aside until morning, as Moses commanded them; and it did not become foul, and there were no worms in it. 25Moses said, "Eat it today, for today is a sabbath to the LORD; today you will not find it in the field. 26Six days you shall gather it; but on the seventh day, which is a sabbath, there will be none."

27 On the seventh day some of the people went out to gather, and they found none. 28The LORD said to Moses, "How long will you refuse to keep my commandments and instructions? 29See! The LORD has given you the sabbath, therefore on the sixth day he gives you food for two days; each of you stay where you are; do not leave your place on the seventh day." 30So the people rested on the seventh day.

---

d 16:16 *about two quarts*, literally, "an omer." The exact measure is not known.

e Or "*It is manna*" (Heb *man hu*, see verse 31)

King James

31And the house of Israel called the name thereof Manna: and it *was* like coriander seed, white; and the taste of it *was* like wafers *made* with honey.

32¶ And Moses said, This *is* the thing which the LORD commandeth, Fill an omer of it to be kept for your generations; that they may see the bread wherewith I have fed you in the wilderness, when I brought you forth from the land of Egypt.

33And Moses said unto Aaron, Take a pot, and put an omer full of manna therein, and lay it up before the LORD, to be kept for your generations.

34As the LORD commanded Moses, so Aaron laid it up before the Testimony, to be kept.

35And the children of Israel did eat manna forty years, until they came to a land inhabited; they did eat manna, until they came unto the borders of the land of Canaan.

36Now an omer *is* the tenth *part* of an ephah.

17 AND ALL the congregation of the children of Israel journeyed from the wilderness of Sin, after their journeys, according to the commandment of the LORD, and pitched in Rephidim: and *there was* no water for the people to drink.

2Wherefore the people did chide with Moses, and said, Give us water that we may drink. And Moses said unto them, Why chide ye with me? wherefore do ye tempt the LORD?

3And the people thirsted there for water; and the people murmured against Moses, and said, Wherefore *is* this *that* thou hast brought us up out of Egypt, to kill us and our children and our cattle with thirst?

4And Moses cried unto the LORD, saying, What shall I do unto this people? they be almost ready to stone me.

5And the LORD said unto Moses, Go on before the people, and take with thee of the elders of Israel; and thy rod, wherewith thou smotest the river, take in thine hand, and go.

6Behold, I will stand before thee there upon the rock in Horeb; and thou shalt smite the rock, and there shall come water out of it, that the people may drink. And Moses did so in the sight of the elders of Israel.

7And he called the name of the place Massah, and Meribah, because of the chiding of the children of Israel, and because they tempted the LORD, saying, Is the LORD among us, or not?

8¶ Then came Amalek, and fought with Israel in Rephidim.

9And Moses said unto Joshua, Choose us out men, and go out, fight with Amalek: tomorrow I will stand on the top of the hill with the rod of God in mine hand.

10So Joshua did as Moses had said to him, and fought with Amalek: and Moses, Aaron, and Hur went up to the top of the hill.

11And it came to pass, when Moses held up his hand, that Israel prevailed: and when he let down his hand, Amalek prevailed.

12But Moses' hands *were* heavy; and they took a stone, and put *it* under him, and he sat thereon; and Aaron and Hur stayed up his hands, the one on the one side, and the other on the other side; and his hands were steady until the going down of the sun.

13And Joshua discomfited Amalek and his people with the edge of the sword.

14And the LORD said unto Moses, Write this *for* a memorial in a book, and rehearse *it* in the ears of Joshua: for I will utterly put out the remembrance of Amalek from under heaven.

New International

31The people of Israel called the bread manna.a It was white like coriander seed and tasted like wafers made with honey. 32Moses said, "This is what the LORD has commanded: 'Take an omer of manna and keep it for the generations to come, so they can see the bread I gave you to eat in the desert when I brought you out of Egypt.' "

33So Moses said to Aaron, "Take a jar and put an omer of manna in it. Then place it before the LORD to be kept for the generations to come."

34As the LORD commanded Moses, Aaron put the manna in front of the Testimony, that it might be kept. 35The Israelites ate manna forty years, until they came to a land that was settled; they ate manna until they reached the border of Canaan.

36(An omer is one tenth of an ephah.)

Water From the Rock

17 THE WHOLE Israelite community set out from the Desert of Sin, traveling from place to place as the LORD commanded. They camped at Rephidim, but there was no water for the people to drink. 2So they quarreled with Moses and said, "Give us water to drink."

Moses replied, "Why do you quarrel with me? Why do you put the LORD to the test?"

3But the people were thirsty for water there, and they grumbled against Moses. They said, "Why did you bring us up out of Egypt to make us and our children and livestock die of thirst?"

4Then Moses cried out to the LORD, "What am I to do with these people? They are almost ready to stone me."

5The LORD answered Moses, "Walk on ahead of the people. Take with you some of the elders of Israel and take in your hand the staff with which you struck the Nile, and go. 6I will stand there before you by the rock at Horeb. Strike the rock, and water will come out of it for the people to drink." So Moses did this in the sight of the elders of Israel. 7And he called the place Massahb and Meribahc because the Israelites quarreled and because they tested the LORD saying, "Is the LORD among us or not?"

The Amalekites Defeated

8The Amalekites came and attacked the Israelites at Rephidim. 9Moses said to Joshua, "Choose some of our men and go out to fight the Amalekites. Tomorrow I will stand on top of the hill with the staff of God in my hands."

10So Joshua fought the Amalekites as Moses had ordered, and Moses, Aaron and Hur went to the top of the hill. 11As long as Moses held up his hands, the Israelites were winning, but whenever he lowered his hands, the Amalekites were winning. 12When Moses' hands grew tired, they took a stone and put it under him and he sat on it. Aaron and Hur held his hands up—one on one side, one on the other—so that his hands remained steady till sunset. 13So Joshua overcame the Amalekite army with the sword.

14Then the LORD said to Moses, "Write this on a scroll as something to be remembered and make sure that Joshua hears it, because I will completely blot out the memory of Amalek from under heaven."

---

a 31 *Manna* means *What is it?* (see verse 15). b 7 *Massah* means *testing*.
c 7 *Meribah* means *quarreling*.

Living Bible

31And the food became known as "manna" (meaning "What is it?"); it was white, like coriander seed, and flat, and tasted like honey bread.

32Then Moses gave them this further instruction from the Lord: they were to take two quarts of it to be kept as a museum specimen forever, so that later generations could see the bread the Lord had fed them with in the wilderness, when he brought them from Egypt. 33Moses told Aaron to get a container and put two quarts of manna in it and to keep it in a sacred place from generation to generation. 34Aaron did this, just as the Lord had instructed Moses, and eventually it was kept in the Ark in the Tabernacle.

35So the people of Israel ate the manna forty years until they arrived in the land of Canaan, where there were crops to eat. 36The omer—the container used to measure the manna—held about two quarts; it is approximately a tenth of a bushel.

17 NOW, AT God's command, the people of Israel left the Sihn desert, going by easy stages to Rephidim. But upon arrival, there was no water!

2So once more the people growled and complained to Moses. "Give us water!" they wailed.

"Quiet!" Moses commanded. "Are you trying to test God's patience with you?"

3But, tormented by thirst, they cried out, "Why did you ever take us out of Egypt? Why did you bring us here to die, with our children and cattle too?"

4Then Moses pleaded with Jehovah. "What shall I do? For they are almost ready to stone me."

5, 6Then Jehovah said to Moses, "Take the elders of Israel with you and lead the people out to Mt. Horeb. I will meet you there at the rock. Strike it with your rodd—the same one you struck the Nile with—and water will come pouring out, enough for everyone!" Moses did as he was told, and the water gushed out! 7Moses named the place Massah (meaning "tempting Jehovah to slay us"), and sometimes they referred to it as Meribah (meaning "argument" and "strife!")—for it was there that the people of Israel argued against God and tempted him to slaye them by saying, "Is Jehovah going to take care of us or not?"

8But now the warriors of Amalek came to fight against the people of Israel at Rephidim. 9Moses instructed Joshua to issue a call to arms to the Israelites, to fight the army of Amalek.

"Tomorrow," Moses told him, "I will stand at the top of the hill, with the rod of God in my hand!"

10So Joshua and his men went out to fight the army of Amalek. Meanwhile Moses, Aaron, and Hurf went up to the top of the hill. 11And as long as Moses held up the rod in his hands, Israel was winning; but whenever he rested his arms at his sides, the soldiers of Amalek were winning. 12Moses' arms finally became too tired to hold up the rod any longer; so Aaron and Hur rolled a stone for him to sit on, and they stood on each side, holding up his hands until sunset. 13As a result, Joshua and his troops crushed the army of Amalek, putting them to the sword.

14Then the Lord instructed Moses, "Write this into a permanent record, to be remembered forever, and announce to Joshua that I will utterly blot out every trace of Amalek." 15, 16Moses built an altar there and called

New Revised Standard

31 The house of Israel called it manna; it was like coriander seed, white, and the taste of it was like wafers made with honey. 32Moses said, "This is what the LORD has commanded: 'Let an omer of it be kept throughout your generations, in order that they may see the food with which I fed you in the wilderness, when I brought you out of the land of Egypt.' " 33And Moses said to Aaron, "Take a jar, and put an omer of manna in it, and place it before the LORD, to be kept throughout your generations." 34As the LORD commanded Moses, so Aaron placed it before the covenant,g for safekeeping. 35The Israelites ate manna forty years, until they came to a habitable land; they ate manna, until they came to the border of the land of Canaan. 36An omer is a tenth of an ephah.

Water from the Rock

17 FROM THE wilderness of Sin the whole congregation of the Israelites journeyed by stages, as the LORD commanded. They camped at Rephidim, but there was no water for the people to drink. 2The people quarreled with Moses, and said, "Give us water to drink." Moses said to them, "Why do you quarrel with me? Why do you test the LORD?" 3But the people thirsted there for water; and the people complained against Moses and said, "Why did you bring us out of Egypt, to kill us and our children and livestock with thirst?" 4So Moses cried out to the LORD, "What shall I do with this people? They are almost ready to stone me." 5The LORD said to Moses, "Go on ahead of the people, and take some of the elders of Israel with you; take in your hand the staff with which you struck the Nile, and go. 6I will be standing there in front of you on the rock at Horeb. Strike the rock, and water will come out of it, so that the people may drink." Moses did so, in the sight of the elders of Israel. 7He called the place Massahh and Meribah,i because the Israelites quarreled and tested the LORD, saying, "Is the LORD among us or not?"

Amalek Attacks Israel and Is Defeated

8 Then Amalek came and fought with Israel at Rephidim. 9Moses said to Joshua, "Choose some men for us and go out, fight with Amalek. Tomorrow I will stand on the top of the hill with the staff of God in my hand." 10So Joshua did as Moses told him, and fought with Amalek, while Moses, Aaron, and Hur went up to the top of the hill. 11Whenever Moses held up his hand, Israel prevailed; and whenever he lowered his hand, Amalek prevailed. 12But Moses' hands grew weary; so they took a stone and put it under him, and he sat on it. Aaron and Hur held up his hands, one on one side, and the other on the other side; so his hands were steady until the sun set. 13And Joshua defeated Amalek and his people with the sword.

14 Then the LORD said to Moses, "Write this as a reminder in a book and recite it in the hearing of Joshua: I will utterly blot out the remembrance of Amalek from under heaven." 15And Moses built an altar and called it,

---

d 17:5, 6 Strike it with your rod, implied.   e 17:7 to slay them, implied.
f 17:10 Hur. Hur was a man of Judah, of the family of Hezron, house of Caleb (1 Chron 2:18, 19). He was the grandfather of Bezalel (31:1, 2).   g Or treaty or testimony; Heb eduth   h That is Test   i That is Quarrel

King James

15And Moses built an altar, and called the name of it Jehovah-nissi:

16For he said, Because the LORD hath sworn *that* the LORD *will have* war with Amalek from generation to generation.

18 WHEN JETHRO, the priest of Midian, Moses' father-in-law, heard of all that God had done for Moses, and for Israel his people, *and* that the LORD had brought Israel out of Egypt;

2Then Jethro, Moses' father-in-law, took Zipporah, Moses' wife, after he had sent her back,

3And her two sons; of which the name of the one *was* Gershom; for he said, I have been an alien in a strange land:

4And the name of the other *was* Eliezer; for the God of my father, *said he, was* mine help, and delivered me from the sword of Pharaoh:

5And Jethro, Moses' father-in-law, came with his sons and his wife unto Moses into the wilderness, where he encamped at the mount of God:

6And he said unto Moses, I thy father-in-law Jethro am come unto thee, and thy wife, and her two sons with her.

7¶ And Moses went out to meet his father-in-law, and did obeisance, and kissed him; and they asked each other of *their* welfare; and they came into the tent.

8And Moses told his father-in-law all that the LORD had done unto Pharaoh and to the Egyptians for Israel's sake, *and* all the travail that had come upon them by the way, and *how* the LORD delivered them.

9And Jethro rejoiced for all the goodness which the LORD had done to Israel, whom he had delivered out of the hand of the Egyptians.

10And Jethro said, Blessed *be* the LORD, who hath delivered you out of the hand of the Egyptians, and out of the hand of Pharaoh, who hath delivered the people from under the hand of the Egyptians.

11Now I know that the LORD *is* greater than all gods: for in the thing wherein they dealt proudly *he was* above them.

12And Jethro, Moses' father-in-law, took a burnt offering and sacrifices for God: and Aaron came, and all the elders of Israel, to eat bread with Moses' father-in-law before God.

13¶ And it came to pass on the morrow, that Moses sat to judge the people: and the people stood by Moses from the morning unto the evening.

14And when Moses' father-in-law saw all that he did to the people, he said, What *is* this thing that thou doest to the people? why sittest thou thyself alone, and all the people stand by thee from morning unto even?

15And Moses said unto his father-in-law, Because the people come unto me to inquire of God:

16When they have a matter, they come unto me; and I judge between one and another, and I do make *them* know the statutes of God, and his laws.

17And Moses' father-in-law said unto him, The thing that thou doest *is* not good.

18Thou wilt surely wear away, both thou, and this people that *is* with thee: for this thing *is* too heavy for thee; thou art not able to perform it thyself alone.

19Hearken now unto my voice, I will give thee counsel, and God shall be with thee: Be thou for the people to God-ward, that thou mayest bring the causes unto God:

20And thou shalt teach them ordinances and laws, and shalt show them the way wherein they must walk, and the work that they must do.

New International

15Moses built an altar and called it The LORD is my Banner. 16He said, "For hands were lifted up to the throne of the LORD. Thea LORD will be at war against the Amalekites from generation to generation."

Jethro Visits Moses

18 NOW JETHRO, the priest of Midian and father-in-law of Moses, heard of everything God had done for Moses and for his people Israel, and how the LORD had brought Israel out of Egypt.

2After Moses had sent away his wife Zipporah, his father-in-law Jethro received her 3and her two sons. One son was named Gershom,b for Moses said, "I have become an alien in a foreign land"; 4and the other was named Eliezer,c for he said, "My father's God was my helper; he saved me from the sword of Pharaoh."

5Jethro, Moses' father-in-law, together with Moses' sons and wife, came to him in the desert, where he was camped near the mountain of God. 6Jethro had sent word to him, "I, your father-in-law Jethro, am coming to you with your wife and her two sons."

7So Moses went out to meet his father-in-law and bowed down and kissed him. They greeted each other and then went into the tent. 8Moses told his father-in-law about everything the LORD had done to Pharaoh and the Egyptians for Israel's sake and about all the hardships they had met along the way and how the LORD had saved them.

9Jethro was delighted to hear about all the good things the LORD had done for Israel in rescuing them from the hand of the Egyptians. 10He said, "Praise be to the LORD, who rescued you from the hand of the Egyptians and of Pharaoh, and who rescued the people from the hand of the Egyptians. 11Now I know that the LORD is greater than all other gods, for he did this to those who had treated Israel arrogantly." 12Then Jethro, Moses' father-in-law, brought a burnt offering and other sacrifices to God, and Aaron came with all the elders of Israel to eat bread with Moses' father-in-law in the presence of God.

13The next day Moses took his seat to serve as judge for the people, and they stood around him from morning till evening. 14When his father-in-law saw all that Moses was doing for the people, he said, "What is this you are doing for the people? Why do you alone sit as judge, while all these people stand around you from morning till evening?"

15Moses answered him, "Because the people come to me to seek God's will. 16Whenever they have a dispute, it is brought to me, and I decide between the parties and inform them of God's decrees and laws."

17Moses' father-in-law replied, "What you are doing is not good. 18You and these people who come to you will only wear yourselves out. The work is too heavy for you; you cannot handle it alone. 19Listen now to me and I will give you some advice, and may God be with you. You must be the people's representative before God and bring their disputes to him. 20Teach them the decrees and laws, and show them the way to live and the duties they are to perform. 21But select capable men from all

---

a 16 Or *"Because a hand was against the throne of the LORD, the*
b 3 *Gershom* sounds like the Hebrew for *an alien there.*   c 4 *Eliezer* means *my God is helper.*

Living Bible

it "Jehovah-nissi" (meaning "Jehovah is my flag").

"Raise the banner of the Lord!" Moses said. "For the Lord will be at war with Amalek generation after generation."

18 WORD SOON reached Jethro, Moses' father-in-law, the priest of Midian, about all the wonderful things God had done for his people and for Moses, and how the Lord had brought them out of Egypt.

2Then Jethro took Moses' wife, Zipporah, to him (for he had sent her home), 3along with Moses' two sons, Gershom (meaning "foreigner," for Moses said when he was born, "I have been wandering in a foreign land") 4and Eliezer (meaning "God is my help," for Moses said at his birth, "The God of my fathers was my helper, and delivered me from the sword of Pharaoh"). 5, 6They arrived while Moses and the people were camped at Mt. Sinai.d

"Jethro, your father-in-law, has come to visit you," Moses was told, "and he has brought your wife and your two sons."

7Moses went out to meet his father-in-law and greeted him warmly; they asked about each other's health and then went into Moses' tent to talk further. 8Moses related to his father-in-law all that had been happening and what the Lord had done to Pharaoh and the Egyptians in order to deliver Israel, and all the problems there had been along the way, and how the Lord had delivered his people from all of them. 9Jethro was very happy about everything the Lord had done for Israel, and about his bringing them out of Egypt.

10"Bless the Lord," Jethro said, "for he has saved you from the Egyptians and from Pharaoh, and has rescued Israel. 11I know now that the Lord is greater than any other god because he delivered his people from the proud and cruel Egyptians.

12Jethro offered sacrificese to God, and afterwards Aaron and the leaders of Israel came to meet Jethro, and they all ate the sacrificial meal together before the Lord.

13The next day Moses sat as usual to hear the people's complaints against each other, from morning to evening.

14When Moses' father-in-law saw how much time this was taking, he said, "Why are you trying to do all this alone, with people standing here all day long to get your help?"

15, 16"Well, because the people come to me with their disputes, to ask for God's decisions," Moses told him. "I am their judge, deciding who is right and who is wrong, and instructing them in God's ways. I apply the laws of God to their particular disputes."

17"It's not right!" his father-in-law exclaimed. 18"You're going to wear yourself out—and if you do, what will happen to the people? Moses, this job is too heavy a burden for you to try to handle all by yourself. 19, 20Now listen, and let me give you a word of advice, and God will bless you: Be these people's lawyer—their representative before God—bringing him their questions to decide; you will tell them his decisions, teaching them God's laws, and showing them the principles of godly living.

New Revised Standard

The Lord is my banner. 16He said, "A hand upon the banner of the Lordf The Lord will have war with Amalek from generation to generation."

Jethro's Advice

18 JETHRO, THE priest of Midian, Moses' father-in-law, heard of all that God had done for Moses and for his people Israel, how the Lord had brought Israel out of Egypt. 2After Moses had sent away his wife Zipporah, his father-in-law Jethro took her back, 3along with her two sons. The name of the one was Gershom (for he said, "I have been an alien in a foreign land"), 4and the name of the other, Eliezerh (for he said, "The God of my father was my help, and delivered me from the sword of Pharaoh"). 5Jethro, Moses' father-in-law, came into the wilderness where Moses was encamped at the mountain of God, bringing Moses' sons and wife to him. 6He sent word to Moses, "I, your father-in-law Jethro, am coming to you, with your wife and her two sons." 7Moses went out to meet his father-in-law; he bowed down and kissed him; each asked after the other's welfare, and they went into the tent. 8Then Moses told his father-in-law all that the Lord had done to Pharaoh and to the Egyptians for Israel's sake, all the hardship that had beset them on the way, and how the Lord had delivered them. 9Jethro rejoiced for all the good that the Lord had done to Israel, in delivering them from the Egyptians.

10 Jethro said, "Blessed be the Lord, who has delivered you from the Egyptians and from Pharaoh. 11Now I know that the Lord is greater than all gods,i because he delivered the people from the Egyptians, when they dealt arrogantly with them." 12And Jethro, Moses' father-in-law, brought a burnt offering and sacrifices to God; and Aaron came with all the elders of Israel to eat bread with Moses' father-in-law in the presence of God.

13 The next day Moses sat as judge for the people, while the people stood around him from morning until evening. 14When Moses' father-in-law saw all that he was doing for the people, he said, "What is this that you are doing for the people? Why do you sit alone, while all the people stand around you from morning until evening?" 15Moses said to his father-in-law, "Because the people come to me to inquire of God. 16When they have a dispute, they come to me and I decide between one person and another, and I make known to them the statutes and instructions of God." 17Moses' father-in-law said to him, "What you are doing is not good. 18You will surely wear yourself out, both you and these people with you. For the task is too heavy for you; you cannot do it alone. 19Now listen to me. I will give you counsel, and God be with you! You should represent the people before God, and you should bring their cases before God; 20teach them the statutes and instructions and make known to them the way they are to go and the things they are to do. 21You should also look for able men among

---

d 18:5, 6 Mt. Sinai, or, "Mt. Horeb." Literally, "the mountain of God."
e 18:12 sacrifices, literally, "a burnt offering and sacrifices for God."

f Cn: Meaning of Heb uncertain   g Heb ger   h Heb Eli, my God; ezer, help
i The clause because . . . Egyptians has been transposed from verse 10

King James

21Moreover thou shalt provide out of all the people able men, such as fear God, men of truth, hating covetousness; and place *such* over them, *to be* rulers of thousands, *and* rulers of hundreds, rulers of fifties, and rulers of tens:

22And let them judge the people at all seasons: and it shall be, *that* every great matter they shall bring unto thee, but every small matter they shall judge: so shall it be easier for thyself, and they shall bear *the burden* with thee.

23If thou shalt do this thing, and God command thee *so,* then thou shalt be able to endure, and all this people shall also go to their place in peace.

24So Moses hearkened to the voice of his father-in-law, and did all that he had said.

25And Moses chose able men out of all Israel, and made them heads over the people, rulers of thousands, rulers of hundreds, rulers of fifties, and rulers of tens.

26And they judged the people at all seasons: the hard causes they brought unto Moses, but every small matter they judged themselves.

27¶ And Moses let his father-in-law depart; and he went his way into his own land.

19 IN THE third month, when the children of Israel were gone forth out of the land of Egypt, the same day came they *into* the wilderness of Sinai.

2For they were departed from Rephidim, and were come *to* the desert of Sinai, and had pitched in the wilderness; and there Israel camped before the mount.

3And Moses went up unto God, and the LORD called unto him out of the mountain, saying, Thus shalt thou say to the house of Jacob, and tell the children of Israel;

4Ye have seen what I did unto the Egyptians, and *how* I bare you on eagles' wings, and brought you unto myself.

5Now therefore, if ye will obey my voice indeed, and keep my covenant, then ye shall be a peculiar treasure unto me above all people: for all the earth *is* mine:

6And ye shall be unto me a kingdom of priests, and an holy nation. These *are* the words which thou shalt speak unto the children of Israel.

7¶ And Moses came and called for the elders of the people, and laid before their faces all these words which the LORD commanded him.

8And all the people answered together, and said, All that the LORD hath spoken we will do. And Moses returned the words of the people unto the LORD.

9And the LORD said unto Moses, Lo, I come unto thee in a thick cloud, that the people may hear when I speak with thee, and believe thee for ever. And Moses told the words of the people unto the LORD.

10¶ And the LORD said unto Moses, Go unto the people, and sanctify them today and tomorrow, and let them wash their clothes,

11And be ready against the third day: for the third day the LORD will come down in the sight of all the people upon mount Sinai.

12And thou shalt set bounds unto the people round about, saying, Take heed to yourselves, *that ye* go *not* up into the mount, or touch the border of it: whosoever toucheth the mount shall be surely put to death:

13There shall not an hand touch it, but he shall surely be stoned, or shot through; whether *it be* beast or man, it shall not live: when the trumpet soundeth long, they shall come up to the mount.

14¶ And Moses went down from the mount unto the people, and sanctified the people; and they washed their clothes.

15And he said unto the people, Be ready against the third day: come not at *your* wives.

New International

the people—men who fear God, trustworthy men who hate dishonest gain—and appoint them as officials over thousands, hundreds, fifties and tens. 22Have them serve as judges for the people at all times, but have them bring every difficult case to you; the simple cases they can decide themselves. That will make your load lighter, because they will share it with you. 23If you do this and God so commands, you will be able to stand the strain, and all these people will go home satisfied."

24Moses listened to his father-in-law and did everything he said. 25He chose capable men from all Israel and made them leaders of the people, officials over thousands, hundreds, fifties and tens. 26They served as judges for the people at all times. The difficult cases they brought to Moses, but the simple ones they decided themselves.

27Then Moses sent his father-in-law on his way, and Jethro returned to his own country.

At Mount Sinai

19 IN THE third month after the Israelites left Egypt—on the very day—they came to the Desert of Sinai. 2After they set out from Rephidim, they entered the Desert of Sinai, and Israel camped there in the desert in front of the mountain.

3Then Moses went up to God, and the LORD called to him from the mountain and said, "This is what you are to say to the house of Jacob and what you are to tell the people of Israel: 4'You yourselves have seen what I did to Egypt, and how I carried you on eagles' wings and brought you to myself. 5Now if you obey me fully and keep my covenant, then out of all nations you will be my treasured possession. Although the whole earth is mine, 6youa will be for me a kingdom of priests and a holy nation.' These are the words you are to speak to the Israelites."

7So Moses went back and summoned the elders of the people and set before them all the words the LORD had commanded him to speak. 8The people all responded together, "We will do everything the LORD has said." So Moses brought their answer back to the LORD.

9The LORD said to Moses, "I am going to come to you in a dense cloud, so that the people will hear me speaking with you and will always put their trust in you." Then Moses told the LORD what the people had said.

10And the LORD said to Moses, "Go to the people and consecrate them today and tomorrow. Have them wash their clothes 11and be ready by the third day, because on that day the LORD will come down on Mount Sinai in the sight of all the people. 12Put limits for the people around the mountain and tell them, 'Be careful that you do not go up the mountain or touch the foot of it. Whoever touches the mountain shall surely be put to death. 13He shall surely be stoned or shot with arrows; not a hand is to be laid on him. Whether man or animal, he shall not be permitted to live.' Only when the ram's horn sounds a long blast may they go up to the mountain."

14After Moses had gone down the mountain to the people, he consecrated them, and they washed their clothes. 15Then he said to the people, "Prepare yourselves for the third day. Abstain from sexual relations."

---

a 5,6 Or *possession, for the whole earth is mine.* 6You

Living Bible

21"Find some capable, godly, honest men who hate bribes, and appoint them as judges, one judge for each 1000 people; he in turn will have ten judges under him, each in charge of a hundred; and under each of them will be two judges, each responsible for the affairs of fifty people; and each of these will have five judges beneath him, each counseling ten persons. 22Let these men be responsible to serve the people with justice at all times. Anything that is too important or complicated can be brought to you. But the smaller matters they can take care of themselves. That way it will be easier for you because you will share the burden with them. 23If you follow this advice, and if the Lord agrees, you will be able to endure the pressures, and there will be peace and harmony in the camp."

24Moses listened to his father-in-law's advice, and followed this suggestion. 25He chose able men from all over Israel and made them judges over the people—thousands, hundreds, fifties, and tens. 26They were constantly available to administer justice. They brought the hard cases to Moses but judged the smaller matters themselves.

27Soon afterwards Moses let his father-in-law return to his own land.

19 THE ISRAELIS arrived in the Sinai peninsula three months after the night of their departure from Egypt. 2, 3After breaking camp at Rephidim, they came to the base of Mt. Sinai and set up camp there. Moses climbed the rugged mountain to meet with God, and from somewhere in the mountain God called to him and said,

"Give these instructions to the people of Israel. Tell them, 4'You have seen what I did to the Egyptians, and how I brought you to myself as though on eagle's wings. 5Now if you will obey me and keep your part of my contract with you, you shall be my own little flock from among all the nations of the earth; for all the earth is mine. 6And you shall be a kingdom of priests to God, a holy nation.' "

7Moses returned from the mountain and called together the leaders of the people and told them what the Lord had said.

8They all responded in unison, "We will certainly do everything he asks of us." Moses reported the words of the people to the Lord.

9Then he said to Moses, "I am going to come to you in the form of a dark cloud, so that the people themselves can hear me when I talk with you, and then they will always believe you. 10Go down now and see that the people are ready for my visit. Sanctify them today and tomorrow, and have them wash their clothes. 11Then, the day after tomorrow, I will come down upon Mt. Sinai as all the people watch. 12Set boundary lines the people may not pass, and tell them, 'Beware! Do not go up into the mountain, or even touch its boundaries; whoever does shall die— 13no hand shall touch him, but he shall be stoned or shot to death with arrows, whether man or animal.' Stay away from the mountain entirely until you hear a ram's horn sounding one long blast; then gather at the foot of the mountain!"

14So Moses went down to the people and sanctified them and they washed their clothing.

15He told them, "Get ready for God's appearance two days from now, and do not have sexual intercourse with your wives."

New Revised Standard

all the people, men who fear God, are trustworthy, and hate dishonest gain; set such men over them as officers over thousands, hundreds, fifties and tens. 22Let them sit as judges for the people at all times; let them bring every important case to you, but decide every minor case themselves. So it will be easier for you, and they will bear the burden with you. 23If you do this, and God so commands you, then you will be able to endure, and all these people will go to their home in peace."

24 So Moses listened to his father-in-law and did all that he had said. 25Moses chose able men from all Israel and appointed them as heads over the people, as officers over thousands, hundreds, fifties, and tens. 26And they judged the people at all times; hard cases they brought to Moses, but any minor case they decided themselves. 27Then Moses let his father-in-law depart, and he went off to his own country.

The Israelites Reach Mount Sinai

19 ON THE third new moon after the Israelites had gone out of the land of Egypt, on that very day, they came into the wilderness of Sinai. 2They had journeyed from Rephidim, entered the wilderness of Sinai, and camped in the wilderness; Israel camped there in front of the mountain. 3Then Moses went up to God; the LORD called to him from the mountain, saying, "Thus you shall say to the house of Jacob, and tell the Israelites: 4You have seen what I did to the Egyptians, and how I bore you on eagles' wings and brought you to myself. 5Now therefore, if you obey my voice and keep my covenant, you shall be my treasured possession out of all the peoples. Indeed, the whole earth is mine, 6but you shall be for me a priestly kingdom and a holy nation. These are the words that you shall speak to the Israelites."

7 So Moses came, summoned the elders of the people, and set before them all these words that the LORD had commanded him. 8The people all answered as one: "Everything that the LORD has spoken we will do." Moses reported the words of the people to the LORD. 9Then the LORD said to Moses, "I am going to come to you in a dense cloud, in order that the people may hear when I speak with you and so trust you ever after."

The People Consecrated

When Moses had told the words of the people to the LORD, 10the LORD said to Moses: "Go to the people and consecrate them today and tomorrow. Have them wash their clothes 11and prepare for the third day, because on the third day the LORD will come down upon Mount Sinai in the sight of all the people. 12You shall set limits for the people all around, saying, 'Be careful not to go up the mountain or to touch the edge of it. Any who touch the mountain shall be put to death. 13No hand shall touch them, but they shall be stoned or shot with arrows;b whether animal or human being, they shall not live.' When the trumpet sounds a long blast, they may go up on the mountain." 14So Moses went down from the mountain to the people. He consecrated the people, and they washed their clothes. 15And he said to the people, "Prepare for the third day; do not go near a woman."

b Heb lacks *with arrows*

King James

16¶ And it came to pass on the third day in the morning, that there were thunders and lightnings, and a thick cloud upon the mount, and the voice of the trumpet exceeding loud; so that all the people that *was* in the camp trembled.

17And Moses brought forth the people out of the camp to meet with God; and they stood at the nether part of the mount.

18And mount Sinai was altogether on a smoke, because the LORD descended upon it in fire: and the smoke thereof ascended as the smoke of a furnace, and the whole mount quaked greatly.

19And when the voice of the trumpet sounded long, and waxed louder and louder, Moses spake, and God answered him by a voice.

20And the LORD came down upon mount Sinai, on the top of the mount: and the LORD called Moses *up* to the top of the mount; and Moses went up.

21And the LORD said unto Moses, Go down, charge the people, lest they break through unto the LORD to gaze, and many of them perish.

22And let the priests also, which come near to the LORD, sanctify themselves, lest the LORD break forth upon them.

23And Moses said unto the LORD, The people cannot come up to mount Sinai: for thou chargedst us, saying, Set bounds about the mount, and sanctify it.

24And the LORD said unto him, Away, get thee down, and thou shalt come up, thou, and Aaron with thee: but let not the priests and the people break through to come up unto the LORD, lest he break forth upon them.

25So Moses went down unto the people, and spake unto them.

20 AND GOD spake all these words, saying, 2I *am* the LORD thy God, which have brought thee out of the land of Egypt, out of the house of bondage.

3Thou shalt have no other gods before me.

4Thou shalt not make unto thee any graven image, or any likeness *of any thing* that *is* in heaven above, or that *is* in the earth beneath, or that *is* in the water under the earth:

5Thou shalt not bow down thyself to them, nor serve them: for I the LORD thy God *am* a jealous God, visiting the iniquity of the fathers upon the children unto the third and fourth *generation* of them that hate me;

6And showing mercy unto thousands of them that love me, and keep my commandments.

7Thou shalt not take the name of the LORD thy God in vain; for the LORD will not hold him guiltless that taketh his name in vain.

8Remember the sabbath day, to keep it holy.

9Six days shalt thou labour, and do all thy work:

10But the seventh day *is* the sabbath of the LORD thy God: *in it* thou shalt not do any work, thou, nor thy son, nor thy daughter, thy manservant, nor thy maidservant, nor thy cattle, nor thy stranger that *is* within thy gates:

11For *in* six days the LORD made heaven and earth, the sea, and all that in them *is,* and rested the seventh day: wherefore the LORD blessed the sabbath day, and hallowed it.

12¶ Honour thy father and thy mother: that thy days may be long upon the land which the LORD thy God giveth thee.

13Thou shalt not kill.

New International

16On the morning of the third day there was thunder and lightning, with a thick cloud over the mountain, and a very loud trumpet blast. Everyone in the camp trembled. 17Then Moses led the people out of the camp to meet with God, and they stood at the foot of the mountain. 18Mount Sinai was covered with smoke, because the LORD descended on it in fire. The smoke billowed up from it like smoke from a furnace, the whole mountain[a] trembled violently, 19and the sound of the trumpet grew louder and louder. Then Moses spoke and the voice of God answered him.[b]

20The LORD descended to the top of Mount Sinai and called Moses to the top of the mountain. So Moses went up 21and the LORD said to him, "Go down and warn the people so they do not force their way through to see the LORD and many of them perish. 22Even the priests, who approach the LORD, must consecrate themselves, or the LORD will break out against them."

23Moses said to the LORD, "The people cannot come up Mount Sinai, because you yourself warned us, 'Put limits around the mountain and set it apart as holy.'"

24The LORD replied, "Go down and bring Aaron up with you. But the priests and the people must not force their way through to come up to the LORD, or he will break out against them."

25So Moses went down to the people and told them.

The Ten Commandments

20 AND GOD spoke all these words:

2"I am the LORD your God, who brought you out of Egypt, out of the land of slavery.

3"You shall have no other gods before[c] me.

4"You shall not make for yourself an idol in the form of anything in heaven above or on the earth beneath or in the waters below. 5You shall not bow down to them or worship them; for I, the LORD your God, am a jealous God, punishing the children for the sin of the fathers to the third and fourth generation of those who hate me, 6but showing love to a thousand ₍generations₎ of those who love me and keep my commandments.

7"You shall not misuse the name of the LORD your God, for the LORD will not hold anyone guiltless who misuses his name.

8"Remember the Sabbath day by keeping it holy. 9Six days you shall labor and do all your work, 10but the seventh day is a Sabbath to the LORD your God. On it you shall not do any work, neither you, nor your son or daughter, nor your manservant or maidservant, nor your animals, nor the alien within your gates. 11For in six days the LORD made the heavens and the earth, the sea, and all that is in them, but he rested on the seventh day. Therefore the LORD blessed the Sabbath day and made it holy.

12"Honor your father and your mother, so that you may live long in the land the LORD your God is giving you.

13"You shall not murder.

a *18* Most Hebrew manuscripts; a few Hebrew manuscripts and Septuagint *all the people*   b *19* Or *and God answered him with thunder*   c *3* Or *besides*

Living Bible

16On the morning of the third day there was a terrific thunder and lightning storm, and a huge cloud came down upon the mountain, and there was a long, loud blast as from a ram's horn; and all the people trembled. 17Moses led them out from the camp to meet God, and they stood at the foot of the mountain. 18All Mt. Sinai was covered with smoke because Jehovah descended upon it in the form of fire; the smoke billowed into the sky as from a furnace, and the whole mountain shook with a violent earthquake. 19As the trumpet blast grew louder and louder, Moses spoke and God thundered his reply. 20So the Lord came down upon the top of Mt. Sinai and called Moses up to the top of the mountain, and Moses ascended to God.

21But the Lord told Moses, "Go back down and warn the people not to cross the boundaries. They must not come up here to try to see God, for if they do, many of them will die. 22Even the priests on dutyd must sanctify themselves, or else I will destroy them."

23"But the people won't come up into the mountain!" Moses protested. "You told them not to! You told me to set boundaries around the mountain, and to declare it off limits because it is reserved for God.

24But Jehovah said, "Go down, and bring Aaron back with you, and don't let the priests and the people break across the boundaries to try to come up here, or I will punish them."

25So Moses went down to the people and told them what God had said.

20

THEN GOD issued this edict:

2"I am Jehovah your God who liberated you from your slavery in Egypt.

3"You may worship no other god than me.

4"You shall not make yourselves any idols: no images of animals, birds, or fish. 5You must never bow or worship it in any way; for I, the Lord your God, am very possessive. I will not share your affection with any other god!

"And when I punish people for their sins, the punishment continues upon the children, grandchildren, and great-grandchildren of those who hate me; 6but I lavish my love upon thousands of those who love me and obey my commandments.

7"You shall not use the name of Jehovah your God irreverently,e nor use it to swear to a falsehood. You will not escape punishment if you do.

8"Remember to observe the Sabbath as a holy day. 9Six days a week are for your daily duties and your regular work, 10but the seventh day is a day of Sabbath rest before the Lord your God. On that day you are to do no work of any kind, nor shall your son, daughter, or slaves—whether men or women—or your cattle or your house guests. 11For in six days the Lord made the heaven, earth, and sea, and everything in them, and rested the seventh day; so he blessed the Sabbath day and set it aside for rest.f

12"Honor your father and mother, that you may have a long, good life in the land the Lord your God will give you.

13"You must not murder.

New Revised Standard

16 On the morning of the third day there was thunder and lightning, as well as a thick cloud on the mountain, and a blast of a trumpet so loud that all the people who were in the camp trembled. 17Moses brought the people out of the camp to meet God. They took their stand at the foot of the mountain. 18Now Mount Sinai was wrapped in smoke, because the LORD had descended upon it in fire; the smoke went up like the smoke of a kiln, while the whole mountain shook violently. 19As the blast of the trumpet grew louder and louder, Moses would speak and God would answer him in thunder. 20When the LORD descended upon Mount Sinai, to the top of the mountain, the LORD summoned Moses to the top of the mountain, and Moses went up. 21Then the LORD said to Moses, "Go down and warn the people not to break through to the LORD to look; otherwise many of them will perish. 22Even the priests who approach the LORD must consecrate themselves or the LORD will break out against them." 23Moses said to the LORD, "The people are not permitted to come up to Mount Sinai; for you yourself warned us, saying, 'Set limits around the mountain and keep it holy.'" 24The LORD said to him, "Go down, and come up bringing Aaron with you; but do not let either the priests or the people break through to come up to the LORD; otherwise he will break out against them." 25So Moses went down to the people and told them.

The Ten Commandments

20

THEN GOD spoke all these words:

2 I am the LORD your God, who brought you out of the land of Egypt, out of the house of slavery; 3you shall have no other gods beforeg me.

4 You shall not make for yourself an idol, whether in the form of anything that is in heaven above, or that is on the earth beneath, or that is in the water under the earth. 5You shall not bow down to them or worship them; for I the LORD your God am a jealous God, punishing children for the iniquity of parents, to the third and the fourth generation of those who reject me, 6but showing steadfast love to the thousandth generationh of those who love me and keep my commandments.

7 You shall not make wrongful use of the name of the LORD your God, for the LORD will not acquit anyone who misuses his name.

8 Remember the sabbath day, and keep it holy. 9Six days you shall labor and do all your work. 10But the seventh day is a sabbath to the LORD your God; you shall not do any work—you, your son or your daughter, your male or female slave, your livestock, or the alien resident in your towns. 11For in six days the LORD made heaven and earth, the sea, and all that is in them, but rested the seventh day; therefore the LORD blessed the sabbath day and consecrated it.

12 Honor your father and your mother, so that your days may be long in the land that the LORD your God is giving you.

13 You shall not murder.i

---

d 19:22 the priests on duty, literally, "the priests who come near to Jehovah."
e 20:7 use the name of Jehovah your God irreverently, or, "you must not use the name of the Lord your God to swear falsely."   f 20:11 blessed the Sabbath day and set it aside for rest, or, "hallowed it."

g Or besides   h Or to thousands   i Or kill

King James

14Thou shalt not commit adultery.

15Thou shalt not steal.

16Thou shalt not bear false witness against thy neighbour.

17Thou shalt not covet thy neighbour's house, thou shalt not covet thy neighbour's wife, nor his manservant, nor his maidservant, nor his ox, nor his ass, nor any thing that *is* thy neighbour's.

18¶ And all the people saw the thunderings, and the lightnings, and the noise of the trumpet, and the mountain smoking: and when the people saw *it,* they removed, and stood afar off.

19And they said unto Moses, Speak thou with us, and we will hear: but let not God speak with us, lest we die.

20And Moses said unto the people, Fear not: for God is come to prove you, and that his fear may be before your faces, that ye sin not.

21And the people stood afar off, and Moses drew near unto the thick darkness where God *was.*

22¶ And the LORD said unto Moses, Thus thou shalt say unto the children of Israel, Ye have seen that I have talked with you from heaven.

23Ye shall not make with me gods of silver, neither shall ye make unto you gods of gold.

24¶ An altar of earth thou shalt make unto me, and shalt sacrifice thereon thy burnt offerings, and thy peace offerings, thy sheep, and thine oxen: in all places where I record my name I will come unto thee, and I will bless thee.

25And if thou wilt make me an altar of stone, thou shalt not build it of hewn stone: for if thou lift up thy tool upon it, thou hast polluted it.

26Neither shalt thou go up by steps unto mine altar, that thy nakedness be not discovered thereon.

21 NOW THESE *are* the judgments which thou shalt set before them.

2If thou buy an Hebrew servant, six years he shall serve: and in the seventh he shall go out free for nothing.

3If he came in by himself, he shall go out by himself: if he were married, then his wife shall go out with him.

4If his master have given him a wife, and she have born him sons or daughters; the wife and her children shall be her master's, and he shall go out by himself.

5And if the servant shall plainly say, I love my master, my wife, and my children; I will not go out free:

6Then his master shall bring him unto the judges; he shall also bring him to the door, or unto the door post; and his master shall bore his ear through with an awl; and he shall serve him for ever.

7¶ And if a man sell his daughter to be a maidservant, she shall not go out as the menservants do.

8If she please not her master, who hath betrothed her to himself, then shall he let her be redeemed: to sell her unto a strange nation he shall have no power, seeing he hath dealt deceitfully with her.

9And if he have betrothed her unto his son, he shall deal with her after the manner of daughters.

10If he take him another *wife;* her food, her raiment, and her duty of marriage, shall he not diminish.

11And if he do not these three unto her, then shall she go out free without money.

12¶ He that smiteth a man, so that he die, shall be surely put to death.

13And if a man lie not in wait, but God deliver *him* into his hand; then I will appoint thee a place whither he shall flee.

New International

14"You shall not commit adultery.

15"You shall not steal.

16"You shall not give false testimony against your neighbor.

17"You shall not covet your neighbor's house. You shall not covet your neighbor's wife, or his manservant or maidservant, his ox or donkey, or anything that belongs to your neighbor."

18When the people saw the thunder and lightning and heard the trumpet and saw the mountain in smoke, they trembled with fear. They stayed at a distance 19and said to Moses, "Speak to us yourself and we will listen. But do not have God speak to us or we will die."

20Moses said to the people, "Do not be afraid. God has come to test you, so that the fear of God will be with you to keep you from sinning."

21The people remained at a distance, while Moses approached the thick darkness where God was.

Idols and Altars

22Then the LORD said to Moses, "Tell the Israelites this: 'You have seen for yourselves that I have spoken to you from heaven: 23Do not make any gods to be alongside me; do not make for yourselves gods of silver or gods of gold.

24" 'Make an altar of earth for me and sacrifice on it your burnt offerings and fellowship offerings,a your sheep and goats and your cattle. Wherever I cause my name to be honored, I will come to you and bless you.

25If you make an altar of stones for me, do not build it with dressed stones, for you will defile it if you use a tool on it. 26And do not go up to my altar on steps, lest your nakedness be exposed on it.'

21 "THESE ARE the laws you are to set before them:

Hebrew Servants

2"If you buy a Hebrew servant, he is to serve you for six years. But in the seventh year, he shall go free, without paying anything. 3If he comes alone, he is to go free alone; but if he has a wife when he comes, she is to go with him. 4If his master gives him a wife and she bears him sons or daughters, the woman and her children shall belong to her master, and only the man shall go free.

5"But if the servant declares, 'I love my master and my wife and children and do not want to go free,' 6then his master must take him before the judges.b He shall take him to the door or the doorpost and pierce his ear with an awl. Then he will be his servant for life.

7"If a man sells his daughter as a servant, she is not to go free as menservants do. 8If she does not please the master who has selected her for himself,c he must let her be redeemed. He has no right to sell her to foreigners, because he has broken faith with her. 9If he selects her for his son, he must grant her the rights of a daughter. 10If he marries another woman, he must not deprive the first one of her food, clothing and marital rights. 11If he does not provide her with these three things, she is to go free, without any payment of money.

Personal Injuries

12"Anyone who strikes a man and kills him shall surely be put to death. 13However, if he does not do it intentionally, but God lets it happen, he is to flee to a place I will designate. 14But if a man schemes and kills another

---

a 24 Traditionally *peace offerings*   b 6 Or *before God*   c 8 Or *master so that he does not choose her*

Living Bible

14"You must not commit adultery.

15"You must not steal.

16"You must not lie.d

17"You must not be envious of your neighbor's house, or want to sleep with his wife, or want to own his slaves, oxen, donkeys, or anything else he has."

18All the people saw the lightning and the smoke billowing from the mountain, and heard the thunder and the long, frightening trumpet blast; and they stood at a distance, shaking with fear.

19They said to Moses, "You tell us what God says and we will obey, but don't let God speak directly to us, or it will kill us."

20"Don't be afraid," Moses told them, "for God has come in this way to show you his awesome power, so that from now on you will be afraid to sin against him!"

21As the people stood in the distance, Moses entered into the deep darkness where God was.

22And the Lord told Moses to be his spokesman to the people of Israel. "You are witnesses to the fact that I have made known my will to you from heaven. 23Remember, you must not make or worship idols made of silver or gold or of anything else!

24"The altars you make for me must be simple altars of earth. Offer upon them your sacrifices to me—your burnt offerings and peace offerings of sheep and oxen. Build altars only where I tell you to, and I will come and bless you there. 25You may also build altars from stone, but if you do, then use only uncut stones and boulders. Don't chip or shape the stones with a tool, for that would make them unfit for my altar. 26And don't make steps for the altar, or someone might look up beneath the skirts of your clothing and see your nakedness.

21 "HERE ARE other laws you must obey:
2"If you buye a Hebrew slave, he shall serve only six years and be freed in the seventh year, and need pay nothing to regain his freedom.

3"If he sold himself as a slave before he married, then if he married afterwards, only he shall be freed; but if he was married before he became a slave, then his wife shall be freed with him at the same time. 4But if his master gave him a wife while he was a slave, and they have sons or daughters, the wife and children shall still belong to the master, and he shall go out by himself free.

5"But if the man shall plainly declare, 'I prefer my master, my wife, and my children, and I would rather not go free,' 6then his master shall bring him before the judges and shall publicly bore his ear with an awl, and after that he will be a slave forever.

7"If a man sells his daughter as a slave, she shall not be freed at the end of six years as the men are. 8If she does not please the man who bought her, then he shall let her be bought back again; but he has no power to sell her to foreigners, since he has wronged her by no longer wanting her after marrying her. 9And if he arranges an engagement between a Hebrew slave-girl and his son, then he may no longer treat her as a slave-girl, but must treat her as a daughter. 10If he himself marries her and then takes another wife, he may not reduce her food or clothing, or fail to sleep with her as his wife. 11If he fails in any of these three things, then she may leave freely without any payment.

12"Anyone who hits a man so hard that he dies shall surely be put to death. 13But if it is accidental—an act of God—and not intentional, then I will appoint a place where he can run and get protection. 14However, if a

New Revised Standard

14 You shall not commit adultery.

15 You shall not steal.

16 You shall not bear false witness against your neighbor.

17 You shall not covet your neighbor's house; you shall not covet your neighbor's wife, or male or female slave, or ox, or donkey, or anything that belongs to your neighbor.

18 When all the people witnessed the thunder and lightning, the sound of the trumpet, and the mountain smoking, they were afraidf and trembled and stood at a distance, 19and said to Moses, "You speak to us, and we will listen; but do not let God speak to us, or we will die." 20Moses said to the people, "Do not be afraid; for God has come only to test you and to put the fear of him upon you so that you do not sin." 21Then the people stood at a distance, while Moses drew near to the thick darkness where God was.

The Law concerning the Altar

22 The LORD said to Moses: Thus you shall say to the Israelites: "You have seen for yourselves that I spoke with you from heaven. 23You shall not make gods of silver alongside me, nor shall you make for yourselves gods of gold. 24You need make for me only an altar of earth and sacrifice on it your burnt offerings and your offerings of well-being, your sheep and your oxen; in every place where I cause my name to be remembered I will come to you and bless you. 25But if you make for me an altar of stone, do not build it of hewn stones; for if you use a chisel upon it you profane it. 26You shall not go up by steps to my altar, so that your nakedness may not be exposed on it."

The Law concerning Slaves

21 THESE ARE the ordinances that you shall set before them:
2 When you buy a male Hebrew slave, he shall serve six years, but in the seventh he shall go out a free person, without debt. 3If he comes in single, he shall go out single; if he comes in married, then his wife shall go out with him. 4If his master gives him a wife and she bears him sons or daughters, the wife and her children shall be her master's and he shall go out alone. 5But if the slave declares, "I love my master, my wife, and my children; I will not go out a free person," 6then his master shall bring him before God.g He shall be brought to the door or the doorpost; and his master shall pierce his ear with an awl; and he shall serve him for life.

7 When a man sells his daughter as a slave, she shall not go out as the male slaves do. 8If she does not please her master, who designated her for himself, then he shall let her be redeemed; he shall have no right to sell her to a foreign people, since he has dealt unfairly with her. 9If he designates her for his son, he shall deal with her as with a daughter. 10If he takes another wife to himself, he shall not diminish the food, clothing, or marital rights of the first wife.h 11And if he does not do these three things for her, she shall go out without debt, without payment of money.

The Law concerning Violence

12 Whoever strikes a person mortally shall be put to death. 13If it was not premeditated, but came about by an act of God, then I will appoint for you a place to which the killer may flee. 14But if someone willfully

---

d 20:16 You must not lie, or, "You must not give false testimony in court."
e 21:2 If you buy a Hebrew slave, that is, "If he owes you money and defaults in the payment, and thus becomes your slave."

f Sam Gk Syr Vg: MT they saw   g Or to the judges   h Heb of her

King James

¹⁴But if a man come presumptuously upon his neighbour, to slay him with guile; thou shalt take him from mine altar, that he may die.

¹⁵¶ And he that smiteth his father, or his mother, shall be surely put to death.

¹⁶¶ And he that stealeth a man, and selleth him, or if he be found in his hand, he shall surely be put to death.

¹⁷¶ And he that curseth his father, or his mother, shall surely be put to death.

¹⁸¶ And if men strive together, and one smite another with a stone, or with *his* fist, and he die not, but keepeth *his* bed:

¹⁹If he rise again, and walk abroad upon his staff, then shall he that smote *him* be quit: only he shall pay *for* the loss of his time, and shall cause *him* to be thoroughly healed.

²⁰¶ And if a man smite his servant, or his maid, with a rod, and he die under his hand; he shall be surely punished.

²¹Notwithstanding, if he continue a day or two, he shall not be punished: for he *is* his money.

²²¶ If men strive, and hurt a woman with child, so that her fruit depart *from her*, and yet no mischief follow: he shall be surely punished, according as the woman's husband will lay upon him; and he shall pay as the judges *determine*.

²³And if *any* mischief follow, then thou shalt give life for life,

²⁴Eye for eye, tooth for tooth, hand for hand, foot for foot,

²⁵Burning for burning, wound for wound, stripe for stripe.

²⁶¶ And if a man smite the eye of his servant, or the eye of his maid, that it perish; he shall let him go free for his eye's sake.

²⁷And if he smite out his manservant's tooth, or his maidservant's tooth; he shall let him go free for his tooth's sake.

²⁸¶ If an ox gore a man or a woman, that they die: then the ox shall be surely stoned, and his flesh shall not be eaten; but the owner of the ox *shall be* quit.

²⁹But if the ox were wont to push with his horn in time past, and it hath been testified to his owner, and he hath not kept him in, but that he hath killed a man or a woman; the ox shall be stoned, and his owner also shall be put to death.

³⁰If there be laid on him a sum of money, then he shall give for the ransom of his life whatsoever is laid upon him.

³¹Whether he have gored a son, or have gored a daughter, according to this judgment shall it be done unto him.

³²If the ox shall push a manservant or a maidservant; he shall give unto their master thirty shekels of silver, and the ox shall be stoned.

³³And if a man shall open a pit, or if a man shall dig a pit, and not cover it, and an ox or an ass fall therein;

³⁴The owner of the pit shall make *it* good, *and* give money unto the owner of them; and the dead *beast* shall be his.

³⁵¶ And if one man's ox hurt another's, that he die; then they shall sell the live ox, and divide the money of it; and the dead *ox* also they shall divide.

³⁶Or if it be known that the ox hath used to push in time past, and his owner hath not kept him in; he shall surely pay ox for ox; and the dead shall be his own.

New International

man deliberately, take him away from my altar and put him to death.

¹⁵"Anyone who attacksᵃ his father or his mother must be put to death.

¹⁶"Anyone who kidnaps another and either sells him or still has him when he is caught must be put to death.

¹⁷"Anyone who curses his father or mother must be put to death.

¹⁸"If men quarrel and one hits the other with a stone or with his fistᵇ and he does not die but is confined to bed, ¹⁹the one who struck the blow will not be held responsible if the other gets up and walks around outside with his staff; however, he must pay the injured man for the loss of his time and see that he is completely healed.

²⁰"If a man beats his male or female slave with a rod and the slave dies as a direct result, he must be punished, ²¹but he is not to be punished if the slave gets up after a day or two, since the slave is his property.

²²"If men who are fighting hit a pregnant woman and she gives birth prematurelyᶜ but there is no serious injury, the offender must be fined whatever the woman's husband demands and the court allows. ²³But if there is serious injury, you are to take life for life, ²⁴eye for eye, tooth for tooth, hand for hand, foot for foot, ²⁵burn for burn, wound for wound, bruise for bruise.

²⁶"If a man hits a manservant or maidservant in the eye and destroys it, he must let the servant go free to compensate for the eye. ²⁷And if he knocks out the tooth of a manservant or maidservant, he must let the servant go free to compensate for the tooth.

²⁸"If a bull gores a man or a woman to death, the bull must be stoned to death, and its meat must not be eaten. But the owner of the bull will not be held responsible. ²⁹If, however, the bull has had the habit of goring and the owner has been warned but has not kept it penned up and it kills a man or woman, the bull must be stoned and the owner also must be put to death. ³⁰However, if payment is demanded of him, he may redeem his life by paying whatever is demanded. ³¹This law also applies if the bull gores a son or daughter. ³²If the bull gores a male or female slave, the owner must pay thirty shekelsᵈ of silver to the master of the slave, and the bull must be stoned.

³³"If a man uncovers a pit or digs one and fails to cover it and an ox or a donkey falls into it, ³⁴the owner of the pit must pay for the loss; he must pay its owner, and the dead animal will be his.

³⁵"If a man's bull injures the bull of another and it dies, they are to sell the live one and divide both the money and the dead animal equally. ³⁶However, if it was known that the bull had the habit of goring, yet the owner did not keep it penned up, the owner must pay, animal for animal, and the dead animal will be his.

ᵃ *15* Or *kills* ᵇ *18* Or *with a tool* ᶜ *22* Or *she has a miscarriage*
ᵈ *32* That is, about 12 ounces (about 0.3 kilogram)

Living Bible

man deliberately attacks another, intending to kill him, drag him even from my altar, and kill him.

¹⁵"Anyone who strikes his father or mother shall surely be put to death.

¹⁶"A kidnapper must be killed, whether he is caught in possession of his victim or has already sold him as a slave.

¹⁷"Anyone who reviles or curses his mother or father shall surely be put to death.

¹⁸"If two men are fighting, and one hits the other with a stone or with his fist and injures him so that he must be confined to bed, but doesn't die, ¹⁹if later he is able to walk again, even with a limp,^e the man who hit him will be innocent except that he must pay for the loss of his time until he is thoroughly healed, and pay any medical expenses.

²⁰"If a man beats his slave to death—whether the slave is male or female—that man shall surely be punished. ²¹However, if the slave does not die for a couple of days, then the man shall not be punished—for the slave is his property.

²²"If two men are fighting, and in the process hurt a pregnant woman so that she has a miscarriage, but she lives, then the man who injured her shall be fined whatever amount the woman's husband shall demand, and as the judges approve. ²³But if any harm comes to the woman and she dies, he shall be executed.

²⁴"If her eye is injured, injure his; if her tooth is knocked out, knock out his; and so on—hand for hand, foot for foot, ²⁵burn for burn, wound for wound, lash for lash.

²⁶"If a man hits his slave in the eye, whether man or woman, and the eye is blinded, then the slave shall go free because of his eye. ²⁷And if a master knocks out his slave's tooth, he shall let him go free to pay for the tooth.

²⁸"If an ox gores a man or woman to death, the ox shall be stoned and its flesh not eaten, but the owner shall not be held— ²⁹unless the ox was known to gore people in the past, and the owner had been notified and still the ox was not kept under control; in that case, if it kills someone, the ox shall be stoned and the owner also shall be killed. ³⁰But the dead man's relatives may accept a fine instead, if they wish. The judges will determine the amount.^f

³¹"The same law holds if the ox gores a boy or a girl. ³²But if the ox gores a slave, whether male or female, the slave's master shall be given thirty pieces of silver, and the ox shall be stoned.

³³"If a man digs a well and doesn't cover it, and an ox or a donkey falls into it, ³⁴the owner of the well shall pay full damages to the owner of the animal, and the dead animal shall belong to him.

³⁵"If a man's ox injures another, and it dies, then the two owners shall sell the live ox and divide the price between them—and each shall also own half of the dead ox. ³⁶But if the ox was known from past experience to gore, and its owner has not kept it under control, then there will not be a division of the income; but the owner of the living ox shall pay in full for the dead ox, and the dead one shall be his.

New Revised Standard

attacks and kills another by treachery, you shall take the killer from my altar for execution.

15   Whoever strikes father or mother shall be put to death.

16   Whoever kidnaps a person, whether that person has been sold or is still held in possession, shall be put to death.

17   Whoever curses father or mother shall be put to death.

18   When individuals quarrel and one strikes the other with a stone or fist so that the injured party, though not dead, is confined to bed, ¹⁹but recovers and walks around outside with the help of a staff, then the assailant shall be free of liability, except to pay for the loss of time, and to arrange for full recovery.

20   When a slaveowner strikes a male or female slave with a rod and the slave dies immediately, the owner shall be punished. ²¹But if the slave survives a day or two, there is no punishment; for the slave is the owner's property.

22   When people who are fighting injure a pregnant woman so that there is a miscarriage, and yet no further harm follows, the one responsible shall be fined what the woman's husband demands, paying as much as the judges determine. ²³If any harm follows, then you shall give life for life, ²⁴eye for eye, tooth for tooth, hand for hand, foot for foot, ²⁵burn for burn, wound for wound, stripe for stripe.

26   When a slaveowner strikes the eye of a male or female slave, destroying it, the owner shall let the slave go, a free person, to compensate for the eye. ²⁷If the owner knocks out a tooth of a male or female slave, the slave shall be let go, a free person, to compensate for the tooth.

Laws concerning Property

28   When an ox gores a man or a woman to death, the ox shall be stoned, and its flesh shall not be eaten; but the owner of the ox shall not be liable. ²⁹If the ox has been accustomed to gore in the past, and its owner has been warned but has not restrained it, and it kills a man or a woman, the ox shall be stoned, and its owner also shall be put to death. ³⁰If a ransom is imposed on the owner, then the owner shall pay whatever is imposed for the redemption of the victim's life. ³¹If it gores a boy or a girl, the owner shall be dealt with according to this same rule. ³²If the ox gores a male or female slave, the owner shall pay to the slaveowner thirty shekels of silver, and the ox shall be stoned.

33   If someone leaves a pit open, or digs a pit and does not cover it, and an ox or a donkey falls into it, ³⁴the owner of the pit shall make restitution, giving money to its owner, but keeping the dead animal.

35   If someone's ox hurts the ox of another, so that it dies, then they shall sell the live ox and divide the price of it; and the dead animal they shall also divide. ³⁶But if it was known that the ox was accustomed to gore in the past, and its owner has not restrained it, the owner shall restore ox for ox, but keep the dead animal.

---

^e *21:19 if later he is able to walk again, even with a limp,* literally, "if he walks abroad with his staff."   ^f *21:30* Literally, verse 30 reads: "But if a ransom is laid upon him, he shall give for the redemption of his life whatever is laid upon him."

King James

New International

22 IF A man shall steal an ox, or a sheep, and kill it, or sell it; he shall restore five oxen for an ox, and four sheep for a sheep.

2¶ If a thief be found breaking up, and be smitten that he die, *there shall* no blood *be shed* for him.

3If the sun be risen upon him, *there shall be* blood *shed* for him; *for* he should make full restitution; if he have nothing, then he shall be sold for his theft.

4If the theft be certainly found in his hand alive, whether it be ox, or ass, or sheep; he shall restore double.

5¶ If a man shall cause a field or vineyard to be eaten, and shall put in his beast, and shall feed in another man's field; of the best of his own field, and of the best of his own vineyard, shall he make restitution.

6¶ If fire break out, and catch in thorns, so that the stacks of corn, or the standing corn, or the field, be consumed *therewith;* he that kindled the fire shall surely make restitution.

7¶ If a man shall deliver unto his neighbour money or stuff to keep, and it be stolen out of the man's house; if the thief be found, let him pay double.

8If the thief be not found, then the master of the house shall be brought unto the judges, *to see* whether he have put his hand unto his neighbour's goods.

9For all manner of trespass, *whether it be* for ox, for ass, for sheep, for raiment, *or* for any manner of lost thing, which *another* challengeth to be his, the cause of both parties shall come before the judges; *and* whom the judges shall condemn, he shall pay double unto his neighbour.

10If a man deliver unto his neighbour an ass, or an ox, or a sheep, or any beast, to keep; and it die, or be hurt, or driven away, no man seeing *it:*

11*Then* shall an oath of the LORD be between them both, that he hath not put his hand unto his neighbour's goods; and the owner of it shall accept *thereof,* and he shall not make *it* good.

12And if it be stolen from him, he shall make restitution unto the owner thereof.

13If it be torn in pieces, *then* let him bring it *for* witness, *and* he shall not make good that which was torn.

14¶ And if a man borrow *aught* of his neighbour, and it be hurt, or die, the owner thereof *being* not with it, he shall surely make *it* good.

15*But* if the owner thereof *be* with it, he shall not make *it* good: if it *be* an hired *thing,* it came for his hire.

16¶ And if a man entice a maid that is not betrothed, and lie with her, he shall surely endow her to be his wife.

17If her father utterly refuse to give her unto him, he shall pay money according to the dowry of virgins.

18¶ Thou shalt not suffer a witch to live.

19¶ Whosoever lieth with a beast shall surely be put to death.

20¶ He that sacrificeth unto *any* god, save unto the LORD only, he shall be utterly destroyed.

21¶ Thou shalt neither vex a stranger, nor oppress him: for ye were strangers in the land of Egypt.

22¶ Ye shall not afflict any widow, or fatherless child.

23If thou afflict them in any wise, and they cry at all unto me, I will surely hear their cry;

Protection of Property

22 "IF A man steals an ox or a sheep and slaughters it or sells it, he must pay back five head of cattle for the ox and four sheep for the sheep.

2"If a thief is caught breaking in and is struck so that he dies, the defender is not guilty of bloodshed; 3but if it happensa after sunrise, he is guilty of bloodshed.

"A thief must certainly make restitution, but if he has nothing, he must be sold to pay for his theft.

4"If the stolen animal is found alive in his possession—whether ox or donkey or sheep—he must pay back double.

5"If a man grazes his livestock in a field or vineyard and lets them stray and they graze in another man's field, he must make restitution from the best of his own field or vineyard.

6"If a fire breaks out and spreads into thornbushes so that it burns shocks of grain or standing grain or the whole field, the one who started the fire must make restitution.

7"If a man gives his neighbor silver or goods for safekeeping and they are stolen from the neighbor's house, the thief, if he is caught, must pay back double. 8But if the thief is not found, the owner of the house must appear before the judgesb to determine whether he has laid his hands on the other man's property. 9In all cases of illegal possession of an ox, a donkey, a sheep, a garment, or any other lost property about which somebody says, 'This is mine,' both parties are to bring their cases before the judges. The one whom the judges declarec guilty must pay back double to his neighbor.

10"If a man gives a donkey, an ox, a sheep or any other animal to his neighbor for safekeeping and it dies or is injured or is taken away while no one is looking, 11the issue between them will be settled by the taking of an oath before the LORD that the neighbor did not lay hands on the other person's property. The owner is to accept this, and no restitution is required. 12But if the animal was stolen from the neighbor, he must make restitution to the owner. 13If it was torn to pieces by a wild animal, he shall bring in the remains as evidence and he will not be required to pay for the torn animal.

14"If a man borrows an animal from his neighbor and it is injured or dies while the owner is not present, he must make restitution. 15But if the owner is with the animal, the borrower will not have to pay. If the animal was hired, the money paid for the hire covers the loss.

Social Responsibility

16"If a man seduces a virgin who is not pledged to be married and sleeps with her, he must pay the bride-price, and she shall be his wife. 17If her father absolutely refuses to give her to him, he must still pay the bride-price for virgins.

18"Do not allow a sorceress to live.

19"Anyone who has sexual relations with an animal must be put to death.

20"Whoever sacrifices to any god other than the LORD must be destroyed.d

21"Do not mistreat an alien or oppress him, for you were aliens in Egypt.

22"Do not take advantage of a widow or an orphan. 23If you do and they cry out to me, I will certainly hear their cry. 24My anger will be aroused, and I will kill you

---

a *3 Or if he strikes him*   b *8 Or before God*; also in verse 9   c *9 Or whom God declares*   d *20 The Hebrew term refers to the irrevocable giving over of things or persons to the LORD, often by totally destroying them.*

Living Bible

22 "IF A man steals an ox or sheep and then kills or sells it, he shall pay a fine of five to one—five oxen shall be returned for each stolen ox. For sheep, the fine shall be four to one—four sheep returned for each sheep stolen.

2"If a thief is caught in the act of breaking into a house and is killed, the one who killed him is not guilty. 3But if it happens in the daylight, it must be presumed to be murder and the man who kills him is guilty.

"If a thief is captured, he must make full restitution; if he can't, then he must be sold as a slave for his debt.

4"If he is caught in the act of stealing a live ox or donkey or sheep or whatever it is, he shall pay double value as his fine.

5"If someone deliberately lets his animal loose and it gets into another man's vineyard; or if he turns it into another man's field to graze, he must pay for all damages by giving the owner of the field or vineyard an equal amount of the best of his own crop.

6"If the field is being burned off and the fire gets out of control and goes into another field so that the shocks of grain, or the standing grain, are destroyed, the one who started the fire shall make full restitution.

7"If someone gives money or goods to anyone to keep for him, and it is stolen, the thief shall pay double if he is found. 8But if no thief is found, then the man to whom the valuables were entrusted shall be brought before God to determine whether or not he himself has stolen his neighbor's property.

9"In every case in which an ox, donkey, sheep, clothing, or anything else is lost, and the owner believes he has found it in the possession of someone else who denies it, both parties to the dispute shall come before God for a decision, and the one whom God declares guilty shall pay double to the other.

10"If a man asks his neighbor to keep a donkey, ox, sheep, or any other animal for him, and it dies, or is hurt, or gets away, and there is no eyewitness to report just what happened to it, 11then the neighbor must take an oath that he has not stolen it, and the owner must accept his word, and no restitution shall be made for it. 12But if the animal or property has been stolen, the neighbor caring for it must repay the owner. 13If it was attacked by some wild animal, he shall bring the torn carcass to confirm the fact, and shall not be required to make restitution.

14"If a man borrows an animal (or anything else) from a neighbor, and it is injured or killed, and the owner is not there at the time, then the man who borrowed it must pay for it. 15But if the owner is there, he need not pay; and if it was rented, then he need not pay, because this possibility was included in the original rental fee.

16"If a man seduces a girl who is not engaged to anyone, and sleeps with her, he must pay the usual dowry[e] and accept her as his wife. 17But if her father utterly refuses to let her marry him, then he shall pay the money anyway.

18"A sorceress shall be put to death.

19"Anyone having sexual relations with an animal shall certainly be executed.

20"Anyone sacrificing to any other god than Jehovah shall be executed.[f]

21"You must not oppress a stranger in any way; remember, you yourselves were foreigners in the land of Egypt.

22"You must not exploit widows or orphans; 23if you do so in any way, and they cry to me for my help, I will surely give it. 24And my anger shall flame out against

New Revised Standard

Laws of Restitution

22[g] WHEN SOMEONE steals an ox or a sheep, and slaughters it or sells it, the thief shall pay five oxen for an ox, and four sheep for a sheep.[h] The thief shall make restitution, but if unable to do so, shall be sold for the theft. 4When the animal, whether ox or donkey or sheep, is found alive in the thief's possession, the thief shall pay double.

2[i] If a thief is found breaking in, and is beaten to death, no bloodguilt is incurred; 3but if it happens after sunrise, bloodguilt is incurred.

5 When someone causes a field or vineyard to be grazed over, or lets livestock loose to graze in someone else's field, restitution shall be made from the best in the owner's field or vineyard.

6 When fire breaks out and catches in thorns so that the stacked grain or the standing grain or the field is consumed, the one who started the fire shall make full restitution.

7 When someone delivers to a neighbor money or goods for safekeeping, and they are stolen from the neighbor's house, then the thief, if caught, shall pay double. 8If the thief is not caught, the owner of the house shall be brought before God,[j] to determine whether or not the owner had laid hands on the neighbor's goods.

9 In any case of disputed ownership involving ox, donkey, sheep, clothing, or any other loss, of which one party says, "This is mine," the case of both parties shall come before God;[j] the one whom God condemns[k] shall pay double to the other.

10 When someone delivers to another a donkey, ox, sheep, or any other animal for safekeeping, and it dies or is injured or is carried off, without anyone seeing it, 11an oath before the LORD shall decide between the two of them that the one has not laid hands on the property of the other; the owner shall accept the oath, and no restitution shall be made. 12But if it was stolen, restitution shall be made to its owner. 13If it was mangled by beasts, let it be brought as evidence; restitution shall not be made for the mangled remains.

14 When someone borrows an animal from another and it is injured or dies, the owner not being present, full restitution shall be made. 15If the owner was present, there shall be no restitution; if it was hired, only the hiring fee is due.

Social and Religious Laws

16 When a man seduces a virgin who is not engaged to be married, and lies with her, he shall give the bride-price for her and make her his wife. 17But if her father refuses to give her to him, he shall pay an amount equal to the bride-price for virgins.

18 You shall not permit a female sorcerer to live.

19 Whoever lies with an animal shall be put to death.

20 Whoever sacrifices to any god, other than the LORD alone, shall be devoted to destruction.

21 You shall not wrong or oppress a resident alien, for you were aliens in the land of Egypt. 22You shall not abuse any widow or orphan. 23If you do abuse them, when they cry out to me, I will surely heed their cry;

---

e 22:16 *girl*, literally, "a virgin." *usual dowry*, more literally, "customary marriage present to the bride's parents."   f 22:20 *shall be executed*, literally, "shall be utterly destroyed."

g Ch 21.37 in Heb   h Verses 2, 3, and 4 rearranged thus: 3b, 4, 2, 3a   i Ch 22.1 in Heb   j Or *before the judges*   k Or *the judges condemn*

King James

24And my wrath shall wax hot, and I will kill you with the sword; and your wives shall be widows, and your children fatherless.

25¶ If thou lend money to *any of* my people *that is* poor by thee, thou shalt not be to him as an usurer, neither shalt thou lay upon him usury.

26If thou at all take thy neighbour's raiment to pledge, thou shalt deliver it unto him by that the sun goeth down:

27For that *is* his covering only, it *is* his raiment for his skin: wherein shall he sleep? and it shall come to pass, when he crieth unto me, that I will hear; for I *am* gracious.

28¶ Thou shalt not revile the gods, nor curse the ruler of thy people.

29¶ Thou shalt not delay *to offer* the first of thy ripe fruits, and of thy liquors: the firstborn of thy sons shalt thou give unto me.

30Likewise shalt thou do with thine oxen, *and* with thy sheep: seven days it shall be with his dam; on the eighth day thou shalt give it me.

31¶ And ye shall be holy men unto me: neither shall ye eat *any* flesh *that is* torn of beasts in the field; ye shall cast it to the dogs.

23 THOU SHALT not raise a false report: put not thine hand with the wicked to be an unrighteous witness.

2¶ Thou shalt not follow a multitude to *do* evil; neither shalt thou speak in a cause to decline after many to wrest *judgment:*

3¶ Neither shalt thou countenance a poor man in his cause.

4¶ If thou meet thine enemy's ox or his ass going astray, thou shalt surely bring it back to him again.

5If thou see the ass of him that hateth thee lying under his burden, and wouldest forbear to help him, thou shalt surely help with him.

6Thou shalt not wrest the judgment of thy poor in his cause.

7Keep thee far from a false matter; and the innocent and righteous slay thou not: for I will not justify the wicked.

8¶ And thou shalt take no gift: for the gift blindeth the wise, and perverteth the words of the righteous.

9¶ Also thou shalt not oppress a stranger: for ye know the heart of a stranger, seeing ye were strangers in the land of Egypt.

10And six years thou shalt sow thy land, and shalt gather in the fruits thereof:

11But the seventh *year* thou shalt let it rest and lie still; that the poor of thy people may eat: and what they leave the beasts of the field shall eat. In like manner thou shalt deal with thy vineyard, *and* with thy oliveyard.

12Six days thou shalt do thy work, and on the seventh day thou shalt rest: that thine ox and thine ass may rest, and the son of thy handmaid, and the stranger, may be refreshed.

13And in all *things* that I have said unto you be circumspect: and make no mention of the name of other gods, neither let it be heard out of thy mouth.

14¶ Three times thou shalt keep a feast unto me in the year.

15Thou shalt keep the feast of unleavened bread: (thou shalt eat unleavened bread seven days, as I commanded thee, in the time appointed of the month Abib; for in it thou camest out from Egypt: and none shall appear before me empty:)

New International

with the sword; your wives will become widows and your children fatherless.

25"If you lend money to one of my people among you who is needy, do not be like a moneylender; charge him no interest.a 26If you take your neighbor's cloak as a pledge, return it to him by sunset, 27because his cloak is the only covering he has for his body. What else will he sleep in? When he cries out to me, I will hear, for I am compassionate.

28"Do not blaspheme Godb or curse the ruler of your people.

29"Do not hold back offerings from your granaries or your vats.c

"You must give me the firstborn of your sons. 30Do the same with your cattle and your sheep. Let them stay with their mothers for seven days, but give them to me on the eighth day.

31"You are to be my holy people. So do not eat the meat of an animal torn by wild beasts; throw it to the dogs.

Laws of Justice and Mercy

23 "DO NOT spread false reports. Do not help a wicked man by being a malicious witness.

2"Do not follow the crowd in doing wrong. When you give testimony in a lawsuit, do not pervert justice by siding with the crowd, 3and do not show favoritism to a poor man in his lawsuit.

4"If you come across your enemy's ox or donkey wandering off, be sure to take it back to him. 5If you see the donkey of someone who hates you fallen down under its load, do not leave it there; be sure you help him with it.

6"Do not deny justice to your poor people in their lawsuits. 7Have nothing to do with a false charge and do not put an innocent or honest person to death, for I will not acquit the guilty.

8"Do not accept a bribe, for a bribe blinds those who see and twists the words of the righteous.

9"Do not oppress an alien; you yourselves know how it feels to be aliens, because you were aliens in Egypt.

Sabbath Laws

10"For six years you are to sow your fields and harvest the crops, 11but during the seventh year let the land lie unplowed and unused. Then the poor among your people may get food from it, and the wild animals may eat what they leave. Do the same with your vineyard and your olive grove.

12"Six days do your work, but on the seventh day do not work, so that your ox and your donkey may rest and the slave born in your household, and the alien as well, may be refreshed.

13"Be careful to do everything I have said to you. Do not invoke the names of other gods; do not let them be heard on your lips.

The Three Annual Festivals

14"Three times a year you are to celebrate a festival to me.

15"Celebrate the Feast of Unleavened Bread; for seven days eat bread made without yeast, as I commanded you. Do this at the appointed time in the month of Abib, for in that month you came out of Egypt.

"No one is to appear before me empty-handed.

---

a 25 Or *excessive interest*　　b 28 Or *Do not revile the judges*　　c 29 The meaning of the Hebrew for this phrase is uncertain.

Living Bible

you, and I will kill you with enemy armies, so that your wives will be widows and your children fatherless.

25"If you lend money to a needy fellow-Hebrew, you are not to handle the transaction in an ordinary way, with interest. 26If you take his clothing as a pledge of his repayment, you must let him have it back at night. 27For it is probably his only warmth; how can he sleep without it? If you don't return it, and he cries to me for help, I will hear and be very gracious to him [at your expensed], for I am very compassionate.

28"You shall not blaspheme God, nor curse government officials—your judges and your rulers.

29"You must be prompt in giving me the tithe of your crops and your wine, and the redemption payment for your oldest son.

30"As to the firstborn of the oxen and the sheep, give it to me on the eighth day, after leaving it with its mother for seven days.

31"And since you yourselves are holy—my special people—do not eat any animal that has been attacked and killed by a wild animal. Leave its carcass for the dogs to eat.

23 "DO NOT pass along untrue reports. Do not cooperate with an evil man by affirming on the witness stand something you know is false.

2, 3"Don't join mobs intent on evil. When on the witness stand, don't be swayed in your testimony by the mood of the majority present, and do not slant your testimony in favor of a man just because he is poor.

4"If you come upon an enemy's ox or donkey that has strayed away, you must take it back to its owner. 5If you see your enemy trying to get his donkey onto its feet beneath a heavy load, you must not go on by, but must help him.

6"A man's poverty is no excuse for twisting justice against him.

7"Keep far away from falsely charging anyone with evil; never let an innocent person be put to death. I will not stand for this.e

8"Take no bribes, for a bribe makes you unaware of what you clearly see! A bribe hurts the cause of the person who is right.

9"Do not oppress foreigners; you know what it's like to be a foreigner; remember your own experience in the land of Egypt.

10"Sow and reap your crops for six years, 11but let the land rest and lie fallow during the seventh year, and let the poor among the people harvest any volunteer crop that may come up; leave the rest for the animals to enjoy. The same rule applies to your vineyards and your olive groves.

12"Work six days only, and rest the seventh; this is to give your oxen and donkeys a rest, as well as the people of your household—your slaves and visitors.

13"Be sure to obey all of these instructions; and remember—never mention the name of any other god.f

14"There are three annual religious pilgrimages you must make.g

15"The first is the Pilgrimage of Unleavened Bread, when for seven days you are not to eat bread with yeast, just as I commanded you before. This celebration is to be an annual event at the regular time in March, the month you left Egypt; everyone must bring me a sacrifice at that time. 16Then there is the Harvest Pilgrimage,

New Revised Standard

24my wrath will burn, and I will kill you with the sword, and your wives shall become widows and your children orphans.

25 If you lend money to my people, to the poor among you, you shall not deal with them as a creditor; you shall not exact interest from them. 26If you take your neighbor's cloak in pawn, you shall restore it before the sun goes down; 27 for it may be your neighbor's only clothing to use as cover; in what else shall that person sleep? And if your neighbor cries out to me, I will listen, for I am compassionate.

28 You shall not revile God, or curse a leader of your people.

29 You shall not delay to make offerings from the fullness of your harvest and from the outflow of your presses.h

The firstborn of your sons you shall give to me. 30 You shall do the same with your oxen and with your sheep: seven days it shall remain with its mother; on the eighth day you shall give it to me.

31 You shall be people consecrated to me; therefore you shall not eat any meat that is mangled by beasts in the field; you shall throw it to the dogs.

Justice for All

23 YOU SHALL not spread a false report. You shall not join hands with the wicked to act as a malicious witness. 2 You shall not follow a majority in wrongdoing; when you bear witness in a lawsuit, you shall not side with the majority so as to pervert justice; 3 nor shall you be partial to the poor in a lawsuit.

4 When you come upon your enemy's ox or donkey going astray, you shall bring it back.

5 When you see the donkey of one who hates you lying under its burden and you would hold back from setting it free, you must help to set it free.h

6 You shall not pervert the justice due to your poor in their lawsuits. 7 Keep far from a false charge, and do not kill the innocent and those in the right, for I will not acquit the guilty. 8 You shall take no bribe, for a bribe blinds the officials, and subverts the cause of those who are in the right.

9 You shall not oppress a resident alien; you know the heart of an alien, for you were aliens in the land of Egypt.

Sabbatical Year and Sabbath

10 For six years you shall sow your land and gather in its yield; 11 but the seventh year you shall let it rest and lie fallow, so that the poor of your people may eat; and what they leave the wild animals may eat. You shall do the same with your vineyard, and with your olive orchard.

12 Six days you shall do your work, but on the seventh day you shall rest, so that your ox and your donkey may have relief, and your homeborn slave and the resident alien may be refreshed. 13 Be attentive to all that I have said to you. Do not invoke the names of other gods; do not let them be heard on your lips.

The Annual Festivals

14 Three times in the year you shall hold a festival for me. 15 You shall observe the festival of unleavened bread; as I commanded you, you shall eat unleavened bread for seven days at the appointed time in the month of Abib, for in it you came out of Egypt.

No one shall appear before me empty-handed.

---

d 22:27 at your expense, implied.   e 23:7 I will not stand for this, literally, "I will not acquit the wicked."   f 23:13 never mention the name of any other god, in prayer, or in taking an oath.   g 23:14 pilgrimages you must make, or, "feasts you must celebrate."

h Meaning of Heb uncertain

King James

16And the feast of harvest, the firstfruits of thy labours, which thou hast sown in the field: and the feast of ingathering, *which is* in the end of the year, when thou hast gathered in thy labours out of the field.

17Three times in the year all thy males shall appear before the Lord GOD.

18Thou shalt not offer the blood of my sacrifice with leavened bread; neither shall the fat of my sacrifice remain until the morning.

19The first of the firstfruits of thy land thou shalt bring into the house of the LORD thy God. Thou shalt not seethe a kid in his mother's milk.

20¶ Behold, I send an Angel before thee, to keep thee in the way, and to bring thee into the place which I have prepared.

21Beware of him, and obey his voice, provoke him not; for he will not pardon your transgressions: for my name *is* in him.

22But if thou shalt indeed obey his voice, and do all that I speak; then I will be an enemy unto thine enemies, and an adversary unto thine adversaries.

23For mine Angel shall go before thee, and bring thee in unto the Amorites, and the Hittites, and the Perizzites, and the Canaanites, the Hivites, and the Jebusites: and I will cut them off.

24Thou shalt not bow down to their gods, nor serve them, nor do after their works: but thou shalt utterly overthrow them, and quite break down their images.

25And ye shall serve the LORD your God, and he shall bless thy bread, and thy water; and I will take sickness away from the midst of thee.

26¶ There shall nothing cast their young, nor be barren, in thy land: the number of thy days I will fulfil.

27I will send my fear before thee, and will destroy all the people to whom thou shalt come, and I will make all thine enemies turn their backs unto thee.

28And I will send hornets before thee, which shall drive out the Hivite, the Canaanite, and the Hittite, from before thee.

29I will not drive them out from before thee in one year; lest the land become desolate, and the beast of the field multiply against thee.

30By little and little I will drive them out from before thee, until thou be increased, and inherit the land.

31And I will set thy bounds from the Red sea even unto the sea of the Philistines, and from the desert unto the river: for I will deliver the inhabitants of the land into your hand; and thou shalt drive them out before thee.

32Thou shalt make no covenant with them, nor with their gods.

33They shall not dwell in thy land, lest they make thee sin against me: for if thou serve their gods, it will surely be a snare unto thee.

24 AND HE said unto Moses, Come up unto the LORD, thou, and Aaron, Nadab, and Abihu, and seventy of the elders of Israel; and worship ye afar off.

2And Moses alone shall come near the LORD: but they shall not come nigh; neither shall the people go up with him.

3¶ And Moses came and told the people all the words of the LORD, and all the judgments: and all the people answered with one voice, and said, All the words which the LORD hath said will we do.

4And Moses wrote all the words of the LORD, and rose up early in the morning, and builded an altar under the hill, and twelve pillars, according to the twelve tribes of Israel.

New International

16"Celebrate the Feast of Harvest with the firstfruits of the crops you sow in your field.

"Celebrate the Feast of Ingathering at the end of the year, when you gather in your crops from the field.

17"Three times a year all the men are to appear before the Sovereign LORD.

18"Do not offer the blood of a sacrifice to me along with anything containing yeast.

"The fat of my festival offerings must not be kept until morning.

19"Bring the best of the firstfruits of your soil to the house of the LORD your God.

"Do not cook a young goat in its mother's milk.

God's Angel to Prepare the Way

20"See, I am sending an angel ahead of you to guard you along the way and to bring you to the place I have prepared. 21Pay attention to him and listen to what he says. Do not rebel against him; he will not forgive your rebellion, since my Name is in him. 22If you listen carefully to what he says and do all that I say, I will be an enemy to your enemies and will oppose those who oppose you. 23My angel will go ahead of you and bring you into the land of the Amorites, Hittites, Perizzites, Canaanites, Hivites and Jebusites, and I will wipe them out. 24Do not bow down before their gods or worship them or follow their practices. You must demolish them and break their sacred stones to pieces. 25Worship the LORD your God, and his blessing will be on your food and water. I will take away sickness from among you, 26and none will miscarry or be barren in your land. I will give you a full life span.

27"I will send my terror ahead of you and throw into confusion every nation you encounter. I will make all your enemies turn their backs and run. 28I will send the hornet ahead of you to drive the Hivites, Canaanites and Hittites out of your way. 29But I will not drive them out in a single year, because the land would become desolate and the wild animals too numerous for you. 30Little by little I will drive them out before you, until you have increased enough to take possession of the land.

31"I will establish your borders from the Red Sea[a] to the Sea of the Philistines,[b] and from the desert to the River.[c] I will hand over to you the people who live in the land and you will drive them out before you. 32Do not make a covenant with them or with their gods. 33Do not let them live in your land, or they will cause you to sin against me, because the worship of their gods will certainly be a snare to you."

The Covenant Confirmed

24 THEN HE said to Moses, "Come up to the LORD, you and Aaron, Nadab and Abihu, and seventy of the elders of Israel. You are to worship at a distance, 2but Moses alone is to approach the LORD; the others must not come near. And the people may not come up with him."

3When Moses went and told the people all the LORD's words and laws, they responded with one voice, "Everything the LORD has said we will do." 4Moses then wrote down everything the LORD had said.

He got up early the next morning and built an altar at the foot of the mountain and set up twelve stone pillars representing the twelve tribes of Israel. 5Then he sent

a *31* Hebrew *Yam Suph*; that is, Sea of Reeds b *31* That is, the Mediterranean   c *31* That is, the Euphrates

Living Bible

when you must bring to me the first of your crops. And, finally, the Pilgrimage of Ingathering at the end of the harvest season. 17At these three times each year, every man in Israel shall appear before the Lord God.

18"No sacrificial blood shall be offered with leavened bread; no sacrificial fat shall be left unoffered until the next morning.

19"As you reap each of your crops, bring me the choicest sample of the first day's harvest; it shall be offeredd to the Lord your God.

"Do not boil a young goat in its mother's milk.

20"See, I am sending an Angel before you to lead you safely to the land I have prepared for you. 21Reverence him and obey all of his instructions; do not rebel against him, for he will not pardon your transgression; he is my representativee—he bears my name. 22But if you are careful to obey him, following all my instructions, then I will be an enemy to your enemies. 23For my Angel shall go before you and bring you into the land of the Amorites, Hittites, Perizzites, Canaanites, Hivites, and Jebusites, to live there. And I will destroy those people before you.

24"You must not worship the gods of these other nations, nor sacrifice to them in any way, and you must not follow the evil example of these heathen people; you must utterly conquer them and break down their shameful idols.

25"You shall serve the Lord your God only; then I will bless you with food and with water, and I will take away sickness from among you. 26There will be no miscarriages nor barrenness throughout your land, and you will live out the full quota of the days of your life.

27"The terror of the Lord shall fall upon all the people whose land you invade, and they will flee before you; 28and I will send hornets to drive out the Hivites, Canaanites, and Hittites from before you. 29I will not do it all in one year, for the land would become a wilderness, and the wild animals would become too many to control. 30But I will drive them out a little at a time, until your population has increased enough to fill the land. 31And I will set your enlarged boundaries from the Red Sea to the Philistine coast, and from the southern deserts as far as the Euphrates River; and I will cause you to defeat the people now living in the land, and you will drive them out ahead of you.

32"You must make no covenant with them, nor have anything to do with their gods. 33Don't let them live among you! For I know that they will infect you with their sin of worshiping false gods, and that would be an utter disaster to you."

24 THE LORD now instructed Moses, "Come up here with Aaron, Nadab, Abihu, and seventy of the elders of Israel. All of you except Moses are to worship at a distance. 2Moses alone shall come near to the Lord; and remember, none of the ordinary people are permitted to come up into the mountain at all."

3Then Moses announced to the people all the laws and regulations God had given him; and the people answered in unison, "We will obey them all."

4Moses wrote down the laws; and early the next morning he built an altar at the foot of the mountain, with twelve pillars around the altar because there were twelve tribes of Israel. 5Then he sent some of the young

New Revised Standard

16 You shall observe the festival of harvest, of the first fruits of your labor, of what you sow in the field. You shall observe the festival of ingathering at the end of the year, when you gather in from the field the fruit of your labor. 17Three times in the year all your males shall appear before the Lord God.

18 You shall not offer the blood of my sacrifice with anything leavened, or let the fat of my festival remain until the morning.

19 The choicest of the first fruits of your ground you shall bring into the house of the LORD your God.

You shall not boil a kid in its mother's milk.

The Conquest of Canaan Promised

20 I am going to send an angel in front of you, to guard you on the way and to bring you to the place that I have prepared. 21Be attentive to him and listen to his voice; do not rebel against him, for he will not pardon your transgression; for my name is in him.

22 But if you listen attentively to his voice and do all that I say, then I will be an enemy to your enemies and a foe to your foes.

23 When my angel goes in front of you, and brings you to the Amorites, the Hittites, the Perizzites, the Canaanites, the Hivites, and the Jebusites, and I blot them out, 24you shall not bow down to their gods, or worship them, or follow their practices, but you shall utterly demolish them and break their pillars in pieces. 25You shall worship the LORD your God, and If will bless your bread and your water; and I will take sickness away from among you. 26No one shall miscarry or be barren in your land; I will fulfill the number of your days. 27I will send my terror in front of you, and will throw into confusion all the people against whom you shall come, and I will make all your enemies turn their backs to you. 28And I will send the pestilenceg in front of you, which shall drive out the Hivites, the Canaanites, and the Hittites from before you. 29I will not drive them out from before you in one year, or the land would become desolate and the wild animals would multiply against you. 30Little by little I will drive them out from before you, until you have increased and possess the land. 31I will set your borders from the Red Seab to the sea of the Philistines, and from the wilderness to the Euphrates; for I will hand over to you the inhabitants of the land, and you shall drive them out before you. 32You shall make no covenant with them and their gods. 33They shall not live in your land, or they will make you sin against me; for if you worship their gods, it will surely be a snare to you.

The Blood of the Covenant

24 THEN HE said to Moses, "Come up to the LORD, you and Aaron, Nadab, and Abihu, and seventy of the elders of Israel, and worship at a distance. 2Moses alone shall come near the LORD; but the others shall not come near, and the people shall not come up with him."

3 Moses came and told the people all the words of the LORD and all the ordinances; and all the people answered with one voice, and said, "All the words that the LORD has spoken we will do." 4And Moses wrote down all the words of the LORD. He rose early in the morning, and built an altar at the foot of the mountain, and set up twelve pillars, corresponding to the twelve tribes of Israel. 5He sent young men of the people of Israel, who

---

d 23:19 it shall be offered to the Lord your God, literally, "you shall bring (it) into the house of Jehovah thy God." e 23:21 he is my representative—he bears my name, literally, "my name is in him."

f Gk Vg: Heb he g Or hornets: Meaning of Heb uncertain h Or Sea of Reeds

King James

5And he sent young men of the children of Israel, which offered burnt offerings, and sacrificed peace offerings of oxen unto the LORD.

6And Moses took half of the blood, and put *it* in basins; and half of the blood he sprinkled on the altar.

7And he took the book of the covenant, and read in the audience of the people: and they said, All that the LORD hath said will we do, and be obedient.

8And Moses took the blood, and sprinkled *it* on the people, and said, Behold the blood of the covenant, which the LORD hath made with you concerning all these words.

9¶ Then went up Moses, and Aaron, Nadab, and Abihu, and seventy of the elders of Israel:

10And they saw the God of Israel: and *there was* under his feet as it were a paved work of a sapphire stone, and as it were the body of heaven in *his* clearness.

11And upon the nobles of the children of Israel he laid not his hand: also they saw God, and did eat and drink.

12¶ And the LORD said unto Moses, Come up to me into the mount, and be there: and I will give thee tables of stone, and a law, and commandments which I have written; that thou mayest teach them.

13And Moses rose up, and his minister Joshua: and Moses went up into the mount of God.

14And he said unto the elders, Tarry ye here for us, until we come again unto you: and, behold, Aaron and Hur *are* with you: if any man have any matters to do, let him come unto them.

15And Moses went up into the mount, and a cloud covered the mount.

16And the glory of the LORD abode upon mount Sinai, and the cloud covered it six days: and the seventh day he called unto Moses out of the midst of the cloud.

17And the sight of the glory of the LORD *was* like devouring fire on the top of the mount in the eyes of the children of Israel.

18And Moses went into the midst of the cloud, and gat him up into the mount: and Moses was in the mount forty days and forty nights.

25 AND THE LORD spake unto Moses, saying, 2Speak unto the children of Israel, that they bring me an offering: of every man that giveth it willingly with his heart ye shall take my offering.

3And this *is* the offering which ye shall take of them; gold, and silver, and brass,

4And blue, and purple, and scarlet, and fine linen, and goats' *hair*,

5And rams' skins dyed red, and badgers' skins, and shittim wood,

6Oil for the light, spices for anointing oil, and for sweet incense,

7Onyx stones, and stones to be set in the ephod, and in the breastplate.

8And let them make me a sanctuary; that I may dwell among them.

9According to all that I show thee, *after* the pattern of the tabernacle, and the pattern of all the instruments thereof, even so shall ye make *it*.

10¶ And they shall make an ark *of* shittim wood: two cubits and a half *shall be* the length thereof, and a cubit and a half the breadth thereof, and a cubit and a half the height thereof.

11And thou shalt overlay it with pure gold, within and without shalt thou overlay it, and shalt make upon it a crown of gold round about.

12And thou shalt cast four rings of gold for it, and put *them* in the four corners thereof; and two rings *shall be* in the one side of it, and two rings in the other side of it.

New International

young Israelite men, and they offered burnt offerings and sacrificed young bulls as fellowship offeringsa to the LORD. 6Moses took half of the blood and put it in bowls, and the other half he sprinkled on the altar. 7Then he took the Book of the Covenant and read it to the people. They responded, "We will do everything the LORD has said; we will obey."

8Moses then took the blood, sprinkled it on the people and said, "This is the blood of the covenant that the LORD has made with you in accordance with all these words."

9Moses and Aaron, Nadab and Abihu, and the seventy elders of Israel went up 10and saw the God of Israel. Under his feet was something like a pavement made of sapphire,b clear as the sky itself. 11But God did not raise his hand against these leaders of the Israelites; they saw God, and they ate and drank.

12The LORD said to Moses, "Come up to me on the mountain and stay here, and I will give you the tablets of stone, with the law and commands I have written for their instruction."

13Then Moses set out with Joshua his aide, and Moses went up on the mountain of God. 14He said to the elders, "Wait here for us until we come back to you. Aaron and Hur are with you, and anyone involved in a dispute can go to them."

15When Moses went up on the mountain, the cloud covered it, 16and the glory of the LORD settled on Mount Sinai. For six days the cloud covered the mountain, and on the seventh day the LORD called to Moses from within the cloud. 17To the Israelites the glory of the LORD looked like a consuming fire on top of the mountain. 18Then Moses entered the cloud as he went on up the mountain. And he stayed on the mountain forty days and forty nights.

Offerings for the Tabernacle

25 THE LORD said to Moses, 2"Tell the Israelites to bring me an offering. You are to receive the offering for me from each man whose heart prompts him to give. 3These are the offerings you are to receive from them: gold, silver and bronze; 4blue, purple and scarlet yarn and fine linen; goat hair; 5ram skins dyed red and hides of sea cowsc; acacia wood; 6olive oil for the light; spices for the anointing oil and for the fragrant incense; 7and onyx stones and other gems to be mounted on the ephod and breastpiece.

8"Then have them make a sanctuary for me, and I will dwell among them. 9Make this tabernacle and all its furnishings exactly like the pattern I will show you.

The Ark

10"Have them make a chest of acacia wood—two and a half cubits long, a cubit and a half wide, and a cubit and a half high.d 11Overlay it with pure gold, both inside and out, and make a gold molding around it. 12Cast four gold rings for it and fasten them to its four feet, with two rings on one side and two rings on the other. 13Then

---

a 5 Traditionally *peace offerings*   b 10 Or *lapis lazuli*   c 5 That is, dugongs   d 10 That is, about 3 3/4 feet (about 1.1 meters) long and 2 1/4 feet (about 0.7 meter) wide and high

Living Bible

men to sacrifice the burnt offerings and peace offerings to the Lord. 6Moses took half of the blood of these animals, and drew it off into basins. The other half he splashed against the altar.

7And he read to the people the Book he had written—the Book of the Covenant—containing God's directions and laws. And the people said again, "We solemnly promise to obey every one of these rules."

8Then Moses threw the blood from the basins towards the people and said, "This blood confirms and seals the covenant the Lord has made with you in giving you these laws."

9Then Moses, Aaron, Nadab, Abihu, and seventy of the elders of Israel went up into the mountain. 10And they saw the God of Israel; under his feet there seemed to be a pavement of brilliant sapphire stones, as clear as the heavens.

11Yet, even though the elders saw God, he did not destroy them; and they had a meal together before the Lord.

12And the Lord said to Moses, "Come up to me into the mountain, and remain until I give you the laws and commandments I have written on tablets of stone, so that you can teach the people from them." 13So Moses and Joshua, his assistant, went up into the mountain of God.

14He told the elders, "Stay here and wait for us until we come back; if there are any problems while I am gone, consult with Aaron and Hur."

15Then Moses went up the mountain and disappeared into the cloud at the top. 16And the glory of the Lord rested upon Mt. Sinai and the cloud covered it six days; the seventh day he called to Moses from the cloud. 17Those at the bottom of the mountain saw the awesome sight: the glory of the Lord on the mountain top looked like a raging fire. 18And Moses disappeared into the cloud-covered mountain top, and was there for forty days and forty nights.

25 JEHOVAH SAID to Moses, "Tell the people of Israel that everyone who wants to may bring me an offering from this list:

Gold, silver, bronze, blue cloth, purple cloth, scarlet cloth, fine linen, goat's hair, red-dyed ram's skins, goat-skins, acacia wood, olive oil for the lamps, spices for the anointing oil and for the fragrant incense, onyx stones, stones to be set in the ephod and in the breastplate.

8"For I want the people of Israel to make me a sacred Temple where I can live among them.

9"This home of mine shall be a tent pavilion—a Tabernacle. I will give you a drawing of the construction plan, and the details of each furnishing.

10"Using acacia wood, make an Ark 3¾ feet long, 2¼ feet wide, and 2¼ feet high. 11Overlay it inside and outside with pure gold, with a molding of gold all around it. 12Cast four rings of gold for it and attach them to the four lower corners, two rings on each side. 13, 14Make

New Revised Standard

offered burnt offerings and sacrificed oxen as offerings of well-being to the LORD. 6Moses took half of the blood and put it in basins, and half of the blood he dashed against the altar. 7Then he took the book of the covenant, and read it in the hearing of the people; and they said, "All that the LORD has spoken we will do, and we will be obedient." 8Moses took the blood and dashed it on the people, and said, "See the blood of the covenant that the LORD has made with you in accordance with all these words."

On the Mountain with God

9 Then Moses and Aaron, Nadab, and Abihu, and seventy of the elders of Israel went up, 10and they saw the God of Israel. Under his feet there was something like a pavement of sapphire stone, like the very heaven for clearness. 11Gode did not lay his hand on the chief men of the people of Israel; also they beheld God, and they ate and drank.

12 The LORD said to Moses, "Come up to me on the mountain, and wait there; and I will give you the tablets of stone, with the law and the commandment, which I have written for their instruction." 13So Moses set out with his assistant Joshua, and Moses went up into the mountain of God. 14To the elders he had said, "Wait here for us, until we come to you again; for Aaron and Hur are with you; whoever has a dispute may go to them."

15 Then Moses went up on the mountain, and the cloud covered the mountain. 16The glory of the LORD settled on Mount Sinai, and the cloud covered it for six days; on the seventh day he called to Moses out of the cloud. 17Now the appearance of the glory of the LORD was like a devouring fire on the top of the mountain in the sight of the people of Israel. 18Moses entered the cloud, and went up on the mountain. Moses was on the mountain for forty days and forty nights.

Offerings for the Tabernacle

25 THE LORD said to Moses: 2Tell the Israelites to take for me an offering; from all whose hearts prompt them to give you shall receive the offering for me. 3This is the offering that you shall receive from them: gold, silver, and bronze, 4blue, purple, and crimson yarns and fine linen, goats' hair, 5tanned rams' skins, fine leather,f acacia wood, 6oil for the lamps, spices for the anointing oil and for the fragrant incense, 7onyx stones and gems to be set in the ephod and for the breastpiece. 8And have them make me a sanctuary, so that I may dwell among them. 9In accordance with all that I show you concerning the pattern of the tabernacle and of all its furniture, so you shall make it.

The Ark of the Covenant

10 They shall make an ark of acacia wood; it shall be two and a half cubits long, a cubit and a half wide, and a cubit and a half high. 11You shall overlay it with pure gold, inside and outside you shall overlay it, and you shall make a molding of gold upon it all around. 12You shall cast four rings of gold for it and put them on its four feet, two rings on the one side of it, and two rings on the other side. 13You shall make poles of acacia

e Heb *He*   f Meaning of Heb uncertain

King James

13And thou shalt make staves *of* shittim wood, and overlay them with gold.

14And thou shalt put the staves into the rings by the sides of the ark, that the ark may be borne with them.

15The staves shall be in the rings of the ark: they shall not be taken from it.

16And thou shalt put into the ark the testimony which I shall give thee.

17And thou shalt make a mercy seat *of* pure gold: two cubits and a half *shall be* the length thereof, and a cubit and a half the breadth thereof.

18And thou shalt make two cherubims *of* gold, *of* beaten work shalt thou make them, in the two ends of the mercy seat.

19And make one cherub on the one end, and the other cherub on the other end: *even* of the mercy seat shall ye make the cherubims on the two ends thereof.

20And the cherubims shall stretch forth *their* wings on high, covering the mercy seat with their wings, and their faces *shall look* one to another; toward the mercy seat shall the faces of the cherubims be.

21And thou shalt put the mercy seat above upon the ark; and in the ark thou shalt put the testimony that I shall give thee.

22And there I will meet with thee, and I will commune with thee from above the mercy seat, from between the two cherubims which *are* upon the ark of the testimony, of all *things* which I will give thee in commandment unto the children of Israel.

23¶ Thou shalt also make a table *of* shittim wood: two cubits *shall be* the length thereof, and a cubit the breadth thereof, and a cubit and a half the height thereof.

24And thou shalt overlay it with pure gold, and make thereto a crown of gold round about.

25And thou shalt make unto it a border of an handbreadth round about, and thou shalt make a golden crown to the border thereof round about.

26And thou shalt make for it four rings of gold, and put the rings in the four corners that *are* on the four feet thereof.

27Over against the border shall the rings be for places of the staves to bear the table.

28And thou shalt make the staves *of* shittim wood, and overlay them with gold, that the table may be borne with them.

29And thou shalt make the dishes thereof, and spoons thereof, and covers thereof, and bowls thereof, to cover withal: *of* pure gold shalt thou make them.

30And thou shalt set upon the table showbread before me always.

31¶ And thou shalt make a candlestick *of* pure gold: *of* beaten work shall the candlestick be made: his shaft, and his branches, his bowls, his knobs, and his flowers, shall be of the same.

32And six branches shall come out of the sides of it; three branches of the candlestick out of the one side, and three branches of the candlestick out of the other side:

33Three bowls made like unto almonds, *with* a knob and a flower in one branch; and three bowls made like almonds in the other branch, *with* a knob and a flower: so in the six branches that come out of the candlestick.

34And in the candlestick *shall be* four bowls made like unto almonds, *with* their knobs and their flowers.

35And *there shall be* a knob under two branches of the same, and a knob under two branches of the same, and a knob under two branches of the same, according to the six branches that proceed out of the candlestick.

36Their knobs and their branches shall be of the same: all it *shall be* one beaten work *of* pure gold.

37And thou shalt make the seven lamps thereof: and they shall light the lamps thereof, that they may give light over against it.

38And the tongs thereof, and the snuffdishes thereof, *shall be of* pure gold.

New International

make poles of acacia wood and overlay them with gold. 14Insert the poles into the rings on the sides of the chest to carry it. 15The poles are to remain in the rings of this ark; they are not to be removed. 16Then put in the ark the Testimony, which I will give you.

17"Make an atonement cover[a] of pure gold—two and a half cubits long and a cubit and a half wide.[b] 18And make two cherubim out of hammered gold at the ends of the cover. 19Make one cherub on one end and the second cherub on the other; make the cherubim of one piece with the cover, at the two ends. 20The cherubim are to have their wings spread upward, overshadowing the cover with them. The cherubim are to face each other, looking toward the cover. 21Place the cover on top of the ark and put in the ark the Testimony, which I will give you. 22There, above the cover between the two cherubim that are over the ark of the Testimony, I will meet with you and give you all my commands for the Israelites.

The Table

23"Make a table of acacia wood—two cubits long, a cubit wide and a cubit and a half high.[c] 24Overlay it with pure gold and make a gold molding around it. 25Also make around it a rim a handbreadth[d] wide and put a gold molding on the rim. 26Make four gold rings for the table and fasten them to the four corners, where the four legs are. 27The rings are to be close to the rim to hold the poles used in carrying the table. 28Make the poles of acacia wood, overlay them with gold and carry the table with them. 29And make its plates and dishes of pure gold, as well as its pitchers and bowls for the pouring out of offerings. 30Put the bread of the Presence on this table to be before me at all times.

The Lampstand

31"Make a lampstand of pure gold and hammer it out, base and shaft; its flowerlike cups, buds and blossoms shall be of one piece with it. 32Six branches are to extend from the sides of the lampstand—three on one side and three on the other. 33Three cups shaped like almond flowers with buds and blossoms are to be on one branch, three on the next branch, and the same for all six branches extending from the lampstand. 34And on the lampstand there are to be four cups shaped like almond flowers with buds and blossoms. 35One bud shall be under the first pair of branches extending from the lampstand, a second bud under the second pair, and a third bud under the third pair—six branches in all. 36The buds and branches shall all be of one piece with the lampstand, hammered out of pure gold.

37"Then make its seven lamps and set them up on it so that they light the space in front of it. 38Its wick trimmers and trays are to be of pure gold. 39A talent[e]

a *17* Traditionally *a mercy seat*   b *17* That is, about 3 3/4 feet (about 1.1 meters) long and 2 1/4 feet (about 0.7 meter) wide   c *23* That is, about 3 feet (about 0.9 meter) long and 1 1/2 feet (about 0.5 meter) wide and 2 1/4 feet (about 0.7 meter) high   d *25* That is, about 3 inches (about 8 centimeters) e *39* That is, about 75 pounds (about 34 kilograms)

Living Bible

poles from acacia wood overlaid with gold, and fit the poles into the rings at the sides of the Ark, to carry it. 15These carrying poles shall never be taken from the rings, but are to be left there permanently. 16When the Ark is finished, place inside it the tablets of stone I will give you, with the Ten Commandments engraved on them.f

17"And make a lid of pure gold, 3¾ feet long and 2¼ feet wide. This is the place of mercy for your sins.g 18Then make two statues of Guardian Angelsh using beaten gold, and place them at the two ends of the lid of the Ark. 19They shall be one piece with the mercy place, one at each end. 20The Guardian Angels shall be facing each other, looking down upon the place of mercy, and shall have wings spread out above the gold lid. 21Install the lid upon the Ark, and place within the Ark the tablets of stone I shall give you. 22And I will meet with you there and talk with you from above the place of mercy between the Guardian Angels; and the Ark will contain the laws of my covenant. There I will tell you my commandments for the people of Israel.

23"Then make a table of acacia wood three feet long, 1½ feet wide, and 2¼ feet high. 24Overlay it with pure gold, and run a rib of gold around it. 25Put a molding four inches wide around the edge of the top, and a gold ridge along the molding, all around. 26, 27Make four gold rings and put the rings at the outside corner of the four legs, close to the top; these are rings for the poles that will be used to carry the table. 28Make the poles from acacia wood overlaid with gold. 29And make gold dishes, spoons, pitchers, and flagons; 30and always keep the special Bread of the Presence on the table before me.

31"Make a lampstand of pure, beaten gold. The entire lampstand and its decorations shall be one piece—the base, shaft, lamps, and blossoms. 32, 33It will have three branches going out from each side of the center shaft, each branch decorated with three almond flowers. 34, 35The central shaft itself will be decorated with four almond flowers—one placed between each set of branches; also, there will be one flower above the top set of branches and one below the bottom set. 36These decorations and branches and the shaft are all to be one piece of pure, beaten gold. 37Then make seven lamps for the lampstand, and set them so that they reflect their light forward. 38The snuffers and trays are to be made of pure gold. 39You will need about 107i pounds of pure gold for the lampstand and its accessories.

New Revised Standard

wood, and overlay them with gold. 14And you shall put the poles into the rings on the sides of the ark, by which to carry the ark. 15The poles shall remain in the rings of the ark; they shall not be taken from it. 16You shall put into the ark the covenantj that I shall give you.

17 Then you shall make a mercy seatk of pure gold; two cubits and a half shall be its length, and a cubit and a half its width. 18You shall make two cherubim of gold; you shall make them of hammered work, at the two ends of the mercy seat.l 19Make one cherub at the one end, and one cherub at the other; of one piece with the mercy seatl you shall make the cherubim at its two ends. 20The cherubim shall spread out their wings above, overshadowing the mercy seatl with their wings. They shall face one to another; the faces of the cherubim shall be turned toward the mercy seat.l 21You shall put the mercy seatl on the top of the ark; and in the ark you shall put the covenanti that I shall give you. 22There I will meet with you, and from above the mercy seat,l from between the two cherubim that are on the ark of the covenant,j I will deliver to you all my commands for the Israelites.

The Table for the Bread of the Presence

23 You shall make a table of acacia wood, two cubits long, one cubit wide, and a cubit and a half high. 24You shall overlay it with pure gold, and make a molding of gold around it. 25You shall make around it a rim a handbreadth wide, and a molding of gold around the rim. 26You shall make for it four rings of gold, and fasten the rings to the four corners at its four legs. 27The rings that hold the poles used for carrying the table shall be close to the rim. 28You shall make the poles of acacia wood, and overlay them with gold, and the table shall be carried with these. 29You shall make its plates and dishes for incense, and its flagons and bowls with which to pour drink offerings; you shall make them of pure gold. 30And you shall set the bread of the Presence on the table before me always.

The Lampstand

31 You shall make a lampstand of pure gold. The base and the shaft of the lampstand shall be made of hammered work; its cups, its calyxes, and its petals shall be of one piece with it; 32and there shall be six branches going out of its sides, three branches of the lampstand out of one side of it and three branches of the lampstand out of the other side of it; 33three cups shaped like almond blossoms, each with calyx and petals, on one branch, and three cups shaped like almond blossoms, each with calyx and petals, on the other branch—so for the six branches going out of the lampstand. 34On the lampstand itself there shall be four cups shaped like almond blossoms, each with its calyxes and petals. 35There shall be a calyx of one piece with it under the first pair of branches, a calyx of one piece with it under the next pair of branches, and a calyx of one piece with it under the last pair of branches—so for the six branches that go out of the lampstand. 36Their calyxes and their branches shall be of one piece with it, the whole of it one hammered piece of pure gold. 37You shall make the seven lamps for it; and the lamps shall be set up so as to give light on the space in front of it. 38Its snuffers and trays shall be of pure gold. 39It, and

---

f 25:16 place inside it the tablets of stone I will give you, with the Ten Commandments engraved on them, implied. Literally, "Put into the Ark the Testimony which I shall give you." g 25:17 the place of mercy for your sins, literally, "mercy seat" or "place of making propitiation for your sins." h 25:18 Guardian Angels, literally, "cherubim." We are not told what they looked like. i 25:39 about 107 pounds of pure gold, literally, "a [gold] talent." The exact weight is not known.

j Or treaty, or testimony; Heb eduth   k Or a cover   l Or the cover

King James

39Of a talent of pure gold shall he make it, with all these vessels.

40And look that thou make *them* after their pattern, which was shown thee in the mount.

26 MOREOVER THOU shalt make the tabernacle *with* ten curtains *of* fine twined linen, and blue, and purple, and scarlet: *with* cherubims of cunning work shalt thou make them.

2The length of one curtain *shall be* eight and twenty cubits, and the breadth of one curtain four cubits: and every one of the curtains shall have one measure.

3The five curtains shall be coupled together one to another; and *other* five curtains *shall be* coupled one to another.

4And thou shalt make loops of blue upon the edge of the one curtain from the selvedge in the coupling; and likewise shalt thou make in the uttermost edge of *another* curtain, in the coupling of the second.

5Fifty loops shalt thou make in the one curtain, and fifty loops shalt thou make in the edge of the curtain that *is* in the coupling of the second; that the loops may take hold one of another.

6And thou shalt make fifty taches of gold, and couple the curtains together with the taches: and it shall be one tabernacle.

7¶ And thou shalt make curtains *of* goats' *hair* to be a covering upon the tabernacle: eleven curtains shalt thou make.

8The length of one curtain *shall be* thirty cubits, and the breadth of one curtain four cubits: and the eleven curtains *shall be all* of one measure.

9And thou shalt couple five curtains by themselves, and six curtains by themselves, and shalt double the sixth curtain in the forefront of the tabernacle.

10And thou shalt make fifty loops on the edge of the one curtain *that is* outmost in the coupling, and fifty loops in the edge of the curtain which coupleth the second.

11And thou shalt make fifty taches of brass, and put the taches into the loops, and couple the tent together, that it may be one.

12And the remnant that remaineth of the curtains of the tent, the half curtain that remaineth, shall hang over the backside of the tabernacle.

13And a cubit on the one side, and a cubit on the other side of that which remaineth in the length of the curtains of the tent, it shall hang over the sides of the tabernacle on this side and on that side, to cover it.

14And thou shalt make a covering for the tent *of* rams' skins dyed red, and a covering above of badgers' skins.

15¶ And thou shalt make boards for the tabernacle *of* shittim wood standing up.

16Ten cubits *shall be* the length of a board, and a cubit and a half *shall be* the breadth of one board.

17Two tenons *shall there be* in one board, set in order one against another: thus shalt thou make for all the boards of the tabernacle.

18And thou shalt make the boards for the tabernacle, twenty boards on the south side southward.

19And thou shalt make forty sockets of silver under the twenty boards; two sockets under one board for his two tenons, and two sockets under another board for his two tenons.

20And for the second side of the tabernacle on the north side *there shall be* twenty boards:

21And their forty sockets *of* silver; two sockets under one board, and two sockets under another board.

New International

of pure gold is to be used for the lampstand and all these accessories. 40See that you make them according to the pattern shown you on the mountain.

The Tabernacle

26 "MAKE THE tabernacle with ten curtains of finely twisted linen and blue, purple and scarlet yarn, with cherubim worked into them by a skilled craftsman. 2All the curtains are to be the same size—twenty-eight cubits long and four cubits wide.a 3Join five of the curtains together, and do the same with the other five. 4Make loops of blue material along the edge of the end curtain in one set, and do the same with the end curtain in the other set. 5Make fifty loops on one curtain and fifty loops on the end curtain of the other set, with the loops opposite each other. 6Then make fifty gold clasps and use them to fasten the curtains together so that the tabernacle is a unit.

7"Make curtains of goat hair for the tent over the tabernacle—eleven altogether. 8All eleven curtains are to be the same size—thirty cubits long and four cubits wide.b 9Join five of the curtains together into one set and the other six into another set. Fold the sixth curtain double at the front of the tent. 10Make fifty loops along the edge of the end curtain in one set and also along the edge of the end curtain in the other set. 11Then make fifty bronze clasps and put them in the loops to fasten the tent together as a unit. 12As for the additional length of the tent curtains, the half curtain that is left over is to hang down at the rear of the tabernacle. 13The tent curtains will be a cubitc longer on both sides; what is left will hang over the sides of the tabernacle so as to cover it. 14Make for the tent a covering of ram skins dyed red, and over that a covering of hides of sea cows.d

15"Make upright frames of acacia wood for the tabernacle. 16Each frame is to be ten cubits long and a cubit and a half wide.e 17with two projections set parallel to each other. Make all the frames of the tabernacle in this way. 18Make twenty frames for the south side of the tabernacle 19and make forty silver bases to go under them—two bases for each frame, one under each projection. 20For the other side, the north side of the tabernacle, make twenty frames 21and forty silver bases—two under each frame. 22Make six frames for the far end, that

---

a 2 That is, about 42 feet (about 12.5 meters) long and 6 feet (about 1.8 meters) wide   b 8 That is, about 45 feet (about 13.5 meters) long and 6 feet (about 1.8 meters) wide   c 13 That is, about 1 1/2 feet (about 0.5 meter)   d 14 That is, dugongs   e 16 That is, about 15 feet (about 4.5 meters) long and 2 1/4 feet (about 0.7 meter) wide

Living Bible

40"Be sure that everything you make follows the pattern I am showing you here on the mountain.

26 "MAKE THE tabernacle-tent from ten colored sheets of fine linen, forty-two feet long and six feet wide, dyed blue, purple, and scarlet, with figures of Guardian Angels embroidered on them. 3Join five sheets end to end for each side of the tent, forming two long pieces, one for each side. 4, 5Use loops at the edges to join these two long pieces together side by side. There are to be fifty loops on each side, opposite each other. 6Then make fifty gold clasps to fasten the loops together, so that the Tabernacle, the dwelling place of God, becomes a single unit.

7, 8"The roof of the Tabernacle is made of goat's hair tarpaulins. There are to be eleven of these tarpaulins, each forty-five feet across and six feet wide. 9Connect five of these tarpaulins into one wide section; and use the other six for another wide section. (The sixth tarpaulin will hang down to form a curtain across the front of the sacred tent.) 10, 11Use fifty loops along the edges of each of these two wide pieces, to join them together with fifty bronze clasps. Thus the two widths become one. 12There will be a 1½-foot length of this roof-covering hanging down from the back of the tent, 13and a 1½-foot length at the front. 14On top of these blankets is placed a layer of rams' skins, dyed red, and over them a top layer of goatskins. This completes the roof-covering.

15, 16"The framework of the sacred tent shall be made from acacia wood, each frame-piece being fifteen feet high and 2¼ feet wide, standing upright, 17with grooves on each side to mortise into the next upright piece. 18, 19Twenty of these frames will form the south side of the sacred tent, with forty silver bases for the frames to fit into—two bases under each piece of the frame. 20On the north side there will also be twenty of these frames, 21with their forty silver bases, two bases for each frame, one under each edge. 22On the west side there will be

New Revised Standard

all these utensils, shall be made from a talent of pure gold. 40 And see that you make them according to the pattern for them, which is being shown you on the mountain.

The Tabernacle

26 MOREOVER YOU shall make the tabernacle with ten curtains of fine twisted linen, and blue, purple, and crimson yarns; you shall make them with cherubim skillfully worked into them. 2 The length of each curtain shall be twenty-eight cubits, and the width of each curtain four cubits; all the curtains shall be of the same size. 3 Five curtains shall be joined to one another; and the other five curtains shall be joined to one another. 4 You shall make loops of blue on the edge of the outermost curtain in the first set; and likewise you shall make loops on the edge of the outermost curtain in the second set. 5 You shall make fifty loops on the one curtain, and you shall make fifty loops on the edge of the curtain that is in the second set; the loops shall be opposite one another. 6 You shall make fifty clasps of gold, and join the curtains to one another with the clasps, so that the tabernacle may be one whole.

7 You shall also make curtains of goats' hair for a tent over the tabernacle; you shall make eleven curtains. 8 The length of each curtain shall be thirty cubits, and the width of each curtain four cubits; the eleven curtains shall be of the same size. 9 You shall join five curtains by themselves, and six curtains by themselves, and the sixth curtain you shall double over at the front of the tent. 10 You shall make fifty loops on the edge of the curtain that is outermost in one set, and fifty loops on the edge of the curtain that is outermost in the second set.

11 You shall make fifty clasps of bronze, and put the clasps into the loops, and join the tent together, so that it may be one whole. 12 The part that remains of the curtains of the tent, the half curtain that remains, shall hang over the back of the tabernacle. 13 The cubit on the one side, and the cubit on the other side, of what remains in the length of the curtains of the tent, shall hang over the sides of the tabernacle, on this side and that side, to cover it. 14 You shall make for the tent a covering of tanned rams' skins and an outer covering of fine leather.f

The Framework

15 You shall make upright frames of acacia wood for the tabernacle. 16 Ten cubits shall be the length of a frame, and a cubit and a half the width of each frame. 17 There shall be two pegs in each frame to fit the frames together; you shall make these for all the frames of the tabernacle. 18 You shall make the frames for the tabernacle: twenty frames for the south side; 19 and you shall make forty bases of silver under the twenty frames, two bases under the first frame for its two pegs, and two bases under the next frame for its two pegs; 20 and for the second side of the tabernacle, on the north side twenty frames, 21 and their forty bases of silver, two bases under the first frame, and two bases under the next frame; 22 and for the rear of the tabernacle westward you

f Meaning of Heb uncertain

King James

22And for the sides of the tabernacle westward thou shalt make six boards.

23And two boards shalt thou make for the corners of the tabernacle in the two sides.

24And they shall be coupled together beneath, and they shall be coupled together above the head of it unto one ring: thus shall it be for them both; they shall be for the two corners.

25And they shall be eight boards, and their sockets *of* silver, sixteen sockets; two sockets under one board, and two sockets under another board.

26¶ And thou shalt make bars *of* shittim wood; five for the boards of the one side of the tabernacle,

27And five bars for the boards of the other side of the tabernacle, and five bars for the boards of the side of the tabernacle, for the two sides westward.

28And the middle bar in the midst of the boards shall reach from end to end.

29And thou shalt overlay the boards with gold, and make their rings *of* gold *for* places for the bars: and thou shalt overlay the bars with gold.

30And thou shalt rear up the tabernacle according to the fashion thereof which was shown thee in the mount.

31¶ And thou shalt make a veil *of* blue, and purple, and scarlet, and fine twined linen of cunning work: with cherubims shall it be made:

32And thou shalt hang it upon four pillars of shittim *wood* overlaid with gold: their hooks *shall be of* gold, upon the four sockets of silver.

33¶ And thou shalt hang up the veil under the taches, that thou mayest bring in thither within the veil the ark of the testimony: and the veil shall divide unto you between the holy *place* and the most holy.

34And thou shalt put the mercy seat upon the ark of the testimony in the most holy *place*.

35And thou shalt set the table without the veil, and the candlestick over against the table on the side of the tabernacle toward the south: and thou shalt put the table on the north side.

36And thou shalt make an hanging for the door of the tent, *of* blue, and purple, and scarlet, and fine twined linen, wrought with needlework.

37And thou shalt make for the hanging five pillars *of* shittim *wood*, and overlay them with gold, *and* their hooks *shall be of* gold: and thou shalt cast five sockets of brass for them.

27 AND THOU shalt make an altar of shittim wood, five cubits long, and five cubits broad; the altar shall be foursquare: and the height thereof *shall be* three cubits.

2And thou shalt make the horns of it upon the four corners thereof: his horns shall be of the same: and thou shalt overlay it with brass.

3And thou shalt make his pans to receive his ashes, and his shovels, and his basins, and his fleshhooks, and his firepans: all the vessels thereof thou shalt make *of* brass.

4And thou shalt make for it a grate of network *of* brass; and upon the net shalt thou make four brasen rings in the four corners thereof.

5And thou shalt put it under the compass of the altar beneath, that the net may be even to the midst of the altar.

6And thou shalt make staves for the altar, staves *of* shittim wood, and overlay them with brass.

7And the staves shall be put into the rings, and the staves shall be upon the two sides of the altar, to bear it.

8Hollow with boards shalt thou make it: as it was shown thee in the mount, so shall they make *it*.

New International

is, the west end of the tabernacle, 23and make two frames for the corners at the far end. 24At these two corners they must be double from the bottom all the way to the top, and fitted into a single ring; both shall be like that. 25So there will be eight frames and sixteen silver bases—two under each frame.

26"Also make crossbars of acacia wood: five for the frames on one side of the tabernacle, 27five for those on the other side, and five for the frames on the west, at the far end of the tabernacle. 28The center crossbar is to extend from end to end at the middle of the frames. 29Overlay the frames with gold and make gold rings to hold the crossbars. Also overlay the crossbars with gold.

30"Set up the tabernacle according to the plan shown you on the mountain.

31"Make a curtain of blue, purple and scarlet yarn and finely twisted linen, with cherubim worked into it by a skilled craftsman. 32Hang it with gold hooks on four posts of acacia wood overlaid with gold and standing on four silver bases. 33Hang the curtain from the clasps and place the ark of the Testimony behind the curtain. The curtain will separate the Holy Place from the Most Holy Place. 34Put the atonement cover on the ark of the Testimony in the Most Holy Place. 35Place the table outside the curtain on the north side of the tabernacle and put the lampstand opposite it on the south side.

36"For the entrance to the tent make a curtain of blue, purple and scarlet yarn and finely twisted linen—the work of an embroiderer. 37Make gold hooks for this curtain and five posts of acacia wood overlaid with gold. And cast five bronze bases for them.

The Altar of Burnt Offering

27 "BUILD AN altar of acacia wood, three cubits[a] high; it is to be square, five cubits long and five cubits wide.[b] 2Make a horn at each of the four corners, so that the horns and the altar are of one piece, and overlay the altar with bronze. 3Make all its utensils of bronze—its pots to remove the ashes, and its shovels, sprinkling bowls, meat forks and firepans. 4Make a grating for it, a bronze network, and make a bronze ring at each of the four corners of the network. 5Put it under the ledge of the altar so that it is halfway up the altar. 6Make poles of acacia wood for the altar and overlay them with bronze. 7The poles are to be inserted into the rings so they will be on two sides of the altar when it is carried. 8Make the altar hollow, out of boards. It is to be made just as you were shown on the mountain.

---

a *1* That is, about 4 1/2 feet (about 1.3 meters)　b *1* That is, about 7 1/2 feet (about 2.3 meters) long and wide

Living Bible

six frames, 23and two frames at each corner. 24These corner frames will be connected at the bottom and top with clasps. 25So, in all, there will be eight frames on that end of the building with sixteen silver bases for the frames—two bases under each frame.

26, 27"Make bars of acacia wood to run across the frames, five bars on each side of the Tabernacle. Also five bars for the rear of the building, facing westward. 28The middle bar, halfway up the frames, runs all the way from end to end of the Tabernacle. 29Overlay the frames with gold, and make gold rings to hold the bars; and also overlay the bars with gold. 30Set up this Tabernacle-tent in the manner I showed you on the mountain.

31"[Inside the Tabernaclec], make a curtain from fine linen, with blue, purple, and scarlet Guardian Angels embroidered into the cloth. 32Hang this curtain on gold hooks set into four pillars made from acacia wood overlaid with gold. The pillars are to be set in silver bases. 33Behind this curtain place the Ark containing the stone tablets engraved with God's laws. The curtain will separate the Holy Place and the Most Holy Place.

34"Now install the mercy place—the golden lid of the Ark—in the Most Holy Place. 35Place the table and lampstand across the room from each other on the outer side of the veil, the lampstand on the south and the table on the north.

36"As a screen for the door of the sacred tent, make another curtain from fine linen, skillfully embroidered in blue, purple, and scarlet. 37Hang this curtain on gold hooks set into posts made from acacia wood overlaid with bronze. The posts are to rest on bronze bases.

New Revised Standard

shall make six frames. 23 You shall make two frames for corners of the tabernacle in the rear; 24they shall be separate beneath, but joined at the top, at the first ring; it shall be the same with both of them; they shall form the two corners. 25 And so there shall be eight frames, with their bases of silver, sixteen bases; two bases under the first frame, and two bases under the next frame.

26 You shall make bars of acacia wood, five for the frames of the one side of the tabernacle, 27 and five bars for the frames of the other side of the tabernacle, and five bars for the frames of the side of the tabernacle at the rear westward. 28 The middle bar, halfway up the frames, shall pass through from end to end. 29 You shall overlay the frames with gold, and shall make their rings of gold to hold the bars; and you shall overlay the bars with gold. 30 Then you shall erect the tabernacle according to the plan for it that you were shown on the mountain.

The Curtain

31 You shall make a curtain of blue, purple, and crimson yarns, and of fine twisted linen; it shall be made with cherubim skillfully worked into it. 32 You shall hang it on four pillars of acacia overlaid with gold, which have hooks of gold and rest on four bases of silver. 33 You shall hang the curtain under the clasps, and bring the ark of the covenantd in there, within the curtain; and the curtain shall separate for you the holy place from the most holy. 34 You shall put the mercy seate on the ark of the covenantd in the most holy place. 35 You shall set the table outside the curtain, and the lampstand on the south side of the tabernacle opposite the table; and you shall put the table on the north side.

36 You shall make a screen for the entrance of the tent, of blue, purple, and crimson yarns, and of fine twisted linen, embroidered with needlework. 37 You shall make for the screen five pillars of acacia, and overlay them with gold; their hooks shall be of gold, and you shall cast five bases of bronze for them.

27 "USING ACACIA wood, make a square altar 7½ feet wide, and 4½ feet high. 2Make horns for the four corners of the altar, attach them firmly, and overlay everything with bronze. 3The ash buckets, shovels, basins, carcass-hooks, and fire pans are all to be made of bronze. 4Make a bronze grating, with a metal ring at each corner, 5and fit the grating halfway down into the fire box, resting it upon the ledge built there. 6For moving the altar, make poles from acacia wood overlaid with bronze. 7To carry it, put the poles into the rings at each side of the altar. 8The altar is to be hollow, made from planks, just as was shown you on the mountain.

The Altar of Burnt Offering

27 YOU SHALL make the altar of acacia wood, five cubits long and five cubits wide; the altar shall be square, and it shall be three cubits high. 2 You shall make horns for it on its four corners; its horns shall be of one piece with it, and you shall overlay it with bronze. 3 You shall make pots for it to receive its ashes, and shovels and basins and forks and firepans; you shall make all its utensils of bronze. 4 You shall also make for it a grating, a network of bronze; and on the net you shall make four bronze rings at its four corners. 5 You shall set it under the ledge of the altar so that the net shall extend halfway down the altar. 6 You shall make poles for the altar, poles of acacia wood, and overlay them with bronze; 7 the poles shall be put through the rings, so that the poles shall be on the two sides of the altar when it is carried. 8 You shall make it hollow, with boards. They shall be made just as you were shown on the mountain.

c 26:31 Inside the Tabernacle, implied.   d Or treaty, or testimony; Heb eduth   e Or the cover

King James

9¶ And thou shalt make the court of the tabernacle: for the south side southward *there shall be* hangings for the court *of* fine twined linen of an hundred cubits long for one side:

10And the twenty pillars thereof and their twenty sockets *shall be of* brass; the hooks of the pillars and their fillets *shall be of* silver.

11And likewise for the north side in length *there shall be* hangings of an hundred *cubits* long, and his twenty pillars and their twenty sockets *of* brass; the hooks of the pillars and their fillets *of* silver.

12¶ And *for* the breadth of the court on the west side *shall be* hangings of fifty cubits: their pillars ten, and their sockets ten.

13And the breadth of the court on the east side eastward *shall be* fifty cubits.

14The hangings of one side *of the gate shall be* fifteen cubits: their pillars three, and their sockets three.

15And on the other side *shall be* hangings fifteen *cubits:* their pillars three, and their sockets three.

16¶ And for the gate of the court *shall be* an hanging of twenty cubits, *of* blue, and purple, and scarlet, and fine twined linen, wrought with needlework: *and* their pillars *shall be* four, and their sockets four.

17All the pillars round about the court *shall be* filleted with silver; their hooks *shall be of* silver, and their sockets *of* brass.

18¶ The length of the court *shall be* an hundred cubits, and the breadth fifty every where, and the height five cubits *of* fine twined linen, and their sockets *of* brass.

19All the vessels of the tabernacle in all the service thereof, and all the pins thereof, and all the pins of the court, *shall be of* brass.

20¶ And thou shalt command the children of Israel, that they bring thee pure oil olive beaten for the light, to cause the lamp to burn always.

21In the tabernacle of the congregation without the veil, which *is* before the testimony, Aaron and his sons shall order it from evening to morning before the LORD: *it shall be* a statute for ever unto their generations on the behalf of the children of Israel.

28 AND TAKE thou unto thee Aaron thy brother, and his sons with him, from among the children of Israel, that he may minister unto me in the priest's office, *even* Aaron, Nadab and Abihu, Eleazar and Ithamar, Aaron's sons.

2And thou shalt make holy garments for Aaron thy brother for glory and for beauty.

3And thou shalt speak unto all *that are* wisehearted, whom I have filled with the spirit of wisdom, that they may make Aaron's garments to consecrate him, that he may minister unto me in the priest's office.

4And these *are* the garments which they shall make; a breastplate, and an ephod, and a robe, and a broidered coat, a mitre, and a girdle: and they shall make holy garments for Aaron thy brother, and his sons, that he may minister unto me in the priest's office.

5And they shall take gold, and blue, and purple, and scarlet, and fine linen.

6¶ And they shall make the ephod *of* gold, *of* blue, and *of* purple, *of* scarlet, and fine twined linen, with cunning work.

7It shall have the two shoulderpieces thereof joined at the two edges thereof; and *so* it shall be joined together.

8And the curious girdle of the ephod, which *is* upon it, shall be of the same, according to the work thereof; *even of* gold, *of* blue, and purple, and scarlet, and fine twined linen.

New International

The Courtyard

9"Make a courtyard for the tabernacle. The south side shall be a hundred cubits[a] long and is to have curtains of finely twisted linen, 10with twenty posts and twenty bronze bases and with silver hooks and bands on the posts. 11The north side shall also be a hundred cubits long and is to have curtains, with twenty posts and twenty bronze bases and with silver hooks and bands on the posts.

12"The west end of the courtyard shall be fifty cubits[b] wide and have curtains, with ten posts and ten bases. 13On the east end, toward the sunrise, the courtyard shall also be fifty cubits wide. 14Curtains fifteen cubits[c] long are to be on one side of the entrance, with three posts and three bases, 15and curtains fifteen cubits long are to be on the other side, with three posts and three bases.

16"For the entrance to the courtyard, provide a curtain twenty cubits[d] long, of blue, purple and scarlet yarn and finely twisted linen—the work of an embroiderer—with four posts and four bases. 17All the posts around the courtyard are to have silver bands and hooks, and bronze bases. 18The courtyard shall be a hundred cubits long and fifty cubits wide,[e] with curtains of finely twisted linen five cubits[f] high, and with bronze bases. 19All the other articles used in the service of the tabernacle, whatever their function, including all the tent pegs for it and those for the courtyard, are to be of bronze.

Oil for the Lampstand

20"Command the Israelites to bring you clear oil of pressed olives for the light so that the lamps may be kept burning. 21In the Tent of Meeting, outside the curtain that is in front of the Testimony, Aaron and his sons are to keep the lamps burning before the LORD from evening till morning. This is to be a lasting ordinance among the Israelites for the generations to come.

The Priestly Garments

28 "HAVE AARON your brother brought to you from among the Israelites, along with his sons Nadab and Abihu, Eleazar and Ithamar, so they may serve me as priests. 2Make sacred garments for your brother Aaron, to give him dignity and honor. 3Tell all the skilled men to whom I have given wisdom in such matters that they are to make garments for Aaron, for his consecration, so he may serve me as priest. 4These are the garments they are to make: a breastpiece, an ephod, a robe, a woven tunic, a turban and a sash. They are to make these sacred garments for your brother Aaron and his sons, so they may serve me as priests. 5Have them use gold, and blue, purple and scarlet yarn, and fine linen.

The Ephod

6"Make the ephod of gold, and of blue, purple and scarlet yarn, and of finely twisted linen—the work of a skilled craftsman. 7It is to have two shoulder pieces attached to two of its corners, so it can be fastened. 8Its skillfully woven waistband is to be like it—of one piece with the ephod and made with gold, and with blue, purple and scarlet yarn, and with finely twisted linen.

---

[a] 9 That is, about 150 feet (about 46 meters); also in verse 11   [b] 12 That is, about 75 feet (about 23 meters); also in verse 13   [c] 14 That is, about 22 1/2 feet (about 6.9 meters); also in verse 15   [d] 16 That is, about 30 feet (about 9 meters)   [e] 18 That is, about 150 feet (about 46 meters) long and 75 feet (about 23 meters) wide   [f] 18 That is, about 7 1/2 feet (about 2.3 meters)

Living Bible

9, 10"Then make a courtyard for the Tabernacle, enclosed with curtains made from fine-twined linen. On the south side the curtains will stretch for 150 feet, and be held up by twenty posts, fitting into twenty bronze post holders. The curtains will be held up with silver hooks attached to silver rods, attached to the posts. 11It will be the same on the north side of the court—150 feet of curtains held up by twenty posts fitted into bronze sockets, with silver hooks and rods. 12The west side of the court will be seventy-five feet wide, with ten posts and ten sockets. 13The east side will also be seventy-five feet. 14, 15On each side of the entrance there will be 22½ feet of curtain, held up by three posts imbedded in three sockets.

16"The entrance to the court will be a thirty-foot-wide curtain, made of beautifully embroidered blue, purple, and scarlet fine-twined linen, and attached to four posts imbedded in their four sockets. 17All the posts around the court are to be connected by silver rods, using silver hooks, the posts being imbedded in solid bronze bases. 18So the entire court will be 150 feet long, and 75 feet wide, with curtain walls 7½ feet high, made from fine-twined linen.

19"All utensils used in the work of the Tabernacle, including all the pins and pegs for hanging the utensils on the walls, will be made of bronze.

20"Instruct the people of Israel to bring you pure olive oil to use in the lamps of the Tabernacle, to burn there continually. 21Aaron and his sons shall place this eternal flame in the outer holy room, tending it day and night before the Lord, so that it never goes out. This is a permanent rule for the people of Israel.

28 "CONSECRATE AARON your brother, and his sons Nadab, Abihu, Eleazar, and Ithamar, to be priests, to minister to me. 2Make special clothes for Aaron, to indicate his separation to God—beautiful garments that will lend dignity to his work. 3Instruct those to whom I have given special skill as tailors to make the garments that will set him apart from others, so that he may minister to me in the priest's office. 4This is the wardrobe they shall make: a chestpiece, an ephod,g a robe, an embroidered shirt, a turban, and a sash. They shall also make special garments for Aaron's sons.

5, 6"The ephod shall be made by the most skilled of the workmen, using gold, blue, purple, and scarlet threads of fine linen. 7It will consist of two pieces, front and back, joined at the shoulders. 8And the sash shall be made of the same material—threads of gold, blue, purple, and scarlet fine-twined linen. 9Take two onyx

New Revised Standard

The Court and Its Hangings

9 You shall make the court of the tabernacle. On the south side the court shall have hangings of fine twisted linen one hundred cubits long for that side; 10its twenty pillars and their twenty bases shall be of bronze, but the hooks of the pillars and their bands shall be of silver. 11Likewise for its length on the north side there shall be hangings one hundred cubits long, their pillars twenty and their bases twenty, of bronze, but the hooks of the pillars and their bands shall be of silver. 12For the width of the court on the west side there shall be fifty cubits of hangings, with ten pillars and ten bases. 13The width of the court on the front to the east shall be fifty cubits. 14There shall be fifteen cubits of hangings on the one side, with three pillars and three bases. 15There shall be fifteen cubits of hangings on the other side, with three pillars and three bases. 16For the gate of the court there shall be a screen twenty cubits long, of blue, purple, and crimson yarns, and of fine twisted linen, embroidered with needlework; it shall have four pillars and with them four bases. 17All the pillars around the court shall be banded with silver; their hooks shall be of silver, and their bases of bronze. 18The length of the court shall be one hundred cubits, the width fifty, and the height five cubits, with hangings of fine twisted linen and bases of bronze. 19All the utensils of the tabernacle for every use, and all its pegs and all the pegs of the court, shall be of bronze.

The Oil for the Lamp

20 You shall further command the Israelites to bring you pure oil of beaten olives for the light, so that a lamp may be set up to burn regularly. 21In the tent of meeting, outside the curtain that is before the covenant,h Aaron and his sons shall tend it from evening to morning before the LORD. It shall be a perpetual ordinance to be observed throughout their generations by the Israelites.

Vestments for the Priesthood

28 THEN BRING near to you your brother Aaron, and his sons with him, from among the Israelites, to serve me as priests—Aaron and Aaron's sons, Nadab and Abihu, Eleazar and Ithamar. 2You shall make sacred vestments for the glorious adornment of your brother Aaron. 3And you shall speak to all who have ability, whom I have endowed with skill, that they make Aaron's vestments to consecrate him for my priesthood. 4These are the vestments that they shall make: a breastpiece, an ephod, a robe, a checkered tunic, a turban, and a sash. When they make these sacred vestments for your brother Aaron and his sons to serve me as priests, 5they shall use gold, blue, purple, and crimson yarns, and fine linen.

The Ephod

6 They shall make the ephod of gold, of blue, purple, and crimson yarns, and of fine twisted linen, skillfully worked. 7It shall have two shoulder-pieces attached to its two edges, so that it may be joined together. 8The decorated band on it shall be of the same workmanship and materials, of gold, of blue, purple, and crimson yarns, and of fine twisted linen. 9You shall take two

---

g 28:4 ephod. Apparently a sort of sleeveless tunic reaching from the shoulders to below the knees.

h Or treaty, or testimony; Heb eduth

King James

9And thou shalt take two onyx stones, and grave on them the names of the children of Israel:

10Six of their names on one stone, and *the other* six names of the rest on the other stone, according to their birth.

11With the work of an engraver in stone, *like* the engravings of a signet, shalt thou engrave the two stones with the names of the children of Israel: thou shalt make them to be set in ouches of gold.

12And thou shalt put the two stones upon the shoulders of the ephod *for* stones of memorial unto the children of Israel: and Aaron shall bear their names before the LORD upon his two shoulders for a memorial.

13¶ And thou shalt make ouches *of* gold;

14And two chains *of* pure gold at the ends; *of* wreathen work shalt thou make them, and fasten the wreathen chains to the ouches.

15¶ And thou shalt make the breastplate of judgment with cunning work; after the work of the ephod thou shalt make it; *of* gold, *of* blue, and *of* purple, and *of* scarlet, and *of* fine twined linen, shalt thou make it.

16Foursquare it shall be *being* doubled; a span *shall be* the length thereof, and a span *shall be* the breadth thereof.

17And thou shalt set in it settings of stones, *even* four rows of stones: *the first* row *shall be* a sardius, a topaz, and a carbuncle: *this shall be* the first row.

18And the second row *shall be* an emerald, a sapphire, and a diamond.

19And the third row a ligure, an agate, and an amethyst.

20And the fourth row a beryl, and an onyx, and a jasper: they shall be set in gold in their inclosings.

21And the stones shall be with the names of the children of Israel, twelve, according to their names, *like* the engravings of a signet; every one with his name shall they be according to the twelve tribes.

22¶ And thou shalt make upon the breastplate chains at the ends *of* wreathen work *of* pure gold.

23And thou shalt make upon the breastplate two rings of gold, and shalt put the two rings on the two ends of the breastplate.

24And thou shalt put the two wreathen *chains* of gold in the two rings *which are* on the ends of the breastplate.

25And *the other* two ends of the two wreathen *chains* thou shalt fasten in the two ouches, and put *them* on the shoulderpieces of the ephod before it.

26¶ And thou shalt make two rings of gold, and thou shalt put them upon the two ends of the breastplate in the border thereof, which *is* in the side of the ephod inward.

27And two *other* rings of gold thou shalt make, and shalt put them on the two sides of the ephod underneath, toward the forepart thereof, over against the *other* coupling thereof, above the curious girdle of the ephod.

28And they shall bind the breastplate by the rings thereof unto the rings of the ephod with a lace of blue, that *it* may be above the curious girdle of the ephod, and that the breastplate be not loosed from the ephod.

29And Aaron shall bear the names of the children of Israel in the breastplate of judgment upon his heart, when he goeth in unto the holy *place,* for a memorial before the LORD continually.

30¶ And thou shalt put in the breastplate of judgment the Urim and the Thummim; and they shall be upon Aaron's heart, when he goeth in before the LORD: and Aaron shall bear the judgment of the children of Israel upon his heart before the LORD continually.

31¶ And thou shalt make the robe of the ephod all *of* blue.

32And there shall be an hole in the top of it, in the midst thereof: it shall have a binding of woven work round about the hole of it, as it were the hole of an habergeon, that it be not rent.

New International

9"Take two onyx stones and engrave on them the names of the sons of Israel 10in the order of their birth— six names on one stone and the remaining six on the other. 11Engrave the names of the sons of Israel on the two stones the way a gem cutter engraves a seal. Then mount the stones in gold filigree settings 12and fasten them on the shoulder pieces of the ephod as memorial stones for the sons of Israel. Aaron is to bear the names on his shoulders as a memorial before the LORD. 13Make gold filigree settings 14and two braided chains of pure gold, like a rope, and attach the chains to the settings.

The Breastpiece

15"Fashion a breastpiece for making decisions—the work of a skilled craftsman. Make it like the ephod: of gold, and of blue, purple and scarlet yarn, and of finely twisted linen. 16It is to be square—a span[a] long and a span wide—and folded double. 17Then mount four rows of precious stones on it. In the first row there shall be a ruby, a topaz and a beryl; 18in the second row a turquoise, a sapphire[b] and an emerald; 19in the third row a jacinth, an agate and an amethyst; 20in the fourth row a chrysolite, an onyx and a jasper.[c] Mount them in gold filigree settings. 21There are to be twelve stones, one for each of the names of the sons of Israel, each engraved like a seal with the name of one of the twelve tribes.

22"For the breastpiece make braided chains of pure gold, like a rope. 23Make two gold rings for it and fasten them to two corners of the breastpiece. 24Fasten the two gold chains to the rings at the corners of the breastpiece, 25and the other ends of the chains to the two settings, attaching them to the shoulder pieces of the ephod at the front. 26Make two gold rings and attach them to the other two corners of the breastpiece on the inside edge next to the ephod. 27Make two more gold rings and attach them to the bottom of the shoulder pieces on the front of the ephod, close to the seam just above the waistband of the ephod. 28The rings of the breastpiece are to be tied to the rings of the ephod with blue cord, connecting it to the waistband, so that the breastpiece will not swing out from the ephod.

29"Whenever Aaron enters the Holy Place, he will bear the names of the sons of Israel over his heart on the breastpiece of decision as a continuing memorial before the LORD. 30Also put the Urim and the Thummim in the breastpiece, so they may be over Aaron's heart whenever he enters the presence of the LORD. Thus Aaron will always bear the means of making decisions for the Israelites over his heart before the LORD.

Other Priestly Garments

31"Make the robe of the ephod entirely of blue cloth, 32with an opening for the head in its center. There shall be a woven edge like a collar[d] around this opening, so that it will not tear. 33Make pomegranates of blue, pur-

---

[a] *16* That is, about 9 inches (about 22 centimeters)   [b] *18* Or *lapis lazuli*
[c] *20* The precise identification of some of these precious stones is uncertain.
[d] *32* The meaning of the Hebrew for this word is uncertain.

Living Bible

stones, and engrave on them the names of the tribes of Israel. 10Six names shall be on each stone, so that all the tribes are named in the order of their births. 11When engraving these names, use the same technique as in making a seal; and mount the stones in gold settings. 12Fasten the two stones upon the shoulders of the ephod, as memorial stones for the people of Israel: Aaron will carry their names before the Lord as a constant reminder. 13, 14Two chains of pure, twisted gold shall be made and attached to gold clasps on the shoulder of the ephod.

15"Then, using the most careful workmanship, make a chestpiece to be used as God's oracle; use the same gold, blue, purple, and scarlet threads of fine-twined linen as you did in the ephod. 16This chestpiece is to be of two folds of cloth, forming a pouch nine inches square. 17Attach to it four rows of stones: A ruby, a topaz, and an emerald shall be in the first row. 18The second row will be carbuncle, a sapphire, and a diamond. 19The third row will be an amber, an agate, and an amethyst. 20The fourth row will be an onyx, a beryl, and a jasper—all set in gold settings. 21Each stone will represent one of the tribes of Israel and the name of that tribe will be engraved upon it like a seal.

22, 23, 24"Attach the top of the chestpiece to the ephod by means of two twisted cords of pure gold. One end of each cord is attached to gold rings placed at the outer top edge of the chestpiece. 25The other ends of the two cords are attached to the front edges of the two settings of the onyx stones on the shoulder of the ephod. 26Then make two more gold rings and place them on the two lower, inside edges of the chestpiece; 27also make two other gold rings for the bottom front edge of the ephod at the sash. 28Now attach the bottom of the chestpiece to the bottom rings of the ephod by means of blue ribbons; this will prevent the chestpiece from coming loose from the ephod. 29In this way Aaron shall carry the names of the tribes of Israel on the chestpiece over his heart (it is God's oracle) when he goes in to the Holy Place; thus Jehovah will be reminded of them continually. 30, 31Insert into the pocket of the chestpiece the Urim and Thummim,e to be carried over Aaron's heart when he goes in before Jehovah. Thus Aaron shall always be carrying the oracle over his heart when he goes in before the Lord.

"The ephod shall be made of blue cloth, 32with an opening for Aaron's head. It shall have a woven band around this opening, just as on the neck of a coat of mail, so that it will not fray. 33, 34The bottom edge of the

New Revised Standard

onyx stones, and engrave on them the names of the sons of Israel, 10six of their names on the one stone, and the names of the remaining six on the other stone, in the order of their birth. 11 As a gem-cutter engraves signets, so you shall engrave the two stones with the names of the sons of Israel; you shall mount them in settings of gold filigree. 12You shall set the two stones on the shoulder-pieces of the ephod, as stones of remembrance for the sons of Israel; and Aaron shall bear their names before the LORD on his two shoulders for remembrance. 13You shall make settings of gold filigree, 14and two chains of pure gold, twisted like cords; and you shall attach the corded chains to the settings.

The Breastplate

15 You shall make a breastpiece of judgment, in skilled work; you shall make it in the style of the ephod; of gold, of blue and purple and crimson yarns, and of fine twisted linen you shall make it. 16It shall be square and doubled, a span in length and a span in width. 17 You shall set in it four rows of stones. A row of carnelian,f chrysolite, and emerald shall be the first row; 18and the second row a turquoise, a sapphire and a moonstone; 19and the third row a jacinth, an agate, and an amethyst; 20and the fourth row a beryl, an onyx, and a jasper; they shall be set in gold filigree. 21There shall be twelve stones with names corresponding to the names of the sons of Israel; they shall be like signets, each engraved with its name, for the twelve tribes. 22You shall make for the breastpiece chains of pure gold, twisted like cords; 23and you shall make for the breastpiece two rings of gold, and put the two rings on the two edges of the breastpiece. 24You shall put the two cords of gold in the two rings at the edges of the breastpiece; 25the two ends of the two cords you shall attach to the two settings, and so attach it in front to the shoulder-pieces of the ephod. 26 You shall make two rings of gold, and put them at the two ends of the breastpiece, on its inside edge next to the ephod. 27You shall make two rings of gold, and attach them in front to the lower part of the two shoulder-pieces of the ephod, at its joining above the decorated band of the ephod. 28The breastpiece shall be bound by its rings to the rings of the ephod with a blue cord, so that it may lie on the decorated band of the ephod, and so that the breastpiece shall not come loose from the ephod. 29So Aaron shall bear the names of the sons of Israel in the breastpiece of judgment on his heart when he goes into the holy place, for a continual remembrance before the LORD. 30In the breastpiece of judgment you shall put the Urim and the Thummim, and they shall be on Aaron's heart when he goes in before the LORD; thus Aaron shall bear the judgment of the Israelites on his heart before the LORD continually.

Other Priestly Vestments

31 You shall make the robe of the ephod all of blue. 32It shall have an opening for the head in the middle of it, with a woven binding around the opening, like the opening in a coat of mail,h so that it may not be torn.

---

e 28:30 *Urim and Thummim.* What they looked like has been lost in antiquity. They were perhaps two gem-stones located in the breastplate of the high priest. They were marked in some way and used by the High Priest to determine God's "yes" or "no" on urgent matters.

f The identity of several of these stones is uncertain   g Or *lapis lazuli*   h Meaning of Heb uncertain

King James

33¶ And *beneath* upon the hem of it thou shalt make pomegranates *of* blue, and *of* purple, and *of* scarlet, round about the hem thereof; and bells of gold between them round about:

34A golden bell and a pomegranate, a golden bell and a pomegranate, upon the hem of the robe round about.

35And it shall be upon Aaron to minister: and his sound shall be heard when he goeth in unto the holy *place* before the LORD, and when he cometh out, that he die not.

36¶ And thou shalt make a plate *of* pure gold, and grave upon it, *like* the engravings of a signet, HOLINESS TO THE LORD.

37And thou shalt put it on a blue lace, that it may be upon the mitre; upon the forefront of the mitre it shall be.

38And it shall be upon Aaron's forehead, that Aaron may bear the iniquity of the holy things, which the children of Israel shall hallow in all their holy gifts; and it shall be always upon his forehead, that they may be accepted before the LORD.

39¶ And thou shalt embroider the coat of fine linen, and thou shalt make the mitre *of* fine linen, and thou shalt make the girdle *of* needlework.

40¶ And for Aaron's sons thou shalt make coats, and thou shalt make for them girdles, and bonnets shalt thou make for them, for glory and for beauty.

41And thou shalt put them upon Aaron thy brother, and his sons with him; and shalt anoint them, and consecrate them, and sanctify them, that they may minister unto me in the priest's office.

42And thou shalt make them linen breeches to cover their nakedness; from the loins even unto the thighs they shall reach:

43And they shall be upon Aaron, and upon his sons, when they come in unto the tabernacle of the congregation, or when they come near unto the altar to minister in the holy *place;* that they bear not iniquity, and die: *it shall be* a statute for ever unto him and his seed after him.

29 AND THIS *is* the thing that thou shalt do unto them to hallow them, to minister unto me in the priest's office: Take one young bullock, and two rams without blemish,

2And unleavened bread, and cakes unleavened tempered with oil, and wafers unleavened anointed with oil: *of* wheaten flour shalt thou make them.

3And thou shalt put them into one basket, and bring them in the basket, with the bullock and the two rams.

4And Aaron and his sons thou shalt bring unto the door of the tabernacle of the congregation, and shalt wash them with water.

5And thou shalt take the garments, and put upon Aaron the coat, and the robe of the ephod, and the ephod, and the breastplate, and gird him with the curious girdle of the ephod:

6And thou shalt put the mitre upon his head, and put the holy crown upon the mitre.

7Then shalt thou take the anointing oil, and pour *it* upon his head, and anoint him.

8And thou shalt bring his sons, and put coats upon them.

9And thou shalt gird them with girdles, Aaron and his sons, and put the bonnets on them: and the priest's office shall be theirs for a perpetual statute: and thou shalt consecrate Aaron and his sons.

10And thou shalt cause a bullock to be brought before the tabernacle of the congregation: and Aaron and his sons shall put their hands upon the head of the bullock.

11And thou shalt kill the bullock before the LORD, *by* the door of the tabernacle of the congregation.

New International

ple and scarlet yarn around the hem of the robe, with gold bells between them. 34The gold bells and the pomegranates are to alternate around the hem of the robe. 35Aaron must wear it when he ministers. The sound of the bells will be heard when he enters the Holy Place before the LORD and when he comes out, so that he will not die.

36"Make a plate of pure gold and engrave on it as on a seal: HOLY TO THE LORD. 37Fasten a blue cord to it to attach it to the turban; it is to be on the front of the turban. 38It will be on Aaron's forehead, and he will bear the guilt involved in the sacred gifts the Israelites consecrate, whatever their gifts may be. It will be on Aaron's forehead continually so that they will be acceptable to the LORD.

39"Weave the tunic of fine linen and make the turban of fine linen. The sash is to be the work of an embroiderer. 40Make tunics, sashes and headbands for Aaron's sons, to give them dignity and honor. 41After you put these clothes on your brother Aaron and his sons, anoint and ordain them. Consecrate them so they may serve me as priests.

42"Make linen undergarments as a covering for the body, reaching from the waist to the thigh. 43Aaron and his sons must wear them whenever they enter the Tent of Meeting or approach the altar to minister in the Holy Place, so that they will not incur guilt and die.

"This is to be a lasting ordinance for Aaron and his descendants.

Consecration of the Priests

29 "THIS IS what you are to do to consecrate them, so they may serve me as priests: Take a young bull and two rams without defect. 2And from fine wheat flour, without yeast, make bread, and cakes mixed with oil, and wafers spread with oil. 3Put them in a basket and present them in it—along with the bull and the two rams. 4Then bring Aaron and his sons to the entrance to the Tent of Meeting and wash them with water. 5Take the garments and dress Aaron with the tunic, the robe of the ephod, the ephod itself and the breastpiece. Fasten the ephod on him by its skillfully woven waistband. 6Put the turban on his head and attach the sacred diadem to the turban. 7Take the anointing oil and anoint him by pouring it on his head. 8Bring his sons and dress them in tunics 9and put headbands on them. Then tie sashes on Aaron and his sons.[a] The priesthood is theirs by a lasting ordinance. In this way you shall ordain Aaron and his sons.

10"Bring the bull to the front of the Tent of Meeting, and Aaron and his sons shall lay their hands on its head. 11Slaughter it in the LORD's presence at the entrance to the Tent of Meeting. 12Take some of the bull's blood and

Living Bible

ephod shall be embroidered with blue, purple, and scarlet pomegranates, alternated with gold bells. ³⁵Aaron shall wear the ephod whenever he goes in to minister to the Lord; the bells will tinkle as he goes in and out of the presence of the Lord in the Holy Place, so that he will not die.

³⁶"Next, make a plate of pure gold and engrave on it, just as you would upon a seal, 'Consecrated to Jehovah.' ³⁷, ³⁸This plate is to be attached by means of a blue ribbon to the front of Aaron's turban. In this way Aaron will be wearing it upon his forehead, and thus bear the guilt connected with any errors regarding the offerings of the people of Israel. It shall always be worn when he goes into the presence of the Lord, so that the people will be accepted and forgiven.

³⁹"Weave Aaron's embroidered shirt from fine-twined linen, using a checkerboard pattern; make the turban, too, of this linen; and make him an embroidered sash.

⁴⁰"Then, for Aaron's sons, make robes, sashes, and turbans to give them honor and respect. ⁴¹Clothe Aaron and his sons with these garments, and then dedicate these men to their ministry by anointing their heads with olive oil, thus sanctifying them as the priests, my ministers. ⁴²Also make linen undershorts for them, to be worn beneath their robes next to their bodies, reaching from hips to knees. ⁴³These are to be worn whenever Aaron and his sons go into the Tabernacle or to the altar in the Holy Place, lest they be guilty and die. This is a permanent ordinance for Aaron and his sons.

29 "THIS IS the ceremony for the dedication of Aaron and his sons as priests: get a young bull and two rams with no defects, ²and bread made without yeast, and thin sheets of sweetened bread mingled with oil, and unleavened wafers with oil poured over them. (The various kinds of bread must be made with finely ground wheat flour.) ³, ⁴Place the bread in a basket and bring it to the entrance of the Tabernacle, along with the young bull and the two rams.

"Bathe Aaron and his sons there at the entrance. ⁵Then put Aaron's robe on him, and the embroidered shirt, ephod, chestpiece, and sash, ⁶and place on his head the turban with the gold plate. ⁷Then take the anointing oil and pour it upon his head. ⁸Next, dress his sons in their robes, ⁹with their woven sashes, and place caps on their heads. They will then be priests forever; thus you shall consecrate Aaron and his sons.

¹⁰"Then bring the young bull to the Tabernacle, and Aaron and his sons shall lay their hands upon its head; ¹¹and you shall kill it before the Lord, at the entrance of the Tabernacle. ¹²Place its blood upon the horns of the

New Revised Standard

³³On its lower hem you shall make pomegranates of blue, purple, and crimson yarns, all around the lower hem, with bells of gold between them all around—³⁴a golden bell and a pomegranate alternating all around the lower hem of the robe. ³⁵Aaron shall wear it when he ministers, and its sound shall be heard when he goes into the holy place before the LORD, and when he comes out, so that he may not die.

36 You shall make a rosette of pure gold, and engrave on it, like the engraving of a signet, "Holy to the LORD." ³⁷You shall fasten it on the turban with a blue cord; it shall be on the front of the turban. ³⁸It shall be on Aaron's forehead, and Aaron shall take on himself any guilt incurred in the holy offering that the Israelites consecrate as their sacred donations; it shall always be on his forehead, in order that they may find favor before the LORD.

39 You shall make the checkered tunic of fine linen, and you shall make a turban of fine linen, and you shall make a sash embroidered with needlework.

40 For Aaron's sons you shall make tunics and sashes and headdresses; you shall make them for their glorious adornment. ⁴¹You shall put them on your brother Aaron, and on his sons with him, and shall anoint them and ordain them and consecrate them, so that they may serve me as priests. ⁴²You shall make for them linen undergarments to cover their naked flesh; they shall reach from the hips to the thighs; ⁴³Aaron and his sons shall wear them when they go into the tent of meeting, or when they come near the altar to minister in the holy place; or they will bring guilt on themselves and die. This shall be a perpetual ordinance for him and for his descendants after him.

The Ordination of the Priests

29 NOW THIS is what you shall do to them to consecrate them, so that they may serve me as priests. Take one young bull and two rams without blemish, ²and unleavened bread, unleavened cakes mixed with oil, and unleavened wafers spread with oil. You shall make them of choice wheat flour. ³You shall put them in one basket and bring them in the basket, and bring the bull and the two rams. ⁴You shall bring Aaron and his sons to the entrance of the tent of meeting, and wash them with water. ⁵Then you shall take the vestments, and put on Aaron the tunic and the robe of the ephod, and the ephod, and the breastpiece, and gird him with the decorated band of the ephod; ⁶and you shall set the turban on his head, and put the holy diadem on the turban. ⁷You shall take the anointing oil, and pour it on his head and anoint him. ⁸Then you shall bring his sons, and put tunics on them, ⁹and you shall gird them with sashesᵇ and tie headdresses on them; and the priesthood shall be theirs by a perpetual ordinance. You shall then ordain Aaron and his sons.

10 You shall bring the bull in front of the tent of meeting. Aaron and his sons shall lay their hands on the head of the bull, ¹¹and you shall slaughter the bull before the LORD, at the entrance of the tent of meeting, ¹²and

---

ᵇ Gk: Heb *sashes, Aaron and his sons*

King James

12And thou shalt take of the blood of the bullock, and put *it* upon the horns of the altar with thy finger, and pour all the blood beside the bottom of the altar.

13And thou shalt take all the fat that covereth the inwards, and the caul *that is* above the liver, and the two kidneys, and the fat that *is* upon them, and burn *them* upon the altar.

14But the flesh of the bullock, and his skin, and his dung, shalt thou burn with fire without the camp: it *is* a sin offering.

15¶ Thou shalt also take one ram; and Aaron and his sons shall put their hands upon the head of the ram.

16And thou shalt slay the ram, and thou shalt take his blood, and sprinkle *it* round about upon the altar.

17And thou shalt cut the ram in pieces, and wash the inwards of him, and his legs, and put *them* unto his pieces, and unto his head.

18And thou shalt burn the whole ram upon the altar: it *is* a burnt offering unto the LORD: it *is* a sweet savour, an offering made by fire unto the LORD.

19¶ And thou shalt take the other ram; and Aaron and his sons shall put their hands upon the head of the ram.

20Then shalt thou kill the ram, and take of his blood, and put *it* upon the tip of the right ear of Aaron, and upon the tip of the right ear of his sons, and upon the thumb of their right hand, and upon the great toe of their right foot, and sprinkle the blood upon the altar round about.

21And thou shalt take of the blood that *is* upon the altar, and of the anointing oil, and sprinkle *it* upon Aaron, and upon his garments, and upon his sons, and upon the garments of his sons with him: and he shall be hallowed, and his garments, and his sons, and his sons' garments with him.

22Also thou shalt take of the ram the fat and the rump, and the fat that covereth the inwards, and the caul *above* the liver, and the two kidneys, and the fat that *is* upon them, and the right shoulder; for it *is* a ram of consecration:

23And one loaf of bread, and one cake of oiled bread, and one wafer out of the basket of the unleavened bread that *is* before the LORD:

24And thou shalt put all in the hands of Aaron, and in the hands of his sons; and shalt wave them *for* a wave offering before the LORD.

25And thou shalt receive them of their hands, and burn *them* upon the altar for a burnt offering, for a sweet savour before the LORD: it *is* an offering made by fire unto the LORD.

26And thou shalt take the breast of the ram of Aaron's consecration, and wave it *for* a wave offering before the LORD: and it shall be thy part.

27And thou shalt sanctify the breast of the wave offering, and the shoulder of the heave offering, which is waved, and which is heaved up, of the ram of the consecration, *even of that* which *is* for Aaron, and of *that* which is for his sons:

28And it shall be Aaron's and his sons' by a statute for ever from the children of Israel: for it *is* an heave offering: and it shall be an heave offering from the children of Israel of the sacrifice of their peace offerings, *even* their heave offering unto the LORD.

29¶ And the holy garments of Aaron shall be his sons' after him, to be anointed therein, and to be consecrated in them.

30*And* that son that is priest in his stead shall put them on seven days, when he cometh into the tabernacle of the congregation to minister in the holy *place.*

31¶ And thou shalt take the ram of the consecration, and seethe his flesh in the holy place.

32And Aaron and his sons shall eat the flesh of the ram, and the bread that *is* in the basket, *by* the door of the tabernacle of the congregation.

New International

put it on the horns of the altar with your finger, and pour out the rest of it at the base of the altar. 13Then take all the fat around the inner parts, the covering of the liver, and both kidneys with the fat on them, and burn them on the altar. 14But burn the bull's flesh and its hide and its offal outside the camp. It is a sin offering.

15"Take one of the rams, and Aaron and his sons shall lay their hands on its head. 16Slaughter it and take the blood and sprinkle it against the altar on all sides. 17Cut the ram into pieces and wash the inner parts and the legs, putting them with the head and the other pieces. 18Then burn the entire ram on the altar. It is a burnt offering to the LORD, a pleasing aroma, an offering made to the LORD by fire.

19"Take the other ram, and Aaron and his sons shall lay their hands on its head. 20Slaughter it, take some of its blood and put it on the lobes of the right ears of Aaron and his sons, on the thumbs of their right hands, and on the big toes of their right feet. Then sprinkle blood against the altar on all sides. 21And take some of the blood on the altar and some of the anointing oil and sprinkle it on Aaron and his garments and on his sons and their garments. Then he and his sons and their garments will be consecrated.

22"Take from this ram the fat, the fat tail, the fat around the inner parts, the covering of the liver, both kidneys with the fat on them, and the right thigh. (This is the ram for the ordination.) 23From the basket of bread made without yeast, which is before the LORD, take a loaf, and a cake made with oil, and a wafer. 24Put all these in the hands of Aaron and his sons and wave them before the LORD as a wave offering. 25Then take them from their hands and burn them on the altar along with the burnt offering for a pleasing aroma to the LORD, an offering made to the LORD by fire. 26After you take the breast of the ram for Aaron's ordination, wave it before the LORD as a wave offering, and it will be your share.

27"Consecrate those parts of the ordination ram that belong to Aaron and his sons: the breast that was waved and the thigh that was presented. 28This is always to be the regular share from the Israelites for Aaron and his sons. It is the contribution the Israelites are to make to the LORD from their fellowship offerings.a

29"Aaron's sacred garments will belong to his descendants so that they can be anointed and ordained in them. 30The son who succeeds him as priest and comes to the Tent of Meeting to minister in the Holy Place is to wear them seven days.

31"Take the ram for the ordination and cook the meat in a sacred place. 32At the entrance to the Tent of Meeting, Aaron and his sons are to eat the meat of the ram and the bread that is in the basket. 33They are to eat these

---

a 28 Traditionally *peace offerings*

Living Bible

altar, smearing it on with your finger, and pour the rest at the base of the altar. 13Then take all the fat that covers the inner parts, also the gall bladder and two kidneys, and the fat on them, and burn them upon the altar. 14Then take the body, including the skin and the dung, outside the camp and burn it as a sin offering.

15, 16"Next, Aaron and his sons shall lay their hands upon the head of one of the rams as it is killed. Its blood shall also be collected and sprinkled upon the altar. 17Cut up the ram and wash off the entrails and the legs; place them with the head and the other pieces of the body, 18and burn it all upon the altar; it is a burnt offering to the Lord, and very pleasant to him.

19, 20"Now take the other ram, and Aaron and his sons shall lay their hands upon its head as it is killed. Collect the blood and place some of it upon the tip of the right ear of Aaron and his sons, and upon their right thumbs and the big toes of their right feet; sprinkle the rest of the blood over the altar. 21Then scrape off some of the blood from the altar and mix it with some of the anointing oil and sprinkle it upon Aaron and his sons and upon their clothes; and they and their clothing shall be sanctified to the Lord.

22"Then take the fat of the ram, including the fat tail and the fat that covers the insides, also the gall bladder and the two kidneys and the fat surrounding them, and the right thigh—this is the ram for ordination of Aaron and his sons— 23and one loaf of bread, one cake of shortening bread, and one wafer from the basket of unleavened bread that was placed before the Lord: 24Place these in the hands of Aaron and his sons, to wave them in a gesture of offering to the Lord. 25Afterwards, take them from their hands and burn them on the altar as a fragrant burnt offering to him. 26Then take the breast of Aaron's ordination ram and wave it before the Lord in a gesture of offering; afterwards, keep it for yourself.

27"Give the breast and thigh of the consecration ram 28to Aaron and his sons. The people of Israel must always contribute this portion of their sacrifices—whether peace offerings or thanksgiving offerings—as their contribution to the Lord.

29"These sacred garments of Aaron shall be preserved for the consecration of his son who succeeds him, from generation to generation, for his anointing ceremony. 30Whoever is the next High Priest after Aaron shall wear these clothes for seven days before beginning to minister in the Tabernacle and the Holy Place.

31"Take the ram of consecration—the ram used in the ordination ceremony—and boil its meat in a sacred area. 32Aaron and his sons shall eat the meat, also the bread in the basket, at the door of the Tabernacle. 33They alone

New Revised Standard

shall take some of the blood of the bull and put it on the horns of the altar with your finger, and all the rest of the blood you shall pour out at the base of the altar. 13 You shall take all the fat that covers the entrails, and the appendage of the liver, and the two kidneys with the fat that is on them, and turn them into smoke on the altar. 14 But the flesh of the bull, and its skin, and its dung, you shall burn with fire outside the camp; it is a sin offering.

15 Then you shall take one of the rams, and Aaron and his sons shall lay their hands on the head of the ram, 16and you shall slaughter the ram, and shall take its blood and dash it against all sides of the altar. 17Then you shall cut the ram into its parts, and wash its entrails and its legs, and put them with its parts and its head, 18and turn the whole ram into smoke on the altar; it is a burnt offering to the Lord; it is a pleasing odor, an offering by fire to the Lord.

19 You shall take the other ram; and Aaron and his sons shall lay their hands on the head of the ram, 20 and you shall slaughter the ram, and take some of its blood and put it on the lobe of Aaron's right ear and on the lobes of the right ears of his sons, and on the thumbs of their right hands, and on the big toes of their right feet, and dash the rest of the blood against all sides of the altar. 21 Then you shall take some of the blood that is on the altar, and some of the anointing oil, and sprinkle it on Aaron and his vestments and on his sons and his sons' vestments with him; then he and his vestments shall be holy, as well as his sons and his sons' vestments.

22 You shall also take the fat of the ram, the fat tail, the fat that covers the entrails, the appendage of the liver, the two kidneys with the fat that is on them, and the right thigh (for it is a ram of ordination), 23 and one loaf of bread, one cake of bread made with oil, and one wafer, out of the basket of unleavened bread that is before the Lord; 24 and you shall place all these on the palms of Aaron and on the palms of his sons, and raise them as an elevation offering before the Lord. 25 Then you shall take them from their hands, and turn them into smoke on the altar on top of the burnt offering of pleasing odor before the Lord; it is an offering by fire to the Lord.

26 You shall take the breast of the ram of Aaron's ordination and raise it as an elevation offering before the Lord; and it shall be your portion. 27 You shall consecrate the breast that was raised as an elevation offering and the thigh that was raised as an elevation offering from the ram of ordination, from that which belonged to Aaron and his sons. 28 These things shall be a perpetual ordinance for Aaron and his sons from the Israelites, for this is an offering; and it shall be an offering by the Israelites from their sacrifice of offerings of well-being, their offering to the Lord.

29 The sacred vestments of Aaron shall be passed on to his sons after him; they shall be anointed in them and ordained in them. 30 The son who is priest in his place shall wear them seven days, when he comes into the tent of meeting to minister in the holy place.

31 You shall take the ram of ordination, and boil its flesh in a holy place; 32 and Aaron and his sons shall eat the flesh of the ram and the bread that is in the basket, at the entrance of the tent of meeting. 33 They themselves

King James

33And they shall eat those things wherewith the atonement was made, to consecrate *and* to sanctify them: but a stranger shall not eat *thereof*, because they *are* holy.

34And if aught of the flesh of the consecrations, or of the bread, remain unto the morning, then thou shalt burn the remainder with fire: it shall not be eaten, because it *is* holy.

35And thus shalt thou do unto Aaron, and to his sons, according to all *things* which I have commanded thee: seven days shalt thou consecrate them.

36And thou shalt offer every day a bullock *for* a sin offering for atonement: and thou shalt cleanse the altar, when thou hast made an atonement for it, and thou shalt anoint it, to sanctify it.

37Seven days thou shalt make an atonement for the altar, and sanctify it; and it shall be an altar most holy: whatsoever toucheth the altar shall be holy.

38¶ Now this *is that* which thou shalt offer upon the altar; two lambs of the first year day by day continually.

39The one lamb thou shalt offer in the morning; and the other lamb thou shalt offer at even:

40And with the one lamb a tenth deal of flour mingled with the fourth part of an hin of beaten oil; and the fourth part of an hin of wine *for* a drink offering.

41And the other lamb thou shalt offer at even, and shalt do thereto according to the meat offering of the morning, and according to the drink offering thereof, for a sweet savour, an offering made by fire unto the LORD.

42*This shall be* a continual burnt offering throughout your generations *at* the door of the tabernacle of the congregation before the LORD: where I will meet you, to speak there unto thee.

43And there I will meet with the children of Israel, and *the* tabernacle shall be sanctified by my glory.

44And I will sanctify the tabernacle of the congregation, and the altar: I will sanctify also both Aaron and his sons, to minister to me in the priest's office.

45¶ And I will dwell among the children of Israel, and will be their God.

46And they shall know that I *am* the LORD their God, that brought them forth out of the land of Egypt, that I may dwell among them: I *am* the LORD their God.

30 AND THOU shalt make an altar to burn incense upon: *of* shittim wood shalt thou make it.

2A cubit *shall be* the length thereof, and a cubit the breadth thereof; foursquare shall it be: and two cubits *shall be* the height thereof: the horns thereof *shall be* of the same.

3And thou shalt overlay it with pure gold, the top thereof, and the sides thereof round about, and the horns thereof; and thou shalt make unto it a crown of gold round about.

4And two golden rings shalt thou make to it under the crown of it, by the two corners thereof, upon the two sides of it shalt thou make *it*; and they shall be for places for the staves to bear it withal.

5And thou shalt make the staves *of* shittim wood, and overlay them with gold.

6And thou shalt put it before the veil that *is* by the ark of the testimony, before the mercy seat that *is* over the testimony, where I will meet with thee.

7And Aaron shall burn thereon sweet incense every morning: when he dresseth the lamps, he shall burn incense upon it.

8And when Aaron lighteth the lamps at even, he shall burn incense upon it, a perpetual incense before the LORD throughout your generations.

9Ye shall offer no strange incense thereon, nor burnt sacrifice, nor meat offering; neither shall ye pour drink offering thereon.

New International

offerings by which atonement was made for their ordination and consecration. But no one else may eat them, because they are sacred. 34And if any of the meat of the ordination ram or any bread is left over till morning, burn it up. It must not be eaten, because it is sacred.

35"Do for Aaron and his sons everything I have commanded you, taking seven days to ordain them. 36Sacrifice a bull each day as a sin offering to make atonement. Purify the altar by making atonement for it, and anoint it to consecrate it. 37For seven days make atonement for the altar and consecrate it. Then the altar will be most holy, and whatever touches it will be holy.

38"This is what you are to offer on the altar regularly each day: two lambs a year old. 39Offer one in the morning and the other at twilight. 40With the first lamb offer a tenth of an ephah[a] of fine flour mixed with a quarter of a hin[b] of oil from pressed olives, and a quarter of a hin of wine as a drink offering. 41Sacrifice the other lamb at twilight with the same grain offering and its drink offering as in the morning—a pleasing aroma, an offering made to the LORD by fire.

42"For the generations to come this burnt offering is to be made regularly at the entrance to the Tent of Meeting before the LORD. There I will meet you and speak to you; 43there also I will meet with the Israelites, and the place will be consecrated by my glory.

44"So I will consecrate the Tent of Meeting and the altar and will consecrate Aaron and his sons to serve me as priests. 45Then I will dwell among the Israelites and be their God. 46They will know that I am the LORD their God, who brought them out of Egypt so that I might dwell among them. I am the LORD their God.

The Altar of Incense

30 "MAKE AN altar of acacia wood for burning incense. 2It is to be square, a cubit long and a cubit wide, and two cubits high[c]—its horns of one piece with it. 3Overlay the top and all the sides and the horns with pure gold, and make a gold molding around it. 4Make two gold rings for the altar below the molding—two on opposite sides—to hold the poles used to carry it. 5Make the poles of acacia wood and overlay them with gold. 6Put the altar in front of the curtain that is before the ark of the Testimony—before the atonement cover that is over the Testimony—where I will meet with you.

7"Aaron must burn fragrant incense on the altar every morning when he tends the lamps. 8He must burn incense again when he lights the lamps at twilight so incense will burn regularly before the LORD for the generations to come. 9Do not offer on this altar any other incense or any burnt offering or grain offering, and do not pour a drink offering on it. 10Once a year Aaron shall

---

a *40* That is, probably about 2 quarts (about 2 liters)   b *40* That is, probably about 1 quart (about 1 liter)   c *2* That is, about 1 1/2 feet (about 0.5 meter) long and wide and about 3 feet (about 0.9 meter) high

Living Bible

shall eat those items used in their atonement (that is, in their consecration ceremony). The ordinary people shall not eat them, for these things are set apart and holy. 34If any of the meat or bread remains until the morning, burn it; it shall not be eaten, for it is holy.

35"This, then, is the way you shall ordain Aaron and his sons to their offices. This ordination shall go on for seven days. 36Every day you shall sacrifice a young bull as a sin offering for atonement; afterwards,d purge the altar by making atonement for it; pour olive oil upon it to sanctify it. 37Make atonement for the altar and consecrate it to God every day for seven days. After this the altar shall be exceedingly holy, so that whatever touches it shall be set apart for God.e

38"Each day offer two yearling lambs upon the altar, 39one in the morning and the other in the evening. 40With one of them offer three quarts of finely ground flour mixed with 2½ pints of oil, pressed from olives; also 2½ pints of wine, as an offering.

41Offer the other lamb in the evening, along with the flour and the wine as in the morning, for a fragrant offering to the Lord, an offering made to the Lord by fire.

42"This shall be a perpetual daily offering at the door of the Tabernacle before the Lord, where I will meet with you and speak with you. 43And I will meet with the people of Israel there, and the Tabernacle shall be sanctified by my glory. 44Yes, I will sanctify the Tabernacle and the altar and Aaron and his sons who are my ministers, the priests. 45And I will live among the people of Israel and be their God, 46and they shall know that I am the Lord their God. I brought them out of Egypt so that I could live among them. I am Jehovah their God.

30 "THEN MAKE a small altar for burning incense. It shall be made from acacia wood. 2It is to be eighteen inches square and three feet high, with horns carved from the wood of the altar—they are not to be merely separate parts that are attached. 3Overlay the top, sides, and horns of the altar with pure gold, and run a gold molding around the entire altar. 4Beneath the molding, on each of two sides, construct two gold rings to hold the carrying poles. 5The poles are to be made of acacia wood overlaid with gold. 6Place the altar just outside the veil, near the place of mercy that is above the Ark containing the Ten Commandments. I will meet with you there.

7"Every morning when Aaron trims the lamps, he shall burn sweet spices on the altar, 8and each evening when he lights the lamps he shall burn the incense before the Lord, and this shall go on from generation to generation. 9Offer no unauthorized incense, burnt offerings, meal offerings, or wine offerings.

New Revised Standard

shall eat the food by which atonement is made, to ordain and consecrate them, but no one else shall eat of them, because they are holy. 34 If any of the flesh for the ordination, or of the bread, remains until the morning, then you shall burn the remainder with fire; it shall not be eaten, because it is holy.

35 Thus you shall do to Aaron and to his sons, just as I have commanded you; through seven days you shall ordain them. 36 Also every day you shall offer a bull as a sin offering for atonement. Also you shall offer a sin offering for the altar, when you make atonement for it, and shall anoint it, to consecrate it. 37 Seven days you shall make atonement for the altar, and consecrate it, and the altar shall be most holy; whatever touches the altar shall become holy.

The Daily Offerings

38 Now this is what you shall offer on the altar: two lambs a year old regularly each day. 39One lamb you shall offer in the morning, and the other lamb you shall offer in the evening; 40and with the first lamb one-tenth of a measure of choice flour mixed with one-fourth of a hin of beaten oil, and one-fourth of a hin of wine for a drink offering. 41And the other lamb you shall offer in the evening, and shall offer with it a grain offering and its drink offering, as in the morning, for a pleasing odor, an offering by fire to the LORD. 42 It shall be a regular burnt offering throughout your generations at the entrance of the tent of meeting before the LORD, where I will meet with you, to speak to you there. 43 I will meet with the Israelites there, and it shall be sanctified by my glory; 44 I will consecrate the tent of meeting and the altar; Aaron also and his sons I will consecrate, to serve me as priests. 45 I will dwell among the Israelites, and I will be their God. 46 And they shall know that I am the LORD their God, who brought them out of the land of Egypt that I might dwell among them; I am the LORD their God.

The Altar of Incense

30 YOU SHALL make an altar on which to offer incense; you shall make it of acacia wood. 2 It shall be one cubit long, and one cubit wide; it shall be square, and shall be two cubits high; its horns shall be of one piece with it. 3 You shall overlay it with pure gold, its top, and its sides all around and its horns; and you shall make for it a molding of gold all around. 4 And you shall make two golden horns for it; under its molding on two opposite sides of it you shall make them, and they shall hold the poles with which to carry it. 5 You shall make the poles of acacia wood, and overlay them with gold. 6 You shall place it in front of the curtain that is above the ark of the covenant,f in front of the mercy seats that is over the covenant,f where I will meet with you. 7 Aaron shall offer fragrant incense on it; every morning when he dresses the lamps he shall offer it, 8 and when Aaron sets up the lamps in the evening, he shall offer it, a regular incense offering before the LORD throughout your generations. 9 You shall not offer unholy incense on it, or a burnt offering, or a grain offering; and you shall not pour a drink offering on it. 10 Once a

---

d 29:36 afterwards, implied.   e 29:37 shall be set apart for God, or, "shall become holy," or, "only those who are holy may touch it."

f Or treaty, or testimony; Heb eduth   g Or the cover

King James

¹⁰And Aaron shall make an atonement upon the horns of it once in a year with the blood of the sin offering of atonements: once in the year shall he make atonement upon it throughout your generations: it *is* most holy unto the LORD.

¹¹¶ And the LORD spake unto Moses, saying,

¹²When thou takest the sum of the children of Israel after their number, then shall they give every man a ransom for his soul unto the LORD, when thou numberest them; that there be no plague among them, when *thou* numberest them.

¹³This they shall give, every one that passeth among them that are numbered, half a shekel after the shekel of the sanctuary: (a shekel *is* twenty gerahs:) an half shekel *shall be* the offering of the LORD.

¹⁴Every one that passeth among them that are numbered, from twenty years old and above, shall give an offering unto the LORD.

¹⁵The rich shall not give more, and the poor shall not give less than half a shekel, when *they* give an offering unto the LORD, to make an atonement for your souls.

¹⁶And thou shalt take the atonement money of the children of Israel, and shalt appoint it for the service of the tabernacle of the congregation; that it may be a memorial unto the children of Israel before the LORD, to make an atonement for your souls.

¹⁷¶ And the LORD spake unto Moses, saying,

¹⁸Thou shalt also make a laver *of* brass, and his foot *also of* brass, to wash *withal:* and thou shalt put it between the tabernacle of the congregation and the altar, and thou shalt put water therein.

¹⁹For Aaron and his sons shall wash their hands and their feet thereat:

²⁰When they go into the tabernacle of the congregation, they shall wash with water, that they die not; or when they come near to the altar to minister, to burn offering made by fire unto the LORD:

²¹So they shall wash their hands and their feet, that they die not: and it shall be a statute for ever to them, *even* to him and to his seed throughout their generations.

²²¶ Moreover the LORD spake unto Moses, saying,

²³Take thou also unto thee principal spices, of pure myrrh five hundred *shekels,* and of sweet cinnamon half so much, *even* two hundred and fifty *shekels,* and of sweet calamus two hundred and fifty *shekels,*

²⁴And of cassia five hundred *shekels,* after the shekel of the sanctuary, and of oil olive an hin:

²⁵And thou shalt make it an oil of holy ointment, an ointment compound after the art of the apothecary: it shall be an holy anointing oil.

²⁶And thou shalt anoint the tabernacle of the congregation therewith, and the ark of the testimony,

²⁷And the table and all his vessels, and the candlestick and his vessels, and the altar of incense,

²⁸And the altar of burnt offering with all his vessels, and the laver and his foot.

²⁹And thou shalt sanctify them, that they may be most holy: whatsoever toucheth them shall be holy.

³⁰And thou shalt anoint Aaron and his sons, and consecrate them, that *they* may minister unto me in the priest's office.

³¹And thou shalt speak unto the children of Israel, saying, This shall be an holy anointing oil unto me throughout your generations.

³²Upon man's flesh shall it not be poured, neither shall ye make *any other* like it, after the composition of it: it *is* holy, *and* it shall be holy unto you.

³³Whosoever compoundeth *any* like it, or whosoever putteth *any* of it upon a stranger, shall even be cut off from his people.

³⁴¶ And the LORD said unto Moses, Take unto thee sweet spices, stacte, and onycha, and galbanum; *these* sweet spices with pure frankincense: of each shall there be a like *weight:*

New International

make atonement on its horns. This annual atonement must be made with the blood of the atoning sin offering for the generations to come. It is most holy to the LORD."

Atonement Money

¹¹Then the LORD said to Moses, ¹²"When you take a census of the Israelites to count them, each one must pay the LORD a ransom for his life at the time he is counted. Then no plague will come on them when you number them. ¹³Each one who crosses over to those already counted is to give a half shekel,ᵃ according to the sanctuary shekel, which weighs twenty gerahs. This half shekel is an offering to the LORD. ¹⁴All who cross over, those twenty years old or more, are to give an offering to the LORD. ¹⁵The rich are not to give more than a half shekel and the poor are not to give less when you make the offering to the LORD to atone for your lives. ¹⁶Receive the atonement money from the Israelites and use it for the service of the Tent of Meeting. It will be a memorial for the Israelites before the LORD, making atonement for your lives."

Basin for Washing

¹⁷Then the LORD said to Moses, ¹⁸"Make a bronze basin, with its bronze stand, for washing. Place it between the Tent of Meeting and the altar, and put water in it. ¹⁹Aaron and his sons are to wash their hands and feet with water from it. ²⁰Whenever they enter the Tent of Meeting, they shall wash with water so that they will not die. Also, when they approach the altar to minister by presenting an offering made to the LORD by fire, ²¹they shall wash their hands and feet so that they will not die. This is to be a lasting ordinance for Aaron and his descendants for the generations to come."

Anointing Oil

²²Then the LORD said to Moses, ²³"Take the following fine spices: 500 shekelsᵇ of liquid myrrh, half as much (that is, 250 shekels) of fragrant cinnamon, 250 shekels of fragrant cane, ²⁴500 shekels of cassia—all according to the sanctuary shekel—and a hinᶜ of olive oil. ²⁵Make these into a sacred anointing oil, a fragrant blend, the work of a perfumer. It will be the sacred anointing oil. ²⁶Then use it to anoint the Tent of Meeting, the ark of the Testimony, ²⁷the table and all its articles, the lampstand and its accessories, the altar of incense, ²⁸the altar of burnt offering and all its utensils, and the basin with its stand. ²⁹You shall consecrate them so they will be most holy, and whatever touches them will be holy.

³⁰"Anoint Aaron and his sons and consecrate them so they may serve me as priests. ³¹Say to the Israelites, 'This is to be my sacred anointing oil for the generations to come. ³²Do not pour it on men's bodies and do not make any oil with the same formula. It is sacred, and you are to consider it sacred. ³³Whoever makes perfume like it and whoever puts it on anyone other than a priest must be cut off from his people.' "

Incense

³⁴Then the LORD said to Moses, "Take fragrant spices—gum resin, onycha and galbanum—and pure frankincense, all in equal amounts, ³⁵and make a fra-

---

ᵃ *13* That is, about 1/5 ounce (about 6 grams); also in verse 15   ᵇ *23* That is, about 12 1/2 pounds (about 6 kilograms)   ᶜ *24* That is, probably about 4 quarts (about 4 liters)

Living Bible

10"Once a year Aaron must sanctify[d] the altar, placing upon its horns the blood of the sin offering for atonement. This shall be a regular, annual event from generation to generation, for this is the Lord's supremely holy altar."

11, 12And Jehovah said to Moses, "Whenever you take a census of the people of Israel, each man who is numbered shall give a ransom to the Lord for his soul, so that there will be no plague among the people when you number them. 13His payment shall be half a dollar.[e] 14All who have reached their twentieth birthday shall give this offering. 15The rich shall not give more and the poor shall not give less, for it is an offering to the Lord to make atonement for yourselves. 16Use this money for the care of the Tabernacle; it is to bring you, the people of Israel, to the Lord's attention, and to make atonement for you."

17, 18And the Lord said to Moses, "Make a bronze basin with a bronze pedestal. Put it between the Tabernacle and the altar, and fill it with water. 19Aaron and his sons shall wash their hands and feet there, 20when they go into the Tabernacle to appear before the Lord, or when they approach the altar to burn offerings to the Lord. They must always wash before doing so, or they will die. 21These are instructions to Aaron and his sons from generation to generation."

22, 23Then the Lord told Moses to collect the choicest of spices—eighteen pounds of pure myrrh; half as much of cinnamon and of sweet cane; 24the same amount of cassia as of myrrh; and 1½ gallons of olive oil. 25The Lord instructed skilled perfumemakers to compound all this into a holy anointing oil.

26, 27"Use this," he said, "to anoint the Tabernacle, the Ark, the table and all its instruments, the lampstand and all its utensils, the incense altar, 28the burnt offering altar with all its instruments, and the washbasin and its pedestal. 29Sanctify them, to make them holy; whatever touches them shall become holy.[f] 30Use it to anoint Aaron and his sons, sanctifying them so that they can minister to me as priests. 31And say to the people of Israel, 'This shall always be my holy anointing oil. 32It must never be poured upon an ordinary person, and you shall never make any of it yourselves, for it is holy, and it shall be treated by you as holy. 33Anyone who compounds any incense like it or puts any of it upon someone who is not a priest shall be excommunicated.' "

34These were the Lord's directions to Moses concerning the incense: "Use sweet spices—stacte, onycha, galbanum, and pure frankincense, weighing out the same amounts of each, 35using the usual techniques of the

New Revised Standard

year Aaron shall perform the rite of atonement on its horns. Throughout your generations he shall perform the atonement for it once a year with the blood of the atoning sin offering. It is most holy to the LORD.

The Half Shekel for the Sanctuary

11 The LORD spoke to Moses: 12When you take a census of the Israelites to register them, at registration all of them shall give a ransom for their lives to the LORD, so that no plague may come upon them for being registered. 13This is what each one who is registered shall give: half a shekel according to the shekel of the sanctuary (the shekel is twenty gerahs), half a shekel as an offering to the LORD. 14Each one who is registered, from twenty years old and upward, shall give the LORD's offering. 15The rich shall not give more, and the poor shall not give less, than the half shekel, when you bring this offering to the LORD to make atonement for your lives. 16You shall take the atonement money from the Israelites and shall designate it for the service of the tent of meeting; before the LORD it will be a reminder to the Israelites of the ransom given for your lives.

The Bronze Basin

17 The LORD spoke to Moses: 18You shall make a bronze basin with a bronze stand for washing. You shall put it between the tent of meeting and the altar, and you shall put water in it; 19with the water[g] Aaron and his sons shall wash their hands and their feet. 20When they go into the tent of meeting, or when they come near the altar to minister, to make an offering by fire to the LORD, they shall wash with water, so that they may not die. 21They shall wash their hands and their feet, so that they may not die: it shall be a perpetual ordinance for them, for him and for his descendants throughout their generations.

The Anointing Oil and Incense

22 The LORD spoke to Moses: 23Take the finest spices: of liquid myrrh five hundred shekels, and of sweet-smelling cinnamon half as much, that is, two hundred fifty, and two hundred fifty of aromatic cane, 24and five hundred of cassia—measured by the sanctuary shekel—and a hin of olive oil; 25and you shall make of these a sacred anointing oil blended as by the perfumer; it shall be a holy anointing oil. 26With it you shall anoint the tent of meeting and the ark of the covenant,[h] 27and the table and all its utensils, and the lampstand and its utensils, and the altar of incense, 28and the altar of burnt offering with all its utensils, and the basin with its stand; 29you shall consecrate them, so that they may be most holy; whatever touches them will become holy. 30You shall anoint Aaron and his sons, and consecrate them, in order that they may serve me as priests. 31You shall say to the Israelites, "This shall be my holy anointing oil throughout your generations. 32It shall not be used in any ordinary anointing of the body, and you shall make no other like it in composition; it is holy, and it shall be holy to you. 33Whoever compounds any like it or whoever puts any of it on an unqualified person shall be cut off from the people."

34 The LORD said to Moses: Take sweet spices, stacte, and onycha, and galbanum, sweet spices with pure frankincense (an equal part of each), 35and make

---

d 30:10 *must sanctify the altar*, literally, "shall make an atonement for the altar." e 30:13 *half a dollar*, literally, "half a shekel after the shekel of the sanctuary [the shekel is twenty gerahs], half a shekel for an offering to Jehovah." f 30:29 *shall become holy*, or, "shall be set apart for God," or, "only what is holy may touch them."

g Heb *it* h Or *treaty*, or *testimony*; Heb *eduth*

King James

35And thou shalt make it a perfume, a confection after the art of the apothecary, tempered together, pure *and* holy:

36And thou shalt beat *some* of it very small, and put of it before the testimony in the tabernacle of the congregation, where I will meet with thee: it shall be unto you most holy.

37And *as for* the perfume which thou shalt make, ye shall not make to yourselves according to the composition thereof: it shall be unto thee holy for the LORD.

38Whosoever shall make like unto that, to smell thereto, shall even be cut off from his people.

31 AND THE LORD spake unto Moses, saying, 2See, I have called by name Bezaleel the son of Uri, the son of Hur, of the tribe of Judah:

3And I have filled him with the spirit of God, in wisdom, and in understanding, and in knowledge, and in all manner of workmanship,

4To devise cunning works, to work in gold, and in silver, and in brass,

5And in cutting of stones, to set *them,* and in carving of timber, to work in all manner of workmanship.

6And I, behold, I have given with him Aholiab, the son of Ahisamach, of the tribe of Dan: and in the hearts of all that are wisehearted I have put wisdom, that they may make all that I have commanded thee;

7The tabernacle of the congregation, and the ark of the testimony, and the mercy seat that *is* thereupon, and all the furniture of the tabernacle,

8And the table and his furniture, and the pure candlestick with all his furniture, and the altar of incense,

9And the altar of burnt offering with all his furniture, and the laver and his foot,

10And the cloths of service, and the holy garments for Aaron the priest, and the garments of his sons, to minister in the priest's office,

11And the anointing oil, and sweet incense for the holy *place:* according to all that I have commanded thee shall they do.

12¶ And the LORD spake unto Moses, saying,

13Speak thou also unto the children of Israel, saying, Verily my sabbaths ye shall keep: for it *is* a sign between me and you throughout your generations; that *ye* may know that I *am* the LORD that doth sanctify you.

14Ye shall keep the sabbath therefore; for it *is* holy unto you: every one that defileth it shall surely be put to death: for whosoever doeth *any* work therein, that soul shall be cut off from among his people.

15Six days may work be done; but in the seventh *is* the sabbath of rest, holy to the LORD: whosoever doeth *any* work in the sabbath day, he shall surely be put to death.

16Wherefore the children of Israel shall keep the sabbath, to observe the sabbath throughout their generations, *for* a perpetual covenant.

17It *is* a sign between me and the children of Israel for ever: for *in* six days the LORD made heaven and earth, and on the seventh day he rested, and was refreshed.

18¶ And he gave unto Moses, when he had made an end of communing with him upon mount Sinai, two tables of testimony, tables of stone, written with the finger of God.

New International

grant blend of incense, the work of a perfumer. It is to be salted and pure and sacred. 36Grind some of it to powder and place it in front of the Testimony in the Tent of Meeting, where I will meet with you. It shall be most holy to you. 37Do not make any incense with this formula for yourselves; consider it holy to the LORD. 38Whoever makes any like it to enjoy its fragrance must be cut off from his people."

Bezalel and Oholiab

31 THEN THE LORD said to Moses, 2"See, I have chosen Bezalel son of Uri, the son of Hur, of the tribe of Judah, 3and I have filled him with the Spirit of God, with skill, ability and knowledge in all kinds of crafts— 4to make artistic designs for work in gold, silver and bronze, 5to cut and set stones, to work in wood, and to engage in all kinds of craftsmanship. 6Moreover, I have appointed Oholiab son of Ahisamach, of the tribe of Dan, to help him. Also I have given skill to all the craftsmen to make everything I have commanded you: 7the Tent of Meeting, the ark of the Testimony with the atonement cover on it, and all the other furnishings of the tent— 8the table and its articles, the pure gold lampstand and all its accessories, the altar of incense, 9the altar of burnt offering and all its utensils, the basin with its stand— 10and also the woven garments, both the sacred garments for Aaron the priest and the garments for his sons when they serve as priests, 11and the anointing oil and fragrant incense for the Holy Place. They are to make them just as I commanded you."

The Sabbath

12Then the LORD said to Moses, 13"Say to the Israelites, 'You must observe my Sabbaths. This will be a sign between me and you for the generations to come, so you may know that I am the LORD, who makes you holy.a

14" 'Observe the Sabbath, because it is holy to you. Anyone who desecrates it must be put to death; whoever does any work on that day must be cut off from his people. 15For six days, work is to be done, but the seventh day is a Sabbath of rest, holy to the LORD. Whoever does any work on the Sabbath day must be put to death. 16The Israelites are to observe the Sabbath, celebrating it for the generations to come as a lasting covenant. 17It will be a sign between me and the Israelites forever, for in six days the LORD made the heavens and the earth, and on the seventh day he abstained from work and rested.' "

18When the LORD finished speaking to Moses on Mount Sinai, he gave him the two tablets of the Testimony, the tablets of stone inscribed by the finger of God.

---

a *13 Or who sanctifies you; or who sets you apart as holy*

Living Bible

incensemaker, and seasoning it with salt; it shall be a pure and holy incense. 36Beat some of it very fine and put some of it in front of the Ark where I meet with you in the Tabernacle; this incense is most holy. 37Never make it for yourselves, for it is reserved for the Lord and you must treat it as holy. 38Anyone making it for himself shall be excommunicated."

31 THE LORD also said to Moses, "See, I have appointed Bezalel (son of Uri, and grandson of Hur, of the tribe of Judah), 3and have filled him with the Spirit of God, giving him great wisdom, ability, and skill in constructing the Tabernacle and everything it contains. 4He is highly capable as an artistic designer of objects made of gold, silver, and bronze. 5He is skilled, too, as a jeweler and in carving wood.

6"And I have appointed Oholiab (son of Ahisamach of the tribe of Dan) to be his assistant; moreover, I have given special skill to all who are known as experts, so that they can make all the things I have instructed you to make: 7the Tabernacle; the Ark with the place of mercy upon it; all the furnishings of the Tabernacle; 8the table and its instruments; the pure gold lampstand with its instruments; the altar of incense; 9the burnt offering altar with its instruments; the laver and its pedestal; 10the beautifully made, holy garments for Aaron the priest, and the garments for his sons, so that they can minister as priests; 11the anointing oil; and the sweet-spice incense for the Holy Place. They are to follow exactly the directions I gave you."

12, 13The Lord then gave these further instructions to Moses: "Tell the people of Israel to rest on my Sabbath day, for the Sabbath is a reminder of the covenant between you and me forever; it helps you to remember that I am Jehovah who makes you holy. 14, 15Yes, rest on the Sabbath, for it is holy. Anyone who does not obey this command must die; anyone who does any work on that day shall be killed. 16, 17Work six days only, for the seventh day is a special day to remind you of my covenant—a weekly reminder forever of my promises to the people of Israel. For in six days the Lord made heaven and earth, and rested on the seventh day, and was refreshed."

18Then, as God finished speaking with Moses on Mount Sinai, he gave him the two tablets of stone on which the Ten Commandments were written with the finger of God.

New Revised Standard

an incense blended as by the perfumer, seasoned with salt, pure and holy; 36and you shall beat some of it into powder, and put part of it before the covenantb in the tent of meeting where I shall meet with you; it shall be for you most holy. 37When you make incense according to this composition, you shall not make it for yourselves; it shall be regarded by you as holy to the LORD. 38Whoever makes any like it to use as perfume shall be cut off from the people.

Bezalel and Oholiab

31 THE LORD spoke to Moses: 2See, I have called by name Bezalel son of Uri son of Hur, of the tribe of Judah: 3and I have filled him with divine spirit,c with ability, intelligence, and knowledge in every kind of craft, 4to devise artistic designs, to work in gold, silver, and bronze, 5in cutting stones for setting, and in carving wood, in every kind of craft. 6Moreover, I have appointed with him Oholiab son of Ahisamach, of the tribe of Dan; and I have given skill to all the skillful, so that they may make all that I have commanded you: 7the tent of meeting, and the ark of the covenant,b and the mercy seatd that is on it, and all the furnishings of the tent, 8the table and its utensils, and the pure lampstand with all its utensils, and the altar of incense, 9and the altar of burnt offering with all its utensils, and the basin with its stand, 10and the finely worked vestments, the holy vestments for the priest Aaron and the vestments of his sons, for their service as priests, 11and the anointing oil and the fragrant incense for the holy place. They shall do just as I have commanded you.

The Sabbath Law

12 The LORD said to Moses: 13You yourself are to speak to the Israelites: "You shall keep my sabbaths, for this is a sign between me and you throughout your generations, given in order that you may know that I, the LORD, sanctify you. 14You shall keep the sabbath, because it is holy for you; everyone who profanes it shall be put to death; whoever does any work on it shall be cut off from among the people. 15Six days shall work be done, but the seventh day is a sabbath of solemn rest, holy to the LORD; whoever does any work on the sabbath day shall be put to death. 16Therefore the Israelites shall keep the sabbath, observing the sabbath throughout their generations, as a perpetual covenant. 17It is a sign forever between me and the people of Israel that in six days the LORD made heaven and earth, and on the seventh day he rested, and was refreshed."

The Two Tablets of the Covenant

18 When Gode finished speaking with Moses on Mount Sinai, he gave him the two tablets of the covenant,b tablets of stone, written with the finger of God.

b Or treaty, or testimony; Heb eduth   c Or with the spirit of God   d Or the cover   e Heb he

King James

32 AND WHEN the people saw that Moses delayed to come down out of the mount, the people gathered themselves together unto Aaron, and said unto him, Up, make us gods, which shall go before us; for *as for* this Moses, the man that brought us up out of the land of Egypt, we wot not what is become of him.

2And Aaron said unto them, Break off the golden earrings, which *are* in the ears of your wives, of your sons, and of your daughters, and bring *them* unto me.

3And all the people brake off the golden earrings which *were* in their ears, and brought *them* unto Aaron.

4And he received *them* at their hand, and fashioned it with a graving tool, after he had made it a molten calf: and they said, These *be* thy gods, O Israel, which brought thee up out of the land of Egypt.

5And when Aaron saw *it*, he built an altar before it; and Aaron made proclamation, and said, Tomorrow *is* a feast to the LORD.

6And they rose up early on the morrow, and offered burnt offerings, and brought peace offerings; and the people sat down to eat and to drink, and rose up to play.

7¶ And the LORD said unto Moses, Go, get thee down; for thy people, which thou broughtest out of the land of Egypt, have corrupted *themselves*:

8They have turned aside quickly out of the way which I commanded them: they have made them a molten calf, and have worshipped it, and have sacrificed thereunto, and said, These *be* thy gods, O Israel, which have brought thee up out of the land of Egypt.

9And the LORD said unto Moses, I have seen this people, and, behold, it *is* a stiffnecked people:

10Now therefore let me alone, that my wrath may wax hot against them, and that I may consume them: and I will make of thee a great nation.

11And Moses besought the LORD his God, and said, LORD, why doth thy wrath wax hot against thy people, which thou hast brought forth out of the land of Egypt with great power, and with a mighty hand?

12Wherefore should the Egyptians speak, and say, For mischief did he bring them out, to slay them in the mountains, and to consume them from the face of the earth? Turn from thy fierce wrath, and repent of this evil against thy people.

13Remember Abraham, Isaac, and Israel, thy servants, to whom thou swarest by thine own self, and saidst unto them, I will multiply your seed as the stars of heaven, and all this land that I have spoken of will I give unto your seed, and they shall inherit *it* for ever.

14And the LORD repented of the evil which he thought to do unto his people.

15¶ And Moses turned, and went down from the mount, and the two tables of the testimony *were* in his hand: the tables *were* written on both their sides; on the one side and on the other *were* they written.

16And the tables *were* the work of God, and the writing *was* the writing of God, graven upon the tables.

17And when Joshua heard the noise of the people as they shouted, he said unto Moses, *There is* a noise of war in the camp.

18And he said, *It is* not the voice of *them that* shout for mastery, neither *is it* the voice of *them that* cry for being overcome: *but* the noise of *them that* sing do I hear.

19¶ And it came to pass, as soon as he came nigh unto the camp, that he saw the calf, and the dancing: and Moses' anger waxed hot, and he cast the tables out of his hands, and brake them beneath the mount.

20And he took the calf which they had made, and burnt *it* in the fire, and ground *it* to powder, and strawed *it* upon the water, and made the children of Israel drink *of it*.

New International

The Golden Calf

32 WHEN THE people saw that Moses was so long in coming down from the mountain, they gathered around Aaron and said, "Come, make us gods[a] who will go before us. As for this fellow Moses who brought us up out of Egypt, we don't know what has happened to him."

2Aaron answered them, "Take off the gold earrings that your wives, your sons and your daughters are wearing, and bring them to me." 3So all the people took off their earrings and brought them to Aaron. 4He took what they handed him and made it into an idol cast in the shape of a calf, fashioning it with a tool. Then they said, "These are your gods,[b] O Israel, who brought you up out of Egypt."

5When Aaron saw this, he built an altar in front of the calf and announced, "Tomorrow there will be a festival to the LORD." 6So the next day the people rose early and sacrificed burnt offerings and presented fellowship offerings.[c] Afterward they sat down to eat and drink and got up to indulge in revelry.

7Then the LORD said to Moses, "Go down, because your people, whom you brought up out of Egypt, have become corrupt. 8They have been quick to turn away from what I commanded them and have made themselves an idol cast in the shape of a calf. They have bowed down to it and sacrificed to it and have said, 'These are your gods, O Israel, who brought you up out of Egypt.'

9"I have seen these people," the LORD said to Moses, "and they are a stiff-necked people. 10Now leave me alone so that my anger may burn against them and that I may destroy them. Then I will make you into a great nation."

11But Moses sought the favor of the LORD his God. "O LORD," he said, "why should your anger burn against your people, whom you brought out of Egypt with great power and a mighty hand? 12Why should the Egyptians say, 'It was with evil intent that he brought them out, to kill them in the mountains and to wipe them off the face of the earth'? Turn from your fierce anger; relent and do not bring disaster on your people. 13Remember your servants Abraham, Isaac and Israel, to whom you swore by your own self: 'I will make your descendants as numerous as the stars in the sky and I will give your descendants all this land I promised them, and it will be their inheritance forever.' " 14Then the LORD relented and did not bring on his people the disaster he had threatened.

15Moses turned and went down the mountain with the two tablets of the Testimony in his hands. They were inscribed on both sides, front and back. 16The tablets were the work of God; the writing was the writing of God, engraved on the tablets.

17When Joshua heard the noise of the people shouting, he said to Moses, "There is the sound of war in the camp."

18Moses replied:

"It is not the sound of victory,
　　it is not the sound of defeat;
　　it is the sound of singing that I hear."

19When Moses approached the camp and saw the calf and the dancing, his anger burned and he threw the tablets out of his hands, breaking them to pieces at the foot of the mountain. 20And he took the calf they had made and burned it in the fire; then he ground it to powder, scattered it on the water and made the Israelites drink it.

---

a *1* Or *a god*; also in verses 23 and 31　　b *4* Or *This is your god*; also in verse 8　　c *6* Traditionally *peace offerings*

Living Bible

32 WHEN MOSES didn't come back down the mountain right away, the people went to Aaron. "Look," they said, "make us a god to lead us, for this fellow Moses who brought us here from Egypt has disappeared; something must have happened to him."

2, 3"Give me your gold earrings," Aaron replied.

So they all did—men and women, boys and girls. 4Aaron melted the gold, then molded and tooled it into the form of a calf. The people exclaimed, "O Israel, this is the god that brought you out of Egypt!"

5When Aaron saw how happy the people were about it, he built an altar before the calf and announced, "Tomorrow there will be a feast to Jehovah!"

6So they were up early the next morning and began offering burnt offerings and peace offerings to the calf-idol; afterwards they sat down to feast and drink at a wild party, followed by sexual immorality.

7Then the Lord told Moses, "Quick! Go on down, for your people that you brought from Egypt have defiled themselves, 8and have quickly abandoned all my laws. They have molded themselves a calf, and worshiped it, and sacrificed to it, and said, 'This is your god, O Israel, that brought you out of Egypt.' "

9Then the Lord said, "I have seen what a stubborn, rebellious lot these people are. 10Now let me alone and my anger shall blaze out against them and destroy them all; and I will make you, Moses, into a great nation instead of them."

11But Moses begged God not to do it. "Lord," he pleaded, "why is your anger so hot against your own people whom you brought from the land of Egypt with such great power and mighty miracles? 12Do you want the Egyptians to say, 'God tricked them into coming to the mountains so that he could slay them, destroying them from off the face of the earth'? Turn back from your fierce wrath. Turn away from this terrible evil you are planning against your people! 13Remember your promise to your servants—to Abraham, Isaac, and Israel. For you swore by your own self, 'I will multiply your posterity as the stars of heaven, and I will give them all of this land I have promised to your descendants, and they shall inherit it forever.' "

14So the Lord changed his mind and spared them. 15Then Moses went down the mountain, holding in his hands the Ten Commandments written on both sides of two stone tablets. 16(God himself had written the commandments on the tablets.)

17When Joshua heard the noise below them, of all the people shouting, he exclaimed to Moses, "It sounds as if they are preparing for war!"

18But Moses replied, "No, it's not a cry of victory or defeat, but singing."

19When they came near the camp, Moses saw the calf and the dancing, and in terrible anger he threw the tablets to the ground and they lay broken at the foot of the mountain. 20He took the calf and melted it in the fire, and when the metal cooled, he ground it into powder and spread it upon the water and made the people drink it.

New Revised Standard

The Golden Calf

32 WHEN THE people saw that Moses delayed to come down from the mountain, the people gathered around Aaron, and said to him, "Come, make gods for us, who shall go before us; as for this Moses, the man who brought us up out of the land of Egypt, we do not know what has become of him." 2Aaron said to them, "Take off the gold rings that are on the ears of your wives, your sons, and your daughters, and bring them to me." 3So all the people took off the gold rings from their ears, and brought them to Aaron. 4He took the gold from them, formed it in a mold,d and cast an image of a calf; and they said, "These are your gods, O Israel, who brought you up out of the land of Egypt!" 5When Aaron saw this, he built an altar before it; and Aaron made proclamation and said, "Tomorrow shall be a festival to the LORD." 6They rose early the next day, and offered burnt offerings and brought sacrifices of well-being; and the people sat down to eat and drink, and rose up to revel.

7 The LORD said to Moses, "Go down at once! Your people, whom you brought up out of the land of Egypt, have acted perversely; 8they have been quick to turn aside from the way that I commanded them; they have cast for themselves an image of a calf, and have worshiped it and sacrificed to it, and said, 'These are your gods, O Israel, who brought you up out of the land of Egypt!' " 9The LORD said to Moses, "I have seen this people, how stiff-necked they are. 10Now let me alone, so that my wrath may burn hot against them and I may consume them; and of you I will make a great nation."

11 But Moses implored the LORD his God, and said, "O LORD, why does your wrath burn hot against your people, whom you brought out of the land of Egypt with great power and with a mighty hand? 12Why should the Egyptians say, 'It was with evil intent that he brought them out to kill them in the mountains, and to consume them from the face of the earth'? Turn from your fierce wrath; change your mind and do not bring disaster on your people. 13Remember Abraham, Isaac, and Israel, your servants, how you swore to them by your own self, saying to them, 'I will multiply your descendants like the stars of heaven, and all this land that I have promised I will give to your descendants, and they shall inherit it forever.' " 14And the LORD changed his mind about the disaster that he planned to bring on his people.

15 Then Moses turned and went down from the mountain, carrying the two tablets of the covenante in his hands, tablets that were written on both sides, written on the front and on the back. 16The tablets were the work of God, and the writing was the writing of God, engraved upon the tablets. 17When Joshua heard the noise of the people as they shouted, he said to Moses, "There is a noise of war in the camp." 18But he said,

"It is not the sound made by victors,
      or the sound made by losers;
   it is the sound of revelers that I hear."

19As soon as he came near the camp and saw the calf and the dancing, Moses' anger burned hot, and he threw the tablets from his hands and broke them at the foot of the mountain. 20He took the calf that they had made, burned it with fire, ground it to powder, scattered it on the water, and made the Israelites drink it.

---

d Or *fashioned it with a graving tool*; Meaning of Heb uncertain   e Or *treaty*, or *testimony*; Heb *eduth*

King James

21And Moses said unto Aaron, What did this people unto thee, that thou hast brought so great a sin upon them?

22And Aaron said, Let not the anger of my lord wax hot: thou knowest the people, that they *are set* on mischief.

23For they said unto me, Make us gods, which shall go before us: for *as for* this Moses, the man that brought us up out of the land of Egypt, we wot not what is become of him.

24And I said unto them, Whosoever hath any gold, let them break *it* off. So they gave *it* me: then I cast it into the fire, and there came out this calf.

25¶ And when Moses saw that the people *were* naked; (for Aaron had made them naked unto *their* shame among their enemies:)

26Then Moses stood in the gate of the camp, and said, Who *is* on the LORD's side? *let him come* unto me. And all the sons of Levi gathered themselves together unto him.

27And he said unto them, Thus saith the LORD God of Israel, Put every man his sword by his side, *and* go in and out from gate to gate throughout the camp, and slay every man his brother, and every man his companion, and every man his neighbour.

28And the children of Levi did according to the word of Moses: and there fell of the people that day about three thousand men.

29For Moses had said, Consecrate yourselves today to the LORD, even every man upon his son, and upon his brother; that he may bestow upon you a blessing this day.

30¶ And it came to pass on the morrow, that Moses said unto the people, Ye have sinned a great sin: and now I will go up unto the LORD; peradventure I shall make an atonement for your sin.

31And Moses returned unto the LORD, and said, Oh, this people have sinned a great sin, and have made them gods of gold.

32Yet now, if thou wilt forgive their sin—; and if not, blot me, I pray thee, out of thy book which thou hast written.

33And the LORD said unto Moses, Whosoever hath sinned against me, him will I blot out of my book.

34Therefore now go, lead the people unto *the place* of which I have spoken unto thee: behold, mine Angel shall go before thee: nevertheless in the day when I visit I will visit their sin upon them.

35And the LORD plagued the people, because they made the calf, which Aaron made.

33 AND THE LORD said unto Moses, Depart, *and* go up hence, thou and the people which thou hast brought up out of the land of Egypt, unto the land which I sware unto Abraham, to Isaac, and to Jacob, saying, Unto thy seed will I give it:

2And I will send an angel before thee; and I will drive out the Canaanite, the Amorite, and the Hittite, and the Perizzite, the Hivite, and the Jebusite:

3Unto a land flowing with milk and honey: for I will not go up in the midst of thee; for thou *art* a stiffnecked people: lest I consume thee in the way.

4¶ And when the people heard these evil tidings, they mourned: and no man did put on him his ornaments.

New International

21He said to Aaron, "What did these people do to you, that you led them into such great sin?"

22"Do not be angry, my lord," Aaron answered. "You know how prone these people are to evil. 23They said to me, 'Make us gods who will go before us. As for this fellow Moses who brought us up out of Egypt, we don't know what has happened to him.' 24So I told them, 'Whoever has any gold jewelry, take it off.' Then they gave me the gold, and I threw it into the fire, and out came this calf!"

25Moses saw that the people were running wild and that Aaron had let them get out of control and so become a laughingstock to their enemies. 26So he stood at the entrance to the camp and said, "Whoever is for the LORD, come to me." And all the Levites rallied to him.

27Then he said to them, "This is what the LORD, the God of Israel, says: 'Each man strap a sword to his side. Go back and forth through the camp from one end to the other, each killing his brother and friend and neighbor.' " 28The Levites did as Moses commanded, and that day about three thousand of the people died. 29Then Moses said, "You have been set apart to the LORD today, for you were against your own sons and brothers, and he has blessed you this day."

30The next day Moses said to the people, "You have committed a great sin. But now I will go up to the LORD; perhaps I can make atonement for your sin."

31So Moses went back to the LORD and said, "Oh, what a great sin these people have committed! They have made themselves gods of gold. 32But now, please forgive their sin—but if not, then blot me out of the book you have written."

33The LORD replied to Moses, "Whoever has sinned against me I will blot out of my book. 34Now go, lead the people to the place I spoke of, and my angel will go before you. However, when the time comes for me to punish, I will punish them for their sin."

35And the LORD struck the people with a plague because of what they did with the calf Aaron had made.

33 THEN THE LORD said to Moses, "Leave this place, you and the people you brought up out of Egypt, and go up to the land I promised on oath to Abraham, Isaac and Jacob, saying, 'I will give it to your descendants.' 2I will send an angel before you and drive out the Canaanites, Amorites, Hittites, Perizzites, Hivites and Jebusites. 3Go up to the land flowing with milk and honey. But I will not go with you, because you are a stiff-necked people and I might destroy you on the way."

4When the people heard these distressing words, they began to mourn and no one put on any ornaments. 5For

Living Bible

21Then he turned to Aaron. "What in the world did the people do to you," he demanded, "to make you bring such a terrible sin upon them?"

22"Don't get so upset," Aaron replied. "You know these people and what a wicked bunch they are. 23They said to me, 'Make us a god to lead us, for something has happened to this fellow Moses who led us out of Egypt.' 24Well, I told them, 'Bring me your gold earrings.' So they brought them to me and I threw them into the fire, and . . . well . . . this calf came out!"

25When Moses saw that the people had been committing adultery—at Aaron's encouragement, and much to the amusement of their enemies— 26he stood at the camp entrance and shouted, "All of you who are on the Lord's side, come over here and join me." And all the Levites came.

27He told them, "Jehovah the God of Israel says, 'Get your swords and go back and forth from one end of the camp to the other and kill even your brothers, friends, and neighbors.' " 28So they did, and about three thousand men died that day.

29Then Moses told the Levites, "Today you have ordained yourselves for the service of the Lord, for you obeyed him even though it meant killing your own sons and brothers; now he will give you a great blessing."

30The next day Moses said to the people, "You have sinned a great sin, but I will return to the Lord on the mountain—perhaps I will be able to obtain his forgiveness for you."

31So Moses returned to the Lord and said, "Oh, these people have sinned a great sin, and have made themselves gods of gold. 32Yet now if you will only forgive their sin—and if not, then blot *me* out of the book you have written."ᵃ

33And the Lord replied to Moses, "Whoever has sinned against me will be blotted out of my book. 34And now go, lead the people to the place I told you about, and I assure you that my Angel shall travel on ahead of you; however, when I come to visit these people, I will punish them for their sins."

35And the Lord sent a great plague upon the people because they had worshiped Aaron's calf.

33 THE LORD said to Moses, "Lead these people you brought from Egypt to the land I promised Abraham, Isaac, and Jacob; for I said, 'I will give this land to your descendants.' 2I will send an Angel before you to drive out the Canaanites, Amorites, Hittites, Perizzites, Hivites, and Jebusites. 3It is a land 'flowing with milk and honey'; but I will not travel among you, for you are a stubborn, unruly people, and I would be tempted to destroy you along the way."

4When the people heard these stern words, they went into mourning and stripped themselves of their jewelry and ornaments.

New Revised Standard

21 Moses said to Aaron, "What did this people do to you that you have brought so great a sin upon them?" 22And Aaron said, "Do not let the anger of my lord burn hot; you know the people, that they are bent on evil. 23They said to me, 'Make us gods, who shall go before us; as for this Moses, the man who brought us up out of the land of Egypt, we do not know what has become of him.' 24So I said to them, 'Whoever has gold, take it off'; so they gave it to me, and I threw it into the fire, and out came this calf!"

25 When Moses saw that the people were running wild (for Aaron had let them run wild, to the derision of their enemies), 26then Moses stood in the gate of the camp, and said, "Who is on the LORD's side? Come to me!" And all the sons of Levi gathered around him. 27He said to them, "Thus says the LORD, the God of Israel, 'Put your sword on your side, each of you! Go back and forth from gate to gate throughout the camp, and each of you kill your brother, your friend, and your neighbor.' " 28The sons of Levi did as Moses commanded, and about three thousand of the people fell on that day. 29Moses said, "Today you have ordained yourselvesᵇ for the service of the LORD, each one at the cost of a son or a brother, and so have brought a blessing on yourselves this day."

30 On the next day Moses said to the people, "You have sinned a great sin. But now I will go up to the LORD; perhaps I can make atonement for your sin." 31So Moses returned to the LORD and said, "Alas, this people has sinned a great sin; they have made for themselves gods of gold. 32But now, if you will only forgive their sin—but if not, blot me out of the book that you have written." 33But the LORD said to Moses, "Whoever has sinned against me I will blot out of my book. 34But now go, lead the people to the place about which I have spoken to you; see, my angel shall go in front of you. Nevertheless, when the day comes for punishment, I will punish them for their sin."

35 Then the LORD sent a plague on the people, because they made the calf—the one that Aaron made.

The Command to Leave Sinai

33 THE LORD said to Moses, "Go, leave this place, you and the people whom you have brought up out of the land of Egypt, and go to the land of which I swore to Abraham, Isaac, and Jacob, saying, 'To your descendants I will give it.' 2I will send an angel before you, and I will drive out the Canaanites, the Amorites, the Hittites, the Perizzites, the Hivites, and the Jebusites. 3Go up to a land flowing with milk and honey; but I will not go up among you, or I would consume you on the way, for you are a stiff-necked people."

4 When the people heard these harsh words, they mourned, and no one put on ornaments. 5For the LORD

ᵃ 32:32 then blot me *out of the book you have written,* or "then kill me instead of them."

ᵇ Gk Vg Compare Tg: Heb *Today ordain yourselves*

King James

5For the LORD had said unto Moses, Say unto the children of Israel, Ye *are* a stiffnecked people: I will come up into the midst of thee in a moment, and consume thee: therefore now put off thy ornaments from thee, that I may know what to do unto thee.

6And the children of Israel stripped themselves of their ornaments by the mount Horeb.

7And Moses took the tabernacle, and pitched it without the camp, afar off from the camp, and called it the Tabernacle of the congregation. And it came to pass, *that* every one which sought the LORD went out unto the tabernacle of the congregation, which *was* without the camp.

8And it came to pass, when Moses went out unto the tabernacle, *that* all the people rose up, and stood every man *at* his tent door, and looked after Moses, until he was gone into the tabernacle.

9And it came to pass, as Moses entered into the tabernacle, the cloudy pillar descended, and stood *at* the door of the tabernacle, and *the* LORD *talked with Moses*.

10And all the people saw the cloudy pillar stand *at* the tabernacle door: and all the people rose up and worshipped, every man *in* his tent door.

11And the LORD spake unto Moses face to face, as a man speaketh unto his friend. And he turned again into the camp: but his servant Joshua, the son of Nun, a young man, departed not out of the tabernacle.

12¶ And Moses said unto the LORD, See, thou sayest unto me, Bring up this people: and thou hast not let me know whom thou wilt send with me. Yet thou hast said, I know thee by name, and thou hast also found grace in my sight.

13Now therefore, I pray thee, if I have found grace in thy sight, show me now thy way, that I may know thee, that I may find grace in thy sight: and consider that this nation *is* thy people.

14And he said, My presence shall go *with thee*, and I will give thee rest.

15And he said unto him, If thy presence go not *with me*, carry us not up hence.

16For wherein shall it be known here that I and thy people have found grace in thy sight? *is it* not in that thou goest with us? so shall we be separated, I and thy people, from all the people that *are* upon the face of the earth.

17And the LORD said unto Moses, I will do this thing also that thou hast spoken: for thou hast found grace in my sight, and I know thee by name.

18And he said, I beseech thee, show me thy glory.

19And he said, I will make all my goodness pass before thee, and I will proclaim the name of the LORD before thee; and will be gracious to whom I will be gracious, and will show mercy on whom I will show mercy.

20And he said, Thou canst not see my face: for there shall no man see me, and live.

21And the LORD said, Behold, *there is* a place by me, and thou shalt stand upon a rock:

22And it shall come to pass, while my glory passeth by, that I will put thee in a cleft of the rock, and will cover thee with my hand while I pass by:

23And I will take away mine hand, and thou shalt see my back parts: but my face shall not be seen.

New International

the LORD had said to Moses, "Tell the Israelites, 'You are a stiff-necked people. If I were to go with you even for a moment, I might destroy you. Now take off your ornaments and I will decide what to do with you.' " 6So the Israelites stripped off their ornaments at Mount Horeb.

The Tent of Meeting

7Now Moses used to take a tent and pitch it outside the camp some distance away, calling it the "tent of meeting." Anyone inquiring of the LORD would go to the tent of meeting outside the camp. 8And whenever Moses went out to the tent, all the people rose and stood at the entrances to their tents, watching Moses until he entered the tent. 9As Moses went into the tent, the pillar of cloud would come down and stay at the entrance, while the LORD spoke with Moses. 10Whenever the people saw the pillar of cloud standing at the entrance to the tent, they all stood and worshiped, each at the entrance to his tent. 11The LORD would speak to Moses face to face, as a man speaks with his friend. Then Moses would return to the camp, but his young aide Joshua son of Nun did not leave the tent.

Moses and the Glory of the LORD

12Moses said to the LORD, "You have been telling me, 'Lead these people,' but you have not let me know whom you will send with me. You have said, 'I know you by name and you have found favor with me.' 13If you are pleased with me, teach me your ways so I may know you and continue to find favor with you. Remember that this nation is your people."

14The LORD replied, "My Presence will go with you, and I will give you rest."

15Then Moses said to him, "If your Presence does not go with us, do not send us up from here. 16How will anyone know that you are pleased with me and with your people unless you go with us? What else will distinguish me and your people from all the other people on the face of the earth?"

17And the LORD said to Moses, "I will do the very thing you have asked, because I am pleased with you and I know you by name."

18Then Moses said, "Now show me your glory."

19And the LORD said, "I will cause all my goodness to pass in front of you, and I will proclaim my name, the LORD, in your presence. I will have mercy on whom I will have mercy, and I will have compassion on whom I will have compassion. 20But," he said, "you cannot see my face, for no one may see me and live."

21Then the LORD said, "There is a place near me where you may stand on a rock. 22When my glory passes by, I will put you in a cleft in the rock and cover you with my hand until I have passed by. 23Then I will remove my hand and you will see my back; but my face must not be seen."

Living Bible

5For the Lord had told Moses to tell them, "You are an unruly, stubborn people. If I were there among you for even a moment, I would exterminate you. Remove your jewelry and ornaments until I decide what to do with you." 6So, after that, they wore no jewelry.

7Moses always erected the sacred tent (the "Tent for Meeting with God," he called it) far outside the camp, and everyone who wanted to consult with Jehovah went out there.

8Whenever Moses went to the Tabernacle, all the people, when they saw it, stood and would rise and stand in their tent doors. 9As he entered, the pillar of cloud would come down and stand at the door while the Lord spoke with Moses. 10Then all the people worshiped from their tent doors, bowing low to the pillar of cloud. 11Inside the tent the Lord spoke to Moses face to face, as a man speaks to his friend. Afterwards Moses would return to the camp, but the young man who assisted him, Joshua (son of Nun), stayed behind in the Tabernacle.

12Moses talked there with the Lord and said to him, "You have been telling me, 'Take these people to the Promised Land,' but you haven't told me whom you will send with me. You say you are my friend,a and that I have found favor before you; 13please, if this is really so, guide me clearly along the way you want me to travelb so that I will understand you and walk acceptably before you. For don't forget that this nation is your people."

14And the Lord replied, "I myself will go with you and give you success."

15For Moses had said, "If you aren't going with us, don't let us move a step from this place. 16If you don't go with us, who will ever know that I and my people have found favor with you, and that we are different from any other people upon the face of the earth?"

17And the Lord replied to Moses, "Yes, I will do what you have asked, for you have certainly found favor with me, and you are my friend."c

18Then Moses asked to see God's glory.

19The Lord replied, "I will make my goodness pass before you, and I will announce to you the meaning of my named Jehovah, the Lord. I show kindness and mercy to anyone I want to. 20But you may not see the glory of my face, for man may not see me and live. 21However, stand here on this rock beside me. 22And when my glory goes by, I will put you in the cleft of the rock and cover you with my hand until I have passed. 23Then I will remove my hand and you shall see my back, but not my face."

New Revised Standard

had said to Moses, "Say to the Israelites, 'You are a stiff-necked people; if for a single moment I should go up among you, I would consume you. So now take off your ornaments, and I will decide what to do to you.' " 6Therefore the Israelites stripped themselves of their ornaments, from Mount Horeb onward.

The Tent outside the Camp

7 Now Moses used to take the tent and pitch it outside the camp, far off from the camp; he called it the tent of meeting. And everyone who sought the LORD would go out to the tent of meeting, which was outside the camp. 8Whenever Moses went out to the tent, all the people would rise and stand, each of them, at the entrance of their tents and watch Moses until he had gone into the tent. 9When Moses entered the tent, the pillar of cloud would descend and stand at the entrance of the tent, and the LORD would speak with Moses. 10When all the people saw the pillar of cloud standing at the entrance of the tent, all the people would rise and bow down, all of them, at the entrance of their tent. 11Thus the LORD used to speak to Moses face to face, as one speaks to a friend. Then he would return to the camp; but his young assistant, Joshua son of Nun, would not leave the tent.

Moses' Intercession

12 Moses said to the LORD, "See, you have said to me, 'Bring up this people'; but you have not let me know whom you will send with me. Yet you have said, 'I know you by name, and you have also found favor in my sight.' 13Now if I have found favor in your sight, show me your ways, so that I may know you and find favor in your sight. Consider too that this nation is your people." 14He said, "My presence will go with you, and I will give you rest." 15And he said to him, "If your presence will not go, do not carry us up from here. 16For how shall it be known that I have found favor in your sight, I and your people, unless you go with us? In this way, we shall be distinct, I and your people, from every people on the face of the earth."

17 The LORD said to Moses, "I will do the very thing that you have asked; for you have found favor in my sight, and I know you by name." 18Moses said, "Show me your glory, I pray." 19And he said, "I will make all my goodness pass before you, and will proclaim before you the name, 'The LORD';e and I will be gracious to whom I will be gracious, and will show mercy on whom I will show mercy. 20But," he said, "you cannot see my face; for no one shall see me and live." 21And the LORD continued, "See, there is a place by me where you shall stand on the rock; 22and while my glory passes by I will put you in a cleft of the rock, and I will cover you with my hand until I have passed by; 23then I will take away my hand, and you shall see my back; but my face shall not be seen."

---

a *33:12 You say you are my friend*, literally, "You have said you know me by name." b *33:13 guide me clearly along the way you want me to travel*, or, "show me your ways," or "show me your majesty." c *33:17 you are my friend*, literally, "I know you by name." d *33:19 I will announce to you the meaning of my name*, literally, "I will proclaim before you my name." His name, *Jehovah*, means, "I will be what I will be." (See Ex 3:14.)

e Heb *YHWH*; see note at 3.15

King James

34 AND THE LORD said unto Moses, Hew thee two tables of stone like unto the first: and I will write upon *these* tables the words that were in the first tables, which thou brakest.

2And be ready in the morning, and come up in the morning unto mount Sinai, and present thyself there to me in the top of the mount.

3And no man shall come up with thee, neither let any man be seen throughout all the mount; neither let the flocks nor herds feed before that mount.

4¶ And he hewed two tables of stone like unto the first; and Moses rose up early in the morning, and went up unto mount Sinai, as the LORD had commanded him, and took in his hand the two tables of stone.

5And the LORD descended in the cloud, and stood with him there, and proclaimed the name of the LORD.

6And the LORD passed by before him, and proclaimed, The LORD, The LORD God, merciful and gracious, longsuffering, and abundant in goodness and truth,

7Keeping mercy for thousands, forgiving iniquity and transgression and sin, and that will by no means clear *the guilty;* visiting the iniquity of the fathers upon the children, and upon the children's children, unto the third and to the fourth *generation.*

8And Moses made haste, and bowed his head toward the earth, and worshipped.

9And he said, If now I have found grace in thy sight, O Lord, let my Lord, I pray thee, go among us; for it *is* a stiffnecked people; and pardon our iniquity and our sin, and take us for thine inheritance.

10¶ And he said, Behold, I make a covenant: before all thy people I will do marvels, such as have not been done in all the earth, nor in any nation: and all the people among which thou *art* shall see the work of the LORD: for it *is* a terrible thing that I will do with thee.

11Observe thou that which I command thee this day: behold, I drive out before thee the Amorite, and the Canaanite, and the Hittite, and the Perizzite, and the Hivite, and the Jebusite.

12Take heed to thyself, lest thou make a covenant with the inhabitants of the land whither thou goest, lest it be for a snare in the midst of thee:

13But ye shall destroy their altars, break their images, and cut down their groves:

14For thou shalt worship no other god: for the LORD, whose name *is* Jealous, *is* a jealous God:

15Lest thou make a covenant with the inhabitants of the land, and they go a-whoring after their gods, and do sacrifice unto their gods, and *one* call thee, and thou eat of his sacrifice;

16And thou take of their daughters unto thy sons, and their daughters go a-whoring after their gods, and make thy sons go a-whoring after their gods.

17Thou shalt make thee no molten gods.

18¶ The feast of unleavened bread shalt thou keep. Seven days thou shalt eat unleavened bread, as I commanded thee, in the time of the month Abib: for in the month Abib thou camest out from Egypt.

19All that openeth the matrix *is* mine; and every firstling among thy cattle, *whether* ox or sheep, *that is male.*

20But the firstling of an ass thou shalt redeem with a lamb: and if thou redeem *him* not, then shalt thou break his neck. All the firstborn of thy sons thou shalt redeem. And none shall appear before me empty.

New International

The New Stone Tablets

34 THE LORD said to Moses, "Chisel out two stone tablets like the first ones, and I will write on them the words that were on the first tablets, which you broke. 2Be ready in the morning, and then come up on Mount Sinai. Present yourself to me there on top of the mountain. 3No one is to come with you or be seen anywhere on the mountain; not even the flocks and herds may graze in front of the mountain."

4So Moses chiseled out two stone tablets like the first ones and went up Mount Sinai early in the morning, as the LORD had commanded him; and he carried the two stone tablets in his hands. 5Then the LORD came down in the cloud and stood there with him and proclaimed his name, the LORD. 6And he passed in front of Moses, proclaiming, "The LORD, the LORD, the compassionate and gracious God, slow to anger, abounding in love and faithfulness, 7maintaining love to thousands, and forgiving wickedness, rebellion and sin. Yet he does not leave the guilty unpunished; he punishes the children and their children for the sin of the fathers to the third and fourth generation."

8Moses bowed to the ground at once and worshiped. 9"O Lord, if I have found favor in your eyes," he said, "then let the Lord go with us. Although this is a stiff-necked people, forgive our wickedness and our sin, and take us as your inheritance."

10Then the LORD said: "I am making a covenant with you. Before all your people I will do wonders never before done in any nation in all the world. The people you live among will see how awesome is the work that I, the LORD, will do for you. 11Obey what I command you today. I will drive out before you the Amorites, Canaanites, Hittites, Perizzites, Hivites and Jebusites. 12Be careful not to make a treaty with those who live in the land where you are going, or they will be a snare among you. 13Break down their altars, smash their sacred stones and cut down their Asherah poles.a 14Do not worship any other god, for the LORD, whose name is Jealous, is a jealous God.

15"Be careful not to make a treaty with those who live in the land; for when they prostitute themselves to their gods and sacrifice to them, they will invite you and you will eat their sacrifices. 16And when you choose some of their daughters as wives for your sons and those daughters prostitute themselves to their gods, they will lead your sons to do the same.

17"Do not make cast idols.

18"Celebrate the Feast of Unleavened Bread. For seven days eat bread made without yeast, as I commanded you. Do this at the appointed time in the month of Abib, for in that month you came out of Egypt.

19"The first offspring of every womb belongs to me, including all the firstborn males of your livestock, whether from herd or flock. 20Redeem the firstborn donkey with a lamb, but if you do not redeem it, break its neck. Redeem all your firstborn sons.

"No one is to appear before me empty-handed.

---

a *13* That is, symbols of the goddess Asherah

Living Bible

34 THE LORD told Moses, "Prepare two stone tablets like the first ones and I will write upon them the same commands that were on the tablets you broke. 2Be ready in the morning to come up into Mount Sinai and present yourself to me on the top of the mountain. 3No one shall come with you and no one must be anywhere on the mountain. Do not let the flocks or herds feed close to the mountain."

4So Moses took two tablets of stone like the first ones, and was up early and climbed Mount Sinai, as the Lord had told him to, taking the two stone tablets in his hands.

5, 6Then the Lord descended in the form of a pillar of cloud and stood there with him, and passed in front of him and announced the meaning of his name.b "I am Jehovah, the merciful and gracious God," he said, "slow to anger and rich in steadfast love and truth. 7I, Jehovah, show this steadfast love to many thousands by forgiving their sins;c or elsed I refuse to clear the guilty, and require that a father's sins be punished in the sons and grandsons, and even later generations."

8Moses fell down before the Lord and worshiped. 9And he said, "If it is true that I have found favor in your sight, O Lord, then please go with us to the Promised Land; yes, it is an unruly, stubborn people, but pardon our iniquity and our sins, and accept us as your own."

10The Lord replied, "All right, this is the contract I am going to make with you. I will do miracles such as have never been done before anywhere in all the earth, and all the people of Israel shall see the power of the Lord—the terrible power I will display through you. 11Your part of the agreement is to obey all of my commandments; then I will drive out from before you the Amorites, Canaanites, Hittites, Perizzites, Hivites, and Jebusites.

12"Be very, very careful never to compromise with the people there in the land where you are going, for if you do, you will soon be following their evil ways. 13Instead, you must break down their heathen altars, smash the obelisks they worship, and cut down their shameful idols.e 14For you must worship no other gods, but only Jehovah, for he is a God who claims absolute loyalty and exclusive devotion.

15"No, do not make a peace treaty of any kind with the people living in the land, for they are spiritual prostitutes, committing adultery against mef by sacrificing to their gods. If you become friendly with them and one of them invites you to go with him and worship his idol, you are apt to do it. 16And you would accept their daughters, who worship other gods, as wives for your sons—and then your sons would commit adultery against me by worshiping their wives' gods. 17You must have nothing to do with idols.

18"Be sure to celebrate the Feast of Unleavened Bread for seven days, just as I instructed you, at the dates appointed each year in March; that was the month you left Egypt.

19"Every firstborn maleg is mine—cattle, sheep, and goats. 20The firstborn colt of a donkey may be redeemed by giving a lamb in its place. If you decide not to redeem it, then its neck must be broken. But your sons must all be redeemed. And no one shall appear before me without a gift.

New Revised Standard

Moses Makes New Tablets

34 THE LORD said to Moses, "Cut two tablets of stone like the former ones, and I will write on the tablets the words that were on the former tablets, which you broke. 2Be ready in the morning, and come up in the morning to Mount Sinai and present yourself there to me, on the top of the mountain. 3No one shall come up with you, and do not let anyone be seen throughout all the mountain; and do not let flocks or herds graze in front of that mountain." 4So Moses cut two tablets of stone like the former ones; and he rose early in the morning and went up on Mount Sinai, as the LORD had commanded him, and took in his hand the two tablets of stone. 5The LORD descended in the cloud and stood with him there, and proclaimed the name, "The LORD."h 6The LORD passed before him, and proclaimed,

"The LORD, the LORD,
a God merciful and gracious,
slow to anger,
and abounding in steadfast love and
        faithfulness,
7 keeping steadfast love for the thousandth
        generation,i
forgiving iniquity and transgression and sin,
yet by no means clearing the guilty,
but visiting the iniquity of the parents
upon the children
and the children's children,
to the third and the fourth generation."

8And Moses quickly bowed his head toward the earth, and worshiped. 9He said, "If now I have found favor in your sight, O Lord, I pray, let the Lord go with us. Although this is a stiff-necked people, pardon our iniquity and our sin, and take us for your inheritance."

The Covenant Renewed

10 He said: I hereby make a covenant. Before all your people I will perform marvels, such as have not been performed in all the earth or in any nation; and all the people among whom you live shall see the work of the LORD; for it is an awesome thing that I will do with you.

11 Observe what I command you today. See, I will drive out before you the Amorites, the Canaanites, the Hittites, the Perizzites, the Hivites, and the Jebusites. 12Take care not to make a covenant with the inhabitants of the land to which you are going, or it will become a snare among you. 13You shall tear down their altars, break their pillars, and cut down their sacred polesj 14(for you shall worship no other god, because the LORD, whose name is Jealous, is a jealous God). 15You shall not make a covenant with the inhabitants of the land, for when they prostitute themselves to their gods and sacrifice to their gods, someone among them will invite you, and you will eat of the sacrifice. 16And you will take wives from among their daughters for your sons, and their daughters who prostitute themselves to their gods will make your sons also prostitute themselves to their gods.

17 You shall not make cast idols.

18 You shall keep the festival of unleavened bread. Seven days you shall eat unleavened bread, as I commanded you, at the time appointed in the month of Abib; for in the month of Abib you came out from Egypt.

19 All that first opens the womb is mine, all your malek livestock, the firstborn of cow and sheep. 20The firstborn of a donkey you shall redeem with a lamb, or if you will not redeem it you shall break its neck. All the firstborn of your sons you shall redeem.

No one shall appear before me empty-handed.

---

b 34:5, 6 announced the meaning of his name, literally, "proclaimed the name of Jehovah." c 34:7 forgiving their sins, literally, "forgiving iniquity and transgression and sin." d 34:7 or else, implied. e 34:13 Asherim, or shameful idols. They were carved statues of male and female genital organs. f 34:15 committing adultery against me, literally, "they play the harlot worshiping their gods." g 34:19 Every firstborn male, literally, "all that opens the womb."

h Heb YHWH; see note at 3.15   i Or for thousands   j Heb Asherim   k Gk Theodotion Vg Tg: Meaning of Heb uncertain

King James

21¶ Six days thou shalt work, but on the seventh day thou shalt rest: in earing time and in harvest thou shalt rest.

22¶ And thou shalt observe the feast of weeks, of the firstfruits of wheat harvest, and the feast of ingathering at the year's end.

23¶ Thrice in the year shall all your menchildren appear before the Lord God, the God of Israel.

24For I will cast out the nations before thee, and enlarge thy borders: neither shall any man desire thy land, when thou shalt go up to appear before the Lord thy God thrice in the year.

25Thou shalt not offer the blood of my sacrifice with leaven; neither shall the sacrifice of the feast of the passover be left unto the morning.

26The first of the firstfruits of thy land thou shalt bring unto the house of the Lord thy God. Thou shalt not seethe a kid in his mother's milk.

27And the Lord said unto Moses, Write thou these words: for after the tenor of these words I have made a covenant with thee and with Israel.

28And he was there with the Lord forty days and forty nights; he did neither eat bread, nor drink water. And he wrote upon the tables the words of the covenant, the ten commandments.

29¶ And it came to pass, when Moses came down from mount Sinai with the two tables of testimony in Moses' hand, when he came down from the mount, that Moses wist not that the skin of his face shone while he talked with him.

30And when Aaron and all the children of Israel saw Moses, behold, the skin of his face shone; and they were afraid to come nigh him.

31And Moses called unto them; and Aaron and all the rulers of the congregation returned unto him: and Moses talked with them.

32And afterward all the children of Israel came nigh: and he gave them in commandment all that the Lord had spoken with him in mount Sinai.

33And *till* Moses had done speaking with them, he put a veil on his face.

34But when Moses went in before the Lord to speak with him, he took the veil off, until he came out. And he came out, and spake unto the children of Israel *that* which he was commanded.

35And the children of Israel saw the face of Moses, that the skin of Moses' face shone: and Moses put the veil upon his face again, until he went in to speak with him.

35 AND MOSES gathered all the congregation of the children of Israel together, and said unto them, These *are* the words which the Lord hath commanded, that *ye* should do them.

2Six days shall work be done, but on the seventh day there shall be to you an holy day, a sabbath of rest to the Lord: whosoever doeth work therein shall be put to death.

3Ye shall kindle no fire throughout your habitations upon the sabbath day.

4¶ And Moses spake unto all the congregation of the children of Israel, saying, This *is* the thing which the Lord commanded, saying,

New International

21"Six days you shall labor, but on the seventh day you shall rest; even during the plowing season and harvest you must rest.

22"Celebrate the Feast of Weeks with the firstfruits of the wheat harvest, and the Feast of Ingathering at the turn of the year.a 23Three times a year all your men are to appear before the Sovereign Lord, the God of Israel. 24I will drive out nations before you and enlarge your territory, and no one will covet your land when you go up three times each year to appear before the Lord your God.

25"Do not offer the blood of a sacrifice to me along with anything containing yeast, and do not let any of the sacrifice from the Passover Feast remain until morning.

26"Bring the best of the firstfruits of your soil to the house of the Lord your God.

"Do not cook a young goat in its mother's milk."

27Then the Lord said to Moses, "Write down these words, for in accordance with these words I have made a covenant with you and with Israel." 28Moses was there with the Lord forty days and forty nights without eating bread or drinking water. And he wrote on the tablets the words of the covenant—the Ten Commandments.

The Radiant Face of Moses

29When Moses came down from Mount Sinai with the two tablets of the Testimony in his hands, he was not aware that his face was radiant because he had spoken with the Lord. 30When Aaron and all the Israelites saw Moses, his face was radiant, and they were afraid to come near him. 31But Moses called to them; so Aaron and all the leaders of the community came back to him, and he spoke to them. 32Afterward all the Israelites came near him, and he gave them all the commands the Lord had given him on Mount Sinai.

33When Moses finished speaking to them, he put a veil over his face. 34But whenever he entered the Lord's presence to speak with him, he removed the veil until he came out. And when he came out and told the Israelites what he had been commanded, 35they saw that his face was radiant. Then Moses would put the veil back over his face until he went in to speak with the Lord.

Sabbath Regulations

35 MOSES ASSEMBLED the whole Israelite community and said to them, "These are the things the Lord has commanded you to do: 2For six days, work is to be done, but the seventh day shall be your holy day, a Sabbath of rest to the Lord. Whoever does any work on it must be put to death. 3Do not light a fire in any of your dwellings on the Sabbath day."

Materials for the Tabernacle

4Moses said to the whole Israelite community, "This is what the Lord has commanded: 5From what you

a 22 That is, in the fall

Living Bible

21"Even during plowing and harvest times, work only six days, and rest on the seventh.

22"And you must remember to celebrate these three annual religious festivals: the Festival of Weeks, the Festival of the First Wheat, and the Harvest Festival. 23On each of these three occasions all the men and boys of Israel shall appear before the Lord. 24No one will attack and conquer your land when you go up to appear before the Lord your God those three times each year. For I will drive out the nations from before you and enlarge your boundaries.

25"You must not use leavened bread with your sacrifices to me, and none of the meat of the Passover lamb may be kept over until the following morning. 26And you must bring the best of the first of each year's crop to the Tabernacle of the Lord your God. You must not cook a young goat in its mother's milk."

27And the Lord said to Moses, "Write down these[b] laws that I have given you, for they represent the terms of my covenant with you and with Israel."

28Moses was up on the mountain with the Lord for forty days and forty nights, and in all that time he neither ate nor drank. At that time God[c] wrote out the Covenant—the Ten Commandments—on the stone tablets.

29Moses didn't realize as he came back down the mountain with the tablets that his face glowed from being in the presence of God. 30Because of this radiance upon his face, Aaron and the people of Israel were afraid to come near him.

31But Moses called them over to him, and Aaron and the leaders of the congregation came and talked with him. 32Afterwards, all the people came to him, and he gave them the commandments the Lord had given him upon the mountain. 33When Moses had finished speaking with them, he put a veil over his face;[d] 34but whenever he went into the Tabernacle to speak with the Lord, he removed the veil until he came out again; then he would pass on to the people whatever instructions God had given him, 35and the people would see his face aglow. Afterwards he would put the veil on again until he returned to speak with God.

35 NOW MOSES called a meeting of all the people and told them, "These are the laws of Jehovah you must obey.

2"Work six days only; the seventh day is a day of solemn rest, a holy day to be used to worship Jehovah; anyone working on that day must die. 3Don't even light the fires in your homes that day."

4Then Moses said to all the people, "This is what the Lord has commanded: 5-9All of you who wish to, all

New Revised Standard

21 Six days you shall work, but on the seventh day you shall rest; even in plowing time and in harvest time you shall rest. 22 You shall observe the festival of weeks, the first fruits of wheat harvest, and the festival of ingathering at the turn of the year. 23 Three times in the year all your males shall appear before the LORD God, the God of Israel. 24 For I will cast out nations before you, and enlarge your borders; no one shall covet your land when you go up to appear before the LORD your God three times in the year.

25 You shall not offer the blood of my sacrifice with leaven, and the sacrifice of the festival of the passover shall not be left until the morning.

26 The best of the first fruits of your ground you shall bring to the house of the LORD your God.

You shall not boil a kid in its mother's milk.

27 The LORD said to Moses: Write these words; in accordance with these words I have made a covenant with you and with Israel. 28 He was there with the LORD forty days and forty nights; he neither ate bread nor drank water. And he wrote on the tablets the words of the covenant, the ten commandments.[e]

The Shining Face of Moses

29 Moses came down from Mount Sinai. As he came down from the mountain with the two tablets of the covenant[f] in his hand, Moses did not know that the skin of his face shone because he had been talking with God. 30 When Aaron and all the Israelites saw Moses, the skin of his face was shining, and they were afraid to come near him. 31 But Moses called to them; and Aaron and all the leaders of the congregation returned to him, and Moses spoke with them. 32 Afterward all the Israelites came near, and he gave them in commandment all that the LORD had spoken with him on Mount Sinai. 33 When Moses had finished speaking with them, he put a veil on his face; 34 but whenever Moses went in before the LORD to speak with him, he would take the veil off, until he came out; and when he came out, and told the Israelites what he had been commanded, 35 the Israelites would see the face of Moses, that the skin of his face was shining; and Moses would put the veil on his face again, until he went in to speak with him.

Sabbath Regulations

35 MOSES ASSEMBLED all the congregation of the Israelites and said to them: These are the things that the LORD has commanded you to do:
2 Six days shall work be done, but on the seventh day you shall have a holy sabbath of solemn rest to the LORD; whoever does any work on it shall be put to death. 3 You shall kindle no fire in all your dwellings on the sabbath day.

Preparations for Making the Tabernacle

4 Moses said to all the congregation of the Israelites: This is the thing that the LORD has commanded: 5 Take

---

b 34:27 Write down these laws, that is, the preceding laws in vss 12-26.
c 34:28 At that time God, implied. See 34:1; Deut 10:1-4.   d 34:33 put a
veil over his face. So that the people would not see the glory fade. See
2 Cor 3:13.

e Heb words   f Or treaty, or testimony; Heb eduth

King James

5Take ye from among you an offering unto the LORD: whosoever *is* of a willing heart, let him bring it, an offering of the LORD; gold, and silver, and brass,

6And blue, and purple, and scarlet, and fine linen, and goats' *hair*,

7And rams' skins dyed red, and badgers' skins, and shittim wood,

8And oil for the light, and spices for anointing oil, and for the sweet incense,

9And onyx stones, and stones to be set for the ephod, and for the breastplate.

10And every wisehearted among you shall come, and make all that the LORD hath commanded;

11The tabernacle, his tent, and his covering, his taches, and his boards, his bars, his pillars, and his sockets,

12The ark, and the staves thereof, *with* the mercy seat, and the veil of the covering,

13The table, and his staves, and all his vessels, and the showbread,

14The candlestick also for the light, and his furniture, and his lamps, with the oil for the light,

15And the incense altar, and his staves, and the anointing oil, and the sweet incense, and the hanging for the door at the entering in of the tabernacle,

16The altar of burnt offering, with his brasen grate, his staves, and all his vessels, the laver and his foot,

17The hangings of the court, his pillars, and their sockets, and the hanging for the door of the court,

18The pins of the tabernacle, and the pins of the court, and their cords,

19The cloths of service, to do service in the holy *place*, the holy garments for Aaron the priest, and the garments of his sons, to minister in the priest's office.

20¶ And all the congregation of the children of Israel departed from the presence of Moses.

21And they came, every one whose heart stirred him up, and every one whom his spirit made willing, *and* they brought the LORD's offering to the work of the tabernacle of the congregation, and for all his service, and for the holy garments.

22And they came, both men and women, as many as were willing-hearted, *and* brought bracelets, and earrings, and rings, and tablets, all jewels of gold: and every man that offered *offered* an offering of gold unto the LORD.

23And every man, with whom was found blue, and purple, and scarlet, and fine linen, and goats' *hair*, and red skins of rams, and badgers' skins, brought *them*.

24Every one that did offer an offering of silver and brass brought the LORD's offering: and every man, with whom was found shittim wood for any work of the service, brought *it*.

25And all the women that were wisehearted did spin with their hands, and brought that which they had spun, *both* of blue, and of purple, *and* of scarlet, and of fine linen.

26And all the women whose heart stirred them up in wisdom spun goats' *hair*.

27And the rulers brought onyx stones, and stones to be set, for the ephod, and for the breastplate;

28And spice, and oil for the light, and for the anointing oil, and for the sweet incense.

29The children of Israel brought a willing offering unto the LORD, every man and woman, whose heart made them willing to bring for all manner of work, which the LORD had commanded to be made by the hand of Moses.

New International

have, take an offering for the LORD. Everyone who is willing is to bring to the LORD an offering of gold, silver and bronze; 6blue, purple and scarlet yarn and fine linen; goat hair; 7ram skins dyed red and hides of sea cowsa; acacia wood; 8olive oil for the light; spices for the anointing oil and for the fragrant incense; 9and onyx stones and other gems to be mounted on the ephod and breastpiece.

10"All who are skilled among you are to come and make everything the LORD has commanded: 11the tabernacle with its tent and its covering, clasps, frames, crossbars, posts and bases; 12the ark with its poles and the atonement cover and the curtain that shields it; 13the table with its poles and all its articles and the bread of the Presence; 14the lampstand that is for light with its accessories, lamps and oil for the light; 15the altar of incense with its poles, the anointing oil and the fragrant incense; the curtain for the doorway at the entrance to the tabernacle; 16the altar of burnt offering with its bronze grating, its poles and all its utensils; the bronze basin with its stand; 17the curtains of the courtyard with its posts and bases, and the curtain for the entrance to the courtyard; 18the tent pegs for the tabernacle and for the courtyard, and their ropes; 19the woven garments worn for ministering in the sanctuary—both the sacred garments for Aaron the priest and the garments for his sons when they serve as priests."

20Then the whole Israelite community withdrew from Moses' presence, 21and everyone who was willing and whose heart moved him came and brought an offering to the LORD for the work on the Tent of Meeting, for all its service, and for the sacred garments. 22All who were willing, men and women alike, came and brought gold jewelry of all kinds: brooches, earrings, rings and ornaments. They all presented their gold as a wave offering to the LORD. 23Everyone who had blue, purple or scarlet yarn or fine linen, or goat hair, ram skins dyed red or hides of sea cows brought them. 24Those presenting an offering of silver or bronze brought it as an offering to the LORD, and everyone who had acacia wood for any part of the work brought it. 25Every skilled woman spun with her hands and brought what she had spun—blue, purple or scarlet yarn or fine linen. 26And all the women who were willing and had the skill spun the goat hair. 27The leaders brought onyx stones and other gems to be mounted on the ephod and breastpiece. 28They also brought spices and olive oil for the light and for the anointing oil and for the fragrant incense. 29All the Israelite men and women who were willing brought to the LORD freewill offerings for all the work the LORD through Moses had commanded them to do.

a 7 That is, dugongs; also in verse 23

Living Bible

those with generous hearts, may bring these offerings to Jehovah:

Gold, silver, and bronze;

Blue, purple, and scarlet cloth, made of fine-twined linen or of goat's hair;

Tanned rams' skins and specially treated goatskins;

Acacia wood;

Olive oil for the lamps;

Spices for the anointing oil and for the incense;

Onyx stones and stones to be used for the ephod and chestpiece.

10-19"Come, all of you who are skilled craftsmen having special talents, and construct what God has commanded us:

The Tabernacle tent, and its coverings, clasps, frames, bars, pillars, and bases;

The Ark and its poles;

The place of mercy;

The curtain to enclose the Holy Place;

The table, its carrying poles, and all of its utensils;

The Bread of the Presence;

Lamp holders, with lamps and oil;

The incense altar and its carrying poles;

The anointing oil and sweet incense;

The curtain for the door of the Tabernacle;

The altar for the burnt offerings;

The bronze grating of the altar, and its carrying poles and utensils;

The basin with its pedestal;

The drapes for the walls of the court;

The pillars and their bases;

Drapes for the entrance to the court;

The posts of the Tabernacle court, and their cords;

The beautiful clothing for the priests, to be used when ministering in the Holy Place;

The holy garments for Aaron the priest, and for his sons."

20So all the people went to their tents to prepare their gifts. 21Those whose hearts were stirred by God's Spirit returned with their offerings of materials for the Tabernacle, its equipment, and for the holy garments. 22Both men and women came, all who were willing-hearted. They brought to the Lord their offerings of gold, jewelry—earrings, rings from their fingers, necklaces—and gold objects of every kind. 23Others brought blue, purple, and scarlet cloth made from the fine-twined linen or goat's hair; and ram skins dyed red, and specially treated goatskins. 24Others brought silver and bronze as their offering to the Lord; and some brought the acacia wood needed in the construction.

25The women skilled in sewing and spinning prepared blue, purple, and scarlet thread and cloth, and fine-twined linen, and brought them in. 26Some other women gladly used their special skill to spin the goat's hair into cloth. 27The leaders brought onyx stones to be used for the ephod and the chestpiece, 28and spices, and oil—for the light, and for compounding the anointing oil and the sweet incense. 29So the people of Israel—every man and woman who wanted to assist in the work given to them by the Lord's command to Moses—brought their freewill offerings to him.

New Revised Standard

from among you an offering to the LORD; let whoever is of a generous heart bring the LORD's offering: gold, silver, and bronze; 6blue, purple, and crimson yarns, and fine linen; goats' hair, 7tanned rams' skins, and fine leather;b acacia wood, 8oil for the light, spices for the anointing oil and for the fragrant incense, 9and onyx stones and gems to be set in the ephod and the breastpiece.

10 All who are skillful among you shall come and make all that the LORD has commanded: the tabernacle, 11its tent and its covering, its clasps and its frames, its bars, its pillars, and its bases; 12the ark with its poles, the mercy seat,c and the curtain for the screen; 13the table with its poles and all its utensils, and the bread of the Presence; 14the lampstand also for the light, with its utensils and its lamps, and the oil for the light; 15and the altar of incense, with its poles, and the anointing oil and the fragrant incense, and the screen for the entrance, the entrance of the tabernacle; 16the altar of burnt offering, with its grating of bronze, its poles, and all its utensils, the basin with its stand; 17the hangings of the court, its pillars and its bases, and the screen for the gate of the court; 18the pegs of the tabernacle and the pegs of the court, and their cords; 19the finely worked vestments for ministering in the holy place, the holy vestments for the priest Aaron, and the vestments of his sons, for their service as priests.

Offerings for the Tabernacle

20 Then all the congregation of the Israelites withdrew from the presence of Moses. 21And they came, everyone whose heart was stirred, and everyone whose spirit was willing, and brought the LORD's offering to be used for the tent of meeting, and for all its service, and for the sacred vestments. 22So they came, both men and women; all who were of a willing heart brought brooches and earrings and signet rings and pendants, all sorts of gold objects, everyone bringing an offering of gold to the LORD. 23And everyone who possessed blue or purple or crimson yarn or fine linen or goats' hair or tanned rams' skins or fine leather,b brought them. 24Everyone who could make an offering of silver or bronze brought it as the LORD's offering; and everyone who possessed acacia wood of any use in the work, brought it. 25All the skillful women spun with their hands, and brought what they had spun in blue and purple and crimson yarns and fine linen; 26all the women whose hearts moved them to use their skill spun the goats' hair. 27And the leaders brought onyx stones and gems to be set in the ephod and the breastpiece, 28and spices and oil for the light, and for the anointing oil, and for the fragrant incense. 29All the Israelite men and women whose hearts made them willing to bring anything for the work that the LORD had commanded by Moses to be done, brought it as a freewill offering to the LORD.

b Meaning of Heb uncertain   c Or the cover

King James

30¶ And Moses said unto the children of Israel, See, the LORD hath called by name Bezaleel the son of Uri, the son of Hur, of the tribe of Judah;

31And he hath filled him with the spirit of God, in wisdom, in understanding, and in knowledge, and in all manner of workmanship;

32And to devise curious works, to work in gold, and in silver, and in brass,

33And in the cutting of stones, to set *them*, and in carving of wood, to make any manner of cunning work.

34And he hath put in his heart that he may teach, *both* he, and Aholiab, the son of Ahisamach, of the tribe of Dan.

35Them hath he filled with wisdom of heart, to work all manner of work, of the engraver, and of the cunning workman, and of the embroiderer, in blue, and in purple, in scarlet, and in fine linen, and of the weaver, *even* of them that do any work, and of those that devise cunning work.

36 THEN WROUGHT Bezaleel and Aholiab, and every wisehearted man, in whom the LORD put wisdom and understanding to know how to work all manner of work for the service of the sanctuary, according to all that the LORD had commanded.

2And Moses called Bezaleel and Aholiab, and every wisehearted man, in whose heart the LORD had put wisdom, *even* every one whose heart stirred him up to come unto the work to do it:

3And they received of Moses all the offering, which the children of Israel had brought for the work of the service of the sanctuary, to make it *withal*. And they brought yet unto him free offerings every morning.

4And all the wise men, that wrought all the work of the sanctuary, came every man from his work which they made;

5¶ And they spake unto Moses, saying, The people bring much more than enough for the service of the work, which the LORD commanded to make.

6And Moses gave commandment, and they caused it to be proclaimed throughout the camp, saying, Let neither man nor woman make any more work for the offering of the sanctuary. So the people were restrained from bringing.

7For the stuff they had was sufficient for all the work to make it, and too much.

8¶ And every wisehearted man among them that wrought the work of the tabernacle made ten curtains of fine twined linen, and blue, and purple, and scarlet: *with* cherubims of cunning work made he them.

9The length of one curtain *was* twenty and eight cubits, and the breadth of one curtain four cubits: the curtains *were* all of one size.

10And he coupled the five curtains one unto another: and *the other* five curtains he coupled one unto another.

11And he made loops of blue on the edge of one curtain from the selvedge in the coupling: likewise he made in the uttermost side of *another* curtain, in the coupling of the second.

12Fifty loops made he in one curtain, and fifty loops made he in the edge of the curtain which *was* in the coupling of the second: the loops held one *curtain* to another.

13And he made fifty taches of gold, and coupled the curtains one unto another with the taches: so it became one tabernacle.

New International

Bezalel and Oholiab

30Then Moses said to the Israelites, "See, the LORD has chosen Bezalel son of Uri, the son of Hur, of the tribe of Judah, 31and he has filled him with the Spirit of God, with skill, ability and knowledge in all kinds of crafts— 32to make artistic designs for work in gold, silver and bronze, 33to cut and set stones, to work in wood and to engage in all kinds of artistic craftsmanship. 34And he has given both him and Oholiab son of Ahisamach, of the tribe of Dan, the ability to teach others. 35He has filled them with skill to do all kinds of work as craftsmen, designers, embroiderers in blue, purple and scarlet yarn and fine linen, and weavers—all of them master craftsmen and designers.

36 SO BEZALEL, Oholiab and every skilled person to whom the LORD has given skill and ability to know how to carry out all the work of constructing the sanctuary are to do the work just as the Lord has commanded."

2Then Moses summoned Bezalel and Oholiab and every skilled person to whom the LORD had given ability and who was willing to come and do the work. 3They received from Moses all the offerings the Israelites had brought to carry out the work of constructing the sanctuary. And the people continued to bring freewill offerings morning after morning. 4So all the skilled craftsmen who were doing all the work on the sanctuary left their work 5and said to Moses, "The people are bringing more than enough for doing the work the LORD commanded to be done."

6Then Moses gave an order and they sent this word throughout the camp: "No man or woman is to make anything else as an offering for the sanctuary." And so the people were restrained from bringing more, 7because what they already had was more than enough to do all the work.

The Tabernacle

8All the skilled men among the workmen made the tabernacle with ten curtains of finely twisted linen and blue, purple and scarlet yarn, with cherubim worked into them by a skilled craftsman. 9All the curtains were the same size—twenty-eight cubits long and four cubits wide.a 10They joined five of the curtains together and did the same with the other five. 11Then they made loops of blue material along the edge of the end curtain in one set, and the same was done with the end curtain in the other set. 12They also made fifty loops on one curtain and fifty loops on the end curtain of the other set, with the loops opposite each other. 13Then they made fifty gold clasps and used them to fasten the two sets of curtains together so that the tabernacle was a unit.

a 9 That is, about 42 feet (about 12.5 meters) long and 6 feet (about 1.8 meters) wide

Living Bible

30, 31And Moses told them, "Jehovah has specifically appointed Bezalel (the son of Uri and grandson of Hur of the tribe of Judah) as general superintendent of the project. 32He will be able to create beautiful workmanship from gold, silver, and bronze; 33he can cut and set stones like a jeweler, and can do beautiful carving; in fact, he has every needed skill. 34And God has made him and Oholiab gifted teachers of their skills to others. (Oholiab is the son of Ahisamach, of the tribe of Dan.) 35God has filled them both with unusual skills as jewelers, carpenters, embroidery designers in blue, purple, and scarlet on linen backgrounds, and as weavers—they excel in all the crafts we will be needing in the work.

36 "ALL THE other craftsmen with God-given abilities are to assist Bezalel and Oholiab in constructing and furnishing the Tabernacle." So Moses told Bezalel and Oholiab and all others who felt called to the work to begin. 3Moses gave them the materials donated by the people and additional gifts were received each morning.

4-7But finally the workmen all left their task to meet with Moses and told him, "We have more than enough materials on hand now to complete the job!" So Moses sent a message throughout the camp announcing that no more donations were needed. Then at last the people were restrained from bringing more!

8, 9The skilled weavers first made ten sheets from fine linen, then embroidered into them blue, purple, and scarlet Guardian Angels. Each sheet was forty-two feet long and six feet wide. 10Five of these sheets were attached end to end, then five others similarly attached, forming two long roofsheets. 11, 12Fifty blue ribbons were looped along the edges of these two long sheets, each loop being opposite its mate on the other long sheet. 13Then fifty clasps of gold were made to connect the loops, thus tying the two long sheets together to form the ceiling of the Tabernacle.

New Revised Standard

Bezalel and Oholiab

30 Then Moses said to the Israelites: See, the LORD has called by name Bezalel son of Uri son of Hur, of the tribe of Judah; 31he has filled him with divine spirit,b with skill, intelligence, and knowledge in every kind of craft, 32to devise artistic designs, to work in gold, silver, and bronze, 33in cutting stones for setting, and in carving wood, in every kind of craft. 34And he has inspired him to teach, both him and Oholiab son of Ahisamach, of the tribe of Dan. 35He has filled them with skill to do every kind of work done by an artisan or by a designer or by an embroiderer in blue, purple, and crimson yarns, and in fine linen, or by a weaver—by any sort of artisan or skilled designer.

36 BEZALEL AND Oholiab and every skillful one to whom the LORD has given skill and understanding to know how to do any work in the construction of the sanctuary shall work in accordance with all that the LORD has commanded.

2 Moses then called Bezalel and Oholiab and every skillful one to whom the LORD had given skill, everyone whose heart was stirred to come to do the work; 3and they received from Moses all the freewill offerings that the Israelites had brought for doing the work on the sanctuary. They still kept bringing him freewill offerings every morning, 4so that all the artisans who were doing every sort of task on the sanctuary came, each from the task being performed, 5and said to Moses, "The people are bringing much more than enough for doing the work that the LORD has commanded us to do." 6So Moses gave command, and word was proclaimed throughout the camp: "No man or woman is to make anything else as an offering for the sanctuary." So the people were restrained from bringing; 7for what they had already brought was more than enough to do all the work.

Construction of the Tabernacle

8 All those with skill among the workers made the tabernacle with ten curtains; they were made of fine twisted linen, and blue, purple, and crimson yarns, with cherubim skillfully worked into them. 9The length of each curtain was twenty-eight cubits, and the width of each curtain four cubits; all the curtains were of the same size.

10 He joined five curtains to one another, and the other five curtains he joined to one another. 11He made loops of blue on the edge of the outermost curtain of the first set; likewise he made them on the edge of the outermost curtain of the second set; 12he made fifty loops on the one curtain, and he made fifty loops on the edge of the curtain that was in the second set; the loops were opposite one another. 13And he made fifty clasps of gold, and joined the curtains one to the other with clasps; so the tabernacle was one whole.

b Or the spirit of God

King James

14¶ And he made curtains *of* goats' *hair* for the tent over the tabernacle: eleven curtains he made them.

15The length of one curtain *was* thirty cubits, and four cubits *was* the breadth of one curtain: the eleven curtains *were* of one size.

16And he coupled five curtains by themselves, and six curtains by themselves.

17And he made fifty loops upon the uttermost edge of the curtain in the coupling, and fifty loops made he upon the edge of the curtain which coupleth the second.

18And he made fifty taches *of* brass to couple the tent together, that it might be one.

19And he made a covering for the tent *of* rams' skins dyed red, and a covering *of* badgers' skins above *that*.

20¶ And he made boards for the tabernacle *of* shittim wood, standing up.

21The length of a board *was* ten cubits, and the breadth of a board one cubit and a half.

22One board had two tenons, equally distant one from another: thus did he make for all the boards of the tabernacle.

23And he made boards for the tabernacle; twenty boards for the south side southward:

24And forty sockets of silver he made under the twenty boards; two sockets under one board for his two tenons, and two sockets under another board for his two tenons.

25And for the other side of the tabernacle, *which is* toward the north corner, he made twenty boards,

26And their forty sockets of silver; two sockets under one board, and two sockets under another board.

27And for the sides of the tabernacle westward he made six boards.

28And two boards made he for the corners of the tabernacle in the two sides.

29And they were coupled beneath, and coupled together at the head thereof, to one ring: thus he did to both of them in both the corners.

30And there were eight boards; and their sockets *were* sixteen sockets of silver, under every board two sockets.

31¶ And he made bars of shittim wood; five for the boards of the one side of the tabernacle,

32And five bars for the boards of the other side of the tabernacle, and five bars for the boards of the tabernacle for the sides westward.

33And he made the middle bar to shoot through the boards from the one end to the other.

34And he overlaid the boards with gold, and made their rings *of* gold *to be* places for the bars, and overlaid the bars with gold.

35¶ And he made a veil *of* blue, and purple, and scarlet, and fine twined linen: *with* cherubims made he it of cunning work.

36And he made thereunto four pillars *of* shittim *wood*, and overlaid them with gold: their hooks *were of* gold; and he cast for them four sockets of silver.

37¶ And he made an hanging for the tabernacle door *of* blue, and purple, and scarlet, and fine twined linen, of needlework;

38And the five pillars of it with their hooks: and he overlaid their chapiters and their fillets with gold: but their five sockets *were of* brass.

37 AND BEZALEEL made the ark *of* shittim wood: two cubits and a half *was* the length of it, and a cubit and a half the breadth of it, and a cubit and a half the height of it:

New International

14They made curtains of goat hair for the tent over the tabernacle—eleven altogether. 15All eleven curtains were the same size—thirty cubits long and four cubits wide.a 16They joined five of the curtains into one set and the other six into another set. 17Then they made fifty loops along the edge of the end curtain in one set and also along the edge of the end curtain in the other set. 18They made fifty bronze clasps to fasten the tent together as a unit. 19Then they made for the tent a covering of ram skins dyed red, and over that a covering of hides of sea cows.b

20They made upright frames of acacia wood for the tabernacle. 21Each frame was ten cubits long and a cubit and a half wide,c 22with two projections set parallel to each other. They made all the frames of the tabernacle in this way. 23They made twenty frames for the south side of the tabernacle 24and made forty silver bases to go under them—two bases for each frame, one under each projection. 25For the other side, the north side of the tabernacle, they made twenty frames 26and forty silver bases—two under each frame. 27They made six frames for the far end, that is, the west end of the tabernacle, 28and two frames were made for the corners of the tabernacle at the far end. 29At these two corners the frames were double from the bottom all the way to the top and fitted into a single ring; both were made alike. 30So there were eight frames and sixteen silver bases—two under each frame.

31They also made crossbars of acacia wood: five for the frames on one side of the tabernacle, 32five for those on the other side, and five for the frames on the west, at the far end of the tabernacle. 33They made the center crossbar so that it extended from end to end at the middle of the frames. 34They overlaid the frames with gold and made gold rings to hold the crossbars. They also overlaid the crossbars with gold.

35They made the curtain of blue, purple and scarlet yarn and finely twisted linen, with cherubim worked into it by a skilled craftsman. 36They made four posts of acacia wood for it and overlaid them with gold. They made gold hooks for them and cast their four silver bases. 37For the entrance to the tent they made a curtain of blue, purple and scarlet yarn and finely twisted linen—the work of an embroiderer; 38and they made five posts with hooks for them. They overlaid the tops of the posts and their bands with gold and made their five bases of bronze.

The Ark

37 BEZALEL MADE the ark of acacia wood— two and a half cubits long, a cubit and a half wide, and a cubit and a half high.d 2He overlaid it with

a *15* That is, about 45 feet (about 13.5 meters) long and 6 feet (about 1.8 meters) wide   b *19* That is, dugongs   c *21* That is, about 15 feet (about 4.5 meters) long and 2 1/4 feet (about 0.7 meter) wide   d *1* That is, about 3 3/4 feet (about 1.1 meters) long and 2 1/4 feet (about 0.7 meter) wide and high

Living Bible

14, 15Above the ceiling was a second layer formed by eleven draperies made of goat's hair (uniformly forty-five feet long and six feet wide). 16Bezalel coupled five of these draperies together to make one long piece, and six others to make another long piece. 17Then he made fifty loops along the end of each, 18and fifty small bronze clasps to couple the loops so that the draperies were firmly attached to each other.

19The top layer of the roof was made of rams' skins, dyed red, and tanned goat skins.

20For the sides of the Tabernacle he used frames of acacia wood standing on end. 21The height of each frame was fifteen feet and the width 2¼ feet. 22Each frame had two clasps joining it to the next. 23There were twenty frames on the south side, 24with the bottoms fitting into forty silver bases. Each frame was connected to its base by two clasps. 25, 26There were also twenty frames on the north side of the Tabernacle, with forty silver bases, two for each frame. 27The west side of the Tabernacle, which was its rear, was made from six frames, 28plus another at each corner. 29These frames, including those at the corners, were linked to each other at both top and bottom by rings. 30So, on the west side, there were a total of eight frames with sixteen silver bases beneath them, two for each frame.

31, 32Then he made five sets of bars from acacia wood to tie the frames together along the sides, five for each side of the Tabernacle. 33The middle bar of the five was halfway up the frames, along each side, running from one end to the other. 34The frames and bars were all overlaid with gold, and the rings were pure gold.

35The blue, purple, and scarlet innere curtain was made from woven linen, with Guardian Angels skillfully embroidered into it. 36The curtain was then attached to four gold hooks set into four posts of acacia wood, overlaid with gold and set into four silver bases.

37Then he made a drapery for the entrance to the Tabernacle; it was woven from finespun linen, embroidered with blue, purple, and scarlet. 38This drapery was connected by five hooks to five posts. The posts and their capitals and rods were overlaid with gold; their five bases were molded from bronze.

37 NEXT BEZALEL made the Ark. This was constructed of acacia wood and was 3¾ feet long, 2¼ feet wide, and 2¼ feet high. 2It was plated with pure

e 36:35 inner, implied.

New Revised Standard

14 He also made curtains of goats' hair for a tent over the tabernacle; he made eleven curtains. 15The length of each curtain was thirty cubits, and the width of each curtain four cubits; the eleven curtains were of the same size. 16He joined five curtains by themselves, and six curtains by themselves. 17He made fifty loops on the edge of the outermost curtain of the one set, and fifty loops on the edge of the other connecting curtain. 18He made fifty clasps of bronze to join the tent together so that it might be one whole. 19And he made for the tent a covering of tanned rams' skins and an outer covering of fine leather.f

20 Then he made the upright frames for the tabernacle of acacia wood. 21Ten cubits was the length of a frame, and a cubit and a half the width of each frame. 22Each frame had two pegs for fitting together; he did this for all the frames of the tabernacle. 23The frames for the tabernacle he made in this way: twenty frames for the south side; 24and he made forty bases of silver under the twenty frames, two bases under the first frame for its two pegs, and two bases under the next frame for its two pegs. 25For the second side of the tabernacle, on the north side, he made twenty frames 26and their forty bases of silver, two bases under the first frame and two bases under the next frame. 27For the rear of the tabernacle westward he made six frames. 28He made two frames for corners of the tabernacle in the rear. 29They were separate beneath, but joined at the top, at the first ring; he made two of them in this way, for the two corners. 30There were eight frames with their bases of silver: sixteen bases, under every frame two bases.

31 He made bars of acacia wood, five for the frames of the one side of the tabernacle, 32and five bars for the frames of the other side of the tabernacle, and five bars for the frames of the tabernacle at the rear westward. 33He made the middle bar to pass through from end to end halfway up the frames. 34And he overlaid the frames with gold, and made rings of gold for them to hold the bars, and overlaid the bars with gold.

35 He made the curtain of blue, purple, and crimson yarns, and fine twisted linen, with cherubim skillfully worked into it. 36For it he made four pillars of acacia, and overlaid them with gold; their hooks were of gold, and he cast for them four bases of silver. 37He also made a screen for the entrance to the tent, of blue, purple, and crimson yarns, and fine twisted linen, embroidered with needlework; 38and its five pillars with their hooks. He overlaid their capitals and their bases with gold, but their five bases were of bronze.

Making the Ark of the Covenant

37 BEZALEL MADE the ark of acacia wood; it was two and a half cubits long, a cubit and a half wide, and a cubit and a half high. 2He overlaid it with

f Meaning of Heb uncertain

King James

2And he overlaid it with pure gold within and without, and made a crown of gold to it round about.

3And he cast for it four rings of gold, *to be set* by the four corners of it; even two rings upon the one side of it, and two rings upon the other side of it.

4And he made staves *of* shittim wood, and overlaid them with gold.

5And he put the staves into the rings by the sides of the ark, to bear the ark.

6¶ And he made the mercy seat *of* pure gold: two cubits and a half *was* the length thereof, and one cubit and a half the breadth thereof.

7And he made two cherubims *of* gold, beaten out of one piece made he them, on the two ends of the mercy seat;

8One cherub on the end on this side, and another cherub on the *other* end on that side: out of the mercy seat made he the cherubims on the two ends thereof.

9And the cherubims spread out *their* wings on high, *and* covered with their wings over the mercy seat, with their faces one to another; *even* to the mercy seatward were the faces of the cherubims.

10¶ And he made the table *of* shittim wood: two cubits *was* the length thereof, and a cubit the breadth thereof, and a cubit and a half the height thereof:

11And he overlaid it with pure gold, and made thereunto a crown of gold round about.

12Also he made thereunto a border of an handbreadth round about; and made a crown of gold for the border thereof round about.

13And he cast for it four rings of gold, and put the rings upon the four corners that *were* in the four feet thereof.

14Over against the border were the rings, the places for the staves to bear the table.

15And he made the staves *of* shittim wood, and overlaid them with gold, to bear the table.

16And he made the vessels which *were* upon the table, his dishes, and his spoons, and his bowls, and his covers to cover withal, *of* pure gold.

17¶ And he made the candlestick *of* pure gold: *of* beaten work made he the candlestick; his shaft, and his branch, his bowls, his knobs, and his flowers, were of the same:

18And six branches going out of the sides thereof; three branches of the candlestick out of the one side thereof, and three branches of the candlestick out of the other side thereof:

19Three bowls made after the fashion of almonds in one branch, a knob and a flower; and three bowls made like almonds in another branch, a knob and a flower: so throughout the six branches going out of the candlestick.

20And in the candlestick *were* four bowls made like almonds, his knobs, and his flowers:

21And a knob under two branches of the same, and a knob under two branches of the same, and a knob under two branches of the same, according to the six branches going out of it.

22Their knobs and their branches were of the same: all of it *was* one beaten work *of* pure gold.

23And he made his seven lamps, and his snuffers, and his snuffdishes, *of* pure gold.

24*Of* a talent of pure gold made he it, and all the vessels thereof.

25¶ And he made the incense altar *of* shittim wood: the length of it *was* a cubit, and the breadth of it a cubit; *it was* foursquare; and two cubits *was* the height of it; the horns thereof were of the same.

26And he overlaid it with pure gold, *both* the top of it, and the sides thereof round about, and the horns of it: also he made unto it a crown of gold round about.

27And he made two rings of gold for it under the crown thereof, by the two corners of it, upon the two sides thereof, to be places for the staves to bear it withal.

New International

pure gold, both inside and out, and made a gold molding around it. 3He cast four gold rings for it and fastened them to its four feet, with two rings on one side and two rings on the other. 4Then he made poles of acacia wood and overlaid them with gold. 5And he inserted the poles into the rings on the sides of the ark to carry it.

6He made the atonement cover of pure gold—two and a half cubits long and a cubit and a half wide.[a] 7Then he made two cherubim out of hammered gold at the ends of the cover. 8He made one cherub on one end and the second cherub on the other; at the two ends he made them of one piece with the cover. 9The cherubim had their wings spread upward, overshadowing the cover with them. The cherubim faced each other, looking toward the cover.

The Table

10They[b] made the table of acacia wood—two cubits long, a cubit wide, and a cubit and a half high.[c] 11Then they overlaid it with pure gold and made a gold molding around it. 12They also made around it a rim a handbreadth[d] wide and put a gold molding on the rim. 13They cast four gold rings for the table and fastened them to the four corners, where the four legs were. 14The rings were put close to the rim to hold the poles used in carrying the table. 15The poles for carrying the table were made of acacia wood and were overlaid with gold. 16And they made from pure gold the articles for the table—its plates and dishes and bowls and its pitchers for the pouring out of drink offerings.

The Lampstand

17They made the lampstand of pure gold and hammered it out, base and shaft; its flowerlike cups, buds and blossoms were of one piece with it. 18Six branches extended from the sides of the lampstand—three on one side and three on the other. 19Three cups shaped like almond flowers with buds and blossoms were on one branch, three on the next branch and the same for all six branches extending from the lampstand. 20And on the lampstand were four cups shaped like almond flowers with buds and blossoms. 21One bud was under the first pair of branches extending from the lampstand, a second bud under the second pair, and a third bud under the third pair—six branches in all. 22The buds and the branches were all of one piece with the lampstand, hammered out of pure gold.

23They made its seven lamps, as well as its wick trimmers and trays, of pure gold. 24They made the lampstand and all its accessories from one talent[e] of pure gold.

The Altar of Incense

25They made the altar of incense out of acacia wood. It was square, a cubit long and a cubit wide, and two cubits high[f]—its horns of one piece with it. 26They overlaid the top and all the sides and the horns with pure gold, and made a gold molding around it. 27They made two gold rings below the molding—two on opposite sides—to hold the poles used to carry it. 28They made

---

[a] *6* That is, about 3 3/4 feet (about 1.1 meters) long and 2 1/4 feet (about 0.7 meter) wide   [b] *10* Or *He*; also in verses 11-29   [c] *10* That is, about 3 feet (about 0.9 meter) long, 1 1/2 feet (about 0.5 meter) wide, and 2 1/4 feet (about 0.7 meter) high   [d] *12* That is, about 3 inches (about 8 centimeters)   [e] *24* That is, about 75 pounds (about 34 kilograms)   [f] *25* That is, about 1 1/2 feet (about 0.5 meter) long and wide, and about 3 feet (about 0.9 meter) high

Living Bible

gold inside and out, and had a molding of gold all the way around the sides. ³There were four gold rings fastened into its four feet, two rings at each end. ⁴Then he made poles from acacia wood, and overlaid them with gold, ⁵and put the poles into the rings at the sides of the Ark, to carry it.

⁶Then, from pure gold, he made a lid called "the place of mercy"; it was 3¾ feet long and 2¼ feet wide. ⁷He made two statues of Guardian Angels of beaten gold, and placed them at the two ends of the gold lid. ⁸They were molded so that they were actually a part of the gold lid—it was all one piece. ⁹The Guardian Angels faced each other, with outstretched wings that overshadowed the place of mercy, looking down upon it.

¹⁰Then he made a table, using acacia wood, three feet long, 1½ feet wide and 2¼ feet high. ¹¹It was overlaid with pure gold, with a gold molding all around the edge. ¹²A rim four inches high was constructed around the edges of the table, with a gold molding along the rim. ¹³Then he cast four rings of gold and placed them into the four table legs, ¹⁴close to the molding, to hold the carrying poles in place. ¹⁵He made the carrying poles of acacia wood covered with gold. ¹⁶Next, using pure gold, he made the bowls, flagons, dishes, and spoons to be placed upon this table.

¹⁷Then he made the lampstand, again using pure, beaten gold. Its base, shaft, lamp-holders, and decorations of almond flowers were all of one piece. ¹⁸The lampstand had six branches, three from each side. ¹⁹Each of the branches was decorated with identical carvings of blossoms. ²⁰, ²¹The main stem of the lampstand was similarly decorated with almond blossoms, a flower on the stem beneath each pair of branches; also a flower below the bottom pair and above the top pair, four in all. ²²The decorations and branches were all one piece of pure, beaten gold. ²³, ²⁴Then he made the seven lamps at the ends of the branches, the snuffers, and the ashtrays, all of pure gold. The entire lampstand weighed 107 pounds, all pure gold.

²⁵The incense altar was made of acacia wood. It was eighteen inches square and three feet high, with its corner-horns made as part of the altar so that it was all one piece. ²⁶He overlaid it all with pure gold and ran a gold molding around the edge. ²⁷Two gold rings were placed on each side, beneath this molding, to hold the carrying

New Revised Standard

pure gold inside and outside, and made a molding of gold around it. ³He cast for it four rings of gold for its four feet, two rings on its one side and two rings on its other side. ⁴He made poles of acacia wood, and overlaid them with gold, ⁵and put the poles into the rings on the sides of the ark, to carry the ark. ⁶He made a mercy seat⁸ of pure gold; two cubits and a half was its length, and a cubit and a half its width. ⁷He made two cherubim of hammered gold; at the two ends of the mercy seatʰ he made them, ⁸one cherub at the one end, and one cherub at the other end; of one piece with the mercy seatʰ he made the cherubim at its two ends. ⁹The cherubim spread out their wings above, overshadowing the mercy seatʰ with their wings. They faced one another; the faces of the cherubim were turned toward the mercy seat.ʰ

Making the Table for the Bread of the Presence

10 He also made the table of acacia wood, two cubits long, one cubit wide, and a cubit and a half high. ¹¹He overlaid it with pure gold, and made a molding of gold around it. ¹²He made around it a rim a handbreadth wide, and made a molding of gold around the rim. ¹³He cast for it four rings of gold, and fastened the rings to the four corners at its four legs. ¹⁴The rings that held the poles used for carrying the table were close to the rim. ¹⁵He made the poles of acacia wood to carry the table, and overlaid them with gold. ¹⁶And he made the vessels of pure gold that were to be on the table, its plates and dishes for incense, and its bowls and flagons with which to pour drink offerings.

Making the Lampstand

17 He also made the lampstand of pure gold. The base and the shaft of the lampstand were made of hammered work; its cups, its calyxes, and its petals were of one piece with it. ¹⁸There were six branches going out of its sides, three branches of the lampstand out of one side of it and three branches of the lampstand out of the other side of it; ¹⁹three cups shaped like almond blossoms, each with calyx and petals, on one branch, and three cups shaped like almond blossoms, each with calyx and petals, on the other branch—so for the six branches going out of the lampstand. ²⁰On the lampstand itself there were four cups shaped like almond blossoms, each with its calyxes and petals. ²¹There was a calyx of one piece with it under the first pair of branches, a calyx of one piece with it under the next pair of branches, and a calyx of one piece with it under the last pair of branches. ²²Their calyxes and their branches were of one piece with it, the whole of it one hammered piece of pure gold. ²³He made its seven lamps and its snuffers and its trays of pure gold. ²⁴He made it and all its utensils of a talent of pure gold.

Making the Altar of Incense

25 He made the altar of incense of acacia wood, one cubit long, and one cubit wide; it was square, and was two cubits high; its horns were of one piece with it. ²⁶He overlaid it with pure gold, its top, and its sides all around, and its horns; and he made for it a molding of gold all around, ²⁷and made two golden rings for it under its molding, on two opposite sides of it, to hold

---

⁸ Or *a cover*   ʰ Or *the cover*

King James

28And he made the staves *of* shittim wood, and overlaid them with gold.

29¶ And he made the holy anointing oil, and the pure incense of sweet spices, according to the work of the apothecary.

38 AND HE made the altar of burnt offering *of* shittim wood: five cubits *was* the length thereof, and five cubits the breadth thereof; *it was* foursquare; and three cubits the height thereof.

2And he made the horns thereof on the four corners of it; the horns thereof were of the same: and he overlaid it with brass.

3And he made all the vessels of the altar, the pots, and the shovels, and the basins, *and* the fleshhooks, and the firepans: all the vessels thereof made he *of* brass.

4And he made for the altar a brasen grate of network under the compass thereof beneath unto the midst of it.

5And he cast four rings for the four ends of the grate of brass, *to be* places for the staves.

6And he made the staves *of* shittim wood, and overlaid them with brass.

7And he put the staves into the rings on the sides of the altar, to bear it withal; he made the altar hollow with boards.

8¶ And he made the laver *of* brass, and the foot of it *of* brass, of the looking glasses of *the women* assembling, which assembled *at* the door of the tabernacle of the congregation.

9¶ And he made the court: on the south side southward the hangings of the court *were of* fine twined linen, an hundred cubits:

10Their pillars *were* twenty, and their brasen sockets twenty; the hooks of the pillars and their fillets *were of* silver.

11And for the north side *the hangings were* an hundred cubits, their pillars *were* twenty, and their sockets of brass twenty; the hooks of the pillars and their fillets *of* silver.

12And for the west side *were* hangings of fifty cubits, their pillars ten, and their sockets ten; the hooks of the pillars and their fillets *of* silver.

13And for the east side eastward fifty cubits.

14The hangings of the one side *of the gate were* fifteen cubits; their pillars three, and their sockets three.

15And for the other side of the court gate, on this hand and that hand, *were* hangings of fifteen cubits; their pillars three, and their sockets three.

16All the hangings of the court round about *were* of fine twined linen.

17And the sockets for the pillars *were of* brass; the hooks of the pillars and their fillets *of* silver; and the overlaying of their chapiters *of* silver; and all the pillars of the court *were* filleted with silver.

18And the hanging for the gate of the court *was* needlework, *of* blue, and purple, and scarlet, and fine twined linen: and twenty cubits *was* the length, and the height in the breadth *was* five cubits, answerable to the hangings of the court.

19And their pillars *were* four, and their sockets *of* brass four; their hooks *of* silver, and the overlaying of their chapiters and their fillets *of* silver.

20And all the pins of the tabernacle, and of the court round about, *were of* brass.

21¶ This is the sum of the tabernacle, *even* of the tabernacle of testimony, as it was counted, according to the commandment of Moses, *for* the service of the Levites, by the hand of Ithamar, son to Aaron the priest.

22And Bezaleel the son of Uri, the son of Hur, of the tribe of Judah, made all that the LORD commanded Moses.

New International

the poles of acacia wood and overlaid them with gold.

29They also made the sacred anointing oil and the pure, fragrant incense—the work of a perfumer.

The Altar of Burnt Offering

38 THEYa BUILT the altar of burnt offering of acacia wood, three cubitsb high; it was square, five cubits long and five cubits wide.c 2They made a horn at each of the four corners, so that the horns and the altar were of one piece, and they overlaid the altar with bronze. 3They made all its utensils of bronze—its pots, shovels, sprinkling bowls, meat forks and firepans. 4They made a grating for the altar, a bronze network, to be under its ledge, halfway up the altar. 5They cast bronze rings to hold the poles for the four corners of the bronze grating. 6They made the poles of acacia wood and overlaid them with bronze. 7They inserted the poles into the rings so they would be on the sides of the altar for carrying it. They made it hollow, out of boards.

Basin for Washing

8They made the bronze basin and its bronze stand from the mirrors of the women who served at the entrance to the Tent of Meeting.

The Courtyard

9Next they made the courtyard. The south side was a hundred cubitsd long and had curtains of finely twisted linen, 10with twenty posts and twenty bronze bases, and with silver hooks and bands on the posts. 11The north side was also a hundred cubits long and had twenty posts and twenty bronze bases, with silver hooks and bands on the posts.

12The west end was fifty cubitse wide and had ten curtains, with ten posts and ten bases, with silver hooks and bands on the posts. 13The east end, toward the sunrise, was also fifty cubits wide. 14Curtains fifteen cubitsf long were on one side of the entrance, with three posts and three bases, 15and curtains fifteen cubits long were on the other side of the entrance to the courtyard, with three posts and three bases. 16All the curtains around the courtyard were of finely twisted linen. 17The bases for the posts were bronze. The hooks and bands on the posts were silver, and their tops were overlaid with silver; so all the posts of the courtyard had silver bands.

18The curtain for the entrance to the courtyard was of blue, purple and scarlet yarn and finely twisted linen—the work of an embroiderer. It was twenty cubitsg long and, like the curtains of the courtyard, five cubitsh high, 19with four posts and four bronze bases. Their hooks and bands were silver, and their tops were overlaid with silver. 20All the tent pegs of the tabernacle and of the surrounding courtyard were bronze.

The Materials Used

21These are the amounts of the materials used for the tabernacle, the tabernacle of the Testimony, which were recorded at Moses' command by the Levites under the direction of Ithamar son of Aaron, the priest. 22(Bezalel son of Uri, the son of Hur, of the tribe of Judah, made everything the LORD commanded Moses; 23with him

---

a *1* Or *He;* also in verses 2-9   b *1* That is, about 4 1/2 feet (about 1.3 meters)   c *1* That is, about 7 1/2 feet (about 2.3 meters) long and wide   d *9* That is, about 150 feet (about 46 meters)   e *12* That is, about 75 feet (about 23 meters)   f *14* That is, about 22 1/2 feet (about 6.9 meters)   g *18* That is, about 30 feet (about 9 meters)   h *18* That is, about 7 1/2 feet (about 2.3 meters)

Living Bible

poles. 28The carrying poles were gold-plated acacia wood.

29Then, from sweet spices, he made the sacred oil for anointing the priests, and the pure incense, using the techniques of the most skilled perfumers.

38 THE BURNT-OFFERING altar was also constructed of acacia wood; it was 7½ feet square at the top, and 4½ feet high. 2There were four horns at the four corners, all of one piece with the rest. This altar was overlaid with bronze. 3Then he made bronze utensils to be used with the altar—the pots, shovels, basins, meat hooks, and fire pans. 4Next he made a bronze grating that rested upon a ledge about halfway up [in the fire box¹]. 5Four rings were cast for each side of the grating, to insert the carrying poles. 6The carrying poles themselves were made of acacia wood, overlaid with bronze. 7The carrying poles were inserted into the rings at the side of the altar. The altar was hollow, with plank siding.

8The bronze washbasin and its bronze pedestal were cast from the solid bronze mirrors donated by the women who assembled at the entrance to the Tabernacle.

9Then he constructed the courtyard. The south wall was 150 feet long; it consisted of drapes woven from fine-twined linen thread. 10There were twenty posts to hold drapes, with bases of bronze and with silver hooks and rods. 11The north wall was also 150 feet long, with twenty bronze posts and bases and with silver hooks and rods. 12The west side was seventy-five feet wide; the walls were made from drapes supported by ten posts and bases, and with silver hooks and rods. 13The east side was also seventy-five feet wide.

14, 15The drapes at either side of the entrance were 22½ feet wide, each with three posts and three bases. 16All the drapes making up the walls of the court were woven of fine-twined linen. 17Each post had a bronze base, and all the hooks and rods were silver; the tops of the posts were overlaid with silver, and the rods to hold up the drapes were solid silver.

18The drapery covering the entrance to the court was made of fine-twined linen, beautifully embroidered with blue, purple, and scarlet thread.

It was thirty feet long and 7½ feet wide, just the same as the drapes composing the walls of the court. 19It was supported by four posts, with four bronze bases, and with silver hooks and rods; the tops of the posts were also silver.

20All the nails used in constructing the Tabernacle and court were bronze.

21This summarizes the various steps in building the Tabernacle to house the Ark, so that the Levites could carry on their ministry. All was done in the order designated by Moses and was supervised by Ithamar, son of Aaron the priest. 22Bezalel (son of Uri and grandson of Hur, of the tribe of Judah) was the master craftsman,

New Revised Standard

the poles with which to carry it. 28 And he made the poles of acacia wood, and overlaid them with gold.

Making the Anointing Oil and the Incense

29 He made the holy anointing oil also, and the pure fragrant incense, blended as by the perfumer.

Making the Altar of Burnt Offering

38 HE MADE the altar of burnt offering also of acacia wood; it was five cubits long, and five cubits wide; it was square, and three cubits high. 2He made horns for it on its four corners; its horns were of one piece with it, and he overlaid it with bronze. 3He made all the utensils of the altar, the pots, the shovels, the basins, the forks, and the firepans: all its utensils he made of bronze. 4He made for the altar a grating, a network of bronze, under its ledge, extending halfway down. 5He cast four rings on the four corners of the bronze grating to hold the poles; 6he made the poles of acacia wood, and overlaid them with bronze. 7And he put the poles through the rings on the sides of the altar, to carry it with them; he made it hollow, with boards.

8 He made the basin of bronze with its stand of bronze, from the mirrors of the women who served at the entrance to the tent of meeting.

Making the Court of the Tabernacle

9 He made the court; for the south side the hangings of the court were of fine twisted linen, one hundred cubits long; 10its twenty pillars and their twenty bases were of bronze, but the hooks of the pillars and their bands were of silver. 11For the north side there were hangings one hundred cubits long; its twenty pillars and their twenty bases were of bronze, but the hooks of the pillars and their bands were of silver. 12For the west side there were hangings fifty cubits long, with ten pillars and ten bases; the hooks of the pillars and their bands were of silver. 13And for the front to the east, fifty cubits. 14The hangings for one side of the gate were fifteen cubits, with three pillars and three bases. 15And so for the other side; on each side of the gate of the court were hangings of fifteen cubits, with three pillars and three bases. 16All the hangings around the court were of fine twisted linen. 17The bases for the pillars were of bronze, but the hooks of the pillars and their bands were of silver; the overlaying of their capitals was also of silver, and all the pillars of the court were banded with silver. 18The screen for the entrance to the court was embroidered with needlework in blue, purple, and crimson yarns and fine twisted linen. It was twenty cubits long and, along the width of it, five cubits high, corresponding to the hangings of the court. 19There were four pillars; their four bases were of bronze, their hooks of silver, and the overlaying of their capitals and their bands of silver. 20All the pegs for the tabernacle and for the court all around were of bronze.

Materials of the Tabernacle

21 These are the records of the tabernacle, the tabernacle of the covenant,ʲ which were drawn up at the commandment of Moses, the work of the Levites being under the direction of Ithamar son of the priest Aaron. 22Bezalel son of Uri son of Hur, of the tribe of Judah, made all that the LORD commanded Moses; 23and with

---

¹ 38:4 in the fire box, implied.

ʲ Or treaty, or testimony; Heb eduth

King James

23And with him *was* Aholiab, son of Ahisamach, of the tribe of Dan, an engraver, and a cunning workman, and an embroiderer in blue, and in purple, and in scarlet, and fine linen.

24All the gold that was occupied for the work in all the work of the holy *place*, even the gold of the offering, was twenty and nine talents, and seven hundred and thirty shekels, after the shekel of the sanctuary.

25And the silver of them that were numbered of the congregation *was* an hundred talents, and a thousand seven hundred and threescore and fifteen shekels, after the shekel of the sanctuary:

26A bekah for every man, *that is,* half a shekel, after the shekel of the sanctuary, for every one that went to be numbered, from twenty years old and upward, for six hundred thousand and three thousand and five hundred and fifty *men.*

27And of the hundred talents of silver were cast the sockets of the sanctuary, and the sockets of the veil; an hundred sockets of the hundred talents, a talent for a socket.

28And of the thousand seven hundred seventy and five *shekels* he made hooks for the pillars, and overlaid their chapiters, and filleted them.

29And the brass of the offering *was* seventy talents, and two thousand and four hundred shekels.

30And therewith he made the sockets to the door of the tabernacle of the congregation, and the brasen altar, and the brasen grate for it, and all the vessels of the altar,

31And the sockets of the court round about, and the sockets of the court gate, and all the pins of the tabernacle, and all the pins of the court round about.

39 AND OF the blue, and purple, and scarlet, they made cloths of service, to do service in the holy *place,* and made the holy garments for Aaron; as the LORD commanded Moses.

2And he made the ephod *of* gold, blue, and purple, and scarlet, and fine twined linen.

3And they did beat the gold into thin plates, and cut *it into* wires, to work *it* in the blue, and in the purple, and in the scarlet, and in the fine linen, *with* cunning work.

4They made shoulderpieces for it, to couple *it* together: by the two edges was it coupled together.

5And the curious girdle of his ephod, that *was* upon it, *was* of the same, according to the work thereof; *of* gold, blue, and purple, and scarlet, and fine twined linen; as the LORD commanded Moses.

6¶ And they wrought onyx stones enclosed in ouches of gold, graven, as signets are graven, with the names of the children of Israel.

7And he put them on the shoulders of the ephod, *that they should be* stones for a memorial to the children of Israel; as the LORD commanded Moses.

8¶ And he made the breastplate *of* cunning work, like the work of the ephod; *of* gold, blue, and purple, and scarlet, and fine twined linen.

9It was foursquare; they made the breastplate double: a span *was* the length thereof, and a span the breadth thereof, *being* doubled.

10And they set in it four rows of stones: *the first* row *was* a sardius, a topaz, and a carbuncle: this *was* the first row.

New International

was Oholiab son of Ahisamach, of the tribe of Dan—a craftsman and designer, and an embroiderer in blue, purple and scarlet yarn and fine linen.) 24The total amount of the gold from the wave offering used for all the work on the sanctuary was 29 talents and 730 shekels,[a] according to the sanctuary shekel.

25The silver obtained from those of the community who were counted in the census was 100 talents and 1,775 shekels,[b] according to the sanctuary shekel— 26one beka per person, that is, half a shekel,[c] according to the sanctuary shekel, from everyone who had crossed over to those counted, twenty years old or more, a total of 603,550 men. 27The 100 talents[d] of silver were used to cast the bases for the sanctuary and for the curtain—100 bases from the 100 talents, one talent for each base. 28They used the 1,775 shekels[e] to make the hooks for the posts, to overlay the tops of the posts, and to make their bands.

29The bronze from the wave offering was 70 talents and 2,400 shekels.[f] 30They used it to make the bases for the entrance to the Tent of Meeting, the bronze altar with its bronze grating and all its utensils, 31the bases for the surrounding courtyard and those for its entrance and all the tent pegs for the tabernacle and those for the surrounding courtyard.

The Priestly Garments

39 FROM THE blue, purple and scarlet yarn they made woven garments for ministering in the sanctuary. They also made sacred garments for Aaron, as the LORD commanded Moses.

The Ephod

2They[g] made the ephod of gold, and of blue, purple and scarlet yarn, and of finely twisted linen. 3They hammered out thin sheets of gold and cut strands to be worked into the blue, purple and scarlet yarn and fine linen—the work of a skilled craftsman. 4They made shoulder pieces for the ephod, which were attached to two of its corners, so it could be fastened. 5Its skillfully woven waistband was like it—of one piece with the ephod and made with gold, and with blue, purple and scarlet yarn, and with finely twisted linen, as the LORD commanded Moses.

6They mounted the onyx stones in gold filigree settings and engraved them like a seal with the names of the sons of Israel. 7Then they fastened them on the shoulder pieces of the ephod as memorial stones for the sons of Israel, as the LORD commanded Moses.

The Breastpiece

8They fashioned the breastpiece—the work of a skilled craftsman. They made it like the ephod: of gold, and of blue, purple and scarlet yarn, and of finely twisted linen. 9It was square—a span[h] long and a span wide—and folded double. 10Then they mounted four rows of precious stones on it. In the first row there was a ruby, a topaz and a beryl; 11in the second row a tur-

---

Living Bible

23assisted by Oholiab (son of Ahisamach of the tribe of Dan); he too was a skilled craftsman and also an expert at engraving, weaving, and at embroidering blue, purple, and scarlet threads into fine linen cloth.

24The people brought gifts of 3,140 pounds of gold, all of which was used throughout the Tabernacle.

25, 26The amount of silver used was 9,575 pounds, which came from the fifty-cent head tax collected from all those registered in the census who were twenty years old or older, a total of 603,550 men. 27The bases for the frames of the sanctuary walls and for the posts supporting the veil required 9,500 pounds of silver, ninety-five poundsⁱ for each socket. 28The silver left over was used for the posts and to overlay their tops, and for the rods and hooks.

29, 30, 31The people brought 7,540 pounds of bronze, which was used for casting the bases for the posts at the entrance to the Tabernacle, and for the bronze altar, the bronze grating, the altar utensils, the bases for the posts supporting the drapes enclosing the court, and for all the nails used in the construction of the Tabernacle and the court.

39 THEN, FOR the priests, the people made beautiful garments of blue, purple, and scarlet cloth—garments to be used while ministering in the Holy Place. This same cloth was used for Aaron's sacred garments, in accordance with the Lord's instructions to Moses. 2The ephod was made from this cloth too, woven from fine-twined linen thread. 3Bezalel beat gold into thin plates and cut it into wire threads, to work into the blue, purple, and scarlet linen; it was a skillful and beautiful piece of workmanship when finished.

4, 5The ephod was held together by shoulder straps at the top, and was tied down by an elaborate one-piece woven sash made of the same gold, blue, purple, and scarlet cloth cut from fine-twined linen thread, just as God had directed Moses. 6, 7The [two]ʲ onyx stones, attached to the [two] shoulder straps of the ephod, were set in gold, and the stones were engraved with the names of the tribes of Israel, just as initials are engraved upon a ring. These stones were reminders to Jehovah concerning the people of Israel;ᵏ all this was done in accordance with the Lord's instructions to Moses.

8The chestpiece was a beautiful piece of work, just like the ephod, made from the finest gold, blue, purple, and scarlet linen. 9It was a piece nine inches square, doubled over to form a pouch; 10there were four rows of stones across it. In the first row were a sardius, a topaz, and a carbuncle; 11in the second row were an emerald,

New Revised Standard

him was Oholiab son of Ahisamach, of the tribe of Dan, engraver, designer, and embroiderer in blue, purple, and crimson yarns, and in fine linen.

24 All the gold that was used for the work, in all the construction of the sanctuary, the gold from the offering, was twenty-nine talents and seven hundred thirty shekels, measured by the sanctuary shekel. 25The silver from those of the congregation who were counted was one hundred talents and one thousand seven hundred seventy-five shekels, measured by the sanctuary shekel; 26a beka a head (that is, half a shekel, measured by the sanctuary shekel), for everyone who was counted in the census, from twenty years old and upward, for six hundred three thousand, five hundred fifty men. 27The hundred talents of silver were for casting the bases of the sanctuary, and the bases of the curtain; one hundred bases for the hundred talents, a talent for a base. 28Of the thousand seven hundred seventy-five shekels he made hooks for the pillars, and overlaid their capitals and made bands for them. 29The bronze that was contributed was seventy talents, and two thousand four hundred shekels; 30with it he made the bases for the entrance of the tent of meeting, the bronze altar and the bronze grating for it and all the utensils of the altar, 31the bases all around the court, and the bases of the gate of the court, all the pegs of the tabernacle, and all the pegs around the court.

Making the Vestments for the Priesthood

39 OF THE blue, purple, and crimson yarns they made finely worked vestments, for ministering in the holy place; they made the sacred vestments for Aaron; as the LORD had commanded Moses.

2 He made the ephod of gold, of blue, purple, and crimson yarns, and of fine twisted linen. 3Gold leaf was hammered out and cut into threads to work into the blue, purple, and crimson yarns and into the fine twisted linen, in skilled design. 4They made for the ephod shoulder-pieces, joined to it at its two edges. 5The decorated band on it was of the same materials and workmanship, of gold, of blue, purple, and crimson yarns, and of fine twisted linen; as the LORD had commanded Moses.

6 The onyx stones were prepared, enclosed in settings of gold filigree and engraved like the engravings of a signet, according to the names of the sons of Israel. 7He set them on the shoulder-pieces of the ephod, to be stones of remembrance for the sons of Israel; as the LORD had commanded Moses.

8 He made the breastpiece, in skilled work, like the work of the ephod, of gold, of blue, purple, and crimson yarns, and of fine twisted linen. 9It was square; the breastpiece was made double, a span in length and a span in width when doubled. 10They set in it four rows of stones. A row of carnelian,ˡ chrysolite, and emerald was the first row; 11and the second row, a turquoise, a

---

ⁱ 38:27 ninety-five pounds, literally, "a [silver] talent." The exact weight cannot be ascertained. ʲ 39:6, 7 two . . . two, implied. ᵏ 39:6, 7 reminders to Jehovah concerning the people of Israel, literally, "to be stones of memorial for the children of Israel."

ˡ The identification of several of these stones is uncertain

King James

11And the second row, an emerald, a sapphire, and a diamond.

12And the third row, a ligure, an agate, and an amethyst.

13And the fourth row, a beryl, an onyx, and a jasper: *they were* enclosed in ouches of gold in their enclosings.

14And the stones *were* according to the names of the children of Israel, twelve, according to their names, *like* the engravings of a signet, every one with his name, according to the twelve tribes.

15And they made upon the breastplate chains at the ends, *of* wreathen work *of* pure gold.

16And they made two ouches *of* gold, and two gold rings; and put the two rings in the two ends of the breastplate.

17And they put the two wreathen chains of gold in the two rings on the ends of the breastplate.

18And the two ends of the two wreathen chains they fastened in the two ouches, and put them on the shoulderpieces of the ephod, before it.

19And they made two rings of gold, and put *them* on the two ends of the breastplate, upon the border of it, which *was* on the side of the ephod inward.

20And they made two *other* golden rings, and put them on the two sides of the ephod underneath, toward the forepart of it, over against the *other* coupling thereof, above the curious girdle of the ephod.

21And they did bind the breastplate by his rings unto the rings of the ephod with a lace of blue, that it might be above the curious girdle of the ephod, and that the breastplate might not be loosed from the ephod; as the LORD commanded Moses.

22¶ And he made the robe of the ephod *of* woven work, all *of* blue.

23And *there was* an hole in the midst of the robe, as the hole of an habergeon, *with* a band round about the hole, that it should not rend.

24And they made upon the hems of the robe pomegranates *of* blue, and purple, and scarlet, *and* twined *linen.*

25And they made bells *of* pure gold, and put the bells between the pomegranates upon the hem of the robe, round about between the pomegranates;

26A bell and a pomegranate, a bell and a pomegranate, round about the hem of the robe to minister *in;* as the LORD commanded Moses.

27¶ And they made coats *of* fine linen *of* woven work for Aaron, and for his sons,

28And a mitre *of* fine linen, and goodly bonnets *of* fine linen, and linen breeches *of* fine twined linen,

29And a girdle *of* fine twined linen, and blue, and purple, and scarlet, *of* needlework; as the LORD commanded Moses.

30¶ And they made the plate of the holy crown *of* pure gold, and wrote upon it a writing, *like to* the engravings of a signet, HOLINESS TO THE LORD.

31And they tied unto it a lace of blue, to fasten *it* on high upon the mitre; as the LORD commanded Moses.

32¶ Thus was all the work of the tabernacle of the tent of the congregation finished: and the children of Israel did according to all that the LORD commanded Moses, so did they.

33¶ And they brought the tabernacle unto Moses, the tent, and all his furniture, his taches, his boards, his bars, and his pillars, and his sockets,

34And the covering of rams' skins dyed red, and the covering of badgers' skins, and the veil of the covering,

35The ark of the testimony, and the staves thereof, and the mercy seat,

36The table, *and* all the vessels thereof, and the showbread,

37The pure candlestick, *with* the lamps thereof, *even with* the lamps to be set in order, and all the vessels thereof, and the oil for light,

New International

quoise, a sapphire[a] and an emerald; 12in the third row a jacinth, an agate and an amethyst; 13in the fourth row a chrysolite, an onyx and a jasper.[b] They were mounted in gold filigree settings. 14There were twelve stones, one for each of the names of the sons of Israel, each engraved like a seal with the name of one of the twelve tribes.

15For the breastpiece they made braided chains of pure gold, like a rope. 16They made two gold filigree settings and two gold rings, and fastened the rings to two of the corners of the breastpiece. 17They fastened the two gold chains to the rings at the corners of the breastpiece, 18and the other ends of the chains to the two settings, attaching them to the shoulder pieces of the ephod at the front. 19They made two gold rings and attached them to the other two corners of the breastpiece on the inside edge next to the ephod. 20Then they made two more gold rings and attached them to the bottom of the shoulder pieces on the front of the ephod, close to the seam just above the waistband of the ephod. 21They tied the rings of the breastpiece to the rings of the ephod with blue cord, connecting it to the waistband so that the breastpiece would not swing out from the ephod—as the LORD commanded Moses.

Other Priestly Garments

22They made the robe of the ephod entirely of blue cloth—the work of a weaver— 23with an opening in the center of the robe like the opening of a collar,[c] and a band around this opening, so that it would not tear. 24They made pomegranates of blue, purple and scarlet yarn and finely twisted linen around the hem of the robe. 25And they made bells of pure gold and attached them around the hem between the pomegranates. 26The bells and pomegranates alternated around the hem of the robe to be worn for ministering, as the LORD commanded Moses.

27For Aaron and his sons, they made tunics of fine linen—the work of a weaver— 28and the turban of fine linen, the linen headbands and the undergarments of finely twisted linen. 29The sash was of finely twisted linen and blue, purple and scarlet yarn—the work of an embroiderer—as the LORD commanded Moses. 30They made the plate, the sacred diadem, out of pure gold and engraved on it, like an inscription on a seal: HOLY TO THE LORD. 31Then they fastened a blue cord to it to attach it to the turban, as the LORD commanded Moses.

Moses Inspects the Tabernacle

32So all the work on the tabernacle, the Tent of Meeting, was completed. The Israelites did everything just as the LORD commanded Moses. 33Then they brought the tabernacle to Moses: the tent and all its furnishings, its clasps, frames, crossbars, posts and bases; 34the covering of ram skins dyed red, the covering of hides of sea cows[d] and the shielding curtain; 35the ark of the Testimony with its poles and the atonement cover; 36the table with all its articles and the bread of the Presence; 37the pure gold lampstand with its row of lamps and all its accessories, and the oil for the light; 38the gold altar, the

a *11* Or *lapis lazuli*   b *13* The precise identification of some of these precious stones is uncertain.   c *23* The meaning of the Hebrew for this word is uncertain.   d *34* That is, dugongs

Living Bible

a sapphire, and a diamond. 12In the third row were a jacinth, an agate, and an amethyst. 13In the fourth row, a beryl, an onyx, and a jasper—all set in gold filigree. 14The stones were engraved like a seal, with the names of the twelve tribes of Israel.

15-18[To attach the chestpiece to the ephode], a gold ring was placed at the top of each shoulder strap of the ephod, and from these gold rings, two strands of twined gold attached to gold clasps on the top corners of the chestpiece. 19Two gold rings were also set at the lower edge of the chestpiece, on the under side, next to the ephod. 20Two other gold rings were placed low on the shoulder straps of the ephod, close to where the ephod joined its beautifully woven sash. 21The chestpiece was held securely above the beautifully woven sash of the ephod by tying the rings of the chestpiece to the rings of the ephod, with a blue ribbon.

All this was commanded to Moses by the Lord.

22The main part of the ephod was woven, all of blue, 23and there was a hole at the center just as in a coat of mail, for the head to go through, reinforced around the edge so that it would not tear. 24Pomegranates were attached to the bottom edge of the robe; these were made of linen cloth, embroideredf with blue, purple, and scarlet. 25, 26Bells of pure gold were placed between the pomegranates along the bottom edge of the skirt, with bells and pomegranates alternating all around the edge. This robe was worn when Aaron ministered to the Lord, just as the Lord had commanded Moses.

27Robes were now made for Aaron and his sons from fine-twined linen thread. 28, 29The chestpiece, the beautiful turbans, and the caps and the underclothes were all made of this linen, and the linen belt was beautifully embroidered with blue, purple, and scarlet threads, just as Jehovah had commanded Moses. 30Finally they made the holy plate of pure gold to wear on the front of the turban, engraved with the words, "Consecrated to Jehovah." 31It was tied to the turban with a blue cord, just as the Lord had instructed.

32And so at last the Tabernacle was finished, following all of the Lord's instructions to Moses.

33-40Then they brought the entire Tabernacle to Moses:

Furniture; clasps; frames; bars;

Posts; bases; layers of covering for the roof and sides—the rams' skins dyed red, the specially tanned goat skins, and the entrance drape; the Ark with the Ten Commandments in it;

The carrying poles;

The place of mercy;

The table and all its utensils;

The Bread of the Presence;

The pure [goldg] lampstand with its lamps, utensils, and oil;

The gold altar;

The anointing oil;

The sweet incense;

The curtain-door of the Tabernacle;

The bronze altar;

The bronze grating;

The poles and the utensils;

The washbasin and its base;

The drapes for the walls of the court and the posts holding them up;

The bases and the drapes at the gate of the court;

The cords and nails;

New Revised Standard

sapphire,h and a moonstone; 12and the third row, a jacinth, an agate, and an amethyst; 13and the fourth row, a beryl, an onyx, and a jasper; they were enclosed in settings of gold filigree. 14There were twelve stones with names corresponding to the names of the sons of Israel; they were like signets, each engraved with its name, for the twelve tribes. 15They made on the breastpiece chains of pure gold, twisted like cords; 16and they made two settings of gold filigree and two gold rings, and put the two rings on the two edges of the breastpiece; 17and they put the two cords of gold in the two rings at the edges of the breastpiece. 18Two ends of the two cords they had attached to the two settings of filigree; in this way they attached it in front to the shoulder-pieces of the ephod. 19Then they made two rings of gold, and put them at the two ends of the breastpiece, on its inside edge next to the ephod. 20They made two rings of gold, and attached them in front to the lower part of the two shoulder-pieces of the ephod, at its joining above the decorated band of the ephod. 21They bound the breastpiece by its rings to the rings of the ephod with a blue cord, so that it should lie on the decorated band of the ephod, and that the breastpiece should not come loose from the ephod; as the LORD had commanded Moses.

22 He also made the robe of the ephod woven all of blue yarn; 23and the opening of the robe in the middle of it was like the opening in a coat of mail,i with a binding around the opening, so that it might not be torn. 24On the lower hem of the robe they made pomegranates of blue, purple, and crimson yarns, and of fine twisted linen. 25They also made bells of pure gold, and put the bells between the pomegranates on the lower hem of the robe all around, between the pomegranates; 26a bell and a pomegranate, a bell and a pomegranate all around on the lower hem of the robe for ministering; as the LORD had commanded Moses.

27 They also made the tunics, woven of fine linen, for Aaron and his sons, 28and the turban of fine linen, and the headdresses of fine linen, and the linen undergarments of fine twisted linen, 29and the sash of fine twisted linen, and of blue, purple, and crimson yarns, embroidered with needlework; as the LORD had commanded Moses.

30 They made the rosette of the holy diadem of pure gold, and wrote on it an inscription, like the engraving of a signet, "Holy to the LORD." 31They tied to it a blue cord, to fasten it on the turban above; as the LORD had commanded Moses.

The Work Completed

32 In this way all the work of the tabernacle of the tent of meeting was finished; the Israelites had done everything just as the LORD had commanded Moses. 33Then they brought the tabernacle to Moses, the tent and all its utensils, its hooks, its frames, its bars, its pillars, and its bases; 34the covering of tanned rams' skins and the covering of fine leather,i and the curtain for the screen; 35the ark of the covenanti with its poles and the mercy seat;k 36the table with all its utensils, and the bread of the Presence; 37the pure lampstand with its lamps set on it and all its utensils, and the oil for the light; 38the golden altar, the anointing oil and the fra-

---

e 39:15-18 to the ephod, implied.   f 39:24 embroidered, implied.   g 39:33-40 gold, implied.

h Or lapis lazuli   i Meaning of Heb uncertain   j Or treaty, or testimony; Heb eduth   k Or the cover

King James

38And the golden altar, and the anointing oil, and the sweet incense, and the hanging for the tabernacle door,

39The brasen altar, and his grate of brass, his staves, and all his vessels, the laver and his foot,

40The hangings of the court, his pillars, and his sockets, and the hanging for the court gate, his cords, and his pins, and all the vessels of the service of the tabernacle, for the tent of the congregation,

41The cloths of service to do service in the holy *place*, and the holy garments for Aaron the priest, and his sons' garments, to minister in the priest's office.

42According to all that the LORD commanded Moses, so the children of Israel made all the work.

43And Moses did look upon all the work, and, behold, they had done it as the LORD had commanded, even so had they done it: and Moses blessed them.

40 AND THE LORD spake unto Moses, saying, 2On the first day of the first month shalt thou set up the tabernacle of the tent of the congregation.

3And thou shalt put therein the ark of the testimony, and cover the ark with the veil.

4And thou shalt bring in the table, and set in order the things that are to be set in order upon it; and thou shalt bring in the candlestick, and light the lamps thereof.

5And thou shalt set the altar of gold for the incense before the ark of the testimony, and put the hanging of the door to the tabernacle.

6And thou shalt set the altar of the burnt offering before the door of the tabernacle of the tent of the congregation.

7And thou shalt set the laver between the tent of the congregation and the altar, and shalt put water therein.

8And thou shalt set up the court round about, and hang up the hanging at the court gate.

9And thou shalt take the anointing oil, and anoint the tabernacle, and all that *is* therein, and shalt hallow it, and all the vessels thereof: and it shall be holy.

10And thou shalt anoint the altar of the burnt offering, and all his vessels, and sanctify the altar: and it shall be an altar most holy.

11And thou shalt anoint the laver and his foot, and sanctify it.

12And thou shalt bring Aaron and his sons unto the door of the tabernacle of the congregation, and wash them with water.

13And thou shalt put upon Aaron the holy garments, and anoint him, and sanctify him; that he may minister unto me in the priest's office.

14And thou shalt bring his sons, and clothe them with coats:

15And thou shalt anoint them, as thou didst anoint their father, that they may minister unto me in the priest's office: for their anointing shall surely be an everlasting priesthood throughout their generations.

16Thus did Moses: according to all that the LORD commanded him, so did he.

17¶ And it came to pass in the first month in the second year, on the first *day* of the month, *that* the tabernacle was reared up.

18And Moses reared up the tabernacle, and fastened his sockets, and set up the boards thereof, and put in the bars thereof, and reared up his pillars.

19And he spread abroad the tent over the tabernacle, and put the covering of the tent above upon it; as the LORD commanded Moses.

20¶ And he took and put the testimony into the ark, and set the staves on the ark, and put the mercy seat above upon the ark:

21And he brought the ark into the tabernacle, and set up the veil of the covering, and covered the ark of the testimony; as the LORD commanded Moses.

New International

anointing oil, the fragrant incense, and the curtain for the entrance to the tent; 39the bronze altar with its bronze grating, its poles and all its utensils; the basin with its stand; 40the curtains of the courtyard with its posts and bases, and the curtain for the entrance to the courtyard; the ropes and tent pegs for the courtyard; all the furnishings for the tabernacle, the Tent of Meeting; 41and the woven garments worn for ministering in the sanctuary, both the sacred garments for Aaron the priest and the garments for his sons when serving as priests.

42The Israelites had done all the work just as the LORD had commanded Moses. 43Moses inspected the work and saw that they had done it just as the LORD had commanded. So Moses blessed them.

Setting Up the Tabernacle

40 THEN THE LORD said to Moses: 2"Set up the tabernacle, the Tent of Meeting, on the first day of the first month. 3Place the ark of the Testimony in it and shield the ark with the curtain. 4Bring in the table and set out what belongs on it. Then bring in the lampstand and set up its lamps. 5Place the gold altar of incense in front of the ark of the Testimony and put the curtain at the entrance to the tabernacle.

6"Place the altar of burnt offering in front of the entrance to the tabernacle, the Tent of Meeting; 7place the basin between the Tent of Meeting and the altar and put water in it. 8Set up the courtyard around it and put the curtain at the entrance to the courtyard.

9"Take the anointing oil and anoint the tabernacle and everything in it; consecrate it and all its furnishings, and it will be holy. 10Then anoint the altar of burnt offering and all its utensils; consecrate the altar, and it will be most holy. 11Anoint the basin and its stand and consecrate them.

12"Bring Aaron and his sons to the entrance to the Tent of Meeting and wash them with water. 13Then dress Aaron in the sacred garments, anoint him and consecrate him so he may serve me as priest. 14Bring his sons and dress them in tunics. 15Anoint them just as you anointed their father, so they may serve me as priests. Their anointing will be to a priesthood that will continue for all generations to come." 16Moses did everything just as the LORD commanded him.

17So the tabernacle was set up on the first day of the first month in the second year. 18When Moses set up the tabernacle, he put the bases in place, erected the frames, inserted the crossbars and set up the posts. 19Then he spread the tent over the tabernacle and put the covering over the tent, as the LORD commanded him.

20He took the Testimony and placed it in the ark, attached the poles to the ark and put the atonement cover over it. 21Then he brought the ark into the tabernacle and hung the shielding curtain and shielded the ark of the Testimony, as the LORD commanded him.

Living Bible

All the utensils used there in the work of the Tabernacle.

41They also brought for his inspection the beautifully tailored garments to be worn while ministering in the Holy Place, and the holy garments for Aaron the priest and those for his sons, to be worn when on duty.

42So the people of Israel followed all the Lord's instructions to Moses. 43And Moses inspected all their work and blessed them because it was all as the Lord had instructed him.

40 THE LORD now said to Moses, 2"Put together the Tabernacle on the first day of the first month. 3In it, place the Ark containing the Ten Commandments; and install the veil to enclose the Ark within the Holy of Holies. 4Then bring in the table and place the utensils on it, and bring in the lampstand and light the lamps.

5"Place the gold altar for the incense in front of the Ark. Set up the drapes at the entrance of the Tabernacle, 6and place the altar for burnt offerings in front of the entrance. 7Set the washbasin between the Tabernacle-tent and the altar, and fill it with water. 8Then make the courtyard around the outside of the tent, and hang the curtain-door at the entrance to the courtyard.

9"Take the anointing oil and sprinkle it here and there upon the Tabernacle and everything in it, upon all of its utensils and parts, and all the furniture, to hallow it; and it shall become holy. 10Sprinkle the anointing oil upon the altar of burnt offering and its utensils, sanctifying it; for the altar shall then become most holy. 11Then anoint the washbasin and its pedestal, sanctifying it.

12"Now bring Aaron and his sons to the entrance of the Tabernacle and wash them with water; 13and clothe Aaron with the holy garments and anoint him, sanctifying him to minister to me as a priest. 14Then bring his sons and put their robes upon them, 15and anoint them as you did their father, that they may minister to me as priests; their anointing shall be permanent from generation to generation: all their children and children's children shall forever be my priests."

16So Moses proceeded to do all as the Lord had commanded him. 17On the first day of the first month, in the second year, the Tabernacle was put together. 18Moses erected it by setting its frames into their bases and attaching the bars. 19Then he spread the coverings over the framework, and put on the top layers, just as the Lord had commanded him.

20Inside the Ark he placed the stones with the Ten Commandments engraved on them, and attached the carrying poles to the Ark and installed the gold lid, the place of mercy. 21Then he brought the Ark into the Tabernacle and set up the curtain to screen it, just as the Lord had commanded.

New Revised Standard

grant incense, and the screen for the entrance of the tent; 39the bronze altar, and its grating of bronze, its poles, and all its utensils; the basin with its stand; 40the hangings of the court, its pillars, and its bases, and the screen for the gate of the court, its cords, and its pegs; and all the utensils for the service of the tabernacle, for the tent of meeting; 41the finely worked vestments for ministering in the holy place, the sacred vestments for the priest Aaron, and the vestments of his sons to serve as priests. 42The Israelites had done all of the work just as the LORD had commanded Moses. 43When Moses saw that they had done all the work just as the LORD had commanded, he blessed them.

The Tabernacle Erected and Its Equipment Installed

40 THE LORD spoke to Moses: 2On the first day of the first month you shall set up the tabernacle of the tent of meeting. 3You shall put in it the ark of the covenant,a and you shall screen the ark with the curtain. 4You shall bring in the table, and arrange its setting; and you shall bring in the lampstand, and set up its lamps. 5You shall put the golden altar for incense before the ark of the covenant,a and set up the screen for the entrance of the tabernacle. 6You shall set the altar of burnt offering before the entrance of the tabernacle of the tent of meeting, 7and place the basin between the tent of meeting and the altar, and put water in it. 8You shall set up the court all around, and hang up the screen for the gate of the court. 9Then you shall take the anointing oil, and anoint the tabernacle and all that is in it, and consecrate it and all its furniture, so that it shall become holy. 10You shall also anoint the altar of burnt offering and all its utensils, and consecrate the altar, so that the altar shall be most holy. 11You shall also anoint the basin with its stand, and consecrate it. 12Then you shall bring Aaron and his sons to the entrance of the tent of meeting, and shall wash them with water, 13and put on Aaron the sacred vestments, and you shall anoint him and consecrate him, so that he may serve me as priest. 14You shall bring his sons also and put tunics on them, 15and anoint them, as you anointed their father, that they may serve me as priests: and their anointing shall admit them to a perpetual priesthood throughout all generations to come.

16 Moses did everything just as the LORD had commanded him. 17In the first month in the second year, on the first day of the month, the tabernacle was set up. 18Moses set up the tabernacle; he laid its bases, and set up its frames, and put in its poles, and raised up its pillars; 19and he spread the tent over the tabernacle, and put the covering of the tent over it; as the LORD had commanded Moses. 20He took the covenanta and put it into the ark, and put the poles on the ark, and set the mercy seatb above the ark; 21and he brought the ark into the tabernacle, and set up the curtain for screening, and screened the ark of the covenant;a as the LORD had commanded Moses. 22He put the table in the tent of

---

a Or treaty, or testimony; Heb eduth   b Or the cover

King James

22¶ And he put the table in the tent of the congregation, upon the side of the tabernacle northward, without the veil.

23And he set the bread in order upon it before the LORD; as the LORD had commanded Moses.

24¶ And he put the candlestick in the tent of the congregation, over against the table, on the side of the tabernacle southward.

25And he lighted the lamps before the LORD; as the LORD commanded Moses.

26¶ And he put the golden altar in the tent of the congregation before the veil:

27And he burnt sweet incense thereon; as the LORD commanded Moses.

28¶ And he set up the hanging *at* the door of the tabernacle.

29And he put the altar of burnt offering *by* the door of the tabernacle of the tent of the congregation, and offered upon it the burnt offering and the meat offering; as the LORD commanded Moses.

30¶ And he set the laver between the tent of the congregation and the altar, and put water there, to wash *withal*.

31And Moses and Aaron and his sons washed their hands and their feet thereat:

32When they went into the tent of the congregation, and when they came near unto the altar, they washed; as the LORD commanded Moses.

33And he reared up the court round about the tabernacle and the altar, and set up the hanging of the court gate. So Moses finished the work.

34¶ Then a cloud covered the tent of the congregation, and the glory of the LORD filled the tabernacle.

35And Moses was not able to enter into the tent of the congregation, because the cloud abode thereon, and the glory of the LORD filled the tabernacle.

36And when the cloud was taken up from over the tabernacle, the children of Israel went onward in all their journeys:

37But if the cloud were not taken up, then they journeyed not till the day that it was taken up.

38For the cloud of the LORD *was* upon the tabernacle by day, and fire was on it by night, in the sight of all the house of Israel, throughout all their journeys.

New International

22Moses placed the table in the Tent of Meeting on the north side of the tabernacle outside the curtain 23and set out the bread on it before the LORD, as the LORD commanded him.

24He placed the lampstand in the Tent of Meeting opposite the table on the south side of the tabernacle 25and set up the lamps before the LORD, as the LORD commanded him.

26Moses placed the gold altar in the Tent of Meeting in front of the curtain 27and burned fragrant incense on it, as the LORD commanded him. 28Then he put up the curtain at the entrance to the tabernacle.

29He set the altar of burnt offering near the entrance to the tabernacle, the Tent of Meeting, and offered on it burnt offerings and grain offerings, as the LORD commanded him.

30He placed the basin between the Tent of Meeting and the altar and put water in it for washing, 31and Moses and Aaron and his sons used it to wash their hands and feet. 32They washed whenever they entered the Tent of Meeting or approached the altar, as the LORD commanded Moses.

33Then Moses set up the courtyard around the tabernacle and altar and put up the curtain at the entrance to the courtyard. And so Moses finished the work.

The Glory of the LORD

34Then the cloud covered the Tent of Meeting, and the glory of the LORD filled the tabernacle. 35Moses could not enter the Tent of Meeting because the cloud had settled upon it, and the glory of the LORD filled the tabernacle.

36In all the travels of the Israelites, whenever the cloud lifted from above the tabernacle, they would set out; 37but if the cloud did not lift, they did not set out—until the day it lifted. 38So the cloud of the LORD was over the tabernacle by day, and fire was in the cloud by night, in the sight of all the house of Israel during all their travels.

Living Bible

22Next he placed the table at the north side of the room outside the curtain, 23and set the Bread of the Presence upon the table before the Lord, just as the Lord had commanded.

24And he placed the lampstand next to the table, on the south side of the Tabernacle. 25Then he lighted the lamps before the Lord, following all the instructions, 26and placed the gold altar in the Tabernacle next to the curtain, 27and burned upon it the incense made from sweet spices, just as the Lord had commanded.

28He attached the curtain at the entrance of the Tabernacle, 29and placed the outside altar for the burnt offerings near the entrance, and offered upon it a burnt offering and a meal offering, just as the Lord had commanded him.

30Next he placed the washbasin between the tent and the altar, and filled it with water so that the priests could use it for washing. 31Moses and Aaron and Aaron's sons washed their hands and feet there. 32Whenever they walked past the altar to enter the Tabernacle, they stopped and washed, just as the Lord had commanded Moses.

33Then he erected the enclosure surrounding the tent and the altar, and set up the curtain-door at the entrance of the enclosure. So at last Moses finished the work. 34Then the cloud covered the Tabernacle and the glory of the Lord filled it. 35Moses was not able to enter because the cloud was standing there, and the glory of the Lord filled the Tabernacle. 36Whenever the cloud lifted and moved, the people of Israel journeyed onward, following it. 37But if the cloud stayed, they stayed until it moved. 38The cloud rested upon the Tabernacle during the daytime, and at night there was fire in the cloud so that all the people of Israel could see it.

This continued throughout all their journeys.

New Revised Standard

meeting, on the north side of the tabernacle, outside the curtain, 23and set the bread in order on it before the LORD; as the LORD had commanded Moses. 24He put the lampstand in the tent of meeting, opposite the table on the south side of the tabernacle, 25and set up the lamps before the LORD; as the LORD had commanded Moses. 26He put the golden altar in the tent of meeting before the curtain, 27and offered fragrant incense on it; as the LORD had commanded Moses. 28He also put in place the screen for the entrance of the tabernacle. 29He set the altar of burnt offering at the entrance of the tabernacle of the tent of meeting, and offered on it the burnt offering and the grain offering as the LORD had commanded Moses. 30He set the basin between the tent of meeting and the altar, and put water in it for washing, 31with which Moses and Aaron and his sons washed their hands and their feet. 32When they went into the tent of meeting, and when they approached the altar, they washed; as the LORD had commanded Moses. 33He set up the court around the tabernacle and the altar, and put up the screen at the gate of the court. So Moses finished the work.

The Cloud and the Glory

34 Then the cloud covered the tent of meeting, and the glory of the LORD filled the tabernacle. 35Moses was not able to enter the tent of meeting because the cloud settled upon it, and the glory of the LORD filled the tabernacle. 36Whenever the cloud was taken up from the tabernacle, the Israelites would set out on each stage of their journey; 37but if the cloud was not taken up, then they did not set out until the day that it was taken up. 38For the cloud of the LORD was on the tabernacle by day, and fire was in the clouda by night, before the eyes of all the house of Israel at each stage of their journey.

---

a Heb it

THE THIRD BOOK OF MOSES, CALLED

Leviticus

Leviticus

1 AND THE LORD called unto Moses, and spake unto him out of the tabernacle of the congregation, saying,

2Speak unto the children of Israel, and say unto them, If any man of you bring an offering unto the LORD, ye shall bring your offering of the cattle, *even* of the herd, and of the flock.

3If his offering *be* a burnt sacrifice of the herd, let him offer a male without blemish: he shall offer it of his own voluntary will at the door of the tabernacle of the congregation before the LORD.

4And he shall put his hand upon the head of the burnt offering; and it shall be accepted for him to make atonement for him.

5And he shall kill the bullock before the LORD: and the priests, Aaron's sons, shall bring the blood, and sprinkle the blood round about upon the altar that *is by* the door of the tabernacle of the congregation.

6And he shall flay the burnt offering, and cut it into his pieces.

7And the sons of Aaron the priest shall put fire upon the altar, and lay the wood in order upon the fire:

8And the priests, Aaron's sons, shall lay the parts, the head, and the fat, in order upon the wood that *is* on the fire which *is* upon the altar:

9But his inwards and his legs shall he wash in water: and the priest shall burn all on the altar, *to be* a burnt sacrifice, an offering made by fire, of a sweet savour unto the LORD.

10¶ And if his offering *be* of the flocks, *namely*, of the sheep, or of the goats, for a burnt sacrifice; he shall bring it a male without blemish.

11And he shall kill it on the side of the altar northward before the LORD: and the priests, Aaron's sons, shall sprinkle his blood round about upon the altar.

12And he shall cut it into his pieces, with his head and his fat: and the priest shall lay them in order on the wood that *is* on the fire which *is* upon the altar:

13But he shall wash the inwards and the legs with water: and the priest shall bring *it* all, and burn *it* upon the altar: it *is* a burnt sacrifice, an offering made by fire, of a sweet savour unto the LORD.

14¶ And if the burnt sacrifice for his offering to the LORD *be* of fowls, then he shall bring his offering of turtledoves, or of young pigeons.

15And the priest shall bring it unto the altar, and wring off his head, and burn *it* on the altar; and the blood thereof shall be wrung out at the side of the altar:

16And he shall pluck away his crop with his feathers, and cast it beside the altar on the east part, by the place of the ashes:

17And he shall cleave it with the wings thereof, *but* shall not divide *it* asunder: and the priest shall burn it upon the altar, upon the wood that *is* upon the fire: it *is* a burnt sacrifice, an offering made by fire, of a sweet savour unto the LORD.

The Burnt Offering

1 THE LORD called to Moses and spoke to him from the Tent of Meeting. He said, 2"Speak to the Israelites and say to them: 'When any of you brings an offering to the LORD, bring as your offering an animal from either the herd or the flock.

3" 'If the offering is a burnt offering from the herd, he is to offer a male without defect. He must present it at the entrance to the Tent of Meeting so that it[a] will be acceptable to the LORD. 4He is to lay his hand on the head of the burnt offering, and it will be accepted on his behalf to make atonement for him. 5He is to slaughter the young bull before the LORD, and then Aaron's sons the priests shall bring the blood and sprinkle it against the altar on all sides at the entrance to the Tent of Meeting. 6He is to skin the burnt offering and cut it into pieces. 7The sons of Aaron the priest are to put fire on the altar and arrange wood on the fire. 8Then Aaron's sons the priests shall arrange the pieces, including the head and the fat, on the burning wood that is on the altar. 9He is to wash the inner parts and the legs with water, and the priest is to burn all of it on the altar. It is a burnt offering, an offering made by fire, an aroma pleasing to the LORD.

10" 'If the offering is a burnt offering from the flock, from either the sheep or the goats, he is to offer a male without defect. 11He is to slaughter it at the north side of the altar before the LORD, and Aaron's sons the priests shall sprinkle its blood against the altar on all sides. 12He is to cut it into pieces, and the priest shall arrange them, including the head and the fat, on the burning wood that is on the altar. 13He is to wash the inner parts and the legs with water, and the priest is to bring all of it and burn it on the altar. It is a burnt offering, an offering made by fire, an aroma pleasing to the LORD.

14" 'If the offering to the LORD is a burnt offering of birds, he is to offer a dove or a young pigeon. 15The priest shall bring it to the altar, wring off the head and burn it on the altar; its blood shall be drained out on the side of the altar. 16He is to remove the crop with its contents[b] and throw it to the east side of the altar, where the ashes are. 17He shall tear it open by the wings, not severing it completely, and then the priest shall burn it on the wood that is on the fire on the altar. It is a burnt offering, an offering made by fire, an aroma pleasing to the LORD.

a 3 Or *he*   b 16 Or *crop and the feathers*; the meaning of the Hebrew for this word is uncertain.

Living Bible

Leviticus

1 THE LORD now spoke to Moses from the Tabernacle, 2, 3and commanded him to give the following instructions to the people of Israel: "When you sacrifice to the Lord, use animals from your herds and flocks.

"If your sacrifice is to be an ox given as a burnt offering, use only a bull with no physical defects. Bring the animal to the entrance of the Tabernacle where the priests will accept your gift for the Lord. 4The person bringing it is to lay his hand upon its head, and it then becomes his substitute: the death of the animal will be accepted by God instead of the death of the man who brings it, as the penalty for his sins.c 5The man shall then kill the animal there before the Lord, and Aaron's sons, the priests, will present the blood before the Lord, sprinkling it upon all sides of the altar at the entrance of the Tabernacle. 6, 7Then the priests will skin the animald and quarter it, and build a wood fire upon the altar, 8and put the sections of the animal and its head and fat upon the wood. 9The internal organs and the legs are to be washed, then the priests will burn them upon the altar, and they will be an acceptable burnt offering with which the Lord is pleased.e

10"If the animal used as a burnt offering is a sheep or a goat, it too must be a male, and without any blemishes. 11The man who brings it will kill it before the Lord on the north side of the altar, and Aaron's sons, the priests, will sprinkle its blood back and forth upon the altar. 12Then the man will quarter it, and the priests will lay the pieces, with the head and the fat, on top of the wood on the altar. 13But the internal organs and the legs shall first be washed with water. Then the priests shall burn it all upon the altar as an offering to the Lord; for burnt offerings give much pleasure to the Lord.

14"If anyone wishes to use a bird as his burnt offering, he may choose either turtledoves or young pigeons. 15, 16, 17A priest will take the bird to the altar and wring off its head, and the blood shall be drained out at the side of the altar. Then the priest will remove the crop and the feathers and throw them on the east side of the altar with the ashes. Then, grasping it by the wings, he shall tear it apart, but not completely. And the priest shall burn it upon the altar, and the Lord will have pleasure in this sacrifice.f

New Revised Standard

Leviticus

The Burnt Offering

1 THE LORD summoned Moses and spoke to him from the tent of meeting, saying: 2Speak to the people of Israel and say to them: When any of you bring an offering of livestock to the LORD, you shall bring your offering from the herd or from the flock.

3 If the offering is a burnt offering from the herd, you shall offer a male without blemish; you shall bring it to the entrance of the tent of meeting, for acceptance in your behalf before the LORD. 4You shall lay your hand on the head of the burnt offering, and it shall be acceptable in your behalf as atonement for you. 5The bull shall be slaughtered before the LORD; and Aaron's sons the priests shall offer the blood, dashing the blood against all sides of the altar that is at the entrance of the tent of meeting. 6The burnt offering shall be flayed and cut up into its parts. 7The sons of the priest Aaron shall put fire on the altar and arrange wood on the fire. 8Aaron's sons the priests shall arrange the parts, with the head and the suet, on the wood that is on the fire on the altar; 9but its entrails and its legs shall be washed with water. Then the priest shall turn the whole into smoke on the altar as a burnt offering, an offering by fire of pleasing odor to the LORD.

10 If your gift for a burnt offering is from the flock, from the sheep or goats, your offering shall be a male without blemish. 11It shall be slaughtered on the north side of the altar before the LORD, and Aaron's sons the priests shall dash its blood against all sides of the altar. 12It shall be cut up into its parts, with its head and its suet, and the priest shall arrange them on the wood that is on the fire on the altar; 13but the entrails and the legs shall be washed with water. Then the priest shall offer the whole and turn it into smoke on the altar; it is a burnt offering, an offering by fire of pleasing odor to the LORD.

14 If your offering to the LORD is a burnt offering of birds, you shall choose your offering from turtledoves or pigeons. 15The priest shall bring it to the altar and wring off its head, and turn it into smoke on the altar; and its blood shall be drained out against the side of the altar. 16He shall remove its crop with its contentsg and throw it at the east side of the altar, in the place for ashes. 17He shall tear it open by its wings without severing it. Then the priest shall turn it into smoke on the altar, on the wood that is on the fire; it is a burnt offering, an offering by fire of pleasing odor to the LORD.

---

c 1:4 as the penalty for his sins, literally, "to make atonement for him."
d 1:6, 7 the priests will skin, literally, "he shall skin . . ." e 1:9 they will be an acceptable burnt offering with which the Lord is pleased, literally, "it will be a sweet savor unto the Lord." f 1:17 the Lord will have pleasure in this sacrifice, literally, "it will be a sweet savor unto the Lord."

g Meaning of Heb uncertain

King James

2 AND WHEN any will offer a meat offering unto the LORD, his offering shall be *of* fine flour; and he shall pour oil upon it, and put frankincense thereon:

2And he shall bring it to Aaron's sons the priests: and he shall take thereout his handful of the flour thereof, and of the oil thereof, with all the frankincense thereof; and the priest shall burn the memorial of it upon the altar, *to be* an offering made by fire, of a sweet savour unto the LORD:

3And the remnant of the meat offering *shall be* Aaron's and his sons': *it is* a thing most holy of the offerings of the LORD made by fire.

4¶ And if thou bring an oblation of a meat offering baked in the oven, *it shall be* unleavened cakes of fine flour mingled with oil, or unleavened wafers anointed with oil.

5¶ And if thy oblation *be* a meat offering *baked* in a pan, it shall be *of* fine flour unleavened, mingled with oil.

6Thou shalt part it in pieces, and pour oil thereon: it *is* a meat offering.

7¶ And if thy oblation *be* a meat offering *baked* in the fryingpan, it shall be made *of* fine flour with oil.

8And thou shalt bring the meat offering that is made of these things unto the LORD: and when it is presented unto the priest, he shall bring it unto the altar.

9And the priest shall take from the meat offering a memorial thereof, and shall burn *it* upon the altar: *it is* an offering made by fire, of a sweet savour unto the LORD.

10And that which is left of the meat offering *shall be* Aaron's and his sons': *it is* a thing most holy of the offerings of the LORD made by fire.

11No meat offering, which ye shall bring unto the LORD, shall be made with leaven: for ye shall burn no leaven, nor any honey, in any offering of the LORD made by fire.

12¶ As for the oblation of the firstfruits, ye shall offer them unto the LORD: but they shall not be burnt on the altar for a sweet savour.

13And every oblation of thy meat offering shalt thou season with salt; neither shalt thou suffer the salt of the covenant of thy God to be lacking from thy meat offering: with all thine offerings thou shalt offer salt.

14And if thou offer a meat offering of thy firstfruits unto the LORD, thou shalt offer for the meat offering of thy firstfruits green ears of corn dried by the fire, *even* corn beaten out of full ears.

15And thou shalt put oil upon it, and lay frankincense thereon: it *is* a meat offering.

16And the priest shall burn the memorial of it, *part* of the beaten corn thereof, and *part* of the oil thereof, with all the frankincense thereof: *it is* an offering made by fire unto the LORD.

3 AND IF his oblation *be* a sacrifice of peace offering, if he offer *it* of the herd; whether *it be* a male or female, he shall offer it without blemish before the LORD.

2And he shall lay his hand upon the head of his offering, and kill it *at* the door of the tabernacle of the congregation: and Aaron's sons the priests shall sprinkle the blood upon the altar round about.

New International

The Grain Offering

2 " 'WHEN SOMEONE brings a grain offering to the LORD, his offering is to be of fine flour. He is to pour oil on it, put incense on it 2and take it to Aaron's sons the priests. The priest shall take a handful of the fine flour and oil, together with all the incense, and burn this as a memorial portion on the altar, an offering made by fire, an aroma pleasing to the LORD. 3The rest of the grain offering belongs to Aaron and his sons; it is a most holy part of the offerings made to the LORD by fire.

4" 'If you bring a grain offering baked in an oven, it is to consist of fine flour: cakes made without yeast and mixed with oil, or[a] wafers made without yeast and spread with oil. 5If your grain offering is prepared on a griddle, it is to be made of fine flour mixed with oil, and without yeast. 6Crumble it and pour oil on it; it is a grain offering. 7If your grain offering is cooked in a pan, it is to be made of fine flour and oil. 8Bring the grain offering made of these things to the LORD; present it to the priest, who shall take it to the altar. 9He shall take out the memorial portion from the grain offering and burn it on the altar as an offering made by fire, an aroma pleasing to the LORD. 10The rest of the grain offering belongs to Aaron and his sons; it is a most holy part of the offerings made to the LORD by fire.

11" 'Every grain offering you bring to the LORD must be made without yeast, for you are not to burn any yeast or honey in an offering made to the LORD by fire. 12You may bring them to the LORD as an offering of the firstfruits, but they are not to be offered on the altar as a pleasing aroma. 13Season all your grain offerings with salt. Do not leave the salt of the covenant of your God out of your grain offerings; add salt to all your offerings.

14" 'If you bring a grain offering of firstfruits to the LORD, offer crushed heads of new grain roasted in the fire. 15Put oil and incense on it; it is a grain offering. 16The priest shall burn the memorial portion of the crushed grain and the oil, together with all the incense, as an offering made to the LORD by fire.

The Fellowship Offering

3 " 'IF SOMEONE'S offering is a fellowship offering,[b] and he offers an animal from the herd, whether male or female, he is to present before the LORD an animal without defect. 2He is to lay his hand on the head of his offering and slaughter it at the entrance to the Tent of Meeting. Then Aaron's sons the priests shall sprinkle the blood against the altar on all sides. 3From

---

a *4* Or *and*   b *1* Traditionally *peace offering;* also in verses 3, 6 and 9

Living Bible

2 "ANYONE WHO wishes to sacrifice a grain offering to the Lord is to bring fine flour and is to
pour olive oil and incense upon it. 2Then he is to take
a handful, representing the entire amount,c to one of the
priests to burn, and the Lord will be fully pleased. 3The
remainder of the flour is to be given to Aaron and his
sons as their food; but all of it is counted as a holy burnt
offering to the Lord.

4"If bread baked in the oven is brought as an offering
to the Lord, it must be made from finely ground flour,
baked with olive oil but without yeast. Wafers made
without yeast and spread with olive oil may also be used
as an offering. 5If the offering is something from the
griddle, it shall be made of finely ground flour without
yeast, and mingled with olive oil. 6Break it into pieces
and pour oil upon it—it is a form of grain offering. 7If
your offering is cooked in a pan, it too shall be made of
fine flour mixed with olive oil.

8"However it is prepared—whether baked, fried, or
grilled—you are to bring this grain offering to the priest
and he shall take it to the altar to present it to the Lord.

9"The priests are to burn only a representative por-
tiond of the offering, but all of it will be fully appreciated by the Lord. 10The remainder belongs to the priests
for their own use, but it is all counted as a holy burnt
offering to the Lord.

11"Use no yeast with your offerings of flour; for no
yeast or honey is permitted in burnt offerings to the
Lord. 12You may offer yeast bread and honey as thanksgiving offerings at harvest time, but not as burnt offer-
ings.e

13"Every offering must be seasoned with salt,f because the salt is a reminder of God's covenant.

14"If you are offering from the first of your harvest,
remove the kernels from a fresh ear, crush and roast
them, then offer them to the Lord. 15Put olive oil and
incense on the offering, for it is a grain offering. 16Then
the priests shall burn part of the bruised grain mixed with
oil and all of the incense as a representative portion
before the Lord.

3 "WHEN ANYONE wants to give an offering of
thanksgiving to the Lord, he may use either a bull
or a cow, but the animal must be entirely without defect
if it is to be offered to the Lord! 2The man who brings
the animal shall lay his hand upon its head and kill it at
the door of the Tabernacle. Then Aaron's sons shall
throw the blood against the sides of the altar, 3, 4, 5and

New Revised Standard

Grain Offerings

2 WHEN ANYONE presents a grain offering to the
LORD, the offering shall be of choice flour; the
worshiper shall pour oil on it, and put frankincense on
it, 2 and bring it to Aaron's sons the priests. After taking
from it a handful of the choice flour and oil, with all its
frankincense, the priest shall turn this token portion into
smoke on the altar, an offering by fire of pleasing odor
to the LORD. 3 And what is left of the grain offering shall
be for Aaron and his sons, a most holy part of the offerings by fire to the LORD.

4 When you present a grain offering baked in the
oven, it shall be of choice flour: unleavened cakes mixed
with oil, or unleavened wafers spread with oil. 5 If your
offering is grain prepared on a griddle, it shall be of
choice flour mixed with oil, unleavened; 6 break it in
pieces, and pour oil on it; it is a grain offering. 7 If your
offering is grain prepared in a pan, it shall be made of
choice flour in oil. 8 You shall bring to the LORD the
grain offering that is prepared in any of these ways; and
when it is presented to the priest, he shall take it to the
altar. 9 The priest shall remove from the grain offering
its token portion and turn this into smoke on the altar,
an offering by fire of pleasing odor to the LORD. 10 And
what is left of the grain offering shall be for Aaron and
his sons; it is a most holy part of the offerings by fire
to the LORD.

11 No grain offering that you bring to the LORD shall
be made with leaven, for you must not turn any leaven
or honey into smoke as an offering by fire to the LORD.
12 You may bring them to the LORD as an offering of
choice products, but they shall not be offered on the altar
for a pleasing odor. 13 You shall not omit from your grain
offerings the salt of the covenant with your God; with
all your offerings you shall offer salt.

14 If you bring a grain offering of first fruits to the
LORD, you shall bring as the grain offering of your first
fruits coarse new grain from fresh ears, parched with
fire. 15 You shall add oil to it and lay frankincense on it;
it is a grain offering. 16 And the priest shall turn a token
portion of it into smoke—some of the coarse grain and
oil with all its frankincense; it is an offering by fire to
the LORD.

Offerings of Well-Being

3 IF THE offering is a sacrifice of well-being, if you
offer an animal of the herd, whether male or female, you shall offer one without blemish before the
LORD. 2 You shall lay your hand on the head of the
offering and slaughter it at the entrance of the tent of
meeting; and Aaron's sons the priests shall dash the
blood against all sides of the altar. 3 You shall offer from

---

c 2:2 *representing the entire amount*, literally, "shall burn the memorial portion
thereof upon the altar, an offering made by fire." d 2:9 *a representative
portion*, literally, "the memorial." e 2:12 *but not as burnt offerings*,
literally, "but not for a sweet savor on the altar." f 2:13 *seasoned with salt*.
In many of the languages of the ancient Near East, the word "salt" is a homonym
of the word "good." It was used symbolically for "goodness" in making
covenants.

King James

3And he shall offer of the sacrifice of the peace offering an offering made by fire unto the LORD; the fat that covereth the inwards, and all the fat that *is* upon the inwards,

4And the two kidneys, and the fat that *is* on them, which *is* by the flanks, and the caul above the liver, with the kidneys, it shall he take away.

5And Aaron's sons shall burn it on the altar upon the burnt sacrifice, which *is* upon the wood that *is* on the fire: *it is* an offering made by fire, of a sweet savour unto the LORD.

6¶ And if his offering for a sacrifice of peace offering unto the LORD *be* of the flock; male or female, he shall offer it without blemish.

7If he offer a lamb for his offering, then shall he offer it before the LORD.

8And he shall lay his hand upon the head of his offering, and kill it before the tabernacle of the congregation: and Aaron's sons shall sprinkle the blood thereof round about upon the altar.

9And he shall offer of the sacrifice of the peace offering an offering made by fire unto the LORD; the fat thereof, *and* the whole rump, it shall he take off hard by the backbone; and the fat that covereth the inwards, and all the fat that *is* upon the inwards,

10And the two kidneys, and the fat that *is* upon them, which *is* by the flanks, and the caul above the liver, with the kidneys, it shall he take away.

11And the priest shall burn it upon the altar: *it is* the food of the offering made by fire unto the LORD.

12¶ And if his offering *be* a goat, then he shall offer it before the LORD.

13And he shall lay his hand upon the head of it, and kill it before the tabernacle of the congregation: and the sons of Aaron shall sprinkle the blood thereof upon the altar round about.

14And he shall offer thereof his offering, *even* an offering made by fire unto the LORD; the fat that covereth the inwards, and all the fat that *is* upon the inwards,

15And the two kidneys, and the fat that *is* upon them, which *is* by the flanks, and the caul above the liver, with the kidneys, it shall he take away.

16And the priest shall burn them upon the altar: *it is* the food of the offering made by fire for a sweet savour: all the fat *is* the LORD's.

17*It shall be* a perpetual statute for your generations throughout all your dwellings, that ye eat neither fat nor blood.

4 AND THE LORD spake unto Moses, saying, 2Speak unto the children of Israel, saying, If a soul shall sin through ignorance against any of the commandments of the LORD *concerning things* which ought not to be done, and shall do against any of them:

3If the priest that is anointed do sin according to the sin of the people; then let him bring for his sin, which he hath sinned, a young bullock without blemish unto the LORD for a sin offering.

4And he shall bring the bullock unto the door of the tabernacle of the congregation before the LORD; and shall lay his hand upon the bullock's head, and kill the bullock before the LORD.

5And the priest that is anointed shall take of the bullock's blood, and bring it to the tabernacle of the congregation:

6And the priest shall dip his finger in the blood, and sprinkle of the blood seven times before the LORD, before the veil of the sanctuary.

New International

the fellowship offering he is to bring a sacrifice made to the LORD by fire: all the fat that covers the inner parts or is connected to them, 4both kidneys with the fat on them near the loins, and the covering of the liver, which he will remove with the kidneys. 5Then Aaron's sons are to burn it on the altar on top of the burnt offering that is on the burning wood, as an offering made by fire, an aroma pleasing to the LORD.

6" 'If he offers an animal from the flock as a fellowship offering to the LORD, he is to offer a male or female without defect. 7If he offers a lamb, he is to present it before the LORD. 8He is to lay his hand on the head of his offering and slaughter it in front of the Tent of Meeting. Then Aaron's sons shall sprinkle its blood against the altar on all sides. 9From the fellowship offering he is to bring a sacrifice made to the LORD by fire: its fat, the entire fat tail cut off close to the backbone, all the fat that covers the inner parts or is connected to them, 10both kidneys with the fat on them near the loins, and the covering of the liver, which he will remove with the kidneys. 11The priest shall burn them on the altar as food, an offering made to the LORD by fire.

12" 'If his offering is a goat, he is to present it before the LORD. 13He is to lay his hand on its head and slaughter it in front of the Tent of Meeting. Then Aaron's sons shall sprinkle its blood against the altar on all sides. 14From what he offers he is to make this offering to the LORD by fire: all the fat that covers the inner parts or is connected to them, 15both kidneys with the fat on them near the loins, and the covering of the liver, which will remove with the kidneys. 16The priest shall burn them on the altar as food, an offering made by fire, a pleasing aroma. All the fat is the LORD's.

17" 'This is a lasting ordinance for the generations to come, wherever you live: You must not eat any fat or any blood.' "

The Sin Offering

4 THE LORD said to Moses, 2"Say to the Israelites: 'When anyone sins unintentionally and does what is forbidden in any of the LORD's commands—

3" 'If the anointed priest sins, bringing guilt on the people, he must bring to the LORD a young bull without defect as a sin offering for the sin he has committed. 4He is to present the bull at the entrance to the Tent of Meeting before the LORD. He is to lay his hand on its head and slaughter it before the LORD. 5Then the anointed priest shall take some of the bull's blood and carry it into the Tent of Meeting. 6He is to dip his finger into the blood and sprinkle some of it seven times before the LORD, in front of the curtain of the sanctuary. 7The priest

Living Bible

shall burn before the Lord the fat that covers the inward parts, the two kidneys and the loin-fat on them, and the gall bladder. And it will give the Lord much pleasure.

6"If a goat or sheep is used as a thank-offering to the Lord, it must have no defect and may be either a male or female.

7, 8"If it is a lamb, the man who brings it shall lay his hand upon its head and kill it at the entrance of the Tabernacle; the priests shall throw the blood against the sides of the altar, 9, 10, 11and shall offer upon the altar the fat, the tail removed close to the backbone, the fat covering the internal organs, the two kidneys with the loin-fat on them, and the gall bladder, as a burnt offering to the Lord.

12"If anyone brings a goat as his offering to the Lord, 13he shall lay his hand upon its head and kill it at the entrance of the Tabernacle. The priest shall throw its blood against the sides of the altar, 14and shall offer upon the altar, as a burnt offering to the Lord, the fat which covers the insides, 15, 16the two kidneys and the loin-fat on them, and the gall bladder. This burnt offering is very pleasing to the Lord. All the fat is Jehovah's. 17This is a permanent law throughout your land, that you shall eat neither fat nor blood."

4 THEN THE Lord gave these further instructions to Moses:

2"Tell the people of Israel that these are the laws concerning anyone who unintentionally breaks any of my commandments. 3If a priest sins unintentionally, and so brings guilt upon the people, he must offer a young bull without defect as a sin offering to the Lord. 4He shall bring it to the door of the Tabernacle, and shall lay his hand upon its head and kill it there before Jehovah. 5Then the priest shall take the animal's blood into the Tabernacle, 6and shall dip his finger in the blood and sprinkle it seven times before the Lord in front of the veil that bars the way to the Holy of Holies. 7Then the priest

New Revised Standard

the sacrifice of well-being, as an offering by fire to the LORD, the fat that covers the entrails and all the fat that is around the entrails; 4the two kidneys with the fat that is on them at the loins, and the appendage of the liver, which he shall remove with the kidneys. 5Then Aaron's sons shall turn these into smoke on the altar, with the burnt offering that is on the wood on the fire, as an offering by fire of pleasing odor to the LORD.

6 If your offering for a sacrifice of well-being to the LORD is from the flock, male or female, you shall offer one without blemish. 7If you present a sheep as your offering, you shall bring it before the LORD 8and lay your hand on the head of the offering. It shall be slaughtered before the tent of meeting, and Aaron's sons shall dash its blood against all sides of the altar. 9You shall present its fat from the sacrifice of well-being, as an offering by fire to the LORD: the whole broad tail, which shall be removed close to the backbone, the fat that covers the entrails, and all the fat that is around the entrails; 10the two kidneys with the fat that is on them at the loins, and the appendage of the liver, which you shall remove with the kidneys. 11Then the priest shall turn these into smoke on the altar as a food offering by fire to the LORD.

12 If your offering is a goat, you shall bring it before the LORD 13and lay your hand on its head; it shall be slaughtered before the tent of meeting; and the sons of Aaron shall dash its blood against all sides of the altar. 14You shall present as your offering from it, as an offering by fire to the LORD, the fat that covers the entrails, and all the fat that is around the entrails; 15the two kidneys with the fat that is on them at the loins, and the appendage of the liver, which you shall remove with the kidneys. 16Then the priest shall turn these into smoke on the altar as a food offering by fire for a pleasing odor.

All fat is the LORD's. 17It shall be a perpetual statute throughout your generations, in all your settlements: you must not eat any fat or any blood.

Sin Offerings

4 THE LORD spoke to Moses, saying, 2Speak to the people of Israel, saying: When anyone sins unintentionally in any of the LORD's commandments about things not to be done, and does any one of them:

3 If it is the anointed priest who sins, thus bringing guilt on the people, he shall offer for the sin that he has committed a bull of the herd without blemish as a sin offering to the LORD. 4He shall bring the bull to the entrance of the tent of meeting before the LORD and lay his hand on the head of the bull; the bull shall be slaughtered before the LORD. 5The anointed priest shall take some of the blood of the bull and bring it into the tent of meeting. 6The priest shall dip his finger in the blood and sprinkle some of the blood seven times before the LORD in front of the curtain of the sanctuary. 7The priest

King James

7And the priest shall put *some* of the blood upon the horns of the altar of sweet incense before the LORD, which *is* in the tabernacle of the congregation; and shall pour all the blood of the bullock at the bottom of the altar of the burnt offering, which *is at* the door of the tabernacle of the congregation.

8And he shall take off from it all the fat of the bullock for the sin offering; the fat that covereth the inwards, and all the fat that *is* upon the inwards,

9And the two kidneys, and the fat that *is* upon them, which *is* by the flanks, and the caul above the liver, with the kidneys, it shall he take away,

10As it was taken off from the bullock of the sacrifice of peace offerings: and the priest shall burn them upon the altar of the burnt offering.

11And the skin of the bullock, and all his flesh, with his head, and with his legs, and his inwards, and his dung,

12Even the whole bullock shall he carry forth without the camp unto a clean place, where the ashes are poured out, and burn him on the wood with fire: where the ashes are poured out shall he be burnt.

13¶ And if the whole congregation of Israel sin through ignorance, and the thing be hid from the eyes of the assembly, and they have done *somewhat against* any of the commandments of the LORD *concerning things* which should not be done, and are guilty;

14When the sin, which they have sinned against it, is known, then the congregation shall offer a young bullock for the sin, and bring him before the tabernacle of the congregation.

15And the elders of the congregation shall lay their hands upon the head of the bullock before the LORD: and the bullock shall be killed before the LORD.

16And the priest that is anointed shall bring of the bullock's blood to the tabernacle of the congregation:

17And the priest shall dip his finger *in some* of the blood, and sprinkle *it* seven times before the LORD, *even* before the veil.

18And he shall put *some* of the blood upon the horns of the altar which *is* before the LORD, that *is in* the tabernacle of the congregation, and shall pour out all the blood at the bottom of the altar of the burnt offering, which *is at* the door of the tabernacle of the congregation.

19And he shall take all his fat from him, and burn *it* upon the altar.

20And he shall do with the bullock as he did with the bullock for a sin offering, so shall he do with this: and the priest shall make an atonement for them, and it shall be forgiven them.

21And he shall carry forth the bullock without the camp, and burn him as he burned the first bullock: it *is* a sin offering for the congregation.

22¶ When a ruler hath sinned, and done *somewhat* through ignorance *against* any of the commandments of the LORD his God *concerning things* which should not be done, and is guilty;

23Or if his sin, wherein he hath sinned, come to his knowledge; he shall bring his offering, a kid of the goats, a male without blemish.

24And he shall lay his hand upon the head of the goat, and kill it in the place where they kill the burnt offering before the LORD: it *is* a sin offering.

25And the priest shall take of the blood of the sin offering with his finger, and put *it* upon the horns of the altar of burnt offering, and shall pour out his blood at the bottom of the altar of burnt offering.

26And he shall burn all his fat upon the altar, as the fat of the sacrifice of peace offerings: and the priest shall make an atonement for him as concerning his sin, and it shall be forgiven him.

New International

shall then put some of the blood on the horns of the altar of fragrant incense that is before the LORD in the Tent of Meeting. The rest of the bull's blood he shall pour out at the base of the altar of burnt offering at the entrance to the Tent of Meeting. 8He shall remove all the fat from the bull of the sin offering—the fat that covers the inner parts or is connected to them, 9both kidneys with the fat on them near the loins, and the covering of the liver, which he will remove with the kidneys— 10just as the fat is removed from the ox[a] sacrificed as a fellowship offering.[b] Then the priest shall burn them on the altar of burnt offering. 11But the hide of the bull and all its flesh, as well as the head and legs, the inner parts and offal— 12that is, all the rest of the bull—he must take outside the camp to a place ceremonially clean, where the ashes are thrown, and burn it in a wood fire on the ash heap.

13" 'If the whole Israelite community sins unintentionally and does what is forbidden in any of the LORD's commands, even though the community is unaware of the matter, they are guilty. 14When they become aware of the sin they committed, the assembly must bring a young bull as a sin offering and present it before the Tent of Meeting. 15The elders of the community are to lay their hands on the bull's head before the LORD, and the bull shall be slaughtered before the LORD. 16Then the anointed priest is to take some of the bull's blood into the Tent of Meeting. 17He shall dip his finger into the blood and sprinkle it before the LORD seven times in front of the curtain. 18He is to put some of the blood on the horns of the altar that is before the LORD in the Tent of Meeting. The rest of the blood he shall pour out at the base of the altar of burnt offering at the entrance to the Tent of Meeting. 19He shall remove all the fat from it and burn it on the altar, 20and do with this bull just as he did with the bull for the sin offering. In this way the priest will make atonement for them, and they will be forgiven. 21Then he shall take the bull outside the camp and burn it as he burned the first bull. This is the sin offering for the community.

22" 'When a leader sins unintentionally and does what is forbidden in any of the commands of the LORD his God, he is guilty. 23When he is made aware of the sin he committed, he must bring as his offering a male goat without defect. 24He is to lay his hand on the goat's head and slaughter it at the place where the burnt offering is slaughtered before the LORD. It is a sin offering. 25Then the priest shall take some of the blood of the sin offering with his finger and put it on the horns of the altar of burnt offering and pour out the rest of the blood at the base of the altar. 26He shall burn all the fat on the altar as he burned the fat of the fellowship offering. In this way the priest will make atonement for the man's sin, and he will be forgiven.

---

a 10 The Hebrew word can include both male and female.
b 10 Traditionally *peace offering*; also in verses 26, 31 and 35

Living Bible

shall put some of the blood upon the horns of the incense altar before the Lord in the Tabernacle; the remainder of the blood shall be poured out at the base of the altar for burnt offerings, at the entrance to the Tabernacle. 8Then he shall take all the fat on the entrails, 9the two kidneys and the loin-fat on them, and the gall bladder, 10and shall burn them on the altar of burnt offering, just as in the case of a bull or cow sacrificed as a thank-offering. 11, 12But the remainder of the young bull—the skin, meat, head, legs, internal organs, and intestines—shall be carried to a ceremonially clean place outside the camp—a place where the ashes are brought from the altar—and burned there on a wood fire.

13"If the entire nation of Israel sins without realizing it, and does something that Jehovah has said not to do, all the people are guilty. 14When they realize it, they shall offer a young bull for a sin offering, bringing it to the Tabernacle 15where the leadersc of the nation shall lay their hands upon the animal's head and kill it before the Lord. 16Then the priest shall bring its blood into the Tabernacle, 17and shall dip his finger in the blood and sprinkle it seven times before the Lord, in front of the veil. 18Then he shall put blood upon the horns of the altar there in the Tabernacle before the Lord, and all the remainder of the blood shall be poured out at the base of the burnt offering altar, at the entrance to the Tabernacle. 19All the fat shall be removed and burned upon the altar. 20He shall follow the same procedure as for a sin offering; in this way the priest shall make atonement for the nation, and everyone will be forgiven. 21The priest shall then cart the young bull outside the camp and burn it there, just as though it were a sin offering for an individual, only this time it is a sin offering for the entire nation.

22"If one of the leaders sins without realizing it and is guilty of disobeying one of God's laws, 23as soon as it is called to his attention he must bring as his sacrifice a male goat without any physical defect. 24He shall lay his hand upon its head and kill it at the place where the burnt offerings are killed, and present it to the Lord. This is his sin offering. 25Then the priest shall take some of the blood of this sin offering and place it with his finger upon the horns of the altar of burnt offerings, and the rest of the blood shall be poured out at the base of the altar. 26All the fat shall be burned upon the altar, just as if it were the fat of the sacrifice of a thank-offering;d thus the priest shall make atonement for the leader concerning his sin, and he shall be forgiven.

New Revised Standard

shall put some of the blood on the horns of the altar of fragrant incense that is in the tent of meeting before the LORD; and the rest of the blood of the bull he shall pour out at the base of the altar of burnt offering, which is at the entrance of the tent of meeting. 8 He shall remove all the fat from the bull of sin offering: the fat that covers the entrails and all the fat that is around the entrails; 9the two kidneys with the fat that is on them at the loins; and the appendage of the liver, which he shall remove with the kidneys, 10just as these are removed from the ox of the sacrifice of well-being. The priest shall turn them into smoke upon the altar of burnt offering. 11But the skin of the bull and all its flesh, as well as its head, its legs, its entrails, and its dung— 12all the rest of the bull—he shall carry out to a clean place outside the camp, to the ash heap, and shall burn it on a wood fire; at the ash heap it shall be burned.

13 If the whole congregation of Israel errs unintentionally and the matter escapes the notice of the assembly, and they do any one of the things that by the LORD's commandments ought not to be done and incur guilt; 14when the sin that they have committed becomes known, the assembly shall offer a bull of the herd for a sin offering and bring it before the tent of meeting. 15The elders of the congregation shall lay their hands on the head of the bull before the LORD, and the bull shall be slaughtered before the LORD. 16The anointed priest shall bring some of the blood of the bull into the tent of meeting, 17and the priest shall dip his finger in the blood and sprinkle it seven times before the LORD, in front of the curtain. 18He shall put some of the blood on the horns of the altar that is before the LORD in the tent of meeting; and the rest of the blood he shall pour out at the base of the altar of burnt offering that is at the entrance of the tent of meeting. 19He shall remove all its fat and turn it into smoke on the altar. 20He shall do with the bull just as is done with the bull of sin offering; he shall do the same with this. The priest shall make atonement for them, and they shall be forgiven. 21He shall carry the bull outside the camp, and burn it as he burned the first bull; it is the sin offering for the assembly.

22 When a ruler sins, doing unintentionally any one of all the things that by commandments of the LORD his God ought not to be done and incurs guilt, 23once the sin that he has committed is made known to him, he shall bring as his offering a male goat without blemish. 24He shall lay his hand on the head of the goat; it shall be slaughtered at the spot where the burnt offering is slaughtered before the LORD; it is a sin offering. 25The priest shall take some of the blood of the sin offering with his finger and put it on the horns of the altar of burnt offering, and pour out the rest of its blood at the base of the altar of burnt offering. 26All its fat he shall turn into smoke on the altar, like the fat of the sacrifice of well-being. Thus the priest shall make atonement on his behalf for his sin, and he shall be forgiven.

---

c 4:15 leaders, literally, "elders."   d 4:26 thank-offering, literally, "peace offering." Also in vss 31, 35.

King James

27¶ And if any one of the common people sin through ignorance, while he doeth *somewhat against* any of the commandments of the LORD *concerning things* which ought not to be done, and be guilty;

28Or if his sin, which he hath sinned, come to his knowledge: then he shall bring his offering, a kid of the goats, a female without blemish, for his sin which he hath sinned.

29And he shall lay his hand upon the head of the sin offering, and slay the sin offering in the place of the burnt offering.

30And the priest shall take of the blood thereof with his finger, and put *it* upon the horns of the altar of burnt offering, and shall pour out all the blood thereof at the bottom of the altar.

31And he shall take away all the fat thereof, as the fat is taken away from off the sacrifice of peace offerings; and the priest shall burn *it* upon the altar for a sweet savour unto the LORD; and the priest shall make an atonement for him, and it shall be forgiven him.

32And if he bring a lamb for a sin offering, he shall bring it a female without blemish.

33And he shall lay his hand upon the head of the sin offering, and slay it for a sin offering in the place where they kill the burnt offering.

34And the priest shall take of the blood of the sin offering with his finger, and put *it* upon the horns of the altar of burnt offering, and shall pour out all the blood thereof at the bottom of the altar:

35And he shall take away all the fat thereof, as the fat of the lamb is taken away from the sacrifice of the peace offerings; and the priest shall burn them upon the altar, according to the offerings made by fire unto the LORD: and the priest shall make an atonement for his sin that he hath committed, and it shall be forgiven him.

5 AND IF a soul sin, and hear the voice of swearing, and *is* a witness, whether he hath seen or known *of it*; if he do not utter *it*, then he shall bear his iniquity.

2Or if a soul touch any unclean thing, whether *it be* a carcase of an unclean beast, or a carcase of unclean cattle, or the carcase of unclean creeping things, and *if* it be hidden from him; he also shall be unclean, and guilty.

3Or if he touch the uncleanness of man, whatsoever uncleanness *it be* that a man shall be defiled withal, and it be hid from him; when he knoweth *of it*, then he shall be guilty.

4Or if a soul swear, pronouncing with *his* lips to do evil, or to do good, whatsoever *it be* that a man shall pronounce with an oath, and it be hid from him; when he knoweth *of it*, then he shall be guilty in one of these.

5And it shall be, when he shall be guilty in one of these *things*, that he shall confess that he hath sinned in that *thing*:

6And he shall bring his trespass offering unto the LORD for his sin which he hath sinned, a female from the flock, a lamb or a kid of the goats, for a sin offering; and the priest shall make an atonement for him concerning his sin.

7And if he be not able to bring a lamb, then he shall bring for his trespass, which he hath committed, two turtledoves, or two young pigeons, unto the LORD; one for a sin offering, and the other for a burnt offering.

8And he shall bring them unto the priest, who shall offer *that* which *is* for the sin offering first, and wring off his head from his neck, but shall not divide *it* asunder:

9And he shall sprinkle of the blood of the sin offering upon the side of the altar; and the rest of the blood shall be wrung out at the bottom of the altar: it *is* a sin offering.

New International

27" 'If a member of the community sins unintentionally and does what is forbidden in any of the LORD's commands, he is guilty. 28When he is made aware of the sin he committed, he must bring as his offering for the sin he committed a female goat without defect. 29He is to lay his hand on the head of the sin offering and slaughter it at the place of the burnt offering. 30Then the priest is to take some of the blood with his finger and put it on the horns of the altar of burnt offering and pour out the rest of the blood at the base of the altar. 31He shall remove all the fat, just as the fat is removed from the fellowship offering, and the priest shall burn it on the altar as an aroma pleasing to the LORD. In this way the priest will make atonement for him, and he will be forgiven.

32" 'If he brings a lamb as his sin offering, he is to bring a female without defect. 33He is to lay his hand on its head and slaughter it for a sin offering at the place where the burnt offering is slaughtered. 34Then the priest shall take some of the blood of the sin offering with his finger and put it on the horns of the altar of burnt offering and pour out the rest of the blood at the base of the altar. 35He shall remove all the fat, just as the fat is removed from the lamb of the fellowship offering, and the priest shall burn it on the altar on top of the offerings made to the LORD by fire. In this way the priest will make atonement for him for the sin he has committed, and he will be forgiven.

5 " 'IF A person sins because he does not speak up when he hears a public charge to testify regarding something he has seen or learned about, he will be held responsible.

2" 'Or if a person touches anything ceremonially unclean—whether the carcasses of unclean wild animals or of unclean livestock or of unclean creatures that move along the ground—even though he is unaware of it, he has become unclean and is guilty.

3" 'Or if he touches human uncleanness—anything that would make him unclean—even though he is unaware of it, when he learns of it he will be guilty.

4" 'Or if a person thoughtlessly takes an oath to do anything, whether good or evil—in any matter one might carelessly swear about—even though he is unaware of it, in any case when he learns of it he will be guilty.

5" 'When anyone is guilty in any of these ways, he must confess in what way he has sinned 6and, as a penalty for the sin he has committed, he must bring to the LORD a female lamb or goat from the flock as a sin offering; and the priest shall make atonement for him for his sin.

7" 'If he cannot afford a lamb, he is to bring two doves or two young pigeons to the LORD as a penalty for his sin—one for a sin offering and the other for a burnt offering. 8He is to bring them to the priest, who shall first offer the one for the sin offering. He is to wring its head from its neck, not severing it completely, 9and is to sprinkle some of the blood of the sin offering against the side of the altar; the rest of the blood must be drained out at the base of the altar. It is a sin offering. 10The

Living Bible

27"If any one of the common people sins and doesn't realize it, he is guilty. 28But as soon as he does realize it, he is to bring as his sacrifice a female goat without defect to atone for his sin. 29He shall bring it to the place where the animals for burnt offerings are killed, and there lay his hand upon the head of the sin offering and kill it. 30And the priest shall take some of the blood with his finger and smear it upon the horns of the burnt offering altar. Then the priest shall pour out the remainder of the blood at the base of the altar. 31All the fat shall be taken off, just as in the procedure for the thank-offering sacrifice, and the priest shall burn it upon the altar; and the Lord will appreciate it. Thus the priest shall make atonement for that man, and he shall be forgiven.

32"However, if he chooses to bring a lamb as his sin offering, it must be a female without physical defect. 33He shall bring it to the place where the burnt offerings are killed, and lay his hand upon its head and kill it there as a sin offering. 34The priest shall take some of the blood with his finger and smear it upon the horns of the burnt offering altar, and all the rest of the blood shall be poured out at the base of the altar. 35The fat shall be used just as in the case of a thank-offering lamb—the priest shall burn the fat on the altar as in any other sacrifice made to Jehovah by fire; and the priest shall make atonement for the man, and his sin shall be forgiven.

5 "ANYONE REFUSING to give testimony concerning what he knows about a crime is guilty.

2"Anyone touching anything ceremonially unclean—such as the dead body of an animal forbidden for food, wild or domesticated, or the dead body of some forbidden insect—is guilty, even though he wasn't aware of touching it. 3Or if he touches human discharge of any kind, he becomes guilty as soon as he realizes that he has touched it.

4"If anyone makes a rash vow, whether the vow is good or bad, when he realizes what a foolish vow he has taken, he is guilty.

5"In any of these cases, he shall confess his sin 6and bring his guilt offering to the Lord, a female lamb or goat, and the priest shall make atonement for him, and he shall be freed from his sin, and need not fulfill the vow.a

7"If he is too poor to bring a lamb to the Lord, then he shall bring two turtledoves or two young pigeons as his guilt offering; one of the birds shall be his sin offering and the other his burnt offering. 8The priest shall offer as the sin sacrifice whichever bird is handed to him first, breaking its neck, but not severing its head from its body. 9Then he shall sprinkle some of the blood at the side of the altar and the rest shall be drained out at the base of the altar; this is the sin offering. 10He shall

New Revised Standard

27 If anyone of the ordinary people among you sins unintentionally in doing any one of the things that by the Lord's commandments ought not to be done and incurs guilt, 28 when the sin that you have committed is made known to you, you shall bring a female goat without blemish as your offering, for the sin that you have committed. 29 You shall lay your hand on the head of the sin offering; and the sin offering shall be slaughtered at the place of the burnt offering. 30 The priest shall take some of its blood with his finger and put it on the horns of the altar of burnt offering, and he shall pour out the rest of its blood at the base of the altar. 31 He shall remove all its fat, as the fat is removed from the offering of well-being, and the priest shall turn it into smoke on the altar for a pleasing odor to the Lord. Thus the priest shall make atonement on your behalf, and you shall be forgiven.

32 If the offering you bring as a sin offering is a sheep, you shall bring a female without blemish. 33 You shall lay your hand on the head of the sin offering; and it shall be slaughtered as a sin offering at the spot where the burnt offering is slaughtered. 34 The priest shall take some of the blood of the sin offering with his finger and put it on the horns of the altar of burnt offering, and pour out the rest of its blood at the base of the altar. 35 You shall remove all its fat, as the fat of the sheep is removed from the sacrifice of well-being, and the priest shall turn it into smoke on the altar, with the offerings by fire to the Lord. Thus the priest shall make atonement on your behalf for the sin that you have committed, and you shall be forgiven.

5 WHEN ANY of you sin in that you have heard a public adjuration to testify and—though able to testify as one who has seen or learned of the matter—does not speak up, you are subject to punishment. 2 Or when any of you touch any unclean thing—whether the carcass of an unclean beast or the carcass of unclean livestock or the carcass of an unclean swarming thing—and are unaware of it, you have become unclean, and are guilty. 3 Or when you touch human uncleanness—any uncleanness by which one can become unclean—and are unaware of it, when you come to know it, you shall be guilty. 4 Or when any of you utter aloud a rash oath for a bad or a good purpose, whatever people utter in an oath, and are unaware of it, when you come to know it, you shall in any of these be guilty. 5 When you realize your guilt in any of these, you shall confess the sin that you have committed. 6 And you shall bring to the Lord, as your penalty for the sin that you have committed, a female from the flock, a sheep or a goat, as a sin offering; and the priest shall make atonement on your behalf for your sin.

7 But if you cannot afford a sheep, you shall bring to the Lord, as your penalty for the sin that you have committed, two turtledoves or two pigeons, one for a sin offering and the other for a burnt offering. 8 You shall bring them to the priest, who shall offer first the one for the sin offering, wringing its head at the nape without severing it. 9 He shall sprinkle some of the blood of the sin offering on the side of the altar, while the rest of the blood shall be drained out at the base of the altar; it is a sin offering. 10 And the second he shall offer for a burnt

a 5:6 *he shall be freed from his sin, and need not fulfill the vow,* implied.

King James

10And he shall offer the second *for* a burnt offering, according to the manner: and the priest shall make an atonement for him for his sin which he hath sinned, and it shall be forgiven him.

11¶ But if he be not able to bring two turtledoves, or two young pigeons, then he that sinned shall bring for his offering the tenth part of an ephah of fine flour for a sin offering; he shall put no oil upon it, neither shall he put *any* frankincense thereon: for it *is* a sin offering.

12Then shall he bring it to the priest, and the priest shall take his handful of it, *even* a memorial thereof, and burn *it* on the altar, according to the offerings made by fire unto the LORD: it *is* a sin offering.

13And the priest shall make an atonement for him as touching his sin that he hath sinned in one of these, and it shall be forgiven him: and *the remnant* shall be the priest's, as a meat offering.

14¶ And the LORD spake unto Moses, saying,

15If a soul commit a trespass, and sin through ignorance, in the holy things of the LORD; then he shall bring for his trespass unto the LORD a ram without blemish out of the flocks, with thy estimation by shekels of silver, after the shekel of the sanctuary, for a trespass offering:

16And he shall make amends for the harm that he hath done in the holy thing, and shall add the fifth part thereto, and give it unto the priest: and the priest shall make an atonement for him with the ram of the trespass offering, and it shall be forgiven him.

17¶ And if a soul sin, and commit any of these things which are forbidden to be done by the commandments of the LORD; though he wist *it* not, yet is he guilty, and shall bear his iniquity.

18And he shall bring a ram without blemish out of the flock, with thy estimation, for a trespass offering, unto the priest: and the priest shall make an atonement for him concerning his ignorance wherein he erred and wist *it* not, and it shall be forgiven him.

19It *is* a trespass offering: he hath certainly trespassed against the LORD.

6 AND THE LORD spake unto Moses, saying,
2If a soul sin, and commit a trespass against the LORD, and lie unto his neighbour in that which was delivered him to keep, or in fellowship, or in a thing taken away by violence, or hath deceived his neighbour;

3Or have found that which was lost, and lieth concerning it, and sweareth falsely; in any of all these that a man doeth, sinning therein:

4Then it shall be, because he hath sinned, and is guilty, that he shall restore that which he took violently away, or the thing which he hath deceitfully gotten, or that which was delivered him to keep, or the lost thing which he found,

5Or all that about which he hath sworn falsely; he shall even restore it in the principal, and shall add the fifth part more thereto, *and* give it unto him to whom it appertaineth, in the day of his trespass offering.

6And he shall bring his trespass offering unto the LORD, a ram without blemish out of the flock, with thy estimation, for a trespass offering, unto the priest:

7And the priest shall make an atonement for him before the LORD: and it shall be forgiven him for any thing of all that he hath done in trespassing therein.

8¶ And the LORD spake unto Moses, saying,

9Command Aaron and his sons, saying, This *is* the law of the burnt offering: It *is* the burnt offering, because of the burning upon the altar all night unto the morning, and the fire of the altar shall be burning in it.

New International

priest shall then offer the other as a burnt offering in the prescribed way and make atonement for him for the sin he has committed, and he will be forgiven.

11" 'If, however, he cannot afford two doves or two young pigeons, he is to bring as an offering for his sin a tenth of an ephah[a] of fine flour for a sin offering. He must not put oil or incense on it, because it is a sin offering. 12He is to bring it to the priest, who shall take a handful of it as a memorial portion and burn it on the altar on top of the offerings made to the LORD by fire. It is a sin offering. 13In this way the priest will make atonement for him for any of these sins he has committed, and he will be forgiven. The rest of the offering will belong to the priest, as in the case of the grain offering.' "

The Guilt Offering

14The LORD said to Moses: 15"When a person commits a violation and sins unintentionally in regard to any of the LORD's holy things, he is to bring to the LORD as a penalty a ram from the flock, one without defect and of the proper value in silver, according to the sanctuary shekel.[b] It is a guilt offering. 16He must make restitution for what he has failed to do in regard to the holy things, add a fifth of the value to that and give it all to the priest, who will make atonement for him with the ram as a guilt offering, and he will be forgiven.

17"If a person sins and does what is forbidden in any of the LORD's commands, even though he does not know it, he is guilty and will be held responsible. 18He is to bring to the priest as a guilt offering a ram from the flock, one without defect and of the proper value. In this way the priest will make atonement for him for the wrong he has committed unintentionally, and he will be forgiven. 19It is a guilt offering; he has been guilty of[c] wrongdoing against the LORD."

6 THE LORD said to Moses: 2"If anyone sins and is unfaithful to the LORD by deceiving his neighbor about something entrusted to him or left in his care or stolen, or if he cheats him, 3or if he finds lost property and lies about it, or if he swears falsely, or if he commits any such sin that people may do— 4when he thus sins and becomes guilty, he must return what he has stolen or taken by extortion, or what was entrusted to him, or the lost property he found, 5or whatever it was he swore falsely about. He must make restitution in full, add a fifth of the value to it and give it all to the owner on the day he presents his guilt offering. 6And as a penalty he must bring to the priest, that is, to the LORD, his guilt offering, a ram from the flock, one without defect and of the proper value. 7In this way the priest will make atonement for him before the LORD, and he will be forgiven for any of these things he did that made him guilty."

The Burnt Offering

8The LORD said to Moses: 9"Give Aaron and his sons this command: 'These are the regulations for the burnt offering: The burnt offering is to remain on the altar hearth throughout the night, till morning, and the fire must be kept burning on the altar. 10The priest shall then

---

Living Bible

offer the second bird as a burnt offering, following the customary procedures that have been set forth; so the priest shall make atonement for him concerning his sin and he shall be forgiven.

11"If he is too poor to bring turtledoves or young pigeons as his sin offering, then he shall bring a tenth of a bushel of fine flour. He must not mix it with olive oil or put any incense on it, because it is a sin offering. 12He shall bring it to the priest and the priest shall take out a handful as a representative portion, and burn it on the altar just as any other offering to Jehovah made by fire; this shall be his sin offering. 13In this way the priest shall make atonement for him for any sin of this kind, and he shall be forgiven. The rest of the flour shall belong to the priest, just as was the case with the grain offering."

14And the Lord said to Moses,

15"If anyone sins by unintentionally defiling what is holy, then he shall bring a ram without defect, worth whatever fined you charge against him, as his guilt offering to the Lord. 16And he shall make restitution for the holy thing he has defiled, or the tithe omitted,e by paying for the loss, plus a twenty percent penalty; he shall bring it to the priest, and the priest shall make atonement for him with the ram of the guilt offering, and he shall be forgiven.

17, 18"Anyone who disobeys some law of God without realizing it is guilty anyway, and must bring his sacrifice of a value determined by Moses. This sacrifice shall be a ram without blemish taken to the priest as a guilt offering; with it the priest shall make atonement for him, so that he will be forgiven for whatever it is he has done without realizing it. 19It must be offered as a guilt offering, for he is certainly guilty before the Lord."

6 AND THE Lord said to Moses, 2"If anyone sins against me by refusing to return a deposit on something borrowed or rented, or by refusing to return something entrusted to him, or by robbery, or by oppressing his neighbor, 3or by finding a lost article and lying about it, swearing that he doesn't have it— 4, 5on the day he is found guilty of any such sin, he shall restore what he took, adding a twenty percent fine, and give it to the one he has harmed; and on the same day he shall bring his guilt offering to the Tabernacle. 6His guilt offering shall be a ram without defect, and must be worth whatever value you demand. He shall bring it to the priest, 7and the priest shall make atonement for him before the Lord, and he shall be forgiven."

8Then the Lord said to Moses, 9"*Give Aaron and his sons these regulations concerning the burnt offering:*

"The burnt offering shall be left upon the hearth of the altar all night, with the altar fire kept burning. 10(The

New Revised Standard

offering according to the regulation. Thus the priest shall make atonement on your behalf for the sin that you have committed, and you shall be forgiven.

11 But if you cannot afford two turtledoves or two pigeons, you shall bring as your offering for the sin that you have committed one-tenth of an ephah of choice flour for a sin offering; you shall not put oil on it or lay frankincense on it, for it is a sin offering. 12You shall bring it to the priest, and the priest shall scoop up a handful of it as its memorial portion, and turn this into smoke on the altar, with the offerings by fire to the Lord; it is a sin offering. 13Thus the priest shall make atonement on your behalf for whichever of these sins you have committed, and you shall be forgiven. Like the grain offering, the rest shall be for the priest.

Offerings with Restitution

14 The Lord spoke to Moses, saying: 15When any of you commit a trespass and sins unintentionally in any of the holy things of the Lord, you shall bring, as your guilt offering to the Lord, a ram without blemish from the flock, convertible into silver by the sanctuary shekel; it is a guilt offering. 16And you shall make restitution for the holy thing in which you were remiss, and shall add one-fifth to it and give it to the priest. The priest shall make atonement on your behalf with the ram of the guilt offering, and you shall be forgiven.

17 If any of you sin without knowing it, doing any of the things that by the Lord's commandments ought not to be done, you have incurred guilt, and are subject to punishment. 18You shall bring to the priest a ram without blemish from the flock, or the equivalent, as a guilt offering; and the priest shall make atonement on your behalf for the error that you committed unintentionally, and you shall be forgiven. 19It is a guilt offering; you have incurred guilt before the Lord.

6f THE LORD spoke to Moses, saying: 2When any of you sin and commit a trespass against the Lord by deceiving a neighbor in a matter of a deposit or a pledge, or by robbery, or if you have defrauded a neighbor, 3or have found something lost and lied about it—if you swear falsely regarding any of the various things that one may do and sin thereby— 4when you have sinned and realize your guilt, and would restore what you took by robbery or by fraud or the deposit that was committed to you, or the lost thing that you found, 5or anything else about which you have sworn falsely, you shall repay the principal amount and shall add one-fifth to it. You shall pay it to its owner when you realize your guilt. 6And you shall bring to the priest, as your guilt offering to the Lord, a ram without blemish from the flock, or its equivalent, for a guilt offering. 7The priest shall make atonement on your behalf before the Lord, and you shall be forgiven for any of the things that one may do and incur guilt thereby.

Instructions concerning Sacrifices

8g The Lord spoke to Moses, saying: 9Command Aaron and his sons, saying: This is the ritual of the burnt offering. The burnt offering itself shall remain on the hearth upon the altar all night until the morning, while the fire on the altar shall be kept burning. 10The priest

---

d *5:15 worth whatever fine*, literally, "using the standard of the shekel of the sanctuary." e *5:16 guilt offering (asham)*. or *the tithe omitted*, implied in remainder of the verse.

f Ch 5.20 in Heb   g Ch 6.1 in Heb

King James

10And the priest shall put on his linen garment, and his linen breeches shall he put upon his flesh, and take up the ashes which the fire hath consumed with the burnt offering on the altar, and he shall put them beside the altar.

11And he shall put off his garments, and put on other garments, and carry forth the ashes without the camp unto a clean place.

12And the fire upon the altar shall be burning in it; it shall not be put out: and the priest shall burn wood on it every morning, and lay the burnt offering in order upon it; and he shall burn thereon the fat of the peace offerings.

13The fire shall ever be burning upon the altar; it shall never go out.

14¶ And this is the law of the meat offering: the sons of Aaron shall offer it before the LORD, before the altar.

15And he shall take of it his handful, of the flour of the meat offering, and of the oil thereof, and all the frankincense which is upon the meat offering, and shall burn it upon the altar for a sweet savour, even the memorial of it, unto the LORD.

16And the remainder thereof shall Aaron and his sons eat: with unleavened bread shall it be eaten in the holy place; in the court of the tabernacle of the congregation they shall eat it.

17It shall not be baken with leaven. I have given it unto them for their portion of my offerings made by fire; it is most holy, as is the sin offering, and as the trespass offering.

18All the males among the children of Aaron shall eat of it. It shall be a statute for ever in your generations concerning the offerings of the LORD made by fire: every one that toucheth them shall be holy.

19¶ And the LORD spake unto Moses, saying,

20This is the offering of Aaron and of his sons, which they shall offer unto the LORD in the day when he is anointed; the tenth part of an ephah of fine flour for a meat offering perpetual, half of it in the morning, and half thereof at night.

21In a pan it shall be made with oil; and when it is baken, thou shalt bring it in: and the baken pieces of the meat offering shalt thou offer for a sweet savour unto the LORD.

22And the priest of his sons that is anointed in his stead shall offer it: it is a statute for ever unto the LORD; it shall be wholly burnt.

23For every meat offering for the priest shall be wholly burnt: it shall not be eaten.

24¶ And the LORD spake unto Moses, saying,

25Speak unto Aaron and to his sons, saying, This is the law of the sin offering: In the place where the burnt offering is killed shall the sin offering be killed before the LORD: it is most holy.

26The priest that offereth it for sin shall eat it: in the holy place shall it be eaten, in the court of the tabernacle of the congregation.

27Whatsoever shall touch the flesh thereof shall be holy: and when there is sprinkled of the blood thereof upon any garment, thou shalt wash that whereon it was sprinkled in the holy place.

28But the earthen vessel wherein it is sodden shall be broken: and if it be sodden in a brasen pot, it shall be both scoured, and rinsed in water.

29All the males among the priests shall eat thereof: it is most holy.

30And no sin offering, whereof any of the blood is brought into the tabernacle of the congregation to reconcile withal in the holy place, shall be eaten: it shall be burnt in the fire.

New International

put on his linen clothes, with linen undergarments next to his body, and shall remove the ashes of the burnt offering that the fire has consumed on the altar and place them beside the altar. 11Then he is to take off these clothes and put on others, and carry the ashes outside the camp to a place that is ceremonially clean. 12The fire on the altar must be kept burning; it must not go out. Every morning the priest is to add firewood and arrange the burnt offering on the fire and burn the fat of the fellowship offeringsa on it. 13The fire must be kept burning on the altar continuously; it must not go out.

The Grain Offering

14" 'These are the regulations for the grain offering: Aaron's sons are to bring it before the LORD, in front of the altar. 15The priest is to take a handful of fine flour and oil, together with all the incense on the grain offering, and burn the memorial portion on the altar as an aroma pleasing to the LORD. 16Aaron and his sons shall eat the rest of it, but it is to be eaten without yeast in a holy place; they are to eat it in the courtyard of the Tent of Meeting. 17It must not be baked with yeast; I have given it as their share of the offerings made to me by fire. Like the sin offering and the guilt offering, it is most holy. 18Any male descendant of Aaron may eat it. It is his regular share of the offerings made to the LORD by fire for the generations to come. Whatever touches them will become holy.b' "

19The LORD also said to Moses, 20"This is the offering Aaron and his sons are to bring to the LORD on the day hec is anointed: a tenth of an ephahd of fine flour as a regular grain offering, half of it in the morning and half in the evening. 21Prepare it with oil on a griddle; bring it well-mixed and present the grain offering brokene in pieces as an aroma pleasing to the LORD. 22The son who is to succeed him as anointed priest shall prepare it. It is the LORD's regular share and is to be burned completely. 23Every grain offering of a priest shall be burned completely; it must not be eaten."

The Sin Offering

24The LORD said to Moses, 25"Say to Aaron and his sons: 'These are the regulations for the sin offering: The sin offering is to be slaughtered before the LORD in the place the burnt offering is slaughtered; it is most holy. 26The priest who offers it shall eat it; it is to be eaten in a holy place, in the courtyard of the Tent of Meeting. 27Whatever touches any of the flesh will become holy, and if any of the blood is spattered on a garment, you must wash it in a holy place. 28The clay pot the meat is cooked in must be broken; but if it is cooked in a bronze pot, the pot is to be scoured and rinsed with water. 29Any male in a priest's family may eat it; it is most holy. 30But any sin offering whose blood is brought into the Tent of Meeting to make atonement in the Holy Place must not be eaten; it must be burned.

---

a 12 Traditionally peace offerings   b 18 Or Whoever touches them must be holy; similarly in verse 27   c 20 Or each   d 20 That is, probably about 2 quarts (about 2 liters)   e 21 The meaning of the Hebrew for this word is uncertain.

Living Bible

next morning) the priest shall put on his linen undergarments and his linen outer garments and clean out the ashes of the burnt offering and put them beside the altar. 11Then he shall change his clothes and carry the ashes outside the camp to a place that is ceremonially clean. 12Meanwhile, the fire on the altar must be kept burning—it must not go out. The priest shall put on fresh wood each morning, and lay the daily burnt offering on it, and burn the fat of the daily peace offering. 13The fire must be kept burning upon the altar continually. It must never go out.

14"These are the regulations concerning the grain offering:

"Aaron's sons shall stand in front of the altar to offer it before the Lord. 15The priest shall then take out a handful of the finely ground flour with the olive oil and the incense mixed into it, and burn it upon the altar as a representative portion for the Lord; and it will be received with pleasure by the Lord. 16After taking out this handful, the remainder of the flour will belong to Aaron and his sons for their food; it shall be eaten without yeast in the courtyard of the Tabernacle. 17(Stress this instruction, that if it is baked it must be without yeast.) I have given to the priests this part of the burnt offerings made to me. However, all of it is most holy, just as is the entire sin offering and the entire guilt offering. 18It may be eaten by any male descendant of Aaron, any priest, generation after generation. But onlyf the priests may eat these offerings made by fire to the Lord."

19, 20And Jehovah said to Moses, "On the day Aaron and his sons are anointed and inducted into the priesthood, they shall bring to the Lord a regular grain offering—a tenth of a bushel of fine flour, half to be offered in the morning and half in the evening. 21It shall be cooked on a griddle, using olive oil, and should be well cooked, then brought to the Lord as an offering that pleases him very much. 22, 23As the sons of the priests replace their fathers, they shall be inducted into office by offering this same sacrifice on the day of their anointing. This is a perpetual law. These offerings shall be entirely burned up before the Lord; none of it shall be eaten."

24Then the Lord said to Moses, 25"Tell Aaron and his sons that these are the instructions concerning the sin offering:

"This sacrifice is most holy, and shall be killed before the Lord at the place where the burnt offerings are killed. 26The priest who performs the ceremony shall eat it in the courtyard of the Tabernacle. 27Only those who are sanctified—the priests—may touch this meat; if any blood sprinkles onto their clothing, it must be washed in a holy place. 28Then the clay pot in which the clothing is boiled shall be broken; or if a bronze kettle is used, it must be scoured and rinsed out thoroughly. 29Every male among the priests may eat this offering, but only they, for it is most holy. 30No sin offering may be eaten by the priests if any of its blood is taken into the Tabernacle, to make atonement in the Holy Place. That carcass must be entirely burned with fire before the Lord.

New Revised Standard

shall put on his linen vestments after putting on his linen undergarments next to his body; and he shall take up the ashes to which the fire has reduced the burnt offering on the altar, and place them beside the altar. 11Then he shall take off his vestments and put on other garments, and carry the ashes out to a clean place outside the camp. 12The fire on the altar shall be kept burning; it shall not go out. Every morning the priest shall add wood to it, lay out the burnt offering on it, and turn into smoke the fat pieces of the offerings of well-being. 13A perpetual fire shall be kept burning on the altar; it shall not go out.

14 This is the ritual of the grain offering: The sons of Aaron shall offer it before the LORD, in front of the altar. 15They shall take from it a handful of the choice flour and oil of the grain offering, with all the frankincense that is on the offering, and they shall turn its memorial portion into smoke on the altar as a pleasing odor to the LORD. 16Aaron and his sons shall eat what is left of it; it shall be eaten as unleavened cakes in a holy place; in the court of the tent of meeting they shall eat it. 17It shall not be baked with leaven. I have given it as their portion of my offerings by fire; it is most holy, like the sin offering and the guilt offering. 18Every male among the descendants of Aaron shall eat of it, as their perpetual due throughout your generations, from the LORD's offerings by fire; anything that touches them shall become holy.

19 The LORD spoke to Moses, saying: 20This is the offering that Aaron and his sons shall offer to the LORD on the day when he is anointed: one-tenth of an ephah of choice flour as a regular offering, half of it in the morning and half in the evening. 21It shall be made with oil on a griddle; you shall bring it well soaked, as a grain offering of bakedg pieces, and you shall present it as a pleasing odor to the LORD. 22And so the priest, anointed from among Aaron's descendants as a successor, shall prepare it; it is the LORD's—a perpetual due—to be turned entirely into smoke. 23Every grain offering of a priest shall be wholly burned; it shall not be eaten.

24 The LORD spoke to Moses, saying: 25Speak to Aaron and his sons, saying: This is the ritual of the sin offering. The sin offering shall be slaughtered before the LORD at the spot where the burnt offering is slaughtered; it is most holy. 26The priest who offers it as a sin offering shall eat of it; it shall be eaten in a holy place, in the court of the tent of meeting. 27Whatever touches its flesh shall become holy; and when any of its blood is spattered on a garment, you shall wash the bespattered part in a holy place. 28An earthen vessel in which it was boiled shall be broken; but if it is boiled in a bronze vessel, that shall be scoured and rinsed in water. 29Every male among the priests shall eat of it; it is most holy. 30But no sin offering shall be eaten from which any blood is brought into the tent of meeting for atonement in the holy place; it shall be burned with fire.

---

f 6:18 But only the priests, literally, "[only] whoever is holy may touch them," or "whoever touches them shall become holy."

g Meaning of Heb uncertain

King James

7 LIKEWISE THIS *is* the law of the trespass offering: it *is* most holy.

2In the place where they kill the burnt offering shall they kill the trespass offering: and the blood thereof shall he sprinkle round about upon the altar.

3And he shall offer of it all the fat thereof; the rump, and the fat that covereth the inwards.

4And the two kidneys, and the fat that *is* on them, which *is* by the flanks, and the caul *that is* above the liver, with the kidneys, it shall he take away:

5And the priest shall burn them upon the altar *for* an offering made by fire unto the LORD: it *is* a trespass offering.

6Every male among the priests shall eat thereof: it shall be eaten in the holy place: it *is* most holy.

7As the sin offering *is*, so *is* the trespass offering: *there is* one law for them: the priest that maketh atonement therewith shall have *it*.

8And the priest that offereth any man's burnt offering, *even* the priest shall have to himself the skin of the burnt offering which he hath offered.

9And all the meat offering that is baked in the oven, and all that is dressed in the fryingpan, and in the pan, shall be the priest's that offereth it.

10And every meat offering, mingled with oil, and dry, shall all the sons of Aaron have, one *as much* as another.

11And this *is* the law of the sacrifice of peace offerings, which he shall offer unto the LORD.

12If he offer it for a thanksgiving, then he shall offer with the sacrifice of thanksgiving unleavened cakes mingled with oil, and unleavened wafers anointed with oil, and cakes mingled with oil, of fine flour, fried.

13Besides the cakes, he shall offer *for* his offering leavened bread with the sacrifice of thanksgiving of his peace offerings.

14And of it he shall offer one out of the whole oblation *for* an heave offering unto the LORD, *and* it shall be the priest's that sprinkleth the blood of the peace offerings.

15And the flesh of the sacrifice of his peace offerings for thanksgiving shall be eaten the same day that it is offered; he shall not leave any of it until the morning.

16But if the sacrifice of his offering *be* a vow, or a voluntary offering, it shall be eaten the same day that he offereth his sacrifice: and on the morrow also the remainder of it shall be eaten:

17But the remainder of the flesh of the sacrifice on the third day shall be burnt with fire.

18And if *any* of the flesh of the sacrifice of his peace offerings be eaten at all on the third day, it shall not be accepted, neither shall it be imputed unto him that offereth it: it shall be an abomination, and the soul that eateth of it shall bear his iniquity.

19And the flesh that toucheth any unclean *thing* shall not be eaten; it shall be burnt with fire: and as for the flesh, all that be clean shall eat thereof.

20But the soul that eateth *of* the flesh of the sacrifice of peace offerings, that *pertain* unto the LORD, having his uncleanness upon him, even that soul shall be cut off from his people.

21Moreover the soul that shall touch any unclean *thing, as* the uncleanness of man, or *any* unclean beast, or any abominable unclean *thing*, and eat of the flesh of the sacrifice of peace offerings, which *pertain* unto the LORD, even that soul shall be cut off from his people.

22¶ And the LORD spake unto Moses, saying,

23Speak unto the children of Israel, saying, Ye shall eat no manner of fat, of ox, or of sheep, or of goat.

24And the fat of the beast that dieth of itself, and the fat of that which is torn with beasts, may be used in any other use: but ye shall in no wise eat of it.

New International

The Guilt Offering

7 " 'THESE ARE the regulations for the guilt offering, which is most holy: 2The guilt offering is to be slaughtered in the place where the burnt offering is slaughtered, and its blood is to be sprinkled against the altar on all sides. 3All its fat shall be offered: the fat tail and the fat that covers the inner parts, 4both kidneys with the fat on them near the loins, and the covering of the liver, which is to be removed with the kidneys. 5The priest shall burn them on the altar as an offering made to the LORD by fire. It is a guilt offering. 6Any male in a priest's family may eat it, but it must be eaten in a holy place; it is most holy.

7" 'The same law applies to both the sin offering and the guilt offering: They belong to the priest who makes atonement with them. 8The priest who offers a burnt offering for anyone may keep its hide for himself. 9Every grain offering baked in an oven or cooked in a pan or on a griddle belongs to the priest who offers it, 10and every grain offering, whether mixed with oil or dry, belongs equally to all the sons of Aaron.

The Fellowship Offering

11" 'These are the regulations for the fellowship offering[a] a person may present to the LORD:

12" 'If he offers it as an expression of thankfulness, then along with this thank offering he is to offer cakes of bread made without yeast and mixed with oil, wafers made without yeast and spread with oil, and cakes of fine flour well-kneaded and mixed with oil. 13Along with his fellowship offering of thanksgiving he is to present an offering with cakes of bread made with yeast. 14He is to bring one of each kind as an offering, a contribution to the LORD; it belongs to the priest who sprinkles the blood of the fellowship offerings. 15The meat of his fellowship offering of thanksgiving must be eaten on the day it is offered; he must leave none of it till morning.

16" 'If, however, his offering is the result of a vow or is a freewill offering, the sacrifice shall be eaten on the day he offers it, but anything left over may be eaten on the next day. 17Any meat of the sacrifice left over till the third day must be burned up. 18If any meat of the fellowship offering is eaten on the third day, it will not be accepted. It will not be credited to the one who offered it, for it is impure; the person who eats any of it will be held responsible.

19" 'Meat that touches anything ceremonially unclean must not be eaten; it must be burned up. As for other meat, anyone ceremonially clean may eat it. 20But if anyone who is unclean eats any meat of the fellowship offering belonging to the LORD, that person must be cut off from his people. 21If anyone touches something unclean—whether human uncleanness or an unclean animal or any unclean, detestable thing—and then eats any of the meat of the fellowship offering belonging to the LORD, that person must be cut off from his people.' "

Eating Fat and Blood Forbidden

22The LORD said to Moses, 23"Say to the Israelites: 'Do not eat any of the fat of cattle, sheep or goats. 24The fat of an animal found dead or torn by wild animals may be used for any other purpose, but you must not eat it.

---

a *11* Traditionally *peace offering*; also in verses 13-37

Living Bible

7 "HERE ARE the instructions concerning the most holy offering for guilt:

2"The sacrificial animal shall be killed at the place where the burnt offering sacrifices are slain, and its blood shall be sprinkled back and forth upon the altar. 3The priest will offer upon the altar all its fat, including the tail, the fat that covers the insides, 4the two kidneys and the loin-fat, and the gall bladder—all shall be set aside for sacrificing. 5The priests will burn them upon the altar as a guilt offering to the Lord. 6Only males among the priests may then eat the carcass, and it must be eaten in a holy place, for this is a most holy sacrifice.

7"The same instructions apply to both the sin offering and the guilt offering—the carcass shall be given to the priest who is in charge of the atonement ceremony, for his food. 8(When the offering is a burnt sacrifice, the priest who is in charge shall also be given the animal's hide.) 9The priests who present the people's grain offerings to the Lord shall be given whatever remains of the sacrifice after the ceremony is completed. This rule applies whether the sacrifice is baked, fried, or grilled. 10All other grain offerings, whether mixed with olive oil or dry, are the common property of all sons of Aaron.

11"Here are the instructions concerning the sacrifices given to the Lord as special peace offerings:

12"If it is an offering of thanksgiving, unleavened short breadb shall be included with the sacrifice, along with unleavened wafers spread with olive oil and loaves from a batter of flour mixed with olive oil. 13This thanksgiving peace offering shall be accompanied with loaves of leavened bread. 14Part of this sacrifice shall be presented to the Lord by a gesture of waving it before the altar, then it shall be given to the assisting priest, the one who sprinkles the blood of the animal presented for the sacrifice. 15After the animal has been sacrificed and presented to the Lord as a peace offering to show special appreciation and thanksgiving to him, its meat is to be eaten that same day, and none left to be eaten the next day.

16"However, if someone brings a sacrifice that is not for thanksgiving, but is because of a vow or is simply a voluntary offering to the Lord, any portion of the sacrifice that is not eaten the day it is sacrificed may be eaten the next day. 17, 18But anything left over until the third day shall be burned. For if any of it is eaten on the third day, the Lord will not accept it; it will have no value as a sacrifice, and there will be no credit to the one who brought it to be offered; and the priest who eats it shall be guilty, for it is detestable to the Lord, and the person who eats it must answer for his sin.

19"Any meat that comes into contact with anything that is ceremonially unclean shall not be eaten, but burned; and as for the meat that may be eaten, it may be eaten only by a person who is ceremonially clean. 20Any priest who is ceremonially unclean but eats the thanksgiving offering anyway, shall be cut off from his people, for he has defiled what is sacred.c 21Anyone who touches anything that is ceremonially unclean, whether it is uncleanness from man or beast, and then eats the peace offering, shall be cut off from his people, for he has defiled what is holy."

22Then the Lord said to Moses, 23"Tell the people of Israel never to eat fat, whether from oxen, sheep, or goats. 24The fat of an animal that dies of disease, or is attacked and killed by wild animals, may be used for other purposes, but never eaten. 25Anyone who eats fat

New Revised Standard

7 THIS IS the ritual of the guilt offering. It is most holy; 2at the spot where the burnt offering is slaughtered, they shall slaughter the guilt offering, and its blood shall be dashed against all sides of the altar. 3All its fat shall be offered: the broad tail, the fat that covers the entrails, 4the two kidneys with the fat that is on them at the loins, and the appendage of the liver, which shall be removed with the kidneys. 5The priest shall turn them into smoke on the altar as an offering by fire to the LORD; it is a guilt offering. 6Every male among the priests shall eat of it; it shall be eaten in a holy place; it is most holy.

7 The guilt offering is like the sin offering, there is the same ritual for them; the priest who makes atonement with it shall have it. 8So, too, the priest who offers anyone's burnt offering shall keep the skin of the burnt offering that he has offered. 9And every grain offering baked in the oven, and all that is prepared in a pan or on a griddle, shall belong to the priest who offers it. 10But every other grain offering, mixed with oil or dry, shall belong to all the sons of Aaron equally.

Further Instructions

11 This is the ritual of the sacrifice of the offering of well-being that one may offer to the LORD. 12If you offer it for thanksgiving, you shall offer with the thank offering unleavened cakes mixed with oil, unleavened wafers spread with oil, and cakes of choice flour well soaked in oil. 13With your thanksgiving sacrifice of well-being you shall bring your offering with cakes of leavened bread. 14From this you shall offer one cake from each offering, as a gift to the LORD; it shall belong to the priest who dashes the blood of the offering of well-being. 15And the flesh of your thanksgiving sacrifice of well-being shall be eaten on the day it is offered; you shall not leave any of it until morning. 16But if the sacrifice you offer is a votive offering or a freewill offering, it shall be eaten on the day that you offer your sacrifice, and what is left of it shall be eaten the next day; 17but what is left of the flesh of the sacrifice shall be burned up on the third day. 18If any of the flesh of your sacrifice of well-being is eaten on the third day, it shall not be acceptable, nor shall it be credited to the one who offers it; it shall be an abomination, and the one who eats of it shall incur guilt.

19 Flesh that touches any unclean thing shall not be eaten; it shall be burned up. As for other flesh, all who are clean may eat such flesh. 20But those who eat flesh from the LORD's sacrifice of well-being while in a state of uncleanness shall be cut off from their kin. 21When any one of you touches any unclean thing—human uncleanness or an unclean animal or any unclean creature—and then eats flesh from the LORD's sacrifice of well-being, you shall be cut off from your kin.

22 The LORD spoke to Moses, saying: 23Speak to the people of Israel, saying: You shall eat no fat of ox or sheep or goat. 24The fat of an animal that died or was torn by wild animals may be put to any use, but you must not eat it. 25If any one of you eats the fat from an animal

---

b 7:12 unleavened short bread, literally, "unleavened loaves mingled with oil." c 7:20 he has defiled what is sacred, literally, "it pertains unto Jehovah."

King James

25For whosoever eateth the fat of the beast, of which men offer an offering made by fire unto the LORD, even the soul that eateth *it* shall be cut off from his people.

26Moreover ye shall eat no manner of blood, *whether it be* of fowl or of beast, in any of your dwellings.

27Whatsoever soul *it be* that eateth any manner of blood, even that soul shall be cut off from his people.

28¶ And the LORD spake unto Moses, saying,

29Speak unto the children of Israel, saying, He that offereth the sacrifice of his peace offerings unto the LORD shall bring his oblation unto the LORD of the sacrifice of his peace offerings.

30His own hands shall bring the offerings of the LORD made by fire, the fat with the breast, it shall he bring, that the breast may be waved *for* a wave offering before the LORD.

31And the priest shall burn the fat upon the altar: but the breast shall be Aaron's and his sons'.

32And the right shoulder shall ye give unto the priest *for* an heave offering of the sacrifices of your peace offerings.

33He among the sons of Aaron, that offereth the blood of the peace offerings, and the fat, shall have the right shoulder for *his* part.

34For the wave breast and the heave shoulder have I taken of the children of Israel from off the sacrifices of their peace offerings, and have given them unto Aaron the priest and unto his sons by a statute for ever from among the children of Israel.

35¶ This *is the portion* of the anointing of Aaron, and of the anointing of his sons, out of the offerings of the LORD made by fire, in the day *when* he presented them to minister unto the LORD in the priest's office;

36Which the LORD commanded to be given them of the children of Israel, in the day that he anointed them, *by* a statute for ever throughout their generations.

37This *is* the law of the burnt offering, of the meat offering, and of the sin offering, and of the trespass offering, and of the consecrations, and of the sacrifice of the peace offerings;

38Which the LORD commanded Moses in mount Sinai, in the day that he commanded the children of Israel to offer their oblations unto the LORD, in the wilderness of Sinai.

8 AND THE LORD spake unto Moses, saying, 2Take Aaron and his sons with him, and the garments, and the anointing oil, and a bullock for the sin offering, and two rams, and a basket of unleavened bread;

3And gather thou all the congregation together unto the door of the tabernacle of the congregation.

4And Moses did as the LORD commanded him; and the assembly was gathered together unto the door of the tabernacle of the congregation.

5And Moses said unto the congregation, This *is* the thing which the LORD commanded to be done.

6And Moses brought Aaron and his sons, and washed them with water.

7And he put upon him the coat, and girded him with the girdle, and clothed him with the robe, and put the ephod upon him, and he girded him with the curious girdle of the ephod, and bound *it* unto him therewith.

8And he put the breastplate upon him: also he put in the breastplate the Urim and the Thummim.

9And he put the mitre upon his head; also upon the mitre, *even* upon his forefront, did he put the golden plate, the holy crown; as the LORD commanded Moses.

10And Moses took the anointing oil, and anointed the tabernacle and all that *was* therein, and sanctified them.

New International

25Anyone who eats the fat of an animal from which an offering by fire may be[a] made to the LORD must be cut off from his people. 26And wherever you live, you must not eat the blood of any bird or animal. 27If anyone eats blood, that person must be cut off from his people.' "

The Priests' Share

28The LORD said to Moses, 29"Say to the Israelites: 'Anyone who brings a fellowship offering to the LORD is to bring part of it as his sacrifice to the LORD. 30With his own hands he is to bring the offering made to the LORD by fire; he is to bring the fat, together with the breast, and wave the breast before the LORD as a wave offering. 31The priest shall burn the fat on the altar, but the breast belongs to Aaron and his sons. 32You are to give the right thigh of your fellowship offerings to the priest as a contribution. 33The son of Aaron who offers the blood and the fat of the fellowship offering shall have the right thigh as his share. 34From the fellowship offerings of the Israelites, I have taken the breast that is waved and the thigh that is presented and have given them to Aaron the priest and his sons as their regular share from the Israelites.' "

35This is the portion of the offerings made to the LORD by fire that were allotted to Aaron and his sons on the day they were presented to serve the LORD as priests. 36On the day they were anointed, the LORD commanded that the Israelites give this to them as their regular share for the generations to come.

37These, then, are the regulations for the burnt offering, the grain offering, the sin offering, the guilt offering, the ordination offering and the fellowship offering, 38which the LORD gave Moses on Mount Sinai on the day he commanded the Israelites to bring their offerings to the LORD, in the Desert of Sinai.

The Ordination of Aaron and His Sons

8 THE LORD said to Moses, 2"Bring Aaron and his sons, their garments, the anointing oil, the bull for the sin offering, the two rams and the basket containing bread made without yeast, 3and gather the entire assembly at the entrance to the Tent of Meeting." 4Moses did as the LORD commanded him, and the assembly gathered at the entrance to the Tent of Meeting.

5Moses said to the assembly, "This is what the LORD has commanded to be done." 6Then Moses brought Aaron and his sons forward and washed them with water. 7He put the tunic on Aaron, tied the sash around him, clothed him with the robe and put the ephod on him. He also tied the ephod to him by its skillfully woven waistband; so it was fastened on him. 8He placed the breastpiece on him and put the Urim and Thummim in the breastpiece. 9Then he placed the turban on Aaron's head and set the gold plate, the sacred diadem, on the front of it, as the LORD commanded Moses.

10Then Moses took the anointing oil and anointed the tabernacle and everything in it, and so consecrated them. 11He sprinkled some of the oil on the altar seven

---

Living Bible

from an offering sacrificed by fire to the Lord shall be outlawed from his people.

26, 27"Never eat blood, whether of birds or animals. Anyone who does shall be excommunicated from his people."

28And the Lord said to Moses, 29"Tell the people of Israel that anyone bringing a thanksgiving offering to the Lord must bring it personally with his own hands. 30He shall bring the offering of the fat and breast, which is to be presented to the Lord by waving it before the altar. 31Then the priest shall burn the fat upon the altar, but the breast shall belong to Aaron and his sons, 32, 33while the right thigh shall be given to the officiating priest. 34For I have designated the breast and thigh as donations from the people of Israel to the sons of Aaron. Aaron and his sons must always be given this portion of the sacrifice. 35This is their pay! It is to be set apart from the burnt offerings, and given to all who have been appointed to minister to the Lord as priests—to Aaron and to his sons. 36For on the day the Lord anointed them, he commanded that the people of Israel give these portions to them; it is their right forever throughout all their generations."

37These were the instructions concerning the burnt offering, grain offering, sin offering, and guilt offering, and concerning the consecration offering and the peace offering; 38these instructions were given to Moses by the Lord on Mount Sinai, to be passed on to the people of Israel so that they would know how to offer their sacrifices to God in the Sinai desert.

8 THE LORD said to Moses, "Now bring Aaron and his sons to the entrance of the Tabernacle, together with their garments, the anointing oil, the young bull for the sin offering, the two rams, and the basket of bread made without yeast; and summon all Israel to a meeting there."

4So all the people assembled, 5and Moses said to them, "What I am now going to do has been commanded by Jehovah."

6Then he took Aaron and his sons and washed them with water, 7and he clothed Aaron with the special coat, sash, robe, and the ephod-jacket with its beautifully woven belt. 8Then he put on him the chestpiece and deposited the Urim and the Thummimb inside its pouch; 9and placed on Aaron's head the turban with the sacred gold plate at its front—the holy crown—as the Lord had commanded Moses.

10Then Moses took the anointing oil and sprinkled it upon the Tabernacle itself and on each item in it, sanctifying them. 11When he came to the altar he sprinkled it

New Revised Standard

of which an offering by fire may be made to the LORD, you who eat it shall be cut off from your kin. 26You must not eat any blood whatever, either of bird or of animal, in any of your settlements. 27Any one of you who eats any blood shall be cut off from your kin.

28 The LORD spoke to Moses, saying: 29Speak to the people of Israel, saying: Any one of you who would offer to the LORD your sacrifice of well-being must yourself bring to the LORD your offering from your sacrifice of well-being. 30Your own hands shall bring the LORD's offering by fire; you shall bring the fat with the breast, so that the breast may be raised as an elevation offering before the LORD. 31The priest shall turn the fat into smoke on the altar, but the breast shall belong to Aaron and his sons. 32And the right thigh from your sacrifices of well-being you shall give to the priest as an offering; 33the one among the sons of Aaron who offers the blood and fat of the offering of well-being shall have the right thigh for a portion. 34For I have taken the breast of the elevation offering, and the thigh that is offered, from the people of Israel, from their sacrifices of well-being, and have given them to Aaron the priest and to his sons, as a perpetual due from the people of Israel. 35This is the portion allotted to Aaron and to his sons from the offerings made by fire to the LORD, once they have been brought forward to serve the LORD as priests; 36these the LORD commanded to be given them, when he anointed them, as a perpetual due from the people of Israel throughout their generations.

37 This is the ritual of the burnt offering, the grain offering, the sin offering, the guilt offering, the offering of ordination, and the sacrifice of well-being, 38 which the LORD commanded Moses on Mount Sinai, when he commanded the people of Israel to bring their offerings to the LORD, in the wilderness of Sinai.

The Rites of Ordination

8 THE LORD spoke to Moses, saying: 2Take Aaron and his sons with him, the vestments, the anointing oil, the bull of sin offering, the two rams, and the basket of unleavened bread; 3and assemble the whole congregation at the entrance of the tent of meeting. 4And Moses did as the LORD commanded him. When the congregation was assembled at the entrance of the tent of meeting, 5Moses said to the congregation, "This is what the LORD has commanded to be done."

6 Then Moses brought Aaron and his sons forward, and washed them with water. 7He put the tunic on him, fastened the sash around him, clothed him with the robe, and put the ephod on him. He then put the decorated band of the ephod around him, tying the ephod to him with it. 8He placed the breastpiece on him, and in the breastpiece he put the Urim and the Thummim. 9And he set the turban on his head, and on the turban, in front, he set the golden ornament, the holy crown, as the LORD commanded Moses.

10 Then Moses took the anointing oil and anointed the tabernacle and all that was in it, and consecrated them. 11He sprinkled some of it on the altar seven times,

---

b 8:8 *Urim and Thummim.* Apparently a kind of sacred lot used to determine the Lord's will by simple "yes" or "no" alternatives.

King James

11And he sprinkled thereof upon the altar seven times, and anointed the altar and all his vessels, both the laver and his foot, to sanctify them.

12And he poured of the anointing oil upon Aaron's head, and anointed him, to sanctify him.

13And Moses brought Aaron's sons, and put coats upon them, and girded them with girdles, and put bonnets upon them; as the LORD commanded Moses.

14And he brought the bullock for the sin offering: and Aaron and his sons laid their hands upon the head of the bullock for the sin offering.

15And he slew *it*; and Moses took the blood, and put *it* upon the horns of the altar round about with his finger, and purified the altar, and poured the blood at the bottom of the altar, and sanctified it, to make reconciliation upon it.

16And he took all the fat that *was* upon the inwards, and the caul *above* the liver, and the two kidneys, and their fat, and Moses burned *it* upon the altar.

17But the bullock, and his hide, his flesh, and his dung, he burnt with fire without the camp; as the LORD commanded Moses.

18¶ And he brought the ram for the burnt offering: and Aaron and his sons laid their hands upon the head of the ram.

19And he killed *it*; and Moses sprinkled the blood upon the altar round about.

20And he cut the ram into pieces; and Moses burnt the head, and the pieces, and the fat.

21And he washed the inwards and the legs in water; and Moses burnt the whole ram upon the altar: it *was* a burnt sacrifice for a sweet savour, *and* an offering made by fire unto the LORD; as the LORD commanded Moses.

22¶ And he brought the other ram, the ram of consecration: and Aaron and his sons laid their hands upon the head of the ram.

23And he slew *it*; and Moses took of the blood of it, and put *it* upon the tip of Aaron's right ear, and upon the thumb of his right hand, and upon the great toe of his right foot.

24And he brought Aaron's sons, and Moses put of the blood upon the tip of their right ear, and upon the thumbs of their right hands, and upon the great toes of their right feet: and Moses sprinkled the blood upon the altar round about.

25And he took the fat, and the rump, and all the fat that *was* upon the inwards, and the caul *above* the liver, and the two kidneys, and their fat, and the right shoulder:

26And out of the basket of unleavened bread, that *was* before the LORD, he took one unleavened cake, and a cake of oiled bread, and one wafer, and put *them* on the fat, and upon the right shoulder:

27And he put all upon Aaron's hands, and upon his sons' hands, and waved them *for* a wave offering before the LORD.

28And Moses took them from off their hands, and burnt *them* on the altar upon the burnt offering: they *were* consecrations for a sweet savour: it *is* an offering made by fire unto the LORD.

29And Moses took the breast, and waved it *for* a wave offering before the LORD: *for* of the ram of consecration it was Moses' part; as the LORD commanded Moses.

30And Moses took of the anointing oil, and of the blood which *was* upon the altar, and sprinkled *it* upon Aaron, *and* upon his garments, and upon his sons, and upon his sons' garments with him; and sanctified Aaron, *and* his garments, and his sons, and his sons' garments with him.

31¶ And Moses said unto Aaron and to his sons, Boil the flesh *at* the door of the tabernacle of the congregation: and there eat it with the bread that *is* in the basket of consecrations, as I commanded, saying, Aaron and his sons shall eat it.

New International

times, anointing the altar and all its utensils and the basin with its stand, to consecrate them. 12He poured some of the anointing oil on Aaron's head and anointed him to consecrate him. 13Then he brought Aaron's sons forward, put tunics on them, tied sashes around them and put headbands on them, as the LORD commanded Moses.

14He then presented the bull for the sin offering, and Aaron and his sons laid their hands on its head. 15Moses slaughtered the bull and took some of the blood, and with his finger he put it on all the horns of the altar to purify the altar. He poured out the rest of the blood at the base of the altar. So he consecrated it to make atonement for it. 16Moses also took all the fat around the inner parts, the covering of the liver, and both kidneys and their fat, and burned it on the altar. 17But the bull with its hide and its flesh and its offal he burned up outside the camp, as the LORD commanded Moses.

18He then presented the ram for the burnt offering, and Aaron and his sons laid their hands on its head. 19Then Moses slaughtered the ram and sprinkled the blood against the altar on all sides. 20He cut the ram into pieces and burned the head, the pieces and the fat. 21He washed the inner parts and the legs with water and burned the whole ram on the altar as a burnt offering, a pleasing aroma, an offering made to the LORD by fire, as the LORD commanded Moses.

22He then presented the other ram, the ram for the ordination, and Aaron and his sons laid their hands on its head. 23Moses slaughtered the ram and took some of its blood and put it on the lobe of Aaron's right ear, on the thumb of his right hand and on the big toe of his right foot. 24Moses also brought Aaron's sons forward and put some of the blood on the lobes of their right ears, on the thumbs of their right hands and on the big toes of their right feet. Then he sprinkled blood against the altar on all sides. 25He took the fat, the fat tail, all the fat around the inner parts, the covering of the liver, both kidneys and their fat and the right thigh. 26Then from the basket of bread made without yeast, which was before the LORD, he took a cake of bread, and one made with oil, and a wafer; he put these on the fat portions and on the right thigh. 27He put all these in the hands of Aaron and his sons and waved them before the LORD as a wave offering. 28Then Moses took them from their hands and burned them on the altar on top of the burnt offering as an ordination offering, a pleasing aroma, an offering made to the LORD by fire. 29He also took the breast—Moses' share of the ordination ram—and waved it before the LORD as a wave offering, as the LORD commanded Moses.

30Then Moses took some of the anointing oil and some of the blood from the altar and sprinkled them on Aaron and his garments and on his sons and their garments. So he consecrated Aaron and his garments and his sons and their garments.

31Moses then said to Aaron and his sons, "Cook the meat at the entrance to the Tent of Meeting and eat it there with the bread from the basket of ordination offerings, as I commanded, saying,[a] 'Aaron and his sons are to eat it.' 32Then burn up the rest of the meat and the

---

a 31 Or *I was commanded*:

Living Bible

seven times, and also sprinkled the utensils of the altar and the washbasin and its pedestal, to sanctify them. 12Then he poured the anointing oil upon Aaron's head, thus setting him apart for his work. 13Next Moses placed the robes on Aaron's sons, with the belts and caps, as the Lord had commanded him.

14Then he took the young bull for the sin offering, and Aaron and his sons laid their hands upon its head 15. 16as Moses killed it. He smeared some of the blood with his finger upon the four horns of the altar, and upon the altar itself, to sanctify it, and poured out the rest of the blood at the base of the altar; thus he sanctified the altar, making atonement for it. He took all the fat covering the entrails, the fatty mass above the liver, and the two kidneys and their fat, and burned them all on the altar. 17The carcass of the young bull, with its hide and dung, was burned outside the camp, as the Lord had commanded Moses.

18Then he presented to the Lord the ram for the burnt offering. Aaron and his sons laid their hands upon its head, 19and Moses killed it and sprinkled the blood back and forth upon the altar. 20Next he quartered the ram and burned the pieces, the head and the fat. 21He then washed the insides and the legs with water, and burned them upon the altar, so that the entire ram was consumed before the Lord; it was a burnt offering that pleased the Lord very much, for Jehovah's directions to Moses were followed in every detail.

22Then Moses presented the other ram, the ram of consecration; Aaron and his sons laid their hands upon its head. 23Moses killed it and took some of its blood and smeared it upon the lobe of Aaron's right ear, and the thumb of his right hand and upon the big toe of his right foot. 24Next he smeared some of the blood upon Aaron's sons—upon the lobes of their right ears, upon their right thumbs, and upon the big toes of their right feet. The rest of the blood he sprinkled back and forth upon the altar.b

25Then he took the fat, the tail, the fat upon the inner organs, the gall bladder, the two kidneys with their fat, and the right shoulder, 26and placed on top of these one unleavened wafer, one wafer spread with olive oil, and a slice of bread, all taken from the basket which had been placed there before the Lord. 27All this was placed in the hands of Aaron and his sons to present to the Lord by a gesture of waving before the altar. 28Moses then took it all back from them and burned it upon the altar, along with the burnt offeringc to the Lord; and Jehovah was pleased by the offering. 29Now Moses took the breast and presented it to the Lord by waving it before the altar; this was Moses' portion of the ram of consecration, just as the Lord had instructed him.

30Next he took some of the anointing oil and some of the blood that had been sprinkled upon the altar, and sprinkled it upon Aaron and upon his clothes and upon his sons and upon their clothes, thus consecrating to the Lord's use Aaron and his sons and their clothes.

31Then Moses said to Aaron and his sons, "Boil the meat at the entrance of the Tabernacle, and eat it along with the bread that is in the basket of consecration, just

New Revised Standard

and anointed the altar and all its utensils, and the basin and its base, to consecrate them. 12He poured some of the anointing oil on Aaron's head and anointed him, to consecrate him. 13And Moses brought forward Aaron's sons, and clothed them with tunics, and fastened sashes around them, and tied headdresses on them, as the LORD commanded Moses.

14 He led forward the bull of sin offering; and Aaron and his sons laid their hands upon the head of the bull of sin offering, 15and it was slaughtered. Moses took the blood and with his finger put some on each of the horns of the altar, purifying the altar; then he poured out the blood at the base of the altar. Thus he consecrated it, to make atonement for it. 16Moses took all the fat that was around the entrails, and the appendage of the liver, and the two kidneys with their fat, and turned them into smoke on the altar. 17But the bull itself, its skin and flesh and its dung, he burned with fire outside the camp, as the LORD commanded Moses.

18 Then he brought forward the ram of burnt offering. Aaron and his sons laid their hands on the head of the ram, 19and it was slaughtered. Moses dashed the blood against all sides of the altar. 20The ram was cut into its parts, and Moses turned into smoke the head and the parts and the suet. 21And after the entrails and the legs were washed with water, Moses turned into smoke the whole ram on the altar; it was a burnt offering for a pleasing odor, an offering by fire to the LORD, as the LORD commanded Moses.

22 Then he brought forward the second ram, the ram of ordination. Aaron and his sons laid their hands on the head of the ram, 23and it was slaughtered. Moses took some of its blood and put it on the lobe of Aaron's right ear and on the thumb of his right hand and on the big toe of his right foot. 24After Aaron's sons were brought forward, Moses put some of the blood on the lobes of their right ears and on the thumbs of their right hands and on the big toes of their right feet; and Moses dashed the rest of the blood against all sides of the altar. 25He took the fat—the broad tail, all the fat that was around the entrails, the appendage of the liver, and the two kidneys with their fat—and the right thigh. 26From the basket of unleavened bread that was before the LORD, he took one cake of unleavened bread, one cake of bread with oil, and one wafer, and placed them on the fat and on the right thigh. 27He placed all these on the palms of Aaron and on the palms of his sons, and raised them as an elevation offering before the LORD. 28Then Moses took them from their hands and turned them into smoke on the altar with the burnt offering. This was an ordination offering for a pleasing odor, an offering by fire to the LORD. 29Moses took the breast and raised it as an elevation offering before the LORD; it was Moses' portion of the ram of ordination, as the LORD commanded Moses.

30 Then Moses took some of the anointing oil and some of the blood that was on the altar and sprinkled them on Aaron and his vestments, and also on his sons and their vestments. Thus he consecrated Aaron and his vestments, and also his sons and their vestments.

31 And Moses said to Aaron and his sons, "Boil the flesh at the entrance of the tent of meeting, and eat it there with the bread that is in the basket of ordination offerings, as I was commanded, 'Aaron and his sons shall eat it'; 32and what remains of the flesh and the

---

b 8:24 *The rest of the blood he sprinkled back and forth upon the altar,* literally, "Moses threw the blood upon the altar round about."   c 8:28 *along with the burnt offering,* literally, "upon the burnt offering."

King James

32And that which remaineth of the flesh and of the bread shall ye burn with fire.

33And ye shall not go out of the door of the tabernacle of the congregation *in* seven days, until the days of your consecration be at an end: for seven days shall he consecrate you.

34As he hath done this day, *so* the LORD hath commanded to do, to make an atonement for you.

35Therefore shall ye abide *at* the door of the tabernacle of the congregation day and night seven days, and keep the charge of the LORD, that ye die not: for so I am commanded.

36So Aaron and his sons did all things which the LORD commanded by the hand of Moses.

9 AND IT came to pass on the eighth day, *that* Moses called Aaron and his sons, and the elders of Israel;

2And he said unto Aaron, Take thee a young calf for a sin offering, and a ram for a burnt offering, without blemish, and offer *them* before the LORD.

3And unto the children of Israel thou shalt speak, saying, Take ye a kid of the goats for a sin offering; and a calf and a lamb, *both* of the first year, without blemish, for a burnt offering;

4Also a bullock and a ram for peace offerings, to sacrifice before the LORD; and a meat offering mingled with oil: for today the LORD will appear unto you.

5¶ And they brought *that* which Moses commanded before the tabernacle of the congregation: and all the congregation drew near and stood before the LORD.

6And Moses said, This *is* the thing which the LORD commanded that ye should do: and the glory of the LORD shall appear unto you.

7And Moses said unto Aaron, Go unto the altar, and offer thy sin offering, and thy burnt offering, and make an atonement for thyself, and for the people: and offer the offering of the people, and make an atonement for them; as the LORD commanded.

8¶ Aaron therefore went unto the altar, and slew the calf of the sin offering, which *was* for himself.

9And the sons of Aaron brought the blood unto him: and he dipped his finger in the blood, and put *it* upon the horns of the altar, and poured out the blood at the bottom of the altar:

10But the fat, and the kidneys, and the caul above the liver of the sin offering, he burnt upon the altar; as the LORD commanded Moses.

11And the flesh and the hide he burnt with fire without the camp.

12And he slew the burnt offering; and Aaron's sons presented unto him the blood, which he sprinkled round about upon the altar.

13And they presented the burnt offering unto him, with the pieces thereof, and the head: and he burnt *them* upon the altar.

14And he did wash the inwards and the legs, and burnt *them* upon the burnt offering on the altar.

15¶ And he brought the people's offering, and took the goat, which *was* the sin offering for the people, and slew it, and offered it for sin, as the first.

16And he brought the burnt offering, and offered it according to the manner.

17And he brought the meat offering, and took an handful thereof, and burnt *it* upon the altar, beside the burnt sacrifice of the morning.

18He slew also the bullock and the ram *for* a sacrifice of peace offerings, which *was* for the people: and Aaron's sons presented unto him the blood, which he sprinkled upon the altar round about,

New International

bread. 33Do not leave the entrance to the Tent of Meeting for seven days, until the days of your ordination are completed, for your ordination will last seven days. 34What has been done today was commanded by the LORD to make atonement for you. 35You must stay at the entrance to the Tent of Meeting day and night for seven days and do what the LORD requires, so you will not die; for that is what I have been commanded." 36So Aaron and his sons did everything the LORD commanded through Moses.

The Priests Begin Their Ministry

9 ON THE eighth day Moses summoned Aaron and his sons and the elders of Israel. 2He said to Aaron, "Take a bull calf for your sin offering and a ram for your burnt offering, both without defect, and present them before the LORD. 3Then say to the Israelites: 'Take a male goat for a sin offering, a calf and a lamb—both a year old and without defect—for a burnt offering, 4and an ox[a] and a ram for a fellowship offering[b] to sacrifice before the LORD, together with a grain offering mixed with oil. For today the LORD will appear to you.'"

5They took the things Moses commanded to the front of the Tent of Meeting, and the entire assembly came near and stood before the LORD. 6Then Moses said, "This is what the LORD has commanded you to do, so that the glory of the LORD may appear to you."

7Moses said to Aaron, "Come to the altar and sacrifice your sin offering and your burnt offering and make atonement for yourself and the people; sacrifice the offering that is for the people and make atonement for them, as the LORD has commanded."

8So Aaron came to the altar and slaughtered the calf as a sin offering for himself. 9His sons brought the blood to him, and he dipped his finger into the blood and put it on the horns of the altar; the rest of the blood he poured out at the base of the altar. 10On the altar he burned the fat, the kidneys and the covering of the liver from the sin offering, as the LORD commanded Moses; 11the flesh and the hide he burned up outside the camp.

12Then he slaughtered the burnt offering. His sons handed him the blood, and he sprinkled it against the altar on all sides. 13They handed him the burnt offering piece by piece, including the head, and he burned them on the altar. 14He washed the inner parts and the legs and burned them on top of the burnt offering on the altar.

15Aaron then brought the offering that was for the people. He took the goat for the people's sin offering and slaughtered it and offered it for a sin offering as he did with the first one.

16He brought the burnt offering and offered it in the prescribed way. 17He also brought the grain offering, took a handful of it and burned it on the altar in addition to the morning's burnt offering.

18He slaughtered the ox and the ram as the fellowship offering for the people. His sons handed him the blood, and he sprinkled it against the altar on all sides. 19But

---

[a] *4* The Hebrew word can include both male and female; also in verses 18 and 19.   [b] *4* Traditionally *peace offering*; also in verses 18 and 22

Living Bible

as I instructed you to do. 32Anything left of the meat and bread must be burned."

33Next he told them not to leave the Tabernacle entrance for seven days, after which time their consecration would be completed—for it takes seven days. 34Then Moses stated again that all he had done that day had been commanded by the Lord in order to make atonement for them. 35And again he warned Aaron and his sons to stay at the entrance of the Tabernacle day and night for seven days. "If you leave," he told them, "you will die—this is what the Lord has said."

36So Aaron and his sons did all that the Lord had commanded Moses.

9 ON THE eighth day (of the consecration ceremonies), Moses summoned Aaron and Aaron's sons and the elders of Israel, 2and told Aaron to take a bull calf from the herd for a sin offering, and a ram without bodily defect for a burnt offering, and to offer them before the Lord.

3"And tell the people of Israel," Moses instructed, "to select a male goat for their sin offering, also a yearling calf and a yearling lamb, all without bodily defect, for their burnt offering. 4In addition, the people are to bring to the Lord a peace offering sacrifice—an ox and a ram, and a grain offering—flour mingled with olive oil. For today," Moses said, "Jehovah will appear to them."

5So they brought all these things to the entrance of the Tabernacle, as Moses had commanded, and the people came and stood there before the Lord.

6Moses told them, "When you have followed the Lord's instructions, his glory will appear to you."

7Moses then told Aaron to proceed to the altar and to offer the sin offering and the burnt offering, making atonement for himself first, and then for the people, as the Lord had commanded. 8So Aaron went up to the altar and killed the calf as a sacrifice for his own sin; 9his sons caught the blood for him, and he dipped his finger in it and smeared it upon the horns of the altar, and poured out the rest at the base of the altar. 10Then he burned upon the altar the fat, kidneys, and gall bladder from this sin offering, as the Lord had commanded Moses, 11but he burned the meat and hide outside the camp.

12Next he killed the burnt offering animal, and his sons caught the blood and he sprinkled it back and forth upon the altar; 13they brought the animal to him piece by piece, including the head, and he burned each part upon the altar. 14Then he washed the insides and the legs, and offered these also upon the altar as a burnt offering.

15Next he sacrificed the people's offering; he killed the goat and offered it in just the same way as he had the sin offering for himself.c 16Thus he sacrificed their burnt offering to the Lord, in accordance with the instructions God had given.

17Then he presented the grain offering, taking a handful and burning it upon the altar in addition to the regular morning offering.

18Next he killed the ox and ram—the people's peace offering sacrifice; and Aaron's sons brought the blood to him and he sprinkled it back and forth upon the altar.

New Revised Standard

bread you shall burn with fire. 33You shall not go outside the entrance of the tent of meeting for seven days, until the day when your period of ordination is completed. For it will take seven days to ordain you; 34as has been done today, the LORD has commanded to be done to make atonement for you. 35You shall remain at the entrance of the tent of meeting day and night for seven days, keeping the LORD's charge so that you do not die; for so I am commanded." 36Aaron and his sons did all the things that the LORD commanded through Moses.

Aaron's Priesthood Inaugurated

9 ON THE eighth day Moses summoned Aaron and his sons and the elders of Israel. 2He said to Aaron, "Take a bull calf for a sin offering and a ram for a burnt offering, without blemish, and offer them before the LORD. 3And say to the people of Israel, 'Take a male goat for a sin offering; a calf and a lamb, yearlings without blemish, for a burnt offering; 4and an ox and a ram for an offering of well-being to sacrifice before the LORD; and a grain offering mixed with oil. For today the LORD will appear to you.'" 5They brought what Moses commanded to the front of the tent of meeting; and the whole congregation drew near and stood before the LORD. 6And Moses said, "This is the thing that the LORD commanded you to do, so that the glory of the LORD may appear to you." 7Then Moses said to Aaron, "Draw near to the altar and sacrifice your sin offering and your burnt offering, and make atonement for yourself and for the people; and sacrifice the offering of the people, and make atonement for them; as the LORD has commanded."

8 Aaron drew near to the altar, and slaughtered the calf of the sin offering, which was for himself. 9The sons of Aaron presented the blood to him, and he dipped his finger in the blood and put it on the horns of the altar; and the rest of the blood he poured out at the base of the altar. 10But the fat, the kidneys, and the appendage of the liver from the sin offering he turned into smoke on the altar, as the LORD commanded Moses; 11and the flesh and the skin he burned with fire outside the camp.

12 Then he slaughtered the burnt offering. Aaron's sons brought him the blood, and he dashed it against all sides of the altar. 13And they brought him the burnt offering piece by piece, and the head, which he turned into smoke on the altar. 14He washed the entrails and the legs and, with the burnt offering, turned them into smoke on the altar.

15 Next he presented the people's offering. He took the goat of the sin offering that was for the people, and slaughtered it, and presented it as a sin offering like the first one. 16He presented the burnt offering, and sacrificed it according to regulation. 17He presented the grain offering, and, taking a handful of it, he turned it into smoke on the altar, in addition to the burnt offering of the morning.

18 He slaughtered the ox and the ram as a sacrifice of well-being for the people. Aaron's sons brought him the blood, which he dashed against all sides of the altar,

---

c 9:15 the sin offering for himself. See vss 8-11.

King James

19And the fat of the bullock and of the ram, the rump, and that which covereth *the inwards,* and the kidneys, and the caul *above* the liver:

20And they put the fat upon the breasts, and he burnt the fat upon the altar:

21And the breasts and the right shoulder Aaron waved *for* a wave offering before the LORD; as Moses commanded.

22And Aaron lifted up his hand toward the people, and blessed them, and came down from offering of the sin offering, and the burnt offering, and peace offerings.

23And Moses and Aaron went into the tabernacle of the congregation, and came out, and blessed the people: and the glory of the LORD appeared unto all the people.

24And there came a fire out from before the LORD, and consumed upon the altar the burnt offering and the fat: *which* when all the people saw, they shouted, and fell on their faces.

10 AND NADAB and Abihu, the sons of Aaron, took either of them his censer, and put fire therein, and put incense thereon, and offered strange fire before the LORD, which he commanded them not.

2And there went out fire from the LORD, and devoured them, and they died before the LORD.

3Then Moses said unto Aaron, This *is it* that the LORD spake, saying, I will be sanctified in them that come nigh me, and before all the people I will be glorified. And Aaron held his peace.

4And Moses called Mishael and Elzaphan, the sons of Uzziel the uncle of Aaron, and said unto them, Come near, carry your brethren from before the sanctuary out of the camp.

5So they went near, and carried them in their coats out of the camp; as Moses had said.

6And Moses said unto Aaron, and unto Eleazar and unto Ithamar, his sons, Uncover not your heads, neither rend your clothes; lest ye die, and lest wrath come upon all the people: but let your brethren, the whole house of Israel, bewail the burning which the LORD hath kindled.

7And ye shall not go out from the door of the tabernacle of the congregation, lest ye die: for the anointing oil of the LORD *is* upon you. And they did according to the word of Moses.

8¶ And the LORD spake unto Aaron, saying,

9Do not drink wine nor strong drink, thou, nor thy sons with thee, when ye go into the tabernacle of the congregation, lest ye die: *it shall be* a statute for ever throughout your generations:

10And that ye may put difference between holy and unholy, and between unclean and clean;

11And that ye may teach the children of Israel all the statutes which the LORD hath spoken unto them by the hand of Moses.

12¶ And Moses spake unto Aaron, and unto Eleazar and unto Ithamar, his sons that were left, Take the meat offering that remaineth of the offerings of the LORD made by fire, and eat it without leaven beside the altar: for it *is* most holy:

13And ye shall eat it in the holy place, because it *is* thy due, and thy sons' due, of the sacrifices of the LORD made by fire: for so I am commanded.

14And the wave breast and heave shoulder shall ye eat in a clean place; thou, and thy sons, and thy daughters with thee: for *they be* thy due, and thy sons' due, *which* are given out of the sacrifices of peace offerings of the children of Israel.

New International

the fat portions of the ox and the ram—the fat tail, the layer of fat, the kidneys and the covering of the liver—20these they laid on the breasts, and then Aaron burned the fat on the altar. 21Aaron waved the breasts and the right thigh before the LORD as a wave offering, as Moses commanded.

22Then Aaron lifted his hands toward the people and blessed them. And having sacrificed the sin offering, the burnt offering and the fellowship offering, he stepped down.

23Moses and Aaron then went into the Tent of Meeting. When they came out, they blessed the people; and the glory of the LORD appeared to all the people. 24Fire came out from the presence of the LORD and consumed the burnt offering and the fat portions on the altar. And when all the people saw it, they shouted for joy and fell facedown.

The Death of Nadab and Abihu

10 AARON'S SONS Nadab and Abihu took their censers, put fire in them and added incense; and they offered unauthorized fire before the LORD, contrary to his command. 2So fire came out from the presence of the LORD and consumed them, and they died before the LORD. 3Moses then said to Aaron, "This is what the LORD spoke of when he said:

" 'Among those who approach me
  I will show myself holy;
 in the sight of all the people
  I will be honored.' "

Aaron remained silent.

4Moses summoned Mishael and Elzaphan, sons of Aaron's uncle Uzziel, and said to them, "Come here; carry your cousins outside the camp, away from the front of the sanctuary." 5So they came and carried them, still in their tunics, outside the camp, as Moses ordered.

6Then Moses said to Aaron and his sons Eleazar and Ithamar, "Do not let your hair become unkempt,[a] and do not tear your clothes, or you will die and the LORD will be angry with the whole community. But your relatives, all the house of Israel, may mourn for those the LORD has destroyed by fire. 7Do not leave the entrance to the Tent of Meeting or you will die, because the LORD's anointing oil is on you." So they did as Moses said.

8Then the LORD said to Aaron, 9"You and your sons are not to drink wine or other fermented drink whenever you go into the Tent of Meeting, or you will die. This is a lasting ordinance for the generations to come. 10You must distinguish between the holy and the common, between the unclean and the clean, 11and you must teach the Israelites all the decrees the LORD has given them through Moses."

12Moses said to Aaron and his remaining sons, Eleazar and Ithamar, "Take the grain offering left over from the offerings made to the LORD by fire and eat it prepared without yeast beside the altar, for it is most holy. 13Eat it in a holy place, because it is your share and your sons' share of the offerings made to the LORD by fire; for so I have been commanded. 14But you and your sons and your daughters may eat the breast that was waved and the thigh that was presented. Eat them in a ceremonially clean place; they have been given to you and your children as your share of the Israelites' fellowship offerings.[b] 15The thigh that was presented and the breast that

a 6 Or *Do not uncover your heads*   b 14 Traditionally *peace offerings*

Living Bible

19Then he collected the fat of the ox and the ram—the fat from their tails and the fat covering the inner organs—and the kidneys and gall bladders. 20The fat was placed upon the breasts of these animals, and Aaron burned it upon the altar; 21but he waved the breasts and right shoulders slowly before the Lord as a gesture of offering it to him, just as Moses had commanded.

22Then, with hands spread out towards the people, Aaron blessed them and came down from the altar. 23Moses and Aaron went into the Tabernacle, and when they came out again they blessed the people; and the glory of the Lord appeared to the whole assembly. 24Then fire came from the Lord and consumed the burnt offering and fat on the altar; and when the people saw it, they all shouted and fell flat upon the ground before the Lord.

10 BUT NADAB and Abihu, the sons of Aaron, placed unholy fire in their censers, laid incense on the fire, and offered the incense before the Lordc—contrary to what the Lord had just commanded them! 2So fire blazed forth from the presence of the Lord and destroyed them.

3Then Moses said to Aaron, "This is what the Lord meant when he said, 'I will show myself holy among those who approach me, and I will be glorified before all the people.' " And Aaron was speechless.

4Then Moses called for Misha-el and Elzaphon, Aaron's cousins, the sons of Uzziel, and told them, "Go and get the charred bodies from before the Tabernacle, and carry them outside the camp."

5So they went over and got them, and carried them out in their coats as Moses had told them to.

6Then Moses said to Aaron and his sons Eleazar and Ithamar, "Do not mourn—do not let your hair hang loose as a sign of your mourning, and do not tear your clothes. If you do, God will strike you dead too, and his wrath will come upon all the people of Israel. But the rest of the people of Israel may lament the death of Nadab and Abihu, and mourn because of the terrible fire the Lord has sent. 7But you are not to leave the Tabernacle under penalty of death, for the anointing oil of Jehovah is upon you." And they did as Moses commanded.

8, 9Now the Lord instructed Aaron, "Never drink wine or strong drink when you go into the Tabernacle, lest you die; and this rule applies to your sons and to all your descendants from generation to generation. 10Your duties will be to arbitrate for the people, to teach them the difference between what is holy and what is ordinary, what is pure and what is impure; 11and to teach them all the laws Jehovah has given through Moses."

12Then Moses said to Aaron and to his sons who were left, Eleazar and Ithamar, "Take the grain offering—the food that remains after the handful has been offered to the Lord by burning it on the altar—make sure there is no leaven in it, and eat it beside the altar. The offering is most holy; 13therefore you must eat it in the sanctuary, in a holy place. It belongs to you and to your sons, from the offerings to Jehovah made by fire; for so I am commanded. 14But the breast and the thigh, which have been offered to the Lord by the gesture of waving it before him, may be eaten in any holy place. It belongs to you and to your sons and daughters for your food. It is your portion of the peace offering sacrifices of the people of Israel.

New Revised Standard

19and the fat of the ox and of the ram—the broad tail, the fat that covers the entrails, the two kidneys and the fat on them,d and the appendage of the liver. 20They first laid the fat on the breasts, and the fat was turned into smoke on the altar; 21and the breasts and the right thigh Aaron raised as an elevation offering before the Lord, as Moses had commanded.

22 Aaron lifted his hands toward the people and blessed them; and he came down after sacrificing the sin offering, the burnt offering, and the offering of well-being. 23Moses and Aaron entered the tent of meeting, and then came out and blessed the people; and the glory of the Lord appeared to all the people. 24Fire came out from the Lord and consumed the burnt offering and the fat on the altar; and when all the people saw it, they shouted and fell on their faces.

Nadab and Abihu

10 NOW AARON'S sons, Nadab and Abihu, each took his censer, put fire in it, and laid incense on it; and they offered unholy fire before the Lord, such as he had not commanded them. 2And fire came out from the presence of the Lord and consumed them, and they died before the Lord. 3Then Moses said to Aaron, "This is what the Lord meant when he said,

'Through those who are near me
     I will show myself holy,
and before all the people
     I will be glorified.' "

And Aaron was silent.

4 Moses summoned Mishael and Elzaphan, sons of Uzziel the uncle of Aaron, and said to them, "Come forward, and carry your kinsmen away from the front of the sanctuary to a place outside the camp." 5They came forward and carried them by their tunics out of the camp, as Moses had ordered. 6And Moses said to Aaron and to his sons Eleazar and Ithamar, "Do not dishevel your hair, and do not tear your vestments, or you will die and wrath will strike all the congregation; but your kindred, the whole house of Israel, may mourn the burning that the Lord has sent. 7You shall not go outside the entrance of the tent of meeting, or you will die; for the anointing oil of the Lord is on you." And they did as Moses had ordered.

8 And the Lord spoke to Aaron: 9Drink no wine or strong drink, neither you nor your sons, when you enter the tent of meeting, that you may not die; it is a statute forever throughout your generations. 10You are to distinguish between the holy and the common, and between the unclean and the clean; 11and you are to teach the people of Israel all the statutes that the Lord has spoken to them through Moses.

12 Moses spoke to Aaron and to his remaining sons, Eleazar and Ithamar: Take the grain offering that is left from the Lord's offerings by fire, and eat it unleavened beside the altar, for it is most holy; 13you shall eat it in a holy place, because it is your due and your sons' due, from the offerings by fire to the Lord; for so I am commanded. 14But the breast that is elevated and the thigh that is raised, you and your sons and daughters as well may eat in any clean place; for they have been assigned to you and your children from the sacrifices of the offerings of well-being of the people of Israel. 15The

c 10:1 and offered the incense before the Lord, or "placed fire in their censors . . . and offered unholy fire . . ." Their fatal error is not clearly identified.

d Gk: Heb the broad tail, and that which covers, and the kidneys

King James

15The heave shoulder and the wave breast shall they bring with the offerings made by fire of the fat, to wave *it for* a wave offering before the LORD; and it shall be thine, and thy sons' with thee, by a statute for ever; as the LORD hath commanded.

16¶ And Moses diligently sought the goat of the sin offering, and, behold, it was burnt: and he was angry with Eleazar and Ithamar, the sons of Aaron *which were* left *alive,* saying,

17Wherefore have ye not eaten the sin offering in the holy place, seeing it *is* most holy, and *God* hath given it you to bear the iniquity of the congregation, to make atonement for them before the LORD?

18Behold, the blood of it was not brought in within the holy *place:* ye should indeed have eaten it in the holy *place,* as I commanded.

19And Aaron said unto Moses, Behold, this day have they offered their sin offering and their burnt offering before the LORD; and such things have befallen me: and *if* I had eaten the sin offering today, should it have been accepted in the sight of the LORD?

20And when Moses heard *that,* he was content.

11 AND THE LORD spake unto Moses and to Aaron, saying unto them,

2Speak unto the children of Israel, saying, These *are* the beasts which ye shall eat among all the beasts that *are* on the earth.

3Whatsoever parteth the hoof, and is clovenfooted, *and* cheweth the cud, among the beasts, that shall ye eat.

4Nevertheless these shall ye not eat of them that chew the cud, or of them that divide the hoof: *as* the camel, because he cheweth the cud, but divideth not the hoof; he *is* unclean unto you.

5And the coney, because he cheweth the cud, but divideth not the hoof; he *is* unclean unto you.

6And the hare, because he cheweth the cud, but divideth not the hoof; he *is* unclean unto you.

7And the swine, though he divide the hoof, and be clovenfooted, yet he cheweth not the cud; he *is* unclean to you.

8Of their flesh shall ye not eat, and their carcase shall ye not touch; they *are* unclean to you.

9¶ These shall ye eat of all that *are* in the waters: whatsoever hath fins and scales in the waters, in the seas, and in the rivers, them shall ye eat.

10And all that have not fins and scales in the seas, and in the rivers, of all that move in the waters, and of any living thing which *is* in the waters, they *shall be* an abomination unto you:

11They shall be even an abomination unto you; ye shall not eat of their flesh, but ye shall have their carcases in abomination.

12Whatsoever hath no fins nor scales in the waters, that *shall be* an abomination unto you.

13¶ And these *are they which* ye shall have in abomination among the fowls; they shall not be eaten, they *are* an abomination: the eagle, and the ossifrage, and the ospray,

14And the vulture, and the kite after his kind;

15Every raven after his kind;

16And the owl, and the night hawk, and the cuckoo, and the hawk after his kind,

17And the little owl, and the cormorant, and the great owl,

18And the swan, and the pelican, and the gier eagle,

19And the stork, the heron after her kind, and the lapwing, and the bat.

20All fowls that creep, going upon *all* four, *shall be* an abomination unto you.

New International

was waved must be brought with the fat portions of the offerings made by fire, to be waved before the LORD as a wave offering. This will be the regular share for you and your children, as the LORD has commanded."

16When Moses inquired about the goat of the sin offering and found that it had been burned up, he was angry with Eleazar and Ithamar, Aaron's remaining sons, and asked, 17"Why didn't you eat the sin offering in the sanctuary area? It is most holy; it was given to you to take away the guilt of the community by making atonement for them before the LORD. 18Since its blood was not taken into the Holy Place, you should have eaten the goat in the sanctuary area, as I commanded."

19Aaron replied to Moses, "Today they sacrificed their sin offering and their burnt offering before the LORD, but such things as this have happened to me. Would the LORD have been pleased if I had eaten the sin offering today?" 20When Moses heard this, he was satisfied.

Clean and Unclean Food

11 THE LORD said to Moses and Aaron, 2"Say to the Israelites: 'Of all the animals that live on land, these are the ones you may eat: 3You may eat any animal that has a split hoof completely divided and that chews the cud.

4" 'There are some that only chew the cud or only have a split hoof, but you must not eat them. The camel, though it chews the cud, does not have a split hoof; it is ceremonially unclean for you. 5The coney,a though it chews the cud, does not have a split hoof; it is unclean for you. 6The rabbit, though it chews the cud, does not have a split hoof; it is unclean for you. 7And the pig, though it has a split hoof completely divided, does not chew the cud; it is unclean for you. 8You must not eat their meat or touch their carcasses; they are unclean for you.

9" 'Of all the creatures living in the water of the seas and the streams, you may eat any that have fins and scales. 10But all creatures in the seas or streams that do not have fins and scales—whether among all the swarming things or among all the other living creatures in the water—you are to detest. 11And since you are to detest them, you must not eat their meat and you must detest their carcasses. 12Anything living in the water that does not have fins and scales is to be detestable to you.

13" 'These are the birds you are to detest and not eat because they are detestable: the eagle, the vulture, the black vulture, 14the red kite, any kind of black kite, 15any kind of raven, 16the horned owl, the screech owl, the gull, any kind of hawk, 17the little owl, the cormorant, the great owl, 18the white owl, the desert owl, the osprey, 19the stork, any kind of heron, the hoopoe and the bat.b

20" 'All flying insects that walk on all fours are to be detestable to you. 21There are, however, some winged

---

a *5* That is, the hyrax or rock badger   b *19* The precise identification of some of the birds, insects and animals in this chapter is uncertain.

Living Bible

15"The people are to bring the thigh that was set aside, along with the breast that was offered when the fat was burned, and they shall be presented before the Lord by the gesture of waving them. And afterwards they shall belong to you and your family, for the Lord has commanded this."

16Then Moses searched everywhere for the goat of the sin offering and discovered that it had been burned! He was very angry about this with Eleazar and Ithamar, the remaining sons of Aaron.

17"Why haven't you eaten the sin offering in the sanctuary, since it is most holy, and God has given it to you to take away the iniquity and guilt of the people, to make atonement for them before the Lord?" he demanded. 18"Since its blood was not taken inside the sanctuary, you should certainly have eaten it there, as I ordered you."

19But Aaron interceded with Moses. "They offered their sin offering and burnt offering before the Lord," he said, "but if I had eaten the sin offering on such a day as this, would it have pleased the Lord?" 20And when Moses heard that, he was satisfied.

11 THEN THE Lord said to Moses and Aaron, 2,3"Tell the people of Israel that the animals which may be used for food include any animal with cloven hooves which chews its cud. 4-7This means that the following may *not* be eaten:

The camel (it chews the cud but does not have cloven hooves);

The coney, or rock badger (because although it chews the cud, it does not have cloven hooves);

The hare (because although it chews the cud, it does not have cloven hooves);

The swine (because although it has cloven hooves, it does not chew the cud).

8"You may not eat their meat or even touch their dead bodies; they are forbidden foods for you.

9"As to fish, you may eat whatever has fins and scales, whether taken from rivers or from the sea; 10but all other water creatures are strictly forbidden to you. 11You mustn't eat their meat or even touch their dead bodies. 12I'll repeat it again—any water creature that does not have fins or scales is forbidden to you.

13-19"Among the birds, these are the ones you may *not* eat:

The eagle, the metire, the osprey,
The falcon (all kinds), the kite,
The raven (all kinds), the ostrich,
The nighthawk, the seagull,
The hawk (all kinds), the owl,
The cormorant, the ibis,
The marsh hen,
The pelican,
The vulture, the stork,
The heron (all kinds),
The hoopoe, the bat.

20"No insects may be eaten, 21, 22with the exception

New Revised Standard

thigh that is raised and the breast that is elevated they shall bring, together with the offerings by fire of the fat, to raise for an elevation offering before the Lord; they are to be your due and that of your children forever, as the Lord has commanded.

16 Then Moses made inquiry about the goat of the sin offering, and—it had already been burned! He was angry with Eleazar and Ithamar, Aaron's remaining sons, and said, 17"Why did you not eat the sin offering in the sacred area? For it is most holy, and Godc has given it to you that you may remove the guilt of the congregation, to make atonement on their behalf before the Lord. 18Its blood was not brought into the inner part of the sanctuary. You should certainly have eaten it in the sanctuary, as I commanded." 19And Aaron spoke to Moses, "See, today they offered their sin offering and their burnt offering before the Lord; and yet such things as these have befallen me! If I had eaten the sin offering today, would it have been agreeable to the Lord?" 20And when Moses heard that, he agreed.

Clean and Unclean Foods

11 THE LORD spoke to Moses and Aaron, saying to them: 2Speak to the people of Israel, saying:

From among all the land animals, these are the creatures that you may eat. 3Any animal that has divided hoofs and is cleft-footed and chews the cud—such you may eat. 4But among those that chew the cud or have divided hoofs, you shall not eat the following: the camel, for even though it chews the cud, it does not have divided hoofs; it is unclean for you. 5The rock badger, for even though it chews the cud, it does not have divided hoofs; it is unclean for you. 6The hare, for even though it chews the cud, it does not have divided hoofs; it is unclean for you. 7The pig, for even though it has divided hoofs and is cleft-footed, it does not chew the cud; it is unclean for you. 8Of their flesh you shall not eat, and their carcasses you shall not touch; they are unclean for you.

9 These you may eat, of all that are in the waters. Everything in the waters that has fins and scales, whether in the seas or in the streams—such you may eat. 10But anything in the seas or the streams that does not have fins and scales, of the swarming creatures in the waters and among all the other living creatures that are in the waters—they are detestable to you 11and detestable they shall remain. Of their flesh you shall not eat, and their carcasses you shall regard as detestable. 12Everything in the waters that does not have fins and scales is detestable to you.

13 These you shall regard as detestable among the birds. They shall not be eaten; they are an abomination: the eagle, the vulture, the osprey, 14the buzzard, the kite of any kind; 15every raven of any kind; 16the ostrich, the nighthawk, the sea gull, the hawk of any kind; 17the little owl, the cormorant, the great owl, 18the water hen, the desert owl,d the carrion vulture, 19the stork, the heron of any kind, the hoopoe, and the bat.e

20 All winged insects that walk upon all fours are detestable to you. 21But among the winged insects that

c Heb *he*   d Or *pelican*   e Identification of several of the birds in verses 13-19 is uncertain

King James

21Yet these may ye eat of every flying creeping thing that goeth upon *all* four, which have legs above their feet, to leap withal upon the earth;

22*Even* these of them ye may eat; the locust after his kind, and the bald locust after his kind, and the beetle after his kind, and the grasshopper after his kind.

23But all *other* flying creeping things, which have four feet, *shall be* an abomination unto you.

24And for these ye shall be unclean: whosoever toucheth the carcase of them shall be unclean until the even.

25And whosoever beareth *aught* of the carcase of them shall wash his clothes, and be unclean until the even.

26*The carcases* of every beast which divideth the hoof, and *is* not clovenfooted, nor cheweth the cud, *are* unclean unto you: every one that toucheth them shall be unclean.

27And whatsoever goeth upon his paws, among all manner of beasts that go on *all* four, those *are* unclean unto you: whoso toucheth their carcase shall be unclean until the even.

28And he that beareth the carcase of them shall wash his clothes, and be unclean until the even: they *are* unclean unto you.

29¶ These also *shall be* unclean unto you among the creeping things that creep upon the earth; the weasel, and the mouse, and the tortoise after his kind,

30And the ferret, and the chameleon, and the lizard, and the snail, and the mole.

31These *are* unclean to you among all that creep: whosoever doth touch them, when they be dead, shall be unclean until the even.

32And upon whatsoever *any* of them, when they are dead, doth fall, it shall be unclean; whether *it be* any vessel of wood, or raiment, or skin, or sack, whatsoever vessel *it be*, wherein *any* work is done, it must be put into water, and it shall be unclean until the even; so it shall be cleansed.

33And every earthen vessel, whereinto *any* of them falleth, whatsoever *is* in it shall be unclean; and ye shall break it.

34Of all meat which may be eaten, *that* on which *such* water cometh shall be unclean: and all drink that may be drunk in every *such* vessel shall be unclean.

35And every *thing* whereupon *any part* of their carcase falleth shall be unclean; *whether it be* oven, or ranges for pots, they shall be broken down: *for* they *are* unclean, and shall be unclean unto you.

36Nevertheless a fountain or pit, *wherein there is* plenty of water, shall be clean: but that which toucheth their carcase shall be unclean.

37And if *any part* of their carcase fall upon any sowing seed which is to be sown, it *shall be* clean.

38But if *any* water be put upon the seed, and *any part* of their carcase fall thereon, it *shall be* unclean unto you.

39And if any beast, of which ye may eat, die; he that toucheth the carcase thereof shall be unclean until the even.

40And he that eateth of the carcase of it shall wash his clothes, and be unclean until the even: he also that beareth the carcase of it shall wash his clothes, and be unclean until the even.

41And every creeping thing that creepeth upon the earth *shall be* an abomination; it shall not be eaten.

42Whatsoever goeth upon the belly, and whatsoever goeth upon *all* four, or whatsoever hath more feet among all creeping things that creep upon the earth, them ye shall not eat; for they *are* an abomination.

43Ye shall not make your selves abominable with any creeping thing that creepeth, neither shall ye make yourselves unclean with them, that ye should be defiled thereby.

New International

creatures that walk on all fours that you may eat: those that have jointed legs for hopping on the ground. 22Of these you may eat any kind of locust, katydid, cricket or grasshopper. 23But all other winged creatures that have four legs you are to detest.

24" 'You will make yourselves unclean by these; whoever touches their carcasses will be unclean till evening. 25Whoever picks up one of their carcasses must wash his clothes, and he will be unclean till evening.

26" 'Every animal that has a split hoof not completely divided or that does not chew the cud is unclean for you; whoever touches the carcass of any of them will be unclean. 27Of all the animals that walk on all fours, those that walk on their paws are unclean for you; whoever touches their carcasses will be unclean till evening. 28Anyone who picks up their carcasses must wash his clothes, and he will be unclean till evening. They are unclean for you.

29" 'Of the animals that move about on the ground, these are unclean for you: the weasel, the rat, any kind of great lizard, 30the gecko, the monitor lizard, the wall lizard, the skink and the chameleon. 31Of all those that move along the ground, these are unclean for you. Whoever touches them when they are dead will be unclean till evening. 32When one of them dies and falls on something, that article, whatever its use, will be unclean, whether it is made of wood, cloth, hide or sackcloth. Put it in water; it will be unclean till evening, and then it will be clean. 33If one of them falls into a clay pot, everything in it will be unclean, and you must break the pot. 34Any food that could be eaten but has water on it from such a pot is unclean, and any liquid that could be drunk from it is unclean. 35Anything that one of their carcasses falls on becomes unclean; an oven or cooking pot must be broken up. They are unclean, and you are to regard them as unclean. 36A spring, however, or a cistern for collecting water remains clean, but anyone who touches one of these carcasses is unclean. 37If a carcass falls on any seeds that are to be planted, they remain clean. 38But if water has been put on the seed and a carcass falls on it, it is unclean for you.

39" 'If an animal that you are allowed to eat dies, anyone who touches the carcass will be unclean till evening. 40Anyone who eats some of the carcass must wash his clothes, and he will be unclean till evening. Anyone who picks up the carcass must wash his clothes, and he will be unclean till evening.

41" 'Every creature that moves about on the ground is detestable; it is not to be eaten. 42You are not to eat any creature that moves about on the ground, whether it moves on its belly or walks on all fours or on many feet; it is detestable. 43Do not defile yourselves by any of these creatures. Do not make yourselves unclean by means of them or be made unclean by them. 44I am the

Living Bible

of those that jump; locusts of all varieties—ordinary locusts, bald locusts, crickets, and grasshoppers—may be eaten. 23All insects that fly and walk or crawl are forbidden to you.

24"Anyone touching their dead bodies shall be defiled until the evening, 25and must wash his clothes immediately. He must also quarantine himself until nightfall, as being ceremonially defiled.

26"You are also defiled by touching any animal with only semi-parted hoofs, or any animal that does not chew the cud. 27Any animal that walks on paws is forbidden to you as food. Anyone touching the dead body of such an animal shall be defiled until evening. 28Anyone carrying away the carcass shall wash his clothes and be ceremonially defiled until evening; for it is forbidden to you.

29, 30"These are the forbidden small animals which scurry about your feet or crawl upon the ground:

The mole, the rat,
The great lizard, the gecko,
The mouse, the lizard,
The snail, the chameleon.

31"Anyone touching their dead bodies shall be defiled until evening, 32and anything upon which the carcass falls shall be defiled—any article of wood, or of clothing, a rug, or a sack; anything it touches must be put into water, and is defiled until evening. After that it may be used again. 33If it falls into a pottery bowl, anything in the bowl is defiled, and you shall smash the bowl. 34If the water used to cleanse the defiled article touches any food, all of it is defiled. Any drink which is in the defiled bowl is also contaminated.

35"If the dead body of such an animal touches any clay oven, it is defiled and must be smashed. 36If the body falls into a spring or cistern where there is water, that water is not defiled; yet anyone who pulls out the carcass is defiled. 37And if the carcass touches grain to be sown in the field, it is not contaminated; 38but if the seeds are wet and the carcass falls upon it, the seed is defiled.

39"If an animal which you are permitted to eat dies of disease, anyone touching the carcass shall be defiled until evening. 40Also, anyone eating its meat or carrying away its carcass shall wash his clothes and be defiled until evening.

41, 42"Animals that crawl shall not be eaten. This includes all reptiles that slither along upon their bellies as well as those that have legs. No crawling thing with many feet may be eaten, for it is defiled. 43Do not defile yourselves by touching it.

New Revised Standard

walk on all fours you may eat those that have jointed legs above their feet, with which to leap on the ground. 22Of them you may eat: the locust according to its kind, the bald locust according to its kind, the cricket according to its kind, and the grasshopper according to its kind. 23But all other winged insects that have four feet are detestable to you.

Unclean Animals

24 By these you shall become unclean; whoever touches the carcass of any of them shall be unclean until the evening, 25and whoever carries any part of the carcass of any of them shall wash his clothes and be unclean until the evening. 26Every animal that has divided hoofs but is not cleft-footed or does not chew the cud is unclean for you; everyone who touches one of them shall be unclean. 27All that walk on their paws, among the animals that walk on all fours, are unclean for you; whoever touches the carcass of any of them shall be unclean until the evening, 28and the one who carries the carcass shall wash his clothes and be unclean until the evening; they are unclean for you.

29 These are unclean for you among the creatures that swarm upon the earth: the weasel, the mouse, the great lizard according to its kind, 30the gecko, the land crocodile, the lizard, the sand lizard, and the chameleon. 31These are unclean for you among all that swarm; whoever touches one of them when they are dead shall be unclean until the evening. 32And anything upon which any of them falls when they are dead shall be unclean, whether an article of wood or cloth or skin or sacking, any article that is used for any purpose; it shall be dipped into water, and it shall be unclean until the evening, and then it shall be clean. 33And if any of them falls into any earthen vessel, all that is in it shall be unclean, and you shall break the vessel. 34Any food that could be eaten shall be unclean if water from any such vessel comes upon it; and any liquid that could be drunk shall be unclean if it was in any such vessel. 35Everything on which any part of the carcass falls shall be unclean; whether an oven or stove, it shall be broken in pieces; they are unclean, and shall remain unclean for you. 36But a spring or a cistern holding water shall be clean, while whatever touches the carcass in it shall be unclean. 37If any part of their carcass falls upon any seed set aside for sowing, it is clean; 38but if water is put on the seed and any part of their carcass falls on it, it is unclean for you.

39 If an animal of which you may eat dies, anyone who touches its carcass shall be unclean until the evening. 40Those who eat of its carcass shall wash their clothes and be unclean until the evening; and those who carry the carcass shall wash their clothes and be unclean until the evening.

41 All creatures that swarm upon the earth are detestable; they shall not be eaten. 42Whatever moves on its belly, and whatever moves on all fours, or whatever has many feet, all the creatures that swarm upon the earth, you shall not eat; for they are detestable. 43You shall not make yourselves detestable with any creature that swarms; you shall not defile yourselves with them, and so become unclean. 44For I am the LORD your God;

King James

44For I *am* the LORD your God: ye shall therefore sanctify yourselves, and ye shall be holy; for I *am* holy: neither shall ye defile yourselves with any manner of creeping thing that creepeth upon the earth.

45For I *am* the LORD that bringeth you up out of the land of Egypt, to be your God: ye shall therefore be holy, for I *am* holy.

46This *is* the law of the beasts, and of the fowl, and of every living creature that moveth in the waters, and of every creature that creepeth upon the earth:

47To make a difference between the unclean and the clean, and between the beast that may be eaten and the beast that may not be eaten.

12 AND THE LORD spake unto Moses, saying, 2Speak unto the children of Israel, saying, If a woman have conceived seed, and born a man child: then she shall be unclean seven days; according to the days of the separation for her infirmity shall she be unclean.

3And in the eighth day the flesh of his foreskin shall be circumcised.

4And she shall then continue in the blood of her purifying three and thirty days; she shall touch no hallowed thing, nor come into the sanctuary, until the days of her purifying be fulfilled.

5But if she bear a maid child, then she shall be unclean two weeks, as in her separation: and she shall continue in the blood of her purifying threescore and six days.

6And when the days of her purifying are fulfilled, for a son, or for a daughter, she shall bring a lamb of the first year for a burnt offering, and a young pigeon, or a turtledove, for a sin offering, unto the door of the tabernacle of the congregation, unto the priest:

7Who shall offer it before the LORD, and make an atonement for her; and she shall be cleansed from the issue of her blood. This *is* the law for her that hath born a male or a female.

8And if she be not able to bring a lamb, then she shall bring two turtles, or two young pigeons; the one for the burnt offering, and the other for a sin offering: and the priest shall make an atonement for her, and she shall be clean.

13 AND THE LORD spake unto Moses and Aaron, saying,

2When a man shall have in the skin of his flesh a rising, a scab, or bright spot, and it be in the skin of his flesh *like* the plague of leprosy; then he shall be brought unto Aaron the priest, or unto one of his sons the priests:

3And the priest shall look on the plague in the skin of the flesh: and *when* the hair in the plague is turned white, and the plague in sight *be* deeper than the skin of his flesh, it *is* a plague of leprosy: and the priest shall look on him, and pronounce him unclean.

4If the bright spot *be* white in the skin of his flesh, and in sight *be* not deeper than the skin, and the hair thereof be not turned white; then the priest shall shut up *him that hath* the plague seven days:

5And the priest shall look on him the seventh day: and, behold, *if* the plague in his sight be at a stay, *and* the plague spread not in the skin; then the priest shall shut him up seven days more:

6And the priest shall look on him again the seventh day: and, behold, *if* the plague *be* somewhat dark, *and* the plague spread not in the skin, the priest shall pronounce him clean: it *is but* a scab: and he shall wash his clothes, and be clean.

New International

LORD your God; consecrate yourselves and be holy, because I am holy. Do not make yourselves unclean by any creature that moves about on the ground. 45I am the LORD who brought you up out of Egypt to be your God; therefore be holy, because I am holy.

46" 'These are the regulations concerning animals, birds, every living thing that moves in the water and every creature that moves about on the ground. 47You must distinguish between the unclean and the clean, between living creatures that may be eaten and those that may not be eaten.' "

Purification After Childbirth

12 THE LORD said to Moses, 2"Say to the Israelites: 'A woman who becomes pregnant and gives birth to a son will be ceremonially unclean for seven days, just as she is unclean during her monthly period. 3On the eighth day the boy is to be circumcised. 4Then the woman must wait thirty-three days to be purified from her bleeding. She must not touch anything sacred or go to the sanctuary until the days of her purification are over. 5If she gives birth to a daughter, for two weeks the woman will be unclean, as during her period. Then she must wait sixty-six days to be purified from her bleeding.

6" 'When the days of her purification for a son or daughter are over, she is to bring to the priest at the entrance to the Tent of Meeting a year-old lamb for a burnt offering and a young pigeon or a dove for a sin offering. 7He shall offer them before the LORD to make atonement for her, and then she will be ceremonially clean from her flow of blood.

" 'These are the regulations for the woman who gives birth to a boy or a girl. 8If she cannot afford a lamb, she is to bring two doves or two young pigeons, one for a burnt offering and the other for a sin offering. In this way the priest will make atonement for her, and she will be clean.' "

Regulations About Infectious Skin Diseases

13 THE LORD said to Moses and Aaron, 2"When anyone has a swelling or a rash or a bright spot on his skin that may become an infectious skin disease,a he must be brought to Aaron the priest or to one of his sonsb who is a priest. 3The priest is to examine the sore on his skin, and if the hair in the sore has turned white and the sore appears to be more than skin deep,c it is an infectious skin disease. When the priest examines him, he shall pronounce him ceremonially unclean. 4If the spot on his skin is white but does not appear to be more than skin deep and the hair in it has not turned white, the priest is to put the infected person in isolation for seven days. 5On the seventh day the priest is to examine him, and if he sees that the sore is unchanged and has not spread in the skin, he is to keep him in isolation another seven days. 6On the seventh day the priest is to examine him again, and if the sore has faded and has not spread in the skin, the priest shall pronounce him clean; it is only a rash. The man must wash his clothes, and he will be clean. 7But if the rash does spread

---

a 2 Traditionally *leprosy*; the Hebrew word was used for various diseases affecting the skin—not necessarily leprosy; also elsewhere in this chapter.
b 2 Or *descendants*   c 3 Or *be lower than the rest of the skin*; also elsewhere in this chapter

Living Bible

44"I am the Lord your God. Keep yourselves pure concerning these things, and be holy, for I am holy; therefore do not defile yourselves by touching any of these things that crawl upon the earth. 45For I am the Lord who brought you out of the land of Egypt to be your God. You must therefore be holy, for I am holy." 46These are the laws concerning animals, birds, and whatever swims in the water or crawls upon the ground. 47These are the distinctions between what is ceremonially clean and may be eaten, and what is ceremonially defiled and may not be eaten, among all animal life upon the earth.

12 THE LORD told Moses to give these instructions to the people of Israel:
2"When a baby boy is born, the mother shall be ceremonially defiled for seven days, and under the same restrictions as during her monthly menstrual periods. 3On the eighth day, her son must be circumcised. 4Then, for the next thirty-three days, while she is recovering from her ceremonial impurity, she must not touch anything sacred, nor enter the Tabernacle.
5"When a baby girl is born, the mother's ceremonial impurity shall last two weeks, during which time she will be under the same restrictions as during menstruation. Then for a further sixty-six days she shall continue her recovery.d
6"When these days of purification are ended (the following instructions are applicable whether her baby is a boy or girl), she must bring a yearling lamb as a burnt offering, and a young pigeon or a turtledove for a sin offering.
"She must take them to the door of the Tabernacle to the priest; 7and the priest will offer them before the Lord and make atonement for her; then she will be ceremonially clean again after her bleeding at childbirth.
"These then, are the procedures after childbirth. 8But if she is too poor to bring a lamb, then she must bring two turtledoves or two young pigeons. One will be for a burnt offering and the other for a sin offering. The priest will make atonement for her with these, so that she will be ceremonially pure again."

13 THE LORD said to Moses and Aaron, "If anyone notices a swelling in his skin, or a scab or boil or pimple with transparent skin, leprosy is to be suspected. He must be brought to Aaron the priest or to one of his sons 3for the spot to be examined. If the hair in this spot turns white, and if the spot looks to be more than skin-deep, it is leprosy, and the priest must declare him a leper.e
4"But if the white spot in the skin does not seem to be deeper than the skin, and the hair in the spot has not turned white, the priest shall quarantine him for seven days. 5At the end of that time, on the seventh day, the priest will examine him again, and if the spot has not changed and has not spread in the skin, then the priest must quarantine him seven days more. 6Again on the seventh day the priest will examine him, and if the marks of the disease have become fainter and have not spread, then the priest shall pronounce him cured; it was only a scab, and the man need only wash his clothes and everything will be normal again. 7But if the spot spreads

New Revised Standard

sanctify yourselves therefore, and be holy, for I am holy. You shall not defile yourselves with any swarming creature that moves on the earth. 45For I am the LORD who brought you up from the land of Egypt, to be your God; you shall be holy, for I am holy.
46 This is the law pertaining to land animal and bird and every living creature that moves through the waters and every creature that swarms upon the earth, 47to make a distinction between the unclean and the clean, and between the living creature that may be eaten and the living creature that may not be eaten.

Purification of Women after Childbirth

12 THE LORD spoke to Moses, saying: 2Speak to the people of Israel, saying:
If a woman conceives and bears a male child, she shall be ceremonially unclean seven days; as at the time of her menstruation, she shall be unclean. 3On the eighth day the flesh of his foreskin shall be circumcised. 4Her time of blood purification shall be thirty-three days; she shall not touch any holy thing, or come into the sanctuary, until the days of her purification are completed. 5If she bears a female child, she shall be unclean two weeks, as in her menstruation; her time of blood purification shall be sixty-six days.
6 When the days of her purification are completed, whether for a son or for a daughter, she shall bring to the priest at the entrance of the tent of meeting a lamb in its first year for a burnt offering, and a pigeon or a turtledove for a sin offering. 7He shall offer it before the LORD, and make atonement on her behalf; then she shall be clean from her flow of blood. This is the law for her who bears a child, male or female. 8If she cannot afford a sheep, she shall take two turtledoves or two pigeons, one for a burnt offering and the other for a sin offering; and the priest shall make atonement on her behalf, and she shall be clean.

Leprosy, Varieties and Symptoms

13 THE LORD spoke to Moses and Aaron, saying:
2 When a person has on the skin of his body a swelling or an eruption or a spot, and it turns into a leprousf disease on the skin of his body, he shall be brought to Aaron the priest or to one of his sons the priests. 3The priest shall examine the disease on the skin of his body, and if the hair in the diseased area has turned white and the disease appears to be deeper than the skin of his body, it is a leprousf disease; after the priest has examined him he shall pronounce him ceremonially unclean. 4But if the spot is white in the skin of his body, and appears no deeper than the skin, and the hair in it has not turned white, the priest shall confine the diseased person for seven days. 5The priest shall examine him on the seventh day, and if he sees that the disease is checked and the disease has not spread in the skin, then the priest shall confine him seven days more. 6The priest shall examine him again on the seventh day, and if the disease has abated and the disease has not spread in the skin, the priest shall pronounce him clean; it is only an eruption; and he shall wash his clothes, and be clean. 7But if the

---

d 12:5 shall continue her recovery, literally, "shall continue in her blood of purification." e 13:3 must declare him a leper, literally, "shall declare him unclean."

f A term for several skin diseases; precise meaning uncertain

King James

7But if the scab spread much abroad in the skin, after that he hath been seen of the priest for his cleansing, he shall be seen of the priest again:

8And *if* the priest see that, behold, the scab spreadeth in the skin, then the priest shall pronounce him unclean: it *is* a leprosy.

9¶ When the plague of leprosy is in a man, then he shall be brought unto the priest;

10And the priest shall see *him:* and, behold, *if* the rising *be* white in the skin, and it have turned the hair white, and *there be* quick raw flesh in the rising;

11It is an old leprosy in the skin of his flesh, and the priest shall pronounce him unclean, and shall not shut him up: for he *is* unclean.

12And if a leprosy break out abroad in the skin, and the leprosy cover all the skin of *him that hath* the plague from his head even to his foot, wheresoever the priest looketh;

13Then the priest shall consider: and, behold, *if* the leprosy have covered all his flesh, he shall pronounce *him clean that hath* the plague: it is all turned white: he *is* clean.

14But when raw flesh appeareth in him, he shall be unclean.

15And the priest shall see the raw flesh, and pronounce him to be unclean: *for* the raw flesh *is* unclean: it *is* a leprosy.

16Or if the raw flesh turn again, and be changed unto white, he shall come unto the priest;

17And the priest shall see him: and, behold, *if* the plague be turned into white; then the priest shall pronounce *him clean that hath* the plague: he *is* clean.

18¶ The flesh also, in which, *even* in the skin thereof, was a boil, and is healed,

19And in the place of the boil there be a white rising, or a bright spot, white, and somewhat reddish, and it be shown to the priest;

20And if, when the priest seeth it, behold, it *be* in sight lower than the skin, and the hair thereof be turned white; the priest shall pronounce him unclean: it *is* a plague of leprosy broken out of the boil.

21But if the priest look on it, and, behold, *there be* no white hairs therein, and *if* it *be* not lower than the skin, but *be* somewhat dark; then the priest shall shut him up seven days:

22And if it spread much abroad in the skin, then the priest shall pronounce him unclean: it *is* a plague.

23But if the bright spot stay in his place, *and* spread not, it *is* a burning boil; and the priest shall pronounce him clean.

24¶ Or if there be *any* flesh, in the skin whereof *there is* a hot burning, and the quick *flesh* that burneth have a white bright spot, somewhat reddish, or white;

25Then the priest shall look upon it: and, behold, *if* the hair in the bright spot be turned white, and it *be in* sight deeper than the skin; it *is* a leprosy broken out of the burning: wherefore the priest shall pronounce him unclean: it *is* the plague of leprosy.

26But if the priest look on it, and, behold, *there be* no white hair in the bright spot, and it *be* no lower than the *other* skin, but *be* somewhat dark; then the priest shall shut him up seven days:

27And the priest shall look upon him the seventh day: *and* if it be spread much abroad in the skin, then the priest shall pronounce him unclean: it *is* the plague of leprosy.

28And if the bright spot stay in his place, *and* spread not in the skin, but it *be* somewhat dark; it *is* a rising of the burning, and the priest shall pronounce him clean: for it *is* an inflammation of the burning.

New International

in his skin after he has shown himself to the priest to be pronounced clean, he must appear before the priest again. 8The priest is to examine him, and if the rash has spread in the skin, he shall pronounce him unclean; it is an infectious disease.

9"When anyone has an infectious skin disease, he must be brought to the priest. 10The priest is to examine him, and if there is a white swelling in the skin that has turned the hair white and if there is raw flesh in the swelling, 11it is a chronic skin disease and the priest shall pronounce him unclean. He is not to put him in isolation, because he is already unclean.

12"If the disease breaks out all over his skin and, so far as the priest can see, it covers all the skin of the infected person from head to foot, 13the priest is to examine him, and if the disease has covered his whole body, he shall pronounce that person clean. Since it has all turned white, he is clean. 14But whenever raw flesh appears on him, he will be unclean. 15When the priest sees the raw flesh, he shall pronounce him unclean. The raw flesh is unclean; he has an infectious disease. 16Should the raw flesh change and turn white, he must go to the priest. 17The priest is to examine him, and if the sores have turned white, the priest shall pronounce the infected person clean; then he will be clean.

18"When someone has a boil on his skin and it heals, 19and in the place where the boil was, a white swelling or reddish-white spot appears, he must present himself to the priest. 20The priest is to examine it, and if it appears to be more than skin deep and the hair in it has turned white, the priest shall pronounce him unclean. It is an infectious skin disease that has broken out where the boil was. 21But if, when the priest examines it, there is no white hair in it and it is not more than skin deep and has faded, then the priest is to put him in isolation for seven days. 22If it is spreading in the skin, the priest shall pronounce him unclean; it is infectious. 23But if the spot is unchanged and has not spread, it is only a scar from the boil, and the priest shall pronounce him clean.

24"When someone has a burn on his skin and a reddish-white or white spot appears in the raw flesh of the burn, 25the priest is to examine the spot, and if the hair in it has turned white, and it appears to be more than skin deep, it is an infectious disease that has broken out in the burn. The priest shall pronounce him unclean; it is an infectious skin disease. 26But if the priest examines it and there is no white hair in the spot and if it is not more than skin deep and has faded, then the priest is to put him in isolation for seven days. 27On the seventh day the priest is to examine him, and if it is spreading in the skin, the priest shall pronounce him unclean; it is an infectious skin disease. 28If, however, the spot is unchanged and has not spread in the skin but has faded, it is a swelling from the burn, and the priest shall pronounce him clean; it is only a scar from the burn.

Living Bible

in the skin after he has come to the priest to be examined, he must come back to the priest again, 8and the priest shall look again, and if the spot has spread, then the priest must pronounce him a leper.

9, 10"When anyone suspected of having leprosy is brought to the priest, the priest is to look to see if there is a white swelling in the skin with white hairs in the spot, and an ulcer developing. 11If he finds these symptoms, it is an established case of leprosy, and the priest must pronounce him defiled. The man is not to be quarantined for further observation, for he is definitely diseased. 12But if the priest sees that the leprosy has erupted and spread all over his body from head to foot wherever he looks, 13then the priest shall pronounce him cured of leprosy, for it has all turned white; he is cured. 14, 15But if there is raw flesh anywhere, the man shall be declared a leper. It is proved by the raw flesh. 16, 17But if the raw flesh later changes to white, the leper will return to the priest to be examined again. If the spot has indeed turned completely white, then the priest will pronounce him cured.

18"In the case of a man who has a boil in his skin which heals, 19but which leaves a white swelling or a bright spot, sort of reddish white, the man must go to the priest for examination. 20If the priest sees that the trouble seems to be down under the skin, and if the hair at the spot has turned white, then the priest shall declare him defiled, for leprosy has broken out from the boil. 21But if the priest sees that there are no white hairs in this spot, and the spot does not appear to be deeper than the skin, and if the color is gray, then the priest shall quarantine him for seven days. 22If during that time the spot spreads, the priest must declare him a leper. 23But if the bright spot grows no larger and does not spread, it is merely the scar from the boil, and the priest shall declare that all is well.

24"If a man is burned in some way, and the burned place becomes bright reddish white or white, 25then the priest must examine the spot. If the hair in the bright spot turns white, and the problem seems to be more than skin-deep, it is leprosy that has broken out from the burn, and the priest must pronounce him a leper.a 26But if the priest sees that there are no white hairs in the bright spot, and the brightness appears to be no deeper than the skin and is fading, the priest shall quarantine him for seven days, 27and examine him again the seventh day. If the spot spreads in the skin, the priest must pronounce him a leper. 28But if the bright spot does not move or spread in the skin, and is fading, it is simply a scar from the burn, and the priest shall declare that he does not have leprosy.

New Revised Standard

eruption spreads in the skin after he has shown himself to the priest for his cleansing, he shall appear again before the priest. 8 The priest shall make an examination, and if the eruption has spread in the skin, the priest shall pronounce him unclean; it is a leprousb disease.

9 When a person contracts a leprousb disease, he shall be brought to the priest. 10 The priest shall make an examination, and if there is a white swelling in the skin that has turned the hair white, and there is quick raw flesh in the swelling, 11 it is a chronic leprousb disease in the skin of his body. The priest shall pronounce him unclean; he shall not confine him, for he is unclean. 12 But if the disease breaks out in the skin, so that it covers all the skin of the diseased person from head to foot, so far as the priest can see, 13 then the priest shall make an examination, and if the disease has covered all his body, he shall pronounce him clean of the disease; since it has all turned white, he is clean. 14 But if raw flesh ever appears on him, he shall be unclean; 15 the priest shall examine the raw flesh and pronounce him unclean. Raw flesh is unclean, for it is a leprousb disease. 16 But if the raw flesh again turns white, he shall come to the priest; 17 the priest shall examine him, and if the disease has turned white, the priest shall pronounce the diseased person clean. He is clean.

18 When there is on the skin of one's body a boil that has healed, 19 and in the place of the boil there appears a white swelling or a reddish-white spot, it shall be shown to the priest. 20 The priest shall make an examination, and if it appears deeper than the skin and its hair has turned white, the priest shall pronounce him unclean; this is a leprousb disease, broken out in the boil. 21 But if the priest examines it and the hair on it is not white, nor is it deeper than the skin but has abated, the priest shall confine him seven days. 22 If it spreads in the skin, the priest shall pronounce him unclean; it is diseased. 23 But if the spot remains in one place and does not spread, it is the scar of the boil; the priest shall pronounce him clean.

24 Or, when the body has a burn on the skin and the raw flesh of the burn becomes a spot, reddish-white or white, 25 the priest shall examine it. If the hair in the spot has turned white and it appears deeper than the skin, it is a leprousb disease; it has broken out in the burn, and the priest shall pronounce him unclean. This is a leprousb disease. 26 But if the priest examines it and the hair in the spot is not white, and it is no deeper than the skin but has abated, the priest shall confine him seven days. 27 The priest shall examine him the seventh day; if it is spreading in the skin, the priest shall pronounce him unclean. This is a leprousb disease. 28 But if the spot remains in one place and does not spread in the skin but has abated, it is a swelling from the burn, and the priest shall pronounce him clean; for it is the scar of the burn.

---

a 13:25 must pronounce him a leper, literally, "pronounce him unclean." Also vs 27.

b A term for several skin diseases; precise meaning uncertain

King James

29¶ If a man or woman have a plague upon the head or the beard;

30Then the priest shall see the plague: and, behold, if it *be* in sight deeper than the skin; *and there be* in it a yellow thin hair; then the priest shall pronounce him unclean: it *is* a dry scall, *even* a leprosy upon the head or beard.

31And if the priest look on the plague of the scall, and, behold, it *be* not in sight deeper than the skin, and *that there is* no black hair in it; then the priest shall shut up *him that hath* the plague of the scall seven days:

32And in the seventh day the priest shall look on the plague: and, behold, *if* the scall spread not, and there be in it no yellow hair, and the scall *be* not in sight deeper than the skin;

33He shall be shaven, but the scall shall he not shave; and the priest shall shut up *him that hath* the scall seven days more:

34And in the seventh day the priest shall look on the scall: and, behold, *if* the scall *be* not spread in the skin, nor *be* in sight deeper than the skin; then the priest shall pronounce him clean: and he shall wash his clothes, and be clean.

35But if the scall spread much in the skin after his cleansing;

36Then the priest shall look on him: and, behold, if the scall *be* spread in the skin, the priest shall not seek for yellow hair; he *is* unclean.

37But if the scall be in his sight at a stay, and *that* there is black hair grown up therein; the scall is healed, he *is* clean: and the priest shall pronounce him clean.

38¶ If a man also or a woman have in the skin of their flesh bright spots, *even* white bright spots;

39Then the priest shall look: and, behold, *if* the bright spots in the skin of their flesh *be* darkish white; it *is* a freckled spot *that* groweth in the skin; he *is* clean.

40And the man whose hair is fallen off his head, he *is* bald; *yet is* he clean.

41And he that hath his hair fallen off from the part of his head toward his face, he *is* forehead bald: *yet is* he clean.

42And if there be in the bald head, or bald forehead, a white reddish sore; it *is* a leprosy sprung up in his bald head, or his bald forehead.

43Then the priest shall look upon it: and, behold, *if* the rising of the sore *be* white reddish in his bald head, or in his bald forehead, as the leprosy appeareth in the skin of the flesh;

44He is a leprous man, he *is* unclean: the priest shall pronounce him utterly unclean; his plague *is* in his head.

45And the leper in whom the plague *is*, his clothes shall be rent, and his head bare, and he shall put a covering upon his upper lip, and shall cry, Unclean, unclean.

46All the days wherein the plague *shall be* in him he shall be defiled; he *is* unclean: he shall dwell alone; without the camp *shall* his habitation *be*.

47¶ The garment also that the plague of leprosy is in, *whether it be* a woollen garment, or a linen garment;

48Whether *it be* in the warp, or woof; of linen, or of woollen; whether in a skin, or in any thing made of skin;

49And if the plague be greenish or reddish in the garment, or in the skin, either in the warp, or in the woof, or in any thing of skin; it *is* a plague of leprosy, and shall be shown unto the priest:

50And the priest shall look upon the plague, and shut up *it that hath* the plague seven days:

51And he shall look on the plague on the seventh day: if the plague be spread in the garment, either in the warp, or in the woof, or in a skin, *or* in any work that is made of skin; the plague *is* a fretting leprosy; it *is* unclean.

52He shall therefore burn that garment, whether warp or woof, in woollen or in linen, or any thing of skin, wherein the plague is: for it *is* a fretting leprosy; it shall be burnt in the fire.

New International

29"If a man or woman has a sore on the head or on the chin, 30the priest is to examine the sore, and if it appears to be more than skin deep and the hair in it is yellow and thin, the priest shall pronounce that person unclean; it is an itch, an infectious disease of the head or chin. 31But if, when the priest examines this kind of sore, it does not seem to be more than skin deep and there is no black hair in it, then the priest is to put the infected person in isolation for seven days. 32On the seventh day the priest is to examine the sore, and if the itch has not spread and there is no yellow hair in it and it does not appear to be more than skin deep, 33he must be shaved except for the diseased area, and the priest is to keep him in isolation another seven days. 34On the seventh day the priest is to examine the itch, and if it has not spread in the skin and appears to be no more than skin deep, the priest shall pronounce him clean. He must wash his clothes, and he will be clean. 35But if the itch does spread in the skin after he is pronounced clean, 36the priest is to examine him, and if the itch has spread in the skin, the priest does not need to look for yellow hair; the person is unclean. 37If, however, in his judgment it is unchanged and black hair has grown in it, the itch is healed. He is clean, and the priest shall pronounce him clean.

38"When a man or woman has white spots on the skin, 39the priest is to examine them, and if the spots are dull white, it is a harmless rash that has broken out on the skin; that person is clean.

40"When a man has lost his hair and is bald, he is clean. 41If he has lost his hair from the front of his scalp and has a bald forehead, he is clean. 42But if he has a reddish-white sore on his bald head or forehead, it is an infectious disease breaking out on his head or forehead. 43The priest is to examine him, and if the swollen sore on his head or forehead is reddish-white like an infectious skin disease, 44the man is diseased and is unclean. The priest shall pronounce him unclean because of the sore on his head.

45"The person with such an infectious disease must wear torn clothes, let his hair be unkempt,[a] cover the lower part of his face and cry out, 'Unclean! Unclean!' 46As long as he has the infection he remains unclean. He must live alone; he must live outside the camp.

Regulations About Mildew

47"If any clothing is contaminated with mildew—any woolen or linen clothing, 48any woven or knitted material of linen or wool, any leather or anything made of leather— 49and if the contamination in the clothing, or leather, or woven or knitted material, or any leather article, is greenish or reddish, it is a spreading mildew and must be shown to the priest. 50The priest is to examine the mildew and isolate the affected article for seven days. 51On the seventh day he is to examine it, and if the mildew has spread in the clothing, or the woven or knitted material, or the leather, whatever its use, it is a destructive mildew; the article is unclean. 52He must burn up the clothing, or the woven or knitted material of wool or linen, or any leather article that has the contamination in it, because the mildew is destructive; the article must be burned up.

---

a 45 Or *clothes, uncover his head*

Living Bible

29, 30"If a man or woman has a sore on the head or chin, the priest must examine him; if the infection seems to be below the skin and yellow hair is found in the sore, the priest must pronounce him a leper. 31But if the priest's examination reveals that the spot seems to be only in the skin but there is healthy hair in it, then he shall be quarantined for seven days, 32and examined again on the seventh day. If the spot has not spread and no yellow hair has appeared, and if the infection does not seem to be deeper than the skin, 33he shall shave off all the hair around the spot (but not on the spot itself) and the priest shall quarantine him for another seven days. 34He shall be examined again on the seventh day, and if the spot has not spread, and it appears to be no deeper than the skin, the priest shall pronounce him well, and after washing his clothes, he is free.b 35But if, later on, this spot begins to spread, 36then the priest must examine him again and, without waiting to see if any yellow hair develops, declare him a leper. 37But if it appears that the spreading has stopped and black hairs are found in the spot, then he is healed and is not a leper, and the priest shall declare him healed.

38"If a man or a woman has white, transparent areas in the skin, 39but these spots are growing dimmer, this is not leprosy, but an ordinary infection that has broken out in the skin.

40"If a man's hair is gone, this does not make him a leper even though he is bald! 41If the hair is gone from the front part of his head, he simply has a bald forehead, but this is not leprosy. 42However, if in the baldness there is a reddish white spot, it may be leprosy breaking out. 43In that case the priest shall examine him, and if there is a reddish white lump that looks like leprosy, 44then he is a leper, and the priest must pronounce him such.

45"Anyone who is discovered to have leprosy must tear his clothes and let his hair grow in wild disarray, and cover his upper lip and call out as he goes, "I am a leper, I am a leper."c 46As long as the disease lasts, he is defiled and must live outside the camp.

47, 48"If leprosy is suspected in a woolen or linen garment or fabric, or in a piece of leather or leather-work, 49and there is a greenish or a reddish spot in it, it is probably leprosy, and must be taken to the priest to be examined. 50The priest will put it away for seven days 51and look at it again on the seventh day. If the spot has spread, it is a contagious leprosy, 52and he must burn the clothing, fabric, linen or woolen covering, or leather article, for it is contagious and must be destroyed by fire.

New Revised Standard

29 When a man or woman has a disease on the head or in the beard, 30the priest shall examine the disease. If it appears deeper than the skin and the hair in it is yellow and thin, the priest shall pronounce him unclean; it is an itch, a leprousd disease of the head or the beard. 31If the priest examines the itching disease, and it appears no deeper than the skin and there is no black hair in it, the priest shall confine the person with the itching disease for seven days. 32On the seventh day the priest shall examine the itch; if the itch has not spread, and there is no yellow hair in it, and the itch appears to be no deeper than the skin, 33he shall shave, but the itch he shall not shave. The priest shall confine the person with the itch for seven days more. 34On the seventh day the priest shall examine the itch; if the itch has not spread in the skin and it appears to be no deeper than the skin, the priest shall pronounce him clean. He shall wash his clothes and be clean. 35But if the itch spreads in the skin after he was pronounced clean, 36the priest shall examine him. If the itch has spread in the skin, the priest need not seek for the yellow hair; he is unclean. 37But if in his eyes the itch is checked, and black hair has grown in it, the itch is healed; he is clean; and the priest shall pronounce him clean.

38 When a man or a woman has spots on the skin of the body, white spots, 39the priest shall make an examination, and if the spots on the skin of the body are of a dull white, it is a rash that has broken out on the skin; he is clean.

40 If anyone loses the hair from his head, he is bald but he is clean. 41If he loses the hair from his forehead and temples, he has baldness of the forehead but he is clean. 42But if there is on the bald head or the bald forehead a reddish-white diseased spot, it is a leprousd disease breaking out on his bald head or his bald forehead. 43The priest shall examine him; if the diseased swelling is reddish-white on his bald head or on his bald forehead, which resembles a leprousd disease in the skin of the body, 44he is leprous,d he is unclean. The priest shall pronounce him unclean; the disease is on his head.

45 The person who has the leprousd disease shall wear torn clothes and let the hair of his head be disheveled; and he shall cover his upper lip and cry out, "Unclean, unclean." 46He shall remain unclean as long as he has the disease; he is unclean. He shall live alone; his dwelling shall be outside the camp.

47 Concerning clothing: when a leprousd disease appears in it, in woolen or linen cloth, 48in warp or woof of linen or wool, or in a skin or in anything made of skin, 49if the disease shows greenish or reddish in the garment, whether in warp or woof or in skin or in anything made of skin, it is a leprousd disease and shall be shown to the priest. 50The priest shall examine the disease, and put the diseased article aside for seven days. 51He shall examine the disease on the seventh day. If the disease has spread in the cloth, in warp or woof, or in the skin, whatever be the use of the skin, this is a spreading leprousd disease; it is unclean. 52He shall burn the clothing, whether diseased in warp or woof, woolen or linen, or anything of skin, for it is a spreading leprousd disease; it shall be burned in fire.

---

b 13:34 he is free, literally, "he is clean."   c 13:45 I am a leper, I am a leper, literally, "unclean, unclean."

d A term for several skin diseases; precise meaning uncertain

King James

53And if the priest shall look, and, behold, the plague be not spread in the garment, either in the warp, or in the woof, or in any thing of skin;

54Then the priest shall command that they wash *the thing* wherein the plague *is,* and he shall shut it up seven days more:

55And the priest shall look on the plague, after that it is washed: and, behold, if the plague have not changed his colour, and the plague be not spread; it *is* unclean; thou shalt burn it in the fire; it *is* fret inward, *whether* it *be* bare within or without.

56And if the priest look, and, behold, the plague *be* somewhat dark after the washing of it; then he shall rend it out of the garment, or out of the skin, or out of the warp, or out of the woof:

57And if it appear still in the garment, either in the warp, or in the woof, or in any thing of skin; it *is* a spreading *plague:* thou shalt burn that wherein the plague *is* with fire.

58And the garment, either warp, or woof, or whatsoever thing of skin it *be,* which thou shalt wash, if the plague be departed from them, then it shall be washed the second time, and shall be clean.

59This *is* the law of the plague of leprosy in a garment of woollen or linen, either in the warp, or woof, or any thing of skins, to pronounce it clean, or to pronounce it unclean.

14 AND THE LORD spake unto Moses, saying, 2This shall be the law of the leper in the day of his cleansing: He shall be brought unto the priest:

3And the priest shall go forth out of the camp; and the priest shall look, and, behold, *if* the plague of leprosy be healed in the leper;

4Then shall the priest command to take for him that is to be cleansed two birds alive *and* clean, and cedar wood, and scarlet, and hyssop:

5And the priest shall command that one of the birds be killed in an earthen vessel over running water:

6As for the living bird, he shall take it, and the cedar wood, and the scarlet, and the hyssop, and shall dip them and the living bird in the blood of the bird *that was* killed over the running water:

7And he shall sprinkle upon him that is to be cleansed from the leprosy seven times, and shall pronounce him clean, and shall let the living bird loose into the open field.

8And he that is to be cleansed shall wash his clothes, and shave off all his hair, and wash himself in water, that he may be clean: and after that he shall come into the camp, and shall tarry abroad out of his tent seven days.

9But it shall be on the seventh day, that he shall shave all his hair off his head and his beard and his eyebrows, even all his hair he shall shave off: and he shall wash his clothes, also he shall wash his flesh in water, and he shall be clean.

10And on the eighth day he shall take two he lambs without blemish, and one ewe lamb of the first year without blemish, and three tenth deals of fine flour *for* a meat offering, mingled with oil, and one log of oil.

11And the priest that maketh *him* clean shall present the man that is to be made clean, and those things, before the LORD, *at* the door of the tabernacle of the congregation:

12And the priest shall take one he lamb, and offer him for a trespass offering, and the log of oil, and wave them *for* a wave offering before the LORD:

13And he shall slay the lamb in the place where he shall kill the sin offering and the burnt offering, in the holy place: for as the sin offering *is* the priest's, *so is* the trespass offering: it *is* most holy:

New International

53"But if, when the priest examines it, the mildew has not spread in the clothing, or the woven or knitted material, or the leather article, 54he shall order that the contaminated article be washed. Then he is to isolate it for another seven days. 55After the affected article has been washed, the priest is to examine it, and if the mildew has not changed its appearance, even though it has not spread, it is unclean. Burn it with fire, whether the mildew has affected one side or the other. 56If, when the priest examines it, the mildew has faded after the article has been washed, he is to tear the contaminated part out of the clothing, or the leather, or the woven or knitted material. 57But if it reappears in the clothing, or in the woven or knitted material, or in the leather article, it is spreading, and whatever has the mildew must be burned with fire. 58The clothing, or the woven or knitted material, or any leather article that has been washed and is rid of the mildew, must be washed again, and it will be clean."

59These are the regulations concerning contamination by mildew in woolen or linen clothing, woven or knitted material, or any leather article, for pronouncing them clean or unclean.

Cleansing From Infectious Skin Diseases

14 THE LORD said to Moses, 2"These are the regulations for the diseased person at the time of his ceremonial cleansing, when he is brought to the priest: 3The priest is to go outside the camp and examine him. If the person has been healed of his infectious skin disease,a 4the priest shall order that two live clean birds and some cedar wood, scarlet yarn and hyssop be brought for the one to be cleansed. 5Then the priest shall order that one of the birds be killed over fresh water in a clay pot. 6He is then to take the live bird and dip it, together with the cedar wood, the scarlet yarn and the hyssop, into the blood of the bird that was killed over the fresh water. 7Seven times he shall sprinkle the one to be cleansed of the infectious disease and pronounce him clean. Then he is to release the live bird in the open fields.

8"The person to be cleansed must wash his clothes, shave off all his hair and bathe with water; then he will be ceremonially clean. After this he may come into the camp, but he must stay outside his tent for seven days. 9On the seventh day he must shave off all his hair; he must shave his head, his beard, his eyebrows and the rest of his hair. He must wash his clothes and bathe himself with water, and he will be clean.

10"On the eighth day he must bring two male lambs and one ewe lamb a year old, each without defect, along with three-tenths of an ephahb of fine flour mixed with oil for a grain offering, and one logc of oil. 11The priest who pronounces him clean shall present both the one to be cleansed and his offerings before the LORD at the entrance to the Tent of Meeting.

12"Then the priest is to take one of the male lambs and offer it as a guilt offering, along with the log of oil; he shall wave them before the LORD as a wave offering. 13He is to slaughter the lamb in the holy place where the sin offering and the burnt offering are slaughtered. Like the sin offering, the guilt offering belongs to the priest; it is most holy. 14The priest is to take some of the blood

---

a *3* Traditionally *leprosy;* the Hebrew word was used for various diseases affecting the skin—not necessarily leprosy; also elsewhere in this chapter. b *10* That is, probably about 6 quarts (about 6.5 liters)　c *10* That is, probably about 2/3 pint (about 0.3 liter); also in verses 12, 15, 21 and 24

Living Bible

53"But if when he examines it again on the seventh day the spot has not spread, 54the priest shall order the suspected article to be washed, then isolated for seven more days. 55If after that time the spot has not changed its color, even though it has not spread, it is leprosy and shall be burned, for the article is infected through and through.d 56But if the priest sees that the spot has faded after the washing, then he shall cut it out from the garment or leather goods or whatever it is in. 57However, if it then reappears, it is leprosy and he must burn it. 58But if after washing it there is no further trouble, it can be put back into service after another washing."

59These are the regulations concerning leprosy in a garment or anything made of skin or leather, indicating whether to pronounce it leprous or not.

14 AND THE Lord gave Moses these regulations concerning a person whose leprosy disappears: 3"The priest shall go out of the camp to examine him. If the priest sees that the leprosy is gone, 4he shall require two living birds of a kind permitted for food, and shall take some cedar wood, a scarlet string, and some hyssop branches, to be used for the purification ceremony of the one who is healed. 5The priest shall then order one of the birds killed in an earthenware pot held above running water. 6The other bird, still living, shall be dipped in the blood, along with the cedar wood, the scarlet thread, and the hyssop branch. 7Then the priest shall sprinkle the blood seven times upon the man cured of his leprosy, and the priest shall pronounce him cured, and shall let the living bird fly into the open field.

8"Then the man who is cured shall wash his clothes, shave off all his hair, and bathe himself, and return to live inside the camp; however, he must stay outside his tent for seven days. 9The seventh day he shall again shave all the hair from his head, beard, and eyebrows, and wash his clothes and bathe, and shall then be declared fully cured of his leprosy.

10"The next day, the eighth day, he shall take two male lambs without physical defect, one yearling ewe-lamb without physical defect, ten quarts of finely ground flour mixed with olive oil, and a pint of olive oil; 11then the priest who examines him shall place the man and his offerings before the Lord at the entrance of the Tabernacle. 12The priest shall take one of the lambs and the pint of olive oil and offer them to the Lord as a guilt offering by the gesture of waving them before the altar. 13Then he shall kill the lamb at the place where sin offerings and burnt offerings are killed, there at the Tabernacle; this guilt offering shall then be given to the priest for food, as in the case of a sin offering. It is a most holy offering.

New Revised Standard

53 If the priest makes an examination, and the disease has not spread in the clothing, in warp or woof or in anything of skin, 54the priest shall command them to wash the article in which the disease appears, and he shall put it aside seven days more. 55The priest shall examine the diseased article after it has been washed. If the diseased spot has not changed color, though the disease has not spread, it is unclean; you shall burn it in fire, whether the leprouse spot is on the inside or on the outside.

56 If the priest makes an examination, and the disease has abated after it is washed, he shall tear the spot out of the cloth, in warp or woof, or out of skin. 57If it appears again in the garment, in warp or woof, or in anything of skin, it is spreading; you shall burn with fire that in which the disease appears. 58But the cloth, warp or woof, or anything of skin from which the disease disappears when you have washed it, shall then be washed a second time, and it shall be clean.

59 This is the ritual for a leprous disease in a cloth of wool or linen, either in warp or woof, or in anything of skin, to decide whether it is clean or unclean.

Purification of Lepers and Leprous Houses

14 THE LORD spoke to Moses, saying: 2This shall be the ritual for the leprouse person at the time of his cleansing:

He shall be brought to the priest; 3the priest shall go out of the camp, and the priest shall make an examination. If the disease is healed in the leprous person, 4the priest shall command that two living clean birds and cedarwood and crimson yarn and hyssop be brought for the one who is to be cleansed. 5The priest shall command that one of the birds be slaughtered over fresh water in an earthen vessel. 6He shall take the living bird with the cedarwood and the crimson yarn and the hyssop, and dip them and the living bird in the blood of the bird that was slaughtered over the fresh water. 7He shall sprinkle it seven times upon the one who is to be cleansed of the leprous disease; then he shall pronounce him clean, and he shall let the living bird go into the open field. 8The one who is to be cleansed shall wash his clothes, and shave off all his hair, and bathe himself in water, and he shall be clean. After that he shall come into the camp, but shall live outside his tent seven days. 9On the seventh day he shall shave all his hair: of head, beard, eyebrows; he shall shave all his hair. Then he shall wash his clothes, and bathe his body in water, and he shall be clean.

10 On the eighth day he shall take two male lambs without blemish, and one ewe lamb in its first year without blemish, and a grain offering of three-tenths of an ephah of choice flour mixed with oil, and one logf of oil. 11The priest who cleanses shall set the person to be cleansed, along with these things, before the LORD, at the entrance of the tent of meeting. 12The priest shall take one of the lambs, and offer it as a guilt offering, along with the logf of oil, and raise them as an elevation offering before the LORD. 13He shall slaughter the lamb in the place where the sin offering and the burnt offering are slaughtered in the holy place; for the guilt offering, like the sin offering, belongs to the priest: it is most holy. 14The priest shall take some of the blood of the

d 13:55 through and through, literally, "whether the bareness be within or without," or "whether it be bald in the head thereof or in the forehead thereof."

e A term for several skin diseases; precise meaning uncertain   f A liquid measure

King James

14And the priest shall take *some* of the blood of the trespass offering, and the priest shall put *it* upon the tip of the right ear of him that is to be cleansed, and upon the thumb of his right hand, and upon the great toe of his right foot:

15And the priest shall take *some* of the log of oil, and pour *it* into the palm of his own left hand:

16And the priest shall dip his right finger in the oil that *is* in his left hand, and shall sprinkle of the oil with his finger seven times before the LORD:

17And of the rest of the oil that *is* in his hand shall the priest put upon the tip of the right ear of him that is to be cleansed, and upon the thumb of his right hand, and upon the great toe of his right foot, upon the blood of the trespass offering:

18And the remnant of the oil that *is* in the priest's hand he shall pour upon the head of him that is to be cleansed: and the priest shall make an atonement for him before the LORD.

19And the priest shall offer the sin offering, and make an atonement for him that is to be cleansed from his uncleanness; and afterward he shall kill the burnt offering:

20And the priest shall offer the burnt offering and the meat offering upon the altar: and the priest shall make an atonement for him, and he shall be clean.

21And if he *be* poor, and cannot get so much; then he shall take one lamb *for* a trespass offering to be waved, to make an atonement for him, and one tenth deal of fine flour mingled with oil for a meat offering, and a log of oil;

22And two turtledoves, or two young pigeons, such as he is able to get; and the one shall be a sin offering, and the other a burnt offering.

23And he shall bring them on the eighth day for his cleansing unto the priest, unto the door of the tabernacle of the congregation, before the LORD.

24And the priest shall take the lamb of the trespass offering, and the log of oil, and the priest shall wave them *for* a wave offering before the LORD:

25And he shall kill the lamb of the trespass offering, and the priest shall take *some* of the blood of the trespass offering, and put *it* upon the tip of the right ear of him that is to be cleansed, and upon the thumb of his right hand, and upon the great toe of his right foot:

26And the priest shall pour of the oil into the palm of his own left hand:

27And the priest shall sprinkle with his right finger *some* of the oil that *is* in his left hand seven times before the LORD:

28And the priest shall put of the oil that *is* in his hand upon the tip of the right ear of him that is to be cleansed, and upon the thumb of his right hand, and upon the great toe of his right foot, upon the place of the blood of the trespass offering:

29And the rest of the oil that *is* in the priest's hand he shall put upon the head of him that is to be cleansed, to make an atonement for him before the LORD.

30And he shall offer the one of the turtledoves, or of the young pigeons, such as he can get;

31*Even* such as he is able to get, the one *for* a sin offering, and the other *for* a burnt offering, with the meat offering: and the priest shall make an atonement for him that is to be cleansed before the LORD.

32This *is* the law *of him* in whom *is* the plague of leprosy, whose hand is not able to get *that which pertaineth* to his cleansing.

33¶ And the LORD spake unto Moses and unto Aaron, saying,

34When ye be come into the land of Canaan, which I give to you for a possession, and I put the plague of leprosy in a house of the land of your possession;

35And he that owneth the house shall come and tell the priest, saying, It seemeth to me *there is* as it were a plague in the house:

New International

of the guilt offering and put it on the lobe of the right ear of the one to be cleansed, on the thumb of his right hand and on the big toe of his right foot. 15The priest shall then take some of the log of oil, pour it in the palm of his own left hand, 16dip his right forefinger into the oil in his palm, and with his finger sprinkle some of it before the LORD seven times. 17The priest is to put some of the oil remaining in his palm on the lobe of the right ear of the one to be cleansed, on the thumb of his right hand and on the big toe of his right foot, on top of the blood of the guilt offering. 18The rest of the oil in his palm the priest shall put on the head of the one to be cleansed and make atonement for him before the LORD.

19"Then the priest is to sacrifice the sin offering and make atonement for the one to be cleansed from his uncleanness. After that, the priest shall slaughter the burnt offering 20and offer it on the altar, together with the grain offering, and make atonement for him, and he will be clean.

21"If, however, he is poor and cannot afford these, he must take one male lamb as a guilt offering to be waved to make atonement for him, together with a tenth of an ephaha of fine flour mixed with oil for a grain offering, a log of oil, 22and two doves or two young pigeons, which he can afford, one for a sin offering and the other for a burnt offering.

23"On the eighth day he must bring them for his cleansing to the priest at the entrance to the Tent of Meeting, before the LORD. 24The priest is to take the lamb for the guilt offering, together with the log of oil, and wave them before the LORD as a wave offering. 25He shall slaughter the lamb for the guilt offering and take some of its blood and put it on the lobe of the right ear of the one to be cleansed, on the thumb of his right hand and on the big toe of his right foot. 26The priest is to pour some of the oil into the palm of his own left hand, 27and with his right forefinger sprinkle some of the oil from his palm seven times before the LORD. 28Some of the oil in his palm he is to put on the same places he put the blood of the guilt offering—on the lobe of the right ear of the one to be cleansed, on the thumb of his right hand and on the big toe of his right foot. 29The rest of the oil in his palm the priest shall put on the head of the one to be cleansed, to make atonement for him before the LORD. 30Then he shall sacrifice the doves or the young pigeons, which the person can afford, 31oneb as a sin offering and the other as a burnt offering, together with the grain offering. In this way the priest will make atonement before the LORD on behalf of the one to be cleansed."

32These are the regulations for anyone who has an infectious skin disease and who cannot afford the regular offerings for his cleansing.

Cleansing From Mildew

33The LORD said to Moses and Aaron, 34"When you enter the land of Canaan, which I am giving you as your possession, and I put a spreading mildew in a house in that land, 35the owner of the house must go and tell the priest, 'I have seen something that looks like mildew in my house.' 36The priest is to order the house to be emp-

---

a *21* That is, probably about 2 quarts (about 2 liters)   b *31* Septuagint and Syriac; Hebrew *31such as the person can afford,* one

Living Bible

¹⁴The priest shall take the blood from this guilt offering and smear some of it upon the tip of the right ear of the man being cleansed, and upon the thumb of his right hand, and upon the big toe of his right foot.

¹⁵"Then the priest shall take the olive oil and pour it into the palm of his left hand, ¹⁶and dip his right finger into it, and sprinkle it with his finger seven times before the Lord. ¹⁷Some of the oil remaining in his left hand shall then be placed by the priest upon the tip of the man's right ear and the thumb of his right hand and the big toe of his right foot—just as he did with the blood of the guilt offering. ¹⁸The remainder of the oil in his hand shall be used to anoint the man's head. Thus the priest shall make atonement for him before the Lord.

¹⁹"Then the priest must offer the sin offering and again^c perform the rite of atonement for the person being cleansed from his leprosy; and afterwards the priest shall kill the burnt offering, ²⁰and offer it along with the grain offering upon the altar, making atonement for the man, who shall then be pronounced finally cleansed.

²¹"If he is so poor that he cannot afford two lambs, then he shall bring only one, a male lamb for the guilt offering, to be presented to the Lord in the rite of atonement by waving it before the altar; and only three quarts of fine white flour, mixed with olive oil, for a grain offering, and a pint of olive oil.

²²"He shall also bring two turtledoves or two young pigeons—whichever he is able to afford—and use one of the pair for a sin offering and the other for a burnt offering. ²³He shall bring them to the priest at the entrance of the Tabernacle on the eighth day, for his ceremony of cleansing before the Lord. ²⁴The priest shall take the lamb for the guilt offering, and the pint of oil, and wave them before the altar as a gesture of offering to the Lord. ²⁵Then he shall kill the lamb for the guilt offering and smear some of its blood upon the tip of the man's right ear—the man on whose behalf the ceremony is being performed—and upon the thumb of his right hand and on the big toe of his right foot.

²⁶"The priest shall then pour the olive oil into the palm of his own left hand, ²⁷and with his right finger he is to sprinkle some of it seven times before the Lord. ²⁸Then he must put some of the olive oil from his hand upon the tip of the man's right ear, and upon the thumb of his right hand, and upon the big toe of his right foot, just as he did with the blood of the guilt offering. ²⁹The remaining oil in his hand shall be placed upon the head of the man being cleansed, to make atonement for him before the Lord.

³⁰"Then he must offer the two turtledoves or two young pigeons (whichever pair he is able to afford). ³¹One of the pair is for a sin offering and the other for a burnt offering, to be sacrificed along with the grain offering; and the priest shall make atonement for the man before the Lord."

³²These, then, are the laws concerning those who are cleansed of leprosy but are not able to bring the sacrifices normally required for the ceremony of cleansing.

^{33, 34}Then the Lord said to Moses and Aaron, "When you arrive in the land of Canaan which I have given you, and I place leprosy in some house there, ³⁵then the owner of the house shall come and report to the priest, 'It seems to me that there may be leprosy in my house!'

New Revised Standard

guilt offering and put it on the lobe of the right ear of the one to be cleansed, and on the thumb of the right hand, and on the big toe of the right foot. ¹⁵The priest shall take some of the log^d of oil and pour it into the palm of his own left hand, ¹⁶and dip his right finger in the oil that is in his left hand and sprinkle some oil with his finger seven times before the Lord. ¹⁷Some of the oil that remains in his hand the priest shall put on the lobe of the right ear of the one to be cleansed, and on the thumb of the right hand, and on the big toe of the right foot, on top of the blood of the guilt offering. ¹⁸The rest of the oil that is in the priest's hand he shall put on the head of the one to be cleansed. Then the priest shall make atonement on his behalf before the Lord: ¹⁹the priest shall offer the sin offering, to make atonement for the one to be cleansed from his uncleanness. Afterward he shall slaughter the burnt offering; ²⁰and the priest shall offer the burnt offering and the grain offering on the altar. Thus the priest shall make atonement on his behalf and he shall be clean.

²¹But if he is poor and cannot afford so much, he shall take one male lamb for a guilt offering to be elevated, to make atonement on his behalf, and one-tenth of an ephah of choice flour mixed with oil for a grain offering and a log^d of oil; ²²also two turtledoves or two pigeons, such as he can afford, one for a sin offering and the other for a burnt offering. ²³On the eighth day he shall bring them for his cleansing to the priest, to the entrance of the tent of meeting, before the Lord; ²⁴and the priest shall take the lamb of the guilt offering and the log^d of oil, and the priest shall raise them as an elevation offering before the Lord. ²⁵The priest shall slaughter the lamb of the guilt offering and shall take some of the blood of the guilt offering, and put it on the lobe of the right ear of the one to be cleansed, and on the thumb of the right hand, and on the big toe of the right foot. ²⁶The priest shall pour some of the oil into the palm of his own left hand, ²⁷and shall sprinkle with his right finger some of the oil that is in his left hand seven times before the Lord. ²⁸The priest shall put some of the oil that is in his hand on the lobe of the right ear of the one to be cleansed, and on the thumb of the right hand, and the big toe of the right foot, where the blood of the guilt offering was placed. ²⁹The rest of the oil that is in the priest's hand he shall put on the head of the one to be cleansed, to make atonement on his behalf before the Lord. ³⁰And he shall offer, of the turtledoves or pigeons such as he can afford, ³¹one^e for a sin offering and the other for a burnt offering, along with a grain offering; and the priest shall make atonement before the Lord on behalf of the one being cleansed. ³²This is the ritual for the one who has a leprous^f disease, who cannot afford the offerings for his cleansing.

33   The Lord spoke to Moses and Aaron, saying:

34   When you come into the land of Canaan, which I give you for a possession, and I put a leprous^f disease in a house in the land of your possession, ³⁵the owner of the house shall come and tell the priest, saying, "There seems to me to be some sort of disease in my house." ³⁶The priest shall command that they empty the

---

^c 14:19 and again, implied.

^d A liquid measure   ^e Gk Syr: Heb afford, ³¹such as he can afford, one   ^f A term for several skin diseases; precise meaning uncertain

King James

New International

King James

36Then the priest shall command that they empty the house, before the priest go *into it* to see the plague, that all that *is* in the house be not made unclean: and afterward the priest shall go in to see the house:

37And he shall look on the plague, and, behold, *if* the plague *be* in the walls of the house with hollow strakes, greenish or reddish, which in sight *are* lower than the wall;

38Then the priest shall go out of the house to the door of the house, and shut up the house seven days:

39And he shall come again the seventh day, and shall look: and, behold, *if* the plague be spread in the walls of the house;

40Then the priest shall command that they take away the stones in which the plague *is,* and they shall cast them into an unclean place without the city:

41And he shall cause the house to be scraped within round about, and they shall pour out the dust that they scrape off without the city into an unclean place:

42And they shall take other stones, and put *them* in the place of those stones; and he shall take other mortar, and shall plaster the house.

43And if the plague come again, and break out in the house, after that he hath taken away the stones, and after he hath scraped the house, and after it is plastered;

44Then the priest shall come and look, and, behold, *if* the plague be spread in the house, it *is* a fretting leprosy in the house: it *is* unclean.

45And he shall break down the house, the stones of it, and the timber thereof, and all the mortar of the house; and he shall carry *them* forth out of the city into an unclean place.

46Moreover he that goeth into the house all the while that it is shut up shall be unclean until the even.

47And he that lieth in the house shall wash his clothes; and he that eateth in the house shall wash his clothes.

48And if the priest shall come in, and look *upon it,* and, behold, the plague hath not spread in the house, after the house was plastered: then the priest shall pronounce the house clean, because the plague is healed.

49And he shall take to cleanse the house two birds, and cedar wood, and scarlet, and hyssop:

50And he shall kill the one of the birds in an earthen vessel over running water:

51And he shall take the cedar wood, and the hyssop, and the scarlet, and the living bird, and dip them in the blood of the slain bird, and in the running water, and sprinkle the house seven times:

52And he shall cleanse the house with the blood of the bird, and with the running water, and with the living bird, and with the cedar wood, and with the hyssop, and with the scarlet:

53But he shall let go the living bird out of the city into the open fields, and make an atonement for the house: and it shall be clean.

54This *is* the law for all manner of plague of leprosy, and scall,

55And for the leprosy of a garment, and of a house,

56And for a rising, and for a scab, and for a bright spot:

57To teach when *it is* unclean, and when *it is* clean: this *is* the law of leprosy.

New International

tied before he goes in to examine the mildew, so that nothing in the house will be pronounced unclean. After this the priest is to go in and inspect the house. 37He is to examine the mildew on the walls, and if it has greenish or reddish depressions that appear to be deeper than the surface of the wall, 38the priest shall go out the doorway of the house and close it up for seven days. 39On the seventh day the priest shall return to inspect the house. If the mildew has spread on the walls, 40he is to order that the contaminated stones be torn out and thrown into an unclean place outside the town. 41He must have all the inside walls of the house scraped and the material that is scraped off dumped into an unclean place outside the town. 42Then they are to take other stones to replace these and take new clay and plaster the house.

43"If the mildew reappears in the house after the stones have been torn out and the house scraped and plastered, 44the priest is to go and examine it and, if the mildew has spread in the house, it is a destructive mildew; the house is unclean. 45It must be torn down—its stones, timbers and all the plaster—and taken out of the town to an unclean place.

46"Anyone who goes into the house while it is closed up will be unclean till evening. 47Anyone who sleeps or eats in the house must wash his clothes.

48"But if the priest comes to examine it and the mildew has not spread after the house has been plastered, he shall pronounce the house clean, because the mildew is gone. 49To purify the house he is to take two birds and some cedar wood, scarlet yarn and hyssop. 50He shall kill one of the birds over fresh water in a clay pot. 51Then he is to take the cedar wood, the hyssop, the scarlet yarn and the live bird, dip them into the blood of the dead bird and the fresh water, and sprinkle the house seven times. 52He shall purify the house with the bird's blood, the fresh water, the live bird, the cedar wood, the hyssop and the scarlet yarn. 53Then he is to release the live bird in the open fields outside the town. In this way he will make atonement for the house, and it will be clean."

54These are the regulations for any infectious skin disease, for an itch, 55for mildew in clothing or in a house, 56and for a swelling, a rash or a bright spot, 57to determine when something is clean or unclean.

These are the regulations for infectious skin diseases and mildew.

Discharges Causing Uncleanness

15 AND THE LORD spake unto Moses and to Aaron, saying,

2Speak unto the children of Israel, and say unto them, When any man hath a running issue out of his flesh, *because of* his issue he *is* unclean.

15 THE LORD said to Moses and Aaron, 2"Speak to the Israelites and say to them: 'When any man has a bodily discharge, the discharge is unclean.

Living Bible

36"The priest shall order the house to be emptied before he examines it, so that everything in the house will not be declared contaminated if he decides that there is leprosy there. 37If he finds greenish or reddish streaks in the walls of the house which seem to be beneath the surface of the wall, 38he shall close up the house for seven days, 39and return the seventh day to look at it again. If the spots have spread in the wall, 40then the priest shall order the removal of the spotted section of wall, and the material must be thrown into a defiled place outside the city. 41Then he shall order the inside walls of the house scraped thoroughly, and the scrapings dumped in a defiled place outside the city. 42Other stones shall be brought to replace those that have been removed, new mortar used, and the house replastered.

43"But if the spots appear again, 44the priest shall come again and look, and if he sees that the spots have spread, it is leprosy, and the house is defiled. 45Then he shall order the destruction of the house—all its stones, timbers, and mortar shall be carried out of the city to a defiled place. 46Anyone entering the house while it is closed shall be defiled until evening. 47Anyone who lies down or eats in the house shall wash his clothing.

48"But if, when the priest comes again to look, the spots have not reappeared after the fresh plastering, then he will pronounce the house cleansed, and declare the leprosy gone. 49He shall also perform the ceremony of cleansing, using two birds, cedar wood, scarlet thread, and hyssop branches. 50He shall kill one of the birds over fresh water in an earthenware bowl, 51, 52and dip the cedar wood, hyssop branch, and scarlet thread, as well as the living bird, into the blood of the bird that was killed over the fresh water, and shall sprinkle the house seven times. In this way the house shall be cleansed. 53Then he shall let the live bird fly away into an open field outside the city. This is the method for making atonement for the house and cleansing it."

54These, then, are the laws concerning the various places where leprosy may appear: 55in a garment or in a house, 56or in any swelling in one's skin, or a scab from a burn, or a bright spot. 57In this way you will know whether or not it is actually leprosy. That is why these laws are given.

15   THE LORD told Moses and Aaron to give the people of Israel these further instructions: "Any man who has a genital dischargeª is ceremonially defiled. 3This applies not only while the discharge

New Revised Standard

house before the priest goes to examine the disease, or all that is in the house will become unclean; and afterward the priest shall go in to inspect the house. 37He shall examine the disease; if the disease is in the walls of the house with greenish or reddish spots, and if it appears to be deeper than the surface, 38the priest shall go outside to the door of the house and shut up the house seven days. 39The priest shall come again on the seventh day and make an inspection; if the disease has spread in the walls of the house, 40the priest shall command that the stones in which the disease appears be taken out and thrown into an unclean place outside the city. 41He shall have the inside of the house scraped thoroughly, and the plaster that is scraped off shall be dumped in an unclean place outside the city. 42They shall take other stones and put them in the place of those stones, and take other plaster and plaster the house.

43 If the disease breaks out again in the house, after he has taken out the stones and scraped the house and plastered it, 44the priest shall go and make inspection; if the disease has spread in the house, it is a spreading leprousᵇ disease in the house; it is unclean. 45He shall have the house torn down, its stones and timber and all the plaster of the house, and taken outside the city to an unclean place. 46All who enter the house while it is shut up shall be unclean until the evening; 47and all who sleep in the house shall wash their clothes; and all who eat in the house shall wash their clothes.

48 If the priest comes and makes an inspection, and the disease has not spread in the house after the house was plastered, the priest shall pronounce the house clean; the disease is healed. 49For the cleansing of the house he shall take two birds, with cedarwood and crimson yarn and hyssop, 50and shall slaughter one of the birds over fresh water in an earthen vessel, 51and shall take the cedarwood and the hyssop and the crimson yarn, along with the living bird, and dip them in the blood of the slaughtered bird and the fresh water, and sprinkle the house seven times. 52Thus he shall cleanse the house with the blood of the bird, and with the fresh water, and with the living bird, and with the cedarwood and hyssop and crimson yarn; 53and he shall let the living bird go out of the city into the open field; so he shall make atonement for the house, and it shall be clean.

54 This is the ritual for any leprousᵇ disease: for an itch, 55for leprousᵇ diseases in clothing and houses, 56and for a swelling or an eruption or a spot, 57to determine when it is unclean and when it is clean. This is the ritual for leprousᵇ diseases.

Concerning Bodily Discharges

15   THE LORD spoke to Moses and Aaron, saying: 2Speak to the people of Israel and say to them: When any man has a discharge from his member,ᶜ his discharge makes him ceremonially unclean. 3The

---

ª 15:2 a genital discharge, literally, "an issue out of his flesh."   ᵇ A term for several skin diseases; precise meaning uncertain   ᶜ Heb flesh

King James

3And this shall be his uncleanness in his issue: whether his flesh run with his issue, or his flesh be stopped from his issue, it *is* his uncleanness.

4Every bed, whereon he lieth that hath the issue, is unclean: and every thing, whereon he sitteth, shall be unclean.

5And whosoever toucheth his bed shall wash his clothes, and bathe *himself* in water, and be unclean until the even.

6And he that sitteth on *any* thing whereon he sat that hath the issue shall wash his clothes, and bathe *himself* in water, and be unclean until the even.

7And he that toucheth the flesh of him that hath the issue shall wash his clothes, and bathe *himself* in water, and be unclean until the even.

8And if he that hath the issue spit upon him that is clean; then he shall wash his clothes, and bathe *himself* in water, and be unclean until the even.

9And what saddle soever he rideth upon that hath the issue shall be unclean.

10And whosoever toucheth any thing that was under him shall be unclean until the even: and he that beareth *any of* those things shall wash his clothes, and bathe *himself* in water, and be unclean until the even.

11And whomsoever he toucheth that hath the issue, and hath not rinsed his hands in water, he shall wash his clothes, and bathe *himself* in water, and be unclean until the even.

12And the vessel of earth, that he toucheth which hath the issue, shall be broken: and every vessel of wood shall be rinsed in water.

13And when he that hath an issue is cleansed of his issue; then he shall number to himself seven days for his cleansing, and wash his clothes, and bathe his flesh in running water, and shall be clean.

14And on the eighth day he shall take to him two turtledoves, or two young pigeons, and come before the LORD unto the door of the tabernacle of the congregation, and give them unto the priest:

15And the priest shall offer them, the one *for* a sin offering, and the other *for* a burnt offering; and the priest shall make an atonement for him before the LORD for his issue.

16And if any man's seed of copulation go out from him, then he shall wash all his flesh in water, and be unclean until the even.

17And every garment, and every skin, whereon is the seed of copulation, shall be washed with water, and be unclean until the even.

18The woman also with whom man shall lie *with* seed of copulation, they shall *both* bathe *themselves* in water, and be unclean until the even.

19¶ And if a woman have an issue, *and* her issue in her flesh be blood, she shall be put apart seven days: and whosoever toucheth her shall be unclean until the even.

20And every thing that she lieth upon in her separation shall be unclean: every thing also that she sitteth upon shall be unclean.

21And whosoever toucheth her bed shall wash his clothes, and bathe *himself* in water, and be unclean until the even.

22And whosoever toucheth any thing that she sat upon shall wash his clothes, and bathe *himself* in water, and be unclean until the even.

23And if it *be* on *her* bed, or on any thing whereon she sitteth, when he toucheth it, he shall be unclean until the even.

24And if any man lie with her at all, and her flowers be upon him, he shall be unclean seven days; and all the bed whereon he lieth shall be unclean.

25And if a woman have an issue of her blood many days out of the time of her separation, or if it run beyond the time of her separation; all the days of the issue of her uncleanness shall be as the days of her separation: she *shall be* unclean.

New International

3Whether it continues flowing from his body or is blocked, it will make him unclean. This is how his discharge will bring about uncleanness:

4" 'Any bed the man with a discharge lies on will be unclean, and anything he sits on will be unclean. 5Anyone who touches his bed must wash his clothes and bathe with water, and he will be unclean till evening. 6Whoever sits on anything that the man with a discharge sat on must wash his clothes and bathe with water, and he will be unclean till evening.

7" 'Whoever touches the man who has a discharge must wash his clothes and bathe with water, and he will be unclean till evening.

8" 'If the man with the discharge spits on someone who is clean, that person must wash his clothes and bathe with water, and he will be unclean till evening.

9" 'Everything the man sits on when riding will be unclean, 10and whoever touches any of the things that were under him will be unclean till evening; whoever picks up those things must wash his clothes and bathe with water, and he will be unclean till evening.

11" 'Anyone the man with a discharge touches without rinsing his hands with water must wash his clothes and bathe with water, and he will be unclean till evening.

12" 'A clay pot that the man touches must be broken, and any wooden article is to be rinsed with water.

13" 'When a man is cleansed from his discharge, he is to count off seven days for his ceremonial cleansing; he must wash his clothes and bathe himself with fresh water, and he will be clean. 14On the eighth day he must take two doves or two young pigeons and come before the LORD to the entrance to the Tent of Meeting and give them to the priest. 15The priest is to sacrifice them, the one for a sin offering and the other for a burnt offering. In this way he will make atonement before the LORD for the man because of his discharge.

16" 'When a man has an emission of semen, he must bathe his whole body with water, and he will be unclean till evening. 17Any clothing or leather that has semen on it must be washed with water, and it will be unclean till evening. 18When a man lies with a woman and there is an emission of semen, both must bathe with water, and they will be unclean till evening.

19" 'When a woman has her regular flow of blood, the impurity of her monthly period will last seven days, and anyone who touches her will be unclean till evening.

20" 'Anything she lies on during her period will be unclean, and anything she sits on will be unclean. 21Whoever touches her bed must wash his clothes and bathe with water, and he will be unclean till evening. 22Whoever touches anything she sits on must wash his clothes and bathe with water, and he will be unclean till evening. 23Whether it is the bed or anything she was sitting on, when anyone touches it, he will be unclean till evening.

24" 'If a man lies with her and her monthly flow touches him, he will be unclean for seven days; any bed he lies on will be unclean.

25" 'When a woman has a discharge of blood for many days at a time other than her monthly period or has a discharge that continues beyond her period, she will be unclean as long as she has the discharge, just as in the days of her period. 26Any bed she lies on while her

Living Bible

is active, but also for a time after it heals. 4Any bed he lies on and anything he sits on is contaminated: 5so anyone touching the man's bed is ceremonially defiled until evening, and must wash his clothes and bathe himself. 6Anyone sitting on a seat the man has sat upon while defiled is himself ceremonially impure until evening, and must wash his clothes and bathe himself. 7The same instructions apply to anyone touching him. 8Anyone he spits on is ceremonially impure until evening, and must wash his clothes and bathe himself. 9Any saddle he rides on is defiled. 10Anyone touching or carrying anything else that was beneath him shall be defiled until evening, and must wash his clothes and bathe himself. 11If the defiled man touches anyone without first rinsing his hands, that person must wash his clothes and bathe himself and be defiled until evening. 12Any earthen pot touched by the defiled man must be broken, and every wooden utensil must be rinsed in water.

13"When the discharge stops, he shall begin a seven-day cleansing ceremony by washing his clothes and bathing in running water. 14On the eighth day he shall take two turtledoves or two young pigeons and come before the Lord at the entrance of the Tabernacle, and give them to the priest. 15The priest shall sacrifice them there, one for a sin offering and the other for a burnt offering; thus the priest shall make atonement before the Lord for the man because of his discharge.

16"Whenever a man's semen goes out from him, he shall take a complete bath and be ceremonially impure until the evening. 17Any clothing or bedding the semen spills on must be washed and remain ceremonially defiled until evening. 18After sexual intercourse, the woman as well as the man must bathe, and they are ceremonially defiled until the next evening.

19"Whenever a woman menstruates, she shall be in a state of ceremonial defilement for seven days afterwards, and during that time anyone touching her shall be defiled until evening. 20Anything she lies on or sits on during that time shall be defiled. 21, 22, 23Anyone touching her bed or anything she sits upon shall wash his clothes and bathe himself and be ceremonially defiled until evening. 24A man having sexual intercourse with her during this time is ceremonially defiled for seven days, and every bed he lies upon shall be defiled.

25"If the menstrual flow continues after the normal time, or at some irregular time during the month, the same rules apply as indicated above, 26so that anything

New Revised Standard

uncleanness of his discharge is this: whether his member[a] flows with his discharge, or his member[a] is stopped from discharging, it is uncleanness for him. 4Every bed on which the one with the discharge lies shall be unclean; and everything on which he sits shall be unclean. 5Anyone who touches his bed shall wash his clothes, and bathe in water, and be unclean until the evening. 6All who sit on anything on which the one with the discharge has sat shall wash their clothes, and bathe in water, and be unclean until the evening. 7All who touch the body of the one with the discharge shall wash their clothes, and bathe in water, and be unclean until the evening. 8If the one with the discharge spits on persons who are clean, then they shall wash their clothes, and bathe in water, and be unclean until the evening. 9Any saddle on which the one with the discharge rides shall be unclean. 10All who touch anything that was under him shall be unclean until the evening, and all who carry such a thing shall wash their clothes, and bathe in water, and be unclean until the evening. 11All those whom the one with the discharge touches without his having rinsed his hands in water shall wash their clothes, and bathe in water, and be unclean until the evening. 12Any earthen vessel that the one with the discharge touches shall be broken; and every vessel of wood shall be rinsed in water.

13 When the one with a discharge is cleansed of his discharge, he shall count seven days for his cleansing; he shall wash his clothes and bathe his body in fresh water, and he shall be clean. 14On the eighth day he shall take two turtledoves or two pigeons and come before the LORD to the entrance of the tent of meeting and give them to the priest. 15The priest shall offer them, one for a sin offering and the other for a burnt offering; and the priest shall make atonement on his behalf before the LORD for his discharge.

16 If a man has an emission of semen, he shall bathe his whole body in water, and be unclean until the evening. 17Everything made of cloth or of skin on which the semen falls shall be washed with water, and be unclean until the evening. 18If a man lies with a woman and has an emission of semen, both of them shall bathe in water, and be unclean until the evening.

19 When a woman has a discharge of blood that is her regular discharge from her body, she shall be in her impurity for seven days, and whoever touches her shall be unclean until the evening. 20Everything upon which she lies during her impurity shall be unclean; everything also upon which she sits shall be unclean. 21Whoever touches her bed shall wash his clothes, and bathe in water, and be unclean until the evening. 22Whoever touches anything upon which she sits shall wash his clothes, and bathe in water, and be unclean until the evening; 23whether it is the bed or anything upon which she sits, when he touches it he shall be unclean until the evening. 24If any man lies with her, and her impurity falls on him, he shall be unclean seven days; and every bed on which he lies shall be unclean.

25 If a woman has a discharge of blood for many days, not at the time of her impurity, or if she has a discharge beyond the time of her impurity, all the days of the discharge she shall continue in uncleanness; as in the days of her impurity, she shall be unclean. 26Every

---

[a] Heb *flesh*

King James

26Every bed whereon she lieth all the days of her issue shall be unto her as the bed of her separation: and whatsoever she sitteth upon shall be unclean, as the uncleanness of her separation.

27And whosoever toucheth those things shall be unclean, and shall wash his clothes, and bathe *himself* in water, and be unclean until the even.

28But if she be cleansed of her issue, then she shall number to herself seven days, and after that she shall be clean.

29And on the eighth day she shall take unto her two turtles, or two young pigeons, and bring them unto the priest, to the door of the tabernacle of the congregation.

30And the priest shall offer the one *for* a sin offering, and the other *for* a burnt offering; and the priest shall make an atonement for her before the LORD for the issue of her uncleanness.

31Thus shall ye separate the children of Israel from their uncleanness; that they die not in their uncleanness, when they defile my tabernacle that *is* among them.

32This *is* the law of him that hath an issue, and *of him* whose seed goeth from him, and is defiled therewith;

33And of her that is sick of her flowers, and of him that hath an issue, of the man, and of the woman, and of him that lieth with her that is unclean.

16 AND THE LORD spake unto Moses after the death of the two sons of Aaron, when they offered before the LORD, and died;

2And the LORD said unto Moses, Speak unto Aaron thy brother, that he come not at all times into the holy *place* within the veil before the mercy seat, which *is* upon the ark; that he die not: for I will appear in the cloud upon the mercy seat.

3Thus shall Aaron come into the holy *place:* with a young bullock for a sin offering, and a ram for a burnt offering.

4He shall put on the holy linen coat, and he shall have the linen breeches upon his flesh, and shall be girded with a linen girdle, and with the linen mitre shall he be attired: these *are* holy garments; therefore shall he wash his flesh in water, and *so* put them on.

5And he shall take of the congregation of the children of Israel two kids of the goats for a sin offering, and one ram for a burnt offering.

6And Aaron shall offer his bullock of the sin offering, which *is* for himself, and make an atonement for himself, and for his house.

7And he shall take the two goats, and present them before the LORD *at* the door of the tabernacle of the congregation.

8And Aaron shall cast lots upon the two goats; one lot for the LORD, and the other lot for the scapegoat.

9And Aaron shall bring the goat upon which the LORD's lot fell, and offer him *for* a sin offering.

10But the goat, on which the lot fell to be the scapegoat, shall be presented alive before the LORD, to make an atonement with him, *and* to let him go for a scapegoat into the wilderness.

11And Aaron shall bring the bullock of the sin offering, which *is* for himself, and shall make an atonement for himself, and for his house, and shall kill the bullock of the sin offering which *is* for himself:

12And he shall take a censer full of burning coals of fire from off the altar before the LORD, and his hands full of sweet incense beaten small, and bring *it* within the veil:

13And he shall put the incense upon the fire before the LORD, that the cloud of the incense may cover the mercy seat that *is* upon the testimony, that he die not:

New International

discharge continues will be unclean, as is her bed during her monthly period, and anything she sits on will be unclean, as during her period. 27Whoever touches them will be unclean; he must wash his clothes and bathe with water, and he will be unclean till evening.

28" 'When she is cleansed from her discharge, she must count off seven days, and after that she will be ceremonially clean. 29On the eighth day she must take two doves or two young pigeons and bring them to the priest at the entrance to the Tent of Meeting. 30The priest is to sacrifice one for a sin offering and the other for a burnt offering. In this way he will make atonement for her before the LORD for the uncleanness of her discharge.

31" 'You must keep the Israelites separate from things that make them unclean, so they will not die in their uncleanness for defiling my dwelling place,a which is among them.' "

32These are the regulations for a man with a discharge, for anyone made unclean by an emission of semen, 33for a woman in her monthly period, for a man or a woman with a discharge, and for a man who lies with a woman who is ceremonially unclean.

The Day of Atonement

16 THE LORD spoke to Moses after the death of the two sons of Aaron who died when they approached the LORD. 2The LORD said to Moses: "Tell your brother Aaron not to come whenever he chooses into the Most Holy Place behind the curtain in front of the atonement cover on the ark, or else he will die, because I appear in the cloud over the atonement cover.

3"This is how Aaron is to enter the sanctuary area: with a young bull for a sin offering and a ram for a burnt offering. 4He is to put on the sacred linen tunic, with linen undergarments next to his body; he is to tie the linen sash around him and put on the linen turban. These are sacred garments; so he must bathe himself with water before he puts them on. 5From the Israelite community he is to take two male goats for a sin offering and a ram for a burnt offering.

6"Aaron is to offer the bull for his own sin offering to make atonement for himself and his household. 7Then he is to take the two goats and present them before the LORD at the entrance to the Tent of Meeting. 8He is to cast lots for the two goats—one lot for the LORD and the other for the scapegoat.b 9Aaron shall bring the goat whose lot falls to the LORD and sacrifice it for a sin offering. 10But the goat chosen by lot as the scapegoat shall be presented alive before the LORD to be used for making atonement by sending it into the desert as a scapegoat.

11"Aaron shall bring the bull for his own sin offering to make atonement for himself and his household, and he is to slaughter the bull for his own sin offering. 12He is to take a censer full of burning coals from the altar before the LORD and two handfuls of finely ground fragrant incense and take them behind the curtain. 13He is to put the incense on the fire before the LORD, and the smoke of the incense will conceal the atonement cover above the Testimony, so that he will not die. 14He is to

---

a 31 Or *my tabernacle*   b 8 That is, the goat of removal; Hebrew *azazel*; also in verses 10 and 26

Living Bible

she lies upon during that time is defiled, just as it would be during her normal menstrual period, and everything she sits on is in a similar state of defilement. 27Anyone touching her bed or anything she sits on shall be defiled, and shall wash his clothes and bathe and be defiled until evening. 28Seven days after the menstruating stops, she is no longer ceremonially defiled.

29"On the eighth day, she shall take two turtledoves or two young pigeons and bring them to the priest at the entrance of the Tabernacle, 30and the priest shall offer one for a sin offering and the other for a burnt offering, and make atonement for her before the Lord, for her menstrual defilement. 31In this way you shall cleanse the people of Israel from their defilement, lest they die because of defiling my Tabernacle that is among them."

32This, then, is the law for the man who is defiled by a genital diseasec or by a seminal emission; 33and for a woman's menstrual period; and for anyone who has sexual intercourse with her while she is in her period of defilement afterwards.

16 AFTER AARON'S two sons died before the Lord, the Lord said to Moses, "Warn your brother Aaron not to enter into the Holy Place behind the veil, where the Ark and the place of mercy are, just whenever he chooses. The penalty for intrusion is death. For I myself am present in the cloud above the place of mercy.

3"Here are the conditions for his entering there: He must bring a young bull for a sin offering, and a ram for a burnt offering. 4He must bathe himself and put on the sacred linen coat, shorts, belt, and turban. 5The people of Israel shall then bring him two male goats for their sin offering, and a ram for their burnt offering. 6First he shall present to the Lord the young bull as a sin offering for himself, making atonement for himself and his family. 7Then he shall bring the two goats before the Lord at the entrance of the Tabernacle, 8and cast lots to determine which is the Lord's and which is to be sent away.d 9The goat allotted to the Lord shall then be sacrificed by Aaron as a sin offering. 10The other goat shall be kept alive and placed before the Lord. The rite of atonement shall be performed over it, and it shall then be sent out into the desert as a scapegoat.

11"After Aaron has sacrificed the young bull as a sin offering for himself and his family, 12he shall take a censer full of live coals from the altar of the Lord, and fill his hands with sweet incense beaten into fine powder, and bring it inside the veil. 13There before the Lord he shall put the incense upon the coals, so that a cloud of incense will cover the mercy place above the Ark (containing the stone tablets of the Ten Commandments); thus he will not die. 14And he shall bring some

New Revised Standard

bed on which she lies during all the days of her discharge shall be treated as the bed of her impurity; and everything on which she sits shall be unclean, as in the uncleanness of her impurity. 27Whoever touches these things shall be unclean, and shall wash his clothes, and bathe in water, and be unclean until the evening. 28If she is cleansed of her discharge, she shall count seven days, and after that she shall be clean. 29On the eighth day she shall take two turtledoves or two pigeons and bring them to the priest to the entrance of the tent of meeting. 30The priest shall offer one for a sin offering and the other for a burnt offering; and the priest shall make atonement on her behalf before the LORD for her unclean discharge.

31 Thus you shall keep the people of Israel separate from their uncleanness, so that they do not die in their uncleanness by defiling my tabernacle that is in their midst.

32 This is the ritual for those who have a discharge: for him who has an emission of semen, becoming unclean thereby, 33for her who is in the infirmity of her period, for anyone, male or female, who has a discharge, and for the man who lies with a woman who is unclean.

The Day of Atonement

16 THE LORD spoke to Moses after the death of the two sons of Aaron, when they drew near before the LORD and died. 2The LORD said to Moses: Tell your brother Aaron not to come just at any time into the sanctuary inside the curtain before the mercy seate that is upon the ark, or he will die; for I appear in the cloud upon the mercy seat.e 3Thus shall Aaron come into the holy place: with a young bull for a sin offering and a ram for a burnt offering. 4He shall put on the holy linen tunic, and shall have the linen undergarments next to his body, fasten the linen sash, and wear the linen turban; these are the holy vestments. He shall bathe his body in water, and then put them on. 5He shall take from the congregation of the people of Israel two male goats for a sin offering, and one ram for a burnt offering.

6 Aaron shall offer the bull as a sin offering for himself, and shall make atonement for himself and for his house. 7He shall take the two goats and set them before the LORD at the entrance of the tent of meeting; 8and Aaron shall cast lots on the two goats, one lot for the LORD and the other lot for Azazel.f 9Aaron shall present the goat on which the lot fell for the LORD, and offer it as a sin offering; 10but the goat on which the lot fell for Azazelf shall be presented alive before the LORD to make atonement over it, that it may be sent away into the wilderness to Azazel.f

11 Aaron shall present the bull as a sin offering for himself, and shall make atonement for himself and for his house; he shall slaughter the bull as a sin offering for himself. 12He shall take a censer full of coals of fire from the altar before the LORD, and two handfuls of crushed sweet incense, and he shall bring it inside the curtain 13and put the incense on the fire before the LORD, that the cloud of the incense may cover the mercy seate that is upon the covenant,g or he will die. 14He shall

c 15:32 is defiled by a genital disease, literally, "has an issue."
d 16:8, 10 sent away and sent out . . . as a scapegoat, literally, "for Azazel" or "for removing."

e Or the cover   f Traditionally rendered a scapegoat   g Or treaty, or testament; Heb eduth

King James

14And he shall take of the blood of the bullock, and sprinkle *it* with his finger upon the mercy seat eastward; and before the mercy seat shall he sprinkle of the blood with his finger seven times.

15¶ Then shall he kill the goat of the sin offering, that *is* for the people, and bring his blood within the veil, and do with that blood as he did with the blood of the bullock, and sprinkle it upon the mercy seat, and before the mercy seat:

16And he shall make an atonement for the holy *place,* because of the uncleanness of the children of Israel, and because of their transgressions in all their sins: and so shall he do for the tabernacle of the congregation, that remaineth among them in the midst of their uncleanness.

17And there shall be no man in the tabernacle of the congregation when he goeth in to make an atonement in the holy *place,* until he come out, and have made an atonement for himself, and for his household, and for all the congregation of Israel.

18And he shall go out unto the altar that *is* before the LORD, and make an atonement for it; and shall take of the blood of the bullock, and of the blood of the goat, and put *it* upon the horns of the altar round about.

19And he shall sprinkle of the blood upon it with his finger seven times, and cleanse it, and hallow it from the uncleanness of the children of Israel.

20¶ And when he hath made an end of reconciling the holy *place,* and the tabernacle of the congregation, and the altar, he shall bring the live goat:

21And Aaron shall lay both his hands upon the head of the live goat, and confess over him all the iniquities of the children of Israel, and all their transgressions in all their sins, putting them upon the head of the goat, and shall send *him* away by the hand of a fit man into the wilderness:

22And the goat shall bear upon him all their iniquities unto a land not inhabited: and he shall let go the goat in the wilderness.

23And Aaron shall come into the tabernacle of the congregation, and shall put off the linen garments, which he put on when he went into the holy *place,* and shall leave them there:

24And he shall wash his flesh with water in the holy place, and put on his garments, and come forth, and offer his burnt offering, and the burnt offering of the people, and make an atonement for himself, and for the people.

25And the fat of the sin offering shall he burn upon the altar.

26And he that let go the goat for the scapegoat shall wash his clothes, and bathe his flesh in water, and afterward come into the camp.

27And the bullock *for* the sin offering, and the goat *for* the sin offering, whose blood was brought in to make atonement in the holy *place,* shall *one* carry forth without the camp; and they shall burn in the fire their skins, and their flesh, and their dung.

28And he that burneth them shall wash his clothes, and bathe his flesh in water, and afterward he shall come into the camp.

29¶ And *this* shall be a statute for ever unto you: *that* in the seventh month, on the tenth *day* of the month, ye shall afflict your souls, and do no work at all, *whether it be* one of your own country, or a stranger that sojourneth among you:

30For on that day shall *the priest* make an atonement for you, to cleanse you, *that* ye may be clean from all your sins before the LORD.

31It *shall be* a sabbath of rest unto you, and ye shall afflict your souls, by a statute for ever.

32And the priest, whom he shall anoint, and whom he shall consecrate to minister in the priest's office in his father's stead, shall make the atonement, and shall put on the linen clothes, *even* the holy garments:

New International

take some of the bull's blood and with his finger sprinkle it on the front of the atonement cover; then he shall sprinkle some of it with his finger seven times before the atonement cover.

15"He shall then slaughter the goat for the sin offering for the people and take its blood behind the curtain and do with it as he did with the bull's blood: He shall sprinkle it on the atonement cover and in front of it. 16In this way he will make atonement for the Most Holy Place because of the uncleanness and rebellion of the Israelites, whatever their sins have been. He is to do the same for the Tent of Meeting, which is among them in the midst of their uncleanness. 17No one is to be in the Tent of Meeting from the time Aaron goes in to make atonement in the Most Holy Place until he comes out, having made atonement for himself, his household and the whole community of Israel.

18"Then he shall come out to the altar that is before the LORD and make atonement for it. He shall take some of the bull's blood and some of the goat's blood and put it on all the horns of the altar. 19He shall sprinkle some of the blood on it with his finger seven times to cleanse it and to consecrate it from the uncleanness of the Israelites.

20"When Aaron has finished making atonement for the Most Holy Place, the Tent of Meeting and the altar, he shall bring forward the live goat. 21He is to lay both hands on the head of the live goat and confess over it all the wickedness and rebellion of the Israelites—all their sins—and put them on the goat's head. He shall send the goat away into the desert in the care of a man appointed for the task. 22The goat will carry on itself all their sins to a solitary place; and the man shall release it in the desert.

23"Then Aaron is to go into the Tent of Meeting and take off the linen garments he put on before he entered the Most Holy Place, and he is to leave them there. 24He shall bathe himself with water in a holy place and put on his regular garments. Then he shall come out and sacrifice the burnt offering for himself and the burnt offering for the people, to make atonement for himself and for the people. 25He shall also burn the fat of the sin offering on the altar.

26"The man who releases the goat as a scapegoat must wash his clothes and bathe himself with water; afterward he may come into the camp. 27The bull and the goat for the sin offerings, whose blood was brought into the Most Holy Place to make atonement, must be taken outside the camp; their hides, flesh and offal are to be burned up. 28The man who burns them must wash his clothes and bathe himself with water; afterward he may come into the camp.

29"This is to be a lasting ordinance for you: On the tenth day of the seventh month you must deny yourselvesᵃ and not do any work—whether native-born or an alien living among you— 30because on this day atonement will be made for you, to cleanse you. Then, before the LORD, you will be clean from all your sins. 31It is a sabbath of rest, and you must deny yourselves; it is a lasting ordinance. 32The priest who is anointed and ordained to succeed his father as high priest is to make atonement. He is to put on the sacred linen garments

---

ᵃ 29 Or *must fast*; also in verse 31

Living Bible

of the blood of the young bull and sprinkle it with his finger upon the east side of the mercy place, and then seven times in front of it.

15"Then he must go out[b] and sacrifice the people's sin offering goat, and bring its blood within the veil, and sprinkle it upon the place of mercy and in front of it, just as he did with the blood of the young bull. 16Thus he shall make atonement for the holy place because it is defiled by the sins of the people of Israel, and for the Tabernacle, located right among them and surrounded by their defilement. 17Not another soul shall be inside the Tabernacle when Aaron enters to make atonement in the Holy Place—not until after he comes out again and has made atonement for himself and his household and for all the people of Israel. 18Then he shall go out to the altar before the Lord and make atonement for it. He must smear the blood of the young bull and the goat on the horns of the altar, 19and sprinkle blood upon the altar seven times with his finger, thus cleansing it from the sinfulness of Israel, and making it holy.[c]

20"When he has completed the rite of atonement for the Holy Place, the entire Tabernacle, and the altar, he shall bring the live goat, and 21laying both hands upon its head, confess over it all the sins of the people of Israel. He shall lay all their sins upon the head of the goat and send it into the desert, led by a man appointed for the task. 22So the goat shall carry all the sins of the people into a land where no one lives,[d] and the man shall let it loose in the wilderness.

23"Then Aaron shall go into the Tabernacle again and take off the linen garments he wore when he went behind the veil, and leave them there in the Tabernacle. 24Then he shall bathe in a sacred place, put on his clothes again, and go out and sacrifice his own burnt offering for the people, making atonement for himself and for them. 25He shall also burn upon the altar the fat for the sin offering.

26"(The man who took the goat out into the desert[e] shall afterwards wash his clothes and bathe himself and then come back into the camp.) 27And the young bull and the goat used for the sin offering (their blood was taken into the Holy Place by Aaron, to make atonement) shall be carried outside the camp and burned, including the hides and internal organs. 28Afterwards, the person doing the burning shall wash his clothes and bathe himself and then return to camp.

29, 30"This is a permanent law: You must do no work on the twenty-fifth day of September,[f] but must spend the day in self-examination and humility. This applies whether you are born in the land or are a foreigner living among the people of Israel; for this is the day commemorating the atonement, cleansing you in the Lord's eyes for all of your sins. 31It is a Sabbath of solemn rest for you, and you shall spend the day in quiet humility;[g] this is a permanent law. 32This ceremony, in later generations, shall be performed by the anointed High Priest, consecrated in place of his ancestor Aaron; he shall be the one to put on the holy linen garments, 33and

New Revised Standard

take some of the blood of the bull, and sprinkle it with his finger on the front of the mercy seat,[h] and before the mercy seat[h] he shall sprinkle the blood with his finger seven times.

15 He shall slaughter the goat of the sin offering that is for the people and bring its blood inside the curtain, and do with its blood as he did with the blood of the bull, sprinkling it upon the mercy seat[h] and before the mercy seat.[h] 16Thus he shall make atonement for the sanctuary, because of the uncleannesses of the people of Israel, and because of their transgressions, all their sins; and so he shall do for the tent of meeting, which remains with them in the midst of their uncleannesses. 17No one shall be in the tent of meeting from the time he enters to make atonement in the sanctuary until he comes out and has made atonement for himself and for his house and for all the assembly of Israel. 18 Then he shall go out to the altar that is before the LORD and make atonement on its behalf, and shall take some of the blood of the bull and of the blood of the goat, and put it on each of the horns of the altar. 19 He shall sprinkle some of the blood on it with his finger seven times, and cleanse it and hallow it from the uncleannesses of the people of Israel.

20 When he has finished atoning for the holy place and the tent of meeting and the altar, he shall present the live goat. 21 Then Aaron shall lay both his hands on the head of the live goat, and confess over it all the iniquities of the people of Israel, and all their transgressions, all their sins, putting them on the head of the goat, and sending it away into the wilderness by means of someone designated for the task.[i] 22 The goat shall bear on itself all their iniquities to a barren region; and the goat shall be set free in the wilderness.

23 Then Aaron shall enter the tent of meeting, and shall take off the linen vestments that he put on when he went into the holy place, and shall leave them there. 24 He shall bathe his body in water in a holy place, and put on his vestments; then he shall come out and offer his burnt offering and the burnt offering of the people, making atonement for himself and for the people. 25 The fat of the sin offering he shall turn into smoke on the altar. 26 The one who sets the goat free for Azazel[j] shall wash his clothes and bathe his body in water, and afterward may come into the camp. 27 The bull of the sin offering and the goat of the sin offering, whose blood was brought in to make atonement in the holy place, shall be taken outside the camp; their skin and their flesh and their dung shall be consumed in fire. 28 The one who burns them shall wash his clothes and bathe his body in water, and afterward may come into the camp.

29 This shall be a statute to you forever: In the seventh month, on the tenth day of the month, you shall deny yourselves,[k] and shall do no work, neither the citizen nor the alien who resides among you. 30 For on this day atonement shall be made for you, to cleanse you; from all your sins you shall be clean before the LORD. 31 It is a sabbath of complete rest to you, and you shall deny yourselves;[k] it is a statute forever. 32 The priest who is anointed and consecrated as priest in his father's place shall make atonement, wearing the linen vestments, the holy vestments. 33 He shall make atone-

---

b *16:15 Then he must go out,* implied.   c *16:19 making it holy,* literally, "hallowing it."   d *16:22 where no one lives,* literally, "a solitary land."   e *16:26 the goat out into the desert,* literally, "for Azazel" or "for removal."   f *16:29, 30 on the twenty-fifth day of September* (which was "on the tenth day of the seventh month" of the Hebrew calendar).   g *16:31 in quiet humility,* or, "in fasting."

h Or *the cover*   i Meaning of Heb uncertain   j Traditionally rendered *a scapegoat*   k Or *shall fast*

King James

33And he shall make an atonement for the holy sanctuary, and he shall make an atonement for the tabernacle of the congregation, and for the altar, and he shall make an atonement for the priests, and for all the people of the congregation.

34And this shall be an everlasting statute unto you, to make an atonement for the children of Israel for all their sins once a year. And he did as the LORD commanded Moses.

17 AND THE LORD spake unto Moses, saying, 2Speak unto Aaron, and unto his sons, and unto all the children of Israel, and say unto them; This *is* the thing which the LORD hath commanded, saying,

3What man soever *there be* of the house of Israel, that killeth an ox, or lamb, or goat, in the camp, or that killeth *it* out of the camp,

4And bringeth it not unto the door of the tabernacle of the congregation, to offer an offering unto the LORD before the tabernacle of the LORD; blood shall be imputed unto that man; he hath shed blood; and that man shall be cut off from among his people:

5To the end that the children of Israel may bring their sacrifices, which they offer in the open field, even that they may bring them unto the LORD, unto the door of the tabernacle of the congregation, unto the priest, and offer them *for* peace offerings unto the LORD.

6And the priest shall sprinkle the blood upon the altar of the LORD *at* the door of the tabernacle of the congregation, and burn the fat for a sweet savour unto the LORD.

7And they shall no more offer their sacrifices unto devils, after whom they have gone a-whoring. This shall be a statute for ever unto them throughout their generations.

8¶ And thou shalt say unto them, Whatsoever man *there be* of the house of Israel, or of the strangers which sojourn among you, that offereth a burnt offering or sacrifice,

9And bringeth it not unto the door of the tabernacle of the congregation, to offer it unto the LORD; even that man shall be cut off from among his people.

10¶ And whatsoever man *there be* of the house of Israel, or of the strangers that sojourn among you, that eateth any manner of blood; I will even set my face against that soul that eateth blood, and will cut him off from among his people.

11For the life of the flesh *is* in the blood: and I have given it to you upon the altar to make an atonement for your souls: for it *is* the blood *that* maketh an atonement for the soul.

12Therefore I said unto the children of Israel, No soul of you shall eat blood, neither shall any stranger that sojourneth among you eat blood.

13And whatsoever man *there be* of the children of Israel, or of the strangers that sojourn among you, which hunteth and catcheth any beast or fowl that may be eaten; he shall even pour out the blood thereof, and cover it with dust.

14For *it is* the life of all flesh; the blood of it *is* for the life thereof: therefore I said unto the children of Israel, Ye shall eat the blood of no manner of flesh: for the life of all flesh *is* the blood thereof: whosoever eateth it shall be cut off.

15And every soul that eateth that which died *of itself*, or that which was torn *with beasts, whether it be* one of your own country, or a stranger, he shall both wash his clothes, and bathe *himself* in water, and be unclean until the even: then shall he be clean.

16But if he wash *them* not, nor bathe his flesh; then he shall bear his iniquity.

New International

33and make atonement for the Most Holy Place, for the Tent of Meeting and the altar, and for the priests and all the people of the community.

34"This is to be a lasting ordinance for you: Atonement is to be made once a year for all the sins of the Israelites."

And it was done, as the LORD commanded Moses.

Eating Blood Forbidden

17 THE LORD said to Moses, 2"Speak to Aaron and his sons and to all the Israelites and say to them: 'This is what the LORD has commanded: 3Any Israelite who sacrifices an ox,[a] a lamb or a goat in the camp or outside of it 4instead of bringing it to the entrance to the Tent of Meeting to present it as an offering to the LORD in front of the tabernacle of the LORD—that man shall be considered guilty of bloodshed; he has shed blood and must be cut off from his people. 5This is so the Israelites will bring to the LORD the sacrifices they are now making in the open fields. They must bring them to the priest, that is, to the LORD, at the entrance to the Tent of Meeting and sacrifice them as fellowship offerings.[b] 6The priest is to sprinkle the blood against the altar of the LORD at the entrance to the Tent of Meeting and burn the fat as an aroma pleasing to the LORD. 7They must no longer offer any of their sacrifices to the goat idols[c] to whom they prostitute themselves. This is to be a lasting ordinance for them and for the generations to come.'

8"Say to them: 'Any Israelite or any alien living among them who offers a burnt offering or sacrifice 9and does not bring it to the entrance to the Tent of Meeting to sacrifice it to the LORD—that man must be cut off from his people.

10"'Any Israelite or any alien living among them who eats any blood—I will set my face against that person who eats blood and will cut him off from his people. 11For the life of a creature is in the blood, and I have given it to you to make atonement for yourselves on the altar; it is the blood that makes atonement for one's life. 12Therefore I say to the Israelites, "None of you may eat blood, nor may an alien living among you eat blood."

13"'Any Israelite or any alien living among you who hunts any animal or bird that may be eaten must drain out the blood and cover it with earth, 14because the life of every creature is its blood. That is why I have said to the Israelites, "You must not eat the blood of any creature, because the life of every creature is its blood; anyone who eats it must be cut off."

15"'Anyone, whether native-born or alien, who eats anything found dead or torn by wild animals must wash his clothes and bathe with water, and he will be ceremonially unclean till evening; then he will be clean. 16But if he does not wash his clothes and bathe himself, he will be held responsible.'"

---

[a] 3 The Hebrew word can include both male and female. [b] 5 Traditionally peace offerings [c] 7 Or demons

Living Bible

make atonement for the holy sanctuary, the Tabernacle, the altar, the priests, and the people. 34This shall be an everlasting law for you, to make atonement for the people of Israel once each year, because of their sins."

And Aaron followed all these instructions that the Lord gave to Moses.

17 THE LORD gave to Moses these additional instructions for Aaron and the priests and for all the people of Israel:

3,4"Any Israelite who sacrificesd an ox, lamb, or goat anywhere except at the Tabernacle is guilty of murder and shall be excommunicated from his nation. 5The purpose of this law is to stop the people of Israel from sacrificing in the open fields, and to cause them to bring their sacrifices to the priest at the entrance of the Tabernacle, and to burn the fat as a savor the Lord will appreciate and enjoy— 6for in this way the priest will be able to sprinkle the blood upon the altar of the Lord at the entrance of the Tabernacle, and to burn the fat as a savor the Lord will appreciate and enjoy— 7instead of the people's sacrificing to evil spiritse out in the fields. This shall be a permanent law for you, from generation to generation. 8,9I repeat: Anyone, whether an Israelite or a foreigner living among you who offers a burnt offering or a sacrifice anywhere other than at the entrance of the Tabernacle, where it will be sacrificed to the Lord, shall be excommunicated.

10"And I will turn my face against anyone, whether an Israelite or a foreigner living among you, who eats blood in any form. I will excommunicate him from his people. 11For the life of the flesh is in the blood, and I have given you the blood to sprinkle upon the altar as an atonement for your souls; it is the blood that makes atonement, because it is the life.f 12That is the reasoning behind my decree to the people of Israel, that neither they, nor any foreigner living among them, may eat blood. 13Anyone, whether an Israelite or a foreigner living among you, who goes hunting and kills an animal or bird of a kind permitted for food, must pour out the blood and cover it with dust, 14for the blood is the life. That is why I told the people of Israel never to eat it, for the life of every bird and animalg is its blood. Therefore, anyone who eats blood must be excommunicated.

15"And anyone—native born or foreigner—who eats the dead body of an animal that dies a natural death, or is killed by wild animals, must wash his clothes and bathe himself and be defiled until evening; after that he shall be declared cleansed. 16But if he does not wash his clothes and bathe, he shall suffer the consequence."

New Revised Standard

ment for the sanctuary, and he shall make atonement for the tent of meeting and for the altar, and he shall make atonement for the priests and for all the people of the assembly. 34 This shall be an everlasting statute for you, to make atonement for the people of Israel once in the year for all their sins. And Moses did as the Lord had commanded him.

The Slaughtering of Animals

17 THE LORD spoke to Moses:
2 Speak to Aaron and his sons and to all the people of Israel and say to them: This is what the Lord has commanded. 3If anyone of the house of Israel slaughters an ox or a lamb or a goat in the camp, or slaughters it outside the camp, 4and does not bring it to the entrance of the tent of meeting, to present it as an offering to the Lord before the tabernacle of the Lord, he shall be held guilty of bloodshed; he has shed blood, and he shall be cut off from the people. 5This is in order that the people of Israel may bring their sacrifices that they offer in the open field, that they may bring them to the Lord, to the priest at the entrance of the tent of meeting, and offer them as sacrifices of well-being to the Lord. 6The priest shall dash the blood against the altar of the Lord at the entrance of the tent of meeting, and turn the fat into smoke as a pleasing odor to the Lord, 7so that they may no longer offer their sacrifices for goat-demons, to whom they prostitute themselves. This shall be a statute forever to them throughout their generations.

8 And say to them further: Anyone of the house of Israel or of the aliens who reside among them who offers a burnt offering or sacrifice, 9and does not bring it to the entrance of the tent of meeting, to sacrifice it to the Lord, shall be cut off from the people.

Eating Blood Prohibited

10 If anyone of the house of Israel or of the aliens who reside among them eats any blood, I will set my face against that person who eats blood, and will cut that person off from the people. 11For the life of the flesh is in the blood; and I have given it to you for making atonement for your lives on the altar; for, as life, it is the blood that makes atonement. 12Therefore I have said to the people of Israel: No person among you shall eat blood, nor shall any alien who resides among you eat blood. 13And anyone of the people of Israel, or of the aliens who reside among them, who hunts down an animal or bird that may be eaten shall pour out its blood and cover it with earth.

14 For the life of every creature—its blood is its life; therefore I have said to the people of Israel: You shall not eat the blood of any creature, for the life of every creature is its blood; whoever eats it shall be cut off. 15All persons, citizens or aliens, who eat what dies of itself or what has been torn by wild animals, shall wash their clothes, and bathe themselves in water, and be unclean until the evening; then they shall be clean. 16But if they do not wash themselves or bathe their body, they shall bear their guilt.

---

d 17:3, 4 sacrifices, literally, "slaughters."   e 17:7 evil spirits, literally, "hairy ones."   f 17:11 because it is the life, implied.   g 17:14 every bird and animal, literally, "every creature."

King James

18 AND THE LORD spake unto Moses, saying, 2Speak unto the children of Israel, and say unto them, I am the LORD your God.

3After the doings of the land of Egypt, wherein ye dwelt, shall ye not do: and after the doings of the land of Canaan, whither I bring you, shall ye not do: neither shall ye walk in their ordinances.

4Ye shall do my judgments, and keep mine ordinances, to walk therein: I *am* the LORD your God.

5Ye shall therefore keep my statutes, and my judgments: which if a man do, he shall live in them: I *am* the LORD.

6¶ None of you shall approach to any that is near of kin to him, to uncover *their* nakedness: I *am* the LORD.

7The nakedness of thy father, or the nakedness of thy mother, shalt thou not uncover: she *is* thy mother; thou shalt not uncover her nakedness.

8The nakedness of thy father's wife shalt thou not uncover: it *is* thy father's nakedness.

9The nakedness of thy sister, the daughter of thy father, or daughter of thy mother, *whether she be* born at home, or born abroad, *even* their nakedness thou shalt not uncover.

10The nakedness of thy son's daughter, or of thy daughter's daughter, *even* their nakedness thou shalt not uncover: for theirs *is* thine own nakedness.

11The nakedness of thy father's wife's daughter, begotten of thy father, she *is* thy sister, thou shalt not uncover her nakedness.

12Thou shalt not uncover the nakedness of thy father's sister: she *is* thy father's near kinswoman.

13Thou shalt not uncover the nakedness of thy mother's sister: for she *is* thy mother's near kinswoman.

14Thou shalt not uncover the nakedness of thy father's brother, thou shalt not approach to his wife: she *is* thine aunt.

15Thou shalt not uncover the nakedness of thy daughter-in-law: she *is* thy son's wife; thou shalt not uncover her nakedness.

16Thou shalt not uncover the nakedness of thy brother's wife: it *is* thy brother's nakedness.

17Thou shalt not uncover the nakedness of a woman and her daughter, neither shalt thou take her son's daughter, or her daughter's daughter, to uncover her nakedness; *for* they *are* her near kinswomen: it *is* wickedness.

18Neither shalt thou take a wife to her sister, to vex *her*, to uncover her nakedness, beside the other in her life *time.*

19Also thou shalt not approach unto a woman to uncover her nakedness, as long as she is put apart for her uncleanness.

20Moreover thou shalt not lie carnally with thy neighbour's wife, to defile thyself with her.

21And thou shalt not let any of thy seed pass through *the fire* to Molech, neither shalt thou profane the name of thy God: I *am* the LORD.

22Thou shalt not lie with mankind, as with womankind: it *is* abomination.

23Neither shalt thou lie with any beast to defile thyself therewith: neither shall any woman stand before a beast to lie down thereto: it *is* confusion.

24Defile not ye yourselves in any of these things: for in all these the nations are defiled which I cast out before you:

25And the land is defiled: therefore I do visit the iniquity thereof upon it, and the land itself vomiteth out her inhabitants.

26Ye shall therefore keep my statutes and my judgments, and shall not commit *any* of these abominations; *neither* any of your own nation, nor any stranger that sojourneth among you:

New International

Unlawful Sexual Relations

18 THE LORD said to Moses, 2"Speak to the Israelites and say to them: 'I am the LORD your God. 3You must not do as they do in Egypt, where you used to live, and you must not do as they do in the land of Canaan, where I am bringing you. Do not follow their practices. 4You must obey my laws and be careful to follow my decrees. I am the LORD your God. 5Keep my decrees and laws, for the man who obeys them will live by them. I am the LORD.

6" 'No one is to approach any close relative to have sexual relations. I am the LORD.

7" 'Do not dishonor your father by having sexual relations with your mother. She is your mother; do not have relations with her.

8" 'Do not have sexual relations with your father's wife; that would dishonor your father.

9" 'Do not have sexual relations with your sister, either your father's daughter or your mother's daughter, whether she was born in the same home or elsewhere.

10" 'Do not have sexual relations with your son's daughter or your daughter's daughter; that would dishonor you.

11" 'Do not have sexual relations with the daughter of your father's wife, born to your father; she is your sister.

12" 'Do not have sexual relations with your father's sister; she is your father's close relative.

13" 'Do not have sexual relations with your mother's sister, because she is your mother's close relative.

14" 'Do not dishonor your father's brother by approaching his wife to have sexual relations; she is your aunt.

15" 'Do not have sexual relations with your daughter-in-law. She is your son's wife; do not have relations with her.

16" 'Do not have sexual relations with your brother's wife; that would dishonor your brother.

17" 'Do not have sexual relations with both a woman and her daughter. Do not have sexual relations with either her son's daughter or her daughter's daughter; they are her close relatives. That is wickedness.

18" 'Do not take your wife's sister as a rival wife and have sexual relations with her while your wife is living.

19" 'Do not approach a woman to have sexual relations during the uncleanness of her monthly period.

20" 'Do not have sexual relations with your neighbor's wife and defile yourself with her.

21" 'Do not give any of your children to be sacrificed[a] to Molech, for you must not profane the name of your God. I am the LORD.

22" 'Do not lie with a man as one lies with a woman; that is detestable.

23" 'Do not have sexual relations with an animal and defile yourself with it. A woman must not present herself to an animal to have sexual relations with it; that is a perversion.

24" 'Do not defile yourselves in any of these ways, because this is how the nations that I am going to drive out before you became defiled. 25Even the land was defiled; so I punished it for its sin, and the land vomited out its inhabitants. 26But you must keep my decrees and my laws. The native-born and the aliens living among you must not do any of these detestable things, 27for all

---

a *21 Or to be passed through the fire*

Living Bible

18 THE LORD then told Moses to tell the people of Israel,

"I am Jehovah your God, 3so don't act like heathen— like the people of Egypt where you lived so long, or the people of Canaan where I am going to take you. 4. 5You must obey only my laws, and you must carry them out in detail, for I am the Lord your God. If you obey them you shall live.b I am the Lord.

6"None of you shall marryc a near relative, for I am the Lord. 7Do not disgrace your father by having intercourse with your mother, 8nor any other of your father's wives. 9Do not have intercourse with your sister or half-sister, whether the daughter of your father or your mother, whether brought up in the same household or elsewhere.

10"You shall not have intercourse with your granddaughter—the daughter of either your son or your daughter—for she is a close relative.d 11You may not have intercourse with a half-sister—your father's wife's daughter; 12nor your aunt—your father's sister—because she is so closely related to your father; 13nor your aunt—your mother's sister—because she is a close relative of your mother; 14nor your aunt—the wife of your father's brother.e

15"You may not marry your daughter-in-law—your son's wife; 16nor your brother's wife, for she is your brother's.f 17You may not marry both a woman and her daughter or granddaughter, for they are near relatives, and to do so is horrible wickedness. 18You shall not marry two sisters, for they will be rivals. However, if your wife dies, then it is all right to marry her sister.

19"There must be no sexual relationship with a woman who is menstruating; 20nor with anyone else's wife, to defile yourself with her.

21"You shall not give any of your children to Molech, burning them upon his altar; never profane the name of your God, for I am Jehovah.

22"Homosexuality is absolutely forbidden, for it is an enormous sin. 23A man shall have no sexual intercourse with any female animal, thus defiling himself; and a woman must never give herself to a male animal, to mate with it; this is a terrible perversion.

24"Do not defile yourselves in any of these ways, for these are the things the heathen do; and because they do them I am going to cast them out from the land into which you are going. 25That entire country is defiled with this kind of activity; that is why I am punishing the people living there, and will throw them out of the land.g 26You must strictly obey all of my laws and ordinances, and you must not do any of these abominable things; these laws apply both to you who are born in the nation of Israel and to foreigners living among you.

New Revised Standard

Sexual Relations

18 THE LORD spoke to Moses, saying: 2 Speak to the people of Israel and say to them: I am the LORD your God. 3 You shall not do as they do in the land of Egypt, where you lived, and you shall not do as they do in the land of Canaan, to which I am bringing you. You shall not follow their statutes. 4 My ordinances you shall observe and my statutes you shall keep, following them: I am the LORD your God. 5 You shall keep my statutes and my ordinances; by doing so one shall live: I am the LORD.

6 None of you shall approach anyone near of kin to uncover nakedness: I am the LORD. 7 You shall not uncover the nakedness of your father, which is the nakedness of your mother; she is your mother, you shall not uncover her nakedness. 8 You shall not uncover the nakedness of your father's wife; it is the nakedness of your father. 9 You shall not uncover the nakedness of your sister, your father's daughter or your mother's daughter, whether born at home or born abroad. 10 You shall not uncover the nakedness of your son's daughter or of your daughter's daughter, for their nakedness is your own nakedness. 11 You shall not uncover the nakedness of your father's wife's daughter, begotten by your father, since she is your sister. 12 You shall not uncover the nakedness of your father's sister; she is your father's flesh. 13 You shall not uncover the nakedness of your mother's sister, for she is your mother's flesh. 14 You shall not uncover the nakedness of your father's brother, that is, you shall not approach his wife; she is your aunt. 15 You shall not uncover the nakedness of your daughter-in-law: she is your son's wife; you shall not uncover her nakedness. 16 You shall not uncover the nakedness of your brother's wife; it is your brother's nakedness. 17 You shall not uncover the nakedness of a woman and her daughter, and you shall not takeh her son's daughter or her daughter's daughter to uncover her nakedness; they are your flesh; it is depravity. 18 And you shall not takeh a woman as a rival to her sister, uncovering her nakedness while her sister is still alive.

19 You shall not approach a woman to uncover her nakedness while she is in her menstrual uncleanness. 20 You shall not have sexual relations with your kinsman's wife, and defile yourself with her. 21 You shall not give any of your offspring to sacrifice themi to Molech, and so profane the name of your God: I am the LORD. 22 You shall not lie with a male as with a woman; it is an abomination. 23 You shall not have sexual relations with any animal and defile yourself with it, nor shall any woman give herself to an animal to have sexual relations with it: it is perversion.

24 Do not defile yourselves in any of these ways, for by all these practices the nations I am casting out before you have defiled themselves. 25 Thus the land became defiled; and I punished it for its iniquity, and the land vomited out its inhabitants. 26 But you shall keep my statutes and my ordinances and commit none of these abominations, either the citizen or the alien who resides among you 27 (for the inhabitants of the land, who were

---

b *18:4, 5 shall live,* literally, "shall live in them" or "shall live by them."
c *18:6 marry,* literally, "uncover the nakedness of," that is "have sexual intercourse with." d *18:10 for she is a close relative,* literally, "for theirs is your own nakedness." e *18:14 nor your aunt—the wife of your father's brother.* This prohibition applied not only while her husband lived, but also after his death. f *18:16 for she is your brother's.* Except when the brother died and left no heir, in which case his wife was left to a brother to beget children for her to carry on the name and inheritance of the deceased. See Deut 25:5. g *18:25 and will throw them out of the land,* literally, "the land vomits out her inhabitants."

h Or *marry*   i Gk: Heb lacks *your*   j Heb *to pass them over*

King James

27(For all these abominations have the men of the land done, which *were* before you, and the land is defiled;)

28That the land spew not you out also, when ye defile it, as it spewed out the nations that *were* before you.

29For whosoever shall commit any of these abominations, even the souls that commit *them* shall be cut off from among their people.

30Therefore shall ye keep mine ordinance, that *ye* commit not *any one* of these abominable customs, which were committed before you, and that ye defile not yourselves therein: I *am* the LORD your God.

19 AND THE LORD spake unto Moses, saying, 2Speak unto all the congregation of the children of Israel, and say unto them, Ye shall be holy: for I the LORD your God *am* holy.

3¶ Ye shall fear every man his mother, and his father, and keep my sabbaths: I *am* the LORD your God.

4¶ Turn ye not unto idols, nor make to yourselves molten gods: I *am* the LORD your God.

5¶ And if ye offer a sacrifice of peace offerings unto the LORD, ye shall offer it at your own will.

6It shall be eaten the same day ye offer it, and on the morrow: and if aught remain until the third day, it shall be burnt in the fire.

7And if it be eaten at all on the third day, it *is* abominable; it shall not be accepted.

8Therefore *every one* that eateth it shall bear his iniquity, because he hath profaned the hallowed thing of the LORD: and that soul shall be cut off from among his people.

9¶ And when ye reap the harvest of your land, thou shalt not wholly reap the corners of thy field, neither shalt thou gather the gleanings of thy harvest.

10And thou shalt not glean thy vineyard, neither shalt thou gather *every* grape of thy vineyard; thou shalt leave them for the poor and stranger: I *am* the LORD your God.

11¶ Ye shall not steal, neither deal falsely, neither lie one to another.

12¶ And ye shall not swear by my name falsely, neither shalt thou profane the name of thy God: I *am* the LORD.

13¶ Thou shalt not defraud thy neighbour, neither rob *him:* the wages of him that is hired shall not abide with thee all night until the morning.

14¶ Thou shalt not curse the deaf, nor put a stumbling-block before the blind, but shalt fear thy God: I *am* the LORD.

15¶ Ye shall do no unrighteousness in judgment: thou shalt not respect the person of the poor, nor honour the person of the mighty: *but* in righteousness shalt thou judge thy neighbour.

16¶ Thou shalt not go up and down *as* a talebearer among thy people: neither shalt thou stand against the blood of thy neighbour: I *am* the LORD.

17¶ Thou shalt not hate thy brother in thine heart: thou shalt in any wise rebuke thy neighbour, and not suffer sin upon him.

18¶ Thou shalt not avenge, nor bear any grudge against the children of thy people, but thou shalt love thy neighbour as thyself: I *am* the LORD.

19¶ Ye shall keep my statutes. Thou shalt not let thy cattle gender with a diverse kind: thou shalt not sow thy field with mingled seed: neither shall a garment mingled of linen and woollen come upon thee.

20¶ And whosoever lieth carnally with a woman, that *is* a bondmaid, betrothed to an husband, and not at all redeemed, nor freedom given her; she shall be scourged; they shall not be put to death, because she was not free.

New International

these things were done by the people who lived in the land before you, and the land became defiled. 28And if you defile the land, it will vomit you out as it vomited out the nations that were before you.

29" 'Everyone who does any of these detestable things—such persons must be cut off from their people. 30Keep my requirements and do not follow any of the detestable customs that were practiced before you came and do not defile yourselves with them. I am the LORD your God.' "

Various Laws

19 THE LORD said to Moses, 2"Speak to the entire assembly of Israel and say to them: 'Be holy because I, the LORD your God, am holy.

3" 'Each of you must respect his mother and father, and you must observe my Sabbaths. I am the LORD your God.

4" 'Do not turn to idols or make gods of cast metal for yourselves. I am the LORD your God.

5" 'When you sacrifice a fellowship offeringa to the LORD, sacrifice it in such a way that it will be accepted on your behalf. 6It shall be eaten on the day you sacrifice it or on the next day; anything left over until the third day must be burned up. 7If any of it is eaten on the third day, it is impure and will not be accepted. 8Whoever eats it will be held responsible because he has desecrated what is holy to the LORD; that person must be cut off from his people.

9" 'When you reap the harvest of your land, do not reap to the very edges of your field or gather the gleanings of your harvest. 10Do not go over your vineyard a second time or pick up the grapes that have fallen. Leave them for the poor and the alien. I am the LORD your God.

11" 'Do not steal.

" 'Do not lie.

" 'Do not deceive one another.

12" 'Do not swear falsely by my name and so profane the name of your God. I am the LORD.

13" 'Do not defraud your neighbor or rob him.

" 'Do not hold back the wages of a hired man overnight.

14" 'Do not curse the deaf or put a stumbling block in front of the blind, but fear your God. I am the LORD.

15" 'Do not pervert justice; do not show partiality to the poor or favoritism to the great, but judge your neighbor fairly.

16" 'Do not go about spreading slander among your people.

" 'Do not do anything that endangers your neighbor's life. I am the LORD.

17" 'Do not hate your brother in your heart. Rebuke your neighbor frankly so you will not share in his guilt.

18" 'Do not seek revenge or bear a grudge against one of your people, but love your neighbor as yourself. I am the LORD.

19" 'Keep my decrees.

" 'Do not mate different kinds of animals.

" 'Do not plant your field with two kinds of seed.

" 'Do not wear clothing woven of two kinds of material.

20" 'If a man sleeps with a woman who is a slave girl promised to another man but who has not been ransomed or given her freedom, there must be due punishment. Yet they are not to be put to death, because she had not been freed. 21The man, however, must bring a ram to

---

a 5 Traditionally *peace offering*

Living Bible

27"Yes, all these abominations have been done continually by the people of the land where I am taking you, and the land is defiled. 28Do not do these things or I will throw you out of the land, just as I will throw outb the nations that live there now. 29, 30Whoever does any of these terrible deeds shall be excommunicated from this nation. So be very sure to obey my laws, and do not practice any of these horrible customs. Do not defile yourselves with the evil deeds of those living in the land where you are going. For I am Jehovah your God."

19 THE LORD also told Moses to tell the people of Israel, "You must be holy because I, the Lord your God, am holy. You must respect your mothers and fathers, and obey my Sabbath law, for I am the Lord your God. 3, 4Do not make or worship idols, for I am Jehovah your God.

5"When you sacrifice a peace offering to the Lord, offer it correctly so that it will be accepted: 6Eat it the same day you offer it, or the next day at the latest; any remaining until the third day must be burned. 7For any of it eaten on the third day is repulsive to me, and will not be accepted. 8If you eat it on the third day you are guilty, for you profane the holiness of Jehovah, and you shall be excommunicated from Jehovah's people.

9"When you harvest your crops, don't reap the corners of your fields, and don't pick up stray grains of wheat from the ground. 10It is the same with your grape crop—don't strip every last piece of fruit from the vines, and don't pick up the grapes that fall to the ground. Leave them for the poor and for those traveling through, for I am Jehovah your God.

11"You must not steal nor lie nor defraud. 12You must not swear to a falsehood, thus bringing reproach upon the name of your God, for I am Jehovah.

13"You shall not rob nor oppress anyone, and you shall pay your hired workers promptly. If something is due them, don't even keep it overnight.

14"You must not curse the deaf nor trip up a blind man as he walks. Fear your God; I am Jehovah!

15"Judges must always be just in their sentences, not noticing whether a person is poor or rich; they must always be perfectly fair.

16"Don't gossip. Don't falsely accuse your neighbor of some crime,c for I am Jehovah.

17"Don't hate your brother. Rebuke anyone who sins; don't let him get away with it, or you will be equally guilty. 18Don't seek vengeance. Don't bear a grudge; but love your neighbor as yourself, for I am Jehovah.

19"Obey my laws: Do not mate your cattle with a different kind; don't sow your field with two kinds of seed; don't wear clothes made of half wool and half linen.

20"If a man seduces a slaved girl who is engaged to be married, they shall be tried in a court but not put to death, because she is not free. 21The man involved shall

New Revised Standard

before you, committed all of these abominations, and the land became defiled); 28 otherwise the land will vomit you out for defiling it, as it vomited out the nation that was before you. 29 For whoever commits any of these abominations shall be cut off from their people. 30 So keep my charge not to commit any of these abominations that were done before you, and not to defile yourselves by them: I am the LORD your God.

Ritual and Moral Holiness

19 THE LORD spoke to Moses, saying: 2 Speak to all the congregation of the people of Israel and say to them: You shall be holy, for I the LORD your God am holy. 3 You shall each revere your mother and father, and you shall keep my sabbaths: I am the LORD your God. 4 Do not turn to idols or make cast images for yourselves: I am the LORD your God.

5 When you offer a sacrifice of well-being to the LORD, offer it in such a way that it is acceptable on your behalf. 6 It shall be eaten on the same day you offer it, or on the next day; and anything left over until the third day shall be consumed in fire. 7 If it is eaten at all on the third day, it is an abomination; it will not be acceptable. 8 All who eat it shall be subject to punishment, because they have profaned what is holy to the LORD; and any such person shall be cut off from the people.

9 When you reap the harvest of your land, you shall not reap to the very edges of your field, or gather the gleanings of your harvest. 10 You shall not strip your vineyard bare, or gather the fallen grapes of your vineyard; you shall leave them for the poor and the alien: I am the LORD your God.

11 You shall not steal; you shall not deal falsely; and you shall not lie to one another. 12 And you shall not swear falsely by my name, profaning the name of your God: I am the LORD.

13 You shall not defraud your neighbor; you shall not steal; and you shall not keep for yourself the wages of a laborer until morning. 14 You shall not revile the deaf or put a stumbling block before the blind; you shall fear your God: I am the LORD.

15 You shall not render an unjust judgment; you shall not be partial to the poor or defer to the great: with justice you shall judge your neighbor. 16 You shall not go around as a slanderere among your people, and you shall not profit by the bloodf of your neighbor: I am the LORD.

17 You shall not hate in your heart anyone of your kin; you shall reprove your neighbor, or you will incur guilt yourself. 18 You shall not take vengeance or bear a grudge against any of your people, but you shall love your neighbor as yourself: I am the LORD.

19 You shall keep my statutes. You shall not let your animals breed with a different kind; you shall not sow your field with two kinds of seed; nor shall you put on a garment made of two different materials.

20 If a man has sexual relations with a woman who is a slave, designated for another man but not ransomed or given her freedom, an inquiry shall be held. They shall not be put to death, since she has not been freed;

---

b 18:28 *or I will throw you out of the land, just as I will throw out,* literally, "that the land vomit not you out also . . . as it vomited out . . ." c 19:16 *Don't falsely accuse your neighbor of some crime,* literally, "neither shall you stand against the blood of your neighbor." d 19:20 *slave girl,* literally, "not yet redeemed, nor given her freedom."

e Meaning of Heb uncertain   f Heb *stand against the blood*

King James

21And he shall bring his trespass offering unto the LORD, unto the door of the tabernacle of the congregation, *even* a ram for a trespass offering.

22And the priest shall make an atonement for him with the ram of the trespass offering before the LORD for his sin which he hath done: and the sin which he hath done shall be forgiven him.

23¶ And when ye shall come into the land, and shall have planted all manner of trees for food, then ye shall count the fruit thereof as uncircumcised: three years shall it be as uncircumcised unto you: it shall not be eaten of.

24But in the fourth year all the fruit thereof shall be holy to praise the LORD *withal*.

25And in the fifth year shall ye eat of the fruit thereof, that it may yield unto you the increase thereof: I *am* the LORD your God.

26¶ Ye shall not eat *any thing* with the blood: neither shall ye use enchantment, nor observe times.

27Ye shall not round the corners of your heads, neither shalt thou mar the corners of thy beard.

28Ye shall not make any cuttings in your flesh for the dead, nor print any marks upon you: I *am* the LORD.

29¶ Do not prostitute thy daughter, to cause her to be a whore; lest the land fall to whoredom, and the land become full of wickedness.

30¶ Ye shall keep my sabbaths, and reverence my sanctuary: I *am* the LORD.

31¶ Regard not them that have familiar spirits, neither seek after wizards, to be defiled by them: I *am* the LORD your God.

32¶ Thou shalt rise up before the hoary head, and honour the face of the old man, and fear thy God: I *am* the LORD.

33¶ And if a stranger sojourn with thee in your land, ye shall not vex him.

34*But* the stranger that dwelleth with you shall be unto you as one born among you, and thou shalt love him as thyself; for ye were strangers in the land of Egypt: I *am* the LORD your God.

35¶ Ye shall do no unrighteousness in judgment, in meteyard, in weight, or in measure.

36Just balances, just weights, a just ephah, and a just hin, shall ye have: I *am* the LORD your God, which brought you out of the land of Egypt.

37Therefore shall ye observe all my statutes, and all my judgments, and do them: I *am* the LORD.

20 AND THE LORD spake unto Moses, saying, 2Again, thou shalt say to the children of Israel, Whosoever *he be* of the children of Israel, or of the strangers that sojourn in Israel, that giveth *any* of his seed unto Molech; he shall surely be put to death: the people of the land shall stone him with stones.

3And I will set my face against that man, and will cut him off from among his people; because he hath given of his seed unto Molech, to defile my sanctuary, and to profane my holy name.

4And if the people of the land do any ways hide their eyes from the man, when he giveth of his seed unto Molech, and kill him not:

5Then I will set my face against that man, and against his family, and will cut him off, and all that go a-whoring after him, to commit whoredom with Molech, from among their people.

6¶ And the soul that turneth after such as have familiar spirits, and after wizards, to go a-whoring after them, I will even set my face against that soul, and will cut him off from among his people.

7¶ Sanctify yourselves therefore, and be ye holy: for I *am* the LORD your God.

New International

the entrance to the Tent of Meeting for a guilt offering to the LORD. 22With the ram of the guilt offering the priest is to make atonement for him before the LORD for the sin he has committed, and his sin will be forgiven.

23" 'When you enter the land and plant any kind of fruit tree, regard its fruit as forbidden.a For three years you are to consider it forbiddena; it must not be eaten. 24In the fourth year all its fruit will be holy, an offering of praise to the LORD. 25But in the fifth year you may eat its fruit. In this way your harvest will be increased. I am the LORD your God.

26" 'Do not eat any meat with the blood still in it.
" 'Do not practice divination or sorcery.

27" 'Do not cut the hair at the sides of your head or clip off the edges of your beard.

28" 'Do not cut your bodies for the dead or put tattoo marks on yourselves. I am the LORD.

29" 'Do not degrade your daughter by making her a prostitute, or the land will turn to prostitution and be filled with wickedness.

30" 'Observe my Sabbaths and have reverence for my sanctuary. I am the LORD.

31" 'Do not turn to mediums or seek out spiritists, for you will be defiled by them. I am the LORD your God.

32" 'Rise in the presence of the aged, show respect for the elderly and revere your God. I am the LORD.

33" 'When an alien lives with you in your land, do not mistreat him. 34The alien living with you must be treated as one of your native-born. Love him as yourself, for you were aliens in Egypt. I am the LORD your God.

35" 'Do not use dishonest standards when measuring length, weight or quantity. 36Use honest scales and honest weights, an honest ephahb and an honest hin.c I am the LORD your God, who brought you out of Egypt.

37" 'Keep all my decrees and all my laws and follow them. I am the LORD.' "

Punishments for Sin

20 THE LORD said to Moses, 2"Say to the Israelites: 'Any Israelite or any alien living in Israel who givesd any of his children to Molech must be put to death. The people of the community are to stone him. 3I will set my face against that man and I will cut him off from his people; for by giving his children to Molech, he has defiled my sanctuary and profaned my holy name. 4If the people of the community close their eyes when that man gives one of his children to Molech and they fail to put him to death, 5I will set my face against that man and his family and will cut off from their people both him and all who follow him in prostituting themselves to Molech.

6" 'I will set my face against the person who turns to mediums and spiritists to prostitute himself by following them, and I will cut him off from his people.

7" 'Consecrate yourselves and be holy, because I am

---

a *23* Hebrew *uncircumcised*   b *36* An ephah was a dry measure.   c *36* A hin was a liquid measure.   d *2* Or *sacrifices*; also in verses 3 and 4

Living Bible

bring his guilt offering to the Lord at the entrance of the Tabernacle; the offering shall be a ram. 22The priest shall make atonement with the ram for the sin the man has committed, and it shall be forgiven him.

23"When you enter the land and have planted all kinds of fruit trees, do not eat the first three crops, for they are considered ceremonially defiled.e 24And the fourth year the entire crop shall be devoted to the Lord, and shall be given to the Lord in praise to him. 25Finally, in the fifth year, the crop is yours.

26"I am Jehovah your God! You must not eat meat with undrained blood nor use fortune telling or witchcraft.

27"You must not trim off your hair on your temples or clip the edges of your beard, as the heathen do.f 28You shall not cut yourselves nor put tattoo marks upon yourselves in connection with funeral rites; I am the Lord.

29"Do not violate your daughter's sanctity by making her a prostitute, lest the land become full of enormous wickedness.

30"Keep my Sabbath laws and reverence my Tabernacle, for I am the Lord.

31"Do not defile yourselves by consulting mediums and wizards, for I am Jehovah your God.

32"You shall give due honor and respect to the elderly, in the fear of God. I am Jehovah.

33"Do not take advantage of foreigners in your land; do not wrong them. 34They must be treated like any other citizen; love them as yourself, for remember that you too were foreigners in the land of Egypt. I am Jehovah your God.

35, 36"You must be impartial in judgment. Use accurate measurements—lengths, weights, and volumes—and give full measure, for I am Jehovah your God who brought you from the land of Egypt. 37You must heed all of my commandments and ordinances, carefully obeying them, for I am Jehovah."

20 THE LORD gave Moses these further instructions for the people of Israel:

"Anyone—whether an Israelite or a foreigner living among you—who sacrifices his child as a burnt offering to Molech shall without fail be stoned by his peers. 3And I myself will turn against that man and cut him off from all his people, because he has given his child to Molech, thus making my Tabernacleg unfit for me to live in, and insulting my holy name. 4And if the people of the land pretend they do not know what the man has done, and refuse to put him to death, 5then I myself will set my face against that man and his family and cut him off, along with all others who turn to other gods than me.

6"I will set my face against anyone who consults mediums and wizards instead of me and I will cut that person off from his people. 7So sanctify yourselves and be holy, for I am the Lord your God. 8You must obey

New Revised Standard

21but he shall bring a guilt offering for himself to the LORD, at the entrance of the tent of meeting, a ram as guilt offering. 22 And the priest shall make atonement for him with the ram of guilt offering before the LORD for his sin that he committed; and the sin he committed shall be forgiven him.

23 When you come into the land and plant all kinds of trees for food, then you shall regard their fruit as forbidden;h three years it shall be forbiddeni to you, it must not be eaten. 24 In the fourth year all their fruit shall be set apart for rejoicing in the LORD. 25 But in the fifth year you may eat of their fruit, that their yield may be increased for you: I am the LORD your God.

26 You shall not eat anything with its blood. You shall not practice augury or witchcraft. 27 You shall not round off the hair on your temples or mar the edges of your beard. 28 You shall not make any gashes in your flesh for the dead or tattoo any marks upon you: I am the LORD.

29 Do not profane your daughter by making her a prostitute, that the land not become prostituted and full of depravity. 30 You shall keep my sabbaths and reverence my sanctuary: I am the LORD.

31 Do not turn to mediums or wizards; do not seek them out, to be defiled by them: I am the LORD your God.

32 You shall rise before the aged, and defer to the old; and you shall fear your God: I am the LORD.

33 When an alien resides with you in your land, you shall not oppress the alien. 34 The alien who resides with you shall be to you as the citizen among you; you shall love the alien as yourself, for you were aliens in the land of Egypt: I am the LORD your God.

35 You shall not cheat in measuring length, weight, or quantity. 36 You shall have honest balances, honest weights, an honest ephah, and an honest hin: I am the LORD your God, who brought you out of the land of Egypt. 37 You shall keep all my statutes and all my ordinances, and observe them: I am the LORD.

Penalties for Violations of Holiness

20 THE LORD spoke to Moses, saying: 2 Say further to the people of Israel:

Any of the people of Israel, or of the aliens who reside in Israel, who give any of their offspring to Molech shall be put to death; the people of the land shall stone them to death. 3 I myself will set my face against them, and will cut them off from the people, because they have given of their offspring to Molech, defiling my sanctuary and profaning my holy name. 4 And if the people of the land should ever close their eyes to them, when they give of their offspring to Molech, and do not put them to death, 5 I myself will set my face against them and against their family, and will cut them off from among their people, them and all who follow them in prostituting themselves to Molech.

6 If any turn to mediums and wizards, prostituting themselves to them, I will set my face against them, and will cut them off from the people. 7 Consecrate yourselves therefore, and be holy; for I am the LORD your God. 8 Keep my statutes, and observe them; I am the

---

e 19:23 for they are considered ceremonially defiled, literally, "you shall count the fruit thereof as their uncircumcision." f 19:27 as the heathen do, implied. g 20:3 my Tabernacle, literally, "my sanctuary . . ."

h Heb as their uncircumcision i Heb uncircumcision

King James

8And ye shall keep my statutes, and do them: I *am* the LORD which sanctify you.

9¶ For every one that curseth his father or his mother shall be surely put to death: he hath cursed his father or his mother; his blood *shall be* upon him.

10¶ And the man that committeth adultery with *another* man's wife, *even he* that committeth adultery with his neighbour's wife, the adulterer and the adulteress shall surely be put to death.

11And the man that lieth with his father's wife hath uncovered his father's nakedness: both of them shall surely be put to death; their blood *shall be* upon them.

12And if a man lie with his daughter-in-law, both of them shall surely be put to death: they have wrought confusion; their blood *shall be* upon them.

13If a man also lie with mankind, as he lieth with a woman, both of them have committed an abomination: they shall surely be put to death; their blood *shall be* upon them.

14And if a man take a wife and her mother, it *is* wickedness: they shall be burnt with fire, both he and they; that there be no wickedness among you.

15And if a man lie with a beast, he shall surely be put to death: and ye shall slay the beast.

16And if a woman approach unto any beast, and lie down thereto, thou shalt kill the woman, and the beast: they shall surely be put to death; their blood *shall be* upon them.

17And if a man shall take his sister, his father's daughter, or his mother's daughter, and see her nakedness, and she see his nakedness; it *is* a wicked thing; and they shall be cut off in the sight of their people; he hath uncovered his sister's nakedness; he shall bear his iniquity.

18And if a man shall lie with a woman having her sickness, and shall uncover her nakedness; he hath discovered her fountain, and she hath uncovered the fountain of her blood: and both of them shall be cut off from among their people.

19And thou shalt not uncover the nakedness of thy mother's sister, nor of thy father's sister: for he uncovereth his near kin: they shall bear their iniquity.

20And if a man shall lie with his uncle's wife, he hath uncovered his uncle's nakedness: they shall bear their sin; they shall die childless.

21And if a man shall take his brother's wife, it *is* an unclean thing: he hath uncovered his brother's nakedness; they shall be childless.

22¶ Ye shall therefore keep all my statutes, and all my judgments, and do them: that the land, whither I bring you to dwell therein, spew you not out.

23And ye shall not walk in the manners of the nation, which I cast out before you: for they committed all these things, and therefore I abhorred them.

24But I have said unto you, Ye shall inherit their land, and I will give it unto you to possess it, a land that floweth with milk and honey: I *am* the LORD your God, which have separated you from *other* people.

25Ye shall therefore put difference between clean beasts and unclean, and between unclean fowls and clean: and ye shall not make your souls abominable by beast, or by fowl, or by any manner of living thing that creepeth on the ground, which I have separated from you as unclean.

26And ye shall be holy unto me: for I the LORD *am* holy, and have severed you from *other* people, that ye should be mine.

27¶ A man also or woman that hath a familiar spirit, or that is a wizard, shall surely be put to death: they shall stone them with stones: their blood *shall be* upon them.

New International

the LORD your God. 8Keep my decrees and follow them. I am the LORD, who makes you holy.a

9" 'If anyone curses his father or mother, he must be put to death. He has cursed his father or his mother, and his blood will be on his own head.

10" 'If a man commits adultery with another man's wife—with the wife of his neighbor—both the adulterer and the adulteress must be put to death.

11" 'If a man sleeps with his father's wife, he has dishonored his father. Both the man and the woman must be put to death; their blood will be on their own heads.

12" 'If a man sleeps with his daughter-in-law, both of them must be put to death. What they have done is a perversion; their blood will be on their own heads.

13" 'If a man lies with a man as one lies with a woman, both of them have done what is detestable. They must be put to death; their blood will be on their own heads.

14" 'If a man marries both a woman and her mother, it is wicked. Both he and they must be burned in the fire, so that no wickedness will be among you.

15" 'If a man has sexual relations with an animal, he must be put to death, and you must kill the animal.

16" 'If a woman approaches an animal to have sexual relations with it, kill both the woman and the animal. They must be put to death; their blood will be on their own heads.

17" 'If a man marries his sister, the daughter of either his father or his mother, and they have sexual relations, it is a disgrace. They must be cut off before the eyes of their people. He has dishonored his sister and will be held responsible.

18" 'If a man lies with a woman during her monthly period and has sexual relations with her, he has exposed the source of her flow, and she has also uncovered it. Both of them must be cut off from their people.

19" 'Do not have sexual relations with the sister of either your mother or your father, for that would dishonor a close relative; both of you would be held responsible.

20" 'If a man sleeps with his aunt, he has dishonored his uncle. They will be held responsible; they will die childless.

21" 'If a man marries his brother's wife, it is an act of impurity; he has dishonored his brother. They will be childless.

22" 'Keep all my decrees and laws and follow them, so that the land where I am bringing you to live may not vomit you out. 23You must not live according to the customs of the nations I am going to drive out before you. Because they did all these things, I abhorred them. 24But I said to you, "You will possess their land; I will give it to you as an inheritance, a land flowing with milk and honey." I am the LORD your God, who has set you apart from the nations.

25" 'You must therefore make a distinction between clean and unclean animals and between unclean and clean birds. Do not defile yourselves by any animal or bird or anything that moves along the ground—those which I have set apart as unclean for you. 26You are to be holy to meb because I, the LORD, am holy, and I have set you apart from the nations to be my own.

27" 'A man or woman who is a medium or spiritist among you must be put to death. You are to stone them; their blood will be on their own heads.' "

---

a 8 Or *who sanctifies you;* or *who sets you apart as holy*   b 26 Or *be my holy ones*

Living Bible

all of my commandments, for I am the Lord who sanctifies you.

9"Anyone who curses his father or mother shall surely be put to death—for he has cursed his own flesh and blood.

10"If a man commits adultery with another man's wife, both the man and woman shall be put to death. 11If a man sleeps with his father's wife, he has defiled what is his father's; both the man and the woman must die, for it is their own fault. 12And if a man has sexual intercourse with his daughter-in-law, both shall be executed: they have brought it upon themselves by defiling each other. 13The penalty for homosexual acts is death to both parties. They have brought it upon themselves. 14If a man has sexual intercourse with a woman and with her mother, it is a great evil. All three shall be burned alive to wipe out wickedness from among you.

15"If a man has sexual intercourse with an animal, he shall be executed and the animal killed. 16If a woman has sexual intercourse with an animal, kill the woman and the animal, for they deserve their punishment.c

17"If a man has sexual intercourse with his sister, whether the daughter of his father or of his mother, it is a shameful thing, and they shall publicly be cut off from the people of Israel. He shall bear his guilt. 18If a man has sexual intercourse with a woman during her period of menstruation, both shall be excommunicated, for he has uncovered the source of her flow, and she has permitted it.

19"Sexual intercourse is outlawed between a man and his maiden aunt—whether the sister of his mother or of his father—for they are near of kin; they shall bear their guilt. 20If a man has intercourse with his uncle's wife, he has taken what belongs to his uncle; their punishment is that they shall bear their sin and die childless. 21If a man marries his brother's wife,d this is impurity; for he has taken what belongs to his brother, and they shall be childless.

22"You must obey all of my laws and ordinances so that I will not throw you out of your new land.e 23You must not follow the customs of the nations I cast out before you, for they do all these things I have warned you against; that is the reason I abhor them. 24I have promised you their land; I will give it to you to possess it. It is a land 'flowing with milk and honey.' I am the Lord your God who has made a distinction between you and the people of other nations.

25"You shall therefore make a distinction between the birds and animals I have given you permission to eat and those you may not eat. You shall not contaminate yourselves and make yourselves hateful to me by eating any animal or bird which I have forbidden, though the land teem with them. 26You shall be holy to me, for I the Lord am holy, and I have set you apart from all other peoples, to be mine.

27"A medium or a wizard—whether man or woman—shall surely be stoned to death. They have caused their own doom."

New Revised Standard

LORD; I sanctify you. 9All who curse father or mother shall be put to death; having cursed father or mother, their blood is upon them.

10 If a man commits adultery with the wife off his neighbor, both the adulterer and the adulteress shall be put to death. 11The man who lies with his father's wife has uncovered his father's nakedness; both of them shall be put to death; their blood is upon them. 12If a man lies with his daughter-in-law, both of them shall be put to death; they have committed perversion, their blood is upon them. 13If a man lies with a male as with a woman, both of them have committed an abomination; they shall be put to death; their blood is upon them. 14If a man takes a wife and her mother also, it is depravity; they shall be burned to death, both he and they, that there may be no depravity among you. 15If a man has sexual relations with an animal, he shall be put to death; and you shall kill the animal. 16If a woman approaches any animal and has sexual relations with it, you shall kill the woman and the animal; they shall be put to death, their blood is upon them.

17 If a man takes his sister, a daughter of his father or a daughter of his mother, and sees her nakedness, and she sees his nakedness, it is a disgrace, and they shall be cut off in the sight of their people; he has uncovered his sister's nakedness, he shall be subject to punishment. 18If a man lies with a woman having her sickness and uncovers her nakedness, he has laid bare her flow and she has laid bare her flow of blood; both of them shall be cut off from their people. 19You shall not uncover the nakedness of your mother's sister or of your father's sister, for that is to lay bare one's own flesh; they shall be subject to punishment. 20If a man lies with his uncle's wife, he has uncovered his uncle's nakedness; they shall be subject to punishment; they shall die childless. 21If a man takes his brother's wife, it is impurity; he has uncovered his brother's nakedness; they shall be childless.

22 You shall keep all my statutes and all my ordinances, and observe them, so that the land to which I bring you to settle in may not vomit you out. 23You shall not follow the practices of the nation that I am driving out before you. Because they did all these things, I abhorred them. 24But I have said to you: You shall inherit their land, and I will give it to you to possess, a land flowing with milk and honey. I am the LORD your God; I have separated you from the peoples. 25You shall therefore make a distinction between the clean animal and the unclean, and between the unclean bird and the clean; you shall not bring abomination on yourselves by animal or by bird or by anything with which the ground teems, which I have set apart for you to hold unclean. 26You shall be holy to me; for I the LORD am holy, and I have separated you from the other peoples to be mine.

27 A man or a woman who is a medium or a wizard shall be put to death; they shall be stoned to death, their blood is upon them.

---

c 20:16 for they deserve their punishment, literally, "their blood shall be upon them." d 20:21 his brother's wife. However, marriage to his brother's widow was required if she had no children. See Deut 25:5. e 20:22 so that I will not throw you out of your new land, literally, "that the land I give you will not vomit you out again."

f Heb repeats if a man commits adultery with the wife of

King James

21 AND THE LORD said unto Moses, Speak unto the priests the sons of Aaron, and say unto them, There shall none be defiled for the dead among his people:

2But for his kin, that is near unto him, *that is,* for his mother, and for his father, and for his son, and for his daughter, and for his brother,

3And for his sister a virgin, that is nigh unto him, which hath had no husband; for her may he be defiled.

4*But* he shall not defile himself, *being* a chief man among his people, to profane himself.

5They shall not make baldness upon their head, neither shall they shave off the corner of their beard, nor make any cuttings in their flesh.

6They shall be holy unto their God, and not profane the name of their God: for the offerings of the LORD made by fire, *and* the bread of their God, they do offer: therefore they shall be holy.

7They shall not take a wife *that is* a whore, or profane; neither shall they take a woman put away from her husband: for he *is* holy unto his God.

8Thou shalt sanctify him therefore; for he offereth the bread of thy God: he shall be holy unto thee: for I the LORD, which sanctify you, *am* holy.

9¶ And the daughter of any priest, if she profane herself by playing the whore, she profaneth her father: she shall be burnt with fire.

10And *he that is* the high priest among his brethren, upon whose head the anointing oil was poured, and that is consecrated to put on the garments, shall not uncover his head, nor rend his clothes;

11Neither shall he go in to any dead body, nor defile himself for his father, or for his mother;

12Neither shall he go out of the sanctuary, nor profane the sanctuary of his God; for the crown of the anointing oil of his God *is* upon him: I *am* the LORD.

13And he shall take a wife in her virginity.

14A widow, or a divorced woman, or profane, *or* an harlot, these shall he not take: but he shall take a virgin of his own people to wife.

15Neither shall he profane his seed among his people: for I the LORD do sanctify him.

16¶ And the LORD spake unto Moses, saying,

17Speak unto Aaron, saying, Whosoever *he be* of thy seed in their generations that hath *any* blemish, let him not approach to offer the bread of his God.

18For whatsoever man *he be* that hath a blemish, he shall not approach: a blind man, or a lame, or he that hath a flat nose, or any thing superfluous,

19Or a man that is brokenfooted, or brokenhanded,

20Or crookbacked, or a dwarf, or that hath a blemish in his eye, or be scurvy, or scabbed, or hath his stones broken;

21No man that hath a blemish of the seed of Aaron the priest shall come nigh to offer the offerings of the LORD made by fire: he hath a blemish; he shall not come nigh to offer the bread of his God.

22He shall eat the bread of his God, *both* of the most holy, and of the holy.

23Only he shall not go in unto the veil, nor come nigh unto the altar, because he hath a blemish; that he profane not my sanctuaries: for I the LORD do sanctify them.

24And Moses told *it* unto Aaron, and to his sons, and unto all the children of Israel.

New International

Rules for Priests

21 THE LORD said to Moses, "Speak to the priests, the sons of Aaron, and say to them: 'A priest must not make himself ceremonially unclean for any of his people who die, 2except for a close relative, such as his mother or father, his son or daughter, his brother, 3or an unmarried sister who is dependent on him since she has no husband—for her he may make himself unclean. 4He must not make himself unclean for people related to him by marriage,[a] and so defile himself.

5" 'Priests must not shave their heads or shave off the edges of their beards or cut their bodies. 6They must be holy to their God and must not profane the name of their God. Because they present the offerings made to the LORD by fire, the food of their God, they are to be holy.

7" 'They must not marry women defiled by prostitution or divorced from their husbands, because priests are holy to their God. 8Regard them as holy, because they offer up the food of your God. Consider them holy, because I the LORD am holy—I who make you holy.[b]

9" 'If a priest's daughter defiles herself by becoming a prostitute, she disgraces her father; she must be burned in the fire.

10" 'The high priest, the one among his brothers who has had the anointing oil poured on his head and who has been ordained to wear the priestly garments, must not let his hair become unkempt[c] or tear his clothes. 11He must not enter a place where there is a dead body. He must not make himself unclean, even for his father or mother, 12nor leave the sanctuary of his God or desecrate it, because he has been dedicated by the anointing oil of his God. I am the LORD.

13" 'The woman he marries must be a virgin. 14He must not marry a widow, a divorced woman, or a woman defiled by prostitution, but only a virgin from his own people, 15so he will not defile his offspring among his people. I am the LORD, who makes him holy.[d]' "

16The LORD said to Moses, 17"Say to Aaron: 'For the generations to come none of your descendants who has a defect may come near to offer the food of his God. 18No man who has any defect may come near: no man who is blind or lame, disfigured or deformed; 19no man with a crippled foot or hand, 20or who is hunchbacked or dwarfed, or who has any eye defect, or who has festering or running sores or damaged testicles. 21No descendant of Aaron the priest who has any defect is to come near to present the offerings made to the LORD by fire. He has a defect; he must not come near to offer the food of his God. 22He may eat the most holy food of his God, as well as the holy food; 23yet because of his defect, he must not go near the curtain or approach the altar, and so desecrate my sanctuary. I am the LORD, who makes them holy.[e]' "

24So Moses told this to Aaron and his sons and to all the Israelites.

[a] 4 Or *unclean as a leader among his people* [b] 8 Or *who sanctify you; or who set you apart as holy* [c] 10 Or *not uncover his head* [d] 15 Or *who sanctifies him; or who sets him apart as holy* [e] 23 Or *who sanctifies them; or who sets them apart as holy*

Living Bible

21 THE LORD said to Moses: "Tell the priests never to defile themselves by touching a dead person, 2, 3unless it is a near relative—a mother, father, son, daughter, brother, or unmarriedᶠ sister for whom he has special responsibility since she has no husband. 4For the priest is a leader among his people and he may not ceremonially defile himself as an ordinary person can.

5"The priests shall not clip bald spots in their hair or beards, nor cut their flesh. 6They shall be holy unto their God, and shall not dishonor and profane his name; otherwise they will be unfit to make food offerings by fire to the Lord their God. 7A priest shall not marry a prostitute, nor a woman of another tribe, and he shall not marry a divorced woman, for he is a holy man of God. 8The priest is set apart to offer the sacrifices of your God; he is holy, for I, the Lord who sanctifies you, am holy. 9The daughter of any priest who becomes a prostitute, thus violating her father's holiness as well as her own, shall be burned alive.

10"The High Priest—anointed with the special anointing oil and wearing the special garments—must not let his hair hang loose in mourning, nor tear his clothing, 11nor be in the presence of any dead person—not even his father or mother.g 12He shall not leave the sanctuary [when on dutyh], nor treat my Tabernacle like an ordinary house, for the consecration of the anointing oil of his God is upon him; I am Jehovah. 13He must marry a virgin. 14, 15He may not marry a widow, nor a woman who is divorced, nor a prostitute. She must be a virgin from his own tribe, for he must not be the father of children of mixed blood—half priestly and half ordinary."ᶦ

16, 17And the Lord said to Moses, "Tell Aaron that any of his descendants from generation to generation who have any bodily defect may not offer the sacrifices to God. 18For instance, if a man is blind or lame, or has a broken nose or any extra fingers or toes, 19or has a broken foot or hand, 20or has a humped back, or is a dwarf, or has a defect in his eye, or has pimples or scabby skin, or has imperfect testicles— 21although he is a descendant of Aaron—he is not permitted to offer the fire sacrifices to the Lord because of his physical defect. 22However, he shall be fed with the food of the priests from the offerings sacrificed to God, both from the holy and most holy offerings. 23But he shall not go in behind the veil, nor come near the altar, because of the physical defect; this would defile my sanctuary, for it is Jehovah who sanctifies it."

24So Moses gave these instructions to Aaron and his sons and to all the people of Israel.

New Revised Standard

The Holiness of Priests

21 THE LORD said to Moses: Speak to the priests, the sons of Aaron, and say to them:

No one shall defile himself for a dead person among his relatives, 2except for his nearest kin: his mother, his father, his son, his daughter, his brother; 3likewise, for a virgin sister, close to him because she has had no husband, he may defile himself for her. 4But he shall not defile himself as a husband among his people and so profane himself. 5They shall not make bald spots upon their heads, or shave off the edges of their beards, or make any gashes in their flesh. 6They shall be holy to their God, and not profane the name of their God; for they offer the LORD's offerings by fire, the food of their God; therefore they shall be holy. 7They shall not marry a prostitute or a woman who has been defiled; neither shall they marry a woman divorced from her husband. For they are holy to their God, 8and you shall treat them as holy, since they offer the food of your God; they shall be holy to you, for I the LORD, I who sanctify you, am holy. 9When the daughter of a priest profanes herself through prostitution, she profanes her father; she shall be burned to death.

10 The priest who is exalted above his fellows, on whose head the anointing oil has been poured and who has been consecrated to wear the vestments, shall not dishevel his hair, nor tear his vestments. 11He shall not go where there is a dead body; he shall not defile himself even for his father or mother. 12He shall not go outside the sanctuary and thus profane the sanctuary of his God; for the consecration of the anointing oil of his God is upon him: I am the LORD. 13He shall marry only a woman who is a virgin. 14A widow, or a divorced woman, or a woman who has been defiled, a prostitute, these he shall not marry. He shall marry a virgin of his own kin, 15that he may not profane his offspring among his kin; for I am the LORD; I sanctify him.

16 The LORD spoke to Moses, saying: 17Speak to Aaron and say: No one of your offspring throughout their generations who has a blemish may approach to offer the food of his God. 18For no one who has a blemish shall draw near, one who is blind or lame, or one who has a mutilated face or a limb too long, 19or one who has a broken foot or a broken hand, 20or a hunchback, or a dwarf, or a man with a blemish in his eyes or an itching disease or scabs or crushed testicles. 21No descendant of Aaron the priest who has a blemish shall come near to offer the LORD's offerings by fire; since he has a blemish, he shall not come near to offer the food of his God. 22He may eat the food of his God, of the most holy as well as of the holy. 23But he shall not come near the curtain or approach the altar, because he has a blemish, that he may not profane my sanctuaries; for I am the LORD; I sanctify them. 24Thus Moses spoke to Aaron and to his sons and to all the people of Israel.

ᶠ 21:2, 3 *unmarried*, literally, "a virgin." ᵍ 21:11 *not even his father or mother.* Note this rule applied to the High Priest, while the contrary instructions in vs 1 applied to ordinary priests. ʰ 21:12 *when on duty*, implied. ᶦ 21:15 *for he must not be the father of children of mixed blood—half priestly and half ordinary*, literally, "he must not profane his offspring among his people."

King James

22 AND THE Lord spake unto Moses, saying, [2]Speak unto Aaron and to his sons, that they separate themselves from the holy things of the children of Israel, and that they profane not my holy name *in those things* which they hallow unto me: I *am* the Lord.

[3]Say unto them, Whosoever *he be* of all your seed among your generations, that goeth unto the holy things, which the children of Israel hallow unto the Lord, having his uncleanness upon him, that soul shall be cut off from my presence: I *am* the Lord.

[4]What man soever of the seed of Aaron *is* a leper, or hath a running issue; he shall not eat of the holy things, until he be clean. And whoso toucheth any thing *that is* unclean *by* the dead, or a man whose seed goeth from him;

[5]Or whosoever toucheth any creeping thing, whereby he may be made unclean, or a man of whom he may take uncleanness, whatsoever uncleanness he hath;

[6]The soul which hath touched any such thing shall be unclean until even, and shall not eat of the holy things, unless he wash his flesh with water.

[7]And when the sun is down, he shall be clean, and shall afterward eat of the holy things; because it *is* his food.

[8]That which dieth of itself, or is torn *with beasts,* he shall not eat to defile himself therewith: I *am* the Lord.

[9]They shall therefore keep mine ordinance, lest they bear sin for it, and die therefore, if they profane it: I the Lord do sanctify them.

[10]There shall no stranger eat *of* the holy thing: a sojourner of the priest, or an hired servant, shall not eat *of* the holy thing.

[11]But if the priest buy *any* soul with his money, he shall eat of it, and he that is born in his house: they shall eat of his meat.

[12]If the priest's daughter also be *married* unto a stranger, she may not eat of an offering of the holy things.

[13]But if the priest's daughter be a widow, or divorced, and have no child, and is returned unto her father's house, as in her youth, she shall eat of her father's meat: but there shall no stranger eat thereof.

[14]¶ And if a man eat *of* the holy thing unwittingly, then he shall put the fifth *part* thereof unto it, and shall give *it* unto the priest with the holy thing.

[15]And they shall not profane the holy things of the children of Israel, which they offer unto the Lord;

[16]Or suffer them to bear the iniquity of trespass, when they eat their holy things: for I the Lord do sanctify them.

[17]¶ And the Lord spake unto Moses, saying,

[18]Speak unto Aaron, and to his sons, and unto all the children of Israel, and say unto them, Whatsoever *he be* of the house of Israel, or of the strangers in Israel, that will offer his oblation for all his vows, and for all his freewill offerings, which they will offer unto the Lord for a burnt offering;

[19]Ye shall offer at your own will a male without blemish, of the beeves, of the sheep, or of the goats.

[20]But whatsoever hath a blemish, *that* shall ye not offer: for it shall not be acceptable for you.

[21]And whosoever offereth a sacrifice of peace offerings unto the Lord to accomplish *his* vow, or a freewill offering in beeves or sheep, it shall be perfect to be accepted; there shall be no blemish therein.

[22]Blind, or broken, or maimed, or having a wen, or scurvy, or scabbed, ye shall not offer these unto the Lord, nor make an offering by fire of them upon the altar unto the Lord.

[23]Either a bullock or a lamb that hath any thing superfluous or lacking in his parts, that mayest thou offer *for* a freewill offering; but for a vow it shall not be accepted.

New International

22 THE LORD said to Moses, [2]"Tell Aaron and his sons to treat with respect the sacred offerings the Israelites consecrate to me, so they will not profane my holy name. I am the Lord.

[3]"Say to them: 'For the generations to come, if any of your descendants is ceremonially unclean and yet comes near the sacred offerings that the Israelites consecrate to the Lord, that person must be cut off from my presence. I am the Lord.

[4]" 'If a descendant of Aaron has an infectious skin disease[a] or a bodily discharge, he may not eat the sacred offerings until he is cleansed. He will also be unclean if he touches something defiled by a corpse or by anyone who has an emission of semen, [5]or if he touches any crawling thing that makes him unclean, or any person who makes him unclean, whatever the uncleanness may be. [6]The one who touches any such thing will be unclean till evening. He must not eat any of the sacred offerings unless he has bathed himself with water. [7]When the sun goes down, he will be clean, and after that he may eat the sacred offerings, for they are his food. [8]He must not eat anything found dead or torn by wild animals, and so become unclean through it. I am the Lord.

[9]" 'The priests are to keep my requirements so that they do not become guilty and die for treating them with contempt. I am the Lord, who makes them holy.[b]

[10]" 'No one outside a priest's family may eat the sacred offering, nor may the guest of a priest or his hired worker eat it. [11]But if a priest buys a slave with money, or if a slave is born in his household, that slave may eat his food. [12]If a priest's daughter marries anyone other than a priest, she may not eat any of the sacred contributions. [13]But if a priest's daughter becomes a widow or is divorced, yet has no children, and she returns to live in her father's house as in her youth, she may eat of her father's food. No unauthorized person, however, may eat any of it.

[14]" 'If anyone eats a sacred offering by mistake, he must make restitution to the priest for the offering and add a fifth of the value to it. [15]The priests must not desecrate the sacred offerings the Israelites present to the Lord [16]by allowing them to eat the sacred offerings and so bring upon them guilt requiring payment. I am the Lord, who makes them holy.' "

Unacceptable Sacrifices

[17]The Lord said to Moses, [18]"Speak to Aaron and his sons and to all the Israelites and say to them: 'If any of you—either an Israelite or an alien living in Israel—presents a gift for a burnt offering to the Lord, either to fulfill a vow or as a freewill offering, [19]you must present a male without defect from the cattle, sheep or goats in order that it may be accepted on your behalf. [20]Do not bring anything with a defect, because it will not be accepted on your behalf. [21]When anyone brings from the herd or flock a fellowship offering[c] to the Lord to fulfill a special vow or as a freewill offering, it must be without defect or blemish to be acceptable. [22]Do not offer to the Lord the blind, the injured or the maimed, or anything with warts or festering or running sores. Do not place any of these on the altar as an offering made to the Lord by fire. [23]You may, however, present as a freewill offering an ox[d] or a sheep that is deformed or stunted, but it will not be accepted in fulfillment of a vow. [24]You must not offer to the Lord an animal whose

a 4 Traditionally *leprosy*; the Hebrew word was used for various diseases affecting the skin—not necessarily leprosy.   b 9 Or *who sanctifies them*; or *who sets them apart as holy*; also in verse 16   c 21 Traditionally *peace offering*   d 23 The Hebrew word can include both male and female.

Living Bible

22 THE LORD told Moses, "Instruct Aaron and his sons to be very careful not to defile my holy name by desecrating the people's sacred gifts; for I am Jehovah. 3From now on and forever, if a priest who is ceremonially defiled sacrifices the animals brought by the people or handles the gifts dedicated to Jehovah, he shall be discharged from the priesthood. For I am Jehovah!

4"No priest who is a leper or who has a running sore may eat the holy sacrifices until healed. And any priest who touches a dead person, or who is defiled by a seminal emission, 5or who touches any reptile or other forbidden thing, or who touches anyone who is ceremonially defiled for any reason— 6that priest shall be defiled until evening, and shall not eat of the holy sacrifices until after he has bathed that evening. 7When the sun is down, then he shall be purified again and may eat the holy food, for it is his source of life. 8He may not eat any animal that dies of itself or is torn by wild animals, for this will defile him. I am Jehovah. 9Warn the priests to follow these instructions carefully, lest they be declared guilty and die for violating these rules. I am the Lord who sanctifies them.

10"No one may eat of the holy sacrifices unless he is a priest; no one visiting the priest, for instance, nor a hired servant, may eat this food. 11However, there is one exception—if the priest buys a slave with his own money, that slave may eat it, and any slave children born in his household may eat it. 12If a priest's daughter is married outside the tribe, she may not eat the sacred offerings.e 13But if she is a widow or divorced and has no son to support her, and has returned home to her father's household, she may eat of her father's food again. But otherwise, no one who is not in the priestly families may eat this food.

14"If someone should eat of the holy sacrifices without realizing it, he shall return to the priest the amount he has used, with twenty percent added; 15for the holy sacrifices brought by the people of Israel must not be defiled by being eaten by unauthorized persons, for these sacrifices have been offered to the Lord. 16Anyone who violates this law is guilty and is in great danger because he has eaten the sacred offerings; for I am Jehovah who sanctifies the offerings."

17, 18And the Lord said to Moses, "Tell Aaron and his sons and all the people of Israel that if an Israelite or other person living among you offers a burnt offering sacrifice to the Lord—whether it is to fulfill a promise or is a spontaneous free will offering— 19it will only be acceptable to the Lord if it is a male animal without defect; it must be a young bull or a sheep or a goat. 20Anything that has a defect must not be offered, for it will not be accepted.

21"Anyone sacrificing a peace offering to the Lord from the herd or flock, whether to fulfill a vow or as a voluntary offering, must sacrifice an animal that has no defect, or it will not be accepted. 22An animal that is blind or disabled or mutilated, or which has sores or itch or any other skin disease, must not be offered to the Lord; it is not a fit burnt offering for the altar of the Lord. 23If the young bull or lamb presented to the Lord has anything superfluous or lacking in its body parts, it may be offered as a free will offering, but not for a vow. 24An

New Revised Standard

The Use of Holy Offerings

22 THE LORD spoke to Moses, saying: 2Direct Aaron and his sons to deal carefully with the sacred donations of the people of Israel, which they dedicate to me, so that they may not profane my holy name; I am the LORD. 3Say to them: If anyone among all your offspring throughout your generations comes near the sacred donations, which the people of Israel dedicate to the LORD, while he is in a state of uncleanness, that person shall be cut off from my presence: I am the LORD. 4No one of Aaron's offspring who has a leprousf disease or suffers a discharge may eat of the sacred donations until he is clean. Whoever touches anything made unclean by a corpse or a man who has had an emission of semen, 5and whoever touches any swarming thing by which he may be made unclean or any human being by whom he may be made unclean— whatever his uncleanness may be— 6the person who touches any such shall be unclean until evening and shall not eat of the sacred donations unless he has washed his body in water. 7When the sun sets he shall be clean; and afterward he may eat of the sacred donations, for they are his food. 8That which died or was torn by wild animals he shall not eat, becoming unclean by it: I am the LORD. 9They shall keep my charge, so that they may not incur guilt and die in the sanctuaryg for having profaned it: I am the LORD; I sanctify them.

10 No lay person shall eat of the sacred donations. No bound or hired servant of the priest shall eat of the sacred donations; 11but if a priest acquires anyone by purchase, the person may eat of them; and those that are born in his house may eat of his food. 12If a priest's daughter marries a layman, she shall not eat of the offering of the sacred donations; 13but if a priest's daughter is widowed or divorced, without offspring, and returns to her father's house, as in her youth, she may eat of her father's food. No lay person shall eat of it. 14If a man eats of the sacred donation unintentionally, he shall add one-fifth of its value to it, and give the sacred donation to the priest. 15No one shall profane the sacred donations of the people of Israel, which they offer to the LORD, 16causing them to bear guilt requiring a guilt offering, by eating their sacred donations: for I am the LORD; I sanctify them.

Acceptable Offerings

17 The LORD spoke to Moses, saying: 18Speak to Aaron and his sons and all the people of Israel and say to them: When anyone of the house of Israel or of the aliens residing in Israel presents an offering, whether in payment of a vow or as a freewill offering that is offered to the LORD as a burnt offering, 19to be acceptable in your behalf it shall be a male without blemish, of the cattle or the sheep or the goats. 20You shall not offer anything that has a blemish, for it will not be acceptable in your behalf.

21 When anyone offers a sacrifice of well-being to the LORD, in fulfillment of a vow or as a freewill offering, from the herd or from the flock, to be acceptable it must be perfect; there shall be no blemish in it. 22Anything blind, or injured, or maimed, or having a discharge or an itch or scabs—these you shall not offer to the LORD or put any of them on the altar as offerings by fire to the LORD. 23An ox or a lamb that has a limb too long or too short you may present for a freewill offering; but it will not be accepted for a vow. 24Any animal that has its

---

e 22:12 the sacred offerings, literally, "the elevation of the holy things."

f A term for several skin diseases; precise meaning uncertain   g Vg: Heb incur guilt for it and die in it

King James

24Ye shall not offer unto the LORD that which is bruised, or crushed, or broken, or cut; neither shall ye make *any offering thereof* in your land.

25Neither from a stranger's hand shall ye offer the bread of your God of any of these; because their corruption *is* in them, *and* blemishes *be* in them: they shall not be accepted for you.

26¶ And the LORD spake unto Moses, saying,

27When a bullock, or a sheep, or a goat, is brought forth, then it shall be seven days under the dam; and from the eighth day and thenceforth it shall be accepted for an offering made by fire unto the LORD.

28And *whether it be* cow or ewe, ye shall not kill it and her young both in one day.

29And when ye will offer a sacrifice of thanksgiving unto the LORD, offer *it* at your own will.

30On the same day it shall be eaten up; ye shall leave none of it until the morrow: I *am* the LORD.

31Therefore shall ye keep my commandments, and do them: I *am* the LORD.

32Neither shall ye profane my holy name; but I will be hallowed among the children of Israel: I *am* the LORD which hallow you,

33That brought you out of the land of Egypt, to be your God: I *am* the LORD.

23 AND THE LORD spake unto Moses, saying, 2Speak unto the children of Israel, and say unto them, *Concerning* the feasts of the LORD, which ye shall proclaim *to be* holy convocations, *even* these *are* my feasts.

3Six days shall work be done: but the seventh day *is* the sabbath of rest, an holy convocation; ye shall do no work *therein:* it *is* the sabbath of the LORD in all your dwellings.

4¶ These *are* the feasts of the LORD, *even* holy convocations, which ye shall proclaim in their seasons.

5In the fourteenth *day* of the first month at even *is* the LORD's passover.

6And on the fifteenth day of the same month *is* the feast of unleavened bread unto the LORD: seven days ye must eat unleavened bread.

7In the first day ye shall have an holy convocation: ye shall do no servile work therein.

8But ye shall offer an offering made by fire unto the LORD seven days: in the seventh day *is* an holy convocation: ye shall do no servile work *therein*.

9¶ And the LORD spake unto Moses, saying,

10Speak unto the children of Israel, and say unto them, When ye be come into the land which I give unto you, and shall reap the harvest thereof, then ye shall bring a sheaf of the firstfruits of your harvest unto the priest:

11And he shall wave the sheaf before the LORD, to be accepted for you: on the morrow after the sabbath the priest shall wave it.

12And ye shall offer that day when ye wave the sheaf an he lamb without blemish of the first year for a burnt offering unto the LORD.

13And the meat offering thereof *shall be* two tenth deals of fine flour mingled with oil, an offering made by fire unto the LORD *for* a sweet savour: and the drink offering thereof *shall be* of wine, the fourth *part* of an hin.

14And ye shall eat neither bread, nor parched corn, nor green ears, until the selfsame day that ye have brought an offering unto your God: *it shall be* a statute for ever throughout your generations in all your dwellings.

New International

testicles are bruised, crushed, torn or cut. You must not do this in your own land, 25and you must not accept such animals from the hand of a foreigner and offer them as the food of your God. They will not be accepted on your behalf, because they are deformed and have defects.' "

26The LORD said to Moses, 27"When a calf, a lamb or a goat is born, it is to remain with its mother for seven days. From the eighth day on, it will be acceptable as an offering made to the LORD by fire. 28Do not slaughter a cow or a sheep and its young on the same day.

29"When you sacrifice a thank offering to the LORD, sacrifice it in such a way that it will be accepted on your behalf. 30It must be eaten that same day; leave none of it till morning. I am the LORD.

31"Keep my commands and follow them. I am the LORD. 32Do not profane my holy name. I must be acknowledged as holy by the Israelites. I am the LORD, who makesa you holyb 33and who brought you out of Egypt to be your God. I am the LORD."

23 THE LORD said to Moses, 2"Speak to the Israelites and say to them: 'These are my appointed feasts, the appointed feasts of the LORD, which you are to proclaim as sacred assemblies.

The Sabbath

3" 'There are six days when you may work, but the seventh day is a Sabbath of rest, a day of sacred assembly. You are not to do any work; wherever you live, it is a Sabbath to the LORD.

The Passover and Unleavened Bread

4" 'These are the LORD's appointed feasts, the sacred assemblies you are to proclaim at their appointed times: 5The LORD's Passover begins at twilight on the fourteenth day of the first month. 6On the fifteenth day of that month the LORD's Feast of Unleavened Bread begins; for seven days you must eat bread made without yeast. 7On the first day hold a sacred assembly and do no regular work. 8For seven days present an offering made to the LORD by fire. And on the seventh day hold a sacred assembly and do no regular work.' "

Firstfruits

9The LORD said to Moses, 10"Speak to the Israelites and say to them: 'When you enter the land I am going to give you and you reap its harvest, bring to the priest a sheaf of the first grain you harvest. 11He is to wave the sheaf before the LORD so it will be accepted on your behalf; the priest is to wave it on the day after the Sabbath. 12On the day you wave the sheaf, you must sacrifice as a burnt offering to the LORD a lamb a year old without defect, 13together with its grain offering of two-tenths of an ephahc of fine flour mixed with oil—an offering made to the LORD by fire, a pleasing aroma—and its drink offering of a quarter of a hind of wine. 14You must not eat any bread, or roasted or new grain, until the very day you bring this offering to your God. This is to be a lasting ordinance for the generations to come, wherever you live.

---

a *32 Or made*   b *32 Or who sanctifies you; or who sets you apart as holy*
c *13 That is, probably about 4 quarts (about 4.5 liters); also in verse 17*
d *13 That is, probably about 1 quart (about 1 liter)*

Living Bible

animal that has injured genitals—crushed or castrated—shall not be offered to the Lord at any time. 25This restriction applies to the sacrifices made by foreigners among you as well as those made by yourselves, for no defective animal is acceptable for this sacrifice."

26, 27And the Lord said to Moses, "When a bullock, sheep, or goat is born, it shall be left with its mother for seven days, but from the eighth day onward it is acceptable as a sacrifice by fire to the Lord. 28You shall not slaughter a mother animal and her offspring the same day, whether she is a cow or ewe. 29, 30When you offer the Lord a sacrifice of thanksgiving, you must do it in the right way, eating the sacrificial animal the same day it is slain. Leave none of it for the following day. I am the Lord.

31"You must keep all of my commandments, for I am the Lord. 32, 33You must not treat me as common and ordinary. Revere me and hallow me, for I, the Lord, made you holy to myself and rescued you from Egypt to be my own people! I am Jehovah!"

23 THE LORD said to Moses, "Announce to the people of Israel that they are to celebrate several annual festivals of the Lord—times when all Israel will assemble and worship me. 3(These are in addition to your Sabbathse—the seventh day of every week—which are always days of rest in every home, times for assembling to worship, and for resting from the normal business of the week.)

4These are the holy festivals which are to be observed each year:

5"The Passover of the Lord: This is to be celebrated on the first day of April, beginning at sundown.f

6"The Festival of Unleavened Bread: This is to be celebrated beginning the day following the Passover, and for seven days you must not eat any bread made with yeast. 7On the first day of this festival, you shall gather the people for worship, and all ordinary work shall cease.g 8You shall do the same on the seventh day of the festival. On each of the intervening days you shall make an offering by fire to the Lord.

9, 10, 11"The Festival of First Fruits: When you arrive in the land I will give you, and you reap your first harvest, bring the first sheaf of the harvest to the priest on the day after the Sabbath. He shall wave it before the Lord in a gesture of offering, and it will be accepted by the Lord as your gift. 12That same day you shall sacrifice to the Lord a male yearling lamb without defect as a burnt offering. 13A grain offering shall accompany it, consisting of a fifth of a bushel of finely ground flour mixed with olive oil, to be offered by fire to the Lord; this will be very pleasant to him. Also offer a drink offering consisting of three pints of wine. 14Until this is done you must not eat any of the harvest for yourselves—neither fresh kernels nor bread nor parched grain. This is a permanent law throughout your nation.

New Revised Standard

testicles bruised or crushed or torn or cut, you shall not offer to the LORD; such you shall not do within your land, 25nor shall you accept any such animals from a foreigner to offer as food to your God; since they are mutilated, with a blemish in them, they shall not be accepted in your behalf.

26 The LORD spoke to Moses, saying: 27When an ox or a sheep or a goat is born, it shall remain seven days with its mother, and from the eighth day on it shall be acceptable as the LORD's offering by fire. 28But you shall not slaughter, from the herd or the flock, an animal with its young on the same day. 29When you sacrifice a thanksgiving offering to the LORD, you shall sacrifice it so that it may be acceptable in your behalf. 30It shall be eaten on the same day; you shall not leave any of it until morning: I am the LORD.

31 Thus you shall keep my commandments and observe them: I am the LORD. 32You shall not profane my holy name, that I may be sanctified among the people of Israel: I am the LORD; I sanctify you, 33I who brought you out of the land of Egypt to be your God: I am the LORD.

Appointed Festivals

23 THE LORD spoke to Moses, saying: 2Speak to the people of Israel and say to them: These are the appointed festivals of the LORD that you shall proclaim as holy convocations, my appointed festivals.

The Sabbath, Passover, and Unleavened Bread

3 Six days shall work be done; but the seventh day is a sabbath of complete rest, a holy convocation; you shall do no work: it is a sabbath to the LORD throughout your settlements.

4 These are the appointed festivals of the LORD, the holy convocations, which you shall celebrate at the time appointed for them. 5In the first month, on the fourteenth day of the month, at twilight,h there shall be a passover offering to the LORD, 6and on the fifteenth day of the same month is the festival of unleavened bread to the LORD; seven days you shall eat unleavened bread. 7On the first day you shall have a holy convocation; you shall not work at your occupations. 8For seven days you shall present the LORD's offerings by fire; on the seventh day there shall be a holy convocation: you shall not work at your occupations.

The Offering of First Fruits

9 The LORD spoke to Moses: 10Speak to the people of Israel and say to them: When you enter the land that I am giving you and you reap its harvest, you shall bring the sheaf of the first fruits of your harvest to the priest. 11He shall raise the sheaf before the LORD, that you may find acceptance; on the day after the sabbath the priest shall raise it. 12On the day when you raise the sheaf, you shall offer a lamb a year old, without blemish, as a burnt offering to the LORD. 13And the grain offering with it shall be two-tenths of an ephah of choice flour mixed with oil, an offering by fire of pleasing odor to the LORD; and the drink offering with it shall be of wine, one-fourth of a hin. 14You shall eat no bread or parched grain or fresh ears until that very day, until you have brought the offering of your God: it is a statute forever throughout your generations in all your settlements.

---

e 23:3 your Sabbaths, implied.   f 23:5 This is to be celebrated on the first day of April, literally, "on the fourteenth day of the first month" (of the Hebrew calendar). This corresponds approximately to our April first.   g 23:7 all ordinary work shall cease, literally, "you shall do no hard work."

h Heb between the two evenings

King James

15¶ And ye shall count unto you from the morrow after the sabbath, from the day that ye brought the sheaf of the wave offering; seven sabbaths shall be complete:

16Even unto the morrow after the seventh sabbath shall ye number fifty days; and ye shall offer a new meat offering unto the LORD.

17Ye shall bring out of your habitations two wave loaves of two tenth deals: they shall be of fine flour; they shall be baked with leaven; *they are* the firstfruits unto the LORD.

18And ye shall offer with the bread seven lambs without blemish of the first year, and one young bullock, and two rams: they shall be *for* a burnt offering unto the LORD, with their meat offering, and their drink offerings, *even* an offering made by fire, of sweet savour unto the LORD.

19Then ye shall sacrifice one kid of the goats for a sin offering, and two lambs of the first year for a sacrifice of peace offerings.

20And the priest shall wave them with the bread of the firstfruits *for* a wave offering before the LORD, with the two lambs: they shall be holy to the LORD for the priest.

21And ye shall proclaim on the selfsame day, *that* it may be an holy convocation unto you: ye shall do no servile work *therein: it shall be* a statute for ever in all your dwellings throughout your generations.

22¶ And when ye reap the harvest of your land, thou shalt not make clean riddance of the corners of thy field when thou reapest, neither shalt thou gather any gleaning of thy harvest: thou shalt leave them unto the poor, and to the stranger: I *am* the LORD your God.

23¶ And the LORD spake unto Moses, saying,

24Speak unto the children of Israel, saying, In the seventh month, in the first *day* of the month, shall ye have a sabbath, a memorial of blowing of trumpets, an holy convocation.

25Ye shall do no servile work *therein:* but ye shall offer an offering made by fire unto the LORD.

26¶ And the LORD spake unto Moses, saying,

27Also on the tenth *day* of this seventh month *there shall be* a day of atonement: it shall be an holy convocation unto you; and ye shall afflict your souls, and offer an offering made by fire unto the LORD.

28And ye shall do no work in that same day: for it *is* a day of atonement, to make an atonement for you before the LORD your God.

29For whatsoever soul *it be* that shall not be afflicted in that same day, he shall be cut off from among his people.

30And whatsoever soul *it be* that doeth any work in that same day, the same soul will I destroy from among his people.

31Ye shall do no manner of work: *it shall be* a statute for ever throughout your generations in all your dwellings.

32It *shall be* unto you a sabbath of rest, and ye shall afflict your souls: in the ninth *day* of the month at even, from even unto even, shall ye celebrate your sabbath.

33¶ And the LORD spake unto Moses, saying,

34Speak unto the children of Israel, saying, The fifteenth day of this seventh month *shall be* the feast of tabernacles *for* seven days unto the LORD.

35On the first day *shall be* an holy convocation: ye shall do no servile work *therein.*

36Seven days ye shall offer an offering made by fire unto the LORD: on the eighth day shall be an holy convocation unto you; and ye shall offer an offering made by fire unto the LORD: it *is* a solemn assembly; *and* ye shall do no servile work *therein.*

37These *are* the feasts of the LORD, which ye shall proclaim *to be* holy convocations, to offer an offering made by fire unto the LORD, a burnt offering, and a meat offering, a sacrifice, and drink offerings, every thing upon his day:

New International

Feast of Weeks

15" 'From the day after the Sabbath, the day you brought the sheaf of the wave offering, count off seven full weeks. 16Count off fifty days up to the day after the seventh Sabbath, and then present an offering of new grain to the LORD. 17From wherever you live, bring two loaves made of two-tenths of an ephah of fine flour, baked with yeast, as a wave offering of firstfruits to the LORD. 18Present with this bread seven male lambs, each a year old and without defect, one young bull and two rams. They will be a burnt offering to the LORD, together with their grain offerings and drink offerings—an offering made by fire, an aroma pleasing to the LORD. 19Then sacrifice one male goat for a sin offering and two lambs, each a year old, for a fellowship offering.[a] 20The priest is to wave the two lambs before the LORD as a wave offering, together with the bread of the firstfruits. They are a sacred offering to the LORD for the priest. 21On that same day you are to proclaim a sacred assembly and do no regular work. This is to be a lasting ordinance for the generations to come, wherever you live.

22" 'When you reap the harvest of your land, do not reap to the very edges of your field or gather the gleanings of your harvest. Leave them for the poor and the alien. I am the LORD your God.' "

Feast of Trumpets

23The LORD said to Moses, 24"Say to the Israelites: 'On the first day of the seventh month you are to have a day of rest, a sacred assembly commemorated with trumpet blasts. 25Do no regular work, but present an offering made to the LORD by fire.' "

Day of Atonement

26The LORD said to Moses, 27"The tenth day of this seventh month is the Day of Atonement. Hold a sacred assembly and deny yourselves,[b] and present an offering made to the LORD by fire. 28Do no work on that day, because it is the Day of Atonement, when atonement is made for you before the LORD your God. 29Anyone who does not deny himself on that day must be cut off from his people. 30I will destroy from among his people anyone who does any work on that day. 31You shall do no work at all. This is to be a lasting ordinance for the generations to come, wherever you live. 32It is a sabbath of rest for you, and you must deny yourselves. From the evening of the ninth day of the month until the following evening you are to observe your sabbath."

Feast of Tabernacles

33The LORD said to Moses, 34"Say to the Israelites: 'On the fifteenth day of the seventh month the LORD's Feast of Tabernacles begins, and it lasts for seven days. 35The first day is a sacred assembly; do no regular work. 36For seven days present offerings made to the LORD by fire, and on the eighth day hold a sacred assembly and present an offering made to the LORD by fire. It is the closing assembly; do no regular work.

37(" 'These are the LORD's appointed feasts, which you are to proclaim as sacred assemblies for bringing offerings made to the LORD by fire—the burnt offerings and grain offerings, sacrifices and drink offerings required for each day. 38These offerings are in addition to

---

a *19* Traditionally *peace offering*   b *27* Or *and fast*; also in verses 29 and 32

Living Bible

15, 16 *"The Harvest Festival (Festival of Pentecost):* Fifty days later you shall bring to the Lord an offering of a sample of the new grain of your later crops. 17This shall consist of two loaves of bread from your homes to be waved before the Lord in a gesture of offering. Bake this bread from a fifth of a bushel of fine flour containing yeast. It is an offering to the Lord of the first sampling of your later crops.c 18Along with the bread and the wine, you shall sacrifice as burnt offerings to the Lord seven yearling lambs without defects, one young bull, and two rams. All are fire offerings, very acceptable to Jehovah.d 19And you shall offer one male goat for a sin offering, and two male yearling lambs for a peace offering.

20"The priests shall wave these offerings before the Lord along with the loaves representing the first sampling of your later crops. They are holy to the Lord, and will be given to the priests as food. 21That day shall be announced as a time of sacred convocation of all the people; don't do any work that day. This is a law to be honored from generation to generation. 22(When you reap your harvests, you must not thoroughly reap all the corners of the fields, nor pick up the fallen grain; leave it for the poor and for foreigners living among you who have no land of their own; I am Jehovah your God!)

23, 24 *"The Festival of Trumpets:* Mid-Septembere is a time for all the people to meet together for worship; it is a time of remembrance, and is to be announced by loud blowing of trumpets. 25Don't do any hard work on that day, but offer a sacrifice by fire to the Lord.

26, 27 *"The Day of Atonement* follows nine days later:f All the people are to come together before the Lord, saddened by their sin; and they shall offer sacrifices by fire to the Lord. 28Don't do any work that day, for it is a special day for making atonement before the Lord your God. 29Anyone who does not spend the day in repentance and sorrow for sin shall be excommunicated from his people. 30, 31And I will put to death anyone who does any kind of work that day. This is a law of Israel from generation to generation. 32For this is a Sabbath of rest, and in it you shall go without food and be filled with sorrow; this time for atonement begins in the evening and continues through the next day.

33, 34 *"The Festival of Shelters:* Five days later, on the last day of September, is the Festival of Shelters to be celebrated before the Lord for seven days.g 35On the first day there will be a sacred assembly of all the people; don't do any hard work that day. 36On each of the seven days of the festival you are to sacrifice an offering by fire to the Lord. The eighth day requires another sacred convocation of all the people, at which time there will again be an offering by fire to the Lord. It is the closing assembly, and no regular work is permitted.

37"(These, then, are the regular annual festivals—sacred convocations of all people—when offerings to the Lord are to be made by fire. 38These annual festivals are

---

c 23:17 It is an offering to the Lord of the first sampling of your later crops, literally, "as first fruits to the Lord."   d 23:18 very acceptable to Jehovah, literally, "of a sweet odor to the Lord."   e 23:23, 24 Mid-September, literally, "the first day of the seventh month" (of the Hebrew calendar). f 23:26, 27 nine days later, literally, "on the tenth day of the seventh month" (of the Hebrew calendar).   g 23:33, 34 on the last day of September, literally, "on the fifteenth day of the seventh month" (of the Hebrew calendar). Festival of Shelters, literally, "Feast of Tabernacles."

New Revised Standard

The Festival of Weeks

15 And from the day after the sabbath, from the day on which you bring the sheaf of the elevation offering, you shall count off seven weeks; they shall be complete. 16You shall count until the day after the seventh sabbath, fifty days; then you shall present an offering of new grain to the LORD. 17You shall bring from your settlements two loaves of bread as an elevation offering, each made of two-tenths of an ephah; they shall be of choice flour, baked with leaven, as first fruits to the LORD. 18You shall present with the bread seven lambs a year old without blemish, one young bull, and two rams; they shall be a burnt offering to the LORD, along with their grain offering and their drink offerings, an offering by fire of pleasing odor to the LORD. 19You shall also offer one male goat for a sin offering, and two male lambs a year old as a sacrifice of well-being. 20The priest shall raise them with the bread of the first fruits as an elevation offering before the LORD, together with the two lambs; they shall be holy to the LORD for the priest. 21On that same day you shall make proclamation; you shall hold a holy convocation; you shall not work at your occupations. This is a statute forever in all your settlements throughout your generations.

22 When you reap the harvest of your land, you shall not reap to the very edges of your field, or gather the gleanings of your harvest; you shall leave them for the poor and for the alien: I am the LORD your God.

The Festival of Trumpets

23 The LORD spoke to Moses, saying: 24Speak to the people of Israel, saying: In the seventh month, on the first day of the month, you shall observe a day of complete rest, a holy convocation commemorated with trumpet blasts. 25You shall not work at your occupations; and you shall present the LORD's offering by fire.

The Day of Atonement

26 The LORD spoke to Moses, saying: 27Now, the tenth day of this seventh month is the day of atonement; it shall be a holy convocation for you: you shall deny yourselvesh and present the LORD's offering by fire; 28and you shall do no work during that entire day; for it is a day of atonement, to make atonement on your behalf before the LORD your God. 29For anyone who does not practice self-deniali during that entire day shall be cut off from the people. 30And anyone who does any work during that entire day, such a one I will destroy from the midst of the people. 31You shall do no work: it is a statute forever throughout your generations in all your settlements. 32It shall be to you a sabbath of complete rest, and you shall deny yourselves;h on the ninth day of the month at evening, from evening to evening you shall keep your sabbath.

The Festival of Booths

33 The LORD spoke to Moses, saying: 34Speak to the people of Israel, saying: On the fifteenth day of this seventh month, and lasting seven days, there shall be the festival of boothsj to the LORD. 35The first day shall be a holy convocation; you shall not work at your occupations. 36Seven days you shall present the LORD's offerings by fire; on the eighth day you shall observe a holy convocation and present the LORD's offerings by fire; it is a solemn assembly; you shall not work at your occupations.

37 These are the appointed festivals of the LORD, which you shall celebrate as times of holy convocation, for presenting to the LORD offerings by fire—burnt offerings and grain offerings, sacrifices and drink offerings, each on its proper day— 38apart from the sabbaths

---

h Or shall fast   i Or does not fast   j Or tabernacles: Heb succoth

King James

38Beside the sabbaths of the LORD, and beside your gifts, and beside all your vows, and beside all your freewill offerings, which ye give unto the LORD.

39Also in the fifteenth day of the seventh month, when ye have gathered in the fruit of the land, ye shall keep a feast unto the LORD seven days: on the first day *shall be* a sabbath, and on the eighth day *shall be* a sabbath.

40And ye shall take you on the first day the boughs of goodly trees, branches of palm trees, and the boughs of thick trees, and willows of the brook; and ye shall rejoice before the LORD your God seven days.

41And ye shall keep it a feast unto the LORD seven days in the year. *It shall be* a statute for ever in your generations: ye shall celebrate it in the seventh month.

42Ye shall dwell in booths seven days; all that are Israelites born shall dwell in booths:

43That your generations may know that I made the children of Israel to dwell in booths, when I brought them out of the land of Egypt: I *am* the LORD your God.

44And Moses declared unto the children of Israel the feasts of the LORD.

24 AND THE LORD spake unto Moses, saying, 2Command the children of Israel, that they bring unto thee pure oil olive beaten for the light, to cause the lamps to burn continually.

3Without the veil of the testimony, in the tabernacle of the congregation, shall Aaron order it from the evening unto the morning before the LORD continually: *it shall be* a statute for ever in your generations.

4He shall order the lamps upon the pure candlestick before the LORD continually.

5¶ And thou shalt take fine flour, and bake twelve cakes thereof: two tenth deals shall be in one cake.

6And thou shalt set them in two rows, six on a row, upon the pure table before the LORD.

7And thou shalt put pure frankincense upon *each* row, that it may be on the bread for a memorial, *even* an offering made by fire unto the LORD.

8Every sabbath he shall set it in order before the LORD continually, *being taken* from the children of Israel by an everlasting covenant.

9And it shall be Aaron's and his sons'; and they shall eat it in the holy place: for it *is* most holy unto him of the offerings of the LORD made by fire by a perpetual statute.

10¶ And the son of an Israelitish woman, whose father *was* an Egyptian, went out among the children of Israel: and this son of the Israelitish *woman* and a man of Israel strove together in the camp;

11And the Israelitish woman's son blasphemed the name *of the LORD*, and cursed. And they brought him unto Moses: (and his mother's name *was* Shelomith, the daughter of Dibri, of the tribe of Dan:)

12And they put him in ward, that the mind of the LORD might be shown them.

13And the LORD spake unto Moses, saying,

14Bring forth him that hath cursed without the camp; and let all that heard *him* lay their hands upon his head, and let all the congregation stone him.

15And thou shalt speak unto the children of Israel, saying, Whosoever curseth his God shall bear his sin.

16And he that blasphemeth the name of the LORD, he shall surely be put to death, *and* all the congregation shall certainly stone him: as well the stranger, as he that is born in the land, when he blasphemeth the name *of the LORD*, shall be put to death.

17¶ And he that killeth any man shall surely be put to death.

18And he that killeth a beast shall make it good; beast for beast.

New International

those for the LORD's Sabbaths and[a] in addition to your gifts and whatever you have vowed and all the freewill offerings you give to the LORD.)

39"'So beginning with the fifteenth day of the seventh month, after you have gathered the crops of the land, celebrate the festival to the LORD for seven days; the first day is a day of rest, and the eighth day also is a day of rest. 40On the first day you are to take choice fruit from the trees, and palm fronds, leafy branches and poplars, and rejoice before the LORD your God for seven days. 41Celebrate this as a festival to the LORD for seven days each year. This is to be a lasting ordinance for the generations to come; celebrate it in the seventh month. 42Live in booths for seven days: All native-born Israelites are to live in booths 43so your descendants will know that I had the Israelites live in booths when I brought them out of Egypt. I am the LORD your God.'"

44So Moses announced to the Israelites the appointed feasts of the LORD.

Oil and Bread Set Before the LORD

24 THE LORD said to Moses, 2"Command the Israelites to bring you clear oil of pressed olives for the light so that the lamps may be kept burning continually. 3Outside the curtain of the Testimony in the Tent of Meeting, Aaron is to tend the lamps before the LORD from evening till morning, continually. This is to be a lasting ordinance for the generations to come. 4The lamps on the pure gold lampstand before the LORD must be tended continually.

5"Take fine flour and bake twelve loaves of bread, using two-tenths of an ephah[b] for each loaf. 6Set them in two rows, six in each row, on the table of pure gold before the LORD. 7Along each row put some pure incense as a memorial portion to represent the bread and to be an offering made to the LORD by fire. 8This bread is to be set out before the LORD regularly, Sabbath after Sabbath, on behalf of the Israelites, as a lasting covenant. 9It belongs to Aaron and his sons, who are to eat it in a holy place, because it is a most holy part of their regular share of the offerings made to the LORD by fire."

A Blasphemer Stoned

10Now the son of an Israelite mother and an Egyptian father went out among the Israelites, and a fight broke out in the camp between him and an Israelite. 11The son of the Israelite woman blasphemed the Name with a curse; so they brought him to Moses. (His mother's name was Shelomith, the daughter of Dibri the Danite.) 12They put him in custody until the will of the LORD should be made clear to them.

13Then the LORD said to Moses: 14"Take the blasphemer outside the camp. All those who heard him are to lay their hands on his head, and the entire assembly is to stone him. 15Say to the Israelites: 'If anyone curses his God, he will be held responsible; 16anyone who blasphemes the name of the LORD must be put to death. The entire assembly must stone him. Whether an alien or native-born, when he blasphemes the Name, he must be put to death.

17"'If anyone takes the life of a human being, he must be put to death. 18Anyone who takes the life of someone's animal must make restitution—life for life.

---

[a] 38 Or *These feasts are in addition to the LORD's Sabbaths, and these offerings are* [b] 5 That is, probably about 4 quarts (about 4.5 liters)

Living Bible

in addition to your regular Sabbaths—the weekly days of holy rest. The sacrifices made during the festivals are to be in addition to your regular giving and normal fulfillment of your vows.)

39"This last day of September, at the end of your harvesting, is the time to begin to celebrate this seven-day festival before the Lord. Remember that the first and last days of the festival are special days of rest. 40On the first day, take boughs of fruit trees laden with fruit, and palm fronds, and the boughs of leafy trees—such as willows that grow by the brooks—and [build shelters with themc], rejoicing before the Lord your God for seven days. 41This seven-day annual feast is a law from generation to generation. 42During those seven days, all of you who are native Israelites are to live in these shelters. 43The purpose of this is to remind the people of Israel, generation after generation, that I rescued you from Egypt, and caused you to live in shelters. I am Jehovah your God."

44So Moses announced these annual festivals of the Lord to the people of Israel.

24 THE LORD said to Moses, "Tell the people of Israel to bring you pure olive oil for an eternal flame 3, 4in the lampstand of pure gold which stands outside the veil that secludes the Holy of Holies. Each morning and evening Aaron shall supply it with fresh oil and trim the wicks. It will be an eternal flame before the Lord from generation to generation.

5-8"Every Sabbath day the High Priest shall place twelve loaves of bread in two rows upon the gold table that stands before the Lord. These loaves shall be baked from finely ground flour, using a fifth of a bushel for each. Pure frankincense shall be sprinkled along each row. This will be a memorial offering made by fire to the Lord, in memory of his everlasting covenant with the people of Israel. 9The bread shall be eaten by Aaron and his sons, in a place set apart for the purpose. For these are offerings made by fire to the Lord under a permanent law of God, and are most holy."

10Out in the camp one day, a young man whose mother was an Israelite and whose father was an Egyptian, got into a fight with one of the men of Israel. 11During the fight the Egyptian man's son cursed God,d and was brought to Moses for judgment. (His mother's name was Shelomith, daughter of Dibri of the tribe of Dan.) 12He was put in jail until the Lord would indicate what to do with him.

13, 14And the Lord said to Moses, "Take him outside the camp and tell all who heard him to lay their hands upon his head; then all the people are to execute him by stoning. 15, 16And tell the people of Israel that anyone who curses his God must pay the penalty: he must die. All the congregation shall stone him; this law applies to the foreigner as well as to the Israelite who blasphemes the name of Jehovah. He must die.

17"Also, all murderers must be executed. 18Anyone who kills an animal [that isn't his] shall replace it.e

New Revised Standard

of the LORD, and apart from your gifts, and apart from all your votive offerings, and apart from all your freewill offerings, which you give to the LORD.

39 Now, the fifteenth day of the seventh month, when you have gathered in the produce of the land, you shall keep the festival of the LORD, lasting seven days; a complete rest on the first day, and a complete rest on the eighth day. 40On the first day you shall take the fruit of majesticf trees, branches of palm trees, boughs of leafy trees, and willows of the brook; and you shall rejoice before the LORD your God for seven days. 41You shall keep it as a festival to the LORD seven days in the year; you shall keep it in the seventh month as a statute forever throughout your generations. 42You shall live in booths for seven days; all that are citizens in Israel shall live in booths, 43so that your generations may know that I made the people of Israel live in booths when I brought them out of the land of Egypt: I am the LORD your God.

44 Thus Moses declared to the people of Israel the appointed festivals of the LORD.

The Lamp

24 THE LORD spoke to Moses, saying: 2Command the people of Israel to bring you pure oil of beaten olives for the lamp, that a light may be kept burning regularly. 3Aaron shall set it up in the tent of meeting, outside the curtain of the covenant,g to burn from evening to morning before the LORD regularly; it shall be a statute forever throughout your generations. 4He shall set up the lamps on the lampstand of pure goldh before the LORD regularly.

The Bread for the Tabernacle

5 You shall take choice flour, and bake twelve loaves of it; two-tenths of an ephah shall be in each loaf. 6You shall place them in two rows, six in a row, on the table of pure gold.i 7You shall put pure frankincense with each row, to be a token offering for the bread, as an offering by fire to the LORD. 8Every sabbath day Aaron shall set them in order before the LORD regularly as a commitment of the people of Israel, as a covenant forever. 9They shall be for Aaron and his descendants, who shall eat them in a holy place, for they are most holy portions for him from the offerings by fire to the LORD, a perpetual due.

Blasphemy and Its Punishment

10 A man whose mother was an Israelite and whose father was an Egyptian came out among the people of Israel; and the Israelite woman's son and a certain Israelite began fighting in the camp. 11The Israelite woman's son blasphemed the Name in a curse. And they brought him to Moses—now his mother's name was Shelomith, daughter of Dibri, of the tribe of Dan— 12and they put him in custody, until the decision of the LORD should be made clear to them.

13 The LORD said to Moses, saying: 14Take the blasphemer outside the camp; and let all who were within hearing lay their hands on his head, and let the whole congregation stone him. 15And speak to the people of Israel, saying: Anyone who curses God shall bear the sin. 16One who blasphemes the name of the LORD shall be put to death; the whole congregation shall stone the blasphemer. Aliens as well as citizens, when they blaspheme the Name, shall be put to death. 17Anyone who kills a human being shall be put to death. 18Anyone who kills an animal shall make restitution for it, life for life.

---

c 23:40 build shelters with them, implied.   d 24:11 the Egyptian man's son, literally, "the Israelite woman's son." cursed God, literally, "blasphemed the Name."   e 24:18 that isn't his, implied. shall replace it, literally, "shall make it good, life for life."

f Meaning of Heb uncertain   g Or treaty, or testament; Heb eduth   h Heb pure lampstand   i Heb pure table

King James

19And if a man cause a blemish in his neighbour; as he hath done, so shall it be done to him;

20Breach for breach, eye for eye, tooth for tooth: as he hath caused a blemish in a man, so shall it be done to him *again*.

21And he that killeth a beast, he shall restore it: and he that killeth a man, he shall be put to death.

22Ye shall have one manner of law, as well for the stranger, as for one of your own country: for I *am* the LORD your God.

23¶ And Moses spake to the children of Israel, that they should bring forth him that had cursed out of the camp, and stone him with stones. And the children of Israel did as the LORD commanded Moses.

25 AND THE LORD spake unto Moses in mount Sinai, saying,

2Speak unto the children of Israel, and say unto them, When ye come into the land which I give you, then shall the land keep a sabbath unto the LORD.

3Six years thou shalt sow thy field, and six years thou shalt prune thy vineyard, and gather in the fruit thereof;

4But in the seventh year shall be a sabbath of rest unto the land, a sabbath for the LORD: thou shalt neither sow thy field, nor prune thy vineyard.

5That which groweth of its own accord of thy harvest thou shalt not reap, neither gather the grapes of thy vine undressed: *for* it is a year of rest unto the land.

6And the sabbath of the land shall be meat for you; for thee, and for thy servant, and for thy maid, and for thy hired servant, and for thy stranger that sojourneth with thee,

7And for thy cattle, and for the beast that *are* in thy land, shall all the increase thereof be meat.

8¶ And thou shalt number seven sabbaths of years unto thee, seven times seven years; and the space of the seven sabbaths of years shall be unto thee forty and nine years.

9Then shalt thou cause the trumpet of the jubilee to sound on the tenth *day* of the seventh month, in the day of atonement shall ye make the trumpet sound throughout all your land.

10And ye shall hallow the fiftieth year, and proclaim liberty throughout *all* the land unto all the inhabitants thereof: it shall be a jubilee unto you; and ye shall return every man unto his possession, and ye shall return every man unto his family.

11A jubilee shall that fiftieth year be unto you: ye shall not sow, neither reap that which groweth of itself in it, nor gather *the grapes* in it of thy vine undressed.

12For it *is* the jubilee; it shall be holy unto you: ye shall eat the increase thereof out of the field.

13In the year of this jubilee ye shall return every man unto his possession.

14And if thou sell aught unto thy neighbour, or buyest *aught* of thy neighbour's hand, ye shall not oppress one another:

15According to the number of years after the jubilee thou shalt buy of thy neighbour, *and* according unto the number of years of the fruits he shall sell unto thee:

16According to the multitude of years thou shalt increase the price thereof, and according to the fewness of years thou shalt diminish the price of it: for *according* to the number *of the years* of the fruits doth he sell unto thee.

17Ye shall not therefore oppress one another; but thou shalt fear thy God: for I *am* the LORD your God.

18¶ Wherefore ye shall do my statutes, and keep my judgments, and do them; and ye shall dwell in the land in safety.

19And the land shall yield her fruit, and ye shall eat your fill, and dwell therein in safety.

New International

19If anyone injures his neighbor, whatever he has done must be done to him: 20fracture for fracture, eye for eye, tooth for tooth. As he has injured the other, so he is to be injured. 21Whoever kills an animal must make restitution, but whoever kills a man must be put to death. 22You are to have the same law for the alien and the native-born. I am the LORD your God.' "

23Then Moses spoke to the Israelites, and they took the blasphemer outside the camp and stoned him. The Israelites did as the LORD commanded Moses.

The Sabbath Year

25 THE LORD said to Moses on Mount Sinai, 2"Speak to the Israelites and say to them: 'When you enter the land I am going to give you, the land itself must observe a sabbath to the LORD. 3For six years sow your fields, and for six years prune your vineyards and gather their crops. 4But in the seventh year the land is to have a sabbath of rest, a sabbath to the LORD. Do not sow your fields or prune your vineyards. 5Do not reap what grows of itself or harvest the grapes of your untended vines. The land is to have a year of rest. 6Whatever the land yields during the sabbath year will be food for you—for yourself, your manservant and maidservant, and the hired worker and temporary resident who live among you, 7as well as for your livestock and the wild animals in your land. Whatever the land produces may be eaten.

The Year of Jubilee

8" 'Count off seven sabbaths of years—seven times seven years—so that the seven sabbaths of years amount to a period of forty-nine years. 9Then have the trumpet sounded everywhere on the tenth day of the seventh month; on the Day of Atonement sound the trumpet throughout your land. 10Consecrate the fiftieth year and proclaim liberty throughout the land to all its inhabitants. It shall be a jubilee for you; each one of you is to return to his family property and each to his own clan. 11The fiftieth year shall be a jubilee for you; do not sow and do not reap what grows of itself or harvest the untended vines. 12For it is a jubilee and is to be holy for you; eat only what is taken directly from the fields.

13" 'In this Year of Jubilee everyone is to return to his own property.

14" 'If you sell land to one of your countrymen or buy any from him, do not take advantage of each other. 15You are to buy from your countryman on the basis of the number of years since the Jubilee. And he is to sell to you on the basis of the number of years left for harvesting crops. 16When the years are many, you are to increase the price, and when the years are few, you are to decrease the price, because what he is really selling you is the number of crops. 17Do not take advantage of each other, but fear your God. I am the LORD your God.

18" 'Follow my decrees and be careful to obey my laws, and you will live safely in the land. 19Then the land will yield its fruit, and you will eat your fill and live there in safety. 20You may ask, "What will we eat in the

Living Bible

¹⁹The penalty for injuring anyone is to be injured in exactly the same way: ²⁰fracture for fracture, eye for eye, tooth for tooth. Whatever anyone does to another shall be done to him.

²¹"To repeat, whoever kills an animal must replace it, and whoever kills a man must die. ²²You shall have the same law for the foreigner as for the home-born citizen, for I am Jehovah your God.

²³So they took the youth out of the camp and stoned him until he died, as Jehovah had commanded Moses.

25 WHILE MOSES was on Mount Sinai, the Lord gave him these instructions for the people of Israel:

"When you come into the land I am going to give you, you must let the land rest before the Lord every seventh year. ³For six years you may sow your field and prune your vineyards and harvest your crops, ⁴but during the seventh year the land is to lie fallow before the Lord, uncultivated. Don't sow your crops and don't prune your vineyards during that entire year. ⁵Don't even reap for yourself the volunteer crops that come up, and don't gather the grapes for yourself; for it is a year of rest for the land. 6. ⁷Any crops that do grow that year shall be free to all—for you, your servants, your slaves, and any foreigners living among you. Cattle and wild animals alike shall be allowed to graze there.

⁸"Every fiftieth year, ⁹on the Day of Atonement,^a let the trumpets blow loud and long throughout the land. ¹⁰For the fiftieth year shall be holy, a time to proclaim liberty throughout the land to all enslaved debtors, and a time for the canceling of all public and private debts. It shall be a year when all the family estates sold to others shall be returned to the original owners or their heirs.

¹¹"What a happy year it will be! In it you shall not sow, nor gather crops nor grapes; ¹²for it is a holy Year of Jubilee for you. That year your food shall be the volunteer crops that grow wild in the fields. ¹³Yes, during the Year of Jubilee everyone shall return home to his original family possession; if he has sold it, it shall be his again! 14, 15, ¹⁶Because of this, if the land is sold or bought during the preceding forty-nine years, a fair price shall be arrived at by counting the number of years until the Jubilee. If the Jubilee is many years away, the price will be high; if few years, the price will be low; for what you are really doing is selling the number of crops the new owner will get from the land before it is returned to you.

17, ¹⁸"You must fear your God and not overcharge! For I am Jehovah. Obey my laws if you want to live safely in the land. ¹⁹When you obey, the land will yield bumper crops and you can eat your fill in safety. ²⁰But

New Revised Standard

¹⁹Anyone who maims another shall suffer the same injury in return: ²⁰fracture for fracture, eye for eye, tooth for tooth; the injury inflicted is the injury to be suffered. ²¹One who kills an animal shall make restitution for it; but one who kills a human being shall be put to death. ²²You shall have one law for the alien and for the citizen: for I am the LORD your God. ²³Moses spoke thus to the people of Israel; and they took the blasphemer outside the camp, and stoned him to death. The people of Israel did as the LORD had commanded Moses.

The Sabbatical Year

25 THE LORD spoke to Moses on Mount Sinai, saying: ²Speak to the people of Israel and say to them: When you enter the land that I am giving you, the land shall observe a sabbath for the LORD. ³Six years you shall sow your field, and six years you shall prune your vineyard, and gather in their yield; ⁴but in the seventh year there shall be a sabbath of complete rest for the land, a sabbath for the LORD: you shall not sow your field or prune your vineyard. ⁵You shall not reap the aftergrowth of your harvest or gather the grapes of your unpruned vine: it shall be a year of complete rest for the land. ⁶You may eat what the land yields during its sabbath—you, your male and female slaves, your hired and your bound laborers who live with you; ⁷for your livestock also, and for the wild animals in your land all its yield shall be for food.

The Year of Jubilee

⁸ You shall count off seven weeks^b of years, seven times seven years, so that the period of seven weeks of years gives forty-nine years. ⁹Then you shall have the trumpet sounded loud; on the tenth day of the seventh month—on the day of atonement—you shall have the trumpet sounded throughout all your land. ¹⁰And you shall hallow the fiftieth year and you shall proclaim liberty throughout the land to all its inhabitants. It shall be a jubilee for you: you shall return, every one of you, to your property and every one of you to your family. ¹¹That fiftieth year shall be a jubilee for you: you shall not sow, or reap the aftergrowth, or harvest the unpruned vines. ¹²For it is a jubilee; it shall be holy to you: you shall eat only what the field itself produces.

¹³ In this year of jubilee you shall return, every one of you, to your property. ¹⁴When you make a sale to your neighbor or buy from your neighbor, you shall not cheat one another. ¹⁵When you buy from your neighbor, you shall pay only for the number of years since the jubilee; the seller shall charge you only for the remaining crop years. ¹⁶If the years are more, you shall increase the price, and if the years are fewer, you shall diminish the price; for it is a certain number of harvests that are being sold to you. ¹⁷You shall not cheat one another, but you shall fear your God; for I am the LORD your God.

¹⁸ You shall observe my statutes and faithfully keep my ordinances, so that you may live on the land securely. ¹⁹The land will yield its fruit, and you will eat your fill and live on it securely. ²⁰Should you ask, What shall

---

^a 25:9 on the Day of Atonement, literally, "the tenth day of the seventh month (of the Hebrew calendar).

^b Or sabbaths

King James

20And if ye shall say, What shall we eat the seventh year? behold, we shall not sow, nor gather in our increase:

21Then I will command my blessing upon you in the sixth year, and it shall bring forth fruit for three years.

22And ye shall sow the eighth year, and eat *yet* of old fruit until the ninth year; until her fruits come in ye shall eat *of* the old *store*.

23¶ The land shall not be sold for ever: for the land *is* mine; for ye *are* strangers and sojourners with me.

24And in all the land of your possession ye shall grant a redemption for the land.

25¶ If thy brother be waxen poor, and hath sold away *some* of his possession, and if any of his kin come to redeem it, then shall he redeem that which his brother sold.

26And if the man have none to redeem it, and himself be able to redeem it;

27Then let him count the years of the sale thereof, and restore the overplus unto the man to whom he sold it; that he may return unto his possession.

28But if he be not able to restore *it* to him, then that which is sold shall remain in the hand of him that hath bought it until the year of jubilee: and in the jubilee it shall go out, and he shall return unto his possession.

29And if a man sell a dwelling house in a walled city, then he may redeem it within a whole year after it is sold; *within* a full year may he redeem it.

30And if it be not redeemed within the space of a full year, then the house that *is* in the walled city shall be established for ever to him that bought it throughout his generations: it shall not go out in the jubilee.

31But the houses of the villages which have no wall round about them shall be counted as the fields of the country: they may be redeemed, and they shall go out in the jubilee.

32Notwithstanding the cities of the Levites, *and* the houses of the cities of their possession, may the Levites redeem at any time.

33And if a man purchase of the Levites, then the house that was sold, and the city of his possession, shall go out in *the year of* jubilee: for the houses of the cities of the Levites *are* their possession among the children of Israel.

34But the field of the suburbs of their cities may not be sold; for it *is* their perpetual possession.

35¶ And if thy brother be waxen poor, and fallen in decay with thee; then thou shalt relieve him: *yea, though he be* a stranger, or a sojourner; that he may live with thee.

36Take thou no usury of him, or increase: but fear thy God; that thy brother may live with thee.

37Thou shalt not give him thy money upon usury, nor lend him thy victuals for increase.

38I *am* the LORD your God, which brought you forth out of the land of Egypt, to give you the land of Canaan, *and* to be your God.

39¶ And if thy brother *that dwelleth* by thee be waxen poor, and be sold unto thee; thou shalt not compel him to serve as a bondservant:

40*But* as an hired servant, *and* as a sojourner, he shall be with thee, *and* shall serve thee unto the year of jubilee:

41And *then* shall he depart from thee, *both* he and his children with him, and shall return unto his own family, and unto the possession of his fathers shall he return.

42For they *are* my servants, which I brought forth out of the land of Egypt: they shall not be sold as bondmen.

43Thou shalt not rule over him with rigour; but shalt fear thy God.

44Both thy bondmen, and thy bondmaids, which thou shalt have, *shall be* of the heathen that are round about you; of them shall ye buy bondmen and bondmaids.

New International

seventh year if we do not plant or harvest our crops?" 21I will send you such a blessing in the sixth year that the land will yield enough for three years. 22While you plant during the eighth year, you will eat from the old crop and will continue to eat from it until the harvest of the ninth year comes in.

23" 'The land must not be sold permanently, because the land is mine and you are but aliens and my tenants. 24Throughout the country that you hold as a possession, you must provide for the redemption of the land.

25" 'If one of your countrymen becomes poor and sells some of his property, his nearest relative is to come and redeem what his countryman has sold. 26If, however, a man has no one to redeem it for him but he himself prospers and acquires sufficient means to redeem it, 27he is to determine the value for the years since he sold it and refund the balance to the man to whom he sold it; he can then go back to his own property. 28But if he does not acquire the means to repay him, what he sold will remain in the possession of the buyer until the Year of Jubilee. It will be returned in the Jubilee, and he can then go back to his property.

29" 'If a man sells a house in a walled city, he retains the right of redemption a full year after its sale. During that time he may redeem it. 30If it is not redeemed before a full year has passed, the house in the walled city shall belong permanently to the buyer and his descendants. It is not to be returned in the Jubilee. 31But houses in villages without walls around them are to be considered as open country. They can be redeemed, and they are to be returned in the Jubilee.

32" 'The Levites always have the right to redeem their houses in the Levitical towns, which they possess. 33So the property of the Levites is redeemable—that is, a house sold in any town they hold—and is to be returned in the Jubilee, because the houses in the towns of the Levites are their property among the Israelites. 34But the pastureland belonging to their towns must not be sold; it is their permanent possession.

35" 'If one of your countrymen becomes poor and is unable to support himself among you, help him as you would an alien or a temporary resident, so he can continue to live among you. 36Do not take interest of any kind[a] from him, but fear your God, so that your countryman may continue to live among you. 37You must not lend him money at interest or sell him food at a profit. 38I am the LORD your God, who brought you out of Egypt to give you the land of Canaan and to be your God.

39" 'If one of your countrymen becomes poor among you and sells himself to you, do not make him work as a slave. 40He is to be treated as a hired worker or a temporary resident among you; he is to work for you until the Year of Jubilee. 41Then he and his children are to be released, and he will go back to his own clan and to the property of his forefathers. 42Because the Israelites are my servants, whom I brought out of Egypt, they must not be sold as slaves. 43Do not rule over them ruthlessly, but fear your God.

44" 'Your male and female slaves are to come from the nations around you; from them you may buy slaves.

---

^a *36 Or* take excessive interest; *similarly in verse* 37

Living Bible

you will ask, 'What shall we eat the seventh year, since we are not allowed to plant or harvest crops that year?' 21, 22The answer is, 'I will bless you with bumper crops the sixth year that will last you until the crops of the eighth year are harvested!' 23And remember, the land is mine, so you may not sell it permanently. You are merely my tenants and sharecroppers!

24"In every contract of sale there must be a stipulation that the land can be redeemed at any time by the seller. 25If anyone becomes poor and sells some of his land, then his nearest relatives may redeem it. 26If there is no one else to redeem it, and he himself gets together enough money, 27then he may always buy it back at a price proportionate to the number of harvests until the Jubilee, and the owner must accept the money and return the land to him. 28But if the original owner is not able to redeem it, then it shall belong to the new owner until the Year of Jubilee; but at the Jubilee year it must be returned again.

29"If a man sells a house in the city,b he has up to one year to redeem it, with full right of redemption during that time. 30But if it is not redeemed within the year, then it will belong permanently to the new owner—it does not return to the original owner in the Year of Jubilee. 31But village houses—a village is a settlement without fortifying walls around it—are like farmland, redeemable at any time, and are always returned to the original owner in the Year of Jubilee.

32"There is one exception: The homes of the Levites, even though in walled cities, may be redeemed at any time, 33and must be returned to the original owners in the Year of Jubilee; for the Levites will not be given farmland like the other tribes, but will receive only houses in their cities, and the surrounding fields.c 34The Levites are not permitted to sell the fields of common land surrounding their cities, for these are their permanent possession, and they must belong to no one else.

35"If your brother becomes poor, you are responsible to help him; invite him to live with you as a guest in your home. 36Fear your God and let your brother live with you; and don't charge him interest on the money you lend him. 37Remember—no interest; and give him what he needs, at your cost: don't try to make a profit! 38For I, the Lord your God, brought you out of the land of Egypt to *give* you the land of Canaan, and to be your God.

39"If a fellow Israelite becomes poor and sells himself to you, you must not treat him as an ordinary slave, 40but rather as a hired servant or as a guest; and he shall serve you only until the Year of Jubilee. 41At that time he can leave with his children, and return to his own family and possessions. 42For I brought you from the land of Egypt, and you are my servants; so you may not be sold as ordinary slaves, 43or treated harshly; fear your God.

44"However, you may purchase slaves from the foreign nations living around you, 45and you may purchase

New Revised Standard

we eat in the seventh year, if we may not sow or gather in our crop? 21I will order my blessing for you in the sixth year, so that it will yield a crop for three years. 22When you sow in the eighth year, you will be eating from the old crop; until the ninth year, when its produce comes in, you shall eat the old. 23The land shall not be sold in perpetuity, for the land is mine; with me you are but aliens and tenants. 24Throughout the land that you hold, you shall provide for the redemption of the land.

25 If anyone of your kin falls into difficulty and sells a piece of property, then the next of kin shall come and redeem what the relative has sold. 26If the person has no one to redeem it, but then prospers and finds sufficient means to do so, 27the years since its sale shall be computed and the difference shall be refunded to the person to whom it was sold, and the property shall be returned. 28But if there is not sufficient means to recover it, what was sold shall remain with the purchaser until the year of jubilee; in the jubilee it shall be released, and the property shall be returned.

29 If anyone sells a dwelling house in a walled city, it may be redeemed until a year has elapsed since its sale; the right of redemption shall be one year. 30If it is not redeemed before a full year has elapsed, a house that is in a walled city shall pass in perpetuity to the purchaser, throughout the generations; it shall not be released in the jubilee. 31But houses in villages that have no walls around them shall be classed as open country; they may be redeemed, and they shall be released in the jubilee. 32As for the cities of the Levites, the Levites shall forever have the right of redemption of the houses in the cities belonging to them. 33Such property as may be redeemed from the Levites—houses sold in a city belonging to them—shall be released in the jubilee; because the houses in the cities of the Levites are their possession among the people of Israel. 34But the open land around their cities may not be sold; for that is their possession for all time.

35 If any of your kin fall into difficulty and become dependent on you,d you shall support them; they shall live with you as though resident aliens. 36Do not take interest in advance or otherwise make a profit from them, but fear your God; let them live with you. 37You shall not lend them your money at interest taken in advance, or provide them food at a profit. 38I am the LORD your God, who brought you out of the land of Egypt, to give you the land of Canaan, to be your God.

39 If any who are dependent on you become so impoverished that they sell themselves to you, you shall not make them serve as slaves. 40They shall remain with you as hired or bound laborers. They shall serve with you until the year of the jubilee. 41Then they and their children with them shall be free from your authority; they shall go back to their own family and return to their ancestral property. 42For they are my servants, whom I brought out of the land of Egypt; they shall not be sold as slaves are sold. 43You shall not rule over them with harshness, but shall fear your God. 44As for the male and female slaves whom you may have, it is from the nations around you that you may acquire male and female slaves. 45You may also acquire them from among

---

b 25:29 *in the city*, literally, "in a walled city."   c 25:33 *and the surrounding fields*, implied.

d Meaning of Heb uncertain

King James

45Moreover of the children of the strangers that do sojourn among you, of them shall ye buy, and of their families that *are* with you, which they begat in your land: and they shall be your possession.

46And ye shall take them as an inheritance for your children after you, to inherit *them for* a possession; they shall be your bondmen for ever: but over your brethren the children of Israel, ye shall not rule one over another with rigour.

47¶ And if a sojourner or stranger wax rich by thee, and thy brother *that dwelleth* by him wax poor, and sell himself unto the stranger *or* sojourner by thee, or to the stock of the stranger's family:

48After that he is sold he may be redeemed again; one of his brethren may redeem him:

49Either his uncle, or his uncle's son, may redeem him, or *any* that is nigh of kin unto him of his family may redeem him; or if he be able, he may redeem himself.

50And he shall reckon with him that bought him from the year that he was sold to him unto the year of jubilee: and the price of his sale shall be according unto the number of years, according to the time of an hired servant shall it be with him.

51If *there be* yet many years *behind,* according unto them he shall give again the price of his redemption out of the money that he was bought for.

52And if there remain but few years unto the year of jubilee, then he shall count with him, *and* according unto his years shall he give him again the price of his redemption.

53*And* as a yearly hired servant shall he be with him: *and the other* shall not rule with rigour over him in thy sight.

54And if he be not redeemed in these *years,* then he shall go out in the year of jubilee, *both* he, and his children with him.

55For unto me the children of Israel *are* servants; they *are* my servants whom I brought forth out of the land of Egypt: I *am* the LORD your God.

26 YE SHALL make you no idols nor graven image, neither rear you up a standing image, neither shall ye set up *any* image of stone in your land, to bow down unto it: for I *am* the LORD your God.

2¶ Ye shall keep my sabbaths, and reverence my sanctuary: I *am* the LORD.

3¶ If ye walk in my statutes, and keep my commandments, and do them;

4Then I will give you rain in due season, and the land shall yield her increase, and the trees of the field shall yield their fruit.

5And your threshing shall reach unto the vintage, and the vintage shall reach unto the sowing time: and ye shall eat your bread to the full, and dwell in your land safely.

6And I will give peace in the land, and ye shall lie down, and none shall make *you* afraid: and I will rid evil beasts out of the land, neither shall the sword go through your land.

7And ye shall chase your enemies, and they shall fall before you by the sword.

8And five of you shall chase an hundred, and an hundred of you shall put ten thousand to flight: and your enemies shall fall before you by the sword.

9For I will have respect unto you, and make you fruitful, and multiply you, and establish my covenant with you.

10And ye shall eat old store, and bring forth the old because of the new.

11And I will set my tabernacle among you: and my soul shall not abhor you.

New International

45You may also buy some of the temporary residents living among you and members of their clans born in your country, and they will become your property. 46You can will them to your children as inherited property and can make them slaves for life, but you must not rule over your fellow Israelites ruthlessly.

47" 'If an alien or a temporary resident among you becomes rich and one of your countrymen becomes poor and sells himself to the alien living among you or to a member of the alien's clan, 48he retains the right of redemption after he has sold himself. One of his relatives may redeem him: 49an uncle or a cousin or any blood relative in his clan may redeem him. Or if he prospers, he may redeem himself. 50He and his buyer are to count the time from the year he sold himself up to the Year of Jubilee. The price for his release is to be based on the rate paid to a hired man for that number of years. 51If many years remain, he must pay for his redemption a larger share of the price paid for him. 52If only a few years remain until the Year of Jubilee, he is to compute that and pay for his redemption accordingly. 53He is to be treated as a man hired from year to year; you must see to it that his owner does not rule over him ruthlessly.

54" 'Even if he is not redeemed in any of these ways, he and his children are to be released in the Year of Jubilee, 55for the Israelites belong to me as servants. They are my servants, whom I brought out of Egypt. I am the LORD your God.

Reward for Obedience

26 " 'DO NOT make idols or set up an image or a sacred stone for yourselves, and do not place a carved stone in your land to bow down before it. I am the LORD your God.

2" 'Observe my Sabbaths and have reverence for my sanctuary. I am the LORD.

3" 'If you follow my decrees and are careful to obey my commands, 4I will send you rain in its season, and the ground will yield its crops and the trees of the field their fruit. 5Your threshing will continue until grape harvest and the grape harvest will continue until planting, and you will eat all the food you want and live in safety in your land.

6" 'I will grant peace in the land, and you will lie down and no one will make you afraid. I will remove savage beasts from the land, and the sword will not pass through your country. 7You will pursue your enemies, and they will fall by the sword before you. 8Five of you will chase a hundred, and a hundred of you will chase ten thousand, and your enemies will fall by the sword before you.

9" 'I will look on you with favor and make you fruitful and increase your numbers, and I will keep my covenant with you. 10You will still be eating last year's harvest when you will have to move it out to make room for the new. 11I will put my dwelling placea among you, and I will not abhor you. 12I will walk among you and

---

a 11 Or *my tabernacle*

Living Bible

the children of the foreigners living among you, even though they have been born in your land. 46They will be permanent slaves for you to pass on to your children after you; but your brothers, the people of Israel, shall not be treated so.

47"If a foreigner living among you becomes rich, and an Israelite becomes poor and sells himself to the foreigner or to the foreigner's family, 48he may be redeemed by one of his brothers, 49his uncle, nephew, or anyone else who is a near relative. He may also redeem himself if he can find the money. 50The price of his freedom shall be in proportion to the number of years left before the Year of Jubilee—whatever it would cost to hire a servant for that number of years. 51If there are still many years until the Jubilee, he shall pay almost the amount he received when he sold himself; 52if the years have passed and only a few remain until the Jubilee, then he will repay only a small part of the amount he received when he sold himself. 53If he sells himself to a foreigner, the foreigner must treat him as a hired servant rather than as a slave or as property. 54If he has not been redeemed by the time the Year of Jubilee arrives, then he and his children shall be freed at that time. 55For the people of Israel are *my* servants; I brought them from the land of Egypt; I am the Lord your God.

26 "YOU MUST have no idols; you must never worship carved images, obelisks, or shaped stones, for I am the Lord your God. 2You must obey my Sabbath laws of rest, and reverence my Tabernacle, for I am the Lord.

3"If you obey all of my commandments, 4, 5I will give you regular rains, and the land will yield bumper crops, and the trees will be loaded with fruit long after the normal time!b And grapes will still be ripening when sowing time comes again. You shall eat your fill, and live safely in the land, 6for I will give you peace, and you will go to sleep without fear. I will chase away the dangerous animals. 7You will chase your enemies; they will die beneath your swords. 8Five of you will chase a hundred, and a hundred of you, ten thousand! You will defeat all of your enemies. 9I will look after you, and multiply you, and fulfill my covenant with you. 10You will have such a surplus of crops that you won't know what to do with them when the new harvest is ready! 11And I will live among you, and not despise you. 12I

New Revised Standard

the aliens residing with you, and from their families that are with you, who have been born in your land; and they may be your property. 46You may keep them as a possession for your children after you, for them to inherit as property. These you may treat as slaves, but as for your fellow Israelites, no one shall rule over the other with harshness.

47 If resident aliens among you prosper, and if any of your kin fall into difficulty with one of them and sell themselves to an alien, or to a branch of the alien's family, 48after they have sold themselves they shall have the right of redemption; one of their brothers may redeem them, 49or their uncle or their uncle's son may redeem them, or anyone of their family who is of their own flesh may redeem them; or if they prosper they may redeem themselves. 50They shall compute with the purchaser the total from the year when they sold themselves to the alien until the jubilee year; the price of the sale shall be applied to the number of years: the time they were with the owner shall be rated as the time of a hired laborer. 51If many years remain, they shall pay for their redemption in proportion to the purchase price; 52and if few years remain until the jubilee year, they shall compute thus: according to the years involved they shall make payment for their redemption. 53As a laborer hired by the year they shall be under the alien's authority, who shall not, however, rule with harshness over them in your sight. 54And if they have not been redeemed in any of these ways, they and their children with them shall go free in the jubilee year. 55For to me the people of Israel are servants; they are my servants whom I brought out from the land of Egypt: I am the Lord your God.

Rewards for Obedience

26 YOU SHALL make for yourselves no idols and erect no carved images or pillars, and you shall not place figured stones in your land, to worship at them; for I am the Lord your God. 2You shall keep my sabbaths and reverence my sanctuary: I am the Lord.

3 If you follow my statutes and keep my commandments and observe them faithfully, 4I will give you your rains in their season, and the land shall yield its produce, and the trees of the field shall yield their fruit. 5Your threshing shall overtake the vintage, and the vintage shall overtake the sowing; you shall eat your bread to the full, and live securely in your land. 6And I will grant peace in the land, and you shall lie down, and no one shall make you afraid; I will remove dangerous animals from the land, and no sword shall go through your land. 7You shall give chase to your enemies, and they shall fall before you by the sword. 8Five of you shall give chase to a hundred, and a hundred of you shall give chase to ten thousand; your enemies shall fall before you by the sword. 9I will look with favor upon you and make you fruitful and multiply you; and I will maintain my covenant with you. 10You shall eat old grain long stored, and you shall have to clear out the old to make way for the new. 11I will place my dwelling in your midst, and I shall not abhor you. 12And I will walk

---

b 26:4, 5 long after the normal time, literally, "until the grape harvest."

King James

12And I will walk among you, and will be your God, and ye shall be my people.

13I *am* the LORD your God, which brought you forth out of the land of Egypt, that ye should not be their bondmen; and I have broken the bands of your yoke, and made you go upright.

14¶ But if ye will not hearken unto me, and will not do all these commandments;

15And if ye shall despise my statutes, or if your soul abhor my judgments, so that ye will not do all my commandments, *but* that ye break my covenant:

16I also will do this unto you; I will even appoint over you terror, consumption, and the burning ague, that shall consume the eyes, and cause sorrow of heart: and ye shall sow your seed in vain, for your enemies shall eat it.

17And I will set my face against you, and ye shall be slain before your enemies: they that hate you shall reign over you; and ye shall flee when none pursueth you.

18And if ye will not yet for all this hearken unto me, then I will punish you seven times more for your sins.

19And I will break the pride of your power; and I will make your heaven as iron, and your earth as brass:

20And your strength shall be spent in vain: for your land shall not yield her increase, neither shall the trees of the land yield their fruits.

21¶ And if ye walk contrary unto me, and will not hearken unto me; I will bring seven times more plagues upon you according to your sins.

22I will also send wild beasts among you, which shall rob you of your children, and destroy your cattle, and make you few in number; and your *high* ways shall be desolate.

23And if ye will not be reformed by me by these things, but will walk contrary unto me;

24Then will I also walk contrary unto you, and will punish you yet seven times for your sins.

25And I will bring a sword upon you, that shall avenge the quarrel of *my* covenant: and when ye are gathered together within your cities, I will send the pestilence among you; and ye shall be delivered into the hand of the enemy.

26*And* when I have broken the staff of your bread, ten women shall bake your bread in one oven, and they shall deliver *you* your bread again by weight: and ye shall eat, and not be satisfied.

27And if ye will not for all this hearken unto me, but walk contrary unto me;

28Then I will walk contrary unto you also in fury; and I, even I, will chastise you seven times for your sins.

29And ye shall eat the flesh of your sons, and the flesh of your daughters shall ye eat.

30And I will destroy your high places, and cut down your images, and cast your carcases upon the carcases of your idols, and my soul shall abhor you.

31And I will make your cities waste, and bring your sanctuaries unto desolation, and I will not smell the savour of your sweet odours.

32And I will bring the land into desolation: and your enemies which dwell therein shall be astonished at it.

33And I will scatter you among the heathen, and will draw out a sword after you: and your land shall be desolate, and your cities waste.

34Then shall the land enjoy her sabbaths, as long as it lieth desolate, and ye *be* in your enemies' land; *even* then shall the land rest, and enjoy her sabbaths.

35As long as it lieth desolate it shall rest; because it did not rest in your sabbaths, when ye dwelt upon it.

36And upon them that are left *alive* of you I will send a faintness into their hearts in the lands of their enemies; and the sound of a shaken leaf shall chase them; and they shall flee, as fleeing from a sword; and they shall fall when none pursueth.

New International

be your God, and you will be my people. 13I am the LORD your God, who brought you out of Egypt so that you would no longer be slaves to the Egyptians; I broke the bars of your yoke and enabled you to walk with heads held high.

Punishment for Disobedience

14" 'But if you will not listen to me and carry out all these commands, 15and if you reject my decrees and abhor my laws and fail to carry out all my commands and so violate my covenant, 16then I will do this to you: I will bring upon you sudden terror, wasting diseases and fever that will destroy your sight and drain away your life. You will plant seed in vain, because your enemies will eat it. 17I will set my face against you so that you will be defeated by your enemies; those who hate you will rule over you, and you will flee even when no one is pursuing you.

18" 'If after all this you will not listen to me, I will punish you for your sins seven times over. 19I will break down your stubborn pride and make the sky above you like iron and the ground beneath you like bronze. 20Your strength will be spent in vain, because your soil will not yield its crops, nor will the trees of the land yield their fruit.

21" 'If you remain hostile toward me and refuse to listen to me, I will multiply your afflictions seven times over, as your sins deserve. 22I will send wild animals against you, and they will rob you of your children, destroy your cattle and make you so few in number that your roads will be deserted.

23" 'If in spite of these things you do not accept my correction but continue to be hostile toward me, 24I myself will be hostile toward you and will afflict you for your sins seven times over. 25And I will bring the sword upon you to avenge the breaking of the covenant. When you withdraw into your cities, I will send a plague among you, and you will be given into enemy hands. 26When I cut off your supply of bread, ten women will be able to bake your bread in one oven, and they will dole out the bread by weight. You will eat, but you will not be satisfied.

27" 'If in spite of this you still do not listen to me but continue to be hostile toward me, 28then in my anger I will be hostile toward you, and I myself will punish you for your sins seven times over. 29You will eat the flesh of your sons and the flesh of your daughters. 30I will destroy your high places, cut down your incense altars and pile your dead bodies on the lifeless forms of your idols, and I will abhor you. 31I will turn your cities into ruins and lay waste your sanctuaries, and I will take no delight in the pleasing aroma of your offerings. 32I will lay waste the land, so that your enemies who live there will be appalled. 33I will scatter you among the nations and will draw out my sword and pursue you. Your land will be laid waste, and your cities will lie in ruins. 34Then the land will enjoy its sabbath years all the time that it lies desolate and you are in the country of your enemies; then the land will rest and enjoy its sabbaths. 35All the time that it lies desolate, the land will have the rest it did not have during the sabbaths you lived in it.

36" 'As for those of you who are left, I will make their hearts so fearful in the lands of their enemies that the sound of a windblown leaf will put them to flight. They will run as though fleeing from the sword, and they will fall, even though no one is pursuing them. 37They will

Living Bible

will walk among you and be your God, and you shall be my people. ¹³For I am the Lord your God who brought you out of the land of Egypt, so that you would be slaves no longer; I have broken your chains so that you can walk with dignity.ª

¹⁴"But if you will not listen to me or obey me, ¹⁵but reject my laws, ¹⁶this is what I will do to you: I will punish you with sudden terrors and panic, and with tuberculosis and burning fever; your eyes shall be consumed and your life shall ebb away; you will sow your crops in vain, for your enemies will eat them. ¹⁷I will set my face against you and you will flee before your attackers; those who hate you will rule you; you will even run when no one is chasing you!

¹⁸"And if you still disobey me, I will punish you seven times more severely for your sins. ¹⁹I will break your proud power and make your heavens as iron, and your earth as bronze. ²⁰Your strength shall be spent in vain; for your land shall not yield its crops, nor your trees their fruit.

²¹"And if even then you will not obey me and listen to me, I will send you seven times more plagues because of your sins. ²²I will send wild animals to kill your children and destroy your cattle and reduce your numbers so that your roads shall be deserted.

²³"And if even this will not reform you, but you continue to walk against my wishes, ²⁴then I will walk against your wishes, and I, even I, will personally smite you seven times for your sin. ²⁵I will revenge the breaking of my covenant by bringing war against you. You will flee to your cities, and I will send a plague among you there; and you will be conquered by your enemies. ²⁶I will destroy your food supply so that one oven will be large enough to bake all the bread available for ten entire families; and you will still be hungry after your pittance has been doled out to you.

²⁷"And if you still won't listen to me or obey me, ²⁸then I will let loose my great anger and send you seven times greater punishment for your sins. ²⁹You shall eat your own sons and daughters, ³⁰and I will destroy the altars on the hills where you worship your idols, and I will cut down your incense altars, leaving your dead bodies to rot among your idols; and I will abhor you. ³¹I will make your cities desolate, and destroy your places of worship, and will not respond to your incense offerings. ³²Yes, I will desolate your land; your enemies shall live in it, utterly amazed at what I have done to you.

³³"I will scatter you out among the nations, destroying you with war as you go. Your land shall be desolate and your cities destroyed. ³⁴, ³⁵Then at last the land will rest and make up for the many years you refused to let it lie idle; for it will lie desolate all the years that you are captives in enemy lands. Yes, then the land will rest and enjoy its Sabbaths! It will make up for the rest you didn't give it every seventh year when you lived upon it.

³⁶"And for those who are left alive, I will cause them to be dragged away to distant lands as prisoners of war, and slaves. There they will live in constant fear. The sound of a leaf driven in the wind will send them fleeing as though chased by a man with a sword; they shall fall when no one is pursuing them. ³⁷Yes, though none pur-

New Revised Standard

among you, and will be your God, and you shall be my people. ¹³I am the LORD your God who brought you out of the land of Egypt, to be their slaves no more; I have broken the bars of your yoke and made you walk erect.

Penalties for Disobedience

14 But if you will not obey me, and do not observe all these commandments, ¹⁵if you spurn my statutes, and abhor my ordinances, so that you will not observe all my commandments, and you break my covenant, ¹⁶I in turn will do this to you: I will bring terror on you; consumption and fever that waste the eyes and cause life to pine away. You shall sow your seed in vain, for your enemies shall eat it. ¹⁷I will set my face against you, and you shall be struck down by your enemies; your foes shall rule over you, and you shall flee though no one pursues you. ¹⁸And if in spite of this you will not obey me, I will continue to punish you sevenfold for your sins. ¹⁹I will break your proud glory, and I will make your sky like iron and your earth like copper. ²⁰Your strength shall be spent to no purpose: your land shall not yield its produce, and the trees of the land shall not yield their fruit.

21 If you continue hostile to me, and will not obey me, I will continue to plague you sevenfold for your sins. ²²I will let loose wild animals against you, and they shall bereave you of your children and destroy your livestock; they shall make you few in number, and your roads shall be deserted.

23 If in spite of these punishments you have not turned back to me, but continue hostile to me, ²⁴then I too will continue hostile to you: I myself will strike you sevenfold for your sins. ²⁵I will bring the sword against you, executing vengeance for the covenant; and if you withdraw within your cities, I will send pestilence among you, and you shall be delivered into enemy hands. ²⁶When I break your staff of bread, ten women shall bake your bread in a single oven, and they shall dole out your bread by weight; and though you eat, you shall not be satisfied.

27 But if, despite this, you disobey me, and continue hostile to me, ²⁸I will continue hostile to you in fury; I in turn will punish you myself sevenfold for your sins. ²⁹You shall eat the flesh of your sons, and you shall eat the flesh of your daughters. ³⁰I will destroy your high places and cut down your incense altars; I will heap your carcasses on the carcasses of your idols. I will abhor you. ³¹I will lay your cities waste, will make your sanctuaries desolate, and I will not smell your pleasing odors. ³²I will devastate the land, so that your enemies who come to settle in it shall be appalled at it. ³³And you I will scatter among the nations, and I will unsheathe the sword against you; your land shall be a desolation, and your cities a waste.

34 Then the land shall enjoyᵇ its sabbath years as long as it lies desolate, while you are in the land of your enemies; then the land shall rest, and enjoyᵇ its sabbath years. ³⁵As long as it lies desolate, it shall have the rest it did not have on your sabbaths when you were living on it. ³⁶And as for those of you who survive, I will send faintness into their hearts in the lands of their enemies; the sound of a driven leaf shall put them to flight, and they shall flee as one flees from the sword, and they shall fall though no one pursues. ³⁷They shall stumble over

---

ª *26:13 so that you can walk with dignity*, literally, "and make you go upright," or "walk with heads held high."

ᵇ Or *make up for*

King James

37And they shall fall one upon another, as it were before a sword, when none pursueth: and ye shall have no power to stand before your enemies.

38And ye shall perish among the heathen, and the land of your enemies shall eat you up.

39And they that are left of you shall pine away in their iniquity in your enemies' lands; and also in the iniquities of their fathers shall they pine away with them.

40If they shall confess their iniquity, and the iniquity of their fathers, with their trespass which they trespassed against me, and that also they have walked contrary unto me;

41And that I also have walked contrary unto them, and have brought them into the land of their enemies; if then their uncircumcised hearts be humbled, and they then accept of the punishment of their iniquity:

42Then will I remember my covenant with Jacob, and also my covenant with Isaac, and also my covenant with Abraham will I remember; and I will remember the land.

43The land also shall be left of them, and shall enjoy her sabbaths, while she lieth desolate without them: and they shall accept of the punishment of their iniquity: because, even because they despised my judgments, and because their soul abhorred my statutes.

44And yet for all that, when they be in the land of their enemies, I will not cast them away, neither will I abhor them, to destroy them utterly, and to break my covenant with them: for I am the LORD their God.

45But I will for their sakes remember the covenant of their ancestors, whom I brought forth out of the land of Egypt in the sight of the heathen, that I might be their God: I am the LORD.

46These are the statutes and judgments and laws, which the LORD made between him and the children of Israel in mount Sinai by the hand of Moses.

27 AND THE LORD spake unto Moses, saying, 2Speak unto the children of Israel, and say unto them, When a man shall make a singular vow, the persons shall be for the LORD by thy estimation.

3And thy estimation shall be of the male from twenty years old even unto sixty years old, even thy estimation shall be fifty shekels of silver, after the shekel of the sanctuary.

4And if it be a female, then thy estimation shall be thirty shekels.

5And if it be from five years old even unto twenty years old, then thy estimation shall be of the male twenty shekels, and for the female ten shekels.

6And if it be from a month old even unto five years old, then thy estimation shall be of the male five shekels of silver, and for the female thy estimation shall be three shekels of silver.

7And if it be from sixty years old and above; if it be a male, then thy estimation shall be fifteen shekels, and for the female ten shekels.

8But if he be poorer than thy estimation, then he shall present himself before the priest, and the priest shall value him; according to his ability that vowed shall the priest value him.

9And if it be a beast, whereof men bring an offering unto the LORD, all that any man giveth of such unto the LORD shall be holy.

10He shall not alter it, nor change it, a good for a bad, or a bad for a good: and if he shall at all change beast for beast, then it and the exchange thereof shall be holy.

New International

stumble over one another as though fleeing from the sword, even though no one is pursuing. So you will not be able to stand before your enemies. 38You will perish among the nations; the land of your enemies will devour you. 39Those of you who are left will waste away in the lands of their enemies because of their sins; also because of their fathers' sins they will waste away.

40" 'But if they will confess their sins and the sins of their fathers—their treachery against me and their hostility toward me, 41which made me hostile toward them so that I sent them into the land of their enemies—then when their uncircumcised hearts are humbled and they pay for their sin, 42I will remember my covenant with Jacob and my covenant with Isaac and my covenant with Abraham, and I will remember the land. 43For the land will be deserted by them and will enjoy its sabbaths while it lies desolate without them. They will pay for their sins because they rejected my laws and abhorred my decrees. 44Yet in spite of this, when they are in the land of their enemies, I will not reject them or abhor them so as to destroy them completely, breaking my covenant with them. I am the LORD their God. 45But for their sake I will remember the covenant with their ancestors whom I brought out of Egypt in the sight of the nations to be their God. I am the LORD.' "

46These are the decrees, the laws and the regulations that the LORD established on Mount Sinai between himself and the Israelites through Moses.

Redeeming What Is the LORD's

27 THE LORD said to Moses, 2"Speak to the Israelites and say to them: 'If anyone makes a special vow to dedicate persons to the LORD by giving equivalent values, 3set the value of a male between the ages of twenty and sixty at fifty shekelsa of silver, according to the sanctuary shekelb; 4and if it is a female, set her value at thirty shekels.c 5If it is a person between the ages of five and twenty, set the value of a male at twenty shekelsd and of a female at ten shekels.e 6If it is a person between one month and five years, set the value of a male at five shekelsf of silver and that of a female at three shekelsg of silver. 7If it is a person sixty years old or more, set the value of a male at fifteen shekelsh and of a female at ten shekels. 8If anyone making the vow is too poor to pay the specified amount, he is to present the person to the priest, who will set the value for him according to what the man making the vow can afford.

9" 'If what he vowed is an animal that is acceptable as an offering to the LORD, such an animal given to the LORD becomes holy. 10He must not exchange it or substitute a good one for a bad one, or a bad one for a good one; if he should substitute one animal for another, both it and the substitute become holy. 11If what he vowed

---

a 3 That is, about 1 1/4 pounds (about 0.6 kilogram); also in verse 16   b 3 That is, about 2/5 ounce (about 11.5 grams); also in verse 25   c 4 That is, about 12 ounces (about 0.3 kilogram)   d 5 That is, about 8 ounces (about 0.2 kilogram)   e 5 That is, about 4 ounces (about 110 grams); also in verse 7   f 6 That is, about 2 ounces (about 55 grams)   g 6 That is, about 1 1/4 ounces (about 35 grams)   h 7 That is, about 6 ounces (about 170 grams)

Living Bible

sue they shall stumble over each other in flight, as though fleeing in battle, with no power to stand before their enemies. 38You shall perish among the nations and be destroyed among your enemies. 39Those left shall pine away in enemy lands because of their sins, the same sins as those of their fathers.

40, 41"But at last they shall confess their sins and their fathers' sins of treachery against me. (Because they were against me, I was against them, and brought them into the land of their enemies.) When at last their evil hearts are humbled and they accept the punishment I send them for their sins, 42then I will remember again my promises to Abraham, Isaac, and Jacob, and I will remember the land (and its desolation). 43For the land shall enjoy its Sabbaths as it lies desolate. But then at last they shall accept their punishment for rejecting my laws and for despising my rule. 44But despite all they have done, I will not utterly destroy them and my covenant with them, for I am Jehovah their God. 45For their sakes I will remember my promises to their ancestors, to be their God. For I brought their forefathers out of Egypt as all the nations watched in wonder. I am Jehovah."

46These were the laws, ordinances, and instructions that Jehovah gave to the people of Israel, through Moses, on Mount Sinai.

27 THE LORD said to Moses, "Tell the people of Israel that when a person makes a special vow to give himself to the Lord, he shall give these payments instead: 3A man from the age of twenty to sixty shall pay twenty-five dollars;i 4a woman from the age of twenty to sixty shall pay fifteen dollars; 5a boy from five to twenty shall pay ten dollars; a girl, five dollars. 6A boy one month to five years old shall have paid for him two and a half dollars; a girl, one and a half dollars. 7A man over sixty shall pay seven and a half dollars; a woman, five dollars. 8But if the person is too poor to pay this amount, he shall be brought to the priest and the priest shall talk it over with him, and he shall pay as the priest shall decide.

9"But if it is an animal that is vowed to be given to the Lord as a sacrifice, it must be given. 10The vow may not be changed; the donor may neither change his mind about giving it to the Lord, nor substitute good for bad or bad for good; if he does, both the first and the second shall belong to the Lord! 11, 12But if the animal given to

New Revised Standard

one another, as if to escape a sword, though no one pursues; and you shall have no power to stand against your enemies. 38You shall perish among the nations, and the land of your enemies shall devour you. 39And those of you who survive shall languish in the land of your enemies because of their iniquities; also they shall languish because of the iniquities of their ancestors.

40 But if they confess their iniquity and the iniquity of their ancestors, in that they committed treachery against me and, moreover, that they continued hostile to me— 41so that I, in turn, continued hostile to them and brought them into the land of their enemies; if then their uncircumcised heart is humbled and they make amends for their iniquity, 42then will I remember my covenant with Jacob; I will remember also my covenant with Isaac and also my covenant with Abraham, and I will remember the land. 43For the land shall be deserted by them, and enjoyj its sabbath years by lying desolate without them, while they shall make amends for their iniquity, because they dared to spurn my ordinances, and they abhorred my statutes. 44Yet for all that, when they are in the land of their enemies, I will not spurn them, or abhor them so as to destroy them utterly and break my covenant with them; for I am the LORD their God; 45but I will remember in their favor the covenant with their ancestors whom I brought out of the land of Egypt in the sight of the nations, to be their God: I am the LORD.

46 These are the statutes and ordinances and laws that the LORD established between himself and the people of Israel on Mount Sinai through Moses.

Votive Offerings

27 THE LORD spoke to Moses, saying: 2Speak to the people of Israel and say to them: When a person makes an explicit vow to the LORD concerning the equivalent for a human being, 3the equivalent for a male shall be: from twenty to sixty years of age the equivalent shall be fifty shekels of silver by the sanctuary shekel. 4If the person is a female, the equivalent is thirty shekels. 5If the age is from five to twenty years of age, the equivalent is twenty shekels for a male and ten shekels for a female. 6If the age is from one month to five years, the equivalent for a male is five shekels of silver, and for a female the equivalent is three shekels of silver. 7And if the person is sixty years old or over, then the equivalent for a male is fifteen shekels, and for a female ten shekels. 8If any cannot afford the equivalent, they shall be brought before the priest and the priest shall assess them; the priest shall assess them according to what each one making a vow can afford.

9 If it concerns an animal that may be brought as an offering to the LORD, any such that may be given to the LORD shall be holy. 10Another shall not be exchanged or substituted for it, either good for bad or bad for good; and if one animal is substituted for another, both that one and its substitute shall be holy. 11If it concerns any

i 27:3 shall pay twenty-five dollars. Note: The actual value by today's standards is uncertain. The above figures are approximate.

j Or make up for

King James

11And if *it be* any unclean beast, of which they do not offer a sacrifice unto the LORD, then he shall present the beast before the priest:

12And the priest shall value it, whether it be good or bad: as thou valuest it, *who art* the priest, so shall it be.

13But if he will at all redeem it, then he shall add a fifth *part* thereof unto thy estimation.

14¶ And when a man shall sanctify his house *to be* holy unto the LORD, then the priest shall estimate it, whether it be good or bad: as the priest shall estimate it, so shall it stand.

15And if he that sanctified it will redeem his house, then he shall add the fifth *part* of the money of thy estimation unto it, and it shall be his.

16And if a man shall sanctify unto the LORD *some part* of a field of his possession, then thy estimation shall be according to the seed thereof: an homer of barley seed *shall be valued* at fifty shekels of silver.

17If he sanctify his field from the year of jubilee, according to thy estimation it shall stand.

18But if he sanctify his field after the jubilee, then the priest shall reckon unto him the money according to the years that remain, even unto the year of the jubilee, and it shall be abated from thy estimation.

19And if he that sanctified the field will in any wise redeem it, then he shall add the fifth *part* of the money of thy estimation unto it, and it shall be assured to him.

20And if he will not redeem the field, or if he have sold the field to another man, it shall not be redeemed any more.

21But the field, when it goeth out in the jubilee, shall be holy unto the LORD, as a field devoted; the possession thereof shall be the priest's.

22And if *a man* sanctify unto the LORD a field which he hath bought, which *is* not of the fields of his possession;

23Then the priest shall reckon unto him the worth of thy estimation, *even* unto the year of the jubilee: and he shall give thine estimation in that day, *as* a holy thing unto the LORD.

24In the year of the jubilee the field shall return unto him of whom it was bought, *even* to him to whom the possession of the land *did belong*.

25And all thy estimations shall be according to the shekel of the sanctuary: twenty gerahs shall be the shekel.

26¶ Only the firstling of the beasts, which should be the LORD's firstling, no man shall sanctify it; whether *it be* ox, or sheep: it *is* the LORD's.

27And if *it be* of an unclean beast, then he shall redeem *it* according to thine estimation, and shall add a fifth *part* of it thereto: or if it be not redeemed, then it shall be sold according to thy estimation.

28Notwithstanding no devoted thing, that a man shall devote unto the LORD of all that he hath, *both* of man and beast, and of the field of his possession, shall be sold or redeemed: every devoted thing *is* most holy unto the LORD.

29None devoted, which shall be devoted of men, shall be redeemed; *but* shall surely be put to death.

30And all the tithe of the land, *whether* of the seed of the land, *or* of the fruit of the tree, *is* the LORD's: *it is* holy unto the LORD.

31And if a man will at all redeem *aught* of his tithes, he shall add thereto the fifth *part* thereof.

32And concerning the tithe of the herd, or of the flock, *even* of whatsoever passeth under the rod, the tenth shall be holy unto the LORD.

33He shall not search whether it be good or bad, neither shall he change it: and if he change it at all, then both it and the change thereof shall be holy; it shall not be redeemed.

34These *are* the commandments, which the LORD commanded Moses for the children of Israel in mount Sinai.

New International

is a ceremonially unclean animal—one that is not acceptable as an offering to the LORD—the animal must be presented to the priest, 12who will judge its quality as good or bad. Whatever value the priest then sets, that is what it will be. 13If the owner wishes to redeem the animal, he must add a fifth to its value.

14" 'If a man dedicates his house as something holy to the LORD, the priest will judge its quality as good or bad. Whatever value the priest then sets, so it will remain. 15If the man who dedicates his house redeems it, he must add a fifth to its value, and the house will again become his.

16" 'If a man dedicates to the LORD part of his family land, its value is to be set according to the amount of seed required for it—fifty shekels of silver to a homer[a] of barley seed. 17If he dedicates his field during the Year of Jubilee, the value that has been set remains. 18But if he dedicates his field after the Jubilee, the priest will determine the value according to the number of years that remain until the next Year of Jubilee, and its set value will be reduced. 19If the man who dedicates the field wishes to redeem it, he must add a fifth to its value, and the field will again become his. 20If, however, he does not redeem the field, or if he has sold it to someone else, it can never be redeemed. 21When the field is released in the Jubilee, it will become holy, like a field devoted to the LORD; it will become the property of the priests.[b]

22" 'If a man dedicates to the LORD a field he has bought, which is not part of his family land, 23the priest will determine its value up to the Year of Jubilee, and the man must pay its value on that day as something holy to the LORD. 24In the Year of Jubilee the field will revert to the person from whom he bought it, the one whose land it was. 25Every value is to be set according to the sanctuary shekel, twenty gerahs to the shekel.

26" 'No one, however, may dedicate the firstborn of an animal, since the firstborn already belongs to the LORD; whether an ox[c] or a sheep, it is the LORD's. 27If it is one of the unclean animals, he may buy it back at its set value, adding a fifth of the value to it. If he does not redeem it, it is to be sold at its set value.

28" 'But nothing that a man owns and devotes[d] to the LORD—whether man or animal or family land—may be sold or redeemed; everything so devoted is most holy to the LORD.

29" 'No person devoted to destruction[e] may be ransomed; he must be put to death.

30" 'A tithe of everything from the land, whether grain from the soil or fruit from the trees, belongs to the LORD; it is holy to the LORD. 31If a man redeems any of his tithe, he must add a fifth of the value to it. 32The entire tithe of the herd and flock—every tenth animal that passes under the shepherd's rod—will be holy to the LORD. 33He must not pick out the good from the bad or make any substitution. If he does make a substitution, both the animal and its substitute become holy and cannot be redeemed.' "

34These are the commands the LORD gave Moses on Mount Sinai for the Israelites.

a 16 That is, probably about 6 bushels (about 220 liters)   b 21 Or *priest*
c 26 The Hebrew word can include both male and female.   d 28 The Hebrew term refers to the irrevocable giving over of things or persons to the LORD.
e 29 The Hebrew term refers to the irrevocable giving over of things or persons to the LORD, often by totally destroying them.

Living Bible

the Lord is not a kind that is permitted as a sacrifice, the owner shall bring it to the priest to value it, and he shall be told how much to pay instead. 13If the animal is a kind that may be offered as a sacrifice,f but the man wants to redeem it, then he shall pay twenty percent more than the value set by the priest.

14, 15"If someone donates his home to the Lord and then wishes to redeem it, the priest will decide its value and the man shall pay that amount plus twenty percent, and the house will be his again.

16"If a man dedicates any part of his field to the Lord, value it in proportion to its size, as indicated by the amount of seed required to sow it. A section of land that requires ten bushels of barley seed for sowing is valued at twenty-five dollars. 17If a man dedicates his field in the Year of Jubilee, then the whole estimate shall stand; 18but if it is after the Year of Jubilee, then the value shall be in proportion to the number of years remaining until the next Year of Jubilee. 19If the man decides to redeem the field, he shall pay twenty percent in addition to the priest's valuation, and the field will be his again. 20But if he decides not to redeem the field, or if he has sold the field to someone else [and has given to the Lord his rights to it at the Year of Jubileeg], it shall not be returned to him again. 21When it is freed in the Year of Jubilee, it shall belong to the Lord as a field devoted to him, and it shall be given to the priests.

22"If a man dedicates to the Lord a field he has bought, but which is not part of his family possession, 23the priest shall estimate the value until the Year of Jubilee, and he shall immediately give that estimated value to the Lord, 24and in the Year of Jubilee the field shall return to the original owner from whom it was bought. 25All the valuations shall be stated in standard money.h

26"You may not dedicate to the Lord the firstborn of any ox or sheep, for it is already his. 27But if it is the firstborn of an animal that cannot be sacrificed because it is not on the list of those acceptable to the Lord, then the owner shall pay the priest's estimate of its worth, plus twenty percent; or if the owner does not redeem it, the priest may sell it to someone else. 28However, anything utterly devoted to the Lord—people, animals, or inherited fields—shall not be sold or redeemed, for they are most holy to the Lord. 29No one sentenced by the courts to die may pay a fine instead; he shall surely be put to death.i

30"A tenth of the produce of the land, whether grain or fruit, is the Lord's, and is holy. 31If anyone wants to buy back this fruit or grain, he must add a fifth to its value. 32And the Lord owns every tenth animal of your herds and flocks and other domestic animals, as they pass by for counting. 33The tenth given to the Lord shall not be selected on the basis of whether it is good or bad, and there shall be no substitutions; for if there is any change made, then both the original and the substitution shall belong to the Lord, and may not be bought back!"

34These are the commandments the Lord gave to Moses for the people of Israel on Mount Sinai.

New Revised Standard

unclean animal that may not be brought as an offering to the LORD, the animal shall be presented before the priest. 12The priest shall assess it: whether good or bad, according to the assessment of the priest, so it shall be. 13But if it is to be redeemed, one-fifth must be added to the assessment.

14 If a person consecrates a house to the LORD, the priest shall assess it: whether good or bad, as the priest assesses it, so it shall stand. 15And if the one who consecrates the house wishes to redeem it, one-fifth shall be added to its assessed value, and it shall revert to the original owner.

16 If a person consecrates to the LORD any inherited landholding, its assessment shall be in accordance with its seed requirements: fifty shekels of silver to a homer of barley seed. 17If the person consecrates the field as of the year of jubilee, that assessment shall stand; 18but if the field is consecrated after the jubilee, the priest shall compute the price for it according to the years that remain until the year of jubilee, and the assessment shall be reduced. 19And if the one who consecrates the field wishes to redeem it, then one-fifth shall be added to its assessed value, and it shall revert to the original owner; 20but if the field is not redeemed, or if it has been sold to someone else, it shall no longer be redeemable. 21But when the field is released in the jubilee, it shall be holy to the LORD as a devoted field; it becomes the priest's holding. 22If someone consecrates to the LORD a field that has been purchased, which is not a part of the inherited landholding, 23the priest shall compute for it the proportionate assessment up to the year of jubilee, and the assessment shall be paid as of that day, a sacred donation to the LORD. 24In the year of jubilee the field shall return to the one from whom it was bought, whose holding the land is. 25All assessments shall be by the sanctuary shekel: twenty gerahs shall make a shekel.

26 A firstling of animals, however, which as a firstling belongs to the LORD, cannot be consecrated by anyone; whether ox or sheep, it is the LORD's. 27If it is an unclean animal, it shall be ransomed at its assessment, with one-fifth added; if it is not redeemed, it shall be sold at its assessment.

28 Nothing that a person owns that has been devoted to destruction for the LORD, be it human or animal, or inherited landholding, may be sold or redeemed; every devoted thing is most holy to the LORD. 29No human beings who have been devoted to destruction can be ransomed; they shall be put to death.

30 All tithes from the land, whether the seed from the ground or the fruit from the tree, are the LORD's; they are holy to the LORD. 31If persons wish to redeem any of their tithes, they must add one-fifth to them. 32All tithes of herd and flock, every tenth one that passes under the shepherd's staff, shall be holy to the LORD. 33Let no one inquire whether it is good or bad, or make substitution for it; if one makes substitution for it, then both it and the substitute shall be holy and cannot be redeemed.

34 These are the commandments that the LORD gave to Moses for the people of Israel on Mount Sinai.

---

f 27:13 If the animal is a kind that may be offered as a sacrifice, implied. g 27:20 and has given to the Lord his rights to it at the Year of Jubilee, implied. h 27:25 All the valuations shall be stated in standard money, literally, "and all your estimations shall be according to the shekel of the sanctuary: twenty gerahs shall be the shekel." i 27:29 No one sentenced by the courts to die may pay a fine instead; he shall surely be put to death, literally, "no one who is under the ban of God to be put to death may be ransomed."

THE FOURTH BOOK OF MOSES, CALLED

Numbers

Numbers

1 AND THE LORD spake unto Moses in the wilderness of Sinai, in the tabernacle of the congregation, on the first *day* of the second month, in the second year after they were come out of the land of Egypt, saying,

2Take ye the sum of all the congregation of the children of Israel, after their families, by the house of their fathers, with the number of *their* names, every male by their polls;

3From twenty years old and upward, all that are able to go forth to war in Israel: thou and Aaron shall number them by their armies.

4And with you there shall be a man of every tribe; every one head of the house of his fathers.

5¶ And these *are* the names of the men that shall stand with you: of *the tribe of* Reuben; Elizur the son of Shedeur.

6Of Simeon; Shelumiel the son of Zurishaddai.

7Of Judah; Nahshon the son of Amminadab.

8Of Issachar; Nethaneel the son of Zuar.

9Of Zebulun; Eliab the son of Helon.

10Of the children of Joseph: of Ephraim; Elishama the son of Ammihud: of Manasseh; Gamaliel the son of Pedahzur.

11Of Benjamin; Abidan the son of Gideoni.

12Of Dan; Ahiezer the son of Ammishaddai.

13Of Asher; Pagiel the son of Ocran.

14Of Gad; Eliasaph the son of Deuel.

15Of Naphtali; Ahira the son of Enan.

16These *were* the renowned of the congregation, princes of the tribes of their fathers, heads of thousands in Israel.

17¶ And Moses and Aaron took these men which are expressed by *their* names:

18And they assembled all the congregation together on the first *day* of the second month, and they declared their pedigrees after their families, by the house of their fathers, according to the number of the names, from twenty years old and upward, by their polls.

19As the LORD commanded Moses, so he numbered them in the wilderness of Sinai.

20And the children of Reuben, Israel's eldest son, by their generations, after their families, by the house of their fathers, according to the number of the names, by their polls, every male from twenty years old and upward, all that were able to go forth to war;

21Those that were numbered of them, *even* of the tribe of Reuben, *were* forty and six thousand and five hundred.

22¶ Of the children of Simeon, by their generations, after their families, by the house of their fathers, those that were numbered of them, according to the number of the names, by their polls, every male from twenty years old and upward, all that were able to go forth to war;

23Those that were numbered of them, *even* of the tribe of Simeon, *were* fifty and nine thousand and three hundred.

The Census

1 THE LORD spoke to Moses in the Tent of Meeting in the Desert of Sinai on the first day of the second month of the second year after the Israelites came out of Egypt. He said: 2"Take a census of the whole Israelite community by their clans and families, listing every man by name, one by one. 3You and Aaron are to number by their divisions all the men in Israel twenty years old or more who are able to serve in the army. 4One man from each tribe, each the head of his family, is to help you. 5These are the names of the men who are to assist you:

from Reuben, Elizur son of Shedeur;
6from Simeon, Shelumiel son of Zurishaddai;
7from Judah, Nahshon son of Amminadab;
8from Issachar, Nethanel son of Zuar;
9from Zebulun, Eliab son of Helon;
10from the sons of Joseph:
　from Ephraim, Elishama son of Ammihud;
　from Manasseh, Gamaliel son of Pedahzur;
11from Benjamin, Abidan son of Gideoni;
12from Dan, Ahiezer son of Ammishaddai;
13from Asher, Pagiel son of Ocran;
14from Gad, Eliasaph son of Deuel;
15from Naphtali, Ahira son of Enan."

16These were the men appointed from the community, the leaders of their ancestral tribes. They were the heads of the clans of Israel.

17Moses and Aaron took these men whose names had been given, 18and they called the whole community together on the first day of the second month. The people indicated their ancestry by their clans and families, and the men twenty years old or more were listed by name, one by one, 19as the LORD commanded Moses. And so he counted them in the Desert of Sinai:

20From the descendants of Reuben the firstborn son of Israel:

All the men twenty years old or more who were able to serve in the army were listed by name, one by one, according to the records of their clans and families. 21The number from the tribe of Reuben was 46,500.

22From the descendants of Simeon:

All the men twenty years old or more who were able to serve in the army were counted and listed by name, one by one, according to the records of their clans and families. 23The number from the tribe of Simeon was 59,300.

Numbers

Numbers

The First Census of Israel

1 IT WAS on the fifteenth day of April[a] of the second year after the Israelis left Egypt that the Lord issued the following instructions to Moses. (He was in the Tabernacle at the camp of Israel on the Sinai peninsula at the time.)

2-15"Take a census of all the men twenty years old and older who are able to go to war, indicating their tribe and family. You and Aaron are to direct the project, assisted by these leaders from each tribe:"

Tribe	Leader
Reuben	Elizur (son of Shedeur)
Simeon	Shelumi-el (son of Zurishaddai)
Judah	Nahshon (son of Amminadab)
Issachar	Nethanel (son of Zuar)
Zebulun	Eliab (son of Helon)
Ephraim (son of Joseph)	Elishama (son of Ammihud)
Manasseh (son of Joseph)	Gamaliel (son of Pedahzur)
Benjamin	Abidan (son of Gideoni)
Dan	Ahiezer (son of Ammishaddai)
Asher	Pagiel (son of Ochran)
Gad	Eliasaph (son of Deuel)
Naphtali	Ahira (son of Enan)

16These were the tribal leaders elected from among the people.

17, 18, 19On the same day[b] Moses and Aaron and the above-named leaders summoned all the men of Israel who were twenty years old or older to come and register, each man indicating his tribe and family, as the Lord had commanded Moses. 20-46Here is the final tabulation:

Tribe	Total
Reuben (the oldest son of Jacob)	46,500
Simeon	59,300

1 THE LORD spoke to Moses in the wilderness of Sinai, in the tent of meeting, on the first day of the second month, in the second year after they had come out of the land of Egypt, saying: 2Take a census of the whole congregation of Israelites, in their clans, by ancestral houses, according to the number of names, every male individually; 3from twenty years old and upward, everyone in Israel able to go to war. You and Aaron shall enroll them, company by company. 4A man from each tribe shall be with you, each man the head of his ancestral house. 5These are the names of the men who shall assist you:

> From Reuben, Elizur son of Shedeur.
> 6 From Simeon, Shelumiel son of Zurishaddai.
> 7 From Judah, Nahshon son of Amminadab.
> 8 From Issachar, Nethanel son of Zuar.
> 9 From Zebulun, Eliab son of Helon.
> 10 From the sons of Joseph:
>   from Ephraim, Elishama son of Ammihud;
>   from Manasseh, Gamaliel son of Pedahzur.
> 11 From Benjamin, Abidan son of Gideoni.
> 12 From Dan, Ahiezer son of Ammishaddai.
> 13 From Asher, Pagiel son of Ochran.
> 14 From Gad, Eliasaph son of Deuel.
> 15 From Naphtali, Ahira son of Enan.

16These were the ones chosen from the congregation, the leaders of their ancestral tribes, the heads of the divisions of Israel.

17 Moses and Aaron took these men who had been designated by name, 18and on the first day of the second month they assembled the whole congregation together. They registered themselves in their clans, by their ancestral houses, according to the number of names from twenty years old and upward, individually, 19as the LORD commanded Moses. So he enrolled them in the wilderness of Sinai.

20 The descendants of Reuben, Israel's firstborn, their lineage, in their clans, by their ancestral houses, according to the number of names, individually, every male from twenty years old and upward, everyone able to go to war: 21those enrolled of the tribe of Reuben were forty-six thousand five hundred.

22 The descendants of Simeon, their lineage, in their clans, by their ancestral houses, those of them that were numbered, according to the number of names, individually, every male from twenty years old and upward, everyone able to go to war: 23those enrolled of the tribe of Simeon were fifty-nine thousand three hundred.

---

[a] 1:1 *fifteenth day of April*, literally, "on the first day of the second month" (of the Jewish calendar). So also for verse 17, *On the same day*.
[b] 1:17-19 Added in the Hebrew text is this sentence: "So he numbered them in the wilderness of Sinai."

King James

24¶ Of the children of Gad, by their generations, after their families, by the house of their fathers, according to the number of the names, from twenty years old and upward, all that were able to go forth to war;

25Those that were numbered of them, *even* of the tribe of Gad, *were* forty and five thousand six hundred and fifty.

26¶ Of the children of Judah, by their generations, after their families, by the house of their fathers, according to the number of the names, from twenty years old and upward, all that were able to go forth to war;

27Those that were numbered of them, *even* of the tribe of Judah, *were* threescore and fourteen thousand and six hundred.

28¶ Of the children of Issachar, by their generations, after their families, by the house of their fathers, according to the number of the names, from twenty years old and upward, all that were able to go forth to war;

29Those that were numbered of them, *even* of the tribe of Issachar, *were* fifty and four thousand and four hundred.

30¶ Of the children of Zebulun, by their generations, after their families, by the house of their fathers, according to the number of the names, from twenty years old and upward, all that were able to go forth to war;

31Those that were numbered of them, *even* of the tribe of Zebulun, *were* fifty and seven thousand and four hundred.

32¶ Of the children of Joseph, *namely,* of the children of Ephraim, by their generations, after their families, by the house of their fathers, according to the number of the names, from twenty years old and upward, all that were able to go forth to war;

33Those that were numbered of them, *even* of the tribe of Ephraim, *were* forty thousand and five hundred.

34¶ Of the children of Manasseh, by their generations, after their families, by the house of their fathers, according to the number of the names, from twenty years old and upward, all that were able to go forth to war;

35Those that were numbered of them, *even* of the tribe of Manasseh, *were* thirty and two thousand and two hundred.

36¶ Of the children of Benjamin, by their generations, after their families, by the house of their fathers, according to the number of the names, from twenty years old and upward, all that were able to go forth to war;

37Those that were numbered of them, *even* of the tribe of Benjamin, *were* thirty and five thousand and four hundred.

38¶ Of the children of Dan, by their generations, after their families, by the house of their fathers, according to the number of the names, from twenty years old and upward, all that were able to go forth to war;

39Those that were numbered of them, *even* of the tribe of Dan, *were* threescore and two thousand and seven hundred.

40¶ Of the children of Asher, by their generations, after their families, by the house of their fathers, according to the number of the names, from twenty years old and upward, all that were able to go forth to war;

41Those that were numbered of them, *even* of the tribe of Asher, *were* forty and one thousand and five hundred.

42¶ Of the children of Naphtali, throughout their generations, after their families, by the house of their fathers, according to the number of the names, from twenty years old and upward, all that were able to go forth to war;

43Those that were numbered of them, *even* of the tribe of Naphtali, *were* fifty and three thousand and four hundred.

44These *are* those that were numbered, which Moses and Aaron numbered, and the princes of Israel, *being* twelve men: each one was for the house of his fathers.

New International

24From the descendants of Gad:
All the men twenty years old or more who were able to serve in the army were listed by name, according to the records of their clans and families. 25The number from the tribe of Gad was 45,650.

26From the descendants of Judah:
All the men twenty years old or more who were able to serve in the army were listed by name, according to the records of their clans and families. 27The number from the tribe of Judah was 74,600.

28From the descendants of Issachar:
All the men twenty years old or more who were able to serve in the army were listed by name, according to the records of their clans and families. 29The number from the tribe of Issachar was 54,400.

30From the descendants of Zebulun:
All the men twenty years old or more who were able to serve in the army were listed by name, according to the records of their clans and families. 31The number from the tribe of Zebulun was 57,400.

32From the sons of Joseph:
From the descendants of Ephraim:
All the men twenty years old or more who were able to serve in the army were listed by name, according to the records of their clans and families. 33The number from the tribe of Ephraim was 40,500.

34From the descendants of Manasseh:
All the men twenty years old or more who were able to serve in the army were listed by name, according to the records of their clans and families. 35The number from the tribe of Manasseh was 32,200.

36From the descendants of Benjamin:
All the men twenty years old or more who were able to serve in the army were listed by name, according to the records of their clans and families. 37The number from the tribe of Benjamin was 35,400.

38From the descendants of Dan:
All the men twenty years old or more who were able to serve in the army were listed by name, according to the records of their clans and families. 39The number from the tribe of Dan was 62,700.

40From the descendants of Asher:
All the men twenty years old or more who were able to serve in the army were listed by name, according to the records of their clans and families. 41The number from the tribe of Asher was 41,500.

42From the descendants of Naphtali:
All the men twenty years old or more who were able to serve in the army were listed by name, according to the records of their clans and families. 43The number from the tribe of Naphtali was 53,400.

44These were the men counted by Moses and Aaron and the twelve leaders of Israel, each one representing his family. 45All the Israelites twenty years old or more

Living Bible

Gad	45,650
Judah	74,600
Issachar	54,400
Zebulun	57,400
Joseph: Ephraim (son of Joseph)	40,500
Joseph: Manasseh (son of Joseph)	32,200
Benjamin	35,400
Dan	62,700
Asher	41,500
Naphtali	53,400
Grand Total:	603,550

New Revised Standard

24 The descendants of Gad, their lineage, in their clans, by their ancestral houses, according to the number of the names, from twenty years old and upward, everyone able to go to war: 25 those enrolled of the tribe of Gad were forty-five thousand six hundred fifty.

26 The descendants of Judah, their lineage, in their clans, by their ancestral houses, according to the number of names, from twenty years old and upward, everyone able to go to war: 27 those enrolled of the tribe of Judah were seventy-four thousand six hundred.

28 The descendants of Issachar, their lineage, in their clans, by their ancestral houses, according to the number of names, from twenty years old and upward, everyone able to go to war: 29 those enrolled of the tribe of Issachar were fifty-four thousand four hundred.

30 The descendants of Zebulun, their lineage, in their clans, by their ancestral houses, according to the number of names, from twenty years old and upward, everyone able to go to war: 31 those enrolled of the tribe of Zebulun were fifty-seven thousand four hundred.

32 The descendants of Joseph, namely, the descendants of Ephraim, their lineage, in their clans, by their ancestral houses, according to the number of names, from twenty years old and upward, everyone able to go to war: 33 those enrolled of the tribe of Ephraim were forty thousand five hundred.

34 The descendants of Manasseh, their lineage, in their clans, by their ancestral houses, according to the number of names, from twenty years old and upward, everyone able to go to war: 35 those enrolled of the tribe of Manasseh were thirty-two thousand two hundred.

36 The descendants of Benjamin, their lineage, in their clans, by their ancestral houses, according to the number of names, from twenty years old and upward, everyone able to go to war: 37 those enrolled of the tribe of Benjamin were thirty-five thousand four hundred.

38 The descendants of Dan, their lineage, in their clans, by their ancestral houses, according to the number of names, from twenty years old and upward, everyone able to go to war: 39 those enrolled of the tribe of Dan were sixty-two thousand seven hundred.

40 The descendants of Asher, their lineage, in their clans, by their ancestral houses, according to the number of names, from twenty years old and upward, everyone able to go to war: 41 those enrolled of the tribe of Asher were forty-one thousand five hundred.

42 The descendants of Naphtali, their lineage, in their clans, by their ancestral houses, according to the number of names, from twenty years old and upward, everyone able to go to war: 43 those enrolled of the tribe of Naphtali were fifty-three thousand four hundred.

44 These are those who were enrolled, whom Moses and Aaron enrolled with the help of the leaders of Israel, twelve men, each representing his ancestral house. 45 So

King James

45So were all those that were numbered of the children of Israel, by the house of their fathers, from twenty years old and upward, all that were able to go forth to war in Israel;

46Even all they that were numbered were six hundred thousand and three thousand and five hundred and fifty.

47¶ But the Levites after the tribe of their fathers were not numbered among them.

48For the LORD had spoken unto Moses, saying,

49Only thou shalt not number the tribe of Levi, neither take the sum of them among the children of Israel:

50But thou shalt appoint the Levites over the tabernacle of testimony, and over all the vessels thereof, and over all things that *belong* to it: they shall bear the tabernacle, and all the vessels thereof; and they shall minister unto it, and shall encamp round about the tabernacle.

51And when the tabernacle setteth forward, the Levites shall take it down: and when the tabernacle is to be pitched, the Levites shall set it up: and the stranger that cometh nigh shall be put to death.

52And the children of Israel shall pitch their tents, every man by his own camp, and every man by his own standard, throughout their hosts.

53But the Levites shall pitch round about the tabernacle of testimony, that there be no wrath upon the congregation of the children of Israel: and the Levites shall keep the charge of the tabernacle of testimony.

54And the children of Israel did according to all that the LORD commanded Moses, so did they.

2 AND THE LORD spake unto Moses and unto Aaron, saying,

2Every man of the children of Israel shall pitch by his own standard, with the ensign of their father's house: far off about the tabernacle of the congregation shall they pitch.

3And on the east side toward the rising of the sun shall they of the standard of the camp of Judah pitch throughout their armies: and Nahshon the son of Amminadab *shall be* captain of the children of Judah.

4And his host, and those that were numbered of them, *were* threescore and fourteen thousand and six hundred.

5And those that do pitch next unto him *shall be* the tribe of Issachar: and Nethaneel the son of Zuar *shall be* captain of the children of Issachar.

6And his host, and those that were numbered thereof, *were* fifty and four thousand and four hundred.

7*Then* the tribe of Zebulun: and Eliab the son of Helon *shall be* captain of the children of Zebulun.

8And his host, and those that were numbered thereof, *were* fifty and seven thousand and four hundred.

9All that were numbered in the camp of Judah *were* an hundred thousand and fourscore thousand and six thousand and four hundred, throughout their armies. These shall first set forth.

10¶ On the south side *shall be* the standard of the camp of Reuben according to their armies: and the captain of the children of Reuben *shall be* Elizur the son of Shedeur.

11And his host, and those that were numbered thereof, *were* forty and six thousand and five hundred.

12And those which pitch by him *shall be* the tribe of Simeon: and the captain of the children of Simeon *shall be* Shelumiel the son of Zurishaddai.

13And his host, and those that were numbered of them, *were* fifty and nine thousand and three hundred.

14Then the tribe of Gad: and the captain of the sons of Gad *shall be* Eliasaph the son of Reuel.

15And his host, and those that were numbered of them, *were* forty and five thousand and six hundred and fifty.

New International

who were able to serve in Israel's army were counted according to their families. 46The total number was 603,550.

47The families of the tribe of Levi, however, were not counted along with the others. 48The LORD had said to Moses: 49"You must not count the tribe of Levi or include them in the census of the other Israelites. 50Instead, appoint the Levites to be in charge of the tabernacle of the Testimony—over all its furnishings and everything belonging to it. They are to carry the tabernacle and all its furnishings; they are to take care of it and encamp around it. 51Whenever the tabernacle is to move, the Levites are to take it down, and whenever the tabernacle is to be set up, the Levites shall do it. Anyone else who goes near it shall be put to death. 52The Israelites are to set up their tents by divisions, each man in his own camp under his own standard. 53The Levites, however, are to set up their tents around the tabernacle of the Testimony so that wrath will not fall on the Israelite community. The Levites are to be responsible for the care of the tabernacle of the Testimony."

54The Israelites did all this just as the LORD commanded Moses.

The Arrangement of the Tribal Camps

2 THE LORD said to Moses and Aaron: 2"The Israelites are to camp around the Tent of Meeting some distance from it, each man under his standard with the banners of his family."

3On the east, toward the sunrise, the divisions of the camp of Judah are to encamp under their standard. The leader of the people of Judah is Nahshon son of Amminadab. 4His division numbers 74,600.

5The tribe of Issachar will camp next to them. The leader of the people of Issachar is Nethanel son of Zuar. 6His division numbers 54,400.

7The tribe of Zebulun will be next. The leader of the people of Zebulun is Eliab son of Helon. 8His division numbers 57,400.

9All the men assigned to the camp of Judah, according to their divisions, number 186,400. They will set out first.

10On the south will be the divisions of the camp of Reuben under their standard. The leader of the people of Reuben is Elizur son of Shedeur. 11His division numbers 46,500.

12The tribe of Simeon will camp next to them. The leader of the people of Simeon is Shelumiel son of Zurishaddai. 13His division numbers 59,300.

14The tribe of Gad will be next. The leader of the people of Gad is Eliasaph son of Deuel.a 15His division numbers 45,650.

a *14* Many manuscripts of the Masoretic Text, Samaritan Pentateuch and Vulgate (see also Num. 1:14); most manuscripts of the Masoretic Text *Reuel*

Living Bible

47, 48, 49This total does not include the Levites, for the Lord had said to Moses, "Exempt the entire tribe of Levi from the draft, and do not include their number in the census. 50For the Levites are assigned for the work connected with the Tabernacle and its transportation. They are to live near the Tabernacle, 51and whenever the Tabernacle is moved, the Levites are to take it down and set it up again; anyone else touching it shall be executed. 52Each tribe of Israel shall have a separate camping area with its own flag. 53The Levites' tents shall be clustered around the Tabernacle as a wall between the people of Israel and God's wrath—to protect them from his fierce anger against their sins."

54So all these instructions of the Lord to Moses were put into effect.

2 THE LORD gave these further instructions to Moses and Aaron: "Each tribe will have its own tent area, with its flagpole and tribal banner; and at the center of these tribal compounds will be the Tabernacle." 3-31Here are the tribal locations:b

Tribe:	Leader:	Location:	Census:
Judah	Nahshon (son of Amminadab)	East side of the Tabernacle	74,600
Issachar	Nethanel (son of Zuar)	Next to Judah	54,400
Zebulun	Eliab (son of Helon)	Next to Issachar	57,400

So the total of all those on Judah's side of the camp was 186,400. These three tribes led the way whenever the Israelites traveled to a new campsite.

Reuben	Elizur (son of Shedeur)	South side of the Tabernacle	46,500
Simeon	Shelumi-el (son of Zuri-shaddai)	Next to Reuben	59,300
Gad	Eliasaph (son of Reuel)	Next to Simeon	45,650

New Revised Standard

the whole number of the Israelites, by their ancestral houses, from twenty years old and upward, everyone able to go to war in Israel— 46their whole number was six hundred three thousand five hundred fifty. 47The Levites, however, were not numbered by their ancestral tribe along with them.

48 The LORD had said to Moses: 49Only the tribe of Levi you shall not enroll, and you shall not take a census of them with the other Israelites. 50Rather you shall appoint the Levites over the tabernacle of the covenant,c and over all its equipment, and over all that belongs to it; they are to carry the tabernacle and all its equipment, and they shall tend it, and shall camp around the tabernacle. 51When the tabernacle is to be set out, the Levites shall take it down; and when the tabernacle is to be pitched, the Levites shall set it up. And any outsider who comes near shall be put to death. 52The other Israelites shall camp in their respective regimental camps, by companies; 53but the Levites shall camp around the tabernacle of the covenant,c that there may be no wrath on the congregation of the Israelites; and the Levites shall perform the guard duty of the tabernacle of the covenant.c 54The Israelites did so; they did just as the LORD commanded Moses.

The Order of Encampment and Marching

2 THE LORD spoke to Moses and Aaron, saying: 2The Israelites shall camp each in their respective regiments, under ensigns by their ancestral houses; they shall camp facing the tent of meeting on every side. 3Those to camp on the east side toward the sunrise shall be of the regimental encampment of Judah by companies. The leader of the people of Judah shall be Nahshon son of Amminadab, 4with a company as enrolled of seventy-four thousand six hundred. 5Those to camp next to him shall be the tribe of Issachar. The leader of the Issacharites shall be Nethanel son of Zuar, 6with a company as enrolled of fifty-four thousand four hundred. 7Then the tribe of Zebulun: The leader of the Zebulunites shall be Eliab son of Helon, 8with a company as enrolled of fifty-seven thousand four hundred. 9The total enrollment of the camp of Judah, by companies, is one hundred eighty-six thousand four hundred. They shall set out first on the march.

10 On the south side shall be the regimental encampment of Reuben by companies. The leader of the Reubenites shall be Elizur son of Shedeur, 11with a company as enrolled of forty-six thousand five hundred. 12And those to camp next to him shall be the tribe of Simeon. The leader of the Simeonites shall be Shelumiel son of Zurishaddai, 13with a company as enrolled of fifty-nine thousand three hundred. 14Then the tribe of Gad: The leader of the Gadites shall be Eliasaph son of Reuel, 15with a company as enrolled of forty-five thousand six hundred fifty. 16The total enrollment of the

---

b 2:3-31 Here are the tribal locations, implied. Reuel. Deuel in chapter 1.   c Or treaty, or testimony; Heb eduth

King James

16All that were numbered in the camp of Reuben *were* an hundred thousand and fifty and one thousand and four hundred and fifty, throughout their armies. And they shall set forth in the second rank.

17¶ Then the tabernacle of the congregation shall set forward with the camp of the Levites in the midst of the camp: as they encamp, so shall they set forward, every man in his place by their standards.

18¶ On the west side *shall be* the standard of the camp of Ephraim according to their armies: and the captain of the sons of Ephraim *shall be* Elishama the son of Ammihud.

19And his host, and those that were numbered of them, *were* forty thousand and five hundred.

20And by him *shall be* the tribe of Manasseh: and the captain of the children of Manasseh *shall be* Gamaliel the son of Pedahzur.

21And his host, and those that were numbered of them, *were* thirty and two thousand and two hundred.

22Then the tribe of Benjamin: and the captain of the sons of Benjamin *shall be* Abidan the son of Gideoni.

23And his host, and those that were numbered of them, *were* thirty and five thousand and four hundred.

24All that were numbered of the camp of Ephraim *were* an hundred thousand and eight thousand and an hundred, throughout their armies. And they shall go forward in the third rank.

25¶ The standard of the camp of Dan *shall be* on the north side by their armies: and the captain of the children of Dan *shall be* Ahiezer the son of Ammishaddai.

26And his host, and those that were numbered of them, *were* threescore and two thousand and seven hundred.

27And those that encamp by him *shall be* the tribe of Asher: and the captain of the children of Asher *shall be* Pagiel the son of Ocran.

28And his host, and those that were numbered of them, *were* forty and one thousand and five hundred.

29¶ Then the tribe of Naphtali: and the captain of the children of Naphtali *shall be* Ahira the son of Enan.

30And his host, and those that were numbered of them, *were* fifty and three thousand and four hundred.

31All they that were numbered in the camp of Dan *were* an hundred thousand and fifty and seven thousand and six hundred. They shall go hindmost with their standards.

32¶ These *are* those which were numbered of the children of Israel by the house of their fathers: all those that were numbered of the camps throughout their hosts *were* six hundred thousand and three thousand and five hundred and fifty.

33But the Levites were not numbered among the children of Israel; as the LORD commanded Moses.

34And the children of Israel did according to all that the LORD commanded Moses: so they pitched by their standards, and so they set forward, every one after their families, according to the house of their fathers.

3 THESE ALSO *are* the generations of Aaron and Moses in the day *that* the LORD spake with Moses in mount Sinai.

2And these *are* the names of the sons of Aaron; Nadab the firstborn, and Abihu, Eleazar, and Ithamar.

3These *are* the names of the sons of Aaron, the priests which were anointed, whom he consecrated to minister in the priest's office.

4And Nadab and Abihu died before the LORD, when they offered strange fire before the LORD, in the wilderness of Sinai, and they had no children: and Eleazar and Ithamar ministered in the priest's office in the sight of Aaron their father.

New International

16All the men assigned to the camp of Reuben, according to their divisions, number 151,450. They will set out second.

17Then the Tent of Meeting and the camp of the Levites will set out in the middle of the camps. They will set out in the same order as they encamp, each in his own place under his standard.

18On the west will be the divisions of the camp of Ephraim under their standard. The leader of the people of Ephraim is Elishama son of Ammihud. 19His division numbers 40,500.

20The tribe of Manasseh will be next to them. The leader of the people of Manasseh is Gamaliel son of Pedahzur. 21His division numbers 32,200.

22The tribe of Benjamin will be next. The leader of the people of Benjamin is Abidan son of Gideoni. 23His division numbers 35,400.

24All the men assigned to the camp of Ephraim, according to their divisions, number 108,100. They will set out third.

25On the north will be the divisions of the camp of Dan, under their standard. The leader of the people of Dan is Ahiezer son of Ammishaddai. 26His division numbers 62,700.

27The tribe of Asher will camp next to them. The leader of the people of Asher is Pagiel son of Ocran. 28His division numbers 41,500.

29The tribe of Naphtali will be next. The leader of the people of Naphtali is Ahira son of Enan. 30His division numbers 53,400.

31All the men assigned to the camp of Dan number 157,600. They will set out last, under their standards.

32These are the Israelites, counted according to their families. All those in the camps, by their divisions, number 603,550. 33The Levites, however, were not counted along with the other Israelites, as the LORD commanded Moses.

34So the Israelites did everything the LORD commanded Moses; that is the way they encamped under their standards, and that is the way they set out, each with his clan and family.

The Levites

3 THIS IS the account of the family of Aaron and Moses at the time the LORD talked with Moses on Mount Sinai.

2The names of the sons of Aaron were Nadab the firstborn and Abihu, Eleazar and Ithamar. 3Those were the names of Aaron's sons, the anointed priests, who were ordained to serve as priests. 4Nadab and Abihu, however, fell dead before the LORD when they made an offering with unauthorized fire before him in the Desert of Sinai. They had no sons; so only Eleazar and Ithamar served as priests during the lifetime of their father Aaron.

Living Bible

So the total of the Reuben side of the camp was 151,450. These three tribes were next in line whenever the Israelis traveled.

Next in the line of march was the Tabernacle, with the Levites. When traveling, each tribe stayed together under its own flag, just as each was separate from the others in camp.

Ephraim	Elishama (son of Ammihud)	West side of Tabernacle	40,500
Manasseh	Gamaliel (son of Pedahzur)	Next to Ephraim	32,200
Benjamim	Abidan (son of Gideoni)	Next to Manasseh	35,400

So the total on the Ephraim side of the camp was 108,100, and they were next in the line of march.

Dan	Ahiezer (son of Ammi-shaddai)	North side of the Tabernacle	62,700
Asher	Pagiel (son of Ochran)	Next to Dan	41,500
Naphtali	Ahira (son of Enan)	Next to Asher	53,400

So the total on Dan's side of the camp was 157,600. They brought up the rear whenever Israel traveled. 32, 33In summary, the armies of Israel totaled 603,550 (not including the Levites, who were exempted by Jehovah's commandment to Moses). 34So the people of Israel set up their camps, each tribe under its own banner, in the locations indicated by the Lord to Moses.

3 AT THE time when the Lord spoke to Moses on Mount Sinai, 2Aaron'sa sons were:
Nadab (his oldest), Abihu, Eleazar, Ithamar.

3All were anointed as priests and set apart to minister at the Tabernacle. 4But Nadab and Abihu died before the Lord in the wilderness of Sinai when they used unholy fire. And since they had no children, this left only Eleazar and Ithamar to assist their father Aaron.

New Revised Standard

camp of Reuben, by companies, is one hundred fifty-one thousand four hundred fifty. They shall set out second.

17 The tent of meeting, with the camp of the Levites, shall set out in the center of the camps; they shall set out just as they camp, each in position, by their regiments.

18 On the west side shall be the regimental encampment of Ephraim by companies. The leader of the people of Ephraim shall be Elishama son of Ammihud, 19with a company as enrolled of forty thousand five hundred. 20Next to him shall be the tribe of Manasseh. The leader of the people of Manasseh shall be Gamaliel son of Pedahzur, 21with a company as enrolled of thirty-two thousand two hundred. 22Then the tribe of Benjamin: The leader of the Benjaminites shall be Abidan son of Gideoni, 23with a company as enrolled of thirty-five thousand four hundred. 24The total enrollment of the camp of Ephraim, by companies, is one hundred eight thousand one hundred. They shall set out third on the march.

25 On the north side shall be the regimental encampment of Dan by companies. The leader of the Danites shall be Ahiezer son of Ammishaddai, 26with a company as enrolled of sixty-two thousand seven hundred. 27Those to camp next to him shall be the tribe of Asher. The leader of the Asherites shall be Pagiel son of Ochran, 28with a company as enrolled of forty-one thousand five hundred. 29Then the tribe of Naphtali: The leader of the Naphtalites shall be Ahira son of Enan, 30with a company as enrolled of fifty-three thousand four hundred. 31The total enrollment of the camp of Dan is one hundred fifty-seven thousand six hundred. They shall set out last, by companies.b

32 This was the enrollment of the Israelites by their ancestral houses; the total enrollment in the camps by their companies was six hundred three thousand five hundred fifty. 33Just as the LORD had commanded Moses, the Levites were not enrolled among the other Israelites.

34 The Israelites did just as the LORD had commanded Moses: They camped by regiments, and they set out the same way, everyone by clans, according to ancestral houses.

The Sons of Aaron

3 THIS IS the lineage of Aaron and Moses at the time when the LORD spoke with Moses on Mount Sinai. 2These are the names of the sons of Aaron: Nadab the firstborn, and Abihu, Eleazar, and Ithamar; 3these are the names of the sons of Aaron, the anointed priests, whom he ordained to minister as priests. 4Nadab and Abihu died before the LORD when they offered illicit fire before the LORD in the wilderness of Sinai, and they had no children. Eleazar and Ithamar served as priests in the lifetime of their father Aaron.

---

a 3:2 Aaron's sons were, literally, "these are the generations of Aaron and Moses."

b Compare verses 9, 16, 24: Heb by their regiments

King James

5¶ And the LORD spake unto Moses, saying,

6Bring the tribe of Levi near, and present them before Aaron the priest, that they may minister unto him.

7And they shall keep his charge, and the charge of the whole congregation before the tabernacle of the congregation, to do the service of the tabernacle.

8And they shall keep all the instruments of the tabernacle of the congregation, and the charge of the children of Israel, to do the service of the tabernacle.

9And thou shalt give the Levites unto Aaron and to his sons: they *are* wholly given unto him out of the children of Israel.

10And thou shalt appoint Aaron and his sons, and they shall wait on their priest's office: and the stranger that cometh nigh shall be put to death.

11And the LORD spake unto Moses, saying,

12And I, behold, I have taken the Levites from among the children of Israel instead of all the firstborn that openeth the matrix among the children of Israel: therefore the Levites shall be mine;

13Because all the firstborn *are* mine; *for* on the day that I smote all the firstborn in the land of Egypt I hallowed unto me all the firstborn in Israel, both man and beast: mine shall they be: I *am* the LORD.

14¶ And the LORD spake unto Moses in the wilderness of Sinai, saying,

15Number the children of Levi after the house of their fathers, by their families: every male from a month old and upward shalt thou number them.

16And Moses numbered them according to the word of the LORD, as he was commanded.

17And these were the sons of Levi by their names; Gershon, and Kohath, and Merari.

18And these *are* the names of the sons of Gershon by their families; Libni, and Shimei.

19And the sons of Kohath by their families; Amram, and Izehar, Hebron, and Uzziel.

20And the sons of Merari by their families; Mahli, and Mushi. These *are* the families of the Levites according to the house of their fathers.

21Of Gershon *was* the family of the Libnites, and the family of the Shimites: these *are* the families of the Gershonites.

22Those that were numbered of them, according to the number of all the males, from a month old and upward, *even* those that were numbered of them *were* seven thousand and five hundred.

23The families of the Gershonites shall pitch behind the tabernacle westward.

24And the chief of the house of the father of the Gershonites *shall be* Eliasaph the son of Lael.

25And the charge of the sons of Gershon in the tabernacle of the congregation *shall be* the tabernacle, and the tent, the covering thereof, and the hanging for the door of the tabernacle of the congregation,

26And the hangings of the court, and the curtain for the door of the court, which *is* by the tabernacle, and by the altar round about, and the cords of it for all the service thereof.

27¶ And of Kohath *was* the family of the Amramites, and the family of the Izeharites, and the family of the Hebronites, and the family of the Uzzielites: these *are* the families of the Kohathites.

28In the number of all the males, from a month old and upward, *were* eight thousand and six hundred, keeping the charge of the sanctuary.

29The families of the sons of Kohath shall pitch on the side of the tabernacle southward.

30And the chief of the house of the father of the families of the Kohathites *shall be* Elizaphan the son of Uzziel.

31And their charge *shall be* the ark, and the table, and the candlestick, and the altars, and the vessels of the sanctuary wherewith they minister, and the hanging, and all the service thereof.

New International

5The LORD said to Moses, 6"Bring the tribe of Levi and present them to Aaron the priest to assist him. 7They are to perform duties for him and for the whole community at the Tent of Meeting by doing the work of the tabernacle. 8They are to take care of all the furnishings of the Tent of Meeting, fulfilling the obligations of the Israelites by doing the work of the tabernacle. 9Give the Levites to Aaron and his sons; they are the Israelites who are to be given wholly to him.[a] 10Appoint Aaron and his sons to serve as priests; anyone else who approaches the sanctuary must be put to death."

11The LORD also said to Moses, 12"I have taken the Levites from among the Israelites in place of the first male offspring of every Israelite woman. The Levites are mine, 13for all the firstborn are mine. When I struck down all the firstborn in Egypt, I set apart for myself every firstborn in Israel, whether man or animal. They are to be mine. I am the LORD."

14The LORD said to Moses in the Desert of Sinai, 15"Count the Levites by their families and clans. Count every male a month old or more." 16So Moses counted them, as he was commanded by the word of the LORD.

17These were the names of the sons of Levi:

Gershon, Kohath and Merari.

18These were the names of the Gershonite clans:

Libni and Shimei.

19The Kohathite clans:

Amram, Izhar, Hebron and Uzziel.

20The Merarite clans:

Mahli and Mushi.

These were the Levite clans, according to their families.

21To Gershon belonged the clans of the Libnites and Shimeites; these were the Gershonite clans. 22The number of all the males a month old or more who were counted was 7,500. 23The Gershonite clans were to camp on the west, behind the tabernacle. 24The leader of the families of the Gershonites was Eliasaph son of Lael. 25At the Tent of Meeting the Gershonites were responsible for the care of the tabernacle and tent, its coverings, the curtain at the entrance to the Tent of Meeting, 26the curtains of the courtyard, the curtain at the entrance to the courtyard surrounding the tabernacle and altar, and the ropes—and everything related to their use.

27To Kohath belonged the clans of the Amramites, Izharites, Hebronites and Uzzielites; these were the Kohathite clans. 28The number of all the males a month old or more was 8,600.[b] The Kohathites were responsible for the care of the sanctuary. 29The Kohathite clans were to camp on the south side of the tabernacle. 30The leader of the families of the Kohathite clans was Elizaphan son of Uzziel. 31They were responsible for the care of the ark, the table, the lampstand, the altars, the articles of the sanctuary used in ministering, the curtain, and everything related to their use. 32The chief leader of the

---

a 9 Most manuscripts of the Masoretic Text; some manuscripts of the Masoretic Text, Samaritan Pentateuch and Septuagint (see also Num. 8:16) *to me*
b 28 Hebrew; some Septuagint manuscripts *8,300*

Living Bible

5Then the Lord said to Moses, 6"Summon the tribe of Levi and present them to Aaron as his assistants. 7, 8, 9They will follow his instructions and perform the sacred duties at the Tabernacle on behalf of all the people of Israel. For they are assigned to him as representatives of all the people of Israel. They are in charge of all the furnishings and maintenance of the Tabernacle. 10However, only Aaron and his sons may carry out the duties of the priesthood; anyone else who presumes to assume this office shall be executed."

11, 12And the Lord said to Moses, "I have accepted the Levites in substitution for all the oldest sons of the people of Israel. The Levites are mine 13in exchange for all the oldest sons. From the day I killed all the oldest sons of the Egyptians, I took for myself all the firstborn in Israel of both men and animals! They are mine; I am Jehovah."

14, 15The Lord now spoke again to Moses at the Sinai peninsula, telling him, "Take a census of the tribe of Levi, indicating each person's clan; count every male down to one month old." 16–24So Moses did:

Levi's son	Levi's grand-sons (clan names)	Census	Leader	Camp Location
Gershon		7,500	Elisaph (son of Lael)	West side of Tabernacle
	Libni			
	Shime-i			

25-30Responsibilities:

The responsibility of these two clans of Levites was the care of the Tabernacle: its coverings, its entry drapes, the drapes covering the fence surrounding the courtyard, the screen at the entrance of the courtyard surrounding the Tabernacle, the altar, and all the ropes used in tying the Tabernacle together.

Levi's son	Levi's grand-sons (clan names)	Census	Leader	Camp Location
Kohath		8,600	Eliza-phan (son of Uzziel)	South side of Tabernacle
	Amran			
	Izhar			
	Hebron			
	Uzziel)			

31-35Responsibilities:

The responsibility of these four clans of Levites was the care of the Ark, the table, the lampstand, the altars, the various utensils used in the Tabernacle, the veil, and any repairs needed on any of these items. (Note: Eleazar, Aaron's son, shall be the chief administrator over the leaders of the Levites, with special responsibility for the oversight of the sanctuary.)

New Revised Standard

The Duties of the Levites

5 Then the LORD spoke to Moses, saying: 6Bring the tribe of Levi near, and set them before Aaron the priest, so that they may assist him. 7They shall perform duties for him and for the whole congregation in front of the tent of meeting, doing service at the tabernacle; 8they shall be in charge of all the furnishings of the tent of meeting, and attend to the duties for the Israelites as they do service at the tabernacle. 9You shall give the Levites to Aaron and his descendants; they are unreservedly given to him from among the Israelites. 10But you shall make a register of Aaron and his descendants; it is they who shall attend to the priesthood, and any outsider who comes near shall be put to death.

11 Then the LORD spoke to Moses, saying: 12I hereby accept the Levites from among the Israelites as substitutes for all the firstborn that open the womb among the Israelites. The Levites shall be mine, 13for all the firstborn are mine; when I killed all the firstborn in the land of Egypt, I consecrated for my own all the firstborn in Israel, both human and animal; they shall be mine. I am the LORD.

A Census of the Levites

14 Then the LORD spoke to Moses in the wilderness of Sinai, saying: 15Enroll the Levites by ancestral houses and by clans. You shall enroll every male from a month old and upward. 16So Moses enrolled them according to the word of the LORD, as he was commanded. 17The following were the sons of Levi, by their names: Gershon, Kohath, and Merari. 18These are the names of the sons of Gershon by their clans: Libni and Shimei. 19The sons of Kohath by their clans: Amram, Izhar, Hebron, and Uzziel. 20The sons of Merari by their clans: Mahli and Mushi. These are the clans of the Levites, by their ancestral houses.

21 To Gershon belonged the clan of the Libnites and the clan of the Shimeites; these were the clans of the Gershonites. 22Their enrollment, counting all the males from a month old and upward, was seven thousand five hundred. 23The clans of the Gershonites were to camp behind the tabernacle on the west, 24with Eliasaph son of Lael as head of the ancestral house of the Gershonites. 25The responsibility of the sons of Gershon in the tent of meeting was to be the tabernacle, the tent with its covering, the screen for the entrance of the tent of meeting, 26the hangings of the court, the screen for the entrance of the court that is around the tabernacle and the altar, and its cords—all the service pertaining to these.

27 To Kohath belonged the clan of the Amramites, the clan of the Izharites, the clan of the Hebronites, and the clan of the Uzzielites; these are the clans of the Kohathites. 28Counting all the males, from a month old and upward, there were eight thousand six hundred, attending to the duties of the sanctuary. 29The clans of the Kohathites were to camp on the south side of the tabernacle, 30with Elizaphan son of Uzziel as head of the ancestral house of the clans of the Kohathites. 31Their responsibility was to be the ark, the table, the lampstand, the altars, the vessels of the sanctuary with which the priests minister, and the screen—all the service pertaining to these. 32Eleazar son of Aaron the priest was

King James

32And Eleazar the son of Aaron the priest *shall be* chief over the chief of the Levites, *and have* the oversight of them that keep the charge of the sanctuary.

33¶ Of Merari *was* the family of the Mahlites, and the family of the Mushites: these *are* the families of Merari.

34And those that were numbered of them, according to the number of all the males, from a month old and upward, *were* six thousand and two hundred.

35And the chief of the house of the father of the families of Merari *was* Zuriel the son of Abihail: *these* shall pitch on the side of the tabernacle northward.

36And *under* the custody and charge of the sons of Merari *shall be* the boards of the tabernacle, and the bars thereof, and the pillars thereof, and the sockets thereof, and all the vessels thereof, and all that serveth thereto,

37And the pillars of the court round about, and their sockets, and their pins, and their cords.

38¶ But those that encamp before the tabernacle toward the east, *even* before the tabernacle of the congregation eastward, *shall be* Moses, and Aaron and his sons, keeping the charge of the sanctuary for the charge of the children of Israel; and the stranger that cometh nigh shall be put to death.

39All that were numbered of the Levites, which Moses and Aaron numbered at the commandment of the LORD, throughout their families, all the males from a month old and upward, *were* twenty and two thousand.

40¶ And the LORD said unto Moses, Number all the firstborn of the males of the children of Israel from a month old and upward, and take the number of their names.

41And thou shalt take the Levites for me (I *am* the LORD) instead of all the firstborn among the children of Israel; and the cattle of the Levites instead of all the firstlings among the cattle of the children of Israel.

42And Moses numbered, as the LORD commanded him, all the firstborn among the children of Israel.

43And all the firstborn males by the number of names, from a month old and upward, of those that were numbered of them, were twenty and two thousand two hundred and threescore and thirteen.

44¶ And the LORD spake unto Moses, saying,

45Take the Levites instead of all the firstborn among the children of Israel, and the cattle of the Levites instead of their cattle; and the Levites shall be mine: I *am* the LORD.

46And for those that are to be redeemed of the two hundred and threescore and thirteen of the firstborn of the children of Israel, which are more than the Levites;

47Thou shalt even take five shekels apiece by the poll, after the shekel of the sanctuary shalt thou take *them:* (the shekel *is* twenty gerahs:)

48And thou shalt give the money, wherewith the odd number of them is to be redeemed, unto Aaron and to his sons.

49And Moses took the redemption money of them that were over and above them that were redeemed by the Levites:

50Of the firstborn of the children of Israel took he the money; a thousand three hundred and threescore and five *shekels,* after the shekel of the sanctuary:

51And Moses gave the money of them that were redeemed unto Aaron and to his sons, according to the word of the LORD, as the LORD commanded Moses.

4 AND THE LORD spake unto Moses and unto Aaron, saying,

2Take the sum of the sons of Kohath from among the sons of Levi, after their families, by the house of their fathers,

New International

Levites was Eleazar son of Aaron, the priest. He was appointed over those who were responsible for the care of the sanctuary.

33To Merari belonged the clans of the Mahlites and the Mushites; these were the Merarite clans. 34The number of all the males a month old or more who were counted was 6,200. 35The leader of the families of the Merarite clans was Zuriel son of Abihail; they were to camp on the north side of the tabernacle. 36The Merarites were appointed to take care of the frames of the tabernacle, its crossbars, posts, bases, all its equipment, and everything related to their use, 37as well as the posts of the surrounding courtyard with their bases, tent pegs and ropes.

38Moses and Aaron and his sons were to camp to the east of the tabernacle, toward the sunrise, in front of the Tent of Meeting. They were responsible for the care of the sanctuary on behalf of the Israelites. Anyone else who approached the sanctuary was to be put to death.

39The total number of Levites counted at the LORD's command by Moses and Aaron according to their clans, including every male a month old or more, was 22,000.

40The LORD said to Moses, "Count all the firstborn Israelite males who are a month old or more and make a list of their names. 41Take the Levites for me in place of all the firstborn of the Israelites, and the livestock of the Levites in place of all the firstborn of the livestock of the Israelites. I am the LORD."

42So Moses counted all the firstborn of the Israelites, as the LORD commanded him. 43The total number of firstborn males a month old or more, listed by name, was 22,273.

44The LORD also said to Moses, 45"Take the Levites in place of all the firstborn of Israel, and the livestock of the Levites in place of their livestock. The Levites are to be mine. I am the LORD. 46To redeem the 273 firstborn Israelites who exceed the number of the Levites, 47collect five shekels[a] for each one, according to the sanctuary shekel, which weighs twenty gerahs. 48Give the money for the redemption of the additional Israelites to Aaron and his sons."

49So Moses collected the redemption money from those who exceeded the number redeemed by the Levites. 50From the firstborn of the Israelites he collected silver weighing 1,365 shekels,[b] according to the sanctuary shekel. 51Moses gave the redemption money to Aaron and his sons, as he was commanded by the word of the LORD.

The Kohathites

4 THE LORD said to Moses and Aaron: 2"Take a census of the Kohathite branch of the Levites by their clans and families. 3Count all the men from thirty

---

a *47* That is, about 2 ounces (about 55 grams)   b *50* That is, about 35 pounds (about 15.5 kilograms)

Living Bible

Levi's son	Levi's grand-	Census	Leader	Camp
Merari	sons	6,200	Zuriel	Location
	(clan		(son of	North
	names)		Abihail)	side of
	Mahli			Tabernacle
	Mushi			

36, 37*Responsibilities:*

The responsibility of these two clans was the care of the frames of the Tabernacle building; the posts; the bases for the posts, and all of the equipment needed for their use; the posts around the courtyard and their bases, pegs, and ropes. 38The area east of the Tabernacle was reserved for the tents of Moses and of Aaron and his sons, who had the final responsibility for the Tabernacle on behalf of the people of Israel. (Anyone who was not a priest or Levite, but came into the Tabernacle, was to be executed.)

39So all the Levites, as numbered by Moses and Aaron at the command of the Lord, were 22,000 males one month old and older.

40Then the Lord said to Moses, "Now take a census of all the eldest sons in Israel who are one month old and older, and register each name. 41The Levites shall be mine (I am Jehovah) as substitutes for the eldest sons of Israel; and the Levites' cattle are mine as substitutes for the firstborn cattle of the whole nation."

42So Moses took a census of the eldest sons of the people of Israel, as the Lord had commanded, 43and found the total number of eldest sons one month old and older to be 22,273.

44Now the Lord said to Moses, 45"Give me the Levites instead of the eldest sons of the people of Israel; and give me the cattle of the Levites instead of the firstborn cattle of the people of Israel; yes, the Levites shall be mine; I am Jehovah. 46To redeem the 273 eldest sons in excess of the number of Levites, 47. 48pay five dollars for each one to Aaron and his sons."

49So Moses received redemption money for the 273 eldest sons of Israel who were in excess of the number of Levites. (All the others were redeemed because the Levites had been given to the Lord in their place.) 50The money collected came to a total of $1,365.c 51And Moses gave it to Aaron and his sons as the Lord had commanded.

4 THEN THE Lord said to Moses and Aaron, "Take a census of the Kohath division of the Levite tribe.

New Revised Standard

to be chief over the leaders of the Levites, and to have oversight of those who had charge of the sanctuary.

33 To Merari belonged the clan of the Mahlites and the clan of the Mushites: these are the clans of Merari. 34Their enrollment, counting all the males from a month old and upward, was six thousand two hundred. 35The head of the ancestral house of the clans of Merari was Zuriel son of Abihail; they were to camp on the north side of the tabernacle. 36The responsibility assigned to the sons of Merari was to be the frames of the tabernacle, the bars, the pillars, the bases, and all their accessories—all the service pertaining to these; 37also the pillars of the court all around, with their bases and pegs and cords.

38 Those who were to camp in front of the tabernacle on the east—in front of the tent of meeting toward the east—were Moses and Aaron and Aaron's sons, having charge of the rites within the sanctuary, whatever had to be done for the Israelites; and any outsider who came near was to be put to death. 39The total enrollment of the Levites whom Moses and Aaron enrolled at the commandment of the LORD, by their clans, all the males from a month old and upward, was twenty-two thousand.

The Redemption of the Firstborn

40 Then the LORD said to Moses: Enroll all the firstborn males of the Israelites, from a month old and upward, and count their names. 41But you shall accept the Levites for me—I am the LORD—as substitutes for all the firstborn among the Israelites, and the livestock of the Levites as substitutes for all the firstborn among the livestock of the Israelites. 42So Moses enrolled all the firstborn among the Israelites, as the LORD commanded him. 43The total enrollment, all the firstborn males from a month old and upward, counting the number of names, was twenty-two thousand two hundred seventy-three.

44 Then the LORD spoke to Moses, saying: 45Accept the Levites as substitutes for all the firstborn among the Israelites, and the livestock of the Levites as substitutes for their livestock; and the Levites shall be mine. I am the LORD. 46As the price of redemption of the two hundred seventy-three of the firstborn of the Israelites, over and above the number of the Levites, 47you shall accept five shekels apiece, reckoning by the shekel of the sanctuary, a shekel of twenty gerahs. 48Give to Aaron and his sons the money by which the excess number of them is redeemed. 49So Moses took the redemption money from those who were over and above those redeemed by the Levites; 50from the firstborn of the Israelites he took the money, one thousand three hundred sixty-five shekels, reckoned by the shekel of the sanctuary; 51and Moses gave the redemption money to Aaron and his sons, according to the word of the LORD, as the LORD had commanded Moses.

The Kohathites

4 THE LORD spoke to Moses and Aaron, saying: 2Take a census of the Kohathites separate from the other Levites, by their clans and their ancestral houses,

c 3:50 *$1,365,* literally, "1365 shekels after the shekel of the sanctuary."

King James

3From thirty years old and upward even until fifty years old, all that enter into the host, to do the work in the tabernacle of the congregation.

4This *shall be* the service of the sons of Kohath in the tabernacle of the congregation, *about* the most holy things:

5¶ And when the camp setteth forward, Aaron shall come, and his sons, and they shall take down the covering veil, and cover the ark of testimony with it:

6And shall put thereon the covering of badgers' skins, and shall spread over *it* a cloth wholly of blue, and shall put in the staves thereof.

7And upon the table of showbread they shall spread a cloth of blue, and put thereon the dishes, and the spoons, and the bowls, and covers to cover withal: and the continual bread shall be thereon:

8And they shall spread upon them a cloth of scarlet, and cover the same with a covering of badgers' skins, and shall put in the staves thereof.

9And they shall take a cloth of blue, and cover the candlestick of the light, and his lamps, and his tongs, and his snuffdishes, and all the oil vessels thereof, wherewith they minister unto it:

10And they shall put it and all the vessels thereof within a covering of badgers' skins, and shall put *it* upon a bar.

11And upon the golden altar they shall spread a cloth of blue, and cover it with a covering of badgers' skins, and shall put to the staves thereof:

12And they shall take all the instruments of ministry, wherewith they minister in the sanctuary, and put *them* in a cloth of blue, and cover them with a covering of badgers' skins, and shall put *them* on a bar:

13And they shall take away the ashes from the altar, and spread a purple cloth thereon:

14And they shall put upon it all the vessels thereof, wherewith they minister about it, *even* the censers, the fleshhooks, and the shovels, and the basins, all the vessels of the altar; and they shall spread upon it a covering of badgers' skins, and put to the staves of it.

15And when Aaron and his sons have made an end of covering the sanctuary, and all the vessels of the sanctuary, as the camp is to set forward; after that the sons of Kohath shall come to bear *it:* but they shall not touch *any* holy thing, lest they die. These *things are* the burden of the sons of Kohath in the tabernacle of the congregation.

16¶ And to the office of Eleazar the son of Aaron the priest *pertaineth* the oil for the light, and the sweet incense, and the daily meat offering, and the anointing oil, *and* the oversight of all the tabernacle, and of all that therein *is,* in the sanctuary, and in the vessels thereof.

17¶ And the LORD spake unto Moses and unto Aaron, saying,

18Cut ye not off the tribe of the families of the Kohathites from among the Levites:

19But thus do unto them, that they may live, and not die, when they approach unto the most holy things: Aaron and his sons shall go in, and appoint them every one to his service and to his burden:

20But they shall not go in to see when the holy things are covered, lest they die.

21¶ And the LORD spake unto Moses, saying,

22Take also the sum of the sons of Gershon, throughout the houses of their fathers, by their families;

23From thirty years old and upward until fifty years old shalt thou number them; all that enter in to perform the service, to do the work in the tabernacle of the congregation.

24This *is* the service of the families of the Gershonites, to serve, and for burdens:

25And they shall bear the curtains of the tabernacle, and the tabernacle of the congregation, his covering, and the covering of the badgers' skins that *is* above upon it, and the hanging for the door of the tabernacle of the congregation,

New International

to fifty years of age who come to serve in the work in the Tent of Meeting.

4"This is the work of the Kohathites in the Tent of Meeting: the care of the most holy things. 5When the camp is to move, Aaron and his sons are to go in and take down the shielding curtain and cover the ark of the Testimony with it. 6Then they are to cover this with hides of sea cows,[a] spread a cloth of solid blue over that and put the poles in place.

7"Over the table of the Presence they are to spread a blue cloth and put on it the plates, dishes and bowls, and the jars for drink offerings; the bread that is continually there is to remain on it. 8Over these they are to spread a scarlet cloth, cover that with hides of sea cows and put its poles in place.

9"They are to take a blue cloth and cover the lampstand that is for light, together with its lamps, its wick trimmers and trays, and all its jars for the oil used to supply it. 10Then they are to wrap it and all its accessories in a covering of hides of sea cows and put it on a carrying frame.

11"Over the gold altar they are to spread a blue cloth and cover that with hides of sea cows and put its poles in place.

12"They are to take all the articles used for ministering in the sanctuary, wrap them in a blue cloth, cover that with hides of sea cows and put them on a carrying frame.

13"They are to remove the ashes from the bronze altar and spread a purple cloth over it. 14Then they are to place on it all the utensils used for ministering at the altar, including the firepans, meat forks, shovels and sprinkling bowls. Over it they are to spread a covering of hides of sea cows and put its poles in place.

15"After Aaron and his sons have finished covering the holy furnishings and all the holy articles, and when the camp is ready to move, the Kohathites are to come to do the carrying. But they must not touch the holy things or they will die. The Kohathites are to carry those things that are in the Tent of Meeting.

16"Eleazar son of Aaron, the priest, is to have charge of the oil for the light, the fragrant incense, the regular grain offering and the anointing oil. He is to be in charge of the entire tabernacle and everything in it, including its holy furnishings and articles."

17The LORD said to Moses and Aaron, 18"See that the Kohathite tribal clans are not cut off from the Levites. 19So that they may live and not die when they come near the most holy things, do this for them: Aaron and his sons are to go into the sanctuary and assign to each man his work and what he is to carry. 20But the Kohathites must not go in to look at the holy things, even for a moment, or they will die."

The Gershonites

21The LORD said to Moses, 22"Take a census also of the Gershonites by their families and clans. 23Count all the men from thirty to fifty years of age who come to serve in the work at the Tent of Meeting.

24"This is the service of the Gershonite clans as they work and carry burdens: 25They are to carry the curtains of the tabernacle, the Tent of Meeting, its covering and the outer covering of hides of sea cows, the curtains for the entrance to the Tent of Meeting, 26the curtains of the

---

[a] 6 That is, dugongs; also in verses 8, 10, 11, 12, 14 and 25

Living Bible

3This census will be of all males from ages thirty to fifty who are able to work in the Tabernacle. 4These are their sacred duties:

5"When the camp moves, Aaron and his sons will enter the Tabernacle first and take down the veil and cover the Ark with it. 6Then they will cover the veil with goatskin leather, cover the goatskins with a blue cloth, and place the carrying poles of the Ark in their rings.

7"Next they must spread a blue cloth over the table where the Bread of the Presence is displayed, and place the dishes, spoons, bowls, cups, and the Bread upon the cloth. 8They will spread a scarlet cloth over that, and finally a covering of goatskin leather on top of the scarlet cloth. Then they shall insert the carrying poles into the table.

9"Next they must cover with a blue cloth the lamp-stand, the lamps, snuffers, trays, and the reservoir of olive oil. 10This entire group of objects shall then be covered with goatskin leather, and the bundle shall be placed upon a carrying frame.

11"They must then spread a blue cloth over the gold altar, cover it with a covering of goatskin leather, and insert the carrying poles into the altar. 12All of the remaining utensils of the Tabernacle are to be wrapped in a blue cloth, covered with goatskin leather, and placed on the carrying frame.

13"The ashes are to be removed from the altar, and the altar shall be covered with a purple cloth. 14All of the altar utensils are to be placed upon the cloth—the firepans, hooks, shovels, basins, and other containers—and a cover of goatskin leather will be spread over them. Finally, the carrying poles are to be put in place. 15When Aaron and his sons have finished packing the sanctuary and all the utensils, the clan of Kohath shall come and carry the units to wherever the camp is traveling; but they must not touch the holy items, lest they die. This, then, is the sacred work of the sons of Kohath.

16"Aaron's son Eleazar shall be responsible for the oil for the light, the sweet incense, the daily grain offering, and the anointing oil—in fact, the supervision of the entire Tabernacle and everything in it will be his responsibility."

17, 18, 19Then the Lord said to Moses and Aaron, "Don't let the families of Kohath destroy themselves! This is what you must do so that they will not die when they carry the most holy things: Aaron and his sons shall go in with them and point out what each is to carry. 20Otherwise they must never enter the sanctuary for even a moment, lest they look at the sacred objects there and die."

21, 22, 23And the Lord said to Moses, "Take a census of the Gershonite division of the tribe of Levi, all of the men between the ages of thirty and fifty who are eligible for the sacred work of the Tabernacle. 24These will be their duties:

25"They will carry the curtains of the Tabernacle, the Tabernacle itself with its coverings, the goatskin leather roof, and the curtain for the Tabernacle entrance. 26They

New Revised Standard

3from thirty years old up to fifty years old, all who qualify to do work relating to the tent of meeting. 4The service of the Kohathites relating to the tent of meeting concerns the most holy things.

5 When the camp is to set out, Aaron and his sons shall go in and take down the screening curtain, and cover the ark of the covenant[b] with it; 6then they shall put on it a covering of fine leather,[c] and spread over that a cloth all of blue, and shall put its poles in place. 7Over the table of the bread of the Presence they shall spread a blue cloth, and put on it the plates, the dishes for incense, the bowls, and the flagons for the drink offering; the regular bread also shall be on it; 8then they shall spread over them a crimson cloth, and cover it with a covering of fine leather,[c] and shall put its poles in place. 9They shall take a blue cloth, and cover the lampstand for the light, with its lamps, its snuffers, its trays, and all the vessels for oil with which it is supplied; 10and they shall put it with all its utensils in a covering of fine leather,[c] and put it on the carrying frame. 11Over the golden altar they shall spread a blue cloth, and cover it with a covering of fine leather,[c] and shall put its poles in place; 12and they shall take all the utensils of the service that are used in the sanctuary, and put them in a blue cloth, and cover them with a covering of fine leather,[c] and put them on the carrying frame. 13They shall take away the ashes from the altar, and spread a purple cloth over it; 14and they shall put on it all the utensils of the altar, which are used for the service there, the firepans, the forks, the shovels, and the basins, all the utensils of the altar; and they shall spread on it a covering of fine leather,[c] and shall put its poles in place. 15When Aaron and his sons have finished covering the sanctuary and all the furnishings of the sanctuary, as the camp sets out, after that the Kohathites shall come to carry these, but they must not touch the holy things, or they will die. These are the things of the tent of meeting that the Kohathites are to carry.

16 Eleazar son of Aaron the priest shall have charge of the oil for the light, the fragrant incense, the regular grain offering, and the anointing oil, the oversight of all the tabernacle and all that is in it, in the sanctuary and in its utensils.

17 Then the Lord spoke to Moses and Aaron, saying: 18You must not let the tribe of the clans of the Kohathites be destroyed from among the Levites. 19This is how you must deal with them in order that they may live and not die when they come near to the most holy things: Aaron and his sons shall go in and assign each to a particular task or burden. 20But the Kohathites[d] must not go in to look on the holy things even for a moment; otherwise they will die.

The Gershonites and Merarites

21 Then the Lord spoke to Moses, saying: 22Take a census of the Gershonites also, by their ancestral houses and by their clans; 23from thirty years old up to fifty years old you shall enroll them, all who qualify to do work in the tent of meeting. 24This is the service of the clans of the Gershonites, in serving and bearing burdens: 25They shall carry the curtains of the tabernacle, and the tent of meeting with its covering, and the outer covering of fine leather[c] that is on top of it, and the screen for the entrance of the tent of meeting, 26and the

b Or treaty, or testimony; Heb eduth   c Meaning of Heb uncertain   d Heb they

King James

26And the hangings of the court, and the hanging for the door of the gate of the court, which *is* by the tabernacle and by the altar round about, and their cords, and all the instruments of their service, and all that is made for them: so shall they serve.

27At the appointment of Aaron and his sons shall be all the service of the sons of the Gershonites, in all their burdens, and in all their service: and ye shall appoint unto them in charge all their burdens.

28This *is* the service of the families of the sons of Gershon in the tabernacle of the congregation: and their charge *shall be* under the hand of Ithamar the son of Aaron the priest.

29¶ As for the sons of Merari, thou shalt number them after their families, by the house of their fathers;

30From thirty years old and upward even unto fifty years old shalt thou number them, every one that entereth into the service, to do the work of the tabernacle of the congregation.

31And this *is* the charge of their burden, according to all their service in the tabernacle of the congregation; the boards of the tabernacle, and the bars thereof, and the pillars thereof, and sockets thereof,

32And the pillars of the court round about, and their sockets, and their pins, and their cords, with all their instruments, and with all their service: and by name ye shall reckon the instruments of the charge of their burden.

33This *is* the service of the families of the sons of Merari, according to all their service, in the tabernacle of the congregation, under the hand of Ithamar the son of Aaron the priest.

34¶ And Moses and Aaron and the chief of the congregation numbered the sons of the Kohathites after their families, and after the house of their fathers,

35From thirty years old and upward even unto fifty years old, every one that entereth into the service, for the work in the tabernacle of the congregation:

36And those that were numbered of them by their families were two thousand seven hundred and fifty.

37These *were* they that were numbered of the families of the Kohathites, all that might do service in the tabernacle of the congregation, which Moses and Aaron did number according to the commandment of the LORD by the hand of Moses.

38And those that were numbered of the sons of Gershon, throughout their families, and by the house of their fathers,

39From thirty years old and upward even unto fifty years old, every one that entereth into the service, for the work in the tabernacle of the congregation,

40Even those that were numbered of them, throughout their families, by the house of their fathers, were two thousand and six hundred and thirty.

41These *are* they that were numbered of the families of the sons of Gershon, of all that might do service in the tabernacle of the congregation, whom Moses and Aaron did number according to the commandment of the LORD.

42¶ And those that were numbered of the families of the sons of Merari, throughout their families, by the house of their fathers,

New International

courtyard surrounding the tabernacle and altar, the curtain for the entrance, the ropes and all the equipment used in its service. The Gershonites are to do all that needs to be done with these things. 27All their service, whether carrying or doing other work, is to be done under the direction of Aaron and his sons. You shall assign to them as their responsibility all they are to carry. 28This is the service of the Gershonite clans at the Tent of Meeting. Their duties are to be under the direction of Ithamar son of Aaron, the priest.

The Merarites

29"Count the Merarites by their clans and families. 30Count all the men from thirty to fifty years of age who come to serve in the work at the Tent of Meeting. 31This is their duty as they perform service at the Tent of Meeting: to carry the frames of the tabernacle, its crossbars, posts and bases, 32as well as the posts of the surrounding courtyard with their bases, tent pegs, ropes, all their equipment and everything related to their use. Assign to each man the specific things he is to carry. 33This is the service of the Merarite clans as they work at the Tent of Meeting under the direction of Ithamar son of Aaron, the priest."

The Numbering of the Levite Clans

34Moses, Aaron and the leaders of the community counted the Kohathites by their clans and families. 35All the men from thirty to fifty years of age who came to serve in the work in the Tent of Meeting, 36counted by clans, were 2,750. 37This was the total of all those in the Kohathite clans who served in the Tent of Meeting. Moses and Aaron counted them according to the LORD's command through Moses.

38The Gershonites were counted by their clans and families. 39All the men from thirty to fifty years of age who came to serve in the work at the Tent of Meeting, 40counted by their clans and families, were 2,630. 41This was the total of those in the Gershonite clans who served at the Tent of Meeting. Moses and Aaron counted them according to the LORD's command.

42The Merarites were counted by their clans and families. 43All the men from thirty to fifty years of age who

Living Bible

are also to carry the drapes covering the courtyard fence, and the curtain across the entrance to the courtyard that surrounds the altar and the Tabernacle. They will also carry the altar, the ropes, and all of the accessories. They are fully responsible for the transportation of these items. 27Aaron or any of his sons may assign the Gershonites' tasks to them, 28but the Gershonites will be directly responsible to Aaron's son Ithamar.

29"Now take a census of the Merari division of the Levite tribe, all of the men from thirty to fifty who are eligible for the Tabernacle service. 30, 31When the Tabernacle is moved, they are to carry the frames of the Tabernacle, the bars, the bases, 32the frames for the courtyard fence with their bases, pegs, cords, and everything else connected with their use and repair.

"Assign duties to each man by name. 33The Merari division will also report to Aaron's son Ithamar."

34So Moses and Aaron and the other leaders took a census of the Kohath division, 35including all of the men thirty to fifty years of age who were eligible for the Tabernacle service, 36and found that the total number was 2,750. 37All this was done to carry out the Lord's instructions to Moses. 38–41A similar census of the Gershon division totaled 2,630. 42–45And of the Merari divi-

New Revised Standard

hangings of the court, and the screen for the entrance of the gate of the court that is around the tabernacle and the altar, and their cords, and all the equipment for their service; and they shall do all that needs to be done with regard to them. 27 All the service of the Gershonites shall be at the command of Aaron and his sons, in all that they are to carry, and in all that they have to do; and you shall assign to their charge all that they are to carry. 28 This is the service of the clans of the Gershonites relating to the tent of meeting, and their responsibilities are to be under the oversight of Ithamar son of Aaron the priest.

29 As for the Merarites, you shall enroll them by their clans and their ancestral houses; 30 from thirty years old up to fifty years old you shall enroll them, everyone who qualifies to do the work of the tent of meeting. 31 This is what they are charged to carry, as the whole of their service in the tent of meeting: the frames of the tabernacle, with its bars, pillars, and bases, 32 and the pillars of the court all around with their bases, pegs, and cords, with all their equipment and all their related service; and you shall assign by name the objects that they are required to carry. 33 This is the service of the clans of the Merarites, the whole of their service relating to the tent of meeting, under the hand of Ithamar son of Aaron the priest.

Census of the Levites

34 So Moses and Aaron and the leaders of the congregation enrolled the Kohathites, by their clans and their ancestral houses, 35 from thirty years old up to fifty years old, everyone who qualified for work relating to the tent of meeting; 36 and their enrollment by clans was two thousand seven hundred fifty. 37 This was the enrollment of the clans of the Kohathites, all who served at the tent of meeting, whom Moses and Aaron enrolled according to the commandment of the LORD by Moses.

38 The enrollment of the Gershonites, by their clans and their ancestral houses, 39 from thirty years old up to fifty years old, everyone who qualified for work relating to the tent of meeting— 40 their enrollment by their clans and their ancestral houses was two thousand six hundred thirty. 41 This was the enrollment of the clans of the Gershonites, all who served at the tent of meeting, whom Moses and Aaron enrolled according to the commandment of the LORD.

42 The enrollment of the clans of the Merarites, by their clans and their ancestral houses, 43 from thirty years

King James

43From thirty years old and upward even unto fifty years old, every one that entereth into the service, for the work in the tabernacle of the congregation,

44Even those that were numbered of them after their families, were three thousand and two hundred.

45These *be* those that were numbered of the families of the sons of Merari, whom Moses and Aaron numbered according to the word of the LORD by the hand of Moses.

46All those that were numbered of the Levites, whom Moses and Aaron and the chief of Israel numbered, after their families, and after the house of their fathers,

47From thirty years old and upward even unto fifty years old, every one that came to do the service of the ministry, and the service of the burden in the tabernacle of the congregation,

48Even those that were numbered of them, were eight thousand and five hundred and fourscore.

49According to the commandment of the LORD they were numbered by the hand of Moses, every one according to his service, and according to his burden: thus were they numbered of him, as the LORD commanded Moses.

5 AND THE LORD spake unto Moses, saying, 2Command the children of Israel, that they put out of the camp every leper, and every one that hath an issue, and whosoever is defiled by the dead:

3Both male and female shall ye put out, without the camp shall ye put them; that they defile not their camps, in the midst whereof I dwell.

4And the children of Israel did so, and put them out without the camp: as the LORD spake unto Moses, so did the children of Israel.

5¶ And the LORD spake unto Moses, saying,

6Speak unto the children of Israel, When a man or woman shall commit any sin that men commit, to do a trespass against the LORD, and that person be guilty;

7Then they shall confess their sin which they have done: and he shall recompense his trespass with the principal thereof, and add unto it the fifth *part* thereof, and give *it* unto *him* against whom he hath trespassed.

8But if the man have no kinsman to recompense the trespass unto, let the trespass be recompensed unto the LORD, *even* to the priest; beside the ram of the atonement, whereby an atonement shall be made for him.

9And every offering of all the holy things of the children of Israel, which they bring unto the priest, shall be his.

10And every man's hallowed things shall be his: whatsoever any man giveth the priest, it shall be his.

11¶ And the LORD spake unto Moses, saying,

12Speak unto the children of Israel, and say unto them, If any man's wife go aside, and commit a trespass against him,

13And a man lie with her carnally, and it be hid from the eyes of her husband, and be kept close, and she be defiled, and *there be* no witness against her, neither she be taken *with the manner;*

14And the spirit of jealousy come upon him, and he be jealous of his wife, and she be defiled: or if the spirit of jealousy come upon him, and he be jealous of his wife, and she be not defiled:

15Then shall the man bring his wife unto the priest, and he shall bring her offering for her, the tenth *part* of an ephah of barley meal; he shall pour no oil upon it, nor put frankincense thereon; for it *is* an offering of jealousy, an offering of memorial, bringing iniquity to remembrance.

16And the priest shall bring her near, and set her before the LORD:

New International

came to serve in the work at the Tent of Meeting, 44counted by their clans, were 3,200. 45This was the total of those in the Merarite clans. Moses and Aaron counted them according to the LORD's command through Moses.

46So Moses, Aaron and the leaders of Israel counted all the Levites by their clans and families. 47All the men from thirty to fifty years of age who came to do the work of serving and carrying the Tent of Meeting 48numbered 8,580. 49At the LORD's command through Moses, each was assigned his work and told what to carry.

Thus they were counted, as the LORD commanded Moses.

The Purity of the Camp

5 THE LORD said to Moses, 2"Command the Israelites to send away from the camp anyone who has an infectious skin diseasea or a discharge of any kind, or who is ceremonially unclean because of a dead body. 3Send away male and female alike; send them outside the camp so they will not defile their camp, where I dwell among them." 4The Israelites did this; they sent them outside the camp. They did just as the LORD had instructed Moses.

Restitution for Wrongs

5The LORD said to Moses, 6"Say to the Israelites: 'When a man or woman wrongs another in any wayb and so is unfaithful to the LORD, that person is guilty 7and must confess the sin he has committed. He must make full restitution for his wrong, add one fifth to it and give it all to the person he has wronged. 8But if that person has no close relative to whom restitution can be made for the wrong, the restitution belongs to the LORD and must be given to the priest, along with the ram with which atonement is made for him. 9All the sacred contributions the Israelites bring to a priest will belong to him. 10Each man's sacred gifts are his own, but what he gives to the priest will belong to the priest.' "

The Test for an Unfaithful Wife

11Then the LORD said to Moses, 12"Speak to the Israelites and say to them: 'If a man's wife goes astray and is unfaithful to him 13by sleeping with another man, and this is hidden from her husband and her impurity is undetected (since there is no witness against her and she has not been caught in the act), 14and if feelings of jealousy come over her husband and he suspects his wife and she is impure—or if he is jealous and suspects her even though she is not impure— 15then he is to take his wife to the priest. He must also take an offering of a tenth of an ephahc of barley flour on her behalf. He must not pour oil on it or put incense on it, because it is a grain offering for jealousy, a reminder offering to draw attention to guilt.

16" 'The priest shall bring her and have her stand before the LORD. 17Then he shall take some holy water

Living Bible

sion, 3,200. 46, 47, 48Thus Moses and Aaron and the leaders of Israel found that the total of all the Levites who were thirty to fifty years old and who were eligible for the Tabernacle service and transportation, was 8,580. 49This census was taken in response to the Lord's instructions to Moses.

5 THESE ARE further instructions from the Lord to Moses: "Inform the people of Israel that they must expel all lepers from the camp, and all who have open sores, or who have been defiled by touching a dead person. 3This applies to men and women alike. Remove them so that they will not defile the camp where I live among you." 4These instructions were put into effect.

5, 6Then the Lord said to Moses, "Tell the people of Israel that when anyone, man or woman, betrays the Lord by betraying a trust, it is sin. 7He must confess his sin and make full repayment for what he has stolen,d adding twenty percent and returning it to the person he took it from. 8But if the person he wronged is dead,e and there is no near relative to whom the payment can be made, it must be given to the priest, along with a lamb for atonement. 9, 10When the people of Israel bring a gift to the Lord it shall go to the priests."

11, 12And the Lord said to Moses, "Tell the people of Israel that if a man's wife commits adultery, 13but there is no proof, there being no witness, 14and he is jealous and suspicious, 15the man shall bring his wife to the priest with an offering for her of a tenth of a bushel of barley meal without oil or frankincense mingled with it—for it is a suspicion offering—to bring out the truthf as to whether or not she is guilty.

16"The priest shall bring her before the Lord, 17and

New Revised Standard

old up to fifty years old, everyone who qualified for work relating to the tent of meeting— 44their enrollment by their clans was three thousand two hundred. 45This is the enrollment of the clans of the Merarites, whom Moses and Aaron enrolled according to the commandment of the LORD by Moses.

46 All those who were enrolled of the Levites, whom Moses and Aaron and the leaders of Israel enrolled, by their clans and their ancestral houses, 47from thirty years old up to fifty years old, everyone who qualified to do the work of service and the work of bearing burdens relating to the tent of meeting, 48their enrollment was eight thousand five hundred eighty. 49According to the commandment of the LORD through Moses they were appointed to their several tasks of serving or carrying; thus they were enrolled by him, as the LORD commanded Moses.

Unclean Persons

5 THE LORD spoke to Moses, saying: 2Command the Israelites to put out of the camp everyone who is leprous,g or has a discharge, and everyone who is unclean through contact with a corpse; 3you shall put out both male and female, putting them outside the camp; they must not defile their camp, where I dwell among them. 4The Israelites did so, putting them outside the camp; as the LORD had spoken to Moses, so the Israelites did.

Confession and Restitution

5 The LORD spoke to Moses, saying: 6Speak to the Israelites: When a man or a woman wrongs another, breaking faith with the LORD, that person incurs guilt 7and shall confess the sin that has been committed. The person shall make full restitution for the wrong, adding one fifth to it, and giving it to the one who was wronged. 8If the injured party has no next of kin to whom restitution may be made for the wrong, the restitution for wrong shall go to the LORD for the priest, in addition to the ram of atonement with which atonement is made for the guilty party. 9Among all the sacred donations of the Israelites, every gift that they bring to the priest shall be his. 10The sacred donations of all are their own; whatever anyone gives to the priest shall be his.

Concerning an Unfaithful Wife

11 The LORD spoke to Moses, saying: 12Speak to the Israelites and say to them: If any man's wife goes astray and is unfaithful to him, 13if a man has had intercourse with her but it is hidden from her husband, so that she is undetected though she has defiled herself, and there is no witness against her since she was not caught in the act; 14if a spirit of jealousy comes on him, and he is jealous of his wife who has defiled herself; or if a spirit of jealousy comes on him, and he is jealous of his wife, though she has not defiled herself; 15then the man shall bring his wife to the priest. And he shall bring the offering required for her, one-tenth of an ephah of barley flour. He shall pour no oil on it and put no frankincense on it, for it is a grain offering of jealousy, a grain offering of remembrance, bringing iniquity to remembrance.

16 Then the priest shall bring her near, and set her before the LORD; 17the priest shall take holy water in an

---

d 5:7 for what he has stolen, literally, "for his wrong."   e 5:8 But if the person he wronged is dead, implied.   f 5:15 a suspicion offering—to bring out the truth, literally, "an offering of remembrance."

g A term for several skin diseases; precise meaning uncertain

King James

17And the priest shall take holy water in an earthen vessel; and of the dust that is in the floor of the tabernacle the priest shall take, and put *it* into the water:

18And the priest shall set the woman before the LORD, and uncover the woman's head, and put the offering of memorial in her hands, which *is* the jealousy offering: and the priest shall have in his hand the bitter water that causeth the curse:

19And the priest shall charge her by an oath, and say unto the woman, If no man have lain with thee, and if thou hast not gone aside to uncleanness *with another* instead of thy husband, be thou free from this bitter water that causeth the curse:

20But if thou hast gone aside *to another* instead of thy husband, and if thou be defiled, and some man have lain with thee beside thine husband:

21Then the priest shall charge the woman with an oath of cursing, and the priest shall say unto the woman, The LORD make thee a curse and an oath among thy people, when the LORD doth make thy thigh to rot, and thy belly to swell;

22And this water that causeth the curse shall go into thy bowels, to make *thy* belly to swell, and *thy* thigh to rot: And the woman shall say, Amen, amen.

23And the priest shall write these curses in a book, and he shall blot *them* out with the bitter water:

24And he shall cause the woman to drink the bitter water that causeth the curse: and the water that causeth the curse shall enter into her, *and become* bitter.

25Then the priest shall take the jealousy offering out of the woman's hand, and shall wave the offering before the LORD, and offer it upon the altar:

26And the priest shall take an handful of the offering, *even* the memorial thereof, and burn *it* upon the altar, and afterward shall cause the woman to drink the water.

27And when he hath made her to drink the water, then it shall come to pass, *that,* if she be defiled, and have done trespass against her husband, that the water that causeth the curse shall enter into her, *and become* bitter, and her belly shall swell, and her thigh shall rot: and the woman shall be a curse among her people.

28And if the woman be not defiled, but be clean; then she shall be free, and shall conceive seed.

29This *is* the law of jealousies, when a wife goeth aside *to another* instead of her husband, and is defiled;

30Or when the spirit of jealousy cometh upon him, and he be jealous over his wife, and shall set the woman before the LORD, and the priest shall execute upon her all this law.

31Then shall the man be guiltless from iniquity, and this woman shall bear her iniquity.

6 AND THE LORD spake unto Moses, saying, 2Speak unto the children of Israel, and say unto them, When either man or woman shall separate *themselves* to vow a vow of a Nazarite, to separate *themselves* unto the LORD:

3He shall separate *himself* from wine and strong drink, and shall drink no vinegar of wine, or vinegar of strong drink, neither shall he drink any liquor of grapes, nor eat moist grapes, or dried.

4All the days of his separation shall he eat nothing that is made of the vine tree, from the kernels even to the husk.

5All the days of the vow of his separation there shall no razor come upon his head: until the days be fulfilled, in the which he separateth *himself* unto the LORD, he shall be holy, *and* shall let the locks of the hair of his head grow.

New International

in a clay jar and put some dust from the tabernacle floor into the water. 18After the priest has had the woman stand before the LORD, he shall loosen her hair and place in her hands the reminder offering, the grain offering for jealousy, while he himself holds the bitter water that brings a curse. 19Then the priest shall put the woman under oath and say to her, "If no other man has slept with you and you have not gone astray and become impure while married to your husband, may this bitter water that brings a curse not harm you. 20But if you have gone astray while married to your husband and you have defiled yourself by sleeping with a man other than your husband"— 21here the priest is to put the woman under this curse of the oath—"may the LORD cause your people to curse and denounce you when he causes your thigh to waste away and your abdomen to swell.[a] 22May this water that brings a curse enter your body so that your abdomen swells and your thigh wastes away.[b]"

" 'Then the woman is to say, "Amen. So be it." '

23" 'The priest is to write these curses on a scroll and then wash them off into the bitter water. 24He shall have the woman drink the bitter water that brings a curse, and this water will enter her and cause bitter suffering. 25The priest is to take from her hands the grain offering for jealousy, wave it before the LORD and bring it to the altar. 26The priest is then to take a handful of the grain offering as a memorial offering and burn it on the altar; after that, he is to have the woman drink the water. 27If she has defiled herself and been unfaithful to her husband, then when she is made to drink the water that brings a curse, it will go into her and cause bitter suffering; her abdomen will swell and her thigh waste away,[c] and she will become accursed among her people. 28If, however, the woman has not defiled herself and is free from impurity, she will be cleared of guilt and will be able to have children.

29" 'This, then, is the law of jealousy when a woman goes astray and defiles herself while married to her husband, 30or when feelings of jealousy come over a man because he suspects his wife. The priest is to have her stand before the LORD and is to apply this entire law to her. 31The husband will be innocent of any wrongdoing, but the woman will bear the consequences of her sin.' "

The Nazirite

6 THE LORD said to Moses, 2"Speak to the Israelites and say to them: 'If a man or woman wants to make a special vow, a vow of separation to the LORD as a Nazirite, 3he must abstain from wine and other fermented drink and must not drink vinegar made from wine or from other fermented drink. He must not drink grape juice or eat grapes or raisins. 4As long as he is a Nazirite, he must not eat anything that comes from the grapevine, not even the seeds or skins.

5" 'During the entire period of his vow of separation no razor may be used on his head. He must be holy until the period of his separation to the LORD is over; he must let the hair of his head grow long. 6Throughout the peri-

---

a 21 Or *causes you to have a miscarrying womb and barrenness*   b 22 Or *body and cause you to be barren and have a miscarrying womb*   c 27 Or *suffering; she will have barrenness and a miscarrying womb*

Living Bible

take holy water in a clay jar and mix into it dust from the floor of the Tabernacle. 18He shall unbind her hair and place the suspicion offering in her hands to determine whether or not her husband's suspicions are justified. The priest shall stand before her holding the jar of bitter water that brings a curse. 19He shall require her to swear that she is innocent, and then he shall say to her, 'If no man has slept with you except your husband, be free from the effects of this bitter water that causes the curse. 20But if you have committed adultery, 21, 22then Jehovah shall make you a curse among your people, for he will make your thigh rot away and your body swell.' And the woman shall be required to say, 'Yes, let it be so.' 23Then the priest shall write these curses in a book and wash them off into the bitter water. 24(When he requires the woman to drink the water, it becomes bitter within her [if she is guiltyd].)

25"Then the priest shall take the suspicion offering from the woman's hand and wave it before Jehovah, and carry it to the altar. 26He shall take a handful, representing all of it, and burn the handful upon the altar, and then require the woman to drink the water. 27If she has been defiled, having committed adultery against her husband, the water will become bitter within her, and her body will swell and her thigh will rot, and she shall be a curse among her people. 28But if she is pure and has not committed adultery, she shall be unharmed and will soon become pregnant. 29"This, then, is the law concerning a wayward wife—or a husband's suspicions against his wife—

30to determine whether or not she has been unfaithful to him. He shall bring her before the Lord and the priest shall handle the situation as outlined above. 31Her husband shall not be brought to trial for causing her horrible disease, for she is responsible."

6 THE LORD gave Moses these further instructions for the people of Israel: "When either a man or a woman takes the special vow of a Nazirite, consecrating himself to the Lord in a special way, 3, 4he must not thereafter, during the entire period of his special consecration to the Lord, taste strong drink or wine or even fresh wine, grape juice, grapes, or raisins! He may eat nothing that comes from grape vines, not even the seeds or skins!

5"Throughout that time he must never cut his hair, for he is holy and consecrated to the Lord; that is why he must let his hair grow.

New Revised Standard

earthen vessel, and take some of the dust that is on the floor of the tabernacle and put it into the water. 18The priest shall set the woman before the LORD, dishevel the woman's hair, and place in her hands the grain offering of remembrance, which is the grain offering of jealousy. In his own hand the priest shall have the water of bitterness that brings the curse. 19Then the priest shall make her take an oath, saying, "If no man has lain with you, if you have not turned aside to uncleanness while under your husband's authority, be immune to this water of bitterness that brings the curse. 20But if you have gone astray while under your husband's authority, if you have defiled yourself and some man other than your husband has had intercourse with you," 21—let the priest make the woman take the oath of the curse and say to the woman—"the LORD make you an execration and an oath among your people, when the LORD makes your uterus drop, your womb discharge; 22now may this water that brings the curse enter your bowels and make your womb discharge, your uterus drop!" And the woman shall say, "Amen. Amen."

23 Then the priest shall put these curses in writing, and wash them off into the water of bitterness. 24He shall make the woman drink the water of bitterness that brings the curse, and the water that brings the curse shall enter her and cause bitter pain. 25The priest shall take the grain offering of jealousy out of the woman's hand, and shall elevate the grain offering before the LORD and bring it to the altar; 26and the priest shall take a handful of the grain offering, as its memorial portion, and turn it into smoke on the altar, and afterward shall make the woman drink the water. 27When he has made her drink the water, then, if she has defiled herself and has been unfaithful to her husband, the water that brings the curse shall enter into her and cause bitter pain, and her womb shall discharge, her uterus drop, and the woman shall become an execration among her people. 28But if the woman has not defiled herself and is clean, then she shall be immune and be able to conceive children.

29 This is the law in cases of jealousy, when a wife, while under her husband's authority, goes astray and defiles herself, 30or when a spirit of jealousy comes on a man and he is jealous of his wife; then he shall set the woman before the LORD, and the priest shall apply this entire law to her. 31The man shall be free from iniquity, but the woman shall bear her iniquity.

The Nazirites

6 THE LORD spoke to Moses, saying: 2Speak to the Israelites and say to them: When either men or women make a special vow, the vow of a nazirite,e to separate themselves to the LORD, 3they shall separate themselves from wine and strong drink; they shall drink no wine vinegar or other vinegar, and shall not drink any grape juice or eat grapes, fresh or dried. 4All their days as naziritesf they shall eat nothing that is produced by the grapevine, not even the seeds or the skins.

5 All the days of their nazirite vow no razor shall come upon the head; until the time is completed for which they separate themselves to the LORD, they shall be holy; they shall let the locks of the head grow long.

---

d 5:24 if she is guilty, implied.

e That is one separated or one consecrated   f That is those separated or those consecrated

King James

6All the days that he separateth *himself* unto the LORD he shall come at no dead body.

7He shall not make himself unclean for his father, or for his mother, for his brother, or for his sister, when they die: because the consecration of his God *is* upon his head.

8All the days of his separation he *is* holy unto the LORD.

9And if any man die very suddenly by him, and he hath defiled the head of his consecration; then he shall shave his head in the day of his cleansing, on the seventh day shall he shave it.

10And on the eighth day he shall bring two turtles, or two young pigeons, to the priest, to the door of the tabernacle of the congregation:

11And the priest shall offer the one for a sin offering, and the other for a burnt offering, and make an atonement for him, for that he sinned by the dead, and shall hallow his head that same day.

12And he shall consecrate unto the LORD the days of his separation, and shall bring a lamb of the first year for a trespass offering: but the days that were before shall be lost, because his separation was defiled.

13¶ And this *is* the law of the Nazarite, when the days of his separation are fulfilled: he shall be brought unto the door of the tabernacle of the congregation:

14And he shall offer his offering unto the LORD, one he lamb of the first year without blemish for a burnt offering, and one ewe lamb of the first year without blemish for a sin offering, and one ram without blemish for peace offerings,

15And a basket of unleavened bread, cakes of fine flour mingled with oil, and wafers of unleavened bread anointed with oil, and their meat offering, and their drink offerings.

16And the priest shall bring *them* before the LORD, and shall offer his sin offering, and his burnt offering:

17And he shall offer the ram *for* a sacrifice of peace offerings unto the LORD, with the basket of unleavened bread: the priest shall offer also his meat offering, and his drink offering.

18And the Nazarite shall shave the head of his separation *at* the door of the tabernacle of the congregation, and shall take the hair of the head of his separation, and put *it* in the fire which *is* under the sacrifice of the peace offerings.

19And the priest shall take the sodden shoulder of the ram, and one unleavened cake out of the basket, and one unleavened wafer, and shall put *them* upon the hands of the Nazarite, after *the hair of* his separation is shaven:

20And the priest shall wave them *for* a wave offering before the LORD: this *is* holy for the priest, with the wave breast and heave shoulder: and after that the Nazarite may drink wine.

21This *is* the law of the Nazarite who hath vowed, *and of* his offering unto the LORD for his separation, beside *that* that his hand shall get: according to the vow which he vowed, so he must do after the law of his separation.

22¶ And the LORD spake unto Moses, saying,

23Speak unto Aaron and unto his sons, saying, On this wise ye shall bless the children of Israel, saying unto them,

24The LORD bless thee, and keep thee:

25The LORD make his face shine upon thee, and be gracious unto thee:

26The LORD lift up his countenance upon thee, and give thee peace.

27And they shall put my name upon the children of Israel; and I will bless them.

New International

od of his separation to the LORD he must not go near a dead body. 7Even if his own father or mother or brother or sister dies, he must not make himself ceremonially unclean on account of them, because the symbol of his separation to God is on his head. 8Throughout the period of his separation he is consecrated to the LORD.

9" 'If someone dies suddenly in his presence, thus defiling the hair he has dedicated, he must shave his head on the day of his cleansing—the seventh day. 10Then on the eighth day he must bring two doves or two young pigeons to the priest at the entrance to the Tent of Meeting. 11The priest is to offer one as a sin offering and the other as a burnt offering to make atonement for him because he sinned by being in the presence of the dead body. That same day he is to consecrate his head. 12He must dedicate himself to the LORD for the period of his separation and must bring a year-old male lamb as a guilt offering. The previous days do not count, because he became defiled during his separation.

13" 'Now this is the law for the Nazirite when the period of his separation is over. He is to be brought to the entrance to the Tent of Meeting. 14There he is to present his offerings to the LORD: a year-old male lamb without defect for a burnt offering, a year-old ewe lamb without defect for a sin offering, a ram without defect for a fellowship offering,a 15together with their grain offerings and drink offerings, and a basket of bread made without yeast—cakes made of fine flour mixed with oil, and wafers spread with oil.

16" 'The priest is to present them before the LORD and make the sin offering and the burnt offering. 17He is to present the basket of unleavened bread and is to sacrifice the ram as a fellowship offering to the LORD, together with its grain offering and drink offering.

18" 'Then at the entrance to the Tent of Meeting, the Nazirite must shave off the hair that he dedicated. He is to take the hair and put it in the fire that is under the sacrifice of the fellowship offering.

19" 'After the Nazirite has shaved off the hair of his dedication, the priest is to place in his hands a boiled shoulder of the ram, and a cake and a wafer from the basket, both made without yeast. 20The priest shall then wave them before the LORD as a wave offering; they are holy and belong to the priest, together with the breast that was waved and the thigh that was presented. After that, the Nazirite may drink wine.

21" 'This is the law of the Nazirite who vows his offering to the LORD in accordance with his separation, in addition to whatever else he can afford. He must fulfill the vow he has made, according to the law of the Nazirite.' "

The Priestly Blessing

22The LORD said to Moses, 23"Tell Aaron and his sons, 'This is how you are to bless the Israelites. Say to them:

24" ' "The LORD bless you
    and keep you;
25the LORD make his face shine upon you
    and be gracious to you;
26the LORD turn his face toward you
    and give you peace." '

27"So they will put my name on the Israelites, and I will bless them."

---

a *14* Traditionally *peace offering*; also in verses 17 and 18

Living Bible

6, 7"And he may not go near any dead body during the entire period of his vow, even if it is the body of his father, mother, brother, or sister; for his vow of consecration remains in effect, 8and he is consecrated to the Lord throughout the entire period. 9If he is defiled by having someone fall dead beside him, then seven days later he shall shave his defiled head; he will then be cleansed from the contamination of being in the presence of death. 10The next day, the eighth day, he must bring two turtledoves or two young pigeons to the priest at the entrance of the Tabernacle. 11The priest shall offer one of the birds for a sin offering, and the other for a burnt offering, and make atonement for his defilement. And he must renew his vows that day and let his hair begin to grow again. 12The days of his vow that were fulfilled before his defilement no longer count. He must begin all over again with a new vow, and must bring a male lamb a year old for a guilt offering.

13"At the conclusion of the period of his vow of separation to the Lord, he must go to the entrance of the Tabernacle 14and offer a burnt sacrifice to the Lord, a year-old lamb without defect. He must also offer a sin offering, a yearling ewe lamb without defect; a peace offering, a ram without defect; 15a basket of bread made without yeast; pancakes made of fine flour mixed with olive oil; unleavened wafers spread with oil; and the accompanying grain offering and drink offerings. 16The priest shall present these offerings before the Lord: first the sin offering and the burnt offering; 17then the ram for a peace offering, along with the basket of bread made without yeast; and finally the grain offering along with the drink offering.

18"Then the Nazirite shall shave his long hair—the sign of his vow of separation. This shall be done at the entrance of the Tabernacle, after which the hair shall be put in the fire under the peace offering sacrifice. 19After the man's head has been shaved, the priest shall take the roasted shoulder of the lamb, one of the pancakes (made without yeast), and one of the wafers (also made without yeast), and put them all into the man's hands. 20The priest shall then wave it all back and forth before the Lord in a gesture of offering; all of it is a holy portion for the priest, as are the rib piece and shoulder that were waved before the Lord. After that the Nazirite may again drink wine, for he is freed from his vow.

21"These are the regulations concerning a Nazirite and his sacrifices at the conclusion of his period of special dedication. In addition to these sacrifices he must bring any further offering he promised at the time he took his vow to become a Nazirite."

22, 23Now the Lord said to Moses, "Tell Aaron and his sons that they are to give this special blessing to the people of Israel: 24, 25, 26'May the Lord bless and protect you; may the Lord's face radiate with joy because of you; may he be gracious to you, show you his favor, and give you his peace.' 27This is how Aaron and his sons shall call down my blessingsb upon the people of Israel; and I myself will personally bless them."

New Revised Standard

6 All the days that they separate themselves to the Lord they shall not go near a corpse. 7Even if their father or mother, brother or sister, should die, they may not defile themselves; because their consecration to God is upon the head. 8All their days as naziritesc they are holy to the Lord.

9 If someone dies very suddenly nearby, defiling the consecrated head, then they shall shave the head on the day of their cleansing; on the seventh day they shall shave it. 10On the eighth day they shall bring two turtledoves or two young pigeons to the priest at the entrance of the tent of meeting, 11and the priest shall offer one as a sin offering and the other as a burnt offering, and make atonement for them, because they incurred guilt by reason of the corpse. They shall sanctify the head that same day, 12and separate themselves to the Lord for their days as nazirites,c and bring a male lamb a year old as a guilt offering. The former time shall be void, because the consecrated head was defiled.

13 This is the law for the naziritesc when the time of their consecration has been completed: they shall be brought to the entrance of the tent of meeting, 14and they shall offer their gift to the Lord, one male lamb a year old without blemish as a burnt offering, one ewe lamb a year old without blemish as a sin offering, one ram without blemish as an offering of well-being, 15and a basket of unleavened bread, cakes of choice flour mixed with oil and unleavened wafers spread with oil, with their grain offering and their drink offerings. 16The priest shall present them before the Lord and offer their sin offering and burnt offering, 17and shall offer the ram as a sacrifice of well-being to the Lord, with the basket of unleavened bread; the priest also shall make the accompanying grain offering and drink offering. 18Then the naziritesc shall shave the consecrated head at the entrance of the tent of meeting, and shall take the hair from the consecrated head and put it on the fire under the sacrifice of well-being. 19The priest shall take the shoulder of the ram, when it is boiled, and one unleavened cake out of the basket, and one unleavened wafer, and shall put them in the palms of the nazirites,c after they have shaved the consecrated head. 20Then the priest shall elevate them as an elevation offering before the Lord; they are a holy portion for the priest, together with the breast that is elevated and the thigh that is offered. After that the naziritesc may drink wine.

21 This is the law for the naziritesc who take a vow. Their offering to the Lord must be in accordance with the nazirited vow, apart from what else they can afford. In accordance with whatever vow they take, so they shall do, following the law for their consecration.

The Priestly Benediction

22 The Lord spoke to Moses, saying: 23Speak to Aaron and his sons, saying, Thus you shall bless the Israelites: You shall say to them,
24 The Lord bless you and keep you;
25 the Lord make his face to shine upon you,
          and be gracious to you;
26 the Lord lift up his countenance upon you,
          and give you peace.
27 So they shall put my name on the Israelites, and I will bless them.

---

b 6:27 shall call down my blessings, literally, "shall put my name upon the people of Israel."

c That is those separated or those consecrated   d That is one separated or one consecrated

King James

7 AND IT came to pass on the day that Moses had fully set up the tabernacle, and had anointed it, and sanctified it, and all the instruments thereof, both the altar and all the vessels thereof, and had anointed them, and sanctified them;

2That the princes of Israel, heads of the house of their fathers, who *were* the princes of the tribes, and were over them that were numbered, offered:

3And they brought their offering before the LORD, six covered wagons, and twelve oxen; a wagon for two of the princes, and for each one an ox: and they brought them before the tabernacle.

4And the LORD spake unto Moses, saying,

5Take *it* of them, that they may be to do the service of the tabernacle of the congregation; and thou shalt give them unto the Levites, to every man according to his service.

6And Moses took the wagons and the oxen, and gave them unto the Levites.

7Two wagons and four oxen he gave unto the sons of Gershon, according to their service:

8And four wagons and eight oxen he gave unto the sons of Merari, according unto their service, under the hand of Ithamar the son of Aaron the priest.

9But unto the sons of Kohath he gave none: because the service of the sanctuary belonging unto them *was that* they should bear upon their shoulders.

10¶ And the princes offered for dedicating of the altar in the day that it was anointed, even the princes offered their offering before the altar.

11And the LORD said unto Moses, They shall offer their offering, each prince on his day, for the dedicating of the altar.

12¶ And he that offered his offering the first day was Nahshon the son of Amminadab, of the tribe of Judah:

13And his offering *was* one silver charger, the weight thereof *was* an hundred and thirty *shekels*, one silver bowl of seventy shekels, after the shekel of the sanctuary; both of them *were* full of fine flour mingled with oil for a meat offering:

14One spoon of ten *shekels* of gold, full of incense:

15One young bullock, one ram, one lamb of the first year, for a burnt offering:

16One kid of the goats for a sin offering:

17And for a sacrifice of peace offerings, two oxen, five rams, five he goats, five lambs of the first year: this *was* the offering of Nahshon the son of Amminadab.

18¶ On the second day Nethaneel the son of Zuar, prince of Issachar, did offer:

19He offered *for* his offering one silver charger, the weight whereof *was* an hundred and thirty *shekels*, one silver bowl of seventy shekels, after the shekel of the sanctuary; both of them full of fine flour mingled with oil for a meat offering:

20One spoon of gold of ten *shekels*, full of incense:

21One young bullock, one ram, one lamb of the first year, for a burnt offering:

22One kid of the goats for a sin offering:

23And for a sacrifice of peace offerings, two oxen, five rams, five he goats, five lambs of the first year: this *was* the offering of Nethaneel the son of Zuar.

New International

Offerings at the Dedication of the Tabernacle

7 WHEN MOSES finished setting up the tabernacle, he anointed it and consecrated it and all its furnishings. He also anointed and consecrated the altar and all its utensils. 2Then the leaders of Israel, the heads of families who were the tribal leaders in charge of those who were counted, made offerings. 3They brought as their gifts before the LORD six covered carts and twelve oxen—an ox from each leader and a cart from every two. These they presented before the tabernacle.

4The LORD said to Moses, 5"Accept these from them, that they may be used in the work at the Tent of Meeting. Give them to the Levites as each man's work requires."

6So Moses took the carts and oxen and gave them to the Levites. 7He gave two carts and four oxen to the Gershonites, as their work required, 8and he gave four carts and eight oxen to the Merarites, as their work required. They were all under the direction of Ithamar son of Aaron, the priest. 9But Moses did not give any to the Kohathites, because they were to carry on their shoulders the holy things, for which they were responsible.

10When the altar was anointed, the leaders brought their offerings for its dedication and presented them before the altar. 11For the LORD had said to Moses, "Each day one leader is to bring his offering for the dedication of the altar."

12The one who brought his offering on the first day was Nahshon son of Amminadab of the tribe of Judah.

13His offering was one silver plate weighing a hundred and thirty shekels,a and one silver sprinkling bowl weighing seventy shekels,b both according to the sanctuary shekel, each filled with fine flour mixed with oil as a grain offering; 14one gold dish weighing ten shekels,c filled with incense; 15one young bull, one ram and one male lamb a year old, for a burnt offering; 16one male goat for a sin offering; 17and two oxen, five rams, five male goats and five male lambs a year old, to be sacrificed as a fellowship offering.d This was the offering of Nahshon son of Amminadab.

18On the second day Nethanel son of Zuar, the leader of Issachar, brought his offering.

19The offering he brought was one silver plate weighing a hundred and thirty shekels, and one silver sprinkling bowl weighing seventy shekels, both according to the sanctuary shekel, each filled with fine flour mixed with oil as a grain offering; 20one gold dish weighing ten shekels, filled with incense; 21one young bull, one ram and one male lamb a year old, for a burnt offering; 22one male goat for a sin offering; 23and two oxen, five rams, five male goats and five male lambs a year old, to be sacrificed as a fellowship offering. This was the offering of Nethanel son of Zuar.

---

a *13* That is, about 3 1/4 pounds (about 1.5 kilograms); also elsewhere in this chapter   b *13* That is, about 1 3/4 pounds (about 0.8 kilogram); also elsewhere in this chapter   c *14* That is, about 4 ounces (about 110 grams); also elsewhere in this chapter   d *17* Traditionally *peace offering*; also elsewhere in this chapter

Living Bible

7 MOSES ANOINTED and sanctified each part of the Tabernacle, including the altar and its utensils, on the day he finished setting it up. 2Then the leaders of Israel—the chiefs of the tribes, the men who had organized the census—brought their offerings. 3They brought six covered wagons, each drawn by two oxen—a wagon for every two leaders and an ox for each one; and they presented them to the Lord in front of the Tabernacle.

4, 5"Accept their gifts," the Lord told Moses, "and use these wagons for the work of the Tabernacle. Give them to the Levites for whatever needs they may have."

6So Moses presented the wagons and the oxen to the Levites. 7Two wagons and four oxen were given to the Gershon division for their use, 8and four wagons and eight oxen were given to the Merari division, which was under the leadership of Ithamar, Aaron's son. 9None of the wagons or teams was given to the Kohath division, for they were required to carry their portion of the Tabernacle upon their shoulders.

10The leaders also presented dedication gifts on the day the altar was anointed, placing them before the altar. 11The Lord said to Moses, "Let each of them bring his gift on a different day for the dedication of the altar."

12So Nahshon, the son of Amminadab of the tribe of Judah, brought his gift the first day. 13It consisted of a silver platter weighing three pounds and a silver bowl of about two pounds, both filled with grain offerings of fine flour mixed with oil. 14He also brought a tinye gold box of incense which weighed only about four ounces. 15He brought a young bull, a ram, and a male yearling lamb as burnt offerings; 16male goat for a sin offering; 17and for the peace offerings two oxen, five rams, five male goats, and five male yearling lambs.

18-23The next day Nethanel, the son of Zuar, chief of the tribe of Issachar, brought his gifts and offerings. They were exactly the same as Nahshon had presented on the previous day.f

New Revised Standard

Offerings of the Leaders

7 ON THE day when Moses had finished setting up the tabernacle, and had anointed and consecrated it with all its furnishings, and had anointed and consecrated the altar with all its utensils, 2the leaders of Israel, heads of their ancestral houses, the leaders of the tribes, who were over those who were enrolled, made offerings. 3They brought their offerings before the LORD, six covered wagons and twelve oxen, a wagon for every two of the leaders, and for each one an ox; they presented them before the tabernacle. 4Then the LORD said to Moses: 5Accept these from them, that they may be used in doing the service of the tent of meeting, and give them to the Levites, to each according to his service. 6So Moses took the wagons and the oxen, and gave them to the Levites. 7Two wagons and four oxen he gave to the Gershonites, according to their service; 8and four wagons and eight oxen he gave to the Merarites, according to their service, under the direction of Ithamar son of Aaron the priest. 9But to the Kohathites he gave none, because they were charged with the care of the holy things that had to be carried on the shoulders.

10 The leaders also presented offerings for the dedication of the altar at the time when it was anointed; the leaders presented their offering before the altar. 11The LORD said to Moses: They shall present their offerings, one leader each day, for the dedication of the altar.

12 The one who presented his offering the first day was Nahshon son of Amminadab, of the tribe of Judah; 13his offering was one silver plate weighing one hundred thirty shekels, one silver basin weighing seventy shekels, according to the shekel of the sanctuary, both of them full of choice flour mixed with oil for a grain offering; 14one golden dish weighing ten shekels, full of incense; 15one young bull, one ram, one male lamb a year old, for a burnt offering; 16one male goat for a sin offering; 17and for the sacrifice of well-being, two oxen, five rams, five male goats, and five male lambs a year old. This was the offering of Nahshon son of Amminadab.

18 On the second day Nethanel son of Zuar, the leader of Issachar, presented an offering; 19he presented for his offering one silver plate weighing one hundred thirty shekels, one silver basin weighing seventy shekels, according to the shekel of the sanctuary, both of them full of choice flour mixed with oil for a grain offering; 20one golden dish weighing ten shekels, full of incense; 21one young bull, one ram, one male lamb a year old, as a burnt offering; 22one male goat as a sin offering; 23and for the sacrifice of well-being, two oxen, five rams, five male goats, and five male lambs a year old. This was the offering of Nethanel son of Zuar.

---

e 7:14 tiny, implied.   f 7:18-83 The original text repeats the lists of the offerings recorded in verses 13-17.

King James

24¶ On the third day Eliab the son of Helon, prince of the children of Zebulun, *did offer:*

25His offering *was* one silver charger, the weight whereof *was* an hundred and thirty *shekels*, one silver bowl of seventy shekels, after the shekel of the sanctuary; both of them full of fine flour mingled with oil for a meat offering:

26One golden spoon of ten *shekels*, full of incense:

27One young bullock, one ram, one lamb of the first year, for a burnt offering:

28One kid of the goats for a sin offering:

29And for a sacrifice of peace offerings, two oxen, five rams, five he goats, five lambs of the first year: this *was* the offering of Eliab the son of Helon.

30¶ On the fourth day Elizur the son of Shedeur, prince of the children of Reuben, *did offer:*

31His offering *was* one silver charger of the weight of an hundred and thirty *shekels*, one silver bowl of seventy shekels, after the shekel of the sanctuary; both of them full of fine flour mingled with oil for a meat offering:

32One golden spoon of ten *shekels*, full of incense:

33One young bullock, one ram, one lamb of the first year, for a burnt offering:

34One kid of the goats for a sin offering:

35And for a sacrifice of peace offerings, two oxen, five rams, five he goats, five lambs of the first year: this *was* the offering of Elizur the son of Shedeur.

36¶ On the fifth day Shelumiel the son of Zurishaddai, prince of the children of Simeon, *did offer:*

37His offering *was* one silver charger, the weight whereof *was* an hundred and thirty *shekels*, one silver bowl of seventy shekels, after the shekel of the sanctuary; both of them full of fine flour mingled with oil for a meat offering:

38One golden spoon of ten *shekels*, full of incense:

39One young bullock, one ram, one lamb of the first year, for a burnt offering:

40One kid of the goats for a sin offering:

41And for a sacrifice of peace offerings, two oxen, five rams, five he goats, five lambs of the first year: this *was* the offering of Shelumiel the son of Zurishaddai.

42¶ On the sixth day Eliasaph the son of Deuel, prince of the children of Gad, *offered:*

43His offering *was* one silver charger of the weight of an hundred and thirty *shekels*, a silver bowl of seventy shekels, after the shekel of the sanctuary; both of them full of fine flour mingled with oil for a meat offering:

44One golden spoon of ten *shekels*, full of incense:

45One young bullock, one ram, one lamb of the first year, for a burnt offering:

46One kid of the goats for a sin offering:

47And for a sacrifice of peace offerings, two oxen, five rams, five he goats, five lambs of the first year: this *was* the offering of Eliasaph the son of Deuel.

48¶ On the seventh day Elishama the son of Ammihud, prince of the children of Ephraim, *offered:*

49His offering *was* one silver charger, the weight whereof *was* an hundred and thirty *shekels*, one silver bowl of seventy shekels, after the shekel of the sanctuary; both of them full of fine flour mingled with oil for a meat offering:

50One golden spoon of ten *shekels*, full of incense:

51One young bullock, one ram, one lamb of the first year, for a burnt offering:

52One kid of the goats for a sin offering:

53And for a sacrifice of peace offerings, two oxen, five rams, five he goats, five lambs of the first year: this *was* the offering of Elishama the son of Ammihud.

54¶ On the eighth day *offered* Gamaliel the son of Pedahzur, prince of the children of Manasseh:

New International

24On the third day, Eliab son of Helon, the leader of the people of Zebulun, brought his offering.

25His offering was one silver plate weighing a hundred and thirty shekels, and one silver sprinkling bowl weighing seventy shekels, both according to the sanctuary shekel, each filled with fine flour mixed with oil as a grain offering; 26one gold dish weighing ten shekels, filled with incense; 27one young bull, one ram and one male lamb a year old, for a burnt offering; 28one male goat for a sin offering; 29and two oxen, five rams, five male goats and five male lambs a year old, to be sacrificed as a fellowship offering. This was the offering of Eliab son of Helon.

30On the fourth day Elizur son of Shedeur, the leader of the people of Reuben, brought his offering.

31His offering was one silver plate weighing a hundred and thirty shekels, and one silver sprinkling bowl weighing seventy shekels, both according to the sanctuary shekel, each filled with fine flour mixed with oil as a grain offering; 32one gold dish weighing ten shekels, filled with incense; 33one young bull, one ram and one male lamb a year old, for a burnt offering; 34one male goat for a sin offering; 35and two oxen, five rams, five male goats and five male lambs a year old, to be sacrificed as a fellowship offering. This was the offering of Elizur son of Shedeur.

36On the fifth day Shelumiel son of Zurishaddai, the leader of the people of Simeon, brought his offering.

37His offering was one silver plate weighing a hundred and thirty shekels, and one silver sprinkling bowl weighing seventy shekels, both according to the sanctuary shekel, each filled with fine flour mixed with oil as a grain offering; 38one gold dish weighing ten shekels, filled with incense; 39one young bull, one ram and one male lamb a year old, for a burnt offering; 40one male goat for a sin offering; 41and two oxen, five rams, five male goats and five male lambs a year old, to be sacrificed as a fellowship offering. This was the offering of Shelumiel son of Zurishaddai.

42On the sixth day Eliasaph son of Deuel, the leader of the people of Gad, brought his offering.

43His offering was one silver plate weighing a hundred and thirty shekels, and one silver sprinkling bowl weighing seventy shekels, both according to the sanctuary shekel, each filled with fine flour mixed with oil as a grain offering; 44one gold dish weighing ten shekels, filled with incense; 45one young bull, one ram and one male lamb a year old, for a burnt offering; 46one male goat for a sin offering; 47and two oxen, five rams, five male goats and five male lambs a year old, to be sacrificed as a fellowship offering. This was the offering of Eliasaph son of Deuel.

48On the seventh day Elishama son of Ammihud, the leader of the people of Ephraim, brought his offering.

49His offering was one silver plate weighing a hundred and thirty shekels, and one silver sprinkling bowl weighing seventy shekels, both according to the sanctuary shekel, each filled with fine flour mixed with oil as a grain offering; 50one gold dish weighing ten shekels, filled with incense; 51one young bull, one ram and one male lamb a year old, for a burnt offering; 52one male goat for a sin offering; 53and two oxen, five rams, five male goats and five male lambs a year old, to be sacrificed as a fellowship offering. This was the offering of Elishama son of Ammihud.

54On the eighth day Gamaliel son of Pedahzur, the leader of the people of Manasseh, brought his offering.

Living Bible

24-29On the third day Eliab, the son of Helon, chief of the tribe of Zebulun, came with his offerings—the same as those presented on the previous days.

30-35On the fourth day the gifts were presented by Elizur, son of Shedeur, chief of the tribe of Reuben; his gifts and offerings were the same as those given on the previous days.

36-41On the fifth day came Shelumi-el, the son of Zuri-shaddai, chief of the tribe of Simeon, with the same gifts.

42-47The next day it was Eliasaph's turn, son of Deuel, chief of the tribe of Gad. He, too, offered the same gifts and sacrifices.

48-53On the seventh day, Elishama, the son of Ammihud, chief of the tribe of Ephraim, brought his gifts, the same as those presented on the previous days.

54-59Gamaliel, son of Pedahzur, prince of the tribe of Manasseh, came the eighth day with the same offerings.

New Revised Standard

24 On the third day Eliab son of Helon, the leader of the Zebulunites: 25his offering was one silver plate weighing one hundred thirty shekels, one silver basin weighing seventy shekels, according to the shekel of the sanctuary, both of them full of choice flour mixed with oil for a grain offering; 26one golden dish weighing ten shekels, full of incense; 27one young bull, one ram, one male lamb a year old, for a burnt offering; 28one male goat for a sin offering; 29and for the sacrifice of well-being, two oxen, five rams, five male goats, and five male lambs a year old. This was the offering of Eliab son of Helon.

30 On the fourth day Elizur son of Shedeur, the leader of the Reubenites: 31his offering was one silver plate weighing one hundred thirty shekels, one silver basin weighing seventy shekels, according to the shekel of the sanctuary, both of them full of choice flour mixed with oil for a grain offering; 32one golden dish weighing ten shekels, full of incense; 33one young bull, one ram, one male lamb a year old, for a burnt offering; 34one male goat for a sin offering; 35and for the sacrifice of well-being, two oxen, five rams, five male goats, and five male lambs a year old. This was the offering of Elizur son of Shedeur.

36 On the fifth day Shelumiel son of Zurishaddai, the leader of the Simeonites: 37his offering was one silver plate weighing one hundred thirty shekels, one silver basin weighing seventy shekels, according to the shekel of the sanctuary, both of them full of choice flour mixed with oil for a grain offering; 38one golden dish weighing ten shekels, full of incense; 39one young bull, one ram, one male lamb a year old, for a burnt offering; 40one male goat for a sin offering; 41and for the sacrifice of well-being, two oxen, five rams, five male goats, and five male lambs a year old. This was the offering of Shelumiel son of Zurishaddai.

42 On the sixth day Eliasaph son of Deuel, the leader of the Gadites: 43his offering was one silver plate weighing one hundred thirty shekels, one silver basin weighing seventy shekels, according to the shekel of the sanctuary, both of them full of choice flour mixed with oil for a grain offering; 44one golden dish weighing ten shekels, full of incense; 45one young bull, one ram, one male lamb a year old, for a burnt offering; 46one male goat for a sin offering; 47and for the sacrifice of well-being, two oxen, five rams, five male goats, and five male lambs a year old. This was the offering of Eliasaph son of Deuel.

48 On the seventh day Elishama son of Ammihud, the leader of the Ephraimites: 49his offering was one silver plate weighing one hundred thirty shekels, one silver basin weighing seventy shekels, according to the shekel of the sanctuary, both of them full of choice flour mixed with oil for a grain offering; 50one golden dish weighing ten shekels, full of incense; 51one young bull, one ram, one male lamb a year old, for a burnt offering; 52one male goat for a sin offering; 53and for the sacrifice of well-being, two oxen, five rams, five male goats, and five male lambs a year old. This was the offering of Elishama son of Ammihud.

54 On the eighth day Gamaliel son of Pedahzur, the leader of the Manassites: 55his offering was one silver

King James

⁵⁵His offering *was* one silver charger of the weight of an hundred and thirty *shekels,* one silver bowl of seventy shekels, after the shekel of the sanctuary; both of them full of fine flour mingled with oil for a meat offering:

⁵⁶One golden spoon of ten *shekels,* full of incense:

⁵⁷One young bullock, one ram, one lamb of the first year, for a burnt offering:

⁵⁸One kid of the goats for a sin offering:

⁵⁹And for a sacrifice of peace offerings, two oxen, five rams, five he goats, five lambs of the first year: this *was* the offering of Gamaliel the son of Pedahzur.

⁶⁰¶ On the ninth day Abidan the son of Gideoni, prince of the children of Benjamin, *offered:*

⁶¹His offering *was* one silver charger, the weight whereof *was* an hundred and thirty *shekels,* one silver bowl of seventy shekels, after the shekel of the sanctuary; both of them full of fine flour mingled with oil for a meat offering:

⁶²One golden spoon of ten *shekels,* full of incense:

⁶³One young bullock, one ram, one lamb of the first year, for a burnt offering:

⁶⁴One kid of the goats for a sin offering:

⁶⁵And for a sacrifice of peace offerings, two oxen, five rams, five he goats, five lambs of the first year: this *was* the offering of Abidan the son of Gideoni.

⁶⁶¶ On the tenth day Ahiezer the son of Ammishaddai, prince of the children of Dan, *offered:*

⁶⁷His offering *was* one silver charger, the weight whereof *was* an hundred and thirty *shekels,* one silver bowl of seventy shekels, after the shekel of the sanctuary; both of them full of fine flour mingled with oil for a meat offering:

⁶⁸One golden spoon of ten *shekels,* full of incense:

⁶⁹One young bullock, one ram, one lamb of the first year, for a burnt offering:

⁷⁰One kid of the goats for a sin offering:

⁷¹And for a sacrifice of peace offerings, two oxen, five rams, five he goats, five lambs of the first year: this *was* the offering of Ahiezer the son of Ammishaddai.

⁷²¶ On the eleventh day Pagiel the son of Ocran, prince of the children of Asher, *offered:*

⁷³His offering *was* one silver charger, the weight whereof *was* an hundred and thirty *shekels,* one silver bowl of seventy shekels, after the shekel of the sanctuary; both of them full of fine flour mingled with oil for a meat offering:

⁷⁴One golden spoon of ten *shekels,* full of incense:

⁷⁵One young bullock, one ram, one lamb of the first year, for a burnt offering:

⁷⁶One kid of the goats for a sin offering:

⁷⁷And for a sacrifice of peace offerings, two oxen, five rams, five he goats, five lambs of the first year: this *was* the offering of Pagiel the son of Ocran.

⁷⁸¶ On the twelfth day Ahira the son of Enan, prince of the children of Naphtali, *offered:*

⁷⁹His offering *was* one silver charger, the weight whereof *was* an hundred and thirty *shekels,* one silver bowl of seventy shekels, after the shekel of the sanctuary; both of them full of fine flour mingled with oil for a meat offering:

⁸⁰One golden spoon of ten *shekels,* full of incense:

⁸¹One young bullock, one ram, one lamb of the first year, for a burnt offering:

⁸²One kid of the goats for a sin offering:

⁸³And for a sacrifice of peace offerings, two oxen, five rams, five he goats, five lambs of the first year: this *was* the offering of Ahira the son of Enan.

⁸⁴This *was* the dedication of the altar, in the day when it was anointed, by the princes of Israel: twelve chargers of silver, twelve silver bowls, twelve spoons of gold:

New International

⁵⁵His offering was one silver plate weighing a hundred and thirty shekels, and one silver sprinkling bowl weighing seventy shekels, both according to the sanctuary shekel, each filled with fine flour mixed with oil as a grain offering; ⁵⁶one gold dish weighing ten shekels, filled with incense; ⁵⁷one young bull, one ram and one male lamb a year old, for a burnt offering; ⁵⁸one male goat for a sin offering; ⁵⁹and two oxen, five rams, five male goats and five male lambs a year old, to be sacrificed as a fellowship offering. This was the offering of Gamaliel son of Pedahzur.

⁶⁰On the ninth day Abidan son of Gideoni, the leader of the people of Benjamin, brought his offering.

⁶¹His offering was one silver plate weighing a hundred and thirty shekels, and one silver sprinkling bowl weighing seventy shekels, both according to the sanctuary shekel, each filled with fine flour mixed with oil as a grain offering; ⁶²one gold dish weighing ten shekels, filled with incense; ⁶³one young bull, one ram and one male lamb a year old, for a burnt offering; ⁶⁴one male goat for a sin offering; ⁶⁵and two oxen, five rams, five male goats and five male lambs a year old, to be sacrificed as a fellowship offering. This was the offering of Abidan son of Gideoni.

⁶⁶On the tenth day Ahiezer son of Ammishaddai, the leader of the people of Dan, brought his offering.

⁶⁷His offering was one silver plate weighing a hundred and thirty shekels, and one silver sprinkling bowl weighing seventy shekels, both according to the sanctuary shekel, each filled with fine flour mixed with oil as a grain offering; ⁶⁸one gold dish weighing ten shekels, filled with incense; ⁶⁹one young bull, one ram and one male lamb a year old, for a burnt offering; ⁷⁰one male goat for a sin offering; ⁷¹and two oxen, five rams, five male goats and five male lambs a year old, to be sacrificed as a fellowship offering. This was the offering of Ahiezer son of Ammishaddai.

⁷²On the eleventh day Pagiel son of Ocran, the leader of the people of Asher, brought his offering.

⁷³His offering was one silver plate weighing a hundred and thirty shekels, and one silver sprinkling bowl weighing seventy shekels, both according to the sanctuary shekel, each filled with fine flour mixed with oil as a grain offering; ⁷⁴one gold dish weighing ten shekels, filled with incense; ⁷⁵one young bull, one ram and one male lamb a year old, for a burnt offering; ⁷⁶one male goat for a sin offering; ⁷⁷and two oxen, five rams, five male goats and five male lambs a year old, to be sacrificed as a fellowship offering. This was the offering of Pagiel son of Ocran.

⁷⁸On the twelfth day Ahira son of Enan, the leader of the people of Naphtali, brought his offering.

⁷⁹His offering was one silver plate weighing a hundred and thirty shekels, and one silver sprinkling bowl weighing seventy shekels, both according to the sanctuary shekel, each filled with fine flour mixed with oil as a grain offering; ⁸⁰one gold dish weighing ten shekels, filled with incense; ⁸¹one young bull, one ram and one male lamb a year old, for a burnt offering; ⁸²one male goat for a sin offering; ⁸³and two oxen, five rams, five male goats and five male lambs a year old, to be sacrificed as a fellowship offering. This was the offering of Ahira son of Enan.

⁸⁴These were the offerings of the Israelite leaders for the dedication of the altar when it was anointed: twelve silver plates, twelve silver sprinkling bowls and twelve gold dishes. ⁸⁵Each silver plate weighed a hundred and

Living Bible

60-65On the ninth day it was Abidan the son of Gideoni, chief of the tribe of Benjamin, with his gifts, the same as those offered by the others.

66-71Ahiezer, the son of Ammishaddai, brought his gifts on the tenth day. He was the chief of the tribe of Dan and his offerings were the same as those on the previous days.

72-77Pagiel, son of Ochran, chief of the tribe of Asher, brought his gifts on the eleventh day—the same gifts and offerings as the others.

78-83On the twelfth day came Ahira, son of Enan, chief of the tribe of Naphtali, with his offerings; they were identical to those brought by the others.

New Revised Standard

plate weighing one hundred thirty shekels, one silver basin weighing seventy shekels, according to the shekel of the sanctuary, both of them full of choice flour mixed with oil for a grain offering; 56one golden dish weighing ten shekels, full of incense; 57one young bull, one ram, one male lamb a year old, for a burnt offering; 58one male goat for a sin offering; 59and for the sacrifice of well-being, two oxen, five rams, five male goats, and five male lambs a year old. This was the offering of Gamaliel son of Pedahzur.

60 On the ninth day Abidan son of Gideoni, the leader of the Benjaminites: 61his offering was one silver plate weighing one hundred thirty shekels, one silver basin weighing seventy shekels, according to the shekel of the sanctuary, both of them full of choice flour mixed with oil for a grain offering; 62one golden dish weighing ten shekels, full of incense; 63one young bull, one ram, one male lamb a year old, for a burnt offering; 64one male goat for a sin offering; 65and for the sacrifice of well-being, two oxen, five rams, five male goats, and five male lambs a year old. This was the offering of Abidan son of Gideoni.

66 On the tenth day Ahiezer son of Ammishaddai, the leader of the Danites: 67his offering was one silver plate weighing one hundred thirty shekels, one silver basin weighing seventy shekels, according to the shekel of the sanctuary, both of them full of choice flour mixed with oil for a grain offering; 68one golden dish weighing ten shekels, full of incense; 69one young bull, one ram, one male lamb a year old, for a burnt offering; 70one male goat for a sin offering; 71and for the sacrifice of well-being, two oxen, five rams, five male goats, and five male lambs a year old. This was the offering of Ahiezer son of Ammishaddai.

72 On the eleventh day Pagiel son of Ochran, the leader of the Asherites: 73his offering was one silver plate weighing one hundred thirty shekels, one silver basin weighing seventy shekels, according to the shekel of the sanctuary, both of them full of choice flour mixed with oil for a grain offering; 74one golden dish weighing ten shekels, full of incense; 75one young bull, one ram, one male lamb a year old, for a burnt offering; 76one male goat for a sin offering; 77and for the sacrifice of well-being, two oxen, five rams, five male goats, and five male lambs a year old. This was the offering of Pagiel son of Ochran.

78 On the twelfth day Ahira son of Enan, the leader of the Naphtalites: 79his offering was one silver plate weighing one hundred thirty shekels, one silver basin weighing seventy shekels, according to the shekel of the sanctuary, both of them full of choice flour mixed with oil for a grain offering; 80one golden dish weighing ten shekels, full of incense; 81one young bull, one ram, one male lamb a year old, for a burnt offering; 82one male goat for a sin offering; 83and for the sacrifice of well-being, two oxen, five rams, five male goats, and five male lambs a year old. This was the offering of Ahira son of Enan.

84 This was the dedication offering for the altar, at the time when it was anointed, from the leaders of Israel: twelve silver plates, twelve silver basins, twelve golden dishes, 85each silver plate weighing one hundred thirty

King James

85Each charger of silver *weighing* an hundred and thirty *shekels*, each bowl seventy: all the silver vessels *weighed* two thousand and four hundred *shekels*, after the shekel of the sanctuary:

86The golden spoons *were* twelve, full of incense, *weighing* ten *shekels* apiece, after the shekel of the sanctuary: all the gold of the spoons *was* an hundred and twenty *shekels*.

87All the oxen for the burnt offering *were* twelve bullocks, the rams twelve, the lambs of the first year twelve, with their meat offering: and the kids of the goats for sin offering twelve.

88And all the oxen for the sacrifice of the peace offerings *were* twenty and four bullocks, the rams sixty, the he goats sixty, the lambs of the first year sixty. This *was* the dedication of the altar, after that it was anointed.

89And when Moses was gone into the tabernacle of the congregation to speak with him, then he heard the voice of one speaking unto him from off the mercy seat that *was* upon the ark of testimony, from between the two cherubims: and he spake unto him.

8 AND THE LORD spake unto Moses, saying, 2Speak unto Aaron, and say unto him, When thou lightest the lamps, the seven lamps shall give light over against the candlestick.

3And Aaron did so; he lighted the lamps thereof over against the candlestick, as the LORD commanded Moses.

4And this work of the candlestick *was of* beaten gold, unto the shaft thereof, unto the flowers thereof, *was* beaten work: according unto the pattern which the LORD had shown Moses, so he made the candlestick.

5¶ And the LORD spake unto Moses, saying,

6Take the Levites from among the children of Israel, and cleanse them.

7And thus shalt thou do unto them, to cleanse them: Sprinkle water of purifying upon them, and let them shave all their flesh, and let them wash their clothes, and *so* make themselves clean.

8Then let them take a young bullock with his meat offering, *even* fine flour mingled with oil, and another young bullock shalt thou take for a sin offering.

9And thou shalt bring the Levites before the tabernacle of the congregation: and thou shalt gather the whole assembly of the children of Israel together:

10And thou shalt bring the Levites before the LORD: and the children of Israel shall put their hands upon the Levites:

11And Aaron shall offer the Levites before the LORD *for* an offering of the children of Israel, that they may execute the service of the LORD.

12And the Levites shall lay their hands upon the heads of the bullocks: and thou shalt offer the one *for* a sin offering, and the other *for* a burnt offering, unto the LORD, to make an atonement for the Levites.

13And thou shalt set the Levites before Aaron, and before his sons, and offer them *for* an offering unto the LORD.

14Thus shalt thou separate the Levites from among the children of Israel: and the Levites shall be mine.

15And after that shall the Levites go in to do the service of the tabernacle of the congregation: and thou shalt cleanse them, and offer them *for* an offering.

16For they *are* wholly given unto me from among the children of Israel; instead of such as open every womb, *even instead of* the firstborn of all the children of Israel, have I taken them unto me.

New International

thirty shekels, and each sprinkling bowl seventy shekels. Altogether, the silver dishes weighed two thousand four hundred shekels,[a] according to the sanctuary shekel. 86The twelve gold dishes filled with incense weighed ten shekels each, according to the sanctuary shekel. Altogether, the gold dishes weighed a hundred and twenty shekels.[b] 87The total number of animals for the burnt offering came to twelve young bulls, twelve rams and twelve male lambs a year old, together with their grain offering. Twelve male goats were used for the sin offering. 88The total number of animals for the sacrifice of the fellowship offering came to twenty-four oxen, sixty rams, sixty male goats and sixty male lambs a year old. These were the offerings for the dedication of the altar after it was anointed.

89When Moses entered the Tent of Meeting to speak with the LORD, he heard the voice speaking to him from between the two cherubim above the atonement cover on the ark of the Testimony. And he spoke with him.

Setting Up the Lamps

8 THE LORD said to Moses, 2"Speak to Aaron and say to him, 'When you set up the seven lamps, they are to light the area in front of the lampstand.' "

3Aaron did so; he set up the lamps so that they faced forward on the lampstand, just as the LORD commanded Moses. 4This is how the lampstand was made: It was made of hammered gold—from its base to its blossoms. The lampstand was made exactly like the pattern the LORD had shown Moses.

The Setting Apart of the Levites

5The LORD said to Moses: 6"Take the Levites from among the other Israelites and make them ceremonially clean. 7To purify them, do this: Sprinkle the water of cleansing on them; then have them shave their whole bodies and wash their clothes, and so purify themselves. 8Have them take a young bull with its grain offering of fine flour mixed with oil; then you are to take a second young bull for a sin offering. 9Bring the Levites to the front of the Tent of Meeting and assemble the whole Israelite community. 10You are to bring the Levites before the LORD, and the Israelites are to lay their hands on them. 11Aaron is to present the Levites before the LORD as a wave offering from the Israelites, so that they may be ready to do the work of the LORD.

12"After the Levites lay their hands on the heads of the bulls, use the one for a sin offering to the LORD and the other for a burnt offering, to make atonement for the Levites. 13Have the Levites stand in front of Aaron and his sons and then present them as a wave offering to the LORD. 14In this way you are to set the Levites apart from the other Israelites, and the Levites will be mine.

15"After you have purified the Levites and presented them as a wave offering, they are to come to do their work at the Tent of Meeting. 16They are the Israelites who are to be given wholly to me. I have taken them as my own in place of the firstborn, the first male offspring from every Israelite woman. 17Every firstborn male in

---

a 85 That is, about 60 pounds (about 28 kilograms)   b 86 That is, about 3 pounds (about 1.4 kilograms)

Living Bible

84, 85, 86So, beginning the day the altar was anointed, it was dedicated by these gifts from the chiefs of the tribes of Israel. Their combined offerings were as follows:

12 silver platters (each weighing about three pounds);
12 silver bowls (each weighing about two pounds); (so the total weight of the silver was about sixty pounds);
12 gold trays (the trays weighing about four ounces apiece); (so the total weight of gold was about three pounds).

87For the burnt offerings they brought:
12 bulls, 12 rams,
12 yearling male goats (with the grain offerings that accompanied them).

For sin offerings they brought:
12 male goats.

88For the peace offerings they brought:
24 young bulls,
60 rams, 60 male goats,
60 male lambs one year old.

89When Moses went into the Tabernacle to speak with God, he heard the Voice speaking to him from above the place of mercy over the Ark, between the statues of the two Guardian Angels.

8 THE LORD said to Moses, 2"Tell Aaron that when he lights the seven lamps in the lampstand, he is to set them so that they will throw their light forward."

3So Aaron did this. 4The lampstand, including the floral decorations on the base and branches, was made entirely of beaten gold. It was constructed according to the exact design the Lord had shown Moses.

5, 6Then the Lord said to Moses, "Now set apart the Levites from the other people of Israel. 7Do this by sprinkling water of purification upon them, then having them shave their entire bodies and wash their clothing and themselves. 8Have them bring a young bull and a grain offering of fine flour mingled with oil, along with another young bull for a sin offering. 9Then bring the Levites to the door of the Tabernacle as all the people watch. 10There the leadersc of the tribes shall lay their hands upon them, 11and Aaron, with a gesture of offering, shall present them to the Lord as a gift from the entire nation of Israel. The Levites will represent all the people in serving the Lord.

12"Next, the Levite leaders shall lay their hands upon the heads of the young bulls and offer them before the Lord; one for a sin offering and the other for a burnt offering, to make atonement for the Levites. 13Then the Levites are to be presented to Aaron and his sons, just as any other gift to the Lord is given to the priests! 14In this way you will dedicate the Levites from among the rest of the people of Israel, and the Levites shall be mine. 15After you have sanctified them and presented them in this way, they shall go in and out of the Tabernacle to do their work.

16"They are mine from among all the people of Israel, and I have accepted them in place of all the firstborn children of the Israelites: I have taken the Levites as their substitutes. 17For all the firstborn among the people of

New Revised Standard

shekels and each basin seventy, all the silver of the vessels two thousand four hundred shekels according to the shekel of the sanctuary, 86the twelve golden dishes, full of incense, weighing ten shekels apiece according to the shekel of the sanctuary, all the gold of the dishes being one hundred twenty shekels; 87all the livestock for the burnt offering twelve bulls, twelve rams, twelve male lambs a year old, with their grain offering; and twelve male goats for a sin offering; 88and all the livestock for the sacrifice of well-being twenty-four bulls, the rams sixty, the male goats sixty, the male lambs a year old sixty. This was the dedication offering for the altar, after it was anointed.

89 When Moses went into the tent of meeting to speak with the LORD,d he would hear the voice speaking to him from above the mercy seate that was on the ark of the covenantf from between the two cherubim; thus it spoke to him.

The Seven Lamps

8 THE LORD spoke to Moses, saying: 2Speak to Aaron and say to him: When you set up the lamps, the seven lamps shall give light in front of the lampstand. 3Aaron did so; he set up its lamps to give light in front of the lampstand, as the LORD had commanded Moses. 4Now this was how the lampstand was made, out of hammered work of gold. From its base to its flowers, it was hammered work; according to the pattern that the LORD had shown Moses, so he made the lampstand.

Consecration and Service of the Levites

5 The LORD spoke to Moses, saying: 6Take the Levites from among the Israelites and cleanse them. 7Thus you shall do to them, to cleanse them: sprinkle the water of purification on them, have them shave their whole body with a razor and wash their clothes, and so cleanse themselves. 8Then let them take a young bull and its grain offering of choice flour mixed with oil, and you shall take another young bull for a sin offering. 9You shall bring the Levites before the tent of meeting, and assemble the whole congregation of the Israelites. 10When you bring the Levites before the LORD, the Israelites shall lay their hands on the Levites, 11and Aaron shall present the Levites before the LORD as an elevation offering from the Israelites, that they may do the service of the LORD. 12The Levites shall lay their hands on the heads of the bulls, and he shall offer the one for a sin offering and the other for a burnt offering to the LORD, to make atonement for the Levites. 13Then you shall have the Levites stand before Aaron and his sons, and you shall present them as an elevation offering to the LORD.

14 Thus you shall separate the Levites from among the other Israelites, and the Levites shall be mine. 15Thereafter the Levites may go in to do service at the tent of meeting, once you have cleansed them and presented them as an elevation offering. 16For they are unreservedly given to me from among the Israelites; I have taken them for myself, in place of all that open the womb, the firstborn of all the Israelites. 17For all the

---

c *8:10 There the leaders,* implied. Also in vs 12.

d Heb *him*   e Or *the cover*   f Or *treaty,* or *testimony;* Heb *eduth*

King James

17For all the firstborn of the children of Israel *are* mine, *both* man and beast: on the day that I smote every firstborn in the land of Egypt I sanctified them for myself.

18And I have taken the Levites for all the firstborn of the children of Israel.

19And I have given the Levites *as* a gift to Aaron and to his sons from among the children of Israel, to do the service of the children of Israel in the tabernacle of the congregation, and to make an atonement for the children of Israel: that there be no plague among the children of Israel, when the children of Israel come nigh unto the sanctuary.

20And Moses, and Aaron, and all the congregation of the children of Israel, did to the Levites according unto all that the LORD commanded Moses concerning the Levites, so did the children of Israel unto them.

21And the Levites were purified, and they washed their clothes; and Aaron offered them *as* an offering before the LORD; and Aaron made an atonement for them to cleanse them.

22And after that went the Levites in to do their service in the tabernacle of the congregation before Aaron, and before his sons: as the LORD had commanded Moses concerning the Levites, so did they unto them.

23¶ And the LORD spake unto Moses, saying,

24This *is it* that *belongeth* unto the Levites: from twenty and five years old and upward they shall go in to wait upon the service of the tabernacle of the congregation:

25And from the age of fifty years they shall cease waiting upon the service *thereof*, and shall serve no more:

26But shall minister with their brethren in the tabernacle of the congregation, to keep the charge, and shall do no service. Thus shalt thou do unto the Levites touching their charge.

9 AND THE LORD spake unto Moses in the wilderness of Sinai, in the first month of the second year after they were come out of the land of Egypt, saying,

2Let the children of Israel also keep the passover at his appointed season.

3In the fourteenth day of this month, at even, ye shall keep it in his appointed season: according to all the rites of it, and according to all the ceremonies thereof, shall ye keep it.

4And Moses spake unto the children of Israel, that they should keep the passover.

5And they kept the passover on the fourteenth day of the first month at even in the wilderness of Sinai: according to all that the LORD commanded Moses, so did the children of Israel.

6¶ And there were certain men, who were defiled by the dead body of a man, that they could not keep the passover on that day: and they came before Moses and before Aaron on that day:

7And those men said unto him, We *are* defiled by the dead body of a man: wherefore are we kept back, that we may not offer an offering of the LORD in his appointed season among the children of Israel?

8And Moses said unto them, Stand still, and I will hear what the LORD will command concerning you.

9¶ And the LORD spake unto Moses, saying,

10Speak unto the children of Israel, saying, If any man of you or of your posterity shall be unclean by reason of a dead body, or *be* in a journey afar off, yet he shall keep the passover unto the LORD.

11The fourteenth day of the second month at even they shall keep it, *and* eat it with unleavened bread and bitter *herbs*.

New International

Israel, whether man or animal, is mine. When I struck down all the firstborn in Egypt, I set them apart for myself. 18And I have taken the Levites in place of all the firstborn sons in Israel. 19Of all the Israelites, I have given the Levites as gifts to Aaron and his sons to do the work at the Tent of Meeting on behalf of the Israelites and to make atonement for them so that no plague will strike the Israelites when they go near the sanctuary."

20Moses, Aaron and the whole Israelite community did with the Levites just as the LORD commanded Moses. 21The Levites purified themselves and washed their clothes. Then Aaron presented them as a wave offering before the LORD and made atonement for them to purify them. 22After that, the Levites came to do their work at the Tent of Meeting under the supervision of Aaron and his sons. They did with the Levites just as the LORD commanded Moses.

23The LORD said to Moses, 24"This applies to the Levites: Men twenty-five years old or more shall come to take part in the work at the Tent of Meeting, 25but at the age of fifty, they must retire from their regular service and work no longer. 26They may assist their brothers in performing their duties at the Tent of Meeting, but they themselves must not do the work. This, then, is how you are to assign the responsibilities of the Levites."

The Passover

9 THE LORD spoke to Moses in the Desert of Sinai in the first month of the second year after they came out of Egypt. He said, 2"Have the Israelites celebrate the Passover at the appointed time. 3Celebrate it at the appointed time, at twilight on the fourteenth day of this month, in accordance with all its rules and regulations."

4So Moses told the Israelites to celebrate the Passover, 5and they did so in the Desert of Sinai at twilight on the fourteenth day of the first month. The Israelites did everything just as the LORD commanded Moses.

6But some of them could not celebrate the Passover on that day because they were ceremonially unclean on account of a dead body. So they came to Moses and Aaron that same day 7and said to Moses, "We have become unclean because of a dead body, but why should we be kept from presenting the LORD's offering with the other Israelites at the appointed time?"

8Moses answered them, "Wait until I find out what the LORD commands concerning you."

9Then the LORD said to Moses, 10"Tell the Israelites: 'When any of you or your descendants are unclean because of a dead body or are away on a journey, they may still celebrate the LORD's Passover. 11They are to celebrate it on the fourteenth day of the second month at twilight. They are to eat the lamb, together with unleavened bread and bitter herbs. 12They must not leave any

Living Bible

Israel are mine, both men and animals; I claimed them for myself the night I killed all the firstborn Egyptians. 18Yes, I have accepted the Levites in place of all the eldest sons of Israel. 19And I will give the Levites as a gift to Aaron and his sons. The Levites will carry out the sacred duties required of the people of Israel in the Tabernacle, and will offer the people's sacrifices, making atonement for them. There will be no plague among the Israelites—as there would be if the ordinary people entered the Tabernacle."

20So Moses and Aaron and all the people of Israel dedicated the Levites, carefully following Jehovah's instructions to Moses. 21The Levites purified themselves and washed their clothes, and Aaron presented them to the Lord in a gesture of offering. He then performed the rite of atonement over them to purify them. 22After that they went into the Tabernacle as assistants to Aaron and his sons; everything was done just as the Lord had commanded Moses.

23, 24The Lord also instructed Moses, "The Levites are to begin serving in the Tabernacle at the age of twenty-five, and are to retire at the age of fifty. 25, 26After retirement they can assist with various light duties in the Tabernacle, but will have no regular responsibilities."

9 JEHOVAH GAVE these instructions to Moses while he and the rest of the Israelis were on the Sinai peninsula, during the first month of the second year after leaving Egypt:

2, 3"The people of Israel must celebrate the Passover annually on April first,a beginning in the evening. Be sure to follow all of my instructions concerning this celebration."

4, 5So Moses announced that the Passover celebration would begin on the evening of April first, there in the Sinai peninsula, just as the Lord had commanded. 6, 7But as it happened, some of the men had just attended a funeral, and were ceremonially defiled by having touched the dead, so they couldn't eat the Passover lamb that night. They came to Moses and Aaron and explained their problem and protested at being forbidden from offering their sacrifice to the Lord at the time he had appointed.

8Moses said he would ask the Lord about it, 9and this was God's reply:

10"If any of the people of Israel, now or in the generations to come, are defiled at Passover time because of touching a dead body, or if they are on a journey and cannot be present, they may still celebrate the Passover, but one month later, 11on May first,b beginning in the evening. They are to eat the lamb at that time, with unleavened bread and bitter herbs. 12They must not

New Revised Standard

firstborn among the Israelites are mine, both human and animal. On the day that I struck down all the firstborn in the land of Egypt I consecrated them for myself, 18but I have taken the Levites in place of all the firstborn among the Israelites. 19Moreover, I have given the Levites as a gift to Aaron and his sons from among the Israelites, to do the service for the Israelites at the tent of meeting, and to make atonement for the Israelites, in order that there may be no plague among the Israelites for coming too close to the sanctuary.

20 Moses and Aaron and the whole congregation of the Israelites did with the Levites accordingly; the Israelites did with the Levites just as the LORD had commanded Moses concerning them. 21The Levites purified themselves from sin and washed their clothes; then Aaron presented them as an elevation offering before the LORD, and Aaron made atonement for them to cleanse them. 22Thereafter the Levites went in to do their service in the tent of meeting in attendance on Aaron and his sons. As the LORD had commanded Moses concerning the Levites, so they did with them.

23 The LORD spoke to Moses, saying: 24This applies to the Levites: from twenty-five years old and upward they shall begin to do duty in the service of the tent of meeting; 25and from the age of fifty years they shall retire from the duty of the service and serve no more. 26They may assist their brothers in the tent of meeting in carrying out their duties, but they shall perform no service. Thus you shall do with the Levites in assigning their duties.

The Passover at Sinai

9 THE LORD spoke to Moses in the wilderness of Sinai, in the first month of the second year after they had come out of the land of Egypt, saying: 2Let the Israelites keep the passover at its appointed time. 3On the fourteenth day of this month, at twilight,c you shall keep it at its appointed time; according to all its statutes and all its regulations you shall keep it. 4So Moses told the Israelites that they should keep the passover. 5They kept the passover in the first month, on the fourteenth day of the month, at twilight,c in the wilderness of Sinai. Just as the LORD had commanded Moses, so the Israelites did. 6Now there were certain people who were unclean through touching a corpse, so that they could not keep the passover on that day. They came before Moses and Aaron on that day, 7and said to him, "Although we are unclean through touching a corpse, why must we be kept from presenting the LORD's offering at its appointed time among the Israelites?" 8Moses spoke to them, "Wait, so that I may hear what the LORD will command concerning you."

9 The LORD spoke to Moses, saying: 10Speak to the Israelites, saying: Anyone of you or your descendants who is unclean through touching a corpse, or is away on a journey, shall still keep the passover to the LORD. 11In the second month on the fourteenth day, at twilight,c they shall keep it; they shall eat it with unleavened bread and bitter herbs. 12They shall leave none of it until

---

a 9:2, 3 on April first, literally, "on the fourteenth day of the first month" (of the Hebrew calendar). This corresponds approximately to our first day of April.   b 9:11 May first, literally, "on the fourteenth day of the second month" (of the Hebrew calendar).

c Heb between the two evenings

King James

¹²They shall leave none of it unto the morning, nor break any bone of it: according to all the ordinances of the passover they shall keep it.

¹³But the man that *is* clean, and is not in a journey, and forbeareth to keep the passover, even the same soul shall be cut off from among his people: because he brought not the offering of the LORD in his appointed season, that man shall bear his sin.

¹⁴And if a stranger shall sojourn among you, and will keep the passover unto the LORD; according to the ordinance of the passover, and according to the manner thereof, so shall he do: ye shall have one ordinance, both for the stranger, and for him that was born in the land.

¹⁵¶ And on the day that the tabernacle was reared up the cloud covered the tabernacle, *namely,* the tent of the testimony: and at even there was upon the tabernacle as it were the appearance of fire, until the morning.

¹⁶So it was always: the cloud covered it *by day,* and the appearance of fire by night.

¹⁷And when the cloud was taken up from the tabernacle, then after that the children of Israel journeyed: and in the place where the cloud abode, there the children of Israel pitched their tents.

¹⁸At the commandment of the LORD the children of Israel journeyed, and at the commandment of the LORD they pitched: as long as the cloud abode upon the tabernacle they rested in their tents.

¹⁹And when the cloud tarried long upon the tabernacle many days, then the children of Israel kept the charge of the LORD, and journeyed not.

²⁰And *so* it was, when the cloud was a few days upon the tabernacle; according to the commandment of the LORD they abode in their tents, and according to the commandment of the LORD they journeyed.

²¹And *so* it was, when the cloud abode from even unto the morning, and *that* the cloud was taken up in the morning, then they journeyed: whether *it was* by day or by night that the cloud was taken up, they journeyed.

²²Or *whether it were* two days, or a month, or a year, that the cloud tarried upon the tabernacle, remaining thereon, the children of Israel abode in their tents, and journeyed not: but when it was taken up, they journeyed.

²³At the commandment of the LORD they rested in the tents, and at the commandment of the LORD they journeyed: they kept the charge of the LORD, at the commandment of the LORD by the hand of Moses.

10 AND THE LORD spake unto Moses, saying, ²Make thee two trumpets of silver; of a whole piece shalt thou make them: that thou mayest use them for the calling of the assembly, and for the journeying of the camps.

³And when they shall blow with them, all the assembly shall assemble themselves to thee at the door of the tabernacle of the congregation.

⁴And if they blow *but* with one *trumpet,* then the princes, *which are* heads of the thousands of Israel, shall gather themselves unto thee.

⁵When ye blow an alarm, then the camps that lie on the east parts shall go forward.

⁶When ye blow an alarm the second time, then the camps that lie on the south side shall take their journey: they shall blow an alarm for their journeys.

⁷But when the congregation is to be gathered together, ye shall blow, but ye shall not sound an alarm.

⁸And the sons of Aaron, the priests, shall blow with the trumpets; and they shall be to you for an ordinance for ever throughout your generations.

⁹And if ye go to war in your land against the enemy that oppresseth you, then ye shall blow an alarm with the trumpets; and ye shall be remembered before the LORD your God, and ye shall be saved from your enemies.

New International

of it till morning or break any of its bones. When they celebrate the Passover, they must follow all the regulations. ¹³But if a man who is ceremonially clean and not on a journey fails to celebrate the Passover, that person must be cut off from his people because he did not present the LORD's offering at the appointed time. That man will bear the consequences of his sin.

¹⁴"'An alien living among you who wants to celebrate the LORD's Passover must do so in accordance with its rules and regulations. You must have the same regulations for the alien and the native-born.'"

The Cloud Above the Tabernacle

¹⁵On the day the tabernacle, the Tent of the Testimony, was set up, the cloud covered it. From evening till morning the cloud above the tabernacle looked like fire. ¹⁶That is how it continued to be; the cloud covered it, and at night it looked like fire. ¹⁷Whenever the cloud lifted from above the Tent, the Israelites set out; wherever the cloud settled, the Israelites encamped. ¹⁸At the LORD's command the Israelites set out, and at his command they encamped. As long as the cloud stayed over the tabernacle, they remained in camp. ¹⁹When the cloud remained over the tabernacle a long time, the Israelites obeyed the LORD's order and did not set out. ²⁰Sometimes the cloud was over the tabernacle only a few days; at the LORD's command they would encamp, and then at his command they would set out. ²¹Sometimes the cloud stayed only from evening till morning, and when it lifted in the morning, they set out. Whether by day or by night, whenever the cloud lifted, they set out. ²²Whether the cloud stayed over the tabernacle for two days or a month or a year, the Israelites would remain in camp and not set out; but when it lifted, they would set out. ²³At the LORD's command they encamped, and at the LORD's command they set out. They obeyed the LORD's order, in accordance with his command through Moses.

The Silver Trumpets

10 THE LORD said to Moses: ²"Make two trumpets of hammered silver, and use them for calling the community together and for having the camps set out. ³When both are sounded, the whole community is to assemble before you at the entrance to the Tent of Meeting. ⁴If only one is sounded, the leaders—the heads of the clans of Israel—are to assemble before you. ⁵When a trumpet blast is sounded, the tribes camping on the east are to set out. ⁶At the sounding of a second blast, the camps on the south are to set out. The blast will be the signal for setting out. ⁷To gather the assembly, blow the trumpets, but not with the same signal.

⁸"The sons of Aaron, the priests, are to blow the trumpets. This is to be a lasting ordinance for you and the generations to come. ⁹When you go into battle in your own land against an enemy who is oppressing you, sound a blast on the trumpets. Then you will be remembered by the LORD your God and rescued from your enemies. ¹⁰Also at your times of rejoicing—your ap-

Living Bible

leave any of it until the next morning, and must not break a bone of it, and must follow all the regular instructions concerning the Passover.

13"But anyone who is not defiled, and anyone who is not away on a trip, and yet refuses to celebrate the Passover at the regular time, shall be excommunicated from the people of Israel for refusing to sacrifice to Jehovah at the proper time; he must bear his guilt. 14And if a foreigner is living among you and wants to celebrate the Passover to the Lord, he shall follow all these same instructions. There is one law for all."

15On the day the Tabernacle was raised, the Cloud covered it; and that evening the Cloud changed to the appearance of fire, and stayed that way throughout the night. 16It was always so—the daytime Cloud changing to the appearance of fire at night. 17When the Cloud lifted, the people of Israel moved on to wherever it stopped, and camped there. 18In this way they journeyed at the command of the Lord and stopped where he told them to, then remained there as long as the Cloud stayed. 19If it stayed a long time, then they stayed a long time. But if it stayed only a few days, then they remained only a few days; for so the Lord had instructed them. 20, 21Sometimes the fire-cloud stayed only during the night and moved on the next morning. But day or night, when it moved, the people broke camp and followed. 22If the Cloud stayed above the Tabernacle two days, a month, or a year, that is how long the people of Israel stayed; but as soon as it moved, they moved. 23So it was that they camped or traveled at the commandment of the Lord; and whatever the Lord told Moses they should do, they did.

10 NOW THE Lord said to Moses, "Make two trumpets of beaten silver to be used for summoning the people to assemble and for signaling the breaking of camp. 3When both trumpets are blown, the people will know that they are to gather at the entrance of the Tabernacle. 4But if only one is blown, then only the chiefs of the tribes of Israel shall come to you. 5, 6, 7"Different trumpet blasts will be necessary to distinguish between the summons to assemble and the signal to break camp and move onward.ᵃ When the travel signal is blown, the tribes camped on the east side of the Tabernacle shall leave first; at the second signal, the tribes on the south shall go. 8Only the priests are permitted to blow the trumpets. This is a permanent instruction to be followed from generation to generation.

9"When you arrive in the Promised Land and go to war against your enemies, God will hear you and save you from your enemies when you sound the alarm with these trumpets. 10Use the trumpets in times of gladness,

New Revised Standard

morning, nor break a bone of it; according to all the statute for the passover they shall keep it. 13But anyone who is clean and is not on a journey, and yet refrains from keeping the passover, shall be cut off from the people for not presenting the LORD's offering at its appointed time; such a one shall bear the consequences for the sin. 14Any alien residing among you who wishes to keep the passover to the LORD shall do so according to the statute of the passover and according to its regulation; you shall have one statute for both the resident alien and the native.

The Cloud and the Fire

15 On the day the tabernacle was set up, the cloud covered the tabernacle, the tent of the covenant;ᵇ and from evening until morning it was over the tabernacle, having the appearance of fire. 16It was always so: the cloud covered it by dayᶜ and the appearance of fire by night. 17Whenever the cloud lifted from over the tent, then the Israelites would set out; and in the place where the cloud settled down, there the Israelites would camp. 18At the command of the LORD the Israelites would set out, and at the command of the LORD they would camp. As long as the cloud rested over the tabernacle, they would remain in camp. 19Even when the cloud continued over the tabernacle many days, the Israelites would keep the charge of the LORD, and would not set out. 20Sometimes the cloud would remain a few days over the tabernacle, and according to the command of the LORD they would remain in camp; then according to the command of the LORD they would set out. 21Sometimes the cloud would remain from evening until morning; and when the cloud lifted in the morning, they would set out, or if it continued for a day and a night, when the cloud lifted they would set out. 22Whether it was two days, or a month, or a longer time, that the cloud continued over the tabernacle, resting upon it, the Israelites would remain in camp and would not set out; but when it lifted they would set out. 23At the command of the LORD they would camp, and at the command of the LORD they would set out. They kept the charge of the LORD, at the command of the LORD by Moses.

The Silver Trumpets

10 THE LORD spoke to Moses, saying: 2Make two silver trumpets; you shall make them of hammered work; and you shall use them for summoning the congregation, and for breaking camp. 3When both are blown, the whole congregation shall assemble before you at the entrance of the tent of meeting. 4But if only one is blown, then the leaders, the heads of the tribes of Israel, shall assemble before you. 5When you blow an alarm, the camps on the east side shall set out; 6when you blow a second alarm, the camps on the south side shall set out. An alarm is to be blown whenever they are to set out. 7But when the assembly is to be gathered, you shall blow, but you shall not sound an alarm. 8The sons of Aaron, the priests, shall blow the trumpets; this shall be a perpetual institution for you throughout your generations. 9When you go to war in your land against the adversary who oppresses you, you shall sound an alarm with the trumpets, so that you may be remembered before the LORD your God and be saved from your enemies. 10Also on your days of rejoicing, at your appoint-

---

ᵃ 10:5-7 and the signal to break the camp and move onward, more literally, vs 7 reads: "But when the Assembly is to be gathered together, you shall blow but you shall not sound the alarm."

ᵇ Or treaty, or testimony; Heb eduth   ᶜ Gk Syr Vg: Heb lacks by day

King James

10Also in the day of your gladness, and in your solemn days, and in the beginnings of your months, ye shall blow with the trumpets over your burnt offerings, and over the sacrifices of your peace offerings; that they may be to you for a memorial before your God: I *am* the LORD your God.

11¶ And it came to pass on the twentieth *day* of the second month, in the second year, that the cloud was taken up from off the tabernacle of the testimony.

12And the children of Israel took their journeys out of the wilderness of Sinai; and the cloud rested in the wilderness of Paran.

13And they first took their journey according to the commandment of the LORD by the hand of Moses.

14¶ In the first *place* went the standard of the camp of the children of Judah according to their armies: and over his host *was* Nahshon the son of Amminadab.

15And over the host of the tribe of the children of Issachar *was* Nethaneel the son of Zuar.

16And over the host of the tribe of the children of Zebulun *was* Eliab the son of Helon.

17And the tabernacle was taken down; and the sons of Gershon and the sons of Merari set forward, bearing the tabernacle.

18¶ And the standard of the camp of Reuben set forward according to their armies: and over his host *was* Elizur the son of Shedeur.

19And over the host of the tribe of the children of Simeon *was* Shelumiel the son of Zurishaddai.

20And over the host of the tribe of the children of Gad *was* Eliasaph the son of Deuel.

21And the Kohathites set forward, bearing the sanctuary: and *the other* did set up the tabernacle against they came.

22¶ And the standard of the camp of the children of Ephraim set forward according to their armies: and over his host *was* Elishama the son of Ammihud.

23And over the host of the tribe of the children of Manasseh *was* Gamaliel the son of Pedahzur.

24And over the host of the tribe of the children of Benjamin *was* Abidan the son of Gideoni.

25¶ And the standard of the camp of the children of Dan set forward, *which was* the rearward of all the camps throughout their hosts: and over his host *was* Ahiezer the son of Ammishaddai.

26And over the host of the tribe of the children of Asher *was* Pagiel the son of Ocran.

27And over the host of the tribe of the children of Naphtali *was* Ahira the son of Enan.

28Thus *were* the journeyings of the children of Israel according to their armies, when they set forward.

29¶ And Moses said unto Hobab, the son of Raguel the Midianite, Moses' father-in-law, We are journeying unto the place of which the LORD said, I will give it you: come thou with us, and we will do thee good: for the LORD hath spoken good concerning Israel.

30And he said unto him, I will not go; but I will depart to mine own land, and to my kindred.

31And he said, Leave us not, I pray thee; forasmuch as thou knowest how we are to encamp in the wilderness, and thou mayest be to us instead of eyes.

32And it shall be, if thou go with us, yea, it shall be, that what goodness the LORD shall do unto us, the same will we do unto thee.

33¶ And they departed from the mount of the LORD three days' journey: and the ark of the covenant of the LORD went before them in the three days' journey, to search out a resting place for them.

34And the cloud of the LORD *was* upon them by day, when they went out of the camp.

35And it came to pass, when the ark set forward, that Moses said, Rise up, LORD, and let thine enemies be scattered; and let them that hate thee flee before thee.

36And when it rested, he said, Return, O LORD, unto the many thousands of Israel.

New International

pointed feasts and New Moon festivals—you are to sound the trumpets over your burnt offerings and fellowship offerings,a and they will be a memorial for you before your God. I am the LORD your God."

The Israelites Leave Sinai

11On the twentieth day of the second month of the second year, the cloud lifted from above the tabernacle of the Testimony. 12Then the Israelites set out from the Desert of Sinai and traveled from place to place until the cloud came to rest in the Desert of Paran. 13They set out, this first time, at the LORD's command through Moses.

14The divisions of the camp of Judah went first, under their standard. Nahshon son of Amminadab was in command. 15Nethanel son of Zuar was over the division of the tribe of Issachar, 16and Eliab son of Helon was over the division of the tribe of Zebulun. 17Then the tabernacle was taken down, and the Gershonites and Merarites, who carried it, set out.

18The divisions of the camp of Reuben went next, under their standard. Elizur son of Shedeur was in command. 19Shelumiel son of Zurishaddai was over the division of the tribe of Simeon, 20and Eliasaph son of Deuel was over the division of the tribe of Gad. 21Then the Kohathites set out, carrying the holy things. The tabernacle was to be set up before they arrived.

22The divisions of the camp of Ephraim went next, under their standard. Elishama son of Ammihud was in command. 23Gamaliel son of Pedahzur was over the division of the tribe of Manasseh, 24and Abidan son of Gideoni was over the division of the tribe of Benjamin.

25Finally, as the rear guard for all the units, the divisions of the camp of Dan set out, under their standard. Ahiezer son of Ammishaddai was in command. 26Pagiel son of Ocran was over the division of the tribe of Asher, 27and Ahira son of Enan was over the division of the tribe of Naphtali. 28This was the order of march for the Israelite divisions as they set out.

29Now Moses said to Hobab son of Reuel the Midianite, Moses' father-in-law, "We are setting out for the place about which the LORD said, 'I will give it to you.' Come with us and we will treat you well, for the LORD has promised good things to Israel."

30He answered, "No, I will not go; I am going back to my own land and my own people."

31But Moses said, "Please do not leave us. You know where we should camp in the desert, and you can be our eyes. 32If you come with us, we will share with you whatever good things the LORD gives us."

33So they set out from the mountain of the LORD and traveled for three days. The ark of the covenant of the LORD went before them during those three days to find them a place to rest. 34The cloud of the LORD was over them by day when they set out from the camp.

35Whenever the ark set out, Moses said,

"Rise up, O LORD!
 May your enemies be scattered;
 may your foes flee before you."

36Whenever it came to rest, he said,

"Return, O LORD,
 to the countless thousands of Israel."

a 10 Traditionally *peace offerings*

Living Bible

too, blowing them at your annual festivals and at the beginning of each month to rejoice over your burnt offerings and peace offerings. And God will be reminded of his covenant with you. For I am Jehovah, your God."

11The Cloud lifted from the Tabernacle on the twentieth day of the second month[b] of the second year of Israel's leaving Egypt; 12so the Israelites left the Sinai wilderness, and followed the Cloud until it stopped in the wilderness of Paran. 13This was their first journey after having received the Lord's travel instructions to Moses.

14At the head of the march was the tribe of Judah grouped behind its flag, and led by Nahshon, the son of Amminadab. 15Next came the tribe of Issachar, led by Nethanel, the son of Zuar, 16and the tribe of Zebulun, led by Eliab, the son of Helon.

17The Tabernacle was taken down and the men of the Gershon and Merari divisions of the tribe of Levi were next in the line of march, carrying the Tabernacle upon their shoulders. 18Then came the flag of the camp of Reuben, with Elizur the son of Shedeur leading his people. 19Next was the tribe of Simeon headed by Shelumiel, the son of Zuri-shaddai; 20and the tribe of Gad led by Eliasaph, the son of Deuel.

21Next came the Kohathites carrying the items from the inner sanctuary. (The Tabernacle was already erected in its new location by the time they arrived.) 22Next in line was the tribe of Ephraim behind its flag, led by Elishama, the son of Ammihud, 23and the tribe of Manasseh led by Gamaliel the son of Pedahzur; 24and the tribe of Benjamin, led by Abidan the son of Gideoni. 25Last of all were the tribes headed by the flag of the tribe of Dan under the leadership of Ahiezer, son of Ammishaddai; 26the tribe of Asher, led by Pagiel, the son of Ochran; 27and the tribe of Naphtali, led by Ahira, the son of Enan. 28That was the order in which the tribes traveled.

29One day Moses said to his brother-in-law Hobab (son of Reuel, the Midianite), "At last we are on our way to the Promised Land. Come with us and we will do you good; for the Lord has given wonderful promises to Israel!"

30But his brother-in-law replied, "No, I must return to my own land and kinfolk."

31"Stay with us," Moses pleaded, "for you know the ways of the wilderness and will be a great help to us.[c] 32If you come, you will share in all the good things the Lord does for us."

33They traveled for three days after leaving Mount Sinai,[d] with the Ark at the front of the column to choose a place for them to stop. 34It was daytime when they left, with the Cloud moving along ahead of them as they began their march. 35As the Ark was carried forward, Moses cried out, "Arise, O Lord, and scatter your enemies; let them flee before you." 36And when the Ark was set down he said, "Return, O Lord, to the millions of Israel."

New Revised Standard

ed festivals, and at the beginnings of your months, you shall blow the trumpets over your burnt offerings and over your sacrifices of well-being; they shall serve as a reminder on your behalf before the LORD your God: I am the LORD your God.

Departure from Sinai

11 In the second year, in the second month, on the twentieth day of the month, the cloud lifted from over the tabernacle of the covenant.[e] 12Then the Israelites set out by stages from the wilderness of Sinai, and the cloud settled down in the wilderness of Paran. 13They set out for the first time at the command of the LORD by Moses. 14The standard of the camp of Judah set out first, company by company, and over the whole company was Nahshon son of Amminadab. 15Over the company of the tribe of Issachar was Nethanel son of Zuar; 16and over the company of the tribe of Zebulun was Eliab son of Helon.

17 Then the tabernacle was taken down, and the Gershonites and the Merarites, who carried the tabernacle, set out. 18Next the standard of the camp of Reuben set out, company by company; and over the whole company was Elizur son of Shedeur. 19Over the company of the tribe of Simeon was Shelumiel son of Zurishaddai, 20and over the company of the tribe of Gad was Eliasaph son of Deuel.

21 Then the Kohathites, who carried the holy things, set out; and the tabernacle was set up before their arrival. 22Next the standard of the Ephraimite camp set out, company by company, and over the whole company was Elishama son of Ammihud. 23Over the company of the tribe of Manasseh was Gamaliel son of Pedahzur, 24and over the company of the tribe of Benjamin was Abidan son of Gideoni.

25 Then the standard of the camp of Dan, acting as the rear guard of all the camps, set out, company by company, and over the whole company was Ahiezer son of Ammishaddai. 26Over the company of the tribe of Asher was Pagiel son of Ochran, 27and over the company of the tribe of Naphtali was Ahira son of Enan. 28This was the order of march of the Israelites, company by company, when they set out.

29 Moses said to Hobab son of Reuel the Midianite, Moses' father-in-law, "We are setting out for the place of which the LORD said, 'I will give it to you'; come with us, and we will treat you well; for the LORD has promised good to Israel." 30But he said to him, "I will not go, but I will go back to my own land and to my kindred." 31He said, "Do not leave us, for you know where we should camp in the wilderness, and you will serve as eyes for us. 32Moreover, if you go with us, whatever good the LORD does for us, the same we will do for you."

33 So they set out from the mount of the LORD three days' journey with the ark of the covenant of the LORD going before them three days' journey, to seek out a resting place for them, 34the cloud of the LORD being over them by day when they set out from the camp.

35 Whenever the ark set out, Moses would say,
"Arise, O LORD, let your enemies be
 scattered,
 and your foes flee before you."
36And whenever it came to rest, he would say,
"Return, O LORD of the ten thousand
 thousands of Israel."[f]

---

b 10:11 on the twentieth day of the second month, (of the Hebrew Calendar), this was approximately May 5. c 10:31 for you know the ways of the wilderness and will be a great help to us, literally, "you know how we are to encamp in the wilderness, and you will serve as eyes for us." d 10:33 Mount Sinai, literally, "the mount of Jehovah."

e Or treaty, or testimony; Heb eduth f Meaning of Heb uncertain

King James

11 AND *WHEN* the people complained, it displeased the LORD: and the LORD heard *it;* and his anger was kindled; and the fire of the LORD burnt among them, and consumed *them that were* in the uttermost parts of the camp.

2And the people cried unto Moses; and when Moses prayed unto the LORD, the fire was quenched.

3And he called the name of the place Taberah: because the fire of the LORD burnt among them.

4¶ And the mixed multitude that *was* among them fell a-lusting: and the children of Israel also wept again, and said, Who shall give us flesh to eat?

5We remember the fish, which we did eat in Egypt freely; the cucumbers, and the melons, and the leeks, and the onions, and the garlic:

6But now our soul *is* dried away: *there is* nothing at all, beside this manna, *before* our eyes.

7And the manna *was* as coriander seed, and the colour thereof as the colour of bdellium.

8*And* the people went about, and gathered *it,* and ground *it* in mills, or beat *it* in a mortar, and baked *it* in pans, and made cakes of it: and the taste of it was as the taste of fresh oil.

9And when the dew fell upon the camp in the night, the manna fell upon it.

10¶ Then Moses heard the people weep throughout their families, every man in the door of his tent: and the anger of the LORD was kindled greatly; Moses also was displeased.

11And Moses said unto the LORD, Wherefore hast thou afflicted thy servant? and wherefore have I not found favour in thy sight, that thou layest the burden of all this people upon me?

12Have I conceived all this people? have I begotten them, that thou shouldest say unto me, Carry them in thy bosom, as a nursing father beareth the sucking child, unto the land which thou swarest unto their fathers?

13Whence should I have flesh to give unto all this people? for they weep unto me, saying, Give us flesh, that we may eat.

14I am not able to bear all this people alone, because *it is* too heavy for me.

15And if thou deal thus with me, kill me, I pray thee, out of hand, if I have found favour in thy sight; and let me not see my wretchedness.

16¶ And the LORD said unto Moses, Gather unto me seventy men of the elders of Israel, whom thou knowest to be the elders of the people, and officers over them; and bring them unto the tabernacle of the congregation, that they may stand there with thee.

17And I will come down and talk with thee there: and I will take of the spirit which *is* upon thee, and will put *it* upon them; and they shall bear the burden of the people with thee, that thou bear *it* not thyself alone.

18And say thou unto the people, Sanctify yourselves against tomorrow, and ye shall eat flesh: for ye have wept in the ears of the LORD, saying, Who shall give us flesh to eat? for *it was* well with us in Egypt: therefore the LORD will give you flesh, and ye shall eat.

19Ye shall not eat one day, nor two days, nor five days, neither ten days, nor twenty days;

20*But* even a whole month, until it come out at your nostrils, and it be loathsome unto you: because that ye have despised the LORD which *is* among you, and have wept before him, saying, Why came we forth out of Egypt?

21And Moses said, The people, among whom I *am, are* six hundred thousand footmen; and thou hast said, I will give them flesh, that they may eat a whole month.

22Shall the flocks and the herds be slain for them, to suffice them? or shall all the fish of the sea be gathered together for them, to suffice them?

New International

Fire From the LORD

11 NOW THE people complained about their hardships in the hearing of the LORD, and when he heard them his anger was aroused. Then fire from the LORD burned among them and consumed some of the outskirts of the camp. 2When the people cried out to Moses, he prayed to the LORD and the fire died down. 3So that place was called Taberah,[a] because fire from the LORD had burned among them.

Quail From the LORD

4The rabble with them began to crave other food, and again the Israelites started wailing and said, "If only we had meat to eat! 5We remember the fish we ate in Egypt at no cost—also the cucumbers, melons, leeks, onions and garlic. 6But now we have lost our appetite; we never see anything but this manna!"

7The manna was like coriander seed and looked like resin. 8The people went around gathering it, and then ground it in a handmill or crushed it in a mortar. They cooked it in a pot or made it into cakes. And it tasted like something made with olive oil. 9When the dew settled on the camp at night, the manna also came down.

10Moses heard the people of every family wailing, each at the entrance to his tent. The LORD became exceedingly angry, and Moses was troubled. 11He asked the LORD, "Why have you brought this trouble on your servant? What have I done to displease you that you put the burden of all these people on me? 12Did I conceive all these people? Did I give them birth? Why do you tell me to carry them in my arms, as a nurse carries an infant, to the land you promised on oath to their forefathers? 13Where can I get meat for all these people? They keep wailing to me, 'Give us meat to eat!' 14I cannot carry all these people by myself; the burden is too heavy for me. 15If this is how you are going to treat me, put me to death right now—if I have found favor in your eyes—and do not let me face my own ruin."

16The LORD said to Moses: "Bring me seventy of Israel's elders who are known to you as leaders and officials among the people. Have them come to the Tent of Meeting, that they may stand there with you. 17I will come down and speak with you there, and I will take of the Spirit that is on you and put the Spirit on them. They will help you carry the burden of the people so that you will not have to carry it alone.

18"Tell the people: 'Consecrate yourselves in preparation for tomorrow, when you will eat meat. The LORD heard you when you wailed, "If only we had meat to eat! We were better off in Egypt!" Now the LORD will give you meat, and you will eat it. 19You will not eat it for just one day, or two days, or five, ten or twenty days, 20but for a whole month—until it comes out of your nostrils and you loathe it—because you have rejected the LORD, who is among you, and have wailed before him, saying, "Why did we ever leave Egypt?" ' "

21But Moses said, "Here I am among six hundred thousand men on foot, and you say, 'I will give them meat to eat for a whole month!' 22Would they have enough if flocks and herds were slaughtered for them? Would they have enough if all the fish in the sea were caught for them?"

Living Bible

11 THE PEOPLE were soon complaining about all their misfortunes, and the Lord heard them. His anger flared out against them because of their complaints, so the fire of the Lord began destroying those at the far end of the camp. ²They screamed to Moses for help, and when he prayed for them the fire stopped. ³Ever after, the area was known as "The Place of Burning,"ᵇ because the fire from the Lord burned among them there.

⁴, ⁵Then the Egyptians who had come with them began to long for the good things of Egypt. This added to the discontent of the people of Israel and they wept, "Oh, for a few bites of meat! Oh, that we had some of the delicious fish we enjoyed so much in Egypt, and the wonderful cucumbers and melons, leeks, onions, and garlic! ⁶But now our strength is gone, and day after day we have to face this manna!"

⁷The manna was the size of small seeds, whitish yellow in color. ⁸The people gathered it from the ground and pounded it into flour, then boiled it, and then made pancakes from it—they tasted like pancakes fried in vegetable oil.ᶜ ⁹The manna fell with the dew during the night.

¹⁰Moses heard all the families standing around their tent doors weeping, and the anger of the Lord grew hot; Moses too was highly displeased.

¹¹Moses said to the Lord, "Why pick on me, to give me the burden of a people like this? ¹²Are they *my* children? Am I their father? Is that why you have given me the job of nursing them along like babies until we get to the land you promised their ancestors? ¹³Where am I supposed to get meat for all these people? For they weep to me saying, 'Give us meat!' ¹⁴I can't carry this nation by myself! The load is far too heavy! ¹⁵If you are going to treat me like this, please kill me right now; it will be a kindness! Let me out of this impossible situation!"

¹⁶Then the Lord said to Moses, "Summon before me seventy of the leaders of Israel; bring them to the Tabernacle, to stand there with you. ¹⁷I will come down and talk with you there and I will take of the Spirit which is on you and will put it upon them also; they shall bear the burden of the people along with you, so that you will not have the task alone.

¹⁸"And tell the people to purify themselves, for tomorrow they shall have meat to eat. Tell them, 'The Lord has heard your tearful complaints about all you left behind in Egypt, and he is going to give you meat. You shall eat it, ¹⁹, ²⁰not for just a day or two, or five or ten or even twenty! For one whole month you will have meat until you vomit it from your noses; for you have rejected the Lord who is here among you, and you have wept for Egypt.' "

²¹But Moses said, "There are 600,000 men alone [besides all the women and childrenᵈ], and yet you promise them meat for a whole month! ²²If we butcher all our flocks and herds it won't be enough! We would have to catch every fish in the ocean to fulfill your promise!"

New Revised Standard

Complaining in the Desert

11 NOW WHEN the people complained in the hearing of the LORD about their misfortunes, the LORD heard it and his anger was kindled. Then the fire of the LORD burned against them, and consumed some outlying parts of the camp. ²But the people cried out to Moses; and Moses prayed to the LORD, and the fire abated. ³So that place was called Taberah,ᵉ because the fire of the LORD burned against them.

4 The rabble among them had a strong craving; and the Israelites also wept again, and said, "If only we had meat to eat! ⁵We remember the fish we used to eat in Egypt for nothing, the cucumbers, the melons, the leeks, the onions, and the garlic; ⁶but now our strength is dried up, and there is nothing at all but this manna to look at."

7 Now the manna was like coriander seed, and its color was like the color of gum resin. ⁸The people went around and gathered it, ground it in mills or beat it in mortars, then boiled it in pots and made cakes of it; and the taste of it was like the taste of cakes baked with oil. ⁹When the dew fell on the camp in the night, the manna would fall with it.

10 Moses heard the people weeping throughout their families, all at the entrances of their tents. Then the LORD became very angry, and Moses was displeased. ¹¹So Moses said to the LORD, "Why have you treated your servant so badly? Why have I not found favor in your sight, that you lay the burden of all this people on me? ¹²Did I conceive all this people? Did I give birth to them, that you should say to me, 'Carry them in your bosom, as a nurse carries a sucking child,' to the land that you promised on oath to their ancestors? ¹³Where am I to get meat to give to all this people? For they come weeping to me and say, 'Give us meat to eat!' ¹⁴I am not able to carry all this people alone, for they are too heavy for me. ¹⁵If this is the way you are going to treat me, put me to death at once—if I have found favor in your sight—and do not let me see my misery."

The Seventy Elders

16 So the LORD said to Moses, "Gather for me seventy of the elders of Israel, whom you know to be the elders of the people and officers over them; bring them to the tent of meeting, and have them take their place there with you. ¹⁷I will come down and talk with you there; and I will take some of the spirit that is on you and put it on them; and they shall bear the burden of the people along with you so that you will not bear it all by yourself. ¹⁸And say to the people: Consecrate yourselves for tomorrow, and you shall eat meat; for you have wailed in the hearing of the LORD, saying, 'If only we had meat to eat! Surely it was better for us in Egypt.' Therefore the LORD will give you meat, and you shall eat. ¹⁹You shall eat not only one day, or two days, or five days, or ten days, or twenty days, ²⁰but for a whole month—until it comes out of your nostrils and becomes loathsome to you—because you have rejected the LORD who is among you, and have wailed before him, saying, 'Why did we ever leave Egypt?' " ²¹But Moses said, "The people I am with number six hundred thousand on foot; and you say, 'I will give them meat, that they may eat for a whole month'! ²²Are there enough flocks and herds to slaughter for them? Are there enough fish in the sea to catch for them?" ²³The LORD said to Moses, "Is

ᵇ 11:3 *The Place of Burning,* literally, "Taberah."   ᶜ *11:8 vegetable oil,* literally, "olive oil."   ᵈ *11:21 besides all the women and children,* implied.   ᵉ That is *Burning*

King James

23And the LORD said unto Moses, Is the LORD's hand waxed short? thou shalt see now whether my word shall come to pass unto thee or not.

24¶ And Moses went out, and told the people the words of the LORD, and gathered the seventy men of the elders of the people, and set them round about the tabernacle.

25And the LORD came down in a cloud, and spake unto him, and took of the spirit that *was* upon him, and gave *it* unto the seventy elders: and it came to pass, *that,* when the spirit rested upon them, they prophesied, and did not cease.

26But there remained two *of the* men in the camp, the name of the one *was* Eldad, and the name of the other Medad: and the spirit rested upon them; and they *were* of them that were written, but went not out unto the tabernacle: and they prophesied in the camp.

27And there ran a young man, and told Moses, and said, Eldad and Medad do prophesy in the camp.

28And Joshua the son of Nun, the servant of Moses, *one* of his young men, answered and said, My lord Moses, forbid them.

29And Moses said unto him, Enviest thou for my sake? would God that all the LORD's people were prophets, *and* that the LORD would put his spirit upon them!

30And Moses gat him into the camp, he and the elders of Israel.

31¶ And there went forth a wind from the LORD, and brought quails from the sea, and let *them* fall by the camp, as it were a day's journey on this side, and as it were a day's journey on the other side, round about the camp, and as it were two cubits *high* upon the face of the earth.

32And the people stood up all that day, and all *that* night, and all the next day, and they gathered the quails: he that gathered least gathered ten homers: and they spread *them* all abroad for themselves round about the camp.

33And while the flesh *was* yet between their teeth, ere it was chewed, the wrath of the LORD was kindled against the people, and the LORD smote the people with a very great plague.

34And he called the name of that place Kibroth-hattaavah: because there they buried the people that lusted.

35*And* the people journeyed from Kibroth-hattaavah unto Hazeroth; and abode at Hazeroth.

12 AND MIRIAM and Aaron spake against Moses because of the Ethiopian woman whom he had married: for he had married an Ethiopian woman.

2And they said, Hath the LORD indeed spoken only by Moses? hath he not spoken also by us? And the LORD heard *it.*

3(Now the man Moses *was* very meek, above all the men which *were* upon the face of the earth.)

4And the LORD spake suddenly unto Moses, and unto Aaron, and unto Miriam, Come out ye three unto the tabernacle of the congregation. And they three came out.

5And the LORD came down in the pillar of the cloud, and stood *in* the door of the tabernacle, and called Aaron and Miriam: and they both came forth.

6And he said, Hear now my words: If there be a prophet among you, *I* the LORD will make myself known unto him in a vision, *and* will speak unto him in a dream.

New International

23The LORD answered Moses, "Is the LORD's arm too short? You will now see whether or not what I say will come true for you."

24So Moses went out and told the people what the LORD had said. He brought together seventy of their elders and had them stand around the Tent. 25Then the LORD came down in the cloud and spoke with him, and he took of the Spirit that was on him and put the Spirit on the seventy elders. When the Spirit rested on them, they prophesied, but they did not do so again.[a]

26However, two men, whose names were Eldad and Medad, had remained in the camp. They were listed among the elders, but did not go out to the Tent. Yet the Spirit also rested on them, and they prophesied in the camp. 27A young man ran and told Moses, "Eldad and Medad are prophesying in the camp."

28Joshua son of Nun, who had been Moses' aide since youth, spoke up and said, "Moses, my lord, stop them!"

29But Moses replied, "Are you jealous for my sake? I wish that all the LORD's people were prophets and that the LORD would put his Spirit on them!" 30Then Moses and the elders of Israel returned to the camp.

31Now a wind went out from the LORD and drove quail in from the sea. It brought them[b] down all around the camp to about three feet[c] above the ground, as far as a day's walk in any direction. 32All that day and night and all the next day the people went out and gathered quail. No one gathered less than ten homers.[d] Then they spread them out all around the camp. 33But while the meat was still between their teeth and before it could be consumed, the anger of the LORD burned against the people, and he struck them with a severe plague. 34Therefore the place was named Kibroth Hattaavah,[e] because there they buried the people who had craved other food.

35From Kibroth Hattaavah the people traveled to Hazeroth and stayed there.

Miriam and Aaron Oppose Moses

12 MIRIAM AND Aaron began to talk against Moses because of his Cushite wife, for he had married a Cushite. 2"Has the LORD spoken only through Moses?" they asked. "Hasn't he also spoken through us?" And the LORD heard this.

3(Now Moses was a very humble man, more humble than anyone else on the face of the earth.)

4At once the LORD said to Moses, Aaron and Miriam, "Come out to the Tent of Meeting, all three of you." So the three of them came out. 5Then the LORD came down in a pillar of cloud; he stood at the entrance to the Tent and summoned Aaron and Miriam. When both of them stepped forward, 6he said, "Listen to my words:

"When a prophet of the LORD is among you,
   I reveal myself to him in visions,
   I speak to him in dreams.

a 25 Or *prophesied and continued to do so* b 31 Or *They flew* c 31 Hebrew *two cubits* (about 1 meter) d 32 That is, probably about 60 bushels (about 2.2 kiloliters) e 34 *Kibroth Hattaavah* means *graves of craving.*

Living Bible

23Then the Lord said to Moses, "When did I become weak? Now you shall see whether my word comes true or not!"

24So Moses left the Tabernacle and reported Jehovah's words to the people; and he gathered the seventy elders and placed them around the Tabernacle. 25And the Lord came down in the Cloud and talked with Moses, and the Lord took of the Spirit that was upon Moses and put it upon the seventy elders; and when the Spirit rested upon them, they prophesied for some time.

26But two of the seventy—Eldad and Medad—were still in the camp, and when the Spirit rested upon them, they prophesied there. 27Some young men ran and told Moses what was happening, 28and Joshua (the son of Nun), one of Moses' personally chosen assistants, protested, "Sir, make them stop!"

29But Moses replied, "Are you jealous for my sake? I only wish that all of the Lord's people were prophets, and that the Lord would put his Spirit upon them all!" 30Then Moses returned to the camp with the elders of Israel.

31The Lord sent a wind that brought quail from the sea, and let them fall into the camp and all around it! As far as one could walk in a day in any direction, there were quail flying three or four feet above the ground.f 32So the people caught and killed quail all that day and through the night and all the next day too! The least anyone gathered was 100 bushels! Quail were spread out all aroundg the camp. 33But as everyone began eating the meat, the anger of the Lord rose against the people and he killed large numbers of them with a plague. 34So the name of that place was called, "The Place of the Graves Caused by Lust,"h because they buried the people there who had lusted for meat and for Egypt. 35And from that place they journeyed to Hazeroth, where they stayed awhile.

12 ONE DAY Miriam and Aaron were criticizing Moses because his wife was a Cushitei woman, 2and they said, "Has the Lord spoken only through Moses? Hasn't he spoken through us, too?"

But the Lord heard them. 3, 4Immediately he summoned Moses, Aaron, and Miriam to the Tabernacle: "Come here, you three," he commanded. So they stood before the Lord. (Now Moses was the humblest man on earth.)

5Then the Lord descended in the Cloud and stood at the entrance of the Tabernacle. "Aaron and Miriam, step forward," he commanded; and they did. 6And the Lord said to them, "Even with a prophet, I would communicate by visions and dreams; 7, 8but that is not how I

f 11:31 there were quail flying three or four feet above the ground, or, "The ground was covered with them, three feet thick." g 11:32 quail were spread out all around. To cure them by drying. h 11:34 The Place of the Graves caused by Lust, literally, "Kibroth-hattaavah." i 12:1 Cushite woman, literally "because of the Cushite woman he had married." Apparently they were referring to his wife Zipporah, the Midianite daughter of Reuel (Ex 2:21); for the land of Midian from which she came was sometimes called Cush. But areas of Ethiopia and Babylon were also known as Cush, so it is possible that the reference is to a second wife of Moses. It is indeterminate from the text whether she was criticized for being a Gentile, or (if she was a Cushite from Ethiopia) because of her color.

New Revised Standard

the LORD's power limited?j Now you shall see whether my word will come true for you or not."

24 So Moses went out and told the people the words of the LORD; and he gathered seventy elders of the people, and placed them all around the tent. 25Then the LORD came down in the cloud and spoke to him, and took some of the spirit that was on him and put it on the seventy elders; and when the spirit rested upon them, they prophesied. But they did not do so again.

26 Two men remained in the camp, one named Eldad, and the other named Medad, and the spirit rested on them; they were among those registered, but they had not gone out to the tent, and so they prophesied in the camp. 27And a young man ran and told Moses, "Eldad and Medad are prophesying in the camp." 28And Joshua son of Nun, the assistant of Moses, one of his chosen men,k said, "My lord Moses, stop them!" 29But Moses said to him, "Are you jealous for my sake? Would that all the LORD's people were prophets, and that the LORD would put his spirit on them!" 30And Moses and the elders of Israel returned to the camp.

The Quails

31 Then a wind went out from the LORD, and it brought quails from the sea and let them fall beside the camp, about a day's journey on this side and a day's journey on the other side, all around the camp, about two cubits deep on the ground. 32So the people worked all that day and night and all the next day, gathering the quails; the least anyone gathered was ten homers; and they spread them out for themselves all around the camp. 33But while the meat was still between their teeth, before it was consumed, the anger of the LORD was kindled against the people, and the LORD struck the people with a very great plague. 34So that place was called Kibroth-hattaavah,l because there they buried the people who had the craving. 35From Kibroth-hattaavah the people journeyed to Hazeroth.

Aaron and Miriam Jealous of Moses

12 WHILE THEY were at Hazeroth, Miriam and Aaron spoke against Moses because of the Cushite woman whom he had married (for he had indeed married a Cushite woman); 2and they said, "Has the LORD spoken only through Moses? Has he not spoken through us also?" And the LORD heard it. 3Now the man Moses was very humble,m more so than anyone else on the face of the earth. 4Suddenly the LORD said to Moses, Aaron, and Miriam, "Come out, you three, to the tent of meeting." So the three of them came out. 5Then the LORD came down in a pillar of cloud, and stood at the entrance of the tent, and called Aaron and Miriam; and they both came forward. 6And he said, "Hear my words:

When there are prophets among you,
I the LORD make myself known to them in visions;
I speak to them in dreams.

j Heb LORD's hand too short? k Or of Moses from his youth l That is Graves of craving m Or devout

King James

7My servant Moses *is* not so, who *is* faithful in all mine house.

8With him will I speak mouth to mouth, even apparently, and not in dark speeches; and the similitude of the LORD shall he behold: wherefore then were ye not afraid to speak against my servant Moses?

9And the anger of the LORD was kindled against them; and he departed.

10And the cloud departed from off the tabernacle; and, behold, Miriam *became* leprous, *white* as snow: and Aaron looked upon Miriam, and, behold, *she was* leprous.

11And Aaron said unto Moses, Alas, my lord, I beseech thee, lay not the sin upon us, wherein we have done foolishly, and wherein we have sinned.

12Let her not be as one dead, of whom the flesh is half consumed when he cometh out of his mother's womb.

13And Moses cried unto the LORD, saying, Heal her now, O God, I beseech thee.

14¶ And the LORD said unto Moses, If her father had but spit in her face, should she not be ashamed seven days? let her be shut out from the camp seven days, and after that let her be received in *again*.

15And Miriam was shut out from the camp seven days: and the people journeyed not till Miriam was brought in *again*.

16And afterward the people removed from Hazeroth, and pitched in the wilderness of Paran.

13 AND THE LORD spake unto Moses, saying, 2Send thou men, that they may search the land of Canaan, which I give unto the children of Israel: of every tribe of their fathers shall ye send a man, every one a ruler among them.

3And Moses by the commandment of the LORD sent them from the wilderness of Paran: all those men *were* heads of the children of Israel.

4And these *were* their names: of the tribe of Reuben, Shammua the son of Zaccur.

5Of the tribe of Simeon, Shaphat the son of Hori.

6Of the tribe of Judah, Caleb the son of Jephunneh.

7Of the tribe of Issachar, Igal the son of Joseph.

8Of the tribe of Ephraim, Oshea the son of Nun.

9Of the tribe of Benjamin, Palti the son of Raphu.

10Of the tribe of Zebulun, Gaddiel the son of Sodi.

11Of the tribe of Joseph, *namely*, of the tribe of Manasseh, Gaddi the son of Susi.

12Of the tribe of Dan, Ammiel the son of Gemalli.

13Of the tribe of Asher, Sethur the son of Michael.

14Of the tribe of Naphtali, Nahbi the son of Vophsi.

15Of the tribe of Gad, Geuel the son of Machi.

16These *are* the names of the men which Moses sent to spy out the land. And Moses called Oshea the son of Nun Jehoshua.

17¶ And Moses sent them to spy out the land of Canaan, and said unto them, Get you up this *way* southward, and go up into the mountain:

18And see the land, what it *is;* and the people that dwelleth therein, whether they *be* strong or weak, few or many;

19And what the land *is* that they dwell in, whether it *be* good or bad; and what cities *they be* that they dwell in, whether in tents, or in strong holds;

20And what the land *is*, whether it *be* fat or lean, whether there be wood therein, or not. And be ye of good courage, and bring of the fruit of the land. Now the time *was* the time of the firstripe grapes.

21¶ So they went up, and searched the land from the wilderness of Zin unto Rehob, as men come to Hamath.

New International

7But this is not true of my servant Moses;
he is faithful in all my house.
8With him I speak face to face,
clearly and not in riddles;
he sees the form of the LORD.
Why then were you not afraid
to speak against my servant Moses?"

9The anger of the LORD burned against them, and he left them.

10When the cloud lifted from above the Tent, there stood Miriam—leprous,a like snow. Aaron turned toward her and saw that she had leprosy; 11and he said to Moses, "Please, my lord, do not hold against us the sin we have so foolishly committed. 12Do not let her be like a stillborn infant coming from its mother's womb with its flesh half eaten away."

13So Moses cried out to the LORD, "O God, please heal her!"

14The LORD replied to Moses, "If her father had spit in her face, would she not have been in disgrace for seven days? Confine her outside the camp for seven days; after that she can be brought back." 15So Miriam was confined outside the camp for seven days, and the people did not move on till she was brought back.

16After that, the people left Hazeroth and encamped in the Desert of Paran.

Exploring Canaan

13 THE LORD said to Moses, 2"Send some men to explore the land of Canaan, which I am giving to the Israelites. From each ancestral tribe send one of its leaders."

3So at the LORD's command Moses sent them out from the Desert of Paran. All of them were leaders of the Israelites. 4These are their names:

from the tribe of Reuben, Shammua son of Zaccur;
5from the tribe of Simeon, Shaphat son of Hori;
6from the tribe of Judah, Caleb son of Jephunneh;
7from the tribe of Issachar, Igal son of Joseph;
8from the tribe of Ephraim, Hoshea son of Nun;
9from the tribe of Benjamin, Palti son of Raphu;
10from the tribe of Zebulun, Gaddiel son of Sodi;
11from the tribe of Manasseh (a tribe of Joseph),
Gaddi son of Susi;
12from the tribe of Dan, Ammiel son of Gemalli;
13from the tribe of Asher, Sethur son of Michael;
14from the tribe of Naphtali, Nahbi son of Vophsi;
15from the tribe of Gad, Geuel son of Maki.

16These are the names of the men Moses sent to explore the land. (Moses gave Hoshea son of Nun the name Joshua.)

17When Moses sent them to explore Canaan, he said, "Go up through the Negev and on into the hill country. 18See what the land is like and whether the people who live there are strong or weak, few or many. 19What kind of land do they live in? Is it good or bad? What kind of towns do they live in? Are they unwalled or fortified? 20How is the soil? Is it fertile or poor? Are there trees on it or not? Do your best to bring back some of the fruit of the land." (It was the season for the first ripe grapes.)

21So they went up and explored the land from the Desert of Zin as far as Rehob, toward Lebob Hamath.

---

a *10* The Hebrew word was used for various diseases affecting the skin—not necessarily leprosy.   b *21* Or *toward the entrance to*

Living Bible

communicate with my servant Moses. He is completely at home in my house! With him I speak face to face! And he shall see the very form of God! Why then were you not afraid to criticize him?"

9Then the anger of the Lord grew hot against them, and he departed. 10As the Cloud moved from above the Tabernacle, Miriam suddenly became white with leprosy. When Aaron saw what had happened, 11he cried out to Moses, "Oh, sir, do not punish us for this sin; we were fools to do such a thing. 12Don't let her be as one dead, whose body is half rotted away at birth."

13And Moses cried out to the Lord, "Heal her, O God, I beg you!"

14And the Lord said to Moses, "If her father had but spit in her face she would be defiled seven days. Let her be banished from the camp for seven days, and after that she can come back again."

15So Miriam was excluded from the camp for seven days, and the people waited until she was brought back in before they traveled again. 16Afterwards they left Hazeroth and camped in the wilderness of Paran.

13 JEHOVAH NOW instructed Moses, 2"Send spies into the land of Canaan—the land I am giving to Israel; send one leader from each tribe."

3-15(The Israelis were camped in the wilderness of Paran at the time.) Moses did as the Lord had commanded and sent these twelve tribal leaders:

Shammu-a, son of Zaccur, from the tribe of Reuben;
Shaphat, son of Hori, from the tribe of Simeon;
Caleb, son of Jephunneh, from the tribe of Judah;
Igal, son of Joseph, from the tribe of Issachar;
Hoshea,c son of Nun, from the half-tribe of Ephraim;
Palti, son of Raphu, from the tribe of Benjamin;
Gaddiel, son of Sodi, from the tribe of Zebulun;
Gaddi, son of Susi, from the tribe of Joseph (actually, the half-tribe of Manasseh);
Ammiel, son of Gemalli, from the tribe of Dan;
Sethur, son of Michael, from the tribe of Asher;
Nahbi, son of Vophsi, from the tribe of Naphtali;
Geuel, son of Machi, from the tribe of Gad.

16It was at this time that Moses changed Hoshea's name to Joshua.d

17Moses sent them out with these instructions: "Go northward into the hill country of the Negeb, 18and see what the land is like; see also what the people are like who live there, whether they are strong or weak, many or few; 19and whether the land is fertile or not; and what cities there are, and whether they are villages or are fortified; 20whether the land is rich or poor, and whether there are many trees. Don't be afraid, and bring back some samples of the crops you see." (The first of the grapes were being harvested at that time.)

21So they spied the land all the way from the wilderness of Zin to Rehob near Hamath. 22Going north-

New Revised Standard

7 Not so with my servant Moses;
  he is entrusted with all my house.
8 With him I speak face to face—
  clearly, not in riddles;
  and he beholds the form of the LORD.
Why then were you not afraid to speak against my servant Moses?" 9And the anger of the LORD was kindled against them, and he departed.

10 When the cloud went away from over the tent, Miriam had become leprous,e as white as snow. And Aaron turned towards Miriam and saw that she was leprous. 11Then Aaron said to Moses, "Oh, my lord, do not punish usf for a sin that we have so foolishly committed. 12Do not let her be like one stillborn, whose flesh is half consumed when it comes out of its mother's womb." 13And Moses cried to the LORD, "O God, please heal her." 14But the LORD said to Moses, "If her father had but spit in her face, would she not bear her shame for seven days? Let her be shut out of the camp for seven days, and after that she may be brought in again." 15So Miriam was shut out of the camp for seven days; and the people did not set out on the march until Miriam had been brought in again. 16After that the people set out from Hazeroth, and camped in the wilderness of Paran.

Spies Sent into Canaan

13 THE LORD said to Moses, 2"Send men to spy out the land of Canaan, which I am giving to the Israelites; from each of their ancestral tribes you shall send a man, every one a leader among them." 3So Moses sent them from the wilderness of Paran, according to the command of the LORD, all of them leading men among the Israelites. 4These were their names: From the tribe of Reuben, Shammua son of Zaccur; 5from the tribe of Simeon, Shaphat son of Hori; 6from the tribe of Judah, Caleb son of Jephunneh; 7from the tribe of Issachar, Igal son of Joseph; 8from the tribe of Ephraim, Hoshea son of Nun; 9from the tribe of Benjamin, Palti son of Raphu; 10from the tribe of Zebulun, Gaddiel son of Sodi; 11from the tribe of Joseph (that is, from the tribe of Manasseh), Gaddi son of Susi; 12from the tribe of Dan, Ammiel son of Gemalli; 13from the tribe of Asher, Sethur son of Michael; 14from the tribe of Naphtali, Nahbi son of Vophsi; 15from the tribe of Gad, Geuel son of Machi. 16These were the names of the men whom Moses sent to spy out the land. And Moses changed the name of Hoshea son of Nun to Joshua.

17 Moses sent them to spy out the land of Canaan, and said to them, "Go up there into the Negeb, and go up into the hill country, 18and see what the land is like, and whether the people who live in it are strong or weak, whether they are few or many, 19and whether the land they live in is good or bad, and whether the towns that they live in are unwalled or fortified, 20and whether the land is rich or poor, and whether there are trees in it or not. Be bold, and bring some of the fruit of the land." Now it was the season of the first ripe grapes.

21 So they went up and spied out the land from the wilderness of Zin to Rehob, near Lebo-hamath. 22They

---

c 13:3-15 Hoshea, or, "Joshua." See verse 16.   d 13:16 Moses changed Hoshea's name to Joshua. "Hoshea" means "salvation;" "Joshua" means "Jehovah is salvation." Joshua is the same name in Hebrew as the Greek name "Jesus."

e A term for several skin diseases; precise meaning uncertain   f Heb do not lay sin upon us

King James

22And they ascended by the south, and came unto Hebron; where Ahiman, Sheshai, and Talmai, the children of Anak, *were*. (Now Hebron was built seven years before Zoan in Egypt.)

23And they came unto the brook of Eshcol, and cut down from thence a branch with one cluster of grapes, and they bare it between two upon a staff; and *they brought* of the pomegranates, and of the figs.

24The place was called the brook Eshcol, because of the cluster of grapes which the children of Israel cut down from thence.

25And they returned from searching of the land after forty days.

26¶ And they went and came to Moses, and to Aaron, and to all the congregation of the children of Israel, unto the wilderness of Paran, to Kadesh; and brought back word unto them, and unto all the congregation, and showed them the fruit of the land.

27And they told him, and said, We came unto the land whither thou sentest us, and surely it floweth with milk and honey; and this *is* the fruit of it.

28Nevertheless the people *be* strong that dwell in the land, and the cities *are* walled, *and* very great: and moreover we saw the children of Anak there.

29The Amalekites dwell in the land of the south: and the Hittites, and the Jebusites, and the Amorites, dwell in the mountains: and the Canaanites dwell by the sea, and by the coast of Jordan.

30And Caleb stilled the people before Moses, and said, Let us go up at once, and possess it; for we are well able to overcome it.

31But the men that went up with him said, We be not able to go up against the people; for they *are* stronger than we.

32And they brought up an evil report of the land which they had searched unto the children of Israel, saying, The land, through which we have gone to search it, *is* a land that eateth up the inhabitants thereof; and all the people that we saw in it *are* men of a great stature.

33And there we saw the giants, the sons of Anak, *which come* of the giants: and we were in our own sight as grasshoppers, and so we were in their sight.

14 AND ALL the congregation lifted up their voice, and cried; and the people wept that night.

2And all the children of Israel murmured against Moses and against Aaron: and the whole congregation said unto them, Would God that we had died in the land of Egypt! or would God we had died in this wilderness!

3And wherefore hath the LORD brought us unto this land, to fall by the sword, that our wives and our children should be a prey? were it not better for us to return into Egypt?

4And they said one to another, Let us make a captain, and let us return into Egypt.

5Then Moses and Aaron fell on their faces before all the assembly of the congregation of the children of Israel.

6¶ And Joshua the son of Nun, and Caleb the son of Jephunneh, *which were* of them that searched the land, rent their clothes:

7And they spake unto all the company of the children of Israel, saying, The land, which we passed through to search it, *is* an exceeding good land.

8If the LORD delight in us, then he will bring us into this land, and give us; a land which floweth with milk and honey.

9Only rebel not ye against the LORD, neither fear ye the people of the land; for they *are* bread for us: their defence is departed from them, and the LORD *is* with us: fear them not.

New International

22They went up through the Negev and came to Hebron, where Ahiman, Sheshai and Talmai, the descendants of Anak, lived. (Hebron had been built seven years before Zoan in Egypt.) 23When they reached the Valley of Eshcol,a they cut off a branch bearing a single cluster of grapes. Two of them carried it on a pole between them, along with some pomegranates and figs. 24That place was called the Valley of Eshcol because of the cluster of grapes the Israelites cut off there. 25At the end of forty days they returned from exploring the land.

Report on the Exploration

26They came back to Moses and Aaron and the whole Israelite community at Kadesh in the Desert of Paran. There they reported to them and to the whole assembly and showed them the fruit of the land. 27They gave Moses this account: "We went into the land to which you sent us, and it does flow with milk and honey! Here is its fruit. 28But the people who live there are powerful, and the cities are fortified and very large. We even saw descendants of Anak there. 29The Amalekites live in the Negev; the Hittites, Jebusites and Amorites live in the hill country; and the Canaanites live near the sea and along the Jordan."

30Then Caleb silenced the people before Moses and said, "We should go up and take possession of the land, for we can certainly do it."

31But the men who had gone up with him said, "We can't attack those people; they are stronger than we are." 32And they spread among the Israelites a bad report about the land they had explored. They said, "The land we explored devours those living in it. All the people we saw there are of great size. 33We saw the Nephilim there (the descendants of Anak come from the Nephilim). We seemed like grasshoppers in our own eyes, and we looked the same to them."

The People Rebel

14 THAT NIGHT all the people of the community raised their voices and wept aloud. 2All the Israelites grumbled against Moses and Aaron, and the whole assembly said to them, "If only we had died in Egypt! Or in this desert! 3Why is the LORD bringing us to this land only to let us fall by the sword? Our wives and children will be taken as plunder. Wouldn't it be better for us to go back to Egypt?" 4And they said to each other, "We should choose a leader and go back to Egypt."

5Then Moses and Aaron fell facedown in front of the whole Israelite assembly gathered there. 6Joshua son of Nun and Caleb son of Jephunneh, who were among those who had explored the land, tore their clothes 7and said to the entire Israelite assembly, "The land we passed through and explored is exceedingly good. 8If the LORD is pleased with us, he will lead us into that land, a land flowing with milk and honey, and will give it to us. 9Only do not rebel against the LORD. And do not be afraid of the people of the land, because we will swallow them up. Their protection is gone, but the LORD is with us. Do not be afraid of them."

a 23 *Eshcol* means *cluster*; also in verse 24.

Living Bible

ward, they passed first through the Negeb and arrived at Hebron. There they saw the Ahimanites, Sheshites, and Talmites, all families descended from Anak. (By the way, Hebron was very ancient, having been founded seven years before Tanis[b] in Egypt). 23Then they came to what is now known as the Valley of Eshcol where they cut down a single cluster of grapes so large that it took two of them to carry it on a pole between them! They also took some samples of the pomegranates and figs. 24The Israelis named the valley "Eshcol" at that time (meaning "Cluster") because of the cluster of grapes they found!

25After forty days of exploration they returned from their tour. 26They made their report to Moses, Aaron, and all the people of Israel in the wilderness of Paran at Kadesh, and they showed the fruit they had brought with them.

27This was their report: "We arrived in the land you sent us to see, and it is indeed a magnificent country—a land 'flowing with milk and honey.' Here is some fruit we have brought as proof. 28But the people living there are powerful, and their cities are fortified and very large; and what's more, we saw Anakim giants there! 29The Amalekites live in the south, while in the hill country there are the Hittites, Jebusites, and Amorites; down along the coast of the Mediterranean Sea and in the Jordan River valley are the Canaanites."

30But Caleb reassured the people as they stood before Moses. "Let us go up at once and possess it," he said, "for we are well able to conquer it!"

31"Not against people as strong as they are!" the other spies said. "They would crush us!"

32So the majority report of the spies was negative: "The land is full of warriors, the people are powerfully built, 33and we saw some of the Anakim there, descendants of the ancient race of giants. We felt like grasshoppers before them, they were so tall!"

14 THEN ALL the people began weeping aloud, and they carried on all night. 2Their voices rose in a great chorus of complaint against Moses and Aaron.

"We wish we had died in Egypt," they wailed, "or even here in the wilderness, 3rather than be taken into this country ahead of us. Jehovah will kill us there, and our wives and little ones will become slaves. Let's get out of here and return to Egypt!"

4The idea swept the camp. "Let's elect a leader to take us back to Egypt!" they shouted.

5Then Moses and Aaron fell face downward on the ground before the people of Israel. 6Two of the spies, Joshua (the son of Nun), and Caleb (the son of Jephunneh), ripped their clothing 7and said to all the people, "It is a wonderful country ahead, 8and the Lord loves us. He will bring us safely into the land and give it to us. It is *very* fertile, a land 'flowing with milk and honey'! 9Oh, do not rebel against the Lord, and do not fear the people of the land. For they are but bread for us to eat! The Lord is with us and he has removed his protection from them! Don't be afraid of them!"

New Revised Standard

went up into the Negeb, and came to Hebron; and Ahiman, Sheshai, and Talmai, the Anakites, were there. (Hebron was built seven years before Zoan in Egypt.) 23And they came to the Wadi Eshcol, and cut down from there a branch with a single cluster of grapes, and they carried it on a pole between two of them. They also brought some pomegranates and figs. 24That place was called the Wadi Eshcol,[c] because of the cluster that the Israelites cut down from there.

The Report of the Spies

25 At the end of forty days they returned from spying out the land. 26And they came to Moses and Aaron and to all the congregation of the Israelites in the wilderness of Paran, at Kadesh; they brought back word to them and to all the congregation, and showed them the fruit of the land. 27And they told him, "We came to the land to which you sent us; it flows with milk and honey, and this is its fruit. 28Yet the people who live in the land are strong, and the towns are fortified and very large; and besides, we saw the descendants of Anak there. 29The Amalekites live in the land of the Negeb; the Hittites, the Jebusites, and the Amorites live in the hill country; and the Canaanites live by the sea, and along the Jordan."

30 But Caleb quieted the people before Moses, and said, "Let us go up at once and occupy it, for we are well able to overcome it." 31Then the men who had gone up with him said, "We are not able to go up against this people, for they are stronger than we." 32So they brought to the Israelites an unfavorable report of the land that they had spied out, saying, "The land that we have gone through as spies is a land that devours its inhabitants; and all the people that we saw in it are of great size. 33There we saw the Nephilim (the Anakites come from the Nephilim); and to ourselves we seemed like grasshoppers, and so we seemed to them."

The People Rebel

14 THEN ALL the congregation raised a loud cry, and the people wept that night. 2And all the Israelites complained against Moses and Aaron; the whole congregation said to them, "Would that we had died in the land of Egypt! Or would that we had died in this wilderness! 3Why is the LORD bringing us into this land to fall by the sword? Our wives and our little ones will become booty; would it not be better for us to go back to Egypt?" 4So they said to one another, "Let us choose a captain, and go back to Egypt."

5 Then Moses and Aaron fell on their faces before all the assembly of the congregation of the Israelites. 6And Joshua son of Nun and Caleb son of Jephunneh, who were among those who had spied out the land, tore their clothes 7and said to all the congregation of the Israelites, "The land that we went through as spies is an exceedingly good land. 8If the LORD is pleased with us, he will bring us into this land and give it to us, a land that flows with milk and honey. 9Only, do not rebel against the LORD; and do not fear the people of the land, for they are no more than bread for us; their protection is removed from them, and the LORD is with us; do not fear them." 10But the whole congregation threatened to stone them.

[b] 13:22 Zoan or Tanis, also known as Avaris, was built ca. 1700 B.C.   [c] That is Cluster

King James

10But all the congregation bade stone them with stones. And the glory of the LORD appeared in the tabernacle of the congregation before all the children of Israel.

11¶ And the LORD said unto Moses, How long will this people provoke me? and how long will it be ere they believe me, for all the signs which I have shown among them?

12I will smite them with the pestilence, and disinherit them, and will make of thee a greater nation and mightier than they.

13¶ And Moses said unto the LORD, Then the Egyptians shall hear *it*, (for thou broughtest up this people in thy might from among them;)

14And they will tell *it* to the inhabitants of this land: *for* they have heard that thou LORD *art* among this people, that thou LORD art seen face to face, and *that* thy cloud standeth over them, and *that* thou goest before them, by day time in a pillar of a cloud, and in a pillar of fire by night.

15¶ Now *if* thou shalt kill *all* this people as one man, then the nations which have heard the fame of thee will speak, saying,

16Because the LORD was not able to bring this people into the land which he sware unto them, therefore he hath slain them in the wilderness.

17And now, I beseech thee, let the power of my LORD be great, according as thou hast spoken, saying,

18The LORD *is* longsuffering, and of great mercy, forgiving iniquity and transgression, and by no means clearing *the guilty,* visiting the iniquity of the fathers upon the children unto the third and fourth *generation.*

19Pardon, I beseech thee, the iniquity of this people according unto the greatness of thy mercy, and as thou hast forgiven this people, from Egypt even until now.

20And the LORD said, I have pardoned according to thy word:

21But *as* truly *as* I live, all the earth shall be filled with the glory of the LORD.

22Because all those men which have seen my glory, and my miracles, which I did in Egypt and in the wilderness, and have tempted me now these ten times, and have not hearkened to my voice;

23Surely they shall not see the land which I sware unto their fathers, neither shall any of them that provoked me see it:

24But my servant Caleb, because he had another spirit with him, and hath followed me fully, him will I bring into the land whereinto he went; and his seed shall possess it.

25(Now the Amalekites and the Canaanites dwelt in the valley.) Tomorrow turn you, and get you into the wilderness by the way of the Red sea.

26¶ And the LORD spake unto Moses and unto Aaron, saying,

27How long *shall I bear with* this evil congregation, which murmur against me? I have heard the murmurings of the children of Israel, which they murmur against me.

28Say unto them, *As truly as* I live, saith the LORD, as ye have spoken in mine ears, so will I do to you:

29Your carcases shall fall in this wilderness; and all that were numbered of you, according to your whole number, from twenty years old and upward, which have murmured against me,

30Doubtless ye shall not come into the land, *concerning* which I sware to make you dwell therein, save Caleb the son of Jephunneh, and Joshua the son of Nun.

31But your little ones, which ye said should be a prey, them will I bring in, and they shall know the land which ye have despised.

32But *as for* you, your carcases, they shall fall in this wilderness.

33And your children shall wander in the wilderness forty years, and bear your whoredoms, until your carcases be wasted in the wilderness.

New International

10But the whole assembly talked about stoning them. Then the glory of the LORD appeared at the Tent of Meeting to all the Israelites. 11The LORD said to Moses, "How long will these people treat me with contempt? How long will they refuse to believe in me, in spite of all the miraculous signs I have performed among them? 12I will strike them down with a plague and destroy them, but I will make you into a nation greater and stronger than they."

13Moses said to the LORD, "Then the Egyptians will hear about it! By your power you brought these people up from among them. 14And they will tell the inhabitants of this land about it. They have already heard that you, O LORD, are with these people and that you, O LORD, have been seen face to face, that your cloud stays over them, and that you go before them in a pillar of cloud by day and a pillar of fire by night. 15If you put these people to death all at one time, the nations who have heard this report about you will say, 16'The LORD was not able to bring these people into the land he promised them on oath; so he slaughtered them in the desert.'

17"Now may the Lord's strength be displayed, just as you have declared: 18'The LORD is slow to anger, abounding in love and forgiving sin and rebellion. Yet he does not leave the guilty unpunished; he punishes the children for the sin of the fathers to the third and fourth generation.' 19In accordance with your great love, forgive the sin of these people, just as you have pardoned them from the time they left Egypt until now."

20The LORD replied, "I have forgiven them, as you asked. 21Nevertheless, as surely as I live and as surely as the glory of the LORD fills the whole earth, 22not one of the men who saw my glory and the miraculous signs I performed in Egypt and in the desert but who disobeyed me and tested me ten times— 23not one of them will ever see the land I promised on oath to their forefathers. No one who has treated me with contempt will ever see it. 24But because my servant Caleb has a different spirit and follows me wholeheartedly, I will bring him into the land he went to, and his descendants will inherit it. 25Since the Amalekites and Canaanites are living in the valleys, turn back tomorrow and set out toward the desert along the route to the Red Sea.ᵃ"

26The LORD said to Moses and Aaron: 27"How long will this wicked community grumble against me? I have heard the complaints of these grumbling Israelites. 28So tell them, 'As surely as I live, declares the LORD, I will do to you the very things I heard you say: 29In this desert your bodies will fall—every one of you twenty years old or more who was counted in the census and who has grumbled against me. 30Not one of you will enter the land I swore with uplifted hand to make your home, except Caleb son of Jephunneh and Joshua son of Nun. 31As for your children that you said would be taken as plunder, I will bring them in to enjoy the land you have rejected. 32But you—your bodies will fall in this desert. 33Your children will be shepherds here for forty years, suffering for your unfaithfulness, until the last of your bodies lies in the desert. 34For forty years—one year for

ᵃ 25 Hebrew *Yam Suph*; that is, Sea of Reeds

Living Bible

10, 11But the only response of the people was to talk of stoning them. Then the glory of the Lord appeared, and the Lord said to Moses, "How long will these people despise me? Will they *never* believe me, even after all the miracles I have done among them? 12I will disinherit them and destroy them with a plague, and I will make you into a nation far greater and mightier than they are!"

13"But what will the Egyptians think when they hear about it?" Moses pleaded with the Lord. "They know full well the power you displayed in rescuing your people. 14They have told this to the inhabitants of this land, who are well aware that you are with Israel and that you talk with her face to face. They see the pillar of cloud and fire standing above us, and they know that you lead and protect us day and night. 15Now if you kill all your people, the nations that have heard your fame will say, 16'The Lord had to kill them because he wasn't able to take care of them in the wilderness. He wasn't strong enough to bring them into the land he swore he would give them.'

17, 18"Oh, please, show the great power [of your patience b] by forgiving our sins and showing us your steadfast love. Forgive us, even though you have said that you don't let sin go unpunished, and that you punish the father's fault in the children to the third and fourth generation. 19Oh, I plead with you, pardon the sins of this people because of your magnificent, steadfast love, just as you have forgiven them all the time from when we left Egypt until now."

20, 21Then the Lord said, "All right, I will pardon them as you have requested. But I vow by my own name that just as it is true that all the earth shall be filled with the glory of the Lord, 22so it is true that not one of the men who has seen my glory and the miracles I did both in Egypt and in the wilderness—and ten times refused to trust me and obey me— 23shall even see the land I promised to this people's ancestors. 24But my servant Caleb is a different kind of man—he has obeyed me fully. I will bring him into the land he entered as a spy, and his descendants shall have their full share in it. 25But now, since the people of Israel are so afraid of the Amalekites and the Canaanites living in the valleys, tomorrow you must turn back into the wilderness in the direction of the Red Sea."

26, 27Then the Lord said to Moses and to Aaron, "How long will this wicked nation complain about me? For I have heard all that they have been saying. 28Tell them, 'The Lord vows to do to you what you feared: 29You will all die here in this wilderness! Not a single one of you twenty years old and older, who has complained against me, 30shall enter the Promised Land. Only Caleb (son of Jephunneh) and Joshua (son of Nun) are permitted to enter it.

31"'You said your children would become slaves of the people of the land. Well, instead I will bring *them* safely into the land and they shall inherit what you have despised. 32But as for you, your dead bodies shall fall in this wilderness. 33You must wander in the desert like nomads for forty years. In this way you will pay for your faithlessness, until the last of you lies dead in the desert.

New Revised Standard

Then the glory of the LORD appeared at the tent of meeting to all the Israelites. 11And the LORD said to Moses, "How long will this people despise me? And how long will they refuse to believe in me, in spite of all the signs that I have done among them? 12I will strike them with pestilence and disinherit them, and I will make of you a nation greater and mightier than they."

Moses Intercedes for the People

13 But Moses said to the LORD, "Then the Egyptians will hear of it, for in your might you brought up this people from among them, 14and they will tell the inhabitants of this land. They have heard that you, O LORD, are in the midst of this people; for you, O LORD, are seen face to face, and your cloud stands over them and you go in front of them, in a pillar of cloud by day and in a pillar of fire by night. 15Now if you kill this people all at one time, then the nations who have heard about you will say, 16'It is because the LORD was not able to bring this people into the land he swore to give them that he has slaughtered them in the wilderness.' 17And now, therefore, let the power of the LORD be great in the way that you promised when you spoke, saying,

18 'The LORD is slow to anger,
and abounding in steadfast love,
forgiving iniquity and transgression,
but by no means clearing the guilty,
visiting the iniquity of the parents
upon the children
to the third and the fourth generation.'

19Forgive the iniquity of this people according to the greatness of your steadfast love, just as you have pardoned this people, from Egypt even until now."

20 Then the LORD said, "I do forgive, just as you have asked; 21nevertheless—as I live, and as all the earth shall be filled with the glory of the LORD— 22none of the people who have seen my glory and the signs that I did in Egypt and in the wilderness, and yet have tested me these ten times and have not obeyed my voice, 23shall see the land that I swore to give to their ancestors; none of those who despised me shall see it. 24But my servant Caleb, because he has a different spirit and has followed me wholeheartedly, I will bring into the land into which he went, and his descendants shall possess it. 25Now, since the Amalekites and the Canaanites live in the valleys, turn tomorrow and set out for the wilderness by the way to the Red Sea."c

An Attempted Invasion is Repulsed

26 And the LORD spoke to Moses and to Aaron, saying: 27How long shall this wicked congregation complain against me? I have heard the complaints of the Israelites, which they complain against me. 28Say to them, "As I live," says the LORD, "I will do to you the very things I heard you say: 29your dead bodies shall fall in this very wilderness; and of all your number, included in the census, from twenty years old and upward, who have complained against me, 30not one of you shall come into the land in which I swore to settle you, except Caleb son of Jephunneh and Joshua son of Nun. 31But your little ones, who you said would become booty, I will bring in, and they shall know the land that you have despised. 32But as for you, your dead bodies shall fall in this wilderness. 33And your children shall be shepherds in the wilderness for forty years, and shall suffer for your faithlessness, until the last of your dead bodies lies in the wilderness. 34According to the number of the

---

b *14:17 of your patience,* implied.

c Or *Sea of Reeds*

King James

34After the number of the days in which ye searched the land, *even* forty days, each day for a year, shall ye bear your iniquities, *even* forty years, and ye shall know my breach of promise.

35I the LORD have said, I will surely do it unto all this evil congregation, that are gathered together against me: in this wilderness they shall be consumed, and there they shall die.

36And the men, which Moses sent to search the land, who returned, and made all the congregation to murmur against him, by bringing up a slander upon the land,

37Even those men that did bring up the evil report upon the land, died by the plague before the LORD.

38But Joshua the son of Nun, and Caleb the son of Jephunneh, *which were* of the men that went to search the land, lived *still*.

39And Moses told these sayings unto all the children of Israel: and the people mourned greatly.

40¶ And they rose up early in the morning, and gat them up into the top of the mountain, saying, Lo, we *be here*, and will go up unto the place which the LORD hath promised: for we have sinned.

41And Moses said, Wherefore now do ye transgress the commandment of the LORD? but it shall not prosper.

42Go not up, for the LORD *is* not among you; that ye be not smitten before your enemies.

43For the Amalekites and the Canaanites *are* there before you, and ye shall fall by the sword: because ye are turned away from the LORD, therefore the LORD will not be with you.

44But they presumed to go up unto the hill top: nevertheless the ark of the covenant of the LORD, and Moses, departed not out of the camp.

45Then the Amalekites came down, and the Canaanites which dwelt in that hill, and smote them, and discomfited them, *even* unto Hormah.

15 AND THE LORD spake unto Moses, saying, 2Speak unto the children of Israel, and say unto them, When ye be come into the land of your habitations, which I give unto you,

3And will make an offering by fire unto the LORD, a burnt offering, or a sacrifice in performing a vow, or in a freewill offering, or in your solemn feasts, to make a sweet savour unto the LORD, of the herd, or of the flock:

4Then shall he that offereth his offering unto the LORD bring a meat offering of a tenth deal of flour mingled with the fourth *part* of an hin of oil.

5And the fourth *part* of an hin of wine for a drink offering shalt thou prepare with the burnt offering or sacrifice, for one lamb.

6Or for a ram, thou shalt prepare *for* a meat offering two tenth deals of flour mingled with the third *part* of an hin of oil.

7And for a drink offering thou shalt offer the third *part* of an hin of wine, *for* a sweet savour unto the LORD.

8And when thou preparest a bullock *for* a burnt offering, or *for* a sacrifice in performing a vow, or peace offerings unto the LORD:

9Then shall he bring with a bullock a meat offering of three tenth deals of flour mingled with half an hin of oil.

10And thou shalt bring for a drink offering half an hin of wine, *for* an offering made by fire, of a sweet savour unto the LORD.

11Thus shall it be done for one bullock, or for one ram, or for a lamb, or for a kid.

12According to the number that ye shall prepare, so shall ye do to every one according to their number.

New International

each of the forty days you explored the land—you will suffer for your sins and know what it is like to have me against you.' 35I, the LORD, have spoken, and I will surely do these things to this whole wicked community, which has banded together against me. They will meet their end in this desert; here they will die."

36So the men Moses had sent to explore the land, who returned and made the whole community grumble against him by spreading a bad report about it— 37these men responsible for spreading the bad report about the land were struck down and died of a plague before the LORD. 38Of the men who went to explore the land, only Joshua son of Nun and Caleb son of Jephunneh survived.

39When Moses reported this to all the Israelites, they mourned bitterly. 40Early the next morning they went up toward the high hill country. "We have sinned," they said. "We will go up to the place the LORD promised."

41But Moses said, "Why are you disobeying the LORD's command? This will not succeed! 42Do not go up, because the LORD is not with you. You will be defeated by your enemies, 43for the Amalekites and Canaanites will face you there. Because you have turned away from the LORD, he will not be with you and you will fall by the sword."

44Nevertheless, in their presumption they went up toward the high hill country, though neither Moses nor the ark of the LORD's covenant moved from the camp. 45Then the Amalekites and Canaanites who lived in that hill country came down and attacked them and beat them down all the way to Hormah.

Supplementary Offerings

15 THE LORD said to Moses, 2"Speak to the Israelites and say to them: 'After you enter the land I am giving you as a home 3and you present to the LORD offerings made by fire, from the herd or the flock, as an aroma pleasing to the LORD—whether burnt offerings or sacrifices, for special vows or freewill offerings or festival offerings— 4then the one who brings his offering shall present to the LORD a grain offering of a tenth of an ephah[a] of fine flour mixed with a quarter of a hin[b] of oil. 5With each lamb for the burnt offering or the sacrifice, prepare a quarter of a hin of wine as a drink offering.

6" 'With a ram prepare a grain offering of two-tenths of an ephah[c] of fine flour mixed with a third of a hin[d] of oil, 7and a third of a hin of wine as a drink offering. Offer it as an aroma pleasing to the LORD.

8" 'When you prepare a young bull as a burnt offering or sacrifice, for a special vow or a fellowship offering[e] to the LORD, 9bring with the bull a grain offering of three-tenths of an ephah[f] of fine flour mixed with half a hin[g] of oil. 10Also bring half a hin of wine as a drink offering. It will be an offering made by fire, an aroma pleasing to the LORD. 11Each bull or ram, each lamb or young goat, is to be prepared in this manner. 12Do this for each one, for as many as you prepare.

a 4 That is, probably about 2 quarts (about 2 liters)   b 4 That is, probably about 1 quart (about 1 liter); also in verse 5   c 6 That is, probably about 4 quarts (about 4.5 liters)   d 6 That is, probably about 1 1/4 quarts (about 1.2 liters); also in verse 7   e 8 Traditionally *peace offering*   f 9 That is, probably about 6 quarts (about 6.5 liters)   g 9 That is, probably about 2 quarts (about 2 liters); also in verse 10

Living Bible

34, 35" 'Since the spies were in the land for forty days, you must wander in the wilderness for forty years—a year for each day, bearing the burden of your sins. I will teach you what it means to reject me. I, Jehovah, have spoken. Every one of you who has conspired against me shall die here in this wilderness.' "

36, 37, 38Then the ten spies who had incited the rebellion against Jehovah by striking fear into the hearts of the people were struck dead before the Lord. Of all the spies, only Joshua and Caleb remained alive. 39What sorrow there was throughout the camp when Moses reported God's words to the people!

40They were up early the next morning, and started towards the Promised Land.

"Here we are!" they said. "We realize that we have sinned, but now we are ready to go on into the land the Lord has promised us."

41But Moses said, "It's too late. Now you are disobeying the Lord's orders to return to the wilderness. 42Don't go ahead with your plan or you will be crushed by your enemies, for the Lord is not with you. 43Don't you remember? The Amalekites and the Canaanites are there! You have deserted the Lord, and now he will desert you."

44But they went ahead into the hill country, despite the fact that neither the Ark nor Moses left the camp. 45Then the Amalekites and the Canaanites who lived in the hills came down and attacked them and chased them to Hormah.

15 THE LORD told Moses to give these instructions to the people of Israel: "When your children finally live in the land I am going to give them, 3, 4and they want to please the Lord with a burnt offering or any other offering by fire, their sacrifice must be an animal from their flocks of sheep and goats, or from their herds of cattle. Each sacrifice—whether an ordinary one, or a sacrifice to fulfill a vow, or a free-will offering, or a special sacrifice at any of the annual festivals—must be accompanied by a grain offering. If a lamb is being sacrificed, use three quarts of fine flour mixed with three pints of oil, 5accompanied by three pints of wine for a drink offering.

6"If the sacrifice is a ram, use six quarts of fine flour mixed with four pints of oil, 7and four pints of wine for a drink offering. This will be a sacrifice that is a pleasing fragrance to the Lord.

8, 9"If the sacrifice is a young bull, then the grain offering accompanying it must consist of nine quarts of fine flour mixed with three quarts of oil, 10plus three quarts of wine for the drink offering. This shall be offered by fire as a pleasing fragrance to the Lord.

11, 12"These are the instructions for what is to accompany each sacrificial bull, ram, lamb, or young goat.

New Revised Standard

days in which you spied out the land, forty days, for every day a year, you shall bear your iniquity, forty years, and you shall know my displeasure." 35 I the LORD have spoken; surely I will do thus to all this wicked congregation gathered together against me: in this wilderness they shall come to a full end, and there they shall die.

36 And the men whom Moses sent to spy out the land, who returned and made all the congregation complain against him by bringing a bad report about the land— 37 the men who brought an unfavorable report about the land died by a plague before the LORD. 38 But Joshua son of Nun and Caleb son of Jephunneh alone remained alive, of those men who went to spy out the land.

39 When Moses told these words to all the Israelites, the people mourned greatly. 40 They rose early in the morning and went up to the heights of the hill country, saying, "Here we are. We will go up to the place that the LORD has promised, for we have sinned." 41 But Moses said, "Why do you continue to transgress the command of the LORD? That will not succeed. 42 Do not go up, for the LORD is not with you; do not let yourselves be struck down before your enemies. 43 For the Amalekites and the Canaanites will confront you there, and you shall fall by the sword; because you have turned back from following the LORD, the LORD will not be with you." 44 But they presumed to go up to the heights of the hill country, even though the ark of the covenant of the LORD, and Moses, had not left the camp. 45 Then the Amalekites and the Canaanites who lived in that hill country came down and defeated them, pursuing them as far as Hormah.

Various Offerings

15 THE LORD spoke to Moses, saying: 2 Speak to the Israelites and say to them: When you come into the land you are to inhabit, which I am giving you, 3 and you make an offering by fire to the LORD from the herd or from the flock—whether a burnt offering or a sacrifice, to fulfill a vow or as a freewill offering or at your appointed festivals—to make a pleasing odor for the LORD, 4 then whoever presents such an offering to the LORD shall present also a grain offering, one-tenth of an ephah of choice flour, mixed with one-fourth of a hin of oil. 5 Moreover, you shall offer one-fourth of a hin of wine as a drink offering with the burnt offering or the sacrifice, for each lamb. 6 For a ram, you shall offer a grain offering, two-tenths of an ephah of choice flour mixed with one-third of a hin of oil; 7 and as a drink offering you shall offer one-third of a hin of wine, a pleasing odor to the LORD. 8 When you offer a bull as a burnt offering or a sacrifice, to fulfill a vow or as an offering of well-being to the LORD, 9 then you shall present with the bull a grain offering, three-tenths of an ephah of choice flour, mixed with half a hin of oil, 10 and you shall present as a drink offering half a hin of wine, as an offering by fire, a pleasing odor to the LORD.

11 Thus it shall be done for each ox or ram, or for each of the male lambs or the kids. 12 According to the number that you offer, so you shall do with each and every one. 13 Every native Israelite shall do these things

King James

13All that are born of the country shall do these things after this manner, in offering an offering made by fire, of a sweet savour unto the LORD.

14And if a stranger sojourn with you, or whosoever *be* among you in your generations, and will offer an offering made by fire, of a sweet savour unto the LORD; as ye do, so he shall do.

15One ordinance *shall be both* for you of the congregation, and also for the stranger that sojourneth *with you*, an ordinance for ever in your generations: as ye *are*, so shall the stranger be before the LORD.

16One law and one manner shall be for you, and for the stranger that sojourneth with you.

17¶ And the LORD spake unto Moses, saying,

18Speak unto the children of Israel, and say unto them, When ye come into the land whither I bring you,

19Then it shall be, that, when ye eat of the bread of the land, ye shall offer up an heave offering unto the LORD.

20Ye shall offer up a cake of the first of your dough *for* an heave offering: as *ye do* the heave offering of the threshingfloor, so shall ye heave it.

21Of the first of your dough ye shall give unto the LORD an heave offering in your generations.

22¶ And if ye have erred, and not observed all these commandments, which the LORD hath spoken unto Moses,

23*Even* all that the LORD hath commanded you by the hand of Moses, from the day that the LORD commanded *Moses,* and henceforward among your generations;

24Then it shall be, if *aught* be committed by ignorance without the knowledge of the congregation, that all the congregation shall offer one young bullock for a burnt offering, for a sweet savour unto the LORD, with his meat offering, and his drink offering, according to the manner, and one kid of the goats for a sin offering.

25And the priest shall make an atonement for all the congregation of the children of Israel, and it shall be forgiven them; for it *is* ignorance: and they shall bring their offering, a sacrifice made by fire unto the LORD, and their sin offering before the LORD, for their ignorance:

26And it shall be forgiven all the congregation of the children of Israel, and the stranger that sojourneth among them; seeing all the people *were* in ignorance.

27¶ And if any soul sin through ignorance, then he shall bring a she goat of the first year for a sin offering.

28And the priest shall make an atonement for the soul that sinneth ignorantly, when he sinneth by ignorance before the LORD, to make an atonement for him; and it shall be forgiven him.

29Ye shall have one law for him that sinneth through ignorance, *both for* him that is born among the children of Israel, and for the stranger that sojourneth among them.

30¶ But the soul that doeth *aught* presumptuously, *whether he be* born in the land, or a stranger, the same reproacheth the LORD; and that soul shall be cut off from among his people.

31Because he hath despised the word of the LORD, and hath broken his commandment, that soul shall utterly be cut off; his iniquity *shall be* upon him.

32¶ And while the children of Israel were in the wilderness, they found a man that gathered sticks upon the sabbath day.

33And they that found him gathering sticks brought him unto Moses and Aaron, and unto all the congregation.

34And they put him in ward, because it was not declared what should be done to him.

35And the LORD said unto Moses, The man shall be surely put to death: all the congregation shall stone him with stones without the camp.

New International

13"Everyone who is native-born must do these things in this way when he brings an offering made by fire as an aroma pleasing to the LORD. 14For the generations to come, whenever an alien or anyone else living among you presents an offering made by fire as an aroma pleasing to the LORD, he must do exactly as you do. 15The community is to have the same rules for you and for the alien living among you; this is a lasting ordinance for the generations to come. You and the alien shall be the same before the LORD: 16The same laws and regulations will apply both to you and to the alien living among you.' "

17The LORD said to Moses, 18"Speak to the Israelites and say to them: 'When you enter the land to which I am taking you 19and you eat the food of the land, present a portion as an offering to the LORD. 20Present a cake from the first of your ground meal and present it as an offering from the threshing floor. 21Throughout the generations to come you are to give this offering to the LORD from the first of your ground meal.

Offerings for Unintentional Sins

22"'Now if you unintentionally fail to keep any of these commands the LORD gave Moses— 23any of the LORD's commands to you through him, from the day the LORD gave them and continuing through the generations to come— 24and if this is done unintentionally without the community being aware of it, then the whole community is to offer a young bull for a burnt offering as an aroma pleasing to the LORD, along with its prescribed grain offering and drink offering, and a male goat for a sin offering. 25The priest is to make atonement for the whole Israelite community, and they will be forgiven, for it was not intentional and they have brought to the LORD for their wrong an offering made by fire and a sin offering. 26The whole Israelite community and the aliens living among them will be forgiven, because all the people were involved in the unintentional wrong.

27"'But if just one person sins unintentionally, he must bring a year-old female goat for a sin offering. 28The priest is to make atonement before the LORD for the one who erred by sinning unintentionally, and when atonement has been made for him, he will be forgiven. 29One and the same law applies to everyone who sins unintentionally, whether he is a native-born Israelite or an alien.

30"'But anyone who sins defiantly, whether native-born or alien, blasphemes the LORD, and that person must be cut off from his people. 31Because he has despised the LORD's word and broken his commands, that person must surely be cut off; his guilt remains on him.' "

The Sabbath-Breaker Put to Death

32While the Israelites were in the desert, a man was found gathering wood on the Sabbath day. 33Those who found him gathering wood brought him to Moses and Aaron and the whole assembly, 34and they kept him in custody, because it was not clear what should be done to him. 35Then the LORD said to Moses, "The man must die. The whole assembly must stone him outside the camp." 36So the assembly took him outside the camp

Living Bible

13, 14These instructions apply both to native-born Israelis and to foreigners living among you who want to please the Lord with sacrifices offered by fire; 15, 16for there is the same law for all, native-born or foreigner, and this shall be true forever from generation to generation; all are the same before the Lord.a Yes, one law for all!"

17, 18The Lord also said to Moses at this time, "Instruct the people of Israel that when they arrive in the land that I am going to give them, 19, 20, 21they must present to the Lord a sample of each year's new crops by making a loaf, using coarse flour from the first grain that is cut each year. This loaf must be waved back and forth before the altar in a gesture of offering to the Lord. It is an annual offering from your threshing floor, and must be observed from generation to generation.

22"If by mistake you or future generations fail to carry out all of these regulations which the Lord has given you over the years through Moses, 23, 24then when the people realize their error, they must offer one young bull for a burnt offering. It will be a pleasant odor before the Lord, and must be offered along with the usual grain offering and drink offering, and one male goat for a sin offering. 25And the priest shall make atonement for all of the people of Israel and they shall be forgiven; for it was an error, and they have corrected it with their sacrifice made by fire before the Lord, and by their sin offering. 26All the people shall be forgiven, including the foreigners living among them, for the entire population is involved in such error and forgiveness.

27"If the error is made by a single individual, then he shall sacrifice a one-year-old female goat for a sin offering, 28and the priest shall make atonement for him before the Lord, and he shall be forgiven. 29This same law applies to individual foreigners who are living among you.

30"But anyone who deliberately makes the 'mistake,' whether he is a native Israeli or a foreigner, is blaspheming Jehovah, and shall be cut off from among his people. 31For he has despised the commandment of the Lord and deliberately failed to obey his law; he must be executed,b and die in his sin."

32One day while the people of Israel were in the wilderness, one of them was caught gathering wood on the Sabbath day. 33He was arrested and taken before Moses and Aaron and the other judges.c 34They jailed him until they could find out the Lord's mind concerning him.

35Then the Lord said to Moses, "The man must die—all the people shall stone him to death outside the camp."

New Revised Standard

in this way, in presenting an offering by fire, a pleasing odor to the LORD. 14An alien who lives with you, or who takes up permanent residence among you, and wishes to offer an offering by fire, a pleasing odor to the LORD, shall do as you do. 15As for the assembly, there shall be for both you and the resident alien a single statute, a perpetual statute throughout your generations; you and the alien shall be alike before the LORD. 16You and the alien who resides with you shall have the same law and the same ordinance.

17 The LORD spoke to Moses, saying: 18Speak to the Israelites and say to them: After you come into the land to which I am bringing you, 19whenever you eat of the bread of the land, you shall present a donation to the LORD. 20From your first batch of dough you shall present a loaf as a donation; you shall present it just as you present a donation from the threshing floor. 21Throughout your generations you shall give to the LORD a donation from the first of your batch of dough.

22 But if you unintentionally fail to observe all these commandments that the LORD has spoken to Moses—23everything that the LORD has commanded you by Moses, from the day the LORD gave commandment and thereafter, throughout your generations— 24then if it was done unintentionally without the knowledge of the congregation, the whole congregation shall offer one young bull for a burnt offering, a pleasing odor to the LORD, together with its grain offering and its drink offering, according to the ordinance, and one male goat for a sin offering. 25The priest shall make atonement for all the congregation of the Israelites, and they shall be forgiven; it was unintentional, and they have brought their offering, an offering by fire to the LORD, and their sin offering before the LORD, for their error. 26All the congregation of the Israelites shall be forgiven, as well as the aliens residing among them, because the whole people was involved in the error.

27 An individual who sins unintentionally shall present a female goat a year old for a sin offering. 28And the priest shall make atonement before the LORD for the one who commits an error, when it is unintentional, to make atonement for the person, who then shall be forgiven. 29For both the native among the Israelites and the alien residing among them—you shall have the same law for anyone who acts in error. 30But whoever acts high-handedly, whether a native or an alien, affronts the LORD, and shall be cut off from among the people. 31Because of having despised the word of the LORD and broken his commandment, such a person shall be utterly cut off and bear the guilt.

Penalty for Violating the Sabbath

32 When the Israelites were in the wilderness, they found a man gathering sticks on the sabbath day. 33Those who found him gathering sticks brought him to Moses, Aaron, and to the whole congregation. 34They put him in custody, because it was not clear what should be done to him. 35Then the LORD said to Moses, "The man shall be put to death; all the congregation shall stone him outside the camp." 36The whole congregation

---

a 15:15, 16 all are the same before the Lord, literally, "as you are, so shall the foreigner be before Jehovah." b 15:31 he must be executed, literally, "that soul shall be utterly cut off; his iniquity shall be upon him." c 15:33 before Moses and Aaron and the other judges, literally, "to all the congregation."

King James

36And all the congregation brought him without the camp, and stoned him with stones, and he died; as the LORD commanded Moses.

37¶ And the LORD spake unto Moses, saying,

38Speak unto the children of Israel, and bid them that they make them fringes in the borders of their garments throughout their generations, and that they put upon the fringe of the borders a ribband of blue:

39And it shall be unto you for a fringe, that ye may look upon it, and remember all the commandments of the LORD, and do them; and that ye seek not after your own heart and your own eyes, after which ye use to go a-whoring:

40That ye may remember, and do all my commandments, and be holy unto your God.

41I *am* the LORD your God, which brought you out of the land of Egypt, to be your God: I *am* the LORD your God.

16 NOW KORAH, the son of Izhar, the son of Kohath, the son of Levi, and Dathan and Abiram, the sons of Eliab, and On, the son of Peleth, sons of Reuben, took *men:*

2And they rose up before Moses, with certain of the children of Israel, two hundred and fifty princes of the assembly, famous in the congregation, men of renown:

3And they gathered themselves together against Moses and against Aaron, and said unto them, *Ye take* too much upon you, seeing all the congregation *are* holy, every one of them, and the LORD *is* among them: wherefore then lift ye up yourselves above the congregation of the LORD?

4And when Moses heard *it,* he fell upon his face:

5And he spake unto Korah and unto all his company, saying, Even tomorrow the LORD will show who *are* his, and *who is* holy; and will cause *him* to come near unto him: even *him* whom he hath chosen will he cause to come near unto him.

6This do; Take you censers, Korah, and all his company;

7And put fire therein, and put incense in them before the LORD tomorrow: and it shall be *that* the man whom the LORD doth choose, he *shall be* holy: *ye take* too much upon you, ye sons of Levi.

8And Moses said unto Korah, Hear, I pray you, ye sons of Levi:

9*Seemeth it but* a small thing unto you, that the God of Israel hath separated you from the congregation of Israel, to bring you near to himself to do the service of the tabernacle of the LORD, and to stand before the congregation to minister unto them?

10And he hath brought thee near *to him,* and all thy brethren the sons of Levi with thee: and seek ye the priesthood also?

11For which cause *both* thou and all thy company *are* gathered together against the LORD: and what *is* Aaron, that ye murmur against him?

12¶ And Moses sent to call Dathan and Abiram, the sons of Eliab: which said, We will not come up:

13*Is it* a small thing that thou hast brought us up out of a land that floweth with milk and honey, to kill us in the wilderness, except thou make thyself altogether a prince over us?

14Moreover thou hast not brought us into a land that floweth with milk and honey, or given us inheritance of fields and vineyards: wilt thou put out the eyes of these men? we will not come up.

15And Moses was very wroth, and said unto the LORD, Respect not thou their offering: I have not taken one ass from them, neither have I hurt one of them.

New International

and stoned him to death, as the LORD commanded Moses.

Tassels on Garments

37The LORD said to Moses, 38"Speak to the Israelites and say to them: 'Throughout the generations to come you are to make tassels on the corners of your garments, with a blue cord on each tassel. 39You will have these tassels to look at and so you will remember all the commands of the LORD, that you may obey them and not prostitute yourselves by going after the lusts of your own hearts and eyes. 40Then you will remember to obey all my commands and will be consecrated to your God. 41I am the LORD your God, who brought you out of Egypt to be your God. I am the LORD your God.' "

Korah, Dathan and Abiram

16 KORAH SON of Izhar, the son of Kohath, the son of Levi, and certain Reubenites—Dathan and Abiram, sons of Eliab, and On son of Peleth—became insolent[a] 2and rose up against Moses. With them were 250 Israelite men, well-known community leaders who had been appointed members of the council. 3They came as a group to oppose Moses and Aaron and said to them, "You have gone too far! The whole community is holy, every one of them, and the LORD is with them. Why then do you set yourselves above the LORD's assembly?"

4When Moses heard this, he fell facedown. 5Then he said to Korah and all his followers: "In the morning the LORD will show who belongs to him and who is holy, and he will have that person come near him. The man he chooses he will cause to come near him. 6You, Korah, and all your followers are to do this: Take censers 7and tomorrow put fire and incense in them before the LORD. The man the LORD chooses will be the one who is holy. You Levites have gone too far!"

8Moses also said to Korah, "Now listen, you Levites! 9Isn't it enough for you that the God of Israel has separated you from the rest of the Israelite community and brought you near himself to do the work at the LORD's tabernacle and to stand before the community and minister to them? 10He has brought you and all your fellow Levites near himself, but now you are trying to get the priesthood too. 11It is against the LORD that you and all your followers have banded together. Who is Aaron that you should grumble against him?"

12Then Moses summoned Dathan and Abiram, the sons of Eliab. But they said, "We will not come! 13Isn't it enough that you have brought us up out of a land flowing with milk and honey to kill us in the desert? And now you also want to lord it over us? 14Moreover, you haven't brought us into a land flowing with milk and honey or given us an inheritance of fields and vineyards. Will you gouge out the eyes of[b] these men? No, we will not come!"

15Then Moses became very angry and said to the LORD, "Do not accept their offering. I have not taken so much as a donkey from them, nor have I wronged any of them."

---

a *1 Or Peleth—took men,*   b *14 Or you make slaves of; or you deceive*

Living Bible

36So they took him outside the camp and killed him as the Lord had commanded.

37, 38The Lord said to Moses, "Tell the people of Israel to make tassels for the hems of their clothes (this is a permanent regulation from generation to generation) and to attach the tassels to their clothes with a blue cord. 39The purpose of this regulation is to remind you, whenever you notice the tassels, of the commandments of the Lord, and that you are to obey his laws instead of following your own desires and going your own ways, as you used to do in serving other gods. 40It will remind you to be holy to your God. 41For I am Jehovah your God who brought you out of the land of Egypt; yes, I am the Lord, your God."

16 ONE DAY Korah (son of Izhar, grandson of Kohath, and a descendant of Levi) conspired with Dathan and Abiram (the sons of Eliab) and On (the son of Peleth), all three from the tribe of Reuben, 2to incite a rebellion against Moses. Two hundred and fifty popular leaders, all members of the Assembly, were involved.

3They went to Moses and Aaron and said, "We have had enough of your presumption; you are no better than anyone else; everyone in Israel has been chosen of the Lord, and he is with all of us. What right do you have to put yourselves forward, claiming that we must obey you, and acting as though you were greater than anyone else among all these people of the Lord?"

4When Moses heard what they were saying he fell face downward to the ground. 5Then he said to Korah and to those who were with him, "In the morning the Lord will show you who are his, and who is holy, and whom he has chosen as his priest. 6, 7Do this: You, Korah, and all those with you, take censers tomorrow and light them, and put incense upon them before the Lord, and we will find out whom the Lord has chosen.c You are the presumptuous ones, you sons of Levi."

8, 9Then Moses spoke again to Korah: "Does it seem a small thing to you that the God of Israel has chosen you from among all the people of Israel to be near to himself as you work in the Tabernacle of Jehovah, and to stand before the people to minister to them? 10Is it nothing to you that he has given this task to only you Levites? And now are you demanding the priesthood also? 11, 12That is what you are really after! That is why you are revolting against Jehovah. And what has Aaron done, that you are dissatisfied with him?" Then Moses summoned Dathan and Abiram (the sons of Eliab), but they refused to come.

13"Is it a small thing," they mimicked,d "that you brought us out of lovely Egypt to kill us here in this terrible wilderness, and that now you want to make yourself our king? 14What's more, you haven't brought us into the wonderful country you promised, nor given us fields and vineyards. Whom are you trying to fool? We refuse to come."

15Then Moses was very angry and said to the Lord, "Do not accept their sacrifices! I have never stolen so much as a donkey from them, and have not hurt one of them."

New Revised Standard

brought him outside the camp and stoned him to death, just as the LORD had commanded Moses.

Fringes on Garments

37 The LORD said to Moses: 38Speak to the Israelites, and tell them to make fringes on the corners of their garments throughout their generations and to put a blue cord on the fringe at each corner. 39You have the fringe so that, when you see it, you will remember all the commandments of the LORD and do them, and not follow the lust of your own heart and your own eyes. 40So you shall remember and do all my commandments, and you shall be holy to your God. 41I am the LORD your God, who brought you out of the land of Egypt, to be your God: I am the LORD your God.

Revolt of Korah, Dathan, and Abiram

16 NOW KORAH son of Izhar son of Kohath son of Levi, along with Dathan and Abiram sons of Eliab, and On son of Peleth—descendants of Reuben— took 2two hundred fifty Israelite men, leaders of the congregation, chosen from the assembly, well-known men,e and they confronted Moses. 3They assembled against Moses and against Aaron, and said to them, "You have gone too far! All the congregation are holy, everyone of them, and the LORD is among them. So why then do you exalt yourselves above the assembly of the LORD?" 4When Moses heard it, he fell on his face. 5Then he said to Korah and all his company, "In the morning the LORD will make known who is his, and who is holy, and who will be allowed to approach him; the one whom he will choose he will allow to approach him. 6Do this: take censers, Korah and all yourf company, 7and tomorrow put fire in them, and lay incense on them before the LORD; and the man whom the LORD chooses shall be the holy one. You Levites have gone too far!" 8Then Moses said to Korah, "Hear now, you Levites! 9Is it too little for you that the God of Israel has separated you from the congregation of Israel, to allow you to approach him in order to perform the duties of the LORD's tabernacle, and to stand before the congregation and serve them? 10He has allowed you to approach him, and all your brother Levites with you; yet you seek the priesthood as well! 11Therefore you and all your company have gathered together against the LORD. What is Aaron that you rail against him?"

12 Moses sent for Dathan and Abiram sons of Eliab; but they said, "We will not come! 13Is it too little that you have brought us up out of a land flowing with milk and honey to kill us in the wilderness, that you must also lord it over us? 14It is clear you have not brought us into a land flowing with milk and honey, or given us an inheritance of fields and vineyards. Would you put out the eyes of these men? We will not come!"

15 Moses was very angry and said to the LORD, "Pay no attention to their offering. I have not taken one donkey from them, and I have not harmed any one of them." 16And Moses said to Korah, "As for you and all

---

c 16:6, 7 whom the Lord has chosen, literally, "whom Jehovah chooses to be the holy one." d 16:13 mimicked, literally, "said."

e Cn: Heb and they confronted Moses, and two hundred fifty men . . . well-known men f Heb his

King James

16And Moses said unto Korah, Be thou and all thy company before the LORD, thou, and they, and Aaron, tomorrow:

17And take every man his censer, and put incense in them, and bring ye before the LORD every man his censer, two hundred and fifty censers; thou also, and Aaron, each *of you* his censer.

18And they took every man his censer, and put fire in them, and laid incense thereon, and stood in the door of the tabernacle of the congregation with Moses and Aaron.

19And Korah gathered all the congregation against them unto the door of the tabernacle of the congregation: and the glory of the LORD appeared unto all the congregation.

20And the LORD spake unto Moses and unto Aaron, saying,

21Separate yourselves from among this congregation, that I may consume them in a moment.

22And they fell upon their faces, and said, O God, the God of the spirits of all flesh, shall one man sin, and wilt thou be wroth with all the congregation?

23¶ And the LORD spake unto Moses, saying,

24Speak unto the congregation, saying, Get you up from about the tabernacle of Korah, Dathan, and Abiram.

25And Moses rose up and went unto Dathan and Abiram; and the elders of Israel followed him.

26And he spake unto the congregation, saying, Depart, I pray you, from the tents of these wicked men, and touch nothing of theirs, lest ye be consumed in all their sins.

27So they gat up from the tabernacle of Korah, Dathan, and Abiram, on every side: and Dathan and Abiram came out, and stood in the door of their tents, and their wives, and their sons, and their little children.

28And Moses said, Hereby ye shall know that the LORD hath sent me to do all these works; for *I have* not *done them* of mine own mind.

29If these men die the common death of all men, or if they be visited after the visitation of all men; *then* the LORD hath not sent me.

30But if the LORD make a new thing, and the earth open her mouth, and swallow them up, with all that *appertain* unto them, and they go down quick into the pit; then ye shall understand that these men have provoked the LORD.

31¶ And it came to pass, as he had made an end of speaking all these words, that the ground clave asunder that *was* under them:

32And the earth opened her mouth, and swallowed them up, and their houses, and all the men that *appertained* unto Korah, and all *their* goods.

33They, and all that *appertained* to them, went down alive into the pit, and the earth closed upon them: and they perished from among the congregation.

34And all Israel that *were* round about them fled at the cry of them: for they said, Lest the earth swallow us up *also.*

35And there came out a fire from the LORD, and consumed the two hundred and fifty men that offered incense.

36¶ And the LORD spake unto Moses, saying,

37Speak unto Eleazar the son of Aaron the priest, that he take up the censers out of the burning, and scatter thou the fire yonder; for they are hallowed.

38The censers of these sinners against their own souls, let them make them broad plates *for* a covering of the altar: for they offered them before the LORD, therefore they are hallowed: and they shall be a sign unto the children of Israel.

39And Eleazar the priest took the brasen censers, wherewith they that were burnt had offered; and they were made broad *plates for* a covering of the altar:

New International

16Moses said to Korah, "You and all your followers are to appear before the LORD tomorrow—you and they and Aaron. 17Each man is to take his censer and put incense in it—250 censers in all—and present it before the LORD. You and Aaron are to present your censers also." 18So each man took his censer, put fire and incense in it, and stood with Moses and Aaron at the entrance to the Tent of Meeting. 19When Korah had gathered all his followers in opposition to them at the entrance to the Tent of Meeting, the glory of the LORD appeared to the entire assembly. 20The LORD said to Moses and Aaron, 21"Separate yourselves from this assembly so I can put an end to them at once."

22But Moses and Aaron fell facedown and cried out, "O God, God of the spirits of all mankind, will you be angry with the entire assembly when only one man sins?"

23Then the LORD said to Moses, 24"Say to the assembly, 'Move away from the tents of Korah, Dathan and Abiram.' "

25Moses got up and went to Dathan and Abiram, and the elders of Israel followed him. 26He warned the assembly, "Move back from the tents of these wicked men! Do not touch anything belonging to them, or you will be swept away because of all their sins." 27So they moved away from the tents of Korah, Dathan and Abiram. Dathan and Abiram had come out and were standing with their wives, children and little ones at the entrances to their tents.

28Then Moses said, "This is how you will know that the LORD has sent me to do all these things and that it was not my idea: 29If these men die a natural death and experience only what usually happens to men, then the LORD has not sent me. 30But if the LORD brings about something totally new, and the earth opens its mouth and swallows them, with everything that belongs to them, and they go down alive into the grave,[a] then you will know that these men have treated the LORD with contempt."

31As soon as he finished saying all this, the ground under them split apart 32and the earth opened its mouth and swallowed them, with their households and all Korah's men and all their possessions. 33They went down alive into the grave, with everything they owned; the earth closed over them, and they perished and were gone from the community. 34At their cries, all the Israelites around them fled, shouting, "The earth is going to swallow us too!"

35And fire came out from the LORD and consumed the 250 men who were offering the incense.

36The LORD said to Moses, 37"Tell Eleazar son of Aaron, the priest, to take the censers out of the smoldering remains and scatter the coals some distance away, for the censers are holy— 38the censers of the men who sinned at the cost of their lives. Hammer the censers into sheets to overlay the altar, for they were presented before the LORD and have become holy. Let them be a sign to the Israelites."

39So Eleazar the priest collected the bronze censers brought by those who had been burned up, and he had them hammered out to overlay the altar, 40as the LORD

---

a 30 Hebrew *Sheol*; also in verse 33

Living Bible

16And Moses said to Korah, "Come here tomorrow before the Lord with all your friends; Aaron will be here too. 17Be sure to bring your censers with incense on them; a censer for each man, 250 in all; and Aaron will also be here with his."

18So they did. They came with their censers and lit them and placed the incense on them, and stood at the entrance of the Tabernacle with Moses and Aaron. 19Meanwhile, Korah had stirred up the entire nation against Moses and Aaron, and they all assembled to watch. Then the glory of Jehovah appeared to all the people, 20and Jehovah said to Moses and Aaron, 21"Get away from these people so that I may instantly destroy them."

22But Moses and Aaron fell face downward to the ground before the Lord. "O God, the God of all mankind," they pleaded, "must you be angry with all the people when one man sins?"

23, 24And the Lord said to Moses, "Then tell the people to get away from the tents of Korah, Dathan, and Abiram."

25So Moses rushed over to the tents of Dathan and Abiram, followed closely by the 250 Israeli leaders. 26"Quick!" he told the people, "get away from the tents of these wicked men, and don't touch anything that belongs to them, lest you be included in their sins [and be destroyed with themb]."

27So all the people stood back from the tents of Korah, Dathan, and Abiram. And Dathan and Abiram came out and stood at the entrances of their tents with their wives and sons and little ones.

28And Moses said, "By this you shall know that Jehovah has sent me to do all these things that I have done—for I have not done them on my own. 29If these men die a natural death or from some ordinary accident or disease, then Jehovah has not sent me. 30But if the Lord does a miracle and the ground opens up and swallows them and everything that belongs to them, and they go down alive into Sheol, then you will know that these men have despised the Lord."

31He had hardly finished speaking the words when the ground suddenly split open beneath them, 32and a great fissure swallowed them up, along with their tents and families and the friends who were standing with them, and everything they owned. 33So they went down alive into Sheol and the earth closed upon them, and they perished. 34All of the people of Israel fled at their screams, fearing that the earth would swallow them too. 35Then fire came from Jehovah and burned up the 250 men who were offering incense.

36, 37And the Lord said to Moses, "Tell Eleazar the son of Aaron the priest to pull those censers from the fire; for they are holy, dedicated to the Lord. He must also scatter the burning incense 38from the censers of these men who have sinned at the cost of their lives. He shall then beat the metal into a sheet as a covering for the altar, for these censers are holy because they were used before the Lord; and the altar sheet shall be a reminder to the people of Israel."

39So Eleazar the priest took the 250 bronze censers and beat them out into a sheet of metal to cover the altar,

New Revised Standard

your company, be present tomorrow before the LORD, you and they and Aaron; 17and let each one of you take his censer, and put incense on it, and each one of you present his censer before the LORD, two hundred fifty censers; you also, and Aaron, each his censer." 18So each man took his censer, and they put fire in the censers and laid incense on them, and they stood at the entrance of the tent of meeting with Moses and Aaron. 19Then Korah assembled the whole congregation against them at the entrance of the tent of meeting. And the glory of the LORD appeared to the whole congregation.

20 Then the LORD spoke to Moses and to Aaron, saying: 21Separate yourselves from this congregation, so that I may consume them in a moment. 22They fell on their faces, and said, "O God, the God of the spirits of all flesh, shall one person sin and you become angry with the whole congregation?"

23 And the LORD spoke to Moses, saying: 24Say to the congregation: Get away from the dwellings of Korah, Dathan, and Abiram. 25So Moses got up and went to Dathan and Abiram; the elders of Israel followed him. 26He said to the congregation, "Turn away from the tents of these wicked men, and touch nothing of theirs, or you will be swept away for all their sins." 27So they got away from the dwellings of Korah, Dathan, and Abiram; and Dathan and Abiram came out and stood at the entrance of their tents, together with their wives, their children, and their little ones. 28And Moses said, "This is how you shall know that the LORD has sent me to do all these works; it has not been of my own accord: 29If these people die a natural death, or if a natural fate comes on them, then the LORD has not sent me. 30But if the LORD creates something new, and the ground opens its mouth and swallows them up, with all that belongs to them, and they go down alive into Sheol, then you shall know that these men have despised the LORD."

31 As soon as he finished speaking all these words, the ground under them was split apart. 32The earth opened its mouth and swallowed them up, along with their households—everyone who belonged to Korah and all their goods. 33So they with all that belonged to them went down alive into Sheol; the earth closed over them, and they perished from the midst of the assembly. 34All Israel around them fled at their outcry, for they said, "The earth will swallow us too!" 35And fire came out from the LORD and consumed the two hundred fifty men offering the incense.

36c Then the LORD spoke to Moses, saying: 37Tell Eleazar son of Aaron the priest to take the censers out of the blaze; then scatter the fire far and wide. 38For the censers of these sinners have become holy at the cost of their lives. Make them into hammered plates as a covering for the altar, for they presented them before the LORD and they became holy. Thus they shall be a sign to the Israelites. 39So Eleazar the priest took the bronze censers that had been presented by those who were burned; and they were hammered out as a covering for the altar— 40a reminder to the Israelites that no outsider,

b 16:26 and be destroyed with them, implied.   c Ch 17.1 in Heb

King James

40*To be* a memorial unto the children of Israel, that no stranger, which *is* not of the seed of Aaron, come near to offer incense before the LORD; that he be not as Korah, and as his company: as the LORD said to him by the hand of Moses.

41¶ But on the morrow all the congregation of the children of Israel murmured against Moses and against Aaron, saying, Ye have killed the people of the LORD.

42And it came to pass, when the congregation was gathered against Moses and against Aaron, that they looked toward the tabernacle of the congregation: and, behold, the cloud covered it, and the glory of the LORD appeared.

43And Moses and Aaron came before the tabernacle of the congregation.

44¶ And the LORD spake unto Moses, saying,

45Get you up from among this congregation, that I may consume them as in a moment. And they fell upon their faces.

46¶ And Moses said unto Aaron, Take a censer, and put fire therein from off the altar, and put on incense, and go quickly unto the congregation, and make an atonement for them: for there is wrath gone out from the LORD; the plague is begun.

47And Aaron took as Moses commanded, and ran into the midst of the congregation; and, behold, the plague was begun among the people: and he put on incense, and made an atonement for the people.

48And he stood between the dead and the living; and the plague was stayed.

49Now they that died in the plague were fourteen thousand and seven hundred, beside them that died about the matter of Korah.

50And Aaron returned unto Moses unto the door of the tabernacle of the congregation: and the plague was stayed.

17 AND THE LORD spake unto Moses, saying, 2Speak unto the children of Israel, and take of every one of them a rod according to the house of *their* fathers, of all their princes according to the house of their fathers twelve rods: write thou every man's name upon his rod.

3And thou shalt write Aaron's name upon the rod of Levi: for one rod *shall be* for the head of the house of their fathers.

4And thou shalt lay them up in the tabernacle of the congregation before the testimony, where I will meet with you.

5And it shall come to pass, *that* the man's rod, whom I shall choose, shall blossom: and I will make to cease from me the murmurings of the children of Israel, whereby they murmur against you.

6¶ And Moses spake unto the children of Israel, and every one of their princes gave him a rod apiece, for each prince one, according to their fathers' houses, *even* twelve rods: and the rod of Aaron *was* among their rods.

7And Moses laid up the rods before the LORD in the tabernacle of witness.

8And it came to pass, that on the morrow Moses went into the tabernacle of witness; and, behold, the rod of Aaron for the house of Levi was budded, and brought forth buds, and bloomed blossoms, and yielded almonds.

9And Moses brought out all the rods from before the LORD unto all the children of Israel: and they looked, and took every man his rod.

10¶ And the LORD said unto Moses, Bring Aaron's rod again before the testimony, to be kept for a token against the rebels; and thou shalt quite take away their murmurings from me, that they die not.

New International

directed him through Moses. This was to remind the Israelites that no one except a descendant of Aaron should come to burn incense before the LORD, or he would become like Korah and his followers.

41The next day the whole Israelite community grumbled against Moses and Aaron. "You have killed the LORD's people," they said.

42But when the assembly gathered in opposition to Moses and Aaron and turned toward the Tent of Meeting, suddenly the cloud covered it and the glory of the LORD appeared. 43Then Moses and Aaron went to the front of the Tent of Meeting, 44and the LORD said to Moses, 45"Get away from this assembly so I can put an end to them at once." And they fell facedown.

46Then Moses said to Aaron, "Take your censer and put incense in it, along with fire from the altar, and hurry to the assembly to make atonement for them. Wrath has come out from the LORD; the plague has started." 47So Aaron did as Moses said, and ran into the midst of the assembly. The plague had already started among the people, but Aaron offered the incense and made atonement for them. 48He stood between the living and the dead, and the plague stopped. 49But 14,700 people died from the plague, in addition to those who had died because of Korah. 50Then Aaron returned to Moses at the entrance to the Tent of Meeting, for the plague had stopped.

The Budding of Aaron's Staff

17 THE LORD said to Moses, 2"Speak to the Israelites and get twelve staffs from them, one from the leader of each of their ancestral tribes. Write the name of each man on his staff. 3On the staff of Levi write Aaron's name, for there must be one staff for the head of each ancestral tribe. 4Place them in the Tent of Meeting in front of the Testimony, where I meet with you. 5The staff belonging to the man I choose will sprout, and I will rid myself of this constant grumbling against you by the Israelites."

6So Moses spoke to the Israelites, and their leaders gave him twelve staffs, one for the leader of each of their ancestral tribes, and Aaron's staff was among them. 7Moses placed the staffs before the LORD in the Tent of the Testimony.

8The next day Moses entered the Tent of the Testimony and saw that Aaron's staff, which represented the house of Levi, had not only sprouted but had budded, blossomed and produced almonds. 9Then Moses brought out all the staffs from the LORD's presence to all the Israelites. They looked at them, and each man took his own staff.

10The LORD said to Moses, "Put back Aaron's staff in front of the Testimony, to be kept as a sign to the rebellious. This will put an end to their grumbling

Living Bible

40to be a reminder to the people of Israel that no unauthorized person—no one who is not a descendant of Aaron—may come before the Lord to burn incense, lest the same thing happen to him as happened to Korah and his associates. Thus the Lord's directions to Moses were carried out.

41But the very next morning all the people began muttering again against Moses and Aaron, saying, "You have killed the Lord's people."

42Soon a great, sullen mob formed; suddenly, as they looked toward the Tabernacle, the Cloud appeared and the awesome glory of the Lord was seen. 43, 44Moses and Aaron came and stood at the entrance of the Tabernacle, and the Lord said to Moses,

45"Get away from these people so that I can instantly destroy them." But Moses and Aaron fell face downward to the earth before the Lord.

46And Moses said to Aaron, "Quick, take a censer and place fire in it from the altar; lay incense on it, and carry it quickly among the people and make atonement for them; for God's anger has gone out among them—the plague has already begun.

47Aaron did as Moses had told him to, and ran among the people, for the plague had indeed already begun; and he put on the incense and made atonement for them. 48And he stood between the living and the dead, and the plague was stopped, 49but not before 14,700 people had died (in addition to those who had died the previous day with Korah). 50Then Aaron returned to Moses at the entrance of the Tabernacle; and so the plague was stopped.

17 THEN THE Lord said to Moses, "Tell the people of Israel that each of their tribal chiefs is to bring you a wooden rod with his name inscribed upon it. Aaron's name is to be on the rod of the tribe of Levi. 4Put these rods in the inner room of the Tabernacle where I meet with you, in front of the Ark. 5I will use these rods to identify the man I have chosen! for buds will grow on his rod! Then at last this murmuring and complaining against you will stop!"

6So Moses gave the instructions to the people, and each of the twelve chiefs (including Aaron) brought him a rod. 7He put them before the Lord in the inner room of the Tabernacle, 8and when he went in the next day, he found that Aaron's rod, representing the tribe of Levi, had budded and was blossoming, and had ripe almonds hanging from it!

9When Moses brought them out to show the others, they stared in disbelief! Then each man except Aaron claimed his rod. 10The Lord told Moses to place Aaron's rod permanently beside the Ark as a reminder of this rebellion. He was to [bring it out and show it to the people again[a]] if there were any further complaints about Aaron's authority; this would ward off further

New Revised Standard

who is not of the descendants of Aaron, shall approach to offer incense before the LORD, so as not to become like Korah and his company—just as the LORD had said to him through Moses.

41 On the next day, however, the whole congregation of the Israelites rebelled against Moses and against Aaron, saying, "You have killed the people of the LORD." 42And when the congregation had assembled against them, Moses and Aaron turned toward the tent of meeting; the cloud had covered it and the glory of the LORD appeared. 43Then Moses and Aaron came to the front of the tent of meeting, 44and the LORD spoke to Moses, saying, 45"Get away from this congregation, so that I may consume them in a moment." And they fell on their faces. 46Moses said to Aaron, "Take your censer, put fire on it from the altar and lay incense on it, and carry it quickly to the congregation and make atonement for them. For wrath has gone out from the LORD; the plague has begun." 47So Aaron took it as Moses had ordered, and ran into the middle of the assembly, where the plague had already begun among the people. He put on the incense, and made atonement for the people. 48He stood between the dead and the living; and the plague was stopped. 49Those who died by the plague were fourteen thousand seven hundred, besides those who died in the affair of Korah. 50When the plague was stopped, Aaron returned to Moses at the entrance of the tent of meeting.

The Budding of Aaron's Rod

17b THE LORD spoke to Moses, saying: 2Speak to the Israelites, and get twelve staffs from them, one for each ancestral house, from all the leaders of their ancestral houses. Write each man's name on his staff, 3and write Aaron's name on the staff of Levi. For there shall be one staff for the head of each ancestral house. 4Place them in the tent of meeting before the covenant,c where I meet with you. 5And the staff of the man whom I choose shall sprout; thus I will put a stop to the complaints of the Israelites that they continually make against you. 6Moses spoke to the Israelites; and all their leaders gave him staffs, one for each leader, according to their ancestral houses, twelve staffs; and the staff of Aaron was among theirs. 7So Moses placed the staffs before the LORD in the tent of the covenant.c

8 When Moses went into the tent of the covenantc on the next day, the staff of Aaron for the house of Levi had sprouted. It put forth buds, produced blossoms, and bore ripe almonds. 9Then Moses brought out all the staffs from before the LORD to all the Israelites; and they looked, and each man took his staff. 10And the LORD said to Moses, "Put back the staff of Aaron before the covenant,c to be kept as a warning to rebels, so that you may make an end of their complaints against me, or else

---

a 17:10 bring it out and show it to the people again, implied. b Ch 17.16 in Heb c Or treaty, or testimony; Heb eduth

King James

11And Moses did *so:* as the LORD commanded him, so did he.

12And the children of Israel spake unto Moses, saying, Behold, we die, we perish, we all perish.

13Whosoever cometh any thing near unto the tabernacle of the LORD shall die: shall we be consumed with dying?

18 AND THE LORD said unto Aaron, Thou and thy sons and thy father's house with thee shall bear the iniquity of the sanctuary: and thou and thy sons with thee shall bear the iniquity of your priesthood.

2And thy brethren also of the tribe of Levi, the tribe of thy father, bring thou with thee, that they may be joined unto thee, and minister unto thee: but thou and thy sons with thee *shall minister* before the tabernacle of witness.

3And they shall keep thy charge, and the charge of all the tabernacle: only they shall not come nigh the vessels of the sanctuary and the altar, that neither they, nor ye also, die.

4And they shall be joined unto thee, and keep the charge of the tabernacle of the congregation, for all the service of the tabernacle: and a stranger shall not come nigh unto you.

5And ye shall keep the charge of the sanctuary, and the charge of the altar: that there be no wrath any more upon the children of Israel.

6And I, behold, I have taken your brethren the Levites from among the children of Israel: to you *they are* given *as* a gift for the LORD, to do the service of the tabernacle of the congregation.

7Therefore thou and thy sons with thee shall keep your priest's office for every thing of the altar, and within the veil; and ye shall serve: I have given your priest's office *unto you as* a service of gift: and the stranger that cometh nigh shall be put to death.

8¶ And the LORD spake unto Aaron, Behold, I also have given thee the charge of mine heave offerings of all the hallowed things of the children of Israel; unto thee have I given them by reason of the anointing, and to thy sons, by an ordinance for ever.

9This shall be thine of the most holy things, *reserved* from the fire: every oblation of theirs, every meat offering of theirs, and every sin offering of theirs, and every trespass offering of theirs, which they shall render unto me, *shall be* most holy for thee and for thy sons.

10In the most holy *place* shalt thou eat it; every male shall eat it: it shall be holy unto thee.

11And this *is* thine; the heave offering of their gift, with all the wave offerings of the children of Israel: I have given them unto thee, and to thy sons and to thy daughters with thee, by a statute for ever: every one that is clean in thy house shall eat of it.

12All the best of the oil, and all the best of the wine, and of the wheat, the firstfruits of them which they shall offer unto the LORD, them have I given thee.

13*And* whatsoever is first ripe in the land, which they shall bring unto the LORD, shall be thine; every one that is clean in thine house shall eat *of* it.

14Every thing devoted in Israel shall be thine.

15Every thing that openeth the matrix in all flesh, which they bring unto the LORD, *whether it be* of men or beasts, shall be thine: nevertheless the firstborn of man shalt thou surely redeem, and the firstling of unclean beasts shalt thou redeem.

16And those that are to be redeemed from a month old shalt thou redeem, according to thine estimation, for the money of five shekels, after the shekel of the sanctuary, which *is* twenty gerahs.

New International

against me, so that they will not die." 11Moses did just as the LORD commanded him.

12The Israelites said to Moses, "We will die! We are lost, we are all lost! 13Anyone who even comes near the tabernacle of the LORD will die. Are we all going to die?"

Duties of Priests and Levites

18 THE LORD said to Aaron, "You, your sons and your father's family are to bear the responsibility for offenses against the sanctuary, and you and your sons alone are to bear the responsibility for offenses against the priesthood. 2Bring your fellow Levites from your ancestral tribe to join you and assist you when you and your sons minister before the Tent of the Testimony. 3They are to be responsible to you and are to perform all the duties of the Tent, but they must not go near the furnishings of the sanctuary or the altar, or both they and you will die. 4They are to join you and be responsible for the care of the Tent of Meeting—all the work at the Tent—and no one else may come near where you are.

5"You are to be responsible for the care of the sanctuary and the altar, so that wrath will not fall on the Israelites again. 6I myself have selected your fellow Levites from among the Israelites as a gift to you, dedicated to the LORD to do the work at the Tent of Meeting. 7But only you and your sons may serve as priests in connection with everything at the altar and inside the curtain. I am giving you the service of the priesthood as a gift. Anyone else who comes near the sanctuary must be put to death."

Offerings for Priests and Levites

8Then the LORD said to Aaron, "I myself have put you in charge of the offerings presented to me; all the holy offerings the Israelites give me I give to you and your sons as your portion and regular share. 9You are to have the part of the most holy offerings that is kept from the fire. From all the gifts they bring me as most holy offerings, whether grain or sin or guilt offerings, that part belongs to you and your sons. 10Eat it as something most holy; every male shall eat it. You must regard it as holy.

11"This also is yours: whatever is set aside from the gifts of all the wave offerings of the Israelites. I give this to you and your sons and daughters as your regular share. Everyone in your household who is ceremonially clean may eat it.

12"I give you all the finest olive oil and all the finest new wine and grain they give the LORD as the firstfruits of their harvest. 13All the land's firstfruits that they bring to the LORD will be yours. Everyone in your household who is ceremonially clean may eat it.

14"Everything in Israel that is devoteda to the LORD is yours. 15The first offspring of every womb, both man and animal, that is offered to the LORD is yours. But you must redeem every firstborn son and every firstborn male of unclean animals. 16When they are a month old, you must redeem them at the redemption price set at five shekelsb of silver, according to the sanctuary shekel, which weighs twenty gerahs.

---

a *14* The Hebrew term refers to the irrevocable giving over of things or persons to the LORD.   b *16* That is, about 2 ounces (about 55 grams)

Living Bible

catastrophe to the people. 11So Moses did as the Lord commanded him.

12, 13But the people of Israel only grumbled the more. "We are as good as dead," they whined. "Everyone who even comes close to the Tabernacle dies. Must we all perish?"

18 THE LORD now spoke to Aaron: "You and your sons and your family are responsible for any desecration of the sanctuary," he said, "and will be held liable for any impropriety in your priestly work.

2, 3"Your kinsmen, the tribe of Levi, are your assistants; but only you and your sons may perform the sacred duties in the Tabernacle itself. The Levites must be careful not to touch any of the sacred articles or the altar, lest I destroy both them and you. 4No one who is not a member of the tribe of Levi shall assist you in any way. 5Remember, only the priests are to perform the sacred duties within the sanctuary and at the altar. If you follow these instructions the wrath of God will never again fall upon any of the people of Israel for violating this law. 6I say it again—your kinsmen the Levites are your assistants for the work of the Tabernacle. They are a gift to you from the Lord. 7But you and your sons, the priests, shall personally handle all the sacred service, including the altar and all that is within the veil, for the priesthood is your special gift of service. Anyone else who attempts to perform these duties shall die."

8The Lord gave these further instructions to Aaron: "I have given the priests all the gifts which are brought to the Lord by the people; all these offerings presented to the Lord by the gesture of waving them before the altar belong to you and your sons, by permanent law. 9The grain offerings, the sin offerings, and the guilt offerings are yours, except for the sample presented to the Lord by burning upon the altar. All these are most holy offerings. 10They are to be eaten only in a most holy place, and only by males. 11All other gifts presented to me by the gesture of waving them before the altar are for you and your families, sons and daughters alike. For all the members of your families may eat these unless anyone is ceremonially impure at the time.

12"Yours also are the first-of-the-harvest gifts the people bring as offerings to the Lord—the best of the olive oil, wine, grain, 13and every other crop. Your families may eat these unless they are ceremonially defiled at the time. 14, 15So everything that is dedicated to the Lord shall be yours, including the firstborn sons of the people of Israel, and the firstborn of their animals. 16However, you may never accept the firstborn sons, nor the firstborn of any animals that I do not permit for food. Instead, there must be a payment of two and a half dollars made for each firstborn child. It is to be brought when he is one month old.

New Revised Standard

they will die." 11Moses did so; just as the LORD commanded him, so he did.

12 The Israelites said to Moses, "We are perishing; we are lost, all of us are lost! 13Everyone who approaches the tabernacle of the LORD will die. Are we all to perish?"

Responsibility of Priests and Levites

18 THE LORD said to Aaron: You and your sons and your ancestral house with you shall bear responsibility for offenses connected with the sanctuary, while you and your sons alone shall bear responsibility for offenses connected with the priesthood. 2So bring with you also your brothers of the tribe of Levi, your ancestral tribe, in order that they may be joined to you, and serve you while you and your sons with you are in front of the tent of the covenant.c 3They shall perform duties for you and for the whole tent. But they must not approach either the utensils of the sanctuary or the altar, otherwise both they and you will die. 4They are attached to you in order to perform the duties of the tent of meeting, for all the service of the tent; no outsider shall approach you. 5You yourselves shall perform the duties of the sanctuary and the duties of the altar, so that wrath may never again come upon the Israelites. 6It is I who now take your brother Levites from among the Israelites; they are now yours as a gift, dedicated to the LORD, to perform the service of the tent of meeting. 7But you and your sons with you shall diligently perform your priestly duties in all that concerns the altar and the area behind the curtain. I give your priesthood as a gift;d any outsider who approaches shall be put to death.

The Priests' Portion

8 The LORD spoke to Aaron: I have given you charge of the offerings made to me, all the holy gifts of the Israelites; I have given them to you and your sons as a priestly portion due you in perpetuity. 9This shall be yours from the most holy things, reserved from the fire: every offering of theirs that they render to me as a most holy thing, whether grain offering, sin offering, or guilt offering, shall belong to you and your sons. 10As a most holy thing you shall eat it; every male may eat it; it shall be holy to you. 11This also is yours: I have given to you, together with your sons and daughters, as a perpetual due, whatever is set aside from the gifts of all the elevation offerings of the Israelites; everyone who is clean in your house may eat them. 12All the best of the oil and all the best of the wine and of the grain, the choice produce that they give to the LORD, I have given to you. 13The first fruits of all that is in their land, which they bring to the LORD, shall be yours; everyone who is clean in your house may eat of it. 14Every devoted thing in Israel shall be yours. 15The first issue of the womb of all creatures, human and animal, which is offered to the LORD, shall be yours; but the firstborn of human beings you shall redeem, and the firstborn of unclean animals you shall redeem. 16Their redemption price, reckoned from one month of age, you shall fix at five shekels of silver, according to the shekel of the sanctuary (that is, twenty gerahs). 17But the firstborn of a cow,

c Or treaty. or testimony; Heb eduth   d Heb as a service of gift

King James

17But the firstling of a cow, or the firstling of a sheep, or the firstling of a goat, thou shalt not redeem; they *are* holy: thou shalt sprinkle their blood upon the altar, and shalt burn their fat *for* an offering made by fire, for a sweet savour unto the LORD.

18And the flesh of them shall be thine, as the wave breast and as the right shoulder are thine.

19All the heave offerings of the holy things, which the children of Israel offer unto the LORD, have I given thee, and thy sons and thy daughters with thee, by a statute for ever: it *is* a covenant of salt for ever before the LORD unto thee and to thy seed with thee.

20¶ And the LORD spake unto Aaron, Thou shalt have no inheritance in their land, neither shalt thou have any part among them: I *am* thy part and thine inheritance among the children of Israel.

21And, behold, I have given the children of Levi all the tenth in Israel for an inheritance, for their service which they serve, *even* the service of the tabernacle of the congregation.

22Neither must the children of Israel henceforth come nigh the tabernacle of the congregation, lest they bear sin, and die.

23But the Levites shall do the service of the tabernacle of the congregation, and they shall bear their iniquity: *it shall be* a statute for ever throughout your generations, that among the children of Israel they have no inheritance.

24But the tithes of the children of Israel, which they offer *as* an heave offering unto the LORD, I have given to the Levites to inherit: therefore I have said unto them, Among the children of Israel they shall have no inheritance.

25¶ And the LORD spake unto Moses, saying,

26Thus speak unto the Levites, and say unto them, When ye take of the children of Israel the tithes which I have given you from them for your inheritance, then ye shall offer up an heave offering of it for the LORD, *even* a tenth *part* of the tithe.

27And *this* your heave offering shall be reckoned unto you, as though *it were* the corn of the threshingfloor, and as the fulness of the winepress.

28Thus ye also shall offer an heave offering unto the LORD of all your tithes, which ye receive of the children of Israel; and ye shall give thereof the LORD's heave offering to Aaron the priest.

29Out of all your gifts ye shall offer every heave offering of the LORD, of all the best thereof, *even* the hallowed part thereof out of it.

30Therefore thou shalt say unto them, When ye have heaved the best thereof from it, then it shall be counted unto the Levites as the increase of the threshingfloor, and as the increase of the winepress.

31And ye shall eat it in every place, ye and your households: for it *is* your reward for your service in the tabernacle of the congregation.

32And ye shall bear no sin by reason of it, when ye have heaved from it the best of it: neither shall ye pollute the holy things of the children of Israel, lest ye die.

19 AND THE LORD spake unto Moses and unto Aaron, saying,

2This *is* the ordinance of the law which the LORD hath commanded, saying, Speak unto the children of Israel, that they bring thee a red heifer without spot, wherein *is* no blemish, *and* upon which never came yoke:

3And ye shall give her unto Eleazar the priest, that he may bring her forth without the camp, and *one* shall slay her before his face:

4And Eleazar the priest shall take of her blood with his finger, and sprinkle of her blood directly before the tabernacle of the congregation seven times:

New International

17"But you must not redeem the firstborn of an ox, a sheep or a goat; they are holy. Sprinkle their blood on the altar and burn their fat as an offering made by fire, an aroma pleasing to the LORD. 18Their meat is to be yours, just as the breast of the wave offering and the right thigh are yours. 19Whatever is set aside from the holy offerings the Israelites present to the LORD I give to you and your sons and daughters as your regular share. It is an everlasting covenant of salt before the LORD for both you and your offspring."

20The LORD said to Aaron, "You will have no inheritance in their land, nor will you have any share among them; I am your share and your inheritance among the Israelites.

21"I give to the Levites all the tithes in Israel as their inheritance in return for the work they do while serving at the Tent of Meeting. 22From now on the Israelites must not go near the Tent of Meeting, or they will bear the consequences of their sin and will die. 23It is the Levites who are to do the work at the Tent of Meeting and bear the responsibility for offenses against it. This is a lasting ordinance for the generations to come. They will receive no inheritance among the Israelites. 24Instead, I give to the Levites as their inheritance the tithes that the Israelites present as an offering to the LORD. That is why I said concerning them: 'They will have no inheritance among the Israelites.' "

25The LORD said to Moses, 26"Speak to the Levites and say to them: 'When you receive from the Israelites the tithe I give you as your inheritance, you must present a tenth of that tithe as the LORD's offering. 27Your offering will be reckoned to you as grain from the threshing floor or juice from the winepress. 28In this way you also will present an offering to the LORD from all the tithes you receive from the Israelites. From these tithes you must give the LORD's portion to Aaron the priest. 29You must present as the LORD's portion the best and holiest part of everything given to you.'

30"Say to the Levites: 'When you present the best part, it will be reckoned to you as the product of threshing floor or the winepress. 31You and your households may eat the rest of it anywhere, for it is your wages for your work at the Tent of Meeting. 32By presenting the best part of it you will not be guilty in this matter; then you will not defile the holy offerings of the Israelites, and you will not die.' "

The Water of Cleansing

19 THE LORD said to Moses and Aaron: 2"This is a requirement of the law that the LORD has commanded: Tell the Israelites to bring you a red heifer without defect or blemish and that has never been under a yoke. 3Give it to Eleazar the priest; it is to be taken outside the camp and slaughtered in his presence. 4Then Eleazar the priest is to take some of its blood on his finger and sprinkle it seven times toward the front of the Tent of Meeting. 5While he watches, the heifer is to be

Living Bible

17"However, the firstborn of cows, sheep, or goats may not be bought back; they must be sacrificed to the Lord.ᵃ Their blood is to be sprinkled upon the altar, and their fat shall be burned as a fire offering; it is very pleasant to the Lord. 18The meat of these animals shall be yours, including the breast and right thigh that are presented to the Lord by the gesture of waving before the altar. 19Yes, I have given to you all of these 'wave offerings' brought by the people of Israel to the Lord; they are for you and your families as food; this is a permanent contractᵇ between the Lord and you and your descendants.

20"You priests may own no property, nor have any other income, for I am all that you need.

21As for the tribe of Levi, your relatives, they shall be paid for their service with the tithes from the entire land of Israel.

22"From now on, Israelites other than the priests and Levites shall not enter the sanctuary, lest they be judged guilty and die. 23Only the Levites shall do the work there, and they shall be guilty if they fail. This is a permanent law among you, that the Levites shall own no property in Israel, 24for the people's tithes, offered to the Lord by the gesture of waving before the altar, shall belong to the Levites; these are their inheritance, and so they have no need for property."

25, 26The Lord also said to Moses, "Tell the Levites to give to the Lord a tenth of the tithes they receive—a tithe of the tithe, to be presented to the Lord by the gesture of waving before the altar. 27The Lord will consider this as your first-of-the-harvest offering to him of grain and wine, as though it were from your own property. 28, 29This tithe of the tithe shall be selected from the choicest part of the tithes you receive as the Lord's portion, and shall be given to Aaron the priest. 30It shall be credited to you just as though it were from your own threshing floor and wine press. 31Aaron and his sons and their families may eat it in their homes or anywhere they wish, for it is their compensation for their service in the Tabernacle. 32You Levites will not be held guilty for accepting the Lord's tithes if you then give the best tenth to the priests. But beware that you do not treat the holy gifts of the people of Israel as though they were common, lest you die."

New Revised Standard

or the firstborn of a sheep, or the firstborn of a goat, you shall not redeem; they are holy. You shall dash their blood on the altar, and shall turn their fat into smoke as an offering by fire for a pleasing odor to the LORD; 18but their flesh shall be yours, just as the breast that is elevated and as the right thigh are yours. 19All the holy offerings that the Israelites present to the LORD I have given to you, together with your sons and daughters, as a perpetual due; it is a covenant of salt forever before the LORD for you and your descendants as well. 20Then the LORD said to Aaron: You shall have no allotment in their land, nor shall you have any share among them; I am your share and your possession among the Israelites.

21 To the Levites I have given every tithe in Israel for a possession in return for the service that they perform, the service in the tent of meeting. 22From now on the Israelites shall no longer approach the tent of meeting, or else they will incur guilt and die. 23But the Levites shall perform the service of the tent of meeting, and they shall bear responsibility for their own offenses; it shall be a perpetual statute throughout your generations. But among the Israelites they shall have no allotment, 24because I have given to the Levites as their portion the tithe of the Israelites, which they set apart as an offering to the LORD. Therefore I have said of them that they shall have no allotment among the Israelites.

25 Then the LORD spoke to Moses, saying: 26You shall speak to the Levites, saying: When you receive from the Israelites the tithe that I have given you from them for your portion, you shall set apart an offering from it to the LORD, a tithe of the tithe. 27It shall be reckoned to you as your gift, the same as the grain of the threshing floor and the fullness of the wine press. 28Thus you also shall set apart an offering to the LORD from all the tithes that you receive from the Israelites; and from them you shall give the LORD's offering to the priest Aaron. 29Out of all the gifts to you, you shall set apart every offering due to the LORD; the best of all of them is the part to be consecrated. 30Say also to them: When you have set apart the best of it, then the rest shall be reckoned to the Levites as produce of the threshing floor, and as produce of the wine press. 31You may eat it in any place, you and your households; for it is your payment for your service in the tent of meeting. 32You shall incur no guilt by reason of it, when you have offered the best of it. But you shall not profane the holy gifts of the Israelites, on pain of death.

Ceremony of the Red Heifer

19 THE LORD said to Moses and Aaron, "Here is another of my laws:

"Tell the people of Israel to bring you a red heifer without defect, one that has never been yoked. Give her to Eleazar the priest and he shall take her outside the camp and someone shall kill her as he watches. 4Eleazar shall take some of her blood upon his finger and sprinkle it seven times towards the front of the Tabernacle. 5Then

19 THE LORD spoke to Moses and Aaron, saying: 2This is a statute of the law that the LORD has commanded: Tell the Israelites to bring you a red heifer without defect, in which there is no blemish and on which no yoke has been laid. 3You shall give it to the priest Eleazar, and it shall be taken outside the camp and slaughtered in his presence. 4The priest Eleazar shall take some of its blood with his finger and sprinkle it seven times towards the front of the tent of meeting.

ᵃ *18:17 they must be sacrificed to the Lord,* literally, "they are holy."
ᵇ *18:19 a permanent contract,* literally, "a covenant of salt."

King James

5And *one* shall burn the heifer in his sight; her skin, and her flesh, and her blood, with her dung, shall he burn:

6And the priest shall take cedar wood, and hyssop, and scarlet, and cast *it* into the midst of the burning of the heifer.

7Then the priest shall wash his clothes, and he shall bathe his flesh in water, and afterward he shall come into the camp, and the priest shall be unclean until the even.

8And he that burneth her shall wash his clothes in water, and bathe his flesh in water, and shall be unclean until the even.

9And a man *that is* clean shall gather up the ashes of the heifer, and lay *them* up without the camp in a clean place, and it shall be kept for the congregation of the children of Israel for a water of separation: it *is* a purification for sin.

10And he that gathereth the ashes of the heifer shall wash his clothes, and be unclean until the even: and it shall be unto the children of Israel, and unto the stranger that sojourneth among them, for a statute for ever.

11¶ He that toucheth the dead body of any man shall be unclean seven days.

12He shall purify himself with it on the third day, and on the seventh day he shall be clean: but if he purify not himself the third day, then the seventh day he shall not be clean.

13Whosoever toucheth the dead body of any man that is dead, and purifieth not himself, defileth the tabernacle of the LORD; and that soul shall be cut off from Israel: because the water of separation was not sprinkled upon him, he shall be unclean; his uncleanness *is* yet upon him.

14This *is* the law, when a man dieth in a tent: all that come into the tent, and all that *is* in the tent, shall be unclean seven days.

15And every open vessel, which hath no covering bound upon it, *is* unclean.

16And whosoever toucheth one that is slain with a sword in the open fields, or a dead body, or a bone of a man, or a grave, shall be unclean seven days.

17And for an unclean *person* they shall take of the ashes of the burnt heifer of purification for sin, and running water shall be put thereto in a vessel:

18And a clean person shall take hyssop, and dip *it* in the water, and sprinkle *it* upon the tent, and upon all the vessels, and upon the persons that were there, and upon him that touched a bone, or one slain, or one dead, or a grave:

19And the clean *person* shall sprinkle upon the unclean on the third day, and on the seventh day: and on the seventh day he shall purify himself, and wash his clothes, and bathe himself in water, and shall be clean at even.

20But the man that shall be unclean, and shall not purify himself, that soul shall be cut off from among the congregation, because he hath defiled the sanctuary of the LORD: the water of separation hath not been sprinkled upon him; he *is* unclean.

21And it shall be a perpetual statute unto them, that he that sprinkleth the water of separation shall wash his clothes; and he that toucheth the water of separation shall be unclean until even.

22And whatsoever the unclean *person* toucheth shall be unclean; and the soul that toucheth *it* shall be unclean until even.

New International

burned—its hide, flesh, blood and offal. 6The priest is to take some cedar wood, hyssop and scarlet wool and throw them onto the burning heifer. 7After that, the priest must wash his clothes and bathe himself with water. He may then come into the camp, but he will be ceremonially unclean till evening. 8The man who burns it must also wash his clothes and bathe with water, and he too will be unclean till evening.

9"A man who is clean shall gather up the ashes of the heifer and put them in a ceremonially clean place outside the camp. They shall be kept by the Israelite community for use in the water of cleansing; it is for purification from sin. 10The man who gathers up the ashes of the heifer must also wash his clothes, and he too will be unclean till evening. This will be a lasting ordinance both for the Israelites and for the aliens living among them.

11"Whoever touches the dead body of anyone will be unclean for seven days. 12He must purify himself with the water on the third day and on the seventh day; then he will be clean. But if he does not purify himself on the third and seventh days, he will not be clean. 13Whoever touches the dead body of anyone and fails to purify himself defiles the LORD's tabernacle. That person must be cut off from Israel. Because the water of cleansing has not been sprinkled on him, he is unclean; his uncleanness remains on him.

14"This is the law that applies when a person dies in a tent: Anyone who enters the tent and anyone who is in it will be unclean for seven days, 15and every open container without a lid fastened on it will be unclean.

16"Anyone out in the open who touches someone who has been killed with a sword or someone who has died a natural death, or anyone who touches a human bone or a grave, will be unclean for seven days.

17"For the unclean person, put some ashes from the burned purification offering into a jar and pour fresh water over them. 18Then a man who is ceremonially clean is to take some hyssop, dip it in the water and sprinkle the tent and all the furnishings and the people who were there. He must also sprinkle anyone who has touched a human bone or a grave or someone who has been killed or someone who has died a natural death. 19The man who is clean is to sprinkle the unclean person on the third and seventh days, and on the seventh day he is to purify him. The person being cleansed must wash his clothes and bathe with water, and that evening he will be clean. 20But if a person who is unclean does not purify himself, he must be cut off from the community, because he has defiled the sanctuary of the LORD. The water of cleansing has not been sprinkled on him, and he is unclean. 21This is a lasting ordinance for them.

"The man who sprinkles the water of cleansing must also wash his clothes, and anyone who touches the water of cleansing will be unclean till evening. 22Anything that an unclean person touches becomes unclean, and anyone who touches it becomes unclean till evening."

Living Bible

someone shall burn the heifer as he watches—her hide, meat, blood, and dung. 6Eleazar shall take cedar wood and hyssop branches and scarlet thread, and throw them into the burning pile.

7"Then he must wash his clothes, and bathe, and afterwards return to the camp and be ceremonially defiled until the evening. 8And the one who burns the animal must wash his clothes, and bathe, and he too shall be defiled until evening. 9Then someone who is not ceremonially defiled shall gather up the ashes of the heifer and place them in some purified place outside the camp, where they shall be kept for the people of Israel as a source of water for the purification ceremonies, for removal of sin. 10And the one who gathers up the ashes of the heifer must wash his clothes and be defiled until evening; this is a permanent law for the benefit of the people of Israel and any foreigners living among them.

11"Anyone who touches a dead human body shall be defiled for seven days, 12and must purify himself the third and seventh days with water [run through the ashes of the red heifer^a]; then he will be purified; but if he does not do this on the third day, he will continue to be defiled even after the seventh day. 13Anyone who touches a dead person and does not purify himself in the manner specified, has defiled the Tabernacle of the Lord, and shall be excommunicated from Israel. The cleansing water was not sprinkled upon him, so the defilement continues.

14"When a man dies in a tent, these are the various regulations: Everyone who enters the tent, and those who are in it at the time, shall be defiled seven days. 15Any container in the tent without a lid over it is defiled.

16"If someone out in a field touches the corpse of someone who has been killed in battle, or who has died in any other way, or if he even touches a bone or a grave, he shall be defiled seven days. 17To become purified again, ashes from the red heifer sin offering^b are to be added to spring water in a kettle. 18Then a person who is not defiled shall take hyssop branches and dip them into the water and sprinkle the water upon the tent and upon all the pots and pans in the tent, and upon anyone who has been defiled by being in the tent, or by touching a bone, or touching someone who has been killed or is otherwise dead, or has touched a grave. 19This shall take place on the third and seventh days; then the defiled person must wash his clothes and bathe himself, and that evening he will be out from under the defilement.

20"But anyone who is defiled and doesn't purify himself shall be excommunicated, for he has defiled the sanctuary of the Lord, and the water to cleanse him has not been sprinkled upon him; so he remains defiled. 21This is a permanent law. The man who sprinkles the water must afterwards wash his clothes; and anyone touching the water shall be defiled until evening. 22And anything a defiled person touches shall be defiled until evening."

New Revised Standard

5Then the heifer shall be burned in his sight; its skin, its flesh, and its blood, with its dung, shall be burned. 6The priest shall take cedarwood, hyssop, and crimson material, and throw them into the fire in which the heifer is burning. 7Then the priest shall wash his clothes and bathe his body in water, and afterwards he may come into the camp; but the priest shall remain unclean until evening. 8The one who burns the heifer^c shall wash his clothes in water and bathe his body in water; he shall remain unclean until evening. 9Then someone who is clean shall gather up the ashes of the heifer, and deposit them outside the camp in a clean place; and they shall be kept for the congregation of the Israelites for the water for cleansing. It is a purification offering. 10The one who gathers the ashes of the heifer shall wash his clothes and be unclean until evening.

This shall be a perpetual statute for the Israelites and for the alien residing among them. 11Those who touch the dead body of any human being shall be unclean seven days. 12They shall purify themselves with the water on the third day and on the seventh day, and so be clean; but if they do not purify themselves on the third day and on the seventh day, they will not become clean. 13All who touch a corpse, the body of a human being who has died, and do not purify themselves, defile the tabernacle of the LORD; such persons shall be cut off from Israel. Since water for cleansing was not dashed on them, they remain unclean; their uncleanness is still on them.

14 This is the law when someone dies in a tent: everyone who comes into the tent, and everyone who is in the tent, shall be unclean seven days. 15And every open vessel with no cover fastened on it is unclean. 16Whoever in the open field touches one who has been killed by a sword, or who has died naturally,^{d} or a human bone, or a grave, shall be unclean seven days. 17For the unclean they shall take some ashes of the burnt purification offering, and running water shall be added in a vessel; 18then a clean person shall take hyssop, dip it in the water, and sprinkle it on the tent, on all the furnishings, on the persons who were there, and on whoever touched the bone, the slain, the corpse, or the grave. 19The clean person shall sprinkle the unclean ones on the third day and on the seventh day, thus purifying them on the seventh day. Then they shall wash their clothes and bathe themselves in water, and at evening they shall be clean. 20Any who are unclean but do not purify themselves, those persons shall be cut off from the assembly, for they have defiled the sanctuary of the LORD. Since the water for cleansing has not been dashed on them, they are unclean.

21 It shall be a perpetual statute for them. The one who sprinkles the water for cleansing shall wash his clothes, and whoever touches the water for cleansing shall be unclean until evening. 22Whatever the unclean person touches shall be unclean, and anyone who touches it shall be unclean until evening.

---

^{a} 19:12 *run through the ashes of the red heifer,* implied. See verse 17.
^{b} 19:17 *ashes from the red heifer sin offering,* literally, "ashes of the burnt sin offering."

^{c} Heb *it* ^{d} Heb lacks *naturally*

King James

20 THEN CAME the children of Israel, *even* the whole congregation, into the desert of Zin in the first month: and the people abode in Kadesh; and Miriam died there, and was buried there.

2And there was no water for the congregation: and they gathered themselves together against Moses and against Aaron.

3And the people chode with Moses, and spake, saying, Would God that we had died when our brethren died before the LORD!

4And why have ye brought up the congregation of the LORD into this wilderness, that we and our cattle should die there?

5And wherefore have ye made us to come up out of Egypt, to bring us in unto this evil place? it *is* no place of seed, or of figs, or of vines, or of pomegranates; neither *is* there any water to drink.

6And Moses and Aaron went from the presence of the assembly unto the door of the tabernacle of the congregation, and they fell upon their faces: and the glory of the LORD appeared unto them.

7¶ And the LORD spake unto Moses, saying,

8Take the rod, and gather thou the assembly together, thou, and Aaron thy brother, and speak ye unto the rock before their eyes; and it shall give forth his water, and thou shalt bring forth to them water out of the rock: so thou shalt give the congregation and their beasts drink.

9And Moses took the rod from before the LORD, as he commanded him.

10And Moses and Aaron gathered the congregation together before the rock, and he said unto them, Hear now, ye rebels; must we fetch you water out of this rock?

11And Moses lifted up his hand, and with his rod he smote the rock twice: and the water came out abundantly, and the congregation drank, and their beasts *also*.

12¶ And the LORD spake unto Moses and Aaron, Because ye believed me not, to sanctify me in the eyes of the children of Israel, therefore ye shall not bring this congregation into the land which I have given them.

13This *is* the water of Meribah; because the children of Israel strove with the LORD, and he was sanctified in them.

14¶ And Moses sent messengers from Kadesh unto the king of Edom, Thus saith thy brother Israel, Thou knowest all the travail that hath befallen us:

15How our fathers went down into Egypt, and we have dwelt in Egypt a long time; and the Egyptians vexed us, and our fathers:

16And when we cried unto the LORD, he heard our voice, and sent an angel, and hath brought us forth out of Egypt: and, behold, we *are* in Kadesh, a city in the uttermost of thy border:

17Let us pass, I pray thee, through thy country: we will not pass through the fields, or through the vineyards, neither will we drink *of* the water of the wells: we will go by the king's *high* way, we will not turn to the right hand nor to the left, until we have passed thy borders.

18And Edom said unto him, Thou shalt not pass by me, lest I come out against thee with the sword.

19And the children of Israel said unto him, We will go by the high way: and if I and my cattle drink of thy water, then I will pay for it: I will only, without *doing* any thing *else*, go through on my feet.

20And he said, Thou shalt not go through. And Edom came out against him with much people, and with a strong hand.

21Thus Edom refused to give Israel passage through his border: wherefore Israel turned away from him.

New International

Water From the Rock

20 IN THE first month the whole Israelite community arrived at the Desert of Zin, and they stayed at Kadesh. There Miriam died and was buried.

2Now there was no water for the community, and the people gathered in opposition to Moses and Aaron. 3They quarreled with Moses and said, "If only we had died when our brothers fell dead before the LORD! 4Why did you bring the LORD's community into this desert, that we and our livestock should die here? 5Why did you bring us up out of Egypt to this terrible place? It has no grain or figs, grapevines or pomegranates. And there is no water to drink!"

6Moses and Aaron went from the assembly to the entrance to the Tent of Meeting and fell facedown, and the glory of the LORD appeared to them. 7The LORD said to Moses, 8"Take the staff, and you and your brother Aaron gather the assembly together. Speak to that rock before their eyes and it will pour out its water. You will bring water out of the rock for the community so they and their livestock can drink."

9So Moses took the staff from the LORD's presence, just as he commanded him. 10He and Aaron gathered the assembly together in front of the rock and Moses said to them, "Listen, you rebels, must we bring you water out of this rock?" 11Then Moses raised his arm and struck the rock twice with his staff. Water gushed out, and the community and their livestock drank.

12But the LORD said to Moses and Aaron, "Because you did not trust in me enough to honor me as holy in the sight of the Israelites, you will not bring this community into the land I give them."

13These were the waters of Meribah,ᵃ where the Israelites quarreled with the LORD and where he showed himself holy among them.

Edom Denies Israel Passage

14Moses sent messengers from Kadesh to the king of Edom, saying:

"This is what your brother Israel says: You know about all the hardships that have come upon us. 15Our forefathers went down into Egypt, and we lived there many years. The Egyptians mistreated us and our fathers, 16but when we cried out to the LORD, he heard our cry and sent an angel and brought us out of Egypt.

"Now we are here at Kadesh, a town on the edge of your territory. 17Please let us pass through your country. We will not go through any field or vineyard, or drink water from any well. We will travel along the king's highway and not turn to the right or to the left until we have passed through your territory."

18But Edom answered:

"You may not pass through here; if you try, we will march out and attack you with the sword."

19The Israelites replied:

"We will go along the main road, and if we or our livestock drink any of your water, we will pay for it. We only want to pass through on foot—nothing else."

20Again they answered:

"You may not pass through."

Then Edom came out against them with a large and powerful army. 21Since Edom refused to let them go through their territory, Israel turned away from them.

ᵃ *13 Meribah* means *quarreling.*

Living Bible

20 THE PEOPLE of Israel arrived in the wilderness of Zin in April[b] and camped at Kadesh, where Miriam died and was buried. 2There was not enough water to drink at that place, so the people again rebelled against Moses and Aaron. A great mob formed, 3and they held a protest meeting.

"Would that we too had died with our dear brothers the Lord killed!" they shouted at Moses. 4"You have deliberately brought us into this wilderness to get rid of us, along with our flocks and herds. 5Why did you ever make us leave Egypt and bring us here to this evil place? Where is the fertile land of wonderful crops—the figs, vines, and pomegranates you told us about? Why, there isn't even water enough to drink!"

6Moses and Aaron turned away and went to the entrance of the Tabernacle, where they fell face downward before the Lord; and the glory of Jehovah appeared to them.

7And he said to Moses, 8"Get Aaron's[c] rod; then you and Aaron must summon the people. As they watch, speak to that rock over there and tell it to pour out its water! You will give them water from a rock, enough for all the people and all their cattle!"

9So Moses did as instructed. He took the rod from the place where it was kept before the Lord; 10then Moses and Aaron summoned the people to come and gather at the rock; and he said to them, "Listen, you rebels! Must we bring you water from this rock?"

11Then Moses lifted the rod and struck the rock twice, and water gushed out; and the people and their cattle drank.

12But the Lord said to Moses and Aaron, "Because you did not believe me[d] and did not sanctify me in the eyes of the people of Israel, you shall not bring them into the land I have promised them!"

13This place was named Meribah (meaning "Rebel Waters"), because it was where the people of Israel fought against Jehovah, and where he showed himself to be holy before them.

14While Moses was at Kadesh he sent messengers to the king of Edom: "We are the descendants of your brother[e] Israel," he declared. "You know our sad history, 15how our ancestors went down to visit Egypt and stayed there so long, and became slaves of the Egyptians. 16But when we cried to the Lord he heard us and sent an Angel who brought us out of Egypt, and now we are here at Kadesh, encamped on the borders of your land. 17Please let us pass through your country. We will be careful not to go through your planted fields, nor through your vineyards; we won't even drink water from your wells, but will stay on the main road and not leave it until we have crossed your border on the other side."

18But the king of Edom said, "Stay out! If you attempt to enter my land I will meet you with an army!"

19"But, sir," protested the Israeli ambassadors, "we will stay on the main road and will not even drink your water unless we pay whatever you demand for it. We only want to pass through, and nothing else."

20But the king of Edom was adamant. "Stay out!" he warned, and, mobilizing his army, he marched to the frontier with a great force. 21, 22Because Edom refused to allow Israel to pass through their country, Israel turned back and journeyed from Kadesh to Mount Hor.

New Revised Standard

The Waters of Meribah

20 THE ISRAELITES, the whole congregation, came into the wilderness of Zin in the first month, and the people stayed in Kadesh. Miriam died there, and was buried there.

2 Now there was no water for the congregation; so they gathered together against Moses and against Aaron. 3The people quarreled with Moses and said, "Would that we had died when our kindred died before the LORD! 4Why have you brought the assembly of the LORD into this wilderness for us and our livestock to die here? 5Why have you brought us up out of Egypt, to bring us to this wretched place? It is no place for grain, or figs, or vines, or pomegranates; and there is no water to drink." 6Then Moses and Aaron went away from the assembly to the entrance of the tent of meeting; they fell on their faces, and the glory of the LORD appeared to them. 7The LORD spoke to Moses, saying: 8Take the staff, and assemble the congregation, you and your brother Aaron, and command the rock before their eyes to yield its water. Thus you shall bring water out of the rock for them; thus you shall provide drink for the congregation and their livestock.

9 So Moses took the staff from before the LORD, as he had commanded him. 10Moses and Aaron gathered the assembly together before the rock, and he said to them, "Listen, you rebels, shall we bring water for you out of this rock?" 11Then Moses lifted up his hand and struck the rock twice with his staff; water came out abundantly, and the congregation and their livestock drank. 12But the LORD said to Moses and Aaron, "Because you did not trust in me, to show my holiness before the eyes of the Israelites, therefore you shall not bring this assembly into the land that I have given them." 13These are the waters of Meribah,[f] where the people of Israel quarreled with the LORD, and by which he showed his holiness.

Passage through Edom Refused

14 Moses sent messengers from Kadesh to the king of Edom, "Thus says your brother Israel: You know all the adversity that has befallen us: 15how our ancestors went down to Egypt, and we lived in Egypt a long time; and the Egyptians oppressed us and our ancestors; 16and when we cried to the LORD, he heard our voice, and sent an angel and brought us out of Egypt; and here we are in Kadesh, a town on the edge of your territory. 17Now let us pass through your land. We will not pass through field or vineyard, or drink water from any well; we will go along the King's Highway, not turning aside to the right hand or to the left until we have passed through your territory."

18 But Edom said to him, "You shall not pass through, or we will come out with the sword against you." 19The Israelites said to him, "We will stay on the highway; and if we drink of your water, we and our livestock, then we will pay for it. It is only a small matter; just let us pass through on foot." 20But he said, "You shall not pass through." And Edom came out against them with a large force, heavily armed. 21Thus Edom refused to give Israel passage through their territory; so Israel turned away from them.

---

[b] 20:1 in April, literally, "the first month." [c] 20:8 Get Aaron's rod, literally, "get the rod." [d] 20:12 did not believe me, literally, "did not sanctify me." The Lord had said to speak to the rock. Moses struck it, not once, but twice. [e] 20:14 your brother Israel. The people of Edom were descended from Esau, while the people of Israel were descended from his brother Jacob, whose name was later changed to Israel.

[f] That is Quarrel

King James

22¶ And the children of Israel, *even* the whole congregation, journeyed from Kadesh, and came unto mount Hor.

23And the LORD spake unto Moses and Aaron in mount Hor, by the coast of the land of Edom, saying,

24Aaron shall be gathered unto his people: for he shall not enter into the land which I have given unto the children of Israel, because ye rebelled against my word at the water of Meribah.

25Take Aaron and Eleazar his son, and bring them up unto mount Hor:

26And strip Aaron of his garments, and put them upon Eleazar his son: and Aaron shall be gathered *unto his people*, and shall die there.

27And Moses did as the LORD commanded: and they went up into mount Hor in the sight of all the congregation.

28And Moses stripped Aaron of his garments, and put them upon Eleazar his son; and Aaron died there in the top of the mount: and Moses and Eleazar came down from the mount.

29And when all the congregation saw that Aaron was dead, they mourned for Aaron thirty days, *even* all the house of Israel.

21 AND *WHEN* king Arad the Canaanite, which dwelt in the south, heard tell that Israel came by the way of the spies; then he fought against Israel, and took *some* of them prisoners.

2And Israel vowed a vow unto the LORD, and said, If thou wilt indeed deliver this people into my hand, then I will utterly destroy their cities.

3And the LORD hearkened to the voice of Israel, and delivered up the Canaanites; and they utterly destroyed them and their cities: and he called the name of the place Hormah.

4¶ And they journeyed from mount Hor by the way of the Red sea, to compass the land of Edom: and the soul of the people was much discouraged because of the way.

5And the people spake against God, and against Moses, Wherefore have ye brought us up out of Egypt to die in the wilderness? for *there is* no bread, neither *is there any* water; and our soul loatheth this light bread.

6And the LORD sent fiery serpents among the people, and they bit the people; and much people of Israel died.

7¶ Therefore the people came to Moses, and said, We have sinned, for we have spoken against the LORD, and against thee; pray unto the LORD, that he take away the serpents from us. And Moses prayed for the people.

8And the LORD said unto Moses, Make thee a fiery serpent, and set it upon a pole: and it shall come to pass, that every one that is bitten, when he looketh upon it, shall live.

9And Moses made a serpent of brass, and put it upon a pole, and it came to pass, that if a serpent had bitten any man, when he beheld the serpent of brass, he lived.

10¶ And the children of Israel set forward, and pitched in Oboth.

11And they journeyed from Oboth, and pitched in Ije-abarim, in the wilderness which *is* before Moab, toward the sunrising.

12¶ From thence they removed, and pitched in the valley of Zared.

13From thence they removed, and pitched on the other side of Arnon, which *is* in the wilderness that cometh out of the coasts of the Amorites: for Arnon *is* the border of Moab, between Moab and the Amorites.

New International

The Death of Aaron

22The whole Israelite community set out from Kadesh and came to Mount Hor. 23At Mount Hor, near the border of Edom, the LORD said to Moses and Aaron, 24"Aaron will be gathered to his people. He will not enter the land I give the Israelites, because both of you rebelled against my command at the waters of Meribah. 25Get Aaron and his son Eleazar and take them up Mount Hor. 26Remove Aaron's garments and put them on his son Eleazar, for Aaron will be gathered to his people; he will die there."

27Moses did as the LORD commanded: They went up Mount Hor in the sight of the whole community. 28Moses removed Aaron's garments and put them on his son Eleazar. And Aaron died there on top of the mountain. Then Moses and Eleazar came down from the mountain, 29and when the whole community learned that Aaron had died, the entire house of Israel mourned for him thirty days.

Arad Destroyed

21 WHEN THE Canaanite king of Arad, who lived in the Negev, heard that Israel was coming along the road to Atharim, he attacked the Israelites and captured some of them. 2Then Israel made this vow to the LORD: "If you will deliver these people into our hands, we will totally destroy[a] their cities." 3The LORD listened to Israel's plea and gave the Canaanites over to them. They completely destroyed them and their towns; so the place was named Hormah.[b]

The Bronze Snake

4They traveled from Mount Hor along the route to the Red Sea,[c] to go around Edom. But the people grew impatient on the way; 5they spoke against God and against Moses, and said, "Why have you brought us up out of Egypt to die in the desert? There is no bread! There is no water! And we detest this miserable food!"

6Then the LORD sent venomous snakes among them; they bit the people and many Israelites died. 7The people came to Moses and said, "We sinned when we spoke against the LORD and against you. Pray that the LORD will take the snakes away from us." So Moses prayed for the people.

8The LORD said to Moses, "Make a snake and put it up on a pole; anyone who is bitten can look at it and live." 9So Moses made a bronze snake and put it up on a pole. Then when anyone was bitten by a snake and looked at the bronze snake, he lived.

The Journey to Moab

10The Israelites moved on and camped at Oboth. 11Then they set out from Oboth and camped in Iye Abarim, in the desert that faces Moab toward the sunrise. 12From there they moved on and camped in the Zered Valley. 13They set out from there and camped alongside the Arnon, which is in the desert extending into Amorite territory. The Arnon is the border of Moab, between

---

a 2 The Hebrew term refers to the irrevocable giving over of things or persons to the LORD, often by totally destroying them; also in verse 3.   b 3 *Hormah* means *destruction*.   c 4 Hebrew *Yam Suph*; that is, Sea of Reeds

Living Bible

23Then the Lord said to Moses and Aaron at the border of the land of Edom, 24"The time has come for Aaron to die—for he shall not enter the land I have given the people of Israel, for the two of you rebelled against my instructions concerning the water at Meribah. 25Now take Aaron and his son Eleazar and lead them up onto Mount Hor. 26There you shall remove Aaron's priestly garments from him and put them on Eleazar his son; and Aaron shall die there."

27So Moses did as the Lord commanded him. The threed of them went up together into Mount Hor as all the people watched. 28When they reached the summit, Moses removed the priestly garments from Aaron and put them on his son Eleazar; and Aaron died on the top of the mountain. Moses and Eleazar returned, 29and when the people were informed of Aaron's death, they mourned for him for thirty days.

21 WHEN THE king of Arad heard that the Israelis were approaching (for they were traveling the same route as the spies), he mobilized his army and attacked Israel, taking some of the men as prisoners. 2Then the people of Israel vowed to the Lord that if he would help them conquer the king of Arad and his people, they would completely annihilate all the cities of that area. 3The Lord heeded their request and defeated the Canaanites; and the Israelis completely destroyed them and their cities. The name of the region was thereafter called Hormah (meaning "Utterly Destroyed").

4Then the people of Israel returned to Mount Hor, and from there continued southward along the road to the Red Sea in order to go around the land of Edom. The people were very discouraged; 5they began to murmur against God and to complain against Moses. "Why have you brought us out of Egypt to die here in the wilderness?" they whined. "There is nothing to eat here, and nothing to drink, and we hate this insipid manna."

6So the Lord sent poisonous snakes among them to punish them, and many of them were bitten and died.

7Then the people came to Moses and cried out, "We have sinned, for we have spoken against Jehovah and against you. Pray to him to take away the snakes." So Moses prayed for the people.

8Then the Lord told him, "Make a bronze replicae of one of these snakes and attach it to the top of a pole; anyone who is bitten shall live if he simply looks at it!"

9So Moses made the replica, and whenever anyone who had been bitten looked at the bronze snake, he recovered!

10Israel journeyed next to Oboth and camped there. 11Then they went on to Iyeabarim, in the wilderness, a short distance east of Moab, 12and from there they traveled to the valley of the brook Zared and set up camp. 13Then they moved to the far side of the Arnon River, near the borders of the Amorites. (The Arnon River is the boundary line between the Moabites and the Amorites. 14This fact is mentioned in *The Book of the Wars*

New Revised Standard

The Death of Aaron

22 They set out from Kadesh, and the Israelites, the whole congregation, came to Mount Hor. 23Then the LORD said to Moses and Aaron at Mount Hor, on the border of the land of Edom, 24"Let Aaron be gathered to his people. For he shall not enter the land that I have given to the Israelites, because you rebelled against my command at the waters of Meribah. 25Take Aaron and his son Eleazar, and bring them up Mount Hor; 26strip Aaron of his vestments, and put them on his son Eleazar. But Aaron shall be gathered to his people,f and shall die there." 27Moses did as the LORD had commanded; they went up Mount Hor in the sight of the whole congregation. 28Moses stripped Aaron of his vestments, and put them on his son Eleazar; and Aaron died there on the top of the mountain. Moses and Eleazar came down from the mountain. 29When all the congregation saw that Aaron had died, all the house of Israel mourned for Aaron thirty days.

The Bronze Serpent

21 WHEN THE Canaanite, the king of Arad, who lived in the Negeb, heard that Israel was coming by the way of Atharim, he fought against Israel and took some of them captive. 2Then Israel made a vow to the LORD and said, "If you will indeed give this people into our hands, then we will utterly destroy their towns." 3The LORD listened to the voice of Israel, and handed over the Canaanites; and they utterly destroyed them and their towns; so the place was called Hormah.g

4 From Mount Hor they set out by the way to the Red Sea,h to go around the land of Edom; but the people became impatient on the way. 5The people spoke against God and against Moses, "Why have you brought us up out of Egypt to die in the wilderness? For there is no food and no water, and we detest this miserable food." 6Then the LORD sent poisonousi serpents among the people, and they bit the people, so that many Israelites died. 7The people came to Moses and said, "We have sinned by speaking against the LORD and against you; pray to the LORD to take away the serpents from us." So Moses prayed for the people. 8And the LORD said to Moses, "Make a poisonousj serpent, and set it on a pole; and everyone who is bitten shall look at it and live." 9So Moses made a serpent of bronze, and put it upon a pole; and whenever a serpent bit someone, that person would look at the serpent of bronze and live.

The Journey to Moab

10 The Israelites set out, and camped in Oboth. 11They set out from Oboth, and camped at Iye-abarim, in the wilderness bordering Moab toward the sunrise. 12From there they set out, and camped in the Wadi Zered. 13From there they set out, and camped on the other side of the Arnon, ink the wilderness that extends from the boundary of the Amorites; for the Arnon is the boundary of Moab, between Moab and the Amorites.

---

d 20:27 *the three,* implied.   e 21:8 *Make a bronze replica,* literally, "Make a fiery serpent."

f Heb lacks *to his people*   g Heb *Destruction*   h Or *Sea of Reeds*   i Or *fiery*; Heb *seraphim*   j Or *fiery*; Heb *seraph*   k Gk: Heb *which is in*

King James

14Wherefore it is said in the book of the wars of the LORD, What he did in the Red sea, and in the brooks of Arnon,

15And at the stream of the brooks that goeth down to the dwelling of Ar, and lieth upon the border of Moab.

16And from thence *they went* to Beer: that *is* the well whereof the LORD spake unto Moses, Gather the people together, and I will give them water.

17¶ Then Israel sang this song, Spring up, O well; sing ye unto it:

18The princes digged the well, the nobles of the people digged it, by *the direction of* the lawgiver, with their staves. And from the wilderness *they went* to Mattanah:

19And from Mattanah to Nahaliel: and from Nahaliel to Bamoth:

20And from Bamoth *in* the valley, that *is* in the country of Moab, to the top of Pisgah, which looketh toward Jeshimon.

21¶ And Israel sent messengers unto Sihon king of the Amorites, saying,

22Let me pass through thy land: we will not turn into the fields, or into the vineyards; we will not drink *of* the waters of the well: *but* we will go along by the king's *high* way, until we be past thy borders.

23And Sihon would not suffer Israel to pass through his border: but Sihon gathered all his people together, and went out against Israel into the wilderness: and he came to Jahaz, and fought against Israel.

24And Israel smote him with the edge of the sword, and possessed his land from Arnon unto Jabbok, even unto the children of Ammon: for the border of the children of Ammon *was* strong.

25And Israel took all these cities: and Israel dwelt in all the cities of the Amorites, in Heshbon, and in all the villages thereof.

26For Heshbon *was* the city of Sihon the king of the Amorites, who had fought against the former king of Moab, and taken all his land out of his hand, even unto Arnon.

27Wherefore they that speak in proverbs say, Come into Heshbon, let the city of Sihon be built and prepared:

28For there is a fire gone out of Heshbon, a flame from the city of Sihon: it hath consumed Ar of Moab, *and* the lords of the high places of Arnon.

29Woe to thee, Moab! thou art undone, O people of Chemosh: he hath given his sons that escaped, and his daughters, into captivity unto Sihon king of the Amorites.

30We have shot at them; Heshbon is perished even unto Dibon, and we have laid them waste even unto Nophah, which *reacheth* unto Medeba.

31¶ Thus Israel dwelt in the land of the Amorites.

32And Moses sent to spy out Jaazer, and they took the villages thereof, and drove out the Amorites that *were* there.

33¶ And they turned and went up by the way of Bashan: and Og the king of Bashan went out against them, he, and all his people, to the battle at Edrei.

34And the LORD said unto Moses, Fear him not: for I have delivered him into thy hand, and all his people, and his land; and thou shalt do to him as thou didst unto Sihon king of the Amorites, which dwelt at Heshbon.

New International

Moab and the Amorites. 14That is why the Book of the Wars of the LORD says:

"... Waheb in Suphaha and the ravines,
    the Arnon 15andb the slopes of the ravines
that lead to the site of Ar
    and lie along the border of Moab."

16From there they continued on to Beer, the well where the LORD said to Moses, 'Gather the people together and I will give them water."

17Then Israel sang this song:

"Spring up, O well!
    Sing about it,
18about the well that the princes dug,
    that the nobles of the people sank—
    the nobles with scepters and staffs."

Then they went from the desert to Mattanah, 19from Mattanah to Nahaliel, from Nahaliel to Bamoth, 20and from Bamoth to the valley in Moab where the top of Pisgah overlooks the wasteland.

Defeat of Sihon and Og

21Israel sent messengers to say to Sihon king of the Amorites:

22"Let us pass through your country. We will not turn aside into any field or vineyard, or drink water from any well. We will travel along the king's highway until we have passed through your territory."

23But Sihon would not let Israel pass through his territory. He mustered his entire army and marched out into the desert against Israel. When he reached Jahaz, he fought with Israel. 24Israel, however, put him to the sword and took over his land from the Arnon to the Jabbok, but only as far as the Ammonites, because their border was fortified. 25Israel captured all the cities of the Amorites and occupied them, including Heshbon and all its surrounding settlements. 26Heshbon was the city of Sihon king of the Amorites, who had fought against the former king of Moab and had taken from him all his land as far as the Arnon.

27That is why the poets say:

"Come to Heshbon and let it be rebuilt;
    let Sihon's city be restored.

28"Fire went out from Heshbon,
    a blaze from the city of Sihon.
It consumed Ar of Moab,
    the citizens of Arnon's heights.
29Woe to you, O Moab!
    You are destroyed, O people of Chemosh!
He has given up his sons as fugitives
    and his daughters as captives
    to Sihon king of the Amorites.

30"But we have overthrown them;
    Heshbon is destroyed all the way to Dibon.
We have demolished them as far as Nophah,
    which extends to Medeba."

31So Israel settled in the land of the Amorites.

32After Moses had sent spies to Jazer, the Israelites captured its surrounding settlements and drove out the Amorites who were there. 33Then they turned and went up along the road toward Bashan, and Og king of Bashan and his whole army marched out to meet them in battle at Edrei.

34The LORD said to Moses, "Do not be afraid of him, for I have handed him over to you, with his whole army and his land. Do to him what you did to Sihon king of the Amorites, who reigned in Heshbon."

---

a *14* The meaning of the Hebrew for this phrase is uncertain.   b *14,15* Or
"I have been given from Suphah and the ravines / of the Arnon 15*to*

Living Bible

of Jehovah, where it is stated that the valley of the Arnon River, and the city of Waheb, 15lie between the Amorites and the people of Moab.)

16Then Israel traveled to Beer (meaning "A Well"). This is the place where the Lord told Moses, "Summon the people, and I will give them water." 17, 18What happened is described in this song the people sang:

Spring up, O well!
Sing of the water!
This is a well
The leaders dug.
It was hollowed
With their staves
And shovels.

Then they left the desert and proceeded on through Mattanah, 19Naha-liel, and Bamoth; 20then to the valley in the plateau of Moab, which overlooks the desert with Mount Pisgah in the distance.

21Israel now sent ambassadors to King Sihon of the Amorites.

22"Let us travel through your land," they requested. "We will not leave the road until we have passed beyond your borders. We won't trample your fields or touch your vineyards or drink your water."

23But King Sihon refused. Instead he mobilized his army and attacked Israel in the wilderness, battling them at Jahaz. 24But Israel slaughtered them and occupied their land from the Arnon River to the Jabbok River, as far as the borders of the Ammonites; but they were stopped there by the rugged terrain.c

25, 26So Israel captured all the cities of the Amorites and lived in them, including the city of Heshbon, which had been King Sihon's capital. 27-30The ancient poets had referred to King Sihon in this poem:

Come to Heshbon,
King Sihon's capital,
For a fire has flamed forth
And devoured
The city of Ar in Moab,
On the heights of the Arnon River.
Woe to Moab!
You are finished,
O people of Chemosh;
Your sons have fled,
And your daughters are captured
By King Sihon of the Amorites.
He has destroyed
The little children
And the men and women
As far as Dibon, Nophah, and Medeba.

31, 32While Israel was there in the Amorite country, Moses sent spies to look over the Jazer area; he followed up with an armed attack, capturing all of the towns and driving out the Amorites. 33They next turned their attention to the city of Bashan, but King Og of Bashan met them with his army at Edrei. 34The Lord told Moses not to fear—that the enemy was already conquered! "The same thing will happen to King Og as happened to King Sihon at Heshbon," the Lord assured him. 35And sure

New Revised Standard

14Wherefore it is said in the Book of the Wars of the Lord,

"Waheb in Suphah and the wadis.
The Arnon 15and the slopes of the wadis
that extend to the seat of Ar,
and lie along the border of Moab."d

16 From there they continued to Beer;e that is the well of which the Lord said to Moses, "Gather the people together, and I will give them water." 17Then Israel sang this song:

"Spring up, O well!—Sing to it!—
18 the well that the leaders sank,
that the nobles of the people dug,
with the scepter, with the staff."

From the wilderness to Mattanah, 19from Mattanah to Nahaliel, from Nahaliel to Bamoth, 20and from Bamoth to the valley lying in the region of Moab by the top of Pisgah that overlooks the wasteland.f

King Sihon Defeated

21 Then Israel sent messengers to King Sihon of the Amorites, saying, 22"Let me pass through your land; we will not turn aside into field or vineyard; we will not drink the water of any well; we will go by the King's Highway until we have passed through your territory." 23But Sihon would not allow Israel to pass through his territory. Sihon gathered all his people together, and went out against Israel to the wilderness; he came to Jahaz, and fought against Israel. 24Israel put him to the sword, and took possession of his land from the Arnon to the Jabbok, as far as to the Ammonites; for the boundary of the Ammonites was strong. 25Israel took all these towns, and Israel settled in all the towns of the Amorites, in Heshbon, and in all its villages. 26For Heshbon was the city of King Sihon of the Amorites, who had fought against the former king of Moab and captured all his land as far as the Arnon. 27Therefore the ballad singers say,

"Come to Heshbon, let it be built;
let the city of Sihon be established.
28 For fire came out from Heshbon,
flame from the city of Sihon.
It devoured Ar of Moab,
and swallowed upg the heights of the
Arnon.
29 Woe to you, O Moab!
You are undone, O people of Chemosh!
He has made his sons fugitives,
and his daughters captives,
to an Amorite king, Sihon.
30 So their posterity perished
from Heshbonh to Dibon,
and we laid waste until fire spread to
Medeba."i

31 Thus Israel settled in the land of the Amorites. 32Moses sent to spy out Jazer; and they captured its villages, and dispossessed the Amorites who were there.

King Og Defeated

33 Then they turned and went up the road to Bashan; and King Og of Bashan came out against them, he and all his people, to battle at Edrei. 34But the Lord said to Moses, "Do not be afraid of him; for I have given him into your hand, with all his people, and all his land. You shall do to him as you did to King Sihon of the Amorites, who ruled in Heshbon." 35So they killed him, his sons,

---

c 21:24 *but they were stopped there by the rugged terrain*, literally, "For the border of the children of Ammon was strong." Deuteronomy 2:19 indicates that God had promised the land of the Ammonites to the descendants of Lot.

d Meaning of Heb uncertain   e That is *Well*   f Or *Jeshimon*   g Gk: Heb *and the lords of*   h Gk: Heb *we have shot at them; Heshbon has perished*   i Compare Sam Gk: Meaning of MT uncertain

King James

35So they smote him, and his sons, and all his people, until there was none left him alive: and they possessed his land.

22 AND THE children of Israel set forward, and pitched in the plains of Moab on this side Jordan *by* Jericho.

2¶ And Balak the son of Zippor saw all that Israel had done to the Amorites.

3And Moab was sore afraid of the people, because they *were* many: and Moab was distressed because of the children of Israel.

4And Moab said unto the elders of Midian, Now shall this company lick up all *that are* round about us, as the ox licketh up the grass of the field. And Balak the son of Zippor *was* king of the Moabites at that time.

5He sent messengers therefore unto Balaam the son of Beor to Pethor, which *is* by the river of the land of the children of his people, to call him, saying, Behold, there is a people come out from Egypt: behold, they cover the face of the earth, and they abide over against me:

6Come now therefore, I pray thee, curse me this people; for they *are* too mighty for me: peradventure I shall prevail, *that* we may smite them, and *that* I may drive them out of the land: for I wot that he whom thou blessest *is* blessed, and he whom thou cursest is cursed.

7And the elders of Moab and the elders of Midian departed with the rewards of divination in their hand; and they came unto Balaam, and spake unto him the words of Balak.

8And he said unto them, Lodge here this night, and I will bring you word again, as the LORD shall speak unto me: and the princes of Moab abode with Balaam.

9And God came unto Balaam, and said, What men *are* these with thee?

10And Balaam said unto God, Balak the son of Zippor, king of Moab, hath sent unto me, *saying,*

11Behold, *there is* a people come out of Egypt, which covereth the face of the earth: come now, curse me them; peradventure I shall be able to overcome them, and drive them out.

12And God said unto Balaam, Thou shalt not go with them; thou shalt not curse the people: for they *are* blessed.

13And Balaam rose up in the morning, and said unto the princes of Balak, Get you into your land: for the LORD refuseth to give me leave to go with you.

14And the princes of Moab rose up, and they went unto Balak, and said, Balaam refuseth to come with us.

15¶ And Balak sent yet again princes, more, and more honourable than they.

16And they came to Balaam, and said to him, Thus saith Balak the son of Zippor, Let nothing, I pray thee, hinder thee from coming unto me:

17For I will promote thee unto very great honour, and I will do whatsoever thou sayest unto me: come therefore, I pray thee, curse me this people.

18And Balaam answered and said unto the servants of Balak, If Balak would give me his house full of silver and gold, I cannot go beyond the word of the LORD my God, to do less or more.

19Now therefore, I pray you, tarry ye also here this night, that I may know what the LORD will say unto me more.

20And God came unto Balaam at night, and said unto him, If the men come to call thee, rise up, *and* go with them; but yet the word which I shall say unto thee, that shalt thou do.

21And Balaam rose up in the morning, and saddled his ass, and went with the princes of Moab.

New International

35So they struck him down, together with his sons and his whole army, leaving them no survivors. And they took possession of his land.

Balak Summons Balaam

22 THEN THE Israelites traveled to the plains of Moab and camped along the Jordan across from Jericho.[a]

2Now Balak son of Zippor saw all that Israel had done to the Amorites, 3and Moab was terrified because there were so many people. Indeed, Moab was filled with dread because of the Israelites.

4The Moabites said to the elders of Midian, "This horde is going to lick up everything around us, as an ox licks up the grass of the field."

So Balak son of Zippor, who was king of Moab at that time, 5sent messengers to summon Balaam son of Beor, who was at Pethor, near the River,[b] in his native land. Balak said:

"A people has come out of Egypt; they cover the face of the land and have settled next to me. 6Now come and put a curse on these people, because they are too powerful for me. Perhaps then I will be able to defeat them and drive them out of the country. For I know that those you bless are blessed, and those you curse are cursed."

7The elders of Moab and Midian left, taking with them the fee for divination. When they came to Balaam, they told him what Balak had said.

8"Spend the night here," Balaam said to them, "and I will bring you back the answer the LORD gives me." So the Moabite princes stayed with him.

9God came to Balaam and asked, "Who are these men with you?"

10Balaam said to God, "Balak son of Zippor, king of Moab, sent me this message: 11'A people that has come out of Egypt covers the face of the land. Now come and put a curse on them for me. Perhaps then I will be able to fight them and drive them away.'"

12But God said to Balaam, "Do not go with them. You must not put a curse on those people, because they are blessed."

13The next morning Balaam got up and said to Balak's princes, "Go back to your own country, for the LORD has refused to let me go with you."

14So the Moabite princes returned to Balak and said, "Balaam refused to come with us."

15Then Balak sent other princes, more numerous and more distinguished than the first. 16They came to Balaam and said:

"This is what Balak son of Zippor says: Do not let anything keep you from coming to me, 17because I will reward you handsomely and do whatever you say. Come and put a curse on these people for me."

18But Balaam answered them, "Even if Balak gave me his palace filled with silver and gold, I could not do anything great or small to go beyond the command of the LORD my God. 19Now stay here tonight as the others did, and I will find out what else the LORD will tell me."

20That night God came to Balaam and said, "Since these men have come to summon you, go with them, but do only what I tell you."

Balaam's Donkey

21Balaam got up in the morning, saddled his donkey and went with the princes of Moab. 22But God was very

---

<small>a *1* Hebrew *Jordan of Jericho*; possibly an ancient name for the Jordan River</small>
<small>b *5* That is, the Euphrates</small>

Living Bible

enough, Israel was victorious and killed King Og, his sons, and his subjects, so that not a single survivor remained; and Israel occupied the land.

22 THE PEOPLE of Israel now traveled to the plains of Moab and camped east of the Jordan River opposite Jericho. 2, 3When King Balak of Moab (the son of Zippor) realized how many of them there were, and when he learned what they had done to the Amorites, he and his people were terrified. 4They quickly consulted with the leaders of Midian.

"This mob will eat us like an ox eats grass," they exclaimed.

So King Balak 5, 6sent messengers to Balaam (son of Beor) who was living in his native land of Pethor, near the Euphrates River. He begged Balaam to come and help him.

"A vast horde of people has arrived from Egypt, and they cover the face of the earth and are headed toward me," he frantically explained. "Please come and curse them for me, so that I can drive them out of my land; for I know what fantastic blessings fall on those whom you bless, and I also know that those whom you curse are doomed."

7The messengers he sent were some of the top leaders of Moab and Midian. They went to Balaam with money in hand, and urgently explained to him what Balak wanted.

8"Stay here overnight," Balaam said, "and I'll tell you in the morning whatever the Lord directs me to say." So they did.

9That night God came to Balaam and asked him, "Who are these men?"

10"They have come from King Balak of Moab," he replied. 11"The king says that a vast horde of people from Egypt has arrived at his border, and he wants me to go at once and curse them, in the hope that he can battle them successfully."

12"Don't do it!" God told him. "You are not to curse them, for I have blessed them!

13The next morning Balaam told the men, "Go on home! The Lord won't let me do it."

14So King Balak's ambassadors returned without him and reported his refusal. 15Balak tried again. This time he sent a larger number of even more distinguished ambassadors than the former group. 16, 17They came to Balaam with this message:

"King Balak pleads with you to come. He promises you great honors plus any payment you ask. Name your own figure! Only come and curse these people for us."

18But Balaam replied, "If he were to give me a palace filled with silver and gold, I could do nothing contrary to the command of the Lord my God. 19However, stay here tonight so that I can find out whether the Lord will add anything to what he said before."

20That night God told Balaam, "You may get up and go with these men, but be sure to say only what I tell you to."

21So the next morning he saddled his donkey and started off with them. 22, 23But God was angry about

New Revised Standard

and all his people, until there was no survivor left; and they took possession of his land.

Balak Summons Balaam to Curse Israel

22 THE ISRAELITES set out, and camped in the plains of Moab across the Jordan from Jericho. 2Now Balak son of Zippor saw all that Israel had done to the Amorites. 3Moab was in great dread of the people, because they were so numerous; Moab was overcome with fear of the people of Israel. 4And Moab said to the elders of Midian, "This horde will now lick up all that is around us, as an ox licks up the grass of the field." Now Balak son of Zippor was king of Moab at that time. 5He sent messengers to Balaam son of Beor at Pethor, which is on the Euphrates, in the land of Amaw,c to summon him, saying, "A people has come out of Egypt; they have spread over the face of the earth, and they have settled next to me. 6Come now, curse this people for me, since they are stronger than I; perhaps I shall be able to defeat them and drive them from the land; for I know that whomever you bless is blessed, and whomever you curse is cursed."

7 So the elders of Moab and the elders of Midian departed with the fees for divination in their hand; and they came to Balaam, and gave him Balak's message. 8He said to them, "Stay here tonight, and I will bring back word to you, just as the LORD speaks to me"; so the officials of Moab stayed with Balaam. 9God came to Balaam and said, "Who are these men with you?" 10Balaam said to God, "King Balak son of Zippor of Moab, has sent me this message: 11'A people has come out of Egypt and has spread over the face of the earth; now come, curse them for me; perhaps I shall be able to fight against them and drive them out.' " 12God said to Balaam, "You shall not go with them; you shall not curse the people, for they are blessed." 13So Balaam rose in the morning, and said to the officials of Balak, "Go to your own land, for the LORD has refused to let me go with you." 14So the officials of Moab rose and went to Balak, and said, "Balaam refuses to come with us."

15 Once again Balak sent officials, more numerous and more distinguished than these. 16They came to Balaam and said to him, "Thus says Balak son of Zippor: 'Do not let anything hinder you from coming to me; 17for I will surely do you great honor, and whatever you say to me I will do; come, curse this people for me.' " 18But Balaam replied to the servants of Balak, "Although Balak were to give me his house full of silver and gold, I could not go beyond the command of the LORD my God, to do less or more. 19You remain here, as the others did, so that I may learn what more the LORD may say to me." 20That night God came to Balaam and said to him, "If the men have come to summon you, get up and go with them; but do only what I tell you to do." 21So Balaam got up in the morning, saddled his donkey, and went with the officials of Moab.

c Or land of his kinsfolk

King James

22¶ And God's anger was kindled because he went: and the angel of the LORD stood in the way for an adversary against him. Now he was riding upon his ass, and his two servants *were* with him.

23And the ass saw the angel of the LORD standing in the way, and his sword drawn in his hand: and the ass turned aside out of the way, and went into the field: and Balaam smote the ass, to turn her into the way.

24But the angel of the LORD stood in a path of the vineyards, a wall *being* on this side, and a wall on that side.

25And when the ass saw the angel of the LORD, she thrust herself unto the wall, and crushed Balaam's foot against the wall: and he smote her again.

26And the angel of the LORD went further, and stood in a narrow place, where *was* no way to turn either to the right hand or to the left.

27And when the ass saw the angel of the LORD, she fell down under Balaam: and Balaam's anger was kindled, and he smote the ass with a staff.

28And the LORD opened the mouth of the ass, and she said unto Balaam, What have I done unto thee, that thou hast smitten me these three times?

29And Balaam said unto the ass, Because thou hast mocked me: I would there were a sword in mine hand, for now would I kill thee.

30And the ass said unto Balaam, *Am* not I thine ass, upon which thou hast ridden ever since *I was* thine unto this day? was I ever wont to do so unto thee? And he said, Nay.

31Then the LORD opened the eyes of Balaam, and he saw the angel of the LORD standing in the way, and his sword drawn in his hand: and he bowed down his head, and fell flat on his face.

32And the angel of the LORD said unto him, Wherefore hast thou smitten thine ass these three times? behold, I went out to withstand thee, because *thy* way is perverse before me:

33And the ass saw me, and turned from me these three times: unless she had turned from me, surely now also I had slain thee, and saved her alive.

34And Balaam said unto the angel of the LORD, I have sinned; for I knew not that thou stoodest in the way against me: now therefore, if it displease thee, I will get me back again.

35And the angel of the LORD said unto Balaam, Go with the men: but only the word that I shall speak unto thee, that thou shalt speak. So Balaam went with the princes of Balak.

36¶ And when Balak heard that Balaam was come, he went out to meet him unto a city of Moab, which *is* in the border of Arnon, which *is* in the utmost coast.

37And Balak said unto Balaam, Did I not earnestly send unto thee to call thee? wherefore camest thou not unto me? am I not able indeed to promote thee to honour?

38And Balaam said unto Balak, Lo, I am come unto thee: have I now any power at all to say any thing? the word that God putteth in my mouth, that shall I speak.

39And Balaam went with Balak, and they came unto Kirjath-huzoth.

40And Balak offered oxen and sheep, and sent to Balaam, and to the princes that *were* with him.

41And it came to pass on the morrow, that Balak took Balaam, and brought him up into the high places of Baal, that thence he might see the utmost *part* of the people.

New International

angry when he went, and the angel of the LORD stood in the road to oppose him. Balaam was riding on his donkey, and his two servants were with him. 23When the donkey saw the angel of the LORD standing in the road with a drawn sword in his hand, she turned off the road into a field. Balaam beat her to get her back on the road.

24Then the angel of the LORD stood in a narrow path between two vineyards, with walls on both sides. 25When the donkey saw the angel of the LORD, she pressed close to the wall, crushing Balaam's foot against it. So he beat her again.

26Then the angel of the LORD moved on ahead and stood in a narrow place where there was no room to turn, either to the right or to the left. 27When the donkey saw the angel of the LORD, she lay down under Balaam, and he was angry and beat her with his staff. 28Then the LORD opened the donkey's mouth, and she said to Balaam, "What have I done to you to make you beat me these three times?"

29Balaam answered the donkey, "You have made a fool of me! If I had a sword in my hand, I would kill you right now."

30The donkey said to Balaam, "Am I not your own donkey, which you have always ridden, to this day? Have I been in the habit of doing this to you?"

"No," he said.

31Then the LORD opened Balaam's eyes, and he saw the angel of the LORD standing in the road with his sword drawn. So he bowed low and fell facedown.

32The angel of the LORD asked him, "Why have you beaten your donkey these three times? I have come here to oppose you because your path is a reckless one before me.[a] 33The donkey saw me and turned away from me these three times. If she had not turned away, I would certainly have killed you by now, but I would have spared her."

34Balaam said to the angel of the LORD, "I have sinned. I did not realize you were standing in the road to oppose me. Now if you are displeased, I will go back."

35The angel of the LORD said to Balaam, "Go with the men, but speak only what I tell you." So Balaam went with the princes of Balak.

36When Balak heard that Balaam was coming, he went out to meet him at the Moabite town on the Arnon border, at the edge of his territory. 37Balak said to Balaam, "Did I not send you an urgent summons? Why didn't you come to me? Am I really not able to reward you?"

38"Well, I have come to you now," Balaam replied. "But can I say just anything? I must speak only what God puts in my mouth."

39Then Balaam went with Balak to Kiriath Huzoth. 40Balak sacrificed cattle and sheep, and gave some to Balaam and the princes who were with him. 41The next morning Balak took Balaam up to Bamoth Baal, and from there he saw part of the people.

---

a 32 The meaning of the Hebrew for this clause is uncertain.

Living Bible

Balaam's eager attitude,[b] so he sent an angel to stand in the road to kill him. As Balaam and two servants were riding along, Balaam's donkey suddenly saw the angel of the Lord standing in the road with a drawn sword. She bolted off the road into a field, but Balaam beat her back onto the road. 24Now the angel of the Lord stood at a place where the road went between two vineyard walls. 25When the donkey saw him standing there, she squirmed past by pressing against the wall, crushing Balaam's foot in the process. So he beat her again. 26Then the angel of the Lord moved farther down the road and stood in a place so narrow that the donkey couldn't get by at all.

27So she lay down in the road! In a great fit of temper Balaam beat her again with his staff.

28Then the Lord caused the donkey to speak! "What have I done that deserves your beating me these three times?" she asked.

29"Because you have made me look like a fool!" Balaam shouted. "I wish I had a sword with me, for I would kill you."

30"Have I ever done anything like this before in my entire life?" the donkey asked.

"No," he admitted.

31Then the Lord opened Balaam's eyes and he saw the angel standing in the roadway with drawn sword, and he fell flat on the ground before him.

32"Why did you beat your donkey those three times?" the angel demanded. "I have come to stop you because you are headed for destruction. 33Three times the donkey saw me and shied away from me; otherwise I would certainly have killed you by now, and spared her."

34Then Balaam confessed, "I have sinned. I didn't realize you were there. I will go back home if you don't want me to go on."

35But the angel told him, "Go with the men, but say only what I tell you to say." So Balaam went on with them. 36When King Balak heard that Balaam was on the way, he left the capital and went out to meet him at the Arnon River, at the border of his land.

37"Why did you delay so long?" he asked Balaam. "Didn't you believe me when I said I would give you great honors?"

38Balaam replied, "I have come, but I have no power to say anything except what God tells me to say; and that is what I shall speak." 39Balaam accompanied the king to Kiriathhuzoth, 40where King Balak sacrificed oxen and sheep, and gave animals to Balaam and the ambassadors for their sacrifices. 41The next morning Balak took Balaam to the top of Mount Bamoth-baal, from which he could see the people of Israel spread out before him.

New Revised Standard

Balaam, the Donkey, and the Angel

22 God's anger was kindled because he was going, and the angel of the LORD took his stand in the road as his adversary. Now he was riding on the donkey, and his two servants were with him. 23 The donkey saw the angel of the LORD standing in the road, with a drawn sword in his hand; so the donkey turned off the road, and went into the field; and Balaam struck the donkey, to turn it back onto the road. 24 Then the angel of the LORD stood in a narrow path between the vineyards, with a wall on either side. 25 When the donkey saw the angel of the LORD, it scraped against the wall, and scraped Balaam's foot against the wall; so he struck it again. 26 Then the angel of the LORD went ahead, and stood in a narrow place, where there was no way to turn either to the right or to the left. 27 When the donkey saw the angel of the LORD, it lay down under Balaam; and Balaam's anger was kindled, and he struck the donkey with his staff. 28 Then the LORD opened the mouth of the donkey, and it said to Balaam, "What have I done to you, that you have struck me these three times?" 29 Balaam said to the donkey, "Because you have made a fool of me! I wish I had a sword in my hand! I would kill you right now!" 30 But the donkey said to Balaam, "Am I not your donkey, which you have ridden all your life to this day? Have I been in the habit of treating you this way?" And he said, "No."

31 Then the LORD opened the eyes of Balaam, and he saw the angel of the LORD standing in the road, with his drawn sword in his hand; and he bowed down, falling on his face. 32 The angel of the LORD said to him, "Why have you struck your donkey these three times? I have come out as an adversary, because your way is perverse[c] before me. 33 The donkey saw me, and turned away from me these three times. If it had not turned away from me, surely just now I would have killed you and let it live." 34 Then Balaam said to the angel of the LORD, "I have sinned, for I did not know that you were standing in the road to oppose me. Now therefore, if it is displeasing to you, I will return home." 35 The angel of the LORD said to Balaam, "Go with the men; but speak only what I tell you to speak." So Balaam went on with the officials of Balak.

36 When Balak heard that Balaam had come, he went out to meet him at Ir-moab, on the boundary formed by the Arnon, at the farthest point of the boundary. 37 Balak said to Balaam, "Did I not send to summon you? Why did you not come to me? Am I not able to honor you?" 38 Balaam said to Balak, "I have come to you now, but do I have power to say just anything? The word God puts in my mouth, that is what I must say." 39 Then Balaam went with Balak, and they came to Kiriath-huzoth. 40 Balak sacrificed oxen and sheep, and sent them to Balaam and to the officials who were with him.

Balaam's First Oracle

41 On the next day Balak took Balaam and brought him up to Bamoth-baal; and from there he could see part of the people of Israel.[d]

---

[b] 22:22, 23 *God was angry about Balaam's eager attitude,* literally, "God was angry because he went." He said much more than God had told him to. See Num 25:1-3; 31:16.

[c] Meaning of Heb uncertain   [d] Heb lacks *of Israel*

King James

23 AND BALAAM said unto Balak, Build me here seven altars, and prepare me here seven oxen and seven rams.

2And Balak did as Balaam had spoken; and Balak and Balaam offered on *every* altar a bullock and a ram.

3And Balaam said unto Balak, Stand by thy burnt offering, and I will go: peradventure the LORD will come to meet me: and whatsoever he showeth me I will tell thee. And he went to an high place.

4And God met Balaam: and he said unto him, I have prepared seven altars, and I have offered upon *every* altar a bullock and a ram.

5And the LORD put a word in Balaam's mouth, and said, Return unto Balak, and thus thou shalt speak.

6And he returned unto him, and, lo, he stood by his burnt sacrifice, he, and all the princes of Moab.

7And he took up his parable, and said, Balak the king of Moab hath brought me from Aram, out of the mountains of the east, *saying,* Come, curse me Jacob, and come, defy Israel.

8How shall I curse, whom God hath not cursed? or how shall I defy, *whom* the LORD hath not defied?

9For from the top of the rocks I see him, and from the hills I behold him: lo, the people shall dwell alone, and shall not be reckoned among the nations.

10Who can count the dust of Jacob, and the number of the fourth *part* of Israel? Let me die the death of the righteous, and let my last end be like his!

11And Balak said unto Balaam, What hast thou done unto me? I took thee to curse mine enemies, and, behold, thou hast blessed *them* altogether.

12And he answered and said, Must I not take heed to speak that which the LORD hath put in my mouth?

13And Balak said unto him, Come, I pray thee, with me unto another place, from whence thou mayest see them: thou shalt see but the utmost part of them, and shalt not see them all: and curse me them from thence.

14¶ And he brought him into the field of Zophim, to the top of Pisgah, and built seven altars, and offered a bullock and a ram on *every* altar.

15And he said unto Balak, Stand here by thy burnt offering, while I meet *the LORD* yonder.

16And the LORD met Balaam, and put a word in his mouth, and said, Go again unto Balak, and say thus.

17And when he came to him, behold, he stood by his burnt offering, and the princes of Moab with him. And Balak said unto him, What hath the LORD spoken?

18And he took up his parable, and said, Rise up, Balak, and hear; hearken unto me, thou son of Zippor:

19God *is* not a man, that he should lie; neither the son of man, that he should repent: hath he said, and shall he not do *it?* or hath he spoken, and shall he not make it good?

20Behold, I have received *commandment* to bless: and he hath blessed; and I cannot reverse it.

21He hath not beheld iniquity in Jacob, neither hath he seen perverseness in Israel; the LORD his God *is* with him, and the shout of a king *is* among them.

New International

Balaam's First Oracle

23 BALAAM SAID, "Build me seven altars here, and prepare seven bulls and seven rams for me." 2Balak did as Balaam said, and the two of them offered a bull and a ram on each altar.

3Then Balaam said to Balak, "Stay here beside your offering while I go aside. Perhaps the LORD will come to meet with me. Whatever he reveals to me I will tell you." Then he went off to a barren height.

4God met with him, and Balaam said, "I have prepared seven altars, and on each altar I have offered a bull and a ram."

5The LORD put a message in Balaam's mouth and said, "Go back to Balak and give him this message."

6So he went back to him and found him standing beside his offering, with all the princes of Moab. 7Then Balaam uttered his oracle:

"Balak brought me from Aram,
　the king of Moab from the eastern mountains.
'Come,' he said, 'curse Jacob for me;
　come, denounce Israel.'
8How can I curse
　those whom God has not cursed?
How can I denounce
　those whom the LORD has not denounced?
9From the rocky peaks I see them,
　from the heights I view them.
I see a people who live apart
　and do not consider themselves one of the
　　nations.
10Who can count the dust of Jacob
　or number the fourth part of Israel?
Let me die the death of the righteous,
　and may my end be like theirs!"

11Balak said to Balaam, "What have you done to me? I brought you to curse my enemies, but you have done nothing but bless them!"

12He answered, "Must I not speak what the LORD puts in my mouth?"

Balaam's Second Oracle

13Then Balak said to him, "Come with me to another place where you can see them; you will see only a part but not all of them. And from there, curse them for me." 14So he took him to the field of Zophim on the top of Pisgah, and there he built seven altars and offered a bull and a ram on each altar.

15Balaam said to Balak, "Stay here beside your offering while I meet with him over there."

16The LORD met with Balaam and put a message in his mouth and said, "Go back to Balak and give him this message."

17So he went to him and found him standing beside his offering, with the princes of Moab. Balak asked him, "What did the LORD say?"

18Then he uttered his oracle:

"Arise, Balak, and listen;
　hear me, son of Zippor.
19God is not a man, that he should lie,
　nor a son of man, that he should change his
　　mind.
Does he speak and then not act?
　Does he promise and not fulfill?
20I have received a command to bless;
　he has blessed, and I cannot change it.

21"No misfortune is seen in Jacob,
　no misery observed in Israel.[a]
The LORD their God is with them;
　the shout of the King is among them.

---

[a] *21 Or He has not looked on Jacob's offenses / or on the wrongs found in Israel.*

Living Bible

23 BALAAM SAID to the king, "Build seven altars here, and prepare seven young bulls and seven rams for sacrifice."

²Balak followed his instructions, and a young bull and a ram were sacrificed on each altar.

³, ⁴Then Balaam said to the king, "Stand here by your burnt offerings and I will see if the Lord will meet me; and I will tell you what he says to me." So he went up to a barren height, and God met him there. Balaam told the Lord, "I have prepared seven altars, and have sacrificed a young bull and a ram on each." ⁵Then the Lord gave Balaam a message for King Balak.

⁶When Balaam returned, the king was standing beside the burnt offerings with all the princes of Moab. ⁷⁻¹⁰This was Balaam's message:

"King Balak, king of Moab, has brought me
From the land of Aram,
From the eastern mountains.
'Come,' he told me, 'curse Jacob for me!
Let your anger rise on Israel.'
But how can I curse
What God has not cursed?
How can I denounce
A people God has not denounced?
I see them from the cliff tops,
I watch them from the hills.
They live alone,
And prefer to remain distinct
From every other nation.
They are as numerous as dust!
They are beyond numbering.
If only I could die as happy as an Israelite!
Oh, that my end might be like theirs!"

¹¹"What have you done to me?" demanded King Balak. "I told you to curse my enemies, and now you have blessed them!

¹²But Balaam replied, "Can I say anything except what Jehovah tells me to?"

¹³Then Balak told him, "Come with me to another place; there you will see only a portion of the nation of Israel. Curse at least that many!"

¹⁴So King Balak took Balaam into the fields of Zophim at the top of Mount Pisgah, and built seven altars there; and he offered up a young bull and a ram on each altar.

¹⁵Then Balaam said to the king, "Stand here by your burnt offering while I go to meet the Lord." ¹⁶And the Lord met Balaam and told him what to say. ¹⁷So he returned to where the king and the princes of Moab were standing beside their burnt offerings.

"What has Jehovah said?" the king eagerly inquired.

¹⁸⁻²⁴And he replied,

"Rise up, Balak, and hear!
Listen to me, you son of Zippor.
God is not a man, that he should lie;
He doesn't change his mind like humans do.
Has he ever promised,
Without doing what he said?
Look! I have received a command to bless them,
For God has blessed them,
And I cannot reverse it!
He has not seen sin in Jacob.
He will not trouble Israel!
Jehovah their God is with them.
He is their king!
God has brought them out of Egypt.
Israel has the strength of a wild ox.
No curse can be placed on Jacob,
And no magic shall be done against him.
For now it shall be said of Israel,

New Revised Standard

23 THEN BALAAM said to Balak, "Build me seven altars here, and prepare seven bulls and seven rams for me." ²Balak did as Balaam had said; and Balak and Balaam offered a bull and a ram on each altar. ³Then Balaam said to Balak, "Stay here beside your burnt offerings while I go aside. Perhaps the LORD will come to meet me. Whatever he shows me I will tell you." And he went to a bare height.

4 Then God met Balaam; and Balaam said to him, "I have arranged the seven altars, and have offered a bull and a ram on each altar." ⁵The LORD put a word in Balaam's mouth, and said, "Return to Balak, and this is what you must say." ⁶So he returned to Balak,ᵇ who was standing beside his burnt offerings with all the officials of Moab. ⁷Then Balaamᶜ uttered his oracle, saying:

"Balak has brought me from Aram,
     the king of Moab from the eastern
        mountains:
'Come, curse Jacob for me;
     Come, denounce Israel!'
⁸ How can I curse whom God has not cursed?
     How can I denounce those whom the LORD
        has not denounced?
⁹ For from the top of the crags I see him,
     from the hills I behold him;
Here is a people living alone,
     and not reckoning itself among the nations!
¹⁰ Who can count the dust of Jacob,
     or number the dust-cloudᵈ of Israel?
Let me die the death of the upright,
     and let my end be like his!"

11 Then Balak said to Balaam, "What have you done to me? I brought you to curse my enemies, but now you have done nothing but bless them." ¹²He answered, "Must I not take care to say what the LORD puts into my mouth?"

Balaam's Second Oracle

13 So Balak said to him, "Come with me to another place from which you may see them; you shall see only part of them, and shall not see them all; then curse them for me from there." ¹⁴So he took him to the field of Zophim, to the top of Pisgah. He built seven altars, and offered a bull and a ram on each altar. ¹⁵Balaam said to Balak, "Stand here beside your burnt offerings, while I meet the LORD over there. ¹⁶The LORD met Balaam, put a word into his mouth, and said, "Return to Balak, and this is what you shall say." ¹⁷When he came to him, he was standing beside his burnt offerings with the officials of Moab. Balak said to him, "What has the LORD said?" ¹⁸Then Balaam uttered his oracle, saying:

"Rise, Balak, and hear;
     listen to me, O son of Zippor:
¹⁹ God is not a human being, that he should lie,
     or a mortal, that he should change his mind.
Has he promised, and will he not do it?
     Has he spoken, and will he not fulfill it?
²⁰ See, I received a command to bless;
     he has blessed, and I cannot revoke it.
²¹ He has not beheld misfortune in Jacob;
     nor has he seen trouble in Israel.
The LORD their God is with them,
     acclaimed as a king among them.

ᵇ Heb *him*   ᶜ Heb *he*   ᵈ Or *fourth part*

King James

22God brought them out of Egypt; he hath as it were the strength of an unicorn.

23Surely *there is* no enchantment against Jacob, neither *is there* any divination against Israel: according to this time it shall be said of Jacob and of Israel, What hath God wrought!

24Behold, the people shall rise up as a great lion, and lift up himself as a young lion: he shall not lie down until he eat *of* the prey, and drink the blood of the slain.

25¶ And Balak said unto Balaam, Neither curse them at all, nor bless them at all.

26But Balaam answered and said unto Balak, Told not I thee, saying, All that the LORD speaketh, that I must do?

27¶ And Balak said unto Balaam, Come, I pray thee, I will bring thee unto another place; peradventure it will please God that thou mayest curse me them from thence.

28And Balak brought Balaam unto the top of Peor, that looketh toward Jeshimon.

29And Balaam said unto Balak, Build me here seven altars, and prepare me here seven bullocks and seven rams.

30And Balak did as Balaam had said, and offered a bullock and a ram on *every* altar.

24 AND WHEN Balaam saw that it pleased the LORD to bless Israel, he went not, as at other times, to seek for enchantments, but he set his face toward the wilderness.

2And Balaam lifted up his eyes, and he saw Israel abiding *in his tents* according to their tribes; and the spirit of God came upon him.

3And he took up his parable, and said, Balaam the son of Beor hath said, and the man whose eyes are open hath said:

4He hath said, which heard the words of God, which saw the vision of the Almighty, falling *into a trance*, but having his eyes open:

5How goodly are thy tents, O Jacob, *and* thy tabernacles, O Israel!

6As the valleys are they spread forth, as gardens by the river's side, as the trees of lign aloes which the LORD hath planted, *and* as cedar trees beside the waters.

7He shall pour the water out of his buckets, and his seed *shall be* in many waters, and his king shall be higher than Agag, and his kingdom shall be exalted.

8God brought him forth out of Egypt; he hath as it were the strength of an unicorn: he shall eat up the nations his enemies, and shall break their bones, and pierce *them* through with his arrows.

9He couched, he lay down as a lion, and as a great lion: who shall stir him up? Blessed *is* he that blesseth thee, and cursed *is* he that curseth thee.

10¶ And Balak's anger was kindled against Balaam, and he smote his hands together: and Balak said unto Balaam, I called thee to curse mine enemies, and, behold, thou hast altogether blessed *them* these three times.

11Therefore now flee thou to thy place: I thought to promote thee unto great honour; but, lo, the LORD hath kept thee back from honour.

12And Balaam said unto Balak, Spake I not also to thy messengers which thou sentest unto me, saying,

New International

22God brought them out of Egypt;
    they have the strength of a wild ox.
23There is no sorcery against Jacob,
    no divination against Israel.
It will now be said of Jacob
    and of Israel, 'See what God has done!'
24The people rise like a lioness;
    they rouse themselves like a lion
that does not rest till he devours his prey
    and drinks the blood of his victims."

25Then Balak said to Balaam, "Neither curse them at all nor bless them at all!"

26Balaam answered, "Did I not tell you I must do whatever the LORD says?"

Balaam's Third Oracle

27Then Balak said to Balaam, "Come, let me take you to another place. Perhaps it will please God to let you curse them for me from there." 28And Balak took Balaam to the top of Peor, overlooking the wasteland.

29Balaam said, "Build me seven altars here, and prepare seven bulls and seven rams for me." 30Balak did as Balaam had said, and offered a bull and a ram on each altar.

24 NOW WHEN Balaam saw that it pleased the LORD to bless Israel, he did not resort to sorcery as at other times, but turned his face toward the desert. 2When Balaam looked out and saw Israel encamped tribe by tribe, the Spirit of God came upon him 3and he uttered his oracle:

"The oracle of Balaam son of Beor,
    the oracle of one whose eye sees clearly,
4the oracle of one who hears the words of God,
    who sees a vision from the Almighty,[a]
    who falls prostrate, and whose eyes are
    opened:

5"How beautiful are your tents, O Jacob,
    your dwelling places, O Israel!

6"Like valleys they spread out,
    like gardens beside a river,
like aloes planted by the LORD,
    like cedars beside the waters.
7Water will flow from their buckets;
    their seed will have abundant water.

"Their king will be greater than Agag;
    their kingdom will be exalted.

8"God brought them out of Egypt;
    they have the strength of a wild ox.
They devour hostile nations
    and break their bones in pieces;
    with their arrows they pierce them.
9Like a lion they crouch and lie down,
    like a lioness—who dares to rouse them?

"May those who bless you be blessed
    and those who curse you be cursed!"

10Then Balak's anger burned against Balaam. He struck his hands together and said to him, "I summoned you to curse my enemies, but you have blessed them these three times. 11Now leave at once and go home! I said I would reward you handsomely, but the LORD has kept you from being rewarded."

12Balaam answered Balak, "Did I not tell the messengers you sent me, 13'Even if Balak gave me his palace

---

a 4 Hebrew *Shaddai*; also in verse 16

Living Bible

'What wonders God has done for them!'
These people rise up as a lion;
They shall not lie down
Until they have eaten what they capture
And have drunk the blood of the slain!

25"If you aren't going to curse them, at least don't *bless* them!" the king exclaimed to Balaam.

26But Balaam replied, "Didn't I tell you that I must say whatever Jehovah tells me to?"

27Then the king said to Balaam, "I will take you to yet another place. Perhaps it will please God to let you curse them from there."

28So King Balak took Balaam to the top of Mount Peor, overlooking the desert. 29Balaam again told the king to build seven altars, and to prepare seven young bulls and seven rams for the sacrifice. 30The king did as Balaam said, and offered a young bull and ram on every altar.

24 BALAAM REALIZED by now that Jehovah planned to bless Israel, so he didn't even go to meet the Lord as he had earlier. Instead, he went at once and looked out toward the camp of Israel 2which stretched away across the plains, divided by tribal areas.

Then the Spirit of God came upon him, 3–9and he spoke this prophecy concerning them:

"Balaam the son of Beor says—
The man whose eyes are open says—
'I have listened to the word of God,
I have seen what God Almighty showed me;
I fell, and my eyes were opened:
Oh, the joys awaiting Israel,
Joys in the homes of Jacob.
I see them spread before me as green valleys,
And fruitful gardens by the riverside;
As aloes planted by the Lord himself;
As cedar trees beside the waters.
They shall be blessed with an abundance of water,
And they shall live in many places.
Their king will be greater than Agag;
Their kingdom is exalted.
God has brought them from Egypt.
Israel has the strength of a wild ox,
And shall eat up the nations that oppose him;
He shall break their bones in pieces,
And shall shoot them with many arrows.
Israel sleeps as a lion or a lioness—
Who dares arouse him?
Blessed is everyone who blesses you, O Israel,
And curses shall fall upon everyone who curses you.'

10King Balak was livid with rage by now. Striking his hands together in anger and disgust he shouted, "I called you to curse my enemies and instead you have blessed them three times. 11Get out of here! Go back home! I had planned to promote you to great honor, but Jehovah has kept you from it!"

12Balaam replied, "Didn't I tell your messengers

New Revised Standard

22 God, who brings them out of Egypt,
   is like the horns of a wild ox for them.
23 Surely there is no enchantment against Jacob,
   no divination against Israel;
now it shall be said of Jacob and Israel,
   'See what God has done!'
24 Look, a people rising up like a lioness,
   and rousing itself like a lion!
It does not lie down until it has eaten the prey
   and drunk the blood of the slain."

25 Then Balak said to Balaam, "Do not curse them at all, and do not bless them at all." 26But Balaam answered Balak, "Did I not tell you, 'Whatever the LORD says, that is what I must do'?"

27 So Balak said to Balaam, "Come now, I will take you to another place; perhaps it will please God that you may curse them for me from there." 28So Balak took Balaam to the top of Peor, which overlooks the wasteland.b 29Balaam said to Balak, "Build me seven altars here, and prepare seven bulls and seven rams for me." 30So Balak did as Balaam had said, and offered a bull and a ram on each altar.

Balaam's Third Oracle

24 NOW BALAAM saw that it pleased the LORD to bless Israel, so he did not go, as at other times, to look for omens, but set his face toward the wilderness. 2Balaam looked up and saw Israel camping tribe by tribe. Then the spirit of God came upon him, 3and he uttered his oracle, saying:
"The oracle of Balaam son of Beor,
   the oracle of the man whose eye is clear,c
4 the oracle of one who hears the words of God,
   who sees the vision of the Almighty,d
   who falls down, but with eyes uncovered:
5 how fair are your tents, O Jacob,
   your encampments, O Israel!
6 Like palm groves that stretch far away,
   like gardens beside a river,
like aloes that the LORD has planted,
   like cedar trees beside the waters.
7 Water shall flow from his buckets,
   and his seed shall have abundant water,
his king shall be higher than Agag,
   and his kingdom shall be exalted.
8 God who brings him out of Egypt,
   is like the horns of a wild ox for him;
he shall devour the nations that are his foes
   and break their bones.
   He shall strike with his arrows.e
9 He crouched, he lay down like a lion,
   and like a lioness; who will rouse him up?
Blessed is everyone who blesses you,
   and cursed is everyone who curses you."

10 Then Balak's anger was kindled against Balaam, and he struck his hands together. Balak said to Balaam, "I summoned you to curse my enemies, but instead you have blessed them these three times. 11Now be off with you! Go home! I said, 'I will reward you richly,' but the LORD has denied you any reward." 12And Balaam said to Balak, "Did I not tell your messengers whom you sent to me, 13'If Balak should give me his house full of silver

---

b Or overlooks Jeshimon   c Or closed or open   d Traditional rendering of Heb Shaddai   e Meaning of Heb uncertain

King James

13If Balak would give me his house full of silver and gold, I cannot go beyond the commandment of the LORD, to do *either* good or bad of mine own mind; *but* what the LORD saith, that will I speak?

14And now, behold, I go unto my people: come *therefore, and* I will advertise thee what this people shall do to thy people in the latter days.

15¶ And he took up his parable, and said, Balaam the son of Beor hath said, and the man whose eyes are open hath said:

16He hath said, which heard the words of God, and knew the knowledge of the most High, *which* saw the vision of the Almighty, falling *into a trance*, but having his eyes open:

17I shall see him, but not now: I shall behold him, but not nigh: there shall come a Star out of Jacob, and a Sceptre shall rise out of Israel, and shall smite the corners of Moab, and destroy all the children of Sheth.

18And Edom shall be a possession, Seir also shall be a possession for his enemies; and Israel shall do valiantly.

19Out of Jacob shall come he that shall have dominion, and shall destroy him that remaineth of the city.

20¶ And when he looked on Amalek, he took up his parable, and said, Amalek *was* the first of the nations; but his latter end *shall be* that he perish for ever.

21And he looked on the Kenites, and took up his parable, and said, Strong is thy dwellingplace, and thou puttest thy nest in a rock.

22Nevertheless the Kenite shall be wasted, until Asshur shall carry thee away captive.

23And he took up his parable, and said, Alas, who shall live when God doeth this!

24And ships *shall come* from the coast of Chittim, and shall afflict Asshur, and shall afflict Eber, and he also shall perish for ever.

25And Balaam rose up, and went and returned to his place: and Balak also went his way.

25 AND ISRAEL abode in Shittim, and the people began to commit whoredom with the daughters of Moab.

2And they called the people unto the sacrifices of their gods: and the people did eat, and bowed down to their gods.

3And Israel joined himself unto Baal-peor: and the anger of the LORD was kindled against Israel.

4And the LORD said unto Moses, Take all the heads of the people, and hang them up before the LORD against the sun, that the fierce anger of the LORD may be turned away from Israel.

5And Moses said unto the judges of Israel, Slay ye every one his men that were joined unto Baal-peor.

6¶ And, behold, one of the children of Israel came and brought unto his brethren a Midianitish woman in the sight of Moses, and in the sight of all the congregation of the children of Israel, who *were* weeping *before* the door of the tabernacle of the congregation.

New International

filled with silver and gold, I could not do anything of my own accord, good or bad, to go beyond the command of the LORD—and I must say only what the LORD says'? 14Now I am going back to my people, but come, let me warn you of what this people will do to your people in days to come."

Balaam's Fourth Oracle

15Then he uttered his oracle:

"The oracle of Balaam son of Beor,
 the oracle of one whose eye sees clearly,
16the oracle of one who hears the words of God,
 who has knowledge from the Most High,
 who sees a vision from the Almighty,
 who falls prostrate, and whose eyes are
  opened:
17"I see him, but not now;
 I behold him, but not near.
A star will come out of Jacob;
 a scepter will rise out of Israel.
He will crush the foreheads of Moab,
 the skulls[a] of[b] all the sons of Sheth.[c]
18Edom will be conquered;
 Seir, his enemy, will be conquered,
 but Israel will grow strong.
19A ruler will come out of Jacob
 and destroy the survivors of the city."

Balaam's Final Oracles

20Then Balaam saw Amalek and uttered his oracle:

"Amalek was first among the nations,
 but he will come to ruin at last."

21Then he saw the Kenites and uttered his oracle:

"Your dwelling place is secure,
 your nest is set in a rock;
22yet you Kenites will be destroyed
 when Asshur takes you captive."

23Then he uttered his oracle:

"Ah, who can live when God does this?[d]
24 Ships will come from the shores of Kittim;
 they will subdue Asshur and Eber,
 but they too will come to ruin."

25Then Balaam got up and returned home, and Balak went his own way.

Moab Seduces Israel

25 WHILE ISRAEL was staying in Shittim, the men began to indulge in sexual immorality with Moabite women, 2who invited them to the sacrifices to their gods. The people ate and bowed down before these gods. 3So Israel joined in worshiping the Baal of Peor. And the LORD's anger burned against them.

4The LORD said to Moses, "Take all the leaders of these people, kill them and expose them in broad daylight before the LORD, so that the LORD's fierce anger may turn away from Israel."

5So Moses said to Israel's judges, "Each of you must put to death those of your men who have joined in worshiping the Baal of Peor."

6Then an Israelite man brought to his family a Midianite woman right before the eyes of Moses and the whole assembly of Israel while they were weeping at the entrance to the Tent of Meeting. 7When Phinehas son of

---

a *17* Samaritan Pentateuch (see also Jer. 48:45); the meaning of the word in the Masoretic Text is uncertain.   b *17* Or possibly *Moab, / batter*   c *17* Or *all the noisy boasters*   d *23* Masoretic Text; with a different word division of the Hebrew *A people will gather from the north.*

Living Bible

13that even if you gave me a palace filled with silver and gold, I could not go beyond the words of Jehovah, and could not say a word of my own? I said that I would say only what Jehovah says! 14Yes, I shall return now to my own people. But first, let me tell you what the Israelites are going to do to your people!"

15-19So he spoke this prophecy to him:
"Balaam the son of Beor is the man
Whose eyes are open!
He hears the words of God
And has knowledge from the Most High;
He sees what Almighty God has shown him;
He fell, and his eyes were opened:
I see in the future of Israel,
Far down the distant trail,
That there shall come a star from Jacob!
This ruler of Israel
Shall smite the people of Moab,
And destroy the sons of Sheth.
Israel shall possess all Edom and Seir.
They shall overcome their enemies.
Jacob shall arise in power
And shall destroy many cities."
20Then Balaam looked over at the homes of the people of Amalek and prophesied:
"Amalek was the first of the nations,
But its destiny is destruction!"
21, 22Then he looked over at the Kenites:
"Yes, you are strongly situated,
Your nest is set in the rocks!
But the Kenites shall be destroyed,
And the mighty army of the king of Assyria shall
    deport you from this land!"
23, 24He concluded his prophecies by saying:
"Alas, who can live when God does this?
Ships shall come from the coasts of Cyprus,
And shall oppress both Eber and Assyria.
They too must be destroyed."
25So Balaam and Balak returned to their homes.e

25 WHILE ISRAEL was camped at Acacia, some of the young men began going to wild parties with the local Moabite girls. 2These girls also invited them to attend the sacrifices to their gods, and soon the men were not only attending the feasts, but also bowing down and worshiping the idols. 3Before long all Israel was joining freely in the worship of Baal, the god of Moab; and the anger of the Lord was hot against his people.

4He issued the following command to Moses: "Execute all the tribal leaders of Israel. Hang them up before the Lord in broad daylight, so that his fierce anger will turn away from the people."

5So Moses ordered the judges to execute all who had worshiped Baal.

6But one of the Israeli men insolently brought a Midianite girl into the camp, right before the eyes of Moses and all the people, as they were weeping at the door of the Tabernacle. 7When Phinehas (son of Eleazar and

New Revised Standard

and gold, I would not be able to go beyond the word of the LORD, to do either good or bad of my own will; what the LORD says, that is what I will say'? 14So now, I am going to my people; let me advise you what this people will do to your people in days to come."

Balaam's Fourth Oracle

15 So he uttered his oracle, saying:
"The oracle of Balaam son of Beor,
    the oracle of the man whose eye is clear,f
16 the oracle of one who hears the words of God,
    and knows the knowledge of the Most
        High,g
    who sees the vision of the Almighty,h
    who falls down, but with his eyes
        uncovered:
17 I see him, but not now;
    I behold him, but not near—
    a star shall come out of Jacob,
    and a scepter shall rise out of Israel;
    it shall crush the borderlandsi of Moab,
    and the territoryj of all the Shethites.
18 Edom will become a possession,
    Seir a possession of its enemies,k
    while Israel does valiantly.
19 One out of Jacob shall rule,
    and destroy the survivors of Ir."

20 Then he looked on Amalek, and uttered his oracle, saying:
"First among the nations was Amalek,
    but its end is to perish forever."
21 Then he looked on the Kenite, and uttered his oracle, saying:
"Enduring is your dwelling place,
    and your nest is set in the rock;
22 yet Kain is destined for burning.
    How long shall Asshur take you away
        captive?"
23 Again he uttered his oracle, saying:
"Alas, who shall live when God does this?
24   But ships shall come from Kittim
    and shall afflict Asshur and Eber;
    and he also shall perish forever."
25 Then Balaam got up and went back to his place, and Balak also went his way.

Worship of Baal of Peor

25 WHILE ISRAEL was staying at Shittim, the people began to have sexual relations with the women of Moab. 2These invited the people to the sacrifices of their gods, and the people ate and bowed down to their gods. 3Thus Israel yoked itself to the Baal of Peor, and the LORD's anger was kindled against Israel. 4The LORD said to Moses, "Take all the chiefs of the people, and impale them in the sun before the LORD, in order that the fierce anger of the LORD may turn away from Israel." 5And Moses said to the judges of Israel, "Each of you shall kill any of your people who have yoked themselves to the Baal of Peor."

6 Just then one of the Israelites came and brought a Midianite woman into his family, in the sight of Moses and in the sight of the whole congregation of the Israelites, while they were weeping at the entrance of the tent of meeting. 7When Phinehas son of Eleazar, son of Aar-

---

c 24:25 So Balaam and Balak returned to their homes. But not before Balaam gave insidious advice that brought about the situation described in 25:1-3. See 31:16.

f Or closed or open   g Or of Elyon   h Traditional rendering of Heb Shaddai   i Or forehead   j Some Mss read skull   k Heb Seir, its enemies, a possession

King James

7And when Phinehas, the son of Eleazar, the son of Aaron the priest, saw *it*, he rose up from among the congregation, and took a javelin in his hand;

8And he went after the man of Israel into the tent, and thrust both of them through, the man of Israel, and the woman through her belly. So the plague was stayed from the children of Israel.

9And those that died in the plague were twenty and four thousand.

10¶ And the LORD spake unto Moses, saying,

11Phinehas, the son of Eleazar, the son of Aaron the priest, hath turned my wrath away from the children of Israel, while he was zealous for my sake among them, that I consumed not the children of Israel in my jealousy.

12Wherefore say, Behold, I give unto him my covenant of peace:

13And he shall have it, and his seed after him, *even* the covenant of an everlasting priesthood; because he was zealous for his God, and made an atonement for the children of Israel.

14Now the name of the Israelite that was slain, *even* that was slain with the Midianitish woman, *was* Zimri, the son of Salu, a prince of a chief house among the Simeonites.

15And the name of the Midianitish woman that was slain *was* Cozbi, the daughter of Zur; he *was* head over a people, *and* of a chief house in Midian.

16¶ And the LORD spake unto Moses, saying,

17Vex the Midianites, and smite them:

18For they vex you with their wiles, wherewith they have beguiled you in the matter of Peor, and in the matter of Cozbi, the daughter of a prince of Midian, their sister, which was slain in the day of the plague for Peor's sake.

26 AND IT came to pass after the plague, that the LORD spake unto Moses and unto Eleazar the son of Aaron the priest, saying,

2Take the sum of all the congregation of the children of Israel, from twenty years old and upward, throughout their fathers' house, all that are able to go to war in Israel.

3And Moses and Eleazar the priest spake with them in the plains of Moab by Jordan *near* Jericho, saying,

4*Take the sum of the people*, from twenty years old and upward; as the LORD commanded Moses and the children of Israel, which went forth out of the land of Egypt.

5¶ Reuben, the eldest son of Israel: the children of Reuben; Hanoch, *of whom cometh* the family of the Hanochites: of Pallu, the family of the Palluites:

6Of Hezron, the family of the Hezronites: of Carmi, the family of the Carmites.

7These *are* the families of the Reubenites: and they that were numbered of them were forty and three thousand and seven hundred and thirty.

8And the sons of Pallu; Eliab.

9And the sons of Eliab; Nemuel, and Dathan, and Abiram. This *is that* Dathan and Abiram, *which were* famous in the congregation, who strove against Moses and against Aaron in the company of Korah, when they strove against the LORD:

10And the earth opened her mouth, and swallowed them up together with Korah, when that company died, what time the fire devoured two hundred and fifty men: and they became a sign.

11Notwithstanding the children of Korah died not.

New International

Eleazar, the son of Aaron, the priest, saw this, he left the assembly, took a spear in his hand 8and followed the Israelite into the tent. He drove the spear through both of them—through the Israelite and into the woman's body. Then the plague against the Israelites was stopped; 9but those who died in the plague numbered 24,000.

10The LORD said to Moses, 11"Phinehas son of Eleazar, the son of Aaron, the priest, has turned my anger away from the Israelites; for he was as zealous as I am for my honor among them, so that in my zeal I did not put an end to them. 12Therefore tell him I am making my covenant of peace with him. 13He and his descendants will have a covenant of a lasting priesthood, because he was zealous for the honor of his God and made atonement for the Israelites."

14The name of the Israelite who was killed with the Midianite woman was Zimri son of Salu, the leader of a Simeonite family. 15And the name of the Midianite woman who was put to death was Cozbi daughter of Zur, a tribal chief of a Midianite family.

16The LORD said to Moses, 17"Treat the Midianites as enemies and kill them, 18because they treated you as enemies when they deceived you in the affair of Peor and their sister Cozbi, the daughter of a Midianite leader, the woman who was killed when the plague came as a result of Peor."

The Second Census

26 AFTER THE plague the LORD said to Moses and Eleazar son of Aaron, the priest, 2"Take a census of the whole Israelite community by families— all those twenty years old or more who are able to serve in the army of Israel." 3So on the plains of Moab by the Jordan across from Jericho,[a] Moses and Eleazar the priest spoke with them and said, 4"Take a census of the men twenty years old or more, as the LORD commanded Moses."

These were the Israelites who came out of Egypt:

5The descendants of Reuben, the firstborn son of Israel, were:

through Hanoch, the Hanochite clan;
through Pallu, the Palluite clan;
6through Hezron, the Hezronite clan;
through Carmi, the Carmite clan.

7These were the clans of Reuben; those numbered were 43,730.

8The son of Pallu was Eliab, 9and the sons of Eliab were Nemuel, Dathan and Abiram. The same Dathan and Abiram were the community officials who rebelled against Moses and Aaron and were among Korah's followers when they rebelled against the LORD. 10The earth opened its mouth and swallowed them along with Korah, whose followers died when the fire devoured the 250 men. And they served as a warning sign. 11The line of Korah, however, did not die out.

a 3 Hebrew *Jordan of Jericho*; possibly an ancient name for the Jordan River; also in verse 63

Living Bible

grandson of Aaron the priest) saw this, he jumped up, grabbed a spear, 8and rushed after the man into his tent, where he had taken the girl. He thrust the spear all the way through the man's body and into her stomach. So the plague was stopped, 9but only after 24,000 people had already died.

10, 11Then the Lord said to Moses, "Phinehas (son of Eleazar and grandson of Aaron the priest) has turned away my anger for he was angry with my anger, and would not tolerate the worship of any God but me. So I have stopped destroying all Israel as I had intended. 12, 13Now because of what he has done—because of his zeal for his God, and because he has made atonement for the people of Israel by what he did—I promise that he and his descendants shall be priests forever."

14The name of the man who was killed with the Midianite girl was Zimri, son of Salu, a leader of the tribe of Simeon. 15The girl's name was Cozbi, daughter of Zur, a Midianite prince.

16, 17Then the Lord said to Moses, "Destroy the Midianites, 18for they are destroying you with their wiles. They are causing you to worship Baal, and they are leading you astray, as you have just seen by the death of Cozbi."

26 AFTER THE plague had ended, Jehovah said to Moses and to Eleazar (son of Aaron the priest), 2"Take a census of all the men of Israel who are twenty years old or older, to find out how many of each tribe and clan are able to go to war."

3, 4So Moses and Eleazar issued census instructions to the leaders of Israel. (The entire nation was camped in the plains of Moab beside the Jordan River, opposite Jericho.) Here are the results of the census:

5-11The tribe of Reuben: 43,730.

(Reuben was Israel's oldest son.) In this tribe were the following clans, named after Reuben's sons:

The Hanochites, named after their ancestor Hanoch.
The Palluites, named after their ancestor Pallu. (In the sub-clan of Eliab—who was one of the sons of Pallu—were the families of Nemu-el, Abiram, and Dathan. This Dathan and Abiram were the two leaders who conspired with Korah against Moses and Aaron, and in fact challenged the very authority of God! But the earth opened and swallowed them; and 250 men were destroyed by fire from the Lord that day, as a warning to the entire nation.)
The Hezronites, named after their ancestor Hezron.
The Carmites, named after their ancestor Carmi.

New Revised Standard

on the priest, saw it, he got up and left the congregation. Taking a spear in his hand, 8he went after the Israelite man into the tent, and pierced the two of them, the Israelite and the woman, through the belly. So the plague was stopped among the people of Israel. 9Nevertheless those that died by the plague were twenty-four thousand.

10 The LORD spoke to Moses, saying: 11"Phinehas son of Eleazar, son of Aaron the priest, has turned back my wrath from the Israelites by manifesting such zeal among them on my behalf that in my jealousy I did not consume the Israelites. 12Therefore say, 'I hereby grant him my covenant of peace. 13It shall be for him and for his descendants after him a covenant of perpetual priesthood, because he was zealous for his God, and made atonement for the Israelites.' "

14 The name of the slain Israelite man, who was killed with the Midianite woman, was Zimri son of Salu, head of an ancestral house belonging to the Simeonites. 15The name of the Midianite woman who was killed was Cozbi daughter of Zur, who was the head of a clan, an ancestral house in Midian.

16 The LORD said to Moses, 17"Harass the Midianites, and defeat them; 18for they have harassed you by the trickery with which they deceived you in the affair of Peor, and in the affair of Cozbi, the daughter of a leader of Midian, their sister; she was killed on the day of the plague that resulted from Peor."

A Census of the New Generation

26 AFTER THE plague the LORD said to Moses and to Eleazar son of Aaron the priest, 2"Take a census of the whole congregation of the Israelites, from twenty years old and upward, by their ancestral houses, everyone in Israel able to go to war." 3Moses and Eleazar the priest spoke with them in the plains of Moab by the Jordan opposite Jericho, saying, 4"Take a census of the people,b from twenty years old and upward," as the LORD commanded Moses.

The Israelites, who came out of the land of Egypt, were:

5 Reuben, the firstborn of Israel. The descendants of Reuben: of Hanoch, the clan of the Hanochites; of Pallu, the clan of the Palluites; 6of Hezron, the clan of the Hezronites; of Carmi, the clan of the Carmites. 7These are the clans of the Reubenites; the number of those enrolled was forty-three thousand seven hundred thirty. 8And the descendants of Pallu: Eliab. 9The descendants of Eliab: Nemuel, Dathan, and Abiram. These are the same Dathan and Abiram, chosen from the congregation, who rebelled against Moses and Aaron in the company of Korah, when they rebelled against the LORD, 10and the earth opened its mouth and swallowed them up along with Korah, when that company died, when the fire devoured two hundred fifty men; and they became a warning. 11Notwithstanding, the sons of Korah did not die.

b Heb lacks take a census of the people: Compare verse 2

King James

12¶ The sons of Simeon after their families: of Nemuel, the family of the Nemuelites: of Jamin, the family of the Jaminites: of Jachin, the family of the Jachinites:

13Of Zerah, the family of the Zarhites: of Shaul, the family of the Shaulites.

14These *are* the families of the Simeonites, twenty and two thousand and two hundred.

15¶ The children of Gad after their families: of Zephon, the family of the Zephonites: of Haggi, the family of the Haggites: of Shuni, the family of the Shunites:

16Of Ozni, the family of the Oznites: of Eri, the family of the Erites:

17Of Arod, the family of the Arodites: of Areli, the family of the Arelites.

18These *are* the families of the children of Gad according to those that were numbered of them, forty thousand and five hundred.

19¶ The sons of Judah *were* Er and Onan: and Er and Onan died in the land of Canaan.

20And the sons of Judah after their families were; of Shelah, the family of the Shelanites: of Pharez, the family of the Pharzites: of Zerah, the family of the Zarhites.

21And the sons of Pharez were; of Hezron, the family of the Hezronites: of Hamul, the family of the Hamulites.

22These *are* the families of Judah according to those that were numbered of them, threescore and sixteen thousand and five hundred.

23¶ *Of* the sons of Issachar after their families: *of* Tola, the family of the Tolaites: of Pua, the family of the Punites:

24Of Jashub, the family of the Jashubites: of Shimron, the family of the Shimronites.

25These *are* the families of Issachar according to those that were numbered of them, threescore and four thousand and three hundred.

26¶ *Of* the sons of Zebulun after their families: of Sered, the family of the Sardites: of Elon, the family of the Elonites: of Jahleel, the family of the Jahleelites.

27These *are* the families of the Zebulunites according to those that were numbered of them, threescore thousand and five hundred.

28¶ The sons of Joseph after their families *were* Manasseh and Ephraim.

29Of the sons of Manasseh: of Machir, the family of the Machirites: and Machir begat Gilead: of Gilead *come* the family of the Gileadites.

30These *are* the sons of Gilead: *of* Jeezer, the family of the Jeezerites: of Helek, the family of the Helekites:

31And *of* Asriel, the family of the Asrielites: and *of* Shechem, the family of the Shechemites:

32And *of* Shemida, the family of the Shemidaites: and *of* Hepher, the family of the Hepherites.

33¶ And Zelophehad the son of Hepher had no sons, but daughters: and the names of the daughters of Zelophehad *were* Mahlah, and Noah, Hoglah, Milcah, and Tirzah.

34These *are* the families of Manasseh, and those that were numbered of them, fifty and two thousand and seven hundred.

35¶ These *are* the sons of Ephraim after their families: of Shuthelah, the family of the Shuthalhites: of Becher, the family of the Bachrites: of Tahan, the family of the Tahanites.

36And these *are* the sons of Shuthelah: of Eran, the family of the Eranites.

New International

12The descendants of Simeon by their clans were:
through Nemuel, the Nemuelite clan;
through Jamin, the Jaminite clan;
through Jakin, the Jakinite clan;
13through Zerah, the Zerahite clan;
through Shaul, the Shaulite clan.

14These were the clans of Simeon; there were 22,200 men.

15The descendants of Gad by their clans were:
through Zephon, the Zephonite clan;
through Haggi, the Haggite clan;
through Shuni, the Shunite clan;
16through Ozni, the Oznite clan;
through Eri, the Erite clan;
17through Arodi,[a] the Arodite clan;
through Areli, the Arelite clan.

18These were the clans of Gad; those numbered were 40,500.

19Er and Onan were sons of Judah, but they died in Canaan.

20The descendants of Judah by their clans were:
through Shelah, the Shelanite clan;
through Perez, the Perezite clan;
through Zerah, the Zerahite clan.

21The descendants of Perez were:
through Hezron, the Hezronite clan;
through Hamul, the Hamulite clan.

22These were the clans of Judah; those numbered were 76,500.

23The descendants of Issachar by their clans were:
through Tola, the Tolaite clan;
through Puah, the Puite[b] clan;
24through Jashub, the Jashubite clan;
through Shimron, the Shimronite clan.

25These were the clans of Issachar; those numbered were 64,300.

26The descendants of Zebulun by their clans were:
through Sered, the Seredite clan;
through Elon, the Elonite clan;
through Jahleel, the Jahleelite clan.

27These were the clans of Zebulun; those numbered were 60,500.

28The descendants of Joseph by their clans through Manasseh and Ephraim were:

29The descendants of Manasseh:
through Makir, the Makirite clan (Makir was the father of Gilead);
through Gilead, the Gileadite clan.

30These were the descendants of Gilead:
through Iezer, the Iezerite clan;
through Helek, the Helekite clan;
31through Asriel, the Asrielite clan;
through Shechem, the Shechemite clan;
32through Shemida, the Shemidaite clan;
through Hepher, the Hepherite clan.

33(Zelophehad son of Hepher had no sons; he had only daughters, whose names were Mahlah, Noah, Hoglah, Milcah and Tirzah.)

34These were the clans of Manasseh; those numbered were 52,700.

35These were the descendants of Ephraim by their clans:
through Shuthelah, the Shuthelahite clan;
through Beker, the Bekerite clan;
through Tahan, the Tahanite clan.

36These were the descendants of Shuthelah:
through Eran, the Eranite clan.

---

a *17* Samaritan Pentateuch and Syriac (see also Gen. 46:16); Masoretic Text *Arod*   b *23* Samaritan Pentateuch, Septuagint, Vulgate and Syriac (see also 1 Chron. 7:1); Masoretic Text *through Puvah, the Punite*

Living Bible

12, 13, 14*The tribe of Simeon:* 22,200.

In this tribe were the following clans, founded by Simeon's sons:

The Nemu-elites, named after their ancestor Nemu-el.

The Jaminites, named after their ancestor Jamin.

The Jachinites, named after their ancestor Jachin.

The Zerahites, named after their ancestor Zerah.

The Shaulites, named after their ancestor Shaul.

15-18*The tribe of Gad:* 40,500

In this tribe were the following clans founded by the sons of Gad:

The Zephonites, named after their ancestor Zephon.

The Haggites, named after their ancestor Haggi.

The Shunites, named after their ancestor Shuni.

The Oznites, named after their ancestor Ozni.

The Erites, named after their ancestor Eri.

The Arodites, named after their ancestor Arod.

The Arelites, named after their ancestor Areli.

19-22*The tribe of Judah:* 76,500

In this tribe were the following clans named after the sons of Judah—but not including Er and Onan who died in the land of Canaan:

The Shelanites, named after their ancestor Shelah.

The Perezites, named after their ancestor Perez.

The Zerahites, named after their ancestor Zerah.

This census also included the subclans of Perez: The Hezronites, named after their ancestor Hezron.

The Hamulites, named after their ancestor Hamul.

23, 24, 25*The tribe of Issachar:* 64,300.

In this tribe were the following clans named after the sons of Issachar:

The Tolaites, named after their ancestor Tola.

The Punites, named after their ancestor Puvah.

The Jashubites, named after their ancestor Jashub.

The Shimronites, named after their ancestor Shimron.

26, 27*The tribe of Zebulun:* 60,500.

In this tribe were the following clans named after the sons of Zebulun:

The Seredites, named after their ancestor Sered.

The Elonites, named after their ancestor Elon.

The Jahleelites, named after their ancestor Jahleel.

28-37*The tribe of Joseph:* 32,500 *in the half-tribe of Ephraim; and* 52,700 *in the half-tribe of Manasseh.*

In the half-tribe of Manasseh was the following clan of Machirites, named after their ancestor Machir.

The sub-clan of the Machirites was the Gileadites, named after their ancestor Gilead.

The tribes of the Gileadites: The Jezerites, named after their ancestor Jezer. The Helekites, named after their ancestor Helek. The Asrielites, named after their ancestor Asriel. The Shechemites, named after their ancestor Shechem. The Shemidaites, named after their ancestor Shemida. The Hepherites, named after their ancestor Hepher. (Hepher's son, Zelophehad, had no sons. Here are the names of his daughters: Mahlah, Noah, Hoglah, Milcah, Tirzah.

The 32,500 registered in the half-tribe of Ephraim included the following clans, named after the sons of Ephraim:

The Shuthelahites, named after their ancestor Shuthelah. (A sub-clan of the Shuthelahites was the Eranites, named after their ancestor Eran, a son of Shuthelah.)

New Revised Standard

12 The descendants of Simeon by their clans: of Nemuel, the clan of the Nemuelites; of Jamin, the clan of the Jaminites; of Jachin, the clan of the Jachinites; 13 of Zerah, the clan of the Zerahites; of Shaul, the clan of the Shaulites.c 14 These are the clans of the Simeonites, twenty-two thousand two hundred.

15 The children of Gad by their clans: of Zephon, the clan of the Zephonites; of Haggi, the clan of the Haggites; of Shuni, the clan of the Shunites; 16 of Ozni, the clan of the Oznites; of Eri, the clan of the Erites; 17 of Arod, the clan of the Arodites; of Areli, the clan of the Arelites. 18 These are the clans of the Gadites: the number of those enrolled was forty thousand five hundred.

19 The sons of Judah: Er and Onan; Er and Onan died in the land of Canaan. 20 The descendants of Judah by their clans were: of Shelah, the clan of the Shelanites; of Perez, the clan of the Perezites; of Zerah, the clan of the Zerahites. 21 The descendants of Perez were: of Hezron, the clan of the Hezronites; of Hamul, the clan of the Hamulites. 22 These are the clans of Judah: the number of those enrolled was seventy-six thousand five hundred.

23 The descendants of Issachar by their clans: of Tola, the clan of the Tolaites; of Puvah, the clan of the Punites; 24 of Jashub, the clan of the Jashubites; of Shimron, the clan of the Shimronites. 25 These are the clans of Issachar: sixty-four thousand three hundred enrolled.

26 The descendants of Zebulun by their clans: of Sered, the clan of the Seredites; of Elon, the clan of the Elonites; of Jahleel, the clan of the Jahleelites. 27 These are the clans of the Zebulunites; the number of those enrolled was sixty thousand five hundred.

28 The sons of Joseph by their clans: Manasseh and Ephraim. 29 The descendants of Manasseh: of Machir, the clan of the Machirites; and Machir was the father of Gilead; of Gilead, the clan of the Gileadites. 30 These are the descendants of Gilead: of Iezer, the clan of the Iezerites; of Helek, the clan of the Helekites; 31 and of Asriel, the clan of the Asrielites; and of Shechem, the clan of the Shechemites; 32 and of Shemida, the clan of the Shemidaites; and of Hepher, the clan of the Hepherites. 33 Now Zelophehad son of Hepher had no sons, but daughters: and the names of the daughters of Zelophehad were Mahlah, Noah, Hoglah, Milcah, and Tirzah. 34 These are the clans of Manasseh; the number of those enrolled was fifty-two thousand seven hundred.

35 These are the descendants of Ephraim according to their clans: of Shuthelah, the clan of the Shuthelahites; of Becher, the clan of the Becherites; of Tahan, the clan of the Tahanites. 36 And these are the descendants of Shuthelah: of Eran, the clan of the Eranites.

c Or Saul ... Saulites

King James

37These *are* the families of the sons of Ephraim according to those that were numbered of them, thirty and two thousand and five hundred. These *are* the sons of Joseph after their families.

38¶ The sons of Benjamin after their families: of Bela, the family of the Belaites: of Ashbel, the family of the Ashbelites: of Ahiram, the family of the Ahiramites:

39Of Shupham, the family of the Shuphamites: of Hupham, the family of the Huphamites.

40And the sons of Bela were Ard and Naaman: *of Ard*, the family of the Ardites: *and* of Naaman, the family of the Naamites.

41These *are* the sons of Benjamin after their families: and they that were numbered of them *were* forty and five thousand and six hundred.

42¶ These *are* the sons of Dan after their families: of Shuham, the family of the Shuhamites. These *are* the families of Dan after their families.

43All the families of the Shuhamites, according to those that were numbered of them, *were* threescore and four thousand and four hundred.

44¶ *Of* the children of Asher after their families: of Jimna, the family of the Jimnites: of Jesui, the family of the Jesuites: of Beriah, the family of the Beriites.

45Of the sons of Beriah: of Heber, the family of the Heberites: of Malchiel, the family of the Malchielites.

46And the name of the daughter of Asher *was* Sarah.

47These *are* the families of the sons of Asher according to those that were numbered of them; *who were* fifty and three thousand and four hundred.

48¶ *Of* the sons of Naphtali after their families: of Jahzeel, the family of the Jahzeelites: of Guni, the family of the Gunites:

49Of Jezer, the family of the Jezerites: of Shillem, the family of the Shillemites.

50These *are* the families of Naphtali according to their families: and they that were numbered of them *were* forty and five thousand and four hundred.

51These *were* the numbered of the children of Israel, six hundred thousand and a thousand seven hundred and thirty.

52¶ And the LORD spake unto Moses, saying,

53Unto these the land shall be divided for an inheritance according to the number of names.

54To many thou shalt give the more inheritance, and to few thou shalt give the less inheritance: to every one shall his inheritance be given according to those that were numbered of him.

55Notwithstanding the land shall be divided by lot: according to the names of the tribes of their fathers they shall inherit.

56According to the lot shall the possession thereof be divided between many and few.

57¶ And these *are* they that were numbered of the Levites after their families: of Gershon, the family of the Gershonites: of Kohath, the family of the Kohathites: of Merari, the family of the Merarites.

58These *are* the families of the Levites: the family of the Libnites, the family of the Hebronites, the family of the Mahlites, the family of the Mushites, the family of the Korathites. And Kohath begat Amram.

59And the name of Amram's wife *was* Jochebed, the daughter of Levi, whom *her mother* bare to Levi in Egypt: and she bare unto Amram Aaron and Moses, and Miriam their sister.

60And unto Aaron was born Nadab, and Abihu, Eleazar, and Ithamar.

New International

37These were the clans of Ephraim; those numbered were 32,500.

These were the descendants of Joseph by their clans.

38The descendants of Benjamin by their clans were:
    through Bela, the Belaite clan;
    through Ashbel, the Ashbelite clan;
    through Ahiram, the Ahiramite clan;
39through Shupham,[a] the Shuphamite clan;
    through Hupham, the Huphamite clan.
40The descendants of Bela through Ard and Naaman were:
    through Ard,[b] the Ardite clan;
    through Naaman, the Naamite clan.
41These were the clans of Benjamin; those numbered were 45,600.

42These were the descendants of Dan by their clans:
    through Shuham, the Shuhamite clan.
These were the clans of Dan: 43All of them were Shuhamite clans; and those numbered were 64,400.

44The descendants of Asher by their clans were:
    through Imnah, the Imnite clan;
    through Ishvi, the Ishvite clan;
    through Beriah, the Beriite clan;
45and through the descendants of Beriah:
    through Heber, the Heberite clan;
    through Malkiel, the Malkielite clan.
46(Asher had a daughter named Serah.)
47These were the clans of Asher; those numbered were 53,400.

48The descendants of Naphtali by their clans were:
    through Jahzeel, the Jahzeelite clan;
    through Guni, the Gunite clan;
49through Jezer, the Jezerite clan;
    through Shillem, the Shillemite clan.
50These were the clans of Naphtali; those numbered were 45,400.

51The total number of the men of Israel was 601,730.

52The LORD said to Moses, 53"The land is to be allotted to them as an inheritance based on the number of names. 54To a larger group give a larger inheritance, and to a smaller group a smaller one; each is to receive its inheritance according to the number of those listed. 55Be sure that the land is distributed by lot. What each group inherits will be according to the names for its ancestral tribe. 56Each inheritance is to be distributed by lot among the larger and smaller groups."

57These were the Levites who were counted by their clans:
    through Gershon, the Gershonite clan;
    through Kohath, the Kohathite clan;
    through Merari, the Merarite clan.
58These also were Levite clans:
    the Libnite clan,
    the Hebronite clan,
    the Mahlite clan,
    the Mushite clan,
    the Korahite clan.
(Kohath was the forefather of Amram; 59the name of Amram's wife was Jochebed, a descendant of Levi, who was born to the Levites[c] in Egypt. To Amram she bore Aaron, Moses and their sister Miriam. 60Aaron was the father of Nadab and Abihu, Eleazar and Ithamar. 61But Nadab and Abihu died

Living Bible

The Becherites, named after their ancestor Becher.
The Tahanites, named after their ancestor Tahan.
38-41*The tribe of Benjamin:* 45,600.
In this tribe were the following clans named after the sons of Benjamin:
The Bela-ites, named after their ancestor Bela.
Sub-clans named after sons of Bela were: The Ardites, named after their ancestor Ard. The Naamites, named after their ancestor Naaman. The Ashbelites, named after their ancestor Ashbel. The Ahiramites, named after their ancestor Ahiram. The Shuphamites, named after their ancestor Shephupham. The Huphamites, named after their ancestor Hupham.
42, 43*The tribe of Dan:* 64,400.
In this tribe was the clan of the Shuhamites, named after Shuham, the son of Dan.
44-47*The tribe of Asher:* 53,400.
In this tribe were the following clans named after the sons of Asher:
The Imnites, named after their ancestor Imnah.
The Ishvites, named after their ancestor Ishvi.
The Beriites, named after their ancestor Beriah.
Sub-clans named after the sons of Beriah were: The Heberites, named after their ancestor Heber. The Malchi-elites, named after their ancestor Malchi-el.
Asher also had a daughter named Serah.
48, 49, 50*The tribe of Naphtali:* 45,400.
In this tribe were the following clans, named after the sons of Naphtali:
The Jahzeelites, named after their ancestor Jahzeel.
The Gunites, named after their ancestor Guni.
The Jezerites, named after their ancestor Jezer.
The Shillemites, named after their ancestor Shillem.
51So the total number of the men of draft age throughout Israel was 601,730.
52, 53Then the Lord told Moses to divide the land among the tribes in proportion to their population, as indicated by the census— 54the larger tribes to be given more land, the smaller tribes less land.
55, 56"Let the representatives of the larger tribes have a lottery, drawing for the larger sections," the Lord instructed, "and let the smaller tribes draw for the smaller sections."
57These are the clans of the Levites numbered in the census:
The Gershonites, named after their ancestor Gershon.
The Kohathites, named after their ancestor Kohath.
The Merarites, named after their ancestor Merari.
58, 59These are the families of the tribe of Levi:
The Libnites, the Hebronites,
The Mahlites, the Mushites,
The Korahites.
While Levi was in Egypt, a daughter, Jochebed, was born to him and she became the wife of Amram, son of Kohath. They were the parents of Aaron, Moses, and Miriam. 60To Aaron were born Nadab, Abihu, Eleazar, and Ithamar. 61But Nadab and Abihu died when they offered unauthorized incense before the Lord.

New Revised Standard

37These are the clans of the Ephraimites: the number of those enrolled was thirty-two thousand five hundred. These are the descendants of Joseph by their clans.
38 The descendants of Benjamin by their clans: of Bela, the clan of the Belaites; of Ashbel, the clan of the Ashbelites; of Ahiram, the clan of the Ahiramites; 39of Shephupham, the clan of the Shuphamites; of Hupham, the clan of the Huphamites. 40And the sons of Bela were Ard and Naaman: of Ard, the clan of the Ardites; of Naaman, the clan of the Naamites. 41These are the descendants of Benjamin by their clans; the number of those enrolled was forty-five thousand six hundred.
42 These are the descendants of Dan by their clans: of Shuham, the clan of the Shuhamites. These are the clans of Dan by their clans. 43All the clans of the Shuhamites: sixty-four thousand four hundred enrolled.
44 The descendants of Asher by their families: of Imnah, the clan of the Imnites; of Ishvi, the clan of the Ishvites; of Beriah, the clan of the Beriites. 45Of the descendants of Beriah: of Heber, the clan of the Heberites; of Malchiel, the clan of the Malchielites. 46And the name of the daughter of Asher was Serah. 47These are the clans of the Asherites: the number of those enrolled was fifty-three thousand four hundred.
48 The descendants of Naphtali by their clans: of Jahzeel, the clan of the Jahzeelites; of Guni, the clan of the Gunites; 49of Jezer, the clan of the Jezerites; of Shillem, the clan of the Shillemites. 50These are the Naphtalites[d] by their clans: the number of those enrolled was forty-five thousand four hundred.
51 This was the number of the Israelites enrolled: six hundred and one thousand seven hundred thirty.
52 The LORD spoke to Moses, saying: 53To these the land shall be apportioned for inheritance according to the number of names. 54To a large tribe you shall give a large inheritance, and to a small tribe you shall give a small inheritance; every tribe shall be given its inheritance according to its enrollment. 55But the land shall be apportioned by lot; according to the names of their ancestral tribes they shall inherit. 56Their inheritance shall be apportioned according to lot between the larger and the smaller.
57 This is the enrollment of the Levites by their clans: of Gershon, the clan of the Gershonites; of Kohath, the clan of the Kohathites; of Merari, the clan of the Merarites. 58These are the clans of Levi: the clan of the Libnites, the clan of the Hebronites, the clan of the Mahlites, the clan of the Mushites, the clan of the Korahites. Now Kohath was the father of Amram. 59The name of Amram's wife was Jochebed daughter of Levi, who was born to Levi in Egypt; and she bore to Amram: Aaron, Moses, and their sister Miriam. 60To Aaron were born Nadab, Abihu, Eleazar, and Ithamar. 61But

---

d Heb *clans of Naphtali*

King James

61And Nadab and Abihu died, when they offered strange fire before the LORD.

62And those that were numbered of them were twenty and three thousand, all males from a month old and upward: for they were not numbered among the children of Israel, because there was no inheritance given them among the children of Israel.

63¶ These *are* they that were numbered by Moses and Eleazar the priest, who numbered the children of Israel in the plains of Moab by Jordan *near* Jericho.

64But among these there was not a man of them whom Moses and Aaron the priest numbered, when they numbered the children of Israel in the wilderness of Sinai.

65For the LORD had said of them, They shall surely die in the wilderness. And there was not left a man of them, save Caleb the son of Jephunneh, and Joshua the son of Nun.

27 THEN CAME the daughters of Zelophehad, the son of Hepher, the son of Gilead, the son of Machir, the son of Manasseh, of the families of Manasseh the son of Joseph: and these *are* the names of his daughters; Mahlah, Noah, and Hoglah, and Milcah, and Tirzah.

2And they stood before Moses, and before Eleazar the priest, and before the princes and all the congregation, *by* the door of the tabernacle of the congregation, saying,

3Our father died in the wilderness, and he was not in the company of them that gathered themselves together against the LORD in the company of Korah; but died in his own sin, and had no sons.

4Why should the name of our father be done away from among his family, because he hath no son? Give unto us *therefore* a possession among the brethren of our father.

5And Moses brought their cause before the LORD.

6¶ And the LORD spake unto Moses, saying,

7The daughters of Zelophehad speak right: thou shalt surely give them a possession of an inheritance among their father's brethren; and thou shalt cause the inheritance of their father to pass unto them.

8And thou shalt speak unto the children of Israel, saying, If a man die, and have no son, then ye shall cause his inheritance to pass unto his daughter.

9And if he have no daughter, then ye shall give his inheritance unto his brethren.

10And if he have no brethren, then ye shall give his inheritance unto his father's brethren.

11And if his father have no brethren, then ye shall give his inheritance unto his kinsman that is next to him of his family, and he shall possess it: and it shall be unto the children of Israel a statute of judgment, as the LORD commanded Moses.

12¶ And the LORD said unto Moses, Get thee up into this mount Abarim, and see the land which I have given unto the children of Israel.

13And when thou hast seen it, thou also shalt be gathered unto thy people, as Aaron thy brother was gathered.

14For ye rebelled against my commandment in the desert of Zin, in the strife of the congregation, to sanctify me at the water before their eyes: that *is* the water of Meribah in Kadesh in the wilderness of Zin.

15¶ And Moses spake unto the LORD, saying,

16Let the LORD, the God of the spirits of all flesh, set a man over the congregation,

17Which may go out before them, and which may go in before them, and which may lead them out, and which may bring them in; that the congregation of the LORD be not as sheep which have no shepherd.

New International

when they made an offering before the LORD with unauthorized fire.)

62All the male Levites a month old or more numbered 23,000. They were not counted along with the other Israelites because they received no inheritance among them.

63These are the ones counted by Moses and Eleazar the priest when they counted the Israelites on the plains of Moab by the Jordan across from Jericho. 64Not one of them was among those counted by Moses and Aaron the priest when they counted the Israelites in the Desert of Sinai. 65For the LORD had told those Israelites they would surely die in the desert, and not one of them was left except Caleb son of Jephunneh and Joshua son of Nun.

Zelophehad's Daughters

27 THE DAUGHTERS of Zelophehad son of Hepher, the son of Gilead, the son of Makir, the son of Manasseh, belonged to the clans of Manasseh son of Joseph. The names of the daughters were Mahlah, Noah, Hoglah, Milcah and Tirzah. They approached 2the entrance to the Tent of Meeting and stood before Moses, Eleazar the priest, the leaders and the whole assembly, and said, 3"Our father died in the desert. He was not among Korah's followers, who banded together against the LORD, but he died for his own sin and left no sons. 4Why should our father's name disappear from his clan because he had no son? Give us property among our father's relatives."

5So Moses brought their case before the LORD 6and the LORD said to him, 7"What Zelophehad's daughters are saying is right. You must certainly give them property as an inheritance among their father's relatives and turn their father's inheritance over to them.

8"Say to the Israelites, 'If a man dies and leaves no son, turn his inheritance over to his daughter. 9If he has no daughter, give his inheritance to his brothers. 10If he has no brothers, give his inheritance to his father's brothers. 11If his father had no brothers, give his inheritance to the nearest relative in his clan, that he may possess it. This is to be a legal requirement for the Israelites, as the LORD commanded Moses.' "

Joshua to Succeed Moses

12Then the LORD said to Moses, "Go up this mountain in the Abarim range and see the land I have given the Israelites. 13After you have seen it, you too will be gathered to your people, as your brother Aaron was, 14for when the community rebelled at the waters in the Desert of Zin, both of you disobeyed my command to honor me as holy before their eyes." (These were the waters of Meribah Kadesh, in the Desert of Zin.)

15Moses said to the LORD, 16"May the LORD, the God of the spirits of all mankind, appoint a man over this community 17to go out and come in before them, one who will lead them out and bring them in, so the LORD's people will not be like sheep without a shepherd."

Living Bible

62*The total number of Levites in the census* was 23,000, counting all the males a month old and upward. But the Levites were not included in the total census figure of the people of Israel, for the Levites were given no land when it was divided among the tribes.

63So these are the census figures as prepared by Moses and Eleazar the priest, in the plains of Moab beside the Jordan River, across from Jericho. 64, 65Not one person in this entire census had been counteda in the previous census taken in the wilderness of Sinai! For all who had been counted then had died, as the Lord had decreed when he said of them, "They shall die in the wilderness." The only exceptions were Caleb (son of Jephunneh) and Joshua (son of Nun).

27 ONE DAY the daughters of Zelophehad came to the entrance of the Tabernacle to give a petition to Moses, Eleazar the priest, the tribal leaders, and others who were there. The names of these women were Mahlah, Noah, Hoglah, Milcah and Tirzah. They were members of the half-tribe of Manasseh (a son of Joseph). Their ancestor was Machir, son of Manasseh. Manasseh's son Gilead was their great-grandfather, his son Hepher was their grandfather, and his son Zelophehad was their father.

3, 4"Our father died in the wilderness," they said, "and he was not one of those who perished in Korah's revolt against the Lord—it was a natural death, but he had no sons. Why should the name of our father disappear just because he had no son? We feel that we should be given property along with our father's brothers."

5So Moses brought their case before the Lord.

6, 7And the Lord replied to Moses, "The daughters of Zelophehad are correct. Give them land along with their uncles; give them the property that would have been given to their father if he had lived. 8Moreover, this is a general law among you, that if a man dies and has no sons, then his inheritance shall be passed on to his daughters. 9And if he has no daughter, it shall belong to his brothers. 10And if he has no brother, then it shall go to his uncles. 11But if he has no uncles, then it shall go to the nearest relative."

12One day the Lord said to Moses, "Go up into Mount Abarim and look across the river to the land I have given to the people of Israel. 13After you have seen it, you shall die as Aaron your brother did, 14for you rebelled against my instructions in the wilderness of Zin. When the people of Israel rebelled, you did not glorify meb before them by following my instructions to order water to come out of the rock." He was referring to the incident at the waters of Meribah ("Place of Strife") in Kadesh, in the wilderness of Zin.

15Then Moses said to the Lord, 16"O Jehovah, the God of the spirits of all mankind, [before I am taken awayc] please appoint a new leader for the people, 17a man who will lead them into battle and care for them, so that the people of the Lord will not be as sheep without a shepherd."

New Revised Standard

Nadab and Abihu died when they offered illicit fire before the LORD. 62The number of those enrolled was twenty-three thousand, every male one month old and up; for they were not enrolled among the Israelites because there was no allotment given to them among the Israelites.

63 These were those enrolled by Moses and Eleazar the priest, who enrolled the Israelites in the plains of Moab by the Jordan opposite Jericho. 64Among these there was not one of those enrolled by Moses and Aaron the priest, who had enrolled the Israelites in the wilderness of Sinai. 65For the LORD had said of them, "They shall die in the wilderness." Not one of them was left, except Caleb son of Jephunneh and Joshua son of Nun.

The Daughters of Zelophehad

27 THEN THE daughters of Zelophehad came forward. Zelophehad was son of Hepher son of Gilead son of Machir son of Manasseh son of Joseph, a member of the Manassite clans. The names of his daughters were: Mahlah, Noah, Hoglah, Milcah, and Tirzah. 2They stood before Moses, Eleazar the priest, the leaders, and all the congregation, at the entrance of the tent of meeting, and they said, 3"Our father died in the wilderness; he was not among the company of those who gathered themselves together against the LORD in the company of Korah, but died for his own sin; and he had no sons. 4Why should the name of our father be taken away from his clan because he had no son? Give to us a possession among our father's brothers."

5 Moses brought their case before the LORD. 6And the LORD spoke to Moses, saying: 7The daughters of Zelophehad are right in what they are saying; you shall indeed let them possess an inheritance among their father's brothers and pass the inheritance of their father on to them. 8You shall also say to the Israelites, "If a man dies, and has no son, then you shall pass his inheritance on to his daughter. 9If he has no daughter, then you shall give his inheritance to his brothers. 10If he has no brothers, then you shall give his inheritance to his father's brothers. 11And if his father has no brothers, then you shall give his inheritance to the nearest kinsman of his clan, and he shall possess it. It shall be for the Israelites a statute and ordinance, as the LORD commanded Moses."

Joshua Appointed Moses' Successor

12 The LORD said to Moses, "Go up this mountain of the Abarim range, and see the land that I have given to the Israelites. 13When you have seen it, you also shall be gathered to your people, as your brother Aaron was, 14because you rebelled against my word in the wilderness of Zin when the congregation quarreled with me.d You did not show my holiness before their eyes at the waters." (These are the waters of Meribath-kadesh in the wilderness of Zin.) 15Moses spoke to the LORD, saying, 16"Let the LORD, the God of the spirits of all flesh, appoint someone over the congregation 17who shall go out before them and come in before them, who shall lead them out and bring them in, so that the congregation of the LORD may not be like sheep without a shepherd." 18So the LORD said to Moses, "Take Joshua

---

a *26:64, 65 Not one person . . . had been counted in the previous census . . .* Forty years earlier, at the time of the first census, they had been under twenty years of age, and so were not counted. All who at that time were older than twenty years of age were now dead.   b *27:14 you did not glorify me,* implied.   c *27:16 before I am taken away,* implied.

d Heb lacks *with me*

King James

18¶ And the LORD said unto Moses, Take thee Joshua the son of Nun, a man in whom *is* the spirit, and lay thine hand upon him;

19And set him before Eleazar the priest, and before all the congregation; and give him a charge in their sight.

20And thou shalt put *some* of thine honour upon him, that all the congregation of the children of Israel may be obedient.

21And he shall stand before Eleazar the priest, who shall ask *counsel* for him after the judgment of Urim before the LORD: at his word shall they go out, and at his word they shall come in, *both* he, and all the children of Israel with him, even all the congregation.

22And Moses did as the LORD commanded him: and he took Joshua, and set him before Eleazar the priest, and before all the congregation:

23And he laid his hands upon him, and gave him a charge, as the LORD commanded by the hand of Moses.

28 AND THE LORD spake unto Moses, saying, 2Command the children of Israel, and say unto them, My offering, *and* my bread for my sacrifices made by fire, *for* a sweet savour unto me, shall ye observe to offer unto me in their due season.

3And thou shalt say unto them, This *is* the offering made by fire which ye shall offer unto the LORD; two lambs of the first year without spot day by day, *for* a continual burnt offering.

4The one lamb shalt thou offer in the morning, and the other lamb shalt thou offer at even;

5And a tenth *part* of an ephah of flour for a meat offering, mingled with the fourth *part* of an hin of beaten oil.

6*It is* a continual burnt offering, which was ordained in mount Sinai for a sweet savour, a sacrifice made by fire unto the LORD.

7And the drink offering thereof *shall be* the fourth *part* of an hin for the one lamb: in the holy *place* shalt thou cause the strong wine to be poured unto the LORD *for* a drink offering.

8And the other lamb shalt thou offer at even: as the meat offering of the morning, and as the drink offering thereof, thou shalt offer *it*, a sacrifice made by fire, of a sweet savour unto the LORD.

9¶ And on the sabbath day two lambs of the first year without spot, and two tenth deals of flour *for* a meat offering, mingled with oil, and the drink offering thereof:

10*This is* the burnt offering of every sabbath, beside the continual burnt offering, and his drink offering.

11¶ And in the beginnings of your months ye shall offer a burnt offering unto the LORD; two young bullocks, and one ram, seven lambs of the first year without spot;

12And three tenth deals of flour *for* a meat offering, mingled with oil, for one bullock; and two tenth deals of flour *for* a meat offering, mingled with oil, for one ram;

13And a several tenth deal of flour mingled with oil *for* a meat offering unto one lamb; *for* a burnt offering of a sweet savour, a sacrifice made by fire unto the LORD.

14And their drink offerings shall be half an hin of wine unto a bullock, and the third *part* of an hin unto a ram, and a fourth *part* of an hin unto a lamb: this *is* the burnt offering of every month throughout the months of the year.

15And one kid of the goats for a sin offering unto the LORD shall be offered, beside the continual burnt offering, and his drink offering.

New International

18So the LORD said to Moses, "Take Joshua son of Nun, a man in whom is the spirit,[a] and lay your hand on him. 19Have him stand before Eleazar the priest and the entire assembly and commission him in their presence. 20Give him some of your authority so the whole Israelite community will obey him. 21He is to stand before Eleazar the priest, who will obtain decisions for him by inquiring of the Urim before the LORD. At his command he and the entire community of the Israelites will go out, and at his command they will come in."

22Moses did as the LORD commanded him. He took Joshua and had him stand before Eleazar the priest and the whole assembly. 23Then he laid his hands on him and commissioned him, as the LORD instructed through Moses.

Daily Offerings

28 THE LORD said to Moses, 2"Give this command to the Israelites and say to them: 'See that you present to me at the appointed time the food for my offerings made by fire, as an aroma pleasing to me.' 3Say to them: 'This is the offering made by fire that you are to present to the LORD: two lambs a year old without defect, as a regular burnt offering each day. 4Prepare one lamb in the morning and the other at twilight, 5together with a grain offering of a tenth of an ephah[b] of fine flour mixed with a quarter of a hin[c] of oil from pressed olives. 6This is the regular burnt offering instituted at Mount Sinai as a pleasing aroma, an offering made to the LORD by fire. 7The accompanying drink offering is to be a quarter of a hin of fermented drink with each lamb. Pour out the drink offering to the LORD at the sanctuary. 8Prepare the second lamb at twilight, along with the same kind of grain offering and drink offering that you prepare in the morning. This is an offering made by fire, an aroma pleasing to the LORD.

Sabbath Offerings

9" 'On the Sabbath day, make an offering of two lambs a year old without defect, together with its drink offering and a grain offering of two-tenths of an ephah[d] of fine flour mixed with oil. 10This is the burnt offering for every Sabbath, in addition to the regular burnt offering and its drink offering.

Monthly Offerings

11" 'On the first of every month, present to the LORD a burnt offering of two young bulls, one ram and seven male lambs a year old, all without defect. 12With each bull there is to be a grain offering of three-tenths of an ephah[e] of fine flour mixed with oil; with the ram, a grain offering of two-tenths of an ephah of fine flour mixed with oil; 13and with each lamb, a grain offering of a tenth of an ephah of fine flour mixed with oil. This is for a burnt offering, a pleasing aroma, an offering made to the LORD by fire. 14With each bull there is to be a drink offering of half a hin[f] of wine; with the ram, a third of a hin[g]; and with each lamb, a quarter of a hin. This is the monthly burnt offering to be made at each new moon during the year. 15Besides the regular burnt offering with its drink offering, one male goat is to be presented to the LORD as a sin offering.

Living Bible

18The Lord replied, "Go and get Joshua (son of Nun), who has the Spirit in him, 19and take him to Eleazar the priest, and as all the people watch, charge him with the responsibility of leading the people. 20Publicly give him your authority so that all the people of Israel will obey him. 21He shall be the one to consult with Eleazar the priest in order to get directions from the Lord. The Lord will speak to Eleazar through the use of the Urim, and Eleazar will pass on these instructions to Joshua and the people. In this way the Lord will continue to give them guidance."

22So Moses did as Jehovah commanded, and took Joshua to Eleazar the priest. As the people watched, 23Moses laid his hands upon him and dedicated him to his responsibilities, as the Lord had commanded.

28 THE LORD gave Moses these instructions to give to the people of Israel: "The offerings which you burn on the altar for me are my food, and are a pleasure to me; so see to it that they are brought regularly and are offered as I have instructed you.

3"When you make offerings by fire, you shall use yearling male lambs—each without defect. Two of them shall be offered each day as a regular burnt offering. 4One lamb shall be sacrificed in the morning, the other in the evening. 5With them shall be offered a grain offering of three quarts of finely ground flour mixed with three pints of oil. 6This is the burnt offering ordained at Mount Sinai, to be regularly offered as a fragrant odor, an offering made by fire to the Lord. 7Along with it shall be the drink offering, consisting of three pints of strong wine with each lamb, poured out in the holy place before the Lord. 8Offer the second lamb in the evening with the same grain offering and drink offering. It too is a fragrant odor to the Lord, an offering made by fire.

9, 10"On the Sabbath day, sacrifice two yearling male lambs—both without defect—in addition to the regular offerings. They are to be accompanied by a grain offering of six quarts of fine flour mixed with oil, and the usual drink offering.

11"Also, on the first day of each month there shall be an extra burnt offering to the Lord of two young bulls, one ram, and seven male yearling lambs—all without defect. 12Accompany them with nine quarts of finely ground flour mixed with oil as a grain offering with each bull; and six quarts of finely ground flour mixed with oil as a grain offering for the ram; 13and for each lamb, three quarts of finely ground flour mixed with oil for a grain offering. This burnt offering shall be presented by fire, and will please the Lord very much. 14Along with each sacrifice shall be a drink offering—six pints of wine with each bull, four pints for a ram, and three pints for a lamb. This, then, will be the burnt offering each month throughout the year.

15"Also on the first day of each month you shall offer one male goat for a sin offering to the Lord. This is in addition to the regular daily burnt offering and its drink offering.

New Revised Standard

son of Nun, a man in whom is the spirit, and lay your hand upon him; 19have him stand before Eleazar the priest and all the congregation, and commission him in their sight. 20You shall give him some of your authority, so that all the congregation of the Israelites may obey. 21But he shall stand before Eleazar the priest, who shall inquire for him by the decision of the Urim before the LORD; at his word they shall go out, and at his word they shall come in, both he and all the Israelites with him, the whole congregation." 22So Moses did as the LORD commanded him. He took Joshua and had him stand before Eleazar the priest and the whole congregation; 23he laid his hands on him and commissioned him—as the LORD had directed through Moses.

Daily Offerings

28 THE LORD spoke to Moses, saying: 2Command the Israelites, and say to them: My offering, the food for my offerings by fire, my pleasing odor, you shall take care to offer to me at its appointed time. 3And you shall say to them, This is the offering by fire that you shall offer to the LORD: two male lambs a year old without blemish, daily, as a regular offering. 4One lamb you shall offer in the morning, and the other lamb you shall offer at twilighth 5also one-tenth of an ephah of choice flour for a grain offering, mixed with one-fourth of a hin of beaten oil. 6It is a regular burnt offering, ordained at Mount Sinai for a pleasing odor, an offering by fire to the LORD. 7Its drink offering shall be one-fourth of a hin for each lamb; in the sanctuary you shall pour out a drink offering of strong drink to the LORD. 8The other lamb you shall offer at twilighth with a grain offering and a drink offering like the one in the morning; you shall offer it as an offering by fire, a pleasing odor to the LORD.

Sabbath Offerings

9 On the sabbath day: two male lambs a year old without blemish, and two-tenths of an ephah of choice flour for a grain offering, mixed with oil, and its drink offering— 10this is the burnt offering for every sabbath, in addition to the regular burnt offering and its drink offering.

Monthly Offerings

11 At the beginnings of your months you shall offer a burnt offering to the LORD: two young bulls, one ram, seven male lambs a year old without blemish; 12also three-tenths of an ephah of choice flour for a grain offering, mixed with oil, for each bull; and two-tenths of choice flour for a grain offering, mixed with oil, for the one ram; 13and one-tenth of choice flour mixed with oil as a grain offering for every lamb—a burnt offering of pleasing odor, an offering by fire to the LORD. 14Their drink offerings shall be half a hin of wine for a bull, one-third of a hin for a ram, and one-fourth of a hin for a lamb. This is the burnt offering of every month throughout the months of the year. 15And there shall be one male goat for a sin offering to the LORD; it shall be offered in addition to the regular burnt offering and its drink offering.

h Heb *between the two evenings*

King James

16And in the fourteenth day of the first month *is* the passover of the LORD.

17And in the fifteenth day of this month *is* the feast: seven days shall unleavened bread be eaten.

18In the first day *shall be* an holy convocation; ye shall do no manner of servile work *therein:*

19But ye shall offer a sacrifice made by fire *for* a burnt offering unto the LORD; two young bullocks, and one ram, and seven lambs of the first year: they shall be unto you without blemish:

20And their meat offering *shall be of* flour mingled with oil: three tenth deals shall ye offer for a bullock, and two tenth deals for a ram;

21A several tenth deal shalt thou offer for every lamb, throughout the seven lambs:

22And one goat *for* a sin offering, to make an atonement for you.

23Ye shall offer these beside the burnt offering in the morning, which *is* for a continual burnt offering.

24After this manner ye shall offer daily, throughout the seven days, the meat of the sacrifice made by fire, of a sweet savour unto the LORD: it shall be offered beside the continual burnt offering, and his drink offering.

25And on the seventh day ye shall have an holy convocation; ye shall do no servile work.

26¶ Also in the day of the firstfruits, when ye bring a new meat offering unto the LORD, after your weeks *be out,* ye shall have an holy convocation; ye shall do no servile work:

27But ye shall offer the burnt offering for a sweet savour unto the LORD; two young bullocks, one ram, seven lambs of the first year;

28And their meat offering of flour mingled with oil, three tenth deals unto one bullock, two tenth deals unto one ram,

29A several tenth deal unto one lamb, throughout the seven lambs;

30*And* one kid of the goats, to make an atonement for you.

31Ye shall offer *them* beside the continual burnt offering, and his meat offering, (they shall be unto you without blemish) and their drink offerings.

29 AND IN the seventh month, on the first *day* of the month, ye shall have an holy convocation; ye shall do no servile work: it is a day of blowing the trumpets unto you.

2And ye shall offer a burnt offering for a sweet savour unto the LORD; one young bullock, one ram, *and* seven lambs of the first year without blemish:

3And their meat offering *shall be of* flour mingled with oil, three tenth deals for a bullock, *and* two tenth deals for a ram,

4And one tenth deal for one lamb, throughout the seven lambs:

5And one kid of the goats *for* a sin offering, to make an atonement for you:

6Beside the burnt offering of the month, and his meat offering, and the daily burnt offering, and his meat offering, and their drink offerings, according unto their manner, for a sweet savour, a sacrifice made by fire unto the LORD.

New International

The Passover

16" 'On the fourteenth day of the first month the LORD's Passover is to be held. 17On the fifteenth day of this month there is to be a festival; for seven days eat bread made without yeast. 18On the first day hold a sacred assembly and do no regular work. 19Present to the LORD an offering made by fire, a burnt offering of two young bulls, one ram and seven male lambs a year old, all without defect. 20With each bull prepare a grain offering of three-tenths of an ephah of fine flour mixed with oil; with the ram, two-tenths; 21and with each of the seven lambs, one-tenth. 22Include one male goat as a sin offering to make atonement for you. 23Prepare these in addition to the regular morning burnt offering. 24In this way prepare the food for the offering made by fire every day for seven days as an aroma pleasing to the LORD; it is to be prepared in addition to the regular burnt offering and its drink offering. 25On the seventh day hold a sacred assembly and do no regular work.

Feast of Weeks

26" 'On the day of firstfruits, when you present to the LORD an offering of new grain during the Feast of Weeks, hold a sacred assembly and do no regular work. 27Present a burnt offering of two young bulls, one ram and seven male lambs a year old as an aroma pleasing to the LORD. 28With each bull there is to be a grain offering of three-tenths of an ephah of fine flour mixed with oil; with the ram, two-tenths; 29and with each of the seven lambs, one-tenth. 30Include one male goat to make atonement for you. 31Prepare these together with their drink offerings, in addition to the regular burnt offering and its grain offering. Be sure the animals are without defect.

Feast of Trumpets

29 " 'ON THE first day of the seventh month hold a sacred assembly and do no regular work. It is a day for you to sound the trumpets. 2As an aroma pleasing to the LORD, prepare a burnt offering of one young bull, one ram and seven male lambs a year old, all without defect. 3With the bull prepare a grain offering of three-tenths of an ephah[a] of fine flour mixed with oil; with the ram, two-tenths[b]; 4and with each of the seven lambs, one-tenth.[c] 5Include one male goat as a sin offering to make atonement for you. 6These are in addition to the monthly and daily burnt offerings with their grain offerings and drink offerings as specified. They are offerings made to the LORD by fire—a pleasing aroma.

a *3* That is, probably about 6 quarts (about 6.5 liters); also in verses 9 and 14   b *3* That is, probably about 4 quarts (about 4.5 liters); also in verses 9 and 14   c *4* That is, probably about 2 quarts (about 2 liters); also in verses 10 and 15

Living Bible

16"On April first[d], you shall celebrate the Passover—[when the death angel passed over the oldest sons of the Israelites in Egypt, leaving them unharmed[e]]. 17On the following day, a great, joyous seven-day festival will begin, but no leavened bread shall be served. 18On the first day of the festival all the people shall be called together before the Lord. No hard work shall be done on that day. 19You shall offer as burnt sacrifices to the Lord two young bulls, one ram, and seven yearling male lambs—all without defect. 20, 21With each bull there shall be a grain offering of nine quarts of fine flour mixed with oil; with the ram there shall be six quarts; and with each of the seven lambs there shall be three quarts of fine flour. 22You must also offer a male goat as a sin offering, to make atonement for yourselves. 23These offerings shall be in addition to the usual daily sacrifices. 24This same sacrifice shall be offered on each of the seven days of the feast; they will be very pleasant to the Lord. 25On the seventh day there shall again be a holy and solemn assembly of all the people, and during that day you may do no hard work.

26"On the first day of the Harvest Festival[f], all the people must come before the Lord for a special, solemn assembly to celebrate the new harvest. On that day you are to present the first of the new crop of grain as a grain offering to the Lord; there is to be no regular work by anyone on that day. 27A special burnt offering, very pleasant to the Lord, shall be offered that day. It shall consist of two young bulls, one ram, and seven yearling male lambs. 28, 29These shall be accompanied by your grain offering of nine quarts of fine flour mixed with oil with each bull, six quarts with the ram, and three quarts with each of the seven lambs. 30Also offer one male goat to make atonement for yourselves. 31These special offerings are in addition to the regular daily burnt offerings and grain offerings and drink offerings. Make sure that the animals you sacrifice are without defect.

29 THE FESTIVAL of Trumpets shall be celebrated on the fifteenth day of September[g] each year; there shall be a solemn assembly of all the people on that day, and no hard work may be done. 2On that day you shall offer a burnt sacrifice consisting of one young bull, one ram, and seven yearling male lambs—all without defect. These are sacrifices which the Lord will appreciate and enjoy. 3, 4A grain offering of nine quarts of fine flour mingled with oil shall be offered with the bull, six quarts with the ram, and three quarts with each of the seven lambs. 5In addition, there shall be a male goat sacrificed as a sin offering, to make atonement for you. 6These special sacrifices are in addition to the regular monthly burnt offering for that day,[h] and also in addition to the regular daily burnt sacrifices, which are to be offered with the respective grain offerings and drink offerings, as specified by the ordinances governing them.

New Revised Standard

Offerings at Passover

16 On the fourteenth day of the first month there shall be a passover offering to the LORD. 17And on the fifteenth day of this month is a festival; seven days shall unleavened bread be eaten. 18On the first day there shall be a holy convocation. You shall not work at your occupations. 19You shall offer an offering by fire, a burnt offering to the LORD: two young bulls, one ram, and seven male lambs a year old; see that they are without blemish. 20Their grain offering shall be of choice flour mixed with oil: three-tenths of an ephah shall you offer for a bull, and two-tenths for a ram; 21one-tenth shall you offer for each of the seven lambs; 22also one male goat for a sin offering, to make atonement for you. 23You shall offer these in addition to the burnt offering of the morning, which belongs to the regular burnt offering. 24In the same way you shall offer daily, for seven days, the food of an offering by fire, a pleasing odor to the LORD; it shall be offered in addition to the regular burnt offering and its drink offering. 25And on the seventh day you shall have a holy convocation; you shall not work at your occupations.

Offerings at the Festival of Weeks

26 On the day of the first fruits, when you offer a grain offering of new grain to the LORD at your festival of weeks, you shall have a holy convocation; you shall not work at your occupations. 27You shall offer a burnt offering, a pleasing odor to the LORD: two young bulls, one ram, seven male lambs a year old. 28Their grain offering shall be of choice flour mixed with oil, three-tenths of an ephah for each bull, two-tenths for one ram, 29one-tenth for each of the seven lambs; 30with one male goat, to make atonement for you. 31In addition to the regular burnt offering with its grain offering, you shall offer them and their drink offering. They shall be without blemish.

Offerings at the Festival of Trumpets

29 ON THE first day of the seventh month you shall have a holy convocation; you shall not work at your occupations. It is a day for you to blow the trumpets, 2and you shall offer a burnt offering, a pleasing odor to the LORD: one young bull, one ram, seven male lambs a year old without blemish. 3Their grain offering shall be of choice flour mixed with oil, three-tenths of one ephah for the bull, two-tenths for the ram, 4and one-tenth for each of the seven lambs; 5with one male goat for a sin offering, to make atonement for you. 6These are in addition to the burnt offering of the new moon and its grain offering, and the regular burnt offering and its grain offering, and their drink offerings, according to the ordinance for them, a pleasing odor, an offering by fire to the LORD.

---

[d] 28:16 on April first, literally, "on the fourteenth day of the first month" (of the Hebrew calendar).   [e] 28:16 when the death angel passed over . . . leaving them unharmed, implied.   [f] 28:26 The Harvest Festival, also called Pentecost, the Feast of Weeks, and the Day of Firstfruits.   [g] 29:1 fifteenth day of September, literally, "upon the first day of the seventh month" (of the Hebrew calendar).   [h] 29:6 regular monthly burnt offering for that day, literally, "burnt offerings of the new moon."

King James

7¶ And ye shall have on the tenth *day* of this seventh month an holy convocation; and ye shall afflict your souls: ye shall not do any work *therein*:

8But ye shall offer a burnt offering unto the LORD *for* a sweet savour; one young bullock, one ram, *and* seven lambs of the first year; they shall be unto you without blemish:

9And their meat offering *shall be of* flour mingled with oil, three tenth deals to a bullock, *and* two tenth deals to one ram,

10A several tenth deal for one lamb, throughout the seven lambs:

11One kid of the goats *for* a sin offering; beside the sin offering of atonement, and the continual burnt offering, and the meat offering of it, and their drink offerings.

12¶ And on the fifteenth day of the seventh month ye shall have an holy convocation; ye shall do no servile work, and ye shall keep a feast unto the LORD seven days:

13And ye shall offer a burnt offering, a sacrifice made by fire, of a sweet savour unto the LORD; thirteen young bullocks, two rams, *and* fourteen lambs of the first year; they shall be without blemish:

14And their meat offering *shall be of* flour mingled with oil, three tenth deals unto every bullock of the thirteen bullocks, two tenth deals to each ram of the two rams,

15And a several tenth deal to each lamb of the fourteen lambs:

16And one kid of the goats *for* a sin offering; beside the continual burnt offering, his meat offering, and his drink offering.

17¶ And on the second day *ye shall offer* twelve young bullocks, two rams, fourteen lambs of the first year without spot:

18And their meat offering and their drink offerings for the bullocks, for the rams, and for the lambs, *shall be* according to their number, after the manner:

19And one kid of the goats *for* a sin offering; beside the continual burnt offering, and the meat offering thereof, and their drink offerings.

20¶ And on the third day eleven bullocks, two rams, fourteen lambs of the first year without blemish;

21And their meat offering and their drink offerings for the bullocks, for the rams, and for the lambs, *shall be* according to their number, after the manner:

22And one goat *for* a sin offering; beside the continual burnt offering, and his meat offering, and his drink offering.

23¶ And on the fourth day ten bullocks, two rams, *and* fourteen lambs of the first year without blemish:

24Their meat offering and their drink offerings for the bullocks, for the rams, and for the lambs, *shall be* according to their number, after the manner:

25And one kid of the goats *for* a sin offering; beside the continual burnt offering, his meat offering, and his drink offering.

26¶ And on the fifth day nine bullocks, two rams, *and* fourteen lambs of the first year without spot:

27And their meat offering and their drink offerings for the bullocks, for the rams, and for the lambs, *shall be* according to their number, after the manner:

28And one goat *for* a sin offering; beside the continual burnt offering, and his meat offering, and his drink offering.

29¶ And on the sixth day eight bullocks, two rams, *and* fourteen lambs of the first year without blemish:

30And their meat offering and their drink offerings for the bullocks, for the rams, and for the lambs, *shall be* according to their number, after the manner:

31And one goat *for* a sin offering; beside the continual burnt offering, his meat offering, and his drink offering.

32¶ And on the seventh day seven bullocks, two rams, *and* fourteen lambs of the first year without blemish:

New International

Day of Atonement

7" 'On the tenth day of this seventh month hold a sacred assembly. You must deny yourselvesa and do no work. 8Present as an aroma pleasing to the LORD a burnt offering of one young bull, one ram and seven male lambs a year old, all without defect. 9With the bull prepare a grain offering of three-tenths of an ephah of fine flour mixed with oil; with the ram, two-tenths; 10and with each of the seven lambs, one-tenth. 11Include one male goat as a sin offering, in addition to the sin offering for atonement and the regular burnt offering with its grain offering, and their drink offerings.

Feast of Tabernacles

12" 'On the fifteenth day of the seventh month, hold a sacred assembly and do no regular work. Celebrate a festival to the LORD for seven days. 13Present an offering made by fire as an aroma pleasing to the LORD, a burnt offering of thirteen young bulls, two rams and fourteen male lambs a year old, all without defect. 14With each of the thirteen bulls prepare a grain offering of three-tenths of an ephah of fine flour mixed with oil; with each of the two rams, two-tenths; 15and with each of the fourteen lambs, one-tenth. 16Include one male goat as a sin offering, in addition to the regular burnt offering with its grain offering and drink offering.

17" 'On the second day prepare twelve young bulls, two rams and fourteen male lambs a year old, all without defect. 18With the bulls, rams and lambs, prepare their grain offerings and drink offerings according to the number specified. 19Include one male goat as a sin offering, in addition to the regular burnt offering with its grain offering, and their drink offerings.

20" 'On the third day prepare eleven bulls, two rams and fourteen male lambs a year old, all without defect. 21With the bulls, rams and lambs, prepare their grain offerings and drink offerings according to the number specified. 22Include one male goat as a sin offering, in addition to the regular burnt offering with its grain offering and drink offering.

23" 'On the fourth day prepare ten bulls, two rams and fourteen male lambs a year old, all without defect. 24With the bulls, rams and lambs, prepare their grain offerings and drink offerings according to the number specified. 25Include one male goat as a sin offering, in addition to the regular burnt offering with its grain offering and drink offering.

26" 'On the fifth day prepare nine bulls, two rams and fourteen male lambs a year old, all without defect. 27With the bulls, rams and lambs, prepare their grain offerings and drink offerings according to the number specified. 28Include one male goat as a sin offering, in addition to the regular burnt offering with its grain offering and drink offering.

29" 'On the sixth day prepare eight bulls, two rams and fourteen male lambs a year old, all without defect. 30With the bulls, rams and lambs, prepare their grain offerings and drink offerings according to the number specified. 31Include one male goat as a sin offering, in addition to the regular burnt offering with its grain offering and drink offering.

32" 'On the seventh day prepare seven bulls, two rams and fourteen male lambs a year old, all without defect.

---

a 7 Or *must fast*

Living Bible

7"Ten days later[b] another convocation of all the people shall be held. This will be a day of solemn humility before the Lord, and no work of any kind may be done. 8On that day you shall offer a burnt sacrifice to the Lord—it will be very pleasant to him—of one young bull, one ram, seven yearling male lambs—each without defect— 9, 10and their accompanying grain offerings. Nine quarts of fine flour mixed with oil are to be offered with the bull; six with the ram; and three with each of the seven lambs. 11You are also to sacrifice one male goat for a sin offering. This is in addition to the sin offering of the Day of Atonement [offered annually on that day[c]], and in addition to the regular daily burnt sacrifices, grain offerings, and drink offerings.

12"Five days later[d] there shall be yet another assembly of all the people, and on that day no hard work shall be done; it is the beginning of a seven-day festival before the Lord. 13Your special burnt sacrifice that day, which will give much pleasure to the Lord, shall be thirteen young bulls, two rams, and fourteen male yearling lambs—each without defect— 14accompanied by the usual grain offerings—nine quarts of fine flour mingled with oil for each of the thirteen young bulls; six quarts for each of the two rams; 15and three quarts for each of the fourteen lambs. 16There must also be a male goat sacrificed for a sin offering, in addition to the regular daily burnt sacrifice with its accompanying grain offerings and drink offerings.

17"On the second day of this seven-day festival you shall sacrifice twelve young bulls, two rams, and fourteen male yearling lambs—each without defect— 18accompanied by the usual grain offerings and drink offerings. 19Also, in addition to the regular daily burnt sacrifice, you are to sacrifice a male goat with its accompanying grain offering and drink offering for a sin offering.

20"On the third day of the festival, offer eleven young bulls, two rams, fourteen male yearling lambs—each without defect— 21and the usual grain offering and drink offering with each sacrifice. 22And in addition to the regular daily burnt sacrifices, sacrifice a male goat for a sin offering, with its accompanying grain offering and drink offering.

23"On the fourth day of the festival, you are to sacrifice ten young bulls, two rams, and fourteen male yearling lambs—each without defect— 24each with its accompanying grain offering and drink offering; 25also a male goat as a sin offering (along with the usual grain and drink offerings) in addition to the regular daily sacrifices.

26, 27"On the fifth day of the festival, sacrifice nine young bulls, two rams, and fourteen male yearling lambs—each without defect—accompanied by the usual grain offerings and drink offerings; 28also sacrifice a male goat with the usual grain and drink offerings, as a special sin offering, in addition to the usual daily sacrifices.

29"On the sixth day of the festival, you must sacrifice eight young bulls, two rams, and fourteen male yearling lambs—each without defect— 30along with their usual grain and drink offerings. 31In addition to the usual daily sacrifices, sacrifice a male goat and the usual grain and drink offerings as a sin offering.

32"On the seventh day of the festival, sacrifice seven young bulls, two rams, and fourteen male yearling lambs—each without defect— 33each with its custom-

New Revised Standard

Offerings on the Day of Atonement

7 On the tenth day of this seventh month you shall have a holy convocation, and deny yourselves;[e] you shall do no work. 8You shall offer a burnt offering to the Lord, a pleasing odor: one young bull, one ram, seven male lambs a year old. They shall be without blemish. 9Their grain offering shall be of choice flour mixed with oil, three-tenths of an ephah for the bull, two-tenths for the one ram, 10one-tenth for each of the seven lambs; 11with one male goat for a sin offering, in addition to the sin offering of atonement, and the regular burnt offering and its grain offering, and their drink offerings.

Offerings at the Festival of Booths

12 On the fifteenth day of the seventh month you shall have a holy convocation; you shall not work at your occupations. You shall celebrate a festival to the Lord seven days. 13You shall offer a burnt offering, an offering by fire, a pleasing odor to the Lord: thirteen young bulls, two rams, fourteen male lambs a year old. They shall be without blemish. 14Their grain offering shall be of choice flour mixed with oil, three-tenths of an ephah for each of the thirteen bulls, two-tenths for each of the two rams, 15and one-tenth for each of the fourteen lambs; 16also one male goat for a sin offering, in addition to the regular burnt offering, its grain offering and its drink offering.

17 On the second day: twelve young bulls, two rams, fourteen male lambs a year old without blemish, 18with the grain offering and the drink offerings for the bulls, for the rams, and for the lambs, as prescribed in accordance with their number; 19also one male goat for a sin offering, in addition to the regular burnt offering and its grain offering, and their drink offerings.

20 On the third day: eleven bulls, two rams, fourteen male lambs a year old without blemish, 21with the grain offering and the drink offerings for the bulls, for the rams, and for the lambs, as prescribed in accordance with their number; 22also one male goat for a sin offering, in addition to the regular burnt offering and its grain offering and its drink offering.

23 On the fourth day: ten bulls, two rams, fourteen male lambs a year old without blemish, 24with the grain offering and the drink offerings for the bulls, for the rams, and for the lambs, as prescribed in accordance with their number; 25also one male goat for a sin offering, in addition to the regular burnt offering, its grain offering and its drink offering.

26 On the fifth day: nine bulls, two rams, fourteen male lambs a year old without blemish, 27with the grain offering and the drink offerings for the bulls, for the rams, and for the lambs, as prescribed in accordance with their number; 28also one male goat for a sin offering, in addition to the regular burnt offering and its grain offering and its drink offering.

29 On the sixth day: eight bulls, two rams, fourteen male lambs a year old without blemish, 30with the grain offering and the drink offerings for the bulls, for the rams, and for the lambs, as prescribed in accordance with their number; 31also one male goat for a sin offering, in addition to the regular burnt offering and its grain offering, and its drink offerings.

32 On the seventh day: seven bulls, two rams, fourteen male lambs a year old without blemish, 33with the

---

b 29:7 Ten days later, literally, "On the tenth day of the seventh month" (of the Hebrew calendar). c 29:11 offered annually on that day, implied. d 29:12 Five days later, literally, "On the fifteenth day of the seventh month" (of the Hebrew calendar).

e Or and fast

King James

33And their meat offering and their drink offerings for the bullocks, for the rams, and for the lambs, *shall be* according to their number, after the manner:

34And one goat *for* a sin offering; beside the continual burnt offering, his meat offering, and his drink offering.

35¶ On the eighth day ye shall have a solemn assembly: ye shall do no servile work *therein:*

36But ye shall offer a burnt offering, a sacrifice made by fire, of a sweet savour unto the LORD: one bullock, one ram, seven lambs of the first year without blemish:

37Their meat offering and their drink offerings for the bullock, for the ram, and for the lambs, *shall be* according to their number, after the manner:

38And one goat *for* a sin offering; beside the continual burnt offering, and his meat offering, and his drink offering.

39These *things* ye shall do unto the LORD in your set feasts, beside your vows, and your freewill offerings, for your burnt offerings, and for your meat offerings, and for your drink offerings, and for your peace offerings.

40And Moses told the children of Israel according to all that the LORD commanded Moses.

30 AND MOSES spake unto the heads of the tribes concerning the children of Israel, saying, This *is* the thing which the LORD hath commanded.

2If a man vow a vow unto the LORD, or swear an oath to bind his soul with a bond; he shall not break his word, he shall do according to all that proceedeth out of his mouth.

3If a woman also vow a vow unto the LORD, and bind *herself* by a bond, *being* in her father's house in her youth;

4And her father hear her vow, and her bond wherewith she hath bound her soul, and her father shall hold his peace at her: then all her vows shall stand, and every bond wherewith she hath bound her soul shall stand.

5But if her father disallow her in the day that he heareth; not any of her vows, or of her bonds wherewith she hath bound her soul, shall stand: and the LORD shall forgive her, because her father disallowed her.

6And if she had at all an husband, when she vowed, or uttered aught out of her lips, wherewith she bound her soul;

7And her husband heard *it*, and held his peace at her in the day that he heard *it:* then her vows shall stand, and her bonds wherewith she bound her soul shall stand.

8But if her husband disallowed her on the day that he heard *it;* then he shall make her vow which she vowed, and that which she uttered with her lips, wherewith she bound her soul, of none effect: and the LORD shall forgive her.

9But every vow of a widow, and of her that is divorced, wherewith they have bound their souls, shall stand against her.

10And if she vowed in her husband's house, or bound her soul by a bond with an oath;

11And her husband heard *it*, and held his peace at her, *and* disallowed her not: then all her vows shall stand, and every bond wherewith she bound her soul shall stand.

12But if her husband hath utterly made them void on the day he heard *them; then* whatsoever proceeded out of her lips concerning her vows, or concerning the bond of her soul, shall not stand: her husband hath made them void; and the LORD shall forgive her.

13Every vow, and every binding oath to afflict the soul, her husband may establish it, or her husband may make it void.

New International

33With the bulls, rams and lambs, prepare their grain offerings and drink offerings according to the number specified. 34Include one male goat as a sin offering, in addition to the regular burnt offering with its grain offering and drink offering.

35" 'On the eighth day hold an assembly and do no regular work. 36Present an offering made by fire as an aroma pleasing to the LORD, a burnt offering of one bull, one ram and seven male lambs a year old, all without defect. 37With the bull, the ram and the lambs, prepare their grain offerings and drink offerings according to the number specified. 38Include one male goat as a sin offering, in addition to the regular burnt offering with its grain offering and drink offering.

39" 'In addition to what you vow and your freewill offerings, prepare these for the LORD at your appointed feasts: your burnt offerings, grain offerings, drink offerings and fellowship offerings.a' "

40Moses told the Israelites all that the LORD commanded him.

Vows

30 MOSES SAID to the heads of the tribes of Israel: "This is what the LORD commands: 2When a man makes a vow to the LORD or takes an oath to obligate himself by a pledge, he must not break his word but must do everything he said.

3"When a young woman still living in her father's house makes a vow to the LORD or obligates herself by a pledge 4and her father hears about her vow or pledge but says nothing to her, then all her vows and every pledge by which she obligated herself will stand. 5But if her father forbids her when he hears about it, none of her vows or the pledges by which she obligated herself will stand; the LORD will release her because her father has forbidden her.

6"If she marries after she makes a vow or after her lips utter a rash promise by which she obligates herself 7and her husband hears about it but says nothing to her, then her vows or the pledges by which she obligated herself will stand. 8But if her husband forbids her when he hears about it, he nullifies the vow that obligates her or the rash promise by which she obligates herself, and the LORD will release her.

9"Any vow or obligation taken by a widow or divorced woman will be binding on her.

10"If a woman living with her husband makes a vow or obligates herself by a pledge under oath 11and her husband hears about it but says nothing to her and does not forbid her, then all her vows or the pledges by which she obligated herself will stand. 12But if her husband nullifies them when he hears about them, then none of the vows or pledges that came from her lips will stand. Her husband has nullified them, and the LORD will release her. 13Her husband may confirm or nullify any vow she makes or any sworn pledge to deny herself.

---

a *39 Traditionally* peace offerings

Living Bible

ary grain and drink offerings; 34also sacrifice an extra sin offering of one male goat, with the usual grain and drink offerings, in addition to the regular daily sacrifices.

35"On the eighth day summon the people to another solemn assembly; you must do no hard work that day. 36Sacrifice a burnt offering—they are very pleasant to the Lord—of one young bull, one ram, seven male yearling lambs—each without defect— 37and the customary grain and drink offerings. 38Sacrifice also one male goat with the usual grain and drink offerings for a sin offering, in addition to the regular daily sacrifices. 39These offerings are compulsory at the times of your annual feasts, and are in addition to sacrifices and offerings you present in connection with vows, or as free-will offerings, burnt sacrifices, grain offerings, drink offerings, or peace offerings."

40So Moses gave all of these instructions to the people of Israel.

30 NOW MOSES summoned the leaders of the tribes and told them, "The Lord has commanded that when anyone makes a promise to the Lord, either to do something or to quit doing something, that vow must not be broken: the person making the vow must do exactly as he has promised.

3"If a woman promises the Lord to do or not do something, and she is still a girl at home in her father's home, 4and her father hears that she has made a vow with penalties, but says nothing, then her vow shall stand. 5But if her father refuses to let her make the vow, or feels that the penalties she has agreed to are too harsh, then her promise will automatically become invalid. Her father must state his disagreement on the first day he hears about it; and then Jehovah will forgive her because her father would not let her do it.

6"If she takes a vow or makes a foolish pledge, and later marries, 7and her husband learns of her vow and says nothing on the day he hears of it, her vow shall stand. 8But if her husband refuses to accept her vow or foolish pledge, his disagreement makes it void, and Jehovah will forgive her.

9"But if the woman is a widow or is divorced, she must fulfill her vow.

10"If she is married and living in her husband's home when she makes the vow, 11and her husband hears of it and does nothing, the vow shall stand; 12but if he refuses to allow it on the first day he hears of it, her vow is void and Jehovah will forgive her. 13So her husband may either confirm or nullify her vow, 14but if he says noth-

New Revised Standard

grain offering and the drink offerings for the bulls, for the rams, and for the lambs, as prescribed in accordance with their number; 34also one male goat for a sin offering, besides the regular burnt offering, its grain offering, and its drink offering.

35 On the eighth day you shall have a solemn assembly; you shall not work at your occupations. 36You shall offer a burnt offering, an offering by fire, a pleasing odor to the LORD: one bull, one ram, seven male lambs a year old without blemish, 37and the grain offering and the drink offerings for the bull, for the ram, and for the lambs, as prescribed in accordance with their number; 38also one male goat for a sin offering, in addition to the regular burnt offering and its grain offering and its drink offering.

39 These you shall offer to the LORD at your appointed festivals, in addition to your votive offerings and your freewill offerings, as your burnt offerings, your grain offerings, your drink offerings, and your offerings of well-being.

40b So Moses told the Israelites everything just as the LORD had commanded Moses.

Vows Made by Women

30 THEN MOSES said to the heads of the tribes of the Israelites: This is what the LORD has commanded. 2When a man makes a vow to the LORD, or swears an oath to bind himself by a pledge, he shall not break his word; he shall do according to all that proceeds out of his mouth.

3 When a woman makes a vow to the LORD, or binds herself by a pledge, while within her father's house, in her youth, 4and her father hears of her vow or her pledge by which she has bound herself, and says nothing to her; then all her vows shall stand, and any pledge by which she has bound herself shall stand. 5But if her father expresses disapproval to her at the time that he hears of it, no vow of hers, and no pledge by which she has bound herself, shall stand; and the LORD will forgive her, because her father had expressed to her his disapproval.

6 If she marries, while obligated by her vows or any thoughtless utterance of her lips by which she has bound herself, 7and her husband hears of it and says nothing to her at the time that he hears, then her vows shall stand, and her pledges by which she has bound herself shall stand. 8But if, at the time that her husband hears of it, he expresses disapproval to her, then he shall nullify the vow by which she was obligated, or the thoughtless utterance of her lips, by which she bound herself; and the LORD will forgive her. 9(But every vow of a widow or of a divorced woman, by which she has bound herself, shall be binding upon her.) 10And if she made a vow in her husband's house, or bound herself by a pledge with an oath, 11and her husband heard it and said nothing to her, and did not express disapproval to her, then all her vows shall stand, and any pledge by which she bound herself shall stand. 12But if her husband nullifies them at the time that he hears them, then whatever proceeds out of her lips concerning her vows, or concerning her pledge of herself, shall not stand. Her husband has nullified them, and the LORD will forgive her. 13Any vow or any binding oath to deny herself,c her husband may allow to stand, or her husband may nullify.

b Ch 30.1 in Heb   c Or to fast

King James

14But if her husband altogether hold his peace at her from day to day; then he establisheth all her vows, or all her bonds, which *are* upon her: he confirmeth them, because he held his peace at her in the day that he heard *them*.

15But if he shall any ways make them void after that he hath heard *them;* then he shall bear her iniquity.

16These *are* the statutes, which the LORD commanded Moses, between a man and his wife, between the father and his daughter, *being yet* in her youth in her father's house.

31 AND THE LORD spake unto Moses, saying, 2Avenge the children of Israel of the Midianites: afterward shalt thou be gathered unto thy people.

3And Moses spake unto the people, saying, Arm some of yourselves unto the war, and let them go against the Midianites, and avenge the LORD of Midian.

4Of every tribe a thousand, throughout all the tribes of Israel, shall ye send to the war.

5So there were delivered out of the thousands of Israel, a thousand of *every* tribe, twelve thousand armed for war.

6And Moses sent them to the war, a thousand of *every* tribe, them and Phinehas the son of Eleazar the priest, to the war, with the holy instruments, and the trumpets to blow in his hand.

7And they warred against the Midianites, as the LORD commanded Moses; and they slew all the males.

8And they slew the kings of Midian, beside the rest of them that were slain; *namely*, Evi, and Rekem, and Zur, and Hur, and Reba, five kings of Midian: Balaam also the son of Beor they slew with the sword.

9And the children of Israel took *all* the women of Midian captives, and their little ones, and took the spoil of all their cattle, and all their flocks, and all their goods.

10And they burnt all their cities wherein they dwelt, and all their goodly castles, with fire.

11And they took all the spoil, and all the prey, *both* of men and of beasts.

12And they brought the captives, and the prey, and the spoil, unto Moses, and Eleazar the priest, and unto the congregation of the children of Israel, unto the camp at the plains of Moab, which *are* by Jordan *near* Jericho.

13¶ And Moses, and Eleazar the priest, and all the princes of the congregation, went forth to meet them without the camp.

14And Moses was wroth with the officers of the host, *with* the captains over thousands, and captains over hundreds, which came from the battle.

15And Moses said unto them, Have ye saved all the women alive?

16Behold, these caused the children of Israel, through the counsel of Balaam, to commit trespass against the LORD in the matter of Peor, and there was a plague among the congregation of the LORD.

17Now therefore kill every male among the little ones, and kill every woman that hath known man by lying with him.

18But all the women children, that have not known a man by lying with him, keep alive for yourselves.

19And do ye abide without the camp seven days: whosoever hath killed any person, and whosoever hath touched any slain, purify *both* yourselves and your captives on the third day, and on the seventh day.

20And purify all *your* raiment, and all that is made of skins, and all work of goats' *hair,* and all things made of wood.

21¶ And Eleazar the priest said unto the men of war which went to the battle, This *is* the ordinance of the law which the LORD commanded Moses;

New International

14But if her husband says nothing to her about it from day to day, then he confirms all her vows or the pledges binding on her. He confirms them by saying nothing to her when he hears about them. 15If, however, he nullifies them some time after he hears about them, then he is responsible for her guilt."

16These are the regulations the LORD gave Moses concerning relationships between a man and his wife, and between a father and his young daughter still living in his house.

Vengeance on the Midianites

31 THE LORD said to Moses, 2"Take vengeance on the Midianites for the Israelites. After that, you will be gathered to your people."

3So Moses said to the people, "Arm some of your men to go to war against the Midianites and to carry out the LORD's vengeance on them. 4Send into battle a thousand men from each of the tribes of Israel." 5So twelve thousand men armed for battle, a thousand from each tribe, were supplied from the clans of Israel. 6Moses sent them into battle, a thousand from each tribe, along with Phinehas son of Eleazar, the priest, who took with him articles from the sanctuary and the trumpets for signaling.

7They fought against Midian, as the LORD commanded Moses, and killed every man. 8Among their victims were Evi, Rekem, Zur, Hur and Reba—the five kings of Midian. They also killed Balaam son of Beor with the sword. 9The Israelites captured the Midianite women and children and took all the Midianite herds, flocks and goods as plunder. 10They burned all the towns where the Midianites had settled, as well as all their camps. 11They took all the plunder and spoils, including the people and animals, 12and brought the captives, spoils and plunder to Moses and Eleazar the priest and the Israelite assembly at their camp on the plains of Moab, by the Jordan across from Jericho.[a]

13Moses, Eleazar the priest and all the leaders of the community went to meet them outside the camp. 14Moses was angry with the officers of the army—the commanders of thousands and commanders of hundreds—who returned from the battle.

15"Have you allowed all the women to live?" he asked them. 16"They were the ones who followed Balaam's advice and were the means of turning the Israelites away from the LORD in what happened at Peor, so that a plague struck the LORD's people. 17Now kill all the boys. And kill every woman who has slept with a man, 18but save for yourselves every girl who has never slept with a man.

19"All of you who have killed anyone or touched anyone who was killed must stay outside the camp seven days. On the third and seventh days you must purify yourselves and your captives. 20Purify every garment as well as everything made of leather, goat hair or wood."

21Then Eleazar the priest said to the soldiers who had gone into battle, "This is the requirement of the law that the LORD gave Moses: 22Gold, silver, bronze, iron, tin,

---

a 12 Hebrew *Jordan of Jericho*; possibly an ancient name for the Jordan River

Living Bible

ing for a day, then he has already agreed to it. 15If he waits more than a day and then refuses to permit the vow, whatever penalties to which she agreed shall come upon him—he shall be responsible."

16These, then, are the commandments the Lord gave Moses concerning relationships between a man and his wife and between a father and his daughter who is living at home.

31 THEN THE Lord said to Moses, "Take vengeance on the Midianites for leading you into idolatry, and then you must die."

3Moses said to the people, "Some of you must take arms to wage Jehovah's war against Midian. 4, 5Conscript 1,000 men from each tribe." So this was done; and out of the many thousands of Israel, 12,000 armed men were sent to battle by Moses. 6Phinehas (son of Eleazar the priest) led them into battle, accompanied by the Ark,b with trumpets blaring. 7And every man of Midian was killed. 8Among those killed were all five of the Midianite kings—Evi, Rekem, Zur, Hur, and Reba. Balaam, the son of Beor, was also killed.

9, 10, 11Then the Israeli army took as captives all the women and children, and seized the cattle and flocks and a lot of miscellaneous booty. All of the cities, towns, and villages of Midian were then burned. 12The captives and other war loot were brought to Moses and Eleazar the priest, and to the rest of the people of Israel who were camped on the plains of Moab beside the Jordan River, across from Jericho. 13Moses and Eleazar the priest and all the leaders of the people went out to meet the victorious army, 14but Moses was very angry with the army officers and battalion leaders.

15"Why have you let all the women live?" he demanded. 16"These are the very ones who followed Balaam's advice and caused the people of Israel to worship idols on Mount Peor, and they are the cause of the plague that destroyed us. 17Now kill all the boys and all the women who have had sexual intercourse. 18Only the little girls may live; you may keep them for yourselves. 19Now stay outside of the camp for seven days, all of you who have killed anyone or touched a dead body. Then purify yourselves and your captives on the third and seventh days. 20Remember also to purify all your garments and everything made of leather, goat's hair, or wood."

21Then Eleazar the priest said to the men who were in the battle, "This is the commandment Jehovah has given Moses: 22'Anything that will stand heat—such as

New Revised Standard

14But if her husband says nothing to her from day to day,c then he validates all her vows, or all her pledges, by which she is obligated; he has validated them, because he said nothing to her at the time that he heard of them. 15But if he nullifies them some time after he has heard of them, then he shall bear her guilt.

16 These are the statutes that the LORD commanded Moses concerning a husband and his wife, and a father and his daughter while she is still young and in her father's house.

War against Midian

31 THE LORD spoke to Moses, saying, 2"Avenge the Israelites on the Midianites; afterward you shall be gathered to your people." 3So Moses said to the people, "Arm some of your number for the war, so that they may go against Midian, to execute the LORD's vengeance on Midian. 4You shall send a thousand from each of the tribes of Israel to the war." 5So out of the thousands of Israel, a thousand from each tribe were conscripted, twelve thousand armed for battle. 6Moses sent them to the war, a thousand from each tribe, along with Phinehas son of Eleazar the priest,d with the vessels of the sanctuary and the trumpets for sounding the alarm in his hand. 7They did battle against Midian, as the LORD had commanded Moses, and killed every male. 8They killed the kings of Midian: Evi, Rekem, Zur, Hur, and Reba, the five kings of Midian, in addition to others who were slain by them; and they also killed Balaam son of Beor with the sword. 9The Israelites took the women of Midian and their little ones captive; and they took all their cattle, their flocks, and all their goods as booty. 10All their towns where they had settled, and all their encampments, they burned, 11but they took all the spoil and all the booty, both people and animals. 12Then they brought the captives and the booty and the spoil to Moses, to Eleazar the priest, and to the congregation of the Israelites, at the camp on the plains of Moab by the Jordan at Jericho.

Return from the War

13 Moses, Eleazar the priest, and all the leaders of the congregation went to meet them outside the camp. 14Moses became angry with the officers of the army, the commanders of thousands and the commanders of hundreds, who had come from service in the war. 15Moses said to them, "Have you allowed all the women to live? 16These women here, on Balaam's advice, made the Israelites act treacherously against the LORD in the affair of Peor, so that the plague came among the congregation of the LORD. 17Now therefore, kill every male among the little ones, and kill every woman who has known a man by sleeping with him. 18But all the young girls who have not known a man by sleeping with him, keep alive for yourselves. 19Camp outside the camp seven days; whoever of you has killed any person or touched a corpse, purify yourselves and your captives on the third and on the seventh day. 20You shall purify every garment, every article of skin, everything made of goats' hair, and every article of wood."

21 Eleazar the priest said to the troops who had gone to battle: "This is the statute of the law that the LORD has commanded Moses: 22gold, silver, bronze, iron, tin,

b 31:6 accompanied by the Ark, literally, "with the vessels of the sanctuary."   c Or from that day to the next   d Gk: Heb adds to the war

King James

22Only the gold, and the silver, the brass, the iron, the tin, and the lead,

23Every thing that may abide the fire, ye shall make it go through the fire, and it shall be clean: nevertheless it shall be purified with the water of separation: and all that abideth not the fire ye shall make go through the water.

24And ye shall wash your clothes on the seventh day, and ye shall be clean, and afterward ye shall come into the camp.

25¶ And the LORD spake unto Moses, saying,

26Take the sum of the prey that was taken, both of man and of beast, thou, and Eleazar the priest, and the chief fathers of the congregation:

27And divide the prey into two parts; between them that took the war upon them, who went out to battle, and between all the congregation:

28And levy a tribute unto the LORD of the men of war which went out to battle: one soul of five hundred, both of the persons, and of the beeves, and of the asses, and of the sheep:

29Take it of their half, and give it unto Eleazar the priest, for an heave offering of the LORD.

30And of the children of Israel's half, thou shalt take one portion of fifty, of the persons, of the beeves, of the asses, and of the flocks, of all manner of beasts, and give them unto the Levites, which keep the charge of the tabernacle of the LORD.

31And Moses and Eleazar the priest did as the LORD commanded Moses.

32And the booty, being the rest of the prey which the men of war had caught, was six hundred thousand and seventy thousand and five thousand sheep,

33And threescore and twelve thousand beeves,

34And threescore and one thousand asses,

35And thirty and two thousand persons in all, of women that had not known man by lying with him.

36And the half, which was the portion of them that went out to war, was in number three hundred thousand and seven and thirty thousand and five hundred sheep:

37And the LORD's tribute of the sheep was six hundred and threescore and fifteen.

38And the beeves were thirty and six thousand; of which the LORD's tribute was threescore and twelve.

39And the asses were thirty thousand and five hundred; of which the LORD's tribute was threescore and one.

40And the persons were sixteen thousand; of which the LORD's tribute was thirty and two persons.

41And Moses gave the tribute, which was the LORD's heave offering, unto Eleazar the priest, as the LORD commanded Moses.

42And of the children of Israel's half, which Moses divided from the men that warred,

43(Now the half that pertained unto the congregation was three hundred thousand and thirty thousand and seven thousand and five hundred sheep,

44And thirty and six thousand beeves,

45And thirty thousand asses and five hundred,

46And sixteen thousand persons;)

47Even of the children of Israel's half, Moses took one portion of fifty, both of man and of beast, and gave them unto the Levites, which kept the charge of the tabernacle of the LORD; as the LORD commanded Moses.

48¶ And the officers which were over thousands of the host, the captains of thousands, and captains of hundreds, came near unto Moses:

49And they said unto Moses, Thy servants have taken the sum of the men of war which are under our charge, and there lacketh not one man of us.

50We have therefore brought an oblation for the LORD, what every man hath gotten, of jewels of gold, chains, and bracelets, rings, earrings, and tablets, to make an atonement for our souls before the LORD.

New International

lead 23and anything else that can withstand fire must be put through the fire, and then it will be clean. But it must also be purified with the water of cleansing. And whatever cannot withstand fire must be put through that water. 24On the seventh day wash your clothes and you will be clean. Then you may come into the camp."

Dividing the Spoils

25The LORD said to Moses, 26"You and Eleazar the priest and the family heads of the community are to count all the people and animals that were captured. 27Divide the spoils between the soldiers who took part in the battle and the rest of the community. 28From the soldiers who fought in the battle, set apart as tribute for the LORD one out of every five hundred, whether persons, cattle, donkeys, sheep or goats. 29Take this tribute from their half share and give it to Eleazar the priest as the LORD's part. 30From the Israelites' half, select one out of every fifty, whether persons, cattle, donkeys, sheep, goats or other animals. Give them to the Levites, who are responsible for the care of the LORD's tabernacle." 31So Moses and Eleazar the priest did as the LORD commanded Moses.

32The plunder remaining from the spoils that the soldiers took was 675,000 sheep, 33 72,000 cattle, 34 61,000 donkeys 35and 32,000 women who had never slept with a man.

36The half share of those who fought in the battle was:

337,500 sheep, 37of which the tribute for the LORD was 675;

3836,000 cattle, of which the tribute for the LORD was 72;

3930,500 donkeys, of which the tribute for the LORD was 61;

4016,000 people, of which the tribute for the LORD was 32.

41Moses gave the tribute to Eleazar the priest as the LORD's part, as the LORD commanded Moses.

42The half belonging to the Israelites, which Moses set apart from that of the fighting men— 43the community's half—was 337,500 sheep, 44436,000 cattle, 4530,500 donkeys 46and 16,000 people. 47From the Israelites' half, Moses selected one out of every fifty persons and animals, as the LORD commanded him, and gave them to the Levites, who were responsible for the care of the LORD's tabernacle.

48Then the officers who were over the units of the army—the commanders of thousands and commanders of hundreds—went to Moses 49and said to him, "Your servants have counted the soldiers under our command, and not one is missing. 50So we have brought as an offering to the LORD the gold articles each of us acquired—armlets, bracelets, signet rings, earrings and necklaces—to make atonement for ourselves before the LORD."

Living Bible

gold, silver, bronze, iron, tin, or lead— 23shall be passed through fire in order to be made ceremonially pure; it must then be further purified with the purification water. But anything that won't stand heat shall be purified by the water alone.' 24On the seventh day you must wash your clothes and be purified, and then you may come back into the camp."

25And the Lord said to Moses, 26"You and Eleazar the priest and the leaders of the tribes are to make a list of all the loot, including the people and animals; 27then divide it into two parts. Half of it is for the men who were in the battle, and the other half is to be given to the people of Israel. 28But first, the Lord gets a share of all the captives, oxen, donkeys, and flocks kept by the army. His share is one out of every five hundred. 29Give this share to Eleazar the priest to be presented to the Lord by the gesture of waving before the altar. 30Also levy a two percent tribute of all the captives, flocks, and cattle that are given to the people of Israel. Present this to the Levites in charge of the Tabernacle, for it is the Lord's portion."

31So Moses and Eleazar the priest did as the Lord commanded. 32–35The total booty (besides the jewelry, clothing, etc., which the soldiers kept for themselves) was 675,000 sheep; 72,000 oxen; 61,000 donkeys; and 32,000 young girls.

36–40So the half given to the army totaled:

337,500 sheep (of which 675 were given to the Lord);
36,000 oxen (of which 72 were given to the Lord);
30,500 donkeys (of which 61 were given to the Lord);
16,000 girls (of whom 32 went to the Levites).a

41All of the Lord's portion was given to Eleazar the priest, as the Lord had directed Moses.

42–46The half of the booty assigned to the people of Israel—Moses had separated it from the half belonging to the warriors—amounted to:

337,500 sheep,
36,000 oxen,
30,500 donkeys, and
16,000 girls

47In accordance with the Lord's directions, Moses gave two percent of these to the Levites.

48, 49Then the officers and battalion leaders came to Moses and said, "We have accounted for all the men who went out to battle, and not one of us is missing! 50So we have brought a special thank-offering to the Lord from our loot—gold jewelry, bracelets, anklets, rings, earrings, and necklaces. This is to make atonement for our souls before the Lord."

New Revised Standard

and lead— 23everything that can withstand fire, shall be passed through fire, and it shall be clean. Nevertheless it shall also be purified with the water for purification; and whatever cannot withstand fire, shall be passed through the water. 24You must wash your clothes on the seventh day, and you shall be clean; afterward you may come into the camp."

Disposition of Captives and Booty

25 The Lord spoke to Moses, saying, 26"You and Eleazar the priest and the heads of the ancestral houses of the congregation make an inventory of the booty captured, both human and animal. 27Divide the booty into two parts, between the warriors who went out to battle and all the congregation. 28From the share of the warriors who went out to battle, set aside as tribute for the Lord, one item out of every five hundred, whether persons, oxen, donkeys, sheep, or goats. 29Take it from their half and give it to Eleazar the priest as an offering to the Lord. 30But from the Israelites' half you shall take one out of every fifty, whether persons, oxen, donkeys, sheep, or goats—all the animals—and give them to the Levites who have charge of the tabernacle of the Lord."

31 Then Moses and Eleazar the priest, as the Lord had commanded Moses:

32 The booty remaining from the spoil that the troops had taken totaled six hundred seventy-five thousand sheep, 33seventy-two thousand oxen, 34sixty-one thousand donkeys, 35and thirty-two thousand persons in all, women who had not known a man by sleeping with him.

36 The half-share, the portion of those who had gone out to war, was in number three hundred thirty-seven thousand five hundred sheep and goats, 37and the Lord's tribute of sheep and goats was six hundred seventy-five. 38The oxen were thirty-six thousand, of which the Lord's tribute was seventy-two. 39The donkeys were thirty thousand five hundred, of which the Lord's tribute was sixty-one. 40The persons were sixteen thousand, of which the Lord's tribute was thirty-two persons. 41Moses gave the tribute, the offering for the Lord, to Eleazar the priest, as the Lord had commanded Moses.

42 As for the Israelites' half, which Moses separated from that of the troops, 43the congregation's half was three hundred thirty-seven thousand five hundred sheep and goats, 44thirty-six thousand oxen, 45thirty thousand five hundred donkeys, 46and sixteen thousand persons. 47From the Israelites' half Moses took one of every fifty, both of persons and of animals, and gave them to the Levites who had charge of the tabernacle of the Lord; as the Lord had commanded Moses.

48 Then the officers who were over the thousands of the army, the commanders of thousands and the commanders of hundreds, approached Moses, 49and said to Moses, "Your servants have counted the warriors who are under our command, and not one of us is missing. 50And we have brought the Lord's offering, what each of us found, articles of gold, armlets and bracelets, signet rings, earrings, and pendants, to make atonement for ourselves before the Lord." 51Moses and Eleazar the

---

a *31:36-40 of whom 32 went to the Levites,* literally, "were the Lord's portion."

King James

51And Moses and Eleazar the priest took the gold of them, *even* all wrought jewels.

52And all the gold of the offering that they offered up to the LORD, of the captains of thousands, and of the captains of hundreds, was sixteen thousand seven hundred and fifty shekels.

53(*For* the men of war had taken spoil, every man for himself.)

54And Moses and Eleazar the priest took the gold of the captains of thousands and of hundreds, and brought it into the tabernacle of the congregation, *for* a memorial for the children of Israel before the LORD.

32 NOW THE children of Reuben and the children of Gad had a very great multitude of cattle: and when they saw the land of Jazer, and the land of Gilead, that, behold, the place *was* a place for cattle;

2The children of Gad and the children of Reuben came and spake unto Moses, and to Eleazar the priest, and unto the princes of the congregation, saying,

3Ataroth, and Dibon, and Jazer, and Nimrah, and Heshbon, and Elealeh, and Shebam, and Nebo, and Beon,

4*Even* the country which the LORD smote before the congregation of Israel, *is* a land for cattle, and thy servants have cattle:

5Wherefore, said they, if we have found grace in thy sight, let this land be given unto thy servants for a possession, *and* bring us not over Jordan.

6¶ And Moses said unto the children of Gad and to the children of Reuben, Shall your brethren go to war, and shall ye sit here?

7And wherefore discourage ye the heart of the children of Israel from going over into the land which the LORD hath given them?

8Thus did your fathers, when I sent them from Kadesh-barnea to see the land.

9For when they went up unto the valley of Eshcol, and saw the land, they discouraged the heart of the children of Israel, that they should not go into the land which the LORD had given them.

10And the LORD's anger was kindled the same time, and he sware, saying,

11Surely none of the men that came up out of Egypt, from twenty years old and upward, shall see the land which I sware unto Abraham, unto Isaac, and unto Jacob; because they have not wholly followed me:

12Save Caleb the son of Jephunneh the Kenezite, and Joshua the son of Nun: for they have wholly followed the LORD.

13And the LORD's anger was kindled against Israel, and he made them wander in the wilderness forty years, until all the generation, that had done evil in the sight of the LORD, was consumed.

14And, behold, ye are risen up in your fathers' stead, an increase of sinful men, to augment yet the fierce anger of the LORD toward Israel.

15For if ye turn away from after him, he will yet again leave them in the wilderness; and ye shall destroy all this people.

16¶ And they came near unto him, and said, We will build sheepfolds here for our cattle, and cities for our little ones:

17But we ourselves will go ready armed before the children of Israel, until we have brought them unto their place: and our little ones shall dwell in the fenced cities because of the inhabitants of the land.

18We will not return unto our houses, until the children of Israel have inherited every man his inheritance.

19For we will not inherit with them on yonder side Jordan, or forward; because our inheritance is fallen to us on this side Jordan eastward.

New International

51Moses and Eleazar the priest accepted from them the gold—all the crafted articles. 52All the gold from the commanders of thousands and commanders of hundreds that Moses and Eleazar presented as a gift to the LORD weighed 16,750 shekels.ᵃ 53Each soldier had taken plunder for himself. 54Moses and Eleazar the priest accepted the gold from the commanders of thousands and commanders of hundreds and brought it into the Tent of Meeting as a memorial for the Israelites before the LORD.

The Transjordan Tribes

32 THE REUBENITES and Gadites, who had very large herds and flocks, saw that the lands of Jazer and Gilead were suitable for livestock. 2So they came to Moses and Eleazar the priest and to the leaders of the community, and said, 3"Ataroth, Dibon, Jazer, Nimrah, Heshbon, Elealeh, Sebam, Nebo and Beon— 4the land the LORD subdued before the people of Israel— are suitable for livestock, and your servants have livestock. 5If we have found favor in your eyes," they said, "let this land be given to your servants as our possession. Do not make us cross the Jordan."

6Moses said to the Gadites and Reubenites, "Shall your countrymen go to war while you sit here? 7Why do you discourage the Israelites from going over into the land the LORD has given them? 8This is what your fathers did when I sent them from Kadesh Barnea to look over the land. 9After they went up to the Valley of Eshcol and viewed the land, they discouraged the Israelites from entering the land the LORD had given them. 10The LORD's anger was aroused that day and he swore this oath: 11'Because they have not followed me wholeheartedly, not one of the men twenty years old or more who came up out of Egypt will see the land I promised on oath to Abraham, Isaac and Jacob— 12not one except Caleb son of Jephunneh the Kenizzite and Joshua son of Nun, for they followed the LORD wholeheartedly.' 13The LORD's anger burned against Israel and he made them wander in the desert forty years, until the whole generation of those who had done evil in his sight was gone.

14"And here you are, a brood of sinners, standing in the place of your fathers and making the LORD even more angry with Israel. 15If you turn away from following him, he will again leave all this people in the desert, and you will be the cause of their destruction."

16Then they came up to him and said, "We would like to build pens here for our livestock and cities for our women and children. 17But we are ready to arm ourselves and go ahead of the Israelites until we have brought them to their place. Meanwhile our women and children will live in fortified cities, for protection from the inhabitants of the land. 18We will not return to our homes until every Israelite has received his inheritance. 19We will not receive any inheritance with them on the other side of the Jordan, because our inheritance has come to us on the east side of the Jordan."

ᵃ 52 That is, about 420 pounds (about 190 kilograms)

Living Bible

51, 52Moses and Eleazar the priest received this special offering from the captains and battalion leaders and company commanders, and found its total value to be more than $300,000. 53(The soldiers had also kept personal loot for themselves.) 54The offering was taken into the Tabernacle and kept there before the Lord as a memorial of the people of Israel.

32 WHEN ISRAEL arrived in the land of Jazar and Gilead, the tribes of Reuben and Gad (who had large flocks of sheep) noticed what wonderful sheep country it was. 2So they came to Moses and Eleazar the priest and the other tribal leaders and said, 3, 4"The Lord has used Israel to destroy the population of this whole countryside—Ataroth, Dibon, Jazer, Nimrah, Heshbon, Elealeh, Sebam, Nebo, and Beon. And it is all wonderful sheep country, ideal for our flocks. 5Please let us have this land as our portion instead of the land on the other side of the Jordan River."

6"You mean you want to sit here while your brothers go across and do all the fighting?" Moses demanded. 7"Are you trying to discourage the rest of the people from going across to the land that the Lord has given them? 8This is the same kind of thing your fathers did! I sent them from Kadesh-barnea to spy out the land, 9but when they finished their survey and returned from the valley of Eshcol, they discouraged the people from going on into the Promised Land. 10, 11And the Lord's anger was hot against them, and he swore that of all those he had rescued from Egypt, no one over twenty years of age would ever see the land he promised Abraham, Isaac, and Jacob, for they had refused to do what he wanted them to.

12"The only exceptions were Caleb (son of Jephunneh the Kenizzite) and Joshua (son of Nun)—for they wholeheartedly followed the Lord and urged the people to go on into the Promised Land.

13"The Lord made us wander back and forth in the wilderness for forty years until all that evil generation died. 14But here you are, a brood of sinners doing exactly the same thing! Only there are more of you, so Jehovah's anger against Israel will be even fiercer this time. 15If you turn away from God like this, he will make the people stay even longer in the wilderness, and you will be responsible for destroying his people and bringing disaster to this entire nation!"

16"Not at all!" they explained. "We will build sheepfolds for our flocks and cities for our little ones, 17but we ourselves will go over armed, ahead of the rest of the people of Israel, until we have brought them safely to their inheritance. But first we will need to build walled cities here for our families, to keep them safe from attack by the local inhabitants. 18We will not settle down here until all the people of Israel have received their inheritance. 19We don't want land on the other side of the Jordan; we would rather have it on this side, on the east."

New Revised Standard

priest received the gold from them, all in the form of crafted articles. 52And all the gold of the offering that they offered to the LORD, from the commanders of thousands and the commanders of hundreds, was sixteen thousand seven hundred fifty shekels. 53(The troops had all taken plunder for themselves.) 54So Moses and Eleazar the priest received the gold from the commanders of thousands and of hundreds, and brought it into the tent of meeting as a memorial for the Israelites before the LORD.

Conquest and Division of Transjordan

32 NOW THE Reubenites and the Gadites owned a very great number of cattle. When they saw that the land of Jazer and the land of Gilead was a good place for cattle, 2the Gadites and the Reubenites came and spoke to Moses, to Eleazar the priest, and to the leaders of the congregation, saying, 3"Ataroth, Dibon, Jazer, Nimrah, Heshbon, Elealeh, Sebam, Nebo, and Beon— 4the land that the LORD subdued before the congregation of Israel—is a land for cattle; and your servants have cattle." 5They continued, "If we have found favor in your sight, let this land be given to your servants for a possession; do not make us cross the Jordan."

6 But Moses said to the Gadites and to the Reubenites, "Shall your brothers go to war while you sit here? 7Why will you discourage the hearts of the Israelites from going over into the land that the LORD has given them? 8Your fathers did this, when I sent them from Kadesh-barnea to see the land. 9When they went up to the Wadi Eshcol and saw the land, they discouraged the hearts of the Israelites from going into the land that the LORD had given them. 10The LORD's anger was kindled on that day and he swore, saying, 11'Surely none of the people who came up out of Egypt, from twenty years old and upward, shall see the land that I swore to give to Abraham, to Isaac, and to Jacob, because they have not unreservedly followed me— 12none except Caleb son of Jephunneh the Kenizzite and Joshua son of Nun, for they have unreservedly followed the LORD.' 13And the LORD's anger was kindled against Israel, and he made them wander in the wilderness for forty years, until all the generation that had done evil in the sight of the LORD had disappeared. 14And now you, a brood of sinners, have risen in place of your fathers, to increase the LORD's fierce anger against Israel! 15If you turn away from following him, he will again abandon them in the wilderness; and you will destroy all this people."

16 Then they came up to him and said, "We will build sheepfolds here for our flocks, and towns for our little ones, 17but we will take up arms as a vanguardb before the Israelites, until we have brought them to their place. Meanwhile our little ones will stay in the fortified towns because of the inhabitants of the land. 18We will not return to our homes until all the Israelites have obtained their inheritance. 19We will not inherit with them on the other side of the Jordan and beyond, because our inheritance has come to us on this side of the Jordan to the east."

b Cn: Heb hurrying

King James

20¶ And Moses said unto them, If ye will do this thing, if ye will go armed before the LORD to war,

21And will go all of you armed over Jordan before the LORD, until he hath driven out his enemies from before him,

22And the land be subdued before the LORD: then afterward ye shall return, and be guiltless before the LORD, and before Israel; and this land shall be your possession before the LORD.

23But if ye will not do so, behold, ye have sinned against the LORD: and be sure your sin will find you out.

24Build you cities for your little ones, and folds for your sheep; and do that which hath proceeded out of your mouth.

25And the children of Gad and the children of Reuben spake unto Moses, saying, Thy servants will do as my lord commandeth.

26Our little ones, our wives, our flocks, and all our cattle, shall be there in the cities of Gilead:

27But thy servants will pass over, every man armed for war, before the LORD to battle, as my lord saith.

28So concerning them Moses commanded Eleazar the priest, and Joshua the son of Nun, and the chief fathers of the tribes of the children of Israel:

29And Moses said unto them, If the children of Gad and the children of Reuben will pass with you over Jordan, every man armed to battle, before the LORD, and the land shall be subdued before you; then ye shall give them the land of Gilead for a possession:

30But if they will not pass over with you armed, they shall have possessions among you in the land of Canaan.

31And the children of Gad and the children of Reuben answered, saying, As the LORD hath said unto thy servants, so will we do.

32We will pass over armed before the LORD into the land of Canaan, that the possession of our inheritance on this side Jordan *may be* ours.

33And Moses gave unto them, *even* to the children of Gad, and to the children of Reuben, and unto half the tribe of Manasseh the son of Joseph, the kingdom of Sihon king of the Amorites, and the kingdom of Og king of Bashan, the land, with the cities thereof in the coasts, *even* the cities of the country round about.

34¶ And the children of Gad built Dibon, and Ataroth, and Aroer,

35And Atroth, Shophan, and Jaazer, and Jogbehah,

36And Beth-nimrah, and Beth-haran, fenced cities: and folds for sheep.

37And the children of Reuben built Heshbon, and Elealeh, and Kirjathaim,

38And Nebo and Baal-meon, (their names being changed,) and Shibmah: and gave other names unto the cities which they builded.

39And the children of Machir the son of Manasseh went to Gilead, and took it, and dispossessed the Amorite which *was* in it.

40And Moses gave Gilead unto Machir the son of Manasseh; and he dwelt therein.

41And Jair the son of Manasseh went and took the small towns thereof, and called them Havoth-jair.

42And Nobah went and took Kenath, and the villages thereof, and called it Nobah, after his own name.

33 THESE *ARE* the journeys of the children of Israel, which went forth out of the land of Egypt with their armies under the hand of Moses and Aaron.

2And Moses wrote their goings out according to their journeys by the commandment of the LORD: and these *are* their journeys according to their goings out.

New International

20Then Moses said to them, "If you will do this—if you will arm yourselves before the LORD for battle, 21and if all of you will go armed over the Jordan before the LORD until he has driven his enemies out before him— 22then when the land is subdued before the LORD, you may return and be free from your obligation to the LORD and to Israel. And this land will be your possession before the LORD.

23"But if you fail to do this, you will be sinning against the LORD; and you may be sure that your sin will find you out. 24Build cities for your women and children, and pens for your flocks, but do what you have promised."

25The Gadites and Reubenites said to Moses, "We your servants will do as our lord commands. 26Our children and wives, our flocks and herds will remain here in the cities of Gilead. 27But your servants, every man armed for battle, will cross over to fight before the LORD, just as our lord says."

28Then Moses gave orders about them to Eleazar the priest and Joshua son of Nun and to the family heads of the Israelite tribes. 29He said to them, "If the Gadites and Reubenites, every man armed for battle, cross over the Jordan with you before the LORD, then when the land is subdued before you, give them the land of Gilead as their possession. 30But if they do not cross over with you armed, they must accept their possession with you in Canaan."

31The Gadites and Reubenites answered, "Your servants will do what the LORD has said. 32We will cross over before the LORD into Canaan armed, but the property we inherit will be on this side of the Jordan."

33Then Moses gave to the Gadites, the Reubenites and the half-tribe of Manasseh son of Joseph the kingdom of Sihon king of the Amorites and the kingdom of Og king of Bashan—the whole land with its cities and the territory around them.

34The Gadites built up Dibon, Ataroth, Aroer, 35Atroth Shophan, Jazer, Jogbehah, 36Beth Nimrah and Beth Haran, as fortified cities, and built pens for their flocks. 37And the Reubenites rebuilt Heshbon, Elealeh and Kiriathaim, 38as well as Nebo and Baal Meon (these names were changed) and Sibmah. They gave names to the cities they rebuilt.

39The descendants of Makir son of Manasseh went to Gilead, captured it and drove out the Amorites who were there. 40So Moses gave Gilead to the Makirites, the descendants of Manasseh, and they settled there. 41Jair, a descendant of Manasseh, captured their settlements and called them Havvoth Jair.[a] 42And Nobah captured Kenath and its surrounding settlements and called it Nobah after himself.

Stages in Israel's Journey

33 HERE ARE the stages in the journey of the Israelites when they came out of Egypt by divisions under the leadership of Moses and Aaron. 2At the LORD's command Moses recorded the stages in their journey. This is their journey by stages:

---

a 41 Or *them the settlements of Jair*

Living Bible

20Then Moses said, "All right, if you will do what you have said and arm yourselves for Jehovah's war, 21and keep your troops across the Jordan until the Lord has driven out his enemies, 22then, when the land is finally subdued before the Lord, you may return. Then you will have discharged your duty to the Lord and to the rest of the people of Israel. And the land on the eastern side shall be your possession from the Lord. 23But if you don't do as you have said, then you will have sinned against the Lord, and you may be sure that your sin will catch up with you. 24Go ahead and build cities for your families and sheepfolds for your sheep, and do all you have said."

25"We will follow your instructions exactly," the people of Gad and Reuben replied. 26"Our children, wives, flocks, and cattle shall stay here in the cities of Gilead. 27But all of us who are conscripted will go over to battle for the Lord, just as you have said."

28So Moses gave his approval by saying to Eleazar, Joshua, and the tribal leaders of Israel, 29"If all the men of the tribes of Gad and Reuben who are conscripted for the Lord's battles go with you over Jordan, then, when the land is conquered, you must give them the land of Gilead; 30but if they refuse, then they must accept land among the rest of you in the land of Canaan."

31The tribes of Gad and Reuben said again, "As the Lord has commanded, so we will do— 32we will follow the Lord fully armed into Canaan, but our own land shall be here on this side of the Jordan."

33So Moses assigned the territory of King Sihon of the Amorites, and of King Og of Bashan—all the land and cities—to the tribes of Gad, Reuben, and the half-tribe of Manasseh (son of Joseph).

34, 35, 36The people of Gad built these cities:

Dibon, Ataroth, Aroer, Atroth-shophan, Jazer, Jogbehah, Beth-nimrah, Beth-haran.

They were all fortified cities with sheepfolds.

37, 38The children of Reuben built the following cities: Heshbon, Elealeh, Kiriathaim, Nebo, Baal-meon, Sibmah.

(The Israelites later changed the names of some of these cities they had conquered and rebuilt.)

39Then the clan of Machir of the tribe of Manasseh went to Gilead and conquered it, and drove out the Amorites who were living there. 40So Moses gave Gilead to the Machirites, and they lived there. 41The men of Jair, another clan of the tribe of Manasseh, occupied many of the towns in Gilead, and changed the name of their area to Havroth-jair. 42Meanwhile, a man named Nobah led an army[b] to Kenath and its surrounding villages, and occupied them, and he called the area Nobah, after his own name.

New Revised Standard

20 So Moses said to them, "If you do this—if you take up arms to go before the Lord for the war, 21and all those of you who bear arms cross the Jordan before the Lord, until he has driven out his enemies from before him 22and the land is subdued before the Lord—then after that you may return and be free of obligation to the Lord and to Israel, and this land shall be your possession before the Lord. 23But if you do not do this, you have sinned against the Lord; and be sure your sin will find you out. 24Build towns for your little ones, and folds for your flocks; but do what you have promised."

25 Then the Gadites and the Reubenites said to Moses, "Your servants will do as my lord commands. 26Our little ones, our wives, our flocks, and all our livestock shall remain there in the towns of Gilead; 27but your servants will cross over, everyone armed for war, to do battle for the Lord, just as my lord orders."

28 So Moses gave command concerning them to Eleazar the priest, to Joshua son of Nun, and to the heads of the ancestral houses of the Israelite tribes. 29And Moses said to them, "If the Gadites and the Reubenites, everyone armed for battle before the Lord, will cross over the Jordan with you and the land shall be subdued before you, then you shall give them the land of Gilead for a possession; 30but if they will not cross over with you armed, they shall have possessions among you in the land of Canaan." 31The Gadites and the Reubenites answered, "As the Lord has spoken to your servants, so we will do. 32We will cross over armed before the Lord into the land of Canaan, but the possession of our inheritance shall remain with us on this side ofc the Jordan."

33 Moses gave to them—to the Gadites and to the Reubenites and to the half-tribe of Manasseh son of Joseph—the kingdom of King Sihon of the Amorites and the kingdom of King Og of Bashan, the land and its towns, with the territories of the surrounding towns. 34And the Gadites rebuilt Dibon, Ataroth, Aroer, 35Atroth-shophan, Jazer, Jogbehah, 36Beth-nimrah, and Beth-haran, fortified cities, and folds for sheep. 37And the Reubenites rebuilt Heshbon, Elealeh, Kiriathaim, 38Nebo, and Baal-meon (some names being changed), and Sibmah; and they gave names to the towns that they rebuilt. 39The descendants of Machir son of Manasseh went to Gilead, captured it, and dispossessed the Amorites who were there; 40so Moses gave Gilead to Machir son of Manasseh, and he settled there. 41Jair son of Manasseh went and captured their villages, and renamed them Havvoth-jair.d 42And Nobah went and captured Kenath and its villages, and renamed it Nobah after himself.

The Stages of Israel's Journey from Egypt

33 THIS IS the itinerary of the nation of Israel from the time Moses and Aaron led them out of Egypt. 2Moses had written down their movements as the Lord had instructed him. 3, 4They left the city of Rame-

33 THESE ARE the stages by which the Israelites went out of the land of Egypt in military formation under the leadership of Moses and Aaron. 2Moses wrote down their starting points, stage by stage, by command of the Lord; and these are their stages according to their starting places. 3They set out from Rameses in

b 32:42 *led an army*, implied.

c Heb *beyond*   d That is *the villages of Jair*

King James

3And they departed from Rameses in the first month, on the fifteenth day of the first month; on the morrow after the passover the children of Israel went out with an high hand in the sight of all the Egyptians.

4For the Egyptians buried all *their* firstborn, which the LORD had smitten among them: upon their gods also the LORD executed judgments.

5And the children of Israel removed from Rameses, and pitched in Succoth.

6And they departed from Succoth, and pitched in Etham, which *is* in the edge of the wilderness.

7And they removed from Etham, and turned again unto Pi-hahiroth, which *is* before Baal-zephon: and they pitched before Migdol.

8And they departed from before Pi-hahiroth, and passed through the midst of the sea into the wilderness, and went three days' journey in the wilderness of Etham, and pitched in Marah.

9And they removed from Marah, and came unto Elim: and in Elim *were* twelve fountains of water, and threescore and ten palm trees; and they pitched there.

10And they removed from Elim, and encamped by the Red sea.

11And they removed from the Red sea, and encamped in the wilderness of Sin.

12And they took their journey out of the wilderness of Sin, and encamped in Dophkah.

13And they departed from Dophkah, and encamped in Alush.

14And they removed from Alush, and encamped at Rephidim, where was no water for the people to drink.

15And they departed from Rephidim, and pitched in the wilderness of Sinai.

16And they removed from the desert of Sinai, and pitched at Kibroth-hattaavah.

17And they departed from Kibroth-hattaavah, and encamped at Hazeroth.

18And they departed from Hazeroth, and pitched in Rithmah.

19And they departed from Rithmah, and pitched at Rimmon-parez.

20And they departed from Rimmon-parez, and pitched in Libnah.

21And they removed from Libnah, and pitched at Rissah.

22And they journeyed from Rissah, and pitched in Kehelathah.

23And they went from Kehelathah, and pitched in mount Shapher.

24And they removed from mount Shapher, and encamped in Haradah.

25And they removed from Haradah, and pitched in Makheloth.

26And they removed from Makheloth, and encamped at Tahath.

27And they departed from Tahath, and pitched at Tarah.

28And they removed from Tarah, and pitched in Mithcah.

29And they went from Mithcah, and pitched in Hashmonah.

30And they departed from Hashmonah, and encamped at Moseroth.

31And they departed from Moseroth, and pitched in Bene-jaakan.

32And they removed from Bene-jaakan, and encamped at Hor-hagidgad.

33And they went from Hor-hagidgad, and pitched in Jotbathah.

34And they removed from Jotbathah, and encamped at Ebronah.

35And they departed from Ebronah, and encamped at Ezion-geber.

36And they removed from Ezion-geber, and pitched in the wilderness of Zin, which *is* Kadesh.

New International

3The Israelites set out from Rameses on the fifteenth day of the first month, the day after the Passover. They marched out boldly in full view of all the Egyptians, 4who were burying all their firstborn, whom the LORD had struck down among them; for the LORD had brought judgment on their gods.

5The Israelites left Rameses and camped at Succoth.

6They left Succoth and camped at Etham, on the edge of the desert.

7They left Etham, turned back to Pi Hahiroth, to the east of Baal Zephon, and camped near Migdol.

8They left Pi Hahirotha and passed through the sea into the desert, and when they had traveled for three days in the Desert of Etham, they camped at Marah.

9They left Marah and went to Elim, where there were twelve springs and seventy palm trees, and they camped there.

10They left Elim and camped by the Red Sea.b

11They left the Red Sea and camped in the Desert of Sin.

12They left the Desert of Sin and camped at Dophkah.

13They left Dophkah and camped at Alush.

14They left Alush and camped at Rephidim, where there was no water for the people to drink.

15They left Rephidim and camped in the Desert of Sinai.

16They left the Desert of Sinai and camped at Kibroth Hattaavah.

17They left Kibroth Hattaavah and camped at Hazeroth.

18They left Hazeroth and camped at Rithmah.

19They left Rithmah and camped at Rimmon Perez.

20They left Rimmon Perez and camped at Libnah.

21They left Libnah and camped at Rissah.

22They left Rissah and camped at Kehelathah.

23They left Kehelathah and camped at Mount Shepher.

24They left Mount Shepher and camped at Haradah.

25They left Haradah and camped at Makheloth.

26They left Makheloth and camped at Tahath.

27They left Tahath and camped at Terah.

28They left Terah and camped at Mithcah.

29They left Mithcah and camped at Hashmonah.

30They left Hashmonah and camped at Moseroth.

31They left Moseroth and camped at Bene Jaakan.

32They left Bene Jaakan and camped at Hor Haggidgad.

33They left Hor Haggidgad and camped at Jotbathah.

34They left Jotbathah and camped at Abronah.

35They left Abronah and camped at Ezion Geber.

36They left Ezion Geber and camped at Kadesh, in the Desert of Zin.

---

a 8 Many manuscripts of the Masoretic Text, Samaritan Pentateuch and Vulgate; most manuscripts of the Masoretic Text *left from before Hahiroth*
b 10 Hebrew *Yam Suph*; that is, Sea of Reeds; also in verse 11

Living Bible

ses, Egypt, on the first day of April,c the day after the night of the Passover. They left proudly, hurried along by the Egyptians who were burying all their eldest sons, killed by the Lord the night before. The Lord had certainly defeated all the gods of Egypt that night!

5, 6After leaving Rameses, they stayed in Succoth, Etham (at the edge of the wilderness), and 7Pihahiroth (near Baal-zephon, where they camped at the foot of Mount Migdol). 8From there they went through the middle of the Red Sea and on for three days into the Etham wilderness, camping at Marah.

9Leaving Marah, they came to Elim, where there are twelve springs of water and seventy palm trees; they stayed there for quite a long time.

10Leaving Elim, they camped beside the Red Sea, 11and then in the wilderness of Sihn.

12Next was Dophkah, 13and then Alush; 14then on to Rephidim (where there was no water for the people to drink).

15-37From Rephidim they went to the wilderness of Sinai; from the wilderness of Sinai to Kibroth-hattaavah;

From Kibroth-hattaavah to Hazeroth;
From Hazeroth to Rithmah;
From Rithmah to Rimmon-parez;
From Rimmon-parez to Libnah;
From Libnah to Rissah;
From Rissah to Kehelathah;
From Kehelathah to Mount Shepher;
From Mount Shepher to Haradah;
From Haradah to Makheloth;
From Makheloth to Tahath;
From Tahath to Terah;
From Terah to Mithkah;
From Mithkah to Hashmonah;
From Hashmonah to Moseroth;
From Moseroth to Bene-jaakan;
From Bene-jaakan to Hor-haggidgad;
From Hor-haggidgad to Jotbathah;
From Jotbathah to Abronah;
From Abronah to Ezion-geber;
From Ezion-geber to Kadesh (in the wilderness of Zin);

New Revised Standard

the first month, on the fifteenth day of the first month; on the day after the passover the Israelites went out boldly in the sight of all the Egyptians, 4 while the Egyptians were burying all their firstborn, whom the LORD had struck down among them. The LORD executed judgments even against their gods.

5 So the Israelites set out from Rameses, and camped at Succoth. 6They set out from Succoth, and camped at Etham, which is on the edge of the wilderness. 7They set out from Etham, and turned back to Pi-hahiroth, which faces Baal-zephon; and they camped before Migdol. 8They set out from Pi-hahiroth, passed through the sea into the wilderness, went a three days' journey in the wilderness of Etham, and camped at Marah. 9They set out from Marah and came to Elim; at Elim there were twelve springs of water and seventy palm trees, and they camped there. 10They set out from Elim and camped by the Red Sea.d 11They set out from the Red Sead and camped in the wilderness of Sin. 12They set out from the wilderness of Sin and camped at Dophkah. 13They set out from Dophkah and camped at Alush. 14They set out from Alush and camped at Rephidim, where there was no water for the people to drink. 15They set out from Rephidim and camped in the wilderness of Sinai. 16They set out from the wilderness of Sinai and camped at Kibroth-hattaavah. 17They set out from Kibroth-hattaavah and camped at Hazeroth. 18They set out from Hazeroth and camped at Rithmah. 19They set out from Rithmah and camped at Rimmon-perez. 20They set out from Rimmon-perez and camped at Libnah. 21They set out from Libnah and camped at Rissah. 22They set out from Rissah and camped at Kehelathah. 23They set out from Kehelathah and camped at Mount Shepher. 24They set out from Mount Shepher and camped at Haradah. 25They set out from Haradah and camped at Makheloth. 26They set out from Makheloth and camped at Tahath. 27They set out from Tahath and camped at Terah. 28They set out from Terah and camped at Mithkah. 29They set out from Mithkah and camped at Hashmonah. 30They set out from Hashmonah and camped at Moseroth. 31They set out from Moseroth and camped at Bene-jaakan. 32They set out from Bene-jaakan and camped at Hor-haggidgad. 33They set out from Hor-haggidgad and camped at Jotbathah. 34They set out from Jotbathah and camped at Abronah. 35They set out from Abronah and camped at Ezion-geber. 36They set out from Ezion-geber and camped in the wilderness of Zin (that is, Kadesh). 37They set out from

---

c 33:3, 4 on the first day of April, literally, "on the fifteenth day of the first month" (of the Hebrew calendar).

d Or Sea of Reeds

King James

37And they removed from Kadesh, and pitched in mount Hor, in the edge of the land of Edom.

38And Aaron the priest went up into mount Hor at the commandment of the LORD, and died there, in the fortieth year after the children of Israel were come out of the land of Egypt, in the first *day* of the fifth month.

39And Aaron *was* an hundred and twenty and three years old when he died in mount Hor.

40And king Arad the Canaanite, which dwelt in the south in the land of Canaan, heard of the coming of the children of Israel.

41And they departed from mount Hor, and pitched in Zalmonah.

42And they departed from Zalmonah, and pitched in Punon.

43And they departed from Punon, and pitched in Oboth.

44And they departed from Oboth, and pitched in Ijeabarim, in the border of Moab.

45And they departed from Iim, and pitched in Dibongad.

46And they removed from Dibon-gad, and encamped in Almon-diblathaim.

47And they removed from Almon-diblathaim, and pitched in the mountains of Abarim, before Nebo.

48And they departed from the mountains of Abarim, and pitched in the plains of Moab by Jordan *near* Jericho.

49And they pitched by Jordan, from Beth-jeshimoth *even* unto Abel-shittim in the plains of Moab.

50¶ And the LORD spake unto Moses in the plains of Moab by Jordan *near* Jericho, saying,

51Speak unto the children of Israel, and say unto them, When ye are passed over Jordan into the land of Canaan;

52Then ye shall drive out all the inhabitants of the land from before you, and destroy all their pictures, and destroy all their molten images, and quite pluck down all their high places:

53And ye shall dispossess *the inhabitants of* the land, and dwell therein: for I have given you the land to possess it.

54And ye shall divide the land by lot for an inheritance among your families: *and* to the more ye shall give the more inheritance, and to the fewer ye shall give the less inheritance: every man's *inheritance* shall be in the place where his lot falleth; according to the tribes of your fathers ye shall inherit.

55But if ye will not drive out the inhabitants of the land from before you; then it shall come to pass, that those which ye let remain of them *shall be* pricks in your eyes, and thorns in your sides, and shall vex you in the land wherein ye dwell.

56Moreover it shall come to pass, *that* I shall do unto you, as I thought to do unto them.

34 AND THE LORD spake unto Moses, saying, 2Command the children of Israel, and say unto them, When ye come into the land of Canaan; (this *is* the land that shall fall unto you for an inheritance, *even* the land of Canaan with the coasts thereof:)

3Then your south quarter shall be from the wilderness of Zin along by the coast of Edom, and your south border shall be the outmost coast of the salt sea eastward:

4And your border shall turn from the south to the ascent of Akrabbim, and pass on to Zin: and the going forth thereof shall be from the south to Kadesh-barnea, and shall go on to Hazar-addar, and pass on to Azmon:

New International

37They left Kadesh and camped at Mount Hor, on the border of Edom. 38At the LORD's command Aaron the priest went up Mount Hor, where he died on the first day of the fifth month of the fortieth year after the Israelites came out of Egypt. 39Aaron was a hundred and twenty-three years old when he died on Mount Hor.

40The Canaanite king of Arad, who lived in the Negev of Canaan, heard that the Israelites were coming.

41They left Mount Hor and camped at Zalmonah. 42They left Zalmonah and camped at Punon. 43They left Punon and camped at Oboth. 44They left Oboth and camped at Iye Abarim, on the border of Moab. 45They left Iyima and camped at Dibon Gad. 46They left Dibon Gad and camped at Almon Diblathaim.

47They left Almon Diblathaim and camped in the mountains of Abarim, near Nebo. 48They left the mountains of Abarim and camped on the plains of Moab by the Jordan across from Jericho.b 49There on the plains of Moab they camped along the Jordan from Beth Jeshimoth to Abel Shittim.

50On the plains of Moab by the Jordan across from Jericho the LORD said to Moses, 51"Speak to the Israelites and say to them: 'When you cross the Jordan into Canaan, 52drive out all the inhabitants of the land before you. Destroy all their carved images and their cast idols, and demolish all their high places. 53Take possession of the land and settle in it, for I have given you the land to possess. 54Distribute the land by lot, according to your clans. To a larger group give a larger inheritance, and to a smaller group a smaller one. Whatever falls to them by lot will be theirs. Distribute it according to your ancestral tribes.

55" 'But if you do not drive out the inhabitants of the land, those you allow to remain will become barbs in your eyes and thorns in your sides. They will give you trouble in the land where you will live. 56And then I will do to you what I plan to do to them.' "

Boundaries of Canaan

34 THE LORD said to Moses, 2"Command the Israelites and say to them: 'When you enter Canaan, the land that will be allotted to you as an inheritance will have these boundaries:

3" 'Your southern side will include some of the Desert of Zin along the border of Edom. On the east, your southern boundary will start from the end of the Salt Sea,c 4cross south of Scorpiond Pass, continue on to Zin and go south of Kadesh Barnea. Then it will go

---

a 45 That is, Iye Abarim   b 48 Hebrew *Jordan of Jericho*; possibly an ancient name for the Jordan River; also in verse 50   c 3 That is, the Dead Sea; also in verse 12   d 4 Hebrew *Akrabbim*

Living Bible

From Kadesh to Mount Hor (at the edge of the land of Edom).

38, 39While they were at the foot of Mount Hor, Aaron the priest was directed by the Lord to go up into the mountain, and there he died. This occurred during the fortieth year after the people of Israel had left Egypt. The date of his death was July 15,e when he was 123 years old.

40It was then that the Canaanite king of Arad, who lived in the Negeb, in the land of Canaan, heard that the people of Israel were approaching his land. 41After dealing with him, the Israelis journeyed from Mount Hor and camped in Zalmonah, 42then at Punon, 43then at Oboth, 44then Iyeabarim (at the border of Moab). 45From there they went to Dibon-gad, 46and then to Almon-diblathaim, 47and on into the mountains of Abarim, near Mount Nebo, 48and finally to the plains of Moab beside the river Jordan, opposite Jericho. 49While in that area they camped at various places along the Jordan River, from Bethjeshimoth as far as Abel-shittim, on the plains of Moab.

50, 51It was while they were camped there that the Lord told Moses to tell the people of Israel, "When you pass across the Jordan River into the land of Canaan, 52you must drive out all the people living there and destroy all their idols—their carved stones, molten images, and the open-air sanctuaries in the hills where they worship their idols. 53I have given the land to you; take it and live there. 54You will be given land in proportion to the size of your tribes. The larger sections of land will be divided by lot among the larger tribes, and the smaller sections will be allotted to the smaller tribes. 55But if you refuse to drive out the people living there, those who remain will be as cinders in your eyes and thorns in your sides. 56And I will destroy you as I had planned for you to destroy them."

34 THE LORD told Moses to tell the people of Israel, "When you come into the land of Canaan (I am giving you the entire land as your homeland), 3the southern portion of the country will be the wilderness of Zin, along the edge of Edom. The southern boundary will begin at the Dead Sea, 4and will continue south past Scorpion Passf in the direction of Zin. Its southernmost point will be Kadesh-barnea, from which it will go to Hazaraddar, and on to Azmon. 5From Azmon the

New Revised Standard

Kadesh and camped at Mount Hor, on the edge of the land of Edom.

38 Aaron the priest went up Mount Hor at the command of the LORD and died there in the fortieth year after the Israelites had come out of the land of Egypt, on the first day of the fifth month. 39Aaron was one hundred twenty-three years old when he died on Mount Hor.

40 The Canaanite, the king of Arad, who lived in the Negeb in the land of Canaan, heard of the coming of the Israelites.

41 They set out from Mount Hor and camped at Zalmonah. 42They set out from Zalmonah and camped at Punon. 43They set out from Punon and camped at Oboth. 44They set out from Oboth and camped at Iyeabarim, in the territory of Moab. 45They set out from Iyim and camped at Dibon-gad. 46They set out from Dibon-gad and camped at Almon-diblathaim. 47They set out from Almon-diblathaim and camped in the mountains of Abarim, before Nebo. 48They set out from the mountains of Abarim and camped in the plains of Moab by the Jordan at Jericho; 49they camped by the Jordan from Beth-jeshimoth as far as Abel-shittim in the plains of Moab.

Directions for the Conquest of Canaan

50 In the plains of Moab by the Jordan at Jericho, the LORD spoke to Moses, saying: 51Speak to the Israelites, and say to them: When you cross over the Jordan into the land of Canaan, 52you shall drive out all the inhabitants of the land from before you, destroy all their figured stones, destroy all their cast images, and demolish all their high places. 53You shall take possession of the land and settle in it, for I have given you the land to possess. 54You shall apportion the land by lot according to your clans; to a large one you shall give a large inheritance, and to a small one you shall give a small inheritance; the inheritance shall belong to the person on whom the lot falls; according to your ancestral tribes you shall inherit. 55But if you do not drive out the inhabitants of the land from before you, then those whom you let remain shall be as barbs in your eyes and thorns in your sides; they shall trouble you in the land where you are settling. 56And I will do to you as I thought to do to them.

The Boundaries of the Land

34 THE LORD spoke to Moses, saying: 2Command the Israelites, and say to them: When you enter the land of Canaan (this is the land that shall fall to you for an inheritance, the land of Canaan, defined by its boundaries), 3your south sector shall extend from the wilderness of Zin along the side of Edom. Your southern boundary shall begin from the end of the Dead Seag on the east; 4your boundary shall turn south of the ascent of Akrabbim, and cross to Zin, and its outer limit shall be south of Kadesh-barnea; then it shall go on to Hazar-addar, and cross to Azmon; 5the boundary shall

e 33:38, 39 The date of his death was July 15, literally, "the first day of the fifth month" (of the Hebrew calendar). f 34:4 Scorpion Pass, literally, "ascent of Akrabbim."

g Heb Salt Sea

King James

5And the border shall fetch a compass from Azmon unto the river of Egypt, and the goings out of it shall be at the sea.

6And as for the western border, ye shall even have the great sea for a border: this shall be your west border.

7And this shall be your north border: from the great sea ye shall point out for you mount Hor:

8From mount Hor ye shall point out your border unto the entrance of Hamath; and the goings forth of the border shall be to Zedad:

9¶ And the border shall go on to Ziphron, and the goings out of it shall be at Hazar-enan: this shall be your north border.

10And ye shall point out your east border from Hazar-enan to Shepham:

11And the coast shall go down from Shepham to Riblah, on the east side of Ain; and the border shall descend, and shall reach unto the side of the sea of Chinnereth eastward:

12And the border shall go down to Jordan, and the goings out of it shall be at the salt sea: this shall be your land with the coasts thereof round about.

13And Moses commanded the children of Israel, saying, This is the land which ye shall inherit by lot, which the LORD commanded to give unto the nine tribes, and to the half tribe:

14For the tribe of the children of Reuben according to the house of their fathers, and the tribe of the children of Gad according to the house of their fathers, have received their inheritance; and half the tribe of Manasseh have received their inheritance:

15The two tribes and the half tribe have received their inheritance on this side Jordan near Jericho eastward, toward the sunrising.

16And the LORD spake unto Moses, saying,

17These are the names of the men which shall divide the land unto you: Eleazar the priest, and Joshua the son of Nun.

18And ye shall take one prince of every tribe, to divide the land by inheritance.

19And the names of the men are these: Of the tribe of Judah, Caleb the son of Jephunneh.

20And of the tribe of the children of Simeon, Shemuel the son of Ammihud.

21Of the tribe of Benjamin, Elidad the son of Chislon.

22And the prince of the tribe of the children of Dan, Bukki the son of Jogli.

23The prince of the children of Joseph, for the tribe of the children of Manasseh, Hanniel the son of Ephod.

24And the prince of the tribe of the children of Ephraim, Kemuel the son of Shiphtan.

25And the prince of the tribe of the children of Zebulun, Elizaphan the son of Parnach.

26And the prince of the tribe of the children of Issachar, Paltiel the son of Azzan.

27And the prince of the tribe of the children of Asher, Ahihud the son of Shelomi.

28And the prince of the tribe of the children of Naphtali, Pedahel the son of Ammihud.

29These are they whom the LORD commanded to divide the inheritance unto the children of Israel in the land of Canaan.

35 AND THE LORD spake unto Moses in the plains of Moab by Jordan near Jericho, saying,

New International

to Hazar Addar and over to Azmon, 5where it will turn, join the Wadi of Egypt and end at the Sea.[a]

6" 'Your western boundary will be the coast of the Great Sea. This will be your boundary on the west.

7" 'For your northern boundary, run a line from the Great Sea to Mount Hor 8and from Mount Hor to Lebo[b] Hamath. Then the boundary will go to Zedad, 9continue to Ziphron and end at Hazar Enan. This will be your boundary on the north.

10" 'For your eastern boundary, run a line from Hazar Enan to Shepham. 11The boundary will go down from Shepham to Riblah on the east side of Ain and continue along the slopes east of the Sea of Kinnereth.[c] 12Then the boundary will go down along the Jordan and end at the Salt Sea.

" 'This will be your land, with its boundaries on every side.' "

13Moses commanded the Israelites: "Assign this land by lot as an inheritance. The LORD has ordered that it be given to the nine and a half tribes, 14because the families of the tribe of Reuben, the tribe of Gad and the half-tribe of Manasseh have received their inheritance. 15These two and a half tribes have received their inheritance on the east side of the Jordan of Jericho,[d] toward the sunrise."

16The LORD said to Moses, 17"These are the names of the men who are to assign the land for you as an inheritance: Eleazar the priest and Joshua son of Nun. 18And appoint one leader from each tribe to help assign the land. 19These are their names:

Caleb son of Jephunneh,
    from the tribe of Judah;
20Shemuel son of Ammihud,
    from the tribe of Simeon;
21Elidad son of Kislon,
    from the tribe of Benjamin;
22Bukki son of Jogli,
    the leader from the tribe of Dan;
23Hanniel son of Ephod,
    the leader from the tribe of Manasseh son of Joseph;
24Kemuel son of Shiphtan,
    the leader from the tribe of Ephraim son of Joseph;
25Elizaphan son of Parnach,
    the leader from the tribe of Zebulun;
26Paltiel son of Azzan,
    the leader from the tribe of Issachar;
27Ahihud son of Shelomi,
    the leader from the tribe of Asher;
28Pedahel son of Ammihud,
    the leader from the tribe of Naphtali."

29These are the men the LORD commanded to assign the inheritance to the Israelites in the land of Canaan.

Towns for the Levites

35 ON THE plains of Moab by the Jordan across from Jericho,[e] the LORD said to Moses, 2"Com-

---

[a] 5 That is, the Mediterranean; also in verses 6 and 7   [b] 8 Or to the entrance to   [c] 11 That is, Galilee   [d] 15 Jordan of Jericho was possibly an ancient name for the Jordan River.   [e] 1 Hebrew Jordan of Jericho; possibly an ancient name for the Jordan River

Living Bible

boundary will follow the Brook of Egypt down to the Mediterranean Sea.

6"Your western boundary will be the coastline of the Mediterranean Sea.

7, 8, 9"Your northern border will begin at the Mediterranean Sea and will proceed eastward to Mount Hor, then to Lebo-Hamath, and on through Zedad and Ziphron to Hazar-enan.

10, 11"The eastern border will be from Hazar-enan south to Shepham, then on to Riblah at the east side of Ain. From there it will make a large half-circle, first going south and then westward until it touches the southernmost tip of the Sea of Galilee, 12and then along the Jordan River, ending at the Dead Sea."

13"This is the territory you are to apportion among yourselves by lot," Moses said. "It is to be divided up among the nine and one-half tribes, 14, 15for the tribes of Reuben and Gad and the half-tribe of Manasseh have already been assigned land on the east side of the Jordan, opposite Jericho."

16-28And the Lord said to Moses, "These are the names of the men I have appointed to handle the dividing up of the land: Eleazar the priest, Joshua (son of Nun), and one leader from each tribe, as listed below:

Tribe	Leader
Judah	Caleb (son of Jephunneh)
Simeon	Shemuel (son of Ammihud)
Benjamin	Elidad (son of Chislon)
Dan	Bukki (son of Jogli)
Manasseh	Hanniel (son of Ephod)
Ephraim	Kemuel (son of Shiphtan)
Zebulun	Elizaphan (son of Parnach)
Issachar	Paltiel (son of Azzan)
Asher	Ahihud (son of Shelomi)
Naphtali	Pedahel (son of Ammihud)

29These are the names of the men I have appointed to oversee the dividing of the land among the tribes."

New Revised Standard

turn from Azmon to the Wadi of Egypt, and its termination shall be at the Sea.

6 For the western boundary, you shall have the Great Sea and its[f] coast; this shall be your western boundary.

7 This shall be your northern boundary: from the Great Sea you shall mark out your line to Mount Hor; 8from Mount Hor you shall mark it out to Lebo-hamath, and the outer limit of the boundary shall be at Zedad; 9then the boundary shall extend to Ziphron, and its end shall be at Hazar-enan; this shall be your northern boundary.

10 You shall mark out your eastern boundary from Hazar-enan to Shepham; 11and the boundary shall continue down from Shepham to Riblah on the east side of Ain; and the boundary shall go down, and reach the eastern slope of the sea of Chinnereth; 12and the boundary shall go down to the Jordan, and its end shall be at the Dead Sea.[g] This shall be your land with its boundaries all around.

13 Moses commanded the Israelites, saying: This is the land that you shall inherit by lot, which the LORD has commanded to give to the nine tribes and to the half-tribe; 14for the tribe of the Reubenites by their ancestral houses and the tribe of the Gadites by their ancestral houses have taken their inheritance, and also the half-tribe of Manasseh; 15the two tribes and the half-tribe have taken their inheritance beyond the Jordan at Jericho eastward, toward the sunrise.

Tribal Leaders

16 The LORD spoke to Moses, saying: 17These are the names of the men who shall apportion the land to you for inheritance: the priest Eleazar and Joshua son of Nun. 18You shall take one leader of every tribe to apportion the land for inheritance. 19These are the names of the men: Of the tribe of Judah, Caleb son of Jephunneh. 20Of the tribe of the Simeonites, Shemuel son of Ammihud. 21Of the tribe of Benjamin, Elidad son of Chislon. 22Of the tribe of the Danites a leader, Bukki son of Jogli. 23Of the Josephites: of the tribe of the Manassites a leader, Hanniel son of Ephod, 24and of the tribe of the Ephraimites a leader, Kemuel son of Shiphtan. 25Of the tribe of the Zebulunites a leader, Eli-zaphan son of Parnach. 26Of the tribe of the Issacharites a leader, Paltiel son of Azzan. 27And of the tribe of the Asherites a leader, Ahihud son of Shelomi. 28Of the tribe of the Naphtalites a leader, Pedahel son of Ammihud. 29These were the ones whom the LORD commanded to apportion the inheritance for the Israelites in the land of Canaan.

Cities for the Levites

35 IN THE plains of Moab by the Jordan at Jericho, the LORD spoke to Moses, saying: 2Com-

35 WHILE ISRAEL was camped beside the Jordan on the plains of Moab, opposite Jericho, the Lord said to Moses,

---

f Syr: Heb lacks *its*   g Heb *Salt Sea*

King James

2Command the children of Israel, that they give unto the Levites of the inheritance of their possession cities to dwell in; and ye shall give *also* unto the Levites suburbs for the cities round about them.

3And the cities shall they have to dwell in; and the suburbs of them shall be for their cattle, and for their goods, and for all their beasts.

4And the suburbs of the cities, which ye shall give unto the Levites, *shall reach* from the wall of the city and outward a thousand cubits round about.

5And ye shall measure from without the city on the east side two thousand cubits, and on the south side two thousand cubits, and on the west side two thousand cubits, and on the north side two thousand cubits; and the city *shall be* in the midst: this shall be to them the suburbs of the cities.

6And among the cities which ye shall give unto the Levites *there shall be* six cities for refuge, which ye shall appoint for the manslayer, that he may flee thither: and to them ye shall add forty and two cities.

7So all the cities which ye shall give to the Levites *shall be* forty and eight cities: them *shall ye give* with their suburbs.

8And the cities which ye shall give *shall be* of the possession of the children of Israel: from *them that have* many ye shall give many; but from *them that have* few ye shall give few: every one shall give of his cities unto the Levites according to his inheritance which he inheriteth.

9¶ And the LORD spake unto Moses, saying,

10Speak unto the children of Israel, and say unto them, When ye be come over Jordan into the land of Canaan;

11Then ye shall appoint you cities to be cities of refuge for you; that the slayer may flee thither, which killeth any person at unawares.

12And they shall be unto you cities for refuge from the avenger; that the manslayer die not, until he stand before the congregation in judgment.

13And of these cities which ye shall give six cities shall ye have for refuge.

14Ye shall give three cities on this side Jordan, and three cities shall ye give in the land of Canaan, *which* shall be cities of refuge.

15These six cities shall be a refuge, *both* for the children of Israel, and for the stranger, and for the sojourner among them: that every one that killeth any person unawares may flee thither.

16And if he smite him with an instrument of iron, so that he die, he *is* a murderer: the murderer shall surely be put to death.

17And if he smite him with throwing a stone, wherewith he may die, and he die, he *is* a murderer: the murderer shall surely be put to death.

18Or *if* he smite him with an handweapon of wood, wherewith he may die, and he die, he *is* a murderer: the murderer shall surely be put to death.

19The revenger of blood himself shall slay the murderer: when he meeteth him, he shall slay him.

20But if he thrust him of hatred, or hurl at him by laying of wait, that he die;

21Or in enmity smite him with his hand, that he die: he that smote *him* shall surely be put to death; *for* he *is* a murderer: the revenger of blood shall slay the murderer, when he meeteth him.

22But if he thrust him suddenly without enmity, or have cast upon him any thing without laying of wait,

23Or with any stone, wherewith a man may die, seeing *him* not, and cast *it* upon him, that he die, and *was* not his enemy, neither sought his harm:

24Then the congregation shall judge between the slayer and the revenger of blood according to these judgments:

New International

mand the Israelites to give the Levites towns to live in from the inheritance the Israelites will possess. And give them pasturelands around the towns. 3Then they will have towns to live in and pasturelands for their cattle, flocks and all their other livestock.

4"The pasturelands around the towns that you give the Levites will extend out fifteen hundred feet[a] from the town wall. 5Outside the town, measure three thousand feet[b] on the east side, three thousand on the south side, three thousand on the west and three thousand on the north, with the town in the center. They will have this area as pastureland for the towns.

Cities of Refuge

6"Six of the towns you give the Levites will be cities of refuge, to which a person who has killed someone may flee. In addition, give them forty-two other towns. 7In all you must give the Levites forty-eight towns, together with their pasturelands. 8The towns you give the Levites from the land the Israelites possess are to be given in proportion to the inheritance of each tribe: Take many towns from a tribe that has many, but few from one that has few."

9Then the LORD said to Moses: 10"Speak to the Israelites and say to them: 'When you cross the Jordan into Canaan, 11select some towns to be your cities of refuge, to which a person who has killed someone accidentally may flee. 12They will be places of refuge from the avenger, so that a person accused of murder may not die before he stands trial before the assembly. 13These six towns you give will be your cities of refuge. 14Give three on this side of the Jordan and three in Canaan as cities of refuge. 15These six towns will be a place of refuge for Israelites, aliens and any other people living among them, so that anyone who has killed another accidentally can flee there.

16" 'If a man strikes someone with an iron object so that he dies, he is a murderer; the murderer shall be put to death. 17Or if anyone has a stone in his hand that could kill, and he strikes someone so that he dies, he is a murderer; the murderer shall be put to death. 18Or if anyone has a wooden object in his hand that could kill, and he hits someone so that he dies, he is a murderer; the murderer shall be put to death. 19The avenger of blood shall put the murderer to death; when he meets him, he shall put him to death. 20If anyone with malice aforethought shoves another or throws something at him intentionally so that he dies 21or if in hostility he hits him with his fist so that he dies, that person shall be put to death; he is a murderer. The avenger of blood shall put the murderer to death when he meets him.

22" 'But if without hostility someone suddenly shoves another or throws something at him unintentionally 23or, without seeing him, drops a stone on him that could kill him, and he dies, then since he was not his enemy and he did not intend to harm him, 24the assembly must judge between him and the avenger of blood according to these regulations. 25The assembly must protect the

---

a *4 Hebrew a thousand cubits* (about 450 meters)   b *5 Hebrew two thousand cubits* (about 900 meters)

Living Bible

2"Instruct the people of Israel to give to the Levites as their inheritance certain cities and surrounding pasture lands. 3These cities are for their homes, and the surrounding lands for their cattle, flocks, and other livestock. 4, 5Their gardens and vineyards shall extend 1500 feet out from the city walls in each direction, with an additional 1500 feet beyond that for pastureland.

6"You shall give the Levites the six Cities of Refuge where a person who has accidentally killed someone can run and be safe, and forty-two other cities besides. 7In all, there shall be forty-eight cities with the surrounding pastureland given to the Levites. 8These cities shall be in various parts of the nation; the larger tribes with many cities will give several to the Levites, while the smaller tribes will give fewer."

9, 10And the Lord said to Moses, "Tell the people that when they arrive in the land, 11Cities of Refuge shall be designated for anyone to flee into if he has killed someone accidentally. 12These Cities will be places of protection from the dead man's relatives who want to avenge his death; for the slayer must not be killed unless a fair trial establishes his guilt. 13, 14Three of these six Cities of Refuge are to be located in the land of Canaan, and three on the east side of the Jordan River. 15There are not only for the protection of Israelites, but also for foreigners and travelers.

16"But if someone is struck and killed by a piece of iron, it must be presumed to be murder, and the murderer must be executed. 17Or if the slain man was struck down with a large stone, it is murder, and the murderer shall die. 18The same is true if he is killed with a wooden weapon. 19The avenger of his death shall personally kill the murderer when he meets him. 20So, if anyone kills another out of hatred by throwing something at him, or ambushing him, 21or angrily striking him with his fist so that he dies, he is a murderer; and the murderer shall be executed by the avenger.

22, 23"But if it is an accident—a case in which something is thrown unintentionally, or in which a stone is thrown without anger, without realizing it will hit anyone, and without wanting to harm an enemy—yet the man dies, 24then the people shall judge whether or not it was an accident, and whether or not to hand the killer over to the avenger of the dead man. 25If it is decided

New Revised Standard

mand the Israelites to give, from the inheritance that they possess, towns for the Levites to live in; you shall also give to the Levites pasture lands surrounding the towns. 3The towns shall be theirs to live in, and their pasture lands shall be for their cattle, for their livestock, and for all their animals. 4The pasture lands of the towns, which you shall give to the Levites, shall reach from the wall of the town outward a thousand cubits all around. 5You shall measure, outside the town, for the east side two thousand cubits, for the south side two thousand cubits, for the west side two thousand cubits, and for the north side two thousand cubits, with the town in the middle; this shall belong to them as pasture land for their towns.

6 The towns that you give to the Levites shall include the six cities of refuge, where you shall permit a slayer to flee, and in addition to them you shall give forty-two towns. 7The towns that you give to the Levites shall total forty-eight, with their pasture lands. 8And as for the towns that you shall give from the possession of the Israelites, from the larger tribes you shall take many, and from the smaller tribes you shall take few; each, in proportion to the inheritance that it obtains, shall give of its towns to the Levites.

Cities of Refuge

9 The LORD spoke to Moses, saying: 10Speak to the Israelites, and say to them: When you cross the Jordan into the land of Canaan, 11then you shall select cities to be cities of refuge for you, so that a slayer who kills a person without intent may flee there. 12The cities shall be for you a refuge from the avenger, so that the slayer may not die until there is a trial before the congregation.

13 The cities that you designate shall be six cities of refuge for you: 14you shall designate three cities beyond the Jordan, and three cities in the land of Canaan, to be cities of refuge. 15These six cities shall serve as refuge for the Israelites, for the resident or transient alien among them, so that anyone who kills a person without intent may flee there.

Concerning Murder and Blood Revenge

16 But anyone who strikes another with an iron object, and death ensues, is a murderer; the murderer shall be put to death. 17Or anyone who strikes another with a stone in hand that could cause death, and death ensues, is a murderer; the murderer shall be put to death. 18Or anyone who strikes another with a weapon of wood in hand that could cause death, and death ensues, is a murderer; the murderer shall be put to death. 19The avenger of blood is the one who shall put the murderer to death; when they meet, the avenger of blood shall execute the sentence. 20Likewise, if someone pushes another from hatred, or hurls something at another, lying in wait, and death ensues, 21or in enmity strikes another with the hand, and death ensues, then the one who struck the blow shall be put to death; that person is a murderer; the avenger of blood shall put the murderer to death, when they meet.

22 But if someone pushes another suddenly without enmity, or hurls any object without lying in wait, 23or, while handling any stone that could cause death, unintentionally[c] drops it on another and death ensues, though they were not enemies, and no harm was intended, 24then the congregation shall judge between the slayer and the avenger of blood, in accordance with these ordinances; 25and the congregation shall rescue the

---

c Heb without seeing

King James

25And the congregation shall deliver the slayer out of the hand of the revenger of blood, and the congregation shall restore him to the city of his refuge, whither he was fled: and he shall abide in it unto the death of the high priest, which was anointed with the holy oil.

26But if the slayer shall at any time come without the border of the city of his refuge, whither he was fled;

27And the revenger of blood find him without the borders of the city of his refuge, and the revenger of blood kill the slayer; he shall not be guilty of blood:

28Because he should have remained in the city of his refuge until the death of the high priest: but after the death of the high priest the slayer shall return into the land of his possession.

29So these *things* shall be for a statute of judgment unto you throughout your generations in all your dwellings.

30Whoso killeth any person, the murderer shall be put to death by the mouth of witnesses: but one witness shall not testify against any person *to cause him* to die.

31Moreover ye shall take no satisfaction for the life of a murderer, which *is* guilty of death: but he shall be surely put to death.

32And ye shall take no satisfaction for him that is fled to the city of his refuge, that he should come again to dwell in the land, until the death of the priest.

33So ye shall not pollute the land wherein ye *are:* for blood it defileth the land: and the land cannot be cleansed of the blood that is shed therein, but by the blood of him that shed it.

34Defile not therefore the land which ye shall inhabit, wherein I dwell: for I the LORD dwell among the children of Israel.

36 AND THE chief fathers of the families of the children of Gilead, the son of Machir, the son of Manasseh, of the families of the sons of Joseph, came near, and spake before Moses, and before the princes, the chief fathers of the children of Israel:

2And they said, The LORD commanded my lord to give the land for an inheritance by lot to the children of Israel: and my lord was commanded by the LORD to give the inheritance of Zelophehad our brother unto his daughters.

3And if they be married to any of the sons of the *other* tribes of the children of Israel, then shall their inheritance be taken from the inheritance of our fathers, and shall be put to the inheritance of the tribe whereunto they are received: so shall it be taken from the lot of our inheritance.

4And when the jubilee of the children of Israel shall be, then shall their inheritance be put unto the inheritance of the tribe whereunto they are received: so shall their inheritance be taken away from the inheritance of the tribe of our fathers.

5And Moses commanded the children of Israel according to the word of the LORD, saying, The tribe of the sons of Joseph hath said well.

6This *is* the thing which the LORD doth command concerning the daughters of Zelophehad, saying, Let them marry to whom they think best; only to the family of the tribe of their father shall they marry.

7So shall not the inheritance of the children of Israel remove from tribe to tribe: for every one of the children of Israel shall keep himself to the inheritance of the tribe of his fathers.

8And every daughter, that possesseth an inheritance in any tribe of the children of Israel, shall be wife unto one of the family of the tribe of her father, that the children of Israel may enjoy every man the inheritance of his fathers.

New International

one accused of murder from the avenger of blood and send him back to the city of refuge to which he fled. He must stay there until the death of the high priest, who was anointed with the holy oil.

26" 'But if the accused ever goes outside the limits of the city of refuge to which he has fled 27and the avenger of blood finds him outside the city, the avenger of blood may kill the accused without being guilty of murder. 28The accused must stay in his city of refuge until the death of the high priest; only after the death of the high priest may he return to his own property.

29" 'These are to be legal requirements for you throughout the generations to come, wherever you live.

30" 'Anyone who kills a person is to be put to death as a murderer only on the testimony of witnesses. But no one is to be put to death on the testimony of only one witness.

31" 'Do not accept a ransom for the life of a murderer, who deserves to die. He must surely be put to death.

32" 'Do not accept a ransom for anyone who has fled to a city of refuge and so allow him to go back and live on his own land before the death of the high priest.

33" 'Do not pollute the land where you are. Bloodshed pollutes the land, and atonement cannot be made for the land on which blood has been shed, except by the blood of the one who shed it. 34Do not defile the land where you live and where I dwell, for I, the LORD, dwell among the Israelites.' "

Inheritance of Zelophehad's Daughters

36 THE FAMILY heads of the clan of Gilead son of Makir, the son of Manasseh, who were from the clans of the descendants of Joseph, came and spoke before Moses and the leaders, the heads of the Israelite families. 2They said, "When the LORD commanded my lord to give the land as an inheritance to the Israelites by lot, he ordered you to give the inheritance of our brother Zelophehad to his daughters. 3Now suppose they marry men from other Israelite tribes; then their inheritance will be taken from our ancestral inheritance and added to that of the tribe they marry into. And so part of the inheritance allotted to us will be taken away. 4When the Year of Jubilee for the Israelites comes, their inheritance will be added to that of the tribe into which they marry, and their property will be taken from the tribal inheritance of our forefathers."

5Then at the LORD's command Moses gave this order to the Israelites: "What the tribe of the descendants of Joseph is saying is right. 6This is what the LORD commands for Zelophehad's daughters: They may marry anyone they please as long as they marry within the tribal clan of their father. 7No inheritance in Israel is to pass from tribe to tribe, for every Israelite shall keep the tribal land inherited from his forefathers. 8Every daughter who inherits land in any Israelite tribe must marry someone in her father's tribal clan, so that every Israelite will possess the inheritance of his fathers. 9No inheri-

Living Bible

that it was accidental, then the people shall save the killer from the avenger; the killer shall be permitted to stay in the City of Refuge; and he must live there until the death of the High Priest.

26"If the slayer leaves the City, 27and the avenger finds him outside and kills him, it is not murder, 28for the man should have stayed inside the City until the death of the High Priest. But after the death of the High Priest, the man may return to his own land and home. 29These are permanent laws for all Israel from generation to generation.

30"All murderers must be executed, but only if there is more than one witness; no man shall die with only one person testifying against him. 31Whenever anyone is judged guilty of murder, he must die—no ransom may be accepted for him. 32Nor may a payment be accepted from a refugee in a City of Refuge, permitting him to return to his home before the death of the High Priest. 33In this way the land will not be polluted, for murder pollutes the land, and no atonement can be made for murder except by the execution of the murderer. 34You shall not defile the land where you are going to live, for I, Jehovah, will be living there."

36 THEN THE heads of the sub-clan of Gilead (of the clan of Machir, of the tribe of Manasseh, one of the sons of Joseph) came to Moses and the leaders of Israel with a petition: "The Lord instructed you to divide the land by lot among the people of Israel," they reminded Moses, "and to give the inheritance of our brother Zelophehad to his daughters. 3But if they marry into another tribe, their land will go with them to the tribe into which they marry. In this way the total area of our tribe will be reduced, 4and will not be returned at the Year of Jubilee."

5Then Moses replied publicly, giving them these instructions from the Lord: "The men of the tribe of Joseph have a proper complaint. 6This is what the Lord has further commanded concerning the daughters of Zelophehad: 'Let them be married to anyone they like, so long as it is within their own tribe. 7In this way none of the land of the tribe will shift to any other tribe, for the inheritance of every tribe is to remain permanently as it was first allotted. 8The girls throughout the tribes of Israel who are heiresses must marry within their own tribe, so that their land won't leave the tribe. 9In this way

New Revised Standard

slayer from the avenger of blood. Then the congregation shall send the slayer back to the original city of refuge. The slayer shall live in it until the death of the high priest who was anointed with the holy oil. 26But if the slayer shall at any time go outside the bounds of the original city of refuge, 27and is found by the avenger of blood outside the bounds of the city of refuge, and is killed by the avenger, no bloodguilt shall be incurred. 28For the slayer must remain in the city of refuge until the death of the high priest; but after the death of the high priest the slayer may return home.

29 These things shall be a statute and ordinance for you throughout your generations wherever you live.

30 If anyone kills another, the murderer shall be put to death on the evidence of witnesses; but no one shall be put to death on the testimony of a single witness. 31Moreover you shall accept no ransom for the life of a murderer who is subject to the death penalty; a murderer must be put to death. 32Nor shall you accept ransom for one who has fled to a city of refuge, enabling the fugitive to return to live in the land before the death of the high priest. 33You shall not pollute the land in which you live; for blood pollutes the land, and no expiation can be made for the land, for the blood that is shed in it, except by the blood of the one who shed it. 34You shall not defile the land in which you live, in which I also dwell; for I the LORD dwell among the Israelites.

Marriage of Female Heirs

36 THE HEADS of the ancestral houses of the clans of the descendants of Gilead son of Machir son of Manasseh, of the Josephite clans, came forward and spoke in the presence of Moses and the leaders, the heads of the ancestral houses of the Israelites; 2they said, "The LORD commanded my lord to give the land for inheritance by lot to the Israelites; and my lord was commanded by the LORD to give the inheritance of our brother Zelophehad to his daughters. 3But if they are married into another Israelite tribe, then their inheritance will be taken from the inheritance of our ancestors and added to the inheritance of the tribe into which they marry; so it will be taken away from the allotted portion of our inheritance. 4And when the jubilee of the Israelites comes, then their inheritance will be added to the inheritance of the tribe into which they have married; and their inheritance will be taken from the inheritance of our ancestral tribe."

5 Then Moses commanded the Israelites according to the word of the LORD, saying, "The descendants of the tribe of Joseph are right in what they are saying. 6This is what the LORD commands concerning the daughters of Zelophehad, 'Let them marry whom they think best; only it must be into a clan of their father's tribe that they are married, 7so that no inheritance of the Israelites shall be transferred from one tribe to another; for all Israelites shall retain the inheritance of their ancestral tribes. 8Every daughter who possesses an inheritance in any tribe of the Israelites shall marry one from the clan of her father's tribe, so that all Israelites may continue to possess their ancestral inheritance. 9No in-

King James

9Neither shall the inheritance remove from *one* tribe to another tribe; but every one of the tribes of the children of Israel shall keep himself to his own inheritance.

10Even as the LORD commanded Moses, so did the daughters of Zelophehad:

11For Mahlah, Tirzah, and Hoglah, and Milcah, and Noah, the daughters of Zelophehad, were married unto their father's brothers' sons:

12*And* they were married into the families of the sons of Manasseh the son of Joseph, and their inheritance remained in the tribe of the family of their father.

13These *are* the commandments and the judgments, which the LORD commanded by the hand of Moses unto the children of Israel in the plains of Moab by Jordan *near* Jericho.

New International

tance may pass from tribe to tribe, for each Israelite tribe is to keep the land it inherits."

10So Zelophehad's daughters did as the LORD commanded Moses. 11Zelophehad's daughters—Mahlah, Tirzah, Hoglah, Milcah and Noah—married their cousins on their father's side. 12They married within the clans of the descendants of Manasseh son of Joseph, and their inheritance remained in their father's clan and tribe.

13These are the commands and regulations the LORD gave through Moses to the Israelites on the plains of Moab by the Jordan across from Jericho.[a]

---

[a] *13* Hebrew *Jordan of Jericho*; possibly an ancient name for the Jordan River

Living Bible

no inheritance shall move from one tribe to another.' "

10The daughters of Zelophehad did as the Lord commanded Moses. 11, 12These girls, Mahlah, Tirzah, Hoglah, Milcah, and Noah, were married to men in their own tribe of Manasseh (son of Joseph); so their inheritance remained in their tribe.

13These are the commandments and ordinances which the Lord gave to the people of Israel through Moses, while they were camped on the plains of Moab beside the Jordan River, across from Jericho.

New Revised Standard

heritance shall be transferred from one tribe to another; for each of the tribes of the Israelites shall retain its own inheritance.' "

10 The daughters of Zelophehad did as the LORD had commanded Moses. 11Mahlah, Tirzah, Hoglah, Milcah, and Noah, the daughters of Zelophehad, married sons of their father's brothers. 12They were married into the clans of the descendants of Manasseh son of Joseph, and their inheritance remained in the tribe of their father's clan.

13 These are the commandments and the ordinances that the LORD commanded through Moses to the Israelites in the plains of Moab by the Jordan at Jericho.

THE FIFTH BOOK OF MOSES, CALLED

Deuteronomy

Deuteronomy

The Command to Leave Horeb

1 THESE *BE* the words which Moses spake unto all Israel on this side Jordan in the wilderness, in the plain over against the Red *sea,* between Paran, and Tophel, and Laban, and Hazeroth, and Dizahab.

2(*There are* eleven days' *journey* from Horeb by the way of mount Seir unto Kadesh-barnea.)

3And it came to pass in the fortieth year, in the eleventh month, on the first *day* of the month, *that* Moses spake unto the children of Israel, according unto all that the LORD had given him in commandment unto them;

4After he had slain Sihon the king of the Amorites, which dwelt in Heshbon, and Og the king of Bashan, which dwelt at Astaroth in Edrei:

5On this side Jordan, in the land of Moab, began Moses to declare this law, saying,

6The LORD our God spake unto us in Horeb, saying, Ye have dwelt long enough in this mount:

7Turn you, and take your journey, and go to the mount of the Amorites, and unto all *the places* nigh thereunto, in the plain, in the hills, and in the vale, and in the south, and by the sea side, to the land of the Canaanites, and unto Lebanon, unto the great river, the river Euphrates.

8Behold, I have set the land before you: go in and possess the land which the LORD sware unto your fathers, Abraham, Isaac, and Jacob, to give unto them and to their seed after them.

9¶ And I spake unto you at that time, saying, I am not able to bear you myself alone:

10The LORD your God hath multiplied you, and, behold, ye *are* this day as the stars of heaven for multitude.

11(The LORD God of your fathers make you a thousand times so many more as ye *are,* and bless you, as he hath promised you!)

12How can I myself alone bear your cumbrance, and your burden, and your strife?

13Take you wise men, and understanding, and known among your tribes, and I will make them rulers over you.

14And ye answered me, and said, The thing which thou hast spoken *is* good *for us* to do.

15So I took the chief of your tribes, wise men, and known, and made them heads over you, captains over thousands, and captains over hundreds, and captains over fifties, and captains over tens, and officers among your tribes.

16And I charged your judges at that time, saying, Hear *the causes* between your brethren, and judge righteously between *every* man and his brother, and the stranger *that is* with him.

17Ye shall not respect persons in judgment; *but* ye shall hear the small as well as the great; ye shall not be afraid of the face of man; for the judgment *is* God's: and the cause that is too hard for you, bring *it* unto me, and I will hear it.

18And I commanded you at that time all the things which ye should do.

1 THESE ARE the words Moses spoke to all Israel in the desert east of the Jordan—that is, in the Arabah—opposite Suph, between Paran and Tophel, Laban, Hazeroth and Dizahab. 2(It takes eleven days to go from Horeb to Kadesh Barnea by the Mount Seir road.)

3In the fortieth year, on the first day of the eleventh month, Moses proclaimed to the Israelites all that the LORD had commanded him concerning them. 4This was after he had defeated Sihon king of the Amorites, who reigned in Heshbon, and at Edrei had defeated Og king of Bashan, who reigned in Ashtaroth.

5East of the Jordan in the territory of Moab, Moses began to expound this law, saying:

6The LORD our God said to us at Horeb, "You have stayed long enough at this mountain. 7Break camp and advance into the hill country of the Amorites; go to all the neighboring peoples in the Arabah, in the mountains, in the western foothills, in the Negev and along the coast, to the land of the Canaanites and to Lebanon, as far as the great river, the Euphrates. 8See, I have given you this land. Go in and take possession of the land that the LORD swore he would give to your fathers—to Abraham, Isaac and Jacob—and to their descendants after them."

The Appointment of Leaders

9At that time I said to you, "You are too heavy a burden for me to carry alone. 10The LORD your God has increased your numbers so that today you are as many as the stars in the sky. 11May the LORD, the God of your fathers, increase you a thousand times and bless you as he has promised! 12But how can I bear your problems and your burdens and your disputes all by myself? 13Choose some wise, understanding and respected men from each of your tribes, and I will set them over you."

14You answered me, "What you propose to do is good."

15So I took the leading men of your tribes, wise and respected men, and appointed them to have authority over you—as commanders of thousands, of hundreds, of fifties and of tens and as tribal officials. 16And I charged your judges at that time: Hear the disputes between your brothers and judge fairly, whether the case is between brother Israelites or between one of them and an alien. 17Do not show partiality in judging; hear both small and great alike. Do not be afraid of any man, for judgment belongs to God. Bring me any case too hard for you, and I will hear it. 18And at that time I told you everything you were to do.

Deuteronomy

Deuteronomy

Living Bible

1 THIS BOOK records Moses' address to the people of Israel when they were camped in the valley of the Arabah in the wilderness of Moab, east of the Jordan River. (Cities in the area included Suph, Paran, Tophel, Laban, Hazeroth, and Dizahab.) The speech was given on February 15,[a] forty years after the people of Israel left Mount Horeb—though it takes only eleven days to travel by foot from Mount Horeb to Kadesh-barnea,[b] going by way of Mount Seir! At the time of this address, King Sihon of the Amorites had already been defeated at Heshbon, and King Og of Bashan had been defeated at Ashtaroth, near Edre-i. Here, then, is Moses' address to Israel, stating all the laws God had commanded him to pass on to them:

6"It was forty years ago, at Mount Horeb, that Jehovah our God told us, 'You have stayed here long enough. 7Now go and occupy the hill country of the Amorites, the valley of the Arabah, and the Negeb, and all the land of Canaan and Lebanon—the entire area from the shores of the Mediterranean Sea to the Euphrates River. 8I am giving all of it to you! Go in and possess it, for it is the land the Lord promised to your ancestors Abraham, Isaac, and Jacob, and all of their descendants.'

9"At that time I told the people, 'I need help! You are a great burden for me to carry all by myself, 10for the Lord has multiplied you to become as many as the stars! 11And may he multiply you a thousand times more, and bless you as he promised, 12but what can one man do to settle all your quarrels and problems? 13So choose some men from each tribe who are wise, experienced, and understanding, and I will appoint them as your leaders.'

14"They agreed to this; 15I took the men they selected, some from every tribe, and appointed them as administrative assistants in charge of thousands, hundreds, fifties, and tens to decide their quarrels and assist them in every way. 16I instructed them to be perfectly fair at all times, even to foreigners. 17'When giving your decisions,' I told them, 'never favor a man because he is rich; be fair to great and small alike. Don't fear their displeasure, for you are judging in the place of God. Bring me any cases too difficult for you, and I will handle them.' 18And I gave them other instructions at that time, also.

New Revised Standard

Events at Horeb Recalled

1 THESE ARE the words that Moses spoke to all Israel beyond the Jordan—in the wilderness, on the plain opposite Suph, between Paran and Tophel, Laban, Hazeroth, and Di-zahab. 2(By the way of Mount Seir it takes eleven days to reach Kadesh-barnea from Horeb.) 3In the fortieth year, on the first day of the eleventh month, Moses spoke to the Israelites just as the LORD had commanded him to speak to them. 4This was after he had defeated King Sihon of the Amorites, who reigned in Heshbon, and King Og of Bashan, who reigned in Ashtaroth and[c] in Edrei. 5Beyond the Jordan in the land of Moab, Moses undertook to expound this law as follows:

6 The LORD our God spoke to us at Horeb, saying, "You have stayed long enough at this mountain. 7Resume your journey, and go into the hill country of the Amorites as well as into the neighboring regions—the Arabah, the hill country, the Shephelah, the Negeb, and the seacoast—the land of the Canaanites and the Lebanon, as far as the great river, the river Euphrates. 8See, I have set the land before you; go in and take possession of the land that I[d] swore to your ancestors, to Abraham, to Isaac, and to Jacob, to give to them and to their descendants after them."

Appointment of Tribal Leaders

9 At that time I said to you, "I am unable by myself to bear you. 10The LORD your God has multiplied you, so that today you are as numerous as the stars of heaven. 11May the LORD, the God of your ancestors, increase you a thousand times more and bless you, as he has promised you! 12But how can I bear the heavy burden of your disputes all by myself? 13Choose for each of your tribes individuals who are wise, discerning, and reputable to be your leaders." 14You answered me, "The plan you have proposed is a good one." 15So I took the leaders of your tribes, wise and reputable individuals, and installed them as leaders over you, commanders of thousands, commanders of hundreds, commanders of fifties, commanders of tens, and officials, throughout your tribes. 16I charged your judges at that time: "Give the members of your community a fair hearing, and judge rightly between one person and another, whether citizen or resident alien. 17You must not be partial in judging: hear out the small and the great alike; you shall not be intimidated by anyone, for the judgment is God's. Any case that is too hard for you, bring to me, and I will hear it." 18So I charged you at that time with all the things that you should do.

a 1:1-5 *February 15th*, literally, "the first day of the eleventh month" (of the Hebrew calendar).   b 1:1-5 *eleven days to travel by foot from Mount Horeb to Kadesh-barnea.* Kadesh-barnea was at the southern edge of the Promised Land.

c Gk Syr Vg Compare Josh 12.4: Heb lacks *and*   d Sam Gk: MT *the LORD*

King James

19¶ And when we departed from Horeb, we went through all that great and terrible wilderness, which ye saw by the way of the mountain of the Amorites, as the LORD our God commanded us; and we came to Kadesh-barnea.

20And I said unto you, Ye are come unto the mountain of the Amorites, which the LORD our God doth give unto us.

21Behold, the LORD thy God hath set the land before thee: go up *and* possess *it,* as the LORD God of thy fathers hath said unto thee; fear not, neither be discouraged.

22¶ And ye came near unto me every one of you, and said, We will send men before us, and they shall search us out the land, and bring us word again by what way we must go up, and into what cities we shall come.

23And the saying pleased me well: and I took twelve men of you, one of a tribe:

24And they turned and went up into the mountain, and came unto the valley of Eshcol, and searched it out.

25And they took of the fruit of the land in their hands, and brought *it* down unto us, and brought us word again, and said, *It is* a good land which the LORD our God doth give us.

26Notwithstanding ye would not go up, but rebelled against the commandment of the LORD your God:

27And ye murmured in your tents, and said, Because the LORD hated us, he hath brought us forth out of the land of Egypt, to deliver us into the hand of the Amorites, to destroy us.

28Whither shall we go up? our brethren have discouraged our heart, saying, The people *is* greater and taller than we; the cities *are* great and walled up to heaven; and moreover we have seen the sons of the Anakims there.

29Then I said unto you, Dread not, neither be afraid of them.

30The LORD your God which goeth before you, he shall fight for you, according to all that he did for you in Egypt before your eyes;

31And in the wilderness, where thou hast seen how that the LORD thy God bare thee, as a man doth bear his son, in all the way that ye went, until ye came into this place.

32Yet in this thing ye did not believe the LORD your God,

33Who went in the way before you, to search you out a place to pitch your tents *in,* in fire by night, to show you by what way ye should go, and in a cloud by day.

34And the LORD heard the voice of your words, and was wroth, and sware, saying,

35Surely there shall not one of these men of this evil generation see that good land, which I sware to give unto your fathers,

36Save Caleb the son of Jephunneh; he shall see it, and to him will I give the land that he hath trodden upon, and to his children, because he hath wholly followed the LORD.

37Also the LORD was angry with me for your sakes, saying, Thou also shalt not go in thither.

38*But* Joshua the son of Nun, which standeth before thee, he shall go in thither: encourage him: for he shall cause Israel to inherit it.

39Moreover your little ones, which ye said should be a prey, and your children, which in that day had no knowledge between good and evil, they shall go in thither, and unto them will I give it, and they shall possess it.

40But *as for* you, turn you, and take your journey into the wilderness by the way of the Red sea.

41Then ye answered and said unto me, We have sinned against the LORD, we will go up and fight, according to all that the LORD our God commanded us. And when ye had girded on every man his weapons of war, ye were ready to go up into the hill.

New International

Spies Sent Out

19Then, as the LORD our God commanded us, we set out from Horeb and went toward the hill country of the Amorites through all that vast and dreadful desert that you have seen, and so we reached Kadesh Barnea. 20Then I said to you, "You have reached the hill country of the Amorites, which the LORD our God is giving us. 21See, the LORD your God has given you the land. Go up and take possession of it as the LORD, the God of your fathers, told you. Do not be afraid; do not be discouraged."

22Then all of you came to me and said, "Let us send men ahead to spy out the land for us and bring back a report about the route we are to take and the towns we will come to."

23The idea seemed good to me; so I selected twelve of you, one man from each tribe. 24They left and went up into the hill country, and came to the Valley of Eshcol and explored it. 25Taking with them some of the fruit of the land, they brought it down to us and reported, "It is a good land that the LORD our God is giving us."

Rebellion Against the LORD

26But you were unwilling to go up; you rebelled against the command of the LORD your God. 27You grumbled in your tents and said, "The LORD hates us; so he brought us out of Egypt to deliver us into the hands of the Amorites to destroy us. 28Where can we go? Our brothers have made us lose heart. They say, 'The people are stronger and taller than we are; the cities are large, with walls up to the sky. We even saw the Anakites there.'"

29Then I said to you, "Do not be terrified; do not be afraid of them. 30The LORD your God, who is going before you, will fight for you, as he did for you in Egypt, before your very eyes, 31and in the desert. There you saw how the LORD your God carried you, as a father carries his son, all the way you went until you reached this place."

32In spite of this, you did not trust in the LORD your God, 33who went ahead of you on your journey, in fire by night and in a cloud by day, to search out places for you to camp and to show you the way you should go.

34When the LORD heard what you said, he was angry and solemnly swore: 35"Not a man of this evil generation shall see the good land I swore to give your forefathers, 36except Caleb son of Jephunneh. He will see it, and I will give him and his descendants the land he set his feet on, because he followed the LORD wholeheartedly."

37Because of you the LORD became angry with me also and said, "You shall not enter it, either. 38But your assistant, Joshua son of Nun, will enter it. Encourage him, because he will lead Israel to inherit it. 39And the little ones that you said would be taken captive, your children who do not yet know good from bad—they will enter the land. I will give it to them and they will take possession of it. 40But as for you, turn around and set out toward the desert along the route to the Red Sea.a"

41Then you replied, "We have sinned against the LORD. We will go up and fight, as the LORD our God commanded us." So every one of you put on his weapons, thinking it easy to go up into the hill country.

---

a *40* Hebrew *Yam Suph;* that is, Sea of Reeds

Living Bible

19, 20, 21"Then we left Mount Horeb and traveled through the great and terrible desert, finally arriving among the Amorite hills to which the Lord our God had directed us. We were then at Kadesh-barnea [on the border of the Promised Landᵇ] and I said to the people, 'The Lord God has given us this land. Go and possess it as he told us to. Don't be afraid! Don't even doubt!'

22"But they replied, 'First let's send out spies to discover the best route of entry, and to decide which cities we should capture first.'

23"This seemed like a good idea, so I chose twelve spies, one from each tribe. 24, 25They crossed into the hills and came to the Valley of Eshcol, and returned with samples of the local fruit. One look was enough to convince us that it was indeed a good land the Lord our God had given us. 26But the people refused to go in, and rebelled against the Lord's command.

27"They murmured and complained in their tents and said, 'The Lord must hate us, bringing us here from Egypt to be slaughtered by these Amorites. 28What are we getting into? Our brothers who spied out the land have frightened us with their report. They say that the people of the land are tall and powerful, and that the walls of their cities rise high into the sky! They have even seen giants there—the descendants of the Anakim!'

29"But I said to them, 'Don't be afraid! 30The Lord God is your leader, and he will fight for you with his mighty miracles, just as you saw him do in Egypt. 31And you know how he has cared for you again and again here in the wilderness, just as a father cares for his child!' 32But nothing I said did any good.

"They refused to believe the Lord our God 33who had led them all the way, and had selected the best places for them to camp, and had guided them by a pillar of fire at night and a pillar of cloud during the day.

34, 35"Well, the Lord heard their complaining and was very angry. He vowed that not one person in that entire generation would live to see the good land he had promised their fathers, 36except Caleb (the son of Jephunneh), who, because he had wholly followed the Lord, would receive as his personal inheritance some of the land he had walked over.

37"And the Lord was even angry with me because of them and said to me, 'You shall not enter the Promised Land! 38Instead, your assistant, Joshua (the son of Nun), shall lead the people. Encourage him as he prepares to take over the leadership. 39I will give the land to the children they said would die in the wilderness. 40But as for you of the older generation, turn around now and go on back across the desert toward the Red Sea.'

41"Then they confessed, 'We have sinned! We will go into the land and fight for it as the Lord our God has told us to.' So they strapped on their weapons and thought it would be easy to conquer the whole area.

New Revised Standard

Israel's Refusal to Enter the Land

19 Then, just as the LORD our God had ordered us, we set out from Horeb and went through all that great and terrible wilderness that you saw, on the way to the hill country of the Amorites, until we reached Kadesh-barnea. 20I said to you, "You have reached the hill country of the Amorites, which the LORD our God is giving us. 21See, the LORD your God has given the land to you; go up, take possession, as the LORD, the God of your ancestors, has promised you; do not fear or be dismayed."

22 All of you came to me and said, "Let us send men ahead of us to explore the land for us and bring back a report to us regarding the route by which we should go up and the cities we will come to." 23The plan seemed good to me, and I selected twelve of you, one from each tribe. 24They set out and went up into the hill country, and when they reached the Valley of Eshcol they spied it out 25and gathered some of the land's produce, which they brought down to us. They brought back a report to us, and said, "It is a good land that the LORD our God is giving us."

26 But you were unwilling to go up. You rebelled against the command of the LORD your God; 27you grumbled in your tents and said, "It is because the LORD hates us that he has brought us out of the land of Egypt, to hand us over to the Amorites to destroy us. 28Where are we headed? Our kindred have made our hearts melt by reporting, 'The people are stronger and taller than we; the cities are large and fortified up to heaven! We actually saw there the offspring of the Anakim!' " 29I said to you, "Have no dread or fear of them. 30The LORD your God, who goes before you, is the one who will fight for you, just as he did for you in Egypt before your very eyes, 31and in the wilderness, where you saw how the LORD your God carried you, just as one carries a child, all the way that you traveled until you reached this place. 32But in spite of this, you have no trust in the LORD your God, 33who goes before you on the way to seek out a place for you to camp, in fire by night, and in the cloud by day, to show you the route you should take."

The Penalty for Israel's Rebellion

34 When the LORD heard your words, he was wrathful and swore: 35"Not one of these—not one of this evil generation—shall see the good land that I swore to give to your ancestors, 36except Caleb son of Jephunneh. He shall see it, and to him and to his descendants I will give the land on which he set foot, because of his complete fidelity to the LORD." 37Even with me the LORD was angry on your account, saying, "You also shall not enter there. 38Joshua son of Nun, your assistant, shall enter there; encourage him, for he is the one who will secure Israel's possession of it. 39And as for your little ones, who you thought would become booty, your children, who today do not yet know right from wrong, they shall enter there; to them I will give it, and they shall take possession of it. 40But as for you, journey back into the wilderness, in the direction of the Red Sea."ᶜ

41 You answered me, "We have sinned against the LORD! We are ready to go up and fight, just as the LORD our God commanded us." So all of you strapped on your battle gear, and thought it easy to go up into the hill country. 42The LORD said to me, "Say to them, 'Do not

---

ᵇ 1:19-21 on the border of the Promised Land, implied.   ᶜ Or Sea of Reeds

King James

42And the LORD said unto me, Say unto them, Go not up, neither fight; for I *am* not among you; lest ye be smitten before your enemies.

43So I spake unto you; and ye would not hear, but rebelled against the commandment of the LORD, and went presumptuously up into the hill.

44And the Amorites, which dwelt in that mountain, came out against you, and chased you, as bees do, and destroyed you in Seir, *even* unto Hormah.

45And ye returned and wept before the LORD; but the LORD would not hearken to your voice, nor give ear unto you.

46So ye abode in Kadesh many days, according unto the days that ye abode *there*.

2 THEN WE turned, and took our journey into the wilderness by the way of the Red sea, as the LORD spake unto me: and we compassed mount Seir many days.

2And the LORD spake unto me, saying,

3Ye have compassed this mountain long enough: turn you northward.

4And command thou the people, saying, Ye *are* to pass through the coast of your brethren the children of Esau, which dwell in Seir; and they shall be afraid of you: take ye good heed unto yourselves therefore:

5Meddle not with them; for I will not give you of their land, no, not so much as a footbreadth; because I have given mount Seir unto Esau *for* a possession.

6Ye shall buy meat of them for money, that ye may eat; and ye shall also buy water of them for money, that ye may drink.

7For the LORD thy God hath blessed thee in all the works of thy hand: he knoweth thy walking through this great wilderness: these forty years the LORD thy God *hath been* with thee; thou hast lacked nothing.

8And when we passed by from our brethren the children of Esau, which dwelt in Seir, through the way of the plain from Elath, and from Ezion-geber, we turned and passed by the way of the wilderness of Moab.

9And the LORD said unto me, Distress not the Moabites, neither contend with them in battle: for I will not give thee of their land *for* a possession; because I have given Ar unto the children of Lot *for* a possession.

10The Emims dwelt therein in times past, a people great, and many, and tall, as the Anakims;

11Which also were accounted giants, as the Anakims; but the Moabites call them Emims.

12The Horims also dwelt in Seir beforetime; but the children of Esau succeeded them, when they had destroyed them from before them, and dwelt in their stead; as Israel did unto the land of his possession, which the LORD gave unto them.

13Now rise up, *said I*, and get you over the brook Zered. And we went over the brook Zered.

14And the space in which we came from Kadesh-barnea, until we were come over the brook Zered, *was* thirty and eight years; until all the generation of the men of war was wasted out from among the host, as the LORD sware unto them.

15For indeed the hand of the LORD was against them, to destroy them from among the host, until they were consumed.

16¶ So it came to pass, when all the men of war were consumed and dead from among the people,

17That the LORD spake unto me, saying,

18Thou art to pass over through Ar, the coast of Moab, this day:

New International

42But the LORD said to me, "Tell them, 'Do not go up and fight, because I will not be with you. You will be defeated by your enemies.' "

43So I told you, but you would not listen. You rebelled against the LORD's command and in your arrogance you marched up into the hill country. 44The Amorites who lived in those hills came out against you; they chased you like a swarm of bees and beat you down from Seir all the way to Hormah. 45You came back and wept before the LORD, but he paid no attention to your weeping and turned a deaf ear to you. 46And so you stayed in Kadesh many days—all the time you spent there.

Wanderings in the Desert

2 THEN WE turned back and set out toward the desert along the route to the Red Sea,a as the LORD had directed me. For a long time we made our way around the hill country of Seir.

2Then the LORD said to me, 3"You have made your way around this hill country long enough; now turn north. 4Give the people these orders: 'You are about to pass through the territory of your brothers the descendants of Esau, who live in Seir. They will be afraid of you, but be very careful. 5Do not provoke them to war, for I will not give you any of their land, not even enough to put your foot on. I have given Esau the hill country of Seir as his own. 6You are to pay them in silver for the food you eat and the water you drink.' "

7The LORD your God has blessed you in all the work of your hands. He has watched over your journey through this vast desert. These forty years the LORD your God has been with you, and you have not lacked anything.

8So we went on past our brothers the descendants of Esau, who live in Seir. We turned from the Arabah road, which comes up from Elath and Ezion Geber, and traveled along the desert road of Moab.

9Then the LORD said to me, "Do not harass the Moabites or provoke them to war, for I will not give you any part of their land. I have given Ar to the descendants of Lot as a possession."

10(The Emites used to live there—a people strong and numerous, and as tall as the Anakites. 11Like the Anakites, they too were considered Rephaites, but the Moabites called them Emites. 12Horites used to live in Seir, but the descendants of Esau drove them out. They destroyed the Horites from before them and settled in their place, just as Israel did in the land the LORD gave them as their possession.)

13And the LORD said, "Now get up and cross the Zered Valley." So we crossed the valley.

14Thirty-eight years passed from the time we left Kadesh Barnea until we crossed the Zered Valley. By then, that entire generation of fighting men had perished from the camp, as the LORD had sworn to them. 15The LORD's hand was against them until he had completely eliminated them from the camp.

16Now when the last of these fighting men among the people had died, 17the LORD said to me, 18"Today you are to pass by the region of Moab at Ar. 19When you

a *1* Hebrew *Yam Suph*; that is, Sea of Reeds

Living Bible

42"But the Lord said to me, 'Tell them not to do it, for I will not go with them; they will be struck down before their enemies.'

43"I told them, but they wouldn't listen. Instead, they rebelled again against the Lord's commandment and went on up into the hill country to fight. 44But the Amorites who lived there came out against them, and chased them like bees and killed them from Seir to Hormah. 45Then they returned and wept before the Lord, but he wouldn't listen. 46So they stayed there at Kadesh for a long time.

2 "THEN WE turned back across the wilderness toward the Red Sea, for so the Lord had instructed me. For many years we wandered around in the area of Mount Seir. 2Then at last the Lord said,

3" 'You have stayed here long enough. Turn northward. 4Inform the people that they will be passing through the country belonging to their brothers the Edomites, the descendants of Esau who live in Seir; the Edomites will be nervous, so be careful. 5Don't start a fight! For I have given them all the Mount Seir hill country as their permanent possession, and I will not give you even a tiny piece of their land. 6Pay them for whatever food or water you use. 7The Lord your God has watched over you and blessed you every step of the way for all these forty years as you have wandered around in this great wilderness; and you have lacked nothing in all that time.'

8"So we passed through Edom where our brothers lived, crossing the Arabah Road that goes south to Elath and Ezi-on-geber, and traveling northward toward the Moab desert.

9"Then the Lord warned us, 'Don't attack the Moabites either, for I will not give you any of their land; I have given it to the descendants of Lot.'

10"(The Emim used to live in that area, a very large tribe, tall as the giants of Anakim; 11both the Emim and the Anakim are often referred to as the Rephaim, but the Moabites call them Emim. 12In earlier days the Horites lived in Seir, but they were driven out and displaced by the Edomites, the descendants of Esau, just as Israel would displace the peoples of Canaan, whose land had been assigned to Israel by the Lord.)

13" 'Now cross Zered Brook,' the Lord said; and we did.

14, 15"So it took us thirty-eight years to finally get across Zered Brook from Kadesh! For the Lord had decreed that this could not happen until all the men, who thirty-eight years earlier were old enough to bear arms, had died. Yes, the hand of the Lord was against them until finally all were dead.

16, 17"Then at last the Lord said to me,

18" 'Today Israel shall cross the borders of Moab at Ar, 19into the land of the Ammonites. But do not attack

New Revised Standard

go up and do not fight, for I am not in the midst of you; otherwise you will be defeated by your enemies.' " 43Although I told you, you would not listen. You rebelled against the command of the LORD and presumptuously went up into the hill country. 44The Amorites who lived in that hill country then came out against you and chased you as bees do. They beat you down in Seir as far as Hormah. 45When you returned and wept before the LORD, the LORD would neither heed your voice nor pay you any attention.

The Desert Years

46 After you had stayed at Kadesh as many days as you did,

2 WE JOURNEYED back into the wilderness, in the direction of the Red Sea,b as the LORD had told me and skirted Mount Seir for many days. 2Then the LORD said to me: 3"You have been skirting this hill country long enough. Head north, 4and charge the people as follows: You are about to pass through the territory of your kindred, the descendants of Esau, who live in Seir. They will be afraid of you, so, be very careful 5not to engage in battle with them, for I will not give you even so much as a foot's length of their land, since I have given Mount Seir to Esau as a possession. 6You shall purchase food from them for money, so that you may eat; and you shall also buy water from them for money, so that you may drink. 7Surely the LORD your God has blessed you in all your undertakings; he knows your going through this great wilderness. These forty years the LORD your God has been with you; you have lacked nothing." 8So we passed by our kin, the descendants of Esau who live in Seir, leaving behind the route of the Arabah, and leaving behind Elath and Ezion-geber.

When we had headed out along the route of the wilderness of Moab, 9the LORD said to me: "Do not harass Moab or engage them in battle, for I will not give you any of its land as a possession, since I have given Ar as a possession to the descendants of Lot." 10(The Emim—a large and numerous people, as tall as the Anakim—had formerly inhabited it. 11Like the Anakim, they are usually reckoned as Rephaim, though the Moabites call them Emim. 12Moreover, the Horim had formerly inhabited Seir, but the descendants of Esau dispossessed them, destroying them and settling in their place, as Israel has done in the land that the LORD gave them as a possession.) 13"Now then, proceed to cross over the Wadi Zered."

So we crossed over the Wadi Zered. 14And the length of time we had traveled from Kadesh-barnea until we crossed the Wadi Zered was thirty-eight years, until the entire generation of warriors had perished from the camp, as the LORD had sworn concerning them. 15Indeed, the LORD's own hand was against them, to root them out from the camp, until all had perished.

16 Just as soon as all the warriors had died off from among the people, 17the LORD spoke to me, saying, 18"Today you are going to cross the boundary of Moab at Ar. 19When you approach the frontier of the Ammon-

b Or Sea of Reeds

King James

19And *when* thou comest nigh over against the children of Ammon, distress them not, nor meddle with them: for I will not give thee of the land of the children of Ammon *any* possession; because I have given it unto the children of Lot *for* a possession.

20(That also was accounted a land of giants: giants dwelt therein in old time; and the Ammonites call them Zamzummims;

21A people great, and many, and tall, as the Anakims; but the LORD destroyed them before them; and they succeeded them, and dwelt in their stead:

22As he did to the children of Esau, which dwelt in Seir, when he destroyed the Horims from before them; and they succeeded them, and dwelt in their stead even unto this day:

23And the Avims which dwelt in Hazerim, *even* unto Azzah, the Caphtorims, which came forth out of Caphtor, destroyed them, and dwelt in their stead.)

24¶ Rise ye up, take your journey, and pass over the river Arnon: behold, I have given into thine hand Sihon the Amorite, king of Heshbon, and his land: begin to possess *it*, and contend with him in battle.

25This day will I begin to put the dread of thee and the fear of thee upon the nations *that are* under the whole heaven, who shall hear report of thee, and shall tremble, and be in anguish because of thee.

26¶ And I sent messengers out of the wilderness of Kedemoth unto Sihon king of Heshbon with words of peace, saying,

27Let me pass through thy land: I will go along by the high way, I will neither turn unto the right hand nor to the left.

28Thou shalt sell me meat for money, that I may eat; and give me water for money, that I may drink: only I will pass through on my feet;

29(As the children of Esau which dwell in Seir, and the Moabites which dwell in Ar, did unto me;) until I shall pass over Jordan into the land which the LORD our God giveth us.

30But Sihon king of Heshbon would not let us pass by him: for the LORD thy God hardened his spirit, and made his heart obstinate, that he might deliver him into thy hand, as *appeareth* this day.

31And the LORD said unto me, Behold, I have begun to give Sihon and his land before thee: begin to possess, that thou mayest inherit his land.

32Then Sihon came out against us, he and all his people, to fight at Jahaz.

33And the LORD our God delivered him before us; and we smote him, and his sons, and all his people.

34And we took all his cities at that time, and utterly destroyed the men, and the women, and the little ones, of every city, we left none to remain:

35Only the cattle we took for a prey unto ourselves, and the spoil of the cities which we took.

36From Aroer, which *is* by the brink of the river of Arnon, and *from* the city that *is* by the river, even unto Gilead, there was not one city too strong for us: the LORD our God delivered all unto us:

37Only unto the land of the children of Ammon thou camest not, *nor* unto any place of the river Jabbok, nor unto the cities in the mountains, nor unto whatsoever the LORD our God forbad us.

New International

come to the Ammonites, do not harass them or provoke them to war, for I will not give you possession of any land belonging to the Ammonites. I have given it as a possession to the descendants of Lot."

20(That too was considered a land of the Rephaites, who used to live there; but the Ammonites called them Zamzummites. 21They were a people strong and numerous, and as tall as the Anakites. The LORD destroyed them from before the Ammonites, who drove them out and settled in their place. 22The LORD had done the same for the descendants of Esau, who lived in Seir, when he destroyed the Horites from before them. They drove them out and have lived in their place to this day. 23And as for the Avvites who lived in villages as far as Gaza, the Caphtorites coming out from Caphtora destroyed them and settled in their place.)

Defeat of Sihon King of Heshbon

24"Set out now and cross the Arnon Gorge. See, I have given into your hand Sihon the Amorite, king of Heshbon, and his country. Begin to take possession of it and engage him in battle. 25This very day I will begin to put the terror and fear of you on all the nations under heaven. They will hear reports of you and will tremble and be in anguish because of you."

26From the desert of Kedemoth I sent messengers to Sihon king of Heshbon offering peace and saying, 27"Let us pass through your country. We will stay on the main road; we will not turn aside to the right or to the left. 28Sell us food to eat and water to drink for their price in silver. Only let us pass through on foot— 29as the descendants of Esau, who live in Seir, and the Moabites, who live in Ar, did for us—until we cross the Jordan into the land the LORD our God is giving us." 30But Sihon king of Heshbon refused to let us pass through. For the LORD your God had made his spirit stubborn and his heart obstinate in order to give him into your hands, as he has now done.

31The LORD said to me, "See, I have begun to deliver Sihon and his country over to you. Now begin to conquer and possess his land."

32When Sihon and all his army came out to meet us in battle at Jahaz, 33the LORD our God delivered him over to us and we struck him down, together with his sons and his whole army. 34At that time we took all his towns and completely destroyedb them—men, women and children. We left no survivors. 35But the livestock and the plunder from the towns we had captured we carried off for ourselves. 36From Aroer on the rim of the Arnon Gorge, and from the town in the gorge, even as far as Gilead, not one town was too strong for us. The LORD our God gave us all of them. 37But in accordance with the command of the LORD our God, you did not encroach on any of the land of the Ammonites, neither the land along the course of the Jabbok nor that around the towns in the hills.

---

a 23 That is, Crete   b 34 The Hebrew term refers to the irrevocable giving over of things or persons to the LORD, often by totally destroying them.

Living Bible

them, for I will not give you any of their land. I have given it to the descendants of Lot.'

20"(That area, too, used to be inhabited by the Rephaim, called 'Zamzummim' by the Ammonites. 21They were a large and powerful tribe, as tall as the Anakim; but Jehovah destroyed them as the Ammonites came in, and the Ammonites lived there in their place. 22The Lord had similarly helped the descendants of Esau at Mount Seir, for he destroyed the Horites who were living there before them. 23Another similar situation occurred when the people of Caphtor invaded and destroyed the tribe of Avvim living in villages scattered across the countryside as far away as Gaza.)

24"Then the Lord said, 'Cross the Arnon River into the land of King Sihon the Amorite, king of Heshbon. War against him and begin to take possession of his land. 25Beginning today I will make people throughout the whole earth tremble with fear because of you, and dread your arrival.'

26"Then from the wilderness of Kedemoth I sent ambassadors to King Sihon of Heshbon with a proposal of peace. 27'Let us pass through your land,' we said. 'We will stay on the main road and won't turn off into the fields on either side. 28We will not steal food as we go, but will purchase every bite we eat and everything we drink; all we want is permission to pass through. 29The Edomites at Seir allowed us to go through their country, and so did the Moabites, whose capital is at Ar. We are on our way across the Jordan into the land the Lord our God has given us.'

30"But King Sihon refused because Jehovah your God made him obstinate, so that he could destroy Sihon by the hands of Israel, as has now been done.

31"Then the Lord said to me, 'I have begun to give you the land of King Sihon; when you possess it, it shall belong to Israel forever.'

32"King Sihon then declared war on us and mobilized his forces at Jahaz. 33, 34But the Lord our God crushed him, and we conquered all his cities, and utterly destroyed everything, including the women and babies. We left nothing alive 35, 36except the cattle, which we took as our reward, along with the booty gained from ransacking the cities we had taken. We conquered everything from Aroer to Gilead—from the edge of the Arnon River valley, and including all the cities in the valley. Not one city was too strong for us, for the Lord our God gave all of them to us. 37However, we stayed away from the people of Ammon and from the Jabbok River and the hill country cities, the places Jehovah our God had forbidden us to enter.

New Revised Standard

ites, do not harass them or engage them in battle, for I will not give the land of the Ammonites to you as a possession, because I have given it to the descendants of Lot." 20 (It also is usually reckoned as a land of Rephaim. Rephaim formerly inhabited it, though the Ammonites call them Zamzummim, 21a strong and numerous people, as tall as the Anakim. But the LORD destroyed them from before the Ammonites so that they could dispossess them and settle in their place. 22He did the same for the descendants of Esau, who live in Seir, by destroying the Horim before them so that they could dispossess them and settle in their place even to this day. 23As for the Avvim, who had lived in settlements in the vicinity of Gaza, the Caphtorim, who came from Caphtor, destroyed them and settled in their place.) 24"Proceed on your journey and cross the Wadi Arnon. See, I have handed over to you King Sihon the Amorite of Heshbon, and his land. Begin to take possession by engaging him in battle. 25This day I will begin to put the dread and fear of you upon the peoples everywhere under heaven; when they hear report of you, they will tremble and be in anguish because of you."

Defeat of King Sihon

26 So I sent messengers from the wilderness of Kedemoth to King Sihon of Heshbon with the following terms of peace: 27"If you let me pass through your land, I will travel only along the road; I will turn aside neither to the right nor to the left. 28 You shall sell me food for money, so that I may eat, and supply me water for money, so that I may drink. Only allow me to pass through on foot— 29just as the descendants of Esau who live in Seir have done for me and likewise the Moabites who live in Ar—until I cross the Jordan into the land that the LORD our God is giving us." 30But King Sihon of Heshbon was not willing to let us pass through, for the LORD your God had hardened his spirit and made his heart defiant in order to hand him over to you, as he has now done.

31 The LORD said to me, "See, I have begun to give Sihon and his land over to you. Begin now to take possession of his land." 32So when Sihon came out against us, he and all his people for battle at Jahaz, 33the LORD our God gave him over to us; and we struck him down, along with his offspring and all his people. 34At that time we captured all his towns, and in each town we utterly destroyed men, women, and children. We left not a single survivor. 35Only the livestock we kept as spoil for ourselves, as well as the plunder of the towns that we had captured. 36From Aroer on the edge of the Wadi Arnon (including the town that is in the wadi itself) as far as Gilead, there was no citadel too high for us. The LORD our God gave everything to us. 37You did not encroach, however, on the land of the Ammonites, avoiding the whole upper region of the Wadi Jabbok as well as the towns of the hill country, just as[c] the LORD our God had charged.

---

[c] Gk Tg: Heb *and all*

King James

3 THEN WE turned, and went up the way to Bashan: and Og the king of Bashan came out against us, he and all his people, to battle at Edrei.

2And the LORD said unto me, Fear him not: for I will deliver him, and all his people, and his land, into thy hand; and thou shalt do unto him as thou didst unto Sihon king of the Amorites, which dwelt at Heshbon.

3So the LORD our God delivered into our hands Og also, the king of Bashan, and all his people: and we smote him until none was left to him remaining.

4And we took all his cities at that time, there was not a city which we took not from them, threescore cities, all the region of Argob, the kingdom of Og in Bashan.

5All these cities *were* fenced with high walls, gates, and bars; beside unwalled towns a great many.

6And we utterly destroyed them, as we did unto Sihon king of Heshbon, utterly destroying the men, women, and children, of every city.

7But all the cattle, and the spoil of the cities, we took for a prey to ourselves.

8And we took at that time out of the hand of the two kings of the Amorites the land that *was* on this side Jordan, from the river of Arnon unto mount Hermon;

9(*Which* Hermon the Sidonians call Sirion; and the Amorites call it Shenir;)

10All the cities of the plain, and all Gilead, and all Bashan, unto Salchah and Edrei, cities of the kingdom of Og in Bashan.

11For only Og king of Bashan remained of the remnant of giants; behold, his bedstead *was* a bedstead of iron; *is* it not in Rabbath of the children of Ammon? nine cubits *was* the length thereof, and four cubits the breadth of it, after the cubit of a man.

12And this land, *which* we possessed at that time, from Aroer, which *is* by the river Arnon, and half mount Gilead, and the cities thereof, gave I unto the Reubenites and to the Gadites.

13And the rest of Gilead, and all Bashan, *being* the kingdom of Og, gave I unto the half tribe of Manasseh; all the region of Argob, with all Bashan, which was called the land of giants.

14Jair the son of Manasseh took all the country of Argob unto the coasts of Geshuri and Maachathi; and called them after his own name, Bashan-havoth-jair, unto this day.

15And I gave Gilead unto Machir.

16And unto the Reubenites and unto the Gadites I gave from Gilead even unto the river Arnon half the valley, and the border even unto the river Jabbok, *which is* the border of the children of Ammon;

17The plain also, and Jordan, and the coast *thereof*, from Chinnereth even unto the sea of the plain, *even* the salt sea, under Ashdoth-pisgah eastward.

18¶ And I commanded you at that time, saying, The LORD your God hath given you this land to possess it: ye shall pass over armed before your brethren the children of Israel, all *that are* meet for the war.

19But your wives, and your little ones, and your cattle, (*for* I know that ye have much cattle,) shall abide in your cities which I have given you;

20Until the LORD have given rest unto your brethren, as well as unto you, and *until* they also possess the land which the LORD your God hath given them beyond Jordan: and *then* shall ye return every man unto his possession, which I have given you.

21¶ And I commanded Joshua at that time, saying, Thine eyes have seen all that the LORD your God hath done unto these two kings: so shall the LORD do unto all the kingdoms whither thou passest.

22Ye shall not fear them: for the LORD your God he shall fight for you.

New International

Defeat of Og King of Bashan

3 NEXT WE turned and went up along the road toward Bashan, and Og king of Bashan with his whole army marched out to meet us in battle at Edrei. 2The LORD said to me, "Do not be afraid of him, for I have handed him over to you with his whole army and his land. Do to him what you did to Sihon king of the Amorites, who reigned in Heshbon."

3So the LORD our God also gave into our hands Og king of Bashan and all his army. We struck them down, leaving no survivors. 4At that time we took all his cities. There was not one of the sixty cities that we did not take from them—the whole region of Argob, Og's kingdom in Bashan. 5All these cities were fortified with high walls and with gates and bars, and there were also a great many unwalled villages. 6We completely destroyeda them, as we had done with Sihon king of Heshbon, destroyinga every city—men, women and children. 7But all the livestock and the plunder from their cities we carried off for ourselves.

8So at that time we took from these two kings of the Amorites the territory east of the Jordan, from the Arnon Gorge as far as Mount Hermon. 9(Hermon is called Sirion by the Sidonians; the Amorites call it Senir.) 10We took all the towns on the plateau, and all Gilead, and all Bashan as far as Salecah and Edrei, towns of Og's kingdom in Bashan. 11(Only Og king of Bashan was left of the remnant of the Rephaites. His bedb was made of iron and was more than thirteen feet long and six feet wide.c It is still in Rabbah of the Ammonites.)

Division of the Land

12Of the land that we took over at that time, I gave the Reubenites and the Gadites the territory north of Aroer by the Arnon Gorge, including half the hill country of Gilead, together with its towns. 13The rest of Gilead and also all of Bashan, the kingdom of Og, I gave to the half tribe of Manasseh. (The whole region of Argob in Bashan used to be known as a land of the Rephaites. 14Jair, a descendant of Manasseh, took the whole region of Argob as far as the border of the Geshurites and the Maacathites; it was named after him, so that to this day Bashan is called Havvoth Jair.d) 15And I gave Gilead to Makir. 16But to the Reubenites and the Gadites I gave the territory extending from Gilead down to the Arnon Gorge (the middle of the gorge being the border) and out to the Jabbok River, which is the border of the Ammonites. 17Its western border was the Jordan in the Arabah, from Kinnereth to the Sea of the Arabah (the Salt Seae), below the slopes of Pisgah.

18I commanded you at that time: "The LORD your God has given you this land to take possession of it. But all your able-bodied men, armed for battle, must cross over ahead of your brother Israelites. 19However, your wives, your children and your livestock (I know you have much livestock) may stay in the towns I have given you, 20until the LORD gives rest to your brothers as he has to you, and they too have taken over the land that the LORD your God is giving them, across the Jordan. After that, each of you may go back to the possession I have given you."

Moses Forbidden to Cross the Jordan

21At that time I commanded Joshua: "You have seen with your own eyes all that the LORD your God has done to these two kings. The LORD will do the same to all the kingdoms over there where you are going. 22Do not be afraid of them; the LORD your God himself will fight for you."

---

a 6 The Hebrew term refers to the irrevocable giving over of things or persons to the LORD, often by totally destroying them.   b 11 Or *sarcophagus*   c 11 Hebrew *nine cubits long and four cubits wide* (about 4 meters long and 1.8 meters wide)   d 14 Or *called the settlements of Jair*   e 17 That is, the Dead Sea

Living Bible

3 "NEXT WE turned toward King Og's land of Bashan. He immediately mobilized his army and attacked us at Edre-i. But the Lord told me not to be afraid of him. 'All his people and his land are yours,' the Lord told me. 'You will do to him as you did to King Sihon of the Amorites, at Heshbon.' 3So the Lord helped us fight against King Og and his people, and we killed them all. 4We conquered all sixty of his cities, the entire Argob region of Bashan. 5These were well-fortified cities with high walls and barred gates. Of course we also took all of the unwalled towns. 6We utterly destroyed the kingdom of Bashan just as we had destroyed King Sihon's kingdom at Heshbon, killing the entire population—men, women, and children alike. 7But we kept the cattle and loot for ourselves.

8"We now possessed all the land of the two kings of the Amorites east of the Jordan River—all the land from the valley of the Arnon to Mount Hermon. 9(The Sidonians called Mount Hermon 'Sirion,' while the Amorites called it 'Senir.') 10We had now conquered all the cities on the plateau, and all of Gilead and Bashan as far as the cities of Salecah and Edre-i.

11"Incidentally, King Og of Bashan was the last of the giant Rephaim. His iron bedstead is kept in a museum at Rabbah, one of the cities of the Ammonites, and measures thirteen and a half feet long by six feet wide.

12"At that time I gave the conquered land to the tribes of Reuben, Gad, and the half-tribe of Manasseh. To the tribes of Reuben and Gad I gave the area beginning at Aroer on the Arnon River, plus half of Mount Gilead, including its cities. 13The half-tribe of Manasseh received the remainder of Gilead and all of the former kingdom of King Og, the Argob region. (Bashan is sometimes called 'The Land of the Rephaim.') 14The clan of Jair, of the tribe of Manasseh, took over the whole Argob region (Bashan) to the borders of the Geshurites and Ma-acathites. They renamed their country after themselves, calling it Havvoth-jair (meaning 'Jair's Villages') as it is still known today. 15Then I gave Gilead to the clan of Machir. 16The tribes of Reuben and Gad received the area extending from the Jabbok River in Gilead (which was the Ammonite frontier) to the middle of the valley of the Arnon River. 17They also received the Arabah (or, wasteland), bounded by the Jordan River on the west, from Chinnereth to Mount Pisgah and the Dead Sea (also called the Sea of the Arabah).

18"At that time I reminded the tribes of Reuben and Gad and the half-tribe of Manasseh, that although the Lord had given them the land, they could not begin settling down until their armed men led the other tribes across the Jordan to the land the Lord was giving them.

19" 'But your wives and children,' I told them, 'may live here in the cities the Lord has given you, caring for your many cattle 20until you return after the Lord has given victory to the other tribes, too. When they conquer the land the Lord your God has given them across the Jordan River, then you may return here to your own land.'

21"Then I said to Joshua, 'You have seen what the Lord your God has done to those two kings. You will do the same to all the kingdoms on the other side of the Jordan. 22Don't be afraid of the nations there, for the Lord your God will fight for you.'

New Revised Standard

Defeat of King Og

3 WHEN WE headed up the road to Bashan, King Og of Bashan came out against us, he and all his people, for battle at Edrei. 2The LORD said to me, "Do not fear him, for I have handed him over to you, along with his people and his land. Do to him as you did to King Sihon of the Amorites, who reigned in Heshbon." 3So the LORD our God also handed over to us King Og of Bashan and all his people. We struck him down until not a single survivor was left. 4At that time we captured all his towns; there was no citadel that we did not take from them—sixty towns, the whole region of Argob, the kingdom of Og in Bashan. 5All these were fortress towns with high walls, double gates, and bars, besides a great many villages. 6And we utterly destroyed them, as we had done to King Sihon of Heshbon, in each city utterly destroying men, women, and children. 7But all the livestock and the plunder of the towns we kept as spoil for ourselves.

8 So at that time we took from the two kings of the Amorites the land beyond the Jordan, from the Wadi Arnon to Mount Hermon 9(the Sidonians call Hermon Sirion, while the Amorites call it Senir), 10all the towns of the tableland, the whole of Gilead, and all of Bashan, as far as Salecah and Edrei, towns of Og's kingdom in Bashan. 11(Now only King Og of Bashan was left of the remnant of the Rephaim. In fact his bed, an iron bed, can still be seen in Rabbah of the Ammonites. By the common cubit it is nine cubits long and four cubits wide.) 12As for the land that we took possession of at that time, I gave to the Reubenites and Gadites the territory north of Aroer,f that is on the edge of the Wadi Arnon, as well as half the hill country of Gilead with its towns, 13and I gave to the half-tribe of Manasseh the rest of Gilead and all of Bashan, Og's kingdom. (The whole region of Argob: all that portion of Bashan used to be called a land of Rephaim; 14Jair the Manassite acquired the whole region of Argob as far as the border of the Geshurites and the Maacathites, and he named them—that is, Bashan—after himself, Havvoth-jair,g as it is to this day.) 15To Machir I gave Gilead. 16And to the Reubenites and the Gadites I gave the territory from Gilead as far as the Wadi Arnon, with the middle of the wadi as a boundary, and up to the Jabbok, the wadi being boundary of the Ammonites; 17the Arabah also, with the Jordan and its banks, from Chinnereth down to the sea of the Arabah, the Dead Sea,h with the lower slopes of Pisgah on the east.

18 At that time, I charged you as follows: "Although the LORD your God has given you this land to occupy, all your troops shall cross over armed as the vanguard of your Israelite kin. 19Only your wives, your children, and your livestock—I know that you have much livestock—shall stay behind in the towns that I have given to you. 20When the LORD gives rest to your kindred, as to you, and they too have occupied the land that the LORD your God is giving them beyond the Jordan, then each of you may return to the property that I have given to you." 21And I charged Joshua as well at that time, saying: "Your own eyes have seen everything that the LORD your God has done to these two kings; so the LORD will do to all the kingdoms into which you are about to cross. 22Do not fear them, for it is the LORD your God who fights for you."

---

f Heb territory from Aroer   g That is Settlement of Jair   h Heb Salt Sea

King James

23And I besought the LORD at that time, saying,

24O Lord GOD, thou hast begun to show thy servant thy greatness, and thy mighty hand: for what God *is there* in heaven or in earth, that can do according to thy works, and according to thy might?

25I pray thee, let me go over, and see the good land that *is* beyond Jordan, that goodly mountain, and Lebanon.

26But the LORD was wroth with me for your sakes, and would not hear me: and the LORD said unto me, Let it suffice thee; speak no more unto me of this matter.

27Get thee up into the top of Pisgah, and lift up thine eyes westward, and northward, and southward, and eastward, and behold *it* with thine eyes: for thou shalt not go over this Jordan.

28But charge Joshua, and encourage him, and strengthen him: for he shall go over before this people, and he shall cause them to inherit the land which thou shalt see.

29So we abode in the valley over against Beth-peor.

4 NOW THEREFORE hearken, O Israel, unto the statutes and unto the judgments, which I teach you, for to do *them,* that ye may live, and go in and possess the land which the LORD God of your fathers giveth you.

2Ye shall not add unto the word which I command you, neither shall ye diminish *aught* from it, that ye may keep the commandments of the LORD your God which I command you.

3Your eyes have seen what the LORD did because of Baal-peor: for all the men that followed Baal-peor, the LORD thy God hath destroyed them from among you.

4But ye that did cleave unto the LORD your God *are* alive every one of you this day.

5Behold, I have taught you statutes and judgments, even as the LORD my God commanded me, that ye should do so in the land whither ye go to possess it.

6Keep therefore and do *them;* for this *is* your wisdom and your understanding in the sight of the nations, which shall hear all these statutes, and say, Surely this great nation *is* a wise and understanding people.

7For what nation *is there* so great, who *hath* God *so* nigh unto them, as the LORD our God *is* in all *things that* we call upon him *for?*

8And what nation *is there* so great, that hath statutes and judgments *so* righteous as all this law, which I set before you this day?

9Only take heed to thyself, and keep thy soul diligently, lest thou forget the things which thine eyes have seen, and lest they depart from thy heart all the days of thy life: but teach them thy sons, and thy sons' sons;

10*Specially* the day that thou stoodest before the LORD thy God in Horeb, when the LORD said unto me, Gather me the people together, and I will make them hear my words, that they may learn to fear me all the days that they shall live upon the earth, and *that* they may teach their children.

11And ye came near and stood under the mountain; and the mountain burned with fire unto the midst of heaven, with darkness, clouds, and thick darkness.

12And the LORD spake unto you out of the midst of the fire: ye heard the voice of the words, but saw no similitude; only *ye heard* a voice.

13And he declared unto you his covenant, which he commanded you to perform, *even* ten commandments; and he wrote them upon two tables of stone.

14¶ And the LORD commanded me at that time to teach you statutes and judgments, that ye might do them in the land whither ye go over to possess it.

New International

23At that time I pleaded with the LORD: 24"O Sovereign LORD, you have begun to show to your servant your greatness and your strong hand. For what god is there in heaven or on earth who can do the deeds and mighty works you do? 25Let me go over and see the good land beyond the Jordan—that fine hill country and Lebanon."

26But because of you the LORD was angry with me and would not listen to me. "That is enough," the LORD said. "Do not speak to me anymore about this matter. 27Go up to the top of Pisgah and look west and north and south and east. Look at the land with your own eyes, since you are not going to cross this Jordan. 28But commission Joshua, and encourage and strengthen him, for he will lead this people across and will cause them to inherit the land that you will see." 29So we stayed in the valley near Beth Peor.

Obedience Commanded

4 HEAR NOW, O Israel, the decrees and laws I am about to teach you. Follow them so that you may live and may go in and take possession of the land that the LORD, the God of your fathers, is giving you. 2Do not add to what I command you and do not subtract from it, but keep the commands of the LORD your God that I give you.

3You saw with your own eyes what the LORD did at Baal Peor. The LORD your God destroyed from among you everyone who followed the Baal of Peor, 4but all of you who held fast to the LORD your God are still alive today.

5See, I have taught you decrees and laws as the LORD my God commanded me, so that you may follow them in the land you are entering to take possession of it. 6Observe them carefully, for this will show your wisdom and understanding to the nations, who will hear about all these decrees and say, "Surely this great nation is a wise and understanding people." 7What other nation is so great as to have their gods near them the way the LORD our God is near us whenever we pray to him? 8And what other nation is so great as to have such righteous decrees and laws as this body of laws I am setting before you today?

9Only be careful, and watch yourselves closely so that you do not forget the things your eyes have seen or let them slip from your heart as long as you live. Teach them to your children and to their children after them. 10Remember the day you stood before the LORD your God at Horeb, when he said to me, "Assemble the people before me to hear my words so that they may learn to revere me as long as they live in the land and may teach them to their children." 11You came near and stood at the foot of the mountain while it blazed with fire to the very heavens, with black clouds and deep darkness. 12Then the LORD spoke to you out of the fire. You heard the sound of words but saw no form; there was only a voice. 13He declared to you his covenant, the Ten Commandments, which he commanded you to follow and then wrote them on two stone tablets. 14And the LORD directed me at that time to teach you the decrees and laws you are to follow in the land that you are crossing the Jordan to possess.

Living Bible

23, 24, 25"At that time I made this plea to God: 'O Lord God, please let me cross over into the Promised Land—the good land beyond the Jordan River with its rolling hills—and Lebanon. I want to see the result of all the greatness and power you have been showing us; for what God in all of heaven or earth can do what you have done for us?'

26"But the Lord was angry with me because of you, and would not let me cross over. 'Speak of it no more,' he ordered, 27'but go to the top of Mount Pisgah where you can look out in every direction, and there you will see the land in the distance. But you shall not cross the Jordan River. 28Commission Joshua to replace you, and then encourage him, for he shall lead the people across to conquer the land you will see from the mountaintop.'

29"So we remained in the valley near Beth-peor.

4 "AND NOW, O Israel, listen carefully to these laws I teach you, and obey them if you want to live and enter into and possess the land given you by the Lord God of your ancestors. 2Do not add other laws or subtract from these; just obey them, for they are from the Lord your God. 3You have seen what the Lord did to you at Baalpeor, where he destroyed many people for worshiping idols. 4But all of you who were faithful to the Lord your God are still alive today.

5"These are the laws for you to obey when you arrive in the land where you will live. They are from the Lord our God. He has given them to me to pass on to you. 6If you obey them they will give you a reputation for wisdom and intelligence. When the surrounding nations hear these laws they will exclaim, 'What other nation is as wise and prudent as Israel!' 7For what other nation, great or small, has God among them, as the Lord our God is here among us whenever we call upon him? 8And what nation, no matter how great, has laws as fair as these I am giving you today?

9"But watch out! Be very careful never to forget what you have seen God doing for you. May his miracles have a deep and permanent effect upon your lives! Tell your children and your grandchildren about the glorious miracles he did. 10Tell them especially about the day you stood before the Lord at Mount Horeb, and he told me, 'Summon the people before me and I will instruct them, so that they will learn always to reverence me, and so that they can teach my laws to their children.' 11You stood at the foot of the mountain, and the mountain burned with fire; flames shot far into the sky, surrounded by black clouds and deep darkness. 12And the Lord spoke to you from the fire; you heard his words but didn't see him. 13He proclaimed the laws you must obey—the Ten Commandments—and wrote them on two stone tablets. 14Yes, it was at that time that the Lord commanded me to issue the laws you must obey when you arrive in the Promised Land.

New Revised Standard

Moses Views Canaan from Pisgah

23 At that time, too, I entreated the LORD, saying: 24"O Lord GOD, you have only begun to show your servant your greatness and your might; what god in heaven or on earth can perform deeds and mighty acts like yours! 25Let me cross over to see the good land beyond the Jordan, that good hill country and the Lebanon." 26But the LORD was angry with me on your account and would not heed me. The LORD said to me, "Enough from you! Never speak to me of this matter again! 27Go up to the top of Pisgah and look around you to the west, to the north, to the south, and to the east. Look well, for you shall not cross over this Jordan. 28But charge Joshua, and encourage and strengthen him, because it is he who shall cross over at the head of this people and who shall secure their possession of the land that you will see." 29So we remained in the valley opposite Beth-peor.

Moses Commands Obedience

4 SO NOW, Israel, give heed to the statutes and ordinances that I am teaching you to observe, so that you may live to enter and occupy the land that the LORD, the God of your ancestors, is giving you. 2 You must neither add anything to what I command you nor take away anything from it, but keep the commandments of the LORD your God with which I am charging you. 3 You have seen for yourselves what the LORD did with regard to the Baal of Peor—how the LORD your God destroyed from among you everyone who followed the Baal of Peor, 4 while those of you who held fast to the LORD your God are all alive today.

5 See, just as the LORD my God has charged me, I now teach you statutes and ordinances for you to observe in the land that you are about to enter and occupy. 6 You must observe them diligently, for this will show your wisdom and discernment to the peoples, who, when they hear all these statutes, will say, "Surely this great nation is a wise and discerning people!" 7 For what other great nation has a god so near to it as the LORD our God is whenever we call to him? 8 And what other great nation has statutes and ordinances as just as this entire law that I am setting before you today?

9 But take care and watch yourselves closely, so as neither to forget the things that your eyes have seen nor to let them slip from your mind all the days of your life; make them known to your children and your children's children— 10 how you once stood before the LORD your God at Horeb, when the LORD said to me, "Assemble the people for me, and I will let them hear my words, so that they may learn to fear me as long as they live on the earth, and may teach their children so"; 11 you approached and stood at the foot of the mountain while the mountain was blazing up to the very heavens, shrouded in dark clouds. 12 Then the LORD spoke to you out of the fire. You heard the sound of words but saw no form; there was only a voice. 13 He declared to you his covenant, which he charged you to observe, that is, the ten commandments;a and he wrote them on two stone tablets. 14 And the LORD charged me at that time to teach you statutes and ordinances for you to observe in the land that you are about to cross into and occupy.

a Heb the ten words

King James

15Take ye therefore good heed unto yourselves; for ye saw no manner of similitude on the day *that* the LORD spake unto you in Horeb out of the midst of the fire:

16Lest ye corrupt *yourselves,* and make you a graven image, the similitude of any figure, the likeness of male or female,

17The likeness of any beast that *is* on the earth, the likeness of any winged fowl that flieth in the air,

18The likeness of any thing that creepeth on the ground, the likeness of any fish that *is* in the waters beneath the earth:

19And lest thou lift up thine eyes unto heaven, and when thou seest the sun, and the moon, and the stars, *even* all the host of heaven, shouldest be driven to worship them, and serve them, which the LORD thy God hath divided unto all nations under the whole heaven.

20But the LORD hath taken you, and brought you forth out of the iron furnace, *even* out of Egypt, to be unto him a people of inheritance, as *ye are* this day.

21Furthermore the LORD was angry with me for your sakes, and sware that I should not go over Jordan, and that I should not go in unto that good land, which the LORD thy God giveth thee *for* an inheritance:

22But I must die in this land, I must not go over Jordan: but ye shall go over, and possess that good land.

23Take heed unto yourselves, lest ye forget the covenant of the LORD your God, which he made with you, and make you a graven image, *or* the likeness of any *thing,* which the LORD thy God hath forbidden thee.

24For the LORD thy God *is* a consuming fire, *even* a jealous God.

25¶ When thou shalt beget children, and children's children, and ye shall have remained long in the land, and shall corrupt *yourselves,* and make a graven image, *or* the likeness of any *thing,* and shall do evil in the sight of the LORD thy God, to provoke him to anger:

26I call heaven and earth to witness against you this day, that ye shall soon utterly perish from off the land whereunto ye go over Jordan to possess it; ye shall not prolong *your* days upon it, but shall utterly be destroyed.

27And the LORD shall scatter you among the nations, and ye shall be left few in number among the heathen, whither the LORD shall lead you.

28And there ye shall serve gods, the work of men's hands, wood and stone, which neither see, nor hear, nor eat, nor smell.

29But if from thence thou shalt seek the LORD thy God, thou shalt find *him,* if thou seek him with all thy heart and with all thy soul.

30When thou art in tribulation, and all these things are come upon thee, *even* in the latter days, if thou turn to the LORD thy God, and shalt be obedient unto his voice;

31(For the LORD thy God *is* a merciful God;) he will not forsake thee, neither destroy thee, nor forget the covenant of thy fathers which he sware unto them.

32For ask now of the days that are past, which were before thee, since the day that God created man upon the earth, and *ask* from the one side of heaven unto the other, whether there hath been *any such thing* as this great thing *is,* or hath been heard like it?

33Did *ever* people hear the voice of God speaking out of the midst of the fire, as thou hast heard, and live?

34Or hath God assayed to go *and* take him a nation from the midst of *another* nation, by temptations, by signs, and by wonders, and by war, and by a mighty hand, and by a stretched out arm, and by great terrors, according to all that the LORD your God did for you in Egypt before your eyes?

35Unto thee it was shown, that thou mightest know that the LORD he *is* God; *there is* none else beside him.

36Out of heaven he made thee to hear his voice, that he might instruct thee: and upon earth he showed thee his great fire; and thou heardest his words out of the midst of the fire.

New International

Idolatry Forbidden

15You saw no form of any kind the day the LORD spoke to you at Horeb out of the fire. Therefore watch yourselves very carefully, 16so that you do not become corrupt and make for yourselves an idol, an image of any shape, whether formed like a man or a woman, 17or like any animal on earth or any bird that flies in the air, 18or like any creature that moves along the ground or any fish in the waters below. 19And when you look up to the sky and see the sun, the moon and the stars—all the heavenly array—do not be enticed into bowing down to them and worshiping things the LORD your God has apportioned to all the nations under heaven. 20But as for you, the LORD took you and brought you out of the iron-smelting furnace, out of Egypt, to be the people of his inheritance, as you now are.

21The LORD was angry with me because of you, and he solemnly swore that I would not cross the Jordan and enter the good land the LORD your God is giving you as your inheritance. 22I will die in this land; I will not cross the Jordan; but you are about to cross over and take possession of that good land. 23Be careful not to forget the covenant of the LORD your God that he made with you; do not make for yourselves an idol in the form of anything the LORD your God has forbidden. 24For the LORD your God is a consuming fire, a jealous God.

25After you have had children and grandchildren and have lived in the land a long time—if you then become corrupt and make any kind of idol, doing evil in the eyes of the LORD your God and provoking him to anger, 26I call heaven and earth as witnesses against you this day that you will quickly perish from the land that you are crossing the Jordan to possess. You will not live there long but will certainly be destroyed. 27The LORD will scatter you among the peoples, and only a few of you will survive among the nations to which the LORD will drive you. 28There you will worship man-made gods of wood and stone, which cannot see or hear or eat or smell. 29But if from there you seek the LORD your God, you will find him if you look for him with all your heart and with all your soul. 30When you are in distress and all these things have happened to you, then in later days you will return to the LORD your God and obey him. 31For the LORD your God is a merciful God; he will not abandon or destroy you or forget the covenant with your forefathers, which he confirmed to them by oath.

The LORD Is God

32Ask now about the former days, long before your time, from the day God created man on the earth; ask from one end of the heavens to the other. Has anything so great as this ever happened, or has anything like it ever been heard of? 33Has any other people heard the voice of God[a] speaking out of fire, as you have, and lived? 34Has any god ever tried to take for himself one nation out of another nation, by testings, by miraculous signs and wonders, by war, by a mighty hand and an outstretched arm, or by great and awesome deeds, like all the things the LORD your God did for you in Egypt before your very eyes?

35You were shown these things so that you might know that the LORD is God; besides him there is no other. 36From heaven he made you hear his voice to discipline you. On earth he showed you his great fire, and you heard his words from out of the fire. 37Because

Living Bible

15"But beware! You didn't see the form of God that day as he spoke to you from the fire at Mount Horeb, 16, 17so do not defile yourselves by trying to make a statue of God—an idol in any form, whether of a man, woman, animal, bird, 18a small animal that runs along the ground, or a fish. 19And do not look up into the sky to worship the sun, moon, or stars. The Lord may permit other nations to get away with this, but not you. 20The Lord has rescued you from prison—Egypt—to be his special people, his own inheritance; this is what you are today. 21, 22But he was angry with me because of you; he vowed that I could not go over the Jordan River into the good land he has given you as your inheritance. I must die here on this side of the river. 23Beware lest you break the contract the Lord your God has made with you! You will break it if you make any idols, for the Lord your God has utterly forbidden this. 24He is a devouring fire, a jealous God.

25"In the future, when your children and grandchildren are born and you have been in the land a long time, and you have defiled yourselves by making idols, and the Lord your God is very angry because of your sin, 26heaven and earth are witnesses that you shall be quickly destroyed from the land. Soon, now, you will cross the Jordan River and conquer that land. But your days there will be brief; you will then be utterly destroyed. 27For the Lord will scatter you among the nations, and you will be but few in number. 28There, far away, you will worship idols made from wood and stone, idols that neither see nor hear nor eat nor smell.

29"But you will also begin to search again for Jehovah your God, and you should find him when you search for him with all your hearts and souls. 30When those bitter days have come upon you in the latter times, you will finally return to the Lord your God and listen to what he tells you. 31For the Lord your God is merciful—he will not abandon you nor destroy you nor forget the promises he has made to your ancestors.

32"In all history, going back to the time when God created man upon the earth, search from one end of the heavens to the other to see if you can find anything like this: 33An entire nation heard the voice of God speaking to it from fire, as you did, and lived! 34Where else will you ever find another example of God's removing a nation from its slavery by sending terrible plagues, mighty miracles, war, and terror? Yet that is what the Lord your God did for you in Egypt, right before your very eyes. 35He did these things so you would realize that Jehovah is God, and that there is no one else like him. 36He let you hear his voice instructing you from heaven, and he let you see his great pillar of fire upon the earth; you even heard his words from the center of the fire.

New Revised Standard

15 Since you saw no form when the LORD spoke to you at Horeb out of the fire, take care and watch yourselves closely, 16so that you do not act corruptly by making an idol for yourselves, in the form of any figure—the likeness of male or female, 17the likeness of any animal that is on the earth, the likeness of any winged bird that flies in the air, 18the likeness of anything that creeps on the ground, the likeness of any fish that is in the water under the earth. 19And when you look up to the heavens and see the sun, the moon, and the stars, all the host of heaven, do not be led astray and bow down to them and serve them, things that the LORD your God has allotted to all the peoples everywhere under heaven. 20But the LORD has taken you and brought you out of the iron-smelter, out of Egypt, to become a people of his very own possession, as you are now.

21 The LORD was angry with me because of you, and he vowed that I should not cross the Jordan and that I should not enter the good land that the LORD your God is giving for your possession. 22For I am going to die in this land without crossing over the Jordan, but you are going to cross over to take possession of that good land. 23So be careful not to forget the covenant that the LORD your God made with you, and not to make for yourselves an idol in the form of anything that the LORD your God has forbidden you. 24For the LORD your God is a devouring fire, a jealous God.

25 When you have had children and children's children, and become complacent in the land, if you act corruptly by making an idol in the form of anything, thus doing what is evil in the sight of the LORD your God, and provoking him to anger, 26I call heaven and earth to witness against you today that you will soon utterly perish from the land that you are crossing the Jordan to occupy; you will not live long on it, but will be utterly destroyed. 27The LORD will scatter you among the peoples; only a few of you will be left among the nations where the LORD will lead you. 28There you will serve other gods made by human hands, objects of wood and stone that neither see, nor hear, nor eat, nor smell. 29From there you will seek the LORD your God, and you will find him if you search after him with all your heart and soul. 30In your distress, when all these things have happened to you in time to come, you will return to the LORD your God and heed him. 31Because the LORD your God is a merciful God, he will neither abandon you nor destroy you; he will not forget the covenant with your ancestors that he swore to them.

32 For ask now about former ages, long before your own, ever since the day that God created human beings on the earth; ask from one end of heaven to the other: has anything so great as this ever happened or has its like ever been heard of? 33Has any people ever heard the voice of a god speaking out of a fire, as you have heard, and lived? 34Or has any god ever attempted to go and take a nation for himself from the midst of another nation, by trials, by signs and wonders, by war, by a mighty hand and an outstretched arm, and by terrifying displays of power, as the LORD your God did for you in Egypt before your very eyes? 35To you it was shown so that you would acknowledge that the LORD is God; there is no other besides him. 36From heaven he made you hear his voice to discipline you. On earth he showed you his great fire, while you heard his words coming out of the fire. 37And because he loved your ancestors, he

King James

37And because he loved thy fathers, therefore he chose their seed after them, and brought thee out in his sight with his mighty power out of Egypt;

38To drive out nations from before thee greater and mightier than thou *art*, to bring thee in, to give thee their land *for* an inheritance, as *it is* this day.

39Know therefore this day, and consider *it* in thine heart, that the LORD he *is* God in heaven above, and upon the earth beneath: *there is* none else.

40Thou shalt keep therefore his statutes, and his commandments, which I command thee this day, that it may go well with thee, and with thy children after thee, and that thou mayest prolong *thy* days upon the earth, which the LORD thy God giveth thee, for ever.

41¶ Then Moses severed three cities on this side Jordan toward the sunrising;

42That the slayer might flee thither, which should kill his neighbour unawares, and hated him not in times past; and that fleeing unto one of these cities he might live:

43*Namely*, Bezer in the wilderness, in the plain country, of the Reubenites; and Ramoth in Gilead, of the Gadites; and Golan in Bashan, of the Manassites.

44¶ And this *is* the law which Moses set before the children of Israel:

45These *are* the testimonies, and the statutes, and the judgments, which Moses spake unto the children of Israel, after they came forth out of Egypt,

46On this side Jordan, in the valley over against Bethpeor, in the land of Sihon king of the Amorites, who dwelt at Heshbon, whom Moses and the children of Israel smote, after they were come forth out of Egypt:

47And they possessed his land, and the land of Og king of Bashan, two kings of the Amorites, which *were* on this side Jordan toward the sunrising;

48From Aroer, which *is* by the bank of the river Arnon, even unto mount Sion, which *is* Hermon,

49And all the plain on this side Jordan eastward, even unto the sea of the plain, under the springs of Pisgah.

5 AND MOSES called all Israel, and said unto them, Hear, O Israel, the statutes and judgments which I speak in your ears this day, that ye may learn them, and keep, and do them.

2The LORD our God made a covenant with us in Horeb.

3The LORD made not this covenant with our fathers, but with us, *even* us, who *are* all of us here alive this day.

4The LORD talked with you face to face in the mount out of the midst of the fire,

5(I stood between the LORD and you at that time, to show you the word of the LORD: for ye were afraid by reason of the fire, and went not up into the mount;) saying,

6¶ I *am* the LORD thy God, which brought thee out of the land of Egypt, from the house of bondage.

7Thou shalt have none other gods before me.

8Thou shalt not make thee *any* graven image, *or* any likeness *of any thing* that *is* in heaven above, or that *is* in the earth beneath, or that *is* in the waters beneath the earth:

9Thou shalt not bow down thyself unto them, nor serve them: for I the LORD thy God *am* a jealous God, visiting the iniquity of the fathers upon the children unto the third and fourth *generation* of them that hate me,

10And showing mercy unto thousands of them that love me and keep my commandments.

11Thou shalt not take the name of the LORD thy God in vain: for the LORD will not hold *him* guiltless that taketh his name in vain.

New International

he loved your forefathers and chose their descendants after them, he brought you out of Egypt by his Presence and his great strength, 38to drive out before you nations greater and stronger than you and to bring you into their land to give it to you for your inheritance, as it is today.

39Acknowledge and take to heart this day that the LORD is God in heaven above and on the earth below. There is no other. 40Keep his decrees and commands, which I am giving you today, so that it may go well with you and your children after you and that you may live long in the land the LORD your God gives you for all time.

Cities of Refuge

41Then Moses set aside three cities east of the Jordan, 42to which anyone who had killed a person could flee if he had unintentionally killed his neighbor without malice aforethought. He could flee into one of these cities and save his life. 43The cities were these: Bezer in the desert plateau, for the Reubenites; Ramoth in Gilead, for the Gadites; and Golan in Bashan, for the Manassites.

Introduction to the Law

44This is the law Moses set before the Israelites. 45These are the stipulations, decrees and laws Moses gave them when they came out of Egypt 46and were in the valley near Beth Peor east of the Jordan, in the land of Sihon king of the Amorites, who reigned in Heshbon and was defeated by Moses and the Israelites as they came out of Egypt. 47They took possession of his land and the land of Og king of Bashan, the two Amorite kings east of the Jordan. 48This land extended from Aroer on the rim of the Arnon Gorge to Mount Siyon[a] (that is, Hermon), 49and included all the Arabah east of the Jordan, as far as the Sea of the Arabah,[b] below the slopes of Pisgah.

The Ten Commandments

5 MOSES SUMMONED all Israel and said: Hear, O Israel, the decrees and laws I declare in your hearing today. Learn them and be sure to follow them. 2The LORD our God made a covenant with us at Horeb. 3It was not with our fathers that the LORD made this covenant, but with us, with all of us who are alive here today. 4The LORD spoke to you face to face out of the fire on the mountain. 5(At that time I stood between the LORD and you to declare to you the word of the LORD, because you were afraid of the fire and did not go up the mountain.) And he said:

6"I am the LORD your God, who brought you out of Egypt, out of the land of slavery.

7"You shall have no other gods before[c] me.

8"You shall not make for yourself an idol in the form of anything in heaven above or on the earth beneath or in the waters below. 9You shall not bow down to them or worship them; for I, the LORD your God, am a jealous God, punishing the children for the sin of the fathers to the third and fourth generation of those who hate me, 10but showing love to a thousand ⌊generations⌋ of those who love me and keep my commandments.

11"You shall not misuse the name of the LORD your God, for the LORD will not hold anyone guiltless who misuses his name.

---

a 48 Hebrew; Syriac (see also Deut. 3:9) *Sirion*   b 49 That is, the Dead Sea
c 7 Or *besides*

Living Bible

37"It was because he loved your ancestors and chose to bless their descendants that he personally brought you out from Egypt with a great display of power. 38He drove away other nations greater by far than you, and gave you their land as an inheritance, as it is today. 39This is your wonderful thought for the day: Jehovah is God both in heaven and down here upon the earth; and there is no God other than him! 40You must obey these laws that I will tell you today, so that all will be well with you and your children, and so that you will live forever in the land the Lord your God is giving you."

41Then Moses instructed the people of Israel to set apart three cities east of the Jordan River, 42where anyone who accidentally killed someone could flee for safety. 43These cities were Bezer, on the plateau in the wilderness, for the tribe of Reuben; Ramoth, in Gilead, for the tribe of Gad; and Golan, in Bashan, for the tribe of Manasseh.

44, 45, 46Listed below are the laws Moses issued to the people of Israel when they left Egypt, and as they were camped east of the Jordan River near the city of Beth-peor. (This was the land formerly occupied by the Amorites under King Sihon, whose capital was Heshbon; he and his people were destroyed by Moses and the Israelis. 47Israel conquered his land and that of King Og of Bashan—they were two Amorite kings east of the Jordan. 48Israel also conquered all the area from Aroer at the edge of the Arnon River valley to Mount Sirion, or Mount Hermon, as it is sometimes called; 49and all the Arabah east of the Jordan River over to the Dead Sea, below the slopes of Mount Pisgah.)

5 MOSES CONTINUED speaking to the people of Israel and said, "Listen carefully now to all these laws God has given you; learn them, and be sure to obey them!

2, 3"The Lord our God made a contract with you at Mount Horeb—*not with your ancestors, but with you who are here alive today*. 4He spoke with you face to face from the center of the fire, there at the mountain. 5I stood as an intermediary between you and Jehovah, for you were afraid of the fire and did not go up to him on the mountain. He spoke to me and I passed on his laws to you. This is what he said:

6" 'I am Jehovah your God who rescued you from slavery in Egypt.

7" 'Never worship any god but me.

8" 'Never make idols; don't worship images, whether of birds, animals, or fish. 9, 10You shall not bow down to any images nor worship them in any way, for I am the Lord your God. I am a jealous God, and I will bring the curse of a father's sins upon even the third and fourth generation of the children of those who hate me; but I will show kindness to a thousand generations of those who love me and keep my commandments.

11" 'You must never use my name to make a vow you don't intend to keep.d I will not overlook that.

New Revised Standard

chose their descendants after them. He brought you out of Egypt with his own presence, by his great power, 38driving out before you nations greater and mightier than yourselves, to bring you in, giving you their land for a possession, as it is still today. 39So acknowledge today and take to heart that the Lord is God in heaven above and on the earth beneath; there is no other. 40Keep his statutes and his commandments, which I am commanding you today for your own well-being and that of your descendants after you, so that you may long remain in the land that the Lord your God is giving you for all time.

Cities of Refuge East of the Jordan

41 Then Moses set apart on the east side of the Jordan three cities 42to which a homicide could flee, someone who unintentionally kills another person, the two not having been at enmity before; the homicide could flee to one of these cities and live: 43 Bezer in the wilderness on the tableland belonging to the Reubenites, Ramoth in Gilead belonging to the Gadites, and Golan in Bashan belonging to the Manassites.

Transition to the Second Address

44 This is the law that Moses set before the Israelites. 45These are the decrees and the statutes and ordinances that Moses spoke to the Israelites when they had come out of Egypt, 46beyond the Jordan in the valley opposite Beth-peor, in the land of King Sihon of the Amorites, who reigned at Heshbon, whom Moses and the Israelites defeated when they came out of Egypt. 47They occupied his land and the land of King Og of Bashan, the two kings of the Amorites on the eastern side of the Jordan: 48from Aroer, which is on the edge of the Wadi Arnon, as far as Mount Sirione (that is, Hermon), 49together with all the Arabah on the east side of the Jordan as far as the Sea of the Arabah, under the slopes of Pisgah.

The Ten Commandments

5 MOSES CONVENED all Israel, and said to them: Hear, O Israel, the statutes and ordinances that I am addressing to you today; you shall learn them and observe them diligently. 2The Lord our God made a covenant with us at Horeb. 3Not with our ancestors did the Lord make this covenant, but with us, who are all of us here alive today. 4The Lord spoke with you face to face at the mountain, out of the fire. 5(At that time I was standing between the Lord and you to declare to you the wordsf of the Lord; for you were afraid because of the fire and did not go up the mountain.) And he said:

6 I am the Lord your God, who brought you out of the land of Egypt, out of the house of slavery; 7you shall have no other gods beforeg me.

8 You shall not make for yourself an idol, whether in the form of anything that is in heaven above, or that is on the earth beneath, or that is in the water under the earth. 9You shall not bow down to them or worship them; for I the Lord your God am a jealous God, punishing children for the iniquity of parents, to the third and fourth generation of those who reject me, 10but showing steadfast love to the thousandth generationh of those who love me and keep my commandments.

11 You shall not make wrongful use of the name of the Lord your God, for the Lord will not acquit anyone who misuses his name.

---

d 5:11 *never use my name to make a vow you don't intend to keep*, literally, "You must not utter the name of the Lord your God to misuse it."

e Syr: Heb *Sion* f Q Mss Sam Gk Syr Vg Tg: MT *word* g Or *besides* h Or *to thousands*

King James

12Keep the sabbath day to sanctify it, as the LORD thy God hath commanded thee.

13Six days thou shalt labour, and do all thy work:

14But the seventh day *is* the sabbath of the LORD thy God: *in it* thou shalt not do any work, thou, nor thy son, nor thy daughter, nor thy manservant, nor thy maidservant, nor thine ox, nor thine ass, nor any of thy cattle, nor thy stranger that *is* within thy gates; that thy manservant and thy maidservant may rest as well as thou.

15And remember that thou wast a servant in the land of Egypt, and *that* the LORD thy God brought thee out thence through a mighty hand and by a stretched out arm: therefore the LORD thy God commanded thee to keep the sabbath day.

16¶ Honour thy father and thy mother, as the LORD thy God hath commanded thee; that thy days may be prolonged, and that it may go well with thee, in the land which the LORD thy God giveth thee.

17Thou shalt not kill.

18Neither shalt thou commit adultery.

19Neither shalt thou steal.

20Neither shalt thou bear false witness against thy neighbour.

21Neither shalt thou desire thy neighbour's wife, neither shalt thou covet thy neighbour's house, his field, or his manservant, or his maidservant, his ox, or his ass, or any *thing* that *is* thy neighbour's.

22¶ These words the LORD spake unto all your assembly in the mount out of the midst of the fire, of the cloud, and of the thick darkness, with a great voice: and he added no more. And he wrote them in two tables of stone, and delivered them unto me.

23And it came to pass, when ye heard the voice out of the midst of the darkness, (for the mountain did burn with fire,) that ye came near unto me, *even* all the heads of your tribes, and your elders;

24And ye said, Behold, the LORD our God hath shown us his glory and his greatness, and we have heard his voice out of the midst of the fire: we have seen this day that God doth talk with man, and he liveth.

25Now therefore why should we die? for this great fire will consume us: if we hear the voice of the LORD our God any more, then we shall die.

26For who *is there of* all flesh, that hath heard the voice of the living God speaking out of the midst of the fire, as we *have*, and lived?

27Go thou near, and hear all that the LORD our God shall say: and speak thou unto us all that the LORD our God shall speak unto thee; and we will hear *it*, and do *it*.

28And the LORD heard the voice of your words, when ye spake unto me; and the LORD said unto me, I have heard the voice of the words of this people, which they have spoken unto thee: they have well said all that they have spoken.

29O that there were such an heart in them, that they would fear me, and keep all my commandments always, that it might be well with them, and with their children for ever!

30Go say to them, Get you into your tents again.

31But as for thee, stand thou here by me, and I will speak unto thee all the commandments, and the statutes, and the judgments, which thou shalt teach them, that they may do *them* in the land which I give them to possess it.

32Ye shall observe to do therefore as the LORD your God hath commanded you: ye shall not turn aside to the right hand or to the left.

33Ye shall walk in all the ways which the LORD your God hath commanded you, that ye may live, and *that it may be* well with you, and *that* ye may prolong *your* days in the land which ye shall possess.

New International

12"Observe the Sabbath day by keeping it holy, as the LORD your God has commanded you. 13Six days you shall labor and do all your work, 14but the seventh day is a Sabbath to the LORD your God. On it you shall not do any work, neither you, nor your son or daughter, nor your manservant or maidservant, nor your ox, your donkey or any of your animals, nor the alien within your gates, so that your manservant and maidservant may rest, as you do.

15Remember that you were slaves in Egypt and that the LORD your God brought you out of there with a mighty hand and an outstretched arm. Therefore the LORD your God has commanded you to observe the Sabbath day.

16"Honor your father and your mother, as the LORD your God has commanded you, so that you may live long and that it may go well with you in the land the LORD your God is giving you.

17"You shall not murder.

18"You shall not commit adultery.

19"You shall not steal.

20"You shall not give false testimony against your neighbor.

21"You shall not covet your neighbor's wife. You shall not set your desire on your neighbor's house or land, his manservant or maidservant, his ox or donkey, or anything that belongs to your neighbor."

22These are the commandments the LORD proclaimed in a loud voice to your whole assembly there on the mountain from out of the fire, the cloud and the deep darkness; and he added nothing more. Then he wrote them on two stone tablets and gave them to me.

23When you heard the voice out of the darkness, while the mountain was ablaze with fire, all the leading men of your tribes and your elders came to me. 24And you said, "The LORD our God has shown us his glory and his majesty, and we have heard his voice from the fire. Today we have seen that a man can live even if God speaks with him. 25But now, why should we die? This great fire will consume us, and we will die if we hear the voice of the LORD our God any longer. 26For what mortal man has ever heard the voice of the living God speaking out of fire, as we have, and survived? 27Go near and listen to all that the LORD our God says. Then tell us whatever the LORD our God tells you. We will listen and obey."

28The LORD heard you when you spoke to me and the LORD said to me, "I have heard what this people said to you. Everything they said was good. 29Oh, that their hearts would be inclined to fear me and keep all my commands always, so that it might go well with them and their children forever!

30"Go, tell them to return to their tents. 31But you stay here with me so that I may give you all the commands, decrees and laws you are to teach them to follow in the land I am giving them to possess."

32So be careful to do what the LORD your God has commanded you; do not turn aside to the right or to the left. 33Walk in all the way that the LORD your God has commanded you, so that you may live and prosper and prolong your days in the land that you will possess.

Living Bible

12" 'Keep the Sabbath day holy. This is my command. 13Work the other six days, 14but the seventh day is the Sabbath of the Lord your God; no work shall be done that day by you or by any of your household—your sons, daughters, servants, oxen, donkeys, or cattle; even foreigners living among you must obey this law. Everybody must rest as you do. 15Why should you keep the Sabbath? It is because you were slaves in Egypt, and the Lord your God brought you out with a great display of miracles.

16" 'Honor your father and mother (remember, this is a commandment of the Lord your God); if you do so, you shall have a long, prosperous life in the land he is giving you.

17" 'You must not murder.

18" 'You must not commit adultery.

19" 'You must not steal.

20" 'You must not tell lies.

21" 'You must not burn with desire for another man's wife, nor envy him for his home, land, servants, oxen, donkeys, nor anything else he owns.'

22"The Lord has given these laws to each one of you from the heart of the fire, surrounded by the clouds and thick darkness that engulfed Mount Sinai. Those were the only commandments he gave you at that time,a and he wrote them out on two stone tablets and gave them to me. 23But when you heard the loud voice from the darkness, and saw the terrible fire at the top of the mountain, all your tribal leaders came to me 24and pleaded, 'Today the Lord our God has shown us his glory and greatness; we have even heard his voice from the heart of the fire. Now we know that a man may speak to God and not die; 25but we will surely die if he speaks to us again. This awesome fire will consume us. 26, 27What man can hear, as we have, the voice of the living God speaking from the heart of the fire, and live? You go and listen to all that God says, then come and tell us, and we will listen and obey.'

28"And the Lord agreed to your request, and said to me, 'I have heard what the people have said to you, and I agree. 29Oh, that they would always have such a heart for me, wanting to obey my commandments. Then all would go well with them in the future, and with their children throughout all generations! 30Go and tell them to return to their tents. 31Then you come back and stand here beside me, and I will give you all my commandments, and you shall teach them to the people; and they will obey them in the land I am giving to them.' "

32So Moses told the people, "You must obey all the commandments of the Lord your God, following his directions in every detail, going the whole way he has laid out for you; 33only then will you live long and prosperous lives in the land you are to enter and possess.

New Revised Standard

12 Observe the sabbath day and keep it holy, as the LORD your God commanded you. 13 Six days you shall labor and do all your work. 14 But the seventh day is a sabbath to the LORD your God; you shall not do any work—you, or your son or your daughter, or your male or female slave, or your ox or your donkey, or any of your livestock, or the resident alien in your towns, so that your male and female slave may rest as well as you. 15 Remember that you were a slave in the land of Egypt, and the LORD your God brought you out from there with a mighty hand and an outstretched arm; therefore the LORD your God commanded you to keep the sabbath day.

16 Honor your father and your mother, as the LORD your God commanded you, so that your days may be long and that it may go well with you in the land that the LORD your God is giving you.

17 You shall not murder.b

18 Neither shall you commit adultery.

19 Neither shall you steal.

20 Neither shall you bear false witness against your neighbor.

21 Neither shall you covet your neighbor's wife.

Neither shall you desire your neighbor's house, or field, or male or female slave, or ox, or donkey, or anything that belongs to your neighbor.

Moses the Mediator of God's Will

22 These words the LORD spoke with a loud voice to your whole assembly at the mountain, out of the fire, the cloud, and the thick darkness, and he added no more. He wrote them on two stone tablets, and gave them to me. 23 When you heard the voice out of the darkness, while the mountain was burning with fire, you approached me, all the heads of your tribes and your elders; 24 and you said, "Look, the LORD our God has shown us his glory and greatness, and we have heard his voice out of the fire. Today we have seen that God may speak to someone and the person may still live. 25 So now why should we die? For this great fire will consume us; if we hear the voice of the LORD our God any longer, we shall die. 26 For who is there of all flesh that has heard the voice of the living God speaking out of fire, as we have, and remained alive? 27 Go near, you yourself, and hear all that the LORD our God will say. Then tell us everything that the LORD our God tells you, and we will listen and do it."

28 The LORD heard your words when you spoke to me, and the LORD said to me: "I have heard the words of this people, which they have spoken to you; they are right in all that they have spoken. 29 If only they had such a mind as this, to fear me and to keep all my commandments always, so that it might go well with them and with their children forever! 30 Go say to them, 'Return to your tents.' 31 But you, stand here by me, and I will tell you all the commandments, the statutes and the ordinances, that you shall teach them, so that they may do them in the land that I am giving them to possess." 32 You must therefore be careful to do as the LORD your God has commanded you; you shall not turn to the right or to the left. 33 You must follow exactly the path that the LORD your God has commanded you, so that you may live, and that it may go well with you, and that you may live long in the land that you are to possess.

---

a 5:22 *the only commandments he gave you at that time,* literally, "and he added no more."

b Or *kill*

King James

6 NOW THESE *are* the commandments, the statutes, and the judgments, which the LORD your God
commanded to teach you, that ye might do *them* in the
land whither ye go to possess it:

2That thou mightest fear the LORD thy God, to keep
all his statutes and his commandments, which I command thee, thou, and thy son, and thy son's son, all the
days of thy life; and that thy days may be prolonged.

3¶ Hear therefore, O Israel, and observe to do *it;* that
it may be well with thee, and that ye may increase mightily, as the LORD God of thy fathers hath promised thee,
in the land that floweth with milk and honey.

4Hear, O Israel: The LORD our God *is* one LORD:

5And thou shalt love the LORD thy God with all thine
heart, and with all thy soul, and with all thy might.

6And these words, which I command thee this day,
shall be in thine heart:

7And thou shalt teach them diligently unto thy children, and shalt talk of them when thou sittest in thine
house, and when thou walkest by the way, and when
thou liest down, and when thou risest up.

8And thou shalt bind them for a sign upon thine hand,
and they shall be as frontlets between thine eyes.

9And thou shalt write them upon the posts of thy
house, and on thy gates.

10And it shall be, when the LORD thy God shall have
brought thee into the land which he sware unto thy fathers, to Abraham, to Isaac, and to Jacob, to give thee
great and goodly cities, which thou buildest not,

11And houses full of all good *things,* which thou filledst not, and wells digged, which thou diggedst not,
vineyards and olive trees, which thou plantedst not;
when thou shalt have eaten and be full;

12*Then* beware lest thou forget the LORD, which
brought thee forth out of the land of Egypt, from the
house of bondage.

13Thou shalt fear the LORD thy God, and serve him,
and shalt swear by his name.

14Ye shall not go after other gods, of the gods of the
people which *are* round about you;

15(For the LORD thy God *is* a jealous God among you)
lest the anger of the LORD thy God be kindled against
thee, and destroy thee from off the face of the earth.

16¶ Ye shall not tempt the LORD your God, as ye
tempted *him* in Massah.

17Ye shall diligently keep the commandments of the
LORD your God, and his testimonies, and his statutes,
which he hath commanded thee.

18And thou shalt do *that which is* right and good in
the sight of the LORD: that it may be well with thee, and
that thou mayest go in and possess the good land which
the LORD sware unto thy fathers,

19To cast out all thine enemies from before thee, as
the LORD hath spoken.

20*And* when thy son asketh thee in time to come,
saying, What *mean* the testimonies, and the statutes, and
the judgments, which the LORD our God hath commanded you?

21Then thou shalt say unto thy son, We were Pharaoh's bondmen in Egypt; and the LORD brought us out
of Egypt with a mighty hand:

22And the LORD showed signs and wonders, great and
sore, upon Egypt, upon Pharaoh, and upon all his household, before our eyes:

23And he brought us out from thence, that he might
bring us in, to give us the land which he sware unto our
fathers.

24And the LORD commanded us to do all these statutes, to fear the LORD our God, for our good always, that
he might preserve us alive, as *it is* at this day.

25And it shall be our righteousness, if we observe to
do all these commandments before the LORD our God,
as he hath commanded us.

New International

Love the LORD Your God

6 THESE ARE the commands, decrees and laws the
LORD your God directed me to teach you to observe in the land that you are crossing the Jordan to
possess, 2so that you, your children and their children
after them may fear the LORD your God as long as you
live by keeping all his decrees and commands that I give
you, and so that you may enjoy long life. 3Hear, O
Israel, and be careful to obey so that it may go well with
you and that you may increase greatly in a land flowing
with milk and honey, just as the LORD, the God of your
fathers, promised you.

4Hear, O Israel: The LORD our God, the LORD is
one.[a] 5Love the LORD your God with all your heart and
with all your soul and with all your strength. 6These
commandments that I give you today are to be upon your
hearts. 7Impress them on your children. Talk about them
when you sit at home and when you walk along the road,
when you lie down and when you get up. 8Tie them as
symbols on your hands and bind them on your foreheads. 9Write them on the doorframes of your houses
and on your gates.

10When the LORD your God brings you into the land
he swore to your fathers, to Abraham, Isaac and Jacob,
to give you—a land with large, flourishing cities you did
not build, 11houses filled with all kinds of good things
you did not provide, wells you did not dig, and vineyards and olive groves you did not plant—then when
you eat and are satisfied, 12be careful that you do not
forget the LORD, who brought you out of Egypt, out of
the land of slavery.

13Fear the LORD your God, serve him only and take
your oaths in his name. 14Do not follow other gods, the
gods of the peoples around you; 15for the LORD your
God, who is among you, is a jealous God and his anger
will burn against you, and he will destroy you from the
face of the land. 16Do not test the LORD your God as you
did at Massah. 17Be sure to keep the commands of the
LORD your God and the stipulations and decrees he has
given you. 18Do what is right and good in the LORD's
sight, so that it may go well with you and you may go
in and take over the good land that the LORD promised
on oath to your forefathers, 19thrusting out all your enemies before you, as the LORD said.

20In the future, when your son asks you, "What is the
meaning of the stipulations, decrees and laws the LORD
our God has commanded you?" 21tell him: "We were
slaves of Pharaoh in Egypt, but the LORD brought us out
of Egypt with a mighty hand. 22Before our eyes the
LORD sent miraculous signs and wonders—great and
terrible—upon Egypt and Pharaoh and his whole household. 23But he brought us out from there to bring us in
and give us the land that he promised on oath to our
forefathers. 24The LORD commanded us to obey all these
decrees and to fear the LORD our God, so that we might
always prosper and be kept alive, as is the case today.
25And if we are careful to obey all this law before the
LORD our God, as he has commanded us, that will be our
righteousness."

---

[a] 4 Or *The LORD our God is one LORD*; or *The LORD is our God, the LORD
is one*; or *The LORD is our God, the LORD alone*

Living Bible

6 "THE LORD your God told me to give you all these commandments which you are to obey in the land you will soon be entering, where you will live. 2The purpose of these laws is to cause you, your sons, and your grandsons to reverence the Lord your God by obeying all of his instructions as long as you live; if you do, you will have long, prosperous years ahead of you. 3Therefore, O Israel, listen closely to each command and be careful to obey it, so that all will go well with you, and so that you will have many children. If you obey these commands you will become a great nation in a glorious land 'flowing with milk and honey,' even as the God of your fathers promised you.

4"O Israel, listen: Jehovah is our God, Jehovah alone. 5You must love him with *all* your heart, soul, and might. 6And you must think constantly about these commandments I am giving you today. 7You must teach them to your children and talk about them when you are at home or out for a walk; at bedtime and the first thing in the morning. 8Tie them on your finger, wear them on your forehead, 9and write them on the doorposts of your house!

10, 11, 12"When the Lord your God has brought you into the land he promised you, Abraham, Isaac, and Jacob, and when he has given you great cities full of good things—cities you didn't build, wells you didn't dig, and vineyards and olive trees you didn't plant—and when you have eaten until you can hold no more, then beware lest you forget the Lord who brought you out of the land of Egypt, the land of slavery. 13When you are full, don't forget to be reverent to him and to serve him and to use *his* name alone to endorse your promises.

14"You must not worship the gods of the neighboring nations, 15for Jehovah your God who lives among you is a jealous God, and his anger may rise quickly against you, and wipe you off the face of the earth. 16You must not provoke him and try his patience as you did when you complained against him at Massah. 17You must actively obey him in everything he commands. 18Only then will you be doing what is right and good in the Lord's eyes. If you obey him, all will go well for you, and you will be able to go in and possess the good land which the Lord promised your ancestors. 19You will also be able to throw out all the enemies living in your land, as the Lord agreed to help you do.

20"In the years to come when your son asks you, 'What is the purpose of these laws which the Lord our God has given us?' 21you must tell him, 'We were Pharaoh's slaves in Egypt, and the Lord brought us out of Egypt with great power 22and mighty miracles—with terrible blows against Egypt and Pharaoh and all his people. We saw it all with our own eyes. 23He brought us out of Egypt so that he could give us this land he had promised to our ancestors. 24And he has commanded us to obey all of these laws and to reverence him so that he can preserve us alive as he has until now. 25For it always goes well with us when we obey all the laws of the Lord our God.'

New Revised Standard

The Great Commandment

6 NOW THIS is the commandment—the statutes and the ordinances—that the LORD your God charged me to teach you to observe in the land that you are about to cross into and occupy, 2 so that you and your children and your children's children may fear the LORD your God all the days of your life, and keep all his decrees and his commandments that I am commanding you, so that your days may be long. 3 Hear therefore, O Israel, and observe them diligently, so that it may go well with you, and so that you may multiply greatly in a land flowing with milk and honey, as the LORD, the God of your ancestors, has promised you.

4 Hear, O Israel: The LORD is our God, the LORD alone.b 5 You shall love the LORD your God with all your heart, and with all your soul, and with all your might. 6 Keep these words that I am commanding you today in your heart. 7 Recite them to your children and talk about them when you are at home and when you are away, when you lie down and when you rise. 8 Bind them as a sign on your hand, fix them as an emblemc on your forehead, 9 and write them on the doorposts of your house and on your gates.

Caution against Disobedience

10 When the LORD your God has brought you into the land that he swore to your ancestors, to Abraham, to Isaac, and to Jacob, to give you—a land with fine, large cities that you did not build, 11 houses filled with all sorts of goods that you did not fill, hewn cisterns that you did not hew, vineyards and olive groves that you did not plant—and when you have eaten your fill, 12 take care that you do not forget the LORD, who brought you out of the land of Egypt, out of the house of slavery. 13 The LORD your God you shall fear; him you shall serve, and by his name alone you shall swear. 14 Do not follow other gods, any of the gods of the peoples who are all around you, 15 because the LORD your God, who is present with you, is a jealous God. The anger of the LORD your God would be kindled against you and he would destroy you from the face of the earth.

16 Do not put the LORD your God to the test, as you tested him at Massah. 17 You must diligently keep the commandments of the LORD your God, and his decrees, and his statutes that he has commanded you. 18 Do what is right and good in the sight of the LORD, so that it may go well with you, and so that you may go in and occupy the good land that the LORD swore to your ancestors to give you, 19 thrusting out all your enemies from before you, as the LORD has promised.

20 When your children ask you in time to come, "What is the meaning of the decrees and the statutes and the ordinances that the LORD our God has commanded you?" 21 then you shall say to your children, "We were Pharaoh's slaves in Egypt, but the LORD brought us out of Egypt with a mighty hand. 22 The LORD displayed before our eyes great and awesome signs and wonders against Egypt, against Pharaoh and all his household. 23 He brought us out from there in order to bring us in, to give us the land that he promised on oath to our ancestors. 24 Then the LORD commanded us to observe all these statutes, to fear the LORD our God, for our lasting good, so as to keep us alive, as is now the case. 25 If we diligently observe this entire commandment before the LORD our God, as he has commanded us, we will be in the right."

b Or The LORD our God is one LORD, or The LORD our God, the LORD is one, or The LORD is our God, the LORD is one   c Or as a frontlet

King James

7 WHEN THE LORD thy God shall bring thee into the land whither thou goest to possess it, and hath cast out many nations before thee, the Hittites, and the Girgashites, and the Amorites, and the Canaanites, and the Perizzites, and the Hivites, and the Jebusites, seven nations greater and mightier than thou;

2And when the LORD thy God shall deliver them before thee; thou shalt smite them, *and* utterly destroy them; thou shalt make no covenant with them, nor show mercy unto them:

3Neither shalt thou make marriages with them; thy daughter thou shalt not give unto his son, nor his daughter shalt thou take unto thy son.

4For they will turn away thy son from following me, that they may serve other gods: so will the anger of the LORD be kindled against you, and destroy thee suddenly.

5But thus shall ye deal with them; ye shall destroy their altars, and break down their images, and cut down their groves, and burn their graven images with fire.

6For thou *art* an holy people unto the LORD thy God: the LORD thy God hath chosen thee to be a special people unto himself, above all people that *are* upon the face of the earth.

7The LORD did not set his love upon you, nor choose you, because ye were more in number than any people; for ye *were* the fewest of all people:

8But because the LORD loved you, and because he would keep the oath which he had sworn unto your fathers, hath the LORD brought you out with a mighty hand, and redeemed you out of the house of bondmen, from the hand of Pharaoh king of Egypt.

9Know therefore that the LORD thy God, he *is* God, the faithful God, which keepeth covenant and mercy with them that love him and keep his commandments to a thousand generations;

10And repayeth them that hate him to their face, to destroy them: he will not be slack to him that hateth him, he will repay him to his face.

11Thou shalt therefore keep the commandments, and the statutes, and the judgments, which I command thee this day, to do them.

12¶ Wherefore it shall come to pass, if ye hearken to these judgments, and keep, and do them, that the LORD thy God shall keep unto thee the covenant and the mercy which he sware unto thy fathers:

13And he will love thee, and bless thee, and multiply thee: he will also bless the fruit of thy womb, and the fruit of thy land, thy corn, and thy wine, and thine oil, the increase of thy kine, and the flocks of thy sheep, in the land which he sware unto thy fathers to give thee.

14Thou shalt be blessed above all people: there shall not be male or female barren among you, or among your cattle.

15And the LORD will take away from thee all sickness, and will put none of the evil diseases of Egypt, which thou knowest, upon thee; but will lay them upon all *them* that hate thee.

16And thou shalt consume all the people which the LORD thy God shall deliver thee; thine eye shall have no pity upon them: neither shalt thou serve their gods; for that *will be* a snare unto thee.

17If thou shalt say in thine heart, These nations *are* more than I; how can I dispossess them?

18Thou shalt not be afraid of them: *but* shalt well remember what the LORD thy God did unto Pharaoh, and unto all Egypt;

19The great temptations which thine eyes saw, and the signs, and the wonders, and the mighty hand, and the stretched out arm, whereby the LORD thy God brought thee out: so shall the LORD thy God do unto all the people of whom thou art afraid.

New International

Driving Out the Nations

7 WHEN THE LORD your God brings you into the land you are entering to possess and drives out before you many nations—the Hittites, Girgashites, Amorites, Canaanites, Perizzites, Hivites and Jebusites, seven nations larger and stronger than you— 2and when the LORD your God has delivered them over to you and you have defeated them, then you must destroy them totally.[a] Make no treaty with them, and show them no mercy. 3Do not intermarry with them. Do not give your daughters to their sons or take their daughters for your sons, 4for they will turn your sons away from following me to serve other gods, and the LORD's anger will burn against you and will quickly destroy you. 5This is what you are to do to them: Break down their altars, smash their sacred stones, cut down their Asherah poles[b] and burn their idols in the fire. 6For you are a people holy to the LORD your God. The LORD your God has chosen you out of all the peoples on the face of the earth to be his people, his treasured possession.

7The LORD did not set his affection on you and choose you because you were more numerous than other peoples, for you were the fewest of all peoples. 8But it was because the LORD loved you and kept the oath he swore to your forefathers that he brought you out with a mighty hand and redeemed you from the land of slavery, from the power of Pharaoh king of Egypt. 9Know therefore that the LORD your God is God; he is the faithful God, keeping his covenant of love to a thousand generations of those who love him and keep his commands. 10But

> those who hate him he will repay to their face
>   by destruction;
>   he will not be slow to repay to their face
>   those who hate him.

11Therefore, take care to follow the commands, decrees and laws I give you today.

12If you pay attention to these laws and are careful to follow them, then the LORD your God will keep his covenant of love with you, as he swore to your forefathers. 13He will love you and bless you and increase your numbers. He will bless the fruit of your womb, the crops of your land—your grain, new wine and oil—the calves of your herds and the lambs of your flocks in the land that he swore to your forefathers to give you. 14You will be blessed more than any other people; none of your men or women will be childless, nor any of your livestock without young. 15The LORD will keep you free from every disease. He will not inflict on you the horrible diseases you knew in Egypt, but he will inflict them on all who hate you. 16You must destroy all the peoples the LORD your God gives over to you. Do not look on them with pity and do not serve their gods, for that will be a snare to you.

17You may say to yourselves, "These nations are stronger than we are. How can we drive them out?" 18But do not be afraid of them; remember well what the LORD your God did to Pharaoh and to all Egypt. 19You saw with your own eyes the great trials, the miraculous signs and wonders, the mighty hand and outstretched arm, with which the LORD your God brought you out. The LORD your God will do the same to all the peoples you now fear. 20Moreover, the LORD your God will send

---

a 2 The Hebrew term refers to the irrevocable giving over of things or persons to the LORD, often by totally destroying them; also in verse 26.   b 5 That is, symbols of the goddess Asherah; here and elsewhere in Deuteronomy

Living Bible

7 "WHEN THE Lord brings you into the Promised Land, as he soon will, he will destroy the following seven nations, all greater and mightier than you are:
The Hittites, the Girgashites,
The Amorites, the Canaanites,
The Perizzites, the Hivites,
The Jebusites.
²"When the Lord your God delivers them over to you to be destroyed, do a complete job of it—don't make any treaties or show them mercy; utterly wipe them out. ³Do not intermarry with them, nor let your sons and daughters marry their sons and daughters. ⁴That would surely result in your young people's beginning to worship their gods. Then the anger of the Lord would be hot against you and he would surely destroy you.

⁵"You must break down the heathen altars and shatter the obelisks and cut up the shameful images and burn the idols.

⁶"For you are a holy people, dedicated to the Lord your God. He has chosen you from all the people on the face of the whole earth to be his own chosen ones. ⁷He didn't choose you and pour out his love upon you because you were a larger nation than any other, for you were the smallest of all! ⁸It was just because he loves you, and because he kept his promise to your ancestors. That is why he brought you out of slavery in Egypt with such amazing power and mighty miracles.

⁹"Understand, therefore, that the Lord your God is the faithful God who for a thousand generations keeps his promises and constantly loves those who love him and who obey his commands. ¹⁰But those who hate him shall be punished publicly and destroyed. He will deal with them personally. ¹¹Therefore, obey all these commandments I am giving you today. ¹²Because of your obedience, the Lord your God will keep his part of the contract which, in his tender love, he made with your fathers. ¹³And he will love you and bless you and make you into a great nation. He will make you fertile and give fertility to your ground and to your animals, so that you will have large crops of grain, grapes, and olives, and great flocks of cattle, sheep, and goats when you arrive in the land he promised your fathers to give you. ¹⁴You will be blessed above all the nations of the earth; not one of you, whether male or female, shall be barren, not even your cattle. ¹⁵And the Lord will take away all your sickness and will not let you suffer any of the diseases of Egypt you remember so well; he will give them all to your enemies!

¹⁶"You must destroy all the nations which the Lord your God delivers into your hands. Have no pity, and do not worship their gods; if you do, it will be a sad day for you. ¹⁷Perhaps you will think to yourself, 'How can we ever conquer these nations that are so much more powerful than we are?' ¹⁸But don't be afraid of them! Just remember what the Lord your God did to Pharoah and to all the land of Egypt. ¹⁹Do you remember the terrors the Lord sent upon them—your parents saw it with their own eyes—and the mighty miracles and wonders, and the power and strength of Almighty God which he used to bring you out of Egypt? Well, the Lord your God will use this same might against the people you

New Revised Standard

A Chosen People

7 WHEN THE Lord your God brings you into the land that you are about to enter and occupy, and he clears away many nations before you—the Hittites, the Girgashites, the Amorites, the Canaanites, the Perizzites, the Hivites, and the Jebusites, seven nations mightier and more numerous than you— ²and when the Lord your God gives them over to you and you defeat them, then you must utterly destroy them. Make no covenant with them and show them no mercy. ³Do not intermarry with them, giving your daughters to their sons or taking their daughters for your sons, ⁴for that would turn away your children from following me, to serve other gods. Then the anger of the Lord would be kindled against you, and he would destroy you quickly. ⁵But this is how you must deal with them: break down their altars, smash their pillars, hew down their sacred poles,ᶜ and burn their idols with fire. ⁶For you are a people holy to the Lord your God; the Lord your God has chosen you out of all the peoples on earth to be his people, his treasured possession.

⁷ It was not because you were more numerous than any other people that the Lord set his heart on you and chose you—for you were the fewest of all peoples. ⁸It was because the Lord loved you and kept the oath that he swore to your ancestors, that the Lord has brought you out with a mighty hand, and redeemed you from the house of slavery, from the hand of Pharaoh king of Egypt. ⁹Know therefore that the Lord your God is God, the faithful God who maintains covenant loyalty with those who love him and keep his commandments, to a thousand generations, ¹⁰and who repays in their own person those who reject him. He does not delay but repays in their own person those who reject him. ¹¹Therefore, observe diligently the commandment—the statutes, and the ordinances—that I am commanding you today.

Blessings for Obedience

12 If you heed these ordinances, by diligently observing them, the Lord your God will maintain with you the covenant loyalty that he swore to your ancestors; ¹³he will love you, bless you, and multiply you; he will bless the fruit of your womb and the fruit of your ground, your grain and your wine and your oil, the increase of your cattle and the issue of your flock, in the land that he swore to your ancestors to give you. ¹⁴You shall be the most blessed of peoples, with neither sterility nor barrenness among you or your livestock. ¹⁵The Lord will turn away from you every illness; all the dread diseases of Egypt that you experienced, he will not inflict on you, but he will lay them on all who hate you. ¹⁶You shall devour all the peoples that the Lord your God is giving over to you, showing them no pity; you shall not serve their gods, for that would be a snare to you.

17 If you say to yourself, "These nations are more numerous than I; how can I dispossess them?" ¹⁸do not be afraid of them. Just remember what the Lord your God did to Pharaoh and to all Egypt, ¹⁹the great trials that your eyes saw, the signs and wonders, the mighty hand and the outstretched arm by which the Lord your God brought you out. The Lord your God will do the same to all the peoples of whom you are afraid. ²⁰More-

ᶜ Heb *Asherim*

King James

20Moreover the LORD thy God will send the hornet among them, until they that are left, and hide themselves from thee, be destroyed.

21Thou shalt not be affrighted at them: for the LORD thy God *is* among you, a mighty God and terrible.

22And the LORD thy God will put out those nations before thee by little and little: thou mayest not consume them at once, lest the beasts of the field increase upon thee.

23But the LORD thy God shall deliver them unto thee, and shall destroy them with a mighty destruction, until they be destroyed.

24And he shall deliver their kings into thine hand, and thou shalt destroy their name from under heaven: there shall no man be able to stand before thee, until thou have destroyed them.

25The graven images of their gods shall ye burn with fire: thou shalt not desire the silver or gold *that is* on them, nor take *it* unto thee, lest thou be snared therein: for it *is* an abomination to the LORD thy God.

26Neither shalt thou bring an abomination into thine house, lest thou be a cursed thing like it: *but* thou shalt utterly detest it, and thou shalt utterly abhor it; for it *is* a cursed thing.

8 ALL THE commandments which I command thee this day shall ye observe to do, that ye may live, and multiply, and go in and possess the land which the LORD sware unto your fathers.

2And thou shalt remember all the way which the LORD thy God led thee these forty years in the wilderness, to humble thee, *and* to prove thee, to know what *was* in thine heart, whether thou wouldest keep his commandments, or no.

3And he humbled thee, and suffered thee to hunger, and fed thee with manna, which thou knewest not, neither did thy fathers know; that he might make thee know that man doth not live by bread only, but by every *word* that proceedeth out of the mouth of the LORD doth man live.

4Thy raiment waxed not old upon thee, neither did thy foot swell, these forty years.

5Thou shalt also consider in thine heart, that, as a man chasteneth his son, *so* the LORD thy God chasteneth thee.

6Therefore thou shalt keep the commandments of the LORD thy God, to walk in his ways, and to fear him.

7For the LORD thy God bringeth thee into a good land, a land of brooks of water, of fountains and depths that spring out of valleys and hills;

8A land of wheat, and barley, and vines, and fig trees, and pomegranates; a land of oil olive, and honey;

9A land wherein thou shalt eat bread without scarceness, thou shalt not lack any *thing* in it; a land whose stones *are* iron, and out of whose hills thou mayest dig brass.

10When thou hast eaten and art full, then thou shalt bless the LORD thy God for the good land which he hath given thee.

11Beware that thou forget not the LORD thy God, in not keeping his commandments, and his judgments, and his statutes, which I command thee this day:

12Lest *when* thou hast eaten and art full, and hast built goodly houses, and dwelt *therein;*

13And *when* thy herds and thy flocks multiply, and thy silver and thy gold is multiplied, and all that thou hast is multiplied;

14Then thine heart be lifted up, and thou forget the LORD thy God, which brought thee forth out of the land of Egypt, from the house of bondage;

New International

the hornet among them until even the survivors who hide from you have perished. 21Do not be terrified by them, for the LORD your God, who is among you, is a great and awesome God. 22The LORD your God will drive out those nations before you, little by little. You will not be allowed to eliminate them all at once, or the wild animals will multiply around you. 23But the LORD your God will deliver them over to you, throwing them into great confusion until they are destroyed. 24He will give their kings into your hand, and you will wipe out their names from under heaven. No one will be able to stand up against you; you will destroy them. 25The images of their gods you are to burn in the fire. Do not covet the silver and gold on them, and do not take it for yourselves, or you will be ensnared by it, for it is detestable to the LORD your God. 26Do not bring a detestable thing into your house or you, like it, will be set apart for destruction. Utterly abhor and detest it, for it is set apart for destruction.

Do Not Forget the LORD

8 BE CAREFUL to follow every command I am giving you today, so that you may live and increase and may enter and possess the land that the LORD promised on oath to your forefathers. 2Remember how the LORD your God led you all the way in the desert these forty years, to humble you and to test you in order to know what was in your heart, whether or not you would keep his commands. 3He humbled you, causing you to hunger and then feeding you with manna, which neither you nor your fathers had known, to teach you that man does not live on bread alone but on every word that comes from the mouth of the LORD. 4Your clothes did not wear out and your feet did not swell during these forty years. 5Know then in your heart that as a man disciplines his son, so the LORD your God disciplines you.

6Observe the commands of the LORD your God, walking in his ways and revering him. 7For the LORD your God is bringing you into a good land—a land with streams and pools of water, with springs flowing in the valleys and hills; 8a land with wheat and barley, vines and fig trees, pomegranates, olive oil and honey; 9a land where bread will not be scarce and you will lack nothing; a land where the rocks are iron and you can dig copper out of the hills.

10When you have eaten and are satisfied, praise the LORD your God for the good land he has given you. 11Be careful that you do not forget the LORD your God, failing to observe his commands, his laws and his decrees that I am giving you this day. 12Otherwise, when you eat and are satisfied, when you build fine houses and settle down, 13and when your herds and flocks grow large and your silver and gold increase and all you have is multiplied, 14then your heart will become proud and you will forget the LORD your God, who brought you out of Egypt, out of the land of slavery. 15He led you through

Living Bible

fear. 20Moreover, the Lord your God will send hornets to drive out those who hide from you!

21"No, do not be afraid of those nations, for the Lord your God is among you, and he is a great and awesome God. 22He will cast them out a little at a time; he will not do it all at once, for if he did, the wild animals would multiply too quickly and become dangerous. 23He will do it gradually, and you will move in against those nations and destroy them. 24He will deliver their kings into your hands, and you will erase their names from the face of the earth. No one will be able to stand against you.

25"Burn their idols and do not touch the silver or gold they are made of. Do not take it or it will be a snare to you, for it is horrible to the Lord your God. 26Do not bring an idol into your home and worship it, for then your doom is sealed. Utterly detest it, for it is a cursed thing.

8 "YOU MUST obey all the commandments I give you today. If you do, you will not only live, you will multiply and will go in and take over the land promised to your fathers by the Lord. 2Do you remember how the Lord led you through the wilderness for all those forty years, humbling you and testing you to find out how you would respond, and whether or not you would really obey him? 3Yes, he humbled you by letting you go hungry and then feeding you with manna, a food previously unknown to both you and your ancestors. He did it to help you realize that food isn't everything, and that real life comes by obeying every command of God. 4For all these forty years your clothes haven't grown old, and your feet haven't been blistered or swollen. 5So you should realize that, as a man punishes his son, the Lord punishes you to help you.

6"Obey the laws of the Lord your God. Walk in his ways and fear him. 7For the Lord your God is bringing you into a good land of brooks, pools, gushing springs, valleys, and hills; 8it is a land of wheat and barley, of grape vines, fig trees, pomegranates, olives, and honey; 9it is a land where food is plentiful, and nothing is lacking; it is a land where iron is as common as stone, and copper is abundant in the hills. 10When you have eaten your fill, bless the Lord your God for the good land he has given you.

11"But that is the time to be careful! Beware that in your plentya you don't forget the Lord your God and begin to disobey him. 12, 13For when you have become full and prosperous and have built fine homes to live in, and when your flocks and herds have become very large, and your silver and gold have multiplied, 14that is the time to watch out that you don't become proud, and forget the Lord your God who brought you out of your slavery in the land of Egypt. 15Beware that you don't

New Revised Standard

over, the LORD your God will send the pestilenceb against them, until even the survivors and the fugitives are destroyed. 21Have no dread of them, for the LORD your God, who is present with you, is a great and awesome God. 22The LORD your God will clear away these nations before you little by little; you will not be able to make a quick end of them, otherwise the wild animals would become too numerous for you. 23But the LORD your God will give them over to you, and throw them into great panic, until they are destroyed. 24He will hand their kings over to you and you shall blot out their name from under heaven; no one will be able to stand against you, until you have destroyed them. 25The images of their gods you shall burn with fire. Do not covet the silver or the gold that is on them and take it for yourself, because you could be ensnared by it; for it is abhorrent to the LORD your God. 26Do not bring an abhorrent thing into your house, or you will be set apart for destruction like it. You must utterly detest and abhor it, for it is set apart for destruction.

A Warning Not to Forget God in Prosperity

8 THIS ENTIRE commandment that I command you today you must diligently observe, so that you may live and increase, and go in and occupy the land that the LORD promised on oath to your ancestors. 2Remember the long way that the LORD your God has led you these forty years in the wilderness, in order to humble you, testing you to know what was in your heart, whether or not you would keep his commandments. 3He humbled you by letting you hunger, then by feeding you with manna, with which neither you nor your ancestors were acquainted, in order to make you understand that one does not live by bread alone, but by every word that comes from the mouth of the LORD.c 4The clothes on your back did not wear out and your feet did not swell these forty years. 5Know then in your heart that as a parent disciplines a child so the LORD your God disciplines you. 6Therefore keep the commandments of the LORD your God, by walking in his ways and by fearing him. 7For the LORD your God is bringing you into a good land, a land with flowing streams, with springs and underground waters welling up in valleys and hills, 8a land of wheat and barley, of vines and fig trees and pomegranates, a land of olive trees and honey, 9a land where you may eat bread without scarcity, where you will lack nothing, a land whose stones are iron and from whose hills you may mine copper. 10You shall eat your fill and bless the LORD your God for the good land that he has given you.

11 Take care that you do not forget the LORD your God, by failing to keep his commandments, his ordinances, and his statutes, which I am commanding you today. 12When you have eaten your fill and have built fine houses and live in them, 13and when your herds and flocks have multiplied, and your silver and gold is multiplied, and all that you have is multiplied, 14then do not exalt yourself, forgetting the LORD your God, who brought you out of the land of Egypt, out of the house of slavery, 15who led you through the great and terrible

---

a 8:11 Beware that in your plenty, implied.

b Or hornets: Meaning of Heb uncertain   c Or by anything that the LORD decrees

King James

¹⁵Who led thee through that great and terrible wilderness, *wherein were* fiery serpents, and scorpions, and drought, where *there was* no water; who brought thee forth water out of the rock of flint;

¹⁶Who fed thee in the wilderness with manna, which thy fathers knew not, that he might humble thee, and that he might prove thee, to do thee good at thy latter end;

¹⁷And thou say in thine heart, My power and the might of *mine* hand hath gotten me this wealth.

¹⁸But thou shalt remember the LORD thy God: for *it is* he that giveth thee power to get wealth, that he may establish his covenant which he sware unto thy fathers, as *it is* this day.

¹⁹And it shall be, if thou do at all forget the LORD thy God, and walk after other gods, and serve them, and worship them, I testify against you this day that ye shall surely perish.

²⁰As the nations which the LORD destroyeth before your face, so shall ye perish; because ye would not be obedient unto the voice of the LORD your God.

9 HEAR, O Israel: Thou *art* to pass over Jordan this day, to go in to possess nations greater and mightier than thyself, cities great and fenced up to heaven,

²A people great and tall, the children of the Anakims, whom thou knowest, and *of whom* thou hast heard *say*, Who can stand before the children of Anak!

³Understand therefore this day, that the LORD thy God *is* he which goeth over before thee; *as* a consuming fire he shall destroy them, and he shall bring them down before thy face: so shalt thou drive them out, and destroy them quickly, as the LORD hath said unto thee.

⁴Speak not thou in thine heart, after that the LORD thy God hath cast them out from before thee, saying, For my righteousness the LORD hath brought me in to possess this land: but for the wickedness of these nations the LORD doth drive them out from before thee.

⁵Not for thy righteousness, or for the uprightness of thine heart, dost thou go to possess their land: but for the wickedness of these nations the LORD thy God doth drive them out from before thee, and that he may perform the word which the LORD sware unto thy fathers, Abraham, Isaac, and Jacob.

⁶Understand therefore, that the LORD thy God giveth thee not this good land to possess it for thy righteousness; for thou *art* a stiffnecked people.

⁷¶ Remember, *and* forget not, how thou provokedst the LORD thy God to wrath in the wilderness: from the day that thou didst depart out of the land of Egypt, until ye came unto this place, ye have been rebellious against the LORD.

⁸Also in Horeb ye provoked the LORD to wrath, so that the LORD was angry with you to have destroyed you.

⁹When I was gone up into the mount to receive the tables of stone, *even* the tables of the covenant which the LORD made with you, then I abode in the mount forty days and forty nights, I neither did eat bread nor drink water:

¹⁰And the LORD delivered unto me two tables of stone written with the finger of God; and on them *was* written according to all the words, which the LORD spake with you in the mount out of the midst of the fire in the day of the assembly.

¹¹And it came to pass at the end of forty days and forty nights, *that* the LORD gave me the two tables of stone, *even* the tables of the covenant.

¹²And the LORD said unto me, Arise, get thee down quickly from hence; for thy people which thou hast brought forth out of Egypt have corrupted *themselves;* they are quickly turned aside out of the way which I commanded them; they have made them a molten image.

New International

the vast and dreadful desert, that thirsty and waterless land, with its venomous snakes and scorpions. He brought you water out of hard rock. ¹⁶He gave you manna to eat in the desert, something your fathers had never known, to humble and to test you so that in the end it might go well with you. ¹⁷You may say to yourself, "My power and the strength of my hands have produced this wealth for me." ¹⁸But remember the LORD your God, for it is he who gives you the ability to produce wealth, and so confirms his covenant, which he swore to your forefathers, as it is today.

¹⁹If you ever forget the LORD your God and follow other gods and worship and bow down to them, I testify against you today that you will surely be destroyed. ²⁰Like the nations the LORD destroyed before you, so you will be destroyed for not obeying the LORD your God.

Not Because of Israel's Righteousness

9 HEAR, O Israel. You are now about to cross the Jordan to go in and dispossess nations greater and stronger than you, with large cities that have walls up to the sky. ²The people are strong and tall—Anakites! You know about them and have heard it said: "Who can stand up against the Anakites?" ³But be assured today that the LORD your God is the one who goes across ahead of you like a devouring fire. He will destroy them; he will subdue them before you. And you will drive them out and annihilate them quickly, as the LORD has promised you.

⁴After the LORD your God has driven them out before you, do not say to yourself, "The LORD has brought me here to take possession of this land because of my righteousness." No, it is on account of the wickedness of these nations that the LORD is going to drive them out before you. ⁵It is not because of your righteousness or your integrity that you are going in to take possession of their land; but on account of the wickedness of these nations, the LORD your God will drive them out before you, to accomplish what he swore to your fathers, to Abraham, Isaac and Jacob. ⁶Understand, then, that it is not because of your righteousness that the LORD your God is giving you this good land to possess, for you are a stiff-necked people.

The Golden Calf

⁷Remember this and never forget how you provoked the LORD your God to anger in the desert. From the day you left Egypt until you arrived here, you have been rebellious against the LORD. ⁸At Horeb you aroused the LORD's wrath so that he was angry enough to destroy you. ⁹When I went up on the mountain to receive the tablets of stone, the tablets of the covenant that the LORD had made with you, I stayed on the mountain forty days and forty nights; I ate no bread and drank no water. ¹⁰The LORD gave me two stone tablets inscribed by the finger of God. On them were all the commandments the LORD proclaimed to you on the mountain out of the fire, on the day of the assembly.

¹¹At the end of the forty days and forty nights, the LORD gave me the two stone tablets, the tablets of the covenant. ¹²Then the LORD told me, "Go down from here at once, because your people whom you brought out of Egypt have become corrupt. They have turned away quickly from what I commanded them and have made a cast idol for themselves."

Living Bible

forget the God who led you through the great and terrible wilderness with the dangerous snakes and scorpions, where it was so hot and dry. He gave you water from the rock! 16He fed you with manna in the wilderness (it was a kind of bread unknown before) so that you would become humble and so that your trust in him would grow, and he could do you good. 17He did it so that you would never feel that it was your own power and might that made you wealthy. 18Always remember that it is the Lord your God who gives you power to become rich, and he does it to fulfill his promise to your ancestors.

19"But if you forget about the Lord your God and worship other gods instead, and follow evil ways, you shall certainly perish, 20just as the Lord has caused other nations in the past to perish. That will be your fate, too, if you don't obey the Lord your God.

9 "O ISRAEL, listen! Today you are to cross the Jordan River and begin to dispossess the nations on the other side. Those nations are much greater and more powerful than you are! They live in high walled cities. Among them are the famed Anak giants, against whom none can stand! 3But the Lord your God will go before you as a devouring fire to destroy them, so that you will quickly conquer them and drive them out.

4"Then, when the Lord has done this for you, don't say to yourselves, 'The Lord has helped us because we are so good!' No, it is because of the wickedness of the other nations that he is doing it. 5It is not at all because you are such fine, upright people that the Lord will drive them out from before you! I say it again, it is only because of the wickedness of the other nations, and because of his promises to your ancestors, Abraham, Isaac, and Jacob, that he will do it. 6I say it yet again: *Jehovah your God is not giving you this good land because you are good, for you are not*—you are a wicked, stubborn people.

7"Don't you remember (oh, never forget it!) how continually angry you made the Lord your God out in the wilderness, from the day you left Egypt until now? For all this time you have constantly rebelled against him.

8"Don't you remember how angry you made him at Mount Horeb? He was ready to destroy you. 9I was on the mountain at the time, receiving the contract which Jehovah had made with you—the stone tablets with the laws inscribed upon them. I was there for forty days and forty nights, and all that time I ate nothing. I didn't even take a drink of water. 10, 11At the end of those forty days and nights the Lord gave me the contract, the tablets on which he had written the commandments he had spoken from the fire-covered mountain while the people had watched below. 12He told me to go down quickly because the people I had led out of Egypt had defiled themselves, quickly turning away from the laws of God, and had made an idol from molten metal.

New Revised Standard

wilderness, an arid wasteland with poisonousa snakes and scorpions. He made water flow for you from flint rock, 16and fed you in the wilderness with manna that your ancestors did not know, to humble you and to test you, and in the end to do you good. 17Do not say to yourself, "My power and the might of my own hand have gotten me this wealth." 18But remember the LORD your God, for it is he who gives you power to get wealth, so that he may confirm his covenant that he swore to your ancestors, as he is doing today. 19If you do forget the LORD your God and follow other gods to serve and worship them, I solemnly warn you today that you shall surely perish. 20Like the nations that the LORD is destroying before you, so shall you perish, because you would not obey the voice of the LORD your God.

The Consequences of Rebelling against God

9 HEAR, O Israel! You are about to cross the Jordan today, to go in and dispossess nations larger and mightier than you, great cities, fortified to the heavens, 2a strong and tall people, the offspring of the Anakim, whom you know. You have heard it said of them, "Who can stand up to the Anakim?" 3Know then today that the LORD your God is the one who crosses over before you as a devouring fire; he will defeat them and subdue them before you, so that you may dispossess and destroy them quickly, as the LORD has promised you.

4 When the LORD your God thrusts them out before you, do not say to yourself, "It is because of my righteousness that the LORD has brought me in to occupy this land"; it is rather because of the wickedness of these nations that the LORD is dispossessing them before you. 5It is not because of your righteousness or the uprightness of your heart that you are going in to occupy their land; but because of the wickedness of these nations the LORD your God is dispossessing them before you, in order to fulfill the promise that the LORD made on oath to your ancestors, to Abraham, to Isaac, and to Jacob.

6 Know, then, that the LORD your God is not giving you this good land to occupy because of your righteousness; for you are a stubborn people. 7Remember and do not forget how you provoked the LORD your God to wrath in the wilderness; you have been rebellious against the LORD from the day you came out of the land of Egypt until you came to this place.

8 Even at Horeb you provoked the LORD to wrath, and the LORD was so angry with you that he was ready to destroy you. 9When I went up the mountain to receive the stone tablets, the tablets of the covenant that the LORD made with you, I remained on the mountain forty days and forty nights; I neither ate bread nor drank water. 10And the LORD gave me the two stone tablets written with the finger of God; on them were all the words that the LORD had spoken to you at the mountain out of the fire on the day of the assembly. 11At the end of forty days and forty nights the LORD gave me the two stone tablets, the tablets of the covenant. 12Then the LORD said to me, "Get up, go down quickly from here, for your people whom you have brought from Egypt have acted corruptly. They have been quick to turn from the way that I commanded them; they have cast an image for themselves." 13Furthermore the LORD said to me, "I

---

a Or *fiery*; Heb *seraph*

King James

13Furthermore the LORD spake unto me, saying, I have seen this people, and, behold, it *is* a stiffnecked people:

14Let me alone, that I may destroy them, and blot out their name from under heaven: and I will make of thee a nation mightier and greater than they.

15So I turned and came down from the mount, and the mount burned with fire: and the two tables of the covenant *were* in my two hands.

16And I looked, and, behold, ye had sinned against the LORD your God, *and* had made you a molten calf: ye had turned aside quickly out of the way which the LORD had commanded you.

17And I took the two tables, and cast them out of my two hands, and brake them before your eyes.

18And I fell down before the LORD, as at the first, forty days and forty nights: I did neither eat bread, nor drink water, because of all your sins which ye sinned, in doing wickedly in the sight of the LORD, to provoke him to anger.

19For I was afraid of the anger and hot displeasure, wherewith the LORD was wroth against you to destroy you. But the LORD hearkened unto me at that time also.

20And the LORD was very angry with Aaron to have destroyed him: and I prayed for Aaron also the same time.

21And I took your sin, the calf which ye had made, and burnt it with fire, and stamped it, *and* ground *it* very small, *even* until it was as small as dust: and I cast the dust thereof into the brook that descended out of the mount.

22And at Taberah, and at Massah, and at Kibroth-hattaavah, ye provoked the LORD to wrath.

23Likewise when the LORD sent you from Kadeshbarnea, saying, Go up and possess the land which I have given you; then ye rebelled against the commandment of the LORD your God, and ye believed him not, nor hearkened to his voice.

24Ye have been rebellious against the LORD from the day that I knew you.

25Thus I fell down before the LORD forty days and forty nights, as I fell down *at the first;* because the LORD had said he would destroy you.

26I prayed therefore unto the LORD, and said, O Lord GOD, destroy not thy people and thine inheritance, which thou hast redeemed through thy greatness, which thou hast brought forth out of Egypt with a mighty hand.

27Remember thy servants, Abraham, Isaac, and Jacob; look not unto the stubbornness of this people, nor to their wickedness, nor to their sin:

28Lest the land whence thou broughtest us out say, Because the LORD was not able to bring them into the land which he promised them, and because he hated them, he hath brought them out to slay them in the wilderness.

29Yet they *are* thy people and thine inheritance, which thou broughtest out by thy mighty power and by thy stretched out arm.

10 AT THAT time the LORD said unto me, Hew thee two tables of stone like unto the first, and come up unto me into the mount, and make thee an ark of wood.

2And I will write on the tables the words that were in the first tables which thou brakest, and thou shalt put them in the ark.

3And I made an ark of shittim wood, and hewed two tables of stone like unto the first, and went up into the mount, having the two tables in mine hand.

New International

13And the LORD said to me, "I have seen this people, and they are a stiff-necked people indeed! 14Let me alone, so that I may destroy them and blot out their name from under heaven. And I will make you into a nation stronger and more numerous than they."

15So I turned and went down from the mountain while it was ablaze with fire. And the two tablets of the covenant were in my hands.a 16When I looked, I saw that you had sinned against the LORD your God; you had made for yourselves an idol cast in the shape of a calf. You had turned aside quickly from the way that the LORD had commanded you. 17So I took the two tablets and threw them out of my hands, breaking them to pieces before your eyes.

18Then once again I fell prostrate before the LORD for forty days and forty nights; I ate no bread and drank no water, because of all the sin you had committed, doing what was evil in the LORD's sight and so provoking him to anger. 19I feared the anger and wrath of the LORD, for he was angry enough with you to destroy you. But again the LORD listened to me. 20And the LORD was angry enough with Aaron to destroy him, but at that time I prayed for Aaron too. 21Also I took that sinful thing of yours, the calf you had made, and burned it in the fire. Then I crushed it and ground it to powder as fine as dust and threw the dust into a stream that flowed down the mountain.

22You also made the LORD angry at Taberah, at Massah and at Kibroth Hattaavah.

23And when the LORD sent you out from Kadesh Barnea, he said, "Go up and take possession of the land I have given you." But you rebelled against the command of the LORD your God. You did not trust him or obey him. 24You have been rebellious against the LORD ever since I have known you.

25I lay prostrate before the LORD those forty days and forty nights because the LORD had said he would destroy you. 26I prayed to the LORD and said, "O Sovereign LORD, do not destroy your people, your own inheritance that you redeemed by your great power and brought out of Egypt with a mighty hand. 27Remember your servants Abraham, Isaac and Jacob. Overlook the stubbornness of this people, their wickedness and their sin. 28Otherwise, the country from which you brought us will say, 'Because the LORD was not able to take them into the land he had promised them, and because he hated them, he brought them out to put them to death in the desert.' 29But they are your people, your inheritance that you brought out by your great power and your outstretched arm."

Tablets Like the First Ones

10 AT THAT time the LORD said to me, "Chisel out two stone tablets like the first ones and come up to me on the mountain. Also make a wooden chest.b 2I will write on the tablets the words that were on the first tablets, which you broke. Then you are to put them in the chest."

3So I made the ark out of acacia wood and chiseled out two stone tablets like the first ones, and I went up on the mountain with the two tablets in my hands. 4The

---

a *15* Or *And I had the two tablets of the covenant with me, one in each hand*
b *1* That is, an ark

Living Bible

13, 14" 'Let me alone that I may destroy this evil, stubborn people!' the Lord told me, 'and I will blot out their name from under heaven, and I will make a mighty nation of you, mightier and greater than they are.'

15"I came down from the burning mountain, holding in my hands the two tablets inscribed with the laws of God. 16There below me I could see the calf you had made in your terrible sin against the Lord your God. How quickly you turned away from him! 17I lifted the tablets high above my head and dashed them to the ground! I smashed them before your eyes! 18Then, for another forty days and nights I lay before the Lord, neither eating bread nor drinking water, for you had done what the Lord hated most, thus provoking him to great anger. 19How I feared for you—for the Lord was ready to destroy you. But that time, too, he listened to me. 20Aaron was in great danger because the Lord was so angry with him; but I prayed, and the Lord spared him. 21I took your sin—the calf you had made—and burned it and ground it into fine dust, and threw it into the stream that cascaded out of the mountain.

22"Again at Taberah and once again at Massah you angered the Lord, and yet again at Kibroth-hattaavah. 23At Kadesh-barnea, when the Lord told you to enter the land he had given you, you rebelled and wouldn't believe that he would help you; you refused to obey him. 24Yes, you have been rebellious against the Lord from the first day I knew you. 25That is why I fell down before him for forty days and nights when the Lord was ready to destroy you.

26"I prayed to him, 'O Lord God, don't destroy your own people. They are your inheritance saved from Egypt by your mighty power and glorious strength. 27Don't notice the rebellion and stubbornness of these people, but remember instead your promises to your servants Abraham, Isaac, and Jacob. Oh, please overlook the awful wickedness and sin of these people. 28For if you destroy them the Egyptians will say, "It is because the Lord wasn't able to bring them to the land he promised them," or "He destroyed them because he hated them: he brought them into the wilderness to slay them." 29They are your people and your inheritance which you brought from Egypt by your great power and your mighty arm.'

10 "AT THAT time the Lord told me to cut two more stone tablets like the first ones, and to make a wooden Ark to keep them in, and to return to God on the mountain. 2He said he would rewrite on the tablets the same commandments that were on the tablets I had smashed, and that I should place them in the Ark. 3So I made an Ark of acacia wood and hewed out two stone tablets like the first two, and took the tablets up on the mountain to God. 4He again wrote the Ten Com-

New Revised Standard

have seen that this people is indeed a stubborn people. 14Let me alone that I may destroy them and blot out their name from under heaven; and I will make of you a nation mightier and more numerous than they."

15 So I turned and went down from the mountain, while the mountain was ablaze; the two tablets of the covenant were in my two hands. 16Then I saw that you had indeed sinned against the LORD your God, by casting for yourselves an image of a calf; you had been quick to turn from the way that the LORD had commanded you. 17So I took hold of the two tablets and flung them from my two hands, smashing them before your eyes. 18Then I lay prostrate before the LORD as before, forty days and forty nights; I neither ate bread nor drank water, because of all the sin you had committed, provoking the LORD by doing what was evil in his sight. 19For I was afraid that the anger that the LORD bore against you was so fierce that he would destroy you. But the LORD listened to me that time also. 20The LORD was so angry with Aaron that he was ready to destroy him, but I interceded also on behalf of Aaron at that same time. 21Then I took the sinful thing you had made, the calf, and burned it with fire and crushed it, grinding it thoroughly, until it was reduced to dust; and I threw the dust of it into the stream that runs down the mountain.

22 At Taberah also, and at Massah, and at Kibroth-hattaavah, you provoked the LORD to wrath. 23And when the LORD sent you from Kadesh-barnea, saying, "Go up and occupy the land that I have given you," you rebelled against the command of the LORD your God, neither trusting him nor obeying him. 24You have been rebellious against the LORD as long as he hasc known you.

25 Throughout the forty days and forty nights that I lay prostrate before the LORD when the LORD intended to destroy you, 26I prayed to the LORD and said, "Lord GOD, do not destroy the people who are your very own possession, whom you redeemed in your greatness, whom you brought out of Egypt with a mighty hand. 27Remember your servants, Abraham, Isaac, and Jacob; pay no attention to the stubbornness of this people, their wickedness and their sin, 28otherwise the land from which you have brought us might say, 'Because the LORD was not able to bring them into the land that he promised them, and because he hated them, he has brought them out to let them die in the wilderness.' 29For they are the people of your very own possession, whom you brought out by your great power and by your outstretched arm."

The Second Pair of Tablets

10 AT THAT time the LORD said to me, "Carve out two tablets of stone like the former ones, and come up to me on the mountain, and make an ark of wood. 2I will write on the tablets the words that were on the former tablets, which you smashed, and you shall put them in the ark." 3So I made an ark of acacia wood, cut two tablets of stone like the former ones, and went up the mountain with the two tablets in my hand. 4Then

c Sam Gk: MT I have

King James

4And he wrote on the tables, according to the first writing, the ten commandments, which the LORD spake unto you in the mount out of the midst of the fire in the day of the assembly: and the LORD gave them unto me.

5And I turned myself and came down from the mount, and put the tables in the ark which I had made; and there they be, as the LORD commanded me.

6¶ And the children of Israel took their journey from Beeroth of the children of Jaakan to Mosera: there Aaron died, and there he was buried; and Eleazar his son ministered in the priest's office in his stead.

7From thence they journeyed unto Gudgodah; and from Gudgodah to Jotbath, a land of rivers of waters.

8¶ At that time the LORD separated the tribe of Levi, to bear the ark of the covenant of the LORD, to stand before the LORD to minister unto him, and to bless in his name, unto this day.

9Wherefore Levi hath no part nor inheritance with his brethren; the LORD is his inheritance, according as the LORD thy God promised him.

10And I stayed in the mount, according to the first time, forty days and forty nights; and the LORD hearkened unto me at that time also, and the LORD would not destroy thee.

11And the LORD said unto me, Arise, take thy journey before the people, that they may go in and possess the land, which I sware unto their fathers to give unto them.

12¶ And now, Israel, what doth the LORD thy God require of thee, but to fear the LORD thy God, to walk in all his ways, and to love him, and to serve the LORD thy God with all thy heart and with all thy soul,

13To keep the commandments of the LORD, and his statutes, which I command thee this day for thy good?

14Behold, the heaven and the heaven of heavens is the LORD's thy God, the earth also, with all that therein is.

15Only the LORD had a delight in thy fathers to love them, and he chose their seed after them, even you above all people, as it is this day.

16Circumcise therefore the foreskin of your heart, and be no more stiffnecked.

17For the LORD your God is God of gods, and Lord of lords, a great God, a mighty, and a terrible, which regardeth not persons, nor taketh reward:

18He doth execute the judgment of the fatherless and widow, and loveth the stranger, in giving him food and raiment.

19Love ye therefore the stranger: for ye were strangers in the land of Egypt.

20Thou shalt fear the LORD thy God; him shalt thou serve, and to him shalt thou cleave, and swear by his name.

21He is thy praise, and he is thy God, that hath done for thee these great and terrible things, which thine eyes have seen.

22Thy fathers went down into Egypt with threescore and ten persons; and now the LORD thy God hath made thee as the stars of heaven for multitude.

11 THEREFORE THOU shalt love the LORD thy God, and keep his charge, and his statutes, and his judgments, and his commandments, always.

2And know ye this day: for I speak not with your children which have not known, and which have not seen the chastisement of the LORD your God, his greatness, his mighty hand, and his stretched out arm,

3And his miracles, and his acts, which he did in the midst of Egypt unto Pharaoh the king of Egypt, and unto all his land;

New International

LORD wrote on these tablets what he had written before, the Ten Commandments he had proclaimed to you on the mountain, out of the fire, on the day of the assembly. And the LORD gave them to me. 5Then I came back down the mountain and put the tablets in the ark I had made, as the LORD commanded me, and they are there now.

6(The Israelites traveled from the wells of the Jaakanites to Moserah. There Aaron died and was buried, and Eleazar his son succeeded him as priest. 7From there they traveled to Gudgodah and on to Jotbathah, a land with streams of water. 8At that time the LORD set apart the tribe of Levi to carry the ark of the covenant of the LORD, to stand before the LORD to minister and to pronounce blessings in his name, as they still do today. 9That is why the Levites have no share or inheritance among their brothers; the LORD is their inheritance, as the LORD your God told them.)

10Now I had stayed on the mountain forty days and nights, as I did the first time, and the LORD listened to me at this time also. It was not his will to destroy you. 11"Go," the LORD said to me, "and lead the people on their way, so that they may enter and possess the land that I swore to their fathers to give them."

Fear the LORD

12And now, O Israel, what does the LORD your God ask of you but to fear the LORD your God, to walk in all his ways, to love him, to serve the LORD your God with all your heart and with all your soul, 13and to observe the LORD's commands and decrees that I am giving you today for your own good?

14To the LORD your God belong the heavens, even the highest heavens, the earth and everything in it. 15Yet the LORD set his affection on your forefathers and loved them, and he chose you, their descendants, above all the nations, as it is today. 16Circumcise your hearts, therefore, and do not be stiff-necked any longer. 17For the LORD your God is God of gods and Lord of lords, the great God, mighty and awesome, who shows no partiality and accepts no bribes. 18He defends the cause of the fatherless and the widow, and loves the alien, giving him food and clothing. 19And you are to love those who are aliens, for you yourselves were aliens in Egypt. 20Fear the LORD your God and serve him. Hold fast to him and take your oaths in his name. 21He is your praise; he is your God, who performed for you those great and awesome wonders you saw with your own eyes. 22Your forefathers who went down into Egypt were seventy in all, and now the LORD your God has made you as numerous as the stars in the sky.

Love and Obey the LORD

11 LOVE THE LORD your God and keep his requirements, his decrees, his laws and his commands always. 2Remember today that your children were not the ones who saw and experienced the discipline of the LORD your God: his majesty, his mighty hand, his outstretched arm; 3the signs he performed and the things he did in the heart of Egypt, both to Pharaoh king of Egypt and to his whole country; 4what he did to

Living Bible

mandments on them and gave them to me. (They were the same commandments he had given you from the heart of the fire on the mountain as you all watched below.) 5Then I came down and placed the tablets in the Ark I had made, where they are to this day, just as the Lord commanded me.

6"The people of Israel then journeyed from Be-eroth of Bene-jaakan to Moserah, where Aaron died and was buried. His son Eleazar became the next priest. 7"Then they journeyed to Gudgodah, and from there to Jotbathah, a land of brooks and water. 8It was there that Jehovah set apart the tribe of Levi to carry the Ark containing the Ten Commandments of Jehovah, and to stand before the Lord and to do his work and to bless his name, just as is done today. 9(That is why the tribe of Levi does not have a portion of land reserved for it in the Promised Land, as their brother tribes do; for as the Lord told them, he himself is their inheritance.)

10"As I said before, I stayed on the mountain before the Lord for forty days and nights the second time, just as I had the first, and the Lord again yielded to my pleas and didn't destroy you. 11"But he said to me, 'Arise and lead the people to the land I promised their fathers. It is time to go in and possess it.'

12, 13"And now, Israel, what does the Lord your God require of you except to listen carefully to all he says to you, and to obey for your own good the commandments I am giving you today, and to love him, and to worship him with all your hearts and souls? 14Earth and highest heaven belong to the Lord your God. 15And yet he rejoiced in your fathers and loved them so much that he chose you, their children, to be above every other nation, as is evident today. 16Therefore, cleanse your sinful hearts and stop your stubbornness.

17"Jehovah your God is God of gods and Lord of lords. He is the great and mighty God, the God of terror who shows no partiality and takes no bribes. 18He gives justice to the fatherless and widows. He loves foreigners and gives them food and clothing. 19(You too must love foreigners, for you yourselves were foreigners in the land of Egypt.) 20You must fear the Lord your God and worship him and cling to him and take oaths by his name alone. 21He is your praise and he is your God, the one who has done mighty miracles you yourselves have seen. 22When your ancestors went down into Egypt there were only seventy of them, but now the Lord your God has made you as many as the stars in the sky!

11 "YOU MUST love the Lord your God and obey every one of his commands. 2Listen! I am not talking now to your children who have never experienced the Lord's punishments or seen his greatness and his awesome power. 3They weren't there to see the miracles he did in Egypt against Pharaoh and all his land.

New Revised Standard

he wrote on the tablets the same words as before, the ten commandmentsa that the LORD had spoken to you on the mountain out of the fire on the day of the assembly; and the LORD gave them to me. 5So I turned and came down from the mountain, and put the tablets in the ark that I had made; and there they are, as the LORD commanded me.

6 (The Israelites journeyed from Beeroth-bene-jaakanb to Moserah. There Aaron died, and there he was buried; his son Eleazar succeeded him as priest. 7From there they journeyed to Gudgodah, and from Gudgodah to Jotbathah, a land with flowing streams. 8At that time the LORD set apart the tribe of Levi to carry the ark of the covenant of the LORD, to stand before the LORD to minister to him, and to bless in his name, to this day. 9Therefore Levi has no allotment or inheritance with his kindred; the LORD is his inheritance, as the LORD your God promised him.)

10 I stayed on the mountain forty days and forty nights, as I had done the first time. And once again the LORD listened to me. The LORD was unwilling to destroy you. 11The LORD said to me, "Get up, go on your journey at the head of the people, that they may go in and occupy the land that I swore to their ancestors to give them."

The Essence of the Law

12 So now, O Israel, what does the LORD your God require of you? Only to fear the LORD your God, to walk in all his ways, to love him, to serve the LORD your God with all your heart and with all your soul, 13and to keep the commandments of the LORD your Godc and his decrees that I am commanding you today, for your own well-being. 14Although heaven and the heaven of heavens belong to the LORD your God, the earth with all that is in it, 15yet the LORD set his heart in love on your ancestors alone and chose you, their descendants after them, out of all the peoples, as it is today. 16Circumcise, then, the foreskin of your heart, and do not be stubborn any longer. 17For the LORD your God is God of gods and Lord of lords, the great God, mighty and awesome, who is not partial and takes no bribe, 18who executes justice for the orphan and the widow, and who loves the strangers, providing them food and clothing. 19You shall also love the stranger, for you were strangers in the land of Egypt. 20You shall fear the LORD your God; him alone you shall worship; to him you shall hold fast, and by his name you shall swear. 21He is your praise; he is your God, who has done for you these great and awesome things that your own eyes have seen. 22Your ancestors went down to Egypt seventy persons; and now the LORD your God has made you as numerous as the stars in heaven.

Rewards for Obedience

11 YOU SHALL love the LORD your God, therefore, and keep his charge, his decrees, his ordinances, and his commandments always. 2Remember today that it was not your children (who have not known or seen the discipline of the LORD your God), but it is you who must acknowledge his greatness, his mighty hand and his outstretched arm, 3his signs and his deeds that he did in Egypt to Pharaoh, the king of Egypt, and to all his land; 4what he did to the Egyptian army, to

a Heb the ten words   b Or the wells of the Bene-jaakan   c Q Ms Gk Syr: MT lacks your God

King James

4And what he did unto the army of Egypt, unto their horses, and to their chariots; how he made the water of the Red sea to overflow them as they pursued after you, and *how* the LORD hath destroyed them unto this day;

5And what he did unto you in the wilderness, until ye came into this place;

6And what he did unto Dathan and Abiram, the sons of Eliab, the son of Reuben: how the earth opened her mouth, and swallowed them up, and their households, and their tents, and all the substance that *was* in their possession, in the midst of all Israel:

7But your eyes have seen all the great acts of the LORD which he did.

8Therefore shall ye keep all the commandments which I command you this day, that ye may be strong, and go in and possess the land, whither ye go to possess it;

9And that ye may prolong *your* days in the land, which the LORD sware unto your fathers to give unto them and to their seed, a land that floweth with milk and honey.

10¶ For the land, whither thou goest in to possess it, *is* not as the land of Egypt, from whence ye came out, where thou sowedst thy seed, and wateredst *it* with thy foot, as a garden of herbs:

11But the land, whither ye go to possess it, *is* a land of hills and valleys, *and* drinketh water of the rain of heaven:

12A land which the LORD thy God careth for: the eyes of the LORD thy God *are* always upon it, from the beginning of the year even unto the end of the year.

13¶ And it shall come to pass, if ye shall hearken diligently unto my commandments which I command you this day, to love the LORD your God, and to serve him with all your heart and with all your soul,

14That I will give *you* the rain of your land in his due season, the first rain and the latter rain, that thou mayest gather in thy corn, and thy wine, and thine oil.

15And I will send grass in thy fields for thy cattle, that thou mayest eat and be full.

16Take heed to yourselves, that your heart be not deceived, and ye turn aside, and serve other gods, and worship them;

17And *then* the LORD's wrath be kindled against you, and he shut up the heaven, that there be no rain, and that the land yield not her fruit; and *lest* ye perish quickly from off the good land which the LORD giveth you.

18¶ Therefore shall ye lay up these my words in your heart and in your soul, and bind them for a sign upon your hand, that they may be as frontlets between your eyes.

19And ye shall teach them your children, speaking of them when thou sittest in thine house, and when thou walkest by the way, when thou liest down, and when thou risest up.

20And thou shalt write them upon the door posts of thine house, and upon thy gates:

21That your days may be multiplied, and the days of your children, in the land which the LORD sware unto your fathers to give them, as the days of heaven upon the earth.

22¶ For if ye shall diligently keep all these commandments which I command you, to do them, to love the LORD your God, to walk in all his ways, and to cleave unto him;

23Then will the LORD drive out all these nations from before you, and ye shall possess greater nations and mightier than yourselves.

24Every place whereon the soles of your feet shall tread shall be yours: from the wilderness and Lebanon, from the river, the river Euphrates, even unto the uttermost sea shall your coast be.

New International

the Egyptian army, to its horses and chariots, how he overwhelmed them with the waters of the Red Sea[a] as they were pursuing you, and how the LORD brought lasting ruin on them. 5It was not your children who saw what he did for you in the desert until you arrived at this place, 6and what he did to Dathan and Abiram, sons of Eliab the Reubenite, when the earth opened its mouth right in the middle of all Israel and swallowed them up with their households, their tents and every living thing that belonged to them. 7But it was your own eyes that saw all these great things the LORD has done.

8Observe therefore all the commands I am giving you today, so that you may have the strength to go in and take over the land that you are crossing the Jordan to possess, 9and so that you may live long in the land that the LORD swore to your forefathers to give to them and their descendants, a land flowing with milk and honey. 10The land you are entering to take over is not like the land of Egypt, from which you have come, where you planted your seed and irrigated it by foot as in a vegetable garden. 11But the land you are crossing the Jordan to take possession of is a land of mountains and valleys that drinks rain from heaven. 12It is a land the LORD your God cares for; the eyes of the LORD your God are continually on it from the beginning of the year to its end.

13So if you faithfully obey the commands I am giving you today—to love the LORD your God and to serve him with all your heart and with all your soul— 14then I will send rain on your land in its season, both autumn and spring rains, so that you may gather in your grain, new wine and oil. 15I will provide grass in the fields for your cattle, and you will eat and be satisfied.

16Be careful, or you will be enticed to turn away and worship other gods and bow down to them. 17Then the LORD's anger will burn against you, and he will shut the heavens so that it will not rain and the ground will yield no produce, and you will soon perish from the good land the LORD is giving you. 18Fix these words of mine in your hearts and minds; tie them as symbols on your hands and bind them on your foreheads. 19Teach them to your children, talking about them when you sit at home and when you walk along the road, when you lie down and when you get up. 20Write them on the doorframes of your houses and on your gates, 21so that your days and the days of your children may be many in the land that the LORD swore to give your forefathers, as many as the days that the heavens are above the earth.

22If you carefully observe all these commands I am giving you to follow—to love the LORD your God, to walk in all his ways and to hold fast to him— 23then the LORD will drive out all these nations before you, and you will dispossess nations larger and stronger than you. 24Every place where you set your foot will be yours: Your territory will extend from the desert to Lebanon, and from the Euphrates River to the western sea.[b] 25No

a 4 Hebrew *Yam Suph*; that is, Sea of Reeds   b 24 That is, the Mediterranean

Living Bible

4They didn't see what God did to the armies of Egypt and to their horses and chariots—how he drowned them in the Red Sea as they were chasing you, and how the Lord has kept them powerless against you until this very day! 5They didn't see how the Lord cared for you time and again through all the years you were wandering in the wilderness, until your arrival here. 6They weren't there when Dathan and Abiram (the sons of Eliab, descendantsᶜ of Reuben) sinned, and the earth opened up and swallowed them, with their households and tents and all their belongings, as all Israel watched!

7"But *you* have seen these mighty miracles! 8How carefully, then, you should obey these commandments I am going to give you today, so that you may have the strength to go in and possess the land you are about to enter. 9If you obey the commandments, you will have a long and good life in the land the Lord promised to your ancestors and to you, their descendants—a wonderful land 'flowing with milk and honey'! 10For the land you are about to enter and possess is not like the land of Egypt where you have come from, where irrigation is necessary. 11It is a land of hills and valleys with plenty of rain— 12a land that the Lord your God personally cares for! His eyes are always upon it, day after day throughout the year!

13"And if you will carefully obey all of his commandments that I am going to give you today, and if you will love the Lord your God with all your hearts and souls, and will worship him, 14then he will continue to send both the early and late rains that will produce wonderful crops of grain, grapes for your wine, and olive oil. 15He will give you lush pastureland for your cattle to graze in, and you yourselves shall have plenty to eat and be fully content.

16"But beware that your hearts do not turn from God to worship other gods. 17For if you do, the anger of the Lord will be hot against you, and he will shut the heavens—there will be no rain and no harvest, and you will quickly perish from the good land the Lord has given you. 18So keep these commandments carefully in mind. Tie them to your hand to remind you to obey them, and tie them to your forehead between your eyes! 19Teach them to your children. Talk about them when you are sitting at home, when you are out walking, at bedtime, and before breakfast! 20Write them upon the doors of your houses and upon your gates, 21so that as long as there is sky above the earth, you and your children will enjoy the good life awaiting you in the land the Lord has promised you.ᵈ

22"If you carefully obey all the commandments I give you, loving the Lord your God, walking in all his ways, and clinging to him, 23then the Lord will drive out all the nations in your land, no matter how much greater and stronger than you they might be. 24Wherever you go, the land is yours. Your frontiers will stretch from the southern Negeb to Lebanon, and from the Euphrates River to the Mediterranean Sea. 25No one will be able to stand

New Revised Standard

their horses and chariots, how he made the water of the Red Seaᵉ flow over them as they pursued you, so that the LORD has destroyed them to this day; 5what he did to you in the wilderness, until you came to this place; 6and what he did to Dathan and Abiram, sons of Eliab son of Reuben, how in the midst of all Israel the earth opened its mouth and swallowed them up, along with their households, their tents, and every living being in their company; 7for it is your own eyes that have seen every great deed that the LORD did.

8 Keep, then, this entire commandment that I am commanding you today, so that you may have strength to go in and occupy the land that you are crossing over to occupy, 9and so that you may live long in the land that the LORD swore to your ancestors to give them and to their descendants, a land flowing with milk and honey. 10For the land that you are about to enter to occupy is not like the land of Egypt, from which you have come, where you sow your seed and irrigate by foot like a vegetable garden. 11But the land that you are crossing over to occupy is a land of hills and valleys, watered by rain from the sky, 12a land that the LORD your God looks after. The eyes of the LORD your God are always on it, from the beginning of the year to the end of the year.

13 If you will only heed his every commandmentᶠ that I am commanding you today—loving the LORD your God, and serving him with all your heart and with all your soul— 14then heᵍ will give the rain for your land in its season, the early rain and the later rain, and you will gather in your grain, your wine, and your oil; 15and heᵍ will give grass in your fields for your livestock, and you will eat your fill. 16Take care, or you will be seduced into turning away, serving other gods and worshiping them, 17for then the anger of the LORD will be kindled against you and he will shut up the heavens, so that there will be no rain and the land will yield no fruit; then you will perish quickly off the good land that the LORD is giving you.

18 You shall put these words of mine in your heart and soul, and you shall bind them as a sign on your hand, and fix them as an emblemʰ on your forehead. 19Teach them to your children, talking about them when you are at home and when you are away, when you lie down and when you rise. 20Write them on the doorposts of your house and on your gates, 21so that your days and the days of your children may be multiplied in the land that the LORD swore to your ancestors to give them, as long as the heavens are above the earth.

22 If you will diligently observe this entire commandment that I am commanding you, loving the LORD your God, walking in all his ways, and holding fast to him, 23then the LORD will drive out all these nations before you, and you will dispossess nations larger and mightier than yourselves. 24Every place on which you set foot shall be yours; your territory shall extend from the wilderness to the Lebanon and from the River, the river Euphrates, to the Western Sea. 25No one will be

---

ᶜ *11:6 descendants,* literally, "sons." ᵈ *11:21 promised you,* literally, "your fathers."

ᵉ Or *Sea of Reeds* ᶠ Compare Gk: Heb *my commandments* ᵍ Sam Gk Vg: MT *I* ʰ Or *as a frontlet*

King James

25There shall no man be able to stand before you: for the LORD your God shall lay the fear of you and the dread of you upon all the land that ye shall tread upon. as he hath said unto you.

26¶ Behold, I set before you this day a blessing and a curse;

27A blessing, if ye obey the commandments of the LORD your God, which I command you this day:

28And a curse, if ye will not obey the commandments of the LORD your God, but turn aside out of the way which I command you this day, to go after other gods, which ye have not known.

29And it shall come to pass, when the LORD thy God hath brought thee in unto the land whither thou goest to possess it, that thou shalt put the blessing upon mount Gerizim, and the curse upon mount Ebal.

30Are they not on the other side Jordan, by the way where the sun goeth down, in the land of the Canaanites, which dwell in the champaign over against Gilgal, beside the plains of Moreh?

31For ye shall pass over Jordan to go in to possess the land which the LORD your God giveth you, and ye shall possess it, and dwell therein.

32And ye shall observe to do all the statutes and judgments which I set before you this day.

12 THESE *ARE* the statutes and judgments, which ye shall observe to do in the land, which the LORD God of thy fathers giveth thee to possess it, all the days that ye live upon the earth.

2Ye shall utterly destroy all the places, wherein the nations which ye shall possess served their gods, upon the high mountains, and upon the hills, and under every green tree:

3And ye shall overthrow their altars, and break their pillars, and burn their groves with fire; and ye shall hew down the graven images of their gods, and destroy the names of them out of that place.

4Ye shall not do so unto the LORD your God.

5But unto the place which the LORD your God shall choose out of all your tribes to put his name there, *even* unto his habitation shall ye seek, and thither thou shalt come:

6And thither ye shall bring your burnt offerings, and your sacrifices, and your tithes, and heave offerings of your hand, and your vows, and your freewill offerings, and the firstlings of your herds and of your flocks:

7And there ye shall eat before the LORD your God, and ye shall rejoice in all that ye put your hand unto, ye and your households, wherein the LORD thy God hath blessed thee.

8Ye shall not do after all *the things* that we do here this day, every man whatsoever *is* right in his own eyes.

9For ye are not as yet come to the rest and to the inheritance, which the LORD your God giveth you.

10But *when* ye go over Jordan, and dwell in the land which the LORD your God giveth you to inherit, and *when* he giveth you rest from all your enemies round about, so that ye dwell in safety;

11Then there shall be a place which the LORD your God shall choose to cause his name to dwell there; thither shall ye bring all that I command you; your burnt offerings, and your sacrifices, your tithes, and the heave offering of your hand, and all your choice vows which ye vow unto the LORD:

12And ye shall rejoice before the LORD your God, ye, and your sons, and your daughters, and your menservants, and your maidservants, and the Levite that *is* within your gates; forasmuch as he hath no part nor inheritance with you.

13Take heed to thyself that thou offer not thy burnt offerings in every place that thou seest:

New International

man will be able to stand against you. The LORD your God, as he promised you, will put the terror and fear of you on the whole land, wherever you go.

26See, I am setting before you today a blessing and a curse— 27the blessing if you obey the commands of the LORD your God that I am giving you today; 28the curse if you disobey the commands of the LORD your God and turn from the way that I command you today by following other gods, which you have not known. 29When the LORD your God has brought you into the land you are entering to possess, you are to proclaim on Mount Gerizim the blessings, and on Mount Ebal the curses. 30As you know, these mountains are across the Jordan, west of the road,[a] toward the setting sun, near the great trees of Moreh, in the territory of those Canaanites living in the Arabah in the vicinity of Gilgal. 31You are about to cross the Jordan to enter and take possession of the land the LORD your God is giving you. When you have taken it over and are living there, 32be sure that you obey all the decrees and laws I am setting before you today.

The One Place of Worship

12 THESE ARE the decrees and laws you must be careful to follow in the land that the LORD, the God of your fathers, has given you to possess—as long as you live in the land. 2Destroy completely all the places on the high mountains and on the hills and under every spreading tree where the nations you are dispossessing worship their gods. 3Break down their altars, smash their sacred stones and burn their Asherah poles in the fire; cut down the idols of their gods and wipe out their names from those places.

4You must not worship the LORD your God in their way. 5But you are to seek the place the LORD your God will choose from among all your tribes to put his Name there for his dwelling. To that place you must go; 6there bring your burnt offerings and sacrifices, your tithes and special gifts, what you have vowed to give and your freewill offerings, and the firstborn of your herds and flocks. 7There, in the presence of the LORD your God, you and your families shall eat and shall rejoice in everything you have put your hand to, because the LORD your God has blessed you.

8You are not to do as we do here today, everyone as he sees fit, 9since you have not yet reached the resting place and the inheritance the LORD your God is giving you. 10But you will cross the Jordan and settle in the land the LORD your God is giving you as an inheritance, and he will give you rest from all your enemies around you so that you will live in safety. 11Then to the place the LORD your God will choose as a dwelling for his Name—there you are to bring everything I command you: your burnt offerings and sacrifices, your tithes and special gifts, and all the choice possessions you have vowed to the LORD. 12And there rejoice before the LORD your God, you, your sons and daughters, your menservants and maidservants, and the Levites from your towns, who have no allotment or inheritance of their own. 13Be careful not to sacrifice your burnt offerings anywhere you please. 14Offer them only at the place the

---

a 30 Or *Jordan, westward*

Living Bible

against you, for the Lord your God will send fear and dread ahead of you wherever you go, just as he has promised.

26"I am giving you the choice today between God's blessing or God's curse! 27There will be blessing if you obey the commandments of the Lord your God which I am giving you today, 28and a curse if you refuse them and worship the gods of these other nations. 29When the Lord your God brings you into the land to possess it, a blessing shall be proclaimed from Mount Gerizim, and a curse from Mount Ebal! 30(Gerizim and Ebal are mountains west of the Jordan River, where the Canaanites live, in the wasteland near Gilgal, where the oaks of Moreh are.) 31For you are to cross the Jordan and live in the land the Lord is giving you. 32But you must obey all the laws I am giving you today.

12 "THESE ARE the laws you must obey when you arrive in the land which Jehovah, the God of your fathers, has given you forever:

2"You must destroy all the heathen altars wherever you find them—high in the mountains, up in the hills, or under the trees. 3Break the altars, smash the obelisks, burn the shameful images, cut down the metal idols, and leave nothing even to remind you of them!

4, 5"You must not make sacrifices to your God just anywhere, as the heathen sacrifice to their gods. Rather, you must build a sanctuary for him at a place he himself will select as his home. 6There you shall bring to the Lord your burnt offerings and other sacrifices—your tithes, your offerings presented by the gesture of waving before the altar, your offerings to fulfill your vows, your free-will offerings, and your offerings of the firstborn animals of your flocks and herds. 7There you and your families shall feast before the Lord your God, and shall rejoice in all he has done for you.

8"You will no longer go your own way as you do now, everyone doing whatever he thinks is right; 9(for these laws don't go into effect until you arrive in the place of rest the Lord will give to you). 10But when you cross the Jordan River and live in the Promised Land, and the Lord gives you rest and keeps you safe from all your enemies, 11then you must bring all your burnt sacrifices and other offerings to his sanctuary, the place he will choose as his home. 12You shall rejoice there before the Lord with your sons and daughters and servants; and remember to invite the Levites to feast with you, for they have no land of their own.

13"You are not to sacrifice your burnt offerings just anywhere; 14you may only do so in the place the Lord

New Revised Standard

able to stand against you; the LORD your God will put the fear and dread of you on all the land on which you set foot, as he promised you.

26 See, I am setting before you today a blessing and a curse: 27the blessing, if you obey the commandments of the LORD your God that I am commanding you today; 28and the curse, if you do not obey the commandments of the LORD your God, but turn from the way that I am commanding you today, to follow other gods that you have not known.

29 When the LORD your God has brought you into the land that you are entering to occupy, you shall set the blessing on Mount Gerizim and the curse on Mount Ebal. 30As you know, they are beyond the Jordan, some distance to the west, in the land of the Canaanites who live in the Arabah, opposite Gilgal, beside the oak[b] of Moreh.

31 When you cross the Jordan to go in to occupy the land that the LORD your God is giving you, and when you occupy it and live in it, 32you must diligently observe all the statutes and ordinances that I am setting before you today.

Pagan Shrines to Be Destroyed

12 THESE ARE the statutes and ordinances that you must diligently observe in the land that the LORD, the God of your ancestors, has given you to occupy all the days that you live on the earth.

2 You must demolish completely all the places where the nations whom you are about to dispossess served their gods, on the mountain heights, on the hills, and under every leafy tree. 3Break down their altars, smash their pillars, burn their sacred poles[c] with fire, and hew down the idols of their gods, and thus blot out their name from their places. 4You shall not worship the LORD your God in such ways. 5But you shall seek the place that the LORD your God will choose out of all your tribes as his habitation to put his name there. You shall go there, 6bringing there your burnt offerings and your sacrifices, your tithes and your donations, your votive gifts, your freewill offerings, and the firstlings of your herds and flocks. 7And you shall eat there in the presence of the LORD your God, you and your households together, rejoicing in all the undertakings in which the LORD your God has blessed you.

8 You shall not act as we are acting here today, all of us according to our own desires, 9for you have not yet come into the rest and the possession that the LORD your God is giving you. 10When you cross over the Jordan and live in the land that the LORD your God is allotting to you, and when he gives you rest from your enemies all around so that you live in safety, 11then you shall bring everything that I command you to the place that the LORD your God will choose as a dwelling for his name: your burnt offerings and your sacrifices, your tithes and your donations, and all your choice votive gifts that you vow to the LORD. 12And you shall rejoice before the LORD your God, you together with your sons and your daughters, your male and female slaves, and the Levites who reside in your towns (since they have no allotment or inheritance with you).

A Prescribed Place of Worship

13 Take care that you do not offer your burnt offerings at any place you happen to see. 14But only at the

b Gk Syr: Compare Gen 12.6; Heb oaks or terebinths   c Heb Asherim

King James

14But in the place which the LORD shall choose in one of thy tribes, there thou shalt offer thy burnt offerings, and there thou shalt do all that I command thee.

15Notwithstanding thou mayest kill and eat flesh in all thy gates, whatsoever thy soul lusteth after, according to the blessing of the LORD thy God which he hath given thee: the unclean and the clean may eat thereof, as of the roebuck, and as of the hart.

16Only ye shall not eat the blood; ye shall pour it upon the earth as water.

17¶ Thou mayest not eat within thy gates the tithe of thy corn, or of thy wine, or of thy oil, or the firstlings of thy herds or of thy flock, nor any of thy vows which thou vowest, nor thy freewill offerings, or heave offering of thine hand:

18But thou must eat them before the LORD thy God in the place which the LORD thy God shall choose, thou, and thy son, and thy daughter, and thy manservant, and thy maidservant, and the Levite that is within thy gates: and thou shalt rejoice before the LORD thy God in all that thou puttest thine hands unto.

19Take heed to thyself that thou forsake not the Levite as long as thou livest upon the earth.

20¶ When the LORD thy God shall enlarge thy border, as he hath promised thee, and thou shalt say, I will eat flesh, because thy soul longeth to eat flesh; thou mayest eat flesh, whatsoever thy soul lusteth after.

21If the place which the LORD thy God hath chosen to put his name there be too far from thee, then thou shalt kill of thy herd and of thy flock, which the LORD hath given thee, as I have commanded thee, and thou shalt eat in thy gates whatsoever thy soul lusteth after.

22Even as the roebuck and the hart is eaten, so thou shalt eat them: the unclean and the clean shall eat of them alike.

23Only be sure that thou eat not the blood: for the blood is the life; and thou mayest not eat the life with the flesh.

24Thou shalt not eat it; thou shalt pour it upon the earth as water.

25Thou shalt not eat it; that it may go well with thee, and with thy children after thee, when thou shalt do that which is right in the sight of the LORD.

26Only thy holy things which thou hast, and thy vows, thou shalt take, and go unto the place which the LORD shall choose:

27And thou shalt offer thy burnt offerings, the flesh and the blood, upon the altar of the LORD thy God: and the blood of thy sacrifices shall be poured out upon the altar of the LORD thy God, and thou shalt eat the flesh.

28Observe and hear all these words which I command thee, that it may go well with thee, and with thy children after thee for ever, when thou doest that which is good and right in the sight of the LORD thy God.

29¶ When the LORD thy God shall cut off the nations from before thee, whither thou goest to possess them, and thou succeedest them, and dwellest in their land;

30Take heed to thyself that thou be not snared by following them, after that they be destroyed from before thee; and that thou inquire not after their gods, saying, How did these nations serve their gods? even so will I do likewise.

31Thou shalt not do so unto the LORD thy God: for every abomination to the LORD, which he hateth, have they done unto their gods; for even their sons and their daughters they have burnt in the fire to their gods.

32What thing soever I command you, observe to do it: thou shalt not add thereto, nor diminish from it.

New International

LORD will choose in one of your tribes, and there observe everything I command you.

15Nevertheless, you may slaughter your animals in any of your towns and eat as much of the meat as you want, as if it were gazelle or deer, according to the blessing the LORD your God gives you. Both the ceremonially unclean and the clean may eat it. 16But you must not eat the blood; pour it out on the ground like water. 17You must not eat in your own towns the tithe of your grain and new wine and oil, or the firstborn of your herds and flocks, or whatever you have vowed to give, or your freewill offerings or special gifts. 18Instead, you are to eat them in the presence of the LORD your God at the place the LORD your God will choose— you, your sons and daughters, your menservants and maidservants, and the Levites from your towns—and you are to rejoice before the LORD your God in everything you put your hand to. 19Be careful not to neglect the Levites as long as you live in your land.

20When the LORD your God has enlarged your territory as he promised you, and you crave meat and say, "I would like some meat," then you may eat as much of it as you want. 21If the place where the LORD your God chooses to put his Name is too far away from you, you may slaughter animals from the herds and flocks the LORD has given you, as I have commanded you, and in your own towns you may eat as much of them as you want. 22Eat them as you would gazelle or deer. Both the ceremonially unclean and the clean may eat. 23But be sure you do not eat the blood, because the blood is the life, and you must not eat the life with the meat. 24You must not eat the blood; pour it out on the ground like water. 25Do not eat it, so that it may go well with you and your children after you, because you will be doing what is right in the eyes of the LORD.

26But take your consecrated things and whatever you have vowed to give, and go to the place the LORD will choose. 27Present your burnt offerings on the altar of the LORD your God, both the meat and the blood. The blood of your sacrifices must be poured beside the altar of the LORD your God, but you may eat the meat. 28Be careful to obey all these regulations I am giving you, so that it may always go well with you and your children after you, because you will be doing what is good and right in the eyes of the LORD your God.

29The LORD your God will cut off before you the nations you are about to invade and dispossess. But when you have driven them out and settled in their land, 30and after they have been destroyed before you, be careful not to be ensnared by inquiring about their gods, saying, "How do these nations serve their gods? We will do the same." 31You must not worship the LORD your God in their way, because in worshiping their gods, they do all kinds of detestable things the LORD hates. They even burn their sons and daughters in the fire as sacrifices to their gods.

32See that you do all I command you; do not add to it or take away from it.

Living Bible

will choose. He will pick a place in the territory allotted to one of the tribes. Only there may you offer your sacrifices and bring your offerings. 15However, the meat you eat may be butchered anywhere, just as you do now with gazelle and deer. Eat as much of this meat as you wish and as often as you are able to obtain it, because the Lord has prospered you. Those who are ceremonially defiled may eat it, too. 16The only restriction is that you are not to eat the blood—pour it out on the ground, like water.

17"But none of the offerings may be eaten at home. Neither the tithe of your grain and new wine and olive oil, nor the firstborn of your flocks and herds, nor anything you have vowed to give the Lord, nor your freewill offerings, nor the offerings to be presented to the Lord by waving them before his altar. 18All these must be brought to the central altar where you, your children, and the Levites shall eat them before the Lord your God. He will tell you where this altar must be located. Rejoice before the Lord your God in everything you do. 19(By the way, be very careful not to forget about the Levites. Share with them.)

20-23"If, when the Lord enlarges your borders, the central altar is too far away from you, then your flocks and herds may be butchered on your own farms, just as you do now with gazelle and deer. And even persons who are ceremonially defiled may eat them. The only restriction is never to eat the blood, for the blood is the life, and you shall not eat the life with the meat. 24, 25Instead, pour the blood out upon the earth. If you do, all will be well with you and your children. 26, 27Only your gifts to the Lord, and the offerings you have promised in your vows, and your burnt offerings need be taken to the central altar. These may only be sacrificed upon the altar of the Lord your God. The blood will be poured out upon the altar, and you will eat the meat.

28"Be careful to obey all of these commandments. If you do what is right in the eyes of the Lord your God, all will go well with you and your children forever. 29When he destroys the nations in the land where you will live, 30don't follow their example in worshiping their gods. Do not ask, 'How do these nations worship their gods?' and then go and worship as they do! 31You must not insult the Lord your God like that! These nations have done horrible things that he hates, all in the name of their religion. They have even roasted their sons and daughters in front of their gods. 32Obey all the commandments I give you. Do not add to or subtract from them.

New Revised Standard

place that the LORD will choose in one of your tribes—there you shall offer your burnt offerings and there you shall do everything I command you.

15 Yet whenever you desire you may slaughter and eat meat within any of your towns, according to the blessing that the LORD your God has given you; the unclean and the clean may eat of it, as they would of gazelle or deer. 16The blood, however, you must not eat; you shall pour it out on the ground like water. 17Nor may you eat within your towns the tithe of your grain, your wine, and your oil, the firstlings of your herds and your flocks, any of your votive gifts that you vow, your freewill offerings, or your donations; 18these you shall eat in the presence of the LORD your God at the place that the LORD your God will choose, you together with your son and your daughter, your male and female slaves, and the Levites resident in your towns, rejoicing in the presence of the LORD your God in all your undertakings. 19Take care that you do not neglect the Levite as long as you live in your land.

20 When the LORD your God enlarges your territory, as he has promised you, and you say, "I am going to eat some meat," because you wish to eat meat, you may eat meat whenever you have the desire. 21If the place where the LORD your God will choose to put his name is too far from you, and you slaughter as I have commanded you any of your herd or flock that the LORD has given you, then you may eat within your towns whenever you desire. 22Indeed, just as gazelle or deer is eaten, so you may eat it; the unclean and the clean alike may eat it. 23Only be sure that you do not eat the blood; for the blood is the life, and you shall not eat the life with the meat. 24Do not eat it; you shall pour it out on the ground like water. 25Do not eat it, so that all may go well with you and your children after you, because you do what is right in the sight of the LORD. 26But the sacred donations that are due from you, and your votive gifts, you shall bring to the place that the LORD will choose. 27You shall present your burnt offerings, both the meat and the blood, on the altar of the LORD your God; the blood of your other sacrifices shall be poured out beside[a] the altar of the LORD your God, but the meat you may eat.

28 Be careful to obey all these words that I command you today,[b] so that it may go well with you and with your children after you forever, because you will be doing what is good and right in the sight of the LORD your God.

Warning against Idolatry

29 When the LORD your God has cut off before you the nations whom you are about to enter to dispossess them, when you have dispossessed them and live in their land, 30take care that you are not snared into imitating them, after they have been destroyed before you: do not inquire concerning their gods, saying, "How did these nations worship their gods? I also want to do the same." 31You must not do the same for the LORD your God, because every abhorrent thing that the LORD hates they have done for their gods. They would even burn their sons and their daughters in the fire to their gods. 32c You must diligently observe everything that I command you; do not add to it or take anything from it.

a Or on   b Gk Sam Syr: MT lacks today   c Ch 13.1 in Heb

King James

13 IF THERE arise among you a prophet, or a dreamer of dreams, and giveth thee a sign or a wonder,

2And the sign or the wonder come to pass, whereof he spake unto thee, saying, Let us go after other gods, which thou hast not known, and let us serve them;

3Thou shalt not hearken unto the words of that prophet, or that dreamer of dreams: for the LORD your God proveth you, to know whether ye love the LORD your God with all your heart and with all your soul.

4Ye shall walk after the LORD your God, and fear him, and keep his commandments, and obey his voice, and ye shall serve him, and cleave unto him.

5And that prophet, or that dreamer of dreams, shall be put to death; because he hath spoken to turn *you* away from the LORD your God, which brought you out of the land of Egypt, and redeemed you out of the house of bondage, to thrust thee out of the way which the LORD thy God commanded thee to walk in. So shalt thou put the evil away from the midst of thee.

6¶ If thy brother, the son of thy mother, or thy son, or thy daughter, or the wife of thy bosom, or thy friend, which *is* as thine own soul, entice thee secretly, saying, Let us go and serve other gods, which thou hast not known, thou, nor thy fathers;

7*Namely,* of the gods of the people which *are* round about you, nigh unto thee, or far off from thee, from the *one* end of the earth even unto the *other* end of the earth;

8Thou shalt not consent unto him, nor hearken unto him; neither shall thine eye pity him, neither shalt thou spare, neither shalt thou conceal him:

9But thou shalt surely kill him; thine hand shall be first upon him to put him to death, and afterwards the hand of all the people.

10And thou shalt stone him with stones, that he die; because he hath sought to thrust thee away from the LORD thy God, which brought thee out of the land of Egypt, from the house of bondage.

11And all Israel shall hear, and fear, and shall do no more any such wickedness as this is among you.

12¶ If thou shalt hear *say* in one of thy cities, which the LORD thy God hath given thee to dwell there, saying,

13*Certain* men, the children of Belial, are gone out from among you, and have withdrawn the inhabitants of their city, saying, Let us go and serve other gods, which ye have not known;

14Then shalt thou inquire, and make search, and ask diligently; and, behold, *if it be* truth, *and* the thing certain, *that* such abomination is wrought among you;

15Thou shalt surely smite the inhabitants of that city with the edge of the sword, destroying it utterly, and all that *is* therein, and the cattle thereof, with the edge of the sword.

16And thou shalt gather all the spoil of it into the midst of the street thereof, and shalt burn with fire the city, and all the spoil thereof every whit, for the LORD thy God: and it shall be an heap for ever; it shall not be built again.

17And there shall cleave nought of the cursed thing to thine hand: that the LORD may turn from the fierceness of his anger, and show thee mercy, and have compassion upon thee, and multiply thee, as he hath sworn unto thy fathers;

18When thou shalt hearken to the voice of the LORD thy God, to keep all his commandments which I command thee this day, to do *that which is* right in the eyes of the LORD thy God.

New International

Worshiping Other Gods

13 IF A prophet, or one who foretells by dreams, appears among you and announces to you a miraculous sign or wonder, 2and if the sign or wonder of which he has spoken takes place, and he says, "Let us follow other gods" (gods you have not known) "and let us worship them," 3you must not listen to the words of that prophet or dreamer. The LORD your God is testing you to find out whether you love him with all your heart and with all your soul. 4It is the LORD your God you must follow, and him you must revere. Keep his commands and obey him; serve him and hold fast to him. 5That prophet or dreamer must be put to death, because he preached rebellion against the LORD your God, who brought you out of Egypt and redeemed you from the land of slavery; he has tried to turn you from the way the LORD your God commanded you to follow. You must purge the evil from among you.

6If your very own brother, or your son or daughter, or the wife you love, or your closest friend secretly entices you, saying, "Let us go and worship other gods" (gods that neither you nor your fathers have known, 7gods of the peoples around you, whether near or far, from one end of the land to the other), 8do not yield to him or listen to him. Show him no pity. Do not spare him or shield him. 9You must certainly put him to death. Your hand must be the first in putting him to death, and then the hands of all the people. 10Stone him to death, because he tried to turn you away from the LORD your God, who brought you out of Egypt, out of the land of slavery. 11Then all Israel will hear and be afraid, and no one among you will do such an evil thing again.

12If you hear it said about one of the towns the LORD your God is giving you to live in 13that wicked men have arisen among you and have led the people of their town astray, saying, "Let us go and worship other gods" (gods you have not known), 14then you must inquire, probe and investigate it thoroughly. And if it is true and it has been proved that this detestable thing has been done among you, 15you must certainly put to the sword all who live in that town. Destroy it completely,a both its people and its livestock. 16Gather all the plunder of the town into the middle of the public square and completely burn the town and all its plunder as a whole burnt offering to the LORD your God. It is to remain a ruin forever, never to be rebuilt. 17None of those condemned thingsa shall be found in your hands, so that the LORD will turn from his fierce anger; he will show you mercy, have compassion on you, and increase your numbers, as he promised on oath to your forefathers, 18because you obey the LORD your God, keeping all his commands that I am giving you today and doing what is right in his eyes.

---

a *15,17* The Hebrew term refers to the irrevocable giving over of things or persons to the LORD, often by totally destroying them.

Living Bible

13 "IF THERE is a prophet among you, or one who claims to foretell the future by dreams, 2and if his predictions come true but he says, 'Come, let us worship the gods of the other nations,' 3don't listen to him. For the Lord is testing you to find out whether or not you really love him with all your heart and soul. 4You must *never* worship any God but Jehovah; obey only his commands and cling to him.

5"The prophet who tries to lead you astray must be executed, for he has attempted to foment rebellion against the Lord your God who brought you out of slavery in the land of Egypt. By executing him you will clear out the evil from among you.

6,7If your nearest relative or closest friend, even a brother, son, daughter, or beloved wife whispers to you to come and worship these foreign gods, 8do not consent nor listen, and have no pity: Do not spare that person from the penalty; don't conceal his horrible suggestion. 9Execute him! Your own hand shall be the first upon him to put him to death, then the hands of all the people. 10Stone him to death because he has tried to draw you away from the Lord your God who brought you from the land of Egypt, the place of slavery. 11Then all Israel will hear about his evil deed, and will fear such wickedness as this among you.

12, 13, 14"If you ever hear it said about one of the cities of Israel that some worthless rabble have led their fellow citizens astray with the suggestion that they worship foreign gods, first check the facts to see if the rumor is true. If you find that it is, that it is certain that such a horrible thing is happening among you in one of the cities the Lord has given you, 15you must without fail declare war against that city and utterly destroy all of its inhabitants, and even all of the cattle. 16Afterwards you must pile all the booty into the middle of the street and burn it, then put the entire city to the torch, as a burnt offering to Jehovah your God. That city shall forever remain a lifeless mound and may never be rebuilt. 17Keep none of the booty! Then the Lord will turn from his fierce anger and be merciful to you, and have compassion upon you, and make you a great nation just as he promised your ancestors.

18"Of course, the Lord your God will be merciful only if you have been obedient to him and to his commandments which I am giving you today, and if you have been doing that which is right in the eyes of the Lord.

New Revised Standard

13[b] IF PROPHETS or those who divine by dreams appear among you and promise you omens or portents, 2and the omens or the portents declared by them take place, and they say, "Let us follow other gods" (whom you have not known) "and let us serve them," 3you must not heed the words of those prophets or those who divine by dreams; for the LORD your God is testing you, to know whether you indeed love the LORD your God with all your heart and soul. 4The LORD your God you shall follow, him alone you shall fear, his commandments you shall keep, his voice you shall obey, him you shall serve, and to him you shall hold fast. 5But those prophets or those who divine by dreams shall be put to death for having spoken treason against the LORD your God—who brought you out of the land of Egypt and redeemed you from the house of slavery—to turn you from the way in which the LORD your God commanded you to walk. So you shall purge the evil from your midst.

6 If anyone secretly entices you—even if it is your brother, your father's son or[c] your mother's son, or your own son or daughter, or the wife you embrace, or your most intimate friend—saying, "Let us go worship other gods," whom neither you nor your ancestors have known, 7any of the gods of the peoples that are around you, whether near you or far away from you, from one end of the earth to the other, 8you must not yield to or heed any such persons. Show them no pity or compassion and do not shield them. 9But you shall surely kill them; your own hand shall be first against them to execute them, and afterwards the hand of all the people. 10Stone them to death for trying to turn you away from the LORD your God, who brought you out of the land of Egypt, out of the house of slavery. 11Then all Israel shall hear and be afraid, and never again do any such wickedness.

12 If you hear it said about one of the towns that the LORD your God is giving you to live in, 13that scoundrels from among you have gone out and led the inhabitants of the town astray, saying, "Let us go and worship other gods," whom you have not known, 14then you shall inquire and make a thorough investigation. If the charge is established that such an abhorrent thing has been done among you, 15you shall put the inhabitants of that town to the sword, utterly destroying it and everything in it—even putting its livestock to the sword. 16All of its spoil you shall gather into its public square; then burn the town and all its spoil with fire, as a whole burnt offering to the LORD your God. It shall remain a perpetual ruin, never to be rebuilt. 17Do not let anything devoted to destruction stick to your hand, so that the LORD may turn from his fierce anger and show you compassion, and in his compassion multiply you, as he swore to your ancestors, 18if you obey the voice of the LORD your God by keeping all his commandments that I am commanding you today, doing what is right in the sight of the LORD your God.

King James

14 YE *ARE* the children of the LORD your God: ye shall not cut yourselves, nor make any baldness between your eyes for the dead.

2For thou *art* an holy people unto the LORD thy God, and the LORD hath chosen thee to be a peculiar people unto himself, above all the nations that *are* upon the earth.

3¶ Thou shalt not eat any abominable thing.

4These *are* the beasts which ye shall eat: the ox, the sheep, and the goat,

5The hart, and the roebuck, and the fallow deer, and the wild goat, and the pygarg, and the wild ox, and the chamois.

6And every beast that parteth the hoof, and cleaveth the cleft into two claws, *and* cheweth the cud among the beasts, that ye shall eat.

7Nevertheless these ye shall not eat of them that chew the cud, or of them that divide the cloven hoof; *as* the camel, and the hare, and the coney: for they chew the cud, but divide not the hoof; *therefore* they *are* unclean unto you.

8And the swine, because it divideth the hoof, yet cheweth not the cud, it *is* unclean unto you: ye shall not eat of their flesh, nor touch their dead carcase.

9¶ These ye shall eat of all that *are* in the waters: all that have fins and scales shall ye eat:

10And whatsoever hath not fins and scales ye may not eat; it *is* unclean unto you.

11¶ *Of* all clean birds ye shall eat.

12But these *are* they of which ye shall not eat: the eagle, and the ossifrage, and the ospray,

13And the glede, and the kite, and the vulture after his kind,

14And every raven after his kind,

15And the owl, and the night hawk, and the cuckoo, and the hawk after his kind,

16The little owl, and the great owl, and the swan,

17And the pelican, and the gier eagle, and the cormorant,

18And the stork, and the heron after her kind, and the lapwing, and the bat.

19And every creeping thing that flieth *is* unclean unto you: they shall not be eaten.

20*But of* all clean fowls ye may eat.

21¶ Ye shall not eat *of* any thing that dieth of itself: thou shalt give it unto the stranger that *is* in thy gates, that he may eat it; or thou mayest sell it unto an alien: for thou *art* an holy people unto the LORD thy God. Thou shalt not seethe a kid in his mother's milk.

22Thou shalt truly tithe all the increase of thy seed, that the field bringeth forth year by year.

23And thou shalt eat before the LORD thy God, in the place which he shall choose to place his name there, the tithe of thy corn, of thy wine, and of thine oil, and the firstlings of thy herds and of thy flocks; that thou mayest learn to fear the LORD thy God always.

24And if the way be too long for thee, so that thou art not able to carry it; *or* if the place be too far from thee, which the LORD thy God shall choose to set his name there, when the LORD thy God hath blessed thee:

25Then shalt thou turn *it* into money, and bind up the money in thine hand, and shalt go unto the place which the LORD thy God shall choose:

26And thou shalt bestow that money for whatsoever thy soul lusteth after, for oxen, or for sheep, or for wine, or for strong drink, or for whatsoever thy soul desireth: and thou shalt eat there before the LORD thy God, and thou shalt rejoice, thou, and thine household.

27And the Levite that *is* within thy gates; thou shalt not forsake him; for he hath no part nor inheritance with thee.

New International

Clean and Unclean Food

14 YOU ARE the children of the LORD your God. Do not cut yourselves or shave the front of your heads for the dead, 2for you are a people holy to the LORD your God. Out of all the peoples on the face of the earth, the LORD has chosen you to be his treasured possession.

3Do not eat any detestable thing. 4These are the animals you may eat: the ox, the sheep, the goat, 5the deer, the gazelle, the roe deer, the wild goat, the ibex, the antelope and the mountain sheep.a 6You may eat any animal that has a split hoof divided in two and that chews the cud. 7However, of those that chew the cud or that have a split hoof completely divided you may not eat the camel, the rabbit or the coney.b Although they chew the cud, they do not have a split hoof; they are ceremonially unclean for you. 8The pig is also unclean; although it has a split hoof, it does not chew the cud. You are not to eat their meat or touch their carcasses.

9Of all the creatures living in the water, you may eat any that has fins and scales. 10But anything that does not have fins and scales you may not eat; for you it is unclean.

11You may eat any clean bird. 12But these you may not eat: the eagle, the vulture, the black vulture, 13the red kite, the black kite, any kind of falcon, 14any kind of raven, 15the horned owl, the screech owl, the gull, any kind of hawk, 16the little owl, the great owl, the white owl, 17the desert owl, the osprey, the cormorant, 18the stork, any kind of heron, the hoopoe and the bat.

19All flying insects that swarm are unclean to you; do not eat them. 20But any winged creature that is clean you may eat.

21Do not eat anything you find already dead. You may give it to an alien living in any of your towns, and he may eat it, or you may sell it to a foreigner. But you are a people holy to the LORD your God.

Do not cook a young goat in its mother's milk.

Tithes

22Be sure to set aside a tenth of all that your fields produce each year. 23Eat the tithe of your grain, new wine and oil, and the firstborn of your herds and flocks in the presence of the LORD your God at the place he will choose as a dwelling for his Name, so that you may learn to revere the LORD your God always. 24But if that place is too distant and you have been blessed by the LORD your God and cannot carry your tithe (because the place where the LORD will choose to put his Name is so far away), 25then exchange your tithe for silver, and take the silver with you and go to the place the LORD your God will choose. 26Use the silver to buy whatever you like: cattle, sheep, wine or other fermented drink, or anything you wish. Then you and your household shall eat there in the presence of the LORD your God and rejoice. 27And do not neglect the Levites living in your towns, for they have no allotment or inheritance of their own.

---

a 5 The precise identification of some of the birds and animals in this chapter is uncertain.   b 7 That is, the hyrax or rock badger

Living Bible

14 "SINCE YOU are the people of God, never cut yourselves [as the heathen do when they worship their idols^c] nor shave the front halves of your heads for funerals. 2You belong exclusively to the Lord your God, and he has chosen you to be his own possession, more so than any other nation on the face of the earth.

3, 4, 5"You are not to eat any animal I have declared to be ceremonially defiled. These are the animals you may eat:

The ox, the sheep, the goat,
The deer, the gazelle, the roebuck,
The wild goat, the ibex,
The antelope, and the mountain sheep.

6"Any animal that has cloven hooves and chews the cud may be eaten, 7but if the animal doesn't have both, it may not be eaten. So you may not eat the camel, the hare, or the coney.

"They chew the cud but do not have cloven hooves. 8Pigs may not be eaten because, although they have cloven hooves, they don't chew the cud. You may not even touch the dead bodies of such animals.

9"Only sea animals with fins and scales may be eaten; 10all other kinds are ceremonially defiled.

11-18"You may eat any bird except the following:

The eagle, the vulture,
The osprey, the buzzard,
The falcon (any variety),
The raven (any variety),
The ostrich, the nighthawk,
The sea gull, the hawk (any variety),
The screech owl, the great owl,
The horned owl, the pelican,
The vulture, the cormorant,
The stork, the heron (any variety),
The hoopoe, the bat.

19, 20"With certain exceptions,^d insects are a defilement to you and may not be eaten.

21"Don't eat anything that has died a natural death. However, a foreigner among you may eat it. You may give it or sell it to him, but don't eat it yourself, for you are holy to the Lord your God.

"You must not boil a young goat in its mother's milk.

22"You must tithe all of your crops every year. 23Bring this tithe to eat before the Lord your God at the place he shall choose as his sanctuary; this applies to your tithes of grain, new wine, olive oil, and the firstborn of your flocks and herds. The purpose of tithing is to teach you always to put God first in your lives. 24If the place the Lord chooses for his sanctuary is so far away that it isn't convenient to carry your tithes to that place, 25then you may sell the tithe portion of your crops and herds and take the money to the Lord's sanctuary. 26When you arrive, use the money to buy an ox, a sheep, some wine, or beer, to feast there before the Lord your God, and to rejoice with your household.

27"Don't forget to share your income with the Levites in your community, for they have no property or crops as you do.

New Revised Standard

Pagan Practices Forbidden

14 YOU ARE children of the LORD your God. You must not lacerate yourselves or shave your forelocks for the dead. 2For you are a people holy to the LORD your God; it is you the LORD has chosen out of all the peoples on earth to be his people, his treasured possession.

Clean and Unclean Foods

3 You shall not eat any abhorrent thing. 4These are the animals you may eat: the ox, the sheep, the goat, 5the deer, the gazelle, the roebuck, the wild goat, the ibex, the antelope, and the mountain-sheep. 6Any animal that divides the hoof and has the hoof cleft in two, and chews the cud, among the animals, you may eat. 7Yet of those that chew the cud or have the hoof cleft you shall not eat these: the camel, the hare, and the rock badger, because they chew the cud but do not divide the hoof; they are unclean for you. 8And the pig, because it divides the hoof but does not chew the cud, is unclean for you. You shall not eat their meat, and you shall not touch their carcasses.

9 Of all that live in water you may eat these: whatever has fins and scales you may eat. 10And whatever does not have fins and scales you shall not eat; it is unclean for you.

11 You may eat any clean birds. 12But these are the ones that you shall not eat: the eagle, the vulture, the osprey, 13the buzzard, the kite, of any kind; 14every raven of any kind; 15the ostrich, the nighthawk, the sea gull, the hawk, of any kind; 16the little owl and the great owl, the water hen 17and the desert owl,^e the carrion vulture and the cormorant, 18the stork, the heron, of any kind; the hoopoe and the bat.^f 19And all winged insects are unclean for you; they shall not be eaten. 20You may eat any clean winged creature.

21 You shall not eat anything that dies of itself; you may give it to aliens residing in your towns for them to eat, or you may sell it to a foreigner. For you are a people holy to the LORD your God.

You shall not boil a kid in its mother's milk.

Regulations concerning Tithes

22 Set apart a tithe of all the yield of your seed that is brought in yearly from the field. 23In the presence of the LORD your God, in the place that he will choose as a dwelling for his name, you shall eat the tithe of your grain, your wine, and your oil, as well as the firstlings of your herd and flock, so that you may learn to fear the LORD your God always. 24But if, when the LORD your God has blessed you, the distance is so great that you are unable to transport it, because the place where the LORD your God will choose to set his name is too far away from you, 25then you may turn it into money. With the money secure in hand, go to the place that the LORD your God will choose; 26spend the money for whatever you wish—oxen, sheep, wine, strong drink, or whatever you desire. And you shall eat there in the presence of the LORD your God, you and your household rejoicing together. 27As for the Levites resident in your towns, do not neglect them, because they have no allotment or inheritance with you.

---

^c 14:1 as the heathen do when they worship idols, implied.
^d 14:19, 20 With certain exceptions. See Lev 11:20-23.

^e Or pelican ^f Identification of several of the birds in verses 12-18 is uncertain

King James

28¶ At the end of three years thou shalt bring forth all the tithe of thine increase the same year, and shalt lay *it* up within thy gates:

29And the Levite, (because he hath no part nor inheritance with thee,) and the stranger, and the fatherless, and the widow, which *are* within thy gates, shall come, and shall eat and be satisfied; that the LORD thy God may bless thee in all the work of thine hand which thou doest.

15 AT THE end of *every* seven years thou shalt make a release.

2And this *is* the manner of the release: Every creditor that lendeth *aught* unto his neighbour shall release *it;* he shall not exact *it* of his neighbour, or of his brother; because it is called the LORD's release.

3Of a foreigner thou mayest exact *it again:* but *that* which is thine with thy brother thine hand shall release;

4Save when there shall be no poor among you; for the LORD shall greatly bless thee in the land which the LORD thy God giveth thee *for* an inheritance to possess it:

5Only if thou carefully hearken unto the voice of the LORD thy God, to observe to do all these commandments which I command thee this day.

6For the LORD thy God blesseth thee, as he promised thee: and thou shalt lend unto many nations, but thou shalt not borrow; and thou shalt reign over many nations, but they shall not reign over thee.

7¶ If there be among you a poor man of one of thy brethren within any of thy gates in thy land which the LORD thy God giveth thee, thou shalt not harden thine heart, nor shut thine hand from thy poor brother:

8But thou shalt open thine hand wide unto him, and shalt surely lend him sufficient for his need, *in that* which he wanteth.

9Beware that there be not a thought in thy wicked heart, saying, The seventh year, the year of release, is at hand; and thine eye be evil against thy poor brother, and thou givest him nought; and he cry unto the LORD against thee, and it be sin unto thee.

10Thou shalt surely give him, and thine heart shall not be grieved when thou givest unto him: because that for this thing the LORD thy God shall bless thee in all thy works, and in all that thou puttest thine hand unto.

11For the poor shall never cease out of the land: therefore I command thee, saying, Thou shalt open thine hand wide unto thy brother, to thy poor, and to thy needy, in thy land.

12¶ *And* if thy brother, an Hebrew man, or an Hebrew woman, be sold unto thee, and serve thee six years; then in the seventh year thou shalt let him go free from thee.

13And when thou sendest him out free from thee, thou shalt not let him go away empty:

14Thou shalt furnish him liberally out of thy flock, and out of thy floor, and out of thy winepress: *of that* wherewith the LORD thy God hath blessed thee thou shalt give unto him.

15And thou shalt remember that thou wast a bondman in the land of Egypt, and the LORD thy God redeemed thee: therefore I command thee this thing today.

16And it shall be, if he say unto thee, I will not go away from thee; because he loveth thee and thine house, because he is well with thee;

17Then thou shalt take an awl, and thrust *it* through his ear unto the door, and he shall be thy servant for ever. And also unto thy maidservant thou shalt do likewise.

18It shall not seem hard unto thee, when thou sendest him away free from thee; for he hath been worth a double hired servant *to thee,* in serving thee six years: and the LORD thy God shall bless thee in all that thou doest.

New International

28At the end of every three years, bring all the tithes of that year's produce and store it in your towns, 29so that the Levites (who have no allotment or inheritance of their own) and the aliens, the fatherless and the widows who live in your towns may come and eat and be satisfied, and so that the LORD your God may bless you in all the work of your hands.

The Year for Canceling Debts

15 AT THE end of every seven years you must cancel debts. 2This is how it is to be done: Every creditor shall cancel the loan he has made to his fellow Israelite. He shall not require payment from his fellow Israelite or brother, because the LORD's time for canceling debts has been proclaimed. 3You may require payment from a foreigner, but you must cancel any debt your brother owes you. 4However, there should be no poor among you, for in the land the LORD your God is giving you to possess as your inheritance, he will richly bless you, 5if only you fully obey the LORD your God and are careful to follow all these commands I am giving you today. 6For the LORD your God will bless you as he has promised, and you will lend to many nations but will borrow from none. You will rule over many nations but none will rule over you.

7If there is a poor man among your brothers in any of the towns of the land that the LORD your God is giving you, do not be hardhearted or tightfisted toward your poor brother. 8Rather be openhanded and freely lend him whatever he needs. 9Be careful not to harbor this wicked thought: "The seventh year, the year for canceling debts, is near," so that you do not show ill will toward your needy brother and give him nothing. He may then appeal to the LORD against you, and you will be found guilty of sin. 10Give generously to him and do so without a grudging heart; then because of this the LORD your God will bless you in all your work and in everything you put your hand to. 11There will always be poor people in the land. Therefore I command you to be openhanded toward your brothers and toward the poor and needy in your land.

Freeing Servants

12If a fellow Hebrew, a man or a woman, sells himself to you and serves you six years, in the seventh year you must let him go free. 13And when you release him, do not send him away empty-handed. 14Supply him liberally from your flock, your threshing floor and your winepress. Give to him as the LORD your God has blessed you. 15Remember that you were slaves in Egypt and the LORD your God redeemed you. That is why I give you this command today.

16But if your servant says to you, "I do not want to leave you," because he loves you and your family and is well off with you, 17then take an awl and push it through his ear lobe into the door, and he will become your servant for life. Do the same for your maidservant.

18Do not consider it a hardship to set your servant free, because his service to you these six years has been worth twice as much as that of a hired hand. And the LORD your God will bless you in everything you do.

Living Bible

28"Every third year you are to use your entire tithe for local welfare programs: 29Give it to the Levites who have no inheritance among you, or to foreigners, or to widows and orphans within your city, so that they can eat and be satisfied; and then Jehovah your God will bless you and your work.

15 "AT THE end of every seventh year there is to be a canceling of all debts! 2Every creditor shall write 'Paid in full' on any promissory note he holds against a fellow Israelite, for the Lord has released everyone from his obligation. 3(This release does not apply to foreigners.) 4, 5No one will become poor because of this, for the Lord will greatly bless you in the land he is giving you if you obey this command. The only prerequisite for his blessing is that you carefully heed all the commands of the Lord your God that I am giving you today. 6He will bless you as he has promised. You shall lend money to many nations but will never need to borrow! You shall rule many nations, but they shall not rule over you!

7"But if, when you arrive in the land the Lord will give you, there are any among you who are poor, you must not shut your heart or hand against them; 8you must lend them as much as they need. 9Beware! Don't refuse a loan because the year of debt cancellation is close at hand! If you refuse to make the loan and the needy man cries out to the Lord, it will be counted against you as a sin. 10You must lend him what he needs, and don't moan about it either! For the Lord will prosper you in everything you do because of this! 11There will always be some among you who are poor; that is why this commandment is necessary. You must lend to them liberally.

12"If you buy a Hebrew slave, whether a man or woman, you must free him at the end of the sixth year you have owned him, 13and don't send him away empty-handed! 14Give him a large farewell present from your flock, your olive press, and your wine press. Share with him in proportion as the Lord your God has blessed you. 15Remember that you were slaves in the land of Egypt and the Lord your God rescued you! That is why I am giving you this command.

16"But if your Hebrew slave doesn't want to leave—if he says he loves you and enjoys your pleasant home and gets along well with you— 17then take an awl and pierce his ear into the door, and after that he shall be your slave forever. Do the same with your women slaves. 18But when you free a slave you must not feel bad, for remember that for six years he has cost you less than half the price of a hired hand! And the Lord your God will prosper all you do because you have released him!

New Revised Standard

28 Every third year you shall bring out the full tithe of your produce for that year, and store it within your towns; 29 the Levites, because they have no allotment or inheritance with you, as well as the resident aliens, the orphans, and the widows in your towns, may come and eat their fill so that the LORD your God may bless you in all the work that you undertake.

Laws concerning the Sabbatical Year

15 EVERY SEVENTH year you shall grant a remission of debts. 2And this is the manner of the remission: every creditor shall remit the claim that is held against a neighbor, not exacting it of a neighbor who is a member of the community, because the LORD's remission has been proclaimed. 3Of a foreigner you may exact it, but you must remit your claim on whatever any member of your community owes you. 4There will, however, be no one in need among you, because the LORD is sure to bless you in the land that the LORD your God is giving you as a possession to occupy, 5if only you will obey the LORD your God by diligently observing this entire commandment that I command you today. 6When the LORD your God has blessed you, as he promised you, you shall lend to many nations, but you will not borrow; you will rule over many nations, but they will not rule over you.

7 If there is among you anyone in need, a member of your community in any of your towns within the land that the LORD your God is giving you, do not be hardhearted or tight-fisted toward your needy neighbor. 8You should rather open your hand, willingly lending enough to meet the need, whatever it may be. 9Be careful that you do not entertain a mean thought, thinking, "The seventh year, the year of remission, is near," and therefore view your needy neighbor with hostility and give nothing; your neighbor might cry to the LORD against you, and you would incur guilt. 10Give liberally and be ungrudging when you do so, for on this account the LORD your God will bless you in all your work and in all that you undertake. 11Since there will never cease to be some in need on the earth, I therefore command you, "Open your hand to the poor and needy neighbor in your land."

12 If a member of your community, whether a Hebrew man or a Hebrew woman, is solda to you and works for you six years, in the seventh year you shall set that person free. 13 And when you send a male slaveb out from you a free person, you shall not send him out empty-handed. 14Provide liberally out of your flock, your threshing floor, and your wine press, thus giving to him some of the bounty with which the LORD your God has blessed you. 15Remember that you were a slave in the land of Egypt, and the LORD your God redeemed you; for this reason I lay this command upon you today. 16But if he says to you, "I will not go out from you," because he loves you and your household, since he is well off with you, 17then you shall take an awl and thrust it through his earlobe into the door, and he shall be your slavec forever.

You shall do the same with regard to your female slave.d

18 Do not consider it a hardship when you send them out from you free persons, because for six years they have given you services worth the wages of hired laborers; and the LORD your God will bless you in all that you do.

---

a Or *sells himself or herself*   b Heb *him*   c Or *bondman*   d Or *bondwoman*

King James

19¶ All the firstling males that come of thy herd and of thy flock thou shalt sanctify unto the LORD thy God: thou shalt do no work with the firstling of thy bullock, nor shear the firstling of thy sheep.

20Thou shalt eat *it* before the LORD thy God year by year in the place which the LORD shall choose, thou and thy household.

21And if there be *any* blemish therein, *as if it be* lame, or blind, *or have* any ill blemish, thou shalt not sacrifice it unto the LORD thy God.

22Thou shalt eat it within thy gates: the unclean and the clean *person shall eat it* alike, as the roebuck, and as the hart.

23Only thou shalt not eat the blood thereof; thou shalt pour it upon the ground as water.

16 OBSERVE THE month of Abib, and keep the passover unto the LORD thy God: for in the month of Abib the LORD thy God brought thee forth out of Egypt by night.

2Thou shalt therefore sacrifice the passover unto the LORD thy God, of the flock and the herd, in the place which the LORD shall choose to place his name there.

3Thou shalt eat no leavened bread with it; seven days shalt thou eat unleavened bread therewith, *even* the bread of affliction; for thou camest forth out of the land of Egypt in haste: that thou mayest remember the day when thou camest forth out of the land of Egypt all the days of thy life.

4And there shall be no leavened bread seen with thee in all thy coast seven days; neither shall there *any thing* of the flesh, which thou sacrificedst the first day at even, remain all night until the morning.

5Thou mayest not sacrifice the passover within any of thy gates, which the LORD thy God giveth thee:

6But at the place which the LORD thy God shall choose to place his name in, there thou shalt sacrifice the passover at even, at the going down of the sun, at the season that thou camest forth out of Egypt.

7And thou shalt roast and eat *it* in the place which the LORD thy God shall choose: and thou shalt turn in the morning, and go unto thy tents.

8Six days thou shalt eat unleavened bread: and on the seventh day *shall be* a solemn assembly to the LORD thy God: thou shalt do no work *therein.*

9¶ Seven weeks shalt thou number unto thee: begin to number the seven weeks from *such time as* thou beginnest *to put* the sickle to the corn.

10And thou shalt keep the feast of weeks unto the LORD thy God with a tribute of a freewill offering of thine hand, which thou shalt give *unto the LORD thy God,* according as the LORD thy God hath blessed thee:

11And thou shalt rejoice before the LORD thy God, thou, and thy son, and thy daughter, and thy manservant, and thy maidservant, and the Levite that *is* within thy gates, and the stranger, and the fatherless, and the widow, that *are* among you, in the place which the LORD thy God hath chosen to place his name there.

12And thou shalt remember that thou wast a bondman in Egypt: and thou shalt observe and do these statutes.

13¶ Thou shalt observe the feast of tabernacles seven days, after that thou hast gathered in thy corn and thy wine:

14And thou shalt rejoice in thy feast, thou, and thy son, and thy daughter, and thy manservant, and thy maidservant, and the Levite, the stranger, and the fatherless, and the widow, that *are* within thy gates.

New International

The Firstborn Animals

19Set apart for the LORD your God every firstborn male of your herds and flocks. Do not put the firstborn of your oxen to work, and do not shear the firstborn of your sheep. 20Each year you and your family are to eat them in the presence of the LORD your God at the place he will choose. 21If an animal has a defect, is lame or blind, or has any serious flaw, you must not sacrifice it to the LORD your God. 22You are to eat it in your own towns. Both the ceremonially unclean and the clean may eat it, as if it were gazelle or deer. 23But you must not eat the blood; pour it out on the ground like water.

Passover

16 OBSERVE THE month of Abib and celebrate the Passover of the LORD your God, because in the month of Abib he brought you out of Egypt by night. 2Sacrifice as the Passover to the LORD your God an animal from your flock or herd at the place the LORD will choose as a dwelling for his Name. 3Do not eat it with bread made with yeast, but for seven days eat unleavened bread, the bread of affliction, because you left Egypt in haste—so that all the days of your life you may remember the time of your departure from Egypt. 4Let no yeast be found in your possession in all your land for seven days. Do not let any of the meat you sacrifice on the evening of the first day remain until morning.

5You must not sacrifice the Passover in any town the LORD your God gives you 6except in the place he will choose as a dwelling for his Name. There you must sacrifice the Passover in the evening, when the sun goes down, on the anniversary[a] of your departure from Egypt. 7Roast it and eat it at the place the LORD your God will choose. Then in the morning return to your tents. 8For six days eat unleavened bread and on the seventh day hold an assembly to the LORD your God and do no work.

Feast of Weeks

9Count off seven weeks from the time you begin to put the sickle to the standing grain. 10Then celebrate the Feast of Weeks to the LORD your God by giving a freewill offering in proportion to the blessings the LORD your God has given you. 11And rejoice before the LORD your God at the place he will choose as a dwelling for his Name—you, your sons and daughters, your menservants and maidservants, the Levites in your towns, and the aliens, the fatherless and the widows living among you. 12Remember that you were slaves in Egypt, and follow carefully these decrees.

Feast of Tabernacles

13Celebrate the Feast of Tabernacles for seven days after you have gathered the produce of your threshing floor and your winepress. 14Be joyful at your Feast—you, your sons and daughters, your menservants and maidservants, and the Levites, the aliens, the fatherless and the widows who live in your towns. 15For seven

---

^a 6 Or *down, at the time of day*

Living Bible

19"You shall set aside for God all the firstborn males from your flocks and herds. Do not use the firstborn of your herds to work your fields, and do not shear the firstborn of your flocks of sheep and goats. 20Instead, you and your family shall eat these animals before the Lord your God each year at his sanctuary. 21However, if this firstborn animal has any defect such as being lame or blind, or if anything else is wrong with it, you shall not sacrifice it. 22Instead, use it for food for your family at home. Anyone, even if ceremonially defiled at the time, may eat it, just as anyone may eat a gazelle or deer. 23But don't eat the blood; pour it out upon the ground like water.

16 "ALWAYS REMEMBER to celebrate the Passover during the month of April,b for that was when Jehovah your God brought you out of Egypt by night. 2Your Passover sacrifice shall be either a lamb or an ox, sacrificed to the Lord your God at his sanctuary. 3Eat the sacrifice with unleavened bread. Eat unleavened bread for seven days as a reminder of the bread you ate as you escaped from Egypt. This is to remind you that you left Egypt in such a hurry that there was no time for the bread to rise.c Remember that day all the rest of your lives! 4For seven days no trace of yeast shall be in your homes, and none of the Passover lamb shall be left until the next morning.

5"The Passover is not to be eaten in your homes. 6It must be eaten at the place the Lord shall choose as his sanctuary. Sacrifice it there on the anniversary evening just as the sun goes down. 7Roast the lamb and eat it, then start back to your homes the next morning. 8For the following six days you shall eat no bread made with yeast. On the seventh day there shall be a quiet gathering of the people of each city before the Lord your God. Don't do any work that day.

9"Seven weeks after the harvest begins, 10there shall be another festival before the Lord your God called the Festival of Weeks. At that time bring to him a free-will offering proportionate in size to his blessing upon you as judged by the amount of your harvest. 11It is a time to rejoice before the Lord with your family and household. And don't forget to include the local Levites, foreigners, widows, and orphans. Invite them to accompany you to the celebration at the sanctuary. 12Remember! You were a slave in Egypt, so be sure to carry out this command.

13"Another celebration, the Festival of Shelters, must be observed for seven days at the end of the harvest season, after the grain is threshed and the grapes have been pressed. 14This will be a happy time of rejoicing together with your family and servants. And don't forget to include the Levites, foreigners, orphans, and widows of your town.

New Revised Standard

The Firstborn of Livestock

19 Every firstling male born of your herd and flock you shall consecrate to the Lord your God; you shall not do work with your firstling ox nor shear the firstling of your flock. 20You shall eat it, you together with your household, in the presence of the Lord your God year by year at the place that the Lord will choose. 21But if it has any defect—any serious defect, such as lameness or blindness—you shall not sacrifice it to the Lord your God; 22within your towns you may eat it, the unclean and the clean alike, as you would a gazelle or deer. 23Its blood, however, you must not eat; you shall pour it out on the ground like water.

The Passover Reviewed

16 OBSERVE THE monthd of Abib by keeping the passover for the Lord your God, for in the month of Abib the Lord your God brought you out of Egypt by night. 2You shall offer the passover sacrifice for the Lord your God, from the flock and the herd, at the place that the Lord will choose as a dwelling for his name. 3You must not eat with it anything leavened. For seven days you shall eat unleavened bread with it—the bread of affliction—because you came out of the land of Egypt in great haste, so that all the days of your life you may remember the day of your departure from the land of Egypt. 4No leaven shall be seen with you in all your territory for seven days; and none of the meat of what you slaughter on the evening of the first day shall remain until morning. 5You are not permitted to offer the passover sacrifice within any of your towns that the Lord your God is giving you. 6But at the place that the Lord your God will choose as a dwelling for his name, only there shall you offer the passover sacrifice, in the evening at sunset, the time of day when you departed from Egypt. 7You shall cook it and eat it at the place that the Lord your God will choose; the next morning you may go back to your tents. 8For six days you shall continue to eat unleavened bread, and on the seventh day there shall be a solemn assembly for the Lord your God, when you shall do no work.

The Festival of Weeks Reviewed

9 You shall count seven weeks; begin to count the seven weeks from the time the sickle is first put to the standing grain. 10Then you shall keep the festival of weeks for the Lord your God, contributing a freewill offering in proportion to the blessing that you have received from the Lord your God. 11Rejoice before the Lord your God—you and your sons and your daughters, your male and female slaves, the Levites resident in your towns, as well as the strangers, the orphans, and the widows who are among you—at the place that the Lord your God will choose as a dwelling for his name. 12Remember that you were a slave in Egypt, and diligently observe these statutes.

The Festival of Booths Reviewed

13 You shall keep the festival of boothse for seven days, when you have gathered in the produce from your threshing floor and your wine press. 14Rejoice during your festival, you and your sons and your daughters, your male and female slaves, as well as the Levites, the strangers, the orphans, and the widows resident in your towns. 15Seven days you shall keep the festival for the

---

b 16:1 the month of April, literally, "Abib"—the first month of the Hebrew calendar.   c 16:3 you left Egypt in such a hurry that there was no time for the bread to rise, literally, "for you left Egypt in hurried flight."

d Or new moon   e Or tabernacles; Heb succoth

King James

15Seven days shalt thou keep a solemn feast unto the LORD thy God in the place which the LORD shall choose: because the LORD thy God shall bless thee in all thine increase, and in all the works of thine hands, therefore thou shalt surely rejoice.

16¶ Three times in a year shall all thy males appear before the LORD thy God in the place which he shall choose; in the feast of unleavened bread, and in the feast of weeks, and in the feast of tabernacles: and they shall not appear before the LORD empty:

17Every man *shall give* as he is able, according to the blessing of the LORD thy God which he hath given thee.

18¶ Judges and officers shalt thou make thee in all thy gates, which the LORD thy God giveth thee, throughout thy tribes: and they shall judge the people with just judgment.

19Thou shalt not wrest judgment; thou shalt not respect persons, neither take a gift: for a gift doth blind the eyes of the wise, and pervert the words of the righteous.

20That which is altogether just shalt thou follow, that thou mayest live, and inherit the land which the LORD thy God giveth thee.

21¶ Thou shalt not plant thee a grove of any trees near unto the altar of the LORD thy God, which thou shalt make thee.

22Neither shalt thou set thee up *any* image; which the LORD thy God hateth.

17 THOU SHALT not sacrifice unto the LORD thy God *any* bullock, or sheep, wherein is blemish, *or* any evilfavouredness: for that *is* an abomination unto the LORD thy God.

2¶ If there be found among you, within any of thy gates which the LORD thy God giveth thee, man or woman, that hath wrought wickedness in the sight of the LORD thy God, in transgressing his covenant,

3And hath gone and served other gods, and worshipped them, either the sun, or moon, or any of the host of heaven, which I have not commanded;

4And it be told thee, and thou hast heard *of it,* and inquired diligently, and, behold, *it be* true, *and* the thing certain, *that* such abomination is wrought in Israel:

5Then shalt thou bring forth that man or that woman, which have committed that wicked thing, unto thy gates, *even* that man or that woman, and shalt stone them with stones, till they die.

6At the mouth of two witnesses, or three witnesses, shall he that is worthy of death be put to death; *but* at the mouth of one witness he shall not be put to death.

7The hands of the witnesses shall be first upon him to put him to death, and afterward the hands of all the people. So thou shalt put the evil away from among you.

8¶ If there arise a matter too hard for thee in judgment, between blood and blood, between plea and plea, and between stroke and stroke, *being* matters of controversy within thy gates: then shalt thou arise, and get thee up into the place which the LORD thy God shall choose;

9And thou shalt come unto the priests the Levites, and unto the judge that shall be in those days, and inquire; and they shall show thee the sentence of judgment:

10And thou shalt do according to the sentence, which they of that place which the LORD shall choose shall show thee; and thou shalt observe to do according to all that they inform thee:

11According to the sentence of the law which they shall teach thee, and according to the judgment which they shall tell thee, thou shalt do: thou shalt not decline from the sentence which they shall show thee, *to* the right hand, nor *to* the left.

New International

days celebrate the Feast to the LORD your God at the place the LORD will choose. For the LORD your God will bless you in all your harvest and in all the work of your hands, and your joy will be complete.

16Three times a year all your men must appear before the LORD your God at the place he will choose: at the Feast of Unleavened Bread, the Feast of Weeks and the Feast of Tabernacles. No man should appear before the LORD empty-handed: 17Each of you must bring a gift in proportion to the way the LORD your God has blessed you.

Judges

18Appoint judges and officials for each of your tribes in every town the LORD your God is giving you, and they shall judge the people fairly. 19Do not pervert justice or show partiality. Do not accept a bribe, for a bribe blinds the eyes of the wise and twists the words of the righteous. 20Follow justice and justice alone, so that you may live and possess the land the LORD your God is giving you.

Worshiping Other Gods

21Do not set up any wooden Asherah pole[a] beside the altar you build to the LORD your God, 22and do not erect a sacred stone, for these the LORD your God hates.

17 DO NOT sacrifice to the LORD your God an ox or a sheep that has any defect or flaw in it, for that would be detestable to him.

2If a man or woman living among you in one of the towns the LORD gives you is found doing evil in the eyes of the LORD your God in violation of his covenant, 3and contrary to my command has worshiped other gods, bowing down to them or to the sun or the moon or the stars of the sky, 4and this has been brought to your attention, then you must investigate it thoroughly. If it is true and it has been proved that this detestable thing has been done in Israel, 5take the man or woman who has done this evil deed to your city gate and stone that person to death. 6On the testimony of two or three witnesses a man shall be put to death, but no one shall be put to death on the testimony of only one witness. 7The hands of the witnesses must be the first in putting him to death, and then the hands of all the people. You must purge the evil from among you.

Law Courts

8If cases come before your courts that are too difficult for you to judge—whether bloodshed, lawsuits or assaults—take them to the place the LORD your God will choose. 9Go to the priests, who are Levites, and to the judge who is in office at that time. Inquire of them and they will give you the verdict. 10You must act according to the decisions they give you at the place the LORD will choose. Be careful to do everything they direct you to do. 11Act according to the law they teach you and the decisions they give you. Do not turn aside from what they tell you, to the right or to the left. 12The man who

---

a 21 Or *Do not plant any tree dedicated to Asherah*

Living Bible

15"This feast will be held at the sanctuary, which will be located at the place the Lord will designate. It is a time of deep thanksgiving to the Lord for blessing you with a good harvest and in so many other ways; it shall be a time of great joy.

16"Every man in Israel shall appear before the Lord your God three times a year at the sanctuary for these festivals:

The Festival of Unleavened Bread,
The Festival of Weeks,
The Festival of Shelters.

"On each of these occasions bring a gift to the Lord. 17Give as you are able, according as the Lord has blessed you.

18"Appoint judges and administrative officials for all the cities the Lord your God is giving you. They will administer justice in every part of the land. 19Never twist justice to benefit a rich man, and never accept bribes. For bribes blind the eyes of the wisest and corrupt their decisions. 20Justice must prevail.

"That is the only way you will be successful in the land which the Lord your God is giving you.

21"Never, under any circumstances, are you to erect shameful images beside the altar of the Lord your God. 22And never set up stone pillars to worship them, for the Lord hates them!

17 "NEVER SACRIFICE a sick or defective ox or sheep to the Lord your God. He doesn't feel honored by such gifts!

2, 3"If anyone, whether man or woman, in any village throughout your land violates your covenant with God by worshiping other gods, the sun, moon, or stars— which I have strictly forbidden— 4first check the rumor very carefully; if there is no doubt it is true, 5then that man or woman shall be taken outside the city and shall be stoned to death. 6However, never put a man to death on the testimony of only one witness; there must be at least two or three. 7The witnesses shall throw the first stones, and then all the people shall join in. In this way you will purge all evil from among you.

8"If a case arises that is too hard for you to decide— for instance, whether someone is guilty of murder when there is insufficient evidence, or whether someone's rights have been violated—you shall take the case to the sanctuary of the Lord your God, 9to the priests and Levites, and the chief judge on duty at the time will make the decision. 10His decision is without appeal and is to be followed to the letter. 11The sentence he imposes is to be fully executed. 12If the defendant refuses to accept

New Revised Standard

LORD your God at the place that the LORD will choose; for the LORD your God will bless you in all your produce and in all your undertakings, and you shall surely celebrate.

16 Three times a year all your males shall appear before the LORD your God at the place that he will choose: at the festival of unleavened bread, at the festival of weeks, and at the festival of booths.b They shall not appear before the LORD empty-handed; 17all shall give as they are able, according to the blessing of the LORD your God that he has given you.

Municipal Judges and Officers

18 You shall appoint judges and officials throughout your tribes, in all your towns that the LORD your God is giving you, and they shall render just decisions for the people. 19You must not distort justice; you must not show partiality; and you must not accept bribes, for a bribe blinds the eyes of the wise and subverts the cause of those who are in the right. 20Justice, and only justice, you shall pursue, so that you may live and occupy the land that the LORD your God is giving you.

Forbidden Forms of Worship

21 You shall not plant any tree as a sacred polec beside the altar that you make for the LORD your God; 22nor shall you set up a stone pillar—things that the LORD your God hates.

17 YOU MUST not sacrifice to the LORD your God an ox or a sheep that has a defect, anything seriously wrong; for that is abhorrent to the LORD your God.

2 If there is found among you, in one of your towns that the LORD your God is giving you, a man or woman who does what is evil in the sight of the LORD your God, and transgresses his covenant 3by going to serve other gods and worshiping them—whether the sun or the moon or any of the host of heaven, which I have forbidden— 4and if it is reported to you or you hear of it, and you make a thorough inquiry, and the charge is proved true that such an abhorrent thing has occurred in Israel, 5then you shall bring out to your gates that man or that woman who has committed this crime and you shall stone the man or woman to death. 6On the evidence of two or three witnesses the death sentence shall be executed; a person must not be put to death on the evidence of only one witness. 7The hands of the witnesses shall be the first raised against the person to execute the death penalty, and afterward the hands of all the people. So you shall purge the evil from your midst.

Legal Decisions by Priests and Judges

8 If a judicial decision is too difficult for you to make between one kind of bloodshed and another, one kind of legal right and another, or one kind of assault and another—any such matters of dispute in your towns— then you shall immediately go up to the place that the LORD your God will choose, 9where you shall consult with the levitical priests and the judge who is in office in those days; they shall announce to you the decision in the case. 10Carry out exactly the decision that they announce to you from the place that the LORD will choose, diligently observing everything that they instruct you. 11You must carry out fully the law that they interpret for you or the ruling that they announce to you; do not turn aside from the decision that they announce to you, either to the right or to the left. 12As for anyone

b Or tabernacles; Heb succoth   c Heb Asherah

King James

12And the man that will do presumptuously, and will not hearken unto the priest that standeth to minister there before the LORD thy God, or unto the judge, even that man shall die: and thou shalt put away the evil from Israel.

13And all the people shall hear, and fear, and do no more presumptuously.

14¶ When thou art come unto the land which the LORD thy God giveth thee, and shalt possess it, and shalt dwell therein, and shalt say, I will set a king over me, like as all the nations that *are* about me;

15Thou shalt in any wise set *him* king over thee, whom the LORD thy God shall choose: *one* from among thy brethren shalt thou set king over thee: thou mayest not set a stranger over thee, which *is* not thy brother.

16But he shall not multiply horses to himself, nor cause the people to return to Egypt, to the end that he should multiply horses: forasmuch as the LORD hath said unto you, Ye shall henceforth return no more that way.

17Neither shall he multiply wives to himself, that his heart turn not away: neither shall he greatly multiply to himself silver and gold.

18And it shall be, when he sitteth upon the throne of his kingdom, that he shall write him a copy of this law in a book out of *that which is* before the priests the Levites:

19And it shall be with him, and he shall read therein all the days of his life: that he may learn to fear the LORD his God, to keep all the words of this law and these statutes, to do them:

20That his heart be not lifted up above his brethren, and that he turn not aside from the commandment, *to* the right hand, or *to* the left: to the end that he may prolong *his* days in his kingdom, he, and his children, in the midst of Israel.

18 THE PRIESTS the Levites, *and* all the tribe of Levi, shall have no part nor inheritance with Israel: they shall eat the offerings of the LORD made by fire, and his inheritance.

2Therefore shall they have no inheritance among their brethren: the LORD *is* their inheritance, as he hath said unto them.

3¶ And this shall be the priest's due from the people, from them that offer a sacrifice, whether *it be* ox or sheep; and they shall give unto the priest the shoulder, and the two cheeks, and the maw.

4The firstfruit *also* of thy corn, of thy wine, and of thine oil, and the first of the fleece of thy sheep, shalt thou give him.

5For the LORD thy God hath chosen him out of all thy tribes, to stand to minister in the name of the LORD, him and his sons for ever.

6¶ And if a Levite come from any of thy gates out of all Israel, where he sojourned, and come with all the desire of his mind unto the place which the LORD shall choose;

7Then he shall minister in the name of the LORD his God, as all his brethren the Levites *do*, which stand there before the LORD.

8They shall have like portions to eat, beside that which cometh of the sale of his patrimony.

9¶ When thou art come into the land which the LORD thy God giveth thee, thou shalt not learn to do after the abominations of those nations.

10There shall not be found among you *any one* that maketh his son or his daughter to pass through the fire, *or* that useth divination, *or* an observer of times, or an enchanter, or a witch,

11Or a charmer, or a consulter with familiar spirits, or a wizard, or a necromancer.

New International

shows contempt for the judge or for the priest who stands ministering there to the LORD your God must be put to death. You must purge the evil from Israel. 13All the people will hear and be afraid, and will not be contemptuous again.

The King

14When you enter the land the LORD your God is giving you and have taken possession of it and settled in it, and you say, "Let us set a king over us like all the nations around us," 15be sure to appoint over you the king the LORD your God chooses. He must be from among your own brothers. Do not place a foreigner over you, one who is not a brother Israelite. 16The king, moreover, must not acquire great numbers of horses for himself or make the people return to Egypt to get more of them, for the LORD has told you, "You are not to go back that way again." 17He must not take many wives, or his heart will be led astray. He must not accumulate large amounts of silver and gold.

18When he takes the throne of his kingdom, he is to write for himself on a scroll a copy of this law, taken from that of the priests, who are Levites. 19It is to be with him, and he is to read it all the days of his life so that he may learn to revere the LORD his God and follow carefully all the words of this law and these decrees 20and not consider himself better than his brothers and turn from the law to the right or to the left. Then he and his descendants will reign a long time over his kingdom in Israel.

Offerings for Priests and Levites

18 THE PRIESTS, who are Levites—indeed the whole tribe of Levi—are to have no allotment or inheritance with Israel. They shall live on the offerings made to the LORD by fire, for that is their inheritance. 2They shall have no inheritance among their brothers; the LORD is their inheritance, as he promised them.

3This is the share due the priests from the people who sacrifice a bull or a sheep: the shoulder, the jowls and the inner parts. 4You are to give them the firstfruits of your grain, new wine and oil, and the first wool from the shearing of your sheep, 5for the LORD your God has chosen them and their descendants out of all your tribes to stand and minister in the LORD's name always.

6If a Levite moves from one of your towns anywhere in Israel where he is living, and comes in all earnestness to the place the LORD will choose, 7he may minister in the name of the LORD his God like all his fellow Levites who serve there in the presence of the LORD. 8He is to share equally in their benefits, even though he has received money from the sale of family possessions.

Detestable Practices

9When you enter the land the LORD your God is giving you, do not learn to imitate the detestable ways of the nations there. 10Let no one be found among you who sacrifices his son or daughter ina the fire, who practices divination or sorcery, interprets omens, engages in witchcraft, 11or casts spells, or who is a medium or spiritist or who consults the dead. 12Anyone who does

---

a 10 Or *who makes his son or daughter pass through*

Living Bible

the decision of the priest or judge appointed by God for this purpose, the penalty is death. Such sinners must be purged from Israel. 13Then everyone will hear about what happened to the man who refused God's verdict, and they will be afraid to defy a court's judgment.

14"When you arrive in the land the Lord your God will give you, and have conquered it, and begin to think, 'We ought to have a king like the other nations around us'— 15be sure that you select as king the man the Lord your God shall choose. He must be an Israelite, not a foreigner. 16Be sure that he doesn't build up a large stable of horses for himself, nor send his men to Egypt to raise horses for him there, for the Lord has told you, 'Never return to Egypt again.' 17He must not have too many wives, lest his heart be turned away from the Lord, neither shall he be excessively rich.

18"And when he has been crowned and sits upon his throne as king, then he must copy these laws from the book kept by the Levite-priests. 19That copy of the laws shall be his constant companion. He must read from it every day of his life so that he will learn to respect the Lord his God by obeying all of his commands. 20This regular reading of God's laws will prevent him from feeling that he is better than his fellow citizens. It will also prevent him from turning away from God's laws in the slightest respect, and will ensure his having a long, good reign. His sons will then follow him upon the throne.

18 "REMEMBER THAT the priests and all the other members of the Levite tribe will not be given property like the other tribes. So the priests and Levites are to be supported by the sacrifices brought to the altar of the Lord and by the other offerings the people bring to him. 2They don't need to own property, for the Lord is their property! That is what he promised them! 3The shoulder, the cheeks, and the stomach of every ox or sheep brought for sacrifice must be given to the priests. 4In addition, the priests shall receive the harvest samples brought in thanksgiving to the Lord—the first of the grain, the new wine, the olive oil, and of the fleece at shearing time. 5For the Lord your God has chosen the tribe of Levi, of all the tribes, to minister to the Lord from generation to generation.

6, 7"Any Levite, no matter where he lives in the land of Israel, has the right to come to the sanctuary at any time and minister in the name of the Lord, just like his brother Levites who work there regularly. 8He shall be given his share of the sacrifices and offerings as his right, not just if he is in need.

9"When you arrive in the Promised Land you must be very careful lest you be corrupted by the horrible customs of the nations now living there. 10For example, any Israeli who presents his child to be burned to death as a sacrifice to heathen gods, must be killed.b No Israeli may practice black magic, or call on the evil spirits for aid, or be a fortune teller, 11or be a serpent charmer, medium, or wizard, or call forth the spirits of the dead.

New Revised Standard

who presumes to disobey the priest appointed to minister there to the Lord your God, or the judge, that person shall die. So you shall purge the evil from Israel. 13 All the people will hear and be afraid, and will not act presumptuously again.

Limitations of Royal Authority

14 When you have come into the land that the Lord your God is giving you, and have taken possession of it and settled in it, and you say, "I will set a king over me, like all the nations that are around me," 15 you may indeed set over you a king whom the Lord your God will choose. One of your own community you may set as king over you; you are not permitted to put a foreigner over you, who is not of your own community. 16 Even so, he must not acquire many horses for himself, or return the people to Egypt in order to acquire more horses, since the Lord has said to you, "You must never return that way again." 17 And he must not acquire many wives for himself, or else his heart will turn away; also silver and gold he must not acquire in great quantity for himself. 18 When he has taken the throne of his kingdom, he shall have a copy of this law written for him in the presence of the levitical priests. 19 It shall remain with him and he shall read in it all the days of his life, so that he may learn to fear the Lord his God, diligently observing all the words of this law and these statutes, 20 neither exalting himself above other members of the community nor turning aside from the commandment, either to the right or to the left, so that he and his descendants may reign long over his kingdom in Israel.

Privileges of Priests and Levites

18 THE LEVITICAL priests, the whole tribe of Levi, shall have no allotment or inheritance within Israel. They may eat the sacrifices that are the Lord's portionc 2 but they shall have no inheritance among the other members of the community; the Lord is their inheritance, as he promised them.

3 This shall be the priests' due from the people, from those offering a sacrifice, whether an ox or a sheep: they shall give to the priest the shoulder, the two jowls, and the stomach. 4 The first fruits of your grain, your wine, and your oil, as well as the first of the fleece of your sheep, you shall give him. 5 For the Lord your God has chosen Levid out of all your tribes, to stand and minister in the name of the Lord, him and his sons for all time.

6 If a Levite leaves any of your towns, from wherever he has been residing in Israel, and comes to the place that the Lord will choose (and he may come whenever he wishes), 7 then he may minister in the name of the Lord his God, like all his fellow-Levites who stand to minister there before the Lord. 8 They shall have equal portions to eat, even though they have income from the sale of family possessions.c

Child-Sacrifice, Divination, and Magic Prohibited

9 When you come into the land that the Lord your God is giving you, you must not learn to imitate the abhorrent practices of those nations. 10 No one shall be found among you who makes a son or daughter pass through fire, or who practices divination, or is a soothsayer, or an augur, or a sorcerer, 11 or one who casts spells, or who consults ghosts or spirits, or who seeks oracles from the dead. 12 For whoever does these things

---

b 18:10 Implied.   c Meaning of Heb uncertain   d Heb him

King James

12For all that do these things *are* an abomination unto the LORD: and because of these abominations the LORD thy God doth drive them out from before thee.

13Thou shalt be perfect with the LORD thy God.

14For these nations, which thou shalt possess, hearkened unto observers of times, and unto diviners: but as for thee, the LORD thy God hath not suffered thee so *to do*.

15¶ The LORD thy God will raise up unto thee a Prophet from the midst of thee, of thy brethren, like unto me; unto him ye shall hearken;

16According to all that thou desiredst of the LORD thy God in Horeb in the day of the assembly, saying, Let me not hear again the voice of the LORD my God, neither let me see this great fire any more, that I die not.

17And the LORD said unto me, They have well *spoken that* which they have spoken.

18I will raise them up a Prophet from among their brethren, like unto thee, and will put my words in his mouth; and he shall speak unto them all that I shall command him.

19And it shall come to pass, *that* whosoever will not hearken unto my words which he shall speak in my name, I will require *it* of him.

20But the prophet, which shall presume to speak a word in my name, which I have not commanded him to speak, or that shall speak in the name of other gods, even that prophet shall die.

21And if thou say in thine heart, How shall we know the word which the LORD hath not spoken?

22When a prophet speaketh in the name of the LORD, if the thing follow not, nor come to pass, that *is* the thing which the LORD hath not spoken, *but* the prophet hath spoken it presumptuously: thou shalt not be afraid of him.

19 WHEN THE LORD thy God hath cut off the nations, whose land the LORD thy God giveth thee, and thou succeedest them, and dwellest in their cities, and in their houses;

2Thou shalt separate three cities for thee in the midst of thy land, which the LORD thy God giveth thee to possess it.

3Thou shalt prepare thee a way, and divide the coasts of thy land, which the LORD thy God giveth thee to inherit, into three parts, that every slayer may flee thither.

4¶ And this *is* the case of the slayer, which shall flee thither, that he may live: Whoso killeth his neighbour ignorantly, whom he hated not in time past;

5As when a man goeth into the wood with his neighbour to hew wood, and his hand fetcheth a stroke with the axe to cut down the tree, and the head slippeth from the helve, and lighteth upon his neighbour, that he die; he shall flee unto one of those cities, and live:

6Lest the avenger of the blood pursue the slayer, while his heart is hot, and overtake him, because the way is long, and slay him; whereas he *was* not worthy of death, inasmuch as he hated him not in time past.

7Wherefore I command thee, saying, Thou shalt separate three cities for thee.

8And if the LORD thy God enlarge thy coast, as he hath sworn unto thy fathers, and give thee all the land which he promised to give unto thy fathers;

9If thou shalt keep all these commandments to do them, which I command thee this day, to love the LORD thy God, and to walk ever in his ways; then shalt thou add three cities more for thee, beside these three:

10That innocent blood be not shed in thy land, which the LORD thy God giveth thee *for* an inheritance, and *so* blood be upon thee.

New International

these things is detestable to the LORD, and because of these detestable practices the LORD your God will drive out those nations before you. 13You must be blameless before the LORD your God.

The Prophet

14The nations you will dispossess listen to those who practice sorcery or divination. But as for you, the LORD your God has not permitted you to do so. 15The LORD your God will raise up for you a prophet like me from among your own brothers. You must listen to him. 16For this is what you asked of the LORD your God at Horeb on the day of the assembly when you said, "Let us not hear the voice of the LORD our God nor see this great fire anymore, or we will die."

17The LORD said to me: "What they say is good. 18I will raise up for them a prophet like you from among their brothers; I will put my words in his mouth, and he will tell them everything I command him. 19If anyone does not listen to my words that the prophet speaks in my name, I myself will call him to account. 20But a prophet who presumes to speak in my name anything I have not commanded him to say, or a prophet who speaks in the name of other gods, must be put to death."

21You may say to yourselves, "How can we know when a message has not been spoken by the LORD?" 22If what a prophet proclaims in the name of the LORD does not take place or come true, that is a message the LORD has not spoken. That prophet has spoken presumptuously. Do not be afraid of him.

Cities of Refuge

19 WHEN THE LORD your God has destroyed the nations whose land he is giving you, and when you have driven them out and settled in their towns and houses, 2then set aside for yourselves three cities centrally located in the land the LORD your God is giving you to possess. 3Build roads to them and divide into three parts the land the LORD your God is giving you as an inheritance, so that anyone who kills a man may flee there.

4This is the rule concerning the man who kills another and flees there to save his life—one who kills his neighbor unintentionally, without malice aforethought. 5For instance, a man may go into the forest with his neighbor to cut wood, and as he swings his ax to fell a tree, the head may fly off and hit his neighbor and kill him. That man may flee to one of these cities and save his life. 6Otherwise, the avenger of blood might pursue him in a rage, overtake him if the distance is too great, and kill him even though he is not deserving of death, since he did it to his neighbor without malice aforethought. 7This is why I command you to set aside for yourselves three cities.

8If the LORD your God enlarges your territory, as he promised on oath to your forefathers, and gives you the whole land he promised them, 9because you carefully follow all these laws I command you today—to love the LORD your God and to walk always in his ways—then you are to set aside three more cities. 10Do this so that innocent blood will not be shed in your land, which the LORD your God is giving you as your inheritance, and so that you will not be guilty of bloodshed.

Living Bible

12Anyone doing these things is an object of horror and disgust to the Lord, and it is because the nations do these things that the Lord your God will displace them. 13You must walk blamelessly before the Lord your God. 14The nations you replace all do these evil things, but the Lord your God will not permit you to do such things.

15"Instead, he will raise up for you a Prophet like me, an Israeli, a man to whom you must listen and whom you must obey. 16For this is what you yourselves begged of God at Mount Horeb. There at the foot of the mountain you begged that you might not have to listen to the terrifying voice of God again, or see the awesome fire on the mountain, lest you die.

17"'All right,' the Lord said to me, 'I will do as they have requested. 18I will raise up from among them a Prophet, an Israeli like you. I will tell him what to say, and he shall be my spokesman to the people. 19I will personally deal with anyone who will not listen to him and heed his messages from me. 20But any prophet who falsely claims that his message is from me, shall die. And any prophet who claims to give a message from other gods must die.' 21If you wonder, 'How shall we know whether the prophecy is from the Lord or not?' 22this is the way to know: If the thing he prophesies doesn't happen, it is not the Lord who has given him the message; he has made it up himself. You have nothing to fear from him.

19 "WHEN THE Lord your God has destroyed the nations you will displace, and when you are living in their cities and homes, 2, 3you must set apart three Cities of Refuge so that anyone who accidentally kills someone may flee to safety. Divide the country into three districts, with one of these cities in each district; and keep the roads to these cities in good repair.

4"Here is an example of the purpose of these cities: 5If a man goes into the forest with his neighbor to chop wood, and the axe head flies off the handle and kills the man's neighbor, he may flee to one of those cities and be safe. 6, 7Anyone seeking to avenge the death will not be able to. These cities must be scattered so that one of them will be reasonably close to everyone; otherwise the angry avenger might catch and kill the innocent slayer, even though he should not have died since he had not killed deliberately.

8"If the Lord enlarges your boundaries as he promised your ancestors, and gives you all the land he promised 9(whether he does this depends on your obedience to all these commandments I am giving you today—loving the Lord your God and walking his paths), then you must designate three additional Cities of Refuge. 10In this way you will be able to avoid the death of innocent people, and you will not be held responsible for unjustified bloodshed.

New Revised Standard

is abhorrent to the LORD; it is because of such abhorrent practices that the LORD your God is driving them out before you. 13You must remain completely loyal to the LORD your God. 14Although these nations that you are about to dispossess do give heed to soothsayers and diviners, as for you, the LORD your God does not permit you to do so.

A New Prophet Like Moses

15 The LORD your God will raise up for you a prophet[a] like me from among your own people; you shall heed such a prophet.[b] 16This is what you requested of the LORD your God at Horeb on the day of the assembly when you said: "If I hear the voice of the LORD my God any more, or ever again see this great fire, I will die." 17Then the LORD replied to me: "They are right in what they have said. 18I will raise up for them a prophet[a] like you from among their own people; I will put my words in the mouth of the prophet,[c] who shall speak to them everything that I command. 19Anyone who does not heed the words that the prophet[d] shall speak in my name, I myself will hold accountable. 20But any prophet who speaks in the name of other gods, or who presumes to speak in my name a word that I have not commanded the prophet to speak—that prophet shall die." 21You may say to yourself, "How can we recognize a word that the LORD has not spoken?" 22If a prophet speaks in the name of the LORD but the thing does not take place or prove true, it is a word that the LORD has not spoken. The prophet has spoken it presumptuously; do not be frightened by it.

Laws concerning the Cities of Refuge

19 WHEN THE LORD your God has cut off the nations whose land the LORD your God is giving you, and you have dispossessed them and settled in their towns and in their houses, 2you shall set apart three cities in the land that the LORD your God is giving you to possess. 3You shall calculate the distances[e] and divide into three regions the land that the LORD your God gives you as a possession, so that any homicide can flee to one of them.

4 Now this is the case of a homicide who might flee there and live, that is, someone who has killed another person unintentionally when the two had not been at enmity before: 5Suppose someone goes into the forest with another to cut wood, and when one of them swings the ax to cut down a tree, the head slips from the handle and strikes the other person who then dies; the killer may flee to one of these cities and live. 6But if the distance is too great, the avenger of blood in hot anger might pursue and overtake and put the killer to death, although a death sentence was not deserved, since the two had not been at enmity before. 7Therefore I command you: You shall set apart three cities.

8 If the LORD your God enlarges your territory, as he swore to your ancestors—and he will give you all the land that he promised your ancestors to give you, 9provided you diligently observe this entire commandment that I command you today, by loving the LORD your God and walking always in his ways—then you shall add three more cities to these three, 10so that the blood of an innocent person may not be shed in the land that the LORD your God is giving you as an inheritance, thereby bringing bloodguilt upon you.

a Or prophets   b Or such prophets   c Or mouths of the prophets   d Heb he   e Or prepare roads to them

King James

11¶ But if any man hate his neighbour, and lie in wait for him, and rise up against him, and smite him mortally that he die, and fleeth into one of these cities:

12Then the elders of his city shall send and fetch him thence, and deliver him into the hand of the avenger of blood, that he may die.

13Thine eye shall not pity him, but thou shalt put away *the guilt of* innocent blood from Israel, that it may go well with thee.

14¶ Thou shalt not remove thy neighbour's landmark, which they of old time have set in thine inheritance, which thou shalt inherit in the land that the LORD thy God giveth thee to possess it.

15¶ One witness shall not rise up against a man for any iniquity, or for any sin, in any sin that he sinneth: at the mouth of two witnesses, or at the mouth of three witnesses, shall the matter be established.

16¶ If a false witness rise up against any man to testify against him *that which is* wrong;

17Then both the men, between whom the controversy *is*, shall stand before the LORD, before the priests and the judges, which shall be in those days;

18And the judges shall make diligent inquisition: and, behold, *if* the witness *be* a false witness, *and* hath testified falsely against his brother;

19Then shall ye do unto him, as he had thought to have done unto his brother: so shalt thou put the evil away from among you.

20And those which remain shall hear, and fear, and shall henceforth commit no more any such evil among you.

21And thine eye shall not pity; *but* life *shall go* for life, eye for eye, tooth for tooth, hand for hand, foot for foot.

20 WHEN THOU goest out to battle against thine enemies, and seest horses, and chariots, *and* a people more than thou, be not afraid of them: for the LORD thy God *is* with thee, which brought thee up out of the land of Egypt.

2And it shall be, when ye are come nigh unto the battle, that the priest shall approach and speak unto the people,

3And shall say unto them, Hear, O Israel, ye approach this day unto battle against your enemies: let not your hearts faint, fear not, and do not tremble, neither be ye terrified because of them;

4For the LORD your God *is* he that goeth with you, to fight for you against your enemies, to save you.

5¶ And the officers shall speak unto the people, saying, What man *is there* that hath built a new house, and hath not dedicated it? let him go and return to his house, lest he die in the battle, and another man dedicate it.

6And what man *is he* that hath planted a vineyard, and hath not *yet* eaten of it? let him *also* go and return unto his house, lest he die in the battle, and another man eat of it.

7And what man *is there* that hath betrothed a wife, and hath not taken her? let him go and return unto his house, lest he die in the battle, and another man take her.

8And the officers shall speak further unto the people, and they shall say, What man *is there that is* fearful and fainthearted? let him go and return unto his house, lest his brethren's heart faint as well as his heart.

9And it shall be, when the officers have made an end of speaking unto the people, that they shall make captains of the armies to lead the people.

10¶ When thou comest nigh unto a city to fight against it, then proclaim peace unto it.

New International

11But if a man hates his neighbor and lies in wait for him, assaults and kills him, and then flees to one of these cities, 12the elders of his town shall send for him, bring him back from the city, and hand him over to the avenger of blood to die. 13Show him no pity. You must purge from Israel the guilt of shedding innocent blood, so that it may go well with you.

14Do not move your neighbor's boundary stone set up by your predecessors in the inheritance you receive in the land the LORD your God is giving you to possess.

Witnesses

15One witness is not enough to convict a man accused of any crime or offense he may have committed. A matter must be established by the testimony of two or three witnesses.

16If a malicious witness takes the stand to accuse a man of a crime, 17the two men involved in the dispute must stand in the presence of the LORD before the priests and the judges who are in office at the time. 18The judges must make a thorough investigation, and if the witness proves to be a liar, giving false testimony against his brother, 19then do to him as he intended to do to his brother. You must purge the evil from among you. 20The rest of the people will hear of this and be afraid, and never again will such an evil thing be done among you. 21Show no pity: life for life, eye for eye, tooth for tooth, hand for hand, foot for foot.

Going to War

20 WHEN YOU go to war against your enemies and see horses and chariots and an army greater than yours, do not be afraid of them, because the LORD your God, who brought you up out of Egypt, will be with you. 2When you are about to go into battle, the priest shall come forward and address the army. 3He shall say: "Hear, O Israel, today you are going into battle against your enemies. Do not be fainthearted or afraid; do not be terrified or give way to panic before them. 4For the LORD your God is the one who goes with you to fight for you against your enemies to give you victory."

5The officers shall say to the army: "Has anyone built a new house and not dedicated it? Let him go home, or he may die in battle and someone else may dedicate it. 6Has anyone planted a vineyard and not begun to enjoy it? Let him go home, or he may die in battle and someone else enjoy it. 7Has anyone become pledged to a woman and not married her? Let him go home, or he may die in battle and someone else marry her." 8Then the officers shall add, "Is any man afraid or fainthearted? Let him go home so that his brothers will not become disheartened too." 9When the officers have finished speaking to the army, they shall appoint commanders over it.

10When you march up to attack a city, make its people an offer of peace. 11If they accept and open their gates,

Living Bible

11"But if anyone hates his neighbor and springs out of hiding and kills him, and then flees into one of the Cities of Refuge, 12the elders of his home town shall send for him and shall bring him home and deliver him over to the dead man's avenger, to kill him. 13Don't pity him! Purge all murderers from Israel! Only then will all go well with you.

14"When you arrive in the land the Lord your God is giving you, remember that you must never steal a man's land by moving the boundary marker.

15"Never convict anyone on the testimony of one witness. There must be at least two, and three is even better. 16If anyone gives false witness, claiming he has seen someone do wrong when he hasn't, 17both men shall be brought before the priests and judges on duty before the Lord at the time. 18They must be closely questioned, and if the witness is lying, 19his penalty shall be the punishment he thought the other man would get. In this way you will purge out evil from among you. 20Then those who hear about it will be afraid to tell lies on the witness stand. Life for life, eye for eye, tooth for tooth, hand for hand, foot for foot; this is your rule in such cases.

20 "WHEN YOU go to war and see before you vast numbers of horses and chariots, an army far greater than yours, don't be frightened! The Lord your God is with you—the same God who brought you safely out of Egypt! 2Before you begin the battle, a priest shall stand before the Israeli army and say,

3"'Listen to me, all you men of Israel! Don't be afraid as you go out to fight today! 4For the Lord your God is going with you! He will fight for you against your enemies, and he will give you the victory!'

5"Then the officers of the army shall address the men in this manner: 'Has anyone just built a new house, but not yet dedicated it? If so, go home! For you might be killed in the battle, and someone else would dedicate it! 6Has anyone just planted a vineyard but not yet eaten any of its fruit? If so, go home! You might die in battle and someone else would eat it! 7Has anyone just become engaged? Well, go home and get married! For you might die in the battle, and someone else would marry your fiancée. 8And now, is anyone afraid? If you are, go home before you frighten the rest of us!' 9When the officers have finished saying this to their men, they will announce the names of the battalion leaders.

10"As you approach a city to fight against it, first offer it a truce. 11If it accepts the truce and opens its gates to

New Revised Standard

11 But if someone at enmity with another lies in wait and attacks and takes the life of that person, and flees into one of these cities, 12then the elders of the killer's city shall send to have the culprit taken from there and handed over to the avenger of blood to be put to death. 13Show no pity; you shall purge the guilt of innocent blood from Israel, so that it may go well with you.

Property Boundaries

14 You must not move your neighbor's boundary marker, set up by former generations, on the property that will be allotted to you in the land that the LORD your God is giving you to possess.

Law concerning Witnesses

15 A single witness shall not suffice to convict a person of any crime or wrongdoing in connection with any offense that may be committed. Only on the evidence of two or three witnesses shall a charge be sustained. 16If a malicious witness comes forward to accuse someone of wrongdoing, 17then both parties to the dispute shall appear before the LORD, before the priests and the judges who are in office in those days, 18and the judges shall make a thorough inquiry. If the witness is a false witness, having testified falsely against another, 19then you shall do to the false witness just as the false witness had meant to do to the other. So you shall purge the evil from your midst. 20The rest shall hear and be afraid, and a crime such as this shall never again be committed among you. 21Show no pity: life for life, eye for eye, tooth for tooth, hand for hand, foot for foot.

Rules of Warfare

20 WHEN YOU go out to war against your enemies, and see horses and chariots, an army larger than your own, you shall not be afraid of them; for the LORD your God is with you, who brought you up from the land of Egypt. 2Before you engage in battle, the priest shall come forward and speak to the troops, 3and shall say to them: "Hear, O Israel! Today you are drawing near to do battle against your enemies. Do not lose heart, or be afraid, or panic, or be in dread of them; 4for it is the LORD your God who goes with you, to fight for you against your enemies, to give you victory." 5Then the officials shall address the troops, saying, "Has anyone built a new house but not dedicated it? He should go back to his house, or he might die in the battle and another dedicate it. 6Has anyone planted a vineyard but not yet enjoyed its fruit? He should go back to his house, or he might die in the battle and another be first to enjoy its fruit. 7Has anyone become engaged to a woman but not yet married her? He should go back to his house, or he might die in the battle and another marry her." 8The officials shall continue to address the troops, saying, "Is anyone afraid or disheartened? He should go back to his house, or he might cause the heart of his comrades to melt like his own." 9When the officials have finished addressing the troops, then the commanders shall take charge of them.

10 When you draw near to a town to fight against it, offer it terms of peace. 11If it accepts your terms of

King James

11And it shall be, if it make thee answer of peace, and open unto thee, then it shall be, *that* all the people *that is* found therein shall be tributaries unto thee, and they shall serve thee.

12And if it will make no peace with thee, but will make war against thee, then thou shalt besiege it:

13And when the LORD thy God hath delivered it into thine hands, thou shalt smite every male thereof with the edge of the sword:

14But the women, and the little ones, and the cattle, and all that is in the city, *even* all the spoil thereof, shalt thou take unto thyself; and thou shalt eat the spoil of thine enemies, which the LORD thy God hath given thee.

15Thus shalt thou do unto all the cities *which are* very far off from thee, which *are* not of the cities of these nations.

16But of the cities of these people, which the LORD thy God doth give thee *for* an inheritance, thou shalt save alive nothing that breatheth:

17But thou shalt utterly destroy them; *namely,* the Hittites, and the Amorites, the Canaanites, and the Perizzites, the Hivites, and the Jebusites; as the LORD thy God hath commanded thee:

18That they teach you not to do after all their abominations, which they have done unto their gods; so should ye sin against the LORD your God.

19¶ When thou shalt besiege a city a long time, in making war against it to take it, thou shalt not destroy the trees thereof by forcing an axe against them: for thou mayest eat of them, and thou shalt not cut them down (for the tree of the field *is* man's *life*) to employ *them* in the siege:

20Only the trees which thou knowest that they *be* not trees for meat, thou shalt destroy and cut them down; and thou shalt build bulwarks against the city that maketh war with thee, until it be subdued.

21 IF *ONE* be found slain in the land which the LORD thy God giveth thee to possess it, lying in the field, *and* it be not known who hath slain him:

2Then thy elders and thy judges shall come forth, and they shall measure unto the cities which *are* round about him that is slain:

3And it shall be, *that* the city *which is* next unto the slain man, even the elders of that city shall take an heifer, which hath not been wrought with, *and* which hath not drawn in the yoke;

4And the elders of that city shall bring down the heifer unto a rough valley, which is neither eared nor sown, and shall strike off the heifer's neck there in the valley:

5And the priests the sons of Levi shall come near; for them the LORD thy God hath chosen to minister unto him, and to bless in the name of the LORD; and by their word shall every controversy and every stroke be *tried:*

6And all the elders of that city, *that are* next unto the slain *man,* shall wash their hands over the heifer that is beheaded in the valley:

7And they shall answer and say, Our hands have not shed this blood, neither have our eyes seen *it.*

8Be merciful, O LORD, unto thy people Israel, whom thou hast redeemed, and lay not innocent blood unto thy people of Israel's charge. And the blood shall be forgiven them.

9So shalt thou put away the *guilt* of innocent blood from among you, when thou shalt do *that which is* right in the sight of the LORD.

10¶ When thou goest forth to war against thine enemies, and the LORD thy God hath delivered them into thine hands, and thou hast taken them captive,

11And seest among the captives a beautiful woman, and hast a desire unto her, that thou wouldest have her to thy wife;

New International

all the people in it shall be subject to forced labor and shall work for you. 12If they refuse to make peace and they engage you in battle, lay siege to that city. 13When the LORD your God delivers it into your hand, put to the sword all the men in it. 14As for the women, the children, the livestock and everything else in the city, you may take these as plunder for yourselves. And you may use the plunder the LORD your God gives you from your enemies. 15This is how you are to treat all the cities that are at a distance from you and do not belong to the nations nearby.

16However, in the cities of the nations the LORD your God is giving you as an inheritance, do not leave alive anything that breathes. 17Completely destroy[a] them— the Hittites, Amorites, Canaanites, Perizzites, Hivites and Jebusites—as the LORD your God has commanded you. 18Otherwise, they will teach you to follow all the detestable things they do in worshiping their gods, and you will sin against the LORD your God.

19When you lay siege to a city for a long time, fighting against it to capture it, do not destroy its trees by putting an ax to them, because you can eat their fruit. Do not cut them down. Are the trees of the field people, that you should besiege them?[b] 20However, you may cut down trees that you know are not fruit trees and use them to build siege works until the city at war with you falls.

Atonement for an Unsolved Murder

21 IF A man is found slain, lying in a field in the land the LORD your God is giving you to possess, and it is not known who killed him, 2your elders and judges shall go out and measure the distance from the body to the neighboring towns. 3Then the elders of the town nearest the body shall take a heifer that has never been worked and has never worn a yoke 4and lead her down to a valley that has not been plowed or planted and where there is a flowing stream. There in the valley they are to break the heifer's neck. 5The priests, the sons of Levi, shall step forward, for the LORD your God has chosen them to minister and to pronounce blessings in the name of the LORD and to decide all cases of dispute and assault. 6Then all the elders of the town nearest the body shall wash their hands over the heifer whose neck was broken in the valley, 7and they shall declare: "Our hands did not shed this blood, nor did our eyes see it done. 8Accept this atonement for your people Israel, whom you have redeemed, O LORD, and do not hold your people guilty of the blood of an innocent man." And the bloodshed will be atoned for. 9So you will purge from yourselves the guilt of shedding innocent blood, since you have done what is right in the eyes of the LORD.

Marrying a Captive Woman

10When you go to war against your enemies and the LORD your God delivers them into your hands and you take captives, 11if you notice among the captives a beautiful woman and are attracted to her, you may take her as your wife. 12Bring her into your home and have her

---

[a] *17* The Hebrew term refers to the irrevocable giving over of things or persons to the LORD, often by totally destroying them.   [b] *19* Or *down to use in the siege, for the fruit trees are for the benefit of man.*

Living Bible

you, then all its people shall become your servants. 12But if it refuses and won't make peace with you, you must besiege it. 13When the Lord your God has given it to you, kill every male in the city; 14but you may keep for yourselves all the women, children, cattle, and booty. 15These instructions apply only to distant cities, not to those in the Promised Landc itself.

16"For in the cities within the boundaries of the Promised Land you are to save no one; destroy every living thing. 17Utterly destroy the Hittites, the Amorites, the Canaanites, the Perizzites, the Hivites, and the Jebusites. This is the commandment of the Lord your God. 18The purpose of this command is to prevent the people of the land from luring you into idol worship and into participation in their loathsome customs, thus sinning deeply against the Lord your God.

19"When you besiege a city, don't destroy the fruit trees. Eat all the fruit you wish; just don't cut down the trees. They aren't enemies who need to be slaughtered! 20But you may cut down trees that aren't valuable for food. Use them for the siege [to make ladders, portable towers, and battering ramsd].

21 "IF, WHEN you arrive in the Promised Land, a murder victim is found lying in a field and no one has seen the murder, 2the elders and judges shall measure from the body to the nearest city. 3Then the elders of that city shall take a heifer that has never been yoked, 4and lead it to a valley where there is running water—a valley neither plowed nor sowed—and there break its neck.

5"Then the priests shall come (for the Lord your God has chosen them to minister before him and to pronounce his blessings and decide lawsuits and punishments), 6and shall wash their hands over the heifer, 7and say, 'Our hands have not shed this blood, neither have our eyes seen it. 8O Lord, forgive your people Israel whom you have redeemed, and do not charge them with murdering an innocent man. Forgive us the guilt of this man's blood.' 9In this way you will put away the guilt from among you by following the Lord's directions.

10"When you go to war and the Lord your God delivers your enemies to you, 11and you see among the captives a beautiful girl you want as your wife, 12take her

New Revised Standard

peace and surrenders to you, then all the people in it shall serve you at forced labor. 12If it does not submit to you peacefully, but makes war against you, then you shall besiege it; 13and when the LORD your God gives it into your hand, you shall put all its males to the sword. 14You may, however, take as your booty the women, the children, livestock, and everything else in the town, all its spoil. You may enjoy the spoil of your enemies, which the LORD your God has given you. 15Thus you shall treat all the towns that are very far from you, which are not towns of the nations here. 16But as for the towns of these peoples that the LORD your God is giving you as an inheritance, you must not let anything that breathes remain alive. 17You shall annihilate them—the Hittites and the Amorites, the Canaanites and the Perizzites, the Hivites and the Jebusites—just as the LORD your God has commanded, 18so that they may not teach you to do all the abhorrent things that they do for their gods, and you thus sin against the LORD your God.

19 If you besiege a town for a long time, making war against it in order to take it, you must not destroy its trees by wielding an ax against them. Although you may take food from them, you must not cut them down. Are trees in the field human beings that they should come under siege from you? 20You may destroy only the trees that you know do not produce food; you may cut them down for use in building siegeworks against the town that makes war with you, until it falls.

Law concerning Murder by Persons Unknown

21 IF, IN the land that the LORD your God is giving you to possess, a body is found lying in open country, and it is not known who struck the person down, 2then your elders and your judges shall come out to measure the distances to the towns that are near the body. 3The elders of the town nearest the body shall take a heifer that has never been worked, one that has not pulled in the yoke; 4the elders of that town shall bring the heifer down to a wadi with running water, which is neither plowed nor sown, and shall break the heifer's neck there in the wadi. 5Then the priests, the sons of Levi, shall come forward, for the LORD your God has chosen them to minister to him and to pronounce blessings in the name of the LORD, and by their decision all cases of dispute and assault shall be settled. 6All the elders of that town nearest the body shall wash their hands over the heifer whose neck was broken in the wadi, 7and they shall declare: "Our hands did not shed this blood, nor were we witnesses to it. 8Absolve, O LORD, your people Israel, whom you redeemed; do not let the guilt of innocent blood remain in the midst of your people Israel." Then they will be absolved of bloodguilt. 9So you shall purge the guilt of innocent blood from your midst, because you must do what is right in the sight of the LORD.

Female Captives

10 When you go out to war against your enemies, and the LORD your God hands them over to you and you take them captive, 11suppose you see among the captives a beautiful woman whom you desire and want to marry, 12and so you bring her home to your house: she

c 20:15 *not to those in the Promised Land itself*, literally, "which are not of the cities of these nations."   d 20:20 *to make ladders, portable towers, and battering rams*, implied.

King James

12Then thou shalt bring her home to thine house; and she shall shave her head, and pare her nails;

13And she shall put the raiment of her captivity from off her, and shall remain in thine house, and bewail her father and her mother a full month: and after that thou shalt go in unto her, and be her husband, and she shall be thy wife.

14And it shall be, if thou have no delight in her, then thou shalt let her go whither she will; but thou shalt not sell her at all for money, thou shalt not make merchandise of her, because thou hast humbled her.

15¶ If a man have two wives, one beloved, and another hated, and they have born him children, *both* the beloved and the hated; and *if* the firstborn son be hers that was hated:

16Then it shall be, when he maketh his sons to inherit *that* which he hath, *that* he may not make the son of the beloved firstborn before the son of the hated, *which is indeed* the firstborn:

17But he shall acknowledge the son of the hated *for* the firstborn, by giving him a double portion of all that he hath: for he *is* the beginning of his strength; the right of the firstborn *is* his.

18¶ If a man have a stubborn and rebellious son, which will not obey the voice of his father, or the voice of his mother, and *that*, when they have chastened him, will not hearken unto them:

19Then shall his father and his mother lay hold on him, and bring him out unto the elders of his city, and unto the gate of his place;

20And they shall say unto the elders of his city, This our son *is* stubborn and rebellious, he will not obey our voice; *he is* a glutton, and a drunkard.

21And all the men of his city shall stone him with stones, that he die: so shalt thou put evil away from among you; and all Israel shall hear, and fear.

22¶ And if a man have committed a sin worthy of death, and he be to be put to death, and thou hang him on a tree:

23His body shall not remain all night upon the tree, but thou shalt in any wise bury him that day; (for he that is hanged *is* accursed of God;) that thy land be not defiled, which the LORD thy God giveth thee *for* an inheritance.

22 THOU SHALT not see thy brother's ox or his sheep go astray, and hide thyself from them: thou shalt in any case bring them again unto thy brother.

2And if thy brother *be* not nigh unto thee, or if thou know him not, then thou shalt bring it unto thine own house, and it shall be with thee until thy brother seek after it, and thou shalt restore it to him again.

3In like manner shalt thou do with his ass; and so shalt thou do with his raiment; and with all lost thing of thy brother's, which he hath lost, and thou hast found, shalt thou do likewise: thou mayest not hide thyself.

4¶ Thou shalt not see thy brother's ass or his ox fall down by the way, and hide thyself from them: thou shalt surely help him to lift *them* up again.

5¶ The woman shall not wear that which pertaineth unto a man, neither shall a man put on a woman's garment: for all that do so *are* abomination unto the LORD thy God.

6¶ If a bird's nest chance to be before thee in the way in any tree, or on the ground, *whether they be* young ones, or eggs, and the dam sitting upon the young, or upon the eggs, thou shalt not take the dam with the young:

7*But* thou shalt in any wise let the dam go, and take the young to thee; that it may be well with thee, and *that* thou mayest prolong *thy* days.

New International

shave her head, trim her nails 13and put aside the clothes she was wearing when captured. After she has lived in your house and mourned her father and mother for a full month, then you may go to her and be her husband and she shall be your wife. 14If you are not pleased with her, let her go wherever she wishes. You must not sell her or treat her as a slave, since you have dishonored her.

The Right of the Firstborn

15If a man has two wives, and he loves one but not the other, and both bear him sons but the firstborn is the son of the wife he does not love, 16when he wills his property to his sons, he must not give the rights of the firstborn to the son of the wife he loves in preference to his actual firstborn, the son of the wife he does not love. 17He must acknowledge the son of his unloved wife as the firstborn by giving him a double share of all he has. That son is the first sign of his father's strength. The right of the firstborn belongs to him.

A Rebellious Son

18If a man has a stubborn and rebellious son who does not obey his father and mother and will not listen to them when they discipline him, 19his father and mother shall take hold of him and bring him to the elders at the gate of his town. 20They shall say to the elders, "This son of ours is stubborn and rebellious. He will not obey us. He is a profligate and a drunkard." 21Then all the men of his town shall stone him to death. You must purge the evil from among you. All Israel will hear of it and be afraid.

Various Laws

22If a man guilty of a capital offense is put to death and his body is hung on a tree, 23you must not leave his body on the tree overnight. Be sure to bury him that same day, because anyone who is hung on a tree is under God's curse. You must not desecrate the land the LORD your God is giving you as an inheritance.

22 IF YOU see your brother's ox or sheep straying, do not ignore it but be sure to take it back to him. 2If the brother does not live near you or if you do not know who he is, take it home with you and keep it until he comes looking for it. Then give it back to him. 3Do the same if you find your brother's donkey or his cloak or anything he loses. Do not ignore it.

4If you see your brother's donkey or his ox fallen on the road, do not ignore it. Help him get it to its feet.

5A woman must not wear men's clothing, nor a man wear women's clothing, for the LORD your God detests anyone who does this.

6If you come across a bird's nest beside the road, either in a tree or on the ground, and the mother is sitting on the young or on the eggs, do not take the mother with the young. 7You may take the young, but be sure to let the mother go, so that it may go well with you and you may have a long life.

Living Bible

home with you. She must shave her head and pare her nails [13]and change her clothing, laying aside that which she was wearing when she was captured, then remain in your home in mourning for her father and mother for a full month. After that you may marry her. [14]However, if after marrying her you decide you don't like her, you must let her go free—you may not sell her or treat her as a slave, for you have humiliated her.

[15]"If a man has two wives but loves one and not the other, and both have borne him children, and the mother of his oldest son is the wife he doesn't love, [16]he may not give a larger inheritance to his younger son, the son of the wife he loves. [17]He must give the customary double portion to his oldest son, who is the beginning of his strength and who owns the rights of a firstborn son, even though he is the son of the wife his father doesn't love.

[18]"If a man has a stubborn, rebellious son who will not obey his father or mother, even though they punish him, [19]then his father and mother shall take him before the elders of the city [20]and declare, 'This son of ours is stubborn and rebellious and won't obey; he is a worthless drunkard.' [21]Then the men of the city shall stone him to death. In this way you shall put away this evil from among you, and all the young men of Israel will hear about what happened and will be afraid.

[22]"If a man has committed a crime worthy of death, and is executed and then hanged on a tree, [23]his body shall not remain on the tree overnight. You must bury him the same day, for anyone hanging on a tree is cursed of God. Don't defile the land the Lord your God has given you.

22 "IF YOU see someone's ox or sheep wandering away, don't pretend you didn't see it; take it back to its owner. [2]If you don't know who the owner is, take it to your farm and keep it there until the owner comes looking for it, and then give it to him. [3]The same applies to donkeys, clothing, or anything else you find. Keep it for its owner.

[4]"If you see someone trying to get an ox or donkey onto its feet when it has slipped beneath its load,[a] don't look the other way. Go and help!

[5]"A woman must not wear men's clothing, and a man must not wear women's clothing. This is abhorrent to the Lord your God.

[6]"If a bird's nest is lying on the ground, or if you spy one in a tree, and there are young ones or eggs in it with the mother sitting in the nest, don't take the mother with the young. [7]Let her go, and take only the young. The Lord will bless you for it.

New Revised Standard

shall shave her head, pare her nails, [13]discard her captive's garb, and shall remain in your house a full month, mourning for her father and mother; after that you may go in to her and be her husband, and she shall be your wife. [14]But if you are not satisfied with her, you shall let her go free and not sell her for money. You must not treat her as a slave, since you have dishonored her.

The Right of the Firstborn

15 If a man has two wives, one of them loved and the other disliked, and if both the loved and the disliked have borne him sons, the firstborn being the son of the one who is disliked, [16]then on the day when he wills his possessions to his sons, he is not permitted to treat the son of the loved as the firstborn in preference to the son of the disliked, who is the firstborn. [17]He must acknowledge as firstborn the son of the one who is disliked, giving him a double portion[b] of all that he has; since he is the first issue of his virility, the right of the firstborn is his.

Rebellious Children

18 If someone has a stubborn and rebellious son who will not obey his father and mother, who does not heed them when they discipline him, [19]then his father and his mother shall take hold of him and bring him out to the elders of his town at the gate of that place. [20]They shall say to the elders of his town, "This son of ours is stubborn and rebellious. He will not obey us. He is a glutton and a drunkard." [21]Then all the men of the town shall stone him to death. So you shall purge the evil from your midst; and all Israel will hear, and be afraid.

Miscellaneous Laws

22 When someone is convicted of a crime punishable by death and is executed, and you hang him on a tree, [23]his corpse must not remain all night upon the tree; you shall bury him that same day, for anyone hung on a tree is under God's curse. You must not defile the land that the Lord your God is giving you for possession.

22 YOU SHALL not watch your neighbor's ox or sheep straying away and ignore them; you shall take them back to their owner. [2]If the owner does not reside near you or you do not know who the owner is, you shall bring it to your own house, and it shall remain with you until the owner claims it; then you shall return it. [3]You shall do the same with a neighbor's donkey; you shall do the same with a neighbor's garment; and you shall do the same with anything else that your neighbor loses and you find. You may not withhold your help.

4 You shall not see your neighbor's donkey or ox fallen on the road and ignore it; you shall help to lift it up.

5 A woman shall not wear a man's apparel, nor shall a man put on a woman's garment; for whoever does such things is abhorrent to the Lord your God.

6 If you come on a bird's nest, in any tree or on the ground, with fledglings or eggs, with the mother sitting on the fledglings or on the eggs, you shall not take the mother with the young. [7]Let the mother go, taking only the young for yourself, in order that it may go well with you and you may live long.

---

[a] 22:4 *when it has slipped beneath its load,* implied.

[b] Heb *two-thirds*

King James

8¶ When thou buildest a new house, then thou shalt make a battlement for thy roof, that thou bring not blood upon thine house, if any man fall from thence.

9¶ Thou shalt not sow thy vineyard with divers seeds: lest the fruit of thy seed which thou hast sown, and the fruit of thy vineyard, be defiled.

10¶ Thou shalt not plow with an ox and an ass together.

11¶ Thou shalt not wear a garment of divers sorts, *as* of woollen and linen together.

12¶ Thou shalt make thee fringes upon the four quarters of thy vesture, wherewith thou coverest *thyself*.

13¶ If any man take a wife, and go in unto her, and hate her,

14And give occasions of speech against her, and bring up an evil name upon her, and say, I took this woman, and when I came to her, I found her not a maid:

15Then shall the father of the damsel, and her mother, take and bring forth *the tokens of* the damsel's virginity unto the elders of the city in the gate:

16And the damsel's father shall say unto the elders, I gave my daughter unto this man to wife, and he hateth her;

17And, lo, he hath given occasions of speech *against her,* saying, I found not thy daughter a maid; and yet these *are the tokens of* my daughter's virginity. And they shall spread the cloth before the elders of the city.

18And the elders of that city shall take that man and chastise him;

19And they shall amerce him in an hundred *shekels* of silver, and give *them* unto the father of the damsel, because he hath brought up an evil name upon a virgin of Israel: and she shall be his wife; he may not put her away all his days.

20But if this thing be true, *and the tokens of* virginity be not found for the damsel:

21Then they shall bring out the damsel to the door of her father's house, and the men of her city shall stone her with stones that she die: because she hath wrought folly in Israel, to play the whore in her father's house: so shalt thou put evil away from among you.

22¶ If a man be found lying with a woman married to an husband, then they shall both of them die, *both* the man that lay with the woman, and the woman: so shalt thou put away evil from Israel.

23¶ If a damsel *that is* a virgin be betrothed unto an husband, and a man find her in the city, and lie with her;

24Then ye shall bring them both out unto the gate of that city, and ye shall stone them with stones that they die; the damsel, because she cried not, *being* in the city; and the man, because he hath humbled his neighbour's wife: so thou shalt put away evil from among you.

25¶ But if a man find a betrothed damsel in the field, and the man force her, and lie with her: then the man only that lay with her shall die:

26But unto the damsel thou shalt do nothing; *there is* in the damsel no sin *worthy* of death: for as when a man riseth against his neighbour, and slayeth him, even so *is* this matter:

27For he found her in the field, *and* the betrothed damsel cried, and *there was* none to save her.

28¶ If a man find a damsel *that is* a virgin, which is not betrothed, and lay hold on her, and lie with her, and they be found;

29Then the man that lay with her shall give unto the damsel's father fifty *shekels* of silver, and she shall be his wife; because he hath humbled her, he may not put her away all his days.

30¶ A man shall not take his father's wife, nor discover his father's skirt.

New International

8When you build a new house, make a parapet around your roof so that you may not bring the guilt of bloodshed on your house if someone falls from the roof.

9Do not plant two kinds of seed in your vineyard; if you do, not only the crops you plant but also the fruit of the vineyard will be defiled.[a]

10Do not plow with an ox and a donkey yoked together.

11Do not wear clothes of wool and linen woven together.

12Make tassels on the four corners of the cloak you wear.

Marriage Violations

13If a man takes a wife and, after lying with her, dislikes her 14and slanders her and gives her a bad name, saying, "I married this woman, but when I approached her, I did not find proof of her virginity," 15then the girl's father and mother shall bring proof that she was a virgin to the town elders at the gate. 16The girl's father will say to the elders, "I gave my daughter in marriage to this man, but he dislikes her. 17Now he has slandered her and said, 'I did not find your daughter to be a virgin.' But here is the proof of my daughter's virginity." Then her parents shall display the cloth before the elders of the town, 18and the elders shall take the man and punish him. 19They shall fine him a hundred shekels of silver[b] and give them to the girl's father, because this man has given an Israelite virgin a bad name. She shall continue to be his wife; he must not divorce her as long as he lives.

20If, however, the charge is true and no proof of the girl's virginity can be found, 21she shall be brought to the door of her father's house and there the men of her town shall stone her to death. She has done a disgraceful thing in Israel by being promiscuous while still in her father's house. You must purge the evil from among you.

22If a man is found sleeping with another man's wife, both the man who slept with her and the woman must die. You must purge the evil from Israel.

23If a man happens to meet in a town a virgin pledged to be married and he sleeps with her, 24you shall take both of them to the gate of that town and stone them to death—the girl because she was in a town and did not scream for help, and the man because he violated another man's wife. You must purge the evil from among you.

25But if out in the country a man happens to meet a girl pledged to be married and rapes her, only the man who has done this shall die. 26Do nothing to the girl; she has committed no sin deserving death. This case is like that of someone who attacks and murders his neighbor, 27for the man found the girl out in the country, and though the betrothed girl screamed, there was no one to rescue her.

28If a man happens to meet a virgin who is not pledged to be married and rapes her and they are discovered, 29he shall pay the girl's father fifty shekels of silver.[c] He must marry the girl, for he has violated her. He can never divorce her as long as he lives.

30A man is not to marry his father's wife; he must not dishonor his father's bed.

---

a 9 Or *be forfeited to the sanctuary*　b 19 That is, about 2 1/2 pounds (about 1 kilogram)　c 29 That is, about 1 1/4 pounds (about 0.6 kilogram)

Living Bible

8"Every new house must have a guardrail around the edge of the flat rooftop to prevent anyone from falling off and bring guilt to both the house and its owner.

9"Do not sow other crops in the rows of your vineyard. If you do, both the crops and the grapes shall be confiscated by the priests.d

10"Don't plow with an ox and a donkey harnessed together.

11"Don't wear clothing woven from two kinds of thread: for instance, wool and linen.

12"You must sew tassels on the four corners of your cloaks.

13, 14"If a man marries a girl, then after sleeping with her accuses her of having had premarital intercourse with another man, saying, 'She was not a virgin when I married her,' 15then the girl's father and mother shall bring the proof of her virginity to the city judges.

16"Her father shall tell them, 'I gave my daughter to this man to be his wife, and now he despises her, 17, 18and has accused her of shameful things, claiming that she was not a virgin when she married; yet here is the proof.' And they shall spread before the judges the blood-stained sheet from her marriage bed. The judges shall sentence the man to be whipped, 19and fine him one hundred dollarse to be given to the girl's father, for he has falsely accused a virgin of Israel. She shall remain his wife and he may never divorce her. 20But if the man's accusations are true, and she was not a virgin, 21the judges shall take the girl to the door of her father's home where the men of the city shall stone her to death. She has defiled Israel by flagrant crime, being a prostitute while living at home with her parents; and such evil must be cleansed from among you.

22"If a man is discovered committing adultery, both he and the other man's wife must be killed; in this way evil will be cleansed from Israel. 23, 24If a girl who is engaged is seduced within the walls of a city, both she and the man who seduced her shall be taken outside the gates and stoned to death—the girl because she didn't scream for help, and the man because he has violated the virginity of another man's fiancée. 25, 26, 27In this way you will reduce crime among you. But if this deed takes place out in the country, only the man shall die. The girl is as innocent as a murder victim; for it must be assumed that she screamed, but there was no one to hear and rescue her out in the field. 28, 29If a man rapes a girl who is not engaged, and is caught in the act, he must pay a finef to the girl's father and marry her; he may never divorce her. 30A man shall not sleep with his father's widowg since she belonged to his father.

New Revised Standard

8 When you build a new house, you shall make a parapet for your roof; otherwise you might have blood-guilt on your house, if anyone should fall from it.

9 You shall not sow your vineyard with a second kind of seed, or the whole yield will have to be forfeited, both the crop that you have sown and the yield of the vineyard itself.

10 You shall not plow with an ox and a donkey yoked together.

11 You shall not wear clothes made of wool and linen woven together.

12 You shall make tassels on the four corners of the cloak with which you cover yourself.

Laws concerning Sexual Relations

13 Suppose a man marries a woman, but after going in to her, he dislikes her 14and makes up charges against her, slandering her by saying, "I married this woman; but when I lay with her, I did not find evidence of her virginity." 15The father of the young woman and her mother shall then submit the evidence of the young woman's virginity to the elders of the city at the gate. 16The father of the young woman shall say to the elders: "I gave my daughter in marriage to this man but he dislikes her; 17now he has made up charges against her, saying, 'I did not find evidence of your daughter's virginity.' But here is the evidence of my daughter's virginity." Then they shall spread out the cloth before the elders of the town. 18The elders of that town shall take the man and punish him; 19they shall fine him one hundred shekels of silver (which they shall give to the young woman's father) because he has slandered a virgin of Israel. She shall remain his wife; he shall not be permitted to divorce her as long as he lives.

20 If, however, this charge is true, that evidence of the young woman's virginity was not found, 21then they shall bring the young woman out to the entrance of her father's house and the men of her town shall stone her to death, because she committed a disgraceful act in Israel by prostituting herself in her father's house. So you shall purge the evil from your midst.

22 If a man is caught lying with the wife of another man, both of them shall die, the man who lay with the woman as well as the woman. So you shall purge the evil from Israel.

23 If there is a young woman, a virgin already engaged to be married, and a man meets her in the town and lies with her, 24you shall bring both of them to the gate of that town and stone them to death, the young woman because she did not cry for help in the town and the man because he violated his neighbor's wife. So you shall purge the evil from your midst.

25 But if the man meets the engaged woman in the open country, and the man seizes her and lies with her, then only the man who lay with her shall die. 26You shall do nothing to the young woman; the young woman has not committed an offense punishable by death, because this case is like that of someone who attacks and murders a neighbor. 27Since he found her in the open country, the engaged woman may have cried for help, but there was no one to rescue her.

28 If a man meets a virgin who is not engaged, and seizes her and lies with her, and they are caught in the act, 29the man who lay with her shall give fifty shekels of silver to the young woman's father, and she shall become his wife. Because he violated her he shall not be permitted to divorce her as long as he lives.

30h A man shall not marry his father's wife, thereby violating his father's rights.i

---

d 22:9 *the grapes shall be confiscated by the priests,* literally, "lest the fulness of the fruit be consecrated."   e 22:19 *one hundred dollars,* literally, "a hundred shekels of silver." The exact value cannot be determined.   f 22:28, 29 *he must pay a fine,* literally, "shall pay her father fifty shekels of silver."   g 22:30 *a man shall not sleep with his father's widow,* literally, "his father's wife." The general law against adultery protected her and other wives while their husbands were living.

h Ch 23.1 in Heb   i Heb *uncovering his father's skirt*

King James

23 HE THAT is wounded in the stones, or hath his privy member cut off, shall not enter into the congregation of the LORD.

2A bastard shall not enter into the congregation of the LORD; even to his tenth generation shall he not enter into the congregation of the LORD.

3An Ammonite or Moabite shall not enter into the congregation of the LORD; even to their tenth generation shall they not enter into the congregation of the LORD for ever:

4Because they met you not with bread and with water in the way, when ye came forth out of Egypt; and because they hired against thee Balaam the son of Beor of Pethor of Mesopotamia, to curse thee.

5Nevertheless the LORD thy God would not hearken unto Balaam; but the LORD thy God turned the curse into a blessing unto thee, because the LORD thy God loved thee.

6Thou shalt not seek their peace nor their prosperity all thy days for ever.

7¶ Thou shalt not abhor an Edomite; for he *is* thy brother: thou shalt not abhor an Egyptian; because thou wast a stranger in his land.

8The children that are begotten of them shall enter into the congregation of the LORD in their third generation.

9¶ When the host goeth forth against thine enemies, then keep thee from every wicked thing.

10¶ If there be among you any man, that is not clean by reason of uncleanness that chanceth him by night, then shall he go abroad out of the camp, he shall not come within the camp:

11But it shall be, when evening cometh on, he shall wash *himself* with water: and when the sun is down, he shall come into the camp *again*.

12¶ Thou shalt have a place also without the camp, whither thou shalt go forth abroad:

13And thou shalt have a paddle upon thy weapon; and it shall be, when thou wilt ease thyself abroad, thou shalt dig therewith, and shalt turn back and cover that which cometh from thee:

14For the LORD thy God walketh in the midst of thy camp, to deliver thee, and to give up thine enemies before thee; therefore shall thy camp be holy: that he see no unclean thing in thee, and turn away from thee.

15¶ Thou shalt not deliver unto his master the servant which is escaped from his master unto thee:

16He shall dwell with thee, *even* among you, in that place which he shall choose in one of thy gates, where it liketh him best: thou shalt not oppress him.

17¶ There shall be no whore of the daughters of Israel, nor a sodomite of the sons of Israel.

18Thou shalt not bring the hire of a whore, or the price of a dog, into the house of the LORD thy God for any vow: for even both these *are* abomination unto the LORD thy God.

19¶ Thou shalt not lend upon usury to thy brother; usury of money, usury of victuals, usury of any thing that is lent upon usury:

20Unto a stranger thou mayest lend upon usury; but unto thy brother thou shalt not lend upon usury: that the LORD thy God may bless thee in all that thou settest thine hand to in the land whither thou goest to possess it.

21¶ When thou shalt vow a vow unto the LORD thy God, thou shalt not slack to pay it: for the LORD thy God will surely require it of thee; and it would be sin in thee.

22But if thou shalt forbear to vow, it shall be no sin in thee.

23That which is gone out of thy lips thou shalt keep and perform; *even* a freewill offering, according as thou hast vowed unto the LORD thy God, which thou hast promised with thy mouth.

New International

Exclusion From the Assembly

23 NO ONE who has been emasculated by crushing or cutting may enter the assembly of the LORD.

2No one born of a forbidden marriagea nor any of his descendants may enter the assembly of the LORD, even down to the tenth generation.

3No Ammonite or Moabite or any of his descendants may enter the assembly of the LORD, even down to the tenth generation. 4For they did not come to meet you with bread and water on your way when you came out of Egypt, and they hired Balaam son of Beor from Pethor in Aram Naharaimb to pronounce a curse on you. 5However, the LORD your God would not listen to Balaam but turned the curse into a blessing for you, because the LORD your God loves you. 6Do not seek a treaty of friendship with them as long as you live.

7Do not abhor an Edomite, for he is your brother. Do not abhor an Egyptian, because you lived as an alien in his country. 8The third generation of children born to them may enter the assembly of the LORD.

Uncleanness in the Camp

9When you are encamped against your enemies, keep away from everything impure. 10If one of your men is unclean because of a nocturnal emission, he is to go outside the camp and stay there. 11But as evening approaches he is to wash himself, and at sunset he may return to the camp.

12Designate a place outside the camp where you can go to relieve yourself. 13As part of your equipment have something to dig with, and when you relieve yourself, dig a hole and cover up your excrement. 14For the LORD your God moves about in your camp to protect you and to deliver your enemies to you. Your camp must be holy, so that he will not see among you anything indecent and turn away from you.

Miscellaneous Laws

15If a slave has taken refuge with you, do not hand him over to his master. 16Let him live among you wherever he likes and in whatever town he chooses. Do not oppress him.

17No Israelite man or woman is to become a shrine prostitute. 18You must not bring the earnings of a female prostitute or of a male prostitutec into the house of the LORD your God to pay any vow, because the LORD your God detests them both.

19Do not charge your brother interest, whether on money or food or anything else that may earn interest. 20You may charge a foreigner interest, but not a brother Israelite, so that the LORD your God may bless you in everything you put your hand to in the land you are entering to possess.

21If you make a vow to the LORD your God, do not be slow to pay it, for the LORD your God will certainly demand it of you and you will be guilty of sin. 22But if you refrain from making a vow, you will not be guilty. 23Whatever your lips utter you must be sure to do, because you made your vow freely to the LORD your God with your own mouth.

a 2 Or *one of illegitimate birth*   b 4 That is, Northwest Mesopotamia
c 18 Hebrew *of a dog*

Living Bible

23 "IF A man's testicles are crushed or his penis cut off, he shall not enter the sanctuary. 2A bastard may not enter the sanctuary, nor any of his descendants for ten generations.

3"No Ammonite or Moabite may ever enter the sanctuary, even after the tenth generation. 4The reason for this law is that these nations did not welcome you with food and water when you came out of Egypt; they even tried to hire Balaam, the son of Beor from Pethor, Mesopotamia, to curse you. 5But the Lord wouldn't listen to Balaam; instead, he turned the intended curse into a blessing for you, because the Lord loves you. 6You must never, as long as you live, try to help the Ammonites or the Moabites in any way. 7But don't look down on the Edomites and the Egyptians; the Edomites are your brothers and you lived among the Egyptians. 8The grandchildren of the Egyptians who came with you from Egypt may enter the sanctuary of the Lord.

9, 10"When you are at war, the men in the camps must stay away from all evil. Any man who becomes ceremonially defiled because of a seminal emission during the night must leave the camp, 11and stay outside until the evening; then he shall bathe himself and return at sunset. 12The toilet area shall be outside the camp. 13Each man must have a spade as part of his equipment; after every bowel movement he must dig a hole with the spade and cover the excrement. 14The camp must be holy, for the Lord walks among you to protect you and to cause your enemies to fall before you; and the Lord does not want to see anything indecent lest he turn away from you.

15, 16"If a slave escapes from his master, you must not force him to return; let him live among you in whatever town he shall choose, and do not oppress him.

17, 18"No prostitutes are permitted in Israel, either men or women; you must not bring to the Lord any offering from the earnings of a prostitute or a homosexual, for both are detestable to the Lord your God.

19"Don't demand interest on loans you make to a brother Israelite, whether it is in the form of money, food, or anything else. 20You may take interest from a foreigner, but not from an Israeli. For if you take interest from a brother, an Israeli, the Lord your God won't bless you when you arrive in the Promised Land.

21"When you make a vow to the Lord, be prompt in doing whatever it is you promised him, for the Lord demands that you promptly fulfill your vows; it is a sin if you don't. 22(But it is not a sin if you refrain from vowing!) 23Once you make the vow, you must be careful to do as you have said, for it was your own choice, and you have vowed to the Lord your God.

New Revised Standard

Those Excluded from the Assembly

23 NO ONE whose testicles are crushed or whose penis is cut off shall be admitted to the assembly of the LORD.

2 Those born of an illicit union shall not be admitted to the assembly of the LORD. Even to the tenth generation, none of their descendants shall be admitted to the assembly of the LORD.

3 No Ammonite or Moabite shall be admitted to the assembly of the LORD. Even to the tenth generation, none of their descendants shall be admitted to the assembly of the LORD, 4because they did not meet you with food and water on your journey out of Egypt, and because they hired against you Balaam son of Beor, from Pethor of Mesopotamia, to curse you. 5(Yet the LORD your God refused to heed Balaam; the LORD your God turned the curse into a blessing for you, because the LORD your God loved you.) 6You shall never promote their welfare or their prosperity as long as you live.

7 You shall not abhor any of the Edomites, for they are your kin. You shall not abhor any of the Egyptians, because you were an alien residing in their land. 8The children of the third generation that are born to them may be admitted to the assembly of the LORD.

Sanitary, Ritual, and Humanitarian Precepts

9 When you are encamped against your enemies you shall guard against any impropriety.

10 If one of you becomes unclean because of a nocturnal emission, then he shall go outside the camp; he must not come within the camp. 11When evening comes, he shall wash himself with water, and when the sun has set, he may come back into the camp.

12 You shall have a designated area outside the camp to which you shall go. 13With your utensils you shall have a trowel; when you relieve yourself outside, you shall dig a hole with it and then cover up your excrement. 14Because the LORD your God travels along with your camp, to save you and to hand over your enemies to you, therefore your camp must be holy, so that he may not see anything indecent among you and turn away from you.

15 Slaves who have escaped to you from their owners shall not be given back to them. 16They shall reside with you, in your midst, in any place they choose in any one of your towns, wherever they please; you shall not oppress them.

17 None of the daughters of Israel shall be a temple prostitute; none of the sons of Israel shall be a temple prostitute. 18You shall not bring the fee of a prostitute or the wages of a male prostitute[d] into the house of the LORD your God in payment for any vow, for both of these are abhorrent to the LORD your God.

19 You shall not charge interest on loans to another Israelite, interest on money, interest on provisions, interest on anything that is lent. 20On loans to a foreigner you may charge interest, but on loans to another Israelite you may not charge interest, so that the LORD your God may bless you in all your undertakings in the land that you are about to enter and possess.

21 If you make a vow to the LORD your God, do not postpone fulfilling it; for the LORD your God will surely require it of you, and you would incur guilt. 22But if you refrain from vowing, you will not incur guilt. 23Whatever your lips utter you must diligently perform, just as you have freely vowed to the LORD your God with your own mouth.

[d] Heb a dog

King James

24¶ When thou comest into thy neighbour's vineyard, then thou mayest eat grapes thy fill at thine own pleasure; but thou shalt not put *any* in thy vessel.

25When thou comest into the standing corn of thy neighbour, then thou mayest pluck the ears with thine hand; but thou shalt not move a sickle unto thy neighbour's standing corn.

24

WHEN A man hath taken a wife, and married her, and it come to pass that she find no favour in his eyes, because he hath found some uncleanness in her: then let him write her a bill of divorcement, and give *it* in her hand, and send her out of his house.

2And when she is departed out of his house, she may go and be another man's *wife*.

3And *if* the latter husband hate her, and write her a bill of divorcement, and giveth *it* in her hand, and sendeth her out of his house; or if the latter husband die, which took her *to be* his wife;

4Her former husband, which sent her away, may not take her again to be his wife, after that she is defiled; for that *is* abomination before the LORD: and thou shalt not cause the land to sin, which the LORD thy God giveth thee *for* an inheritance.

5¶ When a man hath taken a new wife, he shall not go out to war, neither shall he be charged with any business: *but* he shall be free at home one year, and shall cheer up his wife which he hath taken.

6¶ No man shall take the nether or the upper millstone to pledge: for he taketh *a man's* life to pledge.

7¶ If a man be found stealing any of his brethren of the children of Israel, and maketh merchandise of him, or selleth him; then that thief shall die; and thou shalt put evil away from among you.

8¶ Take heed in the plague of leprosy, that thou observe diligently, and do according to all that the priests the Levites shall teach you: as I commanded them, *so* ye shall observe to do.

9Remember what the LORD thy God did unto Miriam by the way, after that ye were come forth out of Egypt.

10¶ When thou dost lend thy brother any thing, thou shalt not go into his house to fetch his pledge.

11Thou shalt stand abroad, and the man to whom thou dost lend shall bring out the pledge abroad unto thee.

12And if the man *be* poor, thou shalt not sleep with his pledge:

13In any case thou shalt deliver him the pledge again when the sun goeth down, that he may sleep in his own raiment, and bless thee: and it shall be righteousness unto thee before the LORD thy God.

14¶ Thou shalt not oppress an hired servant *that is* poor and needy, *whether he be* of thy brethren, or of thy strangers that *are* in thy land within thy gates:

15At his day thou shalt give *him* his hire, neither shall the sun go down upon it; for he *is* poor, and setteth his heart upon it: lest he cry against thee unto the LORD, and it be sin unto thee.

16The fathers shall not be put to death for the children, neither shall the children be put to death for the fathers: every man shall be put to death for his own sin.

17¶ Thou shalt not pervert the judgment of the stranger, *nor* of the fatherless; nor take a widow's raiment to pledge:

18But thou shalt remember that thou wast a bondman in Egypt, and the LORD thy God redeemed thee thence: therefore I command thee to do this thing.

19¶ When thou cuttest down thine harvest in thy field, and hast forgot a sheaf in the field, thou shalt not go again to fetch it: it shall be for the stranger, for the fatherless, and for the widow: that the LORD thy God may bless thee in all the work of thine hands.

New International

24If you enter your neighbor's vineyard, you may eat all the grapes you want, but do not put any in your basket. 25If you enter your neighbor's grainfield, you may pick kernels with your hands, but you must not put a sickle to his standing grain.

24

IF A man marries a woman who becomes displeasing to him because he finds something indecent about her, and he writes her a certificate of divorce, gives it to her and sends her from his house, 2and if after she leaves his house she becomes the wife of another man, 3and her second husband dislikes her and writes her a certificate of divorce, gives it to her and sends her from his house, or if he dies, 4then her first husband, who divorced her, is not allowed to marry her again after she has been defiled. That would be detestable in the eyes of the LORD. Do not bring sin upon the land the LORD your God is giving you as an inheritance.

5If a man has recently married, he must not be sent to war or have any other duty laid on him. For one year he is to be free to stay at home and bring happiness to the wife he has married.

6Do not take a pair of millstones—not even the upper one—as security for a debt, because that would be taking a man's livelihood as security.

7If a man is caught kidnapping one of his brother Israelites and treats him as a slave or sells him, the kidnapper must die. You must purge the evil from among you.

8In cases of leprous[a] diseases be very careful to do exactly as the priests, who are Levites, instruct you. You must follow carefully what I have commanded them. 9Remember what the LORD your God did to Miriam along the way after you came out of Egypt.

10When you make a loan of any kind to your neighbor, do not go into his house to get what he is offering as a pledge. 11Stay outside and let the man to whom you are making the loan bring the pledge out to you. 12If the man is poor, do not go to sleep with his pledge in your possession. 13Return his cloak to him by sunset so that he may sleep in it. Then he will thank you, and it will be regarded as a righteous act in the sight of the LORD your God.

14Do not take advantage of a hired man who is poor and needy, whether he is a brother Israelite or an alien living in one of your towns. 15Pay him his wages each day before sunset, because he is poor and is counting on it. Otherwise he may cry to the LORD against you, and you will be guilty of sin.

16Fathers shall not be put to death for their children, nor children put to death for their fathers; each is to die for his own sin.

17Do not deprive the alien or the fatherless of justice, or take the cloak of the widow as a pledge. 18Remember that you were slaves in Egypt and the LORD your God redeemed you from there. That is why I command you to do this.

19When you are harvesting in your field and you overlook a sheaf, do not go back to get it. Leave it for the alien, the fatherless and the widow, so that the LORD your God may bless you in all the work of your hands.

---

[a] 8 The Hebrew word was used for various diseases affecting the skin—not necessarily leprosy.

Living Bible

24"You may eat your fill of the grapes from another man's vineyard, but do not take any away in a container. 25It is the same with someone else's grain—you may eat a few handfuls of it, but don't use a sickle.

24 "IF A man doesn't like something about his wife, he may write a letter stating that he has divorced her, give her the letter, and send her away. 2If she then remarries, 3and the second husband also divorces her, or dies, 4the former husband may not marry her again, for she has been defiled; this would bring guilt upon the land the Lord your God is giving you.

5"A newly married man is not to be drafted into the army nor given any other special responsibilities; for a year he shall be free to be at home, happy with his wife.

6"It is illegal to take a millstone as a pledge, for it is a tool by which its owner gains his livelihood. 7If anyone kidnaps a brother Israelite, and treats him as a slave or sells him, the kidnapper must die, in order to purge the evil from among you.

8"Be very careful to follow the instructions of the priest in cases of leprosy, for I have given him rules and guidelines you must obey to the letter: 9Remember what the Lord your God did to Miriam as you were coming from Egypt.

10"If you lend anything to another man, you must not enter his house to get his security. 11Stand outside! The owner will bring it out to you. 12, 13If the man is poor and gives you his cloak as security, you are not to sleep in it. Take it back to him at sundown so that he can use it through the night and bless you; and the Lord your God will count it as righteousness for you.

14, 15"Never oppress a poor hired man, whether a fellow Israelite or a foreigner living in your town. Pay him his wage each day before sunset, for since he is poor he needs it right away; otherwise he may cry out to the Lord against you and it should be counted as a sin against you.

16"Fathers shall not be put to death for the sins of their sons nor the sons for the sins of their fathers; every man worthy of death shall be executed for his own crime.

17"Justice must be given to migrants and orphans and you must never accept a widow's garment in pledge of her debt. 18Always remember that you were slaves in Egypt, and that the Lord your God rescued you; that is why I have given you this command. 19If, when reaping your harvest, you forget to bring in a sheaf from the field, don't go back after it. Leave it for the migrants, orphans, and widows; then the Lord your God will bless and prosper all you do. 20When you beat the olives from

New Revised Standard

24 If you go into your neighbor's vineyard, you may eat your fill of grapes, as many as you wish, but you shall not put any in a container.

25 If you go into your neighbor's standing grain, you may pluck the ears with your hand, but you shall not put a sickle to your neighbor's standing grain.

Laws concerning Marriage and Divorce

24 SUPPOSE A man enters into marriage with a woman, but she does not please him because he finds something objectionable about her, and so he writes her a certificate of divorce, puts it in her hand, and sends her out of his house; she then leaves his house 2and goes off to become another man's wife. 3Then suppose the second man dislikes her, writes her a bill of divorce, puts it in her hand, and sends her out of his house (or the second man who married her dies); 4her first husband, who sent her away, is not permitted to take her again to be his wife after she has been defiled; for that would be abhorrent to the LORD, and you shall not bring guilt on the land that the LORD your God is giving you as a possession.

Miscellaneous Laws

5 When a man is newly married, he shall not go out with the army or be charged with any related duty. He shall be free at home one year, to be happy with the wife whom he has married.

6 No one shall take a mill or an upper millstone in pledge, for that would be taking a life in pledge.

7 If someone is caught kidnaping another Israelite, enslaving or selling the Israelite, then that kidnaper shall die. So you shall purge the evil from your midst.

8 Guard against an outbreak of a leprousᵇ skin disease by being very careful; you shall carefully observe whatever the levitical priests instruct you, just as I have commanded them. 9Remember what the LORD your God did to Miriam on your journey out of Egypt.

10 When you make your neighbor a loan of any kind, you shall not go into the house to take the pledge. 11You shall wait outside, while the person to whom you are making the loan brings the pledge out to you. 12If the person is poor, you shall not sleep in the garment given you asᶜ the pledge. 13You shall give the pledge back by sunset, so that your neighbor may sleep in the cloak and bless you; and it will be to your credit before the LORD your God.

14 You shall not withhold the wages of poor and needy laborers, whether other Israelites or aliens who reside in your land in one of your towns. 15You shall pay them their wages daily before sunset, because they are poor and their livelihood depends on them; otherwise they might cry to the LORD against you, and you would incur guilt.

16 Parents shall not be put to death for their children, nor shall children be put to death for their parents; only for their own crimes may persons be put to death.

17 You shall not deprive a resident alien or an orphan of justice; you shall not take a widow's garment in pledge. 18Remember that you were a slave in Egypt and the LORD your God redeemed you from there; therefore I command you to do this.

19 When you reap your harvest in your field and forget a sheaf in the field, you shall not go back to get it; it shall be left for the alien, the orphan, and the widow, so that the LORD your God may bless you in all your undertakings. 20When you beat your olive trees, do not

---

ᵇ A term for several skin diseases; precise meaning uncertain   ᶜ Heb lacks *the garment given you as*

King James

20When thou beatest thine olive tree, thou shalt not go over the boughs again: it shall be for the stranger, for the fatherless, and for the widow.

21When thou gatherest the grapes of thy vineyard, thou shalt not glean *it* afterward: it shall be for the stranger, for the fatherless, and for the widow.

22And thou shalt remember that thou wast a bondman in the land of Egypt: therefore I command thee to do this thing.

25 IF THERE be a controversy between men, and they come unto judgment, that *the judges* may judge them; then they shall justify the righteous, and condemn the wicked.

2And it shall be, if the wicked man *be* worthy to be beaten, that the judge shall cause him to lie down, and to be beaten before his face, according to his fault, by a certain number.

3Forty stripes he may give him, *and* not exceed: lest, *if* he should exceed, and beat him above these with many stripes, then thy brother should seem vile unto thee.

4¶ Thou shalt not muzzle the ox when he treadeth out *the corn.*

5¶ If brethren dwell together, and one of them die, and have no child, the wife of the dead shall not marry without unto a stranger: her husband's brother shall go in unto her, and take her to him to wife, and perform the duty of an husband's brother unto her.

6And it shall be, *that* the firstborn which she beareth shall succeed in the name of his brother *which is* dead, that his name be not put out of Israel.

7And if the man like not to take his brother's wife, then let his brother's wife go up to the gate unto the elders, and say, My husband's brother refuseth to raise up unto his brother a name in Israel, he will not perform the duty of my husband's brother.

8Then the elders of his city shall call him, and speak unto him: and *if* he stand *to it,* and say, I like not to take her;

9Then shall his brother's wife come unto him in the presence of the elders, and loose his shoe from off his foot, and spit in his face, and shall answer and say, So shall it be done unto that man that will not build up his brother's house.

10And his name shall be called in Israel, The house of him that hath his shoe loosed.

11¶ When men strive together one with another, and the wife of the one draweth near for to deliver her husband out of the hand of him that smiteth him, and putteth forth her hand, and taketh him by the secrets:

12Then thou shalt cut off her hand, thine eye shall not pity *her.*

13¶ Thou shalt not have in thy bag divers weights, a great and a small.

14Thou shalt not have in thine house divers measures, a great and a small.

15*But* thou shalt have a perfect and just weight, a perfect and just measure shalt thou have: that thy days may be lengthened in the land which the LORD thy God giveth thee.

16For all that do such things, *and* all that do unrighteously, *are* an abomination unto the LORD thy God.

17¶ Remember what Amalek did unto thee by the way, when ye were come forth out of Egypt;

18How he met thee by the way, and smote the hindmost of thee, *even* all *that were* feeble behind thee, when thou *wast* faint and weary; and he feared not God.

New International

20When you beat the olives from your trees, do not go over the branches a second time. Leave what remains for the alien, the fatherless and the widow. 21When you harvest the grapes in your vineyard, do not go over the vines again. Leave what remains for the alien, the fatherless and the widow. 22Remember that you were slaves in Egypt. That is why I command you to do this.

25 WHEN MEN have a dispute, they are to take it to court and the judges will decide the case, acquitting the innocent and condemning the guilty. 2If the guilty man deserves to be beaten, the judge shall make him lie down and have him flogged in his presence with the number of lashes his crime deserves, 3but he must not give him more than forty lashes. If he is flogged more than that, your brother will be degraded in your eyes.

4Do not muzzle an ox while it is treading out the grain.

5If brothers are living together and one of them dies without a son, his widow must not marry outside the family. Her husband's brother shall take her and marry her and fulfill the duty of a brother-in-law to her. 6The first son she bears shall carry on the name of the dead brother so that his name will not be blotted out from Israel.

7However, if a man does not want to marry his brother's wife, she shall go to the elders at the town gate and say, "My husband's brother refuses to carry on his brother's name in Israel. He will not fulfill the duty of a brother-in-law to me." 8Then the elders of his town shall summon him and talk to him. If he persists in saying, "I do not want to marry her," 9his brother's widow shall go up to him in the presence of the elders, take off one of his sandals, spit in his face and say, "This is what is done to the man who will not build up his brother's family line." 10That man's line shall be known in Israel as The Family of the Unsandaled.

11If two men are fighting and the wife of one of them comes to rescue her husband from his assailant, and she reaches out and seizes him by his private parts, 12you shall cut off her hand. Show her no pity.

13Do not have two differing weights in your bag—one heavy, one light. 14Do not have two differing measures in your house—one large, one small. 15You must have accurate and honest weights and measures, so that you may live long in the land the LORD your God is giving you. 16For the LORD your God detests anyone who does these things, anyone who deals dishonestly.

17Remember what the Amalekites did to you along the way when you came out of Egypt. 18When you were weary and worn out, they met you on your journey and cut off all who were lagging behind; they had no fear of God. 19When the LORD your God gives you rest from all

Living Bible

your olive trees, don't go over the boughs twice; leave anything remaining for the migrants, orphans, and widows. 21It is the same for the grapes in your vineyard; don't glean the vines after they are picked, but leave what's left for those in need. 22Remember that you were slaves in the land of Egypt—that is why I am giving you this command.

25 "IF A man is guilty of a crime, and the penalty is a beating, the judge shall command him to lie down and be beaten in his presence with up to forty stripes in proportion to the seriousness of the crime; but no more than forty stripes may be given lest the punishment seem too severe, and your brother be degraded in your eyes.

4"Don't muzzle an ox as it treads out the grain.

5"If a man's brother dies without a son, his widow must not marry outside the family; instead, her husband's brother must marry her and sleep with her. 6The first son she bears to him shall be counted as the son of the dead brother, so that his name will not be forgotten. 7But if the dead man's brother refuses to do his duty in this matter, refusing to marry the widow, then she shall go to the city elders and say to them, 'My husband's brother refuses to let his brother's name continue—he refuses to marry me.' 8The elders of the city will then summon him and talk it over with him, and if he still refuses, 9the widow shall walk over to him in the presence of the elders, pull his sandal from his foot and spit in his face. She shall then say, 'This is what happens to a man who refuses to build his brother's house.' 10And ever afterwards his house shall be referred to as 'the home of the man who had his sandal pulled off!'

11"If two men are fighting and the wife of one intervenes to help her husband by grabbing the testicles of the other man, 12her hand shall be cut off without pity.

13, 14, 15"In all your transactions you must use accurate scales and honest measurements, so that you will have a long, good life in the land the Lord your God is giving you. 16All who cheat with unjust weights and measurements are detestable to the Lord your God.

17"You must never forget what the people of Amalek did to you as you came from Egypt. 18Remember that they fought with you and struck down those who were faint and weary and lagging behind, with no respect or fear of God. 19Therefore, when the Lord your God has

New Revised Standard

strip what is left; it shall be for the alien, the orphan, and the widow.

21 When you gather the grapes of your vineyard, do not glean what is left; it shall be for the alien, the orphan, and the widow. 22Remember that you were a slave in the land of Egypt; therefore I am commanding you to do this.

25 SUPPOSE TWO persons have a dispute and enter into litigation, and the judges decide between them, declaring one to be in the right and the other to be in the wrong. 2If the one in the wrong deserves to be flogged, the judge shall make that person lie down and be beaten in his presence with the number of lashes proportionate to the offense. 3Forty lashes may be given but not more; if more lashes than these are given, your neighbor will be degraded in your sight.

4 You shall not muzzle an ox while it is treading out the grain.

Levirate Marriage

5 When brothers reside together, and one of them dies and has no son, the wife of the deceased shall not be married outside the family to a stranger. Her husband's brother shall go in to her, taking her in marriage, and performing the duty of a husband's brother to her, 6and the firstborn whom she bears shall succeed to the name of the deceased brother, so that his name may not be blotted out of Israel. 7But if the man has no desire to marry his brother's widow, then his brother's widow shall go up to the elders at the gate and say, "My husband's brother refuses to perpetuate his brother's name in Israel; he will not perform the duty of a husband's brother to me." 8Then the elders of his town shall summon him and speak to him. If he persists, saying, "I have no desire to marry her," 9then his brother's wife shall go up to him in the presence of the elders, pull his sandal off his foot, spit in his face, and declare, "This is what is done to the man who does not build up his brother's house." 10Throughout Israel his family shall be known as "the house of him whose sandal was pulled off."

Various Commands

11 If men get into a fight with one another, and the wife of one intervenes to rescue her husband from the grip of his opponent by reaching out and seizing his genitals, 12you shall cut off her hand; show no pity.

13 You shall not have in your bag two kinds of weights, large and small. 14You shall not have in your house two kinds of measures, large and small. 15You shall have only a full and honest weight; you shall have only a full and honest measure, so that your days may be long in the land that the Lord your God is giving you. 16For all who do such things, all who act dishonestly, are abhorrent to the Lord your God.

17 Remember what Amalek did to you on your journey out of Egypt, 18how he attacked you on the way, when you were faint and weary, and struck down all who lagged behind you; he did not fear God. 19Therefore

King James

New International

[19]Therefore it shall be, when the LORD thy God hath given thee rest from all thine enemies round about, in the land which the LORD thy God giveth thee *for* an inheritance to possess it, *that* thou shalt blot out the remembrance of Amalek from under heaven; thou shalt not forget *it*.

26 AND IT shall be, when thou *art* come in unto the land which the LORD thy God giveth thee *for* an inheritance, and possessest it, and dwellest therein;

[2]That thou shalt take of the first of all the fruit of the earth, which thou shalt bring of thy land that the LORD thy God giveth thee, and shalt put *it* in a basket, and shalt go unto the place which the LORD thy God shall choose to place his name there.

[3]And thou shalt go unto the priest that shall be in those days, and say unto him, I profess this day unto the LORD thy God, that I am come unto the country which the LORD sware unto our fathers for to give us.

[4]And the priest shall take the basket out of thine hand, and set it down before the altar of the LORD thy God.

[5]And thou shalt speak and say before the LORD thy God, A Syrian ready to perish *was* my father, and he went down into Egypt, and sojourned there with a few, and became there a nation, great, mighty, and populous:

[6]And the Egyptians evil entreated us, and afflicted us, and laid upon us hard bondage:

[7]And when we cried unto the LORD God of our fathers, the LORD heard our voice, and looked on our affliction, and our labour, and our oppression:

[8]And the LORD brought us forth out of Egypt with a mighty hand, and with an outstretched arm, and with great terribleness, and with signs, and with wonders:

[9]And he hath brought us into this place, and hath given us this land, *even* a land that floweth with milk and honey.

[10]And now, behold, I have brought the firstfruits of the land, which thou, O LORD, hast given me. And thou shalt set it before the LORD thy God, and worship before the LORD thy God:

[11]And thou shalt rejoice in every good *thing* which the LORD thy God hath given unto thee, and unto thine house, thou, and the Levite, and the stranger that *is* among you.

[12]¶ When thou hast made an end of tithing all the tithes of thine increase the third year, *which is* the year of tithing, and hast given *it* unto the Levite, the stranger, the fatherless, and the widow, that they may eat within thy gates, and be filled;

[13]Then thou shalt say before the LORD thy God, I have brought away the hallowed things out of *mine* house, and also have given them unto the Levite, and unto the stranger, to the fatherless, and to the widow, according to all thy commandments which thou hast commanded me: I have not transgressed thy commandments, neither have I forgotten *them*:

[14]I have not eaten thereof in my mourning, neither have I taken away *aught* thereof for *any* unclean *use*, nor given *aught* thereof for the dead: *but* I have hearkened to the voice of the LORD my God, *and* have done according to all that thou hast commanded me.

[15]Look down from thy holy habitation, from heaven, and bless thy people Israel, and the land which thou hast given us, as thou swarest unto our fathers, a land that floweth with milk and honey.

[16]¶ This day the LORD thy God hath commanded thee to do these statutes and judgments: thou shalt therefore keep and do them with all thine heart, and with all thy soul.

the enemies around you in the land he is giving you to possess as an inheritance, you shall blot out the memory of Amalek from under heaven. Do not forget!

Firstfruits and Tithes

26 WHEN YOU have entered the land the LORD your God is giving you as an inheritance and have taken possession of it and settled in it, [2]take some of the firstfruits of all that you produce from the soil of the land the LORD your God is giving you and put them in a basket. Then go to the place the LORD your God will choose as a dwelling for his Name [3]and say to the priest in office at the time, "I declare today to the LORD your God that I have come to the land the LORD swore to our forefathers to give us." [4]The priest shall take the basket from your hands and set it down in front of the altar of the LORD your God. [5]Then you shall declare before the LORD your God: "My father was a wandering Aramean, and he went down into Egypt with a few people and lived there and became a great nation, powerful and numerous. [6]But the Egyptians mistreated us and made us suffer, putting us to hard labor. [7]Then we cried out to the LORD, the God of our fathers, and the LORD heard our voice and saw our misery, toil and oppression. [8]So the LORD brought us out of Egypt with a mighty hand and an outstretched arm, with great terror and with miraculous signs and wonders. [9]He brought us to this place and gave us this land, a land flowing with milk and honey; [10]and now I bring the firstfruits of the soil that you, O LORD, have given me." Place the basket before the LORD your God and bow down before him. [11]And you and the Levites and the aliens among you shall rejoice in all the good things the LORD your God has given to you and your household.

[12]When you have finished setting aside a tenth of all your produce in the third year, the year of the tithe, you shall give it to the Levite, the alien, the fatherless and the widow, so that they may eat in your towns and be satisfied. [13]Then say to the LORD your God: "I have removed from my house the sacred portion and have given it to the Levite, the alien, the fatherless and the widow, according to all you commanded. I have not turned aside from your commands nor have I forgotten any of them. [14]I have not eaten any of the sacred portion while I was in mourning, nor have I removed any of it while I was unclean, nor have I offered any of it to the dead. I have obeyed the LORD my God; I have done everything you commanded me. [15]Look down from heaven, your holy dwelling place, and bless your people Israel and the land you have given us as you promised on oath to our forefathers, a land flowing with milk and honey."

Follow the LORD's Commands

[16]The LORD your God commands you this day to follow these decrees and laws; carefully observe them with all your heart and with all your soul. [17]You have

Living Bible

given you rest from all your enemies in the Promised Land, you are utterly to destroy the name of Amalek from under heaven. Never forget this.

26 "WHEN YOU arrive in the land and have conquered it and are living there, 2, 3you must present to the Lord at his sanctuary the first sample from each annuala harvest. Bring it in a basket and hand it to the priest on duty and say to him, 'This gift is my acknowledgment that the Lord my God has brought me to the land he promised our ancestors.' 4The priest will then take the basket from your hand and set it before the altar. 5You shall then say before the Lord your God, 'My ancestors were migrant Arameans who went to Egypt for refuge. They were few in number, but in Egypt they became a mighty nation. 6, 7The Egyptians mistreated us and we cried to the Lord God. He heard us and saw our hardship, toil, and oppression, 8and brought us out of Egypt with mighty miracles and a powerful hand. He did great and awesome miracles before the Egyptians, 9and has brought us to this place and given us this land "flowing with milk and honey!" 10And now, O Lord, see, I have brought you a token of the first of the crops from the ground you have given me.' Then place the samples before the Lord your God, and worship him. 11Afterwards, go and feast on all the good things he has given you. Celebrate with your family and with any Levites or migrants living among you.

12"Every third year is a year of special tithing. That year you are to give all your tithes to the Levites, migrants, orphans, and widows, so that they will be well fed. 13Then you shall declare before the Lord your God, 'I have given all of my tithes to the Levites, the migrants, the orphans, and the widows, just as you commanded me; I have not violated or forgotten any of your rules. 14I have not touched the tithe while I was ceremonially defiled (for instance, while I was in mourning), nor have I offered any of it to the dead. I have obeyed the Lord my God and have done everything you commanded me. 15Look down from your holy home in heaven and bless your people and the land you have given us, as you promised our ancestors; make it a land "flowing with milk and honey"!'

16"You must wholeheartedly obey all of these commandments and ordinances which the Lord your God is giving you today. 17You have declared today that he is

New Revised Standard

when the LORD your God has given you rest from all your enemies on every hand, in the land that the LORD your God is giving you as an inheritance to possess, you shall blot out the remembrance of Amalek from under heaven; do not forget.

First Fruits and Tithes

26 WHEN YOU have come into the land that the LORD your God is giving you as an inheritance to possess, and you possess it, and settle in it, 2you shall take some of the first of all the fruit of the ground, which you harvest from the land that the LORD your God is giving you, and you shall put it in a basket and go to the place that the LORD your God will choose as a dwelling for his name. 3You shall go to the priest who is in office at that time, and say to him, "Today I declare to the LORD your God that I have come into the land that the LORD swore to our ancestors to give us." 4When the priest takes the basket from your hand and sets it down before the altar of the LORD your God, 5you shall make this response before the LORD your God: "A wandering Aramean was my ancestor; he went down into Egypt and lived there as an alien, few in number, and there he became a great nation, mighty and populous. 6When the Egyptians treated us harshly and afflicted us, by imposing hard labor on us, 7we cried to the LORD, the God of our ancestors; the LORD heard our voice and saw our affliction, our toil, and our oppression. 8The LORD brought us out of Egypt with a mighty hand and an outstretched arm, with a terrifying display of power, and with signs and wonders; 9and he brought us into this place and gave us this land, a land flowing with milk and honey. 10So now I bring the first of the fruit of the ground that you, O LORD, have given me." You shall set it down before the LORD your God and bow down before the LORD your God. 11Then you, together with the Levites and the aliens who reside among you, shall celebrate with all the bounty that the LORD your God has given to you and to your house.

12 When you have finished paying all the tithe of your produce in the third year (which is the year of the tithe), giving it to the Levites, the aliens, the orphans, and the widows, so that they may eat their fill within your towns, 13then you shall say before the LORD your God: "I have removed the sacred portion from the house, and I have given it to the Levites, the resident aliens, the orphans, and the widows, in accordance with your entire commandment that you commanded me; I have neither transgressed nor forgotten any of your commandments: 14I have not eaten of it while in mourning; I have not removed any of it while I was unclean; and I have not offered any of it to the dead. I have obeyed the LORD my God, doing just as you commanded me. 15Look down from your holy habitation, from heaven, and bless your people Israel and the ground that you have given us, as you swore to our ancestors—a land flowing with milk and honey."

Concluding Exhortation

16 This very day the LORD your God is commanding you to observe these statutes and ordinances; so observe them diligently with all your heart and with all your soul.

---

a 26:2,3 *from each annual*, implied.

King James

17Thou hast avouched the LORD this day to be thy God, and to walk in his ways, and to keep his statutes, and his commandments, and his judgments, and to hearken unto his voice:

18And the LORD hath avouched thee this day to be his peculiar people, as he hath promised thee, and that *thou* shouldest keep all his commandments;

19And to make thee high above all nations which he hath made, in praise, and in name, and in honour; and that thou mayest be an holy people unto the LORD thy God, as he hath spoken.

27 AND MOSES with the elders of Israel commanded the people, saying, Keep all the commandments which I command you this day.

2And it shall be on the day when ye shall pass over Jordan unto the land which the LORD thy God giveth thee, that thou shalt set thee up great stones, and plaster them with plaster:

3And thou shalt write upon them all the words of this law, when thou art passed over, that thou mayest go in unto the land which the LORD thy God giveth thee, a land that floweth with milk and honey; as the LORD God of thy fathers hath promised thee.

4Therefore it shall be when ye be gone over Jordan, *that* ye shall set up these stones, which I command you this day, in mount Ebal, and thou shalt plaster them with plaster.

5And there shalt thou build an altar unto the LORD thy God, an altar of stones: thou shalt not lift up *any* iron *tool* upon them.

6Thou shalt build the altar of the LORD thy God of whole stones: and thou shalt offer burnt offerings thereon unto the LORD thy God:

7And thou shalt offer peace offerings, and shalt eat there, and rejoice before the LORD thy God.

8And thou shalt write upon the stones all the words of this law very plainly.

9¶ And Moses and the priests the Levites spake unto all Israel, saying, Take heed, and hearken, O Israel; this day thou art become the people of the LORD thy God.

10Thou shalt therefore obey the voice of the LORD thy God, and do his commandments and his statutes, which I command thee this day.

11¶ And Moses charged the people the same day, saying,

12These shall stand upon mount Gerizim to bless the people, when ye are come over Jordan; Simeon, and Levi, and Judah, and Issachar, and Joseph, and Benjamin:

13And these shall stand upon mount Ebal to curse; Reuben, Gad, and Asher, and Zebulun, Dan, and Naphtali.

14¶ And the Levites shall speak, and say unto all the men of Israel with a loud voice,

15Cursed *be* the man that maketh *any* graven or molten image, an abomination unto the LORD, the work of the hands of the craftsman, and putteth *it* in *a* secret *place*. And all the people shall answer and say, Amen.

16Cursed *be* he that setteth light by his father or his mother. And all the people shall say, Amen.

17Cursed *be* he that removeth his neighbour's landmark. And all the people shall say, Amen.

18Cursed *be* he that maketh the blind to wander out of the way. And all the people shall say, Amen.

19Cursed *be* he that perverteth the judgment of the stranger, fatherless, and widow. And all the people shall say, Amen.

20Cursed *be* he that lieth with his father's wife; because he uncovereth his father's skirt. And all the people shall say, Amen.

New International

declared this day that the LORD is your God and that you will walk in his ways, that you will keep his decrees, commands and laws, and that you will obey him. 18And the LORD has declared this day that you are his people, his treasured possession as he promised, and that you are to keep all his commands. 19He has declared that he will set you in praise, fame and honor high above all the nations he has made and that you will be a people holy to the LORD your God, as he promised.

The Altar on Mount Ebal

27 MOSES AND the elders of Israel commanded the people: "Keep all these commands that I give you today. 2When you have crossed the Jordan into the land the LORD your God is giving you, set up some large stones and coat them with plaster. 3Write on them all the words of this law when you have crossed over to enter the land the LORD your God is giving you, a land flowing with milk and honey, just as the LORD, the God of your fathers, promised you. 4And when you have crossed the Jordan, set up these stones on Mount Ebal, as I command you today, and coat them with plaster. 5Build there an altar to the LORD your God, an altar of stones. Do not use any iron tool upon them. 6Build the altar of the LORD your God with fieldstones and offer burnt offerings on it to the LORD your God. 7Sacrifice fellowship offeringsa there, eating them and rejoicing in the presence of the LORD your God. 8And you shall write very clearly all the words of this law on these stones you have set up."

Curses From Mount Ebal

9Then Moses and the priests, who are Levites, said to all Israel, "Be silent, O Israel, and listen! You have now become the people of the LORD your God. 10Obey the LORD your God and follow his commands and decrees that I give you today."

11On the same day Moses commanded the people:

12When you have crossed the Jordan, these tribes shall stand on Mount Gerizim to bless the people: Simeon, Levi, Judah, Issachar, Joseph and Benjamin. 13And these tribes shall stand on Mount Ebal to pronounce curses: Reuben, Gad, Asher, Zebulun, Dan and Naphtali.

14The Levites shall recite to all the people of Israel in a loud voice:

15"Cursed is the man who carves an image or casts an idol—a thing detestable to the LORD, the work of the craftsman's hands—and sets it up in secret."

Then all the people shall say, "Amen!"

16"Cursed is the man who dishonors his father or his mother."

Then all the people shall say, "Amen!"

17"Cursed is the man who moves his neighbor's boundary stone."

Then all the people shall say, "Amen!"

18"Cursed is the man who leads the blind astray on the road."

Then all the people shall say, "Amen!"

19"Cursed is the man who withholds justice from the alien, the fatherless or the widow."

Then all the people shall say, "Amen!"

20"Cursed is the man who sleeps with his father's wife, for he dishonors his father's bed."

Then all the people shall say, "Amen!"

---

a 7 Traditionally *peace offerings*

Living Bible

your God, and you have promised to obey and keep his laws and ordinances, and to heed all he tells you to do. 18And the Lord has declared today that you are his very own people, just as he promised, and that you must obey all of his laws. 19If you do, he will make you greater than any other nation, allowing you to receive praise, honor, and renown; but to attain this honor and renown you must be a holy people to the Lord your God, as he requires."

27 THEN MOSES and the elders of Israel gave the people these further instructions to obey:b

2, 3, 4"When you cross the Jordan River and go into the Promised Land—a land 'flowing with milk and honey'—take out boulders from the river bottom and immediately pile them into a monument on the other side, at Mount Ebal. Face the stones with a coating of limec and then write the laws of God in the lime. 5, 6And build an altar there to the Lord your God. Use uncut boulders, and on the altar offer burnt offerings to the Lord your God. 7Sacrifice peace offerings upon it also, and feast there with great joy before the Lord your God. 8Write all of these laws plainly [upon the monumentd]."

9Then Moses and the Levite-priests addressed all Israel as follows: "O Israel, listen! Today you have become the people of the Lord your God, 10so today you must begin to obey all of these commandments I have given you."

11That same day Moses gave this charge to the people:

12"When you cross into the Promised Land, the tribes of Simeon, Levi, Judah, Issachar, Joseph, and Benjamin shall stand upon Mount Gerizim to proclaim a blessing, 13and the tribes of Reuben, Gad, Asher, Zebulun, Dan, and Naphtali shall stand upon Mount Ebal to proclaim a curse. 14Then the Levites standing betweene them shall shout to all Israel,

15" 'The curse of God be upon anyone who makes and worships an idol, even in secret, whether carved of wood or made from molten metal—for these handmade gods are hated by the Lord.' And all the people shall reply, 'Amen.'

16" 'Cursed is anyone who despises his father or mother.' And all the people shall reply, 'Amen.'

17" 'Cursed is he who moves the boundary marker between his land and his neighbor's.' And all the people shall reply, 'Amen.'

18" 'Cursed is he who takes advantage of a blind man.' And all the people shall reply, 'Amen.'

19" 'Cursed is he who is unjust to the foreigner, the orphan, and the widow.' And all the people shall reply, 'Amen.'

20" 'Cursed is he who commits adultery with one of his father's wives, for she belongs to his father.' And all the people shall reply, 'Amen.'

New Revised Standard

17Today you have obtained the LORD's agreement: to be your God; and for you to walk in his ways, to keep his statutes, his commandments, and his ordinances, and to obey him. 18Today the LORD has obtained your agreement: to be his treasured people, as he promised you, and to keep his commandments; 19for him to set you high above all nations that he has made, in praise and in fame and in honor; and for you to be a people holy to the LORD your God, as he promised.

The Inscribed Stones and Altar on Mount Ebal

27 THEN MOSES and the elders of Israel charged all the people as follows: Keep the entire commandment that I am commanding you today. 2On the day that you cross over the Jordan into the land that the LORD your God is giving you, you shall set up large stones and cover them with plaster. 3You shall write on them all the words of this law when you have crossed over, to enter the land that the LORD your God is giving you, a land flowing with milk and honey, as the LORD, the God of your ancestors, promised you. 4So when you have crossed over the Jordan, you shall set up these stones, about which I am commanding you today, on Mount Ebal, and you shall cover them with plaster. 5And you shall build an altar there to the LORD your God, an altar of stones on which you have not used an iron tool. 6You must build the altar of the LORD your God of unhewnf stones. Then offer up burnt offerings on it to the LORD your God, 7make sacrifices of well-being, and eat them there, rejoicing before the LORD your God. 8You shall write on the stones all the words of this law very clearly.

9 Then Moses and the levitical priests spoke to all Israel, saying: Keep silence and hear, O Israel! This very day you have become the people of the LORD your God. 10Therefore obey the LORD your God, observing his commandments and his statutes that I am commanding you today.

Twelve Curses

11 The same day Moses charged the people as follows: 12When you have crossed over the Jordan, these shall stand on Mount Gerizim for the blessing of the people: Simeon, Levi, Judah, Issachar, Joseph, and Benjamin. 13And these shall stand on Mount Ebal for the curse: Reuben, Gad, Asher, Zebulun, Dan, and Naphtali. 14Then the Levites shall declare in a loud voice to all the Israelites:

15 "Cursed be anyone who makes an idol or casts an image, anything abhorrent to the LORD, the work of an artisan, and sets it up in secret." All the people shall respond, saying, "Amen!"

16 "Cursed be anyone who dishonors father or mother." All the people shall say, "Amen!"

17 "Cursed be anyone who moves a neighbor's boundary marker." All the people shall say, "Amen!"

18 "Cursed be anyone who misleads a blind person on the road." All the people shall say, "Amen!"

19 "Cursed be anyone who deprives the alien, the orphan, and the widow of justice." All the people shall say, "Amen!"

20 "Cursed be anyone who lies with his father's wife, because he has violated his father's rights."g All the people shall say, "Amen!"

---

b 27:1 gave the people these further instructions to obey, literally, "Keep all the commandments I enjoin on you today." c 27:2-4 with a coating of lime, literally, "plaster them with plaster." d 27:8 upon the monument, implied. See vss 1-4. e 27:14 Then the Levites standing between, implied.

f Heb whole   g Heb uncovered his father's skirt

King James

21Cursed *be* he that lieth with any manner of beast. And all the people shall say, Amen.

22Cursed *be* he that lieth with his sister, the daughter of his father, or the daughter of his mother. And all the people shall say, Amen.

23Cursed *be* he that lieth with his mother-in-law. And all the people shall say, Amen.

24Cursed *be* he that smiteth his neighbour secretly. And all the people shall say, Amen.

25Cursed *be* he that taketh reward to slay an innocent person. And all the people shall say, Amen.

26Cursed *be* he that confirmeth not *all* the words of this law to do them. And all the people shall say, Amen.

28 AND IT shall come to pass, if thou shalt hearken diligently unto the voice of the LORD thy God, to observe *and* to do all his commandments which I command thee this day, that the LORD thy God will set thee on high above all nations of the earth:

2And all these blessings shall come on thee, and overtake thee, if thou shalt hearken unto the voice of the LORD thy God.

3Blessed *shalt* thou *be* in the city, and blessed *shalt* thou *be* in the field.

4Blessed *shall be* the fruit of thy body, and the fruit of thy ground, and the fruit of thy cattle, the increase of thy kine, and the flocks of thy sheep.

5Blessed *shall be* thy basket and thy store.

6Blessed *shalt* thou *be* when thou comest in, and blessed *shalt* thou *be* when thou goest out.

7The LORD shall cause thine enemies that rise up against thee to be smitten before thy face: they shall come out against thee one way, and flee before thee seven ways.

8The LORD shall command the blessing upon thee in thy storehouses, and in all that thou settest thine hand unto; and he shall bless thee in the land which the LORD thy God giveth thee.

9The LORD shall establish thee an holy people unto himself, as he hath sworn unto thee, if thou shalt keep the commandments of the LORD thy God, and walk in his ways.

10And all people of the earth shall see that thou art called by the name of the LORD; and they shall be afraid of thee.

11And the LORD shall make thee plenteous in goods, in the fruit of thy body, and in the fruit of thy cattle, and in the fruit of thy ground, in the land which the LORD sware unto thy fathers to give thee.

12The LORD shall open unto thee his good treasure, the heaven to give the rain unto thy land in his season, and to bless all the work of thine hand: and thou shalt lend unto many nations, and thou shalt not borrow.

13And the LORD shall make thee the head, and not the tail; and thou shalt be above only, and thou shalt not be beneath; if that thou hearken unto the commandments of the LORD thy God, which I command thee this day, to observe and to do *them*:

14And thou shalt not go aside from any of the words which I command thee this day, *to* the right hand, or *to* the left, to go after other gods to serve them.

New International

21"Cursed is the man who has sexual relations with any animal."

Then all the people shall say, "Amen!"

22"Cursed is the man who sleeps with his sister, the daughter of his father or the daughter of his mother."

Then all the people shall say, "Amen!"

23"Cursed is the man who sleeps with his mother-in-law."

Then all the people shall say, "Amen!"

24"Cursed is the man who kills his neighbor secretly."

Then all the people shall say, "Amen!"

25"Cursed is the man who accepts a bribe to kill an innocent person."

Then all the people shall say, "Amen!"

26"Cursed is the man who does not uphold the words of this law by carrying them out."

Then all the people shall say, "Amen!"

Blessings for Obedience

28 IF YOU fully obey the LORD your God and carefully follow all his commands I give you today, the LORD your God will set you high above all the nations on earth. 2All these blessings will come upon you and accompany you if you obey the LORD your God:

3You will be blessed in the city and blessed in the country.

4The fruit of your womb will be blessed, and the crops of your land and the young of your livestock—the calves of your herds and the lambs of your flocks.

5Your basket and your kneading trough will be blessed.

6You will be blessed when you come in and blessed when you go out.

7The LORD will grant that the enemies who rise up against you will be defeated before you. They will come at you from one direction but flee from you in seven.

8The LORD will send a blessing on your barns and on everything you put your hand to. The LORD your God will bless you in the land he is giving you.

9The LORD will establish you as his holy people, as he promised you on oath, if you keep the commands of the LORD your God and walk in his ways. 10Then all the peoples on earth will see that you are called by the name of the LORD, and they will fear you. 11The LORD will grant you abundant prosperity—in the fruit of your womb, the young of your livestock and the crops of your ground—in the land he swore to your forefathers to give you.

12The LORD will open the heavens, the storehouse of his bounty, to send rain on your land in season and to bless all the work of your hands. You will lend to many nations but will borrow from none. 13The LORD will make you the head, not the tail. If you pay attention to the commands of the LORD your God that I give you this day and carefully follow them, you will always be at the top, never at the bottom. 14Do not turn aside from any of the commands I give you today, to the right or to the left, following other gods and serving them.

Living Bible

21 "'Cursed is he who has sexual intercourse with an animal.' And all the people shall reply, 'Amen.'

22 "'Cursed is he who has sexual intercourse with his sister, whether she be a full sister or a half-sister.' And all the people shall reply, 'Amen.'

23 "'Cursed is he who has sexual intercourse with his widoweda mother-in-law.' And all the people shall reply, 'Amen.'

24 "'Cursed is he who secretly slays another.' And all the people shall reply, 'Amen.'

25 "'Cursed is he who accepts a bribe to kill an innocent person.' And all the people shall reply, 'Amen.'

26 "'Cursed is anyone who does not obey these laws.' And all the people shall reply, 'Amen.'

28 "IF YOU fully obey all of these commandments of the Lord your God, the laws I am declaring to you today, God will transform you into the greatest nation in the world. 2-6These are the blessings that will come upon you:

Blessings in the city,
Blessings in the field;
Many children,
Ample crops,
Large flocks and herds;
Blessings of fruit and bread;
Blessings when you come in,
Blessings when you go out.

7"The Lord will defeat your enemies before you; they will march out together against you but scatter before you in seven directions! 8The Lord will bless you with good crops and healthy cattle, and prosper everything you do when you arrive in the land the Lord your God is giving you. 9He will change you into a holy people dedicated to himself; this he has promised to do if you will only obey him and walk in his ways. 10All the nations in the world shall see that you belong to the Lord, and they will stand in awe.

11"The Lord will give you an abundance of good things in the land, just as he promised: many children, many cattle, and abundant crops. 12He will open to you his wonderful treasury of rain in the heavens, to give you fine crops every season. He will bless everything you do; and you shall lend to many nations, but shall not borrow from them. 13If you will only listen and obey the commandments of the Lord your God that I am giving you today, he will make you the head and not the tail, and you shall always have the upper hand. 14But each of these blessings depends on your not turning aside in any way from the laws I have given you; and you must never worship other gods.

New Revised Standard

21 "Cursed be anyone who lies with any animal." All the people shall say, "Amen!"

22 "Cursed be anyone who lies with his sister, whether the daughter of his father or the daughter of his mother." All the people shall say, "Amen!"

23 "Cursed be anyone who lies with his mother-in-law." All the people shall say, "Amen!"

24 "Cursed be anyone who strikes down a neighbor in secret." All the people shall say, "Amen!"

25 "Cursed be anyone who takes a bribe to shed innocent blood." All the people shall say, "Amen!"

26 "Cursed be anyone who does not uphold the words of this law by observing them." All the people shall say, "Amen!"

Blessings for Obedience

28 IF YOU will only obey the LORD your God, by diligently observing all his commandments that I am commanding you today, the LORD your God will set you high above all the nations of the earth; 2 all these blessings shall come upon you and overtake you, if you obey the LORD your God:

3 Blessed shall you be in the city, and blessed shall you be in the field.

4 Blessed shall be the fruit of your womb, the fruit of your ground, and the fruit of your livestock, both the increase of your cattle and the issue of your flock.

5 Blessed shall be your basket and your kneading bowl.

6 Blessed shall you be when you come in, and blessed shall you be when you go out.

7 The LORD will cause your enemies who rise against you to be defeated before you; they shall come out against you one way, and flee before you seven ways. 8 The LORD will command the blessing upon you in your barns, and in all that you undertake; he will bless you in the land that the LORD your God is giving you. 9 The LORD will establish you as his holy people, as he has sworn to you, if you keep the commandments of the LORD your God and walk in his ways. 10 All the peoples of the earth shall see that you are called by the name of the LORD, and they shall be afraid of you. 11 The LORD will make you abound in prosperity, in the fruit of your womb, in the fruit of your livestock, and in the fruit of your ground in the land that the LORD swore to your ancestors to give you. 12 The LORD will open for you his rich storehouse, the heavens, to give the rain of your land in its season and to bless all your undertakings. You will lend to many nations, but you will not borrow. 13 The LORD will make you the head, and not the tail; you shall be only at the top, and not at the bottom—if you obey the commandments of the LORD your God, which I am commanding you today, by diligently observing them, 14 and if you do not turn aside from any of the words that I am commanding you today, either to the right or to the left, following other gods to serve them.

---

a 27:23 widowed, implied. If she were still married, no special law would be needed to prohibit adultery.

King James

15¶ But it shall come to pass, if thou wilt not hearken unto the voice of the LORD thy God, to observe to do all his commandments and his statutes which I command thee this day; that all these curses shall come upon thee, and overtake thee:

16Cursed *shalt* thou *be* in the city, and cursed *shalt* thou *be* in the field.

17Cursed *shall be* thy basket and thy store.

18Cursed *shall be* the fruit of thy body, and the fruit of thy land, the increase of thy kine, and the flocks of thy sheep.

19Cursed *shalt* thou *be* when thou comest in, and cursed *shalt* thou *be* when thou goest out.

20The LORD shall send upon thee cursing, vexation, and rebuke, in all that thou settest thine hand unto for to do, until thou be destroyed, and until thou perish quickly; because of the wickedness of thy doings, whereby thou hast forsaken me.

21The LORD shall make the pestilence cleave unto thee, until he have consumed thee from off the land, whither thou goest to possess it.

22The LORD shall smite thee with a consumption, and with a fever, and with an inflammation, and with an extreme burning, and with the sword, and with blasting, and with mildew; and they shall pursue thee until thou perish.

23And thy heaven that *is* over thy head shall be brass, and the earth that *is* under thee *shall be* iron.

24The LORD shall make the rain of thy land powder and dust: from heaven shall it come down upon thee, until thou be destroyed.

25The LORD shall cause thee to be smitten before thine enemies: thou shalt go out one way against them, and flee seven ways before them: and shalt be removed into all the kingdoms of the earth.

26And thy carcase shall be meat unto all fowls of the air, and unto the beasts of the earth, and no man shall fray *them* away.

27The LORD will smite thee with the botch of Egypt, and with the emerods, and with the scab, and with the itch, whereof thou canst not be healed.

28The LORD shall smite thee with madness, and blindness, and astonishment of heart:

29And thou shalt grope at noonday, as the blind gropeth in darkness, and thou shalt not prosper in thy ways: and thou shalt be only oppressed and spoiled evermore, and no man shall save *thee*.

30Thou shalt betroth a wife, and another man shall lie with her: thou shalt build an house, and thou shalt not dwell therein: thou shalt plant a vineyard, and shalt not gather the grapes thereof.

31Thine ox *shall be* slain before thine eyes, and thou shalt not eat thereof: thine ass *shall be* violently taken away from before thy face, and shall not be restored to thee: thy sheep *shall be* given unto thine enemies, and thou shalt have none to rescue *them*.

32Thy sons and thy daughters *shall be* given unto another people, and thine eyes shall look, and fail *with longing* for them all the day long: and *there shall be* no might in thine hand.

33The fruit of thy land, and all thy labours, shall a nation which thou knowest not eat up; and thou shalt be only oppressed and crushed always:

34So that thou shalt be mad for the sight of thine eyes which thou shalt see.

35The LORD shall smite thee in the knees, and in the legs, with a sore botch that cannot be healed, from the sole of thy foot unto the top of thy head.

36The LORD shall bring thee, and thy king which thou shalt set over thee, unto a nation which neither thou nor thy fathers have known; and there shalt thou serve other gods, wood and stone.

37And thou shalt become an astonishment, a proverb, and a byword, among all nations whither the LORD shall lead thee.

New International

Curses for Disobedience

15However, if you do not obey the LORD your God and do not carefully follow all his commands and decrees I am giving you today, all these curses will come upon you and overtake you:

16You will be cursed in the city and cursed in the country.

17Your basket and your kneading trough will be cursed.

18The fruit of your womb will be cursed, and the crops of your land, and the calves of your herds and the lambs of your flocks.

19You will be cursed when you come in and cursed when you go out.

20The LORD will send on you curses, confusion and rebuke in everything you put your hand to, until you are destroyed and come to sudden ruin because of the evil you have done in forsaking him.a 21The LORD will plague you with diseases until he has destroyed you from the land you are entering to possess. 22The LORD will strike you with wasting disease, with fever and inflammation, with scorching heat and drought, with blight and mildew, which will plague you until you perish. 23The sky over your head will be bronze, the ground beneath you iron. 24The LORD will turn the rain of your country into dust and powder; it will come down from the skies until you are destroyed.

25The LORD will cause you to be defeated before your enemies. You will come at them from one direction but flee from them in seven, and you will become a thing of horror to all the kingdoms on earth. 26Your carcasses will be food for all the birds of the air and the beasts of the earth, and there will be no one to frighten them away. 27The LORD will afflict you with the boils of Egypt and with tumors, festering sores and the itch, from which you cannot be cured. 28The LORD will afflict you with madness, blindness and confusion of mind. 29At midday you will grope about like a blind man in the dark. You will be unsuccessful in everything you do; day after day you will be oppressed and robbed, with no one to rescue you.

30You will be pledged to be married to a woman, but another will take her and ravish her. You will build a house, but you will not live in it. You will plant a vineyard, but you will not even begin to enjoy its fruit. 31Your ox will be slaughtered before your eyes, but you will eat none of it. Your donkey will be forcibly taken from you and will not be returned. Your sheep will be given to your enemies, and no one will rescue them. 32Your sons and daughters will be given to another nation, and you will wear out your eyes watching for them day after day, powerless to lift a hand. 33A people that you do not know will eat what your land and labor produce, and you will have nothing but cruel oppression all your days. 34The sights you see will drive you mad. 35The LORD will afflict your knees and legs with painful boils that cannot be cured, spreading from the soles of your feet to the top of your head.

36The LORD will drive you and the king you set over you to a nation unknown to you or your fathers. There you will worship other gods, gods of wood and stone. 37You will become a thing of horror and an object of scorn and ridicule to all the nations where the LORD will drive you.

ᵃ *20 Hebrew* me

Living Bible

15-19"If you won't listen to the Lord your God and won't obey these laws I am giving you today, then all of these curses shall come upon you:
Curses in the city,
Curses in the fields,
Curses on your fruit and bread,
The curse of barren wombs,
Curses upon your crops,
Curses upon the fertility of your cattle and flocks,
Curses when you come in,
Curses when you go out.

20"For the Lord himself will send his personal curse upon you. You will be confused and a failure in everything you do, until at last you are destroyed because of the sin of forsaking him. 21He will send disease among you until you are destroyed from the face of the land which you are about to enter and possess. 22He will send tuberculosis, fever, infections, plague, and war. He will blight your crops, covering them with mildew. All these devastations shall pursue you until you perish.

23"The heavens above you will be as unyielding as bronze, and the earth beneath will be as iron. 24The land will become as dry as dust for lack of rain, and dust storms shall destroy you.

25"The Lord will cause you to be defeated by your enemies. You will march out to battle gloriously, but flee before your enemies in utter confusion; and you will be tossed to and fro among all the nations of the earth. 26Your dead bodies will be food to the birds and wild animals, and no one will be there to chase them away.

27"He will send upon you Egyptian boils, tumors, scurvy, and itch, for none of which will there be a remedy. 28He will send madness, blindness, fear, and panic upon you. 29You shall grope in the bright sunlight just as the blind man gropes in darkness. You shall not prosper in anything you do; you will be oppressed and robbed continually, and nothing will save you.

30"Someone else will marry your fiancée; someone else will live in the house you build; someone else will eat the fruit of the vineyard you plant. 31Your oxen shall be butchered before your eyes, but you won't get a single bite of the meat. Your donkeys will be driven away as you watch, and will never return to you again. Your sheep will be given to your enemies. And there will be no one to protect you. 32You will watch as your sons and daughters are taken away as slaves. Your heart will break with longing for them, but you will not be able to help them. 33A foreign nation you have not even heard of will eat the crops you will have worked so hard to grow. You will always be oppressed and crushed. 34You will go mad because of all the tragedy you see around you. 35The Lord will cover you with boils from head to foot.

36"He will exile you and the king you will choose, to a nation to whom neither you nor your ancestors gave a second thought; and while in exile you shall worship gods of wood and stone! 37You will become an object of horror, a proverb and a byword among all the nations, for the Lord will thrust you away.

New Revised Standard

Warnings against Disobedience

15 But if you will not obey the LORD your God by diligently observing all his commandments and decrees, which I am commanding you today, then all these curses shall come upon you and overtake you:

16 Cursed shall you be in the city, and cursed shall you be in the field.

17 Cursed shall be your basket and your kneading bowl.

18 Cursed shall be the fruit of your womb, the fruit of your ground, the increase of your cattle and the issue of your flock.

19 Cursed shall you be when you come in, and cursed shall you be when you go out.

20 The LORD will send upon you disaster, panic, and frustration in everything you attempt to do, until you are destroyed and perish quickly, on account of the evil of your deeds, because you have forsaken me. 21 The LORD will make the pestilence cling to you until it has consumed you off the land that you are entering to possess. 22 The LORD will afflict you with consumption, fever, inflammation, with fiery heat and drought, and with blight and mildew; they shall pursue you until you perish. 23 The sky over your head shall be bronze, and the earth under you iron. 24 The LORD will change the rain of your land into powder, and only dust shall come down upon you from the sky until you are destroyed.

25 The LORD will cause you to be defeated before your enemies; you shall go out against them one way and flee before them seven ways. You shall become an object of horror to all the kingdoms of the earth. 26 Your corpses shall be food for every bird of the air and animal of the earth, and there shall be no one to frighten them away. 27 The LORD will afflict you with the boils of Egypt, with ulcers, scurvy, and itch, of which you cannot be healed. 28 The LORD will afflict you with madness, blindness, and confusion of mind; 29 you shall grope about at noon as blind people grope in darkness, but you shall be unable to find your way; and you shall be continually abused and robbed, without anyone to help. 30 You shall become engaged to a woman, but another man shall lie with her. You shall build a house, but not live in it. You shall plant a vineyard, but not enjoy its fruit. 31 Your ox shall be butchered before your eyes, but you shall not eat of it. Your donkey shall be stolen in front of you, and shall not be restored to you. Your sheep shall be given to your enemies, without anyone to help you. 32 Your sons and daughters shall be given to another people, while you look on; you will strain your eyes looking for them all day but be powerless to do anything. 33 A people whom you do not know shall eat up the fruit of your ground and of all your labors; you shall be continually abused and crushed, 34 and driven mad by the sight that your eyes shall see. 35 The LORD will strike you on the knees and on the legs with grievous boils of which you cannot be healed, from the sole of your foot to the crown of your head. 36 The LORD will bring you, and the king whom you set over you, to a nation that neither you nor your ancestors have known, where you shall serve other gods, of wood and stone. 37 You shall become an object of horror, a proverb, and a byword among all the peoples where the LORD will lead you.

King James

38Thou shalt carry much seed out into the field, and shalt gather *but* little in; for the locust shall consume it.

39Thou shalt plant vineyards, and dress *them,* but shalt neither drink *of* the wine, nor gather *the grapes;* for the worms shall eat them.

40Thou shalt have olive trees throughout all thy coasts, but thou shalt not anoint *thyself* with the oil; for thine olive shall cast *his fruit.*

41Thou shalt beget sons and daughters, but thou shalt not enjoy them; for they shall go into captivity.

42All thy trees and fruit of thy land shall the locust consume.

43The stranger that *is* within thee shall get up above thee very high; and thou shalt come down very low.

44He shall lend to thee, and thou shalt not lend to him: he shall be the head, and thou shalt be the tail.

45Moreover all these curses shall come upon thee, and shall pursue thee, and overtake thee, till thou be destroyed; because thou hearkenedst not unto the voice of the LORD thy God, to keep his commandments and his statutes which he commanded thee:

46And they shall be upon thee for a sign and for a wonder, and upon thy seed for ever.

47Because thou servedst not the LORD thy God with joyfulness, and with gladness of heart, for the abundance of all *things;*

48Therefore shalt thou serve thine enemies which the LORD shall send against thee, in hunger, and in thirst, and in nakedness, and in want of all *things:* and he shall put a yoke of iron upon thy neck, until he have destroyed thee.

49The LORD shall bring a nation against thee from far, from the end of the earth, *as swift* as the eagle flieth; a nation whose tongue thou shalt not understand;

50A nation of fierce countenance, which shall not regard the person of the old, nor show favour to the young:

51And he shall eat the fruit of thy cattle, and the fruit of thy land, until thou be destroyed: which *also* shall not leave thee *either* corn, wine, or oil, *or* the increase of thy kine, or flocks of thy sheep, until he have destroyed thee.

52And he shall besiege thee in all thy gates, until thy high and fenced walls come down, wherein thou trustedst, throughout all thy land: and he shall besiege thee in all thy gates throughout all thy land, which the LORD thy God hath given thee.

53And thou shalt eat the fruit of thine own body, the flesh of thy sons and of thy daughters, which the LORD thy God hath given thee, in the siege, and in the straitness, wherewith thine enemies shall distress thee:

54*So that* the man *that is* tender among you, and very delicate, his eye shall be evil toward his brother, and toward the wife of his bosom, and toward the remnant of his children which he shall leave:

55So that he will not give to any of them of the flesh of his children whom he shall eat: because he hath nothing left him in the siege, and in the straitness, wherewith thine enemies shall distress thee in all thy gates.

56The tender and delicate woman among you, which would not adventure to set the sole of her foot upon the ground for delicateness and tenderness, her eye shall be evil toward the husband of her bosom, and toward her son, and toward her daughter,

57And toward her young one that cometh out from between her feet, and toward her children which she shall bear: for she shall eat them for want of all *things* secretly in the siege and straitness, wherewith thine enemy shall distress thee in thy gates.

New International

38You will sow much seed in the field but you will harvest little, because locusts will devour it. 39You will plant vineyards and cultivate them but you will not drink the wine or gather the grapes, because worms will eat them. 40You will have olive trees throughout your country but you will not use the oil, because the olives will drop off. 41You will have sons and daughters but you will not keep them, because they will go into captivity. 42Swarms of locusts will take over all your trees and the crops of your land.

43The alien who lives among you will rise above you higher and higher, but you will sink lower and lower. 44He will lend to you, but you will not lend to him. He will be the head, but you will be the tail.

45All these curses will come upon you. They will pursue you and overtake you until you are destroyed, because you did not obey the LORD your God and observe the commands and decrees he gave you. 46They will be a sign and a wonder to you and your descendants forever. 47Because you did not serve the LORD your God joyfully and gladly in the time of prosperity, 48therefore in hunger and thirst, in nakedness and dire poverty, you will serve the enemies the LORD sends against you. He will put an iron yoke on your neck until he has destroyed you.

49The LORD will bring a nation against you from far away, from the ends of the earth, like an eagle swooping down, a nation whose language you will not understand, 50a fierce-looking nation without respect for the old or pity for the young. 51They will devour the young of your livestock and the crops of your land until you are destroyed. They will leave you no grain, new wine or oil, nor any calves of your herds or lambs of your flocks until you are ruined. 52They will lay siege to all the cities throughout your land until the high fortified walls in which you trust fall down. They will besiege all the cities throughout the land the LORD your God is giving you.

53Because of the suffering that your enemy will inflict on you during the siege, you will eat the fruit of the womb, the flesh of the sons and daughters the LORD your God has given you. 54Even the most gentle and sensitive man among you will have no compassion on his own brother or the wife he loves or his surviving children, 55and he will not give to one of them any of the flesh of his children that he is eating. It will be all he has left because of the suffering your enemy will inflict on you during the siege of all your cities. 56The most gentle and sensitive woman among you—so sensitive and gentle that she would not venture to touch the ground with the sole of her foot—will begrudge the husband she loves and her own son or daughter 57the afterbirth from her womb and the children she bears. For she intends to eat them secretly during the siege and in the distress that your enemy will inflict on you in your cities.

Living Bible

38"You will sow much but reap little, for the locusts will eat your crops. 39You will plant vineyards and care for them, but you won't eat the grapes or drink the wine, for worms will destroy the vines. 40Olive trees will be growing everywhere, but there won't be enough olive oil to anoint yourselves! For the trees will drop their fruit before it is matured. 41Your sons and daughters will be snatched away from you as slaves. 42The locusts shall destroy your trees and vines. 43Foreigners living among you shall become richer and richer while you become poorer and poorer. 44They shall lend to you, not you to them! They shall be the head and you shall be the tail!

45"All these curses shall pursue and overtake you until you are destroyed—all because you refuse to listen to the Lord your God. 46These horrors shall befall you and your descendants as a warning: 47, 48You will become slaves to your enemies because of your failure to praise God for all that he has given you. The Lord will send your enemies against you, and you will be hungry, thirsty, naked, and in want of everything. A yoke of iron shall be placed around your neck until you are destroyed!

49"The Lord will bring a distant nation against you, swooping down upon you like an eagle; a nation whose language you don't understand— 50a nation of fierce and angry men who will have no mercy upon young or old. 51They will eat you out of house and home until your cattle and crops are gone. Your grain, new wine, olive oil, calves, and lambs will all disappear. 52That nation will lay siege to your cities and knock down your highest walls—the walls you will trust to protect you. 53You will even eat the flesh of your own sons and daughters in the terrible days of siege that lie ahead. 54The most tenderhearted man among you will be utterly callous toward his own brother and his beloved wife and his children who are still alive. 55He will refuse to give them a share of the flesh he is devouring—the flesh of his own children—because he is starving in the midst of the siege of your cities. 56, 57The most tender and delicate woman among you—the one who would not so much as touch her feet to the ground—will refuse to share with her beloved husband, son, and daughter. She will hide from them the afterbirth and the new baby she has borne, so that she herself can eat them: so terrible will be the hunger during the siege and the awful distress caused by your enemies at your gates.

New Revised Standard

38 You shall carry much seed into the field but shall gather little in, for the locust shall consume it. 39You shall plant vineyards and dress them, but you shall neither drink the wine nor gather the grapes, for the worm shall eat them. 40You shall have olive trees throughout all your territory, but you shall not anoint yourself with the oil, for your olives shall drop off. 41You shall have sons and daughters, but they shall not remain yours, for they shall go into captivity. 42All your trees and the fruit of your ground the cicada shall take over. 43Aliens residing among you shall ascend above you higher and higher, while you shall descend lower and lower. 44They shall lend to you but you shall not lend to them; they shall be the head and you shall be the tail.

45 All these curses shall come upon you, pursuing and overtaking you until you are destroyed, because you did not obey the LORD your God, by observing the commandments and the decrees that he commanded you. 46They shall be among you and your descendants as a sign and a portent forever.

47 Because you did not serve the LORD your God joyfully and with gladness of heart for the abundance of everything, 48therefore you shall serve your enemies whom the LORD will send against you, in hunger and thirst, in nakedness and lack of everything. He will put an iron yoke on your neck until he has destroyed you. 49The LORD will bring a nation from far away, from the end of the earth, to swoop down on you like an eagle, a nation whose language you do not understand, 50a grim-faced nation showing no respect to the old or favor to the young. 51It shall consume the fruit of your livestock and the fruit of your ground until you are destroyed, leaving you neither grain, wine, and oil, nor the increase of your cattle and the issue of your flock, until it has made you perish. 52It shall besiege you in all your towns until your high and fortified walls, in which you trusted, come down throughout your land; it shall besiege you in all your towns throughout the land that the LORD your God has given you. 53In the desperate straits to which the enemy siege reduces you, you will eat the fruit of your womb, the flesh of your own sons and daughters whom the LORD your God has given you. 54Even the most refined and gentle of men among you will begrudge food to his own brother, to the wife whom he embraces, and to the last of his remaining children, 55giving to none of them any of the flesh of his children whom he is eating, because nothing else remains to him, in the desperate straits to which the enemy siege will reduce you in all your towns. 56She who is the most refined and gentle among you, so gentle and refined that she does not venture to set the sole of her foot on the ground, will begrudge food to the husband whom she embraces, to her own son, and to her own daughter, 57begrudging even the afterbirth that comes out from between her thighs, and the children that she bears, because she is eating them in secret for lack of anything else, in the desperate straits to which the enemy siege will reduce you in your towns.

King James

58If thou wilt not observe to do all the words of this law that are written in this book, that thou mayest fear this glorious and fearful name, THE LORD THY GOD;

59Then the LORD will make thy plagues wonderful, and the plagues of thy seed, *even* great plagues, and of long continuance, and sore sicknesses, and of long continuance.

60Moreover he will bring upon thee all the diseases of Egypt, which thou wast afraid of; and they shall cleave unto thee.

61Also every sickness, and every plague, which *is* not written in the book of this law, them will the LORD bring upon thee, until thou be destroyed.

62And ye shall be left few in number, whereas ye were as the stars of heaven for multitude; because thou wouldest not obey the voice of the LORD thy God.

63And it shall come to pass, *that* as the LORD rejoiced over you to do you good, and to multiply you; so the LORD will rejoice over you to destroy you, and to bring you to nought; and ye shall be plucked from off the land whither thou goest to possess it.

64And the LORD shall scatter thee among all people, from the one end of the earth even unto the other; and there thou shalt serve other gods, which neither thou nor thy fathers have known, *even* wood and stone.

65And among these nations shalt thou find no ease, neither shall the sole of thy foot have rest: but the LORD shall give thee there a trembling heart, and failing of eyes, and sorrow of mind:

66And thy life shall hang in doubt before thee; and thou shalt fear day and night, and shalt have none assurance of thy life:

67In the morning thou shalt say, Would God it were even! and at even thou shalt say, Would God it were morning! for the fear of thine heart wherewith thou shalt fear, and for the sight of thine eyes which thou shalt see.

68And the LORD shall bring thee into Egypt again with ships, by the way whereof I spake unto thee, Thou shalt see it no more again: and there ye shall be sold unto your enemies for bondmen and bondwomen, and no man shall buy *you.*

29 THESE *ARE* the words of the covenant, which the LORD commanded Moses to make with the children of Israel in the land of Moab, beside the covenant which he made with them in Horeb.

2¶ And Moses called unto all Israel, and said unto them, Ye have seen all that the LORD did before your eyes in the land of Egypt unto Pharaoh, and unto all his servants, and unto all his land;

3The great temptations which thine eyes have seen, the signs, and those great miracles:

4Yet the LORD hath not given you an heart to perceive, and eyes to see, and ears to hear, unto this day.

5And I have led you forty years in the wilderness: your clothes are not waxen old upon you, and thy shoe is not waxen old upon thy foot.

6Ye have not eaten bread, neither have ye drunk wine or strong drink: that ye might know that I *am* the LORD your God.

7And when ye came unto this place, Sihon the king of Heshbon, and Og the king of Bashan, came out against us unto battle, and we smote them:

8And we took their land, and gave it for an inheritance unto the Reubenites, and to the Gadites, and to the half tribe of Manasseh.

9Keep therefore the words of this covenant, and do them, that ye may prosper in all that ye do.

New International

58If you do not carefully follow all the words of this law, which are written in this book, and do not revere this glorious and awesome name—the LORD your God— 59the LORD will send fearful plagues on you and your descendants, harsh and prolonged disasters, and severe and lingering illnesses. 60He will bring upon you all the diseases of Egypt that you dreaded, and they will cling to you. 61The LORD will also bring on you every kind of sickness and disaster not recorded in this Book of the Law, until you are destroyed. 62You who were as numerous as the stars in the sky will be left but few in number, because you did not obey the LORD your God. 63Just as it pleased the LORD to make you prosper and increase in number, so it will please him to ruin and destroy you. You will be uprooted from the land you are entering to possess.

64Then the LORD will scatter you among all nations, from one end of the earth to the other. There you will worship other gods—gods of wood and stone, which neither you nor your fathers have known. 65Among those nations you will find no repose, no resting place for the sole of your foot. There the LORD will give you an anxious mind, eyes weary with longing, and a despairing heart. 66You will live in constant suspense, filled with dread both night and day, never sure of your life. 67In the morning you will say, "If only it were evening!" and in the evening, "If only it were morning!"—because of the terror that will fill your hearts and the sights that your eyes will see. 68The LORD will send you back in ships to Egypt on a journey I said you should never make again. There you will offer yourselves for sale to your enemies as male and female slaves, but no one will buy you.

Renewal of the Covenant

29 THESE ARE the terms of the covenant the LORD commanded Moses to make with the Israelites in Moab, in addition to the covenant he had made with them at Horeb.

2Moses summoned all the Israelites and said to them:

Your eyes have seen all that the LORD did in Egypt to Pharaoh, to all his officials and to all his land. 3With your own eyes you saw those great trials, those miraculous signs and great wonders. 4But to this day the LORD has not given you a mind that understands or eyes that see or ears that hear. 5During the forty years that I led you through the desert, your clothes did not wear out, nor did the sandals on your feet. 6You ate no bread and drank no wine or other fermented drink. I did this so that you might know that I am the LORD your God.

7When you reached this place, Sihon king of Heshbon and Og king of Bashan came out to fight against us, but we defeated them. 8We took their land and gave it as an inheritance to the Reubenites, the Gadites and the half-tribe of Manasseh.

9Carefully follow the terms of this covenant, so that you may prosper in everything you do. 10All of you are

Living Bible

58, 59"If you refuse to obey all the laws written in this book, thus refusing reverence to the glorious and fearful name of Jehovah your God, then Jehovah will send perpetual plagues upon you and upon your children. 60He will bring upon you all the diseases of Egypt which you feared so much, and they shall plague the land. 61And that is not all! The Lord will bring upon you every sickness and plague there is, even those not mentioned in this book, until you are destroyed. 62There will be few of you left, though before you were as numerous as stars. All this if you do not listen to the Lord your God.

63"Just as the Lord has rejoiced over you and has done such wonderful things for you and has multiplied you, so the Lord at that time will rejoice in destroying you; and you shall disappear from the land. 64For the Lord will scatter you among all the nations from one end of the earth to the other. There you will worship heathen gods that neither you nor your ancestors have known, gods made of wood and stone! 65There among those nations you shall find no rest, but the Lord will give you trembling hearts, darkness, and bodies wasted from sorrow and fear. 66Your lives will hang in doubt. You will live night and day in fear, and will have no reason to believe that you will see the morning light. 67In the morning you will say, 'Oh, that night were here!' And in the evening you will say, 'Oh, that morning were here!' You will say this because of the awesome horrors surrounding you. 68Then the Lord will send you back to Egypt in ships, a journey I promised you would never need to make again; and there you will offer to sell yourselves to your enemies as slaves—but no one will even want to buy you."

29 IT WAS on the plains of Moab that Moses restated the covenant which the Lord had made with the people of Israel at Mount Horeb. 2, 3He summoned all Israel before him and told them,

"You have seen with your own eyes the great plagues and mighty miracles that the Lord brought upon Pharaoh and his people in the land of Egypt. 4But even yet the Lord hasn't given you hearts that understand or eyes that see or ears that hear! 5For forty years God has led you through the wilderness, yet your clothes haven't become old, and your shoes haven't worn out! 6The reason he hasn't let you settle down to grow grain for bread or grapes for wine and strong drink, is so that you would realize that it is the Lord your God who has been caring for you.

7"When we came here, King Sihon of Heshbon and King Og of Bashan came out against us in battle, but we destroyed them, 8and took their land and gave it to the tribes of Reuben and Gad and to the half-tribe of Manasseh as their inheritance. 9Therefore, obey the terms of this covenant so that you will prosper in everything you do. 10All of you—your leaders, the people, your judges,

New Revised Standard

58 If you do not diligently observe all the words of this law that are written in this book, fearing this glorious and awesome name, the LORD your God, 59then the LORD will overwhelm both you and your offspring with severe and lasting afflictions and grievous and lasting maladies. 60He will bring back upon you all the diseases of Egypt, of which you were in dread, and they shall cling to you. 61Every other malady and affliction, even though not recorded in the book of this law, the LORD will inflict on you until you are destroyed. 62Although once you were as numerous as the stars in heaven, you shall be left few in number, because you did not obey the LORD your God. 63And just as the LORD took delight in making you prosperous and numerous, so the LORD will take delight in bringing you to ruin and destruction; you shall be plucked off the land that you are entering to possess. 64The LORD will scatter you among all peoples, from one end of the earth to the other; and there you shall serve other gods, of wood and stone, which neither you nor your ancestors have known. 65Among those nations you shall find no ease, no resting place for the sole of your foot. There the LORD will give you a trembling heart, failing eyes, and a languishing spirit. 66Your life shall hang in doubt before you; night and day you shall be in dread, with no assurance of your life. 67In the morning you shall say, "If only it were evening!" and at evening you shall say, "If only it were morning!"—because of the dread that your heart shall feel and the sights that your eyes shall see. 68The LORD will bring you back in ships to Egypt, by a route that I promised you would never see again; and there you shall offer yourselves for sale to your enemies as male and female slaves, but there will be no buyer.

29[a] THESE ARE the words of the covenant that the LORD commanded Moses to make with the Israelites in the land of Moab, in addition to the covenant that he had made with them at Horeb.

The Covenant Renewed in Moab

2b Moses summoned all Israel and said to them: You have seen all that the LORD did before your eyes in the land of Egypt, to Pharaoh and to all his servants and to all his land, 3the great trials that your eyes saw, the signs, and those great wonders. 4But to this day the LORD has not given you a mind to understand, or eyes to see, or ears to hear. 5I have led you forty years in the wilderness. The clothes on your back have not worn out, and the sandals on your feet have not worn out; 6you have not eaten bread, and you have not drunk wine or strong drink—so that you may know that I am the LORD your God. 7When you came to this place, King Sihon of Heshbon and King Og of Bashan came out against us for battle, but we defeated them. 8We took their land and gave it as an inheritance to the Reubenites, the Gadites, and the half-tribe of Manasseh. 9Therefore diligently observe the words of this covenant, in order that you may succeed[c] in everything that you do.

a Ch 28.69 in Heb   b Ch 29.1 in Heb   c Or *deal wisely*

King James

10¶ Ye stand this day all of you before the LORD your God; your captains of your tribes, your elders, and your officers, *with* all the men of Israel,

11Your little ones, your wives, and thy stranger that *is* in thy camp, from the hewer of thy wood unto the drawer of thy water:

12That thou shouldest enter into covenant with the LORD thy God, and into his oath, which the LORD thy God maketh with thee this day:

13That he may establish thee today for a people unto himself, and *that* he may be unto thee a God, as he hath said unto thee, and as he hath sworn unto thy fathers, to Abraham, to Isaac, and to Jacob.

14Neither with you only do I make this covenant and this oath;

15But with *him* that standeth here with us this day before the LORD our God, and also with *him* that *is* not here with us this day:

16(For ye know how we have dwelt in the land of Egypt; and how we came through the nations which ye passed by;

17And ye have seen their abominations, and their idols, wood and stone, silver and gold, which *were* among them:)

18Lest there should be among you man, or woman, or family, or tribe, whose heart turneth away this day from the LORD our God, to go *and* serve the gods of these nations; lest there should be among you a root that beareth gall and wormwood;

19And it come to pass, when he heareth the words of this curse, that he bless himself in his heart, saying, I shall have peace, though I walk in the imagination of mine heart, to add drunkenness to thirst:

20The LORD will not spare him, but then the anger of the LORD and his jealousy shall smoke against that man, and all the curses that are written in this book shall lie upon him, and the LORD shall blot out his name from under heaven.

21And the LORD shall separate him unto evil out of all the tribes of Israel, according to all the curses of the covenant that are written in this book of the law:

22So that the generation to come of your children that shall rise up after you, and the stranger that shall come from a far land, shall say, when they see the plagues of that land, and the sicknesses which the LORD hath laid upon it;

23And that the whole land thereof *is* brimstone, and salt, *and* burning, *that* it is not sown, nor beareth, nor any grass groweth therein, like the overthrow of Sodom, and Gomorrah, Admah, and Zeboim, which the LORD overthrew in his anger, and in his wrath:

24Even all nations shall say, Wherefore hath the LORD done thus unto this land? what *meaneth* the heat of this great anger?

25Then men shall say, Because they have forsaken the covenant of the LORD God of their fathers, which he made with them when he brought them forth out of the land of Egypt:

26For they went and served other gods, and worshipped them, gods whom they knew not, and *whom* he had not given unto them:

27And the anger of the LORD was kindled against this land, to bring upon it all the curses that are written in this book:

28And the LORD rooted them out of their land in anger, and in wrath, and in great indignation, and cast them into another land, as *it is* this day.

29The secret *things belong* unto the LORD our God: but those *things which are* revealed *belong* unto us and to our children for ever, that *we* may do all the words of this law.

New International

standing today in the presence of the LORD your God— your leaders and chief men, your elders and officials, and all the other men of Israel, 11together with your children and your wives, and the aliens living in your camps who chop your wood and carry your water. 12You are standing here in order to enter into a covenant with the LORD your God, a covenant the LORD is making with you this day and sealing with an oath, 13to confirm you this day as his people, that he may be your God as he promised you and as he swore to your fathers, Abraham, Isaac and Jacob. 14I am making this covenant, with its oath, not only with you 15who are standing here with us today in the presence of the LORD our God but also with those who are not here today.

16You yourselves know how we lived in Egypt and how we passed through the countries on the way here. 17You saw among them their detestable images and idols of wood and stone, of silver and gold. 18Make sure there is no man or woman, clan or tribe among you today whose heart turns away from the LORD our God to go and worship the gods of those nations; make sure there is no root among you that produces such bitter poison.

19When such a person hears the words of this oath, he invokes a blessing on himself and therefore thinks, "I will be safe, even though I persist in going my own way." This will bring disaster on the watered land as well as the dry.[a] 20The LORD will never be willing to forgive him; his wrath and zeal will burn against that man. All the curses written in this book will fall upon him, and the LORD will blot out his name from under heaven. 21The LORD will single him out from all the tribes of Israel for disaster, according to all the curses of the covenant written in this Book of the Law.

22Your children who follow you in later generations and foreigners who come from distant lands will see the calamities that have fallen on the land and the diseases with which the LORD has afflicted it. 23The whole land will be a burning waste of salt and sulfur—nothing planted, nothing sprouting, no vegetation growing on it. It will be like the destruction of Sodom and Gomorrah, Admah and Zeboiim, which the LORD overthrew in fierce anger. 24All the nations will ask: "Why has the LORD done this to this land? Why this fierce, burning anger?"

25And the answer will be: "It is because this people abandoned the covenant of the LORD, the God of their fathers, the covenant he made with them when he brought them out of Egypt. 26They went off and worshiped other gods and bowed down to them, gods they did not know, gods he had not given them. 27Therefore the LORD's anger burned against this land, so that he brought on it all the curses written in this book. 28In furious anger and in great wrath the LORD uprooted them from their land and thrust them into another land, as it is now."

29The secret things belong to the LORD our God, but the things revealed belong to us and to our children forever, that we may follow all the words of this law.

---

a *19 Or way, in order to add drunkenness to thirst."*

Living Bible

and your administrative officers—are standing today before the Lord your God, 11along with your little ones and your wives and the foreigners that are among you—those who chop your wood and carry your water. 12You are standing here to enter into a contract with Jehovah your God, a contract he is making with you today. 13He wants to confirm you today as his people, and to confirm that he is your God, just as he promised your ancestors, Abraham, Isaac, and Jacob. 14, 15This contract is not with you alone as you stand before him today, but with all future generations of Israel as well.

16"Surely you remember how we lived in the land of Egypt, and how as we left, we came safely through the territory of enemy nations. 17And you have seen their heathen idols made of wood, stone, silver, and gold. 18The day that any of you—man or woman, family or tribe of Israel—begins to turn away from the Lord our God and desires to worship these gods of other nations, that day a root will be planted that will grow bitter and poisonous fruit.

19"Let no one blithely think, when he hears the warnings of this curse, 'I shall prosper even though I walk in my own stubborn way!' 20For the Lord will not pardon! His anger and jealousy will be hot against that man. And all the curses written in this book shall lie heavily upon him, and the Lord will blot out his name from under heaven. 21The Lord will separate that man from all the tribes of Israel, to pour out upon him all the curses (which are recorded in this book) that befall those who break this contract. 22Then your children and the generations to come and the foreigners that pass by from distant lands shall see the devastation of the land and the diseases the Lord will have sent upon it. 23They will see that the whole land is alkali and salt, a burned over wasteland, unsown, without crops, without a shred of vegetation—just like Sodom and Gomorrah and Admah and Zeboiim, destroyed by the Lord in his anger.

24" 'Why has the Lord done this to his land?' the nations will ask. 'Why was he so angry?'

25"And they will be told, 'Because the people of the land broke the contract made with them by Jehovah, the God of their ancestors, when he brought them out of the land of Egypt. 26For they worshiped other gods, violating his express command. 27That is why the anger of the Lord was hot against this land, so that all his curses (which are recorded in this book) broke forth upon them. 28In great anger the Lord rooted them out of their land and threw them away into another land, where they still live today!'

29"There are secrets the Lord your God has not revealed to us, but these words which he has revealed are for us and our children to obey forever.

New Revised Standard

10 You stand assembled today, all of you, before the LORD your God—the leaders of your tribes,[b] your elders, and your officials, all the men of Israel, 11your children, your women, and the aliens who are in your camp, both those who cut your wood and those who draw your water— 12to enter into the covenant of the LORD your God, sworn by an oath, which the LORD your God is making with you today; 13in order that he may establish you today as his people, and that he may be your God, as he promised you and as he swore to your ancestors, to Abraham, to Isaac, and to Jacob. 14I am making this covenant, sworn by an oath, not only with you who stand here with us today before the LORD our God, 15but also with those who are not here with us today. 16You know how we lived in the land of Egypt, and how we came through the midst of the nations through which you passed. 17You have seen their detestable things, the filthy idols of wood and stone, of silver and gold, that were among them. 18It may be that there is among you a man or woman, or a family or tribe, whose heart is already turning away from the LORD our God to serve the gods of those nations. It may be that there is among you a root sprouting poisonous and bitter growth. 19All who hear the words of this oath and bless themselves, thinking in their hearts, "We are safe even though we go our own stubborn ways" (thus bringing disaster on moist and dry alike)[c]— 20the LORD will be unwilling to pardon them, for the LORD's anger and passion will smoke against them. All the curses written in this book will descend on them, and the LORD will blot out their names from under heaven. 21The LORD will single them out from all the tribes of Israel for calamity, in accordance with all the curses of the covenant written in this book of the law. 22The next generation, your children who rise up after you, as well as the foreigner who comes from a distant country, will see the devastation of that land and the afflictions with which the LORD has afflicted it— 23all its soil burned out by sulfur and salt, nothing planted, nothing sprouting, unable to support any vegetation, like the destruction of Sodom and Gomorrah, Admah and Zeboiim, which the LORD destroyed in his fierce anger— 24they and indeed all the nations will wonder, "Why has the LORD done thus to this land? What caused this great display of anger?" 25They will conclude, "It is because they abandoned the covenant of the LORD, the God of their ancestors, which he made with them when he brought them out of the land of Egypt. 26They turned and served other gods, worshiping them, gods whom they had not known and whom he had not allotted to them; 27so the anger of the LORD was kindled against that land, bringing on it every curse written in this book. 28The LORD uprooted them from their land in anger, fury, and great wrath, and cast them into another land, as is now the case." 29The secret things belong to the LORD our God, but the revealed things belong to us and to our children forever, to observe all the words of this law.

King James

30 AND IT shall come to pass, when all these things are come upon thee, the blessing and the curse, which I have set before thee, and thou shalt call *them* to mind among all the nations, whither the LORD thy God hath driven thee,

2And shalt return unto the LORD thy God, and shalt obey his voice according to all that I command thee this day, thou and thy children, with all thine heart, and with all thy soul;

3That then the LORD thy God will turn thy captivity, and have compassion upon thee, and will return and gather thee from all the nations, whither the LORD thy God hath scattered thee.

4If *any* of thine be driven out unto the outmost *parts* of heaven, from thence will the LORD thy God gather thee, and from thence will he fetch thee:

5And the LORD thy God will bring thee into the land which thy fathers possessed, and thou shalt possess it; and he will do thee good, and multiply thee above thy fathers.

6And the LORD thy God will circumcise thine heart, and the heart of thy seed, to love the LORD thy God with all thine heart, and with all thy soul, that thou mayest live.

7And the LORD thy God will put all these curses upon thine enemies, and on them that hate thee, which persecuted thee.

8And thou shalt return and obey the voice of the LORD, and do all his commandments which I command thee this day.

9And the LORD thy God will make thee plenteous in every work of thine hand, in the fruit of thy body, and in the fruit of thy cattle, and in the fruit of thy land, for good: for the LORD will again rejoice over thee for good, as he rejoiced over thy fathers:

10If thou shalt hearken unto the voice of the LORD thy God, to keep his commandments and his statutes which are written in this book of the law, *and* if thou turn unto the LORD thy God with all thine heart, and with all thy soul.

11¶ For this commandment which I command thee this day, it *is* not hidden from thee, neither *is* it far off.

12It *is* not in heaven, that thou shouldest say, Who shall go up for us to heaven, and bring it unto us, that we may hear it, and do it?

13Neither *is* it beyond the sea, that thou shouldest say, Who shall go over the sea for us, and bring it unto us, that we may hear it, and do it?

14But the word *is* very nigh unto thee, in thy mouth, and in thy heart, that thou mayest do it.

15¶ See, I have set before thee this day life and good, and death and evil;

16In that I command thee this day to love the LORD thy God, to walk in his ways, and to keep his commandments and his statutes and his judgments, that thou mayest live and multiply: and the LORD thy God shall bless thee in the land whither thou goest to possess it.

17But if thine heart turn away, so that thou wilt not hear, but shalt be drawn away, and worship other gods, and serve them;

18I denounce unto you this day, that ye shall surely perish, *and that* ye shall not prolong *your* days upon the land, whither thou passest over Jordan to go to possess it.

19I call heaven and earth to record this day against you, *that* I have set before you life and death, blessing and cursing: therefore choose life, that both thou and thy seed may live:

New International

Prosperity After Turning to the LORD

30 WHEN ALL these blessings and curses I have set before you come upon you and you take them to heart wherever the LORD your God disperses you among the nations, 2and when you and your children return to the LORD your God and obey him with all your heart and with all your soul according to everything I command you today, 3then the LORD your God will restore your fortunesa and have compassion on you and gather you again from all the nations where he scattered you. 4Even if you have been banished to the most distant land under the heavens, from there the LORD your God will gather you and bring you back. 5He will bring you to the land that belonged to your fathers, and you will take possession of it. He will make you more prosperous and numerous than your fathers. 6The LORD your God will circumcise your hearts and the hearts of your descendants, so that you may love him with all your heart and with all your soul, and live. 7The LORD your God will put all these curses on your enemies who hate and persecute you. 8You will again obey the LORD and follow all his commands I am giving you today. 9Then the LORD your God will make you most prosperous in all the work of your hands and in the fruit of your womb, the young of your livestock and the crops of your land. The LORD will again delight in you and make you prosperous, just as he delighted in your fathers, 10if you obey the LORD your God and keep his commands and decrees that are written in this Book of the Law and turn to the LORD your God with all your heart and with all your soul.

The Offer of Life or Death

11Now what I am commanding you today is not too difficult for you or beyond your reach. 12It is not up in heaven, so that you have to ask, "Who will ascend into heaven to get it and proclaim it to us so we may obey it?" 13Nor is it beyond the sea, so that you have to ask, "Who will cross the sea to get it and proclaim it to us so we may obey it?" 14No, the word is very near you; it is in your mouth and in your heart so you may obey it.

15See, I set before you today life and prosperity, death and destruction. 16For I command you today to love the LORD your God, to walk in his ways, and to keep his commands, decrees and laws; then you will live and increase, and the LORD your God will bless you in the land you are entering to possess.

17But if your heart turns away and you are not obedient, and if you are drawn away to bow down to other gods and worship them, 18I declare to you this day that you will certainly be destroyed. You will not live long in the land you are crossing the Jordan to enter and possess.

19This day I call heaven and earth as witnesses against you that I have set before you life and death, blessings and curses. Now choose life, so that you and your children may live 20and that you may love the LORD your

---

a *3 Or will bring you back from captivity*

Living Bible

30 "WHEN ALL these things have happened to you—the blessings and the curses I have listed—you will meditate upon them as you are living among the nations where the Lord your God will have driven you. 2If at that time you want to return to the Lord your God, and you and your children have begun wholeheartedly to obey all of the commandments I have given you today, 3then the Lord your God will rescue you from your captivity! He will have mercy upon you and come and gather you out of all the nations where he will have scattered you. 4Though you are at the ends of the earth, he will go and find you and bring you back again 5to the land of your ancestors. You shall possess the land again, and he will do you good and bless you even more than he did your ancestors! 6He will cleanse your hearts and the hearts of your children and of your children's children so that you will love the Lord your God with all your hearts and souls, and Israel shall come alive again!

7, 8"If you return to the Lord and obey all the commandments that I command you today, the Lord your God will take his curses and turn them against your enemies—against those who hate you and persecute you. 9The Lord your God will prosper everything you do and give you many children and much cattle and wonderful crops; for the Lord will again rejoice over you as he did over your fathers. 10He will rejoice if you but obey the commandments written in this book of the law, and if you turn to the Lord your God with all your hearts and souls.

11"Obeying these commandments is not something beyond your strength and reach; 12for these laws are not in the far heavens, so distant that you can't hear and obey them, and with no one to bring them down to you; 13nor are they beyond the ocean, so far that no one can bring you their message; 14but they are very close at hand—in your hearts and on your lips—so obey them.

15"Look, today I have set before you life and death, depending on whether you obey or disobey. 16I have commanded you today to love the Lord your God and to follow his paths and to keep his laws, so that you will live and become a great nation, and so that the Lord your God will bless you and the land you are about to possess. 17But if your hearts turn away and you won't listen—if you are drawn away to worship other gods— 18then I declare to you this day that you shall surely perish; you will not have a long, good life in the land you are going in to possess.

19"I call heaven and earth to witness against you that today I have set before you life or death, blessing or curse. Oh, that you would choose life; that you and your children might live! 20Choose to love the Lord your God

New Revised Standard

God's Fidelity Assured

30 WHEN ALL these things have happened to you, the blessings and the curses that I have set before you, if you call them to mind among all the nations where the LORD your God has driven you, 2 and return to the LORD your God, and you and your children obey him with all your heart and with all your soul, just as I am commanding you today, 3 then the LORD your God will restore your fortunes and have compassion on you, gathering you again from all the peoples among whom the LORD your God has scattered you. 4 Even if you are exiled to the ends of the world,b from there the LORD your God will gather you, and from there he will bring you back. 5 The LORD your God will bring you into the land that your ancestors possessed, and you will possess it; he will make you more prosperous and numerous than your ancestors.

6 Moreover, the LORD your God will circumcise your heart and the heart of your descendants, so that you will love the LORD your God with all your heart and with all your soul, in order that you may live. 7 The LORD your God will put all these curses on your enemies and on the adversaries who took advantage of you. 8 Then you shall again obey the LORD, observing all his commandments that I am commanding you today, 9 and the LORD your God will make you abundantly prosperous in all your undertakings, in the fruit of your body, in the fruit of your livestock, and in the fruit of your soil. For the LORD will again take delight in prospering you, just as he delighted in prospering your ancestors, 10 when you obey the LORD your God by observing his commandments and decrees that are written in this book of the law, because you turn to the LORD your God with all your heart and with all your soul.

Exhortation to Choose Life

11 Surely, this commandment that I am commanding you today is not too hard for you, nor is it too far away. 12 It is not in heaven, that you should say, "Who will go up to heaven for us, and get it for us so that we may hear it and observe it?" 13 Neither is it beyond the sea, that you should say, "Who will cross to the other side of the sea for us, and get it for us so that we may hear it and observe it?" 14 No, the word is very near to you; it is in your mouth and in your heart for you to observe.

15 See, I have set before you today life and prosperity, death and adversity. 16 If you obey the commandments of the LORD your Godc that I am commanding you today, by loving the LORD your God, walking in his ways, and observing his commandments, decrees, and ordinances, then you shall live and become numerous, and the LORD your God will bless you in the land that you are entering to possess. 17 But if your heart turns away and you do not hear, but are led astray to bow down to other gods and serve them, 18 I declare to you today that you shall perish; you shall not live long in the land that you are crossing the Jordan to enter and possess. 19 I call heaven and earth to witness against you today that I have set before you life and death, blessings and curses. Choose life so that you and your descendants may live, 20 loving the LORD your God, obeying him,

b Heb of heaven   c Gk: Heb lacks If you obey the commandments of the LORD your God

King James

20That thou mayest love the LORD thy God, *and* that thou mayest obey his voice, and that thou mayest cleave unto him: for he *is* thy life, and the length of thy days: that thou mayest dwell in the land which the LORD sware unto thy fathers, to Abraham, to Isaac, and to Jacob, to give them.

31 AND MOSES went and spake these words unto all Israel.

2And he said unto them, I *am* an hundred and twenty years old this day; I can no more go out and come in: also the LORD hath said unto me, Thou shalt not go over this Jordan.

3The LORD thy God, he will go over before thee, *and* he will destroy these nations from before thee, and thou shalt possess them: *and* Joshua, he shall go over before thee, as the LORD hath said.

4And the LORD shall do unto them as he did to Sihon and to Og, kings of the Amorites, and unto the land of them, whom he destroyed.

5And the LORD shall give them up before your face, that ye may do unto them according unto all the commandments which I have commanded you.

6Be strong and of a good courage, fear not, nor be afraid of them: for the LORD thy God, he *it is* that doth go with thee; he will not fail thee, nor forsake thee.

7¶ And Moses called unto Joshua, and said unto him in the sight of all Israel, Be strong and of a good courage: for thou must go with this people unto the land which the LORD hath sworn unto their fathers to give them; and thou shalt cause them to inherit it.

8And the LORD, he *it is* that doth go before thee; he will be with thee, he will not fail thee, neither forsake thee: fear not, neither be dismayed.

9¶ And Moses wrote this law, and delivered it unto the priests the sons of Levi, which bare the ark of the covenant of the LORD, and unto all the elders of Israel.

10And Moses commanded them, saying, At the end of *every* seven years, in the solemnity of the year of release, in the feast of tabernacles,

11When all Israel is come to appear before the LORD thy God in the place which he shall choose, thou shalt read this law before all Israel in their hearing.

12Gather the people together, men, and women, and children, and thy stranger that *is* within thy gates, that they may hear, and that they may learn, and fear the LORD your God, and observe to do all the words of this law:

13And *that* their children, which have not known *any thing*, may hear, and learn to fear the LORD your God, as long as ye live in the land whither ye go over Jordan to possess it.

14¶ And the LORD said unto Moses, Behold, thy days approach that thou must die: call Joshua, and present yourselves in the tabernacle of the congregation, that I may give him a charge. And Moses and Joshua went, and presented themselves in the tabernacle of the congregation.

15And the LORD appeared in the tabernacle in a pillar of a cloud: and the pillar of the cloud stood over the door of the tabernacle.

16¶ And the LORD said unto Moses, Behold, thou shalt sleep with thy fathers; and this people will rise up, and go a-whoring after the gods of the strangers of the land, whither they go *to be* among them, and will forsake me, and break my covenant which I have made with them.

New International

God, listen to his voice, and hold fast to him. For the LORD is your life, and he will give you many years in the land he swore to give to your fathers, Abraham, Isaac and Jacob.

Joshua to Succeed Moses

31 THEN MOSES went out and spoke these words to all Israel: 2"I am now a hundred and twenty years old and I am no longer able to lead you. The LORD has said to me, 'You shall not cross the Jordan.' 3The LORD your God himself will cross over ahead of you. He will destroy these nations before you, and you will take possession of their land. Joshua also will cross over ahead of you, as the LORD said. 4And the LORD will do to them what he did to Sihon and Og, the kings of the Amorites, whom he destroyed along with their land. 5The LORD will deliver them to you, and you must do to them all that I have commanded you. 6Be strong and courageous. Do not be afraid or terrified because of them, for the LORD your God goes with you; he will never leave you nor forsake you."

7Then Moses summoned Joshua and said to him in the presence of all Israel, "Be strong and courageous, for you must go with this people into the land that the LORD swore to their forefathers to give them, and you must divide it among them as their inheritance. 8The LORD himself goes before you and will be with you; he will never leave you nor forsake you. Do not be afraid; do not be discouraged."

The Reading of the Law

9So Moses wrote down this law and gave it to the priests, the sons of Levi, who carried the ark of the covenant of the LORD, and to all the elders of Israel. 10Then Moses commanded them: "At the end of every seven years, in the year for canceling debts, during the Feast of Tabernacles, 11when all Israel comes to appear before the LORD your God at the place he will choose, you shall read this law before them in their hearing. 12Assemble the people—men, women and children, and the aliens living in your towns—so they can listen and learn to fear the LORD your God and follow carefully all the words of this law. 13Their children, who do not know this law, must hear it and learn to fear the LORD your God as long as you live in the land you are crossing the Jordan to possess."

Israel's Rebellion Predicted

14The LORD said to Moses, "Now the day of your death is near. Call Joshua and present yourselves at the Tent of Meeting, where I will commission him." So Moses and Joshua came and presented themselves at the Tent of Meeting.

15Then the LORD appeared at the Tent in a pillar of cloud, and the cloud stood over the entrance to the Tent. 16And the LORD said to Moses: "You are going to rest with your fathers, and these people will soon prostitute themselves to the foreign gods of the land they are entering. They will forsake me and break the covenant I made with them. 17On that day I will become angry with them

Living Bible

and to obey him and to cling to him, for he is your life and the length of your days. You will then be able to live safely in the land the Lord promised your ancestors, Abraham, Isaac, and Jacob."

31 AFTER MOSES had said all these things to the people of Israel, 2he told them, "I am now 120 years old! I am no longer able to lead you,a for the Lord has told me that I shall not cross the Jordan River. 3But the Lord himself will lead you, and will destroy the nations living there, and you shall overcome them. Joshua is your new commander, as the Lord has instructed. 4The Lord will destroy the nations living in the land, just as he destroyed Sihon and Og, the kings of the Amorites. 5The Lord will deliver over to you the people living there, and you shall destroy them as I have commanded you. 6Be strong! Be courageous! Do not be afraid of them! For the Lord your God will be with you. He will neither fail you nor forsake you."

7Then Moses called for Joshua and said to him, as all Israel watched, "Be strong! Be courageous! For you shall lead these people into the land promised by the Lord to their ancestors; see to it that they conquer it. 8Don't be afraid, for the Lord will go before you and will be with you; he will not fail nor forsake you."

9Then Moses wrote out the laws he had already delivered to the people and gave them to the priests, the sons of Levi, who carried the Ark containing the Ten Commandments of the Lord. Moses also gave copies of the laws to the elders of Israel. 10, 11The Lord commanded that these laws be read to all the people at the end of every seventh year—the Year of Release—at the Festival of Tabernacles, when all Israel would assemble before the Lord at the sanctuary.

12"Call them all together," the Lord instructed, "—men, women, children, and foreigners living among you—to hear the laws of God and to learn his will, so that you will reverence the Lord your God and obey his laws. 13Do this so that your little children who have not known these laws will hear them and learn how to revere the Lord your God as long as you live in the Promised Land."

14Then the Lord said to Moses, "The time has come when you must die. Summon Joshua and come into the Tabernacle where I can give him his instructions." So Moses and Joshua came and stood before the Lord.

15He appeared to them in a great cloud at the Tabernacle entrance, 16and said to Moses, "You shall die and join your ancestors. After you are gone, these people will begin worshiping foreign gods in the Promised Land. They will forget about me and break the contract I have made with them. 17Then my anger will flame out

New Revised Standard

and holding fast to him; for that means life to you and length of days, so that you may live in the land that the LORD swore to give to your ancestors, to Abraham, to Isaac, and to Jacob.

Joshua Becomes Moses' Successor

31 WHEN MOSES had finished speaking allb these words to all Israel, 2he said to them: "I am now one hundred twenty years old. I am no longer able to get about, and the LORD has told me, 'You shall not cross over this Jordan.' 3The LORD your God himself will cross over before you. He will destroy these nations before you, and you shall dispossess them. Joshua also will cross over before you, as the LORD promised. 4The LORD will do to them as he did to Sihon and Og, the kings of the Amorites, and to their land, when he destroyed them. 5The LORD will give them over to you and you shall deal with them in full accord with the command that I have given to you. 6Be strong and bold; have no fear or dread of them, because it is the LORD your God who goes with you; he will not fail you or forsake you."

7 Then Moses summoned Joshua and said to him in the sight of all Israel: "Be strong and bold, for you are the one who will go with this people into the land that the LORD has sworn to their ancestors to give them; and you will put them in possession of it. 8 It is the LORD who goes before you. He will be with you; he will not fail you or forsake you. Do not fear or be dismayed."

The Law to Be Read Every Seventh Year

9 Then Moses wrote down this law, and gave it to the priests, the sons of Levi, who carried the ark of the covenant of the LORD, and to all the elders of Israel. 10Moses commanded them: "Every seventh year, in the scheduled year of remission, during the festival of booths,c 11when all Israel comes to appear before the LORD your God at the place that he will choose, you shall read this law before all Israel in their hearing. 12Assemble the people—men, women, and children, as well as the aliens residing in your towns—so that they may hear and learn to fear the LORD your God and to observe diligently all the words of this law, 13and so that their children, who have not known it, may hear and learn to fear the LORD your God, as long as you live in the land that you are crossing over the Jordan to possess."

Moses and Joshua Receive God's Charge

14 The LORD said to Moses, "Your time to die is near; call Joshua and present yourselves in the tent of meeting, so that I may commission him." So Moses and Joshua went and presented themselves in the tent of meeting, 15and the LORD appeared at the tent in a pillar of cloud; the pillar of cloud stood at the entrance to the tent.

16 The LORD said to Moses, "Soon you will lie down with your ancestors. Then this people will begin to prostitute themselves to the foreign gods in their midst, the gods of the land into which they are going; they will forsake me, breaking my covenant that I have made with them. 17My anger will be kindled against

---

a 31:2 *I am no longer able to lead you,* literally, "I am no longer able to go out and come in."

b Q Ms Gk: MT *Moses went and spoke* c Or *tabernacles;* Heb *succoth*

King James

17Then my anger shall be kindled against them in that day, and I will forsake them, and I will hide my face from them, and they shall be devoured, and many evils and troubles shall befall them; so that they will say in that day, Are not these evils come upon us, because our God *is* not among us?

18And I will surely hide my face in that day for all the evils which they shall have wrought, in that they are turned unto other gods.

19Now therefore write ye this song for you, and teach it the children of Israel: put it in their mouths, that this song may be a witness for me against the children of Israel.

20For when I shall have brought them into the land which I sware unto their fathers, that floweth with milk and honey; and they shall have eaten and filled themselves, and waxen fat; then will they turn unto other gods, and serve them, and provoke me, and break my covenant.

21And it shall come to pass, when many evils and troubles are befallen them, that this song shall testify against them as a witness; for it shall not be forgotten out of the mouths of their seed: for I know their imagination which they go about, even now, before I have brought them into the land which I sware.

22¶ Moses therefore wrote this song the same day, and taught it the children of Israel.

23And he gave Joshua the son of Nun a charge, and said, Be strong and of a good courage: for thou shalt bring the children of Israel into the land which I sware unto them: and I will be with thee.

24¶ And it came to pass, when Moses had made an end of writing the words of this law in a book, until they were finished,

25That Moses commanded the Levites, which bare the ark of the covenant of the LORD, saying,

26Take this book of the law, and put it in the side of the ark of the covenant of the LORD your God, that it may be there for a witness against thee.

27For I know thy rebellion, and thy stiff neck: behold, while I am yet alive with you this day, ye have been rebellious against the LORD; and how much more after my death?

28¶ Gather unto me all the elders of your tribes, and your officers, that I may speak these words in their ears, and call heaven and earth to record against them.

29For I know that after my death ye will utterly corrupt *yourselves*, and turn aside from the way which I have commanded you; and evil will befall you in the latter days; because ye will do evil in the sight of the LORD, to provoke him to anger through the work of your hands.

30And Moses spake in the ears of all the congregation of Israel the words of this song, until they were ended.

32 GIVE EAR, O ye heavens, and I will speak; and hear, O earth, the words of my mouth.

2My doctrine shall drop as the rain, my speech shall distil as the dew, as the small rain upon the tender herb, and as the showers upon the grass:

3Because I will publish the name of the LORD: ascribe ye greatness unto our God.

4*He is* the Rock, his work *is* perfect: for all his ways *are* judgment: a God of truth and without iniquity, just and right *is* he.

New International

and forsake them; I will hide my face from them, and they will be destroyed. Many disasters and difficulties will come upon them, and on that day they will ask, 'Have not these disasters come upon us because our God is not with us?' 18And I will certainly hide my face on that day because of all their wickedness in turning to other gods.

19"Now write down for yourselves this song and teach it to the Israelites and have them sing it, so that it may be a witness for me against them. 20When I have brought them into the land flowing with milk and honey, the land I promised on oath to their forefathers, and when they eat their fill and thrive, they will turn to other gods and worship them, rejecting me and breaking my covenant. 21And when many disasters and difficulties come upon them, this song will testify against them, because it will not be forgotten by their descendants. I know what they are disposed to do, even before I bring them into the land I promised them on oath." 22So Moses wrote down this song that day and taught it to the Israelites.

23The LORD gave this command to Joshua son of Nun: "Be strong and courageous, for you will bring the Israelites into the land I promised them on oath, and I myself will be with you."

24After Moses finished writing in a book the words of this law from beginning to end, 25he gave this command to the Levites who carried the ark of the covenant of the LORD: 26"Take this Book of the Law and place it beside the ark of the covenant of the LORD your God. There it will remain as a witness against you. 27For I know how rebellious and stiff-necked you are. If you have been rebellious against the LORD while I am still alive and with you, how much more will you rebel after I die! 28Assemble before me all the elders of your tribes and all your officials, so that I can speak these words in their hearing and call heaven and earth to testify against them. 29For I know that after my death you are sure to become utterly corrupt and to turn from the way I have commanded you. In days to come, disaster will fall upon you because you will do evil in the sight of the LORD and provoke him to anger by what your hands have made."

The Song of Moses

30And Moses recited the words of this song from beginning to end in the hearing of the whole assembly of Israel:

32 LISTEN, O heavens, and I will speak; hear, O earth, the words of my mouth.

2Let my teaching fall like rain
and my words descend like dew,
like showers on new grass,
like abundant rain on tender plants.

3I will proclaim the name of the LORD.
Oh, praise the greatness of our God!
4He is the Rock, his works are perfect,
and all his ways are just.
A faithful God who does no wrong,
upright and just is he.

Living Bible

against them and I will abandon them, hiding my face from them, and they shall be destroyed. Terrible trouble will come upon them, so that they will say, 'God is no longer among us!' 18I will turn away from them because of their sins in worshiping other gods.

19"Now write down the words of this song, and teach it to the people of Israel as my warning to them. 20When I have brought them into the land I promised their ancestors—a land 'flowing with milk and honey'—and when they have become fat and prosperous, and worship other gods and despise me and break my contract, 21and great disasters come upon them, then this song will remind them of the reason for their woes. (For this song will live from generation to generation.) I know now, even before they enter the land, what these people are like."

22So, on that very day, Moses wrote down the words of the song and taught it to the Israelites. 23Then he charged Joshua (son of Nun) to be strong and courageous, and said to him, "You must bring the people of Israel into the land the Lord promised them; for the Lord says, 'I will be with you.' "

24When Moses had finished writing down all the laws that are recorded in this book, 25he instructed the Levites who carried the Ark containing the Ten Commandments 26to put this book of the law beside the Ark, as a solemn warning to the people of Israel.

27"For I know how rebellious and stubborn you are," Moses told them. "If even today, while I am still here with you, you are defiant rebels against the Lord, how much more rebellious will you be after my death! 28Now summon all the elders and officers of your tribes so that I can speak to them, and call heaven and earth to witness against them. 29I know that after my death you will utterly defile yourselves and turn away from God and his commands; and in the days to come evil will crush you for you will do what the Lord says is evil, making him very angry."

30So Moses recited this entire song to the whole assembly of Israel:

32 "LISTEN, O heavens and earth! Listen to what I say! 2My words shall fall upon you Like the gentle rain and dew, Like rain upon the tender grass, Like showers on the hillside. 3I will proclaim the greatness of the Lord. How glorious he is! 4He is the Rock. His work is perfect. Everything he does is just and fair. He is faithful, without sin.

New Revised Standard

them in that day. I will forsake them and hide my face from them; they will become easy prey, and many terrible troubles will come upon them. In that day they will say, 'Have not these troubles come upon us because our God is not in our midst?' 18On that day I will surely hide my face on account of all the evil they have done by turning to other gods. 19Now therefore write this song, and teach it to the Israelites; put it in their mouths, in order that this song may be a witness for me against the Israelites. 20For when I have brought them into the land flowing with milk and honey, which I promised on oath to their ancestors, and they have eaten their fill and grown fat, they will turn to other gods and serve them, despising me and breaking my covenant. 21And when many terrible troubles come upon them, this song will confront them as a witness, because it will not be lost from the mouths of their descendants. For I know what they are inclined to do even now, before I have brought them into the land that I promised them on oath." 22That very day Moses wrote this song and taught it to the Israelites.

23 Then the LORD commissioned Joshua son of Nun and said, "Be strong and bold, for you shall bring the Israelites into the land that I promised them; I will be with you."

24 When Moses had finished writing down in a book the words of this law to the very end, 25Moses commanded the Levites who carried the ark of the covenant of the LORD, saying, 26"Take this book of the law and put it beside the ark of the covenant of the LORD your God; let it remain there as a witness against you. 27For I know well how rebellious and stubborn you are. If you already have been so rebellious toward the LORD while I am still alive among you, how much more after my death! 28Assemble to me all the elders of your tribes and your officials, so that I may recite these words in their hearing and call heaven and earth to witness against them. 29For I know that after my death you will surely act corruptly, turning aside from the way that I have commanded you. In time to come trouble will befall you, because you will do what is evil in the sight of the LORD, provoking him to anger through the work of your hands."

The Song of Moses

30 Then Moses recited the words of this song, to the very end, in the hearing of the whole assembly of Israel:

32 GIVE EAR, O heavens, and I will speak; let the earth hear the words of my mouth. 2 May my teaching drop like the rain, my speech condense like the dew; like gentle rain on grass, like showers on new growth. 3 For I will proclaim the name of the LORD; ascribe greatness to our God!

4 The Rock, his work is perfect, and all his ways are just. A faithful God, without deceit, just and upright is he;

King James

5They have corrupted themselves, their spot *is* not *the spot* of his children: *they are* a perverse and crooked generation.

6Do ye thus requite the LORD, O foolish people and unwise? *is* not he thy father *that* hath bought thee? hath he not made thee, and established thee?

7¶ Remember the days of old, consider the years of many generations: ask thy father, and he will show thee; thy elders, and they will tell thee.

8When the Most High divided to the nations their inheritance, when he separated the sons of Adam, he set the bounds of the people according to the number of the children of Israel.

9For the LORD's portion *is* his people; Jacob *is* the lot of his inheritance.

10He found him in a desert land, and in the waste howling wilderness; he led him about, he instructed him, he kept him as the apple of his eye.

11As an eagle stirreth up her nest, fluttereth over her young, spreadeth abroad her wings, taketh them, beareth them on her wings:

12So the LORD alone did lead him, and *there was* no strange god with him.

13He made him ride on the high places of the earth, that he might eat the increase of the fields; and he made him to suck honey out of the rock, and oil out of the flinty rock;

14Butter of kine, and milk of sheep, with fat of lambs, and rams of the breed of Bashan, and goats, with the fat of kidneys of wheat; and thou didst drink the pure blood of the grape.

15¶ But Jeshurun waxed fat, and kicked: thou art waxen fat, thou art grown thick, thou art covered *with fatness;* then he forsook God *which* made him, and lightly esteemed the Rock of his salvation.

16They provoked him to jealousy with strange *gods,* with abominations provoked they him to anger.

17They sacrificed unto devils, not to God; to gods whom they knew not, to new *gods that* came newly up, whom your fathers feared not.

18Of the Rock *that* begat thee thou art unmindful, and hast forgotten God that formed thee.

19And when the LORD saw *it,* he abhorred *them,* because of the provoking of his sons, and of his daughters.

20And he said, I will hide my face from them, I will see what their end *shall be:* for they *are* a very froward generation, children in whom *is* no faith.

21They have moved me to jealousy with *that which is* not God; they have provoked me to anger with their vanities: and I will move them to jealousy with *those which are* not a people; I will provoke them to anger with a foolish nation.

New International

5They have acted corruptly toward him;
  to their shame they are no longer his children,
  but a warped and crooked generation.[a]
6Is this the way you repay the LORD,
  O foolish and unwise people?
Is he not your Father, your Creator,[b]
  who made you and formed you?

7Remember the days of old;
  consider the generations long past.
Ask your father and he will tell you,
  your elders, and they will explain to you.
8When the Most High gave the nations their
    inheritance,
  when he divided all mankind,
he set up boundaries for the peoples
  according to the number of the sons of
    Israel.[c]
9For the LORD's portion is his people,
  Jacob his allotted inheritance.

10In a desert land he found him,
  in a barren and howling waste.
He shielded him and cared for him;
  he guarded him as the apple of his eye,
11like an eagle that stirs up its nest
  and hovers over its young,
that spreads its wings to catch them
  and carries them on its pinions.
12The LORD alone led him;
  no foreign god was with him.

13He made him ride on the heights of the land
  and fed him with the fruit of the fields.
He nourished him with honey from the rock,
  and with oil from the flinty crag,
14with curds and milk from herd and flock
  and with fattened lambs and goats,
with choice rams of Bashan
  and the finest kernels of wheat.
You drank the foaming blood of the grape.

15Jeshurun[d] grew fat and kicked;
  filled with food, he became heavy and sleek.
He abandoned the God who made him
  and rejected the Rock his Savior.
16They made him jealous with their foreign gods
  and angered him with their detestable idols.
17They sacrificed to demons, which are not
    God—
  gods they had not known,
  gods that recently appeared,
  gods your fathers did not fear.
18You deserted the Rock, who fathered you;
  you forgot the God who gave you birth.

19The LORD saw this and rejected them
  because he was angered by his sons and
    daughters.
20"I will hide my face from them," he said,
  "and see what their end will be;
for they are a perverse generation,
  children who are unfaithful.
21They made me jealous by what is no god
  and angered me with their worthless idols.
I will make them envious by those who are not
    a people;
  I will make them angry by a nation that has
    no understanding.

---

a 5 Or *Corrupt are they and not his children,* / *a generation warped and twisted to their shame*   b 6 Or *Father, who bought you*   c 8 Masoretic Text; Dead Sea Scrolls (see also Septuagint) *sons of God*   d 15 *Jeshurun* means *the upright one,* that is, Israel.

Living Bible

5But Israel has become corrupt,
Smeared with sin. They are no longer his;
They are a stubborn, twisted generation.
6Is this the way you treat Jehovah?
O foolish people,
Is not God your Father?
Has he not created you?
Has he not established you and made you strong?
7Remember the days of long ago!
(Ask your father and the aged men;
They will tell you all about it.)
8When God divided up the world among the nations,
He gave each of them a supervising angel!
9But he appointed none for Israel;
For Israel was God's own personal possession!
10God protected them in the howling wilderness
As though they were the apple of his eye.
11He spreads his wings over them,
Even as an eagle overspreads her young.
She carries them upon her wings—
As does the Lord his people!
12When the Lord alone was leading them,
And they lived without foreign gods,
13God gave them fertile hilltops,
Rolling, fertile fields,
Honey from the rock,
And olive oil from stony ground!e
14He gave them milk and meat—
Choice Bashan rams, and goats—
And the finest of the wheat;
They drank the sparkling wine.
15But Israelf was soon overfed;
Yes, fat and bloated;
Then, in plenty, they forsook their God.
They shrugged away the Rock of their salvation.
16Israel began to follow foreign gods,
And Jehovah was very angry;
He was jealous of his people.
17They sacrificed to heathen gods,
To new gods never before worshiped.
18They spurned the Rock who had made them,
Forgetting it was God who had given them birth.
19God saw what they were doing,
And detested them!
His sons and daughters were insulting him.
20He said, 'I will abandon them;
See what happens to them then!
For they are a stubborn, faithless generation.
21They have made me very jealous of their idols,
Which are not gods at all.
Now I, in turn, will make them jealous
By giving my affections
To the foolish Gentile nations of the world.

New Revised Standard

5 yet his degenerate children have dealt falsely
        with him,g
    a perverse and crooked generation.
6 Do you thus repay the LORD,
        O foolish and senseless people?
    Is not he your father, who created you,
        who made you and established you?
7 Remember the days of old,
        consider the years long past;
    ask your father, and he will inform you;
        your elders, and they will tell you.
8 When the Most Highh apportioned the
        nations,
        when he divided humankind,
    he fixed the boundaries of the peoples
        according to the number of the gods;i
9 the LORD's own portion was his people,
        Jacob his allotted share.

10 He sustainedj him in a desert land,
        in a howling wilderness waste;
    he shielded him, cared for him,
        guarded him as the apple of his eye.
11 As an eagle stirs up its nest,
        and hovers over its young;
    as it spreads its wings, takes them up,
        and bears them aloft on its pinions,
12 the LORD alone guided him;
        no foreign god was with him.
13 He set him atop the heights of the land,
        and fed him withk produce of the field;
    he nursed him with honey from the crags,
        with oil from flinty rock;
14 curds from the herd, and milk from the flock,
        with fat of lambs and rams;
    Bashan bulls and goats,
        together with the choicest wheat—
    you drank fine wine from the blood of
        grapes.
15 Jacob ate his fill;l
        Jeshurun grew fat, and kicked.
    You grew fat, bloated, and gorged!
    He abandoned God who made him,
        and scoffed at the Rock of his salvation.
16 They made him jealous with strange gods,
        with abhorrent things they provoked him.
17 They sacrificed to demons, not God,
        to deities they had never known,
    to new ones recently arrived,
        whom your ancestors had not feared.
18 You were unmindful of the Rock that bore
        you;m
        you forgot the God who gave you birth.

19 The LORD saw it, and was jealousn
        he spurnedo his sons and daughters.
20 He said: I will hide my face from them,
        I will see what their end will be;
    for they are a perverse generation,
        children in whom there is no faithfulness.
21 They made me jealous with what is no god,
        provoked me with their idols.
    So I will make them jealous with what is no
        people,
        provoke them with a foolish nation.

---

g Meaning of Heb uncertain   h Traditional rendering of Heb Elyon   i Q Ms
Compare Gk Tg: MT the Israelites   j Sam Gk Compare Tg: MT found
k Sam Gk Syr Tg: MT he ate   l Q Mss Sam Gk: MT lacks Jacob ate his
fill   m Or that begot you   n Q Mss Gk: MT lacks was jealous   o Cn: Heb
he spurned because of provocation

e 32:13 oil from stony ground, or, "oil from flinty rocks."   f 32:15 Israel,
literally, "Jeshurun."

King James

22For a fire is kindled in mine anger, and shall burn unto the lowest hell, and shall consume the earth with her increase, and set on fire the foundations of the mountains.

23I will heap mischiefs upon them; I will spend mine arrows upon them.

24*They shall be* burnt with hunger, and devoured with burning heat, and with bitter destruction: I will also send the teeth of beasts upon them, with the poison of serpents of the dust.

25The sword without, and terror within, shall destroy both the young man and the virgin, the suckling *also* with the man of gray hairs.

26I said, I would scatter them into corners, I would make the remembrance of them to cease from among men:

27Were it not that I feared the wrath of the enemy, lest their adversaries should behave themselves strangely, *and* lest they should say, Our hand *is* high, and the LORD hath not done all this.

28For they *are* a nation void of counsel, neither *is there any* understanding in them.

29O that they were wise, *that* they understood this, *that* they would consider their latter end!

30How should one chase a thousand, and two put ten thousand to flight, except their Rock had sold them, and the LORD had shut them up?

31For their rock *is* not as our Rock, even our enemies themselves *being* judges.

32For their vine *is* of the vine of Sodom, and of the fields of Gomorrah: their grapes *are* grapes of gall, their clusters *are* bitter:

33Their wine *is* the poison of dragons, and the cruel venom of asps.

34*Is* not this laid up in store with me, *and* sealed up among my treasures?

35To me *belongeth* vengeance, and recompence; their foot shall slide in *due* time: for the day of their calamity *is* at hand, and the things that shall come upon them make haste.

36For the LORD shall judge his people, and repent himself for his servants, when he seeth that *their* power is gone, and *there is* none shut up, or left.

37And he shall say, Where *are* their gods, *their* rock in whom they trusted,

38Which did eat the fat of their sacrifices, *and* drank the wine of their drink offerings? let them rise up and help you, *and* be your protection.

39See now that I, *even* I, *am* he, and *there is* no god with me: I kill, and I make alive; I wound, and I heal: neither *is there any* that can deliver out of my hand.

40For I lift up my hand to heaven, and say, I live for ever.

41If I whet my glittering sword, and mine hand take hold on judgment; I will render vengeance to mine enemies, and will reward them that hate me.

New International

22For a fire has been kindled by my wrath,
  one that burns to the realm of death[a] below.
It will devour the earth and its harvests
  and set afire the foundations of the
    mountains.

23"I will heap calamities upon them
  and spend my arrows against them.
24I will send wasting famine against them,
  consuming pestilence and deadly plague;
I will send against them the fangs of wild
    beasts,
  the venom of vipers that glide in the dust.
25In the street the sword will make them childless;
  in their homes terror will reign.
Young men and young women will perish,
  infants and gray-haired men.
26I said I would scatter them
  and blot out their memory from mankind,
27but I dreaded the taunt of the enemy,
  lest the adversary misunderstand
and say, 'Our hand has triumphed;
  the LORD has not done all this.' "

28They are a nation without sense,
  there is no discernment in them.
29If only they were wise and would understand
    this
  and discern what their end will be!
30How could one man chase a thousand,
  or two put ten thousand to flight,
unless their Rock had sold them,
  unless the LORD had given them up?
31For their rock is not like our Rock,
  as even our enemies concede.
32Their vine comes from the vine of Sodom
  and from the fields of Gomorrah.
Their grapes are filled with poison,
  and their clusters with bitterness.
33Their wine is the venom of serpents,
  the deadly poison of cobras.

34"Have I not kept this in reserve
  and sealed it in my vaults?
35It is mine to avenge; I will repay.
  In due time their foot will slip;
their day of disaster is near
  and their doom rushes upon them."

36The LORD will judge his people
  and have compassion on his servants
when he sees their strength is gone
  and no one is left, slave or free.
37He will say: "Now where are their gods,
  the rock they took refuge in,
38the gods who ate the fat of their sacrifices
  and drank the wine of their drink offerings?
Let them rise up to help you!
  Let them give you shelter!

39"See now that I myself am He!
  There is no god besides me.
I put to death and I bring to life,
  I have wounded and I will heal,
  and no one can deliver out of my hand.
40I lift my hand to heaven and declare:
  As surely as I live forever,
41when I sharpen my flashing sword
  and my hand grasps it in judgment,
I will take vengeance on my adversaries
  and repay those who hate me.

---

[a] 22 Hebrew *to Sheol*

Living Bible

22For my anger has kindled a fire
That burns to the depths of the underworld,
Consuming the earth and all of its crops,
And setting its mountains on fire.
23I will heap evils upon them
And shoot them down with my arrows.
24I will waste them with hunger,
Burning fever, and fatal disease.
I will devour them! I will set wild beasts upon them,
To rip them apart with their teeth;
And deadly serpents
Crawling in the dust.
25Outside, the enemies' sword—
Inside, the plagueb—
Shall terrorize young men and girls alike;
The baby nursing at the breast,
And aged men.
26I had decided to scatter them to distant lands,
So that even the memory of them
Would disappear.
27But then I thought,
"My enemies will boast,
'Israel is destroyed by our own might;
It was not the Lord
Who did it!' "'
28Israel is a stupid nation;
Foolish, without understanding.
29Oh, that they were wise!
Oh, that they could understand!
Oh, that they would know what they are getting into!
30How could one single enemy chase a thousand of
   them,
And two put ten thousand to flight,
Unless their Rock had abandoned them,
Unless the Lord had destroyed them?
31But the rock of other nations
Is not like our Rock;
Prayers to their gods are valueless.
32They act like men of Sodom and Gomorrah:
Their deedsc are bitter with poison;
33They drink the wine of serpent venom.
34But Israeld is my special people,
Sealed as jewels within my treasury.
35Vengeance is mine,
And I decree the punishment of all her enemies:
Their doom is sealed.
36The Lord will see his people righted,
And will have compassion on them when they slip.
He will watch their power ebb away,
Both slave and free.
37Then God will ask,
'Where are their gods—
The rocks they claimed to be their refuge?
38Where are these gods now,
To whom they sacrificed their fat and wine?
Let those gods arise,
And help them!
39Don't you see that I alone am God?
I kill and make live.
I wound and heal—
No one delivers from my power.
40, 41I raise my hand to heaven
And vow by my existence,
That I will whet the lightning of my sword!
And hurl my punishments upon my enemies!

New Revised Standard

22 For a fire is kindled by my anger,
       and burns to the depths of Sheol;
    it devours the earth and its increase,
       and sets on fire the foundations of the
          mountains.
23 I will heap disasters upon them,
       spend my arrows against them:
24 wasting hunger,
       burning consumption,
       bitter pestilence.
    The teeth of beasts I will send against them,
       with venom of things crawling in the dust.
25 In the street the sword shall bereave,
       and in the chambers terror,
    for young man and woman alike,
       nursing child and old gray head.
26 I thought to scatter theme
       and blot out the memory of them from
          humankind;
27 but I feared provocation by the enemy,
       for their adversaries might misunderstand
    and say, "Our hand is triumphant;
       it was not the LORD who did all this."

28 They are a nation void of sense;
       there is no understanding in them.
29 If they were wise, they would understand this;
       they would discern what the end would be.
30 How could one have routed a thousand,
       and two put a myriad to flight,
    unless their Rock had sold them,
       the LORD had given them up?
31 Indeed their rock is not like our Rock;
       our enemies are fools.e
32 Their vine comes from the vinestock of
          Sodom,
       from the vineyards of Gomorrah;
    their grapes are grapes of poison,
       their clusters are bitter;
33 their wine is the poison of serpents,
       the cruel venom of asps.

34 Is not this laid up in store with me,
       sealed up in my treasuries?
35 Vengeance is mine, and recompense,
       for the time when their foot shall slip;
    because the day of their calamity is at hand,
       their doom comes swiftly.

36 Indeed the LORD will vindicate his people,
       have compassion on his servants,
    when he sees that their power is gone,
       neither bond nor free remaining.
37 Then he will say: Where are their gods,
       the rock in which they took refuge,
38 who ate the fat of their sacrifices,
       and drank the wine of their libations?
    Let them rise up and help you,
       let them be your protection!

39 See now that I, even I, am he;
       there is no god besides me.
    I kill and I make alive;
       I wound and I heal;
       and no one can deliver from my hand.
40 For I lift up my hand to heaven,
       and swear: As I live forever,
41 when I whet my flashing sword,
       and my hand takes hold on judgment;
    I will take vengeance on my adversaries,
       and will repay those who hate me.

---

b 32:25 the plague, implied.   c 32:32 deeds, literally, "grapes."
d 32:34 Implied.

e Gk: Meaning of Heb uncertain

King James

42I will make mine arrows drunk with blood, and my sword shall devour flesh; *and that* with the blood of the slain and of the captives, from the beginning of revengers upon the enemy.

43Rejoice, O ye nations, *with* his people: for he will avenge the blood of his servants, and will render vengeance to his adversaries, and will be merciful unto his land, *and* to his people.

44¶ And Moses came and spake all the words of this song in the ears of the people, he, and Hoshea the son of Nun.

45And Moses made an end of speaking all these words to all Israel:

46And he said unto them, Set your hearts unto all the words which I testify among you this day, which ye shall command your children to observe to do, all the words of this law.

47For it *is* not a vain thing for you; because it *is* your life: and through this thing ye shall prolong *your* days in the land, whither ye go over Jordan to possess it.

48And the LORD spake unto Moses that selfsame day, saying,

49Get thee up into this mountain Abarim, *unto* mount Nebo, which *is* in the land of Moab, that *is* over against Jericho; and behold the land of Canaan, which I give unto the children of Israel for a possession:

50And die in the mount whither thou goest up, and be gathered unto thy people; as Aaron thy brother died in mount Hor, and was gathered unto his people:

51Because ye trespassed against me among the children of Israel at the waters of Meribah-Kadesh, in the wilderness of Zin; because ye sanctified me not in the midst of the children of Israel.

52Yet thou shalt see the land before *thee;* but thou shalt not go thither unto the land which I give the children of Israel.

33 AND THIS *is* the blessing, wherewith Moses the man of God blessed the children of Israel before his death.

2And he said, The LORD came from Sinai, and rose up from Seir unto them; he shined forth from mount Paran, and he came with ten thousands of saints: from his right hand *went* a fiery law for them.

3Yea, he loved the people; all his saints *are* in thy hand: and they sat down at thy feet; *every* one shall receive of thy words.

4Moses commanded us a law, *even* the inheritance of the congregation of Jacob.

5And he was king in Jeshurun, when the heads of the people *and* the tribes of Israel were gathered together.

6¶ Let Reuben live, and not die; and let *not* his men be few.

7¶ And this *is the blessing* of Judah: and he said, Hear, LORD, the voice of Judah, and bring him unto his people: let his hands be sufficient for him; and be thou an help *to him* from his enemies.

New International

42I will make my arrows drunk with blood,
  while my sword devours flesh:
 the blood of the slain and the captives,
  the heads of the enemy leaders."

43Rejoice, O nations, with his people,[a,b]
  for he will avenge the blood of his servants;
 he will take vengeance on his enemies
  and make atonement for his land and people.

44Moses came with Joshua[c] son of Nun and spoke all the words of this song in the hearing of the people. 45When Moses finished reciting all these words to all Israel, 46he said to them, "Take to heart all the words I have solemnly declared to you this day, so that you may command your children to obey carefully all the words of this law. 47They are not just idle words for you—they are your life. By them you will live long in the land you are crossing the Jordan to possess."

Moses to Die on Mount Nebo

48On that same day the LORD told Moses, 49"Go up into the Abarim Range to Mount Nebo in Moab, across from Jericho, and view Canaan, the land I am giving the Israelites as their own possession. 50There on the mountain that you have climbed you will die and be gathered to your people, just as your brother Aaron died on Mount Hor and was gathered to his people. 51This is because both of you broke faith with me in the presence of the Israelites at the waters of Meribah Kadesh in the Desert of Zin and because you did not uphold my holiness among the Israelites. 52Therefore, you will see the land only from a distance; you will not enter the land I am giving to the people of Israel."

Moses Blesses the Tribes

33 THIS IS the blessing that Moses the man of God pronounced on the Israelites before his death.
2He said:

"The LORD came from Sinai
  and dawned over them from Seir;
 he shone forth from Mount Paran.
 He came with[d] myriads of holy ones
  from the south, from his mountain slopes.[e]
3Surely it is you who love the people;
  all the holy ones are in your hand.
 At your feet they all bow down,
  and from you receive instruction,
4the law that Moses gave us,
  the possession of the assembly of Jacob.
5He was king over Jeshurun[f]
  when the leaders of the people assembled,
  along with the tribes of Israel.

6"Let Reuben live and not die,
  nor[g] his men be few."

7And this he said about Judah:

"Hear, O LORD, the cry of Judah;
  bring him to his people.
 With his own hands he defends his cause.
  Oh, be his help against his foes!"

a 43 Or *Make his people rejoice, O nations*   b 43 Masoretic Text; Dead Sea Scrolls (see also Septuagint) *people, / and let all the angels worship him /*   c 44 Hebrew *Hoshea,* a variant of *Joshua*   d 2 Or *from*   e 2 The meaning of the Hebrew for this phrase is uncertain.   f 5 *Jeshurun* means *the upright one,* that is, Israel; also in verse 26.   g 6 Or *but let*

Living Bible

42My arrows shall be drunk with blood!
My sword devours the flesh and blood
Of all the slain and captives.
The heads of the enemy
Are gory with blood.'
43Praise his people,
Gentile nations,
For he will avenge his people,
Taking vengeance on his enemies,
Purifying his land
And his people.

44, 45When Moses and Joshua had recited all the words of this song to the people, 46Moses made these comments:

"Meditate upon all the laws I have given you today, and pass them on to your children. 47These laws are not mere words—they are your life! Through obeying them you will live long, plentiful lives in the land you are going to possess across the Jordan River.

48That same day, the Lord said to Moses, 49"Go to Mount Nebo in the Abarim mountains, in the land of Moab across from Jericho. Climb to its heights, and look out across the land of Canaan, the land I am giving to the people of Israel. 50After you see the land you must die and join your ancestors, just as Aaron your brother died in Mount Hor and joined them. 51For you dishonored me among the people of Israel at the springs of Meribah-kadesh, in the wilderness of Zin. 52You will see spread out before you the land I am giving the people of Israel, but you will not enter it."

33 THIS IS the blessing Moses, the man of God, gave to the people of Israel before his death:
2"The Lord came to us at Mount Sinai,
And dawned upon us from Mount Seir;
He shone from Mount Paran,
Surrounded by ten thousands of holy angels,h
And with flaming fire at his right hand.
3How he loves his people—
His holy ones are in his hands.
They followed in your steps, O Lord.
They have received their directions from you.
4The laws I have given
Are your precious possession.
5The Lord became king in Jerusalem,
Elected by a convocation of the leaders of the tribes!
6Let Reuben live forever
And may his tribe increase!"
7And Moses said of Judah:
"O Lord, hear the cry of Judah
And unite him with Israel;
Fight for him against his enemies."

New Revised Standard

42 I will make my arrows drunk with blood,
and my sword shall devour flesh—
with the blood of the slain and the captives,
from the long-haired enemy.

43 Praise, O heavens,i his people,
worship him, all you gods!j
For he will avenge the blood of his children,k
and take vengeance on his adversaries;
he will repay those who hate him,j
and cleanse the land for his people.l

44 Moses came and recited all the words of this song in the hearing of the people, he and Joshuam son of Nun. 45When Moses had finished reciting all these words to all Israel, 46he said to them: "Take to heart all the words that I am giving in witness against you today; give them as a command to your children, so that they may diligently observe all the words of this law. 47This is no trifling matter for you, but rather your very life; through it you may live long in the land that you are crossing over the Jordan to possess."

Moses' Death Foretold

48 On that very day the LORD addressed Moses as follows: 49"Ascend this mountain of the Abarim, Mount Nebo, which is in the land of Moab, across from Jericho, and view the land of Canaan, which I am giving to the Israelites for a possession; 50you shall die there on the mountain that you ascend and shall be gathered to your kin, as your brother Aaron died on Mount Hor and was gathered to his kin; 51because both of you broke faith with me among the Israelites at the waters of Meribath-kadesh in the wilderness of Zin, by failing to maintain my holiness among the Israelites. 52Although you may view the land from a distance, you shall not enter it—the land that I am giving to the Israelites."

Moses' Final Blessing on Israel

33 THIS IS the blessing with which Moses, the man of God, blessed the Israelites before his death. 2He said:
The LORD came from Sinai,
and dawned from Seir upon us;n
he shone forth from Mount Paran.
With him were myriads of holy ones;o
at his right, a host of his own.p
3 Indeed, O favorite amongq peoples,
all his holy ones were in your charge;
they marched at your heels,
accepted direction from you.
4 Moses charged us with the law,
as a possession for the assembly of Jacob.
5 There arose a king in Jeshurun,
when the leaders of the people assembled—
the united tribes of Israel.

6 May Reuben live, and not die out,
even though his numbers are few.

7And this he said of Judah:
O LORD, give heed to Judah,
and bring him to his people;
strengthen his hands for him,r
and be a help against his adversaries.

i Q Ms Gk: MT nations   j Q Ms Gk: MT lacks this line   k Q Ms Gk: MT his servants   l Q Ms Sam Gk Vg: MT his land his people   m Sam Gk Syr Vg: MT Hoshea   n Gk Syr Vg Compare Tg: Heb upon them   o Cn Compare Gk Sam Syr Vg: MT He came from Riboboth-kadesh.   p Cn Compare Gk: meaning of Heb uncertain   q Or O lover of the   r Cn: Heb with his hands he contended

h 33:2 holy angels, literally, "holy ones."

King James

8¶ And of Levi he said, *Let* thy Thummim and thy Urim *be* with thy holy one, whom thou didst prove at Massah, *and with* whom thou didst strive at the waters of Meribah;

9Who said unto his father and to his mother, I have not seen him; neither did he acknowledge his brethren, nor knew his own children: for they have observed thy word, and kept thy covenant.

10They shall teach Jacob thy judgments, and Israel thy law: they shall put incense before thee, and whole burnt sacrifice upon thine altar.

11Bless, LORD, his substance, and accept the work of his hands: smite through the loins of them that rise against him, and of them that hate him, that they rise not again.

12¶ *And* of Benjamin he said, The beloved of the LORD shall dwell in safety by him; *and the* LORD shall cover him all the day long, and he shall dwell between his shoulders.

13¶ And of Joseph he said, Blessed of the LORD *be* his land, for the precious things of heaven, for the dew, and for the deep that coucheth beneath,

14And for the precious fruits *brought forth* by the sun, and for the precious things put forth by the moon,

15And for the chief things of the ancient mountains, and for the precious things of the lasting hills,

16And for the precious things of the earth and fulness thereof, and *for* the good will of him that dwelt in the bush: let *the blessing* come upon the head of Joseph, and upon the top of the head of him *that was* separated from his brethren.

17His glory *is like* the firstling of his bullock, and his horns *are like* the horns of unicorns: with them he shall push the people together to the ends of the earth: and they *are* the ten thousands of Ephraim, and they *are* the thousands of Manasseh.

18¶ And of Zebulun he said, Rejoice, Zebulun, in thy going out; and, Issachar, in thy tents.

19They shall call the people unto the mountain; there they shall offer sacrifices of righteousness: for they shall suck *of* the abundance of the seas, and *of* treasures hid in the sand.

20¶ And of Gad he said, Blessed *be* he that enlargeth Gad: he dwelleth as a lion, and teareth the arm with the crown of the head.

21And he provided the first part for himself, because there, *in* a portion of the lawgiver, *was he* seated; and he came with the heads of the people, he executed the justice of the LORD, and his judgments with Israel.

New International

8About Levi he said:

"Your Thummim and Urim belong
　to the man you favored.
You tested him at Massah;
　you contended with him at the waters of
　　Meribah.
9He said of his father and mother,
　'I have no regard for them.'
He did not recognize his brothers
　or acknowledge his own children,
but he watched over your word
　and guarded your covenant.
10He teaches your precepts to Jacob
　and your law to Israel.
He offers incense before you
　and whole burnt offerings on your altar.
11Bless all his skills, O LORD,
　and be pleased with the work of his hands.
Smite the loins of those who rise up against
　　him;
　strike his foes till they rise no more."

12About Benjamin he said:

"Let the beloved of the LORD rest secure in
　　him,
　for he shields him all day long,
and the one the LORD loves rests between his
　　shoulders."

13About Joseph he said:

"May the LORD bless his land
　with the precious dew from heaven above
　and with the deep waters that lie below;
14with the best the sun brings forth
　and the finest the moon can yield;
15with the choicest gifts of the ancient mountains
　and the fruitfulness of the everlasting hills;
16with the best gifts of the earth and its fullness
　and the favor of him who dwelt in the
　　burning bush.
Let all these rest on the head of Joseph,
　on the brow of the prince among[a] his
　　brothers.
17In majesty he is like a firstborn bull;
　his horns are the horns of a wild ox.
With them he will gore the nations,
　even those at the ends of the earth.
Such are the ten thousands of Ephraim;
　such are the thousands of Manasseh."

18About Zebulun he said:

"Rejoice, Zebulun, in your going out,
　and you, Issachar, in your tents.
19They will summon peoples to the mountain
　and there offer sacrifices of righteousness;
they will feast on the abundance of the seas,
　on the treasures hidden in the sand."

20About Gad he said:

"Blessed is he who enlarges Gad's domain!
　Gad lives there like a lion,
　tearing at arm or head.
21He chose the best land for himself;
　the leader's portion was kept for him.
When the heads of the people assembled,
　he carried out the LORD's righteous will,
　and his judgments concerning Israel."

ᵃ 16 Or *of the one separated from*

Living Bible

8Then Moses said concerning the tribe of Levi:
"Give to godly Levi
Your Urim and your Thummim.
You tested Levi at Massah and at Meribah;
9He obeyed your instructions
[and destroyed many sinnersb],
Even his own children, brothers, fathers, and
    mothers.
10The Levites shall teach God's laws to Israel
And shall work before you at the incense altar
And the altar of burnt offering.
11O Lord, prosper the Levites
And accept the work they do for you.
Crush those who are their enemies;
Don't let them rise again."
12Concerning the tribe of Benjamin, Moses said:
"He is beloved of God
And lives in safety beside him.
God surrounds him with his loving care,
And preserves him from every harm."
13Concerning the tribe of Joseph, he said:
"May his land be blessed by God
With the choicest gifts of heaven
And of the earth that lies below.
14May he be blessed
With the best of what the sun makes grow;
Growing richly month by month,
15With the finest of mountain crops
And of the everlasting hills.
16May he be blessed with the best gifts
Of the earth and its fullness,
And with the favor of God who appeared
In the burning bush.
Let all these blessings come upon Joseph,
The prince among his brothers.
17He is a young bull in strength and splendor,
With the strong horns of a wild ox
To push against the nations everywhere;
This is my blessing on the multitudes of Ephraim
And the thousands of Manasseh."
18Of the tribe of Zebulun, Moses said:
"Rejoice, O Zebulun, you outdoorsmen,
And Issachar, you lovers of your tents;
19They shall summon the people
To celebrate their sacrifices with them.
Lo, they taste the riches of the sea
And the treasures of the sand."
20Concerning the tribe of Gad, Moses said:
"A blessing upon those who help Gad.
He crouches like a lion,
With savage arm and face and head.
21He chose the best of the land for himself
Because it is reserved for a leader.
He led the people
Because he carried out God's penalties for Israel."

b 33:9 and destroyed many sinners, implied.

New Revised Standard

8And of Levi he said:
Give to Levic your Thummim,
    and your Urim to your loyal one,
whom you tested at Massah,
    with whom you contended at the waters of
        Meribah;
9 who said of his father and mother,
    "I regard them not";
he ignored his kin,
    and did not acknowledge his children.
For they observed your word,
    and kept your covenant.
10 They teach Jacob your ordinances,
    and Israel your law;
they place incense before you,
    and whole burnt offerings on your altar.
11 Bless, O LORD, his substance,
    and accept the work of his hands;
crush the loins of his adversaries,
    of those that hate him, so that they do not
        rise again.

12Of Benjamin he said:
The beloved of the LORD rests in safety—
    the High Godd surrounds him all day long—
    the belovede rests between his shoulders.

13And of Joseph he said:
Blessed by the LORD be his land,
    with the choice gifts of heaven above,
    and of the deep that lies beneath;
14 with the choice fruits of the sun,
    and the rich yield of the months;
15 with the finest produce of the ancient
        mountains,
    and the abundance of the everlasting hills;
16 with the choice gifts of the earth and its
        fullness,
    and the favor of the one who dwells on
        Sinai.f
Let these come on the head of Joseph,
    on the brow of the prince among his
        brothers.
17 A firstborng bull—majesty is his!
    His horns are the horns of a wild ox;
with them he gores the peoples,
    driving them toh the ends of the earth;
such are the myriads of Ephraim,
    such the thousands of Manasseh.

18And of Zebulun he said:
Rejoice, Zebulun, in your going out;
    and Issachar, in your tents.
19 They call peoples to the mountain;
    there they offer the right sacrifices;
for they suck the affluence of the seas
    and the hidden treasures of the sand.

20And of Gad he said:
Blessed be the enlargement of Gad!
    Gad lives like a lion;
    he tears at arm and scalp.
21 He chose the best for himself,
    for there a commander's allotment was
        reserved;
he came at the head of the people,
    he executed the justice of the LORD,
    and his ordinances for Israel.

c Q Ms Gk: MT lacks Give to Levi   d Heb above him   e Heb he   f Cn:
Heb in the bush   g Q Ms Gk Syr Vg: MT His firstborn   h Cn: Heb the
peoples, together

King James

22¶ And of Dan he said, Dan *is* a lion's whelp: he shall leap from Bashan.

23¶ And of Naphtali he said, O Naphtali, satisfied with favour, and full with the blessing of the LORD: possess thou the west and the south.

24¶ And of Asher he said, *Let* Asher *be* blessed with children; let him be acceptable to his brethren, and let him dip his foot in oil.

25Thy shoes *shall be* iron and brass; and as thy days, *so shall* thy strength *be*.

26¶ *There is* none like unto the God of Jeshurun, *who* rideth upon the heaven in thy help, and in his excellency on the sky.

27The eternal God *is thy* refuge, and underneath *are* the everlasting arms: and he shall thrust out the enemy from before thee; and shall say, Destroy *them*.

28Israel then shall dwell in safety alone: the fountain of Jacob *shall be* upon a land of corn and wine; also his heavens shall drop down dew.

29Happy *art* thou, O Israel: who *is* like unto thee, O people saved by the LORD, the shield of thy help, and who *is* the sword of thy excellency! and thine enemies shall be found liars unto thee; and thou shalt tread upon their high places.

34 AND MOSES went up from the plains of Moab unto the mountain of Nebo, to the top of Pisgah, that *is* over against Jericho. And the LORD showed him all the land of Gilead, unto Dan,

2And all Naphtali, and the land of Ephraim, and Manasseh, and all the land of Judah, unto the utmost sea,

3And the south, and the plain of the valley of Jericho, the city of palm trees, unto Zoar.

4And the LORD said unto him, This *is* the land which I sware unto Abraham, unto Isaac, and unto Jacob, saying, I will give it unto thy seed: I have caused thee to see *it* with thine eyes, but thou shalt not go over thither.

5¶ So Moses the servant of the LORD died there in the land of Moab, according to the word of the LORD.

6And he buried him in a valley in the land of Moab, over against Beth-peor: but no man knoweth of his sepulchre unto this day.

7¶ And Moses *was* an hundred and twenty years old when he died: his eye was not dim, nor his natural force abated.

8¶ And the children of Israel wept for Moses in the plains of Moab thirty days: so the days of weeping *and* mourning for Moses were ended.

9¶ And Joshua the son of Nun was full of the spirit of wisdom; for Moses had laid his hands upon him: and the children of Israel hearkened unto him, and did as the LORD commanded Moses.

10¶ And there arose not a prophet since in Israel like unto Moses, whom the LORD knew face to face,

11In all the signs and the wonders, which the LORD sent him to do in the land of Egypt to Pharaoh, and to all his servants, and to all his land,

12And in all that mighty hand, and in all the great terror which Moses showed in the sight of all Israel.

New International

22About Dan he said:

"Dan is a lion's cub,
    springing out of Bashan."

23About Naphtali he said:

"Naphtali is abounding with the favor of the
        LORD
    and is full of his blessing;
he will inherit southward to the lake."

24About Asher he said:

"Most blessed of sons is Asher;
    let him be favored by his brothers,
    and let him bathe his feet in oil.
25The bolts of your gates will be iron and bronze,
    and your strength will equal your days.

26"There is no one like the God of Jeshurun,
    who rides on the heavens to help you
    and on the clouds in his majesty.
27The eternal God is your refuge,
    and underneath are the everlasting arms.
He will drive out your enemy before you,
    saying, 'Destroy him!'
28So Israel will live in safety alone;
    Jacob's spring is secure
in a land of grain and new wine,
    where the heavens drop dew.
29Blessed are you, O Israel!
    Who is like you,
    a people saved by the LORD?
He is your shield and helper
    and your glorious sword.
Your enemies will cower before you,
    and you will trample down their high
        places.a"

The Death of Moses

34 THEN MOSES climbed Mount Nebo from the plains of Moab to the top of Pisgah, across from Jericho. There the LORD showed him the whole land—from Gilead to Dan, 2all of Naphtali, the territory of Ephraim and Manasseh, all the land of Judah as far as the western sea,b 3the Negev and the whole region from the Valley of Jericho, the City of Palms, as far as Zoar. 4Then the LORD said to him, "This is the land I promised on oath to Abraham, Isaac and Jacob when I said, 'I will give it to your descendants.' I have let you see it with your eyes, but you will not cross over into it."

5And Moses the servant of the LORD died there in Moab, as the LORD had said. 6He buried himc in Moab, in the valley opposite Beth Peor, but to this day no one knows where his grave is. 7Moses was a hundred and twenty years old when he died, yet his eyes were not weak nor his strength gone. 8The Israelites grieved for Moses in the plains of Moab thirty days, until the time of weeping and mourning was over.

9Now Joshua son of Nun was filled with the spiritd of wisdom because Moses had laid his hands on him. So the Israelites listened to him and did what the LORD had commanded Moses.

10Since then, no prophet has risen in Israel like Moses, whom the LORD knew face to face, 11who did all those miraculous signs and wonders the LORD sent him to do in Egypt—to Pharaoh and to all his officials and to his whole land. 12For no one has ever shown the mighty power or performed the awesome deeds that Moses did in the sight of all Israel.

a 29 Or *will tread upon their bodies*   b 2 That is, the Mediterranean
c 6 Or *He was buried*   d 9 Or *Spirit*

Living Bible

22Of the tribe of Dan, Moses said:
"Dan is like a lion's cub
Leaping out from Bashan."
23Of the tribe of Naphtali, Moses said:
"O Naphtali, you are satisfied
With all the blessings of the Lord;
The Mediterranean coast and the Negeb
Are your home."
24Of the tribe of Asher:
"Asher is a favorite son,
Esteemed above his brothers;
He bathes his feet in oil.
25May you be protected with strong bolts
Of iron and bronze,
And may your strength match the length of your days!
26There is none like the God of Jerusalem—
He descends from the heavens
In majestic splendor to help you.
27The eternal God is your Refuge,
And underneath are the everlasting arms.
He thrusts out your enemies before you;
It is he who cries, 'Destroy them!'
28So Israel dwells safely,
Prospering in a land of corn and wine,
While the gentle rains descend from heaven.
29What blessings are yours, O Israel!
Who else has been saved by the Lord?
He is your shield and your helper!
He is your excellent sword!
Your enemies shall bow low before you,
And you shall trample on their backs!"

34 THEN MOSES climbed from the plains of
Moab to Pisgah Peak in Mount Nebo, across
from Jericho. And the Lord pointed out to him the Promised Land, as they gazed out across Gilead as far as Dan:
2"There is Naphtali; and there is Ephraim and Manasseh; and across there, Judah, extending to the Mediterranean Sea; 3there is the Negeb; and the Jordan Valley;
and Jericho, the city of palm trees; and Zoar," the Lord
told him.
4"It is the Promised Land," the Lord told Moses. "I
promised Abraham, Isaac, and Jacob that I would give
it to their descendants. Now you have seen it, but you
will not enter it."
5So Moses, the disciple of the Lord, died in the land
of Moab as the Lord had said. 6The Lord buried him in
a valley near Beth-Peor in Moab, but no one knows the
exact place.
7Moses was 120 years old when he died, yet his eyesight was perfect and he was as strong as a young man.
8The people of Israel mourned for him for thirty days on
the plains of Moab.
9Joshua (son of Nun) was full of the spirit of wisdom,
for Moses had laid his hands upon him; so the people of
Israel obeyed him, and followed the commandments the
Lord had given to Moses.
10There has never been another prophet like Moses,
for the Lord talked to him face to face. 11, 12And at
God's command he performed amazing miracles which
have never been equaled.

New Revised Standard

22 And of Dan he said:
Dan is a lion's whelp
that leaps forth from Bashan.

23 And of Naphtali he said:
O Naphtali, sated with favor,
full of the blessing of the LORD,
possess the west and the south.

24 And of Asher he said:
Most blessed of sons be Asher;
may he be the favorite of his brothers,
and may he dip his foot in oil.
25 Your bars are iron and bronze;
and as your days, so is your strength.

26 There is none like God, O Jeshurun,
who rides through the heavens to your help,
majestic through the skies.
27 He subdues the ancient gods,e
shattersf the forces of old;g
he drove out the enemy before you,
and said, "Destroy!"
28 So Israel lives in safety,
untroubled is Jacob's abodeh
in a land of grain and wine,
where the heavens drop down dew.
29 Happy are you, O Israel! Who is like you,
a people saved by the LORD,
the shield of your help,
and the sword of your triumph!
Your enemies shall come fawning to you,
and you shall tread on their backs.

Moses Dies and Is Buried in the Land of Moab

34 THEN MOSES went up from the plains of
Moab to Mount Nebo, to the top of Pisgah,
which is opposite Jericho, and the LORD showed him the
whole land: Gilead as far as Dan, 2all Naphtali, the land
of Ephraim and Manasseh, all the land of Judah as far
as the Western Sea, 3the Negeb, and the Plain—that is,
the valley of Jericho, the city of palm trees—as far as
Zoar. 4The LORD said to him, "This is the land of which
I swore to Abraham, to Isaac, and to Jacob, saying, 'I
will give it to your descendants'; I have let you see it
with your eyes, but you shall not cross over there."
5Then Moses, the servant of the LORD, died there in the
land of Moab, at the LORD's command. 6He was buried
in a valley in the land of Moab, opposite Beth-peor, but
no one knows his burial place to this day. 7Moses was
one hundred twenty years old when he died; his sight
was unimpaired and his vigor had not abated. 8The Israelites wept for Moses in the plains of Moab thirty days;
then the period of mourning for Moses was ended.
9 Joshua son of Nun was full of the spirit of wisdom,
because Moses had laid his hands on him; and the Israelites obeyed him, doing as the LORD had commanded
Moses.
10 Never since has there arisen a prophet in Israel
like Moses, whom the LORD knew face to face. 11He
was unequaled for all the signs and wonders that the
LORD sent him to perform in the land of Egypt, against
Pharaoh and all his servants and his entire land, 12and
for all the mighty deeds and all the terrifying displays
of power that Moses performed in the sight of all Israel.

e Or The eternal God is a dwelling place   f Cn: Heb from underneath   g Or
the everlasting arms   h Or fountain

THE BOOK OF

Joshua

Joshua

The LORD Commands Joshua

1 NOW AFTER the death of Moses the servant of the LORD it came to pass, that the LORD spake unto Joshua the son of Nun, Moses' minister, saying,

2Moses my servant is dead; now therefore arise, go over this Jordan, thou, and all this people, unto the land which I do give to them, *even* to the children of Israel.

3Every place that the sole of your foot shall tread upon, that have I given unto you, as I said unto Moses.

4From the wilderness and this Lebanon even unto the great river, the river Euphrates, all the land of the Hittites, and unto the great sea toward the going down of the sun, shall be your coast.

5There shall not any man be able to stand before thee all the days of thy life: as I was with Moses, *so* I will be with thee: I will not fail thee, nor forsake thee.

6Be strong and of a good courage: for unto this people shalt thou divide for an inheritance the land, which I sware unto their fathers to give them.

7Only be thou strong and very courageous, that thou mayest observe to do according to all the law, which Moses my servant commanded thee: turn not from it *to* the right hand or *to* the left, that thou mayest prosper whithersoever thou goest.

8This book of the law shall not depart out of thy mouth; but thou shalt meditate therein day and night, that thou mayest observe to do according to all that is written therein: for then thou shalt make thy way prosperous, and then thou shalt have good success.

9Have not I commanded thee? Be strong and of a good courage; be not afraid, neither be thou dismayed: for the LORD thy God *is* with thee whithersoever thou goest.

10¶ Then Joshua commanded the officers of the people, saying,

11Pass through the host, and command the people, saying, Prepare you victuals; for within three days ye shall pass over this Jordan, to go in to possess the land, which the LORD your God giveth you to possess it.

12¶ And to the Reubenites, and to the Gadites, and to half the tribe of Manasseh, spake Joshua, saying,

13Remember the word which Moses the servant of the LORD commanded you, saying, The LORD your God hath given you rest, and hath given you this land.

14Your wives, your little ones, and your cattle, shall remain in the land which Moses gave you on this side Jordan; but ye shall pass before your brethren armed, all the mighty men of valour, and help them;

15Until the LORD have given your brethren rest, as *he hath given* you, and they also have possessed the land which the LORD your God giveth them: then ye shall return unto the land of your possession, and enjoy it, which Moses the LORD's servant gave you on this side Jordan toward the sunrising.

16¶ And they answered Joshua, saying, All that thou commandest us we will do, and whithersoever thou sendest us, we will go.

1 AFTER THE death of Moses the servant of the LORD, the LORD said to Joshua son of Nun, Moses' aide: 2"Moses my servant is dead. Now then, you and all these people, get ready to cross the Jordan River into the land I am about to give to them—to the Israelites. 3I will give you every place where you set your foot, as I promised Moses. 4Your territory will extend from the desert to Lebanon, and from the great river, the Euphrates—all the Hittite country—to the Great Sea[a] on the west. 5No one will be able to stand up against you all the days of your life. As I was with Moses, so I will be with you; I will never leave you nor forsake you.

6"Be strong and courageous, because you will lead these people to inherit the land I swore to their forefathers to give them. 7Be strong and very courageous. Be careful to obey all the law my servant Moses gave you; do not turn from it to the right or to the left, that you may be successful wherever you go. 8Do not let this Book of the Law depart from your mouth; meditate on it day and night, so that you may be careful to do everything written in it. Then you will be prosperous and successful. 9Have I not commanded you? Be strong and courageous. Do not be terrified; do not be discouraged, for the LORD your God will be with you wherever you go."

10So Joshua ordered the officers of the people: 11"Go through the camp and tell the people, 'Get your supplies ready. Three days from now you will cross the Jordan here to go in and take possession of the land the LORD your God is giving you for your own.'"

12But to the Reubenites, the Gadites and the half-tribe of Manasseh, Joshua said, 13"Remember the command that Moses the servant of the LORD gave you: 'The LORD your God is giving you rest and has granted you this land.' 14Your wives, your children and your livestock may stay in the land that Moses gave you east of the Jordan, but all your fighting men, fully armed, must cross over ahead of your brothers. You are to help your brothers 15until the LORD gives them rest, as he has done for you, and until they too have taken possession of the land that the LORD your God is giving them. After that, you may go back and occupy your own land, which Moses the servant of the LORD gave you east of the Jordan toward the sunrise."

16Then they answered Joshua, "Whatever you have commanded us we will do, and wherever you send us we will go. 17Just as we fully obeyed Moses, so we will

---

a 4 That is, the Mediterranean

Joshua   Joshua

Living Bible

1 AFTER THE death of Moses, the Lord's disciple, God spoke to Moses' assistant, whose name was Joshua (the son of Nun), and said to him,

2"Now that my disciple is dead, [you are the new leader of Israelb]. Lead my people across the Jordan River into the Promised Land. 3I say to you what I said to Moses: 'Wherever you go will be part of the land of Israel— 4all the way from Negeb desert in the south to the Lebanon mountains in the north, and from the Mediterranean Sea in the west to the Euphrates River in the east, including all the land of the Hittites.' 5No one will be able to oppose you as long as you live, for I will be with you just as I was with Moses; I will not abandon you or fail to help you.

6"Be strong and brave, for you will be a successful leader of my people; and they shall conquer all the land I promised to their ancestors. 7You need only to be strong and courageous and to obey to the letter every law Moses gave you, for if you are careful to obey every one of them you will be successful in everything you do. 8Constantly remind the people about these laws, and you yourself must think about them every day and every night so that you will be sure to obey all of them. For only then will you succeed. 9Yes, be bold and strong! Banish fear and doubt! For remember, the Lord your God is with you wherever you go."

10, 11Then Joshua issued instructions to the leaders of Israel to tell the people to get ready to cross the Jordan River. "In three days we will go across and conquer and live in the land which God has given us!" he told them.

12, 13Then he summoned the leaders of the tribes of Reuben, Gad, and the half-tribe of Manasseh and reminded them of their agreement with Moses: "The Lord your God has given you a homeland here on the east side of the Jordan River," Moses had told them, 14"so your wives and children and cattle may remain here, but your troops, fully armed, must lead the other tribes across the Jordan River to help them conquer their territory on the other side; 15stay with them until they complete the conquest. Only then may you settle down here on the east side of the Jordan."

16To this they fully agreed, and pledged themselves to obey Joshua as their commander-in-chief.

New Revised Standard

God's Commission to Joshua

1 AFTER THE death of Moses the servant of the LORD, the LORD spoke to Joshua son of Nun, Moses' assistant, saying, 2"My servant Moses is dead. Now proceed to cross the Jordan, you and all this people, into the land that I am giving to them, to the Israelites. 3Every place that the sole of your foot will tread upon I have given to you, as I promised to Moses. 4From the wilderness and the Lebanon as far as the great river, the river Euphrates, all the land of the Hittites, to the Great Sea in the west shall be your territory. 5No one shall be able to stand against you all the days of your life. As I was with Moses, so I will be with you; I will not fail you or forsake you. 6Be strong and courageous; for you shall put this people in possession of the land that I swore to their ancestors to give them. 7Only be strong and very courageous, being careful to act in accordance with all the law that my servant Moses commanded you; do not turn from it to the right hand or to the left, so that you may be successful wherever you go. 8This book of the law shall not depart out of your mouth; you shall meditate on it day and night, so that you may be careful to act in accordance with all that is written in it. For then you shall make your way prosperous, and then you shall be successful. 9I hereby command you: Be strong and courageous; do not be frightened or dismayed, for the LORD your God is with you wherever you go."

Preparations for the Invasion

10 Then Joshua commanded the officers of the people, 11"Pass through the camp, and command the people: 'Prepare your provisions; for in three days you are to cross over the Jordan, to go in to take possession of the land that the LORD your God gives you to possess.' "

12 To the Reubenites, the Gadites, and the half-tribe of Manasseh Joshua said, 13"Remember the word that Moses the servant of the LORD commanded you, saying, 'The LORD your God is providing you a place of rest, and will give you this land.' 14Your wives, your little ones, and your livestock shall remain in the land that Moses gave you beyond the Jordan. But all the warriors among you shall cross over armed before your kindred and shall help them, 15until the LORD gives rest to your kindred as well as to you, and they too take possession of the land that the LORD your God is giving them. Then you shall return to your own land and take possession of it, the land that Moses the servant of the LORD gave you beyond the Jordan to the east."

16 They answered Joshua: "All that you have commanded us we will do, and wherever you send us we will go. 17Just as we obeyed Moses in all things, so we will

---

b *1:2 you are the new leader of Israel,* implied.

King James

17According as we hearkened unto Moses in all things, so will we hearken unto thee: only the LORD thy God be with thee, as he was with Moses.

18Whosoever *he be* that doth rebel against thy commandment, and will not hearken unto thy words in all that thou commandest him, he shall be put to death: only be strong and of a good courage.

2 AND JOSHUA the son of Nun sent out of Shittim two men to spy secretly, saying, Go view the land, even Jericho. And they went, and came into an harlot's house, named Rahab, and lodged there.

2And it was told the king of Jericho, saying, Behold, there came men in hither tonight of the children of Israel to search out the country.

3And the king of Jericho sent unto Rahab, saying, Bring forth the men that are come to thee, which are entered into thine house: for they be come to search out all the country.

4And the woman took the two men, and hid them, and said thus, There came men unto me, but I wist not whence they *were:*

5And it came to pass *about the time* of shutting of the gate, when it was dark, that the men went out: whither the men went I wot not: pursue after them quickly; for ye shall overtake them.

6But she had brought them up to the roof of the house, and hid them with the stalks of flax, which she had laid in order upon the roof.

7And the men pursued after them the way to Jordan unto the fords: and as soon as they which pursued after them were gone out, they shut the gate.

8¶ And before they were laid down, she came up unto them upon the roof;

9And she said unto the men, I know that the LORD hath given you the land, and that your terror is fallen upon us, and that all the inhabitants of the land faint because of you.

10For we have heard how the LORD dried up the water of the Red sea for you, when ye came out of Egypt; and what ye did unto the two kings of the Amorites, that *were* on the other side Jordan, Sihon and Og, whom ye utterly destroyed.

11And as soon as we had heard *these things,* our hearts did melt, neither did there remain any more courage in any man, because of you: for the LORD your God, he *is* God in heaven above, and in earth beneath.

12Now therefore, I pray you, swear unto me by the LORD, since I have shown you kindness, that ye will also show kindness unto my father's house, and give me a true token:

13And *that* ye will save alive my father, and my mother, and my brethren, and my sisters, and all that they have, and deliver our lives from death.

14And the men answered her, Our life for yours, if ye utter not this our business. And it shall be, when the LORD hath given us the land, that we will deal kindly and truly with thee.

15Then she let them down by a cord through the window: for her house *was* upon the town wall, and she dwelt upon the wall.

16And she said unto them, Get you to the mountain, lest the pursuers meet you; and hide yourselves there three days, until the pursuers be returned: and afterward may ye go your way.

New International

obey you. Only may the LORD your God be with you as he was with Moses. 18Whoever rebels against your word and does not obey your words, whatever you may command them, will be put to death. Only be strong and courageous!"

Rahab and the Spies

2 THEN JOSHUA son of Nun secretly sent two spies from Shittim. "Go, look over the land," he said, "especially Jericho." So they went and entered the house of a prostitutea named Rahab and stayed there.

2The king of Jericho was told, "Look! Some of the Israelites have come here tonight to spy out the land." 3So the king of Jericho sent this message to Rahab: "Bring out the men who came to you and entered your house, because they have come to spy out the whole land."

4But the woman had taken the two men and hidden them. She said, "Yes, the men came to me, but I did not know where they had come from. 5At dusk, when it was time to close the city gate, the men left. I don't know which way they went. Go after them quickly. You may catch up with them." 6(But she had taken them up to the roof and hidden them under the stalks of flax she had laid out on the roof.) 7So the men set out in pursuit of the spies on the road that leads to the fords of the Jordan, and as soon as the pursuers had gone out, the gate was shut.

8Before the spies lay down for the night, she went up on the roof 9and said to them, "I know that the LORD has given this land to you and that a great fear of you has fallen on us, so that all who live in this country are melting in fear because of you. 10We have heard how the LORD dried up the water of the Red Seab for you when you came out of Egypt, and what you did to Sihon and Og, the two kings of the Amorites east of the Jordan, whom you completely destroyed.c 11When we heard of it, our hearts melted and everyone's courage failed because of you, for the LORD your God is God in heaven above and on the earth below. 12Now then, please swear to me by the LORD that you will show kindness to my family, because I have shown kindness to you. Give me a sure sign 13that you will spare the lives of my father and mother, my brothers and sisters, and all who belong to them, and that you will save us from death."

14"Our lives for your lives!" the men assured her. "If you don't tell what we are doing, we will treat you kindly and faithfully when the LORD gives us the land."

15So she let them down by a rope through the window, for the house she lived in was part of the city wall. 16Now she had said to them, "Go to the hills so the pursuers will not find you. Hide yourselves there three days until they return, and then go on your way."

---

a *1* Or possibly *an innkeeper*   b *10* Hebrew *Yam Suph;* that is, Sea of Reeds
c *10* The Hebrew term refers to the irrevocable giving over of things or persons to the LORD, often by totally destroying them.

Living Bible

17, 18"We will obey you just as we obeyed Moses," they assured him, "and may the Lord your God be with you as he was with Moses. If anyone, no matter who, rebels against your commands, he shall die. So lead on with courage and strength!"

2 THEN JOSHUA sent two spies from the Israeli camp at Acacia to cross the river and check out the situation on the other side, especially at Jericho. They arrived at an inn operated by a woman named Rahab, who was a prostitute. They were planning to spend the night there, 2but someone informed the king of Jericho that two Israelis who were suspected of being spies had arrived in the city that evening. 3He dispatched a police squadron to Rahab's home, demanding that she surrender them.

"They are spies," he explained. "They have been sent by the Israeli leaders to discover the best way to attack us."

4But she had hidden them, so she told the officer in charge, "The men were here earlier, but I didn't know they were spies. 5They left the city at dusk as the city gates were about to close, and I don't know where they went. If you hurry you can probably catch up with them!"

6But actually she had taken them up to the roof and hidden them beneath piles of flax that were drying there. 7So the constable and his men went all the way to the Jordan River looking for them; meanwhile, the city gates were kept shut. 8Rahab went up to talk to the men before they retired for the night.

9"I know perfectly well that your God is going to give my country to you," she told them. "We are all afraid of you; everyone is terrified if the word *Israel* is even mentioned. 10For we have heard how the Lord made a path through the Red Sea for you when you left Egypt! And we know what you did to Sihon and Og, the two Amorite kings east of the Jordan, and how you ruined their land and completely destroyed their people. 11No wonder we are afraid of you! No one has any fight left in him after hearing things like that, for your God is the supreme God of heaven, not just an ordinary god. 12, 13Now I beg for this one thing: Swear to me by the sacred name of your God that when Jericho is conquered you will let me live, along with my father and mother, my brothers and sisters, and all their families. This is only fair after the way I have helped you."

14The men agreed. "If you won't betray us, we'll see to it that you and your family aren't harmed," they promised. 15"We'll defend you with our lives." Then, since her house was on top of the city wall, she let them down by a rope from a window.

16"Escape to the mountains," she told them. "Hide there for three days until the men who are searching for you have returned; then go on your way."

New Revised Standard

obey you. Only may the LORD your God be with you, as he was with Moses! 18Whoever rebels against your orders and disobeys your words, whatever you command, shall be put to death. Only be strong and courageous."

Spies Sent to Jericho

2 THEN JOSHUA son of Nun sent two men secretly from Shittim as spies, saying, "Go, view the land, especially Jericho." So they went, and entered the house of a prostitute whose name was Rahab, and spent the night there. 2The king of Jericho was told, "Some Israelites have come here tonight to search out the land." 3Then the king of Jericho sent orders to Rahab, "Bring out the men who have come to you, who entered your house, for they have come only to search out the whole land." 4But the woman took the two men and hid them. Then she said, "True, the men came to me, but I did not know where they came from. 5And when it was time to close the gate at dark, the men went out. Where the men went I do not know. Pursue them quickly, for you can overtake them." 6She had, however, brought them up to the roof and hidden them with the stalks of flax that she had laid out on the roof. 7So the men pursued them on the way to the Jordan as far as the fords. As soon as the pursuers had gone out, the gate was shut.

8 Before they went to sleep, she came up to them on the roof 9and said to the men: "I know that the LORD has given you the land, and that dread of you has fallen on us, and that all the inhabitants of the land melt in fear before you. 10For we have heard how the LORD dried up the water of the Red Sead before you when you came out of Egypt, and what you did to the two kings of the Amorites that were beyond the Jordan, to Sihon and Og, whom you utterly destroyed. 11As soon as we heard it, our hearts melted, and there was no courage left in any of us because of you. The LORD your God is indeed God in heaven above and on earth below. 12Now then, since I have dealt kindly with you, swear to me by the LORD that you in turn will deal kindly with my family. Give me a sign of good faith 13that you will spare my father and mother, my brothers and sisters, and all who belong to them, and deliver our lives from death." 14The men said to her, "Our life for yours! If you do not tell this business of ours, then we will deal kindly and faithfully with you when the LORD gives us the land."

15 Then she let them down by a rope through the window, for her house was on the outer side of the city wall and she resided within the wall itself. 16She said to them, "Go toward the hill country, so that the pursuers may not come upon you. Hide yourselves there three days, until the pursuers have returned; then afterward you may go your way." 17The men said to her, "We will

d Or *Sea of Reeds*

King James

17And the men said unto her, We *will be* blameless of this thine oath which thou hast made us swear.

18Behold, *when* we come into the land, thou shalt bind this line of scarlet thread in the window which thou didst let us down by: and thou shalt bring thy father, and thy mother, and thy brethren, and all thy father's household, home unto thee.

19And it shall be, *that* whosoever shall go out of the doors of thy house into the street, his blood *shall be* upon his head, and we *will be* guiltless: and whosoever shall be with thee in the house, his blood *shall be* on our head, if *any* hand be upon him.

20And if thou utter this our business, then we will be quit of thine oath which thou hast made us to swear.

21And she said, According unto your words, so *be* it. And she sent them away, and they departed: and she bound the scarlet line in the window.

22And they went, and came unto the mountain, and abode there three days, until the pursuers were returned: and the pursuers sought *them* throughout all the way, but found *them* not.

23¶ So the two men returned, and descended from the mountain, and passed over, and came to Joshua the son of Nun, and told him all *things* that befell them:

24And they said unto Joshua, Truly the LORD hath delivered into our hands all the land; for even all the inhabitants of the country do faint because of us.

3 AND JOSHUA rose early in the morning; and they removed from Shittim, and came to Jordan, he and all the children of Israel, and lodged there before they passed over.

2And it came to pass after three days, that the officers went through the host;

3And they commanded the people, saying, When ye see the ark of the covenant of the LORD your God, and the priests the Levites bearing it, then ye shall remove from your place, and go after it.

4Yet there shall be a space between you and it, about two thousand cubits by measure: come not near unto it, that ye may know the way by which ye must go: for ye have not passed *this* way heretofore.

5And Joshua said unto the people, Sanctify yourselves: for tomorrow the LORD will do wonders among you.

6And Joshua spake unto the priests, saying, Take up the ark of the covenant, and pass over before the people. And they took up the ark of the covenant, and went before the people.

7¶ And the LORD said unto Joshua, This day will I begin to magnify thee in the sight of all Israel, that they may know that, as I was with Moses, *so* I will be with thee.

8And thou shalt command the priests that bear the ark of the covenant, saying, When ye are come to the brink of the water of Jordan, ye shall stand still in Jordan.

9¶ And Joshua said unto the children of Israel, Come hither, and hear the words of the LORD your God.

10And Joshua said, Hereby ye shall know that the living God *is* among you, and *that* he will without fail drive out from before you the Canaanites, and the Hittites, and the Hivites, and the Perizzites, and the Girgashites, and the Amorites, and the Jebusites.

11Behold, the ark of the covenant of the Lord of all the earth passeth over before you into Jordan.

12Now therefore take you twelve men out of the tribes of Israel, out of every tribe a man.

New International

17The men said to her, "This oath you made us swear will not be binding on us 18unless, when we enter the land, you have tied this scarlet cord in the window through which you let us down, and unless you have brought your father and mother, your brothers and all your family into your house. 19If anyone goes outside your house into the street, his blood will be on his own head; we will not be responsible. As for anyone who is in the house with you, his blood will be on our head if a hand is laid on him. 20But if you tell what we are doing, we will be released from the oath you made us swear."

21"Agreed," she replied. "Let it be as you say." So she sent them away and they departed. And she tied the scarlet cord in the window.

22When they left, they went into the hills and stayed there three days, until the pursuers had searched all along the road and returned without finding them. 23Then the two men started back. They went down out of the hills, forded the river and came to Joshua son of Nun and told him everything that had happened to them. 24They said to Joshua, "The LORD has surely given the whole land into our hands; all the people are melting in fear because of us."

Crossing the Jordan

3 EARLY IN the morning Joshua and all the Israelites set out from Shittim and went to the Jordan, where they camped before crossing over. 2After three days the officers went throughout the camp, 3giving orders to the people: "When you see the ark of the covenant of the LORD your God, and the priests, who are Levites, carrying it, you are to move out from your positions and follow it. 4Then you will know which way to go, since you have never been this way before. But keep a distance of about a thousand yardsª between you and the ark; do not go near it."

5Joshua told the people, "Consecrate yourselves, for tomorrow the LORD will do amazing things among you."

6Joshua said to the priests, "Take up the ark of the covenant and pass on ahead of the people." So they took it up and went ahead of them.

7And the LORD said to Joshua, "Today I will begin to exalt you in the eyes of all Israel, so they may know that I am with you as I was with Moses. 8Tell the priests who carry the ark of the covenant: 'When you reach the edge of the Jordan's waters, go and stand in the river.' "

9Joshua said to the Israelites, "Come here and listen to the words of the LORD your God. 10This is how you will know that the living God is among you and that he will certainly drive out before you the Canaanites, Hittites, Hivites, Perizzites, Girgashites, Amorites and Jebusites. 11See, the ark of the covenant of the Lord of all the earth will go into the Jordan ahead of you. 12Now then, choose twelve men from the tribes of Israel, one from each tribe. 13And as soon as the priests who carry

ª *4* Hebrew *about two thousand cubits* (about 900 meters)

Living Bible

17, 18But before they left, the men had said to her, "We cannot be responsible for what happens to you unless this rope is hanging from this window and unless all your relatives—your father, mother, brothers, and anyone else—are here inside the house. 19If they go out into the street we assume no responsibility whatsoever; but we swear that no one inside this house will be killed or injured. 20However, if you betray us, then this oath will no longer bind us in any way."

21"I accept your terms," she replied. And she left the scarlet rope hanging from the window.

22The spies went up into the mountains and stayed there three days, until the men who were chasing them had returned to the city after searching everywhere along the road without success. 23Then the two spies came down from the mountain and crossed the river and reported to Joshua all that had happened to them. 24"The Lord will certainly give us the entire land," they said, "for all the people over there are scared to death of us."

3 EARLY THE next morning Joshua and all the people of Israel left Acacia, and arrived that evening at the banks of the Jordan River, where they camped for a few days before crossing.

2, 3, 4On the third day, officers went through the camp giving these instructions: "When you see the priests carrying the Ark of God,b follow them. You have never before been where we are going now, so they will guide you. However, stay about a half mile behind, with a clear space between you and the Ark; be sure that you don't get any closer."

5Then Joshua told the people to purify themselves. "For tomorrow," he said, "the Lord will do a great miracle."

6In the morning Joshua ordered the priests, "Take up the Ark and lead us across the river!" And so they started out.

7"Today," the Lord told Joshua, "I will give you great honor, so that all Israel will know that I am with you just as I was with Moses. 8Instruct the priests who are carrying the Ark to stop at the edge of the river."

9Then Joshua summoned all the people and told them, "Come and listen to what the Lord your God has said. 10Today you are going to know for sure that the living God is among you and that he will, without fail, drive out the Canaanites, Hittites, Hivites, Perizzites, Girgashites, Amorites, and Jebusites—all the people who now live in the land you will soon occupy. 11Think of it! The Ark of God, who is Lord of the whole earth, will lead you across the river!

12"Now select twelve men, one from each tribe, for a special task.c 13, 14When the priests who are carrying

New Revised Standard

be released from this oath that you have made us swear to you 18if we invade the land and you do not tie this crimson cord in the window through which you let us down, and you do not gather into your house your father and mother, your brothers, and all your family. 19If any of you go out of the doors of your house into the street, they shall be responsible for their own death, and we shall be innocent; but if a hand is laid upon any who are with you in the house, we shall bear the responsibility for their death. 20But if you tell this business of ours, then we shall be released from this oath that you made us swear to you." 21She said, "According to your words, so be it." She sent them away and they departed. Then she tied the crimson cord in the window.

22   They departed and went into the hill country and stayed there three days, until the pursuers returned. The pursuers had searched all along the way and found nothing. 23Then the two men came down again from the hill country. They crossed over, came to Joshua son of Nun, and told him all that had happened to them. 24They said to Joshua, "Truly the LORD has given all the land into our hands; moreover all the inhabitants of the land melt in fear before us."

Israel Crosses the Jordan

3 EARLY IN the morning Joshua rose and set out from Shittim with all the Israelites, and they came to the Jordan. They camped there before crossing over. 2At the end of three days the officers went through the camp 3and commanded the people, "When you see the ark of the covenant of the LORD your God being carried by the levitical priests, then you shall set out from your place. Follow it, 4so that you may know the way you should go, for you have not passed this way before. Yet there shall be a space between you and it, a distance of about two thousand cubits; do not come any nearer to it." 5Then Joshua said to the people, "Sanctify yourselves; for tomorrow the LORD will do wonders among you." 6To the priests Joshua said, "Take up the ark of the covenant, and pass on in front of the people." So they took up the ark of the covenant and went in front of the people.

7   The LORD said to Joshua, "This day I will begin to exalt you in the sight of all Israel, so that they may know that I will be with you as I was with Moses. 8You are the one who shall command the priests who bear the ark of the covenant, 'When you come to the edge of the waters of the Jordan, you shall stand still in the Jordan.' " 9Joshua then said to the Israelites, "Draw near and hear the words of the LORD your God." 10Joshua said, "By this you shall know that among you is the living God who without fail will drive out from before you the Canaanites, Hittites, Hivites, Perizzites, Girgashites, Amorites, and Jebusites: 11the ark of the covenant of the Lord of all the earth is going to pass before you into the Jordan. 12So now select twelve men from the tribes of Israel, one from each tribe. 13When the

---

b 3:2-4 the Ark of God, literally, "the Ark of the covenant of the Lord."
c 3:12 for a special task. Their duties are explained in 4:2-7.

King James

13And it shall come to pass, as soon as the soles of the feet of the priests that bear the ark of the LORD, the Lord of all the earth, shall rest in the waters of Jordan, *that* the waters of Jordan shall be cut off *from* the waters that come down from above; and they shall stand upon an heap.

14¶ And it came to pass, when the people removed from their tents, to pass over Jordan, and the priests bearing the ark of the covenant before the people;

15And as they that bare the ark were come unto Jordan, and the feet of the priests that bare the ark were dipped in the brim of the water, (for Jordan overfloweth all his banks all the time of harvest,)

16That the waters which came down from above stood *and* rose up upon an heap very far from the city Adam, that *is* beside Zaretan: and those that came down toward the sea of the plain, *even* the salt sea, failed, *and* were cut off: and the people passed over right against Jericho.

17And the priests that bare the ark of the covenant of the LORD stood firm on dry ground in the midst of Jordan, and all the Israelites passed over on dry ground, until all the people were passed clean over Jordan.

4 AND IT came to pass, when all the people were clean passed over Jordan, that the LORD spake unto Joshua, saying,

2Take you twelve men out of the people, out of every tribe a man,

3And command ye them, saying, Take ye hence out of the midst of Jordan, out of the place where the priests' feet stood firm, twelve stones, and ye shall carry them over with you, and leave them in the lodging place, where ye shall lodge this night.

4Then Joshua called the twelve men, whom he had prepared of the children of Israel, out of every tribe a man:

5And Joshua said unto them, Pass over before the ark of the LORD your God into the midst of Jordan, and take you up every man of you a stone upon his shoulder, according unto the number of the tribes of the children of Israel:

6That this may be a sign among you, *that* when your children ask *their fathers* in time to come, saying, What *mean* ye by these stones?

7Then ye shall answer them, That the waters of Jordan were cut off before the ark of the covenant of the LORD; when it passed over Jordan, the waters of Jordan were cut off: and these stones shall be for a memorial unto the children of Israel for ever.

8And the children of Israel did so as Joshua commanded, and took up twelve stones out of the midst of Jordan, as the LORD spake unto Joshua, according to the number of the tribes of the children of Israel, and carried them over with them unto the place where they lodged, and laid them down there.

9And Joshua set up twelve stones in the midst of Jordan, in the place where the feet of the priests which bare the ark of the covenant stood: and they are there unto this day.

10¶ For the priests which bare the ark stood in the midst of Jordan, until every thing was finished that the LORD commanded Joshua to speak unto the people, according to all that Moses commanded Joshua: and the people hasted and passed over.

11And it came to pass, when all the people were clean passed over, that the ark of the LORD passed over, and the priests, in the presence of the people.

12And the children of Reuben, and the children of Gad, and half the tribe of Manasseh, passed over armed before the children of Israel, as Moses spake unto them:

13About forty thousand prepared for war passed over before the LORD unto battle, to the plains of Jericho.

New International

the ark of the LORD—the Lord of all the earth—set foot in the Jordan, its waters flowing downstream will be cut off and stand up in a heap."

14So when the people broke camp to cross the Jordan, the priests carrying the ark of the covenant went ahead of them. 15Now the Jordan is at flood stage all during harvest. Yet as soon as the priests who carried the ark reached the Jordan and their feet touched the water's edge, 16the water from upstream stopped flowing. It piled up in a heap a great distance away, at a town called Adam in the vicinity of Zarethan, while the water flowing down to the Sea of the Arabah (the Salt Sea a) was completely cut off. So the people crossed over opposite Jericho. 17The priests who carried the ark of the covenant of the LORD stood firm on dry ground in the middle of the Jordan, while all Israel passed by until the whole nation had completed the crossing on dry ground.

4 WHEN THE whole nation had finished crossing the Jordan, the LORD said to Joshua, 2"Choose twelve men from among the people, one from each tribe, 3and tell them to take up twelve stones from the middle of the Jordan from right where the priests stood and to carry them over with you and put them down at the place where you stay tonight."

4So Joshua called together the twelve men he had appointed from the Israelites, one from each tribe, 5and said to them, "Go over before the ark of the LORD your God into the middle of the Jordan. Each of you is to take up a stone on his shoulder, according to the number of the tribes of the Israelites, 6to serve as a sign among you. In the future, when your children ask you, 'What do these stones mean?' 7tell them that the flow of the Jordan was cut off before the ark of the covenant of the LORD. When it crossed the Jordan, the waters of the Jordan were cut off. These stones are to be a memorial to the people of Israel forever."

8So the Israelites did as Joshua commanded them. They took twelve stones from the middle of the Jordan, according to the number of the tribes of the Israelites, as the LORD had told Joshua; and they carried them over with them to their camp, where they put them down. 9Joshua set up the twelve stones that had beenb in the middle of the Jordan at the spot where the priests who carried the ark of the covenant had stood. And they are there to this day.

10Now the priests who carried the ark remained standing in the middle of the Jordan until everything the LORD had commanded Joshua was done by the people, just as Moses had directed Joshua. The people hurried over, 11and as soon as all of them had crossed, the ark of the LORD and the priests came to the other side while the people watched. 12The men of Reuben, Gad and the half-tribe of Manasseh crossed over, armed, in front of the Israelites, as Moses had directed them. 13About forty thousand armed for battle crossed over before the LORD to the plains of Jericho for war.

a *16* That is, the Dead Sea   b *9* Or *Joshua also set up twelve stones*

Living Bible

the Ark touch the water with their feet, the river will stop flowing as though held back by a dam, and will pile up as though against an invisible wall!" Now it was the harvest season and the Jordan was overflowing all its banks; but as the people set out to cross the river and as the feet of the priests who were carrying the Ark touched the water at the river's edge, 15, 16suddenly, far up the river at the city of Adam, near Zarethan, the water began piling up as though against a dam! And the water below that point flowed on to the Dead Sea until the riverbed was empty. Then all the people crossed at a spot where the river was close to the city of Jericho, 17and the priests who were carrying the Ark stood on dry ground in the middle of the Jordan and waited as all the people passed by.

4 WHEN ALL the people were safely across, the Lord said to Joshua,

2, 3"Tell the twelve men chosen for a special task, one from each tribe, each to take a stone from where the priests are standing in the middle of the Jordan, and to carry them out and pile them up as a monument at the place where you camp tonight."

4So Joshua summoned the twelve men, 5and told them, "Go out into the middle of the Jordan where the Ark is. Each of you is to carry out a stone on your shoulder—twelve stones in all, one for each of the twelve tribes. 6We will use them to build a monument so that in the future, when your children ask, 'What is this monument for?' 7you can tell them, 'It is to remind us that the Jordan River stopped flowing when the Ark of God went across!' The monument will be a permanent reminder to the people of Israel of this amazing miracle."

8So the men did as Joshua told them. They took twelve stones from the middle of the Jordan river—one for each tribe, just as the Lord had commanded Joshua. They carried them to the place where they were camped for the night and constructed a monument there. 9Joshua also built another monument of twelve stones in the middle of the river, at the place where the priests were standing; and it is there to this day. 10The priests who were carrying the Ark stood in the middle of the river until all these instructions of the Lord, which had been given to Joshua by Moses, had been carried out. Meanwhile, the people had hurried across the riverbed, 11and when everyone was over, the people watched the priests carry the Ark up out of the riverbed.

12, 13The troops of Reuben, Gad, and the half-tribe of Manasseh—fully armed as Moses had instructed, and forty thousand strong—led the other tribes of the Lord's army across to the plains of Jericho.

New Revised Standard

soles of the feet of the priests who bear the ark of the LORD, the Lord of all the earth, rest in the waters of the Jordan, the waters of the Jordan flowing from above shall be cut off; they shall stand in a single heap."

14 When the people set out from their tents to cross over the Jordan, the priests bearing the ark of the covenant were in front of the people. 15Now the Jordan overflows all its banks throughout the time of harvest. So when those who bore the ark had come to the Jordan, and the feet of the priests bearing the ark were dipped in the edge of the water, 16the waters flowing from above stood still, rising up in a single heap far off at Adam, the city that is beside Zarethan, while those flowing toward the sea of the Arabah, the Dead Sea,c were wholly cut off. Then the people crossed over opposite Jericho. 17While all Israel were crossing over on dry ground, the priests who bore the ark of the covenant of the LORD stood on dry ground in the middle of the Jordan, until the entire nation finished crossing over the Jordan.

Twelve Stones Set Up at Gilgal

4 WHEN THE entire nation had finished crossing over the Jordan, the LORD said to Joshua: 2"Select twelve men from the people, one from each tribe, 3and command them, 'Take twelve stones from here out of the middle of the Jordan, from the place where the priests' feet stood, carry them over with you, and lay them down in the place where you camp tonight.'" 4Then Joshua summoned the twelve men from the Israelites, whom he had appointed, one from each tribe. 5Joshua said to them, "Pass on before the ark of the LORD your God into the middle of the Jordan, and each of you take up a stone on his shoulder, one for each of the tribes of the Israelites, 6so that this may be a sign among you. When your children ask in time to come, 'What do those stones mean to you?' 7then you shall tell them that the waters of the Jordan were cut off in front of the ark of the covenant of the LORD. When it crossed over the Jordan, the waters of the Jordan were cut off. So these stones shall be to the Israelites a memorial forever."

8 The Israelites did as Joshua commanded. They took up twelve stones out of the middle of the Jordan, according to the number of the tribes of the Israelites, as the LORD told Joshua, carried them over with them to the place where they camped, and laid them down there. 9(Joshua set up twelve stones in the middle of the Jordan, in the place where the feet of the priests bearing the ark of the covenant had stood; and they are there to this day.)

10 The priests who bore the ark remained standing in the middle of the Jordan, until everything was finished that the LORD commanded Joshua to tell the people, according to all that Moses had commanded Joshua. The people crossed over in haste. 11As soon as all the people had finished crossing over, the ark of the LORD, and the priests, crossed over in front of the people. 12The Reubenites, the Gadites, and the half-tribe of Manasseh crossed over armed before the Israelites, as Moses had ordered them. 13About forty thousand armed for war crossed over before the LORD to the plains of Jericho for battle.

c Heb *Salt Sea*

King James

14¶ On that day the LORD magnified Joshua in the sight of all Israel; and they feared him, as they feared Moses, all the days of his life.

15And the LORD spake unto Joshua, saying,

16Command the priests that bear the ark of the testimony, that they come up out of Jordan.

17Joshua therefore commanded the priests, saying, Come ye up out of Jordan.

18And it came to pass, when the priests that bare the ark of the covenant of the LORD were come up out of the midst of Jordan, *and* the soles of the priests' feet were lifted up unto the dry land, that the waters of Jordan returned unto their place, and flowed over all his banks, as *they did* before.

19¶ And the people came up out of Jordan on the tenth *day* of the first month, and encamped in Gilgal, in the east border of Jericho.

20And those twelve stones, which they took out of Jordan, did Joshua pitch in Gilgal.

21And he spake unto the children of Israel, saying, When your children shall ask their fathers in time to come, saying, What *mean* these stones?

22Then ye shall let your children know, saying, Israel came over this Jordan on dry land.

23For the LORD your God dried up the waters of Jordan from before you, until ye were passed over, as the LORD your God did to the Red sea, which he dried up from before us, until we were gone over:

24That all the people of the earth might know the hand of the LORD, that it *is* mighty: that ye might fear the LORD your God for ever.

5　　AND IT came to pass, when all the kings of the Amorites, which *were* on the side of Jordan westward, and all the kings of the Canaanites, which *were* by the sea, heard that the LORD had dried up the waters of the Jordan from before the children of Israel, until we were passed over, that their heart melted, neither was there spirit in them any more, because of the children of Israel.

2¶ At that time the LORD said unto Joshua, Make thee sharp knives, and circumcise again the children of Israel the second time.

3And Joshua made him sharp knives, and circumcised the children of Israel at the hill of the foreskins.

4And this *is* the cause why Joshua did circumcise: All the people that came out of Egypt, *that were* males, *even* all the men of war, died in the wilderness by the way, after they came out of Egypt.

5Now all the people that came out were circumcised: but all the people *that were* born in the wilderness by the way as they came forth out of Egypt, *them* they had not circumcised.

6For the children of Israel walked forty years in the wilderness, till all the people *that were* men of war, which came out of Egypt, were consumed, because they obeyed not the voice of the LORD: unto whom the LORD sware that he would not show them the land, which the LORD sware unto their fathers that he would give us, a land that floweth with milk and honey.

7And their children, *whom* he raised up in their stead, them Joshua circumcised: for they were uncircumcised, because they had not circumcised them by the way.

8And it came to pass, when they had done circumcising all the people, that they abode in their places in the camp, till they were whole.

9And the LORD said unto Joshua, This day have I rolled away the reproach of Egypt from off you. Wherefore the name of the place is called Gilgal unto this day.

New International

14That day the LORD exalted Joshua in the sight of all Israel; and they revered him all the days of his life, just as they had revered Moses.

15Then the LORD said to Joshua, 16"Command the priests carrying the ark of the Testimony to come up out of the Jordan."

17So Joshua commanded the priests, "Come up out of the Jordan."

18And the priests came up out of the river carrying the ark of the covenant of the LORD. No sooner had they set their feet on the dry ground than the waters of the Jordan returned to their place and ran at flood stage as before.

19On the tenth day of the first month the people went up from the Jordan and camped at Gilgal on the eastern border of Jericho. 20And Joshua set up at Gilgal the twelve stones they had taken out of the Jordan. 21He said to the Israelites, "In the future when your descendants ask their fathers, 'What do these stones mean?' 22tell them, 'Israel crossed the Jordan on dry ground.' 23For the LORD your God dried up the Jordan before you until you had crossed over. The LORD your God did to the Jordan just what he had done to the Red Sea[a] when he dried it up before us until we had crossed over. 24He did this so that all the peoples of the earth might know that the hand of the LORD is powerful and so that you might always fear the LORD your God."

Circumcision at Gilgal

5　　NOW WHEN all the Amorite kings west of the Jordan and all the Canaanite kings along the coast heard how the LORD had dried up the Jordan before the Israelites until we had crossed over, their hearts melted and they no longer had the courage to face the Israelites.

2At that time the LORD said to Joshua, "Make flint knives and circumcise the Israelites again." 3So Joshua made flint knives and circumcised the Israelites at Gibeath Haaraloth.[b]

4Now this is why he did so: All those who came out of Egypt—all the men of military age—died in the desert on the way after leaving Egypt. 5All the people that came out had been circumcised, but all the people born in the desert during the journey from Egypt had not. 6The Israelites had moved about in the desert forty years until all the men who were of military age when they left Egypt had died, since they had not obeyed the LORD. For the LORD had sworn to them that they would not see the land that he had solemnly promised their fathers to give us, a land flowing with milk and honey. 7So he raised up their sons in their place, and these were the ones Joshua circumcised. They were still uncircumcised because they had not been circumcised on the way. 8And after the whole nation had been circumcised, they remained where they were in camp until they were healed.

9Then the LORD said to Joshua, "Today I have rolled away the reproach of Egypt from you." So the place has been called Gilgal[c] to this day.

---

a 23 Hebrew *Yam Suph*; that is, Sea of Reeds　　b 3 *Gibeath Haaraloth* means *hill of foreskins*.　　c 9 *Gilgal* sounds like the Hebrew for *roll*.

Living Bible

14It was a tremendous day for Joshua! The Lord made him great in the eyes of all the people of Israel, and they revered him as much as they had Moses, and respected him deeply all the rest of his life. 15, 16For it was Joshua who, at the Lord's command, issued the orders to the priests carrying the Ark.

"Come up from the riverbed," the Lord now told him to command them.

17So Joshua issued the order. 18And as soon as the priests came out, the water poured down again as usual and overflowed the banks of the river as before! 19This miracle occurred on the 25th of March.d That day the entire nation crossed the Jordan River and camped in Gilgal at the eastern edge of the city of Jericho; 20and there the twelve stones from the Jordan were piled up as a monument.

21Then Joshua explained again the purpose of the stones: "In the future," he said, "when your children ask you why these stones are here and what they mean, 22you are to tell them that these stones are a reminder of this amazing miracle—that the nation of Israel crossed the Jordan River on dry ground! 23Tell them how the Lord our God dried up the river right before our eyes, and then kept it dry until we were all across! It is the same thing the Lord did forty years agoe at the Red Sea! 24He did this so that all the nations of the earth will realize that Jehovah is the mighty God, and so that all of you will worship him forever."

5 WHEN THE nations west of the Jordan River— the Amorites and Canaanites who lived along the Mediterranean coast—heard that the Lord had dried up the Jordan River so the people of Israel could cross, their courage melted away completely and they were paralyzed with fear.

2, 3The Lord then told Joshua to set aside a day to circumcise the entire male population of Israel. (It was the second time in Israel's history that this was done.) The Lord instructed them to manufacture flint knives for this purpose. The place where the circumcision rite took place was named "The Hill of the Foreskins." 4, 5The reason for this second circumcision ceremony was that although when Israel left Egypt all of the men who had been old enough to bear arms had been circumcised, that entire generation had died during the years in the wilderness, and none of the boys born since that time had been circumcised. 6For the nation of Israel had traveled back and forth across the wilderness for forty years until all the men who had been old enough to bear arms when they left Egypt were dead; they had not obeyed the Lord, and he vowed that he wouldn't let them enter the land he had promised to Israel—a land that "flowed with milk and honey." 7So now Joshua circumcised their children—the men who had grown up to take their fathers' places.

8, 9And the Lord said to Joshua, "Today I have ended your shame of not being circumcised." So the place where this was done was called Gilgal (meaning, "to end"f), and is still called that today. After the ceremony the entire nation rested in camp until the raw flesh of their wounds had been healed.

New Revised Standard

14 On that day the LORD exalted Joshua in the sight of all Israel; and they stood in awe of him, as they had stood in awe of Moses, all the days of his life.

15 The LORD said to Joshua, 16"Command the priests who bear the ark of the covenant,g to come up out of the Jordan." 17Joshua therefore commanded the priests, "Come up out of the Jordan." 18When the priests bearing the ark of the covenant of the LORD came up from the middle of the Jordan, and the soles of the priests' feet touched dry ground, the waters of the Jordan returned to their place and overflowed all its banks, as before.

19 The people came up out of the Jordan on the tenth day of the first month, and they camped in Gilgal on the east border of Jericho. 20Those twelve stones, which they had taken out of the Jordan, Joshua set up in Gilgal, 21saying to the Israelites, "When your children ask their parents in time to come, 'What do these stones mean?' 22then you shall let your children know, 'Israel crossed over the Jordan here on dry ground.' 23For the LORD your God dried up the waters of the Jordan for you until you crossed over, as the LORD your God did to the Red Sea,h which he dried up for us until we crossed over, 24so that all the peoples of the earth may know that the hand of the LORD is mighty, and so that you may fear the LORD your God forever."

The New Generation Circumcised

5 WHEN ALL the kings of the Amorites beyond the Jordan to the west, and all the kings of the Canaanites by the sea, heard that the LORD had dried up the waters of the Jordan for the Israelites until they had crossed over, their hearts melted, and there was no longer any spirit in them, because of the Israelites.

2 At that time the LORD said to Joshua, "Make flint knives and circumcise the Israelites a second time." 3So Joshua made flint knives, and circumcised the Israelites at Gibeath-haaraloth.i 4This is the reason why Joshua circumcised them: all the males of the people who came out of Egypt, all the warriors, had died during the journey through the wilderness after they had come out of Egypt. 5Although all the people who came out had been circumcised, yet all the people born on the journey through the wilderness after they had come out of Egypt had not been circumcised. 6For the Israelites traveled forty years in the wilderness, until all the nation, the warriors who came out of Egypt, perished, not having listened to the voice of the LORD. To them the LORD swore that he would not let them see the land that he had sworn to their ancestors to give us, a land flowing with milk and honey. 7So it was their children, whom he raised up in their place, that Joshua circumcised; for they were uncircumcised, because they had not been circumcised on the way.

8 When the circumcising of all the nation was done, they remained in their places in the camp until they were healed. 9The LORD said to Joshua, "Today I have rolled away from you the disgrace of Egypt." And so that place is called Gilgalj to this day.

---

d 4:19 the 25th of March, literally, "The tenth day of the first month" (of the Jewish calendar).   e 4:23 forty years ago, implied.   f 5:8, 9 your shame of not being circumcised, literally "the shame of Egypt." to end, literally, "to roll" (away).

g Or treaty, or testimony; Heb eduth   h Or Sea of Reeds   i That is the Hill of the Foreskins   j Related to Heb galal to roll

King James

10¶ And the children of Israel encamped in Gilgal, and kept the passover on the fourteenth day of the month at even in the plains of Jericho.

11And they did eat of the old corn of the land on the morrow after the passover, unleavened cakes, and parched *corn* in the selfsame day.

12¶ And the manna ceased on the morrow after they had eaten of the old corn of the land; neither had the children of Israel manna any more; but they did eat of the fruit of the land of Canaan that year.

13¶ And it came to pass, when Joshua was by Jericho, that he lifted up his eyes and looked, and, behold, there stood a man over against him with his sword drawn in his hand: and Joshua went unto him, and said unto him, *Art* thou for us, or for our adversaries?

14And he said, Nay; but *as* captain of the host of the LORD am I now come. And Joshua fell on his face to the earth, and did worship, and said unto him, What saith my lord unto his servant?

15And the captain of the LORD's host said unto Joshua, Loose thy shoe from off thy foot; for the place whereon thou standest *is* holy. And Joshua did so.

6   NOW JERICHO was straitly shut up because of the children of Israel: none went out, and none came in.

2And the LORD said unto Joshua, See, I have given into thine hand Jericho, and the king thereof, *and* the mighty men of valour.

3And ye shall compass the city, all *ye* men of war, *and* go round about the city once. Thus shalt thou do six days.

4And seven priests shall bear before the ark seven trumpets of rams' horns: and the seventh day ye shall compass the city seven times, and the priests shall blow with the trumpets.

5And it shall come to pass, that when they make a long *blast* with the ram's horn, *and* when ye hear the sound of the trumpet, all the people shall shout with a great shout; and the wall of the city shall fall down flat, and the people shall ascend up every man straight before him.

6¶ And Joshua the son of Nun called the priests, and said unto them, Take up the ark of the covenant, and let seven priests bear seven trumpets of rams' horns before the ark of the LORD.

7And he said unto the people, Pass on, and compass the city, and let him that is armed pass on before the ark of the LORD.

8¶ And it came to pass, when Joshua had spoken unto the people, that the seven priests bearing the seven trumpets of rams' horns passed on before the LORD, and blew with the trumpets: and the ark of the covenant of the LORD followed them.

9¶ And the armed men went before the priests that blew with the trumpets, and the rearward came after the ark, *the priests* going on, and blowing with the trumpets.

10And Joshua had commanded the people, saying, Ye shall not shout, nor make any noise with your voice, neither shall *any* word proceed out of your mouth, until the day I bid you shout; then shall ye shout.

11So the ark of the LORD compassed the city, going about *it* once: and they came into the camp, and lodged in the camp.

New International

10On the evening of the fourteenth day of the month, while camped at Gilgal on the plains of Jericho, the Israelites celebrated the Passover. 11The day after the Passover, that very day, they ate some of the produce of the land: unleavened bread and roasted grain. 12The manna stopped the day after^a they ate this food from the land; there was no longer any manna for the Israelites, but that year they ate of the produce of Canaan.

The Fall of Jericho

13Now when Joshua was near Jericho, he looked up and saw a man standing in front of him with a drawn sword in his hand. Joshua went up to him and asked, "Are you for us or for our enemies?"

14"Neither," he replied, "but as commander of the army of the LORD I have now come." Then Joshua fell facedown to the ground in reverence, and asked him, "What message does my Lord^b have for his servant?"

15The commander of the LORD's army replied, "Take off your sandals, for the place where you are standing is holy." And Joshua did so.

6   NOW JERICHO was tightly shut up because of the Israelites. No one went out and no one came in.

2Then the LORD said to Joshua, "See, I have delivered Jericho into your hands, along with its king and its fighting men. 3March around the city once with all the armed men. Do this for six days. 4Have seven priests carry trumpets of rams' horns in front of the ark. On the seventh day, march around the city seven times, with the priests blowing the trumpets. 5When you hear them sound a long blast on the trumpets, have all the people give a loud shout; then the wall of the city will collapse and the people will go up, every man straight in."

6So Joshua son of Nun called the priests and said to them, "Take up the ark of the covenant of the LORD and have seven priests carry trumpets in front of it." 7And he ordered the people, "Advance! March around the city, with the armed guard going ahead of the ark of the LORD."

8When Joshua had spoken to the people, the seven priests carrying the seven trumpets before the LORD went forward, blowing their trumpets, and the ark of the LORD's covenant followed them. 9The armed guard marched ahead of the priests who blew the trumpets, and the rear guard followed the ark. All this time the trumpets were sounding. 10But Joshua had commanded the people, "Do not give a war cry, do not raise your voices, do not say a word until the day I tell you to shout. Then shout!" 11So he had the ark of the LORD carried around the city, circling it once. Then the people returned to camp and spent the night there.

Living Bible

¹⁰While they were camped at Gilgal on the plains of Jericho, they celebrated the Passover during the evening of April first.ᶜ ¹¹, ¹²The next day they began to eat from the gardens and grain fields which they invaded, and they made unleavened bread. The following day no manna fell, and it was never seen again! So from that time on they lived on the crops of Canaan.

¹³As Joshua was sizing up the city of Jericho, a man appeared nearby with a drawn sword. Joshua strode over to him and demanded, "Are you friend or foe?"

¹⁴"I am the Commander-in-Chief of the Lord's army," he replied.

Joshua fell to the ground before him and worshiped him and said, "Give me your commands."

¹⁵"Take off your shoes," the Commander told him, "for this is holy ground." And Joshua did.

6 THE GATES of Jericho were kept tightly shut because the people were afraid of the Israelis; no one was allowed to go in or out.

²But the Lord said to Joshua, "Jericho and its king and all its mighty warriors are already defeated, for I have given them to you! ³, ⁴Your entire army is to walk around the city once a day for six days, followed by seven priests walking ahead of the Ark, each carrying a trumpet made from a ram's horn. On the seventh day you are to walk around the city seven times, with the priests blowing their trumpets. ⁵Then, when they give one long, loud blast, all the people are to give a mighty shout and the walls of the city will fall down; then move in upon the city from every direction."

⁶⁻⁹So Joshua summoned the priests and gave them their instructions: the armed men would lead the procession followed by seven priests blowing continually on their trumpets. Behind them would come the priests carrying the Ark, followed by a rear guard.

¹⁰"Let there be complete silence except for the trumpets," Joshua commanded. "Not a single word from any of you until I tell you to shout; then *shout!*"

¹¹The Ark was carried around the city once that day, after which everyone returned to the camp again and spent the night there. ¹², ¹³, ¹⁴At dawn the next morning

New Revised Standard

The Passover at Gilgal

10 While the Israelites were camped in Gilgal they kept the passover in the evening on the fourteenth day of the month in the plains of Jericho. ¹¹On the day after the passover, on that very day, they ate the produce of the land, unleavened cakes and parched grain. ¹²The manna ceased on the day they ate the produce of the land, and the Israelites no longer had manna; they ate the crops of the land of Canaan that year.

Joshua's Vision

13 Once when Joshua was by Jericho, he looked up and saw a man standing before him with a drawn sword in his hand. Joshua went to him and said to him, "Are you one of us, or one of our adversaries?" ¹⁴He replied, "Neither; but as commander of the army of the LORD I have now come." And Joshua fell on his face to the earth and worshiped, and he said to him, "What do you command your servant, my lord?" ¹⁵The commander of the army of the LORD said to Joshua, "Remove the sandals from your feet, for the place where you stand is holy." And Joshua did so.

Jericho Taken and Destroyed

6 NOW JERICHO was shut up inside and out because of the Israelites; no one came out and no one went in. ²The LORD said to Joshua, "See, I have handed Jericho over to you, along with its king and soldiers. ³You shall march around the city, all the warriors circling the city once. Thus you shall do for six days, ⁴with seven priests bearing seven trumpets of rams' horns before the ark. On the seventh day you shall march around the city seven times, the priests blowing the trumpets. ⁵When they make a long blast with the ram's horn, as soon as you hear the sound of the trumpet, then all the people shall shout with a great shout; and the wall of the city will fall down flat, and all the people shall charge straight ahead." ⁶So Joshua son of Nun summoned the priests and said to them, "Take up the ark of the covenant, and have seven priests carry seven trumpets of rams' horns in front of the ark of the LORD." ⁷To the people he said, "Go forward and march around the city; have the armed men pass on before the ark of the LORD."

8 As Joshua had commanded the people, the seven priests carrying the seven trumpets of rams' horns before the LORD went forward, blowing the trumpets, with the ark of the covenant of the LORD following them. ⁹And the armed men went before the priests who blew the trumpets; the rear guard came after the ark, while the trumpets blew continually. ¹⁰To the people Joshua gave this command: "You shall not shout or let your voice be heard, nor shall you utter a word, until the day I tell you to shout. Then you shall shout." ¹¹So the ark of the LORD went around the city, circling it once; and they came into the camp, and spent the night in the camp.

ᶜ *5:10 April first,* literally, "the fourteenth day of the first month" (of the Hebrew calendar).

King James

12¶ And Joshua rose early in the morning, and the priests took up the ark of the LORD.

13And seven priests bearing seven trumpets of rams' horns before the ark of the LORD went on continually, and blew with the trumpets: and the armed men went before them; but the rearward came after the ark of the LORD, *the priests* going on, and blowing with the trumpets.

14And the second day they compassed the city once, and returned into the camp: so they did six days.

15And it came to pass on the seventh day, that they rose early about the dawning of the day, and compassed the city after the same manner seven times: only on that day they compassed the city seven times.

16And it came to pass at the seventh time, when the priests blew with the trumpets, Joshua said unto the people, Shout; for the LORD hath given you the city.

17¶ And the city shall be accursed, *even* it, and all that *are* therein, to the LORD: only Rahab the harlot shall live, she and all that *are* with her in the house, because she hid the messengers that we sent.

18And ye, in any wise keep *yourselves* from the accursed thing, lest ye make *yourselves* accursed, when ye take of the accursed thing, and make the camp of Israel a curse, and trouble it.

19But all the silver, and gold, and vessels of brass and iron, *are* consecrated unto the LORD: they shall come into the treasury of the LORD.

20So the people shouted when *the priests* blew with the trumpets: and it came to pass, when the people heard the sound of the trumpet, and the people shouted with a great shout, that the wall fell down flat, so that the people went up into the city, every man straight before him, and they took the city.

21And they utterly destroyed all that *was* in the city, both man and woman, young and old, and ox, and sheep, and ass, with the edge of the sword.

22But Joshua had said unto the two men that had spied out the country, Go into the harlot's house, and bring out thence the woman, and all that she hath, as ye sware unto her.

23And the young men that were spies went in, and brought out Rahab, and her father, and her mother, and her brethren, and all that she had; and they brought out all her kindred, and left them without the camp of Israel.

24And they burnt the city with fire, and all that *was* therein: only the silver, and the gold, and the vessels of brass and of iron, they put into the treasury of the house of the LORD.

25And Joshua saved Rahab the harlot alive, and her father's household, and all that she had; and she dwelleth in Israel *even* unto this day; because she hid the messengers, which Joshua sent to spy out Jericho.

26¶ And Joshua adjured *them* at that time, saying, Cursed *be* the man before the LORD, that riseth up and buildeth this city Jericho: he shall lay the foundation thereof in his firstborn, and in his youngest *son* shall he set up the gates of it.

27So the LORD was with Joshua; and his fame was *noised* throughout all the country.

New International

12Joshua got up early the next morning and the priests took up the ark of the LORD. 13The seven priests carrying the seven trumpets went forward, marching before the ark of the LORD and blowing the trumpets. The armed men went ahead of them and the rear guard followed the ark of the LORD, while the trumpets kept sounding. 14So on the second day they marched around the city once and returned to the camp. They did this for six days.

15On the seventh day, they got up at daybreak and marched around the city seven times in the same manner, except that on that day they circled the city seven times. 16The seventh time around, when the priests sounded the trumpet blast, Joshua commanded the people, "Shout! For the LORD has given you the city! 17The city and all that is in it are to be devoteda to the LORD. Only Rahab the prostituteb and all who are with her in her house shall be spared, because she hid the spies we sent. 18But keep away from the devoted things, so that you will not bring about your own destruction by taking any of them. Otherwise you will make the camp of Israel liable to destruction and bring trouble on it. 19All the silver and gold and the articles of bronze and iron are sacred to the LORD and must go into his treasury."

20When the trumpets sounded, the people shouted, and at the sound of the trumpet, when the people gave a loud shout, the wall collapsed; so every man charged straight in, and they took the city. 21They devoted the city to the LORD and destroyed with the sword every living thing in it—men and women, young and old, cattle, sheep and donkeys.

22Joshua said to the two men who had spied out the land, "Go into the prostitute's house and bring her out and all who belong to her, in accordance with your oath to her." 23So the young men who had done the spying went in and brought out Rahab, her father and mother and brothers and all who belonged to her. They brought out her entire family and put them in a place outside the camp of Israel.

24Then they burned the whole city and everything in it, but they put the silver and gold and the articles of bronze and iron into the treasury of the LORD's house. 25But Joshua spared Rahab the prostitute, with her family and all who belonged to her, because she hid the men Joshua had sent as spies to Jericho—and she lives among the Israelites to this day.

26At that time Joshua pronounced this solemn oath: "Cursed before the LORD is the man who undertakes to rebuild this city, Jericho:

"At the cost of his firstborn son
   will he lay its foundations;
at the cost of his youngest
   will he set up its gates."

27So the LORD was with Joshua, and his fame spread throughout the land.

---

a *17* The Hebrew term refers to the irrevocable giving over of things or persons to the LORD, often by totally destroying them; also in verses 18 and 21.
b *17* Or possibly *innkeeper*; also in verses 22 and 25

Living Bible

they went around again, and returned again to the camp. They followed this pattern for six days.

15At dawn of the seventh day they started out again, but this time they went around the city not once, but seven times. 16The seventh time, as the priests blew a long, loud trumpet blast, Joshua yelled to the people, *"Shout!* The Lord has given us the city!"

17(He had told them previously, "Kill everyone except Rahab the prostitute and anyone in her house, for she protected our spies. 18Don't take any loot, for everything is to be destroyed. If it isn't, disaster will fall upon the entire nation of Israel. 19But all the silver and gold and the utensils of bronze and iron will be dedicated to the Lord, and must be brought into his treasury.")

20So when the people heard the trumpet blast, they shouted as loud as they could. And suddenly the walls of Jericho crumbled and fell before them, and the people of Israel poured into the city from every side and captured it! 21They destroyed everything in it—men and women, young and old; oxen; sheep; donkeys—everything.

22Meanwhile Joshua had said to the two spies, "Keep your promise. Go and rescue the prostitute and everyone with her."

23The young men found her and rescued her, along with her father, mother, brothers, and other relatives who were with her. Arrangements were made for them to live outside the camp of Israel. 24Then the Israelis burned the city and everything in it except that the silver and gold and the bronze and iron utensils were kept for the Lord's treasury. 25Thus Joshua saved Rahab the prostitute and her relatives who were with her in the house, and they still live among the Israelites because she hid the spies sent to Jericho by Joshua.

26Then Joshua declared a terrible curse upon anyone who might rebuild Jericho, warning that when the foundation was laid, the builder's oldest son would die, and when the gates were set up, his youngest son would die.c

27So the Lord was with Joshua, and his name became famous everywhere.

New Revised Standard

12 Then Joshua rose early in the morning, and the priests took up the ark of the Lord. 13The seven priests carrying the seven trumpets of rams' horns before the ark of the Lord passed on, blowing the trumpets continually. The armed men went before them, and the rear guard came after the ark of the Lord, while the trumpets blew continually. 14On the second day they marched around the city once and then returned to the camp. They did this for six days.

15 On the seventh day they rose early, at dawn, and marched around the city in the same manner seven times. It was only on that day that they marched around the city seven times. 16And at the seventh time, when the priests had blown the trumpets, Joshua said to the people, "Shout! For the Lord has given you the city. 17The city and all that is in it shall be devoted to the Lord for destruction. Only Rahab the prostitute and all who are with her in her house shall live because she hid the messengers we sent. 18As for you, keep away from the things devoted to destruction, so as not to covetd and take any of the devoted things and make the camp of Israel an object for destruction, bringing trouble upon it. 19But all silver and gold, and vessels of bronze and iron, are sacred to the Lord; they shall go into the treasury of the Lord." 20So the people shouted, and the trumpets were blown. As soon as the people heard the sound of the trumpets, they raised a great shout, and the wall fell down flat; so the people charged straight ahead into the city and captured it. 21Then they devoted to destruction by the edge of the sword all in the city, both men and women, young and old, oxen, sheep, and donkeys.

22 Joshua said to the two men who had spied out the land, "Go into the prostitute's house, and bring the woman out of it and all who belong to her, as you swore to her." 23So the young men who had been spies went in and brought Rahab out, along with her father, her mother, her brothers, and all who belonged to her—they brought all her kindred out—and set them outside the camp of Israel. 24They burned down the city, and everything in it; only the silver and gold, and the vessels of bronze and iron, they put into the treasury of the house of the Lord. 25But Rahab the prostitute, with her family and all who belonged to her, Joshua spared. Her familye has lived in Israel ever since. For she hid the messengers whom Joshua sent to spy out Jericho.

26 Joshua then pronounced this oath, saying,
"Cursed before the Lord be anyone who tries
    to build this city—this Jericho!
At the cost of his firstborn he shall lay its
    foundation,
    and at the cost of his youngest he shall set
    up its gates!"

27 So the Lord was with Joshua; and his fame was in all the land.

---

c 6:26 See 1 Kings 16:34 for the fulfillment of this curse.   d Gk: Heb *devote to destruction* Compare 7.21   e Heb *She*

King James

7 BUT THE children of Israel committed a trespass in the accursed thing: for Achan, the son of Carmi, the son of Zabdi, the son of Zerah, of the tribe of Judah, took of the accursed thing: and the anger of the LORD was kindled against the children of Israel.

2And Joshua sent men from Jericho to Ai, which *is* beside Beth-aven, on the east side of Beth-el, and spake unto them, saying, Go up and view the country. And the men went up and viewed Ai.

3And they returned to Joshua, and said unto him, Let not all the people go up; but let about two or three thousand men go up and smite Ai; *and* make not all the people to labour thither; for they *are but* few.

4So there went up thither of the people about three thousand men: and they fled before the men of Ai.

5And the men of Ai smote of them about thirty and six men: for they chased them *from* before the gate *even* unto Shebarim, and smote them in the going down: wherefore the hearts of the people melted, and became as water.

6¶ And Joshua rent his clothes, and fell to the earth upon his face before the ark of the LORD until the eventide, he and the elders of Israel, and put dust upon their heads.

7And Joshua said, Alas, O Lord GOD, wherefore hast thou at all brought this people over Jordan, to deliver us into the hand of the Amorites, to destroy us? would to God we had been content, and dwelt on the other side Jordan!

8O Lord, what shall I say, when Israel turneth their backs before their enemies!

9For the Canaanites and all the inhabitants of the land shall hear *of it,* and shall environ us round, and cut off our name from the earth: and what wilt thou do unto thy great name?

10¶ And the LORD said unto Joshua, Get thee up; wherefore liest thou thus upon thy face?

11Israel hath sinned, and they have also transgressed my covenant which I commanded them: for they have even taken of the accursed thing, and have also stolen, and dissembled also, and they have put *it* even among their own stuff.

12Therefore the children of Israel could not stand before their enemies, *but* turned *their* backs before their enemies, because they were accursed: neither will I be with you any more, except ye destroy the accursed from among you.

13Up, sanctify the people, and say, Sanctify yourselves against tomorrow: for thus saith the LORD God of Israel, *There is* an accursed thing in the midst of thee, O Israel: thou canst not stand before thine enemies, until ye take away the accursed thing from among you.

14In the morning therefore ye shall be brought according to your tribes: and it shall be, *that* the tribe which the LORD taketh shall come according to the families *thereof;* and the family which the LORD shall take shall come by households; and the household which the LORD shall take shall come man by man.

15And it shall be, *that* he that is taken with the accursed thing shall be burnt with fire, he and all that he hath: because he hath transgressed the covenant of the LORD, and because he hath wrought folly in Israel.

16¶ So Joshua rose up early in the morning, and brought Israel by their tribes; and the tribe of Judah was taken:

17And he brought the family of Judah; and he took the family of the Zarhites: and he brought the family of the Zarhites man by man; and Zabdi was taken:

18And he brought his household man by man; and Achan, the son of Carmi, the son of Zabdi, the son of Zerah, of the tribe of Judah, was taken.

New International

Achan's Sin

7 BUT THE Israelites acted unfaithfully in regard to the devoted things[a]; Achan son of Carmi, the son of Zimri,[b] the son of Zerah, of the tribe of Judah, took some of them. So the LORD's anger burned against Israel.

2Now Joshua sent men from Jericho to Ai, which is near Beth Aven to the east of Bethel, and told them, "Go up and spy out the region." So the men went up and spied out Ai.

3When they returned to Joshua, they said, "Not all the people will have to go up against Ai. Send two or three thousand men to take it and do not weary all the people, for only a few men are there." 4So about three thousand men went up; but they were routed by the men of Ai, 5who killed about thirty-six of them. They chased the Israelites from the city gate as far as the stone quarries[c] and struck them down on the slopes. At this the hearts of the people melted and became like water.

6Then Joshua tore his clothes and fell facedown to the ground before the ark of the LORD, remaining there till evening. The elders of Israel did the same, and sprinkled dust on their heads. 7And Joshua said, "Ah, Sovereign LORD, why did you ever bring this people across the Jordan to deliver us into the hands of the Amorites to destroy us? If only we had been content to stay on the other side of the Jordan! 8O Lord, what can I say, now that Israel has been routed by its enemies? 9The Canaanites and the other people of the country will hear about this and they will surround us and wipe out our name from the earth. What then will you do for your own great name?"

10The LORD said to Joshua, "Stand up! What are you doing down on your face? 11Israel has sinned; they have violated my covenant, which I commanded them to keep. They have taken some of the devoted things; they have stolen, they have lied, they have put them with their own possessions. 12That is why the Israelites cannot stand against their enemies; they turn their backs and run because they have been made liable to destruction. I will not be with you anymore unless you destroy whatever among you is devoted to destruction.

13"Go, consecrate the people. Tell them, 'Consecrate yourselves in preparation for tomorrow; for this is what the LORD, the God of Israel, says: That which is devoted is among you, O Israel. You cannot stand against your enemies until you remove it.

14" 'In the morning, present yourselves tribe by tribe. The tribe that the LORD takes shall come forward clan by clan; the clan that the LORD takes shall come forward family by family; and the family that the LORD takes shall come forward man by man. 15He who is caught with the devoted things shall be destroyed by fire, along with all that belongs to him. He has violated the covenant of the LORD and has done a disgraceful thing in Israel!' "

16Early the next morning Joshua had Israel come forward by tribes, and Judah was taken. 17The clans of Judah came forward, and he took the Zerahites. He had the clan of the Zerahites come forward by families, and Zimri was taken. 18Joshua had his family come forward man by man, and Achan son of Carmi, the son of Zimri, the son of Zerah, of the tribe of Judah, was taken.

---

a *1* The Hebrew term refers to the irrevocable giving over of things or persons to the LORD, often by totally destroying them; also in verses 11, 12, 13 and 15.   b *1* See Septuagint and 1 Chron. 2:6; Hebrew *Zabdi*; also in verses 17 and 18.   c *5* Or *as far as Shebarim*

Living Bible

7 BUT THERE was sin among the Israelis. God's command to destroy everything except that which was reserved for the Lord's treasury was disobeyed. For Achan (the son of Carmi, grandson of Zabdi, and great-grandson of Zerah, of the tribe of Judah) took some loot for himself, and the Lord was very angry with the entire nation of Israel because of this.

2Soon after Jericho's defeat, Joshua sent some of his men to spy on the city of Ai, east of Bethel.

3Upon their return they told Joshua, "It's a small city and it won't take more than two or three thousand of us to destroy it; there's no point in all of us going there."

4So approximately three thousand soldiers were sent—and they were soundly defeated. 5About thirty-six of the Israelis were killed during the attack, and many others died while being chased by the men of Ai as far as the quarries. The Israeli army was paralyzed with fear at this turn of events. 6Joshua and the elders of Israel tore their clothing and lay prostrate before the Ark of the Lord until evening, with dust on their heads.

7Joshua cried out to the Lord, "O Jehovah, why have you brought us over the Jordan River if you are going to let the Amorites kill us? Why weren't we content with what we had? Why didn't we stay on the other side? 8O Lord, what am I to do now that Israel has fled from her enemies! 9For when the Canaanites and the other nearby nations hear about it, they will surround us and attack us and wipe us out. And then what will happen to the honor of your great name?"

10, 11But the Lord said to Joshua, "Get up off your face! Israel has sinned and disobeyed my commandment and has taken loot when I said it was not to be taken; and they have not only taken it, they have lied about it and have hidden it among their belongings. 12That is why the people of Israel are being defeated. That is why your men are running from their enemies—for they are cursed.d I will not stay with you any longer unless you completely rid yourselves of this sin.

13"Get up! Tell the people, 'Each of you must undergo purification rites in preparation for tomorrow, for the Lord your God of Israel says that someone has stolen from him, and you cannot defeat your enemies until you deal with this sin. 14In the morning you must come by tribes, and the Lord will point out the tribe to which the guilty man belongs. And that tribe must come by its clans and the Lord will point out the guilty clan; and the clan must come by its families, and then each member of the guilty family must come one by one. 15And the one who has stolen that which belongs to the Lord shall be burned with fire, along with everything he has, for he has violated the covenant of the Lord and has brought calamity upon all of Israel.'"

16So, early the next morning, Joshua brought the tribes of Israel before the Lord, and the tribe of Judah was indicated. 17Then he brought the clans of Judah, and the clan of Zerah was singled out. Then the families of that clan were brought before the Lord and the family of Zabdi was indicated. 18Zabdi's family was brought man by man, and his grandson Achan was found to be the guilty one.

New Revised Standard

The Sin of Achan and Its Punishment

7 BUT THE Israelites broke faith in regard to the devoted things: Achan son of Carmi son of Zabdi son of Zerah, of the tribe of Judah, took some of the devoted things; and the anger of the Lord burned against the Israelites.

2 Joshua sent men from Jericho to Ai, which is near Beth-aven, east of Bethel, and said to them, "Go up and spy out the land." And the men went up and spied out Ai. 3Then they returned to Joshua and said to him, "Not all the people need go up; about two or three thousand men should go up and attack Ai. Since they are so few, do not make the whole people toil up there." 4So about three thousand of the people went up there; and they fled before the men of Ai. 5The men of Ai killed about thirty-six of them, chasing them from outside the gate as far as Shebarim and killing them on the slope. The hearts of the people melted and turned to water.

6 Then Joshua tore his clothes, and fell to the ground on his face before the ark of the Lord until the evening, he and the elders of Israel; and they put dust on their heads. 7Joshua said, "Ah, Lord God! Why have you brought this people across the Jordan at all, to hand us over to the Amorites so as to destroy us? Would that we had been content to settle beyond the Jordan! 8O Lord, what can I say, now that Israel has turned their backs to their enemies! 9The Canaanites and all the inhabitants of the land will hear of it, and surround us, and cut off our name from the earth. Then what will you do for your great name?"

10 The Lord said to Joshua, "Stand up! Why have you fallen upon your face? 11Israel has sinned; they have transgressed my covenant that I imposed on them. They have taken some of the devoted things; they have stolen, they have acted deceitfully, and they have put them among their own belongings. 12Therefore the Israelites are unable to stand before their enemies; they turn their backs to their enemies, because they have become a thing devoted for destruction themselves. I will be with you no more, unless you destroy the devoted things from among you. 13Proceed to sanctify the people, and say, 'Sanctify yourselves for tomorrow; for thus says the Lord, the God of Israel, "There are devoted things among you, O Israel; you will be unable to stand before your enemies until you take away the devoted things from among you." 14In the morning therefore you shall come forward tribe by tribe. The tribe that the Lord takes shall come near by clans, the clan that the Lord takes shall come near by households, and the household that the Lord takes shall come near one by one. 15And the one who is taken as having the devoted things shall be burned with fire, together with all that he has, for having transgressed the covenant of the Lord, and for having done an outrageous thing in Israel.'"

16 So Joshua rose early in the morning, and brought Israel near tribe by tribe, and the tribe of Judah was taken. 17He brought near the clans of Judah, and the clan of the Zerahites was taken; and he brought near the clan of the Zerahites, family by family,e and Zabdi was taken. 18And he brought near his household one by one, and Achan son of Carmi son of Zabdi son of Zerah, of the tribe of Judah, was taken. 19Then Joshua said to

---

d 7:12 *for they are cursed,* literally, they have become "something which must be totally destroyed" or else become totally God's.

e Mss Syr: MT *man by man*

King James

19And Joshua said unto Achan, My son, give, I pray thee, glory to the LORD God of Israel, and make confession unto him; and tell me now what thou hast done; hide *it* not from me.

20And Achan answered Joshua, and said, Indeed I have sinned against the LORD God of Israel, and thus and thus have I done:

21When I saw among the spoils a goodly Babylonish garment, and two hundred shekels of silver, and a wedge of gold of fifty shekels weight, then I coveted them, and took them; and, behold, they *are* hid in the earth in the midst of my tent, and the silver under it.

22¶ So Joshua sent messengers, and they ran unto the tent; and, behold, *it was* hid in his tent, and the silver under it.

23And they took them out of the midst of the tent, and brought them unto Joshua, and unto all the children of Israel, and laid them out before the LORD.

24And Joshua, and all Israel with him, took Achan the son of Zerah, and the silver, and the garment, and the wedge of gold, and his sons, and his daughters, and his oxen, and his asses, and his sheep, and his tent, and all that he had: and they brought them unto the valley of Achor.

25And Joshua said, Why hast thou troubled us? the LORD shall trouble thee this day. And all Israel stoned him with stones, and burned them with fire, after they had stoned them with stones.

26And they raised over him a great heap of stones unto this day. So the LORD turned from the fierceness of his anger. Wherefore the name of that place was called, The valley of Achor, unto this day.

8 AND THE LORD said unto Joshua, Fear not, neither be thou dismayed: take all the people of war with thee, and arise, go up to Ai: see, I have given into thy hand the king of Ai, and his people, and his city, and his land:

2And thou shalt do to Ai and her king as thou didst unto Jericho and her king: only the spoil thereof, and the cattle thereof, shall ye take for a prey unto yourselves: lay thee an ambush for the city behind it.

3¶ So Joshua arose, and all the people of war, to go up against Ai: and Joshua chose out thirty thousand mighty men of valour, and sent them away by night.

4And he commanded them, saying, Behold, ye shall lie in wait against the city, *even* behind the city: go not very far from the city, but be ye all ready:

5And I, and all the people that *are* with me, will approach unto the city: and it shall come to pass, when they come out against us, as at the first, that we will flee before them,

6(For they will come out after us) till we have drawn them from the city; for they will say, They flee before us, as at the first: therefore we will flee before them.

7Then ye shall rise up from the ambush, and seize upon the city: for the LORD your God will deliver it into your hand.

8And it shall be, when ye have taken the city, *that* ye shall set the city on fire: according to the commandment of the LORD shall ye do. See, I have commanded you.

9¶ Joshua therefore sent them forth: and they went to lie in ambush, and abode between Beth-el and Ai, on the west side of Ai: but Joshua lodged that night among the people.

10And Joshua rose up early in the morning, and numbered the people, and went up, he and the elders of Israel, before the people to Ai.

New International

19Then Joshua said to Achan, "My son, give glory to the LORD,[a] the God of Israel, and give him the praise.[b] Tell me what you have done; do not hide it from me."

20Achan replied, "It is true! I have sinned against the LORD, the God of Israel. This is what I have done: 21When I saw in the plunder a beautiful robe from Babylonia,[c] two hundred shekels[d] of silver and a wedge of gold weighing fifty shekels,[e] I coveted them and took them. They are hidden in the ground inside my tent, with the silver underneath."

22So Joshua sent messengers, and they ran to the tent, and there it was, hidden in his tent, with the silver underneath. 23They took the things from the tent, brought them to Joshua and all the Israelites and spread them out before the LORD.

24Then Joshua, together with all Israel, took Achan son of Zerah, the silver, the robe, the gold wedge, his sons and daughters, his cattle, donkeys and sheep, his tent and all that he had, to the Valley of Achor. 25Joshua said, "Why have you brought this trouble on us? The LORD will bring trouble on you today."

Then all Israel stoned him, and after they had stoned the rest, they burned them. 26Over Achan they heaped up a large pile of rocks, which remains to this day. Then the LORD turned from his fierce anger. Therefore that place has been called the Valley of Achor[f] ever since.

Ai Destroyed

8 THEN THE LORD said to Joshua, "Do not be afraid; do not be discouraged. Take the whole army with you, and go up and attack Ai. For I have delivered into your hands the king of Ai, his people, his city and his land. 2You shall do to Ai and its king as you did to Jericho and its king, except that you may carry off their plunder and livestock for yourselves. Set an ambush behind the city."

3So Joshua and the whole army moved out to attack Ai. He chose thirty thousand of his best fighting men and sent them out at night 4with these orders: "Listen carefully. You are to set an ambush behind the city. Don't go very far from it. All of you be on the alert. 5I and all those with me will advance on the city, and when the men come out against us, as they did before, we will flee from them. 6They will pursue us until we have lured them away from the city, for they will say, 'They are running away from us as they did before.' So when we flee from them, 7you are to rise up from ambush and take the city. The LORD your God will give it into your hand. 8When you have taken the city, set it on fire. Do what the LORD has commanded. See to it; you have my orders."

9Then Joshua sent them off, and they went to the place of ambush and lay in wait between Bethel and Ai, to the west of Ai—but Joshua spent that night with the people.

10Early the next morning Joshua mustered his men, and he and the leaders of Israel marched before them to Ai. 11The entire force that was with him marched up and

a *19* A solemn charge to tell the truth   b *19* Or *and confess to him*
c *21* Hebrew *Shinar*   d *21* That is, about 5 pounds (about 2.3 kilograms)
e *21* That is, about 1 1/4 pounds (about 0.6 kilogram)   f *26 Achor* means *trouble*.

Living Bible

19Joshua said to Achan, "My son, give glory to the God of Israel and make your confession. Tell me what you have done."

20Achan replied, "I have sinned against the Lord, the God of Israel. 21For I saw a beautiful robe imported from Babylon, and some silver worth $200, and a bar of gold worth $500. I wanted them so much that I took them, and they are hidden in the ground beneath my tent, with the silver buried deeper than the rest."

22So Joshua sent some men to search for the loot. They ran to the tent and found the stolen goods hidden there just as Achan had said, with the silver buried beneath the rest. 23They brought it all to Joshua and laid it on the ground in front of him. 24Then Joshua and all the Israelites took Achan, the silver, the robe, the wedge of gold, his sons, his daughters, his oxen, donkeys, sheep, his tent, and everything he had, and brought them to the valley of Achor.

25Then Joshua said to Achan, "Why have you brought calamity upon us? The Lord will now bring calamity upon you."

And the men of Israel stoned them to death and burned their bodies, 26and piled a great heap of stones upon them. The stones are still there to this day, and even today that place is called "The Valley of Calamity." And so the fierce anger of the Lord was ended.

8 THEN THE Lord said to Joshua, "Don't be afraid or discouraged; take the entire army and go to Ai, for it is now yours to conquer. I have given the king of Ai and all of his people to you. 2You shall do to them as you did to Jericho and her king; but this time you may keep the loot and the cattle for yourselves. Set an ambush behind the city."

3, 4Before the main army left for Ai, Joshua sent thirty thousand of his bravest troops to hide in ambush close behind the city, alert for action.

5"This is the plan," he explained to them. "When our main army attacks, the men of Ai will come out to fight as they did before, and we will run away. 6We will let them chase us until they have all left the city; for they will say, 'The Israelis are running away again just as they did before!' 7Then you will jump up from your ambush and enter the city, for the Lord will give it to you. 8Set the city on fire, as the Lord has commanded. You now have your instructions."

9So they left that night and lay in ambush between Bethel and the west side of Ai; but Joshua and the rest of the army remained in the camp at Jericho. 10Early the next morning Joshua roused his men and started toward Ai, accompanied by the elders of Israel, 11, 12, 13and

New Revised Standard

Achan, "My son, give glory to the LORD God of Israel and make confession to him. Tell me now what you have done; do not hide it from me." 20And Achan answered Joshua, "It is true; I am the one who sinned against the LORD God of Israel. This is what I did: 21when I saw among the spoil a beautiful mantle from Shinar, and two hundred shekels of silver, and a bar of gold weighing fifty shekels, then I coveted them and took them. They now lie hidden in the ground inside my tent, with the silver underneath."

22 So Joshua sent messengers, and they ran to the tent; and there it was, hidden in his tent with the silver underneath. 23They took them out of the tent and brought them to Joshua and all the Israelites; and they spread them out before the LORD. 24Then Joshua and all Israel with him took Achan son of Zerah, with the silver, the mantle, and the bar of gold, with his sons and daughters, with his oxen, donkeys, and sheep, and his tent and all that he had; and they brought them up to the Valley of Achor. 25Joshua said, "Why did you bring trouble on us? The LORD is bringing trouble on you today." And all Israel stoned him to death; they burned them with fire, cast stones on them, 26and raised over him a great heap of stones that remains to this day. Then the LORD turned from his burning anger. Therefore that place to this day is called the Valley of Achor.g

Ai Captured by a Stratagem and Destroyed

8 THEN THE LORD said to Joshua, "Do not fear or be dismayed; take all the fighting men with you, and go up now to Ai. See, I have handed over to you the king of Ai with his people, his city, and his land. 2You shall do to Ai and its king as you did to Jericho and its king; only its spoil and its livestock you may take as booty for yourselves. Set an ambush against the city, behind it."

3 So Joshua and all the fighting men set out to go up against Ai. Joshua chose thirty thousand warriors and sent them out by night 4with the command, "You shall lie in ambush against the city, behind it; do not go very far from the city, but all of you stay alert. 5I and all the people who are with me will approach the city. When they come out against us, as before, we shall flee from them. 6They will come out after us until we have drawn them away from the city; for they will say, 'They are fleeing from us, as before.' While we flee from them, 7you shall rise up from the ambush and seize the city; for the LORD your God will give it into your hand. 8And when you have taken the city, you shall set the city on fire, doing as the LORD has ordered; see, I have commanded you." 9So Joshua sent them out; and they went to the place of ambush, and lay between Bethel and Ai, to the west of Ai; but Joshua spent that night in the camp.h

10 In the morning Joshua rose early and mustered the people, and went up, with the elders of Israel, before the people to Ai. 11All the fighting men who were with

g That is Trouble   h Heb among the people

King James

11And all the people, *even the people* of war that *were* with him, went up, and drew nigh, and came before the city, and pitched on the north side of Ai: now *there was* a valley between them and Ai.

12And he took about five thousand men, and set them to lie in ambush between Beth-el and Ai, on the west side of the city.

13And when they had set the people, *even* all the host that *was* on the north of the city, and their liers in wait on the west of the city, Joshua went that night into the midst of the valley.

14¶ And it came to pass, when the king of Ai saw *it*, that they hasted and rose up early, and the men of the city went out against Israel to battle, he and all his people, at a time appointed, before the plain; but he wist not that *there were* liers in ambush against him behind the city.

15And Joshua and all Israel made as if they were beaten before them, and fled by the way of the wilderness.

16And all the people that *were* in Ai were called together to pursue after them: and they pursued after Joshua, and were drawn away from the city.

17And there was not a man left in Ai or Beth-el, that went not out after Israel: and they left the city open, and pursued after Israel.

18And the LORD said unto Joshua, Stretch out the spear that *is* in thy hand toward Ai; for I will give it into thine hand. And Joshua stretched out the spear that *he had* in his hand toward the city.

19And the ambush arose quickly out of their place, and they ran as soon as he had stretched out his hand: and they entered into the city, and took it, and hasted and set the city on fire.

20And when the men of Ai looked behind them, they saw, and, behold, the smoke of the city ascended up to heaven, and they had no power to flee this way or that way: and the people that fled to the wilderness turned back upon the pursuers.

21And when Joshua and all Israel saw that the ambush had taken the city, and that the smoke of the city ascended, then they turned again, and slew the men of Ai.

22And the other issued out of the city against them; so they were in the midst of Israel, some on this side, and some on that side: and they smote them, so that they let none of them remain or escape.

23And the king of Ai they took alive, and brought him to Joshua.

24And it came to pass, when Israel had made an end of slaying all the inhabitants of Ai in the field, in the wilderness wherein they chased them, and when they were all fallen on the edge of the sword, until they were consumed, that all the Israelites returned unto Ai, and smote it with the edge of the sword.

25And *so* it was, *that* all that fell that day, both of men and women, *were* twelve thousand, *even* all the men of Ai.

26For Joshua drew not his hand back, wherewith he stretched out the spear, until he had utterly destroyed all the inhabitants of Ai.

27Only the cattle and the spoil of that city Israel took for a prey unto themselves, according unto the word of the LORD which he commanded Joshua.

28And Joshua burnt Ai, and made it an heap for ever, *even* a desolation unto this day.

29And the king of Ai he hanged on a tree until eventide: and as soon as the sun was down, Joshua commanded that they should take his carcase down from the tree, and cast it at the entering of the gate of the city, and raise thereon a great heap of stones, *that remaineth* unto this day.

30¶ Then Joshua built an altar unto the LORD God of Israel in mount Ebal,

New International

approached the city and arrived in front of it. They set up camp north of Ai, with the valley between them and the city. 12Joshua had taken about five thousand men and set them in ambush between Bethel and Ai, to the west of the city. 13They had the soldiers take up their positions—all those in the camp to the north of the city and the ambush to the west of it. That night Joshua went into the valley.

14When the king of Ai saw this, he and all the men of the city hurried out early in the morning to meet Israel in battle at a certain place overlooking the Arabah. But he did not know that an ambush had been set against him behind the city. 15Joshua and all Israel let themselves be driven back before them, and they fled toward the desert. 16All the men of Ai were called to pursue them, and they pursued Joshua and were lured away from the city. 17Not a man remained in Ai or Bethel who did not go after Israel. They left the city open and went in pursuit of Israel.

18Then the LORD said to Joshua, "Hold out toward Ai the javelin that is in your hand, for into your hand I will deliver the city." So Joshua held out his javelin toward Ai. 19As soon as he did this, the men in the ambush rose quickly from their position and rushed forward. They entered the city and captured it and quickly set it on fire.

20The men of Ai looked back and saw the smoke of the city rising against the sky, but they had no chance to escape in any direction, for the Israelites who had been fleeing toward the desert had turned back against their pursuers. 21For when Joshua and all Israel saw that the ambush had taken the city and that smoke was going up from the city, they turned around and attacked the men of Ai. 22The men of the ambush also came out of the city against them, so that they were caught in the middle, with Israelites on both sides. Israel cut them down, leaving them neither survivors nor fugitives. 23But they took the king of Ai alive and brought him to Joshua.

24When Israel had finished killing all the men of Ai in the fields and in the desert where they had chased them, and when every one of them had been put to the sword, all the Israelites returned to Ai and killed those who were in it. 25Twelve thousand men and women fell that day—all the people of Ai. 26For Joshua did not draw back the hand that held out his javelin until he had destroyed[a] all who lived in Ai. 27But Israel did carry off for themselves the livestock and plunder of this city, as the LORD had instructed Joshua.

28So Joshua burned Ai and made it a permanent heap of ruins, a desolate place to this day. 29He hung the king of Ai on a tree and left him there until evening. At sunset, Joshua ordered them to take his body from the tree and throw it down at the entrance of the city gate. And they raised a large pile of rocks over it, which remains to this day.

The Covenant Renewed at Mount Ebal

30Then Joshua built on Mount Ebal an altar to the LORD, the God of Israel, 31as Moses the servant of the

---

a 26 The Hebrew term refers to the irrevocable giving over of things or persons to the LORD, often by totally destroying them.

Living Bible

stopped at the edge of a valley north of the city. That night Joshua sent another five thousand men[b] to join the troops in ambush on the west side of the city. He himself spent the night in the valley.

14The King of Ai, seeing the Israelis across the valley, went out early the next morning and attacked at the Plain of Arabah. But of course he didn't realize that there was an ambush behind the city. 15Joshua and the Israeli army fled across the wilderness as though badly beaten, 16and all the soldiers in the city were called out to chase after them; so the city was left defenseless; 17there was not a soldier left in Ai or Bethel and the city gates were left wide open.

18Then the Lord said to Joshua, "Point your spear toward Ai, for I will give you the city." Joshua did. 19And when the men in ambush saw his signal, they jumped up and poured into the city and set it on fire. 20, 21When the men of Ai looked behind them, smoke from the city was filling the sky, and they had nowhere to go. When Joshua and the troops who were with him saw the smoke, they knew that their men who had been in ambush were inside the city, so they turned upon their pursuers and began killing them. 22Then the Israelis who were inside the city came out and began destroying the enemy from the rear. So the men of Ai were caught in a trap and all of them died; not one man survived or escaped, 23except for the king of Ai, who was captured and brought to Joshua.

24When the army of Israel had finished slaughtering all the men outside the city, they went back and finished off everyone left inside. 25So the entire population of Ai, twelve thousand in all, was wiped out that day. 26For Joshua kept his spear pointed toward Ai until the last person was dead. 27Only the cattle and the loot were not destroyed, for the armies of Israel kept these for themselves. (The Lord had told Joshua they could.) 28So Ai became a desolate mound of refuse, as it still is today.

29Joshua hanged the king of Ai on a tree until evening, but as the sun was going down, he took down the body and threw it in front of the city gate. There he piled a great heap of stones over it, which can still be seen.

30Then Joshua built an altar to the Lord God of Israel at Mount Ebal, 31as Moses had commanded[c] in the book

New Revised Standard

him went up, and drew near before the city, and camped on the north side of Ai, with a ravine between them and Ai. 12Taking about five thousand men, he set them in ambush between Bethel and Ai, to the west of the city. 13So they stationed the forces, the main encampment that was north of the city and its rear guard west of the city. But Joshua spent that night in the valley. 14When the king of Ai saw this, he and all his people, the inhabitants of the city, hurried out early in the morning to the meeting place facing the Arabah to meet Israel in battle; but he did not know that there was an ambush against him behind the city. 15And Joshua and all Israel made a pretense of being beaten before them, and fled in the direction of the wilderness. 16So all the people who were in the city were called together to pursue them, and as they pursued Joshua they were drawn away from the city. 17There was not a man left in Ai or Bethel who did not go out after Israel; they left the city open, and pursued Israel.

18 Then the Lord said to Joshua, "Stretch out the sword that is in your hand toward Ai; for I will give it into your hand." And Joshua stretched out the sword that was in his hand toward the city. 19As soon as he stretched out his hand, the troops in ambush rose quickly out of their place and rushed forward. They entered the city, took it, and at once set the city on fire. 20So when the men of Ai looked back, the smoke of the city was rising to the sky. They had no power to flee this way or that, for the people who fled to the wilderness turned back against the pursuers. 21When Joshua and all Israel saw that the ambush had taken the city and that the smoke of the city was rising, then they turned back and struck down the men of Ai. 22And the others came out from the city against them; so they were surrounded by Israelites, some on one side, and some on the other; and Israel struck them down until no one was left who survived or escaped. 23But the king of Ai was taken alive and brought to Joshua.

24 When Israel had finished slaughtering all the inhabitants of Ai in the open wilderness where they pursued them, and when all of them to the very last had fallen by the edge of the sword, all Israel returned to Ai, and attacked it with the edge of the sword. 25The total of those who fell that day, both men and women, was twelve thousand—all the people of Ai. 26For Joshua did not draw back his hand, with which he stretched out the sword, until he had utterly destroyed all the inhabitants of Ai. 27Only the livestock and the spoil of that city Israel took as their booty, according to the word of the Lord that he had issued to Joshua. 28So Joshua burned Ai, and made it forever a heap of ruins, as it is to this day. 29And he hanged the king of Ai on a tree until evening; and at sunset Joshua commanded, and they took his body down from the tree, threw it down at the entrance of the gate of the city, and raised over it a great heap of stones, which stands there to this day.

Joshua Renews the Covenant

30 Then Joshua built on Mount Ebal an altar to the Lord, the God of Israel, 31just as Moses the servant of

---

[b] 8:11-13 another five thousand men. These were evidently additional to the thirty thousand men already hiding there. Perhaps the additional five thousand were to intercept the forces expected from Bethel (vs 17). [c] 8:31 as Moses had commanded. See Deut 27:2-8.

King James

31As Moses the servant of the LORD commanded the children of Israel, as it is written in the book of the law of Moses, an altar of whole stones, over which no man hath lift up *any* iron: and they offered thereon burnt offerings unto the LORD, and sacrificed peace offerings.

32¶ And he wrote there upon the stones a copy of the law of Moses, which he wrote in the presence of the children of Israel.

33And all Israel, and their elders, and officers, and their judges, stood on this side the ark and on that side before the priests the Levites, which bare the ark of the covenant of the LORD, as well the stranger, as he that was born among them; half of them over against mount Gerizim, and half of them over against mount Ebal; as Moses the servant of the LORD had commanded before, that they should bless the people of Israel.

34And afterward he read all the words of the law, the blessings and cursings, according to all that is written in the book of the law.

35There was not a word of all that Moses commanded, which Joshua read not before all the congregation of Israel, with the women, and the little ones, and the strangers that were conversant among them.

9 AND IT came to pass, when all the kings which *were* on this side Jordan, in the hills, and in the valleys, and in all the coasts of the great sea over against Lebanon, the Hittite, and the Amorite, the Canaanite, the Perizzite, the Hivite, and the Jebusite, heard *thereof;*

2That they gathered themselves together, to fight with Joshua and with Israel, with one accord.

3¶ And when the inhabitants of Gibeon heard what Joshua had done unto Jericho and to Ai,

4They did work wilily, and went and made as if they had been ambassadors, and took old sacks upon their asses, and wine bottles, old, and rent, and bound up;

5And old shoes and clouted upon their feet, and old garments upon them; and all the bread of their provision was dry *and* mouldy.

6And they went to Joshua unto the camp at Gilgal, and said unto him, and to the men of Israel, We be come from a far country: now therefore make ye a league with us.

7And the men of Israel said unto the Hivites, Peradventure ye dwell among us; and how shall we make a league with you?

8And they said unto Joshua, We *are* thy servants. And Joshua said unto them, Who *are* ye? and from whence come ye?

9And they said unto him, From a very far country thy servants are come because of the name of the LORD thy God: for we have heard the fame of him, and all that he did in Egypt,

10And all that he did to the two kings of the Amorites, that *were* beyond Jordan, to Sihon king of Heshbon, and to Og king of Bashan, which *was* at Ashtaroth.

11Wherefore our elders and all the inhabitants of our country spake to us, saying, Take victuals with you for the journey, and go to meet them, and say unto them, We *are* your servants: therefore now make ye a league with us.

12This our bread we took hot *for* our provision out of our houses on the day we came forth to go unto you; but now, behold, it is dry, and it is mouldy:

13And these bottles of wine, which we filled, *were* new; and, behold, they be rent: and these our garments and our shoes are become old by reason of the very long journey.

New International

LORD had commanded the Israelites. He built it according to what is written in the Book of the Law of Moses—an altar of uncut stones, on which no iron tool had been used. On it they offered to the LORD burnt offerings and sacrificed fellowship offerings.[a] 32There, in the presence of the Israelites, Joshua copied on stones the law of Moses, which he had written. 33All Israel, aliens and citizens alike, with their elders, officials and judges, were standing on both sides of the ark of the covenant of the LORD, facing those who carried it—the priests, who were Levites. Half of the people stood in front of Mount Gerizim and half of them in front of Mount Ebal, as Moses the servant of the LORD had formerly commanded when he gave instructions to bless the people of Israel.

34Afterward, Joshua read all the words of the law—the blessings and the curses—just as it is written in the Book of the Law. 35There was not a word of all that Moses had commanded that Joshua did not read to the whole assembly of Israel, including the women and children, and the aliens who lived among them.

The Gibeonite Deception

9 NOW WHEN all the kings west of the Jordan heard about these things—those in the hill country, in the western foothills, and along the entire coast of the Great Sea[b] as far as Lebanon (the kings of the Hittites, Amorites, Canaanites, Perizzites, Hivites and Jebusites)— 2they came together to make war against Joshua and Israel.

3However, when the people of Gibeon heard what Joshua had done to Jericho and Ai, 4they resorted to a ruse: They went as a delegation whose donkeys were loaded[c] with worn-out sacks and old wineskins, cracked and mended. 5The men put worn and patched sandals on their feet and wore old clothes. All the bread of their food supply was dry and moldy. 6Then they went to Joshua in the camp at Gilgal and said to him and the men of Israel, "We have come from a distant country; make a treaty with us."

7The men of Israel said to the Hivites, "But perhaps you live near us. How then can we make a treaty with you?"

8"We are your servants," they said to Joshua.

But Joshua asked, "Who are you and where do you come from?"

9They answered: "Your servants have come from a very distant country because of the fame of the LORD your God. For we have heard reports of him: all that he did in Egypt, 10and all that he did to the two kings of the Amorites east of the Jordan—Sihon king of Heshbon, and Og king of Bashan, who reigned in Ashtaroth. 11And our elders and all those living in our country said to us, 'Take provisions for your journey; go and meet them and say to them, "We are your servants; make a treaty with us." ' 12This bread of ours was warm when we packed it at home on the day we left to come to you. But now see how dry and moldy it is. 13And these wineskins that we filled were new, but see how cracked they are. And our clothes and sandals are worn out by the very long journey."

Living Bible

of his laws: "Make me an altar of boulders that have neither been broken nor carved," the Lord had said concerning Mount Ebal. Then the priests offered burnt sacrifices and peace offerings to the Lord on the altar. 32And as the people of Israel watched, Joshua carved upon the stones of the altar each of the Ten Commandments.d

33Then all the people of Israel—including the elders, officers, judges, and the foreigners living among them—divided into two groups, half of them standing at the foot of Mount Gerizim and half at the foot of Mount Ebal. Between them stood the priests with the Ark, ready to pronounce their blessing. (This was all done in accordance with the instructions given long before by Moses.) 34Joshua then read to them all of the statements of blessing and curses that Moses had written in the book of God's laws. 35Every commandment Moses had ever given was read before the entire assembly, including the women and children and the foreigners who lived among the Israelis.

9 WHEN THE kings of the surrounding area heard what had happened to Jericho, they quickly combined their armies to fight for their lives against Joshua and the Israelis. These were the kings of the nations west of the Jordan River, along the shores of the Mediterranean as far north as the Lebanon mountains—the Hittites, Amorites, Canaanites, Perizzites, Hivites, and Jebusites.

3, 4, 5But when the people of Gibeon heard what had happened to Jericho and Ai, they resorted to trickery to save themselves. They sent ambassadors to Joshua wearing worn-out clothing, as though from a long journey, with patched shoes, weatherworn saddlebags on their donkeys, old, patched wine-skins and dry, moldy bread. 6When they arrived at the camp of Israel at Gilgal, they told Joshua and the men of Israel, "We have come from a distant land to ask for a peace treaty with you."

7The Israelis replied to these Hivites, "How do we know you don't live nearby? For if you do, we cannot make a treaty with you."

8They replied, "We will be your slaves."

"But who are you?" Joshua demanded. "Where do you come from?"

9And they told him, "We are from a very distant country; we have heard of the might of the Lord your God and of all that he did in Egypt, 10and what you did to the two kings of the Amorites—Sihon, king of Heshbon, and Og, king of Bashan. 11So our elders and our people instructed us, 'Prepare for a long journey; go to the people of Israel and declare our nation to be their servants, and ask for peace.' 12This bread was hot from the ovens when we left, but now as you see, it is dry and moldy; 13these wineskins were new, but now they are old and cracked; our clothing and shoes have become worn out from our long, hard trip."

New Revised Standard

the LORD had commanded the Israelites, as it is written in the book of the law of Moses, "an altar of unhewne stones, on which no iron tool has been used"; and they offered on it burnt offerings to the LORD, and sacrificed offerings of well-being. 32And there, in the presence of the Israelites, Joshuaf wrote on the stones a copy of the law of Moses, which he had written. 33All Israel, alien as well as citizen, with their elders and officers and their judges, stood on opposite sides of the ark in front of the levitical priests who carried the ark of the covenant of the LORD, half of them in front of Mount Gerizim and half of them in front of Mount Ebal, as Moses the servant of the LORD had commanded at the first, that they should bless the people of Israel. 34And afterward he read all the words of the law, blessings and curses, according to all that is written in the book of the law. 35There was not a word of all that Moses commanded that Joshua did not read before all the assembly of Israel, and the women, and the little ones, and the aliens who resided among them.

The Gibeonites Save Themselves by Trickery

9 NOW WHEN all the kings who were beyond the Jordan in the hill country and in the lowland all along the coast of the Great Sea toward Lebanon—the Hittites, the Amorites, the Canaanites, the Perizzites, the Hivites, and the Jebusites—heard of this, 2they gathered together with one accord to fight Joshua and Israel.

3 But when the inhabitants of Gibeon heard what Joshua had done to Jericho and to Ai, 4they on their part acted with cunning: they went and prepared provisions,g and took worn-out sacks for their donkeys, and wineskins, worn-out and torn and mended, 5with worn-out, patched sandals on their feet, and worn-out clothes; and all their provisions were dry and moldy. 6They went to Joshua in the camp at Gilgal, and said to him and to the Israelites, "We have come from a far country; so now make a treaty with us." 7But the Israelites said to the Hivites, "Perhaps you live among us; then how can we make a treaty with you?" 8They said to Joshua, "We are your servants." And Joshua said to them, "Who are you? And where do you come from?" 9They said to him, "Your servants have come from a very far country, because of the name of the LORD your God; for we have heard a report of him, of all that he did in Egypt, 10and of all that he did to the two kings of the Amorites who were beyond the Jordan, King Sihon of Heshbon, and King Og of Bashan who lived in Ashtaroth. 11So our elders and all the inhabitants of our country said to us, 'Take provisions in your hand for the journey; go to meet them, and say to them, "We are your servants; come now, make a treaty with us."' 12Here is our bread; it was still warm when we took it from our houses as our food for the journey, on the day we set out to come to you, but now, see, it is dry and moldy; 13these wineskins were new when we filled them, and see, they are burst; and these garments and sandals of ours are worn out from the very long journey." 14So the leadersh partook

---

d 8:32 each of the Ten Commandments, literally, "the law of Moses."   e Heb whole   f Heb he   g Cn: Meaning of Heb uncertain   h Gk: Heb men

King James

14And the men took of their victuals, and asked not *counsel* at the mouth of the LORD.

15And Joshua made peace with them, and made a league with them, to let them live: and the princes of the congregation sware unto them.

16¶ And it came to pass at the end of three days after they had made a league with them, that they heard that they *were* their neighbours, and *that* they dwelt among them.

17And the children of Israel journeyed, and came unto their cities on the third day. Now their cities *were* Gibeon, and Chephirah, and Beeroth, and Kirjath-jearim.

18And the children of Israel smote them not, because the princes of the congregation had sworn unto them by the LORD God of Israel. And all the congregation murmured against the princes.

19But all the princes said unto all the congregation, We have sworn unto them by the LORD God of Israel: now therefore we may not touch them.

20This we will do to them; we will even let them live, lest wrath be upon us, because of the oath which we sware unto them.

21And the princes said unto them, Let them live; but let them be hewers of wood and drawers of water unto all the congregation; as the princes had promised them.

22¶ And Joshua called for them, and he spake unto them, saying, Wherefore have ye beguiled us, saying, We *are* very far from you; when ye dwell among us?

23Now therefore ye *are* cursed, and there shall none of you be freed from being bondmen, and hewers of wood and drawers of water for the house of my God.

24And they answered Joshua, and said, Because it was certainly told thy servants, how that the LORD thy God commanded his servant Moses to give you all the land, and to destroy all the inhabitants of the land from before you, therefore we were sore afraid of our lives because of you, and have done this thing.

25And now, behold, we *are* in thine hand: as it seemeth good and right unto thee to do unto us, do.

26And so did he unto them, and delivered them out of the hand of the children of Israel, that they slew them not.

27And Joshua made them that day hewers of wood and drawers of water for the congregation, and for the altar of the LORD, even unto this day, in the place which he should choose.

10 NOW IT came to pass, when Adoni-zedec king of Jerusalem had heard how Joshua had taken Ai, and had utterly destroyed it; as he had done to Jericho and her king, so he had done to Ai and her king; and how the inhabitants of Gibeon had made peace with Israel, and were among them;

2That they feared greatly, because Gibeon *was* a great city, as one of the royal cities, and because it *was* greater than Ai, and all the men thereof *were* mighty.

3Wherefore Adoni-zedec king of Jerusalem sent unto Hoham king of Hebron, and unto Piram king of Jarmuth, and unto Japhia king of Lachish, and unto Debir king of Eglon, saying,

4Come up unto me, and help me, that we may smite Gibeon: for it hath made peace with Joshua and with the children of Israel.

5Therefore the five kings of the Amorites, the king of Jerusalem, the king of Hebron, the king of Jarmuth, the king of Lachish, the king of Eglon, gathered themselves together, and went up, they and all their hosts, and encamped before Gibeon, and made war against it.

New International

14The men of Israel sampled their provisions but did not inquire of the LORD. 15Then Joshua made a treaty of peace with them to let them live, and the leaders of the assembly ratified it by oath.

16Three days after they made the treaty with the Gibeonites, the Israelites heard that they were neighbors, living near them. 17So the Israelites set out and on the third day came to their cities: Gibeon, Kephirah, Beeroth and Kiriath Jearim. 18But the Israelites did not attack them, because the leaders of the assembly had sworn an oath to them by the LORD, the God of Israel.

The whole assembly grumbled against the leaders, 19but all the leaders answered, "We have given them our oath by the LORD, the God of Israel, and we cannot touch them now. 20This is what we will do to them: We will let them live, so that wrath will not fall on us for breaking the oath we swore to them." 21They continued, "Let them live, but let them be woodcutters and water carriers for the entire community." So the leaders' promise to them was kept.

22Then Joshua summoned the Gibeonites and said, "Why did you deceive us by saying, 'We live a long way from you,' while actually you live near us? 23You are now under a curse: You will never cease to serve as woodcutters and water carriers for the house of my God."

24They answered Joshua, "Your servants were clearly told how the LORD your God had commanded his servant Moses to give you the whole land and to wipe out all its inhabitants from before you. So we feared for our lives because of you, and that is why we did this. 25We are now in your hands. Do to us whatever seems good and right to you."

26So Joshua saved them from the Israelites, and they did not kill them. 27That day he made the Gibeonites woodcutters and water carriers for the community and for the altar of the LORD at the place the LORD would choose. And that is what they are to this day.

The Sun Stands Still

10 NOW ADONI-ZEDEK king of Jerusalem heard that Joshua had taken Ai and totally destroyeda it, doing to Ai and its king as he had done to Jericho and its king, and that the people of Gibeon had made a treaty of peace with Israel and were living near them. 2He and his people were very much alarmed at this, because Gibeon was an important city, like one of the royal cities; it was larger than Ai, and all its men were good fighters. 3So Adoni-Zedek king of Jerusalem appealed to Hoham king of Hebron, Piram king of Jarmuth, Japhia king of Lachish and Debir king of Eglon. 4"Come up and help me attack Gibeon," he said, "because it has made peace with Joshua and the Israelites."

5Then the five kings of the Amorites—the kings of Jerusalem, Hebron, Jarmuth, Lachish and Eglon—joined forces. They moved up with all their troops and took up positions against Gibeon and attacked it.

---

a *1* The Hebrew term refers to the irrevocable giving over of things or persons to the LORD, often by totally destroying them; also in verses 28, 35, 37, 39 and 40.

Living Bible

14, 15Joshua and the other leaders finally believed them. They did not bother to ask the Lord, but went ahead and signed a peace treaty. And the leaders of Israel ratified the agreement with a binding oath.

16Three days later the facts came out—these men were close neighbors. 17The Israeli army set out at once to investigate, and reached their cities in three days. (The names of the cities were Gibeon, Chephirah, Beeroth, and Kiriath-jearim.) 18But the cities were not harmed because of the vow which the leaders of Israel had made before the Lord God. The people of Israel were angry with their leaders because of the peace treaty.

19But the leaders replied, "We have sworn before the Lord God of Israel that we will not touch them, and we won't. 20We must let them live, for if we break our oath the wrath of Jehovah will be upon us."

21So they became servants of the Israelis, chopping their wood and carrying their water.

22Joshua summoned their leaders and demanded, "Why have you lied to us by saying that you lived in a distant land, when you were actually living right here among us? 23Now a curse shall be upon you! From this moment you must always furnish us with servants to chop wood and carry water for the service of our God."

24They replied, "We did it because we were told that Jehovah instructed his disciple Moses to conquer this entire land and destroy all the people living in it. So we feared for our lives because of you; that is why we have done it. 25But now we are in your hands; you may do with us as you wish."

26So Joshua would not allow the people of Israel to kill them, 27but they became wood-choppers and water-carriers for the people of Israel and for the altar of the Lord—wherever it would be built (for the Lord hadn't yet told them where to build it). This arrangement is still in force at the time of this writing.

10 WHEN ADONI-ZEDEK, the king of Jerusalem, heard how Joshua had captured and destroyed Ai and had killed its king, the same as he had done at Jericho, and how the people of Gibeon had made peace with Israel and were now their allies, 2he was very frightened. For Gibeon was a great city—as great as the royal cities and much larger than Ai—and its men were known as hard fighters. 3So King Adoni-zedek of Jerusalem sent messengers to several other kings:

King Hoham of Hebron,
King Piram of Jarmuth,
King Japhia of Lachish,
King Debir of Eglon.

4"Come and help me destroy Gibeon," he urged them, "for they have made peace with Joshua and the people of Israel."

5So these five Amorite kings combined their armies

New Revised Standard

of their provisions, and did not ask direction from the LORD. 15And Joshua made peace with them, guaranteeing their lives by a treaty; and the leaders of the congregation swore an oath to them.

16 But when three days had passed after they had made a treaty with them, they heard that they were their neighbors and were living among them. 17So the Israelites set out and reached their cities on the third day. Now their cities were Gibeon, Chephirah, Beeroth, and Kiriath-jearim. 18But the Israelites did not attack them, because the leaders of the congregation had sworn to them by the LORD, the God of Israel. Then all the congregation murmured against the leaders. 19But all the leaders said to all the congregation, "We have sworn to them by the LORD, the God of Israel, and now we must not touch them. 20This is what we will do to them: We will let them live, so that wrath may not come upon us, because of the oath that we swore to them." 21The leaders said to them, "Let them live." So they became hewers of wood and drawers of water for all the congregation, as the leaders had decided concerning them.

22 Joshua summoned them, and said to them, "Why did you deceive us, saying, 'We are very far from you,' while in fact you are living among us? 23Now therefore you are cursed, and some of you shall always be slaves, hewers of wood and drawers of water for the house of my God." 24They answered Joshua, "Because it was told to your servants for a certainty that the LORD your God had commanded his servant Moses to give you all the land, and to destroy all the inhabitants of the land before you; so we were in great fear for our lives because of you, and did this thing. 25And now we are in your hand: do as it seems good and right in your sight to do to us." 26This is what he did for them: he saved them from the Israelites; and they did not kill them. 27But on that day Joshua made them hewers of wood and drawers of water for the congregation and for the altar of the LORD, to continue to this day, in the place that he should choose.

The Sun Stands Still

10 WHEN KING Adoni-zedek of Jerusalem heard how Joshua had taken Ai, and had utterly destroyed it, doing to Ai and its king as he had done to Jericho and its king, and how the inhabitants of Gibeon had made peace with Israel and were among them, 2heb became greatly frightened, because Gibeon was a large city, like one of the royal cities, and was larger than Ai, and all its men were warriors. 3So King Adoni-zedek of Jerusalem sent a message to King Hoham of Hebron, to King Piram of Jarmuth, to King Japhia of Lachish, and to King Debir of Eglon, saying, 4"Come up and help me, and let us attack Gibeon; for it has made peace with Joshua and with the Israelites." 5Then the five kings of the Amorites—the king of Jerusalem, the king of Hebron, the king of Jarmuth, the king of Lachish, and the king of Eglon—gathered their forces, and went up with all their armies and camped against Gibeon, and made war against it.

b Heb they

King James

6¶ And the men of Gibeon sent unto Joshua to the camp to Gilgal, saying, Slack not thy hand from thy servants; come up to us quickly, and save us, and help us: for all the kings of the Amorites that dwell in the mountains are gathered together against us.

7So Joshua ascended from Gilgal, he, and all the people of war with him, and all the mighty men of valour.

8¶ And the LORD said unto Joshua, Fear them not: for I have delivered them into thine hand; there shall not a man of them stand before thee.

9Joshua therefore came unto them suddenly, *and* went up from Gilgal all night.

10And the LORD discomfited them before Israel, and slew them with a great slaughter at Gibeon, and chased them along the way that goeth up to Beth-horon, and smote them to Azekah, and unto Makkedah.

11And it came to pass, as they fled from before Israel, *and* were in the going down to Beth-horon, that the LORD cast down great stones from heaven upon them unto Azekah, and they died: *they were* more which died with hailstones than *they* whom the children of Israel slew with the sword.

12¶ Then spake Joshua to the LORD in the day when the LORD delivered up the Amorites before the children of Israel, and he said in the sight of Israel, Sun, stand thou still upon Gibeon; and thou, Moon, in the valley of Ajalon.

13And the sun stood still, and the moon stayed, until the people had avenged themselves upon their enemies. *Is* not this written in the book of Jasher? So the sun stood still in the midst of heaven, and hasted not to go down about a whole day.

14And there was no day like that before it or after it, that the LORD hearkened unto the voice of a man: for the LORD fought for Israel.

15¶ And Joshua returned, and all Israel with him, unto the camp to Gilgal.

16But these five kings fled, and hid themselves in a cave at Makkedah.

17And it was told Joshua, saying, The five kings are found hid in a cave at Makkedah.

18And Joshua said, Roll great stones upon the mouth of the cave, and set men by it for to keep them:

19And stay ye not, *but* pursue after your enemies, and smite the hindmost of them; suffer them not to enter into their cities: for the LORD your God hath delivered them into your hand.

20And it came to pass, when Joshua and the children of Israel had made an end of slaying them with a very great slaughter, till they were consumed, that the rest *which* remained of them entered into fenced cities.

21And all the people returned to the camp to Joshua at Makkedah in peace: none moved his tongue against any of the children of Israel.

22Then said Joshua, Open the mouth of the cave, and bring out those five kings unto me out of the cave.

23And they did so, and brought forth those five kings unto him out of the cave, the king of Jerusalem, the king of Hebron, the king of Jarmuth, the king of Lachish, *and* the king of Eglon.

24And it came to pass, when they brought out those kings unto Joshua, that Joshua called for all the men of Israel, and said unto the captains of the men of war which went with him, Come near, put your feet upon the necks of these kings. And they came near, and put their feet upon the necks of them.

25And Joshua said unto them, Fear not, nor be dismayed, be strong and of good courage: for thus shall the LORD do to all your enemies against whom ye fight.

26And afterward Joshua smote them, and slew them, and hanged them on five trees: and they were hanging upon the trees until the evening.

New International

6The Gibeonites then sent word to Joshua in the camp at Gilgal: "Do not abandon your servants. Come up to us quickly and save us! Help us, because all the Amorite kings from the hill country have joined forces against us."

7So Joshua marched up from Gilgal with his entire army, including all the best fighting men. 8The LORD said to Joshua, "Do not be afraid of them; I have given them into your hand. Not one of them will be able to withstand you."

9After an all-night march from Gilgal, Joshua took them by surprise. 10The LORD threw them into confusion before Israel, who defeated them in a great victory at Gibeon. Israel pursued them along the road going up to Beth Horon and cut them down all the way to Azekah and Makkedah. 11As they fled before Israel on the road down from Beth Horon to Azekah, the LORD hurled large hailstones down on them from the sky, and more of them died from the hailstones than were killed by the swords of the Israelites.

12On the day the LORD gave the Amorites over to Israel, Joshua said to the LORD in the presence of Israel:

"O sun, stand still over Gibeon,
　O moon, over the Valley of Aijalon."
13So the sun stood still,
　and the moon stopped,
　till the nation avenged itself on[a] its enemies,

as it is written in the Book of Jashar.

The sun stopped in the middle of the sky and delayed going down about a full day. 14There has never been a day like it before or since, a day when the LORD listened to a man. Surely the LORD was fighting for Israel!

15Then Joshua returned with all Israel to the camp at Gilgal.

Five Amorite Kings Killed

16Now the five kings had fled and hidden in the cave at Makkedah. 17When Joshua was told that the five kings had been found hiding in the cave at Makkedah, 18he said, "Roll large rocks up to the mouth of the cave, and post some men there to guard it. 19But don't stop! Pursue your enemies, attack them from the rear and don't let them reach their cities, for the LORD your God has given them into your hand."

20So Joshua and the Israelites destroyed them completely—almost to a man—but the few who were left reached their fortified cities. 21The whole army then returned safely to Joshua in the camp at Makkedah, and no one uttered a word against the Israelites.

22Joshua said, "Open the mouth of the cave and bring those five kings out to me." 23So they brought the five kings out of the cave—the kings of Jerusalem, Hebron, Jarmuth, Lachish and Eglon. 24When they had brought these kings to Joshua, he summoned all the men of Israel and said to the army commanders who had come with him, "Come here and put your feet on the necks of these kings." So they came forward and placed their feet on their necks.

25Joshua said to them, "Do not be afraid; do not be discouraged. Be strong and courageous. This is what the LORD will do to all the enemies you are going to fight." 26Then Joshua struck and killed the kings and hung them on five trees, and they were left hanging on the trees until evening.

---

a *13 Or nation triumphed over*

Living Bible

for a united attack on Gibeon. 6The men of Gibeon hurriedly sent messengers to Joshua at Gilgal.

"Come and help your servants!" they demanded. "Come quickly and save us! For all the kings of the Amorites who live in the hills are here with their armies."

7So Joshua and the Israeli army left Gilgal and went to rescue Gibeon.

8"Don't be afraid of them," the Lord said to Joshua, "for they are already defeated! I have given them to you to destroy. Not a single one of them will be able to stand up to you."

9Joshua traveled all night from Gilgal and took the enemy armies by surprise. 10Then the Lord threw them into a panic so that the army of Israel slaughtered great numbers of them at Gibeon and chased the others all the way to Beth-horon and Azekah and Makkedah, killing them along the way. 11And as the enemy was racing down the hill to Beth-horon, the Lord destroyed them with a great hailstorm that continued all the way to Azekah; in fact, more men died from the hail than by the swords of the Israelites.

12As the men of Israel were pursuing and harassing the foe, Joshua prayed aloud, "Let the sun stand still over Gibeon, and let the moon stand in its place over the valley of Aijalon!"

13And the sun and the moon didn't move until the Israeli army had finished the destruction of its enemies! This is described in greater detail in *The Book of Jashar*. So the sun stopped in the heavens and stayed there for almost twenty-four hours! 14There had never been such a day before, and there has never been another since, when the Lord stopped the sun and moon—all because of the prayer of one man. But the Lord was fighting for Israel. 15(Afterwards Joshua and the Israeli army returned to Gilgal.)

16During the battle the five kings escaped and hid in a cave at Makkedah. 17When the news was brought to Joshua that they had been found, 18he issued a command that a great stone be rolled against the mouth of the cave and that guards be placed there to keep the kings inside.

19Then Joshua commanded the rest of the army, "Go on chasing the enemy and cut them down from the rear. Don't let them get back to their cities, for the Lord will help you to completely destroy them."

20So Joshua and the Israeli army continued the slaughter and wiped out the five armies except for a tiny remnant that managed to reach their fortified cities. 21Then the Israelis returned to their camp at Makkedah without having lost a single man! And after that no one dared to attack Israel.

22, 23Joshua now instructed his men to remove the stone from the mouth of the cave and to bring out the five kings—of Jerusalem, Hebron, Jarmuth, Lachish, and Eglon. 24Joshua told the captains of his army to put their feet on the kings' necks.

25"Don't ever be afraid or discouraged," Joshua said to his men. "Be strong and courageous, for the Lord is going to do this to all of your enemies."

26With that, Joshua plunged his sword into each of the five kings, killing them. He then hanged them on five trees until evening.

New Revised Standard

6 And the Gibeonites sent to Joshua at the camp in Gilgal, saying, "Do not abandon your servants; come up to us quickly, and save us, and help us; for all the kings of the Amorites who live in the hill country are gathered against us." 7So Joshua went up from Gilgal, he and all the fighting force with him, all the mighty warriors. 8The LORD said to Joshua, "Do not fear them, for I have handed them over to you; not one of them shall stand before you." 9So Joshua came upon them suddenly, having marched up all night from Gilgal. 10And the LORD threw them into a panic before Israel, who inflicted a great slaughter on them at Gibeon, chased them by the way of the ascent of Beth-horon, and struck them down as far as Azekah and Makkedah. 11As they fled before Israel, while they were going down the slope of Beth-horon, the LORD threw down huge stones from heaven on them as far as Azekah, and they died; there were more who died because of the hailstones than the Israelites killed with the sword.

12 On the day when the LORD gave the Amorites over to the Israelites, Joshua spoke to the LORD; and he said in the sight of Israel,
"Sun, stand still at Gibeon,
    and Moon, in the valley of Aijalon."
13 And the sun stood still, and the moon
        stopped,
    until the nation took vengeance on their
        enemies.
Is this not written in the Book of Jashar? The sun stopped in midheaven, and did not hurry to set for about a whole day. 14There has been no day like it before or since, when the LORD heeded a human voice; for the LORD fought for Israel.

15 Then Joshua returned, and all Israel with him, to the camp at Gilgal.

Five Kings Defeated

16 Meanwhile, these five kings fled and hid themselves in the cave at Makkedah. 17And it was told Joshua, "The five kings have been found, hidden in the cave at Makkedah." 18Joshua said, "Roll large stones against the mouth of the cave, and set men by it to guard them; 19but do not stay there yourselves; pursue your enemies, and attack them from the rear. Do not let them enter their towns, for the LORD your God has given them into your hand." 20When Joshua and the Israelites had finished inflicting a very great slaughter on them, until they were wiped out, and when the survivors had entered into the fortified towns, 21all the people returned safe to Joshua in the camp at Makkedah; no one dared to speakb against any of the Israelites.

22 Then Joshua said, "Open the mouth of the cave, and bring those five kings out to me from the cave." 23They did so, and brought the five kings out to him from the cave, the king of Jerusalem, the king of Hebron, the king of Jarmuth, the king of Lachish, and the king of Eglon. 24When they brought the kings out to Joshua, Joshua summoned all the Israelites, and said to the chiefs of the warriors who had gone with him, "Come near, put your feet on the necks of these kings." Then they came near and put their feet on their necks. 25And Joshua said to them, "Do not be afraid or dismayed; be strong and courageous; for thus the LORD will do to all the enemies against whom you fight." 26Afterward Joshua struck them down and put them to death, and he hung them on five trees. And they hung on the trees until evening. 27At sunset Joshua commanded, and

---

b Heb *moved his tongue*

King James

27And it came to pass at the time of the going down of the sun, *that* Joshua commanded, and they took them down off the trees, and cast them into the cave wherein they had been hid, and laid great stones in the cave's mouth, *which remain* until this very day.

28¶ And that day Joshua took Makkedah, and smote it with the edge of the sword, and the king thereof he utterly destroyed, them, and all the souls that *were* therein; he let none remain: and he did to the king of Makkedah as he did unto the king of Jericho.

29Then Joshua passed from Makkedah, and all Israel with him, unto Libnah, and fought against Libnah:

30And the LORD delivered it also, and the king thereof, into the hand of Israel; and he smote it with the edge of the sword, and all the souls that *were* therein; he let none remain in it; but did unto the king thereof as he did unto the king of Jericho.

31¶ And Joshua passed from Libnah, and all Israel with him, unto Lachish, and encamped against it, and fought against it:

32And the LORD delivered Lachish into the hand of Israel, which took it on the second day, and smote it with the edge of the sword, and all the souls that *were* therein, according to all that he had done to Libnah.

33¶ Then Horam king of Gezer came up to help Lachish; and Joshua smote him and his people, until he had left him none remaining.

34¶ And from Lachish Joshua passed unto Eglon, and all Israel with him; and they encamped against it, and fought against it:

35And they took it on that day, and smote it with the edge of the sword, and all the souls that *were* therein he utterly destroyed that day, according to all that he had done to Lachish.

36And Joshua went up from Eglon, and all Israel with him, unto Hebron; and they fought against it:

37And they took it, and smote it with the edge of the sword, and the king thereof, and all the cities thereof, and all the souls that *were* therein; he left none remaining, according to all that he had done to Eglon; but destroyed it utterly, and all the souls that *were* therein.

38¶ And Joshua returned, and all Israel with him, to Debir; and fought against it:

39And he took it, and the king thereof, and all the cities thereof; and they smote them with the edge of the sword, and utterly destroyed all the souls that *were* therein; he left none remaining: as he had done to Hebron, so he did to Debir, and to the king thereof; as he had done also to Libnah, and to her king.

40¶ So Joshua smote all the country of the hills, and of the south, and of the vale, and of the springs, and all their kings: he left none remaining, but utterly destroyed all that breathed, as the LORD God of Israel commanded.

41And Joshua smote them from Kadesh-barnea even unto Gaza, and all the country of Goshen, even unto Gibeon.

42And all these kings and their land did Joshua take at one time, because the LORD God of Israel fought for Israel.

43And Joshua returned, and all Israel with him, unto the camp to Gilgal.

New International

27At sunset Joshua gave the order and they took them down from the trees and threw them into the cave where they had been hiding. At the mouth of the cave they placed large rocks, which are there to this day.

28That day Joshua took Makkedah. He put the city and its king to the sword and totally destroyed everyone in it. He left no survivors. And he did to the king of Makkedah as he had done to the king of Jericho.

Southern Cities Conquered

29Then Joshua and all Israel with him moved on from Makkedah to Libnah and attacked it. 30The LORD also gave that city and its king into Israel's hand. The city and everyone in it Joshua put to the sword. He left no survivors there. And he did to its king as he had done to the king of Jericho.

31Then Joshua and all Israel with him moved on from Libnah to Lachish; he took up positions against it and attacked it. 32The LORD handed Lachish over to Israel, and Joshua took it on the second day. The city and everyone in it he put to the sword, just as he had done to Libnah. 33Meanwhile, Horam king of Gezer had come up to help Lachish, but Joshua defeated him and his army—until no survivors were left.

34Then Joshua and all Israel with him moved on from Lachish to Eglon; they took up positions against it and attacked it. 35They captured it that same day and put it to the sword and totally destroyed everyone in it, just as they had done to Lachish.

36Then Joshua and all Israel with him went up from Eglon to Hebron and attacked it. 37They took the city and put it to the sword, together with its king, its villages and everyone in it. They left no survivors. Just as at Eglon, they totally destroyed it and everyone in it.

38Then Joshua and all Israel with him turned around and attacked Debir. 39They took the city, its king and its villages, and put them to the sword. Everyone in it they totally destroyed. They left no survivors. They did to Debir and its king as they had done to Libnah and its king and to Hebron.

40So Joshua subdued the whole region, including the hill country, the Negev, the western foothills and the mountain slopes, together with all their kings. He left no survivors. He totally destroyed all who breathed, just as the LORD, the God of Israel, had commanded. 41Joshua subdued them from Kadesh Barnea to Gaza and from the whole region of Goshen to Gibeon. 42All these kings and their lands Joshua conquered in one campaign, because the LORD, the God of Israel, fought for Israel.

43Then Joshua returned with all Israel to the camp at Gilgal.

Living Bible

27As the sun was going down, Joshua instructed that their bodies be taken down and thrown into the cave where they had been hiding; and a great pile of stones was placed at the mouth of the cave. (The pile is still there today.)

28On that same day Joshua destroyed the city of Makkedah and killed its king and everyone in it. Not one person in the entire city was left alive. 29Then the Israelis went to Libnah. 30There, too, the Lord gave them the city and its king. Every last person was slaughtered, just as at Jericho.

31From Libnah they went to Lachish and attacked it. 32And the Lord gave it to them on the second day; here, too, the entire population was slaughtered, just as at Libnah.

33During the attack on Lachish, King Horam of Gezer arrived with his army to try to help defend the city, but Joshua's men killed him and destroyed his entire army.

34, 35The Israeli army then captured Eglon on the first day and, as at Lachish, they killed everyone in the city. 36After leaving Eglon they went to Hebron, 37and captured it and all of its surrounding villages, slaughtering the entire population. Not one person was left alive. 38Then they turned back to Debir, 39which they quickly captured with all of its outlying villages. And they killed everyone just as they had at Libnah.

40So Joshua and his army conquered the whole country—the nations and kings of the hill country, the Negeb, the lowlands, and the mountain slopes. They destroyed everyone in the land, just as the Lord God of Israel had commanded, 41slaughtering them from Kadesh-barnea to Gaza, and from Goshen to Gibeon. 42This was all accomplished in one campaign, for the Lord God of Israel was fighting for his people. 43Then Joshua and his army returned to their camp at Gilgal.

New Revised Standard

they took them down from the trees and threw them into the cave where they had hidden themselves; they set large stones against the mouth of the cave, which remain to this very day.

28 Joshua took Makkedah on that day, and struck it and its king with the edge of the sword; he utterly destroyed every person in it; he left no one remaining. And he did to the king of Makkedah as he had done to the king of Jericho.

29 Then Joshua passed on from Makkedah, and all Israel with him, to Libnah, and fought against Libnah. 30The LORD gave it also and its king into the hand of Israel; and he struck it with the edge of the sword, and every person in it; he left no one remaining in it; and he did to its king as he had done to the king of Jericho.

31 Next Joshua passed on from Libnah, and all Israel with him, to Lachish, and laid siege to it, and assaulted it. 32The LORD gave Lachish into the hand of Israel, and he took it on the second day, and struck it with the edge of the sword, and every person in it, as he had done to Libnah.

33 Then King Horam of Gezer came up to help Lachish; and Joshua struck him and his people, leaving him no survivors.

34 From Lachish Joshua passed on with all Israel to Eglon; and they laid siege to it, and assaulted it; 35and they took it that day, and struck it with the edge of the sword; and every person in it he utterly destroyed that day, as he had done to Lachish.

36 Then Joshua went up with all Israel from Eglon to Hebron; they assaulted it, 37and took it, and struck it with the edge of the sword, and its king and its towns, and every person in it; he left no one remaining, just as he had done to Eglon, and utterly destroyed it with every person in it.

38 Then Joshua, with all Israel, turned back to Debir and assaulted it, 39and he took it with its king and all its towns; they struck them with the edge of the sword, and utterly destroyed every person in it; he left no one remaining; just as he had done to Hebron, and, as he had done to Libnah and its king, so he did to Debir and its king.

40 So Joshua defeated the whole land, the hill country and the Negeb and the lowland and the slopes, and all their kings; he left no one remaining, but utterly destroyed all that breathed, as the LORD God of Israel commanded. 41And Joshua defeated them from Kadesh-barnea to Gaza, and all the country of Goshen, as far as Gibeon. 42Joshua took all these kings and their land at one time, because the LORD God of Israel fought for Israel. 43Then Joshua returned, and all Israel with him, to the camp at Gilgal.

King James

11 AND IT came to pass, when Jabin king of Hazor had heard *those things,* that he sent to Jobab king of Madon, and to the king of Shimron, and to the king of Achshaph,

2And to the kings that *were* on the north of the mountains, and of the plains south of Chinneroth, and in the valley, and in the borders of Dor on the west,

3*And to* the Canaanite on the east and on the west, and *to* the Amorite, and the Hittite, and the Perizzite, and the Jebusite in the mountains, and *to* the Hivite under Hermon in the land of Mizpeh.

4And they went out, they and all their hosts with them, much people, even as the sand that *is* upon the sea shore in multitude, with horses and chariots very many.

5And when all these kings were met together, they came and pitched together at the waters of Merom, to fight against Israel.

6¶ And the LORD said unto Joshua, Be not afraid because of them: for tomorrow about this time will I deliver them up all slain before Israel: thou shalt hough their horses, and burn their chariots with fire.

7So Joshua came, and all the people of war with him, against them by the waters of Merom suddenly; and they fell upon them.

8And the LORD delivered them into the hand of Israel, who smote them, and chased them unto great Zidon, and unto Misrephoth-maim, and unto the valley of Mizpeh eastward; and they smote them, until they left them none remaining.

9And Joshua did unto them as the LORD bade him: he houghed their horses, and burnt their chariots with fire.

10¶ And Joshua at that time turned back, and took Hazor, and smote the king thereof with the sword: for Hazor beforetime was the head of all those kingdoms.

11And they smote all the souls that *were* therein with the edge of the sword, utterly destroying *them:* there was not any left to breathe: and he burnt Hazor with fire.

12And all the cities of those kings, and all the kings of them, did Joshua take, and smote them with the edge of the sword, *and* he utterly destroyed them, as Moses the servant of the LORD commanded.

13But *as for* the cities that stood still in their strength, Israel burned none of them, save Hazor only; *that* did Joshua burn.

14And all the spoil of these cities, and the cattle, the children of Israel took for a prey unto themselves; but every man they smote with the edge of the sword, until they had destroyed them, neither left they any to breathe.

15¶ As the LORD commanded Moses his servant, so did Moses command Joshua, and so did Joshua; he left nothing undone of all that the LORD commanded Moses.

16So Joshua took all that land, the hills, and all the south country, and all the land of Goshen, and the valley, and the plain, and the mountain of Israel, and the valley of the same;

17*Even* from the mount Halak, that goeth up to Seir, even unto Baal-gad in the valley of Lebanon under mount Hermon: and all their kings he took, and smote them, and slew them.

18Joshua made war a long time with all those kings.

19There was not a city that made peace with the children of Israel, save the Hivites the inhabitants of Gibeon: all *other* they took in battle.

20For it was of the LORD to harden their hearts, that they should come against Israel in battle, that he might destroy them utterly, *and* that they might have no favour, but that he might destroy them, as the LORD commanded Moses.

New International

Northern Kings Defeated

11 WHEN JABIN king of Hazor heard of this, he sent word to Jobab king of Madon, to the kings of Shimron and Acshaph, 2and to the northern kings who were in the mountains, in the Arabah south of Kinnereth, in the western foothills and in Naphoth Dora on the west; 3to the Canaanites in the east and west; to the Amorites, Hittites, Perizzites and Jebusites in the hill country; and to the Hivites below Hermon in the region of Mizpah. 4They came out with all their troops and a large number of horses and chariots—a huge army, as numerous as the sand on the seashore. 5All these kings joined forces and made camp together at the Waters of Merom, to fight against Israel.

6The LORD said to Joshua, "Do not be afraid of them, because by this time tomorrow I will hand all of them over to Israel, slain. You are to hamstring their horses and burn their chariots."

7So Joshua and his whole army came against them suddenly at the Waters of Merom and attacked them, 8and the LORD gave them into the hand of Israel. They defeated them and pursued them all the way to Greater Sidon, to Misrephoth Maim, and to the Valley of Mizpah on the east, until no survivors were left. 9Joshua did to them as the LORD had directed: He hamstrung their horses and burned their chariots.

10At that time Joshua turned back and captured Hazor and put its king to the sword. (Hazor had been the head of all these kingdoms.) 11Everyone in it they put to the sword. They totally destroyedb them, not sparing anything that breathed, and he burned up Hazor itself.

12Joshua took all these royal cities and their kings and put them to the sword. He totally destroyed them, as Moses the servant of the LORD had commanded. 13Yet Israel did not burn any of the cities built on their mounds—except Hazor, which Joshua burned. 14The Israelites carried off for themselves all the plunder and livestock of these cities, but all the people they put to the sword until they completely destroyed them, not sparing anyone that breathed. 15As the LORD commanded his servant Moses, so Moses commanded Joshua, and Joshua did it; he left nothing undone of all that the LORD commanded Moses.

16So Joshua took this entire land: the hill country, all the Negev, the whole region of Goshen, the western foothills, the Arabah and the mountains of Israel with their foothills, 17from Mount Halak, which rises toward Seir, to Baal Gad in the Valley of Lebanon below Mount Hermon. He captured all their kings and struck them down, putting them to death. 18Joshua waged war against all these kings for a long time. 19Except for the Hivites living in Gibeon, not one city made a treaty of peace with the Israelites, who took them all in battle. 20For it was the LORD himself who hardened their hearts to wage war against Israel, so that he might destroy them totally, exterminating them without mercy, as the LORD had commanded Moses.

---

a 2 Or *in the heights of Dor*   b 11 The Hebrew term refers to the irrevocable giving over of things or persons to the LORD, often by totally destroying them; also in verses 12, 20 and 21.

Living Bible

11 WHEN KING Jabin of Hazor heard what had happened, he sent urgent messages to the following kings:

King Jobab of Madon;
The king of Shimron;
The king of Achshaph;
All the kings of the northern hill country;
The kings in the Arabah, south of Chinneroth;
Those in the lowland;
The kings in the mountain areas of Dor, on the west;
The kings of Canaan, both east and west;
The kings of the Amorites;
The kings of the Hittites;
The kings of the Perizzites;
The kings in the Jebusite hill country;
The Hivite kings in the cities on the slopes of Mount Hermon, in the land of Mizpah.

⁴All these kings responded by mobilizing their armies, and uniting to crush Israel. Their combined troops, along with a vast array of horses and chariots, covered the landscape around the Springs of Merom as far as one could see; ⁵for they established their camp at the Springs of Merom.

⁶But the Lord said to Joshua, "Don't be afraid of them, for by this time tomorrow they will all be dead! Hamstring their horses and burn their chariots." ⁷Joshua and his troops arrived suddenly at the Springs of Merom and attacked. ⁸And the Lord gave all that vast army to the Israelis, who chased them as far as Great Sidon and a place called the Salt Pits, and eastward into the valley of Mizpah; so not one enemy troop survived the battle. ⁹Then Joshua and his men did as the Lord had instructed, for they hamstrung the horses and burned all the chariots.

¹⁰On the way back, Joshua captured Hazor and killed its king. (Hazor had at one time been the capital of the federation of all those kingdoms.) ¹¹Every person there was killed and the city was burned.

¹²Then he attacked and destroyed all the other cities of those kings. All the people were slaughtered, just as Moses had commanded long before. ¹³(However, Joshua did not burn any of the cities built on mounds except for Hazor.) ¹⁴All the loot and cattle of the ravaged cities were taken by the Israelis for themselves, but they killed all the people. ¹⁵For so the Lord had commanded his disciple Moses; and Moses had passed the commandment on to Joshua, who did as he had been told: he carefully obeyed all of the Lord's instructions to Moses.

¹⁶So Joshua conquered the entire land—the hill country, the Negeb, the land of Goshen, the lowlands, the Arabah, and the hills and lowlands of Israel. ¹⁷The Israeli territory now extended all the way from Mount Halak, near Seir, to Baal-gad in the valley of Lebanon, at the foot of Mount Hermon. And Joshua killed all the kings of those territories. ¹⁸It took seven years[c] of war to accomplish all of this. ¹⁹None of the cities was given a peace treaty except the Hivites of Gibeon; all of the others were destroyed. ²⁰For the Lord made the enemy kings want to fight the Israelis instead of asking for peace; so they were mercilessly killed, as the Lord had commanded Moses.

New Revised Standard

The United Kings of Northern Canaan Defeated

11 WHEN KING Jabin of Hazor heard of this, he sent to King Jobab of Madon, to the king of Shimron, to the king of Achshaph, ²and to the kings who were in the northern hill country, and in the Arabah south of Chinneroth, and in the lowland, and in Naphoth-dor on the west, ³to the Canaanites in the east and the west, the Amorites, the Hittites, the Perizzites, and the Jebusites in the hill country, and the Hivites under Hermon in the land of Mizpah. ⁴They came out, with all their troops, a great army, in number like the sand on the seashore, with very many horses and chariots. ⁵All these kings joined their forces, and came and camped together at the waters of Merom, to fight with Israel.

6 And the LORD said to Joshua, "Do not be afraid of them, for tomorrow at this time I will hand over all of them, slain, to Israel; you shall hamstring their horses, and burn their chariots with fire." ⁷So Joshua came suddenly upon them with all his fighting force, by the waters of Merom, and fell upon them. ⁸And the LORD handed them over to Israel, who attacked them and chased them as far as Great Sidon and Misrephoth-maim, and eastward as far as the valley of Mizpeh. They struck them down, until they had left no one remaining. ⁹And Joshua did to them as the LORD commanded him; he hamstrung their horses, and burned their chariots with fire.

10 Joshua turned back at that time, and took Hazor, and struck its king down with the sword. Before that time Hazor was the head of all those kingdoms. 11And they put to the sword all who were in it, utterly destroying them; there was no one left who breathed, and he burned Hazor with fire. 12And all the towns of those kings, and all their kings, Joshua took, and struck them with the edge of the sword, utterly destroying them, as Moses the servant of the LORD had commanded. 13But Israel burned none of the towns that stood on mounds except Hazor, which Joshua did burn. 14All the spoil of these towns, and the livestock, the Israelites took for their booty; but all the people they struck down with the edge of the sword, until they had destroyed them, and they did not leave any who breathed. 15As the LORD had commanded his servant Moses, so Moses commanded Joshua, and so Joshua did; he left nothing undone of all that the LORD had commanded Moses.

Summary of Joshua's Conquests

16 So Joshua took all that land: the hill country and all the Negeb and all the land of Goshen and the lowland and the Arabah and the hill country of Israel and its lowland, 17from Mount Halak, which rises toward Seir, as far as Baal-gad in the valley of Lebanon below Mount Hermon. He took all their kings, struck them down, and put them to death. 18Joshua made war a long time with all those kings. 19There was not a town that made peace with the Israelites, except the Hivites, the inhabitants of Gibeon; all were taken in battle. 20For it was the LORD's doing to harden their hearts so that they would come against Israel in battle, in order that they might be utterly destroyed, and might receive no mercy, but be exterminated, just as the LORD had commanded Moses.

ᶜ 11:18 *It took seven years*, implied in other text. Literally, "a long time."

King James

21¶ And at that time came Joshua, and cut off the Anakims from the mountains, from Hebron, from Debir, from Anab, and from all the mountains of Judah, and from all the mountains of Israel: Joshua destroyed them utterly with their cities.

22There was none of the Anakims left in the land of the children of Israel: only in Gaza, in Gath, and in Ashdod, there remained.

23So Joshua took the whole land, according to all that the LORD said unto Moses; and Joshua gave it for an inheritance unto Israel according to their divisions by their tribes. And the land rested from war.

12 NOW THESE *are* the kings of the land, which the children of Israel smote, and possessed their land on the other side Jordan toward the rising of the sun, from the river Arnon unto mount Hermon, and all the plain on the east:

2Sihon king of the Amorites, who dwelt in Heshbon, *and* ruled from Aroer, which *is* upon the bank of the river Arnon, and from the middle of the river, and from half Gilead, even unto the river Jabbok, *which is* the border of the children of Ammon;

3And from the plain to the sea of Chinneroth on the east, and unto the sea of the plain, *even* the salt sea on the east, the way to Beth-jeshimoth; and from the south, under Ashdoth-pisgah:

4¶ And the coast of Og king of Bashan, *which was* of the remnant of the giants, that dwelt at Ashtaroth and at Edrei,

5And reigned in mount Hermon, and in Salcah, and in all Bashan, unto the border of the Geshurites and the Maachathites, and half Gilead, the border of Sihon king of Heshbon.

6Them did Moses the servant of the LORD and the children of Israel smite: and Moses the servant of the LORD gave it *for* a possession unto the Reubenites, and the Gadites, and the half tribe of Manasseh.

7¶ And these *are* the kings of the country which Joshua and the children of Israel smote on this side Jordan on the west, from Baal-gad in the valley of Lebanon even unto the mount Halak, that goeth up to Seir; which Joshua gave unto the tribes of Israel *for* a possession according to their divisions;

8In the mountains, and in the valleys, and in the plains, and in the springs, and in the wilderness, and in the south country; the Hittites, the Amorites, and the Canaanites, the Perizzites, the Hivites, and the Jebusites:

9¶ The king of Jericho, one; the king of Ai, which *is* beside Beth-el, one;

10The king of Jerusalem, one; the king of Hebron, one;

11The king of Jarmuth, one; the king of Lachish, one;

12The king of Eglon, one; the king of Gezer, one;

13The king of Debir, one; the king of Geder, one;

14The king of Hormah, one; the king of Arad, one;

15The king of Libnah, one; the king of Adullam, one;

16The king of Makkedah, one; the king of Beth-el, one;

17The king of Tappuah, one; the king of Hepher, one;

18The king of Aphek, one; the king of Lasharon, one;

New International

21At that time Joshua went and destroyed the Anakites from the hill country: from Hebron, Debir and Anab, from all the hill country of Judah, and from all the hill country of Israel. Joshua totally destroyed them and their towns. 22No Anakites were left in Israelite territory; only in Gaza, Gath and Ashdod did any survive. 23So Joshua took the entire land, just as the LORD had directed Moses, and he gave it as an inheritance to Israel according to their tribal divisions.

Then the land had rest from war.

List of Defeated Kings

12 THESE ARE the kings of the land whom the Israelites had defeated and whose territory they took over east of the Jordan, from the Arnon Gorge to Mount Hermon, including all the eastern side of the Arabah:

2Sihon king of the Amorites,
  who reigned in Heshbon. He ruled from Aroer on the rim of the Arnon Gorge—from the middle of the gorge—to the Jabbok River, which is the border of the Ammonites. This included half of Gilead. 3He also ruled over the eastern Arabah from the Sea of Kinneretha to the Sea of the Arabah (the Salt Seab), to Beth Jeshimoth, and then southward below the slopes of Pisgah.

4And the territory of Og king of Bashan,
  one of the last of the Rephaites, who reigned in Ashtaroth and Edrei. 5He ruled over Mount Hermon, Salecah, all of Bashan to the border of the people of Geshur and Maacah, and half of Gilead to the border of Sihon king of Heshbon.

6Moses, the servant of the LORD, and the Israelites conquered them. And Moses the servant of the LORD gave their land to the Reubenites, the Gadites and the half-tribe of Manasseh to be their possession.

7These are the kings of the land that Joshua and the Israelites conquered on the west side of the Jordan, from Baal Gad in the Valley of Lebanon to Mount Halak, which rises toward Seir (their lands Joshua gave as an inheritance to the tribes of Israel according to their tribal divisions— 8the hill country, the western foothills, the Arabah, the mountain slopes, the desert and the Negev—the lands of the Hittites, Amorites, Canaanites, Perizzites, Hivites and Jebusites):

9the king of Jericho	one
the king of Ai (near Bethel)	one
10the king of Jerusalem	one
the king of Hebron	one
11the king of Jarmuth	one
the king of Lachish	one
12the king of Eglon	one
the king of Gezer	one
13the king of Debir	one
the king of Geder	one
14the king of Hormah	one
the king of Arad	one
15the king of Libnah	one
the king of Adullam	one
16the king of Makkedah	one
the king of Bethel	one
17the king of Tappuah	one
the king of Hepher	one
18the king of Aphek	one
the king of Lasharon	one

---

a 3 That is, Galilee   b 3 That is, the Dead Sea

Living Bible

21During this period Joshua routed all of the giants—the descendants of Anak who lived in the hill country in Hebron, Debir, Anab, Judah, and Israel; he killed them all and completely destroyed their cities. 22None was left in all the land of Israel, though some still remained in Gaza, Gath, and Ashdod.

23So Joshua took the entire land just as the Lord had instructed Moses; and he gave it to the people of Israel as their inheritance, dividing the land among the tribes. So the land finally rested from its war.

12 HERE IS the list of the kings on the east side of the Jordan River whose cities were destroyed by the Israelis: (The area involved stretched all the way from the valley of the Arnon River to Mount Hermon, including the cities of the eastern desert.)

2King Sihon of the Amorites, who lived in Heshbon. His kingdom extended from Aroer, on the edge of the Arnon Valley, and from the middle of the valley of the Arnon River to the Jabbok River, which is the boundary of the Ammonites. This includes half of the present area of Gilead, which lies north of the Jabbok River. 3Sihon also controlled the Jordan River valley as far north as the western shores of the Lake of Galilee; and as far south as the Dead Sea and the slopes of Mount Pisgah.

4King Og of Bashan, the last of the Rephaim, who lived at Ashtaroth and Edre-i: 5He ruled a territory stretching from Mount Hermon in the north to Salecah on Mount Bashan in the east, and on the west, extending to the boundary of the kingdoms of Geshur and Ma-acah. His kingdom also stretched south to include the northern half of Gilead where the boundary touched the border of the kingdom of Sihon, king of Heshbon. 6Moses and the people of Israel had destroyed these people, and Moses gave the land to the tribes of Reuben and the half-tribe of Manasseh.

7Here is a list of the kings destroyed by Joshua and the armies of Israel on the west side of the Jordan. (This land which lay between Baal-gad in the Valley of Lebanon and Mount Halak, west of Mount Seir, was allotted by Joshua to the other tribes of Israel. 8–24The area included the hill country, the lowlands, the Arabah, the mountain slopes, the Judean Desert, and the Negeb. The people who lived there were the Hittites, the Amorites, the Canaanites, the Perizzites, the Hivites, and the Jebusites):

The king of Jericho;
The king of Ai, near Bethel;
The king of Jerusalem;
The king of Hebron;
The king of Jarmuth;
The king of Lachish;
The king of Eglon;
The king of Gezer;
The king of Debir;
The king of Geder;
The king of Hormah;
The king of Arad;
The king of Libnah;
The king of Adullam;
The king of Makkedah;
The king of Bethel;
The king of Tappu-ah;
The king of Hepher;
The king of Aphek;
The king of Lasharon;

New Revised Standard

21 At that time Joshua came and wiped out the Anakim from the hill country, from Hebron, from Debir, from Anab, and from all the hill country of Judah, and from all the hill country of Israel; Joshua utterly destroyed them with their towns. 22None of the Anakim was left in the land of the Israelites; some remained only in Gaza, in Gath, and in Ashdod. 23So Joshua took the whole land, according to all that the LORD had spoken to Moses; and Joshua gave it for an inheritance to Israel according to their tribal allotments. And the land had rest from war.

The Kings Conquered by Moses

12 NOW THESE are the kings of the land, whom the Israelites defeated, whose land they occupied beyond the Jordan toward the east, from the Wadi Arnon to Mount Hermon, with all the Arabah eastward: 2King Sihon of the Amorites who lived at Heshbon, and ruled from Aroer, which is on the edge of the Wadi Arnon, and from the middle of the valley as far as the river Jabbok, the boundary of the Ammonites, that is, half of Gilead, 3and the Arabah to the Sea of Chinneroth eastward, and in the direction of Beth-jeshimoth, to the sea of the Arabah, the Dead Sea,c southward to the foot of the slopes of Pisgah; 4and King Ogd of Bashan, one of the last of the Rephaim, who lived at Ashtaroth and at Edrei 5and ruled over Mount Hermon and Salecah and all Bashan to the boundary of the Geshurites and the Maacathites, and over half of Gilead to the boundary of King Sihon of Heshbon. 6Moses, the servant of the LORD, and the Israelites defeated them; and Moses the servant of the LORD gave their land for a possession to the Reubenites and the Gadites and the half-tribe of Manasseh.

The Kings Conquered by Joshua

7 The following are the kings of the land whom Joshua and the Israelites defeated on the west side of the Jordan, from Baal-gad in the valley of Lebanon to Mount Halak, that rises toward Seir (and Joshua gave their land to the tribes of Israel as a possession according to their allotments, 8in the hill country, in the lowland, in the Arabah, in the slopes, in the wilderness, and in the Negeb, the land of the Hittites, Amorites, Canaanites, Perizzites, Hivites, and Jebusites):

9	the king of Jericho	one
	the king of Ai, which is next to Bethel	one
10	the king of Jerusalem	one
	the king of Hebron	one
11	the king of Jarmuth	one
	the king of Lachish	one
12	the king of Eglon	one
	the king of Gezer	one
13	the king of Debir	one
	the king of Geder	one
14	the king of Hormah	one
	the king of Arad	one
15	the king of Libnah	one
	the king of Adullam	one
16	the king of Makkedah	one
	the king of Bethel	one
17	the king of Tappuah	one
	the king of Hepher	one
18	the king of Aphek	one
	the king of Lasharon	one

c Heb *Salt Sea*   d Gk: Heb *the boundary of King Og*

King James

19The king of Madon, one; the king of Hazor, one; 20The king of Shimron-meron, one; the king of Achshaph, one; 21The king of Taanach, one; the king of Megiddo, one; 22The king of Kedesh, one; the king of Jokneam of Carmel, one; 23The king of Dor in the coast of Dor, one; the king of the nations of Gilgal, one; 24The king of Tirzah, one: all the kings thirty and one.

13 NOW JOSHUA was old *and* stricken in years; and the LORD said unto him, Thou art old *and* stricken in years, and there remaineth yet very much land to be possessed.

2This *is* the land that yet remaineth: all the borders of the Philistines, and all Geshuri,

3From Sihor, which *is* before Egypt, even unto the borders of Ekron northward, *which* is counted to the Canaanite: five lords of the Philistines; the Gazathites, and the Ashdothites, the Eshkalonites, the Gittites, and the Ekronites; also the Avites:

4From the south, all the land of the Canaanites, and Mearah that *is* beside the Sidonians, unto Aphek, to the borders of the Amorites:

5And the land of the Giblites, and all Lebanon, toward the sunrising, from Baal-gad under mount Hermon unto the entering into Hamath.

6All the inhabitants of the hill country from Lebanon unto Misrephoth-maim, *and* all the Sidonians, them will I drive out from before the children of Israel: only divide thou it by lot unto the Israelites for an inheritance, as I have commanded thee.

7Now therefore divide this land for an inheritance unto the nine tribes, and the half tribe of Manasseh,

8With whom the Reubenites and the Gadites have received their inheritance, which Moses gave them, beyond Jordan eastward, *even* as Moses the servant of the LORD gave them;

9From Aroer, that *is* upon the bank of the river Arnon, and the city that *is* in the midst of the river, and all the plain of Medeba unto Dibon;

10And all the cities of Sihon king of the Amorites, which reigned in Heshbon, unto the border of the children of Ammon;

11And Gilead, and the border of the Geshurites and Maachathites, and all mount Hermon, and all Bashan unto Salcah;

12All the kingdom of Og in Bashan, which reigned in Ashtaroth and in Edrei, who remained of the remnant of the giants: for these did Moses smite, and cast them out.

13Nevertheless the children of Israel expelled not the Geshurites, nor the Maachathites: but the Geshurites and the Maachathites dwell among the Israelites until this day.

14Only unto the tribe of Levi he gave none inheritance; the sacrifices of the LORD God of Israel made by fire *are* their inheritance, as he said unto them.

15¶ And Moses gave unto the tribe of the children of Reuben *inheritance* according to their families.

New International

19the king of Madon   one
the king of Hazor   one
20the king of Shimron Meron   one
the king of Acshaph   one
21the king of Taanach   one
the king of Megiddo   one
22the king of Kedesh   one
the king of Jokneam in Carmel   one
23the king of Dor (in Naphoth Dora)   one
the king of Goyim in Gilgal   one
24the king of Tirzah   one
thirty-one kings in all.

Land Still to Be Taken

13 WHEN JOSHUA was old and well advanced in years, the LORD said to him, "You are very old, and there are still very large areas of land to be taken over.

2"This is the land that remains: all the regions of the Philistines and Geshurites: 3from the Shihor River on the east of Egypt to the territory of Ekron on the north, all of it counted as Canaanite (the territory of the five Philistine rulers in Gaza, Ashdod, Ashkelon, Gath and Ekron—that of the Avvites); 4from the south, all the land of the Canaanites, from Arah of the Sidonians as far as Aphek, the region of the Amorites, 5the area of the Gebalitesb; and all Lebanon to the east, from Baal Gad below Mount Hermon to Leboc Hamath.

6"As for all the inhabitants of the mountain regions from Lebanon to Misrephoth Maim, that is, all the Sidonians, I myself will drive them out before the Israelites. Be sure to allocate this land to Israel for an inheritance, as I have instructed you, 7and divide it as an inheritance among the nine tribes and half of the tribe of Manasseh."

Division of the Land East of the Jordan

8The other half of Manasseh,d the Reubenites and the Gadites had received the inheritance that Moses had given them east of the Jordan, as he, the servant of the LORD, had assigned it to them.

9It extended from Aroer on the rim of the Arnon Gorge, and from the town in the middle of the gorge, and included the whole plateau of Medeba as far as Dibon, 10and all the towns of Sihon king of the Amorites, who ruled in Heshbon, out to the border of the Ammonites. 11It also included Gilead, the territory of the people of Geshur and Maacah, all of Mount Hermon and all Bashan as far as Salecah— 12that is, the whole kingdom of Og in Bashan, who had reigned in Ashtaroth and Edrei and had survived as one of the last of the Rephaites. Moses had defeated them and taken over their land. 13But the Israelites did not drive out the people of Geshur and Maacah, so they continue to live among the Israelites to this day.

14But to the tribe of Levi he gave no inheritance, since the offerings made by fire to the LORD, the God of Israel, are their inheritance, as he promised them.

15This is what Moses had given to the tribe of Reuben, clan by clan:

---

a 23 Or *in the heights of Dor*   b 5 That is, the area of Byblos   c 5 Or *to the entrance to*   d 8 Hebrew *With it* (that is, with the other half of Manasseh)

Living Bible

The king of Madon;
The king of Hazor;
The king of Shimron-meron;
The king of Achshaph;
The king of Taanach;
The king of Megiddo;
The king of Kedesh;
The king of Jokne-am, in Carmel;
The king of Dor in the city of Naphathdor;
The king of Goiim in Gilgal;
The king of Tirzah.

So in all, thirty-one kings and their cities were destroyed.

13 JOSHUA WAS now an old man. "You are growing old," the Lord said to him, "and there are still many nations to be conquered. 2-7Here is a list of the areas still to be occupied:

All the land of the Philistines;
The land of the Geshurites;
The territory now belonging to the Canaanites from the brook of Egypt to the southern boundary of Ekron;
Five cities of the Philistines: Gaza, Ashdod, Ashkelon, Gath, Ekron;
The land of the Avvim in the south;
In the north,e all the land of the Canaanites, including Me-arah (which belongs to the Sidonians), stretching northwardf to Aphek at the boundary of the Amorites;
The land of the Gebalites on the coastg and all of the Lebanon mountain area from Baal-gad beneath Mount Hermon in the south to the entrance of Hamath in the north;
All the hill country from Lebanon to Misrephoth-maim, including all the land of the Sidonians.

I am ready to drive these people out from before the nation of Israel, so include all this territory when you divide the land among the nine tribes and the half-tribe of Manasseh as I have commanded you."

8The other half of the tribe of Manasseh, and the tribes of Reuben and Gad, had already received their inheritance on the east side of the Jordan, for Moses had previously assigned this land to them. 9Their territory ran from Aroer, on the edge of the valley of the Arnon River, included the city in the valley, and crossed the tableland of Medeba to Dibon; 10it also included all the cities of King Sihon of the Amorites, who reigned in Heshbon, and extended as far as the borders of Ammon. 11It included Gilead; the territory of the Geshurites and the Ma-acathites; all of Mount Hermon; Mount Bashan with its city of Salecah; 12and all the territory of King Og of Bashan, who had reigned in Ashtaroth and Edre-i. (He was the last of the Rephaim, for Moses had attacked them and driven them out. 13However, the people of Israel had not driven out the Geshurites or the Ma-acathites, who still live there among the Israelites to this day.)

14The Territorial Assignments
The Land Given to the Tribe of Levi:
Moses hadn't assigned any land to the tribe of Levi: instead, they were given the offerings brought to the Lord.

15*The Land Given to the Tribe of Reuben:*
Fitting the size of its territory to its size of population,h Moses had assigned the following area to the tribe of Reuben: 16Their land extended from Aroer on the

New Revised Standard

19 the king of Madon	one
the king of Hazor	one
20 the king of Shimron-meron	one
the king of Achshaph	one
21 the king of Taanach	one
the king of Megiddo	one
22 the king of Kedesh	one
the king of Jokneam in Carmel	one
23 the king of Dor in Naphath-dor	one
the king of Goiim in Galilee,i	one
24 the king of Tirzah	one

thirty-one kings in all.

The Parts of Canaan Still Unconquered

13 NOW JOSHUA was old and advanced in years; and the LORD said to him, "You are old and advanced in years, and very much of the land still remains to be possessed. 2This is the land that still remains: all the regions of the Philistines, and all those of the Geshurites 3(from the Shihor, which is east of Egypt, northward to the boundary of Ekron, it is reckoned as Canaanite; there are five rulers of the Philistines, those of Gaza, Ashdod, Ashkelon, Gath, and Ekron), and those of the Avvim, 4in the south, all the land of the Canaanites, and Mearah that belongs to the Sidonians, to Aphek, to the boundary of the Amorites, 5and the land of the Gebalites, and all Lebanon, toward the east, from Baal-gad below Mount Hermon to Lebo-hamath, 6all the inhabitants of the hill country from Lebanon to Misrephoth-maim, even all the Sidonians. I will myself drive them out from before the Israelites; only allot the land to Israel for an inheritance, as I have commanded you. 7Now therefore divide this land for an inheritance to the nine tribes and the half-tribe of Manasseh."

The Territory East of the Jordan

8 With the other half-tribe of Manasseh the Reubenites and the Gadites received their inheritance, which Moses gave them, beyond the Jordan eastward, as Moses the servant of the LORD gave them: 9from Aroer, which is on the edge of the Wadi Arnon, and the town that is in the middle of the valley, and all the tableland fromk Medeba as far as Dibon; 10and all the cities of King Sihon of the Amorites, who reigned in Heshbon, as far as the boundary of the Ammonites; 11and Gilead, and the region of the Geshurites and Maacathites, and all Mount Hermon, and all Bashan to Salecah; 12all the kingdom of Og in Bashan, who reigned in Ashtaroth and in Edrei (he alone was left of the survivors of the Rephaim); these Moses had defeated and driven out. 13Yet the Israelites did not drive out the Geshurites or the Maacathites; but Geshur and Maacath live within Israel to this day.

14 To the tribe of Levi alone Moses gave no inheritance; the offerings by fire to the LORD God of Israel are their inheritance, as he said to them.

The Territory of Reuben

15 Moses gave an inheritance to the tribe of the Reubenites according to their clans. 16Their territory

---

e 13:2-7 *In the north* implied.   f 13:2-7 *stretching northward* implied.
g 13:2-7 *on the coast* implied.   h 13:15 *size of population,* literally, "according to its families."

i Gk: Heb *Gilgal*   j Cn: Heb *With it*   k Compare Gk: Heb lacks *from*

King James

16And their coast was from Aroer, that *is* on the bank of the river Arnon, and the city that *is* in the midst of the river, and all the plain by Medeba;

17Heshbon, and all her cities that *are* in the plain; Dibon, and Bamoth-baal, and Beth-baal-meon,

18And Jahaza, and Kedemoth, and Mephaath,

19And Kirjathaim, and Sibmah, and Zareth-shahar in the mount of the valley,

20And Beth-peor, and Ashdoth-pisgah, and Beth-jeshimoth,

21And all the cities of the plain, and all the kingdom of Sihon king of the Amorites, which reigned in Heshbon, whom Moses smote with the princes of Midian, Evi, and Rekem, and Zur, and Hur, and Reba, *which were* dukes of Sihon, dwelling in the country.

22¶ Balaam also the son of Beor, the soothsayer, did the children of Israel slay with the sword among them that were slain by them.

23And the border of the children of Reuben was Jordan, and the border *thereof*. This *was* the inheritance of the children of Reuben after their families, the cities and the villages thereof.

24And Moses gave *inheritance* unto the tribe of Gad, *even* unto the children of Gad according to their families.

25And their coast was Jazer, and all the cities of Gilead, and half the land of the children of Ammon, unto Aroer that *is* before Rabbah;

26And from Heshbon unto Ramath-mizpeh, and Betonim; and from Mahanaim unto the border of Debir;

27And in the valley, Beth-aram, and Beth-nimrah, and Succoth, and Zaphon, the rest of the kingdom of Sihon king of Heshbon, Jordan and *his* border, *even* unto the edge of the sea of Chinnereth on the other side Jordan eastward.

28This *is* the inheritance of the children of Gad after their families, the cities, and their villages.

29¶ And Moses gave *inheritance* unto the half tribe of Manasseh: and *this* was *the possession* of the half tribe of the children of Manasseh by their families.

30And their coast was from Mahanaim, all Bashan, all the kingdom of Og king of Bashan, and all the towns of Jair, which *are* in Bashan, threescore cities:

31And half Gilead, and Ashtaroth, and Edrei, cities of the kingdom of Og in Bashan, *were pertaining* unto the children of Machir the son of Manasseh, *even* to the one half of the children of Machir by their families.

32These *are the countries* which Moses did distribute for inheritance in the plains of Moab, on the other side Jordan, by Jericho, eastward.

33But unto the tribe of Levi Moses gave not *any* inheritance: the LORD God of Israel *was* their inheritance, as he said unto them.

14 AND THESE *are the countries* which the children of Israel inherited in the land of Canaan, which Eleazar the priest, and Joshua the son of Nun, and the heads of the fathers of the tribes of the children of Israel, distributed for inheritance to them.

2By lot *was* their inheritance, as the LORD commanded by the hand of Moses, for the nine tribes, and *for* the half tribe.

New International

16The territory from Aroer on the rim of the Arnon Gorge, and from the town in the middle of the gorge, and the whole plateau past Medeba 17to Heshbon and all its towns on the plateau, including Dibon, Bamoth Baal, Beth Baal Meon, 18Jahaz, Kedemoth, Mephaath, 19Kiriathaim, Sibmah, Zereth Shahar on the hill in the valley, 20Beth Peor, the slopes of Pisgah, and Beth Jeshimoth 21—all the towns on the plateau and the entire realm of Sihon king of the Amorites, who ruled at Heshbon. Moses had defeated him and the Midianite chiefs, Evi, Rekem, Zur, Hur and Reba—princes allied with Sihon—who lived in that country. 22In addition to those slain in battle, the Israelites had put to the sword Balaam son of Beor, who practiced divination. 23The boundary of the Reubenites was the bank of the Jordan. These towns and their villages were the inheritance of the Reubenites, clan by clan.

24This is what Moses had given to the tribe of Gad, clan by clan:

25The territory of Jazer, all the towns of Gilead and half the Ammonite country as far as Aroer, near Rabbah; 26and from Heshbon to Ramath Mizpah and Betonim, and from Mahanaim to the territory of Debir; 27and in the valley, Beth Haram, Beth Nimrah, Succoth and Zaphon with the rest of the realm of Sihon king of Heshbon (the east side of the Jordan, the territory up to the end of the Sea of Kinneretha). 28These towns and their villages were the inheritance of the Gadites, clan by clan.

29This is what Moses had given to the half-tribe of Manasseh, that is, to half the family of the descendants of Manasseh, clan by clan:

30The territory extending from Mahanaim and including all of Bashan, the entire realm of Og king of Bashan—all the settlements of Jair in Bashan, sixty towns, 31half of Gilead, and Ashtaroth and Edrei (the royal cities of Og in Bashan). This was for the descendants of Makir son of Manasseh—for half of the sons of Makir, clan by clan.

32This is the inheritance Moses had given when he was in the plains of Moab across the Jordan east of Jericho. 33But to the tribe of Levi, Moses had given no inheritance; the LORD, the God of Israel, is their inheritance, as he promised them.

Division of the Land West of the Jordan

14 NOW THESE are the areas the Israelites received as an inheritance in the land of Canaan, which Eleazar the priest, Joshua son of Nun and the heads of the tribal clans of Israel allotted to them. 2Their inheritances were assigned by lot to the nine-and-a-half tribes, as the LORD had commanded through Moses.

---

a 27 That is, Galilee

Living Bible

edge of the valley of the Arnon River, past the city of Arnon in the middle of the valley, to beyond the tableland near Medeba. 17It included Heshbon and the other cities on the plain—Dibon, Bamoth-baal, Beth-baal-meon, 18Jahaz, Kedemoth, Mepha-ath, 19Kiriathaim, Sibmah, Zereth-shahar on the mountain above the valley, 20Beth-peor, Beth-jeshimoth, and the slopes of Mount Pisgah.

21The land of Reuben also included the cities of the tableland and the kingdom of Sihon. Sihon was the king who had lived in Heshbon and was killed by Moses along with the other chiefs of Midian—Evi, Rekem, Zur, Hur, and Reba. 22The people of Israel also killed Balaam the magician, the son of Beor. 23The Jordan River was the western boundary of the tribe of Reuben.

24*The Land Given to the Tribe of Gad:*

Moses also assigned land to the tribe of Gad in proportion to its population.b 25This territory included Jazer, all the cities of Gilead and half of the land of Ammon as far as Aroer near Rabbah. 26It also extended from Heshbon to Ramath-mizpeh and Betonim, and from Mahanaim to Lodebar. 27, 28In the valley were Beth-haram, and Beth-nimrah, Succoth, Zaphon, and the rest of the kingdom of King Sihon of Heshbon. The Jordan River was the western border, extending as far as the Lake of Galilee; then the border turned east from the Jordan River.

29*The Land Given to the Half-Tribe of Manasseh:*

Moses had assigned the following territory to the half-tribe of Manasseh in proportion to its needs:c 30Their territory extended north from Mahanaim, included all of Bashan, the former kingdom of King Og, and the sixty cities of Jair in Bashan. 31Half of Gilead and King Og's royal cities of Ashtaroth and Edre-i were given to half of the clan Machir, who was Manasseh's son.

32That was how Moses divided the land east of the Jordan River where the people were camped at that time across from Jericho. 33But Moses had given no land to the tribe of Levi for, as he had explained to them, the Lord God was their inheritance. He was all they needed. He would take care of them in other ways.

14 THE CONQUERED lands of Canaan were allotted to the remaining nine and a half tribes of Israel. The decision as to which tribe would receive which area was decided by throwing dice before the Lord, and he caused them to turn up in the ways he wanted.d Eleazar the priest, Joshua, and the tribal leaders supervised the lottery.

New Revised Standard

was from Aroer, which is on the edge of the Wadi Arnon, and the town that is in the middle of the valley, and all the tableland by Medeba; 17with Heshbon, and all its towns that are in the tableland; Dibon, and Bamoth-baal, and Beth-baal-meon, 18and Jahaz, and Kedemoth, and Mephaath, 19and Kiriathaim, and Sibmah, and Zereth-shahar on the hill of the valley, 20and Beth-peor, and the slopes of Pisgah, and Beth-jeshimoth, 21that is, all the towns of the tableland, and all the kingdom of King Sihon of the Amorites, who reigned in Heshbon, whom Moses defeated with the leaders of Midian, Evi and Rekem and Zur and Hur and Reba, as princes of Sihon, who lived in the land. 22Along with the rest of those they put to death, the Israelites also put to the sword Balaam son of Beor, who practiced divination. 23And the border of the Reubenites was the Jordan and its banks. This was the inheritance of the Reubenites, according to their families with their towns and villages.

The Territory of Gad

24 Moses gave an inheritance also to the tribe of the Gadites, according to their families. 25Their territory was Jazer, and all the towns of Gilead, and half the land of the Ammonites, to Aroer, which is east of Rabbah, 26and from Heshbon to Ramath-mizpeh and Betonim, and from Mahanaim to the territory of Debir,e 27and in the valley Beth-haram, Beth-nimrah, Succoth, and Zaphon, the rest of the kingdom of King Sihon of Heshbon, the Jordan and its banks, as far as the lower end of the Sea of Chinnereth, eastward beyond the Jordan. 28This is the inheritance of the Gadites according to their clans, with their towns and villages.

The Territory of the Half-Tribe of Manasseh (East)

29 Moses gave an inheritance to the half-tribe of Manasseh; it was allotted to the half-tribe of the Manassites according to their families. 30Their territory extended from Mahanaim, through all Bashan, the whole kingdom of King Og of Bashan, and all the settlements of Jair, which are in Bashan, sixty towns, 31and half of Gilead, and Ashtaroth, and Edrei, the towns of the kingdom of Og in Bashan; these were allotted to the people of Machir son of Manasseh according to their clans—for half the Machirites.

32 These are the inheritances that Moses distributed in the plains of Moab, beyond the Jordan east of Jericho. 33But to the tribe of Levi Moses gave no inheritance; the Lord God of Israel is their inheritance, as he said to them.

The Distribution of Territory West of the Jordan

14 THESE ARE the inheritances that the Israelites received in the land of Canaan, which the priest Eleazar, and Joshua son of Nun, and the heads of the families of the tribes of the Israelites distributed to them. 2Their inheritance was by lot, as the Lord had commanded Moses for the nine and one-half tribes. 3For

b 13:24 *in proportion to its population,* literally, "according to its families."
c 13:29 *in proportion to its needs,* literally, "according to its families."
d 14:2 *by throwing dice,* literally, "by lot."

e Gk Syr Vg: Heb *Lidebir*

King James

3For Moses had given the inheritance of two tribes and an half tribe on the other side Jordan: but unto the Levites he gave none inheritance among them. 4For the children of Joseph were two tribes, Manasseh and Ephraim: therefore they gave no part unto the Levites in the land, save cities to dwell *in*, with their suburbs for their cattle and for their substance. 5As the LORD commanded Moses, so the children of Israel did, and they divided the land.

6¶ Then the children of Judah came unto Joshua in Gilgal: and Caleb the son of Jephunneh the Kenezite said unto him, Thou knowest the thing that the LORD said unto Moses the man of God concerning me and thee in Kadesh-barnea. 7Forty years old *was* I when Moses the servant of the LORD sent me from Kadesh-barnea to espy out the land; and I brought him word again as *it was* in mine heart. 8Nevertheless my brethren that went up with me made the heart of the people melt: but I wholly followed the LORD my God. 9And Moses sware on that day, saying, Surely the land whereon thy feet have trodden shall be thine inheritance, and thy children's for ever, because thou hast wholly followed the LORD my God. 10And now, behold, the LORD hath kept me alive, as he said, these forty and five years, even since the LORD spake this word unto Moses, while *the children of* Israel wandered in the wilderness: and now, lo, I *am* this day fourscore and five years old. 11As yet I *am as* strong this day as *I was* in the day that Moses sent me: as my strength *was* then, even so *is* my strength now, for war, both to go out, and to come in. 12Now therefore give me this mountain, whereof the LORD spake in that day; for thou heardest in that day how the Anakims *were* there, and *that* the cities *were* great *and* fenced: if so be the LORD *will be* with me, then I shall be able to drive them out, as the LORD said. 13And Joshua blessed him, and gave unto Caleb the son of Jephunneh Hebron for an inheritance. 14Hebron therefore became the inheritance of Caleb the son of Jephunneh the Kenezite unto this day, because that he wholly followed the LORD God of Israel. 15And the name of Hebron before *was* Kirjath-arba; *which Arba was* a great man among the Anakims. And the land had rest from war.

15 THIS THEN was the lot of the tribe of the children of Judah by their families; *even* to the border of Edom the wilderness of Zin southward *was* the uttermost part of the south coast. 2And their south border was from the shore of the salt sea, from the bay that looketh southward: 3And it went out to the south side to Maaleh-acrabbim, and passed along to Zin, and ascended up on the south side unto Kadesh-barnea, and passed along to Hezron, and went up to Adar, and fetched a compass to Karkaa: 4From thence it passed toward Azmon, and went out unto the river of Egypt; and the goings out of that coast were at the sea: this shall be your south coast. 5And the east border *was* the salt sea, *even* unto the end of Jordan. And *their* border in the north quarter *was* from the bay of the sea at the uttermost part of Jordan: 6And the border went up to Beth-hoglah, and passed along by the north by Beth-arabah; and the border went up to the stone of Bohan the son of Reuben:

New International

3Moses had granted the two-and-a-half tribes their inheritance east of the Jordan but had not granted the Levites an inheritance among the rest, 4for the sons of Joseph had become two tribes—Manasseh and Ephraim. The Levites received no share of the land but only towns to live in, with pasturelands for their flocks and herds. 5So the Israelites divided the land, just as the LORD had commanded Moses.

Hebron Given to Caleb

6Now the men of Judah approached Joshua at Gilgal, and Caleb son of Jephunneh the Kenizzite said to him, "You know what the LORD said to Moses the man of God at Kadesh Barnea about you and me. 7I was forty years old when Moses the servant of the LORD sent me from Kadesh Barnea to explore the land. And I brought him back a report according to my convictions, 8but my brothers who went up with me made the hearts of the people melt with fear. I, however, followed the LORD my God wholeheartedly. 9So on that day Moses swore to me, 'The land on which your feet have walked will be your inheritance and that of your children forever, because you have followed the LORD my God wholeheartedly.'a

10"Now then, just as the LORD promised, he has kept me alive for forty-five years since the time he said this to Moses, while Israel moved about in the desert. So here I am today, eighty-five years old! 11I am still as strong today as the day Moses sent me out; I'm just as vigorous to go out to battle now as I was then. 12Now give me this hill country that the LORD promised me that day. You yourself heard then that the Anakites were there and their cities were large and fortified, but, the LORD helping me, I will drive them out just as he said."

13Then Joshua blessed Caleb son of Jephunneh and gave him Hebron as his inheritance. 14So Hebron has belonged to Caleb son of Jephunneh the Kenizzite ever since, because he followed the LORD, the God of Israel, wholeheartedly. 15(Hebron used to be called Kiriath Arba after Arba, who was the greatest man among the Anakites.)

Then the land had rest from war.

Allotment for Judah

15 THE ALLOTMENT for the tribe of Judah, clan by clan, extended down to the territory of Edom, to the Desert of Zin in the extreme south.

2Their southern boundary started from the bay at the southern end of the Salt Sea,b 3crossed south of Scorpionc Pass, continued on to Zin and went over to the south of Kadesh Barnea. Then it ran past Hezron up to Addar and curved around to Karka. 4It then passed along to Azmon and joined the Wadi of Egypt, ending at the sea. This is theird southern boundary.

5The eastern boundary is the Salt Sea as far as the mouth of the Jordan.

The northern boundary started from the bay of the sea at the mouth of the Jordan, 6went up to Beth Hoglah and continued north of Beth Arabah to the Stone of Bohan son of Reuben. 7The boundary then

Living Bible

3, 4(Moses had already given land to the two and a half tribes on the east side of the Jordan River. The tribe of Joseph had become two separate tribes, Manasseh and Ephraim, and the Levites were given no land at all, except cities in which to live and the surrounding pasturelands for their cattle. 5So the distribution of the land was in strict accordance with the Lord's directions to Moses.)

6*The Land Given to Caleb:*

A delegation from the tribe of Judah, led by Caleb, came to Joshua in Gilgal.

"Remember what the Lord said to Moses about you and me when we were at Kadesh-barnea?" Caleb asked Joshua. 7"I was forty years old at the time, and Moses had sent us from Kadesh-barnea to spy out the land of Canaan. I reported what I felt was the truth, 8but our brothers who went with us frightened the people and discouraged them from entering the Promised Land. But since I had followed the Lord my God, 9Moses told me, 'The section of Canaan you were just in shall belong to you and your descendants forever.'

10"Now, as you see, from that time until now the Lord has kept me alive and well for all these forty-five years since crisscrossing the wilderness, and today I am eighty-five years old. 11I am as strong now as I was when Moses sent us on that journey, and I can still travel and fight as well as I could then! 12So I'm asking that you give me the hill country which the Lord promised me. You will remember that as spies we found the Anakim living there in great, walled cities, but if the Lord is with me I shall drive them out of the land."

13, 14So Joshua blessed him and gave him Hebron as a permanent inheritance because he had followed the Lord God of Israel. 15(Before that time Hebron had been called Kiriath-arba, after a great hero of the Anakim.)

And there was no resistance from the local populations as the Israelis resettled the land.

15 THE LAND given *to the Tribe of Judah* (as assigned by sacred lot):

Judah's southern boundary began at the northern border of Edom, crossed the Wilderness of Zin, and ended at the northern edge of the Negeb. 2, 3, 4More specifically, this boundary began at the south bay of the Dead Sea, ran along the road going south of Mount Akrabbim, on into the Wilderness of Zin to Hezron (south of Kadesh-barnea), and then up through Karka and Azmon, until it finally reached the Brook of Egypt, and along that to the Mediterranean Sea.

5The eastern boundary extended along the Dead Sea to the mouth of the Jordan River.

The northern boundary began at the bay where the Jordan River empties into the Salt Sea, 6crossed to Beth-hoglah, then proceeded north of Beth-arabah to the stone of Bohan (son of Reuben). 7From that point it went

New Revised Standard

Moses had given an inheritance to the two and one-half tribes beyond the Jordan; but to the Levites he gave no inheritance among them. 4For the people of Joseph were two tribes, Manasseh and Ephraim; and no portion was given to the Levites in the land, but only towns to live in, with their pasture lands for their flocks and herds. 5The Israelites did as the LORD commanded Moses; they allotted the land.

Hebron Allotted to Caleb

6 Then the people of Judah came to Joshua at Gilgal; and Caleb son of Jephunneh the Kenizzite said to him, "You know what the LORD said to Moses the man of God in Kadesh-barnea concerning you and me. 7I was forty years old when Moses the servant of the LORD sent me from Kadesh-barnea to spy out the land; and I brought him an honest report. 8But my companions who went up with me made the heart of the people melt; yet I wholeheartedly followed the LORD my God. 9And Moses swore on that day, saying, 'Surely the land on which your foot has trodden shall be an inheritance for you and your children forever, because you have wholeheartedly followed the LORD my God.' 10And now, as you see, the LORD has kept me alive, as he said, these forty-five years since the time that the LORD spoke this word to Moses, while Israel was journeying through the wilderness; and here I am today, eighty-five years old. 11I am still as strong today as I was on the day that Moses sent me; my strength now is as my strength was then, for war, and for going and coming. 12So now give me this hill country of which the LORD spoke on that day; for you heard on that day how the Anakim were there, with great fortified cities; it may be that the LORD will be with me, and I shall drive them out, as the LORD said."

13 Then Joshua blessed him, and gave Hebron to Caleb son of Jephunneh for an inheritance. 14So Hebron became the inheritance of Caleb son of Jephunneh the Kenizzite to this day, because he wholeheartedly followed the LORD, the God of Israel. 15Now the name of Hebron formerly was Kiriath-arba;e this Arba wasf the greatest man among the Anakim. And the land had rest from war.

The Territory of Judah

15 THE LOT for the tribe of the people of Judah according to their families reached southward to the boundary of Edom, to the wilderness of Zin at the farthest south. 2And their south boundary ran from the end of the Dead Sea,g from the bay that faces southward; 3it goes out southward of the ascent of Akrabbim, passes along to Zin, and goes up south of Kadesh-barnea, along by Hezron, up to Addar, makes a turn to Karka, 4passes along to Azmon, goes out by the Wadi of Egypt, and comes to its end at the sea. This shall be your south boundary. 5And the east boundary is the Dead Sea,g to the mouth of the Jordan. And the boundary on the north side runs from the bay of the sea at the mouth of the Jordan; 6and the boundary goes up to Beth-hoglah, and passes along north of Beth-arabah; and the boundary goes up to the Stone of Bohan, Reuben's son;

e That is *the city of Arba*   f Heb lacks *this Arba was*   g Heb *Salt Sea*

King James

7And the border went up toward Debir from the valley of Achor, and so northward, looking toward Gilgal, that *is* before the going up to Adummim, which *is* on the south side of the river: and the border passed toward the waters of En-shemesh, and the goings out thereof were at En-rogel:

8And the border went up by the valley of the son of Hinnom unto the south side of the Jebusite; the same *is* Jerusalem: and the border went up to the top of the mountain that *lieth* before the valley of Hinnom westward, which *is* at the end of the valley of the giants northward:

9And the border was drawn from the top of the hill unto the fountain of the water of Nephtoah, and went out to the cities of mount Ephron; and the border was drawn to Baalah, which *is* Kirjath-jearim:

10And the border compassed from Baalah westward unto mount Seir, and passed along unto the side of mount Jearim, which *is* Chesalon, on the north side, and went down to Beth-shemesh, and passed on to Timnah:

11And the border went out unto the side of Ekron northward: and the border was drawn to Shicron, and passed along to mount Baalah, and went out unto Jabneel; and the goings out of the border were at the sea.

12And the west border *was* to the great sea, and the coast *thereof*. This *is* the coast of the children of Judah round about according to their families.

13¶ And unto Caleb the son of Jephunneh he gave a part among the children of Judah, according to the commandment of the LORD to Joshua, *even* the city of Arba the father of Anak, which *city is* Hebron.

14And Caleb drove thence the three sons of Anak, Sheshai, and Ahiman, and Talmai, the children of Anak.

15And he went up thence to the inhabitants of Debir: and the name of Debir before *was* Kirjath-sepher.

16¶ And Caleb said, He that smiteth Kirjath-sepher, and taketh it, to him will I give Achsah my daughter to wife.

17And Othniel the son of Kenaz, the brother of Caleb, took it: and he gave him Achsah his daughter to wife.

18And it came to pass, as she came *unto him*, that she moved him to ask of her father a field: and she lighted off *her* ass; and Caleb said unto her, What wouldest thou?

19Who answered, Give me a blessing; for thou hast given me a south land; give me also springs of water. And he gave her the upper springs, and the nether springs.

20This *is* the inheritance of the tribe of the children of Judah according to their families.

21And the uttermost cities of the tribe of the children of Judah toward the coast of Edom southward were Kabzeel, and Eder, and Jagur,

22And Kinah, and Dimonah, and Adadah,

23And Kedesh, and Hazor, and Ithnan,

24Ziph, and Telem, and Bealoth,

25And Hazor, Hadattah, and Kerioth, *and* Hezron, which *is* Hazor,

26Amam, and Shema, and Moladah,

27And Hazar-gaddah, and Heshmon, and Beth-palet,

28And Hazar-shual, and Beer-sheba, and Bizjothjah,

29Baalah, and Iim, and Azem,

30And Eltolad, and Chesil, and Hormah,

31And Ziklag, and Madmannah, and Sansannah,

32And Lebaoth, and Shilhim, and Ain, and Rimmon: all the cities *are* twenty and nine, with their villages:

33*And* in the valley, Eshtaol, and Zoreah, and Ashnah,

34And Zanoah, and En-gannim, Tappuah, and Enam,

35Jarmuth, and Adullam, Socoh, and Azekah,

36And Sharaim, and Adithaim, and Gederah, and Gederothaim; fourteen cities with their villages:

New International

went up to Debir from the Valley of Achor and turned north to Gilgal, which faces the Pass of Adummim south of the gorge. It continued along to the waters of En Shemesh and came out at En Rogel. 8Then it ran up the Valley of Ben Hinnom along the southern slope of the Jebusite city (that is, Jerusalem). From there it climbed to the top of the hill west of the Hinnom Valley at the northern end of the Valley of Rephaim. 9From the hilltop the boundary headed toward the spring of the waters of Nephtoah, came out at the towns of Mount Ephron and went down toward Baalah (that is, Kiriath Jearim). 10Then it curved westward from Baalah to Mount Seir, ran along the northern slope of Mount Jearim (that is, Kesalon), continued down to Beth Shemesh and crossed to Timnah. 11It went to the northern slope of Ekron, turned toward Shikkeron, passed along to Mount Baalah and reached Jabneel. The boundary ended at the sea.

12The western boundary is the coastline of the Great Sea.[a]

These are the boundaries around the people of Judah by their clans.

13In accordance with the LORD's command to him, Joshua gave to Caleb son of Jephunneh a portion in Judah—Kiriath Arba, that is, Hebron. (Arba was the forefather of Anak.) 14From Hebron Caleb drove out the three Anakites—Sheshai, Ahiman and Talmai—descendants of Anak. 15From there he marched against the people living in Debir (formerly called Kiriath Sepher). 16And Caleb said, "I will give my daughter Acsah in marriage to the man who attacks and captures Kiriath Sepher." 17Othniel son of Kenaz, Caleb's brother, took it; so Caleb gave his daughter Acsah to him in marriage.

18One day when she came to Othniel, she urged him[b] to ask her father for a field. When she got off her donkey, Caleb asked her, "What can I do for you?"

19She replied, "Do me a special favor. Since you have given me land in the Negev, give me also springs of water." So Caleb gave her the upper and lower springs.

20This is the inheritance of the tribe of Judah, clan by clan:

21The southernmost towns of the tribe of Judah in the Negev toward the boundary of Edom were:

Kabzeel, Eder, Jagur, 22Kinah, Dimonah, Adadah, 23Kedesh, Hazor, Ithnan, 24Ziph, Telem, Bealoth, 25Hazor Hadattah, Kerioth Hezron (that is, Hazor), 26Amam, Shema, Moladah, 27Hazar Gaddah, Heshmon, Beth Pelet, 28Hazar Shual, Beersheba, Biziothiah, 29Baalah, Iim, Ezem, 30Eltolad, Kesil, Hormah, 31Ziklag, Madmannah, Sansannah, 32Lebaoth, Shilhim, Ain and Rimmon—a total of twenty-nine towns and their villages.

33In the western foothills:

Eshtaol, Zorah, Ashnah, 34Zanoah, En Gannim, Tappuah, Enam, 35Jarmuth, Adullam, Socoh, Azekah, 36Shaaraim, Adithaim and Gederah (or Gederothaim)[c]—fourteen towns and their villages.

---

[a] *12* That is, the Mediterranean; also in verse 47　　[b] *18* Hebrew and some Septuagint manuscripts; other Septuagint manuscripts (see also note at Judges 1:14) *Othniel, he urged her*　　[c] *36* Or *Gederah and Gederothaim*

Living Bible

through the Valley of Achor to Debir, where it turned northwest toward Gilgal, opposite the slopes of Adummim on the south side of the valley. From there the border extended to the springs at Enshemesh and on to En-rogel. 8The boundary then passed through the Valley of Hinnom, along the southern shoulder of Jebus (where the city of Jerusalem is located), then west to the top of the mountain above the Valley of Hinnom and on up to the northern end of the Valley of Rephaim. 9From there the border extended from the top of the mountain to the spring of Nephtoah, and from there to the cities of Mount Ephron before it turned northward to circle around Baalah (which is another name for Kiriath-jearim). 10, 11Then the border circled west of Baalah to Mount Seir, passed along to the town of Chesalon on the northern shoulder of Mount Jearim, and went down to Beth-shemesh. Turning northwest again, the boundary line proceeded past the south of Timnah to the shoulder of the hill north of Ekron, where it bent to the left, passing south of Shikkeron and Mount Baalah. Turning again to the north, it passed Jabneel and ended at the Mediterranean Sea.

12The western border was the shoreline of the Mediterranean.

13*The Land Given to Caleb:*

The Lord instructed Joshua to assign some of Judah's territory to Caleb (son of Jephunneh), so he was given the city of Arba (also called Hebron), which had been named after Anak's father. 14Caleb drove out the descendants of the three sons of Anak: Talmai, Sheshai, and Ahiman. 15Then he fought against the people living in the city of Debir (formerly called Kiriath-sepher).

16Caleb said that he would give his daughter Achsah to be the wife of anyone who would go and capture Kiriath-sepher. 17Othni-el (son of Kenaz), Caleb's nephew, was the one who conquered it, so Achsah became Othni-el's wife. 18, 19As she was leaving with him, she urged him to ask her father for an additional field as a wedding present.d She got off her donkey to speak to Caleb about this.

"What is it? What can I do for you?" he asked.

And she replied, "Give me another present! For the land you gave me is a desert. Give us some springs, too!" Then he gave her the upper and lower springs.

20So this was the assignment of land to the tribe of Judah:

21-32The cities of Judah which were situated along the borders of Edom in the Negeb, namely:

Kabzeel, Eder, Jagur, Kinah,
Dimonah, Adadah, Kedesh, Hazor,
Ithnan, Ziph, Telem, Be-aloth,
Hazor-hadattah, Keri-oth-hezron
(or, Hazor), Amam, Shema,
Moladah, Hazar-gaddah, Heshmon,
Beth-pelet, Hazar-shual,
Beer-sheba, Biziothiah, Baalah, Iim,
Ezem, Eltolad, Chesil, Hormah,
Ziklag, Madmannah, Sansannah,
Lebaoth, Shilhim, Ain, and
Rimmon.

In all, there were twenty-nine of these cities with their surrounding villages.

33-36The following cities situated in the lowlands were also given to Judah:

Eshtaol, Zorah, Ashnah, Zanoah,
En-gannim, Tappu-ah, Enam,
Jarmuth, Adullam, Socoh, Azekah,
Sha-araim, Adithaim, Gederah, and
Gederothaim.

In all, there were fourteen of these cities with their surrounding villages.

New Revised Standard

7and the boundary goes up to Debir from the Valley of Achor, and so northward, turning toward Gilgal, which is opposite the ascent of Adummim, which is on the south side of the valley; and the boundary passes along to the waters of En-shemesh, and ends at En-rogel; 8 then the boundary goes up by the valley of the son of Hinnom at the southern slope of the Jebusites (that is, Jerusalem); and the boundary goes up to the top of the mountain that lies over against the valley of Hinnom, on the west, at the northern end of the valley of Rephaim; 9then the boundary extends from the top of the mountain to the spring of the Waters of Nephtoah, and from there to the towns of Mount Ephron; then the boundary bends around to Baalah (that is, Kiriath-jearim); 10and the boundary circles west of Baalah to Mount Seir, passes along to the northern slope of Mount Jearim (that is, Chesalon), and goes down to Beth-shemesh, and passes along by Timnah; 11the boundary goes out to the slope of the hill north of Ekron, then the boundary bends around to Shikkeron, and passes along to Mount Baalah, and goes out to Jabneel; then the boundary comes to an end at the sea. 12 And the west boundary was the Mediterranean with its coast. This is the boundary surrounding the people of Judah according to their families.

Caleb Occupies His Portion

13 According to the commandment of the LORD to Joshua, he gave to Caleb son of Jephunneh a portion among the people of Judah, Kiriath-arba,e that is, Hebron (Arba was the father of Anak). 14 And Caleb drove out from there the three sons of Anak: Sheshai, Ahiman, and Talmai, the descendants of Anak. 15From there he went up against the inhabitants of Debir; now the name of Debir formerly was Kiriath-sepher. 16 And Caleb said, "Whoever attacks Kiriath-sepher and takes it, to him I will give my daughter Achsah as wife." 17Othniel son of Kenaz, the brother of Caleb, took it; and he gave him his daughter Achsah as wife. 18 When she came to him, she urged him to ask her father for a field. As she dismounted from her donkey, Caleb said to her, "What do you wish?" 19She said to him, "Give me a present; since you have set me in the land of the Negeb, give me springs of water as well." So Caleb gave her the upper springs and the lower springs.

The Towns of Judah

20 This is the inheritance of the tribe of the people of Judah according to their families. 21The towns belonging to the tribe of the people of Judah in the extreme South, toward the boundary of Edom, were Kabzeel, Eder, Jagur, 22Kinah, Dimonah, Adadah, 23Kedesh, Hazor, Ithnan, 24Ziph, Telem, Bealoth, 25Hazorhadattah, Kerioth-hezron (that is, Hazor), 26Amam, Shema, Moladah, 27Hazar-gaddah, Heshmon, Bethpelet, 28Hazar-shual, Beer-sheba, Biziothiah, 29Baalah, Iim, Ezem, 30Eltolad, Chesil, Hormah, 31Ziklag, Madmannah, Sansannah, 32Lebaoth, Shilhim, Ain, and Rimmon: in all, twenty-nine towns, with their villages.

33 And in the Lowland, Eshtaol, Zorah, Ashnah, 34Zanoah, En-gannim, Tappuah, Enam, 35Jarmuth, Adullam, Socoh, Azekah, 36Shaaraim, Adithaim, Gederah, Gederothaim: fourteen towns with their villages.

---

d 15:18, 19 *as a wedding present,* implied.   e That is *the city of Arba*

King James

37Zenan, and Hadashah, and Migdal-gad,
38And Dilean, and Mizpeh, and Joktheel,
39Lachish, and Bozkath, and Eglon,
40And Cabbon, and Lahmam, and Kithlish,
41And Gederoth, Beth-dagon, and Naamah, and Makkedah; sixteen cities with their villages:
42Libnah, and Ether, and Ashan,
43And Jiphtah, and Ashnah, and Nezib,
44And Keilah, and Achzib, and Mareshah; nine cities with their villages:
45Ekron, with her towns and her villages:
46From Ekron even unto the sea, all that *lay* near Ashdod, with their villages:
47Ashdod with her towns and her villages, Gaza with her towns and her villages, unto the river of Egypt, and the great sea, and the border *thereof:*
48¶ And in the mountains, Shamir, and Jattir, and Socoh,
49And Dannah, and Kirjath-sannah, which *is* Debir,
50And Anab, and Eshtemoh, and Anim,
51And Goshen, and Holon, and Giloh; eleven cities with their villages:
52Arab, and Dumah, and Eshean,
53And Janum, and Beth-tappuah, and Aphekah,
54And Humtah, and Kirjath-arba, which *is* Hebron, and Zior; nine cities with their villages:
55Maon, Carmel, and Ziph, and Juttah,
56And Jezreel, and Jokdeam, and Zanoah,
57Cain, Gibeah, and Timnah; ten cities with their villages:
58Halhul, Beth-zur, and Gedor,
59And Maarath, and Beth-anoth, and Eltekon; six cities with their villages:
60Kirjath-baal, which *is* Kirjath-jearim, and Rabbah; two cities with their villages:
61In the wilderness, Beth-arabah, Middin, and Secacah,
62And Nibshan, and the city of Salt, and En-gedi; six cities with their villages.
63¶ As for the Jebusites the inhabitants of Jerusalem, the children of Judah could not drive them out: but the Jebusites dwell with the children of Judah at Jerusalem unto this day.

16 AND THE lot of the children of Joseph fell from Jordan by Jericho, unto the water of Jericho on the east, to the wilderness that goeth up from Jericho throughout mount Beth-el,
2And goeth out from Beth-el to Luz, and passeth along unto the borders of Archi to Ataroth,
3And goeth down westward to the coast of Japhleti, unto the coast of Beth-horon the nether, and to Gezer: and the goings out thereof are at the sea.
4So the children of Joseph, Manasseh and Ephraim, took their inheritance.
5¶ And the border of the children of Ephraim according to their families was *thus:* even the border of their inheritance on the east side was Ataroth-addar, unto Beth-horon the upper;
6And the border went out toward the sea to Michmethah on the north side; and the border went about eastward unto Taanath-shiloh, and passed by it on the east to Janohah;
7And it went down from Janohah to Ataroth, and to Naarath, and came to Jericho, and went out at Jordan.
8The border went out from Tappuah westward unto the river Kanah; and the goings out thereof were at the sea. This *is* the inheritance of the tribe of the children of Ephraim by their families.
9And the separate cities for the children of Ephraim *were* among the inheritance of the children of Manasseh, all the cities with their villages.

New International

37Zenan, Hadashah, Migdal Gad, 38Dilean, Mizpah, Joktheel, 39Lachish, Bozkath, Eglon, 40Cabbon, Lahmas, Kitlish, 41Gederoth, Beth Dagon, Naamah and Makkedah—sixteen towns and their villages.
42Libnah, Ether, Ashan, 43Iphtah, Ashnah, Nezib, 44Keilah, Aczib and Mareshah—nine towns and their villages.
45Ekron, with its surrounding settlements and villages; 46west of Ekron, all that were in the vicinity of Ashdod, together with their villages; 47Ashdod, its surrounding settlements and villages; and Gaza, its settlements and villages, as far as the Wadi of Egypt and the coastline of the Great Sea.

48In the hill country:
Shamir, Jattir, Socoh, 49Dannah, Kiriath Sannah (that is, Debir), 50Anab, Eshtemoh, Anim, 51Goshen, Holon and Giloh—eleven towns and their villages.
52Arab, Dumah, Eshan, 53Janim, Beth Tappuah, Aphekah, 54Humtah, Kiriath Arba (that is, Hebron) and Zior—nine towns and their villages.
55Maon, Carmel, Ziph, Juttah, 56Jezreel, Jokdeam, Zanoah, 57Kain, Gibeah and Timnah—ten towns and their villages.
58Halhul, Beth Zur, Gedor, 59Maarath, Beth Anoth and Eltekon—six towns and their villages.
60Kiriath Baal (that is, Kiriath Jearim) and Rabbah—two towns and their villages.

61In the desert:
Beth Arabah, Middin, Secacah, 62Nibshan, the City of Salt and En Gedi—six towns and their villages.
63Judah could not dislodge the Jebusites, who were living in Jerusalem; to this day the Jebusites live there with the people of Judah.

Allotment for Ephraim and Manasseh

16 THE ALLOTMENT for Joseph began at the Jordan of Jericho,[a] east of the waters of Jericho, and went up from there through the desert into the hill country of Bethel. 2It went on from Bethel (that is, Luz),[b] crossed over to the territory of the Arkites in Ataroth, 3descended westward to the territory of the Japhletites as far as the region of Lower Beth Horon and on to Gezer, ending at the sea.
4So Manasseh and Ephraim, the descendants of Joseph, received their inheritance.
5This was the territory of Ephraim, clan by clan:
The boundary of their inheritance went from Ataroth Addar in the east to Upper Beth Horon 6and continued to the sea. From Micmethath on the north it curved eastward to Taanath Shiloh, passing by it to Janoah on the east. 7Then it went down from Janoah to Ataroth and Naarah, touched Jericho and came out at the Jordan. 8From Tappuah the border went west to the Kanah Ravine and ended at the sea. This was the inheritance of the tribe of the Ephraimites, clan by clan. 9It also included all the towns and their villages that were set aside for the Ephraimites within the inheritance of the Manassites.

a 1 *Jordan of Jericho* was possibly an ancient name for the Jordan River.
b 2 Septuagint; Hebrew *Bethel to Luz*

Living Bible

37-44The tribe of Judah also inherited twenty-five oth-
er cities with their villages:c
  Zenan, Hadashah, Migdal-gad,
  Dilean, Mizpeh, Jokthe-el, Lachish,
  Bozkath, Eglon, Cabbon, Lahmam,
  Chitlish, Gederoth, Beth-dagon,
  Naamah, Makkedah, Libnah,
  Ether, Ashan, Iphtah, Ashnah,
  Nezib, Keilah, Achzib, and
  Mareshah.
45The territory of the tribe of Judah also included all
the towns and villages of Ekron. 46From Ekron the
boundary extended to the Mediterranean, and included
the cities along the borders of Ashdod with their nearby
villages; 47also the city of Ashdod with its villages, and
Gaza with its villages as far as the Brook of Egypt; also
the entire Mediterranean coast from the mouth of the
Brook of Egypt on the south, to Tyre on the north.
48-62Judah also received these forty-fourd cities in the
hill country with their surrounding villages:
  Shamir, Jattir, Socoh, Dannah,
  Kiriath-sannah (or Debir), Anab,
  Eshtemoh, Anim, Goshen, Holon,
  Giloh, Arab, Dumah, Eshan,
  Janim, Beth-tappu-ah, Aphekah,
  Humtah, Kiriath-arba (or, Hebron),
  Zior, Maon, Carmel, Ziph, Juttah,
  Jezreel, Jokde-am, Zanoah, Kain,
  Gibe-ah, Timnah, Halhul, Beth-zur,
  Gedor, Maarath, Beth-anoth,
  Eltekon, Kiriath-baal (also known
  as Kiriath-jearim), Rabbah,
  Beth-arabah, Middin, Secacah,
  Nibshan, The City of Salt, and En-gedi.
63But the tribe of Judah could not drive out the Jebu-
sites who lived in the city of Jerusalem, so the Jebusites
live there among the people of Judah to this day.

New Revised Standard

37 Zenan, Hadashah, Migdal-gad, 38Dilan, Mizpeh, Jokthe-el, 39Lachish, Bozkath, Eglon, 40Cabbon,
Lahmam, Chitlish, 41Gederoth, Beth-dagon, Naamah,
and Makkedah: sixteen towns with their villages.
42 Libnah, Ether, Ashan, 43Iphtah, Ashnah, Nezib,
44Keilah, Achzib, and Mareshah: nine towns with their
villages.
45 Ekron, with its dependencies and its villages;
46from Ekron to the sea, all that were near Ashdod, with
their villages.
47 Ashdod, its towns and its villages; Gaza, its
towns and its villages; to the Wadi of Egypt, and the
Great Sea with its coast.
48 And in the hill country, Shamir, Jattir, Socoh,
49Dannah, Kiriath-sannah (that is, Debir), 50Anab, Eshtemoh, Anim, 51Goshen, Holon, and Giloh: eleven
towns with their villages.
52 Arab, Dumah, Eshan, 53Janim, Beth-tappuah,
Aphekah, 54Humtah, Kiriath-arba (that is, Hebron), and
Zior: nine towns with their villages.
55 Maon, Carmel, Ziph, Juttah, 56Jezreel, Jokde-
am, Zanoah, 57Kain, Gibeah, and Timnah: ten towns
with their villages.
58 Halhul, Beth-zur, Gedor, 59Maarath, Beth-
anoth, and Eltekon: six towns with their villages.
60 Kiriath-baal (that is, Kiriath-jearim), and Rabbah: two towns with their villages.
61 In the wilderness, Beth-arabah, Middin, Secacah, 62Nibshan, the City of Salt, and En-gedi: six towns
with their villages.
63 But the people of Judah could not drive out the
Jebusites, the inhabitants of Jerusalem; so the Jebusites
live with the people of Judah in Jerusalem to this day.

The Territory of Ephraim

16 THE SOUTHERN boundary *of the Tribes of
Joseph* (Ephraim and the half-tribe of Manasseh):
  This boundary extended from the Jordan River at
Jericho through the wilderness and the hill country to
Bethel. It then went from Bethel to Luz, then on to
Ataroth, in the territory of the Archites; and west to the
border of the Japhletites as far as Lower Beth-horon,
then to Gezer and on over to the Mediterranean.
5, 6*The Land Given to the Tribe of Ephraim:* The eastern boundary began at Ataroth-addar. From there it ran
to Upper Beth-horon, then on to the Mediterranean Sea.
The northern boundary began at the Sea, ran east past
Michmethath, then continued on past Taanath-shiloh
and Janoah. 7From Janoah it turned southward to Ataroth and Naarah, and touched Jericho, and ended at the
Jordan River. 8[The western half of the northern bound-
arye] went from Tappu-ah, and followed along Kanah
Brook to the Mediterranean Sea. 9Ephraim was also giv-
en some of the cities in the territory of the half-tribe of
Manasseh. 10The Canaanites living in Gezer were never

16 THE ALLOTMENT of the Josephites went
from the Jordan by Jericho, east of the waters
of Jericho, into the wilderness, going up from Jericho
into the hill country to Bethel; 2then going from Bethel
to Luz, it passes along to Ataroth, the territory of the
Archites; 3then it goes down westward to the territory
of the Japhletites, as far as the territory of Lower Beth-
horon, then to Gezer, and it ends at the sea.
4 The Josephites—Manasseh and Ephraim—
received their inheritance.
5 The territory of the Ephraimites by their families
was as follows: the boundary of their inheritance on the
east was Ataroth-addar as far as Upper Beth-horon, 6and
the boundary goes from there to the sea; on the north is
Michmethath; then on the east the boundary makes a
turn toward Taanath-shiloh, and passes along beyond it
on the east to Janoah, 7then it goes down from Janoah
to Ataroth and to Naarah, and touches Jericho, ending
at the Jordan. 8From Tappuah the boundary goes westward to the Wadi Kanah, and ends at the sea. Such is
the inheritance of the tribe of the Ephraimites by their
families, 9together with the towns that were set apart for
the Ephraimites within the inheritance of the Manassites, all those towns with their villages. 10They did not,

c *15:37-44 The tribe of Judah also inherited twenty-five other cities with their
villages, implied. See verses 41 and 44.* d *15:48-62 Judah also received
these forty-four cities in the hill country with their surrounding villages, implied
in vss 51, 54, 57, 59, 60, and 62, where the original text indicates sub-totals
of the number of cities assigned to Judah.* e *16:8 The western half of the
northern boundary, implied.*

King James

10And they drave not out the Canaanites that dwelt in Gezer: but the Canaanites dwell among the Ephraimites unto this day, and serve under tribute.

17 THERE WAS also a lot for the tribe of Manasseh; for he *was* the firstborn of Joseph; *to wit,* for Machir the firstborn of Manasseh, the father of Gilead: because he was a man of war, therefore he had Gilead and Bashan.

2There was also *a lot* for the rest of the children of Manasseh by their families; for the children of Abiezer, and for the children of Helek, and for the children of Asriel, and for the children of Shechem, and for the children of Hepher, and for the children of Shemida: these *were* the male children of Manasseh the son of Joseph by their families.

3¶ But Zelophehad, the son of Hepher, the son of Gilead, the son of Machir, the son of Manasseh, had no sons, but daughters: and these *are* the names of his daughters, Mahlah, and Noah, Hoglah, Milcah, and Tirzah.

4And they came near before Eleazar the priest, and before Joshua the son of Nun, and before the princes, saying, The LORD commanded Moses to give us an inheritance among our brethren. Therefore according to the commandment of the LORD he gave them an inheritance among the brethren of their father.

5And there fell ten portions to Manasseh, beside the land of Gilead and Bashan, which *were* on the other side Jordan;

6Because the daughters of Manasseh had an inheritance among his sons: and the rest of Manasseh's sons had the land of Gilead.

7¶ And the coast of Manasseh was from Asher to Michmethah, that *lieth* before Shechem; and the border went along on the right hand unto the inhabitants of En-tappuah.

8*Now* Manasseh had the land of Tappuah: but Tappuah on the border of Manasseh *belonged* to the children of Ephraim;

9And the coast descended unto the river Kanah, southward of the river: these cities of Ephraim *are* among the cities of Manasseh: the coast of Manasseh also *was* on the north side of the river, and the outgoings of it were at the sea:

10Southward *it was* Ephraim's, and northward *it was* Manasseh's, and the sea is his border; and they met together in Asher on the north, and in Issachar on the east.

11And Manasseh had in Issachar and in Asher Bethshean and her towns, and Ibleam and her towns, and the inhabitants of Dor and her towns, and the inhabitants of En-dor and her towns, and the inhabitants of Taanach and her towns, and the inhabitants of Megiddo and her towns, *even* three countries.

12Yet the children of Manasseh could not drive out *the inhabitants of* those cities; but the Canaanites would dwell in that land.

13Yet it came to pass, when the children of Israel were waxen strong, that they put the Canaanites to tribute; but did not utterly drive them out.

14And the children of Joseph spake unto Joshua, saying, Why hast thou given me *but* one lot and one portion to inherit, seeing I *am* a great people, forasmuch as the LORD hath blessed me hitherto?

15And Joshua answered them, If thou *be* a great people, *then* get thee up to the wood *country,* and cut down for thyself there in the land of the Perizzites, and of the giants, if mount Ephraim be too narrow for thee.

New International

10They did not dislodge the Canaanites living in Gezer; to this day the Canaanites live among the people of Ephraim but are required to do forced labor.

17 THIS WAS the allotment for the tribe of Manasseh as Joseph's firstborn, that is, for Makir, Manasseh's firstborn. Makir was the ancestor of the Gileadites, who had received Gilead and Bashan because the Makirites were great soldiers. 2So this allotment was for the rest of the people of Manasseh—the clans of Abiezer, Helek, Asriel, Shechem, Hepher and Shemida. These are the other male descendants of Manasseh son of Joseph by their clans.

3Now Zelophehad son of Hepher, the son of Gilead, the son of Makir, the son of Manasseh, had no sons but only daughters, whose names were Mahlah, Noah, Hoglah, Milcah and Tirzah. 4They went to Eleazar the priest, Joshua son of Nun, and the leaders and said, "The LORD commanded Moses to give us an inheritance among our brothers." So Joshua gave them an inheritance along with the brothers of their father, according to the LORD's command. 5Manasseh's share consisted of ten tracts of land besides Gilead and Bashan east of the Jordan, 6because the daughters of the tribe of Manasseh received an inheritance among the sons. The land of Gilead belonged to the rest of the descendants of Manasseh.

7The territory of Manasseh extended from Asher to Micmethath east of Shechem. The boundary ran southward from there to include the people living at En Tappuah. 8(Manasseh had the land of Tappuah, but Tappuah itself, on the boundary of Manasseh, belonged to the Ephraimites.) 9Then the boundary continued south to the Kanah Ravine. There were towns belonging to Ephraim lying among the towns of Manasseh, but the boundary of Manasseh was the northern side of the ravine and ended at the sea. 10On the south the land belonged to Ephraim, on the north to Manasseh. The territory of Manasseh reached the sea and bordered Asher on the north and Issachar on the east.

11Within Issachar and Asher, Manasseh also had Beth Shan, Ibleam and the people of Dor, Endor, Taanach and Megiddo, together with their surrounding settlements (the third in the list is Naphotha).

12Yet the Manassites were not able to occupy these towns, for the Canaanites were determined to live in that region. 13However, when the Israelites grew stronger, they subjected the Canaanites to forced labor but did not drive them out completely.

14The people of Joseph said to Joshua, "Why have you given us only one allotment and one portion for an inheritance? We are a numerous people and the LORD has blessed us abundantly."

15"If you are so numerous," Joshua answered, "and if the hill country of Ephraim is too small for you, go up into the forest and clear land for yourselves there in the land of the Perizzites and Rephaites."

a *11* That is, Naphoth Dor

Living Bible

driven out, so they still live as slaves among the people of Ephraim.

17 THE LAND given *to the Half-tribe of Manasseh* (Joseph's oldest son):

The clan of Machir (Manasseh's oldest son who was the father of Gilead) had already been given the land of Gilead and Bashan [on the east side of the Jordan River[b]], for they were great warriors. 2So now, land on the west side of the Jordan[b] was given to the clans of Abiezer, Helek, Asriel, Shechem, Shemida, and Hepher.

3However, Hepher's son Zelophehad (grandson of Gilead, great-grandson of Machir, and great-great-grandson of Manasseh) had no sons. He had only five daughters whose names were Mahlah, Noah, Hoglah, Milcah, and Tirzah. 4These women came to Eleazar the priest and to Joshua and the Israeli leaders and reminded them,

"The Lord told Moses that we were to receive as much property as the men of our tribe."[c]

5, 6So, as the Lord had commanded through Moses, these five women were given an inheritance along with their five great-uncles, and the total inheritance came to ten sections of land (in addition to the land of Gilead and Bashan across the Jordan River).

7The northern boundary of the tribe of Manasseh extended southward from the border of Asher to Michmethath, which is east of Shechem. On the south the boundary went from Michmethath to the Spring of Tappu-ah. 8(The land of Tappu-ah belonged to Manasseh, but the city of Tappu-ah, on the border of Manasseh's land, belonged to the tribe of Ephraim.) 9From the spring of Tappu-ah the border of Manasseh followed the north bank of the Brook of Kanah to the Mediterranean Sea. (Several cities south of the brook belonged to the tribe of Ephraim, though they were located in Manasseh's territory.) 10The land south of the brook and as far west as the Mediterranean Sea was assigned to Ephraim, and the land north of the brook and east of the sea went to Manasseh. Manasseh's northern boundary was the territory of Asher and the eastern boundary was the territory of Issachar.

11The half-tribe of Manasseh was also given the following cities which were situated in the areas assigned to Issachar and Asher: Beth-shean, Ible-am, Dor, Endor, Taanach, Megiddo (where there are the three cliffs), with their respective villages. 12But since the descendants of Manasseh could not drive out the people who lived in those cities, the Canaanites remained. 13Later on, however, when the Israelis became strong enough, they forced the Canaanites to work as slaves.

14Then the two tribes of Joseph came to Joshua and asked, "Why have you given us only one portion of land when the Lord has given us such large populations?"

15"If the hill country of Ephraim is not large enough for you," Joshua replied, "and if you are able to do it, you may clear out the forest land where the Perizzites and Rephaim live."

New Revised Standard

however, drive out the Canaanites who lived in Gezer: so the Canaanites have lived within Ephraim to this day but have been made to do forced labor.

The Other Half-Tribe of Manasseh (West)

17 THEN ALLOTMENT was made to the tribe of Manasseh, for he was the firstborn of Joseph. To Machir the firstborn of Manasseh, the father of Gilead, were allotted Gilead and Bashan, because he was a warrior. 2And allotments were made to the rest of the tribe of Manasseh, by their families, Abiezer, Helek, Asriel, Shechem, Hepher, and Shemida; these were the male descendants of Manasseh son of Joseph, by their families.

3 Now Zelophehad son of Hepher son of Gilead son of Machir son of Manasseh had no sons, but only daughters; and these are the names of his daughters: Mahlah, Noah, Hoglah, Milcah, and Tirzah. 4They came before the priest Eleazar and Joshua son of Nun and the leaders, and said, "The LORD commanded Moses to give us an inheritance along with our male kin." So according to the commandment of the LORD he gave them an inheritance among the kinsmen of their father. 5Thus there fell to Manasseh ten portions, besides the land of Gilead and Bashan, which is on the other side of the Jordan, 6because the daughters of Manasseh received an inheritance along with his sons. The land of Gilead was allotted to the rest of the Manassites.

7 The territory of Manasseh reached from Asher to Michmethath, which is east of Shechem; then the boundary goes along southward to the inhabitants of En-tappuah. 8The land of Tappuah belonged to Manasseh, but the town of Tappuah on the boundary of Manasseh belonged to the Ephraimites. 9Then the boundary went down to the Wadi Kanah. The towns here, to the south of the wadi, among the towns of Manasseh, belong to Ephraim. Then the boundary of Manasseh goes along the north side of the wadi and ends at the sea. 10The land to the south is Ephraim's and that to the north is Manasseh's, with the sea forming its boundary; on the north Asher is reached, and on the east Issachar. 11Within Issachar and Asher, Manasseh had Beth-shean and its villages, Ibleam and its villages, the inhabitants of Dor and its villages, the inhabitants of En-dor and its villages, the inhabitants of Taanach and its villages, and the inhabitants of Megiddo and its villages (the third is Naphath).[d] 12Yet the Manassites could not take possession of those towns; but the Canaanites continued to live in that land. 13But when the Israelites grew strong, they put the Canaanites to forced labor, but did not utterly drive them out.

The Tribe of Joseph Protests

14 The tribe of Joseph spoke to Joshua, saying, "Why have you given me but one lot and one portion as an inheritance, since we are a numerous people, whom all along the LORD has blessed?" 15And Joshua said to them, "If you are a numerous people, go up to the forest, and clear ground there for yourselves in the land of the Perizzites and the Rephaim, since the hill country of Ephraim is too narrow for you." 16The tribe of Joseph

---

b 17:1,2 *on the east side of the Jordan River*, implied.   c 17:4 *as much property as the men of our tribe*, see Num 27:5-7.

d Meaning of Heb uncertain

King James

16And the children of Joseph said, The hill is not enough for us: and all the Canaanites that dwell in the land of the valley have chariots of iron, *both they* who *are* of Beth-shean and her towns, and *they* who *are* of the valley of Jezreel.

17And Joshua spake unto the house of Joseph, *even* to Ephraim and to Manasseh, saying, Thou *art* a great people, and hast great power: thou shalt not have one lot *only:*

18But the mountain shall be thine; for it *is* a wood, and thou shalt cut it down: and the outgoings of it shall be thine: for thou shalt drive out the Canaanites, though they have iron chariots, *and* though they *be* strong.

18 AND THE whole congregation of the children of Israel assembled together at Shiloh, and set up the tabernacle of the congregation there. And the land was subdued before them.

2And there remained among the children of Israel seven tribes, which had not yet received their inheritance.

3And Joshua said unto the children of Israel, How long *are* ye slack to go to possess the land, which the LORD God of your fathers hath given you?

4Give out from among you three men for *each* tribe: and I will send them, and they shall rise, and go through the land, and describe it according to the inheritance of them; and they shall come *again* to me.

5And they shall divide it into seven parts: Judah shall abide in their coast on the south, and the house of Joseph shall abide in their coasts on the north.

6Ye shall therefore describe the land *into* seven parts, and bring *the description* hither to me, that I may cast lots for you here before the LORD our God.

7But the Levites have no part among you; for the priesthood of the LORD *is* their inheritance: and Gad, and Reuben, and half the tribe of Manasseh, have received their inheritance beyond Jordan on the east, which Moses the servant of the LORD gave them.

8¶ And the men arose, and went away: and Joshua charged them that went to describe the land, saying, Go and walk through the land, and describe it, and come again to me, that I may here cast lots for you before the LORD in Shiloh.

9And the men went and passed through the land, and described it by cities into seven parts in a book, and came *again* to Joshua to the host at Shiloh.

10¶ And Joshua cast lots for them in Shiloh before the LORD: and there Joshua divided the land unto the children of Israel according to their divisions.

11¶ And the lot of the tribe of the children of Benjamin came up according to their families: and the coast of their lot came forth between the children of Judah and the children of Joseph.

12And their border on the north side was from Jordan; and the border went up to the side of Jericho on the north side, and went up through the mountains westward; and the goings out thereof were at the wilderness of Beth-aven.

13And the border went over from thence toward Luz, to the side of Luz, which *is* Beth-el, southward; and the border descended to Ataroth-adar, near the hill that *lieth* on the south side of the nether Beth-horon.

14And the border was drawn *thence,* and compassed the corner of the sea southward, from the hill that *lieth* before Beth-horon southward; and the goings out thereof were at Kirjath-baal, which *is* Kirjath-jearim, a city of the children of Judah: this *was* the west quarter.

15And the south quarter *was* from the end of Kirjath-jearim, and the border went out on the west, and went out to the well of waters of Nephtoah:

New International

16The people of Joseph replied, "The hill country is not enough for us, and all the Canaanites who live in the plain have iron chariots, both those in Beth Shan and its settlements and those in the Valley of Jezreel."

17But Joshua said to the house of Joseph—to Ephraim and Manasseh—"You are numerous and very powerful. You will have not only one allotment 18but the forested hill country as well. Clear it, and its farthest limits will be yours; though the Canaanites have iron chariots and though they are strong, you can drive them out."

Division of the Rest of the Land

18 THE WHOLE assembly of the Israelites gathered at Shiloh and set up the Tent of Meeting there. The country was brought under their control, 2but there were still seven Israelite tribes who had not yet received their inheritance.

3So Joshua said to the Israelites: "How long will you wait before you begin to take possession of the land that the LORD, the God of your fathers, has given you? 4Appoint three men from each tribe. I will send them out to make a survey of the land and to write a description of it, according to the inheritance of each. Then they will return to me. 5You are to divide the land into seven parts. Judah is to remain in its territory on the south and the house of Joseph in its territory on the north. 6After you have written descriptions of the seven parts of the land, bring them here to me and I will cast lots for you in the presence of the LORD our God. 7The Levites, however, do not get a portion among you, because the priestly service of the LORD is their inheritance. And Gad, Reuben and the half-tribe of Manasseh have already received their inheritance on the east side of the Jordan. Moses the servant of the LORD gave it to them."

8As the men started on their way to map out the land, Joshua instructed them, "Go and make a survey of the land and write a description of it. Then return to me, and I will cast lots for you here at Shiloh in the presence of the LORD." 9So the men left and went through the land. They wrote its description on a scroll, town by town, in seven parts, and returned to Joshua in the camp at Shiloh. 10Joshua then cast lots for them in Shiloh in the presence of the LORD, and there he distributed the land to the Israelites according to their tribal divisions.

Allotment for Benjamin

11The lot came up for the tribe of Benjamin, clan by clan. Their allotted territory lay between the tribes of Judah and Joseph:

12On the north side their boundary began at the Jordan, passed the northern slope of Jericho and headed west into the hill country, coming out at the desert of Beth Aven. 13From there it crossed to the south slope of Luz (that is, Bethel) and went down to Ataroth Addar on the hill south of Lower Beth Horon.

14From the hill facing Beth Horon on the south the boundary turned south along the western side and came out at Kiriath Baal (that is, Kiriath Jearim), a town of the people of Judah. This was the western side.

15The southern side began at the outskirts of Kiriath Jearim on the west, and the boundary came out at the spring of the waters of Nephtoah. 16The

Living Bible

16, 17, 18"Fine," said the tribes of Joseph, "for the Canaanites in the lowlands around Beth-shean and the Valley of Jezreel have iron chariots and are too strong for us."

"Then you shall have the mountain forests," Joshua replied, "and since you are such a large, strong tribe you will surely be able to clear it all and live there. And I'm sure you can drive out the Canaanites from the valleys, too, even though they are strong and have iron chariots."

18 AFTER THE conquest—although seven of the tribes of Israel had not yet entered and conquered the land God had given them—all Israel gathered at Shiloh to set up the Tabernacle.

3Then Joshua asked them, "How long are you going to wait before clearing out the people living in the land which the Lord your God has given to you? 4Select three men from each tribe and I will send them to scout the unconquered territory and bring back a report of its size and natural divisions so that I can divide it for you. 5, 6The scouts will map it into seven sections, and then I will throw the sacred dice to decide which section will be assigned to each tribe. 7However, remember that the Levites won't receive any land; they are priests of the Lord. That is their wonderful heritage. And of course the tribes of Gad and Reuben and the half-tribe of Manasseh won't receive any more, for they already have land on the east side of the Jordan where Moses promised them that they could settle."

8So the scouts went out to map the country and to bring back their report to Joshua. Then the Lord could assign the sections of land to the tribes by the throw of the sacred dice. 9The men did as they were told and divided the entire territory into seven sections, listing the cities in each section. Then they returned to Joshua and the camp at Shiloh. 10There at the Tabernacle at Shiloh the Lord showed Joshua by the sacred lottery which tribe should have each section:

11The Land Given to the Tribe of Benjamin:
The section of land assigned to the families of the tribe of Benjamin lay between the territory previously assigned to the tribes of Judah and Joseph.

12The northern boundary began at the Jordan River, went north of Jericho, then west through the hill country and the Wilderness of Beth-aven. 13From there the boundary went south to Luz (also called Bethel) and proceeded down to Ataroth-addar in the hill country south of Lower Beth-horon. 14There the border turned south, passing the mountain near Beth-horon and ending at the village of Kiriath-baal (sometimes called Kiriath-jearim), one of the cities of the tribe of Judah. This was the western boundary.

15The southern border ran from the edge of Kiriath-baal, over Mount Ephron to the spring of Naphtoah,

New Revised Standard

said, "The hill country is not enough for us; yet all the Canaanites who live in the plain have chariots of iron, both those in Beth-shean and its villages and those in the Valley of Jezreel." 17Then Joshua said to the house of Joseph, to Ephraim and Manasseh, "You are indeed a numerous people, and have great power; you shall not have one lot only, 18but the hill country shall be yours, for though it is a forest, you shall clear it and possess it to its farthest borders; for you shall drive out the Canaanites, though they have chariots of iron, and though they are strong."

The Territories of the Remaining Tribes

18 THEN THE whole congregation of the Israelites assembled at Shiloh, and set up the tent of meeting there. The land lay subdued before them.

2 There remained among the Israelites seven tribes whose inheritance had not yet been apportioned. 3So Joshua said to the Israelites, "How long will you be slack about going in and taking possession of the land that the LORD, the God of your ancestors, has given you? 4Provide three men from each tribe, and I will send them out that they may begin to go throughout the land, writing a description of it with a view to their inheritances. Then come back to me. 5They shall divide it into seven portions, Judah continuing in its territory on the south, and the house of Joseph in their territory on the north. 6You shall describe the land in seven divisions and bring the description here to me; and I will cast lots for you here before the LORD our God. 7The Levites have no portion among you, for the priesthood of the LORD is their heritage; and Gad and Reuben and the half-tribe of Manasseh have received their inheritance beyond the Jordan eastward, which Moses the servant of the LORD gave them."

8 So the men started on their way; and Joshua charged those who went to write the description of the land, saying, "Go throughout the land and write a description of it, and come back to me; and I will cast lots for you here before the LORD in Shiloh." 9So the men went and traversed the land and set down in a book a description of it by towns in seven divisions; then they came back to Joshua in the camp at Shiloh, 10and Joshua cast lots for them in Shiloh before the LORD; and there Joshua apportioned the land to the Israelites, to each a portion.

The Territory of Benjamin

11 The lot of the tribe of Benjamin according to its families came up, and the territory allotted to it fell between the tribe of Judah and the tribe of Joseph. 12On the north side their boundary began at the Jordan; then the boundary goes up to the slope of Jericho on the north, then up through the hill country westward; and it ends at the wilderness of Beth-aven. 13From there the boundary passes along southward in the direction of Luz, to the slope of Luz (that is, Bethel), then the boundary goes down to Ataroth-addar, on the mountain that lies south of Lower Beth-horon. 14Then the boundary goes in another direction, turning on the western side southward from the mountain that lies to the south, opposite Beth-horon, and it ends at Kiriath-baal (that is, Kiriath-jearim), a town belonging to the tribe of Judah. This forms the western side. 15The southern side begins at the outskirts of Kiriath-jearim; and the boundary goes from there to Ephron,a to the spring of the Waters of Nephtoah; 16then the boundary goes down to the border

a Cn See 15.9. Heb westward

King James

¹⁶And the border came down to the end of the mountain that *lieth* before the valley of the son of Hinnom, *and* which *is* in the valley of the giants on the north, and descended to the valley of Hinnom, to the side of Jebusi on the south, and descended to En-rogel,

¹⁷And was drawn from the north, and went forth to En-shemesh, and went forth toward Geliloth, which *is* over against the going up of Adummim, and descended to the stone of Bohan the son of Reuben,

¹⁸And passed along toward the side over against Arabah northward, and went down unto Arabah:

¹⁹And the border passed along to the side of Beth-hoglah northward: and the outgoings of the border were at the north bay of the salt sea at the south end of Jordan: this *was* the south coast.

²⁰And Jordan was the border of it on the east side. This *was* the inheritance of the children of Benjamin, by the coasts thereof round about, according to their families.

²¹Now the cities of the tribe of the children of Benjamin according to their families were Jericho, and Beth-hoglah, and the valley of Keziz,

²²And Beth-arabah, and Zemaraim, and Beth-el,

²³And Avim, and Parah, and Ophrah,

²⁴And Chephar-haammonai, and Ophni, and Gaba; twelve cities with their villages:

²⁵Gibeon, and Ramah, and Beeroth,

²⁶And Mizpeh, and Chephirah, and Mozah,

²⁷And Rekem, and Irpeel, and Taralah,

²⁸And Zelah, Eleph, and Jebusi, which *is* Jerusalem, Gibeath, *and* Kirjath; fourteen cities with their villages. This *is* the inheritance of the children of Benjamin according to their families.

19 AND THE second lot came forth to Simeon, *even* for the tribe of the children of Simeon according to their families: and their inheritance was within the inheritance of the children of Judah.

²And they had in their inheritance Beer-sheba, or Sheba, and Moladah,

³And Hazar-shual, and Balah, and Azem,

⁴And Eltolad, and Bethul, and Hormah,

⁵And Ziklag, and Beth-marcaboth, and Hazar-susah,

⁶And Beth-lebaoth, and Sharuhen; thirteen cities and their villages:

⁷Ain, Remmon, and Ether, and Ashan; four cities and their villages:

⁸And all the villages that *were* round about these cities to Baalath-beer, Ramath of the south. This *is* the inheritance of the tribe of the children of Simeon according to their families.

⁹Out of the portion of the children of Judah *was* the inheritance of the children of Simeon: for the part of the children of Judah was too much for them: therefore the children of Simeon had their inheritance within the inheritance of them.

¹⁰¶ And the third lot came up for the children of Zebulun according to their families: and the border of their inheritance was unto Sarid:

¹¹And their border went up toward the sea, and Maralah, and reached to Dabbasheth, and reached to the river that *is* before Jokneam;

¹²And turned from Sarid eastward toward the sunrising unto the border of Chisloth-tabor, and then goeth out to Daberath, and goeth up to Japhia,

¹³And from thence passeth on along on the east to Gittah-hepher, to Ittah-kazin, and goeth out to Remmon-methoar to Neah;

¹⁴And the border compasseth it on the north side to Hannathon: and the outgoings thereof are in the valley of Jiphthah-el:

New International

boundary went down to the foot of the hill facing the Valley of Ben Hinnom, north of the Valley of Rephaim. It continued down the Hinnom Valley along the southern slope of the Jebusite city and so to En Rogel. ¹⁷It then curved north, went to En Shemesh, continued to Geliloth, which faces the Pass of Adummim, and ran down to the Stone of Bohan son of Reuben. ¹⁸It continued to the northern slope of Beth Arabah^a and on down into the Arabah. ¹⁹It then went to the northern slope of Beth Hoglah and came out at the northern bay of the Salt Sea,^b at the mouth of the Jordan in the south. This was the southern boundary.

²⁰The Jordan formed the boundary on the eastern side.

These were the boundaries that marked out the inheritance of the clans of Benjamin on all sides.

²¹The tribe of Benjamin, clan by clan, had the following cities:

Jericho, Beth Hoglah, Emek Keziz, ²²Beth Arabah, Zemaraim, Bethel, ²³Avvim, Parah, Ophrah, ²⁴Kephar Ammoni, Ophni and Geba—twelve towns and their villages.

²⁵Gibeon, Ramah, Beeroth, ²⁶Mizpah, Kephirah, Mozah, ²⁷Rekem, Irpeel, Taralah, ²⁸Zelah, Haeleph, the Jebusite city (that is, Jerusalem), Gibeah and Kiriath—fourteen towns and their villages.

This was the inheritance of Benjamin for its clans.

Allotment for Simeon

19 THE SECOND lot came out for the tribe of Simeon, clan by clan. Their inheritance lay within the territory of Judah. ²It included:

Beersheba (or Sheba),^c Moladah, ³Hazar Shual, Balah, Ezem, ⁴Eltolad, Bethul, Hormah, ⁵Ziklag, Beth Marcaboth, Hazar Susah, ⁶Beth Lebaoth and Sharuhen—thirteen towns and their villages;

⁷Ain, Rimmon, Ether and Ashan—four towns and their villages— ⁸and all the villages around these towns as far as Baalath Beer (Ramah in the Negev).

This was the inheritance of the tribe of the Simeonites, clan by clan. ⁹The inheritance of the Simeonites was taken from the share of Judah, because Judah's portion was more than they needed. So the Simeonites received their inheritance within the territory of Judah.

Allotment for Zebulun

¹⁰The third lot came up for Zebulun, clan by clan:

The boundary of their inheritance went as far as Sarid. ¹¹Going west it ran to Maralah, touched Dabbesheth, and extended to the ravine near Jokneam. ¹²It turned east from Sarid toward the sunrise to the territory of Kisloth Tabor and went on to Daberath and up to Japhia. ¹³Then it continued eastward to Gath Hepher and Eth Kazin; it came out at Rimmon and turned toward Neah. ¹⁴There the boundary went around on the north to Hannathon and ended at the Valley of Iphtah El. ¹⁵Included were Kattath,

Living Bible

16and down to the base of the mountain beside the valley of Hinnom, north of the valley of Rephaim. From there it continued across the valley of Hinnom, crossed south of the old city of Jerusalemd where the Jebusites lived, and continued down to En-rogel. 17From En-rogel the boundary proceeded northeast to En-shemesh and on to Geliloth (which is opposite the slope of Adummim). Then it went down to the Stone of Bohan (who was a son of Reuben), 18where it passed along the north edge of the Arabah. The border then went down into the Arabah, 19ran south past Beth-hoglah, and ended at the north bay of the Dead Sea—which is the southern end of the Jordan River.

20The eastern border was the Jordan River. This was the land assigned to the tribe of Benjamin. 21–28These twenty-sixe cities were included in the land given to the tribe of Benjamin:

Jericho, Beth-hoglah, Emek-keziz, Beth-arabah, Zimaraim, Bethel, Avvim, Parah, Ophrah, Chephar-ammoni, Ophni, Geba, Gibeon, Ramah, Beeroth, Mizpeh, Chephirah, Mozah, Rekem, Irpeel, Taralah, Zela, Ha-eleph, Jebus (or Jerusalem), Gibe-ah, and Kiriath-jearim.

All of these cities and their surrounding villages were given to the tribe of Benjamin.

19 THE LAND given *to the Tribe of Simeon:*
The tribe of Simeon received the next assignment of land—including part of the land previously assigned to Judah. 2–7Their inheritance included these seventeenf cities with their respective villages:

Beer-sheba, Sheba, Moladah, Hazar-shual, Balah, Ezem, Eltolad, Bethul, Hormah, Ziklag, Beth-marcaboth, Hazar-susah, Beth-lebaoth, Sharuhen, Enrimmon, Ether, and Ashan.

8The cities as far south as Baalath-beer (also known as Ramah-in-the-Negeb) were also given to the tribe of Simeon. 9So the Simeon tribe's inheritance came from what had earlier been given to Judah, for Judah's section had been too large for them.

10*The Land Given to the Tribe of Zebulun:*
The third tribe to receive its assignment of land was Zebulun. Its boundary started on the south side of Sarid. 11From there it circled to the west, going near Mareal and Dabbesheth until it reached the brook east of Jeokne-am. 12In the other direction, the boundary line went east to the border of Chisloth-tabor, and from there to Daberath and Japhia; 13then it continued east of Gathhepher, Ethkazin, and Rimmon and turned toward Neah. 14The northern boundary of Zebulun passed Hannathon and ended at the Valley of Iphtahel. 15, 16The

New Revised Standard

of the mountain that overlooks the valley of the son of Hinnom, which is at the north end of the valley of Rephaim; and it then goes down the valley of Hinnom, south of the slope of the Jebusites, and downward to En-rogel; 17then it bends in a northerly direction going on to Enshemesh, and from there goes to Geliloth, which is opposite the ascent of Adummim; then it goes down to the Stone of Bohan, Reuben's son; 18and passing on to the north of the slope of Beth-arabahg it goes down to the Arabah; 19then the boundary passes on to the north of the slope of Beth-hoglah; and the boundary ends at the northern bay of the Dead Sea,h at the south end of the Jordan: this is the southern border. 20The Jordan forms its boundary on the eastern side. This is the inheritance of the tribe of Benjamin, according to its families, boundary by boundary all around.

21 Now the towns of the tribe of Benjamin according to their families were Jericho, Beth-hoglah, Emekkeziz, 22Beth-arabah, Zemaraim, Bethel, 23Avvim, Parah, Ophrah, 24Chephar-ammoni, Ophni, and Geba—twelve towns with their villages: 25Gibeon, Ramah, Beeroth, 26Mizpeh, Chephirah, Mozah, 27Rekem, Irpeel, Taralah, 28Zela, Haeleph, Jebusi (that is, Jerusalem), Gibeahi and Kiriath-jearimk—fourteen towns with their villages. This is the inheritance of the tribe of Benjamin according to its families.

The Territory of Simeon

19 THE SECOND lot came out for Simeon, for the tribe of Simeon, according to its families; its inheritance lay within the inheritance of the tribe of Judah. 2It had for its inheritance Beer-sheba, Sheba, Moladah, 3Hazar-shual, Balah, Ezem, 4Eltolad, Bethul, Hormah, 5Ziklag, Beth-marcaboth, Hazar-susah, 6Beth-lebaoth, and Sharuhen—thirteen towns with their villages; 7Ain, Rimmon, Ether, and Ashan—four towns with their villages; 8together with all the villages all around these towns as far as Baalath-beer, Ramah of the Negeb. This was the inheritance of the tribe of Simeon according to its families. 9The inheritance of the tribe of Simeon formed part of the territory of Judah; because the portion of the tribe of Judah was too large for them, the tribe of Simeon obtained an inheritance within their inheritance.

The Territory of Zebulun

10 The third lot came up for the tribe of Zebulun, according to its families. The boundary of its inheritance reached as far as Sarid; 11then its boundary goes up westward, and on to Maralah, and touches Dabbesheth, then the wadi that is east of Jokneam; 12from Sarid it goes in the other direction eastward toward the sunrise to the boundary of Chisloth-tabor; from there it goes to Daberath, then up to Japhia; 13from there it passes along on the east toward the sunrise to Gath-hepher, to Ethkazin, and going on to Rimmon it bends toward Neah; 14then on the north the boundary makes a turn to Hannathon, and it ends at the valley of Iphtah-el; 15and Kat-

---

d 18:16 *the old city of Jerusalem,* implied.   e 18:21-28 *These twenty-six cities,* implied in verses 24 and 28, where the original manuscript indicates sub-totals.   f 19:2-7 *these seventeen cities.* Totaled from verses 6 and 7 of the original manuscripts, where sub-totals are indicated.

g Gk: Heb *to the slope over against the Arabah*   h Heb *Salt Sea*   i Gk Syr Vg: Heb *the Jebusite*   j Heb *Gibeath*   k Gk: Heb *Kiriath*

King James

15And Kattath, and Nahallal, and Shimron, and Idalah, and Bethlehem: twelve cities with their villages.

16This *is* the inheritance of the children of Zebulun according to their families, these cities with their villages.

17¶ *And* the fourth lot came out to Issachar, for the children of Issachar according to their families.

18And their border was toward Jezreel, and Chesulloth, and Shunem,

19And Haphraim, and Shion, and Anaharath,

20And Rabbith, and Kishion, and Abez,

21And Remeth, and En-gannim, and En-haddah, and Beth-pazzez;

22And the coast reacheth to Tabor, and Shahazimah, and Beth-shemesh; and the outgoings of their border were at Jordan: sixteen cities with their villages.

23This *is* the inheritance of the tribe of the children of Issachar according to their families, the cities and their villages.

24¶ And the fifth lot came out for the tribe of the children of Asher according to their families.

25And their border was Helkath, and Hali, and Beten, and Achshaph,

26And Alammelech, and Amad, and Misheal; and reacheth to Carmel westward, and to Shihor-libnath;

27And turneth toward the sunrising to Beth-dagon, and reacheth to Zebulun, and to the valley of Jiphthah-el toward the north side of Beth-emek, and Neiel, and goeth out to Cabul on the left hand,

28And Hebron, and Rehob, and Hammon, and Kanah, *even* unto great Zidon;

29And *then* the coast turneth to Ramah, and to the strong city Tyre; and the coast turneth to Hosah; and the outgoings thereof are at the sea from the coast to Achzib:

30Ummah also, and Aphek, and Rehob: twenty and two cities with their villages.

31This *is* the inheritance of the tribe of the children of Asher according to their families, these cities with their villages.

32¶ The sixth lot came out to the children of Naphtali, *even* for the children of Naphtali according to their families.

33And their coast was from Heleph, from Allon to Zaanannim, and Adami, Nekeb, and Jabneel, unto Lakum; and the outgoings thereof were at Jordan:

34And *then* the coast turneth westward to Aznoth-tabor, and goeth out from thence to Hukkok, and reacheth to Zebulun on the south side, and reacheth to Asher on the west side, and to Judah upon Jordan toward the sunrising.

35And the fenced cities *are* Ziddim, Zer, and Hammath, Rakkath, and Chinnereth,

36And Adamah, and Ramah, and Hazor,

37And Kedesh, and Edrei, and En-hazor,

38And Iron, and Migdal-el, Horem, and Beth-anath, and Beth-shemesh; nineteen cities with their villages.

39This *is* the inheritance of the tribe of the children of Naphtali according to their families, the cities and their villages.

40¶ *And* the seventh lot came out for the tribe of the children of Dan according to their families.

41And the coast of their inheritance was Zorah, and Eshtaol, and Ir-shemesh,

42And Shaalabbin, and Ajalon, and Jethlah,

43And Elon, and Thimnathah, and Ekron,

44And Eltekeh, and Gibbethon, and Baalath,

45And Jehud, and Bene-berak, and Gath-rimmon,

46And Me-jarkon, and Rakkon, with the border before Japho.

New International

Nahalal, Shimron, Idalah and Bethlehem. There were twelve towns and their villages.

16These towns and their villages were the inheritance of Zebulun, clan by clan.

Allotment for Issachar

17The fourth lot came out for Issachar, clan by clan. 18Their territory included:

Jezreel, Kesulloth, Shunem, 19Hapharaim, Shion, Anaharath, 20Rabbith, Kishion, Ebez, 21Remeth, En Gannim, En Haddah and Beth Pazzez. 22The boundary touched Tabor, Shahazumah and Beth Shemesh, and ended at the Jordan. There were sixteen towns and their villages.

23These towns and their villages were the inheritance of the tribe of Issachar, clan by clan.

Allotment for Asher

24The fifth lot came out for the tribe of Asher, clan by clan. 25Their territory included:

Helkath, Hali, Beten, Acshaph, 26Allammelech, Amad and Mishal. On the west the boundary touched Carmel and Shihor Libnath. 27It then turned east toward Beth Dagon, touched Zebulun and the Valley of Iphtah El, and went north to Beth Emek and Neiel, passing Cabul on the left. 28It went to Abdon,[a] Rehob, Hammon and Kanah, as far as Greater Sidon. 29The boundary then turned back toward Ramah and went to the fortified city of Tyre, turned toward Hosah and came out at the sea in the region of Aczib, 30Ummah, Aphek and Rehob. There were twenty-two towns and their villages.

31These towns and their villages were the inheritance of the tribe of Asher, clan by clan.

Allotment for Naphtali

32The sixth lot came out for Naphtali, clan by clan:

33Their boundary went from Heleph and the large tree in Zaanannim, passing Adami Nekeb and Jabneel to Lakkum and ending at the Jordan. 34The boundary ran west through Aznoth Tabor and came out at Hukkok. It touched Zebulun on the south, Asher on the west and the Jordan[b] on the east. 35The fortified cities were Ziddim, Zer, Hammath, Rakkath, Kinnereth, 36Adamah, Ramah, Hazor, 37Kedesh, Edrei, En Hazor, 38Iron, Migdal El, Horem, Beth Anath and Beth Shemesh. There were nineteen towns and their villages.

39These towns and their villages were the inheritance of the tribe of Naphtali, clan by clan.

Allotment for Dan

40The seventh lot came out for the tribe of Dan, clan by clan. 41The territory of their inheritance included:

Zorah, Eshtaol, Ir Shemesh, 42Shaalabbin, Aijalon, Ithlah, 43Elon, Timnah, Ekron, 44Eltekeh, Gibbethon, Baalath, 45Jehud, Bene Berak, Gath Rimmon, 46Me Jarkon and Rakkon, with the area facing Joppa.

---

a 28 Some Hebrew manuscripts (see also Joshua 21:30); most Hebrew manuscripts *Ebron*   b 34 Septuagint; Hebrew *west, and Judah, the Jordan,*

Living Bible

cities in these areas, besides those already mentioned,[c] included Kattath, Nahalal, Shimron, Idalah, Bethlehem, and each of their surrounding villages. Altogether there were twelve of these cities.

17-23*The Land Given to the Tribe of Issachar:*
The fourth tribe to be assigned its land was Issachar. Its boundaries included the following cities:

Jezreel, Chesulloth, Shunem, Hapharaim, Shion, Anaharath, Rabbith, Kishion, Ebez, Remeth, Engannim, En-haddah, Beth-pazzez, Tabor, Shahazumah, and Beth-shemesh—

sixteen cities in all, each with its surrounding villages. The boundary of Issachar ended at the Jordan River.

24, 25, 26*The Land Given to the Tribe of Asher:*
The fifth tribe to be assigned its land was Asher. The boundaries included these cities:

Helkath, Hali, Beten, Achshaph, Allammelech, Amad, and Mishal.

The boundary on the west side went from Carmel to Shihor-libnath, 27turned east toward Beth-dagon, and ran as far as Zebulun in the Valley of Iphtahel, running north of Beth-emek and Neiel. It then passed to the east of Kabul, 28Ebron, Rehob, Hammon, Kanah, and Greater Sidon. 29Then the boundary turned toward Ramah and the fortified city of Tyre and came to the Mediterranean Sea at Hosah. The territory also included Mahalab, Achzib, 30, 31Ummah, Aphek, and Rehob—an overall total of twenty-two cities and their surrounding villages.

32*The Land Given to the Tribe of Naphtali:*
The sixth tribe to receive its assignment was the tribe of Naphtali. 33Its boundary began at Judah, at the oak in Zaanannim, and extended across to Adami-nekeb, Jabneel, and Lakkum, ending at the Jordan River. 34The western boundary began near Heleph and ran past Aznoth-tabor, then to Hukkok, and coincided with the Zebulun boundary in the south, and with the boundary of Asher on the west, and with the Jordan River at the east. 35-39The fortified cities included in this territory were:

Ziddim, Zer, Hammath, Rakkath, Chinnereth, Adamah, Ramah, Hazor, Kedesh, Edre-i, Enhazor, Yiron, Migdal-el, Horem, Beth-anath, and Bethshemesh.

So altogether the territory included nineteen cities with their surrounding villages.

40*The Land Given to the Tribe of Dan:*
The last tribe to be assigned its land was Dan. 41-46The cities within its area included:

Zorah, Eshta-ol, Ir-shemesh, Sha-alabbin, Aijalon, Ithlah, Elon, Timnah, Ekron, Eltekeh, Gibbethon, Baalath, Jehud, Bene-berak, Gath-rimmon, Me-jarkon, and Rakkon, also the territory near Joppa.

New Revised Standard

tath, Nahalal, Shimron, Idalah, and Bethlehem—twelve towns with their villages. 16This is the inheritance of the tribe of Zebulun, according to its families—these towns with their villages.

The Territory of Issachar

17 The fourth lot came out for Issachar, for the tribe of Issachar, according to its families. 18Its territory included Jezreel, Chesulloth, Shunem, 19Hapharaim, Shion, Anaharath, 20Rabbith, Kishion, Ebez, 21Remeth, En-gannim, En-haddah, Beth-pazzez; 22the boundary also touches Tabor, Shahazumah, and Beth-shemesh, and its boundary ends at the Jordan—sixteen towns with their villages. 23This is the inheritance of the tribe of Issachar, according to its families—the towns with their villages.

The Territory of Asher

24 The fifth lot came out for the tribe of Asher according to its families. 25Its boundary included Helkath, Hali, Beten, Achshaph, 26Allammelech, Amad, and Mishal; on the west it touches Carmel and Shihor-libnath, 27then it turns eastward, goes to Beth-dagon, and touches Zebulun and the valley of Iphtah-el northward to Beth-emek and Neiel; then it continues in the north to Cabul, 28Ebron, Rehob, Hammon, Kanah, as far as Great Sidon; 29then the boundary turns to Ramah, reaching to the fortified city of Tyre; then the boundary turns to Hosah, and it ends at the sea; Mahalab,[d] Achzib, 30Ummah, Aphek, and Rehob—twenty-two towns with their villages. 31This is the inheritance of the tribe of Asher according to its families—these towns with their villages.

The Territory of Naphtali

32 The sixth lot came out for the tribe of Naphtali, for the tribe of Naphtali, according to its families. 33And its boundary ran from Heleph, from the oak in Zaanannim, and Adami-nekeb, and Jabneel, as far as Lakkum; and it ended at the Jordan; 34then the boundary turns westward to Aznoth-tabor, and goes from there to Hukkok, touching Zebulun at the south, and Asher on the west, and Judah on the east at the Jordan. 35The fortified towns are Ziddim, Zer, Hammath, Rakkath, Chinnereth, 36Adamah, Ramah, Hazor, 37Kedesh, Edrei, Enhazor, 38Iron, Migdal-el, Horem, Beth-anath, and Beth-shemesh—nineteen towns with their villages. 39This is the inheritance of the tribe of Naphtali according to its families—the towns with their villages.

The Territory of Dan

40 The seventh lot came out for the tribe of Dan, according to its families. 41The territory of its inheritance included Zorah, Eshtaol, Ir-shemesh, 42Shaalabbin, Aijalon, Ithlah, 43Elon, Timnah, Ekron, 44Eltekeh, Gibbethon, Baalath, 45Jehud, Bene-berak, Gathrimmon, 46Me-jarkon, and Rakkon at the border opposite Joppa. 47When the territory of the Danites was lost

---

c 19:15, 16 besides those already mentioned, implied.

d Cn Compare Gk: Heb Mehebel

King James

47And the coast of the children of Dan went out *too little* for them: therefore the children of Dan went up to fight against Leshem, and took it, and smote it with the edge of the sword, and possessed it, and dwelt therein, and called Leshem, Dan, after the name of Dan their father.

48This *is* the inheritance of the tribe of the children of Dan according to their families, these cities with their villages.

49¶ When they had made an end of dividing the land for inheritance by their coasts, the children of Israel gave an inheritance to Joshua the son of Nun among them:

50According to the word of the LORD they gave him the city which he asked, *even* Timnath-serah in mount Ephraim: and he built the city, and dwelt therein.

51These *are* the inheritances, which Eleazar the priest, and Joshua the son of Nun, and the heads of the fathers of the tribes of the children of Israel, divided for an inheritance by lot in Shiloh before the LORD, at the door of the tabernacle of the congregation. So they made an end of dividing the country.

20 THE LORD also spake unto Joshua, saying, 2Speak to the children of Israel, saying, Appoint out for you cities of refuge, whereof I spake unto you by the hand of Moses:

3That the slayer that killeth *any* person unawares *and* unwittingly may flee thither: and they shall be your refuge from the avenger of blood.

4And when he that doth flee unto one of those cities shall stand at the entering of the gate of the city, and shall declare his cause in the ears of the elders of that city, they shall take him into the city unto them, and give him a place, that he may dwell among them.

5And if the avenger of blood pursue after him, then they shall not deliver the slayer up into his hand; because he smote his neighbour unwittingly, and hated him not beforetime.

6And he shall dwell in that city, until he stand before the congregation for judgment, *and* until the death of the high priest that shall be in those days: then shall the slayer return, and come unto his own city, and unto his own house, unto the city from whence he fled.

7¶ And they appointed Kedesh in Galilee in mount Naphtali, and Shechem in mount Ephraim, and Kirjath-arba, which *is* Hebron, in the mountain of Judah.

8And on the other side Jordan by Jericho eastward, they assigned Bezer in the wilderness upon the plain out of the tribe of Reuben, and Ramoth in Gilead out of the tribe of Gad, and Golan in Bashan out of the tribe of Manasseh.

9These were the cities appointed for all the children of Israel, and for the stranger that sojourneth among them, that whosoever killeth *any* person at unawares might flee thither, and not die by the hand of the avenger of blood, until he stood before the congregation.

21 THEN CAME near the heads of the fathers of the Levites unto Eleazar the priest, and unto Joshua the son of Nun, and unto the heads of the fathers of the tribes of the children of Israel;

2And they spake unto them at Shiloh in the land of Canaan, saying, The LORD commanded by the hand of Moses to give us cities to dwell in, with the suburbs thereof for our cattle.

New International

47(But the Danites had difficulty taking possession of their territory, so they went up and attacked Leshem, took it, put it to the sword and occupied it. They settled in Leshem and named it Dan after their forefather.) 48These towns and their villages were the inheritance of the tribe of Dan, clan by clan.

Allotment for Joshua

49When they had finished dividing the land into its allotted portions, the Israelites gave Joshua son of Nun an inheritance among them, 50as the LORD had commanded. They gave him the town he asked for—Timnath Seraha in the hill country of Ephraim. And he built up the town and settled there.

51These are the territories that Eleazar the priest, Joshua son of Nun and the heads of the tribal clans of Israel assigned by lot at Shiloh in the presence of the LORD at the entrance to the Tent of Meeting. And so they finished dividing the land.

Cities of Refuge

20 THEN THE LORD said to Joshua: 2"Tell the Israelites to designate the cities of refuge, as I instructed you through Moses, 3so that anyone who kills a person accidentally and unintentionally may flee there and find protection from the avenger of blood.

4"When he flees to one of these cities, he is to stand in the entrance of the city gate and state his case before the elders of that city. Then they are to admit him into their city and give him a place to live with them. 5If the avenger of blood pursues him, they must not surrender the one accused, because he killed his neighbor unintentionally and without malice aforethought. 6He is to stay in that city until he has stood trial before the assembly and until the death of the high priest who is serving at that time. Then he may go back to his own home in the town from which he fled."

7So they set apart Kedesh in Galilee in the hill country of Naphtali, Shechem in the hill country of Ephraim, and Kiriath Arba (that is, Hebron) in the hill country of Judah. 8On the east side of the Jordan of Jerichob they designated Bezer in the desert on the plateau in the tribe of Reuben, Ramoth in Gilead in the tribe of Gad, and Golan in Bashan in the tribe of Manasseh. 9Any of the Israelites or any alien living among them who killed someone accidentally could flee to these designated cities and not be killed by the avenger of blood prior to standing trial before the assembly.

Towns for the Levites

21 NOW THE family heads of the Levites approached Eleazar the priest, Joshua son of Nun, and the heads of the other tribal families of Israel 2at Shiloh in Canaan and said to them, "The LORD commanded through Moses that you give us towns to live in, with pasturelands for our livestock." 3So, as the LORD

---

a *50* Also known as *Timnath Heres* (see Judges 2:9) b *8 Jordan of Jericho* was possibly an ancient name for the Jordan River.

Living Bible

^{47, 48}But some of this territory proved impossible to conquer, so the tribe of Dan captured the city of Leshem, slaughtered its people, and lived there; and they called the city "Dan," naming it after their ancestor.

⁴⁹So all the land was divided among the tribes, with the boundaries indicated; and the nation of Israel gave a special piece of land to Joshua, ⁵⁰for the Lord had said that he could have any city he wanted. He chose Timnath-serah in the hill country of Ephraim; he rebuilt it and lived there.

⁵¹Eleazar the priest, Joshua, and the leaders of the tribes of Israel supervised the sacred lottery to divide the land among the tribes. This was done in the Lord's presence at the entrance of the Tabernacle at Shiloh.

20 THE LORD said to Joshua, ²"Tell the people of Israel to designate now the Cities of Refuge, as I instructed Moses.^c ³If a man is guilty of killing someone unintentionally, he can run to one of these cities and be protected from the relatives of the dead man, who may try to kill him in revenge. ⁴When the innocent killer reaches any of these cities, he will meet with the city council and explain what happened, and they must let him come in and must give him a place to live among them. ⁵If a relative of the dead man comes to kill him in revenge, the innocent slayer must not be released to him for the death was accidental. ⁶The man who caused the accidental death must stay in that city until he has been tried by the judges and found innocent, and must live there until the death of the High Priest who was in office at the time of the accident. But then he is free to return to his own city and home."

⁷The cities chosen as Cities of Refuge were Kedesh of Galilee in the hill country of Naphtali; Shechem, in the hill country of Ephraim; and Kiriath-arba (also known as Hebron) in the hill country of Judah. ⁸The Lord also instructed that three cities be set aside for this purpose on the east side of the Jordan River, across from Jericho. They were Bezer, in the wilderness of the land of the tribe of Reuben; Ramoth of Gilead, in the territory of the tribe of Gad; and Golan of Bashan, in the land of the tribe of Manasseh. ⁹These Cities of Refuge were for foreigners living in Israel as well as for the Israelis themselves, so that anyone who accidentally killed another man could run to that place for a trial, and not be killed in revenge.

21 THEN THE leaders of the tribe of Levi came to Shiloh to consult with Eleazar the priest and with Joshua and the leaders of the various tribes.

²"The Lord instructed Moses to give cities to us Levites for our homes, and pastureland for our cattle," they said.

New Revised Standard

to them, the Danites went up and fought against Leshem, and after capturing it and putting it to the sword, they took possession of it and settled in it, calling Leshem, Dan, after their ancestor Dan. ⁴⁸This is the inheritance of the tribe of Dan, according to their families—these towns with their villages.

Joshua's Inheritance

⁴⁹ When they had finished distributing the several territories of the land as inheritances, the Israelites gave an inheritance among them to Joshua son of Nun. ⁵⁰By command of the LORD they gave him the town that he asked for, Timnath-serah in the hill country of Ephraim; he rebuilt the town, and settled in it.

⁵¹ These are the inheritances that the priest Eleazar and Joshua son of Nun and the heads of the families of the tribes of the Israelites distributed by lot at Shiloh before the LORD, at the entrance of the tent of meeting. So they finished dividing the land.

The Cities of Refuge

20 THEN THE LORD spoke to Joshua, saying, ²"Say to the Israelites, 'Appoint the cities of refuge, of which I spoke to you through Moses, ³so that anyone who kills a person without intent or by mistake may flee there; they shall be for you a refuge from the avenger of blood. ⁴The slayer shall flee to one of these cities and shall stand at the entrance of the gate of the city, and explain the case to the elders of that city; then the fugitive shall be taken into the city, and given a place, and shall remain with them. ⁵And if the avenger of blood is in pursuit, they shall not give up the slayer, because the neighbor was killed by mistake, there having been no enmity between them before. ⁶The slayer shall remain in that city until there is a trial before the congregation, until the death of the one who is high priest at the time: then the slayer may return home, to the town in which the deed was done.' "

⁷ So they set apart Kedesh in Galilee in the hill country of Naphtali, and Shechem in the hill country of Ephraim, and Kiriath-arba (that is, Hebron) in the hill country of Judah. ⁸ And beyond the Jordan east of Jericho, they appointed Bezer in the wilderness on the tableland, from the tribe of Reuben, and Ramoth in Gilead, from the tribe of Gad, and Golan in Bashan, from the tribe of Manasseh. ⁹ These were the cities designated for all the Israelites, and for the aliens residing among them, that anyone who killed a person without intent could flee there, so as not to die by the hand of the avenger of blood, until there was a trial before the congregation.

Cities Allotted to the Levites

21 THEN THE heads of the families of the Levites came to the priest Eleazar and to Joshua son of Nun and to the heads of the families of the tribes of the Israelites; ²they said to them at Shiloh in the land of Canaan, "The LORD commanded through Moses that we be given towns to live in, along with their pasture lands for our livestock." ³So by command of the LORD the

^c 20:2 *as I instructed Moses.* See Numbers 35 and 1 Chronicles 6.

King James

3And the children of Israel gave unto the Levites out of their inheritance, at the commandment of the LORD, these cities and their suburbs.

4And the lot came out for the families of the Kohathites: and the children of Aaron the priest, which were of the Levites, had by lot out of the tribe of Judah, and out of the tribe of Simeon, and out of the tribe of Benjamin, thirteen cities.

5And the rest of the children of Kohath had by lot out of the families of the tribe of Ephraim, and out of the tribe of Dan, and out of the half tribe of Manasseh, ten cities.

6And the children of Gershon had by lot out of the families of the tribe of Issachar, and out of the tribe of Asher, and out of the tribe of Naphtali, and out of the half tribe of Manasseh in Bashan, thirteen cities.

7The children of Merari by their families had out of the tribe of Reuben, and out of the tribe of Gad, and out of the tribe of Zebulun, twelve cities.

8And the children of Israel gave by lot unto the Levites these cities with their suburbs, as the LORD commanded by the hand of Moses.

9¶ And they gave out of the tribe of the children of Judah, and out of the tribe of the children of Simeon, these cities which are here mentioned by name,

10Which the children of Aaron, being of the families of the Kohathites, who were of the children of Levi, had: for their's was the first lot.

11And they gave them the city of Arba the father of Anak, which city is Hebron, in the hill country of Judah, with the suburbs thereof round about it.

12But the fields of the city, and the villages thereof, gave they to Caleb the son of Jephunneh for his possession.

13¶ Thus they gave to the children of Aaron the priest Hebron with her suburbs, to be a city of refuge for the slayer; and Libnah with her suburbs,

14And Jattir with her suburbs, and Eshtemoa with her suburbs,

15And Holon with her suburbs, and Debir with her suburbs,

16And Ain with her suburbs, and Juttah with her suburbs, and Beth-shemesh with her suburbs; nine cities out of those two tribes.

17And out of the tribe of Benjamin, Gibeon with her suburbs, Geba with her suburbs,

18Anathoth with her suburbs, and Almon with her suburbs; four cities.

19All the cities of the children of Aaron, the priests, were thirteen cities with their suburbs.

20¶ And the families of the children of Kohath, the Levites which remained of the children of Kohath, even they had the cities of their lot out of the tribe of Ephraim.

21For they gave them Shechem with her suburbs in mount Ephraim, to be a city of refuge for the slayer; and Gezer with her suburbs,

22And Kibzaim with her suburbs, and Beth-horon with her suburbs; four cities.

23And out of the tribe of Dan, Eltekeh with her suburbs, Gibbethon with her suburbs,

24Aijalon with her suburbs, Gathrimmon with her suburbs; four cities.

25And out of the half tribe of Manasseh, Tanach with her suburbs, and Gath-rimmon with her suburbs; two cities.

26All the cities were ten with their suburbs for the families of the children of Kohath that remained.

27¶ And unto the children of Gershon, of the families of the Levites, out of the other half tribe of Manasseh they gave Golan in Bashan with her suburbs, to be a city of refuge for the slayer; and Beesh-terah with her suburbs; two cities.

New International

had commanded, the Israelites gave the Levites the following towns and pasturelands out of their own inheritance:

4The first lot came out for the Kohathites, clan by clan. The Levites who were descendants of Aaron the priest were allotted thirteen towns from the tribes of Judah, Simeon and Benjamin. 5The rest of Kohath's descendants were allotted ten towns from the clans of the tribes of Ephraim, Dan and half of Manasseh.

6The descendants of Gershon were allotted thirteen towns from the clans of the tribes of Issachar, Asher, Naphtali and the half-tribe of Manasseh in Bashan.

7The descendants of Merari, clan by clan, received twelve towns from the tribes of Reuben, Gad and Zebulun.

8So the Israelites allotted to the Levites these towns and their pasturelands, as the LORD had commanded through Moses.

9From the tribes of Judah and Simeon they allotted the following towns by name 10(these towns were assigned to the descendants of Aaron who were from the Kohathite clans of the Levites, because the first lot fell to them):

11They gave them Kiriath Arba (that is, Hebron), with its surrounding pastureland, in the hill country of Judah. (Arba was the forefather of Anak.) 12But the fields and villages around the city they had given to Caleb son of Jephunneh as his possession.

13So to the descendants of Aaron the priest they gave Hebron (a city of refuge for one accused of murder), Libnah, 14Jattir, Eshtemoa, 15Holon, Debir, 16Ain, Juttah and Beth Shemesh, together with their pasturelands—nine towns from these two tribes.

17And from the tribe of Benjamin they gave them Gibeon, Geba, 18Anathoth and Almon, together with their pasturelands—four towns.

19All the towns for the priests, the descendants of Aaron, were thirteen, together with their pasturelands.

20The rest of the Kohathite clans of the Levites were allotted towns from the tribe of Ephraim:

21In the hill country of Ephraim they were given Shechem (a city of refuge for one accused of murder) and Gezer, 22Kibzaim and Beth Horon, together with their pasturelands—four towns.

23Also from the tribe of Dan they received Eltekeh, Gibbethon, 24Aijalon and Gath Rimmon, together with their pasturelands—four towns.

25From half the tribe of Manasseh they received Taanach and Gath Rimmon, together with their pasturelands—two towns.

26All these ten towns and their pasturelands were given to the rest of the Kohathite clans.

27The Levite clans of the Gershonites were given:
  from the half-tribe of Manasseh,
  Golan in Bashan (a city of refuge for one accused of murder) and Be Eshtarah, together with their pasturelands—two towns;

Living Bible

3So they were given some of the recently conquered cities with their pasturelands. 4Thirteen of these cities had been assigned originally to the tribes of Judah, Simeon, and Benjamin. These were given to some of the priests of the Kohath division (of the tribe of Levi, descendants of Aaron). 5The other families of the Kohath division were given ten cities from the territories of Ephraim, Dan, and the half-tribe of Manasseh. 6The Gershon division received thirteen cities, selected by sacred lot in the area of Bashan. These cities were given by the tribes of Issachar, Asher, Naphtali, and the half-tribe of Manasseh. 7The Merari division received twelve cities from the tribes of Reuben, Gad, and Zebulun. 8So the Lord's command to Moses was obeyed, and the cities and pasturelands were assigned by the toss of the sacred dice.

9-16First to receive their assignment were the priests—the descendants of Aaron, who was a member of the Kohath division of the Levites. The tribes of Judah and Simeon gave them the ninea cities listed below, with their surrounding pasturelands:

Hebron, in the Judean hills, as a City of Refuge—it was also called Kiriatharba (Arba was the father of Anak)—although the fields beyond the city and the surrounding villages were given to Caleb, the son of Jephunneh;

Libnah, Jattir, Eshtemoa, Holon, Debir, Ain, Juttah, and Beth-shemesh.

17, 18The tribe of Benjamin gave them these four cities and their pasturelands:

Gibeon, Gaba, Anathoth, and Almon.

19So in all, thirteen cities were given to the priests—the descendants of Aaron.

20, 21, 22The other families of the Kohath division received fourb cities and pasturelands from the tribe of Ephraim:

Shechem (a City of Refuge), Gezer, Kibza-im, and Beth-horon.

23, 24The following four cities and pasturelands were given by the tribe of Dan:

Elteke, Gibbethon, Aijalon, and Gath-rimmon.

25The half-tribe of Manasseh gave the cities of Taanach and Gath-rimmon with their surrounding pasturelands. 26So the total number of cities and pasturelands given to the remainder of the Kohath division was ten.

27The descendants of Gershon, another division of the Levites, received two cities and pasturelands from the half-tribe of Manasseh:

Golan, in Bashan (a City of Refuge), and Be-eshterah.

New Revised Standard

Israelites gave to the Levites the following towns and pasture lands out of their inheritance.

4 The lot came out for the families of the Kohathites. So those Levites who were descendants of Aaron the priest received by lot thirteen towns from the tribes of Judah, Simeon, and Benjamin.

5 The rest of the Kohathites received by lot ten towns from the families of the tribe of Ephraim, from the tribe of Dan, and the half-tribe of Manasseh.

6 The Gershonites received by lot thirteen towns from the families of the tribe of Issachar, from the tribe of Asher, from the tribe of Naphtali, and from the half-tribe of Manasseh in Bashan.

7 The Merarites according to their families received twelve towns from the tribe of Reuben, the tribe of Gad, and the tribe of Zebulun.

8 These towns and their pasture lands the Israelites gave by lot to the Levites, as the LORD had commanded through Moses.

9 Out of the tribe of Judah and the tribe of Simeon they gave the following towns mentioned by name, 10which went to the descendants of Aaron, one of the families of the Kohathites who belonged to the Levites, since the lot fell to them first. 11They gave them Kiriath-arba (Arba being the father of Anak), that is Hebron, in the hill country of Judah, along with the pasture lands around it. 12But the fields of the town and its villages had been given to Caleb son of Jephunneh as his holding.

13 To the descendants of Aaron the priest they gave Hebron, the city of refuge for the slayer, with its pasture lands, Libnah with its pasture lands, 14Jattir with its pasture lands, Eshtemoa with its pasture lands, 15Holon with its pasture lands, Debir with its pasture lands, 16Ain with its pasture lands, Juttah with its pasture lands, and Beth-shemesh with its pasture lands—nine towns out of these two tribes. 17Out of the tribe of Benjamin: Gibeon with its pasture lands, Geba with its pasture lands, 18Anathoth with its pasture lands, and Almon with its pasture lands—four towns. 19The towns of the descendants of Aaron—the priests—were thirteen in all, with their pasture lands.

20 As to the rest of the Kohathites belonging to the Kohathite families of the Levites, the towns allotted to them were out of the tribe of Ephraim. 21To them were given Shechem, the city of refuge for the slayer, with its pasture lands in the hill country of Ephraim, Gezer with its pasture lands, 22Kibzaim with its pasture lands, and Beth-horon with its pasture lands—four towns. 23Out of the tribe of Dan: Elteke with its pasture lands, Gibbethon with its pasture lands, 24Aijalon with its pasture lands, Gath-rimmon with its pasture lands—four towns. 25Out of the half-tribe of Manasseh: Taanach with its pasture lands, and Gath-rimmon with its pasture lands—two towns. 26The towns of the families of the rest of the Kohathites were ten in all, with their pasture lands.

27 To the Gershonites, one of the families of the Levites, were given out of the half-tribe of Manasseh, Golan in Bashan with its pasture lands, the city of refuge for the slayer, and Beeshterah with its pasture lands—two towns. 28Out of the tribe of Issachar: Kishion with

---

a 21:9-16 the nine cities, implied in verse 16, where a sub-total is indicated in the original text. b 21:20-22 four cities, implied in verse 22, where the total appears in the text.

King James

28And out of the tribe of Issachar, Kishon with her suburbs, Dabareh with her suburbs,

29Jarmuth with her suburbs, En-gannim with her suburbs; four cities.

30And out of the tribe of Asher, Mishal with her suburbs, Abdon with her suburbs,

31Helkath with her suburbs, and Rehob with her suburbs; four cities.

32And out of the tribe of Naphtali, Kedesh in Galilee with her suburbs, *to be* a city of refuge for the slayer; and Hammoth-dor with her suburbs, and Kartan with her suburbs; three cities.

33All the cities of the Gershonites according to their families *were* thirteen cities with their suburbs.

34¶ And unto the families of the children of Merari, the rest of the Levites, out of the tribe of Zebulun, Jokneam with her suburbs, and Kartah with her suburbs,

35Dimnah with her suburbs, Nahalal with her suburbs; four cities.

36And out of the tribe of Reuben, Bezer with her suburbs, and Jahazah with her suburbs,

37Kedemoth with her suburbs, and Mephaath with her suburbs; four cities.

38And out of the tribe of Gad, Ramoth in Gilead with her suburbs, *to be* a city of refuge for the slayer; and Mahanaim with her suburbs,

39Heshbon with her suburbs, Jazer with her suburbs; four cities in all.

40So all the cities for the children of Merari by their families, which were remaining of the families of the Levites, were *by* their lot twelve cities.

41All the cities of the Levites within the possession of the children of Israel *were* forty and eight cities with their suburbs.

42These cities were every one with their suburbs round about them: thus *were* all these cities.

43¶ And the LORD gave unto Israel all the land which he sware to give unto their fathers; and they possessed it, and dwelt therein.

44And the LORD gave them rest round about, according to all that he sware unto their fathers: and there stood not a man of all their enemies before them; the LORD delivered all their enemies into their hand.

45There failed not aught of any good thing which the LORD had spoken unto the house of Israel; all came to pass.

22 THEN JOSHUA called the Reubenites, and the Gadites, and the half tribe of Manasseh,

2And said unto them, Ye have kept all that Moses the servant of the LORD commanded you, and have obeyed my voice in all that I commanded you:

3Ye have not left your brethren these many days unto this day, but have kept the charge of the commandment of the LORD your God.

4And now the LORD your God hath given rest unto your brethren, as he promised them: therefore now return ye, and get you unto your tents, *and* unto the land of your possession, which Moses the servant of the LORD gave you on the other side Jordan.

5But take diligent heed to do the commandment and the law, which Moses the servant of the LORD charged you, to love the LORD your God, and to walk in all his ways, and to keep his commandments, and to cleave unto him, and to serve him with all your heart and with all your soul.

6So Joshua blessed them, and sent them away: and they went unto their tents.

New International

28from the tribe of Issachar,
   Kishion, Daberath, 29Jarmuth and En Gannim, together with their pasturelands—four towns;
30from the tribe of Asher,
   Mishal, Abdon, 31Helkath and Rehob, together with their pasturelands—four towns;
32from the tribe of Naphtali,
   Kedesh in Galilee (a city of refuge for one accused of murder), Hammoth Dor and Kartan, together with their pasturelands—three towns.
33All the towns of the Gershonite clans were thirteen, together with their pasturelands.

34The Merarite clans (the rest of the Levites) were given:
   from the tribe of Zebulun,
   Jokneam, Kartah, 35Dimnah and Nahalal, together with their pasturelands—four towns;
36from the tribe of Reuben,
   Bezer, Jahaz, 37Kedemoth and Mephaath, together with their pasturelands—four towns;
38from the tribe of Gad,
   Ramoth in Gilead (a city of refuge for one accused of murder), Mahanaim, 39Heshbon and Jazer, together with their pasturelands—four towns in all.
40All the towns allotted to the Merarite clans, who were the rest of the Levites, were twelve.

41The towns of the Levites in the territory held by the Israelites were forty-eight in all, together with their pasturelands. 42Each of these towns had pasturelands surrounding it; this was true for all these towns.

43So the LORD gave Israel all the land he had sworn to give their forefathers, and they took possession of it and settled there. 44The LORD gave them rest on every side, just as he had sworn to their forefathers. Not one of their enemies withstood them; the LORD handed all their enemies over to them. 45Not one of all the LORD's good promises to the house of Israel failed; every one was fulfilled.

Eastern Tribes Return Home

22 THEN JOSHUA summoned the Reubenites, the Gadites and the half-tribe of Manasseh 2and said to them, "You have done all that Moses the servant of the LORD commanded, and you have obeyed me in everything I commanded. 3For a long time now—to this very day—you have not deserted your brothers but have carried out the mission the LORD your God gave you. 4Now that the LORD your God has given your brothers rest as he promised, return to your homes in the land that Moses the servant of the LORD gave you on the other side of the Jordan. 5But be very careful to keep the commandment and the law that Moses the servant of the LORD gave you: to love the LORD your God, to walk in all his ways, to obey his commands, to hold fast to him and to serve him with all your heart and all your soul."

6Then Joshua blessed them and sent them away, and they went to their homes. 7(To the half-tribe of Manas-

Living Bible

28, 29The tribe of Issachar gave four cities:
Kishion, Daberath, Jarmuth, and Engannim.

30, 31The tribe of Asher gave four cities and pasture-lands:
Mishal, Abdon, Helkath, and Rehob.

32The tribe of Naphtali gave:
Kedesh, in Galilee (a City of Refuge), Hammoth-dor, and Kartan.

33So thirteen cities with their pasturelands were assigned to the division of Gershon.

34, 35The remainder of the Levites—the Merari division—were given four cities by the tribe of Zebulun:
Jokne-am, Kartah, Dimnah, and Nahalal.

36, 37Reuben gave them:
Bezer, Jahaz, Kedemoth, and Mepha-ath.

38, 39Gad gave them four cities with pasturelands:
Ramoth (a City of Refuge), Mahanaim, Heshbon, and Jazer.

40So the Merari division of the Levites was given twelve cities in all.

41, 42The total number of cities and pasturelands given to the Levites came to forty-eight.

43So in this way the Lord gave to Israel all the land he had promised to their ancestors, and they went in and conquered it and lived there. 44And the Lord gave them peace, just as he had promised, and no one could stand against them; the Lord helped them destroy all their enemies. 45Every good thing the Lord had promised them came true.

22 JOSHUA NOW called together the troops from the tribes of Reuben, Gad, and the half-tribe of Manasseh, 2, 3and addressed them as follows:

"You have done as the Lord's disciple Moses commanded you, and have obeyed every order I have given you—every order of the Lord your God. You have not deserted your brother tribes, even though the campaign has lasted for such a long time. 4And now the Lord our God has given us success and rest as he promised he would. So go home now to the land given you by the Lord's servant Moses, on the other side of the Jordan River. 5Be sure to continue to obey all of the commandments Moses gave you. Love the Lord and follow his plan for your lives. Cling to him and serve him enthusiastically."

6So Joshua blessed them and sent them home.

New Revised Standard

its pasture lands, Daberath with its pasture lands, 29Jar-muth with its pasture lands, En-gannim with its pasture lands—four towns; 30Out of the tribe of Asher: Mishal with its pasture lands, Abdon with its pasture lands, 31Helkath with its pasture lands, and Rehob with its pasture lands—four towns. 32Out of the tribe of Naphtali: Kedesh in Galilee with its pasture lands, the city of refuge for the slayer, Hammoth-dor with its pasture lands, and Kartan with its pasture lands—three towns. 33The towns of the several families of the Gershonites were in all thirteen, with their pasture lands.

34 To the rest of the Levites—the Merarite families—were given out of the tribe of Zebulun: Jokne-am with its pasture lands, Kartah with its pasture lands, 35Dimnah with its pasture lands, Nahalal with its pasture lands—four towns. 36Out of the tribe of Reuben: Bezer with its pasture lands, Jahzah with its pasture lands, 37Kedemoth with its pasture lands, and Mephaath with its pasture lands—four towns. 38Out of the tribe of Gad: Ramoth in Gilead with its pasture lands, the city of refuge for the slayer, Mahanaim with its pasture lands, 39Heshbon with its pasture lands, Jazer with its pasture lands—four towns in all. 40As for the towns of the several Merarite families, that is, the remainder of the families of the Levites, those allotted to them were twelve in all.

41 The towns of the Levites within the holdings of the Israelites were in all forty-eight towns with their pasture lands. 42Each of these towns had its pasture lands around it; so it was with all these towns.

43 Thus the LORD gave to Israel all the land that he swore to their ancestors that he would give them; and having taken possession of it, they settled there. 44And the LORD gave them rest on every side just as he had sworn to their ancestors; not one of all their enemies had withstood them, for the LORD had given all their enemies into their hands. 45Not one of all the good promises that the LORD had made to the house of Israel had failed; all came to pass.

The Eastern Tribes Return to Their Territory

22 THEN JOSHUA summoned the Reubenites, the Gadites, and the half-tribe of Manasseh, 2and said to them, "You have observed all that Moses the servant of the LORD commanded you, and have obeyed me in all that I have commanded you; 3you have not forsaken your kindred these many days, down to this day, but have been careful to keep the charge of the LORD your God. 4And now the LORD your God has given rest to your kindred, as he promised them; therefore turn and go to your tents in the land where your possession lies, which Moses the servant of the LORD gave you on the other side of the Jordan. 5Take good care to observe the commandment and instruction that Moses the servant of the LORD commanded you, to love the LORD your God, to walk in all his ways, to keep his commandments, and to hold fast to him, and to serve him with all your heart and with all your soul." 6So Joshua blessed them and sent them away, and they went to their tents.

King James

7¶ Now to the *one* half of the tribe of Manasseh Moses had given *possession* in Bashan: but unto the *other* half thereof gave Joshua among their brethren on this side Jordan westward. And when Joshua sent them away also unto their tents, then he blessed them.

8And he spake unto them, saying, Return with much riches unto your tents, and with very much cattle, with silver, and with gold, and with brass, and with iron, and with very much raiment: divide the spoil of your enemies with your brethren.

9¶ And the children of Reuben and the children of Gad and the half tribe of Manasseh returned, and departed from the children of Israel out of Shiloh, which *is* in the land of Canaan, to go unto the country of Gilead, to the land of their possession, whereof they were possessed, according to the word of the Lord by the hand of Moses.

10¶ And when they came unto the borders of Jordan, that *are* in the land of Canaan, the children of Reuben and the children of Gad and the half tribe of Manasseh built there an altar by Jordan, a great altar to see to.

11¶ And the children of Israel heard say, Behold, the children of Reuben and the children of Gad and the half tribe of Manasseh have built an altar over against the land of Canaan, in the borders of Jordan, at the passage of the children of Israel.

12And when the children of Israel heard *of it*, the whole congregation of the children of Israel gathered themselves together at Shiloh, to go up to war against them.

13And the children of Israel sent unto the children of Reuben, and to the children of Gad, and to the half tribe of Manasseh, into the land of Gilead, Phinehas the son of Eleazar the priest,

14And with him ten princes, of each chief house a prince throughout all the tribes of Israel; and each one *was* an head of the house of their fathers among the thousands of Israel.

15¶ And they came unto the children of Reuben, and to the children of Gad, and to the half tribe of Manasseh, unto the land of Gilead, and they spake with them, saying,

16Thus saith the whole congregation of the Lord, What trespass *is* this that ye have committed against the God of Israel, to turn away this day from following the Lord, in that ye have builded you an altar, that ye might rebel this day against the Lord?

17*Is* the iniquity of Peor too little for us, from which we are not cleansed until this day, although there was a plague in the congregation of the Lord,

18But that ye must turn away this day from following the Lord? and it will be, *seeing* ye rebel today against the Lord, that tomorrow he will be wroth with the whole congregation of Israel.

19Notwithstanding, if the land of your possession *be* unclean, *then* pass ye over unto the land of the possession of the Lord, wherein the Lord's tabernacle dwelleth, and take possession among us: but rebel not against the Lord, nor rebel against us, in building you an altar beside the altar of the Lord our God.

20Did not Achan the son of Zerah commit a trespass in the accursed thing, and wrath fell on all the congregation of Israel? and that man perished not alone in his iniquity.

21¶ Then the children of Reuben and the children of Gad and the half tribe of Manasseh answered, and said unto the heads of the thousands of Israel,

New International

seh Moses had given land in Bashan, and to the other half of the tribe Joshua gave land on the west side of the Jordan with their brothers.) When Joshua sent them home, he blessed them, 8saying, "Return to your homes with your great wealth—with large herds of livestock, with silver, gold, bronze and iron, and a great quantity of clothing—and divide with your brothers the plunder from your enemies."

9So the Reubenites, the Gadites and the half-tribe of Manasseh left the Israelites at Shiloh in Canaan to return to Gilead, their own land, which they had acquired in accordance with the command of the Lord through Moses.

10When they came to Geliloth near the Jordan in the land of Canaan, the Reubenites, the Gadites and the half-tribe of Manasseh built an imposing altar there by the Jordan. 11And when the Israelites heard that they had built the altar on the border of Canaan at Geliloth near the Jordan on the Israelite side, 12the whole assembly of Israel gathered at Shiloh to go to war against them.

13So the Israelites sent Phinehas son of Eleazar, the priest, to the land of Gilead—to Reuben, Gad and the half-tribe of Manasseh. 14With him they sent ten of the chief men, one for each of the tribes of Israel, each the head of a family division among the Israelite clans.

15When they went to Gilead—to Reuben, Gad and the half-tribe of Manasseh—they said to them: 16"The whole assembly of the Lord says: 'How could you break faith with the God of Israel like this? How could you turn away from the Lord and build yourselves an altar in rebellion against him now? 17Was not the sin of Peor enough for us? Up to this very day we have not cleansed ourselves from that sin, even though a plague fell on the community of the Lord! 18And are you now turning away from the Lord?

"'If you rebel against the Lord today, tomorrow he will be angry with the whole community of Israel. 19If the land you possess is defiled, come over to the Lord's land, where the Lord's tabernacle stands, and share the land with us. But do not rebel against the Lord or against us by building an altar for yourselves, other than the altar of the Lord our God. 20When Achan son of Zerah acted unfaithfully regarding the devoted things,[a] did not wrath come upon the whole community of Israel? He was not the only one who died for his sin.' "

21Then Reuben, Gad and the half-tribe of Manasseh replied to the heads of the clans of Israel: 22"The Mighty

---

[a] *20* The Hebrew term refers to the irrevocable giving over of things or persons to the Lord, often by totally destroying them.

Living Bible

7, 8(Moses had assigned the land of Bashan to the half-tribe of Manasseh, although the other half of the tribe was given land on the west side of the Jordan.) As Joshua sent away these troops, he blessed them and told them to share their great wealth with their relatives back home—their loot of cattle, silver, gold, bronze, iron, and clothing.

9So the troops of Reuben, Gad, and the half-tribe of Manasseh left the army of Israel at Shiloh in Canaan and crossed the Jordan River to their own homeland of Gilead. 10Before they went across, while they were still in Canaan, they built a large monument for everyone to see, in the shape of an altar.

11But when the rest of Israel heard about what they had done, 12they mustered an army at Shiloh and prepared to go to war against their brother tribes. 13First, however, they sent a delegation led by Phinehas, the son of Eleazar the priest. They crossed the river and talked to the tribes of Reuben, Gad, and Manasseh. 14In this delegation were ten high officials of Israel, one from each of the ten tribes, and each a clan leader. 15When they arrived in the land of Gilead they said to the tribes of Reuben, Gad, and the half-tribe of Manasseh,

16"The whole congregation of the Lord demands to know why you are sinning against the God of Israel by turning away from him and building an altar of rebellion against the Lord. 17, 18Was our guilt at Peor—from which we have not even yet been cleansed despite the plague that tormented us—so little that you must rebel again? For you know that if you rebel today the Lord will be angry with all of us tomorrow. 19If you need the altar because your land is defiled, then join us on our side of the river where the Lord lives among us in his Tabernacle, and we will share our land with you. But do not rebel against the Lord by building another altar in addition to the only true altar of our God. 20Don't you remember that when Achan, the son of Zerah, sinned against the Lord, the entire nation was punished in addition to the one man who had sinned?"

21This was the reply of the people of Reuben, Gad, and the half-tribe of Manasseh to these high officials:

New Revised Standard

7 Now to the one half of the tribe of Manasseh Moses had given a possession in Bashan; but to the other half Joshua had given a possession beside their fellow Israelites in the land west of the Jordan. And when Joshua sent them away to their tents and blessed them, 8 he said to them, "Go back to your tents with much wealth, and with very much livestock, with silver, gold, bronze, and iron, and with a great quantity of clothing; divide the spoil of your enemies with your kindred." 9 So the Reubenites and the Gadites and the half-tribe of Manasseh returned home, parting from the Israelites at Shiloh, which is in the land of Canaan, to go to the land of Gilead, their own land of which they had taken possession by command of the LORD through Moses.

A Memorial Altar East of the Jordan

10 When they came to the region[b] near the Jordan that lies in the land of Canaan, the Reubenites and the Gadites and the half-tribe of Manasseh built there an altar by the Jordan, an altar of great size. 11 The Israelites heard that the Reubenites and the Gadites and the half-tribe of Manasseh had built an altar at the frontier of the land of Canaan, in the region[c] near the Jordan, on the side that belongs to the Israelites. 12 And when the people of Israel heard of it, the whole assembly of the Israelites gathered at Shiloh, to make war against them.

13 Then the Israelites sent the priest Phinehas son of Eleazar to the Reubenites and the Gadites and the half-tribe of Manasseh, in the land of Gilead, 14 and with him ten chiefs, one from each of the tribal families of Israel, every one of them the head of a family among the clans of Israel. 15 They came to the Reubenites, the Gadites, and the half-tribe of Manasseh, in the land of Gilead, and they said to them, 16 "Thus says the whole congregation of the LORD, 'What is this treachery that you have committed against the God of Israel in turning away today from following the LORD, by building yourselves an altar today in rebellion against the LORD? 17 Have we not had enough of the sin at Peor from which even yet we have not cleansed ourselves, and for which a plague came upon the congregation of the LORD, 18 that you must turn away today from following the LORD! If you rebel against the LORD today, he will be angry with the whole congregation of Israel tomorrow. 19 But now, if your land is unclean, cross over into the LORD's land where the LORD's tabernacle now stands, and take for yourselves a possession among us; only do not rebel against the LORD, or rebel against us[d] by building yourselves an altar other than the altar of the LORD our God. 20 Did not Achan son of Zerah break faith in the matter of the devoted things, and wrath fell upon all the congregation of Israel? And he did not perish alone for his iniquity!' "

21 Then the Reubenites, the Gadites, and the half-tribe of Manasseh said in answer to the heads of the families of Israel, 22 "The LORD, God of gods! The

---

b Or to Geliloth   c Or at Geliloth   d Or make rebels of us

King James

22The LORD God of gods, the LORD God of gods, he knoweth, and Israel he shall know; if *it be* in rebellion, or if in transgression against the LORD, (save us not this day,)

23That we have built us an altar to turn from following the LORD, or if to offer thereon burnt offering or meat offering, or if to offer peace offerings thereon, let the LORD himself require *it;*

24And if we have not *rather* done it for fear of *this* thing, saying, In time to come your children might speak unto our children, saying, What have ye to do with the LORD God of Israel?

25For the LORD hath made Jordan a border between us and you, ye children of Reuben and children of Gad; ye have no part in the LORD: so shall your children make our children cease from fearing the LORD.

26Therefore we said, Let us now prepare to build us an altar, not for burnt offering, nor for sacrifice:

27But *that* it *may be* a witness between us, and you, and our generations after us, that we might do the service of the LORD before him with our burnt offerings, and with our sacrifices, and with our peace offerings; that your children may not say to our children in time to come, Ye have no part in the LORD.

28Therefore said we, that it shall be, when they should *so* say to us or to our generations in time to come, that we may say *again,* Behold the pattern of the altar of the LORD, which our fathers made, not for burnt offerings, nor for sacrifices; but it *is* a witness between us and you.

29God forbid that we should rebel against the LORD, and turn this day from following the LORD, to build an altar for burnt offerings, for meat offerings, or for sacrifices, beside the altar of the LORD our God that *is* before his tabernacle.

30¶ And when Phinehas the priest, and the princes of the congregation and heads of the thousands of Israel which *were* with him, heard the words that the children of Reuben and the children of Gad and the children of Manasseh spake, it pleased them.

31And Phinehas the son of Eleazar the priest said unto the children of Reuben, and to the children of Gad, and to the children of Manasseh, This day we perceive that the LORD *is* among us, because ye have not committed this trespass against the LORD: now ye have delivered the children of Israel out of the hand of the LORD.

32¶ And Phinehas the son of Eleazar the priest, and the princes, returned from the children of Reuben, and from the children of Gad, out of the land of Gilead, unto the land of Canaan, to the children of Israel, and brought them word again.

33And the thing pleased the children of Israel; and the children of Israel blessed God, and did not intend to go up against them in battle, to destroy the land wherein the children of Reuben and Gad dwelt.

34And the children of Reuben and the children of Gad called the altar *Ed:* for it *shall be* a witness between us that the LORD *is* God.

23 AND IT came to pass a long time after that the LORD had given rest unto Israel from all their enemies round about, that Joshua waxed old *and* stricken in age.

2And Joshua called for all Israel, *and* for their elders, and for their heads, and for their judges, and for their officers, and said unto them, I am old *and* stricken in age:

3And ye have seen all that the LORD your God hath done unto all these nations because of you; for the LORD your God *is* he that hath fought for you.

New International

One, God, the LORD! The Mighty One, God, the LORD! He knows! And let Israel know! If this has been in rebellion or disobedience to the LORD, do not spare us this day. 23If we have built our own altar to turn away from the LORD and to offer burnt offerings and grain offerings, or to sacrifice fellowship offeringsa on it, may the LORD himself call us to account.

24"No! We did it for fear that some day your descendants might say to ours, 'What do you have to do with the LORD, the God of Israel? 25The LORD has made the Jordan a boundary between us and you—you Reubenites and Gadites! You have no share in the LORD.' So your descendants might cause ours to stop fearing the LORD.

26"That is why we said, 'Let us get ready and build an altar—but not for burnt offerings or sacrifices.' 27On the contrary, it is to be a witness between us and you and the generations that follow, that we will worship the LORD at his sanctuary with our burnt offerings, sacrifices and fellowship offerings. Then in the future your descendants will not be able to say to ours, 'You have no share in the LORD.'

28"And we said, 'If they ever say this to us, or to our descendants, we will answer: Look at the replica of the LORD's altar, which our fathers built, not for burnt offerings and sacrifices, but as a witness between us and you.'

29"Far be it from us to rebel against the LORD and turn away from him today by building an altar for burnt offerings, grain offerings and sacrifices, other than the altar of the LORD our God that stands before his tabernacle."

30When Phinehas the priest and the leaders of the community—the heads of the clans of the Israelites—heard what Reuben, Gad and Manasseh had to say, they were pleased. 31And Phinehas son of Eleazar, the priest, said to Reuben, Gad and Manasseh, "Today we know that the LORD is with us, because you have not acted unfaithfully toward the LORD in this matter. Now you have rescued the Israelites from the LORD's hand."

32Then Phinehas son of Eleazar, the priest, and the leaders returned to Canaan from their meeting with the Reubenites and Gadites in Gilead and reported to the Israelites. 33They were glad to hear the report and praised God. And they talked no more about going to war against them to devastate the country where the Reubenites and the Gadites lived.

34And the Reubenites and the Gadites gave the altar this name: A Witness Between Us that the LORD is God.

Joshua's Farewell to the Leaders

23 AFTER A long time had passed and the LORD had given Israel rest from all their enemies around them, Joshua, by then old and well advanced in years, 2summoned all Israel—their elders, leaders, judges and officials—and said to them: "I am old and well advanced in years. 3You yourselves have seen everything the LORD your God has done to all these nations for your sake; it was the LORD your God who fought for you. 4Remember how I have allotted as an inheritance

a *23* Traditionally *peace offerings*; also in verse 27

Living Bible

22, 23 "We swear by Jehovah, the God of gods, that we have not built the altar in rebellion against the Lord. He knows (and let all Israel know it too) that we have not built the altar to sacrifice burnt offerings or grain offerings or peace offerings—may the curse of God be on us if we did. 24, 25 We have done it because we love the Lord and because we fear that in the future your children will say to ours, 'What right do you have to worship the Lord God of Israel? The Lord has placed the Jordan River as a barrier between our people and your people! You have no part in the Lord.' And your children may make our children stop worshiping him. 26, 27 So we decided to build the altar as a symbol to show our children and your children that we, too, may worship the Lord with our burnt offerings and peace offerings and sacrifices, and your children will not be able to say to ours, 'You have no part in the Lord our God.' 28 If they say this, our children can reply, 'Look at the altar of the Lord which our fathers made, patterned after the altar of Jehovah. It is not for burnt offerings or sacrifices but is a symbol of the relationship with God that both of us have.' 29 Far be it from us to turn away from the Lord or to rebel against him by building our own altar for burnt offerings, grain offerings, or sacrifices. Only the altar in front of the Tabernacle may be used for that."

30 When Phinehas the priest and the high officials heard this from the tribes of Reuben, Gad, and Manasseh, they were very happy.

31 Phinehas replied to them, "Today we know that the Lord is among us because you have not sinned against the Lord as we thought; instead, you have saved us from destruction!"

32 Then Phinehas and the ten ambassadors went back to the people of Israel and told them what had happened, 33 and all Israel rejoiced and praised God and spoke no more of war against Reuben and Gad. 34 The people of Reuben and Gad named the altar "The Altar of Witness," for they said, "It is a witness between us and them that Jehovah is our God, too."

23 LONG AFTER this, when the Lord had given success to the people of Israel against their enemies and when Joshua was very old, 2 he called for the leaders of Israel—the elders, judges, and officers—and said to them, "I am an old man now, 3 and you have seen all that the Lord your God has done for you during my lifetime. He has fought for you against your enemies and has given you their land. 4, 5 And I have divided to you

New Revised Standard

Lord, God of gods! He knows; and let Israel itself know! If it was in rebellion or in breach of faith toward the Lord, do not spare us today 23 for building an altar to turn away from following the Lord; or if we did so to offer burnt offerings or grain offerings or offerings of well-being on it, may the Lord himself take vengeance. 24 No! We did it from fear that in time to come your children might say to our children, 'What have you to do with the Lord, the God of Israel? 25 For the Lord has made the Jordan a boundary between us and you, you Reubenites and Gadites; you have no portion in the Lord.' So your children might make our children cease to worship the Lord. 26 Therefore we said, 'Let us now build an altar, not for burnt offering, nor for sacrifice, 27 but to be a witness between us and you, and between the generations after us, that we do perform the service of the Lord in his presence with our burnt offerings and sacrifices and offerings of well-being; so that your children may never say to our children in time to come, "You have no portion in the Lord." ' 28 And we thought, If this should be said to us or to our descendants in time to come, we could say, 'Look at this copy of the altar of the Lord, which our ancestors made, not for burnt offerings, nor for sacrifice, but to be a witness between us and you.' 29 Far be it from us that we should rebel against the Lord, and turn away this day from following the Lord by building an altar for burnt offering, grain offering, or sacrifice, other than the altar of the Lord our God that stands before his tabernacle!"

30 When the priest Phinehas and the chiefs of the congregation, the heads of the families of Israel who were with him, heard the words that the Reubenites and the Gadites and the Manassites spoke, they were satisfied. 31 The priest Phinehas son of Eleazar said to the Reubenites and the Gadites and the Manassites, "Today we know that the Lord is among us, because you have not committed this treachery against the Lord; now you have saved the Israelites from the hand of the Lord."

32 Then the priest Phinehas son of Eleazar and the chiefs returned from the Reubenites and the Gadites in the land of Gilead to the land of Canaan, to the Israelites, and brought back word to them. 33 The report pleased the Israelites; and the Israelites blessed God and spoke no more of making war against them, to destroy the land where the Reubenites and the Gadites were settled. 34 The Reubenites and the Gadites called the altar Witness;[b] "For," said they, "it is a witness between us that the Lord is God."

Joshua Exhorts the People

23 A LONG time afterward, when the Lord had given rest to Israel from all their enemies all around, and Joshua was old and well advanced in years, 2 Joshua summoned all Israel, their elders and heads, their judges and officers, and said to them, "I am now old and well advanced in years; 3 and you have seen all that the Lord your God has done to all these nations for your sake, for it is the Lord your God who has fought for you. 4 I have allotted to you as an inheritance for your

[b] Cn Compare Syr: Heb lacks *Witness*

King James

4Behold, I have divided unto you by lot these nations that remain, to be an inheritance for your tribes, from Jordan, with all the nations that I have cut off, even unto the great sea westward.

5And the LORD your God, he shall expel them from before you, and drive them from out of your sight; and ye shall possess their land, as the LORD your God hath promised unto you.

6Be ye therefore very courageous to keep and to do all that is written in the book of the law of Moses, that ye turn not aside therefrom *to* the right hand or *to* the left;

7That ye come not among these nations, these that remain among you; neither make mention of the name of their gods, nor cause to swear *by them*, neither serve them, nor bow yourselves unto them:

8But cleave unto the LORD your God, as ye have done unto this day.

9For the LORD hath driven out from before you great nations and strong: but *as for* you, no man hath been able to stand before you unto this day.

10One man of you shall chase a thousand: for the LORD your God, he *it is* that fighteth for you, as he hath promised you.

11Take good heed therefore unto yourselves, that ye love the LORD your God.

12Else if ye do in any wise go back, and cleave unto the remnant of these nations, *even* these that remain among you, and shall make marriages with them, and go in unto them, and they to you:

13Know for a certainty that the LORD your God will no more drive out *any of* these nations from before you; but they shall be snares and traps unto you, and scourges in your sides, and thorns in your eyes, until ye perish from off this good land which the LORD your God hath given you.

14And, behold, this day I *am* going the way of all the earth: and ye know in all your hearts and in all your souls, that not one thing hath failed of all the good things which the LORD your God spake concerning you; all are come to pass unto you, *and* not one thing hath failed thereof.

15Therefore it shall come to pass, *that* as all good things are come upon you, which the LORD your God promised you; so shall the LORD bring upon you all evil things, until he have destroyed you from off this good land which the LORD your God hath given you.

16When ye have transgressed the covenant of the LORD your God, which he commanded you, and have gone and served other gods, and bowed yourselves to them; then shall the anger of the LORD be kindled against you, and ye shall perish quickly from off the good land which he hath given unto you.

24 AND JOSHUA gathered all the tribes of Israel to Shechem, and called for the elders of Israel, and for their heads, and for their judges, and for their officers; and they presented themselves before God.

2And Joshua said unto all the people, Thus saith the LORD God of Israel, Your fathers dwelt on the other side of the flood in old time, *even* Terah, the father of Abraham, and the father of Nachor: and they served other gods.

3And I took your father Abraham from the other side of the flood, and led him throughout all the land of Canaan, and multiplied his seed, and gave him Isaac.

4And I gave unto Isaac Jacob and Esau: and I gave unto Esau mount Seir, to possess it; but Jacob and his children went down into Egypt.

New International

for your tribes all the land of the nations that remain— the nations I conquered—between the Jordan and the Great Sea[a] in the west. 5The LORD your God himself will drive them out of your way. He will push them out before you, and you will take possession of their land, as the LORD your God promised you.

6"Be very strong; be careful to obey all that is written in the Book of the Law of Moses, without turning aside to the right or to the left. 7Do not associate with these nations that remain among you; do not invoke the names of their gods or swear by them. You must not serve them or bow down to them. 8But you are to hold fast to the LORD your God, as you have until now.

9"The LORD has driven out before you great and powerful nations; to this day no one has been able to withstand you. 10One of you routs a thousand, because the LORD your God fights for you, just as he promised. 11So be very careful to love the LORD your God.

12"But if you turn away and ally yourselves with the survivors of these nations that remain among you and if you intermarry with them and associate with them, 13then you may be sure that the LORD your God will no longer drive out these nations before you. Instead, they will become snares and traps for you, whips on your backs and thorns in your eyes, until you perish from this good land, which the LORD your God has given you.

14"Now I am about to go the way of all the earth. You know with all your heart and soul that not one of all the good promises the LORD your God gave you has failed. Every promise has been fulfilled; not one has failed. 15But just as every good promise of the LORD your God has come true, so the LORD will bring on you all the evil he has threatened, until he has destroyed you from this good land he has given you. 16If you violate the covenant of the LORD your God, which he commanded you, and go and serve other gods and bow down to them, the LORD's anger will burn against you, and you will quickly perish from the good land he has given you."

The Covenant Renewed at Shechem

24 THEN JOSHUA assembled all the tribes of Israel at Shechem. He summoned the elders, leaders, judges and officials of Israel, and they presented themselves before God.

2Joshua said to all the people, "This is what the LORD, the God of Israel, says: 'Long ago your forefathers, including Terah the father of Abraham and Nahor, lived beyond the River[b] and worshiped other gods. 3But I took your father Abraham from the land beyond the River and led him throughout Canaan and gave him many descendants. I gave him Isaac, 4and to Isaac I gave Jacob and Esau. I assigned the hill country of Seir to Esau, but Jacob and his sons went down to Egypt.

---

a 4 That is, the Mediterranean   b 2 That is, the Euphrates; also in verses 3, 14 and 15

Living Bible

the land of the nations yet unconquered as well as the land of those you have already destroyed. All the land from the Jordan River to the Mediterranean Sea shall be yours, for the Lord your God will drive out all the people living there now, and you will live there instead, just as he has promised you.

6"But be very sure to follow all the instructions written in the book of the laws of Moses; do not deviate from them the least little bit. 7Be sure that you do not mix with the heathen people still remaining in the land; do not even mention the names of their gods, much less swear by them or worship them. 8But follow the Lord your God just as you have until now. 9He has driven out great, strong nations from before you, and no one has been able to defeat you. 10Each one of you has put to flight a thousand of the enemy, for the Lord your God fights for you, just as he has promised. 11So be very careful to keep on loving him.

12"If you don't, and if you begin to intermarry with the nations around you, 13then know for a certainty that the Lord your God will no longer chase those nations from your land. Instead, they will be a snare and a trap to you, a pain in your side and a thorn in your eyes, and you will disappear from this good land which the Lord your God has given you.

14"Soon I will be going the way of all the earth—I am going to die.

"You know very well that God's promises to you have all come true. 15, 16But as certainly as the Lord has given you the good things he promised, just as certainly he will bring evil upon you if you disobey him. For if you worship other gods he will completely wipe you out from this good land which the Lord has given you. His anger will rise hot against you, and you will quickly perish."

New Revised Standard

tribes those nations that remain, along with all the nations that I have already cut off, from the Jordan to the Great Sea in the west. 5The Lord your God will push them back before you, and drive them out of your sight; and you shall possess their land, as the Lord your God promised you. 6Therefore be very steadfast to observe and do all that is written in the book of the law of Moses, turning aside from it neither to the right nor to the left, 7so that you may not be mixed with these nations left here among you, or make mention of the names of their gods, or swear by them, or serve them, or bow yourselves down to them, 8but hold fast to the Lord your God, as you have done to this day. 9For the Lord has driven out before you great and strong nations; and as for you, no one has been able to withstand you to this day. 10One of you puts to flight a thousand, since it is the Lord your God who fights for you, as he promised you. 11Be very careful, therefore, to love the Lord your God. 12For if you turn back, and join the survivors of these nations left here among you, and intermarry with them, so that you marry their women and they yours, 13know assuredly that the Lord your God will not continue to drive out these nations before you; but they shall be a snare and a trap for you, a scourge on your sides, and thorns in your eyes, until you perish from this good land that the Lord your God has given you.

14 "And now I am about to go the way of all the earth, and you know in your hearts and souls, all of you, that not one thing has failed of all the good things that the Lord your God promised concerning you; all have come to pass for you, not one of them has failed. 15But just as all the good things that the Lord your God promised concerning you have been fulfilled for you, so the Lord will bring upon you all the bad things, until he has destroyed you from this good land that the Lord your God has given you. 16If you transgress the covenant of the Lord your God, which he enjoined on you, and go and serve other gods and bow down to them, then the anger of the Lord will be kindled against you, and you shall perish quickly from the good land that he has given to you."

The Tribes Renew the Covenant

24 THEN JOSHUA summoned all the people of Israel to him at Shechem, along with their leaders—the elders, officers, and judges. So they came and presented themselves before God.

2Then Joshua addressed them as follows: "The Lord God of Israel says, 'Your ancestors, including Terah the father of Abraham and Nahor, lived east of the Euphrates River; and they worshiped other gods. 3But I took your father Abraham from that land across the river and led him into the land of Canaan and gave him many descendants through Isaac his son. 4Isaac's children, whom I gave him, were Jacob and Esau. To Esau I gave the area around Mount Seir while Jacob and his children went into Egypt.

24 THEN JOSHUA gathered all the tribes of Israel to Shechem, and summoned the elders, the heads, the judges, and the officers of Israel; and they presented themselves before God. 2And Joshua said to all the people, "Thus says the Lord, the God of Israel: Long ago your ancestors—Terah and his sons Abraham and Nahor—lived beyond the Euphrates and served other gods. 3Then I took your father Abraham from beyond the River and led him through all the land of Canaan and made his offspring many. I gave him Isaac; 4and to Isaac I gave Jacob and Esau. I gave Esau the hill country of Seir to possess, but Jacob and his children went down to Egypt. 5Then I sent Moses and Aaron, and I plagued

King James

5I sent Moses also and Aaron, and I plagued Egypt, according to that which I did among them: and afterward I brought you out.

6And I brought your fathers out of Egypt: and ye came unto the sea; and the Egyptians pursued after your fathers with chariots and horsemen unto the Red sea.

7And when they cried unto the LORD, he put darkness between you and the Egyptians, and brought the sea upon them, and covered them; and your eyes have seen what I have done in Egypt: and ye dwelt in the wilderness a long season.

8And I brought you into the land of the Amorites, which dwelt on the other side Jordan; and they fought with you: and I gave them into your hand, that ye might possess their land; and I destroyed them from before you.

9Then Balak the son of Zippor, king of Moab, arose and warred against Israel, and sent and called Balaam the son of Beor to curse you:

10But I would not hearken unto Balaam; therefore he blessed you still: so I delivered you out of his hand.

11And ye went over Jordan, and came unto Jericho: and the men of Jericho fought against you, the Amorites, and the Perizzites, and the Canaanites, and the Hittites, and the Girgashites, the Hivites, and the Jebusites; and I delivered them into your hand.

12And I sent the hornet before you, which drave them out from before you, *even* the two kings of the Amorites; *but* not with thy sword, nor with thy bow.

13And I have given you a land for which ye did not labour, and cities which ye built not, and ye dwell in them; of the vineyards and oliveyards which ye planted not do ye eat.

14¶ Now therefore fear the LORD, and serve him in sincerity and in truth: and put away the gods which your fathers served on the other side of the flood, and in Egypt; and serve ye the LORD.

15And if it seem evil unto you to serve the LORD, choose you this day whom ye will serve; whether the gods which your fathers served that *were* on the other side of the flood, or the gods of the Amorites, in whose land ye dwell: but as for me and my house, we will serve the LORD.

16And the people answered and said, God forbid that we should forsake the LORD, to serve other gods;

17For the LORD our God, he *it is* that brought us up and our fathers out of the land of Egypt, from the house of bondage, and which did those great signs in our sight, and preserved us in all the way wherein we went, and among all the people through whom we passed:

18And the LORD drave out from before us all the people, even the Amorites which dwelt in the land: *therefore* will we also serve the LORD; for he *is* our God.

19And Joshua said unto the people, Ye cannot serve the LORD: for he *is* an holy God; he *is* a jealous God; he will not forgive your transgressions nor your sins.

20If ye forsake the LORD, and serve strange gods, then he will turn and do you hurt, and consume you, after that he hath done you good.

21And the people said unto Joshua, Nay; but we will serve the LORD.

22And Joshua said unto the people, Ye *are* witnesses against yourselves that ye have chosen you the LORD, to serve him. And they said, *We are* witnesses.

23Now therefore put away, *said he,* the strange gods which *are* among you, and incline your heart unto the LORD God of Israel.

24And the people said unto Joshua, The LORD our God will we serve, and his voice will we obey.

25So Joshua made a covenant with the people that day, and set them a statute and an ordinance in Shechem.

26¶ And Joshua wrote these words in the book of the law of God, and took a great stone, and set it up there under an oak, that *was* by the sanctuary of the LORD.

New International

5" 'Then I sent Moses and Aaron, and I afflicted the Egyptians by what I did there, and I brought you out. 6When I brought your fathers out of Egypt, you came to the sea, and the Egyptians pursued them with chariots and horsemena as far as the Red Sea.b 7But they cried to the LORD for help, and he put darkness between you and the Egyptians; he brought the sea over them and covered them. You saw with your own eyes what I did to the Egyptians. Then you lived in the desert for a long time.

8" 'I brought you to the land of the Amorites who lived east of the Jordan. They fought against you, but I gave them into your hands. I destroyed them from before you, and you took possession of their land. 9When Balak son of Zippor, the king of Moab, prepared to fight against Israel, he sent for Balaam son of Beor to put a curse on you. 10But I would not listen to Balaam, so he blessed you again and again, and I delivered you out of his hand.

11" 'Then you crossed the Jordan and came to Jericho. The citizens of Jericho fought against you, as did also the Amorites, Perizzites, Canaanites, Hittites, Girgashites, Hivites and Jebusites, but I gave them into your hands. 12I sent the hornet ahead of you, which drove them out before you—also the two Amorite kings. You did not do it with your own sword and bow. 13So I gave you a land on which you did not toil and cities you did not build; and you live in them and eat from vineyards and olive groves that you did not plant.'

14"Now fear the LORD and serve him with all faithfulness. Throw away the gods your forefathers worshiped beyond the River and in Egypt, and serve the LORD. 15But if serving the LORD seems undesirable to you, then choose for yourselves this day whom you will serve, whether the gods your forefathers served beyond the River, or the gods of the Amorites, in whose land you are living. But as for me and my household, we will serve the LORD."

16Then the people answered, "Far be it from us to forsake the LORD to serve other gods! 17It was the LORD our God himself who brought us and our fathers up out of Egypt, from that land of slavery, and performed those great signs before our eyes. He protected us on our entire journey and among all the nations through which we traveled. 18And the LORD drove out before us all the nations, including the Amorites, who lived in the land. We too will serve the LORD, because he is our God."

19Joshua said to the people, "You are not able to serve the LORD. He is a holy God; he is a jealous God. He will not forgive your rebellion and your sins. 20If you forsake the LORD and serve foreign gods, he will turn and bring disaster on you and make an end of you, after he has been good to you."

21But the people said to Joshua, "No! We will serve the LORD."

22Then Joshua said, "You are witnesses against yourselves that you have chosen to serve the LORD."

"Yes, we are witnesses," they replied.

23"Now then," said Joshua, "throw away the foreign gods that are among you and yield your hearts to the LORD, the God of Israel."

24And the people said to Joshua, "We will serve the LORD our God and obey him."

25On that day Joshua made a covenant for the people, and there at Shechem he drew up for them decrees and laws. 26And Joshua recorded these things in the Book of the Law of God. Then he took a large stone and set it up there under the oak near the holy place of the LORD.

---

a 6 Or *charioteers*   b 6 Hebrew *Yam Suph*; that is, Sea of Reeds

Living Bible

5"Then I sent Moses and Aaron to bring terrible plagues upon Egypt; and afterwards I brought my people out as free men. 6But when they arrived at the Red Sea, the Egyptians chased after them with chariots and cavalry. 7Then Israel cried out to me and I put darkness between them and the Egyptians; and I brought the sea crashing in upon the Egyptians, drowning them. You saw what I did. Then Israel lived in the wilderness for many years.

8"Finally I brought you into the land of the Amorites on the other side of the Jordan; and they fought against you, but I destroyed them and gave you their land. 9Then King Balak of Moab started a war against Israel, and he asked Balaam, the son of Beor, to curse you. 10But I wouldn't listen to him. Instead I made him bless you; and so I delivered Israel from him.

11"Then you crossed the Jordan River and came to Jericho. The men of Jericho fought against you, and so did many others—the Perizzites, the Canaanites, the Hittites, the Girgashites, the Hivites, and the Jebusites. Each in turn fought against you but I destroyed them all. 12And I sent hornets ahead of you to drive out the two kings of the Amorites and their people. It was not your swords or bows that brought you victory! 13I gave you land you had not worked for and cities you did not build—these cities where you are now living. I gave you vineyards and olive groves for food, though you did not plant them.'

14"So revere Jehovah and serve him in sincerity and truth. Put away forever the idols your ancestors worshiped when they lived beyond the Euphrates River and in Egypt. Worship the Lord alone. 15But if you are unwilling to obey the Lord, then decide today whom you will obey. Will it be the gods of your ancestors beyond the Euphrates or the gods of the Amorites here in this land? But as for me and my family, we will serve the Lord."

16And the people replied, "We would never forsake the Lord and worship other gods! 17For the Lord our God is the one who rescued our fathers from their slavery in the land of Egypt. He is the God who did mighty miracles before the eyes of Israel, as we traveled through the wilderness, and preserved us from our enemies when we passed through their land. 18It was the Lord who drove out the Amorites and the other nations living here in the land. Yes, we choose the Lord, for he alone is our God."

19But Joshua replied to the people, "You can't worship the Lord God, for he is holy and jealous; he will not forgive your rebellion and sins. 20If you forsake him and worship other gods, he will turn upon you and destroy you, even though he has taken care of you for such a long time."

21But the people answered, "We choose the Lord!"

22"You have heard yourselves say it," Joshua said— "you have chosen to obey the Lord."

"Yes," they replied, "we are witnesses."

23"All right," he said, "then you must destroy all the idols you now own, and you must obey the Lord God of Israel."

24The people replied to Joshua, "Yes, we will worship and obey the Lord alone."

25So Joshua made a covenant with them that day at Shechem, committing them to a permanent and binding contract between themselves and God. 26Joshua recorded the people's reply in the book of the laws of God, and took a huge stone as a reminder and rolled it beneath the oak tree that was beside the Tabernacle.

New Revised Standard

Egypt with what I did in its midst; and afterwards I brought you out. 6When I brought your ancestors out of Egypt, you came to the sea; and the Egyptians pursued your ancestors with chariots and horsemen to the Red Sea.c 7When they cried out to the LORD, he put darkness between you and the Egyptians, and made the sea come upon them and cover them; and your eyes saw what I did to Egypt. Afterwards you lived in the wilderness a long time. 8Then I brought you to the land of the Amorites, who lived on the other side of the Jordan; they fought with you, and I handed them over to you, and you took possession of their land, and I destroyed them before you. 9Then King Balak son of Zippor of Moab, set out to fight against Israel. He sent and invited Balaam son of Beor to curse you, 10but I would not listen to Balaam; therefore he blessed you; so I rescued you out of his hand. 11When you went over the Jordan and came to Jericho, the citizens of Jericho fought against you, and also the Amorites, the Perizzites, the Canaanites, the Hittites, the Girgashites, the Hivites, and the Jebusites; and I handed them over to you. 12I sent the hornetd ahead of you, which drove out before you the two kings of the Amorites; it was not by your sword or by your bow. 13I gave you a land on which you had not labored, and towns that you had not built, and you live in them; you eat the fruit of vineyards and oliveyards that you did not plant.

14 "Now therefore revere the LORD, and serve him in sincerity and in faithfulness; put away the gods that your ancestors served beyond the River and in Egypt, and serve the LORD. 15Now if you are unwilling to serve the LORD, choose this day whom you will serve, whether the gods your ancestors served in the region beyond the River or the gods of the Amorites in whose land you are living; but as for me and my household, we will serve the LORD."

16 Then the people answered, "Far be it from us that we should forsake the LORD to serve other gods; 17for it is the LORD our God who brought us and our ancestors up from the land of Egypt, out of the house of slavery, and who did those great signs in our sight. He protected us along all the way that we went, and among all the peoples through whom we passed; 18and the LORD drove out before us all the peoples, the Amorites who lived in the land. Therefore we also will serve the LORD, for he is our God."

19 But Joshua said to the people, "You cannot serve the LORD, for he is a holy God. He is a jealous God; he will not forgive your transgressions or your sins. 20If you forsake the LORD and serve foreign gods, then he will turn and do you harm, and consume you, after having done you good." 21And the people said to Joshua, "No, we will serve the LORD!" 22Then Joshua said to the people, "You are witnesses against yourselves that you have chosen the LORD, to serve him." And they said, "We are witnesses." 23He said, "Then put away the foreign gods that are among you, and incline your hearts to the LORD, the God of Israel." 24The people said to Joshua, "The LORD our God we will serve, and him we will obey." 25So Joshua made a covenant with the people that day, and made statutes and ordinances for them at Shechem. 26Joshua wrote these words in the book of the law of God; and he took a large stone, and set it up there under the oak in the sanctuary of the LORD. 27Josh-

c Or Sea of Reeds   d Meaning of Heb uncertain

King James

27And Joshua said unto all the people, Behold, this stone shall be a witness unto us; for it hath heard all the words of the LORD which he spake unto us: it shall be therefore a witness unto you, lest ye deny your God.

28So Joshua let the people depart, every man unto his inheritance.

29¶ And it came to pass after these things, that Joshua the son of Nun, the servant of the LORD, died, *being* an hundred and ten years old.

30And they buried him in the border of his inheritance in Timnath-serah, which *is* in mount Ephraim, on the north side of the hill of Gaash.

31And Israel served the LORD all the days of Joshua, and all the days of the elders that overlived Joshua, and which had known all the works of the LORD, that he had done for Israel.

32¶ And the bones of Joseph, which the children of Israel brought up out of Egypt, buried they in Shechem, in a parcel of ground which Jacob bought of the sons of Hamor the father of Shechem for an hundred pieces of silver: and it became the inheritance of the children of Joseph.

33And Eleazar the son of Aaron died; and they buried him in a hill *that pertained to* Phinehas his son, which was given him in mount Ephraim.

New International

27"See!" he said to all the people. "This stone will be a witness against us. It has heard all the words the LORD has said to us. It will be a witness against you if you are untrue to your God."

Buried in the Promised Land

28Then Joshua sent the people away, each to his own inheritance.

29After these things, Joshua son of Nun, the servant of the LORD, died at the age of a hundred and ten. 30And they buried him in the land of his inheritance, at Timnath Serah[a] in the hill country of Ephraim, north of Mount Gaash.

31Israel served the LORD throughout the lifetime of Joshua and of the elders who outlived him and who had experienced everything the LORD had done for Israel.

32And Joseph's bones, which the Israelites had brought up from Egypt, were buried at Shechem in the tract of land that Jacob bought for a hundred pieces of silver[b] from the sons of Hamor, the father of Shechem. This became the inheritance of Joseph's descendants.

33And Eleazar son of Aaron died and was buried at Gibeah, which had been allotted to his son Phinehas in the hill country of Ephraim.

a 30 Also known as *Timnath Heres* (see Judges 2:9)   b 32 Hebrew *hundred kesitahs*; a kesitah was a unit of money of unknown weight and value.

Living Bible

27Then Joshua said to all the people, "This stone has heard everything the Lord said, so it will be a witness to testify against you if you go back on your word."

28Then Joshua sent the people away to their own sections of the country.

29Soon after this he died at the age of 110. 30He was buried on his own estate at Timnath-serah, in the hill country of Ephraim, on the north side of the mountains of Gaash.

31Israel obeyed the Lord throughout the lifetimes of Joshua and the other old men who had personally witnessed the amazing deeds the Lord had done for Israel.

32The bones of Joseph, the people of Israel had brought them along when they left Egypt—were buried in Shechem, in the parcel of ground Jacob had bought^c from the sons of Hamor. (The land was located in the territory assigned to the tribes of Joseph.)

33Eleazar, the son of Aaron, also died; he was buried in the hill country of Ephraim, at Gibe-ah, the city which had been given to his son Phinehas.

New Revised Standard

ua said to all the people, "See, this stone shall be a witness against us; for it has heard all the words of the LORD that he spoke to us; therefore it shall be a witness against you, if you deal falsely with your God." 28 So Joshua sent the people away to their inheritances.

Death of Joshua and Eleazar

29 After these things Joshua son of Nun, the servant of the LORD, died, being one hundred ten years old. 30 They buried him in his own inheritance at Timnath-serah, which is in the hill country of Ephraim, north of Mount Gaash.

31 Israel served the LORD all the days of Joshua, and all the days of the elders who outlived Joshua and had known all the work that the LORD did for Israel.

32 The bones of Joseph, which the Israelites had brought up from Egypt, were buried at Shechem, in the portion of ground that Jacob had bought from the children of Hamor, the father of Shechem, for one hundred pieces of money;^d it became an inheritance of the descendants of Joseph.

33 Eleazar son of Aaron died; and they buried him at Gibeah, the town of his son Phinehas, which had been given him in the hill country of Ephraim.

---

^c 24:32 had bought, literally, "had bought for 100 pieces of silver."   ^d Heb one hundred qesitah

King James

New International

THE BOOK OF

Judges

Judges

1 NOW AFTER the death of Joshua it came to pass, that the children of Israel asked the LORD, saying, Who shall go up for us against the Canaanites first, to fight against them?

2And the LORD said, Judah shall go up: behold, I have delivered the land into his hand.

3And Judah said unto Simeon his brother, Come up with me into my lot, that we may fight against the Canaanites; and I likewise will go with thee into thy lot. So Simeon went with him.

4And Judah went up; and the LORD delivered the Canaanites and the Perizzites into their hand: and they slew of them in Bezek ten thousand men.

5And they found Adoni-bezek in Bezek: and they fought against him, and they slew the Canaanites and the Perizzites.

6But Adoni-bezek fled; and they pursued after him, and caught him, and cut off his thumbs and his great toes.

7And Adoni-bezek said, Threescore and ten kings, having their thumbs and their great toes cut off, gathered *their meat* under my table: as I have done, so God hath requited me. And they brought him to Jerusalem, and there he died.

8Now the children of Judah had fought against Jerusalem, and had taken it, and smitten it with the edge of the sword, and set the city on fire.

9¶ And afterward the children of Judah went down to fight against the Canaanites, that dwelt in the mountain, and in the south, and in the valley.

10And Judah went against the Canaanites that dwelt in Hebron: (now the name of Hebron before *was* Kirjatharba:) and they slew Sheshai, and Ahiman, and Talmai.

11And from thence he went against the inhabitants of Debir: and the name of Debir before *was* Kirjath-sepher:

12And Caleb said, He that smiteth Kirjath-sepher, and taketh it, to him will I give Achsah my daughter to wife.

13And Othniel the son of Kenaz, Caleb's younger brother, took it: and he gave him Achsah his daughter to wife.

14And it came to pass, when she came *to him,* that she moved him to ask of her father a field: and she lighted from off *her* ass; and Caleb said unto her, What wilt thou?

15And she said unto him, Give me a blessing: for thou hast given me a south land; give me also springs of water. And Caleb gave her the upper springs and the nether springs.

16¶ And the children of the Kenite, Moses' father-in-law, went up out of the city of palm trees with the children of Judah into the wilderness of Judah, which *lieth* in the south of Arad; and they went and dwelt among the people.

17And Judah went with Simeon his brother, and they slew the Canaanites that inhabited Zephath, and utterly destroyed it. And the name of the city was called Hormah.

Israel Fights the Remaining Canaanites

1 AFTER THE death of Joshua, the Israelites asked the LORD, "Who will be the first to go up and fight for us against the Canaanites?"

2The LORD answered, "Judah is to go; I have given the land into their hands."

3Then the men of Judah said to the Simeonites their brothers, "Come up with us into the territory allotted to us, to fight against the Canaanites. We in turn will go with you into yours." So the Simeonites went with them.

4When Judah attacked, the LORD gave the Canaanites and Perizzites into their hands and they struck down ten thousand men at Bezek. 5It was there that they found Adoni-Bezek and fought against him, putting to rout the Canaanites and Perizzites. 6Adoni-Bezek fled, but they chased him and caught him, and cut off his thumbs and big toes.

7Then Adoni-Bezek said, "Seventy kings with their thumbs and big toes cut off have picked up scraps under my table. Now God has paid me back for what I did to them." They brought him to Jerusalem, and he died there.

8The men of Judah attacked Jerusalem also and took it. They put the city to the sword and set it on fire.

9After that, the men of Judah went down to fight against the Canaanites living in the hill country, the Negev and the western foothills. 10They advanced against the Canaanites living in Hebron (formerly called Kiriath Arba) and defeated Sheshai, Ahiman and Talmai.

11From there they advanced against the people living in Debir (formerly called Kiriath Sepher). 12And Caleb said, "I will give my daughter Acsah in marriage to the man who attacks and captures Kiriath Sepher." 13Othniel son of Kenaz, Caleb's younger brother, took it; so Caleb gave his daughter Acsah to him in marriage.

14One day when she came to Othniel, she urged hima to ask her father for a field. When she got off her donkey, Caleb asked her, "What can I do for you?"

15She replied, "Do me a special favor. Since you have given me land in the Negev, give me also springs of water." Then Caleb gave her the upper and lower springs.

16The descendants of Moses' father-in-law, the Kenite, went up from the City of Palmsb with the men of Judah to live among the people of the Desert of Judah in the Negev near Arad.

17Then the men of Judah went with the Simeonites their brothers and attacked the Canaanites living in Zephath, and they totally destroyedc the city. Therefore it was called Hormah.d 18The men of Judah also tooke

---

a *14* Hebrew; Septuagint and Vulgate *Othniel, he urged her*   b *16* That is, Jericho   c *17* The Hebrew term refers to the irrevocable giving over of things or persons to the LORD, often by totally destroying them.   d *17 Hormah* means *destruction.*   e *18* Hebrew; Septuagint *Judah did not take*

Living Bible	New Revised Standard

Judges

Judges

1 AFTER JOSHUA died, the nation of Israel went to the Lord to receive his instructions.

"Which of our tribes should be the first to go to war against the Canaanites?" they inquired.

²God's answer came, "Judah. And I will give them a great victory."

³The leaders of the tribe of Judah, however, asked help from the tribe of Simeon. "Join us in clearing out the people living in the territory allotted to us," they said, "and then we will help you conquer yours." So the army of Simeon went with the army of Judah. 4, 5, 6And the Lord helped them defeat the Canaanites and Perizzites, so that ten thousand of the enemy were slain at Bezek. King Adoni-bezek escaped, but the Israeli army soon captured him and cut off his thumbs and big toes.

⁷"I have treated seventy kings in this same manner and have fed them the scraps under my table!" King Adoni-bezek said. "Now God has paid me back." He was taken to Jerusalem, and died there.

⁸(Judah had conquered Jerusalem, and massacred its people, setting the city on fire.) ⁹Afterward the army of Judah fought the Canaanites in the hill country and in the Negeb, as well as on the coastal plains. ¹⁰Then Judah marched against the Canaanites in Hebron (formerly called Kiriath-arba), destroying the cities of Sheshai, Ahiman, and Talmai. ¹¹Later they attacked the city of Debir (formerly called Kiriath-sepher).

¹²"Who will lead the attack against Debir?" Caleb challenged them. "Whoever conquers it shall have my daughter Achsah as his wife!"

¹³Caleb's nephew, Othni-el, son of his younger brother Kenaz, volunteered to lead the attack; and he conquered the city and won Achsah as his bride. ¹⁴As they were leaving for their new home,ᶠ she urged him to ask her father for an additionalᵍ piece of land. She dismounted from her donkey to speak to Caleb about it.

"What do you wish?" he asked.

¹⁵And she replied, "You have been kind enough to give me land in the Negeb, but please give us springs of water too."

So Caleb gave her the upper and lower springs.

¹⁶When the tribe of Judah moved into its new land in the Negeb wilderness south of Arad, the descendants of Moses' father-in-law—members of the Kenite tribe—accompanied them. They left their homes in Jericho, "The City of Palm Trees," and the two tribes lived together after that. ¹⁷Afterwards the army of Judah joined Simeon's and they fought the Canaanites at the city of Zephath and massacred all its people. So now the city is named Hormah (meaning, "massacred"). ¹⁸The army

1 AFTER THE death of Joshua, the Israelites inquired of the LORD, "Who shall go up first for us against the Canaanites, to fight against them?" ²The LORD said, "Judah shall go up. I hereby give the land into his hand." ³Judah said to his brother Simeon, "Come up with me into the territory allotted to me, that we may fight against the Canaanites; then I too will go with you into the territory allotted to you." So Simeon went with him. ⁴Then Judah went up and the LORD gave the Canaanites and the Perizzites into their hand; and they defeated ten thousand of them at Bezek. ⁵They came upon Adoni-bezek at Bezek, and fought against him, and defeated the Canaanites and the Perizzites. ⁶Adoni-bezek fled; but they pursued him, and caught him, and cut off his thumbs and big toes. ⁷Adoni-bezek said, "Seventy kings with their thumbs and big toes cut off used to pick up scraps under my table; as I have done, so God has paid me back." They brought him to Jerusalem, and he died there.

8 Then the people of Judah fought against Jerusalem and took it. They put it to the sword and set the city on fire. ⁹Afterward the people of Judah went down to fight against the Canaanites who lived in the hill country, in the Negeb, and in the lowland. ¹⁰Judah went against the Canaanites who lived in Hebron (the name of Hebron was formerly Kiriath-arba); and they defeated Sheshai and Ahiman and Talmai.

11 From there they went against the inhabitants of Debir (the name of Debir was formerly Kiriath-sepher). ¹²Then Caleb said, "Whoever attacks Kiriath-sepher and takes it, I will give him my daughter Achsah as wife." ¹³And Othniel son of Kenaz, Caleb's younger brother, took it; and he gave him his daughter Achsah as wife. ¹⁴When she came to him, she urged him to ask her father for a field. As she dismounted from her donkey, Caleb said to her, "What do you wish?" ¹⁵She said to him, "Give me a present; since you have set me in the land of the Negeb, give me also Gulloth-mayim."ʰ So Caleb gave her Upper Gulloth and Lower Gulloth.

16 The descendants of Hobabⁱ the Kenite, Moses' father-in-law, went up with the people of Judah from the city of palms into the wilderness of Judah, which lies in the Negeb near Arad. Then they went and settled with the Amalekites.ʲ ¹⁷Judah went with his brother Simeon, and they defeated the Canaanites who inhabited Zephath, and devoted it to destruction. So the city was called Hormah. ¹⁸Judah took Gaza with its territory,

---

ᶠ *1:14 As they were leaving for their new home,* literally, "when she came to him." ᵍ *1:14 for an additional,* implied.

ʰ That is *Basins of Water* ⁱ Gk: Heb lacks *Hobab* ʲ See 1 Sam 15.6: Heb people

King James

18Also Judah took Gaza with the coast thereof, and Askelon with the coast thereof, and Ekron with the coast thereof.

19And the LORD was with Judah; and he drave out *the inhabitants of* the mountain; but could not drive out the inhabitants of the valley, because they had chariots of iron.

20And they gave Hebron unto Caleb, as Moses said: and he expelled thence the three sons of Anak.

21And the children of Benjamin did not drive out the Jebusites that inhabited Jerusalem; but the Jebusites dwell with the children of Benjamin in Jerusalem unto this day.

22¶ And the house of Joseph, they also went up against Beth-el: and the LORD *was* with them.

23And the house of Joseph sent to descry Beth-el. (Now the name of the city before *was* Luz.)

24And the spies saw a man come forth out of the city, and they said unto him, Show us, we pray thee, the entrance into the city, and we will show thee mercy.

25And when he showed them the entrance into the city, they smote the city with the edge of the sword; but they let go the man and all his family.

26And the man went into the land of the Hittites, and built a city, and called the name thereof Luz: which *is* the name thereof unto this day.

27¶ Neither did Manasseh drive out *the inhabitants of* Beth-shean and her towns, nor Taanach and her towns, nor the inhabitants of Dor and her towns, nor the inhabitants of Ibleam and her towns, nor the inhabitants of Megiddo and her towns: but the Canaanites would dwell in that land.

28And it came to pass, when Israel was strong, that they put the Canaanites to tribute, and did not utterly drive them out.

29¶ Neither did Ephraim drive out the Canaanites that dwelt in Gezer; but the Canaanites dwelt in Gezer among them.

30¶ Neither did Zebulun drive out the inhabitants of Kitron, nor the inhabitants of Nahalol; but the Canaanites dwelt among them, and became tributaries.

31¶ Neither did Asher drive out the inhabitants of Accho, nor the inhabitants of Zidon, nor of Ahlab, nor of Achzib, nor of Helbah, nor of Aphik, nor of Rehob:

32But the Asherites dwelt among the Canaanites, the inhabitants of the land: for they did not drive them out.

33¶ Neither did Naphtali drive out the inhabitants of Beth-shemesh, nor the inhabitants of Beth-anath; but he dwelt among the Canaanites, the inhabitants of the land: nevertheless the inhabitants of Beth-shemesh and of Beth-anath became tributaries unto them.

34And the Amorites forced the children of Dan into the mountain: for they would not suffer them to come down to the valley:

35But the Amorites would dwell in mount Heres in Aijalon, and in Shaalbim: yet the hand of the house of Joseph prevailed, so that they became tributaries.

36And the coast of the Amorites *was* from the going up to Akrabbim, from the rock, and upward.

2 AND AN angel of the LORD came up from Gilgal to Bochim, and said, I made you to go up out of Egypt, and have brought you unto the land which I sware unto your fathers; and I said, I will never break my covenant with you.

2And ye shall make no league with the inhabitants of this land; ye shall throw down their altars: but ye have not obeyed my voice: why have ye done this?

New International

Gaza, Ashkelon and Ekron—each city with its territory.

19The LORD was with the men of Judah. They took possession of the hill country, but they were unable to drive the people from the plains, because they had iron chariots. 20As Moses had promised, Hebron was given to Caleb, who drove from it the three sons of Anak. 21The Benjamites, however, failed to dislodge the Jebusites, who were living in Jerusalem; to this day the Jebusites live there with the Benjamites.

22Now the house of Joseph attacked Bethel, and the LORD was with them. 23When they sent men to spy out Bethel (formerly called Luz), 24the spies saw a man coming out of the city and they said to him, "Show us how to get into the city and we will see that you are treated well." 25So he showed them, and they put the city to the sword but spared the man and his whole family. 26He then went to the land of the Hittites, where he built a city and called it Luz, which is its name to this day.

27But Manasseh did not drive out the people of Beth Shan or Taanach or Dor or Ibleam or Megiddo and their surrounding settlements, for the Canaanites were determined to live in that land. 28When Israel became strong, they pressed the Canaanites into forced labor but never drove them out completely. 29Nor did Ephraim drive out the Canaanites living in Gezer, but the Canaanites continued to live there among them. 30Neither did Zebulun drive out the Canaanites living in Kitron or Nahalol, who remained among them; but they did subject them to forced labor. 31Nor did Asher drive out those living in Acco or Sidon or Ahlab or Aczib or Helbah or Aphek or Rehob, 32and because of this the people of Asher lived among the Canaanite inhabitants of the land. 33Neither did Naphtali drive out those living in Beth Shemesh or Beth Anath; but the Naphtalites too lived among the Canaanite inhabitants of the land, and those living in Beth Shemesh and Beth Anath became forced laborers for them. 34The Amorites confined the Danites to the hill country, not allowing them to come down into the plain. 35And the Amorites were determined also to hold out in Mount Heres, Aijalon and Shaalbim, but when the power of the house of Joseph increased, they too were pressed into forced labor. 36The boundary of the Amorites was from Scorpion[a] Pass to Sela and beyond.

The Angel of the LORD at Bokim

2 THE ANGEL of the LORD went up from Gilgal to Bokim and said, "I brought you up out of Egypt and led you into the land that I swore to give to your forefathers. I said, 'I will never break my covenant with you, 2and you shall not make a covenant with the people of this land, but you shall break down their altars.' Yet you have disobeyed me. Why have you done this? 3Now

a 36 Hebrew Akrabbim

Living Bible

of Judah also conquered the cities of Gaza, Ashkelon, and Ekron, with their surrounding villages. 19The Lord helped the tribe of Judah exterminate the people of the hill country, though they failed in their attempt to conquer the people of the valley, who had iron chariots.

20The city of Hebron was given to Caleb as the Lord had promised; so Caleb drove out the inhabitants of the city; they were descendants of the three sons of Anak.

21The tribe of Benjamin failed to exterminate the Jebusites living in their part of the city of Jerusalem, so they still live there today, mingled with the Israelis.

22, 23As for the tribe of Joseph, they attacked the city of Bethel, formerly known as Luz, and the Lord was with them. First they sent scouts, 24who captured a man coming out of the city. They offered to spare his life and that of his family if he would show them the entrance passage through the wall.b 25So he showed them how to get in, and they massacred the entire population except for this man and his family. 26Later the man moved to Syria and founded a city there, naming it Luz, too, as it is still known today.

27The tribe of Manasseh failed to drive out the people living in Beth-shean, Taanach, Dor, Ibleam, Megiddo, with their surrounding towns; so the Canaanites stayed there. 28In later years when the Israelis were stronger they put the Canaanites to work as slaves, but never did force them to leave the country. 29This was also true of the Canaanites living in Gezer; they still live among the tribe of Ephraim.

30And the tribe of Zebulun did not massacre the people of Kitron or Nahalol, but made them their slaves; 31, 32nor did the tribe of Asher drive out the residents of Acco, Sidon, Ahlab, Achzib, Helbah, Aphik, or Rehob; so the Israelis still live among the Canaanites, who were the original people of that land. 33And the tribe of Naphtali did not drive out the people of Beth-shemesh or of Beth-anath, so these people continue to live among them as servants.

34As for the tribe of Dan, the Amorites forced them into the hill country and wouldn't let them come down into the valley; 35but when the Amorites later spread into Mount Heres, Aijalon, and Sha-albim, the tribe of Joseph conquered them and made them their slaves. 36The boundary of the Amorites begins at the ascent of Scorpion Pass, runs to a spot called The Rock, and continues upward from there.

2 ONE DAY the Angel of the Lord arrived at Bochim, coming from Gilgal, and announced to the people of Israel, "I brought you out of Egypt into this land which I promised to your ancestors, and I said that I would never break my covenant with you, 2if you, on your part, would make no peace treaties with the people living in this land; I told you to destroy their heathen altars. Why have you not obeyed? 3And now since you

b 1:24 the passage through the wall, literally, "the way into the city." Obviously, this does not mean via the city gates.

New Revised Standard

Ashkelon with its territory, and Ekron with its territory. 19The LORD was with Judah, and he took possession of the hill country, but could not drive out the inhabitants of the plain, because they had chariots of iron. 20Hebron was given to Caleb, as Moses had said; and he drove out from it the three sons of Anak. 21But the Benjaminites did not drive out the Jebusites who lived in Jerusalem; so the Jebusites have lived in Jerusalem among the Benjaminites to this day.

22 The house of Joseph also went up against Bethel; and the LORD was with them. 23The house of Joseph sent out spies to Bethel (the name of the city was formerly Luz). 24When the spies saw a man coming out of the city, they said to him, "Show us the way into the city, and we will deal kindly with you." 25So he showed them the way into the city; and they put the city to the sword, but they let the man and all his family go. 26So the man went to the land of the Hittites and built a city, and named it Luz; that is its name to this day.

27 Manasseh did not drive out the inhabitants of Beth-shean and its villages, or Taanach and its villages, or the inhabitants of Dor and its villages, or the inhabitants of Ibleam and its villages, or the inhabitants of Megiddo and its villages; but the Canaanites continued to live in that land. 28When Israel grew strong, they put the Canaanites to forced labor, but did not in fact drive them out.

29 And Ephraim did not drive out the Canaanites who lived in Gezer; but the Canaanites lived among them in Gezer.

30 Zebulun did not drive out the inhabitants of Kitron, or the inhabitants of Nahalol; but the Canaanites lived among them, and became subject to forced labor.

31 Asher did not drive out the inhabitants of Acco, or the inhabitants of Sidon, or of Ahlab, or of Achzib, or of Helbah, or of Aphik, or of Rehob; 32but the Asherites lived among the Canaanites, the inhabitants of the land; for they did not drive them out.

33 Naphtali did not drive out the inhabitants of Beth-shemesh, or the inhabitants of Beth-anath, but lived among the Canaanites, the inhabitants of the land; nevertheless the inhabitants of Beth-shemesh and of Beth-anath became subject to forced labor for them.

34 The Amorites pressed the Danites back into the hill country; they did not allow them to come down to the plain. 35The Amorites continued to live in Har-heres, in Aijalon, and in Shaalbim, but the hand of the house of Joseph rested heavily on them, and they became subject to forced labor. 36The border of the Amorites ran from the ascent of Akrabbim, from Sela and upward.

Israel's Disobedience

2 NOW THE angel of the LORD went up from Gilgal to Bochim, and said, "I brought you up from Egypt, and brought you into the land that I had promised to your ancestors. I said, 'I will never break my covenant with you. 2For your part, do not make a covenant with the inhabitants of this land; tear down their altars.' But you have not obeyed my command. See what you have done! 3So now I say, I will not drive them out before

King James

3Wherefore I also said, I will not drive them out from before you; but they shall be *as thorns* in your sides, and their gods shall be a snare unto you.

4And it came to pass, when the angel of the LORD spake these words unto all the children of Israel, that the people lifted up their voice, and wept.

5And they called the name of that place Bochim: and they sacrificed there unto the LORD.

6¶ And when Joshua had let the people go, the children of Israel went every man unto his inheritance to possess the land.

7And the people served the LORD all the days of Joshua, and all the days of the elders that outlived Joshua, who had seen all the great works of the LORD, that he did for Israel.

8And Joshua the son of Nun, the servant of the LORD, died, *being* an hundred and ten years old.

9And they buried him in the border of his inheritance in Timnath-heres, in the mount of Ephraim, on the north side of the hill Gaash.

10And also all that generation were gathered unto their fathers: and there arose another generation after them, which knew not the LORD, nor yet the works which he had done for Israel.

11¶ And the children of Israel did evil in the sight of the LORD, and served Baalim:

12And they forsook the LORD God of their fathers, which brought them out of the land of Egypt, and followed other gods, of the gods of the people that *were* round about them, and bowed themselves unto them, and provoked the LORD to anger.

13And they forsook the LORD, and served Baal and Ashtaroth.

14¶ And the anger of the LORD was hot against Israel, and he delivered them into the hands of spoilers that spoiled them, and he sold them into the hands of their enemies round about, so that they could not any longer stand before their enemies.

15Whithersoever they went out, the hand of the LORD was against them for evil, as the LORD had said, and as the LORD had sworn unto them: and they were greatly distressed.

16¶ Nevertheless the LORD raised up judges, which delivered them out of the hand of those that spoiled them.

17And yet they would not hearken unto their judges, but they went a-whoring after other gods, and bowed themselves unto them: they turned quickly out of the way which their fathers walked in, obeying the commandments of the LORD; *but* they did not so.

18And when the LORD raised up judges, then The LORD was with the judge, and delivered them out of the hand of their enemies all the days of the judge: for it repented the LORD because of their groanings by reason of them that oppressed them and vexed them.

19And it came to pass, when the judge was dead, *that* they returned, and corrupted *themselves* more than their fathers, in following other gods to serve them, and to bow down unto them; they ceased not from their own doings, nor from their stubborn way.

20¶ And the anger of the LORD was hot against Israel; and he said, Because that this people hath transgressed my covenant which I commanded their fathers, and have not hearkened unto my voice;

21I also will not henceforth drive out any from before them of the nations which Joshua left when he died:

22That through them I may prove Israel, whether they will keep the way of the LORD to walk therein, as their fathers did keep *it*, or not.

23Therefore the LORD left those nations, without driving them out hastily; neither delivered he them into the hand of Joshua.

New International

therefore I tell you that I will not drive them out before you; they will be ‹thorns› in your sides and their gods will be a snare to you."

4When the angel of the LORD had spoken these things to all the Israelites, the people wept aloud, 5and they called that place Bokim.[a] There they offered sacrifices to the LORD.

Disobedience and Defeat

6After Joshua had dismissed the Israelites, they went to take possession of the land, each to his own inheritance. 7The people served the LORD throughout the lifetime of Joshua and of the elders who outlived him and who had seen all the great things the LORD had done for Israel.

8Joshua son of Nun, the servant of the LORD, died at the age of a hundred and ten. 9And they buried him in the land of his inheritance, at Timnath Heres[b] in the hill country of Ephraim, north of Mount Gaash.

10After that whole generation had been gathered to their fathers, another generation grew up, who knew neither the LORD nor what he had done for Israel. 11Then the Israelites did evil in the eyes of the LORD and served the Baals. 12They forsook the LORD, the God of their fathers, who had brought them out of Egypt. They followed and worshiped various gods of the peoples around them. They provoked the LORD to anger 13because they forsook him and served Baal and the Ashtoreths. 14In his anger against Israel the LORD handed them over to raiders who plundered them. He sold them to their enemies all around, whom they were no longer able to resist. 15Whenever Israel went out to fight, the hand of the LORD was against them to defeat them, just as he had sworn to them. They were in great distress.

16Then the LORD raised up judges,[c] who saved them out of the hands of these raiders. 17Yet they would not listen to their judges but prostituted themselves to other gods and worshiped them. Unlike their fathers, they quickly turned from the way in which their fathers had walked, the way of obedience to the LORD's commands. 18Whenever the LORD raised up a judge for them, he was with the judge and saved them out of the hands of their enemies as long as the judge lived; for the LORD had compassion on them as they groaned under those who oppressed and afflicted them. 19But when the judge died, the people returned to ways even more corrupt than those of their fathers, following other gods and serving and worshiping them. They refused to give up their evil practices and stubborn ways.

20Therefore the LORD was very angry with Israel and said, "Because this nation has violated the covenant that I laid down for their forefathers and has not listened to me, 21I will no longer drive out before them any of the nations Joshua left when he died. 22I will use them to test Israel and see whether they will keep the way of the LORD and walk in it as their forefathers did." 23The LORD had allowed those nations to remain; he did not drive them out at once by giving them into the hands of Joshua.

---

[a] 5 *Bokim* means *weepers.* [b] 9 Also known as *Timnath Serah* (see Joshua 19:50 and 24:30) [c] 16 Or *leaders;* similarly in verses 17-19

Living Bible

have broken the contract, it is no longer in effect, and I no longer promise to destroy the nations living in your land; rather, they shall be thorns in your sides, and their gods will be a constant temptation to you."

4The people broke into tears as the Angel finished speaking; 5so the name of that place was called "Bochim" (meaning, "the place where people wept"). Then they offered sacrifices to the Lord.

6When Joshua finally disbanded the armies of Israel, the tribes moved into their new territories and took possession of the land. 7, 8, 9Joshua, the man of God, died at the age of 110, and was buried at the edge of his property in Timnath-heres, in the hill country of Ephraim, north of Mount Gaash. The people had remained true to the Lord throughout Joshua's lifetime, and as long afterward as the old men of his generation were still living—those who had seen the mighty miracles the Lord had done for Israel.

10But finally all that generation died; and the next generation did not worship Jehovah as their God, and did not care about the mighty miracles he had done for Israel. 11They did many things which the Lord had expressly forbidden, including the worshiping of heathen gods. 12, 13, 14They abandoned Jehovah, the God loved and worshiped by their ancestors—the God who had brought them out of Egypt. Instead, they were worshiping and bowing low before the idols of the neighboring nations. So the anger of the Lord flamed out against all Israel. He left them to the mercy of their enemies, for they had departed from Jehovah and were worshiping Baal and the Ashtaroth idols.

15So now when the nation of Israel went out to battle against its enemies, the Lord blocked their path. He had warned them about this, and in fact had vowed that he would do it. But when the people were in this terrible plight, 16the Lord raised up judges to save them from their enemies.

17Yet even then Israel would not listen to the judges, but broke faith with Jehovah by worshiping other gods instead. How quickly they turned away from the true faith of their ancestors, for they refused to obey God's commands. 18Each judge rescued the people of Israel from their enemies throughout his lifetime, for the Lord was moved to pity by the groaning of his people under their crushing oppressions; so he helped them as long as that judge lived. 19But when the judge died, the people turned from doing right and behaved even worse than their ancestors had. They prayed to heathen gods again, throwing themselves to the ground in humble worship. They stubbornly returned to the evil customs of the nations around them.

20Then the anger of the Lord would flame out against Israel again. He declared, "Because these people have violated the treaty I made with their ancestors, 21I will no longer drive out the nations left unconquered by Joshua when he died. 22Instead, I will use these nations to test my people, to see whether or not they will obey the Lord as their ancestors did."

23So the Lord left those nations in the land and did not drive them out, nor let Israel destroy them.

New Revised Standard

you; but they shall become adversariesd to you, and their gods shall be a snare to you." 4When the angel of the LORD spoke these words to all the Israelites, the people lifted up their voices and wept. 5So they named that place Bochim,e and there they sacrificed to the LORD.

Death of Joshua

6 When Joshua dismissed the people, the Israelites all went to their own inheritances to take possession of the land. 7The people worshiped the LORD all the days of Joshua, and all the days of the elders who outlived Joshua, who had seen all the great work that the LORD had done for Israel. 8Joshua son of Nun, the servant of the LORD, died at the age of one hundred ten years. 9So they buried him within the bounds of his inheritance in Timnath-heres, in the hill country of Ephraim, north of Mount Gaash. 10Moreover, that whole generation was gathered to their ancestors, and another generation grew up after them, who did not know the LORD or the work that he had done for Israel.

Israel's Unfaithfulness

11 Then the Israelites did what was evil in the sight of the LORD and worshiped the Baals; 12and they abandoned the LORD, the God of their ancestors, who had brought them out of the land of Egypt; they followed other gods, from among the gods of the peoples who were all around them, and bowed down to them; and they provoked the LORD to anger. 13They abandoned the LORD, and worshiped Baal and the Astartes. 14So the anger of the LORD was kindled against Israel, and he gave them over to plunderers who plundered them, and he sold them into the power of their enemies all around, so that they could no longer withstand their enemies. 15Whenever they marched out, the hand of the LORD was against them to bring misfortune, as the LORD had warned them and sworn to them; and they were in great distress.

16 Then the LORD raised up judges, who delivered them out of the power of those who plundered them. 17Yet they did not listen even to their judges; for they lusted after other gods and bowed down to them. They soon turned aside from the way in which their ancestors had walked, who had obeyed the commandments of the LORD; they did not follow their example. 18Whenever the LORD raised up judges for them, the LORD was with the judge, and he delivered them from the hand of their enemies all the days of the judge; for the LORD would be moved to pity by their groaning because of those who persecuted and oppressed them. 19But whenever the judge died, they would relapse and behave worse than their ancestors, following other gods, worshiping them and bowing down to them. They would not drop any of their practices or their stubborn ways. 20So the anger of the LORD was kindled against Israel; and he said, "Because this people have transgressed my covenant that I commanded their ancestors, and have not obeyed my voice, 21I will no longer drive out before them any of the nations that Joshua left when he died." 22In order to test Israel, whether or not they would take care to walk in the way of the LORD as their ancestors did, 23the LORD had left those nations, not driving them out at once, and had not handed them over to Joshua.

d OL Vg Compare Gk: Heb *sides*   e That is *Weepers*

King James

3 NOW THESE *are* the nations which the LORD left, to prove Israel by them, *even* as many *of Israel* as had not known all the wars of Canaan;

2Only that the generations of the children of Israel might know, to teach them war, at the least such as before knew nothing thereof;

3*Namely,* five lords of the Philistines, and all the Canaanites, and the Sidonians, and the Hivites that dwelt in mount Lebanon, from mount Baal-hermon unto the entering in of Hamath.

4And they were to prove Israel by them, to know whether they would hearken unto the commandments of the LORD, which he commanded their fathers by the hand of Moses.

5¶ And the children of Israel dwelt among the Canaanites, Hittites, and Amorites, and Perizzites, and Hivites, and Jebusites:

6And they took their daughters to be their wives, and gave their daughters to their sons, and served their gods.

7And the children of Israel did evil in the sight of the LORD, and forgat the LORD their God, and served Baalim and the groves.

8¶ Therefore the anger of the LORD was hot against Israel, and he sold them into the hand of Chushan-rishathaim king of Mesopotamia: and the children of Israel served Chushan-rishathaim eight years.

9And when the children of Israel cried unto the LORD, the LORD raised up a deliverer to the children of Israel, who delivered them, *even* Othniel the son of Kenaz, Caleb's younger brother.

10And the spirit of the LORD came upon him, and he judged Israel, and went out to war: and the LORD delivered Chushan-rishathaim king of Mesopotamia into his hand; and his hand prevailed against Chushan-rishathaim.

11And the land had rest forty years. And Othniel the son of Kenaz died.

12¶ And the children of Israel did evil again in the sight of the LORD: and the LORD strengthened Eglon the king of Moab against Israel, because they had done evil in the sight of the LORD.

13And he gathered unto him the children of Ammon and Amalek, and went and smote Israel, and possessed the city of palm trees.

14So the children of Israel served Eglon the king of Moab eighteen years.

15But when the children of Israel cried unto the LORD, the LORD raised them up a deliverer, Ehud the son of Gera, a Benjamite, a man lefthanded: and by him the children of Israel sent a present unto Eglon the king of Moab.

16But Ehud made him a dagger which had two edges, of a cubit length; and he did gird it under his raiment upon his right thigh.

17And he brought the present unto Eglon king of Moab: and Eglon *was* a very fat man.

18And when he had made an end to offer the present, he sent away the people that bare the present.

19But he himself turned again from the quarries that *were* by Gilgal, and said, I have a secret errand unto thee, O king: who said, Keep silence. And all that stood by him went out from him.

20And Ehud came unto him; and he was sitting in a summer parlour, which he had for himself alone. And Ehud said, I have a message from God unto thee. And he arose out of *his* seat.

21And Ehud put forth his left hand, and took the dagger from his right thigh, and thrust it into his belly:

22And the haft also went in after the blade; and the fat closed upon the blade, so that he could not draw the dagger out of his belly; and the dirt came out.

23Then Ehud went forth through the porch, and shut the doors of the parlour upon him, and locked them.

New International

3 THESE ARE the nations the LORD left to test all those Israelites who had not experienced any of the wars in Canaan 2(he did this only to teach warfare to the descendants of the Israelites who had not had previous battle experience): 3the five rulers of the Philistines, all the Canaanites, the Sidonians, and the Hivites living in the Lebanon mountains from Mount Baal Hermon to Leboa Hamath. 4They were left to test the Israelites to see whether they would obey the LORD's commands, which he had given their forefathers through Moses.

5The Israelites lived among the Canaanites, Hittites, Amorites, Perizzites, Hivites and Jebusites. 6They took their daughters in marriage and gave their own daughters to their sons, and served their gods.

Othniel

7The Israelites did evil in the eyes of the LORD; they forgot the LORD their God and served the Baals and the Asherahs. 8The anger of the LORD burned against Israel so that he sold them into the hands of Cushan-Rishathaim king of Aram Naharaim,b to whom the Israelites were subject for eight years. 9But when they cried out to the LORD, he raised up for them a deliverer, Othniel son of Kenaz, Caleb's younger brother, who saved them. 10The Spirit of the LORD came upon him, so that he became Israel's judgec and went to war. The LORD gave Cushan-Rishathaim king of Aram into the hands of Othniel, who overpowered him. 11So the land had peace for forty years, until Othniel son of Kenaz died.

Ehud

12Once again the Israelites did evil in the eyes of the LORD, and because they did this evil the LORD gave Eglon king of Moab power over Israel. 13Getting the Ammonites and Amalekites to join him, Eglon came and attacked Israel, and they took possession of the City of Palms.d 14The Israelites were subject to Eglon king of Moab for eighteen years.

15Again the Israelites cried out to the LORD, and he gave them a deliverer—Ehud, a left-handed man, the son of Gera the Benjamite. The Israelites sent him with tribute to Eglon king of Moab. 16Now Ehud had made a double-edged sword about a foot and a halfe long, which he strapped to his right thigh under his clothing. 17He presented the tribute to Eglon king of Moab, who was a very fat man. 18After Ehud had presented the tribute, he sent on their way the men who had carried it. 19At the idolsf near Gilgal he himself turned back and said, "I have a secret message for you, O king."

The king said, "Quiet!" And all his attendants left him.

20Ehud then approached him while he was sitting alone in the upper room of his summer palaceg and said, "I have a message from God for you." As the king rose from his seat, 21Ehud reached with his left hand, drew the sword from his right thigh and plunged it into the king's belly. 22Even the handle sank in after the blade, which came out his back. Ehud did not pull the sword out, and the fat closed in over it. 23Then Ehud went out to the porchh; he shut the doors of the upper room behind him and locked them.

a 3 Or *to the entrance to*   b 8 That is, Northwest Mesopotamia   c 10 Or *leader*   d 13 That is, Jericho   e 16 Hebrew *a cubit* (about 0.5 meter) f 19 Or *the stone quarries*; also in verse 26   g 20 The meaning of the Hebrew for this phrase is uncertain.   h 23 The meaning of the Hebrew for this word is uncertain.

Living Bible

3 HERE IS a list of the nations the Lord left in the land to test the new generation of Israel who had not experienced the wars of Canaan. For God wanted to give opportunity to the youth of Israel to exercise faith and obedience in conquering their enemies:[i]

The Philistines (five cities),
The Canaanites,
The Sidonians,
the Hivites living in Mount Lebanon, from Baal-hermon to the entrance of Hamath.

4These people were a test to the new generation of Israel, to see whether they would obey the commandments the Lord had given to them through Moses.

5So Israel lived among the Canaanites, Hittites, Hivites, Perizzites, Amorites, and Jebusites. 6But instead of destroying them, the people of Israel intermarried with them. The young men of Israel took their girls as wives, and the Israeli girls married their men. And soon Israel was worshiping their gods. 7So the people of Israel were very evil in God's sight, for they turned against Jehovah their God and worshiped Baal and the Asheroth idols.

8Then the anger of the Lord flamed out against Israel, and he let King Cushan-rishathaim of eastern Syria conquer them. They were under his rule for eight years. 9But when Israel cried out to the Lord, he gave them Caleb's nephew, Othni-el (son of Kenaz, Caleb's younger brother) to save them. 10The Spirit of the Lord took control of him and he reformed and purged Israel so that when he led the forces of Israel against the army of King Cushan-rishathaim, the Lord helped Israel conquer him completely.

11Then, for forty years under Othni-el, there was peace in the land. But when Othni-el died, 12the people of Israel turned once again to their sinful ways, so God helped King Eglon of Moab to conquer part of Israel at that time. 13Allied with him were the armies of the Ammonites and the Amalekites. These forces defeated the Israelis and took possession of Jericho, often called "The City of Palm Trees." 14For the next eighteen years the people of Israel were required to pay crushing taxes to King Eglon.

15But when they cried to the Lord, he sent them a savior, Ehud (son of Gera, a Benjaminite), who was left-handed. Ehud was the man chosen to carry Israel's annual tax money to the Moabite capital. 16Before he went on this journey he made himself a double-edged dagger eighteen inches long and hid it in his clothing, strapped against his right thigh. 17, 18, 19After delivering the money to King Eglon (who, by the way, was very fat!) he started home again. But outside the city, at the quarries of Gilgal, he sent his companions on and returned alone to the king.

"I have a secret message for you," he told him.

The king immediately dismissed all those who were with him so that he could have a private interview. 20Ehud walked over to him as he was sitting in a cool upstairs room and said to him, "It is a message from God!"

King Eglon stood up at once to receive it, 21whereupon Ehud reached beneath his robe with his strong left hand, pulled out the double-bladed dagger strapped against his right thigh, and plunged it deep into the king's belly. 22, 23The hilt of the dagger disappeared beneath the flesh, and the fat closed over it as the entrails oozed out. Leaving the dagger there, Ehud locked the doors behind him and escaped across an upstairs porch.

New Revised Standard

Nations Remaining in the Land

3 NOW THESE are the nations that the Lord left to test all those in Israel who had no experience of any war in Canaan 2(it was only that successive generations of Israelites might know war, to teach those who had no experience of it before): 3the five lords of the Philistines, and all the Canaanites, and the Sidonians, and the Hivites who lived on Mount Lebanon, from Mount Baal-hermon as far as Lebo-hamath. 4They were for the testing of Israel, to know whether Israel would obey the commandments of the Lord, which he commanded their ancestors by Moses. 5So the Israelites lived among the Canaanites, the Hittites, the Amorites, the Perizzites, the Hivites, and the Jebusites; 6and they took their daughters as wives for themselves, and their own daughters they gave to their sons; and they worshiped their gods.

Othniel

7 The Israelites did what was evil in the sight of the Lord, forgetting the Lord their God, and worshiping the Baals and the Asherahs. 8Therefore the anger of the Lord was kindled against Israel, and he sold them into the hand of King Cushan-rishathaim of Aram-naharaim; and the Israelites served Cushan-rishathaim eight years. 9But when the Israelites cried out to the Lord, the Lord raised up a deliverer for the Israelites, who delivered them, Othniel son of Kenaz, Caleb's younger brother. 10The spirit of the Lord came upon him, and he judged Israel; he went out to war, and the Lord gave King Cushan-rishathaim of Aram into his hand; and his hand prevailed over Cushan-rishathaim. 11So the land had rest forty years. Then Othniel son of Kenaz died.

Ehud

12 The Israelites again did what was evil in the sight of the Lord; and the Lord strengthened King Eglon of Moab against Israel, because they had done what was evil in the sight of the Lord. 13In alliance with the Ammonites and the Amalekites, he went and defeated Israel; and they took possession of the city of palms. 14So the Israelites served King Eglon of Moab eighteen years.

15 But when the Israelites cried out to the Lord, the Lord raised up for them a deliverer, Ehud son of Gera, the Benjaminite, a left-handed man. The Israelites sent tribute by him to King Eglon of Moab. 16Ehud made for himself a sword with two edges, a cubit in length; and he fastened it on his right thigh under his clothes. 17Then he presented the tribute to King Eglon of Moab. Now Eglon was a very fat man. 18When Ehud had finished presenting the tribute, he sent the people who carried the tribute on their way. 19But he himself turned back at the sculptured stones near Gilgal, and said, "I have a secret message for you, O king." So the king said,[j] "Silence!" and all his attendants went out from his presence. 20Ehud came to him, while he was sitting alone in his cool roof chamber, and said, "I have a message from God for you." So he rose from his seat. 21Then Ehud reached with his left hand, took the sword from his right thigh, and thrust it into Eglon's[k] belly; 22the hilt also went in after the blade, and the fat closed over the blade, for he did not draw the sword out of his belly; and the dirt came out.[l] 23Then Ehud went out into the vestibule,[m] and closed the doors of the roof chamber on him, and locked them.

---

i 3:1-3 *youth of Israel to exercise faith and obedience,* implied in 2:22 and 3:4, *in conquering their enemies,* literally, "that . . . the people might know war . . ."

j Heb *he said*   k Heb *his*   l With Tg Vg: Meaning of Heb uncertain   m Meaning of Heb uncertain

King James

24When he was gone out, his servants came; and when they saw that, behold, the doors of the parlour *were* locked, they said, Surely he covereth his feet in his summer chamber.

25And they tarried till they were ashamed: and, behold, he opened not the doors of the parlour; therefore they took a key, and opened *them:* and, behold, their lord *was* fallen down dead on the earth.

26And Ehud escaped while they tarried, and passed beyond the quarries, and escaped unto Seirath.

27And it came to pass, when he was come, that he blew a trumpet in the mountain of Ephraim, and the children of Israel went down with him from the mount, and he before them.

28And he said unto them, Follow after me: for the LORD hath delivered your enemies the Moabites into your hand. And they went down after him, and took the fords of Jordan toward Moab, and suffered not a man to pass over.

29And they slew of Moab at that time about ten thousand men, all lusty, and all men of valour; and there escaped not a man.

30So Moab was subdued that day under the hand of Israel. And the land had rest fourscore years.

31¶ And after him was Shamgar the son of Anath, which slew of the Philistines six hundred men with an ox goad: and he also delivered Israel.

4 AND THE children of Israel again did evil in the sight of the LORD, when Ehud was dead.

2And the LORD sold them into the hand of Jabin king of Canaan, that reigned in Hazor; the captain of whose host *was* Sisera, which dwelt in Harosheth of the Gentiles.

3And the children of Israel cried unto the LORD: for he had nine hundred chariots of iron; and twenty years he mightily oppressed the children of Israel.

4¶ And Deborah, a prophetess, the wife of Lapidoth, she judged Israel at that time.

5And she dwelt under the palm tree of Deborah between Ramah and Beth-el in mount Ephraim: and the children of Israel came up to her for judgment.

6And she sent and called Barak the son of Abinoam out of Kedesh-naphtali, and said unto him, Hath not the LORD God of Israel commanded, *saying,* Go and draw toward mount Tabor, and take with thee ten thousand men of the children of Naphtali and of the children of Zebulun?

7And I will draw unto thee to the river Kishon Sisera, the captain of Jabin's army, with his chariots and his multitude; and I will deliver him into thine hand.

8And Barak said unto her, If thou wilt go with me, then I will go: but if thou wilt not go with me, *then* I will not go.

9And she said, I will surely go with thee: notwithstanding the journey that thou takest shall not be for thine honour; for the LORD shall sell Sisera into the hand of a woman. And Deborah arose, and went with Barak to Kedesh.

10¶ And Barak called Zebulun and Naphtali to Kedesh; and he went up with ten thousand men at his feet: and Deborah went up with him.

11Now Heber the Kenite, *which was* of the children of Hobab the father-in-law of Moses, had severed himself from the Kenites, and pitched his tent unto the plain of Zaanaim, which *is* by Kedesh.

12And they showed Sisera that Barak the son of Abinoam was gone up to mount Tabor.

13And Sisera gathered together all his chariots, *even* nine hundred chariots of iron, and all the people that *were* with him, from Harosheth of the Gentiles unto the river of Kishon.

New International

24After he had gone, the servants came and found the doors of the upper room locked. They said, "He must be relieving himself in the inner room of the house." 25They waited to the point of embarrassment, but when he did not open the doors of the room, they took a key and unlocked them. There they saw their lord fallen to the floor, dead.

26While they waited, Ehud got away. He passed by the idols and escaped to Seirah. 27When he arrived there, he blew a trumpet in the hill country of Ephraim, and the Israelites went down with him from the hills, with him leading them.

28"Follow me," he ordered, "for the LORD has given Moab, your enemy, into your hands." So they followed him down and, taking possession of the fords of the Jordan that led to Moab, they allowed no one to cross over. 29At that time they struck down about ten thousand Moabites, all vigorous and strong; not a man escaped. 30That day Moab was made subject to Israel, and the land had peace for eighty years.

Shamgar

31After Ehud came Shamgar son of Anath, who struck down six hundred Philistines with an oxgoad. He too saved Israel.

Deborah

4 AFTER EHUD died, the Israelites once again did evil in the eyes of the LORD. 2So the LORD sold them into the hands of Jabin, a king of Canaan, who reigned in Hazor. The commander of his army was Sisera, who lived in Harosheth Haggoyim. 3Because he had nine hundred iron chariots and had cruelly oppressed the Israelites for twenty years, they cried to the LORD for help.

4Deborah, a prophetess, the wife of Lappidoth, was leadinga Israel at that time. 5She held court under the Palm of Deborah between Ramah and Bethel in the hill country of Ephraim, and the Israelites came to her to have their disputes decided. 6She sent for Barak son of Abinoam from Kedesh in Naphtali and said to him, "The LORD, the God of Israel, commands you: 'Go, take with you ten thousand men of Naphtali and Zebulun and lead the way to Mount Tabor. 7I will lure Sisera, the commander of Jabin's army, with his chariots and his troops to the Kishon River and give him into your hands.' "

8Barak said to her, "If you go with me, I will go; but if you don't go with me, I won't go."

9"Very well," Deborah said, "I will go with you. But because of the way you are going about this,b the honor will not be yours, for the LORD will hand Sisera over to a woman." So Deborah went with Barak to Kedesh, 10where he summoned Zebulun and Naphtali. Ten thousand men followed him, and Deborah also went with him.

11Now Heber the Kenite had left the other Kenites, the descendants of Hobab, Moses' brother-in-law,c and pitched his tent by the great tree in Zaanannim near Kedesh.

12When they told Sisera that Barak son of Abinoam had gone up to Mount Tabor, 13Sisera gathered together his nine hundred iron chariots and all the men with him, from Harosheth Haggoyim to the Kishon River.

a 4 Traditionally *judging*   b 9 Or *But on the expedition you are undertaking*
c 11 Or *father-in-law*

Living Bible

24When the king's servants returned and saw that the doors were locked, they waited, thinking that perhaps he was using the bathroom. 25But when, after a long time, he still didn't come out, they became concerned and got a key. And when they opened the door, they found their master dead on the floor.

26Meanwhile Ehud had escaped past the quarries to Se-irah. 27When he arrived in the hill country of Ephraim, he blew a trumpet as a call to arms and mustered an army under his own command.

28"Follow me," he told them, "for the Lord has put your enemies, the Moabites, at your mercy!"

The army then proceeded to seize the fords of the Jordan River near Moab, preventing anyone from crossing. 29Then they attacked the Moabites and killed about ten thousand of the strongest and most skillful of their fighting men, letting not one escape. 30So Moab was conquered by Israel that day, and the land was at peace for the next eighty years.

31The next judge after Ehud was Shamgar (son of Anath). He once killed six hundred Philistines with an ox goad, thereby saving Israel from disaster.

4 AFTER EHUD'S death the people of Israel again sinned against the Lord, 2, 3so the Lord let them be conquered by King Jabin of Hazor, in Canaan. The commander-in-chief of his army was Sisera, who lived in Harosheth-ha-goiim. He had nine hundred iron chariots, and made life unbearable for the Israelis for twenty years. But finally they begged the Lord for help.

4Israel's leader at that time, the one who was responsible for bringing the people back to God, was Deborah, a prophetess, the wife of Lappidoth. 5She held court at a place now called "Deborah's Palm Tree," between Ramah and Bethel, in the hill country of Ephraim; and the Israelites came to her to decide their disputes.d

6One day she summoned Barak (son of Abinoam), who lived in Kedesh, in the land of Naphtali, and said to him, "The Lord God of Israel has commanded you to mobilize ten thousand men from the tribes of Naphtali and Zebulun. Lead them to Mount Tabor, 7to fight King Jabin's mighty army with all his chariots, under General Sisera's command. The Lord says, 'I will draw them to the Kishon River, and you will defeat them there.' "

8"I'll go, but only if you go with me!" Barak told her.

9"All right," she replied, "I'll go with you; but I'm warning you now that the honor of conquering Sisera will go to a woman instead of to you!" So she went with him to Kedesh.

10When Barak summoned the men of Zebulun and Naphtali to mobilize at Kedesh, ten thousand men volunteered. And Deborah marched with them. 11(Heber, the Kenite—the Kenites were the descendants of Moses' father-in-law Hobab—had moved away from the rest of his clan, and had been living in various places as far away as the Oak of Za-anannim, near Kedesh.) 12When General Sisera was told that Barak and his army were camped at Mount Tabor 13he mobilized his entire army, including the nine hundred iron chariots, and marched from Harosheth-ha-goiim to the Kishon River.

New Revised Standard

24 After he had gone, the servants came. When they saw that the doors of the roof chamber were locked, they thought, "He must be relieving himselfe in the cool chamber." 25So they waited until they were embarrassed. When he still did not open the doors of the roof chamber, they took the key and opened them. There was their lord lying dead on the floor.

26 Ehud escaped while they delayed, and passed beyond the sculptured stones, and escaped to Seirah. 27When he arrived, he sounded the trumpet in the hill country of Ephraim; and the Israelites went down with him from the hill country, having him at their head. 28He said to them, "Follow after me; for the LORD has given your enemies the Moabites into your hand." So they went down after him, and seized the fords of the Jordan against the Moabites, and allowed no one to cross over. 29At that time they killed about ten thousand of the Moabites, all strong, able-bodied men; no one escaped. 30So Moab was subdued that day under the hand of Israel. And the land had rest eighty years.

Shamgar

31 After him came Shamgar son of Anath, who killed six hundred of the Philistines with an oxgoad. He too delivered Israel.

Deborah and Barak

4 THE ISRAELITES again did what was evil in the sight of the LORD, after Ehud died. 2So the LORD sold them into the hand of King Jabin of Canaan, who reigned in Hazor; the commander of his army was Sisera, who lived in Harosheth-ha-goiim. 3Then the Israelites cried out to the LORD for help; for he had nine hundred chariots of iron, and had oppressed the Israelites cruelly twenty years.

4 At that time Deborah, a prophetess, wife of Lappidoth, was judging Israel. 5She used to sit under the palm of Deborah between Ramah and Bethel in the hill country of Ephraim; and the Israelites came up to her for judgment. 6She sent and summoned Barak son of Abinoam from Kedesh in Naphtali, and said to him, "The LORD, the God of Israel, commands you, 'Go, take position at Mount Tabor, bringing ten thousand from the tribe of Naphtali and the tribe of Zebulun. 7I will draw out Sisera, the general of Jabin's army, to meet you by the Wadi Kishon with his chariots and his troops; and I will give him into your hand.' " 8Barak said to her, "If you will go with me, I will go; but if you will not go with me, I will not go." 9And she said, "I will surely go with you; nevertheless, the road on which you are going will not lead to your glory, for the LORD will sell Sisera into the hand of a woman." Then Deborah got up and went with Barak to Kedesh. 10Barak summoned Zebulun and Naphtali to Kedesh; and ten thousand warriors went up behind him; and Deborah went up with him.

11 Now Heber the Kenite had separated from the other Kenites,f that is, the descendants of Hobab the father-in-law of Moses, and had encamped as far away as Elon-bezaanannim, which is near Kedesh.

12 When Sisera was told that Barak son of Abinoam had gone up to Mount Tabor, 13Sisera called out all his chariots, nine hundred chariots of iron, and all the troops who were with him, from Harosheth-ha-goiim to the Wadi Kishon. 14Then Deborah said to Barak, "Up! For

d 4:5 came to her to decide their disputes, or, "to listen to her speak to them about God."

e Heb covering his feet   f Heb from the Kain

King James

14And Deborah said unto Barak, Up; for this *is* the day in which the LORD hath delivered Sisera into thine hand: is not the LORD gone out before thee? So Barak went down from mount Tabor, and ten thousand men after him.

15And the LORD discomfited Sisera, and all *his* chariots, and all *his* host, with the edge of the sword before Barak; so that Sisera lighted down off *his* chariot, and fled away on his feet.

16But Barak pursued after the chariots, and after the host, unto Harosheth of the Gentiles: and all the host of Sisera fell upon the edge of the sword; *and* there was not a man left.

17Howbeit Sisera fled away on his feet to the tent of Jael the wife of Heber the Kenite: for *there was* peace between Jabin the king of Hazor and the house of Heber the Kenite.

18¶ And Jael went out to meet Sisera, and said unto him, Turn in, my lord, turn in to me; fear not. And when he had turned in unto her into the tent, she covered him with a mantle.

19And he said unto her, Give me, I pray thee, a little water to drink; for I am thirsty. And she opened a bottle of milk, and gave him drink, and covered him.

20Again he said unto her, Stand in the door of the tent, and it shall be, when any man doth come and inquire of thee, and say, Is there any man here? that thou shalt say, No.

21Then Jael Heber's wife took a nail of the tent, and took an hammer in her hand, and went softly unto him, and smote the nail into his temples, and fastened it into the ground: for he was fast asleep and weary. So he died.

22And, behold, as Barak pursued Sisera, Jael came out to meet him, and said unto him, Come, and I will show thee the man whom thou seekest. And when he came into her *tent,* behold, Sisera lay dead, and the nail *was* in his temples.

23So God subdued on that day Jabin the king of Canaan before the children of Israel.

24And the hand of the children of Israel prospered, and prevailed against Jabin the king of Canaan, until they had destroyed Jabin king of Canaan.

5 THEN SANG Deborah and Barak the son of Abinoam on that day, saying,

2Praise ye the LORD for the avenging of Israel, when the people willingly offered themselves.

3Hear, O ye kings; give ear, O ye princes; I, *even* I, will sing unto the LORD; I will sing *praise* to the LORD God of Israel.

4LORD, when thou wentest out of Seir, when thou marchedst out of the field of Edom, the earth trembled, and the heavens dropped, the clouds also dropped water.

5The mountains melted from before the LORD, *even* that Sinai from before the LORD God of Israel.

6In the days of Shamgar the son of Anath, in the days of Jael, the highways were unoccupied, and the travellers walked through byways.

New International

14Then Deborah said to Barak, "Go! This is the day the LORD has given Sisera into your hands. Has not the LORD gone ahead of you?" So Barak went down Mount Tabor, followed by ten thousand men. 15At Barak's advance, the LORD routed Sisera and all his chariots and army by the sword, and Sisera abandoned his chariot and fled on foot. 16But Barak pursued the chariots and army as far as Harosheth Haggoyim. All the troops of Sisera fell by the sword; not a man was left.

17Sisera, however, fled on foot to the tent of Jael, the wife of Heber the Kenite, because there were friendly relations between Jabin king of Hazor and the clan of Heber the Kenite.

18Jael went out to meet Sisera and said to him, "Come, my lord, come right in. Don't be afraid." So he entered her tent, and she put a covering over him.

19"I'm thirsty," he said. "Please give me some water." She opened a skin of milk, gave him a drink, and covered him up.

20"Stand in the doorway of the tent," he told her. "If someone comes by and asks you, 'Is anyone here?' say 'No.' "

21But Jael, Heber's wife, picked up a tent peg and a hammer and went quietly to him while he lay fast asleep, exhausted. She drove the peg through his temple into the ground, and he died.

22Barak came by in pursuit of Sisera, and Jael went out to meet him. "Come," she said, "I will show you the man you're looking for." So he went in with her, and there lay Sisera with the tent peg through his temple—dead.

23On that day God subdued Jabin, the Canaanite king, before the Israelites. 24And the hand of the Israelites grew stronger and stronger against Jabin, the Canaanite king, until they destroyed him.

The Song of Deborah

5 ON THAT day Deborah and Barak son of Abinoam sang this song:

2"When the princes in Israel take the lead,
    when the people willingly offer themselves—
        praise the LORD!

3"Hear this, you kings! Listen, you rulers!
    I will sing toa the LORD, I will sing;
    I will make music tob the LORD, the God of
        Israel.

4"O LORD, when you went out from Seir,
    when you marched from the land of Edom,
    the earth shook, the heavens poured,
        the clouds poured down water.
5The mountains quaked before the LORD, the
        One of Sinai,
    before the LORD, the God of Israel.

6"In the days of Shamgar son of Anath,
    in the days of Jael, the roads were
        abandoned;
    travelers took to winding paths.

---

a 3 Or *of*   b 3 Or *I with song I will praise*

Living Bible

14Then Deborah said to Barak, "Now is the time for action! The Lord leads on! He has already delivered Sisera into your hand!"

So Barak led his ten thousand men down the slopes of Mount Tabor into battle.

15Then the Lord threw the enemy into a panic, both the soldiers and the charioteers, and Sisera leaped from his chariot and escaped on foot. 16Barak and his men chased the enemy and the chariots as far as Harosheth-ha-goiim, until all of Sisera's army was destroyed; not one man was left alive. 17Meanwhile, Sisera had escaped to the tent of Jael, the wife of Heber the Kenite, for there was a mutual-assistance agreement between King Jabin of Hazor and the clan of Heber.

18Jael went out to meet Sisera and said to him, "Come into my tent, sir. You will be safe here in our protection. Don't be afraid." So he went into her tent and she covered him with a blanket.

19"Please give me some water," he said, "for I am very thirsty." So she gave him some milk and covered him again.

20"Stand in the door of the tent," he told her, "and if anyone comes by, looking for me, tell them that no one is here."

21Then Jael took a sharp tent peg and a hammer and, quietly creeping up to him as he slept, she drove the peg through his temples and into the ground; and so he died, for he was fast asleep from weariness.

22When Barak came by looking for Sisera, Jael went out to meet him and said, "Come, and I will show you the man you are looking for."

So he followed her into the tent and found Sisera lying there dead, with the tent peg through his temples. 23So that day the Lord used Israel to subdue King Jabin of Canaan. 24And from that time on Israel became stronger and stronger against King Jabin, until he and all his people were destroyed.

5 THEN DEBORAH and Barak sang this song about the wonderful victory:
2"Praise the Lord!
Israel's leaders bravely led;
The people gladly followed!
Yes, bless the Lord!
3Listen, O you kings and princes,
For I shall sing about the Lord,
The God of Israel.
4When you led us out from Seir,
Out across the fields of Edom,
The earth trembled
And the sky poured down its rain.
5Yes, even Mount Sinai quaked
At the presence of the God of Israel!
6In the days of Shamgar and of Jael,
The main roads were deserted.
Travelers used the narrow, crooked side paths.

New Revised Standard

this is the day on which the LORD has given Sisera into your hand. The LORD is indeed going out before you." So Barak went down from Mount Tabor with ten thousand warriors following him. 15 And the LORD threw Sisera and all his chariots and all his army into a panicᶜ before Barak; Sisera got down from his chariot and fled away on foot, 16 while Barak pursued the chariots and the army to Harosheth-ha-goiim. All the army of Sisera fell by the sword; no one was left.

17 Now Sisera had fled away on foot to the tent of Jael wife of Heber the Kenite; for there was peace between King Jabin of Hazor and the clan of Heber the Kenite. 18 Jael came out to meet Sisera, and said to him, "Turn aside, my lord, turn aside to me; have no fear." So he turned aside to her into the tent, and she covered him with a rug. 19 Then he said to her, "Please give me a little water to drink; for I am thirsty." So she opened a skin of milk and gave him a drink and covered him. 20 He said to her, "Stand at the entrance of the tent, and if anybody comes and asks you, 'Is anyone here?' say, 'No.'" 21 But Jael wife of Heber took a tent peg, and took a hammer in her hand, and went softly to him and drove the peg into his temple, until it went down into the ground—he was lying fast asleep from weariness—and he died. 22 Then, as Barak came in pursuit of Sisera, Jael went out to meet him, and said to him, "Come, and I will show you the man whom you are seeking." So he went into her tent; and there was Sisera lying dead, with the tent peg in his temple.

23 So on that day God subdued King Jabin of Canaan before the Israelites. 24 Then the hand of the Israelites bore harder and harder on King Jabin of Canaan, until they destroyed King Jabin of Canaan.

The Song of Deborah

5 THEN DEBORAH and Barak son of Abinoam sang on that day, saying:
2 "When locks are long in Israel,
    when the people offer themselves
        willingly—
    blessᵈ the LORD!

3 "Hear, O kings; give ear, O princes;
    to the LORD I will sing,
    I will make melody to the LORD, the God of
        Israel.

4 "LORD, when you went out from Seir,
    when you marched from the region of
        Edom,
the earth trembled,
    and the heavens poured,
    the clouds indeed poured water.
5 The mountains quaked before the LORD, the
        One of Sinai,
    before the LORD, the God of Israel.

6 "In the days of Shamgar son of Anath,
    in the days of Jael, caravans ceased
    and travelers kept to the byways.

ᶜ Heb adds to the sword; compare verse 16   ᵈ Or You who offer yourselves willingly among the people, bless

King James

7The inhabitants of the villages ceased, they ceased in Israel, until that I Deborah arose, that I arose a mother in Israel.

8They chose new gods; then was war in the gates: was there a shield or spear seen among forty thousand in Israel?

9My heart is toward the governors of Israel, that offered themselves willingly among the people. Bless ye the LORD.

10Speak, ye that ride on white asses, ye that sit in judgment, and walk by the way.

11They that are delivered from the noise of archers in the places of drawing water, there shall they rehearse the righteous acts of the LORD, even the righteous acts toward the inhabitants of his villages in Israel: then shall the people of the LORD go down to the gates.

12Awake, awake, Deborah: awake, awake, utter a song: arise, Barak, and lead thy captivity captive, thou son of Abinoam.

13Then he made him that remaineth have dominion over the nobles among the people: the LORD made me have dominion over the mighty.

14Out of Ephraim was there a root of them against Amalek; after thee, Benjamin, among thy people; out of Machir came down governors, and out of Zebulun they that handle the pen of the writer.

15And the princes of Issachar were with Deborah; even Issachar, and also Barak: he was sent on foot into the valley. For the divisions of Reuben there were great thoughts of heart.

16Why abodest thou among the sheepfolds, to hear the bleatings of the flocks? For the divisions of Reuben there were great searchings of heart.

17Gilead abode beyond Jordan: and why did Dan remain in ships? Asher continued on the sea shore, and abode in his breaches.

18Zebulun and Naphtali were a people that jeoparded their lives unto the death in the high places of the field.

19The kings came and fought, then fought the kings of Canaan in Taanach by the waters of Megiddo; they took no gain of money.

20They fought from heaven; the stars in their courses fought against Sisera.

21The river of Kishon swept them away, that ancient river, the river Kishon. O my soul, thou hast trodden down strength.

22Then were the horsehoofs broken by the means of the pransings, the pransings of their mighty ones.

23Curse ye Meroz, said the angel of the LORD, curse ye bitterly the inhabitants thereof; because they came not to the help of the LORD, to the help of the LORD against the mighty.

New International

7Village lifea in Israel ceased,
  ceased until I,b Deborah, arose,
  arose a mother in Israel.
8When they chose new gods,
  war came to the city gates,
and not a shield or spear was seen
  among forty thousand in Israel.
9My heart is with Israel's princes,
  with the willing volunteers among the people.
  Praise the LORD!

10"You who ride on white donkeys,
  sitting on your saddle blankets,
  and you who walk along the road,
consider 11the voice of the singersc at the
    watering places.
  They recite the righteous acts of the LORD,
  the righteous acts of his warriorsd in Israel.

"Then the people of the LORD
  went down to the city gates.
12'Wake up, wake up, Deborah!
  Wake up, wake up, break out in song!
Arise, O Barak!
  Take captive your captives, O son of
    Abinoam.'

13"Then the men who were left
    came down to the nobles;
  the people of the LORD
    came to me with the mighty.
14Some came from Ephraim, whose roots were in
    Amalek;
  Benjamin was with the people who followed
    you.
From Makir captains came down,
  from Zebulun those who bear a commander's
    staff.
15The princes of Issachar were with Deborah;
  yes, Issachar was with Barak,
  rushing after him into the valley.
In the districts of Reuben
  there was much searching of heart.
16Why did you stay among the campfirese
  to hear the whistling for the flocks?
In the districts of Reuben
  there was much searching of heart.
17Gilead stayed beyond the Jordan.
  And Dan, why did he linger by the ships?
Asher remained on the coast
  and stayed in his coves.
18The people of Zebulun risked their very lives;
  so did Naphtali on the heights of the field.

19"Kings came, they fought;
  the kings of Canaan fought
at Taanach by the waters of Megiddo,
  but they carried off no silver, no plunder.
20From the heavens the stars fought,
  from their courses they fought against Sisera.
21The river Kishon swept them away,
  the age-old river, the river Kishon.
  March on, my soul; be strong!
22Then thundered the horses' hoofs—
  galloping, galloping go his mighty steeds.
23'Curse Meroz,' said the angel of the LORD.
  'Curse its people bitterly,
because they did not come to help the LORD,
  to help the LORD against the mighty.'

a 7 Or Warriors b 7 Or you c 11 Or archers; the meaning of the Hebrew for this word is uncertain. d 11 Or villagers e 16 Or saddlebags

Living Bible

7Israel's population dwindled,
Until Deborah became a mother to Israel.
8When Israel chose new gods,
Everything collapsed.
Our masters would not let us have
A shield or spear.
Among forty thousand men of Israel,
Not a weapon could be found!
9How I rejoice
In the leaders of Israel
Who offered themselves so willingly!
Praise the Lord!
10Let all Israel, rich and poor,
Join in his praises—
Those who ride on white donkeys
And sit on rich carpets,
And those who are poor and must walk.
11The village musicians
Gather at the village well
To sing of the triumphs of the Lord.
Again and again they sing the ballad
Of how the Lord saved Israel
With an army of peasants!
The people of the Lord
Marched through the gates!
12Awake, O Deborah, and sing!
Arise, O Barak!
O son of Abino-am, lead away your captives!
13, 14Down from Mount Tabor marched the noble
     remnant.
The people of the Lord
Marched down against great odds.
They came from Ephraim and Benjamin,
From Machir and from Zebulun.
15Down into the valley
Went the princes of Issachar
With Deborah and Barak.
At God's command they rushed into the valley.
(But the tribe of Reuben didn't go.
16Why did you sit at home among the sheepfolds,
Playing your shepherd pipes?
Yes, the tribe of Reuben has an uneasy conscience.
17Why did Gilead remain across the Jordan,
And why did Dan remain with his ships?
And why did Asher sit unmoved
Upon the seashore,
At ease beside his harbors?)
18But the tribes of Zebulun and Naphtali
Dared to die upon the fields of battle.
19The kings of Canaan fought in Taanach
By Megiddo's springs,
But did not win the victory.
20The very stars of heaven
Fought Sisera.
21The rushing Kishon River
Swept them away.
March on, my soul, with strength!
22Hear the stamping
Of the horsehoofs of the enemy!
See the prancing of his steeds!
23But the Angel of Jehovah
Put a curse on Meroz.
'Curse them bitterly,' he said,
'Because they did not come to help the Lord
Against his enemies.'

New Revised Standard

7 The peasantry prospered in Israel,
      they grew fat on plunder,
   because you arose, Deborah,
      arose as a mother in Israel.
8 When new gods were chosen,
      then war was in the gates.
   Was shield or spear to be seen
      among forty thousand in Israel?
9 My heart goes out to the commanders of Israel
      who offered themselves willingly among the
         people.
      Bless the LORD.

10 "Tell of it, you who ride on white donkeys,
      you who sit on rich carpetsf
      and you who walk by the way.
11 To the sound of musiciansf at the watering
         places,
      there they repeat the triumphs of the LORD,
      the triumphs of his peasantry in Israel.

   "Then down to the gates marched the people
      of the LORD.

12 "Awake, awake, Deborah!
      Awake, awake, utter a song!
   Arise, Barak, lead away your captives,
      O son of Abinoam.
13 Then down marched the remnant of the noble;
      the people of the LORD marched down for
         himg against the mighty.
14 From Ephraim they set outh into the valley,i
      following you, Benjamin, with your kin;
   from Machir marched down the commanders,
      and from Zebulun those who bear the
         marshal's staff;
15 the chiefs of Issachar came with Deborah,
      and Issachar faithful to Barak;
   into the valley they rushed out at his heels.
   Among the clans of Reuben
      there were great searchings of heart.
16 Why did you tarry among the sheepfolds,
      to hear the piping for the flocks?
   Among the clans of Reuben
      there were great searchings of heart.
17 Gilead stayed beyond the Jordan;
      and Dan, why did he abide with the ships?
   Asher sat still at the coast of the sea,
      settling down by his landings.
18 Zebulun is a people that scorned death;
      Naphtali too, on the heights of the field.

19 "The kings came, they fought;
      then fought the kings of Canaan,
   at Taanach, by the waters of Megiddo;
      they got no spoils of silver.
20 The stars fought from heaven,
      from their courses they fought against
         Sisera.
21 The torrent Kishon swept them away,
      the onrushing torrent, the torrent Kishon.
   March on, my soul, with might!

22 "Then loud beat the horses' hoofs
      with the galloping, galloping of his steeds.

23 "Curse Meroz, says the angel of the LORD,
      curse bitterly its inhabitants,
   because they did not come to the help of the
      LORD,
      to the help of the LORD against the mighty.

f Meaning of Heb uncertain   g Gk: Heb me   h Cn: Heb From Ephraim their
root   i Gk: Heb in Amalek

King James

24Blessed above women shall Jael the wife of Heber the Kenite be, blessed shall she be above women in the tent.

25He asked water, *and* she gave *him* milk; she brought forth butter in a lordly dish.

26She put her hand to the nail, and her right hand to the workmen's hammer; and with the hammer she smote Sisera, she smote off his head, when she had pierced and stricken through his temples.

27At her feet he bowed, he fell, he lay down: at her feet he bowed, he fell: where he bowed, there he fell down dead.

28The mother of Sisera looked out at a window, and cried through the lattice, Why is his chariot *so* long in coming? why tarry the wheels of his chariot?

29Her wise ladies answered her, yea, she returned answer to herself,

30Have they not sped? have they *not* divided the prey; to every man a damsel *or* two; to Sisera a prey of divers colours, a prey of divers colours of needlework, of divers colours of needlework on both sides, *meet* for the necks of *them that take* the spoil?

31So let all thine enemies perish, O LORD: but *let* them that love him *be* as the sun when he goeth forth in his might. And the land had rest forty years.

6 AND THE children of Israel did evil in the sight of the LORD: and the LORD delivered them into the hand of Midian seven years.

2And the hand of Midian prevailed against Israel: *and* because of the Midianites the children of Israel made them the dens which *are* in the mountains, and caves, and strong holds.

3And *so* it was, when Israel had sown, that the Midianites came up, and the Amalekites, and the children of the east, even they came up against them;

4And they encamped against them, and destroyed the increase of the earth, till thou come unto Gaza, and left no sustenance for Israel, neither sheep, nor ox, nor ass.

5For they came up with their cattle and their tents, and they came as grasshoppers for multitude; *for* both they and their camels were without number: and they entered into the land to destroy it.

6And Israel was greatly impoverished because of the Midianites; and the children of Israel cried unto the LORD.

7¶ And it came to pass, when the children of Israel cried unto the LORD because of the Midianites,

8That the LORD sent a prophet unto the children of Israel, which said unto them, Thus saith the LORD God of Israel, I brought you up from Egypt, and brought you forth out of the house of bondage;

9And I delivered you out of the hand of the Egyptians, and out of the hand of all that oppressed you, and drave them out from before you, and gave you their land;

10And I said unto you, I *am* the LORD your God; fear not the gods of the Amorites, in whose land ye dwell: but ye have not obeyed my voice.

New International

24"Most blessed of women be Jael,
    the wife of Heber the Kenite,
    most blessed of tent-dwelling women.
25He asked for water, and she gave him milk;
    in a bowl fit for nobles she brought him
        curdled milk.
26Her hand reached for the tent peg,
    her right hand for the workman's hammer.
She struck Sisera, she crushed his head,
    she shattered and pierced his temple.
27At her feet he sank,
    he fell; there he lay.
At her feet he sank, he fell;
    where he sank, there he fell—dead.

28"Through the window peered Sisera's mother;
    behind the lattice she cried out,
'Why is his chariot so long in coming?
    Why is the clatter of his chariots delayed?'
29The wisest of her ladies answer her;
    indeed, she keeps saying to herself,
30'Are they not finding and dividing the spoils:
    a girl or two for each man,
    colorful garments as plunder for Sisera,
    colorful garments embroidered,
    highly embroidered garments for my neck—
all this as plunder?'

31"So may all your enemies perish, O LORD!
    But may they who love you be like the sun
    when it rises in its strength."

Then the land had peace forty years.

Gideon

6 AGAIN THE Israelites did evil in the eyes of the LORD, and for seven years he gave them into the hands of the Midianites. 2Because the power of Midian was so oppressive, the Israelites prepared shelters for themselves in mountain clefts, caves and strongholds. 3Whenever the Israelites planted their crops, the Midianites, Amalekites and other eastern peoples invaded the country. 4They camped on the land and ruined the crops all the way to Gaza and did not spare a living thing for Israel, neither sheep nor cattle nor donkeys. 5They came up with their livestock and their tents like swarms of locusts. It was impossible to count the men and their camels; they invaded the land to ravage it. 6Midian so impoverished the Israelites that they cried out to the LORD for help.

7When the Israelites cried to the LORD because of Midian, 8he sent them a prophet, who said, "This is what the LORD, the God of Israel, says: I brought you up out of Egypt, out of the land of slavery. 9I snatched you from the power of Egypt and from the hand of all your oppressors. I drove them from before you and gave you their land. 10I said to you, 'I am the LORD your God; do not worship the gods of the Amorites, in whose land you live.' But you have not listened to me."

Living Bible

24Blessed be Jael,
The wife of Heber the Kenite—
Yes, may she be blessed
Above all women who live in tents.
25He asked for water
And she gave him milk in a beautiful cup!
26Then she took a tent pin and a workman's hammer
And pierced Sisera's temples,
Crushing his head.
She pounded the tent pin through his head.
27He sank, he fell, he lay dead at her feet.
28The mother of Sisera watched through the window
For his return.
'Why is his chariot so long in coming?
Why don't we hear the sound of the wheels?'
29But her ladies-in-waiting—and she herself—re-
   plied,
30'There is much loot to be divided,
And it takes time.
Each man receives a girl or two;
And Sisera will get gorgeous robes,
And he will bring home
Many gifts for me.'
31O Lord, may all your enemies
Perish as Sisera did,
But may those who love the Lord
Shine as the sun!"
After that there was peace in the land for forty years.

6 THEN THE people of Israel began once again to
worship other gods, and once again the Lord let
their enemies harass them. This time it was by the people
of Midian, for seven years. 2The Midianites were so
cruel that the Israelis took to the mountains, living in
caves and dens. 3, 4When they planted their seed, marauders from Midian, Amalek, and other neighboring
nations came and destroyed their crops and plundered
the countryside as far away as Gaza, leaving nothing to
eat, and taking away all their sheep, oxen, and donkeys.
5These enemy hordes arrived on droves of camels too
numerous to count and stayed until the land was completely stripped and devastated. 6, 7So Israel was reduced to abject poverty because of the Midianites. Then
at last the people of Israel began to cry out to the Lord
for help.

8However, the Lord's reply through the prophet he
sent to them was this: "The Lord God of Israel brought
you out of slavery in Egypt, 9and rescued you from the
Egyptians and from all who were cruel to you, and drove
out your enemies before you, and gave you their land.
10He told you he is the Lord your God, and you must
not worship the gods of the Amorites who live around
you on every side. But you have not listened to him."

New Revised Standard

24 "Most blessed of women be Jael,
   the wife of Heber the Kenite,
   of tent-dwelling women most blessed.
25 He asked water and she gave him milk,
   she brought him curds in a lordly bowl.
26 She put her hand to the tent peg
   and her right hand to the workmen's mallet;
she struck Sisera a blow,
   she crushed his head,
   she shattered and pierced his temple.
27 He sank, he fell,
   he lay still at her feet;
at her feet he sank, he fell;
   where he sank, there he fell dead.

28 "Out of the window she peered,
   the mother of Sisera gazeda through the
      lattice:
'Why is his chariot so long in coming?
   Why tarry the hoofbeats of his chariots?'
29 Her wisest ladies make answer,
   indeed, she answers the question herself:
30 'Are they not finding and dividing the
      spoil?—
   A girl or two for every man;
spoil of dyed stuffs for Sisera,
   spoil of dyed stuffs embroidered,
   two pieces of dyed work embroidered for
      my neck as spoil?'

31 "So perish all your enemies, O LORD!
   But may your friends be like the sun as it
      rises in its might."

And the land had rest forty years.

The Midianite Oppression

6 THE ISRAELITES did what was evil in the sight
of the LORD, and the LORD gave them into the hand
of Midian seven years. 2The hand of Midian prevailed
over Israel; and because of Midian the Israelites provided for themselves hiding places in the mountains, caves
and strongholds. 3For whenever the Israelites put in
seed, the Midianites and the Amalekites and the people
of the east would come up against them. 4They would
encamp against them and destroy the produce of the
land, as far as the neighborhood of Gaza, and leave no
sustenance in Israel, and no sheep or ox or donkey. 5For
they and their livestock would come up, and they would
even bring their tents, as thick as locusts; neither they
nor their camels could be counted; so they wasted the
land as they came in. 6Thus Israel was greatly impoverished because of Midian; and the Israelites cried out to
the LORD for help.

7 When the Israelites cried to the LORD on account
of the Midianites, 8the LORD sent a prophet to the Israelites; and he said to them, "Thus says the LORD, the God
of Israel: I led you up from Egypt, and brought you out
of the house of slavery; 9and I delivered you from the
hand of the Egyptians, and from the hand of all who
oppressed you, and drove them out before you, and gave
you their land; 10and I said to you, 'I am the LORD your
God; you shall not pay reverence to the gods of the
Amorites, in whose land you live.' But you have not
given heed to my voice."

a Gk Compare Tg: Heb *exclaimed*

King James

11¶ And there came an angel of the LORD, and sat under an oak which *was* in Ophrah, that *pertained* unto Joash the Abi-ezrite: and his son Gideon threshed wheat by the winepress, to hide *it* from the Midianites.

12And the angel of the LORD appeared unto him, and said unto him, The LORD *is* with thee, thou mighty man of valour.

13And Gideon said unto him, Oh my Lord, if the LORD be with us, why then is all this befallen us? and where *be* all his miracles which our fathers told us of, saying, Did not the LORD bring us up from Egypt? but now the LORD hath forsaken us, and delivered us into the hands of the Midianites.

14And the LORD looked upon him, and said, Go in this thy might, and thou shalt save Israel from the hand of the Midianites: have not I sent thee?

15And he said unto him, Oh my Lord, wherewith shall I save Israel? behold, my family *is* poor in Manasseh, and I *am* the least in my father's house.

16And the LORD said unto him, Surely I will be with thee, and thou shalt smite the Midianites as one man.

17And he said unto him, If now I have found grace in thy sight, then show me a sign that thou talkest with me.

18Depart not hence, I pray thee, until I come unto thee, and bring forth my present, and set *it* before thee. And he said, I will tarry until thou come again.

19¶ And Gideon went in, and made ready a kid, and unleavened cakes of an ephah of flour: the flesh he put in a basket, and he put the broth in a pot, and brought *it* out unto him under the oak, and presented *it*.

20And the angel of God said unto him, Take the flesh and the unleavened cakes, and lay *them* upon this rock, and pour out the broth. And he did so.

21¶ Then the angel of the LORD put forth the end of the staff that *was* in his hand, and touched the flesh and the unleavened cakes; and there rose up fire out of the rock, and consumed the flesh and the unleavened cakes. Then the angel of the LORD departed out of his sight.

22And when Gideon perceived that he *was* an angel of the LORD, Gideon said, Alas, O Lord GOD! for because I have seen an angel of the LORD face to face.

23And the LORD said unto him, Peace *be* unto thee; fear not: thou shalt not die.

24Then Gideon built an altar there unto the LORD, and called it Jehovah-shalom: unto this day it *is* yet in Ophrah of the Abi-ezrites.

25¶ And it came to pass the same night, that the LORD said unto him, Take thy father's young bullock, even the second bullock of seven years old, and throw down the altar of Baal that thy father hath, and cut down the grove that *is* by it:

26And build an altar unto the LORD thy God upon the top of this rock, in the ordered place, and take the second bullock, and offer a burnt sacrifice with the wood of the grove which thou shalt cut down.

27Then Gideon took ten men of his servants, and did as the LORD had said unto him: and *so* it was, because he feared his father's household, and the men of the city, that he could not do *it* by day, that he did *it* by night.

28¶ And when the men of the city arose early in the morning, behold, the altar of Baal was cast down, and the grove was cut down that *was* by it, and the second bullock was offered upon the altar *that was* built.

29And they said one to another, Who hath done this thing? And when they inquired and asked, they said, Gideon the son of Joash hath done this thing.

New International

11The angel of the LORD came and sat down under the oak in Ophrah that belonged to Joash the Abiezrite, where his son Gideon was threshing wheat in a winepress to keep it from the Midianites. 12When the angel of the LORD appeared to Gideon, he said, "The LORD is with you, mighty warrior."

13"But sir," Gideon replied, "if the LORD is with us, why has all this happened to us? Where are all his wonders that our fathers told us about when they said, 'Did not the LORD bring us up out of Egypt?' But now the LORD has abandoned us and put us into the hand of Midian."

14The LORD turned to him and said, "Go in the strength you have and save Israel out of Midian's hand. Am I not sending you?"

15"But Lord,a" Gideon asked, "how can I save Israel? My clan is the weakest in Manasseh, and I am the least in my family."

16The LORD answered, "I will be with you, and you will strike down all the Midianites together."

17Gideon replied, "If now I have found favor in your eyes, give me a sign that it is really you talking to me. 18Please do not go away until I come back and bring my offering and set it before you."

And the LORD said, "I will wait until you return."

19Gideon went in, prepared a young goat, and from an ephahb of flour he made bread without yeast. Putting the meat in a basket and its broth in a pot, he brought them out and offered them to him under the oak.

20The angel of God said to him, "Take the meat and the unleavened bread, place them on this rock, and pour out the broth." And Gideon did so. 21With the tip of the staff that was in his hand, the angel of the LORD touched the meat and the unleavened bread. Fire flared from the rock, consuming the meat and the bread. And the angel of the LORD disappeared. 22When Gideon realized that it was the angel of the LORD, he exclaimed, "Ah, Sovereign LORD! I have seen the angel of the LORD face to face!"

23But the LORD said to him, "Peace! Do not be afraid. You are not going to die."

24So Gideon built an altar to the LORD there and called it The LORD is Peace. To this day it stands in Ophrah of the Abiezrites.

25That same night the LORD said to him, "Take the second bull from your father's herd, the one seven years old.c Tear down your father's altar to Baal and cut down the Asherah poled beside it. 26Then build a proper kind ofe altar to the LORD your God on the top of this height. Using the wood of the Asherah pole that you cut down, offer the secondf bull as a burnt offering."

27So Gideon took ten of his servants and did as the LORD told him. But because he was afraid of his family and the men of the town, he did it at night rather than in the daytime.

28In the morning when the men of the town got up, there was Baal's altar, demolished, with the Asherah pole beside it cut down and the second bull sacrificed on the newly built altar!

29They asked each other, "Who did this?"

When they carefully investigated, they were told, "Gideon son of Joash did it."

---

a *15* Or *sir*   b *19* That is, probably about 3/5 bushel (about 22 liters)
c *25* Or *Take a full-grown, mature bull from your father's herd*   d *25* That is, a symbol of the goddess Asherah; here and elsewhere in Judges   e *26* Or *build with layers of stone an*   f *26* Or *full-grown*; also in verse 28

Living Bible

11But one day the Angel of the Lord came and sat beneath the oak tree at Ophrah, on the farm of Joash the Abiezrite. Joash's son, Gideon, had been threshing wheat by hand in the bottom of a grape press—a pit where grapes were pressed to make wine—for he was hiding from the Midianites.

12The Angel of the Lord appeared to him and said, "Mighty soldier, the Lord is with you!"

13"Stranger," Gideon replied, "if the Lord is with us, why has all this happened to us? And where are all the miracles our ancestors have told us about—such as when God brought them out of Egypt? Now the Lord has thrown us away and has let the Midianites completely ruin us."

14Then the Lord turned to him and said, "I will make you strong! Go and save Israel from the Midianites! I am sending you!"

15But Gideon replied, "Sir, how can I save Israel? My family is the poorest in the whole tribe of Manasseh, and I am the least thought of in the entire family!"

16Whereupon the Lord said to him, "But I, Jehovah,g will be with you! And you shall quickly destroy the Midianite hordes!"

17Gideon replied, "If it is really true that you are going to help me like that, then do some miracle to prove it! Prove that it is really Jehovah who is talking to me! 18But stay here until I go and get a present for you."

"All right," the Angel agreed. "I'll stay here until you return."

19Gideon hurried home and roasted a young goat, and baked some unleavened bread from a bushel of flour. Then, carrying the meat in a basket and broth in a pot, he took it out to the Angel, who was beneath the oak tree, and presented it to him.

20The Angel said to him, "Place the meat and the bread upon that rock over there, and pour the broth over it.

"When Gideon had followed these instructions, 21the Angel touched the meat and bread with his staff, and fire flamed up from the rock and consumed them! And suddenly the Angel was gone!

22When Gideon realized that it had indeed been the Angel of the Lord, he cried out, "Alas, O Lord God, for I have seen the Angel of the Lord face to face!"

23"It's all right," the Lord replied. "Don't be afraid! You shall not die."

24And Gideon built an altar there and named it "The Altar of Peace with Jehovah." (The altar is still there in Ophrah in the land of the Abiezrites.) 25That night the Lord told Gideon to hitch his father's best ox to the family altar of Baal, and pull it down, and to cut down the wooden idol of the goddess Asherah that stood nearby.

26"Replace it with an altar for the Lord your God, built here on this hill, laying the stones carefully. Then sacrifice the ox as a burnt offering to the Lord, using the wooden idol as wood for the fire on the altar."

27So Gideon took ten of his servants and did as the Lord had commanded. But he did it at night for fear of the other members of his father's household, and for fear of the men of the city; for he knew what would happen if they found out who did it! 28Early the next morning, as the city began to stir, someone discovered that the altar of Baal was knocked apart, the idol beside it was gone, and a new altar had been built instead, with the remains of a sacrifice on it.

29"Who did this?" everyone demanded. Finally they learned that it was Gideon, the son of Joash.

New Revised Standard

The Call of Gideon

11 Now the angel of the LORD came and sat under the oak at Ophrah, which belonged to Joash the Abiezrite, as his son Gideon was beating out wheat in the wine press, to hide it from the Midianites. 12The angel of the LORD appeared to him and said to him, "The LORD is with you, you mighty warrior." 13Gideon answered him, "But sir, if the LORD is with us, why then has all this happened to us? And where are all his wonderful deeds that our ancestors recounted to us, saying, 'Did not the LORD bring us up from Egypt?' But now the LORD has cast us off, and given us into the hand of Midian." 14Then the LORD turned to him and said, "Go in this might of yours and deliver Israel from the hand of Midian; I hereby commission you." 15He responded, "But sir, how can I deliver Israel? My clan is the weakest in Manasseh, and I am the least in my family." 16The LORD said to him, "But I will be with you, and you shall strike down the Midianites, every one of them." 17Then he said to him, "If now I have found favor with you, then show me a sign that it is you who speak with me. 18Do not depart from here until I come to you, and bring out my present, and set it before you." And he said, "I will stay until you return."

19 So Gideon went into his house and prepared a kid, and unleavened cakes from an ephah of flour; the meat he put in a basket, and the broth he put in a pot, and brought them to him under the oak and presented them. 20The angel of God said to him, "Take the meat and the unleavened cakes, and put them on this rock, and pour out the broth." And he did so. 21Then the angel of the LORD reached out the tip of the staff that was in his hand, and touched the meat and the unleavened cakes; and fire sprang up from the rock and consumed the meat and the unleavened cakes; and the angel of the LORD vanished from his sight. 22Then Gideon perceived that it was the angel of the LORD; and Gideon said, "Help me, Lord GOD! For I have seen the angel of the LORD face to face." 23But the LORD said to him, "Peace be to you; do not fear, you shall not die." 24Then Gideon built an altar there to the LORD, and called it, The LORD is peace. To this day it still stands at Ophrah, which belongs to the Abiezrites.

25 That night the LORD said to him, "Take your father's bull, the second bull seven years old, and pull down the altar of Baal that belongs to your father, and cut down the sacred poleh that is beside it; 26and build an altar to the LORD your God on the top of the stronghold here, in proper order; then take the second bull, and offer it as a burnt offering with the wood of the sacred poleh that you shall cut down." 27So Gideon took ten of his servants, and did as the LORD had told him; but because he was too afraid of his family and the townspeople to do it by day, he did it by night.

Gideon Destroys the Altar of Baal

28 When the townspeople rose early in the morning, the altar of Baal was broken down, and the sacred poleh beside it was cut down, and the second bull was offered on the altar that had been built. 29So they said to one another, "Who has done this?" After searching and inquiring, they were told, "Gideon son of Joash did it."

---

g 6:16 But I, Jehovah, literally, "I AM will be with you." The same name is used here as in Exodus 3:14. God is telling Gideon that the same one who appeared to Moses and rescued Israel from Egypt (much on Gideon's mind: see vs 13) will now do it again, rescuing Israel from Midian.

h Heb Asherah

King James

30Then the men of the city said unto Joash, Bring out thy son, that he may die: because he hath cast down the altar of Baal, and because he hath cut down the grove that *was* by it.

31And Joash said unto all that stood against him, Will ye plead for Baal? will ye save him? he that will plead for him, let him be put to death whilst *it is yet* morning: if he *be* a god, let him plead for himself, because *one* hath cast down his altar.

32Therefore on that day he called him Jerubbaal, saying, Let Baal plead against him, because he hath thrown down his altar.

33¶ Then all the Midianites and the Amalekites and the children of the east were gathered together, and went over, and pitched in the valley of Jezreel.

34But the spirit of the Lord came upon Gideon, and he blew a trumpet; and Abiezer was gathered after him.

35And he sent messengers throughout all Manasseh; who also was gathered after him: and he sent messengers unto Asher, and unto Zebulun, and unto Naphtali; and they came up to meet them.

36¶ And Gideon said unto God, If thou wilt save Israel by mine hand, as thou hast said,

37Behold, I will put a fleece of wool in the floor; *and* if the dew be on the fleece only, and *it be* dry upon all the earth *beside*, then shall I know that thou wilt save Israel by mine hand, as thou hast said.

38And it was so: for he rose up early on the morrow, and thrust the fleece together, and wringed the dew out of the fleece, a bowl full of water.

39And Gideon said unto God, Let not thine anger be hot against me, and I will speak but this once: let me prove, I pray thee, but this once with the fleece; let it now be dry only upon the fleece, and upon all the ground let there be dew.

40And God did so that night: for it was dry upon the fleece only, and there was dew on all the ground.

7 THEN JERUBBAAL, who *is* Gideon, and all the people that *were* with him, rose up early, and pitched beside the well of Harod: so that the host of the Midianites were on the north side of them, by the hill of Moreh, in the valley.

2And the Lord said unto Gideon, The people that *are* with thee *are* too many for me to give the Midianites into their hands, lest Israel vaunt themselves against me, saying, Mine own hand hath saved me.

3Now therefore go to, proclaim in the ears of the people, saying, Whosoever *is* fearful and afraid, let him return and depart early from mount Gilead. And there returned of the people twenty and two thousand; and there remained ten thousand.

4And the Lord said unto Gideon, The people *are* yet *too* many; bring them down unto the water, and I will try them for thee there: and it shall be, *that* of whom I say unto thee, This shall go with thee, the same shall go with thee; and of whomsoever I say unto thee, This shall not go with thee, the same shall not go.

5So he brought down the people unto the water: and the Lord said unto Gideon, Every one that lappeth of the water with his tongue, as a dog lappeth, him shalt thou set by himself; likewise every one that boweth down upon his knees to drink.

6And the number of them that lapped, *putting* their hand to their mouth, were three hundred men: but all the rest of the people bowed down upon their knees to drink water.

7And the Lord said unto Gideon, By the three hundred men that lapped will I save you, and deliver the Midianites into thine hand: and let all the *other* people go every man unto his place.

New International

30The men of the town demanded of Joash, "Bring out your son. He must die, because he has broken down Baal's altar and cut down the Asherah pole beside it."

31But Joash replied to the hostile crowd around him, "Are you going to plead Baal's cause? Are you trying to save him? Whoever fights for him shall be put to death by morning! If Baal really is a god, he can defend himself when someone breaks down his altar." 32So that day they called Gideon "Jerub-Baal,[a]" saying, "Let Baal contend with him," because he broke down Baal's altar.

33Now all the Midianites, Amalekites and other eastern peoples joined forces and crossed over the Jordan and camped in the Valley of Jezreel. 34Then the Spirit of the Lord came upon Gideon, and he blew a trumpet, summoning the Abiezrites to follow him. 35He sent messengers throughout Manasseh, calling them to arms, and also into Asher, Zebulun and Naphtali, so that they too went up to meet them.

36Gideon said to God, "If you will save Israel by my hand as you have promised— 37look, I will place a wool fleece on the threshing floor. If there is dew only on the fleece and all the ground is dry, then I will know that you will save Israel by my hand, as you said." 38And that is what happened. Gideon rose early the next day; he squeezed the fleece and wrung out the dew—a bowlful of water.

39Then Gideon said to God, "Do not be angry with me. Let me make just one more request. Allow me one more test with the fleece. This time make the fleece dry and the ground covered with dew." 40That night God did so. Only the fleece was dry; all the ground was covered with dew.

Gideon Defeats the Midianites

7 EARLY IN the morning, Jerub-Baal (that is, Gideon) and all his men camped at the spring of Harod. The camp of Midian was north of them in the valley near the hill of Moreh. 2The Lord said to Gideon, "You have too many men for me to deliver Midian into their hands. In order that Israel may not boast against me that her own strength has saved her, 3announce now to the people, 'Anyone who trembles with fear may turn back and leave Mount Gilead.' " So twenty-two thousand men left, while ten thousand remained.

4But the Lord said to Gideon, "There are still too many men. Take them down to the water, and I will sift them for you there. If I say, 'This one shall go with you,' he shall go; but if I say, 'This one shall not go with you,' he shall not go."

5So Gideon took the men down to the water. There the Lord told him, "Separate those who lap the water with their tongues like a dog from those who kneel down to drink." 6Three hundred men lapped with their hands to their mouths. All the rest got down on their knees to drink.

7The Lord said to Gideon, "With the three hundred men that lapped I will save you and give the Midianites into your hands. Let all the other men go, each to his own place." 8So Gideon sent the rest of the Israelites to

---

^a *32 Jerub-Baal means let Baal contend.*

Living Bible

30"Bring out your son," they shouted to Joash. "He must die for insulting the altar of Baal, and for cutting down the Asherah idol."

31But Joash retorted to the whole mob, "Does Baal need *your* help? What an insult to a god! You are the ones who should die for insulting Baal! If Baal is really a god, let him take care of himself and destroy the one who broke apart his altar!"

32From then on Gideon was called "Jerubbaal," a nickname meaning "Let Baal take care of himself!"b

33Soon afterward the armies of Midian, Amalek, and other neighboring nations united in one vast alliance against Israel. They crossed the Jordan and camped in the valley of Jezreel. 34Then the Spirit of the Lord came upon Gideon, and he blew a trumpet as a call to arms, and the men of Abiezer came to him. 35He also sent messengers throughout Manasseh, Asher, Zebulun, and Naphtali, summoning their fighting forces, and all of them responded.

36Then Gideon said to God, "If you are really going to use me to save Israel as you promised, 37prove it to me in this way: I'll put some wool on the threshing floor tonight, and if, in the morning, the fleece is wet and the ground is dry, I will know you are going to help me!"

38And it happened just that way! When he got up the next morning he pressed the fleece together and wrung out a whole bowlful of water!

39Then Gideon said to the Lord, "Please don't be angry with me, but let me make one more test: this time let the fleece remain dry while the ground around it is wet!"

40So the Lord did as he asked; that night the fleece stayed dry, but the ground was covered with dew!

7 JERUBBAAL (THAT is, Gideon—his other name) and his army got an early start and went as far as the spring of Harod. The armies of Midian were camped north of them, down in the valley beside the hill of Moreh.

2The Lord then said to Gideon, "There are too many of you! I can't let all of you fight the Midianites, for then the people of Israel will boast to me that they saved themselves by their own strength! 3Send home any of your men who are timid and frightened."

So twenty-two thousand of them left, and only ten thousand remained who were willing to fight.

4But the Lord told Gideon, "There are still too many! Bring them down to the spring and I'll show you which ones shall go with you and which ones shall not."

5, 6So Gideon assembled them at the water. There the Lord told him, "Divide them into two groups decided by the way they drink. In Group 1 will be all the men who cup the water in their hands to get it to their mouths and lap it like dogs. In Group 2 will be those who kneel, with their mouths in the stream."

Only three hundred of the men drank from their hands; all the others drank with their mouths in the stream.

7"I'll conquer the Midianites with these three hundred!" the Lord told Gideon. "Send all the others home!"

New Revised Standard

30Then the townspeople said to Joash, "Bring out your son, so that he may die, for he has pulled down the altar of Baal and cut down the sacred polec beside it." 31But Joash said to all who were arrayed against him, "Will you contend for Baal? Or will you defend his cause? Whoever contends for him shall be put to death by morning. If he is a god, let him contend for himself, because his altar has been pulled down." 32Therefore on that day Gideond was called Jerubbaal, that is to say, "Let Baal contend against him," because he pulled down his altar.

33 Then all the Midianites and the Amalekites and the people of the east came together, and crossing the Jordan they encamped in the Valley of Jezreel. 34But the spirit of the LORD took possession of Gideon; and he sounded the trumpet, and the Abiezrites were called out to follow him. 35He sent messengers throughout all Manasseh, and they too were called out to follow him. He also sent messengers to Asher, Zebulun, and Naphtali, and they went up to meet them.

The Sign of the Fleece

36 Then Gideon said to God, "In order to see whether you will deliver Israel by my hand, as you have said, 37I am going to lay a fleece of wool on the threshing floor; if there is dew on the fleece alone, and it is dry on all the ground, then I shall know that you will deliver Israel by my hand, as you have said." 38And it was so. When he rose early next morning and squeezed the fleece, he wrung enough dew from the fleece to fill a bowl with water. 39Then Gideon said to God, "Do not let your anger burn against me, let me speak one more time; let me, please, make trial with the fleece just once more; let it be dry only on the fleece, and on all the ground let there be dew." 40And God did so that night. It was dry on the fleece only, and on all the ground there was dew.

Gideon Surprises and Routs the Midianites

7 THEN JERUBBAAL (that is, Gideon) and all the troops that were with him rose early and encamped beside the spring of Harod; and the camp of Midian was north of them, belowe the hill of Moreh, in the valley.

2 The LORD said to Gideon, "The troops with you are too many for me to give the Midianites into their hand. Israel would only take the credit away from me, saying, 'My own hand has delivered me.' 3Now therefore proclaim this in the hearing of the troops, 'Whoever is fearful and trembling, let him return home.'" Thus Gideon sifted them out;f twenty-two thousand returned, and ten thousand remained.

4 Then the LORD said to Gideon, "The troops are still too many; take them down to the water and I will sift them out for you there. When I say, 'This one shall go with you,' he shall go with you; and when I say, 'This one shall not go with you,' he shall not go." 5So he brought the troops down to the water; and the LORD said to Gideon, "All those who lap the water with their tongues, as a dog laps, you shall put to one side; all those who kneel down to drink, putting their hands to their mouths,g you shall put to the other side." 6The number of those that lapped was three hundred; but all the rest of the troops knelt down to drink water. 7Then the LORD said to Gideon, "With the three hundred that lapped I will deliver you, and give the Midianites into your hand. Let all the others go to their homes." 8So he took the jars

---

b 6:32 *Let Baal take care of himself*, literally, "Let Baal bring charges," or used mockingly, "Let Baal be honored!"

c Heb *Asherah*   d Heb *he*   e Heb *from* Mount Gilead' "   f Cn: Heb *home, and depart from* Mount Gilead' "   g Heb places the words *putting their hands to their mouths* after the word *lapped* in verse 6

King James

8So the people took victuals in their hand, and their trumpets: and he sent all *the rest of* Israel every man unto his tent, and retained those three hundred men: and the host of Midian was beneath him in the valley.

9¶ And it came to pass the same night, that the LORD said unto him, Arise, get thee down unto the host; for I have delivered it into thine hand.

10But if thou fear to go down, go thou with Phurah thy servant down to the host:

11And thou shalt hear what they say; and afterward shall thine hands be strengthened to go down unto the host. Then went he down with Phurah his servant unto the outside of the armed men that *were* in the host.

12And the Midianites and the Amalekites and all the children of the east lay along in the valley like grasshoppers for multitude; and their camels *were* without number, as the sand by the sea side for multitude.

13And when Gideon was come, behold, *there was* a man that told a dream unto his fellow, and said, Behold, I dreamed a dream, and, lo, a cake of barley bread tumbled into the host of Midian, and came unto a tent, and smote it that it fell, and overturned it, that the tent lay along.

14And his fellow answered and said, This *is* nothing else save the sword of Gideon the son of Joash, a man of Israel: *for* into his hand hath God delivered Midian, and all the host.

15¶ And it was *so,* when Gideon heard the telling of the dream, and the interpretation thereof, that he worshipped, and returned into the host of Israel, and said, Arise; for the LORD hath delivered into your hand the host of Midian.

16And he divided the three hundred men *into* three companies, and he put a trumpet in every man's hand, with empty pitchers, and lamps within the pitchers.

17And he said unto them, Look on me, and do likewise: and, behold, when I come to the outside of the camp, it shall be *that,* as I do, so shall ye do.

18When I blow with a trumpet, I and all that *are* with me, then blow ye the trumpets also on every side of all the camp, and say, The *sword* of the LORD, and of Gideon.

19¶ So Gideon, and the hundred men that *were* with him, came unto the outside of the camp in the beginning of the middle watch; and they had but newly set the watch: and they blew the trumpets, and brake the pitchers that *were* in their hands.

20And the three companies blew the trumpets, and brake the pitchers, and held the lamps in their left hands, and the trumpets in their right hands to blow *withal:* and they cried, The sword of the LORD, and of Gideon.

21And they stood every man in his place round about the camp: and all the host ran, and cried, and fled.

22And the three hundred blew the trumpets, and the LORD set every man's sword against his fellow, even throughout all the host: and the host fled to Beth-shittah in Zererath, *and* to the border of Abel-meholah, unto Tabbath.

23And the men of Israel gathered themselves together out of Naphtali, and out of Asher, and out of all Manasseh, and pursued after the Midianites.

24¶ And Gideon sent messengers throughout all mount Ephraim, saying, Come down against the Midianites, and take before them the waters unto Beth-barah and Jordan. Then all the men of Ephraim gathered themselves together, and took the waters unto Beth-barah and Jordan.

25And they took two princes of the Midianites, Oreb and Zeeb; and they slew Oreb upon the rock Oreb, and Zeeb they slew at the winepress of Zeeb, and pursued Midian, and brought the heads of Oreb and Zeeb to Gideon on the other side Jordan.

New International

their tents but kept the three hundred, who took over the provisions and trumpets of the others.

Now the camp of Midian lay below him in the valley. 9During that night the LORD said to Gideon, "Get up, go down against the camp, because I am going to give it into your hands. 10If you are afraid to attack, go down to the camp with your servant Purah 11and listen to what they are saying. Afterward, you will be encouraged to attack the camp." So he and Purah his servant went down to the outposts of the camp. 12The Midianites, the Amalekites and all the other eastern peoples had settled in the valley, thick as locusts. Their camels could no more be counted than the sand on the seashore.

13Gideon arrived just as a man was telling a friend his dream. "I had a dream," he was saying. "A round loaf of barley bread came tumbling into the Midianite camp. It struck the tent with such force that the tent overturned and collapsed."

14His friend responded, "This can be nothing other than the sword of Gideon son of Joash, the Israelite. God has given the Midianites and the whole camp into his hands."

15When Gideon heard the dream and its interpretation, he worshiped God. He returned to the camp of Israel and called out, "Get up! The LORD has given the Midianite camp into your hands." 16Dividing the three hundred men into three companies, he placed trumpets and empty jars in the hands of all of them, with torches inside.

17"Watch me," he told them. "Follow my lead. When I get to the edge of the camp, do exactly as I do. 18When I and all who are with me blow our trumpets, then from all around the camp blow yours and shout, 'For the LORD and for Gideon.' "

19Gideon and the hundred men with him reached the edge of the camp at the beginning of the middle watch, just after they had changed the guard. They blew their trumpets and broke the jars that were in their hands. 20The three companies blew the trumpets and smashed the jars. Grasping the torches in their left hands and holding in their right hands the trumpets they were to blow, they shouted, "A sword for the LORD and for Gideon!" 21While each man held his position around the camp, all the Midianites ran, crying out as they fled.

22When the three hundred trumpets sounded, the LORD caused the men throughout the camp to turn on each other with their swords. The army fled to Beth Shittah toward Zererah as far as the border of Abel Meholah near Tabbath. 23Israelites from Naphtali, Asher and all Manasseh were called out, and they pursued the Midianites. 24Gideon sent messengers throughout the hill country of Ephraim, saying, "Come down against the Midianites and seize the waters of the Jordan ahead of them as far as Beth Barah."

So all the men of Ephraim were called out and they took the waters of the Jordan as far as Beth Barah. 25They also captured two of the Midianite leaders, Oreb and Zeeb. They killed Oreb at the rock of Oreb, and Zeeb at the winepress of Zeeb. They pursued the Midianites and brought the heads of Oreb and Zeeb to Gideon, who was by the Jordan.

Living Bible

8, 9So after Gideon had collected all the clay jars and trumpets they had among them, he sent them home, leaving only three hundred men with him.

During the night, with the Midianites camped in the valley just below, the Lord said to Gideon, "Get up! Take your troops and attack the Midianites, for I will cause you to defeat them! 10But if you are afraid, first go down to the camp alone—take along your servant Purah if you like— 11and listen to what they are saying down there! You will be greatly encouraged and be eager to attack!"

So he took Purah and crept down through the darkness to the outposts of the enemy camp. 12, 13The vast armies of Midian, Amalek, and the other nations of the Mideast were crowded across the valley like locusts—yes, like the sand upon the seashore—and there were too many camels even to count! Gideon crept up to one of the tents just as a man inside had wakened from a nightmare and was telling his tent-mate about it.

"I had this strange dream," he was saying, "and there was this huge loaf of barley bread that came tumbling down into our camp. It hit our tent and knocked it flat!"

14The other soldier replied, "Your dream can mean only one thing! Gideon, the son of Joash, the Israeli, is going to come and massacre all the allied forces of Midian!"

15When Gideon heard the dream and the interpretation, all he could do was just stand there worshiping God! Then he returned to his men and shouted, "Get up! For the Lord is going to use you to conquer all the vast armies of Midian!"

16He divided the three hundred men into three groups and gave each man a trumpet and a clay jar with a torch in it. 17Then he explained his plan.

"When we arrive at the outer guardposts of the camp," he told them, "do just as I do. 18As soon as I and the men in my group blow our trumpets, you blow yours on all sides of the camp and shout, 'We fight for God and for Gideon!' "

19, 20It was just after midnight and the change of guards when Gideon and the hundred men with him crept to the outer edge of the camp of Midian.

Suddenly they blew their trumpets and broke their clay jars so that their torches blazed into the night. Then the other two hundred of his men did the same, blowing the trumpets in their right hands, and holding the flaming torches in their left hands, all shouting, "For the Lord and for Gideon!"a

21Then they just stood and watched as the whole vast enemy army began rushing around in a panic, shouting and running away. 22For in the confusion the Lord caused the enemy troops to begin fighting and killing each other from one end of the camp to the other, and they fled into the night to places as far away as Beth-shittah near Zererah, and to the border of Abel-meholah near Tabbath.

23Then Gideon sent for the troops of Naphtali, Asher, and Manasseh and told them to come and chase and destroy the fleeing army of Midian. 24Gideon also sent messengers throughout the hill country of Ephraim summoning troops who seized the fords of the Jordan River at Beth-barah, thus preventing the Midianites from escaping by going across. 25Oreb and Zeeb, the two generals of Midian, were captured. Oreb was killed at the rock now known by his name, and Zeeb at the winepress of Zeeb, as it is now called; and the Israelis took the heads of Oreb and Zeeb across the Jordan to Gideon.

New Revised Standard

of the troops from their hands,b and their trumpets; and he sent all the rest of Israel back to their own tents, but retained the three hundred. The camp of Midian was below him in the valley.

9 That same night the LORD said to him, "Get up, attack the camp; for I have given it into your hand. 10But if you fear to attack, go down to the camp with your servant Purah; 11and you shall hear what they say, and afterward your hands shall be strengthened to attack the camp." Then he went down with his servant Purah to the outposts of the armed men that were in the camp. 12The Midianites and the Amalekites and all the people of the east lay along the valley as thick as locusts; and their camels were without number, countless as the sand on the seashore. 13When Gideon arrived, there was a man telling a dream to his comrade; and he said, "I had a dream, and in it a cake of barley bread tumbled into the camp of Midian, and came to the tent, and struck it so that it fell; it turned upside down, and the tent collapsed." 14And his comrade answered, "This is no other than the sword of Gideon son of Joash, a man of Israel; into his hand God has given Midian and all the army."

15 When Gideon heard the telling of the dream and its interpretation, he worshiped; and he returned to the camp of Israel, and said, "Get up; for the LORD has given the army of Midian into your hand." 16After he divided the three hundred men into three companies, and put trumpets into the hands of all of them, and empty jars, with torches inside the jars, 17he said to them, "Look at me, and do the same; when I come to the outskirts of the camp, do as I do. 18When I blow the trumpet, I and all who are with me, then you also blow the trumpets around the whole camp, and shout, 'For the LORD and for Gideon!' "

19 So Gideon and the hundred who were with him came to the outskirts of the camp at the beginning of the middle watch, when they had just set the watch; and they blew the trumpets and smashed the jars that were in their hands. 20So the three companies blew the trumpets and broke the jars, holding in their left hands the torches, and in their right hands the trumpets to blow; and they cried, "A sword for the LORD and for Gideon!" 21Every man stood in his place all around the camp, and all the men in camp ran; they cried out and fled. 22When they blew the three hundred trumpets, the LORD set every man's sword against his fellow and against all the army; and the army fled as far as Beth-shittah toward Zererah,c as far as the border of Abel-meholah, by Tabbath. 23And the men of Israel were called out from Naphtali and from Asher and from all Manasseh, and they pursued after the Midianites.

24 Then Gideon sent messengers throughout all the hill country of Ephraim, saying, "Come down against the Midianites and seize the waters against them, as far as Beth-barah, and also the Jordan." So all the men of Ephraim were called out, and they seized the waters as far as Beth-barah, and also the Jordan. 25They captured the two captains of Midian, Oreb and Zeeb; they killed Oreb at the rock of Oreb, and Zeeb they killed at the wine press of Zeeb, as they pursued the Midianites. They brought the heads of Oreb and Zeeb to Gideon beyond the Jordan.

---

a 7:19, 20 "For the Lord and for Gideon!" literally, "A sword for the Lord and for Gideon."

b Cn: Heb So the people took provisions in their hands   c Another reading is Zeredah

King James

8 AND THE men of Ephraim said unto him, Why hast thou served us thus, that thou calledst us not, when thou wentest to fight with the Midianites? And they did chide with him sharply.

2And he said unto them, What have I done now in comparison of you? *Is* not the gleaning of the grapes of Ephraim better than the vintage of Abiezer?

3God hath delivered into your hands the princes of Midian, Oreb and Zeeb: and what was I able to do in comparison of you? Then their anger was abated toward him, when he had said that.

4¶ And Gideon came to Jordan, *and* passed over, he, and the three hundred men that *were* with him, faint, yet pursuing *them*.

5And he said unto the men of Succoth, Give, I pray you, loaves of bread unto the people that follow me; for they *be* faint, and I am pursuing after Zebah and Zalmunna, kings of Midian.

6¶ And the princes of Succoth said, *Are* the hands of Zebah and Zalmunna now in thine hand, that we should give bread unto thine army?

7And Gideon said, Therefore when the LORD hath delivered Zebah and Zalmunna into mine hand, then I will tear your flesh with the thorns of the wilderness and with briers.

8¶ And he went up thence to Penuel, and spake unto them likewise: and the men of Penuel answered him as the men of Succoth had answered *him*.

9And he spake also unto the men of Penuel, saying, When I come again in peace, I will break down this tower.

10¶ Now Zebah and Zalmunna *were* in Karkor, and their hosts with them, about fifteen thousand *men*, all that were left of all the hosts of the children of the east: for there fell an hundred and twenty thousand men that drew sword.

11¶ And Gideon went up by the way of them that dwelt in tents on the east of Nobah and Jogbehah, and smote the host: for the host was secure.

12And when Zebah and Zalmunna fled, he pursued after them, and took the two kings of Midian, Zebah and Zalmunna, and discomfited all the host.

13¶ And Gideon the son of Joash returned from battle before the sun *was up*,

14And caught a young man of the men of Succoth, and inquired of him: and he described unto him the princes of Succoth, and the elders thereof, *even* threescore and seventeen men.

15And he came unto the men of Succoth, and said, Behold Zebah and Zalmunna, with whom ye did upbraid me, saying, *Are* the hands of Zebah and Zalmunna now in thine hand, that we should give bread unto thy men *that are* weary?

16And he took the elders of the city, and thorns of the wilderness and briers, and with them he taught the men of Succoth.

17And he beat down the tower of Penuel, and slew the men of the city.

18¶ Then said he unto Zebah and Zalmunna, What manner of men *were they* whom ye slew at Tabor? And they answered, As thou *art*, so *were* they; each one resembled the children of a king.

19And he said, they *were* my brethren, *even* the sons of my mother: as the LORD liveth, if ye had saved them alive, I would not slay you.

20And he said unto Jether his firstborn, Up, *and* slay them. But the youth drew not his sword: for he feared, because he *was* yet a youth.

21Then Zebah and Zalmunna said, Rise thou, and fall upon us: for as the man *is*, *so is* his strength. And Gideon arose, and slew Zebah and Zalmunna, and took away the ornaments that *were* on their camels' necks.

New International

Zebah and Zalmunna

8 NOW THE Ephraimites asked Gideon, "Why have you treated us like this? Why didn't you call us when you went to fight Midian?" And they criticized him sharply.

2But he answered them, "What have I accomplished compared to you? Aren't the gleanings of Ephraim's grapes better than the full grape harvest of Abiezer? 3God gave Oreb and Zeeb, the Midianite leaders, into your hands. What was I able to do compared to you?" At this, their resentment against him subsided.

4Gideon and his three hundred men, exhausted yet keeping up the pursuit, came to the Jordan and crossed it. 5He said to the men of Succoth, "Give my troops some bread; they are worn out, and I am still pursuing Zebah and Zalmunna, the kings of Midian."

6But the officials of Succoth said, "Do you already have the hands of Zebah and Zalmunna in your possession? Why should we give bread to your troops?"

7Then Gideon replied, "Just for that, when the LORD has given Zebah and Zalmunna into my hand, I will tear your flesh with desert thorns and briers."

8From there he went up to Peniel[a] and made the same request of them, but they answered as the men of Succoth had. 9So he said to the men of Peniel, "When I return in triumph, I will tear down this tower."

10Now Zebah and Zalmunna were in Karkor with a force of about fifteen thousand men, all that were left of the armies of the eastern peoples; a hundred and twenty thousand swordsmen had fallen. 11Gideon went up by the route of the nomads east of Nobah and Jogbehah and fell upon the unsuspecting army. 12Zebah and Zalmunna, the two kings of Midian, fled, but he pursued them and captured them, routing their entire army.

13Gideon son of Joash then returned from the battle by the Pass of Heres. 14He caught a young man of Succoth and questioned him, and the young man wrote down for him the names of the seventy-seven officials of Succoth, the elders of the town. 15Then Gideon came and said to the men of Succoth, "Here are Zebah and Zalmunna, about whom you taunted me by saying, 'Do you already have the hands of Zebah and Zalmunna in your possession? Why should we give bread to your exhausted men?' " 16He took the elders of the town and taught the men of Succoth a lesson by punishing them with desert thorns and briers. 17He also pulled down the tower of Peniel and killed the men of the town.

18Then he asked Zebah and Zalmunna, "What kind of men did you kill at Tabor?"

"Men like you," they answered, "each one with the bearing of a prince."

19Gideon replied, "Those were my brothers, the sons of my own mother. As surely as the LORD lives, if you had spared their lives, I would not kill you." 20Turning to Jether, his oldest son, he said, "Kill them!" But Jether did not draw his sword, because he was only a boy and was afraid.

21Zebah and Zalmunna said, "Come, do it yourself. 'As is the man, so is his strength.' " So Gideon stepped forward and killed them, and took the ornaments off their camels' necks.

---

a 8 Hebrew *Penuel*, a variant of *Peniel*; also in verses 9 and 17

Living Bible

8 BUT THE tribal leaders of Ephraim were violently angry with Gideon.

"Why didn't you send for us when you first went out to fight the Midianites?" they demanded.

2, 3But Gideon replied, "God let you capture Oreb and Zeeb, the generals of the army of Midian! What have I done in comparison with that? Your actions at the end of the battle were more important than ours at the beginning!"b So they calmed down.

4Gideon now crossed the Jordan River with his three hundred men. They were very tired, but still chasing the enemy. 5He asked the men of Succoth for food. "We are weary from chasing after Zebah and Zalmunna, the kings of Midian," he said.

6But the leaders of Succoth replied, "You haven't caught them yet! If we feed you and you fail, they'll return and destroy us."c

7Then Gideon warned them, "When the Lord has delivered them to us, I will return and tear your flesh with the thorns and briars of the wilderness."

8Then he went up to Penuel and asked for food there, but got the same answer. 9And he said to them also, "When this is all over, I will return and break down this tower."

10By this time King Zebah and King Zalmunna with a remnant of fifteen thousand troops were in Karkor. That was all that was left of the allied armies of the east; for one hundred twenty thousand had already been killed. 11Then Gideon circled around by the caravan route east of Nobah and Jogbehah, striking at the Midianite army in surprise raids. 12The two kings fled, but Gideon chased and captured them, routing their entire force. 13Later, Gideon returned by way of Heres Pass. 14There he captured a young fellow from Succoth and demanded that he write down the names of all the seventy-seven political and religious leaders of the city.

15He then returned to Succoth. "You taunted me that I would never catch King Zebah and King Zalmunna, and you refused to give us food when we were tired and hungry," he said. "Well, here they are!"

16Then he took the leaders of the city and scraped them to deathd with wild thorns and briars. 17He also went to Penuel and knocked down the city tower and killed the entire male population.

18Then Gideon asked King Zebah and King Zalmunna, "The men you killed at Tabor—what were they like?"

They replied, "They were dressed just like you—like sons of kings!"

19"They must have been my brothers!" Gideon exclaimed. "I swear that if you hadn't killed them I wouldn't kill you."

20Then, turning to Jether, his oldest son, he instructed him to kill them. But the boy was only a lad and was afraid to.

21Then Zebah and Zalmunna said to Gideon, "You do it; we'd rather be killed by a man!"e So Gideon killed them and took the ornaments from their camels' necks.

New Revised Standard

Gideon's Triumph and Vengeance

8 THEN THE Ephraimites said to him, "What have you done to us, not to call us when you went to fight against the Midianites?" And they upbraided him violently. 2So he said to them, "What have I done now in comparison with you? Is not the gleaning of the grapes of Ephraim better than the vintage of Abiezer? 3God has given into your hands the captains of Midian, Oreb and Zeeb; what have I been able to do in comparison with you?" When he said this, their anger against him subsided.

4 Then Gideon came to the Jordan and crossed over, he and the three hundred who were with him, exhausted and famished.f 5So he said to the people of Succoth, "Please give some loaves of bread to my followers, for they are exhausted, and I am pursuing Zebah and Zalmunna, the kings of Midian." 6But the officials of Succoth said, "Do you already have in your possession the hands of Zebah and Zalmunna, that we should give bread to your army?" 7Gideon replied, "Well then, when the LORD has given Zebah and Zalmunna into my hand, I will trample your flesh on the thorns of the wilderness and on briers." 8From there he went up to Penuel, and made the same request of them; and the people of Penuel answered him as the people of Succoth had answered. 9So he said to the people of Penuel, "When I come back victorious, I will break down this tower."

10 Now Zebah and Zalmunna were in Karkor with their army, about fifteen thousand men, all who were left of all the army of the people of the east; for one hundred twenty thousand men bearing arms had fallen. 11So Gideon went up by the caravan route east of Nobah and Jogbehah, and attacked the army; for the army was off its guard. 12Zebah and Zalmunna fled; and he pursued them and took the two kings of Midian, Zebah and Zalmunna, and threw all the army into a panic.

13 When Gideon son of Joash returned from the battle by the ascent of Heres, 14he caught a young man, one of the people of Succoth, and questioned him; and he listed for him the officials and elders of Succoth, seventy-seven people. 15Then he came to the people of Succoth, and said, "Here are Zebah and Zalmunna, about whom you taunted me, saying, 'Do you already have in your possession the hands of Zebah and Zalmunna, that we should give bread to your troops who are exhausted?'" 16So he took the elders of the city and he took thorns of the wilderness and briers and with them he trampledg the people of Succoth. 17He also broke down the tower of Penuel, and killed the men of the city.

18 Then he said to Zebah and Zalmunna, "What about the men whom you killed at Tabor?" They answered, "As you are, so were they, every one of them; they resembled the sons of a king." 19And he replied, "They were my brothers, the sons of my mother; as the LORD lives, if you had saved them alive, I would not kill you." 20So he said to Jether his firstborn, "Go kill them!" But the boy did not draw his sword, for he was afraid, because he was still a boy. 21Then Zebah and Zalmunna said, "You come and kill us; for as the man is, so is his strength." So Gideon proceeded to kill Zebah and Zalmunna; and he took the crescents that were on the necks of their camels.

---

b 8:2, 3 *at the beginning*, more literally, "Are not the last grapes of Ephraim better than the entire crop of Abiezer?"   c 8:6 *they'll return and destroy us*, literally, "are Zebah and Zalmunna already in your hand . . . ?"   d 8:16 *and scraped them to death*, literally, "he taught the men of Succoth."   e 8:21 *we'd rather be killed by a man*, literally, "For as a man is, so is his strength." Perhaps the meaning is, "A quick death is less painful."

f Gk: Heb *pursuing*   g With verse 7, Compare Gk: Heb *he taught*

King James

22¶ Then the men of Israel said unto Gideon, Rule thou over us, both thou, and thy son, and thy son's son also: for thou hast delivered us from the hand of Midian.

23And Gideon said unto them, I will not rule over you, neither shall my son rule over you: the LORD shall rule over you.

24¶ And Gideon said unto them, I would desire a request of you, that ye would give me every man the earrings of his prey. (For they had golden earrings, because they *were* Ishmaelites.)

25And they answered, We will willingly give *them*. And they spread a garment, and did cast therein every man the earrings of his prey.

26And the weight of the golden earrings that he requested was a thousand and seven hundred *shekels* of gold; beside ornaments, and collars, and purple raiment that *was* on the kings of Midian, and beside the chains that *were* about their camels' necks.

27And Gideon made an ephod thereof, and put it in his city, *even* in Ophrah: and all Israel went thither a-whoring after it: which thing became a snare unto Gideon, and to his house.

28¶ Thus was Midian subdued before the children of Israel, so that they lifted up their heads no more. And the country was in quietness forty years in the days of Gideon.

29¶ And Jerubbaal the son of Joash went and dwelt in his own house.

30And Gideon had threescore and ten sons of his body begotten: for he had many wives.

31And his concubine that *was* in Shechem, she also bare him a son, whose name he called Abimelech.

32¶ And Gideon the son of Joash died in a good old age, and was buried in the sepulchre of Joash his father, in Ophrah of the Abi-ezrites.

33And it came to pass, as soon as Gideon was dead, that the children of Israel turned again, and went a-whoring after Baalim, and made Baal-berith their god.

34And the children of Israel remembered not the LORD their God, who had delivered them out of the hands of all their enemies on every side:

35Neither showed they kindness to the house of Jerubbaal, *namely,* Gideon, according to all the goodness which he had shown unto Israel.

9 AND ABIMELECH the son of Jerubbaal went to Shechem unto his mother's brethren, and communed with them, and with all the family of the house of his mother's father, saying,

2Speak, I pray you, in the ears of all the men of Shechem, Whether *is* better for you, either that all the sons of Jerubbaal, *which are* threescore and ten persons, reign over you, or that one reign over you? remember also that I *am* your bone and your flesh.

3And his mother's brethren spake of him in the ears of all the men of Shechem all these words: and their hearts inclined to follow Abimelech; for they said, He *is* our brother.

4And they gave him threescore and ten *pieces* of silver out of the house of Baal-berith, wherewith Abimelech hired vain and light persons, which followed him.

5And he went unto his father's house at Ophrah, and slew his brethren the sons of Jerubbaal, *being* threescore and ten persons, upon one stone: notwithstanding yet Jotham the youngest son of Jerubbaal was left; for he hid himself.

6And all the men of Shechem gathered together, and all the house of Millo, and went, and made Abimelech king, by the plain of the pillar that *was* in Shechem.

New International

Gideon's Ephod

22The Israelites said to Gideon, "Rule over us—you, your son and your grandson—because you have saved us out of the hand of Midian."

23But Gideon told them, "I will not rule over you, nor will my son rule over you. The LORD will rule over you." 24And he said, "I do have one request, that each of you give me an earring from your share of the plunder." (It was the custom of the Ishmaelites to wear gold earrings.)

25They answered, "We'll be glad to give them." So they spread out a garment, and each man threw a ring from his plunder onto it. 26The weight of the gold rings he asked for came to seventeen hundred shekels,[a] not counting the ornaments, the pendants and the purple garments worn by the kings of Midian or the chains that were on their camels' necks. 27Gideon made the gold into an ephod, which he placed in Ophrah, his town. All Israel prostituted themselves by worshiping it there, and it became a snare to Gideon and his family.

Gideon's Death

28Thus Midian was subdued before the Israelites and did not raise its head again. During Gideon's lifetime, the land enjoyed peace forty years.

29Jerub-Baal son of Joash went back home to live. 30He had seventy sons of his own, for he had many wives. 31His concubine, who lived in Shechem, also bore him a son, whom he named Abimelech. 32Gideon son of Joash died at a good old age and was buried in the tomb of his father Joash in Ophrah of the Abiezrites.

33No sooner had Gideon died than the Israelites again prostituted themselves to the Baals. They set up Baal-Berith as their god and 34did not remember the LORD their God, who had rescued them from the hands of all their enemies on every side. 35They also failed to show kindness to the family of Jerub-Baal (that is, Gideon) for all the good things he had done for them.

Abimelech

9 ABIMELECH SON of Jerub-Baal went to his mother's brothers in Shechem and said to them and to all his mother's clan, 2"Ask all the citizens of Shechem, 'Which is better for you: to have all seventy of Jerub-Baal's sons rule over you, or just one man?' Remember, I am your flesh and blood."

3When the brothers repeated all this to the citizens of Shechem, they were inclined to follow Abimelech, for they said, "He is our brother." 4They gave him seventy shekels[b] of silver from the temple of Baal-Berith, and Abimelech used it to hire reckless adventurers, who became his followers. 5He went to his father's home in Ophrah and on one stone murdered his seventy brothers, the sons of Jerub-Baal. But Jotham, the youngest son of Jerub-Baal, escaped by hiding. 6Then all the citizens of Shechem and Beth Millo gathered beside the great tree at the pillar in Shechem to crown Abimelech king.

---

[a] 26 That is, about 43 pounds (about 19.5 kilograms)   [b] 4 That is, about 1 3/4 pounds (about 0.8 kilogram)

Living Bible

22Now the men of Israel said to Gideon, "Be our king! You and your sons and all your descendants shall be our rulers, for you have saved us from Midian."

23, 24But Gideon replied, "I will not be your king, nor shall my son; the Lord is your King! However, I have one request. Give me all the earrings collected from your fallen foes,"—for the troops of Midian, being Ishmaelites, all wore gold earrings.

25"Gladly!" they replied, and spread out a sheet for everyone to throw in the gold earrings he had gathered. 26Their value was estimated at $25,000, not including the crescents and pendants or the royal clothing of the kings, or the chains around the camels' necks. 27Gideon made an ephodc from the gold and put it in Ophrah, his home town. But all Israel soon began worshiping it, so it became an evil deed that Gideon and his family did.

28That is the true account of how Midian was subdued by Israel. Midian never recovered, and the land was at peace for forty years—all during Gideon's lifetime. 29He returned home, 30and eventually had seventy sons, for he married many wives. 31He also had a concubine in Shechem, who presented him with a son named Abimelech. 32Gideon finally died, an old, old man, and was buried in the sepulcher of his father Joash in Ophrah, in the land of the Abiezrites.

33But as soon as Gideon was dead, the Israelis began to worship the idols Baal and Baal-berith. 34They no longer considered the Lord as their God, though he had rescued them from all their enemies on every side. 35Nor did they show any kindness to the family of Gideon despite all he had done for them.

9 ONE DAY Gideon's son Abimelech visited his uncles—his mother's brothers—in Shechem.

2"Go and talk to the leaders of Shechem," he requested, "and ask them whether they want to be ruled by seventy kings—Gideon's seventy sons—or by one man—meaning me, your own flesh and blood!"d

3So his uncles went to the leaders of the city and proposed Abimelech's scheme; and they decided that since his mother was a native of their town they would go along with it. 4They gave him money from the temple offerings of the idol Baal-berith, which he used to hire some worthless loafers who agreed to do whatever he told them to. 5He took them to his father's home at Ophrah and there, upon one stone, they slaughtered all seventy of his half-brothers, except for the youngest, Jotham, who escaped and hid. 6Then the citizens of Shechem and Beth-millo called a meeting under the oak beside the garrison at Shechem, and Abimelech was acclaimed king of Israel.

New Revised Standard

Gideon's Idolatry

22 Then the Israelites said to Gideon, "Rule over us, you and your son and your grandson also; for you have delivered us out of the hand of Midian." 23Gideon said to them, "I will not rule over you, and my son will not rule over you; the LORD will rule over you." 24Then Gideon said to them, "Let me make a request of you; each of you give me an earring he has taken as booty." (For the enemye had golden earrings, because they were Ishmaelites.) 25"We will willingly give them," they answered. So they spread a garment, and each threw into it an earring he had taken as booty. 26The weight of the golden earrings that he requested was one thousand seven hundred shekels of gold (apart from the crescents and the pendants and the purple garments worn by the kings of Midian, and the collars that were on the necks of their camels). 27Gideon made an ephod of it and put it in his town, in Ophrah; and all Israel prostituted themselves to it there, and it became a snare to Gideon and to his family. 28So Midian was subdued before the Israelites, and they lifted up their heads no more. So the land had rest forty years in the days of Gideon.

Death of Gideon

29 Jerubbaal son of Joash went to live in his own house. 30Now Gideon had seventy sons, his own offspring, for he had many wives. 31His concubine who was in Shechem also bore him a son, and he named him Abimelech. 32Then Gideon son of Joash died at a good old age, and was buried in the tomb of his father Joash at Ophrah of the Abiezrites.

33 As soon as Gideon died, the Israelites relapsed and prostituted themselves with the Baals, making Baal-berith their god. 34The Israelites did not remember the LORD their God, who had rescued them from the hand of all their enemies on every side; 35and they did not exhibit loyalty to the house of Jerubbaal (that is, Gideon) in return for all the good that he had done to Israel.

Abimelech Attempts to Establish a Monarchy

9 NOW ABIMELECH son of Jerubbaal went to Shechem to his mother's kinsfolk and said to them and to the whole clan of his mother's family, 2"Say in the hearing of all the lords of Shechem, 'Which is better for you, that all seventy of the sons of Jerubbaal rule over you, or that one rule over you?' Remember also that I am your bone and your flesh." 3So his mother's kinsfolk spoke all these words on his behalf in the hearing of all the lords of Shechem; and their hearts inclined to follow Abimelech, for they said, "He is our brother." 4They gave him seventy pieces of silver out of the temple of Baal-berith with which Abimelech hired worthless and reckless fellows, who followed him. 5He went to his father's house at Ophrah, and killed his brothers the sons of Jerubbaal, seventy men, on one stone; but Jotham, the youngest son of Jerubbaal, survived, for he hid himself. 6Then all the lords of Shechem and all Beth-millo came together, and they went and made Abimelech king, by the oak of the pillarf at Shechem.

---

c 8:27 The ephod was usually a linen pouch worn by the priests on their chests. In this case the ephod evidently was highly decorated with gold, and probably, because of its weight, hung upon a wall.   d 9:2 meaning me, your own flesh and blood. Of all Gideon's wives, only Abimelech's mother was from Shechem (8:30, 31), so Abimelech felt his close kinship there.

e Heb they   f Cn: Meaning of Heb uncertain

King James

7¶ And when they told *it* to Jotham, he went and stood in the top of mount Gerizim, and lifted up his voice, and cried, and said unto them, Hearken unto me, ye men of Shechem, that God may hearken unto you.

8The trees went forth *on a time* to anoint a king over them; and they said unto the olive tree, Reign thou over us.

9But the olive tree said unto them, Should I leave my fatness, wherewith by me they honour God and man, and go to be promoted over the trees?

10And the trees said to the fig tree, Come thou, *and* reign over us.

11But the fig tree said unto them, Should I forsake my sweetness, and my good fruit, and go to be promoted over the trees?

12Then said the trees unto the vine, Come thou, *and* reign over us.

13And the vine said unto them, Should I leave my wine, which cheereth God and man, and go to be promoted over the trees?

14Then said all the trees unto the bramble, Come thou, *and* reign over us.

15And the bramble said unto the trees, If in truth ye anoint me king over you, *then* come *and* put your trust in my shadow: and if not, let fire come out of the bramble, and devour the cedars of Lebanon.

16Now therefore, if ye have done truly and sincerely, in that ye have made Abimelech king, and if ye have dealt well with Jerubbaal and his house, and have done unto him according to the deserving of his hands;

17(For my father fought for you, and adventured his life far, and delivered you out of the hand of Midian:

18And ye are risen up against my father's house this day, and have slain his sons, threescore and ten persons, upon one stone, and have made Abimelech, the son of his maidservant, king over the men of Shechem, because he *is* your brother;)

19If ye then have dealt truly and sincerely with Jerubbaal and with his house this day, *then* rejoice ye in Abimelech, and let him also rejoice in you:

20But if not, let fire come out from Abimelech, and devour the men of Shechem, and the house of Millo; and let fire come out from the men of Shechem, and from the house of Millo, and devour Abimelech.

21And Jotham ran away, and fled, and went to Beer, and dwelt there, for fear of Abimelech his brother.

22¶ When Abimelech had reigned three years over Israel,

23Then God sent an evil spirit between Abimelech and the men of Shechem; and the men of Shechem dealt treacherously with Abimelech:

24That the cruelty *done* to the threescore and ten sons of Jerubbaal might come, and their blood be laid upon Abimelech their brother, which slew them; and upon the men of Shechem, which aided him in the killing of his brethren.

25And the men of Shechem set liers in wait for him in the top of the mountains, and they robbed all that came along that way by them: and it was told Abimelech.

26And Gaal the son of Ebed came with his brethren, and went over to Shechem: and the men of Shechem put their confidence in him.

27And they went out into the fields, and gathered their vineyards, and trode *the grapes,* and made merry, and went into the house of their god, and did eat and drink, and cursed Abimelech.

New International

7When Jotham was told about this, he climbed up on the top of Mount Gerizim and shouted to them, "Listen to me, citizens of Shechem, so that God may listen to you. 8One day the trees went out to anoint a king for themselves. They said to the olive tree, 'Be our king.'

9"But the olive tree answered, 'Should I give up my oil, by which both gods and men are honored, to hold sway over the trees?'

10"Next, the trees said to the fig tree, 'Come and be our king.'

11"But the fig tree replied, 'Should I give up my fruit, so good and sweet, to hold sway over the trees?'

12"Then the trees said to the vine, 'Come and be our king.'

13"But the vine answered, 'Should I give up my wine, which cheers both gods and men, to hold sway over the trees?'

14"Finally all the trees said to the thornbush, 'Come and be our king.'

15"The thornbush said to the trees, 'If you really want to anoint me king over you, come and take refuge in my shade; but if not, then let fire come out of the thornbush and consume the cedars of Lebanon!'

16"Now if you have acted honorably and in good faith when you made Abimelech king, and if you have been fair to Jerub-Baal and his family, and if you have treated him as he deserves— 17and to think that my father fought for you, risked his life to rescue you from the hand of Midian 18(but today you have revolted against my father's family, murdered his seventy sons on a single stone, and made Abimelech, the son of his slave girl, king over the citizens of Shechem because he is your brother)— 19if then you have acted honorably and in good faith toward Jerub-Baal and his family today, may Abimelech be your joy, and may you be his, too! 20But if you have not, let fire come out from Abimelech and consume you, citizens of Shechem and Beth Millo, and let fire come out from you, citizens of Shechem and Beth Millo, and consume Abimelech!"

21Then Jotham fled, escaping to Beer, and he lived there because he was afraid of his brother Abimelech.

22After Abimelech had governed Israel three years, 23God sent an evil spirit between Abimelech and the citizens of Shechem, who acted treacherously against Abimelech. 24God did this in order that the crime against Jerub-Baal's seventy sons, the shedding of their blood, might be avenged on their brother Abimelech and on the citizens of Shechem, who had helped him murder his brothers. 25In opposition to him these citizens of Shechem set men on the hilltops to ambush and rob everyone who passed by, and this was reported to Abimelech.

26Now Gaal son of Ebed moved with his brothers into Shechem, and its citizens put their confidence in him. 27After they had gone out into the fields and gathered the grapes and trodden them, they held a festival in the temple of their god. While they were eating and drinking, they cursed Abimelech. 28Then Gaal son of Ebed

Living Bible

7When Jotham heard about this, he stood at the top of Mount Gerizim and shouted across to the men of Shechem, "If you want God's blessing, listen to me! 8Once upon a time the trees decided to elect a king. First they asked the olive tree, 9but it refused.

" 'Should I quit producing the olive oil that blesses God and man, just to wave to and fro over the other trees?' it asked.

10"Then they said to the fig tree, 'You be our king!' 11"But the fig tree also refused. 'Should I quit producing sweetness and fruit just to lift my head above all the other trees?' it asked.

12"Then they said to the grapevine, 'You reign over us!'

13"But the grapevine replied, 'Shall I quit producing the wine that cheers both God and man, just to be mightier than all the other trees?'

14"Then all the trees finally turned to the thorn bush. 'You be our king!' they explained.

15"And the thorn bush replied, 'If you really want me, come and humble yourselves beneath my shade! If you refuse, let fire flame forth from me and burn down the great cedars of Lebanon!'

16"Now make sure that you have done the right thing in making Abimelech your king, that you have done right by Gideon and all of his descendants. 17For my father fought for you and risked his life and delivered you from the Midianites, 18yet you have revolted against him and killed his seventy sons upon one stone. And now you have chosen his slave girl's son, Abimelech, to be your king just because he is your relative. 19If you are sure that you have done right by Gideon and his descendants, then may you and Abimelech have a long and happy life together. 20But if you have not been fair to Gideon, then may Abimelech destroy the citizens of Shechem and Beth-millo; and may they destroy Abimelech!"

21Then Jotham escaped and lived in Beer for fear of his brother Abimelech. 22, 23Three years later God stirred up trouble between King Abimelech and the citizens of Shechem, and they revolted. 24In the events that followed, both Abimelech and the citizens of Shechem who aided him in butchering Gideon's seventy sons were given their just punishment for these murders. 25For the men of Shechem set an ambush for Abimelech along the trail at the top of the mountain. (While they were waiting for him to come along, they robbed everyone else who passed that way.) But someone warned Abimelech about their plot.

26At that time Gaal (the son of Ebed) moved to Shechem with his brothers, and he became one of the leading citizens. 27During the harvest feast at Shechem that year, held in the temple of the local god, the wine flowed freely and everyone began cursing Abimelech.

New Revised Standard

The Parable of the Trees

7   When it was told to Jotham, he went and stood on the top of Mount Gerizim, and cried aloud and said to them, "Listen to me, you lords of Shechem, so that God may listen to you.
8   The trees once went out
    to anoint a king over themselves.
So they said to the olive tree,
    'Reign over us.'
9   The olive tree answered them,
    'Shall I stop producing my rich oil
      by which gods and mortals are honored,
      and go to sway over the trees?'
10 Then the trees said to the fig tree,
    'You come and reign over us.'
11 But the fig tree answered them,
    'Shall I stop producing my sweetness
      and my delicious fruit,
      and go to sway over the trees?'
12 Then the trees said to the vine,
    'You come and reign over us.'
13 But the vine said to them,
    'Shall I stop producing my wine
      that cheers gods and mortals,
      and go to sway over the trees?'
14 So all the trees said to the bramble,
    'You come and reign over us.'
15 And the bramble said to the trees,
    'If in good faith you are anointing me king
      over you,
    then come and take refuge in my shade;
    but if not, let fire come out of the bramble
      and devour the cedars of Lebanon.'

16   "Now therefore, if you acted in good faith and honor when you made Abimelech king, and if you have dealt well with Jerubbaal and his house, and have done to him as his actions deserved— 17for my father fought for you, and risked his life, and rescued you from the hand of Midian; 18but you have risen up against my father's house this day, and have killed his sons, seventy men on one stone, and have made Abimelech, the son of his slave woman, king over the lords of Shechem, because he is your kinsman— 19if, I say, you have acted in good faith and honor with Jerubbaal and with his house this day, then rejoice in Abimelech, and let him also rejoice in you; 20but if not, let fire come out from Abimelech, and devour the lords of Shechem, and Beth-millo; and let fire come out from the lords of Shechem, and from Beth-millo, and devour Abimelech." 21Then Jotham ran away and fled, going to Beer, where he remained for fear of his brother Abimelech.

The Downfall of Abimelech

22   Abimelech ruled over Israel three years. 23But God sent an evil spirit between Abimelech and the lords of Shechem; and the lords of Shechem dealt treacherously with Abimelech. 24This happened so that the violence done to the seventy sons of Jerubbaal might be avengeda and their blood be laid on their brother Abimelech, who killed them, and on the lords of Shechem, who strengthened his hands to kill his brothers. 25So, out of hostility to him, the lords of Shechem set ambushes on the mountain tops. They robbed all who passed by them along that way; and it was reported to Abimelech.

26   When Gaal son of Ebed moved into Shechem with his kinsfolk, the lords of Shechem put confidence in him. 27They went out into the field and gathered the grapes from their vineyards, trod them, and celebrated. Then they went into the temple of their god, ate and drank, and ridiculed Abimelech. 28Gaal son of Ebed

---

a Heb *might come*

King James

28And Gaal the son of Ebed said, Who *is* Abimelech, and who *is* Shechem, that we should serve him? *is* not *he* the son of Jerubbaal? and Zebul his officer? serve the men of Hamor the father of Shechem: for why should we serve him?

29And would to God this people were under my hand! then would I remove Abimelech. And he said to Abimelech, Increase thine army, and come out.

30¶ And when Zebul the ruler of the city heard the words of Gaal the son of Ebed, his anger was kindled.

31And he sent messengers unto Abimelech privily, saying, Behold, Gaal the son of Ebed and his brethren be come to Shechem; and, behold, they fortify the city against thee.

32Now therefore up by night, thou and the people that *is* with thee, and lie in wait in the field:

33And it shall be, *that* in the morning, as soon as the sun is up, thou shalt rise early, and set upon the city: and, behold, *when* he and the people that *is* with him come out against thee, then mayest thou do to them as thou shalt find occasion.

34¶ And Abimelech rose up, and all the people that *were* with him, by night, and they laid wait against Shechem in four companies.

35And Gaal the son of Ebed went out, and stood in the entering of the gate of the city: and Abimelech rose up, and the people that *were* with him, from lying in wait.

36And when Gaal saw the people, he said to Zebul, Behold, there come people down from the top of the mountains. And Zebul said unto him, Thou seest the shadow of the mountains as *if they were* men.

37And Gaal spake again and said, See there come people down by the middle of the land, and another company come along by the plain of Meonenim.

38Then said Zebul unto him, Where *is* now thy mouth, wherewith thou saidst, Who *is* Abimelech, that we should serve him? *is* not this the people that thou hast despised? go out, I pray now, and fight with them.

39And Gaal went out before the men of Shechem, and fought with Abimelech.

40And Abimelech chased him, and he fled before him, and many were overthrown *and* wounded, *even* unto the entering of the gate.

41And Abimelech dwelt at Arumah: and Zebul thrust out Gaal and his brethren, that they should not dwell in Shechem.

42And it came to pass on the morrow, that the people went out into the field; and they told Abimelech.

43And he took the people, and divided them into three companies, and laid wait in the field, and looked, and, behold, the people *were* come forth out of the city; and he rose up against them, and smote them.

44And Abimelech, and the company that *was* with him, rushed forward, and stood in the entering of the gate of the city: and the two *other* companies ran upon all *the people* that *were* in the fields, and slew them.

45And Abimelech fought against the city all that day; and he took the city, and slew the people that *was* therein, and beat down the city, and sowed it with salt.

46¶ And when all the men of the tower of Shechem heard *that,* they entered into an hold of the house of the god Berith.

New International

said, "Who is Abimelech, and who is Shechem, that we should be subject to him? Isn't he Jerub-Baal's son, and isn't Zebul his deputy? Serve the men of Hamor, Shechem's father! Why should we serve Abimelech? 29If only this people were under my command! Then I would get rid of him. I would say to Abimelech, 'Call out your whole army!' "a

30When Zebul the governor of the city heard what Gaal son of Ebed said, he was very angry. 31Under cover he sent messengers to Abimelech, saying, "Gaal son of Ebed and his brothers have come to Shechem and are stirring up the city against you. 32Now then, during the night you and your men should come and lie in wait in the fields. 33In the morning at sunrise, advance against the city. When Gaal and his men come out against you, do whatever your hand finds to do."

34So Abimelech and all his troops set out by night and took up concealed positions near Shechem in four companies. 35Now Gaal son of Ebed had gone out and was standing at the entrance to the city gate just as Abimelech and his soldiers came out from their hiding place.

36When Gaal saw them, he said to Zebul, "Look, people are coming down from the tops of the mountains!"

Zebul replied, "You mistake the shadows of the mountains for men."

37But Gaal spoke up again: "Look, people are coming down from the center of the land, and a company is coming from the direction of the soothsayers' tree."

38Then Zebul said to him, "Where is your big talk now, you who said, 'Who is Abimelech that we should be subject to him?' Aren't these the men you ridiculed? Go out and fight them!"

39So Gaal ledb the citizens of Shechem and fought Abimelech. 40Abimelech chased him, and many fell wounded in the flight—all the way to the entrance to the gate. 41Abimelech stayed in Arumah, and Zebul drove Gaal and his brothers out of Shechem.

42The next day the people of Shechem went out to the fields, and this was reported to Abimelech. 43So he took his men, divided them into three companies and set an ambush in the fields. When he saw the people coming out of the city, he rose to attack them. 44Abimelech and the companies with him rushed forward to a position at the entrance to the city gate. Then two companies rushed upon those in the fields and struck them down. 45All that day Abimelech pressed his attack against the city until he had captured it and killed its people. Then he destroyed the city and scattered salt over it.

46On hearing this, the citizens in the tower of Shechem went into the stronghold of the temple of El-Berith. 47When Abimelech heard that they had assembled

---

a 29 Septuagint; Hebrew *him." Then he said to Abimelech, "Call out your whole army!"*   b 39 Or *Gaal went out in the sight of*

Living Bible

28"Who is Abimelech," Gaal shouted, "and why should he be our king? Why should we be his servants? He and his friend Zebul should be *our* servants. Down with Abimelech! 29Make me your king and you'll soon see what happens to Abimelech! I'll tell Abimelech, 'Get up an army and come on out and fight!' "

30But when Zebul, the mayor of the city, heard what Gaal was saying, he was furious. 31He sent messengers to Abimelech in Arumah telling him, "Gaal, son of Ebed, and his relatives have come to live in Shechem, and now they are arousing the city to rebellion against you. 32Come by night with an army and hide out in the fields; 33and in the morning, as soon as it is daylight, storm the city. When he and those who are with him come out against you, you can do with them as you wish!"

34So Abimelech and his men marched through the night and split into four groups, stationing themselves around the city. 35The next morning as Gaal sat at the city gates, discussing various issues with the local leaders, Abimelech and his men began their march upon the city.

36When Gaal saw them, he exclaimed to Zebul, "Look over at that mountain! Doesn't it look like people coming down?"

"No!" Zebul said. "You're just seeing shadows that look like men!"

37"No, look over there," Gaal said. "I'm sure I see people coming towards us. And look! There are others coming along the road past the oak of Meonenim!"

38Then Zebul turned on him triumphantly. "Now where is that big mouth of yours?" he demanded. "Who was it who said, 'Who is Abimelech, and why should he be our king?' The men you taunted and cursed are right outside the city! Go on out and fight!"

39So Gaal led the men of Shechem into the battle and fought with Abimelech, 40but was defeated, and many of the men of Shechem were left wounded all the way to the city gate. 41Abimelech was living at Arumah at this time, and Zebul drove Gaal and his relatives out of Shechem, and wouldn't let them live there any longer.

42The next day the men of Shechem went out to battle again. However, someone had told Abimelech about their plans, 43so he had divided his men into three groups hiding in the fields. And when the men of the city went out to attack, he and his men jumped up from their hiding places and began killing them. 44Abimelech stormed the city gate to keep the men of Shechem from getting back in, while his other two groups cut them down in the fields. 45The battle went on all day before Abimelech finally captured the city, killed its people, and leveled it to the ground. 46The people at the nearby town of Migdal saw what was happening and took refuge in the fort next to the temple of Baal-berith.

New Revised Standard

said, "Who is Abimelech, and who are we of Shechem, that we should serve him? Did not the son of Jerubbaal and Zebul his officer serve the men of Hamor father of Shechem? Why then should we serve him? 29If only this people were under my command! Then I would remove Abimelech; I would sayc to him, 'Increase your army, and come out.' "

30 When Zebul the ruler of the city heard the words of Gaal son of Ebed, his anger was kindled. 31He sent messengers to Abimelech at Arumah,d saying, "Look, Gaal son of Ebed and his kinsfolk have come to Shechem, and they are stirring upe the city against you. 32Now therefore, go by night, you and the troops that are with you, and lie in wait in the fields. 33Then early in the morning, as soon as the sun rises, get up and rush on the city; and when he and the troops that are with him come out against you, you may deal with them as best you can."

34 So Abimelech and all the troops with him got up by night and lay in wait against Shechem in four companies. 35When Gaal son of Ebed went out and stood in the entrance of the gate of the city, Abimelech and the troops with him rose from the ambush. 36And when Gaal saw them, he said to Zebul, "Look, people are coming down from the mountain tops!" And Zebul said to him, "The shadows on the mountains look like people to you." 37Gaal spoke again and said, "Look, people are coming down from Tabbur-erez, and one company is coming from the direction of Elon-meonenim."f 38Then Zebul said to him, "Where is your boastg now, you who said, 'Who is Abimelech, that we should serve him?' Are not these the troops you made light of? Go out now and fight with them." 39So Gaal went out at the head of the lords of Shechem, and fought with Abimelech. 40Abimelech chased him, and he fled before him. Many fell wounded, up to the entrance of the gate. 41So Abimelech resided at Arumah; and Zebul drove out Gaal and his kinsfolk, so that they could not live on at Shechem.

42 On the following day the people went out into the fields. When Abimelech was told, 43he took his troops and divided them into three companies, and lay in wait in the fields. When he looked and saw the people coming out of the city, he rose against them and killed them. 44Abimelech and the company that wash with him rushed forward and stood at the entrance of the gate of the city, while the two companies rushed on all who were in the fields and killed them. 45Abimelech fought against the city all that day; he took the city, and killed the people that were in it; and he razed the city and sowed it with salt.

46 When all the lords of the Tower of Shechem heard of it, they entered the stronghold of the temple of El-berith. 47Abimelech was told that all the lords of the

---

c Gk: Heb *and he said*   d Cn See 9.41. Heb *Tormah*   e Cn: Heb *are besieging*   f That is Diviners' Oak   g Heb *mouth*   h Vg and some Gk Mss: Heb *companies that were*

King James

47And it was told Abimelech, that all the men of the tower of Shechem were gathered together.

48And Abimelech gat him up to mount Zalmon, he and all the people that *were* with him; and Abimelech took an axe in his hand, and cut down a bough from the trees, and took it, and laid *it* on his shoulder, and said unto the people that *were* with him, What ye have seen me do, make haste, *and* do as I *have done*.

49And all the people likewise cut down every man his bough, and followed Abimelech, and put *them* to the hold, and set the hold on fire upon them; so that all the men of the tower of Shechem died also, about a thousand men and women.

50¶ Then went Abimelech to Thebez, and encamped against Thebez, and took it.

51But there was a strong tower within the city, and thither fled all the men and women, and all they of the city, and shut *it* to them, and gat them up to the top of the tower.

52And Abimelech came unto the tower, and fought against it, and went hard unto the door of the tower to burn it with fire.

53And a certain woman cast a piece of a millstone upon Abimelech's head, and all to brake his skull.

54Then he called hastily unto the young man his armourbearer, and said unto him, Draw thy sword, and slay me, that men say not of me, A woman slew him. And his young man thrust him through, and he died.

55And when the men of Israel saw that Abimelech was dead, they departed every man unto his place.

56¶ Thus God rendered the wickedness of Abimelech, which he did unto his father, in slaying his seventy brethren:

57And all the evil of the men of Shechem did God render upon their heads: and upon them came the curse of Jotham the son of Jerubbaal.

10 AND AFTER Abimelech there arose to defend Israel Tola the son of Puah, the son of Dodo, a man of Issachar; and he dwelt in Shamir in mount Ephraim.

2And he judged Israel twenty and three years, and died, and was buried in Shamir.

3¶ And after him arose Jair, a Gileadite, and judged Israel twenty and two years.

4And he had thirty sons that rode on thirty ass colts, and they had thirty cities, which are called Havoth-jair unto this day, which *are* in the land of Gilead.

5And Jair died, and was buried in Camon.

6¶ And the children of Israel did evil again in the sight of the LORD, and served Baalim, and Ashtaroth, and the gods of Syria, and the gods of Zidon, and the gods of Moab, and the gods of the children of Ammon, and the gods of the Philistines, and forsook the LORD, and served not him.

7And the anger of the LORD was hot against Israel, and he sold them into the hands of the Philistines, and into the hands of the children of Ammon.

8And that year they vexed and oppressed the children of Israel: eighteen years, all the children of Israel that *were* on the other side Jordan in the land of the Amorites, which *is* in Gilead.

9Moreover the children of Ammon passed over Jordan to fight also against Judah, and against Benjamin, and against the house of Ephraim; so that Israel was sore distressed.

10¶ And the children of Israel cried unto the LORD, saying, We have sinned against thee, both because we have forsaken our God, and also served Baalim.

New International

there, 48he and all his men went up Mount Zalmon. He took an ax and cut off some branches, which he lifted to his shoulders. He ordered the men with him, "Quick! Do what you have seen me do!" 49So all the men cut branches and followed Abimelech. They piled them against the stronghold and set it on fire over the people inside. So all the people in the tower of Shechem, about a thousand men and women, also died.

50Next Abimelech went to Thebez and besieged it and captured it. 51Inside the city, however, was a strong tower, to which all the men and women—all the people of the city—fled. They locked themselves in and climbed up on the tower roof. 52Abimelech went to the tower and stormed it. But as he approached the entrance to the tower to set it on fire, 53a woman dropped an upper millstone on his head and cracked his skull.

54Hurriedly he called to his armor-bearer, "Draw your sword and kill me, so that they can't say, 'A woman killed him.' " So his servant ran him through, and he died. 55When the Israelites saw that Abimelech was dead, they went home.

56Thus God repaid the wickedness that Abimelech had done to his father by murdering his seventy brothers. 57God also made the men of Shechem pay for all their wickedness. The curse of Jotham son of Jerub-Baal came on them.

Tola

10 AFTER THE time of Abimelech a man of Issachar, Tola son of Puah, the son of Dodo, rose to save Israel. He lived in Shamir, in the hill country of Ephraim. 2He led[a] Israel twenty-three years; then he died, and was buried in Shamir.

Jair

3He was followed by Jair of Gilead, who led Israel twenty-two years. 4He had thirty sons, who rode thirty donkeys. They controlled thirty towns in Gilead, which to this day are called Havvoth Jair.[b] 5When Jair died, he was buried in Kamon.

Jephthah

6Again the Israelites did evil in the eyes of the LORD. They served the Baals and the Ashtoreths, and the gods of Aram, the gods of Sidon, the gods of Moab, the gods of the Ammonites and the gods of the Philistines. And because the Israelites forsook the LORD and no longer served him, 7he became angry with them. He sold them into the hands of the Philistines and the Ammonites, 8who that year shattered and crushed them. For eighteen years they oppressed all the Israelites on the east side of the Jordan in Gilead, the land of the Amorites. 9The Ammonites also crossed the Jordan to fight against Judah, Benjamin and the house of Ephraim; and Israel was in great distress. 10Then the Israelites cried out to the LORD, "We have sinned against you, forsaking our God and serving the Baals."

---

[a] 2 Traditionally *judged*; also in verse 3　　[b] 4 Or *called the settlements of Jair*

Living Bible

^{47,48}When Abimelech learned of this, he led his forces to Mount Zalmon where he began chopping a bundle of firewood, and placed it upon his shoulder. "Do as I have done," he told his men. ⁴⁹So each of them quickly cut a bundle and carried it back to the town where, following Abimelech's example, the bundles were piled against the walls of the fort and set on fire. So all the people inside died, about a thousand men and women.

⁵⁰Abimelech next attacked the city of Thebez, and captured it. ⁵¹However, there was a fort inside the city and the entire population fled into it, barricaded the gates, and climbed to the top of the roof to watch. ⁵²But as Abimelech was preparing to burn it, ⁵³a woman on the roof threw down a millstone. It landed on Abimelech's head, crushing his skull.

⁵⁴"Kill me!" he groaned to his youthful armor bearer. "Never let it be said that a woman killed Abimelech!"

So the young man pierced him with his sword, and he died. ⁵⁵When his men saw that he was dead, they disbanded and returned to their homes. ^{56, 57}Thus God punished both Abimelech and the men of Shechem for their sin of murdering Gideon's seventy sons. So the curse of Jotham, Gideon's son, came true.

New Revised Standard

Tower of Shechem were gathered together. ⁴⁸So Abimelech went up to Mount Zalmon, he and all the troops that were with him. Abimelech took an ax in his hand, cut down a bundle of brushwood, and took it up and laid it on his shoulder. Then he said to the troops with him, "What you have seen me do, do quickly, as I have done." ⁴⁹So every one of the troops cut down a bundle and following Abimelech put it against the stronghold, and they set the stronghold on fire over them, so that all the people of the Tower of Shechem also died, about a thousand men and women.

⁵⁰ Then Abimelech went to Thebez, and encamped against Thebez, and took it. ⁵¹But there was a strong tower within the city, and all the men and women and all the lords of the city fled to it and shut themselves in; and they went to the roof of the tower. ⁵²Abimelech came to the tower, and fought against it, and came near to the entrance of the tower to burn it with fire. ⁵³But a certain woman threw an upper millstone on Abimelech's head, and crushed his skull. ⁵⁴Immediately he called to the young man who carried his armor and said to him, "Draw your sword and kill me, so people will not say about me, 'A woman killed him.'" So the young man thrust him through, and he died. ⁵⁵When the Israelites saw that Abimelech was dead, they all went home. ⁵⁶Thus God repaid Abimelech for the crime he committed against his father in killing his seventy brothers; ⁵⁷and God also made all the wickedness of the people of Shechem fall back on their heads, and on them came the curse of Jotham son of Jerubbaal.

Tola and Jair

10 AFTER ABIMELECH, Tola son of Puah son of Dodo, a man of Issachar, who lived at Shamir in the hill country of Ephraim, rose to deliver Israel. ²He judged Israel twenty-three years. Then he died, and was buried at Shamir.

³ After him came Jair the Gileadite, who judged Israel twenty-two years. ⁴He had thirty sons who rode on thirty donkeys; and they had thirty towns, which are in the land of Gilead, and are called Havvoth-jair to this day. ⁵Jair died, and was buried in Kamon.

Oppression by the Ammonites

⁶ The Israelites again did what was evil in the sight of the LORD, worshiping the Baals and the Astartes, the gods of Aram, the gods of Sidon, the gods of Moab, the gods of the Ammonites, and the gods of the Philistines. Thus they abandoned the LORD, and did not worship him. ⁷So the anger of the LORD was kindled against Israel, and he sold them into the hand of the Philistines and into the hand of the Ammonites, ⁸and they crushed and oppressed the Israelites that year. For eighteen years they oppressed all the Israelites that were beyond the Jordan in the land of the Amorites, which is in Gilead. ⁹The Ammonites also crossed the Jordan to fight against Judah and against Benjamin and against the house of Ephraim; so that Israel was greatly distressed.

¹⁰ So the Israelites cried to the LORD, saying, "We have sinned against you, because we have abandoned our God and have worshiped the Baals." ¹¹And the

10 AFTER ABIMELECH'S death, the next judge of Israel was Tola (son of Puah and grandson of Dodo). He was from the tribe of Issachar, but lived in the city of Shamir in the hill country of Ephraim. ²He was Israel's judge for twenty-three years. When he died, he was buried in Shamir, ³and was succeeded by Jair, a man from Gilead, who judged Israel for twenty-two years. ⁴His thirty sons rode around together on thirty donkeys, and they owned thirty cities in the land of Gilead which are still called "The Cities of Jair." ⁵When Jair died he was buried in Kamon.

⁶Then the people of Israel turned away from the Lord again, and worshiped the heathen gods Baal and Ashtaroth, and the gods of Syria, Sidon, Moab, Ammon and Philistia. Not only this, but they no longer worshiped Jehovah at all. ^{7, 8}This made Jehovah very angry with his people, so he immediately permitted the Philistines and the Ammonites to begin tormenting them. These attacks took place east of the Jordan River in the land of the Amorites (that is, in Gilead), ⁹and also in Judah, Benjamin, and Ephraim. For the Ammonites crossed the Jordan to attack the Israelis. This went on for eighteen years. ¹⁰Finally the Israelis turned to Jehovah again and begged him to save them.

"We have sinned against you and have forsaken you as our God and have worshiped idols," they confessed.

King James

11And the LORD said unto the children of Israel, *Did not I deliver you* from the Egyptians, and from the Amorites, from the children of Ammon, and from the Philistines?

12The Zidonians also, and the Amalekites, and the Maonites, did oppress you; and ye cried to me, and I delivered you out of their hand.

13Yet ye have forsaken me, and served other gods: wherefore I will deliver you no more.

14Go and cry unto the gods which ye have chosen; let them deliver you in the time of your tribulation.

15¶ And the children of Israel said unto the LORD, We have sinned: do thou unto us whatsoever seemeth good unto thee; deliver us only, we pray thee, this day.

16And they put away the strange gods from among them, and served the LORD: and his soul was grieved for the misery of Israel.

17Then the children of Ammon were gathered together, and encamped in Gilead. And the children of Israel assembled themselves together, and encamped in Mizpeh.

18And the people *and* princes of Gilead said one to another, What man *is he* that will begin to fight against the children of Ammon? he shall be head over all the inhabitants of Gilead.

11 NOW JEPHTHAH the Gileadite was a mighty man of valour, and he *was* the son of an harlot: and Gilead begat Jephthah.

2And Gilead's wife bare him sons; and his wife's sons grew up, and they thrust out Jephthah, and said unto him, Thou shalt not inherit in our father's house; for thou *art* the son of a strange woman.

3Then Jephthah fled from his brethren, and dwelt in the land of Tob: and there were gathered vain men to Jephthah, and went out with him.

4¶ And it came to pass in process of time, that the children of Ammon made war against Israel.

5And it was so, that when the children of Ammon made war against Israel, the elders of Gilead went to fetch Jephthah out of the land of Tob:

6And they said unto Jephthah, Come, and be our captain, that we may fight with the children of Ammon.

7And Jephthah said unto the elders of Gilead, Did not ye hate me, and expel me out of my father's house? and why are ye come unto me now when ye are in distress?

8And the elders of Gilead said unto Jephthah, Therefore we turn again to thee now, that thou mayest go with us, and fight against the children of Ammon, and be our head over all the inhabitants of Gilead.

9And Jephthah said unto the elders of Gilead, If ye bring me home again to fight against the children of Ammon, and the LORD deliver them before me, shall I be your head?

10And the elders of Gilead said unto Jephthah, The LORD be witness between us, if we do not so according to thy words.

11Then Jephthah went with the elders of Gilead, and the people made him head and captain over them: and Jephthah uttered all his words before the LORD in Mizpeh.

12¶ And Jephthah sent messengers unto the king of the children of Ammon, saying, What hast thou to do with me, that thou art come against me to fight in my land?

13And the king of the children of Ammon answered unto the messengers of Jephthah, Because Israel took away my land, when they came up out of Egypt, from Arnon even unto Jabbok, and unto Jordan: now therefore restore those *lands* again peaceably.

14And Jephthah sent messengers again unto the king of the children of Ammon:

New International

11The LORD replied, "When the Egyptians, the Amorites, the Ammonites, the Philistines, 12the Sidonians, the Amalekites and the Maonites[a] oppressed you and you cried to me for help, did I not save you from their hands? 13But you have forsaken me and served other gods, so I will no longer save you. 14Go and cry out to the gods you have chosen. Let them save you when you are in trouble!"

15But the Israelites said to the LORD, "We have sinned. Do with us whatever you think best, but please rescue us now." 16Then they got rid of the foreign gods among them and served the LORD. And he could bear Israel's misery no longer.

17When the Ammonites were called to arms and camped in Gilead, the Israelites assembled and camped at Mizpah. 18The leaders of the people of Gilead said to each other, "Whoever will launch the attack against the Ammonites will be the head of all those living in Gilead."

11 JEPHTHAH THE Gileadite was a mighty warrior. His father was Gilead; his mother was a prostitute. 2Gilead's wife also bore him sons, and when they were grown up, they drove Jephthah away. "You are not going to get any inheritance in our family," they said, "because you are the son of another woman." 3So Jephthah fled from his brothers and settled in the land of Tob, where a group of adventurers gathered around him and followed him.

4Some time later, when the Ammonites made war on Israel, 5the elders of Gilead went to get Jephthah from the land of Tob. 6"Come," they said, "be our commander, so we can fight the Ammonites."

7Jephthah said to them, "Didn't you hate me and drive me from my father's house? Why do you come to me now, when you're in trouble?"

8The elders of Gilead said to him, "Nevertheless, we are turning to you now; come with us to fight the Ammonites, and you will be our head over all who live in Gilead."

9Jephthah answered, "Suppose you take me back to fight the Ammonites and the LORD gives them to me— will I really be your head?"

10The elders of Gilead replied, "The LORD is our witness; we will certainly do as you say." 11So Jephthah went with the elders of Gilead, and the people made him head and commander over them. And he repeated all his words before the LORD in Mizpah.

12Then Jephthah sent messengers to the Ammonite king with the question: "What do you have against us that you have attacked our country?"

13The king of the Ammonites answered Jephthah's messengers, "When Israel came up out of Egypt, they took away my land from the Arnon to the Jabbok, all the way to the Jordan. Now give it back peaceably."

14Jephthah sent back messengers to the Ammonite king, 15saying:

---

a *12* Hebrew; some Septuagint manuscripts *Midianites*

Living Bible

11But the Lord replied, "Didn't I save you from the Egyptians, the Amorites, the Ammonites, the Philistines, 12the Sidonians, the Amalekites, and the Maonites? Has there ever been a time when you cried out to me that I haven't rescued you? 13Yet you continue to abandon me and to worship other gods. So go away; I won't save you any more. 14Go and cry to the new gods you have chosen! Let them save you in your hour of distress!"

15But they pleaded with him again and said, "We have sinned. Punish us in any way you think best, only save us once more from our enemies."

16Then they destroyed their foreign gods and worshiped only the Lord; and he was grieved by their misery. 17The armies of Ammon were mobilized in Gilead at that time, preparing to attack Israel's army at Mizpah.

18"Who will lead our forces against the Ammonites?" the leaders of Gilead asked each other. "Whoever volunteers shall be our king!"

11 NOW JEPHTHAH was a great warrior from the land of Gilead, but his mother was a prostitute. His father (whose name was Gilead) had several other sons by his legitimate wife, and when these half brothers grew up, they chased Jephthah out of the country.

"You son of a whore!" they said. "You'll not get any of our father's estate."

3So Jephthah fled from his father's home and lived in the land of Tob. Soon he had quite a band of malcontents as his followers, living off the land as bandits. 4It was about this time that the Ammonites began their war against Israel. 5The leaders of Gilead sent for Jephthah, 6begging him to come and lead their army against the Ammonites.

7But Jephthah said to them, "Why do you come to me when you hate me and have driven me out of my father's house? Why come now when you're in trouble?"

8"Because we need you," they replied. "If you will be our commander-in-chief against the Ammonites, we will make you the king of Gilead."

9"Sure!" Jephthah exclaimed. "Do you expect me to believe that?"

10"We swear it," they replied. "We promise with a solemn oath."

11So Jephthah accepted the commission and was made commander-in-chief and king. The contract was ratified before the Lord in Mizpah at a general assembly of all the people. 12Then Jephthah sent messengers to the king of Ammon, demanding to know why Israel was being attacked. 13The king of Ammon replied that the land belonged to the people of Ammon; it had been stolen from them, he said, when the Israelis came from Egypt; the whole territory from the Arnon River to the Jabbok and the Jordan was his, he claimed.

"Give us back our land peaceably," he demanded.

14, 15Jephthah replied, "Israel did not steal the land.

New Revised Standard

Lord said to the Israelites, "Did I not deliver youᵇ from the Egyptians and from the Amorites, from the Ammonites and from the Philistines? 12The Sidonians also, and the Amalekites, and the Maonites, oppressed you; and you cried to me, and I delivered you out of their hand. 13 Yet you have abandoned me and worshiped other gods; therefore I will deliver you no more. 14Go and cry to the gods whom you have chosen; let them deliver you in the time of your distress." 15And the Israelites said to the Lord, "We have sinned; do to us whatever seems good to you; but deliver us this day!" 16So they put away the foreign gods from among them and worshiped the Lord; and he could no longer bear to see Israel suffer.

17 Then the Ammonites were called to arms, and they encamped in Gilead; and the Israelites came together, and they encamped at Mizpah. 18The commanders of the people of Gilead said to one another, "Who will begin the fight against the Ammonites? He shall be head over all the inhabitants of Gilead."

Jephthah

11 NOW JEPHTHAH the Gileadite, the son of a prostitute, was a mighty warrior. Gilead was the father of Jephthah. 2Gilead's wife also bore him sons; and when his wife's sons grew up, they drove Jephthah away, saying to him, "You shall not inherit anything in our father's house; for you are the son of another woman." 3Then Jephthah fled from his brothers and lived in the land of Tob. Outlaws collected around Jephthah and went raiding with him.

4 After a time the Ammonites made war against Israel. 5And when the Ammonites made war against Israel, the elders of Gilead went to bring Jephthah from the land of Tob. 6They said to Jephthah, "Come and be our commander, so that we may fight with the Ammonites." 7But Jephthah said to the elders of Gilead, "Are you not the very ones who rejected me and drove me out of my father's house? So why do you come to me now when you are in trouble?" 8The elders of Gilead said to Jephthah, "Nevertheless, we have now turned back to you, so that you may go with us and fight with the Ammonites, and become head over us, over all the inhabitants of Gilead." 9Jephthah said to the elders of Gilead, "If you bring me home again to fight with the Ammonites, and the Lord gives them over to me, I will be your head." 10And the elders of Gilead said to Jephthah, "The Lord will be witness between us; we will surely do as you say." 11So Jephthah went with the elders of Gilead, and the people made him head and commander over them; and Jephthah spoke all his words before the Lord at Mizpah.

12 Then Jephthah sent messengers to the king of the Ammonites and said, "What is there between you and me, that you have come to me to fight against my land?" 13The king of the Ammonites answered the messengers of Jephthah, "Because Israel, on coming from Egypt, took away my land from the Arnon to the Jabbok and to the Jordan; now therefore restore it peaceably." 14Once again Jephthah sent messengers to the king of the Ammonites 15and said to him: "Thus says Jephthah:

ᵇ Heb lacks *Did I not deliver you*

King James

15And said unto him, Thus saith Jephthah, Israel took not away the land of Moab, nor the land of the children of Ammon:

16But when Israel came up from Egypt, and walked through the wilderness unto the Red sea, and came to Kadesh;

17Then Israel sent messengers unto the king of Edom, saying, Let me, I pray thee, pass through thy land: but the king of Edom would not hearken *thereto.* And in like manner they sent unto the king of Moab: but he would not *consent:* and Israel abode in Kadesh.

18Then they went along through the wilderness, and compassed the land of Edom, and the land of Moab, and came by the east side of the land of Moab, and pitched on the other side of Arnon, but came not within the border of Moab: for Arnon *was* the border of Moab.

19And Israel sent messengers unto Sihon king of the Amorites, the king of Heshbon; and Israel said unto him, Let us pass, we pray thee, through thy land into my place.

20But Sihon trusted not Israel to pass through his coast: but Sihon gathered all his people together, and pitched in Jahaz, and fought against Israel.

21And the LORD God of Israel delivered Sihon and all his people into the hand of Israel, and they smote them: so Israel possessed all the land of the Amorites, the inhabitants of that country.

22And they possessed all the coasts of the Amorites, from Arnon even unto Jabbok, and from the wilderness even unto Jordan.

23So now the LORD God of Israel hath dispossessed the Amorites from before his people Israel, and shouldest thou possess it?

24Wilt not thou possess that which Chemosh thy god giveth thee to possess? So whomsoever the LORD our God shall drive out from before us, them will we possess.

25And now *art* thou any thing better than Balak the son of Zippor, king of Moab? did he ever strive against Israel, or did he ever fight against them,

26While Israel dwelt in Heshbon and her towns, and in Aroer and her towns, and in all the cities that *be* along by the coasts of Arnon, three hundred years? why therefore did ye not recover *them* within that time?

27Wherefore I have not sinned against thee, but thou doest me wrong to war against me: the LORD the Judge be judge this day between the children of Israel and the children of Ammon.

28Howbeit the king of the children of Ammon hearkened not unto the words of Jephthah which he sent him.

29¶ Then the spirit of the LORD came upon Jephthah, and he passed over Gilead, and Manasseh, and passed over Mizpeh of Gilead, and from Mizpeh of Gilead he passed over *unto* the children of Ammon.

30And Jephthah vowed a vow unto the LORD, and said, If thou shalt without fail deliver the children of Ammon into mine hands,

31Then it shall be, that whatsoever cometh forth of the doors of my house to meet me, when I return in peace from the children of Ammon, shall surely be the LORD's, and I will offer it up for a burnt offering.

32¶ So Jephthah passed over unto the children of Ammon to fight against them; and the LORD delivered them into his hands.

33And he smote them from Aroer, even till thou come to Minnith, *even* twenty cities, and unto the plain of the vineyards, with a very great slaughter. Thus the children of Ammon were subdued before the children of Israel.

34¶ And Jephthah came to Mizpeh unto his house, and, behold, his daughter came out to meet him with timbrels and with dances: and she *was his* only child; beside her he had neither son nor daughter.

New International

"This is what Jephthah says: Israel did not take the land of Moab or the land of the Ammonites. 16But when they came up out of Egypt, Israel went through the desert to the Red Sea[a] and on to Kadesh. 17Then Israel sent messengers to the king of Edom, saying, 'Give us permission to go through your country,' but the king of Edom would not listen. They sent also to the king of Moab, and he refused. So Israel stayed at Kadesh.

18"Next they traveled through the desert, skirted the lands of Edom and Moab, passed along the eastern side of the country of Moab, and camped on the other side of the Arnon. They did not enter the territory of Moab, for the Arnon was its border.

19"Then Israel sent messengers to Sihon king of the Amorites, who ruled in Heshbon, and said to him, 'Let us pass through your country to our own place.' 20Sihon, however, did not trust Israel[b] to pass through his territory. He mustered all his men and encamped at Jahaz and fought with Israel.

21"Then the LORD, the God of Israel, gave Sihon and all his men into Israel's hands, and they defeated them. Israel took over all the land of the Amorites who lived in that country, 22capturing all of it from the Arnon to the Jabbok and from the desert to the Jordan.

23"Now since the LORD, the God of Israel, has driven the Amorites out before his people Israel, what right have you to take it over? 24Will you not take what your god Chemosh gives you? Likewise, whatever the LORD our God has given us, we will possess. 25Are you better than Balak son of Zippor, king of Moab? Did he ever quarrel with Israel or fight with them? 26For three hundred years Israel occupied Heshbon, Aroer, the surrounding settlements and all the towns along the Arnon. Why didn't you retake them during that time? 27I have not wronged you, but you are doing me wrong by waging war against me. Let the LORD, the Judge,[c] decide the dispute this day between the Israelites and the Ammonites."

28The king of Ammon, however, paid no attention to the message Jephthah sent him.

29Then the Spirit of the LORD came upon Jephthah. He crossed Gilead and Manasseh, passed through Mizpah of Gilead, and from there he advanced against the Ammonites. 30And Jephthah made a vow to the LORD: "If you give the Ammonites into my hands, 31whatever comes out of the door of my house to meet me when I return in triumph from the Ammonites will be the LORD's, and I will sacrifice it as a burnt offering."

32Then Jephthah went over to fight the Ammonites, and the LORD gave them into his hands. 33He devastated twenty towns from Aroer to the vicinity of Minnith, as far as Abel Keramim. Thus Israel subdued Ammon.

34When Jephthah returned to his home in Mizpah, who should come out to meet him but his daughter, dancing to the sound of tambourines! She was an only child. Except for her he had neither son nor daughter.

Living Bible

16What happened was this: When the people of Israel arrived at Kadesh, on their journey from Egypt after crossing the Red Sea, 17they sent a message to the king of Edom asking permission to pass through his land. But their petition was denied. Then they asked the king of Moab for similar permission. It was the same story there, so the people of Israel stayed in Kadesh.

18"Finally they went around Edom and Moab through the wilderness, and traveled along the eastern border until at last they arrived beyond the boundary of Moab at the Arnon River; but they never once crossed into Moab. 19Then Israel sent messengers to King Sihon of the Amorites, who lived in Heshbon, and asked permission to cross through his land to get to their destination.

20"But King Sihon didn't trust Israel, so he mobilized an army at Jahaz and attacked them. 21, 22But the Lord our God helped Israel defeat King Sihon and all your people, so Israel took over all of your land from the Arnon River to the Jabbok, and from the wilderness to the Jordan River.

23"So you see, it was the Lord God of Israel who took away the land from the Amorites and gave it to Israel. Why, then, should we return it to you? 24You keep whatever your god Chemosh gives you, and we will keep whatever Jehovah our God gives us! 25And besides, just who do you think you are? Are you better than King Balak, the king of Moab? Did he try to recover his land after Israel defeated him? No, of course not. 26But now after three hundred years you make an issue of this! Israel has been living here for all that time, spread across the land from Heshbon to Aroer, and all along the Arnon River. Why have you made no effort to recover it before now? 27No, I have not sinned against you; rather, you have wronged me by coming to war against me; but Jehovah the Judge will soon show which of us is right—Israel or Ammon."

28But the king of Ammon paid no attention to Jephthah's message.

29At that time the Spirit of the Lord came upon Jephthah and he led his army across the land of Gilead and Manasseh, past Mizpah in Gilead, and attacked the army of Ammon. 30, 31Meanwhile Jephthah had vowed to the Lord that if God would help Israel conquer the Ammonites, then when he returned home in peace, the first person coming out of his house to meet him would be sacrificed as a burnt offering to the Lord!

32So Jephthah led his army against the Ammonites, and the Lord gave him the victory. 33He destroyed the Ammonites with a terrible slaughter all the way from Aroer to Minnith, including twenty cities, and as far away as Vineyard Meadow. Thus the Ammonites were subdued by the people of Israel.

34When Jephthah returned home his daughter—his only child—ran out to meet him, playing on a tambou-

New Revised Standard

Israel did not take away the land of Moab or the land of the Ammonites, 16but when they came up from Egypt, Israel went through the wilderness to the Red Sea[d] and came to Kadesh. 17Israel then sent messengers to the king of Edom, saying, 'Let us pass through your land'; but the king of Edom would not listen. They also sent to the king of Moab, but he would not consent. So Israel remained at Kadesh. 18Then they journeyed through the wilderness, went around the land of Edom and the land of Moab, arrived on the east side of the land of Moab, and camped on the other side of the Arnon. They did not enter the territory of Moab, for the Arnon was the boundary of Moab. 19Israel then sent messengers to King Sihon of the Amorites, king of Heshbon; and Israel said to him, 'Let us pass through your land to our country.' 20But Sihon did not trust Israel to pass through his territory; so Sihon gathered all his people together, and encamped at Jahaz, and fought with Israel. 21Then the LORD, the God of Israel, gave Sihon and all his people into the hand of Israel, and they defeated them; so Israel occupied all the land of the Amorites, who inhabited that country. 22They occupied all the territory of the Amorites from the Arnon to the Jabbok and from the wilderness to the Jordan. 23So now the LORD, the God of Israel, has conquered the Amorites for the benefit of his people Israel. Do you intend to take their place? 24Should you not possess what your god Chemosh gives you to possess? And should we not be the ones to possess everything that the LORD our God has conquered for our benefit? 25Now are you any better than King Balak son of Zippor of Moab? Did he ever enter into conflict with Israel, or did he ever go to war with them? 26While Israel lived in Heshbon and its villages, and in Aroer and its villages, and in all the towns that are along the Arnon, three hundred years, why did you not recover them within that time? 27It is not I who have sinned against you, but you are the one who does me wrong by making war on me. Let the LORD, who is judge, decide today for the Israelites or for the Ammonites." 28But the king of the Ammonites did not heed the message that Jephthah sent him.

Jephthah's Vow

29 Then the spirit of the LORD came upon Jephthah, and he passed through Gilead and Manasseh. He passed on to Mizpah of Gilead, and from Mizpah of Gilead he passed on to the Ammonites. 30And Jephthah made a vow to the LORD, and said, "If you will give the Ammonites into my hand, 31then whoever comes out of the doors of my house to meet me, when I return victorious from the Ammonites, shall be the LORD's, to be offered up by me as a burnt offering." 32So Jephthah crossed over to the Ammonites to fight against them; and the LORD gave them into his hand. 33He inflicted a massive defeat on them from Aroer to the neighborhood of Minnith, twenty towns, and as far as Abel-keramim. So the Ammonites were subdued before the people of Israel.

Jephthah's Daughter

34 Then Jephthah came to his home at Mizpah; and there was his daughter coming out to meet him with timbrels and with dancing. She was his only child; he had no son or daughter except her. 35When he saw her,

d Or Sea of Reeds

King James

35And it came to pass, when he saw her, that he rent his clothes, and said, Alas, my daughter! thou hast brought me very low, and thou art one of them that trouble me: for I have opened my mouth unto the LORD, and I cannot go back.

36And she said unto him, My father, *if* thou hast opened thy mouth unto the LORD, do to me according to that which hath proceeded out of thy mouth; forasmuch as the LORD hath taken vengeance for thee of thine enemies, *even* of the children of Ammon.

37And she said unto her father, Let this thing be done for me: let me alone two months, that I may go up and down upon the mountains, and bewail my virginity, I and my fellows.

38And he said, Go. And he sent her away *for* two months: and she went with her companions, and bewailed her virginity upon the mountains.

39And it came to pass at the end of two months, that she returned unto her father, who did with her *according* to his vow which he had vowed: and she knew no man. And it was a custom in Israel,

40*That* the daughters of Israel went yearly to lament the daughter of Jephthah the Gileadite four days in a year.

12 AND THE men of Ephraim gathered themselves together, and went northward, and said unto Jephthah, Wherefore passedst thou over to fight against the children of Ammon, and didst not call us to go with thee? we will burn thine house upon thee with fire.

2And Jephthah said unto them, I and my people were at great strife with the children of Ammon; and when I called you, ye delivered me not out of their hands.

3And when I saw that ye delivered *me* not, I put my life in my hands, and passed over against the children of Ammon, and the LORD delivered them into my hand: wherefore then are ye come up unto me this day, to fight against me?

4Then Jephthah gathered together all the men of Gilead, and fought with Ephraim: and the men of Gilead smote Ephraim, because they said, Ye Gileadites *are* fugitives of Ephraim among the Ephraimites, *and* among the Manassites.

5And the Gileadites took the passages of Jordan before the Ephraimites: and it was *so,* that when those Ephraimites which were escaped said, Let me go over; that the men of Gilead said unto him, *Art* thou an Ephraimite? If he said, Nay;

6Then said they unto him, Say now Shibboleth: and he said Sibboleth: for he could not frame to pronounce *it* right. Then they took him, and slew him at the passages of Jordan: and there fell at that time of the Ephraimites forty and two thousand.

7And Jephthah judged Israel six years. Then died Jephthah the Gileadite, and was buried in *one of* the cities of Gilead.

8¶ And after him Ibzan of Bethlehem judged Israel.

9And he had thirty sons, and thirty daughters, *whom* he sent abroad, and took in thirty daughters from abroad for his sons. And he judged Israel seven years.

10Then died Ibzan, and was buried at Bethlehem.

11¶ And after him Elon, a Zebulonite, judged Israel; and he judged Israel ten years.

12And Elon the Zebulonite died, and was buried in Aijalon in the country of Zebulun.

13¶ And after him Abdon the son of Hillel, a Pirathonite, judged Israel.

14And he had forty sons and thirty nephews, that rode on threescore and ten ass colts: and he judged Israel eight years.

New International

35When he saw her, he tore his clothes and cried, "Oh! My daughter! You have made me miserable and wretched, because I have made a vow to the LORD that I cannot break."

36"My father," she replied, "you have given your word to the LORD. Do to me just as you promised, now that the LORD has avenged you of your enemies, the Ammonites. 37But grant me this one request," she said. "Give me two months to roam the hills and weep with my friends, because I will never marry."

38"You may go," he said. And he let her go for two months. She and the girls went into the hills and wept because she would never marry. 39After the two months, she returned to her father and he did to her as he had vowed. And she was a virgin.

From this comes the Israelite custom 40that each year the young women of Israel go out for four days to commemorate the daughter of Jephthah the Gileadite.

Jephthah and Ephraim

12 THE MEN of Ephraim called out their forces, crossed over to Zaphon and said to Jephthah, "Why did you go to fight the Ammonites without calling us to go with you? We're going to burn down your house over your head."

2Jephthah answered, "I and my people were engaged in a great struggle with the Ammonites, and although I called, you didn't save me out of their hands. 3When I saw that you wouldn't help, I took my life in my hands and crossed over to fight the Ammonites, and the LORD gave me the victory over them. Now why have you come up today to fight me?"

4Jephthah then called together the men of Gilead and fought against Ephraim. The Gileadites struck them down because the Ephraimites had said, "You Gileadites are renegades from Ephraim and Manasseh." 5The Gileadites captured the fords of the Jordan leading to Ephraim, and whenever a survivor of Ephraim said, "Let me cross over," the men of Gilead asked him, "Are you an Ephraimite?" If he replied, "No," 6they said, "All right, say 'Shibboleth.' " If he said, "Sibboleth," because he could not pronounce the word correctly, they seized him and killed him at the fords of the Jordan. Forty-two thousand Ephraimites were killed at that time.

7Jephthah led[a] Israel six years. Then Jephthah the Gileadite died, and was buried in a town in Gilead.

Ibzan, Elon and Abdon

8After him, Ibzan of Bethlehem led Israel. 9He had thirty sons and thirty daughters. He gave his daughters away in marriage to those outside his clan, and for his sons he brought in thirty young women as wives from outside his clan. Ibzan led Israel seven years. 10Then Ibzan died, and was buried in Bethlehem.

11After him, Elon the Zebulunite led Israel ten years. 12Then Elon died, and was buried in Aijalon in the land of Zebulun.

13After him, Abdon son of Hillel, from Pirathon, led Israel. 14He had forty sons and thirty grandsons, who rode on seventy donkeys. He led Israel eight years.

---

a 7 Traditionally *judged*; also in verses 8-14

Living Bible

rine and dancing for joy. 35When he saw her he tore his clothes in anguish.

"Alas, my daughter!" he cried out. "You have brought me to the dust. For I have made a vow to the Lord and I cannot take it back."

36And she said, "Father, you must do whatever you promised the Lord, for he has given you a great victory over your enemies, the Ammonites. 37But first let me go up into the hills and roam with my girl friends for two months, weeping because I'll never marry."

38"Yes," he said. "Go."

And so she did, bewailing her fate with her friends for two months. 39Then she returned to her father, who did as he had vowed. So she was never married.b And after that it became a custom in Israel, 40that the young girls went away for four days each year to lament the fate of Jephthah's daughter.

12 THEN THE tribe of Ephraim mobilized its army at Zaphon and sent this message to Jephthah: "Why didn't you call for us to help you fight against Ammon? We are going to burn down your house, with you in it!"

2"I summoned you, but you refused to come!" Jephthah retorted. "You failed to help us in our time of need, 3so I risked my life and went to battle without you, and the Lord helped me to conquer the enemy. Is that anything for you to fight us about?"

4Then Jephthah, furious at the taunt of Ephraim that the men of Gilead were mere outcastsc and the scum of the earth, mobilized his army and attacked the army of Ephraim. 5He captured the fords of the Jordan behind the army of Ephraim, and whenever a fugitive from Ephraim tried to cross the river, the Gilead guards challenged him.

"Are you a member of the tribe of Ephraim?" they asked. If the man replied that he was not, 6then they demanded, "Say 'Shibboleth.' " But if he couldn't pronounce the H and said, "Sibboleth" instead of "Shibboleth," he was dragged away and killed. So forty-two thousand people of Ephraim died there at that time.

7Jephthah was Israel's judge for six years. At his death he was buried in one of the cities of Gilead.

8The next judge was Ibzan, who lived in Bethlehem. 9, 10He had thirty sons and thirty daughters. He married his daughters to men outside his clan, and brought in thirty girls to marry his sons. He judged Israel for seven years before he died, and was buried at Bethlehem.

11, 12The next judge was Elon from Zebulun. He judged Israel for ten years and was buried at Aijalon in Zebulun.

13Next was Abdon (son of Hillel) from Pirathon. 14He had forty sons and thirty grandsons, who rode on seventy donkeys. He was Israel's judge for eight years.

New Revised Standard

he tore his clothes, and said, "Alas, my daughter! You have brought me very low; you have become the cause of great trouble to me. For I have opened my mouth to the LORD, and I cannot take back my vow." 36She said to him, "My father, if you have opened your mouth to the LORD, do to me according to what has gone out of your mouth, now that the LORD has given you vengeance against your enemies, the Ammonites." 37And she said to her father, "Let this thing be done for me: Grant me two months, so that I may go and wanderd on the mountains, and bewail my virginity, my companions and I." 38"Go," he said and sent her away for two months. So she departed, she and her companions, and bewailed her virginity on the mountains. 39At the end of two months, she returned to her father, who did with her according to the vow he had made. She had never slept with a man. So there arose an Israelite custom that 40for four days every year the daughters of Israel would go out to lament the daughter of Jephthah the Gileadite.

Intertribal Dissension

12 THE MEN of Ephraim were called to arms, and they crossed to Zaphon and said to Jephthah, "Why did you cross over to fight against the Ammonites, and did not call us to go with you? We will burn your house down over you!" 2Jephthah said to them, "My people and I were engaged in conflict with the Ammonites who oppressed use severely. But when I called you, you did not deliver me from their hand. 3When I saw that you would not deliver me, I took my life in my hand, and crossed over against the Ammonites, and the LORD gave them into my hand. Why then have you come up to me this day, to fight against me?" 4Then Jephthah gathered all the men of Gilead and fought with Ephraim; and the men of Gilead defeated Ephraim, because they said, "You are fugitives from Ephraim, you Gileadites—in the heart of Ephraim and Manasseh."f 5Then the Gileadites took the fords of the Jordan against the Ephraimites. Whenever one of the fugitives of Ephraim said, "Let me go over," the men of Gilead would say to him, "Are you an Ephraimite?" When he said, "No," 6they said to him, "Then say Shibboleth," and he said, "Sibboleth," for he could not pronounce it right. Then they seized him and killed him at the fords of the Jordan. Forty-two thousand of the Ephraimites fell at that time.

7 Jephthah judged Israel six years. Then Jephthah the Gileadite died, and was buried in his town in Gilead.g

Ibzan, Elon, and Abdon

8 After him Ibzan of Bethlehem judged Israel. 9He had thirty sons. He gave his thirty daughters in marriage outside his clan and brought in thirty young women from outside for his sons. He judged Israel seven years. 10Then Ibzan died, and was buried at Bethlehem.

11 After him Elon the Zebulunite judged Israel; and he judged Israel ten years. 12Then Elon the Zebulunite died, and was buried at Aijalon in the land of Zebulun.

13 After him Abdon son of Hillel the Pirathonite judged Israel. 14He had forty sons and thirty grandsons, who rode on seventy donkeys; he judged Israel eight years. 15Then Abdon son of Hillel the Pirathonite died,

---

b 11:39 So she was never married. It is not clear whether he killed her or satisfied his vow by consecrating her to perpetual virginity.   c 12:4 the men of Gilead were mere outcasts, literally, "fugitives of Ephraim . . ."

d Cn: Heb go down   e Gk OL, Syr H: Heb lacks who oppressed us   f Meaning of Heb uncertain: Gk omits because . . . Manasseh   g Gk: Heb in the towns of Gilead

King James

15And Abdon the son of Hillel the Pirathonite died, and was buried in Pirathon in the land of Ephraim, in the mount of the Amalekites.

13 AND THE children of Israel did evil again in the sight of the LORD; and the LORD delivered them into the hand of the Philistines forty years.

2¶ And there was a certain man of Zorah, of the family of the Danites, whose name was Manoah; and his wife was barren, and bare not.

3And the angel of the LORD appeared unto the woman, and said unto her, Behold now, thou art barren, and bearest not: but thou shalt conceive, and bear a son.

4Now therefore beware, I pray thee, and drink not wine nor strong drink, and eat not any unclean thing:

5For, lo, thou shalt conceive, and bear a son; and no razor shall come on his head: for the child shall be a Nazarite unto God from the womb: and he shall begin to deliver Israel out of the hand of the Philistines.

6¶ Then the woman came and told her husband, saying, A man of God came unto me, and his countenance was like the countenance of an angel of God, very terrible: but I asked him not whence he was, neither told he me his name:

7But he said unto me, Behold, thou shalt conceive, and bear a son; and now drink no wine nor strong drink, neither eat any unclean thing: for the child shall be a Nazarite to God from the womb to the day of his death.

8¶ Then Manoah entreated the LORD, and said, O my Lord, let the man of God which thou didst send come again unto us, and teach us what we shall do unto the child that shall be born.

9And God hearkened to the voice of Manoah; and the angel of God came again unto the woman as she sat in the field: but Manoah her husband was not with her.

10And the woman made haste, and ran, and showed her husband, and said unto him, Behold, the man hath appeared unto me, that came unto me the other day.

11And Manoah arose, and went after his wife, and came to the man, and said unto him, Art thou the man that spakest unto the woman? And he said, I am.

12And Manoah said, Now let thy words come to pass. How shall we order the child, and how shall we do unto him?

13And the angel of the LORD said unto Manoah, Of all that I said unto the woman let her beware.

14She may not eat of any thing that cometh of the vine, neither let her drink wine or strong drink, nor eat any unclean thing: all that I commanded her let her observe.

15¶ And Manoah said unto the angel of the LORD, I pray thee, let us detain thee, until we shall have made ready a kid for thee.

16And the angel of the LORD said unto Manoah, Though thou detain me, I will not eat of thy bread: and if thou wilt offer a burnt offering, thou must offer it unto the LORD. For Manoah knew not that he was an angel of the LORD.

17And Manoah said unto the angel of the LORD, What is thy name, that when thy sayings come to pass we may do thee honour?

18And the angel of the LORD said unto him, Why askest thou thus after my name, seeing it is secret?

19So Manoah took a kid with a meat offering, and offered it upon a rock unto the LORD: and the angel did wondrously; and Manoah and his wife looked on.

20For it came to pass, when the flame went up toward heaven from off the altar, that the angel of the LORD ascended in the flame of the altar. And Manoah and his wife looked on it, and fell on their faces to the ground.

New International

15Then Abdon son of Hillel died, and was buried in Pirathon in Ephraim, in the hill country of the Amalekites.

The Birth of Samson

13 AGAIN THE Israelites did evil in the eyes of the LORD, so the LORD delivered them into the hands of the Philistines for forty years.

2A certain man of Zorah, named Manoah, from the clan of the Danites, had a wife who was sterile and remained childless. 3The angel of the LORD appeared to her and said, "You are sterile and childless, but you are going to conceive and have a son. 4Now see to it that you drink no wine or other fermented drink and that you do not eat anything unclean, 5because you will conceive and give birth to a son. No razor may be used on his head, because the boy is to be a Nazirite, set apart to God from birth, and he will begin the deliverance of Israel from the hands of the Philistines."

6Then the woman went to her husband and told him, "A man of God came to me. He looked like an angel of God, very awesome. I didn't ask him where he came from, and he didn't tell me his name. 7But he said to me, 'You will conceive and give birth to a son. Now then, drink no wine or other fermented drink and do not eat anything unclean, because the boy will be a Nazirite of God from birth until the day of his death.'"

8Then Manoah prayed to the LORD: "O Lord, I beg you, let the man of God you sent to us come again to teach us how to bring up the boy who is to be born."

9God heard Manoah, and the angel of God came again to the woman while she was out in the field; but her husband Manoah was not with her. 10The woman hurried to tell her husband, "He's here! The man who appeared to me the other day!"

11Manoah got up and followed his wife. When he came to the man, he said, "Are you the one who talked to my wife?"

"I am," he said.

12So Manoah asked him, "When your words are fulfilled, what is to be the rule for the boy's life and work?"

13The angel of the LORD answered, "Your wife must do all that I have told her. 14She must not eat anything that comes from the grapevine, nor drink any wine or other fermented drink nor eat anything unclean. She must do everything I have commanded her."

15Manoah said to the angel of the LORD, "We would like you to stay until we prepare a young goat for you."

16The angel of the LORD replied, "Even though you detain me, I will not eat any of your food. But if you prepare a burnt offering, offer it to the LORD." (Manoah did not realize that it was the angel of the LORD.)

17Then Manoah inquired of the angel of the LORD, "What is your name, so that we may honor you when your word comes true?"

18He replied, "Why do you ask my name? It is beyond understanding.a" 19Then Manoah took a young goat, together with the grain offering, and sacrificed it on a rock to the LORD. And the LORD did an amazing thing while Manoah and his wife watched: 20As the flame blazed up from the altar toward heaven, the angel of the LORD ascended in the flame. Seeing this, Manoah and his wife fell with their faces to the ground. 21When the

a 18 Or is wonderful

Living Bible

15Then he died and was buried in Pirathon, in Ephraim, in the hill country of the Amalekites.

13 ONCE AGAIN Israel sinned by worshiping other gods, so the Lord let them be conquered by the Philistines, who kept them in subjection for forty years.

2, 3Then one day the Angel of the Lord appeared to the wife of Manoah, of the tribe of Dan, who lived in the city of Zorah. She had no children, but the Angel said to her, "Even though you have been barren so long, you will soon conceive and have a son! 4Don't drink any wine or beer, and don't eat any food that isn't kosher. 5Your son's hair must never be cut, for he shall be a Nazirite, a special servant of God from the time of his birth; and he will begin to rescue Israel from the Philistines."

6The woman ran and told her husband, "A man from God appeared to me and I think he must be the Angel of the Lord, for he was almost too glorious to look at. I didn't ask where he was from, and he didn't tell me his name, 7but he told me, 'You are going to have a baby boy!' And he told me not to drink any wine or beer, and not to eat food that isn't kosher, for the baby is going to be a Nazirite—he will be dedicated to God from the moment of his birth until the day of his death!"

8Then Manoah prayed, "O Lord, please let the man from God come back to us again and give us more instructions about the child you are going to give us." 9The Lord answered his prayer, and the Angel of God appeared once again to his wife as she was sitting in the field. But again she was alone—Manoah was not with her— 10so she quickly ran and found her husband and told him, "The same man is here again!"

11Manoah ran back with his wife and asked, "Are you the man who talked to my wife the other day?"

"Yes," he replied, "I am."

12So Manoah asked him, "Can you give us any special instructions about how we should raise the baby after he is born?"

13, 14And the Angel replied, "Be sure that your wife follows the instructions I gave her. She must not eat grapes or raisins, or drink any wine or beer, or eat anything that isn't kosher."

15Then Manoah said to the Angel, "Please stay here until we can get you something to eat."

16"I'll stay," the Angel replied, "but I'll not eat anything. However, if you wish to bring something, bring an offering to sacrifice to the Lord." (Manoah didn't yet realize that he was the Angel of the Lord.)

17Then Manoah asked him for his name. "When all this comes true and the baby is born," he said to the Angel, "we will certainly want to tell everyone that you predicted it!"

18"Don't even ask my name," the Angel replied, "for it is a secret."

19Then Manoah took a young goat and a grain offering and offered it as a sacrifice to the Lord; and the Angel did a strange and wonderful thing, 20for as the flames from the altar were leaping up toward the sky, and as Manoah and his wife watched, the Angel ascended in the fire! Manoah and his wife fell face downward to the ground, 21and that was the last they ever saw of

New Revised Standard

and was buried at Pirathon in the land of Ephraim, in the hill country of the Amalekites.

The Birth of Samson

13 THE ISRAELITES again did what was evil in the sight of the LORD, and the LORD gave them into the hand of the Philistines forty years.

2 There was a certain man of Zorah, of the tribe of the Danites, whose name was Manoah. His wife was barren, having borne no children. 3And the angel of the LORD appeared to the woman and said to her, "Although you are barren, having borne no children, you shall conceive and bear a son. 4Now be careful not to drink wine or strong drink, or to eat anything unclean, 5for you shall conceive and bear a son. No razor is to come on his head, for the boy shall be a naziriteb to God from birth. It is he who shall begin to deliver Israel from the hand of the Philistines." 6Then the woman came and told her husband, "A man of God came to me, and his appearance was like that of an angelc of God, most awe-inspiring; I did not ask him where he came from, and he did not tell me his name; 7but he said to me, 'You shall conceive and bear a son. So then drink no wine or strong drink, and eat nothing unclean, for the boy shall be a naziriteb to God from birth to the day of his death.'"

8 Then Manoah entreated the LORD, and said, "O, LORD, I pray, let the man of God whom you sent come to us again and teach us what we are to do concerning the boy who will be born." 9God listened to Manoah, and the angel of God came again to the woman as she sat in the field; but her husband Manoah was not with her. 10So the woman ran quickly and told her husband, "The man who came to me the other day has appeared to me." 11Manoah got up and followed his wife, and came to the man and said to him, "Are you the man who spoke to this woman?" And he said, "I am." 12Then Manoah said, "Now when your words come true, what is to be the boy's rule of life; what is he to do?" 13The angel of the LORD said to Manoah, "Let the woman give heed to all that I said to her. 14She may not eat of anything that comes from the vine. She is not to drink wine or strong drink, or eat any unclean thing. She is to observe everything that I commanded her."

15 Manoah said to the angel of the LORD, "Allow us to detain you, and prepare a kid for you." 16The angel of the LORD said to Manoah, "If you detain me, I will not eat your food; but if you want to prepare a burnt offering, then offer it to the LORD." (For Manoah did not know that he was the angel of the LORD.) 17Then Manoah said to the angel of the LORD, "What is your name, so that we may honor you when your words come true?" 18But the angel of the LORD said to him, "Why do you ask my name? It is too wonderful."

19 So Manoah took the kid with the grain offering, and offered it on the rock to the LORD, to him who worksd wonders.e 20When the flame went up toward heaven from the altar, the angel of the LORD ascended in the flame of the altar while Manoah and his wife looked on; and they fell on their faces to the ground.

---

b That is one separated or one consecrated   c Or the angel   d Gk Vg: Heb and working   e Heb wonders, while Manoah and his wife looked on

King James

21But the angel of the LORD did no more appear to Manoah and to his wife. Then Manoah knew that he *was* an angel of the LORD.

22And Manoah said unto his wife, We shall surely die, because we have seen God.

23But his wife said unto him, If the LORD were pleased to kill us, he would not have received a burnt offering and a meat offering at our hands, neither would he have shown us all these *things,* nor would as at this time have told us *such things* as these.

24¶ And the woman bare a son, and called his name Samson: and the child grew, and the LORD blessed him.

25And the spirit of the LORD began to move him at times in the camp of Dan between Zorah and Eshtaol.

14 AND SAMSON went down to Timnath, and saw a woman in Timnath of the daughters of the Philistines.

2And he came up, and told his father and his mother, and said, I have seen a woman in Timnath of the daughters of the Philistines: now therefore get her for me to wife.

3Then his father and his mother said unto him, *Is there* never a woman among the daughters of thy brethren, or among all my people, that thou goest to take a wife of the uncircumcised Philistines? And Samson said unto his father, Get her for me; for she pleaseth me well.

4But his father and his mother knew not that it *was* of the LORD, that he sought an occasion against the Philistines: for at that time the Philistines had dominion over Israel.

5¶ Then went Samson down, and his father and his mother, to Timnath, and came to the vineyards of Timnath: and, behold, a young lion roared against him.

6And the spirit of the LORD came mightily upon him, and he rent him as he would have rent a kid, and *he had* nothing in his hand: but he told not his father or his mother what he had done.

7And he went down, and talked with the woman; and she pleased Samson well.

8¶ And after a time he returned to take her, and he turned aside to see the carcase of the lion: and, behold, *there was* a swarm of bees and honey in the carcase of the lion.

9And he took thereof in his hands, and went on eating, and came to his father and mother, and he gave them, and they did eat: but he told not them that he had taken the honey out of the carcase of the lion.

10¶ So his father went down unto the woman: and Samson made there a feast; for so used the young men to do.

11And it came to pass, when they saw him, that they brought thirty companions to be with him.

12¶ And Samson said unto them, I will now put forth a riddle unto you: if ye can certainly declare it me within the seven days of the feast, and find *it* out, then I will give you thirty sheets and thirty change of garments:

13But if ye cannot declare *it* me, then shall ye give me thirty sheets and thirty change of garments. And they said unto him, Put forth thy riddle, that we may hear it.

14And he said unto them, Out of the eater came forth meat, and out of the strong came forth sweetness. And they could not in three days expound the riddle.

15And it came to pass on the seventh day, that they said unto Samson's wife, Entice thy husband, that he may declare unto us the riddle, lest we burn thee and thy father's house with fire: have ye called us to take that we have? *is it* not *so?*

New International

angel of the LORD did not show himself again to Manoah and his wife, Manoah realized that it was the angel of the LORD.

22"We are doomed to die!" he said to his wife. "We have seen God!"

23But his wife answered, "If the LORD had meant to kill us, he would not have accepted a burnt offering and grain offering from our hands, nor shown us all these things or now told us this."

24The woman gave birth to a boy and named him Samson. He grew and the LORD blessed him, 25and the Spirit of the LORD began to stir him while he was in Mahaneh Dan, between Zorah and Eshtaol.

Samson's Marriage

14 SAMSON WENT down to Timnah and saw there a young Philistine woman. 2When he returned, he said to his father and mother, "I have seen a Philistine woman in Timnah; now get her for me as my wife."

3His father and mother replied, "Isn't there an acceptable woman among your relatives or among all our people? Must you go to the uncircumcised Philistines to get a wife?"

But Samson said to his father, "Get her for me. She's the right one for me." 4(His parents did not know that this was from the LORD, who was seeking an occasion to confront the Philistines; for at that time they were ruling over Israel.) 5Samson went down to Timnah together with his father and mother. As they approached the vineyards of Timnah, suddenly a young lion came roaring toward him. 6The Spirit of the LORD came upon him in power so that he tore the lion apart with his bare hands as he might have torn a young goat. But he told neither his father nor his mother what he had done. 7Then he went down and talked with the woman, and he liked her.

8Some time later, when he went back to marry her, he turned aside to look at the lion's carcass. In it was a swarm of bees and some honey, 9which he scooped out with his hands and ate as he went along. When he rejoined his parents, he gave them some, and they too ate it. But he did not tell them that he had taken the honey from the lion's carcass.

10Now his father went down to see the woman. And Samson made a feast there, as was customary for bridegrooms. 11When he appeared, he was given thirty companions.

12"Let me tell you a riddle," Samson said to them. "If you can give me the answer within the seven days of the feast, I will give you thirty linen garments and thirty sets of clothes. 13If you can't tell me the answer, you must give me thirty linen garments and thirty sets of clothes."

"Tell us your riddle," they said. "Let's hear it."

14He replied,

"Out of the eater, something to eat;
 out of the strong, something sweet."

For three days they could not give the answer.

15On the fourth[a] day, they said to Samson's wife, "Coax your husband into explaining the riddle for us, or we will burn you and your father's household to death. Did you invite us here to rob us?"

---

a 15 Some Septuagint manuscripts and Syriac; Hebrew *seventh*

Living Bible

him. It was then that Manoah finally realized that it had been the Angel of the Lord.

22"We will die," Manoah cried out to his wife, "for we have seen God!"

23But his wife said, "If the Lord were going to kill us he wouldn't have accepted our burnt offerings and wouldn't have appeared to us and told us this wonderful thing and done these miracles."

24When her son was born they named him Samson, and the Lord blessed him as he grew up. 25And the Spirit of the Lord began to excite him whenever he visited the parade grounds of the army of the tribe of Dan, located between the cities of Zorah and Eshta-ol.

14 ONE DAY when Samson was in Timnah, he noticed a certain Philistine girl, 2and when he got home he told his father and mother that he wanted to marry her. 3They objected strenuously.

"Why don't you marry a Jewish girl?" they asked. "Why must you go and get a wife from these heathen Philistines? Isn't there one girl among all the people of Israel you could marry?"

But Samson told his father, "She is the one I want. Get her for me."

4His father and mother didn't realize that the Lord was behind the request, for God was setting a trap for the Philistines, who at that time were the rulers of Israel.

5As Samson and his parents were going to Timnah, a young lion attacked Samson in the vineyards on the outskirts of the town. 6At that moment the Spirit of the Lord came mightily upon him and since he had no weapon, he ripped the lion's jaws apart, and did it as easily as though it were a young goat! But he didn't tell his father or mother about it. 7Upon arriving at Timnah he talked with the girl and found her to be just what he wanted, so the arrangements were made.b

8When he returned for the wedding, he turned off the path to look at the carcass of the lion. And he found a swarm of bees in it, and some honey! 9He took some of the honey with him, eating as he went, and gave some of it to his father and mother. But he didn't tell them where he had gotten it.

10, 11As his father was making final arrangements for the marriage, Samson threw a party for thirty young men of the village, as was the custom of the day. 12When Samson asked if they would like to hear a riddle, they replied that they would.

"If you solve my riddle during these seven days of the celebration," he said, "I'll give you thirty plain robes and thirty fancy robes. 13But if you can't solve it, then you must give the robes to me!"

"All right," they agreed, "let's hear it."

14This was his riddle: "Food came out of the eater, and sweetness from the strong!" Three days later they were still trying to figure it out.

15On the fourth day they said to his new wife, "Get the answer from your husband, or we'll burn down your father's house with you in it. Were we invited to this party just to make us poor?"

New Revised Standard

21The angel of the LORD did not appear again to Manoah and his wife. Then Manoah realized that it was the angel of the LORD. 22And Manoah said to his wife, "We shall surely die, for we have seen God." 23But his wife said to him, "If the LORD had meant to kill us, he would not have accepted a burnt offering and a grain offering at our hands, or shown us all these things, or now announced to us such things as these."

24 The woman bore a son, and named him Samson. The boy grew, and the LORD blessed him. 25The spirit of the LORD began to stir him in Mahaneh-dan, between Zorah and Eshtaol.

Samson's Marriage

14 ONCE SAMSON went down to Timnah, and at Timnah he saw a Philistine woman. 2Then he came up, and told his father and mother, "I saw a Philistine woman at Timnah; now get her for me as my wife." 3But his father and mother said to him, "Is there not a woman among your kin, or among all ourc people, that you must go to take a wife from the uncircumcised Philistines?" But Samson said to his father, "Get her for me, because she pleases me." 4His father and mother did not know that this was from the LORD; for he was seeking a pretext to act against the Philistines. At that time the Philistines had dominion over Israel.

5 Then Samson went down with his father and mother to Timnah. When he came to the vineyards of Timnah, suddenly a young lion roared at him. 6The spirit of the LORD rushed on him, and he tore the lion apart barehanded as one might tear apart a kid. But he did not tell his father or his mother what he had done. 7Then he went down and talked with the woman, and she pleased Samson. 8After a while he returned to marry her, and he turned aside to see the carcass of the lion, and there was a swarm of bees in the body of the lion, and honey. 9He scraped it out into his hands, and went on, eating as he went. When he came to his father and mother, he gave some to them, and they ate it. But he did not tell them that he had taken the honey from the carcass of the lion.

10 His father went down to the woman, and Samson made a feast there as the young men were accustomed to do. 11When the people saw him, they brought thirty companions to be with him. 12Samson said to them, "Let me now put a riddle to you. If you can explain it to me within the seven days of the feast, and find it out, then I will give you thirty linen garments and thirty festal garments. 13But if you cannot explain it to me, then you shall give me thirty linen garments and thirty festal garments." So they said to him, "Ask your riddle; let us hear it." 14He said to them,

"Out of the eater came something to eat.
Out of the strong came something sweet."

But for three days they could not explain the riddle.

15 On the fourthd day they said to Samson's wife, "Coax your husband to explain the riddle to us, or we will burn you and your father's house with fire. Have you invited us here to impoverish us?" 16So Samson's

---

b 14:7 *so the arrangements were made,* implied.   c Cn: Heb *my*   d Gk Syr: Heb *seventh*

King James

16And Samson's wife wept before him, and said, Thou dost but hate me, and lovest me not: thou hast put forth a riddle unto the children of my people, and hast not told *it* me. And he said unto her, Behold, I have not told *it* my father nor my mother, and shall I tell *it* thee?

17And she wept before him the seven days, while their feast lasted: and it came to pass on the seventh day, that he told her, because she lay sore upon him: and she told the riddle to the children of her people.

18And the men of the city said unto him on the seventh day before the sun went down, What *is* sweeter than honey? and what *is* stronger than a lion? And he said unto them, If ye had not plowed with my heifer, ye had not found out my riddle.

19¶ And the spirit of the LORD came upon him, and he went down to Ashkelon, and slew thirty men of them, and took their spoil, and gave change of garments unto them which expounded the riddle. And his anger was kindled, and he went up to his father's house.

20But Samson's wife was *given* to his companion, whom he had used as his friend.

15 BUT IT came to pass within a while after, in the time of wheat harvest, that Samson visited his wife with a kid; and he said, I will go in to my wife into the chamber. But her father would not suffer him to go in.

2And her father said, I verily thought that thou hadst utterly hated her; therefore I gave her to thy companion: *is* not her younger sister fairer than she? take her, I pray thee, instead of her.

3¶ And Samson said concerning them, Now shall I be more blameless than the Philistines, though I do them a displeasure.

4And Samson went and caught three hundred foxes, and took firebrands, and turned tail to tail, and put a firebrand in the midst between two tails.

5And when he had set the brands on fire, he let *them* go into the standing corn of the Philistines, and burnt up both the shocks, and also the standing corn, with the vineyards *and* olives.

6¶ Then the Philistines said, Who hath done this? And they answered, Samson, the son-in-law of the Timnite, because he had taken his wife, and given her to his companion. And the Philistines came up, and burnt her and her father with fire.

7¶ And Samson said unto them, Though ye have done this, yet will I be avenged of you, and after that I will cease.

8And he smote them hip and thigh with a great slaughter: and he went down and dwelt in the top of the rock Etam.

9¶ Then the Philistines went up, and pitched in Judah, and spread themselves in Lehi.

10And the men of Judah said, Why are ye come up against us? And they answered, To bind Samson are we come up, to do to him as he hath done to us.

11Then three thousand men of Judah went to the top of the rock Etam, and said to Samson, Knowest thou not that the Philistines *are* rulers over us? what *is* this *that* thou hast done unto us? And he said unto them, As they did unto me, so have I done unto them.

New International

16Then Samson's wife threw herself on him, sobbing, "You hate me! You don't really love me. You've given my people a riddle, but you haven't told me the answer."

"I haven't even explained it to my father or mother," he replied, "so why should I explain it to you?" 17She cried the whole seven days of the feast. So on the seventh day he finally told her, because she continued to press him. She in turn explained the riddle to her people.

18Before sunset on the seventh day the men of the town said to him,

"What is sweeter than honey?
    What is stronger than a lion?"

Samson said to them,

"If you had not plowed with my heifer,
    you would not have solved my riddle."

19Then the Spirit of the LORD came upon him in power. He went down to Ashkelon, struck down thirty of their men, stripped them of their belongings and gave their clothes to those who had explained the riddle. Burning with anger, he went up to his father's house. 20And Samson's wife was given to the friend who had attended him at his wedding.

Samson's Vengeance on the Philistines

15 LATER ON, at the time of wheat harvest, Samson took a young goat and went to visit his wife. He said, "I'm going to my wife's room." But her father would not let him go in.

2"I was so sure you thoroughly hated her," he said, "that I gave her to your friend. Isn't her younger sister more attractive? Take her instead."

3Samson said to them, "This time I have a right to get even with the Philistines; I will really harm them." 4So he went out and caught three hundred foxes and tied them tail to tail in pairs. He then fastened a torch to every pair of tails, 5lit the torches and let the foxes loose in the standing grain of the Philistines. He burned up the shocks and standing grain, together with the vineyards and olive groves.

6When the Philistines asked, "Who did this?" they were told, "Samson, the Timnite's son-in-law, because his wife was given to his friend."

So the Philistines went up and burned her and her father to death. 7Samson said to them, "Since you've acted like this, I won't stop until I get my revenge on you." 8He attacked them viciously and slaughtered many of them. Then he went down and stayed in a cave in the rock of Etam.

9The Philistines went up and camped in Judah, spreading out near Lehi. 10The men of Judah asked, "Why have you come to fight us?"

"We have come to take Samson prisoner," they answered, "to do to him as he did to us."

11Then three thousand men from Judah went down to the cave in the rock of Etam and said to Samson, "Don't you realize that the Philistines are rulers over us? What have you done to us?"

He answered, "I merely did to them what they did to me."

Living Bible

16So Samson's wife broke down in tears before him and said, "You don't love me at all; you hate me, for you have told a riddle to my people and haven't told me the answer!"

"I haven't even told it to my father or mother; why should I tell you?" he replied.

17So she cried whenever she was with him and kept it up for the remainder of the celebration. At last, on the seventh day, he told her the answer and she, of course, gave the answer to the young men. 18So before sunset of the seventh day they gave him their reply.

"What is sweeter than honey?" they asked, "and what is stronger than a lion?"

"If you hadn't plowed with my heifer, you wouldn't have found the answer to my riddle!" he retorted.

19Then the Spirit of the Lord came upon him and he went to the city of Ashkelon, killed thirty men, took their clothing, and gave it to the young men who had told him the answer to his riddle. But he was furious about it and abandoned his wife and went back home to live with his father and mother. 20So his wife was married instead to the fellow who had been best man at Samson's wedding.

15 LATER ON, during the wheat harvest, Samson took a young goat as a present to his wife, intending to sleep with her; but her father wouldn't let him in.

2"I really thought you hated her," he explained, "so I married her to your best man. But look, her sister is prettier than she is. Marry her instead."

3Samson was furious. "You can't blame me for whatever happens now," he shouted.

4So he went out and caught three hundred foxes and tied their tails together in pairs, with a torch between each pair. 5Then he lit the torches and let the foxes run through the fields of the Philistines, burning the grain to the ground along with all the sheaves and shocks of grain, and destroying the olive trees.

6"Who did this?" the Philistines demanded.

"Samson," was the reply, "because his wife's father gave her to another man." So the Philistines came and got the girl and her father and burned them alive.

7"Now my vengeance will strike again!" Samson vowed. 8So he attacked them with great fury and killed many of them. Then he went to live in a cave in the rock of Etam. 9The Philistines in turn sent a huge posse into Judah and raided Lehi.

10"Why have you come here?" the men of Judah asked.

And the Philistines replied, "To capture Samson and do to him as he has done to us."

11So three thousand men of Judah went down to get Samson at the cave in the rock of Etam.

"What are you doing to us?" they demanded of him. "Don't you realize that the Philistines are our rulers?"

But Samson replied, "I only paid them back for what they did to me.

New Revised Standard

wife wept before him, saying, "You hate me; you do not really love me. You have asked a riddle of my people, but you have not explained it to me." He said to her, "Look, I have not told my father or my mother. Why should I tell you?" 17She wept before him the seven days that their feast lasted; and because she nagged him, on the seventh day he told her. Then she explained the riddle to her people. 18The men of the town said to him on the seventh day before the sun went down,

"What is sweeter than honey?
    What is stronger than a lion?"
And he said to them,

"If you had not plowed with my heifer,
    you would not have found out my riddle."

19Then the spirit of the LORD rushed on him, and he went down to Ashkelon. He killed thirty men of the town, took their spoil, and gave the festal garments to those who had explained the riddle. In hot anger he went back to his father's house. 20And Samson's wife was given to his companion, who had been his best man.

Samson Defeats the Philistines

15 AFTER A while, at the time of the wheat harvest, Samson went to visit his wife, bringing along a kid. He said, "I want to go into my wife's room." But her father would not allow him to go in. 2Her father said, "I was sure that you had rejected her; so I gave her to your companion. Is not her younger sister prettier than she? Why not take her instead?" 3Samson said to them, "This time, when I do mischief to the Philistines, I will be without blame." 4So Samson went and caught three hundred foxes, and took some torches; and he turned the foxesa tail to tail, and put a torch between each pair of tails. 5When he had set fire to the torches, he let the foxes go into the standing grain of the Philistines, and burned up the shocks and the standing grain, as well as the vineyards andb olive groves. 6Then the Philistines asked, "Who has done this?" And they said, "Samson, the son-in-law of the Timnite, because he has taken Samson's wife and given her to his companion." So the Philistines came up, and burned her and her father. 7Samson said to them, "If this is what you do, I swear I will not stop until I have taken revenge on you." 8He struck them down hip and thigh with great slaughter; and he went down and stayed in the cleft of the rock of Etam.

9 Then the Philistines came up and encamped in Judah, and made a raid on Lehi. 10The men of Judah said, "Why have you come up against us?" They said, "We have come up to bind Samson, to do to him as he did to us." 11Then three thousand men of Judah went down to the cleft of the rock of Etam, and they said to Samson, "Do you not know that the Philistines are rulers over us? What then have you done to us?" He replied, "As they did to me, so I have done to them." 12They said

---

a Heb *them*   b Gk Tg Vg: Heb lacks *and*

King James

12And they said unto him, We are come down to bind thee, that we may deliver thee into the hand of the Philistines. And Samson said unto them, Swear unto me, that ye will not fall upon me yourselves.

13And they spake unto him, saying, No; but we will bind thee fast, and deliver thee into their hand: but surely we will not kill thee. And they bound him with two new cords, and brought him up from the rock.

14¶ And when he came unto Lehi, the Philistines shouted against him: and the spirit of the LORD came mightily upon him, and the cords that were upon his arms became as flax that was burnt with fire, and his bands loosed from off his hands.

15And he found a new jawbone of an ass, and put forth his hand, and took it, and slew a thousand men therewith.

16And Samson said, With the jawbone of an ass, heaps upon heaps, with the jaw of an ass have I slain a thousand men.

17And it came to pass, when he had made an end of speaking, that he cast away the jawbone out of his hand, and called that place Ramath-lehi.

18¶ And he was sore athirst, and called on the LORD, and said, Thou hast given this great deliverance into the hand of thy servant: and now shall I die for thirst, and fall into the hand of the uncircumcised?

19But God clave an hollow place that was in the jaw, and there came water thereout; and when he had drunk, his spirit came again, and he revived: wherefore he called the name thereof En-hakkore, which is in Lehi unto this day.

20And he judged Israel in the days of the Philistines twenty years.

16 THEN WENT Samson to Gaza, and saw there an harlot, and went in unto her.

2And it was told the Gazites, saying, Samson is come hither. And they compassed him in, and laid wait for him all night in the gate of the city, and were quiet all the night, saying, In the morning, when it is day, we shall kill him.

3And Samson lay till midnight, and arose at midnight, and took the doors of the gate of the city, and the two posts, and went away with them, bar and all, and put them upon his shoulders, and carried them up to the top of an hill that is before Hebron.

4¶ And it came to pass afterward, that he loved a woman in the valley of Sorek, whose name was Delilah.

5And the lords of the Philistines came up unto her, and said unto her, Entice him, and see wherein his great strength lieth, and by what means we may prevail against him, that we may bind him to afflict him: and we will give thee every one of us eleven hundred pieces of silver.

6¶ And Delilah said to Samson, Tell me, I pray thee, wherein thy great strength lieth, and wherewith thou mightest be bound to afflict thee.

7And Samson said unto her, If they bind me with seven green withs that were never dried, then shall I be weak, and be as another man.

8Then the lords of the Philistines brought up to her seven green withs which had not been dried, and she bound him with them.

9Now there were men lying in wait, abiding with her in the chamber. And she said unto him, The Philistines be upon thee, Samson. And he brake the withs, as a thread of tow is broken when it toucheth the fire. So his strength was not known.

New International

12They said to him, "We've come to tie you up and hand you over to the Philistines."

Samson said, "Swear to me that you won't kill me yourselves."

13"Agreed," they answered. "We will only tie you up and hand you over to them. We will not kill you." So they bound him with two new ropes and led him up from the rock. 14As he approached Lehi, the Philistines came toward him shouting. The Spirit of the LORD came upon him in power. The ropes on his arms became like charred flax, and the bindings dropped from his hands. 15Finding a fresh jawbone of a donkey, he grabbed it and struck down a thousand men.

16Then Samson said,

"With a donkey's jawbone
    I have made donkeys of them.a
With a donkey's jawbone
    I have killed a thousand men."

17When he finished speaking, he threw away the jawbone; and the place was called Ramath Lehi.b

18Because he was very thirsty, he cried out to the LORD, "You have given your servant this great victory. Must I now die of thirst and fall into the hands of the uncircumcised?" 19Then God opened up the hollow place in Lehi, and water came out of it. When Samson drank, his strength returned and he revived. So the spring was called En Hakkore,c and it is still there in Lehi.

20Samson ledd Israel for twenty years in the days of the Philistines.

Samson and Delilah

16 ONE DAY Samson went to Gaza, where he saw a prostitute. He went in to spend the night with her. 2The people of Gaza were told, "Samson is here!" So they surrounded the place and lay in wait for him all night at the city gate. They made no move during the night, saying, "At dawn we'll kill him."

3But Samson lay there only until the middle of the night. Then he got up and took hold of the doors of the city gate, together with the two posts, and tore them loose, bar and all. He lifted them to his shoulders and carried them to the top of the hill that faces Hebron.

4Some time later, he fell in love with a woman in the Valley of Sorek whose name was Delilah. 5The rulers of the Philistines went to her and said, "See if you can lure him into showing you the secret of his great strength and how we can overpower him so we may tie him up and subdue him. Each one of us will give you eleven hundred shekelse of silver."

6So Delilah said to Samson, "Tell me the secret of your great strength and how you can be tied up and subdued."

7Samson answered her, "If anyone ties me with seven fresh thongsf that have not been dried, I'll become as weak as any other man."

8Then the rulers of the Philistines brought her seven fresh thongs that had not been dried, and she tied him with them. 9With men hidden in the room, she called to him, "Samson, the Philistines are upon you!" But he snapped the thongs as easily as a piece of string snaps when it comes close to a flame. So the secret of his strength was not discovered.

a 16 Or made a heap or two; the Hebrew for donkey sounds like the Hebrew for heap.   b 17 Ramath Lehi means jawbone hill.   c 19 En Hakkore means caller's spring.   d 20 Traditionally judged   e 5 That is, about 28 pounds (about 13 kilograms)   f 7 Or bowstrings; also in verses 8 and 9

Living Bible

12, 13"We have come to capture you and take you to the Philistines," the men of Judah told him.

"All right," Samson said, "but promise me that you won't kill me yourselves."

"No," they replied, "we won't do that."

So they tied him with two new ropes and led him away. 14As Samson and his captors arrived at Lehi, the Philistines shouted with glee; but then the strength of the Lord came upon Samson, and the ropes with which he was tied snapped like thread and fell from his wrists! 15Then he picked up a donkey's jawbone that was lying on the ground and killed a thousand Philistines with it. 16, 17Tossing away the jawbone, he remarked,

"Heaps upon heaps,
    All with a donkey's jaw!
I've killed a thousand men,
    All with a donkey's jaw!"

(The place has been called "Jawbone Hill" ever since.)

18But now he was very thirsty and he prayed to the Lord and said, "You have given Israel such a wonderful deliverance through me today! Must I now die of thirst, and fall to the mercy of these heathen?" 19So the Lord caused water to gush out from a hollow in the ground and Samson's spirit was revived as he drank. Then he named the place "The Spring of the Man Who Prayed," and the spring is still there today.

20Samson was Israel's leader for the next twenty years, but the Philistines still controlled the land.

16

ONE DAY Samson went to the Philistine city of Gaza and spent the night with a prostitute. 2Word soon spread that he had been seen in the city, so the police were alerted and many men of the city lay in wait all night at the city gate to capture him if he tried to leave.

"In the morning," they thought, "when there is enough light, we'll find him and kill him."

3Samson stayed in bed with the girl until midnight, then went out to the city gates and lifted them, with the two gateposts, right out of the ground. He put them on his shoulders and carried them to the top of the mountain across from Hebron!

4Later on he fell in love with a girl named Delilah over in the valley of Sorek. 5The five heads of the Philistine nation went personally to her and demanded that she find out from Samson what made him so strong, so that they would know how to overpower and subdue him and put him in chains.

"Each of us will give you a thousand dollars for this job," they promised.

6So Delilah begged Samson to tell her his secret. "Please tell me, Samson, why you are so strong," she pleaded. "I don't think anyone could ever capture you!"

7"Well," Samson replied, "if I were tied with seven raw-leather bowstrings, I would become as weak as anyone else."

8So they brought her the seven bowstrings, and while he sleptg she tied them with them. 9Some men were hiding in the next room, so as soon as she had tied him up she exclaimed,

"Samson! The Philistines are here!"

Then he snapped the bowstrings like cotton thread,h and so his secret was not discovered.

New Revised Standard

to him, "We have come down to bind you, so that we may give you into the hands of the Philistines." Samson answered them, "Swear to me that you yourselves will not attack me." 13They said to him, "No, we will only bind you and give you into their hands; we will not kill you." So they bound him with two new ropes, and brought him up from the rock.

14 When he came to Lehi, the Philistines came shouting to meet him; and the spirit of the LORD rushed on him, and the ropes that were on his arms became like flax that has caught fire, and his bonds melted off his hands. 15Then he found a fresh jawbone of a donkey, reached down and took it, and with it he killed a thousand men. 16And Samson said,

"With the jawbone of a donkey,
    heaps upon heaps,
with the jawbone of a donkey
    I have slain a thousand men."

17When he had finished speaking, he threw away the jawbone; and that place was called Ramath-lehi.i

18 By then he was very thirsty, and he called on the LORD, saying, "You have granted this great victory by the hand of your servant. Am I now to die of thirst, and fall into the hands of the uncircumcised?" 19So God split open the hollow place that is at Lehi, and water came from it. When he drank, his spirit returned, and he revived. Therefore it was named En-hakkore,j which is at Lehi to this day. 20And he judged Israel in the days of the Philistines twenty years.

Samson and Delilah

16

ONCE SAMSON went to Gaza, where he saw a prostitute and went in to her. 2The Gazites were told,k "Samson has come here." So they circled around and lay in wait for him all night at the city gate. They kept quiet all night, thinking, "Let us wait until the light of the morning; then we will kill him." 3But Samson lay only until midnight. Then at midnight he rose up, took hold of the doors of the city gate and the two posts, pulled them up, bar and all, put them on his shoulders, and carried them to the top of the hill that is in front of Hebron.

4 After this he fell in love with a woman in the valley of Sorek, whose name was Delilah. 5The lords of the Philistines came to her and said to her, "Coax him, and find out what makes his strength so great, and how we may overpower him, so that we may bind him in order to subdue him; and we will each give you eleven hundred pieces of silver." 6So Delilah said to Samson, "Please tell me what makes your strength so great, and how you could be bound, so that one could subdue you." 7Samson said to her, "If they bind me with seven fresh bowstrings that are not dried out, then I shall become weak, and be like anyone else." 8Then the lords of the Philistines brought her seven fresh bowstrings that had not dried out, and she bound him with them. 9While men were lying in wait in an inner chamber, she said to him, "The Philistines are upon you, Samson!" But he snapped the bowstrings, as a strand of fiber snaps when it touches the fire. So the secret of his strength was not known.

---

g 16:8 and while he slept, implied in vs 14.   h 16:9 he snapped the bowstrings like cotton thread, literally, "like a string of tow snaps when it touches the fire."

i That is The Hill of the Jawbone   j That is The Spring of the One who Called   k Gk: Heb lacks were told

King James

10And Delilah said unto Samson, Behold, thou hast mocked me, and told me lies: now tell me, I pray thee, wherewith thou mightest be bound.

11And he said unto her, If they bind me fast with new ropes that never were occupied, then shall I be weak, and be as another man.

12Delilah therefore took new ropes, and bound him therewith, and said unto him, The Philistines *be* upon thee, Samson. And *there were* liers in wait abiding in the chamber. And he brake them from off his arms like a thread.

13And Delilah said unto Samson, Hitherto thou hast mocked me, and told me lies: tell me wherewith thou mightest be bound. And he said unto her, If thou weavest the seven locks of my head with the web.

14And she fastened *it* with the pin, and said unto him, The Philistines *be* upon thee, Samson. And he awaked out of his sleep, and went away with the pin of the beam, and with the web.

15¶ And she said unto him, How canst thou say, I love thee, when thine heart *is* not with me? thou hast mocked me these three times, and hast not told me wherein thy great strength *lieth*.

16And it came to pass, when she pressed him daily with her words, and urged him, *so* that his soul was vexed unto death;

17That he told her all his heart, and said unto her, There hath not come a razor upon mine head; for I *have been* a Nazarite unto God from my mother's womb: if I be shaven, then my strength will go from me, and I shall become weak, and be like any *other* man.

18And when Delilah saw that he had told her all his heart, she sent and called for the lords of the Philistines, saying, Come up this once, for he hath shown me all his heart. Then the lords of the Philistines came up unto her, and brought money in their hand.

19And she made him sleep upon her knees; and she called for a man, and she caused him to shave off the seven locks of his head; and she began to afflict him, and his strength went from him.

20And she said, The Philistines *be* upon thee, Samson. And he awoke out of his sleep, and said, I will go out as at other times before, and shake myself. And he wist not that the LORD was departed from him.

21¶ But the Philistines took him, and put out his eyes, and brought him down to Gaza, and bound him with fetters of brass; and he did grind in the prison house.

22Howbeit the hair of his head began to grow again after he was shaven.

23Then the lords of the Philistines gathered them together for to offer a great sacrifice unto Dagon their god, and to rejoice: for they said, Our god hath delivered Samson our enemy into our hand.

24And when the people saw him, they praised their god: for they said, Our god hath delivered into our hands our enemy, and the destroyer of our country, which slew many of us.

25And it came to pass, when their hearts were merry, that they said, Call for Samson, that he may make us sport. And they called for Samson out of the prison house; and he made them sport: and they set him between the pillars.

26And Samson said unto the lad that held him by the hand, Suffer me that I may feel the pillars whereupon the house standeth, that I may lean upon them.

New International

10Then Delilah said to Samson, "You have made a fool of me; you lied to me. Come now, tell me how you can be tied."

11He said, "If anyone ties me securely with new ropes that have never been used, I'll become as weak as any other man."

12So Delilah took new ropes and tied him with them. Then, with men hidden in the room, she called to him, "Samson, the Philistines are upon you!" But he snapped the ropes off his arms as if they were threads.

13Delilah then said to Samson, "Until now, you have been making a fool of me and lying to me. Tell me how you can be tied."

He replied, "If you weave the seven braids of my head into the fabric on the loom, and tighten it with the pin, I'll become as weak as any other man." So while he was sleeping, Delilah took the seven braids of his head, wove them into the fabric 14anda tightened it with the pin.

Again she called to him, "Samson, the Philistines are upon you!" He awoke from his sleep and pulled up the pin and the loom, with the fabric.

15Then she said to him, "How can you say, 'I love you,' when you won't confide in me? This is the third time you have made a fool of me and haven't told me the secret of your great strength." 16With such nagging she prodded him day after day until he was tired to death.

17So he told her everything. "No razor has ever been used on my head," he said, "because I have been a Nazirite set apart to God since birth. If my head were shaved, my strength would leave me, and I would become as weak as any other man."

18When Delilah saw that he had told her everything, she sent word to the rulers of the Philistines, "Come back once more; he has told me everything." So the rulers of the Philistines returned with the silver in their hands. 19Having put him to sleep on her lap, she called a man to shave off the seven braids of his hair, and so began to subdue him.b And his strength left him.

20Then she called, "Samson, the Philistines are upon you!"

He awoke from his sleep and thought, "I'll go out as before and shake myself free." But he did not know that the LORD had left him.

21Then the Philistines seized him, gouged out his eyes and took him down to Gaza. Binding him with bronze shackles, they set him to grinding in the prison. 22But the hair on his head began to grow again after it had been shaved.

The Death of Samson

23Now the rulers of the Philistines assembled to offer a great sacrifice to Dagon their god and to celebrate, saying, "Our god has delivered Samson, our enemy, into our hands."

24When the people saw him, they praised their god, saying,

> "Our god has delivered our enemy
>   into our hands,
>   the one who laid waste our land
>   and multiplied our slain."

25While they were in high spirits, they shouted, "Bring out Samson to entertain us." So they called Samson out of the prison, and he performed for them.

When they stood him among the pillars, 26Samson said to the servant who held his hand, "Put me where I can feel the pillars that support the temple, so that I may lean against them." 27Now the temple was crowded with

---

a *13,14* Some Septuagint manuscripts; Hebrew *"I can, if you weave the seven braids of my head into the fabric on the loom." 14So she*   b *19* Hebrew; some Septuagint manuscripts *and he began to weaken*

Living Bible

10Afterward Delilah said to him, "You are making fun of me! You told me a lie! *Please* tell me how you can be captured!"

11"Well," he said, "if I am tied with brand new ropes which have never been used, I will be as weak as other men."

12So that time, as he slept,c Delilah took new ropes and tied him with them. The men were hiding in the next room, as before. Again Delilah exclaimed,

"Samson! The Philistines have come to capture you!" But he broke the ropes from his arms like spiderwebs!

13"You have mocked me again, and told me more lies!" Delilah complained. "Now tell me how you can *really* be captured."

"Well," he said, "if you weave my hair into your loom . . . !"

14So while he slept, she did just that and then screamed, "The Philistines have come, Samson!" And he woke up and yanked his hair away, breaking the loom.

15"How can you say you love me when you don't confide in me?" she whined. "You've made fun of me three times now, and you still haven't told me what makes you so strong!"

16, 17She nagged at him every day until he couldn't stand it any longer and finally told her his secret.

"My hair has never been cut," he confessed, "for I've been a Nazirite to God since before my birth. If my hair were cut, my strength would leave me, and I would become as weak as anyone else."

18Delilah realized that he had finally told her the truth, so she sent for the five Philistine leaders.

"Come just this once more," she said, "for this time he has told me everything."

So they brought the money with them. 19She lulled him to sleep with his head in her lap, and they brought in a barber and cut off his hair. Delilah began to hit him, but she could see that his strength was leaving him.

20Then she screamed, "The Philistines are here to capture you, Samson!" And he woke up and thought, "I will do as before; I'll just shake myself free." But he didn't realize that the Lord had left him. 21So the Philistines captured him and gouged out his eyes and took him to Gaza, where he was bound with bronze chains and made to grind grain in the prison. 22But before long his hair began to grow again.

23, 24The Philistine leaders declared a great festival to celebrate the capture of Samson. The people made sacrifices to their god Dagon and excitedly praised him.

"Our god has delivered our enemy Samson to us!" they gloated as they saw him there in chains. "The scourge of our nation who killed so many of us is now in our power!" 25, 26Half drunk by now, the people demanded, "Bring out Samson so we can have some fun with him!"

So he was brought from the prison and made to stand at the center of the temple, between the two pillars supporting the roof. Samson said to the boy who was leading him by the hand, "Place my hands against the two pillars. I want to rest against them."

New Revised Standard

10 Then Delilah said to Samson, "You have mocked me and told me lies; please tell me how you could be bound." 11He said to her, "If they bind me with new ropes that have not been used, then I shall become weak, and be like anyone else." 12So Delilah took new ropes and bound him with them, and said to him, "The Philistines are upon you, Samson!" (The men lying in wait were in an inner chamber.) But he snapped the ropes off his arms like a thread.

13 Then Delilah said to Samson, "Until now you have mocked me and told me lies; tell me how you could be bound." He said to her, "If you weave the seven locks of my head with the web and make it tight with the pin, then I shall become weak, and be like anyone else." 14So while he slept, Delilah took the seven locks of his head and wove them into the web,d and made them tight with the pin. Then she said to him, "The Philistines are upon you, Samson!" But he awoke from his sleep, and pulled away the pin, the loom, and the web.

15 Then she said to him, "How can you say, 'I love you,' when your heart is not with me? You have mocked me three times now and have not told me what makes your strength so great." 16Finally, after she had nagged him with her words day after day, and pestered him, he was tired to death. 17So he told her his whole secret, and said to her, "A razor has never come upon my head; for I have been a naziritee to God from my mother's womb. If my head were shaved, then my strength would leave me; I would become weak, and be like anyone else."

18 When Delilah realized that he had told her his whole secret, she sent and called the lords of the Philistines, saying, "This time come up, for he has told his whole secret to me." Then the lords of the Philistines came up to her, and brought the money in their hands. 19She let him fall asleep on her lap; and she called a man, and had him shave off the seven locks of his head. He began to weaken,f and his strength left him. 20Then she said, "The Philistines are upon you, Samson!" When he awoke from his sleep, he thought, "I will go out as at other times, and shake myself free." But he did not know that the LORD had left him. 21So the Philistines seized him and gouged out his eyes. They brought him down to Gaza and bound him with bronze shackles; and he ground at the mill in the prison. 22But the hair of his head began to grow again after it had been shaved.

Samson's Death

23 Now the lords of the Philistines gathered to offer a great sacrifice to their god Dagon, and to rejoice; for they said, "Our god has given Samson our enemy into our hand." 24When the people saw him, they praised their god; for they said, "Our god has given our enemy into our hand, the ravager of our country, who has killed many of us." 25And when their hearts were merry, they said, "Call Samson, and let him entertain us." So they called Samson out of the prison, and he performed for them. They made him stand between the pillars; 26and Samson said to the attendant who held him by the hand, "Let me feel the pillars on which the house rests, so that I may lean against them." 27Now the house was full of

---

c *16:12 as he slept,* implied.

d Compare Gk: in verses 13-14, Heb lacks *and make it tight . . . into the web*   e That is *one separated* or *one consecrated*   f Gk: Heb *She began to torment him*

King James

27Now the house was full of men and women; and all the lords of the Philistines *were* there; and *there were* upon the roof about three thousand men and women, that beheld while Samson made sport.

28And Samson called unto the LORD, and said, O Lord GOD, remember me, I pray thee, and strengthen me, I pray thee, only this once, O God, that I may be at once avenged of the Philistines for my two eyes.

29And Samson took hold of the two middle pillars upon which the house stood, and on which it was borne up, of the one with his right hand, and of the other with his left.

30And Samson said, Let me die with the Philistines. And he bowed himself with *all his* might; and the house fell upon the lords, and upon all the people that *were* therein. So the dead which he slew at his death were more than *they* which he slew in his life.

31Then his brethren and all the house of his father came down, and took him, and brought *him* up, and buried him between Zorah and Eshtaol in the burying-place of Manoah his father. And he judged Israel twenty years.

17 AND THERE was a man of mount Ephraim, whose name *was* Micah.

2And he said unto his mother, The eleven hundred *shekels* of silver that were taken from thee, about which thou cursedst, and spakest of also in mine ears, behold, the silver *is* with me; I took it. And his mother said, Blessed *be thou* of the LORD, my son.

3And when he had restored the eleven hundred *shekels* of silver to his mother, his mother said, I had wholly dedicated the silver unto the LORD from my hand for my son, to make a graven image and a molten image: now therefore I will restore it unto thee.

4Yet he restored the money unto his mother; and his mother took two hundred *shekels* of silver, and gave them to the founder, who made thereof a graven image and a molten image: and they were in the house of Micah.

5And the man Micah had an house of gods, and made an ephod, and teraphim, and consecrated one of his sons, who became his priest.

6In those days *there was* no king in Israel, *but* every man did *that which was* right in his own eyes.

7¶ And there was a young man out of Bethlehem-judah of the family of Judah, who *was* a Levite, and he sojourned there.

8And the man departed out of the city from Bethlehem-judah to sojourn where he could find *a place:* and he came to mount Ephraim to the house of Micah, as he journeyed.

9And Micah said unto him, Whence comest thou? And he said unto him, I *am* a Levite of Bethlehem-judah, and I go to sojourn where I may find *a place*.

10And Micah said unto him, Dwell with me, and be unto me a father and a priest, and I will give thee ten *shekels* of silver by the year, and a suit of apparel, and thy victuals. So the Levite went in.

11And the Levite was content to dwell with the man; and the young man was unto him as one of his sons.

12And Micah consecrated the Levite; and the young man became his priest, and was in the house of Micah.

13Then said Micah, Now know I that the LORD will do me good, seeing I have a Levite to *my* priest.

New International

men and women; all the rulers of the Philistines were there, and on the roof were about three thousand men and women watching Samson perform. 28Then Samson prayed to the LORD, "O Sovereign LORD, remember me. O God, please strengthen me just once more, and let me with one blow get revenge on the Philistines for my two eyes." 29Then Samson reached toward the two central pillars on which the temple stood. Bracing himself against them, his right hand on the one and his left hand on the other, 30Samson said, "Let me die with the Philistines!" Then he pushed with all his might, and down came the temple on the rulers and all the people in it. Thus he killed many more when he died than while he lived.

31Then his brothers and his father's whole family went down to get him. They brought him back and buried him between Zorah and Eshtaol in the tomb of Manoah his father. He had leda Israel twenty years.

Micah's Idols

17 NOW A man named Micah from the hill country of Ephraim 2said to his mother, "The eleven hundred shekelsb of silver that were taken from you and about which I heard you utter a curse—I have that silver with me; I took it."

Then his mother said, "The LORD bless you, my son!"

3When he returned the eleven hundred shekels of silver to his mother, she said, "I solemnly consecrate my silver to the LORD for my son to make a carved image and a cast idol. I will give it back to you."

4So he returned the silver to his mother, and she took two hundred shekelsc of silver and gave them to a silversmith, who made them into the image and the idol. And they were put in Micah's house.

5Now this man Micah had a shrine, and he made an ephod and some idols and installed one of his sons as his priest. 6In those days Israel had no king; everyone did as he saw fit.

7A young Levite from Bethlehem in Judah, who had been living within the clan of Judah, 8left that town in search of some other place to stay. On his wayd he came to Micah's house in the hill country of Ephraim.

9Micah asked him, "Where are you from?"

"I'm a Levite from Bethlehem in Judah," he said, "and I'm looking for a place to stay."

10Then Micah said to him, "Live with me and be my father and priest, and I'll give you ten shekelse of silver a year, your clothes and your food." 11So the Levite agreed to live with him, and the young man was to him like one of his sons. 12Then Micah installed the Levite, and the young man became his priest and lived in his house. 13And Micah said, "Now I know that the LORD will be good to me, since this Levite has become my priest."

a 31 Traditionally *judged*   b 2 That is, about 28 pounds (about 13 kilograms)   c 4 That is, about 5 pounds (about 2.3 kilograms)   d 8 Or *To carry on his profession*   e 10 That is, about 4 ounces (about 110 grams)

Living Bible

27By then the temple was completely filled with people. The five Philistine leaders were there as well as three thousand people in the balconies[f] who were watching Samson and making fun of him.

28Then Samson prayed to the Lord and said, "O Lord Jehovah, remember me again—please strengthen me one more time, so that I may pay back the Philistines for the loss of at least one of my eyes."

29Then Samson pushed against the pillars with all his might.

30"Let me die with the Philistines," he prayed.

And the temple crashed down upon the Philistine leaders and all the people. So those he killed at the moment of his death were more than those he had killed during his entire lifetime. 31Later, his brothers and other relatives came down to get his body, and they brought him back home and buried him between Zorah and Esta-ol, where his father, Manoah, was buried. He had led Israel for twenty years.

17 IN THE hill country of Ephraim lived a man named Micah.

2One day he said to his mother, "That thousand dollars you thought was stolen from you, and you were cursing about—well, I stole it!"

"God bless you for confessing it," his mother replied. 3So he returned the money to her.

"I am going to give it to the Lord as a credit for your account," she declared. "I'll have an idol carved for you and plate it with the silver."

4, 5So his mother took a fifth of it to a silversmith, and the idol he made from it was placed in Micah's shrine. Micah had many idols in his collection, also an ephod and some teraphim, and he installed one of his sons as the priest. 6(For in those days Israel had no king, so everyone did whatever he wanted to—whatever seemed right in his own eyes.)

7, 8One day a young priest[g] from the town of Bethlehem, in Judah, arrived in that area of Ephraim, looking for a good place to live. He happened to stop at Micah's house as he was traveling through.

9"Where are you from?" Micah asked him.

And he replied, "I am a priest from Bethlehem, in Judah, and I am looking for a place to live."

10, 11"Well, stay here with me," Micah said, "and you can be my priest. I will give you one hundred dollars a year plus a new suit and your board and room." The young man agreed to this, and became as one of Micah's sons. 12So Micah consecrated him as his personal priest.

13"I know the Lord will really bless me now," Micah exclaimed, "because now I have a genuine priest working for me!"[h]

New Revised Standard

men and women; all the lords of the Philistines were there, and on the roof there were about three thousand men and women, who looked on while Samson performed.

28 Then Samson called to the LORD and said, "Lord GOD, remember me and strengthen me only this once, O God, so that with this one act of revenge I may pay back the Philistines for my two eyes."[i] 29And Samson grasped the two middle pillars on which the house rested, and he leaned his weight against them, his right hand on the one and his left hand on the other. 30Then Samson said, "Let me die with the Philistines." He strained with all his might; and the house fell on the lords and all the people who were in it. So those he killed at his death were more than those he had killed during his life. 31Then his brothers and all his family came down and took him and brought him up and buried him between Zorah and Eshtaol in the tomb of his father Manoah. He had judged Israel twenty years.

Micah and the Levite

17 THERE WAS a man in the hill country of Ephraim whose name was Micah. 2He said to his mother, "The eleven hundred pieces of silver that were taken from you, about which you uttered a curse, and even spoke it in my hearing,—that silver is in my possession; I took it; but now I will return it to you."[j] And his mother said, "May my son be blessed by the LORD!" 3Then he returned the eleven hundred pieces of silver to his mother; and his mother said, "I consecrate the silver to the LORD from my hand for my son, to make an idol of cast metal." 4So when he returned the money to his mother, his mother took two hundred pieces of silver, and gave it to the silversmith, who made it into an idol of cast metal; and it was in the house of Micah. 5This man Micah had a shrine, and he made an ephod and teraphim, and installed one of his sons, who became his priest. 6In those days there was no king in Israel; all the people did what was right in their own eyes.

7 Now there was a young man of Bethlehem in Judah, of the clan of Judah. He was a Levite residing there. 8This man left the town of Bethlehem in Judah, to live wherever he could find a place. He came to the house of Micah in the hill country of Ephraim to carry on his work.[k] 9Micah said to him, "From where do you come?" He replied, "I am a Levite of Bethlehem in Judah, and I am going to live wherever I can find a place." 10Then Micah said to him, "Stay with me, and be to me a father and a priest, and I will give you ten pieces of silver a year, a set of clothes, and your living."[l] 11The Levite agreed to stay with the man; and the young man became to him like one of his sons. 12So Micah installed the Levite, and the young man became his priest, and was in the house of Micah. 13Then Micah said, "Now I know that the LORD will prosper me, because the Levite has become my priest."

---

f 16:27 people in the balconies, literally, "on the roof."   g 17:7, 8 a young man, "a Levite."   h 17:13 now I have a genuine priest working for me, literally, "a Levite as a priest."

i Or so that I may be avenged upon the Philistines for one of my two eyes   j The words but now I will return it to you are transposed from the end of verse 3 in Heb   k Or Ephraim, continuing his journey   l Heb living, and the Levite went

King James

18 IN THOSE days *there was* no king in Israel: and in those days the tribe of the Danites sought them an inheritance to dwell in; for unto that day *all their* inheritance had not fallen unto them among the tribes of Israel.

2And the children of Dan sent of their family five men from their coasts, men of valour, from Zorah, and from Eshtaol, to spy out the land, and to search it; and they said unto them, Go, search the land: who when they came to mount Ephraim, to the house of Micah, they lodged there.

3When they *were* by the house of Micah, they knew the voice of the young man the Levite: and they turned in thither, and said unto him, Who brought thee hither? and what makest thou in this *place?* and what hast thou here?

4And he said unto them, Thus and thus dealeth Micah with me, and hath hired me, and I am his priest.

5And they said unto him, Ask counsel, we pray thee, of God, that we may know whether our way which we go shall be prosperous.

6And the priest said unto them, Go in peace: before the LORD *is* your way wherein ye go.

7¶ Then the five men departed, and came to Laish, and saw the people that *were* therein, how they dwelt careless, after the manner of the Zidonians, quiet and secure; and *there was* no magistrate in the land, that might put *them* to shame in *any* thing; and they *were* far from the Zidonians, and had no business with *any* man.

8And they came unto their brethren to Zorah and Eshtaol: and their brethren said unto them, What *say* ye?

9And they said, Arise, that we may go up against them: for we have seen the land, and, behold, *it is* very good: and *are* ye still? be not slothful to go, *and* to enter to possess the land.

10When ye go, ye shall come unto a people secure, and to a large land: for God hath given it into your hands; a place where *there is* no want of any thing that *is* in the earth.

11¶ And there went from thence of the family of the Danites, out of Zorah and out of Eshtaol, six hundred men appointed with weapons of war.

12And they went up, and pitched in Kirjath-jearim, in Judah: wherefore they called that place Mahaneh-dan unto this day: behold, *it is* behind Kirjath-jearim.

13And they passed thence unto mount Ephraim, and came unto the house of Micah.

14¶ Then answered the five men that went to spy out the country of Laish, and said unto their brethren, Do ye know that there is in these houses an ephod, and teraphim, and a graven image, and a molten image? now therefore consider what ye have to do.

15And they turned thitherward, and came to the house of the young man the Levite, *even* unto the house of Micah, and saluted him.

16And the six hundred men appointed with their weapons of war, which *were* of the children of Dan, stood by the entering of the gate.

17And the five men that went to spy out the land went up, *and* came in thither, *and* took the graven image, and the ephod, and the teraphim, and the molten image: and the priest stood in the entering of the gate with the six hundred men *that were* appointed with weapons of war.

18And these *that* went into Micah's house, and fetched the carved image, the ephod, and the teraphim, and the molten image. Then said the priest unto them, What do ye?

19And they said unto him, Hold thy peace, lay thine hand upon thy mouth, and go with us, and be to us a father and a priest: *is it* better for thee to be a priest unto the house of one man, or that thou be a priest unto a tribe and a family in Israel?

New International

Danites Settle in Laish

18 IN THOSE days Israel had no king.
And in those days the tribe of the Danites was seeking a place of their own where they might settle, because they had not yet come into an inheritance among the tribes of Israel. 2So the Danites sent five warriors from Zorah and Eshtaol to spy out the land and explore it. These men represented all their clans. They told them, "Go, explore the land."

The men entered the hill country of Ephraim and came to the house of Micah, where they spent the night. 3When they were near Micah's house, they recognized the voice of the young Levite; so they turned in there and asked him, "Who brought you here? What are you doing in this place? Why are you here?"

4He told them what Micah had done for him, and said, "He has hired me and I am his priest."

5Then they said to him, "Please inquire of God to learn whether our journey will be successful."

6The priest answered them, "Go in peace. Your journey has the LORD's approval."

7So the five men left and came to Laish, where they saw that the people were living in safety, like the Sidonians, unsuspecting and secure. And since their land lacked nothing, they were prosperous.a Also, they lived a long way from the Sidonians and had no relationship with anyone else.b

8When they returned to Zorah and Eshtaol, their brothers asked them, "How did you find things?"

9They answered, "Come on, let's attack them! We have seen that the land is very good. Aren't you going to do something? Don't hesitate to go there and take it over. 10When you get there, you will find an unsuspecting people and a spacious land that God has put into your hands, a land that lacks nothing whatever."

11Then six hundred men from the clan of the Danites, armed for battle, set out from Zorah and Eshtaol. 12On their way they set up camp near Kiriath Jearim in Judah. This is why the place west of Kiriath Jearim is called Mahaneh Danc to this day. 13From there they went on to the hill country of Ephraim and came to Micah's house.

14Then the five men who had spied out the land of Laish said to their brothers, "Do you know that one of these houses has an ephod, other household gods, a carved image and a cast idol? Now you know what to do." 15So they turned in there and went to the house of the young Levite at Micah's place and greeted him. 16The six hundred Danites, armed for battle, stood at the entrance to the gate. 17The five men who had spied out the land went inside and took the carved image, the ephod, the other household gods and the cast idol while the priest and the six hundred armed men stood at the entrance to the gate.

18When these men went into Micah's house and took the carved image, the ephod, the other household gods and the cast idol, the priest said to them, "What are you doing?"

19They answered him, "Be quiet! Don't say a word. Come with us, and be our father and priest. Isn't it better that you serve a tribe and clan in Israel as priest rather than just one man's household?" 20Then the priest was

a 7 The meaning of the Hebrew for this clause is uncertain.　b 7 Hebrew; some Septuagint manuscripts *with the Arameans*　c 12 *Mahaneh Dan* means *Dan's camp.*

Living Bible

18 AS HAS already been stated, there was no king in Israel at that time. The tribe of Dan was trying to find a place to settle, for they had not yet driven out the people living in the land assigned to them. 2So the men of Dan chose five army heroes from the cities of Zorah and Eshta-ol as scouts to go and spy out the land they were supposed to settle in. Arriving in the hill country of Ephraim, they stayed at Micah's home. 3Noticing the young Levite's accent, they took him aside and asked him, "What are you doing here? Why did you come?" 4He told them about his contract with Micah, and that he was his personal priest.

5"Well, then," they said, "ask God whether or not our trip will be successful."

6"Yes," the priest replied, "all is well. The Lord is taking care of you."

7So the five men went on to the town of Laish, and noticed how secure everyone felt. Their manner of life was Phoenician, and they were wealthy. They lived quietly, and were unprepared for an attack, for there were no tribes in the area strong enough to try it. They lived a great distance from their relatives in Sidon, and had little or no contact with the nearby villages. 8So the spies returned to their people in Zorah and Eshta-ol.

"What about it?" they were asked. "What did you find?"

9, 10And the men replied, "Let's attack! We have seen the land and it is ours for the taking—a broad, fertile, wonderful place—a real paradise. The people aren't even prepared to defend themselves! Come on, let's go! For God has given it to us!"

11So six hundred armed troops of the tribe of Dan set out from Zorah and Eshtaol. 12They camped first at a place west of Kiriath-jearim in Judah (which is still called "The Camp of Dan"), 13then they went on up into the hill country of Ephraim.

As they passed the home of Micah, 14the five spies told the others. "There is a shrine in there with an ephod, some teraphim, and many plated idols. It's obvious what we ought to do!"

15, 16So the five men went over to the house and with all of the armed men standing just outside the gate, they talked to the young priest, and asked him how he was getting along. 17Then the five spies entered the shrine and took the idols, the ephod, and the teraphim.

18"What are you doing?" the young priest demanded when he saw them carrying them out.

19"Be quiet and come with us," they said. "Be a priest to all of us. Isn't it better for you to be a priest to a whole tribe in Israel instead of just to one man in his private home?"

New Revised Standard

The Migration of Dan

18 IN THOSE days there was no king in Israel. And in those days the tribe of the Danites was seeking for itself a territory to live in; for until then no territory among the tribes of Israel had been allotted to them. 2So the Danites sent five valiant men from the whole number of their clan, from Zorah and from Eshta-ol, to spy out the land and to explore it; and they said to them, "Go, explore the land." When they came to the hill country of Ephraim, to the house of Micah, they stayed there. 3While they were at Micah's house, they recognized the voice of the young Levite; so they went over and asked him, "Who brought you here? What are you doing in this place? What is your business here?" 4He said to them, "Micah did such and such for me, and he hired me, and I have become his priest." 5Then they said to him, "Inquire of God that we may know whether the mission we are undertaking will succeed." 6The priest replied, "Go in peace. The mission you are on is under the eye of the LORD."

7 The five men went on, and when they came to Laish, they observed the people who were there living securely, after the manner of the Sidonians, quiet and unsuspecting, lackingd nothing on earth, and possessing wealth.e Furthermore, they were far from the Sidonians and had no dealings with Aram.f 8When they came to their kinsfolk at Zorah and Eshtaol, they said to them, "What do you report?" 9They said, "Come, let us go up against them; for we have seen the land, and it is very good. Will you do nothing? Do not be slow to go, but enter in and possess the land. 10When you go, you will come to an unsuspecting people. The land is broad—God has indeed given it into your hands—a place where there is no lack of anything on earth."

11 Six hundred men of the Danite clan, armed with weapons of war, set out from Zorah and Eshtaol, 12and went up and encamped at Kiriath-jearim in Judah. On this account that place is called Mahaneh-dang to this day; it is west of Kiriath-jearim. 13From there they passed on to the hill country of Ephraim, and came to the house of Micah.

14 Then the five men who had gone to spy out the land (that is, Laish) said to their comrades, "Do you know that in these buildings there are an ephod, teraphim, and an idol of cast metal? Now therefore consider what you will do." 15So they turned in that direction and came to the house of the young Levite, at the home of Micah, and greeted him. 16While the six hundred men of the Danites, armed with their weapons of war, stood by the entrance of the gate, 17the five men who had gone to spy out the land proceeded to enter and take the idol of cast metal, the ephod, and the teraphim.h The priest was standing by the entrance of the gate with the six hundred men armed with weapons of war. 18When the men went into Micah's house and took the idol of cast metal, the ephod, and the teraphim, the priest said to them, "What are you doing?" 19They said to him, "Keep quiet! Put your hand over your mouth, and come with us, and be to us a father and a priest. Is it better for you to be priest to the house of one person, or to be priest to a tribe and clan in Israel?" 20Then the priest accepted

---

d Cn Compare 18.10: Meaning of Heb uncertain   e Meaning of Heb uncertain
f Symmachus: Heb *with anyone*   g That is *Camp of Dan*   h Compare 17.4,
5; 18.14: Heb *teraphim and the cast metal*

King James

20And the priest's heart was glad, and he took the ephod, and the teraphim, and the graven image, and went in the midst of the people.

21So they turned and departed, and put the little ones and the cattle and the carriage before them.

22¶ And when they were a good way from the house of Micah, the men that were in the houses near to Micah's house were gathered together, and overtook the children of Dan.

23And they cried unto the children of Dan. And they turned their faces, and said unto Micah, What aileth thee, that thou comest with such a company?

24And he said, Ye have taken away my gods which I made, and the priest, and ye are gone away: and what have I more? and what is this that ye say unto me, What aileth thee?

25And the children of Dan said unto him, Let not thy voice be heard among us, lest angry fellows run upon thee, and thou lose thy life, with the lives of thy household.

26And the children of Dan went their way: and when Micah saw that they were too strong for him, he turned and went back unto his house.

27And they took the things which Micah had made, and the priest which he had, and came unto Laish, unto a people that were at quiet and secure: and they smote them with the edge of the sword, and burnt the city with fire.

28And there was no deliverer, because it was far from Zidon, and they had no business with any man; and it was in the valley that lieth by Beth-rehob. And they built a city, and dwelt therein.

29And they called the name of the city Dan, after the name of Dan their father, who was born unto Israel: howbeit the name of the city was Laish at the first.

30¶ And the children of Dan set up the graven image: and Jonathan, the son of Gershom, the son of Manasseh, he and his sons were priests to the tribe of Dan until the day of the captivity of the land.

31And they set them up Micah's graven image, which he made, all the time that the house of God was in Shiloh.

19 AND IT came to pass in those days, when there was no king in Israel, that there was a certain Levite sojourning on the side of mount Ephraim, who took to him a concubine out of Bethlehem-judah.

2And his concubine played the whore against him, and went away from him unto her father's house to Bethlehem-judah, and was there four whole months.

3And her husband arose, and went after her, to speak friendly unto her, and to bring her again, having his servant with him, and a couple of asses: and she brought him into her father's house: and when the father of the damsel saw him, he rejoiced to meet him.

4And his father-in-law, the damsel's father, retained him; and he abode with him three days: so they did eat and drink, and lodged there.

5¶ And it came to pass on the fourth day, when they arose early in the morning, that he rose up to depart: and the damsel's father said unto his son-in-law, Comfort thine heart with a morsel of bread, and afterward go your way.

6And they sat down, and did eat and drink both of them together: for the damsel's father had said unto the man, Be content, I pray thee, and tarry all night, and let thine heart be merry.

7And when the man rose up to depart, his father-in-law urged him: therefore he lodged there again.

New International

glad. He took the ephod, the other household gods and the carved image and went along with the people. 21Putting their little children, their livestock and their possessions in front of them, they turned away and left.

22When they had gone some distance from Micah's house, the men who lived near Micah were called together and overtook the Danites. 23As they shouted after them, the Danites turned and said to Micah, "What's the matter with you that you called out your men to fight?"

24He replied, "You took the gods I made, and my priest, and went away. What else do I have? How can you ask, 'What's the matter with you?' "

25The Danites answered, "Don't argue with us, or some hot-tempered men will attack you, and you and your family will lose your lives." 26So the Danites went their way, and Micah, seeing that they were too strong for him, turned around and went back home.

27Then they took what Micah had made, and his priest, and went on to Laish, against a peaceful and unsuspecting people. They attacked them with the sword and burned down their city. 28There was no one to rescue them because they lived a long way from Sidon and had no relationship with anyone else. The city was in a valley near Beth Rehob.

The Danites rebuilt the city and settled there. 29They named it Dan after their forefather Dan, who was born to Israel—though the city used to be called Laish. 30There the Danites set up for themselves the idols, and Jonathan son of Gershom, the son of Moses,[a] and his sons were priests for the tribe of Dan until the time of the captivity of the land. 31They continued to use the idols Micah had made, all the time the house of God was in Shiloh.

A Levite and His Concubine

19 IN THOSE days Israel had no king.
Now a Levite who lived in a remote area in the hill country of Ephraim took a concubine from Bethlehem in Judah. 2But she was unfaithful to him. She left him and went back to her father's house in Bethlehem, Judah. After she had been there four months, 3her husband went to her to persuade her to return. He had with him his servant and two donkeys. She took him into her father's house, and when her father saw him, he gladly welcomed him. 4His father-in-law, the girl's father, prevailed upon him to stay; so he remained with him three days, eating and drinking, and sleeping there.

5On the fourth day they got up early and he prepared to leave, but the girl's father said to his son-in-law, "Refresh yourself with something to eat; then you can go." 6So the two of them sat down to eat and drink together. Afterward the girl's father said, "Please stay tonight and enjoy yourself." 7And when the man got up to go, his father-in-law persuaded him, so he stayed there that night. 8On the morning of the fifth day, when

---

a 30 An ancient Hebrew scribal tradition, some Septuagint manuscripts and Vulgate; Masoretic Text Manasseh

Living Bible

20The young priest was then quite happy to go with them, and he took along the ephod, the teraphim, and the idols. 21They started on their way again, placing their children, cattle, and household goods at the front of the column. 22When they were quite a distance from Micah's home, Micah and some of his neighbors came chasing after them, 23yelling at them to stop.

"What do you want, chasing after us like this?" the men of Dan demanded.

24"What do you mean, 'What do I want'!" Micah retorted. "You've taken away all my gods and my priest, and I have nothing left!"

25"Be careful how you talk, mister," the men of Dan replied. "Somebody's apt to get angry and kill every one of you."

26So the men of Dan kept going. When Micah saw that there were too many of them for him to handle, he turned back home.

27Then, with Micah's idols and the priest, the men of Dan arrived at the city of Laish. There weren't even any guards, so they went in and slaughtered all the people and burned the city to the ground. 28There was no one to help the inhabitants, for they were too far away from Sidon, and they had no local allies, for they had no dealings with anyone. This happened in the valley next to Beth-rehob. Then the people of the tribe of Dan rebuilt the city and lived there. 29The city was named "Dan" after their ancestor, Israel's son, but it had originally been called Laish.

30Then they set up the idols and appointed a man named Jonathan (son of Gershom and grandson of Moses!) and his sons as their priests. This family continued as priests until the city was finally conquered by its enemies. 31So Micah's idols were worshiped by the tribe of Dan as long as the Tabernacle remained at Shiloh.

19 AT THIS time before Israel had a king, there was a man of the tribe of Levi living on the far side of the hill country of Ephraim, who brought home a girl from Bethlehem in Judah to be his concubine. 2But she became angry with him and ran away, and returned to her father's home in Bethlehem, and was there about four months. 3Then her husband, taking along a servant and an extra donkey, went to see her to try to win her back again. When he arrived at her home, she let him in and introduced him to her father, who was delighted to meet him. 4Her father urged him to stay awhile, so he stayed three days, and they all had a very pleasant time.

5On the fourth day they were up early, ready to leave, but the girl's father insisted on their having breakfast first. 6Then he pleaded with him to stay one more day, as they were having such a good time. 7At first the man refused, but his father-in-law kept urging him until finally he gave in. 8The next morning they were up early

New Revised Standard

the offer. He took the ephod, the teraphim, and the idol, and went along with the people.

21 So they resumed their journey, putting the little ones, the livestock, and the goods in front of them. 22When they were some distance from the home of Micah, the men who were in the houses near Micah's house were called out, and they overtook the Danites. 23They shouted to the Danites, who turned around and said to Micah, "What is the matter that you come with such a company?" 24He replied, "You take my gods that I made, and the priest, and go away, and what have I left? How then can you ask me, 'What is the matter?'" 25And the Danites said to him, "You had better not let your voice be heard among us or else hot-tempered fellows will attack you, and you will lose your life and the lives of your household." 26Then the Danites went their way. When Micah saw that they were too strong for him, he turned and went back to his home.

The Danites Settle in Laish

27 The Danites, having taken what Micah had made, and the priest who belonged to him, came to Laish, to a people quiet and unsuspecting, put them to the sword, and burned down the city. 28There was no deliverer, because it was far from Sidon and they had no dealings with Aram.b It was in the valley that belongs to Beth-rehob. They rebuilt the city, and lived in it. 29They named the city Dan, after their ancestor Dan, who was born to Israel; but the name of the city was formerly Laish. 30Then the Danites set up the idol for themselves. Jonathan son of Gershom, son of Moses,c and his sons were priests to the tribe of the Danites until the time the land went into captivity. 31So they maintained as their own Micah's idol that he had made, as long as the house of God was at Shiloh.

The Levite's Concubine

19 IN THOSE days, when there was no king in Israel, a certain Levite, residing in the remote parts of the hill country of Ephraim, took to himself a concubine from Bethlehem in Judah. 2But his concubine became angry withd him, and she went away from him to her father's house at Bethlehem in Judah, and was there some four months. 3Then her husband set out after her, to speak tenderly to her and bring her back. He had with him his servant and a couple of donkeys. When he reachede her father's house, the girl's father saw him and came with joy to meet him. 4His father-in-law, the girl's father, made him stay, and he remained with him three days; so they ate and drank, and hef stayed there. 5On the fourth day they got up early in the morning, and he prepared to go; but the girl's father said to his son-in-law, "Fortify yourself with a bit of food, and after that you may go." 6So the two men sat and ate and drank together; and the girl's father said to the man, "Why not spend the night and enjoy yourself?" 7When the man got up to go, his father-in-law kept urging him until he spent the night there again. 8On the fifth day he got up early

b Cn Compare verse 7: Heb *with anyone*   c Another reading is *son of Manasseh*   d Gk OL: Heb *prostituted herself against*   e Gk: Heb *she brought him*   f Compare verse 7 and Gk: Heb *they*

King James

8And he arose early in the morning on the fifth day to depart: and the damsel's father said, Comfort thine heart, I pray thee. And they tarried until afternoon, and they did eat both of them.

9And when the man rose up to depart, he, and his concubine, and his servant, his father-in-law, the damsel's father, said unto him, Behold, now the day draweth toward evening, I pray you tarry all night: behold, the day groweth to an end, lodge here, that thine heart may be merry; and tomorrow get you early on your way, that thou mayest go home.

10But the man would not tarry that night, but he rose up and departed, and came over against Jebus, which *is* Jerusalem; and *there were* with him two asses saddled, his concubine also *was* with him.

11*And* when they *were* by Jebus, the day was far spent; and the servant said unto his master, Come, I pray thee, and let us turn in into this city of the Jebusites, and lodge in it.

12And his master said unto him, We will not turn aside hither into the city of a stranger, that *is* not of the children of Israel; we will pass over to Gibeah.

13And he said unto his servant, Come, and let us draw near to one of these places to lodge all night, in Gibeah, or in Ramah.

14And they passed on and went their way; and the sun went down upon them *when they were* by Gibeah, which *belongeth* to Benjamin.

15And they turned aside thither, to go in *and* to lodge in Gibeah: and when he went in, he sat him down in a street of the city: for *there was* no man that took them into his house to lodging.

16¶ And, behold, there came an old man from his work out of the field at even, which *was* also of mount Ephraim; and he sojourned in Gibeah: but the men of the place *were* Benjamites.

17And when he had lifted up his eyes, he saw a way-faring man in the street of the city: and the old man said, Whither goest thou? and whence comest thou?

18And he said unto him, We *are* passing from Bethle-hem-judah toward the side of mount Ephraim; from thence *am* I: and I went to Bethlehem-judah, but I *am now* going to the house of the LORD; and there *is* no man that receiveth me to house.

19Yet there is both straw and provender for our asses; and there is bread and wine also for me, and for thy handmaid, and for the young man *which is* with thy servants: *there is* no want of any thing.

20And the old man said, Peace *be* with thee; howsoever *let* all thy wants *lie* upon me; only lodge not in the street.

21So he brought him into his house, and gave provender unto the asses: and they washed their feet, and did eat and drink.

22¶ *Now* as they were making their hearts merry, behold, the men of the city, certain sons of Belial, beset the house round about, *and* beat at the door, and spake to the master of the house, the old man, saying, Bring forth the man that came into thine house, that we may know him.

23And the man, the master of the house, went out unto them, and said unto them, Nay, my brethren, *nay*, I pray you, do not *so* wickedly; seeing that this man is come into mine house, do not this folly.

24Behold, *here is* my daughter a maiden, and his concubine; them I will bring out now, and humble ye them, and do with them what seemeth good unto you: but unto this man do not so vile a thing.

25But the men would not hearken to him: so the man took his concubine, and brought her forth unto them; and they knew her, and abused her all the night until the morning: and when the day began to spring, they let her go.

New International

he rose to go, the girl's father said, "Refresh yourself. Wait till afternoon!" So the two of them ate together.

9Then when the man, with his concubine and his servant, got up to leave, his father-in-law, the girl's father, said, "Now look, it's almost evening. Spend the night here; the day is nearly over. Stay and enjoy yourself. Early tomorrow morning you can get up and be on your way home." 10But, unwilling to stay another night, the man left and went toward Jebus (that is, Jerusalem), with his two saddled donkeys and his concubine.

11When they were near Jebus and the day was almost gone, the servant said to his master, "Come, let's stop at this city of the Jebusites and spend the night."

12His master replied, "No. We won't go into an alien city, whose people are not Israelites. We will go on to Gibeah." 13He added, "Come, let's try to reach Gibeah or Ramah and spend the night in one of those places." 14So they went on, and the sun set as they neared Gibeah in Benjamin. 15There they stopped to spend the night. They went and sat in the city square, but no one took them into his home for the night.

16That evening an old man from the hill country of Ephraim, who was living in Gibeah (the men of the place were Benjamites), came in from his work in the fields. 17When he looked and saw the traveler in the city square, the old man asked, "Where are you going? Where did you come from?"

18He answered, "We are on our way from Bethlehem in Judah to a remote area in the hill country of Ephraim where I live. I have been to Bethlehem in Judah and now I am going to the house of the LORD. No one has taken me into his house. 19We have both straw and fodder for our donkeys and bread and wine for ourselves your servants—me, your maidservant, and the young man with us. We don't need anything."

20"You are welcome at my house," the old man said. "Let me supply whatever you need. Only don't spend the night in the square." 21So he took him into his house and fed his donkeys. After they had washed their feet, they had something to eat and drink.

22While they were enjoying themselves, some of the wicked men of the city surrounded the house. Pounding on the door, they shouted to the old man who owned the house, "Bring out the man who came to your house so we can have sex with him."

23The owner of the house went outside and said to them, "No, my friends, don't be so vile. Since this man is my guest, don't do this disgraceful thing. 24Look, here is my virgin daughter, and his concubine. I will bring them out to you now, and you can use them and do to them whatever you wish. But to this man, don't do such a disgraceful thing."

25But the men would not listen to him. So the man took his concubine and sent her outside to them, and they raped her and abused her throughout the night, and at dawn they let her go. 26At daybreak the woman went

Living Bible

again, and again the girl's father pleaded, "Stay just today and leave sometime this evening." So they had another day of feasting.

9That afternoon as he and his wife and servant were preparing to leave, his father-in-law said, "Look, it's getting late. Stay just tonight, and we will have a pleasant evening together and tomorrow you can get up early and be on your way."

10But this time the man was adamant, so they left, getting as far as Jerusalem (also called Jebus) before dark.

11His servant said to him, "It's getting too late to travel; let's stay here tonight."

12, 13"No," his master said, "we can't stay in this heathen city where there are no Israelites—we will go on to Gibe-ah, or possibly Ramah."

14So they went on. The sun was setting just as they came to Gibe-ah, a village of the tribe of Benjamin, 15so they went there for the night. But as no one invited them in, they camped in the village square. 16Just then an old man came by on his way home from his work in the fields. (He was originally from the hill country of Ephra-im, but was living now in Gibe-ah, even though it was in the territory of Benjamin.) 17When he saw the travelers camped in the square, he asked them where they were from, and where they were going.

18"We're on the way home from Bethlehem, in Judah," the man replied. "I live on the far edge of the Ephraim hill country, near Shiloh. But no one has taken us in for the night, 19even though we have fodder for our donkeys, and plenty of food and wine for ourselves."

20"Don't worry," the old man said, "be my guests; for you mustn't stay here in the square. It's too dangerous."

21So he took them home with him. He fed their donkeys while they rested, and afterward they had supper together. 22Just as they were beginning to warm to the occasion, a gang of sex perverts gathered around the house and began beating at the door and yelling at the old man to bring out the man who was staying with him, so they could rape him. 23The old man stepped outside to talk to them.

"No, my brothers, don't do such a dastardly act," he begged, "for he is my guest. 24Here, take my virgin daughter and this man's wife. I'll bring them out and you can do whatever you like to them—but don't do such a thing to this man."

25But they wouldn't listen to him. Then the girl's husband pushed her out to them, and they abused her all night, taking turns raping her until morning. Finally, just at dawn, they let her go. 26She fell down at the door

New Revised Standard

in the morning to leave; and the girl's father said, "Fortify yourself." So they lingereda until the day declined, and the two of them ate and drank.b 9When the man with his concubine and his servant got up to leave, his father-in-law, the girl's father, said to him, "Look, the day has worn on until it is almost evening. Spend the night. See, the day has drawn to a close. Spend the night here and enjoy yourself. Tomorrow you can get up early in the morning for your journey, and go home."

10 But the man would not spend the night; he got up and departed, and arrived opposite Jebus (that is, Jerusalem). He had with him a couple of saddled donkeys, and his concubine was with him. 11When they were near Jebus, the day was far spent, and the servant said to his master, "Come now, let us turn aside to this city of the Jebusites, and spend the night in it." 12But his master said to him, "We will not turn aside into a city of foreigners, who do not belong to the people of Israel; but we will continue on to Gibeah." 13Then he said to his servant, "Come, let us try to reach one of these places, and spend the night at Gibeah or at Ramah." 14So they passed on and went their way; and the sun went down on them near Gibeah, which belongs to Benjamin. 15They turned aside there, to go in and spend the night at Gibeah. He went in and sat down in the open square of the city, but no one took them in to spend the night.

16 Then at evening there was an old man coming from his work in the field. The man was from the hill country of Ephraim, and he was residing in Gibeah. (The people of the place were Benjaminites.) 17When the old man looked up and saw the wayfarer in the open square of the city, he said, "Where are you going and where do you come from?" 18He answered him, "We are passing from Bethlehem in Judah to the remote parts of the hill country of Ephraim, from which I come. I went to Bethlehem in Judah; and I am going to my home.c Nobody has offered to take me in. 19We your servants have straw and fodder for our donkeys, with bread and wine for me and the woman and the young man along with us. We need nothing more." 20The old man said, "Peace be to you. I will care for all your wants; only do not spend the night in the square." 21So he brought him into his house, and fed the donkeys; they washed their feet, and ate and drank.

Gibeah's Crime

22 While they were enjoying themselves, the men of the city, a perverse lot, surrounded the house, and started pounding on the door. They said to the old man, the master of the house, "Bring out the man who came into your house, so that we may have intercourse with him." 23And the man, the master of the house, went out to them and said to them, "No, my brothers, do not act so wickedly. Since this man is my guest, do not do this vile thing. 24Here are my virgin daughter and his concubine; let me bring them out now. Ravish them and do whatever you want to them; but against this man do not do such a vile thing." 25But the men would not listen to him. So the man seized his concubine, and put her out to them. They wantonly raped her, and abused her all through the night until the morning. And as the dawn began to break, they let her go. 26As morning appeared,

a Cn: Heb Linger   b Gk: Heb lacks and drank   c Gk Compare 19.29. Heb to the house of the LORD

King James

26Then came the woman in the dawning of the day, and fell down at the door of the man's house where her lord *was*, till it was light.

27And her lord rose up in the morning, and opened the doors of the house, and went out to go his way: and, behold, the woman his concubine was fallen down *at* the door of the house, and her hands *were* upon the threshold.

28And he said unto her, Up, and let us be going. But none answered. Then the man took her *up* upon an ass, and the man rose up, and gat him unto his place.

29¶ And when he was come into his house, he took a knife, and laid hold on his concubine, and divided her, *together* with her bones, into twelve pieces, and sent her into all the coasts of Israel.

30And it was so, that all that saw it said, There was no such deed done nor seen from the day that the children of Israel came up out of the land of Egypt unto this day: consider of it, take advice, and speak *your minds*.

20 THEN ALL the children of Israel went out, and the congregation was gathered together as one man, from Dan even to Beer-sheba, with the land of Gilead, unto the LORD in Mizpeh.

2And the chief of all the people, *even* of all the tribes of Israel, presented themselves in the assembly of the people of God, four hundred thousand footmen that drew sword.

3(Now the children of Benjamin heard that the children of Israel were gone up to Mizpeh.) Then said the children of Israel, Tell *us*, how was this wickedness?

4And the Levite, the husband of the woman that was slain, answered and said, I came into Gibeah that *belongeth* to Benjamin, I and my concubine, to lodge.

5And the men of Gibeah rose against me, and beset the house round about upon me by night, *and* thought to have slain me: and my concubine have they forced, that she is dead.

6And I took my concubine, and cut her in pieces, and sent her throughout all the country of the inheritance of Israel: for they have committed lewdness and folly in Israel.

7Behold, ye *are* all children of Israel; give here your advice and counsel.

8¶ And all the people arose as one man, saying, We will not any *of us* go to his tent, neither will we any *of us* turn into his house.

9But now this *shall be* the thing which we will do to Gibeah; *we will go up* by lot against it;

10And we will take ten men of an hundred throughout all the tribes of Israel, and an hundred of a thousand, and a thousand out of ten thousand, to fetch victual for the people, that they may do, when they come to Gibeah of Benjamin, according to all the folly that they have wrought in Israel.

11So all the men of Israel were gathered against the city, knit together as one man.

12¶ And the tribes of Israel sent men through all the tribe of Benjamin, saying, What wickedness *is* this that is done among you?

13Now therefore deliver *us* the men, the children of Belial, which *are* in Gibeah, that we may put them to death, and put away evil from Israel. But the children of Benjamin would not hearken to the voice of their brethren the children of Israel:

New International

back to the house where her master was staying, fell down at the door and lay there until daylight.

27When her master got up in the morning and opened the door of the house and stepped out to continue on his way, there lay his concubine, fallen in the doorway of the house, with her hands on the threshold. 28He said to her, "Get up; let's go." But there was no answer. Then the man put her on his donkey and set out for home.

29When he reached home, he took a knife and cut up his concubine, limb by limb, into twelve parts and sent them into all the areas of Israel. 30Everyone who saw it said, "Such a thing has never been seen or done, not since the day the Israelites came up out of Egypt. Think about it! Consider it! Tell us what to do!"

Israelites Fight the Benjamites

20 THEN ALL the Israelites from Dan to Beersheba and from the land of Gilead came out as one man and assembled before the LORD in Mizpah. 2The leaders of all the people of the tribes of Israel took their places in the assembly of the people of God, four hundred thousand soldiers armed with swords. 3(The Benjamites heard that the Israelites had gone up to Mizpah.) Then the Israelites said, "Tell us how this awful thing happened."

4So the Levite, the husband of the murdered woman, said, "I and my concubine came to Gibeah in Benjamin to spend the night. 5During the night the men of Gibeah came after me and surrounded the house, intending to kill me. They raped my concubine, and she died. 6I took my concubine, cut her into pieces and sent one piece to each region of Israel's inheritance, because they committed this lewd and disgraceful act in Israel. 7Now, all you Israelites, speak up and give your verdict."

8All the people rose as one man, saying, "None of us will go home. No, not one of us will return to his house. 9But now this is what we'll do to Gibeah: We'll go up against it as the lot directs. 10We'll take ten men out of every hundred from all the tribes of Israel, and a hundred from a thousand, and a thousand from ten thousand, to get provisions for the army. Then, when the army arrives at Gibeah[a] in Benjamin, it can give them what they deserve for all this vileness done in Israel." 11So all the men of Israel got together and united as one man against the city.

12The tribes of Israel sent men throughout the tribe of Benjamin, saying, "What about this awful crime that was committed among you? 13Now surrender those wicked men of Gibeah so that we may put them to death and purge the evil from Israel."

But the Benjamites would not listen to their fellow Israelites. 14From their towns they came together at Gib-

---

a 10 One Hebrew manuscript; most Hebrew manuscripts Geba, a variant of Gibeah

Living Bible

of the house and lay there until it was light. 27When her husband opened the door to be on his way, he found her there, fallen down in front of the door with her hands digging into the threshold.

28"Well, come on," he said. "Let's get going."

But there was no answer, for she was dead; so he threw her across the donkey's back and took her home. 29When he got there he took a knife and cut her body into twelve parts and sent one piece to each tribe of Israel. 30Then the entire nation was roused to action against the men of Benjamin because of this awful deed.

"There hasn't been such a horrible crime since Israel left Egypt," everyone said. "We've got to do something about it."

20 THEN THE entire nation of Israel sent their leaders and 450,000 troops to assemble with one mind before the Lord at Mizpah. They came from as far away as Dan and Beersheba, and everywhere between, and from across the Jordan in the land of Gilead. 3(Word of the mobilization of the Israeli forces at Mizpah soon reached the land of Benjamin.) The chiefs of Israel now called for the murdered woman's husband and asked him just what had happened.

4"We arrived one evening at Gibe-ah, a village in Benjamin," he began. 5"That night the men of Gibe-ah surrounded the house, planning to kill me, and they raped my wife until she was dead. 6So I cut her body into twelve pieces and sent the pieces throughout the land of Israel, for these men have committed a terrible crime. 7Now then, sons of Israel, express your mind and give me your counsel!"

8, 9, 10And as one man they replied, "Not one of us will return home until we have punished the village of Gibe-ah. A tenth of the army will be selected by lot as a supply line to bring us food, and the rest of us will destroy Gibe-ah for this horrible deed."

11So the whole nation united in this task.

12Then messengers were sent to the tribe of Benjamin, asking, "Did you know about the terrible thing that was done among you? 13Give up these evil men from the city of Gibe-ah so that we can execute them and purge Israel of her evil." But the people of Benjamin wouldn't listen. 14, 15Instead, twenty-six thousand of them arrived

New Revised Standard

the woman came and fell down at the door of the man's house where her master was, until it was light.

27 In the morning her master got up, opened the doors of the house, and when he went out to go on his way, there was his concubine lying at the door of the house, with her hands on the threshold. 28"Get up," he said to her, "we are going." But there was no answer. Then he put her on the donkey; and the man set out for his home. 29When he had entered his house, he took a knife, and grasping his concubine he cut her into twelve pieces, limb by limb, and sent her throughout all the territory of Israel. 30Then he commanded the men whom he sent, saying, "Thus shall you say to all the Israelites, 'Has such a thing ever happened[b] since the day that the Israelites came up from the land of Egypt until this day? Consider it, take counsel, and speak out.' "

The Other Tribes Attack Benjamin

20 THEN ALL the Israelites came out, from Dan to Beer-sheba, including the land of Gilead, and the congregation assembled in one body before the LORD at Mizpah. 2The chiefs of all the people, of all the tribes of Israel, presented themselves in the assembly of the people of God, four hundred thousand foot-soldiers bearing arms. 3(Now the Benjaminites heard that the people of Israel had gone up to Mizpah.) And the Israelites said, "Tell us, how did this criminal act come about?" 4The Levite, the husband of the woman who was murdered, answered, "I came to Gibeah that belongs to Benjamin, I and my concubine, to spend the night. 5The lords of Gibeah rose up against me, and surrounded the house at night. They intended to kill me, and they raped my concubine until she died. 6Then I took my concubine and cut her into pieces, and sent her throughout the whole extent of Israel's territory; for they have committed a vile outrage in Israel. 7So now, you Israelites, all of you, give your advice and counsel here."

8 All the people got up as one, saying, "We will not any of us go to our tents, nor will any of us return to our houses. 9But now this is what we will do to Gibeah: we will go up[c] against it by lot. 10We will take ten men of a hundred throughout all the tribes of Israel, and a hundred of a thousand, and a thousand of ten thousand, to bring provisions for the troops, who are going to repay[d] Gibeah of Benjamin for all the disgrace that they have done in Israel." 11So all the men of Israel gathered against the city, united as one.

12 The tribes of Israel sent men through all the tribe of Benjamin, saying, "What crime is this that has been committed among you? 13Now then, hand over those scoundrels in Gibeah, so that we may put them to death, and purge the evil from Israel." But the Benjaminites would not listen to their kinsfolk, the Israelites. 14The

b Compare Gk: Heb 30And all who saw it said, "Such a thing has not happened or been seen   c Gk: Heb lacks we will go up   d Compare Gk: Meaning of Heb uncertain

King James

14But the children of Benjamin gathered themselves together out of the cities unto Gibeah, to go out to battle against the children of Israel.

15And the children of Benjamin were numbered at that time out of the cities twenty and six thousand men that drew sword, beside the inhabitants of Gibeah, which were numbered seven hundred chosen men.

16Among all this people *there were* seven hundred chosen men lefthanded; every one could sling stones at an hair *breadth*, and not miss.

17And the men of Israel, beside Benjamin, were numbered four hundred thousand men that drew sword: all these *were* men of war.

18¶ And the children of Israel arose, and went up to the house of God, and asked counsel of God, and said, Which of us shall go up first to the battle against the children of Benjamin? And the LORD said, Judah *shall go up* first.

19And the children of Israel rose up in the morning, and encamped against Gibeah.

20And the men of Israel went out to battle against Benjamin; and the men of Israel put themselves in array to fight against them at Gibeah.

21And the children of Benjamin came forth out of Gibeah, and destroyed down to the ground of the Israelites that day twenty and two thousand men.

22And the people the men of Israel encouraged themselves, and set their battle again in array in the place where they put themselves in array the first day.

23(And the children of Israel went up and wept before the LORD until even, and asked counsel of the LORD, saying, Shall I go up again to battle against the children of Benjamin my brother? And the LORD said, Go up against him.)

24And the children of Israel came near against the children of Benjamin the second day.

25And Benjamin went forth against them out of Gibeah the second day, and destroyed down to the ground of the children of Israel again eighteen thousand men; all these drew the sword.

26¶ Then all the children of Israel, and all the people, went up, and came unto the house of God, and wept, and sat there before the LORD, and fasted that day until even, and offered burnt offerings and peace offerings before the LORD.

27And the children of Israel inquired of the LORD, (for the ark of the covenant of God *was* there in those days,

28And Phinehas, the son of Eleazar, the son of Aaron, stood before it in those days,) saying, Shall I yet again go out to battle against the children of Benjamin my brother, or shall I cease? And the LORD said, Go up; for tomorrow I will deliver them into thine hand.

29And Israel set liers in wait round about Gibeah.

30And the children of Israel went up against the children of Benjamin on the third day, and put themselves in array against Gibeah, as at other times.

31And the children of Benjamin went out against the people, *and* were drawn away from the city; and they began to smite of the people, *and* kill, as at other times, in the highways, of which one goeth up to the house of God, and the other to Gibeah in the field, about thirty men of Israel.

32And the children of Benjamin said, They *are* smitten down before us, as at the first. But the children of Israel said, Let us flee, and draw them from the city unto the highways.

33And all the men of Israel rose up out of their place, and put themselves in array at Baal-tamar: and the liers in wait of Israel came forth out of their places, *even* out of the meadows of Gibeah.

34And there came against Gibeah ten thousand chosen men out of all Israel, and the battle was sore: but they knew not that evil *was* near them.

New International

eah to fight against the Israelites. 15At once the Benjamites mobilized twenty-six thousand swordsmen from their towns, in addition to seven hundred chosen men from those living in Gibeah. 16Among all these soldiers there were seven hundred chosen men who were left-handed, each of whom could sling a stone at a hair and not miss.

17Israel, apart from Benjamin, mustered four hundred thousand swordsmen, all of them fighting men.

18The Israelites went up to Bethel[a] and inquired of God. They said, "Who of us shall go first to fight against the Benjamites?"

The LORD replied, "Judah shall go first."

19The next morning the Israelites got up and pitched camp near Gibeah. 20The men of Israel went out to fight the Benjamites and took up battle positions against them at Gibeah. 21The Benjamites came out of Gibeah and cut down twenty-two thousand Israelites on the battlefield that day. 22But the men of Israel encouraged one another and again took up their positions where they had stationed themselves the first day. 23The Israelites went up and wept before the LORD until evening, and they inquired of the LORD. They said, "Shall we go up again to battle against the Benjamites, our brothers?"

The LORD answered, "Go up against them."

24Then the Israelites drew near to Benjamin the second day. 25This time, when the Benjamites came out from Gibeah to oppose them, they cut down another eighteen thousand Israelites, all of them armed with swords.

26Then the Israelites, all the people, went up to Bethel, and there they sat weeping before the LORD. They fasted that day until evening and presented burnt offerings and fellowship offerings[b] to the LORD. 27And the Israelites inquired of the LORD. (In those days the ark of the covenant of God was there, 28with Phinehas son of Eleazar, the son of Aaron, ministering before it.) They asked, "Shall we go up again to battle with Benjamin our brother, or not?"

The LORD responded, "Go, for tomorrow I will give them into your hands."

29Then Israel set an ambush around Gibeah. 30They went up against the Benjamites on the third day and took up positions against Gibeah as they had done before. 31The Benjamites came out to meet them and were drawn away from the city. They began to inflict casualties on the Israelites as before, so that about thirty men fell in the open field and on the roads—the one leading to Bethel and the other to Gibeah.

32While the Benjamites were saying, "We are defeating them as before," the Israelites were saying, "Let's retreat and draw them away from the city to the roads."

33All the men of Israel moved from their places and took up positions at Baal Tamar, and the Israelite ambush charged out of its place on the west[c] of Gibeah.[d] 34Then ten thousand of Israel's finest men made a frontal attack on Gibeah. The fighting was so heavy that the Benjamites did not realize how near disaster was. 35The

---

[a] 18 Or *to the house of God*; also in verse 26   [b] 26 Traditionally *peace offerings*   [c] 33 Some Septuagint manuscripts and Vulgate; the meaning of the Hebrew for this word is uncertain.   [d] 33 Hebrew *Geba*, a variant of *Gibeah*

Living Bible

in Gibe-ah to join the seven hundred local men in their defense against the rest of Israel. 16(Among all these there were seven hundred men who were left-handed sharpshooters. They could hit a target within a hair's breadth, never missing!) 17The army of Israel, not counting the men of Benjamin, numbered 400,000 men.

18Before the battle the Israeli army went to Bethel first to ask counsel from God. "Which tribe shall lead us against the people of Benjamin?" they asked.

And the Lord replied, "Judah shall go first."

19, 20So the entire army left early the next morning to go to Gibe-ah, to attack the men of Benjamin. 21But the men defending the village stormed out and killed twenty-two thousand Israelis that day. 22, 23, 24Then the Israeli army wept before the Lord until evening and asked him, "Shall we fight further against our brother Benjamin?"

And the Lord said, "Yes." So the men of Israel took courage and went out again the next day to fight at the same place. 25And that day they lost another eighteen thousand men, all experienced swordsmen.

26Then the entire army went up to Bethel and wept before the Lord and fasted until evening, offering burnt sacrifices and peace offerings. 27, 28(The Ark of God was in Bethel in those days. Phinehas, the son of Eleazar and grandson of Aaron, was the priest.)

The men of Israel asked the Lord, "Shall we go out again and fight against our brother Benjamin, or shall we stop?"

And the Lord said, "Go, for tomorrow I will see to it that you defeat the men of Benjamin."

29So the Israeli army set an ambush all around the village, 30and went out again on the third day and set themselves in their usual battle formation. 31When the army of Benjamin came out of the town to attack, the Israeli forces retreated and Benjamin was drawn away from the town as they chased after Israel. And as they had done previously, Benjamin began to kill the men of Israel along the roadway running between Bethel and Gibe-ah, so that about thirty of them died.

32Then the army of Benjamin shouted, "We're defeating them again!" But the armies of Israel had agreed in advance to run away so that the army of Benjamin would chase them and be drawn away from the town. 33But when the main army of Israel reached Baal-tamar, it turned and attacked, and the ten thousand men in ambush west of Geba jumped up from where they were, 34and advanced against the rear of the army of Benjamin, who still didn't realize the impending disaster.

New Revised Standard

Benjaminites came together out of the towns to Gibeah, to go out to battle against the Israelites. 15On that day the Benjaminites mustered twenty-six thousand armed men from their towns, besides the inhabitants of Gibeah. 16Of all this force, there were seven hundred picked men who were left-handed; every one could sling a stone at a hair, and not miss. 17And the Israelites, apart from Benjamin, mustered four hundred thousand armed men, all of them warriors.

18 The Israelites proceeded to go up to Bethel, where they inquired of God, "Which of us shall go up first to battle against the Benjaminites?" And the LORD answered, "Judah shall go up first."

19 Then the Israelites got up in the morning, and encamped against Gibeah. 20The Israelites went out to battle against Benjamin; and the Israelites drew up the battle line against them at Gibeah. 21The Benjaminites came out of Gibeah, and struck down on that day twenty-two thousand of the Israelites. 23eThe Israelites went up and wept before the LORD until the evening; and they inquired of the LORD, "Shall we again draw near to battle against our kinsfolk the Benjaminites?" And the LORD said, "Go up against them." 22The Israelites took courage, and again formed the battle line in the same place where they had formed it on the first day.

24 So the Israelites advanced against the Benjaminites the second day. 25Benjamin moved out against them from Gibeah the second day, and struck down eighteen thousand of the Israelites, all of them armed men. 26Then all the Israelites, the whole army, went back to Bethel and wept, sitting there before the LORD; they fasted that day until evening. Then they offered burnt offerings and sacrifices of well-being before the LORD. 27And the Israelites inquired of the LORD (for the ark of the covenant of God was there in those days, 28and Phinehas son of Eleazar, son of Aaron, ministered before it in those days), saying, "Shall we go out once more to battle against our kinsfolk the Benjaminites, or shall we desist?" The LORD answered, "Go up, for tomorrow I will give them into your hand."

29 So Israel stationed men in ambush around Gibeah. 30Then the Israelites went up against the Benjaminites on the third day, and set themselves in array against Gibeah, as before. 31When the Benjaminites went out against the army, they were drawn away from the city. As before they began to inflict casualties on the troops, along the main roads, one of which goes up to Bethel and the other to Gibeah, as well as in the open country, killing about thirty men of Israel. 32The Benjaminites thought, "They are being routed before us, as previously." But the Israelites said, "Let us retreat and draw them away from the city toward the roads." 33The main body of the Israelites drew back its battle line to Baal-tamar, while those Israelites who were in ambush rushed out of their place westf of Geba. 34There came against Gibeah ten thousand picked men out of all Israel, and the battle was fierce. But the Benjaminites did not realize that disaster was close upon them.

---

e Verses 22 and 23 are transposed   f Gk Vg: Heb in the plain

King James

35And the LORD smote Benjamin before Israel: and the children of Israel destroyed of the Benjamites that day twenty and five thousand and an hundred men: all these drew the sword.

36So the children of Benjamin saw that they were smitten: for the men of Israel gave place to the Benjamites, because they trusted unto the liers in wait which they had set beside Gibeah.

37And the liers in wait hasted, and rushed upon Gibeah; and the liers in wait drew *themselves* along, and smote all the city with the edge of the sword.

38Now there was an appointed sign between the men of Israel and the liers in wait, that they should make a great flame with smoke rise up out of the city.

39And when the men of Israel retired in the battle, Benjamin began to smite *and* kill of the men of Israel about thirty persons: for they said, Surely they are smitten down before us, as *in* the first battle.

40But when the flame began to arise up out of the city with a pillar of smoke, the Benjamites looked behind them, and, behold, the flame of the city ascended up to heaven.

41And when the men of Israel turned again, the men of Benjamin were amazed: for they saw that evil was come upon them.

42Therefore they turned *their backs* before the men of Israel unto the way of the wilderness; but the battle overtook them; and them which *came* out of the cities they destroyed in the midst of them.

43*Thus* they inclosed the Benjamites round about, *and* chased them, *and* trode them down with ease over against Gibeah toward the sunrising.

44And there fell of Benjamin eighteen thousand men; all these *were* men of valour.

45And they turned and fled toward the wilderness unto the rock of Rimmon: and they gleaned of them in the highways five thousand men; and pursued hard after them unto Gidom, and slew two thousand men of them.

46So that all which fell that day of Benjamin were twenty and five thousand men that drew the sword; all these *were* men of valour.

47But six hundred men turned and fled to the wilderness unto the rock Rimmon, and abode in the rock Rimmon four months.

48And the men of Israel turned again upon the children of Benjamin, and smote them with the edge of the sword, as well the men of *every* city, as the beast, and all that came to hand: also they set on fire all the cities that they came to.

21 NOW THE men of Israel had sworn in Mizpeh, saying, There shall not any of us give his daughter unto Benjamin to wife.

2And the people came to the house of God, and abode there till even before God, and lifted up their voices, and wept sore;

3And said, O LORD God of Israel, why is this come to pass in Israel, that there should be today one tribe lacking in Israel?

4And it came to pass on the morrow, that the people rose early, and built there an altar, and offered burnt offerings and peace offerings.

5And the children of Israel said, Who *is there* among all the tribes of Israel that came not up with the congregation unto the LORD? For they had made a great oath concerning him that came not up to the LORD to Mizpeh, saying, He shall surely be put to death.

6And the children of Israel repented them for Benjamin their brother, and said, There is one tribe cut off from Israel this day.

New International

LORD defeated Benjamin before Israel, and on that day the Israelites struck down 25,100 Benjamites, all armed with swords. 36Then the Benjamites saw that they were beaten.

Now the men of Israel had given way before Benjamin, because they relied on the ambush they had set near Gibeah. 37The men who had been in ambush made a sudden dash into Gibeah, spread out and put the whole city to the sword. 38The men of Israel had arranged with the ambush that they should send up a great cloud of smoke from the city, 39and then the men of Israel would turn in the battle.

The Benjamites had begun to inflict casualties on the men of Israel (about thirty), and they said, "We are defeating them as in the first battle." 40But when the column of smoke began to rise from the city, the Benjamites turned and saw the smoke of the whole city going up into the sky. 41Then the men of Israel turned on them, and the men of Benjamin were terrified, because they realized that disaster had come upon them. 42So they fled before the Israelites in the direction of the desert, but they could not escape the battle. And the men of Israel who came out of the towns cut them down there. 43They surrounded the Benjamites, chased them and easily[a] overran them in the vicinity of Gibeah on the east. 44Eighteen thousand Benjamites fell, all of them valiant fighters. 45As they turned and fled toward the desert to the rock of Rimmon, the Israelites cut down five thousand men along the roads. They kept pressing after the Benjamites as far as Gidom and struck down two thousand more.

46On that day twenty-five thousand Benjamite swordsmen fell, all of them valiant fighters. 47But six hundred men turned and fled into the desert to the rock of Rimmon, where they stayed four months. 48The men of Israel went back to Benjamin and put all the towns to the sword, including the animals and everything else they found. All the towns they came across they set on fire.

Wives for the Benjamites

21 THE MEN of Israel had taken an oath at Mizpah: "Not one of us will give his daughter in marriage to a Benjamite."

2The people went to Bethel,[b] where they sat before God until evening, raising their voices and weeping bitterly. 3"O LORD, the God of Israel," they cried, "why has this happened to Israel? Why should one tribe be missing from Israel today?"

4Early the next day the people built an altar and presented burnt offerings and fellowship offerings.[c]

5Then the Israelites asked, "Who from all the tribes of Israel has failed to assemble before the LORD?" For they had taken a solemn oath that anyone who failed to assemble before the LORD at Mizpah should certainly be put to death.

6Now the Israelites grieved for their brothers, the Benjamites. "Today one tribe is cut off from Israel," they said. 7"How can we provide wives for those who

a 43 The meaning of the Hebrew for this word is uncertain.   b 2 Or *to the house of God*   c 4 Traditionally *peace offerings*

Living Bible

35–39So the Lord helped Israel defeat Benjamin, and the Israeli army killed 25,100 men of Benjamin that day, leaving but a tiny remnant of their forces.

Summary of the Battle:

The army of Israel retreated from the men of Benjamin in order to give the ambush more room for maneuvering. When the men of Benjamin had killed about thirty of the Israelis, they were confident of a massive slaughter just as on the previous days. But then the men in ambush rushed into the village and slaughtered everyone in it, and set it on fire. The great cloud of smoke pouring into the sky was the signal for the Israeli army to turn around and attack the army of Benjamin, 40, 41who now looked behind them and were terrified to discover that their city was on fire, and that they were in serious trouble. 42So they ran toward the wilderness, but the Israelis chased after them, and the men who had set the ambush came out and joined the slaughter from the rear. 43They encircled the army of Benjamin east of Gibe-ah, and killed most of them there. 44Eighteen thousand of the Benjamin troops died in that day's battle. 45The rest of the army fled into the wilderness toward the rock of Rimmon, but five thousand were killed along the way, and two thousand more near Gidom.

46, 47So the tribe of Benjamin lost twenty-five thousand brave warriors that day, leaving only six hundred men who escaped to the rock of Rimmon, where they lived for four months. 48Then the Israeli army returned and slaughtered the entire population of the tribe of Benjamin—men, women, children, and cattle—and burned down every city and village in the entire land.

21 THE LEADERS of Israel had vowed at Mizpah never to let their daughters marry a man from the tribe of Benjamin. 2And now the Israeli leaders met at Bethel and sat before God until evening, weeping bitterly.

3"O Lord God of Israel," they cried out, "why has this happened, that now one of our tribes is missing?"

4The next morning they were up early and built an altar, and offered sacrifices and peace offerings on it. 5And they said among themselves, "Was any tribe of Israel not represented when we held our council before the Lord at Mizpah?" For at that time it was agreed by solemn oath that anyone who refused to come must die. 6There was deep sadness throughout all Israel for the loss of their brother tribe, Benjamin.

"Gone," they kept saying to themselves, "gone—an entire tribe of Israel has been cut off, and is gone. 7And

New Revised Standard

35 The LORD defeated Benjamin before Israel; and the Israelites destroyed twenty-five thousand one hundred men of Benjamin that day, all of them armed. 36 Then the Benjaminites saw that they were defeated.d

The Israelites gave ground to Benjamin, because they trusted to the troops in ambush that they had stationed against Gibeah. 37The troops in ambush rushed quickly upon Gibeah. Then they put the whole city to the sword. 38Now the agreement between the main body of Israel and the men in ambush was that when they sent up a cloud of smoke out of the city 39the main body of Israel should turn in battle. But Benjamin had begun to inflict casualties on the Israelites, killing about thirty of them; so they thought, "Surely they are defeated before us, as in the first battle." 40But when the cloud, a column of smoke, began to rise out of the city, the Benjaminites looked behind them—and there was the whole city going up in smoke toward the sky! 41Then the main body of Israel turned, and the Benjaminites were dismayed, for they saw that disaster was close upon them. 42Therefore they turned away from the Israelites in the direction of the wilderness; but the battle overtook them, and those who came out of the citye were slaughtering them in between.f 43Cutting downg the Benjaminites, they pursued them from Nohahh and trod them down as far as a place east of Gibeah. 44Eighteen thousand Benjaminites fell, all of them courageous fighters. 45When they turned and fled toward the wilderness to the rock of Rimmon, five thousand of them were cut down on the main roads, and they were pursued as far as Gidom, and two thousand of them were slain. 46So all who fell that day of Benjamin were twenty-five thousand armsbearing men, all of them courageous fighters. 47But six hundred turned and fled toward the wilderness to the rock of Rimmon, and remained at the rock of Rimmon for four months. 48Meanwhile, the Israelites turned back against the Benjaminites, and put them to the sword— the city, the people, the animals, and all that remained. Also the remaining towns they set on fire.

The Benjaminites Saved from Extinction

21 NOW THE Israelites had sworn at Mizpah, "No one of us shall give his daughter in marriage to Benjamin." 2And the people came to Bethel, and sat there until evening before God, and they lifted up their voices and wept bitterly. 3They said, "O LORD, the God of Israel, why has it come to pass that today there should be one tribe lacking in Israel?" 4On the next day, the people got up early, and built an altar there, and offered burnt offerings and sacrifices of well-being. 5Then the Israelites said, "Which of all the tribes of Israel did not come up in the assembly to the LORD?" For a solemn oath had been taken concerning whoever did not come up to the LORD to Mizpah, saying, "That one shall be put to death." 6But the Israelites had compassion for Benjamin their kin, and said, "One tribe is cut off from Israel this day. 7What shall we do for wives for those

---

d This sentence is continued by verse 45.   e Compare Vg and some Gk Mss:
Heb *cities*   f Compare Syr: Meaning of Heb uncertain   g Gk: Heb
Surrounding   h Gk: Heb *pursued them at their resting place*

King James

7How shall we do for wives for them that remain, seeing we have sworn by the LORD that we will not give them of our daughters to wives?

8¶ And they said, What one *is there* of the tribes of Israel that came not up to Mizpeh to the LORD? And, behold, there came none to the camp from Jabesh-gilead to the assembly.

9For the people were numbered, and, behold, *there were* none of the inhabitants of Jabesh-gilead there.

10And the congregation sent thither twelve thousand men of the valiantest, and commanded them, saying, Go and smite the inhabitants of Jabesh-gilead with the edge of the sword, with the women and the children.

11And this *is* the thing that ye shall do, Ye shall utterly destroy every male, and every woman that hath lain by man.

12And they found among the inhabitants of Jabesh-gilead four hundred young virgins, that had known no man by lying with any male: and they brought them unto the camp to Shiloh, which *is* in the land of Canaan.

13And the whole congregation sent *some* to speak to the children of Benjamin that *were* in the rock Rimmon, and to call peaceably unto them.

14And Benjamin came again at that time; and they gave them wives which they had saved alive of the women of Jabesh-gilead: and yet so they sufficed them not.

15And the people repented them for Benjamin, because that the LORD had made a breach in the tribes of Israel.

16¶ Then the elders of the congregation said, How shall we do for wives for them that remain, seeing the women are destroyed out of Benjamin?

17And they said, *There must be* an inheritance for them that be escaped of Benjamin, that a tribe be not destroyed out of Israel.

18Howbeit we may not give them wives of our daughters: for the children of Israel have sworn, saying, Cursed *be* he that giveth a wife to Benjamin.

19Then they said, Behold, *there is* a feast of the LORD in Shiloh yearly *in a place* which *is* on the north side of Beth-el, on the east side of the highway that goeth up from Beth-el to Shechem, and on the south of Lebonah.

20Therefore they commanded the children of Benjamin, saying, Go and lie in wait in the vineyards;

21And see, and, behold, if the daughters of Shiloh come out to dance in dances, then come ye out of the vineyards, and catch you every man his wife of the daughters of Shiloh, and go to the land of Benjamin.

22And it shall be, when their fathers or their brethren come unto us to complain, that we will say unto them, Be favourable unto them for our sakes: because we reserved not to each man his wife in the war: for ye did not give unto them at this time, *that* ye should be guilty.

23And the children of Benjamin did so, and took *them* wives, according to their number, of them that danced, whom they caught: and they went and returned unto their inheritance, and repaired the cities, and dwelt in them.

24And the children of Israel departed thence at that time, every man to his tribe and to his family, and they went out from thence every man to his inheritance.

25In those days *there was* no king in Israel: every man did *that which was* right in his own eyes.

New International

are left, since we have taken an oath by the LORD not to give them any of our daughters in marriage?" 8Then they asked, "Which one of the tribes of Israel failed to assemble before the LORD at Mizpah?" They discovered that no one from Jabesh Gilead had come to the camp for the assembly. 9For when they counted the people, they found that none of the people of Jabesh Gilead were there.

10So the assembly sent twelve thousand fighting men with instructions to go to Jabesh Gilead and put to the sword those living there, including the women and children. 11"This is what you are to do," they said. "Kill every male and every woman who is not a virgin." 12They found among the people living in Jabesh Gilead four hundred young women who had never slept with a man, and they took them to the camp at Shiloh in Canaan.

13Then the whole assembly sent an offer of peace to the Benjamites at the rock of Rimmon. 14So the Benjamites returned at that time and were given the women of Jabesh Gilead who had been spared. But there were not enough for all of them.

15The people grieved for Benjamin, because the LORD had made a gap in the tribes of Israel. 16And the elders of the assembly said, "With the women of Benjamin destroyed, how shall we provide wives for the men who are left? 17The Benjamite survivors must have heirs," they said, "so that a tribe of Israel will not be wiped out. 18We can't give them our daughters as wives, since we Israelites have taken this oath: 'Cursed be anyone who gives a wife to a Benjamite.' 19But look, there is the annual festival of the LORD in Shiloh, to the north of Bethel, and east of the road that goes from Bethel to Shechem, and to the south of Lebonah."

20So they instructed the Benjamites, saying, "Go and hide in the vineyards 21and watch. When the girls of Shiloh come out to join in the dancing, then rush from the vineyards and each of you seize a wife from the girls of Shiloh and go to the land of Benjamin. 22When their fathers or brothers complain to us, we will say to them, 'Do us a kindness by helping them, because we did not get wives for them during the war, and you are innocent, since you did not give your daughters to them.'"

23So that is what the Benjamites did. While the girls were dancing, each man caught one and carried her off to be his wife. Then they returned to their inheritance and rebuilt the towns and settled in them.

24At that time the Israelites left that place and went home to their tribes and clans, each to his own inheritance.

25In those days Israel had no king; everyone did as he saw fit.

Living Bible

how shall we get wives for the few who remain, since we have sworn by the Lord that we will not give them our daughters?"

8, 9Then they thought again of their oath to kill anyone who refused to come to Mizpah, and discovered that no one had attended from Jabesh-gilead. 10, 11, 12So they sent twelve thousand of their best soldiers to destroy the people of Jabesh-gilead. All the men, married women, and children were slain, but the young virgins of marriageable age were saved. There were four hundred of these, and they were brought to the camp at Shiloh.

13Then Israel sent a peace delegation to the little remnant of the men of Benjamin at Rimmon Rock. 14The four hundred girls were given to them as wives, and they returned to their homes; but there were not enough of these girls for all of them. 15(What a sad time it was in Israel in those days, because the Lord had made a breach in the tribes of Israel.)

16"What shall we do for wives for the others, since all the women of the tribe of Benjamin are dead?" the leaders of Israel asked. 17"There must be some way to get wives for them, so that an entire tribe of Israel will not be lost forever. 18But we can't give them our own daughters. We have sworn with a solemn oath that anyone who does this shall be cursed of God."

19Suddenly someone thought of the annual religious festival held in the fields of Shiloh, between Lebonah and Bethel, along the east side of the road that goes from Bethel to Shechem.

20They told the men of Benjamin who still needed wives, "Go and hide in the vineyards, 21and when the girls of Shiloh come out for their dances, rush out and catch them and take them home with you to be your wives! 22And when their fathers and brothers come to us in protest, we will tell them, 'Please be understanding and let them have your daughters, for we didn't find enough wives for them when we destroyed Jabesh-gilead, and you couldn't have given your daughters to them without being guilty.' "

23So the men of Benjamin did as they were told and kidnapped the girls who took part in the celebration, and carried them off to their own land. Then they rebuilt their cities and lived in them. 24So the people of Israel returned to their homes.

25(There was no king in Israel in those days, and every man did whatever he thought was right.)

New Revised Standard

who are left, since we have sworn by the LORD that we will not give them any of our daughters as wives?"

8 Then they said, "Is there anyone from the tribes of Israel who did not come up to the LORD to Mizpah?" It turned out that no one from Jabesh-gilead had come to the camp, to the assembly. 9For when the roll was called among the people, not one of the inhabitants of Jabesh-gilead was there. 10So the congregation sent twelve thousand soldiers there and commanded them, "Go, put the inhabitants of Jabesh-gilead to the sword, including the women and the little ones. 11This is what you shall do; every male and every woman that has lain with a male you shall devote to destruction." 12And they found among the inhabitants of Jabesh-gilead four hundred young virgins who had never slept with a man and brought them to the camp at Shiloh, which is in the land of Canaan.

13 Then the whole congregation sent word to the Benjaminites who were at the rock of Rimmon, and proclaimed peace to them. 14Benjamin returned at that time; and they gave them the women whom they had saved alive of the women of Jabesh-gilead; but they did not suffice for them.

15 The people had compassion on Benjamin because the LORD had made a breach in the tribes of Israel. 16So the elders of the congregation said, "What shall we do for wives for those who are left, since there are no women left in Benjamin?" 17And they said, "There must be heirs for the survivors of Benjamin, in order that a tribe may not be blotted out from Israel. 18Yet we cannot give any of our daughters to them as wives." For the Israelites had sworn, "Cursed be anyone who gives a wife to Benjamin." 19So they said, "Look, the yearly festival of the LORD is taking place at Shiloh, which is north of Bethel, on the east of the highway that goes up from Bethel to Shechem, and south of Lebonah." 20And they instructed the Benjaminites, saying, "Go and lie in wait in the vineyards, 21and watch; when the young women of Shiloh come out to dance in the dances, then come out of the vineyards and each of you carry off a wife for himself from the young women of Shiloh, and go to the land of Benjamin. 22Then if their fathers or their brothers come to complain to us, we will say to them, 'Be generous and allow us to have them; because we did not capture in battle a wife for each man. But neither did you incur guilt by giving your daughters to them.' " 23The Benjaminites did so; they took wives for each of them from the dancers whom they abducted. Then they went and returned to their territory, and rebuilt the towns, and lived in them. 24So the Israelites departed from there at that time by tribes and families, and they went out from there to their own territories.

25 In those days there was no king in Israel; all the people did what was right in their own eyes.

THE BOOK OF

Ruth   Ruth

Naomi and Ruth

1 NOW IT came to pass in the days when the judges ruled, that there was a famine in the land. And a certain man of Bethlehem-judah went to sojourn in the country of Moab, he, and his wife, and his two sons.

²And the name of the man *was* Elimelech, and the name of his wife Naomi, and the name of his two sons Mahlon and Chilion, Ephrathites of Bethlehem-judah. And they came into the country of Moab, and continued there.

³And Elimelech Naomi's husband died; and she was left, and her two sons.

⁴And they took them wives of the women of Moab; the name of the one *was* Orpah, and the name of the other Ruth: and they dwelled there about ten years.

⁵And Mahlon and Chilion died also both of them; and the woman was left of her two sons and her husband.

⁶¶ Then she arose with her daughters-in-law, that she might return from the country of Moab: for she had heard in the country of Moab how that the LORD had visited his people in giving them bread.

⁷Wherefore she went forth out of the place where she was, and her two daughters-in-law with her; and they went on the way to return unto the land of Judah.

⁸And Naomi said unto her two daughters-in-law, Go, return each to her mother's house: the LORD deal kindly with you, as ye have dealt with the dead, and with me.

⁹The LORD grant you that ye may find rest, each *of you* in the house of her husband. Then she kissed them; and they lifted up their voice, and wept.

¹⁰And they said unto her, Surely we will return with thee unto thy people.

¹¹And Naomi said, Turn again, my daughters: why will ye go with me? *are* there yet *any more* sons in my womb, that they may be your husbands?

¹²Turn again, my daughters, go *your way;* for I am too old to have an husband. If I should say, I have hope, *if* I should have an husband also tonight, and should also bear sons;

¹³Would ye tarry for them till they were grown? would ye stay for them from having husbands? nay, my daughters; for it grieveth me much for your sakes that the hand of the LORD is gone out against me.

¹⁴And they lifted up their voice, and wept again: and Orpah kissed her mother-in-law; but Ruth clave unto her.

¹⁵And she said, Behold, thy sister-in-law is gone back unto her people, and unto her gods: return thou after thy sister-in-law.

¹⁶And Ruth said, Entreat me not to leave thee, *or to* return from following after thee: for whither thou goest, I will go; and where thou lodgest, I will lodge: thy people *shall be* my people, and thy God my God:

¹⁷Where thou diest, will I die, and there will I be buried: the LORD do so to me, and more also, *if aught* but death part thee and me.

¹⁸When she saw that she was stedfastly minded to go with her, then she left speaking unto her.

Naomi and Ruth

1 IN THE days when the judges ruled,[a] there was a famine in the land, and a man from Bethlehem in Judah, together with his wife and two sons, went to live for a while in the country of Moab. ²The man's name was Elimelech, his wife's name Naomi, and the names of his two sons were Mahlon and Kilion. They were Ephrathites from Bethlehem, Judah. And they went to Moab and lived there.

³Now Elimelech, Naomi's husband, died, and she was left with her two sons. ⁴They married Moabite women, one named Orpah and the other Ruth. After they had lived there about ten years, ⁵both Mahlon and Kilion also died, and Naomi was left without her two sons and her husband.

⁶When she heard in Moab that the LORD had come to the aid of his people by providing food for them, Naomi and her daughters-in-law prepared to return home from there. ⁷With her two daughters-in-law she left the place where she had been living and set out on the road that would take them back to the land of Judah.

⁸Then Naomi said to her two daughters-in-law, "Go back, each of you, to your mother's home. May the LORD show kindness to you, as you have shown to your dead and to me. ⁹May the LORD grant that each of you will find rest in the home of another husband."

Then she kissed them and they wept aloud ¹⁰and said to her, "We will go back with you to your people."

¹¹But Naomi said, "Return home, my daughters. Why would you come with me? Am I going to have any more sons, who could become your husbands? ¹²Return home, my daughters; I am too old to have another husband. Even if I thought there was still hope for me— even if I had a husband tonight and then gave birth to sons— ¹³would you wait until they grew up? Would you remain unmarried for them? No, my daughters. It is more bitter for me than for you, because the LORD's hand has gone out against me!"

¹⁴At this they wept again. Then Orpah kissed her mother-in-law good-by, but Ruth clung to her.

¹⁵"Look," said Naomi, "your sister-in-law is going back to her people and her gods. Go back with her."

¹⁶But Ruth replied, "Don't urge me to leave you or to turn back from you. Where you go I will go, and where you stay I will stay. Your people will be my people and your God my God. ¹⁷Where you die I will die, and there I will be buried. May the LORD deal with me, be it ever so severely, if anything but death separates you and me." ¹⁸When Naomi realized that Ruth was determined to go with her, she stopped urging her.

Ruth

Ruth

Living Bible

1 LONG AGO when judges ruled in Israel, a man named Elimelech, from Bethlehem,[b] left the country because of a famine and moved to the land of Moab. With him were his wife, Naomi, and his two sons, Mahlon and Chilion. 3During the time of their residence there, Elimelech died and Naomi was left with her two sons.

4, 5These young men, Mahlon and Chilion, married girls of Moab, Orpah and Ruth. But later, both men died, so that Naomi was left alone, without her husband or sons. 6, 7She decided to return to Israel with her daughters-in-law, for she had heard that the Lord had blessed his people by giving them good crops again.

8But after they had begun their homeward journey, she changed her mind and said to her two daughters-in-law, "Why don't you return to your parents' homes instead of coming with me? And may the Lord reward you for your faithfulness to your husbands and to me. 9And may he bless you with another happy marriage." Then she kissed them and they all broke down and cried.

10"No," they said. "We want to go with you to your people."

11But Naomi replied, "It is better for you to return to your own people. Do I have younger sons who could grow up to be your husbands?[c] 12No, my daughters, return to your parents' homes, for I am too old to have a husband. And even if that were possible, and I became pregnant tonight, and bore sons, 13would you wait for them to grow up? No, of course not, my daughters; oh, how I grieve for you that the Lord has punished me in a way that injures you."

14And again they cried together, and Orpah kissed her mother-in-law good-bye, and returned to her childhood home; but Ruth insisted on staying with Naomi.

15"See," Naomi said to her, "your sister-in-law has gone back to her people and to her gods; you should do the same."

16But Ruth replied, "Don't make me leave you, for I want to go wherever you go, and to live wherever you live; your people shall be my people, and your God shall be my God; 17I want to die where you die, and be buried there. May the Lord do terrible things to me if I allow anything but death to separate us."

18And when Naomi saw that Ruth had made up her mind and could not be persuaded otherwise, she stopped

New Revised Standard

Elimelech's Family Goes to Moab

1 IN THE days when the judges ruled, there was a famine in the land, and a certain man of Bethlehem in Judah went to live in the country of Moab, he and his wife and two sons. 2The name of the man was Elimelech and the name of his wife Naomi, and the names of his two sons were Mahlon and Chilion; they were Ephrathites from Bethlehem in Judah. They went into the country of Moab and remained there. 3But Elimelech, the husband of Naomi, died, and she was left with her two sons. 4These took Moabite wives; the name of the one was Orpah and the name of the other Ruth. When they had lived there about ten years, 5both Mahlon and Chilion also died, so that the woman was left without her two sons and her husband.

Naomi and Her Moabite Daughters-in-Law

6 Then she started to return with her daughters-in-law from the country of Moab, for she had heard in the country of Moab that the LORD had considered his people and given them food. 7So she set out from the place where she had been living, she and her two daughters-in-law, and they went on their way to go back to the land of Judah. 8But Naomi said to her two daughters-in-law, "Go back each of you to your mother's house. May the LORD deal kindly with you, as you have dealt with the dead and with me. 9The LORD grant that you may find security, each of you in the house of your husband." Then she kissed them, and they wept aloud. 10They said to her, "No, we will return with you to your people." 11But Naomi said, "Turn back, my daughters, why will you go with me? Do I still have sons in my womb that they may become your husbands? 12Turn back, my daughters, go your way, for I am too old to have a husband. Even if I thought there was hope for me, even if I should have a husband tonight and bear sons, 13would you then wait until they were grown? Would you then refrain from marrying? No, my daughters, it has been far more bitter for me than for you, because the hand of the LORD has turned against me." 14Then they wept aloud again. Orpah kissed her mother-in-law, but Ruth clung to her.

15 So she said, "See, your sister-in-law has gone back to her people and to her gods; return after your sister-in-law." 16But Ruth said,

"Do not press me to leave you
 or to turn back from following you!
Where you go, I will go;
 where you lodge, I will lodge;
your people shall be my people,
 and your God my God;
17 Where you die, I will die—
 there will I be buried.
May the LORD do thus and so to me,
 and more as well,
if even death parts me from you!"

18When Naomi saw that she was determined to go with her, she said no more to her.

---

[b] 1:1 from Bethlehem, literally, "They were Ephrathites from Bethlehem in Judah."   [c] 1:11 Do I have younger sons . . . to be your husbands? This refers to the custom of the day. Levirate marriage (Deut 25:5-10) was a common practice. The brother of a deceased husband was to marry the widow.

King James

19¶ So they two went until they came to Bethlehem. And it came to pass, when they were come to Bethlehem, that all the city was moved about them, and they said, *Is* this Naomi?

20And she said unto them, Call me not Naomi, call me Mara: for the Almighty hath dealt very bitterly with me.

21I went out full, and the LORD hath brought me home again empty: why *then* call ye me Naomi, seeing the LORD hath testified against me, and the Almighty hath afflicted me?

22So Naomi returned, and Ruth the Moabitess, her daughter-in-law, with her, which returned out of the country of Moab: and they came to Bethlehem in the beginning of barley harvest.

2 AND NAOMI had a kinsman of her husband's, a mighty man of wealth, of the family of Elimelech; and his name *was* Boaz.

2And Ruth the Moabitess said unto Naomi, Let me now go to the field, and glean ears of corn after *him* in whose sight I shall find grace. And she said unto her, Go, my daughter.

3And she went, and came, and gleaned in the field after the reapers: and her hap was to light on a part of the field *belonging* unto Boaz, who *was* of the kindred of Elimelech.

4¶ And, behold, Boaz came from Bethlehem, and said unto the reapers, The LORD *be* with you. And they answered him, The LORD bless thee.

5Then said Boaz unto his servant that was set over the reapers, Whose damsel *is* this?

6And the servant that was set over the reapers answered and said, It *is* the Moabitish damsel that came back with Naomi out of the country of Moab:

7And she said, I pray you, let me glean and gather after the reapers among the sheaves: so she came, and hath continued even from the morning until now, that she tarried a little in the house.

8Then said Boaz unto Ruth, Hearest thou not, my daughter? Go not to glean in another field, neither go from hence, but abide here fast by my maidens:

9*Let* thine eyes *be* on the field that they do reap, and go thou after them: have I not charged the young men that they shall not touch thee? and when thou art athirst, go unto the vessels, and drink of *that* which the young men have drawn.

10Then she fell on her face, and bowed herself to the ground, and said unto him, Why have I found grace in thine eyes, that thou shouldest take knowledge of me, seeing I *am* a stranger?

11And Boaz answered and said unto her, It hath fully been shown me, all that thou hast done unto thy mother-in-law since the death of thine husband: and *how* thou hast left thy father and thy mother, and the land of thy nativity, and art come unto a people which thou knewest not heretofore.

12The LORD recompense thy work, and a full reward be given thee of the LORD God of Israel, under whose wings thou art come to trust.

13Then she said, Let me find favour in thy sight, my lord; for that thou hast comforted me, and for that thou hast spoken friendly unto thine handmaid, though I be not like unto one of thine handmaidens.

14And Boaz said unto her, At mealtime come thou hither, and eat of the bread, and dip thy morsel in the vinegar. And she sat beside the reapers: and he reached her parched *corn,* and she did eat, and was sufficed, and left.

New International

19So the two women went on until they came to Bethlehem. When they arrived in Bethlehem, the whole town was stirred because of them, and the women exclaimed, "Can this be Naomi?"

20"Don't call me Naomi,a" she told them. "Call me Mara,b because the Almightyc has made my life very bitter. 21I went away full, but the LORD has brought me back empty. Why call me Naomi? The LORD has afflicted me, the Almighty has brought misfortune upon me."

22So Naomi returned from Moab accompanied by Ruth the Moabitess, her daughter-in-law, arriving in Bethlehem as the barley harvest was beginning.

Ruth Meets Boaz

2 NOW NAOMI had a relative on her husband's side, from the clan of Elimelech, a man of standing, whose name was Boaz.

2And Ruth the Moabitess said to Naomi, "Let me go to the fields and pick up the leftover grain behind anyone in whose eyes I find favor."

Naomi said to her, "Go ahead, my daughter." 3So she went out and began to glean in the fields behind the harvesters. As it turned out, she found herself working in a field belonging to Boaz, who was from the clan of Elimelech.

4Just then Boaz arrived from Bethlehem and greeted the harvesters, "The LORD be with you!"

"The LORD bless you!" they called back.

5Boaz asked the foreman of his harvesters, "Whose young woman is that?"

6The foreman replied, "She is the Moabitess who came back from Moab with Naomi. 7She said, 'Please let me glean and gather among the sheaves behind the harvesters.' She went into the field and has worked steadily from morning till now, except for a short rest in the shelter."

8So Boaz said to Ruth, "My daughter, listen to me. Don't go and glean in another field and don't go away from here. Stay here with my servant girls. 9Watch the field where the men are harvesting, and follow along after the girls. I have told the men not to touch you. And whenever you are thirsty, go and get a drink from the water jars the men have filled."

10At this, she bowed down with her face to the ground. She exclaimed, "Why have I found such favor in your eyes that you notice me—a foreigner?"

11Boaz replied, "I've been told all about what you have done for your mother-in-law since the death of your husband—how you left your father and mother and your homeland and came to live with a people you did not know before. 12May the LORD repay you for what you have done. May you be richly rewarded by the LORD, the God of Israel, under whose wings you have come to take refuge."

13"May I continue to find favor in your eyes, my lord," she said. "You have given me comfort and have spoken kindly to your servant—though I do not have the standing of one of your servant girls."

14At mealtime Boaz said to her, "Come over here. Have some bread and dip it in the wine vinegar."

When she sat down with the harvesters, he offered her some roasted grain. She ate all she wanted and had some left over. 15As she got up to glean, Boaz gave

---

a *20 Naomi* means *pleasant*; also in verse 21.   b *20 Mara* means *bitter*.
c *20* Hebrew *Shaddai*; also in verse 21   d *21* Or *has testified against*

Living Bible

urging her. 19So they both came to Bethlehem and the entire village was stirred by their arrival.

"Is it really Naomi?" the women asked.

20But she told them, "Don't call me Naomi. Call me Mara," (Naomi means "pleasant"; Mara means "bitter") "for Almighty God has dealt me bitter blows. 21I went out full and the Lord has brought me home empty; why should you call me Naomi when the Lord has turned his back on me and sent such calamity!"

22(Their return from Moab and arrival in Bethlehem was at the beginning of the barley harvest.)

2 NOW NAOMI had an in-law there in Bethlehem who was a very wealthy man. His name was Boaz. 2One day Ruth said to Naomi, "Perhaps I can go out into the fields of some kind man to glean the free graine behind his reapers."

And Naomi said, "All right, dear daughter. Go ahead."

3So she did. And as it happened, the field where she found herself belonged to Boaz, this relative of Naomi's husband.

4, 5Boaz arrived from the city while she was there. After exchanging greetings with the reapers he said to his foreman, "Hey, who's that girl over there?"

6And the foreman replied, "It's that girl from the land of Moab who came back with Naomi. 7She asked me this morning if she could pick up the grains dropped by the reapers, and she has been at it ever since except for a few minutes' rest over there in the shade."

8, 9Boaz went over and talked to her. "Listen, my child," he said to her. "Stay right here with us to glean; don't think of going to any other fields. Stay right behind my women workers; I have warned the young men not to bother you; when you are thirsty, go and help yourself to the water."

10, 11She thanked him warmly. "How can you be so kind to me?" she asked. "You must know I am only a foreigner."

"Yes, I know," Boaz replied, "and I also know about all the love and kindness you have shown your mother-in-law since the death of your husband, and how you left your father and mother in your own land and have come here to live among strangers. 12May the Lord God of Israel, under whose wings you have come to take refuge, bless you for it."

13"Oh, thank you, sir," she replied. "You are so good to me, and I'm not even one of your workers!"

14At lunch time Boaz called to her, "Come and eat with us."

So she sat with his reapers and he gave her food,f more than she could eat. 15And when she went back to

New Revised Standard

19 So the two of them went on until they came to Bethlehem. When they came to Bethlehem, the whole town was stirred because of them; and the women said, "Is this Naomi?" 20She said to them,

"Call me no longer Naomi,g
   call me Mara,h
   for the Almightyi has dealt bitterly with
      me.
21 I went away full,
   but the LORD has brought me back empty;
   why call me Naomi
      when the LORD has dealt harshly withi me,
      and the Almightyi has brought calamity
         upon me?"

22 So Naomi returned together with Ruth the Moabite, her daughter-in-law, who came back with her from the country of Moab. They came to Bethlehem at the beginning of the barley harvest.

Ruth Meets Boaz

2 NOW NAOMI had a kinsman on her husband's side, a prominent rich man, of the family of Elimelech, whose name was Boaz. 2And Ruth the Moabite said to Naomi, "Let me go to the field and glean among the ears of grain, behind someone in whose sight I may find favor." She said to her, "Go, my daughter." 3So she went. She came and gleaned in the field behind the reapers. As it happened, she came to the part of the field belonging to Boaz, who was of the family of Elimelech. 4Just then Boaz came from Bethlehem. He said to the reapers, "The LORD be with you." They answered, "The LORD bless you." 5Then Boaz said to his servant who was in charge of the reapers, "To whom does this young woman belong?" 6The servant who was in charge of the reapers answered, "She is the Moabite who came back with Naomi from the country of Moab. 7She said, 'Please, let me glean and gather among the sheaves behind the reapers.' So she came, and she has been on her feet from early this morning until now, without resting even for a moment."k

8 Then Boaz said to Ruth, "Now listen, my daughter, do not go to glean in another field or leave this one, but keep close to my young women. 9Keep your eyes on the field that is being reaped, and follow behind them. I have ordered the young men not to bother you. If you get thirsty, go to the vessels and drink from what the young men have drawn." 10Then she fell prostrate, with her face to the ground, and said to him, "Why have I found favor in your sight, that you should take notice of me, when I am a foreigner?" 11But Boaz answered her, "All that you have done for your mother-in-law since the death of your husband has been fully told me, and how you left your father and mother and your native land and came to a people that you did not know before. 12May the LORD reward you for your deeds, and may you have a full reward from the LORD, the God of Israel, under whose wings you have come for refuge!" 13Then she said, "May I continue to find favor in your sight, my lord, for you have comforted me and spoken kindly to your servant, even though I am not one of your servants."

14 At mealtime Boaz said to her, "Come here, and eat some of this bread, and dip your morsel in the sour wine." So she sat beside the reapers, and he heaped up for her some parched grain. She ate until she was satisfied, and she had some left over. 15When she got up to

---

e 2:2 glean the free grain. See Lev 19:9 and Deut 24:19, which established this custom.   f 2:14 he gave her food, literally, "ate the parched grain and dipped her morsels of food in the wine."

g That is Pleasant   h That is Bitter   i Traditional rendering of Heb Shaddai   j Or has testified against   k Compare Gk Vg: Meaning of Heb uncertain

King James

15And when she was risen up to glean, Boaz commanded his young men, saying, Let her glean even among the sheaves, and reproach her not:

16And let fall also *some* of the handfuls of purpose for her, and leave *them*, that she may glean *them*, and rebuke her not.

17So she gleaned in the field until even, and beat out that she had gleaned: and it was about an ephah of barley.

18¶ And she took *it* up, and went into the city: and her mother-in-law saw what she had gleaned: and she brought forth, and gave to her that she had reserved after she was sufficed.

19And her mother-in-law said unto her, Where hast thou gleaned today? and where wroughtest thou? blessed be he that did take knowledge of thee. And she showed her mother-in-law with whom she had wrought, and said, The man's name with whom I wrought today *is* Boaz.

20And Naomi said unto her daughter-in-law, Blessed *be* he of the LORD, who hath not left off his kindness to the living and to the dead. And Naomi said unto her, The man *is* near of kin unto us, one of our next kinsmen.

21And Ruth the Moabitess said, He said unto me also, Thou shalt keep fast by my young men, until they have ended all my harvest.

22And Naomi said unto Ruth her daughter-in-law, *It is* good, my daughter, that thou go out with his maidens, that they meet thee not in any other field.

23So she kept fast by the maidens of Boaz to glean unto the end of barley harvest and of wheat harvest; and dwelt with her mother-in-law.

3 THEN NAOMI her mother-in-law said unto her, My daughter, shall I not seek rest for thee, that it may be well with thee?

2And now *is* not Boaz of our kindred, with whose maidens thou wast? Behold, he winnoweth barley tonight in the threshingfloor.

3Wash thyself therefore, and anoint thee, and put thy raiment upon thee, and get thee down to the floor: *but* make not thyself known unto the man, until he shall have done eating and drinking.

4And it shall be, when he lieth down, that thou shalt mark the place where he shall lie, and thou shalt go in, and uncover his feet, and lay thee down; and he will tell thee what thou shalt do.

5And she said unto her, All that thou sayest unto me I will do.

6¶ And she went down unto the floor, and did according to all that her mother-in-law bade her.

7And when Boaz had eaten and drunk, and his heart was merry, he went to lie down at the end of the heap of corn: and she came softly, and uncovered his feet, and laid her down.

8¶ And it came to pass at midnight, that the man was afraid, and turned himself: and, behold, a woman lay at his feet.

9And he said, Who *art* thou? And she answered, I *am* Ruth thine handmaid: spread therefore thy skirt over thine handmaid; for thou *art* a near kinsman.

10And he said, Blessed *be* thou of the LORD, my daughter: *for* thou hast shown more kindness in the latter end than at the beginning, inasmuch as thou followedst not young men, whether poor or rich.

11And now, my daughter, fear not; I will do to thee all that thou requirest: for all the city of my people doth know that thou *art* a virtuous woman.

12And now it is true that I *am thy* near kinsman: howbeit there is a kinsman nearer than I.

New International

orders to his men, "Even if she gathers among the sheaves, don't embarrass her. 16Rather, pull out some stalks for her from the bundles and leave them for her to pick up, and don't rebuke her."

17So Ruth gleaned in the field until evening. Then she threshed the barley she had gathered, and it amounted to about an ephah.a 18She carried it back to town, and her mother-in-law saw how much she had gathered. Ruth also brought out and gave her what she had left over after she had eaten enough.

19Her mother-in-law asked her, "Where did you glean today? Where did you work? Blessed be the man who took notice of you!"

Then Ruth told her mother-in-law about the one at whose place she had been working. "The name of the man I worked with today is Boaz," she said.

20"The LORD bless him!" Naomi said to her daughter-in-law. "He has not stopped showing his kindness to the living and the dead." She added, "That man is our close relative; he is one of our kinsman-redeemers."

21Then Ruth the Moabitess said, "He even said to me, 'Stay with my workers until they finish harvesting all my grain.' "

22Naomi said to Ruth her daughter-in-law, "It will be good for you, my daughter, to go with his girls, because in someone else's field you might be harmed."

23So Ruth stayed close to the servant girls of Boaz to glean until the barley and wheat harvests were finished. And she lived with her mother-in-law.

Ruth and Boaz at the Threshing Floor

3 ONE DAY Naomi her mother-in-law said to her, "My daughter, should I not try to find a homeb for you, where you will be well provided for? 2Is not Boaz, with whose servant girls you have been, a kinsman of ours? Tonight he will be winnowing barley on the threshing floor. 3Wash and perfume yourself, and put on your best clothes. Then go down to the threshing floor, but don't let him know you are there until he has finished eating and drinking. 4When he lies down, note the place where he is lying. Then go and uncover his feet and lie down. He will tell you what to do."

5"I will do whatever you say," Ruth answered. 6So she went down to the threshing floor and did everything her mother-in-law told her to do.

7When Boaz had finished eating and drinking and was in good spirits, he went over to lie down at the far end of the grain pile. Ruth approached quietly, uncovered his feet and lay down. 8In the middle of the night something startled the man, and he turned and discovered a woman lying at his feet.

9"Who are you?" he asked.

"I am your servant Ruth," she said. "Spread the corner of your garment over me, since you are a kinsman-redeemer."

10"The LORD bless you, my daughter," he replied. "This kindness is greater than that which you showed earlier: You have not run after the younger men, whether rich or poor. 11And now, my daughter, don't be afraid. I will do for you all you ask. All my fellow townsmen know that you are a woman of noble character. 12Although it is true that I am near of kin, there is a kinsman-redeemer nearer than I. 13Stay here for the night, and in

---

a *17* That is, probably about 3/5 bushel (about 22 liters)   b *1* Hebrew *find rest* (see Ruth 1:9)

Living Bible

work again, Boaz told his young men to let her glean right among the sheaves without stopping her, 16and to snap off some heads of barley and drop them on purpose for her to glean, and not to make any remarks. 17So she worked there all day, and in the evening when she had beaten out the barley she had gleaned, it came to a whole bushel! 18She carried it back into the city and gave it to her mother-in-law, with what was left of her lunch.

19"So much!" Naomi exclaimed. "Where in the world did you glean today? Praise the Lord for whoever was so kind to you." So Ruth told her mother-in-law all about it, and mentioned that the owner of the field was Boaz.

20"Praise the Lord for a man like that! God has continued his kindness to us as well as to your dead husband!" Naomi cried excitedly. "Why, that man is one of our closest relatives!"c

21"Well," Ruth told her, "he said to come back and stay close behind his reapers until the entire field is harvested."

22"This is wonderful!" Naomi exclaimed. "Do as he has said. Stay with his girls right through the whole harvest; you will be safer there than in any other field!"

23So Ruth did, and gleaned with them until the end of the barley harvest, and then the wheat harvest, too.

3 ONE DAY Naomi said to Ruth, "My dear, isn't it time that I try to find a husband for you, and get you happily married again? 2The man I'm thinking of is Boaz! He has been so kind to us, and is a close relative. I happen to know that he will be winnowing barley tonight out on the threshing-floor. 3Now do what I tell you—bathe and put on some perfume and some nice clothes and go on down to the threshing-floor, but don't let him see you until he has finished his supper. 4Notice where he lies down to sleep; then go and lift the cover off his feet and lie down there, and he will tell you what to do concerning marriage."

5And Ruth replied, "All right. I'll do whatever you say."

6, 7So she went down to the threshing-floor that night and followed her mother-in-law's instructions. After Boaz had finished a good meal, he lay down very contentedly beside a heap of grain and went to sleep. Then Ruth came quietly and lifted the covering off his feet and lay there. 8Suddenly, around midnight, he wakened and sat up, startled. There was a woman lying at his feet!

9"Who are you?" he demanded.

"It's I, sir—Ruth," she replied. "Make me your wife according to God's law, for you are my close relative."

10"Thank God for a girl like you!" he exclaimed. "For you are being even kinder to Naomi now than before. Naturally you'd prefer a younger man, even though poor. But you have put aside your personal desires. 11Now don't worry about a thing, my child; I'll handle all the details, for everyone knows what a wonderful person you are. 12But there is one problem. It's true that I am a close relative, but there is someone else who is more closely related to you than I am. 13Stay here to-

New Revised Standard

glean, Boaz instructed his young men, "Let her glean even among the standing sheaves, and do not reproach her. 16You must also pull out some handfuls for her from the bundles, and leave them for her to glean, and do not rebuke her."

17 So she gleaned in the field until evening. Then she beat out what she had gleaned, and it was about an ephah of barley. 18She picked it up and came into the town, and her mother-in-law saw how much she had gleaned. Then she took out and gave her what was left over after she herself had been satisfied. 19Her mother-in-law said to her, "Where did you glean today? And where have you worked? Blessed be the man who took notice of you." So she told her mother-in-law with whom she had worked, and said, "The name of the man with whom I worked today is Boaz." 20Then Naomi said to her daughter-in-law, "Blessed be he by the LORD, whose kindness has not forsaken the living or the dead!" Naomi also said to her, "The man is a relative of ours, one of our nearest kin."d 21Then Ruth the Moabite said, "He even said to me, 'Stay close by my servants, until they have finished all my harvest.' " 22Naomi said to Ruth, her daughter-in-law, "It is better, my daughter, that you go out with his young women, otherwise you might be bothered in another field." 23So she stayed close to the young women of Boaz, gleaning until the end of the barley and wheat harvests; and she lived with her mother-in-law.

Ruth and Boaz at the Threshing Floor

3 NAOMI HER mother-in-law said to her, "My daughter, I need to seek some security for you, so that it may be well with you. 2Now here is our kinsman Boaz, with whose young women you have been working. See, he is winnowing barley tonight at the threshing floor. 3Now wash and anoint yourself, and put on your best clothes and go down to the threshing floor; but do not make yourself known to the man until he has finished eating and drinking. 4When he lies down, observe the place where he lies; then, go and uncover his feet and lie down; and he will tell you what to do." 5She said to her, "All that you tell me I will do."

6 So she went down to the threshing floor and did just as her mother-in-law had instructed her. 7When Boaz had eaten and drunk, and he was in a contented mood, he went to lie down at the end of the heap of grain. Then she came stealthily and uncovered his feet, and lay down. 8At midnight the man was startled, and turned over, and there, lying at his feet, was a woman! 9He said, "Who are you?" And she answered, "I am Ruth, your servant; spread your cloak over your servant, for you are next-of-kin."d 10He said, "May you be blessed by the LORD, my daughter; this last instance of your loyalty is better than the first; you have not gone after young men, whether poor or rich. 11And now, my daughter, do not be afraid, I will do for you all that you ask, for all the assembly of my people know that you are a worthy woman. 12But now, though it is true that I am a near kinsman, there is another kinsman more closely related than I. 13Remain this night, and in the morning,

---

c 2:20 *that man (Boaz) is one of our closest relatives*, literally, "a near relative, one of our redeemers."

d Or *one with the right to redeem*

King James

13Tarry this night, and it shall be in the morning, *that* if he will perform unto thee the part of a kinsman, well; let him do the kinsman's part: but if he will not do the part of a kinsman to thee, then will I do the part of a kinsman to thee, *as* the LORD liveth: lie down until the morning.

14¶ And she lay at his feet until the morning: and she rose up before one could know another. And he said, Let it not be known that a woman came into the floor.

15Also he said, Bring the veil that *thou hast* upon thee, and hold it. And when she held it, he measured six *measures* of barley, and laid *it* on her: and she went into the city.

16And when she came to her mother-in-law, she said, Who *art* thou, my daughter? And she told her all that the man had done to her.

17And she said, These six *measures* of barley gave he me; for he said to me, Go not empty unto thy mother-in-law.

18Then said she, Sit still, my daughter, until thou know how the matter will fall: for the man will not be in rest, until he have finished the thing this day.

4 THEN WENT Boaz up to the gate, and sat him down there: and, behold, the kinsman of whom Boaz spake came by; unto whom he said, Ho, such a one! turn aside, sit down here. And he turned aside, and sat down.

2And he took ten men of the elders of the city, and said, Sit ye down here. And they sat down.

3And he said unto the kinsman, Naomi, that is come again out of the country of Moab, selleth a parcel of land, which *was* our brother Elimelech's:

4And I thought to advertise thee, saying, Buy *it* before the inhabitants, and before the elders of my people. If thou wilt redeem *it*, redeem *it:* but if thou wilt not redeem *it, then* tell me, that I may know: for *there is* none to redeem *it* beside thee; and I *am* after thee. And he said, I will redeem *it*.

5Then said Boaz, What day thou buyest the field of the hand of Naomi, thou must buy *it* also of Ruth the Moabitess, the wife of the dead, to raise up the name of the dead upon his inheritance.

6¶ And the kinsman said, I cannot redeem *it* for myself, lest I mar mine own inheritance: redeem thou my right to thyself; for I cannot redeem *it*.

7Now this *was the manner* in former time in Israel concerning redeeming and concerning changing, for to confirm all things; a man plucked off his shoe, and gave *it* to his neighbour: and this *was* a testimony in Israel.

8Therefore the kinsman said unto Boaz, Buy *it* for thee. So he drew off his shoe.

9¶ And Boaz said unto the elders, and *unto* all the people, Ye *are* witnesses this day, that I have bought all that *was* Elimelech's, and all that *was* Chilion's and Mahlon's, of the hand of Naomi.

10Moreover Ruth the Moabitess, the wife of Mahlon, have I purchased to be my wife, to raise up the name of the dead upon his inheritance, that the name of the dead be not cut off from among his brethren, and from the gate of his place: ye *are* witnesses this day.

11And all the people that *were* in the gate, and the elders, said, *We are* witnesses. The LORD make the woman that is come into thine house like Rachel and like Leah, which two did build the house of Israel: and do thou worthily in Ephratah, and be famous in Bethlehem:

12And let thy house be like the house of Pharez, whom Tamar bare unto Judah, of the seed which the LORD shall give thee of this young woman.

New International

the morning if he wants to redeem, good; let him redeem. But if he is not willing, as surely as the LORD lives I will do it. Lie here until morning."

14So she lay at his feet until morning, but got up before anyone could be recognized; and he said, "Don't let it be known that a woman came to the threshing floor."

15He also said, "Bring me the shawl you are wearing and hold it out." When she did so, he poured into it six measures of barley and put it on her. Then hea went back to town.

16When Ruth came to her mother-in-law, Naomi asked, "How did it go, my daughter?"

Then she told her everything Boaz had done for her 17and added, "He gave me these six measures of barley, saying, 'Don't go back to your mother-in-law empty-handed.' "

18Then Naomi said, "Wait, my daughter, until you find out what happens. For the man will not rest until the matter is settled today."

Boaz Marries Ruth

4 MEANWHILE BOAZ went up to the town gate and sat there. When the kinsman-redeemer he had mentioned came along, Boaz said, "Come over here, my friend, and sit down." So he went over and sat down.

2Boaz took ten of the elders of the town and said, "Sit here," and they did so. 3Then he said to the kinsman-redeemer, "Naomi, who has come back from Moab, is selling the piece of land that belonged to our brother Elimelech. 4I thought I should bring the matter to your attention and suggest that you buy it in the presence of these seated here and in the presence of the elders of my people. If you will redeem it, do so. But if youb will not, tell me, so I will know. For no one has the right to do it except you, and I am next in line."

"I will redeem it," he said.

5Then Boaz said, "On the day you buy the land from Naomi and from Ruth the Moabitess, you acquirec the dead man's widow, in order to maintain the name of the dead with his property."

6At this, the kinsman-redeemer said, "Then I cannot redeem it because I might endanger my own estate. You redeem it yourself. I cannot do it."

7(Now in earlier times in Israel, for the redemption and transfer of property to become final, one party took off his sandal and gave it to the other. This was the method of legalizing transactions in Israel.)

8So the kinsman-redeemer said to Boaz, "Buy it yourself." And he removed his sandal.

9Then Boaz announced to the elders and all the people, "Today you are witnesses that I have bought from Naomi all the property of Elimelech, Kilion and Mahlon. 10I have also acquired Ruth the Moabitess, Mahlon's widow, as my wife, in order to maintain the name of the dead with his property, so that his name will not disappear from among his family or from the town records. Today you are witnesses!"

11Then the elders and all those at the gate said, "We are witnesses. May the LORD make the woman who is coming into your home like Rachel and Leah, who together built up the house of Israel. May you have standing in Ephrathah and be famous in Bethlehem. 12Through the offspring the LORD gives you by this young woman, may your family be like that of Perez, whom Tamar bore to Judah."

---

a *15* Most Hebrew manuscripts; many Hebrew manuscripts, Vulgate and Syriac *she*   b *4* Many Hebrew manuscripts, Septuagint, Vulgate and Syriac; most Hebrew manuscripts *he*   c *5* Hebrew; Vulgate and Syriac *Naomi, you acquire Ruth the Moabitess,*

Living Bible

night, and in the morning I'll talk to him, and if he will marry you, fine; let him do his duty; but if he won't, then I will, I swear by Jehovah; lie down until the morning."

14So she lay at his feet until the morning and was up early, before daybreak, for he had said to her, "Don't let it be known that a woman was here at the threshing-floor."

15-18"Bring your shawl," he told her. Then he tied up a bushel and a half of barley in it as a present for her mother-in-law, and laid it on her back. Then she returned to the city.

"Well, what happened, dear?" Naomi asked her when she arrived home. She told Naomi everything and gave her the barley from Boaz, and mentioned his remark that she mustn't go home without a present.

Then Naomi said to her, "Just be patient until we hear what happens, for Boaz won't rest until he has followed through on this. He'll settle it today."

4 SO BOAZ went down to the marketplaced and found the relative he had mentioned.

"Say, come over here," he called to him. "I want to talk to you a minute."

So they sat down together. 2Then Boaz called for ten of the chief men of the village, and asked them to sit as witnesses.

3Boaz said to his relative, "You know Naomi, who came back to us from Moab. She is selling our brother Elimelech's property. 4I felt that I should speak to you about it so that you can buy it if you wish, with these respected men as witnesses. If you want it,e let me know right away, for if you don't take it, I will. You have the first right to purchase it and I am next."

The man replied, "All right, I'll buy it."

5Then Boaz told him, "Your purchase of the land from Naomi requires your marriage to Ruth so that she can have children to carry on her husband's name, and to inherit the land."

6"Then I can't do it," the man replied. "For her son would become an heir to my property, too;f you buy it."

7In those days it was the custom in Israel for a man transferring a right of purchase to pull off his sandal and hand it to the other party; this publicly validated the transaction. 8So, as the man said to Boaz, "You buy it for yourself," he drew off his sandal.

9Then Boaz said to the witnesses and to the crowd standing around, "You have seen that today I have bought all the property of Elimelech, Chilion, and Mahlon, from Naomi, 10and that with it I have purchased Ruth the Moabitess, the widow of Mahlon, to be my wife, so that she can have a son to carry on the family name of her dead husband."

11And all the people standing there, and the witnesses replied, "We are witnesses. May the Lord make this woman, who has now come into your home, as fertile as Rachel and Leah, from whom all the nation of Israel descended! May you be a great and successful man in Bethlehem, 12and may the descendants the Lord will give you from this young woman be as numerous and honorable as those of our ancestor Perez, the son of Tamar and Judah."

d 4:1 went down to the marketplace, literally, "the gate" of the city, where legal affairs were usually transacted. e 4:4 if you want it, literally, "if you want to redeem it." f 4:6 "For her son would become an heir to my property, too," or, "that would ruin my own inheritance," i.e., complicate his estate for the children he already had.

New Revised Standard

if he will act as next-of-king for you, good; let him do it. If he is not willing to act as next-of-king for you, then, as the LORD lives, I will act as next-of-king for you. Lie down until the morning."

14 So one lay at his feet until morning, but got up before one person could recognize another; for he said, "It must not be known that the woman came to the threshing floor." 15Then he said, "Bring the cloak you are wearing and hold it out." So she held it, and he measured out six measures of barley, and put it on her back; then he went into the city. 16She came to her mother-in-law, who said, "How did things go with you,h my daughter?" Then she told her all that the man had done for her, 17saying, "He gave me these six measures of barley, for he said, 'Do not go back to your mother-in-law empty-handed.'" 18She replied, "Wait, my daughter, until you learn how the matter turns out, for the man will not rest, but will settle the matter today."

The Marriage of Boaz and Ruth

4 NO SOONER had Boaz gone up to the gate and sat down there than the next-of-kin,g of whom Boaz had spoken, came passing by. So Boaz said, "Come over, friend; sit down here." And he went over and sat down. 2Then Boaz took ten men of the elders of the city, and said, "Sit down here"; so they sat down. 3He then said to the next-of-kin,g "Naomi, who has come back from the country of Moab, is selling the parcel of land that belonged to our kinsman Elimelech. 4So I thought I would tell you of it, and say: Buy it in the presence of those sitting here, and in the presence of the elders of my people. If you will redeem it, redeem it; but if you will not, tell me, so that I may know; for there is no one prior to you to redeem it, and I come after you." So he said, "I will redeem it." 5Then Boaz said, "The day you acquire the field from the hand of Naomi, you are also acquiring Ruthi the Moabite, the widow of the dead man, to maintain the dead man's name on his inheritance." 6At this, the next-of-king said, "I cannot redeem it for myself without damaging my own inheritance. Take my right of redemption yourself, for I cannot redeem it."

7 Now this was the custom in former times in Israel concerning redeeming and exchanging: to confirm a transaction, the one took off a sandal and gave it to the other; this was the manner of attesting in Israel. 8So when the next-of-king said to Boaz, "Acquire it for yourself," he took off his sandal. 9Then Boaz said to the elders and all the people, "Today you are witnesses that I have acquired from the hand of Naomi all that belonged to Elimelech and all that belonged to Chilion and Mahlon. 10I have also acquired Ruth the Moabite, the wife of Mahlon, to be my wife, to maintain the dead man's name on his inheritance, in order that the name of the dead may not be cut off from his kindred and from the gate of his native place; today you are witnesses." 11Then all the people who were at the gate, along with the elders, said, "We are witnesses. May the LORD make the woman who is coming into your house like Rachel and Leah, who together built up the house of Israel. May you produce children in Ephrathah and bestow a name in Bethlehem; 12and, through the children that the LORD will give you by this young woman, may your house be like the house of Perez, whom Tamar bore to Judah."

g Or one with the right to redeem h Or "Who are you, i OL Vg: Heb from the hand of Naomi and from Ruth

King James

13¶ So Boaz took Ruth, and she was his wife: and when he went in unto her, the LORD gave her conception, and she bare a son.

14And the women said unto Naomi, Blessed *be* the LORD, which hath not left thee this day without a kinsman, that his name may be famous in Israel.

15And he shall be unto thee a restorer of *thy* life, and a nourisher of thine old age: for thy daughter-in-law, which loveth thee, which is better to thee than seven sons, hath borne him.

16And Naomi took the child, and laid it in her bosom, and became nurse unto it.

17And the women her neighbours gave it a name, saying, There is a son born to Naomi; and they called his name Obed: he *is* the father of Jesse, the father of David.

18¶ Now these *are* the generations of Pharez: Pharez begat Hezron,

19And Hezron begat Ram, and Ram begat Amminadab,

20And Amminadab begat Nahshon, and Nahshon begat Salmon,

21And Salmon begat Boaz, and Boaz begat Obed,

22And Obed begat Jesse, and Jesse begat David.

New International

The Genealogy of David

13So Boaz took Ruth and she became his wife. Then he went to her, and the LORD enabled her to conceive, and she gave birth to a son. 14The women said to Naomi: "Praise be to the LORD, who this day has not left you without a kinsman-redeemer. May he become famous throughout Israel! 15He will renew your life and sustain you in your old age. For your daughter-in-law, who loves you and who is better to you than seven sons, has given him birth."

16Then Naomi took the child, laid him in her lap and cared for him. 17The women living there said, "Naomi has a son." And they named him Obed. He was the father of Jesse, the father of David.

18This, then, is the family line of Perez:

Perez was the father of Hezron,
19Hezron the father of Ram,
Ram the father of Amminadab,
20Amminadab the father of Nahshon,
Nahshon the father of Salmon,[a]
21Salmon the father of Boaz,
Boaz the father of Obed,
22Obed the father of Jesse,
and Jesse the father of David.

[a] 20 A few Hebrew manuscripts, some Septuagint manuscripts and Vulgate (see also verse 21 and Septuagint of 1 Chron. 2:11); most Hebrew manuscripts *Salma*

Living Bible

13So Boaz married Ruth, and when he slept with her, the Lord gave her a son.

14And the women of the city said to Naomi, "Bless the Lord who has given you this little grandson; may he be famous in Israel. 15May he restore your youth and take care of you in your old age; for he is the son of your daughter-in-law who loves you so much, and who has been kinder to you than seven sons!"

16, 17Naomi took care of the baby, and the neighbor women said, "Now at last Naomi has a son again!" And they named him Obed. He was the father of Jesse and grandfather of King David.

18-22This is the family tree of Boaz, beginning with his ancestor Perez:

Perez, Hezron, Ram, Amminadab,
Nashon, Salmon, Boaz, Obed,
Jesse, David.

New Revised Standard

The Genealogy of David

13 So Boaz took Ruth and she became his wife. When they came together, the LORD made her conceive, and she bore a son. 14Then the women said to Naomi, "Blessed be the LORD, who has not left you this day without next-of-kin;b and may his name be renowned in Israel! 15He shall be to you a restorer of life and a nourisher of your old age; for your daughter-in-law who loves you, who is more to you than seven sons, has borne him." 16Then Naomi took the child and laid him in her bosom, and became his nurse. 17The women of the neighborhood gave him a name, saying, "A son has been born to Naomi." They named him Obed; he became the father of Jesse, the father of David.

18 Now these are the descendants of Perez: Perez became the father of Hezron, 19Hezron of Ram, Ram of Amminadab, 20Amminadab of Nahshon, Nahshon of Salmon, 21Salmon of Boaz, Boaz of Obed, 22Obed of Jesse, and Jesse of David.

b Or *one with the right to redeem*

THE FIRST BOOK OF

Samuel

OTHERWISE CALLED THE FIRST BOOK

OF THE KINGS

1 NOW THERE was a certain man of Ramathaim-zophim, of mount Ephraim, and his name *was* Elkanah, the son of Jeroham, the son of Elihu, the son of Tohu, the son of Zuph, an Ephrathite:

2And he had two wives; the name of the one *was* Hannah, and the name of the other Peninnah: and Peninnah had children, but Hannah had no children.

3And this man went up out of his city yearly to worship and to sacrifice unto the LORD of hosts in Shiloh. And the two sons of Eli, Hophni and Phinehas, the priests of the LORD, *were* there.

4¶ And when the time was that Elkanah offered, he gave to Peninnah his wife, and to all her sons and her daughters, portions:

5But unto Hannah he gave a worthy portion; for he loved Hannah: but the LORD had shut up her womb.

6And her adversary also provoked her sore, for to make her fret, because the LORD had shut up her womb.

7And *as* he did so year by year, when she went up to the house of the LORD, so she provoked her; therefore she wept, and did not eat.

8Then said Elkanah her husband to her, Hannah, why weepest thou? and why eatest thou not? and why is thy heart grieved? *am* not I better to thee than ten sons?

9¶ So Hannah rose up after they had eaten in Shiloh, and after they had drunk. Now Eli the priest sat upon a seat by a post of the temple of the LORD.

10And she *was* in bitterness of soul, and prayed unto the LORD, and wept sore.

11And she vowed a vow, and said, O LORD of hosts, if thou wilt indeed look on the affliction of thine handmaid, and remember me, and not forget thine handmaid, but wilt give unto thine handmaid a man child, then I will give him unto the LORD all the days of his life, and there shall no razor come upon his head.

12And it came to pass, as she continued praying before the LORD, that Eli marked her mouth.

13Now Hannah, she spake in her heart; only her lips moved, but her voice was not heard: therefore Eli thought she had been drunken.

14And Eli said unto her, How long wilt thou be drunken? put away thy wine from thee.

15And Hannah answered and said, No, my lord, I *am* a woman of a sorrowful spirit: I have drunk neither wine nor strong drink, but have poured out my soul before the LORD.

16Count not thine handmaid for a daughter of Belial: for out of the abundance of my complaint and grief have I spoken hitherto.

17Then Eli answered and said, Go in peace: and the God of Israel grant *thee* thy petition that thou hast asked of him.

18And she said, Let thine handmaid find grace in thy sight. So the woman went her way, and did eat, and her countenance was no more *sad*.

1 Samuel

The Birth of Samuel

1 THERE WAS a certain man from Ramathaim, a Zuphite[a] from the hill country of Ephraim, whose name was Elkanah son of Jeroham, the son of Elihu, the son of Tohu, the son of Zuph, an Ephraimite. 2He had two wives; one was called Hannah and the other Peninnah. Peninnah had children, but Hannah had none.

3Year after year this man went up from his town to worship and sacrifice to the LORD Almighty at Shiloh, where Hophni and Phinehas, the two sons of Eli, were priests of the LORD. 4Whenever the day came for Elkanah to sacrifice, he would give portions of the meat to his wife Peninnah and to all her sons and daughters. 5But to Hannah he gave a double portion because he loved her, and the LORD had closed her womb. 6And because the LORD had closed her womb, her rival kept provoking her in order to irritate her. 7This went on year after year. Whenever Hannah went up to the house of the LORD, her rival provoked her till she wept and would not eat. 8Elkanah her husband would say to her, "Hannah, why are you weeping? Why don't you eat? Why are you downhearted? Don't I mean more to you than ten sons?"

9Once when they had finished eating and drinking in Shiloh, Hannah stood up. Now Eli the priest was sitting on a chair by the doorpost of the LORD's temple.[b] 10In bitterness of soul Hannah wept much and prayed to the LORD. 11And she made a vow, saying, "O LORD Almighty, if you will only look upon your servant's misery and remember me, and not forget your servant but give her a son, then I will give him to the LORD for all the days of his life, and no razor will ever be used on his head."

12As she kept on praying to the LORD, Eli observed her mouth. 13Hannah was praying in her heart, and her lips were moving but her voice was not heard. Eli thought she was drunk 14and said to her, "How long will you keep on getting drunk? Get rid of your wine."

15"Not so, my lord," Hannah replied, "I am a woman who is deeply troubled. I have not been drinking wine or beer; I was pouring out my soul to the LORD. 16Do not take your servant for a wicked woman; I have been praying here out of my great anguish and grief."

17Eli answered, "Go in peace, and may the God of Israel grant you what you have asked of him."

18She said, "May your servant find favor in your eyes." Then she went her way and ate something, and her face was no longer downcast.

---

1 Samuel

1 Samuel

1 THIS IS the story of Elkanah, a man of the tribe of Ephraim who lived in Ramathaim-zophim, in the hills of Ephraim.

His father's name was Jeroham,
His grandfather was Elihu,
His great-grandfather was Tohu,
His great-great-grandfather was Zuph.

2He had two wives, Hannah and Peninnah. Peninnah had some children, but Hannah didn't.

3Each year Elkanah and his families journeyed to the Tabernacle at Shiloh to worship the Lord of the heavens and to sacrifice to him. (The priests on duty at that time were the two sons of Eli—Hophni and Phinehas.) 4On the day he presented his sacrifice, Elkanah would celebrate the happy occasion by giving presents to Peninnah and her children; 5but although he loved Hannah very much, he could give her only one present, for the Lord had sealed her womb; so she had no children to give presents to. 6Peninnah made matters worse by taunting Hannah because of her barrenness. 7Every year it was the same—Peninnah scoffing and laughing at her as they went to Shiloh, making her cry so much she couldn't eat.

8"What's the matter, Hannah?" Elkanah would exclaim. "Why aren't you eating? Why make such a fuss over having no children? Isn't having me better than having ten sons?"

9One evening after supper, when they were at Shiloh, Hannah went over to the Tabernacle. Eli the priest was sitting at his customary place beside the entrance. 10She was in deep anguish and was crying bitterly as she prayed to the Lord.

11And she made this vow: "O Lord of heaven, if you will look down upon my sorrow and answer my prayer and give me a son, then I will give him back to you, and he'll be yours for his entire lifetime, and his hair shall never be cut."c

12, 13Eli noticed her mouth moving as she was praying silently and, hearing no sound, thought she had been drinking.

14"Must you come here drunk?" he demanded. "Throw away your bottle."

15, 16"Oh, no, sir!" she replied, "I'm not drunk! But I am very sad and I was pouring out my heart to the Lord. Please don't think that I am just some drunken bum!"

17"In that case," Eli said, "cheer up! May the Lord of Israel grant you your petition, whatever it is!"

18"Oh, thank you, sir!" she exclaimed, and went happily back, and began to take her meals again.

Samuel's Birth and Dedication

1 THERE WAS a certain man of Ramathaim, a Zuphited from the hill country of Ephraim, whose name was Elkanah son of Jeroham son of Elihu son of Tohu son of Zuph, an Ephraimite. 2He had two wives; the name of the one was Hannah, and the name of the other Peninnah. Peninnah had children, but Hannah had no children.

3 Now this man used to go up year by year from his town to worship and to sacrifice to the LORD of hosts at Shiloh, where the two sons of Eli, Hophni and Phinehas, were priests of the LORD. 4On the day when Elkanah sacrificed, he would give portions to his wife Peninnah and to all her sons and daughters; 5but to Hannah he gave a double portion,e because he loved her, though the LORD had closed her womb. 6Her rival used to provoke her severely, to irritate her, because the LORD had closed her womb. 7So it went on year by year; as often as she went up to the house of the LORD, she used to provoke her. Therefore Hannah wept and would not eat. 8Her husband Elkanah said to her, "Hannah, why do you weep? Why do you not eat? Why is your heart sad? Am I not more to you than ten sons?"

9 After they had eaten and drunk at Shiloh, Hannah rose and presented herself before the LORD.f Now Eli the priest was sitting on the seat beside the doorpost of the temple of the LORD. 10She was deeply distressed and prayed to the LORD, and wept bitterly. 11She made this vow: "O LORD of hosts, if only you will look on the misery of your servant, and remember me, and not forget your servant, but will give to your servant a male child, then I will set him before you as a naziriteg until the day of his death. He shall drink neither wine nor intoxicants,h and no razor shall touch his head."

12 As she continued praying before the LORD, Eli observed her mouth. 13Hannah was praying silently; only her lips moved, but her voice was not heard; therefore Eli thought she was drunk. 14So Eli said to her, "How long will you make a drunken spectacle of yourself? Put away your wine." 15But Hannah answered, "No, my lord, I am a woman deeply troubled; I have drunk neither wine nor strong drink, but I have been pouring out my soul before the LORD. 16Do not regard your servant as a worthless woman, for I have been speaking out of my great anxiety and vexation all this time." 17Then Eli answered, "Go in peace; the God of Israel grant the petition you have made to him." 18And she said, "Let your servant find favor in your sight." Then the woman went to her quarters,i ate and drank with her husband,j and her countenance was sad no longer.k

---

d Compare Gk and 1 Chr 6.35-36: Heb *Ramathaim-zophim*   e Syr: Meaning of Heb uncertain   f Gk: Heb lacks *and presented herself before the LORD*   g That is *one separated* or *one consecrated*   h Cn Compare Gk Q Ms 1.22: MT *then I will give him to the LORD all the days of his life*   i Gk: Heb *went her way*   j Gk: Heb lacks *and drank with her husband*   k Gk: Meaning of Heb uncertain

c 1:11 *and his hair shall never be cut.* This was an approved custom for those who were wholly dedicated to God.

King James

19¶ And they rose up in the morning early, and worshipped before the LORD, and returned, and came to their house to Ramah: and Elkanah knew Hannah his wife; and the LORD remembered her.

20Wherefore it came to pass, when the time was come about after Hannah had conceived, that she bare a son, and called his name Samuel, *saying,* Because I have asked him of the LORD.

21And the man Elkanah, and all his house, went up to offer unto the LORD the yearly sacrifice, and his vow.

22But Hannah went not up; for she said unto her husband, *I will not go up* until the child be weaned, and *then* I will bring him, that he may appear before the LORD, and there abide for ever.

23And Elkanah her husband said unto her, Do what seemeth thee good; tarry until thou have weaned him; only the LORD establish his word. So the woman abode, and gave her son suck until she weaned him.

24¶ And when she had weaned him, she took him up with her, with three bullocks, and one ephah of flour, and a bottle of wine, and brought him unto the house of the LORD in Shiloh: and the child *was* young.

25And they slew a bullock, and brought the child to Eli.

26And she said, Oh my lord, *as* thy soul liveth, my lord, I *am* the woman that stood by thee here, praying unto the LORD.

27For this child I prayed; and the LORD hath given me my petition which I asked of him:

28Therefore also I have lent him to the LORD; as long as he liveth he shall be lent to the LORD. And he worshipped the LORD there.

2 AND HANNAH prayed, and said, My heart rejoiceth in the LORD, mine horn is exalted in the LORD: my mouth is enlarged over mine enemies; because I rejoice in thy salvation.

2*There is* none holy as the LORD: for *there is* none beside thee: neither *is there* any rock like our God.

3Talk no more so exceeding proudly; let *not* arrogancy come out of your mouth: for the LORD *is* a God of knowledge, and by him actions are weighed.

4The bows of the mighty men *are* broken, and they that stumbled are girded with strength.

5*They that were* full have hired out themselves for bread; and *they that were* hungry ceased: so that the barren hath born seven; and she that hath many children is waxed feeble.

6The LORD killeth, and maketh alive: he bringeth down to the grave, and bringeth up.

7The LORD maketh poor, and maketh rich: he bringeth low, and lifteth up.

New International

19Early the next morning they arose and worshiped before the LORD and then went back to their home at Ramah. Elkanah lay with Hannah his wife, and the LORD remembered her. 20So in the course of time Hannah conceived and gave birth to a son. She named him Samuel,a saying, "Because I asked the LORD for him."

Hannah Dedicates Samuel

21When the man Elkanah went up with all his family to offer the annual sacrifice to the LORD and to fulfill his vow, 22Hannah did not go. She said to her husband, "After the boy is weaned, I will take him and present him before the LORD, and he will live there always."

23"Do what seems best to you," Elkanah her husband told her. "Stay here until you have weaned him; only may the LORD make good hisb word." So the woman stayed at home and nursed her son until she had weaned him.

24After he was weaned, she took the boy with her, young as he was, along with a three-year-old bull,c an ephahd of flour and a skin of wine, and brought him to the house of the LORD at Shiloh. 25When they had slaughtered the bull, they brought the boy to Eli, 26and she said to him, "As surely as you live, my lord, I am the woman who stood here beside you praying to the LORD. 27I prayed for this child, and the LORD has granted me what I asked of him. 28So now I give him to the LORD. For his whole life he will be given over to the LORD." And he worshiped the LORD there.

Hannah's Prayer

2 THEN HANNAH prayed and said:

"My heart rejoices in the LORD;
  in the LORD my horne is lifted high.
My mouth boasts over my enemies,
  for I delight in your deliverance.

2"There is no one holyf like the LORD;
  there is no one besides you;
  there is no Rock like our God.

3"Do not keep talking so proudly
  or let your mouth speak such arrogance,
for the LORD is a God who knows,
  and by him deeds are weighed.

4"The bows of the warriors are broken,
  but those who stumbled are armed with
    strength.
5Those who were full hire themselves out for
    food,
  but those who were hungry hunger no more.
She who was barren has borne seven children,
  but she who has had many sons pines away.

6"The LORD brings death and makes alive;
  he brings down to the graveg and raises up.
7The LORD sends poverty and wealth;
  he humbles and he exalts.

a 20 *Samuel* sounds like the Hebrew for *heard of God.*   b 23 Masoretic Text; Dead Sea Scrolls, Septuagint and Syriac *your*   c 24 Dead Sea Scrolls, Septuagint and Syriac; Masoretic Text *with three bulls*   d 24 That is, probably about 3/5 bushel (about 22 liters)   e 1 *Horn* here symbolizes strength; also in verse 10.   f 2 Or *no Holy One*   g 6 Hebrew *Sheol*

Living Bible

19, 20The entire family was up early the next morning and went to the Tabernacle to worship the Lord once more. Then they returned home to Ramah, and when Elkanah slept with Hannah, the Lord remembered her petition; in the process of time, a baby boy was born to her. She named him Samuel (meaningh "asked of God") because, as she said, "I asked the Lord for him."

21, 22The next year Elkanah and Peninnah and her children went on the annual trip to the Tabernacle without Hannah, for she told her husband, "Wait until the baby is weaned, and then I will take him to the Tabernacle and leave him there."

23"Well, whatever you think best," Elkanah agreed. "May the Lord's will be done."

So she stayed home until the baby was weaned. 24Then, though he was still so small, they took him to the Tabernacle in Shiloh, along with a three-year-old bull for the sacrifice, and a bushel of flour and some wine. 25After the sacrifice they took the child to Eli.

26"Sir, do you remember me?" Hannah asked him. "I am the woman who stood here that time praying to the Lord! 27I asked him to give me this child, and he has given me my request; 28and now I am giving him to the Lord for as long as he lives." So she left him there at the Tabernacle for the Lord to use.

2 THIS WAS Hannah's prayer:
"How I rejoice in the Lord!
How he has blessed me!
Now I have an answer for my enemies,
For the Lord has solved my problem.
How I rejoice!
2No one is as holy as the Lord!
There is no other God,
Nor any Rock like our God.
3Quit acting so proud and arrogant!
The Lord knows what you have done,
And he will judge your deeds.
4Those who were mighty are mighty no more!
Those who were weak are now strong.
5Those who were well are now starving;
Those who were starving are fed.
The barren woman now has seven children;
She with many children has no more!
6The Lord kills,
The Lord gives life.
7Some he causes to be poor
And others to be rich.
He cuts one down
And lifts another up.

New Revised Standard

19 They rose early in the morning and worshiped before the LORD; then they went back to their house at Ramah. Elkanah knew his wife Hannah, and the LORD remembered her. 20In due time Hannah conceived and bore a son. She named him Samuel, for she said, "I have asked him of the LORD."

21 The man Elkanah and all his household went up to offer to the LORD the yearly sacrifice, and to pay his vow. 22But Hannah did not go up, for she said to her husband, "As soon as the child is weaned, I will bring him, that he may appear in the presence of the LORD, and remain there forever; I will offer him as a naziritei for all time."j 23Her husband Elkanah said to her, "Do what seems best to you, wait until you have weaned him; only—may the LORD establish his word."k So the woman remained and nursed her son, until she weaned him. 24When she had weaned him, she took him up with her, along with a three-year-old bull,l an ephah of flour, and a skin of wine. She brought him to the house of the LORD at Shiloh; and the child was young. 25Then they slaughtered the bull, and they brought the child to Eli. 26And she said, "Oh, my lord! As you live, my lord, I am the woman who was standing here in your presence, praying to the LORD. 27For this child I prayed; and the LORD has granted me the petition that I made to him. 28Therefore I have lent him to the LORD; as long as he lives, he is given to the LORD."

She left him there form the LORD.

Hannah's Prayer

2 HANNAH PRAYED and said,
"My heart exults in the LORD;
my strength is exalted in my God.n
My mouth derides my enemies,
because I rejoice in myo victory.

2 "There is no Holy One like the LORD,
no one besides you;
there is no Rock like our God.
3 Talk no more so very proudly,
let not arrogance come from your mouth;
for the LORD is a God of knowledge,
and by him actions are weighed.
4 The bows of the mighty are broken,
but the feeble gird on strength.
5 Those who were full have hired themselves
out for bread,
but those who were hungry are fat with
spoil.
The barren has borne seven,
but she who has many children is forlorn.
6 The LORD kills and brings to life;
he brings down to Sheol and raises up.
7 The LORD makes poor and makes rich;
he brings low, he also exalts.

---

i That is one separated or one consecrated   j Cn Compare Q Ms: MT lacks I will offer him as a nazirite for all time   k MT: Q Ms Gk Compare Syr that which goes out of your mouth   l Q Ms Gk Syr: MT three bulls   m Gk (Compare Q Ms) and Gk at 2.11: MT And he (that is, Elkanah) worshiped there before   n Gk: Heb the LORD   o Q Ms: MT your

h 1:19, 20 named him Samuel (meaning "asked of God"). This was a play on words. The word Samuel in Hebrew sounds like the word "to ask."

King James

8He raiseth up the poor out of the dust, *and* lifteth up the beggar from the dunghill, to set *them* among princes, and to make them inherit the throne of glory: for the pillars of the earth *are* the LORD'S, and he hath set the world upon them.

9He will keep the feet of his saints, and the wicked shall be silent in darkness; for by strength shall no man prevail.

10The adversaries of the LORD shall be broken to pieces; out of heaven shall he thunder upon them: the LORD shall judge the ends of the earth; and he shall give strength unto his king, and exalt the horn of his anointed.

11And Elkanah went to Ramah to his house. And the child did minister unto the LORD before Eli the priest.

12¶ Now the sons of Eli *were* sons of Belial; they knew not the LORD.

13And the priests' custom with the people *was, that,* when any man offered sacrifice, the priest's servant came, while the flesh was in seething, with a fleshhook of three teeth in his hand;

14And he struck *it* into the pan, or kettle, or caldron, or pot; all that the fleshhook brought up the priest took for himself. So they did in Shiloh unto all the Israelites that came thither.

15Also before they burnt the fat, the priest's servant came, and said to the man that sacrificed, Give flesh to roast for the priest; for he will not have sodden flesh of thee, but raw.

16And *if* any man said unto him, Let them not fail to burn the fat presently, and *then* take *as much* as thy soul desireth; then he would answer him, *Nay;* but thou shalt give *it* me now: and if not, I will take *it* by force.

17Wherefore the sin of the young men was very great before the LORD: for men abhorred the offering of the LORD.

18¶ But Samuel ministered before the LORD, *being* a child, girded with a linen ephod.

19Moreover his mother made him a little coat, and brought *it* to him from year to year, when she came up with her husband to offer the yearly sacrifice.

20¶ And Eli blessed Elkanah and his wife, and said, The LORD give thee seed of this woman for the loan which is lent to the LORD. And they went unto their own home.

21And the LORD visited Hannah, so that she conceived, and bare three sons and two daughters. And the child Samuel grew before the LORD.

22¶ Now Eli was very old, and heard all that his sons did unto all Israel; and how they lay with the women that assembled *at* the door of the tabernacle of the congregation.

23And he said unto them, Why do ye such things? for I hear of your evil dealings by all this people.

24Nay, my sons; for *it is* no good report that I hear: ye make the LORD's people to transgress.

25If one man sin against another, the judge shall judge him: but if a man sin against the LORD, who shall entreat for him? Notwithstanding they hearkened not unto the voice of their father, because the LORD would slay them.

26And the child Samuel grew on, and was in favour both with the LORD, and also with men.

New International

8He raises the poor from the dust
　　and lifts the needy from the ash heap;
he seats them with princes
　　and has them inherit a throne of honor.

"For the foundations of the earth are the
　　　　LORD's;
　　upon them he has set the world.
9He will guard the feet of his saints,
　　but the wicked will be silenced in darkness.

"It is not by strength that one prevails;
10　　those who oppose the LORD will be shattered.
He will thunder against them from heaven;
　　the LORD will judge the ends of the earth.

"He will give strength to his king
　　and exalt the horn of his anointed."

11Then Elkanah went home to Ramah, but the boy ministered before the LORD under Eli the priest.

Eli's Wicked Sons

12Eli's sons were wicked men; they had no regard for the LORD. 13Now it was the practice of the priests with the people that whenever anyone offered a sacrifice and while the meat was being boiled, the servant of the priest would come with a three-pronged fork in his hand. 14He would plunge it into the pan or kettle or caldron or pot, and the priest would take for himself whatever the fork brought up. This is how they treated all the Israelites who came to Shiloh. 15But even before the fat was burned, the servant of the priest would come and say to the man who was sacrificing, "Give the priest some meat to roast; he won't accept boiled meat from you, but only raw."

16If the man said to him, "Let the fat be burned up first, and then take whatever you want," the servant would then answer, "No, hand it over now; if you don't, I'll take it by force."

17This sin of the young men was very great in the LORD's sight, for they[a] were treating the LORD's offering with contempt.

18But Samuel was ministering before the LORD—a boy wearing a linen ephod. 19Each year his mother made him a little robe and took it to him when she went up with her husband to offer the annual sacrifice. 20Eli would bless Elkanah and his wife, saying, "May the LORD give you children by this woman to take the place of the one she prayed for and gave to the LORD." Then they would go home. 21And the LORD was gracious to Hannah; she conceived and gave birth to three sons and two daughters. Meanwhile, the boy Samuel grew up in the presence of the LORD.

22Now Eli, who was very old, heard about everything his sons were doing to all Israel and how they slept with the women who served at the entrance to the Tent of Meeting. 23So he said to them, "Why do you do such things? I hear from all the people about these wicked deeds of yours. 24No, my sons; it is not a good report that I hear spreading among the LORD's people. 25If a man sins against another man, God[b] may mediate for him; but if a man sins against the LORD, who will intercede for him?" His sons, however, did not listen to their father's rebuke, for it was the LORD's will to put them to death.

26And the boy Samuel continued to grow in stature and in favor with the LORD and with men.

---

a 17 Or *men*　　b 25 Or *the judges*

Living Bible

8He lifts the poor from the dust—
Yes, from a pile of ashes—
And treats them as princes
Sitting in the seats of honor.
For all the earth is the Lord's
And he has set the world in order.
9He will protect his godly ones,
But the wicked shall be silenced in darkness.
No one shall succeed by strength alone.
10Those who fight against the Lord shall be broken;
He thunders against them from heaven.
He judges throughout the earth.
He gives mighty strength to his King,
And gives great glory to his anointed one.

11So they returned home to Ramah without Samuel; and the child became the Lord's helper, for he assisted Eli the priest.

12Now the sons of Eli were evil men who didn't love the Lord. 13, 14It was their regular practice to send out a servant whenever anyone was offering a sacrifice, and while the flesh of the sacrificed animal was boiling, the servant would put a three-pronged fleshhook into the pot and demand that whatever it brought up be given to Eli's sons. They treated all of the Israelites in this way when they came to Shiloh to worship. 15Sometimes the servant would come even before the rite of burning the fat on the altar had been performed, and he would demand raw meat before it was boiled, so that it could be used for roasting.

16If the man offering the sacrifice replied, "Take as much as you want, but the fat must first be burned," [as the law requiresc], then the servant would say,

"No, give it to me now or I'll take it by force."

17So the sin of these young men was very great in the eyes of the Lord; for they treated the people's offerings to the Lord with contempt.

18Samuel, though only a child, was the Lord's helper and wore a little linen robe just like the priest's.d 19Each year his mother made a little coat for him and brought it to him when she came with her husband for the sacrifice. 20Before they returned home Eli would bless Elkanah and Hannah and ask God to give them other children to take the place of this one they had given to the Lord. 21And the Lord gave Hannah three sons and two daughters. Meanwhile Samuel grew up in the service of the Lord.

22Eli was now very old, but he was aware of what was going on around him. He knew, for instance, that his sons were seducing the young women who assisted at the entrance of the Tabernacle.

23, 24, 25"I have been hearing terrible reports from the Lord's people about what you are doing," Eli told his sons. "It is an awful thing to make the Lord's people sin. Ordinary sin receives heavy punishment, but how much more this sin of yours which has been committed against the Lord!" But they wouldn't listen to their father, for the Lord was already planning to kill them.

26Little Samuel was growing in two ways—he was getting taller, and he was becoming everyone's favorite (and he was a favorite of the Lord's, too!).

New Revised Standard

8 He raises up the poor from the dust;
     he lifts the needy from the ash heap,
   to make them sit with princes
     and inherit a seat of honor.e
   For the pillars of the earth are the LORD's,
     and on them he has set the world.

9 "He will guard the feet of his faithful ones,
     but the wicked shall be cut off in darkness;
   for not by might does one prevail.
10 The LORD! His adversaries shall be shattered;
     the Most Highf will thunder in heaven.
   The LORD will judge the ends of the earth;
     he will give strength to his king,
     and exalt the power of his anointed."

Eli's Wicked Sons

11 Then Elkanah went home to Ramah, while the boy remained to minister to the LORD, in the presence of the priest Eli.

12 Now the sons of Eli were scoundrels; they had no regard for the LORD 13or for the duties of the priests to the people. When anyone offered sacrifice, the priest's servant would come, while the meat was boiling, with a three-pronged fork in his hand, 14and he would thrust it into the pan, or kettle, or caldron, or pot; all that the fork brought up the priest would take for himself.g This is what they did at Shiloh to all the Israelites who came there. 15Moreover, before the fat was burned, the priest's servant would come and say to the one who was sacrificing, "Give meat for the priest to roast; for he will not accept boiled meat from you, but only raw." 16And if the man said to him, "Let them burn the fat first, and then take whatever you wish," he would say, "No, you must give it now; if not, I will take it by force." 17Thus the sin of the young men was very great in the sight of the LORD; for they treated the offerings of the LORD with contempt.

The Child Samuel at Shiloh

18 Samuel was ministering before the LORD, a boy wearing a linen ephod. 19His mother used to make for him a little robe and take it to him each year, when she went up with her husband to offer the yearly sacrifice. 20Then Eli would bless Elkanah and his wife, and say, "May the LORD repayh you with children by this woman for the gift that she made toi the LORD"; and then they would return to their home.

21 Andi the LORD took note of Hannah; she conceived and bore three sons and two daughters. And the boy Samuel grew up in the presence of the LORD.

Prophecy against Eli's Household

22 Now Eli was very old. He heard all that his sons were doing to all Israel, and how they lay with the women who served at the entrance to the tent of meeting. 23He said to them, "Why do you do such things? For I hear of your evil dealings from all these people. 24No, my sons; it is not a good report that I hear the people of the LORD spreading abroad. 25If one person sins against another, someone can intercede for the sinner with the LORD;k but if someone sins against the LORD, who can make intercession?" But they would not listen to the voice of their father; for it was the will of the LORD to kill them.

26 Now the boy Samuel continued to grow both in stature and in favor with the LORD and with the people.

---

e Gk (Compare Q Ms) adds *He grants the vow of the one who vows, and blesses the years of the just*   f Cn Heb *against him he*   g Gk Syr Vg: Heb *with it*   h Q Ms Gk: MT *give*   i Q Ms Gk: MT *for the petition that she asked of*   j Q Ms Gk: MT *When*   k Gk Compare Q Ms: MT *another, God will mediate for him*

King James

27¶ And there came a man of God unto Eli, and said unto him, Thus saith the LORD, Did I plainly appear unto the house of thy father, when they were in Egypt in Pharaoh's house?

28And did I choose him out of all the tribes of Israel *to be* my priest, to offer upon mine altar, to burn incense, to wear an ephod before me? and did I give unto the house of thy father all the offerings made by fire of the children of Israel?

29Wherefore kick ye at my sacrifice and at mine offering, which I have commanded *in my* habitation; and honourest thy sons above me, to make yourselves fat with the chiefest of all the offerings of Israel my people?

30Wherefore the LORD God of Israel saith, I said indeed *that* thy house, and the house of thy father, should walk before me for ever: but now the LORD saith, Be it far from me; for them that honour me I will honour, and they that despise me shall be lightly esteemed.

31Behold, the days come, that I will cut off thine arm, and the arm of thy father's house, that there shall not be an old man in thine house.

32And thou shalt see an enemy *in my* habitation, in all *the wealth* which *God* shall give Israel: and there shall not be an old man in thine house for ever.

33And the man of thine, *whom* I shall not cut off from mine altar, *shall be* to consume thine eyes, and to grieve thine heart: and all the increase of thine house shall die in the flower of their age.

34And this *shall be* a sign unto thee, that shall come upon thy two sons, on Hophni and Phinehas; in one day they shall die both of them.

35And I will raise me up a faithful priest, *that* shall do according to *that* which *is* in mine heart and in my mind: and I will build him a sure house; and he shall walk before mine anointed for ever.

36And it shall come to pass, *that* every one that is left in thine house shall come *and* crouch to him for a piece of silver and a morsel of bread, and shall say, Put me, I pray thee, into one of the priests' offices, that I may eat a piece of bread.

3 AND THE child Samuel ministered unto the LORD before Eli. And the word of the LORD was precious in those days; *there was* no open vision.

2And it came to pass at that time, when Eli *was* laid down in his place, and his eyes began to wax dim, *that* he could not see;

3And ere the lamp of God went out in the temple of the LORD, where the ark of God *was,* and Samuel was laid down *to sleep;*

4That the LORD called Samuel: and he answered, Here *am* I.

5And he ran unto Eli, and said, Here *am* I; for thou calledst me. And he said, I called not; lie down again. And he went and lay down.

6And the LORD called yet again, Samuel. And Samuel arose and went to Eli, and said, Here *am* I; for thou didst call me. And he answered, I called not, my son; lie down again.

7Now Samuel did not yet know the LORD, neither was the word of the LORD yet revealed unto him.

8And the LORD called Samuel again the third time. And he arose and went to Eli, and said, Here *am* I; for thou didst call me. And Eli perceived that the LORD had called the child.

9Therefore Eli said unto Samuel, Go, lie down: and it shall be, if he call thee, that thou shalt say, Speak, LORD; for thy servant heareth. So Samuel went and lay down in his place.

New International

Prophecy Against the House of Eli

27Now a man of God came to Eli and said to him, "This is what the LORD says: 'Did I not clearly reveal myself to your father's house when they were in Egypt under Pharaoh? 28I chose your father out of all the tribes of Israel to be my priest, to go up to my altar, to burn incense, and to wear an ephod in my presence. I also gave your father's house all the offerings made with fire by the Israelites. 29Why do youa scorn my sacrifice and offering that I prescribed for my dwelling? Why do you honor your sons more than me by fattening yourselves on the choice parts of every offering made by my people Israel?'

30"Therefore the LORD, the God of Israel, declares: 'I promised that your house and your father's house would minister before me forever.' But now the LORD declares: 'Far be it from me! Those who honor me I will honor, but those who despise me will be disdained. 31The time is coming when I will cut short your strength and the strength of your father's house, so that there will not be an old man in your family line 32and you will see distress in my dwelling. Although good will be done to Israel, in your family line there will never be an old man. 33Every one of you that I do not cut off from my altar will be spared only to blind your eyes with tears and to grieve your heart, and all your descendants will die in the prime of life.

34"'And what happens to your two sons, Hophni and Phinehas, will be a sign to you—they will both die on the same day. 35I will raise up for myself a faithful priest, who will do according to what is in my heart and mind. I will firmly establish his house, and he will minister before my anointed one always. 36Then everyone left in your family line will come and bow down before him for a piece of silver and a crust of bread and plead, "Appoint me to some priestly office so I can have food to eat." ' "

The LORD Calls Samuel

3 THE BOY Samuel ministered before the LORD under Eli. In those days the word of the LORD was rare; there were not many visions.

2One night Eli, whose eyes were becoming so weak that he could barely see, was lying down in his usual place. 3The lamp of God had not yet gone out, and Samuel was lying down in the templeb of the LORD, where the ark of God was. 4Then the LORD called Samuel.

Samuel answered, "Here I am." 5And he ran to Eli and said, "Here I am; you called me."

But Eli said, "I did not call; go back and lie down." So he went and lay down.

6Again the LORD called, "Samuel!" And Samuel got up and went to Eli and said, "Here I am; you called me."

"My son," Eli said, "I did not call; go back and lie down."

7Now Samuel did not yet know the LORD: The word of the LORD had not yet been revealed to him.

8The LORD called Samuel a third time, and Samuel got up and went to Eli and said, "Here I am; you called me."

Then Eli realized that the LORD was calling the boy. 9So Eli told Samuel, "Go and lie down, and if he calls you, say, 'Speak, LORD, for your servant is listening.' " So Samuel went and lay down in his place.

---

a 29 The Hebrew is plural.　　b 3 That is, tabernacle

Living Bible

27One day a prophetc came to Eli and gave him this message from the Lord: "Didn't I demonstrate my power when the people of Israel were slaves in Egypt? 28Didn't I choose your ancestor Levi from among all his brothers to be my priest, and to sacrifice upon my altar, and to burn incense, and to wear a priestly robed as he served me? And didn't I assign the sacrificial offerings to you priests? 29Then why are you so greedy for all the other offerings which are brought to me? Why have you honored your sons more than me—for you and they have become fat from the best of the offerings of my people!

30"Therefore, I, the Lord God of Israel, declare that although I promised that your branch of the tribe of Levi could always be my priests, it is ridiculous to think that what you are doing can continue. I will honor only those who honor me, and I will despise those who despise me. 31I will put an end to your family, so that it will no longer serve as priests. Every member will die before his time. None shall live to be old. 32You will envy the prosperity I will give my people, but you and your family will be in distress and need. Not one of them will live out his days. 33Those who are left alive will live in sadness and grief; and their children shall die by the sword. 34And to prove that what I have said will come true, I will cause your two sons, Hophni and Phinehas, to die on the same day!

35"Then I will raise up a faithful priest who will serve me and do whatever I tell him to do. I will bless his descendants, and his family shall be priests to my kings forever. 36Then all of your descendants shall bow before him, begging for money and food. 'Please,' they will say, 'give me a job among the priests so that I will have enough to eat.'"

3 MEANWHILE LITTLE Samuel was helping the Lord by assisting Eli. Messages from the Lord were very rare in those days, 2, 3but one night after Eli had gone to bed (he was almost blind with age by now), and Samuel was sleeping in the Temple near the Ark, 4, 5the Lord called out, "Samuel! Samuel!"

"Yes?" Samuel replied. "What is it?" He jumped up and ran to Eli. "Here I am. What do you want?" he asked.

"I didn't call you," Eli said. "Go on back to bed." So he did. 6Then the Lord called again, "Samuel!" And again Samuel jumped up and ran to Eli.

"Yes?" he asked. "What do you need?"

"No, I didn't call you, my son," Eli said. "Go on back to bed."

7(Samuel had never had a message from Jehovah before.e) 8So now the Lord called the third time, and once more Samuel jumped up and ran to Eli.

"Yes?" he asked. "What do you need?"

Then Eli realized it was the Lord who had spoken to the child. 9So he said to Samuel, "Go and lie down again, and if he calls again, say, 'Yes, Lord, I'm listening.'" So Samuel went back to bed.

New Revised Standard

27 A man of God came to Eli and said to him, "Thus the LORD has said, 'I revealedf myself to the family of your ancestor in Egypt when they were slavesg to the house of Pharaoh. 28I chose him out of all the tribes of Israel to be my priest, to go up to my altar, to offer incense, to wear an ephod before me; and I gave to the family of your ancestor all my offerings by fire from the people of Israel. 29Why then look with greedy eyeh at my sacrifices and my offerings that I commanded, and honor your sons more than me by fattening yourselves on the choicest parts of every offering of my people Israel?' 30Therefore the LORD the God of Israel declares: 'I promised that your family and the family of your ancestor should go in and out before me forever'; but now the LORD declares: 'Far be it from me; for those who honor me I will honor, and those who despise me shall be treated with contempt. 31See, a time is coming when I will cut off your strength and the strength of your ancestor's family, so that no one in your family will live to old age. 32Then in distress you will look with greedy eyei on all the prosperity that shall be bestowed upon Israel; and no one in your family shall ever live to old age. 33The only one of you whom I shall not cut off from my altar shall be spared to weep out hisj eyes and grieve hisk heart; all the members of your household shall die by the sword.l 34The fate of your two sons, Hophni and Phinehas, shall be the sign to you—both of them shall die on the same day. 35I will raise up for myself a faithful priest, who shall do according to what is in my heart and in my mind. I will build him a sure house, and he shall go in and out before my anointed one forever. 36Everyone who is left in your family shall come to implore him for a piece of silver or a loaf of bread, and shall say, Please put me in one of the priest's places, that I may eat a morsel of bread.'"

Samuel's Calling and Prophetic Activity

3 NOW THE boy Samuel was ministering to the LORD under Eli. The word of the LORD was rare in those days; visions were not widespread.

2 At that time Eli, whose eyesight had begun to grow dim so that he could not see, was lying down in his room; 3the lamp of God had not yet gone out, and Samuel was lying down in the temple of the LORD, where the ark of God was. 4Then the LORD called, "Samuel! Samuel!"m and he said, "Here I am!" 5and ran to Eli, and said, "Here I am, for you called me." But he said, "I did not call; lie down again." So he went and lay down. 6The LORD called again, "Samuel!" Samuel got up and went to Eli, and said, "Here I am, for you called me." But he said, "I did not call, my son; lie down again." 7Now Samuel did not yet know the LORD, and the word of the LORD had not yet been revealed to him. 8The LORD called Samuel again, a third time. And he got up and went to Eli, and said, "Here I am, for you called me." Then Eli perceived that the LORD was calling the boy. 9Therefore Eli said to Samuel, "Go, lie down; and if he calls you, you shall say, 'Speak, LORD, for your servant is listening.'" So Samuel went and lay down in his place.

---

c 2:27 a prophet, literally, "a man of God."   d 2:28 wear a priestly robe, literally, "wear an ephod."   e 3:7 Samuel never had a message from God before, literally, "did not yet know Jehovah."

f Gk Tg Syr: Heb Did I reveal   g Q Ms Gk: MT lacks slaves   h Q Ms Gk: MT then kick   i Q Ms Gk: MT will kick   j Q Ms Gk: MT your   k Q Ms Gk: Heb your   l Q Ms See Gk: MT die like mortals   m Q Ms Gk See 3.10: MT the LORD called Samuel

King James

10And the LORD came, and stood, and called as at other times, Samuel, Samuel. Then Samuel answered, Speak; for thy servant heareth.

11¶ And the LORD said to Samuel, Behold, I will do a thing in Israel, at which both the ears of every one that heareth it shall tingle.

12In that day I will perform against Eli all *things* which I have spoken concerning his house: when I begin, I will also make an end.

13For I have told him that I will judge his house for ever for the iniquity which he knoweth; because his sons made themselves vile, and he restrained them not.

14And therefore I have sworn unto the house of Eli, that the iniquity of Eli's house shall not be purged with sacrifice nor offering for ever.

15¶ And Samuel lay until the morning, and opened the doors of the house of the LORD. And Samuel feared to show Eli the vision.

16Then Eli called Samuel, and said, Samuel, my son. And he answered, Here *am* I.

17And he said, What *is* the thing that *the* LORD hath said unto thee? I pray thee hide *it* not from me: God do so to thee, and more also, if thou hide *any* thing from me of all the things that he said unto thee.

18And Samuel told him every whit, and hid nothing from him. And he said, It *is* the LORD: let him do what seemeth him good.

19¶ And Samuel grew, and the LORD was with him, and did let none of his words fall to the ground.

20And all Israel from Dan even to Beer-sheba knew that Samuel *was* established *to be* a prophet of the LORD.

21And the LORD appeared again in Shiloh: for the LORD revealed himself to Samuel in Shiloh by the word of the LORD.

4 AND THE word of Samuel came to all Israel. Now Israel went out against the Philistines to battle, and pitched beside Eben-ezer: and the Philistines pitched in Aphek.

2And the Philistines put themselves in array against Israel: and when they joined battle, Israel was smitten before the Philistines: and they slew of the army in the field about four thousand men.

3¶ And when the people were come into the camp, the elders of Israel said, Wherefore hath the LORD smitten us today before the Philistines? Let us fetch the ark of the covenant of the LORD out of Shiloh unto us, that, when it cometh among us, it may save us out of the hand of our enemies.

4So the people sent to Shiloh, that they might bring from thence the ark of the covenant of the LORD of hosts, which dwelleth *between* the cherubims: and the two sons of Eli, Hophni and Phinehas, *were* there with the ark of the covenant of God.

5And when the ark of the covenant of the LORD came into the camp, all Israel shouted with a great shout, so that the earth rang again.

6And when the Philistines heard the noise of the shout, they said, What *meaneth* the noise of this great shout in the camp of the Hebrews? And they understood that the ark of the LORD was come into the camp.

7And the Philistines were afraid, for they said, God is come into the camp. And they said, Woe unto us! for there hath not been such a thing heretofore.

8Woe unto us! who shall deliver us out of the hand of these mighty Gods? these *are* the Gods that smote the Egyptians with all the plagues in the wilderness.

9Be strong, and quit yourselves like men, O ye Philistines, that ye be not servants unto the Hebrews, as they have been to you: quit yourselves like men, and fight.

New International

10The LORD came and stood there, calling as at the other times, "Samuel! Samuel!"

Then Samuel said, "Speak, for your servant is listening."

11And the LORD said to Samuel: "See, I am about to do something in Israel that will make the ears of everyone who hears of it tingle. 12At that time I will carry out against Eli everything I spoke against his family—from beginning to end. 13For I told him that I would judge his family forever because of the sin he knew about; his sons made themselves contemptible,a and he failed to restrain them. 14Therefore, I swore to the house of Eli, 'The guilt of Eli's house will never be atoned for by sacrifice or offering.' "

15Samuel lay down until morning and then opened the doors of the house of the LORD. He was afraid to tell Eli the vision, 16but Eli called him and said, "Samuel, my son."

Samuel answered, "Here I am."

17"What was it he said to you?" Eli asked. "Do not hide it from me. May God deal with you, be it ever so severely, if you hide from me anything he told you." 18So Samuel told him everything, hiding nothing from him. Then Eli said, "He is the LORD; let him do what is good in his eyes."

19The LORD was with Samuel as he grew up, and he let none of his words fall to the ground. 20And all Israel from Dan to Beersheba recognized that Samuel was attested as a prophet of the LORD. 21The LORD continued to appear at Shiloh, and there he revealed himself to Samuel through his word.

4 AND SAMUEL'S word came to all Israel.

The Philistines Capture the Ark

Now the Israelites went out to fight against the Philistines. The Israelites camped at Ebenezer, and the Philistines at Aphek. 2The Philistines deployed their forces to meet Israel, and as the battle spread, Israel was defeated by the Philistines, who killed about four thousand of them on the battlefield. 3When the soldiers returned to camp, the elders of Israel asked, "Why did the LORD bring defeat upon us today before the Philistines? Let us bring the ark of the LORD's covenant from Shiloh, so that itb may go with us and save us from the hand of our enemies."

4So the people sent men to Shiloh, and they brought back the ark of the covenant of the LORD Almighty, who is enthroned between the cherubim. And Eli's two sons, Hophni and Phinehas, were there with the ark of the covenant of God.

5When the ark of the LORD's covenant came into the camp, all Israel raised such a great shout that the ground shook. 6Hearing the uproar, the Philistines asked, "What's all this shouting in the Hebrew camp?"

When they learned that the ark of the LORD had come into the camp, 7the Philistines were afraid. "A god has come into the camp," they said. "We're in trouble! Nothing like this has happened before. 8Woe to us! Who will deliver us from the hand of these mighty gods? They are the gods who struck the Egyptians with all kinds of plagues in the desert. 9Be strong, Philistines! Be men, or you will be subject to the Hebrews, as they have been to you. Be men, and fight!"

---

a *13* Masoretic Text; an ancient Hebrew scribal tradition and Septuagint *sons blasphemed God*   b *3* Or *he*

Living Bible

10And the Lord came and called as before, "Samuel! Samuel!"

And Samuel replied, "Yes, I'm listening."

11Then the Lord said to Samuel, "I am going to do a shocking thing in Israel. 12I am going to do all of the dreadful things I warned Eli about. 13I have continually threatened him and his entire family with punishment because his sons are blaspheming God, and he doesn't stop them. 14So I have vowed that the sins of Eli and of his sons shall never be forgiven by sacrifices and offerings."

15Samuel stayed in bed until morning, then opened the doors of the Temple as usual, for he was afraid to tell Eli what the Lord had said to him. 16, 17But Eli called him.

"My son," he said, "what did the Lord say to you? Tell me everything. And may God punish you if you hide anything from me!"

18So Samuel told him what the Lord had said.

"It is the Lord's will," Eli replied; "let him do what he thinks best."

19As Samuel grew, the Lord was with him and people listened carefully to his advice. 20And all Israel from one end of the land to the other knew that Samuel was going to be a prophet of the Lord. 21Then the Lord began to give messages to him there at the Tabernacle in Shiloh, and he passed them on to the people of Israel.

4 AT THAT time Israel was at war with the Philistines. The Israeli army was camped near Ebenezer, the Philistines at Aphek. 2And the Philistines defeated Israel, killing four thousand of them. 3After the battle was over, the army of Israel returned to their camp and their leaders discussed why the Lord had let them be defeated.

"Let's bring the Ark here from Shiloh," they said. "If we carry it into battle with us, the Lord will be among us and he will surely save us from our enemies."

4So they sent for the Ark of the Lord of heaven who is enthroned above the angels. Hophni and Phinehas, the sons of Eli, accompanied it into the battle. 5When the Israelis saw the Ark coming, their shout of joy was so loud that it almost made the ground shake!

6"What's going on?" the Philistines asked. "What's all the shouting about over in the camp of the Hebrews?"

When they were told it was because the Ark of the Lord had arrived, 7they panicked.

"God has come into their camp!" they cried out. "Woe upon us, for we have never had to face anything like this before! 8Who can save us from these mighty gods of Israel? They are the same gods who destroyed the Egyptians with plagues when Israel was in the wilderness. 9Fight as you never have before, O Philistines, or we will become their slaves just as they have been ours."

New Revised Standard

10 Now the LORD came and stood there, calling as before, "Samuel! Samuel!" And Samuel said, "Speak, for your servant is listening." 11Then the LORD said to Samuel, "See, I am about to do something in Israel that will make both ears of anyone who hears of it tingle. 12On that day I will fulfill against Eli all that I have spoken concerning his house, from beginning to end. 13For I have told him that I am about to punish his house forever, for the iniquity that he knew, because his sons were blaspheming God,c and he did not restrain them. 14Therefore I swear to the house of Eli that the iniquity of Eli's house shall not be expiated by sacrifice or offering forever."

15 Samuel lay there until morning; then he opened the doors of the house of the LORD. Samuel was afraid to tell the vision to Eli. 16But Eli called Samuel and said, "Samuel, my son." He said, "Here I am." 17Eli said, "What was it that he told you? Do not hide it from me. May God do so to you and more also, if you hide anything from me of all that he told you." 18So Samuel told him everything and hid nothing from him. Then he said, "It is the LORD; let him do what seems good to him."

19 As Samuel grew up, the LORD was with him and let none of his words fall to the ground. 20And all Israel from Dan to Beer-sheba knew that Samuel was a trustworthy prophet of the LORD. 21The LORD continued to appear at Shiloh, for the LORD revealed himself to Samuel at Shiloh by the word of the LORD.

4 AND THE word of Samuel came to all Israel.

The Ark of God Captured

In those days the Philistines mustered for war against Israel,d and Israel went out to battle against them;e they encamped at Ebenezer, and the Philistines encamped at Aphek. 2The Philistines drew up in line against Israel, and when the battle was joined,f Israel was defeated by the Philistines, who killed about four thousand men on the field of battle. 3When the troops came to the camp, the elders of Israel said, "Why has the LORD put us to rout today before the Philistines? Let us bring the ark of the covenant of the LORD here from Shiloh, so that he may come among us and save us from the power of our enemies." 4So the people sent to Shiloh, and brought from there the ark of the covenant of the LORD of hosts, who is enthroned on the cherubim. The two sons of Eli, Hophni and Phinehas, were there with the ark of the covenant of God.

5 When the ark of the covenant of the LORD came into the camp, all Israel gave a mighty shout, so that the earth resounded. 6When the Philistines heard the noise of the shouting, they said, "What does this great shouting in the camp of the Hebrews mean?" When they learned that the ark of the LORD had come to the camp, 7the Philistines were afraid; for they said, "Gods haveg come into the camp." They also said, "Woe to us! For nothing like this has happened before. 8Woe to us! Who can deliver us from the power of these mighty gods? These are the gods who struck the Egyptians with every sort of plague in the wilderness. 9Take courage, and be men, O Philistines, in order not to become slaves to the Hebrews as they have been to you; be men and fight."

---

c Another reading is *for themselves*   d Gk: Heb lacks *In those days the Philistines mustered for war against Israel*   e Gk: Heb *against the Philistines*   f Meaning of Heb uncertain   g Or *A god has*

King James

10¶ And the Philistines fought, and Israel was smitten, and they fled every man into his tent: and there was a very great slaughter; for there fell of Israel thirty thousand footmen.

11And the ark of God was taken; and the two sons of Eli, Hophni and Phinehas, were slain.

12¶ And there ran a man of Benjamin out of the army, and came to Shiloh the same day with his clothes rent, and with earth upon his head.

13And when he came, lo, Eli sat upon a seat by the wayside watching: for his heart trembled for the ark of God. And when the man came into the city, and told it, all the city cried out.

14And when Eli heard the noise of the crying, he said, What meaneth the noise of this tumult? And the man came in hastily, and told Eli.

15Now Eli was ninety and eight years old; and his eyes were dim, that he could not see.

16And the man said unto Eli, I am he that came out of the army, and I fled today out of the army. And he said, What is there done, my son?

17And the messenger answered and said, Israel is fled before the Philistines, and there hath been also a great slaughter among the people, and thy two sons also, Hophni and Phinehas, are dead, and the ark of God is taken.

18And it came to pass, when he made mention of the ark of God, that he fell from off the seat backward by the side of the gate, and his neck brake, and he died: for he was an old man, and heavy. And he had judged Israel forty years.

19¶ And his daughter-in-law, Phinehas' wife, was with child, near to be delivered: and when she heard the tidings that the ark of God was taken, and that her father-in-law and her husband were dead, she bowed herself and travailed; for her pains came upon her.

20And about the time of her death the women that stood by her said unto her, Fear not; for thou hast borne a son. But she answered not, neither did she regard it.

21And she named the child I-chabod, saying, The glory is departed from Israel: because the ark of God was taken, and because of her father-in-law and her husband.

22And she said, The glory is departed from Israel: for the ark of God is taken.

5 AND THE Philistines took the ark of God, and brought it from Eben-ezer unto Ashdod.

2When the Philistines took the ark of God, they brought it into the house of Dagon, and set it by Dagon.

3¶ And when they of Ashdod arose early on the morrow, behold, Dagon was fallen upon his face to the earth before the ark of the LORD. And they took Dagon, and set him in his place again.

4And when they arose early on the morrow morning, behold, Dagon was fallen upon his face to the ground before the ark of the LORD; and the head of Dagon and both the palms of his hands were cut off upon the threshold; only the stump of Dagon was left to him.

5Therefore neither the priests of Dagon, nor any that come into Dagon's house, tread on the threshold of Dagon in Ashdod unto this day.

6But the hand of the LORD was heavy upon them of Ashdod, and he destroyed them, and smote them with emerods, even Ashdod and the coasts thereof.

7And when the men of Ashdod saw that it was so, they said, The ark of the God of Israel shall not abide with us: for his hand is sore upon us, and upon Dagon our god.

New International

10So the Philistines fought, and the Israelites were defeated and every man fled to his tent. The slaughter was very great; Israel lost thirty thousand foot soldiers. 11The ark of God was captured, and Eli's two sons, Hophni and Phinehas, died.

Death of Eli

12That same day a Benjamite ran from the battle line and went to Shiloh, his clothes torn and dust on his head. 13When he arrived, there was Eli sitting on his chair by the side of the road, watching, because his heart feared for the ark of God. When the man entered the town and told what had happened, the whole town sent up a cry.

14Eli heard the outcry and asked, "What is the meaning of this uproar?"

The man hurried over to Eli, 15who was ninety-eight years old and whose eyes were set so that he could not see. 16He told Eli, "I have just come from the battle line; I fled from it this very day."

Eli asked, "What happened, my son?"

17The man who brought the news replied, "Israel fled before the Philistines, and the army has suffered heavy losses. Also your two sons, Hophni and Phinehas, are dead, and the ark of God has been captured."

18When he mentioned the ark of God, Eli fell backward off his chair by the side of the gate. His neck was broken and he died, for he was an old man and heavy. He had led[a] Israel forty years.

19His daughter-in-law, the wife of Phinehas, was pregnant and near the time of delivery. When she heard the news that the ark of God had been captured and that her father-in-law and her husband were dead, she went into labor and gave birth, but was overcome by her labor pains. 20As she was dying, the women attending her said, "Don't despair; you have given birth to a son." But she did not respond or pay any attention.

21She named the boy Ichabod,[b] saying, "The glory has departed from Israel"—because of the capture of the ark of God and the deaths of her father-in-law and her husband. 22She said, "The glory has departed from Israel, for the ark of God has been captured."

The Ark in Ashdod and Ekron

5 AFTER THE Philistines had captured the ark of God, they took it from Ebenezer to Ashdod. 2Then they carried the ark into Dagon's temple and set it beside Dagon. 3When the people of Ashdod rose early the next day, there was Dagon, fallen on his face on the ground before the ark of the LORD! They took Dagon and put him back in his place. 4But the following morning when they rose, there was Dagon, fallen on his face on the ground before the ark of the LORD! His head and hands had been broken off and were lying on the threshold; only his body remained. 5That is why to this day neither the priests of Dagon nor any others who enter Dagon's temple at Ashdod step on the threshold.

6The LORD's hand was heavy upon the people of Ashdod and its vicinity; he brought devastation upon them and afflicted them with tumors.[c] 7When the men of Ashdod saw what was happening, they said, "The ark of the god of Israel must not stay here with us, because his hand is heavy upon us and upon Dagon our god." 8So

---

a 18 Traditionally judged   b 21 Ichabod means no glory.   c 6 Hebrew; Septuagint and Vulgate tumors. And rats appeared in their land, and death and destruction were throughout the city

Living Bible

10So the Philistines fought desperately and Israel was defeated again. Thirty thousand men of Israel died that day and the remainder fled to their tents. 11And the Ark of God was captured and Hophni and Phinehas were killed.

12A man from the tribe of Benjamin ran from the battle and arrived at Shiloh the same day with his clothes torn and dirt on his head.d 13Eli was waiting beside the road to hear the news of the battle, for his heart trembled for the safety of the Ark of God. As the messenger from the battlefront arrived and told what had happened, a great cry arose throughout the city.

14"What is all the noise about?" Eli asked. And the messenger rushed over to Eli and told him what had happened. 15(Eli was ninety-eight years old and was blind.)

16"I have just come from the battle—I was there today," he told Eli, 17"and Israel has been defeated and thousands of the Israeli troops are dead on the battlefield. Hophni and Phinehas were killed too, and the Ark has been captured."

18When the messenger mentioned what had happened to the Ark, Eli fell backward from his seat beside the gate and his neck was broken by the fall and he died (for he was old and fat). He had judged Israel for forty years.

19When Eli's daughter-in-law, Phinehas's wife, who was pregnant, heard that the Ark had been captured and that her husband and father-in-law were dead, her labor pains suddenly began. 20Just before she died, the women who were attending her told her that everything was all right and that the baby was a boy. But she did not reply or respond in any way. 21, 22Then she murmured, "Name the child 'Ichabod,' for Israel's glory is gone." (Ichabod means "there is no glory." She named him this because the Ark of God had been captured and because her husband and her father-in-law were dead.)

5 THE PHILISTINES took the captured Ark of God from the battleground at Ebenezer to the temple of their idol Dagon in the city of Ashdod. 3But when the local citizens went to see it the next morning, Dagon had fallen with his face to the ground before the Ark of Jehovah! They set him up again, 4but the next morning the same thing had happened—the idol had fallen face down before the Ark of the Lord again. This time his head and hands had been cut off and were lying in the doorway; only the trunk of his body was left intact. 5(That is why to this day neither the priests of Dagon nor his worshipers will walk on the threshold of the temple of Dagon in Ashdod.)

6Then the Lord began to destroy the people of Ashdod and the nearby villages with bubonic plague. 7When the people realized what was happening, they exclaimed, "We can't keep the Ark of the God of Israel here any longer. We will all perish along with our god Dagon."

New Revised Standard

10 So the Philistines fought; Israel was defeated, and they fled, everyone to his home. There was a very great slaughter, for there fell of Israel thirty thousand foot soldiers. 11The ark of God was captured; and the two sons of Eli, Hophni and Phinehas, died.

Death of Eli

12 A man of Benjamin ran from the battle line, and came to Shiloh the same day, with his clothes torn and with earth upon his head. 13When he arrived, Eli was sitting upon his seat by the road watching, for his heart trembled for the ark of God. When the man came into the city and told the news, all the city cried out. 14When Eli heard the sound of the outcry, he said, "What is this uproar?" Then the man came quickly and told Eli. 15Now Eli was ninety-eight years old and his eyes were set, so that he could not see. 16The man said to Eli, "I have just come from the battle; I fled from the battle today." He said, "How did it go, my son?" 17The messenger replied, "Israel has fled before the Philistines, and there has also been a great slaughter among the troops; your two sons also, Hophni and Phinehas, are dead, and the ark of God has been captured." 18When he mentioned the ark of God, Elie fell over backward from his seat by the side of the gate; and his neck was broken and he died, for he was an old man, and heavy. He had judged Israel forty years.

19 Now his daughter-in-law, the wife of Phinehas, was pregnant, about to give birth. When she heard the news that the ark of God was captured, and that her father-in-law and her husband were dead, she bowed and gave birth; for her labor pains overwhelmed her. 20As she was about to die, the women attending her said to her, "Do not be afraid, for you have borne a son." But she did not answer or give heed. 21She named the child Ichabod, meaning, "The glory has departed from Israel," because the ark of God had been captured and because of her father-in-law and her husband. 22She said, "The glory has departed from Israel, for the ark of God has been captured."

The Philistines and the Ark

5 WHEN THE Philistines captured the ark of God, they brought it from Ebenezer to Ashdod; 2then the Philistines took the ark of God and brought it into the house of Dagon and placed it beside Dagon. 3When the people of Ashdod rose early the next day, there was Dagon, fallen on his face to the ground before the ark of the Lord. So they took Dagon and put him back in his place. 4But when they rose early on the next morning, Dagon had fallen on his face to the ground before the ark of the Lord, and the head of Dagon and both his hands were lying cut off upon the threshold; only the trunk off Dagon was left to him. 5This is why the priests of Dagon and all who enter the house of Dagon do not step on the threshold of Dagon in Ashdod to this day.

6 The hand of the Lord was heavy upon the people of Ashdod, and he terrified and struck them with tumors, both in Ashdod and in its territory. 7And when the inhabitants of Ashdod saw how things were, they said, "The ark of the God of Israel must not remain with us; for his hand is heavy on us and on our god Dagon." 8So

---

d 4:12 *clothes torn and dirt on his head.* This was a common expression of grief in that day.

e Heb *he*   f Heb lacks *the trunk of*

King James

8They sent therefore and gathered all the lords of the Philistines unto them, and said, What shall we do with the ark of the God of Israel? And they answered, Let the ark of the God of Israel be carried about unto Gath. And they carried the ark of the God of Israel about *thither*.

9And it was *so*, that, after they had carried it about, the hand of the LORD was against the city with a very great destruction: and he smote the men of the city, both small and great, and they had emerods in their secret parts.

10¶ Therefore they sent the ark of God to Ekron. And it came to pass, as the ark of God came to Ekron, that the Ekronites cried out, saying, They have brought about the ark of the God of Israel to us, to slay us and our people.

11So they sent and gathered together all the lords of the Philistines, and said, Send away the ark of the God of Israel, and let it go again to his own place, that it slay us not, and our people: for there was a deadly destruction throughout all the city; the hand of God was very heavy there.

12And the men that died not were smitten with the emerods: and the cry of the city went up to heaven.

6 AND THE ark of the LORD was in the country of the Philistines seven months.

2And the Philistines called for the priests and the diviners, saying, What shall we do to the ark of the LORD? tell us wherewith we shall send it to his place.

3And they said, If ye send away the ark of the God of Israel, send it not empty; but in any wise return him a trespass offering: then ye shall be healed, and it shall be known to you why his hand is not removed from you.

4Then said they, What *shall be* the trespass offering which we shall return to him? They answered, Five golden emerods, and five golden mice, *according to* the number of the lords of the Philistines: for one plague *was* on you all, and on your lords.

5Wherefore ye shall make images of your emerods, and images of your mice that mar the land; and ye shall give glory unto the God of Israel: peradventure he will lighten his hand from off you, and from off your gods, and from off your land.

6Wherefore then do ye harden your hearts, as the Egyptians and Pharaoh hardened their hearts? when he had wrought wonderfully among them, did they not let the people go, and they departed?

7Now therefore make a new cart, and take two milch kine, on which there hath come no yoke, and tie the kine to the cart, and bring their calves home from them:

8And take the ark of the LORD, and lay it upon the cart; and put the jewels of gold, which ye return him *for* a trespass offering, in a coffer by the side thereof; and send it away, that it may go.

9And see, if it goeth up by the way of his own coast to Beth-shemesh, *then* he hath done us this great evil: but if not, then we shall know that *it is* not his hand *that* smote us; it *was* a chance *that* happened to us.

10¶ And the men did so; and took two milch kine, and tied them to the cart, and shut up their calves at home:

11And they laid the ark of the LORD upon the cart, and the coffer with the mice of gold and the images of their emerods.

12And the kine took the straight way to the way of Beth-shemesh, *and* went along the highway, lowing as they went, and turned not aside *to* the right hand or *to* the left; and the lords of the Philistines went after them unto the border of Beth-shemesh.

13And *they of* Beth-shemesh *were* reaping their wheat harvest in the valley: and they lifted up their eyes, and saw the ark, and rejoiced to see *it*.

New International

they called together all the rulers of the Philistines and asked them, "What shall we do with the ark of the god of Israel?"

They answered, "Have the ark of the god of Israel moved to Gath." So they moved the ark of the God of Israel.

9But after they had moved it, the LORD's hand was against that city, throwing it into a great panic. He afflicted the people of the city, both young and old, with an outbreak of tumors.[a] 10So they sent the ark of God to Ekron.

As the ark of God was entering Ekron, the people of Ekron cried out, "They have brought the ark of the god of Israel around to us to kill us and our people." 11So they called together all the rulers of the Philistines and said, "Send the ark of the god of Israel away; let it go back to its own place, or it[b] will kill us and our people." For death had filled the city with panic; God's hand was very heavy upon it. 12Those who did not die were afflicted with tumors, and the outcry of the city went up to heaven.

The Ark Returned to Israel

6 WHEN THE ark of the LORD had been in Philistine territory seven months, 2the Philistines called for the priests and the diviners and said, "What shall we do with the ark of the LORD? Tell us how we should send it back to its place."

3They answered, "If you return the ark of the god of Israel, do not send it away empty, but by all means send a guilt offering to him. Then you will be healed, and you will know why his hand has not been lifted from you."

4The Philistines asked, "What guilt offering should we send to him?"

They replied, "Five gold tumors and five gold rats, according to the number of the Philistine rulers, because the same plague has struck both you and your rulers. 5Make models of the tumors and of the rats that are destroying the country, and pay honor to Israel's god. Perhaps he will lift his hand from you and your gods and your land. 6Why do you harden your hearts as the Egyptians and Pharaoh did? When he[c] treated them harshly, did they not send the Israelites out so they could go on their way?

7"Now then, get a new cart ready, with two cows that have calved and have never been yoked. Hitch the cows to the cart, but take their calves away and pen them up. 8Take the ark of the LORD and put it on the cart, and in a chest beside it put the gold objects you are sending back to him as a guilt offering. Send it on its way, 9but keep watching it. If it goes up to its own territory, toward Beth Shemesh, then the LORD has brought this great disaster on us. But if it does not, then we will know that it was not his hand that struck us and that it happened to us by chance."

10So they did this. They took two such cows and hitched them to the cart and penned up their calves. 11They placed the ark of the LORD on the cart and along with it the chest containing the gold rats and the models of the tumors. 12Then the cows went straight up toward Beth Shemesh, keeping on the road and lowing all the way; they did not turn to the right or to the left. The rulers of the Philistines followed them as far as the border of Beth Shemesh.

13Now the people of Beth Shemesh were harvesting their wheat in the valley, and when they looked up and saw the ark, they rejoiced at the sight. 14The cart came

---

a 9 Or *with tumors in the groin* (see Septuagint)   b 11 Or *he*   c 6 That is, God

Living Bible

8So they called a conference of the mayors of the five cities of the Philistines to decide how to dispose of the Ark. The decision was to take it to Gath. 9But when the Ark arrived at Gath, the Lord began destroying its people, young and old, with the plague, and there was a great panic. 10So they sent the Ark to Ekron, but when the people of Ekron saw it coming they cried out, "They are bringing the Ark of the God of Israel here to kill us too!"

11So they summoned the mayors again and begged them to send the Ark back to its own country, lest the entire city die. For the plague had already begun and great fear was sweeping across the city. 12Those who didn't die were deathly ill; and there was weeping everywhere.

6 THE ARK remained in the Philistine country for seven months in all. 2Then the Philistines called for their priests and diviners and asked them, "What shall we do about the Ark of God? What sort of gift shall we send with it when we return it to its own land?"

3"Yes, send it back with a gift," they were told. "Send a guilt offering so that the plague will stop. Then, if it doesn't, you will know God didn't send the plague upon you after all."

4, 5"What guilt offering shall we send?" they asked.
And they were told, "Send five gold models of the tumor caused by the plague, and five gold models of the rats that have ravaged the whole land—the capital cities and villages alike. If you send these gifts and then praise the God of Israel, perhaps he will stop persecuting you and your god. 6Don't be stubborn and rebellious as Pharaoh and the Egyptians were. They wouldn't let Israel go until God had destroyed them with dreadful plagues. 7Now build a new cart and hitch to it two cows that have just had calves—cows that never before have been yoked—and shut their calves away from them in the barn. 8Place the Ark of God on the cart beside a chest containing the gold models of the rats and tumors, and let the cows go wherever they want to. 9If they cross the border of our land and go into Beth-shemesh, then you will know that it was God who brought this great evil upon us; if they don't, [but return to their calves,d] then we will know that the plague was simply a coincidence and was not sent by God at all."

10So these instructions were carried out. Two cows with newborn calves were hitched to the cart and their calves were shut up in the barn. 11Then the Ark of the Lord and the chest containing the gold rats and tumors were placed upon the cart. 12And sure enough, the cows went straight along the road toward Beth-shemesh, lowing as they went; and the Philistine mayors followed them as far as the border of Beth-shemesh. 13The people of Beth-shemesh were reaping wheat in the valley, and when they saw the Ark they went wild with joy!

New Revised Standard

they sent and gathered together all the lords of the Philistines, and said, "What shall we do with the ark of the God of Israel?" The inhabitants of Gath replied, "Let the ark of God be moved on to us."e So they moved the ark of the God of Israel to Gath.f 9But after they had brought it to Gath,g the hand of the LORD was against the city, causing a very great panic; he struck the inhabitants of the city, both young and old, so that tumors broke out on them. 10So they sent the ark of the God of Israelh to Ekron. But when the ark of God came to Ekron, the people of Ekron cried out, "Whyi have they brought around to usj the ark of the God of Israel to kill usj and ourk people?" 11They sent therefore and gathered together all the lords of the Philistines, and said, "Send away the ark of the God of Israel, and let it return to its own place, that it may not kill us and our people." For there was a deathly panicl throughout the whole city. The hand of God was very heavy there; 12those who did not die were stricken with tumors, and the cry of the city went up to heaven.

The Ark Returned to Israel

6 THE ARK of the LORD was in the country of the Philistines seven months. 2Then the Philistines called for the priests and the diviners and said, "What shall we do with the ark of the LORD? Tell us what we should send with it to its place." 3They said, "If you send away the ark of the God of Israel, do not send it empty, but by all means return him a guilt offering. Then you will be healed and will be ransomed;m will not his hand then turn from you?" 4And they said, "What is the guilt offering that we shall return to him?" They answered, "Five gold tumors and five gold mice, according to the number of the lords of the Philistines; for the same plague was upon all of you and upon your lords. 5So you must make images of your tumors and images of your mice that ravage the land, and give glory to the God of Israel; perhaps he will lighten his hand on you and your gods and your land. 6Why should you harden your hearts as the Egyptians and Pharaoh hardened their hearts? After he had made fools of them, did they not let the people go, and they departed? 7Now then, get ready a new cart and two milch cows that have never borne a yoke, and yoke the cows to the cart, but take their calves home, away from them. 8Take the ark of the LORD and place it on the cart, and put in a box at its side the figures of gold, which you are returning to him as a guilt offering. Then send it off, and let it go its way. 9And watch; if it goes up on the way to its own land, to Beth-shemesh, then it is he who has done us this great harm; but if not, then we shall know that it is not his hand that struck us; it happened to us by chance."

10 The men did so; they took two milch cows and yoked them to the cart, and shut up their calves at home. 11They put the ark of the LORD on the cart, and the box with the gold mice and the images of their tumors. 12The cows went straight in the direction of Beth-shemesh along one highway, lowing as they went; they turned neither to the right nor to the left, and the lords of the Philistines went after them as far as the border of Beth-shemesh.

13 Now the people of Beth-shemesh were reaping their wheat harvest in the valley. When they looked up and saw the ark, they went with rejoicing to meet it.n

e Gk Compare Q Ms: MT They answered, "Let the ark of the God of Israel be brought around to Gath."   f Gk: Heb lacks to Gath   g Q Ms: MT lacks to Gath   h Q Ms Gk: MT lacks of Israel   i Q Ms Gk: MT lacks Why   j Heb me   k Heb my   l Q Ms reads a panic from the LORD   m Q Ms Gk: MT and it will be known to you   n Gk: Heb rejoiced to see it

d 6:9 return to their calves, implied.

King James

14And the cart came into the field of Joshua, a Beth-shemite, and stood there, where *there was* a great stone: and they clave the wood of the cart, and offered the kine a burnt offering unto the LORD.

15And the Levites took down the ark of the LORD, and the coffer that *was* with it, wherein the jewels of gold *were,* and put *them* on the great stone: and the men of Beth-shemesh offered burnt offerings and sacrificed sacrifices the same day unto the LORD.

16And when the five lords of the Philistines had seen *it,* they returned to Ekron the same day.

17And these *are* the golden emerods which the Philistines returned *for* a trespass offering unto the LORD; for Ashdod one, for Gaza one, for Askelon one, for Gath one, for Ekron one;

18And the golden mice, *according to* the number of all the cities of the Philistines *belonging* to the five lords, *both* of fenced cities, and of country villages, even unto the great *stone of* Abel, whereon they set down the ark of the LORD: *which stone remaineth* unto this day in the field of Joshua, the Beth-shemite.

19¶ And he smote the men of Beth-shemesh, because they had looked into the ark of the LORD, even he smote of the people fifty thousand and threescore and ten men: and the people lamented, because the LORD had smitten *many* of the people with a great slaughter.

20And the men of Beth-shemesh said, Who is able to stand before this holy LORD God? and to whom shall he go up from us?

21¶ And they sent messengers to the inhabitants of Kirjath-jearim, saying, The Philistines have brought again the ark of the LORD; come ye down, *and* fetch it up to you.

7 AND THE men of Kirjath-jearim came, and fetched up the ark of the LORD, and brought it into the house of Abinadab in the hill, and sanctified Eleazar his son to keep the ark of the LORD.

2And it came to pass, while the ark abode in Kirjath-jearim, that the time was long; for it was twenty years: and all the house of Israel lamented after the LORD.

3¶ And Samuel spake unto all the house of Israel, saying, If ye do return unto the LORD with all your hearts, *then* put away the strange gods and Ashtaroth from among you, and prepare your hearts unto the LORD, and serve him only: and he will deliver you out of the hand of the Philistines.

4Then the children of Israel did away Baalim and Ashtaroth, and served the LORD only.

5And Samuel said, Gather all Israel to Mizpeh, and I will pray for you unto the LORD.

6And they gathered together to Mizpeh, and drew water, and poured *it* out before the LORD, and fasted on that day, and said there, We have sinned against the LORD. And Samuel judged the children of Israel in Mizpeh.

7And when the Philistines heard that the children of Israel were gathered together to Mizpeh, the lords of the Philistines went up against Israel. And when the children of Israel heard *it,* they were afraid of the Philistines.

8And the children of Israel said to Samuel, Cease not to cry unto the LORD our God for us, that he will save us out of the hand of the Philistines.

9¶ And Samuel took a sucking lamb, and offered *it* *for* a burnt offering wholly unto the LORD: and Samuel cried unto the LORD for Israel; and the LORD heard him.

New International

to the field of Joshua of Beth Shemesh, and there it stopped beside a large rock. The people chopped up the wood of the cart and sacrificed the cows as a burnt offering to the LORD. 15The Levites took down the ark of the LORD, together with the chest containing the gold objects, and placed them on the large rock. On that day the people of Beth Shemesh offered burnt offerings and made sacrifices to the LORD. 16The five rulers of the Philistines saw all this and then returned that same day to Ekron.

17These are the gold tumors the Philistines sent as a guilt offering to the LORD—one each for Ashdod, Gaza, Ashkelon, Gath and Ekron. 18And the number of the gold rats was according to the number of Philistine towns belonging to the five rulers—the fortified towns with their country villages. The large rock, on whicha they set the ark of the LORD, is a witness to this day in the field of Joshua of Beth Shemesh.

19But God struck down some of the men of Beth Shemesh, putting seventyb of them to death because they had looked into the ark of the LORD. The people mourned because of the heavy blow the LORD had dealt them, 20and the men of Beth Shemesh asked, "Who can stand in the presence of the LORD, this holy God? To whom will the ark go up from here?"

21Then they sent messengers to the people of Kiriath Jearim, saying, "The Philistines have returned the ark of the LORD. Come down and take it up to your place."

7 SO THE men of Kiriath Jearim came and took up the ark of the LORD. They took it to Abinadab's house on the hill and consecrated Eleazar his son to guard the ark of the LORD.

Samuel Subdues the Philistines at Mizpah

2It was a long time, twenty years in all, that the ark remained at Kiriath Jearim, and all the people of Israel mourned and sought after the LORD. 3And Samuel said to the whole house of Israel, "If you are returning to the LORD with all your hearts, then rid yourselves of the foreign gods and the Ashtoreths and commit yourselves to the LORD and serve him only, and he will deliver you out of the hand of the Philistines." 4So the Israelites put away their Baals and Ashtoreths, and served the LORD only.

5Then Samuel said, "Assemble all Israel at Mizpah and I will intercede with the LORD for you." 6When they had assembled at Mizpah, they drew water and poured it out before the LORD. On that day they fasted and there they confessed, "We have sinned against the LORD." And Samuel was leaderc of Israel at Mizpah.

7When the Philistines heard that Israel had assembled at Mizpah, the rulers of the Philistines came up to attack them. And when the Israelites heard of it, they were afraid because of the Philistines. 8They said to Samuel, "Do not stop crying out to the LORD our God for us, that he may rescue us from the hand of the Philistines." 9Then Samuel took a suckling lamb and offered it up as a whole burnt offering to the LORD. He cried out to the LORD on Israel's behalf, and the LORD answered him.

a 18 A few Hebrew manuscripts (see also Septuagint); most Hebrew manuscripts *villages as far as Greater Abel, where*   b 19 A few Hebrew manuscripts; most Hebrew manuscripts and Septuagint *50,070*   c 6 Traditionally *judge*

Living Bible

14The cart came into the field of a man named Joshua and stopped beside a large rock. So the people broke up the wood of the cart for a fire and killed the cows and sacrificed them to the Lord as a burnt offering. 15Several men of the tribe of Levi lifted the Ark and the chest containing the gold rats and tumors from the cart and laid them on the rock. And many burnt offerings and sacrifices were offered to the Lord that day by the men of Beth-shemesh.

16After the five Philistine mayors had watched for awhile, they returned to Ekron that same day. 17The five gold models of tumors which had been sent by the Philistines as a guilt offering to the Lord were gifts from the mayors of the capital cities, Ashdod, Gaza, Ashkelon, Gath, and Ekron. 18The gold rats were to placate God for the other Philistine cities, both the fortified cities and the country villages controlled by the five capitals. (By the way, that large rock at Beth-shemesh can still be seen in the field of Joshua.) 19But the Lord killed seventy of the men of Beth-shemesh because they looked into the Ark. And the people mourned because of the many people whom the Lord had killed.

20"Who is able to stand before Jehovah, this holy God?" they cried out. "Where can we send the Ark from here?"

21So they sent messengers to the people at Kiriath-jearim and told them that the Philistines had brought back the Ark of the Lord.

"Come and get it!" they begged.

7 SO THE men of Kiriath-jearim came and took the Ark to the hillside home of Abinadab; and installed his son Eleazar to be in charge of it. 2The Ark remained there for twenty years, and during that time all Israel was in sorrow because the Lord had seemingly abandoned them.

3At that time Samuel said to them, "If you are really serious about wanting to return to the Lord, get rid of your foreign gods and your Ashtaroth idols. Determine to obey only the Lord; then he will rescue you from the Philistines."

4So they destroyed their idols of Baal and Ashtaroth and worshiped only the Lord.

5Then Samuel told them, "Come to Mizpah, all of you, and I will pray to the Lord for you."

6So they gathered there and, in a great ceremony, drew water from the well and poured it out before the Lord. They also went without food all day as a sign of sorrow for their sins. So it was at Mizpah that Samuel became Israel's judge.

7When the Philistine leaders heard about the great crowds at Mizpah, they mobilized their army and advanced. The Israelis were badly frightened when they learned that the Philistines were approaching.

8"Plead with God to save us!" they begged Samuel.

9So Samuel took a suckling lamb and offered it to the Lord as a whole burnt offering and pleaded with him to help Israel. And the Lord responded. 10Just as Samuel

New Revised Standard

14The cart came into the field of Joshua of Beth-shemesh, and stopped there. A large stone was there; so they split up the wood of the cart and offered the cows as a burnt offering to the Lord. 15The Levites took down the ark of the Lord and the box that was beside it, in which were the gold objects, and set them upon the large stone. Then the people of Beth-shemesh offered burnt offerings and presented sacrifices on that day to the Lord. 16When the five lords of the Philistines saw it, they returned that day to Ekron.

17 These are the gold tumors, which the Philistines returned as a guilt offering to the Lord: one for Ashdod, one for Gaza, one for Ashkelon, one for Gath, one for Ekron; 18also the gold mice, according to the number of all the cities of the Philistines belonging to the five lords, both fortified cities and unwalled villages. The great stone, beside which they set down the ark of the Lord, is a witness to this day in the field of Joshua of Beth-shemesh.

The Ark at Kiriath-jearim

19 The descendants of Jeconiah did not rejoice with the people of Beth-shemesh when they greetedd the ark of the Lord; and he killed seventy men of them.e The people mourned because the Lord had made a great slaughter among the people. 20Then the people of Beth-shemesh said, "Who is able to stand before the Lord, this holy God? To whom shall he go so that we may be rid of him?" 21So they sent messengers to the inhabitants of Kiriath-jearim, saying, "The Philistines have returned the ark of the Lord. Come down and take it up to you."

7 AND THE people of Kiriath-jearim came and took up the ark of the Lord, and brought it to the house of Abinadab on the hill. They consecrated his son, Eleazar, to have charge of the ark of the Lord.

2 From the day that the ark was lodged at Kiriath-jearim, a long time passed, some twenty years, and all the house of Israel lamentedf after the Lord.

Samuel as Judge

3 Then Samuel said to all the house of Israel, "If you are returning to the Lord with all your heart, then put away the foreign gods and the Astartes from among you. Direct your heart to the Lord, and serve him only, and he will deliver you out of the hand of the Philistines." 4So Israel put away the Baals and the Astartes, and they served the Lord only.

5 Then Samuel said, "Gather all Israel at Mizpah, and I will pray to the Lord for you." 6So they gathered at Mizpah, and drew water and poured it out before the Lord. They fasted that day, and said, "We have sinned against the Lord." And Samuel judged the people of Israel at Mizpah.

7 When the Philistines heard that the people of Israel had gathered at Mizpah, the lords of the Philistines went up against Israel. And when the people of Israel heard of it they were afraid of the Philistines. 8The people of Israel said to Samuel, "Do not cease to cry out to the Lord our God for us, and pray that he may save us from the hand of the Philistines." 9So Samuel took a sucking lamb and offered it as a whole burnt offering to the Lord; Samuel cried out to the Lord for Israel, and the Lord answered him. 10As Samuel was offering up

d Gk: Heb And he killed some of the people of Beth-shemesh, because they looked into   e Heb killed seventy men, fifty thousand men   f Meaning of Heb uncertain

King James

10And as Samuel was offering up the burnt offering, the Philistines drew near to battle against Israel: but the LORD thundered with a great thunder on that day upon the Philistines, and discomfited them; and they were smitten before Israel.

11And the men of Israel went out of Mizpeh, and pursued the Philistines, and smote them, until *they came* under Beth-car.

12Then Samuel took a stone, and set *it* between Mizpeh and Shen, and called the name of it Eben-ezer, saying, Hitherto hath the LORD helped us.

13¶ So the Philistines were subdued, and they came no more into the coast of Israel: and the hand of the LORD was against the Philistines all the days of Samuel.

14And the cities which the Philistines had taken from Israel were restored to Israel, from Ekron even unto Gath; and the coasts thereof did Israel deliver out of the hands of the Philistines. And there was peace between Israel and the Amorites.

15And Samuel judged Israel all the days of his life.

16And he went from year to year in circuit to Beth-el, and Gilgal, and Mizpeh, and judged Israel in all those places.

17And his return *was* to Ramah; for there *was* his house; and there he judged Israel; and there he built an altar unto the LORD.

8 AND IT came to pass, when Samuel was old, that he made his sons judges over Israel.

2Now the name of his firstborn was Joel; and the name of his second, Abiah: *they were* judges in Beersheba.

3And his sons walked not in his ways, but turned aside after lucre, and took bribes, and perverted judgment.

4Then all the elders of Israel gathered themselves together, and came to Samuel unto Ramah,

5And said unto him, Behold, thou art old, and thy sons walk not in thy ways: now make us a king to judge us like all the nations.

6¶ But the thing displeased Samuel, when they said, Give us a king to judge us. And Samuel prayed unto the LORD.

7And the LORD said unto Samuel, Hearken unto the voice of the people in all that they say unto thee: for they have not rejected thee, but they have rejected me, that I should not reign over them.

8According to all the works which they have done since the day that I brought them up out of Egypt even unto this day, wherewith they have forsaken me, and served other gods, so do they also unto thee.

9Now therefore hearken unto their voice: howbeit yet protest solemnly unto them, and show them the manner of the king that shall reign over them.

10¶ And Samuel told all the words of the LORD unto the people that asked of him a king.

11And he said, This will be the manner of the king that shall reign over you: He will take your sons, and appoint *them* for himself, for his chariots, and *to be* his horsemen; and *some* shall run before his chariots.

12And he will appoint him captains over thousands, and captains over fifties; and *will set them* to ear his ground, and to reap his harvest, and to make his instruments of war, and instruments of his chariots.

13And he will take your daughters *to be* confectionaries, and *to be* cooks, and *to be* bakers.

14And he will take your fields, and your vineyards, and your oliveyards, *even* the best *of them*, and give *them* to his servants.

15And he will take the tenth of your seed, and of your vineyards, and give to his officers, and to his servants.

New International

10While Samuel was sacrificing the burnt offering, the Philistines drew near to engage Israel in battle. But that day the LORD thundered with loud thunder against the Philistines and threw them into such a panic that they were routed before the Israelites. 11The men of Israel rushed out of Mizpah and pursued the Philistines, slaughtering them along the way to a point below Beth Car.

12Then Samuel took a stone and set it up between Mizpah and Shen. He named it Ebenezer,a saying, "Thus far has the LORD helped us." 13So the Philistines were subdued and did not invade Israelite territory again.

Throughout Samuel's lifetime, the hand of the LORD was against the Philistines. 14The towns from Ekron to Gath that the Philistines had captured from Israel were restored to her, and Israel delivered the neighboring territory from the power of the Philistines. And there was peace between Israel and the Amorites.

15Samuel continued as judge over Israel all the days of his life. 16From year to year he went on a circuit from Bethel to Gilgal to Mizpah, judging Israel in all those places. 17But he always went back to Ramah, where his home was, and there he also judged Israel. And he built an altar there to the LORD.

Israel Asks for a King

8 WHEN SAMUEL grew old, he appointed his sons as judges for Israel. 2The name of his firstborn was Joel and the name of his second was Abijah, and they served at Beersheba. 3But his sons did not walk in his ways. They turned aside after dishonest gain and accepted bribes and perverted justice.

4So all the elders of Israel gathered together and came to Samuel at Ramah. 5They said to him, "You are old, and your sons do not walk in your ways; now appoint a king to leadb us, such as all the other nations have."

6But when they said, "Give us a king to lead us," this displeased Samuel; so he prayed to the LORD. 7And the LORD told him: "Listen to all that the people are saying to you; it is not you they have rejected, but they have rejected me as their king. 8As they have done from the day I brought them up out of Egypt until this day, forsaking me and serving other gods, so they are doing to you. 9Now listen to them; but warn them solemnly and let them know what the king who will reign over them will do."

10Samuel told all the words of the LORD to the people who were asking him for a king. 11He said, "This is what the king who will reign over you will do: He will take your sons and make them serve with his chariots and horses, and they will run in front of his chariots. 12Some he will assign to be commanders of thousands and commanders of fifties, and others to plow his ground and reap his harvest, and still others to make weapons of war and equipment for his chariots. 13He will take your daughters to be perfumers and cooks and bakers. 14He will take the best of your fields and vineyards and olive groves and give them to his attendants. 15He will take a tenth of your grain and of your vintage and give it to his officials and attendants. 16Your menservants and

a *12 Ebenezer* means *stone of help.*   b *5 Traditionally *judge*; also in verses 6 and 20

Living Bible

was sacrificing the burnt offering, the Philistines arrived for battle, but the Lord spoke with a mighty voice of thunder from heaven, and they were thrown into confusion, and the Israelis routed them, 11and chased them from Mizpah to Beth-car, killing them all along the way. 12Samuel then took a stone and placed it between Mizpah and Jeshanah and named it Ebenezer (meaning, "the Stone of Help"), for he said, "The Lord has certainly helped us!" 13So the Philistines were subdued and didn't invade Israel again at that time, because the Lord was against them throughout the remainder of Samuel's lifetime. 14The Israeli cities between Ekron and Gath, which had been conquered by the Philistines, were now returned to Israel, for the Israeli army rescued them from their Philistine captors. And there was peace between Israel and the Amorites in those days.

15Samuel continued as Israel's judge for the remainder of his life. 16He rode circuit annually, setting up his court first at Bethel, then Gilgal, and then Mizpah, and cases of dispute were brought to him in each of these three cities from all the surrounding territory. 17Then he would come back to Ramah, for his home was there, and he would hear cases there, too. And he built an altar to the Lord at Ramah.

8 IN HIS old age, Samuel retired and appointed his sons as judges in his place. 2Joel and Abijah, his oldest sons, held court in Beer-sheba; 3but they were not like their father, for they were greedy for money. They accepted bribes and were very corrupt in the administration of justice. 4Finally the leaders of Israel met in Ramah to discuss the matter with Samuel. 5They told him that since his retirement things hadn't been the same, for his sons were not good men.

"Give us a king like all the other nations have," they pleaded. 6Samuel was terribly upset and went to the Lord for advice.

7"Do as they say," the Lord replied, "for I am the one they are rejecting, not you—they don't want me to be their king any longer. 8Ever since I brought them from Egypt they have continually forsaken me and followed other gods. And now they are giving you the same treatment. 9Do as they ask, but warn them about what it will be like to have a king!"

10So Samuel told the people what the Lord had said: 11"If you insist on having a king, he will conscript your sons and make them run before his chariots; 12some will be made to lead his troops into battle, while others will be slave laborers; they will be forced to plow in the royal fields, and harvest his crops without pay; and make his weapons and chariot equipment. 13He will take your daughters from you and force them to cook and bake and make perfumes for him. 14He will take away the best of your fields and vineyards and olive groves and give them to his friends. 15He will take a tenth of your harvest and distribute it to his favorites. 16He will demand your

New Revised Standard

the burnt offering, the Philistines drew near to attack Israel; but the LORD thundered with a mighty voice that day against the Philistines and threw them into confusion; and they were routed before Israel. 11 And the men of Israel went out of Mizpah and pursued the Philistines, and struck them down as far as beyond Beth-car.

12 Then Samuel took a stone and set it up between Mizpah and Jeshanah,c and named it Ebenezer;d for he said, "Thus far the LORD has helped us." 13 So the Philistines were subdued and did not again enter the territory of Israel; the hand of the LORD was against the Philistines all the days of Samuel. 14 The towns that the Philistines had taken from Israel were restored to Israel, from Ekron to Gath; and Israel recovered their territory from the hand of the Philistines. There was peace also between Israel and the Amorites.

15 Samuel judged Israel all the days of his life. 16 He went on a circuit year by year to Bethel, Gilgal, and Mizpah; and he judged Israel in all these places. 17 Then he would come back to Ramah, for his home was there; he administered justice there to Israel, and built there an altar to the LORD.

Israel Demands a King

8 WHEN SAMUEL became old, he made his sons judges over Israel. 2 The name of his firstborn was Joel, and the name of his second, Abijah; they were judges in Beer-sheba. 3 Yet his sons did not follow in his ways, but turned aside after gain; they took bribes and perverted justice.

4 Then all the elders of Israel gathered together and came to Samuel at Ramah, 5 and said to him, "You are old and your sons do not follow in your ways; appoint for us, then, a king to govern us, like other nations." 6 But the thing displeased Samuel when they said, "Give us a king to govern us." Samuel prayed to the LORD, 7 and the LORD said to Samuel, "Listen to the voice of the people in all that they say to you; for they have not rejected you, but they have rejected me from being king over them. 8 Just as they have done to me,e from the day I brought them up out of Egypt to this day, forsaking me and serving other gods, so also they are doing to you. 9 Now then, listen to their voice; only—you shall solemnly warn them, and show them the ways of the king who shall reign over them."

10 So Samuel reported all the words of the LORD to the people who were asking him for a king. 11 He said, "These will be the ways of the king who will reign over you: he will take your sons and appoint them to his chariots and to be his horsemen, and to run before his chariots; 12 and he will appoint for himself commanders of thousands and commanders of fifties, and some to plow his ground and to reap his harvest, and to make his implements of war and the equipment of his chariots. 13 He will take your daughters to be perfumers and cooks and bakers. 14 He will take the best of your fields and vineyards and olive orchards and give them to his courtiers. 15 He will take one-tenth of your grain and of your vineyards and give it to his officers and his courtiers.

---

c Gk Syr: Heb *Shen*   d That is *Stone of Help*   e Gk: Heb lacks *to me*

King James

16And he will take your menservants, and your maidservants, and your goodliest young men, and your asses, and put *them* to his work.

17He will take the tenth of your sheep: and ye shall be his servants.

18And ye shall cry out in that day because of your king which ye shall have chosen you; and the LORD will not hear you in that day.

19¶ Nevertheless the people refused to obey the voice of Samuel; and they said, Nay; but we will have a king over us;

20That we also may be like all the nations; and that our king may judge us, and go out before us, and fight our battles.

21And Samuel heard all the words of the people, and he rehearsed them in the ears of the LORD.

22And the LORD said to Samuel, Hearken unto their voice, and make them a king. And Samuel said unto the men of Israel, Go ye every man unto his city.

9 NOW THERE was a man of Benjamin, whose name *was* Kish, the son of Abiel, the son of Zeror, the son of Bechorath, the son of Aphiah, a Benjamite, a mighty man of power.

2And he had a son, whose name *was* Saul, a choice young man, and a goodly: and *there was* not among the children of Israel a goodlier person than he: from his shoulders and upward *he was* higher than any of the people.

3And the asses of Kish Saul's father were lost. And Kish said to Saul his son, Take now one of the servants with thee, and arise, go seek the asses.

4And he passed through mount Ephraim, and passed through the land of Shalisha, but they found *them* not: then they passed through the land of Shalim, and *there they were* not: and he passed through the land of the Benjamites, but they found *them* not.

5*And* when they were come to the land of Zuph, Saul said to his servant that *was* with him, Come, and let us return; lest my father leave *caring* for the asses, and take thought for us.

6And he said unto him, Behold now, *there is* in this city a man of God, and *he is* an honourable man; all that he saith cometh surely to pass: now let us go thither; peradventure he can show us our way that we should go.

7Then said Saul to his servant, But, behold, *if* we go, what shall we bring the man? for the bread is spent in our vessels, and *there is* not a present to bring to the man of God: what have we?

8And the servant answered Saul again, and said, Behold, I have here at hand the fourth part of a shekel of silver: *that* will I give to the man of God, to tell us our way.

9(Beforetime in Israel, when a man went to inquire of God, thus he spake, Come, and let us go to the seer: for *he that is* now *called* a Prophet was beforetime called a Seer.)

10Then said Saul to his servant, Well said; come, let us go. So they went unto the city where the man of God *was*.

11¶ *And* as they went up the hill to the city, they found young maidens going out to draw water, and said unto them, Is the seer here?

New International

maidservants and the best of your cattle[a] and donkeys he will take for his own use. 17He will take a tenth of your flocks, and you yourselves will become his slaves. 18When that day comes, you will cry out for relief from the king you have chosen, and the LORD will not answer you in that day."

19But the people refused to listen to Samuel. "No!" they said. "We want a king over us. 20Then we will be like all the other nations, with a king to lead us and to go out before us and fight our battles."

21When Samuel heard all that the people said, he repeated it before the LORD. 22The LORD answered, "Listen to them and give them a king."

Then Samuel said to the men of Israel, "Everyone go back to his town."

Samuel Anoints Saul

9 THERE WAS a Benjamite, a man of standing, whose name was Kish son of Abiel, the son of Zeror, the son of Becorath, the son of Aphiah of Benjamin. 2He had a son named Saul, an impressive young man without equal among the Israelites—a head taller than any of the others.

3Now the donkeys belonging to Saul's father Kish were lost, and Kish said to his son Saul, "Take one of the servants with you and go and look for the donkeys." 4So he passed through the hill country of Ephraim and through the area around Shalisha, but they did not find them. They went on into the district of Shaalim, but the donkeys were not there. Then he passed through the territory of Benjamin, but they did not find them.

5When they reached the district of Zuph, Saul said to the servant who was with him, "Come, let's go back, or my father will stop thinking about the donkeys and start worrying about us."

6But the servant replied, "Look, in this town there is a man of God; he is highly respected, and everything he says comes true. Let's go there now. Perhaps he will tell us what way to take."

7Saul said to his servant, "If we go, what can we give the man? The food in our sacks is gone. We have no gift to take to the man of God. What do we have?"

8The servant answered him again. "Look," he said, "I have a quarter of a shekel[b] of silver. I will give it to the man of God so that he will tell us what way to take." 9(Formerly in Israel, if a man went to inquire of God, he would say, "Come, let us go to the seer," because the prophet of today used to be called a seer.)

10"Good," Saul said to his servant. "Come, let's go." So they set out for the town where the man of God was.

11As they were going up the hill to the town, they met some girls coming out to draw water, and they asked them, "Is the seer here?"

---

a 16 Septuagint; Hebrew *young men*   b 8 That is, about 1/10 ounce (about 3 grams)

Living Bible

slaves and the finest of your youth and will use your animals for his personal gain. 17He will demand a tenth of your flocks, and you shall be his slaves. 18You will shed bitter tears because of this king you are demanding, but the Lord will not help you."

19But the people refused to listen to Samuel's warning.

"Even so, we still want a king," they said, 20"for we want to be like the nations around us. He will govern us and lead us to battle."

21So Samuel told the Lord what the people had said, 22and the Lord replied again, "Then do as they say and give them a king."

So Samuel agreed and sent the men home again.

9   KISH WAS a rich, influential man from the tribe of Benjamin. He was the son of Abiel, grandson of Zeror, great-grandson of Becorath, and great-great-grandson of Aphiah. 2His son Saul was the most handsome man in Israel. And he was head and shoulders taller than anyone else in the land!

3One day Kish's donkeys strayed away, so he sent Saul and a servant to look for them. 4They traveled all through the hill country of Ephraim, the land of Shalisha, the Shaalim area, and the entire land of Benjamin, but couldn't find them anywhere. 5Finally, after searching in the land of Zuph, Saul said to the servant, "Let's go home; by now my father will be more worried about us than about the donkeys!"

6But the servant said, "I've just thought of something! There is a prophet who lives here in this city; he is held in high honor by all the people because everything he says comes true; let's go and find him and perhaps he can tell us where the donkeys are."

7"But we don't have anything to pay him with," Saul replied. "Even our food is gone and we don't have a thing to give him."

8"Well," the servant said, "I have a dollar! We can at least offer it to him and see what happens!"

9, 10, 11"All right," Saul agreed, "let's try it!"

So they started into the city where the prophet lived. As they were climbing a hill toward the city, they saw some young girls going out to draw water and asked them if they knew whether the seer was in town. (In those days prophets were called seers. "Let's go and ask the seer," people would say, rather than, "Let's go and ask the prophet," as we would say now.)

New Revised Standard

16He will take your male and female slaves, and the best of your cattlec and donkeys, and put them to his work. 17He will take one-tenth of your flocks, and you shall be his slaves. 18 And in that day you will cry out because of your king, whom you have chosen for yourselves; but the LORD will not answer you in that day."

Israel's Request for a King Granted

19   But the people refused to listen to the voice of Samuel; they said, "No! but we are determined to have a king over us, 20so that we also may be like other nations, and that our king may govern us and go out before us and fight our battles." 21When Samuel had heard all the words of the people, he repeated them in the ears of the LORD. 22The LORD said to Samuel, "Listen to their voice and set a king over them." Samuel then said to the people of Israel, "Each of you return home."

Saul Chosen to Be King

9   THERE WAS a man of Benjamin whose name was Kish son of Abiel son of Zeror son of Becorath son of Aphiah, a Benjaminite, a man of wealth. 2He had a son whose name was Saul, a handsome young man. There was not a man among the people of Israel more handsome than he; he stood head and shoulders above everyone else.

3   Now the donkeys of Kish, Saul's father, had strayed. So Kish said to his son Saul, "Take one of the boys with you; go and look for the donkeys." 4He passed through the hill country of Ephraim and passed through the land of Shalishah, but they did not find them. And they passed through the land of Shaalim, but they were not there. Then he passed through the land of Benjamin, but they did not find them.

5   When they came to the land of Zuph, Saul said to the boy who was with him, "Let us turn back, or my father will stop worrying about the donkeys and worry about us." 6But he said to him, "There is a man of God in this town; he is a man held in honor. Whatever he says always comes true. Let us go there now; perhaps he will tell us about the journey on which we have set out." 7Then Saul replied to the boy, "But if we go, what can we bring the man? For the bread in our sacks is gone, and there is no present to bring to the man of God. What have we?" 8The boy answered Saul again, "Here, I have with me a quarter shekel of silver; I will give it to the man of God, to tell us our way." 9(Formerly in Israel, anyone who went to inquire of God would say, "Come, let us go to the seer"; for the one who is now called a prophet was formerly called a seer.) 10Saul said to the boy, "Good; come, let us go." So they went to the town where the man of God was.

11   As they went up the hill to the town, they met some girls coming out to draw water, and said to them, "Is the seer here?" 12They answered, "Yes, there he is

---

c Gk: Heb young men

King James

¹²And they answered them, and said, He is; behold, *he is* before you: make haste now, for he came today to the city; for *there is* a sacrifice of the people today in the high place:

¹³As soon as ye be come into the city, ye shall straightway find him, before he go up to the high place to eat: for the people will not eat until he come, because he doth bless the sacrifice; *and* afterwards they eat that be bidden. Now therefore get you up; for about this time ye shall find him.

¹⁴And they went up into the city: *and* when they were come into the city, behold, Samuel came out against them, for to go up to the high place.

¹⁵¶ Now the LORD had told Samuel in his ear a day before Saul came, saying,

¹⁶Tomorrow about this time I will send thee a man out of the land of Benjamin, and thou shalt anoint him *to be* captain over my people Israel, that he may save my people out of the hand of the Philistines: for I have looked upon my people, because their cry is come unto me.

¹⁷And when Samuel saw Saul, the LORD said unto him, Behold the man whom I spake to thee of! this same shall reign over my people.

¹⁸Then Saul drew near to Samuel in the gate, and said, Tell me, I pray thee, where the seer's house *is*.

¹⁹And Samuel answered Saul, and said, I *am* the seer: go up before me unto the high place; for ye shall eat with me today, and tomorrow I will let thee go, and will tell thee all that *is* in thine heart.

²⁰And as for thine asses that were lost three days ago, set not thy mind on them; for they are found. And on whom *is* all the desire of Israel? *Is it* not on thee, and on all thy father's house?

²¹And Saul answered and said, *Am* not I a Benjamite, of the smallest of the tribes of Israel? and my family the least of all the families of the tribe of Benjamin? wherefore then speakest thou so to me?

²²And Samuel took Saul and his servant, and brought them into the parlour, and made them sit in the chiefest place among them that were bidden, which *were* about thirty persons.

²³And Samuel said unto the cook, Bring the portion which I gave thee, of which I said unto thee, Set it by thee.

²⁴And the cook took up the shoulder, and *that* which *was* upon it, and set *it* before Saul. And *Samuel* said, Behold that which is left! set *it* before thee, *and* eat: for unto this time hath it been kept for thee since I said, I have invited the people. So Saul did eat with Samuel that day.

²⁵¶ And when they were come down from the high place into the city, *Samuel* communed with Saul upon the top of the house.

²⁶And they arose early: and it came to pass about the spring of the day, that Samuel called Saul to the top of the house, saying, Up, that I may send thee away. And Saul arose, and they went out both of them, he and Samuel, abroad.

²⁷*And* as they were going down to the end of the city, Samuel said to Saul, Bid the servant pass on before us, (and he passed on,) but stand thou still a while, that I may show thee the word of God.

New International

¹²"He is," they answered. "He's ahead of you. Hurry now; he has just come to our town today, for the people have a sacrifice at the high place. ¹³As soon as you enter the town, you will find him before he goes up to the high place to eat. The people will not begin eating until he comes, because he must bless the sacrifice; afterward, those who are invited will eat. Go up now; you should find him about this time."

¹⁴They went up to the town, and as they were entering it, there was Samuel, coming toward them on his way up to the high place.

¹⁵Now the day before Saul came, the LORD had revealed this to Samuel: ¹⁶"About this time tomorrow I will send you a man from the land of Benjamin. Anoint him leader over my people Israel; he will deliver my people from the hand of the Philistines. I have looked upon my people, for their cry has reached me."

¹⁷When Samuel caught sight of Saul, the LORD said to him, "This is the man I spoke to you about; he will govern my people."

¹⁸Saul approached Samuel in the gateway and asked, "Would you please tell me where the seer's house is?"

¹⁹"I am the seer," Samuel replied. "Go up ahead of me to the high place, for today you are to eat with me, and in the morning I will let you go and will tell you all that is in your heart. ²⁰As for the donkeys you lost three days ago, do not worry about them; they have been found. And to whom is all the desire of Israel turned, if not to you and all your father's family?"

²¹Saul answered, "But am I not a Benjamite, from the smallest tribe of Israel, and is not my clan the least of all the clans of the tribe of Benjamin? Why do you say such a thing to me?"

²²Then Samuel brought Saul and his servant into the hall and seated them at the head of those who were invited—about thirty in number. ²³Samuel said to the cook, "Bring the piece of meat I gave you, the one I told you to lay aside."

²⁴So the cook took up the leg with what was on it and set it in front of Saul. Samuel said, "Here is what has been kept for you. Eat, because it was set aside for you for this occasion, from the time I said, 'I have invited guests.'" And Saul dined with Samuel that day.

²⁵After they came down from the high place to the town, Samuel talked with Saul on the roof of his house. ²⁶They rose about daybreak and Samuel called to Saul on the roof, "Get ready, and I will send you on your way." When Saul got ready, he and Samuel went outside together. ²⁷As they were going down to the edge of the town, Samuel said to Saul, "Tell the servant to go on ahead of us"—and the servant did so—"but you stay here awhile, so that I may give you a message from God."

Living Bible

12, 13"Yes," they replied, "stay right on this road. He lives just inside the city gates. He has just arrived back from a trip to take part in a public sacrifice up on the hill. So hurry, because he'll probably be leaving about the time you get there; the guests can't eat until he arrives and blesses the food."

14So they went into the city, and as they were entering the gates they saw Samuel coming out toward them to go up the hill. 15The Lord had told Samuel the previous day,

16"About this time tomorrow I will send you a man from the land of Benjamin. You are to anoint him as the leader of my people. He will save them from the Philistines, for I have looked down on them in mercy and have heard their cry."

17When Samuel saw Saul the Lord said, "That's the man I told you about! He will rule my people."

18Just then Saul approached Samuel and asked, "Can you please tell me where the seer's house is?"

19"I am the seer!" Samuel replied. "Go on up the hill ahead of me and we'll eat together; in the morning I will tell you what you want to know and send you on your way. 20And don't worry about those donkeys that were lost three days ago, for they have been found. And anyway, you own all the wealth of Israel now!"

21"Pardon me, sir," Saul replied. "I'm from the tribe of Benjamin, the smallest in Israel, and my family is the least important of all the families of the tribe! You must have the wrong man!"

22Then Samuel took Saul and his servant into the great hall and placed them at the head of the table, honoring them above the thirty special guests. 23Samuel then instructed the chef to bring Saul the choicest cut of meat, the piece that had been set aside for the guest of honor. 24So the chef brought it in and placed it before Saul.

"Go ahead and eat it," Samuel said, "for I was saving it for you, even before I invited these others!"

So Saul ate with Samuel. 25After the feast, when they had returned to the city, Samuel took Saul up to the porch on the roof and talked with him there. 26, 27At daybreak the next morning, Samuel called up to him, "Get up; it's time you were on your way!"

So Saul got up and Samuel accompanied him to the edge of the city. When they reached the city walls Samuel told Saul to send the servant on ahead. Then he told him, "I have received a special message for you from the Lord."

New Revised Standard

just ahead of you. Hurry; he has come just now to the town, because the people have a sacrifice today at the shrine. 13As soon as you enter the town, you will find him, before he goes up to the shrine to eat. For the people will not eat until he comes, since he must bless the sacrifice; afterward those eat who are invited. Now go up, for you will meet him immediately." 14So they went up to the town. As they were entering the town, they saw Samuel coming out toward them on his way up to the shrine.

15 Now the day before Saul came, the LORD had revealed to Samuel: 16"Tomorrow about this time I will send to you a man from the land of Benjamin, and you shall anoint him to be ruler over my people Israel. He shall save my people from the hand of the Philistines; for I have seen the suffering ofa my people, because their outcry has come to me." 17When Samuel saw Saul, the LORD told him, "Here is the man of whom I spoke to you. He it is who shall rule over my people." 18Then Saul approached Samuel inside the gate, and said, "Tell me, please, where is the house of the seer?" 19Samuel answered Saul, "I am the seer; go up before me to the shrine, for today you shall eat with me, and in the morning I will let you go and will tell you all that is on your mind. 20As for your donkeys that were lost three days ago, give no further thought to them, for they have been found. And on whom is all Israel's desire fixed, if not on you and on all your ancestral house?" 21Saul answered, "I am only a Benjaminite, from the least of the tribes of Israel, and my family is the humblest of all the families of the tribe of Benjamin. Why then have you spoken to me in this way?"

22 Then Samuel took Saul and his servant-boy and brought them into the hall, and gave them a place at the head of those who had been invited, of whom there were about thirty. 23And Samuel said to the cook, "Bring the portion I gave you, the one I asked you to put aside." 24The cook took up the thigh and what went with itb and set them before Saul. Samuel said, "See, what was kept is set before you. Eat; for it is setc before you at the appointed time, so that you might eat with the guests."d

So Saul ate with Samuel that day. 25When they came down from the shrine into the town, a bed was spread for Saule on the roof, and he lay down to sleep.f 26Then at the break of dawng Samuel called to Saul upon the roof, "Get up, so that I may send you on your way." Saul got up, and both he and Samuel went out into the street.

Samuel Anoints Saul

27 As they were going down to the outskirts of the town, Samuel said to Saul, "Tell the boy to go on before us, and when he has passed on, stop here yourself for a while, that I may make known to you the word of God."

---

a Gk: Heb lacks the suffering of   b Meaning of Heb uncertain   c Q Ms Gk: MT it was kept   d Cn: Heb it was kept for you, saying, I have invited the people   e Gk: Heb and he spoke with Saul   f Gk: Heb lacks and he lay down to sleep   g Gk: Heb and they arose early and at break of dawn

King James

10 THEN SAMUEL took a vial of oil, and poured *it* upon his head, and kissed him, and said, *Is it* not because the LORD hath anointed thee *to be* captain over his inheritance?

2When thou art departed from me today, then thou shalt find two men by Rachel's sepulchre in the border of Benjamin at Zelzah; and they will say unto thee, The asses which thou wentest to seek are found: and, lo, thy father hath left the care of the asses, and sorroweth for you, saying, What shall I do for my son?

3Then shalt thou go on forward from thence, and thou shalt come to the plain of Tabor, and there shall meet thee three men going up to God to Beth-el, one carrying three kids, and another carrying three loaves of bread, and another carrying a bottle of wine:

4And they will salute thee, and give thee two *loaves* of bread; which thou shalt receive of their hands.

5After that thou shalt come to the hill of God, where *is* the garrison of the Philistines: and it shall come to pass, when thou art come thither to the city, that thou shalt meet a company of prophets coming down from the high place with a psaltery, and a tabret, and a pipe, and a harp, before them; and they shall prophesy:

6And the spirit of the LORD will come upon thee, and thou shalt prophesy with them, and shalt be turned into another man.

7And let it be, when these signs are come unto thee, *that* thou do as occasion serve thee; for God *is* with thee.

8And thou shalt go down before me to Gilgal; and, behold, I will come down unto thee, to offer burnt offerings, *and* to sacrifice sacrifices of peace offerings: seven days shalt thou tarry, till I come to thee, and show thee what thou shalt do.

9¶ And it was *so*, that when he had turned his back to go from Samuel, God gave him another heart: and all those signs came to pass that day.

10And when they came thither to the hill, behold, a company of prophets met him; and the spirit of God came upon him, and he prophesied among them.

11And it came to pass, when all that knew him before-time saw that, behold, he prophesied among the prophets, then the people said one to another, What *is* this *that* is come unto the son of Kish? *Is* Saul also among the prophets?

12And one of the same place answered and said, But who *is* their father? Therefore it became a proverb, *Is* Saul among the prophets?

13And when he had made an end of prophesying, he came to the high place.

14¶ And Saul's uncle said unto him and to his servant, Whither went ye? And he said, To seek the asses: and when we saw that *they were* no where, we came to Samuel.

15And Saul's uncle said, Tell me, I pray thee, what Samuel said unto you.

16And Saul said unto his uncle, He told us plainly that the asses were found. But of the matter of the kingdom, whereof Samuel spake, he told him not.

17¶ And Samuel called the people together unto the LORD to Mizpeh;

18And said unto the children of Israel, Thus saith the LORD God of Israel, I brought up Israel out of Egypt, and delivered you out of the hand of the Egyptians, and out of the hand of all kingdoms, *and* of them that oppressed you:

19And ye have this day rejected your God, who himself saved you out of all your adversities and your tribulations; and ye have said unto him, *Nay*, but set a king over us. Now therefore present yourselves before the LORD by your tribes, and by your thousands.

20And when Samuel had caused all the tribes of Israel to come near, the tribe of Benjamin was taken.

New International

10 THEN SAMUEL took a flask of oil and poured it on Saul's head and kissed him, saying, "Has not the LORD anointed you leader over his inheritance?a 2When you leave me today, you will meet two men near Rachel's tomb, at Zelzah on the border of Benjamin. They will say to you, 'The donkeys you set out to look for have been found. And now your father has stopped thinking about them and is worried about you. He is asking, "What shall I do about my son?" '

3"Then you will go on from there until you reach the great tree of Tabor. Three men going up to God at Bethel will meet you there. One will be carrying three young goats, another three loaves of bread, and another a skin of wine. 4They will greet you and offer you two loaves of bread, which you will accept from them.

5"After that you will go to Gibeah of God, where there is a Philistine outpost. As you approach the town, you will meet a procession of prophets coming down from the high place with lyres, tambourines, flutes and harps being played before them, and they will be prophesying. 6The Spirit of the LORD will come upon you in power, and you will prophesy with them; and you will be changed into a different person. 7Once these signs are fulfilled, do whatever your hand finds to do, for God is with you.

8"Go down ahead of me to Gilgal. I will surely come down to you to sacrifice burnt offerings and fellowship offerings,b but you must wait seven days until I come to you and tell you what you are to do."

Saul Made King

9As Saul turned to leave Samuel, God changed Saul's heart, and all these signs were fulfilled that day. 10When they arrived at Gibeah, a procession of prophets met him; the Spirit of God came upon him in power, and he joined in their prophesying. 11When all those who had formerly known him saw him prophesying with the prophets, they asked each other, "What is this that has happened to the son of Kish? Is Saul also among the prophets?"

12A man who lived there answered, "And who is their father?" So it became a saying: "Is Saul also among the prophets?" 13After Saul stopped prophesying, he went to the high place.

14Now Saul's uncle asked him and his servant, "Where have you been?"

"Looking for the donkeys," he said. "But when we saw they were not to be found, we went to Samuel."

15Saul's uncle said, "Tell me what Samuel said to you."

16Saul replied, "He assured us that the donkeys had been found." But he did not tell his uncle what Samuel had said about the kingship.

17Samuel summoned the people of Israel to the LORD at Mizpah 18and said to them, "This is what the LORD, the God of Israel, says: 'I brought Israel up out of Egypt, and I delivered you from the power of Egypt and all the kingdoms that oppressed you.' 19But you have now rejected your God, who saves you out of all your calamities and distresses. And you have said, 'No, set a king over us.' So now present yourselves before the LORD by your tribes and clans."

20When Samuel brought all the tribes of Israel near, the tribe of Benjamin was chosen. 21Then he brought

---

a *1* Hebrew; Septuagint and Vulgate *over his people Israel? You will reign over the LORD's people and save them from the power of their enemies round about. And this will be a sign to you that the LORD has anointed you leader over his inheritance.* b *8* Traditionally *peace offerings*

Living Bible

10 THEN SAMUEL took a flask of olive oil and poured it over Saul's head and kissed him on the cheek and said,

"I am doing this because the Lord has appointed you to be the king of his people, Israel! ²When you leave me, you will see two men beside Rachel's tomb at Zelzah, in the land of Benjamin; they will tell you that the donkeys have been found and that your father is worried about you and is asking, 'How am I to find my son?' ³And when you get to the oak of Tabor you will see three men coming toward you who are on their way to worship God at the altar at Bethel; one will be bringing three young goats, another will have three loaves of bread, and the third will have a bottle of wine. ⁴They will greet you and offer you two of the loaves, which you are to accept. ⁵After that you will come to Gibeath-elohim, also known as "God's Hill," where the garrison of the Philistines is. As you arrive there you will meet a band of prophets coming down the hill playing a psaltery, a timbrel, a flute, and a harp, and prophesying as they come.

⁶"At that time the Spirit of the Lord will come mightily upon you, and you will prophesy with them and you will feel and act like a different person. ⁷From that time on your decisions should be based on whatever seems best under the circumstances, for the Lord will guide you. ⁸Go to Gilgal and wait there seven days for me, for I will be coming to sacrifice burnt offerings and peace offerings. I will give you further instructions when I arrive."

⁹As Saul said good-bye and started to go, God gave him a new attitude, and all of Samuel's prophecies came true that day. ¹⁰When Saul and the servant arrived at the Hill of God they saw the prophets coming toward them, and the Spirit of God came upon him, and he too began to prophesy.

¹¹When his friends heard about it, they exclaimed, "What? Saul a prophet?" ¹²And one of the neighbors added, "With a father like his?" So that is the origin of the proverb, "Is Saul a prophet, too?"ᶜ

¹³When Saul had finished prophesying he climbed the hill to the altar.

¹⁴"Where in the world did you go?" Saul's uncle asked him.

And Saul replied, "We went to look for the donkeys, but we couldn't find them; so we went to the prophet Samuel to ask him where they were."

¹⁵"Oh? And what did he say?" his uncle asked.

¹⁶"He said the donkeys had been found!" Saul replied. (But he didn't tell him that he had been anointed as king!)

¹⁷Samuel now called a convocation of all Israel at Mizpah, ¹⁸, ¹⁹and gave them this message from the Lord God: "I brought you from Egypt and rescued you from the Egyptians and from all of the nations that were torturing you. But although I have done so much for you, you have rejected me and have said, 'We want a king instead!' All right, then, present yourselves before the Lord by tribes and clans."

²⁰So Samuel called the tribal leaders together before the Lord, and the tribe of Benjamin was chosen by sacred lot. ²¹Then he brought each family of the tribe of

New Revised Standard

10 SAMUEL TOOK a vial of oil and poured it on his head, and kissed him; he said, "The LORD has anointed you ruler over his people Israel. You shall reign over the people of the LORD and you will save them from the hand of their enemies all around. Now this shall be the sign to you that the LORD has anointed you rulerᵈ over his heritage: ²When you depart from me today you will meet two men by Rachel's tomb in the territory of Benjamin at Zelzah; they will say to you, 'The donkeys that you went to seek are found, and now your father has stopped worrying about them and is worrying about you, saying: What shall I do about my son?' ³Then you shall go on from there further and come to the oak of Tabor; three men going up to God at Bethel will meet you there, one carrying three kids, another carrying three loaves of bread, and another carrying a skin of wine. ⁴They will greet you and give you two loaves of bread, which you shall accept from them. ⁵After that you shall come to Gibeath-elohim,ᵉ at the place where the Philistine garrison is; there, as you come to the town, you will meet a band of prophets coming down from the shrine with harp, tambourine, flute, and lyre playing in front of them; they will be in a prophetic frenzy. ⁶Then the spirit of the LORD will possess you, and you will be in a prophetic frenzy along with them and be turned into a different person. ⁷Now when these signs meet you, do whatever you see fit to do, for God is with you. ⁸And you shall go down to Gilgal ahead of me; then I will come down to you to present burnt offerings and offer sacrifices of well-being. Seven days you shall wait, until I come to you and show you what you shall do."

Saul Prophesies

9 As he turned away to leave Samuel, God gave him another heart; and all these signs were fulfilled that day. ¹⁰When they were going from thereᶠ to Gibeah,ᵍ a band of prophets met him; and the spirit of God possessed him, and he fell into a prophetic frenzy along with them. ¹¹When all who knew him before saw how he prophesied with the prophets, the people said to one another, "What has come over the son of Kish? Is Saul also among the prophets?" ¹²A man of the place answered, "And who is their father?" Therefore it became a proverb, "Is Saul also among the prophets?" ¹³When his prophetic frenzy had ended, he went home.ʰ

14 Saul's uncle said to him and to the boy, "Where did you go?" And he replied, "To seek the donkeys; and when we saw they were not to be found, we went to Samuel." ¹⁵Saul's uncle said, "Tell me what Samuel said to you." ¹⁶Saul said to his uncle, "He told us that the donkeys had been found." But about the matter of the kingship, of which Samuel had spoken, he did not tell him anything.

Saul Proclaimed King

17 Samuel summoned the people to the LORD at Mizpah ¹⁸and said to them,ⁱ "Thus says the LORD, the God of Israel, 'I brought up Israel out of Egypt, and I rescued you from the hand of the Egyptians and from the hand of all the kingdoms that were oppressing you.' ¹⁹But today you have rejected your God, who saves you from all your calamities and your distresses; and you have said, 'No! but set a king over us.' Now therefore present yourselves before the LORD by your tribes and by your clans."

20 Then Samuel brought all the tribes of Israel near, and the tribe of Benjamin was taken by lot. ²¹He brought

---

ᶜ *10:12 Is Saul a prophet, too?* This was an expression of surprise concerning worldly Saul becoming religious, equivalent to our "He got religion."

ᵈ Gk: Heb lacks *over his people Israel. You shall . . . anointed you ruler* ᵉ Or *the Hill of God* ᶠ Gk: Heb *they came there* ᵍ Or *the hill* ʰ Cn: Heb *he came to the shrine* ⁱ Heb *to the people of Israel*

King James

21When he had caused the tribe of Benjamin to come near by their families, the family of Matri was taken, and Saul the son of Kish was taken: and when they sought him, he could not be found.

22Therefore they inquired of the LORD further, if the man should yet come thither. And the LORD answered, Behold, he hath hid himself among the stuff.

23And they ran and fetched him thence: and when he stood among the people, he was higher than any of the people from his shoulders and upward.

24And Samuel said to all the people, See ye him whom the LORD hath chosen, that *there is* none like him among all the people? And all the people shouted, and said, God save the king.

25Then Samuel told the people the manner of the kingdom, and wrote *it* in a book, and laid *it* up before the LORD. And Samuel sent all the people away, every man to his house.

26¶ And Saul also went home to Gibeah; and there went with him a band of men, whose hearts God had touched.

27But the children of Belial said, How shall this man save us? And they despised him, and brought him no presents. But he held his peace.

11 THEN NAHASH the Ammonite came up, and encamped against Jabesh-gilead: and all the men of Jabesh said unto Nahash, Make a covenant with us, and we will serve thee.

2And Nahash the Ammonite answered them, On this *condition* will I make *a covenant* with you, that I may thrust out all your right eyes, and lay it *for* a reproach upon all Israel.

3And the elders of Jabesh said unto him, Give us seven days' respite, that we may send messengers unto all the coasts of Israel: and then, if *there be* no man to save us, we will come out to thee.

4¶ Then came the messengers to Gibeah of Saul, and told the tidings in the ears of the people: and all the people lifted up their voices, and wept.

5And, behold, Saul came after the herd out of the field; and Saul said, What *aileth* the people that they weep? And they told him the tidings of the men of Jabesh.

6And the spirit of God came upon Saul when he heard those tidings, and his anger was kindled greatly.

7And he took a yoke of oxen, and hewed them in pieces, and sent *them* throughout all the coasts of Israel by the hands of messengers, saying, Whosoever cometh not forth after Saul and after Samuel, so shall it be done unto his oxen. And the fear of the LORD fell on the people, and they came out with one consent.

8And when he numbered them in Bezek, the children of Israel were three hundred thousand, and the men of Judah thirty thousand.

9And they said unto the messengers that came, Thus shall ye say unto the men of Jabesh-gilead, Tomorrow, by *that time* the sun be hot, ye shall have help. And the messengers came and showed *it* to the men of Jabesh; and they were glad.

10Therefore the men of Jabesh said, Tomorrow we will come out unto you, and ye shall do with us all that seemeth good unto you.

New International

forward the tribe of Benjamin, clan by clan, and Matri's clan was chosen. Finally Saul son of Kish was chosen. But when they looked for him, he was not to be found.
22So they inquired further of the LORD, "Has the man come here yet?"

And the LORD said, "Yes, he has hidden himself among the baggage."

23They ran and brought him out, and as he stood among the people he was a head taller than any of the others. 24Samuel said to all the people, "Do you see the man the LORD has chosen? There is no one like him among all the people."

Then the people shouted, "Long live the king!"

25Samuel explained to the people the regulations of the kingship. He wrote them down on a scroll and deposited it before the LORD. Then Samuel dismissed the people, each to his own home.

26Saul also went to his home in Gibeah, accompanied by valiant men whose hearts God had touched. 27But some troublemakers said, "How can this fellow save us?" They despised him and brought him no gifts. But Saul kept silent.

Saul Rescues the City of Jabesh

11 NAHASH THE Ammonite went up and besieged Jabesh Gilead. And all the men of Jabesh said to him, "Make a treaty with us, and we will be subject to you."

2But Nahash the Ammonite replied, "I will make a treaty with you only on the condition that I gouge out the right eye of every one of you and so bring disgrace on all Israel."

3The elders of Jabesh said to him, "Give us seven days so we can send messengers throughout Israel; if no one comes to rescue us, we will surrender to you."

4When the messengers came to Gibeah of Saul and reported these terms to the people, they all wept aloud. 5Just then Saul was returning from the fields, behind his oxen, and he asked, "What is wrong with the people? Why are they weeping?" Then they repeated to him what the men of Jabesh had said.

6When Saul heard their words, the Spirit of God came upon him in power, and he burned with anger. 7He took a pair of oxen, cut them into pieces, and sent the pieces by messengers throughout Israel, proclaiming, "This is what will be done to the oxen of anyone who does not follow Saul and Samuel." Then the terror of the LORD fell on the people, and they turned out as one man. 8When Saul mustered them at Bezek, the men of Israel numbered three hundred thousand and the men of Judah thirty thousand.

9They told the messengers who had come, "Say to the men of Jabesh Gilead, 'By the time the sun is hot tomorrow, you will be delivered.' " When the messengers went and reported this to the men of Jabesh, they were elated. 10They said to the Ammonites, "Tomorrow we will surrender to you, and you can do to us whatever seems good to you."

Living Bible

Benjamin before the Lord, and the family of the Matrites was chosen. And finally, the sacred lot selected Saul, the son of Kish. But when they looked for him, he had disappeared!

22So they asked the Lord, "Where is he? Is he here among us?"

And the Lord replied, "He is hiding in the baggage."

23So they found him and brought him out, and he stood head and shoulders above anyone else.

24Then Samuel said to all the people, "This is the man the Lord has chosen as your king. There isn't his equal in all of Israel!"

And all the people shouted, "Long live the king!"

25Then Samuel told the people again what the rights and duties of a king were; he wrote them in a book and put it in a special place before the Lord. Then Samuel sent the people home again.

26When Saul returned to his home at Gibe-ah, a band of men whose hearts the Lord had touched became his constant companions. 27There were, however, some bums and loafers who exclaimed, "How can this man save us?" And they despised him and refused to bring him presents, but he took no notice.

11 AT THIS time Nahash led the army of the Ammonites against the Israeli city of Jabesh-gilead. But the citizens of Jabesh asked for peace. "Leave us alone and we will be your servants," they pleaded.

2"All right," Nahash said, "but only on one condition: I will gouge out the right eye of every one of you as a disgrace upon all Israel!"

3"Give us seven days to see if we can get some help!" replied the elders of Jabesh. "If none of our brothers will come and save us, we will agree to your terms."

4When a messenger came to Gibe-ah, Saul's home town, and told the people about their plight, everyone broke into tears.

5Saul was plowing in the field, and when he returned to town he asked, "What's the matter? Why is everyone crying?"

So they told him about the message from Jabesh. 6Then the Spirit of God came strongly upon Saul and he became very angry. 7He took two oxen and cut them into pieces and sent messengers to carry them throughout all Israel.

"This is what will happen to the oxen of anyone who refuses to follow Saul and Samuel to battle!" he announced. And God caused the people to be afraid of Saul's anger, and they came to him as one man. 8He counted them in Bezek and found that there were three hundred thousand of them in addition to thirty thousand from Judah.

9So he sent the messengers back to Jabesh-gilead to say, "We will rescue you before tomorrow noon!" What joy there was throughout the city when that message arrived!

10The men of Jabesh then told their enemies, "We surrender. Tomorrow we will come out to you and you can do to us as you wish."

New Revised Standard

the tribe of Benjamin near by its families, and the family of the Matrites was taken by lot. Finally he brought the family of the Matrites near man by man,a and Saul the son of Kish was taken by lot. But when they sought him, he could not be found. 22So they inquired again of the LORD, "Did the man come here?"b and the LORD said, "See, he has hidden himself among the baggage." 23Then they ran and brought him from there. When he took his stand among the people, he was head and shoulders taller than any of them. 24Samuel said to all the people, "Do you see the one whom the LORD has chosen? There is no one like him among all the people." And all the people shouted, "Long live the king!"

25 Samuel told the people the rights and duties of the kingship; and he wrote them in a book and laid it up before the LORD. Then Samuel sent all the people back to their homes. 26Saul also went to his home at Gibeah, and with him went warriors whose hearts God had touched. 27But some worthless fellows said, "How can this man save us?" They despised him and brought him no present. But he held his peace.

Now Nahash, king of the Ammonites, had been grievously oppressing the Gadites and the Reubenites. He would gouge out the right eye of each of them and would not grant Israel a deliverer. No one was left of the Israelites across the Jordan whose right eye Nahash, king of the Ammonites, had not gouged out. But there were seven thousand men who had escaped from the Ammonites and had entered Jabesh-gilead.c

Saul Defeats the Ammonites

11 ABOUT A month later,d Nahash the Ammonite went up and besieged Jabesh-gilead; and all the men of Jabesh said to Nahash, "Make a treaty with us, and we will serve you." 2But Nahash the Ammonite said to them, "On this condition I will make a treaty with you, namely that I gouge out everyone's right eye, and thus put disgrace upon all Israel." 3The elders of Jabesh said to him, "Give us seven days' respite that we may send messengers through all the territory of Israel. Then, if there is no one to save us, we will give ourselves up to you." 4When the messengers came to Gibeah of Saul, they reported the matter in the hearing of the people; and all the people wept aloud.

5 Now Saul was coming from the field behind the oxen; and Saul said, "What is the matter with the people, that they are weeping?" So they told him the message from the inhabitants of Jabesh. 6And the spirit of God came upon Saul in power when he heard these words, and his anger was greatly kindled. 7He took a yoke of oxen, and cut them in pieces and sent them throughout all the territory of Israel by messengers, saying, "Whoever does not come out after Saul and Samuel, so shall it be done to his oxen!" Then the dread of the LORD fell upon the people, and they came out as one. 8When he mustered them at Bezek, those from Israel were three hundred thousand, and those from Judah seventye thousand. 9They said to the messengers who had come, "Thus shall you say to the inhabitants of Jabesh-gilead: 'Tomorrow, by the time the sun is hot, you shall have deliverance.' " When the messengers came and told the inhabitants of Jabesh, they rejoiced. 10So the inhabitants of Jabesh said, "Tomorrow we will give ourselves up to you, and you may do to us whatever seems good to you." 11The next day Saul put the people in three com-

---

a Gk: Heb lacks *Finally . . . man by man*   b Gk: Heb *Is there yet a man to come here?*   c Q Ms Compare Josephus, *Antiquities* VI.v.1 (68-71): MT lacks *Now Nahash . . . entered Jabesh-gilead.*   d Q Ms Gk: MT lacks *About a month later*   e Q Ms Gk: MT *thirty*

King James

¹¹And it was *so* on the morrow, that Saul put the people in three companies; and they came into the midst of the host in the morning watch, and slew the Ammonites until the heat of the day: and it came to pass, that they which remained were scattered, so that two of them were not left together.

¹²¶ And the people said unto Samuel, Who *is* he that said, Shall Saul reign over us? bring the men, that we may put them to death.

¹³And Saul said, There shall not a man be put to death this day: for today the LORD hath wrought salvation in Israel.

¹⁴Then said Samuel to the people, Come, and let us go to Gilgal, and renew the kingdom there.

¹⁵And all the people went to Gilgal; and there they made Saul king before the LORD in Gilgal; and there they sacrificed sacrifices of peace offerings before the LORD; and there Saul and all the men of Israel rejoiced greatly.

12 AND SAMUEL said unto all Israel, Behold, I have hearkened unto your voice in all that ye said unto me, and have made a king over you.

²And now, behold, the king walketh before you: and I am old and grayheaded; and, behold, my sons *are* with you: and I have walked before you from my childhood unto this day.

³Behold, here I *am:* witness against me before the LORD, and before his anointed: whose ox have I taken? or whose ass have I taken? or whom have I defrauded? whom have I oppressed? or of whose hand have I received *any* bribe to blind mine eyes therewith? and I will restore it you.

⁴And they said, Thou hast not defrauded us, nor oppressed us, neither hast thou taken aught of any man's hand.

⁵And he said unto them, The LORD *is* witness against you, and his anointed *is* witness this day, that ye have not found aught in my hand. And they answered, *He is* witness.

⁶¶ And Samuel said unto the people, *It is* the LORD that advanced Moses and Aaron, and that brought your fathers up out of the land of Egypt.

⁷Now therefore stand still, that I may reason with you before the LORD of all the righteous acts of the LORD, which he did to you and to your fathers.

⁸When Jacob was come into Egypt, and your fathers cried unto the LORD, then the LORD sent Moses and Aaron, which brought forth your fathers out of Egypt, and made them dwell in this place.

⁹And when they forgat the LORD their God, he sold them into the hand of Sisera, captain of the host of Hazor, and into the hand of the Philistines, and into the hand of the king of Moab, and they fought against them.

¹⁰And they cried unto the LORD, and said, We have sinned, because we have forsaken the LORD, and have served Baalim and Ashtaroth: but now deliver us out of the hand of our enemies, and we will serve thee.

¹¹And the LORD sent Jerubbaal, and Bedan, and Jephthah, and Samuel, and delivered you out of the hand of your enemies on every side, and ye dwelled safe.

¹²And when ye saw that Nahash the king of the children of Ammon came against you, ye said unto me, Nay; but a king shall reign over us: when the LORD your God *was* your king.

¹³Now therefore behold the king whom ye have chosen, *and* whom ye have desired! and, behold, the LORD hath set a king over you.

¹⁴If ye will fear the LORD, and serve him, and obey his voice, and not rebel against the commandment of the LORD, then shall both ye and also the king that reigneth over you continue following the LORD your God:

New International

¹¹The next day Saul separated his men into three divisions; during the last watch of the night they broke into the camp of the Ammonites and slaughtered them until the heat of the day. Those who survived were scattered, so that no two of them were left together.

Saul Confirmed as King

¹²The people then said to Samuel, "Who was it that asked, 'Shall Saul reign over us?' Bring these men to us and we will put them to death."

¹³But Saul said, "No one shall be put to death today, for this day the LORD has rescued Israel."

¹⁴Then Samuel said to the people, "Come, let us go to Gilgal and there reaffirm the kingship." ¹⁵So all the people went to Gilgal and confirmed Saul as king in the presence of the LORD. There they sacrificed fellowship offeringsᵃ before the LORD, and Saul and all the Israelites held a great celebration.

Samuel's Farewell Speech

12 SAMUEL SAID to all Israel, "I have listened to everything you said to me and have set a king over you. ²Now you have a king as your leader. As for me, I am old and gray, and my sons are here with you. I have been your leader from my youth until this day. ³Here I stand. Testify against me in the presence of the LORD and his anointed. Whose ox have I taken? Whose donkey have I taken? Whom have I cheated? Whom have I oppressed? From whose hand have I accepted a bribe to make me shut my eyes? If I have done any of these, I will make it right."

⁴"You have not cheated or oppressed us," they replied. "You have not taken anything from anyone's hand."

⁵Samuel said to them, "The LORD is witness against you, and also his anointed is witness this day, that you have not found anything in my hand."

"He is witness," they said.

⁶Then Samuel said to the people, "It is the LORD who appointed Moses and Aaron and brought your forefathers up out of Egypt. ⁷Now then, stand here, because I am going to confront you with evidence before the LORD as to all the righteous acts performed by the LORD for you and your fathers.

⁸"After Jacob entered Egypt, they cried to the LORD for help, and the LORD sent Moses and Aaron, who brought your forefathers out of Egypt and settled them in this place.

⁹"But they forgot the LORD their God; so he sold them into the hand of Sisera, the commander of the army of Hazor, and into the hands of the Philistines and the king of Moab, who fought against them. ¹⁰They cried out to the LORD and said, 'We have sinned; we have forsaken the LORD and served the Baals and the Ashtoreths. But now deliver us from the hands of our enemies, and we will serve you.' ¹¹Then the LORD sent Jerub-Baal,ᵇ Barak,ᶜ Jephthah and Samuel,ᵈ and he delivered you from the hands of your enemies on every side, so that you lived securely.

¹²"But when you saw that Nahash king of the Ammonites was moving against you, you said to me, 'No, we want a king to rule over us'—even though the LORD your God was your king. ¹³Now here is the king you have chosen, the one you asked for; see, the LORD has set a king over you. ¹⁴If you fear the LORD and serve and obey him and do not rebel against his commands, and if both you and the king who reigns over you follow the LORD your God—good! ¹⁵But if you do not obey the

---

ᵃ *15* Traditionally *peace offerings*   ᵇ *11* Also called *Gideon*   ᶜ *11* Some Septuagint manuscripts and Syriac; Hebrew *Bedan*   ᵈ *11* Hebrew; some Septuagint manuscripts and Syriac *Samson*

Living Bible

11But early the next morning Saul arrived, having divided his army into three detachments, and launched a surprise attack against the Ammonites and slaughtered them all morning. The remnant of their army was so badly scattered that no two of them were left together.

12Then the people exclaimed to Samuel, "Where are those men who said that Saul shouldn't be our king? Bring them here and we will kill them!"

13But Saul replied, "No one will be executed today; for today the Lord has rescued Israel!"

14Then Samuel said to the people, "Come, let us all go to Gilgal and reconfirm Saul as our king."

15So they went to Gilgal and in a solemn ceremony before the Lord they crowned him king. Then they offered peace offerings to the Lord, and Saul and all Israel were very happy.

12 THEN SAMUEL addressed the people again: "Look," he said, "I have done as you asked. I have given you a king. 2I have selected him ahead of my own sons and now I stand here, an old, grey-haired man who has been in public service from the time he was a lad. 3Now tell me as I stand before the Lord and before his anointed king—whose ox or donkey have I stolen? Have I ever defrauded you? Have I ever oppressed you? Have I ever taken a bribe? Tell me and I will make right whatever I have done wrong."

4"No," they replied, "you have never defrauded or oppressed us in any way and you have never taken even one single bribe."

5"The Lord and his anointed king are my witnesses," Samuel declared, "that you can never accuse me of robbing you."

"Yes, it is true," they replied.

6"It was the Lord who appointed Moses and Aaron," Samuel continued. "He brought your ancestors out of the land of Egypt.

7"Now stand here quietly before the Lord as I remind you of all the good things he has done for you and for your ancestors:

8"When the Israelites were in Egypt and cried out to the Lord, he sent Moses and Aaron to bring them into this land. 9But they soon forgot about the Lord their God, so he let them be conquered by Sisera, the general of King Hazor's army, and by the Philistines and the king of Moab.

10"Then they cried to the Lord again and confessed that they had sinned by turning away from him and worshiping the Baal and Ashtaroth idols. And they pleaded, 'We will worship you and you alone if you will only rescue us from our enemies.' 11Then the Lord sent Gideon, Barak, Jephthah, and Samuel to save you, and you lived in safety.

12"But when you were afraid of Nahash, the king of Ammon, you came to me and said that you wanted a king to reign over you. But the Lord your God was already your King, for he has always been your King. 13All right, here is the king you have chosen. Look him over. You have asked for him, and the Lord has answered your request.

14"Now if you will fear and worship the Lord and listen to his commandments and not rebel against the Lord, and if both you and your king follow the Lord your God, then all will be well. 15But if you rebel against the

New Revised Standard

panies. At the morning watch they came into the camp and cut down the Ammonites until the heat of the day; and those who survived were scattered, so that no two of them were left together.

12 The people said to Samuel, "Who is it that said, 'Shall Saul reign over us?' Give them to us so that we may put them to death." 13But Saul said, "No one shall be put to death this day, for today the LORD has brought deliverance to Israel."

14 Samuel said to the people, "Come, let us go to Gilgal and there renew the kingship." 15So all the people went to Gilgal, and there they made Saul king before the LORD in Gilgal. There they sacrificed offerings of well-being before the LORD, and there Saul and all the Israelites rejoiced greatly.

Samuel's Farewell Address

12 SAMUEL SAID to all Israel, "I have listened to you in all that you have said to me, and have set a king over you. 2See, it is the king who leads you now; I am old and gray, but my sons are with you. I have led you from my youth until this day. 3Here I am; testify against me before the LORD and before his anointed. Whose ox have I taken? Or whose donkey have I taken? Or whom have I defrauded? Whom have I oppressed? Or from whose hand have I taken a bribe to blind my eyes with it? Testify against mee and I will restore it to you." 4They said, "You have not defrauded us or oppressed us or taken anything from the hand of anyone." 5He said to them, "The LORD is witness against you, and his anointed is witness this day, that you have not found anything in my hand." And they said, "He is witness."

6 Samuel said to the people, "The LORD is witness, whof appointed Moses and Aaron and brought your ancestors up out of the land of Egypt. 7Now therefore take your stand, so that I may enter into judgment with you before the LORD, and I will declare to youg all the saving deeds of the LORD that he performed for you and for your ancestors. 8When Jacob went into Egypt and the Egyptians oppressed them,h then your ancestors cried to the LORD and the LORD sent Moses and Aaron, who brought forth your ancestors out of Egypt, and settled them in this place. 9But they forgot the LORD their God; and he sold them into the hand of Sisera, commander of the army of King Jabin ofi Hazor, and into the hand of the Philistines, and into the hand of the king of Moab; and they fought against them. 10Then they cried to the LORD, and said, 'We have sinned, because we have forsaken the LORD, and have served the Baals and the Astartes; but now rescue us out of the hand of our enemies, and we will serve you.' 11And the LORD sent Jerubbaal and Barak,j and Jephthah, and Samson,k and rescued you out of the hand of your enemies on every side; and you lived in safety. 12But when you saw that King Nahash of the Ammonites came against you, you said to me, 'No, but a king shall reign over us,' though the LORD your God was your king. 13See, here is the king whom you have chosen, for whom you have asked; see, the LORD has set a king over you. 14If you will fear the LORD and serve him and heed his voice and not rebel against the commandment of the LORD, and if both you and the king who reigns over you will follow the LORD your God, it will be well; 15but if you will not

---

e Gk: Heb lacks *Testify against me*   f Gk: Heb lacks *is witness, who*   g Gk: Heb lacks *and I will declare to you*   h Gk: Heb lacks *and the Egyptians oppressed them*   i Gk: Heb lacks *Jabin king of*   j Gk Syr: Heb *Bedan*   k Gk: Heb *Samuel*

King James

15But if ye will not obey the voice of the LORD, but rebel against the commandment of the LORD, then shall the hand of the LORD be against you, as *it was* against your fathers.

16¶ Now therefore stand and see this great thing, which the LORD will do before your eyes.

17*Is it* not wheat harvest today? I will call unto the LORD, and he shall send thunder and rain; that ye may perceive and see that your wickedness *is* great, which ye have done in the sight of the LORD, in asking you a king.

18So Samuel called unto the LORD; and the LORD sent thunder and rain that day: and all the people greatly feared the LORD and Samuel.

19And all the people said unto Samuel, Pray for thy servants unto the LORD thy God, that we die not: for we have added unto all our sins *this* evil, to ask us a king.

20¶ And Samuel said unto the people, Fear not: ye have done all this wickedness: yet turn not aside from following the LORD, but serve the LORD with all your heart;

21And turn ye not aside: for *then should ye go* after vain *things,* which cannot profit nor deliver; for they *are* vain.

22For the LORD will not forsake his people for his great name's sake: because it hath pleased the LORD to make you his people.

23Moreover as for me, God forbid that I should sin against the LORD in ceasing to pray for you: but I will teach you the good and the right way:

24Only fear the LORD, and serve him in truth with all your heart: for consider how great *things* he hath done for you.

25But if ye shall still do wickedly, ye shall be consumed, both ye and your king.

13 SAUL REIGNED one year; and when he had reigned two years over Israel,

2Saul chose him three thousand *men* of Israel; where-of two thousand were with Saul in Michmash and in mount Beth-el, and a thousand were with Jonathan in Gibeah of Benjamin: and the rest of the people he sent every man to his tent.

3And Jonathan smote the garrison of the Philistines that *was* in Geba, and the Philistines heard *of it.* And Saul blew the trumpet throughout all the land, saying, Let the Hebrews hear.

4And all Israel heard say *that* Saul had smitten a garrison of the Philistines, and *that* Israel also was had in abomination with the Philistines. And the people were called together after Saul to Gilgal.

5¶ And the Philistines gathered themselves together to fight with Israel, thirty thousand chariots, and six thousand horsemen, and people as the sand which *is* on the sea shore in multitude: and they came up, and pitched in Michmash, eastward from Beth-aven.

6When the men of Israel saw that they were in a strait, (for the people were distressed,) then the people did hide themselves in caves, and in thickets, and in rocks, and in high places, and in pits.

7And *some of* the Hebrews went over Jordan to the land of Gad and Gilead. As for Saul, he *was* yet in Gilgal, and all the people followed him trembling.

8¶ And he tarried seven days, according to the set time that Samuel *had appointed:* but Samuel came not to Gilgal; and the people were scattered from him.

9And Saul said, Bring hither a burnt offering to me, and peace offerings. And he offered the burnt offering.

New International

LORD, and if you rebel against his commands, his hand will be against you, as it was against your fathers.

16"Now then, stand still and see this great thing the LORD is about to do before your eyes! 17Is it not wheat harvest now? I will call upon the LORD to send thunder and rain. And you will realize what an evil thing you did in the eyes of the LORD when you asked for a king."

18Then Samuel called upon the LORD, and that same day the LORD sent thunder and rain. So all the people stood in awe of the LORD and of Samuel.

19The people all said to Samuel, "Pray to the LORD your God for your servants so that we will not die, for we have added to all our other sins the evil of asking for a king."

20"Do not be afraid," Samuel replied. "You have done all this evil; yet do not turn away from the LORD, but serve the LORD with all your heart. 21Do not turn away after useless idols. They can do you no good, nor can they rescue you, because they are useless. 22For the sake of his great name the LORD will not reject his people, because the LORD was pleased to make you his own. 23As for me, far be it from me that I should sin against the LORD by failing to pray for you. And I will teach you the way that is good and right. 24But be sure to fear the LORD and serve him faithfully with all your heart; consider what great things he has done for you. 25Yet if you persist in doing evil, both you and your king will be swept away."

Samuel Rebukes Saul

13 SAUL WAS ₜthirty,ª years old when he became king, and he reigned over Israel ₜforty-ᵇ two years.

2Saulᶜ chose three thousand men from Israel; two thousand were with him at Micmash and in the hill country of Bethel, and a thousand were with Jonathan at Gibeah in Benjamin. The rest of the men he sent back to their homes.

3Jonathan attacked the Philistine outpost at Geba, and the Philistines heard about it. Then Saul had the trumpet blown throughout the land and said, "Let the Hebrews hear!" 4So all Israel heard the news: "Saul has attacked the Philistine outpost, and now Israel has become a stench to the Philistines." And the people were summoned to join Saul at Gilgal.

5The Philistines assembled to fight Israel, with three thousandᵈ chariots, six thousand charioteers, and soldiers as numerous as the sand on the seashore. They went up and camped at Micmash, east of Beth Aven. 6When the men of Israel saw that their situation was critical and that their army was hard pressed, they hid in caves and thickets, among the rocks, and in pits and cisterns. 7Some Hebrews even crossed the Jordan to the land of Gad and Gilead.

Saul remained at Gilgal, and all the troops with him were quaking with fear. 8He waited seven days, the time set by Samuel; but Samuel did not come to Gilgal, and Saul's men began to scatter. 9So he said, "Bring me the burnt offering and the fellowship offerings.ᵉ" And Saul offered up the burnt offering. 10Just as he finished mak-

---

ª *1* A few late manuscripts of the Septuagint; Hebrew does not have *thirty.*
ᵇ *1* See the round number in Acts 13:21; Hebrew does not have *forty-.*
ᶜ *1,2* Or *and when he had reigned over Israel two years,* ²he   ᵈ *5* Some Septuagint manuscripts and Syriac; Hebrew *thirty thousand*
ᵉ *9* Traditionally *peace offerings*

Living Bible

Lord's commandments and refuse to listen to him, then his hand will be as heavy upon you as it was upon your ancestors.

16"Now watch as the Lord does great miracles. 17You know that it does not rain at this time of the year, during the wheat harvest; I will pray for the Lord to send thunder and rain today, so that you will realize the extent of your wickedness in asking for a king!"

18So Samuel called to the Lord, and the Lord sent thunder and rain; and all the people were very much afraid of the Lord and of Samuel.

19"Pray for us lest we die!" they cried out to Samuel. "For now we have added to all our other sins by asking for a king."

20"Don't be frightened," Samuel reassured them. "You have certainly done wrong, but make sure now that you worship the Lord with true enthusiasm, and that you don't turn your back on him in any way. 21Other gods can't help you. 22The Lord will not abandon his chosen people, for that would dishonor his great name. He made you a special nation for himself—just because he wanted to!

23"As for me, I will certainly not sin against the Lord by ending my prayers for you; and I will continue to teach you those things which are good and right.

24"Trust the Lord and sincerely worship him; think of all the tremendous things he has done for you. 25But if you continue to sin, you and your king will be destroyed."

13 BY THIS time Saul had reigned for one year.f In the second year of his reign, 2he selected three thousand special troops and took two thousand of them with him to Michmash and Mount Bethel while the other thousand remained with Jonathan, Saul's son, in Gibe-ah in the land of Benjamin. The rest of the army was sent home. 3, 4Then Jonathan attacked and destroyed the garrison of the Philistines at Geba. The news spread quickly throughout the land of the Philistines, and Saul sounded the call to arms throughout Israel. He announced that he had destroyed the Philistine garrison and warned his men that the army of Israel stank to high heaven as far as the Philistines were concerned. So the entire Israeli army mobilized again and joined at Gilgal. 5The Philistines recruited a mighty army of three thousand chariots, six thousand horsemen, and so many soldiers that they were as thick as sand along the seashore; and they camped at Michmash east of Beth-aven.

6When the men of Israel saw the vast mass of enemy troops, they lost their nerve entirely and tried to hide in caves, thickets, coverts, among the rocks, and even in tombs and cisterns. 7Some of them crossed the Jordan River and escaped to the land of Gad and Gilead. Meanwhile, Saul stayed at Gilgal, and those who were with him trembled with fear at what awaited them. 8Samuel had told Saul earlier to wait seven days for his arrival, but when he still didn't come, and Saul's troops were rapidly slipping away, 9he decided to sacrifice the burnt offering and the peace offerings himself. 10But just as

New Revised Standard

heed the voice of the LORD, but rebel against the commandment of the LORD, then the hand of the LORD will be against you and your king.g 16Now therefore take your stand and see this great thing that the LORD will do before your eyes. 17Is it not the wheat harvest today? I will call upon the LORD, that he may send thunder and rain; and you shall know and see that the wickedness that you have done in the sight of the LORD is great in demanding a king for yourselves." 18So Samuel called upon the LORD, and the LORD sent thunder and rain that day; and all the people greatly feared the LORD and Samuel.

19 All the people said to Samuel, "Pray to the LORD your God for your servants, so that we may not die; for we have added to all our sins the evil of demanding a king for ourselves." 20And Samuel said to the people, "Do not be afraid; you have done all this evil, yet do not turn aside from following the LORD, but serve the LORD with all your heart; 21and do not turn aside after useless things that cannot profit or save, for they are useless. 22For the LORD will not cast away his people, for his great name's sake, because it has pleased the LORD to make you a people for himself. 23Moreover as for me, far be it from me that I should sin against the LORD by ceasing to pray for you; and I will instruct you in the good and the right way. 24Only fear the LORD, and serve him faithfully with all your heart; for consider what great things he has done for you. 25But if you still do wickedly, you shall be swept away, both you and your king."

Saul's Unlawful Sacrifice

13 SAUL WAS . . .h years old when he began to reign; and he reigned . . . and twoi years over Israel.

2 Saul chose three thousand out of Israel; two thousand were with Saul in Michmash and the hill country of Bethel, and a thousand were with Jonathan in Gibeah of Benjamin; the rest of the people he sent home to their tents. 3Jonathan defeated the garrison of the Philistines that was at Geba; and the Philistines heard of it. And Saul blew the trumpet throughout all the land, saying, "Let the Hebrews hear!" 4When all Israel heard that Saul had defeated the garrison of the Philistines, and also that Israel had become odious to the Philistines, the people were called out to join Saul at Gilgal.

5 The Philistines mustered to fight with Israel, thirty thousand chariots, and six thousand horsemen, and troops like the sand on the seashore in multitude; they came up and encamped at Michmash, to the east of Beth-aven. 6When the Israelites saw that they were in distress (for the troops were hard pressed), the people hid themselves in caves and in holes and in rocks and in tombs and in cisterns. 7Some Hebrews crossed the Jordan to the land of Gad and Gilead. Saul was still at Gilgal, and all the people followed him trembling.

8 He waited seven days, the time appointed by Samuel; but Samuel did not come to Gilgal, and the people began to slip away from Saul.j 9So Saul said, "Bring the burnt offering here to me, and the offerings of well-being." And he offered the burnt offering. 10As soon as

---

f 13:1 Saul had reigned for one year. The Hebrew, from which the numbers have evidently dropped out in copying, reads: "Saul was . . . years old when he began to reign, and he reigned . . . and two years over Israel."

g Gk: Heb and your ancestors   h The number is lacking in the Heb text (the verse is lacking in the Septuagint).   i Two is not the entire number; something has dropped out.   j Heb him

King James

10And it came to pass, that as soon as he had made an end of offering the burnt offering, behold, Samuel came; and Saul went out to meet him, that he might salute him.

11¶ And Samuel said, What hast thou done? And Saul said, Because I saw that the people were scattered from me, and *that* thou camest not within the days appointed, and *that* the Philistines gathered themselves together at Michmash;

12Therefore said I, The Philistines will come down now upon me to Gilgal, and I have not made supplication unto the LORD: I forced myself therefore, and offered a burnt offering.

13And Samuel said to Saul, Thou hast done foolishly: thou hast not kept the commandment of the LORD thy God, which he commanded thee: for now would the LORD have established thy kingdom upon Israel for ever.

14But now thy kingdom shall not continue: the LORD hath sought him a man after his own heart, and the LORD hath commanded him *to be* captain over his people, because thou hast not kept *that* which the LORD commanded thee.

15And Samuel arose, and gat him up from Gilgal unto Gibeah of Benjamin. And Saul numbered the people *that were* present with him, about six hundred men.

16And Saul, and Jonathan his son, and the people *that were* present with them, abode in Gibeah of Benjamin: but the Philistines encamped in Michmash.

17¶ And the spoilers came out of the camp of the Philistines in three companies: one company turned unto the way *that leadeth to* Ophrah, unto the land of Shual:

18And another company turned the way *to* Beth-horon: and another company turned *to* the way of the border that looketh to the valley of Zeboim toward the wilderness.

19¶ Now there was no smith found throughout all the land of Israel: for the Philistines said, Lest the Hebrews make *them* swords or spears:

20But all the Israelites went down to the Philistines, to sharpen every man his share, and his coulter, and his axe, and his mattock.

21Yet they had a file for the mattocks, and for the coulters, and for the forks, and for the axes, and to sharpen the goads.

22So it came to pass in the day of battle, that there was neither sword nor spear found in the hand of any of the people that *were* with Saul and Jonathan: but with Saul and with Jonathan his son was there found.

23And the garrison of the Philistines went out to the passage of Michmash.

14 NOW IT came to pass upon a day, that Jonathan the son of Saul said unto the young man that bare his armour, Come, and let us go over to the Philistines' garrison, that *is* on the other side. But he told not his father.

2And Saul tarried in the uttermost part of Gibeah under a pomegranate tree which *is* in Migron: and the people that *were* with him *were* about six hundred men;

3And Ahiah, the son of Ahitub, Ichabod's brother, the son of Phinehas, the son of Eli, the LORD's priest in Shiloh, wearing an ephod. And the people knew not that Jonathan was gone.

4¶ And between the passages, by which Jonathan sought to go over unto the Philistines' garrison, *there was* a sharp rock on the one side, and a sharp rock on the other side: and the name of the one *was* Bozez, and the name of the other Seneh.

5The forefront of the one *was* situate northward over against Michmash, and the other southward over against Gibeah.

New International

ing the offering, Samuel arrived, and Saul went out to greet him.

11"What have you done?" asked Samuel.

Saul replied, "When I saw that the men were scattering, and that you did not come at the set time, and that the Philistines were assembling at Micmash, 12I thought, 'Now the Philistines will come down against me at Gilgal, and I have not sought the LORD's favor.' So I felt compelled to offer the burnt offering."

13"You acted foolishly," Samuel said. "You have not kept the command the LORD your God gave you; if you had, he would have established your kingdom over Israel for all time. 14But now your kingdom will not endure; the LORD has sought out a man after his own heart and appointed him leader of his people, because you have not kept the LORD's command."

15Then Samuel left Gilgala and went up to Gibeah in Benjamin, and Saul counted the men who were with him. They numbered about six hundred.

Israel Without Weapons

16Saul and his son Jonathan and the men with them were staying in Gibeahb in Benjamin, while the Philistines camped at Micmash. 17Raiding parties went out from the Philistine camp in three detachments. One turned toward Ophrah in the vicinity of Shual, 18another toward Beth Horon, and the third toward the borderland overlooking the Valley of Zeboim facing the desert.

19Not a blacksmith could be found in the whole land of Israel, because the Philistines had said, "Otherwise the Hebrews will make swords or spears!" 20So all Israel went down to the Philistines to have their plowshares, mattocks, axes and sicklesc sharpened. 21The price was two thirds of a shekeld for sharpening plowshares and mattocks, and a third of a shekele for sharpening forks and axes and for repointing goads.

22So on the day of the battle not a soldier with Saul and Jonathan had a sword or spear in his hand; only Saul and his son Jonathan had them.

Jonathan Attacks the Philistines

23Now a detachment of Philistines had gone out to the pass at Micmash.

14 ONE DAY Jonathan son of Saul said to the young man bearing his armor, "Come, let's go over to the Philistine outpost on the other side." But he did not tell his father.

2Saul was staying on the outskirts of Gibeah under a pomegranate tree in Migron. With him were about six hundred men, 3among whom was Ahijah, who was wearing an ephod. He was a son of Ichabod's brother Ahitub son of Phinehas, the son of Eli, the LORD's priest in Shiloh. No one was aware that Jonathan had left.

4On each side of the pass that Jonathan intended to cross to reach the Philistine outpost was a cliff; one was called Bozez, and the other Seneh. 5One cliff stood to the north toward Micmash, the other to the south toward Geba.

---

a 15 Hebrew; Septuagint *Gilgal and went his way; the rest of the people went after Saul to meet the army, and they went out of Gilgal*   b 16 Two Hebrew manuscripts; most Hebrew manuscripts *Geba*, a variant of *Gibeah*   c 20 Septuagint; Hebrew *plowshares*   d 21 Hebrew *pim*; that is, about 1/4 ounce (about 8 grams)   e 21 That is, about 1/8 ounce (about 4 grams)

Living Bible

he was finishing, Samuel arrived. Saul went out to meet him and to receive his blessing, 11but Samuel said, "What is this you have done?"

"Well," Saul replied, "when I saw that my men were scattering from me, and that you hadn't arrived by the time you said you would, and that the Philistines were at Michmash, ready for battle, 12I said, 'The Philistines are ready to march against us and I haven't even asked for the Lord's help!' So I reluctantly offered the burnt offering without waiting for you to arrive."

13"You fool!" Samuel exclaimed. "You have disobeyed the commandment of the Lord your God. He was planning to make you and your descendants kings of Israel forever, 14but now your dynasty must end; for the Lord wants a man who will obey him. And he has discovered the man he wants and has already appointed him as king over his people; for you have not obeyed the Lord's commandment."

15Samuel then left Gilgal and went to Gibe-ah in the land of Benjamin.

When Saul counted the soldiers who were still with him, he found only six hundred left! 16Saul and Jonathan and these six hundred men set up their camp in Geba in the land of Benjamin; but the Philistines stayed at Michmash. 17Three companies of raiders soon left the camp of the Philistines; one went toward Ophrah in the land of Shual, 18another went to Beth-horon, and the third moved toward the border above the valley of Zeboim near the desert.

19There were no blacksmiths at all in the land of Israel in those days, for the Philistines wouldn't allow them for fear of their making swords and spears for the Hebrews. 20So whenever the Israelites needed to sharpen their plowshares, discs, axes, or sickles, they had to take them to a Philistine blacksmith. 21(The schedule of charges was as follows:

For sharpening a plow point, 60¢
For sharpening a disc, 60¢
For sharpening an axe, 30¢
For sharpening a sickle, 30¢
For sharpening an ox goad, 30¢)

22So there was not a single sword or spear in the entire "army" of Israel that day, except for Saul's and Jonathan's. 23The mountain pass at Michmash had meanwhile been secured by a contingent of the Philistine army.

14 A DAY or so later, Prince Jonathan said to his young bodyguard, "Come on, let's cross the valley to the garrison of the Philistines." But he didn't tell his father that he was leaving.

2Saul and his six hundred men were camped at the edge of Gibe-ah, around the pomegranate tree at Migron. 3Among his men was Ahijah the priest (the son of Ahitub, Ichabod's brother; Ahitub was the son of Phinehas and the grandson of Eli, the priest of the Lord in Shiloh).

No one realized that Jonathan had gone. 4To reach the Philistine garrison, Jonathan had to go over a narrow pass between two rocky crags which had been named Bozez and Seneh. 5The crag on the north was in front of Michmash and the southern one was in front of Geba.

New Revised Standard

he had finished offering the burnt offering, Samuel arrived; and Saul went out to meet him and salute him. 11Samuel said, "What have you done?" Saul replied, "When I saw that the people were slipping away from me, and that you did not come within the days appointed, and that the Philistines were mustering at Michmash, 12I said, 'Now the Philistines will come down upon me at Gilgal, and I have not entreated the favor of the LORD'; so I forced myself, and offered the burnt offering." 13Samuel said to Saul, "You have done foolishly; you have not kept the commandment of the LORD your God, which he commanded you. The LORD would have established your kingdom over Israel forever, 14but now your kingdom will not continue; the LORD has sought out a man after his own heart; and the LORD has appointed him to be ruler over his people, because you have not kept what the LORD commanded you." 15And Samuel left and went on his way from Gilgal.f The rest of the people followed Saul to join the army; they went up from Gilgal toward Gibeah of Benjamin.g

Preparations for Battle

Saul counted the people who were present with him, about six hundred men. 16Saul, his son Jonathan, and the people who were present with them stayed in Geba of Benjamin; but the Philistines encamped at Michmash. 17And raiders came out of the camp of the Philistines in three companies; one company turned toward Ophrah, to the land of Shual, 18another company turned toward Beth-horon, and another company turned toward the mountainh that looks down upon the valley of Zeboim toward the wilderness.

19 Now there was no smith to be found throughout all the land of Israel; for the Philistines said, "The Hebrews must not make swords or spears for themselves"; 20so all the Israelites went down to the Philistines to sharpen their plowshare, mattocks, axes, or sickles;i 21The charge was two-thirds of a shekeli for the plowshares and for the mattocks, and one-third of a shekel for sharpening the axes and for setting the goads.k 22So on the day of the battle neither sword nor spear was to be found in the possession of any of the people with Saul and Jonathan; but Saul and his son Jonathan had them.

Jonathan Surprises and Routs the Philistines

23 Now a garrison of the Philistines had gone out to the pass of Michmash.

14 ONE DAY Jonathan son of Saul said to the young man who carried his armor, "Come, let us go over to the Philistine garrison on the other side." But he did not tell his father. 2Saul was staying in the outskirts of Gibeah under the pomegranate tree that is at Migron; the troops that were with him were about six hundred men, 3along with Ahijah son of Ahitub, Ichabod's brother, son of Phinehas son of Eli, the priest of the LORD in Shiloh, carrying an ephod. Now the people did not know that Jonathan had gone. 4In the pass,l by which Jonathan tried to go over to the Philistine garrison, there was a rocky crag on one side and a rocky crag on the other; the name of the one was Bozez, and the name of the other Seneh. 5One crag rose on the north in front of Michmash, and the other on the south in front of Geba.

---

f Gk: Heb *went up from Gilgal to Gibeah of Benjamin*   g Gk: Heb lacks *The rest . . . of Benjamin*   h Cn Compare Gk: Heb *toward the border*   i Gk: Heb *plowshare*   j Heb *was a pim*   k Cn: Meaning of Heb uncertain   l Heb *Between the passes*

King James

6And Jonathan said to the young man that bare his armour, Come, and let us go over unto the garrison of these uncircumcised: it may be that the LORD will work for us: for *there is* no restraint to the LORD to save by many or by few.

7And his armourbearer said unto him, Do all that *is* in thine heart: turn thee; behold, I *am* with thee according to thy heart.

8Then said Jonathan, Behold, we will pass over unto *these* men, and we will discover ourselves unto them.

9If they say thus unto us, Tarry until we come to you; then we will stand still in our place, and will not go up unto them.

10But if they say thus, Come up unto us; then we will go up: for the LORD hath delivered them into our hand: and this *shall be* a sign unto us.

11And both of them discovered themselves unto the garrison of the Philistines: and the Philistines said, Behold, the Hebrews come forth out of the holes where they had hid themselves.

12And the men of the garrison answered Jonathan and his armourbearer, and said, Come up to us, and we will show you a thing. And Jonathan said unto his armourbearer, Come up after me: for the LORD hath delivered them into the hand of Israel.

13And Jonathan climbed up upon his hands and upon his feet, and his armourbearer after him: and they fell before Jonathan; and his armourbearer slew after him.

14And that first slaughter, which Jonathan and his armourbearer made, was about twenty men, within as it were an half acre of land, *which* a yoke *of oxen might plow.*

15And there was trembling in the host, in the field, and among all the people: the garrison, and the spoilers, they also trembled, and the earth quaked: so it was a very great trembling.

16And the watchmen of Saul in Gibeah of Benjamin looked; and, behold, the multitude melted away, and they went on beating down *one another.*

17Then said Saul unto the people that *were* with him, Number now, and see who is gone from us. And when they had numbered, behold, Jonathan and his armourbearer *were* not *there.*

18And Saul said unto Ahiah, Bring hither the ark of God. For the ark of God was at that time with the children of Israel.

19¶ And it came to pass, while Saul talked unto the priest, that the noise that *was* in the host of the Philistines went on and increased: and Saul said unto the priest, Withdraw thine hand.

20And Saul and all the people that *were* with him assembled themselves, and they came to the battle: and, behold, every man's sword was against his fellow, *and there was* a very great discomfiture.

21Moreover the Hebrews *that* were with the Philistines before that time, which went up with them into the camp *from the country* round about, even they also *turned* to be with the Israelites that *were* with Saul and Jonathan.

22Likewise all the men of Israel which had hid themselves in mount Ephraim, *when* they heard that the Philistines fled, even they also followed hard after them in the battle.

23So the LORD saved Israel that day: and the battle passed over unto Beth-aven.

New International

6Jonathan said to his young armor-bearer, "Come, let's go over to the outpost of those uncircumcised fellows. Perhaps the LORD will act in our behalf. Nothing can hinder the LORD from saving, whether by many or by few."

7"Do all that you have in mind," his armor-bearer said. "Go ahead; I am with you heart and soul."

8Jonathan said, "Come, then; we will cross over toward the men and let them see us. 9If they say to us, 'Wait there until we come to you,' we will stay where we are and not go up to them. 10But if they say, 'Come up to us,' we will climb up, because that will be our sign that the LORD has given them into our hands."

11So both of them showed themselves to the Philistine outpost. "Look!" said the Philistines. "The Hebrews are crawling out of the holes they were hiding in." 12The men of the outpost shouted to Jonathan and his armor-bearer, "Come up to us and we'll teach you a lesson."

So Jonathan said to his armor-bearer, "Climb up after me; the LORD has given them into the hand of Israel."

13Jonathan climbed up, using his hands and feet, with his armor-bearer right behind him. The Philistines fell before Jonathan, and his armor-bearer followed and killed behind him. 14In that first attack Jonathan and his armor-bearer killed some twenty men in an area of about half an acre.[a]

Israel Routs the Philistines

15Then panic struck the whole army—those in the camp and field, and those in the outposts and raiding parties—and the ground shook. It was a panic sent by God.[b]

16Saul's lookouts at Gibeah in Benjamin saw the army melting away in all directions. 17Then Saul said to the men who were with him, "Muster the forces and see who has left us." When they did, it was Jonathan and his armor-bearer who were not there.

18Saul said to Ahijah, "Bring the ark of God." (At that time it was with the Israelites.)[c] 19While Saul was talking to the priest, the tumult in the Philistine camp increased more and more. So Saul said to the priest, "Withdraw your hand."

20Then Saul and all his men assembled and went to the battle. They found the Philistines in total confusion, striking each other with their swords. 21Those Hebrews who had previously been with the Philistines and had gone up with them to their camp went over to the Israelites who were with Saul and Jonathan. 22When all the Israelites who had hidden in the hill country of Ephraim heard that the Philistines were on the run, they joined the battle in hot pursuit. 23So the LORD rescued Israel that day, and the battle moved on beyond Beth Aven.

---

a 14 Hebrew *half a yoke*; a "yoke" was the land plowed by a yoke of oxen in one day. b 15 Or *a terrible panic* c 18 Hebrew; Septuagint *"Bring the ephod." (At that time he wore the ephod before the Israelites.)*

Living Bible

6"Yes, let's go across to those heathen," Jonathan had said to his bodyguard. "Perhaps the Lord will do a miracle for us. For it makes no difference to him how many enemy troops there are!"

7"Fine!" the youth replied. "Do as you think best; I'm with you heart and soul, whatever you decide."

8"All right, then this is what we'll do," Jonathan told him. 9"When they see us, if they say, 'Stay where you are or we'll kill you!' then we will stop and wait for them. 10But if they say, 'Come on up and fight!' then we will do just that; for it will be God's signal that he will help us defeat them!"

11When the Philistines saw them coming they shouted, "Look! The Israelis are crawling out of their holes!" 12Then they shouted to Jonathan, "Come on up here and we'll show you how to fight!"

"Come on, climb right behind me," Jonathan exclaimed to his bodyguard, "for the Lord will help us defeat them!"

13So they clambered up on their hands and knees, and the Philistines fell back as Jonathan and the lad killed them right and left, 14about twenty men in all, and their bodies were scattered over about half an acre of land. 15Suddenly panic broke out throughout the entire Philistine army, and even among the raiders. And just then there was a great earthquake, increasing the terror.

16Saul's lookouts in Gibe-ah saw a strange sight—the vast army of the Philistines began to melt away in all directions.

17"Find out who isn't here," Saul ordered. And when they had checked, they found that Jonathan and his bodyguard were gone. 18"Bring the Ark of God," Saul shouted to Ahijah. (For the Ark was among the people of Israel at that time.) 19But while Saul was talking to the priest, the shouting and the tumult in the camp of the Philistines grew louder and louder. "Quick! What does God say?" Saul demanded.

20Then Saul and his six hundred men rushed out to the battle and found the Philistines killing each other, and there was terrible confusion everywhere. 21And now the Hebrews who had been drafted into the Philistine army revolted and joined with the Israelis. 22Finally even the men hiding in the hills joined the chase when they saw that the Philistines were running away. 23So the Lord saved Israel that day, and the battle continued out beyond Beth-aven.

New Revised Standard

6 Jonathan said to the young man who carried his armor, "Come, let us go over to the garrison of these uncircumcised; it may be that the LORD will act for us; for nothing can hinder the LORD from saving by many or by few." 7His armor-bearer said to him, "Do all that your mind inclines to.d I am with you; as your mind is, so is mine."e 8Then Jonathan said, "Now we will cross over to those men and will show ourselves to them. 9If they say to us, 'Wait until we come to you,' then we will stand still in our place, and we will not go up to them. 10But if they say, 'Come up to us,' then we will go up; for the LORD has given them into our hand. That will be the sign for us." 11So both of them showed themselves to the garrison of the Philistines; and the Philistines said, "Look, Hebrews are coming out of the holes where they have hidden themselves." 12The men of the garrison hailed Jonathan and his armor-bearer, saying, "Come up to us, and we will show you something." Jonathan said to his armor-bearer, "Come up after me; for the LORD has given them into the hand of Israel." 13Then Jonathan climbed up on his hands and feet, with his armor-bearer following after him. The Philistinesf fell before Jonathan, and his armor-bearer, coming after him, killed them. 14In that first slaughter Jonathan and his armor-bearer killed about twenty men within an area about half a furrow long in an acreg of land. 15There was a panic in the camp, in the field, and among all the people; the garrison and even the raiders trembled; the earth quaked; and it became a very great panic.

16 Saul's lookouts in Gibeah of Benjamin were watching as the multitude was surging back and forth.h 17Then Saul said to the troops that were with him, "Call the roll and see who has gone from us." When they had called the roll, Jonathan and his armor-bearer were not there. 18Saul said to Ahijah, "Bring the arki of God here." For at that time the arki of God went with the Israelites. 19While Saul was talking to the priest, the tumult in the camp of the Philistines increased more and more; and Saul said to the priest, "Withdraw your hand." 20Then Saul and all the people who were with him rallied and went into the battle; and every sword was against the other, so that there was very great confusion. 21Now the Hebrews who previously had been with the Philistines and had gone up with them into the camp turned and joined the Israelites who were with Saul and Jonathan. 22Likewise, when all the Israelites who had gone into hiding in the hill country of Ephraim heard that the Philistines were fleeing, they too followed closely after them in the battle. 23So the LORD gave Israel the victory that day.

The battle passed beyond Beth-aven, and the troops with Saul numbered altogether about ten thousand men. The battle spread out over the hill country of Ephraim.

d Gk: Heb Do all that is in your mind. Turn   e Gk: Heb lacks so is mine
f Heb They   g Heb yoke   h Gk: Heb they went and there   i Gk the ephod

King James

24¶ And the men of Israel were distressed that day: for Saul had adjured the people, saying, Cursed *be* the man that eateth *any* food until evening, that I may be avenged on mine enemies. So none of the people tasted *any* food.

25And all *they of* the land came to a wood; and there was honey upon the ground.

26And when the people were come into the wood, behold, the honey dropped; but no man put his hand to his mouth: for the people feared the oath.

27But Jonathan heard not when his father charged the people with the oath: wherefore he put forth the end of the rod that *was* in his hand, and dipped it in an honeycomb, and put his hand to his mouth; and his eyes were enlightened.

28Then answered one of the people, and said, Thy father straitly charged the people with an oath, saying, Cursed *be* the man that eateth *any* food this day. And the people were faint.

29Then said Jonathan, My father hath troubled the land: see, I pray you, how mine eyes have been enlightened, because I tasted a little of this honey.

30How much more, if haply the people had eaten freely today of the spoil of their enemies which they found? for had there not been now a much greater slaughter among the Philistines?

31And they smote the Philistines that day from Michmash to Aijalon: and the people were very faint.

32And the people flew upon the spoil, and took sheep, and oxen, and calves, and slew *them* on the ground: and the people did eat *them* with the blood.

33¶ Then they told Saul, saying, Behold, the people sin against the LORD, in that they eat with the blood. And he said, Ye have transgressed: roll a great stone unto me this day.

34And Saul said, Disperse yourselves among the people, and say unto them, Bring me hither every man his ox, and every man his sheep, and slay *them* here, and eat; and sin not against the LORD in eating with the blood. And all the people brought every man his ox with him that night, and slew *them* there.

35And Saul built an altar unto the LORD: the same was the first altar that he built unto the LORD.

36¶ And Saul said, Let us go down after the Philistines by night, and spoil them until the morning light, and let us not leave a man of them. And they said, Do whatsoever seemeth good unto thee. Then said the priest, Let us draw near hither unto God.

37And Saul asked counsel of God, Shall I go down after the Philistines? wilt thou deliver them into the hand of Israel? But he answered him not that day.

38And Saul said, Draw ye near hither, all the chief of the people: and know and see wherein this sin hath been this day.

39For, *as* the LORD liveth, which saveth Israel, though it be in Jonathan my son, he shall surely die. But *there was* not a man among all the people *that* answered him.

40Then said he unto all Israel, Be ye on one side, and I and Jonathan my son will be on the other side. And the people said unto Saul, Do what seemeth good unto thee.

41Therefore Saul said unto the LORD God of Israel, Give a perfect *lot*. And Saul and Jonathan were taken: but the people escaped.

42And Saul said, Cast *lots* between me and Jonathan my son. And Jonathan was taken.

43Then Saul said to Jonathan, Tell me what thou hast done. And Jonathan told him, and said, I did but taste a little honey with the end of the rod that *was* in mine hand, *and*, lo, I must die.

44And Saul answered, God do so and more also: for thou shalt surely die, Jonathan.

New International

Jonathan Eats Honey

24Now the men of Israel were in distress that day, because Saul had bound the people under an oath, saying, "Cursed be any man who eats food before evening comes, before I have avenged myself on my enemies!" So none of the troops tasted food.

25The entire army[a] entered the woods, and there was honey on the ground. 26When they went into the woods, they saw the honey oozing out, yet no one put his hand to his mouth, because they feared the oath. 27But Jonathan had not heard that his father had bound the people with the oath, so he reached out the end of the staff that was in his hand and dipped it into the honeycomb. He raised his hand to his mouth, and his eyes brightened.[b] 28Then one of the soldiers told him, "Your father bound the army under a strict oath, saying, 'Cursed be any man who eats food today!' That is why the men are faint."

29Jonathan said, "My father has made trouble for the country. See how my eyes brightened[c] when I tasted a little of this honey. 30How much better it would have been if the men had eaten today some of the plunder they took from their enemies. Would not the slaughter of the Philistines have been even greater?"

31That day, after the Israelites had struck down the Philistines from Micmash to Aijalon, they were exhausted. 32They pounced on the plunder and, taking sheep, cattle and calves, they butchered them on the ground and ate them, together with the blood. 33Then someone said to Saul, "Look, the men are sinning against the LORD by eating meat that has blood in it."

"You have broken faith," he said. "Roll a large stone over here at once." 34Then he said, "Go out among the men and tell them, 'Each of you bring me your cattle and sheep, and slaughter them here and eat them. Do not sin against the LORD by eating meat with blood still in it.' "

So everyone brought his ox that night and slaughtered it there. 35Then Saul built an altar to the LORD; it was the first time he had done this.

36Saul said, "Let us go down after the Philistines by night and plunder them till dawn, and let us not leave one of them alive."

"Do whatever seems best to you," they replied.

But the priest said, "Let us inquire of God here."

37So Saul asked God, "Shall I go down after the Philistines? Will you give them into Israel's hand?" But God did not answer him that day.

38Saul therefore said, "Come here, all you who are leaders of the army, and let us find out what sin has been committed today. 39As surely as the LORD who rescues Israel lives, even if it lies with my son Jonathan, he must die." But not one of the men said a word.

40Saul then said to all the Israelites, "You stand over there; I and Jonathan my son will stand over here."

"Do what seems best to you," the men replied.

41Then Saul prayed to the LORD, the God of Israel, "Give me the right answer."[d] And Jonathan and Saul were taken by lot, and the men were cleared. 42Saul said, "Cast the lot between me and Jonathan my son." And Jonathan was taken.

43Then Saul said to Jonathan, "Tell me what you have done."

So Jonathan told him, "I merely tasted a little honey with the end of my staff. And now must I die?"

44Saul said, "May God deal with me, be it ever so severely, if you do not die, Jonathan."

---

[a] 25 Or *Now all the people of the land*   [b] 27 Or *his strength was renewed*   [c] 29 Or *my strength was renewed*   [d] 41 Hebrew; Septuagint *"Why have you not answered your servant today? If the fault is in me or my son Jonathan, respond with Urim, but if the men of Israel are at fault, respond with Thummim."*

Living Bible

24, 25Saul had declared, "A curse upon anyone who eats anything before evening—before I have full revenge on my enemies." So no one ate anything all day, even though they found honeycomb on the ground in the forest, 26for they all feared Saul's curse. 27Jonathan, however, had not heard his father's command; so he dipped a stick into a honeycomb, and when he had eaten the honey he felt much better. 28Then someone told him that his father had laid a curse upon anyone who ate food that day, and everyone was weary and faint as a result.

29"That's ridiculous!" Jonathan exclaimed. "A command like that only hurts us. See how much better I feel now that I have eaten this little bit of honey. 30If the people had been allowed to eat freely from the food they found among our enemies, think how many more we could have slaughtered!"

31But hungry as they were, they chased and killed the Philistines all day from Michmash to Aijalon, growing more and more faint. 32That eveninge they flew upon the battle loot and butchered the sheep, oxen, and calves, and ate the raw, bloody meat. 33Someone reported to Saul what was happening, that the people were sinning against the Lord by eating blood.

"That is very wrong," Saul said. "Roll a great stone over here, 34and go out among the troops and tell them to bring the oxen and sheep here to kill and drain them, and not to sin against the Lord by eating the blood." So that is what they did.

35And Saul built an altar to the Lord—his first.

36Afterwards Saul said, "Let's chase the Philistines all night and destroy every last one of them."

"Fine!" his men replied. "Do as you think best." But the priest said, "Let's ask God first."

37So Saul asked God, "Shall we go after the Philistines? Will you help us defeat them?" But the Lord made no reply all night.

38Then Saul said to the leaders, "Something's wrong!f We must find out what sin was committed today. 39I vow by the name of the God who saved Israel that though the sinner be my own son Jonathan, he shall surely die!" But no one would tell him what the trouble was.

40Then Saul proposed, "Jonathan and I will stand over here, and all of you stand over there." And the people agreed.

41Then Saul said, "O Lord God of Israel, why haven't you answered my question? What is wrong? Are Jonathan and I guilty, or is the sin among the others? O Lord God, show us who is guilty." And Jonathan and Saul were chosen by sacred lot as the guilty ones, and the people were declared innocent.

42Then Saul said, "Now draw lots between me and Jonathan." And Jonathan was chosen as the guilty one.

43"Tell me what you've done," Saul demanded of Jonathan.

"I tasted a little honey," Jonathan admitted. "It was only a little bit on the end of a stick; but now I must die."

44"Yes, Jonathan," Saul said, "you must die; may God strike me dead if you are not executed for this."

New Revised Standard

Saul's Rash Oath

24 Now Saul committed a very rash act on that day.g He had laid an oath on the troops, saying, "Cursed be anyone who eats food before it is evening and I have been avenged on my enemies." So none of the troops tasted food. 25All the troopsh came upon a honeycomb; and there was honey on the ground. 26When the troops came upon the honeycomb, the honey was dripping out; but they did not put their hands to their mouths, for they feared the oath. 27But Jonathan had not heard his father charge the troops with the oath; so he extended the staff that was in his hand, and dipped the tip of it in the honeycomb, and put his hand to his mouth; and his eyes brightened. 28Then one of the soldiers said, "Your father strictly charged the troops with an oath, saying, 'Cursed be anyone who eats food this day.' And so the troops are faint." 29Then Jonathan said, "My father has troubled the land; see how my eyes have brightened because I tasted a little of this honey. 30How much better if today the troops had eaten freely of the spoil taken from their enemies; for now the slaughter among the Philistines has not been great."

31 After they had struck down the Philistines that day from Michmash to Aijalon, the troops were very faint; 32so the troops flew upon the spoil, and took sheep and oxen and calves, and slaughtered them on the ground; and the troops ate them with the blood. 33Then it was reported to Saul, "Look, the troops are sinning against the LORD by eating with the blood." And he said, "You have dealt treacherously; roll a large stone before me here."i 34Saul said, "Disperse yourselves among the troops, and say to them, 'Let all bring their oxen or their sheep, and slaughter them here, and eat; and do not sin against the LORD by eating with the blood.' " So all of the troops brought their oxen with them that night, and slaughtered them there. 35And Saul built an altar to the LORD; it was the first altar that he built to the LORD.

Jonathan in Danger of Death

36 Then Saul said, "Let us go down after the Philistines by night and despoil them until the morning light; let us not leave one of them." They said, "Do whatever seems good to you." But the priest said, "Let us draw near to God here." 37So Saul inquired of God, "Shall I go down after the Philistines? Will you give them into the hand of Israel?" But he did not answer him that day. 38Saul said, "Come here, all you leaders of the people; and let us find out how this sin has arisen today. 39For as the LORD lives who saves Israel, even if it is in my son Jonathan, he shall surely die!" But there was no one among all the people who answered him. 40He said to all Israel, "You shall be on one side, and I and my son Jonathan will be on the other side." The people said to Saul, "Do what seems good to you." 41Then Saul said, "O LORD God of Israel, why have you not answered your servant today? If this guilt is in me or in my son Jonathan, O LORD God of Israel, give Urim; but if this guilt is in your people Israel,j give Thummim." And Jonathan and Saul were indicated by the lot, but the people were cleared. 42Then Saul said, "Cast the lot between me and my son Jonathan." And Jonathan was taken.

43 Then Saul said to Jonathan, "Tell me what you have done." Jonathan told him, "I tasted a little honey with the tip of the staff that was in my hand; here I am, I will die." 44Saul said, "God do so to me and more also; you shall surely die, Jonathan!" 45Then the people said

---

g Gk: Heb *The Israelites were distressed that day*   h Heb *land*   i Gk: Heb *me this day*   j Vg Compare Gk: Heb 41Saul said to the LORD, the God of Israel

King James

45And the people said unto Saul, Shall Jonathan die, who hath wrought this great salvation in Israel? God forbid: *as* the LORD liveth, there shall not one hair of his head fall to the ground; for he hath wrought with God this day. So the people rescued Jonathan, that he died not.

46Then Saul went up from following the Philistines: and the Philistines went to their own place.

47¶ So Saul took the kingdom over Israel, and fought against all his enemies on every side, against Moab, and against the children of Ammon, and against Edom, and against the kings of Zobah, and against the Philistines: and whithersoever he turned himself, he vexed *them*.

48And he gathered an host, and smote the Amalekites, and delivered Israel out of the hands of them that spoiled them.

49Now the sons of Saul were Jonathan, and Ishui, and Melch-ishua: and the names of his two daughters *were these;* the name of the firstborn Merab, and the name of the younger Michal:

50And the name of Saul's wife *was* Ahinoam, the daughter of Ahimaaz: and the name of the captain of his host *was* Abner, the son of Ner, Saul's uncle.

51And Kish *was* the father of Saul; and Ner the father of Abner *was* the son of Abiel.

52And there was sore war against the Philistines all the days of Saul: and when Saul saw any strong man, or any valiant man, he took him unto him.

15 SAMUEL ALSO said unto Saul, The LORD sent me to anoint thee *to be* king over his people, over Israel: now therefore hearken thou unto the voice of the words of the LORD.

2Thus saith the LORD of hosts, I remember *that* which Amalek did to Israel, how he laid *wait* for him in the way, when he came up from Egypt.

3Now go and smite Amalek, and utterly destroy all that they have, and spare them not; but slay both man and woman, infant and suckling, ox and sheep, camel and ass.

4And Saul gathered the people together, and numbered them in Telaim, two hundred thousand footmen, and ten thousand men of Judah.

5And Saul came to a city of Amalek, and laid wait in the valley.

6¶ And Saul said unto the Kenites, Go, depart, get you down from among the Amalekites, lest I destroy you with them: for ye showed kindness to all the children of Israel, when they came up out of Egypt. So the Kenites departed from among the Amalekites.

7And Saul smote the Amalekites from Havilah *until* thou comest to Shur, that *is* over against Egypt.

8And he took Agag the king of the Amalekites alive, and utterly destroyed all the people with the edge of the sword.

9But Saul and the people spared Agag, and the best of the sheep, and of the oxen, and of the fatlings, and the lambs, and all *that was* good, and would not utterly destroy them: but every thing *that was* vile and refuse, that they destroyed utterly.

10¶ Then came the word of the LORD unto Samuel, saying,

11It repenteth me that I have set up Saul *to be* king: for he is turned back from following me, and hath not performed my commandments. And it grieved Samuel; and he cried unto the LORD all night.

12And when Samuel rose early to meet Saul in the morning, it was told Samuel, saying, Saul came to Carmel, and, behold, he set him up a place, and is gone about, and passed on, and gone down to Gilgal.

New International

45But the men said to Saul, "Should Jonathan die— he who has brought about this great deliverance in Israel? Never! As surely as the LORD lives, not a hair of his head will fall to the ground, for he did this today with God's help." So the men rescued Jonathan, and he was not put to death.

46Then Saul stopped pursuing the Philistines, and they withdrew to their own land.

47After Saul had assumed rule over Israel, he fought against their enemies on every side: Moab, the Ammonites, Edom, the kingsa of Zobah, and the Philistines. Wherever he turned, he inflicted punishment on them.b 48He fought valiantly and defeated the Amalekites, delivering Israel from the hands of those who had plundered them.

Saul's Family

49Saul's sons were Jonathan, Ishvi and Malki-Shua. The name of his older daughter was Merab, and that of the younger was Michal. 50His wife's name was Ahinoam daughter of Ahimaaz. The name of the commander of Saul's army was Abner son of Ner, and Ner was Saul's uncle. 51Saul's father Kish and Abner's father Ner were sons of Abiel.

52All the days of Saul there was bitter war with the Philistines, and whenever Saul saw a mighty or brave man, he took him into his service.

The LORD Rejects Saul as King

15 SAMUEL SAID to Saul, "I am the one the LORD sent to anoint you king over his people Israel; so listen now to the message from the LORD. 2This is what the LORD Almighty says: 'I will punish the Amalekites for what they did to Israel when they waylaid them as they came up from Egypt. 3Now go, attack the Amalekites and totally destroyc everything that belongs to them. Do not spare them; put to death men and women, children and infants, cattle and sheep, camels and donkeys.' "

4So Saul summoned the men and mustered them at Telaim—two hundred thousand foot soldiers and ten thousand men from Judah. 5Saul went to the city of Amalek and set an ambush in the ravine. 6Then he said to the Kenites, "Go away, leave the Amalekites so that I do not destroy you along with them; for you showed kindness to all the Israelites when they came up out of Egypt." So the Kenites moved away from the Amalekites.

7Then Saul attacked the Amalekites all the way from Havilah to Shur, to the east of Egypt. 8He took Agag king of the Amalekites alive, and all his people he totally destroyed with the sword. 9But Saul and the army spared Agag and the best of the sheep and cattle, the fat calvesd and lambs—everything that was good. These they were unwilling to destroy completely, but everything that was despised and weak they totally destroyed.

10Then the word of the LORD came to Samuel: 11"I am grieved that I have made Saul king, because he has turned away from me and has not carried out my instructions." Samuel was troubled, and he cried out to the LORD that night.

12Early in the morning Samuel got up and went to meet Saul, but he was told, "Saul has gone to Carmel. There he has set up a monument in his own honor and has turned and gone on down to Gilgal."

---

a 47 Masoretic Text; Dead Sea Scrolls and Septuagint *king*   b 47 Hebrew; Septuagint *he was victorious*   c 3 The Hebrew term refers to the irrevocable giving over of things or persons to the LORD, often by totally destroying them; also in verses 8, 9, 15, 18, 20 and 21.   d 9 Or *the grown bulls*; the meaning of the Hebrew for this phrase is uncertain.

Living Bible

45But the troops retorted, "Jonathan, who saved Israel today, shall die? Far from it! We vow by the life of God that not one hair on his head will be touched, for he has been used of God to do a mighty miracle today." So the people rescued Jonathan.

46Then Saul called back the army, and the Philistines returned home. 47And now, since he was securely in the saddle as king of Israel, Saul sent the Israeli army out in every direction against Moab, Ammon, Edom, the kings of Zobah, and the Philistines. And wherever he turned, he was successful. 48He did great deeds and conquered the Amalekites and saved Israel from all those who had been their conquerors.

49Saul had three sons, Jonathan, Ishvi, and Malchishua; and two daughters, Merab and Michal. 50, 51Saul's wife was Ahino-am, the daughter of Ahima-az. And the general-in-chief of his army was his cousin Abner, his uncle Ner's son. (Abner's father, Ner, and Saul's father, Kish, were brothers; both were the sons of Abiel.)

52The Israelis fought constantly with the Philistines throughout Saul's lifetime. And whenever Saul saw any brave, strong young man, he conscripted him into his army.

15 ONE DAY Samuel said to Saul, "I crowned you king of Israel because God told me to. Now be sure that you obey him. 2Here is his commandment to you: 'I have decided to settle accounts with the nation of Amalek for refusing to allow my people to cross their territory when Israel came from Egypt. 3Now go and completely destroy the entire Amalek nation—men, women, babies, little children, oxen, sheep, camels, and donkeys.' "

4So Saul mobilized his army at Telaim. There were two hundred thousand troops in addition to ten thousand men from Judah. 5The Amalekites were camped in the valley below them. 6Saul sent a message to the Kenites, telling them to get out from among the Amalekites or else die with them. "For you were kind to the people of Israel when they came out of the land of Egypt," he explained. So the Kenites packed up and left.

7Then Saul butchered the Amalekites from Havilah all the way to Shur, east of Egypt. 8He captured Agag, the king of the Amalekites, but killed everyone else. 9However, Saul and his men kept the best of the sheep and oxen and the fattest of the lambs—everything, in fact, that appealed to them. They destroyed only what was worthless or of poor quality.

10Then the Lord said to Samuel, 11"I am sorry that I ever made Saul king, for he has again refused to obey me."

Samuel was so deeply moved when he heard what God was saying, that he cried to the Lord all night. 12Early the next morning he went out to find Saul. Someone said that he had gone to Mount Carmel to erect a monument to himself, and had then gone on to Gilgal.

New Revised Standard

to Saul, "Shall Jonathan die, who has accomplished this great victory in Israel? Far from it! As the LORD lives, not one hair of his head shall fall to the ground; for he has worked with God today." So the people ransomed Jonathan, and he did not die. 46Then Saul withdrew from pursuing the Philistines; and the Philistines went to their own place.

Saul's Continuing Wars

47 When Saul had taken the kingship over Israel, he fought against all his enemies on every side—against Moab, against the Ammonites, against Edom, against the kings of Zobah, and against the Philistines; wherever he turned he routed them. 48He did valiantly, and struck down the Amalekites, and rescued Israel out of the hands of those who plundered them.

49 Now the sons of Saul were Jonathan, Ishvi, and Malchishua; and the names of his two daughters were these: the name of the firstborn was Merab, and the name of the younger, Michal. 50The name of Saul's wife was Ahinoam daughter of Ahimaaz. And the name of the commander of his army was Abner son of Ner, Saul's uncle; 51Kish was the father of Saul, and Ner the father of Abner was the son of Abiel.

52 There was hard fighting against the Philistines all the days of Saul; and when Saul saw any strong or valiant warrior, he took him into his service.

Saul Defeats the Amalekites but Spares Their King

15 SAMUEL SAID to Saul, "The LORD sent me to anoint you king over his people Israel; now therefore listen to the words of the LORD. 2Thus says the LORD of hosts, 'I will punish the Amalekites for what they did in opposing the Israelites when they came up out of Egypt. 3Now go and attack Amalek, and utterly destroy all that they have; do not spare them, but kill both man and woman, child and infant, ox and sheep, camel and donkey.' "

4 So Saul summoned the people, and numbered them in Telaim, two hundred thousand foot soldiers, and ten thousand soldiers of Judah. 5Saul came to the city of the Amalekites and lay in wait in the valley. 6Saul said to the Kenites, "Go! Leave! Withdraw from among the Amalekites, or I will destroy you with them; for you showed kindness to all the people of Israel when they came up out of Egypt." So the Kenites withdrew from the Amalekites. 7Saul defeated the Amalekites, from Havilah as far as Shur, which is east of Egypt. 8He took King Agag of the Amalekites alive, but utterly destroyed all the people with the edge of the sword. 9Saul and the people spared Agag, and the best of the sheep and of the cattle and of the fatlings, and the lambs, and all that was valuable, and would not utterly destroy them; all that was despised and worthless they utterly destroyed.

Saul Rejected as King

10 The word of the LORD came to Samuel: 11"I regret that I made Saul king, for he has turned back from following me, and has not carried out my commands." Samuel was angry; and he cried out to the LORD all night. 12Samuel rose early in the morning to meet Saul, and Samuel was told, "Saul went to Carmel, where he set up a monument for himself, and on returning he passed on down to Gilgal." 13When Samuel came to

King James

13And Samuel came to Saul: and Saul said unto him, Blessed *be* thou of the LORD: I have performed the commandment of the LORD.

14And Samuel said, What *meaneth* then this bleating of the sheep in mine ears, and the lowing of the oxen which I hear?

15And Saul said, They have brought them from the Amalekites: for the people spared the best of the sheep and of the oxen, to sacrifice unto the LORD thy God; and the rest we have utterly destroyed.

16Then Samuel said unto Saul, Stay, and I will tell thee what the LORD hath said to me this night. And he said unto him, Say on.

17And Samuel said, When thou *wast* little in thine own sight, *wast* thou not *made* the head of the tribes of Israel, and the LORD anointed thee king over Israel?

18And the LORD sent thee on a journey, and said, Go and utterly destroy the sinners the Amalekites, and fight against them until they be consumed.

19Wherefore then didst thou not obey the voice of the LORD, but didst fly upon the spoil, and didst evil in the sight of the LORD?

20And Saul said unto Samuel, Yea, I have obeyed the voice of the LORD, and have gone the way which the LORD sent me, and have brought Agag the king of Amalek, and have utterly destroyed the Amalekites.

21But the people took of the spoil, sheep and oxen, the chief of the things which should have been utterly destroyed, to sacrifice unto the LORD thy God in Gilgal.

22And Samuel said, Hath the LORD *as great* delight in burnt offerings and sacrifices, as in obeying the voice of the LORD? Behold, to obey *is* better than sacrifice, *and* to hearken than the fat of rams.

23For rebellion *is as* the sin of witchcraft, and stubbornness *is as* iniquity and idolatry. Because thou hast rejected the word of the LORD, he hath also rejected thee from *being* king.

24¶ And Saul said unto Samuel, I have sinned: for I have transgressed the commandment of the LORD, and thy words: because I feared the people, and obeyed their voice.

25Now therefore, I pray thee, pardon my sin, and turn again with me, that I may worship the LORD.

26And Samuel said unto Saul, I will not return with thee: for thou hast rejected the word of the LORD, and the LORD hath rejected thee from being king over Israel.

27And as Samuel turned about to go away, he laid hold upon the skirt of his mantle, and it rent.

28And Samuel said unto him, The LORD hath rent the kingdom of Israel from thee this day, and hath given it to a neighbour of thine, *that is* better than thou.

29And also the Strength of Israel will not lie nor repent: for he *is* not a man, that he should repent.

30Then he said, I have sinned: *yet* honour me now, I pray thee, before the elders of my people, and before Israel, and turn again with me, that I may worship the LORD thy God.

31So Samuel turned again after Saul; and Saul worshipped the LORD.

32¶ Then said Samuel, Bring ye hither to me Agag the king of the Amalekites. And Agag came unto him delicately. And Agag said, Surely the bitterness of death is past.

33And Samuel said, As thy sword hath made women childless, so shall thy mother be childless among women. And Samuel hewed Agag in pieces before the LORD in Gilgal.

34¶ Then Samuel went to Ramah; and Saul went up to his house to Gibeah of Saul.

New International

13When Samuel reached him, Saul said, "The LORD bless you! I have carried out the LORD's instructions."

14But Samuel said, "What then is this bleating of sheep in my ears? What is this lowing of cattle that I hear?"

15Saul answered, "The soldiers brought them from the Amalekites; they spared the best of the sheep and cattle to sacrifice to the LORD your God, but we totally destroyed the rest."

16"Stop!" Samuel said to Saul. "Let me tell you what the LORD said to me last night."

"Tell me," Saul replied.

17Samuel said, "Although you were once small in your own eyes, did you not become the head of the tribes of Israel? The LORD anointed you king over Israel. 18And he sent you on a mission, saying, 'Go and completely destroy those wicked people, the Amalekites; make war on them until you have wiped them out.' 19Why did you not obey the LORD? Why did you pounce on the plunder and do evil in the eyes of the LORD?"

20"But I did obey the LORD," Saul said. "I went on the mission the LORD assigned me. I completely destroyed the Amalekites and brought back Agag their king. 21The soldiers took sheep and cattle from the plunder, the best of what was devoted to God, in order to sacrifice them to the LORD your God at Gilgal."

22But Samuel replied:

"Does the LORD delight in burnt offerings and
    sacrifices
    as much as in obeying the voice of the LORD?
To obey is better than sacrifice,
    and to heed is better than the fat of rams.
23For rebellion is like the sin of divination,
    and arrogance like the evil of idolatry.
Because you have rejected the word of the
    LORD,
    he has rejected you as king."

24Then Saul said to Samuel, "I have sinned. I violated the LORD's command and your instructions. I was afraid of the people and so I gave in to them. 25Now I beg you, forgive my sin and come back with me, so that I may worship the LORD."

26But Samuel said to him, "I will not go back with you. You have rejected the word of the LORD, and the LORD has rejected you as king over Israel!"

27As Samuel turned to leave, Saul caught hold of the hem of his robe, and it tore. 28Samuel said to him, "The LORD has torn the kingdom of Israel from you today and has given it to one of your neighbors—to one better than you. 29He who is the Glory of Israel does not lie or change his mind; for he is not a man, that he should change his mind."

30Saul replied, "I have sinned. But please honor me before the elders of my people and before Israel; come back with me, so that I may worship the LORD your God." 31So Samuel went back with Saul, and Saul worshiped the LORD.

32Then Samuel said, "Bring me Agag king of the Amalekites."

Agag came to him confidently,[a] thinking, "Surely the bitterness of death is past."

33But Samuel said,

"As your sword has made women childless,
    so will your mother be childless among
    women."

And Samuel put Agag to death before the LORD at Gilgal.

34Then Samuel left for Ramah, but Saul went up to his home in Gibeah of Saul. 35Until the day Samuel died,

a 32 Or *him trembling, yet*

Living Bible

13When Samuel finally found him, Saul greeted him cheerfully.

"Hello there," he said. "Well, I have carried out the Lord's command!"

14"Then what was all the bleating of sheep and lowing of oxen I heard?" Samuel demanded.

15"It's true that the army spared the best of the sheep and oxen," Saul admitted, "but they are going to sacrifice them to the Lord your God; and we have destroyed everything else."

16Then Samuel said to Saul, "Stop! Listen to what the Lord told me last night!"

"What was it?" Saul asked.

17And Samuel told him, "When you didn't think much of yourself, God made you king of Israel. 18And he sent you on an errand and told you, 'Go and completely destroy the sinners, the Amalekites, until they are all dead.' 19Then why didn't you obey the Lord? Why did you rush for the loot and do exactly what God said not to?"

20"But I *have* obeyed the Lord," Saul insisted. "I did what he told me to; and I brought King Agag but killed everyone else. 21And it was only when my troops demanded it that I let them keep the best of the sheep and oxen and loot to sacrifice to the Lord."

22Samuel replied, "Has the Lord as much pleasure in your burnt offerings and sacrifices as in your obedience? Obedience is far better than sacrifice. He is much more interested in your listening to him than in your offering the fat of rams to him. 23For rebellion is as bad as the sin of witchcraft, and stubbornness is as bad as worshiping idols. And now because you have rejected the word of Jehovah, he has rejected you from being king."

24"I have sinned," Saul finally admitted. "Yes, I have disobeyed your instructions and the command of the Lord, for I was afraid of the people and did what they demanded. 25Oh, please pardon my sin now and go with me to worship the Lord."

26But Samuel replied, "It's no use! Since you have rejected the commandment of the Lord, he has rejected you from being the king of Israel."

27As Samuel turned to go, Saul grabbed at him to try to hold him back, and tore his robe.

28And Samuel said to him, "See? The Lord has torn the kingdom of Israel from you today and has given it to a countryman of yours who is better than you are. 29And he who is the glory of Israel is not lying, nor will he change his mind, for he is not a man!"

30Then Saul pleaded again, "I have sinned; but oh, at least honor me before the leaders and before my people by going with me to worship the Lord your God."

31So Samuel finally agreed and went with him.

32Then Samuel said, "Bring King Agag to me." Agag arrived all full of smiles, for he thought, "Surely the worst is over and I have been spared!" 33But Samuel said, "As your sword has killed the sons of many mothers, now your mother shall be childless." And Samuel chopped him in pieces before the Lord at Gilgal. 34Then Samuel went home to Ramah, and Saul returned to Gibe-ah. 35Samuel never saw Saul again, but he

New Revised Standard

Saul, Saul said to him, "May you be blessed by the LORD; I have carried out the command of the LORD." 14But Samuel said, "What then is this bleating of sheep in my ears, and the lowing of cattle that I hear?" 15Saul said, "They have brought them from the Amalekites; for the people spared the best of the sheep and the cattle, to sacrifice to the LORD your God; but the rest we have utterly destroyed." 16Then Samuel said to Saul, "Stop! I will tell you what the LORD said to me last night." He replied, "Speak."

17 Samuel said, "Though you are little in your own eyes, are you not the head of the tribes of Israel? The LORD anointed you king over Israel. 18And the LORD sent you on a mission, and said, 'Go, utterly destroy the sinners, the Amalekites, and fight against them until they are consumed.' 19Why then did you not obey the voice of the LORD? Why did you swoop down on the spoil, and do what was evil in the sight of the LORD?" 20Saul said to Samuel, "I have obeyed the voice of the LORD, I have gone on the mission on which the LORD sent me, I have brought Agag the king of Amalek, and I have utterly destroyed the Amalekites. 21But from the spoil the people took sheep and cattle, the best of the things devoted to destruction, to sacrifice to the LORD your God in Gilgal." 22And Samuel said,

"Has the LORD as great delight in burnt
　　offerings and sacrifices,
　　as in obeying the voice of the LORD?
Surely, to obey is better than sacrifice,
　　and to heed than the fat of rams.
23 For rebellion is no less a sin than divination,
　　and stubbornness is like iniquity and
　　　idolatry.
Because you have rejected the word of the
　　LORD,
　　he has also rejected you from being king."

24 Saul said to Samuel, "I have sinned; for I have transgressed the commandment of the LORD and your words, because I feared the people and obeyed their voice. 25Now therefore, I pray, pardon my sin, and return with me, so that I may worship the LORD." 26Samuel said to Saul, "I will not return with you; for you have rejected the word of the LORD, and the LORD has rejected you from being king over Israel." 27As Samuel turned to go away, Saul caught hold of the hem of his robe, and it tore. 28And Samuel said to him, "The LORD has torn the kingdom of Israel from you this very day, and has given it to a neighbor of yours, who is better than you. 29Moreover the Glory of Israel will not recantb or change his mind; for he is not a mortal, that he should change his mind." 30Then Saulc said, "I have sinned; yet honor me now before the elders of my people and before Israel, and return with me, so that I may worship the LORD your God." 31So Samuel turned back after Saul; and Saul worshiped the LORD.

32 Then Samuel said, "Bring Agag king of the Amalekites here to me." And Agag came to him haltingly.d Agag said, "Surely this is the bitterness of death."e 33But Samuel said,

"As your sword has made women childless,
　　so your mother shall be childless among
　　　women."

And Samuel hewed Agag in pieces before the LORD in Gilgal.

34 Then Samuel went to Ramah; and Saul went up to his house in Gibeah of Saul. 35Samuel did not see

---

b Q Ms Gk: MT *deceive*　c Heb *he*　d Cn Compare Gk: Meaning of Heb uncertain　e Q Ms Gk: MT *Surely the bitterness of death is past*

King James

35And Samuel came no more to see Saul until the day of his death: nevertheless Samuel mourned for Saul: and the LORD repented that he had made Saul king over Israel.

16 AND THE LORD said unto Samuel, How long wilt thou mourn for Saul, seeing I have rejected him from reigning over Israel? fill thine horn with oil, and go, I will send thee to Jesse the Bethlehemite: for I have provided me a king among his sons.

2And Samuel said, How can I go? if Saul hear *it*, he will kill me. And the LORD said, Take an heifer with thee, and say, I am come to sacrifice to the LORD.

3And call Jesse to the sacrifice, and I will show thee what thou shalt do: and thou shalt anoint unto me *him* whom I name unto thee.

4And Samuel did that which the LORD spake, and came to Bethlehem. And the elders of the town trembled at his coming, and said, Comest thou peaceably?

5And he said, Peaceably: I am come to sacrifice unto the LORD: sanctify yourselves, and come with me to the sacrifice. And he sanctified Jesse and his sons, and called them to the sacrifice.

6¶ And it came to pass, when they were come, that he looked on Eliab, and said, Surely the LORD's anointed *is* before him.

7But the LORD said unto Samuel, Look not on his countenance, or on the height of his stature; because I have refused him: for *the LORD seeth* not as man seeth; for man looketh on the outward appearance, but the LORD looketh on the heart.

8Then Jesse called Abinadab, and made him pass before Samuel. And he said, Neither hath the LORD chosen this.

9Then Jesse made Shammah to pass by. And he said, Neither hath the LORD chosen this.

10Again, Jesse made seven of his sons to pass before Samuel. And Samuel said unto Jesse, The LORD hath not chosen these.

11And Samuel said unto Jesse, Are here all thy children? And he said, There remaineth yet the youngest, and, behold, he keepeth the sheep. And Samuel said unto Jesse, Send and fetch him: for we will not sit down till he come hither.

12And he sent, and brought him in. Now he *was* ruddy, *and* withal of a beautiful countenance, and goodly to look to. And the LORD said, Arise, anoint him: for this *is* he.

13Then Samuel took the horn of oil, and anointed him in the midst of his brethren: and the spirit of the LORD came upon David from that day forward. So Samuel rose up, and went to Ramah.

14¶ But the spirit of the LORD departed from Saul, and an evil spirit from the LORD troubled him.

15And Saul's servants said unto him, Behold now, an evil spirit from God troubleth thee.

16Let our lord now command thy servants, *which are* before thee, to seek out a man, *who is* a cunning player on an harp: and it shall come to pass, when the evil spirit from God is upon thee, that he shall play with his hand, and thou shalt be well.

17And Saul said unto his servants, Provide me now a man that can play well, and bring *him* to me.

18Then answered one of the servants, and said, Behold, I have seen a son of Jesse the Bethlehemite, *that is* cunning in playing, and a mighty valiant man, and a man of war, and prudent in matters, and a comely person, and the LORD *is* with him.

19¶ Wherefore Saul sent messengers unto Jesse, and said, Send me David thy son, which *is* with the sheep.

New International

he did not go to see Saul again, though Samuel mourned for him. And the LORD was grieved that he had made Saul king over Israel.

Samuel Anoints David

16 THE LORD said to Samuel, "How long will you mourn for Saul, since I have rejected him as king over Israel? Fill your horn with oil and be on your way; I am sending you to Jesse of Bethlehem. I have chosen one of his sons to be king."

2But Samuel said, "How can I go? Saul will hear about it and kill me."

The LORD said, "Take a heifer with you and say, 'I have come to sacrifice to the LORD.' 3Invite Jesse to the sacrifice, and I will show you what to do. You are to anoint for me the one I indicate."

4Samuel did what the LORD said. When he arrived at Bethlehem, the elders of the town trembled when they met him. They asked, "Do you come in peace?"

5Samuel replied, "Yes, in peace; I have come to sacrifice to the LORD. Consecrate yourselves and come to the sacrifice with me." Then he consecrated Jesse and his sons and invited them to the sacrifice.

6When they arrived, Samuel saw Eliab and thought, "Surely the LORD's anointed stands here before the LORD."

7But the LORD said to Samuel, "Do not consider his appearance or his height, for I have rejected him. The LORD does not look at the things man looks at. Man looks at the outward appearance, but the LORD looks at the heart."

8Then Jesse called Abinadab and had him pass in front of Samuel. But Samuel said, "The LORD has not chosen this one either." 9Jesse then had Shammah pass by, but Samuel said, "Nor has the LORD chosen this one." 10Jesse had seven of his sons pass before Samuel, but Samuel said to him, "The LORD has not chosen these." 11So he asked Jesse, "Are these all the sons you have?"

"There is still the youngest," Jesse answered, "but he is tending the sheep."

Samuel said, "Send for him; we will not sit down[a] until he arrives."

12So he sent and had him brought in. He was ruddy, with a fine appearance and handsome features.

Then the LORD said, "Rise and anoint him; he is the one."

13So Samuel took the horn of oil and anointed him in the presence of his brothers, and from that day on the Spirit of the LORD came upon David in power. Samuel then went to Ramah.

David in Saul's Service

14Now the Spirit of the LORD had departed from Saul, and an evil[b] spirit from the LORD tormented him.

15Saul's attendants said to him, "See, an evil spirit from God is tormenting you. 16Let our lord command his servants here to search for someone who can play the harp. He will play when the evil spirit from God comes upon you, and you will feel better."

17So Saul said to his attendants, "Find someone who plays well and bring him to me."

18One of the servants answered, "I have seen a son of Jesse of Bethlehem who knows how to play the harp. He is a brave man and a warrior. He speaks well and is a fine-looking man. And the LORD is with him."

19Then Saul sent messengers to Jesse and said, "Send me your son David, who is with the sheep." 20So Jesse

---

a *11* Some Septuagint manuscripts; Hebrew *not gather around*   b *14* Or *injurious*; also in verses 15, 16 and 23

Living Bible

mourned constantly for him; and the Lord was sorry that he had ever made Saul king of Israel.

16 FINALLY THE Lord said to Samuel, "You have mourned long enough for Saul, for I have rejected him as king of Israel. Now take a vial of olive oil and go to Bethlehem and find a man named Jesse, for I have selected one of his sons to be the new king."

²But Samuel asked, "How can I do that? If Saul hears about it, he will kill me."

"Take a heifer with you," the Lord replied, "and say that you have come to make a sacrifice to the Lord. ³Then call Jesse to the sacrifice and I will show you which of his sons to anoint."

⁴So Samuel did as the Lord had told him to. When he arrived at Bethlehem, the elders of the city came trembling to meet him.

"What is wrong?" they asked. "Why have you come?"

⁵But he replied, "All is well. I have come to sacrifice to the Lord. Purify yourselves and come with me to the sacrifice."

And he performed the purification rite on Jesse and his sons, and invited them too. ⁶When they arrived, Samuel took one look at Eliab and thought, "Surely this is the man the Lord has chosen!"

⁷But the Lord said to Samuel, "Don't judge by a man's face or height, for this is not the one. I don't make decisions the way you do! Men judge by outward appearance, but I look at a man's thoughts and intentions."

⁸Then Jesse told his son Abinadab to step forward and walk in front of Samuel. But the Lord said, "This is not the right man either."

⁹Next Jesse summoned Shammah, but the Lord said, "No, this is not the one." In the same way all seven of his sons presented themselves to Samuel and were rejected.

10, 11"The Lord has not chosen any of them," Samuel told Jesse. "Are these all there are?"

"Well, there is the youngest," Jesse replied. "But he's out in the fields watching the sheep."

"Send for him at once," Samuel said, "for we will not sit down to eat until he arrives."

¹²So Jesse sent for him. He was a fine looking boy, ruddy-faced, and with pleasant eyes. And the Lord said, "This is the one; anoint him."

¹³So as David stood there among his brothers, Samuel took the olive oil he had brought and poured it upon David's head; and the Spirit of Jehovah came upon him and gave him great power from that day onward. Then Samuel returned to Ramah.

¹⁴But the Spirit of the Lord had left Saul, and instead, the Lord had sent a tormenting spirit that filled him with depression and fear. 15, 16Some of Saul's aides suggested a cure.

"We'll find a good harpist to play for you whenever the tormenting spirit is bothering you," they said. "The harp music will quiet you and you'll soon be well again."

17"All right," Saul said. "Find me a harpist."

18One of them said he knew a young fellow in Bethlehem, the son of a man named Jesse, who was not only a talented harp player, but was handsome, brave, and strong, and had good, solid judgment. "What's more," he added, "the Lord is with him."

19So Saul sent messengers to Jesse, asking that he send his son David the shepherd. 20Jesse responded by

New Revised Standard

Saul again until the day of his death, but Samuel grieved over Saul. And the LORD was sorry that he had made Saul king over Israel.

David Anointed as King

16 THE LORD said to Samuel, "How long will you grieve over Saul? I have rejected him from being king over Israel. Fill your horn with oil and set out; I will send you to Jesse the Bethlehemite, for I have provided for myself a king among his sons." ²Samuel said, "How can I go? If Saul hears of it, he will kill me." And the LORD said, "Take a heifer with you, and say, 'I have come to sacrifice to the LORD.' ³Invite Jesse to the sacrifice, and I will show you what you shall do; and you shall anoint for me the one whom I name to you." ⁴Samuel did what the LORD commanded, and came to Bethlehem. The elders of the city came to meet him trembling, and said, "Do you come peaceably?" ⁵He said, "Peaceably; I have come to sacrifice to the LORD; sanctify yourselves and come with me to the sacrifice." And he sanctified Jesse and his sons and invited them to the sacrifice.

6 When they came, he looked on Eliab and thought, "Surely the LORD's anointed is now before the LORD."ᶜ ⁷But the LORD said to Samuel, "Do not look on his appearance or on the height of his stature, because I have rejected him; for the LORD does not see as mortals see; they look on the outward appearance, but the LORD looks on the heart." ⁸Then Jesse called Abinadab, and made him pass before Samuel. He said, "Neither has the LORD chosen this one." ⁹Then Jesse made Shammah pass by. And he said, "Neither has the LORD chosen this one." 10Jesse made seven of his sons pass before Samuel, and Samuel said to Jesse, "The LORD has not chosen any of these." 11Samuel said to Jesse, "Are all your sons here?" And he said, "There remains yet the youngest, but he is keeping the sheep." And Samuel said to Jesse, "Send and bring him; for we will not sit down until he comes here." 12He sent and brought him in. Now he was ruddy, and had beautiful eyes, and was handsome. The LORD said, "Rise and anoint him; for this is the one." 13Then Samuel took the horn of oil, and anointed him in the presence of his brothers; and the spirit of the LORD came mightily upon David from that day forward. Samuel then set out and went to Ramah.

David Plays the Lyre for Saul

14 Now the spirit of the LORD departed from Saul, and an evil spirit from the LORD tormented him. 15And Saul's servants said to him, "See now, an evil spirit from God is tormenting you. 16Let our lord now command the servants who attend you to look for someone who is skillful in playing the lyre; and when the evil spirit from God is upon you, he will play it, and you will feel better." 17So Saul said to his servants, "Provide for me someone who can play well, and bring him to me." 18One of the young men answered, "I have seen a son of Jesse the Bethlehemite who is skillful in playing, a man of valor, a warrior, prudent in speech, and a man of good presence; and the LORD is with him." 19So Saul sent messengers to Jesse, and said, "Send me your son David who is with the sheep." 20Jesse took a donkey

ᶜ Heb *him*

King James

20And Jesse took an ass *laden* with bread, and a bottle of wine, and a kid, and sent *them* by David his son unto Saul.

21And David came to Saul, and stood before him: and he loved him greatly; and he became his armourbearer.

22And Saul sent to Jesse, saying, Let David, I pray thee, stand before me; for he hath found favour in my sight.

23And it came to pass, when the *evil* spirit from God was upon Saul, that David took an harp, and played with his hand: so Saul was refreshed, and was well, and the evil spirit departed from him.

17 NOW THE Philistines gathered together their armies to battle, and were gathered together at Shochoh, which *belongeth* to Judah, and pitched between Shochoh and Azekah, in Ephes-dammim.

2And Saul and the men of Israel were gathered together, and pitched by the valley of Elah, and set the battle in array against the Philistines.

3And the Philistines stood on a mountain on the one side, and Israel stood on a mountain on the other side: and *there was* a valley between them.

4¶ And there went out a champion out of the camp of the Philistines, named Goliath, of Gath, whose height *was* six cubits and a span.

5And *he had* an helmet of brass upon his head, and he *was* armed with a coat of mail; and the weight of the coat *was* five thousand shekels of brass.

6And *he had* greaves of brass upon his legs, and a target of brass between his shoulders.

7And the staff of his spear *was* like a weaver's beam; and his spear's head *weighed* six hundred shekels of iron: and one bearing a shield went before him.

8And he stood and cried unto the armies of Israel, and said unto them, Why are ye come out to set *your* battle in array? *am* not I a Philistine, and ye servants to Saul? choose you a man for you, and let him come down to me.

9If he be able to fight with me, and to kill me, then will we be your servants: but if I prevail against him, and kill him, then shall ye be our servants, and serve us.

10And the Philistine said, I defy the armies of Israel this day; give me a man, that we may fight together.

11When Saul and all Israel heard those words of the Philistine, they were dismayed, and greatly afraid.

12¶ Now David *was* the son of that Ephrathite of Bethlehem-judah, whose name *was* Jesse; and he had eight sons: and the man went among men *for* an old man in the days of Saul.

13And the three eldest sons of Jesse went *and* followed Saul to the battle: and the names of his three sons that went to the battle *were* Eliab the firstborn, and next unto him Abinadab, and the third Shammah.

14And David *was* the youngest: and the three eldest followed Saul.

15But David went and returned from Saul to feed his father's sheep at Bethlehem.

16And the Philistine drew near morning and evening, and presented himself forty days.

17And Jesse said unto David his son, Take now for thy brethren an ephah of this parched *corn,* and these ten loaves, and run to the camp to thy brethren;

18And carry these ten cheeses unto the captain of *their* thousand, and look how thy brethren fare, and take their pledge.

19Now Saul, and they, and all the men of Israel, *were* in the valley of Elah, fighting with the Philistines.

New International

took a donkey loaded with bread, a skin of wine and a young goat and sent them with his son David to Saul.

21David came to Saul and entered his service. Saul liked him very much, and David became one of his armor-bearers. 22Then Saul sent word to Jesse, saying, "Allow David to remain in my service, for I am pleased with him."

23Whenever the spirit from God came upon Saul, David would take his harp and play. Then relief would come to Saul; he would feel better, and the evil spirit would leave him.

David and Goliath

17 NOW THE Philistines gathered their forces for war and assembled at Socoh in Judah. They pitched camp at Ephes Dammim, between Socoh and Azekah. 2Saul and the Israelites assembled and camped in the Valley of Elah and drew up their battle line to meet the Philistines. 3The Philistines occupied one hill and the Israelites another, with the valley between them.

4A champion named Goliath, who was from Gath, came out of the Philistine camp. He was over nine feet[a] tall. 5He had a bronze helmet on his head and wore a coat of scale armor of bronze weighing five thousand shekels[b]; 6on his legs he wore bronze greaves, and a bronze javelin was slung on his back. 7His spear shaft was like a weaver's rod, and its iron point weighed six hundred shekels.[c] His shield bearer went ahead of him.

8Goliath stood and shouted to the ranks of Israel, "Why do you come out and line up for battle? Am I not a Philistine, and are you not the servants of Saul? Choose a man and have him come down to me. 9If he is able to fight and kill me, we will become your subjects; but if I overcome him and kill him, you will become our subjects and serve us." 10Then the Philistine said, "This day I defy the ranks of Israel! Give me a man and let us fight each other." 11On hearing the Philistine's words, Saul and all the Israelites were dismayed and terrified.

12Now David was the son of an Ephrathite named Jesse, who was from Bethlehem in Judah. Jesse had eight sons, and in Saul's time he was old and well advanced in years. 13Jesse's three oldest sons had followed Saul to the war: The firstborn was Eliab; the second, Abinadab; and the third, Shammah. 14David was the youngest. The three oldest followed Saul, 15but David went back and forth from Saul to tend his father's sheep at Bethlehem.

16For forty days the Philistine came forward every morning and evening and took his stand.

17Now Jesse said to his son David, "Take this ephah[d] of roasted grain and these ten loaves of bread for your brothers and hurry to their camp. 18Take along these ten cheeses to the commander of their unit.[e] See how your brothers are and bring back some assurance[f] from them. 19They are with Saul and all the men of Israel in the Valley of Elah, fighting against the Philistines."

---

a *4* Hebrew *was six cubits and a span* (about 3 meters)   b *5* That is, about 125 pounds (about 57 kilograms)   c *7* That is, about 15 pounds (about 7 kilograms)   d *17* That is, probably about 3/5 bushel (about 22 liters)   e *18* Hebrew *thousand*   f *18* Or *some token*; or *some pledge of spoils*

Living Bible

sending not only David but a young goat and a donkey carrying a load of food and wine. 21From the instant he saw David, Saul admired and loved him; and David became his bodyguard.

22Then Saul wrote to Jesse, "Please let David join my staff, for I am very fond of him."

23And whenever the tormenting spirit from God troubled Saul, David would play the harp and Saul would feel better, and the evil spirit would go away.

17 THE PHILISTINES now mustered their army for battle and camped between Socoh in Judah and Azekah in Ephes-dammim. 2Saul countered with a buildup of forces at Elah Valley. 3So the Philistines and Israelis faced each other on opposite hills, with the valley between them.

4-7Then Goliath, a Philistine champion from Gath, came out of the Philistine ranks to face the forces of Israel. He was a giant of a man, measuring over nine feet tall! He wore a bronze helmet, a two-hundred-pound coat of mail, bronze leggings, and carried a bronze javelin several inches thick, tipped with a twenty-five-pound iron spearhead, and his armor bearer walked ahead of him with a huge shield.

8He stood and shouted across to the Israelis, "Do you need a whole army to settle this? I will represent the Philistines, and you choose someone to represent you, and we will settle this in single combat! 9If your man is able to kill me, then we will be your slaves. But if I kill him, then you must be our slaves! 10I defy the armies of Israel! Send me a man who will fight with me!"

11When Saulg and the Israeli army heard this, they were dismayed and frightened. 12David (the son of aging Jesse, a member of the tribe of Judah who lived in Bethlehem) had seven older brothers. 13The three oldest—Eliab, Abinadab, and Shammah—had already volunteered for Saul's army to fight the Philistines. 14, 15David was the youngest son, and was on Saul's staff on a part-time basis. He went back and forth to Bethlehem to help his father with the sheep. 16For forty days, twice a day, morning and evening the Philistine giant strutted before the armies of Israel.

17One day Jesse said to David, "Take this bushel of roasted grain and these ten loaves of bread to your brothers. 18Give this cheese to their captain and see how the boys are getting along; and bring us back a letterh from them!"

19(Saul and the Israeli army were camped at the valley of Elah.)

New Revised Standard

loaded with bread, a skin of wine, and a kid, and sent them by his son David to Saul. 21And David came to Saul, and entered his service. Saul loved him greatly, and he became his armor-bearer. 22Saul sent to Jesse, saying, "Let David remain in my service, for he has found favor in my sight." 23And whenever the evil spirit from God came upon Saul, David took the lyre and played it with his hand, and Saul would be relieved and feel better, and the evil spirit would depart from him.

David and Goliath

17 NOW THE Philistines gathered their armies for battle; they were gathered at Socoh, which belongs to Judah, and encamped between Socoh and Azekah, in Ephes-dammim. 2Saul and the Israelites gathered and encamped in the valley of Elah, and formed ranks against the Philistines. 3The Philistines stood on the mountain on the one side, and Israel stood on the mountain on the other side, with a valley between them. 4And there came out from the camp of the Philistines a champion named Goliath, of Gath, whose height was sixi cubits and a span. 5He had a helmet of bronze on his head, and he was armed with a coat of mail; the weight of the coat was five thousand shekels of bronze. 6He had greaves of bronze on his legs and a javelin of bronze slung between his shoulders. 7The shaft of his spear was like a weaver's beam, and his spear's head weighed six hundred shekels of iron; and his shield-bearer went before him. 8He stood and shouted to the ranks of Israel, "Why have you come out to draw up for battle? Am I not a Philistine, and are you not servants of Saul? Choose a man for yourselves, and let him come down to me. 9If he is able to fight with me and kill me, then we will be your servants; but if I prevail against him and kill him, then you shall be our servants and serve us." 10And the Philistine said, "Today I defy the ranks of Israel! Give me a man, that we may fight together." 11When Saul and all Israel heard these words of the Philistine, they were dismayed and greatly afraid.

12 Now David was the son of an Ephrathite of Bethlehem in Judah, named Jesse, who had eight sons. In the days of Saul the man was already old and advanced in years.j 13The three eldest sons of Jesse had followed Saul to the battle; the names of his three sons who went to the battle were Eliab the firstborn, and next to him Abinadab, and the third Shammah. 14David was the youngest; the three eldest followed Saul, 15but David went back and forth from Saul to feed his father's sheep at Bethlehem. 16For forty days the Philistine came forward and took his stand, morning and evening.

17 Jesse said to his son David, "Take for your brothers an ephah of this parched grain and these ten loaves, and carry them quickly to the camp to your brothers; 18also take these ten cheeses to the commander of their thousand. See how your brothers fare, and bring some token from them."

19 Now Saul, and they, and all the men of Israel, were in the valley of Elah, fighting with the Philistines.

---

g 17:11 *When Saul.* Probably King Saul was especially worried, for he was tallest of the Israelites, and was obviously the best match! h 17:18 *bring back a letter,* literally, "take their pledge."

i MT: Q Ms Gk *four* j Gk Syr: Heb *among men*

King James

20¶ And David rose up early in the morning, and left the sheep with a keeper, and took, and went, as Jesse had commanded him; and he came to the trench, as the host was going forth to the fight, and shouted for the battle.

21For Israel and the Philistines had put the battle in array, army against army.

22And David left his carriage in the hand of the keeper of the carriage, and ran into the army, and came and saluted his brethren.

23And as he talked with them, behold, there came up the champion, the Philistine of Gath, Goliath by name, out of the armies of the Philistines, and spake according to the same words: and David heard *them*.

24And all the men of Israel, when they saw the man, fled from him, and were sore afraid.

25And the men of Israel said, Have ye seen this man that is come up? surely to defy Israel is he come up: and it shall be, *that* the man who killeth him, the king will enrich him with great riches, and will give him his daughter, and make his father's house free in Israel.

26And David spake to the men that stood by him, saying, What shall be done to the man that killeth this Philistine, and taketh away the reproach from Israel? for who *is* this uncircumcised Philistine, that he should defy the armies of the living God?

27And the people answered him after this manner, saying, So shall it be done to the man that killeth him.

28¶ And Eliab his eldest brother heard when he spake unto the men; and Eliab's anger was kindled against David, and he said, Why camest thou down hither? and with whom hast thou left those few sheep in the wilderness? I know thy pride, and the naughtiness of thine heart; for thou art come down that thou mightest see the battle.

29And David said, What have I now done? *Is there* not a cause?

30¶ And he turned from him toward another, and spake after the same manner: and the people answered him again after the former manner.

31And when the words were heard which David spake, they rehearsed *them* before Saul: and he sent for him.

32¶ And David said to Saul, Let no man's heart fail because of him; thy servant will go and fight with this Philistine.

33And Saul said to David, Thou art not able to go against this Philistine to fight with him: for thou *art but* a youth, and he a man of war from his youth.

34And David said unto Saul, Thy servant kept his father's sheep, and there came a lion, and a bear, and took a lamb out of the flock:

35And I went out after him, and smote him, and delivered *it* out of his mouth: and when he arose against me, I caught *him* by his beard, and smote him, and slew him.

36Thy servant slew both the lion and the bear: and this uncircumcised Philistine shall be as one of them, seeing he hath defied the armies of the living God.

37David said moreover, The LORD that delivered me out of the paw of the lion, and out of the paw of the bear, he will deliver me out of the hand of this Philistine. And Saul said unto David, Go, and the LORD be with thee.

38¶ And Saul armed David with his armour, and he put an helmet of brass upon his head; also he armed him with a coat of mail.

39And David girded his sword upon his armour, and he assayed to go; for he had not proved *it*. And David said unto Saul, I cannot go with these; for I have not proved *them*. And David put them off him.

40And he took his staff in his hand, and chose him five smooth stones out of the brook, and put them in a shepherd's bag which he had, even in a scrip; and his sling *was* in his hand: and he drew near to the Philistine.

New International

20Early in the morning David left the flock with a shepherd, loaded up and set out, as Jesse had directed. He reached the camp as the army was going out to its battle positions, shouting the war cry. 21Israel and the Philistines were drawing up their lines facing each other. 22David left his things with the keeper of supplies, ran to the battle lines and greeted his brothers. 23As he was talking with them, Goliath, the Philistine champion from Gath, stepped out from his lines and shouted his usual defiance, and David heard it. 24When the Israelites saw the man, they all ran from him in great fear.

25Now the Israelites had been saying, "Do you see how this man keeps coming out? He comes out to defy Israel. The king will give great wealth to the man who kills him. He will also give him his daughter in marriage and will exempt his father's family from taxes in Israel."

26David asked the men standing near him, "What will be done for the man who kills this Philistine and removes this disgrace from Israel? Who is this uncircumcised Philistine that he should defy the armies of the living God?"

27They repeated to him what they had been saying and told him, "This is what will be done for the man who kills him."

28When Eliab, David's oldest brother, heard him speaking with the men, he burned with anger at him and asked, "Why have you come down here? And with whom did you leave those few sheep in the desert? I know how conceited you are and how wicked your heart is; you came down only to watch the battle."

29"Now what have I done?" said David. "Can't I even speak?" 30He then turned away to someone else and brought up the same matter, and the men answered him as before. 31What David said was overheard and reported to Saul, and Saul sent for him.

32David said to Saul, "Let no one lose heart on account of this Philistine; your servant will go and fight him."

33Saul replied, "You are not able to go out against this Philistine and fight him; you are only a boy, and he has been a fighting man from his youth."

34But David said to Saul, "Your servant has been keeping his father's sheep. When a lion or a bear came and carried off a sheep from the flock, 35I went after it, struck it and rescued the sheep from its mouth. When it turned on me, I seized it by its hair, struck it and killed it. 36Your servant has killed both the lion and the bear; this uncircumcised Philistine will be like one of them, because he has defied the armies of the living God. 37The LORD who delivered me from the paw of the lion and the paw of the bear will deliver me from the hand of this Philistine."

Saul said to David, "Go, and the LORD be with you."

38Then Saul dressed David in his own tunic. He put a coat of armor on him and a bronze helmet on his head. 39David fastened on his sword over the tunic and tried walking around, because he was not used to them.

"I cannot go in these," he said to Saul, "because I am not used to them." So he took them off. 40Then he took his staff in his hand, chose five smooth stones from the stream, put them in the pouch of his shepherd's bag and, with his sling in his hand, approached the Philistine.

Living Bible

20So David left the sheep with another shepherd and took off early the next morning with the gifts. He arrived at the outskirts of the camp just as the Israeli army was leaving for the battlefield with shouts and battle cries. 21Soon the Israeli and Philistine forces stood facing each other, army against army. 22David left his luggage with a baggage officer and hurried out to the ranks to find his brothers. 23As he was talking with them, he saw Goliath the giant step out from the Philistine troops and shout his challenge to the army of Israel. 24As soon as they saw him the Israeli army began to run away in fright.

25"Have you seen the giant?" the soldiers were asking. "He has insulted the entire army of Israel. And have you heard about the huge reward the king has offered to anyone who kills him? And the king will give him one of his daughters for a wife, and his whole family will be exempted from paying taxes!"

26David talked to some others standing there to verify the report. "What will a man get for killing this Philistine and ending his insults to Israel?" he asked them. "Who is this heathen Philistine, anyway, that he is allowed to defy the armies of the living God?" 27And he received the same reply as before.

28But when David's oldest brother, Eliab, heard David talking like that, he was angry. "What are you doing around here, anyway?" he demanded. "What about the sheep you're supposed to be taking care of? I know what a cocky brat you are; you just want to see the battle!"

29"What have I done now?" David replied. "I was only asking a question!"

30And he walked over to some others and asked them the same thing and received the same answer. 31When it was finally realized what David meant, someone told King Saul, and the king sent for him.

32"Don't worry about a thing," David told him. "I'll take care of this Philistine!"

33"Don't be ridiculous!" Saul replied. "How can a kid like you fight with a man like him? You are only a boy and he has been in the army *since* he was a boy!"

34But David persisted. "When I am taking care of my father's sheep," he said, "and a lion or a bear comes and grabs a lamb from the flock, 35I go after it with a club and take the lamb from its mouth. If it turns on me I catch it by the jaw and club it to death. 36I have done this to both lions and bears, and I'll do it to this heathen Philistine too, for he has defied the armies of the living God! 37The Lord who saved me from the claws and teeth of the lion and the bear will save me from this Philistine!"

Saul finally consented, "All right, go ahead," he said, "and may the Lord be with you!"

38, 39Then Saul gave David his own armor—a bronze helmet and a coat of mail. David put it on, strapped the sword over it, and took a step or two to see what it was like, for he had never worn such things before. "I can hardly move!" he exclaimed, and took them off again. 40Then he picked up five smooth stones from a stream and put them in his shepherd's bag and, armed only with his shepherd's staff and sling, started across to Goliath.

New Revised Standard

20David rose early in the morning, left the sheep with a keeper, took the provisions, and went as Jesse had commanded him. He came to the encampment as the army was going forth to the battle line, shouting the war cry. 21Israel and the Philistines drew up for battle, army against army. 22David left the things in charge of the keeper of the baggage, ran to the ranks, and went and greeted his brothers. 23As he talked with them, the champion, the Philistine of Gath, Goliath by name, came up out of the ranks of the Philistines, and spoke the same words as before. And David heard him.

24 All the Israelites, when they saw the man, fled from him and were very much afraid. 25The Israelites said, "Have you seen this man who has come up? Surely he has come up to defy Israel. The king will greatly enrich the man who kills him, and will give him his daughter and make his family free in Israel." 26David said to the men who stood by him, "What shall be done for the man who kills this Philistine, and takes away the reproach from Israel? For who is this uncircumcised Philistine that he should defy the armies of the living God?" 27The people answered him in the same way, "So shall it be done for the man who kills him."

28 His eldest brother Eliab heard him talking to the men; and Eliab's anger was kindled against David. He said, "Why have you come down? With whom have you left those few sheep in the wilderness? I know your presumption and the evil of your heart; for you have come down just to see the battle." 29David said, "What have I done now? It was only a question." 30He turned away from him toward another and spoke in the same way; and the people answered him again as before.

31 When the words that David spoke were heard, they repeated them before Saul; and he sent for him. 32David said to Saul, "Let no one's heart fail because of him; your servant will go and fight with this Philistine." 33Saul said to David, "You are not able to go against this Philistine to fight with him; for you are just a boy, and he has been a warrior from his youth." 34But David said to Saul, "Your servant used to keep sheep for his father; and whenever a lion or a bear came, and took a lamb from the flock, 35I went after it and struck it down, rescuing the lamb from its mouth; and if it turned against me, I would catch it by the jaw, strike it down, and kill it. 36Your servant has killed both lions and bears; and this uncircumcised Philistine shall be like one of them, since he has defied the armies of the living God." 37David said, "The LORD, who saved me from the paw of the lion and from the paw of the bear, will save me from the hand of this Philistine." So Saul said to David, "Go, and may the LORD be with you!"

38 Saul clothed David with his armor; he put a bronze helmet on his head and clothed him with a coat of mail. 39David strapped Saul's sword over the armor, and he tried in vain to walk, for he was not used to them. Then David said to Saul, "I cannot walk with these; for I am not used to them." So David removed them. 40Then he took his staff in his hand, and chose five smooth stones from the wadi, and put them in his shepherd's bag, in the pouch; his sling was in his hand, and he drew near to the Philistine.

King James

41And the Philistine came on and drew near unto David; and the man that bare the shield *went* before him.

42And when the Philistine looked about, and saw David, he disdained him: for he was *but* a youth, and ruddy, and of a fair countenance.

43And the Philistine said unto David, *Am* I a dog, that thou comest to me with staves? And the Philistine cursed David by his gods.

44And the Philistine said to David, Come to me, and I will give thy flesh unto the fowls of the air, and to the beasts of the field.

45Then said David to the Philistine, Thou comest to me with a sword, and with a spear, and with a shield: but I come to thee in the name of the LORD of hosts, the God of the armies of Israel, whom thou hast defied.

46This day will the LORD deliver thee into mine hand; and I will smite thee, and take thine head from thee; and I will give the carcases of the host of the Philistines this day unto the fowls of the air, and to the wild beasts of the earth; that all the earth may know that there is a God in Israel.

47And all this assembly shall know that the LORD saveth not with sword and spear: for the battle *is* the LORD'S, and he will give you into our hands.

48And it came to pass, when the Philistine arose, and came and drew nigh to meet David, that David hasted, and ran toward the army to meet the Philistine.

49And David put his hand in his bag, and took thence a stone, and slang *it,* and smote the Philistine in his forehead, that the stone sunk into his forehead; and he fell upon his face to the earth.

50So David prevailed over the Philistine with a sling and with a stone, and smote the Philistine, and slew him; but *there was* no sword in the hand of David.

51Therefore David ran, and stood upon the Philistine, and took his sword, and drew it out of the sheath thereof, and slew him, and cut off his head therewith. And when the Philistines saw their champion was dead, they fled.

52And the men of Israel and of Judah arose, and shouted, and pursued the Philistines, until thou come to the valley, and to the gates of Ekron. And the wounded of the Philistines fell down by the way to Shaaraim, even unto Gath, and unto Ekron.

53And the children of Israel returned from chasing after the Philistines, and they spoiled their tents.

54And David took the head of the Philistine, and brought it to Jerusalem; but he put his armour in his tent.

55¶ And when Saul saw David go forth against the Philistine, he said unto Abner, the captain of the host, Abner, whose son *is* this youth? And Abner said, *As* thy soul liveth, O king, I cannot tell.

56And the king said, Inquire thou whose son the stripling *is.*

57And as David returned from the slaughter of the Philistine, Abner took him, and brought him before Saul with the head of the Philistine in his hand.

58And Saul said to him, Whose son *art* thou, *thou* young man? And David answered, *I am* the son of thy servant Jesse the Bethlehemite.

18 AND IT came to pass, when he had made an end of speaking unto Saul, that the soul of Jonathan was knit with the soul of David, and Jonathan loved him as his own soul.

2And Saul took him that day, and would let him go no more home to his father's house.

3Then Jonathan and David made a covenant, because he loved him as his own soul.

New International

41Meanwhile, the Philistine, with his shield bearer in front of him, kept coming closer to David. 42He looked David over and saw that he was only a boy, ruddy and handsome, and he despised him. 43He said to David, "Am I a dog, that you come at me with sticks?" And the Philistine cursed David by his gods. 44"Come here," he said, "and I'll give your flesh to the birds of the air and the beasts of the field!"

45David said to the Philistine, "You come against me with sword and spear and javelin, but I come against you in the name of the LORD Almighty, the God of the armies of Israel, whom you have defied. 46This day the LORD will hand you over to me, and I'll strike you down and cut off your head. Today I will give the carcasses of the Philistine army to the birds of the air and the beasts of the earth, and the whole world will know that there is a God in Israel. 47All those gathered here will know that it is not by sword or spear that the LORD saves; for the battle is the LORD's, and he will give all of you into our hands."

48As the Philistine moved closer to attack him, David ran quickly toward the battle line to meet him. 49Reaching into his bag and taking out a stone, he slung it and struck the Philistine on the forehead. The stone sank into his forehead, and he fell facedown on the ground.

50So David triumphed over the Philistine with a sling and a stone; without a sword in his hand he struck down the Philistine and killed him.

51David ran and stood over him. He took hold of the Philistine's sword and drew it from the scabbard. After he killed him, he cut off his head with the sword.

When the Philistines saw that their hero was dead, they turned and ran. 52Then the men of Israel and Judah surged forward with a shout and pursued the Philistines to the entrance of Gath[a] and to the gates of Ekron. Their dead were strewn along the Shaaraim road to Gath and Ekron. 53When the Israelites returned from chasing the Philistines, they plundered their camp. 54David took the Philistine's head and brought it to Jerusalem, and he put the Philistine's weapons in his own tent.

55As Saul watched David going out to meet the Philistine, he said to Abner, commander of the army, "Abner, whose son is that young man?"

Abner replied, "As surely as you live, O king, I don't know."

56The king said, "Find out whose son this young man is."

57As soon as David returned from killing the Philistine, Abner took him and brought him before Saul, with David still holding the Philistine's head.

58"Whose son are you, young man?" Saul asked him.

David said, "I am the son of your servant Jesse of Bethlehem."

Saul's Jealousy of David

18 AFTER DAVID had finished talking with Saul, Jonathan became one in spirit with David, and he loved him as himself. 2From that day Saul kept David with him and did not let him return to his father's house. 3And Jonathan made a covenant with David because he loved him as himself. 4Jonathan took off the robe he was

---

a 52 Some Septuagint manuscripts; Hebrew *a valley*

Living Bible

41, 42Goliath walked out towards David with his shield bearer ahead of him, sneering in contempt at this nice little red-cheeked boy!

43"Am I a dog," he roared at David, "that you come at me with a stick?" And he cursed David by the names of his gods. 44"Come over here and I'll give your flesh to the birds and wild animals," Goliath yelled.

45David shouted in reply, "You come to me with a sword and a spear, but I come to you in the name of the Lord of the armies of heaven and of Israel—the very God whom you have defied. 46Today the Lord will conquer you and I will kill you and cut off your head; and then I will give the dead bodies of *your* men to the birds and wild animals, and the whole world will know that there is a God in Israel! 47And Israel will learn that the Lord does not depend on weapons to fulfill his plans— he works without regard to human means! He will give you to us!"

48, 49As Goliath approached, David ran out to meet him and, reaching into his shepherd's bag, took out a stone, hurled it from his sling, and hit the Philistine in the forehead. The stone sank in, and the man fell on his face to the ground. 50, 51So David conquered the Philistine giant with a sling and a stone. Since he had no sword, he ran over and pulled Goliath's from its sheath and killed him with it, and then cut off his head. When the Philistines saw that their champion was dead, they turned and ran.

52Then the Israelis gave a great shout of triumph and rushed after the Philistines, chasing them as far as Gath and the gates of Ekron. The bodies of the dead and wounded Philistines were strewn all along the road to Shaaraim. 53Then the Israeli army returned and plundered the deserted Philistine camp.

54(Later David took Goliath's head to Jerusalem, but stored his armor in his tent.)

55As Saul was watching David go out to fight Goliath, he asked Abner, the general of his army, "Abner, what sort of family does this young fellow come from?"b

"I really don't know," Abner said.

56"Well, find out!" the king told him.

57After David had killed Goliath, Abner brought him to Saul with the Philistine's head still in his hand.

58"Tell me about your father, my boy," Saul said.

And David replied, "His name is Jesse and we live in Bethlehem."

18 AFTER KING Saul had finished his conversation with David, David met Jonathan, the king's son, and there was an immediate bond of love between them. Jonathan swore to be his blood brother,

New Revised Standard

41 The Philistine came on and drew near to David, with his shield-bearer in front of him. 42When the Philistine looked and saw David, he disdained him, for he was only a youth, ruddy and handsome in appearance. 43The Philistine said to David, "Am I a dog, that you come to me with sticks?" And the Philistine cursed David by his gods. 44The Philistine said to David, "Come to me, and I will give your flesh to the birds of the air and to the wild animals of the field." 45But David said to the Philistine, "You come to me with sword and spear and javelin; but I come to you in the name of the LORD of hosts, the God of the armies of Israel, whom you have defied. 46This very day the LORD will deliver you into my hand, and I will strike you down and cut off your head; and I will give the dead bodies of the Philistine army this very day to the birds of the air and to the wild animals of the earth, so that all the earth may know that there is a God in Israel, 47and that all this assembly may know that the LORD does not save by sword and spear; for the battle is the LORD's and he will give you into our hand."

48 When the Philistine drew nearer to meet David, David ran quickly toward the battle line to meet the Philistine. 49David put his hand in his bag, took out a stone, slung it, and struck the Philistine on his forehead; the stone sank into his forehead, and he fell face down on the ground.

50 So David prevailed over the Philistine with a sling and a stone, striking down the Philistine and killing him; there was no sword in David's hand. 51Then David ran and stood over the Philistine; he grasped his sword, drew it out of its sheath, and killed him; then he cut off his head with it.

When the Philistines saw that their champion was dead, they fled. 52The troops of Israel and Judah rose up with a shout and pursued the Philistines as far as Gathc and the gates of Ekron, so that the wounded Philistines fell on the way from Shaaraim as far as Gath and Ekron. 53The Israelites came back from chasing the Philistines, and they plundered their camp. 54David took the head of the Philistine and brought it to Jerusalem; but he put his armor in his tent.

55 When Saul saw David go out against the Philistine, he said to Abner, the commander of the army, "Abner, whose son is this young man?" Abner said, "As your soul lives, O king, I do not know." 56The king said, "Inquire whose son the stripling is." 57On David's return from killing the Philistine, Abner took him and brought him before Saul, with the head of the Philistine in his hand. 58Saul said to him, "Whose son are you, young man?" And David answered, "I am the son of your servant Jesse the Bethlehemite."

Jonathan's Covenant with David

18 WHEN DAVIDd had finished speaking to Saul, the soul of Jonathan was bound to the soul of David, and Jonathan loved him as his own soul. 2Saul took him that day and would not let him return to his father's house. 3Then Jonathan made a covenant with David, because he loved him as his own soul. 4Jonathan

---

b *17:55 What sort of family does this young fellow come from?* Literally, "Whose son is this?" Since David was, if successful, scheduled to marry Saul's daughter, Saul wanted to know more about his family! The other explanation of this confusing passage is that Saul's mental condition caused forgetfulness, so that he didn't recognize David.

c Gk Syr: Heb *Gai*   d Heb *he*

King James

4And Jonathan stripped himself of the robe that *was* upon him, and gave it to David, and his garments, even to his sword, and to his bow, and to his girdle.

5¶ And David went out whithersoever Saul sent him, *and* behaved himself wisely: and Saul set him over the men of war, and he was accepted in the sight of all the people, and also in the sight of Saul's servants.

6And it came to pass as they came, when David was returned from the slaughter of the Philistine, that the women came out of all cities of Israel, singing and dancing, to meet king Saul, with tabrets, with joy, and with instruments of music.

7And the women answered *one another* as they played, and said, Saul hath slain his thousands, and David his ten thousands.

8And Saul was very wroth, and the saying displeased him; and he said, They have ascribed unto David ten thousands, and to me they have ascribed *but* thousands: and *what* can he have more but the kingdom?

9And Saul eyed David from that day and forward.

10¶ And it came to pass on the morrow, that the evil spirit from God came upon Saul, and he prophesied in the midst of the house: and David played with his hand, as at other times: and *there was* a javelin in Saul's hand.

11And Saul cast the javelin; for he said, I will smite David even to the wall *with it.* And David avoided out of his presence twice.

12¶ And Saul was afraid of David, because the LORD was with him, and was departed from Saul.

13Therefore Saul removed him from him, and made him his captain over a thousand; and he went out and came in before the people.

14And David behaved himself wisely in all his ways; and the LORD *was* with him.

15Wherefore when Saul saw that he behaved himself very wisely, he was afraid of him.

16But all Israel and Judah loved David, because he went out and came in before them.

17¶ And Saul said to David, Behold my elder daughter Merab, her will I give thee to wife: only be thou valiant for me, and fight the LORD's battles. For Saul said, Let not mine hand be upon him, but let the hand of the Philistines be upon him.

18And David said unto Saul, Who *am* I? and what *is* my life, *or* my father's family in Israel, that I should be son-in-law to the king?

19But it came to pass at the time when Merab Saul's daughter should have been given to David, that she was given unto Adriel the Meholathite to wife.

20And Michal Saul's daughter loved David: and they told Saul, and the thing pleased him.

21And Saul said, I will give him her, that she may be a snare to him, and that the hand of the Philistines may be against him. Wherefore Saul said to David, Thou shalt this day be my son-in-law in *the one of* the twain.

22¶ And Saul commanded his servants, *saying,* Commune with David secretly, and say, Behold, the king hath delight in thee, and all his servants love thee: now therefore be the king's son-in-law.

23And Saul's servants spake those words in the ears of David. And David said, Seemeth it to you *a* light *thing* to be a king's son-in-law, seeing that I *am* a poor man, and lightly esteemed?

24And the servants of Saul told him, saying, On this manner spake David.

25And Saul said, Thus shall ye say to David, The king desireth not any dowry, but an hundred foreskins of the Philistines, to be avenged of the king's enemies. But Saul thought to make David fall by the hand of the Philistines.

26And when his servants told David these words, it pleased David well to be the king's son-in-law: and the days were not expired.

New International

wearing and gave it to David, along with his tunic, and even his sword, his bow and his belt.

5Whatever Saul sent him to do, David did it so successfullya that Saul gave him a high rank in the army. This pleased all the people, and Saul's officers as well.

6When the men were returning home after David had killed the Philistine, the women came out from all the towns of Israel to meet King Saul with singing and dancing, with joyful songs and with tambourines and lutes. 7As they danced, they sang:

"Saul has slain his thousands,
  and David his tens of thousands."

8Saul was very angry; this refrain galled him. "They have credited David with tens of thousands," he thought, "but me with only thousands. What more can he get but the kingdom?" 9And from that time on Saul kept a jealous eye on David.

10The next day an evilb spirit from God came forcefully upon Saul. He was prophesying in his house, while David was playing the harp, as he usually did. Saul had a spear in his hand 11and he hurled it, saying to himself, "I'll pin David to the wall." But David eluded him twice.

12Saul was afraid of David, because the LORD was with David but had left Saul. 13So he sent David away from him and gave him command over a thousand men, and David led the troops in their campaigns. 14In everything he did he had great success,c because the LORD was with him. 15When Saul saw how successfuld he was, he was afraid of him. 16But all Israel and Judah loved David, because he led them in their campaigns.

17Saul said to David, "Here is my older daughter Merab. I will give her to you in marriage; only serve me bravely and fight the battles of the LORD." For Saul said to himself, "I will not raise a hand against him. Let the Philistines do that!"

18But David said to Saul, "Who am I, and what is my family or my father's clan in Israel, that I should become the king's son-in-law?" 19Soe when the time came for Merab, Saul's daughter, to be given to David, she was given in marriage to Adriel of Meholah.

20Now Saul's daughter Michal was in love with David, and when they told Saul about it, he was pleased. 21"I will give her to him," he thought, "so that she may be a snare to him and so that the hand of the Philistines may be against him." So Saul said to David, "Now you have a second opportunity to become my son-in-law."

22Then Saul ordered his attendants: "Speak to David privately and say, 'Look, the king is pleased with you, and his attendants all like you; now become his son-in-law.' "

23They repeated these words to David. But David said, "Do you think it is a small matter to become the king's son-in-law? I'm only a poor man and little known."

24When Saul's servants told him what David had said, 25Saul replied, "Say to David, 'The king wants no other price for the bride than a hundred Philistine foreskins, to take revenge on his enemies.' " Saul's plan was to have David fall by the hands of the Philistines.

26When the attendants told David these things, he was pleased to become the king's son-in-law. So before the allotted time elapsed, 27David and his men went out

---

a *5 Or wisely*   b *10 Or injurious*   c *14 Or he was very wise*   d *15 Or wise*
e *19 Or However,*

Living Bible

4and sealed the pact by giving him his robe, sword, bow, and belt.

King Saul now kept David with him and wouldn't let him return home any more. 5He was Saul's special assistant, and he always carried out his assignments successfully. So Saul made him commander of his troops, an appointment which was applauded by the army and general public alike. 6But something had happened when the victorious Israeli army was returning home after David had killed Goliath. Women came out from all the towns along the way to celebrate and to cheer for King Saul, and were singing and dancing for joy with tambourines and cymbals.

7However, this was their song: "Saul has slain his thousands, and David his ten thousands!"

8Of course Saul was very angry. "What's this?" he said to himself. "They credit David with ten thousands and me with only thousands. Next they'll be making him their king!"

9So from that time on King Saul kept a jealous watch on David. 10The very next day, in fact, a tormenting spirit from God overwhelmed Saul, and he began to rave like a madman. David began to soothe him by playing the harp, as he did whenever this happened. But Saul, who was fiddling with his spear, 11, 12suddenly hurled it at David, intending to pin him to the wall. But David jumped aside and escaped. This happened another time, too, for Saul was afraid of him and jealous because the Lord had left him and was now with David. 13Finally Saul banned him from his presence and demoted him to the rank of captain. But the controversy put David more than ever in the public eye.

14David continued to succeed in everything he undertook, for the Lord was with him. 15, 16When King Saul saw this, he became even more afraid of him; but all Israel and Judah loved him, for he was as one of them.

17One day Saul said to David, "I am ready to give you my oldest daughter Merab as your wife. But first you must prove yourself to be a real soldier by fighting the Lord's battles." For Saul thought to himself, "I'll send him out against the Philistines and let them kill him rather than doing it myself."

18"Who am I that I should be the king's son-in-law?" David exclaimed. "My father's family is nothing!"

19But when the time arrived for the wedding, Saul married her to Adriel, a man from Meholath, instead. 20In the meantime Saul's daughter Michal had fallen in love with David, and Saul was delighted when he heard about it.

21"Here's another opportunity to see him killed by the Philistines!" Saul said to himself. But to David he said, "You can be my son-in-law after all, for I will give you my youngest daughter."

22Then Saul instructed his men to say confidentially to David that the king really liked him a lot, and that they all loved him and thought he should accept the king's proposition and become his son-in-law.

23But David replied, "How can a poor man like me from an unknown family find enough dowry to marry the daughter of a king?"

24When Saul's men reported this back to him, 25he told them, "Tell David that the only dowry I need is one hundred dead Philistines!f Vengeance on my enemies is all I want." But what Saul had in mind was that David would be killed in the fight.

26David was delighted to accept the offer. So, before the time limit expired, 27he and his men went out and

New Revised Standard

stripped himself of the robe that he was wearing, and gave it to David, and his armor, and even his sword and his bow and his belt. 5David went out and was successful wherever Saul sent him; as a result, Saul set him over the army. And all the people, even the servants of Saul, approved.

6 As they were coming home, when David returned from killing the Philistine, the women came out of all the towns of Israel, singing and dancing, to meet King Saul, with tambourines, with songs of joy, and with musical instruments.g 7And the women sang to one another as they made merry,

> "Saul has killed his thousands,
> and David his ten thousands."

8Saul was very angry, for this saying displeased him. He said, "They have ascribed to David ten thousands, and to me they have ascribed thousands; what more can he have but the kingdom?" 9So Saul eyed David from that day on.

Saul Tries to Kill David

10 The next day an evil spirit from God rushed upon Saul, and he raved within his house, while David was playing the lyre, as he did day by day. Saul had his spear in his hand; 11and Saul threw the spear, for he thought, "I will pin David to the wall." But David eluded him twice.

12 Saul was afraid of David, because the LORD was with him but had departed from Saul. 13So Saul removed him from his presence, and made him a commander of a thousand; and David marched out and came in, leading the army. 14David had success in all his undertakings; for the LORD was with him. 15When Saul saw that he had great success, he stood in awe of him. 16But all Israel and Judah loved David; for it was he who marched out and came in leading them.

David Marries Michal

17 Then Saul said to David, "Here is my elder daughter Merab; I will give her to you as a wife; only be valiant for me and fight the LORD's battles." For Saul thought, "I will not raise a hand against him; let the Philistines deal with him." 18David said to Saul, "Who am I and who are my kinsfolk, my father's family in Israel, that I should be son-in-law to the king?" 19But at the time when Saul's daughter Merab should have been given to David, she was given to Adriel the Meholathite as a wife.

20 Now Saul's daughter Michal loved David. Saul was told, and the thing pleased him. 21Saul thought, "Let me give her to him that she may be a snare for him and that the hand of the Philistines may be against him." Therefore Saul said to David a second time,h "You shall now be my son-in-law." 22Saul commanded his servants, "Speak to David in private and say, 'See, the king is delighted with you, and all his servants love you; now then, become the king's son-in-law.' " 23So Saul's servants reported these words to David in private. And David said, "Does it seem to you a little thing to become the king's son-in-law, seeing that I am a poor man and of no repute?" 24The servants of Saul told him, "This is what David said." 25Then Saul said, "Thus shall you say to David, 'The king desires no marriage present except a hundred foreskins of the Philistines, that he may be avenged on the king's enemies.' " Now Saul planned to make David fall by the hand of the Philistines. 26When his servants told David these words, David was well pleased to be the king's son-in-law. Before the time had expired, 27David rose and went, along with his men, and

---

f 18:25 one hundred dead Philistines, literally, "one hundred foreskins of the Philistines."

g Or triangles, or three-stringed instruments   h Heb by two

King James

27Wherefore David arose and went, he and his men, and slew of the Philistines two hundred men; and David brought their foreskins, and they gave them in full tale to the king, that he might be the king's son-in-law. And Saul gave him Michal his daughter to wife.

28¶ And Saul saw and knew that the LORD *was* with David, and *that* Michal Saul's daughter loved him.

29And Saul was yet the more afraid of David; and Saul became David's enemy continually.

30Then the princes of the Philistines went forth: and it came to pass, after they went forth, *that* David behaved himself more wisely than all the servants of Saul; so that his name was much set by.

19 AND SAUL spake to Jonathan his son, and to all his servants, that they should kill David. 2But Jonathan Saul's son delighted much in David: and Jonathan told David, saying, Saul my father seeketh to kill thee: now therefore, I pray thee, take heed to thyself until the morning, and abide in a secret *place,* and hide thyself:

3And I will go out and stand beside my father in the field where thou *art,* and I will commune with my father of thee; and what I see, that I will tell thee.

4¶ And Jonathan spake good of David unto Saul his father, and said unto him, Let not the king sin against his servant, against David; because he hath not sinned against thee, and because his works *have been* to thee-ward very good:

5For he did put his life in his hand, and slew the Philistine, and the LORD wrought a great salvation for all Israel: thou sawest *it,* and didst rejoice: wherefore then wilt thou sin against innocent blood, to slay David without a cause?

6And Saul hearkened unto the voice of Jonathan: and Saul sware, *As* the LORD liveth, he shall not be slain.

7And Jonathan called David, and Jonathan showed him all those things. And Jonathan brought David to Saul, and he was in his presence, as in times past.

8¶ And there was war again: and David went out, and fought with the Philistines, and slew them with a great slaughter; and they fled from him.

9And the evil spirit from the LORD was upon Saul, as he sat in his house with his javelin in his hand: and David played with *his* hand.

10And Saul sought to smite David even to the wall with the javelin; but he slipped away out of Saul's presence, and he smote the javelin into the wall: and David fled, and escaped that night.

11Saul also sent messengers unto David's house, to watch him, and to slay him in the morning: and Michal David's wife told him, saying, If thou save not thy life tonight, tomorrow thou shalt be slain.

12¶ So Michal let David down through a window: and he went, and fled, and escaped.

13And Michal took an image, and laid *it* in the bed, and put a pillow of goats' *hair* for his bolster, and covered *it* with a cloth.

14And when Saul sent messengers to take David, she said, He *is* sick.

15And Saul sent the messengers *again* to see David, saying, Bring him up to me in the bed, that I may slay him.

16And when the messengers were come in, behold, *there was* an image in the bed, with a pillow of goats' hair for his bolster.

17And Saul said unto Michal, Why hast thou deceived me so, and sent away mine enemy, that he is escaped? And Michal answered Saul, He said unto me, Let me go; why should I kill thee?

New International

and killed two hundred Philistines. He brought their foreskins and presented the full number to the king so that he might become the king's son-in-law. Then Saul gave him his daughter Michal in marriage.

28When Saul realized that the LORD was with David and that his daughter Michal loved David, 29Saul became still more afraid of him, and he remained his enemy the rest of his days.

30The Philistine commanders continued to go out to battle, and as often as they did, David met with more successa than the rest of Saul's officers, and his name became well known.

Saul Tries to Kill David

19 SAUL TOLD his son Jonathan and all the attendants to kill David. But Jonathan was very fond of David 2and warned him, "My father Saul is looking for a chance to kill you. Be on your guard tomorrow morning; go into hiding and stay there. 3I will go out and stand with my father in the field where you are. I'll speak to him about you and will tell you what I find out."

4Jonathan spoke well of David to Saul his father and said to him, "Let not the king do wrong to his servant David; he has not wronged you, and what he has done has benefited you greatly. 5He took his life in his hands when he killed the Philistine. The LORD won a great victory for all Israel, and you saw it and were glad. Why then would you do wrong to an innocent man like David by killing him for no reason?"

6Saul listened to Jonathan and took this oath: "As surely as the LORD lives, David will not be put to death."

7So Jonathan called David and told him the whole conversation. He brought him to Saul, and David was with Saul as before.

8Once more war broke out, and David went out and fought the Philistines. He struck them with such force that they fled before him.

9But an evilb spirit from the LORD came upon Saul as he was sitting in his house with his spear in his hand. While David was playing the harp, 10Saul tried to pin him to the wall with his spear, but David eluded him as Saul drove the spear into the wall. That night David made good his escape.

11Saul sent men to David's house to watch it and to kill him in the morning. But Michal, David's wife, warned him, "If you don't run for your life tonight, tomorrow you'll be killed." 12So Michal let David down through a window, and he fled and escaped. 13Then Michal took an idolc and laid it on the bed, covering it with a garment and putting some goats' hair at the head.

14When Saul sent the men to capture David, Michal said, "He is ill."

15Then Saul sent the men back to see David and told them, "Bring him up to me in his bed so that I may kill him." 16But when the men entered, there was the idol in the bed, and at the head was some goats' hair.

17Saul said to Michal, "Why did you deceive me like this and send my enemy away so that he escaped?"

Michal told him, "He said to me, 'Let me get away. Why should I kill you?' "

a *30* Or *David acted more wisely*   b *9* Or *injurious*   c *13* Hebrew *teraphim;* also in verse 16

Living Bible

killed two hundred Philistines and presented their foreskins to King Saul. So Saul gave Michal to him.

28When the king realized how much the Lord was with David and how immensely popular he was with all the people, 29he became even more afraid of him, and grew to hate him more with every passing day. 30Whenever the Philistine army attacked, David was more successful against them than all the rest of Saul's officers. So David's name became very famous throughout the land.

19 SAUL NOW urged his aides and his son Jonathan to assassinate David. But Jonathan, because of his close friendship with David, 2told him what his father was planning. "Tomorrow morning," he warned him, "you must find a hiding place out in the fields. 3I'll ask my father to go out there with me, and I'll talk to him about you; then I'll tell you everything I can find out."

4The next morningd as Jonathan and his father were talking together, he spoke well of David and begged him not to be against David.

"He's never done anything to harm you," Jonathan pleaded. "He has always helped you in any way he could. 5Have you forgotten about the time he risked his life to kill Goliath, and how the Lord brought a great victory to Israel as a result? You were certainly happy about it then. Why should you now murder an innocent man? There is no reason for it at all!"

6Finally Saul agreed, and vowed, "As the Lord lives, he shall not be killed."

7Afterwards Jonathan called David and told him what had happened. Then he took David to Saul and everything was as it had been before. 8War broke out shortly after that and David led his troops against the Philistines and slaughtered many of them, and put to flight their entire army.

9, 10But one day as Saul was sitting at home, listening to David playing the harp, suddenly the tormenting spirit from the Lord attacked him. He had his spear in his hand, and hurled it at David in an attempt to kill him. But David dodged out of the way and fled into the night, leaving the spear imbedded in the timber of the wall. 11Saul sent troops to watch David's house and kill him when he came out in the morning.

"If you don't get away tonight," Michal warned him, "you'll be dead by morning."

12So she helped him get down to the ground through a window. 13Then she took an idole and put it in his bed, and covered it with blankets, with its head on a pillow of goat's hair. 14When the soldiers came to arrest David and take him to Saul,f she told them he was sick and couldn't get out of bed. 15Saul said to bring him in his bed, then, so that he could kill him. 16But when they came to carry him out, they discovered that it was only an idol!

17"Why have you deceived me and let my enemy escape?" Saul demanded of Michal.

"I had to," Michal replied. "He threatened to kill me if I didn't help him."

New Revised Standard

killed one hundredg of the Philistines; and David brought their foreskins, which were given in full number to the king, that he might become the king's son-in-law. Saul gave him his daughter Michal as a wife. 28But when Saul realized that the LORD was with David, and that Saul's daughter Michal loved him, 29Saul was still more afraid of David. So Saul was David's enemy from that time forward.

30 Then the commanders of the Philistines came out to battle; and as often as they came out, David had more success than all the servants of Saul, so that his fame became very great.

Jonathan Intercedes for David

19 SAUL SPOKE with his son Jonathan and with all his servants about killing David. But Saul's son Jonathan took great delight in David. 2Jonathan told David, "My father Saul is trying to kill you; therefore be on guard tomorrow morning; stay in a secret place and hide yourself. 3I will go out and stand beside my father in the field where you are, and I will speak to my father about you; if I learn anything I will tell you." 4Jonathan spoke well of David to his father Saul, saying to him, "The king should not sin against his servant David, because he has not sinned against you, and because his deeds have been of good service to you; 5for he took his life in his hand when he attacked the Philistine, and the LORD brought about a great victory for all Israel. You saw it, and rejoiced; why then will you sin against an innocent person by killing David without cause?" 6Saul heeded the voice of Jonathan; Saul swore, "As the LORD lives, he shall not be put to death." 7So Jonathan called David and related all these things to him. Jonathan then brought David to Saul, and he was in his presence as before.

Michal Helps David Escape from Saul

8 Again there was war, and David went out to fight the Philistines. He launched a heavy attack on them, so that they fled before him. 9Then an evil spirit from the LORD came upon Saul, as he sat in his house with his spear in his hand, while David was playing music. 10Saul sought to pin David to the wall with the spear; but he eluded Saul, so that he struck the spear into the wall. David fled and escaped that night.

11 Saul sent messengers to David's house to keep watch over him, planning to kill him in the morning. David's wife Michal told him, "If you do not save your life tonight, tomorrow you will be killed." 12So Michal let David down through the window; he fled away and escaped. 13Michal took an idolh and laid it on the bed; she put a neti of goats' hair on its head, and covered it with the clothes. 14When Saul sent messengers to take David, she said, "He is sick." 15Then Saul sent the messengers to see David for themselves. He said, "Bring him up to me in the bed, that I may kill him." 16When the messengers came in, the idolj was in the bed, with the coveringi of goats' hair on its head. 17Saul said to Michal, "Why have you deceived me like this, and let my enemy go, so that he has escaped?" Michal answered Saul, "He said to me, 'Let me go; why should I kill you?'"

---

d 19:4 the next morning, implied.   e 19:13 an idol, literally, "teraphim."
f 19:14 When the soldiers came to arrest David and take him to Saul, implied.

g Gk Compare 2 Sam 3.14: Heb two hundred   h Heb took the teraphim
i Meaning of Heb uncertain   j Heb the teraphim

King James

18¶ So David fled, and escaped, and came to Samuel to Ramah, and told him all that Saul had done to him. And he and Samuel went and dwelt in Naioth.

19And it was told Saul, saying, Behold, David *is* at Naioth in Ramah.

20And Saul sent messengers to take David: and when they saw the company of the prophets prophesying, and Samuel standing *as* appointed over them, the spirit of God was upon the messengers of Saul, and they also prophesied.

21And when it was told Saul, he sent other messengers, and they prophesied likewise. And Saul sent messengers again the third time, and they prophesied also.

22Then went he also to Ramah, and came to a great well that *is* in Sechu: and he asked and said, Where *are* Samuel and David? And *one* said, Behold, *they be* at Naioth in Ramah.

23And he went thither to Naioth in Ramah: and the spirit of God was upon him also, and he went on, and prophesied, until he came to Naioth in Ramah.

24And he stripped off his clothes also, and prophesied before Samuel in like manner, and lay down naked all that day and all that night. Wherefore they say, *Is* Saul also among the prophets?

20 AND DAVID fled from Naioth in Ramah, and came and said before Jonathan, What have I done? what *is* mine iniquity? and what *is* my sin before thy father, that he seeketh my life?

2And he said unto him, God forbid; thou shalt not die: behold, my father will do nothing either great or small, but that he will show it me: and why should my father hide this thing from me? it *is* not *so.*

3And David sware moreover, and said, Thy father certainly knoweth that I have found grace in thine eyes; and he saith, Let not Jonathan know this, lest he be grieved: but truly *as* the LORD liveth, and *as* thy soul liveth, *there is* but a step between me and death.

4Then said Jonathan unto David, Whatsoever thy soul desireth, I will even do *it* for thee.

5And David said unto Jonathan, Behold, tomorrow *is* the new moon, and I should not fail to sit with the king at meat: but let me go, that I may hide myself in the field unto the third *day* at even.

6If thy father at all miss me, then say, David earnestly asked *leave* of me that he might run to Bethlehem his city: for *there is* a yearly sacrifice there for all the family.

7If he say thus, *It is* well; thy servant shall have peace: but if he be very wroth, *then* be sure that evil is determined by him.

8Therefore thou shalt deal kindly with thy servant; for thou hast brought thy servant into a covenant of the LORD with thee: notwithstanding, if there be in me iniquity, slay me thyself; for why shouldest thou bring me to thy father?

9And Jonathan said, Far be it from thee: for if I knew certainly that evil were determined by my father to come upon thee, then would not I tell it thee?

10Then said David to Jonathan, Who shall tell me? or what *if* thy father answer thee roughly?

11¶ And Jonathan said unto David, Come, and let us go out into the field. And they went out both of them into the field.

12And Jonathan said unto David, O LORD God of Israel, when I have sounded my father about tomorrow any time, *or* the third *day,* and, behold, *if there be* good toward David, and I then send not unto thee, and show it thee;

New International

18When David had fled and made his escape, he went to Samuel at Ramah and told him all that Saul had done to him. Then he and Samuel went to Naioth and stayed there. 19Word came to Saul: "David is in Naioth at Ramah"; 20so he sent men to capture him. But when they saw a group of prophets prophesying, with Samuel standing there as their leader, the Spirit of God came upon Saul's men and they also prophesied. 21Saul was told about it, and he sent more men, and they prophesied too. Saul sent men a third time, and they also prophesied. 22Finally, he himself left for Ramah and went to the great cistern at Secu. And he asked, "Where are Samuel and David?"

"Over in Naioth at Ramah," they said.

23So Saul went to Naioth at Ramah. But the Spirit of God came even upon him, and he walked along prophesying until he came to Naioth. 24He stripped off his robes and also prophesied in Samuel's presence. He lay that way all that day and night. This is why people say, "Is Saul also among the prophets?"

David and Jonathan

20 THEN DAVID fled from Naioth at Ramah and went to Jonathan and asked, "What have I done? What is my crime? How have I wronged your father, that he is trying to take my life?"

2"Never!" Jonathan replied. "You are not going to die! Look, my father doesn't do anything, great or small, without confiding in me. Why would he hide this from me? It's not so!"

3But David took an oath and said, "Your father knows very well that I have found favor in your eyes, and he has said to himself, 'Jonathan must not know this or he will be grieved.' Yet as surely as the LORD lives and as you live, there is only a step between me and death."

4Jonathan said to David, "Whatever you want me to do, I'll do for you."

5So David said, "Look, tomorrow is the New Moon festival, and I am supposed to dine with the king; but let me go and hide in the field until the evening of the day after tomorrow. 6If your father misses me at all, tell him, 'David earnestly asked my permission to hurry to Bethlehem, his hometown, because an annual sacrifice is being made there for his whole clan.' 7If he says, 'Very well,' then your servant is safe. But if he loses his temper, you can be sure that he is determined to harm me. 8As for you, show kindness to your servant, for you have brought him into a covenant with you before the LORD. If I am guilty, then kill me yourself! Why hand me over to your father?"

9"Never!" Jonathan said. "If I had the least inkling that my father was determined to harm you, wouldn't I tell you?"

10David asked, "Who will tell me if your father answers you harshly?"

11"Come," Jonathan said, "let's go out into the field." So they went there together.

12Then Jonathan said to David: "By the LORD, the God of Israel, I will surely sound out my father by this time the day after tomorrow! If he is favorably disposed toward you, will I not send you word and let you know?

Living Bible

18In that way David got away and went to Ramah to see Samuel, and told him all that Saul had done to him. So Samuel took David with him to live at Naioth. 19When the report reached Saul that David was at Naioth in Ramah, 20he sent soldiers to capture him; but when they arrived and saw Samuel and the other prophets prophesying, the Spirit of God came upon them and they also began to prophesy. 21When Saul heard what had happened, he sent other soldiers, but they too prophesied! The same thing happened a third time! 22Then Saul himself went to Ramah and arrived at the great well in Secu.

"Where are Samuel and David?" he demanded.

Someone told him they were at Naioth. 23But on the way to Naioth the Spirit of God came upon Saul, and he too began to prophesy! 24He tore off his clothes and lay naked all day and all night, prophesying with Samuel's prophets. Saul's men were incredulous!

"What!" they exclaimed. "Is Saul a prophet, too?"a

20 DAVID NOW fled from Naioth in Ramah, and found Jonathan.

"What have I done?" he exclaimed. "Why is your father so determined to kill me?"

2"That's not true!" Jonathan protested. "I'm sure he's not planning any such thing, for he always tells me everything he's going to do, even little things, and I know he wouldn't hide something like this from me. It just isn't so."

3"Of course you don't know about it!" David fumed. "Your father knows perfectly well about our friendship, so he has said to himself, 'I'll not tell Jonathan—why should I hurt him?' But the truth is that I am only a step away from death! I swear it by the Lord and by your own soul!"

4"Tell me what I can do," Jonathan begged.

5And David replied, "Tomorrow is the beginning of the celebration of the new moon. Always before, I've been with your father for this occasion, but tomorrow I'll hide in the field and stay there until the evening of the third day. 6If your father asks where I am, tell him that I asked permission to go home to Bethlehem for an annual family reunion. 7If he says, 'Fine!' then I'll know that all is well. But if he is angry, then I'll know that he is planning to kill me. 8Do this for me as my sworn brother. Or else kill me yourself if I have sinned against your father, but don't betray me to him!"

9"Of course not!" Jonathan exclaimed. "Look, wouldn't I say so if I knew that my father was planning to kill you?"

10Then David asked, "How will I know whether or not your father is angry?"

11"Come out to the field with me," Jonathan replied. And they went out there together.

12Then Jonathan told David, "I promise by the Lord God of Israel that about this time tomorrow, or the next day at the latest, I will talk to my father about you and let you know at once how he feels about you. 13If he is

New Revised Standard

David Joins Samuel in Ramah

18 Now David fled and escaped; he came to Samuel at Ramah, and told him all that Saul had done to him. He and Samuel went and settled at Naioth. 19Saul was told, "David is at Naioth in Ramah." 20Then Saul sent messengers to take David. When they saw the company of the prophets in a frenzy, with Samuel standing in charge ofb them, the spirit of God came upon the messengers of Saul, and they also fell into a prophetic frenzy. 21When Saul was told, he sent other messengers, and they also fell into a frenzy. Saul sent messengers again the third time, and they also fell into a frenzy. 22Then he himself went to Ramah. He came to the great well that is in Secu;c he asked, "Where are Samuel and David?" And someone said, "They are at Naioth in Ramah." 23He went there, toward Naioth in Ramah; and the spirit of God came upon him. As he was going, he fell into a prophetic frenzy, until he came to Naioth in Ramah. 24He too stripped off his clothes, and he too fell into a frenzy before Samuel. He lay naked all that day and all that night. Therefore it is said, "Is Saul also among the prophets?"

The Friendship of David and Jonathan

20 DAVID FLED from Naioth in Ramah. He came before Jonathan and said, "What have I done? What is my guilt? And what is my sin against your father that he is trying to take my life?" 2He said to him, "Far from it! You shall not die. My father does nothing either great or small without disclosing it to me; and why should my father hide this from me? Never!" 3But David also swore, "Your father knows well that you like me; and he thinks, 'Do not let Jonathan know this, or he will be grieved.' But truly, as the LORD lives and as you yourself live, there is but a step between me and death." 4Then Jonathan said to David, "Whatever you say, I will do for you." 5David said to Jonathan, "Tomorrow is the new moon, and I should not fail to sit with the king at the meal; but let me go, so that I may hide in the field until the third evening. 6If your father misses me at all, then say, 'David earnestly asked leave of me to run to Bethlehem his city; for there is a yearly sacrifice there for all the family.' 7If he says, 'Good!' it will be well with your servant; but if he is angry, then know that evil has been determined by him. 8Therefore deal kindly with your servant, for you have brought your servant into a sacred covenantd with you. But if there is guilt in me, kill me yourself; why should you bring me to your father?" 9Jonathan said, "Far be it from you! If I knew that it was decided by my father that evil should come upon you, would I not tell you?" 10Then David said to Jonathan, "Who will tell me if your father answers you harshly?" 11Jonathan replied to David, "Come, let us go out into the field." So they both went out into the field.

12 Jonathan said to David, "By the LORD, the God of Israel! When I have sounded out my father, about this time tomorrow, or on the third day, if he is well disposed toward David, shall I not then send and disclose it to you? 13But if my father intends to do you harm, the

---

a 19:24 Is Saul a prophet, too? implied. Literally, "Hence it is said, 'Is Saul also among the prophets?' " (See 10:10-12.)

b Meaning of Heb uncertain   c Gk reads to the well of the threshing floor on the bare height   d Heb a covenant of the LORD

King James

13The LORD do so and much more to Jonathan: but if it please my father *to do* thee evil, then I will show it thee, and send thee away, that thou mayest go in peace: and the LORD be with thee, as he hath been with my father.

14And thou shalt not only while yet I live show me the kindness of the LORD, that I die not:

15But *also* thou shalt not cut off thy kindness from my house for ever: no, not when the LORD hath cut off the enemies of David every one from the face of the earth.

16So Jonathan made *a covenant* with the house of David, *saying,* Let the LORD even require *it* at the hand of David's enemies.

17And Jonathan caused David to swear again, because he loved him: for he loved him as he loved his own soul.

18Then Jonathan said to David, Tomorrow *is* the new moon: and thou shalt be missed, because thy seat will be empty.

19And *when* thou hast stayed three days, *then* thou shalt go down quickly, and come to the place where thou didst hide thyself when the business was *in hand,* and shalt remain by the stone Ezel.

20And I will shoot three arrows on the side *thereof,* as though I shot at a mark.

21And, behold, I will send a lad, *saying,* Go, find out the arrows. If I expressly say unto the lad, Behold, the arrows *are* on this side of thee, take them; then come thou: for *there is* peace to thee, and no hurt; *as* the LORD liveth.

22But if I say thus unto the young man, Behold, the arrows *are* beyond thee; go thy way: for the LORD hath sent thee away.

23And *as touching* the matter which thou and I have spoken of, behold, the LORD *be* between thee and me for ever.

24¶ So David hid himself in the field: and when the new moon was come, the king sat him down to eat meat.

25And the king sat upon his seat, as at other times, *even* upon a seat by the wall: and Jonathan arose, and Abner sat by Saul's side, and David's place was empty.

26Nevertheless Saul spake not any thing that day: for he thought, Something hath befallen him, he *is* not clean; surely he *is* not clean.

27And it came to pass on the morrow, *which was* the second *day* of the month, that David's place was empty: and Saul said unto Jonathan his son, Wherefore cometh not the son of Jesse to meat, neither yesterday, nor to-day?

28And Jonathan answered Saul, David earnestly asked *leave* of me *to go* to Bethlehem:

29And he said, Let me go, I pray thee; for our family hath a sacrifice in the city; and my brother, he hath commanded me *to be there:* and now, if I have found favour in thine eyes, let me get away, I pray thee, and see my brethren. Therefore he cometh not unto the king's table.

30Then Saul's anger was kindled against Jonathan, and he said unto him, Thou son of the perverse rebellious *woman,* do not I know that thou hast chosen the son of Jesse to thine own confusion, and unto the confusion of thy mother's nakedness?

31For as long as the son of Jesse liveth upon the ground, thou shalt not be established, nor thy kingdom. Wherefore now send and fetch him unto me, for he shall surely die.

32And Jonathan answered Saul his father, and said unto him, Wherefore shall he be slain? what hath he done?

33And Saul cast a javelin at him to smite him: whereby Jonathan knew that it was determined of his father to slay David.

New International

13But if my father is inclined to harm you, may the LORD deal with me, be it ever so severely, if I do not let you know and send you away safely. May the LORD be with you as he has been with my father. 14But show me unfailing kindness like that of the LORD as long as I live, so that I may not be killed, 15and do not ever cut off your kindness from my family—not even when the LORD has cut off every one of David's enemies from the face of the earth.

16So Jonathan made a covenant with the house of David, saying, "May the LORD call David's enemies to account." 17And Jonathan had David reaffirm his oath out of love for him, because he loved him as he loved himself.

18Then Jonathan said to David: "Tomorrow is the New Moon festival. You will be missed, because your seat will be empty. 19The day after tomorrow, toward evening, go to the place where you hid when this trouble began, and wait by the stone Ezel. 20I will shoot three arrows to the side of it, as though I were shooting at a target. 21Then I will send a boy and say, 'Go, find the arrows.' If I say to him, 'Look, the arrows are on this side of you; bring them here,' then come, because, as surely as the LORD lives, you are safe; there is no danger. 22But if I say to the boy, 'Look, the arrows are beyond you,' then you must go, because the LORD has sent you away. 23And about the matter you and I discussed—remember, the LORD is witness between you and me forever."

24So David hid in the field, and when the New Moon festival came, the king sat down to eat. 25He sat in his customary place by the wall, opposite Jonathan,a and Abner sat next to Saul, but David's place was empty. 26Saul said nothing that day, for he thought, "Something must have happened to David to make him ceremonially unclean—surely he is unclean." 27But the next day, the second day of the month, David's place was empty again. Then Saul said to his son Jonathan, "Why hasn't the son of Jesse come to the meal, either yesterday or today?"

28Jonathan answered, "David earnestly asked me for permission to go to Bethlehem. 29He said, 'Let me go, because our family is observing a sacrifice in the town and my brother has ordered me to be there. If I have found favor in your eyes, let me get away to see my brothers.' That is why he has not come to the king's table."

30Saul's anger flared up at Jonathan and he said to him, "You son of a perverse and rebellious woman! Don't I know that you have sided with the son of Jesse to your own shame and to the shame of the mother who bore you? 31As long as the son of Jesse lives on this earth, neither you nor your kingdom will be established. Now send and bring him to me, for he must die!"

32"Why should he be put to death? What has he done?" Jonathan asked his father. 33But Saul hurled his spear at him to kill him. Then Jonathan knew that his father intended to kill David.

---

a 25 Septuagint; Hebrew *wall. Jonathan arose*

Living Bible

angry and wants you killed, then may the Lord kill me if I don't tell you, so you can escape and live. May the Lord be with you as he used to be with my father. ¹⁴And remember, you must demonstrate the love and kindness of the Lord not only to me during my own lifetime, ¹⁵but also to my children after the Lord has destroyed all of your enemies.

¹⁶So Jonathan made a covenant with the family of David, and David swore to it with a terrible curse against himself and his descendants, should he be unfaithful to his promise. ¹⁷But Jonathan made David swear to it again, this time by his love for him, for he loved him as much as he loved himself.

¹⁸Then Jonathan said, "Yes, they will miss you tomorrow when your place at the table is empty. ¹⁹By the day after tomorrow, everyone will be asking about you, so be at the hideout where you were before, over by the stone pile. ²⁰I will come out and shoot three arrows in front of the pile as though I were shooting at a target. ²¹Then I'll send a lad to bring the arrows back. If you hear me tell him, 'They're on this side,' then you will know that all is well and that there is no trouble. ²²But if I tell him, 'Go farther—the arrows are still ahead of you,' then it will mean that you must leave immediately. ²³And may the Lord make us keep our promises to each other, for he has witnessed them."ᵇ

²⁴, ²⁵So David hid himself in the field.

When the new moon celebration began, the king sat down to eat at his usual place against the wall. Jonathan sat opposite him and Abner was sitting beside Saul, but David's place was empty. ²⁶Saul didn't say anything about it that day, for he supposed that something had happened so that David was ceremonially impure. Yes, surely that must be it! ²⁷But when his place was still empty the next day, Saul asked Jonathan, "Why hasn't David been here for dinner either yesterday or today?"

²⁸, ²⁹"He asked me if he could go to Bethlehem to take part in a family celebration," Jonathan replied. "His brother demanded that he be there, so I told him to go ahead."

³⁰Saul boiled with rage. "You fool!"ᶜ he yelled at him. "Do you think I don't know that you want this son of a nobodyᵈ to be king in your place, shaming yourself and your mother? ³¹As long as that fellow is alive, you'll never be king. Now go and get him so I can kill him!"

³²"But what has he done?" Jonathan demanded. "Why should he be put to death?"

³³Then Saul hurled his spear at Jonathan, intending to kill him; so at last Jonathan realized that his father really meant it when he said David must die. ³⁴Jonathan

New Revised Standard

LORD do so to Jonathan, and more also, if I do not disclose it to you, and send you away, so that you may go in safety. May the LORD be with you, as he has been with my father. ¹⁴If I am still alive, show me the faithful love of the LORD; but if I die,ᵉ ¹⁵never cut off your faithful love from my house, even if the LORD were to cut off every one of the enemies of David from the face of the earth." ¹⁶Thus Jonathan made a covenant with the house of David, saying, "May the LORD seek out the enemies of David." ¹⁷Jonathan made David swear again by his love for him; for he loved him as he loved his own life.

18 Jonathan said to him, "Tomorrow is the new moon; you will be missed, because your place will be empty. ¹⁹On the day after tomorrow, you shall go a long way down; go to the place where you hid yourself earlier, and remain beside the stone there.ᵉ ²⁰I will shoot three arrows to the side of it, as though I shot at a mark. ²¹Then I will send the boy, saying, 'Go, find the arrows.' If I say to the boy, 'Look, the arrows are on this side of you, collect them,' then you are to come, for, as the LORD lives, it is safe for you and there is no danger. ²²But if I say to the young man, 'Look, the arrows are beyond you,' then go; for the LORD has sent you away. ²³As for the matter about which you and I have spoken, the LORD is witnessᶠ between you and me forever."

24 So David hid himself in the field. When the new moon came, the king sat at the feast to eat. ²⁵The king sat upon his seat, as at other times, upon the seat by the wall. Jonathan stood, while Abner sat by Saul's side; but David's place was empty.

26 Saul did not say anything that day; for he thought, "Something has befallen him; he is not clean, surely he is not clean." ²⁷But on the second day, the day after the new moon, David's place was empty. And Saul said to his son Jonathan, "Why has the son of Jesse not come to the feast, either yesterday or today?" ²⁸Jonathan answered Saul, "David earnestly asked leave of me to go to Bethlehem; ²⁹he said, 'Let me go; for our family is holding a sacrifice in the city, and my brother has commanded me to be there. So now, if I have found favor in your sight, let me get away, and see my brothers.' For this reason he has not come to the king's table."

30 Then Saul's anger was kindled against Jonathan. He said to him, "You son of a perverse, rebellious woman! Do I not know that you have chosen the son of Jesse to your own shame, and to the shame of your mother's nakedness? ³¹For as long as the son of Jesse lives upon the earth, neither you nor your kingdom shall be established. Now send and bring him to me, for he shall surely die." ³²Then Jonathan answered his father Saul, "Why should he be put to death? What has he done?" ³³But Saul threw his spear at him to strike him; so Jonathan knew that it was the decision of his father to put David to death. ³⁴Jonathan rose from the table in fierce

---

ᵇ 20:23 for he has witnessed them, literally, "The Lord is our mediator forever." ᶜ 20:30 You fool, literally, "Son of a perverse, rebellious woman." The modern equivalent is "son of a bitch." ᵈ 20:30 this son of a nobody, literally, "son of Jesse."

ᵉ Meaning of Heb uncertain   ᶠ Gk: Heb lacks witness

King James

34So Jonathan arose from the table in fierce anger, and did eat no meat the second day of the month: for he was grieved for David, because his father had done him shame.

35¶ And it came to pass in the morning, that Jonathan went out into the field at the time appointed with David, and a little lad with him.

36And he said unto his lad, Run, find out now the arrows which I shoot. *And* as the lad ran, he shot an arrow beyond him.

37And when the lad was come to the place of the arrow which Jonathan had shot, Jonathan cried after the lad, and said, *Is* not the arrow beyond thee?

38And Jonathan cried after the lad, Make speed, haste, stay not. And Jonathan's lad gathered up the arrows, and came to his master.

39But the lad knew not any thing: only Jonathan and David knew the matter.

40And Jonathan gave his artillery unto his lad, and said unto him, Go, carry *them* to the city.

41¶ *And* as soon as the lad was gone, David arose out of *a place* toward the south, and fell on his face to the ground, and bowed himself three times: and they kissed one another, and wept one with another, until David exceeded.

42And Jonathan said to David, Go in peace, forasmuch as we have sworn both of us in the name of the LORD, saying, The LORD be between me and thee, and between my seed and thy seed for ever. And he arose and departed: and Jonathan went into the city.

21 THEN CAME David to Nob to Ahimelech the priest: and Ahimelech was afraid at the meeting of David, and said unto him, Why *art* thou alone, and no man with thee?

2And David said unto Ahimelech the priest, The king hath commanded me a business, and hath said unto me, Let no man know any thing of the business whereabout I send thee, and what I have commanded thee: and I have appointed *my* servants to such and such a place.

3Now therefore what is under thine hand? give *me* five *loaves of* bread in mine hand, or what there is present.

4And the priest answered David, and said, There is no common bread under mine hand, but there is hallowed bread; if the young men have kept themselves at least from women.

5And David answered the priest, and said unto him, Of a truth women *have been* kept from us about these three days, since I came out, and the vessels of the young men are holy, and *the bread is* in a manner common, yea, though it were sanctified this day in the vessel.

6So the priest gave him hallowed *bread:* for there was no bread there but the showbread, that was taken from before the LORD, to put hot bread in the day when it was taken away.

7Now a certain man of the servants of Saul *was* there that day, detained before the LORD; and his name *was* Doeg, an Edomite, the chiefest of the herdmen that *belonged* to Saul.

8¶ And David said unto Ahimelech, And is there not here under thine hand spear or sword? for I have neither brought my sword nor my weapons with me, because the king's business required haste.

9And the priest said, The sword of Goliath the Philistine, whom thou slewest in the valley of Elah, behold, it *is here* wrapped in a cloth behind the ephod: if thou wilt take that, take *it:* for *there is* no other save that here. And David said, *There is* none like that; give it me.

New International

34Jonathan got up from the table in fierce anger; on that second day of the month he did not eat, because he was grieved at his father's shameful treatment of David.

35In the morning Jonathan went out to the field for his meeting with David. He had a small boy with him, 36and he said to the boy, "Run and find the arrows I shoot." As the boy ran, he shot an arrow beyond him. 37When the boy came to the place where Jonathan's arrow had fallen, Jonathan called out after him, "Isn't the arrow beyond you?" 38Then he shouted, "Hurry! Go quickly! Don't stop!" The boy picked up the arrow and returned to his master. 39(The boy knew nothing of all this; only Jonathan and David knew.) 40Then Jonathan gave his weapons to the boy and said, "Go, carry them back to town."

41After the boy had gone, David got up from the south side of the stone, and bowed down before Jonathan three times, with his face to the ground. Then they kissed each other and wept together—but David wept the most.

42Jonathan said to David, "Go in peace, for we have sworn friendship with each other in the name of the LORD, saying, 'The LORD is witness between you and me, and between your descendants and my descendants forever.'" Then David left, and Jonathan went back to the town.

David at Nob

21 DAVID WENT to Nob, to Ahimelech the priest. Ahimelech trembled when he met him, and asked, "Why are you alone? Why is no one with you?"

2David answered Ahimelech the priest, "The king charged me with a certain matter and said to me, 'No one is to know anything about your mission and your instructions.' As for my men, I have told them to meet me at a certain place. 3Now then, what do you have on hand? Give me five loaves of bread, or whatever you can find."

4But the priest answered David, "I don't have any ordinary bread on hand; however, there is some consecrated bread here—provided the men have kept themselves from women."

5David replied, "Indeed women have been kept from us, as usual whenevera I set out. The men's thingsb are holy even on missions that are not holy. How much more so today!" 6So the priest gave him the consecrated bread, since there was no bread there except the bread of the Presence that had been removed from before the LORD and replaced by hot bread on the day it was taken away.

7Now one of Saul's servants was there that day, detained before the LORD; he was Doeg the Edomite, Saul's head shepherd.

8David asked Ahimelech, "Don't you have a spear or a sword here? I haven't brought my sword or any other weapon, because the king's business was urgent."

9The priest replied, "The sword of Goliath the Philistine, whom you killed in the Valley of Elah, is here; it is wrapped in a cloth behind the ephod. If you want it, take it; there is no sword here but that one."

David said, "There is none like it; give it to me."

---

a 5 Or *from us in the past few days since*   b 5 Or *bodies*

Living Bible

left the table in fierce anger and refused to eat all that day, for he was crushed by his father's shameful behavior toward David.

35The next morning, as agreed, Jonathan went out into the field and took a young boy with him to gather his arrows.

36"Start running," he told the boy, "so that you can find the arrows as I shoot them." So the boy ran and Jonathan shot an arrow beyond him. 37When the boy had almost reached the arrow, Jonathan shouted, "The arrow is still ahead of you. 38Hurry, hurry, don't wait." So the boy quickly gathered up the arrows and ran back to his master. 39He, of course, didn't understand what Jonathan meant; only Jonathan and David knew. 40Then Jonathan gave his bow and arrows to the boy and told him to take them back to the city.

41As soon as he was gone, David came out from where he had been hiding near the south edge of the field. Both of them were crying as they said goodbye, especially David.c 42At last Jonathan said to David, "Cheer up, for we have entrusted each other and each other's children into God's hands forever." So they parted, David going away and Jonathan returning to the city.

21 DAVID WENT to the city of Nob to see Ahimelech, the priest. Ahimelech trembled when he saw him.

"Why are you alone?" he asked. "Why is no one with you?"

2"The king has sent me on a private matter," David lied. "He told me not to tell anybody why I am here. I have told my men where to meet me later. 3Now, what is there to eat? Give me five loaves of bread, or anything else you can."

4"We don't have any regular bread," the priest replied, "but there is the holy bread, which I guess you can have if only your young men have not slept with any women for awhile."

5"Rest assured," David replied. "I never let my men run wild when they are on an expedition, and since they stay clean even on ordinary trips, how much more so on this one!"

6So, since there was no other food available, the priest gave him the holy bread—the Bread of the Presence that was placed before the Lord in the Tabernacle. It had just been replaced that day with fresh bread.

7(Incidentally, Doeg the Edomite, Saul's chief herdsman, was there at that time for ceremonial purification.d)

8David asked Ahimelech if he had a spear or sword he could use. "The king's business required such haste, and I left in such a rush that I came away without a weapon!" David explained.

9"Well," the priest replied, "I have the sword of Goliath, the Philistine—the fellow you killed in the valley of Elah. It is wrapped in a cloth in the clothes closet.e Take that if you want it, for there is nothing else here."

"Just the thing!" David replied. "Give it to me!"

New Revised Standard

anger and ate no food on the second day of the month, for he was grieved for David, and because his father had disgraced him.

35 In the morning Jonathan went out into the field to the appointment with David, and with him was a little boy. 36He said to the boy, "Run and find the arrows that I shoot." As the boy ran, he shot an arrow beyond him. 37When the boy came to the place where Jonathan's arrow had fallen, Jonathan called after the boy and said, "Is the arrow not beyond you?" 38Jonathan called after the boy, "Hurry, be quick, do not linger." So Jonathan's boy gathered up the arrows and came to his master. 39But the boy knew nothing; only Jonathan and David knew the arrangement. 40Jonathan gave his weapons to the boy and said to him, "Go and carry them to the city." 41As soon as the boy had gone, David rose from beside the stone heapf and prostrated himself with his face to the ground. He bowed three times, and they kissed each other, and wept with each other; David wept the more.g 42Then Jonathan said to David, "Go in peace, since both of us have sworn in the name of the LORD, saying, 'The LORD shall be between me and you, and between my descendants and your descendants, forever.' " He got up and left; and Jonathan went into the city.h

David and the Holy Bread

21i DAVID CAME to Nob to the priest Ahimelech. Ahimelech came trembling to meet David, and said to him, "Why are you alone, and no one with you?" 2David said to the priest Ahimelech, "The king has charged me with a matter, and said to me, 'No one must know anything of the matter about which I send you, and with which I have charged you.' I have made an appointmenti with the young men for such and such a place. 3Now then, what have you at hand? Give me five loaves of bread, or whatever is here." 4The priest answered David, "I have no ordinary bread at hand, only holy bread—provided that the young men have kept themselves from women." 5David answered the priest, "Indeed women have been kept from us as always when I go on an expedition; the vessels of the young men are holy even when it is a common journey; how much more today will their vessels be holy?" 6So the priest gave him the holy bread; for there was no bread there except the bread of the Presence, which is removed from before the LORD, to be replaced by hot bread on the day it is taken away.

7 Now a certain man of the servants of Saul was there that day, detained before the LORD; his name was Doeg the Edomite, the chief of Saul's shepherds.

8 David said to Ahimelech, "Is there no spear or sword here with you? I did not bring my sword or my weapons with me, because the king's business required haste." 9The priest said, "The sword of Goliath the Philistine, whom you killed in the valley of Elah, is here wrapped in a cloth behind the ephod; if you will take that, take it, for there is none here except that one." David said, "There is none like it; give it to me."

King James

10¶ And David arose, and fled that day for fear of Saul, and went to Achish the king of Gath.

11And the servants of Achish said unto him, *Is* not this David the king of the land? did they not sing one to another of him in dances, saying, Saul hath slain his thousands, and David his ten thousands?

12And David laid up these words in his heart, and was sore afraid of Achish the king of Gath.

13And he changed his behaviour before them, and feigned himself mad in their hands, and scrabbled on the doors of the gate, and let his spittle fall down upon his beard.

14Then said Achish unto his servants, Lo, ye see the man is mad: wherefore *then* have ye brought him to me?

15Have I need of mad men, that ye have brought this *fellow* to play the mad man in my presence? shall this *fellow* come into my house?

22 DAVID THEREFORE departed thence, and escaped to the cave Adullam: and when his brethren and all his father's house heard *it,* they went down thither to him.

2And every one *that was* in distress, and every one that *was* in debt, and every one *that was* discontented, gathered themselves unto him; and he became a captain over them: and there were with him about four hundred men.

3¶ And David went thence to Mizpeh of Moab: and he said unto the king of Moab, Let my father and my mother, I pray thee, come forth, *and be* with you, till I know what God will do for me.

4And he brought them before the king of Moab: and they dwelt with him all the while that David was in the hold.

5¶ And the prophet Gad said unto David, Abide not in the hold; depart, and get thee into the land of Judah. Then David departed, and came into the forest of Hareth.

6¶ When Saul heard that David was discovered, and the men that *were* with him, (now Saul abode in Gibeah under a tree in Ramah, having his spear in his hand, and all his servants *were* standing about him;)

7Then Saul said unto his servants that stood about him, Hear now, ye Benjamites; will the son of Jesse give every one of you fields and vineyards, *and* make you all captains of thousands, and captains of hundreds;

8That all of you have conspired against me, and *there is* none that showeth me that my son hath made a league with the son of Jesse, and *there is* none of you that is sorry for me, or showeth unto me that my son hath stirred up my servant against me, to lie in wait, as at this day?

9¶ Then answered Doeg the Edomite, which was set over the servants of Saul, and said, I saw the son of Jesse coming to Nob, to Ahimelech the son of Ahitub.

10And he inquired of the LORD for him, and gave him victuals, and gave him the sword of Goliath the Philistine.

11Then the king sent to call Ahimelech the priest, the son of Ahitub, and all his father's house, the priests that *were* in Nob: and they came all of them to the king.

12And Saul said, Hear now, thou son of Ahitub. And he answered, Here I *am*, my lord.

13And Saul said unto him, Why have ye conspired against me, thou and the son of Jesse, in that thou hast given him bread, and a sword, and hast inquired of God for him, that he should rise against me, to lie in wait, as at this day?

New International

David at Gath

10That day David fled from Saul and went to Achish king of Gath. 11But the servants of Achish said to him, "Isn't this David, the king of the land? Isn't he the one they sing about in their dances:

" 'Saul has slain his thousands,
and David his tens of thousands'?"

12David took these words to heart and was very much afraid of Achish king of Gath. 13So he pretended to be insane in their presence; and while he was in their hands he acted like a madman, making marks on the doors of the gate and letting saliva run down his beard.

14Achish said to his servants, "Look at the man! He is insane! Why bring him to me? 15Am I so short of madmen that you have to bring this fellow here to carry on like this in front of me? Must this man come into my house?"

David at Adullam and Mizpah

22 DAVID LEFT Gath and escaped to the cave of Adullam. When his brothers and his father's household heard about it, they went down to him there. 2All those who were in distress or in debt or discontented gathered around him, and he became their leader. About four hundred men were with him.

3From there David went to Mizpah in Moab and said to the king of Moab, "Would you let my father and mother come and stay with you until I learn what God will do for me?" 4So he left them with the king of Moab, and they stayed with him as long as David was in the stronghold.

5But the prophet Gad said to David, "Do not stay in the stronghold. Go into the land of Judah." So David left and went to the forest of Hereth.

Saul Kills the Priests of Nob

6Now Saul heard that David and his men had been discovered. And Saul, spear in hand, was seated under the tamarisk tree on the hill at Gibeah, with all his officials standing around him. 7Saul said to them, "Listen, men of Benjamin! Will the son of Jesse give all of you fields and vineyards? Will he make all of you commanders of thousands and commanders of hundreds? 8Is that why you have all conspired against me? No one tells me when my son makes a covenant with the son of Jesse. None of you is concerned about me or tells me that my son has incited my servant to lie in wait for me, as he does today."

9But Doeg the Edomite, who was standing with Saul's officials, said, "I saw the son of Jesse come to Ahimelech son of Ahitub at Nob. 10Ahimelech inquired of the LORD for him; he also gave him provisions and the sword of Goliath the Philistine."

11Then the king sent for the priest Ahimelech son of Ahitub and his father's whole family, who were the priests at Nob, and they all came to the king. 12Saul said, "Listen now, son of Ahitub."

"Yes, my lord," he answered.

13Saul said to him, "Why have you conspired against me, you and the son of Jesse, giving him bread and a sword and inquiring of God for him, so that he has rebelled against me and lies in wait for me, as he does today?"

Living Bible

10Then David hurried on, for he was fearful of Saul, and went to King Achish of Gath. 11But Achish's officers weren't happy about his being there. "Isn't he the top leader of Israel?" they asked.

"Isn't he the one the people honor at their dances, singing, 'Saul has slain his thousands and David his ten thousands'?"

12David heard these comments and was afraid of what King Achish might do to him, 13so he pretended to be insane! He scratched on doors and let his spittle flow down his beard, 14, 15until finally King Achish said to his men.

"Must you bring me a madman? We already have enough of them around here! Should such a fellow as this be my guest?"

22 SO DAVID left Gath and escaped to the cave of Adullam, where his brothers and other relatives soon joined him. 2Then others began coming—those who were in any kind of trouble, such as being in debt, or merely discontented—until David was the leader of about four hundred men.

3(Later David went to Mizpeh in Moab to ask permission of the king for his father and mother to live there under royal protection until David knew what God was going to do for him. 4They stayed in Moab during the entire period when David was living in the cave.)

5One day the prophet Gad told David to leave the cave and return to the land of Judah. So David went to the forest of Hereth. 6The news of his arrival in Judah soon reached Saul. He was in Gibe-ah at the time, sitting beneath an oak tree playing with his spear, surrounded by his officers.

7"Listen here, you men of Benjamin!" Saul exclaimed when he heard the news. "Has David promised you fields and vineyards and commissions in his army? 8Is that why you are against me? For not one of you has ever told me that my own son is on David's side. You're not even sorry for me. Think of it! My own son—encouraging David to come and kill me!"

9, 10Then Doeg the Edomite, who was standing there with Saul's men, spoke up. "When I was at Nob," he said, "I saw David talking to Ahimelech the priest. Ahimelech consulted the Lord to find out what David should do, and then gave him food and the sword of Goliath the Philistine."

11, 12King Saul immediately summoned Ahimelech and all his family and all the other priests at Nob. When they arrived Saul shouted at him, "Listen to me, you son of Ahitub!"

"What is it?" quavered Ahimelech.

13"Why have you and David conspired against me?" Saul demanded. "Why did you give him food and a sword and talk to God for him? Why did you encourage him to revolt against me and to come here and attack me?"

New Revised Standard

David Flees to Gath

10 David rose and fled that day from Saul; he went to King Achish of Gath. 11The servants of Achish said to him, "Is this not David the king of the land? Did they not sing to one another of him in dances,

'Saul has killed his thousands,
and David his ten thousands'?"

12David took these words to heart and was very much afraid of King Achish of Gath. 13So he changed his behavior before them; he pretended to be mad when in their presence.a He scratched marks on the doors of the gate, and let his spittle run down his beard. 14Achish said to his servants, "Look, you see the man is mad; why then have you brought him to me? 15Do I lack madmen, that you have brought this fellow to play the madman in my presence? Shall this fellow come into my house?"

David and His Followers at Adullam

22 DAVID LEFT there and escaped to the cave of Adullam; when his brothers and all his father's house heard of it, they went down there to him. 2Everyone who was in distress, and everyone who was in debt, and everyone who was discontented gathered to him; and he became captain over them. Those who were with him numbered about four hundred.

3 David went from there to Mizpeh of Moab. He said to the king of Moab, "Please let my father and mother comeb to you, until I know what God will do for me." 4He left them with the king of Moab, and they stayed with him all the time that David was in the stronghold. 5Then the prophet Gad said to David, "Do not remain in the stronghold; leave, and go into the land of Judah." So David left, and went into the forest of Hereth.

Saul Slaughters the Priests at Nob

6 Saul heard that David and those who were with him had been located. Saul was sitting at Gibeah, under the tamarisk tree on the height, with his spear in his hand, and all his servants were standing around him. 7Saul said to his servants who stood around him, "Hear now, you Benjaminites; will the son of Jesse give every one of you fields and vineyards, will he make you all commanders of thousands and commanders of hundreds? 8Is that why all of you have conspired against me? No one discloses to me when my son makes a league with the son of Jesse, none of you is sorry for me or discloses to me that my son has stirred up my servant against me, to lie in wait, as he is doing today." 9Doeg the Edomite, who was in charge of Saul's servants, answered, "I saw the son of Jesse coming to Nob, to Ahimelech son of Ahitub; 10he inquired of the LORD for him, gave him provisions, and gave him the sword of Goliath the Philistine."

11 The king sent for the priest Ahimelech son of Ahitub and for all his father's house, the priests who were at Nob; and all of them came to the king. 12Saul said, "Listen now, son of Ahitub." He answered, "Here I am, my lord." 13Saul said to him, "Why have you conspired against me, you and the son of Jesse, by giving him bread and a sword, and by inquiring of God for him, so that he has risen against me, to lie in wait, as he is doing today?"

a Heb *in their hands*   b Syr Vg: Heb *come out*

King James

14Then Ahimelech answered the king, and said, And who *is so* faithful among all thy servants as David, which is the king's son-in-law, and goeth at thy bidding, and is honourable in thine house?

15Did I then begin to inquire of God for him? be it far from me: let not the king impute *any* thing unto his servant, *nor* to all the house of my father: for thy servant knew nothing of all this, less or more.

16And the king said, Thou shalt surely die, Ahimelech, thou, and all thy father's house.

17¶ And the king said unto the footmen that stood about him, Turn, and slay the priests of the LORD; because their hand also *is* with David, and because they knew when he fled, and did not show it to me. But the servants of the king would not put forth their hand to fall upon the priests of the LORD.

18And the king said to Doeg, Turn thou, and fall upon the priests. And Doeg the Edomite turned, and he fell upon the priests, and slew on that day fourscore and five persons that did wear a linen ephod.

19And Nob, the city of the priests, smote he with the edge of the sword, both men and women, children and sucklings, and oxen, and asses, and sheep, with the edge of the sword.

20¶ And one of the sons of Ahimelech the son of Ahitub, named Abiathar, escaped, and fled after David.

21And Abiathar showed David that Saul had slain the LORD's priests.

22And David said unto Abiathar, I knew *it* that day, when Doeg the Edomite *was* there, that he would surely tell Saul: I have occasioned *the death* of all the persons of thy father's house.

23Abide thou with me, fear not: for he that seeketh my life seeketh thy life: but with me thou *shalt be* in safeguard.

23 THEN THEY told David, saying, Behold, the Philistines fight against Keilah, and they rob the threshingfloors.

2Therefore David inquired of the LORD, saying, Shall I go and smite these Philistines? And the LORD said unto David, Go, and smite the Philistines, and save Keilah.

3And David's men said unto him, Behold, we be afraid here in Judah: how much more then if we come to Keilah against the armies of the Philistines?

4Then David inquired of the LORD yet again. And the LORD answered him and said, Arise, go down to Keilah; for I will deliver the Philistines into thine hand.

5So David and his men went to Keilah, and fought with the Philistines, and brought away their cattle, and smote them with a great slaughter. So David saved the inhabitants of Keilah.

6And it came to pass, when Abiathar the son of Ahimelech fled to David to Keilah, *that* he came down *with* an ephod in his hand.

7¶ And it was told Saul that David was come to Keilah. And Saul said, God hath delivered him into mine hand; for he is shut in, by entering into a town that hath gates and bars.

8And Saul called all the people together to war, to go down to Keilah, to besiege David and his men.

9¶ And David knew that Saul secretly practised mischief against him; and he said to Abiathar the priest, Bring hither the ephod.

10Then said David, O LORD God of Israel, thy servant hath certainly heard that Saul seeketh to come to Keilah, to destroy the city for my sake.

11Will the men of Keilah deliver me up into his hand? will Saul come down, as thy servant hath heard? O LORD God of Israel, I beseech thee, tell thy servant. And the LORD said, He will come down.

New International

14Ahimelech answered the king, "Who of all your servants is as loyal as David, the king's son-in-law, captain of your bodyguard and highly respected in your household? 15Was that day the first time I inquired of God for him? Of course not! Let not the king accuse your servant or any of his father's family, for your servant knows nothing at all about this whole affair."

16But the king said, "You will surely die, Ahimelech, you and your father's whole family."

17Then the king ordered the guards at his side: "Turn and kill the priests of the LORD, because they too have sided with David. They knew he was fleeing, yet they did not tell me."

But the king's officials were not willing to raise a hand to strike the priests of the LORD.

18The king then ordered Doeg, "You turn and strike down the priests." So Doeg the Edomite turned and struck them down. That day he killed eighty-five men who wore the linen ephod. 19He also put to the sword Nob, the town of the priests, with its men and women, its children and infants, and its cattle, donkeys and sheep.

20But Abiathar, a son of Ahimelech son of Ahitub, escaped and fled to join David. 21He told David that Saul had killed the priests of the LORD. 22Then David said to Abiathar: "That day, when Doeg the Edomite was there, I knew he would be sure to tell Saul. I am responsible for the death of your father's whole family. 23Stay with me; don't be afraid; the man who is seeking your life is seeking mine also. You will be safe with me."

David Saves Keilah

23 WHEN DAVID was told, "Look, the Philistines are fighting against Keilah and are looting the threshing floors," 2he inquired of the LORD, saying, "Shall I go and attack these Philistines?"

The LORD answered him, "Go, attack the Philistines and save Keilah."

3But David's men said to him, "Here in Judah we are afraid. How much more, then, if we go to Keilah against the Philistine forces!"

4Once again David inquired of the LORD, and the LORD answered him, "Go down to Keilah, for I am going to give the Philistines into your hand." 5So David and his men went to Keilah, fought the Philistines and carried off their livestock. He inflicted heavy losses on the Philistines and saved the people of Keilah. 6(Now Abiathar son of Ahimelech had brought the ephod down with him when he fled to David at Keilah.)

Saul Pursues David

7Saul was told that David had gone to Keilah, and he said, "God has handed him over to me, for David has imprisoned himself by entering a town with gates and bars." 8And Saul called up all his forces for battle, to go down to Keilah to besiege David and his men.

9When David learned that Saul was plotting against him, he said to Abiathar the priest, "Bring the ephod." 10David said, "O LORD, God of Israel, your servant has heard definitely that Saul plans to come to Keilah and destroy the town on account of me. 11Will the citizens of Keilah surrender me to him? Will Saul come down, as your servant has heard? O LORD, God of Israel, tell your servant."

And the LORD said, "He will."

Living Bible

14"But sir," Ahimelech replied, "is there anyone among all your servants who is as faithful as David your son-in-law? Why, he is the captain of your bodyguard and a highly honored member of your own household! 15This was certainly not the first time I had consulted God for him! It's unfair for you to accuse me and my family in this matter, for we knew nothing of any plot against you."

16"You shall die, Ahimelech, along with your entire family!" the king shouted. 17He ordered his bodyguards, "Kill these priests, for they are allies and conspirators with David; they knew he was running away from me, but they didn't tell me!"

But the soldiers refused to harm the clergy.

18Then the king said to Doeg, "You do it."

So Doeg turned on them and killed them, eighty-five priests in all, all wearing their priestly robes. 19Then he went to Nob, the city of the priests, and killed the priests' families—men, women, children, and babies, and also all the oxen, donkeys, and sheep. 20Only Abiathar, one of the sons of Ahimelech, escaped and fled to David.

21When he told him what Saul had done, 22David exclaimed, "I knew it! When I saw Doeg there, I knew he would tell Saul. Now I have caused the death of all of your father's family. 23Stay here with me, and I'll protect you with my own life. Any harm to you will be over my dead body."

23 ONE DAY news came to David that the Philistines were at Keilah robbing the threshing floors. 2David asked the Lord, "Shall I go and attack them?"

"Yes, go and save Keilah," the Lord told him.

3But David's men said, "We're afraid even here in Judah; we certainly don't want to go to Keilah to fight the whole Philistine army!"

4David asked the Lord again, and the Lord again replied, "Go down to Keilah, for I will help you conquer the Philistines."

5They went to Keilah and slaughtered the Philistines and confiscated their cattle, and so the people of Keilah were saved. 6(Abiathar the priest went to Keilah with David, taking his ephod with him to get answers for David from the Lord.) 7Saul soon learned that David was at Keilah.

"Good!" he exclaimed. "We've got him now! God has delivered him to me, for he has trapped himself in a walled city!"

8So Saul mobilized his entire army to march to Keilah and besiege David and his men. 9But David learned of Saul's plan and told Abiathar the priest to bring the ephod and to ask the Lord what he should do.

10"O Lord God of Israel," David said, "I have heard that Saul is planning to come and destroy Keilah because I am here. 11Will the men of Keilah surrender me to him? And will Saul actually come, as I have heard? O Lord God of Israel, please tell me."

And the Lord said, "He will come."

New Revised Standard

14 Then Ahimelech answered the king, "Who among all your servants is so faithful as David? He is the king's son-in-law, and is quicka to do your bidding, and is honored in your house. 15Is today the first time that I have inquired of God for him? By no means! Do not let the king impute anything to his servant or to any member of my father's house; for your servant has known nothing of all this, much or little." 16The king said, "You shall surely die, Ahimelech, you and all your father's house." 17The king said to the guard who stood around him, "Turn and kill the priests of the Lord, because their hand also is with David; they knew that he fled, and did not disclose it to me." But the servants of the king would not raise their hand to attack the priests of the Lord. 18Then the king said to Doeg, "You, Doeg, turn and attack the priests." Doeg the Edomite turned and attacked the priests; on that day he killed eighty-five who wore the linen ephod. 19Nob, the city of the priests, he put to the sword; men and women, children and infants, oxen, donkeys, and sheep, he put to the sword.

20 But one of the sons of Ahimelech son of Ahitub, named Abiathar, escaped and fled after David. 21Abiathar told David that Saul had killed the priests of the Lord. 22David said to Abiathar, "I knew on that day, when Doeg the Edomite was there, that he would surely tell Saul. I am responsibleb for the lives of all your father's house. 23Stay with me, and do not be afraid; for the one who seeks my life seeks your life; you will be safe with me."

David Saves the City of Keilah

23 NOW THEY told David, "The Philistines are fighting against Keilah, and are robbing the threshing floors." 2David inquired of the Lord, "Shall I go and attack these Philistines?" The Lord said to David, "Go and attack the Philistines and save Keilah." 3But David's men said to him, "Look, we are afraid here in Judah; how much more then if we go to Keilah against the armies of the Philistines?" 4Then David inquired of the Lord again. The Lord answered him, "Yes, go down to Keilah; for I will give the Philistines into your hand." 5So David and his men went to Keilah, fought with the Philistines, brought away their livestock, and dealt them a heavy defeat. Thus David rescued the inhabitants of Keilah.

6 When Abiathar son of Ahimelech fled to David at Keilah, he came down with an ephod in his hand. 7Now it was told Saul that David had come to Keilah. And Saul said, "God has givenc him into my hand; for he has shut himself in by entering a town that has gates and bars." 8Saul summoned all the people to war, to go down to Keilah, to besiege David and his men. 9When David learned that Saul was plotting evil against him, he said to the priest Abiathar, "Bring the ephod here." 10David said, "O Lord, the God of Israel, your servant has heard that Saul seeks to come to Keilah, to destroy the city on my account. 11And now, willd Saul come down as your servant has heard? O Lord, the God of Israel, I beseech you, tell your servant." The Lord said, "He will come down." 12Then David said, "Will the men of Keilah

---

a Heb *and turns aside* b Gk Vg: Meaning of Heb uncertain c Gk Tg: Heb *made a stranger of* d Q Ms Compare Gk: MT *Will the men of Keilah surrender me into his hand?* Will

King James

12Then said David, Will the men of Keilah deliver me and my men into the hand of Saul? And the LORD said, They will deliver *thee* up.

13¶ Then David and his men, *which were* about six hundred, arose and departed out of Keilah, and went whithersoever they could go. And it was told Saul that David was escaped from Keilah; and he forbare to go forth.

14And David abode in the wilderness in strong holds, and remained in a mountain in the wilderness of Ziph. And Saul sought him every day, but God delivered him not into his hand.

15And David saw that Saul was come out to seek his life: and David *was* in the wilderness of Ziph in a wood.

16¶ And Jonathan Saul's son arose, and went to David into the wood, and strengthened his hand in God.

17And he said unto him, Fear not: for the hand of Saul my father shall not find thee; and thou shalt be king over Israel, and I shall be next unto thee; and that also Saul my father knoweth.

18And they two made a covenant before the LORD: and David abode in the wood, and Jonathan went to his house.

19¶ Then came up the Ziphites to Saul to Gibeah, saying, Doth not David hide himself with us in strong holds in the wood, in the hill of Hachilah, which *is* on the south of Jeshimon?

20Now therefore, O king, come down according to all the desire of thy soul to come down; and our part *shall be* to deliver him into the king's hand.

21And Saul said, Blessed *be* ye of the LORD; for ye have compassion on me.

22Go, I pray you, prepare yet, and know and see his place where his haunt is, *and* who hath seen him there: for it is told me *that* he dealeth very subtly.

23See therefore, and take knowledge of all the lurking places where he hideth himself, and come ye again to me with the certainty, and I will go with you: and it shall come to pass, if he be in the land, that I will search him out throughout all the thousands of Judah.

24And they arose, and went to Ziph before Saul: but David and his men *were* in the wilderness of Maon, in the plain on the south of Jeshimon.

25Saul also and his men went to seek *him.* And they told David: wherefore he came down into a rock, and abode in the wilderness of Maon. And when Saul heard *that,* he pursued after David in the wilderness of Maon.

26And Saul went on this side of the mountain, and David and his men on that side of the mountain: and David made haste to get away for fear of Saul; for Saul and his men compassed David and his men round about to take them.

27¶ But there came a messenger unto Saul, saying, Haste thee, and come; for the Philistines have invaded the land.

28Wherefore Saul returned from pursuing after David, and went against the Philistines: therefore they called that place Sela-hammahlekoth.

29¶ And David went up from thence, and dwelt in strong holds at En-gedi.

24 AND IT came to pass, when Saul was returned from following the Philistines, that it was told him, saying, Behold, David *is* in the wilderness of En-gedi.

2Then Saul took three thousand chosen men out of all Israel, and went to seek David and his men upon the rocks of the wild goats.

New International

12Again David asked, "Will the citizens of Keilah surrender me and my men to Saul?"

And the LORD said, "They will."

13So David and his men, about six hundred in number, left Keilah and kept moving from place to place. When Saul was told that David had escaped from Keilah, he did not go there.

14David stayed in the desert strongholds and in the hills of the Desert of Ziph. Day after day Saul searched for him, but God did not give David into his hands.

15While David was at Horesh in the Desert of Ziph, he learned that Saul had come out to take his life. 16And Saul's son Jonathan went to David at Horesh and helped him find strength in God. 17"Don't be afraid," he said. "My father Saul will not lay a hand on you. You will be king over Israel, and I will be second to you. Even my father Saul knows this." 18The two of them made a covenant before the LORD. Then Jonathan went home, but David remained at Horesh.

19The Ziphites went up to Saul at Gibeah and said, "Is not David hiding among us in the strongholds at Horesh, on the hill of Hakilah, south of Jeshimon? 20Now, O king, come down whenever it pleases you to do so, and we will be responsible for handing him over to the king."

21Saul replied, "The LORD bless you for your concern for me. 22Go and make further preparation. Find out where David usually goes and who has seen him there. They tell me he is very crafty. 23Find out about all the hiding places he uses and come back to me with definite information.a Then I will go with you; if he is in the area, I will track him down among all the clans of Judah."

24So they set out and went to Ziph ahead of Saul. Now David and his men were in the Desert of Maon, in the Arabah south of Jeshimon. 25Saul and his men began the search, and when David was told about it, he went down to the rock and stayed in the Desert of Maon. When Saul heard this, he went into the Desert of Maon in pursuit of David.

26Saul was going along one side of the mountain, and David and his men were on the other side, hurrying to get away from Saul. As Saul and his forces were closing in on David and his men to capture them, 27a messenger came to Saul, saying, "Come quickly! The Philistines are raiding the land." 28Then Saul broke off his pursuit of David and went to meet the Philistines. That is why they call this place Sela Hammahlekoth.b 29And David went up from there and lived in the strongholds of En Gedi.

David Spares Saul's Life

24 AFTER SAUL returned from pursuing the Philistines, he was told, "David is in the Desert of En Gedi." 2So Saul took three thousand chosen men from all Israel and set out to look for David and his men near the Crags of the Wild Goats.

a 23 Or me at Nacon   b 28 Sela Hammahlekoth means rock of parting.

Living Bible

12"And will these men of Keilah betray me to Saul?" David persisted.

And the Lord replied, "Yes, they will betray you."

13So David and his men—about six hundred of them now—left Keilah and began roaming the countryside. Word soon reached Saul that David had escaped, so he didn't go there after all. 14, 15David now lived in the wilderness caves in the hill country of Ziph. One day near Horesh he received the news that Saul was on the way to Ziph to search for him and kill him. Saul hunted him day after day, but the Lord didn't let him find him.

16(Prince Jonathan now went to find David; he met him at Horesh and encouraged him in his faith in God.

17"Don't be afraid," Jonathan reassured him. "My father will never find you! You are going to be the king of Israel and I will be next to you, as my father is well aware." 18So the two of them renewed their pact of friendship; and David stayed at Horesh while Jonathan returned home.)

19But now the men of Ziph went to Saul in Gibe-ah and betrayed David to him.

"We know where he is hiding," they said. "He is in the caves of Horesh on Hachilah Hill, down in the southern part of the wilderness. 20Come on down, sir, and we will catch him for you and your fondest wish will be fulfilled!"

21"Well, praise the Lord!" Saul said. "At last someone has had pity on me! 22Go and check again to be sure of where he is staying and who has seen him there, for I know that he is very crafty. 23Discover his hiding places and then come back and give me a more definite report. Then I'll go with you. And if he is in the area at all, I'll find him if I have to search every inch of the entire land!"

24, 25So the men of Ziph returned home. But when David heard that Saul was on his way to Ziph, he and his men went even further into the wilderness of Maon in the south of the desert. But Saul followed them there. 26He and David were now on opposite sides of a mountain. As Saul and his men began to close in, David tried his best to escape, but it was no use. 27But just then a message reached Saul that the Philistines were raiding Israel again, 28so Saul quit the chase and returned to fight the Philistines. Ever since that time the place where David was camped has been called, "The Rock of Escape!" 29David then went to live in the caves of Engedi.

24 AFTER SAUL'S return from his battle with the Philistines, he was told that David had gone into the wilderness of Engedi; 2so he took three thousand special troops and went to search for him among the rocks and wild goats of the desert. 3At the place where

New Revised Standard

surrender me and my men into the hand of Saul?" The LORD said, "They will surrender you." 13Then David and his men, who were about six hundred, set out and left Keilah; they wandered wherever they could go. When Saul was told that David had escaped from Keilah, he gave up the expedition. 14David remained in the strongholds in the wilderness, in the hill country of the Wilderness of Ziph. Saul sought him every day, but the LORDc did not give him into his hand.

David Eludes Saul in the Wilderness

15 David was in the Wilderness of Ziph at Horesh when he learned thatd Saul had come out to seek his life. 16Saul's son Jonathan set out and came to David at Horesh; there he strengthened his hand through the LORD.e 17He said to him, "Do not be afraid; for the hand of my father Saul shall not find you; you shall be king over Israel, and I shall be second to you; my father Saul also knows that this is so." 18Then the two of them made a covenant before the LORD; David remained at Horesh, and Jonathan went home.

19 Then some Ziphites went up to Saul at Gibeah and said, "David is hiding among us in the strongholds of Horesh, on the hill of Hachilah, which is south of Jeshimon. 20Now, O king, whenever you wish to come down, do so; and our part will be to surrender him into the king's hand." 21Saul said, "May you be blessed by the LORD for showing me compassion! 22Go and make sure once more; find out exactly where he is, and who has seen him there; for I am told that he is very cunning. 23Look around and learn all the hiding places where he lurks, and come back to me with sure information. Then I will go with you; and if he is in the land, I will search him out among all the thousands of Judah." 24So they set out and went to Ziph ahead of Saul.

David and his men were in the wilderness of Maon, in the Arabah to the south of Jeshimon. 25Saul and his men went to search for him. When David was told, he went down to the rock and stayed in the wilderness of Maon. When Saul heard that, he pursued David into the wilderness of Maon. 26Saul went on one side of the mountain, and David and his men on the other side of the mountain. David was hurrying to get away from Saul, while Saul and his men were closing in on David and his men to capture them. 27Then a messenger came to Saul, saying, "Hurry and come; for the Philistines have made a raid on the land." 28So Saul stopped pursuing David, and went against the Philistines; therefore that place was called the Rock of Escape.f 29gDavid then went up from there, and lived in the strongholds of En-gedi.

David Spares Saul's Life

24 WHEN SAUL returned from following the Philistines, he was told, "David is in the wilderness of En-gedi." 2Then Saul took three thousand chosen men out of all Israel, and went to look for David and his men in the direction of the Rocks of the Wild Goats.

---

c Q Ms Gk: MT God   d Or saw that   e Compare Q Ms Gk: MT God   f Or Rock of Division; Meaning of Heb uncertain   g Ch 24.1 in Heb

King James

3And he came to the sheepcotes by the way, where *was* a cave; and Saul went in to cover his feet: and David and his men remained in the sides of the cave.

4And the men of David said unto him, Behold the day of which the LORD said unto thee, Behold, I will deliver thine enemy into thine hand, that thou mayest do to him as it shall seem good unto thee. Then David arose, and cut off the skirt of Saul's robe privily.

5And it came to pass afterward, that David's heart smote him, because he had cut off Saul's skirt.

6And he said unto his men, The LORD forbid that I should do this thing unto my master, the LORD's anointed, to stretch forth mine hand against him, seeing he *is* the anointed of the LORD.

7So David stayed his servants with these words, and suffered them not to rise against Saul. But Saul rose up out of the cave, and went on *his* way.

8David also arose afterward, and went out of the cave, and cried after Saul, saying, My lord the king. And when Saul looked behind him, David stooped with his face to the earth, and bowed himself.

9¶ And David said to Saul, Wherefore hearest thou men's words, saying, Behold, David seeketh thy hurt?

10Behold, this day thine eyes have seen how that the LORD had delivered thee today into mine hand in the cave: and *some* bade *me* kill thee: but *mine eye* spared thee; and I said, I will not put forth mine hand against my lord; for he *is* the LORD's anointed.

11Moreover, my father, see, yea, see the skirt of thy robe in my hand: for in that I cut off the skirt of thy robe, and killed thee not, know thou and see that *there is* neither evil nor transgression in mine hand, and I have not sinned against thee; yet thou huntest my soul to take it.

12The LORD judge between me and thee, and the LORD avenge me of thee: but mine hand shall not be upon thee.

13As saith the proverb of the ancients, Wickedness proceedeth from the wicked: but mine hand shall not be upon thee.

14After whom is the king of Israel come out? after whom dost thou pursue? after a dead dog, after a flea.

15The LORD therefore be judge, and judge between me and thee, and see, and plead my cause, and deliver me out of thine hand.

16¶ And it came to pass, when David had made an end of speaking these words unto Saul, that Saul said, *Is* this thy voice, my son David? And Saul lifted up his voice, and wept.

17And he said to David, Thou *art* more righteous than I: for thou hast rewarded me good, whereas I have rewarded thee evil.

18And thou hast shown this day how that thou hast dealt well with me: forasmuch as when the LORD had delivered me into thine hand, thou killedst me not.

19For if a man find his enemy, will he let him go well away? wherefore the LORD reward thee good for that thou hast done unto me this day.

20And now, behold, I know well that thou shalt surely be king, and that the kingdom of Israel shall be established in thine hand.

21Swear now therefore unto me by the LORD, that thou wilt not cut off my seed after me, and that thou wilt not destroy my name out of my father's house.

22And David sware unto Saul. And Saul went home; but David and his men gat them up unto the hold.

New International

3He came to the sheep pens along the way; a cave was there, and Saul went in to relieve himself. David and his men were far back in the cave. 4The men said, "This is the day the LORD spoke of when he said[a] to you, 'I will give your enemy into your hands for you to deal with as you wish.' " Then David crept up unnoticed and cut off a corner of Saul's robe.

5Afterward, David was conscience-stricken for having cut off a corner of his robe. 6He said to his men, "The LORD forbid that I should do such a thing to my master, the LORD's anointed, or lift my hand against him; for he is the anointed of the LORD." 7With these words David rebuked his men and did not allow them to attack Saul. And Saul left the cave and went his way.

8Then David went out of the cave and called out to Saul, "My lord the king!" When Saul looked behind him, David bowed down and prostrated himself with his face to the ground. 9He said to Saul, "Why do you listen when men say, 'David is bent on harming you'? 10This day you have seen with your own eyes how the LORD delivered you into my hands in the cave. Some urged me to kill you, but I spared you; I said, 'I will not lift my hand against my master, because he is the LORD's anointed.' 11See, my father, look at this piece of your robe in my hand! I cut off the corner of your robe but did not kill you. Now understand and recognize that I am not guilty of wrongdoing or rebellion. I have not wronged you, but you are hunting me down to take my life. 12May the LORD judge between you and me. And may the LORD avenge the wrongs you have done to me, but my hand will not touch you. 13As the old saying goes, 'From evildoers come evil deeds,' so my hand will not touch you.

14"Against whom has the king of Israel come out? Whom are you pursuing? A dead dog? A flea? 15May the LORD be our judge and decide between us. May he consider my cause and uphold it; may he vindicate me by delivering me from your hand."

16When David finished saying this, Saul asked, "Is that your voice, David my son?" And he wept aloud. 17"You are more righteous than I," he said. "You have treated me well, but I have treated you badly. 18You have just now told me of the good you did to me; the LORD delivered me into your hands, but you did not kill me. 19When a man finds his enemy, does he let him get away unharmed? May the LORD reward you well for the way you treated me today. 20I know that you will surely be king and that the kingdom of Israel will be established in your hands. 21Now swear to me by the LORD that you will not cut off my descendants or wipe out my name from my father's family."

22So David gave his oath to Saul. Then Saul returned home, but David and his men went up to the stronghold.

---

a 4 Or *"Today the LORD is saying*

Living Bible

the road passes some sheepfolds, Saul went into a cave to go to the bathroom, but as it happened, David and his men were hiding in the cave!

4"Now's your time!" David's men whispered to him. "Today is the day the Lord was talking about when he said, 'I will certainly put Saul into your power, to do with as you wish'!" Then David crept forward and quietly slit off the bottom of Saul's robe! 5But then his conscience began bothering him.

6"I shouldn't have done it," he said to his men. "It is a serious sin to attack God's chosen king in any way."

7,8These words of David persuaded his men not to kill Saul.

After Saul had left the cave and gone on his way, David came out and shouted after him, "My lord the king!" And when Saul looked around, David bowed low before him. 9, 10Then he shouted to Saul, "Why do you listen to the people who say I am trying to harm you? This very day you have seen it isn't true. For the Lord placed you at my mercy back there in the cave and some of my men told me to kill you, but I spared you. For I said, 'I will never harm him—he is the Lord's chosen king.' 11See what I have in my hand? It is the hem of your robe! I cut it off, but I didn't kill you! Doesn't this convince you that I am not trying to harm you and that I have not sinned against you, even though you have been hunting for my life?

12"The Lord will decide between us. Perhaps he will kill you for what you are trying to do to me, but I will never harm you. 13As that old proverb says, 'Wicked is as wicked does,' but despite your wickedness, I'll not touch you. 14And who is the king of Israel trying to catch, anyway? Should he spend his time chasing one who is as worthless as a dead dog or a flea? 15May the Lord judge as to which of us is right and punish whichever one of us is guilty. He is my lawyer and defender, and he will rescue me from your power!"

16Saul called back, "Is it really you, my son David?" Then he began to cry. 17And he said to David, "You are a better man than I am, for you have repaid me good for evil. 18Yes, you have been wonderfully kind to me today, for when the Lord delivered me into your hand, you didn't kill me. 19Who else in all the world would let his enemy get away when he had him in his power? May the Lord reward you well for the kindness you have shown me today. 20And now I realize that you are surely going to be king, and Israel shall be yours to rule. 21Oh, swear to me by the Lord that when that happens you will not kill my family and destroy my line of descendants!"

22So David promised, and Saul went home, but David and his men went back to their cave.

New Revised Standard

3He came to the sheepfolds beside the road, where there was a cave; and Saul went in to relieve himself.b Now David and his men were sitting in the innermost parts of the cave. 4The men of David said to him, "Here is the day of which the LORD said to you, 'I will give your enemy into your hand, and you shall do to him as it seems good to you.'" Then David went and stealthily cut off a corner of Saul's cloak. 5Afterward David was stricken to the heart because he had cut off a corner of Saul's cloak. 6He said to his men, "The LORD forbid that I should do this thing to my lord, the LORD's anointed, to raise my hand against him; for he is the LORD's anointed." 7So David scolded his men severely and did not permit them to attack Saul. Then Saul got up and left the cave, and went on his way.

8 Afterwards David also rose up and went out of the cave and called after Saul, "My lord the king!" When Saul looked behind him, David bowed with his face to the ground, and did obeisance. 9David said to Saul, "Why do you listen to the words of those who say, 'David seeks to do you harm'? 10This very day your eyes have seen how the LORD gave you into my hand in the cave; and some urged me to kill you, but I sparedc you. I said, 'I will not raise my hand against my lord; for he is the LORD's anointed.' 11See, my father, see the corner of your cloak in my hand; for by the fact that I cut off the corner of your cloak, and did not kill you, you may know for certain that there is no wrong or treason in my hands. I have not sinned against you, though you are hunting me to take my life. 12May the LORD judge between me and you! May the LORD avenge me on you; but my hand shall not be against you. 13As the ancient proverb says, 'Out of the wicked comes forth wickedness'; but my hand shall not be against you. 14Against whom has the king of Israel come out? Whom do you pursue? A dead dog? A single flea? 15May the LORD therefore be judge, and give sentence between me and you. May he see to it, and plead my cause, and vindicate me against you."

16 When David had finished speaking these words to Saul, Saul said, "Is this your voice, my son David?" Saul lifted up his voice and wept. 17He said to David, "You are more righteous than I; for you have repaid me good, whereas I have repaid you evil. 18 Today you have explained how you have dealt well with me, in that you did not kill me when the LORD put me into your hands. 19For who has ever found an enemy, and sent the enemy safely away? So may the LORD reward you with good for what you have done to me this day. 20Now I know that you shall surely be king, and that the kingdom of Israel shall be established in your hand. 21Swear to me therefore by the LORD that you will not cut off my descendants after me, and that you will not wipe out my name from my father's house." 22So David swore this to Saul. Then Saul went home; but David and his men went up to the stronghold.

---

b Heb *to cover his feet*   c Gk Syr Tg Vg: Heb *it* (my eye) *spared*

King James

25 AND SAMUEL died; and all the Israelites were gathered together, and lamented him, and buried him in his house at Ramah. And David arose, and went down to the wilderness of Paran.

2And *there was* a man in Maon, whose possessions *were* in Carmel; and the man *was* very great, and he had three thousand sheep, and a thousand goats: and he was shearing his sheep in Carmel.

3Now the name of the man *was* Nabal; and the name of his wife Abigail: and *she was* a woman of good understanding, and of a beautiful countenance: but the man *was* churlish and evil in his doings; and he *was* of the house of Caleb.

4¶ And David heard in the wilderness that Nabal did shear his sheep.

5And David sent out ten young men, and David said unto the young men, Get you up to Carmel, and go to Nabal, and greet him in my name:

6And thus shall ye say to him that liveth *in prosperity,* Peace *be* both to thee, and peace *be* to thine house, and peace *be* unto all that thou hast.

7And now I have heard that thou hast shearers: now thy shepherds which were with us, we hurt them not, neither was there aught missing unto them, all the while they were in Carmel.

8Ask thy young men, and they will show thee. Wherefore let the young men find favour in thine eyes: for we come in a good day: give, I pray thee, whatsoever cometh to thine hand unto thy servants, and to thy son David.

9And when David's young men came, they spake to Nabal according to all those words in the name of David, and ceased.

10¶ And Nabal answered David's servants, and said, Who *is* David? and who *is* the son of Jesse? there be many servants now a days that break away every man from his master.

11Shall I then take my bread, and my water, and my flesh that I have killed for my shearers, and give *it* unto men, whom I know not whence they *be?*

12So David's young men turned their way, and went again, and came and told him all those sayings.

13And David said unto his men, Gird ye on every man his sword. And they girded on every man his sword; and David also girded on his sword: and there went up after David about four hundred men; and two hundred abode by the stuff.

14¶ But one of the young men told Abigail, Nabal's wife, saying, Behold, David sent messengers out of the wilderness to salute our master; and he railed on them.

15But the men *were* very good unto us, and we were not hurt, neither missed we any thing, as long as we were conversant with them, when we were in the fields:

16They were a wall unto us both by night and day, all the while we were with them keeping the sheep.

17Now therefore know and consider what thou wilt do; for evil is determined against our master, and against all his household: for he *is such* a son of Belial, that *a man* cannot speak to him.

18¶ Then Abigail made haste, and took two hundred loaves, and two bottles of wine, and five sheep ready dressed, and five measures of parched *corn,* and an hundred clusters of raisins, and two hundred cakes of figs, and laid *them* on asses.

19And she said unto her servants, Go on before me; behold, I come after you. But she told not her husband Nabal.

20And it was *so, as* she rode on the ass, that she came down by the covert of the hill, and, behold, David and his men came down against her; and she met them.

New International

David, Nabal and Abigail

25 NOW SAMUEL died, and all Israel assembled and mourned for him; and they buried him at his home in Ramah.

Then David moved down into the Desert of Maon.[a] 2A certain man in Maon, who had property there at Carmel, was very wealthy. He had a thousand goats and three thousand sheep, which he was shearing in Carmel. 3His name was Nabal and his wife's name was Abigail. She was an intelligent and beautiful woman, but her husband, a Calebite, was surly and mean in his dealings.

4While David was in the desert, he heard that Nabal was shearing sheep. 5So he sent ten young men and said to them, "Go up to Nabal at Carmel and greet him in my name. 6Say to him: 'Long life to you! Good health to you and your household! And good health to all that is yours!

7"'Now I hear that it is sheep-shearing time. When your shepherds were with us, we did not mistreat them, and the whole time they were at Carmel nothing of theirs was missing. 8Ask your own servants and they will tell you. Therefore be favorable toward my young men, since we come at a festive time. Please give your servants and your son David whatever you can find for them.'"

9When David's men arrived, they gave Nabal this message in David's name. Then they waited.

10Nabal answered David's servants, "Who is this David? Who is this son of Jesse? Many servants are breaking away from their masters these days. 11Why should I take my bread and water, and the meat I have slaughtered for my shearers, and give it to men coming from who knows where?"

12David's men turned around and went back. When they arrived, they reported every word. 13David said to his men, "Put on your swords!" So they put on their swords, and David put on his. About four hundred men went up with David, while two hundred stayed with the supplies.

14One of the servants told Nabal's wife Abigail: "David sent messengers from the desert to give our master his greetings, but he hurled insults at them. 15Yet these men were very good to us. They did not mistreat us, and the whole time we were out in the fields near them nothing was missing. 16Night and day they were a wall around us all the time we were herding our sheep near them. 17Now think it over and see what you can do, because disaster is hanging over our master and his whole household. He is such a wicked man that no one can talk to him."

18Abigail lost no time. She took two hundred loaves of bread, two skins of wine, five dressed sheep, five seahs[b] of roasted grain, a hundred cakes of raisins and two hundred cakes of pressed figs, and loaded them on donkeys. 19Then she told her servants, "Go on ahead; I'll follow you." But she did not tell her husband Nabal.

20As she came riding her donkey into a mountain ravine, there were David and his men descending toward her, and she met them. 21David had just said, "It's been

---

Living Bible

25 SHORTLY AFTERWARDS, Samuel died and all Israel gathered for his funeral and buried him in his family plot at Ramah.

Meanwhile David went down to the wilderness of Paran. 2A wealthy man from Maon owned a sheep ranch there, near the village of Carmel. He had three thousand sheep and a thousand goats, and was at his ranch at this time for the sheep shearing. 3His name was Nabal and his wife, a beautiful and very intelligent woman, was named Abigail. But the man, who was a descendant of Caleb, was uncouth, churlish, stubborn, and ill-mannered.

4When David heard that Nabal was shearing his sheep, 5he sent ten of his young men to Carmel to give him this message: 6"May God prosper you and your family and multiply everything you own. 7I am told that you are shearing your sheep and goats. While your shepherds have lived among us, we have never harmed them, nor stolen anything from them the whole time they have been in Carmel. 8Ask your young men and they will tell you whether or not this is true. Now I have sent my men to ask for a little contribution from you, for we have come at a happy time of holiday. Please give us a present of whatever is at hand."

9The young men gave David's message to Nabal and waited for his reply.

10"Who is this fellow David?" he sneered. "Who does this son of Jesse think he is? There are lots of servants these days who run away from their masters. 11Should I take my bread and my water and my meat that I've slaughtered for my shearers and give it to a gang who comes from God knows where?"

12So David's messengers returned and told him what Nabal had said.

13"Get your swords!" was David's reply as he strapped on his own. Four hundred of them started off with David and two hundred remained behind to guard their gear.

14Meanwhile, one of Nabal's men went and told Abigail, "David sent men from the wilderness to talk to our master, but he insulted them and railed at them. 15, 16But David's men were very good to us and we never suffered any harm from them; in fact, day and night they were like a wall of protection to us and the sheep, and nothing was stolen from us the whole time they were with us. 17You'd better think fast, for there is going to be trouble for our master and his whole family—he's such a stubborn lout that no one can even talk to him!"

18Then Abigail hurriedly took two hundred loaves of bread, two barrels of wine, five dressed sheep, two bushels of roasted grain, one hundred raisin cakes, and two hundred fig cakes, and packed them onto donkeys.

19"Go on ahead," she said to her young men, "and I will follow." But she didn't tell her husband what she was doing. 20As she was riding down the trail on her donkey, she met David coming towards her.

New Revised Standard

Death of Samuel

25 NOW SAMUEL died; and all Israel assembled and mourned for him. They buried him at his home in Ramah.

Then David got up and went down to the wilderness of Paran.

David and the Wife of Nabal

2 There was a man in Maon, whose property was in Carmel. The man was very rich; he had three thousand sheep and a thousand goats. He was shearing his sheep in Carmel. 3Now the name of the man was Nabal, and the name of his wife Abigail. The woman was clever and beautiful, but the man was surly and mean; he was a Calebite. 4David heard in the wilderness that Nabal was shearing his sheep. 5So David sent ten young men; and David said to the young men, "Go up to Carmel, and go to Nabal, and greet him in my name. 6Thus you shall salute him: 'Peace be to you, and peace be to your house, and peace be to all that you have. 7I hear that you have shearers; now your shepherds have been with us, and we did them no harm, and they missed nothing, all the time they were in Carmel. 8Ask your young men, and they will tell you. Therefore let my young men find favor in your sight; for we have come on a feast day. Please give whatever you have at hand to your servants and to your son David.' "

9 When David's young men came, they said all this to Nabal in the name of David; and then they waited. 10But Nabal answered David's servants, "Who is David? Who is the son of Jesse? There are many servants today who are breaking away from their masters. 11 Shall I take my bread and my water and the meat that I have butchered for my shearers, and give it to men who come from I do not know where?" 12So David's young men turned away, and came back and told him all this. 13David said to his men, "Every man strap on his sword!" And every one of them strapped on his sword; David also strapped on his sword; and about four hundred men went up after David, while two hundred remained with the baggage.

14 But one of the young men told Abigail, Nabal's wife, "David sent messengers out of the wilderness to salute our master; and he shouted insults at them. 15 Yet the men were very good to us, and we suffered no harm, and we never missed anything when we were in the fields, as long as we were with them; 16they were a wall to us both by night and by day, all the while we were with them keeping the sheep. 17Now therefore know this and consider what you should do; for evil has been decided against our master and against all his house; he is so ill-natured that no one can speak to him."

18 Then Abigail hurried and took two hundred loaves, two skins of wine, five sheep ready dressed, five measures of parched grain, one hundred clusters of raisins, and two hundred cakes of figs. She loaded them on donkeys 19and said to her young men, "Go on ahead of me; I am coming after you." But she did not tell her husband Nabal. 20 As she rode on the donkey and came down under cover of the mountain, David and his men came down toward her; and she met them. 21 Now David

King James

21Now David had said, Surely in vain have I kept all that this *fellow* hath in the wilderness, so that nothing was missed of all that *pertained* unto him: and he hath requited me evil for good.

22So and more also do God unto the enemies of David, if I leave of all that *pertain* to him by the morning light any that pisseth against the wall.

23And when Abigail saw David, she hasted, and lighted off the ass, and fell before David on her face, and bowed herself to the ground,

24And fell at his feet, and said, Upon me, my lord, *upon* me *let this* iniquity *be:* and let thine handmaid, I pray thee, speak in thine audience, and hear the words of thine handmaid.

25Let not my lord, I pray thee, regard this man of Belial, *even* Nabal: for as his name *is,* so *is* he; Nabal *is* his name, and folly *is* with him: but I thine handmaid saw not the young men of my lord, whom thou didst send.

26Now therefore, my lord, *as* the LORD liveth, and *as* thy soul liveth, seeing the LORD hath withholden thee from coming to *shed* blood, and from avenging thyself with thine own hand, now let thine enemies, and they that seek evil to my lord, be as Nabal.

27And now this blessing which thine handmaid hath brought unto my lord, let it even be given unto the young men that follow my lord.

28I pray thee, forgive the trespass of thine handmaid: for the LORD will certainly make my lord a sure house; because my lord fighteth the battles of the LORD, and evil hath not been found in thee *all* thy days.

29Yet a man is risen to pursue thee, and to seek thy soul: but the soul of my lord shall be bound in the bundle of life with the LORD thy God; and the souls of thine enemies, them shall he sling out, *as out* of the middle of a sling.

30And it shall come to pass, when the LORD shall have done to my lord according to all the good that he hath spoken concerning thee, and shall have appointed thee ruler over Israel;

31That this shall be no grief unto thee, nor offence of heart unto my lord, either that thou hast shed blood causeless, or that my lord hath avenged himself: but when the LORD shall have dealt well with my lord, then remember thine handmaid.

32¶ And David said to Abigail, Blessed *be* the LORD God of Israel, which sent thee this day to meet me:

33And blessed *be* thy advice, and blessed *be* thou, which hast kept me this day from coming to *shed* blood, and from avenging myself with mine own hand.

34For in very deed, *as* the LORD God of Israel liveth, which hath kept me back from hurting thee, except thou hadst hasted and come to meet me, surely there had not been left unto Nabal by the morning light any that pisseth against the wall.

35So David received of her hand *that* which she had brought him, and said unto her, Go up in peace to thine house; see, I have hearkened to thy voice, and have accepted thy person.

36¶ And Abigail came to Nabal; and, behold, he held a feast in his house, like the feast of a king; and Nabal's heart *was* merry within him, for he *was* very drunken: wherefore she told him nothing, less or more, until the morning light.

37But it came to pass in the morning, when the wine was gone out of Nabal, and his wife had told him these things, that his heart died within him, and he became *as* a stone.

38And it came to pass about ten days *after,* that the LORD smote Nabal, that he died.

New International

useless—all my watching over this fellow's property in the desert so that nothing of his was missing. He has paid me back evil for good. 22May God deal with David,[a] be it ever so severely, if by morning I leave alive one male of all who belong to him!"

23When Abigail saw David, she quickly got off her donkey and bowed down before David with her face to the ground. 24She fell at his feet and said: "My lord, let the blame be on me alone. Please let your servant speak to you; hear what your servant has to say. 25May my lord pay no attention to that wicked man Nabal. He is just like his name—his name is Fool, and folly goes with him. But as for me, your servant, I did not see the men my master sent.

26"Now since the LORD has kept you, my master, from bloodshed and from avenging yourself with your own hands, as surely as the LORD lives and as you live, may your enemies and all who intend to harm my master be like Nabal. 27And let this gift, which your servant has brought to my master, be given to the men who follow you. 28Please forgive your servant's offense, for the LORD will certainly make a lasting dynasty for my master, because he fights the LORD's battles. Let no wrongdoing be found in you as long as you live. 29Even though someone is pursuing you to take your life, the life of my master will be bound securely in the bundle of the living by the LORD your God. But the lives of your enemies he will hurl away as from the pocket of a sling. 30When the LORD has done for my master every good thing he promised concerning him and has appointed him leader over Israel, 31my master will not have on his conscience the staggering burden of needless bloodshed or of having avenged himself. And when the LORD has brought my master success, remember your servant."

32David said to Abigail, "Praise be to the LORD, the God of Israel, who has sent you today to meet me. 33May you be blessed for your good judgment and for keeping me from bloodshed this day and from avenging myself with my own hands. 34Otherwise, as surely as the LORD, the God of Israel, lives, who has kept me from harming you, if you had not come quickly to meet me, not one male belonging to Nabal would have been left alive by daybreak."

35Then David accepted from her hand what she had brought him and said, "Go home in peace. I have heard your words and granted your request."

36When Abigail went to Nabal, he was in the house holding a banquet like that of a king. He was in high spirits and very drunk. So she told him nothing until daybreak. 37Then in the morning, when Nabal was sober, his wife told him all these things, and his heart failed him and he became like a stone. 38About ten days later, the LORD struck Nabal and he died.

a 22 Some Septuagint manuscripts; Hebrew *with David's enemies*

Living Bible

21David had been saying to himself, "A lot of good it did us to help this fellow. We protected his flocks in the wilderness so that not one thing was lost or stolen, but he has repaid me bad for good. All that I get for my trouble is insults. 22May God curse me if even one of his men remains alive by tomorrow morning!"

23When Abigail saw David, she quickly dismounted and bowed low before him.

24"I accept all blame in this matter, my lord," she said. "Please listen to what I want to say. 25Nabal is a bad-tempered boor, but please don't pay any attention to what he said. He is a fool—just like his name means. But I didn't see the messengers you sent. 26Sir, since the Lord has kept you from murdering and taking vengeance into your own hands, I pray by the life of God, and by your own life too, that all your enemies shall be as cursed as Nabal is. 27And now, here is a present I have brought to you and your young men. 28Forgive me for my boldness in coming out here. The Lord will surely reward you with eternal royalty for your descendants, for you are fighting his battles; and you will never do wrong throughout your entire life. 29Even when you are chased by those who seek your life, you are safe in the care of the Lord your God, just as though you were safe inside his purse! But the lives of your enemies shall disappear like stones from a sling! 30, 31When the Lord has done all the good things he promised you and has made you king of Israel, you won't want the conscience of a murderer who took the law into his own hands! And when the Lord has done these great things for you, please remember me!"

32David replied to Abigail, "Bless the Lord God of Israel who has sent you to meet me today! 33Thank God for your good sense! Bless you for keeping me from murdering the man and carrying out vengeance with my own hands. 34For I swear by the Lord, the God of Israel who has kept me from hurting you, that if you had not come out to meet me, not one of Nabal's men would be alive tomorrow morning."

35Then David accepted her gifts and told her to return home without fear, for he would not kill her husband. 36When she arrived home she found that Nabal had thrown a big party. He was roaring drunk, so she didn't tell him anything about her meeting with David until the next morning. 37, 38By that time he was sober, and when his wife told him what had happened, he had a stroke and lay paralyzedb for about ten days, then died, for the Lord killed him.

New Revised Standard

had said, "Surely it was in vain that I protected all that this fellow has in the wilderness, so that nothing was missed of all that belonged to him; but he has returned me evil for good. 22God do so to Davidc and more also, if by morning I leave so much as one male of all who belong to him."

23 When Abigail saw David, she hurried and alighted from the donkey, fell before David on her face, bowing to the ground. 24She fell at his feet and said, "Upon me alone, my lord, be the guilt; please let your servant speak in your ears, and hear the words of your servant. 25My lord, do not take seriously this ill-natured fellow, Nabal; for as his name is, so is he; Nabald is his name, and folly is with him; but I, your servant, did not see the young men of my lord, whom you sent.

26 Now then, my lord, as the LORD lives, and as you yourself live, since the LORD has restrained you from bloodguilt and from taking vengeance with your own hand, now let your enemies and those who seek to do evil to my lord be like Nabal. 27And now let this present that your servant has brought to my lord be given to the young men who follow my lord. 28Please forgive the trespass of your servant; for the LORD will certainly make my lord a sure house, because my lord is fighting the battles of the LORD; and evil shall not be found in you so long as you live. 29If anyone should rise up to pursue you and to seek your life, the life of my lord shall be bound in the bundle of the living under the care of the LORD your God; but the lives of your enemies he shall sling out as from the hollow of a sling. 30When the LORD has done to my lord according to all the good that he has spoken concerning you, and has appointed you prince over Israel, 31my lord shall have no cause of grief, or pangs of conscience, for having shed blood without cause or for having saved himself. And when the LORD has dealt well with my lord, then remember your servant."

32 David said to Abigail, "Blessed be the LORD, the God of Israel, who sent you to meet me today! 33Blessed be your good sense, and blessed be you, who have kept me today from bloodguilt and from avenging myself by my own hand! 34For as surely as the LORD the God of Israel lives, who has restrained me from hurting you, unless you had hurried and come to meet me, truly by morning there would not have been left to Nabal so much as one male." 35Then David received from her hand what she had brought him; he said to her, "Go up to your house in peace; see, I have heeded your voice, and I have granted your petition."

36 Abigail came to Nabal; he was holding a feast in his house, like the feast of a king. Nabal's heart was merry within him, for he was very drunk; so she told him nothing at all until the morning light. 37In the morning, when the wine had gone out of Nabal, his wife told him these things, and his heart died within him; he became like a stone. 38About ten days later the LORD struck Nabal, and he died.

---

b 25:37, 38 *he had a stroke and lay paralyzed*, literally, "his heart died within him and he became as stone."

c Gk Compare Syr: Heb *the enemies of David*   d That is *Fool*

King James

39¶ And when David heard that Nabal was dead, he said, Blessed *be* the LORD, that hath pleaded the cause of my reproach from the hand of Nabal, and hath kept his servant from evil: for the LORD hath returned the wickedness of Nabal upon his own head. And David sent and communed with Abigail, to take her to him to wife.

40And when the servants of David were come to Abigail to Carmel, they spake unto her, saying, David sent us unto thee, to take thee to him to wife.

41And she arose, and bowed herself on *her* face to the earth, and said, Behold, *let* thine handmaid *be* a servant to wash the feet of the servants of my lord.

42And Abigail hasted, and arose, and rode upon an ass, with five damsels of hers that went after her; and she went after the messengers of David, and became his wife.

43David also took Ahinoam of Jezreel; and they were also both of them his wives.

44¶ But Saul had given Michal his daughter, David's wife, to Phalti the son of Laish, which *was* of Gallim.

26 AND THE Ziphites came unto Saul to Gibeah, saying, Doth not David hide himself in the hill of Hachilah, *which is* before Jeshimon?

2Then Saul arose, and went down to the wilderness of Ziph, having three thousand chosen men of Israel with him, to seek David in the wilderness of Ziph.

3And Saul pitched in the hill of Hachilah, which *is* before Jeshimon, by the way. But David abode in the wilderness, and he saw that Saul came after him into the wilderness.

4David therefore sent out spies, and understood that Saul was come in very deed.

5¶ And David arose, and came to the place where Saul had pitched: and David beheld the place where Saul lay, and Abner the son of Ner, the captain of his host: and Saul lay in the trench, and the people pitched round about him.

6Then answered David and said to Ahimelech the Hittite, and to Abishai the son of Zeruiah, brother to Joab, saying, Who will go down with me to Saul to the camp? And Abishai said, I will go down with thee.

7So David and Abishai came to the people by night: and, behold, Saul lay sleeping within the trench, and his spear stuck in the ground at his bolster: but Abner and the people lay round about him.

8Then said Abishai to David, God hath delivered thine enemy into thine hand this day: now therefore let me smite him, I pray thee, with the spear even to the earth at once, and I will not *smite* him the second time.

9And David said to Abishai, Destroy him not: for who can stretch forth his hand against the LORD's anointed, and be guiltless?

10David said furthermore, *As* the LORD liveth, the LORD shall smite him; or his day shall come to die; or he shall descend into battle, and perish.

11The LORD forbid that I should stretch forth mine hand against the LORD's anointed: but, I pray thee, take thou now the spear that *is* at his bolster, and the cruse of water, and let us go.

12So David took the spear and the cruse of water from Saul's bolster; and they gat them away, and no man saw *it*, nor knew *it*, neither awaked: for they *were* all asleep; because a deep sleep from the LORD was fallen upon them.

13¶ Then David went over to the other side, and stood on the top of an hill afar off; a great space *being* between them:

14And David cried to the people, and to Abner the son of Ner, saying, Answerest thou not, Abner? Then Abner answered and said, Who *art* thou *that* criest to the king?

New International

39When David heard that Nabal was dead, he said, "Praise be to the LORD, who has upheld my cause against Nabal for treating me with contempt. He has kept his servant from doing wrong and has brought Nabal's wrongdoing down on his own head."

Then David sent word to Abigail, asking her to become his wife. 40His servants went to Carmel and said to Abigail, "David has sent us to you to take you to become his wife."

41She bowed down with her face to the ground and said, "Here is your maidservant, ready to serve you and wash the feet of my master's servants." 42Abigail quickly got on a donkey and, attended by her five maids, went with David's messengers and became his wife. 43David had also married Ahinoam of Jezreel, and they both were his wives. 44But Saul had given his daughter Michal, David's wife, to Paltiel[a] son of Laish, who was from Gallim.

David Again Spares Saul's Life

26 THE ZIPHITES went to Saul at Gibeah and said, "Is not David hiding on the hill of Hakilah, which faces Jeshimon?"

2So Saul went down to the Desert of Ziph, with his three thousand chosen men of Israel, to search there for David. 3Saul made his camp beside the road on the hill of Hakilah facing Jeshimon, but David stayed in the desert. When he saw that Saul had followed him there, 4he sent out scouts and learned that Saul had definitely arrived.[b]

5Then David set out and went to the place where Saul had camped. He saw where Saul and Abner son of Ner, the commander of the army, had lain down. Saul was lying inside the camp, with the army encamped around him.

6David then asked Ahimelech the Hittite and Abishai son of Zeruiah, Joab's brother, "Who will go down into the camp with me to Saul?"

"I'll go with you," said Abishai.

7So David and Abishai went to the army by night, and there was Saul, lying asleep inside the camp with his spear stuck in the ground near his head. Abner and the soldiers were lying around him.

8Abishai said to David, "Today God has delivered your enemy into your hands. Now let me pin him to the ground with one thrust of my spear; I won't strike him twice."

9But David said to Abishai, "Don't destroy him! Who can lay a hand on the LORD's anointed and be guiltless? 10As surely as the LORD lives," he said, "the LORD himself will strike him; either his time will come and he will die, or he will go into battle and perish. 11But the LORD forbid that I should lay a hand on the LORD's anointed. Now get the spear and water jug that are near his head, and let's go."

12So David took the spear and water jug near Saul's head, and they left. No one saw or knew about it, nor did anyone wake up. They were all sleeping, because the LORD had put them into a deep sleep.

13Then David crossed over to the other side and stood on top of the hill some distance away; there was a wide space between them. 14He called out to the army and to Abner son of Ner, "Aren't you going to answer me, Abner?"

Abner replied, "Who are you who calls to the king?"

---

[a] 44 Hebrew *Palti*, a variant of *Paltiel*   [b] 4 Or *had come to Nacon*

Living Bible

39When David heard that Nabal was dead, he said, "Praise the Lord! God has paid back Nabal and kept me from doing it myself; he has received his punishment for his sin."

Then David wasted no time in sending messengers to Abigail to ask her to become his wife. 40When the messengers arrived at Carmel and told her why they had come, 41she readily agreed to his request. 42Quickly getting ready, she took along five of her serving girls as attendants, mounted her donkey, and followed the men back to David. So she became his wife.

43David also married Ahino-am from Jezreel. 44King Saul, meanwhile, had forced David's wife Michal, Saul's daughter, to marry a man from Gallim named Palti (the son of Laish).

26 NOW THE men from Ziph came back to Saul at Gibe-ah to tell him that David had returned to the wilderness and was hiding on Hachilah Hill. 2So Saul took his elite corps of three thousand troops and went to hunt him down. 3, 4Saul camped along the road at the edge of the wilderness where David was hiding, but David knew of Saul's arrival and sent out spies to watch his movements.

5, 6, 7David slipped over to Saul's camp one night to look around. King Saul and General Abner were sleeping inside a ring formed by the slumbering soldiers.

"Any volunteers to go down there with me?" David asked Ahimelech (the Hittite) and Abishai (Joab's brother and the son of Zeruiah).

"I'll go with you," Abishai replied. So David and Abishai went to Saul's camp and found him asleep, with his spear in the ground beside his head.

8"God has put your enemy within your power this time for sure," Abishai whispered to David. "Let me go and put that spear through him. I'll pin him to the earth with it—I'll not need to strike a second time!"

9"No," David said. "Don't kill him, for who can remain innocent after attacking the Lord's chosen king? 10Surely God will strike him down some day, or he will die in battle or of old age. 11But God forbid that I should kill the man he has chosen to be king! But I'll tell you what—we'll take his spear and his jug of water and then get out of here!"

12So David took the spear and jug of water, and they got away without anyone seeing them or even waking up, because the Lord had put them sound asleep. 13They climbed the mountain slope opposite the camp until they were at a safe distance.

14Then David shouted down to Abner and Saul, "Wake up, Abner!"

"Who is it?" Abner demanded.

New Revised Standard

39 When David heard that Nabal was dead, he said, "Blessed be the LORD who has judged the case of Nabal's insult to me, and has kept back his servant from evil; the LORD has returned the evildoing of Nabal upon his own head." Then David sent and wooed Abigail, to make her his wife. 40When David's servants came to Abigail at Carmel, they said to her, "David has sent us to you to take you to him as his wife." 41She rose and bowed down, with her face to the ground, and said, "Your servant is a slave to wash the feet of the servants of my lord." 42Abigail got up hurriedly and rode away on a donkey; her five maids attended her. She went after the messengers of David and became his wife.

43 David also married Ahinoam of Jezreel; both of them became his wives. 44Saul had given his daughter Michal, David's wife, to Palti son of Laish, who was from Gallim.

David Spares Saul's Life a Second Time

26 THEN THE Ziphites came to Saul at Gibeah, saying, "David is in hiding on the hill of Hachilah, which is opposite Jeshimon."c 2So Saul rose and went down to the Wilderness of Ziph, with three thousand chosen men of Israel, to seek David in the Wilderness of Ziph. 3Saul encamped on the hill of Hachilah, which is opposite Jeshimonc beside the road. But David remained in the wilderness. When he learned that Saul came after him into the wilderness, 4David sent out spies, and learned that Saul had indeed arrived. 5Then David set out and came to the place where Saul had encamped; and David saw the place where Saul lay, with Abner son of Ner, the commander of his army. Saul was lying within the encampment, while the army was encamped around him.

6 Then David said to Ahimelech the Hittite, and to Joab's brother Abishai son of Zeruiah, "Who will go down with me into the camp to Saul?" Abishai said, "I will go down with you." 7So David and Abishai went to the army by night; there Saul lay sleeping within the encampment, with his spear stuck in the ground at his head; and Abner and the army lay around him. 8Abishai said to David, "God has given your enemy into your hand today; now therefore let me pin him to the ground with one stroke of the spear; I will not strike him twice." 9But David said to Abishai, "Do not destroy him; for who can raise his hand against the LORD's anointed, and be guiltless?" 10David said, "As the LORD lives, the LORD will strike him down; or his day will come to die; or he will go down into battle and perish. 11The LORD forbid that I should raise my hand against the LORD's anointed; but now take the spear that is at his head, and the water jar, and let us go." 12So David took the spear that was at Saul's head and the water jar, and they went away. No one saw it, or knew it, nor did anyone awake; for they were all asleep, because a deep sleep from the LORD had fallen upon them.

13 Then David went over to the other side, and stood on top of a hill far away, with a great distance between them. 14David called to the army and to Abner son of Ner, saying, "Abner! Will you not answer?" Then Abner replied, "Who are you that calls to the king?"

c Or opposite the wasteland

King James

15And David said to Abner, *Art* not thou a *valiant* man? and who *is* like to thee in Israel? wherefore then hast thou not kept thy lord the king? for there came one of the people in to destroy the king thy lord.

16This thing *is* not good that thou hast done. *As* the LORD liveth, ye *are* worthy to die, because ye have not kept your master, the LORD's anointed. And now see where the king's spear *is*, and the cruse of water that *was* at his bolster.

17And Saul knew David's voice, and said, *Is* this thy voice, my son David? And David said, *It is* my voice, my lord, O king.

18And he said, Wherefore doth my lord thus pursue after his servant? for what have I done? or what evil *is* in mine hand?

19Now therefore, I pray thee, let my lord the king hear the words of his servant. If the LORD have stirred thee up against me, let him accept an offering: but if *they be* the children of men, cursed *be* they before the LORD; for they have driven me out this day from abiding in the inheritance of the LORD, saying, Go, serve other gods.

20Now therefore, let not my blood fall to the earth before the face of the LORD: for the king of Israel is come out to seek a flea, as when one doth hunt a partridge in the mountains.

21¶ Then said Saul, I have sinned: return, my son David: for I will no more do thee harm, because my soul was precious in thine eyes this day: behold, I have played the fool, and have erred exceedingly.

22And David answered and said, Behold the king's spear! and let one of the young men come over and fetch it.

23The LORD render to every man his righteousness and his faithfulness: for the LORD delivered thee into *my* hand today, but I would not stretch forth mine hand against the LORD's anointed.

24And, behold, as thy life was much set by this day in mine eyes, so let my life be much set by in the eyes of the LORD, and let him deliver me out of all tribulation.

25Then Saul said to David, Blessed *be* thou, my son David: thou shalt both do great *things,* and also shalt still prevail. So David went on his way, and Saul returned to his place.

27 AND DAVID said in his heart, I shall now perish one day by the hand of Saul: *there is* nothing better for me than that I should speedily escape into the land of the Philistines; and Saul shall despair of me, to seek me any more in any coast of Israel: so shall I escape out of his hand.

2And David arose, and he passed over with the six hundred men that *were* with him unto Achish, the son of Maoch, king of Gath.

3And David dwelt with Achish at Gath, he and his men, every man with his household, *even* David with his two wives, Ahinoam the Jezreelitess, and Abigail the Carmelitess, Nabal's wife.

4And it was told Saul that David was fled to Gath: and he sought no more again for him.

5¶ And David said unto Achish, If I have now found grace in thine eyes, let them give me a place in some town in the country, that I may dwell there: for why should thy servant dwell in the royal city with thee?

6Then Achish gave him Ziklag that day: wherefore Ziklag pertaineth unto the kings of Judah unto this day.

7And the time that David dwelt in the country of the Philistines was a full year and four months.

8¶ And David and his men went up, and invaded the Geshurites, and the Gezrites, and the Amalekites: for those *nations were* of old the inhabitants of the land, as thou goest to Shur, even unto the land of Egypt.

New International

15David said, "You're a man, aren't you? And who is like you in Israel? Why didn't you guard your lord the king? Someone came to destroy your lord the king. 16What you have done is not good. As surely as the LORD lives, you and your men deserve to die, because you did not guard your master, the LORD's anointed. Look around you. Where are the king's spear and water jug that were near his head?"

17Saul recognized David's voice and said, "Is that your voice, David my son?"

David replied, "Yes it is, my lord the king." 18And he added, "Why is my lord pursuing his servant? What have I done, and what wrong am I guilty of? 19Now let my lord the king listen to his servant's words. If the LORD has incited you against me, then may he accept an offering. If, however, men have done it, may they be cursed before the LORD! They have now driven me from my share in the LORD's inheritance and have said, 'Go, serve other gods.' 20Now do not let my blood fall to the ground far from the presence of the LORD. The king of Israel has come out to look for a flea—as one hunts a partridge in the mountains."

21Then Saul said, "I have sinned. Come back, David my son. Because you considered my life precious today, I will not try to harm you again. Surely I have acted like a fool and have erred greatly."

22"Here is the king's spear," David answered. "Let one of your young men come over and get it. 23The LORD rewards every man for his righteousness and faithfulness. The LORD delivered you into my hands today, but I would not lay a hand on the LORD's anointed. 24As surely as I valued your life today, so may the LORD value my life and deliver me from all trouble."

25Then Saul said to David, "May you be blessed, my son David; you will do great things and surely triumph."

So David went on his way, and Saul returned home.

David Among the Philistines

27 BUT DAVID thought to himself, "One of these days I will be destroyed by the hand of Saul. The best thing I can do is to escape to the land of the Philistines. Then Saul will give up searching for me anywhere in Israel, and I will slip out of his hand."

2So David and the six hundred men with him left and went over to Achish son of Maoch king of Gath. 3David and his men settled in Gath with Achish. Each man had his family with him, and David had his two wives: Ahinoam of Jezreel and Abigail of Carmel, the widow of Nabal. 4When Saul was told that David had fled to Gath, he no longer searched for him.

5Then David said to Achish, "If I have found favor in your eyes, let a place be assigned to me in one of the country towns, that I may live there. Why should your servant live in the royal city with you?"

6So on that day Achish gave him Ziklag, and it has belonged to the kings of Judah ever since. 7David lived in Philistine territory a year and four months.

8Now David and his men went up and raided the Geshurites, the Girzites and the Amalekites. (From ancient times these peoples had lived in the land extending to Shur and Egypt.) 9Whenever David attacked an area,

Living Bible

15"Well, Abner, you're a great fellow, aren't you?" David taunted. "Where in all Israel is there anyone as wonderful? So why haven't you guarded your master the king when someone came to kill him? 16This isn't good at all! I swear by the Lord that you ought to die for your carelessness. Where is the king's spear and the jug of water that was beside his head? Look and see!"

17, 18Saul recognized David's voice and said, "Is that you, my son David?"

And David replied, "Yes, sir, it is. Why are you chasing me? What have I done? What is my crime? 19If the Lord has stirred you up against me, then let him accept my peace offering. But if this is simply the scheme of a man, then may he be cursed by God. For you have driven me out of my home so that I can't be with the Lord's people, and you have sent me away to worship heathen gods. 20Must I die on foreign soil, far from the presence of Jehovah? Why should the king of Israel come out to hunt my life like a partridge on the mountains?"

21Then Saul confessed, "I have done wrong. Come back home, my son, and I'll no longer try to harm you; for you saved my life today. I have been a fool, and very, very wrong."

22"Here is your spear, sir," David replied. "Let one of your young men come over and get it. 23The Lord gives his own reward for doing good and for being loyal, and I refused to kill you even when the Lord placed you in my power. 24Now may the Lord save my life, even as I have saved yours today. May he rescue me from all my troubles."

25And Saul said to David, "Blessings on you, my son David. You shall do heroic deeds and be a great conqueror."

Then David went away and Saul returned home.

27 BUT DAVID kept thinking to himself, "Some day Saul is going to get me. I'll try my luck among the Philistines until Saul gives up and quits hunting for me; then I will finally be safe again."

2, 3So David took his six hundred men and their families to live at Gath under the protection of King Achish. He had his two wives with him—Ahino-am of Jezreel and Abigail of Carmel, Nabal's widow. 4Word soon reached Saul that David had fled to Gath, so he quit hunting for him.

5One day David said to Achish, "My lord, if it is all right with you, we would rather live in one of the country towns instead of here in the royal city."

6So Achish gave him Ziklag (which still belongs to the kings of Judah to this day), 7and they lived there among the Philistines for a year and four months. 8He and his men spent their time raiding the Geshurites, the Girzites, and the Amalekites—people who had lived near Shur along the road to Egypt ever since ancient times. 9They didn't leave one person alive in the villages

New Revised Standard

15David said to Abner, "Are you not a man? Who is like you in Israel? Why then have you not kept watch over your lord the king? For one of the people came in to destroy your lord the king. 16This thing that you have done is not good. As the LORD lives, you deserve to die, because you have not kept watch over your lord, the LORD's anointed. See now, where is the king's spear, or the water jar that was at his head?"

17 Saul recognized David's voice, and said, "Is this your voice, my son David?" David said, "It is my voice, my lord, O king." 18And he added, "Why does my lord pursue his servant? For what have I done? What guilt is on my hands? 19Now therefore let my lord the king hear the words of his servant. If it is the LORD who has stirred you up against me, may he accept an offering; but if it is mortals, may they be cursed before the LORD, for they have driven me out today from my share in the heritage of the LORD, saying, 'Go, serve other gods.' 20Now therefore, do not let my blood fall to the ground, away from the presence of the LORD; for the king of Israel has come out to seek a single flea, like one who hunts a partridge in the mountains."

21 Then Saul said, "I have done wrong; come back, my son David, for I will never harm you again, because my life was precious in your sight today; I have been a fool, and have made a great mistake." 22David replied, "Here is the spear, O king! Let one of the young men come over and get it. 23The LORD rewards everyone for his righteousness and his faithfulness; for the LORD gave you into my hand today, but I would not raise my hand against the LORD's anointed. 24As your life was precious today in my sight, so may my life be precious in the sight of the LORD, and may he rescue me from all tribulation." 25Then Saul said to David, "Blessed be you, my son David! You will do many things and will succeed in them." So David went his way, and Saul returned to his place.

David Serves King Achish of Gath

27 DAVID SAID in his heart, "I shall now perish one day by the hand of Saul; there is nothing better for me than to escape to the land of the Philistines; then Saul will despair of seeking me any longer within the borders of Israel, and I shall escape out of his hand." 2So David set out and went over, he and the six hundred men who were with him, to King Achish son of Maoch of Gath. 3David stayed with Achish at Gath, he and his troops, every man with his household, and David with his two wives, Ahinoam of Jezreel, and Abigail of Carmel, Nabal's widow. 4When Saul was told that David had fled to Gath, he no longer sought for him.

5 Then David said to Achish, "If I have found favor in your sight, let a place be given me in one of the country towns, so that I may live there; for why should your servant live in the royal city with you?" 6So that day Achish gave him Ziklag; therefore Ziklag has belonged to the kings of Judah to this day. 7The length of time that David lived in the country of the Philistines was one year and four months.

8 Now David and his men went up and made raids on the Geshurites, the Girzites, and the Amalekites; for these were the landed settlements from Telam[a] on the way to Shur and on to the land of Egypt. 9David struck

a Compare Gk 15.4: Heb *from of old*

King James

9And David smote the land, and left neither man nor woman alive, and took away the sheep, and the oxen, and the asses, and the camels, and the apparel, and returned, and came to Achish.

10And Achish said, Whither have ye made a road today? And David said, Against the south of Judah, and against the south of the Jerahmeelites, and against the south of the Kenites.

11And David saved neither man nor woman alive, to bring *tidings* to Gath, saying, Lest they should tell on us, saying, So did David, and so *will be* his manner all the while he dwelleth in the country of the Philistines.

12And Achish believed David, saying, He hath made his people Israel utterly to abhor him; therefore he shall be my servant for ever.

28 AND IT came to pass in those days, that the Philistines gathered their armies together for warfare, to fight with Israel. And Achish said unto David, Know thou assuredly, that thou shalt go out with me to battle, thou and thy men.

2And David said to Achish, Surely thou shalt know what thy servant can do. And Achish said to David, Therefore will I make thee keeper of mine head for ever.

3¶ Now Samuel was dead, and all Israel had lamented him, and buried him in Ramah, even in his own city. And Saul had put away those that had familiar spirits, and the wizards, out of the land.

4And the Philistines gathered themselves together, and came and pitched in Shunem: and Saul gathered all Israel together, and they pitched in Giboa.

5And when Saul saw the host of the Philistines, he was afraid, and his heart greatly trembled.

6And when Saul inquired of the LORD, the LORD answered him not, neither by dreams, nor by Urim, nor by prophets.

7¶ Then said Saul unto his servants, Seek me a woman that hath a familiar spirit, that I may go to her, and inquire of her. And his servants said to him, Behold, *there is* a woman that hath a familiar spirit at En-dor.

8And Saul disguised himself, and put on other raiment, and he went, and two men with him, and they came to the woman by night: and he said, I pray thee, divine unto me by the familiar spirit, and bring me *him* up, whom I shall name unto thee.

9And the woman said unto him, Behold, thou knowest what Saul hath done, how he hath cut off those that have familiar spirits, and the wizards, out of the land: wherefore then layest thou a snare for my life, to cause me to die?

10And Saul sware to her by the LORD, saying, *As* the LORD liveth, there shall no punishment happen to thee for this thing.

11Then said the woman, Whom shall I bring up unto thee? And he said, Bring me up Samuel.

12And when the woman saw Samuel, she cried with a loud voice: and the woman spake to Saul, saying, Why hast thou deceived me? for thou *art* Saul.

13And the king said unto her, Be not afraid: for what sawest thou? And the woman said unto Saul, I saw gods ascending out of the earth.

14And he said unto her, What form *is* he of? And she said, An old man cometh up; and he *is* covered with a mantle. And Saul perceived that it *was* Samuel, and he stooped with *his* face to the ground, and bowed himself.

15¶ And Samuel said to Saul, Why hast thou disquieted me, to bring me up? And Saul answered, I am sore distressed; for the Philistines make war against me, and God is departed from me, and answereth me no more, neither by prophets, nor by dreams: therefore I have called thee, that thou mayest make known unto me what I shall do.

New International

he did not leave a man or woman alive, but took sheep and cattle, donkeys and camels, and clothes. Then he returned to Achish.

10When Achish asked, "Where did you go raiding today?" David would say, "Against the Negev of Judah" or "Against the Negev of Jerahmeel" or "Against the Negev of the Kenites." 11He did not leave a man or woman alive to be brought to Gath, for he thought, "They might inform on us and say, 'This is what David did.'" And such was his practice as long as he lived in Philistine territory. 12Achish trusted David and said to himself, "He has become so odious to his people, the Israelites, that he will be my servant forever."

Saul and the Witch of Endor

28 IN THOSE days the Philistines gathered their forces to fight against Israel. Achish said to David, "You must understand that you and your men will accompany me in the army."

2David said, "Then you will see for yourself what your servant can do."

Achish replied, "Very well, I will make you my bodyguard for life."

3Now Samuel was dead, and all Israel had mourned for him and buried him in his own town of Ramah. Saul had expelled the mediums and spiritists from the land.

4The Philistines assembled and came and set up camp at Shunem, while Saul gathered all the Israelites and set up camp at Gilboa. 5When Saul saw the Philistine army, he was afraid; terror filled his heart. 6He inquired of the LORD, but the LORD did not answer him by dreams or Urim or prophets. 7Saul then said to his attendants, "Find me a woman who is a medium, so I may go and inquire of her."

"There is one in Endor," they said.

8So Saul disguised himself, putting on other clothes, and at night he and two men went to the woman. "Consult a spirit for me," he said, "and bring up for me the one I name."

9But the woman said to him, "Surely you know what Saul has done. He has cut off the mediums and spiritists from the land. Why have you set a trap for my life to bring about my death?"

10Saul swore to her by the LORD, "As surely as the LORD lives, you will not be punished for this."

11Then the woman asked, "Whom shall I bring up for you?"

"Bring up Samuel," he said.

12When the woman saw Samuel, she cried out at the top of her voice and said to Saul, "Why have you deceived me? You are Saul!"

13The king said to her, "Don't be afraid. What do you see?"

The woman said, "I see a spirita coming up out of the ground."

14"What does he look like?" he asked.

"An old man wearing a robe is coming up," she said.

Then Saul knew it was Samuel, and he bowed down and prostrated himself with his face to the ground.

15Samuel said to Saul, "Why have you disturbed me by bringing me up?"

"I am in great distress," Saul said. "The Philistines are fighting against me, and God has turned away from me. He no longer answers me, either by prophets or by dreams. So I have called on you to tell me what to do."

a *13* Or *see spirits; or see gods*

Living Bible

they hit, and took for themselves the sheep, oxen, don-keys, camels, and clothing before returning to their homes.

10"Where did you make your raid today?" Achish would ask.

And David would reply, "Against the south of Judah and the people of Jerahmeel and the Kenites."

11No one was left alive to come to Gath and tell where he had really been. This happened again and again while he was living among the Philistines. 12Achish believed David and thought that the people of Israel must hate him bitterly by now. "Now he will have to stay here and serve me forever!" the king thought.

28 ABOUT THAT time the Philistines mustered their armies for another war with Israel.

"Come and help us fight," King Achish said to David and his men.

2"Good," David agreed. "You will soon see what a help we can be to you."

"If you are, you shall be my personal bodyguard for life," Achish told him.

3(Meanwhile, Samuel had died and all Israel had mourned for him. He was buried in Ramah, his home town. King Saul had banned all mediums and wizards from the land of Israel.)

4The Philistines set up their camp at Shunem, and Saul and the armies of Israel were at Gilboa. 5, 6When Saul saw the vast army of the Philistines, he was frantic with fear and asked the Lord what he should do. But the Lord refused to answer him, either by dreams, or by Urim,b or by the prophets. 7, 8Saul then instructed his aides to try to find a medium so that he could ask her what to do, and they found one at Endor. Saul disguised himself by wearing ordinary clothing instead of his royal robes. He went to the woman's home at night, accompa-nied by two of his men.

"I've got to talk to a dead man," he pleaded. "Will you bring his spirit up?"

9"Are you trying to get me killed?" the woman demanded. "You know that Saul has had all of the mediums and fortune-tellers executed. You are spying on me."

10But Saul took a solemn oath that he wouldn't betray her.

11Finally the woman said, "Well, whom do you want me to bring up?"

"Bring me Samuel," Saul replied.

12When the woman saw Samuel, she screamed, "You've deceived me! You are Saul!"

13"Don't be frightened!" the king told her. "What do you see?"

"I see a specter coming up out of the earth," she said.

14"What does he look like?"

"He is an old man wrapped in a robe."

Saul realized that it was Samuel and bowed low be-fore him.

15"Why have you disturbed me by bringing me back?" Samuel asked Saul.

"Because I am in deep trouble," he replied. "The Philistines are at war with us, and God has left me and won't reply by prophets or dreams; so I have called for you to ask you what to do."

New Revised Standard

the land, leaving neither man nor woman alive, but took away the sheep, the oxen, the donkeys, the camels, and the clothing, and came back to Achish. 10When Achish asked, "Against whomc have you made a raid today?" David would say, "Against the Negeb of Judah," or "Against the Negeb of the Jerahmeelites," or, "Against the Negeb of the Kenites." 11David left neither man nor woman alive to be brought back to Gath, thinking, "They might tell about us, and say, 'David has done so and so.' " Such was his practice all the time he lived in the country of the Philistines. 12Achish trusted David, thinking, "He has made himself utterly abhorrent to his people Israel; therefore he shall always be my servant."

28 IN THOSE days the Philistines gathered their forces for war, to fight against Israel. Achish said to David, "You know, of course, that you and your men are to go out with me in the army." 2David said to Achish, "Very well, then you shall know what your servant can do." Achish said to David, "Very well, I will make you my bodyguard for life."

Saul Consults a Medium

3 Now Samuel had died, and all Israel had mourned for him and buried him in Ramah, his own city. Saul had expelled the mediums and the wizards from the land. 4The Philistines assembled, and came and encamped at Shunem. Saul gathered all Israel, and they encamped at Gilboa. 5When Saul saw the army of the Philistines, he was afraid, and his heart trembled greatly. 6When Saul inquired of the LORD, the LORD did not answer him, not by dreams, or by Urim, or by prophets. 7Then Saul said to his servants, "Seek out for me a woman who is a medium, so that I may go to her and inquire of her." His servants said to him, "There is a medium at Endor."

8 So Saul disguised himself and put on other clothes and went there, he and two men with him. They came to the woman by night. And he said, "Consult a spirit for me, and bring up for me the one whom I name to you." 9The woman said to him, "Surely you know what Saul has done, how he has cut off the mediums and the wizards from the land. Why then are you laying a snare for my life to bring about my death?" 10But Saul swore to her by the LORD, "As the LORD lives, no punishment shall come upon you for this thing." 11Then the woman said, "Whom shall I bring up for you?" He answered, "Bring up Samuel for me." 12When the woman saw Samuel, she cried out with a loud voice; and the woman said to Saul, "Why have you deceived me? You are Saul!" 13The king said to her, "Have no fear; what do you see?" The woman said to Saul, "I see a divine be-ingd coming up out of the ground." 14He said to her, "What is his appearance?" She said, "An old man is coming up; he is wrapped in a robe." So Saul knew that it was Samuel, and he bowed with his face to the ground, and did obeisance.

15 Then Samuel said to Saul, "Why have you dis-turbed me by bringing me up?" Saul answered, "I am in great distress, for the Philistines are warring against me, and God has turned away from me and answers me no more, either by prophets or by dreams; so I have sum-moned you to tell me what I should do." 16Samuel said,

---

b 28:5, 6 or by Urim. The Urim and Thummim were holy instruments which were used as lots in determining the will of God. See Ex 28:30.

c Q Ms Gk Vg: MT lacks whom   d Or a god; or gods

King James

16Then said Samuel, Wherefore then dost thou ask of me, seeing the LORD is departed from thee, and is become thine enemy?

17And the LORD hath done to him, as he spake by me: for the LORD hath rent the kingdom out of thine hand, and given it to thy neighbour, *even* to David:

18Because thou obeyedst not the voice of the LORD, nor executedst his fierce wrath upon Amalek, therefore hath the LORD done this thing unto thee this day.

19Moreover the LORD will also deliver Israel with thee into the hand of the Philistines: and tomorrow *shalt* thou and thy sons *be* with me: the LORD also shall deliver the host of Israel into the hand of the Philistines.

20Then Saul fell straightway all along on the earth, and was sore afraid, because of the words of Samuel: and there was no strength in him; for he had eaten no bread all the day, nor all the night.

21¶ And the woman came unto Saul, and saw that he was sore troubled, and said unto him, Behold, thine handmaid hath obeyed thy voice, and I have put my life in my hand, and have hearkened unto thy words which thou spakest unto me.

22Now therefore, I pray thee, hearken thou also unto the voice of thine handmaid, and let me set a morsel of bread before thee; and eat, that thou mayest have strength, when thou goest on thy way.

23But he refused, and said, I will not eat. But his servants, together with the woman, compelled him; and he hearkened unto their voice. So he arose from the earth, and sat upon the bed.

24And the woman had a fat calf in the house; and she hasted, and killed it, and took flour, and kneaded *it*, and did bake unleavened bread thereof:

25And she brought *it* before Saul, and before his servants; and they did eat. Then they rose up, and went away that night.

29 NOW THE Philistines gathered together all their armies to Aphek: and the Israelites pitched by a fountain which *is* in Jezreel.

2And the lords of the Philistines passed on by hundreds, and by thousands: but David and his men passed on in the rearward with Achish.

3Then said the princes of the Philistines, What *do* these Hebrews *here?* And Achish said unto the princes of the Philistines, *Is* not this David, the servant of Saul the king of Israel, which hath been with me these days, or these years, and I have found no fault in him since he fell *unto me* unto this day?

4And the princes of the Philistines were wroth with him; and the princes of the Philistines said unto him, Make this fellow return, that he may go again to his place which thou hast appointed him, and let him not go down with us to battle, lest in the battle he be an adversary to us: for wherewith should he reconcile himself unto his master? *should it* not *be* with the heads of these men?

5*Is* not this David, of whom they sang one to another in dances, saying, Saul slew his thousands, and David his ten thousands?

6¶ Then Achish called David, and said unto him, Surely, *as* the LORD liveth, thou hast been upright, and thy going out and thy coming in with me in the host *is* good in my sight: for I have not found evil in thee since the day of thy coming unto me unto this day: nevertheless the lords favour thee not.

7Wherefore now return, and go in peace, that thou displease not the lords of the Philistines.

8¶ And David said unto Achish, But what have I done? and what hast thou found in thy servant so long as I have been with thee unto this day, that I may not go fight against the enemies of my lord the king?

New International

16Samuel said, "Why do you consult me, now that the LORD has turned away from you and become your enemy? 17The LORD has done what he predicted through me. The LORD has torn the kingdom out of your hands and given it to one of your neighbors—to David. 18Because you did not obey the LORD or carry out his fierce wrath against the Amalekites, the LORD has done this to you today. 19The LORD will hand over both Israel and you to the Philistines, and tomorrow you and your sons will be with me. The LORD will also hand over the army of Israel to the Philistines."

20Immediately Saul fell full length on the ground, filled with fear because of Samuel's words. His strength was gone, for he had eaten nothing all that day and night.

21When the woman came to Saul and saw that he was greatly shaken, she said, "Look, your maidservant has obeyed you. I took my life in my hands and did what you told me to do. 22Now please listen to your servant and let me give you some food so you may eat and have the strength to go on your way."

23He refused and said, "I will not eat."

But his men joined the woman in urging him, and he listened to them. He got up from the ground and sat on the couch.

24The woman had a fattened calf at the house, which she butchered at once. She took some flour, kneaded it and baked bread without yeast. 25Then she set it before Saul and his men, and they ate. That same night they got up and left.

Achish Sends David Back to Ziklag

29 THE PHILISTINES gathered all their forces at Aphek, and Israel camped by the spring in Jezreel. 2As the Philistine rulers marched with their units of hundreds and thousands, David and his men were marching at the rear with Achish. 3The commanders of the Philistines asked, "What about these Hebrews?"

Achish replied, "Is this not David, who was an officer of Saul king of Israel? He has already been with me for over a year, and from the day he left Saul until now, I have found no fault in him."

4But the Philistine commanders were angry with him and said, "Send the man back, that he may return to the place you assigned him. He must not go with us into battle, or he will turn against us during the fighting. How better could he regain his master's favor than by taking the heads of our own men? 5Isn't this the David they sang about in their dances:

" 'Saul has slain his thousands,
and David his tens of thousands'?"

6So Achish called David and said to him, "As surely as the LORD lives, you have been reliable, and I would be pleased to have you serve with me in the army. From the day you came to me until now, I have found no fault in you, but the rulers don't approve of you. 7Turn back and go in peace; do nothing to displease the Philistine rulers."

8"But what have I done?" asked David. "What have you found against your servant from the day I came to you until now? Why can't I go and fight against the enemies of my lord the king?"

Living Bible

16But Samuel replied, "Why ask me if the Lord has left you and has become your enemy? 17He has done just as he said he would and has taken the kingdom from you and given it to your rival, David. 18All this has come upon you because you did not obey the Lord's instructions when he was so angry with Amalek. 19What's more, the entire Israeli army will be routed and destroyed by the Philistines tomorrow, and you and your sons will be here with me."

20Saul now fell full length upon the ground, paralyzed with fright because of Samuel's words. He was also faint with hunger, for he had eaten nothing all day. 21When the woman saw how distraught he was, she said, "Sir, I obeyed your command at the risk of my life. 22Now do what I say, and let me give you something to eat so you'll regain your strength for the trip back." 23But he refused. The men who were with him added their pleas to that of the woman until he finally yielded and got up and sat on the bed. 24The woman had been fattening a calf, so she hurried out and killed it and kneaded dough and baked unleavened bread. 25She brought the meal to the king and his men, and they ate it. Then they went out into the night.

29 THE PHILISTINE army now mobilized at Aphek, and the Israelis camped at the springs in Jezreel. 2As the Philistine captains were leading out their troops by battalions and companies, David and his men marched at the rear with King Achish.

3But the Philistine commanders demanded, "What are these Israelis doing here?"

And King Achish told them, "This is David, the runaway servant of King Saul of Israel. He's been with me for years, and I've never found one fault in him since he arrived."

4But the Philistine leaders were angry. "Send them back!" they demanded. "They aren't going into the battle with us—they'll turn against us. Is there any better way for him to reconcile himself with his master than by turning against us in the battle? 5This is the same man the women of Israel sang about in their dances: 'Saul has slain his thousands and David his ten thousands!' "

6So Achish finally summoned David and his men.

"I swear by the Lord," he told them, "you are some of the finest men I've ever met, and I think you should go with us, but my commanders say no. 7Please don't upset them, but go back quietly."

8"What have I done to deserve this treatment?" David demanded. "Why can't I fight your enemies?"

New Revised Standard

"Why then do you ask me, since the LORD has turned from you and become your enemy? 17The LORD has done to you just as he spoke by me; for the LORD has torn the kingdom out of your hand, and given it to your neighbor, David. 18Because you did not obey the voice of the LORD, and did not carry out his fierce wrath against Amalek, therefore the LORD has done this thing to you today. 19Moreover the LORD will give Israel along with you into the hands of the Philistines; and tomorrow you and your sons shall be with me; the LORD will also give the army of Israel into the hands of the Philistines."

20 Immediately Saul fell full length on the ground, filled with fear because of the words of Samuel; and there was no strength in him, for he had eaten nothing all day and all night. 21The woman came to Saul, and when she saw that he was terrified, she said to him, "Your servant has listened to you; I have taken my life in my hand, and have listened to what you have said to me. 22Now therefore, you also listen to your servant; let me set a morsel of bread before you. Eat, that you may have strength when you go on your way." 23He refused, and said, "I will not eat." But his servants, together with the woman, urged him; and he listened to their words. So he got up from the ground and sat on the bed. 24Now the woman had a fatted calf in the house. She quickly slaughtered it, and she took flour, kneaded it, and baked unleavened cakes. 25She put them before Saul and his servants, and they ate. Then they rose and went away that night.

The Philistines Reject David

29 NOW THE Philistines gathered all their forces at Aphek, while the Israelites were encamped by the fountain that is in Jezreel. 2As the lords of the Philistines were passing on by hundreds and by thousands, and David and his men were passing on in the rear with Achish, 3the commanders of the Philistines said, "What are these Hebrews doing here?" Achish said to the commanders of the Philistines, "Is this not David, the servant of King Saul of Israel, who has been with me now for days and years? Since he deserted to me I have found no fault in him to this day." 4But the commanders of the Philistines were angry with him; and the commanders of the Philistines said to him, "Send the man back, so that he may return to the place that you have assigned to him; he shall not go down with us to battle, or else he may become an adversary to us in the battle. For how could this fellow reconcile himself to his lord? Would it not be with the heads of the men here? 5Is this not David, of whom they sing to one another in dances,

'Saul has killed his thousands,
　and David his ten thousands'?"

6 Then Achish called David and said to him, "As the LORD lives, you have been honest, and to me it seems right that you should march out and in with me in the campaign; for I have found nothing wrong in you from the day of your coming to me until today. Nevertheless the lords do not approve of you. 7So go back now; and go peaceably; do nothing to displease the lords of the Philistines." 8David said to Achish, "But what have I done? What have you found in your servant from the day I entered your service until now, that I should not go and fight against the enemies of my lord the king?" 9Achish

King James

9And Achish answered and said to David, I know that thou *art* good in my sight, as an angel of God: notwithstanding the princes of the Philistines have said, He shall not go up with us to the battle.

10Wherefore now rise up early in the morning with thy master's servants that are come with thee: and as soon as ye be up early in the morning, and have light, depart.

11So David and his men rose up early to depart in the morning, to return into the land of the Philistines. And the Philistines went up to Jezreel.

30 AND IT came to pass, when David and his men were come to Ziklag on the third day, that the Amalekites had invaded the south, and Ziklag, and smitten Ziklag, and burned it with fire;

2And had taken the women captives, that *were* therein: they slew not any, either great or small, but carried *them* away, and went on their way.

3¶ So David and his men came to the city, and, behold, *it was* burned with fire; and their wives, and their sons, and their daughters, were taken captives.

4Then David and the people that *were* with him lifted up their voice and wept, until they had no more power to weep.

5And David's two wives were taken captives, Ahinoam the Jezreelitess, and Abigail the wife of Nabal the Carmelite.

6And David was greatly distressed; for the people spake of stoning him, because the soul of all the people was grieved, every man for his sons and for his daughters: but David encouraged himself in the LORD his God.

7And David said to Abiathar the priest, Ahimelech's son, I pray thee, bring me hither the ephod. And Abiathar brought thither the ephod to David.

8And David inquired at the LORD, saying, Shall I pursue after this troop? shall I overtake them? And he answered him, Pursue: for thou shalt surely overtake *them*, and without fail recover *all*.

9So David went, he and the six hundred men that *were* with him, and came to the brook Besor, where those that were left behind stayed.

10But David pursued, he and four hundred men: for two hundred abode behind, which were so faint that they could not go over the brook Besor.

11¶ And they found an Egyptian in the field, and brought him to David, and gave him bread, and he did eat; and they made him drink water;

12And they gave him a piece of a cake of figs, and two clusters of raisins: and when he had eaten, his spirit came again to him: for he had eaten no bread, nor drunk *any* water, three days and three nights.

13And David said unto him, To whom *belongest* thou? and whence *art* thou? And he said, I *am* a young man of Egypt, servant to an Amalekite; and my master left me, because three days agone I fell sick.

14We made an invasion *upon* the south of the Cherethites, and upon *the coast* which *belongeth* to Judah, and upon the south of Caleb; and we burned Ziklag with fire.

15And David said to him, Canst thou bring me down to this company? And he said, Swear unto me by God, that thou wilt neither kill me, nor deliver me into the hands of my master, and I will bring thee down to this company.

16¶ And when he had brought him down, behold, *they were* spread abroad upon all the earth, eating and drinking, and dancing, because of all the great spoil that they had taken out of the land of the Philistines, and out of the land of Judah.

New International

9Achish answered, "I know that you have been as pleasing in my eyes as an angel of God; nevertheless, the Philistine commanders have said, 'He must not go up with us into battle.' 10Now get up early, along with your master's servants who have come with you, and leave in the morning as soon as it is light."

11So David and his men got up early in the morning to go back to the land of the Philistines, and the Philistines went up to Jezreel.

David Destroys the Amalekites

30 DAVID AND his men reached Ziklag on the third day. Now the Amalekites had raided the Negev and Ziklag. They had attacked Ziklag and burned it, 2and had taken captive the women and all who were in it, both young and old. They killed none of them, but carried them off as they went on their way.

3When David and his men came to Ziklag, they found it destroyed by fire and their wives and sons and daughters taken captive. 4So David and his men wept aloud until they had no strength left to weep. 5David's two wives had been captured—Ahinoam of Jezreel and Abigail, the widow of Nabal of Carmel. 6David was greatly distressed because the men were talking of stoning him; each one was bitter in spirit because of his sons and daughters. But David found strength in the LORD his God.

7Then David said to Abiathar the priest, the son of Ahimelech, "Bring me the ephod." Abiathar brought it to him, 8and David inquired of the LORD, "Shall I pursue this raiding party? Will I overtake them?"

"Pursue them," he answered. "You will certainly overtake them and succeed in the rescue."

9David and the six hundred men with him came to the Besor Ravine, where some stayed behind, 10for two hundred men were too exhausted to cross the ravine. But David and four hundred men continued the pursuit. 11They found an Egyptian in a field and brought him to David. They gave him water to drink and food to eat— 12part of a cake of pressed figs and two cakes of raisins. He ate and was revived, for he had not eaten any food or drunk any water for three days and three nights.

13David asked him, "To whom do you belong, and where do you come from?"

He said, "I am an Egyptian, the slave of an Amalekite. My master abandoned me when I became ill three days ago. 14We raided the Negev of the Kerethites and the territory belonging to Judah and the Negev of Caleb. And we burned Ziklag."

15David asked him, "Can you lead me down to this raiding party?"

He answered, "Swear to me before God that you will not kill me or hand me over to my master, and I will take you down to them."

16He led David down, and there they were, scattered over the countryside, eating, drinking and reveling because of the great amount of plunder they had taken from the land of the Philistines and from Judah. 17David

Living Bible

9But Achish insisted, "As far as I'm concerned, you're as perfect as an angel of God. But my commanders are afraid to have you with them in the battle. 10Now get up early in the morning and leave as soon as it is light."

11So David headed back into the land of the Philistines while the Philistine army went on to Jezreel.

30 THREE DAYS later, when David and his men arrived home at their city of Ziklag, they found that the Amalekites had raided the city and burned it to the ground, 2carrying off all the women and children. 3As David and his men looked at the ruins and realized what had happened to their families, 4they wept until they could weep no more. 5(David's two wives, Ahinoam and Abigail, were among those who had been captured.) 6David was seriously worried, for in their bitter grief for their children, his men began talking of killing him. But David took strength from the Lord.

7Then he said to Abiathar the priest, "Bring me the oracle!"a So Abiathar brought it.

8David asked the Lord, "Shall I chase them? Will I catch them?"

And the Lord told him, "Yes, go after them; you will recover everything that was taken from you!"

9, 10So David and his six hundred men set out after the Amalekites. When they reached Besor Brook, two hundred of the men were too exhausted to cross, but the other four hundred kept going. 11, 12Along the way they found an Egyptian youth in a field and brought him to David. He had not had anything to eat or drink for three days and nights, so they gave him part of a fig cake, two clusters of raisins, and some water, and his strength soon returned.

13"Who are you and where do you come from?" David asked him.

"I am an Egyptian—the servant of an Amalekite," he replied. "My master left me behind three days ago because I was sick. 14We were on our way back from raiding the Cherethites in the Negeb, and had raided the south of Judah and the land of Caleb, and had burned Ziklag."

15"Can you tell me where they went?" David asked.

The young man replied, "If you swear by God's name that you will not kill me or give me back to my master, then I will guide you to them."

16So he led them to the Amalekite encampment. They were spread out across the fields, eating and drinking and dancing with joy because of the vast amount of loot they had taken from the Philistines and from the men of Judah. 17David and his men rushed in among them and killed him.

New Revised Standard

replied to David, "I know that you are as blameless in my sight as an angel of God; nevertheless, the commanders of the Philistines have said, 'He shall not go up with us to the battle.' 10Now then rise early in the morning, you and the servants of your lord who came with you, and go to the place that I appointed for you. As for the evil report, do not take it to heart, for you have done well before me.b Start early in the morning, and leave as soon as you have light." 11So David set out with his men early in the morning, to return to the land of the Philistines. But the Philistines went up to Jezreel.

David Avenges the Destruction of Ziklag

30 NOW WHEN David and his men came to Ziklag on the third day, the Amalekites had made a raid on the Negeb and on Ziklag. They had attacked Ziklag, burned it down, 2and taken captive the women and allc who were in it, both small and great; they killed none of them, but carried them off, and went their way. 3When David and his men came to the city, they found it burned down, and their wives and sons and daughters taken captive. 4Then David and the people who were with him raised their voices and wept, until they had no more strength to weep. 5David's two wives also had been taken captive, Ahinoam of Jezreel, and Abigail the widow of Nabal of Carmel. 6David was in great danger; for the people spoke of stoning him, because all the people were bitter in spirit for their sons and daughters. But David strengthened himself in the LORD his God.

7 David said to the priest Abiathar son of Ahimelech, "Bring me the ephod." So Abiathar brought the ephod to David. 8David inquired of the LORD, "Shall I pursue this band? Shall I overtake them?" He answered him, "Pursue; for you shall surely overtake and shall surely rescue." 9So David set out, he and the six hundred men who were with him. They came to the Wadi Besor, where those stayed who were left behind. 10But David went on with the pursuit, he and four hundred men; two hundred stayed behind, too exhausted to cross the Wadi Besor.

11 In the open country they found an Egyptian, and brought him to David. They gave him bread and he ate, they gave him water to drink; 12they also gave him a piece of fig cake and two clusters of raisins. When he had eaten, his spirit revived; for he had not eaten bread or drunk water for three days and three nights. 13Then David said to him, "To whom do you belong? Where are you from?" He said, "I am a young man of Egypt, servant of an Amalekite. My master left me behind because I fell sick three days ago. 14We had made a raid on the Negeb of the Cherethites and on that which belongs to Judah and on the Negeb of Caleb; and we burned Ziklag down." 15David said to him, "Will you take me down to this raiding party?" He said, "Swear to me by God that you will not kill me, or hand me over to my master, and I will take you down to them."

16 When he had taken him down, they were spread out all over the ground, eating and drinking and dancing, because of the great amount of spoil they had taken from the land of the Philistines and from the land of Judah.

---

a 30:7 Bring me the oracle, literally, "Bring me the ephod." See Ex 28.

b Gk: Heb lacks and go to the place . . . done well before me   c Gk: Heb lacks and all

King James

17And David smote them from the twilight even unto the evening of the next day: and there escaped not a man of them, save four hundred young men, which rode upon camels, and fled.

18And David recovered all that the Amalekites had carried away: and David rescued his two wives.

19And there was nothing lacking to them, neither small nor great, neither sons nor daughters, neither spoil, nor any *thing* that they had taken to them: David recovered all.

20And David took all the flocks and the herds, *which* they drave before those *other* cattle, and said, This *is* David's spoil.

21¶ And David came to the two hundred men, which were so faint that they could not follow David, whom they had made also to abide at the brook Besor: and they went forth to meet David, and to meet the people that *were* with him: and when David came near to the people, he saluted them.

22Then answered all the wicked men and *men* of Belial, of those that went with David, and said, Because they went not with us, we will not give them *aught* of the spoil that we have recovered, save to every man his wife and his children, that they may lead *them* away, and depart.

23Then said David, Ye shall not do so, my brethren, with that which the LORD hath given us, who hath preserved us, and delivered the company that came against us into our hand.

24For who will hearken unto you in this matter? but as his part *is* that goeth down to the battle, so *shall* his part *be* that tarrieth by the stuff: they shall part alike.

25And it was *so* from that day forward, that he made it a statute and an ordinance for Israel unto this day.

26¶ And when David came to Ziklag, he sent of the spoil unto the elders of Judah, *even* to his friends, saying, Behold a present for you of the spoil of the enemies of the LORD;

27To *them* which *were* in Beth-el, and to *them* which *were* in south Ramoth, and to *them* which *were* in Jattir,

28And to *them* which *were* in Aroer, and to *them* which *were* in Siphmoth, and to *them* which *were* in Eshtemoa,

29And to *them* which *were* in Rachal, and to *them* which *were* in the cities of the Jerahmeelites, and to *them* which *were* in the cities of the Kenites,

30And to *them* which *were* in Hormah, and to *them* which *were* in Chor-ashan, and to *them* which *were* in Athach,

31And to *them* which *were* in Hebron, and to all the places where David himself and his men were wont to haunt.

31 NOW THE Philistines fought against Israel: and the men of Israel fled from before the Philistines, and fell down slain in mount Gilboa.

2And the Philistines followed hard upon Saul and upon his sons; and the Philistines slew Jonathan, and Abinadab, and Melchi-shua, Saul's sons.

3And the battle went sore against Saul, and the archers hit him; and he was sore wounded of the archers.

4Then said Saul unto his armourbearer, Draw thy sword, and thrust me through therewith; lest these uncircumcised come and thrust me through, and abuse me. But his armourbearer would not; for he was sore afraid. Therefore Saul took a sword, and fell upon it.

5And when his armourbearer saw that Saul was dead, he fell likewise upon his sword, and died with him.

6So Saul died, and his three sons, and his armourbearer, and all his men, that same day together.

New International

fought them from dusk until the evening of the next day, and none of them got away, except four hundred young men who rode off on camels and fled. 18David recovered everything the Amalekites had taken, including his two wives. 19Nothing was missing: young or old, boy or girl, plunder or anything else they had taken. David brought everything back. 20He took all the flocks and herds, and his men drove them ahead of the other livestock, saying, "This is David's plunder."

21Then David came to the two hundred men who had been too exhausted to follow him and who were left behind at the Besor Ravine. They came out to meet David and the people with him. As David and his men approached, he greeted them. 22But all the evil men and troublemakers among David's followers said, "Because they did not go out with us, we will not share with them the plunder we recovered. However, each man may take his wife and children and go."

23David replied, "No, my brothers, you must not do that with what the LORD has given us. He has protected us and handed over to us the forces that came against us. 24Who will listen to what you say? The share of the man who stayed with the supplies is to be the same as that of him who went down to the battle. All will share alike." 25David made this a statute and ordinance for Israel from that day to this.

26When David arrived in Ziklag, he sent some of the plunder to the elders of Judah, who were his friends, saying, "Here is a present for you from the plunder of the LORD's enemies."

27He sent it to those who were in Bethel, Ramoth Negev and Jattir; 28to those in Aroer, Siphmoth, Eshtemoa 29and Racal; to those in the towns of the Jerahmeelites and the Kenites; 30to those in Hormah, Bor Ashan, Athach 31and Hebron; and to those in all the other places where David and his men had roamed.

Saul Takes His Life

31 NOW THE Philistines fought against Israel; the Israelites fled before them, and many fell slain on Mount Gilboa. 2The Philistines pressed hard after Saul and his sons, and they killed his sons Jonathan, Abinadab and Malki-Shua. 3The fighting grew fierce around Saul, and when the archers overtook him, they wounded him critically.

4Saul said to his armor-bearer, "Draw your sword and run me through, or these uncircumcised fellows will come and run me through and abuse me."

But his armor-bearer was terrified and would not do it; so Saul took his own sword and fell on it. 5When the armor-bearer saw that Saul was dead, he too fell on his sword and died with him. 6So Saul and his three sons and his armor-bearer and all his men died together that same day.

Living Bible

slaughtered them all that night and the entire next day until evening. No one escaped except four hundred young men who fled on camels. 18, 19David got back everything they had taken. The men recovered their families and all of their belongings, and David rescued his two wives. 20His troops rounded up all the flocks and herds and drove them on ahead of them. "These are all yours personally, as your reward!" they told David.

21When they reached Besor Brook and the two hundred men who had been too exhausted to go on, David greeted them joyfully. 22But some of the ruffians among David's men declared, "They didn't go with us, so they can't have any of the loot. Give them their wives and their children and tell them to be gone.

23But David said, "No, my brothers! The Lord has kept us safe and helped us defeat the enemy. 24Do you think that anyone will listen to you when you talk like this? We share and share alike—those who go to battle and those who guard the equipment."

25From then on David made this a law for all of Israel, and it is still followed.

26When he arrived at Ziklag, he sent part of the loot to the elders of Judah. "Here is a present for you, taken from the Lord's enemies," he wrote them. 27–31The gifts were sent to the elders in the following cities where David and his men had been: Bethel, South Ramoth, Jattir, Aroer, Siphmoth, Eshtemoa, Racal, the cities of the Jerahmeelites, the cities of the Kenites, Hormah, Borashan, Athach, Hebron.

New Revised Standard

17David attacked them from twilight until the evening of the next day. Not one of them escaped, except four hundred young men, who mounted camels and fled. 18David recovered all that the Amalekites had taken; and David rescued his two wives. 19Nothing was missing, whether small or great, sons or daughters, spoil or anything that had been taken; David brought back everything. 20David also captured all the flocks and herds, which were driven ahead of the other cattle; people said, "This is David's spoil."

21 Then David came to the two hundred men who had been too exhausted to follow David, and who had been left at the Wadi Besor. They went out to meet David and to meet the people who were with him. When David drew near to the people he saluted them. 22Then all the corrupt and worthless fellows among the men who had gone with David said, "Because they did not go with us, we will not give them any of the spoil that we have recovered, except that each man may take his wife and children, and leave." 23But David said, "You shall not do so, my brothers, with what the LORD has given us; he has preserved us and handed over to us the raiding party that attacked us. 24Who would listen to you in this matter? For the share of the one who goes down into the battle shall be the same as the share of the one who stays by the baggage; they shall share alike." 25From that day forward he made it a statute and an ordinance for Israel; it continues to the present day.

26 When David came to Ziklag, he sent part of the spoil to his friends, the elders of Judah, saying, "Here is a present for you from the spoil of the enemies of the LORD"; 27it was for those in Bethel, in Ramoth of the Negeb, in Jattir, 28in Aroer, in Siphmoth, in Eshtemoa, 29in Racal, in the towns of the Jerahmeelites, in the towns of the Kenites, 30in Hormah, in Bor-ashan, in Athach, 31in Hebron, all the places where David and his men had roamed.

The Death of Saul and His Sons

31 MEANWHILE THE Philistines had begun the battle against Israel, and the Israelis fled from them and were slaughtered wholesale on Mount Gilboa. 2The Philistines closed in on Saul, and killed his sons Jonathan, Abinidab, and Malchishua.

3, 4Then the archers overtook Saul and wounded him badly. He groaned to his armor bearer, "Kill me with your sword before these heathen Philistines capture me and torture me." But his armor bearer was afraid to, so Saul took his own sword and fell upon the point of the blade, and it pierced him through. 5When his armor bearer saw that he was dead, he also fell upon his sword and died with him. 6So Saul, his armor bearer, his three sons, and his troops died together that same day.

31 NOW THE Philistines fought against Israel; and the men of Israel fled before the Philistines, and many fella on Mount Gilboa. 2The Philistines overtook Saul and his sons; and the Philistines killed Jonathan and Abinadab and Malchishua, the sons of Saul. 3The battle pressed hard upon Saul; the archers found him, and he was badly wounded by them. 4Then Saul said to his armor-bearer, "Draw your sword and thrust me through with it, so that these uncircumcised may not come and thrust me through, and make sport of me." But his armor-bearer was unwilling; for he was terrified. So Saul took his own sword and fell upon it. 5When his armor-bearer saw that Saul was dead, he also fell upon his sword and died with him. 6So Saul and his three sons and his armor-bearer and all his men died together on the same day. 7When the men of Israel who were on the

a Heb *and they fell slain*

King James

7¶ And when the men of Israel that *were* on the other side of the valley, and *they* that *were* on the other side Jordan, saw that the men of Israel fled, and that Saul and his sons were dead, they forsook the cities, and fled; and the Philistines came and dwelt in them.

8And it came to pass on the morrow, when the Philistines came to strip the slain, that they found Saul and his three sons fallen in mount Gilboa.

9And they cut off his head, and stripped off his armour, and sent into the land of the Philistines round about, to publish *it in* the house of their idols, and among the people.

10And they put his armour in the house of Ashtaroth: and they fastened his body to the wall of Beth-shan.

11¶ And when the inhabitants of Jabesh-gilead heard of that which the Philistines had done to Saul;

12All the valiant men arose, and went all night, and took the body of Saul and the bodies of his sons from the wall of Beth-shan, and came to Jabesh, and burnt them there.

13And they took their bones, and buried *them* under a tree at Jabesh, and fasted seven days.

New International

7When the Israelites along the valley and those across the Jordan saw that the Israelite army had fled and that Saul and his sons had died, they abandoned their towns and fled. And the Philistines came and occupied them.

8The next day, when the Philistines came to strip the dead, they found Saul and his three sons fallen on Mount Gilboa. 9They cut off his head and stripped off his armor, and they sent messengers throughout the land of the Philistines to proclaim the news in the temple of their idols and among their people. 10They put his armor in the temple of the Ashtoreths and fastened his body to the wall of Beth Shan.

11When the people of Jabesh Gilead heard of what the Philistines had done to Saul, 12all their valiant men journeyed through the night to Beth Shan. They took down the bodies of Saul and his sons from the wall of Beth Shan and went to Jabesh, where they burned them. 13Then they took their bones and buried them under a tamarisk tree at Jabesh, and they fasted seven days.

Living Bible

7When the Israelis on the other side of the valley and beyond the Jordan heard that their comrades had fled and that Saul and his sons were dead, they abandoned their cities; and the Philistines lived in them.

8The next day when the Philistines went out to strip the dead, they found the bodies of Saul and his three sons on Mount Gilboa. 9They cut off Saul's head and stripped off his armor and sent the wonderful news of Saul's death to their idols and to the people throughout their land.

10His armor was placed in the temple of Ashtaroth, and his body was fastened to the wall of Beth-shan.

11But when the people of Jabesh-gilead heard what the Philistines had done, 12warriors from that town traveled all night to Beth-shan and took down the bodies of Saul and his sons from the wall and brought them to Jabesh, where they cremated them. 13Then they buried their remains beneath the oak tree at Jabesh and fasted for seven days.

New Revised Standard

other side of the valley and those beyond the Jordan saw that the men of Israel had fled and that Saul and his sons were dead, they forsook their towns and fled; and the Philistines came and occupied them.

8 The next day, when the Philistines came to strip the dead, they found Saul and his three sons fallen on Mount Gilboa. 9They cut off his head, stripped off his armor, and sent messengers throughout the land of the Philistines to carry the good news to the houses of their idols and to the people. 10They put his armor in the temple of Astarte;[a] and they fastened his body to the wall of Beth-shan. 11But when the inhabitants of Jabesh-gilead heard what the Philistines had done to Saul, 12all the valiant men set out, traveled all night long, and took the body of Saul and the bodies of his sons from the wall of Beth-shan. They came to Jabesh and burned them there. 13Then they took their bones and buried them under the tamarisk tree in Jabesh, and fasted seven days.

---

[a] Heb plural

King James   **New International**

THE SECOND BOOK OF

Samuel

OTHERWISE CALLED THE SECOND BOOK

OF THE KINGS

1 NOW IT came to pass after the death of Saul, when David was returned from the slaughter of the Amalekites, and David had abode two days in Ziklag;

2It came even to pass on the third day, that, behold, a man came out of the camp from Saul with his clothes rent, and earth upon his head: and *so* it was, when he came to David, that he fell to the earth, and did obeisance.

3And David said unto him, From whence comest thou? And he said unto him, Out of the camp of Israel am I escaped.

4And David said unto him, How went the matter? I pray thee, tell me. And he answered, That the people are fled from the battle, and many of the people also are fallen and dead; and Saul and Jonathan his son are dead also.

5And David said unto the young man that told him, How knowest thou that Saul and Jonathan his son be dead?

6And the young man that told him said, As I happened by chance upon mount Gilboa, behold, Saul leaned upon his spear; and, lo, the chariots and horsemen followed hard after him.

7And when he looked behind him, he saw me, and called unto me. And I answered, Here *am* I.

8And he said unto me, Who *art* thou? And I answered him, I *am* an Amalekite.

9He said unto me again, Stand, I pray thee, upon me, and slay me: for anguish is come upon me, because my life *is* yet whole in me.

10So I stood upon him, and slew him, because I was sure that he could not live after that he was fallen: and I took the crown that *was* upon his head, and the bracelet that *was* on his arm, and have brought them hither unto my lord.

11Then David took hold on his clothes, and rent them; and likewise all the men that *were* with him:

12And they mourned, and wept, and fasted until even, for Saul, and for Jonathan his son, and for the people of the LORD, and for the house of Israel; because they were fallen by the sword.

13¶ And David said unto the young man that told him, Whence *art* thou? And he answered, I *am* the son of a stranger, an Amalekite.

14And David said unto him, How wast thou not afraid to stretch forth thine hand to destroy the LORD's anointed?

15And David called one of the young men, and said, Go near, *and* fall upon him. And he smote him that he died.

16And David said unto him, Thy blood *be* upon thy head; for thy mouth hath testified against thee, saying, I have slain the LORD's anointed.

17¶ And David lamented with this lamentation over Saul and over Jonathan his son:

18(Also he bade them teach the children of Judah *the use of* the bow: behold, *it is* written in the book of Jasher.)

2 Samuel

David Hears of Saul's Death

1 AFTER THE death of Saul, David returned from defeating the Amalekites and stayed in Ziklag two days. 2On the third day a man arrived from Saul's camp, with his clothes torn and with dust on his head. When he came to David, he fell to the ground to pay him honor.

3"Where have you come from?" David asked him.

He answered, "I have escaped from the Israelite camp."

4"What happened?" David asked. "Tell me."

He said, "The men fled from the battle. Many of them fell and died. And Saul and his son Jonathan are dead."

5Then David said to the young man who brought him the report, "How do you know that Saul and his son Jonathan are dead?"

6"I happened to be on Mount Gilboa," the young man said, "and there was Saul, leaning on his spear, with the chariots and riders almost upon him. 7When he turned around and saw me, he called out to me, and I said, 'What can I do?'

8"He asked me, 'Who are you?'

"'An Amalekite,' I answered.

9"Then he said to me, 'Stand over me and kill me! I am in the throes of death, but I'm still alive.'

10"So I stood over him and killed him, because I knew that after he had fallen he could not survive. And I took the crown that was on his head and the band on his arm and have brought them here to my lord."

11Then David and all the men with him took hold of their clothes and tore them. 12They mourned and wept and fasted till evening for Saul and his son Jonathan, and for the army of the LORD and the house of Israel, because they had fallen by the sword.

13David said to the young man who brought him the report, "Where are you from?"

"I am the son of an alien, an Amalekite," he answered.

14David asked him, "Why were you not afraid to lift your hand to destroy the LORD's anointed?"

15Then David called one of his men and said, "Go, strike him down!" So he struck him down, and he died. 16For David had said to him, "Your blood be on your own head. Your own mouth testified against you when you said, 'I killed the LORD's anointed.' "

David's Lament for Saul and Jonathan

17David took up this lament concerning Saul and his son Jonathan, 18and ordered that the men of Judah be taught this lament of the bow (it is written in the Book of Jashar):

2 Samuel

2 Samuel

Living Bible

1 SAUL WAS dead and David had returned to Ziklag after slaughtering the Amalekites. Three days later a man arrived from the Israeli army with his clothes torn and with dirt on his head as a sign of mourning. He fell to the ground before David in deep respect.

3"Where do you come from?" David asked.

"From the Israeli army," he replied.

4"What happened?" David demanded. "Tell me how the battle went."

And the man replied, "Our entire army fled. Thousands of men are dead and wounded on the field, and Saul and his son Jonathan have been killed."

5"How do you know they are dead?"

6"Because I was on Mount Gilboa and saw Saul leaning against his spear with the enemy chariots closing in upon him. 7When he saw me he cried out for me to come to him.

8" 'Who are you?' he asked.

" 'An Amalekite,' I replied.

9" 'Come and put me out of my misery,' he begged, 'for I am in terrible pain but life lingers on.'

10"So I killed him, for I knew he couldn't live.ᵃ Then I took his crown and one of his bracelets to bring to you, my lord."

11David and his men tore their clothes in sorrow when they heard the news. 12They mourned and wept and fasted all day for Saul and his son Jonathan, and for the Lord's people, and for the men of Israel who had died that day.

13Then David said to the young man who had brought the news, "Where are you from?"

And he replied, "I am an Amalekite."

14"Why did you kill God's chosen king?" David demanded.

15Then he said to one of his young men, "Kill him!" So he ran him through with his sword and he died.

16"You die self-condemned," David said, "for you yourself confessed that you killed God's appointed king."

17, 18Then David composed a dirge for Saul and Jonathan and afterward commanded that it be sung throughout Israel. It is quoted here from the book, _Heroic Ballads._

New Revised Standard

David Mourns for Saul and Jonathan

1 AFTER THE death of Saul, when David had returned from defeating the Amalekites, David remained two days in Ziklag. 2On the third day, a man came from Saul's camp, with his clothes torn and dirt on his head. When he came to David, he fell to the ground and did obeisance. 3David said to him, "Where have you come from?" He said to him, "I have escaped from the camp of Israel." 4David said to him, "How did things go? Tell me!" He answered, "The army fled from the battle, but also many of the army fell and died; and Saul and his son Jonathan also died." 5Then David asked the young man who was reporting to him, "How do you know that Saul and his son Jonathan died?" 6The young man reporting to him said, "I happened to be on Mount Gilboa; and there was Saul leaning on his spear, while the chariots and the horsemen drew close to him. 7When he looked behind him, he saw me, and called to me. I answered, 'Here sir.' 8And he said to me, 'Who are you?' I answered him, 'I am an Amalekite.' 9He said to me, 'Come, stand over me and kill me; for convulsions have seized me, and yet my life still lingers.' 10So I stood over him, and killed him, for I knew that he could not live after he had fallen. I took the crown that was on his head and the armlet that was on his arm, and I have brought them here to my lord."

11 Then David took hold of his clothes and tore them; and all the men who were with him did the same. 12They mourned and wept, and fasted until evening for Saul and for his son Jonathan, and for the army of the LORD and for the house of Israel, because they had fallen by the sword. 13David said to the young man who had reported to him, "Where do you come from?" He answered, "I am the son of a resident alien, an Amalekite." 14David said to him, "Were you not afraid to lift your hand to destroy the LORD's anointed?" 15Then David called one of the young men and said, "Come here and strike him down." So he struck him down and he died. 16David said to him, "Your blood be on your head; for your own mouth has testified against you, saying, 'I have killed the LORD's anointed.' "

17 David intoned this lamentation over Saul and his son Jonathan. 18(He ordered that The Song of the Bowᵇ be taught to the people of Judah; it is written in the Book of Jashar.) He said:

ᵃ 1:10 He was evidently lying. See 1 Sam 31:3 for the true account. Probably he had found Saul dead upon the field and thought David would reward him for killing his rival.

ᵇ Heb _that The Bow_

King James

[19]The beauty of Israel is slain upon thy high places: how are the mighty fallen!

[20]Tell *it* not in Gath, publish *it* not in the streets of Askelon; lest the daughters of the Philistines rejoice, lest the daughters of the uncircumcised triumph.

[21]Ye mountains of Gilboa, *let there be* no dew, neither *let there be* rain, upon you, nor fields of offerings: for there the shield of the mighty is vilely cast away, the shield of Saul, *as though he had* not *been* anointed with oil.

[22]From the blood of the slain, from the fat of the mighty, the bow of Jonathan turned not back, and the sword of Saul returned not empty.

[23]Saul and Jonathan *were* lovely and pleasant in their lives, and in their death they were not divided: they were swifter than eagles, they were stronger than lions.

[24]Ye daughters of Israel, weep over Saul, who clothed you in scarlet, with *other* delights, who put on ornaments of gold upon your apparel.

[25]How are the mighty fallen in the midst of the battle! O Jonathan, *thou wast* slain in thine high places.

[26]I am distressed for thee, my brother Jonathan: very pleasant hast thou been unto me: thy love to me was wonderful, passing the love of women.

[27]How are the mighty fallen, and the weapons of war perished!

2 AND IT came to pass after this, that David inquired of the LORD, saying, Shall I go up into any of the cities of Judah? And the LORD said unto him, Go up. And David said, Whither shall I go up? And he said, Unto Hebron.

[2]So David went up thither, and his two wives also, Ahinoam the Jezreelitess, and Abigail Nabal's wife the Carmelite.

[3]And his men that *were* with him did David bring up, every man with his household: and they dwelt in the cities of Hebron.

[4]And the men of Judah came, and there they anointed David king over the house of Judah. And they told David, saying, *That* the men of Jabesh-gilead *were they* that buried Saul.

[5]¶ And David sent messengers unto the men of Jabesh-gilead, and said unto them, Blessed *be* ye of the LORD, that ye have shown this kindness unto your lord, *even* unto Saul, and have buried him.

[6]And now the LORD show kindness and truth unto you: and I also will requite you this kindness, because ye have done this thing.

[7]Therefore now let your hands be strengthened, and be ye valiant: for your master Saul is dead, and also the house of Judah have anointed me king over them.

[8]¶ But Abner the son of Ner, captain of Saul's host, took Ish-bosheth the son of Saul, and brought him over to Mahanaim;

New International

[19]"Your glory, O Israel, lies slain on your heights.
    How the mighty have fallen!

[20]"Tell it not in Gath,
    proclaim it not in the streets of Ashkelon,
lest the daughters of the Philistines be glad,
    lest the daughters of the uncircumcised rejoice.

[21]"O mountains of Gilboa,
    may you have neither dew nor rain,
    nor fields that yield offerings of grain,.
For there the shield of the mighty was defiled,
    the shield of Saul—no longer rubbed with oil.

[22]From the blood of the slain,
    from the flesh of the mighty,
the bow of Jonathan did not turn back,
    the sword of Saul did not return unsatisfied.

[23]"Saul and Jonathan—
    in life they were loved and gracious,
    and in death they were not parted.
They were swifter than eagles,
    they were stronger than lions.

[24]"O daughters of Israel,
    weep for Saul,
who clothed you in scarlet and finery,
    who adorned your garments with ornaments of gold.

[25]"How the mighty have fallen in battle!
    Jonathan lies slain on your heights.
[26]I grieve for you, Jonathan my brother;
    you were very dear to me.
Your love for me was wonderful,
    more wonderful than that of women.

[27]"How the mighty have fallen!
    The weapons of war have perished!"

David Anointed King Over Judah

2 IN THE course of time, David inquired of the LORD. "Shall I go up to one of the towns of Judah?" he asked.
    The LORD said, "Go up."
    David asked, "Where shall I go?"
    "To Hebron," the LORD answered.

[2]So David went up there with his two wives, Ahinoam of Jezreel and Abigail, the widow of Nabal of Carmel. [3]David also took the men who were with him, each with his family, and they settled in Hebron and its towns. [4]Then the men of Judah came to Hebron and there they anointed David king over the house of Judah.

When David was told that it was the men of Jabesh Gilead who had buried Saul, [5]he sent messengers to the men of Jabesh Gilead to say to them, "The LORD bless you for showing this kindness to Saul your master by burying him. [6]May the LORD now show you kindness and faithfulness, and I too will show you the same favor because you have done this. [7]Now then, be strong and brave, for Saul your master is dead, and the house of Judah has anointed me king over them."

War Between the Houses of David and Saul

[8]Meanwhile, Abner son of Ner, the commander of Saul's army, had taken Ish-Bosheth son of Saul and brought him over to Mahanaim. [9]He made him king over

Living Bible

19O Israel, your pride and joy lies dead upon the hills;
Mighty heroes have fallen.
20Don't tell the Philistines, lest they rejoice.
Hide it from the cities of Gath and Ashkelon,
Lest the heathen nations laugh in triumph.
21O Mount Gilboa,
Let there be no dew nor rain upon you,
Let no crops of grain grow on your slopes.a
For there the mighty Saul has died;
He is God's appointed king no more.
22Both Saul and Jonathan slew their strongest foes,
And did not return from battle empty-handed.
23How much they were loved, how wonderful they
    were—
Both Saul and Jonathan!
They were together in life and in death.
They were swifter than eagles, stronger than lions.
24But now, O women of Israel, weep for Saul;
He enriched you
With fine clothing and gold ornaments.
25These mighty heroes have fallen in the midst of the
    battle.
Jonathan is slain upon the hills.
26How I weep for you, my brother Jonathan;
How much I loved you!
And your love for me was deeper
Than the love of women!
27The mighty ones have fallen,
Stripped of their weapons, and dead.

2 DAVID THEN asked the Lord, "Shall I move back
   to Judah?"
   And the Lord replied, "Yes."
   "Which city shall I go to?"
   And the Lord replied, "Hebron."
   2So David and his wives—Ahino-am from Jezreel
and Abigail the widow of Nabal from Carmel— 3and his
men and their families all moved to Hebron. 4Then the
leaders of Judah came to David and crowned him king
of the Judean confederacy.
   When David heard that the men of Jabesh-gilead had
buried Saul, 5he sent them this message: "May the Lord
bless you for being so loyal to your king and giving him
a decent burial. 6May the Lord be loyal to you in return,
and reward you with many demonstrations of his love!
And I too will be kind to you because of what you have
done. 7And now I ask you to be my strong and loyal
subjects, now that Saul is dead. Be like the tribe of Judah
who have appointed me as their new king."
   8But Abner, Saul's commander-in-chief, had gone to
Mahanaim to crown Saul's son Ish-bosheth as king. 9His

New Revised Standard

19 Your glory, O Israel, lies slain upon your high
        places!
    How the mighty have fallen!
20 Tell it not in Gath,
        proclaim it not in the streets of Ashkelon;
    or the daughters of the Philistines will rejoice,
        the daughters of the uncircumcised will
        exult.

21 You mountains of Gilboa,
        let there be no dew or rain upon you,
        nor bounteous fields!b
    For there the shield of the mighty was defiled,
        the shield of Saul, anointed with oil no
        more.

22 From the blood of the slain,
        from the fat of the mighty,
    the bow of Jonathan did not turn back,
        nor the sword of Saul return empty.

23 Saul and Jonathan, beloved and lovely!
        In life and in death they were not divided;
    they were swifter than eagles,
        they were stronger than lions.

24 O daughters of Israel, weep over Saul,
        who clothed you with crimson, in luxury,
        who put ornaments of gold on your apparel.

25 How the mighty have fallen
        in the midst of the battle!

    Jonathan lies slain upon your high places.
26 I am distressed for you, my brother
        Jonathan;
    greatly beloved were you to me;
        your love to me was wonderful,
        passing the love of women.

27 How the mighty have fallen,
        and the weapons of war perished!

David Anointed King of Judah

2 AFTER THIS David inquired of the LORD, "Shall
   I go up into any of the cities of Judah?" The LORD
said to him, "Go up." David said, "To which shall I go
up?" He said, "To Hebron." 2So David went up there,
along with his two wives, Ahinoam of Jezreel, and Abigail the widow of Nabal of Carmel. 3David brought up
the men who were with him, every one with his household; and they settled in the towns of Hebron. 4Then the
people of Judah came, and there they anointed David
king over the house of Judah.
   When they told David, "It was the people of Jabesh-
gilead who buried Saul," 5David sent messengers to the
people of Jabesh-gilead, and said to them, "May you be
blessed by the LORD, because you showed this loyalty
to Saul your lord, and buried him! 6Now may the LORD
show steadfast love and faithfulness to you! And I too
will reward you because you have done this thing.
7Therefore let your hands be strong, and be valiant; for
Saul your lord is dead, and the house of Judah has
anointed me king over them."

Ishbaal King of Israel

8 But Abner son of Ner, commander of Saul's
army, had taken Ishbaalc son of Saul, and brought him
over to Mahanaim. 9He made him king over Gilead, the

---

a 1:21 let no crops of grain grow on your slopes. The text is uncertain in
the original manuscripts.

b Meaning of Heb uncertain   c Gk Compare 1 Chr 8.33; 9.39: Heb
Ish-bosheth, "man of shame"

King James

9And made him king over Gilead, and over the Ashurites, and over Jezreel, and over Ephraim, and over Benjamin, and over all Israel.

10Ish-bosheth Saul's son *was* forty years old when he began to reign over Israel, and reigned two years. But the house of Judah followed David.

11And the time that David was king in Hebron over the house of Judah was seven years and six months.

12¶ And Abner the son of Ner, and the servants of Ish-bosheth the son of Saul, went out from Mahanaim to Gibeon.

13And Joab the son of Zeruiah, and the servants of David, went out, and met together by the pool of Gibeon: and they sat down, the one on the one side of the pool, and the other on the other side of the pool.

14And Abner said to Joab, Let the young men now arise, and play before us. And Joab said, Let them arise.

15Then there arose and went over by number twelve of Benjamin, which *pertained* to Ish-bosheth the son of Saul, and twelve of the servants of David.

16And they caught every one his fellow by the head, and *thrust* his sword in his fellow's side; so they fell down together: wherefore that place was called Helkath-hazzurim, which *is* in Gibeon.

17And there was a very sore battle that day; and Abner was beaten, and the men of Israel, before the servants of David.

18¶ And there were three sons of Zeruiah there, Joab, and Abishai, and Asahel: and Asahel *was as* light of foot as a wild roe.

19And Asahel pursued after Abner; and in going he turned not to the right hand nor to the left from following Abner.

20Then Abner looked behind him, and said, *Art* thou Asahel? And he answered, I *am*.

21And Abner said to him, Turn thee aside to thy right hand or to thy left, and lay thee hold on one of the young men, and take thee his armour. But Asahel would not turn aside from following of him.

22And Abner said again to Asahel, Turn thee aside from following me: wherefore should I smite thee to the ground? how then should I hold up my face to Joab thy brother?

23Howbeit he refused to turn aside: wherefore Abner with the hinder end of the spear smote him under the fifth *rib*, that the spear came out behind him; and he fell down there, and died in the same place: and it came to pass, *that* as many as came to the place where Asahel fell down and died stood still.

24Joab also and Abishai pursued after Abner: and the sun went down when they were come to the hill of Ammah, that *lieth* before Giah by the way of the wilderness of Gibeon.

25¶ And the children of Benjamin gathered themselves together after Abner, and became one troop, and stood on the top of an hill.

26Then Abner called to Joab, and said, Shall the sword devour for ever? knowest thou not that it will be bitterness in the latter end? how long shall it be then, ere thou bid the people return from following their brethren?

27And Joab said, *As* God liveth, unless thou hadst spoken, surely then in the morning the people had gone up every one from following his brother.

28So Joab blew a trumpet, and all the people stood still, and pursued after Israel no more, neither fought they any more.

29And Abner and his men walked all that night through the plain, and passed over Jordan, and went through all Bithron, and they came to Mahanaim.

30And Joab returned from following Abner: and when he had gathered all the people together, there lacked of David's servants nineteen men and Asahel.

31But the servants of David had smitten of Benjamin, and of Abner's men, *so that* three hundred and threescore men died.

New International

Gilead, Ashuri[a] and Jezreel, and also over Ephraim, Benjamin and all Israel.

10Ish-Bosheth son of Saul was forty years old when he became king over Israel, and he reigned two years. The house of Judah, however, followed David. 11The length of time David was king in Hebron over the house of Judah was seven years and six months.

12Abner son of Ner, together with the men of Ish-Bosheth son of Saul, left Mahanaim and went to Gibeon. 13Joab son of Zeruiah and David's men went out and met them at the pool of Gibeon. One group sat down on one side of the pool and one group on the other side.

14Then Abner said to Joab, "Let's have some of the young men get up and fight hand to hand in front of us."

"All right, let them do it," Joab said.

15So they stood up and were counted off—twelve men for Benjamin and Ish-Bosheth son of Saul, and twelve for David. 16Then each man grabbed his opponent by the head and thrust his dagger into his opponent's side, and they fell down together. So that place in Gibeon was called Helkath Hazzurim.[b]

17The battle that day was very fierce, and Abner and the men of Israel were defeated by David's men.

18The three sons of Zeruiah were there: Joab, Abishai and Asahel. Now Asahel was as fleet-footed as a wild gazelle. 19He chased Abner, turning neither to the right nor to the left as he pursued him. 20Abner looked behind him and asked, "Is that you, Asahel?"

"It is," he answered.

21Then Abner said to him, "Turn aside to the right or to the left; take on one of the young men and strip him of his weapons." But Asahel would not stop chasing him.

22Again Abner warned Asahel, "Stop chasing me! Why should I strike you down? How could I look your brother Joab in the face?"

23But Asahel refused to give up the pursuit; so Abner thrust the butt of his spear into Asahel's stomach, and the spear came out through his back. He fell there and died on the spot. And every man stopped when he came to the place where Asahel had fallen and died.

24But Joab and Abishai pursued Abner, and as the sun was setting, they came to the hill of Ammah, near Giah on the way to the wasteland of Gibeon. 25Then the men of Benjamin rallied behind Abner. They formed themselves into a group and took their stand on top of a hill.

26Abner called out to Joab, "Must the sword devour forever? Don't you realize that this will end in bitterness? How long before you order your men to stop pursuing their brothers?"

27Joab answered, "As surely as God lives, if you had not spoken, the men would have continued the pursuit of their brothers until morning.[c]"

28So Joab blew the trumpet, and all the men came to a halt; they no longer pursued Israel, nor did they fight anymore.

29All that night Abner and his men marched through the Arabah. They crossed the Jordan, continued through the whole Bithron[d] and came to Mahanaim.

30Then Joab returned from pursuing Abner and assembled all his men. Besides Asahel, nineteen of David's men were found missing. 31But David's men had killed three hundred and sixty Benjamites who were with Abner. 32They took Asahel and buried him in his

a 9 Or *Asher* b 16 *Helkath Hazzurim* means *field of daggers* or *field of hostilities*. c 27 Or *spoken this morning, the men would not have taken up the pursuit of their brothers*; or *spoken, the men would have given up the pursuit of their brothers by morning* d 29 Or *morning*; or *ravine*; the meaning of the Hebrew for this word is uncertain.

Living Bible

territory included Gilead, Ashuri, Jezreel, Ephraim, the tribe of Benjamin, and all the rest of Israel. 10, 11Ish-bosheth was forty years old at the time. He reigned in Mahanaim for two years; meanwhile, David was reigning in Hebron and was king of the Judean confederacy for seven and one-half years.

12One day General Abner led some of Ish-bosheth's troops to Gibeon from Mahanaim, 13and General Joab (the son of Zeruiah) led David's troops out to meet them. They met at the pool of Gibeon, where they sat facing each other on opposite sides of the pool. 14Then Abner suggested to Joab, "Let's watch some sword play between our young men!"

Joab agreed, 15so twelve men were chosen from each side to fight in mortal combat. 16Each one grabbed his opponent by the hair and thrust his sword into the other's side, so that all of them died. The place has been known ever since as Sword Field.

17The two armies then began to fight each other, and by the end of the day Abner and the men of Israel had been defeated by Joabe and the forces of David. 18Joab's brothers, Abishai and Asahel, were also in the battle. Asahel could run like a deer, 19and he began chasing Abner. He wouldn't stop for anything, but kept on, singleminded, after Abner alone.

20When Abner looked behind and saw him coming, he called out to him, "Is that you, Asahel?"

"Yes," he called back, "it is."

21"Go after someone else!" Abner warned. But Asahel refused and kept on coming.

22Again Abner shouted to him, "Get away from here. I could never face your brother Joab if I have to kill you!"

23But he refused to turn away, so Abner pierced him through the belly with the butt end of his spear. It went right through his body and came out his back. He stumbled to the ground and died there, and everyone stopped when they came to the place where he lay.

24Now Joab and Abishai set out after Abner. The sun was just going down as they arrived at Ammah Hill near Giah, along the road into the Gibeon desert. 25Abner's troops from the tribe of Benjamin regrouped there at the top of the hill, 26and Abner shouted down to Joab, "Must our swords continue to kill each other forever? How long will it be before you call off your people from chasing their brothers?"

27Joab shouted back, "I swear by God that even if you hadn't spoken, we would all have gone home tomorrow morning." 28Then he blew his trumpet and his men stopped chasing the troops of Israel.

29That night Abner and his men retreated across the Jordan Valley, crossed the river, and traveled all the next morning until they arrived at Mahanaim. 30Joab and the men who were with him returned home too, and when he counted his casualties, he learned that only nineteen men were missing, in addition to Asahel. 31But three hundred and sixty of Abner's men (all from the tribe of Benjamin) were dead. 32Joab and his men took

New Revised Standard

Ashurites, Jezreel, Ephraim, Benjamin, and over all Israel. 10Ishbaal,f Saul's son, was forty years old when he began to reign over Israel, and he reigned two years. But the house of Judah followed David. 11The time that David was king in Hebron over the house of Judah was seven years and six months.

The Battle of Gibeon

12 Abner son of Ner, and the servants of Ishbaalf son of Saul, went out from Mahanaim to Gibeon. 13 Joab son of Zeruiah, and the servants of David, went out and met them at the pool of Gibeon. One group sat on one side of the pool, while the other sat on the other side of the pool. 14Abner said to Joab, "Let the young men come forward and have a contest before us." Joab said, "Let them come forward." 15So they came forward and were counted as they passed by, twelve for Benjamin and Ishbaalf son of Saul, and twelve of the servants of David. 16Each grasped his opponent by the head, and thrust his sword in his opponent's side; so they fell down together. Therefore that place was called Helkath-hazzurim,g which is at Gibeon. 17The battle was very fierce that day; and Abner and the men of Israel were beaten by the servants of David.

18 The three sons of Zeruiah were there, Joab, Abishai, and Asahel. Now Asahel was as swift of foot as a wild gazelle. 19Asahel pursued Abner, turning neither to the right nor to the left as he followed him. 20Then Abner looked back and said, "Is it you, Asahel?" He answered, "Yes, it is." 21Abner said to him, "Turn to your right or to your left, and seize one of the young men, and take his spoil." But Asahel would not turn away from following him. 22Abner said again to Asahel, "Turn away from following me; why should I strike you to the ground? How then could I show my face to your brother Joab?" 23But he refused to turn away. So Abner struck him in the stomach with the butt of his spear, so that the spear came out at his back. He fell there, and died where he lay. And all those who came to the place where Asahel had fallen and died, stood still.

24 But Joab and Abishai pursued Abner. As the sun was going down they came to the hill of Ammah, which lies before Giah on the way to the wilderness of Gibeon. 25The Benjaminites rallied around Abner and formed a single band; they took their stand on the top of a hill. 26Then Abner called to Joab, "Is the sword to keep devouring forever? Do you not know that the end will be bitter? How long will it be before you order your people to turn from the pursuit of their kinsmen?" 27Joab said, "As God lives, if you had not spoken, the people would have continued to pursue their kinsmen, not stopping until morning." 28Joab sounded the trumpet and all the people stopped; they no longer pursued Israel or engaged in battle any further.

29 Abner and his men traveled all that night through the Arabah; they crossed the Jordan, and, marching the whole forenoon,h they came to Mahanaim. 30Joab returned from the pursuit of Abner; and when he had gathered all the people together, there were missing of David's servants nineteen men besides Asahel. 31But the servants of David had killed of Benjamin three hundred sixty of Abner's men. 32They took up Asahel and buried

King James

32¶ And they took up Asahel, and buried him in the sepulchre of his father, which *was in* Bethlehem. And Joab and his men went all night, and they came to Hebron at break of day.

3 NOW THERE was long war between the house of Saul and the house of David: but David waxed stronger and stronger, and the house of Saul waxed weaker and weaker.

2¶ And unto David were sons born in Hebron: and his firstborn was Amnon, of Ahinoam the Jezreelitess;

3And his second, Chileab, of Abigail the wife of Nabal the Carmelite; and the third, Absalom the son of Maacah the daughter of Talmai king of Geshur;

4And the fourth, Adonijah the son of Haggith; and the fifth, Shephatiah the son of Abital;

5And the sixth, Ithream, by Eglah David's wife. These were born to David in Hebron.

6¶ And it came to pass, while there was war between the house of Saul and the house of David, that Abner made himself strong for the house of Saul.

7And Saul had a concubine, whose name *was* Rizpah, the daughter of Aiah: and Ish-bosheth said to Abner, Wherefore hast thou gone in unto my father's concubine?

8Then was Abner very wroth for the words of Ish-bosheth, and said, *Am* I a dog's head, which against Judah do show kindness this day unto the house of Saul thy father, to his brethren, and to his friends, and have not delivered thee into the hand of David, that thou chargest me today with a fault concerning this woman?

9So do God to Abner, and more also, except, as the LORD hath sworn to David, even so I do to him;

10To translate the kingdom from the house of Saul, and to set up the throne of David over Israel and over Judah, from Dan even to Beer-sheba.

11And he could not answer Abner a word again, because he feared him.

12¶ And Abner sent messengers to David on his behalf, saying, Whose *is* the land? saying *also,* Make thy league with me, and, behold, my hand *shall be* with thee, to bring about all Israel unto thee.

13¶ And he said, Well; I will make a league with thee: but one thing I require of thee, that is, Thou shalt not see my face, except thou first bring Michal Saul's daughter, when thou comest to see my face.

14And David sent messengers to Ish-bosheth Saul's son, saying, Deliver *me* my wife Michal, which I espoused to me for an hundred foreskins of the Philistines.

15And Ish-bosheth sent, and took her from *her* husband, *even* from Phaltiel the son of Laish.

16And her husband went with her along weeping behind her to Bahurim. Then said Abner unto him, Go, return. And he returned.

17¶ And Abner had communication with the elders of Israel, saying, Ye sought for David in times past *to be* king over you:

18Now then do *it:* for the LORD hath spoken of David, saying, By the hand of my servant David I will save my people Israel out of the hand of the Philistines, and out of the hand of all their enemies.

19And Abner also spake in the ears of Benjamin: and Abner went also to speak in the ears of David in Hebron all that seemed good to Israel, and that seemed good to the whole house of Benjamin.

20So Abner came to David to Hebron, and twenty men with him. And David made Abner and the men that *were* with him a feast.

New International

father's tomb at Bethlehem. Then Joab and his men marched all night and arrived at Hebron by daybreak.

3 THE WAR between the house of Saul and the house of David lasted a long time. David grew stronger and stronger, while the house of Saul grew weaker and weaker.

2Sons were born to David in Hebron:

His firstborn was Amnon the son of Ahinoam of Jezreel;

3his second, Kileab the son of Abigail the widow of Nabal of Carmel;

the third, Absalom the son of Maacah daughter of Talmai king of Geshur;

4the fourth, Adonijah the son of Haggith;

the fifth, Shephatiah the son of Abital;

5and the sixth, Ithream the son of David's wife Eglah.

These were born to David in Hebron.

Abner Goes Over to David

6During the war between the house of Saul and the house of David, Abner had been strengthening his own position in the house of Saul. 7Now Saul had had a concubine named Rizpah daughter of Aiah. And Ish-Bosheth said to Abner, "Why did you sleep with my father's concubine?"

8Abner was very angry because of what Ish-Bosheth said and he answered, "Am I a dog's head—on Judah's side? This very day I am loyal to the house of your father Saul and to his family and friends. I haven't handed you over to David. Yet now you accuse me of an offense involving this woman! 9May God deal with Abner, be it ever so severely, if I do not do for David what the LORD promised him on oath 10and transfer the kingdom from the house of Saul and establish David's throne over Israel and Judah from Dan to Beersheba." 11Ish-Bosheth did not dare to say another word to Abner, because he was afraid of him.

12Then Abner sent messengers on his behalf to say to David, "Whose land is it? Make an agreement with me, and I will help you bring all Israel over to you."

13"Good," said David. "I will make an agreement with you. But I demand one thing of you: Do not come into my presence unless you bring Michal daughter of Saul when you come to see me." 14Then David sent messengers to Ish-Bosheth son of Saul, demanding, "Give me my wife Michal, whom I betrothed to myself for the price of a hundred Philistine foreskins."

15So Ish-Bosheth gave orders and had her taken away from her husband Paltiel son of Laish. 16Her husband, however, went with her, weeping behind her all the way to Bahurim. Then Abner said to him, "Go back home!" So he went back.

17Abner conferred with the elders of Israel and said, "For some time you have wanted to make David your king. 18Now do it! For the LORD promised David, 'By my servant David I will rescue my people Israel from the hand of the Philistines and from the hand of all their enemies.'"

19Abner also spoke to the Benjamites in person. Then he went to Hebron to tell David everything that Israel and the whole house of Benjamin wanted to do. 20When Abner, who had twenty men with him, came to David at Hebron, David prepared a feast for him and his men.

Living Bible

Asahel's body to Bethlehem and buried him beside his father; then they traveled all night and reached Hebron at daybreak.

3 THAT WAS the beginning of a long war between the followers of Saul and of David. David's position now became stronger and stronger, while Saul's dynasty became weaker and weaker.

2Several sons were born to David while he was at Hebron. The oldest was Amnon, born to his wife Ahinoam. 3His second son, Chileab, was born to Abigail, the widow of Nabal of Carmel. The third was Absalom, born to Maacah, the daughter of King Talmai of Geshur. 4The fourth was Adonijah, who was born to Haggith. Then Shephatiah was born to Abital, and 5Ithream was born to Eglah.

6As the war went on, Abner became a very powerful political leader among the followers of Saul. 7He took advantage of his position by sleeping with one of Saul's concubines, a girl named Rizpah. But when Ish-bosheth accused Abner of this, 8Abner was furious.

"Am I a Judean dog to be kicked around like this?" he shouted. "After all I have done for you and for your father by not betraying you to David, is this my reward—to find fault with me about some woman? 9, 10May God curse me if I don't do everything I can to take away the entire kingdom from you, all the way from Dan to Beersheba, and give it to David, just as the Lord predicted."

11Ish-bosheth made no reply, for he was afraid of Abner.

12Then Abner sent messengers to David to discuss a deal—to surrender the kingdom of Israel to him in exchange for becoming commander-in-chief of the combined armies of Israel and Judah.

13"All right," David replied, "but I will not negotiate with you unless you bring me my wife Michal, Saul's daughter." 14David then sent this message to Ish-bosheth: "Give me back my wife Michal, for I bought her with the lives of one hundred Philistines."

15So Ish-bosheth took her away from her husband Palti.a 16He followed along behind her as far as Behurim, weeping as he went. Then Abner told him, "Go on home now." So he returned.

17Meanwhile, Abner consulted with the leaders of Israel and reminded them that for a long time they had wanted David as their king.

18"Now is the time!" he told them. "For the Lord has said, 'It is David by whom I will save my people from the Philistines and from all their other enemies.' "

19Abner also talked to the leaders of the tribe of Benjamin; then he went to Hebron and reported to David his progress with the people of Israel and Benjamin. 20Twenty men accompanied him, and David entertained them with a feast.

New Revised Standard

him in the tomb of his father, which was at Bethlehem. Joab and his men marched all night, and the day broke upon them at Hebron.

Abner Defects to David

3 THERE WAS a long war between the house of Saul and the house of David; David grew stronger and stronger, while the house of Saul became weaker and weaker.

2 Sons were born to David at Hebron: his firstborn was Amnon, of Ahinoam of Jezreel; 3his second, Chileab, of Abigail the widow of Nabal of Carmel; the third, Absalom son of Maacah, daughter of King Talmai of Geshur; 4the fourth, Adonijah son of Haggith; the fifth, Shephatiah son of Abital; 5and the sixth, Ithream, of David's wife Eglah. These were born to David in Hebron.

6 While there was war between the house of Saul and the house of David, Abner was making himself strong in the house of Saul. 7Now Saul had a concubine whose name was Rizpah daughter of Aiah. And Ishbaalb said to Abner, "Why have you gone in to my father's concubine?" 8The words of Ishbaalc made Abner very angry; he said, "Am I a dog's head for Judah? Today I keep showing loyalty to the house of your father Saul, to his brothers, and to his friends, and have not given you into the hand of David; and yet you charge me now with a crime concerning this woman. 9So may God do to Abner and so may he add to it! For just what the LORD has sworn to David, that will I accomplish for him, 10to transfer the kingdom from the house of Saul, and set up the throne of David over Israel and over Judah, from Dan to Beer-sheba." 11And Ishbaalb could not answer Abner another word, because he feared him.

12 Abner sent messengers to David at Hebron,d saying, "To whom does the land belong? Make your covenant with me, and I will give you my support to bring all Israel over to you." 13He said, "Good; I will make a covenant with you. But one thing I require of you: you shall never appear in my presence unless you bring Saul's daughter Michal when you come to see me." 14Then David sent messengers to Saul's son Ishbaal,e saying, "Give me my wife Michal, to whom I became engaged at the price of one hundred foreskins of the Philistines." 15Ishbaale sent and took her from her husband Paltiel the son of Laish. 16But her husband went with her, weeping as he walked behind her all the way to Bahurim. Then Abner said to him, "Go back home!" So he went back.

17 Abner sent word to the elders of Israel, saying, "For some time past you have been seeking David as king over you. 18Now then bring it about; for the LORD has promised David: Through my servant David I will save my people Israel from the hand of the Philistines, and from all their enemies." 19Abner also spoke directly to the Benjaminites; then Abner went to tell David at Hebron all that Israel and the whole house of Benjamin were ready to do.

20 When Abner came with twenty men to David at Hebron, David made a feast for Abner and the men who were with him. 21Abner said to David, "Let me go and

a 3:15 Palti. See 1 Sam 25:44.

b Heb And he   c Gk Compare 1 Chr 8.33; 9.39; Heb Ish-bosheth, "man of shame"   d Gk: Heb where he was   e Heb Ish-bosheth

King James

21And Abner said unto David, I will arise and go, and will gather all Israel unto my lord the king, that they may make a league with thee, and that thou mayest reign over all that thine heart desireth. And David sent Abner away; and he went in peace.

22¶ And, behold, the servants of David and Joab came from *pursuing* a troop, and brought in a great spoil with them: but Abner *was* not with David in Hebron; for he had sent him away, and he was gone in peace.

23When Joab and all the host that *was* with him were come, they told Joab, saying, Abner the son of Ner came to the king, and he hath sent him away, and he is gone in peace.

24Then Joab came to the king, and said, What hast thou done? behold, Abner came unto thee; why *is* it *that* thou hast sent him away, and he is quite gone?

25Thou knowest Abner the son of Ner, that he came to deceive thee, and to know thy going out and thy coming in, and to know all that thou doest.

26And when Joab was come out from David, he sent messengers after Abner, which brought him again from the well of Sirah: but David knew *it* not.

27And when Abner was returned to Hebron, Joab took him aside in the gate to speak with him quietly, and smote him there under the fifth *rib,* that he died, for the blood of Asahel his brother.

28¶ And afterward when David heard *it,* he said, I and my kingdom *are* guiltless before the LORD for ever from the blood of Abner the son of Ner:

29Let it rest on the head of Joab, and on all his father's house; and let there not fail from the house of Joab one that hath an issue, or that is a leper, or that leaneth on a staff, or that falleth on the sword, or that lacketh bread.

30So Joab and Abishai his brother slew Abner, because he had slain their brother Asahel at Gibeon in the battle.

31¶ And David said to Joab, and to all the people that *were* with him, Rend your clothes, and gird you with sackcloth, and mourn before Abner. And king David *himself* followed the bier.

32And they buried Abner in Hebron: and the king lifted up his voice, and wept at the grave of Abner; and all the people wept.

33And the king lamented over Abner, and said, Died Abner as a fool dieth?

34Thy hands *were* not bound, nor thy feet put into fetters: as a man falleth before wicked men, *so* fellest thou. And all the people wept again over him.

35And when all the people came to cause David to eat meat while it was yet day, David sware, saying, So do God to me, and more also, if I taste bread, or aught else, till the sun be down.

36And all the people took notice *of it,* and it pleased them: as whatsoever the king did pleased all the people.

37For all the people and all Israel understood that day that it was not of the king to slay Abner the son of Ner.

38And the king said unto his servants, Know ye not that there is a prince and a great man fallen this day in Israel?

39And I *am* this day weak, though anointed king; and these men the sons of Zeruiah *be* too hard for me: the LORD shall reward the doer of evil according to his wickedness.

4 AND WHEN Saul's son heard that Abner was dead in Hebron, his hands were feeble, and all the Israelites were troubled.

New International

21Then Abner said to David, "Let me go at once and assemble all Israel for my lord the king, so that they may make a compact with you, and that you may rule over all that your heart desires." So David sent Abner away, and he went in peace.

Joab Murders Abner

22Just then David's men and Joab returned from a raid and brought with them a great deal of plunder. But Abner was no longer with David in Hebron, because David had sent him away, and he had gone in peace. 23When Joab and all the soldiers with him arrived, he was told that Abner son of Ner had come to the king and that the king had sent him away and that he had gone in peace. 24So Joab went to the king and said, "What have you done? Look, Abner came to you. Why did you let him go? Now he is gone! 25You know Abner son of Ner; he came to deceive you and observe your movements and find out everything you are doing."

26Joab then left David and sent messengers after Abner, and they brought him back from the well of Sirah. But David did not know it. 27Now when Abner returned to Hebron, Joab took him aside into the gateway, as though to speak with him privately. And there, to avenge the blood of his brother Asahel, Joab stabbed him in the stomach, and he died.

28Later, when David heard about this, he said, "I and my kingdom are forever innocent before the LORD concerning the blood of Abner son of Ner. 29May his blood fall upon the head of Joab and upon all his father's house! May Joab's house never be without someone who has a running sore or leprosya or who leans on a crutch or who falls by the sword or who lacks food."

30(Joab and his brother Abishai murdered Abner because he had killed their brother Asahel in the battle at Gibeon.)

31Then David said to Joab and all the people with him, "Tear your clothes and put on sackcloth and walk in mourning in front of Abner." King David himself walked behind the bier. 32They buried Abner in Hebron, and the king wept aloud at Abner's tomb. All the people wept also.

33The king sang this lament for Abner:

"Should Abner have died as the lawless die?
34   Your hands were not bound,
   your feet were not fettered.
You fell as one falls before wicked men."

And all the people wept over him again.

35Then they all came and urged David to eat something while it was still day; but David took an oath, saying, "May God deal with me, be it ever so severely, if I taste bread or anything else before the sun sets!"

36All the people took note and were pleased; indeed, everything the king did pleased them. 37So on that day all the people and all Israel knew that the king had no part in the murder of Abner son of Ner.

38Then the king said to his men, "Do you not realize that a prince and a great man has fallen in Israel this day? 39And today, though I am the anointed king, I am weak, and these sons of Zeruiah are too strong for me. May the LORD repay the evildoer according to his evil deeds!"

Ish-Bosheth Murdered

4 WHEN ISH-BOSHETH son of Saul heard that Abner had died in Hebron, he lost courage, and all Israel became alarmed. 2Now Saul's son had two men

---

a 29 The Hebrew word was used for various diseases affecting the skin—not necessarily leprosy.

Living Bible

21As Abner left, he promised David, "When I get back I will call a convention of all the people of Israel, and they will elect you as their king, as you've so long desired." So David let Abner return in safety.

22But just after Abner left, Joab and some of David's troops returned from a raid, bringing much loot with them. 23When Joab was told that Abner had just been there visiting the king and had been sent away in peace, 24, 25he rushed to the king, demanding, "What have you done? What do you mean by letting him get away? You know perfectly well that he came to spy on us and that he plans to return and attack us!"

26Then Joab sent messengers to catch up with Abner and tell him to come back. They found him at the well of Sirah and he returned with them; but David knew nothing about it. 27When Abner arrived at Hebron, Joab took him aside at the city gate as if to speak with him privately; but then he pulled out a dagger and killed him in revenge for the death of his brother Asahel.

28When David heard about it he declared, "I vow by the Lord that I and my people are innocent of this crime against Abner. 29Joab and his family are the guilty ones. May each of his children be victims of cancer, or be lepers, or be sterile, or die of starvation, or be killed by the sword!"

30So Joab and his brother Abishai killed Abner because of the death of their brother Asahel at the battle of Gibeon.

31Then David said to Joab and to all those who were with him, "Go into deep mourning for Abner." And King David accompanied the bier to the cemetery. 32They buried Abner in Hebron. And the king and all the people wept at the graveside.

33, 34"Should Abner have died like a fool?" the king lamented.

"Your hands were not bound,
Your feet were not tied—
You were murdered—
The victim of a wicked plot."

And all the people wept again for him. 35, 36David had refused to eat anything the day of the funeral, and now everyone begged him to take a bite of supper. But David vowed that he would eat nothing until sundown. This pleased his people, just as everything else he did pleased them! 37Thus the whole nation, both Judah and Israel, understood from David's actions that he was in no way responsible for Abner's death.

38And David said to his people, "A great leader and a great man has fallen today in Israel; 39and even though I am God's chosen king, I can do nothing with these two sons of Zeruiah. May the Lord repay wicked men for their wicked deeds."

4 WHEN KING Ish-bosheth heard about Abner's death at Hebron, he was paralyzed with fear, and his people too were badly frightened. 2, 3The command

New Revised Standard

rally all Israel to my lord the king, in order that they may make a covenant with you, and that you may reign over all that your heart desires." So David dismissed Abner, and he went away in peace.

Abner Is Killed by Joab

22 Just then the servants of David arrived with Joab from a raid, bringing much spoil with them. But Abner was not with David at Hebron, for Davidb had dismissed him, and he had gone away in peace. 23When Joab and all the army that was with him came, it was told Joab, "Abner son of Ner came to the king, and he has dismissed him, and he has gone away in peace." 24Then Joab went to the king and said, "What have you done? Abner came to you; why did you dismiss him, so that he got away? 25You know that Abner son of Ner came to deceive you, and to learn your comings and goings and to learn all that you are doing."

26 When Joab came out from David's presence, he sent messengers after Abner, and they brought him back from the cistern of Sirah; but David did not know about it. 27When Abner returned to Hebron, Joab took him aside in the gateway to speak with him privately, and there he stabbed him in the stomach. So he died for sheddingc the blood of Asahel, Joab'sd brother. 28Afterward, when David heard of it, he said, "I and my kingdom are forever guiltless before the LORD for the blood of Abner son of Ner. 29May the guilte fall on the head of Joab, and on all his father's house; and may the house of Joab never be without one who has a discharge, or who is leprous,f or who holds a spindle, or who falls by the sword, or who lacks food!" 30So Joab and his brother Abishai murdered Abner because he had killed their brother Asahel in the battle at Gibeon.

31 Then David said to Joab and to all the people who were with him, "Tear your clothes, and put on sackcloth, and mourn over Abner." And King David followed the bier. 32They buried Abner at Hebron. The king lifted up his voice and wept at the grave of Abner, and all the people wept. 33The king lamented for Abner, saying,

"Should Abner die as a fool dies?
34 Your hands were not bound,
your feet were not fettered;
as one falls before the wicked
you have fallen."

And all the people wept over him again. 35Then all the people came to persuade David to eat something while it was still day; but David swore, saying, "So may God do to me, and more, if I taste bread or anything else before the sun goes down!" 36All the people took notice of it, and it pleased them; just as everything the king did pleased all the people. 37So all the people and all Israel understood that day that the king had no part in the killing of Abner son of Ner. 38And the king said to his servants, "Do you not know that a prince and a great man has fallen this day in Israel? 39Today I am powerless, even though anointed king; these men, the sons of Zeruiah, are too violent for me. The LORD pay back the one who does wickedly in accordance with his wickedness!"

Ishbaal Assassinated

4 WHEN SAUL'S son Ishbaalg heard that Abner had died at Hebron, his courage failed, and all Israel was dismayed. 2Saul's son had two captains of

b Heb he   c Heb lacks shedding   d Heb his   e Heb May it   f A term for several skin diseases; precise meaning uncertain   g Heb lacks Ishbaal

King James

2And Saul's son had two men *that were* captains of bands: the name of the one *was* Baanah, and the name of the other Rechab, the sons of Rimmon a Beerothite, of the children of Benjamin: (for Beeroth also was reckoned to Benjamin:

3And the Beerothites fled to Gittaim, and were sojourners there until this day.)

4And Jonathan, Saul's son, had a son *that was* lame of *his* feet. He was five years old when the tidings came of Saul and Jonathan out of Jezreel, and his nurse took him up, and fled: and it came to pass, as she made haste to flee, that he fell, and became lame. And his name *was* Mephibosheth.

5And the sons of Rimmon the Beerothite, Rechab and Baanah, went, and came about the heat of the day to the house of Ish-bosheth, who lay on a bed at noon.

6And they came thither into the midst of the house, *as though* they would have fetched wheat; and they smote him under the fifth *rib:* and Rechab and Baanah his brother escaped.

7For when they came into the house, he lay on his bed in his bedchamber, and they smote him, and slew him, and beheaded him, and took his head, and gat them away through the plain all night.

8And they brought the head of Ish-bosheth unto David to Hebron, and said to the king, Behold the head of Ish-bosheth the son of Saul thine enemy, which sought thy life; and the LORD hath avenged my lord the king this day of Saul, and of his seed.

9¶ And David answered Rechab and Baanah his brother, the sons of Rimmon the Beerothite, and said unto them, *As* the LORD liveth, who hath redeemed my soul out of all adversity,

10When one told me, saying, Behold, Saul is dead, thinking to have brought good tidings, I took hold of him, and slew him in Ziklag, who *thought* that I would have given him a reward for his tidings:

11How much more, when wicked men have slain a righteous person in his own house upon his bed? shall I not therefore now require his blood of your hand, and take you away from the earth?

12And David commanded his young men, and they slew them, and cut off their hands and their feet, and hanged *them* up over the pool in Hebron. But they took the head of Ish-bosheth, and buried *it* in the sepulchre of Abner in Hebron.

5 THEN CAME all the tribes of Israel to David unto Hebron, and spake, saying, Behold, we *are* thy bone and thy flesh.

2Also in time past, when Saul was king over us, thou wast he that leddest out and broughtest in Israel: and the LORD said to thee, Thou shalt feed my people Israel, and thou shalt be a captain over Israel.

3So all the elders of Israel came to the king to Hebron; and king David made a league with them in Hebron before the LORD: and they anointed David king over Israel.

4¶ David *was* thirty years old when he began to reign, *and* he reigned forty years.

5In Hebron he reigned over Judah seven years and six months: and in Jerusalem he reigned thirty and three years over all Israel and Judah.

6¶ And the king and his men went to Jerusalem unto the Jebusites, the inhabitants of the land: which spake unto David, saying, Except thou take away the blind and the lame, thou shalt not come in hither: thinking, David cannot come in hither.

7Nevertheless David took the strong hold of Zion: the same *is* the city of David.

New International

who were leaders of raiding bands. One was named Baanah and the other Recab; they were sons of Rimmon the Beerothite from the tribe of Benjamin—Beeroth is considered part of Benjamin, 3because the people of Beeroth fled to Gittaim and have lived there as aliens to this day.

4(Jonathan son of Saul had a son who was lame in both feet. He was five years old when the news about Saul and Jonathan came from Jezreel. His nurse picked him up and fled, but as she hurried to leave, he fell and became crippled. His name was Mephibosheth.)

5Now Recab and Baanah, the sons of Rimmon the Beerothite, set out for the house of Ish-Bosheth, and they arrived there in the heat of the day while he was taking his noonday rest. 6They went into the inner part of the house as if to get some wheat, and they stabbed him in the stomach. Then Recab and his brother Baanah slipped away.

7They had gone into the house while he was lying on the bed in his bedroom. After they stabbed and killed him, they cut off his head. Taking it with them, they traveled all night by way of the Arabah. 8They brought the head of Ish-Bosheth to David at Hebron and said to the king, "Here is the head of Ish-Bosheth son of Saul, your enemy, who tried to take your life. This day the LORD has avenged my lord the king against Saul and his offspring."

9David answered Recab and his brother Baanah, the sons of Rimmon the Beerothite, "As surely as the LORD lives, who has delivered me out of all trouble, 10when a man told me, 'Saul is dead,' and thought he was bringing good news, I seized him and put him to death in Ziklag. That was the reward I gave him for his news! 11How much more—when wicked men have killed an innocent man in his own house and on his own bed—should I not now demand his blood from your hand and rid the earth of you!"

12So David gave an order to his men, and they killed them. They cut off their hands and feet and hung the bodies by the pool in Hebron. But they took the head of Ish-Bosheth and buried it in Abner's tomb at Hebron.

David Becomes King Over Israel

5 ALL THE tribes of Israel came to David at Hebron and said, "We are your own flesh and blood. 2In the past, while Saul was king over us, you were the one who led Israel on their military campaigns. And the LORD said to you, 'You will shepherd my people Israel, and you will become their ruler.' "

3When all the elders of Israel had come to King David at Hebron, the king made a compact with them at Hebron before the LORD, and they anointed David king over Israel.

4David was thirty years old when he became king, and he reigned forty years. 5In Hebron he reigned over Judah seven years and six months, and in Jerusalem he reigned over all Israel and Judah thirty-three years.

David Conquers Jerusalem

6The king and his men marched to Jerusalem to attack the Jebusites, who lived there. The Jebusites said to David, "You will not get in here; even the blind and the lame can ward you off." They thought, "David cannot get in here." 7Nevertheless, David captured the fortress of Zion, the City of David.

Living Bible

of the Israeli troops then fell to two brothers, Baanah and Rechab, who were captains of King Ish-bosheth's raiding bands. They were the sons of Rimmon, who was from Be-eroth in Benjamin. (People from Be-eroth are counted as Benjaminites even though they fled to Gittaim,a where they now live.)

4(There was a little lame grandson of King Saul's named Mephibosheth, who was the son of Prince Jonathan. He was five years old at the time Saul and Jonathan were killed at the battle of Jezreel. When the news of the outcome of the battle reached the capital, the child's nurse grabbed him and fled, but she fell and dropped him as she was running, and he became lame.)

5Rechab and Baanah arrived at King Ish-bosheth's home one noon as he was taking a nap. 6, 7They walked into the kitchen as though to get a sack of wheat, but then sneaked into his bedroom and murdered him and cut off his head. Taking his head with them, they fled across the desert that night and escaped. 8They presented the head to David at Hebron.

"Look!" they exclaimed. "Here is the head of Ish-bosheth, the son of your enemy Saul who tried to kill you. Today the Lord has given you revenge upon Saul and upon his entire family!"

9But David replied, "I swear by the Lord who saved me from my enemies, 10that when someone told me, 'Saul is dead,' thinking he was bringing me good news, I killed him; that is how I rewarded him for his 'glad tidings.' 11And how much more shall I do to wicked men who kill a good man in his own house and on his bed! Shall I not demand your lives?"

12So David ordered his young men to kill them, and they did. They cut off their hands and feet and hanged their bodies beside the pool in Hebron. And they took Ish-bosheth's head and buried it in Abner's tomb in Hebron.

5 REPRESENTATIVES OF all the tribes of Israel now came to David at Hebron and gave him their pledge of loyalty.

"We are your blood brothers," they said. 2"And even when Saul was our king you were our real leader. The Lord has said that you should be the shepherd and leader of his people."

3So David made a contract before the Lord with the leaders of Israel there at Hebron, and they crowned him king of Israel. 4, 5(He had already been the king of Judah for seven years, since the age of thirty. He then ruled thirty-three years in Jerusalem as king of both Israel and Judah; so he reigned for forty years altogether.)

6David now led his troops to Jerusalem to fight against the Jebusites who lived there.

"You'll never come in here," they told him. "Even the blind and lame could keep you out!" For they thought they were safe. 7But David and his troops defeated them and captured the stronghold of Zion, now called the City of David.

New Revised Standard

raiding bands; the name of the one was Baanah, and the name of the other Rechab. They were sons of Rimmon a Benjaminite from Beeroth—for Beeroth is considered to belong to Benjamin. 3(Now the people of Beeroth had fled to Gittaim and are there as resident aliens to this day).

4 Saul's son Jonathan had a son who was crippled in his feet. He was five years old when the news about Saul and Jonathan came from Jezreel. His nurse picked him up and fled; and, in her haste to flee, it happened that he fell and became lame. His name was Mephibosheth.b

5 Now the sons of Rimmon the Beerothite, Rechab and Baanah, set out, and about the heat of the day they came to the house of Ishbaal,c while he was taking his noonday rest. 6They came inside the house as though to take wheat, and they struck him in the stomach; then Rechab and his brother Baanah escaped.d 7Now they had come into the house while he was lying on his couch in his bedchamber; they attacked him, killed him, and beheaded him. Then they took his head and traveled by way of the Arabah all night long. 8They brought the head of Ishbaalc to David at Hebron and said to the king, "Here is the head of Ishbaal,c son of Saul, your enemy, who sought your life; the LORD has avenged my lord the king this day on Saul and on his offspring."

9 David answered Rechab and his brother Baanah, the sons of Rimmon the Beerothite, "As the LORD lives, who has redeemed my life out of every adversity, 10when the one who told me, 'See, Saul is dead,' thought he was bringing good news, I seized him and killed him at Ziklag—this was the reward I gave him for his news. 11How much more then, when wicked men have killed a righteous man on his bed in his own house! And now shall I not require his blood at your hand, and destroy you from the earth?" 12So David commanded the young men, and they killed them; they cut off their hands and feet, and hung their bodies beside the pool at Hebron. But the head of Ishbaalc they took and buried in the tomb of Abner at Hebron.

David Anointed King of All Israel

5 THEN ALL the tribes of Israel came to David at Hebron, and said, "Look, we are your bone and flesh. 2For some time, while Saul was king over us, it was you who led out Israel and brought it in. The LORD said to you: It is you who shall be shepherd of my people Israel, you who shall be ruler over Israel." 3So all the elders of Israel came to the king at Hebron; and King David made a covenant with them at Hebron before the LORD, and they anointed David king over Israel. 4David was thirty years old when he began to reign, and he reigned forty years. 5At Hebron he reigned over Judah seven years and six months; and at Jerusalem he reigned over all Israel and Judah thirty-three years.

Jerusalem Made Capital of the United Kingdom

6 The king and his men marched to Jerusalem against the Jebusites, the inhabitants of the land, who said to David, "You will not come in here, even the blind and the lame will turn you back"—thinking, "David cannot come in here." 7Nevertheless David took the stronghold of Zion, which is now the city of David.

---

a 4:3 to Gittaim, which is not in Benjamin.

b In 1 Chr 8.34 and 9.40, Merib-baal   c Heb Ish-bosheth   d Meaning of Heb of verse 6 uncertain

King James

8And David said on that day, Whosoever getteth up to the gutter, and smiteth the Jebusites, and the lame and the blind, *that are* hated of David's soul, *he shall be chief and captain*. Wherefore they said, The blind and the lame shall not come into the house.

9So David dwelt in the fort, and called it the city of David. And David built round about from Millo and inward.

10And David went on, and grew great, and the LORD God of hosts *was* with him.

11¶ And Hiram king of Tyre sent messengers to David, and cedar trees, and carpenters, and masons: and they built David an house.

12And David perceived that the LORD had established him king over Israel, and that he had exalted his kingdom for his people Israel's sake.

13¶ And David took *him* more concubines and wives out of Jerusalem, after he was come from Hebron: and there were yet sons and daughters born to David.

14And these *be* the names of those that were born unto him in Jerusalem; Shammuah, and Shobab, and Nathan, and Solomon,

15Ibhar also, and Elishua, and Nepheg, and Japhia,

16And Elishama, and Eliada, and Eliphalet.

17¶ But when the Philistines heard that they had anointed David king over Israel, all the Philistines came up to seek David; and David heard *of it*, and went down to the hold.

18The Philistines also came and spread themselves in the valley of Rephaim.

19And David inquired of the LORD, saying, Shall I go up to the Philistines? wilt thou deliver them into mine hand? And the LORD said unto David, Go up: for I will doubtless deliver the Philistines into thine hand.

20And David came to Baal-perazim, and David smote them there, and said, The LORD hath broken forth upon mine enemies before me, as the breach of waters. Therefore he called the name of that place Baal-perazim.

21And there they left their images, and David and his men burned them.

22¶ And the Philistines came up yet again, and spread themselves in the valley of Rephaim.

23And when David inquired of the LORD, he said, Thou shalt not go up; *but* fetch a compass behind them, and come upon them over against the mulberry trees.

24And let it be, when thou hearest the sound of a going in the tops of the mulberry trees, that then thou shalt bestir thyself: for then shall the LORD go out before thee, to smite the host of the Philistines.

25And David did so, as the LORD had commanded him; and smote the Philistines from Geba until thou come to Gazer.

6 AGAIN, DAVID gathered together all *the* chosen men of Israel, thirty thousand.

2And David arose, and went with all the people that *were* with him from Baale of Judah, to bring up from thence the ark of God, whose name is called by the name of the LORD of hosts that dwelleth *between* the cherubims.

3And they set the ark of God upon a new cart, and brought it out of the house of Abinadab that *was* in Gibeah: and Uzzah and Ahio, the sons of Abinadab, drave the new cart.

4And they brought it out of the house of Abinadab which *was* at Gibeah, accompanying the ark of God: and Ahio went before the ark.

New International

8On that day, David said, "Anyone who conquers the Jebusites will have to use the water shafta to reach those 'lame and blind' who are David's enemies.b" That is why they say, "The 'blind and lame' will not enter the palace."

9David then took up residence in the fortress and called it the City of David. He built up the area around it, from the supporting terracesc inward. 10And he became more and more powerful, because the LORD God Almighty was with him.

11Now Hiram king of Tyre sent messengers to David, along with cedar logs and carpenters and stonemasons, and they built a palace for David. 12And David knew that the LORD had established him as king over Israel and had exalted his kingdom for the sake of his people Israel.

13After he left Hebron, David took more concubines and wives in Jerusalem, and more sons and daughters were born to him. 14These are the names of the children born to him there: Shammua, Shobab, Nathan, Solomon, 15Ibhar, Elishua, Nepheg, Japhia, 16Elishama, Eliada and Eliphelet.

David Defeats the Philistines

17When the Philistines heard that David had been anointed king over Israel, they went up in full force to search for him, but David heard about it and went down to the stronghold. 18Now the Philistines had come and spread out in the Valley of Rephaim; 19so David inquired of the LORD, "Shall I go and attack the Philistines? Will you hand them over to me?"

The LORD answered him, "Go, for I will surely hand the Philistines over to you."

20So David went to Baal Perazim, and there he defeated them. He said, "As waters break out, the LORD has broken out against my enemies before me." So that place was called Baal Perazim.d 21The Philistines abandoned their idols there, and David and his men carried them off.

22Once more the Philistines came up and spread out in the Valley of Rephaim; 23so David inquired of the LORD, and he answered, "Do not go straight up, but circle around behind them and attack them in front of the balsam trees. 24As soon as you hear the sound of marching in the tops of the balsam trees, move quickly, because that will mean the LORD has gone out in front of you to strike the Philistine army." 25So David did as the LORD commanded him, and he struck down the Philistines all the way from Gibeone to Gezer.

The Ark Brought to Jerusalem

6 DAVID AGAIN brought together out of Israel chosen men, thirty thousand in all. 2He and all his men set out from Baalah of Judahf to bring up from there the ark of God, which is called by the Name,g the name of the LORD Almighty, who is enthroned between the cherubim that are on the ark. 3They set the ark of God on a new cart and brought it from the house of Abinadab, which was on the hill. Uzzah and Ahio, sons of Abinadab, were guiding the new cart 4with the ark of God on it,h and Ahio was walking in front of it. 5David and the

---

a 8 Or *use scaling hooks*   b 8 Or *are hated by David*   c 9 Or *the Millo*
d 20 *Baal Perazim* means *the lord who breaks out*.   e 25 Septuagint (see also 1 Chron. 14:16); Hebrew *Geba*   f 2 That is, Kiriath Jearim; Hebrew *Baale Judah*, a variant of *Baalah of Judah*   g 2 Hebrew; Septuagint and Vulgate do not have *the Name*.   h 3,4 Dead Sea Scrolls and some Septuagint manuscripts; Masoretic Text *cart 4and they brought it with the ark of God from the house of Abinadab, which was on the hill*

Living Bible

8When the insulting message from the defenders of the city reached David, he told his troops, "Go up through the water tunnel into the city and destroy those 'lame' and 'blind' Jebusites. How I hate them." (That is the origin of the saying, "Even the blind and the lame could conquer you!")

9So David made the stronghold of Zion (also called the City of David) his headquarters. Then, beginning at the old Millo section of the city, he built northward toward the present city center. 10So David became greater and greater, for the Lord God of heaven was with him.

11Then King Hiram of Tyre sent cedar lumber, carpenters, and masons to build a palace for David. 12David now realized why the Lord had made him the king and blessed his kingdom so greatly—it was because God wanted to pour out his kindness on Israel, his chosen people.

13After moving from Hebron to Jerusalem, David married additional wives and concubines, and had many sons and daughters. 14, 15, 16These are his children who were born at Jerusalem:

Shammu-a, Shobab, Nathan, Solomon, Ibhar, Elishu-a, Nepheg, Japhia, Elishama, Eliada, Eliphelet.

17When the Philistines heard that David had been crowned king of Israel, they tried to capture him; but David was told that they were coming and went into the stronghold. 18The Philistines arrived and spread out across the valley of Rephaim.

19Then David asked the Lord, "Shall I go out and fight against them? Will you defeat them for me?"

And the Lord replied, "Yes, go ahead, for I will give them to you."

20So David went out and fought with them at Baal-perazim, and defeated them. "The Lord did it!" he exclaimed. "He burst through my enemies like a raging flood." So he named the place "Bursting." 21At that time David and his troops confiscated many idols which had been abandoned by the Philistines. 22But the Philistines returned and again spread out across the valley of Rephaim.

23When David asked the Lord what to do, he replied, "Don't make a frontal attack. Go behind them and come out by the balsam trees. 24When you hear a sound like marching feet in the tops of the balsam trees, attack! For it will signify that the Lord has prepared the way for you and will destroy them."

25So David did as the Lord had instructed him and destroyed the Philistines all the way from Geba to Gezer.

6 THEN DAVID mobilized thirty thousand special troops and led them to Baal-judah to bring home the Ark of the Lord of heaven who is en-throned above the Guardian Angels. 3The Ark was placed upon a new cart and taken from the hillside home of Abinadab. It was driven by Abinadab's sons, Uzzah and Ahio. 4Ahio was walking in front, 5and was followed by David and

New Revised Standard

8David had said on that day, "Whoever would strike down the Jebusites, let him get up the water shaft to attack the lame and the blind, those whom David hates."i Therefore it is said, "The blind and the lame shall not come into the house." 9David occupied the stronghold, and named it the city of David. David built the city all around from the Millo inward. 10And David became greater and greater, for the LORD, the God of hosts, was with him.

11 King Hiram of Tyre sent messengers to David, along with cedar trees, and carpenters and masons who built David a house. 12David then perceived that the LORD had established him king over Israel, and that he had exalted his kingdom for the sake of his people Israel.

13 In Jerusalem, after he came from Hebron, David took more concubines and wives; and more sons and daughters were born to David. 14These are the names of those who were born to him in Jerusalem: Shammua, Shobab, Nathan, Solomon, 15Ibhar, Elishua, Nepheg, Japhia, 16Elishama, Eliada, and Eliphelet.

Philistine Attack Repulsed

17 When the Philistines heard that David had been anointed king over Israel, all the Philistines went up in search of David; but David heard about it and went down to the stronghold. 18Now the Philistines had come and spread out in the valley of Rephaim. 19David inquired of the LORD, "Shall I go up against the Philistines? Will you give them into my hand?" The LORD said to David, "Go up; for I will certainly give the Philistines into your hand." 20So David came to Baal-perazim, and David defeated them there. He said, "The LORD has burst forth against my enemies before me, like a bursting flood." Therefore that place is called Baal-perazim.k 21The Philistines abandoned their idols there, and David and his men carried them away.

22 Once again the Philistines came up, and were spread out in the valley of Rephaim. 23When David inquired of the LORD, he said, "You shall not go up; go around to their rear, and come upon them opposite the balsam trees. 24When you hear the sound of marching in the tops of the balsam trees, then be on the alert; for then the LORD has gone out before you to strike down the army of the Philistines." 25David did just as the LORD had commanded him; and he struck down the Philistines from Geba all the way to Gezer.

David Brings the Ark to Jerusalem

6 DAVID AGAIN gathered all the chosen men of Israel, thirty thousand. 2David and all the people with him set out and went from Baale-judah, to bring up from there the ark of God, which is called by the name of the LORD of hosts is enthroned on the cherubim. 3They carried the ark of God on a new cart, and brought it out of the house of Abinadab, which was on the hill. Uzzah and Ahio,l the sons of Abinadab, were driving the new cart 4with the ark of God;m and Ahiol went in front of the ark. 5David and all the house of Israel were

i Another reading is those who hate David   j Heb paraz   k That is Lord of Bursting Forth   l Or and his brother   m Compare Gk: Heb and brought it out of the house of Abinadab, which was on the hill with the ark of God

King James

5And David and all the house of Israel played before the LORD on all manner of *instruments made of* fir wood, even on harps, and on psalteries, and on timbrels, and on cornets, and on cymbals.

6¶ And when they came to Nachon's threshingfloor, Uzzah put forth *his hand* to the ark of God, and took hold of it; for the oxen shook *it.*

7And the anger of the LORD was kindled against Uzzah; and God smote him there for *his* error; and there he died by the ark of God.

8And David was displeased, because the LORD had made a breach upon Uzzah: and he called the name of the place Perez-uzzah to this day.

9And David was afraid of the LORD that day, and said, How shall the ark of the LORD come to me?

10So David would not remove the ark of the LORD unto him into the city of David: but David carried it aside into the house of Obed-edom the Gittite.

11And the ark of the LORD continued in the house of Obed-edom the Gittite three months: and the LORD blessed Obed-edom, and all his household.

12¶ And it was told king David, saying, The LORD hath blessed the house of Obed-edom, and all that *per-taineth* unto him, because of the ark of God. So David went and brought up the ark of God from the house of Obed-edom into the city of David with gladness.

13And it was *so,* that when they that bare the ark of the LORD had gone six paces, he sacrificed oxen and fatlings.

14And David danced before the LORD with all *his* might; and David *was* girded with a linen ephod.

15So David and all the house of Israel brought up the ark of the LORD with shouting, and with the sound of the trumpet.

16And as the ark of the LORD came into the city of David, Michal Saul's daughter looked through a window, and saw king David leaping and dancing before the LORD; and she despised him in her heart.

17¶ And they brought in the ark of the LORD, and set it in his place, in the midst of the tabernacle that David had pitched for it: and David offered burnt offerings and peace offerings before the LORD.

18And as soon as David had made an end of offering burnt offerings and peace offerings, he blessed the people in the name of the LORD of hosts.

19And he dealt among all the people, *even* among the whole multitude of Israel, as well to the women as men, to every one a cake of bread, and a good piece *of flesh,* and a flagon *of wine.* So all the people departed every one to his house.

20¶ Then David returned to bless his household. And Michal the daughter of Saul came out to meet David, and said, How glorious was the king of Israel today, who uncovered himself today in the eyes of the handmaids of his servants, as one of the vain fellows shamelessly uncovereth himself!

21And David said unto Michal, *It was* before the LORD, which chose me before thy father, and before all his house, to appoint me ruler over the people of the LORD, over Israel: therefore will I play before the LORD.

22And I will yet be more vile than thus, and will be base in mine own sight: and of the maidservants which thou hast spoken of, of them shall I be had in honour.

23Therefore Michal the daughter of Saul had no child unto the day of her death.

New International

whole house of Israel were celebrating with all their might before the LORD, with songs[a] and with harps, lyres, tambourines, sistrums and cymbals.

6When they came to the threshing floor of Nacon, Uzzah reached out and took hold of the ark of God, because the oxen stumbled. 7The LORD's anger burned against Uzzah because of his irreverent act; therefore God struck him down and he died there beside the ark of God.

8Then David was angry because the LORD's wrath had broken out against Uzzah, and to this day that place is called Perez Uzzah.[b]

9David was afraid of the LORD that day and said, "How can the ark of the LORD ever come to me?" 10He was not willing to take the ark of the LORD to be with him in the City of David. Instead, he took it aside to the house of Obed-Edom the Gittite. 11The ark of the LORD remained in the house of Obed-Edom the Gittite for three months, and the LORD blessed him and his entire household.

12Now King David was told, "The LORD has blessed the household of Obed-Edom and everything he has, because of the ark of God." So David went down and brought up the ark of God from the house of Obed-Edom to the City of David with rejoicing. 13When those who were carrying the ark of the LORD had taken six steps, he sacrificed a bull and a fattened calf. 14David, wearing a linen ephod, danced before the LORD with all his might, 15while he and the entire house of Israel brought up the ark of the LORD with shouts and the sound of trumpets.

16As the ark of the LORD was entering the City of David, Michal daughter of Saul watched from a window. And when she saw King David leaping and dancing before the LORD, she despised him in her heart.

17They brought the ark of the LORD and set it in its place inside the tent that David had pitched for it, and David sacrificed burnt offerings and fellowship offerings[c] before the LORD. 18After he had finished sacrificing the burnt offerings and fellowship offerings, he blessed the people in the name of the LORD Almighty. 19Then he gave a loaf of bread, a cake of dates and a cake of raisins to each person in the whole crowd of Israelites, both men and women. And all the people went to their homes.

20When David returned home to bless his household, Michal daughter of Saul came out to meet him and said, "How the king of Israel has distinguished himself today, disrobing in the sight of the slave girls of his servants as any vulgar fellow would!"

21David said to Michal, "It was before the LORD, who chose me rather than your father or anyone from his house when he appointed me ruler over the LORD's people Israel—I will celebrate before the LORD. 22I will become even more undignified than this, and I will be humiliated in my own eyes. But by these slave girls you spoke of, I will be held in honor."

23And Michal daughter of Saul had no children to the day of her death.

[a] 5 See Dead Sea Scrolls, Septuagint and 1 Chronicles 13:8; Masoretic Text *celebrating before the LORD with all kinds of instruments made of pine.* [b] 8 *Perez Uzzah* means *outbreak against Uzzah.* [c] 17 Traditionally *peace offerings;* also in verse 18

Living Bible

the other leaders of Israel, who were joyously waving branches of juniper trees and playing every sort of musical instrument before the Lord—lyres, harps, tambourines, castanets, and cymbals.

6But when they arrived at the threshing floor of Nacon, the oxen stumbled and Uzzah put out his hand to steady the Ark. 7Then the anger of the Lord flared out against Uzzah and he killed him for doing this, so he died there beside the Ark. 8David was angry at what the Lord had done, and named the spot "The Place of Wrath upon Uzzah" (which it is still called to this day).

9David was now afraid of the Lord and asked, "How can I ever bring the Ark home?" 10So he decided against taking it into the City of David, but carried it instead to the home of Obed-edom, who had come from Gath. 11It remained there for three months, and the Lord blessed Obed-edom and all his household.

12When David heard this, he brought the Ark to the City of David with a great celebration. 13After the men who were carrying it had gone six paces, they stopped and waited so that he could sacrifice an ox and a fat lamb. 14And David danced before the Lord with all his might, and was wearing priests' clothing.d 15So Israel brought home the Ark of the Lord with much shouting and blowing of trumpets.

16(But as the procession came into the city, Michal, Saul's daughter, watched from a window and saw King David leaping and dancing before the Lord; and she was filled with contempt for him.)

17The Ark was placed inside the tent which David had prepared for it; and he sacrificed burnt offerings and peace offerings to the Lord. 18Then he blessed the people in the name of the Lord of heaven, 19and gave a present to everyone—men and women alike—of a loaf of bread, some wine, and a cake of raisins. When it was all over, and everyone had gone home, 20David returned to bless his family.

But Michal came out to meet him and exclaimed in disgust, "How glorious the king of Israel looked today! He exposed himself to the girls along the street like a common pervert!"

21David retorted, "I was dancing before the Lord who chose me above your father and his family and who appointed me as leader of Israel, the people of the Lord! So I am willing to act like a fool in order to show my joy in the Lord. 22Yes, and I am willing to look even more foolish than this, but I will be respected by the girls of whom you spoke!"

23So Michal was childless throughout her life.

New Revised Standard

dancing before the Lord with all their might, with songse and lyres and harps and tambourines and castanets and cymbals.

6 When they came to the threshing floor of Nacon, Uzzah reached out his hand to the ark of God and took hold of it, for the oxen shook it. 7The anger of the Lord was kindled against Uzzah; and God struck him there because he reached out his hand to the ark;f and he died there beside the ark of God. 8David was angry because the Lord had burst forth with an outburst upon Uzzah; so that place is called Perez-uzzah,g to this day. 9David was afraid of the Lord that day; he said, "How can the ark of the Lord come into my care?" 10So David was unwilling to take the ark of the Lord into his care in the city of David; instead David took it to the house of Obed-edom the Gittite. 11The ark of the Lord remained in the house of Obed-edom the Gittite three months; and the Lord blessed Obed-edom and all his household.

12 It was told King David, "The Lord has blessed the household of Obed-edom and all that belongs to him, because of the ark of God." So David went and brought up the ark of God from the house of Obed-edom to the city of David with rejoicing; 13and when those who bore the ark of the Lord had gone six paces, he sacrificed an ox and a fatling. 14David danced before the Lord with all his might; David was girded with a linen ephod. 15So David and all the house of Israel brought up the ark of the Lord with shouting, and with the sound of the trumpet.

16 As the ark of the Lord came into the city of David, Michal daughter of Saul looked out of the window, and saw King David leaping and dancing before the Lord; and she despised him in her heart.

17 They brought in the ark of the Lord, and set it in its place, inside the tent that David had pitched for it; and David offered burnt offerings and offerings of well-being before the Lord. 18When David had finished offering the burnt offerings and the offerings of well-being, he blessed the people in the name of the Lord of hosts, 19and distributed food among all the people, the whole multitude of Israel, both men and women, to each a cake of bread, a portion of meat,h and a cake of raisins. Then all the people went back to their homes.

20 David returned to bless his household. But Michal the daughter of Saul came out to meet David, and said, "How the king of Israel honored himself today, uncovering himself today before the eyes of his servants' maids, as any vulgar fellow might shamelessly uncover himself!" 21David said to Michal, "It was before the Lord, who chose me in place of your father and all his household, to appoint me as prince over Israel, the people of the Lord, that I have danced before the Lord. 22I will make myself yet more contemptible than this, and I will be abased in my own eyes; but by the maids of whom you have spoken, by them I shall be held in honor." 23And Michal the daughter of Saul had no child to the day of her death.

---

d 6:14 *was wearing priests' clothing*, literally, "David was girded with a linen ephod."

e Q Ms Gk 1 Chr 13.8: Heb *fir-trees* f 1 Chr 13.10 Compare Q Ms: Meaning of Heb uncertain g That is *Bursting Out Against Uzzah* h Vg: Meaning of Heb uncertain

King James

7 AND IT came to pass, when the king sat in his house, and the LORD had given him rest round about from all his enemies;

2That the king said unto Nathan the prophet, See now, I dwell in an house of cedar, but the ark of God dwelleth within curtains.

3And Nathan said to the king, Go, do all that *is* in thine heart; for the LORD *is* with thee.

4¶ And it came to pass that night, that the word of the LORD came unto Nathan, saying,

5Go and tell my servant David, Thus saith the LORD, Shalt thou build me an house for me to dwell in?

6Whereas I have not dwelt in *any* house since the time that I brought up the children of Israel out of Egypt, even to this day, but have walked in a tent and in a tabernacle.

7In all *the places* wherein I have walked with all the children of Israel spake I a word with any of the tribes of Israel, whom I commanded to feed my people Israel, saying, Why build ye not me an house of cedar?

8Now therefore so shalt thou say unto my servant David, Thus saith the LORD of hosts, I took thee from the sheepcote, from following the sheep, to be ruler over my people, over Israel:

9And I was with thee whithersoever thou wentest, and have cut off all thine enemies out of thy sight, and have made thee a great name, like unto the name of the great *men* that *are* in the earth.

10Moreover I will appoint a place for my people Israel, and will plant them, that they may dwell in a place of their own, and move no more; neither shall the children of wickedness afflict them any more, as beforetime,

11And as since the time that I commanded judges *to be* over my people Israel, and have caused thee to rest from all thine enemies. Also the LORD telleth thee that he will make thee an house.

12¶ And when thy days be fulfilled, and thou shalt sleep with thy fathers, I will set up thy seed after thee, which shall proceed out of thy bowels, and I will establish his kingdom.

13He shall build an house for my name, and I will stablish the throne of his kingdom for ever.

14I will be his father, and he shall be my son. If he commit iniquity, I will chasten him with the rod of men, and with the stripes of the children of men:

15But my mercy shall not depart away from him, as I took *it* from Saul, whom I put away before thee.

16And thine house and thy kingdom shall be established for ever before thee: thy throne shall be established for ever.

17According to all these words, and according to all this vision, so did Nathan speak unto David.

18¶ Then went king David in, and sat before the LORD, and he said, Who *am* I, O Lord GOD? and what *is* my house, that thou hast brought me hitherto?

19And this was yet a small thing in thy sight, O Lord GOD; but thou hast spoken also of thy servant's house for a great while to come. And *is* this the manner of man, O Lord GOD?

20And what can David say more unto thee? for thou, Lord GOD, knowest thy servant.

21For thy word's sake, and according to thine own heart, hast thou done all these great things, to make thy servant know *them*.

22Wherefore thou art great, O LORD God: for *there is* none like thee, neither *is there any* God beside thee, according to all that we have heard with our ears.

New International

God's Promise to David

7 AFTER THE king was settled in his palace and the LORD had given him rest from all his enemies around him, 2he said to Nathan the prophet, "Here I am, living in a palace of cedar, while the ark of God remains in a tent."

3Nathan replied to the king, "Whatever you have in mind, go ahead and do it, for the LORD is with you."

4That night the word of the LORD came to Nathan, saying:

5"Go and tell my servant David, 'This is what the LORD says: Are you the one to build me a house to dwell in? 6I have not dwelt in a house from the day I brought the Israelites up out of Egypt to this day. I have been moving from place to place with a tent as my dwelling. 7Wherever I have moved with all the Israelites, did I ever say to any of their rulers whom I commanded to shepherd my people Israel, "Why have you not built me a house of cedar?" '

8"Now then, tell my servant David, 'This is what the LORD Almighty says: I took you from the pasture and from following the flock to be ruler over my people Israel. 9I have been with you wherever you have gone, and I have cut off all your enemies from before you. Now I will make your name great, like the names of the greatest men of the earth. 10And I will provide a place for my people Israel and will plant them so that they can have a home of their own and no longer be disturbed. Wicked people will not oppress them anymore, as they did at the beginning 11and have done ever since the time I appointed leadersa over my people Israel. I will also give you rest from all your enemies.

" 'The LORD declares to you that the LORD himself will establish a house for you: 12When your days are over and you rest with your fathers, I will raise up your offspring to succeed you, who will come from your own body, and I will establish his kingdom. 13He is the one who will build a house for my Name, and I will establish the throne of his kingdom forever. 14I will be his father, and he will be my son. When he does wrong, I will punish him with the rod of men, with floggings inflicted by men. 15But my love will never be taken away from him, as I took it away from Saul, whom I removed from before you. 16Your house and your kingdom will endure forever before meb; your throne will be established forever.' "

17Nathan reported to David all the words of this entire revelation.

David's Prayer

18Then King David went in and sat before the LORD, and he said:

"Who am I, O Sovereign LORD, and what is my family, that you have brought me this far? 19And as if this were not enough in your sight, O Sovereign LORD, you have also spoken about the future of the house of your servant. Is this your usual way of dealing with man, O Sovereign LORD?

20"What more can David say to you? For you know your servant, O Sovereign LORD. 21For the sake of your word and according to your will, you have done this great thing and made it known to your servant.

22"How great you are, O Sovereign LORD! There is no one like you, and there is no God but you, as we have heard with our own ears. 23And who is like

---

a *11* Traditionally *judges*   b *16* Some Hebrew manuscripts and Septuagint; most Hebrew manuscripts *you*

Living Bible

7 WHEN THE Lord finally sent peace upon the land, and Israel was no longer at war with the surrounding nations, 2David said to Nathan the prophet, "Look! Here I am living in this beautiful cedar palace while the Ark of God is out in a tent!"

3"Go ahead with what you have in mind," Nathan replied, "for the Lord is with you."

4But that night the Lord said to Nathan, 5"Tell my servant David not to do it!c 6For I have never lived in a temple. My home has been a tent ever since the time I brought Israel out of Egypt. 7And I have never once complained to Israel's leaders, the shepherds of my people. Have I ever asked them, 'Why haven't you built me a beautiful cedar temple?'

8"Now go and give this message to David from the Lord of heaven: 'I chose you to be the leader of my people Israel when you were a mere shepherd, tending your sheep in the pastureland. 9I have been with you wherever you have gone and have destroyed your enemies. And I will make your name greater yet, so that you will be one of the most famous men in the world! 10, 11I have selected a homeland for my people from which they will never have to move. It will be their own land where the heathen nations won't bother them as they did when the judges ruled my people. There will be no more wars against you; and your descendants shall rule this land for generations to come! 12For when you die, I will put one of your sons upon your throne and I will make his kingdom strong. 13He is the one who shall build me a temple. And I will continue his kingdom into eternity. 14I will be his father and he shall be my son. If he sins, I will use other nations to punish him, 15but my love and kindness shall not leave him as I took it from Saul, your predecessor. 16Your family shall rule my kingdom forever.' "

17So Nathan went back to David and told him everything the Lord had said.

18Then David went into the Tabernacle and sat before the Lord and prayed, "O Lord God, why have you showered your blessings on such an insignificant person as I am? 19And now, in addition to everything else, you speak of giving me an eternal dynasty! Such generosity is far beyond any human standard! Oh, Lord God! 20What can I say? For you know what I am like! 21You are doing all these things just because you promised to and because you want to! 22How great you are, Lord God! We have never heard of any other god like you. And there is no other god. 23What other nation in all the

New Revised Standard

God's Covenant with David

7 NOW WHEN the king was settled in his house, and the LORD had given him rest from all his enemies around him, 2the king said to the prophet Nathan, "See now, I am living in a house of cedar, but the ark of God stays in a tent." 3Nathan said to the king, "Go, do all that you have in mind; for the LORD is with you."

4 But that same night the word of the LORD came to Nathan: 5Go and tell my servant David: Thus says the LORD: Are you the one to build me a house to live in? 6I have not lived in a house since the day I brought up the people of Israel from Egypt to this day, but I have been moving about in a tent and a tabernacle. 7Wherever I have moved about among all the people of Israel, did I ever speak a word with any of the tribal leadersd of Israel, whom I commanded to shepherd my people Israel, saying, "Why have you not built me a house of cedar?" 8Now therefore thus you shall say to my servant David: Thus says the LORD of hosts: I took you from the pasture, from following the sheep to be prince over my people Israel; 9and I have been with you wherever you went, and have cut off all your enemies from before you; and I will make for you a great name, like the name of the great ones of the earth. 10And I will appoint a place for my people Israel and will plant them, so that they may live in their own place, and be disturbed no more; and evildoers shall afflict them no more, as formerly, 11from the time that I appointed judges over my people Israel; and I will give you rest from all your enemies. Moreover the LORD declares to you that the LORD will make you a house. 12When your days are fulfilled and you lie down with your ancestors, I will raise up your offspring after you, who shall come forth from your body, and I will establish his kingdom. 13He shall build a house for my name, and I will establish the throne of his kingdom forever. 14I will be a father to him, and he shall be a son to me. When he commits iniquity, I will punish him with a rod such as mortals use, with blows inflicted by human beings. 15But I will not takee my steadfast love from him, as I took it from Saul, whom I put away from before you. 16Your house and your kingdom shall be made sure forever before me;f your throne shall be established forever. 17In accordance with all these words and with all this vision, Nathan spoke to David.

David's Prayer

18 Then King David went in and sat before the LORD, and said, "Who am I, O Lord GOD, and what is my house, that you have brought me thus far? 19And yet this was a small thing in your eyes, O Lord GOD; you have spoken also of your servant's house for a great while to come. May this be instruction for the people,g O Lord GOD! 20And what more can David say to you? For you know your servant, O Lord GOD! 21Because of your promise, and according to your own heart, you have wrought all this greatness, so that your servant may know it. 22Therefore you are great, O LORD God; for there is no one like you, and there is no God besides you, according to all that we have heard with our ears. 23Who

---

c 7:5 Tell my servant David not to do it! Literally, "Shall you build me a house to dwell in?"

d Or any of the tribes e Gk Syr Vg 1 Chr 17.13: Heb shall not depart f Gk Heb Mss: MT before you; Compare 2 Sam 7.26, 29 g Meaning of Heb uncertain

King James

23And what one nation in the earth *is* like thy people, *even* like Israel, whom God went to redeem for a people to himself, and to make him a name, and to do for you great things and terrible, for thy land, before thy people, which thou redeemedst to thee from Egypt, *from* the nations and their gods?

24For thou hast confirmed to thyself thy people Israel *to be* a people unto thee for ever: and thou, LORD, art become their God.

25And now, O LORD God, the word that thou hast spoken concerning thy servant, and concerning his house, establish *it* for ever, and do as thou hast said.

26And let thy name be magnified for ever, saying, The LORD of hosts *is* the God over Israel: and let the house of thy servant David be established before thee.

27For thou, O LORD of hosts, God of Israel, hast revealed to thy servant, saying, I will build thee an house: therefore hath thy servant found in his heart to pray this prayer unto thee.

28And now, O Lord GOD, thou *art* that God, and thy words be true, and thou hast promised this goodness unto thy servant:

29Therefore now let it please thee to bless the house of thy servant, that it may continue for ever before thee: for thou, O Lord GOD, hast spoken *it:* and with thy blessing let the house of thy servant be blessed for ever.

8 AND AFTER this it came to pass, that David smote the Philistines, and subdued them: and David took Metheg-ammah out of the hand of the Philistines.

2And he smote Moab, and measured them with a line, casting them down to the ground; even with two lines measured he to put to death, and with one full line to keep alive. And *so* the Moabites became David's servants, *and* brought gifts.

3¶ David smote also Hadadezer, the son of Rehob, king of Zobah, as he went to recover his border at the river Euphrates.

4And David took from him a thousand *chariots,* and seven hundred horsemen, and twenty thousand footmen: and David houghed all the chariot *horses,* but reserved of them *for* an hundred chariots.

5And when the Syrians of Damascus came to succour Hadadezer king of Zobah, David slew of the Syrians two and twenty thousand men.

6Then David put garrisons in Syria of Damascus: and the Syrians became servants to David, *and* brought gifts. And the LORD preserved David whithersoever he went.

7And David took the shields of gold that were on the servants of Hadadezer, and brought them to Jerusalem.

8And from Betah, and from Berothai, cities of Hadadezer, king David took exceeding much brass.

9¶ When Toi king of Hamath heard that David had smitten all the host of Hadadezer,

10Then Toi sent Joram his son unto king David, to salute him, and to bless him, because he had fought against Hadadezer, and smitten him: for Hadadezer had wars with Toi. And *Joram* brought with him vessels of silver, and vessels of gold, and vessels of brass:

11Which also king David did dedicate unto the LORD, with the silver and gold that he had dedicated of all nations which he subdued;

12Of Syria, and of Moab, and of the children of Ammon, and of the Philistines, and of Amalek, and of the spoil of Hadadezer, son of Rehob, king of Zobah.

New International

your people Israel—the one nation on earth that God went out to redeem as a people for himself, and to make a name for himself, and to perform great and awesome wonders by driving out nations and their gods from before your people, whom you redeemed from Egypt?[a] 24You have established your people Israel as your very own forever, and you, O LORD, have become their God.

25"And now, LORD God, keep forever the promise you have made concerning your servant and his house. Do as you promised, 26so that your name will be great forever. Then men will say, 'The LORD Almighty is God over Israel!' And the house of your servant David will be established before you.

27"O LORD Almighty, God of Israel, you have revealed this to your servant, saying, 'I will build a house for you.' So your servant has found courage to offer you this prayer. 28O Sovereign LORD, you are God! Your words are trustworthy, and you have promised these good things to your servant. 29Now be pleased to bless the house of your servant, that it may continue forever in your sight; for you, O Sovereign LORD, have spoken, and with your blessing the house of your servant will be blessed forever."

David's Victories

8 IN THE course of time, David defeated the Philistines and subdued them, and he took Metheg Ammah from the control of the Philistines.

2David also defeated the Moabites. He made them lie down on the ground and measured them off with a length of cord. Every two lengths of them were put to death, and the third length was allowed to live. So the Moabites became subject to David and brought tribute.

3Moreover, David fought Hadadezer son of Rehob, king of Zobah, when he went to restore his control along the Euphrates River. 4David captured a thousand of his chariots, seven thousand charioteers[b] and twenty thousand foot soldiers. He hamstrung all but a hundred of the chariot horses.

5When the Arameans of Damascus came to help Hadadezer king of Zobah, David struck down twenty-two thousand of them. 6He put garrisons in the Aramean kingdom of Damascus, and the Arameans became subject to him and brought tribute. The LORD gave David victory wherever he went.

7David took the gold shields that belonged to the officers of Hadadezer and brought them to Jerusalem. 8From Tebah[c] and Berothai, towns that belonged to Hadadezer, King David took a great quantity of bronze.

9When Tou[d] king of Hamath heard that David had defeated the entire army of Hadadezer, 10he sent his son Joram[e] to King David to greet him and congratulate him on his victory in battle over Hadadezer, who had been at war with Tou. Joram brought with him articles of silver and gold and bronze.

11King David dedicated these articles to the LORD, as he had done with the silver and gold from all the nations he had subdued: 12Edom[f] and Moab, the Ammonites and the Philistines, and Amalek. He also dedicated the plunder taken from Hadadezer son of Rehob, king of Zobah.

---

a *23* See Septuagint and 1 Chron. 17:21; Hebrew *wonders for your land and before your people, whom you redeemed from Egypt, from the nations and their gods.* b *4* Septuagint (see also Dead Sea Scrolls and 1 Chron. 18:4); Masoretic Text *captured seventeen hundred of his charioteers* c *8* See some Septuagint manuscripts (see also 1 Chron. 18:8); Hebrew *Betah.* d *9* Hebrew *Toi,* a variant of *Tou;* also in verse 10 e *10* A variant of *Hadoram* f *12* Some Hebrew manuscripts, Septuagint and Syriac (see also 1 Chron. 18:11); most Hebrew manuscripts *Aram*

Living Bible

earth has received such blessings as Israel, your people? For you have rescued your chosen nation in order to bring glory to your name. You have done great miracles to destroy Egypt and its gods. 24You chose Israel to be your people forever, and you became our God.

25"And now, Lord God, do as you have promised concerning me and my family. 26And may you be eternally honored when you have established Israel as your people and have established my dynasty before you. 27For you have revealed to me, O Lord of heaven, God of Israel, that I am the first of a dynasty which will rule your people forever; that is why I have been bold enough to pray this prayer of acceptance. 28For you are indeed God, and your words are truth; and you have promised me these good things— 29so do as you have promised! Bless me and my family forever! May our dynasty continue on and on before you; for you, Lord God, have promised it."

8 AFTER THIS David subdued and humbled the Philistines by conquering Gath, their largest city. 2He also devastated the land of Moab. He divided his victims by making them lie down side by side in rows. Two-thirds of each row, as measured with a tape, were butchered, and one-third were spared to become David's servants—they paid him tribute each year.

3He also destroyed the forces of King Hadadezer (son of Rehob) of Zobah in a battle at the Euphrates River, for Hadadezer had attempted to regain his power. 4David captured seventeen hundred cavalry and twenty thousand infantry; then he lamed all of the chariot horses except for one hundred teams. 5He also slaughtered twenty-two thousand Syrians from Damascus when they came to help Hadadezer. 6David placed several army garrisons in Damascus, and the Syrians became David's subjects and brought him annual tribute money. So the Lord gave him victories wherever he turned. 7David brought the gold shields to Jerusalem which King Hadadezer's officers had used. 8He also carried back to Jerusalem a very large amount of bronze from Hadadezer's cities of Betah and Berothai.

9When King Toi of Hamath heard about David's victory over the army of Hadadezer, 10he sent his son Joram to congratulate him, for Hadadezer and Toi were enemies. He gave David presents made from silver, gold, and bronze. 11, 12David dedicated all of these to the Lord, along with the silver and gold he had taken from Syria, Moab, Ammon, the Philistines, Amalek, and King Hadadezer.

New Revised Standard

is like your people, like Israel? Is there another[g] nation on earth whose God went to redeem it as a people, and to make a name for himself, doing great and awesome things for them,[h] by driving out[i] before his people nations and their gods?[j] 24And you established your people Israel for yourself to be your people forever; and you, O LORD, became their God. 25And now, O LORD God, as for the word that you have spoken concerning your servant and concerning his house, confirm it forever; do as you have promised. 26Thus your name will be magnified forever in the saying, 'The LORD of hosts is God over Israel'; and the house of your servant David will be established before you. 27For you, O LORD of hosts, the God of Israel, have made this revelation to your servant, saying, 'I will build you a house'; therefore your servant has found courage to pray this prayer to you. 28And now, O Lord GOD, you are God, and your words are true, and you have promised this good thing to your servant; 29now therefore may it please you to bless the house of your servant, so that it may continue forever before you; for you, O Lord GOD, have spoken, and with your blessing shall the house of your servant be blessed forever."

David's Wars

8 SOME TIME afterward, David attacked the Philistines and subdued them; David took Methegammah out of the hand of the Philistines.

2 He also defeated the Moabites and, making them lie down on the ground, measured them off with a cord; he measured two lengths of cord for those who were to be put to death, and one length[k] for those who were to be spared. And the Moabites became servants to David and brought tribute.

3 David also struck down King Hadadezer son of Rehob of Zobah, as he went to restore his monument[l] at the river Euphrates. 4David took from him one thousand seven hundred horsemen, and twenty thousand foot soldiers. David hamstrung all the chariot horses, but left enough for a hundred chariots. 5When the Arameans of Damascus came to help King Hadadezer of Zobah, David killed twenty-two thousand men of the Arameans. 6Then David put garrisons among the Arameans of Damascus; and the Arameans became servants to David and brought tribute. The LORD gave victory to David wherever he went. 7David took the gold shields that were carried by the servants of Hadadezer, and brought them to Jerusalem. 8From Betah and from Berothai, towns of Hadadezer, King David took a great amount of bronze.

9 When King Toi of Hamath heard that David had defeated the whole army of Hadadezer, 10Toi sent his son Joram to King David, to greet him and to congratulate him because he had fought against Hadadezer and defeated him. Now Hadadezer had often been at war with Toi. Joram brought with him articles of silver, gold, and bronze; 11these also King David dedicated to the LORD, together with the silver and gold that he dedicated from all the nations he subdued, 12from Edom, Moab, the Ammonites, the Philistines, Amalek, and from the spoil of King Hadadezer son of Rehob of Zobah.

g Gk: Heb one   h Heb you   i Gk 1 Chr 17.21: Heb for your land   j Cn: Heb before your people, whom you redeemed for yourself from Egypt, nations and its gods   k Heb one full length   l Compare 1 Sam 15.12 and 2 Sam 18.18

King James

¹³And David gat *him* a name when he returned from smiting of the Syrians in the valley of salt, *being* eighteen thousand *men*.

¹⁴¶ And he put garrisons in Edom; throughout all Edom put he garrisons, and all they of Edom became David's servants. And the LORD preserved David whithersoever he went.

¹⁵And David reigned over all Israel; and David executed judgment and justice unto all his people.

¹⁶And Joab the son of Zeruiah *was* over the host; and Jehoshaphat the son of Ahilud *was* recorder;

¹⁷And Zadok the son of Ahitub, and Ahimelech the son of Abiathar, *were* the priests; and Seraiah *was* the scribe;

¹⁸And Benaiah the son of Jehoiada *was over* both the Cherethites and the Pelethites; and David's sons were chief rulers.

9 AND DAVID said, Is there yet any that is left of the house of Saul, that I may show him kindness for Jonathan's sake?

²And *there was* of the house of Saul a servant whose name *was* Ziba. And when they had called him unto David, the king said unto him, Art thou Ziba? And he said, Thy servant *is he.*

³And the king said, *Is* there not yet any of the house of Saul, that I may show the kindness of God unto him? And Ziba said unto the king, Jonathan hath yet a son, *which is* lame on *his* feet.

⁴And the king said unto him, Where *is* he? And Ziba said unto the king, Behold, he *is* in the house of Machir, the son of Ammiel, in Lo-debar.

⁵¶ Then king David sent, and fetched him out of the house of Machir, the son of Ammiel, from Lo-debar.

⁶Now when Mephibosheth, the son of Jonathan, the son of Saul, was come unto David, he fell on his face, and did reverence. And David said, Mephibosheth. And he answered, Behold thy servant!

⁷¶ And David said unto him, Fear not: for I will surely show thee kindness for Jonathan thy father's sake, and will restore thee all the land of Saul thy father; and thou shalt eat bread at my table continually.

⁸And he bowed himself, and said, What *is* thy servant, that thou shouldest look upon such a dead dog as I *am?*

⁹¶ Then the king called to Ziba, Saul's servant, and said unto him, I have given unto thy master's son all that pertained to Saul and to all his house.

¹⁰Thou therefore, and thy sons, and thy servants, shall till the land for him, and thou shalt bring in *the fruits,* that thy master's son may have food to eat: but Mephibosheth thy master's son shall eat bread always at my table. Now Ziba had fifteen sons and twenty servants.

¹¹Then said Ziba unto the king, According to all that my lord the king hath commanded his servant, so shall thy servant do. As for Mephibosheth, *said the king,* he shall eat at my table, as one of the king's sons.

¹²And Mephibosheth had a young son, whose name *was* Micha. And all that dwelt in the house of Ziba *were* servants unto Mephibosheth.

¹³So Mephibosheth dwelt in Jerusalem: for he did eat continually at the king's table; and was lame on both his feet.

New International

¹³And David became famous after he returned from striking down eighteen thousand Edomites^a in the Valley of Salt.

¹⁴He put garrisons throughout Edom, and all the Edomites became subject to David. The LORD gave David victory wherever he went.

David's Officials

¹⁵David reigned over all Israel, doing what was just and right for all his people. ¹⁶Joab son of Zeruiah was over the army; Jehoshaphat son of Ahilud was recorder; ¹⁷Zadok son of Ahitub and Ahimelech son of Abiathar were priests; Seraiah was secretary; ¹⁸Benaiah son of Jehoiada was over the Kerethites and Pelethites; and David's sons were royal advisers.^b

David and Mephibosheth

9 DAVID ASKED, "Is there anyone still left of the house of Saul to whom I can show kindness for Jonathan's sake?"

²Now there was a servant of Saul's household named Ziba. They called him to appear before David, and the king said to him, "Are you Ziba?"

"Your servant," he replied.

³The king asked, "Is there no one still left of the house of Saul to whom I can show God's kindness?"

Ziba answered the king, "There is still a son of Jonathan; he is crippled in both feet."

⁴"Where is he?" the king asked.

Ziba answered, "He is at the house of Makir son of Ammiel in Lo Debar."

⁵So King David had him brought from Lo Debar, from the house of Makir son of Ammiel.

⁶When Mephibosheth son of Jonathan, the son of Saul, came to David, he bowed down to pay him honor.

David said, "Mephibosheth!"

"Your servant," he replied.

⁷"Don't be afraid," David said to him, "for I will surely show you kindness for the sake of your father Jonathan. I will restore to you all the land that belonged to your grandfather Saul, and you will always eat at my table."

⁸Mephibosheth bowed down and said, "What is your servant, that you should notice a dead dog like me?"

⁹Then the king summoned Ziba, Saul's servant, and said to him, "I have given your master's grandson everything that belonged to Saul and his family. ¹⁰You and your sons and your servants are to farm the land for him and bring in the crops, so that your master's grandson may be provided for. And Mephibosheth, grandson of your master, will always eat at my table." (Now Ziba had fifteen sons and twenty servants.)

¹¹Then Ziba said to the king, "Your servant will do whatever my lord the king commands his servant to do." So Mephibosheth ate at David's^c table like one of the king's sons.

¹²Mephibosheth had a young son named Mica, and all the members of Ziba's household were servants of Mephibosheth. ¹³And Mephibosheth lived in Jerusalem, because he always ate at the king's table, and he was crippled in both feet.

^a *13* A few Hebrew manuscripts, Septuagint and Syriac (see also 1 Chron. 18:12); most Hebrew manuscripts *Aram* (that is, Arameans)   ^b *18* Or *were priests*   ^c *11* Septuagint; Hebrew *my*

Living Bible

13So David became very famous. After his return he destroyed eighteen thousand Edomitesd at the Valley of Salt, 14and then placed garrisons throughout Edom, so that the entire nation was forced to pay tribute to Israel—another example of the way the Lord made him victorious wherever he went.

15David reigned with justice over Israel and was fair to everyone. 16The general of his army was Joab (son of Zeruiah), and his secretary of state was Jehoshaphat (son of Ahilud). 17Zadok (son of Ahitub) and Ahimelech (son of Abiathar) were the High Priests, and Seraiah was the king's private secretary. 18Benaiah (son of Jehoiada) was captain of his bodyguard,e and David's sons were his assistants.f

9 ONE DAY David began wondering if any of Saul's family was still living, for he wanted to be kind to them, as he had promised Prince Jonathan. 2He heard about a man named Ziba who had been one of Saul's servants, and summoned him.

"Are you Ziba?" the king asked.

"Yes, sir, I am," he replied.

3The king then asked him, "Is anyone left from Saul's family? If so, I want to fulfill a sacred vow by being kind to him."

"Yes," Ziba replied, "Jonathan's lame son is still alive."

4"Where is he?" the king asked.

"In Lo-debar," Ziba told him. "At the home of Machir."

5,6So King David sent for Mephibosheth—Jonathan's son and Saul's grandson. Mephibosheth arrived in great fear and greeted the king in deep humility, bowing low before him.

7But David said, "Don't be afraid! I've asked you to come so that I can be kind to you because of my vow to your father Jonathan. I will restore to you all the land of your grandfather Saul, and you shall live here at the palace!"

8Mephibosheth fell to the ground before the king. "Should the king show kindness to a dead dog like me?" he exclaimed.

9Then the king summoned Saul's servant Ziba. "I have given your master's grandson everything that belonged to Saul and his family," he said. 10, 11"You and your sons and servants are to farm the land for him, to produce food for his family; but he will live here with me."

Ziba, who had fifteen sons and twenty servants, replied, "Sir, I will do all you have commanded."

And from that time on, Mephibosheth ate regularly with King David, as though he were one of his own sons. 12Mephibosheth had a young son, Mica. All the household of Ziba became Mephibosheth's servants, 13but Mephibosheth (who was lame in both feet) moved to Jerusalem to live at the palace.

New Revised Standard

13 David won a name for himself. When he returned, he killed eighteen thousand Edomitesg in the Valley of Salt. 14He put garrisons in Edom; throughout all Edom he put garrisons, and all the Edomites became David's servants. And the LORD gave victory to David wherever he went.

David's Officers

15 So David reigned over all Israel; and David administered justice and equity to all his people. 16Joab son of Zeruiah was over the army; Jehoshaphat son of Ahilud was recorder; 17Zadok son of Ahitub and Ahimelech son of Abiathar were priests; Seraiah was secretary; 18Benaiah son of Jehoiada was overh the Cherethites and the Pelethites; and David's sons were priests.

David's Kindness to Mephibosheth

9 DAVID ASKED, "Is there still anyone left of the house of Saul to whom I may show kindness for Jonathan's sake?" 2Now there was a servant of the house of Saul whose name was Ziba, and he was summoned to David. The king said to him, "Are you Ziba?" And he said, "At your service!" 3The king said, "Is there anyone remaining of the house of Saul to whom I may show the kindness of God?" Ziba said to the king, "There remains a son of Jonathan; he is crippled in his feet." 4The king said to him, "Where is he?" Ziba said to the king, "He is in the house of Machir son of Ammiel, at Lo-debar." 5Then King David sent and brought him from the house of Machir son of Ammiel, at Lo-debar. 6Mephiboshethi son of Jonathan son of Saul came to David, and fell on his face and did obeisance. David said, "Mephibosheth!"i He answered, "I am your servant." 7David said to him, "Do not be afraid, for I will show you kindness for the sake of your father Jonathan; I will restore to you all the land of your grandfather Saul, and you yourself shall eat at my table always." 8He did obeisance and said, "What is your servant, that you should look upon a dead dog such as I?"

9 Then the king summoned Saul's servant Ziba, and said to him, "All that belonged to Saul and to all his house I have given to your master's grandson. 10You and your sons and your servants shall till the land for him, and shall bring in the produce, so that your master's grandson may have food to eat; but your master's grandson Mephiboshethi shall always eat at my table." Now Ziba had fifteen sons and twenty servants. 11Then Ziba said to the king, "According to all that my lord the king commands his servant, so your servant will do." Mephiboshethi ate at David'sj table, like one of the king's sons. 12Mephiboshethi had a young son whose name was Mica. And all who lived in Ziba's house became Mephibosheth'sk servants. 13Mephiboshethi lived in Jerusalem, for he always ate at the king's table. Now he was lame in both his feet.

---

d 8:13 Edomites, literally, "Syrians."   e 8:18 captain of his bodyguard, literally, "the Cherethites and Pelethites."   f 8:18 were his assistants, literally, "were priests." See 1 Chron 18:17.

g Gk: Heb returned from striking down eighteen thousand Arameans   h Syr Tg Vg 20.23; 1 Chr 18.17: Heb lacks was over   i Or Merib-baal: See 4.4 note   j Gk: Heb my   k Or Merib-baal's: See 4.4 note

King James

10 AND IT came to pass after this, that the king of the children of Ammon died, and Hanun his son reigned in his stead.

2Then said David, I will show kindness unto Hanun the son of Nahash, as his father showed kindness unto me. And David sent to comfort him by the hand of his servants for his father. And David's servants came into the land of the children of Ammon.

3And the princes of the children of Ammon said unto Hanun their lord, Thinkest thou that David doth honour thy father, that he hath sent comforters unto thee? hath not David *rather* sent his servants unto thee, to search the city, and to spy it out, and to overthrow it?

4Wherefore Hanun took David's servants, and shaved off the one half of their beards, and cut off their garments in the middle, *even* to their buttocks, and sent them away.

5When they told *it* unto David, he sent to meet them, because the men were greatly ashamed: and the king said, Tarry at Jericho until your beards be grown, and *then* return.

6¶ And when the children of Ammon saw that they stank before David, the children of Ammon sent and hired the Syrians of Beth-rehob, and the Syrians of Zoba, twenty thousand footmen, and of king Maacah a thousand men, and of Ish-tob twelve thousand men.

7And when David heard of *it,* he sent Joab, and all the host of the mighty men.

8And the children of Ammon came out, and put the battle in array at the entering in of the gate: and the Syrians of Zoba, and of Rehob, and Ish-tob, and Maacah, *were* by themselves in the field.

9When Joab saw that the front of the battle was against him before and behind, he chose of all the choice *men* of Israel, and put *them* in array against the Syrians:

10And the rest of the people he delivered into the hand of Abishai his brother, that he might put *them* in array against the children of Ammon.

11And he said, If the Syrians be too strong for me, then thou shalt help me: but if the children of Ammon be too strong for thee, then I will come and help thee.

12Be of good courage, and let us play the men for our people, and for the cities of our God: and the LORD do that which seemeth him good.

13And Joab drew nigh, and the people that *were* with him, unto the battle against the Syrians: and they fled before him.

14And when the children of Ammon saw that the Syrians were fled, then fled they also before Abishai, and entered into the city. So Joab returned from the children of Ammon, and came to Jerusalem.

15¶ And when the Syrians saw that they were smitten before Israel, they gathered themselves together.

16And Hadarezer sent, and brought out the Syrians that *were* beyond the river: and they came to Helam; and Shobach the captain of the host of Hadarezer *went* before them.

17And when it was told David, he gathered all Israel together, and passed over Jordan, and came to Helam. And the Syrians set themselves in array against David, and fought with him.

18And the Syrians fled before Israel; and David slew *the men of* seven hundred chariots of the Syrians, and forty thousand horsemen, and smote Shobach the captain of their host, who died there.

19And when all the kings *that were* servants to Hadarezer saw that they were smitten before Israel, they made peace with Israel, and served them. So the Syrians feared to help the children of Ammon any more.

New International

David Defeats the Ammonites

10 IN THE course of time, the king of the Ammonites died, and his son Hanun succeeded him as king. 2David thought, "I will show kindness to Hanun son of Nahash, just as his father showed kindness to me." So David sent a delegation to express his sympathy to Hanun concerning his father.

When David's men came to the land of the Ammonites, 3the Ammonite nobles said to Hanun their lord, "Do you think David is honoring your father by sending men to you to express sympathy? Hasn't David sent them to you to explore the city and spy it out and overthrow it?" 4So Hanun seized David's men, shaved off half of each man's beard, cut off their garments in the middle at the buttocks, and sent them away.

5When David was told about this, he sent messengers to meet the men, for they were greatly humiliated. The king said, "Stay at Jericho till your beards have grown, and then come back."

6When the Ammonites realized that they had become a stench in David's nostrils, they hired twenty thousand Aramean foot soldiers from Beth Rehob and Zobah, as well as the king of Maacah with a thousand men, and also twelve thousand men from Tob.

7On hearing this, David sent Joab out with the entire army of fighting men. 8The Ammonites came out and drew up in battle formation at the entrance to their city gate, while the Arameans of Zobah and Rehob and the men of Tob and Maacah were by themselves in the open country.

9Joab saw that there were battle lines in front of him and behind him; so he selected some of the best troops in Israel and deployed them against the Arameans. 10He put the rest of the men under the command of Abishai his brother and deployed them against the Ammonites. 11Joab said, "If the Arameans are too strong for me, then you are to come to my rescue; but if the Ammonites are too strong for you, then I will come to rescue you. 12Be strong and let us fight bravely for our people and the cities of our God. The LORD will do what is good in his sight."

13Then Joab and the troops with him advanced to fight the Arameans, and they fled before him. 14When the Ammonites saw that the Arameans were fleeing, they fled before Abishai and went inside the city. So Joab returned from fighting the Ammonites and came to Jerusalem.

15After the Arameans saw that they had been routed by Israel, they regrouped. 16Hadadezer had Arameans brought from beyond the River[a]; they went to Helam, with Shobach the commander of Hadadezer's army leading them.

17When David was told of this, he gathered all Israel, crossed the Jordan and went to Helam. The Arameans formed their battle lines to meet David and fought against him. 18But they fled before Israel, and David killed seven hundred of their charioteers and forty thousand of their foot soldiers.[b] He also struck down Shobach the commander of their army, and he died there. 19When all the kings who were vassals of Hadadezer saw that they had been defeated by Israel, they made peace with the Israelites and became subject to them.

So the Arameans were afraid to help the Ammonites anymore.

---

a 16 That is, the Euphrates   b 18 Some Septuagint manuscripts (see also 1 Chron. 19:18); Hebrew horsemen

Living Bible

10 SOME TIME after this the Ammonite king died and his son Hanun replaced him.

2"I am going to show special respect for him," David said, "because his father Nahash was always so loyal and kind to me." So David sent ambassadors to express regrets to Hanun about his father's death.

3But Hanun's officers told him, "These men aren't here to honor your father! David has sent them to spy out the city before attacking it!"

4So Hanun took David's men and shaved off half their beards and cut their robes off at the buttocks and sent them home half naked. 5When David heard what had happened he told them to stay at Jericho until their beards grew out; for the men were very embarrassed over their appearance.

6Now the people of Ammon realized how seriously they had angered David, so they hired twenty thousand Syrian mercenaries from the lands of Rehob and Zobah, one thousand from the king of Maacah, and ten thousand from the land of Tob. 7, 8When David heard about this, he sent Joab and the entire Israeli army to attack them. The Ammonites defended the gates of their city while the Syrians from Zobah, Rehob, Tob, and Maacah fought in the fields. 9When Joab realized that he would have to fight on two fronts, he selected the best fighters in his army, placed them under his personal command, and took them out to fight the Syrians in the fields. 10He left the rest of the army to his brother Abishai, who was to attack the city.

11"If I need assistance against the Syrians, come out and help me," Joab instructed him. "And if the Ammonites are too strong for you, I will come and help you. 12Courage! We must really act like men today if we are going to save our people and the cities of our God. May the Lord's will be done."

13And when Joab and his troops attacked, the Syrians began to run away. 14Then, when the Ammonites saw the Syrians running, they ran too, and retreated into the city. Afterwards Joab returned to Jerusalem. 15, 16The Syrians now realized that they were no match for Israel. So when they regrouped, they were joined by additional Syrian troops summoned by Hadadezer from the other side of the Euphrates River. These troops arrived at Helam under the command of Shobach, the commander-in-chief of all of Hadadezer's forces.

17When David heard what was happening, he personally led the Israeli army to Helam, where the Syrians attacked him. 18But again the Syrians fled from the Israelis, this time leaving seven hundred charioteers dead on the field, also forty thousand cavalrymen, including General Shobach. 19When Hadadezer's allies saw that the Syrians had been defeated, they surrendered to David and became his servants. And the Syrians were afraid to help the Ammonites anymore after that.

New Revised Standard

The Ammonites and Arameans Are Defeated

10 SOME TIME afterward, the king of the Ammonites died, and his son Hanun succeeded him. 2David said, "I will deal loyally with Hanun son of Nahash, just as his father dealt loyally with me." So David sent envoys to console him concerning his father. When David's envoys came into the land of the Ammonites, 3the princes of the Ammonites said to their lord Hanun, "Do you really think that David is honoring your father just because he has sent messengers with condolences to you? Has not David sent his envoys to you to search the city, to spy it out, and to overthrow it?" 4So Hanun seized David's envoys, shaved off half the beard of each, cut off their garments in the middle at their hips, and sent them away. 5When David was told, he sent to meet them, for the men were greatly ashamed. The king said, "Remain at Jericho until your beards have grown, and then return."

6 When the Ammonites saw that they had become odious to David, the Ammonites sent and hired the Arameans of Beth-rehob and the Arameans of Zobah, twenty thousand foot soldiers, as well as the king of Maacah, one thousand men, and the men of Tob, twelve thousand men. 7When David heard of it, he sent Joab and all the army with the warriors. 8The Ammonites came out and drew up in battle array at the entrance of the gate; but the Arameans of Zobah and of Rehob, and the men of Tob and Maacah, were by themselves in the open country.

9 When Joab saw that the battle was set against him both in front and in the rear, he chose some of the picked men of Israel, and arrayed them against the Arameans; 10the rest of his men he put in the charge of his brother Abishai, and he arrayed them against the Ammonites. 11He said, "If the Arameans are too strong for me, then you shall help me; but if the Ammonites are too strong for you, then I will come and help you. 12Be strong, and let us be courageous for the sake of our people, and for the cities of our God; and may the Lord do what seems good to him." 13So Joab and the people who were with him moved forward into battle against the Arameans; and they fled before him. 14When the Ammonites saw that the Arameans fled, they likewise fled before Abishai, and entered the city. Then Joab returned from fighting against the Ammonites, and came to Jerusalem.

15 But when the Arameans saw that they had been defeated by Israel, they gathered themselves together. 16Hadadezer sent and brought out the Arameans who were beyond the Euphrates; and they came to Helam, with Shobach the commander of the army of Hadadezer at their head. 17When it was told David, he gathered all Israel together, and crossed the Jordan, and came to Helam. The Arameans arrayed themselves against David and fought with him. 18The Arameans fled before Israel; and David killed of the Arameans seven hundred chariot teams, and forty thousand horsemen,c and wounded Shobach the commander of their army, so that he died there. 19When all the kings who were servants of Hadadezer saw that they had been defeated by Israel, they made peace with Israel, and became subject to them. So the Arameans were afraid to help the Ammonites any more.

---

c 1 Chr 19.18 and some Gk Mss read *foot soldiers*

King James

11 AND IT came to pass, after the year was expired, at the time when kings go forth *to battle*, that David sent Joab, and his servants with him, and all Israel; and they destroyed the children of Ammon, and besieged Rabbah. But David tarried still at Jerusalem.

2¶ And it came to pass in an eveningtide, that David arose from off his bed, and walked upon the roof of the king's house: and from the roof he saw a woman washing herself; and the woman *was* very beautiful to look upon.

3And David sent and inquired after the woman. And *one* said, *Is* not this Bath-sheba, the daughter of Eliam, the wife of Uriah the Hittite?

4And David sent messengers, and took her; and she came in unto him, and he lay with her; for she was purified from her uncleanness: and she returned unto her house.

5And the woman conceived, and sent and told David, and said, I *am* with child.

6¶ And David sent to Joab, *saying*, Send me Uriah the Hittite. And Joab sent Uriah to David.

7And when Uriah was come unto him, David demanded *of him* how Joab did, and how the people did, and how the war prospered.

8And David said to Uriah, Go down to thy house, and wash thy feet. And Uriah departed out of the king's house, and there followed him a mess *of meat* from the king.

9But Uriah slept at the door of the king's house with all the servants of his lord, and went not down to his house.

10And when they had told David, saying, Uriah went not down unto his house, David said unto Uriah, Camest thou not from *thy* journey? why *then* didst thou not go down unto thine house?

11And Uriah said unto David, The ark, and Israel, and Judah, abide in tents; and my lord Joab, and the servants of my lord, are encamped in the open fields; shall I then go into mine house, to eat and to drink, and to lie with my wife? *as* thou livest, and *as* thy soul liveth, I will not do this thing.

12And David said to Uriah, Tarry here today also, and tomorrow I will let thee depart. So Uriah abode in Jerusalem that day, and the morrow.

13And when David had called him, he did eat and drink before him; and he made him drunk: and at even he went out to lie on his bed with the servants of his lord, but went not down to his house.

14¶ And it came to pass in the morning, that David wrote a letter to Joab, and sent *it* by the hand of Uriah.

15And he wrote in the letter, saying, Set ye Uriah in the forefront of the hottest battle, and retire ye from him, that he may be smitten, and die.

16And it came to pass, when Joab observed the city, that he assigned Uriah unto a place where he knew that valiant men *were*.

17And the men of the city went out, and fought with Joab: and there fell *some* of the people of the servants of David; and Uriah the Hittite died also.

18¶ Then Joab sent and told David all the things concerning the war;

19And charged the messenger, saying, When thou hast made an end of telling the matters of the war unto the king,

20And if so be that the king's wrath arise, and he say unto thee, Wherefore approached ye so nigh unto the city when ye did fight? knew ye not that they would shoot from the wall?

21Who smote Abimelech the son of Jerubbesheth? did not a woman cast a piece of a millstone upon him from the wall, that he died in Thebez? why went ye nigh the wall? then say thou, Thy servant Uriah the Hittite is dead also.

New International

David and Bathsheba

11 IN THE spring, at the time when kings go off to war, David sent Joab out with the king's men and the whole Israelite army. They destroyed the Ammonites and besieged Rabbah. But David remained in Jerusalem.

2One evening David got up from his bed and walked around on the roof of the palace. From the roof he saw a woman bathing. The woman was very beautiful, 3and David sent someone to find out about her. The man said, "Isn't this Bathsheba, the daughter of Eliam and the wife of Uriah the Hittite?" 4Then David sent messengers to get her. She came to him, and he slept with her. (She had purified herself from her uncleanness.) Then[a] she went back home. 5The woman conceived and sent word to David, saying, "I am pregnant."

6So David sent this word to Joab: "Send me Uriah the Hittite." And Joab sent him to David. 7When Uriah came to him, David asked him how Joab was, how the soldiers were and how the war was going. 8Then David said to Uriah, "Go down to your house and wash your feet." So Uriah left the palace, and a gift from the king was sent after him. 9But Uriah slept at the entrance to the palace with all his master's servants and did not go down to his house.

10When David was told, "Uriah did not go home," he asked him, "Haven't you just come from a distance? Why didn't you go home?"

11Uriah said to David, "The ark and Israel and Judah are staying in tents, and my master Joab and my lord's men are camped in the open fields. How could I go to my house to eat and drink and lie with my wife? As surely as you live, I will not do such a thing!"

12Then David said to him, "Stay here one more day, and tomorrow I will send you back." So Uriah remained in Jerusalem that day and the next. 13At David's invitation, he ate and drank with him, and David made him drunk. But in the evening Uriah went out to sleep on his mat among his master's servants; he did not go home.

14In the morning David wrote a letter to Joab and sent it with Uriah. 15In it he wrote, "Put Uriah in the front line where the fighting is fiercest. Then withdraw from him so he will be struck down and die."

16So while Joab had the city under siege, he put Uriah at a place where he knew the strongest defenders were. 17When the men of the city came out and fought against Joab, some of the men in David's army fell; moreover, Uriah the Hittite died.

18Joab sent David a full account of the battle. 19He instructed the messenger: "When you have finished giving the king this account of the battle, 20the king's anger may flare up, and he may ask you, 'Why did you get so close to the city to fight? Didn't you know they would shoot arrows from the wall? 21Who killed Abimelech son of Jerub-Besheth[b]? Didn't a woman throw an upper millstone on him from the wall, so that he died in Thebez? Why did you get so close to the wall?' If he asks you this, then say to him, 'Also, your servant Uriah the Hittite is dead.' "

---

[a] 4 Or *with her. When she purified herself from her uncleanness.*   [b] 21 Also known as *Jerub-Baal* (that is, Gideon)

Living Bible

11 IN THE spring of the following year, at the time when wars begin, David sent Joab and the Israeli army to destroy the Ammonites. They began by laying siege to the city of Rabbah. But David stayed in Jerusalem.

²One night he couldn't get to sleep[c] and went for a stroll on the roof of the palace. As he looked out over the city, he noticed a woman of unusual beauty taking her evening bath. ³He sent to find out who she was and was told that she was Bath-sheba, the daughter of Eliam and the wife of Uriah. ⁴Then David sent for her and when she came he slept with her. (She had just completed the purification rites after menstruation.) Then she returned home. ⁵When she found that he had gotten her pregnant she sent a message to inform him.

⁶So David dispatched a memo to Joab: "Send me Uriah the Hittite." ⁷When he arrived, David asked him how Joab and the army were getting along and how the war was prospering. ⁸Then he told him to go home and relax, and he sent a present to him at his home. ⁹But Uriah didn't go there. He stayed that night at the gateway of the palace with the other servants of the king.

¹⁰When David heard what Uriah had done, he summoned him and asked him, "What's the matter with you? Why didn't you go home to your wife last night after being away for so long?"

¹¹Uriah replied, "The Ark and the armies and the general and his officers are camping out in open fields, and should I go home to wine and dine and sleep with my wife? I swear that I will never be guilty of acting like that."

¹²"Well, stay here tonight," David told him, "and tomorrow you may return to the army."

So Uriah stayed around the palace. ¹³David invited him to dinner and got him drunk; but even so he didn't go home that night, but again he slept at the entry to the palace.

¹⁴Finally the next morning David wrote a letter to Joab and gave it to Uriah to deliver. ¹⁵The letter instructed Joab to put Uriah at the front of the hottest part of the battle—and then pull back and leave him there to die! ¹⁶So Joab assigned Uriah to a spot close to the besieged city where he knew that the enemies' best men were fighting; ¹⁷and Uriah was killed along with several other Israeli soldiers.

¹⁸When Joab sent a report to David of how the battle was going, ¹⁹, ²⁰, ²¹he told his messenger, "If the king is angry and asks, 'Why did the troops go so close to the city? Didn't they know there would be shooting from the walls? Wasn't Abimelech killed at Thebez by a woman who threw down a millstone on him?'—then tell him, 'Uriah was killed, too.'"

New Revised Standard

David Commits Adultery with Bathsheba

11 IN THE spring of the year, the time when kings go out to battle, David sent Joab with his officers and all Israel with him; they ravaged the Ammonites, and besieged Rabbah. But David remained at Jerusalem.

2 It happened, late one afternoon, when David rose from his couch and was walking about on the roof of the king's house, that he saw from the roof a woman bathing; the woman was very beautiful. ³David sent someone to inquire about the woman. It was reported, "This is Bathsheba daughter of Eliam, the wife of Uriah the Hittite." ⁴So David sent messengers to get her, and she came to him, and he lay with her. (Now she was purifying herself after her period.) Then she returned to her house. ⁵The woman conceived; and she sent and told David, "I am pregnant."

6 So David sent word to Joab, "Send me Uriah the Hittite." And Joab sent Uriah to David. ⁷When Uriah came to him, David asked how Joab and the people fared, and how the war was going. ⁸Then David said to Uriah, "Go down to your house, and wash your feet." Uriah went out of the king's house, and there followed him a present from the king. ⁹But Uriah slept at the entrance of the king's house with all the servants of his lord, and did not go down to his house. ¹⁰When they told David, "Uriah did not go down to his house," David said to Uriah, "You have just come from a journey. Why did you not go down to your house?" ¹¹Uriah said to David, "The ark and Israel and Judah remain in booths;[d] and my lord Joab and the servants of my lord are camping in the open field; shall I then go to my house, to eat and to drink, and to lie with my wife? As you live, and as your soul lives, I will not do such a thing." ¹²Then David said to Uriah, "Remain here today also, and tomorrow I will send you back." So Uriah remained in Jerusalem that day. On the next day, ¹³David invited him to eat and drink in his presence and made him drunk; and in the evening he went out to lie on his couch with the servants of his lord, but he did not go down to his house.

David Has Uriah Killed

14 In the morning David wrote a letter to Joab, and sent it by the hand of Uriah. ¹⁵In the letter he wrote, "Set Uriah in the forefront of the hardest fighting, and then draw back from him, so that he may be struck down and die." ¹⁶As Joab was besieging the city, he assigned Uriah to the place where he knew there were valiant warriors. ¹⁷The men of the city came out and fought with Joab; and some of the servants of David among the people fell. Uriah the Hittite was killed as well. ¹⁸Then Joab sent and told David all the news about the fighting; ¹⁹and he instructed the messenger, "When you have finished telling the king all the news about the fighting, ²⁰then, if the king's anger rises, and if he says to you, 'Why did you go so near the city to fight? Did you not know that they would shoot from the wall? ²¹Who killed Abimelech son of Jerubbaal?[e] Did not a woman throw an upper millstone on him from the wall, so that he died at Thebez? Why did you go so near the wall?' then you shall say, 'Your servant Uriah the Hittite is dead too.'"

---

c *11:2 he couldn't get to sleep*, literally, "arose from his bed."

d Or *at Succoth*   e Gk Syr Judg 7.1: Heb *Jerubbesheth*

King James

22¶ So the messenger went, and came and showed David all that Joab had sent him for.

23And the messenger said unto David, Surely the men prevailed against us, and came out unto us into the field, and we were upon them even unto the entering of the gate.

24And the shooters shot from off the wall upon thy servants; and *some* of the king's servants be dead, and thy servant Uriah the Hittite is dead also.

25Then David said unto the messenger, Thus shalt thou say unto Joab, Let not this thing displease thee, for the sword devoureth one as well as another: make thy battle more strong against the city, and overthrow it: and encourage thou him.

26¶ And when the wife of Uriah heard that Uriah her husband was dead, she mourned for her husband.

27And when the mourning was past, David sent and fetched her to his house, and she became his wife, and bare him a son. But the thing that David had done displeased the LORD.

12 AND THE LORD sent Nathan unto David. And he came unto him, and said unto him, There were two men in one city; the one rich, and the other poor.

2The rich *man* had exceeding many flocks and herds:

3But the poor *man* had nothing, save one little ewe lamb, which he had bought and nourished up: and it grew up together with him, and with his children; it did eat of his own meat, and drank of his own cup, and lay in his bosom, and was unto him as a daughter.

4And there came a traveller unto the rich man, and he spared to take of his own flock and of his own herd, to dress for the wayfaring man that was come unto him; but took the poor man's lamb, and dressed it for the man that was come to him.

5And David's anger was greatly kindled against the man; and he said to Nathan, *As* the LORD liveth, the man that hath done this *thing* shall surely die:

6And he shall restore the lamb fourfold, because he did this thing, and because he had no pity.

7¶ And Nathan said to David, Thou *art* the man. Thus saith the LORD God of Israel, I anointed thee king over Israel, and I delivered thee out of the hand of Saul;

8And I gave thee thy master's house, and thy master's wives into thy bosom, and gave thee the house of Israel and of Judah; and if *that had been* too little, I would moreover have given unto thee such and such things.

9Wherefore hast thou despised the commandment of the LORD, to do evil in his sight? thou hast killed Uriah the Hittite with the sword, and hast taken his wife *to be* thy wife, and hast slain him with the sword of the children of Ammon.

10Now therefore the sword shall never depart from thine house; because thou hast despised me, and hast taken the wife of Uriah the Hittite to be thy wife.

11Thus saith the LORD, Behold, I will raise up evil against thee out of thine own house, and I will take thy wives before thine eyes, and give *them* unto thy neighbour, and he shall lie with thy wives in the sight of this sun.

12For thou didst *it* secretly: but I will do this thing before all Israel, and before the sun.

13And David said unto Nathan, I have sinned against the LORD. And Nathan said unto David, The LORD also hath put away thy sin; thou shalt not die.

14Howbeit, because by this deed thou hast given great occasion to the enemies of the LORD to blaspheme, the child also *that is* born unto thee shall surely die.

New International

22The messenger set out, and when he arrived he told David everything Joab had sent him to say. 23The messenger said to David, "The men overpowered us and came out against us in the open, but we drove them back to the entrance to the city gate. 24Then the archers shot arrows at your servants from the wall, and some of the king's men died. Moreover, your servant Uriah the Hittite is dead."

25David told the messenger, "Say this to Joab: 'Don't let this upset you; the sword devours one as well as another. Press the attack against the city and destroy it.' Say this to encourage Joab."

26When Uriah's wife heard that her husband was dead, she mourned for him. 27After the time of mourning was over, David had her brought to his house, and she became his wife and bore him a son. But the thing David had done displeased the LORD.

Nathan Rebukes David

12 THE LORD sent Nathan to David. When he came to him, he said, "There were two men in a certain town, one rich and the other poor. 2The rich man had a very large number of sheep and cattle, 3but the poor man had nothing except one little ewe lamb he had bought. He raised it, and it grew up with him and his children. It shared his food, drank from his cup and even slept in his arms. It was like a daughter to him.

4"Now a traveler came to the rich man, but the rich man refrained from taking one of his own sheep or cattle to prepare a meal for the traveler who had come to him. Instead, he took the ewe lamb that belonged to the poor man and prepared it for the one who had come to him."

5David burned with anger against the man and said to Nathan, "As surely as the LORD lives, the man who did this deserves to die! 6He must pay for that lamb four times over, because he did such a thing and had no pity."

7Then Nathan said to David, "You are the man! This is what the LORD, the God of Israel, says: 'I anointed you king over Israel, and I delivered you from the hand of Saul. 8I gave your master's house to you, and your master's wives into your arms. I gave you the house of Israel and Judah. And if all this had been too little, I would have given you even more. 9Why did you despise the word of the LORD by doing what is evil in his eyes? You struck down Uriah the Hittite with the sword and took his wife to be your own. You killed him with the sword of the Ammonites. 10Now, therefore, the sword will never depart from your house, because you despised me and took the wife of Uriah the Hittite to be your own.'

11"This is what the LORD says: 'Out of your own household I am going to bring calamity upon you. Before your very eyes I will take your wives and give them to one who is close to you, and he will lie with your wives in broad daylight. 12You did it in secret, but I will do this thing in broad daylight before all Israel.' "

13Then David said to Nathan, "I have sinned against the LORD."

Nathan replied, "The LORD has taken away your sin. You are not going to die. 14But because by doing this you have made the enemies of the LORD show utter contempt,[a] the son born to you will die."

<hr/>

a *14* Masoretic Text; an ancient Hebrew scribal tradition *this you have shown utter contempt for the LORD*

Living Bible

22So the messenger arrived at Jerusalem, and gave the report to David.

23"The enemy came out against us," he said, "and as we chased them back to the city gates, 24the men on the wall attacked us; and some of our men were killed, and Uriah the Hittite is dead too."

25"Well, tell Joab not to be discouraged," David said. "The sword kills one as well as another!b Fight harder next time, and conquer the city; tell him he is doing well."

26When Bath-sheba heard that her husband was dead, she mourned for him; 27then, when the period of mourning was over, David sent for her and brought her to the palace and she became one of his wives; and she gave birth to his son. But the Lord was very displeased with what David had done.

12 SO THE Lord sent the prophet Nathan to tell David this story:

"There were two men in a certain city, one very rich, owning many flocks of sheep and herds of goats; 3and the other very poor, owning nothing but a little lamb he had managed to buy. It was his children's pet and he fed it from his own plate and let it drink from his own cup; he cuddled it in his arms like a baby daughter. 4Recently a guest arrived at the home of the rich man. But instead of killing a lamb from his own flocks for food for the traveler, he took the poor man's lamb and roasted it and served it."

5David was furious. "I swear by the living God," he vowed, "any man who would do a thing like that should be put to death; 6he shall repay four lambs to the poor man for the one he stole, and for having no pity."

7Then Nathan said to David, "You are that rich man! The Lord God of Israel says, 'I made you king of Israel and saved you from the power of Saul. 8I gave you his palace and his wives and the kingdoms of Israel and Judah; and if that had not been enough, I would have given you much, much more. 9Why, then, have you despised the laws of God and done this horrible deed? For you have murdered Uriah and stolen his wife. 10Therefore murder shall be a constant threat in your family from this time on, because you have insulted me by taking Uriah's wife. 11I vow that because of what you have done I will cause your own household to rebel against you. I will give your wives to another man, and he will go to bed with them in public view.c 12You did it secretly, but I will do this to you openly, in the sight of all Israel.' "

13"I have sinned against the Lord," David confessed to Nathan.

Then Nathan replied, "Yes, but the Lord has forgiven you, and you won't die for this sin. 14But you have given great opportunity to the enemies of the Lord to despise and blaspheme him, so your child shall die."

New Revised Standard

22 So the messenger went, and came and told David all that Joab had sent him to tell. 23The messenger said to David, "The men gained an advantage over us, and came out against us in the field; but we drove them back to the entrance of the gate. 24Then the archers shot at your servants from the wall; some of the king's servants are dead; and your servant Uriah the Hittite is dead also." 25David said to the messenger, "Thus you shall say to Joab, 'Do not let this matter trouble you, for the sword devours now one and now another; press your attack on the city, and overthrow it.' And encourage him."

26 When the wife of Uriah heard that her husband was dead, she made lamentation for him. 27When the mourning was over, David sent and brought her to his house, and she became his wife, and bore him a son.

Nathan Condemns David

But the thing that David had done displeased the LORD,

12 AND THE LORD sent Nathan to David. He came to him, and said to him, "There were two men in a certain city, the one rich and the other poor. 2The rich man had very many flocks and herds; 3but the poor man had nothing but one little ewe lamb, which he had bought. He brought it up, and it grew up with him and with his children; it used to eat of his meager fare, and drink from his cup, and lie in his bosom, and it was like a daughter to him. 4Now there came a traveler to the rich man, and he was loath to take one of his own flock or herd to prepare for the wayfarer who had come to him, but he took the poor man's lamb, and prepared that for the guest who had come to him." 5Then David's anger was greatly kindled against the man. He said to Nathan, "As the LORD lives, the man who has done this deserves to die; 6he shall restore the lamb fourfold, because he did this thing, and because he had no pity."

7 Nathan said to David, "You are the man! Thus says the LORD, the God of Israel: I anointed you king over Israel, and I rescued you from the hand of Saul; 8I gave you your master's house, and your master's wives into your bosom, and gave you the house of Israel and of Judah; and if that had been too little, I would have added as much more. 9Why have you despised the word of the LORD, to do what is evil in his sight? You have struck down Uriah the Hittite with the sword, and have taken his wife to be your wife, and have killed him with the sword of the Ammonites. 10Now therefore the sword shall never depart from your house, for you have despised me, and have taken the wife of Uriah the Hittite to be your wife. 11Thus says the LORD: I will raise up trouble against you from within your own house; and I will take your wives before your eyes, and give them to your neighbor, and he shall lie with your wives in the sight of this very sun. 12For you did it secretly; but I will do this thing before all Israel, and before the sun." 13David said to Nathan, "I have sinned against the LORD." Nathan said to David, "Now the LORD has put away your sin; you shall not die. 14Nevertheless, because by this deed you have utterly scorned the LORD,d the child that

---

b 11:25 The sword kills one as well as another, literally, "the sword devours now one and now another." c 12:11 with them in public view, literally, "under this sun."

d Ancient scribal tradition: Compare 1 Sam 25.22 note: Heb scorned the enemies of the LORD

King James

15¶ And Nathan departed unto his house. And the LORD struck the child that Uriah's wife bare unto David, and it was very sick.

16David therefore besought God for the child; and David fasted, and went in, and lay all night upon the earth.

17And the elders of his house arose, *and went* to him, to raise him up from the earth: but he would not, neither did he eat bread with them.

18And it came to pass on the seventh day, that the child died. And the servants of David feared to tell him that the child was dead: for they said, Behold, while the child was yet alive, we spake unto him, and he would not hearken unto our voice: how will he then vex himself, if we tell him that the child is dead?

19But when David saw that his servants whispered, David perceived that the child was dead: therefore David said unto his servants, Is the child dead? And they said, He is dead.

20Then David arose from the earth, and washed, and anointed *himself*, and changed his apparel, and came into the house of the LORD, and worshipped: then he came to his own house; and when he required, they set bread before him, and he did eat.

21Then said his servants unto him, What thing *is* this that thou hast done? thou didst fast and weep for the child, *while it was* alive; but when the child was dead, thou didst rise and eat bread.

22And he said, While the child was yet alive, I fasted and wept: for I said, Who can tell *whether* GOD will be gracious to me, that the child may live?

23But now he is dead, wherefore should I fast? can I bring him back again? I shall go to him, but he shall not return to me.

24¶ And David comforted Bath-sheba his wife, and went in unto her, and lay with her: and she bare a son, and he called his name Solomon: and the LORD loved him.

25And he sent by the hand of Nathan the prophet; and he called his name Jedidiah, because of the LORD.

26¶ And Joab fought against Rabbah of the children of Ammon, and took the royal city.

27And Joab sent messengers to David, and said, I have fought against Rabbah, and have taken the city of waters.

28Now therefore gather the rest of the people together, and encamp against the city, and take it: lest I take the city, and it be called after my name.

29And David gathered all the people together, and went to Rabbah, and fought against it, and took it.

30And he took their king's crown from off his head, the weight whereof *was* a talent of gold with the precious stones: and it was *set* on David's head. And he brought forth the spoil of the city in great abundance.

31And he brought forth the people that *were* therein, and put *them* under saws, and under harrows of iron, and under axes of iron, and made them pass through the brickkiln: and thus did he unto all the cities of the children of Ammon. So David and all the people returned unto Jerusalem.

13 AND IT came to pass after this, that Absalom the son of David had a fair sister, whose name *was* Tamar; and Amnon the son of David loved her.

New International

15After Nathan had gone home, the LORD struck the child that Uriah's wife had borne to David, and he became ill. 16David pleaded with God for the child. He fasted and went into his house and spent the nights lying on the ground. 17The elders of his household stood beside him to get him up from the ground, but he refused, and he would not eat any food with them.

18On the seventh day the child died. David's servants were afraid to tell him that the child was dead, for they thought, "While the child was still living, we spoke to David but he would not listen to us. How can we tell him the child is dead? He may do something desperate."

19David noticed that his servants were whispering among themselves and he realized the child was dead. "Is the child dead?" he asked.

"Yes," they replied, "he is dead."

20Then David got up from the ground. After he had washed, put on lotions and changed his clothes, he went into the house of the LORD and worshiped. Then he went to his own house, and at his request they served him food, and he ate.

21His servants asked him, "Why are you acting this way? While the child was alive, you fasted and wept, but now that the child is dead, you get up and eat!"

22He answered, "While the child was still alive, I fasted and wept. I thought, 'Who knows? The LORD may be gracious to me and let the child live.' 23But now that he is dead, why should I fast? Can I bring him back again? I will go to him, but he will not return to me."

24Then David comforted his wife Bathsheba, and he went to her and lay with her. She gave birth to a son, and they named him Solomon. The LORD loved him; 25and because the LORD loved him, he sent word through Nathan the prophet to name him Jedidiah.[a]

26Meanwhile Joab fought against Rabbah of the Ammonites and captured the royal citadel. 27Joab then sent messengers to David, saying, "I have fought against Rabbah and taken its water supply. 28Now muster the rest of the troops and besiege the city and capture it. Otherwise I will take the city, and it will be named after me."

29So David mustered the entire army and went to Rabbah, and attacked and captured it. 30He took the crown from the head of their king[b]—its weight was a talent[c] of gold, and it was set with precious stones—and it was placed on David's head. He took a great quantity of plunder from the city 31and brought out the people who were there, consigning them to labor with saws and with iron picks and axes, and he made them work at brickmaking.[d] He did this to all the Ammonite towns. Then David and his entire army returned to Jerusalem.

Amnon and Tamar

13 IN THE course of time, Amnon son of David fell in love with Tamar, the beautiful sister of Absalom son of David.

---

[a] *25 Jedidiah* means *loved by the LORD.*   [b] *30* Or *of Milcom* (that is, Molech)
[c] *30* That is, about 75 pounds (about 34 kilograms)   [d] *31* The meaning of the Hebrew for this clause is uncertain.

Living Bible

15Then Nathan returned to his home. And the Lord made Bath-sheba's baby deathly sick. 16David begged him to spare the child, and went without food and lay all night before the Lord on the bare earth. 17The leaders of the nation pleaded with him to get up and eat with them, but he refused. 18Then, on the seventh day, the baby died. David's aides were afraid to tell him.

"He was so broken up about the baby being sick," they said, "what will he do to himself when we tell him the child is dead?"

19But when David saw them whispering, he realized what had happened.

"Is the baby dead?" he asked.

"Yes," they replied, "he is." 20Then David got up off the ground, washed himself, brushed his hair, changed his clothes, and went into the Tabernacle and worshiped the Lord. Then he returned to the palace and ate. 21His aides were amazed.

"We don't understand you," they told him. "While the baby was still living, you wept and refused to eat; but now that the baby is dead, you have stopped your mourning and are eating again."

22David replied, "I fasted and wept while the child was alive, for I said, 'Perhaps the Lord will be gracious to me and let the child live.' 23But why should I fast when he is dead? Can I bring him back again? I shall go to him, but he shall not return to me."

24Then David comforted Bath-sheba; and when he slept with her, she conceived and gave birth to a son and named him Solomon. And the Lord loved the baby, 25and sent congratulations and blessings through Nathan the prophet. David nicknamed the baby Jedidiah (meaning, "Beloved of Jehovah") because of the Lord's interest.e 26. 27Meanwhile Joab and the Israeli army were successfully ending their siege of Rabbah the capital of Ammon. Joab sent messengers to tell David, "Rabbah and its beautiful harbor are ours!f 28Now bring the rest of the army and finish the job, so that you will get the credit for the victory instead of me."

29, 30So David led his army to Rabbah and captured it. Tremendous amounts of loot were carried back to Jerusalem, and David took the king of Rabbah's crown—a $50,000 treasure made from solid gold set with gems—and placed it on his own head. 31He made slaves of the people of the city and made them labor with saws, picks, and axes and work in the brick kilns;g that is the way he treated all of the cities of the Ammonites. Then David and the army returned to Jerusalem.

13 PRINCE ABSALOM, David's son, had a beautiful sister named Tamar. And Prince Amnon (her half brother) fell desperately in love with her. 2Am-

New Revised Standard

is born to you shall die." 15Then Nathan went to his house.

Bathsheba's Child Dies

The LORD struck the child that Uriah's wife bore to David, and it became very ill. 16David therefore pleaded with God for the child; David fasted, and went in and lay all night on the ground. 17The elders of his house stood beside him, urging him to rise from the ground; but he would not, nor did he eat food with them. 18On the seventh day the child died. And the servants of David were afraid to tell him that the child was dead; for they said, "While the child was still alive, we spoke to him, and he did not listen to us; how then can we tell him the child is dead? He may do himself some harm." 19But when David saw that his servants were whispering together, he perceived that the child was dead; and David said to his servants, "Is the child dead?" They said, "He is dead."

20 Then David rose from the ground, washed, anointed himself, and changed his clothes. He went into the house of the LORD, and worshiped; he then went to his own house; and when he asked, they set food before him and he ate. 21Then his servants said to him, "What is this thing that you have done? You fasted and wept for the child while it was alive; but when the child died, you rose and ate food." 22He said, "While the child was still alive, I fasted and wept; for I said, 'Who knows? The LORD may be gracious to me, and the child may live.' 23But now he is dead; why should I fast? Can I bring him back again? I shall go to him, but he will not return to me."

Solomon Is Born

24 Then David consoled his wife Bathsheba, and went to her, and lay with her; and she bore a son, and he named him Solomon. The LORD loved him, 25and sent a message by the prophet Nathan; so he named him Jedidiah,h because of the LORD.

The Ammonites Crushed

26 Now Joab fought against Rabbah of the Ammonites, and took the royal city. 27Joab sent messengers to David, and said, "I have fought against Rabbah; moreover, I have taken the water city. 28Now, then, gather the rest of the people together, and encamp against the city, and take it; or I myself will take the city, and it will be called by my name." 29So David gathered all the people together and went to Rabbah, and fought against it and took it. 30He took the crown of Milcomi from his head; the weight of it was a talent of gold, and in it was a precious stone; and it was placed on David's head. He also brought forth the spoil of the city, a very great amount. 31He brought out the people who were in it, and set them to work with saws and iron picks and iron axes, or sent them to the brickworks. Thus he did to all the cities of the Ammonites. Then David and all the people returned to Jerusalem.

Amnon and Tamar

13 SOME TIME passed. David's son Absalom had a beautiful sister whose name was Tamar; and David's son Amnon fell in love with her. 2Amnon

---

e 12:25 and sent congratulations, literally, "Jehovah sent word by Nathan the prophet." because of the Lord's interest, literally, "because of the Lord." f 12:26, 27 Rabbah and its beautiful harbor are ours, or, "I have taken the City of Waters." g 12:31 made them labor with saws, picks, and axes and work in the brick kilns, or "killed them with saws and iron harrows, and in the brick kilns."

h That is Beloved of the LORD   i Gk See 1 Kings 11.5, 33: Heb their kings

King James

2And Amnon was so vexed, that he fell sick for his sister Tamar; for she *was* a virgin; and Amnon thought it hard for him to do any thing to her.

3But Amnon had a friend, whose name *was* Jonadab, the son of Shimeah David's brother: and Jonadab *was* a very subtle man.

4And he said unto him, Why *art thou, being* the king's son, lean from day to day? wilt thou not tell me? And Amnon said unto him, I love Tamar, my brother Absalom's sister.

5And Jonadab said unto him, Lay thee down on thy bed, and make thyself sick: and when thy father cometh to see thee, say unto him, I pray thee, let my sister Tamar come, and give me meat, and dress the meat in my sight, that I may see *it,* and eat *it* at her hand.

6¶ So Amnon lay down, and made himself sick: and when the king was come to see him, Amnon said unto the king, I pray thee, let Tamar my sister come, and make me a couple of cakes in my sight, that I may eat at her hand.

7Then David sent home to Tamar, saying, Go now to thy brother Amnon's house, and dress him meat.

8So Tamar went to her brother Amnon's house; and he was laid down. And she took flour, and kneaded *it,* and made cakes in his sight, and did bake the cakes.

9And she took a pan, and poured *them* out before him; but he refused to eat. And Amnon said, Have out all men from me. And they went out every man from him.

10And Amnon said unto Tamar, Bring the meat into the chamber, that I may eat of thine hand. And Tamar took the cakes which she had made, and brought *them* into the chamber to Amnon her brother.

11And when she had brought *them* unto him to eat, he took hold of her, and said unto her, Come lie with me, my sister.

12And she answered him, Nay, my brother, do not force me; for no such thing ought to be done in Israel: do not thou this folly.

13And I, whither shall I cause my shame to go? and as for thee, thou shalt be as one of the fools in Israel. Now therefore, I pray thee, speak unto the king; for he will not withhold me from thee.

14Howbeit he would not hearken unto her voice: but, being stronger than she, forced her, and lay with her.

15¶ Then Amnon hated her exceedingly; so that the hatred wherewith he hated her *was* greater than the love wherewith he had loved her. And Amnon said unto her, Arise, be gone.

16And she said unto him, *There is* no cause: this evil in sending me away *is* greater than the other that thou didst unto me. But he would not hearken unto her.

17Then he called his servant that ministered unto him, and said, Put now this *woman* out from me, and bolt the door after her.

18And *she had* a garment of divers colours upon her: for with such robes were the king's daughters *that were* virgins apparelled. Then his servant brought her out, and bolted the door after her.

19¶ And Tamar put ashes on her head, and rent her garment of divers colours that *was* on her, and laid her hand on her head, and went on crying.

20And Absalom her brother said unto her, Hath Amnon thy brother been with thee? but hold now thy peace, my sister: he *is* thy brother; regard not this thing. So Tamar remained desolate in her brother Absalom's house.

New International

2Amnon became frustrated to the point of illness on account of his sister Tamar, for she was a virgin, and it seemed impossible for him to do anything to her.

3Now Amnon had a friend named Jonadab son of Shimeah, David's brother. Jonadab was a very shrewd man. 4He asked Amnon, "Why do you, the king's son, look so haggard morning after morning? Won't you tell me?"

Amnon said to him, "I'm in love with Tamar, my brother Absalom's sister."

5"Go to bed and pretend to be ill," Jonadab said. "When your father comes to see you, say to him, 'I would like my sister Tamar to come and give me something to eat. Let her prepare the food in my sight so I may watch her and then eat it from her hand.' "

6So Amnon lay down and pretended to be ill. When the king came to see him, Amnon said to him, "I would like my sister Tamar to come and make some special bread in my sight, so I may eat from her hand."

7David sent word to Tamar at the palace: "Go to the house of your brother Amnon and prepare some food for him." 8So Tamar went to the house of her brother Amnon, who was lying down. She took some dough, kneaded it, made the bread in his sight and baked it. 9Then she took the pan and served him the bread, but he refused to eat.

"Send everyone out of here," Amnon said. So everyone left him. 10Then Amnon said to Tamar, "Bring the food here into my bedroom so I may eat from your hand." And Tamar took the bread she had prepared and brought it to her brother Amnon in his bedroom. 11But when she took it to him to eat, he grabbed her and said, "Come to bed with me, my sister."

12"Don't, my brother!" she said to him. "Don't force me. Such a thing should not be done in Israel! Don't do this wicked thing. 13What about me? Where could I get rid of my disgrace? And what about you? You would be like one of the wicked fools in Israel. Please speak to the king; he will not keep me from being married to you." 14But he refused to listen to her, and since he was stronger than she, he raped her.

15Then Amnon hated her with intense hatred. In fact, he hated her more than he had loved her. Amnon said to her, "Get up and get out!"

16"No!" she said to him. "Sending me away would be a greater wrong than what you have already done to me."

But he refused to listen to her. 17He called his personal servant and said, "Get this woman out of here and bolt the door after her." 18So his servant put her out and bolted the door after her. She was wearing a richly ornamented[a] robe, for this was the kind of garment the virgin daughters of the king wore. 19Tamar put ashes on her head and tore the ornamented[b] robe she was wearing. She put her hand on her head and went away, weeping aloud as she went.

20Her brother Absalom said to her, "Has that Amnon, your brother, been with you? Be quiet now, my sister; he is your brother. Don't take this thing to heart." And Tamar lived in her brother Absalom's house, a desolate woman.

---

[a] *18* The meaning of the Hebrew for this phrase is uncertain.　[b] *19* The meaning of the Hebrew for this word is uncertain.

Living Bible

non became so tormented by his love for her that he became ill. He had no way of talking to her, for the girls and young men were kept strictly apart.c 3But Amnon had a very crafty friend—his cousin Jonadab (the son of David's brother Shime-ah).

4One day Jonadab said to Amnon, "What's the trouble? Why should the son of a king look so haggard morning after morning?"

So Amnon told him, "I am in love with Tamar, my half sister."

5"Well," Jonadab said, "I'll tell you what to do. Go back to bed and pretend you are sick; when your father comes to see you, ask him to let Tamar come and prepare some food for you. Tell him you'll feel better if she feeds you."

6So Amnon did. And when the king came to see him, Amnon asked him for this favor—that his sister Tamar be permitted to come and cook a little something for him to eat. 7David agreed, and sent word to Tamar to go to Amnon's quarters and prepare some food for him. 8So she did, and went into his bedroom so that he could watch her mix some dough; then she baked some special bread for him. 9But when she set the serving tray before him, he refused to eat!

"Everyone get out of here," he told his servants; so they all left the apartment.

10Then he said to Tamar, "Now bring me the food again here in my bedroom and feed it to me." So Tamar took it to him. 11But as she was standing there before him, he grabbed her and demanded, "Come to bed with me, my darling."

12"Oh, Amnon," she cried. "Don't be foolish! Don't do this to me! You know what a serious crime it is in Israel.d 13Where could I go in my shame? And you would be called one of the greatest fools in Israel. Please, just speak to the king about it, for he will let you marry me.

14But he wouldn't listen to her; and since he was stronger than she, he forced her. 15Then suddenly his love turned to hate, and now he hated her more than he had loved her.

"Get out of here!" he snarled at her.

16"No, no!" she cried. "To reject me now is a greater crime than the other you did to me."

But he wouldn't listen to her. 17, 18He shouted for his valet and demanded, "Throw this woman out and lock the door behind her."

So he put her out. She was wearing a long robe with sleeves, as was the custom in those days for virgin daughters of the king. 19Now she tore the robe and put ashes on her head and with her head in her hands went away crying.

20Her brother Absalom asked her, "Is it true that Amnon raped you? Don't be so upset, since it's all in the family anyway. It's not anything to worry about!"

So Tamar lived as a desolate woman in her brother Absalom's quarters.

New Revised Standard

was so tormented that he made himself ill because of his sister Tamar, for she was a virgin and it seemed impossible to Amnon to do anything to her. 3But Amnon had a friend whose name was Jonadab, the son of David's brother Shimeah; and Jonadab was a very crafty man. 4He said to him, "O son of the king, why are you so haggard morning after morning? Will you not tell me?" Amnon said to him, "I love Tamar, my brother Absalom's sister." 5Jonadab said to him, "Lie down on your bed, and pretend to be ill; and when your father comes to see you, say to him, 'Let my sister Tamar come and give me something to eat, and prepare the food in my sight, so that I may see it and eat it from her hand.' " 6So Amnon lay down, and pretended to be ill; and when the king came to see him, Amnon said to the king, "Please let my sister Tamar come and make a couple of cakes in my sight, so that I may eat from her hand."

7 Then David sent home to Tamar, saying, "Go to your brother Amnon's house, and prepare food for him." 8So Tamar went to her brother Amnon's house, where he was lying down. She took dough, kneaded it, made cakes in his sight, and baked the cakes. 9Then she took the pan and set theme out before him, but he refused to eat. Amnon said, "Send out everyone from me." So everyone went out from him. 10Then Amnon said to Tamar, "Bring the food into the chamber, so that I may eat from your hand." So Tamar took the cakes she had made, and brought them into the chamber to Amnon her brother. 11But when she brought them near him to eat, he took hold of her, and said to her, "Come, lie with me, my sister." 12She answered him, "No, my brother, do not force me; for such a thing is not done in Israel; do not do anything so vile! 13As for me, where could I carry my shame? And as for you, you would be as one of the scoundrels in Israel. Now therefore, I beg you, speak to the king; for he will not withhold me from you." 14But he would not listen to her; and being stronger than she, he forced her and lay with her.

15 Then Amnon was seized with a very great loathing for her; indeed, his loathing was even greater than the lust he had felt for her. Amnon said to her, "Get out!" 16But she said to him, "No, my brother;f for this wrong in sending me away is greater than the other that you did to me." But he would not listen to her. 17He called the young man who served him and said, "Put this woman out of my presence, and bolt the door after her." 18 (Now she was wearing a long robe with sleeves; for this is how the virgin daughters of the king were clothed in earlier times.g) So his servant put her out, and bolted the door after her. 19But Tamar put ashes on her head, and tore the long robe that she was wearing; she put her hand on her head, and went away, crying aloud as she went.

20 Her brother Absalom said to her, "Has Amnon your brother been with you? Be quiet for now, my sister; he is your brother; do not take this to heart." So Tamar remained, a desolate woman, in her brother Absalom's house. 21When King David heard of all these things, he

---

c 13:2 *for the girls and young men were kept strictly apart,* literally, "for she was a virgin, and it seemed impossible to Amnon to do anything to her."
d 13:12 *You know what a serious crime it is in Israel,* literally, "No such thing ought to be done in Israel; do not this folly."

e Heb *and poured*   f Cn Compare Gk Vg: Meaning of Heb uncertain   g Cn: Heb *were clothed in robes*

King James

²¹¶ But when king David heard of all these things, he was very wroth.

²²And Absalom spake unto his brother Amnon neither good nor bad: for Absalom hated Amnon, because he had forced his sister Tamar.

²³¶ And it came to pass after two full years, that Absalom had sheepshearers in Baal-hazor, which is beside Ephraim: and Absalom invited all the king's sons.

²⁴And Absalom came to the king, and said, Behold now, thy servant hath sheepshearers; let the king, I beseech thee, and his servants go with thy servant.

²⁵And the king said to Absalom, Nay, my son, let us not all now go, lest we be chargeable unto thee. And he pressed him: howbeit he would not go, but blessed him.

²⁶Then said Absalom, If not, I pray thee, let my brother Amnon go with us. And the king said unto him, Why should he go with thee?

²⁷But Absalom pressed him, that he let Amnon and all the king's sons go with him.

²⁸¶ Now Absalom had commanded his servants, saying, Mark ye now when Amnon's heart is merry with wine, and when I say unto you, Smite Amnon; then kill him, fear not: have not I commanded you? be courageous, and be valiant.

²⁹And the servants of Absalom did unto Amnon as Absalom had commanded. Then all the king's sons arose, and every man gat him up upon his mule, and fled.

³⁰¶ And it came to pass, while they were in the way, that tidings came to David, saying, Absalom hath slain all the king's sons, and there is not one of them left.

³¹Then the king arose, and tare his garments, and lay on the earth; and all his servants stood by with their clothes rent.

³²And Jonadab, the son of Shimeah David's brother, answered and said, Let not my lord suppose that they have slain all the young men the king's sons; for Amnon only is dead: for by the appointment of Absalom this hath been determined from the day that he forced his sister Tamar.

³³Now therefore let not my lord the king take the thing to his heart, to think that all the king's sons are dead: for Amnon only is dead.

³⁴But Absalom fled. And the young man that kept the watch lifted up his eyes, and looked, and, behold, there came much people by the way of the hill side behind him.

³⁵And Jonadab said unto the king, Behold, the king's sons come: as thy servant said, so it is.

³⁶And it came to pass, as soon as he had made an end of speaking, that, behold, the king's sons came, and lifted up their voice and wept: and the king also and all his servants wept very sore.

³⁷¶ But Absalom fled, and went to Talmai, the son of Ammihud, king of Geshur. And David mourned for his son every day.

³⁸So Absalom fled, and went to Geshur, and was there three years.

³⁹And the soul of king David longed to go forth unto Absalom: for he was comforted concerning Amnon, seeing he was dead.

14 NOW JOAB the son of Zeruiah perceived that the king's heart was toward Absalom.

New International

²¹When King David heard all this, he was furious. ²²Absalom never said a word to Amnon, either good or bad; he hated Amnon because he had disgraced his sister Tamar.

Absalom Kills Amnon

²³Two years later, when Absalom's sheepshearers were at Baal Hazor near the border of Ephraim, he invited all the king's sons to come there. ²⁴Absalom went to the king and said, "Your servant has had shearers come. Will the king and his officials please join me?"

²⁵"No, my son," the king replied. "All of us should not go; we would only be a burden to you." Although Absalom urged him, he still refused to go, but gave him his blessing.

²⁶Then Absalom said, "If not, please let my brother Amnon come with us."

The king asked him, "Why should he go with you?" ²⁷But Absalom urged him, so he sent with him Amnon and the rest of the king's sons.

²⁸Absalom ordered his men, "Listen! When Amnon is in high spirits from drinking wine and I say to you, 'Strike Amnon down,' then kill him. Don't be afraid. Have not I given you this order? Be strong and brave." ²⁹So Absalom's men did to Amnon what Absalom had ordered. Then all the king's sons got up, mounted their mules and fled.

³⁰While they were on their way, the report came to David: "Absalom has struck down all the king's sons; not one of them is left." ³¹The king stood up, tore his clothes and lay down on the ground; and all his servants stood by with their clothes torn.

³²But Jonadab son of Shimeah, David's brother, said, "My lord should not think that they killed all the princes; only Amnon is dead. This has been Absalom's expressed intention ever since the day Amnon raped his sister Tamar. ³³My lord the king should not be concerned about the report that all the king's sons are dead. Only Amnon is dead."

³⁴Meanwhile, Absalom had fled.

Now the man standing watch looked up and saw many people on the road west of him, coming down the side of the hill. The watchman went and told the king, "I see men in the direction of Horonaim, on the side of the hill."ᵃ

³⁵Jonadab said to the king, "See, the king's sons are here; it has happened just as your servant said."

³⁶As he finished speaking, the king's sons came in, wailing loudly. The king, too, and all his servants wept very bitterly.

³⁷Absalom fled and went to Talmai son of Ammihud, the king of Geshur. But King David mourned for his son every day.

³⁸After Absalom fled and went to Geshur, he stayed there three years. ³⁹And the spirit of the kingᵇ longed to go to Absalom, for he was consoled concerning Amnon's death.

Absalom Returns to Jerusalem

14 JOAB SON of Zeruiah knew that the king's heart longed for Absalom. ²So Joab sent some-

---

ᵃ 34 Septuagint; Hebrew does not have this sentence.   ᵇ 39 Dead Sea Scrolls and some Septuagint manuscripts; Masoretic Text But the spirit of, David the king

Living Bible

21-24When King David heard what had happened, he was very angry, but Absalom said nothing one way or the other about this to Amnon. However, he hated him with a deep hatred because of what he had done to his sister. Then, two years later, when Absalom's sheep were being sheared at Baal-hazor in Ephraim, Absalom invited his father and all his brothers to come to a feast to celebrate the occasion.

25The king replied, "No, my boy; if we all came, we would be too much of a burden on you."

Absalom pressed him, but he wouldn't come, though he sent his thanks.

26"Well, then," Absalom said, "if you can't come, how about sending my brother Amnon instead?"

"Why Amnon?" the king asked.

27Absalom kept on urging the matter until finally the king agreed, and let all of his sons attend, including Amnon.

28Absalom told his men, "Wait until Amnon gets drunk, then, at my signal, kill him! Don't be afraid. I'm the one who gives the orders around here, and this is a command. Take courage and do it!"

29, 30So they murdered Amnon. Then the other sons of the king jumped on their mules and fled. As they were on the way back to Jerusalem, the report reached David: "Absalom has killed all of your sons, and not one is left alive!"

31The king jumped up, ripped off his robe, and fell prostrate to the ground. His aides also tore their clothes in horror and sorrow.

32, 33But just then Jonadab (the son of David's brother Shime-ah) arrived and said, "No, not all have been killed! It was only Amnon! Absalom has been plotting this ever since Amnon raped Tamar. No, no! Your sons aren't all dead! It was only Amnon."

34Meanwhile Absalom escaped. Now the watchman on the Jerusalem wall saw a great crowd coming toward the city along the road at the side of the hill.

35"See!" Jonadab told the king. "There they are now! Your sons are coming, just as I said."

36They soon arrived, weeping and sobbing, and the king and his officials wept with them. 37, 38, 39Absalom fled to King Talmai of Geshurᶜ (the son of Ammihud) and stayed there three years. Meanwhile David, now reconciled to Amnon's death, longed day after day for fellowship with his son Absalom.

14 WHEN GENERAL Joab realized how much the king was longing to see Absalom, 2, 3he

New Revised Standard

became very angry, but he would not punish his son Amnon, because he loved him, for he was his first-born.ᵈ 22But Absalom spoke to Amnon neither good nor bad; for Absalom hated Amnon, because he had raped his sister Tamar.

Absalom Avenges the Violation of His Sister

23 After two full years Absalom had sheepshearers at Baal-hazor, which is near Ephraim, and Absalom invited all the king's sons. 24Absalom came to the king, and said, "Your servant has sheepshearers; will the king and his servants please go with your servant?" 25But the king said to Absalom, "No, my son, let us not all go, or else we will be burdensome to you." He pressed him, but he would not go but gave him his blessing. 26Then Absalom said, "If not, please let my brother Amnon go with us." The king said to him, "Why should he go with you?" 27But Absalom pressed him until he let Amnon and all the king's sons go with him. Absalom made a feast like a king's feast.ᵉ 28Then Absalom commanded his servants, "Watch when Amnon's heart is merry with wine, and when I say to you, 'Strike Amnon,' then kill him. Do not be afraid; have I not myself commanded you? Be courageous and valiant." 29So the servants of Absalom did to Amnon as Absalom had commanded. Then all the king's sons rose, and each mounted his mule and fled.

30 While they were on the way, the report came to David that Absalom had killed all the king's sons, and not one of them was left. 31The king rose, tore his garments, and lay on the ground; and all his servants who were standing by tore their garments. 32But Jonadab, the son of David's brother Shimeah, said, "Let not my lord suppose that they have killed all the young men the king's sons; Amnon alone is dead. This has been determined by Absalom from the day Amnonᶠ raped his sister Tamar. 33Now therefore, do not let my lord the king take it to heart, as if all the king's sons were dead; for Amnon alone is dead."

34 But Absalom fled. When the young man who kept watch looked up, he saw many people coming from the Horonaim roadᵍ by the side of the mountain. 35Jonadab said to the king, "See, the king's sons have come; as your servant said, so it has come about." 36As soon as he had finished speaking, the king's sons arrived, and raised their voices and wept; and the king and all his servants also wept very bitterly.

37 But Absalom fled, and went to Talmai son of Ammihud, king of Geshur. David mourned for his son day after day. 38Absalom, having fled to Geshur, stayed there three years. 39And the heart ofʰ the king went out, yearning for Absalom; for he was now consoled over the death of Amnon.

Absalom Returns to Jerusalem

14 NOW JOAB son of Zeruiah perceived that the king's mind was on Absalom. 2Joab sent to

---

ᶜ 13:37 King Talmai of Geshur. He was Absalom's grandfather—his mother's father.

ᵈ Q Ms Gk: MT lacks but he would not punish . . . firstborn ᵉ Gk Compare Q Ms: MT lacks Absalom made a feast like a king's feast ᶠ Heb he ᵍ Cn Compare Gk: Heb the road behind him ʰ Q Ms Gk: MT And David

King James

2And Joab sent to Tekoah, and fetched thence a wise woman, and said unto her, I pray thee, feign thyself to be a mourner, and put on now mourning apparel, and anoint not thyself with oil, but be as a woman that had a long time mourned for the dead:

3And come to the king, and speak on this manner unto him. So Joab put the words in her mouth.

4¶ And when the woman of Tekoah spake to the king, she fell on her face to the ground, and did obeisance, and said, Help, O king.

5And the king said unto her, What aileth thee? And she answered, I am indeed a widow woman, and mine husband is dead.

6And thy handmaid had two sons, and they two strove together in the field, and there was none to part them, but the one smote the other, and slew him.

7And, behold, the whole family is risen against thine handmaid, and they said, Deliver him that smote his brother, that we may kill him, for the life of his brother whom he slew; and we will destroy the heir also: and so they shall quench my coal which is left, and shall not leave to my husband neither name nor remainder upon the earth.

8And the king said unto the woman, Go to thine house, and I will give charge concerning thee.

9And the woman of Tekoah said unto the king, My lord, O king, the iniquity be on me, and on my father's house: and the king and his throne be guiltless.

10And the king said, Whosoever saith aught unto thee, bring him to me, and he shall not touch thee any more.

11Then said she, I pray thee, let the king remember the LORD thy God, that thou wouldest not suffer the revengers of blood to destroy any more, lest they destroy my son. And he said, As the LORD liveth, there shall not one hair of thy son fall to the earth.

12Then the woman said, Let thine handmaid, I pray thee, speak one word unto my lord the king. And he said, Say on.

13And the woman said, Wherefore then hast thou thought such a thing against the people of God? for the king doth speak this thing as one which is faulty, in that the king doth not fetch home again his banished.

14For we must needs die, and are as water spilt on the ground, which cannot be gathered up again; neither doth God respect any person: yet doth he devise means, that his banished be not expelled from him.

15Now therefore that I am come to speak of this thing unto my lord the king, it is because the people have made me afraid: and thy handmaid said, I will now speak unto the king; it may be that the king will perform the request of his handmaid.

16For the king will hear, to deliver his handmaid out of the hand of the man that would destroy me and my son together out of the inheritance of God.

17Then thine handmaid said, The word of my lord the king shall now be comfortable: for as an angel of God, so is my lord the king to discern good and bad: therefore the LORD thy God will be with thee.

18Then the king answered and said unto the woman, Hide not from me, I pray thee, the thing that I shall ask thee. And the woman said, Let my lord the king now speak.

19And the king said, Is not the hand of Joab with thee in all this? And the woman answered and said, As thy soul liveth, my lord the king, none can turn to the right hand or to the left from aught that my lord the king hath spoken: for thy servant Joab, he bade me, and he put all these words in the mouth of thine handmaid:

20To fetch about this form of speech hath thy servant Joab done this thing: and my lord is wise, according to the wisdom of an angel of God, to know all things that are in the earth.

New International

one to Tekoa and had a wise woman brought from there. He said to her, "Pretend you are in mourning. Dress in mourning clothes, and don't use any cosmetic lotions. Act like a woman who has spent many days grieving for the dead. 3Then go to the king and speak these words to him." And Joab put the words in her mouth.

4When the woman from Tekoa went[a] to the king, she fell with her face to the ground to pay him honor, and she said, "Help me, O king!"

5The king asked her, "What is troubling you?"

She said, "I am indeed a widow; my husband is dead. 6I your servant had two sons. They got into a fight with each other in the field, and no one was there to separate them. One struck the other and killed him. 7Now the whole clan has risen up against your servant; they say, 'Hand over the one who struck his brother down, so that we may put him to death for the life of his brother whom he killed; then we will get rid of the heir as well.' They would put out the only burning coal I have left, leaving my husband neither name nor descendant on the face of the earth."

8The king said to the woman, "Go home, and I will issue an order in your behalf."

9But the woman from Tekoa said to him, "My lord the king, let the blame rest on me and on my father's family, and let the king and his throne be without guilt."

10The king replied, "If anyone says anything to you, bring him to me, and he will not bother you again."

11She said, "Then let the king invoke the LORD his God to prevent the avenger of blood from adding to the destruction, so that my son will not be destroyed."

"As surely as the LORD lives," he said, "not one hair of your son's head will fall to the ground."

12Then the woman said, "Let your servant speak a word to my lord the king."

"Speak," he replied.

13The woman said, "Why then have you devised a thing like this against the people of God? When the king says this, does he not convict himself, for the king has not brought back his banished son? 14Like water spilled on the ground, which cannot be recovered, so we must die. But God does not take away life; instead, he devises ways so that a banished person may not remain estranged from him.

15"And now I have come to say this to my lord the king because the people have made me afraid. Your servant thought, 'I will speak to the king; perhaps he will do what his servant asks. 16Perhaps the king will agree to deliver his servant from the hand of the man who is trying to cut off both me and my son from the inheritance God gave us.'

17"And now your servant says, 'May the word of my lord the king bring me rest, for my lord the king is like an angel of God in discerning good and evil. May the LORD your God be with you.'"

18Then the king said to the woman, "Do not keep from me the answer to what I am going to ask you."

"Let my lord the king speak," the woman said.

19The king asked, "Isn't the hand of Joab with you in all this?"

The woman answered, "As surely as you live, my lord the king, no one can turn to the right or to the left from anything my lord the king says. Yes, it was your servant Joab who instructed me to do this and who put all these words into the mouth of your servant. 20Your servant Joab did this to change the present situation. My lord has wisdom like that of an angel of God—he knows everything that happens in the land."

---

a 4 Many Hebrew manuscripts, Septuagint, Vulgate and Syriac; most Hebrew manuscripts spoke

Living Bible

sent for a woman of Tekoa who had a reputation for great wisdom and told her to ask for an appointment with the king. He told her what to say to him.

"Pretend you are in mourning," Joab instructed her. "Wear mourning clothes, and dishevel your hair as though you have been in deep sorrow for a long time."

4When the woman approached the king, she fell face downward on the floor in front of him, and cried out, "O king! Help me!"

5,6"What's the trouble?" he asked.

"I am a widow," she replied, "and my two sons had a fight out in the field, and since no one was there to part them, one of them was killed. 7Now the rest of the family is demanding that I surrender my other son to them to be executed for murdering his brother. But if I do that, I will have no one left, and my husband's name will be destroyed from the face of the earth."

8"Leave it with me," the king told her, "I'll see to it that no one touches him."

9"Oh, thank you, my lord," she replied. "And I'll take the responsibility if you are criticized for helping me like this."

10"Don't worry about that!" the king replied. "If anyone objects, bring him to me; I can assure you he will never complain again!"

11Then she said, "Please swear to me by God that you won't let anyone harm my son. I want no more bloodshed."

"I vow by God," he replied, "that not a hair of your son's head shall be disturbed!"

12"Please let me ask one more thing of you!" she said.

"Go ahead," he replied. "Speak!"

13"Why don't you do as much for all the people of God as you have promised to do for me?" she asked. "You have convicted yourself in making this decision, because you have refused to bring home your own banished son. 14All of us must die eventually; our lives are like water that is poured out on the ground—it can't be gathered up again. But God will bless you with a longer life if you will find a way to bring your son back from his exile.b 15, 16But I have come to plead with you for my son because my life and my son's life have been threatened, and I said to myself, 'Perhaps the king will listen to me and rescue us from those who would end our existence in Israel. 17Yes, the king will give us peace again.' I know that you are like the angel of God and can discern good from evil. May God be with you."

18"I want to know one thing," the king replied.

"Yes, my lord?" she asked.

19"Did Joab send you here?"

And the woman replied, "How can I deny it? Yes, Joab sent me and told me what to say. 20He did it in order to place the matter before you in a different light. But you are as wise as an angel of God, and you know everything that happens!"

New Revised Standard

Tekoa and brought from there a wise woman. He said to her, "Pretend to be a mourner; put on mourning garments, do not anoint yourself with oil, but behave like a woman who has been mourning many days for the dead. 3Go to the king and speak to him as follows." And Joab put the words into her mouth.

4 When the woman of Tekoa came to the king, she fell on her face to the ground and did obeisance, and said, "Help, O king!" 5The king asked her, "What is your trouble?" She answered, "Alas, I am a widow; my husband is dead. 6Your servant had two sons, and they fought with one another in the field; there was no one to part them, and one struck the other and killed him. 7Now the whole family has risen against your servant. They say, 'Give up the man who struck his brother, so that we may kill him for the life of his brother whom he murdered, even if we destroy the heir as well.' Thus they would quench my one remaining ember, and leave to my husband neither name nor remnant on the face of the earth."

8 Then the king said to the woman, "Go to your house, and I will give orders concerning you." 9The woman of Tekoa said to the king, "On me be the guilt, my lord the king, and on my father's house; let the king and his throne be guiltless." 10The king said, "If anyone says anything to you, bring him to me, and he shall never touch you again." 11Then she said, "Please, may the king keep the Lord your God in mind, so that the avenger of blood may kill no more, and my son not be destroyed." He said, "As the Lord lives, not one hair of your son shall fall to the ground."

12 Then the woman said, "Please let your servant speak a word to my lord the king." He said, "Speak." 13The woman said, "Why then have you planned such a thing against the people of God? For in giving this decision the king convicts himself, inasmuch as the king does not bring his banished one home again. 14We must all die; we are like water spilled on the ground, which cannot be gathered up. But God will not take away a life; he will devise plans so as not to keep an outcast banished forever from his presence.c 15Now I have come to say this to my lord the king because the people have made me afraid; your servant thought, 'I will speak to the king; it may be that the king will perform the request of his servant. 16For the king will hear, and deliver his servant from the hand of the man who would cut both me and my son off from the heritage of God.' 17Your servant thought, 'The word of my lord the king will set me at rest'; for my lord the king is like the angel of God, discerning good and evil. The Lord your God be with you!"

18 Then the king answered the woman, "Do not withhold from me anything I ask you." The woman said, "Let my lord the king speak." 19The king said, "Is the hand of Joab with you in all this?" The woman answered and said, "As surely as you live, my lord the king, one cannot turn right or left from anything that my lord the king has said. For it was your servant Joab who commanded me; it was he who put all these words into the mouth of your servant. 20In order to change the course of affairs your servant Joab did this. But my lord has wisdom like the wisdom of the angel of God to know all things that are on the earth."

---

b 14:14 bring your son back from his exile, or, "God does not sweep life away, but has made provision to bring back those he banishes, so that they will not be forever exiles."

c Meaning of Heb uncertain

King James

21¶ And the king said unto Joab, Behold now, I have done this thing: go therefore, bring the young man Absalom again.

22And Joab fell to the ground on his face, and bowed himself, and thanked the king: and Joab said, Today thy servant knoweth that I have found grace in thy sight, my lord, O king, in that the king hath fulfilled the request of his servant.

23So Joab arose and went to Geshur, and brought Absalom to Jerusalem.

24And the king said, Let him turn to his own house, and let him not see my face. So Absalom returned to his own house, and saw not the king's face.

25¶ But in all Israel there was none to be so much praised as Absalom for his beauty: from the sole of his foot even to the crown of his head there was no blemish in him.

26And when he polled his head, (for it was at every year's end that he polled it: because the hair was heavy on him, therefore he polled it:) he weighed the hair of his head at two hundred shekels after the king's weight.

27And unto Absalom there were born three sons, and one daughter, whose name was Tamar: she was a woman of a fair countenance.

28¶ So Absalom dwelt two full years in Jerusalem, and saw not the king's face.

29Therefore Absalom sent for Joab, to have sent him to the king; but he would not come to him: and when he sent again the second time, he would not come.

30Therefore he said unto his servants, See, Joab's field is near mine, and he hath barley there; go and set it on fire. And Absalom's servants set the field on fire.

31Then Joab arose, and came to Absalom unto his house, and said unto him, Wherefore have thy servants set my field on fire?

32And Absalom answered Joab, Behold, I sent unto thee, saying, Come hither, that I may send thee to the king, to say, Wherefore am I come from Geshur? it had been good for me to have been there still: now therefore let me see the king's face; and if there be any iniquity in me, let him kill me.

33So Joab came to the king, and told him: and when he had called for Absalom, he came to the king, and bowed himself on his face to the ground before the king: and the king kissed Absalom.

15 AND IT came to pass after this, that Absalom prepared him chariots and horses, and fifty men to run before him.

2And Absalom rose up early, and stood beside the way of the gate: and it was so, that when any man that had a controversy came to the king for judgment, then Absalom called unto him, and said, Of what city art thou? And he said, Thy servant is of one of the tribes of Israel.

3And Absalom said unto him, See, thy matters are good and right; but there is no man deputed of the king to hear thee.

4Absalom said moreover, Oh that I were made judge in the land, that every man which hath any suit or cause might come unto me, and I would do him justice!

5And it was so, that when any man came nigh to him to do him obeisance, he put forth his hand, and took him, and kissed him.

6And on this manner did Absalom to all Israel that came to the king for judgment: so Absalom stole the hearts of the men of Israel.

New International

21The king said to Joab, "Very well, I will do it. Go, bring back the young man Absalom."

22Joab fell with his face to the ground to pay him honor, and he blessed the king. Joab said, "Today your servant knows that he has found favor in your eyes, my lord the king, because the king has granted his servant's request."

23Then Joab went to Geshur and brought Absalom back to Jerusalem. 24But the king said, "He must go to his own house; he must not see my face." So Absalom went to his own house and did not see the face of the king.

25In all Israel there was not a man so highly praised for his handsome appearance as Absalom. From the top of his head to the sole of his foot there was no blemish in him. 26Whenever he cut the hair of his head—he used to cut his hair from time to time when it became too heavy for him—he would weigh it, and its weight was two hundred shekelsa by the royal standard.

27Three sons and a daughter were born to Absalom. The daughter's name was Tamar, and she became a beautiful woman.

28Absalom lived two years in Jerusalem without seeing the king's face. 29Then Absalom sent for Joab in order to send him to the king, but Joab refused to come to him. So he sent a second time, but he refused to come. 30Then he said to his servants, "Look, Joab's field is next to mine, and he has barley there. Go and set it on fire." So Absalom's servants set the field on fire.

31Then Joab did go to Absalom's house and he said to him, "Why have your servants set my field on fire?"

32Absalom said to Joab, "Look, I sent word to you and said, 'Come here so I can send you to the king to ask, "Why have I come from Geshur? It would be better for me if I were still there!" ' Now then, I want to see the king's face, and if I am guilty of anything, let him put me to death."

33So Joab went to the king and told him this. Then the king summoned Absalom, and he came in and bowed down with his face to the ground before the king. And the king kissed Absalom.

Absalom's Conspiracy

15 IN THE course of time, Absalom provided himself with a chariot and horses and with fifty men to run ahead of him. 2He would get up early and stand by the side of the road leading to the city gate. Whenever anyone came with a complaint to be placed before the king for a decision, Absalom would call out to him, "What town are you from?" He would answer, "Your servant is from one of the tribes of Israel." 3Then Absalom would say to him, "Look, your claims are valid and proper, but there is no representative of the king to hear you." 4And Absalom would add, "If only I were appointed judge in the land! Then everyone who has a complaint or case could come to me and I would see that he gets justice."

5Also, whenever anyone approached him to bow down before him, Absalom would reach out his hand, take hold of him and kiss him. 6Absalom behaved in this way toward all the Israelites who came to the king asking for justice, and so he stole the hearts of the men of Israel.

Living Bible

21So the king sent for Joab and told him, "All right, go and bring back Absalom."

22Joab fell to the ground before the king and blessed him and said, "At last I know that you like me! For you have granted me this request!"

23Then Joab went to Geshur and brought Absalom back to Jerusalem.

24"He may go to his own quarters," the king ordered, "but he must never come here. I refuse to see him."

25Now no one in Israel was such a handsome specimen of manhood as Absalom, and no one else received such praise. 26He cut his hair only once a year—and then only because it weighed three pounds and was too much of a load to carry around! 27He had three sons and one daughter, Tamar, who was a very beautiful girl.

28After Absalom had been in Jerusalem for two years and had not yet seen the king, 29he sent for Joab to ask him to intercede for him; but Joab wouldn't come. Absalom sent for him again, but again he refused to come.

30So Absalom said to his servants, "Go and set fire to that barley field of Joab's next to mine," and they did.

31Then Joab came to Absalom and demanded, "Why did your servants set my field on fire?"

32And Absalom replied, "Because I wanted you to ask the king why he brought me back from Geshur if he didn't intend to see me. I might as well have stayed there. Let me have an interview with the king; then if he finds that I am guilty of murder, let him execute me."

33So Joab told the king what Absalom had said. Then at last David summoned Absalom, and he came and bowed low before the king, and David kissed him.

15 ABSALOM THEN bought a magnificent chariot and chariot horses, and hired fifty footmen to run ahead of him. 2He got up early every morning and went out to the gate of the city; and when anyone came to bring a case to the king for trial, Absalom called him over and expressed interest in his problem.

3He would say, "I can see that you are right in this matter; it's unfortunate that the king doesn't have anyone to assist him in hearing these cases. 4I surely wish I were the judge; then anyone with a lawsuit could come to me, and I would give him justice!"

5And when anyone came to bow to him, Absalom wouldn't let him, but shook his hand instead!b 6So in this way Absalom stole the hearts of all the people of Israel.

New Revised Standard

21 Then the king said to Joab, "Very well, I grant this; go, bring back the young man Absalom." 22Joab prostrated himself with his face to the ground and did obeisance, and blessed the king; and Joab said, "Today your servant knows that I have found favor in your sight, my lord the king, in that the king has granted the request of his servant." 23So Joab set off, went to Geshur, and brought Absalom to Jerusalem. 24The king said, "Let him go to his own house; he is not to come into my presence." So Absalom went to his own house, and did not come into the king's presence.

David Forgives Absalom

25 Now in all Israel there was no one to be praised so much for his beauty as Absalom; from the sole of his foot to the crown of his head there was no blemish in him. 26When he cut the hair of his head (for at the end of every year he used to cut it; when it was heavy on him, he cut it), he weighed the hair of his head, two hundred shekels by the king's weight. 27There were born to Absalom three sons, and one daughter whose name was Tamar; she was a beautiful woman.

28 So Absalom lived two full years in Jerusalem, without coming into the king's presence. 29Then Absalom sent for Joab to send him to the king; but Joab would not come to him. He sent a second time, but Joab would not come. 30Then he said to his servants, "Look, Joab's field is next to mine, and he has barley there; go and set it on fire." So Absalom's servants set the field on fire. 31Then Joab rose and went to Absalom at his house, and said to him, "Why have your servants set my field on fire?" 32Absalom answered Joab, "Look, I sent word to you: Come here, that I may send you to the king with the question, 'Why have I come from Geshur? It would be better for me to be there still.' Now let me go into the king's presence; if there is guilt in me, let him kill me!" 33Then Joab went to the king and told him; and he summoned Absalom. So he came to the king and prostrated himself with his face to the ground before the king; and the king kissed Absalom.

Absalom Usurps the Throne

15 AFTER THIS Absalom got himself a chariot and horses, and fifty men to run ahead of him. 2Absalom used to rise early and stand beside the road into the gate; and when anyone brought a suit before the king for judgment, Absalom would call out and say, "From what city are you?" When the person said, "Your servant is of such and such a tribe in Israel," 3Absalom would say, "See, your claims are good and right; but there is no one deputed by the king to hear you." 4Absalom said moreover, "If only I were judge in the land! Then all who had a suit or cause might come to me, and I would give them justice." 5Whenever people came near to do obeisance to him, he would put out his hand and take hold of them, and kiss them. 6Thus Absalom did to every Israelite who came to the king for judgment; so Absalom stole the hearts of the people of Israel.

---

b 15:5 *shook his hand instead*, literally, "took hold of him and kissed him."

King James

7¶ And it came to pass after forty years, that Absalom said unto the king, I pray thee, let me go and pay my vow, which I have vowed unto the LORD, in Hebron.

8For thy servant vowed a vow while I abode at Geshur in Syria, saying, If the LORD shall bring me again indeed to Jerusalem, then I will serve the LORD.

9And the king said unto him, Go in peace. So he arose, and went to Hebron.

10¶ But Absalom sent spies throughout all the tribes of Israel, saying, As soon as ye hear the sound of the trumpet, then ye shall say, Absalom reigneth in Hebron.

11And with Absalom went two hundred men out of Jerusalem, *that were* called; and they went in their simplicity, and they knew not any thing.

12And Absalom sent for Ahithophel the Gilonite, David's counsellor, from his city, *even* from Giloh, while he offered sacrifices. And the conspiracy was strong; for the people increased continually with Absalom.

13¶ And there came a messenger to David, saying, The hearts of the men of Israel are after Absalom.

14And David said unto all his servants that *were* with him at Jerusalem, Arise, and let us flee; for we shall not *else* escape from Absalom: make speed to depart, lest he overtake us suddenly, and bring evil upon us, and smite the city with the edge of the sword.

15And the king's servants said unto the king, Behold, thy servants *are ready to do* whatsoever my lord the king shall appoint.

16And the king went forth, and all his household after him. And the king left ten women, *which were* concubines, to keep the house.

17And the king went forth, and all the people after him, and tarried in a place that was far off.

18And all his servants passed on beside him; and all the Cherethites, and all the Pelethites, and all the Gittites, six hundred men which came after him from Gath, passed on before the king.

19¶ Then said the king to Ittai the Gittite, Wherefore goest thou also with us? return to thy place, and abide with the king: for thou *art* a stranger, and also an exile.

20Whereas thou camest *but* yesterday, should I this day make thee go up and down with us? seeing I go whither I may, return thou, and take back thy brethren: mercy and truth *be* with thee.

21And Ittai answered the king, and said, *As* the LORD liveth, and *as* my lord the king liveth, surely in what place my lord the king shall be, whether in death or life, even there also will thy servant be.

22And David said to Ittai, Go and pass over. And Ittai the Gittite passed over, and all his men, and all the little ones that *were* with him.

23And all the country wept with a loud voice, and all the people passed over: the king also himself passed over the brook Kidron, and all the people passed over, toward the way of the wilderness.

24¶ And lo Zadok also, and all the Levites *were* with him, bearing the ark of the covenant of God: and they set down the ark of God; and Abiathar went up, until all the people had done passing out of the city.

25And the king said unto Zadok, Carry back the ark of God into the city: if I shall find favour in the eyes of the LORD, he will bring me again, and show me *both* it, and his habitation:

26But if he thus say, I have no delight in thee; behold, *here am* I, let him do to me as seemeth good unto him.

27The king said also unto Zadok the priest, *Art not* thou a seer? return into the city in peace, and your two sons with you, Ahimaaz thy son, and Jonathan the son of Abiathar.

28See, I will tarry in the plain of the wilderness, until there come word from you to certify me.

New International

7At the end of four[a] years, Absalom said to the king, "Let me go to Hebron and fulfill a vow I made to the LORD. 8While your servant was living at Geshur in Aram, I made this vow: 'If the LORD takes me back to Jerusalem, I will worship the LORD in Hebron.[b]' "

9The king said to him, "Go in peace." So he went to Hebron.

10Then Absalom sent secret messengers throughout the tribes of Israel to say, "As soon as you hear the sound of the trumpets, then say, 'Absalom is king in Hebron.' " 11Two hundred men from Jerusalem had accompanied Absalom. They had been invited as guests and went quite innocently, knowing nothing about the matter. 12While Absalom was offering sacrifices, he also sent for Ahithophel the Gilonite, David's counselor, to come from Giloh, his hometown. And so the conspiracy gained strength, and Absalom's following kept on increasing.

David Flees

13A messenger came and told David, "The hearts of the men of Israel are with Absalom."

14Then David said to all his officials who were with him in Jerusalem, "Come! We must flee, or none of us will escape from Absalom. We must leave immediately, or he will move quickly to overtake us and bring ruin upon us and put the city to the sword."

15The king's officials answered him, "Your servants are ready to do whatever our lord the king chooses."

16The king set out, with his entire household following him; but he left ten concubines to take care of the palace. 17So the king set out, with all the people following him, and they halted at a place some distance away. 18All his men marched past him, along with all the Kerethites and Pelethites; and all the six hundred Gittites who had accompanied him from Gath marched before the king.

19The king said to Ittai the Gittite, "Why should you come along with us? Go back and stay with King Absalom. You are a foreigner, an exile from your homeland. 20You came only yesterday. And today shall I make you wander about with us, when I do not know where I am going? Go back, and take your countrymen. May kindness and faithfulness be with you."

21But Ittai replied to the king, "As surely as the LORD lives, and as my lord the king lives, wherever my lord the king may be, whether it means life or death, there will your servant be."

22David said to Ittai, "Go ahead, march on." So Ittai the Gittite marched on with all his men and the families that were with him.

23The whole countryside wept aloud as all the people passed by. The king also crossed the Kidron Valley, and all the people moved on toward the desert.

24Zadok was there, too, and all the Levites who were with him were carrying the ark of the covenant of God. They set down the ark of God, and Abiathar offered sacrifices[c] until all the people had finished leaving the city.

25Then the king said to Zadok, "Take the ark of God back into the city. If I find favor in the LORD's eyes, he will bring me back and let me see it and his dwelling place again. 26But if he says, 'I am not pleased with you,' then I am ready; let him do to me whatever seems good to him."

27The king also said to Zadok the priest, "Aren't you a seer? Go back to the city in peace, with your son Ahimaaz and Jonathan son of Abiathar. You and Abiathar take your two sons with you. 28I will wait at the fords in the desert until word comes from you to inform

---

[a] 7 Some Septuagint manuscripts, Syriac and Josephus; Hebrew *forty*
[b] 8 Some Septuagint manuscripts; Hebrew does not have *in Hebron.*
[c] 24 Or *Abiathar went up*

Living Bible

7, 8After four years, Absalom said to the king, "Let me go to Hebron to sacrifice to the Lord in fulfillment of a vow I made to him while I was at Geshur—that if he would bring me back to Jerusalem, I would sacrifice to him."

9"All right," the king told him, "go and fulfill your vow."

So Absalom went to Hebron.d 10But while he was there, he sent spies to every part of Israel to incite rebellion against the king. "As soon as you hear the trumpets," his message read, "you will know that Absalom has been crowned in Hebron." 11He took two hundred men from Jerusalem with him as guests, but they knew nothing of his intentions. 12While he was offering the sacrifice, he sent for Ahithophel, one of David's counselors who lived in Giloh. Ahithophel declared for Absalom, as did more and more others. So the conspiracy became very strong.

13A messenger soon arrived in Jerusalem to tell King David, "All Israel has joined Absalom in a conspiracy against you!"

14"Then we must flee at once or it will be too late!" was David's instant response to his men. "If we get out of the city before he arrives, both we and the city of Jerusalem will be saved."

15"We are with you," his aides replied. "Do as you think best."

16So the king and his household set out at once. He left no one behind except ten of his young wives to keep the palace in order. 17, 18David paused at the edge of the city to let his troops move past him to lead the way—six hundred Gittites who had come with him from Gath, and the Cherethites and Pelethites.

19, 20But suddenly the king turned to Ittai, the captain of the six hundred Gittites, and said to him, "What are you doing here? Go on back with your men to Jerusalem, to your king, for you are a guest in Israel, a foreigner in exile. It seems that yesterday that you arrived, and now today should I force you to wander with us, who knows where? Go on back and take your troops with you, and may the Lord be merciful to you."

21But Ittai replied, "I vow by God and by your own life that wherever you go, I will go, no matter what happens—whether it means life or death."

22So David replied, "All right, come with us." Then Ittai and his six hundred men and their families went along.

23There was deep sadness throughout the city as the king and his retinue passed by, crossed Kidron Brook, and went out into the country. 24Abiathar and Zadok and the Levites took the Ark of the Covenant of God and set it down beside the road until everyone had passed. 25, 26Then, following David's instructions, Zadok took the Ark back into the city. "If the Lord sees fit," David said, "he will bring me back to see the Ark and the Tabernacle again. But if he is through with me, well, let him do what seems best to him."

27Then the king told Zadok, "Look, here is my plan. Return quietly to the city with your son Ahima-az and Abiathar's son Jonathan. 28I will stop at the ford of the Jordan River and wait there for a message from you. Let me know what happens in Jerusalem before I disappear into the wilderness."

New Revised Standard

7 At the end of foure years Absalom said to the king, "Please let me go to Hebron and pay the vow that I have made to the LORD. 8For your servant made a vow while I lived at Geshur in Aram: If the LORD will indeed bring me back to Jerusalem, then I will worship the LORD in Hebron."f 9The king said to him, "Go in peace." So he got up, and went to Hebron. 10But Absalom sent secret messengers throughout all the tribes of Israel, saying, "As soon as you hear the sound of the trumpet, then shout: Absalom has become king at Hebron!" 11Two hundred men from Jerusalem went with Absalom; they were invited guests, and they went in their innocence, knowing nothing of the matter. 12While Absalom was offering the sacrifices, he sent forg Ahithophel the Gilonite, David's counselor, from his city Giloh. The conspiracy grew in strength, and the people with Absalom kept increasing.

David Flees from Jerusalem

13 A messenger came to David, saying, "The hearts of the Israelites have gone after Absalom." 14Then David said to all his officials who were with him at Jerusalem, "Get up! Let us flee, or there will be no escape for us from Absalom. Hurry, or he will soon overtake us, and bring disaster down upon us, and attack the city with the edge of the sword." 15The king's officials said to the king, "Your servants are ready to do whatever our lord the king decides." 16So the king left, followed by all his household, except ten concubines whom he left behind to look after the house. 17The king left, followed by all the people; and they stopped at the last house. 18All his officials passed by him; and all the Cherethites, and all the Pelethites, and all the six hundred Gittites who had followed him from Gath, passed on before the king.

19 Then the king said to Ittai the Gittite, "Why are you also coming with us? Go back, and stay with the king; for you are a foreigner, and also an exile from your home. 20You came only yesterday, and shall I today make you wander about with us, while I go wherever I can? Go back, and take your kinsfolk with you; and may the LORD showh steadfast love and faithfulness to you." 21But Ittai answered the king, "As the LORD lives, and as my lord the king lives, wherever my lord the king may be, whether for death or for life, there also your servant will be." 22David said to Ittai, "Go then, march on." So Ittai the Gittite marched on, with all his men and all the little ones who were with him. 23The whole country wept aloud as all the people passed by; the king crossed the Wadi Kidron, and all the people moved on toward the wilderness.

24 Abiathar came up, and Zadok also, with all the Levites, carrying the ark of the covenant of God. They set down the ark of God, until the people had all passed out of the city. 25Then the king said to Zadok, "Carry the ark of God back into the city. If I find favor in the eyes of the LORD, he will bring me back and let me see both it and the place where it stays. 26But if he says, 'I take no pleasure in you,' here I am, let him do to me what seems good to him." 27The king also said to the priest Zadok, "Look,i go back to the city in peace, you and Abiathar,j with your two sons, Ahimaaz your son, and Jonathan son of Abiathar. 28See, I will wait at the fords of the wilderness until word comes from you to

---

d *15:9 So Absalom went to Hebron.* Hebron was King David's first capital, and it was also Absalom's home town whose people doubtless were very proud of him.

e Gk Syr: Heb *forty*   f Gk Mss: Heb lacks *in Hebron*   g Or *he sent*   h Gk
Compare 2.6: Heb lacks *may the LORD show*   i Gk: Heb *Are you a seer* or
Do you see?   j Cn: Heb lacks *and Abiathar*

King James

29Zadok therefore and Abiathar carried the ark of God again to Jerusalem: and they tarried there.

30¶ And David went up by the ascent of *mount* Olivet, and wept as he went up, and had his head covered, and he went barefoot: and all the people that *was* with him covered every man his head, and they went up, weeping as they went up.

31¶ And *one* told David, saying, Ahithophel *is* among the conspirators with Absalom. And David said, O LORD, I pray thee, turn the counsel of Ahithophel into foolishness.

32¶ And it came to pass, that *when* David was come to the top *of the mount,* where he worshipped God, behold, Hushai the Archite came to meet him with his coat rent, and earth upon his head:

33Unto whom David said, If thou passest on with me, then thou shalt be a burden unto me:

34But if thou return to the city, and say unto Absalom, I will be thy servant, O king; *as* I *have been* thy father's servant hitherto, so *will* I now also *be* thy servant: then mayest thou for me defeat the counsel of Ahithophel.

35And *hast thou* not there with thee Zadok and Abiathar the priests? therefore it shall be, *that* what thing soever thou shalt hear out of the king's house, thou shalt tell *it* to Zadok and Abiathar the priests.

36Behold, *they have* there with them their two sons, Ahimaaz Zadok's *son,* and Jonathan Abiathar's *son;* and by them ye shall send unto me every thing that ye can hear.

37So Hushai David's friend came into the city, and Absalom came into Jerusalem.

16 AND WHEN David was a little past the top *of the hill,* behold, Ziba the servant of Mephibosheth met him, with a couple of asses saddled, and upon them two hundred *loaves* of bread, and an hundred bunches of raisins, and an hundred of summer fruits, and a bottle of wine.

2And the king said unto Ziba, What meanest thou by these? And Ziba said, The asses *be* for the king's household to ride on; and the bread and summer fruit for the young men to eat; and the wine, that such as be faint in the wilderness may drink.

3And the king said, And where *is* thy master's son? And Ziba said unto the king, Behold, he abideth at Jerusalem: for he said, Today shall the house of Israel restore me the kingdom of my father.

4Then said the king to Ziba, Behold, thine *are* all that *pertained* unto Mephibosheth. And Ziba said, I humbly beseech thee *that* I may find grace in thy sight, my lord, O king.

5¶ And when king David came to Bahurim, behold, thence came out a man of the family of the house of Saul, whose name *was* Shimei, the son of Gera: he came forth, and cursed still as he came.

6And he cast stones at David, and at all the servants of king David: and all the people and all the mighty men *were* on his right hand and on his left.

7And thus said Shimei when he cursed, Come out, come out, thou bloody man, and thou man of Belial:

8The LORD hath returned upon thee all the blood of the house of Saul, in whose stead thou hast reigned; and the LORD hath delivered the kingdom into the hand of Absalom thy son: and, behold, thou *art taken* in thy mischief, because thou *art* a bloody man.

9¶ Then said Abishai the son of Zeruiah unto the king, Why should this dead dog curse my lord the king? let me go over, I pray thee, and take off his head.

New International

me." 29So Zadok and Abiathar took the ark of God back to Jerusalem and stayed there.

30But David continued up the Mount of Olives, weeping as he went; his head was covered and he was barefoot. All the people with him covered their heads too and were weeping as they went up. 31Now David had been told, "Ahithophel is among the conspirators with Absalom." So David prayed, "O LORD, turn Ahithophel's counsel into foolishness."

32When David arrived at the summit, where people used to worship God, Hushai the Arkite was there to meet him, his robe torn and dust on his head. 33David said to him, "If you go with me, you will be a burden to me. 34But if you return to the city and say to Absalom, 'I will be your servant, O king; I was your father's servant in the past, but now I will be your servant,' then you can help me by frustrating Ahithophel's advice. 35Won't the priests Zadok and Abiathar be there with you? Tell them anything you hear in the king's palace. 36Their two sons, Ahimaaz son of Zadok and Jonathan son of Abiathar, are there with them. Send them to me with anything you hear."

37So David's friend Hushai arrived at Jerusalem as Absalom was entering the city.

David and Ziba

16 WHEN DAVID had gone a short distance beyond the summit, there was Ziba, the steward of Mephibosheth, waiting to meet him. He had a string of donkeys saddled and loaded with two hundred loaves of bread, a hundred cakes of raisins, a hundred cakes of figs and a skin of wine.

2The king asked Ziba, "Why have you brought these?"

Ziba answered, "The donkeys are for the king's household to ride on, the bread and fruit are for the men to eat, and the wine is to refresh those who become exhausted in the desert."

3The king then asked, "Where is your master's grandson?"

Ziba said to him, "He is staying in Jerusalem, because he thinks, 'Today the house of Israel will give me back my grandfather's kingdom.' "

4Then the king said to Ziba, "All that belonged to Mephibosheth is now yours."

"I humbly bow," Ziba said. "May I find favor in your eyes, my lord the king."

Shimei Curses David

5As King David approached Bahurim, a man from the same clan as Saul's family came out from there. His name was Shimei son of Gera, and he cursed as he came out. 6He pelted David and all the king's officials with stones, though all the troops and the special guard were on David's right and left. 7As he cursed, Shimei said, "Get out, get out, you man of blood, you scoundrel! 8The LORD has repaid you for all the blood you have shed in the household of Saul, in whose place you have reigned. The LORD has handed the kingdom over to your son Absalom. You have come to ruin because you are a man of blood!"

9Then Abishai son of Zeruiah said to the king, "Why should this dead dog curse my lord the king? Let me go over and cut off his head."

Living Bible

²⁹So Zadok and Abiathar carried the Ark of God back into the city and stayed there.

³⁰David walked up the road that led to the Mount of Olives, weeping as he went. His head was covered and his feet were bare as a sign of mourning. And the people who were with him covered their heads and wept as they climbed the mountain. ³¹When someone told David that Ahithophel, his advisor, was backing Absalom, David prayed, "O Lord, please make Ahithophel give Absalom foolish advice!" ³²As they reached the spot at the top of the Mount of Olives where people worshiped God, David found Hushai the Archite waiting for him with torn clothing and earth upon his head.

^{33, 34}But David told him, "If you go with me, you will only be a burden; return to Jerusalem and tell Absalom, 'I will counsel you as I did your father.' Then you can frustrate and counter Ahithophel's advice. ^{35, 36}Zadok and Abiathar, the priests, are there. Tell them the plans that are being made to capture me, and they will send their sons Ahima-az and Jonathan to find me and tell me what is going on."

³⁷So David's friend Hushai returned to the city, getting there just as Absalom arrived.

16 DAVID WAS just past the top of the hill when Ziba, the manager of Mephibosheth's household, caught up with him. He was leading two donkeys loaded with two hundred loaves of bread, one hundred clusters of raisins, one hundred bunches of grapes, and a small barrel of wine.

²"What are these for?" the king asked Ziba.

And Ziba replied, "The donkeys are for your people to ride on, and the bread and summer fruit are for the young men to eat; the wine is to be taken with you into the wilderness for any who become faint."

³"And where is Mephibosheth?" the king asked him.

"He stayed at Jerusalem," Ziba replied. "He said, 'Now I'll get to be king! Today I will get back the kingdom of my father, Saul.' "^a

⁴"In that case," the king told Ziba, "I give you everything he owns."

"Thank you, thank you, sir," Ziba replied.

⁵As David and his party passed Bahurim, a man came out of the village cursing them. It was Shime-i, the son of Gera, a member of Saul's family. ⁶He threw stones at the king and the king's officers and all the mighty warriors who surrounded them!

^{7, 8}"Get out of here, you murderer, you scoundrel!" he shouted at David. "The Lord is paying you back for murdering King Saul and his family; you stole his throne and now the Lord has given it to your son Absalom! At last you will taste some of your own medicine, you murderer!"

⁹"Why should this dead dog curse my lord the king?" Abishai demanded. "Let me go over and strike off his head!"

New Revised Standard

inform me." ²⁹So Zadok and Abiathar carried the ark of God back to Jerusalem, and they remained there.

30 But David went up the ascent of the Mount of Olives, weeping as he went, with his head covered and walking barefoot; and all the people who were with him covered their heads and went up, weeping as they went. ³¹David was told that Ahithophel was among the conspirators with Absalom. And David said, "O Lord, I pray you, turn the counsel of Ahithophel into foolishness."

Hushai Becomes David's Spy

32 When David came to the summit, where God was worshiped, Hushai the Archite came to meet him with his coat torn and earth on his head. ³³David said to him, "If you go on with me, you will be a burden to me. ³⁴But if you return to the city and say to Absalom, 'I will be your servant, O king; as I have been your father's servant in time past, so now I will be your servant,' then you will defeat for me the counsel of Ahithophel. ³⁵The priests Zadok and Abiathar will be with you there. So whatever you hear from the king's house, tell it to the priests Zadok and Abiathar. ³⁶Their two sons are with them there, Zadok's son Ahimaaz and Abiathar's son Jonathan; and by them you shall report to me everything you hear." ³⁷So Hushai, David's friend, came into the city, just as Absalom was entering Jerusalem.

David's Adversaries

16 WHEN DAVID had passed a little beyond the summit, Ziba the servant of Mephibosheth^b met him, with a couple of donkeys saddled, carrying two hundred loaves of bread, one hundred bunches of raisins, one hundred of summer fruits, and one skin of wine. ²The king said to Ziba, "Why have you brought these?" Ziba answered, "The donkeys are for the king's household to ride, the bread and summer fruit for the young men to eat, and the wine is for those to drink who faint in the wilderness." ³The king said, "And where is your master's son?" Ziba said to the king, "He remains in Jerusalem; for he said, 'Today the house of Israel will give me back my grandfather's kingdom.' " ⁴Then the king said to Ziba, "All that belonged to Mephibosheth^b is now yours." Ziba said, "I do obeisance; let me find favor in your sight, my lord the king."

Shimei Curses David

5 When King David came to Bahurim, a man of the family of the house of Saul came out whose name was Shimei son of Gera; he came out cursing. ⁶He threw stones at David and at all the servants of King David; now all the people and all the warriors were on his right and on his left. ⁷Shimei shouted while he cursed, "Out! Out! Murderer! Scoundrel! ⁸The Lord has avenged on all of you the blood of the house of Saul, in whose place you have reigned; and the Lord has given the kingdom into the hand of your son Absalom. See, disaster has overtaken you; for you are a man of blood."

9 Then Abishai son of Zeruiah said to the king, "Why should this dead dog curse my lord the king? Let me go over and take off his head." ¹⁰But the king said,

---

^a 16:3 *I will get back the kingdom of my father, Saul.* Saul was Mephibosheth's grandfather.

^b Or *Merib-baal*: See 4.4 note

King James

10And the king said, What have I to do with you, ye sons of Zeruiah? so let him curse, because the LORD hath said unto him, Curse David. Who shall then say, Wherefore hast thou done so?

11And David said to Abishai, and to all his servants, Behold, my son, which came forth of my bowels, seeketh my life: how much more now *may this* Benjamite *do it?* let him alone, and let him curse; for the LORD hath bidden him.

12It may be that the LORD will look on mine affliction, and that the LORD will requite me good for his cursing this day.

13And as David and his men went by the way, Shimei went along on the hill's side over against him, and cursed as he went, and threw stones at him, and cast dust.

14And the king, and all the people that *were* with him, came weary, and refreshed themselves there.

15¶ And Absalom, and all the people the men of Israel, came to Jerusalem, and Ahithophel with him.

16And it came to pass, when Hushai the Archite, David's friend, was come unto Absalom, that Hushai said unto Absalom, God save the king, God save the king.

17And Absalom said to Hushai, *Is* this thy kindness to thy friend? why wentest thou not with thy friend?

18And Hushai said unto Absalom, Nay; but whom the LORD, and this people, and all the men of Israel, choose, his will I be, and with him will I abide.

19And again, whom should I serve? *should I* not *serve* in the presence of his son? as I have served in thy father's presence, so will I be in thy presence.

20¶ Then said Absalom to Ahithophel, Give counsel among you what we shall do.

21And Ahithophel said unto Absalom, Go in unto thy father's concubines, which he hath left to keep the house; and all Israel shall hear that thou art abhorred of thy father: then shall the hands of all that *are* with thee be strong.

22So they spread Absalom a tent upon the top of the house; and Absalom went in unto his father's concubines in the sight of all Israel.

23And the counsel of Ahithophel, which he counselled in those days, *was* as if a man had inquired at the oracle of God: so *was* all the counsel of Ahithophel both with David and with Absalom.

17 MOREOVER AHITHOPHEL said unto Absalom, Let me now choose out twelve thousand men, and I will arise and pursue after David this night:

2And I will come upon him while he *is* weary and weak handed, and will make him afraid: and all the people that *are* with him shall flee; and I will smite the king only:

3And I will bring back all the people unto thee: the man whom thou seekest *is* as if all returned: *so* all the people shall be in peace.

4And the saying pleased Absalom well, and all the elders of Israel.

5Then said Absalom, Call now Hushai the Archite also, and let us hear likewise what he saith.

6And when Hushai was come to Absalom, Absalom spake unto him, saying, Ahithophel hath spoken after this manner: shall we do *after* his saying? if not; speak thou.

7And Hushai said unto Absalom, The counsel that Ahithophel hath given *is* not good at this time.

New International

10But the king said, "What do you and I have in common, you sons of Zeruiah? If he is cursing because the LORD said to him, 'Curse David,' who can ask, 'Why do you do this?' "

11David then said to Abishai and all his officials, "My son, who is of my own flesh, is trying to take my life. How much more, then, this Benjamite! Leave him alone; let him curse, for the LORD has told him to. 12It may be that the LORD will see my distress and repay me with good for the cursing I am receiving today."

13So David and his men continued along the road while Shimei was going along the hillside opposite him, cursing as he went and throwing stones at him and showering him with dirt. 14The king and all the people with him arrived at their destination exhausted. And there he refreshed himself.

The Advice of Hushai and Ahithophel

15Meanwhile, Absalom and all the men of Israel came to Jerusalem, and Ahithophel was with him. 16Then Hushai the Arkite, David's friend, went to Absalom and said to him, "Long live the king! Long live the king!"

17Absalom asked Hushai, "Is this the love you show your friend? Why didn't you go with your friend?"

18Hushai said to Absalom, "No, the one chosen by the LORD, by these people, and by all the men of Israel—his I will be, and I will remain with him. 19Furthermore, whom should I serve? Should I not serve the son? Just as I served your father, so I will serve you."

20Absalom said to Ahithophel, "Give us your advice. What should we do?"

21Ahithophel answered, "Lie with your father's concubines whom he left to take care of the palace. Then all Israel will hear that you have made yourself a stench in your father's nostrils, and the hands of everyone with you will be strengthened." 22So they pitched a tent for Absalom on the roof, and he lay with his father's concubines in the sight of all Israel.

23Now in those days the advice Ahithophel gave was like that of one who inquires of God. That was how both David and Absalom regarded all of Ahithophel's advice.

17 AHITHOPHEL SAID to Absalom, "I woulda choose twelve thousand men and set out tonight in pursuit of David. 2I wouldb attack him while he is weary and weak. I wouldb strike him with terror, and then all the people with him will flee. I wouldb strike down only the king 3and bring all the people back to you. The death of the man you seek will mean the return of all; all the people will be unharmed." 4This plan seemed good to Absalom and to all the elders of Israel.

5But Absalom said, "Summon also Hushai the Arkite, so we can hear what he has to say." 6When Hushai came to him, Absalom said, "Ahithophel has given this advice. Should we do what he says? If not, give us your opinion."

7Hushai replied to Absalom, "The advice Ahithophel has given is not good this time. 8You know your father

Living Bible

10"No!" the king said. "If the Lord has told him to curse me, who am I to say no? 11My own son is trying to kill me, and this Benjaminite is merely cursing me. Let him alone, for no doubt the Lord has told him to do it. 12And perhaps the Lord will see that I am being wronged and will bless me because of these curses."

13So David and his men continued on, and Shime-i kept pace with them on a nearby hillside, cursing as he went and throwing stones at David and tossing dust into the air. 14The king and all those who were with him were weary by the time they reached Bahurim, so they stayed there awhile and rested.

15Meanwhile, Absalom and his men arrived at Jerusalem, accompanied by Ahithophel. 16When David's friend, Hushai the Archite, arrived, he went immediately to see Absalom.

"Long live the king!" he exclaimed. "Long live the king!"

17"Is this the way to treat your friend David?" Absalom asked him. "Why aren't you with him?"

18"Because I work for the man who is chosen by the Lord and by Israel," Hushai replied. 19"And anyway, why shouldn't I? I helped your father and now I will help you!"

20Then Absalom turned to Ahithophel and asked him, "What shall I do next?"

21Ahithophel told him, "Go and sleep with your father's wives, for he has left them here to keep the house. Then all Israel will know that you have insulted him beyond the possibility of reconciliation, and they will all close ranks behind you."c

22So a tent was erected on the roof of the palace where everybody could see it, and Absalom went into the tent to lie with his father's wives. 23(Absalom did whatever Ahithophel told him to, just as David had; for every word Ahithophel spoke seemed as wise as though it had come directly from the mouth of God.)

17 "NOW," AHITHOPHEL said, "give me twelve thousand men to start out after David tonight. 2, 3I will come upon him while he is weary and discouraged, and he and his troops will be thrown into a panic and everyone will run away; and I will kill only the king, and let all those who are with him live, and restore them to you."

4Absalom and all the elders of Israel approved of the plan, 5but Absalom said, "Ask Hushai the Archite what he thinks about this."

6When Hushai arrived, Absalom told him what Ahithophel had said.

"What is your opinion?" Absalom asked him. "Should we follow Ahithophel's advice? If not, speak up."

7"Well," Hushai replied, "this time I think Ahithophel has made a mistake. 8You know your father and his

New Revised Standard

"What have I to do with you, you sons of Zeruiah? If he is cursing because the LORD has said to him, 'Curse David,' who then shall say, 'Why have you done so?'" 11David said to Abishai and to all his servants, "My own son seeks my life; how much more now may this Benjaminite! Let him alone, and let him curse; for the LORD has bidden him. 12It may be that the LORD will look on my distress,d and the LORD will repay me with good for this cursing of me today." 13So David and his men went on the road, while Shimei went along on the hillside opposite him and cursed as he went, throwing stones and flinging dust at him. 14The king and all the people who were with him arrived weary at the Jordan;e and there he refreshed himself.

The Counsel of Ahithophel

15 Now Absalom and all the Israelitesf came to Jerusalem; Ahithophel was with him. 16When Hushai the Archite, David's friend, came to Absalom, Hushai said to Absalom, "Long live the king! Long live the king!" 17Absalom said to Hushai, "Is this your loyalty to your friend? Why did you not go with your friend?" 18Hushai said to Absalom, "No; but the one whom the LORD and this people and all the Israelites have chosen, his I will be, and with him I will remain. 19Moreover, whom should I serve? Should it not be his son? Just as I have served your father, so I will serve you."

20 Then Absalom said to Ahithophel, "Give us your counsel; what shall we do?" 21Ahithophel said to Absalom, "Go in to your father's concubines, the ones he has left to look after the house; and all Israel will hear that you have made yourself odious to your father, and the hands of all who are with you will be strengthened." 22So they pitched a tent for Absalom upon the roof; and Absalom went in to his father's concubines in the sight of all Israel. 23Now in those days the counsel that Ahithophel gave was as if one consulted the oracles of God; so all the counsel of Ahithophel was esteemed, both by David and by Absalom.

17 MOREOVER AHITHOPHEL said to Absalom, "Let me choose twelve thousand men, and I will set out and pursue David tonight. 2I will come upon him while he is weary and discouraged, and throw him into a panic; and all the people who are with him will flee. I will strike down only the king, 3and I will bring all the people back to you as a bride comes home to her husband. You seek the life of only one man,h and all the people will be at peace." 4The advice pleased Absalom and all the elders of Israel.

The Counsel of Hushai

5 Then Absalom said, "Call Hushai the Archite also, and let us hear too what he has to say." 6When Hushai came to Absalom, Absalom said to him, "This is what Ahithophel has said; shall we do as he advises? If not, you tell us." 7Then Hushai said to Absalom, "This time the counsel that Ahithophel has given is not good." 8Hushai continued, "You know that your father

---

c 16:21 they will all close ranks behind you, literally, "the hands of all who are with you will be strengthened."

d Gk Vg: Heb iniquity   e Gk: Heb lacks at the Jordan   f Gk: Heb all the people, the men of Israel   g Heb word   h Gk: Heb like the return of the whole (is) the man whom you seek

King James

8For, said Hushai, thou knowest thy father and his men, that they *be* mighty men, and they *be* chafed in their minds, as a bear robbed of her whelps in the field: and thy father *is* a man of war, and will not lodge with the people.

9Behold, he is hid now in some pit, or in some *other* place: and it will come to pass, when some of them be overthrown at the first, that whosoever heareth it will say, There is a slaughter among the people that follow Absalom.

10And he also *that is* valiant, whose heart *is* as the heart of a lion, shall utterly melt: for all Israel knoweth that thy father *is* a mighty man, and *they* which *be* with him *are* valiant men.

11Therefore I counsel that all Israel be generally gathered unto thee, from Dan even to Beer-sheba, as the sand that *is* by the sea for multitude; and that thou go to battle in thine own person.

12So shall we come upon him in some place where he shall be found, and we will light upon him as the dew falleth on the ground: and of him and of all the men that *are* with him there shall not be left so much as one.

13Moreover, if he be gotten into a city, then shall all Israel bring ropes to that city, and we will draw it into the river, until there be not one small stone found there.

14And Absalom and all the men of Israel said, The counsel of Hushai the Archite *is* better than the counsel of Ahithophel. For the LORD had appointed to defeat the good counsel of Ahithophel, to the intent that the LORD might bring evil upon Absalom.

15¶ Then said Hushai unto Zadok and to Abiathar the priests, Thus and thus did Ahithophel counsel Absalom and the elders of Israel; and thus and thus have I counselled.

16Now therefore send quickly, and tell David, saying, Lodge not this night in the plains of the wilderness, but speedily pass over; lest the king be swallowed up, and all the people that *are* with him.

17Now Jonathan and Ahimaaz stayed by En-rogel; for they might not be seen to come into the city: and a wench went and told them; and they went and told king David.

18Nevertheless a lad saw them, and told Absalom: but they went both of them away quickly, and came to a man's house in Bahurim, which had a well in his court; whither they went down.

19And the woman took and spread a covering over the well's mouth, and spread ground corn thereon; and the thing was not known.

20And when Absalom's servants came to the woman to the house, they said, Where *is* Ahimaaz and Jonathan? And the woman said unto them, They be gone over the brook of water. And when they had sought and could not find *them,* they returned to Jerusalem.

21And it came to pass, after they were departed, that they came up out of the well, and went and told king David, and said unto David, Arise, and pass quickly over the water: for thus hath Ahithophel counselled against you.

22Then David arose, and all the people that *were* with him, and they passed over Jordan: by the morning light there lacked not one of them that was not gone over Jordan.

23¶ And when Ahithophel saw that his counsel was not followed, he saddled *his* ass, and arose, and gat him home to his house, to his city, and put his household in order, and hanged himself, and died, and was buried in the sepulchre of his father.

24Then David came to Mahanaim. And Absalom passed over Jordan, he and all the men of Israel with him.

25¶ And Absalom made Amasa captain of the host instead of Joab: which Amasa *was* a man's son, whose name *was* Ithra an Israelite, that went in to Abigail the daughter of Nahash, sister to Zeruiah Joab's mother.

New International

and his men; they are fighters, and as fierce as a wild bear robbed of her cubs. Besides, your father is an experienced fighter; he will not spend the night with the troops. 9Even now, he is hidden in a cave or some other place. If he should attack your troops first,[a] whoever hears about it will say, 'There has been a slaughter among the troops who follow Absalom.' 10Then even the bravest soldier, whose heart is like the heart of a lion, will melt with fear, for all Israel knows that your father is a fighter and that those with him are brave.

11"So I advise you: Let all Israel, from Dan to Beersheba—as numerous as the sand on the seashore—be gathered to you, with you yourself leading them into battle. 12Then we will attack him wherever he may be found, and we will fall on him as dew settles on the ground. Neither he nor any of his men will be left alive. 13If he withdraws into a city, then all Israel will bring ropes to that city, and we will drag it down to the valley until not even a piece of it can be found."

14Absalom and all the men of Israel said, "The advice of Hushai the Arkite is better than that of Ahithophel." For the LORD had determined to frustrate the good advice of Ahithophel in order to bring disaster on Absalom.

15Hushai told Zadok and Abiathar, the priests, "Ahithophel has advised Absalom and the elders of Israel to do such and such, but I have advised them to do so and so. 16Now send a message immediately and tell David, 'Do not spend the night at the fords in the desert; cross over without fail, or the king and all the people with him will be swallowed up.' "

17Jonathan and Ahimaaz were staying at En Rogel. A servant girl was to go and inform them, and they were to go and tell King David, for they could not risk being seen entering the city. 18But a young man saw them and told Absalom. So the two of them left quickly and went to the house of a man in Bahurim. He had a well in his courtyard, and they climbed down into it. 19His wife took a covering and spread it out over the opening of the well and scattered grain over it. No one knew anything about it.

20When Absalom's men came to the woman at the house, they asked, "Where are Ahimaaz and Jonathan?"

The woman answered them, "They crossed over the brook."[b] The men searched but found no one, so they returned to Jerusalem.

21After the men had gone, the two climbed out of the well and went to inform King David. They said to him, "Set out and cross the river at once; Ahithophel has advised such and such against you." 22So David and all the people with him set out and crossed the Jordan. By daybreak, no one was left who had not crossed the Jordan.

23When Ahithophel saw that his advice had not been followed, he saddled his donkey and set out for his house in his hometown. He put his house in order and then hanged himself. So he died and was buried in his father's tomb.

24David went to Mahanaim, and Absalom crossed the Jordan with all the men of Israel. 25Absalom had appointed Amasa over the army in place of Joab. Amasa was the son of a man named Jether,[c] an Israelite[d] who had married Abigail,[e] the daughter of Nahash and sister

---

a 9 Or *When some of the men fall at the first attack*   b 20 Or *"They passed by the sheep pen toward the water."*   c 25 Hebrew *Ithra,* a variant of *Jether*   d 25 Hebrew and some Septuagint manuscripts; other Septuagint manuscripts (see also 1 Chron. 2:17) *Ishmaelite* or *Jezreelite*   e 25 Hebrew *Abigal,* a variant of *Abigail*

Living Bible

men; they are mighty warriors and are probably as upset as a mother bear who has been robbed of her cubs. And your father is an old soldier and isn't going to be spending the night among the troops; 9he has probably already hidden in some pit or cave. And when he comes out and attacks a few of your men fall, there will be panic among your troops and everyone will start shouting that your men are being slaughtered. 10Then even the bravest of them, though they have hearts of lions, will be paralyzed with fear; for all Israel knows what a mighty man your father is and how courageous his soldiers are.

11"What I suggest is that you mobilize the entire army of Israel, bringing them from as far away as Dan and Beer-sheba, so that you will have a huge force. And I think that you should personally lead the troops. 12Then when we find him we can destroy his entire army so that not one of them is left alive. 13And if David has escaped into some city, you will have the entire army of Israel there at your command, and we can take ropes and drag the walls of the city into the nearest valley until every stone is torn down."

14Then Absalom and all the men of Israel said, "Hushai's advice is better than Ahithophel's." For the Lord had arranged to defeat the counsel of Ahithophel, which really was the better plan, so that he could bring disaster upon Absalom! 15Then Hushai reported to Zadok and Abiathar, the priests, what Ahithophel had said and what he himself had suggested instead.

16"Quick!" he told them. "Find David and urge him not to stay at the ford of the Jordan River tonight. He must go across at once into the wilderness beyond; otherwise he will die, and his entire army with him."

17Jonathan and Ahima-az had been staying at En-rogel so as not to be seen entering and leaving the city. Arrangements had been made for a servant girl to carry to them the messages they were to take to King David. 18But a boy saw them leaving En-rogel to go to David, and he told Absalom about it. Meanwhile, they escaped to Bahurim where a man hid them inside a well in his backyard. 19The man's wife put a cloth over the top of the well with grain on it to dry in the sun; so no one suspected they were there.

20When Absalom's men arrived and asked her if she had seen Ahima-az and Jonathan, she said they had crossed the brook and were gone. They looked for them without success and returned to Jerusalem. 21Then the two men crawled out of the well and hurried on to King David. "Quick!" they told him, "cross the Jordan tonight!" And they told him how Ahithophel had advised that he be captured and killed. 22So David and all the people with him went across during the night and were all on the other bank before dawn.

23Meanwhile, Ahithophel—publicly disgraced when Absalom refused his advice—saddled his donkey, went to his home town, set his affairs in order, and hanged himself; so he died and was buried beside his father.

24David soon arrived at Mahanaim. Meanwhile, Absalom had mobilized the entire army of Israel and was leading the men across the Jordan River. 25Absalom had appointed Amasa as general of the army, replacing Joab. (Amasa was Joab's second cousin; his father was Ithra, an Ishmaelite, and his mother was Abigail, the daughter of Nahash, who was the sister of Joab's mother Zerui-

New Revised Standard

and his men are warriors, and that they are enraged, like a bear robbed of her cubs in the field. Besides, your father is expert in war; he will not spend the night with the troops. 9Even now he has hidden himself in one of the pits, or in some other place. And when some of our troopsf fall at the first attack, whoever hears it will say, 'There has been a slaughter among the troops who follow Absalom.' 10Then even the valiant warrior, whose heart is like the heart of a lion, will utterly melt with fear; for all Israel knows that your father is a warrior, and that those who are with him are valiant warriors. 11But my counsel is that all Israel be gathered to you, from Dan to Beer-sheba, like the sand by the sea for multitude, and that you go to battle in person. 12So we shall come upon him in whatever place he may be found, and we shall light on him as the dew falls on the ground; and he will not survive, nor will any of those with him. 13If he withdraws into a city, then all Israel will bring ropes to that city, and we shall drag it into the valley, until not even a pebble is to be found there." 14Absalom and all the men of Israel said, "The counsel of Hushai the Archite is better than the counsel of Ahithophel." For the LORD had ordained to defeat the good counsel of Ahithophel, so that the LORD might bring ruin on Absalom.

Hushai Warns David to Escape

15 Then Hushai said to the priests Zadok and Abiathar, "Thus and so did Ahithophel counsel Absalom and the elders of Israel; and thus and so I have counseled. 16Therefore send quickly and tell David, 'Do not lodge tonight at the fords of the wilderness, but by all means cross over; otherwise the king and all the people who are with him will be swallowed up.'" 17Jonathan and Ahimaaz were waiting at En-rogel; a servant-girl used to go and tell them, and they would go and tell King David; for they could not risk being seen entering the city. 18But a boy saw them, and told Absalom; so both of them went away quickly, and came to the house of a man at Bahurim, who had a well in his courtyard; and they went down into it. 19The man's wife took a covering, stretched it over the well's mouth, and spread out grain on it; and nothing was known of it. 20When Absalom's servants came to the woman at the house, they said, "Where are Ahimaaz and Jonathan?" The woman said to them, "They have crossed over the brookg of water." And when they had searched and could not find them, they returned to Jerusalem.

21 After they had gone, the men came up out of the well, and went and told King David. They said to David, "Go and cross the water quickly; for thus and so has Ahithophel counseled against you." 22So David and all the people who were with him set out and crossed the Jordan; by daybreak not one was left who had not crossed the Jordan.

23 When Ahithophel saw that his counsel was not followed, he saddled his donkey and went off home to his own city. He set his house in order, and hanged himself; he died and was buried in the tomb of his father.

24 Then David came to Mahanaim, while Absalom crossed the Jordan with all the men of Israel. 25Now Absalom had set Amasa over the army in the place of Joab. Amasa was the son of a man named Ithra the Ishmaelite,h who had married Abigal daughter of Na-

---

f Gk Mss: Heb *some of them*   g Meaning of Heb uncertain   h 1 Chr 2.17: Heb *Israelite*

King James

26So Israel and Absalom pitched in the land of Gilead.

27¶ And it came to pass, when David was come to Mahanaim, that Shobi the son of Nahash of Rabbah of the children of Ammon, and Machir the son of Ammiel of Lo-debar, and Barzillai the Gileadite of Rogelim,

28Brought beds, and basins, and earthen vessels, and wheat, and barley, and flour, and parched *corn*, and beans, and lentiles, and parched *pulse*,

29And honey, and butter, and sheep, and cheese of kine, for David, and for the people that *were* with him, to eat: for they said, The people *is* hungry, and weary, and thirsty, in the wilderness.

18 AND DAVID numbered the people that *were* with him, and set captains of thousands and captains of hundreds over them.

2And David sent forth a third part of the people under the hand of Joab, and a third part under the hand of Abishai the son of Zeruiah, Joab's brother, and a third part under the hand of Ittai the Gittite. And the king said unto the people, I will surely go forth with you myself also.

3But the people answered, Thou shalt not go forth: for if we flee away, they will not care for us; neither if half of us die, will they care for us: but now *thou art* worth ten thousand of us: therefore now *it is* better that thou succour us out of the city.

4And the king said unto them, What seemeth you best I will do. And the king stood by the gate side, and all the people came out by hundreds and by thousands.

5And the king commanded Joab and Abishai and It-tai, saying, *Deal* gently for my sake with the young man, *even* with Absalom. And all the people heard when the king gave all the captains charge concerning Absalom.

6¶ So the people went out into the field against Israel: and the battle was in the wood of Ephraim;

7Where the people of Israel were slain before the servants of David, and there was there a great slaughter that day of twenty thousand *men*.

8For the battle was there scattered over the face of all the country: and the wood devoured more people that day than the sword devoured.

9¶ And Absalom met the servants of David. And Absalom rode upon a mule, and the mule went under the thick boughs of a great oak, and his head caught hold of the oak, and he was taken up between the heaven and the earth; and the mule that *was* under him went away.

10And a certain man saw *it*, and told Joab, and said, Behold, I saw Absalom hanged in an oak.

11And Joab said unto the man that told him, And, behold, thou sawest *him*, and why didst thou not smite him there to the ground? and I would have given thee ten *shekels* of silver, and a girdle.

12And the man said unto Joab, Though I should receive a thousand *shekels* of silver in mine hand, *yet* would I not put forth mine hand against the king's son: for in our hearing the king charged thee and Abishai and Ittai, saying, Beware that none *touch* the young man Absalom.

13Otherwise I should have wrought falsehood against mine own life: for there is no matter hid from the king, and thou thyself wouldest have set thyself against *me*.

14Then said Joab, I may not tarry thus with thee. And he took three darts in his hand, and thrust them through the heart of Absalom, while he *was* yet alive in the midst of the oak.

15And ten young men that bare Joab's armour compassed about and smote Absalom, and slew him.

New International

of Zeruiah the mother of Joab. 26The Israelites and Absalom camped in the land of Gilead.

27When David came to Mahanaim, Shobi son of Nahash from Rabbah of the Ammonites, and Makir son of Ammiel from Lo Debar, and Barzillai the Gileadite from Rogelim 28brought bedding and bowls and articles of pottery. They also brought wheat and barley, flour and roasted grain, beans and lentils,a 29honey and curds, sheep, and cheese from cows' milk for David and his people to eat. For they said, "The people have become hungry and tired and thirsty in the desert."

Absalom's Death

18 DAVID MUSTERED the men who were with him and appointed over them commanders of thousands and commanders of hundreds. 2David sent the troops out—a third under the command of Joab, a third under Joab's brother Abishai son of Zeruiah, and a third under Ittai the Gittite. The king told the troops, "I myself will surely march out with you."

3But the men said, "You must not go out; if we are forced to flee, they won't care about us. Even if half of us die, they won't care; but you are worth ten thousand of us.b It would be better now for you to give us support from the city."

4The king answered, "I will do whatever seems best to you."

So the king stood beside the gate while all the men marched out in units of hundreds and of thousands. 5The king commanded Joab, Abishai and Ittai, "Be gentle with the young man Absalom for my sake." And all the troops heard the king giving orders concerning Absalom to each of the commanders.

6The army marched into the field to fight Israel, and the battle took place in the forest of Ephraim. 7There the army of Israel was defeated by David's men, and the casualties that day were great—twenty thousand men. 8The battle spread out over the whole countryside, and the forest claimed more lives that day than the sword.

9Now Absalom happened to meet David's men. He was riding his mule, and as the mule went under the thick branches of a large oak, Absalom's head got caught in the tree. He was left hanging in midair, while the mule he was riding kept on going.

10When one of the men saw this, he told Joab, "I just saw Absalom hanging in an oak tree."

11Joab said to the man who had told him this, "What! You saw him? Why didn't you strike him to the ground right there? Then I would have had to give you ten shekelsc of silver and a warrior's belt."

12But the man replied, "Even if a thousand shekelsd were weighed out into my hands, I would not lift my hand against the king's son. In our hearing the king commanded you and Abishai and Ittai, 'Protect the young man Absalom for my sake.e' 13And if I had put my life in jeopardyf—and nothing is hidden from the king—you would have kept your distance from me."

14Joab said, "I'm not going to wait like this for you." So he took three javelins in his hand and plunged them into Absalom's heart while Absalom was still alive in the oak tree. 15And ten of Joab's armor-bearers surrounded Absalom, struck him and killed him.

---

a 28 Most Septuagint manuscripts and Syriac; Hebrew *lentils, and roasted grain*   b 3 Two Hebrew manuscripts, some Septuagint manuscripts and Vulgate; most Hebrew manuscripts *care; for now there are ten thousand like us*   c 11 That is, about 4 ounces (about 115 grams)   d 12 That is, about 25 pounds (about 11 kilograms)   e 12 A few Hebrew manuscripts, Septuagint, Vulgate and Syriac; most Hebrew manuscripts may be translated *Absalom, whoever you may be.*   f 13 Or *Otherwise, if I had acted treacherously toward him*

Living Bible

ah.) 26Absalom and the Israeli army now camped in the land of Gilead.

27When David arrived at Mahanaim, he was warmly greeted by Shobi (son of Nahash of Rabbah, an Ammonite) and Machir (son of Ammiel of Lodebar) and Barzillai (a Gileadite of Rogelim). 28, 29They brought him and those who were with him mats to sleep on, cooking pots, serving bowls, wheat and barley flour, parched grain, beans, lentils, honey, butter, and cheese. For they said, "You must be very tired and hungry and thirsty after your long march through the wilderness."

18 DAVID NOW appointed regimental colonels and company commanders over his troops. 2A third were placed under Joab's brother, Abishai (the son of Zeruiah); and a third under Ittai, the Gittite. The king planned to lead the army himself, but his men objected strongly.

3"You mustn't do it," they said, "for if we have to turn and run, and half of us die, it will make no difference to them—they will be looking only for you. You are worth ten thousand of us, and it is better that you stay here in the city and send us help if we need it."

4"Well, whatever you think best," the king finally replied. So he stood at the gate of the city as all the troops passed by.

5And the king commanded Joab, Abishai, and Ittai, "For my sake, deal gently with young Absalom." And all the troops heard the king give them this charge.

6So the battle began in the forest of Ephraim, 7and the Israeli troops were beaten back by David's men. There was a great slaughter and twenty thousand men laid down their lives that day. 8The battle raged all across the countryside, and more men disappeared in the forest than were killed. 9During the battle Absalom came upon some of David's men and as he fledg on his mule, it went beneath the thick boughs of a great oak tree, and his hair caught in the branches. His mule went on, leaving him dangling in the air. 10One of David's men saw him and told Joab.

11"What? You saw him there and didn't kill him?" Joab demanded. "I would have rewarded you handsomely and made you a commissioned officer."h

12"For a million dollars I wouldn't do it," the man replied. "We all heard the king say to you and Abishai and Ittai, 'For my sake, please don't harm young Absalom.' 13And if I had betrayed the king by killing his son (and the king would certainly find out who did it), you yourself would be the first to accuse me."

14"Enough of this nonsense," Joab said. Then he took three daggers and plunged them into the heart of Absalom as he dangled alive from the oak. 15Ten of Joab's young armor bearers then surrounded Absalom and finished him off. 16Then Joab blew the trumpet, and his

New Revised Standard

hash, sister of Zeruiah, Joab's mother. 26The Israelites and Absalom encamped in the land of Gilead.

27 When David came to Mahanaim, Shobi son of Nahash from Rabbah of the Ammonites, and Machir son of Ammiel from Lo-debar, and Barzillai the Gileadite from Rogelim, 28brought beds, basins, and earthen vessels, wheat, barley, meal, parched grain, beans and lentils,i 29honey and curds, sheep, and cheese from the herd, for David and the people with him to eat; for they said, "The troops are hungry and weary and thirsty in the wilderness."

The Defeat and Death of Absalom

18 THEN DAVID mustered the men who were with him, and set over them commanders of thousands and commanders of hundreds. 2And David divided the army into three groups:j one third under the command of Joab, one third under the command of Abishai son of Zeruiah, Joab's brother, and one third under the command of Ittai the Gittite. The king said to the men, "I myself will also go out with you." 3But the men said, "You shall not go out. For if we flee, they will not care about us. If half of us die, they will not care about us. But you are worth ten thousand of us;k therefore it is better that you send us help from the city." 4The king said to them, "Whatever seems best to you I will do." So the king stood at the side of the gate, while all the army marched out by hundreds and by thousands. 5The king ordered Joab and Abishai and Ittai, saying, "Deal gently for my sake with the young man Absalom." And all the people heard when the king gave orders to all the commanders concerning Absalom.

6 So the army went out into the field against Israel; and the battle was fought in the forest of Ephraim. 7The men of Israel were defeated there by the servants of David, and the slaughter there was great on that day, twenty thousand men. 8The battle spread over the face of all the country; and the forest claimed more victims that day than the sword.

9 Absalom happened to meet the servants of David. Absalom was riding on his mule, and the mule went under the thick branches of a great oak. His head caught fast in the oak, and he was left hangingl between heaven and earth, while the mule that was under him went on. 10A man saw it, and told Joab, "I saw Absalom hanging in an oak." 11Joab said to the man who told him, "What, you saw him! Why then did you not strike him there to the ground? I would have been glad to give you ten pieces of silver and a belt." 12But the man said to Joab, "Even if I felt in my hand the weight of a thousand pieces of silver, I would not raise my hand against the king's son; for in our hearing the king commanded you and Abishai and Ittai, saying: For my sake protect the young man Absalom! 13On the other hand, if I had dealt treacherously against his lifem (and there is nothing hidden from the king), then you yourself would have stood aloof." 14Joab said, "I will not waste time like this with you." He took three spears in his hand, and thrust them into the heart of Absalom, while he was still alive in the oak. 15And ten young men, Joab's armor-bearers, surrounded Absalom and struck him, and killed him.

g 18:9 as he fled, implied.   h 18:11 made you a commissioned officer, literally, "given you ten pieces of silver and a belt." There is no way of knowing the value of the silver. The belt was probably that worn by a commissioned officer.

i Heb and lentils and parched grain   j Gk: Heb sent forth the army   k Gk Vg Symmachus: Heb for now there are ten thousand such as we   l Gk Syr Tg: Heb was put   m Another reading is at the risk of my life

King James

16And Joab blew the trumpet, and the people returned from pursuing after Israel: for Joab held back the people.

17And they took Absalom, and cast him into a great pit in the wood, and laid a very great heap of stones upon him: and all Israel fled every one to his tent.

18¶ Now Absalom in his lifetime had taken and reared up for himself a pillar, which *is* in the king's dale: for he said, I have no son to keep my name in remembrance: and he called the pillar after his own name: and it is called unto this day, Absalom's place.

19¶ Then said Ahimaaz the son of Zadok, Let me now run, and bear the king tidings, how that the LORD hath avenged him of his enemies.

20And Joab said unto him, Thou shalt not bear tidings this day, but thou shalt bear tidings another day: but this day thou shalt bear no tidings, because the king's son is dead.

21Then said Joab to Cushi, Go tell the king what thou hast seen. And Cushi bowed himself unto Joab, and ran.

22Then said Ahimaaz the son of Zadok yet again to Joab, But howsoever, let me, I pray thee, also run after Cushi. And Joab said, Wherefore wilt thou run, my son, seeing that thou hast no tidings ready?

23But howsoever, *said he,* let me run. And he said unto him, Run. Then Ahimaaz ran by the way of the plain, and overran Cushi.

24And David sat between the two gates: and the watchman went up to the roof over the gate unto the wall, and lifted up his eyes, and looked, and behold a man running alone.

25And the watchman cried, and told the king. And the king said, If he *be* alone, *there is* tidings in his mouth. And he came apace, and drew near.

26And the watchman saw another man running: and the watchman called unto the porter, and said, Behold *another* man running alone. And the king said, He also bringeth tidings.

27And the watchman said, Me thinketh the running of the foremost is like the running of Ahimaaz the son of Zadok. And the king said, He *is* a good man, and cometh with good tidings.

28And Ahimaaz called, and said unto the king, All is well. And he fell down to the earth upon his face before the king, and said, Blessed *be* the LORD thy God, which hath delivered up the men that lifted up their hand against my lord the king.

29And the king said, Is the young man Absalom safe? And Ahimaaz answered, When Joab sent the king's servant, and *me* thy servant, I saw a great tumult, but I knew not what *it was.*

30And the king said *unto him,* Turn aside, *and* stand here. And he turned aside, and stood still.

31And, behold, Cushi came; and Cushi said, Tidings, my lord the king: for the LORD hath avenged thee this day of all them that rose up against thee.

32And the king said unto Cushi, *Is* the young man Absalom safe? And Cushi answered, The enemies of my lord the king, and all that rise against thee to do *thee* hurt, be as *that* young man *is.*

33¶ And the king was much moved, and went up to the chamber over the gate, and wept: and as he went, thus he said, O my son Absalom, my son, my son Absalom! would God I had died for thee, O Absalom, my son, my son!

New International

16Then Joab sounded the trumpet, and the troops stopped pursuing Israel, for Joab halted them. 17They took Absalom, threw him into a big pit in the forest and piled up a large heap of rocks over him. Meanwhile, all the Israelites fled to their homes.

18During his lifetime Absalom had taken a pillar and erected it in the King's Valley as a monument to himself, for he thought, "I have no son to carry on the memory of my name." He named the pillar after himself, and it is called Absalom's Monument to this day.

David Mourns

19Now Ahimaaz son of Zadok said, "Let me run and take the news to the king that the LORD has delivered him from the hand of his enemies."

20"You are not the one to take the news today," Joab told him. "You may take the news another time, but you must not do so today, because the king's son is dead."

21Then Joab said to a Cushite, "Go, tell the king what you have seen." The Cushite bowed down before Joab and ran off.

22Ahimaaz son of Zadok again said to Joab, "Come what may, please let me run behind the Cushite."

But Joab replied, "My son, why do you want to go? You don't have any news that will bring you a reward."

23He said, "Come what may, I want to run."

So Joab said, "Run!" Then Ahimaaz ran by way of the plaina and outran the Cushite.

24While David was sitting between the inner and outer gates, the watchman went up to the roof of the gateway by the wall. As he looked out, he saw a man running alone. 25The watchman called out to the king and reported it.

The king said, "If he is alone, he must have good news." And the man came closer and closer.

26Then the watchman saw another man running, and he called down to the gatekeeper, "Look, another man running alone!"

The king said, "He must be bringing good news, too."

27The watchman said, "It seems to me that the first one runs like Ahimaaz son of Zadok."

"He's a good man," the king said. "He comes with good news."

28Then Ahimaaz called out to the king, "All is well!" He bowed down before the king with his face to the ground and said, "Praise be to the LORD your God! He has delivered up the men who lifted their hands against my lord the king."

29The king asked, "Is the young man Absalom safe?"

Ahimaaz answered, "I saw great confusion just as Joab was about to send the king's servant and me, your servant, but I don't know what it was."

30The king said, "Stand aside and wait here." So he stepped aside and stood there.

31Then the Cushite arrived and said, "My lord the king, hear the good news! The LORD has delivered you today from all who rose up against you."

32The king asked the Cushite, "Is the young man Absalom safe?"

The Cushite replied, "May the enemies of my lord the king and all who rise up to harm you be like that young man."

33The king was shaken. He went up to the room over the gateway and wept. As he went, he said: "O my son Absalom! My son, my son Absalom! If only I had died instead of you—O Absalom, my son, my son!"

---

a 23 That is, the plain of the Jordan

Living Bible

men returned from chasing the army of Israel. 17They threw Absalom's body into a deep pit in the forest and piled a great heap of stones over it. And the army of Israel fled to their homes.

18(Absalom had built a monument to himself in the King's Valley, for he said, "I have no sons to carry on my name." He called it "Absalom's Monument," as it is still known today.)

19Then Zadok's son Ahima-az said, "Let me run to King David with the good news that the Lord has saved him from his enemy Absalom."

20"No," Joab told him, "it wouldn't be good news to the king that his son is dead. You can be my messenger some other time."

21Then Joab said to a man from Cush, "Go tell the king what you have seen." The man bowed and ran off.

22But Ahima-az pleaded with Joab, "Please let me go, too."

"No, we don't need you now, my boy." Joab replied. "There is no further news to send."

23"Yes, but let me go anyway," he begged.

And Joab finally said, "All right, go ahead." Then Ahima-az took a short cut across the plain and got there ahead of the man from Cush. 24David was sitting at the gate of the city. When the watchman climbed the stairs to his post at the top of the wall, he saw a lone man running towards them.

25He shouted the news down to David, and the king replied, "If he is alone, he has news."

As the messenger came closer, 26the watchman saw another man running towards them. He shouted down, "Here comes another one."

And the king replied, "He will have more news."

27"The first man looks like Ahima-az, the son of Zadok," the watchman said.

"He is a good man and comes with good news," the king replied.

28Then Ahima-az cried out to the king, "All is well!" He bowed low with his face to the ground and said, "Blessed be the Lord your God who has destroyed the rebels who dared to stand against you."

29"What of young Absalom?" the king demanded. "Is he all right?"

"When Joab told me to come, there was a lot of shouting; but I didn't know what was happening,"b Ahima-az answered.

30"Wait here," the king told him. So Ahima-az stepped aside.

31Then the man from Cush arrived and said, "I have good news for my lord the king. Today Jehovah has rescued you from all those who rebelled against you."

32"What about young Absalom? Is he all right?" the king demanded.

And the man replied, "May all of your enemies be as that young man is!"

33Then the king broke into tears, and went up to his room over the gate, crying as he went. "O my son Absalom, my son, my son Absalom. If only I could have died for you! O Absalom, my son, my son."

New Revised Standard

16 Then Joab sounded the trumpet, and the troops came back from pursuing Israel, for Joab restrained the troops. 17They took Absalom, threw him into a great pit in the forest, and raised over him a very great heap of stones. Meanwhile all the Israelites fled to their homes. 18Now Absalom in his lifetime had taken and set up for himself a pillar that is in the King's Valley, for he said, "I have no son to keep my name in remembrance"; he called the pillar by his own name. It is called Absalom's Monument to this day.

David Hears of Absalom's Death

19 Then Ahimaaz son of Zadok said, "Let me run, and carry tidings to the king that the LORD has delivered him from the power of his enemies." 20Joab said to him, "You are not to carry tidings today; you may carry tidings another day, but today you shall not do so, because the king's son is dead." 21Then Joab said to a Cushite, "Go, tell the king what you have seen." The Cushite bowed before Joab, and ran. 22Then Ahimaaz son of Zadok said again to Joab, "Come what may, let me also run after the Cushite." And Joab said, "Why will you run, my son, seeing that you have no rewardᶜ for the tidings?" 23"Come what may," he said, "I will run." So he said to him, "Run." Then Ahimaaz ran by the way of the Plain, and outran the Cushite.

24 Now David was sitting between the two gates. The sentinel went up to the roof of the gate by the wall, and when he looked up, he saw a man running alone. 25The sentinel shouted and told the king. The king said, "If he is alone, there are tidings in his mouth." He kept coming, and drew near. 26Then the sentinel saw another man running; and the sentinel called to the gatekeeper and said, "See, another man running alone!" The king said, "He also is bringing tidings." 27The sentinel said, "I think the running of the first one is like the running of Ahimaaz son of Zadok." The king said, "He is a good man, and comes with good tidings."

28 Then Ahimaaz cried out to the king, "All is well!" He prostrated himself before the king with his face to the ground, and said, "Blessed be the LORD your God, who has delivered up the men who raised their hand against my lord the king." 29The king said, "Is it well with the young man Absalom?" Ahimaaz answered, "When Joab sent your servant,ᵈ I saw a great tumult, but I do not know what it was." 30The king said, "Turn aside, and stand here." So he turned aside, and stood still.

31 Then the Cushite came; and the Cushite said, "Good tidings for my lord the king! For the LORD has vindicated you this day, delivering you from the power of all who rose up against you." 32The king said to the Cushite, "Is it well with the young man Absalom?" The Cushite answered, "May the enemies of my lord the king, and all who rise up to do you harm, be like that young man."

David Mourns for Absalom

33ᵉ The king was deeply moved, and went up to the chamber over the gate, and wept; and as he went, he said, "O my son Absalom, my son, my son Absalom! Would I had died instead of you, O Absalom, my son, my son!"

---

b 18:29 *I didn't know what was happening.* Ahima-az apparently was afraid to tell the king what actually had happened.

c Meaning of Heb uncertain   d Heb *the king's servant, your servant*
e Ch 19.1 in Heb

King James

19 AND IT was told Joab, Behold, the king weepeth and mourneth for Absalom.

2And the victory that day was *turned* into mourning unto all the people: for the people heard say that day how the king was grieved for his son.

3And the people gat them by stealth that day into the city, as people being ashamed steal away when they flee in battle.

4But the king covered his face, and the king cried with a loud voice, O my son Absalom, O Absalom, my son, my son!

5And Joab came into the house to the king, and said, Thou hast shamed this day the faces of all thy servants, which this day have saved thy life, and the lives of thy sons and of thy daughters, and the lives of thy wives, and the lives of thy concubines;

6In that thou lovest thine enemies, and hatest thy friends. For thou hast declared this day, that thou regardest neither princes nor servants: for this day I perceive, that if Absalom had lived, and all we had died this day, then it had pleased thee well.

7Now therefore arise, go forth, and speak comfortably unto thy servants: for I swear by the LORD, if thou go not forth, there will not tarry one with thee this night: and that will be worse unto thee than all the evil that befell thee from thy youth until now.

8Then the king arose, and sat in the gate. And they told unto all the people, saying, Behold, the king doth sit in the gate. And all the people came before the king: for Israel had fled every man to his tent.

9¶ And all the people were at strife throughout all the tribes of Israel, saying, The king saved us out of the hand of our enemies, and he delivered us out of the hand of the Philistines; and now he is fled out of the land for Absalom.

10And Absalom, whom we anointed over us, is dead in battle. Now therefore why speak ye not a word of bringing the king back?

11¶ And king David sent to Zadok and to Abiathar the priests, saying, Speak unto the elders of Judah, saying, Why are ye the last to bring the king back to his house? seeing the speech of all Israel is come to the king, *even* to his house.

12Ye *are* my brethren, ye *are* my bones and my flesh: wherefore then are ye the last to bring back the king?

13And say ye to Amasa, *Art* thou not of my bone, and of my flesh? God do so to me, and more also, if thou be not captain of the host before me continually in the room of Joab.

14And he bowed the heart of all the men of Judah, even as *the heart of* one man; so that they sent *this word* unto the king, Return thou, and all thy servants.

15So the king returned, and came to Jordan. And Judah came to Gilgal, to go to meet the king, to conduct the king over Jordan.

16¶ And Shimei the son of Gera, a Benjamite, which *was* of Bahurim, hasted and came down with the men of Judah to meet king David.

17And *there were* a thousand men of Benjamin with him, and Ziba the servant of the house of Saul, and his fifteen sons and his twenty servants with him; and they went over Jordan before the king.

18And there went over a ferry boat to carry over the king's household, and to do what he thought good. And Shimei the son of Gera fell down before the king, as he was come over Jordan;

19And said unto the king, Let not my lord impute iniquity unto me, neither do thou remember that which thy servant did perversely the day that my lord the king went out of Jerusalem, that the king should take it to his heart.

20For thy servant doth know that I have sinned: therefore, behold, I am come the first this day of all the house of Joseph to go down to meet my lord the king.

New International

19 JOAB WAS told, "The king is weeping and mourning for Absalom." 2And for the whole army the victory that day was turned into mourning, because on that day the troops heard it said, "The king is grieving for his son." 3The men stole into the city that day as men steal in who are ashamed when they flee from battle. 4The king covered his face and cried aloud, "O my son Absalom! O Absalom, my son, my son!"

5Then Joab went into the house to the king and said, "Today you have humiliated all your men, who have just saved your life and the lives of your sons and daughters and the lives of your wives and concubines. 6You love those who hate you and hate those who love you. You have made it clear today that the commanders and their men mean nothing to you. I see that you would be pleased if Absalom were alive today and all of us were dead. 7Now go out and encourage your men. I swear by the LORD that if you don't go out, not a man will be left with you by nightfall. This will be worse for you than all the calamities that have come upon you from your youth till now."

8So the king got up and took his seat in the gateway. When the men were told, "The king is sitting in the gateway," they all came before him.

David Returns to Jerusalem

Meanwhile, the Israelites had fled to their homes. 9Throughout the tribes of Israel, the people were all arguing with each other, saying, "The king delivered us from the hand of our enemies; he is the one who rescued us from the hand of the Philistines. But now he has fled the country because of Absalom; 10and Absalom, whom we anointed to rule over us, has died in battle. So why do you say nothing about bringing the king back?"

11King David sent this message to Zadok and Abiathar, the priests: "Ask the elders of Judah, 'Why should you be the last to bring the king back to his palace, since what is being said throughout Israel has reached the king at his quarters? 12You are my brothers, my own flesh and blood. So why should you be the last to bring back the king?' 13And say to Amasa, 'Are you not my own flesh and blood? May God deal with me, be it ever so severely, if from now on you are not the commander of my army in place of Joab.' "

14He won over the hearts of all the men of Judah as though they were one man. They sent word to the king, "Return, you and all your men." 15Then the king returned and went as far as the Jordan.

Now the men of Judah had come to Gilgal to go out and meet the king and bring him across the Jordan. 16Shimei son of Gera, the Benjamite from Bahurim, hurried down with the men of Judah to meet King David. 17With him were a thousand Benjamites, along with Ziba, the steward of Saul's household, and his fifteen sons and twenty servants. They rushed to the Jordan, where the king was. 18They crossed at the ford to take the king's household over and to do whatever he wished.

When Shimei son of Gera crossed the Jordan, he fell prostrate before the king 19and said to him, "May my lord not hold me guilty. Do not remember how your servant did wrong on the day my lord the king left Jerusalem. May the king put it out of his mind. 20For I your servant know that I have sinned, but today I have come here as the first of the whole house of Joseph to come down and meet my lord the king."

Living Bible

19 WORD SOON reached Joab that the king was weeping and mourning for Absalom. 2As the people heard of the king's deep grief for his son, the joy of that day's wonderful victory was turned into deep sadness. 3The entire army crept back into the city as though they were ashamed and had been beaten in battle.

4The king covered his face with his hands and kept on weeping, "O my son Absalom! O Absalom my son, my son!"

5Then Joab went to the king's room and said to him, "We saved your life today and the lives of your sons, your daughters, your wives and concubines; and yet you act like this, making us feel ashamed, as though we had done something wrong. 6You seem to love those who hate you, and hate those who love you. Apparently we don't mean anything to you; if Absalom had lived and all of us had died, you would be happy. 7Now go out there and congratulate the troops, for I swear by Jehovah that if you don't, not a single one of them will remain here during the night; then you will be worse off than you have ever been in your entire life."

8, 9, 10So the king went out and sat at the city gates, and as the news spread throughout the city that he was there, everyone went to him.

Meanwhile, there was much discussion and argument going on all across the nation: "Why aren't we talking about bringing the king back?" was the great topic everywhere. "For he saved us from our enemies, the Philistines; and Absalom, whom we made our king instead, chased him out of the country, but now Absalom is dead. Let's ask David to return and be our king again."

11, 12Then David sent Zadok and Abiathar the priests to say to the elders of Judah, "Why are you the last ones to reinstate the king? For all Israel is ready, and only you are holding out. Yet you are my own brothers, my own tribe, my own flesh and blood!"

13And he told them to tell Amasa, "Since you are my nephew, may God strike me dead if I do not appoint you as commander-in-chief of my army in place of Joab." 14Then Amasa convinced all the leaders of Judah, and they responded as one man. They sent word to the king, "Return to us and bring back all those who are with you."

15So the king started back to Jerusalem. And when he arrived at the Jordan River, it seemed as if everyone in Judah had come to Gilgal to meet him and escort him across the river! 16Then Shime-i (the son of Gera the Benjaminite), the man from Bahurim, hurried across with the men of Judah to welcome King David. 17A thousand men from the tribe of Benjamin were with him, including Ziba, the servant of Saul, and Ziba's fifteen sons and twenty servants; they rushed down to the Jordan to arrive ahead of the king. 18They all worked hard ferrying the king's household and troops across, and helped them in every way they could.

As the king was crossing, Shime-i fell down before him, 19and pleaded, "My lord the king, please forgive me and forget the terrible thing I did when you left Jerusalem; 20for I know very well how much I sinned. That is why I have come here today, the very first person in all the tribe of Joseph to greet you."

New Revised Standard

19 IT WAS told Joab, "The king is weeping and mourning for Absalom." 2So the victory that day was turned into mourning for all the troops; for the troops heard that day, "The king is grieving for his son." 3The troops stole into the city that day as soldiers steal in who are ashamed when they flee in battle. 4The king covered his face, and the king cried with a loud voice, "O my son Absalom, O Absalom, my son, my son!" 5Then Joab came into the house to the king, and said, "Today you have covered with shame the faces of all your officers who have saved your life today, and the lives of your sons and your daughters, and the lives of your wives and your concubines, 6for love of those who hate you and for hatred of those who love you. You have made it clear today that commanders and officers are nothing to you; for I perceive that if Absalom were alive and all of us were dead today, then you would be pleased. 7So go out at once and speak kindly to your servants; for I swear by the LORD, if you do not go, not a man will stay with you this night; and this will be worse for you than any disaster that has come upon you from your youth until now." 8Then the king got up and took his seat in the gate. The troops were all told, "See, the king is sitting in the gate"; and all the troops came before the king.

David Recalled to Jerusalem

Meanwhile, all the Israelites had fled to their homes. 9All the people were disputing throughout all the tribes of Israel, saying, "The king delivered us from the hand of our enemies, and saved us from the hand of the Philistines; and now he has fled out of the land because of Absalom. 10But Absalom, whom we anointed over us, is dead in battle. Now therefore why do you say nothing about bringing the king back?"

11 King David sent this message to the priests Zadok and Abiathar, "Say to the elders of Judah, 'Why should you be the last to bring the king back to his house? The talk of all Israel has come to the king.a 12You are my kin, you are my bone and my flesh; why then should you be the last to bring back the king?' 13And say to Amasa, 'Are you not my bone and my flesh? So may God do to me, and more, if you are not the commander of my army from now on, in place of Joab.' " 14Amasab swayed the hearts of all the people of Judah as one, and they sent word to the king, "Return, both you and all your servants." 15So the king came back to the Jordan; and Judah came to Gilgal to meet the king and to bring him over the Jordan.

16 Shimei son of Gera, the Benjaminite, from Bahurim, hurried to come down with the people of Judah to meet King David; 17with him were a thousand people from Benjamin. And Ziba, the servant of the house of Saul, with his fifteen sons and his twenty servants, rushed down to the Jordan ahead of the king, 18while the crossing was taking place,c to bring over the king's household, and to do his pleasure.

David's Mercy to Shimei

Shimei son of Gera fell down before the king, as he was about to cross the Jordan, 19and said to the king, "May my lord not hold me guilty or remember how your servant did wrong on the day my lord the king left Jerusalem; may the king not bear it in mind. 20For your servant knows that I have sinned; therefore, see, I have come this day, the first of all the house of Joseph to come down to meet my lord the king." 21Abishai son of Zerui-

a Gk: Heb to the king, to his house   b Heb He   c Cn: Heb the ford crossed

King James

21But Abishai the son of Zeruiah answered and said, Shall not Shimei be put to death for this, because he cursed the LORD's anointed?

22And David said, What have I to do with you, ye sons of Zeruiah, that ye should this day be adversaries unto me? shall there any man be put to death this day in Israel? for do not I know that I *am* this day king over Israel?

23Therefore the king said unto Shimei, Thou shalt not die. And the king sware unto him.

24¶ And Mephibosheth the son of Saul came down to meet the king, and had neither dressed his feet, nor trimmed his beard, nor washed his clothes, from the day the king departed until the day he came *again* in peace.

25And it came to pass, when he was come to Jerusalem to meet the king, that the king said unto him, Wherefore wentest not thou with me, Mephibosheth?

26And he answered, My lord, O king, my servant deceived me: for thy servant said, I will saddle me an ass, that I may ride thereon, and go to the king; because thy servant *is* lame.

27And he hath slandered thy servant unto my lord the king; but my lord the king *is* as an angel of God: do therefore *what is* good in thine eyes.

28For all *of* my father's house were but dead men before my lord the king: yet didst thou set thy servant among them that did eat at thine own table. What right therefore have I yet to cry any more unto the king?

29And the king said unto him, Why speakest thou any more of thy matters? I have said, Thou and Ziba divide the land.

30And Mephibosheth said unto the king, Yea, let him take all, forasmuch as my lord the king is come again in peace unto his own house.

31¶ And Barzillai the Gileadite came down from Rogelim, and went over Jordan with the king, to conduct him over Jordan.

32Now Barzillai was a very aged man, *even* fourscore years old: and he had provided the king of sustenance while he lay at Mahanaim; for he *was* a very great man.

33And the king said unto Barzillai, Come thou over with me, and I will feed thee with me in Jerusalem.

34And Barzillai said unto the king, How long have I to live, that I should go up with the king unto Jerusalem?

35I *am* this day fourscore years old: *and* can I discern between good and evil? can thy servant taste what I eat or what I drink? can I hear any more the voice of singing men and singing women? wherefore then should thy servant be yet a burden unto my lord the king?

36Thy servant will go a little way over Jordan with the king: and why should the king recompense it me with such a reward?

37Let thy servant, I pray thee, turn back again, that I may die in mine own city, *and be buried* by the grave of my father and of my mother. But behold thy servant Chimham; let him go over with my lord the king; and do to him what shall seem good unto thee.

38And the king answered, Chimham shall go over with me, and I will do to him that which shall seem good unto thee: and whatsoever thou shalt require of me, *that* will I do for thee.

39And all the people went over Jordan. And when the king was come over, the king kissed Barzillai, and blessed him; and he returned unto his own place.

40Then the king went on to Gilgal, and Chimham went on with him: and all the people of Judah conducted the king, and also half the people of Israel.

41¶ And, behold, all the men of Israel came to the king, and said unto the king, Why have our brethren the men of Judah stolen thee away, and have brought the king, and his household, and all David's men with him, over Jordan?

New International

21Then Abishai son of Zeruiah said, "Shouldn't Shimei be put to death for this? He cursed the LORD's anointed."

22David replied, "What do you and I have in common, you sons of Zeruiah? This day you have become my adversaries! Should anyone be put to death in Israel today? Do I not know that today I am king over Israel?" 23So the king said to Shimei, "You shall not die." And the king promised him on oath.

24Mephibosheth, Saul's grandson, also went down to meet the king. He had not taken care of his feet or trimmed his mustache or washed his clothes from the day the king left until the day he returned safely. 25When he came from Jerusalem to meet the king, the king asked him, "Why didn't you go with me, Mephibosheth?"

26He said, "My lord the king, since I your servant am lame, I said, 'I will have my donkey saddled and will ride on it, so I can go with the king.' But Ziba my servant betrayed me. 27And he has slandered your servant to my lord the king. My lord the king is like an angel of God; so do whatever pleases you. 28All my grandfather's descendants deserved nothing but death from my lord the king, but you gave your servant a place among those who sat at your table. So what right do I have to make any more appeals to the king?"

29The king said to him, "Why say more? I order you and Ziba to divide the fields."

30Mephibosheth said to the king, "Let him take everything, now that my lord the king has arrived home safely."

31Barzillai the Gileadite also came down from Rogelim to cross the Jordan with the king and to send him on his way from there. 32Now Barzillai was a very old man, eighty years of age. He had provided for the king during his stay in Mahanaim, for he was a very wealthy man. 33The king said to Barzillai, "Cross over with me and stay with me in Jerusalem, and I will provide for you."

34But Barzillai answered the king, "How many more years will I live, that I should go up to Jerusalem with the king? 35I am now eighty years old. Can I tell the difference between what is good and what is not? Can your servant taste what he eats and drinks? Can I still hear the voices of men and women singers? Why should your servant be an added burden to my lord the king? 36Your servant will cross over the Jordan with the king for a short distance, but why should the king reward me in this way? 37Let your servant return, that I may die in my own town near the tomb of my father and mother. But here is your servant Kimham. Let him cross over with my lord the king. Do for him whatever pleases you."

38The king said, "Kimham shall cross over with me, and I will do for him whatever pleases you. And anything you desire from me I will do for you."

39So all the people crossed the Jordan, and then the king crossed over. The king kissed Barzillai and gave him his blessing, and Barzillai returned to his home.

40When the king crossed over to Gilgal, Kimham crossed with him. All the troops of Judah and half the troops of Israel had taken the king over.

41Soon all the men of Israel were coming to the king and saying to him, "Why did our brothers, the men of Judah, steal the king away and bring him and his household across the Jordan, together with all his men?"

Living Bible

21Abishai asked, "Shall not Shime-i die, for he cursed the Lord's chosen king!"

22"Don't talk to me like that!" David exclaimed. "This is not a day for execution but for celebration! I am once more king of Israel!"

23Then, turning to Shime-i, he vowed, "Your life is spared."

24, 25Now Mephibosheth, Saul's grandson, arrived from Jerusalem to meet the king. He had not washed his feet or clothes nor trimmed his beard since the day the king left Jerusalem.

"Why didn't you come with me, Mephibosheth?" the king asked him.

26And he replied, "My lord, O king, my servant Ziba deceived me. I told him, 'Saddle my donkey so that I can go with the king.' For as you know I am lame. 27But Ziba has slandered me by saying that I refused to come.a But I know that you are as an angel of God, so do what you think best. 28I and all my relatives could expect only death from you, but instead you have honored me among all those who eat at your own table! So how can I complain?"

29"All right," David replied. "My decision is that you and Ziba will divide the land equally between you."

30"Give him all of it," Mephibosheth said. "I am content just to have you back again!"

31, 32Barzillai, who had fed the king and his army during their exile in Mahanaim, arrived from Rogelim to conduct the king across the river. He was very old now, about eighty, and very wealthy.

33"Come across with me and live in Jerusalem," the king said to Barzillai. "I will take care of you there."

34"No," he replied, "I am far too old for that. 35I am eighty years old today, and life has lost its excitement.b Food and wine are no longer tasty, and entertainment is not much fun; I would only be a burden to my lord the king. 36Just to go across the river with you is all the honor I need! 37Then let me return again to die in my own city, where my father and mother are buried. But here is Chimham.c Let him go with you and receive whatever good things you want to give him."

38"Good," the king agreed. "Chimham shall go with me, and I will do for him whatever I would have done for you."

39So all the people crossed the Jordan with the king; and after David had kissed and blessed Barzillai, he returned home. 40The king then went on to Gilgal, taking Chimham with him. And most of Judah and half of Israel were there to greet him. 41But the men of Israel complained to the king because only men from Judah had ferried him and his household across the Jordan.

New Revised Standard

ah answered, "Shall not Shimei be put to death for this, because he cursed the LORD's anointed?" 22But David said, "What have I to do with you, you sons of Zeruiah, that you should today become an adversary to me? Shall anyone be put to death in Israel this day? For do I not know that I am this day king over Israel?" 23The king said to Shimei, "You shall not die." And the king gave him his oath.

David and Mephibosheth Meet

24 Mephiboshethd grandson of Saul came down to meet the king; he had not taken care of his feet, or trimmed his beard, or washed his clothes, from the day the king left until the day he came back in safety. 25When he came from Jerusalem to meet the king, the king said to him, "Why did you not go with me, Mephibosheth?"d 26He answered, "My lord, O king, my servant deceived me; for your servant said to him, 'Saddle a donkey for me,e so that I may ride on it and go with the king.' For your servant is lame. 27He has slandered your servant to my lord the king. But my lord the king is like the angel of God; do therefore what seems good to you. 28For all my father's house were doomed to death before my lord the king; but you set your servant among those who eat at your table. What further right have I, then, to appeal to the king?" 29The king said to him, "Why speak any more of your affairs? I have decided: you and Ziba shall divide the land." 30Mephiboshethd said to the king, "Let him take it all, since my lord the king has arrived home safely."

David's Kindness to Barzillai

31 Now Barzillai the Gileadite had come down from Rogelim; he went on with the king to the Jordan, to escort him over the Jordan. 32Barzillai was a very aged man, eighty years old. He had provided the king with food while he stayed at Mahanaim, for he was a very wealthy man. 33The king said to Barzillai, "Come over with me, and I will provide for you in Jerusalem at my side." 34But Barzillai said to the king, "How many years have I still to live, that I should go up with the king to Jerusalem? 35Today I am eighty years old; can I discern what is pleasant and what is not? Can your servant taste what he eats or what he drinks? Can I still listen to the voice of singing men and singing women? Why then should your servant be an added burden to my lord the king? 36Your servant will go a little way over the Jordan with the king. Why should the king recompense me with such a reward? 37Please let your servant return, so that I may die in my own town, near the graves of my father and my mother. But here is your servant Chimham; let him go over with my lord the king; and do for him whatever seems good to you." 38The king answered, "Chimham shall go over with me, and I will do for him whatever seems good to you; and all that you desire of me I will do for you." 39Then all the people crossed over the Jordan, and the king crossed over; the king kissed Barzillai and blessed him, and he returned to his own home. 40The king went on to Gilgal, and Chimham went on with him; all the people of Judah, and also half the people of Israel, brought the king on his way.

41 Then all the people of Israel came to the king, and said to him, "Why have our kindred the people of Judah stolen you away, and brought the king and his household over the Jordan, and all David's men with him?" 42All the people of Judah answered the people of

---

a 19:27 saying that I refused to come, implied.   b 19:35 life has lost its excitement, literally, "can I discern between good and bad?"   c 19:37 Chimham. According to Josephus, Chimham was Barzillai's son.

d Or Merib-baal: See 4.4 note   e Gk Syr Vg: Heb said, I will saddle a donkey for myself

King James

42And all the men of Judah answered the men of Israel, Because the king *is* near of kin to us: wherefore then be ye angry for this matter? have we eaten at all of the king's *cost?* or hath he given us any gift?

43And the men of Israel answered the men of Judah, and said, We have ten parts in the king, and we have also more *right* in David than ye: why then did ye despise us, that our advice should not be first had in bringing back our king? And the words of the men of Judah were fiercer than the words of the men of Israel.

20 AND THERE happened to be there a man of Belial, whose name *was* Sheba, the son of Bichri, a Benjamite: and he blew a trumpet, and said, We have no part in David, neither have we inheritance in the son of Jesse: every man to his tents, O Israel.

2So every man of Israel went up from after David, *and* followed Sheba the son of Bichri: but the men of Judah clave unto their king, from Jordan even to Jerusalem.

3¶ And David came to his house at Jerusalem; and the king took the ten women *his* concubines, whom he had left to keep the house, and put them in ward, and fed them, but went not in unto them. So they were shut up unto the day of their death, living in widowhood.

4¶ Then said the king to Amasa, Assemble me the men of Judah within three days, and be thou here present.

5So Amasa went to assemble *the men of* Judah: but he tarried longer than the set time which he had appointed him.

6And David said to Abishai, Now shall Sheba the son of Bichri do us more harm than *did* Absalom: take thou thy lord's servants, and pursue after him, lest he get him fenced cities, and escape us.

7And there went out after him Joab's men, and the Cherethites, and the Pelethites, and all the mighty men: and they went out of Jerusalem, to pursue after Sheba the son of Bichri.

8When they *were* at the great stone which *is* in Gibeon, Amasa went before them. And Joab's garment that he had put on was girded unto him, and upon it a girdle *with* a sword fastened upon his loins in the sheath thereof; and as he went forth it fell out.

9And Joab said to Amasa, *Art* thou in health, my brother? And Joab took Amasa by the beard with the right hand to kiss him.

10But Amasa took no heed to the sword that *was* in Joab's hand: so he smote him therewith in the fifth *rib,* and shed out his bowels to the ground, and struck him not again; and he died. So Joab and Abishai his brother pursued after Sheba the son of Bichri.

11And one of Joab's men stood by him, and said, He that favoureth Joab, and he that *is* for David, *let him go* after Joab.

12And Amasa wallowed in blood in the midst of the highway. And when the man saw that all the people stood still, he removed Amasa out of the highway into the field, and cast a cloth upon him, when he saw that every one that came by him stood still.

13When he was removed out of the highway, all the people went on after Joab, to pursue after Sheba the son of Bichri.

14¶ And he went through all the tribes of Israel unto Abel, and to Beth-maachah, and all the Berites: and they were gathered together, and went also after him.

15And they came and besieged him in Abel of Beth-maachah, and they cast up a bank against the city, and it stood in the trench: and all the people that *were* with Joab battered the wall, to throw it down.

New International

42All the men of Judah answered the men of Israel, "We did this because the king is closely related to us. Why are you angry about it? Have we eaten any of the king's provisions? Have we taken anything for ourselves?"

43Then the men of Israel answered the men of Judah, "We have ten shares in the king; and besides, we have a greater claim on David than you have. So why do you treat us with contempt? Were we not the first to speak of bringing back our king?"

But the men of Judah responded even more harshly than the men of Israel.

Sheba Rebels Against David

20 NOW A troublemaker named Sheba son of Bicri, a Benjamite, happened to be there. He sounded the trumpet and shouted,

"We have no share in David,
    no part in Jesse's son!
Every man to his tent, O Israel!"

2So all the men of Israel deserted David to follow Sheba son of Bicri. But the men of Judah stayed by their king all the way from the Jordan to Jerusalem.

3When David returned to his palace in Jerusalem, he took the ten concubines he had left to take care of the palace and put them in a house under guard. He provided for them, but did not lie with them. They were kept in confinement till the day of their death, living as widows.

4Then the king said to Amasa, "Summon the men of Judah to come to me within three days, and be here yourself." 5But when Amasa went to summon Judah, he took longer than the time the king had set for him.

6David said to Abishai, "Now Sheba son of Bicri will do us more harm than Absalom did. Take your master's men and pursue him, or he will find fortified cities and escape from us." 7So Joab's men and the Kerethites and Pelethites and all the mighty warriors went out under the command of Abishai. They marched out from Jerusalem to pursue Sheba son of Bicri.

8While they were at the great rock in Gibeon, Amasa came to meet them. Joab was wearing his military tunic, and strapped over it at his waist was a belt with a dagger in its sheath. As he stepped forward, it dropped out of its sheath.

9Joab said to Amasa, "How are you, my brother?" Then Joab took Amasa by the beard with his right hand to kiss him. 10Amasa was not on his guard against the dagger in Joab's hand, and Joab plunged it into his belly, and his intestines spilled out on the ground. Without being stabbed again, Amasa died. Then Joab and his brother Abishai pursued Sheba son of Bicri.

11One of Joab's men stood beside Amasa and said, "Whoever favors Joab, and whoever is for David, let him follow Joab!" 12Amasa lay wallowing in his blood in the middle of the road, and the man saw that all the troops came to a halt there. When he realized that everyone who came up to Amasa stopped, he dragged him from the road into a field and threw a garment over him. 13After Amasa had been removed from the road, all the men went on with Joab to pursue Sheba son of Bicri.

14Sheba passed through all the tribes of Israel to Abel Beth Maacah[a] and through the entire region of the Berites, who gathered together and followed him. 15All the troops with Joab came and besieged Sheba in Abel Beth Maacah. They built a siege ramp up to the city, and it stood against the outer fortifications. While they were battering the wall to bring it down, 16a wise woman

---

a *14* Or *Abel, even Beth Maacah;* also in verse 15

Living Bible

[42]"Why not?" the men of Judah replied. "The king is one of our own tribe. Why should this make you angry? We have charged him nothing—he hasn't fed us or given us gifts!"

[43]"But there are ten tribes in Israel," the others replied, "so we have ten times as much right in the king as you do; why didn't you invite the rest of us? And, remember, we were the first to speak of bringing him back to be our king again."

The argument continued back and forth, and the men of Judah were very rough in their replies.

20 THEN A hot-head whose name was Sheba (son of Bichri, a Benjaminite) blew a trumpet and yelled, "We want nothing to do with David. Come on, you men of Israel, let's get out of here. He's not our king!"

[2]So all except Judah and Benjamin turned around and deserted David and followed Sheba! But the men of Judah stayed with their king, accompanying him from the Jordan to Jerusalem. [3]When he arrived at his palace in Jerusalem, the king instructed that his ten wives he had left to keep house should be placed in seclusion. Their needs were to be cared for, he said, but he would no longer sleep with them as his wives. So they remained in virtual widowhood until their deaths.

[4]Then the king instructed Amasa to mobilize the army of Judah within three days and to report back at that time. [5]So Amasa went out to notify the troops, but it took him longer than the three days he had been given.

[6]Then David said to Abishai, "That fellow Sheba is going to hurt us more than Absalom did. Quick, take my bodyguard and chase after him before he gets into a fortified city where we can't reach him."

[7]So Abishai and Joab set out after Sheba with an elite guard from Joab's army and the king's own bodyguard. [8, 9, 10]As they arrived at the great stone in Gibeon, they came face to face with Amasa. Joab was wearing his uniform with a dagger strapped to his side. As he stepped forward to greet Amasa, he stealthily slipped the dagger from its sheath. "I'm glad to see you, my brother," Joab said, and took him by the beard with his right hand as though to kiss him. Amasa didn't notice the dagger in his left hand, and Joab stabbed him in the stomach with it, so that his bowels gushed out onto the ground. He did not need to strike again, and he died there. Joab and his brother Abishai left him lying there and continued after Sheba.

[11]One of Joab's young officers shouted to Amasa's troops, "If you are for David, come and follow Joab."

[12]But Amasa lay in his blood in the middle of the road, and when Joab's young officers saw that a crowd was gathering around to stare at him, they dragged him off the road into a field and threw a garment over him. [13]With the body out of the way, everyone went on with Joab to capture Sheba.

[14]Meanwhile Sheba had traveled across Israel to mobilize his own clan of Bichri at the city of Abel in Beth-maach. [15]When Joab's forces arrived, they besieged Abel and built a mound to the top of the city wall and began battering it down.

New Revised Standard

Israel, "Because the king is near of kin to us. Why then are you angry over this matter? Have we eaten at all at the king's expense? Or has he given us any gift?" [43]But the people of Israel answered the people of Judah, "We have ten shares in the king, and in David also we have more than you. Why then did you despise us? Were we not the first to speak of bringing back our king?" But the words of the people of Judah were fiercer than the words of the people of Israel.

The Rebellion of Sheba

20 NOW A scoundrel named Sheba son of Bichri, a Benjaminite, happened to be there. He sounded the trumpet and cried out,

"We have no portion in David,
no share in the son of Jesse!
Everyone to your tents, O Israel!"

[2]So all the people of Israel withdrew from David and followed Sheba son of Bichri; but the people of Judah followed their king steadfastly from the Jordan to Jerusalem.

[3] David came to his house at Jerusalem; and the king took the ten concubines whom he had left to look after the house, and put them in a house under guard, and provided for them, but did not go in to them. So they were shut up until the day of their death, living as if in widowhood.

[4] Then the king said to Amasa, "Call the men of Judah together to me within three days, and be here yourself." [5]So Amasa went to summon Judah; but he delayed beyond the set time that had been appointed him. [6]David said to Abishai, "Now Sheba son of Bichri will do us more harm than Absalom; take your lord's servants and pursue him, or he will find fortified cities for himself, and escape from us." [7]Joab's men went out after him, along with the Cherethites, the Pelethites, and all the warriors; they went out from Jerusalem to pursue Sheba son of Bichri. [8]When they were at the large stone that is in Gibeon, Amasa came to meet them. Now Joab was wearing a soldier's garment and over it was a belt with a sword in its sheath fastened at his waist; as he went forward it fell out. [9]Joab said to Amasa, "Is it well with you, my brother?" And Joab took Amasa by the beard with his right hand to kiss him. [10]But Amasa did not notice the sword in Joab's hand; Joab struck him in the belly so that his entrails poured out on the ground, and he died. He did not strike a second blow.

Then Joab and his brother Abishai pursued Sheba son of Bichri. [11]And one of Joab's men took his stand by Amasa, and said, "Whoever favors Joab, and whoever is for David, let him follow Joab." [12]Amasa lay wallowing in his blood on the highway, and the man saw that all the people were stopping. Since he saw that all who came by him were stopping, he carried Amasa from the highway into a field, and threw a garment over him. [13]Once he was removed from the highway, all the people went on after Joab to pursue Sheba son of Bichri.

[14] Sheba[b] passed through all the tribes of Israel to Abel of Beth-maacah;[c] and all the Bichrites[d] assembled, and followed him inside. [15]Joab's forces[e] came and besieged him in Abel of Beth-maacah; they threw up a siege ramp against the city, and it stood against the rampart. Joab's forces were battering the wall to break it down. [16]Then a wise woman called from the city,

[b] Heb *He*   [c] Compare 20.15: Heb *and Beth-maacah*   [d] Compare Gk Vg: Heb *Berites*   [e] Heb *They*

King James

16¶ Then cried a wise woman out of the city, Hear, hear; say, I pray you, unto Joab, Come near hither, that I may speak with thee.

17And when he was come near unto her, the woman said, *Art* thou Joab? And he answered, I *am* he. Then she said unto him, Hear the words of thine handmaid. And he answered, I do hear.

18Then she spake, saying, They were wont to speak in old time, saying, They shall surely ask *counsel* at Abel: and so they ended *the matter*.

19I *am one of them that are* peaceable *and* faithful in Israel: thou seekest to destroy a city and a mother in Israel: why wilt thou swallow up the inheritance of the LORD?

20And Joab answered and said, Far be it, far be it from me, that I should swallow up or destroy.

21The matter *is* not so: but a man of mount Ephraim, Sheba the son of Bichri by name, hath lifted up his hand against the king, *even* against David: deliver him only, and I will depart from the city. And the woman said unto Joab, Behold, his head shall be thrown to thee over the wall.

22Then the woman went unto all the people in her wisdom. And they cut off the head of Sheba the son of Bichri, and cast *it* out to Joab. And he blew a trumpet, and they retired from the city, every man to his tent. And Joab returned to Jerusalem unto the king.

23¶ Now Joab *was* over all the host of Israel: and Benaiah the son of Jehoiada *was* over the Cherethites and over the Pelethites:

24And Adoram *was* over the tribute: and Jehoshaphat the son of Ahilud *was* recorder:

25And Sheva *was* scribe: and Zadok and Abiathar *were* the priests:

26And Ira also the Jairite was a chief ruler about David.

21 THEN THERE was a famine in the days of David three years, year after year; and David inquired of the LORD. And the LORD answered, *It is* for Saul, and for *his* bloody house, because he slew the Gibeonites.

2And the king called the Gibeonites, and said unto them; (now the Gibeonites *were* not of the children of Israel, but of the remnant of the Amorites; and the children of Israel had sworn unto them: and Saul sought to slay them in his zeal to the children of Israel and Judah.)

3Wherefore David said unto the Gibeonites, What shall I do for you? and wherewith shall I make the atonement, that ye may bless the inheritance of the LORD?

4And the Gibeonites said unto him, We will have no silver nor gold of Saul, nor of his house; neither for us shalt thou kill any man in Israel. And he said, What ye shall say, *that* will I do for you.

5And they answered the king, The man that consumed us, and that devised against us *that* we should be destroyed from remaining in any of the coasts of Israel,

6Let seven men of his sons be delivered unto us, and we will hang them up unto the LORD in Gibeah of Saul, *whom* the LORD did choose. And the king said, I will give *them*.

7But the king spared Mephibosheth, the son of Jonathan the son of Saul, because of the LORD's oath that *was* between them, between David and Jonathan the son of Saul.

8But the king took the two sons of Rizpah the daughter of Aiah, whom she bare unto Saul, Armoni and Mephibosheth; and the five sons of Michal the daughter of Saul, whom she brought up for Adriel the son of Barzillai the Meholathite:

New International

called from the city, "Listen! Listen! Tell Joab to come here so I can speak to him." 17He went toward her, and she asked, "Are you Joab?"

"I am," he answered.

She said, "Listen to what your servant has to say."

"I'm listening," he said.

18She continued, "Long ago they used to say, 'Get your answer at Abel,' and that settled it. 19We are the peaceful and faithful in Israel. You are trying to destroy a city that is a mother in Israel. Why do you want to swallow up the LORD's inheritance?"

20"Far be it from me!" Joab replied, "Far be it from me to swallow up or destroy! 21That is not the case. A man named Sheba son of Bicri, from the hill country of Ephraim, has lifted up his hand against the king, against David. Hand over this one man, and I'll withdraw from the city."

The woman said to Joab, "His head will be thrown to you from the wall."

22Then the woman went to all the people with her wise advice, and they cut off the head of Sheba son of Bicri and threw it to Joab. So he sounded the trumpet, and his men dispersed from the city, each returning to his home. And Joab went back to the king in Jerusalem.

23Joab was over Israel's entire army; Benaiah son of Jehoiada was over the Kerethites and Pelethites; 24Adoniram[a] was in charge of forced labor; Jehoshaphat son of Ahilud was recorder; 25Sheva was secretary; Zadok and Abiathar were priests; 26and Ira the Jairite was David's priest.

The Gibeonites Avenged

21 DURING THE reign of David, there was a famine for three successive years; so David sought the face of the LORD. The LORD said, "It is on account of Saul and his blood-stained house; it is because he put the Gibeonites to death."

2The king summoned the Gibeonites and spoke to them. (Now the Gibeonites were not a part of Israel but were survivors of the Amorites; the Israelites had sworn to spare them, but Saul in his zeal for Israel and Judah had tried to annihilate them.) 3David asked the Gibeonites, "What shall I do for you? How shall I make amends so that you will bless the LORD's inheritance?"

4The Gibeonites answered him, "We have no right to demand silver or gold from Saul or his family, nor do we have the right to put anyone in Israel to death."

"What do you want me to do for you?" David asked.

5They answered the king, "As for the man who destroyed us and plotted against us so that we have been decimated and have no place anywhere in Israel, 6let seven of his male descendants be given to us to be killed and exposed before the LORD at Gibeah of Saul—the LORD's chosen one."

So the king said, "I will give them to you."

7The king spared Mephibosheth son of Jonathan, the son of Saul, because of the oath before the LORD between David and Jonathan son of Saul. 8But the king took Armoni and Mephibosheth, the two sons of Aiah's daughter Rizpah, whom she had borne to Saul, together with the five sons of Saul's daughter Merab,[b] whom she had borne to Adriel son of Barzillai the Meholathite. 9He

---

[a] 24 Some Septuagint manuscripts (see also 1 Kings 4:6 and 5:14); Hebrew *Adoram*   [b] 8 Two Hebrew manuscripts, some Septuagint manuscripts and Syriac (see also 1 Samuel 18:19); most Hebrew and Septuagint manuscripts *Michal*

Living Bible

16But a wise woman in the city called out to Joab, "Listen to me, Joab. Come over here so I can talk to you."

17As he approached, the woman asked, "Are you Joab?"

And he replied, "I am."

18So she told him, "There used to be a saying, 'If you want to settle an argument, ask advice at Abel.' For we always give wise counsel. 19You are destroying an ancient, peace-loving city, loyal to Israel. Should you destroy what is the Lord's?"

20And Joab replied, "That isn't it at all. 21All I want is a man named Sheba from the hill country of Ephraim, who has revolted against King David. If you will deliver him to me, we will leave the city in peace."

"All right," the woman replied, "we will throw his head over the wall to you."

22Then the woman went to the people with her wise advice, and they cut off Sheba's head and threw it out to Joab. And he blew the trumpet and called his troops back from the attack, and they returned to the king at Jerusalem.

23Joab was commander-in-chief of the army, and Benaiah was in charge of the king's bodyguard.c 24Adoram was in charge of the forced labor battalions, and Jehoshaphat was the historian who kept the records. 25Sheva was the secretary, and Zadok and Abiathar were the chief priests. 26Ira the Jairite was David's personal chaplain.

21 THERE WAS a famine during David's reign that lasted year after year for three years, and David spent much time in prayer about it. Then the Lord said, "The famine is because of the guilt of Saul and his family, for they murdered the Gibeonites."

2So King David summoned the Gibeonites. They were not part of Israel, but were what was left of the nation of the Amorites. Israel had sworn not to kill them; but Saul, in his nationalistic zeal, had tried to wipe them out.

3David asked them, "What can I do for you, to rid ourselves of this guilt and to induce you to ask God to bless us?"

4"Well, money won't do it," the Gibeonites replied, "and we don't want to see Israelites executed in revenge."

"What can I do, then?" David asked. "Just tell me and I will do it for you."

5, 6"Well, then," they replied, "give us seven of Saul's sons—the sons of the man who did his best to destroy us. We will hang them before the Lord in Gibeon, the city of King Saul."

"All right," the king said, "I will do it."

7He spared Jonathan's son Mephibosheth, who was Saul's grandson, because of the oath between himself and Jonathan. 8But he gave them Saul's two sons Armoni and Mephibosheth, whose mother was Rizpah, the daughter of Aiah. He also gave them the five adopted sons of Michal that she brought up for Saul's daughter Merab, the wife of Adri-el. 9The men of Gibeon impaled

New Revised Standard

"Listen! Listen! Tell Joab, 'Come here, I want to speak to you.'" 17He came near her; and the woman said, "Are you Joab?" He answered, "I am." Then she said to him, "Listen to the words of your servant." He answered, "I am listening." 18Then she said, "They used to say in the old days, 'Let them inquire at Abel'; and so they would settle a matter. 19I am one of those who are peaceable and faithful in Israel; you seek to destroy a city that is a mother in Israel; why will you swallow up the heritage of the Lord?" 20Joab answered, "Far be it from me, far be it, that I should swallow up or destroy! 21That is not the case! But a man of the hill country of Ephraim, called Sheba son of Bichri, has lifted up his hand against King David; give him up alone, and I will withdraw from the city." The woman said to Joab, "His head shall be thrown over the wall to you." 22Then the woman went to all the people with her wise plan. And they cut off the head of Sheba son of Bichri, and threw it out to Joab. So he blew the trumpet, and they dispersed from the city, and all went to their homes, while Joab returned to Jerusalem to the king.

23 Now Joab was in command of all the army of Israel;d Benaiah son of Jehoiada was in command of the Cherethites and the Pelethites; 24Adoram was in charge of the forced labor; Jehoshaphat son of Ahilud was the recorder; 25Sheva was secretary; Zadok and Abiathar were priests; 26and Ira the Jairite was also David's priest.

David Avenges the Gibeonites

21 NOW THERE was a famine in the days of David for three years, year after year; and David inquired of the Lord. The Lord said, "There is bloodguilt on Saul and on his house, because he put the Gibeonites to death." 2So the king called the Gibeonites and spoke to them. (Now the Gibeonites were not of the people of Israel, but of the remnant of the Amorites; although the people of Israel had sworn to spare them, Saul had tried to wipe them out in his zeal for the people of Israel and Judah.) 3David said to the Gibeonites, "What shall I do for you? How shall I make expiation, that you may bless the heritage of the Lord?" 4The Gibeonites said to him, "It is not a matter of silver or gold between us and Saul or his house; neither is it for us to put anyone to death in Israel." He said, "What do you say that I should do for you?" 5They said to the king, "The man who consumed us and planned to destroy us, so that we should have no place in all the territory of Israel— 6let seven of his sons be handed over to us, and we will impale them before the Lord at Gibeon on the mountain of the Lord."e The king said, "I will hand them over."

7 But the king spared Mephibosheth,f the son of Saul's son Jonathan, because of the oath of the Lord that was between them, between David and Jonathan son of Saul. 8The king took the two sons of Rizpah daughter of Aiah, whom she bore to Saul, Armoni and Mephibosheth;f and the five sons of Merabg daughter of Saul, whom she bore to Adriel son of Barzillai the Meholathite; 9he gave them into the hands of the Gibeonites,

---

d Cn: Heb Joab to all the army, Israel   e Cn Compare Gk and 21.9: Heb at Gibeah of Saul, the chosen of the Lord   f Or Merib-baal: See 4.4 note
g Two Heb Mss Syr Compare Gk: MT Michal

King James

9And he delivered them into the hands of the Gibeonites, and they hanged them in the hill before the LORD:
and they fell *all* seven together, and were put to death
in the days of harvest, in the first *days,* in the beginning
of barley harvest.

10¶ And Rizpah the daughter of Aiah took sackcloth,
and spread it for her upon the rock, from the beginning
of harvest until water dropped upon them out of heaven,
and suffered neither the birds of the air to rest on them
by day, nor the beasts of the field by night.

11And it was told David what Rizpah the daughter of
Aiah, the concubine of Saul, had done.

12¶ And David went and took the bones of Saul and
the bones of Jonathan his son from the men of Jabesh-
gilead, which had stolen them from the street of Beth-
shan, where the Philistines had hanged them, when the
Philistines had slain Saul in Gilboa:

13And he brought up from thence the bones of Saul
and the bones of Jonathan his son; and they gathered the
bones of them that were hanged.

14And the bones of Saul and Jonathan his son buried
they in the country of Benjamin in Zelah, in the sepulchre of Kish his father: and they performed all that the
king commanded. And after that God was entreated for
the land.

15¶ Moreover the Philistines had yet war again with
Israel; and David went down, and his servants with him,
and fought against the Philistines: and David waxed
faint.

16And Ishbi-benob, which *was* of the sons of the
giant, the weight of whose spear *weighed* three hundred
shekels of brass in weight, he being girded with a new
sword, thought to have slain David.

17But Abishai the son of Zeruiah succoured him, and
smote the Philistine, and killed him. Then the men of
David sware unto him, saying, Thou shalt go no more
out with us to battle, that thou quench not the light of
Israel.

18And it came to pass after this, that there was again
a battle with the Philistines at Gob: then Sibbechai the
Hushathite slew Saph, which *was* of the sons of the
giant.

19And there was again a battle in Gob with the Philistines, where Elhanan the son of Jaare-oregim, a Bethlehemite, slew *the brother of* Goliath the Gittite, the staff
of whose spear *was* like a weaver's beam.

20And there was yet a battle in Gath, where *was* a man
of *great* stature, that had on every hand six fingers, and
on every foot six toes, four and twenty in number; and
he also was born to the giant.

21And when he defied Israel, Jonathan the son of
Shimeah the brother of David slew him.

22These four were born to the giant in Gath, and fell
by the hand of David, and by the hand of his servants.

22 AND DAVID spake unto the LORD the words
of this song in the day *that* the LORD had delivered him out of the hand of all his enemies, and out of
the hand of Saul:

2And he said, The LORD *is* my rock, and my fortress,
and my deliverer;

3The God of my rock; in him will I trust: *he is* my
shield, and the horn of my salvation, my high tower, and
my refuge, my saviour; thou savest me from violence.

New International

handed them over to the Gibeonites, who killed and
exposed them on a hill before the LORD. All seven of
them fell together; they were put to death during the first
days of the harvest, just as the barley harvest was beginning.

10Rizpah daughter of Aiah took sackcloth and spread
it out for herself on a rock. From the beginning of the
harvest till the rain poured down from the heavens on the
bodies, she did not let the birds of the air touch them by
day or the wild animals by night. 11When David was told
what Aiah's daughter Rizpah, Saul's concubine, had
done, 12he went and took the bones of Saul and his son
Jonathan from the citizens of Jabesh Gilead. (They had
taken them secretly from the public square at Beth Shan,
where the Philistines had hung them after they struck
Saul down on Gilboa.) 13David brought the bones of
Saul and his son Jonathan from there, and the bones of
those who had been killed and exposed were gathered up.

14They buried the bones of Saul and his son Jonathan
in the tomb of Saul's father Kish, at Zela in Benjamin,
and did everything the king commanded. After that,
God answered prayer in behalf of the land.

Wars Against the Philistines

15Once again there was a battle between the Philistines and Israel. David went down with his men to fight
against the Philistines, and he became exhausted. 16And
Ishbi-Benob, one of the descendants of Rapha, whose
bronze spearhead weighed three hundred shekels[a] and
who was armed with a new sword, said he would kill
David. 17But Abishai son of Zeruiah came to David's
rescue; he struck the Philistine down and killed him.
Then David's men swore to him, saying, "Never again
will you go out with us to battle, so that the lamp of
Israel will not be extinguished."

18In the course of time, there was another battle with
the Philistines, at Gob. At that time Sibbecai the Hushathite killed Saph, one of the descendants of Rapha.

19In another battle with the Philistines at Gob, Elhanan son of Jaare-Oregim[b] the Bethlehemite killed Goliath[c] the Gittite, who had a spear with a shaft like a
weaver's rod.

20In still another battle, which took place at Gath,
there was a huge man with six fingers on each hand and
six toes on each foot—twenty-four in all. He also was
descended from Rapha. 21When he taunted Israel, Jonathan son of Shimeah, David's brother, killed him.

22These four were descendants of Rapha in Gath, and
they fell at the hands of David and his men.

David's Song of Praise

22 DAVID SANG to the LORD the words of this
song when the LORD delivered him from the
hand of all his enemies and from the hand of Saul. 2He
said:

"The LORD is my rock, my fortress and my
        deliverer;
3   my God is my rock, in whom I take refuge,
     my shield and the horn[d] of my salvation.
He is my stronghold, my refuge and my
        savior—
    from violent men you save me.

---

a *16* That is, about 7 1/2 pounds (about 3.5 kilograms)   b *19* Or *son of Jair
the weaver*   c *19* Hebrew and Septuagint; 1 Chron. 20:5 *son of Jair killed
Lahmi the brother of Goliath*   d *3* Horn here symbolizes strength.

Living Bible

them in the mountain before the Lord. So all seven of them died together at the beginning of the barley harvest.

¹⁰Then Rizpah, the mother of two of the men,ᵉ spread sackcloth upon a rock and stayed there through the entire harvest seasonᶠ to prevent the vultures from tearing at their bodies during the day and the wild animals from eating them at night. ¹¹When David learned what she had done, ¹², ¹³, ¹⁴he arranged for the men's bones to be buried in the grave of Saul's father, Kish. At the same time he sent a request to the men of Jabesh-gilead, asking them to bring him the bones of Saul and Jonathan. They had stolen their bodies from the public square at Beth-shan where the Philistines had impaled them after they had died in battle on Mount Gilboa. So their bones were brought to him. Then at last God answered prayer and ended the famine.

¹⁵Once when the Philistines were at war with Israel, and David and his men were in the thick of the battle, David became weak and exhausted. ¹⁶Ishbi-benob, a giant whose speartip weighed more than twelve pounds and who was sporting a new suit of armor, closed in on David and was about to kill him. ¹⁷But Abishai the son of Zeruiah came to his rescue and killed the Philistine. After that David's men declared, "You are not going out to battle again! Why should we risk snuffing out the light of Israel?"

¹⁸Later, during a war with the Philistines at Gob, Sibbecai the Hushathite killed Saph, another giant. ¹⁹At still another time and at the same place, Elhanan killed the brother of Goliath the Gittite,ᵍ whose spearhandle was as huge as a weaver's beam! ²⁰, ²¹And once when the Philistines and the Israelis were fighting at Gath, a giant with six fingers on each hand and six toes on each foot defied Israel, and David's nephew Jonathan—the son of David's brother Shime-i—killed him. ²²These four were from the tribe of giants in Gath, and were killed by David's troops.

22 DAVID SANG this song to the Lord after he had rescued him from Saul and from all his other enemies:

²"Jehovah is my rock,
My fortress and my Savior.
³I will hide in God,
Who is my rock and my refuge.
He is my shield
And my salvation,
My refuge and high tower.
Thank you, O my Savior,
For saving me from all my enemies.

New Revised Standard

and they impaled them on the mountain before the LORD. The seven of them perished together. They were put to death in the first days of harvest, at the beginning of barley harvest.

10 Then Rizpah the daughter of Aiah took sackcloth, and spread it on a rock for herself, from the beginning of harvest until rain fell on them from the heavens; she did not allow the birds of the air to come on the bodiesʰ by day, or the wild animals by night. ¹¹When David was told what Rizpah daughter of Aiah, the concubine of Saul, had done, ¹²David went and took the bones of Saul and the bones of his son Jonathan from the people of Jabesh-gilead, who had stolen them from the public square of Beth-shan, where the Philistines had hung them up, on the day the Philistines killed Saul on Gilboa. ¹³He brought up from there the bones of Saul and the bones of his son Jonathan; and they gathered the bones of those who had been impaled. ¹⁴They buried the bones of Saul and of his son Jonathan in the land of Benjamin in Zela, in the tomb of his father Kish; they did all that the king commanded. After that, God heeded supplications for the land.

Exploits of David's Men

15 The Philistines went to war again with Israel, and David went down together with his servants. They fought against the Philistines, and David grew weary. ¹⁶Ishbi-benob, one of the descendants of the giants, whose spear weighed three hundred shekels of bronze, and who was fitted out with new weapons,ⁱ said he would kill David. ¹⁷But Abishai son of Zeruiah came to his aid, and attacked the Philistine and killed him. Then David's men swore to him, "You shall not go out with us to battle any longer, so that you do not quench the lamp of Israel."

18 After this a battle took place with the Philistines, at Gob; then Sibbecai the Hushathite killed Saph, who was one of the descendants of the giants. ¹⁹Then there was another battle with the Philistines at Gob; and Elhanan son of Jaare-oregim, the Bethlehemite, killed Goliath the Gittite, the shaft of whose spear was like a weaver's beam. ²⁰There was again war at Gath, where there was a man of great size, who had six fingers on each hand, and six toes on each foot, twenty-four in number; he too was descended from the giants. ²¹When he taunted Israel, Jonathan son of David's brother Shimei, killed him. ²²These four were descended from the giants in Gath; they fell by the hands of David and his servants.

David's Song of Thanksgiving

22 DAVID SPOKE to the LORD the words of this song on the day when the LORD delivered him from the hand of all his enemies, and from the hand of Saul. ²He said:
The LORD is my rock, my fortress, and my
deliverer,
3   my God, my rock, in whom I take refuge,
my shield and the horn of my salvation,
my stronghold and my refuge,
my savior; you save me from violence.

King James

4I will call on the LORD, *who is* worthy to be praised: so shall I be saved from mine enemies.

5When the waves of death compassed me, the floods of ungodly men made me afraid;

6The sorrows of hell compassed me about; the snares of death prevented me;

7In my distress I called upon the LORD, and cried to my God: and he did hear my voice out of his temple, and my cry *did enter* into his ears.

8Then the earth shook and trembled; the foundations of heaven moved and shook, because he was wroth.

9There went up a smoke out of his nostrils, and fire out of his mouth devoured: coals were kindled by it.

10He bowed the heavens also, and came down; and darkness *was* under his feet.

11And he rode upon a cherub, and did fly: and he was seen upon the wings of the wind.

12And he made darkness pavilions round about him, dark waters, *and* thick clouds of the skies.

13Through the brightness before him were coals of fire kindled.

14The LORD thundered from heaven, and the most High uttered his voice.

15And he sent out arrows, and scattered them; lightning, and discomfited them.

16And the channels of the sea appeared, the foundations of the world were discovered, at the rebuking of the LORD, at the blast of the breath of his nostrils.

17He sent from above, he took me; he drew me out of many waters;

18He delivered me from my strong enemy, *and* from them that hated me: for they were too strong for me.

19They prevented me in the day of my calamity: but the LORD was my stay.

20He brought me forth also into a large place: he delivered me, because he delighted in me.

21The LORD rewarded me according to my righteousness: according to the cleanness of my hands hath he recompensed me.

22For I have kept the ways of the LORD, and have not wickedly departed from my God.

23For all his judgments *were* before me: and *as for* his statutes, I did not depart from them.

24I was also upright before him, and have kept myself from mine iniquity.

25Therefore the LORD hath recompensed me according to my righteousness; according to my cleanness in his eyesight.

26With the merciful thou wilt show thyself merciful, *and* with the upright man thou wilt show thyself upright.

27With the pure thou wilt show thyself pure; and with the froward thou wilt show thyself unsavoury.

28And the afflicted people thou wilt save: but thine eyes *are* upon the haughty, *that* thou mayest bring *them* down.

29For thou *art* my lamp, O LORD: and the LORD will lighten my darkness.

New International

4I call to the LORD, who is worthy of praise,
  and I am saved from my enemies.

5"The waves of death swirled about me;
  the torrents of destruction overwhelmed me.

6The cords of the grave[a] coiled around me;
  the snares of death confronted me.

7In my distress I called to the LORD;
  I called out to my God.
From his temple he heard my voice;
  my cry came to his ears.

8"The earth trembled and quaked,
  the foundations of the heavens[b] shook;
  they trembled because he was angry.

9Smoke rose from his nostrils;
  consuming fire came from his mouth,
  burning coals blazed out of it.

10He parted the heavens and came down;
  dark clouds were under his feet.

11He mounted the cherubim and flew;
  he soared[c] on the wings of the wind.

12He made darkness his canopy around him—
  the dark[d] rain clouds of the sky.

13Out of the brightness of his presence
  bolts of lightning blazed forth.

14The LORD thundered from heaven;
  the voice of the Most High resounded.

15He shot arrows and scattered the enemies,
  bolts of lightning and routed them.

16The valleys of the sea were exposed
  and the foundations of the earth laid bare
at the rebuke of the LORD,
  at the blast of breath from his nostrils.

17"He reached down from on high and took hold
    of me;
  he drew me out of deep waters.

18He rescued me from my powerful enemy,
  from my foes, who were too strong for me.

19They confronted me in the day of my disaster,
  but the LORD was my support.

20He brought me out into a spacious place;
  he rescued me because he delighted in me.

21"The LORD has dealt with me according to my
    righteousness;
  according to the cleanness of my hands he
    has rewarded me.

22For I have kept the ways of the LORD;
  I have not done evil by turning from my God.

23All his laws are before me;
  I have not turned away from his decrees.

24I have been blameless before him
  and have kept myself from sin.

25The LORD has rewarded me according to my
    righteousness,
  according to my cleanness[e] in his sight.

26"To the faithful you show yourself faithful,
  to the blameless you show yourself blameless,

27to the pure you show yourself pure,
  but to the crooked you show yourself shrewd.

28You save the humble,
  but your eyes are on the haughty to bring
    them low.

29You are my lamp, O LORD;
  the LORD turns my darkness into light.

---

a 6 Hebrew *Sheol*   b 8 Hebrew; Vulgate and Syriac (see also Psalm 18:7) *mountains*   c 11 Many Hebrew manuscripts (see also Psalm 18:10); most Hebrew manuscripts *appeared*   d 12 Septuagint and Vulgate (see also Psalm 18:11); Hebrew *massed*   e 25 Hebrew; Septuagint and Vulgate (see also Psalm 18:24) *to the cleanness of my hands*

Living Bible

4I will call upon the Lord,
Who is worthy to be praised;
He will save me from all my enemies.
5The waves of death surrounded me;
Floods of evil burst upon me;
6I was trapped, and bound
By hell and death;
7But I called upon the Lord in my distress,
And he heard me from his Temple.
My cry reached his ears.
8Then the earth shook and trembled;
The foundations of the heavens quaked
Because of his wrath.
9Smoke poured from his nostrils;
Fire leaped from his mouth
And burned up all before him,
Setting fire to the world.f
10He bent the heavens down and came to earth;
He walked upon dark clouds.
11He rode upon the glorious—
On the wings of the wind.
12Darkness surrounded him,
And clouds were thick around him;
13The earth was radiant with his brightness.
14The Lord thundered from heaven;
The God above all gods gave out a mighty shout.
15He shot forth his arrows of lightning
And routed his enemies.
16By the blast of his breath
Was the sea split in two.
The bottom of the sea appeared.
17From above, he rescued me.
He drew me out from the waters;
18He saved me from powerful enemies,
From those who hated me
And from those who were too strong for me.
19They came upon me
In the day of my calamity,
But the Lord was my salvation.
20He set me free and rescued me,
For I was his delight.
21The Lord rewarded me for my goodness,
For my hands were clean;
22And I have not departed from my God.
23I knew his laws,
And I obeyed them.
24I was perfect in obedience
And kept myself from sin.
25That is why the Lord has done so much for me,
For he sees that I am clean.
26You are merciful to the merciful;
You show your perfections
To the blameless.
27To those who are pure,
You show yourself pure;
But you destroy those who are evil.
28You will save those in trouble,
But you bring down the haughty;
For you watch their every move.
29O Lord, you are my light!
You make my darkness bright.

f 22:9 setting fire to the world, literally, "coals were kindled by it."

New Revised Standard

4 I call upon the LORD, who is worthy to be
    praised,
    and I am saved from my enemies.

5 For the waves of death encompassed me,
    the torrents of perdition assailed me;
6 the cords of Sheol entangled me,
    the snares of death confronted me.

7 In my distress I called upon the LORD;
    to my God I called.
    From his temple he heard my voice,
    and my cry came to his ears.

8 Then the earth reeled and rocked;
    the foundations of the heavens trembled
    and quaked, because he was angry.
9 Smoke went up from his nostrils,
    and devouring fire from his mouth;
    glowing coals flamed forth from him.
10 He bowed the heavens, and came down;
    thick darkness was under his feet.
11 He rode on a cherub, and flew;
    he was seen upon the wings of the wind.
12 He made darkness around him a canopy,
    thick clouds, a gathering of water.
13 Out of the brightness before him
    coals of fire flamed forth.
14 The LORD thundered from heaven;
    the Most High uttered his voice.
15 He sent out arrows, and scattered them
    —lightning, and routed them.
16 Then the channels of the sea were seen,
    the foundations of the world were laid bare
at the rebuke of the LORD,
    at the blast of the breath of his nostrils.

17 He reached from on high, he took me,
    he drew me out of mighty waters.
18 He delivered me from my strong enemy,
    from those who hated me;
    for they were too mighty for me.
19 They came upon me in the day of my
    calamity,
    but the LORD was my stay.
20 He brought me out into a broad place;
    he delivered me, because he delighted in
    me.

21 The LORD rewarded me according to my
    righteousness;
    according to the cleanness of my hands he
    recompensed me.
22 For I have kept the ways of the LORD,
    and have not wickedly departed from my
    God.
23 For all his ordinances were before me,
    and from his statutes I did not turn aside.
24 I was blameless before him,
    and I kept myself from guilt.
25 Therefore the LORD has recompensed me
    according to my righteousness,
    according to my cleanness in his sight.

26 With the loyal you show yourself loyal;
    with the blameless you show yourself
    blameless;
27 with the pure you show yourself pure,
    and with the crooked you show yourself
    perverse.
28 You deliver a humble people,
    but your eyes are upon the haughty to bring
    them down.
29 Indeed, you are my lamp, O LORD,
    the LORD lightens my darkness.

King James

30For by thee I have run through a troop: by my God have I leaped over a wall.

31*As for* God, his way *is* perfect; the word of the Lord *is* tried: he *is* a buckler to all them that trust in him.

32For who *is* God, save the Lord? and who *is* a rock, save our God?

33God *is* my strength *and* power: and he maketh my way perfect.

34He maketh my feet like hinds' *feet:* and setteth me upon my high places.

35He teacheth my hands to war; so that a bow of steel is broken by mine arms.

36Thou hast also given me the shield of thy salvation: and thy gentleness hath made me great.

37Thou hast enlarged my steps under me; so that my feet did not slip.

38I have pursued mine enemies, and destroyed them; and turned not again until I had consumed them.

39And I have consumed them, and wounded them, that they could not arise: yea, they are fallen under my feet.

40For thou hast girded me with strength to battle: them that rose up against me hast thou subdued under me.

41Thou hast also given me the necks of mine enemies, that I might destroy them that hate me.

42They looked, but *there was* none to save; *even* unto the Lord, but he answered them not.

43Then did I beat them as small as the dust of the earth, I did stamp them as the mire of the street, *and* did spread them abroad.

44Thou also hast delivered me from the strivings of my people, thou hast kept me *to be* head of the heathen: a people *which* I knew not shall serve me.

45Strangers shall submit themselves unto me: as soon as they hear, they shall be obedient unto me.

46Strangers shall fade away, and they shall be afraid out of their close places.

47The Lord liveth; and blessed *be* my rock; and exalted be the God of the rock of my salvation.

48It *is* God that avengeth me, and that bringeth down the people under me,

49And that bringeth me forth from mine enemies: thou also hast lifted me up on high above them that rose up against me: thou hast delivered me from the violent man.

50Therefore I will give thanks unto thee, O Lord, among the heathen, and I will sing praises unto thy name.

51*He is* the tower of salvation for his king: and showeth mercy to his anointed, unto David, and to his seed for evermore.

New International

30With your help I can advance against a troop[a];
  with my God I can scale a wall.

31"As for God, his way is perfect;
  the word of the Lord is flawless.
He is a shield
  for all who take refuge in him.

32For who is God besides the Lord?
  And who is the Rock except our God?

33It is God who arms me with strength[b]
  and makes my way perfect.

34He makes my feet like the feet of a deer;
  he enables me to stand on the heights.

35He trains my hands for battle;
  my arms can bend a bow of bronze.

36You give me your shield of victory;
  you stoop down to make me great.

37You broaden the path beneath me,
  so that my ankles do not turn.

38"I pursued my enemies and crushed them;
  I did not turn back till they were destroyed.

39I crushed them completely, and they could not rise;
  they fell beneath my feet.

40You armed me with strength for battle;
  you made my adversaries bow at my feet.

41You made my enemies turn their backs in flight,
  and I destroyed my foes.

42They cried for help, but there was no one to save them—
  to the Lord, but he did not answer.

43I beat them as fine as the dust of the earth;
  I pounded and trampled them like mud in the streets.

44"You have delivered me from the attacks of my people;
  you have preserved me as the head of nations.
People I did not know are subject to me,

45 and foreigners come cringing to me;
  as soon as they hear me, they obey me.

46They all lose heart;
  they come trembling[c] from their strongholds.

47"The Lord lives! Praise be to my Rock!
  Exalted be God, the Rock, my Savior!

48He is the God who avenges me,
  who puts the nations under me,

49 who sets me free from my enemies.
You exalted me above my foes;
  from violent men you rescued me.

50Therefore I will praise you, O Lord, among the nations;
  I will sing praises to your name.

51He gives his king great victories;
  he shows unfailing kindness to his anointed,
  to David and his descendants forever."

---

a *30 Or can run through a barricade*   b *33* Dead Sea Scrolls, some Septuagint manuscripts, Vulgate and Syriac (see also Psalm 18:32); Masoretic Text *who is my strong refuge*   c *46* Some Septuagint manuscripts and Vulgate (see also Psalm 18:45); Masoretic Text *they arm themselves.*

Living Bible

30By your power I can crush an army;
By your strength I leap over a wall.
31As for God, his way is perfect;
The word of the Lord is true.
He shields all who hide behind him.
32Our Lord alone is God;
We have no other Savior.d
33God is my strong fortress;
He has made me safe.
34He causes the good to walk a steady tread
Like mountain goats upon the rocks.
35He gives me skill in war
And strength to bend a bow of bronze.
36You have given me the shield of your salvation;
Your gentleness has made me great.
37You have made wide steps for my feet,
To keep them from slipping.
38I have chased my enemies
And destroyed them.
I did not stop till all were gone.
39I have destroyed them
So that none can rise again.
They have fallen beneath my feet.
40For you have given me strength for the battle
And have caused me to subdue
All those who rose against me.
41You have made my enemies
Turn and run away;
I have destroyed them all.
42They looked in vain for help;
They cried to God,
But he refused to answer.
43I beat them into dust;
I crushed and scattered them
Like dust along the streets.
44You have preserved me
From the rebels of my people;
You have preserved me
As the head of the nations.
Foreigners shall serve me
45And shall quickly submit to me
When they hear of my power.
46They shall lose heart
And come, trembling,
From their hiding places.
47The Lord lives.
Blessed be my Rock.
Praise to him—
The Rock of my salvation.
48Blessed be God
Who destroys those who oppose me
49And rescues me from my enemies.
Yes, you hold me safe above their heads.
You deliver me from violence.
50No wonder I give thanks to you, O Lord, among the
nations,
And sing praises to your name.
51He gives wonderful deliverance to his king,
And shows mercy to his anointed—
To David and his family,
Forever."

New Revised Standard

30 By you I can crush a troop,
       and by my God I can leap over a wall.
31 This God—his way is perfect;
       the promise of the LORD proves true;
       he is a shield for all who take refuge in
          him.
32 For who is God, but the LORD?
       And who is a rock, except our God?
33 The God who has girded me with strengthe
       has opened wide my path.f
34 He made myg feet like the feet of deer,
       and set me secure on the heights.
35 He trains my hands for war,
       so that my arms can bend a bow of bronze.
36 You have given me the shield of your
          salvation,
       and your helph has made me great.
37 You have made me stride freely,
       and my feet do not slip;
38 I pursued my enemies and destroyed them,
       and did not turn back until they were
          consumed.
39 I consumed them; I struck them down, so that
          they did not rise;
       they fell under my feet.
40 For you girded me with strength for the battle;
       you made my assailants sink under me.
41 You made my enemies turn their backs to me,
       those who hated me, and I destroyed them.
42 They looked, but there was no one to save
          them;
       they cried to the LORD, but he did not
          answer them.
43 I beat them fine like the dust of the earth,
       I crushed them and stamped them down like
          the mire of the streets.

44 You delivered me from strife with the
          peoples;i
       you kept me as the head of the nations;
       people whom I had not known served me.
45 Foreigners came cringing to me;
       as soon as they heard of me, they obeyed
          me.
46 Foreigners lost heart,
       and came trembling out of their strongholds.

47 The LORD lives! Blessed be my rock,
       and exalted be my God, the rock of my
          salvation,
48 the God who gave me vengeance
       and brought down peoples under me,
49 who brought me out from my enemies;
       you exalted me above my adversaries,
       you delivered me from the violent.

50 For this I will extol you, O LORD, among the
          nations,
       and sing praises to your name.
51 He is a tower of salvation for his king,
       and shows steadfast love to his anointed,
       to David and his descendants forever.

d 22:32 We have no other Savior, literally, "Who is a rock save our God?"

e Q Ms Gk Syr Vg Compare Ps 18.32: MT *God is my strong refuge*
f Meaning of Heb uncertain   g Another reading is *his*   h Q Ms: MT *your
answering*   i Gk: Heb *from strife with my people*

King James

23 NOW THESE *be* the last words of David. David the son of Jesse said, and the man *who was* raised up on high, the anointed of the God of Jacob, and the sweet psalmist of Israel, said,

2The spirit of the LORD spake by me, and his word *was* in my tongue.

3The God of Israel said, the Rock of Israel spake to me, He that ruleth over men *must be* just, ruling in the fear of God.

4And *he shall be* as the light of the morning, *when* the sun riseth, *even* a morning without clouds; *as* the tender grass *springing* out of the earth by clear shining after rain.

5Although my house *be* not so with God; yet he hath made with me an everlasting covenant, ordered in all *things,* and sure: for *this is* all my salvation, and all *my* desire, although he make *it* not to grow.

6¶ But *the sons* of Belial *shall be* all of them as thorns thrust away, because they cannot be taken with hands:

7But the man *that* shall touch them must be fenced with iron and the staff of a spear; and they shall be utterly burned with fire in the *same* place.

8¶ These *be* the names of the mighty men whom David had: The Tachmonite that sat in the seat, chief among the captains; the same *was* Adino the Eznite: *he lift up his spear* against eight hundred, whom he slew at one time.

9And after him *was* Eleazar the son of Dodo the Ahohite, *one* of the three mighty men with David, when they defied the Philistines *that* were there gathered together to battle, and the men of Israel were gone away:

10He arose, and smote the Philistines until his hand was weary, and his hand clave unto the sword: and the LORD wrought a great victory that day; and the people returned after him only to spoil.

11And after him *was* Shammah the son of Agee the Hararite. And the Philistines were gathered together into a troop, where was a piece of ground full of lentiles: and the people fled from the Philistines.

12But he stood in the midst of the ground, and defended it, and slew the Philistines: and the LORD wrought a great victory.

13And three of the thirty chief went down, and came to David in the harvest time unto the cave of Adullam: and the troop of the Philistines pitched in the valley of Rephaim.

14And David *was* then in an hold, and the garrison of the Philistines *was* then *in* Bethlehem.

15And David longed, and said, Oh that one would give me drink of the water of the well of Bethlehem, which *is* by the gate!

16And the three mighty men brake through the host of the Philistines, and drew water out of the well of Bethlehem, that *was* by the gate, and took *it,* and brought *it* to David: nevertheless he would not drink thereof, but poured it out unto the LORD.

17And he said, Be it far from me, O LORD, that I should do this: *is not this* the blood of the men that went in jeopardy of their lives? therefore he would not drink it. These things did these three mighty men.

New International

The Last Words of David

23 THESE ARE the last words of David:

"The oracle of David son of Jesse,
    the oracle of the man exalted by the Most
        High,
the man anointed by the God of Jacob,
    Israel's singer of songsa:

2"The Spirit of the LORD spoke through me;
    his word was on my tongue.
3The God of Israel spoke,
    the Rock of Israel said to me:
'When one rules over men in righteousness,
    when he rules in the fear of God,
4he is like the light of morning at sunrise
    on a cloudless morning,
like the brightness after rain
    that brings the grass from the earth.'

5"Is not my house right with God?
    Has he not made with me an everlasting
        covenant,
    arranged and secured in every part?
Will he not bring to fruition my salvation
    and grant me my every desire?
6But evil men are all to be cast aside like thorns,
    which are not gathered with the hand.
7Whoever touches thorns
    uses a tool of iron or the shaft of a spear;
    they are burned up where they lie."

David's Mighty Men

8These are the names of David's mighty men:

Josheb-Basshebeth,b a Tahkemonite,c was chief of the Three; he raised his spear against eight hundred men, whom he killedd in one encounter.

9Next to him was Eleazar son of Dodai the Ahohite. As one of the three mighty men, he was with David when they taunted the Philistines gathered at Pas Dammim,e for battle. Then the men of Israel retreated, 10but he stood his ground and struck down the Philistines till his hand grew tired and froze to the sword. The LORD brought about a great victory that day. The troops returned to Eleazar, but only to strip the dead.

11Next to him was Shammah son of Agee the Hararite. When the Philistines banded together at a place where there was a field full of lentils, Israel's troops fled from them. 12But Shammah took his stand in the middle of the field. He defended it and struck the Philistines down, and the LORD brought about a great victory.

13During harvest time, three of the thirty chief men came down to David at the cave of Adullam, while a band of Philistines was encamped in the Valley of Rephaim. 14At that time David was in the stronghold, and the Philistine garrison was at Bethlehem. 15David longed for water and said, "Oh, that someone would get me a drink of water from the well near the gate of Bethlehem!" 16So the three mighty men broke through the Philistine lines, drew water from the well near the gate of Bethlehem and carried it back to David. But he refused to drink it; instead, he poured it out before the LORD. 17"Far be it from me, O LORD, to do this!" he said. "Is it not the blood of men who went at the risk of their lives?" And David would not drink it.

Such were the exploits of the three mighty men.

---

a 1 Or *Israel's beloved singer*   b 8 Hebrew; some Septuagint manuscripts suggest *Ish-Bosheth,* that is, *Esh-Baal* (see also 1 Chron. 11:11 *Jashobeam*). c 8 Probably a variant of *Hacmonite* (see 1 Chron. 11:11)   d 8 Some Septuagint manuscripts (see also 1 Chron. 11:11); Hebrew and other Septuagint manuscripts *Three; it was Adino the Eznite who killed eight hundred men* e 9 See 1 Chron. 11:13; Hebrew *gathered there.*

Living Bible

23

THESE ARE the last words of David:
"David, the son of Jesse, speaks.
David, the man to whom God gave such wonderful
success;
David, the anointed of the God of Jacob;
David, sweet psalmist of Israel:
2The Spirit of the Lord spoke by me,
And his word was on my tongue.
3The Rock of Israel said to me:
'One shall come who rules righteously,
Who rules in the fear of God.
4He shall be as the light of the morning;
A cloudless sunrise
When the tender grass
Springs forth upon the earth;
As sunshine after rain.'
5And it is my family
He has chosen!
Yes, God has made
An everlasting covenant with me;
His agreement is eternal, final, sealed.
He will constantly look after
My safety and success.f
6But the godless are as thorns to be thrown away,
For they tear the hand that touches them.
7One must be armed to chop them down;
They shall be burned.

8These are the names of the Top Three—the most heroic men in David's army: the first was Josheb-bas-shebeth from Tah-chemon, known also as Adino, the Eznite. He once killed eight hundred men in one battle. 9Next in rank was Eleazar, the son of Dodo and grandson of Ahohi. He was one of the three men who, with David, held back the Philistines that time when the rest of the Israeli army fled. 10He killed the Philistines until his hand was too tired to hold his sword; and the Lord gave him a great victory. (The rest of the army did not return until it was time to collect the loot!)

11, 12After him was Shammah, the son of Agee from Harar. Once during a Philistine attack, when all his men deserted him and fled, he stood alone at the center of a field of lentils and beat back the Philistines; and God gave him a great victory.

13One time when David was living in the cave of Adullam and the invading Philistines were at the valley of Rephaim, three of The Thirty—the top-ranking officers of the Israeli army—went down at harvest time to visit him. 14David was in the stronghold at the time, for Philistine marauders had occupied the nearby city of Bethlehem. 15David remarked, "How thirsty I am for some of that good water in the city well!" (The well was near the city gate.) 16So the three men broke through the Philistine ranks and drew water from the well and brought it to David. But he refused to drink it! Instead, he poured it out before the Lord.

17"No, my God," he exclaimed, "I cannot do it! This is the blood of these men who have risked their lives."

New Revised Standard

The Last Words of David

23

NOW THESE are the last words of David:
The oracle of David, son of Jesse,
the oracle of the man whom God exalted,g
the anointed of the God of Jacob,
the favorite of the Strong One of Israel:

2 The spirit of the LORD speaks through me,
his word is upon my tongue.
3 The God of Israel has spoken,
the Rock of Israel has said to me:
One who rules over people justly,
ruling in the fear of God,
4 is like the light of morning,
like the sun rising on a cloudless morning,
gleaming from the rain on the grassy land.

5 Is not my house like this with God?
For he has made with me an everlasting
covenant,
ordered in all things and secure.
Will he not cause to prosper
all my help and my desire?
6 But the godless areh all like thorns that are
thrown away;
for they cannot be picked up with the hand;
7 to touch them one uses an iron bar
or the shaft of a spear.
And they are entirely consumed in fire on
the spot.i

David's Mighty Men

8 These are the names of the warriors whom David had: Josheb-basshebeth a Tahchemonite; he was chief of the Three;j he wielded his speark against eight hundred whom he killed at one time.

9 Next to him among the three warriors was Eleazar son of Dodo son of Ahohi. He was with David when they defied the Philistines who were gathered there for battle. The Israelites withdrew, 10but he stood his ground. He struck down the Philistines until his arm grew weary, though his hand clung to the sword. The LORD brought about a great victory that day. Then the people came back to him—but only to strip the dead.

11 Next to him was Shammah son of Agee, the Hararite. The Philistines gathered together at Lehi, where there was a plot of ground full of lentils; and the army fled from the Philistines. 12But he took his stand in the middle of the plot, defended it, and killed the Philistines; and the LORD brought about a great victory.

13 Towards the beginning of harvest three of the thirtyl chiefs went down to join David at the cave of Adullam, while a band of Philistines was encamped in the valley of Rephaim. 14David was then in the stronghold; and the garrison of the Philistines was then at Bethlehem. 15David said longingly, "O that someone would give me water to drink from the well of Bethlehem that is by the gate!" 16Then the three warriors broke through the camp of the Philistines, drew water from the well of Bethlehem that was by the gate, and brought it to David. But he would not drink of it; he poured it out to the LORD, 17for he said, "The LORD forbid that I should do this. Can I drink the blood of the men who went at the risk of their lives?" Therefore he would not drink it. The three warriors did these things.

---

f 23:5 My safety and success, literally, "He will cause my help and my desire to sprout."

g Q Ms: MT who was raised on high   h Heb But worthlessness   i Heb in sitting   j Gk Vg Compare 1 Chr 11:11: Meaning of Heb uncertain   k 1 Chr 11:11: Meaning of Heb uncertain   l Heb adds head

King James

18And Abishai, the brother of Joab, the son of Zeruiah, was chief among three. And he lifted up his spear
against three hundred, *and* slew *them,* and had the name
among three.

19Was he not most honourable of three? therefore he
was their captain: howbeit he attained not unto the *first*
three.

20And Benaiah the son of Jehoiada, the son of a valiant man, of Kabzeel, who had done many acts, he slew
two lionlike men of Moab: he went down also and slew
a lion in the midst of a pit in time of snow:

21And he slew an Egyptian, a goodly man: and the
Egyptian had a spear in his hand; but he went down to
him with a staff, and plucked the spear out of the Egyptian's hand, and slew him with his own spear.

22These *things* did Benaiah the son of Jehoiada, and
had the name among three mighty men.

23He was more honourable than the thirty, but he
attained not to the *first* three. And David set him over
his guard.

24Asahel the brother of Joab *was* one of the thirty;
Elhanan the son of Dodo of Bethlehem,

25Shammah the Harodite, Elika the Harodite,

26Helez the Paltite, Ira the son of Ikkesh the Tekoite,

27Abiezer the Anethothite, Mebunnai the Hushathite,

28Zalmon the Ahohite, Maharai the Netophathite,

29Heleb the son of Baanah, a Netophathite, Ittai the
son of Ribai out of Gibeah of the children of Benjamin,

30Benaiah the Pirathonite, Hiddai of the brooks of
Gaash,

31Abi-albon the Arbathite, Azmaveth the Barhumite,

32Eliahba the Shaalbonite, of the sons of Jashen, Jonathan,

33Shammah the Hararite, Ahiam the son of Sharar the
Hararite,

34Eliphelet the son of Ahasbai, the son of the Maachathite, Eliam the son of Ahithophel the Gilonite,

35Hezrai the Carmelite, Paarai the Arbite,

36Igal the son of Nathan of Zobah, Bani the Gadite,

37Zelek the Ammonite, Nahari the Beerothite, armourbearer to Joab the son of Zeruiah,

38Ira an Ithrite, Gareb an Ithrite,

39Uriah the Hittite: thirty and seven in all.

24 AND AGAIN the anger of the LORD was kindled against Israel, and he moved David against
them to say, Go, number Israel and Judah.

2For the king said to Joab the captain of the host,
which *was* with him, Go now through all the tribes of
Israel, from Dan even to Beer-sheba, and number ye the
people, that I may know the number of the people.

New International

18Abishai the brother of Joab son of Zeruiah was chief
of the Three.[a] He raised his spear against three hundred
men, whom he killed, and so he became as famous as
the Three. 19Was he not held in greater honor than the
Three? He became their commander, even though he
was not included among them.

20Benaiah son of Jehoiada was a valiant fighter from
Kabzeel, who performed great exploits. He struck down
two of Moab's best men. He also went down into a pit
on a snowy day and killed a lion. 21And he struck down
a huge Egyptian. Although the Egyptian had a spear in
his hand, Benaiah went against him with a club. He
snatched the spear from the Egyptian's hand and killed
him with his own spear. 22Such were the exploits of
Benaiah son of Jehoiada; he too was as famous as the
three mighty men. 23He was held in greater honor than
any of the Thirty, but he was not included among the
Three. And David put him in charge of his bodyguard.

24Among the Thirty were:
    Asahel the brother of Joab,
    Elhanan son of Dodo from Bethlehem,
    25Shammah the Harodite,
    Elika the Harodite,
    26Helez the Paltite,
    Ira son of Ikkesh from Tekoa,
    27Abiezer from Anathoth,
    Mebunnai[b] the Hushathite,
    28Zalmon the Ahohite,
    Maharai the Netophathite,
    29Heled[c] son of Baanah the Netophathite,
    Ithai son of Ribai from Gibeah in Benjamin,
    30Benaiah the Pirathonite,
    Hiddai[d] from the ravines of Gaash,
    31Abi-Albon the Arbathite,
    Azmaveth the Barhumite,
    32Eliahba the Shaalbonite,
    the sons of Jashen,
    Jonathan 33son of[e] Shammah the Hararite,
    Ahiam son of Sharar[f] the Hararite,
    34Eliphelet son of Ahasbai the Maacathite,
    Eliam son of Ahithophel the Gilonite,
    35Hezro the Carmelite,
    Paarai the Arbite,
    36Igal son of Nathan from Zobah,
    the son of Hagri,[g]
    37Zelek the Ammonite,
    Naharai the Beerothite, the armor-bearer of Joab
        son of Zeruiah,
    38Ira the Ithrite,
    Gareb the Ithrite
    39and Uriah the Hittite.
    There were thirty-seven in all.

David Counts the Fighting Men

24 AGAIN THE anger of the LORD burned against
Israel, and he incited David against them, saying, "Go and take a census of Israel and Judah."

2So the king said to Joab and the army commanders[h]
with him, "Go throughout the tribes of Israel from Dan
to Beersheba and enroll the fighting men, so that I may
know how many there are."

---

a *18* Most Hebrew manuscripts (see also 1 Chron. 11:20); two Hebrew
manuscripts and Syriac *Thirty*   b *27* Hebrew; some Septuagint manuscripts
(see also 1 Chron. 11:29) *Sibbecai*   c *29* Some Hebrew manuscripts and
Vulgate (see also 1 Chron. 11:30); most Hebrew manuscripts *Heleb*
d *30* Hebrew; some Septuagint manuscripts (see also 1 Chron. 11:32) *Hurai*
e *33* Some Septuagint manuscripts (see also 1 Chron. 11:34); Hebrew does
not have *son of.*   f *33* Hebrew; some Septuagint manuscripts (see also
1 Chron. 11:35) *Sacar*   g *36* Some Septuagint manuscripts (see also 1 Chron.
11:38); Hebrew *Haggadi*   h *2* Septuagint (see also verse 4 and 1 Chron.
21:2); Hebrew *Joab the army commander*

Living Bible

18, 19Of those three men, Abishai, the brother of Joab (son of Zeruiah), was the greatest. Once he took on three hundred of the enemy singlehanded and killed them all. It was by such feats that he earned a reputation equal to The Three, though he was not actually one of them. But he was the greatest of The Thirty—the top-ranking officers of the army—and was their leader.

20There was also Benaiah (son of Jehoiada), a heroic soldier from Kabzeel. Benaiah killed two giants,i sons of Ariel of Moab. Another time he went down into a pit and, despite the slippery snow on the ground, took on a lion that was caught there and killed it. 21Another time, armed only with a staff, he killed an Egyptian warrior who was armed with a spear; he wrenched the spear from the Egyptian's hand and killed him with it. 22These were some of the deeds that gave Benaiah almost as much renown as the Top Three. 23He was one of the greatest of The Thirty, but was not actually one of the Top Three. And David made him chief of his bodyguard.

24-39Asahel, the brother of Joab, was also one of The Thirty. Others were:

Elhanan (son of Dodo) from Bethlehem;
Shammah from Harod;
Elika from Harod;
Helez from Palti;
Ira (son of Ikkesh) from Tekoa;
Abi-ezer from Anathoth;
Mebunnai from Hushath;
Zalmon from Ahoh;
Maharai from Netophah;
Heleb (son of Baanah) from Netophah;
Ittai (son of Ribai) from Gibe-ah, of the tribe of Benjamin;
Benaiah of Pirathon;
Hiddai from the brooks of Gaash;
Abi-albon from Arbath;
Azmaveth from Bahurim;
Eliahba from Sha-albon;
The sons of Jashen;
Jonathan;
Shammah from Harar;
Ahiam (the son of Sharar) from Harar;
Eliphelet (son of Ahasbai) from Maacah;
Eliam (the son of Ahithophel) from Gilo;
Hezro from Carmel;
Paarai from Arba;
Igal (son of Nathan) from Zobah;
Bani from Gad;
Zelek from Ammon;
Naharai from Be-eroth, the armor bearer of Joab (son of Zeruiah);
Ira from Ithra;
Gareb from Ithra;
Uriah the Hittite—thirty-sevenj in all.

24 ONCE AGAIN the anger of the Lord flared against Israel, and he caused David to harm them by taking a national census. "Go and count the people of Israel and Judah," the Lord told him.

2So the king said to Joab, commander-in-chief of his army, "Take a census of all the people from one end of the nation to the other, so that I will know how many of them there are."

New Revised Standard

18 Now Abishai son of Zeruiah, the brother of Joab, was chief of the Thirty.k With his spear he fought against three hundred men and killed them, and won a name beside the Three. 19He was the most renowned of the Thirty,l and became their commander; but he did not attain to the Three.

20 Benaiah son of Jehoiada was a valiant warriorm from Kabzeel, a doer of great deeds; he struck down two sons of Arieln of Moab. He also went down and killed a lion in a pit on a day when snow had fallen. 21And he killed an Egyptian, a handsome man. The Egyptian had a spear in his hand; but Benaiah went against him with a staff, snatched the spear out of the Egyptian's hand, and killed him with his own spear. 22Such were the things Benaiah son of Jehoiada did, and won a name beside the three warriors. 23He was renowned among the Thirty, but he did not attain to the Three. And David put him in charge of his bodyguard.

24 Among the Thirty were Asahel brother of Joab; Elhanan son of Dodo of Bethlehem; 25Shammah of Harod; Elika of Harod; 26Helez the Paltite; Ira son of Ikkesh of Tekoa; 27Abiezer of Anathoth; Mebunnai the Hushathite; 28Zalmon the Ahohite; Maharai of Netophah; 29Heleb son of Baanah of Netophah; Ittai son of Ribai of Gibeah of the Benjaminites; 30Benaiah of Pirathon; Hiddai of the torrents of Gaash; 31Abi-albon the Arbathite; Azmaveth of Bahurim; 32Eliahba of Shaalbon; the sons of Jashen: Jonathan 33son ofo Shammah the Hararite; Ahiam son of Sharar the Hararite; 34Eliphelet son of Ahasbai of Maacah; Eliam son of Ahithophel the Gilonite; 35Hezrop of Carmel; Paarai the Arbite; 36Igal son of Nathan of Zobah; Bani the Gadite; 37Zelek the Ammonite; Naharai of Beeroth, the armor-bearer of Joab son of Zeruiah; 38Ira the Ithrite; Gareb the Ithrite; 39Uriah the Hittite—thirty-seven in all.

David's Census of Israel and Judah

24 AGAIN THE anger of the LORD was kindled against Israel, and he incited David against them, saying, "Go, count the people of Israel and Judah." 2So the king said to Joab and the commanders of the army,q who were with him, "Go through all the tribes of Israel, from Dan to Beer-sheba, and take a census of the people, so that I may know how many there are." 3But Joab said to the king, "May the LORD

---

i 23:20 two giants. The meaning of the Hebrew word is uncertain. j 23:24-39 thirty-seven in all. The Thirty, plus the Top Three, plus Generals Joab, Abishai, Asahel and Benaiah. Apparently new names were elected to this hall of fame to replace those who died.

k Two Heb Mss Syr: MT Three l Syr Compare 1 Chr 11.25: Heb Was he the most renowned of the Three? m Another reading is the son of Ish-hai n Gk: Heb lacks sons of o Gk: Heb lacks son of p Another reading is Hezrai q 1 Chr 21.2 Gk: Heb to Joab the commander of the army

King James

3And Joab said unto the king, Now the LORD thy God add unto the people, how many soever they be, an hundredfold, and that the eyes of my lord the king may see *it:* but why doth my lord the king delight in this thing?

4Notwithstanding the king's word prevailed against Joab, and against the captains of the host. And Joab and the captains of the host went out from the presence of the king, to number the people of Israel.

5¶ And they passed over Jordan, and pitched in Aroer, on the right side of the city that *lieth* in the midst of the river of Gad, and toward Jazer:

6Then they came to Gilead, and to the land of Tahtimhodshi; and they came to Dan-jaan, and about to Zidon,

7And came to the strong hold of Tyre, and to all the cities of the Hivites, and of the Canaanites: and they went out to the south of Judah, *even* to Beer-sheba.

8So when they had gone through all the land, they came to Jerusalem at the end of nine months and twenty days.

9And Joab gave up the sum of the number of the people unto the king: and there were in Israel eight hundred thousand valiant men that drew the sword; and the men of Judah *were* five hundred thousand men.

10¶ And David's heart smote him after that he had numbered the people. And David said unto the LORD, I have sinned greatly in that I have done: and now, I beseech thee, O LORD, take away the iniquity of thy servant; for I have done very foolishly.

11For when David was up in the morning, the word of the LORD came unto the prophet Gad, David's seer, saying,

12Go and say unto David, Thus saith the LORD, I offer thee three *things;* choose thee one of them, that I may *do it* unto thee.

13So Gad came to David, and told him, and said unto him, Shall seven years of famine come unto thee in thy land? or wilt thou flee three months before thine enemies, while they pursue thee? or that there be three days' pestilence in thy land? now advise, and see what answer I shall return to him that sent me.

14And David said unto Gad, I am in a great strait: let us fall now into the hand of the LORD; for his mercies *are* great: and let me not fall into the hand of man.

15¶ So the LORD sent a pestilence upon Israel from the morning even to the time appointed: and there died of the people from Dan even to Beer-sheba seventy thousand men.

16And when the angel stretched out his hand upon Jerusalem to destroy it, the LORD repented him of the evil, and said to the angel that destroyed the people, It is enough: stay now thine hand. And the angel of the LORD was by the threshingplace of Araunah the Jebusite.

17And David spake unto the LORD when he saw the angel that smote the people, and said, Lo, I have sinned, and I have done wickedly: but these sheep, what have they done? let thine hand, I pray thee, be against me, and against my father's house.

18¶ And Gad came that day to David, and said unto him, Go up, rear an altar unto the LORD in the threshingfloor of Araunah the Jebusite.

19And David, according to the saying of Gad, went up as the LORD commanded.

20And Araunah looked, and saw the king and his servants coming on toward him: and Araunah went out, and bowed himself before the king on his face upon the ground.

21And Araunah said, Wherefore is my lord the king come to his servant? And David said, To buy the threshingfloor of thee, to build an altar unto the LORD, that the plague may be stayed from the people.

22And Araunah said unto David, Let my lord the king take and offer up what *seemeth* good unto him: behold, *here be* oxen for burnt sacrifice, and threshing instruments and *other* instruments of the oxen for wood.

New International

3But Joab replied to the king, "May the LORD your God multiply the troops a hundred times over, and may the eyes of my lord the king see it. But why does my lord the king want to do such a thing?"

4The king's word, however, overruled Joab and the army commanders; so they left the presence of the king to enroll the fighting men of Israel.

5After crossing the Jordan, they camped near Aroer, south of the town in the gorge, and then went through Gad and on to Jazer. 6They went to Gilead and the region of Tahtim Hodshi, and on to Dan Jaan and around toward Sidon. 7Then they went toward the fortress of Tyre and all the towns of the Hivites and Canaanites. Finally, they went on to Beersheba in the Negev of Judah.

8After they had gone through the entire land, they came back to Jerusalem at the end of nine months and twenty days.

9Joab reported the number of the fighting men to the king: In Israel there were eight hundred thousand able-bodied men who could handle a sword, and in Judah five hundred thousand.

10David was conscience-stricken after he had counted the fighting men, and he said to the LORD, "I have sinned greatly in what I have done. Now, O LORD, I beg you, take away the guilt of your servant. I have done a very foolish thing."

11Before David got up the next morning, the word of the LORD had come to Gad the prophet, David's seer: 12"Go and tell David, 'This is what the LORD says: I am giving you three options. Choose one of them for me to carry out against you.'"

13So Gad went to David and said to him, "Shall there come upon you three[a] years of famine in your land? Or three months of fleeing from your enemies while they pursue you? Or three days of plague in your land? Now then, think it over and decide how I should answer the one who sent me."

14David said to Gad, "I am in deep distress. Let us fall into the hands of the LORD, for his mercy is great; but do not let me fall into the hands of men."

15So the LORD sent a plague on Israel from that morning until the end of the time designated, and seventy thousand of the people from Dan to Beersheba died. 16When the angel stretched out his hand to destroy Jerusalem, the LORD was grieved because of the calamity and said to the angel who was afflicting the people, "Enough! Withdraw your hand." The angel of the LORD was then at the threshing floor of Araunah the Jebusite.

17When David saw the angel who was striking down the people, he said to the LORD, "I am the one who has sinned and done wrong. These are but sheep. What have they done? Let your hand fall upon me and my family."

David Builds an Altar

18On that day Gad went to David and said to him, "Go up and build an altar to the LORD on the threshing floor of Araunah the Jebusite." 19So David went up, as the LORD had commanded through Gad. 20When Araunah looked and saw the king and his men coming toward him, he went out and bowed down before the king with his face to the ground.

21Araunah said, "Why has my lord the king come to his servant?"

"To buy your threshing floor," David answered, "so I can build an altar to the LORD, that the plague on the people may be stopped."

22Araunah said to David, "Let my lord the king take whatever pleases him and offer it up. Here are oxen for the burnt offering, and here are threshing sledges and ox yokes for the wood. 23O king, Araunah gives all this to

---

a 13 Septuagint (see also 1 Chron. 21:12); Hebrew *seven*

Living Bible

3But Joab replied, "God grant that you will live to see the day when there will be a hundred times as many people in your kingdom as there are now! But you have no right to rejoice in their strength."b

4But the king's command overcame Joab's remonstrance; so Joab and the other army officers went out to count the people of Israel. 5First they crossed the Jordan and camped at Aroer, south of the city that lies in the middle of the valley of Gad, near Jazer; 6then they went to Gilead in the land of Tahtim-hodshi and to Dan-jaan and around to Sidon; 7and then to the stronghold of Tyre, and all the cities of the Hivites and Canaanites, and south to Judah as far as Beer-sheba. 8Having gone through the entire land, they completed their task in nine months and twenty days. 9And Joab reported the number of the people to the king—800,000 men of conscription age in Israel and 500,000 in Judah.

10But after he had taken the census, David's conscience began to bother him, and he said to the Lord, "What I did was very wrong. Please forgive this foolish wickedness of mine."

11The next morning the word of the Lord came to the prophet Gad, who was David's contact with God.

The Lord said to Gad, 12"Tell David that I will give him three choices."

13So Gad came to David and asked him, "Will you choose seven years of famine across the land, or to flee for three months before your enemies, or to submit to three days of plague? Think this over and let me know what answer to give to God."

14"This is a hard decision," David replied, "but it is better to fall into the hand of the Lord (for his mercy is great) than into the hands of men."

15So the Lord sent a plague upon Israel that morning, and it lasted for three days; and seventy thousand men died throughout the nation. 16But as the death angel was preparing to destroy Jerusalem, the Lord was sorry for what was happening and told him to stop. He was by the threshing floor of Araunah the Jebusite at the time.

17When David saw the angel, he said to the Lord, "Look, I am the one who has sinned! What have these sheep done? Let your anger be only against me and my family."

18That day Gad came to David and said to him, "Go and build an altar to the Lord on the threshing floor of Araunah the Jebusite." 19So David went to do what the Lord had commanded him. 20When Araunah saw the king and his men coming towards him, he came forward and fell flat on the ground with his face in the dust.

21"Why have you come?" Araunah asked.

And David replied, "To buy your threshing floor, so that I can build an altar to the Lord, and he will stop the plague."

22"Use anything you like," Araunah told the king. "Here are oxen for the burnt offering, and you can use the threshing instruments and ox yokes for wood to build

New Revised Standard

your God increase the number of the people a hundredfold, while the eyes of my lord the king can still see it! But why does my lord the king want to do this?" 4But the king's word prevailed against Joab and the commanders of the army. So Joab and the commanders of the army went out from the presence of the king to take a census of the people of Israel. 5They crossed the Jordan, and began fromc Aroer and from the city that is in the middle of the valley, toward Gad and on to Jazer. 6Then they came to Gilead, and to Kadesh in the land of the Hittites;d and they came to Dan, and from Dane they went around to Sidon, 7and came to the fortress of Tyre and to all the cities of the Hivites and Canaanites; and they went out to the Negeb of Judah at Beer-sheba. 8So when they had gone through all the land, they came back to Jerusalem at the end of nine months and twenty days. 9Joab reported to the king the number of those who had been recorded: in Israel there were eight hundred thousand soldiers able to draw the sword, and those of Judah were five hundred thousand.

Judgment on David's Sin

10 But afterward, David was stricken to the heart because he had numbered the people. David said to the LORD, "I have sinned greatly in what I have done. But now, O LORD, I pray you, take away the guilt of your servant; for I have done very foolishly." 11When David rose in the morning, the word of the LORD came to the prophet Gad, David's seer, saying, 12"Go and say to David: Thus says the LORD: Three things I offerf you; choose one of them, and I will do it to you." 13So Gad came to David and told him; he asked him, "Shall threeg years of famine come to you on your land? Or will you flee three months before your foes while they pursue you? Or shall there be three days' pestilence in your land? Now consider, and decide what answer I shall return to the one who sent me." 14Then David said to Gad, "I am in great distress; let us fall into the hand of the LORD, for his mercy is great; but let me not fall into human hands."

15 So the LORD sent a pestilence on Israel from that morning until the appointed time; and seventy thousand of the people died, from Dan to Beer-sheba. 16But when the angel stretched out his hand toward Jerusalem to destroy it, the LORD relented concerning the evil, and said to the angel who was bringing destruction among the people, "It is enough; now stay your hand." The angel of the LORD was then by the threshing floor of Araunah the Jebusite. 17When David saw the angel who was destroying the people, he said to the LORD, "I alone have sinned, and I alone have done wickedly; but these sheep, what have they done? Let your hand, I pray, be against me and against my father's house."

David's Altar on the Threshing Floor

18 That day Gad came to David and said to him, "Go up and erect an altar to the LORD on the threshing floor of Araunah the Jebusite." 19Following Gad's instructions, David went up, as the LORD had commanded. 20When Araunah looked down, he saw the king and his servants coming toward him; and Araunah went out and prostrated himself before the king with his face to the ground. 21Araunah said, "Why has my lord the king come to his servant?" David said, "To buy the threshing floor from you in order to build an altar to the LORD, so that the plague may be averted from the people." 22Then Araunah said to David, "Let my lord the king take and offer up what seems good to him; here are the oxen for the burnt offering, and the threshing sledges and the yokes of the oxen for the wood. 23All this, O king,

b 24:3 you have no right to rejoice in their strength, literally, "But why does my lord the king delight in this thing?"

c Gk Mss: Heb encamped in Aroer south of   d Gk: Heb to the land of Tahtim-hodshi   e Cn Compare Gk: Heb they came to Dan-jaan and   f Or hold over   g 1 Chr 21.12 Gk: Heb seven

King James

23All these *things* did Araunah, *as* a king, give unto the king. And Araunah said unto the king, The LORD thy God accept thee.

24And the king said unto Araunah, Nay; but I will surely buy *it* of thee at a price: neither will I offer burnt offerings unto the LORD my God of that which doth cost me nothing. So David bought the threshingfloor and the oxen for fifty shekels of silver.

25And David built there an altar unto the LORD, and offered burnt offerings and peace offerings. So the LORD was entreated for the land, and the plague was stayed from Israel.

New International

the king." Araunah also said to him, "May the LORD your God accept you."

24But the king replied to Araunah, "No, I insist on paying you for it. I will not sacrifice to the LORD my God burnt offerings that cost me nothing."

So David bought the threshing floor and the oxen and paid fifty shekelsa of silver for them. 25David built an altar to the LORD there and sacrificed burnt offerings and fellowship offerings.b Then the LORD answered prayer in behalf of the land, and the plague on Israel was stopped.

---

a *24* That is, about 1 1/4 pounds (about 0.6 kilogram)　　b *25* Traditionally *peace offerings*

Living Bible

a fire on the altar. 23I will give it all to you, and may the Lord God accept your sacrifice."

24But the king said to Araunah, "No, I will not have it as a gift. I will buy it, for I don't want to offer to the Lord my God burnt offerings that have cost me nothing."

So David paid himc for the threshing floor and the oxen. 25And David built an altar there to the Lord and offered burnt offerings and peace offerings. And the Lord answered his prayer, and the plague was stopped.

New Revised Standard

Araunah gives to the king." And Araunah said to the king, "May the LORD your God respond favorably to you."

24 But the king said to Araunah, "No, but I will buy them from you for a price; I will not offer burnt offerings to the LORD my God that cost me nothing." So David bought the threshing floor and the oxen for fifty shekels of silver. 25David built there an altar to the LORD, and offered burnt offerings and offerings of well-being. So the LORD answered his supplication for the land, and the plague was averted from Israel.

---

c 24:24 So David paid him, literally, "paid him fifty shekels of silver."

THE FIRST BOOK OF THE

Kings

COMMONLY CALLED THE THIRD BOOK

OF THE KINGS

1 Kings

Adonijah Sets Himself Up as King

1 NOW KING David was old *and* stricken in years; and they covered him with clothes, but he gat no heat.

2Wherefore his servants said unto him, Let there be sought for my lord the king a young virgin: and let her stand before the king, and let her cherish him, and let her lie in thy bosom, that my lord the king may get heat.

3So they sought for a fair damsel throughout all the coasts of Israel, and found Abishag a Shunammite, and brought her to the king.

4And the damsel *was* very fair, and cherished the king, and ministered to him: but the king knew her not.

5¶ Then Adonijah the son of Haggith exalted himself, saying, I will be king: and he prepared him chariots and horsemen, and fifty men to run before him.

6And his father had not displeased him at any time in saying, Why hast thou done so? and he also *was a* very goodly *man;* and *his mother* bare him after Absalom.

7And he conferred with Joab the son of Zeruiah, and with Abiathar the priest: and they following Adonijah helped *him.*

8But Zadok the priest, and Benaiah the son of Jehoiada, and Nathan the prophet, and Shimei, and Rei, and the mighty men which *belonged* to David, were not with Adonijah.

9And Adonijah slew sheep and oxen and fat cattle by the stone of Zoheleth, which *is* by En-rogel, and called all his brethren the king's sons, and all the men of Judah the king's servants:

10But Nathan the prophet, and Benaiah, and the mighty men, and Solomon his brother, he called not.

11¶ Wherefore Nathan spake unto Bath-sheba the mother of Solomon, saying, Hast thou not heard that Adonijah the son of Haggith doth reign, and David our lord knoweth *it* not?

12Now therefore come, let me, I pray thee, give thee counsel, that thou mayest save thine own life, and the life of thy son Solomon.

13Go and get thee in unto king David, and say unto him, Didst not thou, my lord, O king, swear unto thine handmaid, saying, Assuredly Solomon thy son shall reign after me, and he shall sit upon my throne? why then doth Adonijah reign?

14Behold, while thou yet talkest there with the king, I also will come in after thee, and confirm thy words.

15¶ And Bath-sheba went in unto the king into the chamber: and the king was very old; and Abishag the Shunammite ministered unto the king.

16And Bath-sheba bowed, and did obeisance unto the king. And the king said, What wouldest thou?

17And she said unto him, My lord, thou swarest by the LORD thy God unto thine handmaid, *saying,* Assuredly Solomon thy son shall reign after me, and he shall sit upon my throne.

18And now, behold, Adonijah reigneth; and now, my lord the king, thou knowest *it* not:

1 WHEN KING David was old and well advanced in years, he could not keep warm even when they put covers over him. 2So his servants said to him, "Let us look for a young virgin to attend the king and take care of him. She can lie beside him so that our lord the king may keep warm."

3Then they searched throughout Israel for a beautiful girl and found Abishag, a Shunammite, and brought her to the king. 4The girl was very beautiful; she took care of the king and waited on him, but the king had no intimate relations with her.

5Now Adonijah, whose mother was Haggith, put himself forward and said, "I will be king." So he got chariots and horses[a] ready, with fifty men to run ahead of him. 6(His father had never interfered with him by asking, "Why do you behave as you do?" He was also very handsome and was born next after Absalom.)

7Adonijah conferred with Joab son of Zeruiah and with Abiathar the priest, and they gave him their support. 8But Zadok the priest, Benaiah son of Jehoiada, Nathan the prophet, Shimei and Rei[b] and David's special guard did not join Adonijah.

9Adonijah then sacrificed sheep, cattle and fattened calves at the Stone of Zoheleth near En Rogel. He invited all his brothers, the king's sons, and all the men of Judah who were royal officials, 10but he did not invite Nathan the prophet or Benaiah or the special guard or his brother Solomon.

11Then Nathan asked Bathsheba, Solomon's mother, "Have you not heard that Adonijah, the son of Haggith, has become king without our lord David's knowing it? 12Now then, let me advise you how you can save your own life and the life of your son Solomon. 13Go in to King David and say to him, 'My lord the king, did you not swear to me your servant: "Surely Solomon your son shall be king after me, and he will sit on my throne"? Why then has Adonijah become king?' 14While you are still there talking to the king, I will come in and confirm what you have said."

15So Bathsheba went to see the aged king in his room, where Abishag the Shunammite was attending him. 16Bathsheba bowed low and knelt before the king.

"What is it you want?" the king asked.

17She said to him, "My lord, you yourself swore to me your servant by the LORD your God: 'Solomon your son shall be king after me, and he will sit on my throne.' 18But now Adonijah has become king, and you, my lord the king, do not know about it. 19He has sacrificed great

a 5 Or *charioteers*   b 8 Or *and his friends*

Living Bible

1 Kings

1 IN HIS old age King David was confined to his bed; but no matter how many blankets were heaped upon him, he was always cold.

2"The cure for this," his aides told him, "is to find a young virgin to be your concubine and nurse. She will lie in your arms and keep you warm."

3, 4So they searched the country from one end to the other to find the most beautiful girl in all the land. Abishag, from Shunam, was finally selected. They brought her to the king and she lay in his arms to warm him (but he had no sexual relations with her).

5At about that time, David's son^c Adonijah (his mother was Haggith) decided to crown himself king in place of his aged father. So he hired chariots and drivers and recruited fifty men to run down the streets before him as royal footmen. 6Now his father, King David, had never disciplined him at any time—not so much as by a single scolding! He was a very handsome man, and was Absalom's younger brother. 7He took General Joab and Abiathar the priest into his confidence, and they agreed to help him become king. 8But among those who remained loyal to King David and refused to endorse Adonijah were the priests Zadok and Benaiah, the prophet Nathan, Shime-i, Rei, and David's army chiefs.

9Adonijah went to En-rogel where he sacrificed sheep, oxen, and fat young goats at the Serpent's Stone. Then he summoned all of his brothers—the other sons of King David—and all the royal officials of Judah, requesting that they come to his coronation. 10But he didn't invite Nathan the prophet, Benaiah, the loyal army officers, or his brother Solomon.

11Then Nathan the prophet went to Bath-sheba, Solomon's mother, and asked her, "Do you realize that Haggith's son, Adonijah, is now the king and that our lord David doesn't even know about it? 12If you want to save your own life and the life of your son Solomon—do exactly as I say! 13Go at once to King David and ask him, 'My lord, didn't you promise me that my son Solomon would be the next king and would sit upon your throne? Then why is Adonijah reigning?' 14And while you are still talking with him, I'll come and confirm everything you've said."

15So Bath-sheba went into the king's bedroom. He was an old, old man now, and Abishag was caring for him. 16Bath-sheba bowed low before him.

"What do you want?" he asked her.

17She replied, "My lord, you vowed to me by the Lord your God that my son Solomon would be the next king and would sit upon your throne. 18But instead, Adonijah is the new king, and you don't even know about it. 19He has celebrated his coronation by sacrific-

New Revised Standard

1 Kings

The Struggle for the Succession

1 KING DAVID was old and advanced in years; and although they covered him with clothes, he could not get warm. 2 So his servants said to him, "Let a young virgin be sought for my lord the king, and let her wait on the king, and be his attendant; let her lie in your bosom, so that my lord the king may be warm." 3 So they searched for a beautiful girl throughout all the territory of Israel, and found Abishag the Shunammite, and brought her to the king. 4 The girl was very beautiful. She became the king's attendant and served him, but the king did not know her sexually.

5 Now Adonijah son of Haggith exalted himself, saying, "I will be king"; he prepared for himself chariots and horsemen, and fifty men to run before him. 6 His father had never at any time displeased him by asking, "Why have you done thus and so?" He was also a very handsome man, and he was born next after Absalom. 7 He conferred with Joab son of Zeruiah and with the priest Abiathar, and they supported Adonijah. 8 But the priest Zadok, and Benaiah son of Jehoiada, and the prophet Nathan, and Shimei, and Rei, and David's own warriors did not side with Adonijah.

9 Adonijah sacrificed sheep, oxen, and fatted cattle by the stone Zoheleth, which is beside En-rogel, and he invited all his brothers, the king's sons, and all the royal officials of Judah, 10 but he did not invite the prophet Nathan or Benaiah or the warriors or his brother Solomon.

11 Then Nathan said to Bathsheba, Solomon's mother, "Have you not heard that Adonijah son of Haggith has become king and our lord David does not know it? 12 Now therefore come, let me give you advice, so that you may save your own life and the life of your son Solomon. 13 Go in at once to King David, and say to him, 'Did you not, my lord the king, swear to your servant, saying: Your son Solomon shall succeed me as king, and he shall sit on my throne? Why then is Adonijah king?' 14 Then while you are still there speaking with the king, I will come in after you and confirm your words."

15 So Bathsheba went to the king in his room. The king was very old; Abishag the Shunammite was attending the king. 16 Bathsheba bowed and did obeisance to the king, and the king said, "What do you wish?" 17 She said to him, "My lord, you swore to your servant by the LORD your God, saying: Your son Solomon shall succeed me as king, and he shall sit on my throne. 18 But now suddenly Adonijah has become king, though you, my lord the king, do not know it. 19 He has sacrificed

King James

19And he hath slain oxen and fat cattle and sheep in abundance, and hath called all the sons of the king, and Abiathar the priest, and Joab the captain of the host: but Solomon thy servant hath he not called.

20And thou, my lord, O king, the eyes of all Israel *are* upon thee, that thou shouldest tell them who shall sit on the throne of my lord the king after him.

21Otherwise it shall come to pass, when my lord the king shall sleep with his fathers, that I and my son Solomon shall be counted offenders.

22¶ And, lo, while she yet talked with the king, Nathan the prophet also came in.

23And they told the king, saying, Behold Nathan the prophet. And when he was come in before the king, he bowed himself before the king with his face to the ground.

24And Nathan said, My lord, O king, hast thou said, Adonijah shall reign after me, and he shall sit upon my throne?

25For he is gone down this day, and hath slain oxen and fat cattle and sheep in abundance, and hath called all the king's sons, and the captains of the host, and Abiathar the priest; and, behold, they eat and drink before him, and say, God save king Adonijah.

26But me, *even* me thy servant, and Zadok the priest, and Benaiah the son of Jehoiada, and thy servant Solomon, hath he not called.

27Is this thing done by my lord the king, and thou hast not showed *it* unto thy servant, who should sit on the throne of my lord the king after him?

28¶ Then king David answered and said, Call me Bath-sheba. And she came into the king's presence, and stood before the king.

29And the king sware, and said, As the LORD liveth, that hath redeemed my soul out of all distress,

30Even as I sware unto thee by the LORD God of Israel, saying, Assuredly Solomon thy son shall reign after me, and he shall sit upon my throne in my stead; even so will I certainly do this day.

31Then Bath-sheba bowed with *her* face to the earth, and did reverence to the king, and said, Let my lord king David live for ever.

32¶ And king David said, Call me Zadok the priest, and Nathan the prophet, and Benaiah the son of Jehoiada. And they came before the king.

33The king also said unto them, Take with you the servants of your lord, and cause Solomon my son to ride upon mine own mule, and bring him down to Gihon:

34And let Zadok the priest and Nathan the prophet anoint him there king over Israel: and blow ye with the trumpet, and say, God save king Solomon.

35Then ye shall come up after him, that he may come and sit upon my throne; for he shall be king in my stead: and I have appointed him to be ruler over Israel and over Judah.

36And Benaiah the son of Jehoiada answered the king, and said, Amen: the LORD God of my lord the king say so too.

37As the LORD hath been with my lord the king, even so be he with Solomon, and make his throne greater than the throne of my lord king David.

38So Zadok the priest, and Nathan the prophet, and Benaiah the son of Jehoiada, and the Cherethites, and the Pelethites, went down, and caused Solomon to ride upon king David's mule, and brought him to Gihon.

39And Zadok the priest took an horn of oil out of the tabernacle, and anointed Solomon. And they blew the trumpet; and all the people said, God save king Solomon.

40And all the people came up after him, and the people piped with pipes, and rejoiced with great joy, so that the earth rent with the sound of them.

New International

numbers of cattle, fattened calves, and sheep, and has invited all the king's sons, Abiathar the priest and Joab the commander of the army, but he has not invited Solomon your servant. 20My lord the king, the eyes of all Israel are on you, to learn from you who will sit on the throne of my lord the king after him. 21Otherwise, as soon as my lord the king is laid to rest with his fathers, I and my son Solomon will be treated as criminals."

22While she was still speaking with the king, Nathan the prophet arrived. 23And they told the king, "Nathan the prophet is here." So he went before the king and bowed with his face to the ground.

24Nathan said, "Have you, my lord the king, declared that Adonijah shall be king after you, and that he will sit on your throne? 25Today he has gone down and sacrificed great numbers of cattle, fattened calves, and sheep. He has invited all the king's sons, the commanders of the army and Abiathar the priest. Right now they are eating and drinking with him and saying, 'Long live King Adonijah!' 26But me your servant, and Zadok the priest, and Benaiah son of Jehoiada, and your servant Solomon he did not invite. 27Is this something my lord the king has done without letting his servants know who should sit on the throne of my lord the king after him?"

David Makes Solomon King

28Then King David said, "Call in Bathsheba." So she came into the king's presence and stood before him.

29The king then took an oath: "As surely as the LORD lives, who has delivered me out of every trouble, 30I will surely carry out today what I swore to you by the LORD, the God of Israel: Solomon your son shall be king after me, and he will sit on my throne in my place."

31Then Bathsheba bowed low with her face to the ground and, kneeling before the king, said, "May my lord King David live forever!"

32King David said, "Call in Zadok the priest, Nathan the prophet and Benaiah son of Jehoiada." When they came before the king, 33he said to them: "Take your lord's servants with you and set Solomon my son on my own mule and take him down to Gihon. 34There have Zadok the priest and Nathan the prophet anoint him king over Israel. Blow the trumpet and shout, 'Long live King Solomon!' 35Then you are to go up with him, and he is to come and sit on my throne and reign in my place. I have appointed him ruler over Israel and Judah."

36Benaiah son of Jehoiada answered the king, "Amen! May the LORD, the God of my lord the king, so declare it. 37As the LORD was with my lord the king, so may he be with Solomon to make his throne even greater than the throne of my lord King David!"

38So Zadok the priest, Nathan the prophet, Benaiah son of Jehoiada, the Kerethites and the Pelethites went down and put Solomon on King David's mule and escorted him to Gihon. 39Zadok the priest took the horn of oil from the sacred tent and anointed Solomon. Then they sounded the trumpet and all the people shouted, "Long live King Solomon!" 40And all the people went up after him, playing flutes and rejoicing greatly, so that the ground shook with the sound.

Living Bible

ing oxen, fat goats, and many sheep and has invited all your sons and Abiathar the priest and General Joab. But he didn't invite Solomon. 20And now, my lord the king, all Israel is waiting for your decision as to whether Adonijah is the one you have chosen to succeed you. 21If you don't act, my son Solomon and I will be arrested and executed as criminals as soon as you are dead."

22, 23While she was speaking, the king's aides told him, "Nathan the prophet is here to see you."

Nathan came in and bowed low before the king, 24and asked, "My lord, have you appointed Adonijah to be the next king? Is he the one you have selected to sit upon your throne? 25Today he celebrated his coronation by sacrificing oxen and fat goats and many sheep, and has invited your sons to attend the festivities. He also invited General Joab and Abiathar the priest; and they are feasting and drinking with him and shouting, 'Long live King Adonijah!' 26But Zadok the priest and Benaiah and Solomon and I weren't invited. 27Has this been done with your knowledge? For you haven't said a word as to which of your sons you have chosen to be the next king."

28"Call Bath-sheba," David said. So she came back in and stood before the king.

29And the king vowed, "As the Lord lives who has rescued me from every danger, 30I decree that your son Solomon shall be the next king and shall sit upon my throne, just as I swore to you before by the Lord God of Israel."

31Then Bath-sheba bowed low before him againa and exclaimed, "Oh, thank you, sir. May my lord the king live forever!"

32"Call Zadok the priest," the king ordered, "and Nathan the prophet, and Benaiah."

When they arrived, 33he said to them, "Take Solomon and my officers to Gihon. Solomon is to ride on my personal mule, 34and Zadok the priest and Nathan the prophet are to anoint him there as king of Israel. Then blow the trumpets and shout, 'Long live King Solomon!' 35When you bring him back here, place him upon my throne as the new king; for I have appointed him king of Israel and Judah."

36"Amen! Praise God!" replied Benaiah, and added, 37"May the Lord be with Solomon as he has been with you, and may God make Solomon's reign even greater than yours!"

38So Zadok the priest, Nathan the prophet, Benaiah, and David's bodyguard took Solomon to Gihon, riding on King David's own mule. 39At Gihon, Zadok took a flask of sacred oil from the Tabernacle and poured it over Solomon; and the trumpets were blown and all the people shouted, "Long live King Solomon!"

40Then they all returned with him to Jerusalem, making a joyous and noisy celebration all along the way.

New Revised Standard

oxen, fatted cattle, and sheep in abundance, and has invited all the children of the king, the priest Abiathar, and Joab the commander of the army; but your servant Solomon he has not invited. 20But you, my lord the king—the eyes of all Israel are on you to tell them who shall sit on the throne of my lord the king after him. 21Otherwise it will come to pass, when my lord the king sleeps with his ancestors, that my son Solomon and I will be counted offenders."

22 While she was still speaking with the king, the prophet Nathan came in. 23The king was told, "Here is the prophet Nathan." When he came in before the king, he did obeisance to the king, with his face to the ground. 24Nathan said, "My lord the king, have you said, 'Adonijah shall succeed me as king, and he shall sit on my throne'? 25For today he has gone down and has sacrificed oxen, fatted cattle, and sheep in abundance, and has invited all the king's children, Joab the commanderb of the army, and the priest Abiathar, who are now eating and drinking before him, and saying, 'Long live King Adonijah!' 26But he did not invite me, your servant, and the priest Zadok, and Benaiah son of Jehoiada, and your servant Solomon. 27Has this thing been brought about by my lord the king and you have not let your servants know who should sit on the throne of my lord the king after him?"

The Accession of Solomon

28 King David answered, "Summon Bathsheba to me." So she came into the king's presence, and stood before the king. 29The king swore, saying, "As the LORD lives, who has saved my life from every adversity, 30as I swore to you by the LORD, the God of Israel, 'Your son Solomon shall succeed me as king, and he shall sit on my throne in my place,' so will I do this day." 31Then Bathsheba bowed with her face to the ground, and did obeisance to the king, and said, "May my lord King David live forever!"

32 King David said, "Summon to me the priest Zadok, the prophet Nathan, and Benaiah son of Jehoiada." When they came before the king, 33the king said to them, "Take with you the servants of your lord, and have my son Solomon ride on my own mule, and bring him down to Gihon. 34There let the priest Zadok and the prophet Nathan anoint him king over Israel; then blow the trumpet, and say, 'Long live King Solomon!' 35You shall go up following him. Let him enter and sit on my throne; he shall be king in my place; for I have appointed him to be ruler over Israel and over Judah." 36Benaiah son of Jehoiada answered the king, "Amen! May the LORD, the God of my lord the king, so ordain. 37As the LORD has been with my lord the king, so may he be with Solomon, and make his throne greater than the throne of my lord King David."

38 So the priest Zadok, the prophet Nathan, and Benaiah son of Jehoiada, and the Cherethites and the Pelethites, went down and had Solomon ride on King David's mule, and led him to Gihon. 39There the priest Zadok took the horn of oil from the tent and anointed Solomon. Then they blew the trumpet, and all the people said, "Long live King Solomon!" 40And all the people went up following him, playing on pipes and rejoicing with great joy, so that the earth quaked at their noise.

---

a 1:31 bowed low before him, literally, "did reverence to the king."   b Gk: Heb the commanders

King James

41¶ And Adonijah and all the guests that *were* with him heard *it* as they had made an end of eating. And when Joab heard the sound of the trumpet, he said, Wherefore *is this* noise of the city being in an uproar?

42And while he yet spake, behold, Jonathan the son of Abiathar the priest came: and Adonijah said unto him, Come in; for thou *art* a valiant man, and bringest good tidings.

43And Jonathan answered and said to Adonijah, Verily our lord king David hath made Solomon king.

44And the king hath sent with him Zadok the priest, and Nathan the prophet, and Benaiah the son of Jehoiada, and the Cherethites, and the Pelethites, and they have caused him to ride upon the king's mule:

45And Zadok the priest and Nathan the prophet have anointed him king in Gihon: and they are come up from thence rejoicing, so that the city rang again. This *is* the noise that ye have heard.

46And also Solomon sitteth on the throne of the kingdom.

47And moreover the king's servants came to bless our lord king David, saying, God make the name of Solomon better than thy name, and make his throne greater than thy throne. And the king bowed himself upon the bed.

48And also thus said the king, Blessed *be* the LORD God of Israel, which hath given *one* to sit on my throne this day, mine eyes even seeing *it*.

49And all the guests that *were* with Adonijah were afraid, and rose up, and went every man his way.

50¶ And Adonijah feared because of Solomon, and arose, and went, and caught hold on the horns of the altar.

51And it was told Solomon, saying, Behold, Adonijah feareth king Solomon: for, lo, he hath caught hold on the horns of the altar, saying, Let king Solomon swear unto me today that he will not slay his servant with the sword.

52And Solomon said, If he will show himself a worthy man, there shall not an hair of him fall to the earth: but if wickedness shall be found in him, he shall die.

53So king Solomon sent, and they brought him down from the altar. And he came and bowed himself to king Solomon: and Solomon said unto him, Go to thine house.

2 NOW THE days of David drew nigh that he should die; and he charged Solomon his son, saying,

2I go the way of all the earth: be thou strong therefore, and show thyself a man;

3And keep the charge of the LORD thy God, to walk in his ways, to keep his statutes, and his commandments, and his judgments, and his testimonies, as it is written in the law of Moses, that thou mayest prosper in all that thou doest, and whithersoever thou turnest thyself:

4That the LORD may continue his word which he spake concerning me, saying, If thy children take heed to their way, to walk before me in truth with all their heart and with all their soul, there shall not fail thee (said he) a man on the throne of Israel.

5Moreover thou knowest also what Joab the son of Zeruiah did to me, *and* what he did to the two captains of the hosts of Israel, unto Abner the son of Ner, and unto Amasa the son of Jether, whom he slew, and shed the blood of war in peace, and put the blood of war upon his girdle that *was* about his loins, and in his shoes that *were* on his feet.

6Do therefore according to thy wisdom, and let not his hoar head go down to the grave in peace.

New International

41Adonijah and all the guests who were with him heard it as they were finishing their feast. On hearing the sound of the trumpet, Joab asked, "What's the meaning of all the noise in the city?"

42Even as he was speaking, Jonathan son of Abiathar the priest arrived. Adonijah said, "Come in. A worthy man like you must be bringing good news."

43"Not at all!" Jonathan answered. "Our lord King David has made Solomon king. 44The king has sent with him Zadok the priest, Nathan the prophet, Benaiah son of Jehoiada, the Kerethites and the Pelethites, and they have put him on the king's mule, 45and Zadok the priest and Nathan the prophet have anointed him king at Gihon. From there they have gone up cheering, and the city resounds with it. That's the noise you hear. 46Moreover, Solomon has taken his seat on the royal throne. 47Also, the royal officials have come to congratulate our lord King David, saying, 'May your God make Solomon's name more famous than yours and his throne greater than yours!' And the king bowed in worship on his bed 48and said, 'Praise be to the LORD, the God of Israel, who has allowed my eyes to see a successor on my throne today.' "

49At this, all Adonijah's guests rose in alarm and dispersed. 50But Adonijah, in fear of Solomon, went and took hold of the horns of the altar. 51Then Solomon was told, "Adonijah is afraid of King Solomon and is clinging to the horns of the altar. He says, 'Let King Solomon swear to me today that he will not put his servant to death with the sword.' "

52Solomon replied, "If he shows himself to be a worthy man, not a hair of his head will fall to the ground; but if evil is found in him, he will die." 53Then King Solomon sent men, and they brought him down from the altar. And Adonijah came and bowed down to King Solomon, and Solomon said, "Go to your home."

David's Charge to Solomon

2 WHEN THE time drew near for David to die, he gave a charge to Solomon his son.

2"I am about to go the way of all the earth," he said. "So be strong, show yourself a man, 3and observe what the LORD your God requires: Walk in his ways, and keep his decrees and commands, his laws and requirements, as written in the Law of Moses, so that you may prosper in all you do and wherever you go, 4and that the LORD may keep his promise to me: 'If your descendants watch how they live, and if they walk faithfully before me with all their heart and soul, you will never fail to have a man on the throne of Israel.'

5"Now you yourself know what Joab son of Zeruiah did to me—what he did to the two commanders of Israel's armies, Abner son of Ner and Amasa son of Jether. He killed them, shedding their blood in peacetime as if in battle, and with that blood stained the belt around his waist and the sandals on his feet. 6Deal with him according to your wisdom, but do not let his gray head go down to the gravea in peace.

a 6 Hebrew *Sheol*; also in verse 9

Living Bible

41Adonijah and his guests heard the commotion and shouting just as they were finishing their banquet.

"What's going on?" Joab demanded. "Why is the city in such an uproar?"

42And while he was still speaking, Jonathan, the son of Abiathar the priest, rushed in.

"Come in," Adonijah said to him, "for you are a good man; you must have good news."

43"Our lord King David has declared Solomon as king!" Jonathan shouted. 44, 45"The king sent him to Gihon with Zadok the priest and Nathan the prophet and Benaiah, protected by the king's own bodyguard; and he rode on the king's own mule. And Zadok and Nathan have anointed him as the new king! They have just returned, and the whole city is celebrating and rejoicing. That's what all the noise is. 46, 47Solomon is sitting on the throne, and all the people are congratulating King David, saying, 'May God bless you even more through Solomon than he has blessed you personally! May God make Solomon's reign even greater than yours!' And the king is lying in bed, acknowledging their blessings. 48He is saying, 'Blessed be the Lord God of Israel who has selected one of my sons to sit upon my throne while I am still alive to see it.' "

49, 50Then Adonijah and his guests jumped up from the banquet table and fled in panic; for they were fearful for their lives. Adonijah rushed into the Tabernacle and caught hold of the horns of the sacred altar. 51When word reached Solomon that Adonijah was claiming sanctuary in the Tabernacle, and pleading for clemency, 52Solomon replied, "If he behaves himself, he will not be harmed; but if he does not, he shall die." 53So King Solomon summoned him, and they brought him down from the altar. He came to bow low before the king; and then Solomon curtly dismissed him.

"Go on home," he said.

2 AS THE time of King David's death approached, he gave this charge to his son Solomon:

2"I am going where every man on earth must some day go. I am counting on you to be a strong and worthy successor. 3Obey the laws of God and follow all his ways; keep each of his commands written in the law of Moses so that you will prosper in everything you do, wherever you turn. 4If you do this, then the Lord will fulfill the promise he gave me, that if my children and their descendants watch their step and are faithful to God, one of them shall always be the king of Israel—my dynasty will never end.

5"Now listen to my instructions. You know that Joab murdered my two generals, Abner and Amasa. He pretended that it was an act of war, but it was done in a time of peace. 6You are a wise man and will know what to do—don't let him die in peace. 7But be kind to the sons

New Revised Standard

41 Adonijah and all the guests who were with him heard it as they finished feasting. When Joab heard the sound of the trumpet, he said, "Why is the city in an uproar?" 42While he was still speaking, Jonathan son of the priest Abiathar arrived. Adonijah said, "Come in, for you are a worthy man and surely you bring good news." 43 Jonathan answered Adonijah, "No, for our lord King David has made Solomon king; 44the king has sent with him the priest Zadok, the prophet Nathan, and Benaiah son of Jehoiada, and the Cherethites and the Pelethites; and they had him ride on the king's mule; 45the priest Zadok and the prophet Nathan have anointed him king at Gihon; and they have gone up from there rejoicing, so that the city is in an uproar. This is the noise that you heard. 46Solomon now sits on the royal throne. 47Moreover the king's servants came to congratulate our lord King David, saying, 'May God make the name of Solomon more famous than yours, and make his throne greater than your throne.' The king bowed in worship on the bed 48and went on to pray thus, 'Blessed be the LORD, the God of Israel, who today has granted one of my offspringb to sit on my throne and permitted me to witness it.' "

49 Then all the guests of Adonijah got up trembling and went their own ways. 50Adonijah, fearing Solomon, got up and went to grasp the horns of the altar. 51Solomon was informed, "Adonijah is afraid of King Solomon; see, he has laid hold of the horns of the altar, saying, 'Let King Solomon swear to me first that he will not kill his servant with the sword.' " 52So Solomon responded, "If he proves to be a worthy man, not one of his hairs shall fall to the ground; but if wickedness is found in him, he shall die." 53 Then King Solomon sent to have him brought down from the altar. He came to do obeisance to King Solomon; and Solomon said to him, "Go home."

David's Instruction to Solomon

2 WHEN DAVID'S time to die drew near, he charged his son Solomon, saying: 2"I am about to go the way of all the earth. Be strong, be courageous, 3and keep the charge of the LORD your God, walking in his ways and keeping his statutes, his commandments, his ordinances, and his testimonies, as it is written in the law of Moses, so that you may prosper in all that you do and wherever you turn. 4Then the LORD will establish his word that he spoke concerning me: 'If your heirs take heed to their way, to walk before me in faithfulness with all their heart and with all their soul, there shall not fail you a successor on the throne of Israel.'

5 "Moreover you know also what Joab son of Zeruiah did to me, how he dealt with the two commanders of the armies of Israel, Abner son of Ner, and Amasa son of Jether, whom he murdered, retaliating in time of peace for blood that had been shed in war, and putting the blood of war on the belt around his waist, and on the sandals on his feet. 6Act therefore according to your wisdom, but do not let his gray head go down to Sheol in peace. 7Deal loyally, however, with the sons of Bar-

b Gk: Heb one

King James

7But show kindness unto the sons of Barzillai the Gileadite, and let them be of those that eat at thy table: for so they came to me when I fled because of Absalom thy brother.

8And, behold, *thou hast* with thee Shimei the son of Gera, a Benjamite of Bahurim, which cursed me with a grievous curse in the day when I went to Mahanaim: but he came down to meet me at Jordan, and I sware to him by the LORD, saying, I will not put thee to death with the sword.

9Now therefore hold him not guiltless: for thou *art* a wise man, and knowest what thou oughtest to do unto him; but his hoar head bring thou down to the grave with blood.

10So David slept with his fathers, and was buried in the city of David.

11And the days that David reigned over Israel *were* forty years: seven years reigned he in Hebron, and thirty and three years reigned he in Jerusalem.

12¶ Then sat Solomon upon the throne of David his father; and his kingdom was established greatly.

13¶ And Adonijah the son of Haggith came to Bathsheba the mother of Solomon. And she said, Comest thou peaceably? And he said, Peaceably.

14He said moreover, I have somewhat to say unto thee. And she said, Say on.

15And he said, Thou knowest that the kingdom was mine, and *that* all Israel set their faces on me, that I should reign: howbeit the kingdom is turned about, and is become my brother's: for it was his from the LORD.

16And now I ask one petition of thee, deny me not. And she said unto him, Say on.

17And he said, Speak, I pray thee, unto Solomon the king, (for he will not say thee nay,) that he give me Abishag the Shunammite to wife.

18And Bath-sheba said, Well; I will speak for thee unto the king.

19¶ Bath-sheba therefore went unto king Solomon, to speak unto him for Adonijah. And the king rose up to meet her, and bowed himself unto her, and sat down on his throne, and caused a seat to be set for the king's mother; and she sat on his right hand.

20Then she said, I desire one small petition of thee; *I pray thee,* say me not nay. And the king said unto her, Ask on, my mother: for I will not say thee nay.

21And she said, Let Abishag the Shunammite be given to Adonijah thy brother to wife.

22And king Solomon answered and said unto his mother, And why dost thou ask Abishag the Shunammite for Adonijah? ask for him the kingdom also; for he *is* mine elder brother; even for him, and for Abiathar the priest, and for Joab the son of Zeruiah.

23Then king Solomon sware by the LORD, saying, God do so to me, and more also, if Adonijah have not spoken this word against his own life.

24Now therefore, *as* the LORD liveth, which hath established me, and set me on the throne of David my father, and who hath made me an house, as he promised, Adonijah shall be put to death this day.

25And king Solomon sent by the hand of Benaiah the son of Jehoiada; and he fell upon him that he died.

26¶ And unto Abiathar the priest said the king, Get thee to Anathoth, unto thine own fields; for thou *art* worthy of death: but I will not at this time put thee to death, because thou barest the ark of the Lord GOD before David my father, and because thou hast been afflicted in all wherein my father was afflicted.

27So Solomon thrust out Abiathar from being priest unto the LORD; that he might fulfil the word of the LORD, which he spake concerning the house of Eli in Shiloh.

28¶ Then tidings came to Joab: for Joab had turned after Adonijah, though he turned not after Absalom. And Joab fled unto the tabernacle of the LORD, and caught hold on the horns of the altar.

New International

7"But show kindness to the sons of Barzillai of Gilead and let them be among those who eat at your table. They stood by me when I fled from your brother Absalom.

8"And remember, you have with you Shimei son of Gera, the Benjamite from Bahurim, who called down bitter curses on me the day I went to Mahanaim. When he came down to meet me at the Jordan, I swore to him by the LORD: 'I will not put you to death by the sword.' 9But now, do not consider him innocent. You are a man of wisdom; you will know what to do to him. Bring his gray head down to the grave in blood."

10Then David rested with his fathers and was buried in the City of David. 11He had reigned forty years over Israel—seven years in Hebron and thirty-three in Jerusalem. 12So Solomon sat on the throne of his father David, and his rule was firmly established.

Solomon's Throne Established

13Now Adonijah, the son of Haggith, went to Bathsheba, Solomon's mother. Bathsheba asked him, "Do you come peacefully?"

He answered, "Yes, peacefully." 14Then he added, "I have something to say to you."

"You may say it," she replied.

15"As you know," he said, "the kingdom was mine. All Israel looked to me as their king. But things changed, and the kingdom has gone to my brother; for it has come to him from the LORD. 16Now I have one request to make of you. Do not refuse me."

"You may make it," she said.

17So he continued, "Please ask King Solomon—he will not refuse you—to give me Abishag the Shunammite as my wife."

18"Very well," Bathsheba replied, "I will speak to the king for you."

19When Bathsheba went to King Solomon to speak to him for Adonijah, the king stood up to meet her, bowed down to her and sat down on his throne. He had a throne brought for the king's mother, and she sat down at his right hand.

20"I have one small request to make of you," she said. "Do not refuse me."

The king replied, "Make it, my mother; I will not refuse you."

21So she said, "Let Abishag the Shunammite be given in marriage to your brother Adonijah."

22King Solomon answered his mother, "Why do you request Abishag the Shunammite for Adonijah? You might as well request the kingdom for him—after all, he is my older brother—yes, for him and for Abiathar the priest and Joab son of Zeruiah!"

23Then King Solomon swore by the LORD: "May God deal with me, be it ever so severely, if Adonijah does not pay with his life for this request! 24And now, as surely as the LORD lives—he who has established me securely on the throne of my father David and has founded a dynasty for me as he promised—Adonijah shall be put to death today!" 25So King Solomon gave orders to Benaiah son of Jehoiada, and he struck down Adonijah and he died.

26To Abiathar the priest the king said, "Go back to your fields in Anathoth. You deserve to die, but I will not put you to death now, because you carried the ark of the Sovereign LORD before my father David and shared all my father's hardships." 27So Solomon removed Abiathar from the priesthood of the LORD, fulfilling the word the LORD had spoken at Shiloh about the house of Eli.

28When the news reached Joab, who had conspired with Adonijah though not with Absalom, he fled to the tent of the LORD and took hold of the horns of the altar.

Living Bible

of Barzillai the Gileadite. Make them permanent guests of the king, for they took care of me when I fled from your brother Absalom. 8And do you remember Shime-i, the son of Gera the Benjaminite from Bahurim? He cursed me with a terrible curse as I was going to Mahanaim; but when he came down to meet me at the Jordan River I promised I wouldn't kill him. 9But that promise doesn't bind you! You are a wise man, and you will know how to arrange a bloody death for him."

10Then David died and was buried in Jerusalem. 11He had reigned over Israel for forty years, seven of them in Hebron and thirty-three in Jerusalem. 12And Solomon became the new king, replacing his father David; and his kingdom prospered.

13One day Adonijah the son of Haggith came to see Solomon's mother, Bath-sheba.

"Have you come to make trouble?" she asked him.

"No," he replied, "I come in peace. 14As a matter of fact, I have a favor to ask of you."

"What is it?" she asked.

15"Everything was going well for me," he said, "and the kingdom was mine: everyone expected me to be the next king. But the tables are turned, and everything went to my brother instead; for that is the way the Lord wanted it. 16But now I have just a small favor to ask of you; please don't turn me down."

"What is it?" she asked.

17He replied, "Speak to King Solomon on my behalf (for I know he will do anything you request) and ask him to give me Abishag, the Shunammite, as my wife."

18"All right," Bath-sheba replied, "I'll ask him."

19So she went to ask the favor of King Solomon. The king stood up from his throne as she entered and bowed low to her. He ordered that a throne for his mother be placed beside his; so she sat at his right hand.

20"I have one small request to make of you," she said. "I hope you won't turn me down."

"What is it, my mother?" he asked. "You know I won't refuse you."

21"Then let your brother Adonijah marry Abishag," she replied.

22"Are you crazy?" he demanded. "If I were to give him Abishag, I would be giving him the kingdom too! For he is my older brother! He and Abiathar the priest and General Joab would take over!" 23, 24Then King Solomon swore with a great oath, "May God strike me dead if Adonijah does not die this very day for this plot against me! I swear it by the living God who has given me the throne of my father David and this kingdom he promised me."

25So King Solomon sent Benaiah to execute him, and he killed him with a sword.

26Then the king said to Abiathar the priest, "Go back to your home in Anathoth. You should be killed, too, but I won't do it now. For you carried the Ark of the Lord during my father's reign, and you suffered right along with him in all of his troubles."

27So Solomon forced Abiathar to give up his position as the priest of the Lord, thereby fulfilling the decree of Jehovah at Shiloh concerning the descendants of Eli.[a]

28When Joab heard about Adonijah's death (Joab had joined Adonijah's revolt, though not Absalom's) he ran to the Tabernacle for sanctuary and caught hold of the

New Revised Standard

zillai the Gileadite, and let them be among those who eat at your table; for with such loyalty they met me when I fled from your brother Absalom. 8 There is also with you Shimei son of Gera, the Benjaminite from Bahurim, who cursed me with a terrible curse on the day when I went to Mahanaim; but when he came down to meet me at the Jordan, I swore to him by the LORD, 'I will not put you to death with the sword.' 9 Therefore do not hold him guiltless, for you are a wise man; you will know what you ought to do to him, and you must bring his gray head down with blood to Sheol."

Death of David

10 Then David slept with his ancestors, and was buried in the city of David. 11 The time that David reigned over Israel was forty years; he reigned seven years in Hebron, and thirty-three years in Jerusalem. 12 So Solomon sat on the throne of his father David; and his kingdom was firmly established.

Solomon Consolidates His Reign

13 Then Adonijah son of Haggith came to Bathsheba, Solomon's mother. She asked, "Do you come peaceably?" He said, "Peaceably." 14 Then he said, "May I have a word with you?" She said, "Go on." 15 He said, "You know that the kingdom was mine, and that all Israel expected me to reign; however, the kingdom has turned about and become my brother's, for it was his from the LORD. 16 And now I have one request to make of you; do not refuse me." She said to him, "Go on." 17 He said, "Please ask King Solomon—he will not refuse you—to give me Abishag the Shunammite as my wife." 18 Bathsheba said, "Very well; I will speak to the king on your behalf."

19 So Bathsheba went to King Solomon, to speak to him on behalf of Adonijah. The king rose to meet her, and bowed down to her; then he sat on his throne, and had a throne brought for the king's mother, and she sat on his right. 20 Then she said, "I have one small request to make of you; do not refuse me." And the king said to her, "Make your request, my mother; for I will not refuse you." 21 She said, "Let Abishag the Shunammite be given to your brother Adonijah as his wife." 22 King Solomon answered his mother, "And why do you ask Abishag the Shunammite for Adonijah? Ask for him the kingdom as well! For he is my elder brother; ask not only for him but also for the priest Abiathar and for Joab son of Zeruiah!" 23 Then King Solomon swore by the LORD, "So may God do to me, and more also, for Adonijah has devised this scheme at the risk of his life! 24 Now therefore as the LORD lives, who has established me and placed me on the throne of my father David, and who has made me a house as he promised, today Adonijah shall be put to death." 25 So King Solomon sent Benaiah son of Jehoiada; he struck him down, and he died.

26 The king said to the priest Abiathar, "Go to Anathoth, to your estate; for you deserve death. But I will not at this time put you to death, because you carried the ark of the Lord GOD before my father David, and because you shared in all the hardships my father endured." 27 So Solomon banished Abiathar from being priest to the LORD, thus fulfilling the word of the LORD that he had spoken concerning the house of Eli in Shiloh.

28 When the news came to Joab—for Joab had supported Adonijah though he had not supported Absalom—Joab fled to the tent of the LORD and grasped the horns of the altar. 29 When it was told King Solomon,

---

a 2:27 See 1 Sam 2:31-35.

King James

29And it was told king Solomon that Joab was fled unto the tabernacle of the LORD; and, behold, *he is* by the altar. Then Solomon sent Benaiah the son of Jehoiada, saying, Go, fall upon him.

30And Benaiah came to the tabernacle of the LORD, and said unto him, Thus saith the king, Come forth. And he said, Nay; but I will die here. And Benaiah brought the king word again, saying, Thus said Joab, and thus he answered me.

31And the king said unto him, Do as he hath said, and fall upon him, and bury him; that thou mayest take away the innocent blood, which Joab shed, from me, and from the house of my father.

32And the LORD shall return his blood upon his own head, who fell upon two men more righteous and better than he, and slew them with the sword, my father David not knowing *thereof, to wit*, Abner the son of Ner, captain of the host of Israel, and Amasa the son of Jether, captain of the host of Judah.

33Their blood shall therefore return upon the head of Joab, and upon the head of his seed for ever: but upon David, and upon his seed, and upon his house, and upon his throne, shall there be peace for ever from the LORD.

34So Benaiah the son of Jehoiada went up, and fell upon him, and slew him: and he was buried in his own house in the wilderness.

35¶ And the king put Benaiah the son of Jehoiada in his room over the host: and Zadok the priest did the king put in the room of Abiathar.

36¶ And the king sent and called for Shimei, and said unto him, Build thee an house in Jerusalem, and dwell there, and go not forth thence any whither.

37For it shall be, *that* on the day thou goest out, and passest over the brook Kidron, thou shalt know for certain that thou shalt surely die: thy blood shall be upon thine own head.

38And Shimei said unto the king, The saying *is* good: as my lord the king hath said, so will thy servant do. And Shimei dwelt in Jerusalem many days.

39And it came to pass at the end of three years, that two of the servants of Shimei ran away unto Achish son of Maachah king of Gath. And they told Shimei, saying, Behold, thy servants *be* in Gath.

40And Shimei arose, and saddled his ass, and went to Gath to Achish to seek his servants: and Shimei went, and brought his servants from Gath.

41And it was told Solomon that Shimei had gone from Jerusalem to Gath, and was come again.

42And the king sent and called for Shimei, and said unto him, Did I not make thee to swear by the LORD, and protested unto thee, saying, Know for a certain, on the day thou goest out, and walkest abroad any whither, that thou shalt surely die? and thou saidst unto me, The word *that* I have heard *is* good.

43Why then hast thou not kept the oath of the LORD, and the commandment that I have charged thee with?

44The king said moreover to Shimei, Thou knowest all the wickedness which thine heart is privy to, that thou didst to David my father: therefore the LORD shall return thy wickedness upon thine own head;

45And king Solomon *shall be* blessed, and the throne of David shall be established before the LORD for ever.

46So the king commanded Benaiah the son of Jehoiada; which went out, and fell upon him, that he died. And the kingdom was established in the hand of Solomon.

New International

29King Solomon was told that Joab had fled to the tent of the LORD and was beside the altar. Then Solomon ordered Benaiah son of Jehoiada, "Go, strike him down!"

30So Benaiah entered the tent of the LORD and said to Joab, "The king says, 'Come out!' "

But he answered, "No, I will die here."

Benaiah reported to the king, "This is how Joab answered me."

31Then the king commanded Benaiah, "Do as he says. Strike him down and bury him, and so clear me and my father's house of the guilt of the innocent blood that Joab shed. 32The LORD will repay him for the blood he shed, because without the knowledge of my father David he attacked two men and killed them with the sword. Both of them—Abner son of Ner, commander of Israel's army, and Amasa son of Jether, commander of Judah's army—were better men and more upright than he. 33May the guilt of their blood rest on the head of Joab and his descendants forever. But on David and his descendants, his house and his throne, may there be the LORD's peace forever."

34So Benaiah son of Jehoiada went up and struck down Joab and killed him, and he was buried on his own landa in the desert. 35The king put Benaiah son of Jehoiada over the army in Joab's position and replaced Abiathar with Zadok the priest.

36Then the king sent for Shimei and said to him, "Build yourself a house in Jerusalem and live there, but do not go anywhere else. 37The day you leave and cross the Kidron Valley, you can be sure you will die; your blood will be on your own head."

38Shimei answered the king, "What you say is good. Your servant will do as my lord the king has said." And Shimei stayed in Jerusalem for a long time.

39But three years later, two of Shimei's slaves ran off to Achish son of Maacah, king of Gath, and Shimei was told, "Your slaves are in Gath." 40At this, he saddled his donkey and went to Achish at Gath in search of his slaves. So Shimei went away and brought the slaves back from Gath.

41When Solomon was told that Shimei had gone from Jerusalem to Gath and had returned, 42the king summoned Shimei and said to him, "Did I not make you swear by the LORD and warn you, 'On the day you leave to go anywhere else, you can be sure you will die'? At that time you said to me, 'What you say is good. I will obey.' 43Why then did you not keep your oath to the LORD and obey the command I gave you?"

44The king also said to Shimei, "You know in your heart all the wrong you did to my father David. Now the LORD will repay you for your wrongdoing. 45But King Solomon will be blessed, and David's throne will remain secure before the LORD forever."

46Then the king gave the order to Benaiah son of Jehoiada, and he went out and struck Shimei down and killed him.

The kingdom was now firmly established in Solomon's hands.

---

a 34 Or *buried in his tomb*

Living Bible

horns of the altar. 29When news of this reached King Solomon, he sent Benaiah to execute him.

30Benaiah went into the Tabernacle and said to Joab, "The king says to come out!"

"No," he said, "I'll die here."

So Benaiah returned to the king for further instructions.

31"Do as he says," the king replied. "Kill him there beside the altar and bury him. This will remove the guilt of his senseless murders from me and from my father's family. 32Then Jehovah will hold him personally responsible for the murders of two men who were better than he. For my father was no party to the deaths of General Abner, commander-in-chief of the army of Israel, and General Amasa, commander-in-chief of the army of Judah. 33May Joab and his descendants be forever guilty of these murders, and may the Lord declare David and his descendants guiltless concerning their deaths."

34So Benaiah returned to the Tabernacle and killed Joab; and he was buried beside his house in the desert. 35Then the king appointed Benaiah as commander-in-chief, and Zadok as priest instead of Abiathar.

36, 37The king now sent for Shime-i and told him, "Build a house here in Jerusalem, and don't step outside the city on pain of death. The moment you go beyond Kidron Brook, you die; and it will be your own fault."

38"All right," Shime-i replied, "whatever you say." So he lived in Jerusalem for a long time.

39But three years later two of Shime-i's slaves escaped to King Achish of Gath. When Shime-i learned where they were, 40he saddled a donkey and went to Gath to visit the king. And when he had found his slaves, he took them back to Jerusalem.

41When Solomon heard that Shime-i had left Jerusalem and had gone to Gath and returned, 42he sent for him and demanded, "Didn't I command you in the name of God to stay in Jerusalem or die? You replied, 'Very well, I will do as you say.' 43Then why have you not kept your agreement and obeyed my commandment? 44And what about all the wicked things you did to my father, King David? May the Lord take revenge on you, 45but may I receive God's rich blessings, and may one of David's descendants always sit upon this throne."

46Then, at the king's command, Benaiah took Shime-i outside and killed him.

So Solomon's grip upon the kingdom became secure.

New Revised Standard

"Joab has fled to the tent of the LORD and now is beside the altar," Solomon sent Benaiah son of Jehoiada, saying, "Go, strike him down." 30So Benaiah came to the tent of the LORD and said to him, "The king commands, 'Come out.' " But he said, "No, I will die here." Then Benaiah brought the king word again, saying, "Thus said Joab, and thus he answered me." 31The king replied to him, "Do as he has said, strike him down and bury him; and thus take away from me and from my father's house the guilt for the blood that Joab shed without cause. 32The LORD will bring back his bloody deeds on his own head, because, without the knowledge of my father David, he attacked and killed with the sword two men more righteous and better than himself, Abner son of Ner, commander of the army of Israel, and Amasa son of Jether, commander of the army of Judah. 33So shall their blood come back on the head of Joab and on the head of his descendants forever; but to David, and to his descendants, and to his house, and to his throne, there shall be peace from the LORD forevermore." 34Then Benaiah son of Jehoiada went up and struck him down and killed him; and he was buried at his own house near the wilderness. 35The king put Benaiah son of Jehoiada over the army in his place, and the king put the priest Zadok in the place of Abiathar.

36 Then the king sent and summoned Shimei, and said to him, "Build yourself a house in Jerusalem, and live there, and do not go out from there to any place whatever. 37For on the day you go out, and cross the Wadi Kidron, know for certain that you shall die; your blood shall be on your own head." 38And Shimei said to the king, "The sentence is fair; as my lord the king has said, so will your servant do." So Shimei lived in Jerusalem many days.

39 But it happened at the end of three years that two of Shimei's slaves ran away to King Achish son of Maacah of Gath. When it was told Shimei, "Your slaves are in Gath," 40Shimei arose and saddled a donkey, and went to Achish in Gath, to search for his slaves; Shimei went and brought his slaves from Gath. 41When Solomon was told that Shimei had gone from Jerusalem to Gath and returned, 42the king sent and summoned Shimei, and said to him, "Did I not make you swear by the LORD, and solemnly adjure you, saying, 'Know for certain that on the day you go out and go to any place whatever, you shall die'? And you said to me, 'The sentence is fair; I accept.' 43Why then have you not kept your oath to the LORD and the commandment with which I charged you?" 44The king also said to Shimei, "You know in your own heart all the evil that you did to my father David; so the LORD will bring back your evil on your own head. 45But King Solomon shall be blessed, and the throne of David shall be established before the LORD forever." 46Then the king commanded Benaiah son of Jehoiada; and he went out and struck him down, and he died.

So the kingdom was established in the hand of Solomon.

King James

3 AND SOLOMON made affinity with Pharaoh king of Egypt, and took Pharaoh's daughter, and brought her into the city of David, until he had made an end of building his own house, and the house of the LORD, and the wall of Jerusalem round about.

2Only the people sacrificed in high places, because there was no house built unto the name of the LORD, until those days.

3And Solomon loved the LORD, walking in the statutes of David his father: only he sacrificed and burnt incense in high places.

4And the king went to Gibeon to sacrifice there; for that *was* the great high place: a thousand burnt offerings did Solomon offer upon that altar.

5¶ In Gibeon the LORD appeared to Solomon in a dream by night: and God said, Ask what I shall give thee.

6And Solomon said, Thou hast shown unto thy servant David my father great mercy, according as he walked before thee in truth, and in righteousness, and in uprightness of heart with thee; and thou hast kept for him this great kindness, that thou hast given him a son to sit on his throne, as *it is* this day.

7And now, O LORD my God, thou hast made thy servant king instead of David my father: and I *am but* a little child: I know not *how* to go out or come in.

8And thy servant *is* in the midst of thy people which thou hast chosen, a great people, that cannot be numbered nor counted for multitude.

9Give therefore thy servant an understanding heart to judge thy people, that I may discern between good and bad: for who is able to judge this thy so great a people?

10And the speech pleased the Lord, that Solomon had asked this thing.

11And God said unto him, Because thou hast asked this thing, and hast not asked for thyself long life; neither hast asked riches for thyself, nor hast asked the life of thine enemies; but hast asked for thyself understanding to discern judgment;

12Behold, I have done according to thy words: lo, I have given thee a wise and an understanding heart; so that there was none like thee before thee, neither after thee shall any arise like unto thee.

13And I have also given thee that which thou hast not asked, both riches, and honour: so that there shall not be any among the kings like unto thee all thy days.

14And if thou wilt walk in my ways, to keep my statutes and my commandments, as thy father David did walk, then I will lengthen thy days.

15And Solomon awoke; and, behold, *it was* a dream. And he came to Jerusalem, and stood before the ark of the covenant of the LORD, and offered up burnt offerings, and offered peace offerings, and made a feast to all his servants.

16¶ Then came there two women, *that were* harlots, unto the king, and stood before him.

17And the one woman said, O my lord, I and this woman dwell in one house; and I was delivered of a child with her in the house.

18And it came to pass the third day after that I was delivered, that this woman was delivered also: and we *were* together; *there was* no stranger with us in the house, save we two in the house.

19And this woman's child died in the night; because she overlaid it.

20And she arose at midnight, and took my son from beside me, while thine handmaid slept, and laid it in her bosom, and laid her dead child in my bosom.

21And when I rose in the morning to give my child suck, behold, it was dead: but when I had considered it in the morning, behold, it was not my son, which I did bear.

New International

Solomon Asks for Wisdom

3 SOLOMON MADE an alliance with Pharaoh king of Egypt and married his daughter. He brought her to the City of David until he finished building his palace and the temple of the LORD, and the wall around Jerusalem. 2The people, however, were still sacrificing at the high places, because a temple had not yet been built for the Name of the LORD. 3Solomon showed his love for the LORD by walking according to the statutes of his father David, except that he offered sacrifices and burned incense on the high places.

4The king went to Gibeon to offer sacrifices, for that was the most important high place, and Solomon offered a thousand burnt offerings on that altar. 5At Gibeon the LORD appeared to Solomon during the night in a dream, and God said, "Ask for whatever you want me to give you."

6Solomon answered, "You have shown great kindness to your servant, my father David, because he was faithful to you and righteous and upright in heart. You have continued this great kindness to him and have given him a son to sit on his throne this very day.

7"Now, O LORD my God, you have made your servant king in place of my father David. But I am only a little child and do not know how to carry out my duties. 8Your servant is here among the people you have chosen, a great people, too numerous to count or number. 9So give your servant a discerning heart to govern your people and to distinguish between right and wrong. For who is able to govern this great people of yours?"

10The Lord was pleased that Solomon had asked for this. 11So God said to him, "Since you have asked for this and not for long life or wealth for yourself, nor have asked for the death of your enemies but for discernment in administering justice, 12I will do what you have asked. I will give you a wise and discerning heart, so that there will never have been anyone like you, nor will there ever be. 13Moreover, I will give you what you have not asked for—both riches and honor—so that in your lifetime you will have no equal among kings. 14And if you walk in my ways and obey my statutes and commands as David your father did, I will give you a long life." 15Then Solomon awoke—and he realized it had been a dream.

He returned to Jerusalem, stood before the ark of the Lord's covenant and sacrificed burnt offerings and fellowship offerings.a Then he gave a feast for all his court.

A Wise Ruling

16Now two prostitutes came to the king and stood before him. 17One of them said, "My lord, this woman and I live in the same house. I had a baby while she was there with me. 18The third day after my child was born, this woman also had a baby. We were alone; there was no one in the house but the two of us.

19"During the night this woman's son died because she lay on him. 20So she got up in the middle of the night and took my son from my side while I your servant was asleep. She put him by her breast and put her dead son by my breast. 21The next morning, I got up to nurse my son—and he was dead! But when I looked at him closely in the morning light, I saw that it wasn't the son I had borne."

---

a 15 Traditionally *peace offerings*

Living Bible

3 SOLOMON MADE an alliance with Pharoah, the king of Egypt, and married one of his daughters. He brought her to Jerusalem to live in the City of David until he could finish building his palace and the Temple and the wall around the city.

²At that time the people of Israel sacrificed their offerings on altars in the hills, for the Temple of the Lord hadn't yet been built.

³(Solomon loved the Lord and followed all of his father David's instructions except that he continued to sacrifice in the hills and to offer incense there.) ⁴The most famous of the hilltop altars was at Gibeon and now the king went there and sacrificed one thousand burnt offerings! ⁵The Lord appeared to him in a dream that night and told him to ask for anything he wanted, and it would be given to him!

⁶Solomon replied, "You were wonderfully kind to my father David because he was honest and true and faithful to you, and obeyed your commands. And you have continued your kindness to him by giving him a son to succeed him. ⁷O Lord my God, now you have made me the king instead of my father David, but I am as a little child who doesn't know his way around. ⁸And here I am among your own chosen people, a nation so great that there are almost too many people to count! ⁹Give me an understanding mind so that I can govern your people well and know the difference between what is right and what is wrong. For who by himself is able to carry such a heavy responsibility?"

¹⁰The Lord was pleased with his reply and was glad that Solomon had asked for wisdom. ¹¹So he replied, "Because you have asked for wisdom in governing my people, and haven't asked for a long life or riches for yourself, or the defeat of your enemies— ¹²yes, I'll give you what you asked for! I will give you a wiser mind than anyone else has ever had or ever will have! ¹³And I will also give you what you didn't ask for—riches and honor! And no one in all the world will be as rich and famous as you for the rest of your life! ¹⁴And I will give you a long life if you follow me and obey my laws as your father David did."

¹⁵Then Solomon woke up and realized it had been a dream. He returned to Jerusalem and went into the Tabernacle. And as he stood before the Ark of the Covenant of the Lord, he sacrificed burnt offerings and peace offerings. Then he invited all of his officials to a great banquet.

¹⁶Soon afterwards two young prostitutes came to the king to have an argument settled.

¹⁷, ¹⁸"Sir," one of them began, "we live in the same house, just the two of us, and recently I had a baby. When it was three days old, this woman's baby was born too. ¹⁹But her baby died during the night when she rolled over on it in her sleep and smothered it. ²⁰Then she got up in the night and took my son from beside me while I was asleep, and laid her dead child in my arms and took mine to sleep beside her. ²¹And in the morning when I tried to feed my baby it was dead! But when it became light outside, I saw that it wasn't my son at all."

New Revised Standard

Solomon's Prayer for Wisdom

3 SOLOMON MADE a marriage alliance with Pharaoh king of Egypt; he took Pharaoh's daughter and brought her into the city of David, until he had finished building his own house and the house of the Lord and the wall around Jerusalem. ²The people were sacrificing at the high places, however, because no house had yet been built for the name of the Lord.

3 Solomon loved the Lord, walking in the statutes of his father David; only, he sacrificed and offered incense at the high places. ⁴The king went to Gibeon to sacrifice there, for that was the principal high place; Solomon used to offer a thousand burnt offerings on that altar. ⁵At Gibeon the Lord appeared to Solomon in a dream by night; and God said, "Ask what I should give you." ⁶And Solomon said, "You have shown great and steadfast love to your servant my father David, because he walked before you in faithfulness, in righteousness, and in uprightness of heart toward you; and you have kept for him this great and steadfast love, and have given him a son to sit on his throne today. ⁷And now, O Lord my God, you have made your servant king in place of my father David, although I am only a little child; I do not know how to go out or come in. ⁸And your servant is in the midst of the people whom you have chosen, a great people, so numerous they cannot be numbered or counted. ⁹Give your servant therefore an understanding mind to govern your people, able to discern between good and evil; for who can govern this your great people?"

10 It pleased the Lord that Solomon had asked this. ¹¹God said to him, "Because you have asked this, and have not asked for yourself long life or riches, or for the life of your enemies, but have asked for yourself understanding to discern what is right, ¹²I now do according to your word. Indeed I give you a wise and discerning mind; no one like you has been before you and no one like you shall arise after you. ¹³I give you also what you have not asked, both riches and honor all your life; no other king shall compare with you. ¹⁴If you will walk in my ways, keeping my statutes and my commandments, as your father David walked, then I will lengthen your life."

15 Then Solomon awoke; it had been a dream. He came to Jerusalem where he stood before the ark of the covenant of the Lord. He offered up burnt offerings and offerings of well-being, and provided a feast for all his servants.

Solomon's Wisdom in Judgment

16 Later, two women who were prostitutes came to the king and stood before him. ¹⁷The one woman said, "Please, my lord, this woman and I live in the same house; and I gave birth while she was in the house. ¹⁸Then on the third day after I gave birth, this woman also gave birth. We were together; there was no one else with us in the house, only the two of us were in the house. ¹⁹Then this woman's son died in the night, because she lay on him. ²⁰She got up in the middle of the night and took my son from beside me while your servant slept. She laid him at her breast, and laid her dead son at my breast. ²¹When I rose in the morning to nurse my son, I saw that he was dead; but when I looked at him closely in the morning, clearly it was not the son I had borne." ²²But the other woman said, "No, the living

King James

22And the other woman said, Nay; but the living *is* my son, and the dead *is* thy son. And this said, No; but the dead *is* thy son, and the living *is* my son. Thus they spake before the king.

23Then said the king, The one saith, This *is* my son that liveth, and thy son *is* the dead: and the other saith, Nay; but thy son *is* the dead, and my son *is* the living.

24And the king said, Bring me a sword. And they brought a sword before the king.

25And the king said, Divide the living child in two, and give half to the one, and half to the other.

26Then spake the woman whose the living child *was* unto the king, for her bowels yearned upon her son, and she said, O my lord, give her the living child, and in no wise slay it. But the other said, Let it be neither mine nor thine, *but* divide *it*.

27Then the king answered and said, Give her the living child, and in no wise slay it: she *is* the mother thereof.

28And all Israel heard of the judgment which the king had judged; and they feared the king: for they saw that the wisdom of God *was* in him, to do judgment.

4 SO KING Solomon was king over all Israel.
2And these *were* the princes which he had; Azariah the son of Zadok the priest,

3Elihoreph and Ahiah, the sons of Shisha, scribes; Jehoshaphat the son of Ahilud, the recorder.

4And Benaiah the son of Jehoiada *was* over the host: and Zadok and Abiathar *were* the priests:

5And Azariah the son of Nathan *was* over the officers: and Zabud the son of Nathan *was* principal officer, *and* the king's friend:

6And Ahishar *was* over the household: and Adoniram the son of Abda *was* over the tribute.

7¶ And Solomon had twelve officers over all Israel, which provided victuals for the king and his household: each man his month in a year made provision.

8And these *are* their names: The son of Hur, in mount Ephraim:

9The son of Dekar, in Makaz, and in Shaalbim, and Beth-shemesh, and Elon-beth-hanan:

10The son of Hesed, in Aruboth; to him *pertained* Sochoh, and all the land of Hepher:

11The son of Abinadab, in all the region of Dor; which had Taphath the daughter of Solomon to wife:

12Baana the son of Ahilud; *to him pertained* Taanach and Megiddo, and all Beth-shean, which *is* by Zartanah beneath Jezreel, from Beth-shean to Abel-meholah, *even* unto *the place that is* beyond Jokneam:

13The son of Geber, in Ramoth-gilead; to him *pertained* the towns of Jair the son of Manasseh, which *are* in Gilead; to him *also pertained* the region of Argob, which *is* in Bashan, threescore great cities with walls and brasen bars:

14Ahinadab the son of Iddo *had* Mahanaim:

15Ahimaaz *was* in Naphtali; he also took Basmath the daughter of Solomon to wife:

16Baanah the son of Hushai *was* in Asher and in Aloth:

17Jehoshaphat the son of Paruah, in Issachar:

18Shimei the son of Elah, in Benjamin:

New International

22The other woman said, "No! The living one is my son; the dead one is yours."

But the first one insisted, "No! The dead one is yours; the living one is mine." And so they argued before the king.

23The king said, "This one says, 'My son is alive and your son is dead,' while that one says, 'No! Your son is dead and mine is alive.' "

24Then the king said, "Bring me a sword." So they brought a sword for the king. 25He then gave an order: "Cut the living child in two and give half to one and half to the other."

26The woman whose son was alive was filled with compassion for her son and said to the king, "Please, my lord, give her the living baby! Don't kill him!"

But the other said, "Neither I nor you shall have him. Cut him in two!"

27Then the king gave his ruling: "Give the living baby to the first woman. Do not kill him; she is his mother."

28When all Israel heard the verdict the king had given, they held the king in awe, because they saw that he had wisdom from God to administer justice.

Solomon's Officials and Governors

4 SO KING Solomon ruled over all Israel. 2And these were his chief officials:

Azariah son of Zadok—the priest;
3Elihoreph and Ahijah, sons of Shisha—secretaries;
Jehoshaphat son of Ahilud—recorder;
4Benaiah son of Jehoiada—commander in chief;
Zadok and Abiathar—priests;
5Azariah son of Nathan—in charge of the district officers;
Zabud son of Nathan—a priest and personal adviser to the king;
6Ahishar—in charge of the palace;
Adoniram son of Abda—in charge of forced labor.

7Solomon also had twelve district governors over all Israel, who supplied provisions for the king and the royal household. Each one had to provide supplies for one month in the year. 8These are their names:

Ben-Hur—in the hill country of Ephraim;
9Ben-Deker—in Makaz, Shaalbim, Beth Shemesh and Elon Bethhanan;
10Ben-Hesed—in Arubboth (Socoh and all the land of Hepher were his);
11Ben-Abinadab—in Naphoth Dora (he was married to Taphath daughter of Solomon);
12Baana son of Ahilud—in Taanach and Megiddo, and in all of Beth Shan next to Zarethan below Jezreel, from Beth Shan to Abel Meholah across to Jokmeam;
13Ben-Geber—in Ramoth Gilead (the settlements of Jair son of Manasseh in Gilead were his, as well as the district of Argob in Bashan and its sixty large walled cities with bronze gate bars);
14Ahinadab son of Iddo—in Mahanaim;
15Ahimaaz—in Naphtali (he had married Basemath daughter of Solomon);
16Baana son of Hushai—in Asher and in Aloth;
17Jehoshaphat son of Paruah—in Issachar;
18Shimei son of Ela—in Benjamin;

---

a *11* Or *in the heights of Dor*

Living Bible

22Then the other woman interrupted, "It certainly was her son, and the living child is mine."

"No," the first woman said, "the dead one is yours and the living one is mine." And so they argued back and forth before the king.

23Then the king said, "Let's get the facts straight: both of you claim the living child, and each says that the dead child belongs to the other. 24All right, bring me a sword." So a sword was brought to the king. 25Then he said, "Divide the living child in two and give half to each of these women!"

26Then the woman who really was the mother of the child, and who loved him very much, cried out, "Oh, no, sir! Give her the child—don't kill him!"

But the other woman said, "All right, it will be neither yours nor mine; divide it between us!"

27Then the king said, "Give the baby to the woman who wants him to live, for she is the mother!"

28Word of the king's decision spread quickly throughout the entire nation, and all the people were awed as they realized the great wisdom God had given him.

4 HERE IS a list of King Solomon's cabinet members:

Azariah (son of Zadok) was the High Priest;

Elihoreph and Ahijah (sons of Shisha) were secretaries;

Jehoshaphat (son of Ahilud) was the official historian and in charge of the archives;

Benaiah (son of Jehoiada) was commander-in-chief of the army;

Zadok and Abiathar were priests;

Azariah (son of Nathan) was secretary of state;

Zabud (son of Nathan) was the king's personal priest and special friend;

Ahishar was manager of palace affairs;

Adoniram (son of Abda) was superintendent of public works.

7There were also twelve officials of Solomon's court—one man from each tribe—responsible for requisitioning food from the people for the king's household. Each of them arranged provisions for one month of the year.

8-19The names of these twelve officers were:

Ben-hur, whose area for this taxation was the hill country of Ephraim;

Ben-deker, whose area was Makaz, Sha-albim, Beth-shemesh, and Elon-beth-hanan;

Ben-hesed, whose area was Arubboth, including Socoh and all the land of Hepher;

Ben-abinadab (who married Solomon's daughter, the princess Taphath), whose area was the highlands of Dor;

Baana (son of Ahilud), whose area was Taanach and Megiddo, all of Beth-shean near Zarethan below Jezreel, and all the territory from Beth-shean to Abel-meholah and over to Jokmeam;

Ben-geber, whose area was Ramoth-gilead, including the villages of Jair (the son of Manasseh) in Gilead; and the region of Argob in Bashan, including sixty walled cities with bronze gates;

Ahinadab (the son of Iddo), whose area was Mahanaim;

Ahima-az (who married Princess Basemath, another of Solomon's daughters), whose area was Naphtali;

New Revised Standard

son is mine, and the dead son is yours." The first said, "No, the dead son is yours, and the living son is mine." So they argued before the king.

23 Then the king said, "The one says, 'This is my son that is alive, and your son is dead'; while the other says, 'Not so! Your son is dead, and my son is the living one.' " 24So the king said, "Bring me a sword," and they brought a sword before the king. 25The king said, "Divide the living boy in two; then give half to the one, and half to the other." 26But the woman whose son was alive said to the king—because compassion for her son burned within her—"Please, my lord, give her the living boy; certainly do not kill him!" The other said, "It shall be neither mine nor yours; divide it." 27Then the king responded: "Give the first woman the living boy; do not kill him. She is his mother." 28All Israel heard of the judgment that the king had rendered; and they stood in awe of the king, because they perceived that the wisdom of God was in him, to execute justice.

Solomon's Administrative Officers

4 KING SOLOMON was king over all Israel, 2and these were his high officials: Azariah son of Zadok was the priest; 3Elihoreph and Ahijah sons of Shisha were secretaries; Jehoshaphat son of Ahilud was recorder; 4Benaiah son of Jehoiada was in command of the army; Zadok and Abiathar were priests; 5Azariah son of Nathan was over the officials; Zabud son of Nathan was priest and king's friend; 6Ahishar was in charge of the palace; and Adoniram son of Abda was in charge of the forced labor.

7 Solomon had twelve officials over all Israel, who provided food for the king and his household; each one had to make provision for one month in the year. 8These were their names: Ben-hur, in the hill country of Ephraim; 9Ben-deker, in Makaz, Shaalbim, Beth-shemesh, and Elon-beth-hanan; 10Ben-hesed, in Arubboth (to him belonged Socoh and all the land of Hepher); 11Ben-abinadab, in all Naphath-dor (he had Taphath, Solomon's daughter, as his wife); 12Baana son of Ahilud, in Taanach, Megiddo, and all Beth-shean, which is beside Zarethan below Jezreel, and from Beth-shean to Abel-meholah, as far as the other side of Jokmeam; 13Ben-geber, in Ramoth-gilead (he had the villages of Jair son of Manasseh, which are in Gilead, and he had the region of Argob, which is in Bashan, sixty great cities with walls and bronze bars); 14Ahinadab son of Iddo, in Mahanaim; 15Ahimaaz, in Naphtali (he had taken Basemath, Solomon's daughter, as his wife); 16Baana son of Hushai, in Asher and Bealoth; 17Jehoshaphat son of Paruah, in Issachar; 18Shimei son of Ela, in Benjamin;

King James

19Geber the son of Uri *was* in the country of Gilead, *in* the country of Sihon king of the Amorites, and of Og king of Bashan; and *he was* the only officer which *was* in the land.

20¶ Judah and Israel *were* many, as the sand which *is* by the sea in multitude, eating and drinking, and making merry.

21And Solomon reigned over all kingdoms from the river unto the land of the Philistines, and unto the border of Egypt: they brought presents, and served Solomon all the days of his life.

22¶ And Solomon's provision for one day was thirty measures of fine flour, and threescore measures of meal,

23Ten fat oxen, and twenty oxen out of the pastures, and an hundred sheep, beside harts, and roebucks, and fallowdeer, and fatted fowl.

24For he had dominion over all *the region* on this side the river, from Tiphsah even to Azzah, over all the kings on this side the river: and he had peace on all sides round about him.

25And Judah and Israel dwelt safely, every man under his vine and under his fig tree, from Dan even to Beersheba, all the days of Solomon.

26¶ And Solomon had forty thousand stalls of horses for his chariots, and twelve thousand horsemen.

27And those officers provided victual for king Solomon, and for all that came unto king Solomon's table, every man in his month: they lacked nothing.

28Barley also and straw for the horses and dromedaries brought they unto the place where *the officers* were, every man according to his charge.

29¶ And God gave Solomon wisdom and understanding exceeding much, and largeness of heart, even as the sand that *is* on the sea shore.

30And Solomon's wisdom excelled the wisdom of all the children of the east country, and all the wisdom of Egypt.

31For he was wiser than all men; than Ethan the Ezrahite, and Heman, and Chalcol, and Darda, the sons of Mahol: and his fame was in all nations round about.

32And he spake three thousand proverbs: and his songs were a thousand and five.

33And he spake of trees, from the cedar tree that *is* in Lebanon even unto the hyssop that springeth out of the wall: he spake also of beasts, and of fowl, and of creeping things, and of fishes.

34And there came of all people to hear the wisdom of Solomon, from all kings of the earth, which had heard of his wisdom.

5 AND HIRAM king of Tyre sent his servants unto Solomon; for he had heard that they had anointed him king in the room of his father: for Hiram was ever a lover of David.

2And Solomon sent to Hiram, saying,

3Thou knowest how that David my father could not build an house unto the name of the LORD his God for the wars which were about him on every side, until the LORD put them under the soles of his feet.

4But now the LORD my God hath given me rest on every side, *so that there is* neither adversary nor evil occurrent.

5And, behold, I purpose to build an house unto the name of the LORD my God, as the LORD spake unto David my father, saying, Thy son, whom I will set upon thy throne in thy room, he shall build an house unto my name.

New International

19Geber son of Uri—in Gilead (the country of Sihon king of the Amorites and the country of Og king of Bashan). He was the only governor over the district.

Solomon's Daily Provisions

20The people of Judah and Israel were as numerous as the sand on the seashore; they ate, they drank and they were happy. 21And Solomon ruled over all the kingdoms from the Rivera to the land of the Philistines, as far as the border of Egypt. These countries brought tribute and were Solomon's subjects all his life.

22Solomon's daily provisions were thirty corsb of fine flour and sixty corsc of meal, 23ten head of stall-fed cattle, twenty of pasture-fed cattle and a hundred sheep and goats, as well as deer, gazelles, roebucks and choice fowl. 24For he ruled over all the kingdoms west of the River, from Tiphsah to Gaza, and had peace on all sides. 25During Solomon's lifetime Judah and Israel, from Dan to Beersheba, lived in safety, each man under his own vine and fig tree.

26Solomon had fourd thousand stalls for chariot horses, and twelve thousand horses.e

27The district officers, each in his month, supplied provisions for King Solomon and all who came to the king's table. They saw to it that nothing was lacking. 28They also brought to the proper place their quotas of barley and straw for the chariot horses and the other horses.

Solomon's Wisdom

29God gave Solomon wisdom and very great insight, and a breadth of understanding as measureless as the sand on the seashore. 30Solomon's wisdom was greater than the wisdom of all the men of the East, and greater than all the wisdom of Egypt. 31He was wiser than any other man, including Ethan the Ezrahite—wiser than Heman, Calcol and Darda, the sons of Mahol. And his fame spread to all the surrounding nations. 32He spoke three thousand proverbs and his songs numbered a thousand and five. 33He described plant life, from the cedar of Lebanon to the hyssop that grows out of walls. He also taught about animals and birds, reptiles and fish. 34Men of all nations came to listen to Solomon's wisdom, sent by all the kings of the world, who had heard of his wisdom.

Preparations for Building the Temple

5 WHEN HIRAM king of Tyre heard that Solomon had been anointed king to succeed his father David, he sent his envoys to Solomon, because he had always been on friendly terms with David. 2Solomon sent back this message to Hiram:

3"You know that because of the wars waged against my father David from all sides, he could not build a temple for the Name of the LORD his God until the LORD put his enemies under his feet. 4But now the LORD my God has given me rest on every side, and there is no adversary or disaster. 5I intend, therefore, to build a temple for the Name of the LORD my God, as the LORD told my father David, when he said, 'Your son whom I will put on the throne in your place will build the temple for my Name.'

---

a 21 That is, the Euphrates; also in verse 24   b 22 That is, probably about 185 bushels (about 6.6 kiloliters)   c 22 That is, probably about 375 bushels (about 13.2 kiloliters)   d 26 Some Septuagint manuscripts (see also 2 Chron. 9:25); Hebrew *forty*   e 26 Or *charioteers*

Living Bible

Baana (son of Hushai), whose areas were Asher and Bealoth;

Jehoshaphat (son of Paruah), whose area was Issachar;

Shime-i (son of Ela), whose area was Benjamin;

Geber (son of Uri), whose area was Gilead, including the territories of King Sihon of the Amorites and King Og of Bashan.

A general manager supervised these officials and their work.

20Israel and Judah were a wealthy, populous, contented nation at this time. 21King Solomon ruled the whole area from the Euphrates River to the land of the Philistines, and down to the borders of Egypt. The conquered peoples of those lands sent taxes to Solomon and continued to serve him throughout his lifetime.

22The daily food requirements for the palace were 195 bushels of fine flour, 390 bushels of meal, 2310 oxen from the fattening pens, 20 pasture-fed cattle, 100 sheep, and, from time to time, deer, gazelles, roebucks, and plump fowl.

24His dominion extended over all the kingdoms west of the Euphrates River, from Tiphsah to Gaza. And there was peace throughout the land.

25Throughout the lifetime of Solomon, all of Judah and Israel lived in peace and safety; and each family had its own home and garden.

26Solomon owned forty thousand chariot horses and employed twelve thousand charioteers. 27Each month the tax officials provided food for King Solomon and his court; 28also the barley and straw for the royal horses in the stables.

29God gave Solomon great wisdom and understanding, and a mind with broad interests. 30In fact, his wisdom excelled that of any of the wise men of the East, including those in Egypt. 31He was wiser than Ethan the Ezrahite and Heman, Calcol, and Darda, the sons of Mahol; and he was famous among all the surrounding nations. 32He was the author of 3,000 proverbs and wrote 1,005 songs. 33He was a great naturalist, with interest in animals, birds, snakes, fish, and trees—from the great cedars of Lebanon down to the tiny hyssop which grows in cracks in the wall. 34And kings from many lands sent their ambassadors to him for his advice.

5 KING HIRAM of Tyre had always been a great admirer of David, so when he learned that David's son Solomon was the new king of Israel, he sent ambassadors to extend congratulations and good wishes. 2, 3Solomon replied with a proposal about the Temple of the Lord he wanted to build. His father David, Solomon pointed out to Hiram, had not been able to build it because of the numerous wars going on, and he had been waiting for the Lord to give him peace.

4"But now," Solomon said to Hiram, "the Lord my God has given Israel peace on every side; I have no foreign enemies or internal rebellions. 5So I am planning to build a Temple for the Lord my God, just as he instructed my father that I should do. For the Lord told him, 'Your son, whom I will place upon your throne, shall build me a Temple.' 6Now please assist me with

New Revised Standard

19Geber son of Uri, in the land of Gilead, the country of King Sihon of the Amorites and of King Og of Bashan. And there was one official in the land of Judah.

Magnificence of Solomon's Rule

20 Judah and Israel were as numerous as the sand by the sea; they ate and drank and were happy. 21fSolomon was sovereign over all the kingdoms from the Euphrates to the land of the Philistines, even to the border of Egypt; they brought tribute and served Solomon all the days of his life.

22 Solomon's provision for one day was thirty cors of choice flour, and sixty cors of meal, 23ten fat oxen, and twenty pasture-fed cattle, one hundred sheep, besides deer, gazelles, roebucks, and fatted fowl. 24For he had dominion over all the region west of the Euphrates from Tiphsah to Gaza, over all the kings west of the Euphrates; and he had peace on all sides. 25During Solomon's lifetime Judah and Israel lived in safety, from Dan even to Beer-sheba, all of them under their vines and fig trees. 26Solomon also had forty thousand stalls of horses for his chariots, and twelve thousand horsemen. 27Those officials supplied provisions for King Solomon and for all who came to King Solomon's table, each one in his month; they let nothing be lacking. 28They also brought to the required place barley and straw for the horses and swift steeds, each according to his charge.

Fame of Solomon's Wisdom

29 God gave Solomon very great wisdom, discernment, and breadth of understanding as vast as the sand on the seashore, 30so that Solomon's wisdom surpassed the wisdom of all the people of the east, and all the wisdom of Egypt. 31He was wiser than anyone else, wiser than Ethan the Ezrahite, and Heman, Calcol, and Darda, children of Mahol; his fame spread throughout all the surrounding nations. 32He composed three thousand proverbs, and his songs numbered a thousand and five. 33He would speak of trees, from the cedar that is in the Lebanon to the hyssop that grows in the wall; he would speak of animals, and birds, and reptiles, and fish. 34People came from all the nations to hear the wisdom of Solomon; they came from all the kings of the earth who had heard of his wisdom.

Preparations and Materials for the Temple

5g NOW KING Hiram of Tyre sent his servants to Solomon, when he heard that they had anointed him king in place of his father; for Hiram had always been a friend to David. 2Solomon sent word to Hiram, saying, 3"You know that my father David could not build a house for the name of the LORD his God because of the warfare with which his enemies surrounded him, until the LORD put them under the soles of his feet.h 4But now the LORD my God has given me rest on every side; there is neither adversary nor misfortune. 5So I intend to build a house for the name of the LORD my God, as the LORD said to my father David, 'Your son, whom I will set on your throne in your place, shall build the house for my name.' 6Therefore command that ce-

f Ch 5.1 in Heb   g Ch 5.15 in Heb   h Gk Tg Vg: Heb *my feet* or *his feet*

King James

6Now therefore command thou that they hew me cedar trees out of Lebanon; and my servants shall be with thy servants: and unto thee will I give hire for thy servants according to all that thou shalt appoint: for thou knowest that *there is* not among us any that can skill to hew timber like unto the Sidonians.

7¶ And it came to pass, when Hiram heard the words of Solomon, that he rejoiced greatly, and said, Blessed *be* the LORD this day, which hath given unto David a wise son over this great people.

8And Hiram sent to Solomon, saying, I have considered the things which thou sentest to me for: *and* I will do all thy desire concerning timber of cedar, and concerning timber of fir.

9My servants shall bring *them* down from Lebanon unto the sea: and I will convey them by sea in floats unto the place that thou shalt appoint me, and will cause them to be discharged there, and thou shalt receive *them:* and thou shalt accomplish my desire, in giving food for my household.

10So Hiram gave Solomon cedar trees and fir trees *according to* all his desire.

11And Solomon gave Hiram twenty thousand measures of wheat *for* food to his household, and twenty measures of pure oil: thus gave Solomon to Hiram year by year.

12And the LORD gave Solomon wisdom, as he promised him: and there was peace between Hiram and Solomon; and they two made a league together.

13¶ And king Solomon raised a levy out of all Israel; and the levy was thirty thousand men.

14And he sent them to Lebanon, ten thousand a month by courses: a month they were in Lebanon, *and* two months at home: and Adoniram *was* over the levy.

15And Solomon had threescore and ten thousand that bare burdens, and fourscore thousand hewers in the mountains;

16Beside the chief of Solomon's officers which *were* over the work, three thousand and three hundred, which ruled over the people that wrought in the work.

17And the king commanded, and they brought great stones, costly stones, *and* hewed stones, to lay the foundation of the house.

18And Solomon's builders and Hiram's builders did hew *them,* and the stonesquarers: so they prepared timber and stones to build the house.

6 AND IT came to pass in the four hundred and eightieth year after the children of Israel were come out of the land of Egypt, in the fourth year of Solomon's reign over Israel, in the month Zif, which *is* the second month, that he began to build the house of the LORD.

2And the house which king Solomon built for the LORD, the length thereof *was* threescore cubits, and the breadth thereof twenty *cubits,* and the height thereof thirty cubits.

3And the porch before the temple of the house, twenty cubits *was* the length thereof, according to the breadth of the house; *and* ten cubits *was* the breadth thereof before the house.

4And for the house he made windows of narrow lights.

5¶ And against the wall of the house he built chambers round about, *against* the walls of the house round about, *both* of the temple and of the oracle: and he made chambers round about:

New International

6"So give orders that cedars of Lebanon be cut for me. My men will work with yours, and I will pay you for your men whatever wages you set. You know that we have no one so skilled in felling timber as the Sidonians."

7When Hiram heard Solomon's message, he was greatly pleased and said, "Praise be to the LORD today, for he has given David a wise son to rule over this great nation."

8So Hiram sent word to Solomon:

"I have received the message you sent me and will do all you want in providing the cedar and pine logs. 9My men will haul them down from Lebanon to the sea, and I will float them in rafts by sea to the place you specify. There I will separate them and you can take them away. And you are to grant my wish by providing food for my royal household."

10In this way Hiram kept Solomon supplied with all the cedar and pine logs he wanted, 11and Solomon gave Hiram twenty thousand cors[a] of wheat as food for his household, in addition to twenty thousand baths[b,c] of pressed olive oil. Solomon continued to do this for Hiram year after year. 12The LORD gave Solomon wisdom, just as he had promised him. There were peaceful relations between Hiram and Solomon, and the two of them made a treaty.

13King Solomon conscripted laborers from all Israel—thirty thousand men. 14He sent them off to Lebanon in shifts of ten thousand a month, so that they spent one month in Lebanon and two months at home. Adoniram was in charge of the forced labor. 15Solomon had seventy thousand carriers and eighty thousand stonecutters in the hills, 16as well as thirty-three hundred[d] foremen who supervised the project and directed the workmen. 17At the king's command they removed from the quarry large blocks of quality stone to provide a foundation of dressed stone for the temple. 18The craftsmen of Solomon and Hiram and the men of Gebal[e] cut and prepared the timber and stone for the building of the temple.

Solomon Builds the Temple

6 IN THE four hundred and eightieth[f] year after the Israelites had come out of Egypt, in the fourth year of Solomon's reign over Israel, in the month of Ziv, the second month, he began to build the temple of the LORD.

2The temple that King Solomon built for the LORD was sixty cubits long, twenty wide and thirty high.[g] 3The portico at the front of the main hall of the temple extended the width of the temple, that is twenty cubits,[h] and projected ten cubits[i] from the front of the temple. 4He made narrow clerestory windows in the temple. 5Against the walls of the main hall and inner sanctuary he built a structure around the building, in which there were side rooms. 6The lowest floor was five cubits[j]

---

a *11* That is, probably about 125,000 bushels (about 4,400 kiloliters)
b *11* Septuagint (see also 2 Chron. 2:10); Hebrew *twenty cors*   c *11* That is, about 115,000 gallons (about 440 kiloliters)   d *16* Hebrew; some Septuagint manuscripts (see also 2 Chron. 2:2, 18) *thirty-six hundred*
e *18* That is, Byblos   f *1* Hebrew; Septuagint *four hundred and fortieth*
g *2* That is, about 90 feet (about 27 meters) long and 30 feet (about 9 meters) wide and 45 feet (about 13.5 meters) high   h *3* That is, about 30 feet (about 9 meters)   i *3* That is, about 15 feet (about 4.5 meters)   j *6* That is, about 7 1/2 feet (about 2.3 meters); also in verses 10 and 24

Living Bible

this project. Send your woodsmen to the mountains of Lebanon to cut cedar timber for me, and I will send my men to work beside them, and I will pay your men whatever wages you ask; for as you know, no one in Israel can cut timber like you Sidonians!"

7Hiram was very pleased with the message from Solomon. "Praise God for giving David a wise son to be king of the great nation of Israel," he said. 8Then he sent this reply to Solomon: "I have received your message and I will do as you have asked concerning the timber. I can supply both cedar and cypress. 9My men will bring the logs from the Lebanon mountains to the Mediterranean Sea and build them into rafts. We will float them along the coast to wherever you need them; then we will break the rafts apart and deliver the timber to you. You can pay me with food for my household."

10So Hiram produced for Solomon as much cedar and cypress timber as he desired, 11and in return Solomon sent him an annual payment of 125,000 bushels of wheat for his household and 96 gallons of pure olive oil. 12So the Lord gave great wisdom to Solomon just as he had promised. And Hiram and Solomon made a formal alliance of peace.

13Then Solomon drafted thirty thousand laborers from all over Israel, 14and rotated them to Lebanon, ten thousand a month, so that each man was a month in Lebanon and two months at home. Adoniram was the general superintendent of this labor camp. 15Solomon also had seventy thousand additional laborers, eighty thousand stonecutters in the hill country, 16and thirty-three hundred foremen. 17The stonecutters quarried and shaped huge blocks of stone—a very expensive job—for the foundation of the Temple. 18Men from Gebal helped Solomon's and Hiram's builders in cutting the timber and making the boards, and in preparing the stone for the Temple.

6 IT WAS in the spring of the fourth year of Solomon's reign that he began the actual construction of the Temple. (This was 480 years after the people of Israel left their slavery in Egypt.) 2The Temple was ninety feet long, thirty feet wide, and forty-five feet high. 3All along the front of the Temple was a porch thirty feet long and fifteen feet deep. 4Narrow windows were used throughout.

5An annex of rooms was built along the full length of both sides of the Temple against the outer walls.

New Revised Standard

dars from the Lebanon be cut for me. My servants will join your servants, and I will give you whatever wages you set for your servants; for you know that there is no one among us who knows how to cut timber like the Sidonians."

7 When Hiram heard the words of Solomon, he rejoiced greatly, and said, "Blessed be the LORD today, who has given to David a wise son to be over this great people." 8Hiram sent word to Solomon, "I have heard the message that you have sent to me; I will fulfill all your needs in the matter of cedar and cypress timber. 9My servants shall bring it down to the sea from the Lebanon; I will make it into rafts to go by sea to the place you indicate. I will have them broken up there for you to take away. And you shall meet my needs by providing food for my household." 10So Hiram supplied Solomon's every need for timber of cedar and cypress. 11Solomon in turn gave Hiram twenty thousand cors of wheat as food for his household, and twenty cors of fine oil. Solomon gave this to Hiram year by year. 12So the LORD gave Solomon wisdom, as he promised him. There was peace between Hiram and Solomon; and the two of them made a treaty.

13 King Solomon conscripted forced labor out of all Israel; the levy numbered thirty thousand men. 14He sent them to the Lebanon, ten thousand a month in shifts; they would be a month in the Lebanon and two months at home; Adoniram was in charge of the forced labor. 15Solomon also had seventy thousand laborers and eighty thousand stonecutters in the hill country, 16besides Solomon's three thousand three hundred supervisors who were over the work, having charge of the people who did the work. 17At the king's command, they quarried out great, costly stones in order to lay the foundation of the house with dressed stones. 18So Solomon's builders and Hiram's builders and the Gebalites did the stonecutting and prepared the timber and the stone to build the house.

Solomon Builds the Temple

6 IN THE four hundred eightieth year after the Israelites came out of the land of Egypt, in the fourth year of Solomon's reign over Israel, in the month of Ziv, which is the second month, he began to build the house of the LORD. 2The house that King Solomon built for the LORD was sixty cubits long, twenty cubits wide, and thirty cubits high. 3The vestibule in front of the nave of the house was twenty cubits wide, across the width of the house. Its depth was ten cubits in front of the house. 4For the house he made windows with recessed frames.k 5He also built a structure against the wall of the house, running around the walls of the house, both the nave and the inner sanctuary; and he made side chambers all around. 6The lowest storyl was five cubits

k Gk: Meaning of Heb uncertain   l Gk: Heb structure

King James

6The nethermost chamber *was* five cubits broad, and the middle *was* six cubits broad, and the third *was* seven cubits broad: for without *in the wall* of the house he made narrowed rests round about, that *the beams* should not be fastened in the walls of the house.

7And the house, when it was in building, was built of stone made ready before it was brought thither: so that there was neither hammer nor axe *nor* any tool of iron heard in the house, while it was in building.

8The door for the middle chamber *was* in the right side of the house: and they went up with winding stairs into the middle *chamber*, and out of the middle into the third.

9So he built the house, and finished it; and covered the house with beams and boards of cedar.

10And *then* he built chambers against all the house, five cubits high: and they rested on the house with timber of cedar.

11¶ And the word of the LORD came to Solomon, saying,

12*Concerning* this house which thou art in building, if thou wilt walk in my statutes, and execute my judgments, and keep all my commandments to walk in them; then will I perform my word with thee, which I spake unto David thy father:

13And I will dwell among the children of Israel, and will not forsake my people Israel.

14So Solomon built the house, and finished it.

15And he built the walls of the house within with boards of cedar, both the floor of the house, and the walls of the ceiling: *and* he covered *them* on the inside with wood, and covered the floor of the house with planks of fir.

16And he built twenty cubits on the sides of the house, both the floor and the walls with boards of cedar: he even built *them* for it within, *even* for the oracle, *even* for the most holy *place*.

17And the house, that *is*, the temple before it, was forty cubits *long*.

18And the cedar of the house within *was* carved with knobs and open flowers: all *was* cedar; there was no stone seen.

19And the oracle he prepared in the house within, to set there the ark of the covenant of the LORD.

20And the oracle in the forepart *was* twenty cubits in length, and twenty cubits in breadth, and twenty cubits in the height thereof: and he overlaid it with pure gold; and *so* covered the altar *which was* of cedar.

21So Solomon overlaid the house within with pure gold: and he made a partition by the chains of gold before the oracle; and he overlaid it with gold.

22And the whole house he overlaid with gold, until he had finished all the house: also the whole altar that *was* by the oracle he overlaid with gold.

23¶ And within the oracle he made two cherubims *of* olive tree, *each* ten cubits high.

24And five cubits *was* the one wing of the cherub, and five cubits the other wing of the cherub: from the uttermost part of the one wing unto the uttermost part of the other *were* ten cubits.

25And the other cherub *was* ten cubits: both the cherubims *were* of one measure and one size.

26The height of the one cherub *was* ten cubits, and so *was it* of the other cherub.

27And he set the cherubims within the inner house: and they stretched forth the wings of the cherubims, so that the wing of the one touched the *one* wall, and the wing of the other cherub touched the other wall; and their wings touched one another in the midst of the house.

28And he overlaid the cherubims with gold.

29And he carved all the walls of the house round about with carved figures of cherubims and palm trees and open flowers, within and without.

New International

wide, the middle floor six cubits[a] and the third floor seven.[b] He made offset ledges around the outside of the temple so that nothing would be inserted into the temple walls.

7In building the temple, only blocks dressed at the quarry were used, and no hammer, chisel or any other iron tool was heard at the temple site while it was being built.

8The entrance to the lowest[c] floor was on the south side of the temple; a stairway led up to the middle level and from there to the third. 9So he built the temple and completed it, roofing it with beams and cedar planks. 10And he built the side rooms all along the temple. The height of each was five cubits, and they were attached to the temple by beams of cedar.

11The word of the LORD came to Solomon: 12"As for this temple you are building, if you follow my decrees, carry out my regulations and keep all my commands and obey them, I will fulfill through you the promise I gave to David your father. 13And I will live among the Israelites and will not abandon my people Israel."

14So Solomon built the temple and completed it. 15He lined its interior walls with cedar boards, paneling them from the floor of the temple to the ceiling, and covered the floor of the temple with planks of pine. 16He partitioned off twenty cubits[d] at the rear of the temple with cedar boards from floor to ceiling to form within the temple an inner sanctuary, the Most Holy Place. 17The main hall in front of this room was forty cubits[e] long. 18The inside of the temple was cedar, carved with gourds and open flowers. Everything was cedar; no stone was to be seen.

19He prepared the inner sanctuary within the temple to set the ark of the covenant of the LORD there. 20The inner sanctuary was twenty cubits long, twenty wide and twenty high.[f] He overlaid the inside with pure gold, and he also overlaid the altar of cedar. 21Solomon covered the inside of the temple with pure gold, and he extended gold chains across the front of the inner sanctuary, which was overlaid with gold. 22So he overlaid the whole interior with gold. He also overlaid with gold the altar that belonged to the inner sanctuary.

23In the inner sanctuary he made a pair of cherubim of olive wood, each ten cubits[g] high. 24One wing of the first cherub was five cubits long, and the other wing five cubits—ten cubits from wing tip to wing tip. 25The second cherub also measured ten cubits, for the two cherubim were identical in size and shape. 26The height of each cherub was ten cubits. 27He placed the cherubim inside the innermost room of the temple, with their wings spread out. The wing of one cherub touched one wall, while the wing of the other touched the other wall, and their wings touched each other in the middle of the room. 28He overlaid the cherubim with gold.

29On the walls all around the temple, in both the inner and outer rooms, he carved cherubim, palm trees and

---

a 6 That is, about 9 feet (about 2.7 meters)   b 6 That is, about 10 1/2 feet (about 3.1 meters)   c 8 Septuagint; Hebrew *middle*   d 16 That is, about 30 feet (about 9 meters)   e 17 That is, about 60 feet (about 18 meters)   f 20 That is, about 30 feet (about 9 meters) long, wide and high   g 23 That is, about 15 feet (about 4.5 meters)

Living Bible

6These rooms were three stories high, the lower floor being 7½ feet wide, the second floor 9 feet wide, and the upper floor 10½ feet wide. The rooms were connected to the walls of the Temple by beams resting on blocks built out from the wall—so the beams were not inserted into the walls themselves.

7The stones used in the construction of the Temple were prefinished at the quarry, so the entire structure was built without the sound of hammer, axe, or any other tool at the building site.

8The bottom floor of the side rooms was entered from the right side of the Temple, and there were winding stairs going up to the second floor; another flight of stairs led from the second to the third. 9After completing the Temple, Solomon paneled it all, including the beams and pillars, with cedar. 10As already stated, there was an annex on each side of the building, attached to the Temple walls by cedar timbers. Each story of the annex was 7½ feet high.

11, 12Then the Lord sent this message to Solomon concerning the Temple he was building: "If you do as I tell you to and follow all of my commandments and instructions, I will do what I told your father David I would do: 13I will live among the people of Israel and never forsake them."

14At last the Temple was finished. 15The entire inside, from floor to ceiling, was paneled with cedar, and the floors were made of cypress boards. 16The thirty-foot inner room at the far end of the Temple—the Most Holy Place—was also paneled from the floor to the ceiling with cedar boards. 17The remainder of the Temple—other than the Most Holy Place—was sixty feet long. 18Throughout the Temple the cedar paneling laid over the stone walls was carved with designs of rosebuds and open flowers.

19The inner room was where the Ark of the Covenant of the Lord was placed. 20This inner sanctuary was thirty feet long, thirty feet wide, and thirty feet high. Its walls and ceiling were overlaid with pure gold, and Solomon made a cedar-wood altar for this room. 21, 22Then he overlaid the interior of the remainder of the Temple—including the cedar altar—with pure gold; and he made gold chains to protect the entrance to the Most Holy Place.

23-28Within the inner sanctuary Solomon placed two statues of Guardian Angelsʰ made from olive wood, each fifteen feet high. They were placed so that their outspread wings reached from wall to wall, while their inner wings touched each other at the center of the room; each wing was 7½ feet long, so each angel measured fifteen feet from wing tip to wing tip. The two angels were identical in all dimensions, and each was overlaid with gold.

29Figures of angels, palm trees, and open flowers were carved on all the walls of both rooms of the Tem-

New Revised Standard

wide, the middle one was six cubits wide, and the third was seven cubits wide; for around the outside of the house he made offsets on the wall in order that the supporting beams should not be inserted into the walls of the house.

7 The house was built with stone finished at the quarry, so that neither hammer nor ax nor any tool of iron was heard in the temple while it was being built.

8 The entrance for the middle story was on the south side of the house: one went up by winding stairs to the middle story, and from the middle story to the third. 9So he built the house, and finished it; he roofed the house with beams and planks of cedar. 10He built the structure against the whole house, each storyⁱ five cubits high, and it was joined to the house with timbers of cedar.

11 Now the word of the LORD came to Solomon, 12"Concerning this house that you are building, if you will walk in my statutes, obey my ordinances, and keep all my commandments by walking in them, then I will establish my promise with you, which I made to your father David. 13I will dwell among the children of Israel, and will not forsake my people Israel."

14 So Solomon built the house, and finished it. 15He lined the walls of the house on the inside with boards of cedar; from the floor of the house to the rafters of the ceiling, he covered them on the inside with wood; and he covered the floor of the house with boards of cypress. 16He built twenty cubits of the rear of the house with boards of cedar from the floor to the rafters, and he built this within as an inner sanctuary, as the most holy place. 17The house, that is, the nave in front of the inner sanctuary, was forty cubits long. 18The cedar within the house had carvings of gourds and open flowers; all was cedar, no stone was seen. 19The inner sanctuary he prepared in the innermost part of the house, to set there the ark of the covenant of the LORD. 20The interior of the inner sanctuary was twenty cubits long, twenty cubits wide, and twenty cubits high; he overlaid it with pure gold. He also overlaid the altar with cedar.ʲ 21Solomon overlaid the inside of the house with pure gold, then he drew chains of gold across, in front of the inner sanctuary, and overlaid it with gold. 22Next he overlaid the whole house with gold, in order that the whole house might be perfect; even the whole altar that belonged to the inner sanctuary he overlaid with gold.

The Furnishings of the Temple

23 In the inner sanctuary he made two cherubim of olivewood, each ten cubits high. 24Five cubits was the length of one wing of the cherub, and five cubits the length of the other wing of the cherub; it was ten cubits from the tip of one wing to the tip of the other. 25The other cherub also measured ten cubits; both cherubim had the same measure and the same form. 26The height of one cherub was ten cubits, and so was that of the other cherub. 27He put the cherubim in the innermost part of the house; the wings of the cherubim were spread out so that a wing of one was touching the one wall, and a wing of the other cherub was touching the other wall; their other wings toward the center of the house were touching wing to wing. 28He also overlaid the cherubim with gold.

29 He carved the walls of the house all around about with carved engravings of cherubim, palm trees, and open flowers, in the inner and outer rooms. 30The floor

---

ʰ 6:23-28 *two statues of Guardian Angels*, literally, "he made two cherubim."   ⁱ Heb lacks *each story*   ʲ Meaning of Heb uncertain

King James

30And the floor of the house he overlaid with gold, within and without.

31¶ And for the entering of the oracle he made doors of olive tree: the lintel *and* side posts *were* a fifth part of the wall.

32The two doors also *were of* olive tree; and he carved upon them carvings of cherubims and palm trees and open flowers, and overlaid *them* with gold, and spread gold upon the cherubims, and upon the palm trees.

33So also made he for the door of the temple posts *of* olive tree, a fourth part *of the wall.*

34And the two doors *were of* fir tree: the two leaves of the one door *were* folding, and the two leaves of the other door *were* folding.

35And he carved *thereon* cherubims and palm trees and open flowers: and covered *them* with gold fitted upon the carved work.

36¶ And he built the inner court with three rows of hewed stone, and a row of cedar beams.

37¶ In the fourth year was the foundation of the house of the LORD laid, in the month Zif:

38And in the eleventh year, in the month Bul, which *is* the eighth month, was the house finished throughout all the parts thereof, and according to all the fashion of it. So was he seven years in building it.

7 BUT SOLOMON was building his own house thirteen years, and he finished all his house.

2¶ He built also the house of the forest of Lebanon; the length thereof *was* an hundred cubits, and the breadth thereof fifty cubits, and the height thereof thirty cubits, upon four rows of cedar pillars, with cedar beams upon the pillars.

3And *it was* covered with cedar above upon the beams, that *lay* on forty-five pillars, fifteen *in* a row.

4And *there were* windows *in* three rows, and light *was* against light in three ranks.

5And all the doors and posts *were* square, with the windows: and light *was* against light *in* three ranks.

6¶ And he made a porch of pillars; the length thereof *was* fifty cubits, and the breadth thereof thirty cubits: and the porch *was* before them: and the *other* pillars and the thick beam *were* before them.

7¶ Then he made a porch for the throne where he might judge, *even* the porch of judgment: and *it was* covered with cedar from one side of the floor to the other.

8¶ And his house where he dwelt *had* another court within the porch, *which* was of the like work. Solomon made also an house for Pharaoh's daughter, whom he had taken *to wife*, like unto this porch.

9All these *were of* costly stones, according to the measures of hewed stones, sawed with saws, within and without, even from the foundation unto the coping, and *so* on the outside toward the great court.

10And the foundation *was of* costly stones, even great stones, stones of ten cubits, and stones of eight cubits.

11And above *were* costly stones, after the measures of hewed stones, and cedars.

12And the great court round about *was* with three rows of hewed stones, and a row of cedar beams, both for the inner court of the house of the LORD, and for the porch of the house.

13¶ And king Solomon sent and fetched Hiram out of Tyre.

14He *was* a widow's son of the tribe of Naphtali, and his father *was* a man of Tyre, a worker in brass: and he was filled with wisdom, and understanding, and cunning to work all works in brass. And he came to king Solomon, and wrought all his work.

New International

open flowers. 30He also covered the floors of both the inner and outer rooms of the temple with gold.

31For the entrance of the inner sanctuary he made doors of olive wood with five-sided jambs. 32And on the two olive wood doors he carved cherubim, palm trees and open flowers, and overlaid the cherubim and palm trees with beaten gold. 33In the same way he made four-sided jambs of olive wood for the entrance to the main hall. 34He also made two pine doors, each having two leaves that turned in sockets. 35He carved cherubim, palm trees and open flowers on them and overlaid them with gold hammered evenly over the carvings.

36And he built the inner courtyard of three courses of dressed stone and one course of trimmed cedar beams.

37The foundation of the temple of the LORD was laid in the fourth year, in the month of Ziv. 38In the eleventh year in the month of Bul, the eighth month, the temple was finished in all its details according to its specifications. He had spent seven years building it.

Solomon Builds His Palace

7 IT TOOK Solomon thirteen years, however, to complete the construction of his palace. 2He built the Palace of the Forest of Lebanon a hundred cubits long, fifty wide and thirty high,[a] with four rows of cedar columns supporting trimmed cedar beams. 3It was roofed with cedar above the beams that rested on the columns—forty-five beams, fifteen to a row. 4Its windows were placed high in sets of three, facing each other. 5All the doorways had rectangular frames; they were in the front part in sets of three, facing each other.[b]

6He made a colonnade fifty cubits long and thirty wide.[c] In front of it was a portico, and in front of that were pillars and an overhanging roof.

7He built the throne hall, the Hall of Justice, where he was to judge, and he covered it with cedar from floor to ceiling.[d] 8And the palace in which he was to live, set farther back, was similar in design. Solomon also made a palace like this hall for Pharaoh's daughter, whom he had married.

9All these structures, from the outside to the great courtyard and from foundation to eaves, were made of blocks of high-grade stone cut to size and trimmed with a saw on their inner and outer faces. 10The foundations were laid with large stones of good quality, some measuring ten cubits[e] and some eight.[f] 11Above were high-grade stones, cut to size, and cedar beams. 12The great courtyard was surrounded by a wall of three courses of dressed stone and one course of trimmed cedar beams, as was the inner courtyard of the temple of the LORD with its portico.

The Temple's Furnishings

13King Solomon sent to Tyre and brought Huram,[g] 14whose mother was a widow from the tribe of Naphtali and whose father was a man of Tyre and a craftsman in bronze. Huram was highly skilled and experienced in all kinds of bronze work. He came to King Solomon and did all the work assigned to him.

---

[a] 2 That is, about 150 feet (about 46 meters) long, 75 feet (about 23 meters) wide and 45 feet (about 13.5 meters) high   [b] 5 The meaning of the Hebrew for this verse is uncertain.   [c] 6 That is, about 75 feet (about 23 meters) long and 45 feet (about 13.5 meters) wide   [d] 7 Vulgate and Syriac; Hebrew *floor*   [e] 10 That is, about 15 feet (about 4.5 meters)   [f] 10 That is, about 12 feet (about 3.6 meters)   [g] 13 Hebrew *Hiram*, a variant of *Huram*; also in verses 40 and 45

Living Bible

ple, 30and the floor of both rooms was overlaid with gold.

31The doorway to the inner sanctuary was a five-sided opening, 32and its two olive-wood doors were carved with Guardian Angels, palm trees, and open flowers, all overlaid with gold.

33Then he made square doorposts of olive wood for the entrance to the Temple. 34There were two folding doors of cypress wood, and each door was hinged to fold back upon itself. 35Angels, palm trees, and open flowers were carved on these doors and carefully overlaid with gold.

36The wall of the inner court had three layers of hewn stone and one layer of cedar beams.

37The foundation of the Temple was laid in the month of May in the fourth year of Solomon's reign, 38and the entire building was completed in every detail in November of the eleventh year of his reign. So it took seven years to build.

7 THEN SOLOMON built his own palace, which took thirteen years to construct.

2One of the rooms in the palace was called the Hall of the Forest of Lebanon. It was huge—measuring 150 feet long, 75 feet wide, and 45 feet high. The great cedar ceiling beams rested upon four rows of cedar pillars. 3, 4There were forty-five windows in the hall, set in three tiers, one tier above the other, five to a tier, facing each other from three walls. 5Each of the doorways and windows had a square frame.

6Another room was called the Hall of Pillars. It was seventy-five feet long and forty-five feet wide, with a porch in front covered by a canopy which was supported by pillars.

7There was also the Throne Room or Judgment Hall, where Solomon sat to hear legal matters; it was paneled with cedar from the floor to the rafters.

8His cedar-paneled living quarters surrounded a courtyard behind this hall. (He designed similar living quarters, the same size, in the palace which he built for Pharaoh's daughter—one of his wives.) 9These buildings were constructed entirely from huge, expensive stones, cut to measure. 10The foundation stones were twelve to fifteen feet across. 11The huge stones in the walls were also cut to measure, and were topped with cedar beams. 12The Great Court had three courses of hewn stone in its walls, topped with cedar beams, just like the inner court of the Temple and the porch of the palace.

13King Solomon then asked for a man named Hiram to come from Tyre, for he was a skilled craftsman in bronze work. 14He was half Jewish, being the son of a widow of the tribe of Naphtali, and his father had been a foundry worker from Tyre. So he came to work for King Solomon.

New Revised Standard

of the house he overlaid with gold, in the inner and outer rooms.

31 For the entrance to the inner sanctuary he made doors of olivewood; the lintel and the doorposts were five-sided.h 32He covered the two doors of olivewood with carvings of cherubim, palm trees, and open flowers; he overlaid them with gold, and spread gold on the cherubim and on the palm trees.

33 So also he made for the entrance to the nave doorposts of olivewood, four-sided each, 34and two doors of cypress wood; the two leaves of the one door were folding, and the two leaves of the other door were folding. 35He carved cherubim, palm trees, and open flowers, overlaying them with gold evenly applied upon the carved work. 36He built the inner court with three courses of dressed stone to one course of cedar beams.

37 In the fourth year the foundation of the house of the Lord was laid, in the month of Ziv. 38 In the eleventh year, in the month of Bul, which is the eighth month, the house was finished in all its parts, and according to all its specifications. He was seven years in building it.

Solomon's Palace and Other Buildings

7 SOLOMON WAS building his own house thirteen years, and he finished his entire house.

2 He built the House of the Forest of the Lebanon one hundred cubits long, fifty cubits wide, and thirty cubits high, built on four rows of cedar pillars, with cedar beams on the pillars. 3It was roofed with cedar on the forty-five rafters, fifteen in each row, which were on the pillars. 4There were window frames in the three rows, facing each other in the three rows. 5All the doorways and doorposts had four-sided frames, opposite, facing each other in the three rows.

6 He made the Hall of Pillars fifty cubits long and thirty cubits wide. There was a porch in front with pillars, and a canopy in front of them.

7 He made the Hall of the Throne where he was to pronounce judgment, the Hall of Justice, covered with cedar from floor to floor.

8 His own house where he would reside, in the other court back of the hall, was of the same construction. Solomon also made a house like this hall for Pharaoh's daughter, whom he had taken in marriage.

9 All these were made of costly stones, cut according to measure, sawed with saws, back and front, from the foundation to the coping, and from outside to the great court. 10The foundation was of costly stones, huge stones, stones of eight and ten cubits. 11There were costly stones above, cut to measure, and cedarwood. 12The great court had three courses of dressed stone to one layer of cedar beams all around; so had the inner court of the house of the Lord, and the vestibule of the house.

Products of Hiram the Bronzeworker

13 Now King Solomon invited and received Hiram from Tyre. 14He was the son of a widow of the tribe of Naphtali, whose father, a man of Tyre, had been an artisan in bronze; he was full of skill, intelligence, and knowledge in working bronze. He came to King Solomon, and did all his work.

h Meaning of Heb uncertain

King James

15For he cast two pillars of brass, of eighteen cubits high apiece: and a line of twelve cubits did compass either of them about.

16And he made two chapiters *of* molten brass, to set upon the tops of the pillars: the height of the one chapiter *was* five cubits, and the height of the other chapiter *was* five cubits:

17*And* nets of checker work, and wreaths of chain work, for the chapiters which *were* upon the top of the pillars; seven for the one chapiter, and seven for the other chapiter.

18And he made the pillars, and two rows round about upon the one network, to cover the chapiters that *were* upon the top, with pomegranates: and so did he for the other chapiter.

19And the chapiters that *were* upon the top of the pillars *were* of lily work in the porch, four cubits.

20And the chapiters upon the two pillars had pomegranates also above, over against the belly which *was* by the network: and the pomegranates *were* two hundred in rows round about upon the other chapiter.

21And he set up the pillars in the porch of the temple: and he set up the right pillar, and called the name thereof Jachin: and he set up the left pillar, and called the name thereof Boaz.

22And upon the top of the pillars *was* lily work: so was the work of the pillars finished.

23¶ And he made a molten sea, ten cubits from the one brim to the other: *it was* round all about, and his height *was* five cubits: and a line of thirty cubits did compass it round about.

24And under the brim of it round about *there were* knobs compassing it, ten in a cubit, compassing the sea round about: the knobs *were* cast in two rows, when it was cast.

25It stood upon twelve oxen, three looking toward the north, and three looking toward the west, and three looking toward the south, and three looking toward the east: and the sea *was set* above upon them, and all their hinder parts *were* inward.

26And it *was* an handbreadth thick, and the brim thereof was wrought like the brim of a cup, with flowers of lilies: it contained two thousand baths.

27¶ And he made ten bases of brass; four cubits *was* the length of one base, and four cubits the breadth thereof, and three cubits the height of it.

28And the work of the bases *was* on this *manner:* they had borders, and the borders *were* between the ledges:

29And on the borders that *were* between the ledges *were* lions, oxen, and cherubims: and upon the ledges *there was* a base above: and beneath the lions and oxen *were* certain additions made of thin work.

30And every base had four brasen wheels, and plates of brass: and the four corners thereof had undersetters: under the laver *were* undersetters molten, at the side of every addition.

31And the mouth of it within the chapiter and above *was* a cubit: but the mouth thereof *was* round *after* the work of the base, a cubit and an half: and also upon the mouth of it *were* gravings with their borders, foursquare, not round.

32And under the borders *were* four wheels; and the axletrees of the wheels *were joined* to the base: and the height of a wheel *was* a cubit and half a cubit.

33And the work of the wheels *was* like the work of a chariot wheel: their axletrees, and their naves, and their felloes, and their spokes, *were* all molten.

34And *there were* four undersetters to the four corners of one base: *and* the undersetters *were* of the very base itself.

35And in the top of the base *was there* a round compass of half a cubit high: and on the top of the base the ledges thereof and the borders thereof *were* of the same.

New International

15He cast two bronze pillars, each eighteen cubits high and twelve cubits around,[a] by line. 16He also made two capitals of cast bronze to set on the tops of the pillars; each capital was five cubits[b] high. 17A network of interwoven chains festooned the capitals on top of the pillars, seven for each capital. 18He made pomegranates in two rows[c] encircling each network to decorate the capitals on top of the pillars.[d] He did the same for each capital. 19The capitals on top of the pillars in the portico were in the shape of lilies, four cubits[e] high. 20On the capitals of both pillars, above the bowl-shaped part next to the network, were the two hundred pomegranates in rows all around. 21He erected the pillars at the portico of the temple. The pillar to the south he named Jakin[f] and the one to the north Boaz.[g] 22The capitals on top were in the shape of lilies. And so the work on the pillars was completed.

23He made the Sea of cast metal, circular in shape, measuring ten cubits[h] from rim to rim and five cubits high. It took a line of thirty cubits[i] to measure around it. 24Below the rim, gourds encircled it—ten to a cubit. The gourds were cast in two rows in one piece with the Sea.

25The Sea stood on twelve bulls, three facing north, three facing west, three facing south and three facing east. The Sea rested on top of them, and their hindquarters were toward the center. 26It was a handbreadth[j] in thickness, and its rim was like the rim of a cup, like a lily blossom. It held two thousand baths.[k]

27He also made ten movable stands of bronze; each was four cubits long, four cubits wide and three high.[l] 28This is how the stands were made: They had side panels attached to uprights. 29On the panels between the uprights were lions, bulls and cherubim—and on the uprights as well. Above and below the lions and bulls were wreaths of hammered work. 30Each stand had four bronze wheels with bronze axles, and each had a basin resting on four supports, cast with wreaths on each side. 31On the inside of the stand there was an opening that had a circular frame one cubit[m] deep. This opening was round, and with its basework it measured a cubit and a half.[n] Around its opening there was engraving. The panels of the stands were square, not round. 32The four wheels were under the panels, and the axles of the wheels were attached to the stand. The diameter of each wheel was a cubit and a half. 33The wheels were made like chariot wheels; the axles, rims, spokes and hubs were all of cast metal.

34Each stand had four handles, one on each corner, projecting from the stand. 35At the top of the stand there was a circular band half a cubit[o] deep. The supports and panels were attached to the top of the stand. 36He en-

a *15* That is, about 27 feet (about 8.1 meters) high and 18 feet (about 5.4 meters) around   b *16* That is, about 7 1/2 feet (about 2.3 meters); also in verse 23   c *18* Two Hebrew manuscripts and Septuagint; most Hebrew manuscripts *made the pillars, and there were two rows*   d *18* Many Hebrew manuscripts and Syriac; most Hebrew manuscripts *pomegranates*   e *19* That is, about 6 feet (about 1.8 meters); also in verse 38   f *21 Jakin* probably means *he establishes.*   g *21 Boaz* probably means *in him is strength.*   h *23* That is, about 15 feet (about 4.5 meters)   i *23* That is, about 45 feet (about 13.5 meters)   j *26* That is, about 3 inches (about 8 centimeters)   k *26* That is, probably about 11,500 gallons (about 44 kiloliters); the Septuagint does not have this sentence.   l *27* That is, about 6 feet (about 1.8 meters) long and wide and about 4 1/2 feet (about 1.3 meters) high   m *31* That is, about 1 1/2 feet (about 0.5 meter)   n *31* That is, about 2 1/4 feet (about 0.7 meter); also in verse 32   o *35* That is, about 3/4 foot (about 0.2 meter)

Living Bible

15He cast two hollow bronze pillars, each twenty-seven feet high and eighteen feet around, with three-inch-thick walls. 16–22At the tops of the pillars he made two lily-shaped capitals from molten bronze, each 7½ feet high. The upper part of each capital was shaped like a lily, six feet high. Each capital was decorated with seven sets of bronze, chain-designed lattices and four hundred pomegranates in two rows. Hiram set these pillars at the entrance of the Temple. The one on the south was named the Jachin Pillar, and the one on the north, the Boaz Pillar.P

23Then Hiram cast a round bronze tank, 7½ feet high and 15 feet from brim to brim; 45 feet in circumference. 24On the underside of the rim were two rows of ornaments an inch or two apart,q which were cast along with the tank. 25It rested on twelve bronzer oxen standing tail to tail, three facing north, three west, three south, and three east. 26The sides of the tank were four inches thick; its brim was shaped like a goblet, and it had a twelve thousand gallon capacity.

27–30Then he made ten four-wheeled movable stands, each 6 feet square and 4½ feet high. They were constructed with undercarriages braced with squares crosspieces. These crosspieces were decorated with carved lions, oxen, and angels. Above and below the lions and oxen were wreath decorations. Each of these movable stands had four bronze wheels and bronze axles, and at each corner of the stands were supporting posts made of bronze and decorated with wreaths on each side. 31The top of each stand was a round piece 1½ feet high. Its center was concave, 2¼ feet deep, decorated on the outside with wreaths. Its panels were square, not round.

32The stands rode on four wheels which were connected to axles that had been cast as part of the stands. The wheels were twenty-seven inches high, 33and were similar to chariot wheels. All the parts of the stands were cast from molten bronze, including the axles, spokes, rims, and hubs. 34There were supports at each of the four corners of the stands, and these, too, were cast with the stands. 35A nine-inch rim surrounded the tip of each stand, banded with lugs. All was cast as one unit with the stand. 36Guardian Angels, lions, and palm trees sur-

New Revised Standard

15 He cast two pillars of bronze. Eighteen cubits was the height of the one, and a cord of twelve cubits would encircle it; the second pillar was the same.t 16He also made two capitals of molten bronze, to set on the tops of the pillars; the height of the one capital was five cubits, and the height of the other capital was five cubits. 17There were nets of checker work with wreaths of chain work for the capitals on the tops of the pillars; sevenu for the one capital, and sevenu for the other capital. 18He made the columns with two rows around each latticework to cover the capitals that were above the pomegranates; he did the same with the other capital. 19Now the capitals that were on the tops of the pillars in the vestibule were of lily-work, four cubits high. 20The capitals were on the two pillars and also above the rounded projection that was beside the latticework; there were two hundred pomegranates in rows all around; and so with the other capital. 21He set up the pillars at the vestibule of the temple; he set up the pillar on the south and called it Jachin; and he set up the pillar on the north and called it Boaz. 22On the tops of the pillars was lily-work. Thus the work of the pillars was finished.

23 Then he made the molten sea; it was round, ten cubits from brim to brim, and five cubits high. A line of thirty cubits would encircle it completely. 24Under its brim were panels all around, each of ten cubits, surrounding the sea; there were two rows of panels, cast when it was cast. 25It stood on twelve oxen, three facing north, three facing west, three facing south, and three facing east; the sea was set on them. The hindquarters of each were toward the inside. 26Its thickness was a handbreadth; its brim was made like the brim of a cup, like the flower of a lily; it held two thousand baths.v

27 He also made the ten stands of bronze; each stand was four cubits long, four cubits wide, and three cubits high. 28This was the construction of the stands: they had borders; the borders were within the frames; 29on the borders that were set in the frames were lions, oxen, and cherubim. On the frames, both above and below the lions and oxen, there were wreaths of beveled work. 30Each stand had four bronze wheels and axles of bronze; at the four corners were supports for a basin. The supports were cast with wreaths at the side of each. 31Its opening was within the crown whose height was one cubit; its opening was round, as a pedestal is made; it was a cubit and a half wide. At its opening there were carvings; its borders were four-sided, not round. 32The four wheels were underneath the borders; the axles of the wheels were in the stands; and the height of a wheel was a cubit and a half. 33The wheels were made like a chariot wheel; their axles, their rims, their spokes, and their hubs were all cast. 34There were four supports at the four corners of each stand; the supports were of one piece with the stands. 35On the top of the stand there was a round band half a cubit high; on the top of the stand, its stays and its borders were of one piece with it. 36On the

---

P *7:22 Jachin Pillar and Boaz Pillar.* Jachin means "to establish," and Boaz means "strength."   q *7:24 an inch or two apart,* literally, "ten in a cubit."   r *7:25 bronze,* implied.   s *7:27 square,* implied in vs 31.

t Cn: Heb *and a cord of twelve cubits encircled the second pillar*; Compare Jer 52.21   u Heb: Gk *a net*   v A Heb measure of volume

King James

36For on the plates of the ledges thereof, and on the borders thereof, he graved cherubims, lions, and palm trees, according to the proportion of every one, and additions round about.

37After this *manner* he made the ten bases; all of them had one casting, one measure, *and* one size.

38¶ Then made he ten lavers of brass: one laver contained forty baths: *and* every laver was four cubits: *and* upon every one of the ten bases one laver.

39And he put five bases on the right side of the house, and five on the left side of the house: and he set the sea on the right side of the house eastward over against the south.

40¶ And Hiram made the lavers, and the shovels, and the basins. So Hiram made an end of doing all the work that he made king Solomon for the house of the LORD:

41The two pillars, and the *two* bowls of the chapiters that *were* on the top of the two pillars; and the two networks, to cover the two bowls of the chapiters which *were* upon the top of the two pillars;

42And four hundred pomegranates for the two networks, *even* two rows of pomegranates for one network, to cover the two bowls of the chapiters that *were* upon the pillars;

43And the ten bases, and ten lavers on the bases;

44And one sea, and twelve oxen under the sea;

45And the pots, and the shovels, and the basins: and all these vessels, which Hiram made to king Solomon for the house of the LORD, *were of* bright brass.

46In the plain of Jordan did the king cast them, in the clay ground between Succoth and Zarthan.

47And Solomon left all the vessels *unweighed*, because they were exceeding many: neither was the weight of the brass found out.

48And Solomon made all the vessels that *pertained* unto the house of the LORD: the altar of gold, and the table of gold, whereupon the showbread *was*,

49And the candlesticks of pure gold, five on the right *side*, and five on the left, before the oracle, with the flowers, and the lamps, and the tongs *of* gold,

50And the bowls, and the snuffers, and the basins, and the spoons, and the censers *of* pure gold; and the hinges *of* gold, *both* for the doors of the inner house, the most holy *place, and* for the doors of the house, *to wit*, of the temple.

51So was ended all the work that king Solomon made for the house of the LORD. And Solomon brought in the things which David his father had dedicated; *even* the silver, and the gold, and the vessels, did he put among the treasures of the house of the LORD.

8 THEN SOLOMON assembled the elders of Israel, and all the heads of the tribes, the chief of the fathers of the children of Israel, unto king Solomon in Jerusalem, that they might bring up the ark of the covenant of the LORD out of the city of David, which *is* Zion.

2And all the men of Israel assembled themselves unto king Solomon at the feast in the month Ethanim, which *is* the seventh month.

3And all the elders of Israel came, and the priests took up the ark.

4And they brought up the ark of the LORD, and the tabernacle of the congregation, and all the holy vessels that *were* in the tabernacle, even those did the priests and the Levites bring up.

5And king Solomon, and all the congregation of Israel, that were assembled unto him, *were* with him before the ark, sacrificing sheep and oxen, that could not be told nor numbered for multitude.

New International

graved cherubim, lions and palm trees on the surfaces of the supports and on the panels, in every available space, with wreaths all around. 37This is the way he made the ten stands. They were all cast in the same molds and were identical in size and shape.

38He then made ten bronze basins, each holding forty bathsa and measuring four cubits across, one basin to go on each of the ten stands. 39He placed five of the stands on the south side of the temple and five on the north. He placed the Sea on the south side, at the southeast corner of the temple. 40He also made the basins and shovels and sprinkling bowls.

So Huram finished all the work he had undertaken for King Solomon in the temple of the LORD:

41the two pillars;
the two bowl-shaped capitals on top of the pillars;
the two sets of network decorating the two bowl-shaped capitals on top of the pillars;

42the four hundred pomegranates for the two sets of network (two rows of pomegranates for each network, decorating the bowl-shaped capitals on top of the pillars);

43the ten stands with their ten basins;

44the Sea and the twelve bulls under it;

45the pots, shovels and sprinkling bowls.

All these objects that Huram made for King Solomon for the temple of the LORD were of burnished bronze. 46The king had them cast in clay molds in the plain of the Jordan between Succoth and Zarethan. 47Solomon left all these things unweighed, because there were so many; the weight of the bronze was not determined.

48Solomon also made all the furnishings that were in the LORD's temple:

the golden altar;
the golden table on which was the bread of the Presence;

49the lampstands of pure gold (five on the right and five on the left, in front of the inner sanctuary);
the gold floral work and lamps and tongs;

50the pure gold basins, wick trimmers, sprinkling bowls, dishes and censers;
and the gold sockets for the doors of the innermost room, the Most Holy Place, and also for the doors of the main hall of the temple.

51When all the work King Solomon had done for the temple of the LORD was finished, he brought in the things his father David had dedicated—the silver and gold and the furnishings—and he placed them in the treasuries of the LORD's temple.

The Ark Brought to the Temple

8 THEN KING Solomon summoned into his presence at Jerusalem the elders of Israel, all the heads of the tribes and the chiefs of the Israelite families, to bring up the ark of the LORD's covenant from Zion, the City of David. 2All the men of Israel came together to King Solomon at the time of the festival in the month of Ethanim, the seventh month.

3When all the elders of Israel had arrived, the priests took up the ark, 4and they brought up the ark of the LORD and the Tent of Meeting and all the sacred furnishings in it. The priests and Levites carried them up, 5and King Solomon and the entire assembly of Israel that had gathered about him were before the ark, sacrificing so many sheep and cattle that they could not be recorded or counted.

---

a *38* That is, about 230 gallons (about 880 liters)

Living Bible

rounded by wreaths were engraved on the borders of the band wherever there was room. 37All ten stands were the same size and were made alike, for each was cast from the same mold.

38Then he made ten brass vats, and placed them on the stands. Each vat was six feet square and contained 240 gallons of water. 39Five of these vats were arranged on the left and five on the right-hand side of the room. The tank was in the southeast corner, on the right-hand side of the room. 40Hiram also made the necessary pots, shovels, and basins and at last completed the work in the Temple of the Lord which had been assigned to him by King Solomon.

41-46Here is a list of the items he made:
Two pillars;
A capital at the top of each pillar;
Latticework covering the bases of the capitals of each pillar;
Four hundred pomegranates in two rows on the latticework, to cover the bases of the two capitals;
Ten movable stands holding ten vats;
One large tank and twelve oxen supporting it;
Pots;
Shovels;
Basins.

All these items were made of burnished bronze, and were cast at the plains of the Jordan River between Succoth and Zarethan. 47The total weight of these pieces was not known because they were too heavy to weigh!

48All the utensils and furniture used in the Temple were made of solid gold. This included the altar, the table where the Bread of the Presence of God was displayed, 49the lampstands (five on the right-hand side and five on the left, in front of the Most Holy Place), the flowers, lamps, tongs, 50cups, snuffers, basins, spoons, firepans, the hinges of the doors to the Most Holy Place, and the main entrance doors of the Temple. Each of these was made of solid gold.

51When the Temple was finally finished, Solomon took into the treasury of the Temple the silver, the gold, and all the vessels dedicated for that purpose by his father David.

8 THEN SOLOMON called a convocation at Jerusalem of all the leaders of Israel—the heads of the tribes and clans—to observe the transferring of the Ark of the Covenant of the Lord from the Tabernacle in Zion, the City of David, to the Temple. 2This celebration occurred at the time of the Tabernacle Festival in the month of October. 3, 4During the festivities the priests carried the Ark to the Temple, along with all the sacred vessels which had previously been in the Tabernacle. 5King Solomon and all the people gathered before the Ark, sacrificing uncounted sheep and oxen.

New Revised Standard

surfaces of its stays and on its borders he carved cherubim, lions, and palm trees, where each had space, with wreaths all around. 37In this way he made the ten stands; all of them were cast alike, with the same size and the same form.

38 He made ten basins of bronze; each basin held forty baths,b each basin measured four cubits; there was a basin for each of the ten stands. 39He set five of the stands on the south side of the house, and five on the north side of the house; he set the sea on the southeast corner of the house.

40 Hiram also made the pots, the shovels, and the basins. So Hiram finished all the work that he did for King Solomon on the house of the LORD: 41the two pillars, the two bowls of the capitals that were on the tops of the pillars, the two latticeworks to cover the two bowls of the capitals that were on the tops of the pillars; 42the four hundred pomegranates for the two latticeworks, two rows of pomegranates for each latticework, to cover the two bowls of the capitals that were on the pillars; 43the ten stands, the ten basins on the stands; 44the one sea, and the twelve oxen underneath the sea.

45 The pots, the shovels, and the basins, all these vessels that Hiram made for King Solomon for the house of the LORD were of burnished bronze. 46In the plain of the Jordan the king cast them, in the clay ground between Succoth and Zarethan. 47Solomon left all the vessels unweighed, because there were so many of them; the weight of the bronze was not determined.

48 So Solomon made all the vessels that were in the house of the LORD: the golden altar, the golden table for the bread of the Presence, 49the lampstands of pure gold, five on the south side and five on the north, in front of the inner sanctuary; the flowers, the lamps, and the tongs, of gold; 50the cups, snuffers, basins, dishes for incense, and firepans, of pure gold; the sockets for the doors of the innermost part of the house, the most holy place, and for the doors of the nave of the temple, of gold.

51 Thus all the work that King Solomon did on the house of the LORD was finished. Solomon brought in the things that his father David had dedicated, the silver, the gold, and the vessels, and stored them in the treasuries of the house of the LORD.

Dedication of the Temple

8 THEN SOLOMON assembled the elders of Israel and all the heads of the tribes, the leaders of the ancestral houses of the Israelites, before King Solomon in Jerusalem, to bring up the ark of the covenant of the LORD out of the city of David, which is Zion. 2All the people of Israel assembled to King Solomon at the festival in the month Ethanim, which is the seventh month. 3And all the elders of Israel came, and the priests carried the ark. 4So they brought up the ark of the LORD, the tent of meeting, and all the holy vessels that were in the tent; the priests and the Levites brought them up. 5King Solomon and all the congregation of Israel, who had assembled before him, were with him before the ark, sacrificing so many sheep and oxen that they could not be counted or numbered. 6Then the priests brought the

b A Heb measure of volume

King James

6And the priests brought in the ark of the covenant of the LORD unto his place, into the oracle of the house, to the most holy *place, even* under the wings of the cherubims.

7For the cherubims spread forth *their* two wings over the place of the ark, and the cherubims covered the ark and the staves thereof above.

8And they drew out the staves, that the ends of the staves were seen out in the holy *place* before the oracle, and they were not seen without: and there they are unto this day.

9*There was* nothing in the ark save the two tables of stone, which Moses put there at Horeb, when the LORD made *a covenant* with the children of Israel, when they came out of the land of Egypt.

10And it came to pass, when the priests were come out of the holy *place,* that the cloud filled the house of the LORD,

11So that the priests could not stand to minister because of the cloud: for the glory of the LORD had filled the house of the LORD.

12¶ Then spake Solomon, The LORD said that he would dwell in the thick darkness.

13I have surely built thee an house to dwell in, a settled place for thee to abide in for ever.

14And the king turned his face about, and blessed all the congregation of Israel: (and all the congregation of Israel stood;)

15And he said, Blessed *be* the LORD God of Israel, which spake with his mouth unto David my father, and hath with his hand fulfilled *it,* saying,

16Since the day that I brought forth my people Israel out of Egypt, I chose no city out of all the tribes of Israel to build an house, that my name might be therein; but I chose David to be over my people Israel.

17And it was in the heart of David my father to build an house for the name of the LORD God of Israel.

18And the LORD said unto David my father, Whereas it was in thine heart to build an house unto my name, thou didst well that it was in thine heart.

19Nevertheless thou shalt not build the house; but thy son that shall come forth out of thy loins, he shall build the house unto my name.

20And the LORD hath performed his word that he spake, and I am risen up in the room of David my father, and sit on the throne of Israel, as the LORD promised, and have built an house for the name of the LORD God of Israel.

21And I have set there a place for the ark, wherein *is* the covenant of the LORD, which he made with our fathers, when he brought them out of the land of Egypt.

22¶ And Solomon stood before the altar of the LORD in the presence of all the congregation of Israel, and spread forth his hands toward heaven:

23And he said, LORD God of Israel, *there is* no God like thee, in heaven above, or on earth beneath, who keepest covenant and mercy with thy servants that walk before thee with all their heart:

24Who hast kept with thy servant David my father that thou promisedst him: thou spakest also with thy mouth, and hast fulfilled *it* with thine hand, as *it is* this day.

25Therefore now, LORD God of Israel, keep with thy servant David my father that thou promisedst him, saying, There shall not fail thee a man in my sight to sit on the throne of Israel; so that thy children take heed to their way, that they walk before me as thou hast walked before me.

26And now, O God of Israel, let thy word, I pray thee, be verified, which thou spakest unto thy servant David my father.

27But will God indeed dwell on the earth? behold, the heaven and heaven of heavens cannot contain thee; how much less this house that I have builded?

New International

6The priests then brought the ark of the LORD's covenant to its place in the inner sanctuary of the temple, the Most Holy Place, and put it beneath the wings of the cherubim. 7The cherubim spread their wings over the place of the ark and overshadowed the ark and its carrying poles. 8These poles were so long that their ends could be seen from the Holy Place in front of the inner sanctuary, but not from outside the Holy Place; and they are still there today. 9There was nothing in the ark except the two stone tablets that Moses had placed in it at Horeb, where the LORD made a covenant with the Israelites after they came out of Egypt.

10When the priests withdrew from the Holy Place, the cloud filled the temple of the LORD. 11And the priests could not perform their service because of the cloud, for the glory of the LORD filled his temple.

12Then Solomon said, "The LORD has said that he would dwell in a dark cloud; 13I have indeed built a magnificent temple for you, a place for you to dwell forever."

14While the whole assembly of Israel was standing there, the king turned around and blessed them. 15Then he said:

"Praise be to the LORD, the God of Israel, who with his own hand has fulfilled what he promised with his own mouth to my father David. For he said, 16'Since the day I brought my people Israel out of Egypt, I have not chosen a city in any tribe of Israel to have a temple built for my Name to be there, but I have chosen David to rule my people Israel.'

17"My father David had it in his heart to build a temple for the Name of the LORD, the God of Israel. 18But the LORD said to my father David, 'Because it was in your heart to build a temple for my Name, you did well to have this in your heart. 19Nevertheless, you are not the one to build the temple, but your son, who is your own flesh and blood—he is the one who will build the temple for my Name.'

20"The LORD has kept the promise he made: I have succeeded David my father and now I sit on the throne of Israel, just as the LORD promised, and I have built the temple for the Name of the LORD, the God of Israel. 21I have provided a place there for the ark, in which is the covenant of the LORD that he made with our fathers when he brought them out of Egypt."

Solomon's Prayer of Dedication

22Then Solomon stood before the altar of the LORD in front of the whole assembly of Israel, spread out his hands toward heaven 23and said:

"O LORD, God of Israel, there is no God like you in heaven above or on earth below—you who keep your covenant of love with your servants who continue wholeheartedly in your way. 24You have kept your promise to your servant David my father; with your mouth you have promised and with your hand you have fulfilled it—as it is today.

25"Now LORD, God of Israel, keep for your servant David my father the promises you made to him when you said, 'You shall never fail to have a man to sit before me on the throne of Israel, if only your sons are careful in all they do to walk before me as you have done.' 26And now, O God of Israel, let your word that you promised your servant David my father come true.

27"But will God really dwell on earth? The heavens, even the highest heaven, cannot contain you. How much less this temple I have built! 28Yet give

Living Bible

6Then the priests took the Ark into the inner sanctuary of the Temple—the Most Holy Place—and placed it under the wings of the statues of the mighty angels. 7The angels had been constructed in such a manner that their wings spread out over the spot where the Ark would be placed; so now their wings overshadowed the Ark and its carrying poles. 8The poles were so long that they stuck out past the angels and could be seen from the next room, but not from the outer court; and they remain there to this day. 9There was nothing in the Ark at that time except the two stone tablets which Moses had placed there at Mount Horeb at the time the Lord made his covenant with the people of Israel after they left Egypt.

10Look! As the priests are returning from the inner sanctuary, a bright cloud fills the Temple! 11The priests have to go outside because the glory of the Lord is filling the entire building!

12, 13Now King Solomon prayed this invocation: "The Lord has said that he would live in the thick darkness;

But, O Lord, I have built you a lovely home on earth, a place for you to live forever.

14Then the king turned around and faced the people as they stood before him, and blessed them.

15"Blessed be the Lord God of Israel," he said, "who has done today what he promised my father David: 16for he said to him, 'When I brought my people from Egypt, I didn't appoint a place for my Temple, but I appointed a man to be my people's leader.' 17This man was my father, David. He wanted to build a Temple for the Lord God of Israel, 18but the Lord told him not to. 'I am glad you want to do it,' he said, 19'but your son is the one who shall build my Temple.' 20And now the Lord has done what he promised; for I have followed my father as king of Israel, and now this Temple has been built for the Lord God of Israel. 21And I have prepared a place in the Temple for the Ark which contains the covenant made by the Lord with our fathers, at the time that he brought them out of the land of Egypt."

22, 23Then, as all the people watched, Solomon stood before the altar of the Lord with his hands spread out towards heaven and said, "O Lord God of Israel, there is no god like you in heaven or earth, for you are loving and kind and you keep your promises to your people if they do their best to do your will. 24Today you have fulfilled your promise to my father David, who was your servant; 25and now, O Lord God of Israel, fulfill your further promise to him: that if his descendants follow your ways and try to do your will as he did, one of them shall always sit upon the throne of Israel. 26Yes, O God of Israel, fulfill this promise too.

27"But is it possible that God would really live on earth? Why, even the skies and the highest heavens cannot contain you, much less this Temple I have built!

New Revised Standard

ark of the covenant of the LORD to its place, in the inner sanctuary of the house, in the most holy place, underneath the wings of the cherubim. 7For the cherubim spread out their wings over the place of the ark, so that the cherubim made a covering above the ark and its poles. 8The poles were so long that the ends of the poles were seen from the holy place in front of the inner sanctuary; but they could not be seen from outside; they are there to this day. 9There was nothing in the ark except the two tablets of stone that Moses had placed there at Horeb, where the LORD made a covenant with the Israelites, when they came out of the land of Egypt. 10And when the priests came out of the holy place, a cloud filled the house of the LORD, 11so that the priests could not stand to minister because of the cloud; for the glory of the LORD filled the house of the LORD.

12   Then Solomon said,
"The LORD has said that he would dwell in thick darkness.

13   I have built you an exalted house,
a place for you to dwell in forever."

Solomon's Speech

14   Then the king turned around and blessed all the assembly of Israel, while all the assembly of Israel stood. 15He said, "Blessed be the LORD, the God of Israel, who with his hand has fulfilled what he promised with his mouth to my father David, saying, 16'Since the day that I brought my people Israel out of Egypt, I have not chosen a city from any of the tribes of Israel in which to build a house, that my name might be there; but I chose David to be over my people Israel.' 17My father David had it in mind to build a house for the name of the LORD, the God of Israel. 18But the LORD said to my father David, 'You did well to consider building a house for my name; 19nevertheless you shall not build the house, but your son who shall be born to you shall build the house for my name.' 20Now the LORD has upheld the promise that he made; for I have risen in the place of my father David; I sit on the throne of Israel, as the LORD promised, and have built the house for the name of the LORD, the God of Israel. 21There I have provided a place for the ark, in which is the covenant of the LORD that he made with our ancestors when he brought them out of the land of Egypt."

Solomon's Prayer of Dedication

22   Then Solomon stood before the altar of the LORD in the presence of all the assembly of Israel, and spread out his hands to heaven. 23He said, "O LORD, God of Israel, there is no God like you in heaven above or on earth beneath, keeping covenant and steadfast love for your servants who walk before you with all their heart, 24the covenant that you kept for your servant my father David as you declared to him; you promised with your mouth and have this day fulfilled with your hand. 25Therefore, O LORD, God of Israel, keep for your servant my father David that which you promised him, saying, 'There shall never fail you a successor before me to sit on the throne of Israel, if only your children look to their way, to walk before me as you have walked before me.' 26Therefore, O God of Israel, let your word be confirmed, which you promised to your servant my father David.

27   "But will God indeed dwell on the earth? Even heaven and the highest heaven cannot contain you, much less this house that I have built! 28Regard your

King James

28Yet have thou respect unto the prayer of thy servant, and to his supplication, O Lord my God, to hearken unto the cry and to the prayer, which thy servant prayeth before thee today:

29That thine eyes may be open toward this house night and day, *even* toward the place of which thou hast said, My name shall be there: that thou mayest hearken unto the prayer which thy servant shall make toward this place.

30And hearken thou to the supplication of thy servant, and of thy people Israel, when they shall pray toward this place: and hear thou in heaven thy dwellingplace: and when thou hearest, forgive.

31¶ If any man trespass against his neighbour, and an oath be laid upon him to cause him to swear, and the oath come before thine altar in this house:

32Then hear thou in heaven, and do, and judge thy servants, condemning the wicked, to bring his way upon his head; and justifying the righteous, to give him according to his righteousness.

33¶ When thy people Israel be smitten down before the enemy, because they have sinned against thee, and shall turn again to thee, and confess thy name, and pray, and make supplication unto thee in this house:

34Then hear thou in heaven, and forgive the sin of thy people Israel, and bring them again unto the land which thou gavest unto their fathers.

35¶ When heaven is shut up, and there is no rain, because they have sinned against thee; if they pray toward this place, and confess thy name, and turn from their sin, when thou afflictest them:

36Then hear thou in heaven, and forgive the sin of thy servants, and of thy people Israel, that thou teach them the good way wherein they should walk, and give rain upon thy land, which thou hast given to thy people for an inheritance.

37¶ If there be in the land famine, if there be pestilence, blasting, mildew, locust, *or* if there be caterpillar; if their enemy besiege them in the land of their cities; whatsoever plague, whatsoever sickness *there be;*

38What prayer and supplication soever be *made* by any man, *or* by all thy people Israel, which shall know every man the plague of his own heart, and spread forth his hands toward this house:

39Then hear thou in heaven thy dwellingplace, and forgive, and do, and give to every man according to his ways, whose heart thou knowest; (for thou, *even* thou only, knowest the hearts of all the children of men;)

40That they may fear thee all the days that they live in the land which thou gavest unto our fathers.

41Moreover concerning a stranger, that *is* not of thy people Israel, but cometh out of a far country for thy name's sake;

42(For they shall hear of thy great name, and of thy strong hand, and of thy stretched out arm;) when he shall come and pray toward this house;

43Hear thou in heaven thy dwellingplace, and do according to all that the stranger calleth to thee for: that all people of the earth may know thy name, to fear thee, as *do* thy people Israel; and that they may know that this house, which I have builded, is called by thy name.

44¶ If thy people go out to battle against their enemy, whithersoever thou shalt send them, and shall pray unto the Lord toward the city which thou hast chosen, and *toward* the house that I have built for thy name:

45Then hear thou in heaven their prayer and their supplication, and maintain their cause.

46If they sin against thee, (for *there is* no man that sinneth not,) and thou be angry with them, and deliver them to the enemy, so that they carry them away captives unto the land of the enemy, far or near;

New International

attention to your servant's prayer and his plea for mercy, O Lord my God. Hear the cry and the prayer that your servant is praying in your presence this day. 29May your eyes be open toward this temple night and day, this place of which you said, 'My Name shall be there,' so that you will hear the prayer your servant prays toward this place. 30Hear the supplication of your servant and of your people Israel when they pray toward this place. Hear from heaven, your dwelling place, and when you hear, forgive.

31"When a man wrongs his neighbor and is required to take an oath and he comes and swears the oath before your altar in this temple, 32then hear from heaven and act. Judge between your servants, condemning the guilty and bringing down on his own head what he has done. Declare the innocent not guilty, and so establish his innocence.

33"When your people Israel have been defeated by an enemy because they have sinned against you, and when they turn back to you and confess your name, praying and making supplication to you in this temple, 34then hear from heaven and forgive the sin of your people Israel and bring them back to the land you gave to their fathers.

35"When the heavens are shut up and there is no rain because your people have sinned against you, and when they pray toward this place and confess your name and turn from their sin because you have afflicted them, 36then hear from heaven and forgive the sin of your servants, your people Israel. Teach them the right way to live, and send rain on the land you gave your people for an inheritance.

37"When famine or plague comes to the land, or blight or mildew, locusts or grasshoppers, or when an enemy besieges them in any of their cities, whatever disaster or disease may come, 38and when a prayer or plea is made by any of your people Israel—each one aware of the afflictions of his own heart, and spreading out his hands toward this temple— 39then hear from heaven, your dwelling place. Forgive and act; deal with each man according to all he does, since you know his heart (for you alone know the hearts of all men), 40so that they will fear you all the time they live in the land you gave our fathers.

41"As for the foreigner who does not belong to your people Israel but has come from a distant land because of your name— 42for men will hear of your great name and your mighty hand and your outstretched arm—when he comes and prays toward this temple, 43then hear from heaven, your dwelling place, and do whatever the foreigner asks of you, so that all the peoples of the earth may know your name and fear you, as do your own people Israel, and may know that this house I have built bears your Name.

44"When your people go to war against their enemies, wherever you send them, and when they pray to the Lord toward the city you have chosen and the temple I have built for your Name, 45then hear from heaven their prayer and their plea, and uphold their cause.

46"When they sin against you—for there is no one who does not sin—and you become angry with them and give them over to the enemy, who takes them captive to his own land, far away or near;

Living Bible

28And yet, O Lord my God, you have heard and answered my request: 29Please watch over this Temple night and day—this place you have promised to live in—and as I face toward the Temple and pray, whether by night or by day, please listen to me and answer my requests. 30Listen to every plea of the people of Israel whenever they face this place to pray; yes, hear in heaven where you live, and when you hear, forgive.

31"If a man is accused of doing something wrong and then, standing here before your altar, swears that he didn't do it, 32hear him in heaven and do what is right; judge whether or not he did it.

33, 34"And when your people sin and their enemies defeat them, hear them from heaven and forgive them if they turn to you again and confess that you are their God. Bring them back again to this land which you have given to their fathers.

35, 36"And when the skies are shut up and there is no rain because of their sin, hear them from heaven and forgive them when they pray toward this place and confess your name. And after you have punished them, help them to follow the good ways in which they should walk, and send rain upon the land which you have given your people.

37"If there is a famine in the land caused by plant disease or locusts or caterpillars, or if Israel's enemies besiege one of her cities, or if the people are struck by an epidemic or plague—or whatever the problem is— 38then when the people realize their sin and pray toward this Temple, 39hear them from heaven and forgive and answer all who have made an honest confession; for you know each heart. 40In this way they will always learn to reverence you as they continue to live in this land which you have given their fathers.

41, 42"And when foreigners hear of your great name and come from distant lands to worship you (for they shall hear of your great name and mighty miracles) and pray toward this Temple, 43hear them from heaven and answer their prayers. And all the nations of the earth will know and fear your name just as your own people Israel do; and all the earth will know that this is your Temple.

44"When you send your people out to battle against their enemies and they pray to you, looking toward your chosen city of Jerusalem and toward this Temple which I have built in your name, 45hear their prayer and help them.

46"If they sin against you (and who doesn't?) and you become angry with them and let their enemies lead them away as captives to some foreign land, whether far or near, 47and they come to their senses and turn to you and

New Revised Standard

servant's prayer and his plea, O Lord my God, heeding the cry and the prayer that your servant prays to you today; 29that your eyes may be open night and day toward this house, the place of which you said, 'My name shall be there,' that you may heed the prayer that your servant prays toward this place. 30Hear the plea of your servant and of your people Israel when they pray toward this place; O hear in heaven your dwelling place; heed and forgive.

31 "If someone sins against a neighbor and is given an oath to swear, and comes and swears before your altar in this house, 32then hear in heaven, and act, and judge your servants, condemning the guilty by bringing their conduct on their own head, and vindicating the righteous by rewarding them according to their righteousness.

33 "When your people Israel, having sinned against you, are defeated before an enemy but turn again to you, confess your name, pray and plead with you in this house, 34then hear in heaven, forgive the sin of your people Israel, and bring them again to the land that you gave to their ancestors.

35 "When heaven is shut up and there is no rain because they have sinned against you, and then they pray toward this place, confess your name, and turn from their sin, because you punisha them, 36then hear in heaven, and forgive the sin of your servants, your people Israel, when you teach them the good way in which they should walk; and grant rain on your land, which you have given to your people as an inheritance.

37 "If there is famine in the land, if there is plague, blight, mildew, locust, or caterpillar; if their enemy besieges them in anyb of their cities; whatever plague, whatever sickness there is; 38whatever prayer, whatever plea there is from any individual or from all your people Israel, all knowing the afflictions of their own hearts so that they stretch out their hands toward this house; 39then hear in heaven your dwelling place, forgive, act, and render to all whose hearts you know—according to all their ways, for only you know what is in every human heart— 40so that they may fear you all the days that they live in the land that you gave to our ancestors.

41 "Likewise when a foreigner, who is not of your people Israel, comes from a distant land because of your name 42—for they shall hear of your great name, your mighty hand, and your outstretched arm—when a foreigner comes and prays toward this house, 43then hear in heaven your dwelling place, and do according to all that the foreigner calls to you, so that all the peoples of the earth may know your name and fear you, as do your people Israel, and so that they may know that your name has been invoked on this house that I have built.

44 "If your people go out to battle against their enemy, by whatever way you shall send them, and they pray to the Lord toward the city that you have chosen and the house that I have built for your name, 45then hear in heaven their prayer and their plea, and maintain their cause.

46 "If they sin against you—for there is no one who does not sin—and you are angry with them and give them to an enemy, so that they are carried away captive to the land of the enemy, far off or near; 47yet if they

---

a Or *when you answer*   b Gk Syr: Heb *in the land*

King James

47Yet if they shall bethink themselves in the land whither they were carried captives, and repent, and make supplication unto thee in the land of them that carried them captives, saying, We have sinned, and have done perversely, we have committed wickedness;

48And so return unto thee with all their heart, and with all their soul, in the land of their enemies, which led them away captive, and pray unto thee toward their land, which thou gavest unto their fathers, the city which thou hast chosen, and the house which I have built for thy name:

49Then hear thou their prayer and their supplication in heaven thy dwellingplace, and maintain their cause,

50And forgive thy people that have sinned against thee, and all their transgressions wherein they have transgressed against thee, and give them compassion before them who carried them captive, that they may have compassion on them:

51For they be thy people, and thine inheritance, which thou broughtest forth out of Egypt, from the midst of the furnace of iron:

52That thine eyes may be open unto the supplication of thy servant, and unto the supplication of thy people Israel, to hearken unto them in all that they call for unto thee.

53For thou didst separate them from among all the people of the earth, to be thine inheritance, as thou spakest by the hand of Moses thy servant, when thou broughtest our fathers out of Egypt, O Lord GOD.

54And it was so, that when Solomon had made an end of praying all this prayer and supplication unto the LORD, he arose from before the altar of the LORD, from kneeling on his knees with his hands spread up to heaven.

55And he stood, and blessed all the congregation of Israel with a loud voice, saying,

56Blessed be the LORD, that hath given rest unto his people Israel, according to all that he promised: there hath not failed one word of all his good promise, which he promised by the hand of Moses his servant.

57The LORD our God be with us, as he was with our fathers: let him not leave us, nor forsake us:

58That he may incline our hearts unto him, to walk in all his ways, and to keep his commandments, and his statutes, and his judgments, which he commanded our fathers.

59And let these my words, wherewith I have made supplication before the LORD, be nigh unto the LORD our God day and night, that he maintain the cause of his servant, and the cause of his people Israel at all times, as the matter shall require:

60That all the people of the earth may know that the LORD is God, and that there is none else.

61Let your heart therefore be perfect with the LORD our God, to walk in his statutes, and to keep his commandments, as at this day.

62¶ And the king, and all Israel with him, offered sacrifice before the LORD.

63And Solomon offered a sacrifice of peace offerings, which he offered unto the LORD, two and twenty thousand oxen, and an hundred and twenty thousand sheep. So the king and all the children of Israel dedicated the house of the LORD.

64The same day did the king hallow the middle of the court that was before the house of the LORD: for there he offered burnt offerings, and meat offerings, and the fat of the peace offerings: because the brasen altar that was before the LORD was too little to receive the burnt offerings, and meat offerings, and the fat of the peace offerings.

65And at that time Solomon held a feast, and all Israel with him, a great congregation, from the entering in of Hamath unto the river of Egypt, before the LORD our God, seven days and seven days, even fourteen days.

New International

47and if they have a change of heart in the land where they are held captive, and repent and plead with you in the land of their conquerors and say, 'We have sinned, we have done wrong, we have acted wickedly'; 48and if they turn back to you with all their heart and soul in the land of their enemies who took them captive, and pray to you toward the land you gave their fathers, toward the city you have chosen and the temple I have built for your Name; 49then from heaven, your dwelling place, hear their prayer and their plea, and uphold their cause. 50And forgive your people, who have sinned against you; forgive all the offenses they have committed against you, and cause their conquerors to show them mercy; 51for they are your people and your inheritance, whom you brought out of Egypt, out of that iron-smelting furnace.

52"May your eyes be open to your servant's plea and to the plea of your people Israel, and may you listen to them whenever they cry out to you. 53For you singled them out from all the nations of the world to be your own inheritance, just as you declared through your servant Moses when you, O Sovereign LORD, brought our fathers out of Egypt."

54When Solomon had finished all these prayers and supplications to the LORD, he rose from before the altar of the LORD, where he had been kneeling with his hands spread out toward heaven. 55He stood and blessed the whole assembly of Israel in a loud voice, saying:

56"Praise be to the LORD, who has given rest to his people Israel just as he promised. Not one word has failed of all the good promises he gave through his servant Moses. 57May the LORD our God be with us as he was with our fathers; may he never leave us nor forsake us. 58May he turn our hearts to him, to walk in all his ways and to keep the commands, decrees and regulations he gave our fathers. 59And may these words of mine, which I have prayed before the LORD, be near to the LORD our God day and night, that he may uphold the cause of his servant and the cause of his people Israel according to each day's need, 60so that all the peoples of the earth may know that the LORD is God and that there is no other. 61But your hearts must be fully committed to the LORD our God, to live by his decrees and obey his commands, as at this time."

The Dedication of the Temple

62Then the king and all Israel with him offered sacrifices before the LORD. 63Solomon offered a sacrifice of fellowship offeringsa to the LORD: twenty-two thousand cattle and a hundred and twenty thousand sheep and goats. So the king and all the Israelites dedicated the temple of the LORD.

64On that same day the king consecrated the middle part of the courtyard in front of the temple of the LORD, and there he offered burnt offerings, grain offerings and the fat of the fellowship offerings, because the bronze altar before the LORD was too small to hold the burnt offerings, the grain offerings and the fat of the fellowship offerings.

65So Solomon observed the festival at that time, and all Israel with him—a vast assembly, people from Lebob Hamath to the Wadi of Egypt. They celebrated it before the LORD our God for seven days and seven days more, fourteen days in all. 66On the following day

---

a 63 Traditionally peace offerings; also in verse 64   b 65 Or from the entrance to

Living Bible

cry to you saying, 'We have sinned, we have done wrong'; 48if they honestly return to you and pray toward this land which you have given their fathers, and toward this city of Jerusalem which you have chosen, and toward this Temple, which I have built for your name, 49hear their prayers and pleadings from heaven where you live, and come to their assistance.

50"Forgive your people for all of their evil deeds, and make their captors merciful to them; 51for they are your people—your inheritance that you brought out from the Egyptian furnace. 52May your eyes be open and your ears listening to their pleas. O Lord, hear and answer them whenever they cry out to you, 53for when you brought our fathers out of the land of Egypt, you told your servant Moses that you had chosen Israel from among all the nations of the earth to be your own special people."

54, 55Solomon had been kneeling with his hands outstretched toward heaven. As he finished this prayer, he rose from before the altar of Jehovah and cried out this blessing upon all the people of Israel:

56"Blessed be the Lord who has fulfilled his promise and given rest to his people Israel; not one word has failed of all the wonderful promises proclaimed by his servant Moses. 57May the Lord our God be with us as he was with our fathers; may he never forsake us. 58May he give us the desire to do his will in everything, and to obey all the commandments and instructions he has given our ancestors. 59And may these words of my prayer be constantly before him day and night, so that he helps me and all of Israel in accordance with our daily needs. 60May people all over the earth know that the Lord is God, and that there is no other god at all. 61O my people, may you live good and perfect lives before the Lord our God; may you always obey his laws and commandments, just as you are doing today."

62, 63Then the king and all the people dedicated the Temple by sacrificing peace offerings to the Lord—a total of 22,000 oxen and 120,000 sheep and goats! 64As a temporary measure the king sanctified the court in front of the Temple for the burnt offerings, grain offerings, and the fat of the peace offerings: for the bronze altar was too small to handle so much. 65The celebration lasted for fourteen days, and a great crowd came from one end of the land to the other. 66Afterwards Solomon

New Revised Standard

come to their senses in the land to which they have been taken captive, and repent, and plead with you in the land of their captors, saying, 'We have sinned, and have done wrong; we have acted wickedly'; 48if they repent with all their heart and soul in the land of their enemies, who took them captive, and pray to you toward their land, which you gave to their ancestors, the city that you have chosen, and the house that I have built for your name; 49then hear in heaven your dwelling place their prayer and their plea, maintain their cause 50and forgive your people who have sinned against you, and all their transgressions that they have committed against you; and grant them compassion in the sight of their captors, so that they may have compassion on them 51(for they are your people and heritage, which you brought out of Egypt, from the midst of the iron-smelter). 52Let your eyes be open to the plea of your servant, and to the plea of your people Israel, listening to them whenever they call to you. 53For you have separated them from among all the peoples of the earth, to be your heritage, just as you promised through Moses, your servant, when you brought our ancestors out of Egypt, O Lord GOD."

Solomon Blesses the Assembly

54 Now when Solomon finished offering all this prayer and this plea to the LORD, he arose from facing the altar of the LORD, where he had knelt with hands outstretched toward heaven; 55he stood and blessed all the assembly of Israel with a loud voice:

56 "Blessed be the LORD, who has given rest to his people Israel according to all that he promised; not one word has failed of all his good promise, which he spoke through his servant Moses. 57The LORD our God be with us, as he was with our ancestors; may he not leave us or abandon us, 58but incline our hearts to him, to walk in all his ways, and to keep his commandments, his statutes, and his ordinances, which he commanded our ancestors. 59Let these words of mine, with which I pleaded before the LORD, be near to the LORD our God day and night, and may he maintain the cause of his servant and the cause of his people Israel, as each day requires; 60so that all the peoples of the earth may know that the LORD is God; there is no other. 61Therefore devote yourselves completely to the LORD our God, walking in his statutes and keeping his commandments, as at this day."

Solomon Offers Sacrifices

62 Then the king, and all Israel with him, offered sacrifice before the LORD. 63Solomon offered as sacrifices of well-being to the LORD twenty-two thousand oxen and one hundred twenty thousand sheep. So the king and all the people of Israel dedicated the house of the LORD. 64The same day the king consecrated the middle of the court that was in front of the house of the LORD; for there he offered the burnt offerings and the grain offerings and the fat pieces of the sacrifices of well-being, because the bronze altar that was before the LORD was too small to receive the burnt offerings and the grain offerings and the fat pieces of the sacrifices of well-being.

65 So Solomon held the festival at that time, and all Israel with him—a great assembly, people from Lebohamath to the Wadi of Egypt—before the LORD our God, seven days.c 66On the eighth day he sent the peo-

---

c Compare Gk: Heb *seven days and seven days, fourteen days*

King James

66On the eighth day he sent the people away: and they blessed the king, and went unto their tents joyful and glad of heart for all the goodness that the LORD had done for David his servant, and for Israel his people.

9 AND IT came to pass, when Solomon had finished the building of the house of the LORD, and the king's house, and all Solomon's desire which he was pleased to do,
2That the LORD appeared to Solomon the second time, as he had appeared unto him at Gibeon.
3And the LORD said unto him, I have heard thy prayer and thy supplication, that thou hast made before me: I have hallowed this house, which thou hast built, to put my name there for ever; and mine eyes and mine heart shall be there perpetually.
4And if thou wilt walk before me, as David thy father walked, in integrity of heart, and in uprightness, to do according to all that I have commanded thee, *and* wilt keep my statutes and my judgments:
5Then I will establish the throne of thy kingdom upon Israel for ever, as I promised to David thy father, saying, There shall not fail thee a man upon the throne of Israel.
6*But* if ye shall at all turn from following me, ye or your children, and will not keep my commandments *and* my statutes which I have set before you, but go and serve other gods, and worship them:
7Then will I cut off Israel out of the land which I have given them; and this house, which I have hallowed for my name, will I cast out of my sight; and Israel shall be a proverb and a byword among all people:
8And at this house, *which* is high, every one that passeth by it shall be astonished, and shall hiss; and they shall say, Why hath the LORD done thus unto this land, and to this house?
9And they shall answer, Because they forsook the LORD their God, who brought forth their fathers out of the land of Egypt, and have taken hold upon other gods, and have worshipped them, and served them: therefore hath the LORD brought upon them all this evil.
10¶ And it came to pass at the end of twenty years, when Solomon had built the two houses, the house of the LORD, and the king's house,
11(*Now* Hiram the king of Tyre had furnished Solomon with cedar trees and fir trees, and with gold, according to all his desire,) that then king Solomon gave Hiram twenty cities in the land of Galilee.
12And Hiram came out from Tyre to see the cities which Solomon had given him; and they pleased him not.
13And he said, What cities *are* these which thou hast given me, my brother? And he called them the land of Cabul unto this day.
14And Hiram sent to the king sixscore talents of gold.
15¶ And this *is* the reason of the levy which king Solomon raised; for to build the house of the LORD, and his own house, and Millo, and the wall of Jerusalem, and Hazor, and Megiddo, and Gezer.
16*For* Pharaoh king of Egypt had gone up, and taken Gezer, and burnt it with fire, and slain the Canaanites that dwelt in the city, and given it *for* a present unto his daughter, Solomon's wife.
17And Solomon built Gezer, and Beth-horon the nether,
18And Baalath, and Tadmor in the wilderness, in the land,
19And all the cities of store that Solomon had, and cities for his chariots, and cities for his horsemen, and that which Solomon desired to build in Jerusalem, and in Lebanon, and in all the land of his dominion.

New International

he sent the people away. They blessed the king and then went home, joyful and glad in heart for all the good things the LORD had done for his servant David and his people Israel.

The LORD Appears to Solomon

9 WHEN SOLOMON had finished building the temple of the LORD and the royal palace, and had achieved all he had desired to do, 2the LORD appeared to him a second time, as he had appeared to him at Gibeon. 3The LORD said to him:

"I have heard the prayer and plea you have made before me; I have consecrated this temple, which you have built, by putting my Name there forever. My eyes and my heart will always be there.

4"As for you, if you walk before me in integrity of heart and uprightness, as David your father did, and do all I command and observe my decrees and laws, 5I will establish your royal throne over Israel forever, as I promised David your father when I said, 'You shall never fail to have a man on the throne of Israel.'

6"But if youa or your sons turn away from me and do not observe the commands and decrees I have given youa and go off to serve other gods and worship them, 7then I will cut off Israel from the land I have given them and will reject this temple I have consecrated for my Name. Israel will then become a byword and an object of ridicule among all peoples. 8And though this temple is now imposing, all who pass by will be appalled and will scoff and say, 'Why has the LORD done such a thing to this land and to this temple?' 9People will answer, 'Because they have forsaken the LORD their God, who brought their fathers out of Egypt, and have embraced other gods, worshiping and serving them—that is why the LORD brought all this disaster on them.'"

Solomon's Other Activities

10At the end of twenty years, during which Solomon built these two buildings—the temple of the LORD and the royal palace— 11King Solomon gave twenty towns in Galilee to Hiram king of Tyre, because Hiram had supplied him with all the cedar and pine and gold he wanted. 12But when Hiram went from Tyre to see the towns that Solomon had given him, he was not pleased with them. 13"What kind of towns are these you have given me, my brother?" he asked. And he called them the Land of Cabul,b a name they have to this day. 14Now Hiram had sent to the king 120 talentsc of gold.

15Here is the account of the forced labor King Solomon conscripted to build the LORD's temple, his own palace, the supporting terraces,d the wall of Jerusalem, and Hazor, Megiddo and Gezer. 16(Pharaoh king of Egypt had attacked and captured Gezer. He had set it on fire. He killed its Canaanite inhabitants and then gave it as a wedding gift to his daughter, Solomon's wife. 17And Solomon rebuilt Gezer.) He built up Lower Beth Horon, 18Baalath, and Tadmore in the desert, within his land, 19as well as all his store cities and the towns for his chariots and for his horsesf—whatever he desired to build in Jerusalem, in Lebanon and throughout all the territory he ruled.

---

a 6 The Hebrew is plural. b 13 Cabul sounds like the Hebrew for good-for-nothing. c 14 That is, about 4 1/2 tons (about 4 metric tons) d 15 Or the Millo; also in verse 24 e 18 The Hebrew may also be read Tamar. f 19 Or charioteers

Living Bible

sent the people home, happy for all the goodness that the Lord had shown to his servant David and to his people Israel. And they blessed the king.

9 WHEN SOLOMON had finished building the Temple and the palace and all the other buildings he had always wanted, 2, 3the Lord appeared to him the second time (the first time had been at Gibeon) and said to him,

"I have heard your prayer. I have hallowed this Temple which you have built and have put my name here forever. I will constantly watch over it and rejoice in it. 4And if you live in honesty and truth as your father David did, always obeying me, 5then I will cause your descendants to be the kings of Israel forever, just as I promised your father David when I told him, 'One of your sons shall always be upon the throne of Israel.'

6"However, if you or your children turn away from me and worship other gods and do not obey my laws, 7then I will take away the people of Israel from this land which I have given them. I will take them from this Temple which I have hallowed for my name and I will cast them out of my sight; and Israel will become a joke to the nations and an example and proverb of sudden disaster. 8This Temple will become a heap of ruins, and everyone passing by will be amazed and will whistle with astonishment, asking, 'Why has the Lord done such things to this land and this Temple?' 9And the answer will be, 'The people of Israel abandoned the Lord their God who brought them out of the land of Egypt; they worshiped other gods instead. That is why the Lord has brought this evil upon them.'"

10At the end of the twenty years during which Solomon built the Temple and the palace, 11, 12he gave twenty cities in the land of Galilee to King Hiram of Tyre as payment for all the cedar and cypress lumber and gold he had furnished for the construction of the palace and Temple. Hiram came from Tyre to see the cities, but he wasn't at all pleased with them.

13"What sort of deal is this, my brother?" he asked. "These cities are a wasteland!" (And they are still known as "The Wasteland" today.) 14For Hiram had sent gold to Solomon valued at $3,500,000!

15Solomon had conscripted forced labor to build the Temple, his palace, Fort Millo, the wall of Jerusalem, and the cities of Hazor, Megiddo, and Gezer. 16Gezer was the city the king of Egypt conquered and burned, killing the Israeli population; later he had given the city to his daughter as a dowry—she was one of Solomon's wives. 17, 18So now Solomon rebuilt Gezer along with Lower Beth-horon, Baalath, and Tamar, a desert city. 19He also built cities for grain storage, cities in which to keep his chariots, cities for homes for his cavalry and chariot drivers, and resort cities near Jerusalem and in the Lebanon mountains and elsewhere throughout the land.

New Revised Standard

ple away; and they blessed the king, and went to their tents, joyful and in good spirits because of all the goodness that the LORD had shown to his servant David and to his people Israel.

God Appears Again to Solomon

9 WHEN SOLOMON had finished building the house of the LORD and the king's house and all that Solomon desired to build, 2the LORD appeared to Solomon a second time, as he had appeared to him at Gibeon. 3The LORD said to him, "I have heard your prayer and your plea, which you made before me; I have consecrated this house that you have built, and put my name there forever; my eyes and my heart will be there for all time. 4As for you, if you will walk before me, as David your father walked, with integrity of heart and uprightness, doing according to all that I have commanded you, and keeping my statutes and my ordinances, 5then I will establish your royal throne over Israel forever, as I promised your father David, saying, 'There shall not fail you a successor on the throne of Israel.'

6 "If you turn aside from following me, you or your children, and do not keep my commandments and my statutes that I have set before you, but go and serve other gods and worship them, 7then I will cut Israel off from the land that I have given them; and the house that I have consecrated for my name I will cast out of my sight; and Israel will become a proverb and a taunt among all peoples. 8This house will become a heap of ruins;g everyone passing by it will be astonished, and will hiss; and they will say, 'Why has the LORD done such a thing to this land and to this house?' 9Then they will say, 'Because they have forsaken the LORD their God, who brought their ancestors out of the land of Egypt, and embraced other gods, worshiping them and serving them; therefore the LORD has brought this disaster upon them.'"

10 At the end of twenty years, in which Solomon had built the two houses, the house of the LORD and the king's house, 11King Hiram of Tyre having supplied Solomon with cedar and cypress timber and gold, as much as he desired, King Solomon gave to Hiram twenty cities in the land of Galilee. 12But when Hiram came from Tyre to see the cities that Solomon had given him, they did not please him. 13Therefore he said, "What kind of cities are these that you have given me, my brother?" So they are called the land of Cabulh to this day. 14But Hiram had sent to the king one hundred twenty talents of gold.

Other Acts of Solomon

15 This is the account of the forced labor that King Solomon conscripted to build the house of the LORD and his own house, the Millo and the wall of Jerusalem, Hazor, Megiddo, Gezer 16(Pharaoh king of Egypt had gone up and captured Gezer and burned it down, had killed the Canaanites who lived in the city, and had given it as dowry to his daughter, Solomon's wife; 17so Solomon rebuilt Gezer), Lower Beth-horon, 18Baalath, Tamar in the wilderness, within the land, 19as well as all of Solomon's storage cities, the cities for his chariots, the cities for his cavalry, and whatever Solomon desired to build, in Jerusalem, in Lebanon, and in all the land of his dominion. 20All the people who were left of the

g Syr Old Latin: Heb *will become high*   h Perhaps meaning *a land good for nothing*

King James

20And all the people *that were* left of the Amorites, Hittites, Perizzites, Hivites, and Jebusites, which *were* not of the children of Israel,

21Their children that were left after them in the land, whom the children of Israel also were not able utterly to destroy, upon those did Solomon levy a tribute of bondservice unto this day.

22But of the children of Israel did Solomon make no bondmen: but they *were* men of war, and his servants, and his princes, and his captains, and rulers of his chariots, and his horsemen.

23These *were* the chief of the officers that *were* over Solomon's work, five hundred and fifty, which bare rule over the people that wrought in the work.

24¶ But Pharaoh's daughter came up out of the city of David unto her house which *Solomon* had built for her: then did he build Millo.

25¶ And three times in a year did Solomon offer burnt offerings and peace offerings upon the altar which he built unto the LORD, and he burnt incense upon the altar that *was* before the LORD. So he finished the house.

26¶ And king Solomon made a navy of ships in Eziongeber, which *is* beside Eloth, on the shore of the Red sea, in the land of Edom.

27And Hiram sent in the navy his servants, shipmen that had knowledge of the sea, with the servants of Solomon.

28And they came to Ophir, and fetched from thence gold, four hundred and twenty talents, and brought *it* to king Solomon.

10 AND WHEN the queen of Sheba heard of the fame of Solomon concerning the name of the LORD, she came to prove him with hard questions.

2And she came to Jerusalem with a very great train, with camels that bare spices, and very much gold, and precious stones: and when she was come to Solomon, she communed with him of all that was in her heart.

3And Solomon told her all her questions: there was not *any* thing hid from the king, which he told her not.

4And when the queen of Sheba had seen all Solomon's wisdom, and the house that he had built,

5And the meat of his table, and the sitting of his servants, and the attendance of his ministers, and their apparel, and his cupbearers, and his ascent by which he went up unto the house of the LORD; there was no more spirit in her.

6And she said to the king, It was a true report that I heard in mine own land of thy acts and of thy wisdom.

7Howbeit I believed not the words, until I came, and mine eyes had seen *it:* and, behold, the half was not told me: thy wisdom and prosperity exceedeth the fame which I heard.

8Happy *are* thy men, happy *are* these thy servants, which stand continually before thee, *and* that hear thy wisdom.

9Blessed be the LORD thy God, which delighted in thee, to set thee on the throne of Israel: because the LORD loved Israel for ever, therefore made he thee king, to do judgment and justice.

10And she gave the king an hundred and twenty talents of gold, and of spices very great store, and precious stones: there came no more such abundance of spices as these which the queen of Sheba gave to king Solomon.

11And the navy also of Hiram, that brought gold from Ophir, brought in from Ophir great plenty of almug trees, and precious stones.

New International

20All the people left from the Amorites, Hittites, Perizzites, Hivites and Jebusites (these peoples were not Israelites), 21that is, their descendants remaining in the land, whom the Israelites could not exterminatea— these Solomon conscripted for his slave labor force, as it is to this day. 22But Solomon did not make slaves of any of the Israelites; they were his fighting men, his government officials, his officers, his captains, and the commanders of his chariots and charioteers. 23They were also the chief officials in charge of Solomon's projects—550 officials supervising the men who did the work.

24After Pharaoh's daughter had come up from the City of David to the palace Solomon had built for her, he constructed the supporting terraces.

25Three times a year Solomon sacrificed burnt offerings and fellowship offeringsb on the altar he had built for the LORD, burning incense before the LORD along with them, and so fulfilled the temple obligations.

26King Solomon also built ships at Ezion Geber, which is near Elath in Edom, on the shore of the Red Sea.c 27And Hiram sent his men—sailors who knew the sea—to serve in the fleet with Solomon's men. 28They sailed to Ophir and brought back 420 talentsd of gold, which they delivered to King Solomon.

The Queen of Sheba Visits Solomon

10 WHEN THE queen of Sheba heard about the fame of Solomon and his relation to the name of the LORD, she came to test him with hard questions. 2Arriving at Jerusalem with a very great caravan—with camels carrying spices, large quantities of gold, and precious stones—she came to Solomon and talked with him about all that she had on her mind. 3Solomon answered all her questions; nothing was too hard for the king to explain to her. 4When the queen of Sheba saw all the wisdom of Solomon and the palace he had built, 5the food on his table, the seating of his officials, the attending servants in their robes, his cupbearers, and the burnt offerings he made ate the temple of the LORD, she was overwhelmed.

6She said to the king, "The report I heard in my own country about your achievements and your wisdom is true. 7But I did not believe these things until I came and saw with my own eyes. Indeed, not even half was told me; in wisdom and wealth you have far exceeded the report I heard. 8How happy your men must be! How happy your officials, who continually stand before you and hear your wisdom! 9Praise be to the LORD your God, who has delighted in you and placed you on the throne of Israel. Because of the LORD's eternal love for Israel, he has made you king, to maintain justice and righteousness."

10And she gave the king 120 talentsf of gold, large quantities of spices, and precious stones. Never again were so many spices brought in as those the queen of Sheba gave to King Solomon.

11(Hiram's ships brought gold from Ophir; and from there they brought great cargoes of almugwoodg and precious stones. 12The king used the almugwood to

a 21 The Hebrew term refers to the irrevocable giving over of things or persons to the LORD, often by totally destroying them.   b 25 Traditionally *peace offerings*   c 26 Hebrew *Yam Suph*; that is, Sea of Reeds   d 28 That is, about 16 tons (about 14.5 metric tons)   e 5 Or *the ascent by which he went up to*   f 10 That is, about 4 1/2 tons (about 4 metric tons)   g 11 Probably a variant of *algumwood*; also in verse 12

Living Bible

20, 21Solomon conscripted his labor forces from those who survived in the nations he conquered—the Amorites, Hittites, Perizzites, Hivites, and Jebusites. For the people of Israel had not been able to wipe them out completely at the time of the invasion and conquest of Israel, and they continue as slaves even today. 22Solomon didn't conscript any Israelis for this work, although they became soldiers, officials, army officers, chariot commanders, and cavalrymen. 23And there were 550 men of Israel who were overseers of the labor forces.

Miscellaneous Notes:

24King Solomon moved Pharaoh's daughter from the City of David—the old sector of Jerusalem—to the new quarters he had built for her in the palace. Then he built Fort Millo.

25After the Temple was completed, Solomon offered burnt offerings and peace offerings three times a year on the altar he had built. And he also burned incense upon it.

26King Solomon had a shipyard in Ezion-geber near Eloth on the Red Sea in the land of Edom, where he built a fleet of ships.

27, 28King Hiram supplied experienced sailors to accompany Solomon's crews. They used to sail back and forth from Ophir, bringing gold to King Solomon, the total value of which was several million dollars each trip.

10 WHEN THE Queen of Sheba heard how wonderfully the Lord had blessed Solomon with wisdom,h she decided to test him with some hard questions. 2She arrived in Jerusalem with a long train of camels carrying spices, gold, and jewels; and she told him all her problems. 3Solomon answered all her questions; nothing was too difficult for him, for the Lord gave him the right answers every time.i 4She soon realized that everything she had ever heard about his great wisdom was true. She also saw the beautiful palace he had built, 5and when she saw the wonderful foods on his table, the great number of servants and aides who stood around in splendid uniforms, his cupbearers, and the many offerings he sacrificed by fire to the Lord—well, there was no more spirit in her!

6She exclaimed to him, "Everything I heard in my own country about your wisdom and about the wonderful things going on here is all true. 7I didn't believe it until I came, but now I have seen it for myself! And really! The half had not been told me! Your wisdom and prosperity are far greater than anything I've ever heard of! 8Your people are happy and your palace aides are content—but how could it be otherwise, for they stand here day after day listening to your wisdom! 9Blessed be the Lord your God who chose you and set you on the throne of Israel. How the Lord must love Israel—for he gave you to them as their king! And you give your people a just, good government!"

10Then she gave the king a gift of $3,500,000 in gold, along with a huge quantity of spices and precious gems; in fact, it was the largest single gift of spices King Solomon had ever received.

11(And when King Hiram's ships brought gold to Solomon from Ophir, they also brought along a great supply of algum trees and gems. 12Solomon used the algum

New Revised Standard

Amorites, the Hittites, the Perizzites, the Hivites, and the Jebusites, who were not of the people of Israel— 21their descendants who were still left in the land, whom the Israelites were unable to destroy completely—these Solomon conscripted for slave labor, and so they are to this day. 22But of the Israelites Solomon made no slaves; they were the soldiers, they were his officials, his commanders, his captains, and the commanders of his chariotry and cavalry.

23 These were the chief officers who were over Solomon's work: five hundred fifty, who had charge of the people who carried on the work.

24 But Pharaoh's daughter went up from the city of David to her own house that Solomon had built for her; then he built the Millo.

25 Three times a year Solomon used to offer up burnt offerings and sacrifices of well-being on the altar that he built for the Lord, offering incensej before the Lord. So he completed the house.

Solomon's Commercial Activity

26 King Solomon built a fleet of ships at Eziongeber, which is near Eloth on the shore of the Red Sea,k in the land of Edom. 27Hiram sent his servants with the fleet, sailors who were familiar with the sea, together with the servants of Solomon. 28They went to Ophir, and imported from there four hundred twenty talents of gold, which they delivered to King Solomon.

Visit of the Queen of Sheba

10 WHEN THE queen of Sheba heard of the fame of Solomon, (fame due tol the name of the Lord), she came to test him with hard questions. 2She came to Jerusalem with a very great retinue, with camels bearing spices, and very much gold, and precious stones; and when she came to Solomon, she told him all that was on her mind. 3Solomon answered all her questions; there was nothing hidden from the king that he could not explain to her. 4When the queen of Sheba had observed all the wisdom of Solomon, the house that he had built, 5the food of his table, the seating of his officials, and the attendance of his servants, their clothing, his valets, and his burnt offerings that he offered at the house of the Lord, there was no more spirit in her.

6 So she said to the king, "The report was true that I heard in my own land of your accomplishments and of your wisdom, 7but I did not believe the reports until I came and my own eyes had seen it. Not even half had been told me; your wisdom and prosperity far surpass the report that I had heard. 8Happy are your wives!m Happy are these your servants, who continually attend you and hear your wisdom! 9Blessed be the Lord your God, who has delighted in you and set you on the throne of Israel! Because the Lord loved Israel forever, he has made you king to execute justice and righteousness."

10Then she gave the king one hundred twenty talents of gold, a great quantity of spices, and precious stones; never again did spices come in such quantity as that which the queen of Sheba gave to King Solomon.

11 Moreover, the fleet of Hiram, which carried gold from Ophir, brought from Ophir a great quantity of almug wood and precious stones. 12From the almug wood

---

h *10:1 the Lord had blessed Solomon with wisdom,* literally, "heard of the fame of Solomon concerning the name of the Lord."   i *10:3 the Lord gave him the right answers every time,* literally, "there was nothing hidden from the king which he could not explain to her."

j Gk: Heb *offering incense with it that was*   k Or *Sea of Reeds*   l *Meaning of Heb uncertain*   m Gk Syr: Heb *men*

King James

12And the king made of the almug trees pillars for the house of the LORD, and for the king's house, harps also and psalteries for singers: there came no such almug trees, nor were seen unto this day.

13And king Solomon gave unto the queen of Sheba all her desire, whatsoever she asked, beside that which Solomon gave her of his royal bounty. So she turned and went to her own country, she and her servants.

14¶ Now the weight of gold that came to Solomon in one year was six hundred threescore and six talents of gold,

15Beside that he had of the merchantmen, and of the traffic of the spice merchants, and of all the kings of Arabia, and of the governors of the country.

16¶ And king Solomon made two hundred targets of beaten gold: six hundred shekels of gold went to one target.

17And he made three hundred shields of beaten gold; three pound of gold went to one shield: and the king put them in the house of the forest of Lebanon.

18¶ Moreover the king made a great throne of ivory, and overlaid it with the best gold.

19The throne had six steps, and the top of the throne was round behind: and there were stays on either side on the place of the seat, and two lions stood beside the stays.

20And twelve lions stood there on the one side and on the other upon the six steps: there was not the like made in any kingdom.

21¶ And all king Solomon's drinking vessels were of gold, and all the vessels of the house of the forest of Lebanon were of pure gold; none were of silver: it was nothing accounted of in the days of Solomon.

22For the king had at sea a navy of Tharshish with the navy of Hiram: once in three years came the navy of Tharshish, bringing gold, and silver, ivory, and apes, and peacocks.

23So king Solomon exceeded all the kings of the earth for riches and for wisdom.

24¶ And all the earth sought to Solomon, to hear his wisdom, which God had put in his heart.

25And they brought every man his present, vessels of silver, and vessels of gold, and garments, and armour, and spices, horses, and mules, a rate year by year.

26¶ And Solomon gathered together chariots and horsemen: and he had a thousand and four hundred chariots, and twelve thousand horsemen, whom he bestowed in the cities for chariots, and with the king at Jerusalem.

27And the king made silver to be in Jerusalem as stones, and cedars made he to be as the sycamore trees that are in the vale, for abundance.

28¶ And Solomon had horses brought out of Egypt, and linen yarn: the king's merchants received the linen yarn at a price.

29And a chariot came up and went out of Egypt for six hundred shekels of silver, and an horse for an hundred and fifty: and so for all the kings of the Hittites, and for the kings of Syria, did they bring them out by their means.

11 BUT KING Solomon loved many strange women, together with the daughter of Pharaoh, women of the Moabites, Ammonites, Edomites, Zidonians, and Hittites;

New International

make supports for the temple of the LORD and for the royal palace, and to make harps and lyres for the musicians. So much almugwood has never been imported or seen since that day.)

13King Solomon gave the queen of Sheba all she desired and asked for, besides what he had given her out of his royal bounty. Then she left and returned with her retinue to her own country.

Solomon's Splendor

14The weight of the gold that Solomon received yearly was 666 talents,a 15not including the revenues from merchants and traders and from all the Arabian kings and the governors of the land.

16King Solomon made two hundred large shields of hammered gold; six hundred bekasb of gold went into each shield. 17He also made three hundred small shields of hammered gold, with three minasc of gold in each shield. The king put them in the Palace of the Forest of Lebanon.

18Then the king made a great throne inlaid with ivory and overlaid with fine gold. 19The throne had six steps, and its back had a rounded top. On both sides of the seat were armrests, with a lion standing beside each of them. 20Twelve lions stood on the six steps, one at either end of each step. Nothing like it had ever been made for any other kingdom. 21All King Solomon's goblets were gold, and all the household articles in the Palace of the Forest of Lebanon were pure gold. Nothing was made of silver, because silver was considered of little value in Solomon's days. 22The king had a fleet of trading shipsd at sea along with the ships of Hiram. Once every three years it returned, carrying gold, silver and ivory, and apes and baboons.

23King Solomon was greater in riches and wisdom than all the other kings of the earth. 24The whole world sought audience with Solomon to hear the wisdom God had put in his heart. 25Year after year, everyone who came brought a gift—articles of silver and gold, robes, weapons and spices, and horses and mules.

26Solomon accumulated chariots and horses; he had fourteen hundred chariots and twelve thousand horses,e which he kept in the chariot cities and also with him in Jerusalem. 27The king made silver as common in Jerusalem as stones, and cedar as plentiful as sycamore-fig trees in the foothills. 28Solomon's horses were imported from Egyptf and from Kueg—the royal merchants purchased them from Kue. 29They imported a chariot from Egypt for six hundred shekelsh of silver, and a horse for a hundred and fifty.i They also exported them to all the kings of the Hittites and of the Arameans.

Solomon's Wives

11 KING SOLOMON, however, loved many foreign women besides Pharaoh's daughter—Moabites, Ammonites, Edomites, Sidonians and Hittites.

---

a 14 That is, about 25 tons (about 23 metric tons)   b 16 That is, about 7 1/2 pounds (about 3.5 kilograms)   c 17 That is, about 3 3/4 pounds (about 1.5 kilograms)   d 22 Hebrew of ships of Tarshish   e 26 Or charioteers   f 28 Or possibly Muzur, a region in Cilicia; also in verse 29   g 28 Probably Cilicia   h 29 That is, about 15 pounds (about 7 kilograms)   i 29 That is, about 3 3/4 pounds (about 1.7 kilograms)

Living Bible

New Revised Standard

wood to make pillars for the Temple and the palace, and for harps and harpsichords for his choirs. Never before or since has there been such a supply of beautiful wood.)

13In exchange for the gifts from the queen of Sheba, King Solomon gave her everything she asked him for, besides the presents he had already planned. Then she and her servants returned to their own land.

14Each year Solomon received gold worth a quarter of a billion, 15besides sales taxes and profits from trade with the kings of Arabia and the other surrounding territories. 16, 17Solomon had some of the gold beaten into two hundred pieces of armor (gold worth $6,000 went into each piece) and three hundred shields ($1,800 worth of gold in each). And he kept them in his palace in the Hall of the Forest of Lebanon.

18He also made a huge ivory throne and overlaid it with pure gold. 19It had six steps and a rounded back, with arm rests; and a lion standing on each side. 20And there were two lions on each step—twelve in all. There was no other throne in all the world so splendid as that one.

21All of King Solomon's cups were of solid gold, and in the Hall of the Forest of Lebanon his entire dining service was made of solid gold. (Silver wasn't used because it wasn't considered to be of much value!)

22King Solomon's merchant fleet was in partnership with King Hiram's, and once every three years a great load of gold, silver, ivory, apes, and peacocks arrived at the Israeli ports.

23So King Solomon was richer and wiser than all the kings of the earth. 24Great men from many lands came to interview him and listen to his God-given wisdom. 25They brought him annual tribute of silver and gold dishes, beautiful cloth, myrrh, spices, horses, and mules.

26Solomon built up a great stable of horses with a vast number of chariots and cavalry—1,400 chariots in all, and 12,000 cavalrymen who lived in the chariot cities and with the king at Jerusalem. 27Silver was as common as stones in Jerusalem in those days, and cedar was of no greater value than the common sycamore! 28Solomon's horses were brought to him from Egypt and southern Turkey, where his agents purchased them at wholesale prices. 29An Egyptian chariot delivered to Jerusalem cost $400, and the horses were valued at $150 each. Many of these were then resold to the Hittite and Syrian kings.

the king made supports for the house of the LORD, and for the king's house, lyres also and harps for the singers; no such almug wood has come or been seen to this day.

13 Meanwhile King Solomon gave to the queen of Sheba every desire that she expressed, as well as what he gave her out of Solomon's royal bounty. Then she returned to her own land, with her servants.

14 The weight of gold that came to Solomon in one year was six hundred sixty-six talents of gold, 15besides that which came from the traders and from the business of the merchants, and from all the kings of Arabia and the governors of the land. 16King Solomon made two hundred large shields of beaten gold; six hundred shekels of gold went into each large shield. 17He made three hundred shields of beaten gold; three minas of gold went into each shield; and the king put them in the House of the Forest of Lebanon. 18The king also made a great ivory throne, and overlaid it with the finest gold. 19The throne had six steps. The top of the throne was rounded in the back, and on each side of the seat were arm rests and two lions standing beside the arm rests, 20while twelve lions were standing, one on each end of a step on the six steps. Nothing like it was ever made in any kingdom. 21All King Solomon's drinking vessels were of gold, and all the vessels of the House of the Forest of Lebanon were of pure gold; none were of silver—it was not considered as anything in the days of Solomon. 22For the king had a fleet of ships of Tarshish at sea with the fleet of Hiram. Once every three years the fleet of ships of Tarshish used to come bringing gold, silver, ivory, apes, and peacocks.k

23 Thus King Solomon excelled all the kings of the earth in riches and in wisdom. 24The whole earth sought the presence of Solomon to hear his wisdom, which God had put into his mind. 25Every one of them brought a present, objects of silver and gold, garments, weaponry, spices, horses, and mules, so much year by year.

26 Solomon gathered together chariots and horses; he had fourteen hundred chariots and twelve thousand horses, which he stationed in the chariot cities and with the king in Jerusalem. 27The king made silver as common in Jerusalem as stones, and he made cedars as numerous as the sycamores of the Shephelah. 28Solomon's import of horses was from Egypt and Kue, and the king's traders received them from Kue at a price. 29A chariot could be imported from Egypt for six hundred shekels of silver, and a horse for one hundred fifty; so through the king's traders they were exported to all the kings of the Hittites and the kings of Aram.

Solomon's Errors

11 KING SOLOMON married many other girls besides the Egyptian princess. Many of them came from nations where idols were worshiped!— Moab, Ammon, Edom, Sidon, and from the Hittites—

11 KING SOLOMON loved many foreign women along with the daughter of Pharaoh: Moabite, Ammonite, Edomite, Sidonian, and Hittite women,

---

j 11:1 *where idols were worshiped,* implied.

k Or *baboons*

King James

2Of the nations *concerning* which the LORD said unto the children of Israel, Ye shall not go in to them, neither shall they come in unto you: *for* surely they will turn away your heart after their gods: Solomon clave unto these in love.

3And he had seven hundred wives, princesses, and three hundred concubines: and his wives turned away his heart.

4For it came to pass, when Solomon was old, *that* his wives turned away his heart after other gods: and his heart was not perfect with the LORD his God, as *was* the heart of David his father.

5For Solomon went after Ashtoreth the goddess of the Zidonians, and after Milcom the abomination of the Ammonites.

6And Solomon did evil in the sight of the LORD, and went not fully after the LORD, as *did* David his father.

7Then did Solomon build an high place for Chemosh, the abomination of Moab, in the hill that *is* before Jerusalem, and for Molech, the abomination of the children of Ammon.

8And likewise did he for all his strange wives, which burnt incense and sacrificed unto their gods.

9¶ And the LORD was angry with Solomon, because his heart was turned from the LORD God of Israel, which had appeared unto him twice,

10And had commanded him concerning this thing, that he should not go after other gods: but he kept not that which the LORD commanded.

11Wherefore the LORD said unto Solomon, Forasmuch as this is done of thee, and thou hast not kept my covenant and my statutes, which I have commanded thee, I will surely rend the kingdom from thee, and will give it to thy servant.

12Notwithstanding in thy days I will not do it for David thy father's sake: *but* I will rend it out of the hand of thy son.

13Howbeit I will not rend away all the kingdom; *but* will give one tribe to thy son for David my servant's sake, and for Jerusalem's sake which I have chosen.

14¶ And the LORD stirred up an adversary unto Solomon, Hadad the Edomite: he *was* of the king's seed in Edom.

15For it came to pass, when David was in Edom, and Joab the captain of the host was gone up to bury the slain, after he had smitten every male in Edom;

16(For six months did Joab remain there with all Israel, until he had cut off every male in Edom:)

17That Hadad fled, he and certain Edomites of his father's servants with him, to go into Egypt; Hadad *being* yet a little child.

18And they arose out of Midian, and came to Paran: and they took men with them out of Paran, and they came to Egypt, unto Pharaoh king of Egypt; which gave him an house, and appointed him victuals, and gave him land.

19And Hadad found great favour in the sight of Pharaoh, so that he gave him to wife the sister of his own wife, the sister of Tahpenes the queen.

20And the sister of Tahpenes bare him Genubath his son, whom Tahpenes weaned in Pharaoh's house: and Genubath was in Pharaoh's household among the sons of Pharaoh.

21And when Hadad heard in Egypt that David slept with his fathers, and that Joab the captain of the host was dead, Hadad said to Pharaoh, Let me depart, that I may go to mine own country.

22Then Pharaoh said unto him, But what hast thou lacked with me, that, behold, thou seekest to go to thine own country? And he answered, Nothing: howbeit let me go in any wise.

23¶ And God stirred him up *another* adversary, Rezon the son of Eliadah, which fled from his lord Hadadezer king of Zobah:

New International

2They were from nations about which the LORD had told the Israelites, "You must not intermarry with them, because they will surely turn your hearts after their gods." Nevertheless, Solomon held fast to them in love. 3He had seven hundred wives of royal birth and three hundred concubines, and his wives led him astray. 4As Solomon grew old, his wives turned his heart after other gods, and his heart was not fully devoted to the LORD his God, as had been the heart of David his father. 5He followed Ashtoreth the goddess of the Sidonians, and Molecha the detestable god of the Ammonites. 6So Solomon did evil in the eyes of the LORD; he did not follow the LORD completely, as David his father had done. 7On a hill east of Jerusalem, Solomon built a high place for Chemosh the detestable god of Moab, and for Molech the detestable god of the Ammonites. 8He did the same for all his foreign wives, who burned incense and offered sacrifices to their gods.

9The LORD became angry with Solomon because his heart had turned away from the LORD, the God of Israel, who had appeared to him twice. 10Although he had forbidden Solomon to follow other gods, Solomon did not keep the LORD's command. 11So the LORD said to Solomon, "Since this is your attitude and you have not kept my covenant and my decrees, which I commanded you, I will most certainly tear the kingdom away from you and give it to one of your subordinates. 12Nevertheless, for the sake of David your father, I will not do it during your lifetime. I will tear it out of the hand of your son. 13Yet I will not tear the whole kingdom from him, but will give him one tribe for the sake of David my servant and for the sake of Jerusalem, which I have chosen."

Solomon's Adversaries

14Then the LORD raised up against Solomon an adversary, Hadad the Edomite, from the royal line of Edom. 15Earlier when David was fighting with Edom, Joab the commander of the army, who had gone up to bury the dead, had struck down all the men in Edom. 16Joab and all the Israelites stayed there for six months, until they had destroyed all the men in Edom. 17But Hadad, still only a boy, fled to Egypt with some Edomite officials who had served his father. 18They set out from Midian and went to Paran. Then taking men from Paran with them, they went to Egypt, to Pharaoh king of Egypt, who gave Hadad a house and land and provided him with food.

19Pharaoh was so pleased with Hadad that he gave him a sister of his own wife, Queen Tahpenes, in marriage. 20The sister of Tahpenes bore him a son named Genubath, whom Tahpenes brought up in the royal palace. There Genubath lived with Pharaoh's own children.

21While he was in Egypt, Hadad heard that David rested with his fathers and that Joab the commander of the army was also dead. Then Hadad said to Pharaoh, "Let me go, that I may return to my own country."

22"What have you lacked here that you want to go back to your own country?" Pharaoh asked.

"Nothing," Hadad replied, "but do let me go!"

23And God raised up against Solomon another adversary, Rezon son of Eliada, who had fled from his master, Hadadezer king of Zobah. 24He gathered men around

a 5 Hebrew *Milcom*; also in verse 33

Living Bible

2even though the Lord had clearly instructed his people not to marry into those nations, because the women they married would get them started worshiping their gods. Yet Solomon did it anyway. 3He had seven hundred wives and three hundred concubines; and sure enough, they turned his heart away from the Lord, 4especially in his old age. They encouraged him to worship their gods instead of trusting completely in the Lord as his father David had done. 5Solomon worshiped Ashtoreth, the goddess of the Sidonians, and Milcom, the horrible god of the Ammonites. 6Thus Solomon did what was clearly wrong and refused to follow the Lord as his father David did. 7He even built a temple on the Mount of Olives, across the valley from Jerusalem, for Chemosh, the depraved god of Moab, and another for Molech, the unutterably vile god of the Ammonites. 8Solomon built temples for these foreign wives to use for burning incense and sacrificing to their gods.

9, 10Jehovah was very angry with Solomon about this, for now Solomon was no longer interested in the Lord God of Israel who had appeared to him twice to warn him specifically against worshiping other gods. But he hadn't listened, 11so now the Lord said to him, "Since you have not kept our agreement and have not obeyed my laws, I will tear the kingdom away from you and your family and give it to someone else. 12, 13However, for the sake of your father David, I won't do this while you are still alive. I will take the kingdom away from your son. And even so I will let him be king of one tribe, for David's sake and for the sake of Jerusalem, my chosen city."

14So the Lord caused Hadad the Edomite to grow in power. And Solomon became apprehensive, for Hadad was a member of the royal family of Edom. 15Years before, when David had been in Edom with Joab to arrange for the burial of some Israeli soldiers who had died in battle, the Israeli army had killed nearly every male in the entire country. 16, 17, 18It took six months to accomplish this, but they finally killed all except Hadad and a few royal officials who took him to Egypt (he was a very small child at the time). They slipped out of Midian and went to Paran, where others joined them and accompanied them to Egypt, and Pharaoh had given them homes and food.

19Hadad became one of Pharaoh's closest friends, and he gave him a wife—the sister of Queen Tahpenes. 20She presented him with a son, Genubath, who was brought up in Pharaoh's palace among Pharaoh's own sons. 21When Hadad, there in Egypt, heard that David and Joab were both dead, he asked Pharaoh for permission to return to Edom.

22"Why?" Pharaoh asked him. "What do you lack here? How have we disappointed you?"

"Everything is wonderful," he replied "but even so, I'd like to go back home."

23Another of Solomon's enemies whom God raised to power was Rezon, one of the officials of King Hadadezer of Zobah who had deserted his post and fled the country. 24He had become the leader of a gang of ban-

New Revised Standard

2from the nations concerning which the LORD had said to the Israelites, "You shall not enter into marriage with them, neither shall they with you; for they will surely incline your heart to follow their gods"; Solomon clung to these in love. 3Among his wives were seven hundred princesses and three hundred concubines; and his wives turned away his heart. 4For when Solomon was old, his wives turned away his heart after other gods; and his heart was not true to the LORD his God, as was the heart of his father David. 5For Solomon followed Astarte the goddess of the Sidonians, and Milcom the abomination of the Ammonites. 6So Solomon did what was evil in the sight of the LORD, and did not completely follow the LORD, as his father David had done. 7Then Solomon built a high place for Chemosh the abomination of Moab, and for Molech the abomination of the Ammonites, on the mountain east of Jerusalem. 8He did the same for all his foreign wives, who offered incense and sacrificed to their gods.

9 Then the LORD was angry with Solomon, because his heart had turned away from the LORD, the God of Israel, who had appeared to him twice, 10and had commanded him concerning this matter, that he should not follow other gods; but he did not observe what the LORD commanded. 11Therefore the LORD said to Solomon, "Since this has been your mind and you have not kept my covenant and my statutes that I have commanded you, I will surely tear the kingdom from you and give it to your servant. 12Yet for the sake of your father David I will not do it in your lifetime; I will tear it out of the hand of your son. 13I will not, however, tear away the entire kingdom; I will give one tribe to your son, for the sake of my servant David and for the sake of Jerusalem, which I have chosen."

Adversaries of Solomon

14 Then the LORD raised up an adversary against Solomon, Hadad the Edomite; he was of the royal house in Edom. 15For when David was in Edom, and Joab the commander of the army went up to bury the dead, he killed every male in Edom 16(for Joab and all Israel remained there six months, until he had eliminated every male in Edom); 17but Hadad fled to Egypt with some Edomites who were servants of his father. He was a young boy at that time. 18They set out from Midian and came to Paran; they took people with them from Paran and came to Egypt, to Pharaoh king of Egypt, who gave him a house, assigned him an allowance of food, and gave him land. 19Hadad found great favor in the sight of Pharaoh, so that he gave him his sister-in-law for a wife, the sister of Queen Tahpenes. 20The sister of Tahpenes gave birth by him to his son Genubath, whom Tahpenes weaned in Pharaoh's house; Genubath was in Pharaoh's house among the children of Pharaoh. 21When Hadad heard in Egypt that David slept with his ancestors and that Joab the commander of the army was dead, Hadad said to Pharaoh, "Let me depart, that I may go to my own country." 22But Pharaoh said to him, "What do you lack with me that you now seek to go to your own country?" And he said, "No, do let me go."

23 God raised up another adversary against Solomon,[b] Rezon son of Eliada, who had fled from his master, King Hadadezer of Zobah. 24He gathered followers

_____
b Heb *him*

King James

24And he gathered men unto him, and became captain over a band, when David slew them *of Zobah:* and they went to Damascus, and dwelt therein, and reigned in Damascus.

25And he was an adversary to Israel all the days of Solomon, beside the mischief that Hadad *did:* and he abhorred Israel, and reigned over Syria.

26¶ And Jeroboam the son of Nebat, an Ephrathite of Zereda, Solomon's servant, whose mother's name *was* Zeruah, a widow woman, even he lifted up *his* hand against the king.

27And this *was* the cause that he lifted up *his* hand against the king: Solomon built Millo, *and* repaired the breaches of the city of David his father.

28And the man Jeroboam *was* a mighty man of valour: and Solomon seeing the young man that he was industrious, he made him ruler over all the charge of the house of Joseph.

29And it came to pass at that time when Jeroboam went out of Jerusalem, that the prophet Ahijah the Shilonite found him in the way; and he had clad himself with a new garment; and they two *were* alone in the field:

30And Ahijah caught the new garment that *was* on him, and rent it *in* twelve pieces:

31And he said to Jeroboam, Take thee ten pieces: for thus saith the LORD, the God of Israel, Behold, I will rend the kingdom out of the hand of Solomon, and will give ten tribes to thee:

32(But he shall have one tribe for my servant David's sake, and for Jerusalem's sake, the city which I have chosen out of all the tribes of Israel:)

33Because that they have forsaken me, and have worshipped Ashtoreth the goddess of the Zidonians, Chemosh the god of the Moabites, and Milcom the god of the children of Ammon, and have not walked in my ways, to do *that which is* right in mine eyes, and *to keep* my statutes and my judgments, as *did* David his father.

34Howbeit I will not take the whole kingdom out of his hand: but I will make him prince all the days of his life for David my servant's sake, whom I chose, because he kept my commandments and my statutes:

35But I will take the kingdom out of his son's hand, and will give it unto thee, *even* ten tribes.

36And unto his son will I give one tribe, that David my servant may have a light alway before me in Jerusalem, the city which I have chosen me to put my name there.

37And I will take thee, and thou shalt reign according to all that thy soul desireth, and shalt be king over Israel.

38And it shall be, if thou wilt hearken unto all that I command thee, and wilt walk in my ways, and do *that is* right in my sight, to keep my statutes and my commandments, as David my servant did; that I will be with thee, and build thee a sure house, as I built for David, and will give Israel unto thee.

39And I will for this afflict the seed of David, but not for ever.

40Solomon sought therefore to kill Jeroboam. And Jeroboam arose, and fled into Egypt, unto Shishak king of Egypt, and was in Egypt until the death of Solomon.

41¶ And the rest of the acts of Solomon, and all that he did, and his wisdom, *are* they not written in the book of the acts of Solomon?

42And the time that Solomon reigned in Jerusalem over all Israel *was* forty years.

43And Solomon slept with his fathers, and was buried in the city of David his father: and Rehoboam his son reigned in his stead.

New International

him and became the leader of a band of rebels when David destroyed the forces[a] of Zobah,; the rebels went to Damascus, where they settled and took control. 25Rezon was Israel's adversary as long as Solomon lived, adding to the trouble caused by Hadad. So Rezon ruled in Aram and was hostile toward Israel.

Jeroboam Rebels Against Solomon

26Also, Jeroboam son of Nebat rebelled against the king. He was one of Solomon's officials, an Ephraimite from Zeredah, and his mother was a widow named Zeruah.

27Here is the account of how he rebelled against the king: Solomon had built the supporting terraces[b] and had filled in the gap in the wall of the city of David his father. 28Now Jeroboam was a man of standing, and when Solomon saw how well the young man did his work, he put him in charge of the whole labor force of the house of Joseph.

29About that time Jeroboam was going out of Jerusalem, and Ahijah the prophet of Shiloh met him on the way, wearing a new cloak. The two of them were alone out in the country, 30and Ahijah took hold of the new cloak he was wearing and tore it into twelve pieces. 31Then he said to Jeroboam, "Take ten pieces for yourself, for this is what the LORD, the God of Israel, says: 'See, I am going to tear the kingdom out of Solomon's hand and give you ten tribes. 32But for the sake of my servant David and the city of Jerusalem, which I have chosen out of all the tribes of Israel, he will have one tribe. 33I will do this because they have[c] forsaken me and worshiped Ashtoreth the goddess of the Sidonians, Chemosh the god of the Moabites, and Molech the god of the Ammonites, and have not walked in my ways, nor done what is right in my eyes, nor kept my statutes and laws as David, Solomon's father, did.

34" 'But I will not take the whole kingdom out of Solomon's hand; I have made him ruler all the days of his life for the sake of David my servant, whom I chose and who observed my commands and statutes. 35I will take the kingdom from his son's hands and give you ten tribes. 36I will give one tribe to his son so that David my servant may always have a lamp before me in Jerusalem, the city where I chose to put my Name. 37However, as for you, I will take you, and you will rule over all that your heart desires; you will be king over Israel. 38If you do whatever I command you and walk in my ways and do what is right in my eyes by keeping my statutes and commands, as David my servant did, I will be with you. I will build you a dynasty as enduring as the one I built for David and will give Israel to you. 39I will humble David's descendants because of this, but not forever.' "

40Solomon tried to kill Jeroboam, but Jeroboam fled to Egypt, to Shishak the king, and stayed there until Solomon's death.

Solomon's Death

41As for the other events of Solomon's reign—all he did and the wisdom he displayed—are they not written in the book of the annals of Solomon? 42Solomon reigned in Jerusalem over all Israel forty years. 43Then he rested with his fathers and was buried in the city of David his father. And Rehoboam his son succeeded him as king.

---

a 24 Hebrew *destroyed them*   b 27 Or *the Millo*   c 33 Hebrew; Septuagint, Vulgate and Syriac *because he has*

Living Bible

dits—men who fled with him to Damascus (where he later became king) when David destroyed Zobah. 25During Solomon's entire lifetime, Rezon and Hadad were his enemies, for they hated Israel intensely.

26Another rebel leader was Jeroboam (the son of Nebat), who came from the city of Zeredah in Ephraim; his mother was Zeruah, a widow. 27, 28Here is the story back of his rebellion: Solomon was rebuilding Fort Millo, repairing the walls of this city his father had built. Jeroboam was very able, and when Solomon saw how industrious he was, he put him in charge of his labor battalions from the tribe of Joseph.

29One day as Jeroboam was leaving Jerusalem, the prophet Ahijah from Shiloh (who had put on a new robe for the occasion) met him and called him aside to talk to him. And as the two of them were alone in the field, 30Ahijah tore his new robe into twelve parts, 31and said to Jeroboam, "Take ten of these pieces, for the Lord God of Israel says, 'I will tear the kingdom from the hand of Solomon and give ten of the tribes to you! 32But I will leave him one tribed for the sake of my servant David and for the sake of Jerusalem, which I have chosen above all the other cities of Israel. 33For Solomon has forsaken me and worships Ashtoreth, the goddess of the Sidonians; and Chemosh, the god of Moab; and Milcom, the god of the Ammonites. He has not followed my paths and has not done what I consider right; he has not kept my laws and instructions as his father David did. 34I will not take the kingdom from him now, however; for the sake of my servant David, my chosen one who obeyed my commandments, I will let Solomon reign for the rest of his life.

35" 'But I will take away the kingdom from his son and give ten of the tribes to you. 36His son shall have the other one so that the descendants of David will continue to reign in Jerusalem, the city I have chosen to be the place for my name to be enshrined. 37And I will place you on the throne of Israel, and give you absolute power. 38If you listen to what I tell you and walk in my path and do whatever I consider right, obeying my commandments as my servant David did, then I will bless you; and your descendants shall rule Israel forever. (I once made this same promise to David. 39But because of Solomon's sin I will punish the descendants of David—though not forever.)' "

40Solomon tried to kill Jeroboam, but he fled to King Shishak of Egypt and stayed there until the death of Solomon.

41The rest of what Solomon did and said is written in the book The Acts of Solomon. 42He ruled in Jerusalem for forty years, 43and then died and was buried in the city of his father David; and his son Rehoboam reigned in his place.

New Revised Standard

around him and became leader of a marauding band, after the slaughter by David; they went to Damascus, settled there, and made him king in Damascus. 25He was an adversary of Israel all the days of Solomon, making trouble as Hadad did; he despised Israel and reigned over Aram.

Jeroboam's Rebellion

26 Jeroboam son of Nebat, an Ephraimite of Zeredah, a servant of Solomon, whose mother's name was Zeruah, a widow, rebelled against the king. 27The following was the reason he rebelled against the king. Solomon built the Millo, and closed up the gape of the city of his father David. 28The man Jeroboam was very able, and when Solomon saw that the young man was industrious he gave him charge over all the forced labor of the house of Joseph. 29About that time, when Jeroboam was leaving Jerusalem, the prophet Ahijah the Shilonite found him on the road. Ahijah had clothed himself with a new garment. The two of them were alone in the open country 30when Ahijah laid hold of the new garment he was wearing and tore it into twelve pieces. 31He then said to Jeroboam: Take for yourself ten pieces; for thus says the LORD, the God of Israel, "See, I am about to tear the kingdom from the hand of Solomon, and will give you ten tribes. 32One tribe will remain his, for the sake of my servant David and for the sake of Jerusalem, the city that I have chosen out of all the tribes of Israel. 33This is because he hasf forsaken me, worshiped Astarte the goddess of the Sidonians, Chemosh the god of Moab, and Milcom the god of the Ammonites, and hasf not walked in my ways, doing what is right in my sight and keeping my statutes and my ordinances, as his father David did. 34Nevertheless I will not take the whole kingdom away from him but will make him ruler all the days of his life, for the sake of my servant David whom I chose and who did keep my commandments and my statutes; 35but I will take the kingdom away from his son and give it to you—that is, the ten tribes. 36Yet to his son I will give one tribe, so that my servant David may always have a lamp before me in Jerusalem, the city where I have chosen to put my name. 37I will take you, and you shall reign over all that your soul desires; you shall be king over Israel. 38If you will listen to all that I command you, walk in my ways, and do what is right in my sight by keeping my statutes and my commandments, as David my servant did, I will be with you, and will build you an enduring house, as I built for David, and I will give Israel to you. 39For this reason I will punish the descendants of David, but not forever." 40Solomon sought therefore to kill Jeroboam; but Jeroboam promptly fled to Egypt, to King Shishak of Egypt, and remained in Egypt until the death of Solomon.

Death of Solomon

41 Now the rest of the acts of Solomon, all that he did as well as his wisdom, are they not written in the Book of the Acts of Solomon? 42The time that Solomon reigned in Jerusalem over all Israel was forty years. 43Solomon slept with his ancestors and was buried in the city of his father David; and his son Rehoboam succeeded him.

---

d 11:32 I will leave him one tribe. Of the twelve tribes, Judah and Benjamin were left to Solomon's son. These two tribes were often called "Judah," the larger of the two.

e Heb lacks in the wall   f Gk Syr Vg: Heb they have

King James

12 AND REHOBOAM went to Shechem: for all Israel were come to Shechem to make him king.

2And it came to pass, when Jeroboam the son of Nebat, who was yet in Egypt, heard *of it,* (for he was fled from the presence of king Solomon, and Jeroboam dwelt in Egypt;)

3That they sent and called him. And Jeroboam and all the congregation of Israel came, and spake unto Rehoboam, saying,

4Thy father made our yoke grievous: now therefore make thou the grievous service of thy father, and his heavy yoke which he put upon us, lighter, and we will serve thee.

5And he said unto them, Depart yet *for* three days, then come again to me. And the people departed.

6¶ And king Rehoboam consulted with the old men, that stood before Solomon his father while he yet lived, and said, How do ye advise that I may answer this people?

7And they spake unto him, saying, If thou wilt be a servant unto this people this day, and wilt serve them, and answer them, and speak good words to them, then they will be thy servants for ever.

8But he forsook the counsel of the old men, which they had given him, and consulted with the young men that were grown up with him, *and* which stood before him:

9And he said unto them, What counsel give ye that we may answer this people, who have spoken to me, saying, Make the yoke which thy father did put upon us lighter?

10And the young men that were grown up with him spake unto him, saying, Thus shalt thou speak unto this people that spake unto thee, saying, Thy father made our yoke heavy, but make thou *it* lighter unto us; thus shalt thou say unto them, My little *finger* shall be thicker than my father's loins.

11And now whereas my father did lade you with a heavy yoke, I will add to your yoke: my father hath chastised you with whips, but I will chastise you with scorpions.

12¶ So Jeroboam and all the people came to Rehoboam the third day, as the king had appointed, saying, Come to me again the third day.

13And the king answered the people roughly, and forsook the old men's counsel that they gave him;

14And spake to them after the counsel of the young men, saying, My father made your yoke heavy, and I will add to your yoke: my father *also* chastised you with whips, but I will chastise you with scorpions.

15Wherefore the king hearkened not unto the people; for the cause was from the LORD, that he might perform his saying, which the LORD spake by Ahijah the Shilonite unto Jeroboam the son of Nebat.

16¶ So when all Israel saw that the king hearkened not unto them, the people answered the king, saying, What portion have we in David? neither *have we* inheritance in the son of Jesse: to your tents, O Israel: now see to thine own house, David. So Israel departed unto their tents.

17But *as for* the children of Israel which dwelt in the cities of Judah, Rehoboam reigned over them.

18Then king Rehoboam sent Adoram, who *was* over the tribute; and all Israel stoned him with stones, that he died. Therefore king Rehoboam made speed to get him up to his chariot, to flee to Jerusalem.

19So Israel rebelled against the house of David unto this day.

20And it came to pass, when all Israel heard that Jeroboam was come again, that they sent and called him unto the congregation, and made him king over all Israel: there was none that followed the house of David, but the tribe of Judah only.

New International

Israel Rebels Against Rehoboam

12 REHOBOAM WENT to Shechem, for all the Israelites had gone there to make him king. 2When Jeroboam son of Nebat heard this (he was still in Egypt, where he had fled from King Solomon), he returned froma Egypt. 3So they sent for Jeroboam, and he and the whole assembly of Israel went to Rehoboam and said to him: 4"Your father put a heavy yoke on us, but now lighten the harsh labor and the heavy yoke he put on us, and we will serve you."

5Rehoboam answered, "Go away for three days and then come back to me." So the people went away.

6Then King Rehoboam consulted the elders who had served his father Solomon during his lifetime. "How would you advise me to answer these people?" he asked.

7They replied, "If today you will be a servant to these people and serve them and give them a favorable answer, they will always be your servants."

8But Rehoboam rejected the advice the elders gave him and consulted the young men who had grown up with him and were serving him. 9He asked them, "What is your advice? How should we answer these people who say to me, 'Lighten the yoke your father put on us'?"

10The young men who had grown up with him replied, "Tell these people who have said to you, 'Your father put a heavy yoke on us, but make our yoke lighter'—tell them, 'My little finger is thicker than my father's waist. 11My father laid on you a heavy yoke; I will make it even heavier. My father scourged you with whips; I will scourge you with scorpions.' "

12Three days later Jeroboam and all the people returned to Rehoboam, as the king had said, "Come back to me in three days." 13The king answered the people harshly. Rejecting the advice given him by the elders, 14he followed the advice of the young men and said, "My father made your yoke heavy; I will make it even heavier. My father scourged you with whips; I will scourge you with scorpions." 15So the king did not listen to the people, for this turn of events was from the LORD, to fulfill the word the LORD had spoken to Jeroboam son of Nebat through Ahijah the Shilonite.

16When all Israel saw that the king refused to listen to them, they answered the king:

"What share do we have in David,
    what part in Jesse's son?
To your tents, O Israel!
    Look after your own house, O David!"

So the Israelites went home. 17But as for the Israelites who were living in the towns of Judah, Rehoboam still ruled over them.

18King Rehoboam sent out Adoniram,b who was in charge of forced labor, but all Israel stoned him to death. King Rehoboam, however, managed to get into his chariot and escape to Jerusalem. 19So Israel has been in rebellion against the house of David to this day.

20When all the Israelites heard that Jeroboam had returned, they sent and called him to the assembly and made him king over all Israel. Only the tribe of Judah remained loyal to the house of David.

---

a *2* Or *he remained in*   b *18* Some Septuagint manuscripts and Syriac (see also 1 Kings 4:6 and 5:14); Hebrew *Adoram*

Living Bible

12 REHOBOAM'S INAUGURATION was at Shechem, and all Israel came for the coronation ceremony. 2, 3, 4Jeroboam, who was still in Egypt where he had fled from King Solomon, heard about the plans from his friends. They urged him to attend, so he joined the rest of Israel at Shechem, and was the ringleader in getting the people to make certain demands upon Rehoboam.

"Your father was a hard master," they told Rehoboam. "We don't want you as our king unless you promise to treat us better than he did."

5"Give me three days to think this over," Rehoboam replied. "Come back then for my answer." So the people left.

6Rehoboam talked it over with the old men who had counseled his father Solomon.

"What do you think I should do?" he asked them.

7And they replied, "If you give them a pleasant reply and agree to be good to them and serve them well, you can be their king forever."

8But Rehoboam refused the old men's counsel and called in the young men with whom he had grown up.

9"What do you think I should do?" he asked them.

10And the young men replied, "Tell them, 'If you think my father was hard on you, well, I'll be harder! 11Yes, my father was harsh, but I'll be even harsher! My father used whips on you, but I'll use scorpions!' "

12So when Jeroboam and the people returned three days later, 13, 14the new king answered them roughly. He ignored the old men's advice and followed that of the young men; 15so the king refused the people's demands. (But the Lord's hand was in it—he caused the new king to do this in order to fulfill his promise to Jeroboam, made through Ahijah, the prophet from Shiloh.)

16, 17When the people realized that the king meant what he said and was refusing to listen to them, they began shouting, "Down with David and all his relatives! Let's go home! Let Rehoboam be king of his own family!"

And they all deserted him except for the tribe of Judah, who remained loyal and accepted Rehoboam as their king. 18When King Rehoboam sent Adoram (who was in charge of the draft) to conscript men from the other tribes, a great mob stoned him to death. But King Rehoboam escaped by chariot and fled to Jerusalem. 19And Israel has been in rebellion against the dynasty of David to this day.

20When the people of Israel learned of Jeroboam's return from Egypt, he was asked to come before an open meeting of all the people; and there he was made king of Israel. Only the tribe of Judahc continued under the kingship of the family of David.

New Revised Standard

The Northern Tribes Secede

12 REHOBOAM WENT to Shechem, for all Israel had come to Shechem to make him king. 2When Jeroboam son of Nebat heard of it (for he was still in Egypt, where he had fled from King Solomon), then Jeroboam returned fromd Egypt. 3And they sent and called him; and Jeroboam and all the assembly of Israel came and said to Rehoboam, 4"Your father made our yoke heavy. Now therefore lighten the hard service of your father and his heavy yoke that he placed on us, and we will serve you." 5He said to them, "Go away for three days, then come again to me." So the people went away.

6 Then King Rehoboam took counsel with the older men who had attended his father Solomon while he was still alive, saying, "How do you advise me to answer this people?" 7They answered him, "If you will be a servant to this people today and serve them, and speak good words to them when you answer them, then they will be your servants forever." 8But he disregarded the advice that the older men gave him, and consulted with the young men who had grown up with him and now attended him. 9He said to them, "What do you advise that we answer this people who have said to me, 'Lighten the yoke that your father put on us'?" 10The young men who had grown up with him said to him, "Thus you should say to this people who spoke to you, 'Your father made our yoke heavy, but you must lighten it for us'; thus you should say to them, 'My little finger is thicker than my father's loins. 11Now, whereas my father laid on you a heavy yoke, I will add to your yoke. My father disciplined you with whips, but I will discipline you with scorpions.' "

12 So Jeroboam and all the people came to Rehoboam the third day, as the king had said, "Come to me again the third day." 13The king answered the people harshly. He disregarded the advice that the older men had given him 14and spoke to them according to the advice of the young men, "My father made your yoke heavy, but I will add to your yoke; my father disciplined you with whips, but I will discipline you with scorpions." 15So the king did not listen to the people, because it was a turn of affairs brought about by the LORD that he might fulfill his word, which the LORD had spoken by Ahijah the Shilonite to Jeroboam son of Nebat.

16 When all Israel saw that the king would not listen to them, the people answered the king,

"What share do we have in David?
We have no inheritance in the son of Jesse.
To your tents, O Israel!
Look now to your own house, O David."

So Israel went away to their tents. 17But Rehoboam reigned over the Israelites who were living in the towns of Judah. 18When King Rehoboam sent Adoram, who was taskmaster over the forced labor, all Israel stoned him to death. King Rehoboam then hurriedly mounted his chariot to flee to Jerusalem. 19So Israel has been in rebellion against the house of David to this day.

First Dynasty: Jeroboam Reigns over Israel

20 When all Israel heard that Jeroboam had returned, they sent and called him to the assembly and made him king over all Israel. There was no one who followed the house of David, except the tribe of Judah alone.

---

c 12:20 *Only the tribe of Judah.* Judah and Benjamin were sometimes (as in this instance) counted together as one tribe.

d Gk Vg Compare 2 Chr 10.2: Heb *lived in*

King James

21¶ And when Rehoboam was come to Jerusalem, he assembled all the house of Judah, with the tribe of Benjamin, an hundred and fourscore thousand chosen men, which were warriors, to fight against the house of Israel, to bring the kingdom again to Rehoboam the son of Solomon.

22But the word of God came unto Shemaiah the man of God, saying,

23Speak unto Rehoboam, the son of Solomon, king of Judah, and unto all the house of Judah and Benjamin, and to the remnant of the people, saying,

24Thus saith the LORD, Ye shall not go up, nor fight against your brethren the children of Israel: return every man to his house; for this thing is from me. They hearkened therefore to the word of the LORD, and returned to depart, according to the word of the LORD.

25¶ Then Jeroboam built Shechem in mount Ephraim, and dwelt therein; and went out from thence, and built Penuel.

26And Jeroboam said in his heart, Now shall the kingdom return to the house of David:

27If this people go up to do sacrifice in the house of the LORD at Jerusalem, then shall the heart of this people turn again unto their lord, *even* unto Rehoboam king of Judah, and they shall kill me, and go again to Rehoboam king of Judah.

28Whereupon the king took counsel, and made two calves *of* gold, and said unto them, It is too much for you to go up to Jerusalem: behold thy gods, O Israel, which brought thee up out of the land of Egypt.

29And he set the one in Beth-el, and the other put he in Dan.

30And this thing became a sin: for the people went *to worship* before the one, *even* unto Dan.

31And he made an house of high places, and made priests of the lowest of the people, which were not of the sons of Levi.

32And Jeroboam ordained a feast in the eighth month, on the fifteenth day of the month, like unto the feast that *is* in Judah, and he offered upon the altar. So did he in Beth-el, sacrificing unto the calves that he had made: and he placed in Beth-el the priests of the high places which he had made.

33So he offered upon the altar which he had made in Beth-el the fifteenth day of the eighth month, *even* in the month which he had devised of his own heart; and ordained a feast unto the children of Israel: and he offered upon the altar, and burnt incense.

13 AND, BEHOLD, there came a man of God out of Judah by the word of the LORD unto Beth-el: and Jeroboam stood by the altar to burn incense.

2And he cried against the altar in the word of the LORD, and said, O altar, altar, thus saith the LORD; Behold, a child shall be born unto the house of David, Josiah by name; and upon thee shall he offer the priests of the high places that burn incense upon thee, and men's bones shall be burnt upon thee.

3And he gave a sign the same day, saying, This *is* the sign which the LORD hath spoken; Behold, the altar shall be rent, and the ashes that *are* upon it shall be poured out.

4And it came to pass, when king Jeroboam heard the saying of the man of God, which had cried against the altar in Beth-el, that he put forth his hand from the altar, saying, Lay hold on him. And his hand, which he put forth against him, dried up, so that he could not pull it in again to him.

5The altar also was rent, and the ashes poured out from the altar, according to the sign which the man of God had given by the word of the LORD.

New International

21When Rehoboam arrived in Jerusalem, he mustered the whole house of Judah and the tribe of Benjamin—a hundred and eighty thousand fighting men—to make war against the house of Israel and to regain the kingdom for Rehoboam son of Solomon.

22But this word of God came to Shemaiah the man of God: 23"Say to Rehoboam son of Solomon king of Judah, to the whole house of Judah and Benjamin, and to the rest of the people, 24'This is what the LORD says: Do not go up to fight against your brothers, the Israelites. Go home, every one of you, for this is my doing.'" So they obeyed the word of the LORD and went home again, as the LORD had ordered.

Golden Calves at Bethel and Dan

25Then Jeroboam fortified Shechem in the hill country of Ephraim and lived there. From there he went out and built up Peniel.a

26Jeroboam thought to himself, "The kingdom will now likely revert to the house of David. 27If these people go up to offer sacrifices at the temple of the LORD in Jerusalem, they will again give their allegiance to their lord, Rehoboam king of Judah. They will kill me and return to King Rehoboam."

28After seeking advice, the king made two golden calves. He said to the people, "It is too much for you to go up to Jerusalem. Here are your gods, O Israel, who brought you up out of Egypt." 29One he set up in Bethel, and the other in Dan. 30And this thing became a sin; the people even went as far as Dan to worship the one there.

31Jeroboam built shrines on high places and appointed priests from all sorts of people, even though they were not Levites. 32He instituted a festival on the fifteenth day of the eighth month, like the festival held in Judah, and offered sacrifices on the altar. This he did in Bethel, sacrificing to the calves he had made. And at Bethel he also installed priests at the high places he had made. 33On the fifteenth day of the eighth month, a month of his own choosing, he offered sacrifices on the altar he had built at Bethel. So he instituted the festival for the Israelites and went up to the altar to make offerings.

The Man of God From Judah

13 BY THE word of the LORD a man of God came from Judah to Bethel, as Jeroboam was standing by the altar to make an offering. 2He cried out against the altar by the word of the LORD: "O altar, altar! This is what the LORD says: 'A son named Josiah will be born to the house of David. On you he will sacrifice the priests of the high places who now make offerings here, and human bones will be burned on you.'" 3That same day the man of God gave a sign: "This is the sign the LORD has declared: The altar will be split apart and the ashes on it will be poured out."

4When King Jeroboam heard what the man of God cried out against the altar at Bethel, he stretched out his hand from the altar and said, "Seize him!" But the hand he stretched out toward the man shriveled up, so that he could not pull it back. 5Also, the altar was split apart and its ashes poured out according to the sign given by the man of God by the word of the LORD.

---

a 25 Hebrew *Penuel*, a variant of *Peniel*

Living Bible

21When King Rehoboam arrived in Jerusalem, he summoned his army—all the able-bodied men of Judah and Benjamin: 180,000 special troops—to force the rest of Israel to acknowledge him as their king. 22But God sent this message to Shemaiah, the prophet:

23, 24"Tell Rehoboam the son of Solomon, king of Judah, and all the people of Judah and Benjamin that they must not fight against their brothers, the people of Israel. Tell them to disband and go home, for what has happened to Rehoboam is according to my wish." So the army went home as the Lord had commanded.

25Jeroboam now built the city of Shechem in the hill country of Ephraim, and it became his capital. Later he built Penuel. 26Jeroboam thought, "Unless I'm careful, the people will want a descendant of David as their king. 27When they go to Jerusalem to offer sacrifices at the Temple, they will become friendly with King Rehoboam; then they will kill me and ask him to be their king instead."

28So on the advice of his counselors, the king had two gold calf-idols made and told the people, "It's too much trouble to go to Jerusalem to worship; from now on these will be your gods—they rescued you from your captivity in Egypt!"

29One of these calf-idols was placed in Bethel and the other in Dan. 30This was of course a great sin, for the people worshiped them. 31He also made shrines on the hills and ordained priests from the rank and file of the people—even those who were not from the priest-tribe of Levi. 32, 33Jeroboam also announced that the annual Tabernacle Festival would be held at Bethel on the first of Novemberb (a date he decided upon himself), similar to the annual festival at Jerusalem; he himself offered sacrifices upon the altar to the calves at Bethel, and burned incense to them. And it was there at Bethel that he ordained priests for the shrines on the hills.

13 AS JEROBOAM approached the altar to burn incense to the gold calf-idol, a prophet of the Lord from Judah walked up to him. 2Then, at the Lord's command, the prophet shouted, "O altar, the Lord says that a child named Josiah shall be born into the family line of David, and he shall sacrifice upon you the priests from the shrines on the hills who come here to burn incense; and men's bones shall be burned upon you."

3He gave this proof that his message was from the Lord: "This altar will split apart, and the ashes on it will spill to the ground."

4The king was very angry with the prophet for saying this. He shouted to his guards, "Arrest that man!" and shook his fist at him. Instantly the king's arm became paralyzed in that position; he couldn't pull it back again! 5At the same moment a wide crack appeared in the altar and the ashes poured out, just as the prophet had said would happen. For this was the prophet's proof that God had been speaking through him.

b 12:32, 33 on the first of November, literally, "on the fifteenth day of the eighth month" of the Hebrew calendar. This was a month later than the annual celebration in Jerusalem, which God had ordained.

New Revised Standard

21 When Rehoboam came to Jerusalem, he assembled all the house of Judah and the tribe of Benjamin, one hundred eighty thousand chosen troops to fight against the house of Israel, to restore the kingdom to Rehoboam son of Solomon. 22But the word of God came to Shemaiah the man of God: 23Say to King Rehoboam of Judah, son of Solomon, and to all the house of Judah and Benjamin, and to the rest of the people, 24"Thus says the LORD, You shall not go up or fight against your kindred the people of Israel. Let everyone go home, for this thing is from me." So they heeded the word of the LORD and went home again, according to the word of the LORD.

Jeroboam's Golden Calves

25 Then Jeroboam built Shechem in the hill country of Ephraim, and resided there; he went out from there and built Penuel. 26Then Jeroboam said to himself, "Now the kingdom may well revert to the house of David. 27If this people continues to go up to offer sacrifices in the house of the LORD at Jerusalem, the heart of this people will turn again to their master, King Rehoboam of Judah; they will kill me and return to King Rehoboam of Judah." 28So the king took counsel, and made two calves of gold. He said to the people,c "You have gone up to Jerusalem long enough. Here are your gods, O Israel, who brought you up out of the land of Egypt." 29He set one in Bethel, and the other he put in Dan. 30And this thing became a sin, for the people went to worship before the one at Bethel and before the other as far as Dan.d 31He also made housese on high places, and appointed priests from among all the people, who were not Levites. 32Jeroboam appointed a festival on the fifteenth day of the eighth month like the festival that was in Judah, and he offered sacrifices on the altar; so he did in Bethel, sacrificing to the calves that he had made. And he placed in Bethel the priests of the high places that he had made. 33He went up to the altar that he had made in Bethel on the fifteenth day in the eighth month, in the month that he alone had devised; he appointed a festival for the people of Israel, and he went up to the altar to offer incense.

A Man of God from Judah

13 WHILE JEROBOAM was standing by the altar to offer incense, a man of God came out of Judah by the word of the LORD to Bethel 2and proclaimed against the altar by the word of the LORD, and said, "O altar, altar, thus says the LORD: 'A son shall be born to the house of David, Josiah by name; and he shall sacrifice on you the priests of the high places who offer incense on you, and human bones shall be burned on you.' " 3He gave a sign the same day, saying, "This is the sign that the LORD has spoken: 'The altar shall be torn down, and the ashes that are on it shall be poured out.' " 4When the king heard what the man of God cried out against the altar at Bethel, Jeroboam stretched out his hand from the altar, saying, "Seize him!" But the hand that he stretched out against him withered so that he could not draw it back to himself. 5The altar also was torn down, and the ashes poured out from the altar, according to the sign that the man of God had given by the word of the LORD. 6The king said to the man of God,

c Gk: Heb to them   d Compare Gk: Heb went to the one as far as Dan   e Gk Vg Compare 13.32: Heb a house

King James

6And the king answered and said unto the man of God, Entreat now the face of the Lord thy God, and pray for me, that my hand may be restored me again. And the man of God besought the Lord, and the king's hand was restored him again, and became as *it was* before.

7And the king said unto the man of God, Come home with me, and refresh thyself, and I will give thee a reward.

8And the man of God said unto the king, If thou wilt give me half thine house, I will not go in with thee, neither will I eat bread nor drink water in this place:

9For so was it charged me by the word of the Lord, saying, Eat no bread, nor drink water, nor turn again by the same way that thou camest.

10So he went another way, and returned not by the way that he came to Beth-el.

11¶ Now there dwelt an old prophet in Beth-el; and his sons came and told him all the works that the man of God had done that day in Beth-el: the words which he had spoken unto the king, them they told also to their father.

12And their father said unto them, What way went he? For his sons had seen what way the man of God went, which came from Judah.

13And he said unto his sons, Saddle me the ass. So they saddled him the ass; and he rode thereon,

14And went after the man of God, and found him sitting under an oak: and he said unto him, *Art* thou the man of God that camest from Judah? And he said, I *am.*

15Then he said unto him, Come home with me, and eat bread.

16And he said, I may not return with thee, nor go in with thee: neither will I eat bread nor drink water with thee in this place:

17For it was said to me by the word of the Lord, Thou shalt eat no bread nor drink water there, nor turn again to go by the way that thou camest.

18He said unto him, I *am* a prophet also as thou *art;* and an angel spake unto me by the word of the Lord, saying, Bring him back with thee into thine house, that he may eat bread and drink water. *But* he lied unto him.

19So he went back with him, and did eat bread in his house, and drank water.

20¶ And it came to pass, as they sat at the table, that the word of the Lord came unto the prophet that brought him back:

21And he cried unto the man of God that came from Judah, saying, Thus saith the Lord, Forasmuch as thou hast disobeyed the mouth of the Lord, and hast not kept the commandment which the Lord thy God commanded thee,

22But camest back, and hast eaten bread and drunk water in the place, of the which *the* Lord did say to thee, Eat no bread, and drink no water; thy carcase shall not come unto the sepulchre of thy fathers.

23¶ And it came to pass, after he had eaten bread, and after he had drunk, that he saddled for him the ass, *to wit,* for the prophet whom he had brought back.

24And when he was gone, a lion met him by the way, and slew him: and his carcase was cast in the way, and the ass stood by it, the lion also stood by the carcase.

25And, behold, men passed by, and saw the carcase cast in the way, and the lion standing by the carcase: and they came and told *it* in the city where the old prophet dwelt.

26And when the prophet that brought him back from the way heard *thereof,* he said, It *is* the man of God, who was disobedient unto the word of the Lord: therefore the Lord hath delivered him unto the lion, which hath torn him, and slain him, according to the word of the Lord, which he spake unto him.

27And he spake to his sons, saying, Saddle me the ass. And they saddled *him.*

New International

6Then the king said to the man of God, "Intercede with the Lord your God and pray for me that my hand may be restored." So the man of God interceded with the Lord, and the king's hand was restored and became as it was before.

7The king said to the man of God, "Come home with me and have something to eat, and I will give you a gift."

8But the man of God answered the king, "Even if you were to give me half your possessions, I would not go with you, nor would I eat bread or drink water here. 9For I was commanded by the word of the Lord: 'You must not eat bread or drink water or return by the way you came.' " 10So he took another road and did not return by the way he had come to Bethel.

11Now there was a certain old prophet living in Bethel, whose sons came and told him all that the man of God had done there that day. They also told their father what he had said to the king. 12Their father asked them, "Which way did he go?" And his sons showed him which road the man of God from Judah had taken. 13So he said to his sons, "Saddle the donkey for me." And when they had saddled the donkey for him, he mounted it 14and rode after the man of God. He found him sitting under an oak tree and asked, "Are you the man of God who came from Judah?"

"I am," he replied.

15So the prophet said to him, "Come home with me and eat."

16The man of God said, "I cannot turn back and go with you, nor can I eat bread or drink water with you in this place. 17I have been told by the word of the Lord: 'You must not eat bread or drink water there or return by the way you came.' "

18The old prophet answered, "I too am a prophet, as you are. And an angel said to me by the word of the Lord: 'Bring him back with you to your house so that he may eat bread and drink water.' " (But he was lying to him.) 19So the man of God returned with him and ate and drank in his house.

20While they were sitting at the table, the word of the Lord came to the old prophet who had brought him back. 21He cried out to the man of God who had come from Judah, "This is what the Lord says: 'You have defied the word of the Lord and have not kept the command the Lord your God gave you. 22You came back and ate bread and drank water in the place where he told you not to eat or drink. Therefore your body will not be buried in the tomb of your fathers.' "

23When the man of God had finished eating and drinking, the prophet who had brought him back saddled his donkey for him. 24As he went on his way, a lion met him on the road and killed him, and his body was thrown down on the road, with both the donkey and the lion standing beside it. 25Some people who passed by saw the body thrown down there, with the lion standing beside the body, and they went and reported it in the city where the old prophet lived.

26When the prophet who had brought him back from his journey heard of it, he said, "It is the man of God who defied the word of the Lord. The Lord has given him over to the lion, which has mauled him and killed him, as the word of the Lord had warned him."

27The prophet said to his sons, "Saddle the donkey for me," and they did so. 28Then he went out and found the

Living Bible

6"Oh, please, please," the king cried out to the prophet, "beg the Lord your God to restore my arm again." So he prayed to the Lord, and the king's arm became normal again.

7Then the king said to the prophet, "Come to the palace with me and rest awhile and have some food; and I'll give you a reward because you healed my arm." 8But the prophet said to the king, "Even if you gave me half your palace, I wouldn't go into it; nor would I eat or drink even water in this place! 9For the Lord has given me strict orders not to eat anything or drink any water while I'm here, and not to return to Judah by the road I came on."

10So he went back another way.

11As it happened, there was an old prophet living in Bethel, and his sons went home and told him what the prophet from Judah had done and what he had said to the king.

12"Which way did he go?" the old prophet asked. So they told him.

13"Quick, saddle the donkey," the old man said. And when they had saddled the donkey for him, 14he rode after the prophet and found him sitting under an oak tree.

"Are you the prophet who came from Judah?" he asked him.

"Yes," he replied, "I am."

15Then the old man said to the prophet, "Come home with me and eat."

16, 17"No," he replied, "I can't; for I am not allowed to eat anything or to drink any water at Bethel. The Lord strictly warned me against it; and he also told me not to return home by the same road I came on."

18But the old man said, "I am a prophet too, just as you are; and an angel gave me a message from the Lord. I am to take you home with me and give you food and water."

But the old man was lying to him. 19So they went back together, and the prophet ate some food and drank some water at the old man's home.

20Then, suddenly, while they were sitting at the table, a message from the Lord came to the old man, 21, 22and he shouted at the prophet from Judah, "The Lord says that because you have been disobedient to his clear command, and have come here, and have eaten and drunk water in the place he told you not to, therefore your body shall not be buried in the grave of your fathers."

23After finishing the meal, the old man saddled the prophet's donkey, 24, 25and the prophet started off again. But as he was traveling along, a lion came out and killed him. His body lay there on the road, with the donkey and the lion standing beside it. Those who came by and saw the body lying in the road and the lion standing quietly beside it, reported it in Bethel where the old prophet lived.

26When he heard what had happened he exclaimed, "It is the prophet who disobeyed the Lord's command; the Lord fulfilled his warning by causing the lion to kill him."

27Then he said to his sons, "Saddle my donkey!" And they did.

New Revised Standard

"Entreat now the favor of the LORD your God, and pray for me, so that my hand may be restored to me." So the man of God entreated the LORD; and the king's hand was restored to him, and became as it was before. 7Then the king said to the man of God, "Come home with me and dine, and I will give you a gift." 8But the man of God said to the king, "If you give me half your kingdom, I will not go in with you; nor will I eat food or drink water in this place. 9For thus I was commanded by the word of the LORD: You shall not eat food, or drink water, or return by the way that you came." 10So he went another way, and did not return by the way that he had come to Bethel.

11 Now there lived an old prophet in Bethel. One of his sons came and told him all that the man of God had done that day in Bethel; the words also that he had spoken to the king, they told to their father. 12Their father said to them, "Which way did he go?" And his sons showed him the way that the man of God who came from Judah had gone. 13Then he said to his sons, "Saddle a donkey for me." So they saddled a donkey for him, and he mounted it. 14He went after the man of God, and found him sitting under an oak tree. He said to him, "Are you the man of God who came from Judah?" He answered, "I am." 15Then he said to him, "Come home with me and eat some food." 16But he said, "I cannot return with you, or go in with you; nor will I eat food or drink water with you in this place; 17for it was said to me by the word of the LORD: You shall not eat food or drink water there, or return by the way that you came." 18Then the othera said to him, "I also am a prophet as you are, and an angel spoke to me by the word of the LORD: Bring him back with you into your house so that he may eat food and drink water." But he was deceiving him. 19Then the man of Goda went back with him, and ate food and drank water in his house.

20 As they were sitting at the table, the word of the LORD came to the prophet who had brought him back; 21and he proclaimed to the man of God who came from Judah, "Thus says the LORD: Because you have disobeyed the word of the LORD, and have not kept the commandment that the LORD your God commanded you, 22but have come back and have eaten food and drunk water in the place of which he said to you, 'Eat no food, and drink no water,' your body shall not come to your ancestral tomb." 23After the man of Goda had eaten food and had drunk, they saddled for him a donkey belonging to the prophet who had brought him back. 24Then as he went away, a lion met him on the road and killed him. His body was thrown in the road, and the donkey stood beside it; the lion also stood beside the body. 25People passed by and saw the body thrown in the road, with the lion standing by the body. And they came and told it in the town where the old prophet lived.

26 When the prophet who had brought him back from the way heard of it, he said, "It is the man of God who disobeyed the word of the LORD; therefore the LORD has given him to the lion, which has torn him and killed him according to the word that the LORD spoke to him." 27Then he said to his sons, "Saddle a donkey for me." So they saddled one, 28and he went and found the body

a Heb *he*

King James

28And he went and found his carcase cast in the way, and the ass and the lion standing by the carcase: the lion had not eaten the carcase, nor torn the ass.

29And the prophet took up the carcase of the man of God, and laid it upon the ass, and brought it back: and the old prophet came to the city, to mourn and to bury him.

30And he laid his carcase in his own grave; and they mourned over him, *saying*, Alas, my brother!

31And it came to pass, after he had buried him, that he spake to his sons, saying, When I am dead, then bury me in the sepulchre wherein the man of God *is* buried; lay my bones beside his bones:

32For the saying which he cried by the word of the LORD against the altar in Beth-el, and against all the houses of the high places which *are* in the cities of Samaria, shall surely come to pass.

33¶ After this thing Jeroboam returned not from his evil way, but made again of the lowest of the people priests of the high places: whosoever would, he consecrated him, and he became *one* of the priests of the high places.

34And this thing became sin unto the house of Jeroboam, even to cut *it* off, and to destroy *it* from off the face of the earth.

14 AT THAT time Abijah the son of Jeroboam fell sick.

2And Jeroboam said to his wife, Arise, I pray thee, and disguise thyself, that thou be not known to be the wife of Jeroboam; and get thee to Shiloh: behold, there *is* Ahijah the prophet, which told me that *I should be* king over this people.

3And take with thee ten loaves, and cracknels, and a cruse of honey, and go to him: he shall tell thee what shall become of the child.

4And Jeroboam's wife did so, and arose, and went to Shiloh, and came to the house of Ahijah. But Ahijah could not see; for his eyes were set by reason of his age.

5¶ And the LORD said unto Ahijah, Behold, the wife of Jeroboam cometh to ask a thing of thee for her son; for he *is* sick: thus and thus shalt thou say unto her: for it shall be, when she cometh in, that she shall feign herself *to be* another *woman*.

6And it was *so*, when Ahijah heard the sound of her feet, as she came in at the door, that he said, Come in, thou wife of Jeroboam; why feignest thou thyself *to be* another? for I *am* sent to thee *with* heavy *tidings*.

7Go, tell Jeroboam, Thus saith the LORD God of Israel, Forasmuch as I exalted thee from among the people, and made thee prince over my people Israel,

8And rent the kingdom away from the house of David, and gave it thee: and *yet* thou hast not been as my servant David, who kept my commandments, and who followed me with all his heart, to do *that* only *which was* right in mine eyes;

9But hast done evil above all that were before thee: for thou hast gone and made thee other gods, and molten images, to provoke me to anger, and hast cast me behind thy back:

10Therefore, behold, I will bring evil upon the house of Jeroboam, and will cut off from Jeroboam him that pisseth against the wall, *and* him that is shut up and left in Israel, and will take away the remnant of the house of Jeroboam, as a man taketh away dung, till it be all gone.

11Him that dieth of Jeroboam in the city shall the dogs eat; and him that dieth in the field shall the fowls of the air eat: for the LORD hath spoken *it*.

12Arise thou therefore, get thee to thine own house: *and* when thy feet enter into the city, the child shall die.

New International

body thrown down on the road, with the donkey and the lion standing beside it. The lion had neither eaten the body nor mauled the donkey. 29So the prophet picked up the body of the man of God, laid it on the donkey, and brought it back to his own city to mourn for him and bury him. 30Then he laid the body in his own tomb, and they mourned over him and said, "Oh, my brother!"

31After burying him, he said to his sons, "When I die, bury me in the grave where the man of God is buried; lay my bones beside his bones. 32For the message he declared by the word of the LORD against the altar in Bethel and against all the shrines on the high places in the towns of Samaria will certainly come true."

33Even after this, Jeroboam did not change his evil ways, but once more appointed priests for the high places from all sorts of people. Anyone who wanted to become a priest he consecrated for the high places. 34This was the sin of the house of Jeroboam that led to its downfall and to its destruction from the face of the earth.

Ahijah's Prophecy Against Jeroboam

14 AT THAT time Abijah son of Jeroboam became ill, 2and Jeroboam said to his wife, "Go, disguise yourself, so you won't be recognized as the wife of Jeroboam. Then go to Shiloh. Ahijah the prophet is there—the one who told me I would be king over this people. 3Take ten loaves of bread with you, some cakes and a jar of honey, and go to him. He will tell you what will happen to the boy." 4So Jeroboam's wife did what he said and went to Ahijah's house in Shiloh.

Now Ahijah could not see; his sight was gone because of his age. 5But the LORD had told Ahijah, "Jeroboam's wife is coming to ask you about her son, for he is ill, and you are to give her such and such an answer. When she arrives, she will pretend to be someone else."

6So when Ahijah heard the sound of her footsteps at the door, he said, "Come in, wife of Jeroboam. Why this pretense? I have been sent to you with bad news. 7Go, tell Jeroboam that this is what the LORD, the God of Israel, says: 'I raised you up from among the people and made you a leader over my people Israel. 8I tore the kingdom away from the house of David and gave it to you, but you have not been like my servant David, who kept my commands and followed me with all his heart, doing only what was right in my eyes. 9You have done more evil than all who lived before you. You have made for yourself other gods, idols made of metal; you have provoked me to anger and thrust me behind your back.

10" 'Because of this, I am going to bring disaster on the house of Jeroboam. I will cut off from Jeroboam every last male in Israel—slave or free. I will burn up the house of Jeroboam as one burns dung, until it is all gone. 11Dogs will eat those belonging to Jeroboam who die in the city, and the birds of the air will feed on those who die in the country. The LORD has spoken!'

12"As for you, go back home. When you set foot in your city, the boy will die. 13All Israel will mourn for

Living Bible

28He found the prophet's body lying in the road; and the donkey and lion were still standing there beside it, for the lion had not eaten the body nor attacked the donkey. 29So the prophet laid the body upon the donkey and took it back to the city to mourn over it and bury it.

30He laid the body in his own grave, exclaiming, "Alas, my brother!"

31Afterwards he said to his sons, "When I die, bury me in the grave where the prophet is buried. Lay my bones beside his bones. 32For the Lord told him to shout against the altar in Bethel, and his curse against the shrines in the cities of Samaria shall surely be fulfilled."

33Despite the prophet's warning, Jeroboam did not turn away from his evil ways; instead, he made more priests than ever from the common people, to offer sacrifices to idols in the shrines on the hills. Anyone who wanted to could be a priest. 34This was a great sin, and resulted in the destruction of Jeroboam's kingdom and the death of all of his family.

14 JEROBOAM'S SON Abijah now became very sick. 2Jeroboam told his wife, "Disguise yourself so that no one will recognize you as the queen, and go to Ahijah the prophet at Shiloh—the man who told me that I would become king. 3Take him a gift of ten loaves of bread, some fig bars, and a jar of honey and ask him whether the boy will recover."

4So his wife went to Ahijah's home at Shiloh. He was an old man now, and could no longer see. 5But the Lord told him that the queen, pretending to be someone else, would come to ask about her son, for he was very sick. And the Lord told him what to tell her.

6So when Ahijah heard her at the door, he called out, "Come in, wife of Jeroboam! Why are you pretending to be someone else?" Then he told her, "I have sad news for you. 7Give your husband this message from the Lord God of Israel: 'I promoted you from the ranks of the common people and made you king of Israel. 8I ripped the kingdom away from the family of David and gave it to you, but you have not obeyed my commandments as my servant David did. His heart's desire was always to obey me and to do whatever I wanted him to. 9But you have done more evil than all the other kings before you; you have made other gods and have made me furious with your gold calves. And since you have refused to acknowledge me, 10I will bring disaster upon your home and will destroy all of your sons—this boy who is sick and all those who are well.a I will sweep away your family as a stable hand shovels out manure. 11I vow that those of your family who die in the city shall be eaten by dogs, and those who die in the field shall be eaten by birds.' "

12Then Ahijah said to Jeroboam's wife, "Go on home, and when you step into the city, the child will die.

New Revised Standard

thrown in the road, with the donkey and the lion standing beside the body. The lion had not eaten the body or attacked the donkey. 29The prophet took up the body of the man of God, laid it on the donkey, and brought it back to the city,b to mourn and to bury him. 30He laid the body in his own grave; and they mourned over him, saying, "Alas, my brother!" 31After he had buried him, he said to his sons, "When I die, bury me in the grave in which the man of God is buried; lay my bones beside his bones. 32For the saying that he proclaimed by the word of the LORD against the altar in Bethel, and against all the houses of the high places that are in the cities of Samaria, shall surely come to pass."

33 Even after this event Jeroboam did not turn from his evil way, but made priests for the high places again from among all the people; any who wanted to be priests he consecrated for the high places. 34This matter became sin to the house of Jeroboam, so as to cut it off and to destroy it from the face of the earth.

Judgment on the House of Jeroboam

14 AT THAT time Abijah son of Jeroboam fell sick. 2Jeroboam said to his wife, "Go, disguise yourself, so that it will not be known that you are the wife of Jeroboam, and go to Shiloh; for the prophet Ahijah is there, who said of me that I should be king over this people. 3Take with you ten loaves, some cakes, and a jar of honey, and go to him; he will tell you what shall happen to the child."

4 Jeroboam's wife did so; she set out and went to Shiloh, and came to the house of Ahijah. Now Ahijah could not see, for his eyes were dim because of his age. 5But the LORD said to Ahijah, "The wife of Jeroboam is coming to inquire of you concerning her son; for he is sick. Thus and thus you shall say to her."

When she came, she pretended to be another woman. 6But when Ahijah heard the sound of her feet, as she came in at the door, he said, "Come in, wife of Jeroboam; why do you pretend to be another? For I am charged with heavy tidings for you. 7Go, tell Jeroboam, 'Thus says the LORD, the God of Israel: Because I exalted you from among the people, made you leader over my people Israel, 8and tore the kingdom away from the house of David to give it to you; yet you have not been like my servant David, who kept my commandments and followed me with all his heart, doing only that which was right in my sight, 9but you have done evil above all those who were before you and have gone and made for yourself other gods, and cast images, provoking me to anger, and have thrust me behind your back; 10therefore, I will bring evil upon the house of Jeroboam. I will cut off from Jeroboam every male, both bond and free in Israel, and will consume the house of Jeroboam, just as one burns up dung until it is all gone. 11Anyone belonging to Jeroboam who dies in the city, the dogs shall eat; and anyone who dies in the open country, the birds of the air shall eat; for the LORD has spoken.' 12Therefore set out, go to your house. When your feet enter the city, the child shall die. 13All Israel shall

---

a 14:10 *this boy who is sick and all those who are well*, literally, "every male, both bond and free."

b Gk: Heb *he came to the town of the old prophet*

King James

13And all Israel shall mourn for him, and bury him: for he only of Jeroboam shall come to the grave, because in him there is found *some* good thing toward the LORD God of Israel in the house of Jeroboam.

14Moreover the LORD shall raise him up a king over Israel, who shall cut off the house of Jeroboam that day: but what? even now.

15For the LORD shall smite Israel, as a reed is shaken in the water, and he shall root up Israel out of this good land, which he gave to their fathers, and shall scatter them beyond the river, because they have made their groves, provoking the LORD to anger.

16And he shall give Israel up because of the sins of Jeroboam, who did sin, and who made Israel to sin.

17¶ And Jeroboam's wife arose, and departed, and came to Tirzah: *and* when she came to the threshold of the door, the child died;

18And they buried him; and all Israel mourned for him, according to the word of the LORD, which he spake by the hand of his servant Ahijah the prophet.

19And the rest of the acts of Jeroboam, how he warred, and how he reigned, behold, they *are* written in the book of the chronicles of the kings of Israel.

20And the days which Jeroboam reigned *were* two and twenty years: and he slept with his fathers, and Nadab his son reigned in his stead.

21¶ And Rehoboam the son of Solomon reigned in Judah. Rehoboam *was* forty and one years old when he began to reign, and he reigned seventeen years in Jerusalem, the city which the LORD did choose out of all the tribes of Israel, to put his name there. And his mother's name *was* Naamah an Ammonitess.

22And Judah did evil in the sight of the LORD, and they provoked him to jealousy with their sins which they had committed, above all that their fathers had done.

23For they also built them high places, and images, and groves, on every high hill, and under every green tree.

24And there were also sodomites in the land: *and* they did according to all the abominations of the nations which the LORD cast out before the children of Israel.

25¶ And it came to pass in the fifth year of king Rehoboam, *that* Shishak king of Egypt came up against Jerusalem:

26And he took away the treasures of the house of the LORD, and the treasures of the king's house; he even took away all: and he took away all the shields of gold which Solomon had made.

27And king Rehoboam made in their stead brasen shields, and committed *them* unto the hands of the chief of the guard, which kept the door of the king's house.

28And it was *so*, when the king went into the house of the LORD, that the guard bare them, and brought them back into the guard chamber.

29¶ Now the rest of the acts of Rehoboam, and all that he did, *are* they not written in the book of the chronicles of the kings of Judah?

30And there was war between Rehoboam and Jeroboam all *their* days.

31And Rehoboam slept with his fathers, and was buried with his fathers in the city of David. And his mother's name *was* Naamah an Ammonitess. And Abijam his son reigned in his stead.

New International

him and bury him. He is the only one belonging to Jeroboam who will be buried, because he is the only one in the house of Jeroboam in whom the LORD, the God of Israel, has found anything good.

14"The LORD will raise up for himself a king over Israel who will cut off the family of Jeroboam. This is the day! What? Yes, even now.a 15And the LORD will strike Israel, so that it will be like a reed swaying in the water. He will uproot Israel from this good land that he gave to their forefathers and scatter them beyond the River,b because they provoked the LORD to anger by making Asherah poles.c 16And he will give Israel up because of the sins Jeroboam has committed and has caused Israel to commit."

17Then Jeroboam's wife got up and left and went to Tirzah. As soon as she stepped over the threshold of the house, the boy died. 18They buried him, and all Israel mourned for him, as the LORD had said through his servant the prophet Ahijah.

19The other events of Jeroboam's reign, his wars and how he ruled, are written in the book of the annals of the kings of Israel. 20He reigned for twenty-two years and then rested with his fathers. And Nadab his son succeeded him as king.

Rehoboam King of Judah

21Rehoboam son of Solomon was king in Judah. He was forty-one years old when he became king, and he reigned seventeen years in Jerusalem, the city the LORD had chosen out of all the tribes of Israel in which to put his Name. His mother's name was Naamah; she was an Ammonite.

22Judah did evil in the eyes of the LORD. By the sins they committed they stirred up his jealous anger more than their fathers had done. 23They also set up for themselves high places, sacred stones and Asherah poles on every high hill and under every spreading tree. 24There were even male shrine prostitutes in the land; the people engaged in all the detestable practices of the nations the LORD had driven out before the Israelites.

25In the fifth year of King Rehoboam, Shishak king of Egypt attacked Jerusalem. 26He carried off the treasures of the temple of the LORD and the treasures of the royal palace. He took everything, including all the gold shields Solomon had made. 27So King Rehoboam made bronze shields to replace them and assigned these to the commanders of the guard on duty at the entrance to the royal palace. 28Whenever the king went to the LORD's temple, the guards bore the shields, and afterward they returned them to the guardroom.

29As for the other events of Rehoboam's reign, and all he did, are they not written in the book of the annals of the kings of Judah? 30There was continual warfare between Rehoboam and Jeroboam. 31And Rehoboam rested with his fathers and was buried with them in the City of David. His mother's name was Naamah; she was an Ammonite. And Abijahd his son succeeded him as king.

---

a *14* The meaning of the Hebrew for this sentence is uncertain.   b *15* That is, the Euphrates   c *15* That is, symbols of the goddess Asherah; here and elsewhere in 1 Kings   d *31* Some Hebrew manuscripts and Septuagint (see also 2 Chron. 12:16); most Hebrew manuscripts *Abijam*

Living Bible

13All of Israel will mourn for him and bury him, but he is the only member of your family who will come to a quiet end. For this child is the only good thing which the Lord God of Israel sees in the entire family of Jeroboam. 14And the Lord will raise up a king over Israel who will destroy the family of Jeroboam. 15Then the Lord will shake Israel like a reed whipped about in a stream; he will uproot the people of Israel from this good land of their fathers and scatter them beyond the Euphrates River, for they have angered the Lord by worshiping idolgods. 16He will abandon Israel because Jeroboam sinned and made all of Israel sin along with him."

17So Jeroboam's wife returned to Tirzah; and the child died just as she walked through the door of her home. 18And there was mourning for him throughout the land, just as the Lord had predicted through Ahijah.

19The rest of Jeroboam's activities—his wars and the other events of his reign—are recorded in *The Annals of the Kings of Israel.* 20Jeroboam reigned twenty-two years, and when he died, his son Nadab took the throne.

21Meanwhile, Rehoboam the son of Solomon was king in Judah. He was forty-one years old when he began to reign, and he was on the throne seventeen years in Jerusalem, the city which, among all the cities of Israel, the Lord had chosen to live in. (Rehoboam's mother was Naamah, an Ammonite woman.) 22During his reign the people of Judah, like those in Israel, did wrong and angered the Lord with their sin, for it was even worse than that of their ancestors. 23They built shrines and obelisks and idols on every high hill and under every green tree. 24There was homosexuality throughout the land, and the people of Judah became as depraved as the heathen nations which the Lord drove out to make room for his people.

25In the fifth year of Rehoboam's reign, King Shishak of Egypt attacked and conquered Jerusalem. 26He ransacked the Temple and the palace and stole everything, including all the gold shields Solomon had made. 27Afterwards Rehoboam made bronze shields as substitutes, and the palace guards used these instead. 28Whenever the king went to the Temple, the guards paraded before him and then took the shields back to the guard chamber.

29The other events in Rehoboam's reign are written in *The Annals of the Kings of Judah.* 30There was constant war between Rehoboam and Jeroboam. 31When Rehoboam died—his mother was Naamah the Ammonitess—he was buried among his ancestors in Jerusalem, and his son Abijam took the throne.

New Revised Standard

mourn for him and bury him; for he alone of Jeroboam's family shall come to the grave, because in him there is found something pleasing to the LORD, the God of Israel, in the house of Jeroboam. 14Moreover the LORD will raise up for himself a king over Israel, who shall cut off the house of Jeroboam today, even right now!e

15 "The LORD will strike Israel, as a reed is shaken in the water; he will root up Israel out of this good land that he gave to their ancestors, and scatter them beyond the Euphrates, because they have made their sacred poles,f provoking the LORD to anger. 16He will give Israel up because of the sins of Jeroboam, which he sinned and which he caused Israel to commit."

17 Then Jeroboam's wife got up and went away, and she came to Tirzah. As she came to the threshold of the house, the child died. 18All Israel buried him and mourned for him, according to the word of the LORD, which he spoke by his servant the prophet Ahijah.

Death of Jeroboam

19 Now the rest of the acts of Jeroboam, how he warred and how he reigned, are written in the Book of the Annals of the Kings of Israel. 20The time that Jeroboam reigned was twenty-two years; then he slept with his ancestors, and his son Nadab succeeded him.

Rehoboam Reigns over Judah

21 Now Rehoboam son of Solomon reigned in Judah. Rehoboam was forty-one years old when he began to reign, and he reigned seventeen years in Jerusalem, the city that the LORD had chosen out of all the tribes of Israel, to put his name there. His mother's name was Naamah the Ammonite. 22Judah did what was evil in the sight of the LORD; they provoked him to jealousy with their sins that they committed, more than all that their ancestors had done. 23For they also built for themselves high places, pillars, and sacred polesf on every high hill and under every green tree; 24there were also male temple prostitutes in the land. They committed all the abominations of the nations that the LORD drove out before the people of Israel.

25 In the fifth year of King Rehoboam, King Shishak of Egypt came up against Jerusalem; 26he took away the treasures of the house of the LORD and the treasures of the king's house; he took everything. He also took away all the shields of gold that Solomon had made; 27so King Rehoboam made shields of bronze instead, and committed them to the hands of the officers of the guard, who kept the door of the king's house. 28As often as the king went into the house of the LORD, the guard carried them and brought them back to the guardroom.

29 Now the rest of the acts of Rehoboam, and all that he did, are they not written in the Book of the Annals of the Kings of Judah? 30There was war between Rehoboam and Jeroboam continually. 31Rehoboam slept with his ancestors and was buried with his ancestors in the city of David. His mother's name was Naamah the Ammonite. His son Abijam succeeded him.

e Meaning of Heb uncertain   f Heb *Asherim*

King James

15 NOW IN the eighteenth year of king Jeroboam the son of Nebat reigned Abijam over Judah. ²Three years reigned he in Jerusalem. And his mother's name *was* Maachah, the daughter of Abishalom.

³And he walked in all the sins of his father, which he had done before him: and his heart was not perfect with the LORD his God, as the heart of David his father.

⁴Nevertheless for David's sake did the LORD his God give him a lamp in Jerusalem, to set up his son after him, and to establish Jerusalem:

⁵Because David did *that which was* right in the eyes of the LORD, and turned not aside from any *thing* that he commanded him all the days of his life, save only in the matter of Uriah the Hittite.

⁶And there was war between Rehoboam and Jeroboam all the days of his life.

⁷Now the rest of the acts of Abijam, and all that he did, *are* they not written in the book of the chronicles of the kings of Judah? And there was war between Abijam and Jeroboam.

⁸And Abijam slept with his fathers; and they buried him in the city of David: and Asa his son reigned in his stead.

⁹¶ And in the twentieth year of Jeroboam king of Israel reigned Asa over Judah.

¹⁰And forty and one years reigned he in Jerusalem. And his mother's name *was* Maachah, the daughter of Abishalom.

¹¹And Asa did *that which was* right in the eyes of the LORD, as *did* David his father.

¹²And he took away the sodomites out of the land, and removed all the idols that his fathers had made.

¹³And also Maachah his mother, even her he removed from *being* queen, because she had made an idol in a grove; and Asa destroyed her idol, and burnt *it* by the brook Kidron.

¹⁴But the high places were not removed: nevertheless Asa's heart was perfect with the LORD all his days.

¹⁵And he brought in the things which his father had dedicated, and the things which himself had dedicated, into the house of the LORD, silver, and gold, and vessels.

¹⁶¶ And there was war between Asa and Baasha king of Israel all their days.

¹⁷And Baasha king of Israel went up against Judah, and built Ramah, that he might not suffer any to go out or come in to Asa king of Judah.

¹⁸Then Asa took all the silver and the gold *that were* left in the treasures of the house of the LORD, and the treasures of the king's house, and delivered them into the hand of his servants: and king Asa sent them to Ben-hadad, the son of Tabrimon, the son of Hezion, king of Syria, that dwelt at Damascus, saying,

¹⁹*There is* a league between me and thee, *and* between my father and thy father: behold, I have sent unto thee a present of silver and gold; come and break thy league with Baasha king of Israel, that he may depart from me.

²⁰So Ben-hadad hearkened unto king Asa, and sent the captains of the hosts which he had against the cities of Israel, and smote Ijon, and Dan, and Abel-beth-maachah, and all Cinneroth, with all the land of Naphtali.

²¹And it came to pass, when Baasha heard *thereof,* that he left off building of Ramah, and dwelt in Tirzah.

²²Then king Asa made a proclamation throughout all Judah; none *was* exempted: and they took away the stones of Ramah, and the timber thereof, wherewith Baasha had builded; and king Asa built with them Geba of Benjamin, and Mizpah.

²³The rest of all the acts of Asa, and all his might, and all that he did, and the cities which he built, *are* they not written in the book of the chronicles of the kings of Judah? Nevertheless in the time of his old age he was diseased in his feet.

New International

Abijah King of Judah

15 IN THE eighteenth year of the reign of Jeroboam son of Nebat, Abijah[a] became king of Judah, ²and he reigned in Jerusalem three years. His mother's name was Maacah daughter of Abishalom.[b]

³He committed all the sins his father had done before him; his heart was not fully devoted to the LORD his God, as the heart of David his forefather had been. ⁴Nevertheless, for David's sake the LORD his God gave him a lamp in Jerusalem by raising up a son to succeed him and by making Jerusalem strong. ⁵For David had done what was right in the eyes of the LORD and had not failed to keep any of the LORD's commands all the days of his life—except in the case of Uriah the Hittite.

⁶There was war between Rehoboam and Jeroboam throughout Abijah's lifetime. ⁷As for the other events of Abijah's reign, and all he did, are they not written in the book of the annals of the kings of Judah? There was war between Abijah and Jeroboam. ⁸And Abijah rested with his fathers and was buried in the City of David. And Asa his son succeeded him as king.

Asa King of Judah

⁹In the twentieth year of Jeroboam king of Israel, Asa became king of Judah, ¹⁰and he reigned in Jerusalem forty-one years. His grandmother's name was Maacah daughter of Abishalom.

¹¹Asa did what was right in the eyes of the LORD, as his father David had done. ¹²He expelled the male shrine prostitutes from the land and got rid of all the idols his fathers had made. ¹³He even deposed his grandmother Maacah from her position as queen mother, because she had made a repulsive Asherah pole. Asa cut the pole down and burned it in the Kidron Valley. ¹⁴Although he did not remove the high places, Asa's heart was fully committed to the LORD all his life. ¹⁵He brought into the temple of the LORD the silver and gold and the articles that he and his father had dedicated.

¹⁶There was war between Asa and Baasha king of Israel throughout their reigns. ¹⁷Baasha king of Israel went up against Judah and fortified Ramah to prevent anyone from leaving or entering the territory of Asa king of Judah.

¹⁸Asa then took all the silver and gold that was left in the treasuries of the LORD's temple and of his own palace. He entrusted it to his officials and sent them to Ben-Hadad son of Tabrimmon, the son of Hezion, the king of Aram, who was ruling in Damascus. ¹⁹"Let there be a treaty between me and you," he said, "as there was between my father and your father. See, I am sending you a gift of silver and gold. Now break your treaty with Baasha king of Israel so he will withdraw from me."

²⁰Ben-Hadad agreed with King Asa and sent the commanders of his forces against the towns of Israel. He conquered Ijon, Dan, Abel Beth Maacah and all Kinnereth in addition to Naphtali. ²¹When Baasha heard this, he stopped building Ramah and withdrew to Tirzah. ²²Then King Asa issued an order to all Judah—no one was exempt—and they carried away from Ramah the stones and timber Baasha had been using there. With them King Asa built up Geba in Benjamin, and also Mizpah.

²³As for all the other events of Asa's reign, all his achievements, all he did and the cities he built, are they not written in the book of the annals of the kings of Judah? In his old age, however, his feet became diseased. ²⁴Then Asa rested with his fathers and was buried

---

ª *1* Some Hebrew manuscripts and Septuagint (see also 2 Chron. 12:16); most Hebrew manuscripts *Abijam*; also in verses 7 and 8   ᵇ 2 A variant of *Absalom*; also in verse 10   ᶜ 6 Most Hebrew manuscripts; some Hebrew manuscripts and Syriac *Abijam* (that is, Abijah)

Living Bible

15 ABIJAM BEGAN his three-year reign as king of Judah in Jerusalem during the eighteenth year of Jeroboam's reign in Israel. (Abijam's mother was Maacah, the daughter of Abishalom.) ³He was as great a sinner as his father was, and his heart was not right with God, as King David's was. ⁴But despite Abijam's sin, the Lord remembered David's love[d] and did not end the line of David's royal descendants. ⁵For David had obeyed God during his entire life except for the affair concerning Uriah the Hittite. ⁶During Abijam's reign there was constant war between Israel and Judah.[e] ⁷The rest of Abijam's history is recorded in *The Annals of the Kings of Judah.* ⁸When he died he was buried in Jerusalem, and his son Asa reigned in his place.

⁹Asa became king of Judah, in Jerusalem, in the twentieth year of the reign of Jeroboam over Israel, ¹⁰and reigned forty-one years. (His grandmother was Maacah, the daughter of Abishalom.) ¹¹He pleased the Lord like his ancestor King David. ¹²He executed the male prostitutes and removed all the idols his father had made. ¹³He deposed his grandmother Maacah as queen-mother because she had made an idol—which he cut down and burned at Kidron Brook. ¹⁴However, the shrines on the hills were not removed, for Asa did not realize that these were wrong.[f] ¹⁵He made permanent exhibits in the Temple of the bronze shields his grandfather had dedicated,[g] along with the silver and gold vessels he himself had donated.

¹⁶There was lifelong war between King Asa of Judah and King Baasha of Israel. ¹⁷King Baasha built the fortress city of Ramah in an attempt to cut off all trade with Jerusalem. ¹⁸Then Asa took all the silver and gold left in the Temple treasury and all the treasures of the palace, and gave them to his officials to take to Damascus, to King Ben-hadad of Syria, with this message:

¹⁹"Let us be allies just as our fathers were. I am sending you a present of gold and silver. Now break your alliance with King Baasha of Israel so that he will leave me alone."

²⁰Ben-hadad agreed and sent his armies against some of the cities of Israel; and he destroyed Ijon, Dan, Abel-beth-maacah, all of Chinneroth, and all the cities in the land of Naphtali. ²¹When Baasha received word of the attack, he discontinued building the city of Ramah and returned to Tirzah. ²²Then King Asa made a proclamation to all Judah, asking every able-bodied man to help demolish Ramah and haul away its stones and timbers. And King Asa used these materials to build the city of Geba in Benjamin and the city of Mizpah.

²³The rest of Asa's biography—his conquests and deeds and the names of the cities he built—is found in *The Annals of the Kings of Judah.* In his old age his feet became diseased, ²⁴and when he died he was buried in

New Revised Standard

Abijam Reigns over Judah: Idolatry and War

15 NOW IN the eighteenth year of King Jeroboam son of Nebat, Abijam began to reign over Judah. ²He reigned for three years in Jerusalem. His mother's name was Maacah daughter of Abishalom. ³He committed all the sins that his father did before him; his heart was not true to the LORD his God, like the heart of his father David. ⁴Nevertheless for David's sake the LORD his God gave him a lamp in Jerusalem, setting up his son after him, and establishing Jerusalem; ⁵because David did what was right in the sight of the LORD, and did not turn aside from anything that he commanded him all the days of his life, except in the matter of Uriah the Hittite. ⁶The war begun between Rehoboam and Jeroboam continued all the days of his life. ⁷The rest of the acts of Abijam, and all that he did, are they not written in the Book of the Annals of the Kings of Judah? There was war between Abijam and Jeroboam. ⁸Abijam slept with his ancestors, and they buried him in the city of David. Then his son Asa succeeded him.

Asa Reigns over Judah

9 In the twentieth year of King Jeroboam of Israel, Asa began to reign over Judah; ¹⁰he reigned forty-one years in Jerusalem. His mother's name was Maacah daughter of Abishalom. ¹¹Asa did what was right in the sight of the LORD, as his father David had done. ¹²He put away the male temple prostitutes out of the land, and removed all the idols that his ancestors had made. ¹³He also removed his mother Maacah from being queen mother, because she had made an abominable image for Asherah; Asa cut down her image and burned it at the Wadi Kidron. ¹⁴But the high places were not taken away. Nevertheless the heart of Asa was true to the LORD all his days. ¹⁵He brought into the house of the LORD the votive gifts of his father and his own votive gifts—silver, gold, and utensils.

Alliance with Aram against Israel

16 There was war between Asa and King Baasha of Israel all their days. ¹⁷King Baasha of Israel went up against Judah, and built Ramah, to prevent anyone from going out or coming in to King Asa of Judah. ¹⁸Then Asa took all the silver and the gold that were left in the treasures of the house of the LORD and the treasures of the king's house, and gave them into the hands of his servants. King Asa sent them to King Ben-hadad son of Tabrimmon son of Hezion of Aram, who resided in Damascus, saying, ¹⁹"Let there be an alliance between me and you, like that between my father and your father: I am sending you a present of silver and gold; go, break your alliance with King Baasha of Israel, so that he may withdraw from me." ²⁰Ben-hadad listened to King Asa, and sent the commanders of his armies against the cities of Israel. He conquered Ijon, Dan, Abel-beth-maacah, and all Chinneroth, with all the land of Naphtali. ²¹When Baasha heard of it, he stopped building Ramah and lived in Tirzah. ²²Then King Asa made a proclamation to all Judah, none was exempt: they carried away the stones of Ramah and its timber, with which Baasha had been building; with them King Asa built Geba of Benjamin and Mizpah. ²³Now the rest of all the acts of Asa, all his power, all that he did, and the cities that he built, are they not written in the Book of the Annals of the Kings of Judah? But in his old age he was diseased in his feet. ²⁴Then Asa slept with his ancestors, and was

---

d *15:4 The Lord remembered David's love,* literally, "for David's sake."
e *15:6 between Israel and Judah,* literally, "between Rehoboam and Jeroboam." f *15:14 Asa did not realize that these were wrong,* literally, "nevertheless, the heart of Asa was perfect toward Jehovah all his days." g *15:15 the bronze shields his grandfather had dedicated,* literally, "the dedicated objects of his grandfather." See 14:27.

King James

24And Asa slept with his fathers, and was buried with his fathers in the city of David his father: and Jehoshaphat his son reigned in his stead.

25¶ And Nadab the son of Jeroboam began to reign over Israel in the second year of Asa king of Judah, and reigned over Israel two years.

26And he did evil in the sight of the LORD, and walked in the way of his father, and in his sin wherewith he made Israel to sin.

27¶ And Baasha the son of Ahijah, of the house of Issachar, conspired against him; and Baasha smote him at Gibbethon, which *belonged* to the Philistines; for Nadab and all Israel laid siege to Gibbethon.

28Even in the third year of Asa king of Judah did Baasha slay him, and reigned in his stead.

29And it came to pass, when he reigned, *that* he smote all the house of Jeroboam; he left not to Jeroboam any that breathed, until he had destroyed him, according unto the saying of the LORD, which he spake by his servant Ahijah the Shilonite:

30Because of the sins of Jeroboam which he sinned, and which he made Israel sin, by his provocation wherewith he provoked the LORD God of Israel to anger.

31¶ Now the rest of the acts of Nadab, and all that he did, *are* they not written in the book of the chronicles of the kings of Israel?

32And there was war between Asa and Baasha king of Israel all their days.

33In the third year of Asa king of Judah began Baasha the son of Ahijah to reign over all Israel in Tirzah, twenty and four years.

34And he did evil in the sight of the LORD, and walked in the way of Jeroboam, and in his sin wherewith he made Israel to sin.

16 THEN THE word of the LORD came to Jehu the son of Hanani against Baasha, saying,

2Forasmuch as I exalted thee out of the dust, and made thee prince over my people Israel; and thou hast walked in the way of Jeroboam, and hast made my people Israel to sin, to provoke me to anger with their sins;

3Behold, I will take away the posterity of Baasha, and the posterity of his house; and will make thy house like the house of Jeroboam the son of Nebat.

4Him that dieth of Baasha in the city shall the dogs eat; and him that dieth of his in the fields shall the fowls of the air eat.

5Now the rest of the acts of Baasha, and what he did, and his might, *are* they not written in the book of the chronicles of the kings of Israel?

6So Baasha slept with his fathers, and was buried in Tirzah: and Elah his son reigned in his stead.

7And also by the hand of the prophet Jehu the son of Hanani came the word of the LORD against Baasha, and against his house, even for all the evil that he did in the sight of the LORD, in provoking him to anger with the work of his hands, in being like the house of Jeroboam; and because he killed them.

8¶ In the twenty and sixth year of Asa king of Judah began Elah the son of Baasha to reign over Israel in Tirzah, two years.

9And his servant Zimri, captain of half *his* chariots, conspired against him, as he was in Tirzah, drinking himself drunk in the house of Arza steward of *his* house in Tirzah.

10And Zimri went in and smote him, and killed him, in the twenty and seventh year of Asa king of Judah, and reigned in his stead.

New International

with them in the city of his father David. And Jehoshaphat his son succeeded him as king.

Nadab King of Israel

25Nadab son of Jeroboam became king of Israel in the second year of Asa king of Judah, and he reigned over Israel two years. 26He did evil in the eyes of the LORD, walking in the ways of his father and in his sin, which he had caused Israel to commit.

27Baasha son of Ahijah of the house of Issachar plotted against him, and he struck him down at Gibbethon, a Philistine town, while Nadab and all Israel were besieging it. 28Baasha killed Nadab in the third year of Asa king of Judah and succeeded him as king.

29As soon as he began to reign, he killed Jeroboam's whole family. He did not leave Jeroboam anyone that breathed, but destroyed them all, according to the word of the LORD given through his servant Ahijah the Shilonite— 30because of the sins Jeroboam had committed and had caused Israel to commit, and because he provoked the LORD, the God of Israel, to anger.

31As for the other events of Nadab's reign, and all he did, are they not written in the book of the annals of the kings of Israel? 32There was war between Asa and Baasha king of Israel throughout their reigns.

Baasha King of Israel

33In the third year of Asa king of Judah, Baasha son of Ahijah became king of all Israel in Tirzah, and he reigned twenty-four years. 34He did evil in the eyes of the LORD, walking in the ways of Jeroboam and in his sin, which he had caused Israel to commit.

16 THEN THE word of the LORD came to Jehu son of Hanani against Baasha: 2"I lifted you up from the dust and made you leader of my people Israel, but you walked in the ways of Jeroboam and caused my people Israel to sin and to provoke me to anger by their sins. 3So I am about to consume Baasha and his house, and I will make your house like that of Jeroboam son of Nebat. 4Dogs will eat those belonging to Baasha who die in the city, and the birds of the air will feed on those who die in the country."

5As for the other events of Baasha's reign, what he did and his achievements, are they not written in the book of the annals of the kings of Israel? 6Baasha rested with his fathers and was buried in Tirzah. And Elah his son succeeded him as king.

7Moreover, the word of the LORD came through the prophet Jehu son of Hanani to Baasha and his house, because of all the evil he had done in the eyes of the LORD, provoking him to anger by the things he did, and becoming like the house of Jeroboam—and also because he destroyed it.

Elah King of Israel

8In the twenty-sixth year of Asa king of Judah, Elah son of Baasha became king of Israel, and he reigned in Tirzah two years.

9Zimri, one of his officials, who had command of half his chariots, plotted against him. Elah was in Tirzah at the time, getting drunk in the home of Arza, the man in charge of the palace at Tirzah. 10Zimri came in, struck him down and killed him in the twenty-seventh year of Asa king of Judah. Then he succeeded him as king.

Living Bible

the royal cemetery in Jerusalem. Then his son Jehoshaphat became the new king of Judah.

25Meanwhile, over in Israel, Nadab the son of Jeroboam had become king. He reigned two years, beginning in the second year of the reign of King Asa of Judah. 26But he was not a good king; like his father, he worshiped many idols and led all of Israel into sin.

27Then Baasha (the son of Ahijah, from the tribe of Issachar) plotted against him and assassinated him while he was with the Israeli army laying siege to the Philistine city of Gibbethon. 28So Baasha replaced Nadab as the king of Israel in Tirzah, during the third year of the reign of King Asa of Judah. 29He immediately killed all of the descendants of King Jeroboam, so that not one of the royal family was left, just as the Lord had said would happen when he spoke through Ahijah, the prophet from Shiloh. 30This was done because Jeroboam had angered the Lord God of Israel by sinning and leading the rest of Israel into sin.

31Further details of Baasha's reign are recorded in *The Annals of the Kings of Israel*.

32, 33There was continuous warfare between King Asa of Judah and King Baasha of Israel. Baasha reigned for twenty-four years, 34but all that time he continually disobeyed the Lord. He followed the evil paths of Jeroboam, for he led the people of Israel into the sin of worshiping idols.

16 A MESSAGE of condemnation from the Lord was delivered to King Baasha at this time by the prophet Jehu:

2"I lifted you out of the dust," the message said, "to make you king of my people Israel; but you have walked in the evil paths of Jeroboam. You have made my people sin, and I am angry! 3So now I will destroy you and your family, just as I did the descendants of Jeroboam. 4-7Those of your family who die in the city will be eaten by dogs, and those who die in the fields will be eaten by the birds."

The message was sent to Baasha and his family because he had angered the Lord by all his evil deeds. He was as evil as Jeroboam despite the fact that the Lord had destroyed all of Jeroboam's descendants for their sins.

The rest of Baasha's biography—his deeds and conquests—are written in *The Annals of the Kings of Israel*.

8Elah, Baasha's son, began reigning during the twenty-sixth year of the reign of King Asa of Judah, but he reigned only two years. 9Then General Zimri, who had charge of half the royal chariot troops, plotted against him. One day King Elah was half drunk at the home of Arza, the superintendent of the palace, in the capital city of Tirzah. 10Zimri simply walked in and struck him down and killed him. (This occurred during the twenty-seventh year of the reign of King Asa of Judah.) Then Zimri declared himself to be the new king of Israel.

New Revised Standard

buried with his ancestors in the city of his father David; his son Jehoshaphat succeeded him.

Nadab Reigns over Israel

25 Nadab son of Jeroboam began to reign over Israel in the second year of King Asa of Judah; he reigned over Israel two years. 26He did what was evil in the sight of the LORD, walking in the way of his ancestor and in the sin that he caused Israel to commit.

27 Baasha son of Ahijah, of the house of Issachar, conspired against him; and Baasha struck him down at Gibbethon, which belonged to the Philistines; for Nadab and all Israel were laying siege to Gibbethon. 28 So Baasha killed Nadaba in the third year of King Asa of Judah, and succeeded him. 29 As soon as he was king, he killed all the house of Jeroboam; he left to the house of Jeroboam not one that breathed, until he had destroyed it, according to the word of the LORD that he spoke by his servant Ahijah the Shilonite— 30because of the sins of Jeroboam that he committed and that he caused Israel to commit, and because of the anger to which he provoked the LORD, the God of Israel.

31 Now the rest of the acts of Nadab, and all that he did, are they not written in the Book of the Annals of the Kings of Israel? 32There was war between Asa and King Baasha of Israel all their days.

Second Dynasty: Baasha Reigns over Israel

33 In the third year of King Asa of Judah, Baasha son of Ahijah began to reign over all Israel at Tirzah; he reigned twenty-four years. 34He did what was evil in the sight of the LORD, walking in the way of Jeroboam and in the sin that he caused Israel to commit.

16 THE WORD of the LORD came to Jehu son of Hanani against Baasha, saying, 2"Since I exalted you out of the dust and made you leader over my people Israel, and you have walked in the way of Jeroboam, and have caused my people Israel to sin, provoking me to anger with their sins, 3therefore, I will consume Baasha and his house, and I will make your house like the house of Jeroboam son of Nebat. 4Anyone belonging to Baasha who dies in the city the dogs shall eat; and anyone of his who dies in the field the birds of the air shall eat."

5 Now the rest of the acts of Baasha, what he did, and his power, are they not written in the Book of the Annals of the Kings of Israel? 6Baasha slept with his ancestors, and was buried at Tirzah; and his son Elah succeeded him. 7Moreover the word of the LORD came by the prophet Jehu son of Hanani against Baasha and his house, both because of all the evil that he did in the sight of the LORD, provoking him to anger with the work of his hands, in being like the house of Jeroboam, and also because he destroyed it.

Elah Reigns over Israel

8 In the twenty-sixth year of King Asa of Judah, Elah son of Baasha began to reign over Israel in Tirzah; he reigned two years. 9But his servant Zimri, commander of half his chariots, conspired against him. When he was at Tirzah, drinking himself drunk in the house of Arza, who was in charge of the palace at Tirzah, 10Zimri came in and struck him down and killed him, in the twenty-seventh year of King Asa of Judah, and succeeded him.

a Heb *him*

King James

11¶ And it came to pass, when he began to reign, as soon as he sat on his throne, *that* he slew all the house of Baasha: he left him not one that pisseth against a wall, neither of his kinsfolks, nor of his friends.

12Thus did Zimri destroy all the house of Baasha, according to the word of the LORD, which he spake against Baasha by Jehu the prophet,

13For all the sins of Baasha, and the sins of Elah his son, by which they sinned, and by which they made Israel to sin, in provoking the LORD God of Israel to anger with their vanities.

14Now the rest of the acts of Elah, and all that he did, *are* they not written in the book of the chronicles of the kings of Israel?

15¶ In the twenty and seventh year of Asa king of Judah did Zimri reign seven days in Tirzah. And the people *were* encamped against Gibbethon, which *belonged* to the Philistines.

16And the people *that were* encamped heard say, Zimri hath conspired, and hath also slain the king: wherefore all Israel made Omri, the captain of the host, king over Israel that day in the camp.

17And Omri went up from Gibbethon, and all Israel with him, and they besieged Tirzah.

18And it came to pass, when Zimri saw that the city was taken, that he went into the palace of the king's house, and burnt the king's house over him with fire, and died,

19For his sins which he sinned in doing evil in the sight of the LORD, in walking in the way of Jeroboam, and in his sin which he did, to make Israel to sin.

20Now the rest of the acts of Zimri, and his treason that he wrought, *are* they not written in the book of the chronicles of the kings of Israel?

21¶ Then were the people of Israel divided into two parts: half of the people followed Tibni the son of Ginath, to make him king; and half followed Omri.

22But the people that followed Omri prevailed against the people that followed Tibni the son of Ginath: so Tibni died, and Omri reigned.

23¶ In the thirty and first year of Asa king of Judah began Omri to reign over Israel, twelve years: six years reigned he in Tirzah.

24And he bought the hill Samaria of Shemer for two talents of silver, and built on the hill, and called the name of the city which he built, after the name of Shemer, owner of the hill, Samaria.

25¶ But Omri wrought evil in the eyes of the LORD, and did worse than all that *were* before him.

26For he walked in all the way of Jeroboam the son of Nebat, and in his sin wherewith he made Israel to sin, to provoke the LORD God of Israel to anger with their vanities.

27Now the rest of the acts of Omri which he did, and his might that he showed, *are* they not written in the book of the chronicles of the kings of Israel?

28So Omri slept with his fathers, and was buried in Samaria: and Ahab his son reigned in his stead.

29¶ And in the thirty and eighth year of Asa king of Judah began Ahab the son of Omri to reign over Israel: and Ahab the son of Omri reigned over Israel in Samaria twenty and two years.

30And Ahab the son of Omri did evil in the sight of the LORD above all that *were* before him.

31And it came to pass, as if it had been a light thing for him to walk in the sins of Jeroboam the son of Nebat, that he took to wife Jezebel the daughter of Ethbaal king of the Zidonians, and went and served Baal, and worshipped him.

32And he reared up an altar for Baal in the house of Baal, which he had built in Samaria.

New International

11As soon as he began to reign and was seated on the throne, he killed off Baasha's whole family. He did not spare a single male, whether relative or friend. 12So Zimri destroyed the whole family of Baasha, in accordance with the word of the LORD spoken against Baasha through the prophet Jehu— 13because of all the sins Baasha and his son Elah had committed and had caused Israel to commit, so that they provoked the LORD, the God of Israel, to anger by their worthless idols.

14As for the other events of Elah's reign, and all he did, are they not written in the book of the annals of the kings of Israel?

Zimri King of Israel

15In the twenty-seventh year of Asa king of Judah, Zimri reigned in Tirzah seven days. The army was encamped near Gibbethon, a Philistine town. 16When the Israelites in the camp heard that Zimri had plotted against the king and murdered him, they proclaimed Omri, the commander of the army, king over Israel that very day there in the camp. 17Then Omri and all the Israelites with him withdrew from Gibbethon and laid siege to Tirzah. 18When Zimri saw that the city was taken, he went into the citadel of the royal palace and set the palace on fire around him. So he died, 19because of the sins he had committed, doing evil in the eyes of the LORD and walking in the ways of Jeroboam and in the sin he had committed and had caused Israel to commit.

20As for the other events of Zimri's reign, and the rebellion he carried out, are they not written in the book of the annals of the kings of Israel?

Omri King of Israel

21Then the people of Israel were split into two factions; half supported Tibni son of Ginath for king, and the other half supported Omri. 22But Omri's followers proved stronger than those of Tibni son of Ginath. So Tibni died and Omri became king.

23In the thirty-first year of Asa king of Judah, Omri became king of Israel, and he reigned twelve years, six of them in Tirzah. 24He bought the hill of Samaria from Shemer for two talents[a] of silver and built a city on the hill, calling it Samaria, after Shemer, the name of the former owner of the hill.

25But Omri did evil in the eyes of the LORD and sinned more than all those before him. 26He walked in all the ways of Jeroboam son of Nebat and in his sin, which he had caused Israel to commit, so that they provoked the LORD, the God of Israel, to anger by their worthless idols.

27As for the other events of Omri's reign, what he did and the things he achieved, are they not written in the book of the annals of the kings of Israel? 28Omri rested with his fathers and was buried in Samaria. And Ahab his son succeeded him as king.

Ahab Becomes King of Israel

29In the thirty-eighth year of Asa king of Judah, Ahab son of Omri became king of Israel, and he reigned in Samaria over Israel twenty-two years. 30Ahab son of Omri did more evil in the eyes of the LORD than any of those before him. 31He not only considered it trivial to commit the sins of Jeroboam son of Nebat, but he also married Jezebel daughter of Ethbaal king of the Sidonians, and began to serve Baal and worship him. 32He set up an altar for Baal in the temple of Baal that he built in Samaria. 33Ahab also made an Asherah pole and did

---

a 24 That is, about 150 pounds (about 70 kilograms)

Living Bible

11He immediately killed the entire royal family—leaving not a single male child. He even destroyed distant relatives and friends. 12This destruction of the descendants of Baasha was in line with what the Lord had predicted through the prophet Jehu. 13The tragedy occurred because of the sins of Baasha and his son Elah; for they had led Israel into worshiping idols and the Lord was very angry about it. 14The rest of the history of Elah's reign is written in *The Annals of the Kings of Israel.*

15, 16But Zimri lasted only seven days; for when the army of Israel, which was then engaged in attacking the Philistine city of Gibbethon, heard that Zimri had assassinated the king, they decided on General Omri, commander-in-chief of the army, as their new ruler. 17So Omri led the army of Gibbethon to besiege Tirzah, Israel's capital. 18When Zimri saw that the city had been taken, he went into the palace and burned it over him and died in the flames. 19For he, too, had sinned like Jeroboam; he had worshiped idols and had led the people of Israel to sin with him. 20The rest of the story of Zimri and his treason are written in *The Annals of the Kings of Israel.*

21But now the kingdom of Israel was split in two; half the people were loyal to General Omri, and the other half followed Tibni, the son of Ginath. 22But General Omri won and Tibni was killed; so Omri reigned without opposition.

23King Asa of Judah had been on the throne thirty-one years when Omri began his reign over Israel, which lasted twelve years, six of them in Tirzah. 24Then Omri bought the hill now known as Samaria from its owner, Shemer, for $4,000 and built a city on it, calling it Samaria in honor of Shemer. 25But Omri was worse than any of the kings before him; 26he worshiped idols as Jeroboam had, and led Israel into this same sin. So God was very angry. 27The rest of Omri's history is recorded in *The Annals of the Kings of Israel.* 28When Omri died he was buried in Samaria, and his son Ahab became king in his place.

29King Asa of Judah had been on the throne thirty-eight years when Ahab became the king of Israel; and Ahab reigned for twenty-two years. 30But he was even more wicked than his father Omri; he was worse than any other king of Israel! 31And as though that were not enough, he married Jezebel, the daughter of King Ethbaal of the Sidonians, and then began worshiping Baal. 32First he built a temple and an altar for Baal in Samaria.

New Revised Standard

11 When he began to reign, as soon as he had seated himself on his throne, he killed all the house of Baasha; he did not leave him a single male of his kindred or his friends. 12 Thus Zimri destroyed all the house of Baasha, according to the word of the LORD, which he spoke against Baasha by the prophet Jehu— 13because of all the sins of Baasha and the sins of his son Elah that they committed, and that they caused Israel to commit, provoking the LORD God of Israel to anger with their idols. 14Now the rest of the acts of Elah, and all that he did, are they not written in the Book of the Annals of the Kings of Israel?

Third Dynasty: Zimri Reigns over Israel

15 In the twenty-seventh year of King Asa of Judah, Zimri reigned seven days in Tirzah. Now the troops were encamped against Gibbethon, which belonged to the Philistines, 16and the troops who were encamped heard it said, "Zimri has conspired, and he has killed the king"; therefore all Israel made Omri, the commander of the army, king over Israel that day in the camp. 17So Omri went up from Gibbethon, and all Israel with him, and they besieged Tirzah. 18When Zimri saw that the city was taken, he went into the citadel of the king's house; he burned down the king's house over himself with fire, and died— 19because of the sins that he committed, doing evil in the sight of the LORD, walking in the way of Jeroboam, and for the sin that he committed, causing Israel to sin. 20Now the rest of the acts of Zimri, and the conspiracy that he made, are they not written in the Book of the Annals of the Kings of Israel?

Fourth Dynasty: Omri Reigns over Israel

21 Then the people of Israel were divided into two parts; half of the people followed Tibni son of Ginath, to make him king, and half followed Omri. 22 But the people who followed Omri overcame the people who followed Tibni son of Ginath; so Tibni died, and Omri became king. 23 In the thirty-first year of King Asa of Judah, Omri began to reign over Israel; he reigned for twelve years, six of them in Tirzah.

Samaria the New Capital

24 He bought the hill of Samaria from Shemer for two talents of silver; he fortified the hill, and called the city that he built, Samaria, after the name of Shemer, the owner of the hill.

25 Omri did what was evil in the sight of the LORD; he did more evil than all who were before him. 26For he walked in all the way of Jeroboam son of Nebat, and in the sins that he caused Israel to commit, provoking the LORD, the God of Israel, to anger by their idols. 27Now the rest of the acts of Omri that he did, and the power that he showed, are they not written in the Book of the Annals of the Kings of Israel? 28Omri slept with his ancestors, and was buried in Samaria; his son Ahab succeeded him.

Ahab Reigns over Israel

29 In the thirty-eighth year of King Asa of Judah, Ahab son of Omri began to reign over Israel; Ahab son of Omri reigned over Israel in Samaria twenty-two years. 30Ahab son of Omri did evil in the sight of the LORD more than all who were before him.

Ahab Marries Jezebel and Worships Baal

31 And as if it had been a light thing for him to walk in the sins of Jeroboam son of Nebat, he took as his wife Jezebel daughter of King Ethbaal of the Sidonians, and went and served Baal, and worshiped him. 32He erected an altar for Baal in the house of Baal, which he built in Samaria. 33 Ahab also made a sacred pole.b Ahab did

b Heb *Asherah*

King James

33And Ahab made a grove; and Ahab did more to provoke the LORD God of Israel to anger than all the kings of Israel that were before him.

34¶ In his days did Hiel the Beth-elite build Jericho: he laid the foundation thereof in Abiram his firstborn, and set up the gates thereof in his youngest *son* Segub, according to the word of the LORD, which he spake by Joshua the son of Nun.

17 AND ELIJAH the Tishbite, *who was* of the inhabitants of Gilead, said unto Ahab, As the LORD God of Israel liveth, before whom I stand, there shall not be dew nor rain these years, but according to my word.

2And the word of the LORD came unto him, saying, 3Get thee hence, and turn thee eastward, and hide thyself by the brook Cherith, that *is* before Jordan.

4And it shall be, *that* thou shalt drink of the brook; and I have commanded the ravens to feed thee there.

5So he went and did according unto the word of the LORD: for he went and dwelt by the brook Cherith, that *is* before Jordan.

6And the ravens brought him bread and flesh in the morning, and bread and flesh in the evening; and he drank of the brook.

7And it came to pass after a while, that the brook dried up, because there had been no rain in the land.

8¶ And the word of the LORD came unto him, saying, 9Arise, get thee to Zarephath, which *belongeth* to Zidon, and dwell there: behold, I have commanded a widow woman there to sustain thee.

10So he arose and went to Zarephath. And when he came to the gate of the city, behold, the widow woman *was* there gathering of sticks: and he called to her, and said, Fetch me, I pray thee, a little water in a vessel, that I may drink.

11And as she was going to fetch *it*, he called to her, and said, Bring me, I pray thee, a morsel of bread in thine hand.

12And she said, As the LORD thy God liveth, I have not a cake, but an handful of meal in a barrel, and a little oil in a cruse: and, behold, I *am* gathering two sticks, that I may go in and dress it for me and my son, that we may eat it, and die.

13And Elijah said unto her, Fear not; go *and* do as thou hast said: but make me thereof a little cake first, and bring *it* unto me, and after make for thee and for thy son.

14For thus saith the LORD God of Israel, The barrel of meal shall not waste, neither shall the cruse of oil fail, until the day *that* the LORD sendeth rain upon the earth.

15And she went and did according to the saying of Elijah: and she, and he, and her house, did eat *many* days.

16*And* the barrel of meal wasted not, neither did the cruse of oil fail, according to the word of the LORD, which he spake by Elijah.

17¶ And it came to pass after these things, *that* the son of the woman, the mistress of the house, fell sick; and his sickness was so sore, that there was no breath left in him.

18And she said unto Elijah, What have I to do with thee, O thou man of God? art thou come unto me to call my sin to remembrance, and to slay my son?

19And he said unto her, Give me thy son. And he took him out of her bosom, and carried him up into a loft, where he abode, and laid him upon his own bed.

20And he cried unto the LORD, and said, O LORD my God, hast thou also brought evil upon the widow with whom I sojourn, by slaying her son?

New International

more to provoke the LORD, the God of Israel, to anger than did all the kings of Israel before him.

34In Ahab's time, Hiel of Bethel rebuilt Jericho. He laid its foundations at the cost of his firstborn son Abiram, and he set up its gates at the cost of his youngest son Segub, in accordance with the word of the LORD spoken by Joshua son of Nun.

Elijah Fed by Ravens

17 NOW ELIJAH the Tishbite, from Tishbea in Gilead, said to Ahab, "As the LORD, the God of Israel, lives, whom I serve, there will be neither dew nor rain in the next few years except at my word."

2Then the word of the LORD came to Elijah: 3"Leave here, turn eastward and hide in the Kerith Ravine, east of the Jordan. 4You will drink from the brook, and I have ordered the ravens to feed you there."

5So he did what the LORD had told him. He went to the Kerith Ravine, east of the Jordan, and stayed there. 6The ravens brought him bread and meat in the morning and bread and meat in the evening, and he drank from the brook.

The Widow at Zarephath

7Some time later the brook dried up because there had been no rain in the land. 8Then the word of the LORD came to him: 9"Go at once to Zarephath of Sidon and stay there. I have commanded a widow in that place to supply you with food." 10So he went to Zarephath. When he came to the town gate, a widow was there gathering sticks. He called to her and asked, "Would you bring me a little water in a jar so I may have a drink?" 11As she was going to get it, he called, "And bring me, please, a piece of bread."

12"As surely as the LORD your God lives," she replied, "I don't have any bread—only a handful of flour in a jar and a little oil in a jug. I am gathering a few sticks to take home and make a meal for myself and my son, that we may eat it—and die."

13Elijah said to her, "Don't be afraid. Go home and do as you have said. But first make a small cake of bread for me from what you have and bring it to me, and then make something for yourself and your son. 14For this is what the LORD, the God of Israel, says: 'The jar of flour will not be used up and the jug of oil will not run dry until the day the LORD gives rain on the land.' "

15She went away and did as Elijah had told her. So there was food every day for Elijah and for the woman and her family. 16For the jar of flour was not used up and the jug of oil did not run dry, in keeping with the word of the LORD spoken by Elijah.

17Some time later the son of the woman who owned the house became ill. He grew worse and worse, and finally stopped breathing. 18She said to Elijah, "What do you have against me, man of God? Did you come to remind me of my sin and kill my son?"

19"Give me your son," Elijah replied. He took him from her arms, carried him to the upper room where he was staying, and laid him on his bed. 20Then he cried out to the LORD, "O LORD my God, have you brought tragedy also upon this widow I am staying with, by causing her son to die?" 21Then he stretched himself out

Living Bible

33Then he made other idols and did more to anger the Lord God of Israel than any of the other kings of Israel before him.

34(It was during his reign that Hiel, a man from Bethel, rebuilt Jericho. When he laid the foundations, his oldest son, Abiram, died; and when he finally completed it by setting up the gates, his youngest son, Segub, died. For this was the Lord's curse upon Jericho[b] as declared by Joshua, the son of Nun.)

17 THEN ELIJAH, the prophet[c] from Tishbe in Gilead, told King Ahab, "As surely as the Lord God of Israel lives—the God whom I worship and serve—there won't be any dew or rain for several years until I say the word!"

2Then the Lord said to Elijah, 3"Go to the east and hide by Cherith Brook at a place east of where it enters the Jordan River. 4Drink from the brook and eat what the ravens bring you, for I have commanded them to feed you."

5So he did as the Lord had told him to, and camped beside the brook. 6The ravens brought him bread and meat each morning and evening, and he drank from the brook. 7But after awhile the brook dried up, for there was no rainfall anywhere in the land.

8,9Then the Lord said to him, "Go and live in the village of Zarephath, near the city of Sidon. There is a widow there who will feed you. I have given her my instructions."

10So he went to Zarephath. As he arrived at the gates of the city he saw a widow gathering sticks; and he asked her for a cup of water.

11As she was going to get it, he called to her, "Bring me a bite of bread, too."

12But she said, "I swear by the Lord your God that I haven't a single piece of bread in the house. And I have only a handful of flour left and a little cooking oil in the bottom of the jar. I was just gathering a few sticks to cook this last meal, and then my son and I must die of starvation."

13But Elijah said to her, "Don't be afraid! Go ahead and cook that 'last meal,' but bake me a little loaf of bread first; and afterwards there will still be enough food for you and your son. 14For the Lord God of Israel says that there will always be plenty of flour and oil left in your containers until the time when the Lord sends rain, and the crops grow again!"

15So she did as Elijah said, and she and Elijah and her son continued to eat from her supply of flour and oil as long as it was needed. 16For no matter how much they used, there was always plenty left in the containers, just as the Lord had promised through Elijah!

17But one day the woman's son became sick and died. 18"O man of God," she cried, "what have you done to me? Have you come here to punish my sins by killing my son?"

19"Give him to me," Elijah replied. And he took the boy's body from her and carried it upstairs to the guest room where he lived, and laid the body on his bed, 20and then cried out to the Lord, "O Lord my God, why have you killed the son of this widow with whom I am staying?"

New Revised Standard

more to provoke the anger of the LORD, the God of Israel, than had all the kings of Israel who were before him. 34In his days Hiel of Bethel built Jericho; he laid its foundation at the cost of Abiram his firstborn, and set up its gates at the cost of his youngest son Segub, according to the word of the LORD, which he spoke by Joshua son of Nun.

Elijah Predicts a Drought

17 NOW ELIJAH the Tishbite, of Tishbe[d] in Gilead, said to Ahab, "As the LORD the God of Israel lives, before whom I stand, there shall be neither dew nor rain these years, except by my word." 2The word of the LORD came to him, saying, 3"Go from here and turn eastward, and hide yourself by the Wadi Cherith, which is east of the Jordan. 4You shall drink from the wadi, and I have commanded the ravens to feed you there." 5So he went and did according to the word of the LORD; he went and lived by the Wadi Cherith, which is east of the Jordan. 6The ravens brought him bread and meat in the morning, and bread and meat in the evening; and he drank from the wadi. 7But after a while the wadi dried up, because there was no rain in the land.

The Widow of Zarephath

8 Then the word of the LORD came to him, saying, 9"Go now to Zarephath, which belongs to Sidon, and live there; for I have commanded a widow there to feed you." 10So he set out and went to Zarephath. When he came to the gate of the town, a widow was there gathering sticks; he called to her and said, "Bring me a little water in a vessel, so that I may drink." 11As she was going to bring it, he called to her and said, "Bring me a morsel of bread in your hand." 12But she said, "As the LORD your God lives, I have nothing baked, only a handful of meal in a jar, and a little oil in a jug; I am now gathering a couple of sticks, so that I may go home and prepare it for myself and my son, that we may eat it, and die." 13Elijah said to her, "Do not be afraid; go and do as you have said; but first make me a little cake of it and bring it to me, and afterwards make something for yourself and your son. 14For thus says the LORD the God of Israel: The jar of meal will not be emptied and the jug of oil will not fail until the day that the LORD sends rain on the earth." 15She went and did as Elijah said, so that she as well as he and her household ate for many days. 16The jar of meal was not emptied, neither did the jug of oil fail, according to the word of the LORD that he spoke by Elijah.

Elijah Revives the Widow's Son

17 After this the son of the woman, the mistress of the house, became ill; his illness was so severe that there was no breath left in him. 18She then said to Elijah, "What have you against me, O man of God? You have come to me to bring my sin to remembrance, and to cause the death of my son!" 19But he said to her, "Give me your son." He took him from her bosom, carried him up into the upper chamber where he was lodging, and laid him on his own bed. 20He cried out to the LORD, "O LORD my God, have you brought calamity even upon the widow with whom I am staying, by killing her son?" 21Then he stretched himself upon the child three

---

b 16:34 the Lord's curse upon Jericho. See Joshua 6:26.   c 17:1 The prophet, implied.   d Gk: Heb of the settlers

King James

21And he stretched himself upon the child three times, and cried unto the Lord, and said, O Lord my God, I pray thee, let this child's soul come into him again.

22And the Lord heard the voice of Elijah; and the soul of the child came into him again, and he revived.

23And Elijah took the child, and brought him down out of the chamber into the house, and delivered him unto his mother: and Elijah said, See, thy son liveth.

24¶ And the woman said to Elijah, Now by this I know that thou *art* a man of God, *and* that the word of the Lord in thy mouth *is* truth.

18 AND IT came to pass *after* many days, that the word of the Lord came to Elijah in the third year, saying, Go, show thyself unto Ahab; and I will send rain upon the earth.

2And Elijah went to show himself unto Ahab. And *there was* a sore famine in Samaria.

3And Ahab called Obadiah, which *was* the governor of *his* house. (Now Obadiah feared the Lord greatly:

4For it was *so,* when Jezebel cut off the prophets of the Lord, that Obadiah took an hundred prophets, and hid them by fifty in a cave, and fed them with bread and water.)

5And Ahab said unto Obadiah, Go into the land, unto all fountains of water, and unto all brooks: peradventure we may find grass to save the horses and mules alive, that we lose not all the beasts.

6So they divided the land between them to pass throughout it: Ahab went one way by himself, and Obadiah went another way by himself.

7¶ And as Obadiah was in the way, behold, Elijah met him: and he knew him, and fell on his face, and said, *Art* thou that my lord Elijah?

8And he answered him, I *am:* go, tell thy lord, Behold, Elijah *is here.*

9And he said, What have I sinned, that thou wouldest deliver thy servant into the hand of Ahab, to slay me?

10*As* the Lord thy God liveth, there is no nation or kingdom, whither my lord hath not sent to seek thee: and when they said, *He is* not *there;* he took an oath of the kingdom and nation, that they found thee not.

11And now thou sayest, Go, tell thy lord, Behold, Elijah *is here.*

12And it shall come to pass, *as soon as* I am gone from thee, that the spirit of the Lord shall carry thee whither I know not; and *so* when I come and tell Ahab, and he cannot find thee, he shall slay me: but I thy servant fear the Lord from my youth.

13Was it not told my lord what I did when Jezebel slew the prophets of the Lord, how I hid an hundred men of the Lord's prophets by fifty in a cave, and fed them with bread and water?

14And now thou sayest, Go, tell thy lord, Behold, Elijah *is here:* and he shall slay me.

15And Elijah said, *As* the Lord of hosts liveth, before whom I stand, I will surely show myself unto him today.

16So Obadiah went to meet Ahab, and told him: and Ahab went to meet Elijah.

17¶ And it came to pass, when Ahab saw Elijah, that Ahab said unto him, *Art* thou he that troubleth Israel?

18And he answered, I have not troubled Israel; but thou, and thy father's house, in that ye have forsaken the commandments of the Lord, and thou hast followed Baalim.

19Now therefore send, *and* gather to me all Israel unto mount Carmel, and the prophets of Baal four hundred and fifty, and the prophets of the groves four hundred, which eat at Jezebel's table.

20So Ahab sent unto all the children of Israel, and gathered the prophets together unto mount Carmel.

New International

on the boy three times and cried to the Lord, "O Lord my God, let this boy's life return to him!"

22The Lord heard Elijah's cry, and the boy's life returned to him, and he lived. 23Elijah picked up the child and carried him down from the room into the house. He gave him to his mother and said, "Look, your son is alive!"

24Then the woman said to Elijah, "Now I know that you are a man of God and that the word of the Lord from your mouth is the truth."

Elijah and Obadiah

18 AFTER A long time, in the third year, the word of the Lord came to Elijah: "Go and present yourself to Ahab, and I will send rain on the land." 2So Elijah went to present himself to Ahab.

Now the famine was severe in Samaria, 3and Ahab had summoned Obadiah, who was in charge of his palace. (Obadiah was a devout believer in the Lord. 4While Jezebel was killing off the Lord's prophets, Obadiah had taken a hundred prophets and hidden them in two caves, fifty in each, and had supplied them with food and water.) 5Ahab had said to Obadiah, "Go through the land to all the springs and valleys. Maybe we can find some grass to keep the horses and mules alive so we will not have to kill any of our animals." 6So they divided the land they were to cover, Ahab going in one direction and Obadiah in another.

7As Obadiah was walking along, Elijah met him. Obadiah recognized him, bowed down to the ground, and said, "Is it really you, my lord Elijah?"

8"Yes," he replied. "Go tell your master, 'Elijah is here.' "

9"What have I done wrong," asked Obadiah, "that you are handing your servant over to Ahab to be put to death? 10As surely as the Lord your God lives, there is not a nation or kingdom where my master has not sent someone to look for you. And whenever a nation or kingdom claimed you were not there, he made them swear they could not find you. 11But now you tell me to go to my master and say, 'Elijah is here.' 12I don't know where the Spirit of the Lord may carry you when I leave you. If I go and tell Ahab and he doesn't find you, he will kill me. Yet I your servant have worshiped the Lord since my youth. 13Haven't you heard, my lord, what I did while Jezebel was killing the prophets of the Lord? I hid a hundred of the Lord's prophets in two caves, fifty in each, and supplied them with food and water. 14And now you tell me to go to my master and say, 'Elijah is here.' He will kill me!"

15Elijah said, "As the Lord Almighty lives, whom I serve, I will surely present myself to Ahab today."

Elijah on Mount Carmel

16So Obadiah went to meet Ahab and told him, and Ahab went to meet Elijah. 17When he saw Elijah, he said to him, "Is that you, you troubler of Israel?"

18"I have not made trouble for Israel," Elijah replied. "But you and your father's family have. You have abandoned the Lord's commands and have followed the Baals. 19Now summon the people from all over Israel to meet me on Mount Carmel. And bring the four hundred and fifty prophets of Baal and the four hundred prophets of Asherah, who eat at Jezebel's table."

20So Ahab sent word throughout all Israel and assembled the prophets on Mount Carmel. 21Elijah went be-

Living Bible

21And he stretched himself upon the child three times, and cried out to the Lord, "O Lord my God, please let this child's spirit return to him."

22And the Lord heard Elijah's prayer; and the spirit of the child returned, and he became alive again! 23Then Elijah took him downstairs and gave him to his mother. "See! He's alive!" he beamed.

24"Now I know for sure that you are a prophet," she told him afterward,a "and that whatever you say is from the Lord!"

18 IT WAS three years later that the Lord said to Elijah, "Go and tell King Ahab that I will soon send rain again!"

2So Elijah went to tell him. Meanwhile the famine had become very severe in Samaria.

3, 4The man in charge of Ahab's household affairs was Obadiah, who was a devoted follower of the Lord. Once when Queen Jezebel had tried to kill all of the Lord's prophets, Obadiah had hidden one hundred of them in two caves—fifty in each—and had fed them with bread and water.

5That same day, while Elijah was on the way to see King Ahab,b the king said to Obadiah, "We must check every stream and brook to see if we can find enough grass to save at least some of my horses and mules. You go one way and I'll go the other, and we will search the entire land."

6So they did, each going alone. 7Suddenly Obadiah saw Elijah coming toward him! Obadiah recognized him at once and fell to the ground before him.

"Is it really you, my lord Elijah?" he asked.

8"Yes, it is," Elijah replied. "Now go and tell the king I am here."

9"Oh, sir," Obadiah protested, "what harm have I done to you that you are sending me to my death? 10For I swear by God that the king has searched every nation and kingdom on earth from end to end to find you. And each time when he was told 'Elijah isn't here,' King Ahab forced the king of that nation to swear to the truth of his claim. 11And now you say, 'Go and tell him Elijah is here'! 12But as soon as I leave you, the Spirit of the Lord will carry you away, who knows where, and when Ahab comes and can't find you, he will kill me; yet I have been a true servant of the Lord all my life. 13Has no one told you about the time when Queen Jezebel was trying to kill the Lord's prophets, and I hid a hundred of them in two caves and fed them with bread and water? 14And now you say, 'Go tell the king that Elijah is here'! Sir, if I do that, I'm dead!"

15But Elijah said, "I swear by the Lord God of the armies of heaven, in whose presence I stand, that I myself will present myself to Ahab today."

16So Obadiah went to tell Ahab that Elijah had come; and Ahab went out to meet him.

17"So it's you, is it?—the man who brought this disaster upon Israel!" Ahab exclaimed when he saw him.

18"You're talking about yourself," Elijah answered. "For you and your family have refused to obey the Lord, and have worshiped Baal instead. 19Now bring all the people of Israel to Mount Carmel, with all 450 prophets of Baal and the 400 prophets of Asherah who are supported by Jezebel."

20So Ahab summoned all the people and the prophets to Mount Carmel.

New Revised Standard

times, and cried out to the LORD, "O LORD my God, let this child's life come into him again." 22The LORD listened to the voice of Elijah; the life of the child came into him again, and he revived. 23Elijah took the child, brought him down from the upper chamber into the house, and gave him to his mother; then Elijah said, "See, your son is alive." 24So the woman said to Elijah, "Now I know that you are a man of God, and that the word of the LORD in your mouth is truth."

Elijah's Message to Ahab

18 AFTER MANY days the word of the LORD came to Elijah, in the third year of the drought,c saying, "Go, present yourself to Ahab; I will send rain on the earth." 2So Elijah went to present himself to Ahab. The famine was severe in Samaria. 3Ahab summoned Obadiah, who was in charge of the palace. (Now Obadiah revered the LORD greatly; 4when Jezebel was killing off the prophets of the LORD, Obadiah took a hundred prophets, hid them fifty to a cave, and provided them with bread and water.) 5Then Ahab said to Obadiah, "Go through the land to all the springs of water and to all the wadis; perhaps we may find grass to keep the horses and mules alive, and not lose some of the animals." 6So they divided the land between them to pass through it; Ahab went in one direction by himself, and Obadiah went in another direction by himself.

7 As Obadiah was on the way, Elijah met him; Obadiah recognized him, fell on his face, and said, "Is it you, my lord Elijah?" 8He answered him, "It is I. Go, tell your lord that Elijah is here." 9And he said, "How have I sinned, that you would hand your servant over to Ahab, to kill me? 10As the LORD your God lives, there is no nation or kingdom to which my lord has not sent to seek you; and when they would say, 'He is not here,' he would require an oath of the kingdom or nation, that they had not found you. 11But now you say, 'Go, tell your lord that Elijah is here.' 12As soon as I have gone from you, the spirit of the LORD will carry you I know not where; so, when I come and tell Ahab and he cannot find you, he will kill me, although I your servant have revered the LORD from my youth. 13Has it not been told my lord what I did when Jezebel killed the prophets of the LORD, how I hid a hundred of the LORD's prophets fifty to a cave, and provided them with bread and water? 14Yet now you say, 'Go, tell your lord that Elijah is here'; he will surely kill me." 15Elijah said, "As the LORD of hosts lives, before whom I stand, I will surely show myself to him today." 16So Obadiah went to meet Ahab, and told him; and Ahab went to meet Elijah.

17 When Ahab saw Elijah, Ahab said to him, "Is it you, you troubler of Israel?" 18He answered, "I have not troubled Israel; but you have, and your father's house, because you have forsaken the commandments of the LORD and followed the Baals. 19Now therefore have all Israel assemble for me at Mount Carmel, with the four hundred fifty prophets of Baal and the four hundred prophets of Asherah, who eat at Jezebel's table."

Elijah's Triumph over the Priests of Baal

20 So Ahab sent to all the Israelites, and assembled the prophets at Mount Carmel. 21Elijah then came near

---

a 17:24 she told him afterward, implied.   b 18:5 while Elijah was on the way to see King Ahab, implied.

c Heb lacks of the drought

King James

21And Elijah came unto all the people, and said, How long halt ye between two opinions? if the LORD *be* God, follow him: but if Baal, *then* follow him. And the people answered him not a word.

22Then said Eliajah unto the people, I, *even* I only, remain a prophet of the LORD; but Baal's prophets *are* four hundred and fifty men.

23Let them therefore give us two bullocks; and let them choose one bullock for themselves, and cut it in pieces, and lay *it* on wood, and put no fire *under:* and I will dress the other bullock, and lay *it* on wood, and put no fire *under:*

24And call ye on the name of your gods, and I will call on the name of the LORD: and the God that answereth by fire, let him be God. And all the people answered and said, It is well spoken.

25And Elijah said unto the prophets of Baal, Choose you one bullock for yourselves, and dress *it* first; for ye *are* many; and call on the name of your gods, but put no fire *under*.

26And they took the bullock which was given them, and they dressed *it*, and called on the name of Baal from morning even until noon, saying, O Baal, hear us. But *there was* no voice, nor any that answered. And they leaped upon the altar which was made.

27And it came to pass at noon, that Elijah mocked them, and said, Cry aloud: for he *is* a god; either he is talking, or he is pursuing, or he is in a journey, *or* peradventure he sleepeth, and must be awaked.

28And they cried aloud, and cut themselves after their manner with knives and lancets, till the blood gushed out upon them.

29And it came to pass, when midday was past, and they prophesied until the *time* of the offering of the *evening* sacrifice, that *there was* neither voice, nor any to answer, nor any that regarded.

30And Elijah said unto all the people, Come near unto me. And all the people came near unto him. And he repaired the altar of the LORD *that was* broken down.

31And Elijah took twelve stones, according to the number of the tribes of the sons of Jacob, unto whom the word of the LORD came, saying, Israel shall be thy name:

32And with the stones he built an altar in the name of the LORD: and he made a trench about the altar, as great as would contain two measures of seed.

33And he put the wood in order, and cut the bullock in pieces, and laid *him* on the wood, and said, Fill four barrels with water, and pour *it* on the burnt sacrifice, and on the wood.

34And he said, Do *it* the second time. And they did *it* the second time. And he said, Do *it* the third time. And they did *it* the third time.

35And the water ran round about the altar; and he filled the trench also with water.

36And it came to pass at *the time of* the offering of the *evening* sacrifice, that Elijah the prophet came near, and said, LORD God of Abraham, Isaac, and of Israel, let it be known this day that thou *art* God in Israel, and *that* I *am* thy servant, and *that* I have done all these things at thy word.

37Hear me, O LORD, hear me, that this people may know that thou *art* the LORD God, and *that* thou hast turned their heart back again.

38Then the fire of the LORD fell, and consumed the burnt sacrifice, and the wood, and the stones, and the dust, and licked up the water that *was* in the trench.

39And when all the people saw *it*, they fell on their faces: and they said, The LORD, he *is* the God; the LORD, he *is* the God.

40And Elijah said unto them, Take the prophets of Baal; let not one of them escape. And they took them: and Elijah brought them down to the brook Kishon, and slew them there.

New International

fore the people and said, "How long will you waver between two opinions? If the LORD is God, follow him; but if Baal is God, follow him."

But the people said nothing.

22Then Elijah said to them, "I am the only one of the LORD's prophets left, but Baal has four hundred and fifty prophets. 23Get two bulls for us. Let them choose one for themselves, and let them cut it into pieces and put it on the wood but not set fire to it. I will prepare the other bull and put it on the wood but not set fire to it. 24Then you call on the name of your god, and I will call on the name of the LORD. The god who answers by fire—he is God."

Then all the people said, "What you say is good."

25Elijah said to the prophets of Baal, "Choose one of the bulls and prepare it first, since there are so many of you. Call on the name of your god, but do not light the fire." 26So they took the bull given them and prepared it.

Then they called on the name of Baal from morning till noon. "O Baal, answer us!" they shouted. But there was no response; no one answered. And they danced around the altar they had made.

27At noon Elijah began to taunt them. "Shout louder!" he said. "Surely he is a god! Perhaps he is deep in thought, or busy, or traveling. Maybe he is sleeping and must be awakened." 28So they shouted louder and slashed themselves with swords and spears, as was their custom, until their blood flowed. 29Midday passed, and they continued their frantic prophesying until the time for the evening sacrifice. But there was no response, no one answered, no one paid attention.

30Then Elijah said to all the people, "Come here to me." They came to him, and he repaired the altar of the LORD, which was in ruins. 31Elijah took twelve stones, one for each of the tribes descended from Jacob, to whom the word of the LORD had come, saying, "Your name shall be Israel." 32With the stones he built an altar in the name of the LORD, and he dug a trench around it large enough to hold two seahs[a] of seed. 33He arranged the wood, cut the bull into pieces and laid it on the wood. Then he said to them, "Fill four large jars with water and pour it on the offering and on the wood."

34"Do it again," he said, and they did it again.

"Do it a third time," he ordered, and they did it the third time. 35The water ran down around the altar and even filled the trench.

36At the time of sacrifice, the prophet Elijah stepped forward and prayed: "O LORD, God of Abraham, Isaac and Israel, let it be known today that you are God in Israel and that I am your servant and have done all these things at your command. 37Answer me, O LORD, answer me, so these people will know that you, O LORD, are God, and that you are turning their hearts back again."

38Then the fire of the LORD fell and burned up the sacrifice, the wood, the stones and the soil, and also licked up the water in the trench.

39When all the people saw this, they fell prostrate and cried, "The LORD—he is God! The LORD—he is God!"

40Then Elijah commanded them, "Seize the prophets of Baal. Don't let anyone get away!" They seized them, and Elijah had them brought down to the Kishon Valley and slaughtered there.

---

a 32 That is, probably about 13 quarts (about 15 liters)

Living Bible

21Then Elijah talked to them. "How long are you going to waver between two opinions?" he asked the people. "If the Lord is God, *follow* him! But if Baal is God, then follow *him!*"

22Then Elijah spoke again. "I am the only prophet of the Lord who is left," he told them, "but Baal has 450 prophets. 23Now bring two young bulls. The prophets of Baal may choose whichever one they wish and cut it into pieces and lay it on the wood of their altar, but without putting any fire under the wood; and I will prepare the other young bull and lay it on the wood on the Lord's altar, with no fire under it. 24Then pray to your god, and I will pray to the Lord; and the god who answers by sending fire to light the wood is the true God!" And all the people agreed to this test.

25Then Elijah turned to the prophets of Baal. "You first," he said, "for there are many of you; choose one of the bulls and prepare it and call to your god; but don't put any fire under the wood."

26So they prepared one of the young bulls and placed it on the altar; and they called to Baal all morning, shouting, "O Baal, hear us!" But there was no reply of any kind. Then they began to dance around the altar. 27About noontime, Elijah began mocking them.

"You'll have to shout louder than that," he scoffed, "to catch the attention of your god! Perhaps he is talking to someone, or is out sitting on the toilet, or maybe he is away on a trip, or is asleep and needs to be wakened!"

28So they shouted louder and, as was their custom, cut themselves with knives and swords until the blood gushed out. 29They raved all afternoon until the time of the evening sacrifice, but there was no reply, no voice, no answer.

30Then Elijah called to the people, "Come over here." And they all crowded around him as he repaired the altar of the Lord which had been torn down. 31He took twelve stones, one to represent each of the tribes of Israel,b 32and used the stones to rebuild the Lord's altar. Then he dug a trench about three feet widec around the altar. 33He piled wood upon the altar and cut the young bull into pieces and laid the pieces on the wood.

"Fill four barrels with water," he said, "and pour the water over the carcass and the wood."

After they had done this he said, 34"Do it again." And they did.

"Now, do it once more!" And they did; 35and the water ran off the altar and filled the trench.

36At the customary time for offering the evening sacrifice, Elijah walked up to the altar and prayed, "O Lord God of Abraham, Isaac, and Israel, prove today that you are the God of Israel and that I am your servant; prove that I have done all this at your command. 37O Lord, answer me! Answer me so these people will know that you are God and that you have brought them back to yourself."

38Then, suddenly, fire flashed down from heaven and burned up the young bull, the wood, the stones, the dust, and even evaporated all the water in the ditch!

39And when the people saw it, they fell to their faces upon the ground shouting, "Jehovah is God! Jehovah is God!"

40Then Elijah told them to grab the prophets of Baal. "Don't let a single one escape," he commanded.

So they seized them all, and Elijah took them to Kishon Brook and killed them there.

New Revised Standard

to all the people, and said, "How long will you go limping with two different opinions? If the LORD is God, follow him; but if Baal, then follow him." The people did not answer him a word. 22Then Elijah said to the people, "I, even I only, am left a prophet of the LORD; but Baal's prophets number four hundred fifty. 23Let two bulls be given to us; let them choose one bull for themselves, cut it in pieces, and lay it on the wood, but put no fire to it; I will prepare the other bull and lay it on the wood, but put no fire to it. 24Then you call on the name of your god and I will call on the name of the LORD; the god who answers by fire is indeed God." All the people answered, "Well spoken!" 25Then Elijah said to the prophets of Baal, "Choose for yourselves one bull and prepare it first, for you are many; then call on the name of your god, but put no fire to it." 26So they took the bull that was given them, prepared it, and called on the name of Baal from morning until noon, crying, "O Baal, answer us!" But there was no voice, and no answer. They limped about the altar that they had made. 27At noon Elijah mocked them, saying, "Cry aloud! Surely he is a god; either he is meditating, or he has wandered away, or he is on a journey, or perhaps he is asleep and must be awakened." 28Then they cried aloud and, as was their custom, they cut themselves with swords and lances until the blood gushed out over them. 29As midday passed, they raved on until the time of the offering of the oblation, but there was no voice, no answer, and no response.

30 Then Elijah said to all the people, "Come closer to me"; and all the people came closer to him. First he repaired the altar of the LORD that had been thrown down; 31Elijah took twelve stones, according to the number of the tribes of the sons of Jacob, to whom the word of the LORD came, saying, "Israel shall be your name"; 32with the stones he built an altar in the name of the LORD. Then he made a trench around the altar, large enough to contain two measures of seed. 33Next he put the wood in order, cut the bull in pieces, and laid it on the wood. He said, "Fill four jars with water and pour it on the burnt offering and on the wood." 34Then he said, "Do it a second time"; and they did it a second time. Again he said, "Do it a third time"; and they did it a third time, 35so that the water ran all around the altar, and filled the trench also with water.

36 At the time of the offering of the oblation, the prophet Elijah came near and said, "O LORD, God of Abraham, Isaac, and Israel, let it be known this day that you are God in Israel, that I am your servant, and that I have done all these things at your bidding. 37Answer me, O LORD, answer me, so that this people may know that you, O LORD, are God, and that you have turned their hearts back." 38Then the fire of the LORD fell and consumed the burnt offering, the wood, the stones, and the dust, and even licked up the water that was in the trench. 39When all the people saw it, they fell on their faces and said, "The LORD indeed is God; the LORD indeed is God." 40Elijah said to them, "Seize the prophets of Baal; do not let one of them escape." Then they seized them; and Elijah brought them down to the Wadi Kishon, and killed them there.

---

b *18:31 one to represent each of the tribes of Israel,* literally, "each of the tribes of the sons of Jacob to whom the Lord had said, 'Israel shall be your name.'"   c *18:32 three feet wide,* literally, "as great as would contain two measures of seed."

King James

41¶ And Elijah said unto Ahab, Get thee up, eat and drink; for *there is* a sound of abundance of rain.

42So Ahab went up to eat and to drink. And Elijah went up to the top of Carmel; and he cast himself down upon the earth, and put his face between his knees,

43And said to his servant, Go up now, look toward the sea. And he went up, and looked, and said, *There is* nothing. And he said, Go again seven times.

44And it came to pass at the seventh time, that he said, Behold, there ariseth a little cloud out of the sea, like a man's hand. And he said, Go up, say unto Ahab, Prepare *thy chariot*, and get thee down, that the rain stop thee not.

45And it came to pass in the mean while, that the heaven was black with clouds and wind, and there was a great rain. And Ahab rode, and went to Jezreel.

46And the hand of the LORD was on Elijah; and he girded up his loins, and ran before Ahab to the entrance of Jezreel.

19 AND AHAB told Jezebel all that Elijah had done, and withal how he had slain all the prophets with the sword.

2Then Jezebel sent a messenger unto Elijah, saying, So let the gods do *to me*, and more also, if I make not thy life as the life of one of them by tomorrow about this time.

3And when he saw *that*, he arose, and went for his life, and came to Beer-sheba, which *belongeth* to Judah, and left his servant there.

4¶ But he himself went a day's journey into the wilderness, and came and sat down under a juniper tree: and he requested for himself that he might die; and said, It is enough; now, O LORD, take away my life; for I *am* not better than my fathers.

5And as he lay and slept under a juniper tree, behold, then an angel touched him, and said unto him, Arise *and* eat.

6And he looked, and, behold, *there was* a cake baked on the coals, and a cruse of water at his head. And he did eat and drink, and laid him down again.

7And the angel of the LORD came again the second time, and touched him, and said, Arise *and* eat; because the journey *is* too great for thee.

8And he arose, and did eat and drink, and went in the strength of that meat forty days and forty nights unto Horeb the mount of God.

9¶ And he came thither unto a cave, and lodged there; and, behold, the word of the LORD *came* to him, and he said unto him, What doest thou here, Elijah?

10And he said, I have been very jealous for the LORD God of hosts: for the children of Israel have forsaken thy covenant, thrown down thine altars, and slain thy prophets with the sword; and I, *even* I only, am left; and they seek my life, to take it away.

11And he said, Go forth, and stand upon the mount before the LORD. And, behold, the LORD passed by, and a great and strong wind rent the mountains, and brake in pieces the rocks before the LORD; *but* the LORD *was* not in the wind: and after the wind an earthquake; *but* the LORD *was* not in the earthquake:

12And after the earthquake a fire; *but* the LORD *was* not in the fire: and after the fire a still small voice.

13And it was *so*, when Elijah heard *it*, that he wrapped his face in his mantle, and went out, and stood in the entering in of the cave. And, behold, *there came* a voice unto him, and said, What doest thou here, Elijah?

New International

41And Elijah said to Ahab, "Go, eat and drink, for there is the sound of a heavy rain." 42So Ahab went off to eat and drink, but Elijah climbed to the top of Carmel, bent down to the ground and put his face between his knees.

43"Go and look toward the sea," he told his servant. And he went up and looked.

"There is nothing there," he said.

Seven times Elijah said, "Go back."

44The seventh time the servant reported, "A cloud as small as a man's hand is rising from the sea."

So Elijah said, "Go and tell Ahab, 'Hitch up your chariot and go down before the rain stops you.'"

45Meanwhile, the sky grew black with clouds, the wind rose, a heavy rain came on and Ahab rode off to Jezreel. 46The power of the LORD came upon Elijah and, tucking his cloak into his belt, he ran ahead of Ahab all the way to Jezreel.

Elijah Flees to Horeb

19 NOW AHAB told Jezebel everything Elijah had done and how he had killed all the prophets with the sword. 2So Jezebel sent a messenger to Elijah to say, "May the gods deal with me, be it ever so severely, if by this time tomorrow I do not make your life like that of one of them."

3Elijah was afraid[a] and ran for his life. When he came to Beersheba in Judah, he left his servant there, 4while he himself went a day's journey into the desert. He came to a broom tree, sat down under it and prayed that he might die. "I have had enough, LORD," he said. "Take my life; I am no better than my ancestors." 5Then he lay down under the tree and fell asleep.

All at once an angel touched him and said, "Get up and eat." 6He looked around, and there by his head was a cake of bread baked over hot coals, and a jar of water. He ate and drank and then lay down again.

7The angel of the LORD came back a second time and touched him and said, "Get up and eat, for the journey is too much for you." 8So he got up and ate and drank. Strengthened by that food, he traveled forty days and forty nights until he reached Horeb, the mountain of God. 9There he went into a cave and spent the night.

The LORD Appears to Elijah

And the word of the LORD came to him: "What are you doing here, Elijah?"

10He replied, "I have been very zealous for the LORD God Almighty. The Israelites have rejected your covenant, broken down your altars, and put your prophets to death with the sword. I am the only one left, and now they are trying to kill me too."

11The LORD said, "Go out and stand on the mountain in the presence of the LORD, for the LORD is about to pass by."

Then a great and powerful wind tore the mountains apart and shattered the rocks before the LORD, but the LORD was not in the wind. After the wind there was an earthquake, but the LORD was not in the earthquake. 12After the earthquake came a fire, but the LORD was not in the fire. And after the fire came a gentle whisper. 13When Elijah heard it, he pulled his cloak over his face and went out and stood at the mouth of the cave.

Then a voice said to him, "What are you doing here, Elijah?"

---

a 3 Or Elijah saw

Living Bible

41Then Elijah said to Ahab, "Go and enjoy a good meal! For I hear a mighty rainstorm coming!"

42So Ahab prepared a feast. But Elijah climbed to the top of Mount Carmel and got down on his knees, with his face between his knees, 43and said to his servant, "Go and look out toward the sea."

He did, but returned to Elijah and told him, "I didn't see anything."

Then Elijah told him, "Go again, and again, and again, seven times!"

44Finally, the seventh time, his servant told him, "I saw a little cloud about the size of a man's hand rising from the sea."

Then Elijah shouted, "Hurry to Ahab and tell him to get into his chariot and get down the mountain, or he'll be stopped by the rain!"

45And sure enough, the sky was soon black with clouds, and a heavy wind brought a terrific rainstorm. Ahab left hastily for Jezreel, 46and the Lord gave special strength to Elijah so that he was able to run ahead of Ahab's chariot to the entrance of the city!

19 WHEN AHAB told Queen Jezebel what Elijah had done, and that he had slaughtered the prophets of Baal, 2she sent this message to Elijah: "You killed my prophets, and now I swear by the gods that I am going to kill you by this time tomorrow night."

3So Elijah fled for his life; he went to Beer-sheba, a city of Judah, and left his servant there. 4Then he went on alone into the wilderness, traveling all day, and sat down under a broom bush and prayed that he might die.

"I've had enough," he told the Lord. "Take away my life. I've got to die sometime, and it might as well be now."b

5Then he lay down and slept beneath the broom bush. But as he was sleeping, an angel touched him and told him to get up and eat! 6He looked around and saw some bread baking on hot stones, and a jar of water! So he ate and drank and lay down again.

7Then the angel of the Lord came again and touched him and said, "Get up and eat some more, for there is a long journey ahead of you."

8So he got up and ate and drank, and the food gave him enough strength to travel forty days and forty nights to Mount Horeb, the mountain of God, 9where he lived in a cave.

But the Lord said to him, "What are you doing here, Elijah?"

10He replied, "I have worked very hard for the Lord God of the heavens; but the people of Israel have broken their covenant with you and torn down your altars, and killed your prophets, and only I am left; and now they are trying to kill me, too."

11"Go out and stand before me on the mountain," the Lord told him. And as Elijah stood there the Lord passed by, and a mighty windstorm hit the mountain; it was such a terrible blast that the rocks were torn loose, but the Lord was not in the wind. After the wind, there was an earthquake, but the Lord was not in the earthquake. 12And after the earthquake, there was a fire, but the Lord was not in the fire. And after the fire, there was the sound of a gentle whisper. 13When Elijah heard it, he wrapped his face in his scarf and went out and stood at the entrance of the cave.

And a voice said, "Why are you here, Elijah?"

New Revised Standard

The Drought Ends

41 Elijah said to Ahab, "Go up, eat and drink; for there is a sound of rushing rain." 42So Ahab went up to eat and to drink. Elijah went up to the top of Carmel; there he bowed himself down upon the earth and put his face between his knees. 43He said to his servant, "Go up now, look toward the sea." He went up and looked, and said, "There is nothing." Then he said, "Go again seven times." 44At the seventh time he said, "Look, a little cloud no bigger than a person's hand is rising out of the sea." Then he said, "Go say to Ahab, 'Harness your chariot and go down before the rain stops you.' " 45In a little while the heavens grew black with clouds and wind; there was a heavy rain. Ahab rode off and went to Jezreel. 46But the hand of the LORD was on Elijah; he girded up his loins and ran in front of Ahab to the entrance of Jezreel.

Elijah Flees from Jezebel

19 AHAB TOLD Jezebel all that Elijah had done, and how he had killed all the prophets with the sword. 2Then Jezebel sent a messenger to Elijah, saying, "So may the gods do to me, and more also, if I do not make your life like the life of one of them by this time tomorrow." 3Then he was afraid; he got up and fled for his life, and came to Beer-sheba, which belongs to Judah; he left his servant there.

4 But he himself went a day's journey into the wilderness, and came and sat down under a solitary broom tree. He asked that he might die: "It is enough; now, O LORD, take away my life, for I am no better than my ancestors." 5Then he lay down under the broom tree and fell asleep. Suddenly an angel touched him and said to him, "Get up and eat." 6He looked, and there at his head was a cake baked on hot stones, and a jar of water. He ate and drank, and lay down again. 7The angel of the LORD came a second time, touched him, and said, "Get up and eat, otherwise the journey will be too much for you." 8He got up, and ate and drank; then he went in the strength of that food forty days and forty nights to Horeb the mount of God. 9At that place he came to a cave, and spent the night there.

Then the word of the LORD came to him, saying, "What are you doing here, Elijah?" 10He answered, "I have been very zealous for the LORD, the God of hosts; for the Israelites have forsaken your covenant, thrown down your altars, and killed your prophets with the sword. I alone am left, and they are seeking my life, to take it away."

Elijah Meets God at Horeb

11 He said, "Go out and stand on the mountain before the LORD, for the LORD is about to pass by." Now there was a great wind, so strong that it was splitting mountains and breaking rocks in pieces before the LORD, but the LORD was not in the wind; and after the wind an earthquake, but the LORD was not in the earthquake; 12and after the earthquake a fire, but the LORD was not in the fire; and after the fire a sound of sheer silence. 13When Elijah heard it, he wrapped his face in his mantle and went out and stood at the entrance of the cave. Then there came a voice to him that said, "What are you doing here, Elijah?" 14He answered, "I have

---

b 19:4 and it might as well be now, literally, "I am no better than my fathers."

King James

14And he said, I have been very jealous for the LORD God of hosts: because the children of Israel have forsaken thy covenant, thrown down thine altars, and slain thy prophets with the sword; and I, *even* I only, am left; and they seek my life, to take it away.

15And the LORD said unto him, Go, return on thy way to the wilderness of Damascus: and when thou comest, anoint Hazael *to be* king over Syria:

16And Jehu the son of Nimshi shalt thou anoint *to be* king over Israel: and Elisha the son of Shaphat of Abelmeholah shalt thou anoint *to be* prophet in thy room.

17And it shall come to pass, *that* him that escapeth the sword of Hazael shall Jehu slay: and him that escapeth from the sword of Jehu shall Elisha slay.

18Yet I have left *me* seven thousand in Israel, all the knees which have not bowed unto Baal, and every mouth which hath not kissed him.

19¶ So he departed thence, and found Elisha the son of Shaphat, who *was* plowing *with* twelve yoke *of oxen* before him, and he with the twelfth: and Elijah passed by him, and cast his mantle upon him.

20And he left the oxen, and ran after Elijah, and said, Let me, I pray thee, kiss my father and my mother, and *then* I will follow thee. And he said unto him, Go back again: for what have I done to thee?

21And he returned back from him, and took a yoke of oxen, and slew them, and boiled their flesh with the instruments of the oxen, and gave unto the people, and they did eat. Then he arose, and went after Elijah, and ministered unto him.

20 AND BEN-HADAD the king of Syria gathered all his host together: and *there were* thirty and two kings with him, and horses, and chariots: and he went up and besieged Samaria, and warred against it.

2And he sent messengers to Ahab king of Israel into the city, and said unto him, Thus saith Ben-hadad,

3Thy silver and thy gold *is* mine; thy wives also and thy children, *even* the goodliest, *are* mine.

4And the king of Israel answered and said, My lord, O king, according to thy saying, I *am* thine, and all that I have.

5And the messengers came again, and said, Thus speaketh Ben-hadad, saying, Although I have sent unto thee, saying, Thou shalt deliver me thy silver, and thy gold, and thy wives, and thy children;

6Yet I will send my servants unto thee tomorrow about this time, and they shall search thine house, and the houses of thy servants; and it shall be, *that* whatsoever is pleasant in thine eyes, they shall put *it* in their hand, and take *it* away.

7Then the king of Israel called all the elders of the land, and said, Mark, I pray you, and see how this *man* seeketh mischief: for he sent unto me for my wives, and for my children, and for my silver, and for my gold; and I denied him not.

8And all the elders and all the people said unto him, Hearken not *unto him,* nor consent.

9Wherefore he said unto the messengers of Ben-hadad, Tell my lord the king, All that thou didst send for to thy servant at the first I will do: but this thing I may not do. And the messengers departed, and brought him word again.

10And Ben-hadad sent unto him, and said, The gods do so unto me, and more also, if the dust of Samaria shall suffice for handfuls for all the people that follow me.

11And the king of Israel answered and said, Tell *him,* Let not him that girdeth on *his harness* boast himself as he that putteth it off.

New International

14He replied, "I have been very zealous for the LORD God Almighty. The Israelites have rejected your covenant, broken down your altars, and put your prophets to death with the sword. I am the only one left, and now they are trying to kill me too."

15The LORD said to him, "Go back the way you came, and go to the Desert of Damascus. When you get there, anoint Hazael king over Aram. 16Also, anoint Jehu son of Nimshi king over Israel, and anoint Elisha son of Shaphat from Abel Meholah to succeed you as prophet. 17Jehu will put to death any who escape the sword of Hazael, and Elisha will put to death any who escape the sword of Jehu. 18Yet I reserve seven thousand in Israel—all whose knees have not bowed down to Baal and all whose mouths have not kissed him."

The Call of Elisha

19So Elijah went from there and found Elisha son of Shaphat. He was plowing with twelve yoke of oxen, and he himself was driving the twelfth pair. Elijah went up to him and threw his cloak around him. 20Elisha then left his oxen and ran after Elijah. "Let me kiss my father and mother good-by," he said, "and then I will come with you."

"Go back," Elijah replied. "What have I done to you?"

21So Elisha left him and went back. He took his yoke of oxen and slaughtered them. He burned the plowing equipment to cook the meat and gave it to the people, and they ate. Then he set out to follow Elijah and became his attendant.

Ben-Hadad Attacks Samaria

20 NOW BEN-HADAD king of Aram mustered his entire army. Accompanied by thirty-two kings with their horses and chariots, he went up and besieged Samaria and attacked it. 2He sent messengers into the city to Ahab king of Israel, saying, "This is what Ben-Hadad says: 3'Your silver and gold are mine, and the best of your wives and children are mine.'"

4The king of Israel answered, "Just as you say, my lord the king. I and all I have are yours."

5The messengers came again and said, "This is what Ben-Hadad says: 'I sent to demand your silver and gold, your wives and your children. 6But about this time tomorrow I am going to send my officials to search your palace and the houses of your officials. They will seize everything you value and carry it away.'"

7The king of Israel summoned all the elders of the land and said to them, "See how this man is looking for trouble! When he sent for my wives and my children, my silver and my gold, I did not refuse him."

8The elders and the people all answered, "Don't listen to him or agree to his demands."

9So he replied to Ben-Hadad's messengers, "Tell my lord the king, 'Your servant will do all you demanded the first time, but this demand I cannot meet.'" They left and took the answer back to Ben-Hadad.

10Then Ben-Hadad sent another message to Ahab: "May the gods deal with me, be it ever so severely, if enough dust remains in Samaria to give each of my men a handful."

11The king of Israel answered, "Tell him: 'One who puts on his armor should not boast like one who takes it off.'"

Living Bible

14He replied again, "I have been working very hard for the Lord God of the armies of heaven, but the people have broken their covenant and have torn down your altars; they have killed every one of your prophets except me; and now they are trying to kill me, too."

15Then the Lord told him, "Go back by the desert road to Damascus, and when you arrive, anoint Hazael to be king of Syria. 16Then anoint Jehu (son of Nimshi) to be king of Israel, and anoint Elisha (the son of Shaphat of Abel-meholah) to replace you as my prophet. 17Anyone who escapes from Hazael shall be killed by Jehu, and those who escape Jehu shall be killed by Elisha! 18And incidentally, there are 7,000 men in Israel who have never bowed to Baal nor kissed him!"

19So Elijah went and found Elisha who was plowing a field with eleven other teams ahead of him; he was at the end of the line with the last team. Elijah went over to him and threw his coat across his shoulders and walked away again.a

20Elisha left the oxen standing there and ran after Elijah and said to him, "First let me go and say good-bye to my father and mother, and then I'll go with you!" Elijah replied, "Go on back! Why all the excitement?"

21Elisha then returned to his oxen, killed them, and used wood from the plow to build a fire to roast their flesh. He passed around the meat to the other plowmen, and they all had a great feast. Then he went with Elijah, as his assistant.

20 KING BEN-HADAD of Syria now mobilized his army and, with thirty-two allied nations and their hordes of chariots and horses, besieged Samaria, the Israeli capital. 2, 3He sent this message into the city to King Ahab of Israel: "Your silver and gold are mine, as are your prettiest wives and the best of your children!"

4"All right, my lord," Ahab replied. "All that I have is yours!"

5, 6Soon Ben-hadad's messengers returned again with another message: "You must not only give me your silver, gold, wives, and children, but about this time tomorrow I will send my men to search your palace and the homes of your people, and they will take away whatever they like!"

7Then Ahab summoned his advisors. "Look what this man is doing," he complained to them. "He is stirring up trouble despite the fact that I have already told him he could have my wives and children and silver and gold, just as he demanded."

8"Don't give him anything more," the elders advised.

9So he told the messengers from Ben-hadad, "Tell my lord the king, 'I will give you everything you asked for the first time, but your men may not search the palace and the homes of the people.' "b So the messengers returned to Ben-hadad.

10Then the Syrian king sent this message to Ahab: "May the gods do more to me than I am going to do to you if I don't turn Samaria into handfuls of dust!"

11The king of Israel retorted, "Don't count your chickens before they hatch!"

New Revised Standard

been very zealous for the LORD, the God of hosts; for the Israelites have forsaken your covenant, thrown down your altars, and killed your prophets with the sword. I alone am left, and they are seeking my life, to take it away." 15Then the LORD said to him, "Go, return on your way to the wilderness of Damascus; when you arrive, you shall anoint Hazael as king over Aram. 16Also you shall anoint Jehu son of Nimshi as king over Israel; and you shall anoint Elisha son of Shaphat of Abel-meholah as prophet in your place. 17Whoever escapes from the sword of Hazael, Jehu shall kill; and whoever escapes from the sword of Jehu, Elisha shall kill. 18Yet I will leave seven thousand in Israel, all the knees that have not bowed to Baal, and every mouth that has not kissed him."

Elisha Becomes Elijah's Disciple

19 So he set out from there, and found Elisha son of Shaphat, who was plowing. There were twelve yoke of oxen ahead of him, and he was with the twelfth. Elijah passed by him and threw his mantle over him. 20He left the oxen, ran after Elijah, and said, "Let me kiss my father and my mother, and then I will follow you." Then Elijahc said to him, "Go back again; for what have I done to you?" 21He returned from following him, took the yoke of oxen, and slaughtered them; using the equipment from the oxen, he boiled their flesh, and gave it to the people, and they ate. Then he set out and followed Elijah, and became his servant.

Ahab's Wars with the Arameans

20 KING BEN-HADAD of Aram gathered all his army together; thirty-two kings were with him, along with horses and chariots. He marched against Samaria, laid siege to it, and attacked it. 2Then he sent messengers into the city to King Ahab of Israel, and said to him: "Thus says Ben-hadad: 3Your silver and gold are mine; your fairest wives and children also are mine." 4The king of Israel answered, "As you say, my lord, O king, I am yours, and all that I have." 5The messengers came again and said: "Thus says Ben-hadad: I sent to you, saying, 'Deliver to me your silver and gold, your wives and children'; 6nevertheless I will send my servants to you tomorrow about this time, and they shall search your house and the houses of your servants, and lay hands on whatever pleases them,d and take it away."

7 Then the king of Israel called all the elders of the land, and said, "Look now! See how this man is seeking trouble; for he sent to me for my wives, my children, my silver, and my gold; and I did not refuse him." 8Then all the elders and all the people said to him, "Do not listen or consent." 9So he said to the messengers of Ben-hadad, "Tell my lord the king: All that you first demanded of your servant I will do; but this thing I cannot do." The messengers left and brought him word again. 10Ben-hadad sent to him and said, "The gods do so to me, and more also, if the dust of Samaria will provide a handful for each of the people who follow me." 11The king of Israel answered, "Tell him: One who puts on armor should not brag like one who takes it off."

---

a 19:19 and walked away again, implied. b 20:9 your men may not search the palace and the homes of the people, literally, "this thing I cannot do." c Heb he d Gk Syr Vg: Heb you

King James

12And it came to pass, when *Ben-hadad* heard this message, as he *was* drinking, he and the kings in the pavilions, that he said unto his servants, Set *yourselves in array*. And they set *themselves in array* against the city.

13¶ And, behold, there came a prophet unto Ahab king of Israel, saying, Thus saith the LORD, Hast thou seen all this great multitude? behold, I will deliver it into thine hand this day; and thou shalt know that I *am* the LORD.

14And Ahab said, By whom? And he said, Thus saith the LORD, *Even* by the young men of the princes of the provinces. Then he said, Who shall order the battle? And he answered, Thou.

15Then he numbered the young men of the princes of the provinces, and they were two hundred and thirty two: and after them he numbered all the people, *even* all the children of Israel, *being* seven thousand.

16And they went out at noon. But Ben-hadad *was* drinking himself drunk in the pavilions, he and the kings, the thirty and two kings that helped him.

17And the young men of the princes of the provinces went out first; and Ben-hadad sent out, and they told him, saying, There are men come out of Samaria.

18And he said, Whether they be come out for peace, take them alive; or whether they be come out for war, take them alive.

19So these young men of the princes of the provinces came out of the city, and the army which followed them.

20And they slew every one his man: and the Syrians fled; and Israel pursued them: and Ben-hadad the king of Syria escaped on an horse with the horsemen.

21And the king of Israel went out, and smote the horses and chariots, and slew the Syrians with a great slaughter.

22¶ And the prophet came to the king of Israel, and said unto him, Go, strengthen thyself, and mark, and see what thou doest: for at the return of the year the king of Syria will come up against thee.

23And the servants of the king of Syria said unto him, Their gods *are* gods of the hills; therefore they were stronger than we; but let us fight against them in the plain, and surely we shall be stronger than they.

24And do this thing, Take the kings away, every man out of his place, and put captains in their rooms:

25And number thee an army, like the army that thou hast lost, horse for horse, and chariot for chariot: and we will fight against them in the plain, *and* surely we shall be stronger than they. And he hearkened unto their voice, and did so.

26And it came to pass at the return of the year, that Ben-hadad numbered the Syrians, and went up to Aphek, to fight against Israel.

27And the children of Israel were numbered, and were all present, and went against them: and the children of Israel pitched before them like two little flocks of kids; but the Syrians filled the country.

28¶ And there came a man of God, and spake unto the king of Israel, and said, Thus saith the LORD, Because the Syrians have said, The LORD *is* God of the hills, but he *is* not God of the valleys, therefore will I deliver all this great multitude into thine hand, and ye shall know that I *am* the LORD.

29And they pitched one over against the other seven days. And *so* it was, that in the seventh day the battle was joined: and the children of Israel slew of the Syrians an hundred thousand footmen in one day.

30But the rest fled to Aphek, into the city; and *there* a wall fell upon twenty and seven thousand of the men *that were* left. And Ben-hadad fled, and came into the city, into an inner chamber.

New International

12Ben-Hadad heard this message while he and the kings were drinking in their tents,[a] and he ordered his men: "Prepare to attack." So they prepared to attack the city.

Ahab Defeats Ben-Hadad

13Meanwhile a prophet came to Ahab king of Israel and announced, "This is what the LORD says: 'Do you see this vast army? I will give it into your hand today, and then you will know that I am the LORD.' "

14"But who will do this?" asked Ahab.

The prophet replied, "This is what the LORD says: 'The young officers of the provincial commanders will do it.' "

"And who will start the battle?" he asked.

The prophet answered, "You will."

15So Ahab summoned the young officers of the provincial commanders, 232 men. Then he assembled the rest of the Israelites, 7,000 in all. 16They set out at noon while Ben-Hadad and the 32 kings allied with him were in their tents getting drunk. 17The young officers of the provincial commanders went out first.

Now Ben-Hadad had dispatched scouts, who reported, "Men are advancing from Samaria."

18He said, "If they have come out for peace, take them alive; if they have come out for war, take them alive."

19The young officers of the provincial commanders marched out of the city with the army behind them 20and each one struck down his opponent. At that, the Arameans fled, with the Israelites in pursuit. But Ben-Hadad king of Aram escaped on horseback with some of his horsemen. 21The king of Israel advanced and overpowered the horses and chariots and inflicted heavy losses on the Arameans.

22Afterward, the prophet came to the king of Israel and said, "Strengthen your position and see what must be done, because next spring the king of Aram will attack you again."

23Meanwhile, the officials of the king of Aram advised him, "Their gods are gods of the hills. That is why they were too strong for us. But if we fight them on the plains, surely we will be stronger than they. 24Do this: Remove all the kings from their commands and replace them with other officers. 25You must also raise an army like the one you lost—horse for horse and chariot for chariot—so we can fight Israel on the plains. Then surely we will be stronger than they." He agreed with them and acted accordingly.

26The next spring Ben-Hadad mustered the Arameans and went up to Aphek to fight against Israel. 27When the Israelites were also mustered and given provisions, they marched out to meet them. The Israelites camped opposite them like two small flocks of goats, while the Arameans covered the countryside.

28The man of God came up and told the king of Israel, "This is what the LORD says: 'Because the Arameans think the LORD is a god of the hills and not a god of the valleys, I will deliver this vast army into your hands, and you will know that I am the LORD.' "

29For seven days they camped opposite each other, and on the seventh day the battle was joined. The Israelites inflicted a hundred thousand casualties on the Aramean foot soldiers in one day. 30The rest of them escaped to the city of Aphek, where the wall collapsed on twenty-seven thousand of them. And Ben-Hadad fled to the city and hid in an inner room.

---

a *12 Or in Succoth; also in verse 16*

Living Bible

12This reply of Ahab's reached Ben-hadad and the other kings as they were drinking in their tents.

"Prepare to attack!" Ben-hadad commanded his officers.

13Then a prophet came to see King Ahab and gave him this message from the Lord: "Do you see all these enemy forces? I will deliver them all to you today. Then at last you will know that I am the Lord."

14Ahab asked, "How will he do it?"

And the prophet replied, "The Lord says, 'By the troops from the provinces.' "

"Shall we attack first?" Ahab asked.

"Yes," the prophet answered.

15So he mustered the troops from the provinces, 232 of them, then the rest of his army of 7,000 men. 16About noontime, as Ben-hadad and the thirty-two allied kings were still drinking themselves drunk, the first of Ahab's troops marched out of the city.

17As they approached, Ben-hadad's scouts reported to him, "Some troops are coming!"

18"Take them alive," Ben-hadad commanded, "whether they have come for truce or for war."

19By now Ahab's entire army had joined the attack. 20Each one killed a Syrian soldier, and suddenly the entire Syrian army panicked and fled. The Israelis chased them, but King Ben-hadad and a few others escaped on horses. 21However, the great bulk of the horses and chariots were captured, and most of the Syrian army was killed in a great slaughter.

22Then the prophet approached King Ahab and said, "Get ready for another attack by the king of Syria."

23For after their defeat, Ben-hadad's officers said to him, "The Israeli God is a god of the hills; that is why they won. But we can beat them easily on the plains. 24Only this time replace the kings with generals! 25Recruit another army like the one you lost; give us the same number of horses, chariots, and men, and we will fight against them in the plains; there's not a shadow of a doubt that we will beat them." So King Ben-hadad did as they suggested. 26The following year he called up the Syrian army and marched out against Israel again, this time at Aphek. 27Israel then mustered its army, set up supply lines, and moved into the battle; but the Israeli army looked like two little flocks of baby goats in comparison to the vast Syrian forces that filled the countryside!

28Then a prophet went to the king of Israel with this message from the Lord: "Because the Syrians have declared, 'The Lord is a God of the hills and not of the plains,' I will help you defeat this vast army, and you shall know that I am indeed the Lord.

29The two armies camped opposite each other for seven days, and on the seventh day the battle began. And the Israelis killed 100,000 Syrian infantrymen that first day. 30The rest fled behind the walls of Aphek, but the wall fell on them and killed another 27,000. Ben-hadad fled into the city and hid in the inner room of one of the houses.

New Revised Standard

12When Ben-hadad heard this message—now he had been drinking with the kings in the booths—he said to his men, "Take your positions!" And they took their positions against the city.

Prophetic Opposition to Ahab

13 Then a certain prophet came up to King Ahab of Israel and said, "Thus says the LORD, Have you seen all this great multitude? Look, I will give it into your hand today; and you shall know that I am the LORD." 14Ahab said, "By whom?" He said, "Thus says the LORD, By the young men who serve the district governors." Then he said, "Who shall begin the battle?" He answered, "You." 15Then he mustered the young men who serve the district governors, two hundred thirty-two; after them he mustered all the people of Israel, seven thousand.

16 They went out at noon, while Ben-hadad was drinking himself drunk in the booths, he and the thirty-two kings allied with him. 17The young men who serve the district governors went out first. Ben-hadad had sent out scouts,b and they reported to him, "Men have come out from Samaria." 18He said, "If they have come out for peace, take them alive; if they have come out for war, take them alive."

19 But these had already come out of the city: the young men who serve the district governors, and the army that followed them. 20Each killed his man; the Arameans fled and Israel pursued them, but King Ben-hadad of Aram escaped on a horse with the cavalry. 21The king of Israel went out, attacked the horses and chariots, and defeated the Arameans with a great slaughter.

22 Then the prophet approached the king of Israel and said to him, "Come, strengthen yourself, and consider well what you have to do; for in the spring the king of Aram will come up against you."

The Arameans Are Defeated

23 The servants of the king of Aram said to him, "Their gods are gods of the hills, and so they were stronger than we; but let us fight against them in the plain, and surely we shall be stronger than they. 24Also do this: remove the kings, each from his post, and put commanders in place of them; 25and muster an army like the army that you have lost, horse for horse, and chariot for chariot; then we will fight against them in the plain, and surely we shall be stronger than they." He heeded their voice, and did so.

26 In the spring Ben-hadad mustered the Arameans and went up to Aphek to fight against Israel. 27After the Israelites had been mustered and provisioned, they went out to engage them; the people of Israel encamped opposite them like two little flocks of goats, while the Arameans filled the country. 28A man of God approached and said to the king of Israel, "Thus says the LORD: Because the Arameans have said, 'The LORD is a god of the hills but he is not a god of the valleys,' therefore I will give all this great multitude into your hand, and you shall know that I am the LORD." 29They encamped opposite one another seven days. Then on the seventh day the battle began; the Israelites killed one hundred thousand Aramean foot soldiers in one day. 30The rest fled into the city of Aphek; and the wall fell on twenty-seven thousand men that were left.

Ben-hadad also fled, and entered the city to hide.

b Heb lacks scouts

King James

31¶ And his servants said unto him, Behold now, we have heard that the kings of the house of Israel *are* merciful kings: let us, I pray thee, put sackcloth on our loins, and ropes upon our heads, and go out to the king of Israel: peradventure he will save thy life.

32So they girded sackcloth on their loins, and *put* ropes on their heads, and came to the king of Israel, and said, Thy servant Ben-hadad saith, I pray thee, let me live. And he said, *Is* he yet alive? he *is* my brother.

33Now the men did diligently observe whether *any thing would come* from him, and did hastily catch *it:* and they said, Thy brother Ben-hadad. Then he said, Go ye, bring him. Then Ben-hadad came forth to him; and he caused him to come up into the chariot.

34And *Ben-hadad* said unto him, The cities, which my father took from thy father, I will restore; and thou shalt make streets for thee in Damascus, as my father made in Samaria. Then *said Ahab,* I will send thee away with this covenant. So he made a covenant with him, and sent him away.

35¶ And a certain man of the sons of the prophets said unto his neighbour in the word of the LORD, Smite me, I pray thee. And the man refused to smite him.

36Then said he unto him, Because thou hast not obeyed the voice of the LORD, behold, as soon as thou art departed from me, a lion shall slay thee. And as soon as he was departed from him, a lion found him, and slew him.

37Then he found another man, and said, Smite me, I pray thee. And the man smote him, so that in smiting he wounded *him.*

38So the prophet departed, and waited for the king by the way, and disguised himself with ashes upon his face.

39And as the king passed by, he cried unto the king: and he said, Thy servant went out into the midst of the battle; and, behold, a man turned aside, and brought a man unto me, and said, Keep this man: if by any means he be missing, then shall thy life be for his life, or else thou shalt pay a talent of silver.

40And as thy servant was busy here and there, he was gone. And the king of Israel said unto him, So *shall* thy judgment *be;* thyself hast decided *it.*

41And he hasted, and took the ashes away from his face; and the king of Israel discerned him that he *was* of the prophets.

42And he said unto him, Thus saith the LORD, Because thou hast let go out of *thy* hand a man whom I appointed to utter destruction, therefore thy life shall go for his life, and thy people for his people.

43And the king of Israel went to his house heavy and displeased, and came to Samaria.

21 AND IT came to pass after these things, *that* Naboth the Jezreelite had a vineyard, which *was* in Jezreel, hard by the palace of Ahab king of Samaria.

2And Ahab spake unto Naboth, saying, Give me thy vineyard, that I may have it for a garden of herbs, because it *is* near unto my house: and I will give thee for it a better vineyard than it; *or,* if it seem good to thee, I will give thee the worth of it in money.

3And Naboth said to Ahab, The LORD forbid it me, that I should give the inheritance of my fathers unto thee.

4And Ahab came into his house heavy and displeased because of the word which Naboth the Jezreelite had spoken to him: for he had said, I will not give thee the inheritance of my fathers. And he laid him down upon his bed, and turned away his face, and would eat no bread.

5¶ But Jezebel his wife came to him, and said unto him, Why is thy spirit so sad, that thou eatest no bread?

New International

31His officials said to him, "Look, we have heard that the kings of the house of Israel are merciful. Let us go to the king of Israel with sackcloth around our waists and ropes around our heads. Perhaps he will spare your life."

32Wearing sackcloth around their waists and ropes around their heads, they went to the king of Israel and said, "Your servant Ben-Hadad says: 'Please let me live.' "

The king answered, "Is he still alive? He is my brother."

33The men took this as a good sign and were quick to pick up his word. "Yes, your brother Ben-Hadad!" they said.

"Go and get him," the king said. When Ben-Hadad came out, Ahab had him come up into his chariot.

34"I will return the cities my father took from your father," Ben-Hadad offered. "You may set up your own market areas in Damascus, as my father did in Samaria."

Ahab said, "On the basis of a treaty I will set you free." So he made a treaty with him, and let him go.

A Prophet Condemns Ahab

35By the word of the LORD one of the sons of the prophets said to his companion, "Strike me with your weapon," but the man refused.

36So the prophet said, "Because you have not obeyed the LORD, as soon as you leave me a lion will kill you." And after the man went away, a lion found him and killed him.

37The prophet found another man and said, "Strike me, please." So the man struck him and wounded him.

38Then the prophet went and stood by the road waiting for the king. He disguised himself with his headband down over his eyes. 39As the king passed by, the prophet called out to him, "Your servant went into the thick of the battle, and someone came to me with a captive and said, 'Guard this man. If he is missing, it will be your life for his life, or you must pay a talent[a] of silver.' 40While your servant was busy here and there, the man disappeared."

"That is your sentence," the king of Israel said. "You have pronounced it yourself."

41Then the prophet quickly removed the headband from his eyes, and the king of Israel recognized him as one of the prophets. 42He said to the king, "This is what the LORD says: 'You have set free a man I had determined should die.[b] Therefore it is your life for his life, your people for his people.' " 43Sullen and angry, the king of Israel went to his palace in Samaria.

Naboth's Vineyard

21 SOME TIME later there was an incident involving a vineyard belonging to Naboth the Jezreelite. The vineyard was in Jezreel, close to the palace of Ahab king of Samaria. 2Ahab said to Naboth, "Let me have your vineyard to use for a vegetable garden, since it is close to my palace. In exchange I will give you a better vineyard or, if you prefer, I will pay you whatever it is worth."

3But Naboth replied, "The LORD forbid that I should give you the inheritance of my fathers."

4So Ahab went home, sullen and angry because Naboth the Jezreelite had said, "I will not give you the inheritance of my fathers." He lay on his bed sulking and refused to eat.

5His wife Jezebel came in and asked him, "Why are you so sullen? Why won't you eat?"

---

[a] *39* That is, about 75 pounds (about 34 kilograms)   [b] *42* The Hebrew term refers to the irrevocable giving over of things or persons to the LORD, often by totally destroying them.

Living Bible

31"Sir," his officers said to him, "we have heard that the kings of Israel are very merciful. Let us wear sackcloth and put ropes on our heads and go out to King Ahab to see if he will let you live."

32So they went to the king of Israel and begged, "Your servant Ben-hadad pleads, 'Let me live!' "

"Oh, is he still alive?" the king of Israel asked. "He is my brother!"

33The men were quick to grab this straw of hope and hurried to clinch the matter by exclaiming, "Yes, your brother Ben-hadad!"

"Go and get him," the king of Israel told them. And when Ben-hadad arrived, he invited him up into his chariot!

34Ben-hadad told him, "I will restore the cities my father took from your father, and you may establish trading posts in Damascus, as my father did in Samaria."

35Meanwhile, the Lord instructed one of the prophets to say to another man, "Strike me with your sword!" But the man refused.

36Then the prophet told him, "Because you have not obeyed the voice of the Lord, a lion shall kill you as soon as you leave me." And sure enough, as he turned to go a lion attacked and killed him.

37Then the prophet turned to another man and said, "Strike me with your sword." And he did, wounding him.

38The prophet waited for the king beside the road, having placed a bandage over his eyes to disguise himself.

39As the king passed by, the prophet called out to him, "Sir, I was in the battle, and a man brought me a prisoner and said, 'Keep this man; if he gets away, you must die, or else pay me $2,000!' 40But while I was busy doing something else, the prisoner disappeared!"

"Well, it's your own fault," the king replied. "You'll have to pay."

41Then the prophet yanked off the bandage from his eyes, and the king recognized him as one of the prophets. 42Then the prophet told him, "The Lord says, 'Because you have spared the man I said must die, now you must die in his place, and your people shall perish instead of his.' "

43So the king of Israel went home to Samaria angry and sullen.

21 NABOTH, A man from Jezreel, had a vineyard on the outskirts of the city near King Ahab's palace. 2One day the king talked to him about selling him this land.

"I want it for a garden," the king explained, "because it's so convenient to the palace." He offered cash or, if Naboth preferred, a piece of better land in trade.

3But Naboth replied, "Not on your life! That land has been in my family for generations."

4So Ahab went back to the palace angry and sullen. He refused to eat and went to bed with his face to the wall!

5"What in the world is the matter?" his wife, Jezebel, asked him. "Why aren't you eating? What has made you so upset and angry?"

New Revised Standard

31His servants said to him, "Look, we have heard that the kings of the house of Israel are merciful kings; let us put sackcloth around our waists and ropes on our heads, and go out to the king of Israel; perhaps he will spare your life." 32So they tied sackcloth around their waists, put ropes on their heads, went to the king of Israel, and said, "Your servant Ben-hadad says, 'Please let me live.' " And he said, "Is he still alive? He is my brother." 33Now the men were watching for an omen; they quickly took it up from him and said, "Yes, Ben-hadad is your brother." Then he said, "Go and bring him." So Ben-hadad came out to him; and he had him come up into the chariot. 34Ben-hadad said to him, "I will restore the towns that my father took from your father; and you may establish bazaars for yourself in Damascus, as my father did in Samaria." The king of Israel responded,d "I will let you go on those terms." So he made a treaty with him and let him go.

A Prophet Condemns Ahab

35 At the command of the LORD a certain member of a company of prophetse said to another, "Strike me!" But the man refused to strike him. 36Then he said to him, "Because you have not obeyed the voice of the LORD, as soon as you have left me, a lion will kill you." And when he had left him, a lion met him and killed him. 37Then he found another man and said, "Strike me!" So the man hit him, striking and wounding him. 38Then the prophet departed, and waited for the king along the road, disguising himself with a bandage over his eyes. 39As the king passed by, he cried to the king and said, "Your servant went out into the thick of the battle; then a soldier turned and brought a man to me, and said, 'Guard this man; if he is missing, your life shall be given for his life, or else you shall pay a talent of silver.' 40While your servant was busy here and there, he was gone." The king of Israel said to him, "So shall your judgment be; you yourself have decided it." 41Then he quickly took the bandage away from his eyes. The king of Israel recognized him as one of the prophets. 42Then he said to him, "Thus says the LORD, 'Because you have let the man go whom I had devoted to destruction, therefore your life shall be for his life, and your people for his people.' " 43The king of Israel set out toward home, resentful and sullen, and came to Samaria.

Naboth's Vineyard

21 LATER THE following events took place: Naboth the Jezreelite had a vineyard in Jezreel, beside the palace of King Ahab of Samaria. 2And Ahab said to Naboth, "Give me your vineyard, so that I may have it for a vegetable garden, because it is near my house; I will give you a better vineyard for it; or, if it seems good to you, I will give you its value in money." 3But Naboth said to Ahab, "The LORD forbid that I should give you my ancestral inheritance." 4Ahab went home resentful and sullen because of what Naboth the Jezreelite had said to him; for he had said, "I will not give you my ancestral inheritance." He lay down on his bed, turned away his face, and would not eat.

5 His wife Jezebel came to him and said, "Why are you so depressed that you will not eat?" 6He said to her,

---

c Heb He   d Heb lacks The king of Israel responded   e Heb of the sons
of the prophets

King James

6And he said unto her, Because I spake unto Naboth the Jezreelite, and said unto him, Give me thy vineyard for money; or else, if it please thee, I will give thee *another* vineyard for it: and he answered, I will not give thee my vineyard.

7And Jezebel his wife said unto him, Dost thou now govern the kingdom of Israel? arise, *and* eat bread, and let thine heart be merry: I will give thee the vineyard of Naboth the Jezreelite.

8So she wrote letters in Ahab's name, and sealed *them* with his seal, and sent the letters unto the elders and to the nobles that *were* in his city, dwelling with Naboth.

9And she wrote in the letters, saying, Proclaim a fast, and set Naboth on high among the people:

10And set two men, sons of Belial, before him, to bear witness against him, saying, Thou didst blaspheme God and the king. And *then* carry him out, and stone him, that he may die.

11And the men of his city, *even* the elders and the nobles who were the inhabitants in his city, did as Jezebel had sent unto them, *and* as it *was* written in the letters which she had sent unto them.

12They proclaimed a fast, and set Naboth on high among the people.

13And there came in two men, children of Belial, and sat before him: and the men of Belial witnessed against him, *even* against Naboth, in the presence of the people, saying, Naboth did blaspheme God and the king. Then they carried him forth out of the city, and stoned him with stones, that he died.

14Then they sent to Jezebel, saying, Naboth is stoned, and is dead.

15¶ And it came to pass, when Jezebel heard that Naboth was stoned, and was dead, that Jezebel said to Ahab, Arise, take possession of the vineyard of Naboth the Jezreelite, which he refused to give thee for money: for Naboth is not alive, but dead.

16And it came to pass, when Ahab heard that Naboth was dead, that Ahab rose up to go down to the vineyard of Naboth the Jezreelite, to take possession of it.

17¶ And the word of the LORD came to Elijah the Tishbite, saying,

18Arise, go down to meet Ahab king of Israel, which *is* in Samaria: behold, *he is* in the vineyard of Naboth, whither he is gone down to possess it.

19And thou shalt speak unto him, saying, Thus saith the LORD, Hast thou killed, and also taken possession? And thou shalt speak unto him, saying, Thus saith the LORD, In the place where dogs licked the blood of Naboth shall dogs lick thy blood, even thine.

20And Ahab said to Elijah, Hast thou found me, O mine enemy? And he answered, I have found *thee:* because thou hast sold thyself to work evil in the sight of the LORD.

21Behold, I will bring evil upon thee, and will take away thy posterity, and will cut off from Ahab him that pisseth against the wall, and him that is shut up and left in Israel,

22And will make thine house like the house of Jeroboam the son of Nebat, and like the house of Baasha the son of Ahijah, for the provocation wherewith thou hast provoked *me* to anger, and made Israel to sin.

23And of Jezebel also spake the LORD, saying, The dogs shall eat Jezebel by the wall of Jezreel.

24Him that dieth of Ahab in the city the dogs shall eat; and him that dieth in the field shall the fowls of the air eat.

25¶ But there was none like unto Ahab, which did sell himself to work wickedness in the sight of the LORD, whom Jezebel his wife stirred up.

26And he did very abominably in following idols, according to all *things* as did the Amorites, whom the LORD cast out before the children of Israel.

New International

6He answered her, "Because I said to Naboth the Jezreelite, 'Sell me your vineyard; or if you prefer, I will give you another vineyard in its place.' But he said, 'I will not give you my vineyard.'"

7Jezebel his wife said, "Is this how you act as king over Israel? Get up and eat! Cheer up. I'll get you the vineyard of Naboth the Jezreelite."

8So she wrote letters in Ahab's name, placed his seal on them, and sent them to the elders and nobles who lived in Naboth's city with him. 9In those letters she wrote:

> "Proclaim a day of fasting and seat Naboth in a prominent place among the people. 10But seat two scoundrels opposite him and have them testify that he has cursed both God and the king. Then take him out and stone him to death."

11So the elders and nobles who lived in Naboth's city did as Jezebel directed in the letters she had written to them. 12They proclaimed a fast and seated Naboth in a prominent place among the people. 13Then two scoundrels came and sat opposite him and brought charges against Naboth before the people, saying, "Naboth has cursed both God and the king." So they took him outside the city and stoned him to death. 14Then they sent word to Jezebel: "Naboth has been stoned and is dead."

15As soon as Jezebel heard that Naboth had been stoned to death, she said to Ahab, "Get up and take possession of the vineyard of Naboth the Jezreelite that he refused to sell you. He is no longer alive, but dead." 16When Ahab heard that Naboth was dead, he got up and went down to take possession of Naboth's vineyard.

17Then the word of the LORD came to Elijah the Tishbite: 18"Go down to meet Ahab king of Israel, who rules in Samaria. He is now in Naboth's vineyard, where he has gone to take possession of it. 19Say to him, 'This is what the LORD says: Have you not murdered a man and seized his property?' Then say to him, 'This is what the LORD says: In the place where dogs licked up Naboth's blood, dogs will lick up your blood—yes, yours!'"

20Ahab said to Elijah, "So you have found me, my enemy!"

"I have found you," he answered, "because you have sold yourself to do evil in the eyes of the LORD. 21'I am going to bring disaster on you. I will consume your descendants and cut off from Ahab every last male in Israel—slave or free. 22I will make your house like that of Jeroboam son of Nebat and that of Baasha son of Ahijah, because you have provoked me to anger and have caused Israel to sin.'

23"And also concerning Jezebel the LORD says: 'Dogs will devour Jezebel by the wall of[a] Jezreel.'

24"Dogs will eat those belonging to Ahab who die in the city, and the birds of the air will feed on those who die in the country."

25(There was never a man like Ahab, who sold himself to do evil in the eyes of the LORD, urged on by Jezebel his wife. 26He behaved in the vilest manner by going after idols, like the Amorites the LORD drove out before Israel.)

---

a 23 Most Hebrew manuscripts; a few Hebrew manuscripts, Vulgate and Syriac (see also 2 Kings 9:26) *the plot of ground at*

Living Bible

6"I asked Naboth to sell me his vineyard, or to trade it, and he refused!" Ahab told her.

7"Are you the king of Israel or not?" Jezebel demanded. "Get up and eat and don't worry about it. I'll get you Naboth's vineyard!"

8So she wrote letters in Ahab's name, sealed them with his seal, and addressed them to the civic leaders of Jezreel, where Naboth lived. 9In her letter she commanded: "Call the citizens together for fasting and prayer.b Then summon Naboth, 10and find two scoundrels who will accuse him of cursing God and the king. Then take him out and execute him."

11The city fathers followed the queen's instructions. 12They called the meeting and put Naboth on trial. 13Then two men who had no conscience accused him of cursing God and the king; and he was dragged outside the city and stoned to death. 14The city officials then sent word to Jezebel that Naboth was dead.

15When Jezebel heard the news, she said to Ahab, "You know the vineyard Naboth wouldn't sell you? Well, you can have it now! He's dead!"

16So Ahab went down to the vineyard to claim it.

17But the Lord said to Elijah, 18"Go to Samaria to meet King Ahab. He will be at Naboth's vineyard, taking possession of it. 19Give him this message from me: 'Isn't killing Naboth bad enough? Must you rob him, too? Because you have done this, dogs shall lick your blood outside the city just as they licked the blood of Naboth!'"

20"So my enemy has found me!" Ahab exclaimed to Elijah.

"Yes," Elijah answered, "I have come to place God's curse upon you because you have sold yourself to the devil.c 21The Lord is going to bring great harm to you and sweep you away; he will not let a single one of your male descendants survive! 22He is going to destroy your family as he did the family of King Jeroboam and the family of King Baasha, for you have made him very angry and have led all of Israel into sin. 23The Lord has also told me that the dogs of Jezreel shall tear apart the body of your wife, Jezebel. 24The members of your family who die in the city shall be eaten by dogs and those who die in the country shall be eaten by vultures."

25No one else was so completely sold out to the devil as Ahab, for his wife Jezebel encouraged him to do every sort of evil. 26He was especially guilty because he worshiped idols just as the Amorites did—the people whom the Lord had chased out of the land to make room for the people of Israel. 27When Ahab heard these proph-

New Revised Standard

"Because I spoke to Naboth the Jezreelite and said to him, 'Give me your vineyard for money; or else, if you prefer, I will give you another vineyard for it'; but he answered, 'I will not give you my vineyard.'" 7His wife Jezebel said to him, "Do you now govern Israel? Get up, eat some food, and be cheerful; I will give you the vineyard of Naboth the Jezreelite."

8 So she wrote letters in Ahab's name and sealed them with his seal; she sent the letters to the elders and the nobles who lived with Naboth in his city. 9She wrote in the letters, "Proclaim a fast, and seat Naboth at the head of the assembly; 10seat two scoundrels opposite him, and have them bring a charge against him, saying, 'You have cursed God and the king.' Then take him out, and stone him to death." 11The men of his city, the elders and the nobles who lived in his city, did as Jezebel had sent word to them. Just as it was written in the letters that she had sent to them, 12they proclaimed a fast and seated Naboth at the head of the assembly. 13The two scoundrels came in and sat opposite him; and the scoundrels brought a charge against Naboth, in the presence of the people, saying, "Naboth cursed God and the king." So they took him outside the city, and stoned him to death. 14Then they sent to Jezebel, saying, "Naboth has been stoned; he is dead."

15 As soon as Jezebel heard that Naboth had been stoned and was dead, Jezebel said to Ahab, "Go, take possession of the vineyard of Naboth the Jezreelite, which he refused to give you for money; for Naboth is not alive, but dead." 16As soon as Ahab heard that Naboth was dead, Ahab set out to go down to the vineyard of Naboth the Jezreelite, to take possession of it.

Elijah Pronounces God's Sentence

17 Then the word of the Lord came to Elijah the Tishbite, saying: 18Go down to meet King Ahab of Israel, who ruledd in Samaria; he is now in the vineyard of Naboth, where he has gone to take possession. 19You shall say to him, "Thus says the Lord: Have you killed, and also taken possession?" You shall say to him, "Thus says the Lord: In the place where dogs licked up the blood of Naboth, dogs will also lick up your blood."

20 Ahab said to Elijah, "Have you found me, O my enemy?" He answered, "I have found you. Because you have sold yourself to do what is evil in the sight of the Lord, 21I will bring disaster on you; I will consume you, and will cut off from Ahab every male, bond or free, in Israel; 22and I will make your house like the house of Jeroboam son of Nebat, and like the house of Baasha son of Ahijah, because you have provoked me to anger and have caused Israel to sin. 23Also concerning Jezebel the Lord said, 'The dogs shall eat Jezebel within the bounds of Jezreel.' 24Anyone belonging to Ahab who dies in the city the dogs shall eat; and anyone of his who dies in the open country the birds of the air shall eat."

25 (Indeed, there was no one like Ahab, who sold himself to do what was evil in the sight of the Lord, urged on by his wife Jezebel. 26He acted most abominably in going after idols, as the Amorites had done, whom the Lord drove out before the Israelites.)

---

b 21:9 Call the citizens together for fasting and prayer. This inquiry was perhaps ostensibly to discover whose sins had caused the famine.
c 21:20 because you have sold yourself to the devil, literally, "I have found you because you have sold yourself to that which is evil in the sight of the Lord."

d Heb who is

King James

27And it came to pass, when Ahab heard those words, that he rent his clothes, and put sackcloth upon his flesh, and fasted, and lay in sackcloth, and went softly.

28And the word of the LORD came to Elijah the Tishbite, saying,

29Seest thou how Ahab humbleth himself before me? because he humbleth himself before me, I will not bring the evil in his days: *but* in his son's days will I bring the evil upon his house.

22 AND THEY continued three years without war between Syria and Israel.

2And it came to pass in the third year, that Jehoshaphat the king of Judah came down to the king of Israel.

3And the king of Israel said unto his servants, Know ye that Ramoth in Gilead *is* ours, and we *be* still, *and* take it not out of the hand of the king of Syria?

4And he said unto Jehoshaphat, Wilt thou go with me to battle to Ramoth-gilead? And Jehoshaphat said to the king of Israel, I *am* as thou *art,* my people as thy people, my horses as thy horses.

5And Jehoshaphat said unto the king of Israel, Inquire, I pray thee, at the word of the LORD today.

6Then the king of Israel gathered the prophets together, about four hundred men, and said unto them, Shall I go against Ramoth-gilead to battle, or shall I forbear? And they said, Go up; for the Lord shall deliver *it* into the hand of the king.

7And Jehoshaphat said, *Is there* not here a prophet of the LORD besides, that we might inquire of him?

8And the king of Israel said unto Jehoshaphat, *There is* yet one man, Micaiah the son of Imlah, by whom we may inquire of the LORD: but I hate him; for he doth not prophesy good concerning me, but evil. And Jehoshaphat said, Let not the king say so.

9Then the king of Israel called an officer, and said, Hasten *hither* Micaiah the son of Imlah.

10And the king of Israel and Jehoshaphat the king of Judah sat each on his throne, having put on their robes, in a void place in the entrance of the gate of Samaria; and all the prophets prophesied before them.

11And Zedekiah the son of Chenaanah made him horns of iron: and he said, Thus saith the LORD, With these shalt thou push the Syrians, until thou have consumed them.

12And all the prophets prophesied so, saying, Go up to Ramoth-gilead, and prosper: for the LORD shall deliver *it* into the king's hand.

13And the messenger that was gone to call Micaiah spake unto him, saying, Behold now, the words of the prophets *declare* good unto the king with one mouth: let thy word, I pray thee, be like the word of one of them, and speak *that which is* good.

14And Micaiah said, *As* the LORD liveth, what the LORD saith unto me, that will I speak.

15¶ So he came to the king. And the king said unto him, Micaiah, shall we go against Ramoth-gilead to battle, or shall we forbear? And he answered him, Go, and prosper: for the LORD shall deliver *it* into the hand of the king.

16And the king said unto him, How many times shall I adjure thee that thou tell me nothing but *that which is* true in the name of the LORD?

17And he said, I saw all Israel scattered upon the hills, as sheep that have not a shepherd: and the LORD said, These have no master: let them return every man to his house in peace.

New International

27When Ahab heard these words, he tore his clothes, put on sackcloth and fasted. He lay in sackcloth and went around meekly.

28Then the word of the LORD came to Elijah the Tishbite: 29"Have you noticed how Ahab has humbled himself before me? Because he has humbled himself, I will not bring this disaster in his day, but I will bring it on his house in the days of his son."

Micaiah Prophesies Against Ahab

22 FOR THREE years there was no war between Aram and Israel. 2But in the third year Jehoshaphat king of Judah went down to see the king of Israel. 3The king of Israel had said to his officials, "Don't you know that Ramoth Gilead belongs to us and yet we are doing nothing to retake it from the king of Aram?"

4So he asked Jehoshaphat, "Will you go with me to fight against Ramoth Gilead?"

Jehoshaphat replied to the king of Israel, "I am as you are, my people as your people, my horses as your horses." 5But Jehoshaphat also said to the king of Israel, "First seek the counsel of the LORD."

6So the king of Israel brought together the prophets— about four hundred men—and asked them, "Shall I go to war against Ramoth Gilead, or shall I refrain?"

"Go," they answered, "for the Lord will give it into the king's hand."

7But Jehoshaphat asked, "Is there not a prophet of the LORD here whom we can inquire of?"

8The king of Israel answered Jehoshaphat, "There is still one man through whom we can inquire of the LORD, but I hate him because he never prophesies anything good about me, but always bad. He is Micaiah son of Imlah."

"The king should not say that," Jehoshaphat replied.

9So the king of Israel called one of his officials and said, "Bring Micaiah son of Imlah at once."

10Dressed in their royal robes, the king of Israel and Jehoshaphat king of Judah were sitting on their thrones at the threshing floor by the entrance of the gate of Samaria, with all the prophets prophesying before them. 11Now Zedekiah son of Kenaanah had made iron horns and he declared, "This is what the LORD says: 'With these you will gore the Arameans until they are destroyed.'"

12All the other prophets were prophesying the same thing. "Attack Ramoth Gilead and be victorious," they said, "for the LORD will give it into the king's hand."

13The messenger who had gone to summon Micaiah said to him, "Look, as one man the other prophets are predicting success for the king. Let your word agree with theirs, and speak favorably."

14But Micaiah said, "As surely as the LORD lives, I can tell him only what the LORD tells me."

15When he arrived, the king asked him, "Micaiah, shall we go to war against Ramoth Gilead, or shall I refrain?"

"Attack and be victorious," he answered, "for the LORD will give it into the king's hand."

16The king said to him, "How many times must I make you swear to tell me nothing but the truth in the name of the LORD?"

17Then Micaiah answered, "I saw all Israel scattered on the hills like sheep without a shepherd, and the LORD said, 'These people have no master. Let each one go home in peace.'"

Living Bible

ecies, he tore his clothing, put on rags, fasted, slept in sackcloth, and went about in deep humility.

28Then another message came to Elijah: 29"Do you see how Ahab has humbled himself before me? Because he has done this, I will not do what I promised during his lifetime; it will happen to his sons; I will destroy his descendants."

22 FOR THREE years there was no war between Syria and Israel. 2But during the third year, while King Jehoshaphat of Judah was visiting King Ahab of Israel, 3Ahab said to his officials, "Do you realize that the Syrians are still occupying our city of Ramoth-gilead? And we're sitting here without doing a thing about it!"

4Then he turned to Jehoshaphat and asked him, "Will you send your army with mine to recover Ramoth-gilead?"

And King Jehoshaphat of Judah replied, "Of course! You and I are brothers; my people are yours to command, and my horses are at your service. 5But," he added, "we should ask the Lord first, to be sure of what he wants us to do."

6So King Ahab summoned his four hundred heathena prophets and asked them, "Shall I attack Ramoth-gilead, or not?"

And they all said, "Yes, go ahead, for God will help you conquer it."

7But Jehoshaphat asked, "Isn't there a prophet of the Lord here? I'd like to ask him, too."

8"Well, there's one," King Ahab replied, "but I hate him, for he never prophesies anything good. He always has something gloomy to say. His name is Micaiah, the son of Imlah."

"Oh, come now!" Jehoshaphat replied. "Don't talk like that!"

9So King Ahab called to one of his aides, "Go get Micaiah. Hurry!"

10Meanwhile, all the prophets continued prophesying before the two kings, who were dressed in their royal robes and were sitting on thrones placed on the threshing floor near the city gate. 11One of the prophets, Zedekiah (son of Chenaanah), made some iron horns and declared, "The Lord promises that you will push the Syrians around with these horns until they are destroyed."

12And all the others agreed. "Go ahead and attack Ramoth-gilead," they said, "for the Lord will cause you to triumph!"

13The messenger who went to get Micaiah told him what the other prophets were saying, and urged him to say the same thing.

14But Micaiah told him, "This I vow, that I will say only what the Lord tells me to!"

15When he arrived, the king asked him, "Micaiah, shall we attack Ramoth-gilead, or not?"

"Why, of course! Go right ahead!" Micaiah told him. "You will have a great victory, for the Lord will cause you to conquer!"

16"How many times must I tell you to speak only what the Lord tells you to?" the king demanded.

17Then Micaiah told him, "I saw all Israel scattered upon the mountains as sheep without a shepherd. And the Lord said, 'Their king is dead; send them to their homes.'"

New Revised Standard

27 When Ahab heard those words, he tore his clothes and put sackcloth over his bare flesh; he fasted, lay in the sackcloth, and went about dejectedly. 28Then the word of the LORD came to Elijah the Tishbite: 29"Have you seen how Ahab has humbled himself before me? Because he has humbled himself before me, I will not bring the disaster in his days; but in his son's days I will bring the disaster on his house."

Joint Campaign with Judah against Aram

22 FOR THREE years Aram and Israel continued without war. 2But in the third year King Jehoshaphat of Judah came down to the king of Israel. 3The king of Israel said to his servants, "Do you know that Ramoth-gilead belongs to us, yet we are doing nothing to take it out of the hand of the king of Aram?" 4He said to Jehoshaphat, "Will you go up with me to battle at Ramoth-gilead?" Jehoshaphat replied to the king of Israel, "I am as you are; my people are your people, my horses are your horses."

5 But Jehoshaphat also said to the king of Israel, "Inquire first for the word of the LORD." 6Then the king of Israel gathered the prophets together, about four hundred of them, and said to them, "Shall I go to battle against Ramoth-gilead, or shall I refrain?" They said, "Go up; for the LORD will give it into the hand of the king." 7But Jehoshaphat said, "Is there no other prophet of the LORD here of whom we may inquire?" 8The king of Israel said to Jehoshaphat, "There is still one other by whom we may inquire of the LORD, Micaiah son of Imlah; but I hate him, for he never prophesies anything favorable about me, but only disaster." Jehoshaphat said, "Let the king not say such a thing." 9Then the king of Israel summoned an officer and said, "Bring quickly Micaiah son of Imlah." 10Now the king of Israel and King Jehoshaphat of Judah were sitting on their thrones, arrayed in their robes, at the threshing floor at the entrance of the gate of Samaria; and all the prophets were prophesying before them. 11Zedekiah son of Chenaanah made for himself horns of iron, and he said, "Thus says the LORD: With these you shall gore the Arameans until they are destroyed." 12All the prophets were prophesying the same and saying, "Go up to Ramoth-gilead and triumph; the LORD will give it into the hand of the king."

Micaiah Predicts Failure

13 The messenger who had gone to summon Micaiah said to him, "Look, the words of the prophets with one accord are favorable to the king; let your word be like the word of one of them, and speak favorably." 14But Micaiah said, "As the LORD lives, whatever the LORD says to me, that I will speak."

15 When he had come to the king, the king said to him, "Micaiah, shall we go to Ramoth-gilead to battle, or shall we refrain?" He answered him, "Go up and triumph; the LORD will give it into the hand of the king." 16But the king said to him, "How many times must I make you swear to tell me nothing but the truth in the name of the LORD?" 17Then Micaiahb said, "I saw all Israel scattered on the mountains, like sheep that have no shepherd; and the LORD said, 'These have no master; let each one go home in peace.'" 18The king of Israel

---

a 22:6 *Ahab summoned his four hundred heathen prophets,* implied. These were evidently the 400 Asherah priests left alive by Elijah at Carmel, though the 450 prophets of Baal were slain. See 18:19 and 40.

b *Heb he*

King James

18And the king of Israel said unto Jehoshaphat, Did I not tell thee that he would prophesy no good concerning me, but evil?

19And he said, Hear thou therefore the word of the LORD: I saw the LORD sitting on his throne, and all the host of heaven standing by him on his right hand and on his left.

20And the LORD said, Who shall persuade Ahab, that he may go up and fall at Ramoth-gilead? And one said on this manner, and another said on that manner.

21And there came forth a spirit, and stood before the LORD, and said, I will persuade him.

22And the LORD said unto him, Wherewith? And he said, I will go forth, and I will be a lying spirit in the mouth of all his prophets. And he said, Thou shalt persuade *him,* and prevail also: go forth, and do so.

23Now therefore, behold, the LORD hath put a lying spirit in the mouth of all these thy prophets, and the LORD hath spoken evil concerning thee.

24But Zedekiah the son of Chenaanah went near, and smote Micaiah on the cheek, and said, Which way went the spirit of the LORD from me to speak unto thee?

25And Micaiah said, Behold, thou shalt see in that day, when thou shalt go into an inner chamber to hide thyself.

26And the king of Israel said, Take Micaiah, and carry him back unto Amon the governor of the city, and to Joash the king's son;

27And say, Thus saith the king, Put this *fellow* in the prison, and feed him with bread of affliction and with water of affliction, until I come in peace.

28And Micaiah said, If thou return at all in peace, the LORD hath not spoken by me. And he said, Hearken, O people, every one of you.

29So the king of Israel and Jehoshaphat the king of Judah went up to Ramoth-gilead.

30And the king of Israel said unto Jehoshaphat, I will disguise myself, and enter into the battle; but put thou on thy robes. And the king of Israel disguised himself, and went into the battle.

31But the king of Syria commanded his thirty and two captains that had rule over his chariots, saying, Fight neither with small nor great, save only with the king of Israel.

32And it came to pass, when the captains of the chariots saw Jehoshaphat, that they said, Surely it *is* the king of Israel. And they turned aside to fight against him: and Jehoshaphat cried out.

33And it came to pass, when the captains of the chariots perceived that it *was* not the king of Israel, that they turned back from pursuing him.

34And a *certain* man drew a bow at a venture, and smote the king of Israel between the joints of the harness: wherefore he said unto the driver of his chariot, Turn thine hand, and carry me out of the host; for I am wounded.

35And the battle increased that day: and the king was stayed up in his chariot against the Syrians, and died at even: and the blood ran out of the wound into the midst of the chariot.

36And there went a proclamation throughout the host about the going down of the sun, saying, Every man to his city, and every man to his own country.

37¶ So the king died, and was brought to Samaria; and they buried the king in Samaria.

38And *one* washed the chariot in the pool of Samaria; and the dogs licked up his blood; and they washed his armour; according unto the word of the LORD which he spake.

39Now the rest of the acts of Ahab, and all that he did, and the ivory house which he made, and all the cities that he built, *are* they not written in the book of the chronicles of the kings of Israel?

40So Ahab slept with his fathers; and Ahaziah his son reigned in his stead.

New International

18The king of Israel said to Jehoshaphat, "Didn't I tell you that he never prophesies anything good about me, but only bad?"

19Micaiah continued, "Therefore hear the word of the LORD: I saw the LORD sitting on his throne with all the host of heaven standing around him on his right and on his left. 20And the LORD said, 'Who will entice Ahab into attacking Ramoth Gilead and going to his death there?'

"One suggested this, and another that. 21Finally, a spirit came forward, stood before the LORD and said, 'I will entice him.'

22" 'By what means?' the LORD asked.

" 'I will go out and be a lying spirit in the mouths of all his prophets,' he said.

" 'You will succeed in enticing him,' said the LORD. 'Go and do it.'

23"So now the LORD has put a lying spirit in the mouths of all these prophets of yours. The LORD has decreed disaster for you."

24Then Zedekiah son of Kenaanah went up and slapped Micaiah in the face. "Which way did the spirit from[a] the LORD go when he went from me to speak to you?" he asked.

25Micaiah replied, "You will find out on the day you go to hide in an inner room."

26The king of Israel then ordered, "Take Micaiah and send him back to Amon the ruler of the city and to Joash the king's son 27and say, 'This is what the king says: Put this fellow in prison and give him nothing but bread and water until I return safely.' "

28Micaiah declared, "If you ever return safely, the LORD has not spoken through me." Then he added, "Mark my words, all you people!"

Ahab Killed at Ramoth Gilead

29So the king of Israel and Jehoshaphat king of Judah went up to Ramoth Gilead. 30The king of Israel said to Jehoshaphat, "I will enter the battle in disguise, but you wear your royal robes." So the king of Israel disguised himself and went into battle.

31Now the king of Aram had ordered his thirty-two chariot commanders, "Do not fight with anyone, small or great, except the king of Israel." 32When the chariot commanders saw Jehoshaphat, they thought, "Surely this is the king of Israel." So they turned to attack him, but when Jehoshaphat cried out, 33the chariot commanders saw that he was not the king of Israel and stopped pursuing him.

34But someone drew his bow at random and hit the king of Israel between the sections of his armor. The king told his chariot driver, "Wheel around and get me out of the fighting. I've been wounded." 35All day long the battle raged, and the king was propped up in his chariot facing the Arameans. The blood from his wound ran onto the floor of the chariot, and that evening he died. 36As the sun was setting, a cry spread through the army: "Every man to his town; everyone to his land!"

37So the king died and was brought to Samaria, and they buried him there. 38They washed the chariot at a pool in Samaria (where the prostitutes bathed),[b] and the dogs licked up his blood, as the word of the LORD had declared.

39As for the other events of Ahab's reign, including all he did, the palace he built and inlaid with ivory, and the cities he fortified, are they not written in the book of the annals of the kings of Israel? 40Ahab rested with his fathers. And Ahaziah his son succeeded him as king.

---

a 24 Or Spirit of 	*b 38 Or Samaria and cleaned the weapons*

Living Bible

18Turning to Jehoshaphat, Ahab complained, "Didn't I tell you this would happen? He *never* tells me anything good. It's *always* bad."

19Then Micaiah said, "Listen to this further word from the Lord. I saw the Lord sitting on his throne, and the armies of heaven stood around him.

20"Then the Lord said, 'Who will entice Ahab to go and die at Ramoth-gilead?'

"Various suggestions were made, 21until one angel approached the Lord and said, 'I'll do it!'

22"'How?' the Lord asked.

"And he replied, 'I will go as a lying spirit in the mouths of all his prophets.'

"And the Lord said, 'That will do it; you will succeed. Go ahead.'

23"Don't you see? The Lord has put a lying spirit in the mouths of all these prophets, but the fact of the matter is that the Lord has decreed disaster upon you."

24Then Zedekiah (son of Chenaanah) walked over and slapped Micaiah on the face.

"When did the Spirit of the Lord leave me and speak to you?" he demanded.

25And Micaiah replied, "You will have the answer to your question when you find yourself hiding in an inner room."

26Then King Ahab ordered Micaiah's arrest.

"Take him to Amon, the mayor of the city, and to my son Joash. 27Tell them, 'The king says to put this fellow in jail and feed him with bread and water—and only enough to keep him alivec—until I return in peace.'"

28"If you return in peace," Micaiah replied, "it will prove that the Lord has not spoken through me." Then he turned to the people standing nearby and said, "Take note of what I've said."

29So King Ahab of Israel and King Jehoshaphat of Judah led their armies to Ramoth-gilead.

30Ahab said to Jehoshaphat, "You wear your royal robes, but I'll not wear mine!"

So Ahab went into the battle disguised in an ordinary soldier's uniform. 31For the king of Syria had commanded his thirty-two chariot captains to fight no one except King Ahab himself. 32, 33When they saw King Jehoshaphat in his royal robes, they thought, "That's the man we're after." So they wheeled around to attack him. But when Jehoshaphat shouted out to identify himself,d they turned back! 34However, someone shot an arrow at random and it struck King Ahab between the joints of his armor.

"Take me out of the battle, for I am badly wounded," he groaned to his chariot driver.

35The battle became more and more intense as the day wore on, and King Ahab went back in, propped up in his chariot with the blood from his wound running down onto the floorboards. Finally, toward evening, he died. 36, 37Just as the sun was going down the cry ran through his troops. "It's all over—return home! The king is dead!"

And his body was taken to Samaria and buried there. 38When his chariot and armor were washed beside the pool of Samaria, where the prostitutes bathed, dogs came and licked the king's blood just as the Lord had said would happen.

39The rest of Ahab's history—including the story of the ivory palace and the cities he built—is written in *The Annals of the Kings of Israel.* 40So Ahab was buried among his ancestors, and Ahaziah his son became the new king of Israel.

New Revised Standard

said to Jehoshaphat, "Did I not tell you that he would not prophesy anything favorable about me, but only disaster?"

19 Then Micaiahe said, "Therefore hear the word of the LORD: I saw the LORD sitting on his throne, with all the host of heaven standing beside him to the right and to the left of him. 20And the LORD said, 'Who will entice Ahab, so that he may go up and fall at Ramoth-gilead?' Then one said one thing, and another said another, 21until a spirit came forward and stood before the LORD, saying, 'I will entice him.' 22'How?' the LORD asked him. He replied, 'I will go out and be a lying spirit in the mouth of all his prophets.' Then the LORDe said, 'You are to entice him, and you shall succeed; go out and do it.' 23So you see, the LORD has put a lying spirit in the mouth of all these your prophets; the LORD has decreed disaster for you."

24 Then Zedekiah son of Chenaanah came up to Micaiah, slapped him on the cheek, and said, "Which way did the spirit of the LORD pass from me to speak to you?" 25Micaiah replied, "You will find out on that day when you go in to hide in an inner chamber." 26The king of Israel then ordered, "Take Micaiah, and return him to Amon the governor of the city and to Joash the king's son, 27and say, 'Thus says the king: Put this fellow in prison, and feed him on reduced rations of bread and water until I come in peace.'" 28Micaiah said, "If you return in peace, the LORD has not spoken by me." And he said, "Hear, you peoples, all of you!"

Defeat and Death of Ahab

29 So the king of Israel and King Jehoshaphat of Judah went up to Ramoth-gilead. 30The king of Israel said to Jehoshaphat, "I will disguise myself and go into battle, but you wear your robes." So the king of Israel disguised himself and went into battle. 31Now the king of Aram had commanded the thirty-two captains of his chariots, "Fight with no one small or great, but only with the king of Israel." 32When the captains of the chariots saw Jehoshaphat, they said, "It is surely the king of Israel." So they turned to fight against him; and Jehoshaphat cried out. 33When the captains of the chariots saw that it was not the king of Israel, they turned back from pursuing him. 34But a certain man drew his bow and unknowingly struck the king of Israel between the scale armor and the breastplate; so he said to the driver of his chariot, "Turn around, and carry me out of the battle, for I am wounded." 35The battle grew hot that day, and the king was propped up in his chariot facing the Arameans, until at evening he died; the blood from the wound had flowed into the bottom of the chariot. 36Then about sunset a shout went through the army, "Every man to his city, and every man to his country!"

37 So the king died, and was brought to Samaria; they buried the king in Samaria. 38They washed the chariot by the pool of Samaria; the dogs licked up his blood, and the prostitutes washed themselves in it,f according to the word of the LORD that he had spoken. 39Now the rest of the acts of Ahab, and all that he did, and the ivory house that he built, and all the cities that he built, are they not written in the Book of the Annals of the Kings of Israel? 40So Ahab slept with his ancestors; and his son Ahaziah succeeded him.

---

c *22:27 only enough to keep him alive,* literally, "as though the city were under siege." d *22:32, 33 shouted out to identify himself,* implied.

e Heb *he* f Heb lacks *in it*

King James

41¶ And Jehoshaphat the son of Asa began to reign over Judah in the fourth year of Ahab king of Israel.

42Jehoshaphat *was* thirty and five years old when he began to reign; and he reigned twenty and five years in Jerusalem. And his mother's name *was* Azubah the daughter of Shilhi.

43And he walked in all the ways of Asa his father; he turned not aside from it, doing *that which was* right in the eyes of the LORD: nevertheless the high places were not taken away; *for* the people offered and burnt incense yet in the high places.

44And Jehoshaphat made peace with the king of Israel.

45Now the rest of the acts of Jehoshaphat, and his might that he showed, and how he warred, *are* they not written in the book of the chronicles of the kings of Judah?

46And the remnant of the sodomites, which remained in the days of his father Asa, he took out of the land.

47*There was* then no king in Edom: a deputy *was* king.

48Jehoshaphat made ships of Tharshish to go to Ophir for gold: but they went not; for the ships were broken at Ezion-geber.

49Then said Ahaziah the son of Ahab unto Jehoshaphat, Let my servants go with thy servants in the ships. But Jehoshaphat would not.

50¶ And Jehoshaphat slept with his fathers, and was buried with his fathers in the city of David his father: and Jehoram his son reigned in his stead.

51¶ Ahaziah the son of Ahab began to reign over Israel in Samaria the seventeenth year of Jehoshaphat king of Judah, and reigned two years over Israel.

52And he did evil in the sight of the LORD, and walked in the way of his father, and in the way of his mother, and in the way of Jeroboam the son of Nebat, who made Israel to sin:

53For he served Baal, and worshipped him, and provoked to anger the LORD God of Israel, according to all that his father had done.

New International

Jehoshaphat King of Judah

41Jehoshaphat son of Asa became king of Judah in the fourth year of Ahab king of Israel. 42Jehoshaphat was thirty-five years old when he became king, and he reigned in Jerusalem twenty-five years. His mother's name was Azubah daughter of Shilhi. 43In everything he walked in the ways of his father Asa and did not stray from them; he did what was right in the eyes of the LORD. The high places, however, were not removed, and the people continued to offer sacrifices and burn incense there. 44Jehoshaphat was also at peace with the king of Israel.

45As for the other events of Jehoshaphat's reign, the things he achieved and his military exploits, are they not written in the book of the annals of the kings of Judah? 46He rid the land of the rest of the male shrine prostitutes who remained there even after the reign of his father Asa. 47There was then no king in Edom; a deputy ruled.

48Now Jehoshaphat built a fleet of trading ships[a] to go to Ophir for gold, but they never set sail—they were wrecked at Ezion Geber. 49At that time Ahaziah son of Ahab said to Jehoshaphat, "Let my men sail with your men," but Jehoshaphat refused.

50Then Jehoshaphat rested with his fathers and was buried with them in the city of David his father. And Jehoram his son succeeded him.

Ahaziah King of Israel

51Ahaziah son of Ahab became king of Israel in Samaria in the seventeenth year of Jehoshaphat king of Judah, and he reigned over Israel two years. 52He did evil in the eyes of the LORD, because he walked in the ways of his father and mother and in the ways of Jeroboam son of Nebat, who caused Israel to sin. 53He served and worshiped Baal and provoked the LORD, the God of Israel, to anger, just as his father had done.

---

a 48 Hebrew *of ships of Tarshish*

Living Bible

41Meanwhile, over in Judah, Jehoshaphat the son of Asa had become king during the fourth year of the reign of King Ahab of Israel. 42Jehoshaphat was thirty-five years old when he ascended the throne, and he reigned in Jerusalem for twenty-five years. His mother was Azubah, the daughter of Shilhi. 43He did as his father Asa had done, obeying the Lord in all but one thing: he did not destroy the shrines on the hills, so the people sacrificed and burned incense there. 44He also made peace with Ahab, the king of Israel. 45The rest of the deeds of Jehoshaphat and his heroic achievements and his wars are described in *The Annals of the Kings of Judah*.

46He also closed all the houses of male prostitution that still continued from the days of his father Asa. 47(There was no king in Edom at that time, only a deputy.)

48King Jehoshaphat built great freighters to sail to Ophir for gold; but they never arrived, for they were wrecked at Eziongeber. 49Ahaziah, King Ahab's son and successor, had proposed to Jehoshaphat that his men go too, but Jehoshaphat had refused the offer.

50When King Jehoshaphat died he was buried with his ancestors in Jerusalem, the city of his forefather David; and his son Jehoram took the throne. 51It was during the seventeenth year of the reign of King Jehoshaphat of Judah that Ahaziah, Ahab's son, began to reign over Israel in Samaria; and he reigned two years. 52, 53But he was not a good king, for he followed in the footsteps of his father and mother and of Jeroboam, who had led Israel into the sin of worshiping idols. So Ahaziah made the Lord God of Israel very angry.

New Revised Standard

Jehoshaphat Reigns over Judah

41 Jehoshaphat son of Asa began to reign over Judah in the fourth year of King Ahab of Israel. 42Jehoshaphat was thirty-five years old when he began to reign, and he reigned twenty-five years in Jerusalem. His mother's name was Azubah daughter of Shilhi. 43He walked in all the way of his father Asa; he did not turn aside from it, doing what was right in the sight of the LORD; yet the high places were not taken away, and the people still sacrificed and offered incense on the high places. 44Jehoshaphat also made peace with the king of Israel.

45 Now the rest of the acts of Jehoshaphat, and his power that he showed, and how he waged war, are they not written in the Book of the Annals of the Kings of Judah? 46The remnant of the male temple prostitutes who were still in the land in the days of his father Asa, he exterminated.

47 There was no king in Edom; a deputy was king. 48Jehoshaphat made ships of the Tarshish type to go to Ophir for gold; but they did not go, for the ships were wrecked at Ezion-geber. 49Then Ahaziah son of Ahab said to Jehoshaphat, "Let my servants go with your servants in the ships," but Jehoshaphat was not willing. 50Jehoshaphat slept with his ancestors and was buried with his ancestors in the city of his father David; his son Jehoram succeeded him.

Ahaziah Reigns over Israel

51 Ahaziah son of Ahab began to reign over Israel in Samaria in the seventeenth year of King Jehoshaphat of Judah; he reigned two years over Israel. 52He did what was evil in the sight of the LORD, and walked in the way of his father and mother, and in the way of Jeroboam son of Nebat, who caused Israel to sin. 53He served Baal and worshiped him; he provoked the LORD, the God of Israel, to anger, just as his father had done.

King James

THE SECOND BOOK OF THE

Kings

COMMONLY CALLED THE FOURTH

BOOK OF THE KINGS

1 THEN MOAB rebelled against Israel after the death of Ahab.

2And Ahaziah fell down through a lattice in his upper chamber that *was* in Samaria, and was sick: and he sent messengers, and said unto them, Go, inquire of Baal-zebub the god of Ekron whether I shall recover of this disease.

3But the angel of the LORD said to Elijah the Tishbite, Arise, go up to meet the messengers of the king of Samaria, and say unto them, *Is it* not because *there is* not a God in Israel, *that* ye go to inquire of Baal-zebub the god of Ekron?

4Now therefore thus saith the LORD, Thou shalt not come down from that bed on which thou art gone up, but shalt surely die. And Elijah departed.

5¶ And when the messengers turned back unto him, he said unto them, Why are ye now turned back?

6And they said unto him, There came a man up to meet us, and said unto us, Go, turn again unto the king that sent you, and say unto him, Thus saith the LORD, *Is it* not because *there is* not a God in Israel, *that* thou sendest to inquire of Baal-zebub the god of Ekron? therefore thou shalt not come down from that bed on which thou art gone up, but shalt surely die.

7And he said unto them, What manner of man *was* he which came up to meet you, and told you these words?

8And they answered him, *He was* an hairy man, and girt with a girdle of leather about his loins. And he said, It *is* Elijah the Tishbite.

9Then the king sent unto him a captain of fifty with his fifty. And he went up to him: and, behold, he sat on the top of an hill. And he spake unto him, Thou man of God, the king hath said, Come down.

10And Elijah answered and said to the captain of fifty, If I *be* a man of God, then let fire come down from heaven, and consume thee and thy fifty. And there came down fire from heaven, and consumed him and his fifty.

11Again also he sent unto him another captain of fifty with his fifty. And he answered and said unto him, O man of God, thus hath the king said, Come down quickly.

12And Elijah answered and said unto them, If I *be* a man of God, let fire come down from heaven, and consume thee and thy fifty. And the fire of God came down from heaven, and consumed him and his fifty.

13¶ And he sent again a captain of the third fifty with his fifty. And the third captain of fifty went up, and came and fell on his knees before Elijah, and besought him, and said unto him, O man of God, I pray thee, let my life, and the life of these fifty thy servants, be precious in thy sight.

14Behold, there came fire down from heaven, and burnt up the two captains of the former fifties with their fifties: therefore let my life now be precious in thy sight.

15And the angel of the LORD said unto Elijah, Go down with him: be not afraid of him. And he arose, and went down with him unto the king.

New International

2 Kings

The LORD's Judgment on Ahaziah

1 AFTER AHAB'S death, Moab rebelled against Israel. 2Now Ahaziah had fallen through the lattice of his upper room in Samaria and injured himself. So he sent messengers, saying to them, "Go and consult Baal-Zebub, the god of Ekron, to see if I will recover from this injury."

3But the angel of the LORD said to Elijah the Tishbite, "Go up and meet the messengers of the king of Samaria and ask them, 'Is it because there is no God in Israel that you are going off to consult Baal-Zebub, the god of Ekron?' 4Therefore this is what the LORD says: 'You will not leave the bed you are lying on. You will certainly die!' " So Elijah went.

5When the messengers returned to the king, he asked them, "Why have you come back?"

6"A man came to meet us," they replied. "And he said to us, 'Go back to the king who sent you and tell him, "This is what the LORD says: Is it because there is no God in Israel that you are sending men to consult Baal-Zebub, the god of Ekron? Therefore you will not leave the bed you are lying on. You will certainly die!" ' "

7The king asked them, "What kind of man was it who came to meet you and told you this?"

8They replied, "He was a man with a garment of hair and with a leather belt around his waist."

The king said, "That was Elijah the Tishbite."

9Then he sent to Elijah a captain with his company of fifty men. The captain went up to Elijah, who was sitting on the top of a hill, and said to him, "Man of God, the king says, 'Come down!' "

10Elijah answered the captain, "If I am a man of God, may fire come down from heaven and consume you and your fifty men!" Then fire fell from heaven and consumed the captain and his men.

11At this the king sent to Elijah another captain with his fifty men. The captain said to him, "Man of God, this is what the king says, 'Come down at once!' "

12"If I am a man of God," Elijah replied, "may fire come down from heaven and consume you and your fifty men!" Then the fire of God fell from heaven and consumed him and his fifty men.

13So the king sent a third captain with his fifty men. This third captain went up and fell on his knees before Elijah. "Man of God," he begged, "please have respect for my life and the lives of these fifty men, your servants! 14See, fire has fallen from heaven and consumed the first two captains and all their men. But now have respect for my life!"

15The angel of the LORD said to Elijah, "Go down with him; do not be afraid of him." So Elijah got up and went down with him to the king.

2 Kings

2 Kings

1 AFTER KING Ahab's death the nation of Moab declared its independence and refused to pay tribute to Israel any longer.

2Israel's new king, Ahaziah, had fallen off the upstairs porch of his palace at Samaria and was seriously injured. He sent messengers to the temple of the god Baal-zebub at Ekron to ask whether he would recover.

3But an angel of the Lord told Elijah the prophet,a "Go and meet the messengers and ask them, 'Is it true that there is no God in Israel? Is that why you are going to Baal-zebub, the god of Ekron, to ask whether the king will get well? 4, 5Because King Ahaziah has done this, the Lord says that he will never leave the bed he is lying on; he will surely die.' "

When Elijah told the messengers this, they returned immediately to the king.

"Why have you returned so soon?" he asked them.

6"A man came up to us," they said, "and told us to go back to the king and tell him, 'The Lord wants to know why you are asking questions of Baal-zebub, the god of Ekron. Is it because there is no God in Israel? Now, since you have done this, you will not leave the bed you are lying on; you will surely die.' "

7"Who was this fellow?" the king demanded. "What did he look like?"

8"He was a hairy man," they replied, "with a wide leather belt."

"It was Elijah the prophet!" the king exclaimed. 9Then he sent an army captain with fifty soldiers to arrest him. They found him sitting on top of a hill. The captain said to him, "O man of God, the king has commanded you to come along with us."

10But Elijah replied, "If I am a man of God, let fire come down from heaven and destroy you and your fifty men!" Then lightning struck them and killed them all!

11So the king sent another captain with fifty men to demand, "O man of God, the king says that you must come down right away."

12Elijah replied, "If I am a man of God, let fire come down from heaven and destroy you and your fifty men." And again the fire from God burned them up.

13Once more the king sent fifty men, but this time the captain fell to his knees before Elijah and pleaded with him, "O man of God, please spare my life and the lives of these, your fifty servants. 14Have mercy on us! Don't destroy us as you did the others."

15Then the angel of the Lord said to Elijah, "Don't be afraid. Go with him." So Elijah went to the king.

Elijah Denounces Ahaziah

1 AFTER THE death of Ahab, Moab rebelled against Israel.

2 Ahaziah had fallen through the lattice in his upper chamber in Samaria, and lay injured; so he sent messengers, telling them, "Go, inquire of Baal-zebub, the god of Ekron, whether I shall recover from this injury." 3But the angel of the LORD said to Elijah the Tishbite, "Get up, go to meet the messengers of the king of Samaria, and say to them, 'Is it because there is no God in Israel that you are going to inquire of Baal-zebub, the god of Ekron?' 4Now therefore thus says the LORD, 'You shall not leave the bed to which you have gone, but you shall surely die.' " So Elijah went.

5 The messengers returned to the king, who said to them, "Why have you returned?" 6They answered him, "There came a man to meet us, who said to us, 'Go back to the king who sent you, and say to him: Thus says the LORD: Is it because there is no God in Israel that you are sending to inquire of Baal-zebub, the god of Ekron? Therefore you shall not leave the bed to which you have gone, but shall surely die.' " 7He said to them, "What sort of man was he who came to meet you and told you these things?" 8They answered him, "A hairy man, with a leather belt around his waist." He said, "It is Elijah the Tishbite."

9 Then the king sent to him a captain of fifty with his fifty men. He went up to Elijah, who was sitting on the top of a hill, and said to him, "O man of God, the king says, 'Come down.' " 10But Elijah answered the captain of fifty, "If I am a man of God, let fire come down from heaven and consume you and your fifty." Then fire came down from heaven, and consumed him and his fifty.

11 Again the king sent to him another captain of fifty with his fifty. He went upb and said to him, "O man of God, this is the king's order: Come down quickly!" 12But Elijah answered them, "If I am a man of God, let fire come down from heaven and consume you and your fifty." Then the fire of God came down from heaven and consumed him and his fifty.

13 Again the king sent the captain of a third fifty with his fifty. So the third captain of fifty went up, and came and fell on his knees before Elijah, and entreated him, "O man of God, please let my life, and the life of these fifty servants of yours, be precious in your sight. 14Look, fire came down from heaven and consumed the two former captains of fifty men with their fifties; but now let my life be precious in your sight." 15Then the angel of the LORD said to Elijah, "Go down with him; do not be afraid of him." So he set out and went down with him to the king, 16and said to him, "Thus says the

---

a *1:3 Elijah the prophet*, literally, "Elijah the Tishbite."

b Gk Compare verses 9, 13: Heb *He answered*

King James

16And he said unto him, Thus saith the LORD, Forasmuch as thou hast sent messengers to inquire of Baal-zebub the god of Ekron, *is it* not because *there is* no God in Israel to inquire of his word? therefore thou shalt not come down off that bed on which thou art gone up, but shalt surely die.

17¶ So he died according to the word of the LORD which Elijah had spoken. And Jehoram reigned in his stead in the second year of Jehoram the son of Jehoshaphat king of Judah; because he had no son.

18Now the rest of the acts of Ahaziah which he did, *are* they not written in the book of the chronicles of the kings of Israel?

2 AND IT came to pass, when the LORD would take up Elijah into heaven by a whirlwind, that Elijah went with Elisha from Gilgal.

2And Elijah said unto Elisha, Tarry here, I pray thee; for the LORD hath sent me to Beth-el. And Elisha said *unto him,* As the LORD liveth, and *as* thy soul liveth, I will not leave thee. So they went down to Beth-el.

3And the sons of the prophets that *were* at Beth-el came forth to Elisha, and said unto him, Knowest thou that the LORD will take away thy master from thy head today? And he said, Yea, I know *it;* hold ye your peace.

4And Elijah said unto him, Elisha, tarry here, I pray thee; for the LORD hath sent me to Jericho. And he said, As the LORD liveth, and *as* thy soul liveth, I will not leave thee. So they came to Jericho.

5And the sons of the prophets that *were* at Jericho came to Elisha, and said unto him, Knowest thou that the LORD will take away thy master from thy head today? And he answered, Yea, I know *it;* hold ye your peace.

6And Elijah said unto him, Tarry, I pray thee, here; for the LORD hath sent me to Jordan. And he said, As the LORD liveth, and *as* thy soul liveth, I will not leave thee. And they two went on.

7And fifty men of the sons of the prophets went, and stood to view afar off: and they two stood by Jordan.

8And Elijah took his mantle, and wrapped *it* together, and smote the waters, and they were divided hither and thither, so that they two went over on dry ground.

9¶ And it came to pass, when they were gone over, that Elijah said unto Elisha, Ask what I shall do for thee, before I be taken away from thee. And Elisha said, I pray thee, let a double portion of thy spirit be upon me.

10And he said, Thou hast asked a hard thing: *nevertheless,* if thou see me *when I am* taken from thee, it shall be so unto thee; but if not, it shall not be *so.*

11And it came to pass, as they still went on, and talked, that, behold, *there appeared* a chariot of fire, and horses of fire, and parted them both asunder; and Elijah went up by a whirlwind into heaven.

12¶ And Elisha saw *it,* and he cried, My father, my father, the chariot of Israel, and the horsemen thereof. And he saw him no more: and he took hold of his own clothes, and rent them in two pieces.

13He took up also the mantle of Elijah that fell from him, and went back, and stood by the bank of Jordan;

14And he took the mantle of Elijah that fell from him, and smote the waters, and said, Where *is* the LORD God of Elijah? and when he also had smitten the waters, they parted hither and thither: and Elisha went over.

New International

16He told the king, "This is what the LORD says: Is it because there is no God in Israel for you to consult that you have sent messengers to consult Baal-Zebub, the god of Ekron? Because you have done this, you will never leave the bed you are lying on. You will certainly die!" 17So he died, according to the word of the LORD that Elijah had spoken.

Because Ahaziah had no son, Jorama succeeded him as king in the second year of Jehoram son of Jehoshaphat king of Judah. 18As for all the other events of Ahaziah's reign, and what he did, are they not written in the book of the annals of the kings of Israel?

Elijah Taken Up to Heaven

2 WHEN THE LORD was about to take Elijah up to heaven in a whirlwind, Elijah and Elisha were on their way from Gilgal. 2Elijah said to Elisha, "Stay here; the LORD has sent me to Bethel."

But Elisha said, "As surely as the LORD lives and as you live, I will not leave you." So they went down to Bethel.

3The company of the prophets at Bethel came out to Elisha and asked, "Do you know that the LORD is going to take your master from you today?"

"Yes, I know," Elisha replied, "but do not speak of it."

4Then Elijah said to him, "Stay here, Elisha; the LORD has sent me to Jericho."

And he replied, "As surely as the LORD lives and as you live, I will not leave you." So they went to Jericho.

5The company of the prophets at Jericho went up to Elisha and asked him, "Do you know that the LORD is going to take your master from you today?"

"Yes, I know," he replied, "but do not speak of it."

6Then Elijah said to him, "Stay here; the LORD has sent me to the Jordan."

And he replied, "As surely as the LORD lives and as you live, I will not leave you." So the two of them walked on.

7Fifty men of the company of the prophets went and stood at a distance, facing the place where Elijah and Elisha had stopped at the Jordan. 8Elijah took his cloak, rolled it up and struck the water with it. The water divided to the right and to the left, and the two of them crossed over on dry ground.

9When they had crossed, Elijah said to Elisha, "Tell me, what can I do for you before I am taken from you?"

"Let me inherit a double portion of your spirit," Elisha replied.

10"You have asked a difficult thing," Elijah said, "yet if you see me when I am taken from you, it will be yours—otherwise not."

11As they were walking along and talking together, suddenly a chariot of fire and horses of fire appeared and separated the two of them, and Elijah went up to heaven in a whirlwind. 12Elisha saw this and cried out, "My father! My father! The chariots and horsemen of Israel!" And Elisha saw him no more. Then he took hold of his own clothes and tore them apart.

13He picked up the cloak that had fallen from Elijah and went back and stood on the bank of the Jordan. 14Then he took the cloak that had fallen from him and struck the water with it. "Where now is the LORD, the God of Elijah?" he asked. When he struck the water, it divided to the right and to the left, and he crossed over.

---

a 17 Hebrew *Jehoram*, a variant of *Joram*

Living Bible

16"Why did you send messengers to Baal-zebub, the god of Ekron, to ask about your sickness?" Elijah demanded. "Is it because there is no God in Israel to ask? Because you have done this, you shall not leave this bed; you will surely die."

17So Ahaziah died as the Lord had predicted through Elijah, and his brother Joram became the new king—for Ahaziah did not have a son to succeed him. This occurred in the second year of the reign of King Jehoram (son of Jehoshaphat) of Judah. 18The rest of the history of Ahaziah's reign is recorded in *The Annals of the Kings of Israel*.

2 NOW THE time came for the Lord to take Elijah to heaven—by means of a whirlwind! Elijah said to Elisha as they left Gilgal, "Stay here, for the Lord has told me to go to Bethel."

But Elisha replied, "I swear to God that I won't leave you!"

So they went on together to Bethel. 3There the young prophets of Bethel Seminary came out to meet them and asked Elisha, "Did you know that the Lord is going to take Elijah away from you today?"

"Quiet!" Elisha snapped. "Of course I know it."

4Then Elijah said to Elisha, "Please stay here in Bethel, for the Lord has sent me to Jericho."

But Elisha replied again, "I swear to God that I won't leave you." So they went on together to Jericho.

5Then the students at Jericho Seminary came to Elisha and asked him, "Do you know that the Lord is going to take away your master today?"

"Will you please be quiet?" he commanded. "Of course I know it!"

6, 7Then Elijah said to Elisha, "Please stay here, for the Lord has sent me to the Jordan River."

But Elisha replied as before, "I swear to God that I won't leave you."

So they went on together and stood beside the Jordan River as fifty of the young prophets watched from a distance. 8Then Elijah folded his cloak together and struck the water with it; and the river divided and they went across on dry ground!

9When they arrived on the other side Elijah said to Elisha, "What wish shall I grant you before I am taken away?"

And Elisha replied, "Please grant me twice as much prophetic power as you have had."

10"You have asked a hard thing," Elijah replied. "If you see me when I am taken from you, then you will get your request. But if not, then you won't."

11As they were walking along, talking, suddenly a chariot of fire, drawn by horses of fire, appeared and drove between them, separating them, and Elijah was carried by a whirlwind into heaven.

12Elisha saw it and cried out, "My father! My father! The Chariot of Israel and the charioteers!"

As they disappeared from sight he tore his robe.

13, 14Then he picked up Elijah's cloak and returned to the bank of the Jordan River, and struck the water with it.

"Where is the Lord God of Elijah?" he cried out. And the water parted and Elisha went across!

New Revised Standard

LORD: Because you have sent messengers to inquire of Baal-zebub, the god of Ekron,—is it because there is no God in Israel to inquire of his word?—therefore you shall not leave the bed to which you have gone, but you shall surely die."

Death of Ahaziah

17 So he died according to the word of the LORD that Elijah had spoken. His brother,[b] Jehoram succeeded him as king in the second year of King Jehoram son of Jehoshaphat of Judah, because Ahaziah had no son. 18Now the rest of the acts of Ahaziah that he did, are they not written in the Book of the Annals of the Kings of Israel?

Elijah Ascends to Heaven

2 NOW WHEN the LORD was about to take Elijah up to heaven by a whirlwind, Elijah and Elisha were on their way from Gilgal. 2Elijah said to Elisha, "Stay here; for the LORD has sent me as far as Bethel." But Elisha said, "As the LORD lives, and as you yourself live, I will not leave you." So they went down to Bethel. 3The company of prophets[c] who were in Bethel came out to Elisha, and said to him, "Do you know that today the LORD will take your master away from you?" And he said, "Yes, I know; keep silent."

4 Elijah said to him, "Elisha, stay here; for the LORD has sent me to Jericho." But he said, "As the LORD lives, and as you yourself live, I will not leave you." So they came to Jericho. 5The company of prophets[c] who were at Jericho drew near to Elisha, and said to him, "Do you know that today the LORD will take your master away from you?" And he answered, "Yes, I know; be silent."

6 Then Elijah said to him, "Stay here; for the LORD has sent me to the Jordan." But he said, "As the LORD lives, and as you yourself live, I will not leave you." So the two of them went on. 7Fifty men of the company of prophets[c] also went, and stood at some distance from them, as they both were standing by the Jordan. 8Then Elijah took his mantle and rolled it up, and struck the water; the water was parted to the one side and to the other, until the two of them crossed on dry ground.

9 When they had crossed, Elijah said to Elisha, "Tell me what I may do for you, before I am taken from you." Elisha said, "Please let me inherit a double share of your spirit." 10He responded, "You have asked a hard thing; yet, if you see me as I am being taken from you, it will be granted you; if not, it will not." 11As they continued walking and talking, a chariot of fire and horses of fire separated the two of them, and Elijah ascended in a whirlwind into heaven. 12Elisha kept watching and crying out, "Father, father! The chariots of Israel and its horsemen!" But when he could no longer see him, he grasped his own clothes and tore them in two pieces.

Elisha Succeeds Elijah

13 He picked up the mantle of Elijah that had fallen from him, and went back and stood on the bank of the Jordan. 14He took the mantle of Elijah that had fallen from him, and struck the water, saying, "Where is the LORD, the God of Elijah?" When he had struck the water, it was parted to the one side and to the other, and Elisha went over.

---

b Gk Syr: Heb lacks *His brother*   c Heb *sons of the prophets*

King James

15And when the sons of the prophets which *were* to view at Jericho saw him, they said, The spirit of Elijah doth rest on Elisha. And they came to meet him, and bowed themselves to the ground before him.

16¶ And they said unto him, Behold now, there be with thy servants fifty strong men; let them go, we pray thee, and seek thy master: lest peradventure the spirit of the LORD hath taken him up, and cast him upon some mountain, or into some valley. And he said, Ye shall not send.

17And when they urged him till he was ashamed, he said, Send. They sent therefore fifty men; and they sought three days, but found him not.

18And when they came again to him, (for he tarried at Jericho,) he said unto them, Did I not say unto you, Go not?

19¶ And the men of the city said unto Elisha, Behold, I pray thee, the situation of this city *is* pleasant, as my lord seeth: but the water *is* naught, and the ground barren.

20And he said, Bring me a new cruse, and put salt therein. And they brought *it* to him.

21And he went forth unto the spring of the waters, and cast the salt in there, and said, Thus saith the LORD, I have healed these waters; there shall not be from thence any more death or barren *land*.

22So the waters were healed unto this day, according to the saying of Elisha which he spake.

23¶ And he went up from thence unto Beth-el: and as he was going up by the way, there came forth little children out of the city, and mocked him, and said unto him, Go up, thou bald head; go up, thou bald head.

24And he turned back, and looked on them, and cursed them in the name of the LORD. And there came forth two she bears out of the wood, and tare forty and two children of them.

25And he went from thence to mount Carmel, and from thence he returned to Samaria.

3 NOW JEHORAM the son of Ahab began to reign over Israel in Samaria the eighteenth year of Jehoshaphat king of Judah, and reigned twelve years.

2And he wrought evil in the sight of the LORD; but not like his father, and like his mother: for he put away the image of Baal that his father had made.

3Nevertheless he cleaved unto the sins of Jeroboam the son of Nebat, which made Israel to sin; he departed not therefrom.

4¶ And Mesha king of Moab was a sheepmaster, and rendered unto the king of Israel an hundred thousand lambs, and an hundred thousand rams, with the wool.

5But it came to pass, when Ahab was dead, that the king of Moab rebelled against the king of Israel.

6¶ And king Jehoram went out of Samaria the same time, and numbered all Israel.

7And he went and sent to Jehoshaphat the king of Judah, saying, The king of Moab hath rebelled against me: wilt thou go with me against Moab to battle? And he said, I will go up: I *am* as thou *art*, my people as thy people, *and* my horses as thy horses.

8And he said, Which way shall we go up? And he answered, The way through the wilderness of Edom.

9So the king of Israel went, and the king of Judah, and the king of Edom: and they fetched a compass of seven days' journey: and there was no water for the host, and for the cattle that followed them.

10And the king of Israel said, Alas! that the LORD hath called these three kings together, to deliver them into the hand of Moab!

New International

15The company of the prophets from Jericho, who were watching, said, "The spirit of Elijah is resting on Elisha." And they went to meet him and bowed to the ground before him. 16"Look," they said, "we your servants have fifty able men. Let them go and look for your master. Perhaps the Spirit of the LORD has picked him up and set him down on some mountain or in some valley."

"No," Elisha replied, "do not send them."

17But they persisted until he was too ashamed to refuse. So he said, "Send them." And they sent fifty men, who searched for three days but did not find him. 18When they returned to Elisha, who was staying in Jericho, he said to them, "Didn't I tell you not to go?"

Healing of the Water

19The men of the city said to Elisha, "Look, our lord, this town is well situated, as you can see, but the water is bad and the land is unproductive."

20"Bring me a new bowl," he said, "and put salt in it." So they brought it to him.

21Then he went out to the spring and threw the salt into it, saying, "This is what the LORD says: 'I have healed this water. Never again will it cause death or make the land unproductive.' " 22And the water has remained wholesome to this day, according to the word Elisha had spoken.

Elisha Is Jeered

23From there Elisha went up to Bethel. As he was walking along the road, some youths came out of the town and jeered at him. "Go on up, you baldhead!" they said. "Go on up, you baldhead!" 24He turned around, looked at them and called down a curse on them in the name of the LORD. Then two bears came out of the woods and mauled forty-two of the youths. 25And he went on to Mount Carmel and from there returned to Samaria.

Moab Revolts

3 JORAM[a] A SON of Ahab became king of Israel in Samaria in the eighteenth year of Jehoshaphat king of Judah, and he reigned twelve years. 2He did evil in the eyes of the LORD, but not as his father and mother had done. He got rid of the sacred stone of Baal that his father had made. 3Nevertheless he clung to the sins of Jeroboam son of Nebat, which he had caused Israel to commit; he did not turn away from them.

4Now Mesha king of Moab raised sheep, and he had to supply the king of Israel with a hundred thousand lambs and with the wool of a hundred thousand rams. 5But after Ahab died, the king of Moab rebelled against the king of Israel. 6So at that time King Joram set out from Samaria and mobilized all Israel. 7He also sent this message to Jehoshaphat king of Judah: "The king of Moab has rebelled against me. Will you go with me to fight against Moab?"

"I will go with you," he replied. "I am as you are, my people as your people, my horses as your horses."

8"By what route shall we attack?" he asked.

"Through the Desert of Edom," he answered.

9So the king of Israel set out with the king of Judah and the king of Edom. After a roundabout march of seven days, the army had no more water for themselves or for the animals with them.

10"What!" exclaimed the king of Israel. "Has the LORD called us three kings together only to hand us over to Moab?"

---

a *1* Hebrew *Jehoram*, a variant of *Joram*; also in verse 6

Living Bible

15When the young prophets of Jericho saw what had happened, they exclaimed, "The spirit of Elijah rests upon Elisha!" And they went to meet him and greeted him respectfully.

16"Sir," they said, "just say the word and fifty of our best athletes will search the wilderness for your master; perhaps the Spirit of the Lord has left him on some mountain or in some ravine."

"No," Elisha said, "don't bother."

17But they kept urging until he was embarrassed, and finally said, "All right, go ahead." Then fifty men searched for three days, but didn't find him.

18Elisha was still at Jericho when they returned. "Didn't I tell you not to go?" he growled.

19Now a delegation of the city officials of Jericho visited Elisha. "We have a problem," they told him. "This city is located in beautiful natural surroundings, as you can see; but the water is bad, and causes our women to have miscarriages."b

20"Well," he said, "bring me a new bowl filled with salt." So they brought it to him.

21Then he went out to the city well and threw the salt in and declared, "The Lord has healed these waters. They shall no longer cause death or miscarriage."

22And sure enough! The water was purified, just as Elisha had said.

23From Jericho he went to Bethel. As he was walking along the road, a gang of young men from the city began mocking and making fun of him because of his bald head. 24He turned around and cursed them in the name of the Lord; and two female bears came out of the woods and tore forty-two of them. 25Then he went to Mount Carmel and finally returned to Samaria.

3 AHAB'S SON Jehoram began his reign over Israel during the eighteenth year of the reign of King Jehoshaphatᶜ of Judah; and he reigned twelve years. His capital was Samaria. 2He was a very evil man, but not as wicked as his father and mother had been, for he at least tore down the pillar to Baal that his father had made. 3Nevertheless he still clung to the great sin of Jeroboam (the son of Nebat), who had led the people of Israel into the worship of idols.

4King Mesha of Moab and his people were sheep ranchers. They paid Israel an annual tribute of 100,000 lambs and the wool of 100,000 rams; 5but after Ahab's death, the king of Moab rebelled against Israel. 6, 7, 8So King Jehoram mustered the Israeli army and sent this message to King Jehoshaphat of Judah:

"The king of Moab has rebelled against me. Will you help me fight him?"

"Of course I will," Jehoshaphat replied. "My people and horses are yours to command. What are your battle plans?"

"We'll attack from the wilderness of Edom," Jehoram replied.

9So their two armies, now joined also by troops from Edom, moved along a roundabout route through the wilderness for seven days; but there was no water for the men or their pack animals.

10"Oh, what shall we do?" the king of Israel cried out. "The Lord has brought us here to let the king of Moab defeat us."

b 2:19 causes our women to have miscarriages, implied in vs 21. Literally, "the land is unfruitful." c 3:1 the reign of King Jehoshaphat. 1:17 says King Jehoram was the king of Judah at this time. Possibly there was a co-regency.

New Revised Standard

15 When the company of prophetsᵈ who were at Jericho saw him at a distance, they declared, "The spirit of Elijah rests on Elisha." They came to meet him and bowed to the ground before him. 16They said to him, "See now, we have fifty strong men among your servants; please let them go and seek your master; it may be that the spirit of the LORD has caught him up and thrown him down on some mountain or into some valley." He responded, "No, do not send them." 17But when they urged him until he was ashamed, he said, "Send them." So they sent fifty men who searched for three days but did not find him. 18When they came back to him (he had remained at Jericho), he said to them, "Did I not say to you, Do not go?"

Elisha Performs Miracles

19 Now the people of the city said to Elisha, "The location of this city is good, as my lord sees; but the water is bad, and the land is unfruitful." 20He said, "Bring me a new bowl, and put salt in it." So they brought it to him. 21Then he went to the spring of water and threw the salt into it, and said, "Thus says the LORD, I have made this water wholesome; from now on neither death nor miscarriage shall come from it." 22So the water has been wholesome to this day, according to the word that Elisha spoke.

23 He went up from there to Bethel; and while he was going up on the way, some small boys came out of the city and jeered at him, saying, "Go away, baldhead! Go away, baldhead!" 24When he turned around and saw them, he cursed them in the name of the LORD. Then two she-bears came out of the woods and mauled forty-two of the boys. 25From there he went on to Mount Carmel, and then returned to Samaria.

Jehoram Reigns over Israel

3 IN THE eighteenth year of King Jehoshaphat of Judah, Jehoram son of Ahab became king over Israel in Samaria; he reigned twelve years. 2He did what was evil in the sight of the LORD, though not like his father and mother, for he removed the pillar of Baal that his father had made. 3Nevertheless he clung to the sin of Jeroboam son of Nebat, which he caused Israel to commit; he did not depart from it.

War with Moab

4 Now King Mesha of Moab was a sheep breeder, who used to deliver to the king of Israel one hundred thousand lambs, and the wool of one hundred thousand rams. 5But when Ahab died, the king of Moab rebelled against the king of Israel. 6So King Jehoram marched out of Samaria at that time and mustered all Israel. 7As he went he sent word to King Jehoshaphat of Judah, "The king of Moab has rebelled against me; will you go with me to battle against Moab?" He answered, "I will; I am with you, my people are your people, my horses are your horses." 8Then he asked, "By which way shall we march?" Jehoram answered, "By the way of the wilderness of Edom."

9 So the king of Israel, the king of Judah, and the king of Edom set out; and when they had made a roundabout march of seven days, there was no water for the army or for the animals that were with them. 10Then the king of Israel said, "Alas! The LORD has summoned us, three kings, only to be handed over to Moab." 11But

d Heb sons of the prophets

King James

11But Jehoshaphat said, *Is there* not here a prophet of the LORD, that we may inquire of the LORD by him? And one of the king of Israel's servants answered and said, Here *is* Elisha the son of Shaphat, which poured water on the hands of Elijah.

12And Jehoshaphat said, The word of the LORD is with him. So the king of Israel and Jehoshaphat and the king of Edom went down to him.

13And Elisha said unto the king of Israel, What have I to do with thee? get thee to the prophets of thy father, and to the prophets of thy mother. And the king of Israel said unto him, Nay: for the LORD hath called these three kings together, to deliver them into the hand of Moab.

14And Elisha said, *As* the LORD of hosts liveth, before whom I stand, surely, were it not that I regard the presence of Jehoshaphat the king of Judah, I would not look toward thee, nor see thee.

15But now bring me a minstrel. And it came to pass, when the minstrel played, that the hand of the LORD came upon him.

16And he said, Thus saith the LORD, Make this valley full of ditches.

17For thus saith the LORD, Ye shall not see wind, neither shall ye see rain; yet that valley shall be filled with water, that ye may drink, both ye, and your cattle, and your beasts.

18And this is *but* a light thing in the sight of the LORD: he will deliver the Moabites also into your hand.

19And ye shall smite every fenced city, and every choice city, and shall fell every good tree, and stop all wells of water, and mar every good piece of land with stones.

20And it came to pass in the morning, when the meat offering was offered, that, behold, there came water by the way of Edom, and the country was filled with water.

21¶ And when all the Moabites heard that the kings were come up to fight against them, they gathered all that were able to put on armour, and upward, and stood in the border.

22And they rose up early in the morning, and the sun shone upon the water, and the Moabites saw the water on the other side *as* red as blood:

23And they said, This *is* blood: the kings are surely slain, and they have smitten one another: now therefore, Moab, to the spoil.

24And when they came to the camp of Israel, the Israelites rose up and smote the Moabites, so that they fled before them: but they went forward smiting the Moabites, even in *their* country.

25And they beat down the cities, and on every good piece of land cast every man his stone, and filled it; and they stopped all the wells of water, and felled all the good trees: only in Kir-haraseth left they the stones thereof; howbeit the slingers went about *it*, and smote it.

26¶ And when the king of Moab saw that the battle was too sore for him, he took with him seven hundred men that drew swords, to break through *even* unto the king of Edom: but they could not.

27Then he took his eldest son that should have reigned in his stead, and offered him *for* a burnt offering upon the wall. And there was great indignation against Israel: and they departed from him, and returned to *their own* land.

New International

11But Jehoshaphat asked, "Is there no prophet of the LORD here, that we may inquire of the LORD through him?"

An officer of the king of Israel answered, "Elisha son of Shaphat is here. He used to pour water on the hands of Elijah.a"

12Jehoshaphat said, "The word of the LORD is with him." So the king of Israel and Jehoshaphat and the king of Edom went down to him.

13Elisha said to the king of Israel, "What do we have to do with each other? Go to the prophets of your father and the prophets of your mother."

"No," the king of Israel answered, "because it was the LORD who called us three kings together to hand us over to Moab."

14Elisha said, "As surely as the LORD Almighty lives, whom I serve, if I did not have respect for the presence of Jehoshaphat king of Judah, I would not look at you or even notice you. 15But now bring me a harpist."

While the harpist was playing, the hand of the LORD came upon Elisha 16and he said, "This is what the LORD says: Make this valley full of ditches. 17For this is what the LORD says: You will see neither wind nor rain, yet this valley will be filled with water, and you, your cattle and your other animals will drink. 18This is an easy thing in the eyes of the LORD; he will also hand Moab over to you. 19You will overthrow every fortified city and every major town. You will cut down every good tree, stop up all the springs, and ruin every good field with stones."

20The next morning, about the time for offering the sacrifice, there it was—water flowing from the direction of Edom! And the land was filled with water.

21Now all the Moabites had heard that the kings had come to fight against them; so every man, young and old, who could bear arms was called up and stationed on the border. 22When they got up early in the morning, the sun was shining on the water. To the Moabites across the way, the water looked red—like blood. 23"That's blood!" they said. "Those kings must have fought and slaughtered each other. Now to the plunder, Moab!"

24But when the Moabites came to the camp of Israel, the Israelites rose up and fought them until they fled. And the Israelites invaded the land and slaughtered the Moabites. 25They destroyed the towns, and each man threw a stone on every good field until it was covered. They stopped up all the springs and cut down every good tree. Only Kir Hareseth was left with its stones in place, but men armed with slings surrounded it and attacked it as well.

26When the king of Moab saw that the battle had gone against him, he took with him seven hundred swordsmen to break through to the king of Edom, but they failed. 27Then he took his firstborn son, who was to succeed him as king, and offered him as a sacrifice on the city wall. The fury against Israel was great; they withdrew and returned to their own land.

---

a *11* That is, he was Elijah's personal servant.

Living Bible

11But Jehoshaphat, the king of Judah, asked, "Isn't there a prophet of the Lord with us? If so, we can find out what to do!"

"Elisha is here," one of the king of Israel's officers replied. Then he added, "He was Elijah's assistant."

12"Fine," Jehoshaphat said. "He's just the man we want."b So the kings of Israel, Judah, and Edom went to consult Elisha.

13"I want no part of you," Elisha snarled at King Jehoram of Israel. "Go to the false prophets of your father and mother!"

But King Jehoram replied, "No! For it is the Lord who has called us here to be destroyed by the king of Moab!"

14"I swear by the Lord God that I wouldn't bother with you except for the presence of King Jehoshaphat of Judah," Elisha replied. 15"Now bring me someone to play the lute." And as the lute was played, the message of the Lord came to Elisha:

16"The Lord says to fill this dry valley with trenches to hold the water he will send. 17You won't see wind nor rain, but this valley will be filled with water, and you will have plenty for yourselves and for your animals! 18But this is only the beginning, for the Lord will make you victorious over the army of Moab! 19You will conquer the best of their cities—even those that are fortified—and ruin all the good land with stones."

20And sure enough, the next day at about the time when the morning sacrifice was offered—look! Water! It was flowing from the direction of Edom, and soon there was water everywhere.

21Meanwhile, when the people of Moab heard about the three armies marching against them, they mobilized every man who could fight, old and young, and stationed themselves along their frontier. 22But early the next morning the sun looked red as it shone across the water!

23"Blood!" they exclaimed. "The three armies have attacked and killed each other! Let's go and collect the loot!"

24But when they arrived at the Israeli camp, the army of Israel rushed out and began killing them; and the army of Moab fled. Then the men of Israel moved forward into the land of Moab, destroying everything as they went. 25They destroyed the cities, threw stones on every good piece of land, stopped up the wells, and felled the fruit trees; finally, only Fort Kir-haraseth was left, but even that finally fell to them.c

26When the king of Moab saw that the battle had been lost, he led 700 of his swordsmen in a last desperate attempt to break through to the king of Edom; but he failed. 27Then he took his oldest son, who was to have been the next king, and to the horror of the Israeli army, killed him and sacrificed him as a burnt offering upon the wall. So the army of Israel turned back in disgust to their own land.

New Revised Standard

Jehoshaphat said, "Is there no prophet of the LORD here, through whom we may inquire of the LORD?" Then one of the servants of the king of Israel answered, "Elisha son of Shaphat, who used to pour water on the hands of Elijah, is here." 12Jehoshaphat said, "The word of the LORD is with him." So the king of Israel and Jehoshaphat and the king of Edom went down to him.

13 Elisha said to the king of Israel, "What have I to do with you? Go to your father's prophets or to your mother's." But the king of Israel said to him, "No; it is the LORD who has summoned us, three kings, only to be handed over to Moab." 14Elisha said, "As the LORD of hosts lives, whom I serve, were it not that I have regard for King Jehoshaphat of Judah, I would give you neither a look nor a glance." 15But get me a musician." And then, while the musician was playing, the power of the LORD came on him. 16And he said, "Thus says the LORD, 'I will make this wadi full of pools.' 17For thus says the LORD, 'You shall see neither wind nor rain, but the wadi shall be filled with water, so that you shall drink, you, your cattle, and your animals.' 18This is only a trifle in the sight of the LORD, for he will also hand Moab over to you. 19You shall conquer every fortified city and every choice city; every good tree you shall fell, all springs of water you shall stop up, and every good piece of land you shall ruin with stones." 20The next day, about the time of the morning offering, suddenly water began to flow from the direction of Edom, until the country was filled with water.

21 When all the Moabites heard that the kings had come up to fight against them, all who were able to put on armor, from the youngest to the oldest, were called out and were drawn up at the frontier. 22When they rose early in the morning, and the sun shone upon the water, the Moabites saw the water opposite them as red as blood. 23They said, "This is blood; the kings must have fought together, and killed one another. Now then, Moab, to the spoil!" 24But when they came to the camp of Israel, the Israelites rose up and attacked the Moabites, who fled before them; as they entered Moab they continued the attack.d 25The cities they overturned, and on every good piece of land everyone threw a stone, until it was covered; every spring of water they stopped up, and every good tree they felled. Only at Kir-hareseth did the stone walls remain, until the slingers surrounded and attacked it. 26When the king of Moab saw that the battle was going against him, he took with him seven hundred swordsmen to break through, opposite the king of Edom; but they could not. 27Then he took his firstborn son who was to succeed him, and offered him as a burnt offering on the wall. And great wrath came upon Israel, so they withdrew from him and returned to their own land.

---

b 3:12 He's just the man we want, literally, "the word of the Lord is with him." c 3:25 even that finally fell to them, literally, "the slingers surrounded and conquered it."

d Compare Gk Syr: Meaning of Heb uncertain

King James

4 NOW THERE cried a certain woman of the wives of the sons of the prophets unto Elisha, saying, Thy servant my husband is dead; and thou knowest that thy servant did fear the LORD: and the creditor is come to take unto him my two sons to be bondmen.

2And Elisha said unto her, What shall I do for thee? tell me, what hast thou in the house? And she said, Thine handmaid hath not any thing in the house, save a pot of oil.

3Then he said, Go, borrow thee vessels abroad of all thy neighbours, *even* empty vessels; borrow not a few.

4And when thou art come in, thou shalt shut the door upon thee and upon thy sons, and shalt pour out into all those vessels, and thou shalt set aside that which is full.

5So she went from him, and shut the door upon her and upon her sons, who brought *the vessels* to her; and she poured out.

6And it came to pass, when the vessels were full, that she said unto her son, Bring me yet a vessel. And he said unto her, *There is* not a vessel more. And the oil stayed.

7Then she came and told the man of God. And he said, Go, sell the oil, and pay thy debt, and live thou and thy children of the rest.

8¶ And it fell on a day, that Elisha passed to Shunem, where *was* a great woman; and she constrained him to eat bread. And *so* it was, *that* as oft as he passed by, he turned in thither to eat bread.

9And she said unto her husband, Behold now, I perceive that this *is* an holy man of God, which passeth by us continually.

10Let us make a little chamber, I pray thee, on the wall; and let us set for him there a bed, and a table, and a stool, and a candlestick: and it shall be, when he cometh to us, that he shall turn in thither.

11And it fell on a day, that he came thither, and he turned into the chamber, and lay there.

12And he said to Gehazi his servant, Call this Shunammite. And when he had called her, she stood before him.

13And he said unto him, Say now unto her, Behold, thou hast been careful for us with all this care; what *is* to be done for thee? wouldest thou be spoken for to the king, or to the captain of the host? And she answered, I dwell among mine own people.

14And he said, What then *is* to be done for her? And Gehazi answered, Verily she hath no child, and her husband is old.

15And he said, Call her. And when he had called her, she stood in the door.

16And he said, About this season, according to the time of life, thou shalt embrace a son. And she said, Nay, my lord, *thou* man of God, do not lie unto thine handmaid.

17And the woman conceived, and bare a son at that season that Elisha had said unto her, according to the time of life.

18¶ And when the child was grown, it fell on a day, that he went out to his father to the reapers.

19And he said unto his father, My head, my head. And he said to a lad, Carry him to his mother.

20And when he had taken him, and brought him to his mother, he sat on her knees till noon, and *then* died.

21And she went up, and laid him on the bed of the man of God, and shut *the door* upon him, and went out.

22And she called unto her husband, and said, Send me, I pray thee, one of the young men, and one of the asses, that I may run to the man of God, and come again.

23And he said, Wherefore wilt thou go to him today? *it is* neither new moon, nor sabbath. And she said, *It shall be* well.

24Then she saddled an ass, and said to her servant, Drive, and go forward; slack not *thy* riding for me, except I bid thee.

New International

The Widow's Oil

4 THE WIFE of a man from the company of the prophets cried out to Elisha, "Your servant my husband is dead, and you know that he revered the LORD. But now his creditor is coming to take my two boys as his slaves."

2Elisha replied to her, "How can I help you? Tell me, what do you have in your house?"

"Your servant has nothing there at all," she said, "except a little oil."

3Elisha said, "Go around and ask all your neighbors for empty jars. Don't ask for just a few. 4Then go inside and shut the door behind you and your sons. Pour oil into all the jars, and as each is filled, put it to one side."

5She left him and afterward shut the door behind her and her sons. They brought the jars to her and she kept pouring. 6When all the jars were full, she said to her son, "Bring me another one."

But he replied, "There is not a jar left." Then the oil stopped flowing.

7She went and told the man of God, and he said, "Go, sell the oil and pay your debts. You and your sons can live on what is left."

The Shunammite's Son Restored to Life

8One day Elisha went to Shunem. And a well-to-do woman was there, who urged him to stay for a meal. So whenever he came by, he stopped there to eat. 9She said to her husband, "I know that this man who often comes our way is a holy man of God. 10Let's make a small room on the roof and put in it a bed and a table, a chair and a lamp for him. Then he can stay there whenever he comes to us."

11One day when Elisha came, he went up to his room and lay down there. 12He said to his servant Gehazi, "Call the Shunammite." So he called her, and she stood before him. 13Elisha said to him, "Tell her, 'You have gone to all this trouble for us. Now what can be done for you? Can we speak on your behalf to the king or the commander of the army?'"

She replied, "I have a home among my own people."

14"What can be done for her?" Elisha asked.

Gehazi said, "Well, she has no son and her husband is old."

15Then Elisha said, "Call her." So he called her, and she stood in the doorway. 16"About this time next year," Elisha said, "you will hold a son in your arms."

"No, my lord," she objected. "Don't mislead your servant, O man of God!"

17But the woman became pregnant, and the next year about that same time she gave birth to a son, just as Elisha had told her.

18The child grew, and one day he went out to his father, who was with the reapers. 19"My head! My head!" he said to his father.

His father told a servant, "Carry him to his mother." 20After the servant had lifted him up and carried him to his mother, the boy sat on her lap until noon, and then he died. 21She went up and laid him on the bed of the man of God, then shut the door and went out.

22She called her husband and said, "Please send me one of the servants and a donkey so I can go to the man of God quickly and return."

23"Why go to him today?" he asked. "It's not the New Moon or the Sabbath."

"It's all right," she said.

24She saddled the donkey and said to her servant, "Lead on; don't slow down for me unless I tell you."

Living Bible

4 ONE DAY the wife of one of the seminary students came to Elisha to tell him of her husband's death. He was a man who had loved God, she said. But he had owed some money when he died, and now the creditor was demanding it back. If she didn't pay, he said he would take her two sons as his slaves.

2"What shall I do?" Elisha asked. "How much food do you have in the house?"

"Nothing at all, except a jar of olive oil," she replied. 3"Then borrow many pots and pans from your friends and neighbors!" he instructed. 4"Go into your house with your sons and shut the door behind you. Then pour olive oil from your jar into the pots and pans, setting them aside as they are filled!"

5So she did. Her sons brought the pots and pans to her, and she filled one after another! 6Soon every container was full to the brim!

"Bring me another jar," she said to her sons.

"There aren't any more!" they told her. And then the oil stopped flowing!

7When she told the prophet what had happened, he said to her, "Go and sell the oil and pay your debt, and there will be enough money left for you and your sons to live on!"

8One day Elisha went to Shunem. A prominent woman of the city invited him in to eat, and afterwards, whenever he passed that way, he stopped for dinner.

9She said to her husband, "I'm sure this man who stops in from time to time is a holy prophet. 10Let's make a little room for him on the roof; we can put in a bed, a table, a chair, and a lamp, and he will have a place to stay whenever he comes by."

11, 12Once when he was resting in the room he said to his servant Gehazi, "Tell the woman I want to speak to her."

When she came, 13he said to Gehazi, "Tell her that we appreciate her kindness to us. Now ask her what we can do for her. Does she want me to put in a good word for her to the king or to the general of the army?"

"No," she replied, "I am perfectly content."

14"What can we do for her?" he asked Gehazi afterwards.

He suggested, "She doesn't have a son, and her husband is an old man."

15, 16"Call her back again," Elisha told him.

When she returned, he talked to her as she stood in the doorway. "Next year at about this time you shall have a son!"

"O man of God," she exclaimed, "don't lie to me like that!"

17But it was true; the woman soon conceived and had a baby boy the following year, just as Elisha had predicted.

18One day when her child was older, he went out to visit his father, who was working with the reapers. 19He complained about a headache, and soon was moaning in pain. His father said to one of the servants, "Carry him home to his mother."

20So he took him home, and his mother held him on her lap; but around noontime he died. 21She carried him up to the bed of the prophet and shut the door; 22then she sent a message to her husband: "Send one of the servants and a donkey so that I can hurry to the prophet and come right back."

23"Why today?" he asked. "This isn't a religious holiday."

But she said, "It's important. I must go."

24So she saddled the donkey and said to the servant, "Hurry! Don't slow down for my comfort unless I tell you to."

New Revised Standard

Elisha and the Widow's Oil

4 NOW THE wife of a member of the company of prophets[a] cried to Elisha, "Your servant my husband is dead; and you know that your servant feared the Lord, but a creditor has come to take my two children as slaves." 2 Elisha said to her, "What shall I do for you? Tell me, what do you have in the house?" She answered, "Your servant has nothing in the house, except a jar of oil." 3 He said, "Go outside, borrow vessels from all your neighbors, empty vessels and not just a few. 4 Then go in, and shut the door behind you and your children, and start pouring into all these vessels; when each is full, set it aside." 5 So she left him and shut the door behind her and her children; they kept bringing vessels to her, and she kept pouring. 6 When the vessels were full, she said to her son, "Bring me another vessel." But he said to her, "There are no more." Then the oil stopped flowing. 7 She came and told the man of God, and he said, "Go sell the oil and pay your debts, and you and your children can live on the rest."

Elisha Raises the Shunammite's Son

8 One day Elisha was passing through Shunem, where a wealthy woman lived, who urged him to have a meal. So whenever he passed that way, he would stop there for a meal. 9 She said to her husband, "Look, I am sure that this man who regularly passes our way is a holy man of God. 10 Let us make a small roof chamber with walls, and put there for him a bed, a table, a chair, and a lamp, so that he can stay there whenever he comes to us."

11 One day when he came there, he went up to the chamber and lay down there. 12 He said to his servant Gehazi, "Call the Shunammite woman." When he had called her, she stood before him. 13 He said to him, "Say to her, Since you have taken all this trouble for us, what may be done for you? Would you have a word spoken on your behalf to the king or to the commander of the army?" She answered, "I live among my own people." 14 He said, "What then may be done for her?" Gehazi answered, "Well, she has no son, and her husband is old." 15 He said, "Call her." When he had called her, she stood at the door. 16 He said, "At this season, in due time, you shall embrace a son." She replied, "No, my lord, O man of God; do not deceive your servant."

17 The woman conceived and bore a son at that season, in due time, as Elisha had declared to her.

18 When the child was older, he went out one day to his father among the reapers. 19 He complained to his father, "Oh, my head, my head!" The father said to his servant, "Carry him to his mother." 20 He carried him and brought him to his mother; the child sat on her lap until noon, and he died. 21 She went up and laid him on the bed of the man of God, closed the door on him, and left. 22 Then she called to her husband, and said, "Send me one of the servants and one of the donkeys, so that I may quickly go to the man of God and come back again." 23 He said, "Why go to him today? It is neither new moon nor sabbath." She said, "It will be all right." 24 Then she saddled the donkey and said to her servant, "Urge the animal on; do not hold back for me unless I

---

a Heb *the sons of the prophets*

King James

25So she went and came unto the man of God to mount Carmel. And it came to pass, when the man of God saw her afar off, that he said to Gehazi his servant, Behold, *yonder is* that Shunammite:

26Run now, I pray thee, to meet her, and say unto her, *Is it* well with thee? *is it* well with thy husband? *is it* well with the child? And she answered, *It is* well.

27And when she came to the man of God to the hill, she caught him by the feet: but Gehazi came near to thrust her away. And the man of God said, Let her alone; for her soul *is* vexed within her: and the LORD hath hid *it* from me, and hath not told me.

28Then she said, Did I desire a son of my lord? did I not say, Do not deceive me?

29Then he said to Gehazi, Gird up thy loins, and take my staff in thine hand, and go thy way: if thou meet any man, salute him not; and if any salute thee, answer him not again: and lay my staff upon the face of the child.

30And the mother of the child said, *As* the LORD liveth, and *as* thy soul liveth, I will not leave thee. And he arose, and followed her.

31And Gehazi passed on before them, and laid the staff upon the face of the child; but *there was* neither voice, nor hearing. Wherefore he went again to meet him, and told him, saying, The child is not awaked.

32And when Elisha was come into the house, behold, the child was dead, *and* laid upon his bed.

33He went in therefore, and shut the door upon them twain, and prayed unto the LORD.

34And he went up, and lay upon the child, and put his mouth upon his mouth, and his eyes upon his eyes, and his hands upon his hands: and he stretched himself upon the child; and the flesh of the child waxed warm.

35Then he returned, and walked in the house to and fro; and went up, and stretched himself upon him: and the child sneezed seven times, and the child opened his eyes.

36And he called Gehazi, and said, Call this Shunammite. So he called her. And when she was come in unto him, he said, Take up thy son.

37Then she went in, and fell at his feet, and bowed herself to the ground, and took up her son, and went out.

38¶ And Elisha came again to Gilgal: and *there was* a dearth in the land; and the sons of the prophets *were* sitting before him: and he said unto his servant, Set on the great pot, and seethe pottage for the sons of the prophets.

39And one went out into the field to gather herbs, and found a wild vine, and gathered thereof wild gourds his lap full, and came and shred *them* into the pot of pottage: for they knew *them* not.

40So they poured out for the men to eat. And it came to pass, as they were eating of the pottage, that they cried out, and said, O *thou* man of God, *there is* death in the pot. And they could not eat *thereof*.

41But he said, Then bring meal. And he cast *it* into the pot; and he said, Pour out for the people, that they may eat. And there was no harm in the pot.

42¶ And there came a man from Baal-shalisha, and brought the man of God bread of the firstfruits, twenty loaves of barley, and full ears of corn in the husk thereof. And he said, Give unto the people, that they may eat.

43And his servitor said, What, should I set this before an hundred men? He said again, Give the people, that they may eat: for thus saith the LORD, They shall eat, and shall leave *thereof*.

44So he set *it* before them, and they did eat, and left *thereof*, according to the word of the LORD.

New International

25So she set out and came to the man of God at Mount Carmel.

When he saw her in the distance, the man of God said to his servant Gehazi, "Look! There's the Shunammite! 26Run to meet her and ask her, 'Are you all right? Is your husband all right? Is your child all right?' "

"Everything is all right," she said.

27When she reached the man of God at the mountain, she took hold of his feet. Gehazi came over to push her away, but the man of God said, "Leave her alone! She is in bitter distress, but the LORD has hidden it from me and has not told me why."

28"Did I ask you for a son, my lord?" she said. "Didn't I tell you, 'Don't raise my hopes'?"

29Elisha said to Gehazi, "Tuck your cloak into your belt, take my staff in your hand and run. If you meet anyone, do not greet him, and if anyone greets you, do not answer. Lay my staff on the boy's face."

30But the child's mother said, "As surely as the LORD lives and as you live, I will not leave you." So he got up and followed her.

31Gehazi went on ahead and laid the staff on the boy's face, but there was no sound or response. So Gehazi went back to meet Elisha and told him, "The boy has not awakened."

32When Elisha reached the house, there was the boy lying dead on his couch. 33He went in, shut the door on the two of them and prayed to the LORD. 34Then he got on the bed and lay upon the boy, mouth to mouth, eyes to eyes, hands to hands. As he stretched himself out upon him, the boy's body grew warm. 35Elisha turned away and walked back and forth in the room and then got on the bed and stretched out upon him once more. The boy sneezed seven times and opened his eyes.

36Elisha summoned Gehazi and said, "Call the Shunammite." And he did. When she came, he said, "Take your son." 37She came in, fell at his feet and bowed to the ground. Then she took her son and went out.

Death in the Pot

38Elisha returned to Gilgal and there was a famine in that region. While the company of the prophets was meeting with him, he said to his servant, "Put on the large pot and cook some stew for these men."

39One of them went out into the fields to gather herbs and found a wild vine. He gathered some of its gourds and filled the fold of his cloak. When he returned, he cut them up into the pot of stew, though no one knew what they were. 40The stew was poured out for the men, but as they began to eat it, they cried out, "O man of God, there is death in the pot!" And they could not eat it.

41Elisha said, "Get some flour." He put it into the pot and said, "Serve it to the people to eat." And there was nothing harmful in the pot.

Feeding of a Hundred

42A man came from Baal Shalishah, bringing the man of God twenty loaves of barley bread baked from the first ripe grain, along with some heads of new grain. "Give it to the people to eat," Elisha said.

43"How can I set this before a hundred men?" his servant asked.

But Elisha answered, "Give it to the people to eat. For this is what the LORD says: 'They will eat and have some left over.' " 44Then he set it before them, and they ate and had some left over, according to the word of the LORD.

Living Bible

25As she approached Mount Carmel, Elisha saw her in the distance and said to Gehazi, "Look, that woman from Shunem is coming. 26Run and meet her and ask her what the trouble is. See if her husband is all right and if the child is well."

"Yes," she told Gehazi, "everything is fine."

27But when she came to Elisha at the mountain she fell to the ground before him and caught hold of his feet. Gehazi began to push her away, but the prophet said, "Let her alone; something is deeply troubling her and the Lord hasn't told me what it is."

28Then she said, "It was you who said I'd have a son. And I begged you not to lie to me!"

29Then he said to Gehazi, "Quick, take my staff! Don't talk to anyone along the way. Hurry! Lay the staff upon the child's face."

30But the boy's mother said, "I swear to God that I won't go home without you." So Elisha returned with her.

31Gehazi went on ahead and laid the staff upon the child's face, but nothing happened. There was no sign of life. He returned to meet Elisha and told him, "The child is still dead."

32When Elisha arrived, the child was indeed dead, lying there upon the prophet's bed. 33He went in and shut the door behind him and prayed to the Lord. 34Then he lay upon the child's body, placing his mouth upon the child's mouth, and his eyes upon the child's eyes, and his hands upon the child's hands. And the child's body began to grow warm again! 35Then the prophet went down and walked back and forth in the house a few times; returning upstairs, he stretched himself again upon the child. This time the little boy sneezed seven times and opened his eyes!

36Then the prophet summoned Gehazi. "Call her!" he said. And when she came in, he said, "Here's your son!"

37She fell to the floor at his feet and then picked up her son and went out.

38Elisha now returned to Gilgal, but there was a famine in the land. One day as he was teaching the young prophets, he said to Gehazi, "Make some stew for supper for these men."

39One of the young men went out into the field to gather vegetables and came back with some wild gourds. He shredded them and put them into a kettle without realizing that they were poisonous. 40But after the men had eaten a bite or two they cried out, "Oh, sir, there's poison in this stew!"

41"Bring me some meal," Elisha said. He threw it into the kettle and said, "Now it's all right! Go ahead and eat!" And then it didn't harm them.

42One day a man from Baal-shalishah brought Elisha a sack of fresh corna and twenty individual loaves of barley bread made from the first grain of his harvest. Elisha told Gehazi to use it to feed the young prophets.

43"What?" Gehazi exclaimed. "Feed one hundred men with only this?"

But Elisha said, "Go ahead, for the Lord says there will be plenty for all, and some will even be left over!"

44And sure enough, there was, just as the Lord had said!

New Revised Standard

tell you." 25So she set out, and came to the man of God at Mount Carmel.

When the man of God saw her coming, he said to Gehazi his servant, "Look, there is the Shunammite woman; 26run at once to meet her, and say to her, Are you all right? Is your husband all right? Is the child all right?" She answered, "It is all right." 27When she came to the man of God at the mountain, she caught hold of his feet. Gehazi approached to push her away. But the man of God said, "Let her alone, for she is in bitter distress; the Lord has hidden it from me and has not told me." 28Then she said, "Did I ask my lord for a son? Did I not say, Do not mislead me?" 29He said to Gehazi, "Gird up your loins, and take my staff in your hand, and go. If you meet anyone, give no greeting, and if anyone greets you, do not answer; and lay my staff on the face of the child." 30Then the mother of the child said, "As the Lord lives, and as you yourself live, I will not leave without you." So he rose up and followed her. 31Gehazi went on ahead and laid the staff on the face of the child, but there was no sound or sign of life. He came back to meet him and told him, "The child has not awakened."

32 When Elisha came into the house, he saw the child lying dead on his bed. 33So he went in and closed the door on the two of them, and prayed to the Lord. 34Then he got up on the bedb and lay upon the child, putting his mouth upon his mouth, his eyes upon his eyes, and his hands upon his hands; and while he lay bent over him, the flesh of the child became warm. 35He got down, walked once to and fro in the room, then got up again and bent over him; the child sneezed seven times, and the child opened his eyes. 36Elishac summoned Gehazi and said, "Call the Shunammite woman." So he called her. When she came to him, he said, "Take your son." 37She came and fell at his feet, bowing to the ground; then she took her son and left.

Elisha Purifies the Pot of Stew

38 When Elisha returned to Gilgal, there was a famine in the land. As the company of prophets wasd sitting before him, he said to his servant, "Put the large pot on, and make some stew for the company of prophets."e 39One of them went out into the field to gather herbs; he found a wild vine and gathered from it a lapful of wild gourds, and came and cut them up into the pot of stew, not knowing what they were. 40They served some for the men to eat. But while they were eating the stew, they cried out, "O man of God, there is death in the pot!" They could not eat it. 41He said, "Then bring some flour." He threw it into the pot, and said, "Serve the people and let them eat." And there was nothing harmful in the pot.

Elisha Feeds One Hundred Men

42 A man came from Baal-shalishah, bringing food from the first fruits to the man of God: twenty loaves of barley and fresh ears of grain in his sack. Elisha said, "Give it to the people and let them eat." 43But his servant said, "How can I set this before a hundred people?" So he repeated, "Give it to the people and let them eat, for thus says the Lord, 'They shall eat and have some left.' " 44He set it before them, they ate, and had some left, according to the word of the Lord.

---

a 4:42 a sack of fresh corn, literally, "fresh grain."

b Heb lacks on the bed   c Heb he   d Heb sons of the prophets were   e Heb sons of the prophets

King James

5 NOW NAAMAN, captain of the host of the king of Syria, was a great man with his master, and honourable, because by him the LORD had given deliverance unto Syria: he was also a mighty man in valour, *but he was* a leper.

2And the Syrians had gone out by companies, and had brought away captive out of the land of Israel a little maid; and she waited on Naaman's wife.

3And she said unto her mistress, Would God my lord *were* with the prophet that *is* in Samaria! for he would recover him of his leprosy.

4And *one* went in, and told his lord, saying, Thus and thus said the maid that *is* of the land of Israel.

5And the king of Syria said, Go to, go, and I will send a letter unto the king of Israel. And he departed, and took with him ten talents of silver, and six thousand *pieces* of gold, and ten changes of raiment.

6And he brought the letter to the king of Israel, saying, Now when this letter is come unto thee, behold, I have *therewith* sent Naaman my servant to thee, that thou mayest recover him of his leprosy.

7And it came to pass, when the king of Israel had read the letter, that he rent his clothes, and said, *Am* I God, to kill and to make alive, that this man doth send unto me to recover a man of his leprosy? wherefore consider, I pray you, and see how he seeketh a quarrel against me.

8¶ And it was *so,* when Elisha the man of God had heard that the king of Israel had rent his clothes, that he sent to the king, saying, Wherefore hast thou rent thy clothes? let him come now to me, and he shall know that there is a prophet in Israel.

9So Naaman came with his horses and with his chariot, and stood at the door of the house of Elisha.

10And Elisha sent a messenger unto him, saying, Go and wash in Jordan seven times, and thy flesh shall come again to thee, and thou shalt be clean.

11But Naaman was wroth, and went away, and said, Behold, I thought, He will surely come out to me, and stand, and call on the name of the LORD his God, and strike his hand over the place, and recover the leper.

12*Are* not Abana and Pharpar, rivers of Damascus, better than all the waters of Israel? may I not wash in them, and be clean? So he turned and went away in a rage.

13And his servants came near, and spake unto him, and said, My father, *if* the prophet had bid thee *do some* great thing, wouldest thou not have done *it?* how much rather then, when he saith to thee, Wash, and be clean?

14Then went he down, and dipped himself seven times in Jordan, according to the saying of the man of God: and his flesh came again like unto the flesh of a little child, and he was clean.

15¶ And he returned to the man of God, he and all his company, and came, and stood before him: and he said, Behold, now I know that *there is* no God in all the earth, but in Israel: now therefore, I pray thee, take a blessing of thy servant.

16But he said, As the LORD liveth, before whom I stand, I will receive none. And he urged him to take *it;* but he refused.

17And Naaman said, Shall there not then, I pray thee, be given to thy servant two mules' burden of earth? for thy servant will henceforth offer neither burnt offering nor sacrifice unto other gods, but unto the LORD.

18In this thing the LORD pardon thy servant, *that* when my master goeth into the house of Rimmon to worship there, and he leaneth on my hand, and I bow myself in the house of Rimmon: when I bow down myself in the house of Rimmon, the LORD pardon thy servant in this thing.

19And he said unto him, Go in peace. So he departed from him a little way.

New International

Naaman Healed of Leprosy

5 NOW NAAMAN was commander of the army of the king of Aram. He was a great man in the sight of his master and highly regarded, because through him the LORD had given victory to Aram. He was a valiant soldier, but he had leprosy.a

2Now bands from Aram had gone out and had taken captive a young girl from Israel, and she served Naaman's wife. 3She said to her mistress, "If only my master would see the prophet who is in Samaria! He would cure him of his leprosy."

4Naaman went to his master and told him what the girl from Israel had said. 5"By all means, go," the king of Aram replied. "I will send a letter to the king of Israel." So Naaman left, taking with him ten talentsb of silver, six thousand shekelsc of gold and ten sets of clothing. 6The letter that he took to the king of Israel read: "With this letter I am sending my servant Naaman to you so that you may cure him of his leprosy."

7As soon as the king of Israel read the letter, he tore his robes and said, "Am I God? Can I kill and bring back to life? Why does this fellow send someone to me to be cured of his leprosy? See how he is trying to pick a quarrel with me!"

8When Elisha the man of God heard that the king of Israel had torn his robes, he sent him this message: "Why have you torn your robes? Have the man come to me and he will know that there is a prophet in Israel." 9So Naaman went with his horses and chariots and stopped at the door of Elisha's house. 10Elisha sent a messenger to say to him, "Go, wash yourself seven times in the Jordan, and your flesh will be restored and you will be cleansed."

11But Naaman went away angry and said, "I thought that he would surely come out to me and stand and call on the name of the LORD his God, wave his hand over the spot and cure me of my leprosy. 12Are not Abana and Pharpar, the rivers of Damascus, better than any of the waters of Israel? Couldn't I wash in them and be cleansed?" So he turned and went off in a rage.

13Naaman's servants went to him and said, "My father, if the prophet had told you to do some great thing, would you not have done it? How much more, then, when he tells you, 'Wash and be cleansed'!" 14So he went down and dipped himself in the Jordan seven times, as the man of God had told him, and his flesh was restored and became clean like that of a young boy.

15Then Naaman and all his attendants went back to the man of God. He stood before him and said, "Now I know that there is no God in all the world except in Israel. Please accept now a gift from your servant."

16The prophet answered, "As surely as the LORD lives, whom I serve, I will not accept a thing." And even though Naaman urged him, he refused.

17"If you will not," said Naaman, "please let me, your servant, be given as much earth as a pair of mules can carry, for your servant will never again make burnt offerings and sacrifices to any other god but the LORD. 18But may the LORD forgive your servant for this one thing: When my master enters the temple of Rimmon to bow down and he is leaning on my arm and I bow there also—when I bow down in the temple of Rimmon, may the LORD forgive your servant for this."

19"Go in peace," Elisha said.

After Naaman had traveled some distance, 20Gehazi,

---

a *1* The Hebrew word was used for various diseases affecting the skin—not necessarily leprosy; also in verses 3, 6, 7, 11 and 27.   b *5* That is, about 750 pounds (about 340 kilograms)   c *5* That is, about 150 pounds (about 70 kilograms)

Living Bible

5 THE KING of Syria had high admiration for Naaman, the commander-in-chief of his army, for he had led his troops to many glorious victories. So he was a great hero, but he was a leper. 2Bands of Syrians had invaded the land of Israel and among their captives was a little girl who had been given to Naaman's wife as a maid.

3One day the little girl said to her mistress, "I wish my master would go to see the prophet in Samaria. He would heal him of his leprosy!"

4Naaman told the king what the little girl had said.

5"Go and visit the prophet," the king told him. "I will send a letter of introduction for you to carry to the king of Israel."

So Naaman started out, taking gifts of $20,000 in silver, $60,000 in gold, and ten suits of clothing. 6The letter to the king of Israel said: "The man bringing this letter is my servant Naaman; I want you to heal him of his leprosy."

7When the king of Israel read it, he tore his clothes and said, "This man sends me a leper to heal! Am I God, that I can kill and give life? He is only trying to get an excuse to invade us again."

8But when Elisha the prophet heard about the king of Israel's plight, he sent this message to him: "Why are you so upset? Send Naaman to me, and he will learn that there is a true prophet of God here in Israel."

9So Naaman arrived with his horses and chariots and stood at the door of Elisha's home. 10Elisha sent a messenger out to tell him to go and wash in the Jordan River seven times and he would be healed of every trace of his leprosy! 11But Naaman was angry and stalked away. "Look," he said, "I thought at least he would come out and talk to me! I expected him to wave his hand over the leprosy and call upon the name of the Lord his God, and heal me! 12Aren't the Abana River and Pharpar River of Damascus better than all the rivers of Israel put together? If it's rivers I need, I'll wash at home and get rid of my leprosy." So he went away in a rage.

13But his officers tried to reason with him and said, "If the prophet had told you to do some great thing, wouldn't you have done it? So you should certainly obey him when he says simply to go and wash and be cured!"

14So Naaman went down to the Jordan River and dipped himself seven times, as the prophet had told him to. And his flesh became as healthy as a little child's, and he was healed! 15Then he and his entire party went back to find the prophet; they stood humbly before him and Naaman said, "I know at last that there is no God in all the world except in Israel; now please accept my gifts."

16But Elisha replied, "I swear by Jehovah my God that I will not accept them."

Naaman urged him to take them, but he absolutely refused. 17"Well," Naaman said, "all right. But please give me two muleloads of earth to take back with me, for from now on I will never again offer any burnt offerings or sacrifices to any other God except the Lord.d 18However, may the Lord pardon me this one thing— when my master the king goes into the temple of the god Rimmon to worship there and leans on my arm, may the Lord pardon me when I bow too."

19"All right," Elisha said. So Naaman started home again.

New Revised Standard

The Healing of Naaman

5 NAAMAN, COMMANDER of the army of the king of Aram, was a great man and in high favor with his master, because by him the LORD had given victory to Aram. The man, though a mighty warrior, suffered from leprosy.e 2Now the Arameans on one of their raids had taken a young girl captive from the land of Israel, and she served Naaman's wife. 3She said to her mistress, "If only my lord were with the prophet who is in Samaria! He would cure him of his leprosy."e 4So Naamanf went in and told his lord just what the girl from the land of Israel had said. 5And the king of Aram said, "Go then, and I will send along a letter to the king of Israel."

He went, taking with him ten talents of silver, six thousand shekels of gold, and ten sets of garments. 6He brought the letter to the king of Israel, which read, "When this letter reaches you, know that I have sent to you my servant Naaman, that you may cure him of his leprosy."e 7When the king of Israel read the letter, he tore his clothes and said, "Am I God, to give death or life, that this man sends word to me to cure a man of his leprosy?e Just look and see how he is trying to pick a quarrel with me."

8 But when Elisha the man of God heard that the king of Israel had torn his clothes, he sent a message to the king, "Why have you torn your clothes? Let him come to me, that he may learn that there is a prophet in Israel." 9So Naaman came with his horses and chariots, and halted at the entrance of Elisha's house. 10Elisha sent a messenger to him, saying, "Go, wash in the Jordan seven times, and your flesh shall be restored and you shall be clean." 11But Naaman became angry and went away, saying, "I thought that for me he would surely come out, and stand and call on the name of the LORD his God, and would wave his hand over the spot, and cure the leprosy!e 12Are not Abanag and Pharpar, the rivers of Damascus, better than all the waters of Israel? Could I not wash in them, and be clean?" He turned and went away in a rage. 13But his servants approached and said to him, "Father, if the prophet had commanded you to do something difficult, would you not have done it? How much more, when all he said to you was, 'Wash, and be clean'?" 14So he went down and immersed himself seven times in the Jordan, according to the word of the man of God; his flesh was restored like the flesh of a young boy, and he was clean.

15 Then he returned to the man of God, he and all his company; he came and stood before him and said, "Now I know that there is no God in all the earth except in Israel; please accept a present from your servant." 16But he said, "As the LORD lives, whom I serve, I will accept nothing!" He urged him to accept, but he refused. 17Then Naaman said, "If not, please let two mule-loads of earth be given to your servant; for your servant will no longer offer burnt offering or sacrifice to any god except the LORD. 18But may the LORD pardon your servant on this one count: when my master goes into the house of Rimmon to worship there, leaning on my arm, and I bow down in the house of Rimmon, when I do bow down in the house of Rimmon, may the LORD pardon your servant on this one count." 19He said to him, "Go in peace."

Gehazi's Greed

But when Naaman had gone from him a short distance, 20Gehazi, the servant of Elisha the man of God,

---

d 5:17 two muleloads of earth, etc. Thus even in a foreign land Naaman could worship God on Israel's soil.

e A term for several skin diseases; precise meaning uncertain f Heb he
g Another reading is Amana

King James

20¶ But Gehazi, the servant of Elisha the man of God, said, Behold, my master hath spared Naaman this Syrian, in not receiving at his hands that which he brought: but, *as* the LORD liveth, I will run after him, and take somewhat of him.

21So Gehazi followed after Naaman. And when Naaman saw *him* running after him, he lighted down from the chariot to meet him, and said, *Is* all well?

22And he said, All *is* well. My master hath sent me, saying, Behold, even now there be come to me from mount Ephraim two young men of the sons of the prophets: give them, I pray thee, a talent of silver, and two changes of garments.

23And Naaman said, Be content, take two talents. And he urged him, and bound two talents of silver in two bags, with two changes of garments, and laid *them* upon two of his servants; and they bare *them* before him.

24And when he came to the tower, he took *them* from their hand, and bestowed *them* in the house: and he let the men go, and they departed.

25But he went in, and stood before his master. And Elisha said unto him, Whence *comest thou,* Gehazi? And he said, Thy servant went no whither.

26And he said unto him, Went not mine heart *with thee,* when the man turned again from his chariot to meet thee? *Is it* a time to receive money, and to receive garments, and oliveyards, and vineyards, and sheep, and oxen, and menservants, and maidservants?

27The leprosy therefore of Naaman shall cleave unto thee, and unto thy seed for ever. And he went out from his presence a leper *as white* as snow.

6 AND THE sons of the prophets said unto Elisha, Behold now, the place where we dwell with thee is too strait for us.

2Let us go, we pray thee, unto Jordan, and take thence every man a beam, and let us make us a place there, where we may dwell. And he answered, Go ye.

3And one said, Be content, I pray thee, and go with thy servants. And he answered, I will go.

4So he went with them. And when they came to Jordan, they cut down wood.

5But as one was felling a beam, the axe head fell into the water: and he cried, and said, Alas, master! for it was borrowed.

6And the man of God said, Where fell it? And he showed him the place. And he cut down a stick, and cast *it* in thither; and the iron did swim.

7Therefore said he, Take *it* up to thee. And he put out his hand, and took it.

8¶ Then the king of Syria warred against Israel, and took counsel with his servants, saying, In such and such a place *shall be* my camp.

9And the man of God sent unto the king of Israel, saying, Beware that thou pass not such a place; for thither the Syrians are come down.

10And the king of Israel sent to the place which the man of God told him and warned him of, and saved himself there, not once nor twice.

11Therefore the heart of the king of Syria was sore troubled for this thing; and he called his servants, and said unto them, Will ye not show me which of us *is* for the king of Israel?

12And one of his servants said, None, my lord, O king: but Elisha, the prophet that *is* in Israel, telleth the king of Israel the words that thou speakest in thy bedchamber.

New International

the servant of Elisha the man of God, said to himself, "My master was too easy on Naaman, this Aramean, by not accepting from him what he brought. As surely as the LORD lives, I will run after him and get something from him."

21So Gehazi hurried after Naaman. When Naaman saw him running toward him, he got down from the chariot to meet him. "Is everything all right?" he asked.

22"Everything is all right," Gehazi answered. "My master sent me to say, 'Two young men from the company of the prophets have just come to me from the hill country of Ephraim. Please give them a talent[a] of silver and two sets of clothing.'"

23"By all means, take two talents," said Naaman. He urged Gehazi to accept them, and then tied up the two talents of silver in two bags, with two sets of clothing. He gave them to two of his servants, and they carried them ahead of Gehazi. 24When Gehazi came to the hill, he took the things from the servants and put them away in the house. He sent the men away and they left. 25Then he went in and stood before his master Elisha.

"Where have you been, Gehazi?" Elisha asked.

"Your servant didn't go anywhere," Gehazi answered.

26But Elisha said to him, "Was not my spirit with you when the man got down from his chariot to meet you? Is this the time to take money, or to accept clothes, olive groves, vineyards, flocks, herds, or menservants and maidservants? 27Naaman's leprosy will cling to you and to your descendants forever." Then Gehazi went from Elisha's presence and he was leprous, as white as snow.

An Axhead Floats

6 THE COMPANY of the prophets said to Elisha, "Look, the place where we meet with you is too small for us. 2Let us go to the Jordan, where each of us can get a pole; and let us build a place there for us to live."

And he said, "Go."

3Then one of them said, "Won't you please come with your servants?"

"I will," Elisha replied. 4And he went with them. They went to the Jordan and began to cut down trees. 5As one of them was cutting down a tree, the iron axhead fell into the water. "Oh, my lord," he cried out, "it was borrowed!"

6The man of God asked, "Where did it fall?" When he showed him the place, Elisha cut a stick and threw it there, and made the iron float. 7"Lift it out," he said. Then the man reached out his hand and took it.

Elisha Traps Blinded Arameans

8Now the king of Aram was at war with Israel. After conferring with his officers, he said, "I will set up my camp in such and such a place."

9The man of God sent word to the king of Israel: "Beware of passing that place, because the Arameans are going down there." 10So the king of Israel checked on the place indicated by the man of God. Time and again Elisha warned the king, so that he was on his guard in such places.

11This enraged the king of Aram. He summoned his officers and demanded of them, "Will you not tell me which of us is on the side of the king of Israel?"

12"None of us, my lord the king," said one of his officers, "but Elisha, the prophet who is in Israel, tells the king of Israel the very words you speak in your bedroom."

---

a 22 That is, about 75 pounds (about 34 kilograms)

Living Bible

20But Gehazi, Elisha's servant, said to himself, "My master shouldn't have let this fellow get away without taking his gifts. I will chase after him and get something from him."

21So Gehazi caught up with him. When Naaman saw him coming, he jumped down from his chariot and ran to meet him.

"Is everything all right?" he asked.

22"Yes," he said, "but my master has sent me to tell you that two young prophets from the hills of Ephraim have just arrived, and he would like $2,000 in silver and two suits to give to them."

23"Take $4,000," Naaman insisted. He gave him two expensive robes, tied up the money in two bags, and gave them to two of his servants to carry back with Gehazi. 24But when they arrived at the hill where Elisha lived,b Gehazi took the bags from the servants and sent the men back. Then he hid the money in his house.

25When he went in to his master, Elisha asked him, "Where have you been, Gehazi?"

"I haven't been anywhere," he replied.

26But Elisha asked him, "Don't you realize that I was there in thought when Naaman stepped down from his chariot to meet you? Is this the time to receive money and clothing and olive farms and vineyards and sheep and oxen and servants? 27Because you have done this, Naaman's leprosy shall be upon you and upon your children and your children's children forever."

And Gehazi walked from the room a leper, his skin as white as snow.

6 ONE DAY the seminary students came to Elisha and told him, "As you can see, our dormitory is too small. Tell us, as our president, whether we can build a new one down beside the Jordan River, where there are plenty of logs."

"All right," he told them, "go ahead."

3"Please, sir, come with us," someone suggested.

"I will," he said.

4When they arrived at the Jordan, they began cutting down trees; 5but as one of them was chopping, his ax-head fell into the river.

"Oh, sir," he cried, "it was borrowed!"

6"Where did it fall?" the prophet asked. The youth showed him the place, and Elisha cut a stick and threw it into the water; and the axhead rose to the surface and floated! 7"Grab it," Elisha said to him; and he did.

8Once when the king of Syria was at war with Israel, he said to his officers, "We will mobilize our forces at —" (naming the place).

9Immediately Elisha warned the king of Israel, "Don't go near —" (naming the same place) "for the Syrians are planning to mobilize their troops there!"

10The king sent a scout to see if Elisha was right, and sure enough, he had saved him from disaster. This happened several times.

11The king of Syria was puzzled. He called together his officers and demanded, "Which of you is the traitor? Who has been informing the king of Israel about my plans?"

12"It's not us, sir," one of the officers replied. "Elisha, the prophet, tells the king of Israel even the words you speak in the privacy of your bedroom!"

New Revised Standard

thought, "My master has let that Aramean Naaman off too lightly by not accepting from him what he offered. As the LORD lives, I will run after him and get something out of him." 21So Gehazi went after Naaman. When Naaman saw someone running after him, he jumped down from the chariot to meet him and said, "Is everything all right?" 22He replied, "Yes, but my master has sent me to say, 'Two members of a company of prophetsc have just come to me from the hill country of Ephraim; please give them a talent of silver and two changes of clothing.' " 23Naaman said, "Please accept two talents." He urged him, and tied up two talents of silver in two bags, with two changes of clothing, and gave them to two of his servants, who carried them in front of Gehazi.d 24When he came to the citadel, he took the bagse from them, and stored them inside; he dismissed the men, and they left.

25 He went in and stood before his master; and Elisha said to him, "Where have you been, Gehazi?" He answered, "Your servant has not gone anywhere at all." 26But he said to him, "Did I not go with you in spirit when someone left his chariot to meet you? Is this a time to accept money and to accept clothing, olive orchards and vineyards, sheep and oxen, and male and female slaves? 27Therefore the leprosyf of Naaman shall cling to you, and to your descendants forever." So he left his presence leprous,f as white as snow.

The Miracle of the Ax Head

6 NOW THE company of prophetsc said to Elisha, "As you see, the place where we live under your charge is too small for us. 2Let us go to the Jordan, and let us collect logs there, one for each of us, and build a place there for us to live." He answered, "Do so." 3Then one of them said, "Please come with your servants." And he answered, "I will." 4So he went with them. When they came to the Jordan, they cut down trees. 5But as one was felling a log, his ax head fell into the water; he cried out, "Alas, master! It was borrowed." 6Then the man of God said, "Where did it fall?" When he showed him the place, he cut off a stick, and threw it in there, and made the iron float. 7He said, "Pick it up." So he reached out his hand and took it.

The Aramean Attack Is Thwarted

8 Once when the king of Aram was at war with Israel, he took counsel with his officers. He said, "At such and such a place shall be my camp." 9But the man of God sent word to the king of Israel, "Take care not to pass this place, because the Arameans are going down there." 10The king of Israel sent word to the place of which the man of God spoke. More than once or twice he warned such a placeg so that it was on the alert.

11 The mind of the king of Aram was greatly perturbed because of this; he called his officers and said to them, "Now tell me who among us sides with the king of Israel?" 12Then one of his officers said, "No one, my lord king. It is Elisha, the prophet in Israel, who tells the king of Israel the words that you speak in your bedchamber." 13He said, "Go and find where he is; I will send

---

b 5:24 at the hill where Elisha lived, implied.

c Heb sons of the prophets   d Heb him   e Heb lacks the bags   f A term for several skin diseases; precise meaning uncertain   g Heb warned it

King James

13¶ And he said, Go and spy where he *is,* that I may send and fetch him. And it was told him, saying, Behold, *he is* in Dothan.

14Therefore sent he thither horses, and chariots, and a great host: and they came by night, and compassed the city about.

15And when the servant of the man of God was risen early, and gone forth, behold, an host compassed the city both with horses and chariots. And his servant said unto him, Alas, my master! how shall we do?

16And he answered, Fear not: for they that *be* with us *are* more than they that *be* with them.

17And Elisha prayed, and said, LORD, I pray thee, open his eyes, that he may see. And the LORD opened the eyes of the young man; and he saw: and, behold, the mountain *was* full of horses and chariots of fire round about Elisha.

18And when they came down to him, Elisha prayed unto the LORD, and said, Smite this people, I pray thee, with blindness. And he smote them with blindness according to the word of Elisha.

19¶ And Elisha said unto them, This *is* not the way, neither *is* this the city: follow me, and I will bring you to the man whom ye seek. But he led them to Samaria.

20And it came to pass, when they were come into Samaria, that Elisha said, LORD, open the eyes of these *men,* that they may see. And the LORD opened their eyes, and they saw; and, behold, *they were* in the midst of Samaria.

21And the king of Israel said unto Elisha, when he saw them, My father, shall I smite *them?* shall I smite *them?*

22And he answered, Thou shalt not smite *them:* wouldest thou smite those whom thou hast taken captive with thy sword and with thy bow? set bread and water before them, that they may eat and drink, and go to their master.

23And he prepared great provision for them: and when they had eaten and drunk, he sent them away, and they went to their master. So the bands of Syria came no more into the land of Israel.

24¶ And it came to pass after this, that Ben-hadad king of Syria gathered all his host, and went up, and besieged Samaria.

25And there was a great famine in Samaria: and, behold, they besieged it, until an ass's head was *sold* for fourscore *pieces* of silver, and the fourth part of a cab of dove's dung for five *pieces* of silver.

26And as the king of Israel was passing by upon the wall, there cried a woman unto him, saying, Help, my lord, O king.

27And he said, If the LORD do not help thee, whence shall I help thee? out of the barnfloor, or out of the winepress?

28And the king said unto her, What aileth thee? And she answered, This woman said unto me, Give thy son, that we may eat him today, and we will eat my son tomorrow.

29So we boiled my son, and did eat him: and I said unto her on the next day, Give thy son, that we may eat him: and she hath hid her son.

30¶ And it came to pass, when the king heard the words of the woman, that he rent his clothes; and he passed by upon the wall, and the people looked, and, behold, *he had* sackcloth within upon his flesh.

31Then he said, God do so and more also to me, if the head of Elisha the son of Shaphat shall stand on him this day.

32But Elisha sat in his house, and the elders sat with him; and *the king* sent a man from before him: but ere the messenger came to him, he said to the elders, See ye how this son of a murderer hath sent to take away mine head? look, when the messenger cometh, shut the door, and hold him fast at the door: *is* not the sound of his master's feet behind him?

New International

13"Go, find out where he is," the king ordered, "so I can send men and capture him." The report came back: "He is in Dothan." 14Then he sent horses and chariots and a strong force there. They went by night and surrounded the city.

15When the servant of the man of God got up and went out early the next morning, an army with horses and chariots had surrounded the city. "Oh, my lord, what shall we do?" the servant asked.

16"Don't be afraid," the prophet answered. "Those who are with us are more than those who are with them."

17And Elisha prayed, "O LORD, open his eyes so he may see." Then the LORD opened the servant's eyes, and he looked and saw the hills full of horses and chariots of fire all around Elisha.

18As the enemy came down toward him, Elisha prayed to the LORD, "Strike these people with blindness." So he struck them with blindness, as Elisha had asked.

19Elisha told them, "This is not the road and this is not the city. Follow me, and I will lead you to the man you are looking for." And he led them to Samaria.

20After they entered the city, Elisha said, "LORD, open the eyes of these men so they can see." Then the LORD opened their eyes and they looked, and there they were, inside Samaria.

21When the king of Israel saw them, he asked Elisha, "Shall I kill them, my father? Shall I kill them?"

22"Do not kill them," he answered. "Would you kill men you have captured with your own sword or bow? Set food and water before them so that they may eat and drink and then go back to their master." 23So he prepared a great feast for them, and after they had finished eating and drinking, he sent them away, and they returned to their master. So the bands from Aram stopped raiding Israel's territory.

Famine in Besieged Samaria

24Some time later, Ben-Hadad king of Aram mobilized his entire army and marched up and laid siege to Samaria. 25There was a great famine in the city; the siege lasted so long that a donkey's head sold for eighty shekels[a] of silver, and a quarter of a cab[b] of seed pods[c] for five shekels.[d]

26As the king of Israel was passing by on the wall, a woman cried to him, "Help me, my lord the king!"

27The king replied, "If the LORD does not help you, where can I get help for you? From the threshing floor? From the winepress?" 28Then he asked her, "What's the matter?"

She answered, "This woman said to me, 'Give up your son so we may eat him today, and tomorrow we'll eat my son.' 29So we cooked my son and ate him. The next day I said to her, 'Give up your son so we may eat him,' but she had hidden him."

30When the king heard the woman's words, he tore his robes. As he went along the wall, the people looked, and there, underneath, he had sackcloth on his body. 31He said, "May God deal with me, be it ever so severely, if the head of Elisha son of Shaphat remains on his shoulders today!"

32Now Elisha was sitting in his house, and the elders were sitting with him. The king sent a messenger ahead, but before he arrived, Elisha said to the elders, "Don't you see how this murderer is sending someone to cut off my head? Look, when the messenger comes, shut the door and hold it shut against him. Is not the sound of his master's footsteps behind him?"

---

a 25 That is, about 2 pounds (about 1 kilogram)   b 25 That is, probably about 1/2 pint (about 0.3 liter)   c 25 Or *of dove's dung*   d 25 That is, about 2 ounces (about 55 grams)

Living Bible

13"Go and find out where he is, and we'll send troops to seize him," the king exclaimed.

And the report came back, "Elisha is at Dothan."

14So one night the king of Syria sent a great army with many chariots and horses to surround the city. 15When the prophet's servant got up early the next morning and went outside, there were troops, horses, and chariots everywhere.

"Alas, my master, what shall we do now?" he cried out to Elisha.

16"Don't be afraid!" Elisha told him. "For our army is bigger than theirs!"

17Then Elisha prayed, "Lord, open his eyes and let him see!" And the Lord opened the young man's eyes so that he could see horses of fire and chariots of fire everywhere upon the mountain!

18As the Syrian army advanced upon them, Elisha prayed, "Lord, please make them blind." And he did.

19Then Elisha went out and told them, "You've come the wrong way! This isn't the right city! Follow me and I will take you to the man you're looking for." And he led them to Samaria!

20As soon as they arrived Elisha prayed, "Lord, now open their eyes and let them see." And the Lord did, and they discovered that they were in Samaria, the capital city of Israel!

21When the king of Israel saw them, he shouted to Elisha, "Oh, sir, shall I kill them? Shall I kill them?"

22"Of course not!" Elisha told him. "Do we kill prisoners of war? Give them food and drink and send them home again."

23So the king made a great feast for them, and then sent them home to their king. And after that the Syrian raiders stayed away from the land of Israel.

24Later on, however, King Ben-hadad of Syria mustered his entire army and besieged Samaria. 25As a result there was a great famine in the city, and after a long while even a donkey's head sold for fifty dollars and a pint of dove's dung brought three dollars!

26-30One day as the king of Israel was walking along the wall of the city, a woman called to him, "Help, my lord the king!"

"If the Lord doesn't help you, what can I do?" he retorted. "I have neither food nor wine to give you. However, what's the matter?"

She replied, "This woman proposed that we eat my son one day and her son the next. So we boiled my son and ate him, but the next day when I said, 'Kill your son so we can eat him,' she hid him."

When the king heard this he tore his clothes. (The people watching noticed through the rip he tore in them that he was wearing an inner robe made of sackcloth next to his flesh.)

31"May God kill me if I don't execute Elisha this very day," the king vowed.

32Elisha was sitting in his house at a meeting with the elders of Israel when the king sent a messenger to summon him. But before the messenger arrived Elisha said to the elders, "This murderer has sent a man to kill me. When he arrives, shut the door and keep him out, for his master will soon follow him."

New Revised Standard

and seize him." He was told, "He is in Dothan." 14So he sent horses and chariots there and a great army; they came by night, and surrounded the city.

15 When an attendant of the man of God rose early in the morning and went out, an army with horses and chariots was all around the city. His servant said, "Alas, master! What shall we do?" 16He replied, "Do not be afraid, for there are more with us than there are with them." 17Then Elisha prayed: "O LORD, please open his eyes that he may see." So the LORD opened the eyes of the servant, and he saw; the mountain was full of horses and chariots of fire all around Elisha. 18When the Arameanse came down against him, Elisha prayed to the LORD, and said, "Strike this people, please, with blindness." So he struck them with blindness as Elisha had asked. 19Elisha said to them, "This is not the way, and this is not the city; follow me, and I will bring you to the man whom you seek." And he led them to Samaria.

20 As soon as they entered Samaria, Elisha said, "O LORD, open the eyes of these men so that they may see." The LORD opened their eyes, and they saw that they were inside Samaria. 21When the king of Israel saw them he said to Elisha, "Father, shall I kill them? Shall I kill them?" 22He answered, "No! Did you capture with your sword and your bow those whom you want to kill? Set food and water before them so that they may eat and drink; and let them go to their master." 23So he prepared for them a great feast; after they ate and drank, he sent them on their way, and they went to their master. And the Arameans no longer came raiding into the land of Israel.

Ben-hadad's Siege of Samaria

24 Some time later King Ben-hadad of Aram mustered his entire army; he marched against Samaria and laid siege to it. 25As the siege continued, famine in Samaria became so great that a donkey's head was sold for eighty shekels of silver, and one-fourth of a kab of dove's dung for five shekels of silver. 26Now as the king of Israel was walking on the city wall, a woman cried out to him, "Help, my lord king!" 27He said, "No! Let the LORD help you. How can I help you? From the threshing floor or from the wine press?" 28But then the king asked her, "What is your complaint?" She answered, "This woman said to me, 'Give up your son; we will eat him today, and we will eat my son tomorrow.' 29So we cooked my son and ate him. The next day I said to her, 'Give up your son and we will eat him.' But she has hidden her son." 30When the king heard the words of the woman he tore his clothes—now since he was walking on the city wall, the people could see that he had sackcloth on his body underneath— 31and he said, "So may God do to me, and more, if the head of Elisha son of Shaphat stays on his shoulders today." 32So he dispatched a man from his presence.

Now Elisha was sitting in his house, and the elders were sitting with him. Before the messenger arrived, Elisha said to the elders, "Are you aware that this murderer has sent someone to take off my head? When the messenger comes, see that you shut the door and hold it closed against him. Is not the sound of his master's feet behind him?" 33While he was still speaking with

King James

33And while he yet talked with them, behold, the messenger came down unto him: and he said, Behold, this evil *is* of the LORD; what should I wait for the LORD any longer?

7 THEN ELISHA said, Hear ye the word of the LORD; Thus saith the LORD, Tomorrow about this time *shall* a measure of fine flour *be sold* for a shekel, and two measures of barley for a shekel, in the gate of Samaria.

2Then a lord on whose hand the king leaned answered the man of God, and said, Behold, *if* the LORD would make windows in heaven, might this thing be? And he said, Behold, thou shalt see *it* with thine eyes, but shalt not eat thereof.

3¶ And there were four leprous men at the entering in of the gate: and they said one to another, Why sit we here until we die?

4If we say, We will enter into the city, then the famine *is* in the city, and we shall die there: and if we sit still here, we die also. Now therefore come, and let us fall unto the host of the Syrians: if they save us alive, we shall live; and if they kill us, we shall but die.

5And they rose up in the twilight, to go unto the camp of the Syrians: and when they were come to the uttermost part of the camp of Syria, behold, *there was* no man there.

6For the Lord had made the host of the Syrians to hear a noise of chariots, and a noise of horses, *even* the noise of a great host: and they said one to another, Lo, the king of Israel hath hired against us the kings of the Hittites, and the kings of the Egyptians, to come upon us.

7Wherefore they arose and fled in the twilight, and left their tents, and their horses, and their asses, even the camp as it *was*, and fled for their life.

8And when these lepers came to the uttermost part of the camp, they went into one tent, and did eat and drink, and carried thence silver, and gold, and raiment, and went and hid *it*; and came again, and entered into another tent, and carried thence *also*, and went and hid *it*.

9Then they said one to another, We do not well: this day *is* a day of good tidings, and we hold our peace: if we tarry till the morning light, some mischief will come upon us: now therefore come, that we may go and tell the king's household.

10So they came and called unto the porter of the city: and they told them, saying, We came to the camp of the Syrians, and, behold, *there was* no man there, neither voice of man, but horses tied, and asses tied, and the tents as they *were*.

11And he called the porters; and they told *it* to the king's house within.

12¶ And the king arose in the night, and said unto his servants, I will now show you what the Syrians have done to us. They know that we *be* hungry; therefore are they gone out of the camp to hide themselves in the field, saying, When they come out of the city, we shall catch them alive, and get into the city.

13And one of his servants answered and said, Let *some* take, I pray thee, five of the horses that remain, which are left in the city, (behold, they *are* as all the multitude of Israel that are left in it: behold, *I say*, they *are* even as all the multitude of the Israelites that are consumed:) and let us send and see.

14They took therefore two chariot horses; and the king sent after the host of the Syrians, saying, Go and see.

15And they went after them unto Jordan: and, lo, all the way *was* full of garments and vessels, which the Syrians had cast away in their haste. And the messengers returned, and told the king.

New International

33While he was still talking to them, the messenger came down to him. And the king said, "This disaster is from the LORD. Why should I wait for the LORD any longer?"

7 ELISHA SAID, "Hear the word of the LORD. This is what the LORD says: About this time tomorrow, a seah[a] of flour will sell for a shekel[b] and two seahs[c] of barley for a shekel at the gate of Samaria."

2The officer on whose arm the king was leaning said to the man of God, "Look, even if the LORD should open the floodgates of the heavens, could this happen?"

"You will see it with your own eyes," answered Elisha, "but you will not eat any of it!"

The Siege Lifted

3Now there were four men with leprosy[d] at the entrance of the city gate. They said to each other, "Why stay here until we die? 4If we say, 'We'll go into the city'—the famine is there, and we will die. And if we stay here, we will die. So let's go over to the camp of the Arameans and surrender. If they spare us, we live; if they kill us, then we die."

5At dusk they got up and went to the camp of the Arameans. When they reached the edge of the camp, not a man was there, 6for the Lord had caused the Arameans to hear the sound of chariots and horses and a great army, so that they said to one another, "Look, the king of Israel has hired the Hittite and Egyptian kings to attack us!" 7So they got up and fled in the dusk and abandoned their tents and their horses and donkeys. They left the camp as it was and ran for their lives.

8The men who had leprosy reached the edge of the camp and entered one of the tents. They ate and drank, and carried away silver, gold and clothes, and went off and hid them. They returned and entered another tent and took some things from it and hid them also.

9Then they said to each other, "We're not doing right. This is a day of good news and we are keeping it to ourselves. If we wait until daylight, punishment will overtake us. Let's go at once and report this to the royal palace."

10So they went and called out to the city gatekeepers and told them, "We went into the Aramean camp and not a man was there—not a sound of anyone—only tethered horses and donkeys, and the tents left just as they were." 11The gatekeepers shouted the news, and it was reported within the palace.

12The king got up in the night and said to his officers, "I will tell you what the Arameans have done to us. They know we are starving; so they have left the camp to hide in the countryside, thinking, 'They will surely come out, and then we will take them alive and get into the city.'"

13One of his officers answered, "Have some men take five of the horses that are left in the city. Their plight will be like that of all the Israelites left here—yes, they will only be like all these Israelites who are doomed. So let us send them to find out what happened."

14So they selected two chariots with their horses, and the king sent them after the Aramean army. He commanded the drivers, "Go and find out what has happened." 15They followed them as far as the Jordan, and they found the whole road strewn with the clothing and equipment the Arameans had thrown away in their headlong flight. So the messengers returned and reported to the king. 16Then the people went out and plundered the

---

a 1 That is, probably about 7 quarts (about 7.3 liters); also in verses 16 and 18   b 1 That is, about 2/5 ounce (about 11 grams); also in verses 16 and 18   c 1 That is, probably about 13 quarts (about 15 liters); also in verses 16 and 18   d 3 The Hebrew word is used for various diseases affecting the skin—not necessarily leprosy; also in verse 8.

Living Bible

33While Elisha was still saying this, the messenger arrived [followed by the kinge].

"The Lord has caused this mess," the king stormed. "Why should I expect any help from him?"

7 ELISHA REPLIED, "The Lord says that by this time tomorrow two gallons of flour or four gallons of barley grain will be sold in the markets of Samaria for a dollar!"

2The officer assisting the king said, "That couldn't happen if the Lord made windows in the sky!"

But Elisha replied, "You will see it happen, but you won't be able to buy any of it!"

3Now there were four lepers sitting outside the city gates.

"Why sit here until we die?" they asked each other. 4"We will starve if we stay here and we will starve if we go back into the city; so we might as well go out and surrender to the Syrian army. If they let us live, so much the better; but if they kill us, we would have died anyway."

5So that evening they went out to the camp of the Syrians, but there was no one there! 6(For the Lord had made the whole Syrian army hear the clatter of speeding chariots and a loud galloping of horses and the sounds of a great army approaching. "The king of Israel has hired the Hittites and Egyptians to attack us," they cried out. 7So they panicked and fled into the night, abandoning their tents, horses, donkeys, and everything else.)

8When the lepers arrived at the edge of the camp they went into one tent after another, eating, drinking wine, and carrying out silver and gold and clothing and hiding it. 9Finally they said to each other, "This isn't right. This is wonderful news, and we aren't sharing it with anyone! Even if we wait until morning, some terrible calamity will certainly fall upon us; come on, let's go back and tell the people at the palace."

10So they went back to the city and told the watchmen what had happened—they had gone out to the Syrian camp and no one was there! The horses and donkeys were tethered and the tents were all in order, but there was not a soul around. 11Then the watchmen shouted the news to those in the palace.

12The king got out of bed and told his officers, "I know what has happened. The Syrians know we are starving, so they have left their camp and have hidden in the fields, thinking that we will be lured out of the city. Then they will attack us and make slaves of us and get in."

13One of his officers replied, "We'd better send out scouts to see. Let them take five of the remaining horses—if something happens to the animals it won't be any greater loss than if they stay here and die with the rest of us!"

14Four chariot-horses were found and the king sent out two charioteers to see where the Syrians had gone. 15They followed a trail of clothing and equipment all the way to the Jordan River—thrown away by the Syrians in their haste. The scouts returned and told the king,

New Revised Standard

them, the kingf came down to him and said, "This trouble is from the LORD! Why should I hope in the LORD any longer?"

7 BUT ELISHA said, "Hear the word of the LORD: thus says the LORD, Tomorrow about this time a measure of choice meal shall be sold for a shekel, and two measures of barley for a shekel, at the gate of Samaria." 2Then the captain on whose hand the king leaned said to the man of God, "Even if the LORD were to make windows in the sky, could such a thing happen?" But he said, "You shall see it with your own eyes, but you shall not eat from it."

The Arameans Flee

3 Now there were four leprousg men outside the city gate, who said to one another, "Why should we sit here until we die? 4If we say, 'Let us enter the city,' the famine is in the city, and we shall die there; but if we sit here, we shall also die. Therefore, let us desert to the Aramean camp; if they spare our lives, we shall live; and if they kill us, we shall but die." 5So they arose at twilight to go to the Aramean camp; but when they came to the edge of the Aramean camp, there was no one there at all. 6For the Lord had caused the Aramean army to hear the sound of chariots, and of horses, the sound of a great army, so that they said to one another, "The king of Israel has hired the kings of the Hittites and the kings of Egypt to fight against us." 7So they fled away in the twilight and abandoned their tents, their horses, and their donkeys leaving the camp just as it was, and fled for their lives. 8When these leprousg men had come to the edge of the camp, they went into a tent, ate and drank, carried off silver, gold, and clothing, and went and hid them. Then they came back, entered another tent, carried off things from it, and went and hid them.

9 Then they said to one another, "What we are doing is wrong. This is a day of good news; if we are silent and wait until the morning light, we will be found guilty; therefore let us go and tell the king's household." 10So they came and called to the gatekeepers of the city, and told them, "We went to the Aramean camp, but there was no one to be seen or heard there, nothing but the horses tied, the donkeys tied, and the tents as they were." 11Then the gatekeepers called out and proclaimed it to the king's household. 12The king got up in the night, and said to his servants, "I will tell you what the Arameans have prepared against us. They know that we are starving; so they have left the camp to hide themselves in the open country, thinking, 'When they come out of the city, we shall take them alive and get into the city.'" 13One of his servants said, "Let some men take five of the remaining horses, since those left here will suffer the fate of the whole multitude of Israel that have perished already;h let us send and find out." 14So they took two mounted men, and the king sent them after the Aramean army, saying, "Go and find out." 15So they went after them as far as the Jordan; the whole way was littered with garments and equipment that the Arameans had thrown away in their haste. So the messengers returned, and told the king.

f See 7.2: Heb messenger   g A term for several skin diseases; precise meaning uncertain   h Compare Gk Syr Vg: Meaning of Heb uncertain

King James

16And the people went out, and spoiled the tents of the Syrians. So a measure of fine flour was *sold* for a shekel, and two measures of barley for a shekel, according to the word of the LORD.

17¶ And the king appointed the lord on whose hand he leaned to have the charge of the gate: and the people trode upon him in the gate, and he died, as the man of God had said, who spake when the king came down to him.

18And it came to pass as the man of God had spoken to the king, saying, Two measures of barley for a shekel, and a measure of fine flour for a shekel, shall be tomorrow about this time in the gate of Samaria:

19And that lord answered the man of God, and said, Now, behold, *if* the LORD should make windows in heaven, might such a thing be? And he said, Behold, thou shalt see it with thine eyes, but shalt not eat thereof.

20And so it fell out unto him: for the people trode upon him in the gate, and he died.

8 THEN SPAKE Elisha unto the woman, whose son he had restored to life, saying, Arise, and go thou and thine household, and sojourn wheresoever thou canst sojourn: for the LORD hath called for a famine; and it shall also come upon the land seven years.

2And the woman arose, and did after the saying of the man of God: and she went with her household, and sojourned in the land of the Philistines seven years.

3And it came to pass at the seven years' end, that the woman returned out of the land of the Philistines: and she went forth to cry unto the king for her house and for her land.

4And the king talked with Gehazi the servant of the man of God, saying, Tell me, I pray thee, all the great things that Elisha hath done.

5And it came to pass, as he was telling the king how he had restored a dead body to life, that, behold, the woman, whose son he had restored to life, cried to the king for her house and for her land. And Gehazi said, My lord, O king, this *is* the woman, and this *is* her son, whom Elisha restored to life.

6And when the king asked the woman, she told him. So the king appointed unto her a certain officer, saying, Restore all that *was* hers, and all the fruits of the field since the day that she left the land, even until now.

7¶ And Elisha came to Damascus; and Ben-hadad the king of Syria was sick; and it was told him, saying, The man of God is come hither.

8And the king said unto Hazael, Take a present in thine hand, and go, meet the man of God, and inquire of the LORD by him, saying, Shall I recover of this disease?

9So Hazael went to meet him, and took a present with him, even of every good thing of Damascus, forty camels' burden, and came and stood before him, and said, Thy son Ben-hadad king of Syria hath sent me to thee, saying, Shall I recover of this disease?

10And Elisha said unto him, Go, say unto him, Thou mayest certainly recover: howbeit the LORD hath shown me that he shall surely die.

11And he settled his countenance stedfastly, until he was ashamed: and the man of God wept.

12And Hazael said, Why weepeth my lord? And he answered, Because I know the evil that thou wilt do unto the children of Israel: their strong holds wilt thou set on fire, and their young men wilt thou slay with the sword, and wilt dash their children, and rip up their women with child.

New International

camp of the Arameans. So a seah of flour sold for a shekel, and two seahs of barley sold for a shekel, as the LORD had said.

17Now the king had put the officer on whose arm he leaned in charge of the gate, and the people trampled him in the gateway, and he died, just as the man of God had foretold when the king came down to his house. 18It happened as the man of God had said to the king: "About this time tomorrow, a seah of flour will sell for a shekel and two seahs of barley for a shekel at the gate of Samaria."

19The officer had said to the man of God, "Look, even if the LORD should open the floodgates of the heavens, could this happen?" The man of God had replied, "You will see it with your own eyes, but you will not eat any of it!" 20And that is exactly what happened to him, for the people trampled him in the gateway, and he died.

The Shunammite's Land Restored

8 NOW ELISHA had said to the woman whose son he had restored to life, "Go away with your family and stay for a while wherever you can, because the LORD has decreed a famine in the land that will last seven years." 2The woman proceeded to do as the man of God said. She and her family went away and stayed in the land of the Philistines seven years.

3At the end of the seven years she came back from the land of the Philistines and went to the king to beg for her house and land. 4The king was talking to Gehazi, the servant of the man of God, and had said, "Tell me about all the great things Elisha has done." 5Just as Gehazi was telling the king how Elisha had restored the dead to life, the woman whose son Elisha had brought back to life came to beg the king for her house and land.

Gehazi said, "This is the woman, my lord the king, and this is her son whom Elisha restored to life." 6The king asked the woman about it, and she told him.

Then he assigned an official to her case and said to him, "Give back everything that belonged to her, including all the income from her land from the day she left the country until now."

Hazael Murders Ben-Hadad

7Elisha went to Damascus, and Ben-Hadad king of Aram was ill. When the king was told, "The man of God has come all the way up here," 8he said to Hazael, "Take a gift with you and go to meet the man of God. Consult the LORD through him; ask him, 'Will I recover from this illness?' "

9Hazael went to meet Elisha, taking with him as a gift forty camel-loads of all the finest wares of Damascus. He went in and stood before him, and said, "Your son Ben-Hadad king of Aram has sent me to ask, 'Will I recover from this illness?' "

10Elisha answered, "Go and say to him, 'You will certainly recover'; but*a* the LORD has revealed to me that he will in fact die." 11He stared at him with a fixed gaze until Hazael felt ashamed. Then the man of God began to weep.

12"Why is my lord weeping?" asked Hazael.

"Because I know the harm you will do to the Israelites," he answered. "You will set fire to their fortified places, kill their young men with the sword, dash their little children to the ground, and rip open their pregnant women."

---

a *10* The Hebrew may also be read *Go and say, 'You will certainly not recover,'* for.

Living Bible

16and the people of Samaria rushed out and plundered the camp of the Syrians. So it was true that two gallons of flour and four gallons of barley were sold that day for one dollar, just as the Lord had said!

17The king appointed his special assistant to control the traffic at the gate, but he was knocked down and trampled and killed as the people rushed out. This is what Elisha had predicted on the previous day when the king had come to arrest him, 18and the prophet had told the king that flour and barley would sell for so little on the following day.

19The king's officer had replied, "That couldn't happen even if the Lord opened the windows of heaven!"
And the prophet had said, "You will see it happen, but you won't be able to buy any of it!"

20And he couldn't, for the people trampled him to death at the gate!

8 ELISHA HAD told the woman whose son he had brought back to life, "Take your family and move to some other country, for the Lord has called down a famine on Israel that will last for seven years."

2So the woman took her family and lived in the land of the Philistines for seven years. 3After the famine ended, she returned to the land of Israel and went to see the king about getting back her house and land. 4Just as she came in, the king was talking with Gehazi, Elisha's servant, and saying, "Tell me some stories of the great things Elisha has done." 5And Gehazi was telling the king about the time when Elisha brought a little boy back to life. At that very moment, the mother of the boy walked in!

"Oh, sir!" Gehazi exclaimed. "Here is the woman now, and this is her son—the very one Elisha brought back to life!"

6"Is this true?" the king asked her. And she told him that it was. So he directed one of his officials to see to it that everything she had owned was restored to her, plus the value of any crops that had been harvested during her absence.

7Afterwards Elisha went to Damascus (the capital of Syria), where King Ben-hadad lay sick. Someone told the king that the prophet had come.

8, 9When the king heard the news, he said to Hazael, "Take a present to the man of God and tell him to ask the Lord whether I will get well again."

So Hazael took forty camel-loads of the best produce of the land as presents for Elisha and said to him, "Your son Ben-hadad, the king of Syria, has sent me to ask you whether he will recover."

10And Elisha replied, "Tell him, 'Yes.' But the Lord has shown me that he will surely die!"

11Elisha stared at Hazael until he became embarrassed, and then Elisha started crying.

12"What's the matter, sir?" Hazael asked him.

Elisha replied, "I know the terrible things you will do to the people of Israel: you will burn their forts, kill the young men, dash their babies against the rocks, and rip open the bellies of the pregnant women!"

New Revised Standard

16 Then the people went out, and plundered the camp of the Arameans. So a measure of choice meal was sold for a shekel, and two measures of barley for a shekel, according to the word of the LORD. 17Now the king had appointed the captain on whose hand he leaned to have charge of the gate; the people trampled him to death in the gate, just as the man of God had said when the king came down to him. 18For when the man of God had said to the king, "Two measures of barley shall be sold for a shekel, and a measure of choice meal for a shekel, about this time tomorrow in the gate of Samaria," 19the captain had answered the man of God, "Even if the LORD were to make windows in the sky, could such a thing happen?" And he had answered, "You shall see it with your own eyes, but you shall not eat from it." 20It did indeed happen to him; the people trampled him to death in the gate.

The Shunammite Woman's Land Restored

8 NOW ELISHA had said to the woman whose son he had restored to life, "Get up and go with your household, and settle wherever you can; for the LORD has called for a famine, and it will come on the land for seven years." 2So the woman got up and did according to the word of the man of God; she went with her household and settled in the land of the Philistines seven years. 3At the end of the seven years, when the woman returned from the land of the Philistines, she set out to appeal to the king for her house and her land. 4Now the king was talking with Gehazi the servant of the man of God, saying, "Tell me all the great things that Elisha has done." 5While he was telling the king how Elisha had restored a dead person to life, the woman whose son he had restored to life appealed to the king for her house and her land. Gehazi said, "My lord king, here is the woman, and here is her son whom Elisha restored to life." 6When the king questioned the woman, she told him. So the king appointed an official for her, saying, "Restore all that was hers, together with all the revenue of the fields from the day that she left the land until now."

Death of Ben-hadad

7 Elisha went to Damascus while King Ben-hadad of Aram was ill. When it was told him, "The man of God has come here," 8the king said to Hazael, "Take a present with you and go to meet the man of God. Inquire of the LORD through him, whether I shall recover from this illness." 9So Hazael went to meet him, taking a present with him, all kinds of goods of Damascus, forty camel loads. When he entered and stood before him, he said, "Your son King Ben-hadad of Aram has sent me to you, saying, 'Shall I recover from this illness?'" 10Elisha said to him, "Go, say to him, 'You shall certainly recover'; but the LORD has shown me that he shall certainly die." 11He fixed his gaze and stared at him, until he was ashamed. Then the man of God wept. 12Hazael asked, "Why does my lord weep?" He answered, "Because I know the evil that you will do to the people of Israel; you will set their fortresses on fire, you will kill their young men with the sword, dash in pieces their little ones, and rip up their pregnant women."

King James

13And Hazael said, But what, *is* thy servant a dog, that he should do this great thing? And Elisha answered, The LORD hath shown me that thou *shalt be* king over Syria.

14So he departed from Elisha, and came to his master; who said to him, What said Elisha to thee? And he answered, He told me *that* thou shouldest surely recover.

15And it came to pass on the morrow, that he took a thick cloth, and dipped *it* in water, and spread *it* on his face, so that he died: and Hazael reigned in his stead.

16¶ And in the fifth year of Joram the son of Ahab king of Israel, Jehoshaphat *being* then king of Judah, Jehoram the son of Jehoshaphat king of Judah began to reign.

17Thirty and two years old was he when he began to reign; and he reigned eight years in Jerusalem.

18And he walked in the way of the kings of Israel, as did the house of Ahab: for the daughter of Ahab was his wife: and he did evil in the sight of the LORD.

19Yet the LORD would not destroy Judah for David his servant's sake, as he promised him to give him always a light, *and* to his children.

20¶ In his days Edom revolted from under the hand of Judah, and made a king over themselves.

21So Joram went over to Zair, and all the chariots with him: and he rose by night, and smote the Edomites which compassed him about, and the captains of the chariots: and the people fled into their tents.

22Yet Edom revolted from under the hand of Judah unto this day. Then Libnah revolted at the same time.

23And the rest of the acts of Joram, and all that he did, *are* they not written in the book of the chronicles of the kings of Judah?

24And Joram slept with his fathers, and was buried with his fathers in the city of David: and Ahaziah his son reigned in his stead.

25¶ In the twelfth year of Joram the son of Ahab king of Israel did Ahaziah the son of Jehoram king of Judah begin to reign.

26Two and twenty years old *was* Ahaziah when he began to reign; and he reigned one year in Jerusalem. And his mother's name *was* Athaliah, the daughter of Omri king of Israel.

27And he walked in the way of the house of Ahab, and did evil in the sight of the LORD, as *did* the house of Ahab: for he *was* the son-in-law of the house of Ahab.

28¶ And he went with Joram the son of Ahab to the war against Hazael king of Syria in Ramoth-gilead; and the Syrians wounded Joram.

29And king Joram went back to be healed in Jezreel of the wounds which the Syrians had given him at Ramah, when he fought against Hazael king of Syria. And Ahaziah the son of Jehoram king of Judah went down to see Joram the son of Ahab in Jezreel, because he was sick.

9 AND ELISHA the prophet called one of the children of the prophets, and said unto him, Gird up thy loins, and take this box of oil in thine hand, and go to Ramoth-gilead:

2And when thou comest thither, look out there Jehu the son of Jehoshaphat the son of Nimshi, and go in, and make him arise up from among his brethren, and carry him to an inner chamber;

3Then take the box of oil, and pour *it* on his head, and say, Thus saith the LORD, I have anointed thee king over Israel. Then open the door, and flee, and tarry not.

New International

13Hazael said, "How could your servant, a mere dog, accomplish such a feat?"

"The LORD has shown me that you will become king of Aram," answered Elisha.

14Then Hazael left Elisha and returned to his master. When Ben-Hadad asked, "What did Elisha say to you?" Hazael replied, "He told me that you would certainly recover." 15But the next day he took a thick cloth, soaked it in water and spread it over the king's face, so that he died. Then Hazael succeeded him as king.

Jehoram King of Judah

16In the fifth year of Joram son of Ahab king of Israel, when Jehoshaphat was king of Judah, Jehoram son of Jehoshaphat began his reign as king of Judah. 17He was thirty-two years old when he became king, and he reigned in Jerusalem eight years. 18He walked in the ways of the kings of Israel, as the house of Ahab had done, for he married a daughter of Ahab. He did evil in the eyes of the LORD. 19Nevertheless, for the sake of his servant David, the LORD was not willing to destroy Judah. He had promised to maintain a lamp for David and his descendants forever.

20In the time of Jehoram, Edom rebelled against Judah and set up its own king. 21So Jehorama went to Zair with all his chariots. The Edomites surrounded him and his chariot commanders, but he rose up and broke through by night; his army, however, fled back home. 22To this day Edom has been in rebellion against Judah. Libnah revolted at the same time.

23As for the other events of Jehoram's reign, and all he did, are they not written in the book of the annals of the kings of Judah? 24Jehoram rested with his fathers and was buried with them in the City of David. And Ahaziah his son succeeded him as king.

Ahaziah King of Judah

25In the twelfth year of Joram son of Ahab king of Israel, Ahaziah son of Jehoram king of Judah began to reign. 26Ahaziah was twenty-two years old when he became king, and he reigned in Jerusalem one year. His mother's name was Athaliah, a granddaughter of Omri king of Israel. 27He walked in the ways of the house of Ahab and did evil in the eyes of the LORD, as the house of Ahab had done, for he was related by marriage to Ahab's family.

28Ahaziah went with Joram son of Ahab to war against Hazael king of Aram at Ramoth Gilead. The Arameans wounded Joram; 29so King Joram returned to Jezreel to recover from the wounds the Arameans had inflicted on him at Ramothb in his battle with Hazael king of Aram.

Then Ahaziah son of Jehoram king of Judah went down to Jezreel to see Joram son of Ahab, because he had been wounded.

Jehu Anointed King of Israel

9 THE PROPHET Elisha summoned a man from the company of the prophets and said to him, "Tuck your cloak into your belt, take this flask of oil with you and go to Ramoth Gilead. 2When you get there, look for Jehu son of Jehoshaphat, the son of Nimshi. Go to him, get him away from his companions and take him into an inner room. 3Then take the flask and pour the oil on his head and declare, 'This is what the LORD says: I anoint you king over Israel.' Then open the door and run; don't delay!"

a 21 Hebrew *Joram*, a variant of *Jehoram*; also in verses 23 and 24
b 29 Hebrew *Ramah*, a variant of *Ramoth*

Living Bible

13"Am I a dog?" Hazael asked him. "I would *never* do that sort of thing."

But Elisha replied, "The Lord has shown me that you are going to be the king of Syria."

14When Hazael went back, the king asked him, "What did he tell you?"

And Hazael replied, "He told me that you would recover."

15But the next day Hazael took a blanket and dipped it in water and held it over the king's face until he smothered to death. And Hazael became king instead.

16King Jehoram, the son of King Jehoshaphat of Judah, began his reign during the fifth year of the reign of King Joram of Israel, the son of Ahab. 17Jehoram was thirty-two years old when he became king, and he reigned in Jerusalem for eight years. 18But he was as wicked as Ahab and the other kings of Israel; he even married one of Ahab's daughters. 19Nevertheless, because God had promised his servant David that he would watch over and guide his descendants, he did not destroy Judah.

20During Jehoram's reign, the people in Edom revolted from Judah and appointed their own king. 21King Jehoram tried unsuccessfully to crush the rebellion: he crossed the Jordan River and attacked the city of Zair, but was quickly surrounded by the army of Edom. Under cover of night he broke through their ranks, but his army deserted him and fled. 22So Edom has maintained its independence to this day. Libnah also rebelled at that time.

23The rest of the history of King Jehoram is written in *The Annals of the Kings of Judah*. 24, 25He died and was buried in the royal cemetery in the City of David—the old section of Jerusalem.

Then his son Ahaziah[c] became the new king during the twelfth year of the reign of King Jehoram of Israel, the son of Ahab. 26Ahaziah was twenty-two years old when he began to reign but he reigned only one year, in Jerusalem. His mother was Athaliah, the granddaughter of King Omri of Israel. 27He was an evil king, just as all of King Ahab's descendants were—for he was related to Ahab by marriage.

28He joined King Joram of Israel (son of Ahab) in his war against Hazael, the king of Syria, at Ramoth-gilead. King Joram was wounded in the battle, 29so he went to Jezreel to rest and recover from his wounds. While he was there, King Ahaziah of Judah (son of Jehoram) came to visit him.

9 MEANWHILE ELISHA had summoned one of the young prophets.

"Get ready to go to Ramoth-gilead," he told him. "Take this vial of oil with you, 2and find Jehu (the son of Jehoshaphat, the son of Nimshi). Call him into a private room away from his friends, 3and pour the oil over his head. Tell him that the Lord has anointed him to be the king of Israel; then run for your life!"

New Revised Standard

13Hazael said, "What is your servant, who is a mere dog, that he should do this great thing?" Elisha answered, "The LORD has shown me that you are to be king over Aram." 14Then he left Elisha, and went to his master Ben-hadad,[d] who said to him, "What did Elisha say to you?" And he answered, "He told me that you would certainly recover." 15But the next day he took the bedcover and dipped it in water and spread it over the king's face, until he died. And Hazael succeeded him.

Jehoram Reigns over Judah

16 In the fifth year of King Joram son of Ahab of Israel,[e] Jehoram son of King Jehoshaphat of Judah began to reign. 17He was thirty-two years old when he became king, and he reigned eight years in Jerusalem. 18He walked in the way of the kings of Israel, as the house of Ahab had done, for the daughter of Ahab was his wife. He did what was evil in the sight of the LORD. 19Yet the LORD would not destroy Judah, for the sake of his servant David, since he had promised to give a lamp to him and to his descendants forever.

20 In his days Edom revolted against the rule of Judah, and set up a king of their own. 21Then Joram crossed over to Zair with all his chariots. He set out by night and attacked the Edomites and their chariot commanders who had surrounded him;[f] but his army fled home. 22So Edom has been in revolt against the rule of Judah to this day. Libnah also revolted at the same time. 23Now the rest of the acts of Joram, and all that he did, are they not written in the Book of the Annals of the Kings of Judah? 24So Joram slept with his ancestors, and was buried with them in the city of David; his son Ahaziah succeeded him.

Ahaziah Reigns over Judah

25 In the twelfth year of King Joram son of Ahab of Israel, Ahaziah son of King Jehoram of Judah began to reign. 26Ahaziah was twenty-two years old when he began to reign; he reigned one year in Jerusalem. His mother's name was Athaliah, a granddaughter of King Omri of Israel. 27He also walked in the way of the house of Ahab, doing what was evil in the sight of the LORD, as the house of Ahab had done, for he was son-in-law to the house of Ahab.

28 He went with Joram son of Ahab to wage war against King Hazael of Aram at Ramoth-gilead, where the Arameans wounded Joram. 29King Joram returned to be healed in Jezreel of the wounds that the Arameans had inflicted on him at Ramah, when he fought against King Hazael of Aram. King Ahaziah son of Jehoram of Judah went down to see Joram son of Ahab in Jezreel, because he was wounded.

Anointing of Jehu

9 THEN THE prophet Elisha called a member of the company of prophets[g] and said to him, "Gird up your loins; take this flask of oil in your hand, and go to Ramoth-gilead. 2When you arrive, look there for Jehu son of Jehoshaphat, son of Nimshi; go in and get him to leave his companions, and take him into an inner chamber. 3Then take the flask of oil, pour it on his head, and say, 'Thus says the LORD: I anoint you king over Israel.' Then open the door and flee; do not linger."

---

c 8:25 *his son Ahaziah*. Ahaziah is an alternate form of the name Jehoahaz.

d Heb lacks *Ben-hadad*   e Gk Syr: Heb adds *Jehoshaphat being king of Judah*,
f Meaning of Heb uncertain   g Heb *sons of the prophets*

King James

4¶ So the young man, *even* the young man the prophet, went to Ramoth-gilead.

5And when he came, behold, the captains of the host *were* sitting; and he said, I have an errand to thee, O captain. And Jehu said, Unto which of all us? And he said, To thee, O captain.

6And he arose, and went into the house; and he poured the oil on his head, and said unto him, Thus saith the LORD God of Israel, I have anointed thee king over the people of the LORD, *even* over Israel.

7And thou shalt smite the house of Ahab thy master, that I may avenge the blood of my servants the prophets, and the blood of all the servants of the LORD, at the hand of Jezebel.

8For the whole house of Ahab shall perish: and I will cut off from Ahab him that pisseth against the wall, and him that is shut up and left in Israel:

9And I will make the house of Ahab like the house of Jeroboam the son of Nebat, and like the house of Baasha the son of Ahijah:

10And the dogs shall eat Jezebel in the portion of Jezreel, and *there shall be* none to bury *her*. And he opened the door, and fled.

11¶ Then Jehu came forth to the servants of his lord: and *one* said unto him, *Is* all well? wherefore came this mad *fellow* to thee? And he said unto them, Ye know the man, and his communication.

12And they said, *It is* false; tell us now. And he said, Thus and thus spake he to me, saying, Thus saith the LORD, I have anointed thee king over Israel.

13Then they hasted, and took every man his garment, and put *it* under him on the top of the stairs, and blew with trumpets, saying, Jehu is king.

14So Jehu the son of Jehoshaphat the son of Nimshi conspired against Joram. (Now Joram had kept Ramoth-gilead, he and all Israel, because of Hazael king of Syria.

15But king Joram was returned to be healed in Jezreel of the wounds which the Syrians had given him, when he fought with Hazael king of Syria.) And Jehu said, If it be your minds, *then* let none go forth *nor* escape out of the city to go to tell *it* in Jezreel.

16So Jehu rode in a chariot, and went to Jezreel; for Joram lay there. And Ahaziah king of Judah was come down to see Joram.

17And there stood a watchman on the tower in Jezreel, and he spied the company of Jehu as he came, and said, I see a company. And Joram said, Take an horseman, and send to meet them, and let him say, *Is it* peace?

18So there went one on horseback to meet him, and said, Thus saith the king, *Is it* peace? And Jehu said, What hast thou to do with peace? turn thee behind me. And the watchman told, saying, The messenger came to them, but he cometh not again.

19Then he sent out a second on horseback, which came to them, and said, Thus saith the king, *Is it* peace? And Jehu answered, What hast thou to do with peace? turn thee behind me.

20And the watchman told, saying, He came even unto them, and cometh not again: and the driving *is* like the driving of Jehu the son of Nimshi; for he driveth furiously.

21And Joram said, Make ready. And his chariot was made ready. And Joram king of Israel and Ahaziah king of Judah went out, each in his chariot, and they went out against Jehu, and met him in the portion of Naboth the Jezreelite.

22And it came to pass, when Joram saw Jehu, that he said, *Is it* peace, Jehu? And he answered, What peace, so long as the whoredoms of thy mother Jezebel and her witchcrafts *are so* many?

New International

4So the young man, the prophet, went to Ramoth Gilead. 5When he arrived, he found the army officers sitting together. "I have a message for you, commander," he said.

"For which of us?" asked Jehu.

"For you, commander," he replied.

6Jehu got up and went into the house. Then the prophet poured the oil on Jehu's head and declared, "This is what the LORD, the God of Israel, says: 'I anoint you king over the LORD's people Israel. 7You are to destroy the house of Ahab your master, and I will avenge the blood of my servants the prophets and the blood of all the LORD's servants shed by Jezebel. 8The whole house of Ahab will perish. I will cut off from Ahab every last male in Israel—slave or free. 9I will make the house of Ahab like the house of Jeroboam son of Nebat and like the house of Baasha son of Ahijah. 10As for Jezebel, dogs will devour her on the plot of ground at Jezreel, and no one will bury her.' " Then he opened the door and ran.

11When Jehu went out to his fellow officers, one of them asked him, "Is everything all right? Why did this madman come to you?"

"You know the man and the sort of things he says," Jehu replied.

12"That's not true!" they said. "Tell us."

Jehu said, "Here is what he told me: 'This is what the LORD says: I anoint you king over Israel.' "

13They hurried and took their cloaks and spread them under him on the bare steps. Then they blew the trumpet and shouted, "Jehu is king!"

Jehu Kills Joram and Ahaziah

14So Jehu son of Jehoshaphat, the son of Nimshi, conspired against Joram. (Now Joram and all Israel had been defending Ramoth Gilead against Hazael king of Aram, 15but King Joram[a] had returned to Jezreel to recover from the wounds the Arameans had inflicted on him in the battle with Hazael king of Aram.) Jehu said, "If this is the way you feel, don't let anyone slip out of the city to go and tell the news in Jezreel." 16Then he got into his chariot and rode to Jezreel, because Joram was resting there and Ahaziah king of Judah had gone down to see him.

17When the lookout standing on the tower in Jezreel saw Jehu's troops approaching, he called out, "I see some troops coming."

"Get a horseman," Joram ordered. "Send him to meet them and ask, 'Do you come in peace?' "

18The horseman rode off to meet Jehu and said, "This is what the king says: 'Do you come in peace?' "

"What do you have to do with peace?" Jehu replied. "Fall in behind me."

The lookout reported, "The messenger has reached them, but he isn't coming back."

19So the king sent out a second horseman. When he came to them he said, "This is what the king says: 'Do you come in peace?' "

Jehu replied, "What do you have to do with peace? Fall in behind me."

20The lookout reported, "He has reached them, but he isn't coming back either. The driving is like that of Jehu son of Nimshi—he drives like a madman."

21"Hitch up my chariot," Joram ordered. And when it was hitched up, Joram king of Israel and Ahaziah king of Judah rode out, each in his own chariot, to meet Jehu. They met him at the plot of ground that had belonged to Naboth the Jezreelite. 22When Joram saw Jehu he asked, "Have you come in peace, Jehu?"

"How can there be peace," Jehu replied, "as long as all the idolatry and witchcraft of your mother Jezebel abound?"

---

a *15* Hebrew *Jehoram,* a variant of *Joram*; also in verses 17 and 21-24

Living Bible

4So the young prophet did as he was told. When he arrived in Ramoth-gilead, 5he found Jehu sitting around with the other army officers.

"I have a message for you, sir," he said.

"For which one of us?" Jehu asked.

"For you," he replied.

6So Jehu left the others and went into the house, and the young man poured the oil over his head and said, "The Lord God of Israel says, 'I anoint you king of the Lord's people, Israel. 7You are to destroy the family of Ahab; you will avenge the murder of my prophets and of all my other people who were killed by Jezebel. 8The entire family of Ahab must be wiped out—every male, no matter who. 9I will destroy the family of Ahab as I destroyed the families of Jeroboam (son of Nebat) and of Baasha (son of Ahijah). 10Dogs shall eat Ahab's wife Jezebel at Jezreel, and no one will bury her.'"

Then he opened the door and ran.

11Jehu went back to his friends and one of them asked him, "What did that crazy fellow want? Is everything all right?"

"You know very well who he was and what he wanted," Jehu replied.

12"No, we don't," they said. "Tell us."

So he told them what the man had said and that he had been anointed king of Israel!

13They quickly carpeted the bare steps with their coats and blew a trumpet, shouting, "Jehu is king!"

14That is how Jehu (son of Jehoshaphat, son of Nimshi) rebelled against King Joram. (King Joram had been with the army at Ramoth-gilead, defending Israel against the forces of King Hazael of Syria. 15But he had returned to Jezreel to recover from his wounds.)

"Since you want me to be king," Jehu told the men who were with him, "don't let anyone escape to Jezreel to report what we have done."

16Then Jehu jumped into a chariot and rode to Jezreel himself to find King Joram, who was lying there wounded. (King Ahaziah of Judah was there too, for he had gone to visit him.) 17The watchman on the Tower of Jezreel saw Jehu and his company approaching and shouted, "Someone is coming."

"Send out a rider and find out if he is friend or foe," King Joram shouted back. 18So a soldier rode out to meet Jehu.

"The king wants to know whether you are friend or foe," he demanded. "Do you come in peace?"

Jehu replied, "What do you know about peace? Get behind me!"

The watchman called out to the king that the messenger had met them but was not returning. 19So the king sent out a second rider. He rode up to them and demanded in the name of the king to know whether their intentions were friendly or not.

Jehu answered, "What do you know about friendliness? Get behind me!"

20"He isn't returning either!" the watchman exclaimed. "It must be Jehu, for he is driving so furiously."

21"Quick! Get my chariot ready!" King Joram commanded.

Then he and King Ahaziah of Judah rode out to meet Jehu. They met him at the field of Naboth, 22and King Joram demanded, "Do you come as a friend, Jehu?"

Jehu replied, "How can there be friendship as long as the evils of your mother Jezebel are all around us?"

New Revised Standard

4 So the young man, the young prophet, went to Ramoth-gilead. 5He arrived while the commanders of the army were in council, and he announced, "I have a message for you, commander." "For which one of us?" asked Jehu. "For you, commander." 6So Jehub got up and went inside; the young man poured the oil on his head, saying to him, "Thus says the LORD the God of Israel: I anoint you king over the people of the LORD, over Israel. 7You shall strike down the house of your master Ahab, so that I may avenge on Jezebel the blood of my servants the prophets, and the blood of all the servants of the LORD. 8For the whole house of Ahab shall perish; I will cut off from Ahab every male, bond or free, in Israel. 9I will make the house of Ahab like the house of Jeroboam son of Nebat, and like the house of Baasha son of Ahijah. 10The dogs shall eat Jezebel in the territory of Jezreel, and no one shall bury her." Then he opened the door and fled.

11 When Jehu came back to his master's officers, they said to him, "Is everything all right? Why did that madman come to you?" He answered them, "You know the sort and how they babble." 12They said, "Liar! Come on, tell us!" So he said, "This is just what he said to me: 'Thus says the LORD, I anoint you king over Israel.' " 13Then hurriedly they all took their cloaks and spread them for him on the barec steps; and they blew the trumpet, and proclaimed, "Jehu is king."

Joram of Israel Killed

14 Thus Jehu son of Jehoshaphat son of Nimshi conspired against Joram. Joram with all Israel had been on guard at Ramoth-gilead against King Hazael of Aram; 15but King Joram had returned to be healed in Jezreel of the wounds that the Arameans had inflicted on him, when he fought against King Hazael of Aram. So Jehu said, "If this is your wish, then let no one slip out of the city to go and tell the news in Jezreel." 16Then Jehu mounted his chariot and went to Jezreel, where Joram was lying ill. King Ahaziah of Judah had come down to visit Joram.

17 In Jezreel, the sentinel standing on the tower spied the company of Jehu arriving, and said, "I see a company." Joram said, "Take a horseman; send him to meet them, and let him say, 'Is it peace?' " 18So the horseman went to meet him; he said, "Thus says the king, 'Is it peace?' " Jehu responded, "What have you to do with peace? Fall in behind me." The sentinel reported, saying, "The messenger reached them, but he is not coming back." 19Then he sent out a second horseman, who came to them and said, "Thus says the king, 'Is it peace?' " Jehu answered, "What have you to do with peace? Fall in behind me." 20Again the sentinel reported, "He reached them, but he is not coming back. It looks like the driving of Jehu son of Nimshi; for he drives like a maniac."

21 Joram said, "Get ready." And they got his chariot ready. Then King Joram of Israel and King Ahaziah of Judah set out, each in his chariot, and went to meet Jehu; they met him at the property of Naboth the Jezreelite. 22When Joram saw Jehu, he said, "Is it peace, Jehu?" He answered, "What peace can there be, so long as the many whoredoms and sorceries of your mother Jezebel continue?" 23Then Joram reined about and fled,

b Heb *he*   c Meaning of Heb uncertain

King James

23And Joram turned his hands, and fled, and said to Ahaziah, *There is* treachery, O Ahaziah.

24And Jehu drew a bow with his full strength, and smote Jehoram between his arms, and the arrow went out at his heart, and he sunk down in his chariot.

25Then said *Jehu* to Bidkar his captain, Take up, *and* cast him in the portion of the field of Naboth the Jezreelite: for remember how that, when I and thou rode together after Ahab his father, the LORD laid this burden upon him;

26Surely I have seen yesterday the blood of Naboth, and the blood of his sons, saith the LORD; and I will requite thee in this plat, saith the LORD. Now therefore take *and* cast him into the plat *of ground,* according to the word of the LORD.

27¶ But when Ahaziah the king of Judah saw *this,* he fled by the way of the garden house. And Jehu followed after him, and said, Smite him also in the chariot. *And they did so* at the going up to Gur, which *is* by Ibleam. And he fled to Megiddo, and died there.

28And his servants carried him in a chariot to Jerusalem, and buried him in his sepulchre with his fathers in the city of David.

29And in the eleventh year of Joram the son of Ahab began Ahaziah to reign over Judah.

30¶ And when Jehu was come to Jezreel, Jezebel heard *of it;* and she painted her face, and tired her head, and looked out at a window.

31And as Jehu entered in at the gate, she said, *Had* Zimri peace, who slew his master?

32And he lifted up his face to the window, and said, Who *is* on my side? who? And there looked out to him two *or* three eunuchs.

33And he said, Throw her down. So they threw her down: and *some* of her blood was sprinkled on the wall, and on the horses: and he trode her under foot.

34And when he was come in, he did eat and drink, and said, Go, see now this cursed *woman,* and bury her: for she *is* a king's daughter.

35And they went to bury her: but they found no more of her than the skull, and the feet, and the palms of *her* hands.

36Wherefore they came again, and told him. And he said, This *is* the word of the LORD, which he spake by his servant Elijah the Tishbite, saying, In the portion of Jezreel shall dogs eat the flesh of Jezebel:

37And the carcase of Jezebel shall be as dung upon the face of the field in the portion of Jezreel; *so* that they shall not say, This *is* Jezebel.

10 AND AHAB had seventy sons in Samaria. And Jehu wrote letters, and sent to Samaria, unto the rulers of Jezreel, to the elders, and to them that brought up Ahab's *children,* saying,

2Now as soon as this letter cometh to you, seeing your master's sons *are* with you, and *there are* with you chariots and horses, a fenced city also, and armour;

3Look even out the best and meetest of your master's sons, and set *him* on his father's throne, and fight for your master's house.

4But they were exceedingly afraid, and said, Behold, two kings stood not before him: how then shall we stand?

5And he that *was* over the house, and he that *was* over the city, the elders also, and the bringers up *of the children,* sent to Jehu, saying, *We are* thy servants, and will do all that thou shalt bid us; we will not make any king: do thou *that which is* good in thine eyes.

New International

23Joram turned about and fled, calling out to Ahaziah, "Treachery, Ahaziah!"

24Then Jehu drew his bow and shot Joram between the shoulders. The arrow pierced his heart and he slumped down in his chariot. 25Jehu said to Bidkar, his chariot officer, "Pick him up and throw him on the field that belonged to Naboth the Jezreelite. Remember how you and I were riding together in chariots behind Ahab his father when the LORD made this prophecy about him: 26'Yesterday I saw the blood of Naboth and the blood of his sons, declares the LORD, and I will surely make you pay for it on this plot of ground, declares the LORD.'[a] Now then, pick him up and throw him on that plot, in accordance with the word of the LORD."

27When Ahaziah king of Judah saw what had happened, he fled up the road to Beth Haggan.[b] Jehu chased him, shouting, "Kill him too!" They wounded him in his chariot on the way up to Gur near Ibleam, but he escaped to Megiddo and died there. 28His servants took him by chariot to Jerusalem and buried him with his fathers in his tomb in the City of David. 29(In the eleventh year of Joram son of Ahab, Ahaziah had become king of Judah.)

Jezebel Killed

30Then Jehu went to Jezreel. When Jezebel heard about it, she painted her eyes, arranged her hair and looked out of a window. 31As Jehu entered the gate, she asked, "Have you come in peace, Zimri, you murderer of your master?"[c]

32He looked up at the window and called out, "Who is on my side? Who?" Two or three eunuchs looked down at him. 33"Throw her down!" Jehu said. So they threw her down, and some of her blood spattered the wall and the horses as they trampled her underfoot.

34Jehu went in and ate and drank. "Take care of that cursed woman," he said, "and bury her, for she was a king's daughter." 35But when they went out to bury her, they found nothing except her skull, her feet and her hands. 36They went back and told Jehu, who said, "This is the word of the LORD that he spoke through his servant Elijah the Tishbite: On the plot of ground at Jezreel dogs will devour Jezebel's flesh.[d] 37Jezebel's body will be like refuse on the ground in the plot at Jezreel, so that no one will be able to say, 'This is Jezebel.' "

Ahab's Family Killed

10 NOW THERE were in Samaria seventy sons of the house of Ahab. So Jehu wrote letters and sent them to Samaria: to the officials of Jezreel,[e] to the elders and to the guardians of Ahab's children. He said, 2"As soon as this letter reaches you, since your master's sons are with you and you have chariots and horses, a fortified city and weapons, 3choose the best and most worthy of your master's sons and set him on his father's throne. Then fight for your master's house."

4But they were terrified and said, "If two kings could not resist him, how can we?"

5So the palace administrator, the city governor, the elders and the guardians sent this message to Jehu: "We are your servants and we will do anything you say. We will not appoint anyone as king; you do whatever you think best."

a 26 See 1 Kings 21:19.   b 27 Or *fled by way of the garden house*   c 31 Or *"Did Zimri have peace, who murdered his master?"*   d 36 See 1 Kings 21:23.   e 1 Hebrew; some Septuagint manuscripts and Vulgate *of the city*

Living Bible

23Then King Joram reined the chariot-horses around and fled, shouting to King Ahaziah, "There is treachery, Ahaziah! Treason!"

24Then Jehu drew his bow with his full strength and shot Joram between the shoulders; and the arrow pierced his heart, and he sank down dead in his chariot.

25Jehu said to Bidkar, his assistant, "Throw him into the field of Naboth, for once when you and I were riding along behind his father Ahab, the Lord revealed this prophecy to me: 26'I will repay him here on Naboth's property for the murder of Naboth and his sons.' So throw him out on Naboth's field, just as the Lord said."

27Meanwhile, King Ahaziah of Judah had fled along the road to Beth-haggan. Jehu rode after him, shouting, "Shoot him, too."

So they shot him in his chariot at the place where the road climbs to Gur, near Ibleam. He was able to go on as far as Megiddo, but died there. 28His officials took him by chariot to Jerusalem where they buried him in the royal cemetery. 29(Ahaziah's reign over Judah had begun in the twelfthf year of the reign of King Joram of Israel.)

30When Jezebel heard that Jehu had come to Jezreel, she painted her eyelids and fixed her hair and sat at a window. 31When Jehu entered the gate of the palace, she shouted at him, "How are you today, you murderer! You son of a Zimri who murdered his master!"

32He looked up and saw her at the window and shouted, "Who is on my side?" And two or three eunuchs looked out at him.

33"Throw her down!" he yelled.

So they threw her out the window, and her blood spattered against the wall and on the horses; and she was trampled by the horses' hoofs.

34Then Jehu went into the palace for lunch. Afterwards he said, "Someone go and bury this cursed woman, for she is the daughter of a king."

35But when they went out to bury her, they found only her skull, her feet, and her hands.

36When they returned and told him, he remarked, "That is just what the Lord said would happen. He told Elijah the prophet that dogs would eat her flesh 37and that her body would be scattered like manure upon the field, so that no one could tell whose it was."

10 THEN JEHU wrote a letter to the city council of Samaria and to the guardians of Ahab's seventy sons—all of whom were living there.

2, 3"Upon receipt of this letter, select the best one of Ahab's sons to be your king, and prepare to fight for his throne. For you have chariots and horses and a fortified city and an armory."

4But they were too frightened to do it. "Two kings couldn't stand against this man! What can we do?" they said.

5So the manager of palace affairs and the city manager, together with the city council and the guardians of Ahab's sons, sent him this message:

"Jehu, we are your servants and will do anything you tell us to. We have decided that you should be our king instead of one of Ahab's sons."

New Revised Standard

saying to Ahaziah, "Treason, Ahaziah!" 24Jehu drew his bow with all his strength, and shot Joram between the shoulders, so that the arrow pierced his heart; and he sank in his chariot. 25Jehu said to his aide Bidkar, "Lift him out, and throw him on the plot of ground belonging to Naboth the Jezreelite; for remember, when you and I rode side by side behind his father Ahab how the Lord uttered this oracle against him: 26'For the blood of Naboth and for the blood of his children that I saw yesterday, says the Lord, I swear I will repay you on this very plot of ground.' Now therefore lift him out and throw him on the plot of ground, in accordance with the word of the Lord."

Ahaziah of Judah Killed

27 When King Ahaziah of Judah saw this, he fled in the direction of Beth-haggan. Jehu pursued him, saying, "Shoot him also!" And they shot himg in the chariot at the ascent to Gur, which is by Ibleam. Then he fled to Megiddo, and died there. 28His officers carried him in a chariot to Jerusalem, and buried him in his tomb with his ancestors in the city of David.

29 In the eleventh year of Joram son of Ahab, Ahaziah began to reign over Judah.

Jezebel's Violent Death

30 When Jehu came to Jezreel, Jezebel heard of it; she painted her eyes, and adorned her head, and looked out of the window. 31As Jehu entered the gate, she said, "Is it peace, Zimri, murderer of your master?" 32He looked up to the window and said, "Who is on my side? Who?" Two or three eunuchs looked out at him. 33He said, "Throw her down." So they threw her down; some of her blood spattered on the wall and on the horses, which trampled on her. 34Then he went in and ate and drank; he said, "See to that cursed woman and bury her; for she is a king's daughter." 35But when they went to bury her, they found no more of her than the skull and the feet and the palms of her hands. 36When they came back and told him, he said, "This is the word of the Lord, which he spoke by his servant Elijah the Tishbite, 'In the territory of Jezreel the dogs shall eat the flesh of Jezebel; 37the corpse of Jezebel shall be like dung on the field in the territory of Jezreel, so that no one can say, This is Jezebel.' "

Massacre of Ahab's Descendants

10 NOW AHAB had seventy sons in Samaria. So Jehu wrote letters and sent them to Samaria, to the rulers of Jezreel,h to the elders, and to the guardians of the sons ofi Ahab, saying, 2"Since your master's sons are with you and you have at your disposal chariots and horses, a fortified city, and weapons, 3select the son of your master who is the best qualified, set him on his father's throne, and fight for your master's house." 4But they were utterly terrified and said, "Look, two kings could not withstand him; how then can we stand?" 5So the steward of the palace, and the governor of the city, along with the elders and the guardians, sent word to Jehu: "We are your servants; we will do anything you say. We will not make anyone king; do whatever you think right." 6Then he wrote them a second letter, say-

---

f 9:29 twelfth year, implied in 8:25. Literally, "eleventh."

g Syr Vg Compare Gk: Heb lacks and they shot him   h Or of the city; Vg Compare Gk   i Gk: Heb lacks of the sons of

King James

6Then he wrote a letter the second time to them, saying, If ye *be* mine, and *if* ye will hearken unto my voice, take ye the heads of the men your master's sons, and come to me to Jezreel by tomorrow this time. Now the king's sons, *being* seventy persons, *were* with the great men of the city, which brought them up.

7And it came to pass, when the letter came to them, that they took the king's sons, and slew seventy persons, and put their heads in baskets, and sent him *them* to Jezreel.

8¶ And there came a messenger, and told him, saying, They have brought the heads of the king's sons. And he said, Lay ye them in two heaps at the entering in of the gate until the morning.

9And it came to pass in the morning, that he went out, and stood, and said to all the people, Ye *be* righteous: behold, I conspired against my master, and slew him: but who slew all these?

10Know now that there shall fall unto the earth nothing of the word of the LORD, which the LORD spake concerning the house of Ahab: for the LORD hath done *that* which he spake by his servant Elijah.

11So Jehu slew all that remained of the house of Ahab in Jezreel, and all his great men, and his kinsfolks, and his priests, until he left him none remaining.

12¶ And he arose and departed, and came to Samaria. *And* as he *was* at the shearing house in the way,

13Jehu met with the brethren of Ahaziah king of Judah, and said, Who *are* ye? And they answered, We *are* the brethren of Ahaziah; and we go down to salute the children of the king and the children of the queen.

14And he said, Take them alive. And they took them alive, and slew them at the pit of the shearing house, *even* two and forty men: neither left he any of them.

15¶ And when he was departed thence, He lighted on Jehonadab the son of Rechab *coming* to meet him: and he saluted him, and said to him, Is thine heart right, as my heart *is* with thy heart? And Jehonadab answered, It is. If it be, give *me* thine hand. And he gave *him* his hand; and he took him up to him into the chariot.

16And he said, Come with me, and see my zeal for the LORD. So they made him ride in his chariot.

17And when he came to Samaria, he slew all that remained unto Ahab in Samaria, till he had destroyed him, according to the saying of the LORD, which he spake to Elijah.

18¶ And Jehu gathered all the people together, and said unto them, Ahab served Baal a little; *but* Jehu shall serve him much.

19Now therefore call unto me all the prophets of Baal, all his servants, and all his priests; let none be wanting: for I have a great sacrifice *to do* to Baal; whosoever shall be wanting, he shall not live. But Jehu did *it* in subtlety, to the intent that he might destroy the worshippers of Baal.

20And Jehu said, Proclaim a solemn assembly for Baal. And they proclaimed *it.*

21And Jehu sent through all Israel: and all the worshippers of Baal came, so that there was not a man left that came not. And they came into the house of Baal; and the house of Baal was full from one end to another.

22And he said unto him that *was* over the vestry, Bring forth vestments for all the worshippers of Baal. And he brought them forth vestments.

23And Jehu went, and Jehonadab the son of Rechab, into the house of Baal, and said unto the worshippers of Baal, Search, and look that there be here with you none of the servants of the LORD, but the worshippers of Baal only.

24And when they went in to offer sacrifices and burnt offerings, Jehu appointed fourscore men without, and said, *If* any of the men whom I have brought into your hands escape, *he that letteth him go,* his life *shall be* for the life of him.

New International

6Then Jehu wrote them a second letter, saying, "If you are on my side and will obey me, take the heads of your master's sons and come to me in Jezreel by this time tomorrow."

Now the royal princes, seventy of them, were with the leading men of the city, who were rearing them. 7When the letter arrived, these men took the princes and slaughtered all seventy of them. They put their heads in baskets and sent them to Jehu in Jezreel. 8When the messenger arrived, he told Jehu, "They have brought the heads of the princes."

Then Jehu ordered, "Put them in two piles at the entrance of the city gate until morning."

9The next morning Jehu went out. He stood before all the people and said, "You are innocent. It was I who conspired against my master and killed him, but who killed all these? 10Know then, that not a word the LORD has spoken against the house of Ahab will fail. The LORD has done what he promised through his servant Elijah." 11So Jehu killed everyone in Jezreel who remained of the house of Ahab, as well as all his chief men, his close friends and his priests, leaving him no survivor.

12Jehu then set out and went toward Samaria. At Beth Eked of the Shepherds, 13he met some relatives of Ahaziah king of Judah and asked, "Who are you?"

They said, "We are relatives of Ahaziah, and we have come down to greet the families of the king and of the queen mother."

14"Take them alive!" he ordered. So they took them alive and slaughtered them by the well of Beth Eked— forty-two men. He left no survivor.

15After he left there, he came upon Jehonadab son of Recab, who was on his way to meet him. Jehu greeted him and said, "Are you in accord with me, as I am with you?"

"I am," Jehonadab answered.

"If so," said Jehu, "give me your hand." So he did, and Jehu helped him up into the chariot. 16Jehu said, "Come with me and see my zeal for the LORD." Then he had him ride along in his chariot.

17When Jehu came to Samaria, he killed all who were left there of Ahab's family; he destroyed them, according to the word of the LORD spoken to Elijah.

Ministers of Baal Killed

18Then Jehu brought all the people together and said to them, "Ahab served Baal a little; Jehu will serve him much. 19Now summon all the prophets of Baal, all his ministers and all his priests. See that no one is missing, because I am going to hold a great sacrifice for Baal. Anyone who fails to come will no longer live." But Jehu was acting deceptively in order to destroy the ministers of Baal.

20Jehu said, "Call an assembly in honor of Baal." So they proclaimed it. 21Then he sent word throughout Israel, and all the ministers of Baal came; not one stayed away. They crowded into the temple of Baal until it was full from one end to the other. 22And Jehu said to the keeper of the wardrobe, "Bring robes for all the ministers of Baal." So he brought out robes for them.

23Then Jehu and Jehonadab son of Recab went into the temple of Baal. Jehu said to the ministers of Baal, "Look around and see that no servants of the LORD are here with you—only ministers of Baal." 24So they went in to make sacrifices and burnt offerings. Now Jehu had posted eighty men outside with this warning: "If one of you lets any of the men I am placing in your hands escape, it will be your life for his life."

Living Bible

6Jehu responded with this message: "If you are on my side and are going to obey me, bring the heads of your master's sons to me at Jezreel at about this time tomorrow."

(These seventy sons of King Ahab were living in the homes of the chief men of the city, where they had been raised since childhood.) 7When the letter arrived, all seventy of them were murdered, and their heads were packed into baskets and presented to Jehu at Jezreel. 8When a messenger told Jehu that the heads of the king's sons had arrived, he said to pile them in two heaps at the entrance of the city gate, and to leave them there until the next morning.

9, 10In the morning he went out and spoke to the crowd that had gathered around them. "You aren't to blame," he told them. "I conspired against my master and killed him, but I didn't kill his sons! The Lord has done that, for everything he says comes true. He declared through his servant Elijah that this would happen to Ahab's descendants."

11Jehu then killed all the rest of the members of the family of Ahab who were in Jezreel, as well as all of his important officials, personal friends, and private chaplains. Finally, no one was left who had been close to him in any way.a 12Then he set out for Samaria, and stayed overnight at a shepherd's inn along the way. 13While he was there he met the brothers of King Ahaziah of Judah.

"Who are you?" he asked them.

And they replied, "We are brothersb of King Ahaziah. We are going to Samaria to visit the sons of King Ahab and of the Queen Mother, Jezebel."

14"Grab them!" Jehu shouted to his men. And he took them out to the cistern and killed all forty-two of them.

15As he left the inn, he met Jehonadab, the son of Rechab, who was coming to meet him. After they had greeted each other, Jehu said to him, "Are you as loyal to me as I am to you?"

"Yes," Jehonadab replied.

"Then give me your hand," Jehu said, and he helped him into the royal chariot.

16"Now come along with me," Jehu said, "and see how much I have done for the Lord." So Jehonadab rode along with him. 17When he arrived in Samaria he butchered all of Ahab's friends and relatives, just as Elijah, speaking for the Lord, had predicted.

Then Jehu called a meeting of all the people of the city and said to them, "Ahab hardly worshiped Baal at all in comparison to the way I am going to! 18, 19Summon all the prophets and priests of Baal, and call together all his worshipers. See to it that every one of them comes, for we worshipers of Baal are going to have a great celebration to praise him. Any of Baal's worshipers who don't come will be put to death."

But Jehu's plan was to exterminate them. 20, 21He sent messengers throughout all Israel summoning those who worshiped Baal; and they all came and filled the temple of Baal from one end to the other. 22He instructed the head of the robing room, "Be sure that every worshiper wears one of the special robes."

23Then Jehu and Jehonadab (son of Rechab) went into the temple to address the people: "Check to be sure that only those who worship Baal are here; don't let anyone in who worships the Lord!"

24As the priests of Baal began offering sacrifices and burnt offerings, Jehu surrounded the building with eighty of his men and told them, "If you let anyone escape, you'll pay for it with your own life."

New Revised Standard

ing, "If you are on my side, and if you are ready to obey me, take the heads of your master's sons and come to me at Jezreel tomorrow at this time." Now the king's sons, seventy persons, were with the leaders of the city, who were charged with their upbringing. 7When the letter reached them, they took the king's sons and killed them, seventy persons; they put their heads in baskets and sent them to him at Jezreel. 8When the messenger came and told him, "They have brought the heads of the king's sons," he said, "Lay them in two heaps at the entrance of the gate until the morning." 9Then in the morning when he went out, he stood and said to all the people, "You are innocent. It was I who conspired against my master and killed him; but who struck down all these? 10Know then that there shall fall to the earth nothing of the word of the LORD, which the LORD spoke concerning the house of Ahab; for the LORD has done what he said through his servant Elijah." 11So Jehu killed all who were left of the house of Ahab in Jezreel, all his leaders, close friends, and priests, until he left him no survivor.

12 Then he set out and went to Samaria. On the way, when he was at Beth-eked of the Shepherds, 13Jehu met relatives of King Ahaziah of Judah and said, "Who are you?" They answered, "We are kin of Ahaziah; we have come down to visit the royal princes and the sons of the queen mother." 14He said, "Take them alive." They took them alive, and slaughtered them at the pit of Beth-eked, forty-two in all; he spared none of them.

15 When he left there, he met Jehonadab son of Rechab coming to meet him; he greeted him, and said to him, "Is your heart as true to mine as mine is to yours?"c Jehonadab answered, "It is." Jehu said,d "If it is, give me your hand." So he gave him his hand. Jehu took him up with him into the chariot. 16He said, "Come with me, and see my zeal for the LORD." So hee had him ride in his chariot. 17When he came to Samaria, he killed all who were left to Ahab in Samaria, until he had wiped them out, according to the word of the LORD that he spoke to Elijah.

Slaughter of Worshipers of Baal

18 Then Jehu assembled all the people and said to them, "Ahab offered Baal small service; but Jehu will offer much more. 19Now therefore summon to me all the prophets of Baal, all his worshipers, and all his priests; let none be missing, for I have a great sacrifice to offer to Baal; whoever is missing shall not live." But Jehu was acting with cunning in order to destroy the worshipers of Baal. 20Jehu decreed, "Sanctify a solemn assembly for Baal." So they proclaimed it. 21Jehu sent word throughout all Israel; all the worshipers of Baal came, so that there was no one left who did not come. They entered the temple of Baal, until the temple of Baal was filled from wall to wall. 22He said to the keeper of the wardrobe, "Bring out the vestments for all the worshipers of Baal." So he brought out the vestments for them. 23Then Jehu entered the temple of Baal with Jehonadab son of Rechab; he said to the worshipers of Baal, "Search and see that there is no worshiper of the LORD here among you, but only worshipers of Baal." 24Then they proceeded to offer sacrifices and burnt offerings.

Now Jehu had stationed eighty men outside, saying, "Whoever allows any of those to escape whom I deliver into your hands shall forfeit his life." 25As soon as he

---

a 10:11 no one was left who had been close to him in any way. Apparently Jehu in his zeal exceeded the Lord's command in this bloodbath, for he was blamed for it by the prophet Hosea (1:4). b 10:13 we are brothers, literally, "kinsmen."

c Gk: Heb Is it right with your heart, as my heart is with your heart? d Gk: Heb lacks Jehu said e Gk Syr Tg: Heb they

King James

25And it came to pass, as soon as he had made an end of offering the burnt offering, that Jehu said to the guard and to the captains, Go in, *and* slay them; let none come forth. And they smote them with the edge of the sword; and the guard and the captains cast *them* out, and went to the city of the house of Baal.

26And they brought forth the images out of the house of Baal, and burned them.

27And they brake down the image of Baal, and brake down the house of Baal, and made it a draught house unto this day.

28Thus Jehu destroyed Baal out of Israel.

29¶ Howbeit *from* the sins of Jeroboam the son of Nebat, who made Israel to sin, Jehu departed not from after them, *to wit,* the golden calves that *were* in Beth-el, and that *were* in Dan.

30And the LORD said unto Jehu, Because thou hast done well in executing *that which is* right in mine eyes, *and* hast done unto the house of Ahab according to all that *was* in mine heart, thy children of the fourth *generation* shall sit on the throne of Israel.

31But Jehu took no heed to walk in the law of the LORD God of Israel with all his heart: for he departed not from the sins of Jeroboam, which made Israel to sin.

32¶ In those days the LORD began to cut Israel short: and Hazael smote them in all the coasts of Israel;

33From Jordan eastward, all the land of Gilead, the Gadites, and the Reubenites, and the Manassites, from Aroer, which *is* by the river Arnon, even Gilead and Bashan.

34Now the rest of the acts of Jehu, and all that he did, and all his might, *are* they not written in the book of the chronicles of the kings of Israel?

35And Jehu slept with his fathers: and they buried him in Samaria. And Jehoahaz his son reigned in his stead.

36And the time that Jehu reigned over Israel in Samaria *was* twenty and eight years.

11 AND WHEN Athaliah the mother of Ahaziah saw that her son was dead, she arose and destroyed all the seed royal.

2But Jehosheba, the daughter of king Joram, sister of Ahaziah, took Joash the son of Ahaziah, and stole him from among the king's sons *which were* slain; and they hid him, *even* him and his nurse, in the bedchamber from Athaliah, so that he was not slain.

3And he was with her hid in the house of the LORD six years. And Athaliah did reign over the land.

4¶ And the seventh year Jehoiada sent and fetched the rulers over hundreds, with the captains and the guard, and brought them to him into the house of the LORD, and made a covenant with them, and took an oath of them in the house of the LORD, and showed them the king's son.

5And he commanded them, saying, This *is* the thing that ye shall do; A third part of you that enter in on the sabbath shall even be keepers of the watch of the king's house;

6And a third part *shall be* at the gate of Sur; and a third part at the gate behind the guard: so shall ye keep the watch of the house, that it be not broken down.

7And two parts of all you that go forth on the sabbath, even they shall keep the watch of the house of the LORD about the king.

8And ye shall compass the king round about, every man with his weapons in his hand: and he that cometh within the ranges, let him be slain: and be ye with the king as he goeth out and as he cometh in.

New International

25As soon as Jehu had finished making the burnt offering, he ordered the guards and officers: "Go in and kill them; let no one escape." So they cut them down with the sword. The guards and officers threw the bodies out and then entered the inner shrine of the temple of Baal. 26They brought the sacred stone out of the temple of Baal and burned it. 27They demolished the sacred stone of Baal and tore down the temple of Baal, and people have used it for a latrine to this day.

28So Jehu destroyed Baal worship in Israel. 29However, he did not turn away from the sins of Jeroboam son of Nebat, which he had caused Israel to commit—the worship of the golden calves at Bethel and Dan.

30The LORD said to Jehu, "Because you have done well in accomplishing what is right in my eyes and have done to the house of Ahab all I had in mind to do, your descendants will sit on the throne of Israel to the fourth generation." 31Yet Jehu was not careful to keep the law of the LORD, the God of Israel, with all his heart. He did not turn away from the sins of Jeroboam, which he had caused Israel to commit.

32In those days the LORD began to reduce the size of Israel. Hazael overpowered the Israelites throughout their territory 33east of the Jordan in all the land of Gilead (the region of Gad, Reuben and Manasseh), from Aroer by the Arnon Gorge through Gilead to Bashan.

34As for the other events of Jehu's reign, all he did, and all his achievements, are they not written in the book of the annals of the kings of Israel?

35Jehu rested with his fathers and was buried in Samaria. And Jehoahaz his son succeeded him as king. 36The time that Jehu reigned over Israel in Samaria was twenty-eight years.

Athaliah and Joash

11 WHEN ATHALIAH the mother of Ahaziah saw that her son was dead, she proceeded to destroy the whole royal family. 2But Jehosheba, the daughter of King Jehoram[a] and sister of Ahaziah, took Joash son of Ahaziah and stole him away from among the royal princes, who were about to be murdered. She put him and his nurse in a bedroom to hide him from Athaliah; so he was not killed. 3He remained hidden with his nurse at the temple of the LORD for six years while Athaliah ruled the land.

4In the seventh year Jehoiada sent for the commanders of units of a hundred, the Carites and the guards and had them brought to him at the temple of the LORD. He made a covenant with them and put them under oath at the temple of the LORD. Then he showed them the king's son. 5He commanded them, saying, "This is what you are to do: You who are in the three companies that are going on duty on the Sabbath—a third of you guarding the royal palace, 6a third at the Sur Gate, and a third at the gate behind the guard, who take turns guarding the temple— 7and you who are in the other two companies that normally go off Sabbath duty are all to guard the temple for the king. 8Station yourselves around the king, each man with his weapon in his hand. Anyone who approaches your ranks[b] must be put to death. Stay close to the king wherever he goes."

---

a 2 Hebrew *Joram,* a variant of *Jehoram*   b 8 Or *approaches the precincts*

Living Bible

25As soon as he had finished sacrificing the burnt offering, Jehu went out and told his officers and men, "Go in and kill the whole bunch of them. Don't let a single one escape."

So they slaughtered them all and dragged their bodies outside. Then Jehu's men went into the inner temple, 26dragged out the pillar used for the worship of Baal, and burned it. 27They wrecked the temple and converted it into a public toilet, which it still is today. 28Thus Jehu destroyed every trace of Baal from Israel. 29However, he didn't destroy the gold calves at Bethel and Dan—this was the great sin of Jeroboam (son of Nebat), for it resulted in all Israel sinning.

30Afterwards the Lord said to Jehu, "You have done well in following my instructions to destroy the dynasty of Ahab. Because of this I will cause your son, your grandson, and your great-grandson to be the kings of Israel."

31But Jehu didn't follow the Lord God of Israel with all his heart, for he continued to worship Jeroboam's gold calves that had been the cause of such great sin in Israel.

32, 33At about that time the Lord began to whittle down the size of Israel. King Hazael conquered several sections of the country east of the Jordan River, as well as all of Gilead, Gad, and Reuben; he also conquered parts of Manasseh from the Aroer River in the valley of the Arnon as far as Gilead and Bashan.

34The rest of Jehu's activities are recorded in *The Annals of the Kings of Israel*. 35When Jehu died, he was buried in Samaria; and his son Jehoahaz became the new king. 36In all, Jehu reigned as king of Israel, in Samaria, for twenty-eight years.

11 WHEN ATHALIAH, the mother of King Ahaziah of Judah, learned that her son was dead, she killed all of his children, 2, 3except for his year-oldc son Joash. Joash was rescued by his Aunt Jehosheba, who was a sister of King Ahaziah (for she was a daughter of King Jehoram, Ahaziah's father). She stole him away from among the rest of the king's children who were waiting to be slain, and hid him and his nurse in a storeroom of the Temple.d They lived there for six years while Athaliah reigned as queen.

4In the seventh year of Queen Athaliah's reign, Jehoiada the prieste summoned the officers of the palace guard and the queen's bodyguard. He met them in the Temple, swore them to secrecy, and showed them the king's son.

5Then he gave them their instructions: "A third of those who are on duty on the Sabbath are to guard the palace. 6, 7, 8The other two-thirds shall stand guard at the Temple; surround the king, weapons in hand, and kill anyone who tries to break through. Stay with the king at all times."

New Revised Standard

had finished presenting the burnt offering, Jehu said to the guards and to the officers, "Come in and kill them; let no one escape." So they put them to the sword. The guards and the officers threw them out, and then went into the citadel of the temple of Baal. 26They brought out the pillarf that was in the temple of Baal, and burned it. 27Then they demolished the pillar of Baal, and destroyed the temple of Baal, and made it a latrine to this day.

28 Thus Jehu wiped out Baal from Israel. 29But Jehu did not turn aside from the sins of Jeroboam son of Nebat, which he caused Israel to commit—the golden calves that were in Bethel and in Dan. 30The LORD said to Jehu, "Because you have done well in carrying out what I consider right, and in accordance with all that was in my heart have dealt with the house of Ahab, your sons of the fourth generation shall sit on the throne of Israel." 31But Jehu was not careful to follow the law of the LORD the God of Israel with all his heart; he did not turn from the sins of Jeroboam, which he caused Israel to commit.

Death of Jehu

32 In those days the LORD began to trim off parts of Israel. Hazael defeated them throughout the territory of Israel: 33from the Jordan eastward, all the land of Gilead, the Gadites, the Reubenites, and the Manassites, from Aroer, which is by the Wadi Arnon, that is, Gilead and Bashan. 34Now the rest of the acts of Jehu, all that he did, and all his power, are they not written in the Book of the Annals of the Kings of Israel? 35So Jehu slept with his ancestors, and they buried him in Samaria. His son Jehoahaz succeeded him. 36The time that Jehu reigned over Israel in Samaria was twenty-eight years.

Athaliah Reigns over Judah

11 NOW WHEN Athaliah, Ahaziah's mother, saw that her son was dead, she set about to destroy all the royal family. 2But Jehosheba, King Joram's daughter, Ahaziah's sister, took Joash son of Ahaziah, and stole him away from among the king's children who were about to be killed; she putg him and his nurse in a bedroom. Thus sheh hid him from Athaliah, so that he was not killed; 3he remained with her six years, hidden in the house of the LORD, while Athaliah reigned over the land.

Jehoiada Anoints the Child Joash

4 But in the seventh year Jehoiada summoned the captains of the Carites and of the guards and had them come to him in the house of the LORD. He made a covenant with them and put them under oath in the house of the LORD; then he showed them the king's son. 5He commanded them, "This is what you are to do: one-third of you, those who go off duty on the sabbath and guard the king's house 6(another third being at the gate Sur and a third at the gate behind the guards), shall guard the palace; 7and your two divisions that come on duty in force on the sabbath and guard the house of the LORDi 8shall surround the king, each with weapons in hand; and whoever approaches the ranks is to be killed. Be with the king in his comings and goings."

---

c 11:2 *except for his year-old son*, implied.   d 11:3 *storeroom in the Temple*. This arrangement was practical because Jehosheba was the wife of Jehoiada the High Priest.   e 11:4 *the priest*, implied.

f Gk Vg Syr Tg: Heb *pillars*   g With 2 Chr 22.11: Heb lacks *she put*   h Gk Syr Vg Compare 2 Chr 22.11: Heb *they*   i Heb *the LORD to the king*

King James

9And the captains over the hundreds did according to all *things* that Jehoiada the priest commanded: and they took every man his men that were to come in on the sabbath, with them that should go out on the sabbath, and came to Jehoiada the priest.

10And to the captains over hundreds did the priest give king David's spears and shields, that *were* in the temple of the LORD.

11And the guard stood, every man with his weapons in his hand, round about the king, from the right corner of the temple to the left corner of the temple, *along* by the altar and the temple.

12And he brought forth the king's son, and put the crown upon him, and *gave him* the testimony; and they made him king, and anointed him; and they clapped their hands, and said, God save the king.

13¶ And when Athaliah heard the noise of the guard *and* of the people, she came to the people into the temple of the LORD.

14And when she looked, behold, the king stood by a pillar, as the manner *was,* and the princes and the trumpeters by the king, and all the people of the land rejoiced, and blew with trumpets: and Athaliah rent her clothes, and cried, Treason, Treason.

15But Jehoiada the priest commanded the captains of the hundreds, the officers of the host, and said unto them, Have her forth without the ranges: and him that followeth her kill with the sword. For the priest had said, Let her not be slain in the house of the LORD.

16And they laid hands on her; and she went by the way by the which the horses came into the king's house: and there was she slain.

17¶ And Jehoiada made a covenant between the LORD and the king and the people, that they should be the LORD's people; between the king also and the people.

18And all the people of the land went into the house of Baal, and brake it down; his altars and his images brake they in pieces thoroughly, and slew Mattan the priest of Baal before the altars. And the priest appointed officers over the house of the LORD.

19And he took the rulers over hundreds, and the captains, and the guard, and all the people of the land; and they brought down the king from the house of the LORD, and came by the way of the gate of the guard to the king's house. And he sat on the throne of the kings.

20And all the people of the land rejoiced, and the city was in quiet: and they slew Athaliah with the sword *beside* the king's house.

21Seven years old *was* Jehoash when he began to reign.

12 IN THE seventh year of Jehu Jehoash began to reign; and forty years reigned he in Jerusalem. And his mother's name *was* Zibiah of Beer-sheba.

2And Jehoash did *that which was* right in the sight of the LORD all his days wherein Jehoiada the priest instructed him.

3But the high places were not taken away: the people still sacrificed and burnt incense in the high places.

4¶ And Jehoash said to the priests, All the money of the dedicated things that is brought into the house of the LORD, *even* the money of every one that passeth *the account,* the money that every man is set at, *and* all the money that cometh into any man's heart to bring into the house of the LORD,

5Let the priests take *it* to them, every man of his acquaintance: and let them repair the breaches of the house, wheresoever any breach shall be found.

New International

9The commanders of units of a hundred did just as Jehoiada the priest ordered. Each one took his men— those who were going on duty on the Sabbath and those who were going off duty—and came to Jehoiada the priest. 10Then he gave the commanders the spears and shields that had belonged to King David and that were in the temple of the LORD. 11The guards, each with his weapon in his hand, stationed themselves around the king—near the altar and the temple, from the south side to the north side of the temple.

12Jehoiada brought out the king's son and put the crown on him; he presented him with a copy of the covenant and proclaimed him king. They anointed him, and the people clapped their hands and shouted, "Long live the king!"

13When Athaliah heard the noise made by the guards and the people, she went to the people at the temple of the LORD. 14She looked and there was the king, standing by the pillar, as the custom was. The officers and the trumpeters were beside the king, and all the people of the land were rejoicing and blowing trumpets. Then Athaliah tore her robes and called out, "Treason! Treason!"

15Jehoiada the priest ordered the commanders of units of a hundred, who were in charge of the troops: "Bring her out between the ranksa and put to the sword anyone who follows her." For the priest had said, "She must not be put to death in the temple of the LORD." 16So they seized her as she reached the place where the horses enter the palace grounds, and there she was put to death.

17Jehoiada then made a covenant between the LORD and the king and people that they would be the LORD's people. He also made a covenant between the king and the people. 18All the people of the land went to the temple of Baal and tore it down. They smashed the altars and idols to pieces and killed Mattan the priest of Baal in front of the altars.

Then Jehoiada the priest posted guards at the temple of the LORD. 19He took with him the commanders of hundreds, the Carites, the guards and all the people of the land, and together they brought the king down from the temple of the LORD and went into the palace, entering by way of the gate of the guards. The king then took his place on the royal throne, 20and all the people of the land rejoiced. And the city was quiet, because Athaliah had been slain with the sword at the palace.

21Joashb was seven years old when he began to reign.

Joash Repairs the Temple

12 IN THE seventh year of Jehu, Joashc became king, and he reigned in Jerusalem forty years. His mother's name was Zibiah; she was from Beersheba. 2Joash did what was right in the eyes of the LORD all the years Jehoiada the priest instructed him. 3The high places, however, were not removed; the people continued to offer sacrifices and burn incense there.

4Joash said to the priests, "Collect all the money that is brought as sacred offerings to the temple of the LORD—the money collected in the census, the money received from personal vows and the money brought voluntarily to the temple. 5Let every priest receive the money from one of the treasurers, and let it be used to repair whatever damage is found in the temple."

---

a *15* Or *out from the precincts*   b *21* Hebrew *Jehoash,* a variant of *Joash*
c *1* Hebrew *Jehoash,* a variant of *Joash;* also in verses 2, 4, 6, 7 and 18

Living Bible

9So the officers followed Jehoiada's instructions. They brought to Jehoiada the men who were going off duty on the Sabbath and those who were coming on duty, 10and he armed them from the Temple's supply of spears and shields that had belonged to King David. 11The guards, with weapons ready, stood across the front of the sanctuary, and surrounded the altar, which was near Joash's hideaway.

12Then Jehoiada brought out the young prince and put the crown upon his head and gave him a copy of the Ten Commandments, and anointed him as king. Then everyone clapped and shouted, "Long live the king!"

13, 14When Athaliah heard all the noise, she ran into the Temple and saw the new king standing beside the pillar, as was the custom at times of coronation, surrounded by her bodyguard and many trumpeters; and everyone was rejoicing and blowing trumpets.

"Treason! Treason!" she screamed, and began to tear her clothes.

15"Get her out of here," shouted Jehoiada to the officers of the guard. "Don't kill her here in the Temple. But kill anyone who tries to come to her rescue."

16So they dragged her to the palace stables and killed her there.

17Jehoiada made a treaty between the Lord, the king, and the people, that they would be the Lord's people. He also made a contract between the king and the people. 18Everyone went over to the temple of Baal and tore it down, breaking the altars and images and killing Mattan, the priest of Baal, in front of the altar. And Jehoiada set guards at the Temple of the Lord. 19Then he and the officers and the guard and all the people led the king from the Temple, past the guardhouse, and into the palace. And he sat upon the king's throne.

20So everyone was happy, and the city settled back into quietness after Athaliah's death. 21Joash was seven years old when he became king.

12 IT WAS seven years after Jehu had become the king of Israel that Joash became king of Judah. He reigned in Jerusalem for forty years. (His mother was Zibiah, from Beer-sheba.) 2All his life Joash did what was right because Jehoiada the High Priest instructed him. 3Yet even so he didn't destroy the shrines on the hills—the people still sacrificed and burned incense there.

4, 5One day King Joash said to Jehoiada, "The Temple building needs repairing. Whenever anyone brings a contribution to the Lord, whether it is a regular assessment or some special gift, use it to pay for whatever repairs are needed."

New Revised Standard

9 The captains did according to all that the priest Jehoiada commanded; each brought his men who were to go off duty on the sabbath, with those who were to come on duty on the sabbath, and came to the priest Jehoiada. 10The priest delivered to the captains the spears and shields that had been King David's, which were in the house of the LORD; 11 the guards stood, every man with his weapons in his hand, from the south side of the house to the north side of the house, around the altar and the house, to guard the king on every side. 12Then he brought out the king's son, put the crown on him, and gave him the covenant;d they proclaimed him king, and anointed him; they clapped their hands and shouted, "Long live the king!"

Death of Athaliah

13 When Athaliah heard the noise of the guard and of the people, she went into the house of the LORD to the people; 14when she looked, there was the king standing by the pillar, according to custom, with the captains and the trumpeters beside the king, and all the people of the land rejoicing and blowing trumpets. Athaliah tore her clothes and cried, "Treason! Treason!" 15Then the priest Jehoiada commanded the captains who were set over the army, "Bring her out between the ranks, and kill with the sword anyone who follows her." For the priest said, "Let her not be killed in the house of the LORD." 16So they laid hands on her; she went through the horses' entrance to the king's house, and there she was put to death.

17 Jehoiada made a covenant between the LORD and the king and people, that they should be the LORD's people; also between the king and the people. 18Then all the people of the land went to the house of Baal, and tore it down; his altars and his images they broke in pieces, and they killed Mattan, the priest of Baal, before the altars. The priest posted guards over the house of the LORD. 19He took the captains, the Carites, the guards, and all the people of the land; then they brought the king down from the house of the LORD, marching through the gate of the guards to the king's house. He took his seat on the throne of the kings. 20So all the people of the land rejoiced; and the city was quiet after Athaliah had been killed with the sword at the king's house.

21e Jehoashf was seven years old when he began to reign.

The Temple Repaired

12 IN THE seventh year of Jehu, Jehoash began to reign; he reigned forty years in Jerusalem. His mother's name was Zibiah of Beer-sheba. 2Jehoash did what was right in the sight of the LORD all his days, because the priest Jehoiada instructed him. 3Nevertheless the high places were not taken away; the people continued to sacrifice and make offerings on the high places.

4 Jehoash said to the priests, "All the money offered as sacred donations that is brought into the house of the LORD, the money for which each person is assessed— the money from the assessment of persons—and the money from the voluntary offerings brought into the house of the LORD, 5let the priests receive from each of the donors; and let them repair the house wherever any need of repairs is discovered." 6But by the twenty-third

d Or treaty or testimony; Heb eduth   e Ch 12.1 in Heb   f Another spelling is Joash; see verse 19

King James

6But it was *so, that* in the three and twentieth year of king Jehoash the priests had not repaired the breaches of the house.

7Then king Jehoash called for Jehoiada the priest, and the *other* priests, and said unto them, Why repair ye not the breaches of the house? now therefore receive no *more* money of your acquaintance, but deliver it for the breaches of the house.

8And the priests consented to receive no *more* money of the people, neither to repair the breaches of the house.

9But Jehoiada the priest took a chest, and bored a hole in the lid of it, and set it beside the altar, on the right side as one cometh into the house of the LORD: and the priests that kept the door put therein all the money *that was* brought into the house of the LORD.

10And it was *so,* when they saw that *there was* much money in the chest, that the king's scribe and the high priest came up, and they put up in bags, and told the money that was found in the house of the LORD.

11And they gave the money, being told, into the hands of them that did the work, that had the oversight of the house of the LORD: and they laid it out to the carpenters and builders, that wrought upon the house of the LORD,

12And to masons, and hewers of stone, and to buy timber and hewed stone to repair the breaches of the house of the LORD, and for all that was laid out for the house to repair *it.*

13Howbeit there were not made for the house of the LORD bowls of silver, snuffers, basins, trumpets, any vessels of gold, or vessels of silver, of the money *that was* brought into the house of the LORD:

14But they gave that to the workmen, and repaired therewith the house of the LORD.

15Moreover they reckoned not with the men, into whose hand they delivered the money to be bestowed on workmen: for they dealt faithfully.

16The trespass money and sin money was not brought into the house of the LORD: it was the priests'.

17¶ Then Hazael king of Syria went up, and fought against Gath, and took it: and Hazael set his face to go up to Jerusalem.

18And Jehoash king of Judah took all the hallowed things that Jehoshaphat, and Jehoram, and Ahaziah, his fathers, kings of Judah, had dedicated, and his own hallowed things, and all the gold *that was* found in the treasures of the house of the LORD, and in the king's house, and sent *it* to Hazael king of Syria: and he went away from Jerusalem.

19¶ And the rest of the acts of Joash, and all that he did, *are* they not written in the book of the chronicles of the kings of Judah?

20And his servants arose, and made a conspiracy, and slew Joash in the house of Millo, which goeth down to Silla.

21For Jozachar the son of Shimeath, and Jehozabad the son of Shomer, his servants, smote him, and he died; and they buried him with his fathers in the city of David: and Amaziah his son reigned in his stead.

13 IN THE three and twentieth year of Joash the son of Ahaziah king of Judah Jehoahaz the son of Jehu began to reign over Israel in Samaria, *and reigned* seventeen years.

2And he did *that which was* evil in the sight of the LORD, and followed the sins of Jeroboam the son of Nebat, which made Israel to sin; he departed not therefrom.

3¶ And the anger of the LORD was kindled against Israel, and he delivered them into the hand of Hazael king of Syria, and into the hand of Ben-hadad the son of Hazael, all *their* days.

New International

6But by the twenty-third year of King Joash the priests still had not repaired the temple. 7Therefore King Joash summoned Jehoiada the priest and the other priests and asked them, "Why aren't you repairing the damage done to the temple? Take no more money from your treasurers, but hand it over for repairing the temple." 8The priests agreed that they would not collect any more money from the people and that they would not repair the temple themselves.

9Jehoiada the priest took a chest and bored a hole in its lid. He placed it beside the altar, on the right side as one enters the temple of the LORD. The priests who guarded the entrance put into the chest all the money that was brought to the temple of the LORD. 10Whenever they saw that there was a large amount of money in the chest, the royal secretary and the high priest came, counted the money that had been brought into the temple of the LORD and put it into bags. 11When the amount had been determined, they gave the money to the men appointed to supervise the work on the temple. With it they paid those who worked on the temple of the LORD—the carpenters and builders, 12the masons and stonecutters. They purchased timber and dressed stone for the repair of the temple of the LORD, and met all the other expenses of restoring the temple.

13The money brought into the temple was not spent for making silver basins, wick trimmers, sprinkling bowls, trumpets or any other articles of gold or silver for the temple of the LORD; 14it was paid to the workmen, who used it to repair the temple. 15They did not require an accounting from those to whom they gave the money to pay the workers, because they acted with complete honesty. 16The money from the guilt offerings and sin offerings was not brought into the temple of the LORD; it belonged to the priests.

17About this time Hazael king of Aram went up and attacked Gath and captured it. Then he turned to attack Jerusalem. 18But Joash king of Judah took all the sacred objects dedicated by his fathers—Jehoshaphat, Jehoram and Ahaziah, the kings of Judah—and the gifts he himself had dedicated and all the gold found in the treasuries of the temple of the LORD and of the royal palace, and he sent them to Hazael king of Aram, who then withdrew from Jerusalem.

19As for the other events of the reign of Joash, and all he did, are they not written in the book of the annals of the kings of Judah? 20His officials conspired against him and assassinated him at Beth Millo, on the road down to Silla. 21The officials who murdered him were Jozabad son of Shimeath and Jehozabad son of Shomer. He died and was buried with his fathers in the City of David. And Amaziah his son succeeded him as king.

Jehoahaz King of Israel

13 IN THE twenty-third year of Joash son of Ahaziah king of Judah, Jehoahaz son of Jehu became king of Israel in Samaria, and he reigned seventeen years. 2He did evil in the eyes of the LORD by following the sins of Jeroboam son of Nebat, which he had caused Israel to commit, and he did not turn away from them. 3So the LORD's anger burned against Israel, and for a long time he kept them under the power of Hazael king of Aram and Ben-Hadad his son.

Living Bible

6But in the twenty-third year of his reign the Temple was still in disrepair. 7So Joash called for Jehoiada and the other priests and asked them, "Why haven't you done anything about the Temple? Now don't use any more money for your own needs; from now on it must all be spent on getting the Temple into good condition."

8So the priests agreed to set up a special repair fund that would not go through their hands, lest it be diverted to care for their personal needs. 9Jehoiada the priest bored a hole in the lid of a large chest and set it on the right-hand side of the altar at the Temple entrance. The doorkeepers put all of the people's contributions into it. 10Whenever the chest became full, the king's financial secretary and the High Priest counted it, put it into bags, 11, 12and gave it to the construction superintendents to pay the carpenters, stonemasons, quarrymen, timber dealers, and stone merchants, and to buy the other materials needed to repair the Temple of the Lord. 13, 14It was not used to buy silver cups, gold snuffers, bowls, trumpets, or similar articles, but only for repairs to the building. 15No accounting was required from the construction superintendents, for they were honest and faithful men. 16However, the money that was contributed for guilt offerings and sin offerings was given to the priests for their own use. It was not put into the chest.

17About this time, King Hazael of Syria went to war against Gath and captured it; then he moved on toward Jerusalem to attack it. 18King Joash took all the sacred objects that his ancestors—Jehoshaphat, Jehoram, and Ahaziah, the kings of Judah—had dedicated, along with what he himself had dedicated, and all the gold in the treasuries of the Temple and the palace, and sent it to Hazael. So Hazael called off the attack.

19The rest of the history of Joash is recorded in *The Annals of the Kings of Judah*. 20But his officers plotted against him and assassinated him in his royal residence at Millo on the road to Silla. 21The assassins were Jozachar, the son of Shimeath, and Jehozabad, the son of Shomer—both trusted aides.a He was buried in the royal cemetery in Jerusalem, and his son Amaziah became the new king.

New Revised Standard

year of King Jehoash the priests had made no repairs on the house. 7Therefore King Jehoash summoned the priest Jehoiada with the other priests and said to them, "Why are you not repairing the house? Now therefore do not accept any more money from your donors but hand it over for the repair of the house." 8So the priests agreed that they would neither accept more money from the people nor repair the house.

9 Then the priest Jehoiada took a chest, made a hole in its lid, and set it beside the altar on the right side as one entered the house of the Lord; the priests who guarded the threshold put in it all the money that was brought into the house of the Lord. 10Whenever they saw that there was a great deal of money in the chest, the king's secretary and the high priest went up, counted the money that was found in the house of the Lord, and tied it up in bags. 11They would give the money that was weighed out into the hands of the workers who had the oversight of the house of the Lord; then they paid it out to the carpenters and the builders who worked on the house of the Lord, 12to the masons and the stonecutters, as well as to buy timber and quarried stone for making repairs on the house of the Lord, as well as for any outlay for repairs of the house. 13But for the house of the Lord no basins of silver, snuffers, bowls, trumpets, or any vessels of gold, or of silver, were made from the money that was brought into the house of the Lord, 14for that was given to the workers who were repairing the house of the Lord with it. 15They did not ask an accounting from those into whose hand they delivered the money to pay out to the workers, for they dealt honestly. 16The money from the guilt offerings and the money from the sin offerings was not brought into the house of the Lord; it belonged to the priests.

Hazael Threatens Jerusalem

17 At that time King Hazael of Aram went up, fought against Gath, and took it. But when Hazael set his face to go up against Jerusalem, 18King Jehoash of Judah took all the votive gifts that Jehoshaphat, Jehoram, and Ahaziah, his ancestors, the kings of Judah, had dedicated, as well as his own votive gifts, all the gold that was found in the treasuries of the house of the Lord and of the king's house, and sent these to King Hazael of Aram. Then Hazael withdrew from Jerusalem.

Death of Joash

19 Now the rest of the acts of Joash, and all that he did, are they not written in the Book of the Annals of the Kings of Judah? 20His servants arose, devised a conspiracy, and killed Joash in the house of Millo, on the way that goes down to Silla. 21It was Jozacar son of Shimeath and Jehozabad son of Shomer, his servants, who struck him down, so that he died. He was buried with his ancestors in the city of David; then his son Amaziah succeeded him.

Jehoahaz Reigns over Israel

13 IN THE twenty-third year of King Joash son of Ahaziah of Judah, Jehoahaz son of Jehu began to reign over Israel in Samaria; he reigned seventeen years. 2He did what was evil in the sight of the Lord, and followed the sins of Jeroboam son of Nebat, which he caused Israel to sin; he did not depart from them. 3The anger of the Lord was kindled against Israel, so that he gave them repeatedly into the hand of King Hazael of Aram, then into the hand of Ben-hadad son of Hazael. 4But Jehoahaz entreated the Lord, and the

13 JEHOAHAZ (THE son of Jehu) began a seventeen-year reign over Israel during the twenty-third year of the reign of King Joash of Judah. 2But he was an evil king, and he followed the wicked paths of Jeroboam, who had caused Israel to sin. 3So the Lord was very angry with Israel, and he continually allowed King Hazael of Syria and his son Ben-hadad to conquer them. 4But Jehoahaz prayed for the Lord's help, and the

a 12:21 *both trusted aides*, literally, "his servants."

King James

4And Jehoahaz besought the LORD, and the LORD hearkened unto him: for he saw the oppression of Israel, because the king of Syria oppressed them.

5(And the LORD gave Israel a saviour, so that they went out from under the hand of the Syrians: and the children of Israel dwelt in their tents, as beforetime.)

6Nevertheless they departed not from the sins of the house of Jeroboam, who made Israel sin, *but* walked therein: and there remained the grove also in Samaria.)

7Neither did he leave of the people to Jehoahaz but fifty horsemen, and ten chariots, and ten thousand footmen; for the king of Syria had destroyed them, and had made them like the dust by threshing.

8¶ Now the rest of the acts of Jehoahaz, and all that he did, and his might, *are* they not written in the book of the chronicles of the kings of Israel?

9And Jehoahaz slept with his fathers; and they buried him in Samaria: and Joash his son reigned in his stead.

10¶ In the thirty and seventh year of Joash king of Judah began Jehoash the son of Jehoahaz to reign over Israel in Samaria, *and reigned* sixteen years.

11And he did *that which was* evil in the sight of the LORD; he departed not from all the sins of Jeroboam the son of Nebat, who made Israel sin: *but* he walked therein.

12And the rest of the acts of Joash, and all that he did, and his might wherewith he fought against Amaziah king of Judah, *are* they not written in the book of the chronicles of the kings of Israel?

13And Joash slept with his fathers; and Jeroboam sat upon his throne: and Joash was buried in Samaria with the kings of Israel.

14¶ Now Elisha was fallen sick of his sickness whereof he died. And Joash the king of Israel came down unto him, and wept over his face, and said, O my father, my father, the chariot of Israel, and the horsemen thereof.

15And Elisha said unto him, Take bow and arrows. And he took unto him bow and arrows.

16And he said to the king of Israel, Put thine hand upon the bow. And he put his hand *upon it:* and Elisha put his hands upon the king's hands.

17And he said, Open the window eastward. And he opened *it.* Then Elisha said, Shoot. And he shot. And he said, The arrow of the LORD's deliverance, and the arrow of deliverance from Syria: for thou shalt smite the Syrians in Aphek, till thou have consumed *them.*

18And he said, Take the arrows. And he took *them.* And he said unto the king of Israel, Smite upon the ground. And he smote thrice, and stayed.

19And the man of God was wroth with him, and said, Thou shouldest have smitten five or six times; then hadst thou smitten Syria till thou hadst consumed *it:* whereas now thou shalt smite Syria *but* thrice.

20¶ And Elisha died, and they buried him. And the bands of the Moabites invaded the land at the coming in of the year.

21And it came to pass, as they were burying a man, that, behold, they spied a band *of men;* and they cast the man into the sepulchre of Elisha: and when the man was let down, and touched the bones of Elisha, he revived, and stood up on his feet.

22¶ But Hazael king of Syria oppressed Israel all the days of Jehoahaz.

23And the LORD was gracious unto them, and had compassion on them, and had respect unto them, because of his covenant with Abraham, Isaac, and Jacob, and would not destroy them, neither cast he them from his presence as yet.

24So Hazael king of Syria died; and Ben-hadad his son reigned in his stead.

25And Jehoash the son of Jehoahaz took again out of the hand of Ben-hadad the son of Hazael the cities, which he had taken out of the hand of Jehoahaz his father by war. Three times did Joash beat him, and recovered the cities of Israel.

New International

4Then Jehoahaz sought the LORD's favor, and the LORD listened to him, for he saw how severely the king of Aram was oppressing Israel. 5The LORD provided a deliverer for Israel, and they escaped from the power of Aram. So the Israelites lived in their own homes as they had before. 6But they did not turn away from the sins of the house of Jeroboam, which he had caused Israel to commit; they continued in them. Also, the Asherah pole[a] remained standing in Samaria.

7Nothing had been left of the army of Jehoahaz except fifty horsemen, ten chariots and ten thousand foot soldiers, for the king of Aram had destroyed the rest and made them like the dust at threshing time.

8As for the other events of the reign of Jehoahaz, all he did and his achievements, are they not written in the book of the annals of the kings of Israel? 9Jehoahaz rested with his fathers and was buried in Samaria. And Jehoash[b] his son succeeded him as king.

Jehoash King of Israel

10In the thirty-seventh year of Joash king of Judah, Jehoash son of Jehoahaz became king of Israel in Samaria, and he reigned sixteen years. 11He did evil in the eyes of the LORD and did not turn away from any of the sins of Jeroboam son of Nebat, which he had caused Israel to commit; he continued in them.

12As for the other events of the reign of Jehoash, all he did and his achievements, including his war against Amaziah king of Judah, are they not written in the book of the annals of the kings of Israel? 13Jehoash rested with his fathers, and Jeroboam succeeded him on the throne. Jehoash was buried in Samaria with the kings of Israel.

14Now Elisha was suffering from the illness from which he died. Jehoash king of Israel went down to see him and wept over him. "My father! My father!" he cried. "The chariots and horsemen of Israel!"

15Elisha said, "Get a bow and some arrows," and he did so. 16"Take the bow in your hands," he said to the king of Israel. When he had taken it, Elisha put his hands on the king's hands.

17"Open the east window," he said, and he opened it. "Shoot!" Elisha said, and he shot. "The LORD's arrow of victory, the arrow of victory over Aram!" Elisha declared. "You will completely destroy the Arameans at Aphek."

18Then he said, "Take the arrows," and the king took them. Elisha told him, "Strike the ground." He struck it three times and stopped. 19The man of God was angry with him and said, "You should have struck the ground five or six times; then you would have defeated Aram and completely destroyed it. But now you will defeat it only three times."

20Elisha died and was buried.

Now Moabite raiders used to enter the country every spring. 21Once while some Israelites were burying a man, suddenly they saw a band of raiders; so they threw the man's body into Elisha's tomb. When the body touched Elisha's bones, the man came to life and stood up on his feet.

22Hazael king of Aram oppressed Israel throughout the reign of Jehoahaz. 23But the LORD was gracious to them and had compassion and showed concern for them because of his covenant with Abraham, Isaac and Jacob. To this day he has been unwilling to destroy them or banish them from his presence.

24Hazael king of Aram died, and Ben-Hadad his son succeeded him as king. 25Then Jehoash son of Jehoahaz recaptured from Ben-Hadad son of Hazael the towns he had taken in battle from his father Jehoahaz. Three times Jehoash defeated him, and so he recovered the Israelite towns.

---

a 6 That is, a symbol of the goddess Asherah; here and elsewhere in 2 Kings
b 9 Hebrew *Joash*, a variant of *Jehoash*; also in verses 12-14 and 25

Living Bible

Lord listened to him; for the Lord saw how terribly the king of Syria was oppressing Israel. 5So the Lord raised up leaders among the Israelis to rescue them from the tyranny of the Syrians; and then Israel lived in safety again as they had in former days. 6But they continued to sin, following the evil ways of Jeroboam; and they continued to worship the goddess Asherah at Samaria. 7Finally the Lord reduced Jehoahaz's army to fifty mounted troops, ten chariots, and ten thousand infantry; for the king of Syria had destroyed the others as though they were dust beneath his feet.

8The rest of the history of Jehoahaz is recorded in *The Annals of the Kings of Israel.*

9, 10Jehoahaz died and was buried in Samaria, and his son Joash reigned in Samaria for sixteen years. He came to the throne in the thirty-seventh year of the reign of King Joash of Judah. 11But he was an evil man, for, like Jeroboam, he encouraged the people to worship idols and led them into sin. 12The rest of the history of the reign of Joash, including his wars against King Amaziah of Judah, are written in *The Annals of the Kings of Israel.* 13Joash died and was buried in Samaria with the other kings of Israel; and Jeroboam II became the new king.

14When Elisha was in his last illness, King Joash visited him and wept over him.

"My father! My father! You are the strength of Israel!"c he cried.

15Elisha told him, "Get a bow and some arrows," and he did.

16, 17"Open that eastern window," he instructed.

Then he told the king to put his hand upon the bow, and Elisha laid his own hands upon the king's hands.

"Shoot!" Elisha commanded, and he did.

Then Elisha proclaimed, "This is the Lord's arrow, full of victory over Syria; for you will completely conquer the Syrians at Aphek. 18Now pick up the other arrows and strike them against the floor."

So the king picked them up and struck the floor three times. 19But the prophet was angry with him. "You should have struck the floor five or six times," he exclaimed, "for then you would have beaten Syria until they were entirely destroyed; now you will be victorious only three times."

20, 21So Elisha died and was buried.

In those days bandit gangs of Moabites used to invade the land each spring. Once some men who were burying a friend spied these marauders so they hastily threw his body into the tomb of Elisha. And as soon as the body touched Elisha's bones, the dead man revived and jumped to his feet!

22King Hazael of Syria had oppressed Israel during the entire reign of King Jehoahaz. 23But the Lord was gracious to the people of Israel, and they were not totally destroyed. For God pitied them, and also he was honoring his contract with Abraham, Isaac, and Jacob. And this is still true. 24Then King Hazael of Syria died, and his son Ben-hadad reigned in his place.

25King Joash of Israeld (the son of Jehoahaz) was successful on three occasions in reconquering the cities that his father had lost to Ben-hadad.

New Revised Standard

LORD heeded him; for he saw the oppression of Israel, how the king of Aram oppressed them. 5Therefore the LORD gave Israel a savior, so that they escaped from the hand of the Arameans; and the people of Israel lived in their homes as formerly. 6Nevertheless they did not depart from the sins of the house of Jeroboam, which he caused Israel to sin, but walkede in them; the sacred polef also remained in Samaria. 7So Jehoahaz was left with an army of not more than fifty horsemen, ten chariots and ten thousand footmen; for the king of Aram had destroyed them and made them like the dust at threshing. 8Now the rest of the acts of Jehoahaz and all that he did, including his might, are they not written in the Book of the Annals of the Kings of Israel? 9So Jehoahaz slept with his ancestors, and they buried him in Samaria; then his son Joash succeeded him.

Jehoash Reigns over Israel

10 In the thirty-seventh year of King Joash of Judah, Jehoash son of Jehoahaz began to reign over Israel in Samaria; he reigned sixteen years. 11He also did what was evil in the sight of the LORD; he did not depart from all the sins of Jeroboam son of Nebat, which he caused Israel to sin, but he walked in them. 12Now the rest of the acts of Joash, and all that he did, as well as the might with which he fought against King Amaziah of Judah, are they not written in the Book of the Annals of the Kings of Israel? 13So Joash slept with his ancestors, and Jeroboam sat upon his throne; Joash was buried in Samaria with the kings of Israel.

Death of Elisha

14 Now when Elisha had fallen sick with the illness of which he was to die, King Joash of Israel went down to him, and wept before him, crying, "My father, my father! The chariots of Israel and its horsemen!" 15Elisha said to him, "Take a bow and arrows"; so he took a bow and arrows. 16Then he said to the king of Israel, "Draw the bow"; and he drew it. Elisha laid his hands on the king's hands. 17Then he said, "Open the window eastward"; and he opened it. Elisha said, "Shoot"; and he shot. Then he said, "The LORD's arrow of victory, the arrow of victory over Aram! For you shall fight the Arameans in Aphek until you have made an end of them." 18He continued, "Take the arrows"; and he took them. He said to the king of Israel, "Strike the ground with them"; he struck three times, and stopped. 19Then the man of God was angry with him, and said, "You should have struck five or six times; then you would have struck down Aram until you had made an end of it, but now you will strike down Aram only three times."

20 So Elisha died, and they buried him. Now bands of Moabites used to invade the land in the spring of the year. 21As a man was being buried, a marauding band was seen and the man was thrown into the grave of Elisha; as soon as the man touched the bones of Elisha, he came to life and stood on his feet.

Israel Recaptures Cities from Aram

22 Now King Hazael of Aram oppressed Israel all the days of Jehoahaz. 23But the LORD was gracious to them and had compassion on them; he turned toward them, because of his covenant with Abraham, Isaac, and Jacob, and would not destroy them; nor has he banished them from his presence until now.

24 When King Hazael of Aram died, his son Ben-hadad succeeded him. 25Then Jehoash son of Jehoahaz took again from Ben-hadad son of Hazael the towns that he had taken from his father Jehoahaz in war. Three times Joash defeated him and recovered the towns of Israel.

---

c 13:14 *you are the strength of Israel,* literally, "The chariots of Israel and its horsemen!"   d 13:25 *of Israel,* implied.

e Gk Syr Tg Vg: Heb *he walked*   f Heb *Asherah*

King James

14 IN THE second year of Joash son of Jehoahaz king of Israel reigned Amaziah the son of Joash king of Judah.

2He was twenty and five years old when he began to reign, and reigned twenty and nine years in Jerusalem. And his mother's name *was* Jehoaddan of Jerusalem.

3And he did *that which was* right in the sight of the LORD, yet not like David his father: he did according to all things as Joash his father did.

4Howbeit the high places were not taken away: as yet the people did sacrifice and burnt incense on the high places.

5¶ And it came to pass, as soon as the kingdom was confirmed in his hand, that he slew his servants which had slain the king his father.

6But the children of the murderers he slew not: according unto that which is written in the book of the law of Moses, wherein the LORD commanded, saying, The fathers shall not be put to death for the children, nor the children be put to death for the fathers; but every man shall be put to death for his own sin.

7He slew of Edom in the valley of salt ten thousand, and took Selah by war, and called the name of it Joktheel unto this day.

8¶ Then Amaziah sent messengers to Jehoash, the son of Jehoahaz son of Jehu, king of Israel, saying, Come, let us look one another in the face.

9And Jehoash the king of Israel sent to Amaziah king of Judah, saying, The thistle that *was* in Lebanon sent to the cedar that *was* in Lebanon, saying, Give thy daughter to my son to wife: and there passed by a wild beast that *was* in Lebanon, and trode down the thistle.

10Thou hast indeed smitten Edom, and thine heart hath lifted thee up: glory *of this,* and tarry at home: for why shouldest thou meddle to *thy* hurt, that thou shouldest fall, *even* thou, and Judah with thee?

11But Amaziah would not hear. Therefore Jehoash king of Israel went up; and he and Amaziah king of Judah looked one another in the face at Beth-shemesh, which *belongeth* to Judah.

12And Judah was put to the worse before Israel; and they fled every man to their tents.

13And Jehoash king of Israel took Amaziah king of Judah, the son of Jehoash the son of Ahaziah, at Beth-shemesh, and came to Jerusalem, and brake down the wall of Jerusalem from the gate of Ephraim unto the corner gate, four hundred cubits.

14And he took all the gold and silver, and all the vessels that were found in the house of the LORD, and in the treasures of the king's house, and hostages, and returned to Samaria.

15¶ Now the rest of the acts of Jehoash which he did, and his might, and how he fought with Amaziah king of Judah, *are* they not written in the book of the chronicles of the kings of Israel?

16And Jehoash slept with his fathers, and was buried in Samaria with the kings of Israel; and Jeroboam his son reigned in his stead.

17¶ And Amaziah the son of Joash king of Judah lived after the death of Jehoash son of Jehoahaz king of Israel fifteen years.

18And the rest of the acts of Amaziah, *are* they not written in the book of the chronicles of the kings of Judah?

19Now they made a conspiracy against him in Jerusalem: and he fled to Lachish; but they sent after him to Lachish, and slew him there.

20And they brought him on horses: and he was buried at Jerusalem with his fathers in the city of David.

21¶ And all the people of Judah took Azariah, which *was* sixteen years old, and made him king instead of his father Amaziah.

New International

Amaziah King of Judah

14 IN THE second year of Jehoash[a] son of Jehoahaz king of Israel, Amaziah son of Joash king of Judah began to reign. 2He was twenty-five years old when he became king, and he reigned in Jerusalem twenty-nine years. His mother's name was Jehoaddin; she was from Jerusalem. 3He did what was right in the eyes of the LORD, but not as his father David had done. In everything he followed the example of his father Joash. 4The high places, however, were not removed; the people continued to offer sacrifices and burn incense there.

5After the kingdom was firmly in his grasp, he executed the officials who had murdered his father the king. 6Yet he did not put the sons of the assassins to death, in accordance with what is written in the Book of the Law of Moses where the LORD commanded: "Fathers shall not be put to death for their children, nor children put to death for their fathers; each is to die for his own sins."[b]

7He was the one who defeated ten thousand Edomites in the Valley of Salt and captured Sela in battle, calling it Joktheel, the name it has to this day.

8Then Amaziah sent messengers to Jehoash son of Jehoahaz, the son of Jehu, king of Israel, with the challenge: "Come, meet me face to face."

9But Jehoash king of Israel replied to Amaziah king of Judah: "A thistle in Lebanon sent a message to a cedar in Lebanon, 'Give your daughter to my son in marriage.' Then a wild beast in Lebanon came along and trampled the thistle underfoot. 10You have indeed defeated Edom and now you are arrogant. Glory in your victory, but stay at home! Why ask for trouble and cause your own downfall and that of Judah also?"

11Amaziah, however, would not listen, so Jehoash king of Israel attacked. He and Amaziah king of Judah faced each other at Beth Shemesh in Judah. 12Judah was routed by Israel, and every man fled to his home. 13Jehoash king of Israel captured Amaziah king of Judah, the son of Joash, the son of Ahaziah, at Beth Shemesh. Then Jehoash went to Jerusalem and broke down the wall of Jerusalem from the Ephraim Gate to the Corner Gate—a section about six hundred feet long.[c] 14He took all the gold and silver and all the articles found in the temple of the LORD and in the treasuries of the royal palace. He also took hostages and returned to Samaria.

15As for the other events of the reign of Jehoash, what he did and his achievements, including his war against Amaziah king of Judah, are they not written in the book of the annals of the kings of Israel? 16Jehoash rested with his fathers and was buried in Samaria with the kings of Israel. And Jeroboam his son succeeded him as king.

17Amaziah son of Joash king of Judah lived for fifteen years after the death of Jehoash son of Jehoahaz king of Israel. 18As for the other events of Amaziah's reign, are they not written in the book of the annals of the kings of Judah?

19They conspired against him in Jerusalem, and he fled to Lachish, but they sent men after him to Lachish and killed him there. 20He was brought back by horse and was buried in Jerusalem with his fathers, in the City of David.

21Then all the people of Judah took Azariah,[d] who was sixteen years old, and made him king in place of his father Amaziah. 22He was the one who rebuilt Elath and

a *1* Hebrew *Joash,* a variant of *Jehoash*; also in verses 13, 23 and 27
b *6* Deut. 24:16   c *13* Hebrew *four hundred cubits* (about 180 meters)
d *21* Also called *Uzziah*

Living Bible

14 DURING THE second year of the reign of King Joash of Israel, King Amaziah began his reign over Judah. ²Amaziah was twenty-five years old at the time, and he reigned in Jerusalem for twenty-nine years. (His mother was Jeho-addin, a native of Jerusalem.) ³He was a good king in the Lord's sight, though not quite like his ancestor David; but he was as good a king as his father Joash. ⁴However, he didn't destroy the shrines on the hills, so the people still sacrificed and burned incense there.

⁵As soon as he had a firm grip on the kingdom, he killed the men who had assassinated his father; ⁶but he didn't kill their children, for the Lord had commanded through the law of Moses that fathers shall not be killed for their children, nor children for the sins of their fathers: everyone must pay the penalty for his own sins. ⁷Once Amaziah killed ten thousand Edomites in Salt Valley; he also conquered Sela and changed its name to Jokthe-el, as it is called to this day.

⁸One day he sent a message to King Joash of Israel (the son of Jehoahaz and the grandson of Jehu), daring him to mobilize his army and come out and fight.

⁹But King Joash replied, "The thistle of Lebanon demanded of the mighty cedar tree, 'Give your daughter to be a wife for my son.' But just then a wild animal passed by and stepped on the thistle and trod it into the ground! ¹⁰You have destroyed Edom and are very proud about it; but my advice to you is, be content with your glory and stay home! Why provoke disaster for both yourself and Judah?"

¹¹But Amaziah refused to listen, so King Joash of Israel mustered his army. The battle began at Beth-shemesh, one of the cities of Judah, ¹²and Judah was defeated and the army fled home. ¹³King Amaziah was captured, and the army of Israel marched on Jerusalem and broke down its wall from the Gate of Ephraim to the Corner Gate, a distance of about six hundred feet. ¹⁴King Joash took many hostages and all the gold and silver from the Temple and palace treasury, also the gold cups. Then he returned to Samaria.

¹⁵The rest of the history of Joash and his war with King Amaziah of Judah are recorded in *The Annals of the Kings of Israel*. ¹⁶When Joash died, he was buried in Samaria with the other kings of Israel. And his son Jeroboam became the new king.

¹⁷Amaziah lived fifteen years longer than Joash, ¹⁸and the rest of his biography is recorded in *The Annals of the Kings of Judah*. ¹⁹There was a plot against his life in Jerusalem, and he fled to Lachish; but his enemies sent assassins and killed him there. ²⁰His body was returned on horses, and he was buried in the royal cemetery, in the City of David section of Jerusalem.

²¹Then his son Azariah became the new king at the

New Revised Standard

Amaziah Reigns over Judah

14 IN THE second year of King Joash son of Joahaz of Israel, King Amaziah son of Joash of Judah, began to reign. ²He was twenty-five years old when he began to reign, and he reigned twenty-nine years in Jerusalem. His mother's name was Jehoaddin of Jerusalem. ³He did what was right in the sight of the LORD, yet not like his ancestor David; in all things he did as his father Joash had done. ⁴But the high places were not removed; the people still sacrificed and made offerings on the high places. ⁵As soon as the royal power was firmly in his hand he killed his servants who had murdered his father the king. ⁶But he did not put to death the children of the murderers; according to what is written in the book of the law of Moses, where the LORD commanded, "The parents shall not be put to death for the children, or the children be put to death for the parents; but all shall be put to death for their own sins."

⁷ He killed ten thousand Edomites in the Valley of Salt and took Sela by storm; he called it Jokthe-el, which is its name to this day.

⁸ Then Amaziah sent messengers to King Jehoash son of Jehoahaz, son of Jehu, of Israel, saying, "Come, let us look one another in the face." ⁹King Jehoash of Israel sent word to King Amaziah of Judah, "A thornbush on Lebanon sent to a cedar on Lebanon, saying, 'Give your daughter to my son for a wife'; but a wild animal of Lebanon passed by and trampled down the thornbush. ¹⁰You have indeed defeated Edom, and your heart has lifted you up. Be content with your glory, and stay at home; for why should you provoke trouble so that you fall, you and Judah with you?"

¹¹ But Amaziah would not listen. So King Jehoash of Israel went up; he and King Amaziah of Judah faced one another in battle at Beth-shemesh, which belongs to Judah. ¹²Judah was defeated by Israel; everyone fled home. ¹³King Jehoash of Israel captured King Amaziah of Judah son of Jehoash, son of Ahaziah, at Beth-shemesh; he came to Jerusalem, and broke down the wall of Jerusalem from the Ephraim Gate to the Corner Gate, a distance of four hundred cubits. ¹⁴He seized all the gold and silver, and all the vessels that were found in the house of the LORD and in the treasuries of the king's house, as well as hostages; then he returned to Samaria.

¹⁵ Now the rest of the acts that Jehoash did, his might, and how he fought with King Amaziah of Judah, are they not written in the Book of the Annals of the Kings of Israel? ¹⁶Jehoash slept with his ancestors, and was buried in Samaria with the kings of Israel; then his son Jeroboam succeeded him.

¹⁷ King Amaziah son of Joash of Judah lived fifteen years after the death of King Jehoash son of Jehoahaz of Israel. ¹⁸Now the rest of the deeds of Amaziah, are they not written in the Book of the Annals of the Kings of Judah? ¹⁹They made a conspiracy against him in Jerusalem, and he fled to Lachish. But they sent after him to Lachish, and killed him there. ²⁰They brought him on horses; he was buried in Jerusalem with his ancestors in the city of David. ²¹All the people of Judah took Azariah, who was sixteen years old, and made him king to succeed his father Amaziah. ²²He rebuilt Elath and re-

King James

22He built Elath, and restored it to Judah, after that the king slept with his fathers.

23¶ In the fifteenth year of Amaziah the son of Joash king of Judah Jeroboam the son of Joash king of Israel began to reign in Samaria, *and reigned* forty and one years.

24And he did *that which was* evil in the sight of the LORD: he departed not from all the sins of Jeroboam the son of Nebat, who made Israel to sin.

25He restored the coast of Israel from the entering of Hamath unto the sea of the plain, according to the word of the LORD God of Israel, which he spake by the hand of his servant Jonah, the son of Amittai, the prophet, which *was* of Gath-hepher.

26For the LORD saw the affliction of Israel, *that it was* very bitter: for *there was* not any shut up, nor any left, nor any helper for Israel.

27And the LORD said not that he would blot out the name of Israel from under heaven: but he saved them by the hand of Jeroboam the son of Joash.

28¶ Now the rest of the acts of Jeroboam, and all that he did, and his might, how he warred, and how he recovered Damascus, and Hamath, *which belonged* to Judah, for Israel, *are* they not written in the book of the chronicles of the kings of Israel?

29And Jeroboam slept with his fathers, *even* with the kings of Israel; and Zachariah his son reigned in his stead.

15 IN THE twenty and seventh year of Jeroboam king of Israel began Azariah son of Amaziah king of Judah to reign.

2Sixteen years old was he when he began to reign, and he reigned two and fifty years in Jerusalem. And his mother's name *was* Jecholiah of Jerusalem.

3And he did *that which was* right in the sight of the LORD, according to all that his father Amaziah had done;

4Save that the high places were not removed: the people sacrificed and burnt incense still on the high places.

5¶ And the LORD smote the king, so that he was a leper unto the day of his death, and dwelt in a several house. And Jotham the king's son *was* over the house, judging the people of the land.

6And the rest of the acts of Azariah, and all that he did, *are* they not written in the book of the chronicles of the kings of Judah?

7So Azariah slept with his fathers; and they buried him with his fathers in the city of David: and Jotham his son reigned in his stead.

8¶ In the thirty and eighth year of Azariah king of Judah did Zachariah the son of Jeroboam reign over Israel in Samaria six months.

9And he did *that which was* evil in the sight of the LORD, as his fathers had done: he departed not from the sins of Jeroboam the son of Nebat, who made Israel to sin.

10And Shallum the son of Jabesh conspired against him, and smote him before the people, and slew him, and reigned in his stead.

11And the rest of the acts of Zachariah, behold, they *are* written in the book of the chronicles of the kings of Israel.

12This *was* the word of the LORD which he spake unto Jehu, saying, Thy sons shall sit on the throne of Israel unto the fourth *generation*. And so it came to pass.

13¶ Shallum the son of Jabesh began to reign in the nine and thirtieth year of Uzziah king of Judah; and he reigned a full month in Samaria.

New International

restored it to Judah after Amaziah rested with his fathers.

Jeroboam II King of Israel

23In the fifteenth year of Amaziah son of Joash king of Judah, Jeroboam son of Jehoash king of Israel became king in Samaria, and he reigned forty-one years. 24He did evil in the eyes of the LORD and did not turn away from any of the sins of Jeroboam son of Nebat, which he had caused Israel to commit. 25He was the one who restored the boundaries of Israel from Lebo[a] Hamath to the Sea of the Arabah,[b] in accordance with the word of the LORD, the God of Israel, spoken through his servant Jonah son of Amittai, the prophet from Gath Hepher.

26The LORD had seen how bitterly everyone in Israel, whether slave or free, was suffering; there was no one to help them. 27And since the LORD had not said he would blot out the name of Israel from under heaven, he saved them by the hand of Jeroboam son of Jehoash.

28As for the other events of Jeroboam's reign, all he did, and his military achievements, including how he recovered for Israel both Damascus and Hamath, which had belonged to Yaudi,[c] are they not written in the book of the annals of the kings of Israel? 29Jeroboam rested with his fathers, the kings of Israel. And Zechariah his son succeeded him as king.

Azariah King of Judah

15 IN THE twenty-seventh year of Jeroboam king of Israel, Azariah son of Amaziah king of Judah began to reign. 2He was sixteen years old when he became king, and he reigned in Jerusalem fifty-two years. His mother's name was Jecoliah; she was from Jerusalem. 3He did what was right in the eyes of the LORD, just as his father Amaziah had done. 4The high places, however, were not removed; the people continued to offer sacrifices and burn incense there.

5The LORD afflicted the king with leprosy[d] until the day he died, and he lived in a separate house.[e] Jotham the king's son had charge of the palace and governed the people of the land.

6As for the other events of Azariah's reign, and all he did, are they not written in the book of the annals of the kings of Judah? 7Azariah rested with his fathers and was buried near them in the City of David. And Jotham his son succeeded him as king.

Zechariah King of Israel

8In the thirty-eighth year of Azariah king of Judah, Zechariah son of Jeroboam became king of Israel in Samaria, and he reigned six months. 9He did evil in the eyes of the LORD, as his fathers had done. He did not turn away from the sins of Jeroboam son of Nebat, which he had caused Israel to commit.

10Shallum son of Jabesh conspired against Zechariah. He attacked him in front of the people,[f] assassinated him and succeeded him as king. 11The other events of Zechariah's reign are written in the book of the annals of the kings of Israel. 12So the word of the LORD spoken to Jehu was fulfilled: "Your descendants will sit on the throne of Israel to the fourth generation."[g]

Shallum King of Israel

13Shallum son of Jabesh became king in the thirty-ninth year of Uzziah king of Judah, and he reigned in Samaria one month. 14Then Menahem son of Gadi went

---

a 25 Or *from the entrance to*　b 25 That is, the Dead Sea　c 28 Or *Judah*
d 5 The Hebrew word was used for various diseases affecting the skin—not necessarily leprosy.　e 5 Or *in a house where he was relieved of responsibility*
f 10 Hebrew; some Septuagint manuscripts *in Ibleam*　g 12 2 Kings 10:30

Living Bible

age of sixteen. 22After his father's death he built Elath and restored it to Judah.

23Meanwhile, over in Israel, Jeroboam II had become king during the fifteenth year of the reign of King Amaziah of Judah. Jeroboam's reign lasted forty-one years. 24But he was as evil as Jeroboam I (the son of Nebat), who had led Israel into the sin of worshiping idols. 25Jeroboam II recovered the lost territories of Israel between Hamath and the Dead Sea, just as the Lord God of Israel had predicted through Jonah (son of Amittai) the prophet from Gatthepher. 26For the Lord saw the bitter plight of Israel—she had no one to help her. 27And he had not said that he would blot out the name of Israel, so he used King Jeroboam II to save her.

28The rest of Jeroboam's biography—all that he did, and his great power, and his wars, and how he recovered Damascus and Hamath (which had been captured by Judah)—is recorded in *The Annals of the Kings of Israel*. 29When Jeroboam II died he was buried with the other kings of Israel, and his son Zechariah became the new king of Israel.

15 NEW KING of Judah: Azariah
Name of his father: Amaziah, the former king
Name of his mother: Jecoliah of Jerusalem
Length of his reign: 52 years, in Jerusalem
His age at the beginning of his reign: 16 years old
Reigning in Israel at this time: King Jeroboam, who had been the king there for 27 years.

3Azariah was a good king, and he pleased the Lord just as his father Amaziah had. 4But like his predecessors, he didn't destroy the shrines on the hills where people sacrificed and burned incense. 5Because of this[h] the Lord struck him with leprosy, which lasted until the day of his death; so he lived in a house by himself. And his son Jotham was the acting king. 6The rest of the history of Azariah is recorded in *The Annals of the Kings of Judah*. 7When Azariah died, he was buried with his ancestors in the City of David, and his son Jotham became king.

8New king of Israel: Zechariah
Name of his father: Jeroboam
Length of reign: 6 months
Reigning in Judah at that time: King Azariah, who had been the king there for 38 years

9But Zechariah was an evil king in the Lord's sight, just like his ancestors. Like Jeroboam I (the son of Nebat), he encouraged Israel in the sin of worshiping idols. 10Then Shallum (the son of Jabesh) conspired against him and assassinated him at Ibleam and took the crown himself. 11The rest of the history of Zechariah's reign is found in *The Annals of the Kings of Israel*. 12(So the Lord's statement to Jehu came true, that Jehu's son, grandson, and great-grandson would be kings of Israel[i].)

13New king of Israel: Shallum
Father's name: Jabesh
Length of reign: 1 month
Reigning in Judah at that time: King Uzziah, who had been the king there for 39 years

New Revised Standard

stored it to Judah, after King Amaziah slept with his ancestors.

Jeroboam II Reigns over Israel

23 In the fifteenth year of King Amaziah son of Joash of Judah, King Jeroboam son of Joash of Israel began to reign in Samaria; he reigned forty-one years. 24He did what was evil in the sight of the LORD; he did not depart from all the sins of Jeroboam son of Nebat, which he caused Israel to sin. 25He restored the border of Israel from Lebo-hamath as far as the Sea of the Arabah, according to the word of the LORD, the God of Israel, which he spoke by his servant Jonah son of Amittai, the prophet, who was from Gath-hepher. 26For the LORD saw that the distress of Israel was very bitter; there was no one left, bond or free, and no one to help Israel. 27But the LORD had not said that he would blot out the name of Israel from under heaven, so he saved them by the hand of Jeroboam son of Joash.

28 Now the rest of the acts of Jeroboam, and all that he did, and his might, how he fought, and how he recovered for Israel Damascus and Hamath, which had belonged to Judah, are they not written in the Book of the Annals of the Kings of Israel? 29Jeroboam slept with his ancestors, the kings of Israel; his son Zechariah succeeded him.

Azariah Reigns over Judah

15 IN THE twenty-seventh year of King Jeroboam of Israel King Azariah son of Amaziah of Judah began to reign. 2He was sixteen years old when he began to reign, and he reigned fifty-two years in Jerusalem. His mother's name was Jecoliah of Jerusalem. 3He did what was right in the sight of the LORD, just as his father Amaziah had done. 4Nevertheless the high places were not taken away; the people still sacrificed and made offerings on the high places. 5The LORD struck the king, so that he was leprous[k] to the day of his death, and lived in a separate house. Jotham the king's son was in charge of the palace, governing the people of the land. 6Now the rest of the acts of Azariah, and all that he did, are they not written in the Book of the Annals of the Kings of Judah? 7Azariah slept with his ancestors; they buried him with his ancestors in the city of David; his son Jotham succeeded him.

Zechariah Reigns over Israel

8 In the thirty-eighth year of King Azariah of Judah, Zechariah son of Jeroboam reigned over Israel in Samaria six months. 9He did what was evil in the sight of the LORD, as his ancestors had done. He did not depart from the sins of Jeroboam son of Nebat, which he caused Israel to sin. 10Shallum son of Jabesh conspired against him, and struck him down in public and killed him, and reigned in place of him. 11Now the rest of the deeds of Zechariah are written in the Book of the Annals of the Kings of Israel. 12This was the promise of the LORD that he gave to Jehu, "Your sons shall sit on the throne of Israel to the fourth generation." And so it happened.

Shallum Reigns over Israel

13 Shallum son of Jabesh began to reign in the thirty-ninth year of King Uzziah of Judah; he reigned one month in Samaria. 14Then Menahem son of Gadi

h 15:5 *Because of this*, implied.   i 15:12 *would be kings of Israel*, see 10:30.   j Heb *the king*   k A term for several skin diseases; precise meaning uncertain

King James

14For Menahem the son of Gadi went up from Tirzah, and came to Samaria, and smote Shallum the son of Jabesh in Samaria, and slew him, and reigned in his stead.

15And the rest of the acts of Shallum, and his conspiracy which he made, behold, they *are* written in the book of the chronicles of the kings of Israel.

16¶ Then Menahem smote Tiphsah, and all that *were* therein, and the coasts thereof from Tirzah: because they opened not *to him,* therefore he smote *it; and* all the women therein that were with child he ripped up.

17In the nine and thirtieth year of Azariah king of Judah began Menahem the son of Gadi to reign over Israel, *and reigned* ten years in Samaria.

18And he did *that which was* evil in the sight of the LORD: he departed not all his days from the sins of Jeroboam the son of Nebat, who made Israel to sin.

19*And* Pul the king of Assyria came against the land: and Menahem gave Pul a thousand talents of silver, that his hand might be with him to confirm the kingdom in his hand.

20And Menahem exacted the money of Israel, *even of* all the mighty men of wealth, of each man fifty shekels of silver, to give to the king of Assyria. So the king of Assyria turned back, and stayed not there in the land.

21¶ And the rest of the acts of Menahem, and all that he did, *are* they not written in the book of the chronicles of the kings of Israel?

22And Menahem slept with his fathers; and Pekahiah his son reigned in his stead.

23¶ In the fiftieth year of Azariah king of Judah Pekahiah the son of Menahem began to reign over Israel in Samaria, *and reigned* two years.

24And he did *that which was* evil in the sight of the LORD: he departed not from the sins of Jeroboam the son of Nebat, who made Israel to sin.

25But Pekah the son of Remaliah, a captain of his, conspired against him, and smote him in Samaria, in the palace of the king's house, with Argob and Arieh, and with him fifty men of the Gileadites: and he killed him, and reigned in his room.

26And the rest of the acts of Pekahiah, and all that he did, behold, they *are* written in the book of the chronicles of the kings of Israel.

27¶ In the two and fiftieth year of Azariah king of Judah Pekah the son of Remaliah began to reign over Israel in Samaria, *and reigned* twenty years.

28And he did *that which was* evil in the sight of the LORD: he departed not from the sins of Jeroboam the son of Nebat, who made Israel to sin.

29In the days of Pekah king of Israel came Tiglath-pileser king of Assyria, and took Ijon, and Abel-beth-maachah, and Janoah, and Kedesh, and Hazor, and Gilead, and Galilee, all the land of Naphtali, and carried them captive to Assyria.

30And Hoshea the son of Elah made a conspiracy against Pekah the son of Remaliah, and smote him, and slew him, and reigned in his stead, in the twentieth year of Jotham the son of Uzziah.

31And the rest of the acts of Pekah, and all that he did, behold, they *are* written in the book of the chronicles of the kings of Israel.

32¶ In the second year of Pekah the son of Remaliah king of Israel began Jotham the son of Uzziah king of Judah to reign.

33Five and twenty years old was he when he began to reign, and he reigned sixteen years in Jerusalem. And his mother's name *was* Jerusha, the daughter of Zadok.

New International

from Tirzah up to Samaria. He attacked Shallum son of Jabesh in Samaria, assassinated him and succeeded him as king.

15The other events of Shallum's reign, and the conspiracy he led, are written in the book of the annals of the kings of Israel.

16At that time Menahem, starting out from Tirzah, attacked Tiphsah and everyone in the city and its vicinity, because they refused to open their gates. He sacked Tiphsah and ripped open all the pregnant women.

Menahem King of Israel

17In the thirty-ninth year of Azariah king of Judah, Menahem son of Gadi became king of Israel, and he reigned in Samaria ten years. 18He did evil in the eyes of the LORD. During his entire reign he did not turn away from the sins of Jeroboam son of Nebat, which he had caused Israel to commit.

19Then Pula king of Assyria invaded the land, and Menahem gave him a thousand talentsb of silver to gain his support and strengthen his own hold on the kingdom. 20Menahem exacted this money from Israel. Every wealthy man had to contribute fifty shekelsc of silver to be given to the king of Assyria. So the king of Assyria withdrew and stayed in the land no longer.

21As for the other events of Menahem's reign, and all he did, are they not written in the book of the annals of the kings of Israel? 22Menahem rested with his fathers. And Pekahiah his son succeeded him as king.

Pekahiah King of Israel

23In the fiftieth year of Azariah king of Judah, Pekahiah son of Menahem became king of Israel in Samaria, and he reigned two years. 24Pekahiah did evil in the eyes of the LORD. He did not turn away from the sins of Jeroboam son of Nebat, which he had caused Israel to commit. 25One of his chief officers, Pekah son of Remaliah, conspired against him. Taking fifty men of Gilead with him, he assassinated Pekahiah, along with Argob and Arieh, in the citadel of the royal palace at Samaria. So Pekah killed Pekahiah and succeeded him as king.

26The other events of Pekahiah's reign, and all he did, are written in the book of the annals of the kings of Israel.

Pekah King of Israel

27In the fifty-second year of Azariah king of Judah, Pekah son of Remaliah became king of Israel in Samaria, and he reigned twenty years. 28He did evil in the eyes of the LORD. He did not turn away from the sins of Jeroboam son of Nebat, which he had caused Israel to commit.

29In the time of Pekah king of Israel, Tiglath-Pileser king of Assyria came and took Ijon, Abel Beth Maacah, Janoah, Kedesh and Hazor. He took Gilead and Galilee, including all the land of Naphtali, and deported the people to Assyria. 30Then Hoshea son of Elah conspired against Pekah son of Remaliah. He attacked and assassinated him, and then succeeded him as king in the twentieth year of Jotham son of Uzziah.

31As for the other events of Pekah's reign, and all he did, are they not written in the book of the annals of the kings of Israel?

Jotham King of Judah

32In the second year of Pekah son of Remaliah king of Israel, Jotham son of Uzziah king of Judah began to reign. 33He was twenty-five years old when he became king, and he reigned in Jerusalem sixteen years. His mother's name was Jerusha daughter of Zadok. 34He did

a *19* Also called *Tiglath-Pileser*   b *19* That is, about 37 tons (about 34 metric tons)   c *20* That is, about 1 1/4 pounds (about 0.6 kilogram)

Living Bible

14One month after Shallum became king, Menahem (the son of Gadi) came to Samaria from Tirzah and assassinated him and took the throne. 15Additional details about King Shallum and his conspiracyd are recorded in *The Annals of the Kings of Israel*.

16Menahem destroyed the city of Tappuah and the surrounding countryside, for its citizens refused to accept him as their king; he killed the entire population and ripped open the pregnant women.

17Name of new king of Israel: Menahem
Length of reign: 10 years, in Samaria
Concurrent with: King Azariah of Judah who had been the king there for 39 years

18But Menahem was an evil king. He worshiped idols, as King Jeroboam I had done so long before, and he led the people of Israel into grievous sin. 19, 20Then King Pul of Assyria invaded the land; but King Menahem bought him off with a gift of $2,000,000, so he turned around and returned home. Menahem extorted the money from the rich, assessing each one $2,000 in the form of a special tax. 21The rest of the history of King Menahem is written in *The Annals of the Kings of Israel*. 22When he died, his son Pekahiah became the new king.

23Name of new king of Israel: Pekahiah
Father's name: King Menahem
Length of reign: 2 years, in Samaria
Concurrent with: King Azariah of Judah, who had been the king there for 50 years

24But Pekahiah was an evil king, and he continued the idol-worship begun by Jeroboam I (son of Nebat) who led Israel down that evil trail.

25Then Pekah (son of Remaliah), the commanding general of his army, conspired against him with fifty men from Gilead, and assassinated him in the palace at Samaria (Argob and Arieh were also slain in the revolt). So Pekah became the new king. 26The rest of the history of King Pekahiah is recorded in *The Annals of the Kings of Israel*.

27New king of Israel: Pekah
Father's name: Remaliah
Length of reign: 20 years, in Samaria
Concurrent with: King Azariah of Judah, who had been the king there for 52 years

28Pekah, too, was an evil king, and he continued in the example of Jeroboam I (son of Nebat), who led all of Israel into the sin of worshiping idols. 29It was during his reign that King Tiglathpilesere led an attack against Israel. He captured the cities of Ijon, Abel-beth-maacah, Janoah, Kedesh, Hazor, Gilead, Galilee, and all the land of Naphtali; and he took the people away to Assyria as captives. 30Then Hoshea (the son of Elah) plotted against Pekah and assassinated him; and he took the throne for himself.

New king of Israel: Hoshea
Concurrent with: Jotham (son of Uzziah) king of Judah, who had been the king there for 20 years
31The rest of the history of Pekah's reign is recorded in *The Annals of the Kings of Israel*. 32, 33New king of Judah: Jotham
Father's name: King Uzziah
His age when he became king: 25 years old
Duration of his reign: 16 years, in Jerusalem
Mother's name: Jerusha (daughter of Zadok)
Reigning in Israel at this time: Pekah (son of Remaliah), who had been the king there for 2 years

New Revised Standard

came up from Tirzah and came to Samaria; he struck down Shallum son of Jabesh in Samaria and killed him; he reigned in place of him. 15Now the rest of the deeds of Shallum, including the conspiracy that he made, are written in the Book of the Annals of the Kings of Israel. 16At that time Menahem sacked Tiphsah, all who were in it and its territory from Tirzah on; because they did not open it to him, he sacked it. He ripped open all the pregnant women in it.

Menahem Reigns over Israel

17 In the thirty-ninth year of King Azariah of Judah, Menahem son of Gadi began to reign over Israel; he reigned ten years in Samaria. 18He did what was evil in the sight of the LORD; he did not depart all his days from any of the sins of Jeroboam son of Nebat, which he caused Israel to sin. 19King Pul of Assyria came against the land; Menahem gave Pul a thousand talents of silver, so that he might help him confirm his hold on the royal power. 20Menahem exacted the money from Israel, that is, from all the wealthy, fifty shekels of silver from each one, to give to the king of Assyria. So the king of Assyria turned back, and did not stay there in the land. 21Now the rest of the deeds of Menahem, and all that he did, are they not written in the Book of the Annals of the Kings of Israel? 22Menahem slept with his ancestors, and his son Pekahiah succeeded him.

Pekahiah Reigns over Israel

23 In the fiftieth year of King Azariah of Judah, Pekahiah son of Menahem began to reign over Israel in Samaria; he reigned two years. 24He did what was evil in the sight of the LORD; he did not turn away from the sins of Jeroboam son of Nebat, which he caused Israel to sin. 25Pekah son of Remaliah, his captain, conspired against him with fifty of the Gileadites, and attacked him in Samaria, in the citadel of the palace along with Argob and Arieh; he killed him, and reigned in place of him. 26Now the rest of the deeds of Pekahiah, and all that he did, are written in the Book of the Annals of the Kings of Israel.

Pekah Reigns over Israel

27 In the fifty-second year of King Azariah of Judah, Pekah son of Remaliah began to reign over Israel in Samaria; he reigned twenty years. 28He did what was evil in the sight of the LORD; he did not depart from the sins of Jeroboam son of Nebat, which he caused Israel to sin.

29 In the days of King Pekah of Israel, King Tiglath-pileser of Assyria came and captured Ijon, Abel-beth-maacah, Janoah, Kedesh, Hazor, Gilead, and Galilee, all the land of Naphtali; and he carried the people captive to Assyria. 30Then Hoshea son of Elah made a conspiracy against Pekah son of Remaliah, attacked him, and killed him; he reigned in place of him, in the twentieth year of Jotham son of Uzziah. 31Now the rest of the acts of Pekah, and all that he did, are written in the Book of the Annals of the Kings of Israel.

Jotham Reigns over Judah

32 In the second year of King Pekah son of Remaliah of Israel, King Jotham son of Uzziah of Judah began to reign. 33He was twenty-five years old when he began to reign and reigned sixteen years in Jerusalem. His mother's name was Jerusha daughter of Zadok. 34He did

---

d *15:15 Shallum and his conspiracy*, see vs 10.   e *15:29* Also called Pul, in vs 19 above.

King James

34And he did *that which was* right in the sight of the
LORD: he did according to all that his father Uzziah had
done.

35¶ Howbeit the high places were not removed: the
people sacrificed and burned incense still in the high
places. He built the higher gate of the house of the LORD.

36¶ Now the rest of the acts of Jotham, and all that
he did, *are* they not written in the book of the chronicles
of the kings of Judah?

37In those days the LORD began to send against Judah
Rezin the king of Syria, and Pekah the son of Remaliah.

38And Jotham slept with his fathers, and was buried
with his fathers in the city of David his father: and Ahaz
his son reigned in his stead.

16 IN THE seventeenth year of Pekah the son of
Remaliah Ahaz the son of Jotham king of Judah
began to reign.

2Twenty years old *was* Ahaz when he began to reign,
and reigned sixteen years in Jerusalem, and did not *that
which was* right in the sight of the LORD his God, like
David his father.

3But he walked in the way of the kings of Israel, yea,
and made his son to pass through the fire, according to
the abominations of the heathen, whom the LORD cast
out from before the children of Israel.

4And he sacrificed and burnt incense in the high
places, and on the hills, and under every green tree.

5¶ Then Rezin king of Syria and Pekah son of Remaliah king of Israel came up to Jerusalem to war: and they
besieged Ahaz, but could not overcome *him*.

6At that time Rezin king of Syria recovered Elath to
Syria, and drave the Jews from Elath: and the Syrians
came to Elath, and dwelt there unto this day.

7So Ahaz sent messengers to Tiglath-pileser king of
Assyria, saying, I *am* thy servant and thy son: come up,
and save me out of the hand of the king of Syria, and
out of the hand of the king of Israel, which rise up
against me.

8And Ahaz took the silver and gold that was found
in the house of the LORD, and in the treasures of the
king's house, and sent *it for* a present to the king of
Assyria.

9And the king of Assyria hearkened unto him: for the
king of Assyria went up against Damascus, and took it,
and carried *the people of* it captive to Kir, and slew
Rezin.

10¶ And king Ahaz went to Damascus to meet Tiglath-pileser king of Assyria, and saw an altar that *was*
at Damascus: and king Ahaz sent to Urijah the priest the
fashion of the altar, and the pattern of it, according to
all the workmanship thereof.

11And Urijah the priest built an altar according to all
that king Ahaz had sent from Damascus: so Urijah the
priest made *it* against king Ahaz came from Damascus.

12And when the king was come from Damascus, the
king saw the altar: and the king approached to the altar,
and offered thereon.

13And he burnt his burnt offering and his meat offering, and poured his drink offering, and sprinkled the
blood of his peace offerings, upon the altar.

14And he brought also the brasen altar, which *was*
before the LORD, from the forefront of the house, from
between the altar and the house of the LORD, and put it
on the north side of the altar.

New International

what was right in the eyes of the LORD, just as his father
Uzziah had done. 35The high places, however, were not
removed; the people continued to offer sacrifices and
burn incense there. Jotham rebuilt the Upper Gate of the
temple of the LORD.

36As for the other events of Jotham's reign, and what
he did, are they not written in the book of the annals of
the kings of Judah? 37(In those days the LORD began to
send Rezin king of Aram and Pekah son of Remaliah
against Judah.) 38Jotham rested with his fathers and was
buried with them in the City of David, the city of his
father. And Ahaz his son succeeded him as king.

Ahaz King of Judah

16 IN THE seventeenth year of Pekah son of Remaliah, Ahaz son of Jotham king of Judah began
to reign. 2Ahaz was twenty years old when he became
king, and he reigned in Jerusalem sixteen years. Unlike
David his father, he did not do what was right in the eyes
of the LORD his God. 3He walked in the ways of the
kings of Israel and even sacrificed his son ina the fire,
following the detestable ways of the nations the LORD
had driven out before the Israelites. 4He offered sacrifices and burned incense at the high places, on the hilltops and under every spreading tree.

5Then Rezin king of Aram and Pekah son of Remaliah king of Israel marched up to fight against Jerusalem
and besieged Ahaz, but they could not overpower him.
6At that time, Rezin king of Aram recovered Elath for
Aram by driving out the men of Judah. Edomites then
moved into Elath and have lived there to this day.

7Ahaz sent messengers to say to Tiglath-Pileser king
of Assyria, "I am your servant and vassal. Come up and
save me out of the hand of the king of Aram and of the
king of Israel, who are attacking me." 8And Ahaz took
the silver and gold found in the temple of the LORD and
in the treasuries of the royal palace and sent it as a gift
to the king of Assyria. 9The king of Assyria complied
by attacking Damascus and capturing it. He deported its
inhabitants to Kir and put Rezin to death.

10Then King Ahaz went to Damascus to meet Tiglath-
Pileser king of Assyria. He saw an altar in Damascus and
sent to Uriah the priest a sketch of the altar, with detailed
plans for its construction. 11So Uriah the priest built an
altar in accordance with all the plans that King Ahaz had
sent from Damascus and finished it before King Ahaz
returned. 12When the king came back from Damascus
and saw the altar, he approached it and presented offeringsb on it. 13He offered up his burnt offering and grain
offering, poured out his drink offering, and sprinkled the
blood of his fellowship offeringsc on the altar. 14The
bronze altar that stood before the LORD he brought from
the front of the temple—from between the new altar and
the temple of the LORD—and put it on the north side of
the new altar.

a 3 Or *even made his son pass through*   b 12 Or *and went up*
c 13 Traditionally *peace offerings*

Living Bible

34,35Generally speaking, Jotham was a good king. Like his father Uzziah, he followed the Lord. But he didn't destroy the shrines on the hills where the people sacrificed and burned incense. It was during King Jotham's reign that the upper gate of the Temple of the Lord was built. 36The rest of Jotham's history is written in *The Annals of the Kings of Judah*. 37In those days the Lord caused King Rezin of Syria and King Pekah of Israel to attack Judah. 38When Jotham died he was buried with the other kings of Judah in the royal cemetery, in the City of David section of Jerusalem. Then his son Ahaz became the new king.

16 NEW KING of Judah: Ahaz
Father's name: Jotham
Age: 20 years old
Duration of reign: 16 years, in Jerusalem
Character of his reign: evil
Reigning in Israel at this time: King Pekah (son of Remaliah) who had been the king there for 17 years

2But he did not follow the Lord as his ancestor David had; 3he was as wicked as the kings of Israel. He even killed his own son by offering him as a burnt sacrifice to the gods, following the heathen customs of the nations around Judah—nations which the Lord destroyed when the people of Israel entered the land. 4He also sacrificed and burned incense at the shrines on the hills and at the numerous altars in the groves of trees.

5Then King Rezin of Syria and King Pekah (son of Remaliah) of Israel declared war on Ahaz and besieged Jerusalem; but they did not conquer it. 6However, at that time King Rezin of Syria recovered the city of Elath for Syria; he drove out the Jews and sent new Syrians to live there, as they do to this day. 7King Ahaz sent a messenger to King Tiglath-pileser of Assyria, begging him to help him fight the attacking armies of Syria and Israel.d 8Ahaz took the silver and gold from the Temple and from the royal vaults and sent it as a payment to the Assyrian king. 9So the Assyrians attacked Damascus, the capital of Syria. They took away the population of the city as captives, resettling them in Kir, and King Rezin of Syria was killed.

10King Ahaz now went to Damascus to meet with King Tiglath-pileser, and while he was there he noticed an unusual altar in a heathen temple.e He jotted down its dimensions and made a sketch and sent it back to Uriah the priest with a detailed description. 11,12Uriah built one just like it by following these directions and had it ready for the king, who, upon his return from Damascus, inaugurated it with an offering. 13The king presented a burnt offering and a grain offering, poured a drink offering over it, and sprinkled the blood of peace offerings upon it. 14Then he removed the old bronze altar from the front of the Temple (it had stood between the Temple entrance and the new altar), and placed it on the north side of the new altar. 15He instructed Uriah

New Revised Standard

what was right in the sight of the LORD, just as his father Uzziah had done. 35Nevertheless the high places were not removed; the people still sacrificed and made offerings on the high places. He built the upper gate of the house of the LORD. 36Now the rest of the acts of Jotham, and all that he did, are they not written in the Book of the Annals of the Kings of Judah? 37In those days the LORD began to send King Rezin of Aram and Pekah son of Remaliah against Judah. 38Jotham slept with his ancestors, and was buried with his ancestors in the city of David, his ancestor; his son Ahaz succeeded him.

Ahaz Reigns over Judah

16 IN THE seventeenth year of Pekah son of Remaliah, King Ahaz son of Jotham of Judah began to reign. 2Ahaz was twenty years old when he began to reign; he reigned sixteen years in Jerusalem. He did not do what was right in the sight of the LORD his God, as his ancestor David had done, 3but he walked in the way of the kings of Israel. He even made his son pass through fire, according to the abominable practices of the nations whom the LORD drove out before the people of Israel. 4He sacrificed and made offerings on the high places, on the hills, and under every green tree.

5 Then King Rezin of Aram and King Pekah son of Remaliah of Israel came up to wage war on Jerusalem; they besieged Ahaz but could not conquer him. 6At that time the king of Edomf recovered Elath for Edom,g and drove the Judeans from Elath; and the Edomites came to Elath, where they live to this day. 7Ahaz sent messengers to King Tiglath-pileser of Assyria, saying, "I am your servant and your son. Come up, and rescue me from the hand of the king of Aram and from the hand of the king of Israel, who are attacking me." 8Ahaz also took the silver and gold found in the house of the LORD and in the treasures of the king's house, and sent a present to the king of Assyria. 9The king of Assyria listened to him; the king of Assyria marched up against Damascus, and took it, carrying its people captive to Kir; then he killed Rezin.

10 When King Ahaz went to Damascus to meet King Tiglath-pileser of Assyria, he saw the altar that was at Damascus. King Ahaz sent to the priest Uriah a model of the altar, and its pattern, exact in all its details. 11The priest Uriah built the altar; in accordance with all that King Ahaz had sent from Damascus, just so did the priest Uriah build it, before King Ahaz arrived from Damascus. 12When the king came from Damascus, the king viewed the altar. Then the king drew near to the altar, went up on it, 13and offered his burnt offering and his grain offering, poured his drink offering, and dashed the blood of his offerings of well-being against the altar. 14The bronze altar that was before the LORD he removed from the front of the house, from the place between his altar and the house of the LORD, and put it on the north side of his altar. 15King Ahaz commanded the priest

---

d 16:7 *begging him to . . . fight . . . Syria and Israel,* literally, "saying, 'I am your servant and your son. Come and rescue me.'" e 16:10 *an unusual altar in a heathen temple,* literally, "he saw the altar that was at Damascus."

f Cn: Heb *King Rezin of Aram*   g Cn: Heb *Aram*

King James

15And king Ahaz commanded Urijah the priest, saying, Upon the great altar burn the morning burnt offering, and the evening meat offering, and the king's burnt sacrifice, and his meat offering, with the burnt offering of all the people of the land, and their meat offering, and their drink offerings; and sprinkle upon it all the blood of the burnt offering, and all the blood of the sacrifice: and the brasen altar shall be for me to inquire *by*.

16Thus did Urijah the priest, according to all that king Ahaz commanded.

17¶ And king Ahaz cut off the borders of the bases, and removed the laver from off them; and took down the sea from off the brasen oxen that *were* under it, and put it upon a pavement of stones.

18And the covert for the sabbath that they had built in the house, and the king's entry without, turned he from the house of the LORD for the king of Assyria.

19¶ Now the rest of the acts of Ahaz which he did, *are* they not written in the book of the chronicles of the kings of Judah?

20And Ahaz slept with his fathers, and was buried with his fathers in the city of David: and Hezekiah his son reigned in his stead.

17 IN THE twelfth year of Ahaz king of Judah began Hoshea the son of Elah to reign in Samaria over Israel nine years.

2And he did *that which was* evil in the sight of the LORD, but not as the kings of Israel that were before him.

3¶ Against him came up Shalmaneser king of Assyria; and Hoshea became his servant, and gave him presents.

4And the king of Assyria found conspiracy in Hoshea: for he had sent messengers to So king of Egypt, and brought no present to the king of Assyria, as *he had done* year by year: therefore the king of Assyria shut him up, and bound him in prison.

5¶ Then the king of Assyria came up throughout all the land, and went up to Samaria, and besieged it three years.

6¶ In the ninth year of Hoshea the king of Assyria took Samaria, and carried Israel away into Assyria, and placed them in Halah and in Habor *by* the river of Gozan, and in the cities of the Medes.

7For *so* it was, that the children of Israel had sinned against the LORD their God, which had brought them up out of the land of Egypt, from under the hand of Pharaoh king of Egypt, and had feared other gods,

8And walked in the statutes of the heathen, whom the LORD cast out from before the children of Israel, and of the kings of Israel, which they had made.

9And the children of Israel did secretly *those* things that *were* not right against the LORD their God, and they built them high places in all their cities, from the tower of the watchmen to the fenced city.

10And they set them up images and groves in every high hill, and under every green tree:

11And there they burnt incense in all the high places, as *did* the heathen whom the LORD carried away before them; and wrought wicked things to provoke the LORD to anger:

12For they served idols, whereof the LORD had said unto them, Ye shall not do this thing.

13Yet the LORD testified against Israel, and against Judah, by all the prophets, *and by* all the seers, saying, Turn ye from your evil ways, and keep my commandments *and* my statutes, according to all the law which I commanded your fathers, and which I sent to you by my servants the prophets.

14Notwithstanding they would not hear, but hardened their necks, like to the neck of their fathers, that did not believe in the LORD their God.

New International

15King Ahaz then gave these orders to Uriah the priest: "On the large new altar, offer the morning burnt offering and the evening grain offering, the king's burnt offering and his grain offering, and the burnt offering of all the people of the land, and their grain offering and their drink offering. Sprinkle on the altar all the blood of the burnt offerings and sacrifices. But I will use the bronze altar for seeking guidance." 16And Uriah the priest did just as King Ahaz had ordered.

17King Ahaz took away the side panels and removed the basins from the movable stands. He removed the Sea from the bronze bulls that supported it and set it on a stone base. 18He took away the Sabbath canopya that had been built at the temple and removed the royal entryway outside the temple of the LORD, in deference to the king of Assyria.

19As for the other events of the reign of Ahaz, and what he did, are they not written in the book of the annals of the kings of Judah? 20Ahaz rested with his fathers and was buried with them in the City of David. And Hezekiah his son succeeded him as king.

Hoshea Last King of Israel

17 IN THE twelfth year of Ahaz king of Judah, Hoshea son of Elah became king of Israel in Samaria, and he reigned nine years. 2He did evil in the eyes of the LORD, but not like the kings of Israel who preceded him.

3Shalmaneser king of Assyria came up to attack Hoshea, who had been Shalmaneser's vassal and had paid him tribute. 4But the king of Assyria discovered that Hoshea was a traitor, for he had sent envoys to Sob king of Egypt, and he no longer paid tribute to the king of Assyria, as he had done year by year. Therefore Shalmaneser seized him and put him in prison. 5The king of Assyria invaded the entire land, marched against Samaria and laid siege to it for three years. 6In the ninth year of Hoshea, the king of Assyria captured Samaria and deported the Israelites to Assyria. He settled them in Halah, in Gozan on the Habor River and in the towns of the Medes.

Israel Exiled Because of Sin

7All this took place because the Israelites had sinned against the LORD their God, who had brought them up out of Egypt from under the power of Pharaoh king of Egypt. They worshiped other gods 8and followed the practices of the nations the LORD had driven out before them, as well as the practices that the kings of Israel had introduced. 9The Israelites secretly did things against the LORD their God that were not right. From watchtower to fortified city they built themselves high places in all their towns. 10They set up sacred stones and Asherah poles on every high hill and under every spreading tree. 11At every high place they burned incense, as the nations whom the LORD had driven out before them had done. They did wicked things that provoked the LORD to anger. 12They worshiped idols, though the LORD had said, "You shall not do this."c 13The LORD warned Israel and Judah through all his prophets and seers: "Turn from your evil ways. Observe my commands and decrees, in accordance with the entire Law that I commanded your fathers to obey and that I delivered to you through my servants the prophets."

14But they would not listen and were as stiff-necked as their fathers, who did not trust in the LORD their God.

---

a *18 Or the dais of his throne* (see Septuagint)   b *4 Or to Sais, to the; So* is possibly an abbreviation for *Osorkon.*   c *12 Exodus 20:4, 5*

Living Bible

priest to use the new altar for the sacrifices of burnt offering, the evening grain offering, the king's burnt offering and grain offering, and the offerings of the people, including their drink offerings. The blood from the burnt offerings and sacrifices was also to be sprinkled over the new altar. So the old altar was used only for purposes of divination.

"The old bronze altar," he said, "will be only for my personal use."

16Uriah the priest did as King Ahaz instructed him. 17Then the king dismantled the wheeled stands in the Temple, removed their crosspieces and the water vats they supported, and removed the great tank from the backs of the bronze oxen and placed it upon the stone pavement. 18In deference to the king of Assyria he also removed the festive passageway he had constructed between the palace and the Temple.d

19The rest of the history of the reign of King Ahaz is recorded in *The Annals of the Kings of Judah*. 20When Ahaz died he was buried in the royal cemetery, in the City of David sector of Jerusalem, and his son Hezekiah became the new king.

17 NEW KING of Israel: Hoshea
Father's name: Elah
Length of his reign: 9 years, in Samaria
Character of his reign: evil—but not as bad as some of the other kings of Israel
Reigning in Judah at this time: King Ahaz, who had been the king there for 12 years

3King Shalmaneser of Assyria attacked and defeated King Hoshea, so Israel had to pay heavy annual taxes to Assyria. 4Then Hoshea conspired against the king of Assyria by asking King So of Egypt to help him shake free of Assyria's power, but this treachery was discovered. At the same time he refused to pay the annual tribute to Assyria. So the king of Assyria put him in prison and in chains for his rebellion.

5Now the land of Israel was filled with Assyrian troops for three years besieging Samaria, the capital city of Israel. 6Finally, in the ninth year of King Hoshea's reign, Samaria fell and the people of Israel were exiled to Assyria. They were placed in colonies in the city of Halah and along the banks of the Habor River in Gozan, and among the cities of the Medes.

7This disaster came upon the nation of Israel because the people worshiped other gods, thus sinning against the Lord their God who had brought them safely out of their slavery in Egypt. 8They had followed the evil customs of the nations which the Lord had cast out from before them. 9The people of Israel had also secretly done many things that were wrong, and had built altars to other gods throughout the land.e 10They had placed obelisks and idols at the top of every hill and under every green tree; 11and they had burned incense to the gods of the very nations which the Lord had cleared out of the land when Israel came in. So the people of Israel had done many evil things, and the Lord was very angry. 12Yes, they worshiped idols, despite the Lord's specific and repeated warnings.

13Again and again the Lord had sent prophets to warn both Israel and Judah to turn from their evil ways; he had warned them to obey his commandments which he had given to their ancestors through these prophets, 14but Israel wouldn't listen. The people were as stubborn as their ancestors and refused to believe in the Lord their God. 15They rejected his laws and the covenant he had

New Revised Standard

Uriah, saying, "Upon the great altar offer the morning burnt offering, and the evening grain offering, and the king's burnt offering, and his grain offering, with the burnt offering of all the people of the land, their grain offering, and their drink offering; then dash against it all the blood of the burnt offering, and all the blood of the sacrifice; but the bronze altar shall be for me to inquire by." 16The priest Uriah did everything that King Ahaz commanded.

17 Then King Ahaz cut off the frames of the stands, and removed the laver from them; he removed the sea from the bronze oxen that were under it, and put it on a pediment of stone. 18The covered portal for use on the sabbath that had been built inside the palace, and the outer entrance for the king he removed fromf the house of the LORD. He did this because of the king of Assyria. 19Now the rest of the acts of Ahaz that he did, are they not written in the Book of the Annals of the Kings of Judah? 20Ahaz slept with his ancestors, and was buried with his ancestors in the city of David; his son Hezekiah succeeded him.

Hoshea Reigns over Israel

17 IN THE twelfth year of King Ahaz of Judah, Hoshea son of Elah began to reign in Samaria over Israel; he reigned nine years. 2He did what was evil in the sight of the LORD, yet not like the kings of Israel who were before him. 3King Shalmaneser of Assyria came up against him; Hoshea became his vassal, and paid him tribute. 4But the king of Assyria found treachery in Hoshea; for he had sent messengers to King So of Egypt, and offered no tribute to the king of Assyria, as he had done year by year; therefore the king of Assyria confined him and imprisoned him.

Israel Carried Captive to Assyria

5 Then the king of Assyria invaded all the land and came to Samaria; for three years he besieged it. 6In the ninth year of Hoshea the king of Assyria captured Samaria; he carried the Israelites away to Assyria. He placed them in Halah, on the Habor, the river of Gozan, and in the cities of the Medes.

7 This occurred because the people of Israel had sinned against the LORD their God, who had brought them up out of the land of Egypt from under the hand of Pharaoh king of Egypt. They had worshiped other gods 8and walked in the customs of the nations whom the LORD drove out before the people of Israel, and in the customs that the kings of Israel had introduced.g 9The people of Israel secretly did things that were not right against the LORD their God. They built for themselves high places at all their towns, from watchtower to fortified city; 10they set up for themselves pillars and sacred polesh on every high hill and under every green tree; 11there they made offerings on all the high places, as the nations did whom the LORD carried away before them. They did wicked things, provoking the LORD to anger; 12they served idols, of which the LORD had said to them, "You shall not do this." 13Yet the LORD warned Israel and Judah by every prophet and every seer, saying, "Turn from your evil ways and keep my commandments and my statutes, in accordance with all the law that I commanded your ancestors and that I sent to you by my servants the prophets." 14They would not listen but were stubborn, as their ancestors had been, who did not believe in the LORD their God. 15They despised his

---

d 16:18 The Hebrew is unclear.   e 17:9 *built altars to other gods throughout the land*, literally, "built them high places in all their cities."

f Cn: Heb lacks *from*   g Meaning of Heb uncertain   h Heb *Asherim*

King James

15And they rejected his statutes, and his covenant that he made with their fathers, and his testimonies which he testified against them; and they followed vanity, and became vain, and went after the heathen that *were* round about them, *concerning* whom the LORD had charged them, that they should not do like them.

16And they left all the commandments of the LORD their God, and made them molten images, *even* two calves, and made a grove, and worshipped all the host of heaven, and served Baal.

17And they caused their sons and their daughters to pass through the fire, and used divination and enchantments, and sold themselves to do evil in the sight of the LORD, to provoke him to anger.

18Therefore the LORD was very angry with Israel, and removed them out of his sight: there was none left but the tribe of Judah only.

19Also Judah kept not the commandments of the LORD their God, but walked in the statutes of Israel which they made.

20And the LORD rejected all the seed of Israel, and afflicted them, and delivered them into the hand of spoilers, until he had cast them out of his sight.

21For he rent Israel from the house of David; and they made Jeroboam the son of Nebat king: and Jeroboam drave Israel from following the LORD, and made them sin a great sin.

22For the children of Israel walked in all the sins of Jeroboam which he did; they departed not from them;

23Until the LORD removed Israel out of his sight, as he had said by all his servants the prophets. So was Israel carried away out of their own land to Assyria unto this day.

24¶ And the king of Assyria brought *men* from Babylon, and from Cuthah, and from Ava, and from Hamath, and from Sepharvaim, and placed *them* in the cities of Samaria instead of the children of Israel: and they possessed Samaria, and dwelt in the cities thereof.

25And *so* it was at the beginning of their dwelling there, *that* they feared not the LORD: therefore the LORD sent lions among them, which slew *some* of them.

26Wherefore they spake to the king of Assyria, saying, The nations which thou hast removed, and placed in the cities of Samaria, know not the manner of the God of the land: therefore he hath sent lions among them, and, behold, they slay them, because they know not the manner of the God of the land.

27Then the king of Assyria commanded, saying, Carry thither one of the priests whom ye brought from thence; and let them go and dwell there, and let him teach them the manner of the God of the land.

28Then one of the priests whom they had carried away from Samaria came and dwelt in Beth-el, and taught them how they should fear the LORD.

29Howbeit every nation made gods of their own, and put *them* in the houses of the high places which the Samaritans had made, every nation in their cities wherein they dwelt.

30And the men of Babylon made Succoth-benoth, and the men of Cuth made Nergal, and the men of Hamath made Ashima,

31And the Avites made Nibhaz and Tartak, and the Sepharvites burnt their children in fire to Adrammelech and Anammelech, the gods of Sepharvaim.

32So they feared the LORD, and made unto themselves of the lowest of them priests of the high places, which sacrificed for them in the houses of the high places.

33They feared the LORD, and served their own gods, after the manner of the nations whom they carried away from thence.

34Unto this day they do after the former manners: they fear not the LORD, neither do they after their statutes, or after their ordinances, or after the law and commandment which the LORD commanded the children of Jacob, whom he named Israel;

New International

15They rejected his decrees and the covenant he had made with their fathers and the warnings he had given them. They followed worthless idols and themselves became worthless. They imitated the nations around them although the LORD had ordered them, "Do not do as they do," and they did the things the LORD had forbidden them to do.

16They forsook all the commands of the LORD their God and made for themselves two idols cast in the shape of calves, and an Asherah pole. They bowed down to all the starry hosts, and they worshiped Baal. 17They sacrificed their sons and daughters in[a] the fire. They practiced divination and sorcery and sold themselves to do evil in the eyes of the LORD, provoking him to anger.

18So the LORD was very angry with Israel and removed them from his presence. Only the tribe of Judah was left, 19and even Judah did not keep the commands of the LORD their God. They followed the practices Israel had introduced. 20Therefore the LORD rejected all the people of Israel; he afflicted them and gave them into the hands of plunderers, until he thrust them from his presence.

21When he tore Israel away from the house of David, they made Jeroboam son of Nebat their king. Jeroboam enticed Israel away from following the LORD and caused them to commit a great sin. 22The Israelites persisted in all the sins of Jeroboam and did not turn away from them 23until the LORD removed them from his presence, as he had warned through all his servants the prophets. So the people of Israel were taken from their homeland into exile in Assyria, and they are still there.

Samaria Resettled

24The king of Assyria brought people from Babylon, Cuthah, Avva, Hamath and Sepharvaim and settled them in the towns of Samaria to replace the Israelites. They took over Samaria and lived in its towns. 25When they first lived there, they did not worship the LORD; so he sent lions among them and they killed some of the people. 26It was reported to the king of Assyria: "The people you deported and resettled in the towns of Samaria do not know what the god of that country requires. He has sent lions among them, which are killing them off, because the people do not know what he requires."

27Then the king of Assyria gave this order: "Have one of the priests you took captive from Samaria go back to live there and teach the people what the god of the land requires." 28So one of the priests who had been exiled from Samaria came to live in Bethel and taught them how to worship the LORD.

29Nevertheless, each national group made its own gods in the several towns where they settled, and set them up in the shrines the people of Samaria had made at the high places. 30The men from Babylon made Succoth Benoth, the men from Cuthah made Nergal, and the men from Hamath made Ashima; 31the Avvites made Nibhaz and Tartak, and the Sepharvites burned their children in the fire as sacrifices to Adrammelech and Anammelech, the gods of Sepharvaim. 32They worshiped the LORD, but they also appointed all sorts of their own people to officiate for them as priests in the shrines at the high places. 33They worshiped the LORD, but they also served their own gods in accordance with the customs of the nations from which they had been brought.

34To this day they persist in their former practices. They neither worship the LORD nor adhere to the decrees and ordinances, the laws and commands that the LORD gave the descendants of Jacob, whom he named Israel.

---

a 17 Or *They made their sons and daughters pass through*

Living Bible

made with their ancestors, and despised all his warnings. In their foolishness they worshiped heathen idols despite the Lord's stern warnings. 16They defied all the commandments of the Lord their God and made two calves from molten gold. They made detestable, shameful idols and worshiped Baal and the sun, moon, and stars. 17They even burned their own sons and daughters to death on the altars of Molech;b they consulted fortune-tellers and used magic and sold themselves to evil. So the Lord was very angry. 18He swept them from his sight until only the tribe of Judah remained in the land.

19But even Judah refused to obey the commandments of the Lord their God; they too walked in the same evil paths as Israel had. 20So the Lord rejected all the descendants of Jacob.c He punished them by delivering them to their attackers until they were destroyed. 21For Israel split off from the kingdom of David and chose Jeroboam I (the son of Nebat) as its king. Then Jeroboam drew Israel away from following the Lord. He made them sin a great sin, 22and the people of Israel never quit doing the evil things that Jeroboam led them into, 23until the Lord finally swept them away, just as all his prophets had warned would happen. So Israel was carried off to the land of Assyria where they remain to this day.

24And the king of Assyria transported colonies of people from Babylon, Cuthah, Avva, Hamath, and Sepharvaim and resettled them in the cities of Samaria, replacing the people of Israel. So the Assyrians took over Samaria and the other cities of Israel. 25But since these Assyrian colonists did not worship the Lord when they first arrived, the Lord sent lions among them to kill some of them.

26Then they sent a message to the king of Assyria: "We colonists here in Israel don't know the laws of the god of the land, and he has sent lions among us to destroy us because we have not worshiped him."

27, 28The king of Assyria then decreed that one of the exiled priests from Samaria should return to Israel and teach the new residents the laws of the god of the land. So one of them returned to Bethel and taught the colonists from Babylon how to worship the Lord.

29But these foreigners also worshiped their own gods. They placed them in the shrines on the hills near their cities. 30Those from Babylon worshiped idols of their god Succoth-benoth; those from Cuth worshiped their god Nergal; and the men of Hamath worshiped Ashima. 31The gods Nibhaz and Tartak were worshiped by the Avvites, and the people from Sephar even burned their own children on the altars of their gods Adrammelech and Anammelech.

32They also worshiped the Lord, and they appointed from among themselves priests to sacrifice to the Lord on the hilltop altars. 33But they continued to follow the religious customs of the nations from which they came. 34And this is still going on among them today—they follow their former practices instead of truly worshiping the Lord or obeying the laws he gave to the descendants of Jacob (whose name was later changed to Israel).

New Revised Standard

statutes, and his covenant that he made with their ancestors, and the warnings that he gave them. They went after false idols and became false; they followed the nations that were around them, concerning whom the LORD had commanded them that they should not do as they did. 16They rejected all the commandments of the LORD their God and made for themselves cast images of two calves; they made a sacred pole,d worshiped all the host of heaven, and served Baal. 17They made their sons and their daughters pass through fire; they used divination and augury; and they sold themselves to do evil in the sight of the LORD, provoking him to anger. 18Therefore the LORD was very angry with Israel and removed them out of his sight; none was left but the tribe of Judah alone.

19 Judah also did not keep the commandments of the LORD their God but walked in the customs that Israel had introduced. 20The LORD rejected all the descendants of Israel; he punished them and gave them into the hand of plunderers, until he had banished them from his presence.

21 When he had torn Israel from the house of David, they made Jeroboam son of Nebat king. Jeroboam drove Israel from following the LORD and made them commit great sin. 22The people of Israel continued in all the sins that Jeroboam committed; they did not depart from them 23until the LORD removed Israel out of his sight, as he had foretold through all his servants the prophets. So Israel was exiled from their own land to Assyria until this day.

Assyria Resettles Samaria

24 The king of Assyria brought people from Babylon, Cuthah, Avva, Hamath, and Sepharvaim, and placed them in the cities of Samaria in place of the people of Israel; they took possession of Samaria, and settled in its cities. 25When they first settled there, they did not worship the LORD; therefore the LORD sent lions among them, which killed some of them. 26So the king of Assyria was told, "The nations that you have carried away and placed in the cities of Samaria do not know the law of the god of the land; therefore he has sent lions among them; they are killing them, because they do not know the law of the god of the land." 27Then the king of Assyria commanded, "Send there one of the priests whom you carried away from there; let hime go and live there, and teach them the law of the god of the land." 28So one of the priests whom they had carried away from Samaria came and lived in Bethel; he taught them how they should worship the LORD.

29 But every nation still made gods of its own and put them in the shrines of the high places that the people of Samaria had made, every nation in the cities in which they lived; 30the people of Babylon made Succoth-benoth, the people of Cuth made Nergal, the people of Hamath made Ashima; 31the Avvites made Nibhaz and Tartak; the Sepharvites burned their children in the fire to Adrammelech and Anammelech, the gods of Sepharvaim. 32They also worshiped the LORD and appointed from among themselves all sorts of people as priests of the high places, who sacrificed for them in the shrines of the high places. 33So they worshiped the LORD but also served their own gods, after the manner of the nations from among whom they had been carried away. 34To this day they continue to practice their former customs.

They do not worship the LORD and they do not follow the statutes or the ordinances or the law or the commandment that the LORD commanded the children of Jacob, whom he named Israel. 35The LORD had made a cove-

---

b 17:17 They even burned their own sons and daughters to death on the altars of Molech, literally, "as offerings."   c 17:20 descendants of Jacob, literally, "descendants of Israel."

d Heb Asherah   e Syr Vg: Heb them

King James

35With whom the LORD had made a covenant, and charged them, saying, Ye shall not fear other gods, nor bow yourselves to them, nor serve them, nor sacrifice to them:

36But the LORD, who brought you up out of the land of Egypt with great power and a stretched out arm, him shall ye fear, and him shall ye worship, and to him shall ye do sacrifice.

37And the statutes, and the ordinances, and the law, and the commandment, which he wrote for you, ye shall observe to do for evermore; and ye shall not fear other gods.

38And the covenant that I have made with you ye shall not forget; neither shall ye fear other gods.

39But the LORD your God ye shall fear; and he shall deliver you out of the hand of all your enemies.

40Howbeit they did not hearken, but they did after their former manner.

41So these nations feared the LORD, and served their graven images, both their children, and their children's children: as did their fathers, so do they unto this day.

18 NOW IT came to pass in the third year of Hoshea son of Elah king of Israel, *that* Hezekiah the son of Ahaz king of Judah began to reign.

2Twenty and five years old was he when he began to reign; and he reigned twenty and nine years in Jerusalem. His mother's name also *was* Abi, the daughter of Zachariah.

3And he did *that which was* right in the sight of the LORD, according to all that David his father did.

4¶ He removed the high places, and brake the images, and cut down the groves, and brake in pieces the brasen serpent that Moses had made: for unto those days the children of Israel did burn incense to it: and he called it Nehushtan.

5He trusted in the LORD God of Israel; so that after him was none like him among all the kings of Judah, nor *any* that were before him.

6For he clave to the LORD, *and* departed not from following him, but kept his commandments, which the LORD commanded Moses.

7And the LORD was with him; *and* he prospered whithersoever he went forth: and he rebelled against the king of Assyria, and served him not.

8He smote the Philistines, *even* unto Gaza, and the borders thereof, from the tower of the watchmen to the fenced city.

9¶ And it came to pass in the fourth year of king Hezekiah, which *was* the seventh year of Hoshea son of Elah king of Israel, *that* Shalmaneser king of Assyria came up against Samaria, and besieged it.

10And at the end of three years they took it: *even in* the sixth year of Hezekiah, that *is* the ninth year of Hoshea king of Israel, Samaria was taken.

11And the king of Assyria did carry away Israel unto Assyria, and put them in Halah and in Habor *by* the river of Gozan, and in the cities of the Medes:

12Because they obeyed not the voice of the LORD their God, but transgressed his covenant, *and* all that Moses the servant of the LORD commanded, and would not hear *them*, nor do *them*.

13¶ Now in the fourteenth year of king Hezekiah did Sennacherib king of Assyria come up against all the fenced cities of Judah, and took them.

14And Hezekiah king of Judah sent to the king of Assyria to Lachish, saying, I have offended; return from me: that which thou puttest on me will I bear. And the king of Assyria appointed unto Hezekiah king of Judah three hundred talents of silver and thirty talents of gold.

New International

35When the LORD made a covenant with the Israelites, he commanded them: "Do not worship any other gods or bow down to them, serve them or sacrifice to them. 36But the LORD, who brought you up out of Egypt with mighty power and outstretched arm, is the one you must worship. To him you shall bow down and to him offer sacrifices. 37You must always be careful to keep the decrees and ordinances, the laws and commands he wrote for you. Do not worship other gods. 38Do not forget the covenant I have made with you, and do not worship other gods. 39Rather, worship the LORD your God; it is he who will deliver you from the hand of all your enemies."

40They would not listen, however, but persisted in their former practices. 41Even while these people were worshiping the LORD, they were serving their idols. To this day their children and grandchildren continue to do as their fathers did.

Hezekiah King of Judah

18 IN THE third year of Hoshea son of Elah king of Israel, Hezekiah son of Ahaz king of Judah began to reign. 2He was twenty-five years old when he became king, and he reigned in Jerusalem twenty-nine years. His mother's name was Abijaha daughter of Zechariah. 3He did what was right in the eyes of the LORD, just as his father David had done. 4He removed the high places, smashed the sacred stones and cut down the Asherah poles. He broke into pieces the bronze snake Moses had made, for up to that time the Israelites had been burning incense to it. (It was calledb Nehushtan.c)

5Hezekiah trusted in the LORD, the God of Israel. There was no one like him among all the kings of Judah, either before him or after him. 6He held fast to the LORD and did not cease to follow him; he kept the commands the LORD had given Moses. 7And the LORD was with him; he was successful in whatever he undertook. He rebelled against the king of Assyria and did not serve him. 8From watchtower to fortified city, he defeated the Philistines, as far as Gaza and its territory.

9In King Hezekiah's fourth year, which was the seventh year of Hoshea son of Elah king of Israel, Shalmaneser king of Assyria marched against Samaria and laid siege to it. 10At the end of three years the Assyrians took it. So Samaria was captured in Hezekiah's sixth year, which was the ninth year of Hoshea king of Israel. 11The king of Assyria deported Israel to Assyria and settled them in Halah, in Gozan on the Habor River and in towns of the Medes. 12This happened because they had not obeyed the LORD their God, but had violated his covenant—all that Moses the servant of the LORD commanded. They neither listened to the commands nor carried them out.

13In the fourteenth year of King Hezekiah's reign, Sennacherib king of Assyria attacked all the fortified cities of Judah and captured them. 14So Hezekiah king of Judah sent this message to the king of Assyria at Lachish: "I have done wrong. Withdraw from me, and I will pay whatever you demand of me." The king of Assyria exacted from Hezekiah king of Judah three hundred talentsd of silver and thirty talentse of gold. 15So

---

a 2 Hebrew *Abi*, a variant of *Abijah*   b 4 Or *He called it*   c 4 *Nehushtan* sounds like the Hebrew for *bronze* and *snake* and *unclean thing*.   d 14 That is, about 11 tons (about 10 metric tons)   e 14 That is, about 1 ton (about 1 metric ton)

Living Bible

35, 36For the Lord had made a contract with them—that they were never to worship or make sacrifices to any heathen gods. They were to worship only the Lord who had brought them out of the land of Egypt with such tremendous miracles and power. 37The descendants of Jacob were to obey all of God's laws and *never* worship other gods.

38For God had said, *"You must never forget the covenant I made with you; never worship other gods.* 39*You must worship only the Lord; he will save you from all your enemies."*

40But Israel didn't listen, and the people continued to worship other gods. 41These colonists from Babylon worshiped the Lord, yes—but they also worshiped their idols. And to this day their descendants do the same thing.

18 NEW KING of Judah: Hezekiah
Father's name: Ahaz

Length of his reign: 29 years, in Jerusalem
His age at the beginning of his reign: 25 years old
His mother's name: Abi (daughter of Zechariah)
Character of his reign: good (similar to that of his ancestor David)
Reigning in Israel at this time: King Hoshea (son of Elah), who had been the king there for 3 years
4He removed the shrines on the hills, broke down the obelisks, knocked down the shameful idols of Asherah, and broke up the bronze serpent that Moses had made, because the people of Israel had begun to worship it by burning incense to it; even though, as King Hezekiahf pointed out to them, it was merely a piece of bronze. 5He trusted very strongly in the Lord God of Israel. In fact, none of the kings before or after him were as close to God as he was. 6For he followed the Lord in everything, and carefully obeyed all of God's commands to Moses. 7So the Lord was with him and prospered everything he did. Then he rebelled against the king of Assyria and refused to pay tribute any longer. 8He also conquered the Philistines as far distant as Gaza and its suburbs, destroying cities both large and small.g

9It was during the fourth year of his reign (which was the seventh year of the reign of King Hoshea in Israel) that King Shalmaneser of Assyria attacked Israel and began a siege on the city of Samaria. 10Three years later (during the sixth year of the reign of King Hezekiah and the ninth year of the reign of King Hoshea of Israel) Samaria fell. 11It was at that time that the king of Assyria transported the Israelis to Assyria and put them in colonies in the city of Halath and along the banks of the Habor River in Gozan, and in the cities of the Medes. 12For they had refused to listen to the Lord their God or to do what he wanted them to do. Instead, they had transgressed his covenant and disobeyed all the laws given to them by Moses the servant of the Lord.

13Later, during the fourteenth year of the reign of King Hezekiah, King Sennacherib of Assyria besieged and captured all the fortified cities of Judah. 14King Hezekiah sued for peace and sent this message to the king of Assyria at Lachish: "I have done wrong. I will pay whatever tribute you demand if you will only go away." The king of Assyria then demanded a settlement of $1,500,000. 15To gather this amount, King Hezekiah

New Revised Standard

nant with them and commanded them, "You shall not worship other gods or bow yourselves to them or serve them or sacrifice to them, 36but you shall worship the LORD, who brought you out of the land of Egypt with great power and with an outstretched arm; you shall bow yourselves to him, and to him you shall sacrifice. 37The statutes and the ordinances and the law and the commandment that he wrote for you, you shall always be careful to observe. You shall not worship other gods; 38you shall not forget the covenant that I have made with you. You shall not worship other gods, 39but you shall worship the LORD your God; he will deliver you out of the hand of all your enemies." 40They would not listen, however, but they continued to practice their former custom.

41 So these nations worshiped the LORD, but also served their carved images; to this day their children and their children's children continue to do as their ancestors did.

Hezekiah's Reign over Judah

18 IN THE third year of King Hoshea son of Elah of Israel, Hezekiah son of King Ahaz of Judah began to reign. 2He was twenty-five years old when he began to reign; he reigned twenty-nine years in Jerusalem. His mother's name was Abi daughter of Zechariah. 3He did what was right in the sight of the LORD just as his ancestor David had done. 4He removed the high places, broke down the pillars, and cut down the sacred pole.h He broke in pieces the bronze serpent that Moses had made, for until those days the people of Israel had made offerings to it; it was called Nehushtan. 5He trusted in the LORD the God of Israel; so that there was no one like him among all the kings of Judah after him, or among those who were before him. 6For he held fast to the LORD; he did not depart from following him but kept the commandments that the LORD commanded Moses. 7The LORD was with him; wherever he went, he prospered. He rebelled against the king of Assyria and would not serve him. 8He attacked the Philistines as far as Gaza and its territory, from watchtower to fortified city.

9 In the fourth year of King Hezekiah, which was the seventh year of King Hoshea son of Elah of Israel, King Shalmaneser of Assyria came up against Samaria, besieged it, 10and at the end of three years, took it. In the sixth year of Hezekiah, which was the ninth year of King Hoshea of Israel, Samaria was taken. 11The king of Assyria carried the Israelites away to Assyria, settled them in Halah, on the Habor, the river of Gozan, and in the cities of the Medes, 12because they did not obey the voice of the LORD their God but transgressed his covenant—all that Moses the servant of the LORD had commanded; they neither listened nor obeyed.

Sennacherib Invades Judah

13 In the fourteenth year of King Hezekiah, King Sennacherib of Assyria came up against all the fortified cities of Judah and captured them. 14King Hezekiah of Judah sent to the king of Assyria at Lachish, saying, "I have done wrong; withdraw from me; whatever you impose on me I will bear." The king of Assyria demanded of King Hezekiah of Judah three hundred talents of silver and thirty talents of gold. 15Hezekiah gave him all

---

f 18:4 *King Hezekiah,* implied.   g 18:8 *destroying cities both large and small,* literally, "from the tower of the watchman to the fortified cities."

h Heb *Asherah*

King James

¹⁵And Hezekiah gave *him* all the silver that was found in the house of the LORD, and in the treasures of the king's house.

¹⁶At that time did Hezekiah cut off *the gold from* the doors of the temple of the LORD, and *from* the pillars which Hezekiah king of Judah had overlaid, and gave it to the king of Assyria.

¹⁷¶ And the king of Assyria sent Tartan and Rabsaris and Rab-shakeh from Lachish to king Hezekiah with a great host against Jerusalem. And they went up and came to Jerusalem. And when they were come up, they came and stood by the conduit of the upper pool, which *is* in the highway of the fuller's field.

¹⁸And when they had called to the king, there came out to them Eliakim the son of Hilkiah, which *was* over the household, and Shebna the scribe, and Joah the son of Asaph the recorder.

¹⁹And Rab-shakeh said unto them, Speak ye now to Hezekiah, Thus saith the great king, the king of Assyria, What confidence *is* this wherein thou trustest?

²⁰Thou sayest, (but *they are but* vain words,) *I have* counsel and strength for the war. Now on whom dost thou trust, that thou rebellest against me?

²¹Now, behold, thou trustest upon the staff of this bruised reed, *even* upon Egypt, on which if a man lean, it will go into his hand, and pierce it: so *is* Pharaoh king of Egypt unto all that trust on him.

²²But if ye say unto me, We trust in the LORD our God: *is* not that he, whose high places and whose altars Hezekiah hath taken away, and hath said to Judah and Jerusalem, Ye shall worship before this altar in Jerusalem?

²³Now therefore, I pray thee, give pledges to my lord the king of Assyria, and I will deliver thee two thousand horses, if thou be able on thy part to set riders upon them.

²⁴How then wilt thou turn away the face of one captain of the least of my master's servants, and put thy trust on Egypt for chariots and for horsemen?

²⁵Am I now come up without the LORD against this place to destroy it? The LORD said to me, Go up against this land, and destroy it.

²⁶Then said Eliakim the son of Hilkiah, and Shebna, and Joah, unto Rab-shakeh, Speak, I pray thee, to thy servants in the Syrian language; for we understand *it:* and talk not with us in the Jews' language in the ears of the people that *are* on the wall.

²⁷But Rab-shakeh said unto them, Hath my master sent me to thy master, and to thee, to speak these words? *hath he* not *sent me* to the men which sit on the wall, that they may eat their own dung, and drink their own piss with you?

²⁸Then Rab-shakeh stood and cried with a loud voice in the Jews' language, and spake, saying, Hear the word of the great king, the king of Assyria:

²⁹Thus saith the king, Let not Hezekiah deceive you: for he shall not be able to deliver you out of his hand:

³⁰Neither let Hezekiah make you trust in the LORD, saying, The LORD will surely deliver us, and this city shall not be delivered into the hand of the king of Assyria.

³¹Hearken not to Hezekiah: for thus saith the king of Assyria, Make *an agreement* with me by a present, and come out to me, and *then* eat ye every man of his own vine, and every one of his fig tree, and drink ye every one the waters of his cistern:

³²Until I come and take you away to a land like your own land, a land of corn and wine, a land of bread and vineyards, a land of oil olive and of honey, that ye may live, and not die: and hearken not unto Hezekiah, when he persuadeth you, saying, The LORD will deliver us.

³³Hath any of the gods of the nations delivered at all his land out of the hand of the king of Assyria?

New International

Hezekiah gave him all the silver that was found in the temple of the LORD and in the treasuries of the royal palace.

¹⁶At this time Hezekiah king of Judah stripped off the gold with which he had covered the doors and doorposts of the temple of the LORD, and gave it to the king of Assyria.

Sennacherib Threatens Jerusalem

¹⁷The king of Assyria sent his supreme commander, his chief officer and his field commander with a large army, from Lachish to King Hezekiah at Jerusalem. They came up to Jerusalem and stopped at the aqueduct of the Upper Pool, on the road to the Washerman's Field. ¹⁸They called for the king; and Eliakim son of Hilkiah the palace administrator, Shebna the secretary, and Joah son of Asaph the recorder went out to them.

¹⁹The field commander said to them, "Tell Hezekiah:

" 'This is what the great king, the king of Assyria, says: On what are you basing this confidence of yours? ²⁰You say you have strategy and military strength—but you speak only empty words. On whom are you depending, that you rebel against me? ²¹Look now, you are depending on Egypt, that splintered reed of a staff, which pierces a man's hand and wounds him if he leans on it! Such is Pharaoh king of Egypt to all who depend on him. ²²And if you say to me, "We are depending on the LORD our God"—isn't he the one whose high places and altars Hezekiah removed, saying to Judah and Jerusalem, "You must worship before this altar in Jerusalem"?

²³" 'Come now, make a bargain with my master, the king of Assyria: I will give you two thousand horses—if you can put riders on them! ²⁴How can you repulse one officer of the least of my master's officials, even though you are depending on Egypt for chariots and horsemen^a? ²⁵Furthermore, have I come to attack and destroy this place without word from the LORD? The LORD himself told me to march against this country and destroy it.' "

²⁶Then Eliakim son of Hilkiah, and Shebna and Joah said to the field commander, "Please speak to your servants in Aramaic, since we understand it. Don't speak to us in Hebrew in the hearing of the people on the wall."

²⁷But the commander replied, "Was it only to your master and you that my master sent me to say these things, and not to the men sitting on the wall—who, like you, will have to eat their own filth and drink their own urine?"

²⁸Then the commander stood and called out in Hebrew: "Hear the word of the great king, the king of Assyria! ²⁹This is what the king says: Do not let Hezekiah deceive you. He cannot deliver you from my hand. ³⁰Do not let Hezekiah persuade you to trust in the LORD when he says, 'The LORD will surely deliver us; this city will not be given into the hand of the king of Assyria.'

³¹"Do not listen to Hezekiah. This is what the king of Assyria says: Make peace with me and come out to me. Then every one of you will eat from his own vine and fig tree and drink water from his own cistern, ³²until I come and take you to a land like your own, a land of grain and new wine, a land of bread and vineyards, a land of olive trees and honey. Choose life and not death!

"Do not listen to Hezekiah, for he is misleading you when he says, 'The LORD will deliver us.' ³³Has the god of any nation ever delivered his land from the hand of the king of Assyria? ³⁴Where are the gods of Hamath and

^a 24 Or charioteers

Living Bible

used all the silver stored in the Temple and in the palace treasury. 16He even stripped off the gold from the Temple doors, and from the doorposts he had overlaid with gold, and gave it all to the Assyrian king.

17Nevertheless the king of Assyria sent his field marshal, his chief treasurer, and his chief of staff from Lachish with a great army; and they camped along the highway beside the field where cloth was bleached, near the conduit of the upper pool. 18They demanded that King Hezekiah come out to speak to them, but instead he sent a truce delegation of the following men: Eliakim, his business manager; Shebnah, his secretary; and Joah, his royal historian.

19Then the Assyrian general sent this message to King Hezekiah: "The great King of Assyria says, 'No one can save you from my power! 20, 21You need more than mere promises of help before rebelling against me. But which of your allies will give you more than words? Egypt? If you lean on Egypt, you will find her to be a stick that breaks beneath your weight and pierces your hand. The Egyptian Pharaoh is totally unreliable! 22And if you say, "We're trusting the Lord to rescue us"—just remember that he is the very one whose hilltop altars you've destroyed. For you require everyone to worship at the altar in Jerusalem!' 23I'll tell you what: Make a bet with my master, the king of Assyria! If you have two thousand men left who can ride horses, we'll furnish the horses! 24And with an army as small as yours,b you are no threat to even the least lieutenant in charge of the smallest contingent in my master's army. Even if Egypt supplies you with horses and chariots, it will do no good. 25And do you think we have come here on our own? No! The Lord sent us and told us, 'Go and destroy this nation!'"

26Then Eliakim, Shebnah, and Joah said to them, "Please speak in Aramaic, for we understand it. Don't use Hebrew, for the people standing on the walls will hear you."

27But the Assyrian general replied, "Has my master sent me to speak only to you and to your master? Hasn't he sent me to the people on the walls too? For they are doomed with you to eat their own excrement and drink their own urine!"

28Then the Assyrian ambassador shouted in Hebrew to the people on the wall, "Listen to the great king of Assyria! 29'Don't let King Hezekiah fool you. He will never be able to save you from my power. 30Don't let him fool you into trusting in the Lord to rescue you. 31, 32Don't listen to King Hezekiah. Surrender! You can live in peace here in your own land until I take you to another land just like this one—with plentiful crops, grain, grapes, olive trees, and honey. All of this instead of death! Don't listen to King Hezekiah when he tries to persuade you that the Lord will deliver you. 33Have any of the gods of the other nations ever delivered their people from the king of Assyria? 34What happened to the

New Revised Standard

the silver that was found in the house of the LORD and in the treasuries of the king's house. 16At that time Hezekiah stripped the gold from the doors of the temple of the LORD, and from the doorposts that King Hezekiah of Judah had overlaid and gave it to the king of Assyria. 17The king of Assyria sent the Tartan, the Rabsaris, and the Rabshakeh with a great army from Lachish to King Hezekiah at Jerusalem. They went up and came to Jerusalem. When they arrived, they came and stood by the conduit of the upper pool, which is on the highway to the Fuller's Field. 18When they called for the king, there came out to them Eliakim son of Hilkiah, who was in charge of the palace, and Shebnah the secretary, and Joah son of Asaph, the recorder.

19 The Rabshakeh said to them, "Say to Hezekiah: Thus says the great king, the king of Assyria: On what do you base this confidence of yours? 20Do you think that mere words are strategy and power for war? On whom do you now rely, that you have rebelled against me? 21See, you are relying now on Egypt, that broken reed of a staff, which will pierce the hand of anyone who leans on it. Such is Pharaoh king of Egypt to all who rely on him. 22But if you say to me, 'We rely on the LORD our God,' is it not he whose high places and altars Hezekiah has removed, saying to Judah and to Jerusalem, 'You shall worship before this altar in Jerusalem'? 23Come now, make a wager with my master the king of Assyria: I will give you two thousand horses, if you are able on your part to set riders on them. 24How then can you repulse a single captain among the least of my master's servants, when you rely on Egypt for chariots and for horsemen? 25Moreover, is it without the LORD that I have come up against this place to destroy it? The LORD said to me, Go up against this land, and destroy it."

26 Then Eliakim son of Hilkiah, and Shebnah, and Joah said to the Rabshakeh, "Please speak to your servants in the Aramaic language, for we understand it; do not speak to us in the language of Judah within the hearing of the people who are on the wall." 27But the Rabshakeh said to them, "Has my master sent me to speak these words to your master and to you, and not to the people sitting on the wall, who are doomed with you to eat their own dung and to drink their own urine?"

28 Then the Rabshakeh stood and called out in a loud voice in the language of Judah, "Hear the word of the great king, the king of Assyria! 29Thus says the king: 'Do not let Hezekiah deceive you, for he will not be able to deliver you out of my hand. 30Do not let Hezekiah make you rely on the LORD by saying, The LORD will surely deliver us, and this city will not be given into the hand of the king of Assyria.' 31Do not listen to Hezekiah; for thus says the king of Assyria: 'Make your peace with me and come out to me; then every one of you will eat from your own vine and your own fig tree, and drink water from your own cistern, 32until I come and take you away to a land like your own land, a land of grain and wine, a land of bread and vineyards, a land of olive oil and honey, that you may live and not die. Do not listen to Hezekiah when he misleads you by saying, The LORD will deliver us. 33Has any of the gods of the nations ever delivered its land out of the hand of the king of Assyria?

b 18:24 with an army as small as yours, implied.

King James

34Where *are* the gods of Hamath, and of Arpad? where *are* the gods of Sepharvaim, Hena, and Ivah? have they delivered Samaria out of mine hand?

35Who *are* they among all the gods of the countries, that have delivered their country out of mine hand, that the LORD should deliver Jerusalem out of mine hand?

36But the people held their peace, and answered him not a word: for the king's commandment was, saying, Answer him not.

37Then came Eliakim the son of Hilkiah, which *was* over the household, and Shebna the scribe, and Joah the son of Asaph the recorder, to Hezekiah with *their* clothes rent, and told him the words of Rab-shakeh.

19 AND IT came to pass, when king Hezekiah heard *it,* that he rent his clothes, and covered himself with sackcloth, and went into the house of the LORD.

2And he sent Eliakim, which *was* over the household, and Shebna the scribe, and the elders of the priests, covered with sackcloth, to Isaiah the prophet the son of Amoz.

3And they said unto him, Thus saith Hezekiah, This day *is* a day of trouble, and of rebuke, and blasphemy: for the children are come to the birth, and *there is* not strength to bring forth.

4It may be the LORD thy God will hear all the words of Rab-shakeh, whom the king of Assyria his master hath sent to reproach the living God; and will reprove the words which the LORD thy God hath heard: wherefore lift up *thy* prayer for the remnant that are left.

5So the servants of king Hezekiah came to Isaiah.

6¶ And Isaiah said unto them, Thus shall ye say to your master, Thus saith the LORD, Be not afraid of the words which thou hast heard, with which the servants of the king of Assyria have blasphemed me.

7Behold, I will send a blast upon him, and he shall hear a rumour, and shall return to his own land; and I will cause him to fall by the sword in his own land.

8¶ So Rab-shakeh returned, and found the king of Assyria warring against Libnah: for he had heard that he was departed from Lachish.

9And when he heard say of Tirhakah king of Ethiopia, Behold, he is come out to fight against thee: he sent messengers again unto Hezekiah, saying,

10Thus shall ye speak to Hezekiah king of Judah, saying, Let not thy God in whom thou trustest deceive thee, saying, Jerusalem shall not be delivered into the hand of the king of Assyria.

11Behold, thou hast heard what the kings of Assyria have done to all lands, by destroying them utterly: and shalt thou be delivered?

12Have the gods of the nations delivered them which my fathers have destroyed; *as* Gozan, and Haran, and Rezeph, and the children of Eden which *were* in Thelasar?

13Where *is* the king of Hamath, and the king of Arpad, and the king of the city of Sepharvaim, of Hena, and Ivah?

14¶ And Hezekiah received the letter of the hand of the messengers, and read it: and Hezekiah went up into the house of the LORD, and spread it before the LORD.

15And Hezekiah prayed before the LORD, and said, O LORD God of Israel, which dwellest *between* the cherubims, thou art the God, *even* thou alone, of all the kingdoms of the earth; thou hast made heaven and earth.

16LORD, bow down thine ear, and hear: open, LORD, thine eyes, and see: and hear the words of Sennacherib, which hath sent him to reproach the living God.

17Of a truth, LORD, the kings of Assyria have destroyed the nations and their lands,

New International

Arpad? Where are the gods of Sepharvaim, Hena and Ivvah? Have they rescued Samaria from my hand? 35Who of all the gods of these countries has been able to save his land from me? How then can the LORD deliver Jerusalem from my hand?"

36But the people remained silent and said nothing in reply, because the king had commanded, "Do not answer him."

37Then Eliakim son of Hilkiah the palace administrator, Shebna the secretary and Joah son of Asaph the recorder went to Hezekiah, with their clothes torn, and told him what the field commander had said.

Jerusalem's Deliverance Foretold

19 WHEN KING Hezekiah heard this, he tore his clothes and put on sackcloth and went into the temple of the LORD. 2He sent Eliakim the palace administrator, Shebna the secretary and the leading priests, all wearing sackcloth, to the prophet Isaiah son of Amoz. 3They told him, "This is what Hezekiah says: This day is a day of distress and rebuke and disgrace, as when children come to the point of birth and there is no strength to deliver them. 4It may be that the LORD your God will hear all the words of the field commander, whom his master, the king of Assyria, has sent to ridicule the living God, and that he will rebuke him for the words the LORD your God has heard. Therefore pray for the remnant that still survives."

5When King Hezekiah's officials came to Isaiah, 6Isaiah said to them, "Tell your master, 'This is what the LORD says: Do not be afraid of what you have heard— those words with which the underlings of the king of Assyria have blasphemed me. 7Listen! I am going to put such a spirit in him that when he hears a certain report, he will return to his own country, and there I will have him cut down with the sword.' "

8When the field commander heard that the king of Assyria had left Lachish, he withdrew and found the king fighting against Libnah.

9Now Sennacherib received a report that Tirhakah, the Cushite[a] king of Egypt, was marching out to fight against him. So he again sent messengers to Hezekiah with this word: 10"Say to Hezekiah king of Judah: Do not let the god you depend on deceive you when he says, 'Jerusalem will not be handed over to the king of Assyria.' 11Surely you have heard what the kings of Assyria have done to all the countries, destroying them completely. And will you be delivered? 12Did the gods of the nations that were destroyed by my forefathers deliver them: the gods of Gozan, Haran, Rezeph and the people of Eden who were in Tel Assar? 13Where is the king of Hamath, the king of Arpad, the king of the city of Sepharvaim, or of Hena or Ivvah?"

Hezekiah's Prayer

14Hezekiah received the letter from the messengers and read it. Then he went up to the temple of the LORD and spread it out before the LORD. 15And Hezekiah prayed to the LORD: "O LORD, God of Israel, enthroned between the cherubim, you alone are God over all the kingdoms of the earth. You have made heaven and earth. 16Give ear, O LORD, and hear; open your eyes, O LORD, and see; listen to the words Sennacherib has sent to insult the living God.

17"It is true, O LORD, that the Assyrian kings have laid waste these nations and their lands. 18They have

Living Bible

gods of Hamath, Arpad, Sepharvaim, Hena, and Ivvah? Did they rescue Samaria? 35What god has ever been able to save any nation from my power? So what makes you think the Lord can save Jerusalem?' "

36But the people on the wall remained silent, for the king had instructed them to say nothing. 37Then Eliakim (son of Hilkiah) the business manager, and Shebnah the king's secretary, and Joah (son of Asaph) the historian went to King Hezekiah with their clothes torn and told him what the Assyrian general had said.

19 WHEN KING Hezekiah heard their report he tore his clothes and put on sackcloth and went into the Temple to pray. 2Then he told Eliakim, Shebnah, and some of the older priests to clothe themselves in sackcloth and to go to Isaiah (son of Amoz), the prophet, with this message:

3"King Hezekiah says, 'This is a day of trouble, insult, and dishonor. It is as when a child is ready to be born, but the mother has no strength to deliver it. 4Yet perhaps the Lord your God has heard the Assyrian general defying the living God, and will rebuke him. Oh, pray for the few of us who are left.' "

5,6Isaiah replied, "The Lord says, 'Tell your master not to be troubled by the sneers these Assyrians have made against me.' 7For the king of Assyria will receive bad news from home and will decide to return; and the Lord will see to it that he is killed when he arrives there."

8Then the Assyrian general returned to his king at Libnah (for he received word that he had left Lachish). 9Soon afterwards news reached the king that King Tirhakah of Ethiopia was coming to attack him. Before leaving to meet the attack, he sent back this message to King Hezekiah:

10"Don't be fooled by that god you trust in. Don't believe it when he says that I won't conquer Jerusalem. 11You know perfectly well what the kings of Assyria have done wherever they have gone; they have completely destroyed everything. Why would you be any different? 12Have the gods of the other nations delivered them—such nations as Gozan, Haran, Rezeph, and Eden in the land of Telassar? The former kings of Assyria destroyed them all! 13What happened to the king of Hamoth and the king of Arpad? What happened to the kings of Sepharvaim, Hena, and Ivvah?"

14Hezekiah took the letter from the messengers, read it, and went over to the Temple and spread it out before the Lord. 15Then he prayed this prayer:

"O Lord God of Israel, sitting on your throne high above the angels,b you alone are the God of all the kingdoms of the earth. You created the heavens and the earth. 16Bend low, O Lord, and listen. Open your eyes, O Lord, and see. Listen to this man's defiance of the living God. 17Lord, it is true that the kings of Assyria have destroyed all those nations, 18and have burned their

New Revised Standard

34Where are the gods of Hamath and Arpad? Where are the gods of Sepharvaim, Hena, and Ivvah? Have they delivered Samaria out of my hand? 35 Who among all the gods of the countries have delivered their countries out of my hand, that the LORD should deliver Jerusalem out of my hand?' "

36 But the people were silent and answered him not a word, for the king's command was, "Do not answer him." 37 Then Eliakim son of Hilkiah, who was in charge of the palace, and Shebna the secretary, and Joah son of Asaph, the recorder, came to Hezekiah with their clothes torn and told him the words of the Rabshakeh.

Hezekiah Consults Isaiah

19 WHEN KING Hezekiah heard it, he tore his clothes, covered himself with sackcloth, and went into the house of the LORD. 2 And he sent Eliakim, who was in charge of the palace, and Shebna the secretary, and the senior priests, covered with sackcloth, to the prophet Isaiah son of Amoz. 3 They said to him, "Thus says Hezekiah, This day is a day of distress, of rebuke, and of disgrace; children have come to the birth, and there is no strength to bring them forth. 4 It may be that the LORD your God heard all the words of the Rabshakeh, whom his master the king of Assyria has sent to mock the living God, and will rebuke the words that the LORD your God has heard; therefore lift up your prayer for the remnant that is left." 5 When the servants of King Hezekiah came to Isaiah, 6 Isaiah said to them, "Say to your master, 'Thus says the LORD: Do not be afraid because of the words that you have heard, with which the servants of the king of Assyria have reviled me. 7 I myself will put a spirit in him, so that he shall hear a rumor and return to his own land; I will cause him to fall by the sword in his own land.' "

Sennacherib's Threat

8 The Rabshakeh returned, and found the king of Assyria fighting against Libnah; for he had heard that the king had left Lachish. 9 When the kingc heard concerning King Tirhakah of Ethiopia,d "See, he has set out to fight against you," he sent messengers again to Hezekiah, saying, 10"Thus shall you speak to King Hezekiah of Judah: Do not let your God on whom you rely deceive you by promising that Jerusalem will not be given into the hand of the king of Assyria. 11 See, you have heard what the kings of Assyria have done to all lands, destroying them utterly. Shall you be delivered? 12 Have the gods of the nations delivered them, the nations that my predecessors destroyed, Gozan, Haran, Rezeph, and the people of Eden who were in Telassar? 13 Where is the king of Hamath, the king of Arpad, the king of the city of Sepharvaim, the king of Hena, or the king of Ivvah?"

Hezekiah's Prayer

14 Hezekiah received the letter from the hand of the messengers and read it; then Hezekiah went up to the house of the LORD and spread it before the LORD. 15 And Hezekiah prayed before the LORD, and said: "O LORD the God of Israel, who are enthroned above the cherubim, you are God, you alone, of all the kingdoms of the earth; you have made heaven and earth. 16Incline your ear, O LORD, and hear; open your eyes, O LORD, and see; hear the words of Sennacherib, which he has sent to mock the living God. 17Truly, O LORD, the kings of Assyria have laid waste the nations and their lands,

King James

18And have cast their gods into the fire: for they *were* no gods, but the work of men's hands, wood and stone: therefore they have destroyed them.

19Now therefore, O LORD our God, I beseech thee, save thou us out of his hand, that all the kingdoms of the earth may know that thou *art* the LORD God, *even* thou only.

20¶ Then Isaiah the son of Amoz sent to Hezekiah, saying, Thus saith the LORD God of Israel, *That* which thou hast prayed to me against Sennacherib king of Assyria I have heard.

21This *is* the word that the LORD hath spoken concerning him; The virgin the daughter of Zion hath despised thee, *and* laughed thee to scorn; the daughter of Jerusalem hath shaken her head at thee.

22Whom hast thou reproached and blasphemed? and against whom hast thou exalted *thy* voice, and lifted up thine eyes on high? *even* against the Holy *One* of Israel.

23By thy messengers thou hast reproached the Lord, and hast said, With the multitude of my chariots I am come up to the height of the mountains, to the sides of Lebanon, and will cut down the tall cedar trees thereof, *and* the choice fir trees thereof: and I will enter into the lodgings of his borders, *and into* the forest of his Carmel.

24I have digged and drunk strange waters, and with the sole of my feet have I dried up all the rivers of besieged places.

25Hast thou not heard long ago *how* I have done it, *and* of ancient times that I have formed it? now have I brought it to pass, that thou shouldest be to lay waste fenced cities *into* ruinous heaps.

26Therefore their inhabitants were of small power, they were dismayed and confounded; they were *as* the grass of the field, and *as* the green herb, *as* the grass on the housetops, and *as corn* blasted before it be grown up.

27But I know thy abode, and thy going out, and thy coming in, and thy rage against me.

28Because thy rage against me and thy tumult is come up into mine ears, therefore I will put my hook in thy nose, and my bridle in thy lips, and I will turn thee back by the way by which thou camest.

29And this *shall be* a sign unto thee, Ye shall eat this year such things as grow of themselves, and in the second year that which springeth of the same; and in the third year sow ye, and reap, and plant vineyards, and eat the fruits thereof.

30And the remnant that is escaped of the house of Judah shall yet again take root downward, and bear fruit upward.

31For out of Jerusalem shall go forth a remnant, and they that escape out of mount Zion: the zeal of the LORD *of hosts* shall do this.

32Therefore thus saith the LORD concerning the king of Assyria, He shall not come into this city, nor shoot an arrow there, nor come before it with shield, nor cast a bank against it.

New International

thrown their gods into the fire and destroyed them, for they were not gods but only wood and stone, fashioned by men's hands. 19Now, O LORD our God, deliver us from his hand, so that all kingdoms on earth may know that you alone, O LORD, are God."

Isaiah Prophesies Sennacherib's Fall

20Then Isaiah son of Amoz sent a message to Hezekiah: "This is what the LORD, the God of Israel, says: I have heard your prayer concerning Sennacherib king of Assyria. 21This is the word that the LORD has spoken against him:

> " 'The Virgin Daughter of Zion
>   despises you and mocks you.
> The Daughter of Jerusalem
>   tosses her head as you flee.
> 22Who is it you have insulted and blasphemed?
>   Against whom have you raised your voice
> and lifted your eyes in pride?
>   Against the Holy One of Israel!
> 23By your messengers
>   you have heaped insults on the Lord.
> And you have said,
>   "With my many chariots
> I have ascended the heights of the mountains,
>   the utmost heights of Lebanon.
> I have cut down its tallest cedars,
>   the choicest of its pines.
> I have reached its remotest parts,
>   the finest of its forests.
> 24I have dug wells in foreign lands
>   and drunk the water there.
> With the soles of my feet
>   I have dried up all the streams of Egypt."
>
> 25" 'Have you not heard?
>   Long ago I ordained it.
> In days of old I planned it;
>   now I have brought it to pass,
> that you have turned fortified cities
>   into piles of stone.
> 26Their people, drained of power,
>   are dismayed and put to shame.
> They are like plants in the field,
>   like tender green shoots,
> like grass sprouting on the roof,
>   scorched before it grows up.
>
> 27" 'But I know where you stay
>   and when you come and go
>   and how you rage against me.
> 28Because you rage against me
>   and your insolence has reached my ears,
> I will put my hook in your nose
>   and my bit in your mouth,
> and I will make you return
>   by the way you came.'

29"This will be the sign for you, O Hezekiah:

> "This year you will eat what grows by itself,
>   and the second year what springs from that.
> But in the third year sow and reap,
>   plant vineyards and eat their fruit.
> 30Once more a remnant of the house of Judah
>   will take root below and bear fruit above.
> 31For out of Jerusalem will come a remnant,
>   and out of Mount Zion a band of survivors.

The zeal of the LORD Almighty will accomplish this.

32"Therefore this is what the LORD says concerning the king of Assyria:

> "He will not enter this city
>   or shoot an arrow here.
> He will not come before it with shield
>   or build a siege ramp against it.

Living Bible

idol-gods. But they weren't gods at all; they were destroyed because they were only things that men had made of wood and stone. 19O Lord our God, we plead with you to save us from his power; then all the kingdoms of the earth will know that you alone are God."

20Then Isaiah sent this message to Hezekiah: "The Lord God of Israel says, 'I have heard you! 21And this is my reply to King Sennacherib: The virgin daughter of Zion isn't afraid of you! The daughter of Jerusalem scorns and mocks at you. 22Whom have you defied and blasphemed? And toward whom have you felt so cocky? It is the Holy One of Israel!

23" 'You have boasted, "My chariots have conquered the highest mountains, yes, the peaks of Lebanon. I have cut down the tallest cedars and choicest cypress trees and have conquered the farthest borders. 24I have been refreshed at many conquered wells, and I destroyed the strength of Egypt just by walking by!"

25" 'Why haven't you realized long before this that it is I, the Lord, who lets you do these things? I decreed your conquest of all those fortified cities! 26So of course the nations you conquered had no power against you! They were like grass shriveling beneath the hot sun, and like grain blighted before it is half grown. 27I know everything about you. I know all your plans and where you are going next; and I also know the evil things you have said about me. 28And because of your arrogance against me I am going to put a hook in your nose and a bridle in your mouth and turn you back on the road by which you came. 29And this is the proof that I will do as I have promised: This year my people will eat the volunteer wheat, and use it as seed for next year's crop; and in the third year they will have a bountiful harvest.

30" 'O my people Judah, those of you who have escaped the ravages of the siege shall become a great nation again; you shall be rooted deeply in the soil and bear fruit for God. 31A remnant of my people shall become strong in Jerusalem. The Lord is eager to cause this to happen.

32" 'And my command concerning the king of Assyria is that he shall not enter this city. He shall not stand before it with a shield, nor build a ramp against its wall, nor even shoot an arrow into it. 33He shall return by the

New Revised Standard

18and have hurled their gods into the fire, though they were no gods but the work of human hands—wood and stone—and so they were destroyed. 19So now, O LORD our God, save us, I pray you, from his hand, so that all the kingdoms of the earth may know that you, O LORD, are God alone."

20 Then Isaiah son of Amoz sent to Hezekiah, saying, "Thus says the LORD, the God of Israel: I have heard your prayer to me about King Sennacherib of Assyria. 21This is the word that the LORD has spoken concerning him:

She despises you, she scorns you—
    virgin daughter Zion;
she tosses her head—behind your back,
    daughter Jerusalem.

22 Whom have you mocked and reviled?
      Against whom have you raised your voice
    and haughtily lifted your eyes?
      Against the Holy One of Israel!
23 By your messengers you have mocked the
          Lord,
      and you have said, 'With my many chariots
    I have gone up the heights of the mountains,
      to the far recesses of Lebanon;
    I felled its tallest cedars,
      its choicest cypresses;
    I entered its farthest retreat,
      its densest forest.
24 I dug wells
      and drank foreign waters,
    I dried up with the sole of my foot
      all the streams of Egypt.'

25 Have you not heard
      that I determined it long ago?
    I planned from days of old
      what now I bring to pass,
    that you should make fortified cities
      crash into heaps of ruins,
26 while their inhabitants, shorn of strength,
      are dismayed and confounded;
    they have become like plants of the field
      and like tender grass,
    like grass on the housetops,
      blighted before it is grown.

27 "But I know your risinga and your sitting,
      your going out and coming in,
      and your raging against me.
28 Because you have raged against me
      and your arrogance has come to my ears,
    I will put my hook in your nose
      and my bit in your mouth;
    I will turn you back on the way
      by which you came.

29 "And this shall be the sign for you: This year you shall eat what grows of itself, and in the second year what springs from that; then in the third year sow, reap, plant vineyards, and eat their fruit. 30The surviving remnant of the house of Judah shall again take root downward, and bear fruit upward; 31for from Jerusalem a remnant shall go out, and from Mount Zion a band of survivors. The zeal of the LORD of hosts will do this.

32 "Therefore thus says the LORD concerning the king of Assyria: He shall not come into this city, shoot an arrow there, come before it with a shield, or cast up a siege ramp against it. 33By the way that he came, by

a Gk Compare Isa 37.27 Q Ms: MT lacks *rising*

King James

33By the way that he came, by the same shall he return, and shall not come into this city, saith the LORD.

34For I will defend this city, to save it, for mine own sake, and for my servant David's sake.

35¶ And it came to pass that night, that the angel of the LORD went out, and smote in the camp of the Assyrians an hundred fourscore and five thousand: and when they arose early in the morning, behold, they *were* all dead corpses.

36So Sennacherib king of Assyria departed, and went and returned, and dwelt at Nineveh.

37And it came to pass, as he was worshipping in the house of Nisroch his god, that Adrammelech and Sharezer his sons smote him with the sword: and they escaped into the land of Armenia. And Esar-haddon his son reigned in his stead.

20 IN THOSE days was Hezekiah sick unto death. And the prophet Isaiah the son of Amoz came to him, and said unto him, Thus saith the LORD, Set thine house in order; for thou shalt die, and not live.

2Then he turned his face to the wall, and prayed unto the LORD, saying,

3I beseech thee, O LORD, remember now how I have walked before thee in truth and with a perfect heart, and have done *that which is* good in thy sight. And Hezekiah wept sore.

4And it came to pass, afore Isaiah was gone out into the middle court, that the word of the LORD came to him, saying,

5Turn again, and tell Hezekiah the captain of my people, Thus saith the LORD, the God of David thy father, I have heard thy prayer, I have seen thy tears: behold, I will heal thee: on the third day thou shalt go up unto the house of the LORD.

6And I will add unto thy days fifteen years; and I will deliver thee and this city out of the hand of the king of Assyria; and I will defend this city for mine own sake, and for my servant David's sake.

7And Isaiah said, Take a lump of figs. And they took and laid *it* on the boil, and he recovered.

8¶ And Hezekiah said unto Isaiah, What *shall be* the sign that the LORD will heal me, and that I shall go up into the house of the LORD the third day?

9And Isaiah said, This sign shalt thou have of the LORD, that the LORD will do the thing that he hath spoken: shall the shadow go forward ten degrees, or go back ten degrees?

10And Hezekiah answered, It is a light thing for the shadow to go down ten degrees: nay, but let the shadow return backward ten degrees.

11And Isaiah the prophet cried unto the LORD: and he brought the shadow ten degrees backward, by which it had gone down in the dial of Ahaz.

12¶ At that time Berodach-baladan, the son of Baladan, king of Babylon, sent letters and a present unto Hezekiah: for he had heard that Hezekiah had been sick.

13And Hezekiah hearkened unto them, and showed them all the house of his precious things, the silver, and the gold, and the spices, and the precious ointment, and *all* the house of his armour, and all that was found in his treasures: there was nothing in his house, nor in all his dominion, that Hezekiah showed them not.

14¶ Then came Isaiah the prophet unto king Hezekiah, and said unto him, What said these men? and from whence came they unto thee? And Hezekiah said, They are come from a far country, *even* from Babylon.

New International

33By the way that he came he will return;
he will not enter this city,
                    declares the LORD.
34I will defend this city and save it,
for my sake and for the sake of David my
servant."

35That night the angel of the LORD went out and put to death a hundred and eighty-five thousand men in the Assyrian camp. When the people got up the next morning—there were all the dead bodies! 36So Sennacherib king of Assyria broke camp and withdrew. He returned to Nineveh and stayed there.

37One day, while he was worshiping in the temple of his god Nisroch, his sons Adrammelech and Sharezer cut him down with the sword, and they escaped to the land of Ararat. And Esarhaddon his son succeeded him as king.

Hezekiah's Illness

20 IN THOSE days Hezekiah became ill and was at the point of death. The prophet Isaiah son of Amoz went to him and said, "This is what the LORD says: Put your house in order, because you are going to die; you will not recover."

2Hezekiah turned his face to the wall and prayed to the LORD, 3"Remember, O LORD, how I have walked before you faithfully and with wholehearted devotion and have done what is good in your eyes." And Hezekiah wept bitterly.

4Before Isaiah had left the middle court, the word of the LORD came to him: 5"Go back and tell Hezekiah, the leader of my people, 'This is what the LORD, the God of your father David, says: I have heard your prayer and seen your tears; I will heal you. On the third day from now you will go up to the temple of the LORD. 6I will add fifteen years to your life. And I will deliver you and this city from the hand of the king of Assyria. I will defend this city for my sake and for the sake of my servant David.'"

7Then Isaiah said, "Prepare a poultice of figs." They did so and applied it to the boil, and he recovered.

8Hezekiah had asked Isaiah, "What will be the sign that the LORD will heal me and that I will go up to the temple of the LORD on the third day from now?"

9Isaiah answered, "This is the LORD's sign to you that the LORD will do what he has promised: Shall the shadow go forward ten steps, or shall it go back ten steps?"

10"It is a simple matter for the shadow to go forward ten steps," said Hezekiah. "Rather, have it go back ten steps."

11Then the prophet Isaiah called upon the LORD, and the LORD made the shadow go back the ten steps it had gone down on the stairway of Ahaz.

Envoys From Babylon

12At that time Merodach-Baladan son of Baladan king of Babylon sent Hezekiah letters and a gift, because he had heard of Hezekiah's illness. 13Hezekiah received the messengers and showed them all that was in his storehouses—the silver, the gold, the spices and the fine oil—his armory and everything found among his treasures. There was nothing in his palace or in all his kingdom that Hezekiah did not show them.

14Then Isaiah the prophet went to King Hezekiah and asked, "What did those men say, and where did they come from?"

"From a distant land," Hezekiah replied. "They came from Babylon."

Living Bible

road he came, 34for I will defend and save this city for the sake of my own name and for the sake of my servant David.' "

35That very night the angel of the Lord killed 185,000 Assyrian troops, and dead bodies were seen all across the landscape in the morning.

36Then King Sennacherib returned to Nineveh; 37and as he was worshiping in the temple of his god Nisroch, his sons Adrammelech and Sharezer killed him. They escaped into eastern Turkey—the land of Ararat—and his son Esarhaddon became the new king.

20 HEZEKIAH NOW became deathly sick, and Isaiah the prophet went to visit him. "Set your affairs in order and prepare to die," Isaiah told him. "The Lord says you won't recover."

2Hezekiah turned his face to the wall.

3"O Lord," he pleaded, "remember how I've always tried to obey you and to please you in everything I do. . . ." Then he broke down and cried.

4So before Isaiah had left the courtyard, the Lord spoke to him again.

5"Go back to Hezekiah, the leader of my people, and tell him that the Lord God of his ancestor David has heard his prayer and seen his tears. I will heal him, and three days from now he will be out of bed and at the Temple! 6I will add fifteen years to his life and save him and this city from the king of Assyria. And it will all be done for the glory of my own name and for the sake of my servant David."

7Isaiah then instructed Hezekiah to boil some dried figs and to make a paste of them and spread it on the boil. And he recovered!

8Meanwhile, King Hezekiah had said to Isaiah, "Do a miracle to prove to me that the Lord will heal me and that I will be able to go to the Temple again three days from now."

9"All right, the Lord will give you a proof," Isaiah told him. "Do you want the shadow on the sundial to go forward ten points or backward ten points?"

10"The shadow always moves forward," Hezekiah replied; "make it go backward."

11So Isaiah asked the Lord to do this, and he caused the shadow to move ten points backward on the sundial of Ahaz!a

12At that time Merodach-baladan (the son of King Baladan of Babylon) sent ambassadors with greetings and a present to Hezekiah, for he had learned of his sickness. 13Hezekiah welcomed them and showed them all his treasures—the silver, gold, spices, aromatic oils, the armory—everything.

14Then Isaiah went to King Hezekiah and asked him, "What did these men want? Where are they from?"

"From far away in Babylon," Hezekiah replied.

New Revised Standard

the same he shall return; he shall not come into this city, says the LORD. 34For I will defend this city to save it, for my own sake and for the sake of my servant David."

Sennacherib's Defeat and Death

35 That very night the angel of the LORD set out and struck down one hundred eighty-five thousand in the camp of the Assyrians; when morning dawned, they were all dead bodies. 36Then King Sennacherib of Assyria left, went home, and lived at Nineveh. 37 As he was worshiping in the house of his god Nisroch, his sons Adrammelech and Sharezer killed him with the sword, and they escaped into the land of Ararat. His son Esarhaddon succeeded him.

Hezekiah's Illness

20 IN THOSE days Hezekiah became sick and was at the point of death. The prophet Isaiah son of Amoz came to him, and said to him, "Thus says the LORD: Set your house in order, for you shall die; you shall not recover." 2 Then Hezekiah turned his face to the wall and prayed to the LORD: 3"Remember now, O LORD, I implore you, how I have walked before you in faithfulness with a whole heart, and have done what is good in your sight." Hezekiah wept bitterly. 4Before Isaiah had gone out of the middle court, the word of the LORD came to him: 5"Turn back, and say to Hezekiah prince of my people, Thus says the LORD, the God of your ancestor David: I have heard your prayer, I have seen your tears; indeed, I will heal you; on the third day you shall go up to the house of the LORD. 6I will add fifteen years to your life. I will deliver you and this city out of the hand of the king of Assyria; I will defend this city for my own sake and for my servant David's sake." 7Then Isaiah said, "Bring a lump of figs. Let them take it and apply it to the boil, so that he may recover."

8 Hezekiah said to Isaiah, "What shall be the sign that the LORD will heal me, and that I shall go up to the house of the LORD on the third day?" 9Isaiah said, "This is the sign to you from the LORD, that the LORD will do the thing that he has promised: the shadow has now advanced ten intervals; shall it retreat ten intervals?" 10Hezekiah answered, "It is normal for the shadow to lengthen ten intervals; rather let the shadow retreat ten intervals." 11The prophet Isaiah cried to the LORD; and he brought the shadow back the ten intervals, by which the sunb had declined on the dial of Ahaz.

Envoys from Babylon

12 At that time King Merodach-baladan son of Baladan of Babylon sent envoys with letters and a present to Hezekiah, for he had heard that Hezekiah had been sick. 13Hezekiah welcomed them;c he showed them all his treasure house, the silver, the gold, the spices, the precious oil, his armory, all that was found in his storehouses; there was nothing in his house or in all his realm that Hezekiah did not show them. 14Then the prophet Isaiah came to King Hezekiah, and said to him, "What did these men say? From where did they come to you?" Hezekiah answered, "They have come from a far country, from Babylon." 15He said, "What have they seen in

---

a 20:11 *on the sundial of Ahaz,* or, "on the steps of Ahaz." Egyptian sundials in this period were made in the form of miniature staircases, so that the shadow moved up and down the steps.

b Syr See Isa 38.8 and Tg: Heb *it*   c Gk Vg Syr: Heb *When Hezekiah heard about them*

King James

15And he said, What have they seen in thine house? And Hezekiah answered, All *the things* that *are* in mine house have they seen: there is nothing among my treasures that I have not showed them.

16And Isaiah said unto Hezekiah, Hear the word of the LORD.

17Behold, the days come, that all that *is* in thine house, and that which thy fathers have laid up in store unto this day, shall be carried into Babylon: nothing shall be left, saith the LORD.

18And of thy sons that shall issue from thee, which thou shalt beget, shall they take away; and they shall be eunuchs in the palace of the king of Babylon.

19Then said Hezekiah unto Isaiah, Good *is* the word of the LORD which thou hast spoken. And he said, *Is it* not *good,* if peace and truth be in my days?

20¶ And the rest of the acts of Hezekiah, and all his might, and how he made a pool, and a conduit, and brought water into the city, *are* they not written in the book of the chronicles of the kings of Judah?

21And Hezekiah slept with his fathers: and Manasseh his son reigned in his stead.

21 MANASSEH *WAS* twelve years old when he began to reign, and reigned fifty and five years in Jerusalem. And his mother's name *was* Hephzibah.

2And he did *that which was* evil in the sight of the LORD, after the abominations of the heathen, whom the LORD cast out before the children of Israel.

3For he built up again the high places which Hezekiah his father had destroyed; and he reared up altars for Baal, and made a grove, as did Ahab king of Israel; and worshipped all the host of heaven, and served them.

4And he built altars in the house of the LORD, of which the LORD said, In Jerusalem will I put my name.

5And he built altars for all the host of heaven in the two courts of the house of the LORD.

6And he made his son pass through the fire, and observed times, and used enchantments, and dealt with familiar spirits and wizards: he wrought much wickedness in the sight of the LORD, to provoke *him* to anger.

7And he set a graven image of the grove that he had made in the house, of which the LORD said to David, and to Solomon his son, In this house, and in Jerusalem, which I have chosen out of all tribes of Israel, will I put my name for ever:

8Neither will I make the feet of Israel move any more out of the land which I gave their fathers; only if they will observe to do according to all that I have commanded them, and according to all the law that my servant Moses commanded them.

9But they hearkened not: and Manasseh seduced them to do more evil than did the nations whom the LORD destroyed before the children of Israel.

10¶ And the LORD spake by his servants the prophets, saying,

11Because Manasseh king of Judah hath done these abominations, *and* hath done wickedly above all that the Amorites did, which *were* before him, and hath made Judah also to sin with his idols:

12Therefore thus saith the LORD God of Israel, Behold, I *am* bringing *such* evil upon Jerusalem and Judah, that whosoever heareth of it, both his ears shall tingle.

13And I will stretch over Jerusalem the line of Samaria, and the plummet of the house of Ahab: and I will wipe Jerusalem as *a man* wipeth a dish, wiping *it,* and turning *it* upside down.

14And I will forsake the remnant of mine inheritance, and deliver them into the hand of their enemies; and they shall become a prey and a spoil to all their enemies;

New International

15The prophet asked, "What did they see in your palace?"

"They saw everything in my palace," Hezekiah said. "There is nothing among my treasures that I did not show them."

16Then Isaiah said to Hezekiah, "Hear the word of the LORD: 17The time will surely come when everything in your palace, and all that your fathers have stored up until this day, will be carried off to Babylon. Nothing will be left, says the LORD. 18And some of your descendants, your own flesh and blood, that will be born to you, will be taken away, and they will become eunuchs in the palace of the king of Babylon."

19"The word of the LORD you have spoken is good," Hezekiah replied. For he thought, "Will there not be peace and security in my lifetime?"

20As for the other events of Hezekiah's reign, all his achievements and how he made the pool and the tunnel by which he brought water into the city, are they not written in the book of the annals of the kings of Judah? 21Hezekiah rested with his fathers. And Manasseh his son succeeded him as king.

Manasseh King of Judah

21 MANASSEH WAS twelve years old when he became king, and he reigned in Jerusalem fifty-five years. His mother's name was Hephzibah. 2He did evil in the eyes of the LORD, following the detestable practices of the nations the LORD had driven out before the Israelites. 3He rebuilt the high places his father Hezekiah had destroyed; he also erected altars to Baal and made an Asherah pole, as Ahab king of Israel had done. He bowed down to all the starry hosts and worshiped them. 4He built altars in the temple of the LORD, of which the LORD had said, "In Jerusalem I will put my Name." 5In both courts of the temple of the LORD, he built altars to all the starry hosts. 6He sacrificed his own son ina the fire, practiced sorcery and divination, and consulted mediums and spiritists. He did much evil in the eyes of the LORD, provoking him to anger.

7He took the carved Asherah pole he had made and put it in the temple, of which the LORD had said to David and to his son Solomon, "In this temple and in Jerusalem, which I have chosen out of all the tribes of Israel, I will put my Name forever. 8I will not again make the feet of the Israelites wander from the land I gave their forefathers, if only they will be careful to do everything I commanded them and will keep the whole Law that my servant Moses gave them." 9But the people did not listen. Manasseh led them astray, so that they did more evil than the nations the LORD had destroyed before the Israelites.

10The LORD said through his servants the prophets: 11"Manasseh king of Judah has committed these detestable sins. He has done more evil than the Amorites who preceded him and has led Judah into sin with his idols. 12Therefore this is what the LORD, the God of Israel, says: I am going to bring such disaster on Jerusalem and Judah that the ears of everyone who hears of it will tingle. 13I will stretch out over Jerusalem the measuring line used against Samaria and the plumb line used against the house of Ahab. I will wipe out Jerusalem as one wipes a dish, wiping it and turning it upside down. 14I will forsake the remnant of my inheritance and hand them over to their enemies. They will be looted and plundered by all their foes, 15because they have done

---

a 6 Or *He made his own son pass through*

Living Bible

15"What have they seen in your palace?" Isaiah asked.

And Hezekiah replied, "Everything. I showed them all my treasures."

16Then Isaiah said to Hezekiah, "Listen to the word of the Lord: 17The time will come when everything in this palace shall be carried to Babylon. All the treasures of your ancestors will be taken—nothing shall be left. 18Some of your own sons will be taken away and made into eunuchs who will serve in the palace of the king of Babylon."

19"All right," Hezekiah replied, "if this is what the Lord wants, it is good." But he was really thinking, "At least there will be peace and security during the remainder of my own life!"

20The rest of the history of Hezekiah and his great deeds—including the pool and conduit he made and how he brought water into the city—are recorded in *The Annals of the Kings of Judah*. 21When he died, his son Manasseh became the new king.

21 NEW KING of Judah: Manasseh
His age at beginning of his reign: 12 years
Length of his reign: 55 years, in Jerusalem
Name of his mother: Hephzibah
Character of his reign: evil. He did the same things the nations had done that were thrown out of the land to make room for the people of Israel
3,4,5He rebuilt the hilltop shrines which his father Hezekiah had destroyed. He built altars for Baal and made a shameful Asherah idol, just as Ahab the king of Israel had done. Heathen altars to the sun god, moon god, and the gods of the stars were placed even in the Temple of the Lord—in the very city and building which the Lord had selected to honor his own name. 6And he sacrificed one of his sons as a burnt offering on a heathen altar. He practiced black magic and used fortune-telling, and patronized mediums and wizards. So the Lord was very angry, for Manasseh was an evil man, in God's sight. 7Manasseh even set up a shameful Asherah-idol in the Temple—the very place which the Lord had spoken to David and Solomon about when he said, "I will place my name forever in this Temple, and in Jerusalem—the city I have chosen from among all the cities of the tribes of Israel. 8If the people of Israel will only follow the instructions I gave them through Moses, I will never again expel them from this land of their fathers."

9But the people did not listen to the Lord, and Manasseh enticed them to do even more evil than the surrounding nations had done, even though Jehovah had destroyed those nations for their evil ways when the people of Israel entered the land.

10Then the Lord declared through the prophets,
11"Because King Manasseh has done these evil things and is even more wicked than the Amorites who were in this land long ago, and because he has led the people of Judah into idolatry: 12I will bring such evil upon Jerusalem and Judah that the ears of those who hear about it will tingle with horror. 13I will punish Jerusalem as I did Samaria, and as I did King Ahab of Israel and his descendants. I will wipe away the people of Jerusalem as a man wipes a dish and turns it upside down to dry. 14Then I will reject even those few of my people who are left, and I will hand them over to their enemies. 15For

New Revised Standard

your house?" Hezekiah answered, "They have seen all that is in my house; there is nothing in my storehouses that I did not show them."

16 Then Isaiah said to Hezekiah, "Hear the word of the Lord: 17Days are coming when all that is in your house, and that which your ancestors have stored up until this day, shall be carried to Babylon; nothing shall be left, says the Lord. 18Some of your own sons who are born to you shall be taken away; they shall be eunuchs in the palace of the king of Babylon." 19Then Hezekiah said to Isaiah, "The word of the Lord that you have spoken is good." For he thought, "Why not, if there will be peace and security in my days?"

Death of Hezekiah

20 The rest of the deeds of Hezekiah, all his power, how he made the pool and the conduit and brought water into the city, are they not written in the Book of the Annals of the Kings of Judah? 21 Hezekiah slept with his ancestors; and his son Manasseh succeeded him.

Manasseh Reigns over Judah

21 MANASSEH WAS twelve years old when he began to reign; he reigned fifty-five years in Jerusalem. His mother's name was Hephzibah. 2He did what was evil in the sight of the Lord, following the abominable practices of the nations that the Lord drove out before the people of Israel. 3For he rebuilt the high places that his father Hezekiah had destroyed; he erected altars for Baal, made a sacred pole,[b] as King Ahab of Israel had done, worshiped all the host of heaven, and served them. 4He built altars in the house of the Lord, of which the Lord had said, "In Jerusalem I will put my name." 5He built altars for all the host of heaven in the two courts of the house of the Lord. 6He made his son pass through fire; he practiced soothsaying and augury, and dealt with mediums and with wizards. He did much evil in the sight of the Lord, provoking him to anger. 7The carved image of Asherah that he had made he set in the house of which the Lord said to David and to his son Solomon, "In this house, and in Jerusalem, which I have chosen out of all the tribes of Israel, I will put my name forever; 8I will not cause the feet of Israel to wander any more out of the land that I gave to their ancestors, if only they will be careful to do according to all that I have commanded them, and according to all the law that my servant Moses commanded them." 9But they did not listen; Manasseh misled them to do more evil than the nations had done that the Lord destroyed before the people of Israel.

10 The Lord said by his servants the prophets, 11"Because King Manasseh of Judah has committed these abominations, has done things more wicked than all that the Amorites did, who were before him, and has caused Judah also to sin with his idols; 12therefore thus says the Lord, the God of Israel, I am bringing upon Jerusalem and Judah such evil that the ears of everyone who hears of it will tingle. 13I will stretch over Jerusalem the measuring line for Samaria, and the plummet for the house of Ahab; I will wipe Jerusalem as one wipes a dish, wiping it and turning it upside down. 14I will cast off the remnant of my heritage, and give them into the hand of their enemies; they shall become a prey and a spoil to all their enemies, 15because they have done what

King James

15Because they have done *that which was* evil in my sight, and have provoked me to anger, since the day their fathers came forth out of Egypt, even unto this day.

16Moreover Manasseh shed innocent blood very much, till he had filled Jerusalem from one end to another; beside his sin wherewith he made Judah to sin, in doing *that which was* evil in the sight of the LORD.

17¶ Now the rest of the acts of Manasseh, and all that he did, and his sin that he sinned, *are* they not written in the book of the chronicles of the kings of Judah?

18And Manasseh slept with his fathers, and was buried in the garden of his own house, in the garden of Uzza: and Amon his son reigned in his stead.

19¶ Amon *was* twenty and two years old when he began to reign, and he reigned two years in Jerusalem. And his mother's name *was* Meshullemeth, the daughter of Haruz of Jotbah.

20And he did *that which was* evil in the sight of the LORD, as his father Manasseh did.

21And he walked in all the way that his father walked in, and served the idols that his father served, and worshipped them:

22And he forsook the LORD God of his fathers, and walked not in the way of the LORD.

23¶ And the servants of Amon conspired against him, and slew the king in his own house.

24And the people of the land slew all them that had conspired against king Amon; and the people of the land made Josiah his son king in his stead.

25Now the rest of the acts of Amon which he did, *are* they not written in the book of the chronicles of the kings of Judah?

26And he was buried in his sepulchre in the garden of Uzza: and Josiah his son reigned in his stead.

22 JOSIAH *WAS* eight years old when he began to reign, and he reigned thirty and one years in Jerusalem. And his mother's name *was* Jedidah, the daughter of Adaiah of Boscath.

2And he did *that which was* right in the sight of the LORD, and walked in all the way of David his father, and turned not aside to the right hand or to the left.

3¶ And it came to pass in the eighteenth year of king Josiah, *that* the king sent Shaphan the son of Azaliah, the son of Meshullam, the scribe, to the house of the LORD, saying,

4Go up to Hilkiah the high priest, that he may sum the silver which is brought into the house of the LORD, which the keepers of the door have gathered of the people:

5And let them deliver it into the hand of the doers of the work, that have the oversight of the house of the LORD: and let them give it to the doers of the work which *is* in the house of the LORD, to repair the breaches of the house,

6Unto carpenters, and builders, and masons, and to buy timber and hewn stone to repair the house.

7Howbeit there was no reckoning made with them of the money that was delivered into their hand, because they dealt faithfully.

8¶ And Hilkiah the high priest said unto Shaphan the scribe, I have found the book of the law in the house of the LORD. And Hilkiah gave the book to Shaphan, and he read it.

New International

evil in my eyes and have provoked me to anger from the day their forefathers came out of Egypt until this day."

16Moreover, Manasseh also shed so much innocent blood that he filled Jerusalem from end to end—besides the sin that he had caused Judah to commit, so that they did evil in the eyes of the LORD.

17As for the other events of Manasseh's reign, and all he did, including the sin he committed, are they not written in the book of the annals of the kings of Judah? 18Manasseh rested with his fathers and was buried in his palace garden, the garden of Uzza. And Amon his son succeeded him as king.

Amon King of Judah

19Amon was twenty-two years old when he became king, and he reigned in Jerusalem two years. His mother's name was Meshullemeth daughter of Haruz; she was from Jotbah. 20He did evil in the eyes of the LORD, as his father Manasseh had done. 21He walked in all the ways of his father; he worshiped the idols his father had worshiped, and bowed down to them. 22He forsook the LORD, the God of his fathers, and did not walk in the way of the LORD.

23Amon's officials conspired against him and assassinated the king in his palace. 24Then the people of the land killed all who had plotted against King Amon, and they made Josiah his son king in his place.

25As for the other events of Amon's reign, and what he did, are they not written in the book of the annals of the kings of Judah? 26He was buried in his grave in the garden of Uzza. And Josiah his son succeeded him as king.

The Book of the Law Found

22 JOSIAH WAS eight years old when he became king, and he reigned in Jerusalem thirty-one years. His mother's name was Jedidah daughter of Adaiah; she was from Bozkath. 2He did what was right in the eyes of the LORD and walked in all the ways of his father David, not turning aside to the right or to the left.

3In the eighteenth year of his reign, King Josiah sent the secretary, Shaphan son of Azaliah, the son of Meshullam, to the temple of the LORD. He said: 4"Go up to Hilkiah the high priest and have him get ready the money that has been brought into the temple of the LORD, which the doorkeepers have collected from the people. 5Have them entrust it to the men appointed to supervise the work on the temple. And have these men pay the workers who repair the temple of the LORD— 6the carpenters, the builders and the masons. Also have them purchase timber and dressed stone to repair the temple. 7But they need not account for the money entrusted to them, because they are acting faithfully."

8Hilkiah the high priest said to Shaphan the secretary, "I have found the Book of the Law in the temple of the LORD." He gave it to Shaphan, who read it. 9Then Sha-

Living Bible

they have done great evil and have angered me ever since I brought their ancestors from Egypt."

16In addition to the idolatry which God hated and into which Manasseh led the people of Judah, he murdered great numbers of innocent people. And Jerusalem was filled from one end to the other with the bodies of his victims.

17The rest of the history of Manasseh's sinful reign is recorded in *The Annals of the Kings of Judah*. 18When he died he was buried in the garden of his palace at Uzza, and his son Amon became the new king.

19, 20Name of the new king of Judah: Amon
His age at the beginning of his reign: 22 years old
Length of his reign: 2 years, in Jerusalem
His mother's name: Meshullemeth (daughter of Haruz, of Jotbah)
Character of his reign: evil

21He did all the evil things his father had done: he worshiped the same idols, 22and turned his back on the Lord God of his ancestors. He refused to listen to God's instructions. 23But his aides conspired against him and killed him in the palace. 24Then a posse of civilians killed all the assassins and placed Amon's son Josiah upon the throne. 25The rest of Amon's biography is recorded in *The Annals of the Kings of Judah*. 26He was buried in a crypt in the garden of Uzza, and his son Josiah became the new king.

22 NEW KING of Judah: Josiah
His age at the beginning of his reign: 8 years old
Duration of his reign: 31 years in Jerusalem
Name of his mother: Jedidah (daughter of Adaiah of Bozkath)
Character of his reign: good; for he followed in the steps of his ancestor King David, obeying the Lord completely

3, 4In the eighteenth year of his reign, King Josiah sent his secretary Shaphan (son of Azaliah, son of Meshullam) to the Temple to give instruction to Hilkiah, the High Priest:

"Collect the money given to the priests at the door of the Temple when the people come to worship. 5, 6Give this money to the building superintendents so that they can hire carpenters and masons to repair the Temple, and to buy lumber and stone."

7(The building superintendents were not required to keep account of their expenditures, for they were honest men.)

8One day Hilkiah the High Priest went to Shaphan the secretary and exclaimed, "I have discovered a scroll in the Temple, with God's laws written on it!"

He gave the scroll to Shaphan to read. 9, 10When

New Revised Standard

is evil in my sight and have provoked me to anger, since the day their ancestors came out of Egypt, even to this day."

16 Moreover Manasseh shed very much innocent blood, until he had filled Jerusalem from one end to another, besides the sin that he caused Judah to sin so that they did what was evil in the sight of the LORD.

17 Now the rest of the acts of Manasseh, all that he did, and the sin that he committed, are they not written in the Book of the Annals of the Kings of Judah? 18Manasseh slept with his ancestors, and was buried in the garden of his house, in the garden of Uzza. His son Amon succeeded him.

Amon Reigns over Judah

19 Amon was twenty-two years old when he began to reign; he reigned two years in Jerusalem. His mother's name was Meshullemeth daughter of Haruz of Jotbah. 20He did what was evil in the sight of the LORD, as his father Manasseh had done. 21He walked in all the way in which his father walked, served the idols that his father served, and worshiped them; 22he abandoned the LORD, the God of his ancestors, and did not walk in the way of the LORD. 23The servants of Amon conspired against him, and killed the king in his house. 24But the people of the land killed all those who had conspired against King Amon, and the people of the land made his son Josiah king in place of him. 25Now the rest of the acts of Amon that he did, are they not written in the Book of the Annals of the Kings of Judah? 26He was buried in his tomb in the garden of Uzza; then his son Josiah succeeded him.

Josiah Reigns over Judah

22 JOSIAH WAS eight years old when he began to reign; he reigned thirty-one years in Jerusalem. His mother's name was Jedidah daughter of Adaiah of Bozkath. 2He did what was right in the sight of the LORD, and walked in all the way of his father David; he did not turn aside to the right or to the left.

Hilkiah Finds the Book of the Law

3 In the eighteenth year of King Josiah, the king sent Shaphan son of Azaliah, son of Meshullam, the secretary, to the house of the LORD, saying, 4"Go up to the high priest Hilkiah, and have him count the entire sum of the money that has been brought into the house of the LORD, which the keepers of the threshold have collected from the people; 5let it be given into the hand of the workers who have the oversight of the house of the LORD; let them give it to the workers who are at the house of the LORD, repairing the house, 6that is, to the carpenters, to the builders, to the masons; and let them use it to buy timber and quarried stone to repair the house. 7But no accounting shall be asked from them for the money that is delivered into their hand, for they deal honestly."

8 The high priest Hilkiah said to Shaphan the secretary, "I have found the book of the law in the house of the LORD." When Hilkiah gave the book to Shaphan, he read it. 9Then Shaphan the secretary came to the king,

King James

9And Shaphan the scribe came to the king, and brought the king word again, and said, Thy servants have gathered the money that was found in the house, and have delivered it into the hand of them that do the work, that have the oversight of the house of the LORD.

10And Shaphan the scribe showed the king, saying, Hilkiah the priest hath delivered me a book. And Shaphan read it before the king.

11And it came to pass, when the king had heard the words of the book of the law, that he rent his clothes.

12And the king commanded Hilkiah the priest, and Ahikam the son of Shaphan, and Achbor the son of Michaiah, and Shaphan the scribe, and Asahiah a servant of the king's, saying,

13Go ye, inquire of the LORD for me, and for the people, and for all Judah, concerning the words of this book that is found: for great is the wrath of the LORD that is kindled against us, because our fathers have not hearkened unto the words of this book, to do according unto all that which is written concerning us.

14So Hilkiah the priest, and Ahikam, and Achbor, and Shaphan, and Asahiah, went unto Huldah the prophetess, the wife of Shallum the son of Tikvah, the son of Harhas, keeper of the wardrobe; (now she dwelt in Jerusalem in the college;) and they communed with her.

15¶ And she said unto them, Thus saith the LORD God of Israel, Tell the man that sent you to me,

16Thus saith the LORD, Behold, I will bring evil upon this place, and upon the inhabitants thereof, even all the words of the book which the king of Judah hath read:

17Because they have forsaken me, and have burned incense unto other gods, that they might provoke me to anger with all the works of their hands; therefore my wrath shall be kindled against this place, and shall not be quenched.

18But to the king of Judah which sent you to inquire of the LORD, thus shall ye say to him, Thus saith the LORD God of Israel, As touching the words which thou hast heard;

19Because thine heart was tender, and thou hast humbled thyself before the LORD, when thou heardest what I spake against this place, and against the inhabitants thereof, that they should become a desolation and a curse, and hast rent thy clothes, and wept before me; I also have heard thee, saith the LORD.

20Behold therefore, I will gather thee unto thy fathers, and thou shalt be gathered into thy grave in peace; and thine eyes shall not see all the evil which I will bring upon this place. And they brought the king word again.

23 AND THE king sent, and they gathered unto him all the elders of Judah and of Jerusalem.

2And the king went up into the house of the LORD, and all the men of Judah and all the inhabitants of Jerusalem with him, and the priests, and the prophets, and all the people, both small and great: and he read in their ears all the words of the book of the covenant which was found in the house of the LORD.

3¶ And the king stood by a pillar, and made a covenant before the LORD, to walk after the LORD, and to keep his commandments and his testimonies and his statutes with all their heart and all their soul, to perform the words of this covenant that were written in this book. And all the people stood to the covenant.

4And the king commanded Hilkiah the high priest, and the priests of the second order, and the keepers of the door, to bring forth out of the temple of the LORD all the vessels that were made for Baal, and for the grove, and for all the host of heaven: and he burned them without Jerusalem in the fields of Kidron, and carried the ashes of them unto Beth-el.

New International

phan the secretary went to the king and reported to him: "Your officials have paid out the money that was in the temple of the LORD and have entrusted it to the workers and supervisors at the temple." 10Then Shaphan the secretary informed the king, "Hilkiah the priest has given me a book." And Shaphan read from it in the presence of the king.

11When the king heard the words of the Book of the Law, he tore his robes. 12He gave these orders to Hilkiah the priest, Ahikam son of Shaphan, Acbor son of Micaiah, Shaphan the secretary and Asaiah the king's attendant: 13"Go and inquire of the LORD for me and for the people and for all Judah about what is written in this book that has been found. Great is the LORD's anger that burns against us because our fathers have not obeyed the words of this book; they have not acted in accordance with all that is written there concerning us."

14Hilkiah the priest, Ahikam, Acbor, Shaphan and Asaiah went to speak to the prophetess Huldah, who was the wife of Shallum son of Tikvah, the son of Harhas, keeper of the wardrobe. She lived in Jerusalem, in the Second District.

15She said to them, "This is what the LORD, the God of Israel, says: Tell the man who sent you to me, 16'This is what the LORD says: I am going to bring disaster on this place and its people, according to everything written in the book the king of Judah has read. 17Because they have forsaken me and burned incense to other gods and provoked me to anger by all the idols their hands have made,a my anger will burn against this place and will not be quenched.' 18Tell the king of Judah, who sent you to inquire of the LORD, 'This is what the LORD, the God of Israel, says concerning the words you heard: 19Because your heart was responsive and you humbled yourself before the LORD when you heard what I have spoken against this place and its people, that they would become accursed and laid waste, and because you tore your robes and wept in my presence, I have heard you, declares the LORD. 20Therefore I will gather you to your fathers, and you will be buried in peace. Your eyes will not see all the disaster I am going to bring on this place.' "

So they took her answer back to the king.

Josiah Renews the Covenant

23 THEN THE king called together all the elders of Judah and Jerusalem. 2He went up to the temple of the LORD with the men of Judah, the people of Jerusalem, the priests and the prophets—all the people from the least to the greatest. He read in their hearing all the words of the Book of the Covenant, which had been found in the temple of the LORD. 3The king stood by the pillar and renewed the covenant in the presence of the LORD—to follow the LORD and keep his commands, regulations and decrees with all his heart and all his soul, thus confirming the words of the covenant written in this book. Then all the people pledged themselves to the covenant.

4The king ordered Hilkiah the high priest, the priests next in rank and the doorkeepers to remove from the temple of the LORD all the articles made for Baal and Asherah and all the starry hosts. He burned them outside Jerusalem in the fields of the Kidron Valley and took the ashes to Bethel. 5He did away with the pagan priests

a 17 Or by everything they have done

Living Bible

Shaphan reported to the king about the progress of the repairs at the Temple, he also mentioned the scroll found by Hilkiah. Then Shaphan read it to the king. 11When the king heard what was written in it, he tore his clothes in terror. 12, 13He commanded Hilkiah the priest, and Shaphan, and Asaiah, the king's assistant, and Ahikam (Shaphan's son), and Achbor (Michaiah's son) to ask the Lord, "What shall we do? For we have not been following the instructions of this book: you must be very angry with us, for neither we nor our ancestors have followed your commands."

14So Hilkiah the priest, and Ahikam, and Achbor, and Shaphan, and Asaiah went to the Mishneh section of Jerusalem to find Huldah the prophetess. (She was the wife of Shallum—son of Tikvah, son of Harhas—who was in charge of the palace tailor shop.) 15, 16She gave them this message from the Lord God of Israel:

"Tell the man who sent you to me, that I am going to destroy this city and its people, just as I stated in that book you read. 17For the people of Judah have thrown me aside and have worshiped other gods and have made me very angry; and my anger can't be stopped. 18, 19But because you were sorry and concerned and humbled yourself before the Lord when you read the book and its warnings that this land would be cursed and become desolate, and because you have torn your clothing and wept before me in contrition, I will listen to your plea. 20The death of this nation will not occur until after you die—you will not see the evil which I will bring upon this place."

So they took the message to the king.

23 THEN THE king sent for the elders and other leaders of Judah and Jerusalem to go to the Temple with him. So all the priests and prophets and the people, small and great, of Jerusalem and Judah gathered there at the Temple so that the king could read to them the entire book of God's laws which had been discovered in the Temple. 3He stood beside the pillar in front of the people, and he and they made a solemn promise to the Lord to obey him at all times and to do everything the book commanded.

4Then the king instructed Hilkiah the High Priest and the rest of the priests and the guards of the Temple to destroy all the equipment used in the worship of Baal, Asherah, and the sun, moon, and stars. The king had it all burned in the fields of the Kidron Valley outside Jerusalem, and he carried the ashes to Bethel. 5He killed

New Revised Standard

and reported to the king, "Your servants have emptied out the money that was found in the house, and have delivered it into the hand of the workers who have oversight of the house of the LORD." 10Shaphan the secretary informed the king, "The priest Hilkiah has given me a book." Shaphan then read it aloud to the king.

11 When the king heard the words of the book of the law, he tore his clothes. 12Then the king commanded the priest Hilkiah, Ahikam son of Shaphan, Achbor son of Micaiah, Shaphan the secretary, and the king's servant Asaiah, saying, 13"Go, inquire of the LORD for me, for the people, and for all Judah, concerning the words of this book that has been found; for great is the wrath of the LORD that is kindled against us, because our ancestors did not obey the words of this book, to do according to all that is written concerning us."

14 So the priest Hilkiah, Ahikam, Achbor, Shaphan, and Asaiah went to the prophetess Huldah the wife of Shallum son of Tikvah, son of Harhas, keeper of the wardrobe; she resided in Jerusalem in the Second Quarter, where they consulted her. 15She declared to them, "Thus says the LORD, the God of Israel: Tell the man who sent you to me, 16Thus says the LORD, I will indeed bring disaster on this place and on its inhabitants—all the words of the book that the king of Judah has read. 17Because they have abandoned me and have made offerings to other gods, so that they have provoked me to anger with all the work of their hands, therefore my wrath will be kindled against this place, and it will not be quenched. 18But as to the king of Judah, who sent you to inquire of the LORD, thus shall you say to him, Thus says the LORD, the God of Israel: Regarding the words that you have heard, 19because your heart was penitent, and you humbled yourself before the LORD, when you heard how I spoke against this place, and against its inhabitants, that they should become a desolation and a curse, and because you have torn your clothes and wept before me, I also have heard you, says the LORD. 20Therefore, I will gather you to your ancestors, and you shall be gathered to your grave in peace; your eyes shall not see all the disaster that I will bring on this place." They took the message back to the king.

Josiah's Reformation

23 THEN THE king directed that all the elders of Judah and Jerusalem should be gathered to him. 2The king went up to the house of the LORD, and with him went all the people of Judah, all the inhabitants of Jerusalem, the priests, the prophets, and all the people, both small and great; he read in their hearing all the words of the book of the covenant that had been found in the house of the LORD. 3The king stood by the pillar and made a covenant before the LORD, to follow the LORD, keeping his commandments, his decrees, and his statutes, with all his heart and all his soul, to perform the words of this covenant that were written in this book. All the people joined in the covenant.

4 The king commanded the high priest Hilkiah, the priests of the second order, and the guardians of the threshold, to bring out of the temple of the LORD all the vessels made for Baal, for Asherah, and for all the host of heaven; he burned them outside Jerusalem in the fields of the Kidron, and carried their ashes to Bethel.

King James

5And he put down the idolatrous priests, whom the kings of Judah had ordained to burn incense in the high places in the cities of Judah, and in the places round about Jerusalem; them also that burned incense unto Baal, to the sun, and to the moon, and to the planets, and to all the hosts of heaven.

6And he brought out the grove from the house of the LORD, without Jerusalem, unto the brook Kidron, and burned it at the brook Kidron, and stamped it small to powder, and cast the powder thereof upon the graves of the children of the people.

7And he brake down the houses of the sodomites, that were by the house of the LORD, where the women wove hangings for the grove.

8And he brought all the priests out of the cities of Judah, and defiled the high places where the priests had burned incense, from Geba to Beer-sheba, and brake down the high places of the gates that were in the entering in of the gate of Joshua the governor of the city, which were on a man's left hand at the gate of the city.

9Nevertheless the priests of the high places came not up to the altar of the LORD in Jerusalem, but they did eat of the unleavened bread among their brethren.

10And he defiled Topheth, which is in the valley of the children of Hinnom, that no man might make his son or his daughter to pass through the fire to Molech.

11And he took away the horses that the kings of Judah had given to the sun, at the entering in of the house of the LORD, by the chamber of Nathan-melech the chamberlain, which was in the suburbs, and burned the chariots of the sun with fire.

12And the altars that were on the top of the upper chamber of Ahaz, which the kings of Judah had made, and the altars which Manasseh had made in the two courts of the house of the LORD, did the king beat down, and brake them down from thence, and cast the dust of them into the brook Kidron.

13And the high places that were before Jerusalem, which were on the right hand of the mount of corruption, which Solomon the king of Israel had builded for Ashtoreth the abomination of the Zidonians, and for Chemosh the abomination of the Moabites, and for Milcom the abomination of the children of Ammon, did the king defile.

14And he brake in pieces the images, and cut down the groves, and filled their places with the bones of men.

15¶ Moreover the altar that was at Beth-el, and the high place which Jeroboam the son of Nebat, who made Israel to sin, had made, both that altar and the high place he brake down, and burned the high place, and stamped it small to powder, and burned the grove.

16And as Josiah turned himself, he spied the sepulchres that were there in the mount, and sent, and took the bones out of the sepulchres, and burned them upon the altar, and polluted it, according to the word of the LORD which the man of God proclaimed, who proclaimed these words.

17Then he said, What title is that that I see? And the men of the city told him, It is the sepulchre of the man of God, which came from Judah, and proclaimed these things that thou hast done against the altar of Beth-el.

18And he said, Let him alone; let no man move his bones. So they let his bones alone, with the bones of the prophet that came out of Samaria.

19And all the houses also of the high places that were in the cities of Samaria, which the kings of Israel had made to provoke the LORD to anger, Josiah took away, and did to them according to all the acts that he had done in Beth-el.

20And he slew all the priests of the high places that were there upon the altars, and burned men's bones upon them, and returned to Jerusalem.

21¶ And the king commanded all the people, saying, Keep the passover unto the LORD your God, as it is written in the book of this covenant.

New International

appointed by the kings of Judah to burn incense on the high places of the towns of Judah and on those around Jerusalem—those who burned incense to Baal, to the sun and moon, to the constellations and to all the starry hosts. 6He took the Asherah pole from the temple of the LORD to the Kidron Valley outside Jerusalem and burned it there. He ground it to powder and scattered the dust over the graves of the common people. 7He also tore down the quarters of the male shrine prostitutes, which were in the temple of the LORD and where women did weaving for Asherah.

8Josiah brought all the priests from the towns of Judah and desecrated the high places, from Geba to Beer-sheba, where the priests had burned incense. He broke down the shrinesa at the gates—at the entrance to the Gate of Joshua, the city governor, which is on the left of the city gate. 9Although the priests of the high places did not serve at the altar of the LORD in Jerusalem, they ate unleavened bread with their fellow priests.

10He desecrated Topheth, which was in the Valley of Ben Hinnom, so no one could use it to sacrifice his son or daughter inb the fire to Molech. 11He removed from the entrance to the temple of the LORD the horses that the kings of Judah had dedicated to the sun. They were in the court near the room of an official named Nathan-Melech. Josiah then burned the chariots dedicated to the sun.

12He pulled down the altars the kings of Judah had erected on the roof near the upper room of Ahaz, and the altars Manasseh had built in the two courts of the temple of the LORD. He removed them from there, smashed them to pieces and threw the rubble into the Kidron Valley. 13The king also desecrated the high places that were east of Jerusalem on the south of the Hill of Corruption—the ones Solomon king of Israel had built for Ashtoreth the vile goddess of the Sidonians, for Chemosh the vile god of Moab, and for Molechc the detestable god of the people of Ammon. 14Josiah smashed the sacred stones and cut down the Asherah poles and covered the sites with human bones.

15Even the altar at Bethel, the high place made by Jeroboam son of Nebat, who had caused Israel to sin—even that altar and high place he demolished. He burned the high place and ground it to powder, and burned the Asherah pole also. 16Then Josiah looked around, and when he saw the tombs that were there on the hillside, he had the bones removed from them and burned on the altar to defile it, in accordance with the word of the LORD proclaimed by the man of God who foretold these things.

17The king asked, "What is that tombstone I see?"

The men of the city said, "It marks the tomb of the man of God who came from Judah and pronounced against the altar of Bethel the very things you have done to it."

18"Leave it alone," he said. "Don't let anyone disturb his bones." So they spared his bones and those of the prophet who had come from Samaria.

19Just as he had done at Bethel, Josiah removed and defiled all the shrines at the high places that the kings of Israel had built in the towns of Samaria that had provoked the LORD to anger. 20Josiah slaughtered all the priests of those high places on the altars and burned human bones on them. Then he went back to Jerusalem.

21The king gave this order to all the people: "Celebrate the Passover to the LORD your God, as it is written in this Book of the Covenant." 22Not since the days of

---

a 8 Or high places   b 10 Or to make his son or daughter pass through
c 13 Hebrew Milcom

Living Bible

the heathen priests who had been appointed by the previous kings of Judah, for they had burned incense in the shrines on the hills throughout Judah and even in Jerusalem. They had also offered incense to Baal and to the sun, moon, stars, and planets. 6He removed the shameful idol of Asherah from the Temple and took it outside Jerusalem to Kidron Brook; there he burned it and beat it to dust and threw the dust on the graves of the common people. 7He also tore down the houses of male prostitution around the Temple, where the women wove robes for the Asherah-idol.

8He brought back to Jerusalem the priests of the Lord, who were living in other cities of Judah, and tore down all the shrines on the hills where they had burned incense, even those as far away as Geba and Beersheba. He also destroyed the shrines at the entrance of the palace of Joshua, the former mayor of Jerusalem, located on the left side as one enters the city gate. 9However, these priestsd did not serve at the altar of the Lord in Jerusalem, even though they ate with the other priests.

10Then the king destroyed the altar of Topheth in the Valley of the Sons of Hinnom, so that no one could ever again use it to burn his son or daughter to death as a sacrifice to Molech. 11He tore down the statues of horses and chariots located near the entrance of the Temple, next to the quarters of Nathan-melech the eunuch. These had been dedicated by former kings of Judah to the sun god. 12Then he tore down the altars which the kings of Judah had built on the palace roof above the Ahaz Room. He also destroyed the altars which Manasseh had built in the two courts of the Temple; he smashed them to bits and scattered the pieces in Kidron Valley.

13Next he removed the shrines on the hills east of Jerusalem and south of Destruction Mountain. (Solomon had built these shrines for Ashtoreth, the evil goddess of the Sidonians; and for Chemosh, the evil god of Moab; and for Milcom, the evil god of the Ammonites.) 14He smashed the obelisks and cut down the shameful idols of Asherah; then he defiled these places by scattering human bones over them. 15He also tore down the altar and shrine at Bethel which Jeroboam I had made when he led Israel into sin. He crushed the stones to dust and burned the shameful idol of Asherah.

16As Josiah was looking around, he noticed several graves in the side of the mountain. He ordered his men to bring out the bones in them and to burn them there upon the altar at Bethel to defile it, just as the Lord's prophet had declared would happen to Jeroboam's altar.e

17"What is that monument over there?" he asked.

And the men of the city told him, "It is the grave of the prophet who came from Judah and proclaimed that what you have just done would happen here at the altar at Bethel!"

18So King Josiah replied, "Leave it alone. Don't disturb his bones."

So they didn't burn his bones or those of the prophet from Samaria.f

19Josiah demolished the shrines on the hills in all of Samaria. They had been built by the various kings of Israel and had made the Lord very angry. But now he crushed them into dust, just as he had done at Bethel. 20He executed the priests of the heathen shrines upon their own altars, and he burned human bones upon the altars to defile them. Finally he returned to Jerusalem.

21The king then issued orders for his people to observe the Passover ceremonies as recorded by the Lord their God in The Book of the Covenant. 22There had not

New Revised Standard

5He deposed the idolatrous priests whom the kings of Judah had ordained to make offerings in the high places at the cities of Judah and around Jerusalem; those also who made offerings to Baal, to the sun, the moon, the constellations, and all the host of the heavens. 6He brought out the image ofg Asherah from the house of the LORD, outside Jerusalem, to the Wadi Kidron, burned it at the Wadi Kidron, beat it to dust and threw the dust of it upon the graves of the common people. 7He broke down the houses of the male temple prostitutes that were in the house of the LORD, where the women did weaving for Asherah. 8He brought all the priests out of the towns of Judah, and defiled the high places where the priests had made offerings, from Geba to Beer-sheba; he broke down the high places of the gates that were at the entrance of the gate of Joshua the governor of the city, which were on the left at the gate of the city. 9The priests of the high places, however, did not come up to the altar of the LORD in Jerusalem, but ate unleavened bread among their kindred. 10He defiled Topheth, which is in the valley of Ben-hinnom, so that no one would make a son or a daughter pass through fire as an offering to Molech. 11He removed the horses that the kings of Judah had dedicated to the sun, at the entrance to the house of the LORD, by the chamber of the eunuch Nathan-melech, which was in the precincts;h then he burned the chariots of the sun with fire. 12The altars on the roof of the upper chamber of Ahaz, which the kings of Judah had made, and the altars that Manasseh had made in the two courts of the house of the LORD, he pulled down from there and broke in pieces, and threw the rubble into the Wadi Kidron. 13The king defiled the high places that were east of Jerusalem, to the south of the Mount of Destruction, which King Solomon of Israel had built for Astarte the abomination of the Sidonians, for Chemosh the abomination of Moab, and for Milcom the abomination of the Ammonites. 14He broke the pillars in pieces, cut down the sacred poles,i and covered the sites with human bones.

15 Moreover, the altar at Bethel, the high place erected by Jeroboam son of Nebat, who caused Israel to sin—he pulled down that altar along with the high place. He burned the high place, crushing it to dust; he also burned the sacred pole.j 16As Josiah turned, he saw the tombs there on the mount; and he sent and took the bones out of the tombs, and burned them on the altar, and defiled it, according to the word of the LORD that the man of God proclaimed,k when Jeroboam stood by the altar at the festival; he turned and looked up at the tomb of the man of God who had predicted these things. 17Then he said, "What is that monument that I see?" The people of the city told him, "It is the tomb of the man of God who came from Judah and predicted these things that you have done against the altar at Bethel." 18He said, "Let him rest; let no one move his bones." So they let his bones alone, with the bones of the prophet who came out of Samaria. 19Moreover, Josiah removed all the shrines of the high places that were in the towns of Samaria, which kings of Israel had made, provoking the LORD to anger; he did to them just as he had done at Bethel. 20He slaughtered on the altars all the priests of the high places who were there, and burned human bones on them. Then he returned to Jerusalem.

The Passover Celebrated

21 The king commanded all the people, "Keep the passover to the LORD your God as prescribed in this book of the covenant." 22No such passover had been kept

---

d 23:9 these priests, literally, "the priests of the high places."
e 23:16 Jeroboam's altar, see 1 Kgs 13:2.   f 23:18 See 1 Kgs 13:31, 32.

g Heb lacks image of   h Meaning of Heb uncertain   i Heb Asherim   j Heb
Asherah   k Gk: Heb proclaimed, who had predicted these things

King James

22Surely there was not holden such a passover from the days of the judges that judged Israel, nor in all the days of the kings of Israel, nor of the kings of Judah;

23But in the eighteenth year of king Josiah, *wherein* this passover was holden to the LORD in Jerusalem.

24¶ Moreover the *workers with* familiar spirits, and the wizards, and the images, and the idols, and all the abominations that were spied in the land of Judah and in Jerusalem, did Josiah put away, that he might perform the words of the law which were written in the book that Hilkiah the priest found in the house of the LORD.

25And like unto him was there no king before him, that turned to the LORD with all his heart, and with all his soul, and with all his might, according to all the law of Moses; neither after him arose there *any* like him.

26¶ Notwithstanding the LORD turned not from the fierceness of his great wrath, wherewith his anger was kindled against Judah, because of all the provocations that Manasseh had provoked him withal.

27And the LORD said, I will remove Judah also out of my sight, as I have removed Israel, and will cast off this city Jerusalem which I have chosen, and the house of which I said, My name shall be there.

28Now the rest of the acts of Josiah, and all that he did, *are* they not written in the book of the chronicles of the kings of Judah?

29¶ In his days Pharaoh-nechoh king of Egypt went up against the king of Assyria to the river Euphrates: and king Josiah went against him; and he slew him at Megiddo, when he had seen him.

30And his servants carried him in a chariot dead from Megiddo, and brought him to Jerusalem, and buried him in his own sepulchre. And the people of the land took Jehoahaz the son of Josiah, and anointed him, and made him king in his father's stead.

31¶ Jehoahaz *was* twenty and three years old when he began to reign; and he reigned three months in Jerusalem. And his mother's name *was* Hamutal, the daughter of Jeremiah of Libnah.

32And he did *that which was* evil in the sight of the LORD, according to all that his fathers had done.

33And Pharaoh-nechoh put him in bands at Riblah in the land of Hamath, that he might not reign in Jerusalem; and put the land to a tribute of an hundred talents of silver, and a talent of gold.

34And Pharaoh-nechoh made Eliakim the son of Josiah king in the room of Josiah his father, and turned his name to Johoiakim, and took Jehoahaz away: and he came to Egypt, and died there.

35And Jehoiakim gave the silver and the gold to Pharaoh; but he taxed the land to give the money according to the commandment of Pharaoh: he exacted the silver and the gold of the people of the land, of every one according to his taxation, to give *it* unto Pharaoh-nechoh.

36¶ Jehoiakim *was* twenty and five years old when he began to reign; and he reigned eleven years in Jerusalem. And his mother's name was Zebudah, the daughter of Pedaiah of Rumah.

37And he did *that which was* evil in the sight of the LORD, according to all that his fathers had done.

24 IN HIS days Nebuchadnezzar king of Babylon came up, and Jehoiakim became his servant three years: then he turned and rebelled against him.

New International

the judges who led Israel, nor throughout the days of the kings of Israel and the kings of Judah, had any such Passover been observed. 23But in the eighteenth year of King Josiah, this Passover was celebrated to the LORD in Jerusalem.

24Furthermore, Josiah got rid of the mediums and spiritists, the household gods, the idols and all the other detestable things seen in Judah and Jerusalem. This he did to fulfill the requirements of the law written in the book that Hilkiah the priest had discovered in the temple of the LORD. 25Neither before nor after Josiah was there a king like him who turned to the LORD as he did—with all his heart and with all his soul and with all his strength, in accordance with all the Law of Moses.

26Nevertheless, the LORD did not turn away from the heat of his fierce anger, which burned against Judah because of all that Manasseh had done to provoke him to anger. 27So the LORD said, "I will remove Judah also from my presence as I removed Israel, and I will reject Jerusalem, the city I chose, and this temple, about which I said, 'There shall my Name be.'a"

28As for the other events of Josiah's reign, and all he did, are they not written in the book of the annals of the kings of Judah?

29While Josiah was king, Pharaoh Neco king of Egypt went up to the Euphrates River to help the king of Assyria. King Josiah marched out to meet him in battle, but Neco faced him and killed him at Megiddo. 30Josiah's servants brought his body in a chariot from Megiddo to Jerusalem and buried him in his own tomb. And the people of the land took Jehoahaz son of Josiah and anointed him and made him king in place of his father.

Jehoahaz King of Judah

31Jehoahaz was twenty-three years old when he became king, and he reigned in Jerusalem three months. His mother's name was Hamutal daughter of Jeremiah; she was from Libnah. 32He did evil in the eyes of the LORD, just as his fathers had done. 33Pharaoh Neco put him in chains at Riblah in the land of Hamathb so that he might not reign in Jerusalem, and he imposed on Judah a levy of a hundred talentsc of silver and a talentd of gold. 34Pharaoh Neco made Eliakim son of Josiah king in place of his father Josiah and changed Eliakim's name to Jehoiakim. But he took Jehoahaz and carried him off to Egypt, and there he died. 35Jehoiakim paid Pharaoh Neco the silver and gold he demanded. In order to do so, he taxed the land and exacted the silver and gold from the people of the land according to their assessments.

Jehoiakim King of Judah

36Jehoiakim was twenty-five years old when he became king, and he reigned in Jerusalem eleven years. His mother's name was Zebidah daughter of Pedaiah; she was from Rumah. 37And he did evil in the eyes of the LORD, just as his fathers had done.

24 DURING JEHOIAKIM'S reign, Nebuchadnezzar king of Babylon invaded the land, and Jehoiakim became his vassal for three years. But then he changed his mind and rebelled against Nebuchadnezzar. 2The LORD sent Babylonian,e Aramean, Moabite

---

a 27 1 Kings 8:29   b 33 Hebrew; Septuagint (see also 2 Chron. 36:3) *Neco at Riblah in Hamath removed him*   c 33 That is, about 3 3/4 tons (about 3.4 metric tons)   d 33 That is, about 75 pounds (about 34 kilograms)   e 2 Or Chaldean

Living Bible

been a Passover celebration like that since the days of the judges of Israel, and there was never another like it in all the years of the kings of Israel and Judah. 23This Passover was in the eighteenth year of the reign of King Josiah, and it was celebrated in Jerusalem.

24Josiah also exterminated the mediums and wizards, and every kind of idol worship, both in Jerusalem and throughout the land. For Josiah wanted to follow all the laws which were written in the book that Hilkiah the priest had found in the Temple. 25There was no other king who so completely turned to the Lord and followed all the laws of Moses; and no king since the time of Josiah has approached his record of obedience.

26But the Lord still did not hold back his great anger against Judah, caused by the evils of King Manasseh. 27For the Lord had said, "I will destroy Judah just as I have destroyed Israel; and I will discard my chosen city of Jerusalem and the Temple that I said was mine."

28The rest of the biography of Josiah is written in *The Annals of the Kings of Judah.* 29In those days King Neco of Egypt went out to help the king of Assyria at the Euphrates River. Then King Josiah went out with his troops to fight King Neco; but King Neco withstood him at Meggido and killed him. 30His officers took his body back in a chariot from Megiddo to Jerusalem and buried him in the grave he had selected. And his son Jehoahaz was chosen by the nation as its new king.

31, 32New king of Judah: Jehoahaz
His age when he became king: 23 years old
Length of his reign: 3 months, in Jerusalem
His mother's name: Hamutal (the daughter of Jeremiah of Libnah)
Character of his reign: evil, like the other kings who had preceded him

33Pharaoh-Neco jailed him at Riblah in Hamath to prevent his reigning in Jerusalem, and he levied a tax against Judah totaling $230,000. 34The Egyptian king then chose Eliakim, another of Josiah's sons, to reign in Jerusalem; and he changed his name to Jehoiakim. Then he took King Jehoahaz to Egypt, where he died. 35Jehoiakim taxed the people to get the money that the Pharaoh had demanded.

36, 37New king of Judah: Jehoiakim
His age when he became king: 25 years old
Length of his reign: 11 years, in Jerusalem
His mother's name: Zebidah (daughter of Pedaiah of Rumah)
Character of his reign: evil, like the other kings who had preceded him

24 DURING THE reign of King Jehoiakim, King Nebuchadnezzar of Babylon attacked Jerusalem. Jehoiakim surrendered and paid him tribute for three years, but then rebelled. 2And the Lord sent bands

New Revised Standard

since the days of the judges who judged Israel, or during all the days of the kings of Israel or of the kings of Judah; 23 but in the eighteenth year of King Josiah this passover was kept to the LORD in Jerusalem.

24 Moreover Josiah put away the mediums, wizards, teraphim,f idols, and all the abominations that were seen in the land of Judah and in Jerusalem, so that he established the words of the law that were written in the book that the priest Hilkiah had found in the house of the LORD. 25 Before him there was no king like him, who turned to the LORD with all his heart, with all his soul, and with all his might, according to all the law of Moses; nor did any like him arise after him.

26 Still the LORD did not turn from the fierceness of his great wrath, by which his anger was kindled against Judah, because of all the provocations with which Manasseh had provoked him. 27 The LORD said, "I will remove Judah also out of my sight, as I have removed Israel; and I will reject this city that I have chosen, Jerusalem, and the house of which I said, My name shall be there."

Josiah Dies in Battle

28 Now the rest of the acts of Josiah, and all that he did, are they not written in the Book of the Annals of the Kings of Judah? 29 In his days Pharaoh Neco king of Egypt went up to the king of Assyria to the river Euphrates. King Josiah went to meet him; but when Pharaoh Neco met him at Megiddo, he killed him. 30 His servants carried him dead in a chariot from Megiddo, brought him to Jerusalem, and buried him in his own tomb. The people of the land took Jehoahaz son of Josiah, anointed him, and made him king in place of his father.

Reign and Captivity of Jehoahaz

31 Jehoahaz was twenty-three years old when he began to reign; he reigned three months in Jerusalem. His mother's name was Hamutal daughter of Jeremiah of Libnah. 32 He did what was evil in the sight of the LORD, just as his ancestors had done. 33 Pharaoh Neco confined him at Riblah in the land of Hamath, so that he might not reign in Jerusalem, and imposed tribute on the land of one hundred talents of silver and a talent of gold. 34 Pharaoh Neco made Eliakim son of Josiah king in place of his father Josiah, and changed his name to Jehoiakim. But he took Jehoahaz away; he came to Egypt, and died there. 35 Jehoiakim gave the silver and the gold to Pharaoh, but he taxed the land in order to meet Pharaoh's demand for money. He exacted the silver and the gold from the people of the land, from all according to their assessment, to give it to Pharaoh Neco.

Jehoiakim Reigns over Judah

36 Jehoiakim was twenty-five years old when he began to reign; he reigned eleven years in Jerusalem. His mother's name was Zebidah daughter of Pedaiah of Rumah. 37 He did what was evil in the sight of the LORD, just as all his ancestors had done.

Judah Overrun by Enemies

24 IN HIS days King Nebuchadnezzar of Babylon came up; Jehoiakim became his servant for three years; then he turned and rebelled against him.

---

f Or *household gods*

King James

2And the LORD sent against him bands of the Chaldees, and bands of the Syrians, and bands of the Moabites, and bands of the children of Ammon, and sent them against Judah to destroy it, according to the word of the LORD, which he spake by his servants the prophets.

3Surely at the commandment of the LORD came *this* upon Judah, to remove *them* out of his sight, for the sins of Manasseh, according to all that he did;

4And also for the innocent blood that he shed: for he filled Jerusalem with innocent blood; which the LORD would not pardon.

5¶ Now the rest of the acts of Jehoiakim, and all that he did, *are* they not written in the book of the chronicles of the kings of Judah?

6So Jehoiakim slept with his fathers: and Jehoiachin his son reigned in his stead.

7And the king of Egypt came not again any more out of his land: for the king of Babylon had taken from the river of Egypt unto the river Euphrates all that pertained to the king of Egypt.

8¶ Jehoiachin *was* eighteen years old when he began to reign, and he reigned in Jerusalem three months. And his mother's name *was* Nehushta, the daughter of Elnathan of Jerusalem.

9And he did *that which was* evil in the sight of the LORD, according to all that his father had done.

10¶ At that time the servants of Nebuchadnezzar king of Babylon came up against Jerusalem, and the city was besieged.

11And Nebuchadnezzar king of Babylon came against the city, and his servants did besiege it.

12And Jehoiachin the king of Judah went out to the king of Babylon, he, and his mother, and his servants, and his princes, and his officers: and the king of Babylon took him in the eighth year of his reign.

13And he carried out thence all the treasures of the house of the LORD, and the treasures of the king's house, and cut in pieces all the vessels of gold which Solomon king of Israel had made in the temple of the LORD, as the LORD had said.

14And he carried away all Jerusalem, and all the princes, and all the mighty men of valour, *even* ten thousand captives, and all the craftsmen and smiths: none remained, save the poorest sort of the people of the land.

15And he carried away Jehoiachin to Babylon, and the king's mother, and the king's wives, and his officers, and the mighty of the land, *those* carried he into captivity from Jerusalem to Babylon.

16And all the men of might, *even* seven thousand, and craftsmen and smiths a thousand, all *that were* strong *and* apt for war, even them the king of Babylon brought captive to Babylon.

17¶ And the king of Babylon made Mattaniah his father's brother king in his stead, and changed his name to Zedekiah.

18Zedekiah *was* twenty and one years old when he began to reign, and he reigned eleven years in Jerusalem. And his mother's name *was* Hamutal, the daughter of Jeremiah of Libnah.

19And he did *that which was* evil in the sight of the LORD, according to all that Jehoiakim had done.

20For through the anger of the LORD it came to pass in Jerusalem and Judah, until he had cast them out from his presence, that Zedekiah rebelled against the king of Babylon.

New International

and Ammonite raiders against him. He sent them to destroy Judah, in accordance with the word of the LORD proclaimed by his servants the prophets. 3Surely these things happened to Judah according to the LORD's command, in order to remove them from his presence because of the sins of Manasseh and all he had done, 4including the shedding of innocent blood. For he had filled Jerusalem with innocent blood, and the LORD was not willing to forgive.

5As for the other events of Jehoiakim's reign, and all he did, are they not written in the book of the annals of the kings of Judah? 6Jehoiakim rested with his fathers. And Jehoiachin his son succeeded him as king.

7The king of Egypt did not march out from his own country again, because the king of Babylon had taken all his territory, from the Wadi of Egypt to the Euphrates River.

Jehoiachin King of Judah

8Jehoiachin was eighteen years old when he became king, and he reigned in Jerusalem three months. His mother's name was Nehushta daughter of Elnathan; she was from Jerusalem. 9He did evil in the eyes of the LORD, just as his father had done.

10At that time the officers of Nebuchadnezzar king of Babylon advanced on Jerusalem and laid siege to it, 11and Nebuchadnezzar himself came up to the city while his officers were besieging it. 12Jehoiachin king of Judah, his mother, his attendants, his nobles and his officials all surrendered to him.

In the eighth year of the reign of the king of Babylon, he took Jehoiachin prisoner. 13As the LORD had declared, Nebuchadnezzar removed all the treasures from the temple of the LORD and from the royal palace, and took away all the gold articles that Solomon king of Israel had made for the temple of the LORD. 14He carried into exile all Jerusalem: all the officers and fighting men, and all the craftsmen and artisans—a total of ten thousand. Only the poorest people of the land were left.

15Nebuchadnezzar took Jehoiachin captive to Babylon. He also took from Jerusalem to Babylon the king's mother, his wives, his officials and the leading men of the land. 16The king of Babylon also deported to Babylon the entire force of seven thousand fighting men, strong and fit for war, and a thousand craftsmen and artisans. 17He made Mattaniah, Jehoiachin's uncle, king in his place and changed his name to Zedekiah.

Zedekiah King of Judah

18Zedekiah was twenty-one years old when he became king, and he reigned in Jerusalem eleven years. His mother's name was Hamutal daughter of Jeremiah; she was from Libnah. 19He did evil in the eyes of the LORD, just as Jehoiakim had done. 20It was because of the LORD's anger that all this happened to Jerusalem and Judah, and in the end he thrust them from his presence.

The Fall of Jerusalem

Now Zedekiah rebelled against the king of Babylon.

Living Bible

of Chaldeans, Syrians, Moabites, and Ammonites against Judah in order to destroy the nation, just as the Lord had warned through his prophets that he would. ³, ⁴It is clear that these disasters befell Judah at the direct command of the Lord. He had decided to wipe Judah out of his sight because of the many sins of Manasseh, for he had filled Jerusalem with blood, and the Lord would not pardon it.

⁵The rest of the history of the life of Jehoiakim is recorded in *The Annals of the Kings of Judah*. ⁶When he died, his son Jehoiachin became the new king. ⁷(The Egyptian Pharaoh never returned after that, for the king of Babylon occupied the entire area claimed by Egypt— all of Judah from the Brook of Egypt to the Euphrates River.)

⁸, ⁹New king of Judah, Jehoiachin

His age at the beginning of his reign: 18 years old
Length of his reign: 3 months, in Jerusalem
Name of his mother: Nehushta (daughter of Elnathan, a citizen of Jerusalem)

¹⁰During his reign the armies of King Nebuchadnezzar of Babylon besieged the city of Jerusalem. ¹¹Nebuchadnezzar himself arrived during the siege, ¹²and King Jehoiachin, all of his officials, and the queen mother surrendered to him. The surrender was accepted, and Jehoiachin was imprisoned in Babylon during the eighth year of Nebuchadnezzar's reign.

¹³The Babylonians carried home all the treasures from the Temple and the royal palace; and they cut apart all the gold bowls which King Solomon of Israel had placed in the Temple at the Lord's directions. ¹⁴King Nebuchadnezzar took ten thousand captives from Jerusalem, including all the princes and the best of the soldiers, craftsmen, and smiths. So only the poorest and least skilled people were left in the land. ¹⁵Nebuchadnezzar took King Jehoiachin, his wives and officials, and the queen mother, to Babylon. ¹⁶He also took seven thousand of the best troops and one thousand craftsmen and smiths, all of whom were strong and fit for war. ¹⁷Then the king of Babylon appointed King Jehoiachin's great-uncle,ᵃ Mattaniah, to be the next king; and he changed his name to Zedekiah.

¹⁸, ¹⁹New king of Judah: Zedekiah

His age when he became king: 21 years old
Length of his reign: 11 years, in Jerusalem
His mother's name: Hamutal (daughter of Jeremiah of Libnah)
Character of his reign: evil, like that of Jehoiakim

²⁰So the Lord finally, in his anger, destroyed the people of Jerusalem and Judah. But now King Zedekiah rebelled against the king of Babylon.

New Revised Standard

²The LORD sent against him bands of the Chaldeans, bands of the Arameans, bands of the Moabites, and bands of the Ammonites; he sent them against Judah to destroy it, according to the word of the LORD that he spoke by his servants the prophets. ³Surely this came upon Judah at the command of the LORD, to remove them out of his sight, for the sins of Manasseh, for all that he had committed, ⁴and also for the innocent blood that he had shed; for he filled Jerusalem with innocent blood, and the LORD was not willing to pardon. ⁵Now the rest of the deeds of Jehoiakim, and all that he did, are they not written in the Book of the Annals of the Kings of Judah? ⁶So Jehoiakim slept with his ancestors; then his son Jehoiachin succeeded him. ⁷The king of Egypt did not come again out of his land, for the king of Babylon had taken over all that belonged to the king of Egypt from the Wadi of Egypt to the River Euphrates.

Reign and Captivity of Jehoiachin

8 Jehoiachin was eighteen years old when he began to reign; he reigned three months in Jerusalem. His mother's name was Nehushta daughter of Elnathan of Jerusalem. ⁹He did what was evil in the sight of the LORD, just as his father had done.

10 At that time the servants of King Nebuchadnezzar of Babylon came up to Jerusalem, and the city was besieged. ¹¹King Nebuchadnezzar of Babylon came to the city, while his servants were besieging it; ¹²King Jehoiachin of Judah gave himself up to the king of Babylon, himself, his mother, his servants, his officers, and his palace officials. The king of Babylon took him prisoner in the eighth year of his reign.

Capture of Jerusalem

13 He carried off all the treasures of the house of the LORD, and the treasures of the king's house; he cut in pieces all the vessels of gold in the temple of the LORD, which King Solomon of Israel had made, all this as the LORD had foretold. ¹⁴He carried away all Jerusalem, all the officials, and all the warriors, ten thousand captives, all the artisans and the smiths; no one remained, except the poorest people of the land. ¹⁵He carried away Jehoiachin to Babylon; the king's mother, the king's wives, his officials, and the elite of the land, he took into captivity from Jerusalem to Babylon. ¹⁶The king of Babylon brought captive to Babylon all the men of valor, seven thousand, the artisans and the smiths, one thousand, all of them strong and fit for war. ¹⁷The king of Babylon made Mattaniah, Jehoiachin's uncle, king in his place, and changed his name to Zedekiah.

Zedekiah Reigns over Judah

18 Zedekiah was twenty-one years old when he began to reign; he reigned eleven years in Jerusalem. His mother's name was Hamutal daughter of Jeremiah of Libnah. ¹⁹He did what was evil in the sight of the LORD, just as Jehoiakim had done. ²⁰Indeed, Jerusalem and Judah so angered the LORD that he expelled them from his presence.

The Fall and Captivity of Judah

Zedekiah rebelled against the king of Babylon.

ᵃ *24:17* Implied in 23:31 and 24:18.

King James

25 AND IT came to pass in the ninth year of his reign, in the tenth month, in the tenth *day* of the month, *that* Nebuchadnezzar king of Babylon came, he, and all his host, against Jerusalem, and pitched against it; and they built forts against it round about.

2And the city was besieged unto the eleventh year of king Zedekiah.

3And on the ninth *day* of the *fourth* month the famine prevailed in the city, and there was no bread for the people of the land.

4¶ And the city was broken up, and all the men of war *fled* by night by the way of the gate between two walls, which *is* by the king's garden: (now the Chaldees *were* against the city round about:) and *the king* went the way toward the plain.

5And the army of the Chaldees pursued after the king, and overtook him in the plains of Jericho: and all his army were scattered from him.

6So they took the king, and brought him up to the king of Babylon to Riblah; and they gave judgment upon him.

7And they slew the sons of Zedekiah before his eyes, and put out the eyes of Zedekiah, and bound him with fetters of brass, and carried him to Babylon.

8¶ And in the fifth month, on the seventh *day* of the month, which *is* the nineteenth year of king Nebuchadnezzar king of Babylon, came Nebuzar-adan, captain of the guard, a servant of the king of Babylon, unto Jerusalem:

9And he burnt the house of the LORD, and the king's house, and all the houses of Jerusalem, and every great *man's* house burnt he with fire.

10And all the army of the Chaldees, that *were with* the captain of the guard, brake down the walls of Jerusalem round about.

11Now the rest of the people *that were* left in the city, and the fugitives that fell away to the king of Babylon, with the remnant of the multitude, did Nebuzar-adan the captain of the guard carry away.

12But the captain of the guard left of the poor of the land *to be* vinedressers and husbandmen.

13And the pillars of brass that *were* in the house of the LORD, and the bases, and the brasen sea that *was* in the house of the LORD, did the Chaldees break in pieces, and carried the brass of them to Babylon.

14And the pots, and the shovels, and the snuffers, and the spoons, and all the vessels of brass wherewith they ministered, took they away.

15And the firepans, and the bowls, *and* such things as *were* of gold, *in* gold, and of silver, *in* silver, the captain of the guard took away.

16The two pillars, one sea, and the bases which Solomon had made for the house of the LORD; the brass of all these vessels was without weight.

17The height of the one pillar *was* eighteen cubits, and the chapiter upon it *was* brass: and the height of the chapiter three cubits; and the wreathen work, and pomegranates upon the chapiter round about, all of brass: and like unto these had the second pillar with wreathen work.

18¶ And the captain of the guard took Seraiah the chief priest, and Zephaniah the second priest, and the three keepers of the door:

19And out of the city he took an officer that was set over the men of war, and five men of them that were in the king's presence, which were found in the city, and the principal scribe of the host, which mustered the people of the land, and threescore men of the people of the land *that were* found in the city:

20And Nebuzar-adan captain of the guard took these, and brought them to the king of Babylon to Riblah:

21And the king of Babylon smote them, and slew them at Riblah in the land of Hamath. So Judah was carried away out of their land.

New International

25 SO IN the ninth year of Zedekiah's reign, on the tenth day of the tenth month, Nebuchadnezzar king of Babylon marched against Jerusalem with his whole army. He encamped outside the city and built siege works all around it. 2The city was kept under siege until the eleventh year of King Zedekiah. 3By the ninth day of the ⌞fourth⌟[a] month the famine in the city had become so severe that there was no food for the people to eat. 4Then the city wall was broken through, and the whole army fled at night through the gate between the two walls near the king's garden, though the Babylonians[b] were surrounding the city. They fled toward the Arabah,[c] 5but the Babylonian[d] army pursued the king and overtook him in the plains of Jericho. All his soldiers were separated from him and scattered, 6and he was captured. He was taken to the king of Babylon at Riblah, where sentence was pronounced on him. 7They killed the sons of Zedekiah before his eyes. Then they put out his eyes, bound him with bronze shackles and took him to Babylon.

8On the seventh day of the fifth month, in the nineteenth year of Nebuchadnezzar king of Babylon, Nebuzaradan commander of the imperial guard, an official of the king of Babylon, came to Jerusalem. 9He set fire to the temple of the LORD, the royal palace and all the houses of Jerusalem. Every important building he burned down. 10The whole Babylonian army, under the commander of the imperial guard, broke down the walls around Jerusalem. 11Nebuzaradan the commander of the guard carried into exile the people who remained in the city, along with the rest of the populace and those who had gone over to the king of Babylon. 12But the commander left behind some of the poorest people of the land to work the vineyards and fields.

13The Babylonians broke up the bronze pillars, the movable stands and the bronze Sea that were at the temple of the LORD and they carried the bronze to Babylon. 14They also took away the pots, shovels, wick trimmers, dishes and all the bronze articles used in the temple service. 15The commander of the imperial guard took away the censers and sprinkling bowls—all that were made of pure gold or silver.

16The bronze from the two pillars, the Sea and the movable stands, which Solomon had made for the temple of the LORD, was more than could be weighed. 17Each pillar was twenty-seven feet[e] high. The bronze capital on top of one pillar was four and a half feet[f] high and was decorated with a network and pomegranates of bronze all around. The other pillar, with its network, was similar.

18The commander of the guard took as prisoners Seraiah the chief priest, Zephaniah the priest next in rank and the three doorkeepers. 19Of those still in the city, he took the officer in charge of the fighting men and five royal advisers. He also took the secretary who was chief officer in charge of conscripting the people of the land and sixty of his men who were found in the city. 20Nebuzaradan the commander took them all and brought them to the king of Babylon at Riblah. 21There at Riblah, in the land of Hamath, the king had them executed.

So Judah went into captivity, away from her land.

a *3* See Jer. 52:6.   b *4* Or *Chaldeans*; also in verses 13, 25 and 26   c *4* Or *the Jordan Valley*   d *5* Or *Chaldean*; also in verses 10 and 24   e *17* Hebrew *eighteen cubits* (about 8.1 meters)   f *17* Hebrew *three cubits* (about 1.3 meters)

Living Bible

25 THEN KING Nebuchadnezzar of Babylon mobilized his entire army and laid siege to Jerusalem, arriving on March 25 of the ninth year of the reign of King Zedekiah of Judah. 2The siege continued into the eleventh year of his reign.

3The last food in the city was eaten on July 24, 4, 5and that night the king and his troops made a hole in the inner wall and fled out toward the Arabah through a gate that lay between the double walls near the king's garden. The Babylonian troops surrounding the city took out after him and captured him in the plains of Jericho, and all his men scattered. 6He was taken to Riblah, where he was tried and sentenced before the king of Babylon. 7He was forced to watch as his sons were killed before his eyes; then his eyes were put out and he was bound with chains and taken away to Babylon.

8General Nebuzaradan, the captain of the royal bodyguard, arrived at Jerusalem from Babylon on July 22 of the nineteenth year of the reign of King Nebuchadnezzar. 9He burned down the Temple, the palace, and all the other houses of any worth. 10He then supervised the Babylonian army in tearing down the walls of Jerusalem. 11The remainder of the people in the city and the Jewish deserters who had declared their allegiance to the king of Babylon were all taken as exiles to Babylon. 12But the poorest of the people were left to farm the land.

13The Babylonians broke up the bronze pillars of the Temple and the bronze tank and its bases and carried all the bronze to Babylon. 14, 15They also took all the pots, shovels, firepans, snuffers, spoons, and other bronze instruments used for the sacrifices. The gold and silver bowls, with all the rest of the gold and silver, were melted down to bullion. 16It was impossible to estimate the weight of the two pillars and the great tank and its bases—all made for the Temple by King Solomon—because they were so heavy. 17Each pillar was twenty-seven feet high, with an intricate bronze network of pomegranates decorating the 4½-foot capitals at the tops of the pillars.

18The general took Seraiah, the chief priest, his assistant Zephaniah, and the three Temple guards to Babylon as captives. 19A commander of the army of Judah, the chief recruiting officer, five of the king's counselors, and sixty farmers, all of whom were discovered hiding in the city, 20were taken by General Nebuzaradan to the king of Babylon at Riblah, 21where they were put to the sword and died.

So Judah was exiled from its land.

New Revised Standard

25 AND IN the ninth year of his reign, in the tenth month, on the tenth day of the month, King Nebuchadnezzar of Babylon came with all his army against Jerusalem, and laid siege to it; they built siegeworks against it all around. 2So the city was besieged until the eleventh year of King Zedekiah. 3On the ninth day of the fourth month the famine became so severe in the city that there was no food for the people of the land. 4Then a breach was made in the city wall;g the king with all the soldiers fledh by night by the way of the gate between the two walls, by the king's garden, though the Chaldeans were all around the city. They went in the direction of the Arabah. 5But the army of the Chaldeans pursued the king, and overtook him in the plains of Jericho; all his army was scattered, deserting him. 6Then they captured the king and brought him up to the king of Babylon at Riblah, who passed sentence on him. 7They slaughtered the sons of Zedekiah before his eyes, then put out the eyes of Zedekiah; they bound him in fetters and took him to Babylon.

8 In the fifth month, on the seventh day of the month—which was the nineteenth year of King Nebuchadnezzar—Nebuzaradan, the captain of the bodyguard, a servant of the king of Babylon, came to Jerusalem. 9He burned the house of the LORD, the king's house, and all the houses of Jerusalem; every great house he burned down. 10All the army of the Chaldeans who were with the captain of the guard broke down the walls around Jerusalem. 11Nebuzaradan the captain of the guard carried into exile the rest of the people who were left in the city and the deserters who had defected to the king of Babylon—all the rest of the population. 12But the captain of the guard left some of the poorest people of the land to be vinedressers and tillers of the soil.

13 The bronze pillars that were in the house of the LORD, as well as the stands and the bronze sea that were in the house of the LORD, the Chaldeans broke in pieces, and carried the bronze to Babylon. 14They took away the pots, the shovels, the snuffers, the dishes for incense, and all the bronze vessels used in the temple service, 15as well as the firepans and the basins. What was made of gold the captain of the guard took away for the gold, and what was made of silver, for the silver. 16As for the two pillars, the one sea, and the stands, which Solomon had made for the house of the LORD, the bronze of all these vessels was beyond weighing. 17The height of the one pillar was eighteen cubits, and on it was a bronze capital; the height of the capital was three cubits; latticework and pomegranates, all of bronze, were on the capital all around. The second pillar had the same, with the latticework.

18 The captain of the guard took the chief priest Seraiah, the second priest Zephaniah, and the three guardians of the threshold; 19from the city he took an officer who had been in command of the soldiers, and five men of the king's council who were found in the city; the secretary who was the commander of the army who mustered the people of the land; and sixty men of the people of the land who were found in the city. 20Nebuzaradan the captain of the guard took them, and brought them to the king of Babylon at Riblah. 21The king of Babylon struck them down and put them to death at Riblah in the land of Hamath. So Judah went into exile out of its land.

---

g Heb lacks *wall*   h Gk Compare Jer 39.4; 52.7: Heb lacks *the king* and lacks *fled*

King James

22¶ And *as for* the people that remained in the land of Judah, whom Nebuchadnezzar king of Babylon had left, even over them he made Gedaliah the son of Ahikam, the son of Shaphan, ruler.

23And when all the captains of the armies, they and their men, heard that the king of Babylon had made Gedaliah governor, there came to Gedaliah to Mizpah, even Ishmael the son of Nethaniah, and Johanan the son of Careah, and Seraiah the son of Tanhumeth the Netophathite, and Jaazaniah the son of a Maachathite, they and their men.

24And Gedaliah sware to them, and to their men, and said unto them, Fear not to be the servants of the Chaldees: dwell in the land, and serve the king of Babylon; and it shall be well with you.

25But it came to pass in the seventh month, that Ishmael the son of Nethaniah, the son of Elishama, of the seed royal, came, and ten men with him, and smote Gedaliah, that he died, and the Jews and the Chaldees that were with him at Mizpah.

26And all the people, both small and great, and the captains of the armies, arose, and came to Egypt: for they were afraid of the Chaldees.

27¶ And it came to pass in the seven and thirtieth year of the captivity of Jehoiachin king of Judah, in the twelfth month, on the seven and twentieth *day* of the month, *that* Evil-merodach king of Babylon in the year that he began to reign did lift up the head of Jehoiachin king of Judah out of prison;

28And he spake kindly to him, and set his throne above the throne of the kings that *were* with him in Babylon;

29And changed his prison garments: and he did eat bread continually before him all the days of his life.

30And his allowance *was* a continual allowance given him of the king, a daily rate for every day, all the days of his life.

New International

22Nebuchadnezzar king of Babylon appointed Gedaliah son of Ahikam, the son of Shaphan, to be over the people he had left behind in Judah. 23When all the army officers and their men heard that the king of Babylon had appointed Gedaliah as governor, they came to Gedaliah at Mizpah—Ishmael son of Nethaniah, Johanan son of Kareah, Seraiah son of Tanhumeth the Netophathite, Jaazaniah the son of the Maacathite, and their men. 24Gedaliah took an oath to reassure them and their men. "Do not be afraid of the Babylonian officials," he said. "Settle down in the land and serve the king of Babylon, and it will go well with you."

25In the seventh month, however, Ishmael son of Nethaniah, the son of Elishama, who was of royal blood, came with ten men and assassinated Gedaliah and also the men of Judah and the Babylonians who were with him at Mizpah. 26At this, all the people from the least to the greatest, together with the army officers, fled to Egypt for fear of the Babylonians.

Jehoiachin Released

27In the thirty-seventh year of the exile of Jehoiachin king of Judah, in the year Evil-Merodach[a] became king of Babylon, he released Jehoiachin from prison on the twenty-seventh day of the twelfth month. 28He spoke kindly to him and gave him a seat of honor higher than those of the other kings who were with him in Babylon. 29So Jehoiachin put aside his prison clothes and for the rest of his life ate regularly at the king's table. 30Day by day the king gave Jehoiachin a regular allowance as long as he lived.

---

a 27 Also called *Amel-Marduk*

Living Bible

22Then King Nebuchadnezzar appointed Gedaliah (the son of Ahikam and grandson of Shaphan) as governor over the people left in Judah. 23When the Israeli guerrilla forces learned that the king of Babylon had appointed Gedaliah as governor, some of these underground leaders and their men joined him at Mizpah. These included Ishmael, the son of Nethaniah; Johanan, the son of Kareah; Seraiah, the son of Tanhumeth the Netophathite; and Jaazaniah, son of Maachathite, and their men.

24Gedaliah vowed that if they would give themselves up and submit to the Babylonians, they would be allowed to live in the land and would not be exiled. 25But seven months later, Ishmael, who was a member of the royal line, went to Mizpah with ten men and killed Gedaliah and his court—both the Jews and the Babylonians.

26Then all the men of Judah and the guerrilla leaders fled in panic to Egypt, for they were afraid of what the Babylonians would do to them.

27King Jehoiachin was released from prison on the twenty-seventh day of the last month of the thirty-seventh year of his captivity.

This occurred during the first year of the reign of King Evil-merodach of Babylon. 28He treated Jehoiachin kindly and gave him preferential treatment over all the other kings who were being held as prisoners in Babylon. 29Jehoiachin was given civilian clothing to replace his prison garb, and for as long as he lived, he ate regularly at the king's table. 30The king also gave him a daily cash allowance for the rest of his life.

New Revised Standard

Gedaliah Made Governor of Judah

22 He appointed Gedaliah son of Ahikam son of Shaphan as governor over the people who remained in the land of Judah, whom King Nebuchadnezzar of Babylon had left. 23Now when all the captains of the forces and their men heard that the king of Babylon had appointed Gedaliah as governor, they came with their men to Gedaliah at Mizpah, namely, Ishmael son of Nethaniah, Johanan son of Kareah, Seraiah son of Tanhumeth the Netophathite, and Jaazaniah son of the Maacathite. 24Gedaliah swore to them and their men, saying, "Do not be afraid because of the Chaldean officials; live in the land, serve the king of Babylon, and it shall be well with you." 25But in the seventh month, Ishmael son of Nethaniah son of Elishama, of the royal family, came with ten men; they struck down Gedaliah so that he died, along with the Judeans and Chaldeans who were with him at Mizpah. 26Then all the people, high and low[b] and the captains of the forces set out and went to Egypt; for they were afraid of the Chaldeans.

Jehoiachin Released from Prison

27 In the thirty-seventh year of the exile of King Jehoiachin of Judah, in the twelfth month, on the twenty-seventh day of the month, King Evil-merodach of Babylon, in the year that he began to reign, released King Jehoiachin of Judah from prison; 28he spoke kindly to him, and gave him a seat above the other seats of the kings who were with him in Babylon. 29So Jehoiachin put aside his prison clothes. Every day of his life he dined regularly in the king's presence. 30For his allowance, a regular allowance was given him by the king, a portion every day, as long as he lived.

[b] Or young and old

King James

THE FIRST BOOK OF THE

Chronicles

1 ADAM, SHETH, Enosh,
  2Kenan, Mahalaleel, Jered,
3Henoch, Methuselah, Lamech,
4Noah, Shem, Ham, and Japheth.
  5¶ The sons of Japheth; Gomer, and Magog, and Madai, and Javan, and Tubal, and Meshech, and Tiras.
  6And the sons of Gomer; Ashchenaz, and Riphath, and Togarmah.
  7And the sons of Javan; Elishah, and Tarshish, Kittim, and Dodanim.
  8¶ The sons of Ham; Cush, and Mizraim, Put, and Canaan.
  9And the sons of Cush; Seba, and Havilah, and Sabta, and Raamah, and Sabtecha. And the sons of Raamah; Sheba, and Dedan.
  10And Cush begat Nimrod: he began to be mighty upon the earth.
  11And Mizraim begat Ludim, and Anamim, and Lehabim, and Naphtuhim,
  12And Pathrusim, and Casluhim, (of whom came the Philistines,) and Caphthorim.
  13And Canaan begat Zidon his firstborn, and Heth,
  14The Jebusite also, and the Amorite, and the Girgashite,
  15And the Hivite, and the Arkite, and the Sinite,
  16And the Arvadite, and the Zemarite, and the Hamathite.
  17¶ The sons of Shem; Elam, and Asshur, and Arphaxad, and Lud, and Aram, and Uz, and Hul, and Gether, and Meshech.
  18And Arphaxad begat Shelah, and Shelah begat Eber.
  19And unto Eber were born two sons: the name of the one *was* Peleg; because in his days the earth was divided: and his brother's name *was* Joktan.

New International

1 Chronicles

Historical Records From Adam to Abraham

To Noah's Sons

1 ADAM, SETH, Enosh, 2Kenan, Mahalalel, Jared,
  3Enoch, Methuselah, Lamech, Noah.

  4The sons of Noah:a
    Shem, Ham and Japheth.

The Japhethites

  5The sonsb of Japheth:
    Gomer, Magog, Madai, Javan, Tubal, Meshech and Tiras.
  6The sons of Gomer:
    Ashkenaz, Riphathc and Togarmah.
  7The sons of Javan:
    Elishah, Tarshish, the Kittim and the Rodanim.

The Hamites

  8The sons of Ham:
    Cush, Mizraim,d Put and Canaan.
  9The sons of Cush:
    Seba, Havilah, Sabta, Raamah and Sabteca.
  The sons of Raamah:
    Sheba and Dedan.
  10Cush was the fathere of
    Nimrod, who grew to be a mighty warrior on earth.
  11Mizraim was the father of
    the Ludites, Anamites, Lehabites, Naphtuhites,
  12Pathrusites, Casluhites (from whom the Philistines came) and Caphtorites.
  13Canaan was the father of
    Sidon his firstborn,f and of the Hittites, 14Jebusites, Amorites, Girgashites, 15Hivites, Arkites, Sinites, 16Arvadites, Zemarites and Hamathites.

The Semites

  17The sons of Shem:
    Elam, Asshur, Arphaxad, Lud and Aram.
  The sons of Aramg:
    Uz, Hul, Gether and Meshech.
  18Arphaxad was the father of Shelah,
    and Shelah the father of Eber.
  19Two sons were born to Eber:
    One was named Peleg,h because in his time the earth was divided; his brother was named Joktan.

---

a 4 Septuagint; Hebrew does not have *The sons of Noah:*   b 5 *Sons* may mean *descendants* or *successors* or *nations*; also in verses 6-10, 17 and 20.   c 6 Many Hebrew manuscripts and Vulgate (see also Septuagint and Gen. 10:3); most Hebrew manuscripts *Diphath*   d 8 That is, Egypt; also in verse 11   e 10 *Father* may mean *ancestor* or *predecessor* or *founder*; also in verses 11, 13, 18 and 20.   f 13 Or *of the Sidonians, the foremost*   g 17 One Hebrew manuscript and some Septuagint manuscripts (see also Gen. 10:23); most Hebrew manuscripts do not have this line.   h 19 *Peleg* means *division.*

1 Chronicles

1 Chronicles

From Adam to Abraham

1 THESE ARE the earliest generations of mankind:[i] Adam, Seth, Enosh, Kenan, Mahalalel, Jared, Enoch, Methuselah, Lamech, Noah, **Shem, Ham,** and **Japheth.**[j]

5-9The sons of *Japheth*[k] were:

Gomer, Magog, Madai, **Javan,** Tubal, Meshech, and Tiras.

The sons of *Gomer:*

Ashkenaz, Diphath, and Togarmah.

The sons of *Javan:*

Elishah, Tarshish, Kittim, and Rodanim.

The sons of *Ham:*

Cush, Misream, Canaan, and **Put.**

The sons of *Cush* were:

Seba, Havilah, Sabta, Raama, and Sabteca.

The sons of *Raama* were Sheba and Dedan.

10Another of the sons of *Cush* was Nimrod, who became a great hero.

11, 12The clans named after the sons of *Misream* were: the Ludim, the Anamim, the Lehabim, the Naphtuhim, the Pathrusim, the Caphtorim, and the Casluhim (the ancestors of the Philistines).

13-16Among *Canaan's* sons were:

Sidon (his firstborn) and Heth.

Canaan was also the ancestor of the Jebusites, Amorites, Girgashites, Hivites, Arkites, Sinites, Arvadites, Zemarites, and Hamathites.

17The sons of *Shem:*

Elam, Asshur, **Arpachshad,** Lud, Aram, Uz, Hul, Gether, and Meshech.

18*Arpachshad's* son was **Shelah,** and *Shelah's* son was **Eber.**

19*Eber* had two sons: Peleg (which means "Divided," for it was during his lifetime that the people of the earth were divided into different language groups), and Joktan.

1 ADAM, SETH, Enosh; 2Kenan, Mahalalel, Jared; 3Enoch, Methuselah, Lamech; 4Noah, Shem, Ham, and Japheth.

5 The descendants of Japheth: Gomer, Magog, Madai, Javan, Tubal, Meshech, and Tiras. 6The descendants of Gomer: Ashkenaz, Diphath,[l] and Togarmah. 7The descendants of Javan: Elishah, Tarshish, Kittim, and Rodanim.[m]

8 The descendants of Ham: Cush, Egypt, Put, and Canaan. 9The descendants of Cush: Seba, Havilah, Sabta, Raama, and Sabteca. The descendants of Raamah: Sheba and Dedan. 10Cush became the father of Nimrod; he was the first to be a mighty one on the earth.

11 Egypt became the father of Ludim, Anamim, Lehabim, Naphtuhim, 12Pathrusim, Casluhim, and Caphtorim, from whom the Philistines come.[n]

13 Canaan became the father of Sidon his firstborn, and Heth, 14and the Jebusites, the Amorites, the Girgashites, 15the Hivites, the Arkites, the Sinites, 16the Arvadites, the Zemarites, and the Hamathites.

17 The descendants of Shem: Elam, Asshur, Arpachshad, Lud, Aram, Uz, Hul, Gether, and Meshech.[o] 18Arpachshad became the father of Shelah; and Shelah became the father of Eber. 19To Eber were born two sons: the name of the one was Peleg (for in his days the earth was divided), and the name of his brother Joktan.

---

[i] *1:1-4 These are the earliest generations of mankind,* implied. [j] *1:1-4 Shem, Ham and Japheth.* The names in bold face type are referred to in the following verse or verses. The use of bold type or italic type does not mean that these persons were more important; it is simply a way of easier identification of ancestors and descendants. [k] *1:5-7 Japheth.* Italic means that the name has previously appeared in bold face type.

[l] Gen 10.3 *Ripath;* See Gk Vg   [m] Gen 10.4 *Dodanim;* See Syr Vg   [n] Heb *Casluhim, from which the Philistines come, Caphtorim;* See Am 9.7, Jer 47.4   [o] *Mash* in Gen 10.23

King James

²⁰And Joktan begat Almodad, and Sheleph, and Hazarmaveth, and Jerah,

²¹Hadoram also, and Uzal, and Diklah,

²²And Ebal, and Abimael, and Sheba,

²³And Ophir, and Havilah, and Jobab. All these *were* the sons of Joktan.

²⁴¶ Shem, Arphaxad, Shelah,

²⁵Eber, Peleg, Reu,

²⁶Serug, Nahor, Terah,

²⁷Abram; the same *is* Abraham.

²⁸The sons of Abraham; Isaac, and Ishmael.

²⁹¶ These *are* their generations: The firstborn of Ishmael, Nebaioth; then Kedar, and Adbeel, and Mibsam,

³⁰Mishma, and Dumah, Massa, Hadad, and Tema,

³¹Jetur, Naphish, and Kedemah. These are the sons of Ishmael.

³²¶ Now the sons of Keturah, Abraham's concubine: she bare Zimran, and Jokshan, and Medan, and Midian, and Ishbak, and Shuah. And the sons of Jokshan; Sheba, and Dedan.

³³And the sons of Midian; Ephah, and Epher, and Henoch, and Abida, and Eldaah. All these *are* the sons of Keturah.

³⁴And Abraham begat Isaac. The sons of Isaac; Esau and Israel.

³⁵¶ The sons of Esau; Eliphaz, Reuel, and Jeush, and Jaalam, and Korah.

³⁶The sons of Eliphaz; Teman, and Omar, Zephi, and Gatam, Kenaz, and Timna, and Amalek.

³⁷The sons of Reuel; Nahath, Zerah, Shammah, and Mizzah.

³⁸And the sons of Seir; Lotan, and Shobal, and Zibeon, and Anah, and Dishon, and Ezar, and Dishan.

³⁹And the sons of Lotan; Hori, and Homam: and Timna *was* Lotan's sister.

⁴⁰The sons of Shobal; Alian, and Manahath, and Ebal, Shephi, and Onam. And the sons of Zibeon; Aiah, and Anah.

⁴¹The sons of Anah; Dishon. And the sons of Dishon; Amram, and Eshban, and Ithran, and Cheran.

⁴²The sons of Ezer; Bilhan, and Zavan, *and* Jakan. The sons of Dishan; Uz, and Aran.

New International

²⁰Joktan was the father of
Almodad, Sheleph, Hazarmaveth, Jerah, ²¹Hadoram, Uzal, Diklah, ²²Obal,^a Abimael, Sheba, ²³Ophir, Havilah and Jobab. All these were sons of Joktan.

²⁴Shem, Arphaxad,^b Shelah,

²⁵Eber, Peleg, Reu,

²⁶Serug, Nahor, Terah

²⁷and Abram (that is, Abraham).

The Family of Abraham

²⁸The sons of Abraham:
Isaac and Ishmael.

Descendants of Hagar

²⁹These were their descendants:
Nebaioth the firstborn of Ishmael, Kedar, Adbeel, Mibsam, ³⁰Mishma, Dumah, Massa, Hadad, Tema, ³¹Jetur, Naphish and Kedemah. These were the sons of Ishmael.

Descendants of Keturah

³²The sons born to Keturah, Abraham's concubine:
Zimran, Jokshan, Medan, Midian, Ishbak and Shuah.
The sons of Jokshan:
Sheba and Dedan.

³³The sons of Midian:
Ephah, Epher, Hanoch, Abida and Eldaah.
All these were descendants of Keturah.

Descendants of Sarah

³⁴Abraham was the father of Isaac.
The sons of Isaac:
Esau and Israel.

Esau's Sons

³⁵The sons of Esau:
Eliphaz, Reuel, Jeush, Jalam and Korah.

³⁶The sons of Eliphaz:
Teman, Omar, Zepho,^c Gatam and Kenaz;
by Timna: Amalek.^d

³⁷The sons of Reuel:
Nahath, Zerah, Shammah and Mizzah.

The People of Seir in Edom

³⁸The sons of Seir:
Lotan, Shobal, Zibeon, Anah, Dishon, Ezer and Dishan.

³⁹The sons of Lotan:
Hori and Homam. Timna was Lotan's sister.

⁴⁰The sons of Shobal:
Alvan,^e Manahath, Ebal, Shepho and Onam.
The sons of Zibeon:
Aiah and Anah.

⁴¹The son of Anah:
Dishon.
The sons of Dishon:
Hemdan,^f Eshban, Ithran and Keran.

⁴²The sons of Ezer:
Bilhan, Zaavan and Akan.^g
The sons of Dishan^h:
Uz and Aran.

^a *22* Some Hebrew manuscripts and Syriac (see also Gen. 10:28); most Hebrew manuscripts *Ebal*   ^b *24* Hebrew; some Septuagint manuscripts *Arphaxad, Cainan* (see also note at Gen. 11:10)   ^c *36* Many Hebrew manuscripts and Syriac (see also Gen. 36:11); most Hebrew manuscripts *Zephi*   ^d *36* Some Septuagint manuscripts (see also Gen. 36:12); Hebrew *Gatam, Kenaz, Timna and Amalek*   ^e *40* Many Hebrew manuscripts and some Septuagint manuscripts (see also Gen. 36:23); most Hebrew manuscripts *Alian*   ^f *41* Many Hebrew manuscripts and some Septuagint manuscripts (see also Gen. 36:26); most Hebrew manuscripts *Hamran*   ^g *42* Many Hebrew and Septuagint manuscripts (see also Gen. 36:27); most Hebrew manuscripts *Zaavan, Jaakan*   ^h *42* Hebrew *Dishon*, a variant of *Dishan*

Living Bible

20-23The sons of Joktan:
Almodad, Sheleph, Hazarmaveth, Jerah, Hadoram, Uzal, Diklah, Ebal, Abima-el, Sheba, Ophir, Havilah, and Jobab.

24-27So the son[i] of *Shem* was Arpachshad, the son of Arpachshad was Shelah,
The son of Shelah was Eber,
The son of Eber was Peleg,
The son of Peleg was Reu,
The son of Reu was Serug,
The son of Serug was Nahor,
The son of Nahor was Terah,
The son of Terah was Abram (later known as Abraham).

28-31Abraham's sons were Isaac and Ishmael.
The sons of *Ishmael:*
Nabaioth (the oldest), Kedar, Adbeel, Mibsam, Mishma, Dumah, Massa, Hadad, Tema, Jetur, Naphish, and Kedemah.

32Abraham also had sons by his concubine Keturah: Zimram, **Jokshan,** Medan, **Midian,** Ishbak, and Shuah.
Jokshan's sons were Sheba and Dedan.

33The sons of *Midian:*
Ephah, Epher, Hanoch, Abida, and Eldaah. These were the descendants of Abraham by his concubine Keturah.

34Abraham's son *Isaac* had two sons, Esau and Israel.

35The sons of *Esau:*
Eliphaz, Reuel, Jeush, Jalam, and Korah.

36The sons of *Eliphaz:*
Teman, Omar, Zephi, Gatam, Kenaz, Timna, and Amalek.

37The sons of *Reuel:*
Nahath, Zerah, Shammah, and Mizzah.

38, 39The sons of *Esau*[j] also included **Lotan, Shobal, Zibeon,** Anah, **Dishon, Ezer,** and **Dishan;** and Esau's daughter was named Timna.
Lotan's sons: Hori and Homam.

40The sons of *Shobal:* Alian, Manahath, Ebal, Shephi, and Onam.
Zibeon's sons were Aiah and **Anah.**

41*Anah's* son was **Dishon:**
The sons of *Dishon:* Hamran, Eshban, Ithran, and Cheran.

42The sons of *Ezer:* Bilhan, Zaavan, and Jaakan.
Dishan's sons were Uz and Aran.

New Revised Standard

20Joktan became the father of Almodad, Sheleph, Hazarmaveth, Jerah, 21Hadoram, Uzal, Diklah, 22Ebal, Abimael, Sheba, 23Ophir, Havilah, and Jobab; all these were the descendants of Joktan.

24 Shem, Arpachshad, Shelah; 25Eber, Peleg, Reu; 26Serug, Nahor, Terah; 27Abram, that is, Abraham.

From Abraham to Jacob

28 The sons of Abraham: Isaac and Ishmael. 29These are their genealogies: the firstborn of Ishmael, Nebaioth; and Kedar, Adbeel, Mibsam, 30Mishma, Dumah, Massa, Hadad, Tema, 31Jetur, Naphish, and Kedemah. These are the sons of Ishmael. 32The sons of Keturah, Abraham's concubine: she bore Zimran, Jokshan, Medan, Midian, Ishbak, and Shuah. The sons of Jokshan: Sheba and Dedan. 33The sons of Midian: Ephah, Epher, Hanoch, Abida, and Eldaah. All these were the descendants of Keturah.

34 Abraham became the father of Isaac. The sons of Isaac: Esau and Israel. 35The sons of Esau: Eliphaz, Reuel, Jeush, Jalam, and Korah. 36The sons of Eliphaz: Teman, Omar, Zephi, Gatam, Kenaz, Timna, and Amalek. 37The sons of Reuel: Nahath, Zerah, Shammah, and Mizzah.

38 The sons of Seir: Lotan, Shobal, Zibeon, Anah, Dishon, Ezer, and Dishan. 39The sons of Lotan: Hori and Homam; and Lotan's sister was Timna. 40The sons of Shobal: Alian, Manahath, Ebal, Shephi, and Onam. The sons of Zibeon: Aiah and Anah. 41The sons of Anah: Dishon. The sons of Dishon: Hamran, Eshban, Ithran, and Cheran. 42The sons of Ezer: Bilhan, Zaavan, and Jaakan.[k] The sons of Dishan:[l] Uz and Aran.

---

[i] *1:24-27 son,* or "descendant." The subsequent use of the word "son" could also be interpreted "descendant."   [j] *1:38, 39 Esau,* or "Seir."

[k] Or *and Akan;* See Gen 36.27   [l] See 1.38: Heb *Dishon*

King James

43¶ Now these *are* the kings that reigned in the land of Edom before *any* king reigned over the children of Israel; Bela the son of Beor: and the name of his city *was* Dinhabah.

44And when Bela was dead, Jobab the son of Zerah of Bozrah reigned in his stead.

45And when Jobab was dead, Husham of the land of the Temanites reigned in his stead.

46And when Husham was dead, Hadad the son of Bedad, which smote Midian in the field of Moab, reigned in his stead: and the name of his city *was* Avith.

47And when Hadad was dead, Samlah of Masrekah reigned in his stead.

48And when Samlah was dead, Shaul of Rehoboth by the river reigned in his stead.

49And when Shaul was dead, Baal-hanan the son of Achbor reigned in his stead.

50And when Baal-hanan was dead, Hadad reigned in his stead: and the name of his city *was* Pai; and his wife's name *was* Mehetabel, the daughter of Matred, the daughter of Mezahab.

51¶ Hadad died also. And the dukes of Edom were; duke Timnah, duke Aliah, duke Jetheth,

52Duke Aholibamah, duke Elah, duke Pinon,

53Duke Kenaz, duke Teman, duke Mibzar,

54Duke Magdiel, duke Iram. These *are* the dukes of Edom.

2 THESE *ARE* the sons of Israel; Reuben, Simeon, Levi, and Judah, Issachar, and Zebulun,

2Dan, Joseph, and Benjamin, Naphtali, Gad, and Asher.

3¶ The sons of Judah; Er, and Onan, and Shelah: *which* three were born unto him of the daughter of Shua the Canaanitess. And Er, the firstborn of Judah, was evil in the sight of the LORD; and he slew him.

4And Tamar his daughter-in-law bare him Pharez and Zerah. All the sons of Judah *were* five.

5The sons of Pharez; Hezron, and Hamul.

6And the sons of Zerah; Zimri, and Ethan, and Heman, and Calcol, and Dara: five of them in all.

7And the sons of Carmi; Achar, the troubler of Israel, who transgressed in the thing accursed.

8And the sons of Ethan; Azariah.

9The sons also of Hezron, that were born unto him; Jerahmeel, and Ram, and Chelubai.

10And Ram begat Amminadab; and Amminadab begat Nahshon, prince of the children of Judah;

11And Nahshon begat Salma, and Salma begat Boaz,

New International

The Rulers of Edom

43These were the kings who reigned in Edom before any Israelite king reigned[a]:

Bela son of Beor, whose city was named Dinhabah.

44When Bela died, Jobab son of Zerah from Bozrah succeeded him as king.

45When Jobab died, Husham from the land of the Temanites succeeded him as king.

46When Husham died, Hadad son of Bedad, who defeated Midian in the country of Moab, succeeded him as king. His city was named Avith.

47When Hadad died, Samlah from Masrekah succeeded him as king.

48When Samlah died, Shaul from Rehoboth on the river[b] succeeded him as king.

49When Shaul died, Baal-Hanan son of Acbor succeeded him as king.

50When Baal-Hanan died, Hadad succeeded him as king. His city was named Pau,[c] and his wife's name was Mehetabel daughter of Matred, the daughter of Me-Zahab. 51Hadad also died.

The chiefs of Edom were:

Timna, Alvah, Jetheth, 52Oholibamah, Elah, Pinon, 53Kenaz, Teman, Mibzar, 54Magdiel and Iram. These were the chiefs of Edom.

Israel's Sons

2 THESE WERE the sons of Israel:

Reuben, Simeon, Levi, Judah, Issachar, Zebulun, 2Dan, Joseph, Benjamin, Naphtali, Gad and Asher.

Judah

To Hezron's Sons

3The sons of Judah:

Er, Onan and Shelah. These three were born to him by a Canaanite woman, the daughter of Shua. Er, Judah's firstborn, was wicked in the LORD's sight; so the LORD put him to death. 4Tamar, Judah's daughter-in-law, bore him Perez and Zerah. Judah had five sons in all.

5The sons of Perez:

Hezron and Hamul.

6The sons of Zerah:

Zimri, Ethan, Heman, Calcol and Darda[d]— five in all.

7The son of Carmi:

Achar,[e] who brought trouble on Israel by violating the ban on taking devoted things.[f]

8The son of Ethan:

Azariah.

9The sons born to Hezron were:

Jerahmeel, Ram and Caleb.[g]

From Ram Son of Hezron

10Ram was the father of

Amminadab, and Amminadab the father of Nahshon, the leader of the people of Judah. 11Nahshon was the father of Salmon,[h] Salmon

a 43 Or *before an Israelite king reigned over them*　b 48 Possibly the Euphrates　c 50 Many Hebrew manuscripts, some Septuagint manuscripts, Vulgate and Syriac (see also Gen. 36:39); most Hebrew manuscripts *Pai* d 6 Many Hebrew manuscripts, some Septuagint manuscripts and Syriac (see also 1 Kings 4:31); most Hebrew manuscripts *Dara*　e 7 *Achar* means *trouble; Achar* is called *Achan* in Joshua.　f 7 The Hebrew term refers to the irrevocable giving over of things or persons to the LORD, often by totally destroying them.　g 9 Hebrew *Kelubai*, a variant of *Caleb*　h 11 Septuagint (see also Ruth 4:21); Hebrew *Salma*

Living Bible

43Here is a list of the names of the kings of Edom who reigned before the kingdom of Israel began:

Bela (the son of Beor), who lived in the city of Dinhabah.

44When Bela died, Jobab the son of Zerah from Bozrah became the new king.

45When Jobab died, Husham from the country of the Temanites became the king.

46When Husham died, Hadad the son of Bedad—the one who destroyed the army of Midian in the fields of Moab—became king and ruled from the city of Avith.

47When Hadad died, Samlah from the city of Masrekah came to the throne.

48When Samlah died, Shaul from the river town of Rehoboth became the new king.

49When Shaul died, Baal-hanan the son of Achbor became king.

50When Baal-hanan died, Hadad became king and ruled from the city of Pai (his wife was Mehetabel, the daughter of Matred and granddaughter of Mezahab).

51-54At the time of Hadad's death, the kings of Edom were:

Chief Timna, Chief Aliah, Chief Jetheth, Chief Oholibamah, Chief Elah, Chief Pinon, Chief Kenaz, Chief Teman, Chief Mibzar, Chief Magdi-el, Chief Iram.

2 THE SONS of Israel were:
Reuben, Simeon, Levi, Judah, Issachar, Zebulun, Dan, Joseph, Benjamin, Naphtali, Gad, Asher.

3Judah had three sons by Bath-shua, a girl from Canaan: **Er,** Onan, and Shelah. But the oldest son, *Er,* was so wicked that the Lord killed him.

4Then Er's widow, Tamar, and her father-in-law, Judah, became the parents of twin sons, **Perez** and **Zerah.** So Judah had five sons.

5The sons of *Perez* were Hezron and Hamul.

6The sons of *Zerah* were:
Zimri, **Ethan,** Heman, Calcol, and Dara.

7(Achan, the son of Carmi, was the man who robbed God and was such a troublemaker for his nation.)

8*Ethan's* son was Azariah.

9The sons of *Hezron* were Jerahmeel, Ram, and Chelubai.

10Ram was the father of Amminadab, and Amminadab was the father of Nahshon, a leader of Israel.

11Nahshon was the father of Salma, and Salma was the father of Boaz.

New Revised Standard

43 These are the kings who reigned in the land of Edom before any king reigned over the Israelites: Bela son of Beor, whose city was called Dinhabah. 44When Bela died, Jobab son of Zerah of Bozrah succeeded him. 45When Jobab died, Husham of the land of the Temanites succeeded him. 46When Husham died, Hadad son of Bedad, who defeated Midian in the country of Moab, succeeded him; and the name of his city was Avith. 47When Hadad died, Samlah of Masrekah succeeded him. 48When Samlah died, Shauli of Rehoboth on the Euphrates succeeded him. 49When Shauli died, Baalhanan son of Achbor succeeded him. 50When Baalhanan died, Hadad succeeded him; the name of his city was Pai, and his wife's name Mehetabel daughter of Matred, daughter of Me-zahab. 51And Hadad died.

The clansi of Edom were: clansi Timna, Aliah,k Jetheth, 52Oholibamah, Elah, Pinon, 53Kenaz, Teman, Mibzar, 54Magdiel, and Iram; these are the clansi of Edom.

The Sons of Israel and the Descendants of Judah

2 THESE ARE the sons of Israel: Reuben, Simeon, Levi, Judah, Issachar, Zebulun, 2Dan, Joseph, Benjamin, Naphtali, Gad, and Asher. 3The sons of Judah: Er, Onan, and Shelah; these three the Canaanite woman Bath-shua bore to him. Now Er, Judah's firstborn, was wicked in the sight of the LORD, and he put him to death. 4His daughter-in-law Tamar also bore him Perez and Zerah. Judah had five sons in all.

5 The sons of Perez: Hezron and Hamul. 6The sons of Zerah: Zimri, Ethan, Heman, Calcol, and Dara,l five in all. 7The sons of Carmi: Achar, the troubler of Israel, who transgressed in the matter of the devoted thing; 8and Ethan's son was Azariah.

9 The sons of Hezron, who were born to him: Jerahmeel, Ram, and Chelubai. 10Ram became the father of Amminadab, and Amminadab became the father of Nahshon, prince of the sons of Judah. 11Nahshon became the father of Salma, Salma of Boaz, 12Boaz of

---

i Or *Saul*   j Or *chiefs*   k Or *Alvah*; See Gen 36.40   l Or *Darda*; Compare Syr Tg some Gk Mss; See 1 Kings 4.31

King James

12And Boaz begat Obed, and Obed begat Jesse.

13¶ And Jesse begat his firstborn Eliab, and Abinadab the second, and Shimma the third,

14Nethaneel the fourth, Raddai the fifth.

15Ozem the sixth, David the seventh:

16Whose sisters were Zeruiah, and Abigail. And the sons of Zeruiah; Abishai, and Joab, and Asahel, three.

17And Abigail bare Amasa: and the father of Amasa was Jether the Ishmaelite.

18¶ And Caleb the son of Hezron begat children of Azubah his wife, and of Jerioth: her sons are these; Jesher, and Shobab, and Ardon.

19And when Azubah was dead, Caleb took unto him Ephrath, which bare him Hur.

20And Hur begat Uri, and Uri begat Bezaleel.

21¶ And afterward Hezron went in to the daughter of Machir the father of Gilead, whom he married when he was threescore years old; and she bare him Segub.

22And Segub begat Jair, who had three and twenty cities in the land of Gilead.

23And he took Geshur, and Aram, with the towns of Jair, from them, with Kenath, and the towns thereof, even threescore cities. All these belonged to the sons of Machir the father of Gilead.

24And after that Hezron was dead in Caleb-ephratah, then Abiah Hezron's wife bare him Ashur the father of Tekoa.

25¶ And the sons of Jerahmeel the firstborn of Hezron were, Ram the firstborn, and Bunah, and Oren, and Ozem, and Ahijah.

26Jerahmeel had also another wife, whose name was Atarah; she was the mother of Onam.

27And the sons of Ram the firstborn of Jerahmeel were, Maaz, and Jamin, and Eker.

28And the sons of Onam were, Shammai, and Jada. And the sons of Shammai; Nadab, and Abishur.

29And the name of the wife of Abishur was Abihail, and she bare him Ahban, and Molid.

30And the sons of Nadab; Seled, and Appaim: but Seled died without children.

31And the sons of Appaim; Ishi. And the sons of Ishi; Sheshan. And the children of Sheshan; Ahlai.

32And the sons of Jada the brother of Shammai; Jether, and Jonathan: and Jether died without children.

33And the sons of Jonathan; Peleth, and Zaza. These were the sons of Jerahmeel.

34¶ Now Sheshan had no sons, but daughters. And Sheshan had a servant, an Egyptian, whose name was Jarha.

35And Sheshan gave his daughter to Jarha his servant to wife; and she bare him Attai.

36And Attai begat Nathan, and Nathan begat Zabad,

37And Zabad begat Ephlal, and Ephlal begat Obed,

38And Obed begat Jehu, and Jehu begat Azariah,

39And Azariah begat Helez, and Helez begat Eleasah,

40And Eleasah begat Sisamai, and Sisamai begat Shallum,

41And Shallum begat Jekamiah, and Jekamiah begat Elishama.

New International

the father of Boaz, 12Boaz the father of Obed and Obed the father of Jesse.

13Jesse was the father of

Eliab his firstborn; the second son was Abinadab, the third Shimea, 14the fourth Nethanel, the fifth Raddai, 15the sixth Ozem and the seventh David. 16Their sisters were Zeruiah and Abigail. Zeruiah's three sons were Abishai, Joab and Asahel. 17Abigail was the mother of Amasa, whose father was Jether the Ishmaelite.

Caleb Son of Hezron

18Caleb son of Hezron had children by his wife Azubah (and by Jerioth). These were her sons: Jesher, Shobab and Ardon. 19When Azubah died, Caleb married Ephrath, who bore him Hur. 20Hur was the father of Uri, and Uri the father of Bezalel.

21Later, Hezron lay with the daughter of Makir the father of Gilead (he had married her when he was sixty years old), and she bore him Segub. 22Segub was the father of Jair, who controlled twenty-three towns in Gilead. 23(But Geshur and Aram captured Havvoth Jair,a as well as Kenath with its surrounding settlements—sixty towns.) All these were descendants of Makir the father of Gilead.

24After Hezron died in Caleb Ephrathah, Abijah the wife of Hezron bore him Ashhur the fatherb of Tekoa.

Jerahmeel Son of Hezron

25The sons of Jerahmeel the firstborn of Hezron:
Ram his firstborn, Bunah, Oren, Ozem andc Ahijah. 26Jerahmeel had another wife, whose name was Atarah; she was the mother of Onam.

27The sons of Ram the firstborn of Jerahmeel:
Maaz, Jamin and Eker.

28The sons of Onam:
Shammai and Jada.
The sons of Shammai:
Nadab and Abishur.

29Abishur's wife was named Abihail, who bore him Ahban and Molid.

30The sons of Nadab:
Seled and Appaim. Seled died without children.

31The son of Appaim:
Ishi, who was the father of Sheshan.
Sheshan was the father of Ahlai.

32The sons of Jada, Shammai's brother:
Jether and Jonathan. Jether died without children.

33The sons of Jonathan:
Peleth and Zaza.
These were the descendants of Jerahmeel.

34Sheshan had no sons—only daughters.
He had an Egyptian servant named Jarha. 35Sheshan gave his daughter in marriage to his servant Jarha, and she bore him Attai.

36Attai was the father of Nathan,
Nathan the father of Zabad,

37Zabad the father of Ephlal,
Ephlal the father of Obed,

38Obed the father of Jehu,
Jehu the father of Azariah,

39Azariah the father of Helez,
Helez the father of Eleasah,

40Eleasah the father of Sismai,
Sismai the father of Shallum,

41Shallum the father of Jekamiah,
and Jekamiah the father of Elishama.

a 23 Or captured the settlements of Jair   b 24 Father may mean civic leader or military leader; also in verses 42, 45, 49-52 and possibly elsewhere.   c 25 Or Oren and Ozem, by

Living Bible

12Boaz was the father of Obed, and Obed was the father of Jesse.

13*Jesse's* first son was Eliab, his second was Abinadab, his third was Shimea, 14his fourth was Nethanel, his fifth was Raddai, 15his sixth was Ozem, and his seventh was David. 16He also had two girls (by the same wife) named **Zeruiah** and **Abigail.**

Zeruiah's sons were Abishai, Joab, and Asahel. 17*Abigail,* whose husband was Jether from the land of Ishmael, had a son named Amasa.

18Caleb (the son of **Hezron**) had two wives, **Azubah** and Jerioth. These are the children of *Azubah:*

Jesher, Shobab, and Ardon.

19After Azubah's death, Caleb married Ephrath, who presented him with a son, **Hur.**

20*Hur's* son was **Uri,** and *Uri's* son was Bezalel. 21**Hezron** married Machir's daughter at the age of sixty, and she presented him with a son, **Segub.** (Machir was also the father of Gilead.)

22*Segub* was the father of Jair, who ruledd twenty-three cities in the land of Gilead. 23But Geshur and Aram wrested these cities from him and also took Kenath and its sixty surrounding villages.

24Soon after his father *Hezron's* death, Caleb married Ephrathah, his father's widow, and she gave birth to Ashhur, the father of Tekoa.

25These are the sons of **Jerahmeel** (the oldest son of *Hezron*):

Ram (the oldest), Bunah, Oren, Ozem, and Ahijah. 26*Jerahmeel's* second wife Atarah was the mother of **Onam.**

27The sons of *Ram:*

Maaz, Jamin, and Eker. 28*Onam's* sons were **Shammai** and Jada.

Shammai's sons were **Nadab** and **Abishur.**

29The sons of *Abishur* and his wife Abihail were Ahban and Molid.

30*Nadab's* sons were **Seled** and **Appa-im.** *Seled* died without children, 31but *Appa-im* had a son named **Ishi;** *Ishi's* son was **Sheshan;** and *Sheshan's* son was Ahlai.

32*Shammai's* brother Jada had two sons, **Jether** and **Jonathan.** *Jether* died without children, 33but *Jonathan* had two sons named Peleth and Zaza.

34, 35*Sheshan*e had no sons, although he had several daughters. He gave one of his daughters to be the wife of Jarha, his Egyptian servant. And they had a son whom they named **Attai.**

36*Attai's* son was Nathan; Nathan's son was Zabad; 37Zabad's son was Ephlal; Ephlal's son was Obed; 38Obed's son was Jehu; Jehu's son was Azariah; 39Azariah's son was Helez; Helez's son was Ele-asah; 40Eleasah's son was Sismai; Sismai's son was Shallum; 41Shallum's son was Jekamiah; Jekamiah's son was Elishama.

New Revised Standard

Obed, Obed of Jesse. 13Jesse became the father of Eliab his firstborn, Abinadab the second, Shimea the third, 14Nethanel the fourth, Raddai the fifth, 15Ozem the sixth, David the seventh; 16and their sisters were Zeruiah and Abigail. The sons of Zeruiah: Abishai, Joab, and Asahel, three. 17Abigail bore Amasa, and the father of Amasa was Jether the Ishmaelite.

18 Caleb son of Hezron had children by his wife Azubah, and by Jerioth; these were her sons: Jesher, Shobab, and Ardon. 19When Azubah died, Caleb married Ephrath, who bore him Hur. 20Hur became the father of Uri, and Uri became the father of Bezalel.

21 Afterward Hezron went in to the daughter of Machir father of Gilead, whom he married when he was sixty years old; and she bore him Segub; 22and Segub became the father of Jair, who had twenty-three towns in the land of Gilead. 23But Geshur and Aram took from them Havvoth-jair, Kenath and its villages, sixty towns. All these were descendants of Machir, father of Gilead. 24After the death of Hezron, in Caleb-ephrathah, Abijah wife of Hezron bore Ashhur, father of Tekoa.

25 The sons of Jerahmeel, the firstborn of Hezron: Ram his firstborn, Bunah, Oren, Ozem, and Ahijah. 26Jerahmeel also had another wife, whose name was Atarah; she was the mother of Onam. 27The sons of Ram, the firstborn of Jerahmeel: Maaz, Jamin, and Eker. 28The sons of Onam: Shammai and Jada. The sons of Shammai: Nadab and Abishur. 29The name of Abishur's wife was Abihail, and she bore him Ahban and Molid. 30The sons of Nadab: Seled and Appaim; and Seled died childless. 31The sonf of Appaim: Ishi. The sonf of Ishi: Sheshan. The sonf of Sheshan: Ahlai. 32The sons of Jada, Shammai's brother: Jether and Jonathan; and Jether died childless. 33The sons of Jonathan: Peleth and Zaza. These were the descendants of Jerahmeel. 34Now Sheshan had no sons, only daughters; but Sheshan had an Egyptian slave, whose name was Jarha. 35So Sheshan gave his daughter in marriage to his slave Jarha; and she bore him Attai. 36Attai became the father of Nathan, and Nathan of Zabad. 37Zabad became the father of Ephlal, and Ephlal of Obed. 38Obed became the father of Jehu, and Jehu of Azariah. 39Azariah became the father of Helez, and Helez of Eleasah. 40Eleasah became the father of Sismai, and Sismai of Shallum. 41Shallum became the father of Jekamiah, and Jekamiah of Elishama.

---

d 2:22 *ruled,* literally, "had."   e 2:34, 35 *Sheshan,* apparently a different Sheshan than in vs 31.

f Heb *sons*

King James

42¶ Now the sons of Caleb the brother of Jerahmeel *were,* Mesha his firstborn, which *was* the father of Ziph; and the sons of Mareshah the father of Hebron.

43And the sons of Hebron; Korah, and Tappuah, and Rekem, and Shema.

44And Shema begat Raham, the father of Jorkoam: and Rekem begat Shammai.

45And the son of Shammai *was* Maon: and Maon *was* the father of Beth-zur.

46And Ephah, Caleb's concubine, bare Haran, and Moza, and Gazez: and Haran begat Gazez.

47And the sons of Jahdai; Regem, and Jotham, and Gesham, and Pelet, and Ephah, and Shaaph.

48Maachah, Caleb's concubine, bare Sheber, and Tirhanah.

49She bare also Shaaph the father of Madmannah, Sheva the father of Machbenah, and the father of Gibea: and the daughter of Caleb *was* Achsah.

50¶ These were the sons of Caleb the son of Hur, the firstborn of Ephratah; Shobal the father of Kirjath-jearim,

51Salma the father of Bethlehem, Hareph the father of Beth-gader.

52And Shobal the father of Kirjath-jearim had sons; Haroeh, *and* half of the Manahethites.

53And the families of Kirjath-jearim; the Ithrites, and the Puhites, and the Shumathites, and the Mishraites; of them came the Zareathites, and the Eshtaulites.

54The sons of Salma; Bethlehem, and the Netophathites, Ataroth, the house of Joab, and half of the Manahethites, the Zorites.

55And the families of the scribes which dwelt at Jabez; the Tirathites, the Shimeathites, *and* Suchathites. These *are* the Kenites that came of Hemath, the father of the house of Rechab.

---

3 NOW THESE were the sons of David, which were born unto him in Hebron; the firstborn Amnon, of Ahinoam the Jezreelitess; the second Daniel, of Abigail the Carmelitess:

2The third, Absalom the son of Maachah the daughter of Talmai king of Geshur: the fourth, Adonijah the son of Haggith:

3The fifth, Shephatiah of Abital: the sixth, Ithream by Eglah his wife.

4*These* six were born unto him in Hebron; and there he reigned seven years and six months: and in Jerusalem he reigned thirty and three years.

5And these were born unto him in Jerusalem; Shimea, and Shobab, and Nathan, and Solomon, four, of Bathshua the daughter of Ammiel:

6Ibhar also, and Elishama, and Eliphelet,

7And Nogah, and Nepheg, and Japhia,

8And Elishama, and Eliada, and Eliphelet, nine.

9*These were* all the sons of David, beside the sons of the concubines, and Tamar their sister.

New International

The Clans of Caleb

42The sons of Caleb the brother of Jerahmeel:
Mesha his firstborn, who was the father of Ziph, and his son Mareshah,a who was the father of Hebron.

43The sons of Hebron:
Korah, Tappuah, Rekem and Shema. 44Shema was the father of Raham, and Raham the father of Jorkeam. Rekem was the father of Shammai. 45The son of Shammai was Maon, and Maon was the father of Beth Zur.

46Caleb's concubine Ephah was the mother of Haran, Moza and Gazez. Haran was the father of Gazez.

47The sons of Jahdai:
Regem, Jotham, Geshan, Pelet, Ephah and Shaaph.

48Caleb's concubine Maacah was the mother of Sheber and Tirhanah. 49She also gave birth to Shaaph the father of Madmannah and to Sheva the father of Macbenah and Gibea. Caleb's daughter was Acsah. 50These were the descendants of Caleb.

The sons of Hur the firstborn of Ephrathah:
Shobal the father of Kiriath Jearim, 51Salma the father of Bethlehem, and Hareph the father of Beth Gader.

52The descendants of Shobal the father of Kiriath Jearim were:
Haroeh, half the Manahathites, 53and the clans of Kiriath Jearim: the Ithrites, Puthites, Shumathites and Mishraites. From these descended the Zorathites and Eshtaolites.

54The descendants of Salma:
Bethlehem, the Netophathites, Atroth Beth Joab, half the Manahathites, the Zorites, 55and the clans of scribesb who lived at Jabez: the Tirathites, Shimeathites and Sucathites. These are the Kenites who came from Hammath, the father of the house of Recab.c

The Sons of David

3 THESE WERE the sons of David born to him in Hebron:
The firstborn was Amnon the son of Ahinoam of Jezreel;
the second, Daniel the son of Abigail of Carmel;

2the third, Absalom the son of Maacah daughter of Talmai king of Geshur;
the fourth, Adonijah the son of Haggith;

3the fifth, Shephatiah the son of Abital;
and the sixth, Ithream, by his wife Eglah.

4These six were born to David in Hebron, where he reigned seven years and six months.

David reigned in Jerusalem thirty-three years, 5and these were the children born to him there:
Shammua,d Shobab, Nathan and Solomon. These four were by Bathshebae daughter of Ammiel. 6There were also Ibhar, Elishua,f Eliphelet, 7Nogah, Nepheg, Japhia, 8Elishama, Eliada and Eliphelet—nine in all. 9All these were the sons of David, besides his sons by his concubines. And Tamar was their sister.

---

a *42* The meaning of the Hebrew for this phrase is uncertain.   b *55* Or *of the Sopherites*   c *55* Or *father of Beth Recab*   d *5* Hebrew *Shimea,* a variant of *Shammua*   e *5* One Hebrew manuscript and Vulgate (see also Septuagint and 2 Samuel 11:3); most Hebrew manuscripts *Bathshua*   f *6* Two Hebrew manuscripts (see also 2 Samuel 5:15 and 1 Chron. 14:5); most Hebrew manuscripts *Elishama*

Living Bible

42The oldest son of **Caleb** (Jerahmeel's brother) was Mesha; he was the father of Ziph, who was father of Mareshah, who was the father of **Hebron.**

43The sons of *Hebron:* Korah, Tappuah, **Rekem,** and **Shema.**

44*Shema* was the father of Raham, who was the father of Jorke-am.

Rekem was the father of **Shammai.**

45*Shammai's* son was Maon, the father of Bethzur.

46*Caleb's* concubine Ephah bore him **Haran,** Moza, and Gazez; *Haran* had a son named Gazez.

47The sons of Jahdai:

Regem, Jotham, Geshan, Pelet, Ephah, and Sha-aph.

48, 49Another of *Caleb's* concubines, Maacah, bore him Sheber, Tirhanah, Shaaph (the father of Madmannah), and Sheva (the father of Machbenah and of Gibe-a). *Caleb* also had a daughter, whose name was Achsah.

50The sons of Hur (who was the oldest son of *Caleb*g and Ephrathah) were **Shobal** (the father of Kiriath-jearim), **Salma** (the father of Bethlehem), and Hareph (the father of Beth-gader).

52**Shobal's** sons included **Kiriath-jearim** and Haroeh, the ancestor of half of the Menuhoth tribe.

53The families of *Kiriath-jearim* were the Ithrites, the Puthites, the Shumathites, and the Mishraites (from whom descended the Zorathites and Eshtaolites).

54The descendants of Salma were his son Bethlehem, the Netophathites, Atrothbeth-joab, half the Manahathites, and the Zorites; 55they also included the families of the writers living at Jabez—the Tirathites, Shime-athites, and Sucathites. All these are Kenites who descended from Hammath, the founder of the family of Rechab.

New Revised Standard

42 The sons of Caleb brother of Jerahmeel: Meshai his firstborn, who was father of Ziph. The sons of Mareshah father of Hebron. 43The sons of Hebron: Korah, Tappuah, Rekem, and Shema. 44Shema became father of Raham, father of Jorkeam; and Rekem became the father of Shammai. 45The son of Shammai: Maon; and Maon was the father of Beth-zur. 46Ephah also, Caleb's concubine, bore Haran, Moza, and Gazez; and Haran became the father of Gazez. 47The sons of Jahdai: Regem, Jotham, Geshan, Pelet, Ephah, and Shaaph. 48Maacah, Caleb's concubine, bore Sheber and Tirhanah. 49She also bore Shaaph father of Madmannah, Sheva father of Machbenah and father of Gibea; and the daughter of Caleb was Achsah. 50These were the descendants of Caleb.

The sonsi of Hur the firstborn of Ephrathah: Shobal father of Kiriath-jearim, 51Salma father of Bethlehem, and Hareph father of Beth-gader. 52Shobal father of Kiriath-jearim had other sons: Haroeh, half of the Menuhoth. 53And the families of Kiriath-jearim: the Ithrites, the Puthites, the Shumathites, and the Mishraites; from these came the Zorathites and the Eshtaolites. 54The sons of Salma: Bethlehem, the Netophathites, Atrothbeth-joab, and half of the Manahathites, the Zorites. 55The families also of the scribes that lived at Jabez: the Tirathites, the Shimeathites, and the Sucathites. These are the Kenites who came from Hammath, father of the house of Rechab.

Descendants of David and Solomon

3 KING DAVID'S oldest son was Amnon, who was born to his wife, Ahino-am of Jezreel.

The second was Daniel, whose mother was Abigail from Carmel.

2The third was Absalom, the son of his wife Maacah, who was the daughter of King Talmai of Geshur.

The fourth was Adonijah, the son of Haggith.

3The fifth was Shephatiah, the son of Abital.

The sixth was Ithream, the son of his wife Eglah.

4These six were born to him in Hebron, where he reigned seven and one-half years. Then he moved the capital to Jerusalem, where he reigned another thirty-three years.

5While he was in Jerusalem, his wife Bathshebah (the daughter of Ammi-el) became the mother of his sons Shime-a, Shobab, Nathan, and **Solomon.**

6, 7, 8David also had nine other sons:

Ibhar, Elishama, Eliphelet, Nogah, Nepheg, Japhia, Elishama, Eliada, and Eliphelet.

9(This list does not include the sons of his concubines.) David also had a daughter Tamar.

3 THESE ARE the sons of David who were born to him in Hebron: the firstborn Amnon, by Ahinoam the Jezreelite; the second Daniel, by Abigail the Carmelite; 2the third Absalom, son of Maacah, daughter of King Talmai of Geshur; the fourth Adonijah, son of Haggith; 3the fifth Shephatiah, by Abital; the sixth Ithream, by his wife Eglah; 4six were born to him in Hebron, where he reigned for seven years and six months. And he reigned thirty-three years in Jerusalem. 5These were born to him in Jerusalem: Shimea, Shobab, Nathan, and Solomon, four by Bath-shua, daughter of Ammiel; 6then Ibhar, Elishama, Eliphelet, 7Nogah, Nepheg, Japhia, 8Elishama, Eliada, and Eliphelet, nine. 9All these were David's sons, besides the sons of the concubines; and Tamar was their sister.

---

g 2:50 Caleb, implied in 2:24.   h 3:5 Bathsheba, literally, "Bath-shua."   i Gk reads Mareshah   j Gk Vg: Heb son

King James

10¶ And Solomon's son *was* Rehoboam, Abia his son, Asa his son, Jehoshaphat his son,

11Joram his son, Ahaziah his son, Joash his son,

12Amaziah his son, Azariah his son, Jotham his son,

13Ahaz his son, Hezekiah his son, Manasseh his son,

14Amon his son, Josiah his son.

15And the sons of Josiah *were*, the firstborn Johanan, the second Jehoiakim, the third Zedekiah, the fourth Shallum.

16And the sons of Jehoiakim: Jeconiah his son, Zedekiah his son.

17¶ And the sons of Jeconiah; Assir, Salathiel his son,

18Malchiram also, and Pedaiah, and Shenazar, Jecamiah, Hoshama, and Nedabiah.

19And the sons of Pedaiah *were*, Zerubbabel, and Shimei: and the sons of Zerubbabel; Meshullam, and Hananiah, and Shelomith their sister:

20And Hashubah, and Ohel, and Berechiah, and Hasadiah, Jushab-hesed, five.

21And the sons of Hananiah; Pelatiah, and Jesaiah: the sons of Rephaiah, the sons of Arnan, the sons of Obadiah, the sons of Shechaniah.

22And the sons of Shechaniah; Shemaiah: and the sons of Shemaiah; Hattush, and Igeal, and Bariah, and Neariah, and Shaphat, six.

23And the sons of Neariah; Elioenai, and Hezekiah, and Azrikam, three.

24And the sons of Elioenai *were*, Hodaiah, and Eliashib, and Pelaiah, and Akkub, and Johanan, and Dalaiah, and Anani, seven.

4 THE SONS of Judah; Pharez, Hezron, and Carmi, and Hur, and Shobal.

2And Reaiah the son of Shobal begat Jahath; and Jahath begat Ahumai, and Lahad. These *are* the families of the Zorathites.

3And these *were of* the father of Etam; Jezreel, and Ishma, and Idbash: and the name of their sister *was* Hazelelponi:

4And Penuel the father of Gedor, and Ezer the father of Hushah. These *are* the sons of Hur, the firstborn of Ephratah, the father of Bethlehem.

5¶ And Ashur the father of Tekoa had two wives, Helah and Naarah.

6And Naarah bare him Ahuzam, and Hepher, and Temeni, and Haahashtari. These *were* the sons of Naarah.

New International

The Kings of Judah

10Solomon's son was Rehoboam,
Abijah his son,
Asa his son,
Jehoshaphat his son,

11Jehorama his son,
Ahaziah his son,
Joash his son,

12Amaziah his son,
Azariah his son,
Jotham his son,

13Ahaz his son,
Hezekiah his son,
Manasseh his son,

14Amon his son,
Josiah his son.

15The sons of Josiah:
Johanan the firstborn,
Jehoiakim the second son,
Zedekiah the third,
Shallum the fourth.

16The successors of Jehoiakim:
Jehoiachinb his son,
and Zedekiah.

The Royal Line After the Exile

17The descendants of Jehoiachin the captive:
Shealtiel his son, 18Malkiram, Pedaiah, Shenazzar, Jekamiah, Hoshama and Nedabiah.

19The sons of Pedaiah:
Zerubbabel and Shimei.

The sons of Zerubbabel:
Meshullam and Hananiah.
Shelomith was their sister.

20There were also five others:
Hashubah, Ohel, Berekiah, Hasadiah and Jushab-Hesed.

21The descendants of Hananiah:
Pelatiah and Jeshaiah, and the sons of Rephaiah, of Arnan, of Obadiah and of Shecaniah.

22The descendants of Shecaniah:
Shemaiah and his sons:
Hattush, Igal, Bariah, Neariah and Shaphat—six in all.

23The sons of Neariah:
Elioenai, Hizkiah and Azrikam—three in all.

24The sons of Elioenai:
Hodaviah, Eliashib, Pelaiah, Akkub, Johanan, Delaiah and Anani—seven in all.

Other Clans of Judah

4 THE DESCENDANTS of Judah:
Perez, Hezron, Carmi, Hur and Shobal.

2Reaiah son of Shobal was the father of Jahath, and Jahath the father of Ahumai and Lahad. These were the clans of the Zorathites.

3These were the sonsc of Etam:
Jezreel, Ishma and Idbash. Their sister was named Hazzelelponi. 4Penuel was the father of Gedor, and Ezer the father of Hushah.

These were the descendants of Hur, the firstborn of Ephrathah and fatherd of Bethlehem.

5Ashhur the father of Tekoa had two wives, Helah and Naarah.

6Naarah bore him Ahuzzam, Hepher, Temeni and Haahashtari. These were the descendants of Naarah.

a *11* Hebrew *Joram*, a variant of *Jehoram*　b *16* Hebrew *Jeconiah*, a variant of *Jehoiachin*; also in verse 17　c *3* Some Septuagint manuscripts (see also Vulgate); Hebrew *father*　d *4* Father may mean *civic leader* or *military leader*; also in verses 12, 14, 17, 18 and possibly elsewhere.

Living Bible

10-14These are the descendants of King *Solomon:*
Rehoboam, Abijah, Asa, Jehoshaphat, Joram,e
Ahaziah, Joash, Amaziah, Azariah,f Jotham,
Ahaz, Hezekiah, Manasseh, Amon, Josiah.

15The sons of *Josiah* were:
Johanan, **Jehoiakim,** Zedekiah, Shallum.g

16The sons of *Jehoiakim:*
Jeconiah, Zedekiah.

17,18These are the sons who were born to King *Jeco-niah* during the years that he was under house arrest:
Shealtiel, Malchiram, **Pedaiah,** Shenazzar, Jekami-ah, Hoshama, Nedabiah.

19,20*Pedaiah* was the father of **Zerubbabel** and Shime-i.

Zerubbabel's children were:
Meshullam, **Hananiah,** Hashubah, Ohel, Bere-chiah, Hasadiah, Jushab-hesed, Shelomith (a daughter).

21,22*Hananiah's* sons were Pelatiah and Jeshaiah;
Jeshaiah's son was Rephaiah; Rephaiah's son was
Arnan; Arnan's son was Obadiah; Obadiah's son
was Shecaniah. Shecaniah's son was Shemaiah;
Shemaiah had six sons, including Hattush, Igal, Ba-riah, **Neariah,** and Shaphat.

23*Neariah* had three sons:
Eli-o-enai, Hizkiah, Azrikam.

24*Eli-o-enai* had seven sons:
Hodaviah, Eliashib, Pelaiah, Akkub, Johanan, De-laiah, Anani.

New Revised Standard

10 The descendants of Solomon: Rehoboam, Abi-jah his son, Asa his son, Jehoshaphat his son, 11Joram
his son, Ahaziah his son, Joash his son, 12Amaziah his
son, Azariah his son, Jotham his son, 13Ahaz his son,
Hezekiah his son, Manasseh his son, 14Amon his son,
Josiah his son. 15The sons of Josiah: Johanan the first-born, the second Jehoiakim, the third Zedekiah, the
fourth Shallum. 16The descendants of Jehoiakim: Jeco-niah his son, Zedekiah his son; 17and the sons of Jeconi-ah, the captive: Shealtiel his son, 18Malchiram, Peda-iah, Shenazzar, Jekamiah, Hoshama, and Nedabiah;
19The sons of Pedaiah: Zerubbabel and Shimei; and the
sons of Zerubbabel: Meshullam and Hananiah, and She-lomith was their sister; 20and Hashubah, Ohel, Berechi-ah, Hasadiah, and Jushab-hesed, five. 21The sons of
Hananiah: Pelatiah and Jeshaiah, his sonh Rephaiah, his
sonh Arnan, his sonh Obadiah, his sonh Shecaniah.
22The soni of Shecaniah: Shemaiah. And the sons of
Shemaiah: Hattush, Igal, Bariah, Neariah, and Shaphat,
six. 23The sons of Neariah: Elioenai, Hizkiah, and Azri-kam, three. 24The sons of Elioenai: Hodaviah, Eliashib,
Pelaiah, Akkub, Johanan, Delaiah, and Anani, seven.

---

4   THESE ARE the sons of Judah:
Perez, Hezron, Carmi, Hur, **Shobal.**

2*Shobal's* son Re-aiah was the father of Jahath, the
ancestor of Ahumai and Lahad. These were known as
the Zorathite clans.

3,4The descendants of Etam:
Jezreel, Ishma, Idbash,
Hazzelelponi (his daughter),
Penuel (the ancestor of Gedor),
Ezer (the ancestor of Hushah),
The son of Hur, the oldest son of Ephrathah, who was
the father of Bethlehem.

5Ashhur, the father of Tekoa, had two wives—**He-lah,** and **Naarah.**

6*Naarah* bore him Ahuzzam, Hepher, Temeni, and

Descendants of Judah

4   THE SONS of Judah: Perez, Hezron, Carmi, Hur,
and Shobal. 2Reaiah son of Shobal became the
father of Jahath, and Jahath became the father of Ahu-mai and Lahad. These were the families of the Zorath-ites. 3These were the sonsi of Etam: Jezreel, Ishma, and
Idbash; and the name of their sister was Hazzelelponi,
4and Penuel was the father of Gedor, and Ezer the father
of Hushah. These were the sons of Hur, the firstborn of
Ephrathah, the father of Bethlehem. 5Ashhur father of
Tekoa had two wives, Helah and Naarah; 6Naarah bore
him Ahuzzam, Hepher, Temeni, and Haahashtari.k
These were the sons of Naarah. 7The sons of Helah:

e *3:10-14 Joram,* or "Jehoram." f *3:10-14 Azariah,* or "Uzziah."
g *3:15 Shallum,* that is, *Jehoahaz* (see Jer 22:11).

h Gk Compare Syr Vg: Heb *sons of* i Heb *sons* j Gk Compare Vg: Heb
the father k Or *Ahashtari*

King James

7And the sons of Helah were, Zereth, and Jezoar, and Ethnan.

8And Coz begat Anub, and Zobebah, and the families of Aharhel the son of Harum.

9¶ And Jabez was more honourable than his brethren: and his mother called his name Jabez, saying, Because I bare him with sorrow.

10And Jabez called on the God of Israel, saying, Oh that thou wouldest bless me indeed, and enlarge my coast, and that thine hand might be with me, and that thou wouldest keep me from evil, that it may not grieve me! And God granted him that which he requested.

11¶ And Chelub the brother of Shuah begat Mehir, which was the father of Eshton.

12And Eshton begat Beth-rapha, and Paseah, and Tehinnah the father of Ir-nahash. These are the men of Rechah.

13And the sons of Kenaz; Othniel, and Seraiah: and the sons of Othniel; Hathath.

14And Meonothai begat Ophrah: and Seraiah begat Joab, the father of the valley of Charashim; for they were craftsmen.

15And the sons of Caleb the son of Jephunneh; Iru, Elah, and Naam: and the sons of Elah, even Kenaz.

16And the sons of Jehaleleel; Ziph, and Ziphah, Tiria, and Asareel.

17And the sons of Ezra were, Jether, and Mered, and Epher, and Jalon: and she bare Miriam, and Shammai, and Ishbah the father of Eshtemoa.

18And his wife Jehudijah bare Jered the father of Gedor, and Heber the father of Socho, and Jekuthiel the father of Zanoah. And these are the sons of Bithiah the daughter of Pharaoh, which Mered took.

19And the sons of his wife Hodiah the sister of Naham, the father of Keilah the Garmite, and Eshtemoa the Maachathite.

20And the sons of Shimon were, Amnon, and Rinnah, Ben-hanan, and Tilon. And the sons of Ishi were, Zoheth, and Ben-zoheth.

21¶ The sons of Shelah the son of Judah were, Er the father of Lecah, and Laadah the father of Mareshah, and the families of the house of them that wrought fine linen, of the house of Ashbea,

22And Jokim, and the men of Chozeba, and Joash, and Saraph, who had the dominion in Moab, and Jashubi-lehem. And these are ancient things.

23These were the potters, and those that dwelt among plants and hedges: there they dwelt with the king for his work.

24¶ The sons of Simeon were, Nemuel, and Jamin, Jarib, Zerah, and Shaul:

25Shallum his son, Mibsam his son, Mishma his son.

26And the sons of Mishma; Hamuel his son, Zacchur his son, Shimei his son.

27And Shimei had sixteen sons and six daughters; but his brethren had not many children, neither did all their family multiply, like to the children of Judah.

28And they dwelt at Beer-sheba, and Moladah, and Hazar-shual,

29And at Bilhah, and at Ezem, and at Tolad,

30And at Bethuel, and at Hormah, and at Ziklag,

New International

7The sons of Helah:
Zereth, Zohar, Ethnan, 8and Koz, who was the father of Anub and Hazzobebah and of the clans of Aharhel son of Harum.

9Jabez was more honorable than his brothers. His mother had named him Jabez,a saying, "I gave birth to him in pain." 10Jabez cried out to the God of Israel, "Oh, that you would bless me and enlarge my territory! Let your hand be with me, and keep me from harm so that I will be free from pain." And God granted his request.

11Kelub, Shuhah's brother, was the father of Mehir, who was the father of Eshton. 12Eshton was the father of Beth Rapha, Paseah and Tehinnah the father of Ir Nahash.b These were the men of Recah.

13The sons of Kenaz:
Othniel and Seraiah.
The sons of Othniel:
Hathath and Meonothai.c 14Meonothai was the father of Ophrah.
Seraiah was the father of Joab,
the father of Ge Harashim.d It was called this because its people were craftsmen.

15The sons of Caleb son of Jephunneh:
Iru, Elah and Naam.
The son of Elah:
Kenaz.

16The sons of Jehallelel:
Ziph, Ziphah, Tiria and Asarel.

17The sons of Ezrah:
Jether, Mered, Epher and Jalon. One of Mered's wives gave birth to Miriam, Shammai and Ishbah the father of Eshtemoa. 18(His Judean wife gave birth to Jered the father of Gedor, Heber the father of Soco, and Jekuthiel the father of Zanoah.) These were the children of Pharaoh's daughter Bithiah, whom Mered had married.

19The sons of Hodiah's wife, the sister of Naham:
the father of Keilah the Garmite, and Eshtemoa the Maacathite.

20The sons of Shimon:
Amnon, Rinnah, Ben-Hanan and Tilon.
The descendants of Ishi:
Zoheth and Ben-Zoheth.

21The sons of Shelah son of Judah:
Er the father of Lecah, Laadah the father of Mareshah and the clans of the linen workers at Beth Ashbea, 22Jokim, the men of Cozeba, and Joash and Saraph, who ruled in Moab and Jashubi Lehem. (These records are from ancient times.) 23They were the potters who lived at Netaim and Gederah; they stayed there and worked for the king.

Simeon

24The descendants of Simeon:
Nemuel, Jamin, Jarib, Zerah and Shaul;

25Shallum was Shaul's son, Mibsam his son and Mishma his son.

26The descendants of Mishma:
Hammuel his son, Zaccur his son and Shimei his son.

27Shimei had sixteen sons and six daughters, but his brothers did not have many children; so their entire clan did not become as numerous as the people of Judah.

28They lived in Beersheba, Moladah, Hazar Shual, 29Bilhah, Ezem, Tolad, 30Bethuel, Hormah, Ziklag,

---

a 9 Jabez sounds like the Hebrew for pain.   b 12 Or of the city of Nahash
c 13 Some Septuagint manuscripts and Vulgate; Hebrew does not have and Meonothai.   d 14 Ge Harashim means valley of craftsmen.

Living Bible

Haahashtari; 7and *Helah* bore him Zereth, Izhar, and Ethnan.

8Koz was the father of Anub and Zobebah; he was also the ancestor of the clan named after Aharhel, the son of Harum.

9Jabez was more distinguished than any of his brothers. His mother named him Jabez because she had such a hard time at his birth (Jabez meanse "Distress").

10He was the one who prayed to the God of Israel, "Oh, that you would wonderfully bless me and help me in my work; please be with me in all that I do, and keep me from all evil and disaster!" And God granted him his request.

11, 12The descendants of Recah were:
Chelub (the brother of Shuhah), whose son was Mahir, the father of **Eshton;**
Eshton was the father of Bethrapha, Paseah, and Tehinnah;
Tehinnah was the father of Irnahash.
13The sons of Kenaz were **Othni-el** and **Seraiah.**
Othni-el's sons were Hathath and **Meonothai;**
14*Meonothai* was the father of Ophrah;
Seraiah was the father of Joab, the ancestor of the inhabitants of Craftsman Valley (called that because many craftsmen lived there).
15The sons of Caleb (the son of Jephunneh):
Iru, **Elah,** Naam.
The sons of *Elah* included Kenaz.
16Jehallelel's sons were:
Ziph, Ziphah, Tiri-a, Asarel.
17Ezrah's sons were:
Jether, **Mered,** Epher, Jalon.
Mered married Bithi-ah, an Egyptian princess. She was the mother of Miriam, Shammai, and Ishbah—an ancestor of **Eshtemoa.**
18*Eshtemoa's* wife was a Jewess; she was the mother of Jered, Heber, and Jekuthiel, who were, respectively, the ancestors of the Gedorites, Socoites, and Zanoahites.
19Hodiah's wife was the sister of Naham. One of her sons was the father of Keilah the Garmite, and another was the father of Eshtemoa the Maacathite.
20The sons of Shimon:
Amnon, Rinnah, Ben-hanan, Tilon.
The sons of Ishi:
Zoheth, Ben-zoheth.
21, 22The sons of Shelah (the son of Judah):
Er (the father of Lecah),
Laadah (the father of Mareshah),
The families of the linen workers who worked at Beth-ashbea,
Jokim,
The clans of Cozeba,
Joash,
Saraph (who was a ruler in Moab before he returned to Lehem).
These names all come from very ancient records.
23These clans were noted for their pottery, gardening, and planting; they all worked for the king:
24The sons of Simeon:
Nemu-el, Jamin, Jarib, Zerah, **Shaul.**
25*Shaul's* son was Shallum, his grandson was Mibsam, and his great-grandson was **Mishma.**
26*Mishma's* sons included Hammu-el (the father of Zaccur and grandfather of **Shime-i).**
27*Shime-i* had sixteen sons and six daughters, but none of his brothers had large families—they all had fewer children than was normal in Judah.
28They lived at Beer-sheba, Moladah, Hazar-shual, 29Bilhah, Ezem, Tolad, 30Bethuel, Hormah, Ziklag,

New Revised Standard

Zereth, Izhar,f and Ethnan. 8Koz became the father of Anub, Zobebah, and the families of Aharhel son of Harum. 9Jabez was honored more than his brothers; and his mother named him Jabez, saying, "Because I bore him in pain." 10Jabez called on the God of Israel, saying, "Oh that you would bless me and enlarge my border, and that your hand might be with me, and that you would keep me from hurt and harm!" And God granted what he asked. 11Chelub the brother of Shuhah became the father of Mehir, who was the father of Eshton. 12Eshton became the father of Beth-rapha, Paseah, and Tehinnah the father of Ir-nahash. These are the men of Recah. 13The sons of Kenaz: Othniel and Seraiah; and the sons of Othniel: Hathath and Meonothai.g 14Meonothai became the father of Ophrah; and Seraiah became the father of Joab father of Ge-harashim,h so-called because they were artisans. 15The sons of Caleb son of Jephunneh: Iru, Elah, and Naam; and the soni of Elah: Kenaz. 16The sons of Jehallelel: Ziph, Ziphah, Tiria, and Asarel. 17The sons of Ezrah: Jether, Mered, Epher, and Jalon. These are the sons of Bithiah, daughter of Pharaoh, whom Mered married;j and she conceived and borek Miriam, Shammai, and Ishbah father of Eshtemoa. 18And his Judean wife bore Jered father of Gedor, Heber father of Soco, and Jekuthiel father of Zanoah. 19The sons of the wife of Hodiah, the sister of Naham, were the fathers of Keilah the Garmite and Eshtemoa the Maacathite. 20The sons of Shimon: Amnon, Rinnah, Ben-hanan, and Tilon. The sons of Ishi: Zoheth and Ben-zoheth. 21The sons of Shelah son of Judah: Er father of Lecah, Laadah father of Mareshah, and the families of the guild of linen workers at Beth-ashbea; 22and Jokim, and the men of Cozeba, and Joash, and Saraph, who married into Moab but returned to Lehem[l] (now the recordsm are ancient). 23These were the potters and inhabitants of Netaim and Gederah; they lived there with the king in his service.

Descendants of Simeon

24   The sons of Simeon: Nemuel, Jamin, Jarib, Zerah, Shaul;n 25Shallum was his son, Mibsam his son, Mishma his son. 26The sons of Mishma: Hammuel his son, Zaccur his son, Shimei his son. 27Shimei had sixteen sons and six daughters; but his brothers did not have many children, nor did all their family multiply like the Judeans. 28They lived in Beer-sheba, Moladah, Hazar-shual, 29Bilhah, Ezem, Tolad, 30Bethuel, Hormah, Ziklag, 31Beth-marcaboth, Hazar-susim, Beth-biri, and

---

e *4:9 Jabez means.* A play on words. *Jabez* sounds like *ozeb*, the Hebrew word meaning "distress."

f Another reading is *Zohar*   g Gk Vg: Heb lacks *and Meonothai*   h That is *Valley of artisans*   i Heb *sons*   j The clause: *These are . . . married* is transposed from verse 18   k Heb lacks *and bore*   l Vg Compare Gk: Heb *and Jashubi-lahem*   m Or *matters*   n Or *Saul*

King James

31And at Beth-marcaboth, and Hazar-susim, and at Beth-birei, and at Shaaraim. These *were* their cities unto the reign of David.

32And their villages *were,* Etam, and Ain, Rimmon, and Tochen, and Ashan, five cities:

33And all their villages that *were* round about the same cities, unto Baal. These *were* their habitations, and their genealogy.

34And Meshobab, and Jamlech, and Joshah the son of Amaziah,

35And Joel, and Jehu the son of Josibiah, the son of Seraiah, the son of Asiel,

36And Elioenai, and Jaakobah, and Jeshohaiah, and Asaiah, and Adiel, and Jesimiel, and Benaiah,

37And Ziza the son of Shiphi, the son of Allon, the son of Jedaiah, the son of Shimri, the son of Shemaiah;

38These mentioned by *their* names *were* princes in their families: and the house of their fathers increased greatly.

39¶ And they went to the entrance of Gedor, *even* unto the east side of the valley, to seek pasture for their flocks.

40And they found fat pasture and good, and the land *was* wide, and quiet, and peaceable; for *they* of Ham had dwelt there of old.

41And these written by name came in the days of Hezekiah king of Judah, and smote their tents, and the habitations that were found there, and destroyed them utterly unto this day, and dwelt in their rooms: because *there was* pasture there for their flocks.

42And *some* of them, *even* of the sons of Simeon, five hundred men, went to mount Seir, having for their captains Pelatiah, and Neariah, and Rephaiah, and Uzziel, the sons of Ishi.

43And they smote the rest of the Amalekites that were escaped, and dwelt there unto this day.

5 NOW THE sons of Reuben the firstborn of Israel, (for he *was* the firstborn; but, forasmuch as he defiled his father's bed, his birthright was given unto the sons of Joseph the son of Israel: and the genealogy is not to be reckoned after the birthright.

2For Judah prevailed above his brethren, and of him *came* the chief ruler; but the birthright *was* Joseph's:)

3The sons, *I say,* of Reuben the firstborn of Israel *were,* Hanoch, and Pallu, Hezron, and Carmi.

4The sons of Joel; Shemaiah his son, Gog his son, Shimei his son,

5Micah his son, Reaia his son, Baal his son,

6Beerah his son, whom Tilgath-pilneser king of Assyria carried away *captive:* he *was* prince of the Reubenites.

7And his brethren by their families, when the genealogy of their generations was reckoned, *were* the chief, Jeiel, and Zechariah,

8And Bela the son of Azaz, the son of Shema, the son of Joel, who dwelt in Aroer, even unto Nebo and Baal-meon:

9And eastward he inhabited unto the entering in of the wilderness from the river Euphrates: because their cattle were multiplied in the land of Gilead.

10And in the days of Saul they made war with the Hagarites, who fell by their hand: and they dwelt in their tents throughout all the east *land* of Gilead.

New International

31Beth Marcaboth, Hazar Susim, Beth Biri and Shaaraim. These were their towns until the reign of David. 32Their surrounding villages were Etam, Ain, Rimmon, Token and Ashan—five towns— 33and all the villages around these towns as far as Baalath.ᵃ These were their settlements. And they kept a genealogical record.

34Meshobab, Jamlech, Joshah son of Amaziah, 35Joel, Jehu son of Joshibiah, the son of Seraiah, the son of Asiel, 36also Elioenai, Jaakobah, Jeshohaiah, Asaiah, Adiel, Jesimiel, Benaiah, 37and Ziza son of Shiphi, the son of Allon, the son of Jedaiah, the son of Shimri, the son of Shemaiah.

38The men listed above by name were leaders of their clans. Their families increased greatly, 39and they went to the outskirts of Gedor to the east of the valley in search of pasture for their flocks. 40They found rich, good pasture, and the land was spacious, peaceful and quiet. Some Hamites had lived there formerly.

41The men whose names were listed came in the days of Hezekiah king of Judah. They attacked the Hamites in their dwellings and also the Meunites who were there and completely destroyedᵇ them, as is evident to this day. Then they settled in their place, because there was pasture for their flocks. 42And five hundred of these Simeonites, led by Pelatiah, Neariah, Rephaiah and Uzziel, the sons of Ishi, invaded the hill country of Seir. 43They killed the remaining Amalekites who had escaped, and they have lived there to this day.

Reuben

5 THE SONS of Reuben the firstborn of Israel (he was the firstborn, but when he defiled his father's marriage bed, his rights as firstborn were given to the sons of Joseph son of Israel; so he could not be listed in the genealogical record in accordance with his birthright, 2and though Judah was the strongest of his brothers and a ruler came from him, the rights of the firstborn belonged to Joseph)— 3the sons of Reuben the firstborn of Israel:

Hanoch, Pallu, Hezron and Carmi.

4The descendants of Joel:

Shemaiah his son, Gog his son, Shimei his son, 5Micah his son, Reaiah his son, Baal his son, 6and Beerah his son, whom Tiglath-Pileserᶜ king of Assyria took into exile. Beerah was a leader of the Reubenites.

7Their relatives by clans, listed according to their genealogical records:

Jeiel the chief, Zechariah, 8and Bela son of Azaz, the son of Shema, the son of Joel. They settled in the area from Aroer to Nebo and Baal Meon. 9To the east they occupied the land up to the edge of the desert that extends to the Euphrates River, because their livestock had increased in Gilead.

10During Saul's reign they waged war against the Hagrites, who were defeated at their hands; they occupied the dwellings of the Hagrites throughout the entire region east of Gilead.

ᵃ *33* Some Septuagint manuscripts (see also Joshua 19:8); Hebrew *Baal*
ᵇ *41* The Hebrew term refers to the irrevocable giving over of things or persons to the LORD, often by totally destroying them.   ᶜ *6* Hebrew *Tilgath-Pileser,* a variant of *Tiglath-Pileser*; also in verse 26

Living Bible

31Beth-marcaboth, Hazar-susim, Beth-biri, and Shaaraim. These cities were under their control until the time of David.

32, 33Their descendants also lived in or near Etam, Ain, Rimmon, Tochen, and Ashan; some were as far away as Baal. (These facts are recorded in their genealogies.)

34-39These are the names of some of the princes of wealthy clans who traveled to the east side of Gedor Valley in search of pasture for their flocks:

Meshobab, Jamlech, Joshah, Joel, Jehu, Eli-o-enai, Ja-akobah, Jeshohaiah, Asaiah, Adi-el, Jesimi-el, Benaiah, Ziza (the son of Shiphi, son of Allon, son of Jedaiah, son of Shimri, son of Shemaiah).

40, 41They found good pastures, and everything was quiet and peaceful; but the land belonged to the descendants of Ham.

So during the reign of King Hezekiah of Judah these princes invaded the land and struck down the tents and houses of the descendants of Ham; they killed the inhabitants of the land and took possession of it for themselves.

42Later, five hundred of these invaders from the tribe of Simeon went to Mount Seir. (Their leaders were Pelatiah, Ne-ariah, Rephaiah, and Uzziel—all sons of Ishi.)

43There they destroyed the few surviving members of the tribe of Amalek. And they have lived there ever since.

5 THE OLDEST son of Israel was Reuben, but since he dishonored his father by sleeping with one of his father's wives, his birthright was given to his half brother, Joseph. So the official genealogy doesn't name Reuben as the oldest son.

2Although Joseph received the birthright, yet Judah was a powerful and influential tribe in Israel, and from Judah came a Prince.

3The sons of Reuben, Israel's son, were:

Hanoch, Pallu, Hezron, Carmi.

4Joel's descendants were his son Shemaiah, his grandson Gog, and his great-grandson **Shime-i.**

5*Shime-i's* son was Micah; his grandson was Reaiah; and his great-grandson was **Baal.**

6*Baal's* son was Beerah. He was a prince of the tribe of Reuben and was taken into captivity by King Tilgath-pilneser of Assyria.

7, 8His relatives became heads of clans and were included in the official genealogy:

Je-iel, Zechariah, Bela (the son of Azaz, grandson of Shema, and great-grandson of **Joel**).

These Reubenitesd lived in Aroer and as far distant as Mount Nebo and Baal-meon.

9Joel was a cattle man, and he pastured his animals eastward to the edge of the desert and to the Euphrates River, for there were many cattle in the land of Gilead.

10During the reign of King Saul, the men of Reuben defeated the Hagrites in war and moved into their tents on the eastern edge of Gilead. 11Across from them, in

New Revised Standard

Shaaraim. These were their towns until David became king. 32And their villages were Etam, Ain, Rimmon, Tochen, and Ashan, five towns, 33along with all their villages that were around these towns as far as Baal. These were their settlements. And they kept a genealogical record.

34 Meshobab, Jamlech, Joshah son of Amaziah, 35Joel, Jehu son of Joshibiah son of Seraiah son of Asiel, 36Elioenai, Jaakobah, Jeshohaiah, Asaiah, Adiel, Jesimiel, Benaiah, 37Ziza son of Shiphi son of Allon son of Jedaiah son of Shimri son of Shemaiah— 38these mentioned by name were leaders in their families, and their clans increased greatly. 39They journeyed to the entrance of Gedor, to the east side of the valley, to seek pasture for their flocks, 40where they found rich, good pasture, and the land was very broad, quiet, and peaceful; for the former inhabitants there belonged to Ham. 41These, registered by name, came in the days of King Hezekiah of Judah, and attacked their tents and the Meunim who were found there, and exterminated them to this day, and settled in their place, because there was pasture there for their flocks. 42And some of them, five hundred men of the Simeonites, went to Mount Seir, having as their leaders Pelatiah, Neariah, Rephaiah, and Uzziel, sons of Ishi; 43they destroyed the remnant of the Amalekites that had escaped, and they have lived there to this day.

Descendants of Reuben

5 THE SONS of Reuben the firstborn of Israel. (He was the firstborn, but because he defiled his father's bed his birthright was given to the sons of Joseph son of Israel, so that he is not enrolled in the genealogy according to the birthright; 2though Judah became prominent among his brothers and a ruler came from him, yet the birthright belonged to Joseph.) 3The sons of Reuben, the firstborn of Israel: Hanoch, Pallu, Hezron, and Carmi. 4The sons of Joel: Shemaiah his son, Gog his son, Shimei his son, 5Micah his son, Reaiah his son, Baal his son, 6Beerah his son, whom King Tilgath-pilneser of Assyria carried away into exile; he was a chieftain of the Reubenites. 7And his kindred by their families, when the genealogy of their generations was reckoned: the chief, Jeiel, and Zechariah, 8and Bela son of Azaz, son of Shema, son of Joel, who lived in Aroer, as far as Nebo and Baal-meon. 9He also lived to the east as far as the beginning of the desert this side of the Euphrates, because their cattle had multiplied in the land of Gilead. 10And in the days of Saul they made war on the Hagrites, who fell by their hand; and they lived in their tents throughout all the region east of Gilead.

d 5:7, 8 These Reubenites, implied in 5:1.

King James

11¶ And the children of Gad dwelt over against them, in the land of Bashan unto Salcah:

12Joel the chief, and Shapham the next, and Jaanai, and Shaphat in Bashan.

13And their brethren of the house of their fathers *were*, Michael, and Meshullam, and Sheba, and Jorai, and Jachan, and Zia, and Heber, seven.

14These *are* the children of Abihail the son of Huri, the son of Jaroah, the son of Gilead, the son of Michael, the son of Jeshishai, the son of Jahdo, the son of Buz;

15Ahi the son of Abdiel, the son of Guni, chief of the house of their fathers.

16And they dwelt in Gilead in Bashan, and in her towns, and in all the suburbs of Sharon, upon their borders.

17All these were reckoned by genealogies in the days of Jotham king of Judah, and in the days of Jeroboam king of Israel.

18¶ The sons of Reuben, and the Gadites, and half the tribe of Manasseh, of valiant men, men able to bear buckler and sword, and to shoot with bow, and skilful in war, *were* four and forty thousand seven hundred and threescore, that went out to the war.

19And they made war with the Hagarites, with Jetur, and Nephish, and Nodab.

20And they were helped against them, and the Hagarites were delivered into their hand, and all that *were* with them: for they cried to God in the battle, and he was entreated of them; because they put their trust in him.

21And they took away their cattle; of their camels fifty thousand, and of sheep two hundred and fifty thousand, and of asses two thousand, and of men an hundred thousand.

22For there fell down many slain, because the war *was* of God. And they dwelt in their steads until the captivity.

23¶ And the children of the half tribe of Manasseh dwelt in the land: they increased from Bashan unto Baalhermon and Senir, and unto mount Hermon.

24And these *were* the heads of the house of their fathers, even Epher, and Ishi, and Eliel, and Azriel, and Jeremiah, and Hodaviah, and Jahdiel, mighty men of valour, famous men, *and* heads of the house of their fathers.

25¶ And they transgressed against the God of their fathers, and went a-whoring after the gods of the people of the land, whom God destroyed before them.

26And the God of Israel stirred up the spirit of Pul king of Assyria, and the spirit of Tilgath-pilneser king of Assyria, and he carried them away, even the Reubenites, and the Gadites, and the half tribe of Manasseh, and brought them unto Halah, and Habor, and Hara, and to the river Gozan, unto this day.

6 THE SONS of Levi; Gershon, Kohath, and Merari.

2And the sons of Kohath; Amram, Izhar, and Hebron, and Uzziel.

3And the children of Amram; Aaron, and Moses, and Miriam. The sons also of Aaron; Nadab, and Abihu, Eleazar, and Ithamar.

New International

Gad

11The Gadites lived next to them in Bashan, as far as Salecah:

12Joel was the chief, Shapham the second, then Janai and Shaphat, in Bashan.

13Their relatives, by families, were:

Michael, Meshullam, Sheba, Jorai, Jacan, Zia and Eber—seven in all.

14These were the sons of Abihail son of Huri, the son of Jaroah, the son of Gilead, the son of Michael, the son of Jeshishai, the son of Jahdo, the son of Buz.

15Ahi son of Abdiel, the son of Guni, was head of their family.

16The Gadites lived in Gilead, in Bashan and its outlying villages, and on all the pasturelands of Sharon as far as they extended.

17All these were entered in the genealogical records during the reigns of Jotham king of Judah and Jeroboam king of Israel.

18The Reubenites, the Gadites and the half-tribe of Manasseh had 44,760 men ready for military service—able-bodied men who could handle shield and sword, who could use a bow, and who were trained for battle. 19They waged war against the Hagrites, Jetur, Naphish and Nodab. 20They were helped in fighting them, and God handed the Hagrites and all their allies over to them, because they cried out to him during the battle. He answered their prayers, because they trusted in him. 21They seized the livestock of the Hagrites—fifty thousand camels, two hundred fifty thousand sheep and two thousand donkeys. They also took one hundred thousand people captive, 22and many others fell slain, because the battle was God's. And they occupied the land until the exile.

The Half-Tribe of Manasseh

23The people of the half-tribe of Manasseh were numerous; they settled in the land from Bashan to Baal Hermon, that is, to Senir (Mount Hermon).

24These were the heads of their families: Epher, Ishi, Eliel, Azriel, Jeremiah, Hodaviah and Jahdiel. They were brave warriors, famous men, and heads of their families. 25But they were unfaithful to the God of their fathers and prostituted themselves to the gods of the peoples of the land, whom God had destroyed before them. 26So the God of Israel stirred up the spirit of Pul king of Assyria (that is, Tiglath-Pileser king of Assyria), who took the Reubenites, the Gadites and the half-tribe of Manasseh into exile. He took them to Halah, Habor, Hara and the river of Gozan, where they are to this day.

Levi

6 THE SONS of Levi:

Gershon, Kohath and Merari.

2The sons of Kohath:

Amram, Izhar, Hebron and Uzziel.

3The children of Amram:

Aaron, Moses and Miriam.

The sons of Aaron:

Nadab, Abihu, Eleazar and Ithamar.

Living Bible

the land of Bashan, lived the descendants of Gad, who were spread as far as Salecah.

12Joel was the greatest and was followed by Shapham, also Janai and Shaphat. 13Their relatives, the heads of the seven clans, were Michael, Meshullam, Sheba, Jorai, Jacan, Zia, and Eber.

14The descendants of Buz, in the order of their generations, were:

Jahdo, Jeshishai, Michael, Gilead, Jaroah, Huri, Abihail.

15Ahi, the son of Abdi-el and grandson of Guni, was the leader of the clan. 16The clan lived in and around Gilead (in the land of Bashan) and throughout the entire pasture country of Sharon. 17All were included in the official genealogy at the time of King Jotham of Judah and King Jeroboam of Israel.

18There were 44,760 armed, trained, and brave troops in the army of Reuben, Gad, and the half-tribe of Manasseh. 19They declared war on the Hagrites, the Jeturites, the Naphishites, and the Nodabites. 20They cried out to God to help them, and he did, for they trusted in him. So the Hagrites and all their allies were defeated. 21The booty included 50,000 camels, 250,000 sheep, 2,000 donkeys, and 100,000 captives. 22A great number of the enemy also died in the battle, for God was fighting against them. So the Reubenites lived in the territory of the Hagrites until the time of the exile.

23The half-tribe of Manasseh spread through the land from Bashan to Baal-hermon, Senir, and Mount Hermon. They too were very numerous.

24The chiefs of their clans were the following:

Epher, Ishi, Eliel, Azri-el, Jeremiah, Hodaviah, Jahdi-el.

Each of these men had a great reputation as a warrior and leader. 25But they were not true to the God of their fathers; instead they worshiped the idols of the people whom God had destroyed. 26So God caused King Pul of Assyria (also known as Tilgath-pilneser III) to invade the land and deport the men of Reuben, Gad, and the half-tribe of Manasseh. They took them to Halah, Habor, Hara, and the Gozan River, where they remain to this day.

6 THESE ARE the names of the sons of Levi:
Gershom, Kohath, Merari.
2*Kohath's* sons were:
Amram, Izhar, Hebron, Uzziel.
3*Amram's* descendants included:
Aaron, Moses, Miriam.
Aaron's sons were:
Nadab, Abihu, Eleazar, Ithamar.

New Revised Standard

Descendants of Gad

11 The sons of Gad lived beside them in the land of Bashan as far as Salecah: 12Joel the chief, Shapham the second, Janai, and Shaphat in Bashan. 13And their kindred according to their clans: Michael, Meshullam, Sheba, Jorai, Jacan, Zia, and Eber, seven. 14These were the sons of Abihail son of Huri, son of Jaroah, son of Gilead, son of Michael, son of Jeshishai, son of Jahdo, son of Buz; 15Ahi son of Abdiel, son of Guni, was chief in their clan; 16and they lived in Gilead, in Bashan and in its towns, and in all the pasture lands of Sharon to their limits. 17All of these were enrolled by genealogies in the days of King Jotham of Judah, and in the days of King Jeroboam of Israel.

18 The Reubenites, the Gadites, and the half-tribe of Manasseh had valiant warriors, who carried shield and sword, and drew the bow, expert in war, forty-four thousand seven hundred sixty, ready for service. 19They made war on the Hagrites, Jetur, Naphish, and Nodab; 20and when they received help against them, the Hagrites and all who were with them were given into their hands, for they cried to God in the battle, and he granted their entreaty because they trusted in him. 21They captured their livestock: fifty thousand of their camels, two hundred fifty thousand sheep, two thousand donkeys, and one hundred thousand captives. 22Many fell slain, because the war was of God. And they lived in their territory until the exile.

The Half-Tribe of Manasseh

23 The members of the half-tribe of Manasseh lived in the land; they were very numerous from Bashan to Baal-hermon, Senir, and Mount Hermon. 24These were the heads of their clans: Epher,[a] Ishi, Eliel, Azriel, Jeremiah, Hodaviah, and Jahdiel, mighty warriors, famous men, heads of their clans. 25But they transgressed against the God of their ancestors, and prostituted themselves to the gods of the peoples of the land, whom God had destroyed before them. 26So the God of Israel stirred up the spirit of King Pul of Assyria, the spirit of King Tilgath-pilneser of Assyria, and he carried them away, namely, the Reubenites, the Gadites, and the half-tribe of Manasseh, and brought them to Halah, Habor, Hara, and the river Gozan, to this day.

Descendants of Levi

6[b] THE SONS of Levi: Gershom,[c] Kohath, and Merari. 2The sons of Kohath: Amram, Izhar, Hebron, and Uzziel. 3The children of Amram: Aaron, Moses, and Miriam. The sons of Aaron: Nadab, Abihu, Eleazar, and Ithamar. 4Eleazar became the father of Phinehas,

---

King James

4¶ Eleazar begat Phinehas, Phinehas begat Abishua,
5And Abishua begat Bukki, and Bukki begat Uzzi,
6And Uzzi begat Zerahiah, and Zerahiah begat Meraioth,
7Meraioth begat Amariah, and Amariah begat Ahitub,
8And Ahitub begat Zadok, and Zadok begat Ahimaaz,
9And Ahimaaz begat Azariah, and Azariah begat Johanan,
10And Johanan begat Azariah, (he *it is* that executed the priest's office in the temple that Solomon built in Jerusalem:)
11And Azariah begat Amariah, and Amariah begat Ahitub,
12And Ahitub begat Zadok, and Zadok begat Shallum,
13And Shallum begat Hilkiah, and Hilkiah begat Azariah,
14And Azariah begat Seraiah, and Seraiah begat Jehozadak,
15And Jehozadak went *into captivity,* when the LORD carried away Judah and Jerusalem by the hand of Nebuchadnezzar.
16¶ The sons of Levi; Gershom, Kohath, and Merari.
17And these *be* the names of the sons of Gershom; Libni, and Shimei.
18And the sons of Kohath *were,* Amram, and Izhar, and Hebron, and Uzziel.
19The sons of Merari; Mahli, and Mushi. And these *are* the families of the Levites according to their fathers.
20Of Gershom; Libni his son, Jahath his son, Zimmah his son,
21Joah his son, Iddo his son, Zerah his son, Jeaterai his son.
22The sons of Kohath; Amminadab his son, Korah his son, Assir his son,
23Elkanah his son, and Ebiasaph his son, and Assir his son,
24Tahath his son, Uriel his son, Uzziah his son, and Shaul his son.
25And the sons of Elkanah; Amasai, and Ahimoth.
26*As for* Elkanah: the sons of Elkanah; Zophai his son, and Nahath his son,
27Eliab his son, Jeroham his son, Elkanah his son.
28And the sons of Samuel; the firstborn Vashni, and Abiah.
29The sons of Merari; Mahli, Libni his son, Shimei his son, Uzza his son,
30Shimea his son, Haggiah his son, Asaiah his son.
31And these *are they* whom David set over the service of song in the house of the LORD, after that the ark had rest.

New International

4Eleazar was the father of Phinehas,
   Phinehas the father of Abishua,
5Abishua the father of Bukki,
   Bukki the father of Uzzi,
6Uzzi the father of Zerahiah,
   Zerahiah the father of Meraioth,
7Meraioth the father of Amariah,
   Amariah the father of Ahitub,
8Ahitub the father of Zadok,
   Zadok the father of Ahimaaz,
9Ahimaaz the father of Azariah,
   Azariah the father of Johanan,
10Johanan the father of Azariah (it was he who served as priest in the temple Solomon built in Jerusalem),
11Azariah the father of Amariah,
   Amariah the father of Ahitub,
12Ahitub the father of Zadok,
   Zadok the father of Shallum,
13Shallum the father of Hilkiah,
   Hilkiah the father of Azariah,
14Azariah the father of Seraiah,
   and Seraiah the father of Jehozadak.
15Jehozadak was deported when the LORD sent Judah and Jerusalem into exile by the hand of Nebuchadnezzar.

16The sons of Levi:
   Gershon,ᵃ Kohath and Merari.
17These are the names of the sons of Gershon:
   Libni and Shimei.
18The sons of Kohath:
   Amram, Izhar, Hebron and Uzziel.
19The sons of Merari:
   Mahli and Mushi.
These are the clans of the Levites listed according to their fathers:
20Of Gershon:
   Libni his son, Jehath his son,
   Zimmah his son, 21Joah his son,
   Iddo his son, Zerah his son
   and Jeatherai his son.
22The descendants of Kohath:
   Amminadab his son, Korah his son,
   Assir his son, 23Elkanah his son,
   Ebiasaph his son, Assir his son,
24Tahath his son, Uriel his son,
   Uzziah his son and Shaul his son.
25The descendants of Elkanah:
   Amasai, Ahimoth,
26Elkanah his son,ᵇ Zophai his son,
   Nahath his son, 27Eliab his son,
   Jeroham his son, Elkanah his son
   and Samuel his son.ᶜ
28The sons of Samuel:
   Joelᵈ the firstborn
   and Abijah the second son.
29The descendants of Merari:
   Mahli, Libni his son,
   Shimei his son, Uzzah his son,
30Shimea his son, Haggiah his son
   and Asaiah his son.

The Temple Musicians

31These are the men David put in charge of the music in the house of the LORD after the ark came to rest there.

ᵃ *16* Hebrew *Gershom,* a variant of *Gershon;* also in verses 17, 20, 43, 62 and 71   ᵇ *26* Some Hebrew manuscripts, Septuagint and Syriac; most Hebrew manuscripts *Ahimoth* *26and Elkanah. The sons of Elkanah:*   ᶜ *27* Some Septuagint manuscripts (see also 1 Samuel 1:19,20 and 1 Chron. 6:33,34); Hebrew does not have *and Samuel his son.*   ᵈ *28* Some Septuagint manuscripts and Syriac (see also 1 Samuel 8:2 and 1 Chron. 6:33); Hebrew does not have *Joel.*

Living Bible

4-15The oldest sons of the successive generations of Aaron were as follows:e
Eleazar, the father of
Phinehas, the father of
Abishua, the father of
Bukki, the father of
Uzzi, the father of
Zerahiah, the father of
Meraioth, the father of
Amariah, the father of
Ahitub, the father of
Zadok, the father of
Ahima-az, the father of
Azariah, the father of
Johanan, the father of
Azariah (the High Priest in Solomon's Temple at Jerusalem), the father of
Amariah, the father of
Ahitub, the father of
Zadok, the father of
Shallum, the father of
Hilkiah, the father of
Azariah, the father of
Seraiah, the father of
Jehozadak (who went into exile when the Lord sent the people of Judah and Jerusalem into captivity under Nebuchadnezzar).

16As previously stated,f the sons of Levi were:
Gershom, Kohath, Merari.
17The sons of *Gershom* were:
Libni, Shime-i.
18The sons of *Kohath* were:
Amram, Izhar, Hebron, Uzziel.
19, 20, 21The sons of *Merari* were:
Mahli, Mushi.
The subclans of the Levites were:
In the Gershom clan:
Libni, Jahath, Zimmah, Joah, Iddo, Zerah, Jeatherai.
22, 23, 24In the Kohath clan:
Amminadab, Korah, Assir, **Elkanah,** Ebiasaph, Assir, Tahath, Uriel, Uzziah, Shaul.
25, 26, 27The subclan of *Elkanah* was further divided into the families of his sons:
Amasai, Ahimoth, Elkanah, Zophai, Nahath, Eliab, Jeroham, Elkanah.
28The families of the subclan of Samuel were headed by Samuel's sons:
Joel, the oldest;
Abijah, the second.
29, 30The subclans of the clan of Merari were headed by his sons:
Mahli, Libni, Shime-i, Uzzah, Shime-a, Haggiah, Asaiah.
31King David appointed songleaders and choirs to praise God in the Tabernacle after he had placed the Ark

New Revised Standard

Phinehas of Abishua, 5Abishua of Bukki, Bukki of Uzzi, 6Uzzi of Zerahiah, Zerahiah of Meraioth, 7Meraioth of Amariah, Amariah of Ahitub, 8Ahitub of Zadok, Zadok of Ahimaaz, 9Ahimaaz of Azariah, Azariah of Johanan, 10and Johanan of Azariah (it was he who served as priest in the house that Solomon built in Jerusalem). 11Azariah became the father of Amariah, Amariah of Ahitub, 12Ahitub of Zadok, Zadok of Shallum, 13Shallum of Hilkiah, Hilkiah of Azariah, 14Azariah of Seraiah, Seraiah of Jehozadak; 15and Jehozadak went into exile when the LORD sent Judah and Jerusalem into exile by the hand of Nebuchadnezzar.

16g The sons of Levi: Gershom, Kohath, and Merari. 17These are the names of the sons of Gershom: Libni and Shimei. 18The sons of Kohath: Amram, Izhar, Hebron, and Uzziel. 19The sons of Merari: Mahli and Mushi. These are the clans of the Levites according to their ancestry. 20Of Gershom: Libni his son, Jahath his son, Zimmah his son, 21Joah his son, Iddo his son, Zerah his son, Jeatherai his son. 22The sons of Kohath: Amminadab his son, Korah his son, Assir his son, 23Elkanah his son, Ebiasaph his son, Assir his son, 24Tahath his son, Uriel his son, Uzziah his son, and Shaul his son. 25The sons of Elkanah: Amasai and Ahimoth, 26Elkanah his son, Zophai his son, Nahath his son, 27Eliab his son, Jeroham his son, Elkanah his son. 28The sons of Samuel: Joelh his firstborn, the second Abijah.i 29The sons of Merari: Mahli, Libni his son, Shimei his son, Uzzah his son, 30Shimea his son, Haggiah his son, and Asaiah his son.

Musicians Appointed by David

31 These are the men whom David put in charge of the service of song in the house of the LORD, after the ark came to rest there. 32They ministered with song

---

e 6:4-15 *The oldest sons of the successive generations of Aaron were as follows,* implied.   f *6:16 As previously stated,* implied in 6:1.

g Ch 6.1 in Heb   h Gk Syr Compare verse 33 and 1 Sam 8.2: Heb lacks *Joel*
i Heb reads *Vashni, and Abijah* for *the second Abijah,* taking *the second* as a proper name

King James

32And they ministered before the dwellingplace of the tabernacle of the congregation with singing, until Solomon had built the house of the LORD in Jerusalem: and *then* they waited on their office according to their order.

33And these *are* they that waited with their children. Of the sons of the Kohathites: Heman a singer, the son of Joel, the son of Shemuel,

34The son of Elkanah, the son of Jeroham, the son of Eliel, the son of Toah,

35The son of Zuph, the son of Elkanah, the son of Mahath, the son of Amasai,

36The son of Elkanah, the son of Joel, the son of Azariah, the son of Zephaniah,

37The son of Tahath, the son of Assir, the son of Ebiasaph, the son of Korah,

38The son of Izhar, the son of Kohath, the son of Levi, the son of Israel.

39And his brother Asaph, who stood on his right hand, *even* Asaph the son of Berachiah, the son of Shimea,

40The son of Michael, the son of Baaseiah, the son of Malchiah,

41The son of Ethni, the son of Zerah, the son of Adaiah,

42The son of Ethan, the son of Zimmah, the son of Shimei,

43The son of Jahath, the son of Gershom, the son of Levi.

44And their brethren the sons of Merari *stood* on the left hand: Ethan the son of Kishi, the son of Abdi, the son of Malluch,

45The son of Hashabiah, the son of Amaziah, the son of Hilkiah,

46The son of Amzi, the son of Bani, the son of Shamer,

47The son of Mahli, the son of Mushi, the son of Merari, the son of Levi.

48Their brethren also the Levites *were* appointed unto all manner of service of the tabernacle of the house of God.

49¶ But Aaron and his sons offered upon the altar of the burnt offering, and on the altar of incense, *and were appointed* for all the work of the *place* most holy, and to make an atonement for Israel, according to all that Moses the servant of God had commanded.

50And these *are* the sons of Aaron; Eleazar his son, Phinehas his son, Abishua his son,

51Bukki his son, Uzzi his son, Zerahiah his son,

52Meraioth his son, Amariah his son, Ahitub his son,

53Zadok his son, Ahimaaz his son.

54¶ Now these *are* their dwelling places throughout their castles in their coasts, of the sons of Aaron, of the families of the Kohathites: for theirs was the lot.

55And they gave them Hebron in the land of Judah, and the suburbs thereof round about it.

56But the fields of the city, and the villages thereof, they gave to Caleb the son of Jephunneh.

57And to the sons of Aaron they gave the cities of Judah, *namely,* Hebron, *the city* of refuge, and Libnah with her suburbs, and Jattir, and Eshtemoa, with their suburbs,

58And Hilen with her suburbs, Debir with her suburbs,

59And Ashan with her suburbs, and Beth-shemesh with her suburbs:

New International

32They ministered with music before the tabernacle, the Tent of Meeting, until Solomon built the temple of the LORD in Jerusalem. They performed their duties according to the regulations laid down for them.

33Here are the men who served, together with their sons:

From the Kohathites:
Heman, the musician,
the son of Joel, the son of Samuel,
34the son of Elkanah, the son of Jeroham,
the son of Eliel, the son of Toah,
35the son of Zuph, the son of Elkanah,
the son of Mahath, the son of Amasai,
36the son of Elkanah, the son of Joel,
the son of Azariah, the son of Zephaniah,
37the son of Tahath, the son of Assir,
the son of Ebiasaph, the son of Korah,
38the son of Izhar, the son of Kohath,
the son of Levi, the son of Israel;

39and Heman's associate Asaph, who served at his right hand:
Asaph son of Berekiah, the son of Shimea,
40the son of Michael, the son of Baaseiah,[a]
the son of Malkijah, 41the son of Ethni,
the son of Zerah, the son of Adaiah,
42the son of Ethan, the son of Zimmah,
the son of Shimei, 43the son of Jahath,
the son of Gershon, the son of Levi;

44and from their associates, the Merarites, at his left hand:
Ethan son of Kishi, the son of Abdi,
the son of Malluch, 45the son of Hashabiah,
the son of Amaziah, the son of Hilkiah,
46the son of Amzi, the son of Bani,
the son of Shemer, 47the son of Mahli,
the son of Mushi, the son of Merari,
the son of Levi.

48Their fellow Levites were assigned to all the other duties of the tabernacle, the house of God. 49But Aaron and his descendants were the ones who presented offerings on the altar of burnt offering and on the altar of incense in connection with all that was done in the Most Holy Place, making atonement for Israel, in accordance with all that Moses the servant of God had commanded.

50These were the descendants of Aaron:
Eleazar his son, Phinehas his son,
Abishua his son, 51Bukki his son,
Uzzi his son, Zerahiah his son,
52Meraioth his son, Amariah his son,
Ahitub his son, 53Zadok his son
and Ahimaaz his son.

54These were the locations of their settlements allotted as their territory (they were assigned to the descendants of Aaron who were from the Kohathite clan, because the first lot was for them):

55They were given Hebron in Judah with its surrounding pasturelands. 56But the fields and villages around the city were given to Caleb son of Jephunneh.

57So the descendants of Aaron were given Hebron (a city of refuge), and Libnah,[b] Jattir, Eshtemoa, 58Hilen, Debir, 59Ashan, Juttah[c] and Beth Shemesh, together with their pasturelands. 60And

a *40* Most Hebrew manuscripts; some Hebrew manuscripts, one Septuagint manuscript and Syriac *Maaseiah*   b *57* See Joshua 21:13; Hebrew *given the cities of refuge: Hebron, Libnah.*   c *59* Syriac (see also Septuagint and Joshua 21:16); Hebrew does not have *Juttah.*

Living Bible

in it. 32Then, when Solomon built the Temple at Jerusalem, the choirs carried on their work there.

33-38These are the names and ancestriesd of choir leaders: Heman the Cantor was from the clan of Kohath; his genealogy was traced back through:

Joel, Samuel, Elkanah III, Jeroham, Eliel, Toah, Zuph, Elkanah II, Mahath, Amasai, Elkanah I, Joel, Azariah, Zephaniah, Tahath, Assir, Ebiasaph, Korah, Izhar, Kohath, Levi, Israel.

39-43Heman's assistant was his colleague Asaph, whose genealogy was traced back through:

Berechiah, Shime-a, Michael, Ba-aseiah, Malchijah, Ethni, Zerah, Adaiah, Ethan, Zimmah, Shime-i, Jahath, Gershom, Levi.

44-47Heman's second assistant was Ethan, a representative from the clan of Merari, who stood on his left. Merari's ancestry was traced back through:

Kishi, Abdi, Malluch, Hashabiah, Amaziah, Hilkiah, Amzi, Bani, Shemer, Mahli, Mushi, Merari, Levi.

48Their relatives—all the other Levites—were appointed to various other tasks in the Tabernacle. 49But only Aaron and his descendants were the priests. Their duties included sacrificing burnt offerings and incense, handling all the tasks relating to the inner sanctuary—the Holy of Holies—and the tasks relating to the annual Day of Atonement for Israel. They saw to it that all the details commanded by Moses the servant of God were strictly followed.

50-53The descendants of Aaron were:

Eleazar, Phinehas, Abishua, Bukki, Uzzi, Zerahiah, Meraioth, Amariah, Ahitub, Zadok, Ahima-az.

54This is a record of the cities and land assigned by lot to the descendants of Aaron, all of whom were members of the Kohath clan:

55, 56, 57Hebron and its surrounding pasturelands in Judah (although the fields and suburbs were given to Caleb the son of Jephunneh), 58, 59and the following Cities of Refuge with their surrounding pasturelands:

Libnah, Jattir, Eshtemoa, Hilen, Debir, Ashan, Beth-shemesh.

New Revised Standard

before the tabernacle of the tent of meeting, until Solomon had built the house of the LORD in Jerusalem; and they performed their service in due order. 33These are the men who served; and their sons were: Of the Kohathites: Heman, the singer, son of Joel, son of Samuel, 34son of Elkanah, son of Jeroham, son of Eliel, son of Toah, 35son of Zuph, son of Elkanah, son of Mahath, son of Amasai, 36son of Elkanah, son of Joel, son of Azariah, son of Zephaniah, 37son of Tahath, son of Assir, son of Ebiasaph, son of Korah, 38son of Izhar, son of Kohath, son of Levi, son of Israel; 39and his brother Asaph, who stood on his right, namely, Asaph son of Berechiah, son of Shimea, 40son of Michael, son of Baaseiah, son of Malchijah, 41son of Ethni, son of Zerah, son of Adaiah, 42son of Ethan, son of Zimmah, son of Shimei, 43son of Jahath, son of Gershom, son of Levi. 44On the left were their kindred the sons of Merari: Ethan son of Kishi, son of Abdi, son of Malluch, 45son of Hashabiah, son of Amaziah, son of Hilkiah, 46son of Amzi, son of Bani, son of Shemer, 47son of Mahli, son of Mushi, son of Merari, son of Levi; 48and their kindred the Levites were appointed for all the service of the tabernacle of the house of God.

49 But Aaron and his sons made offerings on the altar of burnt offering and on the altar of incense, doing all the work of the most holy place, to make atonement for Israel, according to all that Moses the servant of God had commanded. 50These are the sons of Aaron: Eleazar his son, Phinehas his son, Abishua his son, 51Bukki his son, Uzzi his son, Zerahiah his son, 52Meraioth his son, Amariah his son, Ahitub his son, 53Zadok his son, Ahimaaz his son.

Settlements of the Levites

54 These are their dwelling places according to their settlements within their borders: to the sons of Aaron of the families of Kohathites—for the lot fell to them first— 55to them they gave Hebron in the land of Judah and its surrounding pasture lands, 56but the fields of the city and its villages they gave to Caleb son of Jephunneh. 57To the sons of Aaron they gave the cities of refuge: Hebron, Libnah with its pasture lands, Jattir, Eshtemoa with its pasture lands, 58Hilenf with its pasture lands, Debir with its pasture lands, 59Ashan with its pasture lands, and Beth-shemesh with its pasture lands.

---

d 6:33-38 ancestries, implied. e 6:39-43 Heman's assistant, literally, "brother," or "kinsman."

f Other readings Hilez, Holon; See Josh 21.15

King James

⁶⁰And out of the tribe of Benjamin; Geba with her suburbs, and Alemeth with her suburbs, and Anathoth with her suburbs. All their cities throughout their families *were* thirteen cities.

⁶¹And unto the sons of Kohath, *which were* left of the family of that tribe, *were cities given* out of the half tribe, *namely, out of* the half *tribe* of Manasseh, by lot, ten cities.

⁶²And to the sons of Gershom throughout their families out of the tribe of Issachar, and out of the tribe of Asher, and out of the tribe of Naphtali, and out of the tribe of Manasseh in Bashan, thirteen cities.

⁶³Unto the sons of Merari *were given* by lot, throughout their families, out of the tribe of Reuben, and out of the tribe of Gad, and out of the tribe of Zebulun, twelve cities.

⁶⁴And the children of Israel gave to the Levites *these* cities with their suburbs.

⁶⁵And they gave by lot out of the tribe of the children of Judah, and out of the tribe of the children of Simeon, and out of the tribe of the children of Benjamin, these cities, which are called by *their* names.

⁶⁶And *the residue* of the families of the sons of Kohath had cities of their coasts out of the tribe of Ephraim.

⁶⁷And they gave unto them, *of* the cities of refuge, Shechem in mount Ephraim with her suburbs; *they gave* also Gezer with her suburbs,

⁶⁸And Jokmeam with her suburbs, and Beth-horon with her suburbs,

⁶⁹And Aijalon with her suburbs, and Gath-rimmon with her suburbs:

⁷⁰And out of the half tribe of Manasseh; Aner with her suburbs, and Bileam with her suburbs, for the family of the remnant of the sons of Kohath.

⁷¹Unto the sons of Gershom *were given* out of the family of the half tribe of Manasseh, Golan in Bashan with her suburbs, and Ashtaroth with her suburbs:

⁷²And out of the tribe of Issachar; Kedesh with her suburbs, Daberath with her suburbs,

⁷³And Ramoth with her suburbs, and Anem with her suburbs:

⁷⁴And out of the tribe of Asher; Mashal with her suburbs, and Abdon with her suburbs,

⁷⁵And Hukok with her suburbs, and Rehob with her suburbs:

⁷⁶And out of the tribe of Naphtali; Kedesh in Galilee with her suburbs, and Hammon with her suburbs, and Kirjathaim with her suburbs.

⁷⁷Unto the rest of the children of Merari *were given* out of the tribe of Zebulun, Rimmon with her suburbs, Tabor with her suburbs:

⁷⁸And on the other side Jordan by Jericho, on the east side of Jordan, *were given them* out of the tribe of Reuben, Bezer in the wilderness with her suburbs, and Jahzah with her suburbs,

⁷⁹Kedemoth also with her suburbs, and Mephaath with her suburbs:

⁸⁰And out of the tribe of Gad; Ramoth in Gilead with her suburbs, and Mahanaim with her suburbs,

⁸¹And Heshbon with her suburbs, and Jazer with her suburbs.

7 NOW THE sons of Issachar *were*, Tola, and Puah, Jashub, and Shimrom, four.

New International

from the tribe of Benjamin they were given Gibeon,ᵃ Geba, Alemeth and Anathoth, together with their pasturelands.

These towns, which were distributed among the Kohathite clans, were thirteen in all.

⁶¹The rest of Kohath's descendants were allotted ten towns from the clans of half the tribe of Manasseh.

⁶²The descendants of Gershon, clan by clan, were allotted thirteen towns from the tribes of Issachar, Asher and Naphtali, and from the part of the tribe of Manasseh that is in Bashan.

⁶³The descendants of Merari, clan by clan, were allotted twelve towns from the tribes of Reuben, Gad and Zebulun.

⁶⁴So the Israelites gave the Levites these towns and their pasturelands. ⁶⁵From the tribes of Judah, Simeon and Benjamin they allotted the previously named towns.

⁶⁶Some of the Kohathite clans were given as their territory towns from the tribe of Ephraim.

⁶⁷In the hill country of Ephraim they were given Shechem (a city of refuge), and Gezer,ᵇ ⁶⁸Jokmeam, Beth Horon, ⁶⁹Aijalon and Gath Rimmon, together with their pasturelands.

⁷⁰And from half the tribe of Manasseh the Israelites gave Aner and Bileam, together with their pasturelands, to the rest of the Kohathite clans.

⁷¹The Gershonites received the following:
From the clan of the half-tribe of Manasseh
    they received Golan in Bashan and also Ashtaroth, together with their pasturelands;
⁷²from the tribe of Issachar
    they received Kedesh, Daberath, ⁷³Ramoth and Anem, together with their pasturelands;
⁷⁴from the tribe of Asher
    they received Mashal, Abdon, ⁷⁵Hukok and Rehob, together with their pasturelands;
⁷⁶and from the tribe of Naphtali
    they received Kedesh in Galilee, Hammon and Kiriathaim, together with their pasturelands.

⁷⁷The Merarites (the rest of the Levites) received the following:
From the tribe of Zebulun
    they received Jokneam, Kartah,ᶜ Rimmono and Tabor, together with their pasturelands;
⁷⁸from the tribe of Reuben across the Jordan east of Jericho
    they received Bezer in the desert, Jahzah, ⁷⁹Kedemoth and Mephaath, together with their pasturelands;
⁸⁰and from the tribe of Gad
    they received Ramoth in Gilead, Mahanaim, ⁸¹Heshbon and Jazer, together with their pasturelands.

Issachar

7 THE SONS of Issachar:
    Tola, Puah, Jashub and Shimron—four in all.

ᵃ *60* See Joshua 21:17; Hebrew does not have *Gibeon*.   ᵇ *67* See Joshua 21:21; Hebrew *given the cities of refuge: Shechem, Gezer*.   ᶜ *77* See Septuagint and Joshua 21:34; Hebrew does not have *Jokneam, Kartah*.

Living Bible

60Thirteen other cities with surrounding pastures—including Geba, Alemeth, and Anathoth—were given to the priests by the tribe of Benjamin. 61Lots were then drawn to assign land to the remaining descendants of Kohath, and they received ten cities in the territory of the half-tribe of Manasseh.

62The subclans of the Gershom clan received by lot thirteen cities in the Bashan area from the tribes of Issachar, Asher, Naphtali, and Manasseh.

63The subclans of Merari received by lot twelve cities from the tribes of Reuben, Gad, and Zebulun.

64,65Cities and pasturelands were also assigned by lot to the Levites (and then renamed) from the tribes of Judah, Simeon, and Benjamin.

66-69The tribe of Ephraim gave these Cities of Refuge with the surrounding pasturelands to the subclans of Kohath:

Shechem, in Mount Ephraim; Gezer; Jokme-am; Beth-horon; Aijalon; Gath-rimmon.

70The following Cities of Refuge and their pasturelands were given to the subclans of the Kohathites by the half-tribe of Manasseh:

Aner, Bile-am.

71Cities of Refuge and pastureland given to the clan of Gershom by the half-tribe of Manasseh were:

Golan, in Bashan; Ashtaroth.

72The tribe of Issachar gave them Kedesh, Daberath, 73Ramoth, and Anem, and the surrounding pastureland of each.

74The tribe of Asher gave them Abdon, Mashal, 75Hukok, and Rehob, with their pasturelands.

76The tribe of Naphtali gave them Kedesh in Galilee, Hammon, and Kiriathaim with pasturelands.

77The tribe of Zebulun gave Rimmono and Tabor to the Merari clan as Cities of Refuge.

78,79And across the Jordan River, opposite Jericho, the tribe of Reuben gave them Bezer (a desert town), Jahzah, Kedemoth and Mepha-ath, along with their pasturelands.

80The tribe of Gad gave them Ramoth in Gilead, Mahanaim, 81Heshbon, and Jazer, each with their surrounding pasturelands.

New Revised Standard

60From the tribe of Benjamin, Geba with its pasture lands, Alemeth with its pasture lands, and Anathoth with its pasture lands. All their towns throughout their families were thirteen.

61 To the rest of the Kohathites were given by lot out of the family of the tribe, out of the half-tribe, the half of Manasseh, ten towns. 62To the Gershomites according to their families were allotted thirteen towns out of the tribes of Issachar, Asher, Naphtali, and Manasseh in Bashan. 63To the Merarites according to their families were allotted twelve towns out of the tribes of Reuben, Gad, and Zebulun. 64So the people of Israel gave the Levites the towns with their pasture lands. 65They also gave them by lot out of the tribes of Judah, Simeon, and Benjamin these towns that are mentioned by name.

66 And some of the families of the sons of Kohath had towns of their territory out of the tribe of Ephraim. 67They were given the cities of refuge: Shechem with its pasture lands in the hill country of Ephraim, Gezer with its pasture lands, 68Jokmeam with its pasture lands, Beth-horon with its pasture lands, 69Aijalon with its pasture lands, Gath-rimmon with its pasture lands; 70and out of the half-tribe of Manasseh, Aner with its pasture lands, and Bileam with its pasture lands, for the rest of the families of the Kohathites.

71 To the Gershomites: out of the half-tribe of Manasseh: Golan in Bashan with its pasture lands and Ashtaroth with its pasture lands; 72and out of the tribe of Issachar: Kedesh with its pasture lands, Daberathd with its pasture lands, 73Ramoth with its pasture lands, and Anem with its pasture lands; 74out of the tribe of Asher: Mashal with its pasture lands, Abdon with its pasture lands, 75Hukok with its pasture lands, and Rehob with its pasture lands; 76and out of the tribe of Naphtali: Kedesh in Galilee with its pasture lands, Hammon with its pasture lands, and Kiriathaim with its pasture lands. 77To the rest of the Merarites out of the tribe of Zebulun: Rimmono with its pasture lands, Tabor with its pasture lands, 78and across the Jordan from Jericho, on the east side of the Jordan, out of the tribe of Reuben: Bezer in the steppe with its pasture lands, Jahzah with its pasture lands, 79Kedemoth with its pasture lands, and Mephaath with its pasture lands; 80and out of the tribe of Gad: Ramoth in Gilead with its pasture lands, Mahanaim with its pasture lands, 81Heshbon with its pasture lands, and Jazer with its pasture lands.

7 THE SONS of Issachar: **Tola,** Puah, Jashub, Shimron.

Descendants of Issachar

7 THE SONSe of Issachar: Tola, Puah, Jashub, and Shimron, four. 2The sons of Tola: Uzzi, Repha-

d Or *Dobrath*   e Syr Compare Vg: Heb *And to the sons*

King James

²And the sons of Tola; Uzzi, and Rephaiah, and Jeriel, and Jahmai, and Jibsam, and Shemuel, heads of their father's house, *to wit*, of Tola: *they were* valiant men of might in their generations; whose number *was* in the days of David two and twenty thousand and six hundred.

³And the sons of Uzzi; Izrahiah: and the sons of Izrahiah; Michael and Obadiah, and Joel, Ishiah, five: all of them chief men.

⁴And with them, by their generations, after the house of their fathers, *were* bands of soldiers for war, six and thirty thousand *men:* for they had many wives and sons.

⁵And their brethren among all the families of Issachar *were* valiant men of might, reckoned in all by their genealogies fourscore and seven thousand.

⁶¶ *The sons* of Benjamin: Bela, and Becher, and Jediael, three.

⁷And the sons of Bela; Ezbon, and Uzzi, and Uzziel, and Jerimoth, and Iri, five; heads of the house of *their* fathers, mighty men of valour; and were reckoned by their genealogies twenty and two thousand and thirty and four.

⁸And the sons of Becher; Zemira, and Joash, and Eliezer, and Elioenai, and Omri, and Jerimoth, and Abiah, and Anathoth, and Alameth. All these *are* the sons of Becher.

⁹And the number of them, after their genealogy by their generations, heads of the house of their fathers, mighty men of valour, *was* twenty thousand and two hundred.

¹⁰The sons also of Jediael; Bilhan: and the sons of Bilhan; Jeush, and Benjamin, and Ehud, and Chenaanah, and Zethan, and Tharshish, and Ahishahar.

¹¹All these the sons of Jediael, by the heads of their fathers, mighty men of valour, *were* seventeen thousand and two hundred *soldiers*, fit to go out for war *and* battle.

¹²Shuppim also, and Huppim, the children of Ir, *and* Hushim, the sons of Aher.

¹³¶ The sons of Naphtali; Jahziel, and Guni, and Jezer, and Shallum, the sons of Bilhah.

¹⁴¶ The sons of Manasseh; Ashriel, whom she bare: (*but* his concubine the Aramitess bare Machir the father of Gilead:

¹⁵And Machir took to wife *the sister* of Huppim and Shuppim, whose sister's name *was* Maachah;) and the name of the second *was* Zelophehad: and Zelophehad had daughters.

¹⁶And Maachah the wife of Machir bare a son, and she called his name Peresh; and the name of his brother *was* Sheresh; and his sons *were* Ulam and Rakem.

¹⁷And the sons of Ulam; Bedan. These *were* the sons of Gilead, the son of Machir, the son of Manasseh.

¹⁸And his sister Hammoleketh bare Ishod, and Abiezer, and Mahalah.

¹⁹And the sons of Shemidah were, Ahian, and Shechem, and Likhi, and Aniam.

New International

²The sons of Tola:
   Uzzi, Rephaiah, Jeriel, Jahmai, Ibsam and Samuel—heads of their families. During the reign of David, the descendants of Tola listed as fighting men in their genealogy numbered 22,600.

³The son of Uzzi:
   Izrahiah.
The sons of Izrahiah:
   Michael, Obadiah, Joel and Isshiah. All five of them were chiefs. ⁴According to their family genealogy, they had 36,000 men ready for battle, for they had many wives and children.

⁵The relatives who were fighting men belonging to all the clans of Issachar, as listed in their genealogy, were 87,000 in all.

Benjamin

⁶Three sons of Benjamin:
   Bela, Beker and Jediael.

⁷The sons of Bela:
   Ezbon, Uzzi, Uzziel, Jerimoth and Iri, heads of families—five in all. Their genealogical record listed 22,034 fighting men.

⁸The sons of Beker:
   Zemirah, Joash, Eliezer, Elioenai, Omri, Jeremoth, Abijah, Anathoth and Alemeth. All these were the sons of Beker. ⁹Their genealogical record listed the heads of families and 20,200 fighting men.

¹⁰The son of Jediael:
   Bilhan.
The sons of Bilhan:
   Jeush, Benjamin, Ehud, Kenaanah, Zethan, Tarshish and Ahishahar. ¹¹All these sons of Jediael were heads of families. There were 17,200 fighting men ready to go out to war.

¹²The Shuppites and Huppites were the descendants of Ir, and the Hushites the descendants of Aher.

Naphtali

¹³The sons of Naphtali:
   Jahziel, Guni, Jezer and Shillemᵃ—the descendants of Bilhah.

Manasseh

¹⁴The descendants of Manasseh:
   Asriel was his descendant through his Aramean concubine. She gave birth to Makir the father of Gilead. ¹⁵Makir took a wife from among the Huppites and Shuppites. His sister's name was Maacah.
   Another descendant was named Zelophehad, who had only daughters.
   ¹⁶Makir's wife Maacah gave birth to a son and named him Peresh. His brother was named Sheresh, and his sons were Ulam and Rakem.

¹⁷The son of Ulam:
   Bedan.
These were the sons of Gilead son of Makir, the son of Manasseh. ¹⁸His sister Hammoleketh gave birth to Ishhod, Abiezer and Mahlah.

¹⁹The sons of Shemida were:
   Ahian, Shechem, Likhi and Aniam.

ᵃ *13* Some Hebrew and Septuagint manuscripts (see also Gen. 46:24 and Num. 26:49); most Hebrew manuscripts *Shallum*

Living Bible

2The sons of *Tola,* each of whom was the head of a subclan:

Uzzi, Rephaiah, Jeri-el, Jahmai, Ibsam, Shemuel.

At the time of King David, the total number of men of war from these families totaled 22,600.

3*Uzzi's* son was Izrahiah among whose five sons were Michael, Obadiah, Joel, and Isshiah, all chiefs of subclans. 4Their descendants, at the time of King David, numbered 36,000 troops; for all five of them had several wives and many sons. 5The total number of men available for military service from all the clans of the tribe of Issachar numbered 87,000 stouthearted warriors, all included in the official genealogy.

6The sons of Benjamin were:

Bela, Becher, Jedia-el.

7The sons of *Bela:*

Ezbon, Uzzi, Uzziel, Jerimoth, Iri.

These five mighty warriors were chiefs of subclans and were the leaders of 22,034 troops (all of whom were recorded in the official genealogies).

8The sons of *Becher* were: Zemirah, Joash, Eliezer, Eli-o-enai, Omri, Jeremoth, Abijah, Anathoth, Alemeth.

9At the time of David there were 22,200 mighty warriors among their descendants; and they were led by their clan chiefs.

10The son of *Jedia-el* was **Bilhan.**

The sons of *Bilhan* were:

Jeush, Benjamin, Ehud, Chenaanah, Zethan, Tarshish, Ahishahar.

11They were the chiefs of the subclans of *Jedia-el,* and their descendants included 17,200 warriors at the time of King David.

12The sons of Ir were Shuppim and Huppim. Hushim was one of the sons of Aher.

13The sons of Naphtali (descendants of Jacob's wife[b] Bilhah) were:

Jahzi-el, Guni, Jezer, Shallum.

14The sons of Manasseh, born to his Aramaean concubine, were Asri-el and Machir (who became the father of Gilead).

15It was Machir who found wives for Huppim and Shuppim.[c] Machir's sister was Maacah. Another descendant was Zelophehad, who had only[d] daughters.

16Machir's wife, also named Maacah, bore him a son whom she named Peresh; his brother's name was Sheresh, and he had sons named Ulam and Rakem.

17Ulam's son was Bedan. So these were the sons of Gilead, the grandsons of Machir, and the great-grandsons of Manasseh.

18Hammolecheth, Machir's sister, bore Ishhod, Abiezer, and Mahlah.

19The sons of Shemida were Ahian, Shechem, Likhi, and Aniam.

New Revised Standard

iah, Jeriel, Jahmai, Ibsam, and Shemuel, heads of their ancestral houses, namely of Tola, mighty warriors of their generations, their number in the days of David being twenty-two thousand six hundred. 3The son[e] of Uzzi: Izrahiah. And the sons of Izrahiah: Michael, Obadiah, Joel, and Isshiah, five, all of them chiefs; 4and along with them, by their generations, according to their ancestral houses, were units of the fighting force, thirty-six thousand, for they had many wives and sons. 5Their kindred belonging to all the families of Issachar were in all eighty-seven thousand mighty warriors, enrolled by genealogy.

Descendants of Benjamin

6 The sons of Benjamin: Bela, Becher, and Jediael, three. 7The sons of Bela: Ezbon, Uzzi, Uzziel, Jerimoth, and Iri, five, heads of ancestral houses, mighty warriors; and their enrollment by genealogies was twenty-two thousand thirty-four. 8The sons of Becher: Zemirah, Joash, Eliezer, Elioenai, Omri, Jeremoth, Abijah, Anathoth, and Alemeth. All these were the sons of Becher; 9and their enrollment by genealogies, according to their generations, as heads of their ancestral houses, mighty warriors, was twenty thousand two hundred. 10The sons of Jediael: Bilhan. And the sons of Bilhan: Jeush, Benjamin, Ehud, Chenaanah, Zethan, Tarshish, and Ahishahar. 11All these were the sons of Jediael according to the heads of their ancestral houses, mighty warriors, seventeen thousand two hundred, ready for service in war. 12And Shuppim and Huppim were the sons of Ir, Hushim the son[e] of Aher.

Descendants of Naphtali

13 The descendants of Naphtali: Jahziel, Guni, Jezer, and Shallum, the descendants of Bilhah.

Descendants of Manasseh

14 The sons of Manasseh: Asriel, whom his Aramean concubine bore; she bore Machir the father of Gilead. 15And Machir took a wife for Huppim and for Shuppim. The name of his sister was Maacah. And the name of the second was Zelophehad; and Zelophehad had daughters. 16Maacah the wife of Machir bore a son, and she named him Peresh; the name of his brother was Sheresh; and his sons were Ulam and Rekem. 17The son[e] of Ulam: Bedan. These were the sons of Gilead son of Machir, son of Manasseh. 18And his sister Hammolecheth bore Ishhod, Abiezer, and Mahlah. 19The sons of Shemida were Ahian, Shechem, Likhi, and Aniam.

---

b *7:13 Jacob's wife,* implied.   c *7:15 Huppim and Shuppim,* see vs 12.
d *7:15 only daughters,* implied. See Numbers 26:33.   e Heb *sons*

King James

20¶ And the sons of Ephraim; Shuthelah, and Bered his son, and Tahath his son, and Eladah his son, and Tahath his son,

21¶ And Zabad his son, and Shuthelah his son, and Ezer, and Elead, whom the men of Gath *that were* born in *that* land slew, because they came down to take away their cattle.

22And Ephraim their father mourned many days, and his brethren came to comfort him.

23¶ And when he went in to his wife, she conceived, and bare a son, and he called his name Beriah, because it went evil with his house.

24(And his daughter *was* Sherah, who built Beth-horon the nether, and the upper, and Uzzen-sherah.)

25And Rephah *was* his son, also Resheph, and Telah his son, and Tahan his son,

26Laadan his son, Ammihud his son, Elishama his son,

27Non his son, Jehoshuah his son.

28¶ And their possessions and habitations *were,* Bethel and the towns thereof, and eastward Naaran, and westward Gezer, with the towns thereof; Shechem also and the towns thereof, unto Gaza and the towns thereof:

29And by the borders of the children of Manasseh, Beth-shean and her towns, Taanach and her towns, Megiddo and her towns, Dor and her towns. In these dwelt the children of Joseph the son of Israel.

30¶ The sons of Asher; Imnah, and Isuah, and Ishuai, and Beriah, and Serah their sister.

31And the sons of Beriah; Heber, and Malchiel, who *is* the father of Birzavith.

32And Heber begat Japhlet, and Shomer, and Hotham, and Shua their sister.

33And the sons of Japhlet; Pasach, and Bimhal, and Ashvath. These *are* the children of Japhlet.

34And the sons of Shamer; Ahi, and Rohgah, Jehubbah, and Aram.

35And the sons of his brother Helem; Zophah, and Imna, and Shelesh, and Amal.

36The sons of Zophah; Suah, and Harnepher, and Shual, and Beri, and Imrah,

37Bezer, and Hod, and Shamma, and Shilshah, and Ithran, and Beera.

38And the sons of Jether; Jephunneh, and Pispah, and Ara.

39And the sons of Ulla; Arah, and Haniel, and Rezia.

40All these *were* the children of Asher, heads of *their* father's house, choice *and* mighty men of valour, chief of the princes. And the number throughout the genealogy of them that were apt to the war *and* to battle *was* twenty and six thousand men.

8 NOW BENJAMIN begat Bela his firstborn, Ashbel the second, and Aharah the third,

2Nohah the fourth, and Rapha the fifth.

3And the sons of Bela were, Addar, and Gera, and Abihud,

4And Abishua, and Naaman, and Ahoah,

5And Gera, and Shephuphan, and Huram.

New International

Ephraim

20The descendants of Ephraim:

Shuthelah, Bered his son,
Tahath his son, Eleadah his son,
Tahath his son, 21Zabad his son
and Shuthelah his son.

Ezer and Elead were killed by the native-born men of Gath, when they went down to seize their livestock. 22Their father Ephraim mourned for them many days, and his relatives came to comfort him. 23Then he lay with his wife again, and she became pregnant and gave birth to a son. He named him Beriah,a because there had been misfortune in his family. 24His daughter was Sheerah, who built Lower and Upper Beth Horon as well as Uzzen Sheerah.

25Rephah was his son, Resheph his son,b
Telah his son, Tahan his son,
26Ladan his son, Ammihud his son,
Elishama his son, 27Nun his son
and Joshua his son.

28Their lands and settlements included Bethel and its surrounding villages, Naaran to the east, Gezer and its villages to the west, and Shechem and its villages all the way to Ayyah and its villages. 29Along the borders of Manasseh were Beth Shan, Taanach, Megiddo and Dor, together with their villages. The descendants of Joseph son of Israel lived in these towns.

Asher

30The sons of Asher:

Imnah, Ishvah, Ishvi and Beriah. Their sister was Serah.

31The sons of Beriah:

Heber and Malkiel, who was the father of Birzaith.

32Heber was the father of Japhlet, Shomer and Hotham and of their sister Shua.

33The sons of Japhlet:

Pasach, Bimhal and Ashvath.
These were Japhlet's sons.

34The sons of Shomer:

Ahi, Rohgah,c Hubbah and Aram.

35The sons of his brother Helem:

Zophah, Imna, Shelesh and Amal.

36The sons of Zophah:

Suah, Harnepher, Shual, Beri, Imrah, 37Bezer, Hod, Shamma, Shilshah, Ithrand and Beera.

38The sons of Jether:

Jephunneh, Pispah and Ara.

39The sons of Ulla:

Arah, Hanniel and Rizia.

40All these were descendants of Asher—heads of families, choice men, brave warriors and outstanding leaders. The number of men ready for battle, as listed in their genealogy, was 26,000.

The Genealogy of Saul the Benjamite

8 BENJAMIN WAS the father of Bela his firstborn, Ashbel the second, Aharah the third,

2Nohah the fourth and Rapha the fifth.

3The sons of Bela were:

Addar, Gera, Abihud,e 4Abishua, Naaman, Ahoah, 5Gera, Shephuphan and Huram.

---

a 23 *Beriah* sounds like the Hebrew for *misfortune.*　　b 25 Some Septuagint manuscripts; Hebrew does not have *his son.*　　c 34 Or *of his brother Shomer: Rohgah*　　d 37 Possibly a variant of *Jether*　　e 3 Or *Gera the father of Ehud*

Living Bible

20, 21The sons of Ephraim:
Shuthelah, Bered, Tahath, Eleadah, Tahath, Zabad,
Shuthelah, **Ezer, Ele-ad.**
Ele-ad and *Ezer* attempted to rustle cattle at Gath, but they were killed by the local farmers. 22Their father Ephraim mourned for them a long time, and his brothers tried to comfort him. 23Afterwards, his wife conceived and bore a son whom he called Beriah (meaning "a tragedy") because of what had happened.

24Ephraim's daughter's name was Sheerah. She built Lower and Upper Beth-horon and Uzzen-sheerah.

25, 26, 27This is Ephraim's line of descent:
Rephah, the father of
Resheph, the father of
Telah, the father of
Tahan, the father of
Ladan, the father of
Ammihud, the father of
Elishama, the father of
Nun, the father of
Joshua.

28They lived in an area bounded on one side by Bethel and its surrounding towns, on the east by Naaran, on the west by Gezer and its villages, and finally by Shechem and its surrounding villages as far as Ayyah and its towns.

29The tribe of Manasseh, descendants of Joseph the son of Israel, controlled the following cities and their surrounding areas: Beth-shean, Taanach, Megiddo, and Dor.

30The children of Asher:
Imnah, Ishvah, Ishvi, **Beriah,** Serah (their sister).

31The sons of *Beriah* were:
Heber, Malchi-el (the father of Birzaith).

32*Heber's* children were:
Japhlet, Shomer, Hotham, Shua (their sister).

33*Japhlet's* sons were:
Pasach, Bimhal, Ashvath.

34His brother *Shomer's*f sons were:
Rohgah, Jehubbah, Aram.

35The sons of his brother *Hotham*g were:
Zophah, Imna, Shelesh, Amal.

36, 37The sons of *Zophah* were:
Suah, Harnepher, Shual, Beri, Imrah, Bezer, Hod, Shamma, Shilshah, **Ithran,** Be-era.

38The sons of *Ithran*h were:
Jephunneh, Pispa, Ara.

39The sons of Ulla were:
Arah, Hanniel, Rizia.

40These descendants of Asher were heads of subclans and were all skilled warriors and chiefs. Their descendants in the official genealogy numbered 36,000 men of war.

8 THE SONS of Benjamin, according to age, were:
Bela, the first,
Ashbel, the second,
Aharah, the third,
Nohah, the fourth,
Rapha, the fifth.

3, 4, 5The sons of *Bela* were:
Addar, Gera, Abihud, Abishua, Naaman, Ahoah,
Gera, Shephuphan, Huram.

New Revised Standard

Descendants of Ephraim

20 The sons of Ephraim: Shuthelah, and Bered his son, Tahath his son, Eleadah his son, Tahath his son, 21Zabad his son, Shuthelah his son, and Ezer and Elead. Now the people of Gath, who were born in the land, killed them, because they came down to raid their cattle. 22And their father Ephraim mourned many days, and his brothers came to comfort him. 23Ephraimi went in to his wife, and she conceived and bore a son; and he named him Beriah, because disasterj had befallen his house. 24His daughter was Sheerah, who built both Lower and Upper Beth-horon, and Uzzen-sheerah. 25Rephah was his son, Resheph his son, Telah his son, Tahan his son, 26Ladan his son, Ammihud his son, Elishama his son, 27Nunk his son, Joshua his son. 28Their possessions and settlements were Bethel and its towns, and eastward Naaran, and westward Gezer and its towns, Shechem and its towns, as far as Ayyah and its towns; 29also along the borders of the Manassites, Beth-shean and its towns, Taanach and its towns, Megiddo and its towns, Dor and its towns. In these lived the sons of Joseph son of Israel.

Descendants of Asher

30 The sons of Asher: Imnah, Ishvah, Ishvi, Beriah, and their sister Serah. 31The sons of Beriah: Heber and Malchiel, who was the father of Birzaith. 32Heber became the father of Japhlet, Shomer, Hotham, and their sister Shua. 33The sons of Japhlet: Pasach, Bimhal, and Ashvath. These are the sons of Japhlet. 34The sons of Shemer: Ahi, Rohgah, Hubbah, and Aram. 35The sons of Heleml his brother: Zophah, Imna, Shelesh, and Amal. 36The sons of Zophah: Suah, Harnepher, Shual, Beri, Imrah, 37Bezer, Hod, Shamma, Shilshah, Ithran, and Beera. 38The sons of Jether: Jephunneh, Pispa, and Ara. 39The sons of Ulla: Arah, Hanniel, and Rizia. 40All of these were men of Asher, heads of ancestral houses, select mighty warriors, chief of the princes. Their number enrolled by genealogies, for service in war, was twenty-six thousand men.

Descendants of Benjamin

8 BENJAMIN BECAME the father of Bela his first-born, Ashbel the second, Aharah the third, 2Nohah the fourth, and Rapha the fifth. 3And Bela had sons: Addar, Gera, Abihud,m 4Abishua, Naaman, Ahoah, 5Gera, Shephuphan, and Huram. 6These are the sons of

---

f 7:34 *Shomer's,* or "Shemer's." g 7:35 *Hotham,* literally, "Helem."
h 7:38 *Ithran,* literally, "Jether."

i Heb *He* j Heb *beraah* k Here spelled *Non;* see Ex 33.11 l Or *Hotham;* see 7.32 m Or *father of Ehud;* see 8.6

King James

6And these *are* the sons of Ehud: these are the heads of the fathers of the inhabitants of Geba, and they removed them to Manahath:

7And Naaman, and Ahiah, and Gera, he removed them, and begat Uzza, and Ahihud.

8And Shaharaim begat *children* in the country of Moab, after he had sent them away; Hushim and Baara *were* his wives.

9And he begat of Hodesh his wife, Jobab, and Zibia, and Mesha, and Malcham,

10And Jeuz, and Shachia, and Mirma. These *were* his sons, heads of the fathers.

11And of Hushim he begat Abitub, and Elpaal.

12The sons of Elpaal; Eber, and Misham, and Shamed, who built Ono, and Lod, with the towns thereof:

13Beriah also, and Shema, who *were* heads of the fathers of the inhabitants of Aijalon, who drove away the inhabitants of Gath:

14And Ahio, Shashak, and Jeremoth,

15And Zebadiah, and Arad, and Ader,

16And Michael, and Ispah, and Joha, the sons of Beriah;

17And Zebadiah, and Meshullam, and Hezeki, and Heber,

18Ishmerai also, and Jezliah, and Jobab, the sons of Elpaal;

19And Jakim, and Zichri, and Zabdi,

20And Elienai, and Zilthai, and Eliel,

21And Adaiah, and Beraiah, and Shimrath, the sons of Shimhi;

22And Ishpan, and Heber, and Eliel,

23And Abdon, and Zichri, and Hanan,

24And Hananiah, and Elam, and Antothijah,

25And Iphedeiah, and Penuel, the sons of Shashak;

26And Shamsherai, and Shehariah, and Athaliah,

27And Jaresiah, and Eliah, and Zichri, the sons of Jeroham.

28These *were* heads of the fathers, by their generations, chief *men*. These dwelt in Jerusalem.

29And at Gibeon dwelt the father of Gibeon; whose wife's name *was* Maachah:

30And his firstborn son Abdon, and Zur, and Kish, and Baal, and Nadab,

31And Gedor, and Ahio, and Zacher.

32And Mikloth begat Shimeah. And these also dwelt with their brethren in Jerusalem, over against them.

33¶ And Ner begat Kish, and Kish begat Saul, and Saul begat Jonathan, and Malchi-shua, and Abinadab, and Esh-baal.

34And the son of Jonathan *was* Merib-baal; and Merib-baal begat Micah.

35And the sons of Micah *were*, Pithon, and Melech, and Tarea, and Ahaz.

36And Ahaz begat Jehoadah; and Jehoadah begat Alemeth, and Azmaveth, and Zimri; and Zimri begat Moza,

37And Moza begat Binea: Rapha *was* his son, Eleasah his son, Azel his son:

38And Azel had six sons, whose names *are* these, Azrikam, Bocheru, and Ishmael, and Sheariah, and Obadiah, and Hanan. All these *were* the sons of Azel.

39And the sons of Eshek his brother *were*, Ulam his firstborn, Jehush the second, and Eliphelet the third.

40And the sons of Ulam were mighty men of valour, archers, and had many sons, and sons' sons, an hundred and fifty. All these *are* of the sons of Benjamin.

New International

6These were the descendants of Ehud, who were heads of families of those living in Geba and were deported to Manahath:

7Naaman, Ahijah, and Gera, who deported them and who was the father of Uzza and Ahihud.

8Sons were born to Shaharaim in Moab after he had divorced his wives Hushim and Baara. 9By his wife Hodesh he had Jobab, Zibia, Mesha, Malcam, 10Jeuz, Sakia and Mirmah. These were his sons, heads of families. 11By Hushim he had Abitub and Elpaal.

12The sons of Elpaal:
Eber, Misham, Shemed (who built Ono and Lod with its surrounding villages), 13and Beriah and Shema, who were heads of families of those living in Aijalon and who drove out the inhabitants of Gath.

14Ahio, Shashak, Jeremoth, 15Zebadiah, Arad, Eder, 16Michael, Ishpah and Joha were the sons of Beriah.

17Zebadiah, Meshullam, Hizki, Heber, 18Ishmerai, Izliah and Jobab were the sons of Elpaal.

19Jakim, Zicri, Zabdi, 20Elienai, Zillethai, Eliel, 21Adaiah, Beraiah and Shimrath were the sons of Shimei.

22Ishpan, Eber, Eliel, 23Abdon, Zicri, Hanan, 24Hananiah, Elam, Anthothijah, 25Iphdeiah and Penuel were the sons of Shashak.

26Shamsherai, Shehariah, Athaliah, 27Jaareshiah, Elijah and Zicri were the sons of Jeroham.

28All these were heads of families, chiefs as listed in their genealogy, and they lived in Jerusalem.

29Jeiel[a] the father[b] of Gibeon lived in Gibeon.
His wife's name was Maacah, 30and his firstborn son was Abdon, followed by Zur, Kish, Baal, Ner,[c] Nadab, 31Gedor, Ahio, Zeker 32and Mikloth, who was the father of Shimeah. They too lived near their relatives in Jerusalem.

33Ner was the father of Kish, Kish the father of Saul, and Saul the father of Jonathan, Malki-Shua, Abinadab and Esh-Baal.[d]

34The son of Jonathan:
Merib-Baal,[e] who was the father of Micah.

35The sons of Micah:
Pithon, Melech, Tarea and Ahaz.

36Ahaz was the father of Jehoaddah, Jehoaddah was the father of Alemeth, Azmaveth and Zimri, and Zimri was the father of Moza. 37Moza was the father of Binea; Raphah was his son, Eleasah his son and Azel his son.

38Azel had six sons, and these were their names:
Azrikam, Bokeru, Ishmael, Sheariah, Obadiah and Hanan. All these were the sons of Azel.

39The sons of his brother Eshek:
Ulam his firstborn, Jeush the second son and Eliphelet the third. 40The sons of Ulam were brave warriors who could handle the bow. They had many sons and grandsons—150 in all.
All these were the descendants of Benjamin.

---

a 29 Some Septuagint manuscripts (see also 1 Chron. 9:35); Hebrew does not have *Jeiel*.   b 29 *Father* may mean *civic leader* or *military leader*.   c 30 Some Septuagint manuscripts (see also 1 Chron. 9:36); Hebrew does not have *Ner*.   d 33 Also known as *Ish-Bosheth*   e 34 Also known as *Mephibosheth*

Living Bible

6, 7The sons of Ehud, chiefs of the subclans living at Geba, were captured in war and exiled to Manahath. They were:

Naaman, Ahijah, Gera (also called Heglam), the father of Uzza and Ahihud.

8, 9, 10Shaharaim divorced his wives **Hushim** and Baara, but he had children in the land of Moab by Hodesh, his new wife:

Jobab, Zibia, Mesha, Malcam, Jeuz, Sachia, Mirmah.

These sons all became chiefs of subclans.

11His wife *Hushim* had borne him Abitub and **Elpaal.**

12The sons of *Elpaal* were:

Eber, Misham, Shemed (who built Ono and Lod and their surrounding villages).

13His other sons were **Beriah** and Shema, chiefs of subclans living in Aijalon; they chased out the inhabitants of Gath.

14*Elpaal's* sons also included:

Ahio, **Shashak,** Jeremoth.

15, 16The sons of *Beriah* were:

Zebadiah, Arad, Eder, Michael, Ishpah, Joha.

17, 18The sons of *Elpaal* also included:

Zebadiah, Meshullam, Hizki, Heber, Ishmerai, Izliah, Jobab.

19, 20, 21The sons of Shime-i were:

Jakim, Zichri, Zabdi, Eli-enai, Zille-thai, Eliel, Adaiah, Beraiah, Shimrath.

22-25The sons of *Shashak* were:

Ishpan, Eber, Eliel, Abdon, Zichri, Hanan, Hananiah, Elam, Anthothijah, Iphdeiah, Penuel.

26, 27The sons of Jeroham were:

Shamsherai, Shehariah, Athaliah, Jaareshiah, Elijah, Zichri.

28These were the chiefs of the subclans living at Jerusalem.

29Je-iel, the father of Gibeon, lived at Gibeon; and his wife's name was Maacah. 30, 31, 32His oldest son was named Abdon, followed by:

Zur, Kish, Baal, Nadab, Gedor, Ahio, Zecher, Mikloth who was the father of Shimeah.

All of these families lived together near Jerusalem.

33Ner was the father of Kish, and Kish was the father of Saul;

Saul's sons included:

Jonathan, Malchishua, Abinadab, Eshbaal.

34The son of *Jonathan* was Mephibosheth;f

The son of Mephiboshethf was Micah.

35The sons of Micah:

Pithon, Melech, Tarea, Ahaz.

36Ahaz was the father of Jehoaddah, Jehoaddah was the father of:

Alemeth, Azmaveth, Zimri.

Zimri's son was Moza.

37Moza was the father of Bine-a, whose sons were:

Raphah, Eleasah, Azel.

38Azel had six sons:

Azrikam, Bocheru, Ishmael, She-ariah, Obadiah, Hanan.

39Azel's brother Eshek had three sons:

Ulam, the first, Jeush, the second, Eliphelet, the third.

40*Ulam's* sons were prominent warriors who were expert marksmen with their bows. These men had 150 sons and grandsons, and they were all from the tribe of Benjamin.

New Revised Standard

Ehud (they were heads of ancestral houses of the inhabitants of Geba, and they were carried into exile to Manahath): 7Naaman,g Ahijah, and Gera, that is, Heglam,h who became the father of Uzza and Ahihud. 8And Shaharaim had sons in the country of Moab after he had sent away his wives Hushim and Baara. 9He had sons by his wife Hodesh: Jobab, Zibia, Mesha, Malcam, 10Jeuz, Sachia, and Mirmah. These were his sons, heads of ancestral houses. 11He also had sons by Hushim: Abitub and Elpaal. 12The sons of Elpaal: Eber, Misham, and Shemed, who built Ono and Lod with its towns, 13and Beriah and Shema (they were heads of ancestral houses of the inhabitants of Aijalon, who put to flight the inhabitants of Gath); 14and Ahio, Shashak, and Jeremoth. 15Zebadiah, Arad, Eder, 16Michael, Ishpah, and Joha were sons of Beriah. 17Zebadiah, Meshullam, Hizki, Heber, 18Ishmerai, Izliah, and Jobab were the sons of Elpaal. 19Jakim, Zichri, Zabdi, 20Elienai, Zillethai, Eliel, 21Adaiah, Beraiah, and Shimrath were the sons of Shimei. 22Ishpan, Eber, Eliel, 23Abdon, Zichri, Hanan, 24Hananiah, Elam, Anthothijah, 25Iphdeiah, and Penuel were the sons of Shashak. 26Shamsherai, Shehariah, Athaliah, 27Jaareshiah, Elijah, and Zichri were the sons of Jeroham. 28These were the heads of ancestral houses, according to their generations, chiefs. These lived in Jerusalem.

29 Jeieli the father of Gibeon lived in Gibeon, and the name of his wife was Maacah. 30His firstborn son: Abdon, then Zur, Kish, Baal,j Nadab, 31Gedor, Ahio, Zecher, 32and Mikloth, who became the father of Shimeah. Now these also lived opposite their kindred in Jerusalem, with their kindred. 33Ner became the father of Kish, Kish of Saul,k Saulk of Jonathan, Malchishua, Abinadab, and Esh-baal; 34and the son of Jonathan was Merib-baal; and Merib-baal became the father of Micah. 35The sons of Micah: Pithon, Melech, Tarea, and Ahaz. 36Ahaz became the father of Jehoaddah; and Jehoaddah became the father of Alemeth, Azmaveth, and Zimri; Zimri became the father of Moza. 37Moza became the father of Binea; Raphah was his son, Eleasah his son, Azel his son. 38Azel had six sons, and these are their names: Azrikam, Bocheru, Ishmael, Sheariah, Obadiah, and Hanan; all these were the sons of Azel. 39The sons of his brother Eshek: Ulam his firstborn, Jeush the second, and Eliphelet the third. 40The sons of Ulam were mighty warriors, archers, having many children and grandchildren, one hundred fifty. All these were Benjaminites.

---

f 8:34 Mephibosheth, or "Merib-baal."

g Heb and Naaman   h Or he carried them into exile   i Compare 9.35: Heb lacks Jeiel   j Gk Ms adds Ner; Compare 8.33 and 9.36   k Or Shaul

King James

9 SO ALL Israel were reckoned by genealogies; and, behold, they *were* written in the book of the kings of Israel and Judah, *who* were carried away to Babylon for their transgression.

2¶ Now the first inhabitants that *dwelt* in their possessions in their cities *were*, the Israelites, the priests, Levites, and the Nethinims.

3And in Jerusalem dwelt of the children of Judah, and of the children of Benjamin, and of the children of Ephraim, and Manasseh;

4Uthai the son of Ammihud, the son of Omri, the son of Imri, the son of Bani, of the children of Pharez the son of Judah.

5And of the Shilonites; Asaiah the firstborn, and his sons.

6And of the sons of Zerah; Jeuel, and their brethren, six hundred and ninety.

7And of the sons of Benjamin; Sallu the son of Meshullam, the son of Hodaviah, the son of Hasenuah,

8And Ibneiah the son of Jeroham, and Elah the son of Uzzi, the son of Michri, and Meshullam the son of Shephathiah, the son of Reuel, the son of Ibnijah;

9And their brethren, according to their generations, nine hundred and fifty and six. All these men *were* chief of the fathers in the house of their fathers.

10¶ And of the priests; Jedaiah, and Jehoiarib, and Jachin,

11And Azariah the son of Hilkiah, the son of Meshullam, the son of Zadok, the son of Meraioth, the son of Ahitub, the ruler of the house of God;

12And Adaiah the son of Jeroham, the son of Pashur, the son of Malchijah, and Maasiai the son of Adiel, the son of Jahzerah, the son of Meshullam, the son of Meshillemith, the son of Immer;

13And their brethren, heads of the house of their fathers, a thousand and seven hundred and threescore; very able men for the work of the service of the house of God.

14And of the Levites; Shemaiah the son of Hasshub, the son of Azrikam, the son of Hashabiah, of the sons of Merari;

15And Bakbakkar, Heresh, and Galal, and Mattaniah the son of Micah, the son of Zichri, the son of Asaph;

16And Obadiah the son of Shemaiah, the son of Galal, the son of Jeduthun, and Berechiah the son of Asa, the son of Elkanah, that dwelt in the villages of the Netophathites.

17And the porters *were,* Shallum, and Akkub, and Talmon, and Ahiman, and their brethren: Shallum *was* the chief;

18Who hitherto *waited* in the king's gate eastward: they *were* porters in the companies of the children of Levi.

19And Shallum the son of Kore, the son of Ebiasaph, the son of Korah, and his brethren, of the house of his father, the Korahites, *were* over the work of the service, keepers of the gates of the tabernacle: and their fathers, *being* over the host of the LORD, *were* keepers of the entry.

20And Phinehas the son of Eleazar was the ruler over them in time past, *and* the LORD *was* with him.

21And Zechariah the son of Meshelemiah *was* porter of the door of the tabernacle of the congregation.

22All these *which were* chosen to be porters in the gates *were* two hundred and twelve. These were reckoned by their genealogy in their villages, whom David and Samuel the seer did ordain in their set office.

23So they and their children *had* the oversight of the gates of the house of the LORD, *namely,* the house of the tabernacle, by wards.

New International

9 ALL ISRAEL was listed in the genealogies recorded in the book of the kings of Israel.

The People in Jerusalem

The people of Judah were taken captive to Babylon because of their unfaithfulness. 2Now the first to resettle on their own property in their own towns were some Israelites, priests, Levites and temple servants.

3Those from Judah, from Benjamin, and from Ephraim and Manasseh who lived in Jerusalem were:

4Uthai son of Ammihud, the son of Omri, the son of Imri, the son of Bani, a descendant of Perez son of Judah.

5Of the Shilonites:
Asaiah the firstborn and his sons.

6Of the Zerahites:
Jeuel.
The people from Judah numbered 690.

7Of the Benjamites:
Sallu son of Meshullam, the son of Hodaviah, the son of Hassenuah;

8Ibneiah son of Jeroham; Elah son of Uzzi, the son of Micri; and Meshullam son of Shephatiah, the son of Reuel, the son of Ibnijah.

9The people from Benjamin, as listed in their genealogy, numbered 956. All these men were heads of their families.

10Of the priests:
Jedaiah; Jehoiarib; Jakin;

11Azariah son of Hilkiah, the son of Meshullam, the son of Zadok, the son of Meraioth, the son of Ahitub, the official in charge of the house of God;

12Adaiah son of Jeroham, the son of Pashhur, the son of Malkijah; and Maasai son of Adiel, the son of Jahzerah, the son of Meshullam, the son of Meshillemith, the son of Immer.

13The priests, who were heads of families, numbered 1,760. They were able men, responsible for ministering in the house of God.

14Of the Levites:
Shemaiah son of Hasshub, the son of Azrikam, the son of Hashabiah, a Merarite; 15Bakbakkar, Heresh, Galal and Mattaniah son of Mica, the son of Zicri, the son of Asaph; 16Obadiah son of Shemaiah, the son of Galal, the son of Jeduthun; and Berekiah son of Asa, the son of Elkanah, who lived in the villages of the Netophathites.

17The gatekeepers:
Shallum, Akkub, Talmon, Ahiman and their brothers, Shallum their chief 18being stationed at the King's Gate on the east, up to the present time. These were the gatekeepers belonging to the camp of the Levites. 19Shallum son of Kore, the son of Ebiasaph, the son of Korah, and his fellow gatekeepers from his family (the Korahites) were responsible for guarding the thresholds of the Tent[a] just as their fathers had been responsible for guarding the entrance to the dwelling of the LORD. 20In earlier times Phinehas son of Eleazar was in charge of the gatekeepers, and the LORD was with him. 21Zechariah son of Meshelemiah was the gatekeeper at the entrance to the Tent of Meeting.

22Altogether, those chosen to be gatekeepers at the thresholds numbered 212. They were registered by genealogy in their villages. The gatekeepers had been assigned to their positions of trust by David and Samuel the seer. 23They and their descendants were in charge of guarding the gates of the house of the LORD—the house called the Tent. 24The gatekeepers were on the four

---

a *19* That is, the temple; also in verses 21 and 23

Living Bible

9 THE FAMILY tree of every person in Israel was carefully recorded in *The Annals of the Kings of Israel*.

Judah was exiled to Babylon because the people worshiped idols.

2The first to return and live again in their former cities were families from the tribes of Israel, and also the priests, the Levites, and the Temple assistants.

3Then some families from the tribes of Judah, Benjamin, Ephraim, and Manasseh arrived in Jerusalem:

4One family was that of Uthai (the son of Ammihud, son of Omri, son of Imri, son of Bani) of the clan of Perez (son of Judah).

5The Shilonites were another family to return, including Asaiah (Shilon's oldest son) and his sons; 6there were also the sons of Zerah, including Jeuel and his relatives: 690 in all.

7, 8Among the members of the tribe of Benjamin who returned were these:

Sallu (the son of Meshullam, the son of Hodaviah, the son of Hassenuah);

Ibneiah (the son of Jeroham);

Elah (the son of Uzzi, the son of Michri);

Meshullam (the son of Shephatiah, the son of Reuel, the son of Ibnijah).

9These men were all chiefs of subclans. A total of 956 Benjaminites returned.

10, 11The priests who returned were:

Jedaiah, Jehoiarib, Jachin,

Azariah (the son of Hilkiah, son of Meshullam, son of Zadok, son of Meraioth, son of Ahitub). He was the chief custodian of the Temple.

12Another of the returning priests was Adaiah (son of Jeroham, son of Pashhur, son of Malchijah).

Another priest was Maasai (son of Adi-el, son of Jahzerah, son of Meshullam, son of Meshillemith, son of Immer).

13In all, 1,760 priests returned.

14Among the Levites who returned was Shemaiah (son of Hasshub, son of Azrikam, son of Hashabiah, who was a descendant of Merari).

15, 16Other Levites who returned included:

Bakbakkar, Heresh, Galal,

Mattaniah (the son of Mica, who was the son of Zichri, who was the son of Asaph).

Obadiah (the son of Shemaiah, son of Galal, son of Jeduthun).

Berechiah (the son of Asa, son of El-kanah, who lived in the area of the Netophathites).

17, 18The gatekeepers were Shallum (the chief gatekeeper), Akkub, Talmon, and Ahiman—all Levites. They are still responsible for the eastern royal gate. 19Shallum's ancestry went back through Kore and Ebiasaph to Korah. He and his close relatives the Korahites were in charge of the sacrifices and the protection of the sanctuary, just as their ancestors had supervised and guarded the Tabernacle. 20Phinehas, the son of Eleazar, was the first director of this division in ancient times. And the Lord was with him.

21At that time Zechariah, the son of Meshelemiah, had been responsible for the protection of the entrance to the Tabernacle. 22There were 212 doorkeepers in those days. They were chosen from their villages on the basis of their genealogies, and they were appointed by David and Samuel because of their reliability. 23They and their descendants were in charge of the Lord's Tabernacle. 24They were assigned to each of the four sides:

New Revised Standard

9 SO ALL Israel was enrolled by genealogies; and these are written in the Book of the Kings of Israel. And Judah was taken into exile in Babylon because of their unfaithfulness. 2Now the first to live again in their possessions in their towns were Israelites, priests, Levites, and temple servants.

Inhabitants of Jerusalem after the Exile

3 And some of the people of Judah, Benjamin, Ephraim, and Manasseh lived in Jerusalem: 4Uthai son of Ammihud, son of Omri, son of Imri, son of Bani, from the sons of Perez son of Judah. 5And of the Shilonites: Asaiah the firstborn, and his sons. 6Of the sons of Zerah: Jeuel and their kin, six hundred ninety. 7Of the Benjaminites: Sallu son of Meshullam, son of Hodaviah, son of Hassenuah, 8Ibneiah son of Jeroham, Elah son of Uzzi, son of Michri, and Meshullam son of Shephatiah, son of Reuel, son of Ibnijah; 9and their kindred according to their generations, nine hundred fifty-six. All these were heads of families according to their ancestral houses.

Priestly Families

10 Of the priests: Jedaiah, Jehoiarib, Jachin, 11and Azariah son of Hilkiah, son of Meshullam, son of Zadok, son of Meraioth, son of Ahitub, the chief officer of the house of God; 12and Adaiah son of Jeroham, son of Pashhur, son of Malchijah, and Maasai son of Adiel, son of Jahzerah, son of Meshullam, son of Meshillemith, son of Immer; 13besides their kindred, heads of their ancestral houses, one thousand seven hundred sixty, qualified for the work of the service of the house of God.

Levitical Families

14 Of the Levites: Shemaiah son of Hasshub, son of Azrikam, son of Hashabiah, of the sons of Merari; 15and Bakbakkar, Heresh, Galal, and Mattaniah son of Mica, son of Zichri, son of Asaph; 16and Obadiah son of Shemaiah, son of Galal, son of Jeduthun, and Berechiah son of Asa, son of Elkanah, who lived in the villages of the Netophathites.

17 The gatekeepers were: Shallum, Akkub, Talmon, Ahiman; and their kindred Shallum was the chief, 18stationed previously in the king's gate on the east side. These were the gatekeepers of the camp of the Levites. 19Shallum son of Kore, son of Ebiasaph, son of Korah, and his kindred of his ancestral house, the Korahites, were in charge of the work of the service, guardians of the thresholds of the tent, as their ancestors had been in charge of the camp of the LORD, guardians of the entrance. 20And Phinehas son of Eleazar was chief over them in former times; the LORD was with him. 21Zechariah son of Meshelemiah was gatekeeper at the entrance of the tent of meeting. 22All these, who were chosen as gatekeepers at the thresholds, were two hundred twelve. They were enrolled by genealogies in their villages. David and the seer Samuel established them in their office of trust. 23So they and their descendants were in charge of the gates of the house of the LORD, that is, the house of the tent, as guards. 24The gatekeepers were on the

King James

24In four quarters were the porters, toward the east, west, north, and south.

25And their brethren, *which were* in their villages, *were* to come after seven days from time to time with them.

26For these Levites, the four chief porters, were in *their* set office, and were over the chambers and treasuries of the house of God.

27¶ And they lodged round about the house of God, because the charge *was* upon them, and the opening thereof every morning *pertained* to them.

28And *certain* of them had the charge of the ministering vessels, that they should bring them in and out by tale.

29*Some* of them also *were* appointed to oversee the vessels, and all the instruments of the sanctuary, and the fine flour, and the wine, and the oil, and the frankincense, and the spices.

30And *some* of the sons of the priests made the ointment of the spices.

31And Mattithiah, *one* of the Levites, who *was* the firstborn of Shallum the Korahite, had the set office over the things that were made in the pans.

32And *other* of their brethren, of the sons of the Kohathites, *were* over the showbread, to prepare *it* every sabbath.

33And these *are* the singers, chief of the fathers of the Levites, *who remaining* in the chambers *were* free: for they were employed in *that* work day and night.

34These chief fathers of the Levites *were* chief throughout their generations; these dwelt at Jerusalem.

35¶ And in Gibeon dwelt the father of Gibeon, Jehiel, whose wife's name *was* Maachah:

36And his firstborn son Abdon, then Zur, and Kish, and Baal, and Ner, and Nadab,

37And Gedor, and Ahio, and Zechariah, and Mikloth.

38And Mikloth begat Shimeam. And they also dwelt with their brethren at Jerusalem, over against their brethren.

39And Ner begat Kish; and Kish begat Saul; and Saul begat Jonathan, and Malchi-shua, and Abinadab, and Esh-baal.

40And the son of Jonathan *was* Merib-baal: and Merib-baal begat Micah.

41And the sons of Micah *were*, Pithon, and Melech, and Tahrea, *and* Ahaz.

42And Ahaz begat Jarah; and Jarah begat Alemeth, and Azmaveth, and Zimri; and Zimri begat Moza;

43And Moza begat Binea; and Rephaiah his son, Eleasah his son, Azel his son.

44And Azel had six sons, whose names *are* these, Azrikam, Bocheru, and Ishmael, and Sheariah, and Obadiah, and Hanan: these *were* the sons of Azel.

10 NOW THE Philistines fought against Israel; and the men of Israel fled from before the Philistines, and fell down slain in mount Gilboa.

2And the Philistines followed hard after Saul, and after his sons; and the Philistines slew Jonathan, and Abinadab, and Malchi-shua, the sons of Saul.

3And the battle went sore against Saul, and the archers hit him, and he was wounded of the archers.

4Then said Saul to his armourbearer, Draw thy sword, and thrust me through therewith; lest these uncircumcised come and abuse me. But his armourbearer would not; for he was sore afraid. So Saul took a sword, and fell upon it.

New International

sides: east, west, north and south. 25Their brothers in their villages had to come from time to time and share their duties for seven-day periods. 26But the four principal gatekeepers, who were Levites, were entrusted with the responsibility for the rooms and treasuries in the house of God. 27They would spend the night stationed around the house of God, because they had to guard it; and they had charge of the key for opening it each morning.

28Some of them were in charge of the articles used in the temple service; they counted them when they were brought in and when they were taken out. 29Others were assigned to take care of the furnishings and all the other articles of the sanctuary, as well as the flour and wine, and the oil, incense and spices. 30But some of the priests took care of mixing the spices. 31A Levite named Mattithiah, the firstborn son of Shallum the Korahite, was entrusted with the responsibility for baking the offering bread. 32Some of their Kohathite brothers were in charge of preparing for every Sabbath the bread set out on the table.

33Those who were musicians, heads of Levite families, stayed in the rooms of the temple and were exempt from other duties because they were responsible for the work day and night.

34All these were heads of Levite families, chiefs as listed in their genealogy, and they lived in Jerusalem.

The Genealogy of Saul

35Jeiel the father[a] of Gibeon lived in Gibeon.

His wife's name was Maacah, 36and his firstborn son was Abdon, followed by Zur, Kish, Baal, Ner, Nadab, 37Gedor, Ahio, Zechariah and Mikloth. 38Mikloth was the father of Shimeam. They too lived near their relatives in Jerusalem.

39Ner was the father of Kish, Kish the father of Saul, and Saul the father of Jonathan, Malki-Shua, Abinadab and Esh-Baal.[b]

40The son of Jonathan:

Merib-Baal,[c] who was the father of Micah.

41The sons of Micah:

Pithon, Melech, Tahrea and Ahaz.[d]

42Ahaz was the father of Jadah, Jadah[e] was the father of Alemeth, Azmaveth and Zimri, and Zimri was the father of Moza. 43Moza was the father of Binea; Rephaiah was his son, Eleasah his son and Azel his son.

44Azel had six sons, and these were their names: Azrikam, Bokeru, Ishmael, Sheariah, Obadiah and Hanan. These were the sons of Azel.

Saul Takes His Life

10 NOW THE Philistines fought against Israel; the Israelites fled before them, and many fell slain on Mount Gilboa. 2The Philistines pressed hard after Saul and his sons, and they killed his sons Jonathan, Abinadab and Malki-Shua. 3The fighting grew fierce around Saul, and when the archers overtook him, they wounded him.

4Saul said to his armor-bearer, "Draw your sword and run me through, or these uncircumcised fellows will come and abuse me."

But his armor-bearer was terrified and would not do it; so Saul took his own sword and fell on it. 5When the

---

a *35 Father* may mean *civic leader* or *military leader.*   b *39 Also known as Ish-Bosheth*   c *40 Also known as Mephibosheth*   d *41 Vulgate and Syriac (see also Septuagint and 1 Chron. 8:35); Hebrew does not have and Ahaz.*   e *42 Some Hebrew manuscripts and Septuagint (see also 1 Chron. 8:36); most Hebrew manuscripts Jarah, Jarah*

Living Bible

east, west, north, and south. 25And their relatives in the villages were assigned to help them from time to time, for seven days at a time.

26The four head gatekeepers, all Levites, were in an office of great trust, for they were responsible for the rooms and treasuries in the Tabernacle of God. 27Because of their important positions they lived near the Tabernacle, and they opened the gates each morning. 28Some of them were assigned to care for the various vessels used in the sacrifices and worship; they checked them in and out to avoid loss. 29Others were responsible for the furniture, the items in the sanctuary, and the supplies such as fine flour, wine, incense, and spices.

30Other priests prepared the spices and incense.

31And Mattithiah (a Levite and the oldest son of Shallum the Korahite) was entrusted with making the flat cakes for grain offerings.

32Some members of the Kohath clan were in charge of the preparation of the special bread[f] each Sabbath.

33, 34The cantors were all prominent Levites. They lived in Jerusalem at the Temple and were on duty at all hours. They were free from other responsibilities and were selected by their genealogies.

35, 36, 37Jeiel (whose wife was Maacah) lived in Gibeon. He had many[g] sons, including:

Gibeon, Abdon (the oldest), Zur, Kish, Baal, **Ner,** Nadab, Gedor, Ahio, Zechariah, Mikloth.

38Mikloth lived with his son Shime-am in Jerusalem near his relatives.

39Ner was the father of Kish, Kish was the father of Saul, Saul was the father of Jonathan, Malchishua, Abinadab, and Eshbaal.

40Jonathan was the father of Mephibosheth;[h] Mephibosheth[h] was the father of Micah;

41Micah was the father of Pithon, Melech, Tahre-a, and Ahaz;

42Ahaz was the father of Jarah;

Jarah was the father of Alemeth, Azmaveth, and Zimri;

Zimri was the father of Moza.

43Moza was the father of Bine-a, Rephaiah, Eleasah, and Azel.

44Azel had six sons:

Azrikam, Bocheru, Ishmael, She-ariah, Obadiah, Hanan.

New Revised Standard

four sides, east, west, north, and south; 25and their kindred who were in their villages were obliged to come in every seven days, in turn, to be with them; 26for the four chief gatekeepers, who were Levites, were in charge of the chambers and the treasures of the house of God. 27And they would spend the night near the house of God; for on them lay the duty of watching, and they had charge of opening it every morning.

28 Some of them had charge of the utensils of service, for they were required to count them when they were brought in and taken out. 29Others of them were appointed over the furniture, and over all the holy utensils, also over the choice flour, the wine, the oil, the incense, and the spices. 30Others, of the sons of the priests, prepared the mixing of the spices, 31and Mattithiah, one of the Levites, the firstborn of Shallum the Korahite, was in charge of making the flat cakes. 32Also some of their kindred of the Kohathites had charge of the rows of bread, to prepare them for each sabbath.

33 Now these are the singers, the heads of ancestral houses of the Levites, living in the chambers of the temple free from other service, for they were on duty day and night. 34These were heads of ancestral houses of the Levites, according to their generations; these leaders lived in Jerusalem.

The Family of King Saul

35 In Gibeon lived the father of Gibeon, Jeiel, and the name of his wife was Maacah. 36His firstborn son was Abdon, then Zur, Kish, Baal, Ner, Nadab, 37Gedor, Ahio, Zechariah, and Mikloth; 38and Mikloth became the father of Shimeam; and these also lived opposite their kindred in Jerusalem, with their kindred. 39Ner became the father of Kish, Kish of Saul, Saul of Jonathan, Malchishua, Abinadab, and Esh-baal; 40and the son of Jonathan was Merib-baal; and Merib-baal became the father of Micah. 41The sons of Micah: Pithon, Melech, Tahrea, and Ahaz;[j] 42and Ahaz became the father of Jarah, and Jarah of Alemeth, Azmaveth, and Zimri; and Zimri became the father of Moza. 43Moza became the father of Binea; and Rephaiah was his son, Eleasah his son, Azel his son. 44Azel had six sons, and these are their names: Azrikam, Bocheru, Ishmael, Sheariah, Obadiah, and Hanan; these were the sons of Azel.

Death of Saul and His Sons

10 NOW THE Philistines fought against Israel; and the men of Israel fled before the Philistines, and fell slain on Mount Gilboa. 2The Philistines overtook Saul and his sons; and the Philistines killed Jonathan and Abinadab and Malchishua, sons of Saul. 3The battle pressed hard on Saul; and the archers found him, and he was wounded by the archers. 4Then Saul said to his armor-bearer, "Draw your sword, and thrust me through with it, so that these uncircumcised may not come and make sport of me." But his armor-bearer was unwilling, for he was terrified. So Saul took his own sword and fell on it. 5When his armor-bearer saw that

10[i] THE PHILISTINES attacked and defeated the Israeli troops, who turned and fled and were slaughtered on the slopes of Mount Gilboa. 2They caught up with Saul and his three sons, Jonathan, Abinadab, and Malchishua, and killed them all. 3Saul had been hard pressed with heavy fighting all around him, when the Philistine archers shot and wounded him.

4He cried out to his bodyguard, "Quick, kill me with your sword before these uncircumcised heathen capture and torture me."

But the man was afraid to do it, so Saul took his own sword and fell against its point; and it pierced his body.

---

f 9:32 *special bread,* literally, "showbread."   g 9:35-37 *many,* implied.
h 9:40 *Mephibosheth,* or "Merib-baal."   i 10:1 The remainder of
1 Chronicles deals with events preceding chapter 9.

j Compare 8.35: Heb lacks *and Ahaz*

King James

5And when his armourbearer saw that Saul was dead, he fell likewise on the sword, and died.

6So Saul died, and his three sons, and all his house died together.

7And when all the men of Israel that *were* in the valley saw that they fled, and that Saul and his sons were dead, then they forsook their cities, and fled: and the Philistines came and dwelt in them.

8¶ And it came to pass on the morrow, when the Philistines came to strip the slain, that they found Saul and his sons fallen in mount Gilboa.

9And when they had stripped him, they took his head, and his armour, and sent into the land of the Philistines round about, to carry tidings unto their idols, and to the people.

10And they put his armour in the house of their gods, and fastened his head in the temple of Dagon.

11¶ And when all Jabesh-gilead heard all that the Philistines had done to Saul.

12They arose, all the valiant men, and took away the body of Saul, and the bodies of his sons, and brought them to Jabesh, and buried their bones under the oak in Jabesh, and fasted seven days.

13¶ So Saul died for his transgression which he committed against the LORD, *even* against the word of the LORD, which he kept not, and also for asking *counsel* of one that had a familiar spirit, to inquire *of it;*

14And inquired not of the LORD: therefore he slew him, and turned the kingdom unto David the son of Jesse.

11 THEN ALL Israel gathered themselves to David unto Hebron, saying, Behold, we *are* thy bone and thy flesh.

2And moreover in time past, even when Saul was king, thou *wast* he that leddest out and broughtest in Israel: and the LORD thy God said unto thee, Thou shalt feed my people Israel, and thou shalt be ruler over my people Israel.

3Therefore came all the elders of Israel to the king to Hebron; and David made a covenant with them in Hebron before the LORD; and they anointed David king over Israel, according to the word of the LORD by Samuel.

4¶ And David and all Israel went to Jerusalem, which *is* Jebus; where the Jebusites *were,* the inhabitants of the land.

5And the inhabitants of Jebus said to David, Thou shalt not come hither. Nevertheless David took the castle of Zion, which *is* the city of David.

6And David said, Whosoever smiteth the Jebusites first shall be chief and captain. So Joab the son of Zeruiah went first up, and was chief.

7And David dwelt in the castle; therefore they called it the city of David.

8And he built the city round about, even from Millo round about: and Joab repaired the rest of the city.

9So David waxed greater and greater: for the LORD of hosts *was* with him.

10¶ These also *are* the chief of the mighty men whom David had, who strengthened themselves with him in his kingdom, *and* with all Israel, to make him king, according to the word of the LORD concerning Israel.

11And this *is* the number of the mighty men whom David had; Jashobeam, an Hachmonite, the chief of the captains: he lifted up his spear against three hundred slain *by him* at one time.

12And after him *was* Eleazar the son of Dodo, the Ahohite, who *was one* of the three mighties.

New International

armor-bearer saw that Saul was dead, he too fell on his sword and died. 6So Saul and his three sons died, and all his house died together.

7When all the Israelites in the valley saw that the army had fled and that Saul and his sons had died, they abandoned their towns and fled. And the Philistines came and occupied them.

8The next day, when the Philistines came to strip the dead, they found Saul and his sons fallen on Mount Gilboa. 9They stripped him and took his head and his armor, and sent messengers throughout the land of the Philistines to proclaim the news among their idols and their people. 10They put his armor in the temple of their gods and hung up his head in the temple of Dagon.

11When all the inhabitants of Jabesh Gilead heard of everything the Philistines had done to Saul, 12all their valiant men went and took the bodies of Saul and his sons and brought them to Jabesh. Then they buried their bones under the great tree in Jabesh, and they fasted seven days.

13Saul died because he was unfaithful to the LORD; he did not keep the word of the LORD and even consulted a medium for guidance, 14and did not inquire of the LORD. So the LORD put him to death and turned the kingdom over to David son of Jesse.

David Becomes King Over Israel

11 ALL ISRAEL came together to David at Hebron and said, "We are your own flesh and blood. 2In the past, even while Saul was king, you were the one who led Israel on their military campaigns. And the LORD your God said to you, 'You will shepherd my people Israel, and you will become their ruler.' "

3When all the elders of Israel had come to King David at Hebron, he made a compact with them at Hebron before the LORD, and they anointed David king over Israel, as the LORD had promised through Samuel.

David Conquers Jerusalem

4David and all the Israelites marched to Jerusalem (that is, Jebus). The Jebusites who lived there 5said to David, "You will not get in here." Nevertheless, David captured the fortress of Zion, the City of David.

6David had said, "Whoever leads the attack on the Jebusites will become commander-in-chief." Joab son of Zeruiah went up first, and so he received the command.

7David then took up residence in the fortress, and so it was called the City of David. 8He built up the city around it, from the supporting terracesª to the surrounding wall, while Joab restored the rest of the city. 9And David became more and more powerful, because the LORD Almighty was with him.

David's Mighty Men

10These were the chiefs of David's mighty men— they, together with all Israel, gave his kingship strong support to extend it over the whole land, as the LORD had promised— 11this is the list of David's mighty men:

Jashobeam,ᵇ a Hacmonite, was chief of the officersᶜ; he raised his spear against three hundred men, whom he killed in one encounter.

12Next to him was Eleazar son of Dodai the Ahohite, one of the three mighty men. 13He was with David at Pas

---

ª *8 Or the Millo*   ᵇ *11 Possibly a variant of Jashob-Baal*   ᶜ *11 Or Thirty;* some Septuagint manuscripts *Three* (see also 2 Samuel 23:8)

Living Bible

5Then his bodyguard, seeing that Saul was dead, killed himself in the same way. 6So Saul and his three sons died together; the entire family was wiped out in one day.

7When the Israelis in the valley below the mountain heard that their troops had been routed and that Saul and his sons were dead, they abandoned their cities and fled. And the Philistines came and lived in them. 8When the Philistines went back the next day to strip the bodies of the men killed in action and to gather the booty from the battlefield, they found the bodies of Saul and his sons. 9So they stripped off Saul's armor and cut off his head; then they displayed them throughout the nation and celebrated the wonderful news before their idols. 10They fastened his armor to the walls of the Temple of the Gods and nailed his head to the wall of Dagon's temple.

11But when the people of Jabesh-gilead heard what the Philistines had done to Saul, 12their heroic warriors went out to the battlefieldd and brought back his body and the bodies of his three sons. Then they buried them beneath the oak tree at Jabesh and mourned and fasted for seven days.

13Saul died for his disobedience to the Lord and because he had consulted a medium,e 14and did not ask the Lord for guidance. So the Lord killed him and gave the kingdom to David, the son of Jesse.

11 THEN THE leaders of Israel went to David at Hebron and told him, "We are your relatives,f 2and even when Saul was king, you were the one who led our armies to battle and brought them safely back again. And the Lord your God has told you, 'You shall be the shepherd of my people Israel. You shall be their king.' "

3So David made a contract with them before the Lord, and they anointed him as king of Israel, just as the Lord had told Samuel. 4Then David and the leaders went to Jerusalem (or Jebus, as it used to be called) where the Jebusites—the original inhabitants of the land—lived. 5, 6But the people of Jebus refused to let them enter the city. So David captured the fortress of Zion, later called the City of David, and said to his men, "The first man to kill a Jebusite shall be made commanderin-chief!" Joab, the son of Zeruiah, was the first, so he became the general of David's army. 7David lived in the fortress and that is why that area of Jerusalem is called the City of David. 8He extended the city out around the fortress while Joab rebuilt the rest of Jerusalem. 9And David became more and more famous and powerful, for the Lord of the heavens was with him.

10These are the names of some of the bravest of David's warriors (who also encouraged the leaders of Israel to make David their king, as the Lord had said would happen):

11Jashobeam (the son of a man from Hachmon) was the leader of The Top Three—the three greatest heroes among David's men. He once killed 300 men with his spear.

12The second of The Top Three was Eleazar, the son of Dodo, a member of the subclan of Ahoh. 13He was

New Revised Standard

Saul was dead, he also fell on his sword and died. 6Thus Saul died; he and his three sons and all his house died together. 7When all the men of Israel who were in the valley saw that the armyg had fled and that Saul and his sons were dead, they abandoned their towns and fled; and the Philistines came and occupied them.

8 The next day when the Philistines came to strip the dead, they found Saul and his sons fallen on Mount Gilboa. 9They stripped him and took his head and his armor, and sent messengers throughout the land of the Philistines to carry the good news to their idols and to the people. 10They put his armor in the temple of their gods, and fastened his head in the temple of Dagon. 11But when all Jabesh-gilead heard everything that the Philistines had done to Saul, 12all the valiant warriors got up and took away the body of Saul and the bodies of his sons, and brought them to Jabesh. Then they buried their bones under the oak in Jabesh, and fasted seven days.

13 So Saul died for his unfaithfulness; he was unfaithful to the Lord in that he did not keep the command of the Lord; moreover, he had consulted a medium, seeking guidance, 14and did not seek guidance from the Lord. Therefore the Lordh put him to death and turned the kingdom over to David son of Jesse.

David Anointed King of All Israel

11 THEN ALL Israel gathered together to David at Hebron and said, "See, we are your bone and flesh. 2For some time now, even while Saul was king, it was you who commanded the army of Israel. The Lord your God said to you: It is you who shall be shepherd of my people Israel, you who shall be ruler over my people Israel." 3So all the elders of Israel came to the king at Hebron, and David made a covenant with them at Hebron before the Lord. And they anointed David king over Israel, according to the word of the Lord by Samuel.

Jerusalem Captured

4 David and all Israel marched to Jerusalem, that is Jebus, where the Jebusites were, the inhabitants of the land. 5The inhabitants of Jebus said to David, "You will not come in here." Nevertheless David took the stronghold of Zion, now the city of David. 6David had said, "Whoever attacks the Jebusites first shall be chief and commander." And Joab son of Zeruiah went up first, so he became chief. 7David resided in the stronghold; therefore it was called the city of David. 8He built the city all around, from the Millo in complete circuit; and Joab repaired the rest of the city. 9And David became greater and greater, for the Lord of hosts was with him.

David's Mighty Men and Their Exploits

10 Now these are the chiefs of David's warriors, who gave him strong support in his kingdom, together with all Israel, to make him king, according to the word of the Lord concerning Israel. 11This is an account of David's mighty warriors: Jashobeam, son of Hachmoni,i was chief of the Three;j he wielded his spear against three hundred whom he killed at one time.

12 And next to him among the three warriors was Eleazar son of Dodo, the Ahohite. 13He was with David

---

d 10:12 *battlefield*, implied.   e 10:13 *medium*.   See 1 Sam 28.
f 11:1 *your relatives*, literally, "your bone and flesh."

g Heb *they*   h Heb *he*   i Or *a Hachmonite*   j Compare 2 Sam 23.8: Heb *Thirty* or *captains*

King James

13He was with David at Pas-dammim, and there the Philistines were gathered together to battle, where was a parcel of ground full of barley; and the people fled from before the Philistines.

14And they set themselves in the midst of *that* parcel, and delivered it, and slew the Philistines; and the LORD saved *them* by a great deliverance.

15¶ Now three of the thirty captains went down to the rock to David, into the cave of Adullam; and the host of the Philistines encamped in the valley of Rephaim.

16And David *was* then in the hold, and the Philistines' garrison *was* then at Bethlehem.

17And David longed, and said, Oh that one would give me drink of the water of the well of Bethlehem, that *is* at the gate!

18And the three brake through the host of the Philistines, and drew water out of the well of Bethlehem, that *was* by the gate, and took *it*, and brought *it* to David: but David would not drink *of* it, but poured it out to the LORD,

19And said, My God forbid it me, that I should do this thing: shall I drink the blood of these men that have put their lives in jeopardy? for with *the jeopardy of* their lives they brought it. Therefore he would not drink it. These things did these three mightiest.

20¶ And Abishai the brother of Joab, he was chief of the three: for lifting up his spear against three hundred, he slew *them*, and had a name among the three.

21Of the three, he was more honourable than the two; for he was their captain: howbeit he attained not to the *first* three.

22Benaiah the son of Jehoiada, the son of a valiant man of Kabzeel, who had done many acts; he slew two lionlike men of Moab: also he went down and slew a lion in a pit in a snowy day.

23And he slew an Egyptian, a man of *great* stature, five cubits high; and in the Egyptian's hand *was* a spear like a weaver's beam; and he went down to him with a staff, and plucked the spear out of the Egyptian's hand, and slew him with his own spear.

24These *things* did Benaiah the son of Jehoiada, and had the name among the three mighties.

25Behold, he was honourable among the thirty, but attained not to the *first* three: and David set him over his guard.

26¶ Also the valiant men of the armies *were*, Asahel the brother of Joab, Elhanan the son of Dodo of Bethlehem,

27Shammoth the Harorite, Helez the Pelonite,

28Ira the son of Ikkesh the Tekoite, Abiezer the Antothite,

29Sibbecai the Hushathite, Ilai the Ahohite,

30Maharai the Netophathite, Heled the son of Baanah the Netophathite,

31Ithai the son of Ribai of Gibeah, *that pertained* to the children of Benjamin, Benaiah the Pirathonite,

32Hurai of the brooks of Gaash, Abiel the Arbathite,

33Azmaveth the Baharumite, Eliahba the Shaalbonite,

34The sons of Hashem the Gizonite, Jonathan the son of Shage the Hararite,

35Ahiam the son of Sacar the Hararite, Eliphal the son of Ur,

36Hepher the Mecherathite, Ahijah the Pelonite,

37Hezro the Carmelite, Naarai the son of Ezbai,

38Joel the brother of Nathan, Mibhar the son of Haggeri,

39Zelek the Ammonite, Naharai the Berothite, the armourbearer of Joab the son of Zeruiah,

40Ira the Ithrite, Gareb the Ithrite,

New International

Dammim when the Philistines gathered there for battle. At a place where there was a field full of barley, the troops fled from the Philistines. 14But they took their stand in the middle of the field. They defended it and struck the Philistines down, and the LORD brought about a great victory.

15Three of the thirty chiefs came down to David to the rock at the cave of Adullam, while a band of Philistines was encamped in the Valley of Rephaim. 16At that time David was in the stronghold, and the Philistine garrison was at Bethlehem. 17David longed for water and said, "Oh, that someone would get me a drink of water from the well near the gate of Bethlehem!" 18So the Three broke through the Philistine lines, drew water from the well near the gate of Bethlehem and carried it back to David. But he refused to drink it; instead, he poured it out before the LORD. 19"God forbid that I should do this!" he said. "Should I drink the blood of these men who went at the risk of their lives?" Because they risked their lives to bring it back, David would not drink it.

Such were the exploits of the three mighty men.

20Abishai the brother of Joab was chief of the Three. He raised his spear against three hundred men, whom he killed, and so he became as famous as the Three. 21He was doubly honored above the Three and became their commander, even though he was not included among them.

22Benaiah son of Jehoiada was a valiant fighter from Kabzeel, who performed great exploits. He struck down two of Moab's best men. He also went down into a pit on a snowy day and killed a lion. 23And he struck down an Egyptian who was seven and a half feet[a] tall. Although the Egyptian had a spear like a weaver's rod in his hand, Benaiah went against him with a club. He snatched the spear from the Egyptian's hand and killed him with his own spear. 24Such were the exploits of Benaiah son of Jehoiada; he too was as famous as the three mighty men. 25He was held in greater honor than any of the Thirty, but he was not included among the Three. And David put him in charge of his bodyguard.

26The mighty men were:
　　Asahel the brother of Joab,
　　Elhanan son of Dodo from Bethlehem,
27Shammah the Harorite,
　　Helez the Pelonite,
28Ira son of Ikkesh from Tekoa,
　　Abiezer from Anathoth,
29Sibbecai the Hushathite,
　　Ilai the Ahohite,
30Maharai the Netophathite,
　　Heled son of Baanah the Netophathite,
31Ithai son of Ribai from Gibeah in Benjamin,
　　Benaiah the Pirathonite,
32Hurai from the ravines of Gaash,
　　Abiel the Arbathite,
33Azmaveth the Baharumite,
　　Eliahba the Shaalbonite,
34the sons of Hashem the Gizonite,
　　Jonathan son of Shagee the Hararite,
35Ahiam son of Sacar the Hararite,
　　Eliphal son of Ur,
36Hepher the Mekerathite,
　　Ahijah the Pelonite,
37Hezro the Carmelite,
　　Naarai son of Ezbai,
38Joel the brother of Nathan,
　　Mibhar son of Hagri,
39Zelek the Ammonite,
　　Naharai the Berothite, the armor-bearer of Joab son of Zeruiah,
40Ira the Ithrite,
　　Gareb the Ithrite,

Living Bible

with David in the battle against the Philistines at Pas-dammim. The Israeli army was in a barley field and had begun to run away, 14but he held his ground in the middle of the field, and recovered it and slaughtered the Philistines; and the Lord saved them with a great victory.

15Another time, three of The Thirtyb went to David while he was hiding in the cave of Adullam. The Philistines were camped in the Valley of Rephaim, 16and David was in the stronghold at the time; an outpost of the Philistines had occupied Bethlehem. 17David wanted a drink from the Bethlehem well beside the gate, and when he mentioned this to his men, 18, 19these three broke through to the Philistine camp, drew some water from the well, and brought it back to David. But he refused to drink it! Instead he poured it out as an offering to the Lord and said, "God forbid that I should drink it! It is the very blood of these men who risked their lives to get it."

20Abishai, Joab's brother, was commander of The Thirty. He had gained his place among The Thirty by killing 300 men at one time with his spear. 21He was the chief and the most famous of The Thirty, but he was not as great as The Three.

22Benaiah, whose father was a mighty warrior from Kabzeel, killed the two famous giantsc from Moab. He also killed a lion in a slippery pit when there was snow on the ground. 23Once he killed an Egyptian who was seven and one-half feet tall, whose spear was as thick as a weaver's beam. But Benaiah went up to him with only a club in his hand and pulled the spear away from him and used it to kill him. 24. 25He was nearly as great as The Three, and he was very famous among The Thirty. David made him captain of his bodyguard.

26-47Other famous warriors among David's men were:
Asahel (Joab's brother);
Elhanan, the son of Dodo from Bethlehem;
Shammoth from Harod;
Helez from Pelon;
Ira (son of Ikkesh) from Tekoa;
Abi-ezer from Anathoth;
Sibbecai from Hushath;
Ilai from Ahoh;
Maharai from Netophah;
Heled (son of Baanah) from Netophah;
Ithai (son of Ribai) a Benjaminite from Gibe-ah;
Benaiah from Pirathon;
Hurai from near the brooks of Gaash;
Abiel from Arbath;
Azmaveth from Baharum;
Eliahba from Sha-albon;
The sonsd of Hashem from Gizon;
Jonathan (son of Shagee) from Harar;
Ahiam (son of Sacher) from Harar;
Eliphal (son of Ur);
Hepher from Mecherath;
Ahijah from Pelon;
Hezro from Carmel;
Naarai (son of Ezbai);
Joel (brother of Nathan);
Mibhar (son of Hagri);
Zelek from Ammon;
Naharai from Be-eroth—he was General Joab's
   armorbearer;
Ira from Ithra;
Gareb from Ithra;
Uriah the Hittite;
Zabad (son of Ahlai);

New Revised Standard

at Pas-dammim when the Philistines were gathered there for battle. There was a plot of ground full of barley. Now the people had fled from the Philistines, 14but he and David took their stand in the middle of the plot, defended it, and killed the Philistines; and the LORD saved them by a great victory.

15 Three of the thirty chiefs went down to the rock to David at the cave of Adullam, while the army of Philistines was encamped in the valley of Rephaim. 16David was then in the stronghold; and the garrison of the Philistines was then at Bethlehem. 17David said longingly, "O that someone would give me water to drink from the well of Bethlehem that is by the gate!" 18Then the Three broke through the camp of the Philistines, and drew water from the well of Bethlehem that was by the gate, and they brought it to David. But David would not drink of it; he poured it out to the LORD, 19and said, "My God forbid that I should do this. Can I drink the blood of these men? For at the risk of their lives they brought it." Therefore he would not drink it. The three warriors did these things.

20 Now Abishai,e the brother of Joab, was chief of the Thirty.f With his spear he fought against three hundred and killed them, and won a name beside the Three. 21He was the most renownedg of the Thirty,f and became their commander; but he did not attain to the Three.

22 Benaiah son of Jehoiada was a valiant manh of Kabzeel, a doer of great deeds; he struck down two sons ofi Ariel of Moab. He also went down and killed a lion in a pit on a day when snow had fallen. 23And he killed an Egyptian, a man of great stature, five cubits tall. The Egyptian had in his hand a spear like a weaver's beam; but Benaiah went against him with a staff, snatched the spear out of the Egyptian's hand, and killed him with his own spear. 24Such were the things Benaiah son of Jehoiada did, and he won a name beside the three warriors. 25He was renowned among the Thirty, but he did not attain to the Three. And David put him in charge of his bodyguard.

26 The warriors of the armies were Asahel brother of Joab, Elhanan son of Dodo of Bethlehem, 27Shammoth of Harod,j Helez the Pelonite, 28Ira son of Ikkesh of Tekoa, Abiezer of Anathoth, 29Sibbecai the Hushathite, Ilai the Ahohite, 30Maharai of Netophah, Heled son of Baanah of Netophah, 31Ithai son of Ribai of Gibeah of the Benjaminites, Benaiah of Pirathon, 32Hurai of the wadis of Gaash, Abiel the Arbathite, 33Azmaveth of Baharum, Eliahba of Shaalbon, 34Hashemk the Gizonite, Jonathan son of Shagee the Hararite, 35Ahiam son of Sachar the Hararite, Eliphal son of Ur, 36Hepher the Mecherathite, Ahijah the Pelonite, 37Hezro of Carmel, Naarai son of Ezbai, 38Joel the brother of Nathan, Mibhar son of Hagri, 39Zelek the Ammonite, Naharai of Beeroth, the armor-bearer of Joab son of Zeruiah, 40Ira the Ithrite, Gareb the Ithrite, 41Uriah the Hittite, Zabad

---

b 11:15 The Thirty were the highest-ranking officers in the army.
c 11:22 giants, literally, "ariels." The meaning of the term is uncertain.
d 11:26-47 sons (of Hashem), implied in 2 Sam. 23:30.

e Gk Vg Tg Compare 2 Sam 23.18: Heb Abshai   f Syr: Heb Three
g Compare 2 Sam 23.19: Heb more renowned among the two   h Syr: Heb the son of a valiant man   i See 2 Sam 23.20: Heb lacks sons of   j Compare 2 Sam 23.25: Heb the Harorite   k Compare Gk and 2 Sam 23.32: Heb the sons of Hashem

King James

41Uriah the Hittite, Zabad the son of Ahlai,

42Adina the son of Shiza the Reubenite, a captain of the Reubenites, and thirty with him,

43Hanan the son of Maachah, and Joshaphat the Mithnite,

44Uzzia the Ashterathite, Shama and Jehiel the sons of Hothan the Aroerite,

45Jediael the son of Shimri, and Joha his brother, the Tizite,

46Eliel the Mahavite, and Jeribai, and Joshaviah, the sons of Elnaam, and Ithmah the Moabite,

47Eliel, and Obed, and Jasiel the Mesobaite.

12 NOW THESE *are* they that came to David to Ziklag, while he yet kept himself close because of Saul the son of Kish: and they *were* among the mighty men, helpers of the war.

2*They were* armed with bows, and could use both the right hand and the left in *hurling* stones and *shooting* arrows out of a bow, *even* of Saul's brethren of Benjamin.

3The chief *was* Ahiezer, then Joash, the sons of Shemaah the Gibeathite; and Jeziel, and Pelet, the sons of Azmaveth; and Berachah, and Jehu the Antothite,

4And Ismaiah the Gibeonite, a mighty man among the thirty, and over the thirty; and Jeremiah, and Jahaziel, and Johanan, and Josabad the Gederathite,

5Eluzai, and Jerimoth, and Bealiah, and Shemariah, and Shephatiah the Haruphite,

6Elkanah, and Jesiah, and Azareel, and Joezer, and Jashobeam, the Korhites,

7And Joelah, and Zebadiah, the sons of Jeroham of Gedor.

8And of the Gadites there separated themselves unto David into the hold to the wilderness men of might, *and* men of war *fit* for the battle, that could handle shield and buckler, whose faces *were like* the faces of lions, and *were* as swift as the roes upon the mountains;

9Ezer the first, Obadiah the second, Eliab the third,

10Mishmannah the fourth, Jeremiah the fifth,

11Attai the sixth, Eliel the seventh,

12Johanan the eighth, Elzabad the ninth,

13Jeremiah the tenth, Machbanai the eleventh.

14These *were* of the sons of Gad, captains of the host: one of the least *was* over an hundred, and the greatest over a thousand.

15These *are* they that went over Jordan in the first month, when it had overflown all his banks; and they put to flight all *them* of the valleys, *both* toward the east, and toward the west.

16And there came of the children of Benjamin and Judah to the hold unto David.

17And David went out to meet them, and answered and said unto them, If ye be come peaceably unto me to help me, mine heart shall be knit unto you: but if *ye be come* to betray me to mine enemies, seeing *there is* no wrong in mine hands, the God of our fathers look *thereon*, and rebuke *it*.

18Then the spirit came upon Amasai, *who was* chief of the captains, *and he said*, Thine *are we*, David, and on thy side, thou son of Jesse: peace, peace *be* unto thee, and peace *be* to thine helpers; for thy God helpeth thee. Then David received them, and made them captains of the band.

New International

41Uriah the Hittite,
Zabad son of Ahlai,

42Adina son of Shiza the Reubenite, who was chief of the Reubenites, and the thirty with him,

43Hanan son of Maacah,
Joshaphat the Mithnite,

44Uzzia the Ashterathite,
Shama and Jeiel the sons of Hotham the Aroerite,

45Jediael son of Shimri,
his brother Joha the Tizite,

46Eliel the Mahavite,
Jeribai and Joshaviah the sons of Elnaam,
Ithmah the Moabite,

47Eliel, Obed and Jaasiel the Mezobaite.

Warriors Join David

12 THESE WERE the men who came to David at Ziklag, while he was banished from the presence of Saul son of Kish (they were among the warriors who helped him in battle; 2they were armed with bows and were able to shoot arrows or to sling stones right-handed or left-handed; they were kinsmen of Saul from the tribe of Benjamin):

3Ahiezer their chief and Joash the sons of Shemaah the Gibeathite; Jeziel and Pelet the sons of Azmaveth; Beracah, Jehu the Anathothite, 4and Ishmaiah the Gibeonite, a mighty man among the Thirty, who was a leader of the Thirty; Jeremiah, Jahaziel, Johanan, Jozabad the Gederathite, 5Eluzai, Jerimoth, Bealiah, Shemariah and Shephatiah the Haruphite; 6Elkanah, Isshiah, Azarel, Joezer and Jashobeam the Korahites; 7and Joelah and Zebadiah the sons of Jeroham from Gedor.

8Some Gadites defected to David at his stronghold in the desert. They were brave warriors, ready for battle and able to handle the shield and spear. Their faces were the faces of lions, and they were as swift as gazelles in the mountains.

9Ezer was the chief,
Obadiah the second in command, Eliab the third,

10Mishmannah the fourth, Jeremiah the fifth,

11Attai the sixth, Eliel the seventh,

12Johanan the eighth, Elzabad the ninth,

13Jeremiah the tenth and Macbannai the eleventh.

14These Gadites were army commanders; the least was a match for a hundred, and the greatest for a thousand. 15It was they who crossed the Jordan in the first month when it was overflowing all its banks, and they put to flight everyone living in the valleys, to the east and to the west.

16Other Benjamites and some men from Judah also came to David in his stronghold. 17David went out to meet them and said to them, "If you have come to me in peace, to help me, I am ready to have you unite with me. But if you have come to betray me to my enemies when my hands are free from violence, may the God of our fathers see it and judge you."

18Then the Spirit came upon Amasai, chief of the Thirty, and he said:

"We are yours, O David!
 We are with you, O son of Jesse!
Success, success to you,
 and success to those who help you,
 for your God will help you."

So David received them and made them leaders of his raiding bands.

Living Bible

Adina (son of Shiza) from the tribe of Reuben—he was among the thirty-one leaders of the tribe of Reuben;
Hanan (son of Maacah);
Joshaphat from Mithna;
Uzza from Ashterath;
Shama and Je-iel (sons of Hotham) from Aroer;
Jedia-el (son of Shimri);
Joha (his brother) from Tiza;
Eliel from Mahavi;
Jeribai and Joshaviah (sons of Elna-am);
Ithmah from Moab;
Eliel; Obed; Ja-asiel from Mezoba.

12 THESE ARE the names of the famous warriors who joined David at Ziklag while he was hiding from King Saul.a 2All of them were expert archers and slingers, and they could use their left hands as readily as their right! Like King Saul, they were all of the tribe of Benjamin.

3-7Their chief was Ahi-ezer, son of Shemaah from Gibe-ah. The others were:

His brother Joash; Jezi-el and Pelet, sons of Azmaveth; Beracah; Jehu from Anathoth; Ishmaiah from Gibeon (a brave warrior rated as high or higher than The Thirty); Jeremiah; Jahaziel; Johanan; Jozabad from Gederah; Eluzai; Jerimoth; Bealiah; Shemariah; Shephatiah from Haruph; Elkanah, Isshiah, Azarel, Jo-ezer, Jashobe-am—all Korahites; Jo-elah and Zebadiah (sons of Jeroham from Gedor).

8-13Great and brave warriors from the tribe of Gad also went to David in the wilderness. They were experts with both shield and spear and were "lion-faced men, swift as deer upon the mountains."

Ezer was the chief;
Obadiah was second in command;
Eliab was third in command;
Mishmannah was fourth in command;
Jeremiah was fifth in command;
Attai was sixth in command;
Eliel was seventh in command;
Johanan was eighth in command;
Elzabad was ninth in command;
Jeremiah was tenth in command;
Machbannai was eleventh in command.

14These men were army officers; the weakest was worth a hundred normal troops, and the greatest was worth a thousand! 15They crossed the Jordan River during its seasonal flooding and conquered the lowlands on both the east and west banks.

16Others came to David from Benjamin and Judah. 17David went out to meet them and said, "If you have come to help me, we are friends; but if you have come to betray me to my enemies when I am innocent, then may the God of our fathers see and judge you."

18Then the Holy Spirit came upon them, and Amasai, a leader of The Thirty, replied,

"We are yours, David;
We are on your side, son of Jesse.
Peace, peace be unto you,
And peace to all who aid you;
For your God is with you."

So David let them join him, and he made them captains of his army.

New Revised Standard

son of Ahlai, 42Adina son of Shiza the Reubenite, a leader of the Reubenites, and thirty with him, 43Hanan son of Maacah, and Joshaphat the Mithnite, 44Uzzia the Ashterathite, Shama and Jeiel sons of Hotham the Aroerite, 45Jediael son of Shimri, and his brother Joha the Tizite, 46Eliel the Mahavite, and Jeribai and Joshaviah sons of Elnaam, and Ithmah the Moabite, 47Eliel, and Obed, and Jaasiel the Mezobaite.

David's Followers in the Wilderness

12 THE FOLLOWING are those who came to David at Ziklag, while he could not move about freely because of Saul son of Kish; they were among the mighty warriors who helped him in war. 2They were archers, and could shoot arrows and sling stones with either the right hand or the left; they were Benjaminites, Saul's kindred. 3The chief was Ahiezer, then Joash, both sons of Shemaah of Gibeah; also Jeziel and Pelet sons of Azmaveth; Beracah, Jehu of Anathoth, 4Ishmaiah of Gibeon, a warrior among the Thirty and a leader over the Thirty; Jeremiah,b Jahaziel, Johanan, Jozabad of Gederah, 5Eluzai,c Jerimoth, Bealiah, Shemariah, Shephatiah the Haruphite; 6Elkanah, Isshiah, Azarel, Joezer, and Jashobeam, the Korahites; 7and Joelah and Zebadiah, sons of Jeroham of Gedor.

8 From the Gadites there went over to David at the stronghold in the wilderness mighty and experienced warriors, expert with shield and spear, whose faces were like the faces of lions, and who were swift as gazelles on the mountains; 9Ezer the chief, Obadiah second, Eliab third, 10Mishmannah fourth, Jeremiah fifth, 11Attai sixth, Eliel seventh, 12Johanan eighth, Elzabad ninth, 13Jeremiah tenth, Machbannai eleventh. 14These Gadites were officers of the army, the least equal to a hundred and the greatest to a thousand. 15These are the men who crossed the Jordan in the first month, when it was overflowing all its banks, and put to flight all those in the valleys, to the east and to the west.

16 Some Benjaminites and Judahites came to the stronghold to David. 17David went out to meet them and said to them, "If you have come to me in friendship, to help me, then my heart will be knit to you; but if you have come to betray me to my adversaries, though my hands have done no wrong, then may the God of our ancestors see and give judgment." 18Then the spirit came upon Amasai, chief of the Thirty, and he said,

"We are yours, O David;
and with you, O son of Jesse!
Peace, peace to you,
and peace to the one who helps you!
For your God is the one who helps you."

Then David received them, and made them officers of his troops.

---

a 12:1 King Saul, literally, "the son of Kish."　　　b Heb verse 5　c Heb verse 6

King James

19And there fell *some* of Manasseh to David, when he came with the Philistines against Saul to battle: but they helped them not: for the lords of the Philistines upon advisement sent him away, saying, He will fall to his master Saul to *the jeopardy of* our heads.

20As he went to Ziklag, there fell to him of Manasseh, Adnah, and Jozabad, and Jediael, and Michael, and Jozabad, and Elihu, and Zilthai, captains of the thousands that *were* of Manasseh.

21And they helped David against the band *of the rovers:* for they *were* all mighty men of valour, and were captains in the host.

22For at *that* time day by day there came to David to help him, until *it was* a great host, like the host of God.

23¶ And these *are* the numbers of the bands *that were* ready armed to the war, *and* came to David to Hebron, to turn the kingdom of Saul to him, according to the word of the LORD.

24The children of Judah that bare shield and spear *were* six thousand and eight hundred, ready armed to the war.

25Of the children of Simeon, mighty men of valour for the war, seven thousand and one hundred.

26Of the children of Levi four thousand and six hundred.

27And Jehoiada *was* the leader of the Aaronites, and with him *were* three thousand and seven hundred;

28And Zadok, a young man mighty of valour, and of his father's house twenty and two captains.

29And of the children of Benjamin, the kindred of Saul, three thousand: for hitherto the greatest part of them had kept the ward of the house of Saul.

30And of the children of Ephraim twenty thousand and eight hundred, mighty men of valour, famous throughout the house of their fathers.

31And of the half tribe of Manasseh eighteen thousand, which were expressed by name, to come and make David king.

32And of the children of Issachar, *which were men* that had understanding of the times, to know what Israel ought to do; the heads of them *were* two hundred; and all their brethren *were* at their commandment.

33Of Zebulun, such as went forth to battle, expert in war, with all instruments of war, fifty thousand, which could keep rank: *they were* not of double heart.

34And of Naphtali a thousand captains, and with them with shield and spear thirty and seven thousand.

35And of the Danites expert in war twenty and eight thousand and six hundred.

36And of Asher, such as went forth to battle, expert in war, forty thousand.

37And on the other side of Jordan, of the Reubenites, and the Gadites, and of the half tribe of Manasseh, with all manner of instruments of war for the battle, an hundred and twenty thousand.

38All these men of war, that could keep rank, came with a perfect heart to Hebron, to make David king over all Israel: and all the rest also of Israel *were* of one heart to make David king.

39And there they were with David three days, eating and drinking: for their brethren had prepared for them.

40Moreover they that were nigh them, *even* unto Issachar and Zebulun and Naphtali, brought bread on asses, and on camels, and on mules, and on oxen, *and* meat, meal, cakes of figs, and bunches of raisins, and wine, and oil, and oxen, and sheep abundantly: for *there was* joy in Israel.

New International

19Some of the men of Manasseh defected to David when he went with the Philistines to fight against Saul. (He and his men did not help the Philistines because, after consultation, their rulers sent him away. They said, "It will cost us our heads if he deserts to his master Saul.") 20When David went to Ziklag, these were the men of Manasseh who defected to him: Adnah, Jozabad, Jediael, Michael, Jozabad, Elihu and Zillethai, leaders of units of a thousand in Manasseh. 21They helped David against raiding bands, for all of them were brave warriors, and they were commanders in his army. 22Day after day men came to help David, until he had a great army, like the army of God.[a]

Others Join David at Hebron

23These are the numbers of the men armed for battle who came to David at Hebron to turn Saul's kingdom over to him, as the LORD had said:

24men of Judah, carrying shield and spear— 6,800 armed for battle;

25men of Simeon, warriors ready for battle— 7,100;

26men of Levi— 4,600, 27including Jehoiada, leader of the family of Aaron, with 3,700 men, 28and Zadok, a brave young warrior, with 22 officers from his family;

29men of Benjamin, Saul's kinsmen— 3,000, most of whom had remained loyal to Saul's house until then;

30men of Ephraim, brave warriors, famous in their own clans—20,800;

31men of half the tribe of Manasseh, designated by name to come and make David king—18,000;

32men of Issachar, who understood the times and knew what Israel should do—200 chiefs, with all their relatives under their command;

33men of Zebulun, experienced soldiers prepared for battle with every type of weapon, to help David with undivided loyalty—50,000;

34men of Naphtali— 1,000 officers, together with 37,000 men carrying shields and spears;

35men of Dan, ready for battle—28,600;

36men of Asher, experienced soldiers prepared for battle—40,000;

37and from east of the Jordan, men of Reuben, Gad and the half-tribe of Manasseh, armed with every type of weapon—120,000.

38All these were fighting men who volunteered to serve in the ranks. They came to Hebron fully determined to make David king over all Israel. All the rest of the Israelites were also of one mind to make David king. 39The men spent three days there with David, eating and drinking, for their families had supplied provisions for them. 40Also, their neighbors from as far away as Issachar, Zebulun and Naphtali came bringing food on donkeys, camels, mules and oxen. There were plentiful supplies of flour, fig cakes, raisin cakes, wine, oil, cattle and sheep, for there was joy in Israel.

---

a 22 Or *a great and mighty army*

Living Bible

19Some men from Manasseh deserted the Israeli army and joined David just as he was going into battle with the Philistines against King Saul. But as it turned out, the Philistine generals refused to let David and his men go with them. After much discussion they sent them back, for they were afraid that David and his men would imperil them by deserting to King Saul.

20Here is a list of the men from Manasseh who deserted to David as he was en route to Ziklag:

Adnah, Jozabad, Jedia-el, Michael, Jozabad, Elihu, Zillethai.

Each was a high-ranking officer of Manasseh's troops. 21They were brave and able warriors, and they assisted David when he fought against the Amalek raiders at Ziklag.b

22More men joined David almost every day until he had a tremendous army—the army of God. 23Here is the registry of recruits who joined David at Hebron. They were all anxious to see David become king instead of Saul, just as the Lord had said would happen.

24-37From Judah, 6,800 troops armed with shields and spears.

From the tribe of Simeon, 7,100 outstanding warriors.

From the Levites, 4,600.

From the priests—descendants of Aaron—there were 3,700 troops under the command of Zadok, a young man of unusual courage, and Jehoiada. (He and twenty-two members of his family were officers of the fighting priests.)

From the tribe of Benjamin, the same tribe Saul was from, there were 3,000. (Most of that tribe retained its allegiance to Saul.)

From the tribe of Ephraim, 20,800 mighty warriors, each famous in his respective clan.

From the half-tribe of Manasseh, 18,000 were sent for the express purpose of helping David become king.

From the tribe of Issachar there were 200 leaders of the tribe with their relatives—all men who understood the temper of the times and knew the best course for Israel to take.

From the tribe of Zebulun there were 50,000 trained warriors; they were fully armed and totally loyal to David.

From Naphtali there were 1,000 officers and 37,000 troops equipped with shields and spears.

From the tribe of Dan there were 28,600 troops, all of them prepared for war.

From the tribe of Asher, there were 40,000 trained and ready troops.

From the other side of the Jordan River—where the tribes of Reuben and Gad and the half-tribe of Manasseh lived—there were 120,000 troops equipped with every kind of weapon.

38All these men came in battle array to Hebron with the single purpose of making David the king of Israel. In fact, all of Israel was ready for this change. 39They feasted and drank with David for three days, for preparations had been made for their arrival. 40People from nearby and from as far away as Issachar, Zebulun, and Naphtali brought food on donkeys, camels, mules, and oxen. Vast supplies of flour, fig cakes, raisins, wine, oil, cattle, and sheep were brought to the celebration, for joy had spread throughout the land.

New Revised Standard

19 Some of the Manassites deserted to David when he came with the Philistines for the battle against Saul. (Yet he did not help them, for the rulers of the Philistines took counsel and sent him away, saying, "He will desert to his master Saul at the cost of our heads.") 20As he went to Ziklag these Manassites deserted to him: Adnah, Jozabad, Jediael, Michael, Jozabad, Elihu, and Zillethai, chiefs of the thousands in Manasseh. 21They helped David against the band of raiders,c for they were all warriors and commanders in the army. 22Indeed from day to day people kept coming to David to help him, until there was a great army, like an army of God.

David's Army at Hebron

23 These are the numbers of the divisions of the armed troops who came to David in Hebron to turn the kingdom of Saul over to him, according to the word of the LORD. 24The people of Judah bearing shield and spear numbered six thousand eight hundred armed troops. 25Of the Simeonites, mighty warriors, seven thousand one hundred. 26Of the Levites four thousand six hundred. 27Jehoiada, leader of the house of Aaron, and with him three thousand seven hundred. 28Zadok, a young warrior, and twenty-two commanders from his own ancestral house. 29Of the Benjaminites, the kindred of Saul, three thousand, of whom the majority had continued to keep their allegiance to the house of Saul. 30Of the Ephraimites, twenty thousand eight hundred, mighty warriors, notables in their ancestral houses. 31Of the half-tribe of Manasseh, eighteen thousand, who were expressly named to come and make David king. 32Of Issachar, those who had understanding of the times, to know what Israel ought to do, two hundred chiefs, and all their kindred under their command. 33Of Zebulun, fifty thousand seasoned troops, equipped for battle with all the weapons of war, to help Davidd with singleness of purpose. 34Of Naphtali, a thousand commanders, with whom there were thirty-seven thousand armed with shield and spear. 35Of the Danites, twenty-eight thousand six hundred equipped for battle. 36Of Asher, forty thousand seasoned troops ready for battle. 37Of the Reubenites and Gadites and the half-tribe of Manasseh from beyond the Jordan, one hundred twenty thousand armed with all the weapons of war.

38 All these, warriors arrayed in battle order, came to Hebron with full intent to make David king over all Israel; likewise all the rest of Israel were of a single mind to make David king. 39They were there with David for three days, eating and drinking, for their kindred had provided for them. 40And also their neighbors, from as far away as Issachar and Zebulun and Naphtali, came bringing food on donkeys, camels, mules, and oxen—abundant provisions of meal, cakes of figs, clusters of raisins, wine, oil, oxen, and sheep, for there was joy in Israel.

---

b 12:21 Ziklag, implied.   c Or as officers of his troops   d Gk: Heb lacks David

King James

13 AND DAVID consulted with the captains of thousands and hundreds, *and* with every leader.

2And David said unto all the congregation of Israel, If *it seem* good unto you, and *that it be* of the LORD our God, let us send abroad unto our brethren every where, *that are* left in all the land of Israel, and with them *also* to the priests and Levites *which are* in their cities *and* suburbs, that they may gather themselves unto us:

3And let us bring again the ark of our God to us: for we inquired not at it in the days of Saul.

4And all the congregation said that they would do so: for the thing was right in the eyes of all the people.

5So David gathered all Israel together, from Shihor of Egypt even unto the entering of Hemath, to bring the ark of God from Kirjath-jearim.

6And David went up, and all Israel, to Baalah, *that is,* to Kirjath-jearim, which *belonged* to Judah, to bring up thence the ark of God the LORD, that dwelleth *between* the cherubims, whose name is called *on it.*

7And they carried the ark of God in a new cart out of the house of Abinadab: and Uzza and Ahio drave the cart.

8And David and all Israel played before God with all *their* might, and with singing, and with harps, and with psalteries, and with timbrels, and with cymbals, and with trumpets.

9¶ And when they came unto the threshingfloor of Chidon, Uzza put forth his hand to hold the ark; for the oxen stumbled.

10And the anger of the LORD was kindled against Uzza, and he smote him, because he put his hand to the ark: and there he died before God.

11And David was displeased, because the LORD had made a breach upon Uzza: wherefore that place is called Perez-uzza to this day.

12And David was afraid of God that day, saying, How shall I bring the ark of God *home* to me?

13So David brought not the ark *home* to himself to the city of David, but carried it aside into the house of Obed-edom the Gittite.

14And the ark of God remained with the family of Obed-edom in his house three months. And the LORD blessed the house of Obed-edom, and all that he had.

14 NOW HIRAM king of Tyre sent messengers to David, and timber of cedars, with masons and carpenters, to build him an house.

2And David perceived that the LORD had confirmed him king over Israel, for his kingdom was lifted up on high, because of his people Israel.

3¶ And David took more wives at Jerusalem: and David begat more sons and daughters.

4Now these *are* the names of *his* children which he had in Jerusalem; Shammua, and Shobab, Nathan, and Solomon,

5And Ibhar, and Elishua, and Elpalet,

6And Nogah, and Nepheg, and Japhia,

7And Elishama, and Beeliada, and Eliphalet.

8¶ And when the Philistines heard that David was anointed king over all Israel, all the Philistines went up to seek David. And David heard *of it,* and went out against them.

9And the Philistines came and spread themselves in the valley of Rephaim.

10And David inquired of God, saying, Shall I go up against the Philistines? and wilt thou deliver them into mine hand? And the LORD said unto him, Go up; for I will deliver them into thine hand.

New International

Bringing Back the Ark

13 DAVID CONFERRED with each of his officers, the commanders of thousands and commanders of hundreds. 2He then said to the whole assembly of Israel, "If it seems good to you and if it is the will of the LORD our God, let us send word far and wide to the rest of our brothers throughout the territories of Israel, and also to the priests and Levites who are with them in their towns and pasturelands, to come and join us. 3Let us bring the ark of our God back to us, for we did not inquire ofᵃ itᵇ during the reign of Saul." 4The whole assembly agreed to do this, because it seemed right to all the people.

5So David assembled all the Israelites, from the Shihor River in Egypt to Leboᶜ Hamath, to bring the ark of God from Kiriath Jearim. 6David and all the Israelites with him went to Baalah of Judah (Kiriath Jearim) to bring up from there the ark of God the LORD, who is enthroned between the cherubim—the ark that is called by the Name.

7They moved the ark of God from Abinadab's house on a new cart, with Uzzah and Ahio guiding it. 8David and all the Israelites were celebrating with all their might before God, with songs and with harps, lyres, tambourines, cymbals and trumpets.

9When they came to the threshing floor of Kidon, Uzzah reached out his hand to steady the ark, because the oxen stumbled. 10The LORD's anger burned against Uzzah, and he struck him down because he had put his hand on the ark. So he died there before God.

11Then David was angry because the LORD's wrath had broken out against Uzzah, and to this day that place is called Perez Uzzah.ᵈ

12David was afraid of God that day and asked, "How can I ever bring the ark of God to me?" 13He did not take the ark to be with him in the City of David. Instead, he took it aside to the house of Obed-Edom the Gittite. 14The ark of God remained with the family of Obed-Edom in his house for three months, and the LORD blessed his household and everything he had.

David's House and Family

14 NOW HIRAM king of Tyre sent messengers to David, along with cedar logs, stonemasons and carpenters to build a palace for him. 2And David knew that the LORD had established him as king over Israel and that his kingdom had been highly exalted for the sake of his people Israel.

3In Jerusalem David took more wives and became the father of more sons and daughters. 4These are the names of the children born to him there: Shammua, Shobab, Nathan, Solomon, 5Ibhar, Elishua, Elpelet, 6Nogah, Nepheg, Japhia, 7Elishama, Beeliadaᵉ and Eliphelet.

David Defeats the Philistines

8When the Philistines heard that David had been anointed king over all Israel, they went up in full force to search for him, but David heard about it and went out to meet them. 9Now the Philistines had come and raided the Valley of Rephaim; 10so David inquired of God: "Shall I go and attack the Philistines? Will you hand them over to me?"

The LORD answered him, "Go, I will hand them over to you."

ᵃ *3 Or we neglected* ᵇ *3 Or him* ᶜ *5 Or to the entrance to* ᵈ *11 Perez Uzzah means outbreak against Uzzah.* ᵉ *7 A variant of Eliada*

Living Bible

13 AFTER DAVID had consulted with all of his army officers, 2he addressed the assembled men of Israel as follows:

"Since you think that I should be your king, and since the Lord our God has given his approval, let us send messages to our brothers throughout the land of Israel, including the priests and Levites, inviting them to come and join us. 3And let us bring back the Ark of our God, for we have been neglecting it ever since Saul became king."

4There was unanimous consent, for everyone agreed with him. 5So David summoned the people of Israel from all across the nationf so that they could be present when the Ark of God was brought from Kiriath-jearim.

6Then David and all Israel went to Baalah (i.e., Kiriath-jearim) in Judah to bring back the Ark of the Lord God enthroned above the angels.g 7It was taken from the house of Abinadab on a new cart. Uzza and Ahio drove the oxen. 8Then David and all the people danced before the Lord with great enthusiasm, accompanied by singing and by zithers, harps, tambourines, cymbals, and trumpets. 9But as they arrived at the threshing-floor of Chidon, the oxen stumbled and Uzza reached out his hand to steady the Ark. 10Then the anger of the Lord blazed out against Uzza, and killed him because he had touched the Ark. And so he died there before God. 11David was angry at the Lord for what he had done to Uzza, and he named the place "The Outbreak Against Uzza." And it is still called that today.

12Now David was afraid of God and asked, "How shall I ever get the Ark of God home?"

13Finally he decided to take it to the home of Obed-edom the Gittite instead of bringing it to the City of David. 14The Ark remained there with the family of Obed-edom for three months, and the Lord blessed him and his family.

14 KING HIRAM of Tyre sent masons and carpenters to help build David's palace and he supplied him with much cedar lumber. 2David now realized why the Lord had made him king and why he had made his kingdom so great; it was for a special reason—to give joy to God's people!

3After David moved to Jerusalem, he married additional wives and became the father of many sons and daughters.

4-7These are the names of the sons born to him in Jerusalem:

Shammua, Shobab, Nathan, Solomon, Ibhar, Elishu-a, Elpelet, Nogah, Nepheg, Japhia, Elishama, Beeliada, Eliphelet.

8When the Philistines heard that David was Israel's new king, they mobilized their forces to capture him. But David learned that they were on the way, so he called together his army. 9The Philistines were raiding the Valley of Rephaim, 10and David asked the Lord, "If I go out and fight them, will you give me the victory?"

And the Lord replied, "Yes, I will."

New Revised Standard

The Ark Brought from Kiriath-jearim

13 DAVID CONSULTED with the commanders of the thousands and of the hundreds, with every leader. 2David said to the whole assembly of Israel, "If it seems good to you, and if it is the will of the LORD our God, let us send abroad to our kindred who remain in all the land of Israel, including the priests and Levites in the cities that have pasture lands, that they may come together to us. 3Then let us bring again the ark of our God to us; for we did not turn to it in the days of Saul." 4The whole assembly agreed to do so, for the thing pleased all the people.

5 So David assembled all Israel from the Shihor of Egypt to Lebo-hamath, to bring the ark of God from Kiriath-jearim. 6And David and all Israel went up to Baalah, that is, to Kiriath-jearim, which belongs to Judah, to bring up from there the ark of God, the LORD, who is enthroned on the cherubim, which is called by hish name. 7They carried the ark of God on a new cart, from the house of Abinadab, and Uzzah and Ahioi were driving the cart. 8David and all Israel were dancing before God with all their might, with song and lyres and harps and tambourines and cymbals and trumpets.

9 When they came to the threshing floor of Chidon, Uzzah put out his hand to hold the ark, for the oxen shook it. 10The anger of the LORD was kindled against Uzzah; he struck him down because he put out his hand to the ark; and he died there before God. 11David was angry because the LORD had burst out against Uzzah; so that place is called Perez-uzzah to this day. 12David was afraid of God that day; he said, "How can I bring the ark of God into my care?" 13So David did not take the ark into his care into the city of David; he took it instead to the house of Obed-edom the Gittite. 14The ark of God remained with the household of Obed-edom in his house three months, and the LORD blessed the household of Obed-edom and all that he had.

David Established at Jerusalem

14 KING HIRAM of Tyre sent messengers to David, along with cedar logs, and masons and carpenters to build a house for him. 2David then perceived that the LORD had established him as king over Israel, and that his kingdom was highly exalted for the sake of his people Israel.

3 David took more wives in Jerusalem, and David became the father of more sons and daughters. 4These are the names of the children whom he had in Jerusalem: Shammua, Shobab, and Nathan; Solomon, 5Ibhar, Elishua, and Elpelet; 6Nogah, Nepheg, and Japhia; 7Elishama, Beeliada, and Eliphelet.

Defeat of the Philistines

8 When the Philistines heard that David had been anointed king over all Israel, all the Philistines went up in search of David; and David heard of it and went out against them. 9Now the Philistines had come and made a raid in the valley of Rephaim. 10David inquired of God, "Shall I go up against the Philistines? Will you give them into my hand?" The LORD said to him, "Go up, and I will give them into your hand." 11So he went

---

f 13:5 from all across the nation, literally, "from Shihor—the Brook of Egypt—to the entrance of Hamath." g 13:6 above the angels, literally "above the cherubim."

h Heb lacks his   i Or and his brother   j That is Bursting Out Against Uzzah

King James

11So they came up to Baal-perazim; and David smote them there. Then David said, God hath broken in upon mine enemies by mine hand like the breaking forth of waters: therefore they called the name of that place Baal-perazim.

12And when they had left their gods there, David gave a commandment, and they were burned with fire.

13And the Philistines yet again spread themselves abroad in the valley.

14Therefore David inquired again of God; and God said unto him, Go not up after them; turn away from them, and come upon them over against the mulberry trees.

15And it shall be, when thou shalt hear a sound of going in the tops of the mulberry trees, *that* then thou shalt go out to battle: for God is gone forth before thee to smite the host of the Philistines.

16David therefore did as God commanded him: and they smote the host of the Philistines from Gibeon even to Gazer.

17And the fame of David went out into all lands; and the LORD brought the fear of him upon all nations.

15 AND *DAVID* made him houses in the city of David, and prepared a place for the ark of God, and pitched for it a tent.

2Then David said, None ought to carry the ark of God but the Levites: for them hath the LORD chosen to carry the ark of God, and to minister unto him for ever.

3And David gathered all Israel together to Jerusalem, to bring up the ark of the LORD unto his place, which he had prepared for it.

4And David assembled the children of Aaron, and the Levites:

5Of the sons of Kohath; Uriel the chief, and his brethren an hundred and twenty:

6Of the sons of Merari; Asaiah the chief, and his brethren two hundred and twenty:

7Of the sons of Gershom; Joel the chief, and his brethren an hundred and thirty:

8Of the sons of Elizaphan; Shemaiah the chief, and his brethren two hundred:

9Of the sons of Hebron; Eliel the chief, and his brethren fourscore:

10Of the sons of Uzziel; Amminadab the chief, and his brethren an hundred and twelve.

11And David called for Zadok and Abiathar the priests, and for the Levites, for Uriel, Asaiah, and Joel, Shemaiah, and Eliel, and Amminadab,

12And said unto them, Ye *are* the chief of the fathers of the Levites: Sanctify yourselves, *both* ye and your brethren, that ye may bring up the ark of the LORD God of Israel unto *the place that* I have prepared for it.

13For because ye *did it* not at the first, the LORD our God made a breach upon us, for that we sought him not after the due order.

14So the priests and the Levites sanctified themselves to bring up the ark of the LORD God of Israel.

15And the children of the Levites bare the ark of God upon their shoulders with the staves thereon, as Moses commanded according to the word of the LORD.

16And David spake to the chief of the Levites to appoint their brethren *to be* the singers with instruments of music, psalteries and harps and cymbals, sounding, by lifting up the voice with joy.

17So the Levites appointed Heman the son of Joel; and of his brethren, Asaph the son of Berechiah; and of the sons of Merari their brethren, Ethan the son of Kushaiah;

New International

11So David and his men went up to Baal Perazim, and there he defeated them. He said, "As waters break out, God has broken out against my enemies by my hand." So that place was called Baal Perazim.a 12The Philistines had abandoned their gods there, and David gave orders to burn them in the fire.

13Once more the Philistines raided the valley; 14so David inquired of God again, and God answered him, "Do not go straight up, but circle around them and attack them in front of the balsam trees. 15As soon as you hear the sound of marching in the tops of the balsam trees, move out to battle, because that will mean God has gone out in front of you to strike the Philistine army." 16So David did as God commanded him, and they struck down the Philistine army, all the way from Gibeon to Gezer.

17So David's fame spread throughout every land, and the LORD made all the nations fear him.

The Ark Brought to Jerusalem

15 AFTER DAVID had constructed buildings for himself in the City of David, he prepared a place for the ark of God and pitched a tent for it. 2Then David said, "No one but the Levites may carry the ark of God, because the LORD chose them to carry the ark of the LORD and to minister before him forever."

3David assembled all Israel in Jerusalem to bring up the ark of the LORD to the place he had prepared for it. 4He called together the descendants of Aaron and the Levites:

5From the descendants of Kohath,
    Uriel the leader and 120 relatives;
6from the descendants of Merari,
    Asaiah the leader and 220 relatives;
7from the descendants of Gershom,b
    Joel the leader and 130 relatives;
8from the descendants of Elizaphan,
    Shemaiah the leader and 200 relatives;
9from the descendants of Hebron,
    Eliel the leader and 80 relatives;
10from the descendants of Uzziel,
    Amminadab the leader and 112 relatives.

11Then David summoned Zadok and Abiathar the priests, and Uriel, Asaiah, Joel, Shemaiah, Eliel and Amminadab the Levites. 12He said to them, "You are the heads of the Levitical families; you and your fellow Levites are to consecrate yourselves and bring up the ark of the LORD, the God of Israel, to the place I have prepared for it. 13It was because you, the Levites, did not bring it up the first time that the LORD our God broke out in anger against us. We did not inquire of him about how to do it in the prescribed way." 14So the priests and Levites consecrated themselves in order to bring up the ark of the LORD, the God of Israel. 15And the Levites carried the ark of God with the poles on their shoulders, as Moses had commanded in accordance with the word of the LORD.

16David told the leaders of the Levites to appoint their brothers as singers to sing joyful songs, accompanied by musical instruments: lyres, harps and cymbals.

17So the Levites appointed Heman son of Joel; from his brothers, Asaph son of Berekiah; and from their brothers the Merarites, Ethan son of Kushaiah; 18and

---

a *11 Baal Perazim means the lord who breaks out.*   b *7 Hebrew Gershom,* a variant of *Gershon*

Living Bible

11So he attacked them at Baal-perazim and wiped them out. He exulted, "God has used me to sweep away my enemies like water bursting through a dam!" That is why the place has been known as Baal-perazim ever since (meaning, "The Place of Breaking Through").

12After the battle the Israelis picked up many idols left by the Philistines, but David ordered them burned.

13Later the Philistines raided the valley again, 14and again David asked God what to do.

The Lord replied, "Go around by the mulberry trees and attack from there. 15When you hear a sound like marching in the tops of the mulberry trees, that is your signal to attack, for God will go before you and destroy the enemy."

16So David did as the Lord commanded him; and he cut down the army of the Philistines all the way from Gibeon to Gezer. 17David's fame spread everywhere, and the Lord caused all the nations to fear him.

15 DAVID NOW built several palaces for himself in Jerusalem, and he also built a new Tabernacle to house the Ark of God, 2and issued these instructions: "[When we transfer the Ark to its new homec], no one except the Levites may carry it, for God has chosen them for this purpose; they are to minister to him forever."

3Then David summoned all Israel to Jerusalem to celebrate the bringing of the Ark into the new Tabernacle. 4–10These were the priests and Levites present:

120 from the clan of Kohath; with Uriel as their leader;
220 from the clan of Merari; with Asaiah as their leader;
130 from the clan of Gershom; with Joel as their leader;
200 from the subclan of Elizaphan; with Shemaiah as their leader;
80 from the subclan of Hebron; with Eliel as their leader;
112 from the subclan of Uzziel; with Amminadab as their leader.

11Then David called for Zadok and Abiathar, the High Priests, and for the Levite leaders: Uriel, Asaiah, Joel, Shemaiah, Eliel, and Amminadab.

12"You are the leaders of the clans of the Levites," he told them. "Now sanctify yourselves with all your brothers so that you may bring the Ark of Jehovah, the God of Israel, to the place I have prepared for it. 13The Lord destroyed us before because we handled the matter improperly—you were not carrying it."

14So the priests and the Levites underwent the ceremonies of sanctification in preparation for bringing home the Ark of Jehovah, the God of Israel. 15Then the Levites carried the Ark on their shoulders with its carrying poles, just as the Lord had instructed Moses.

16King David also ordered the Levite leaders to organize the singers into an orchestra, and they played loudly and joyously upon psalteries, harps, and cymbals. 17Heman (son of Joel), Asaph (son of Berechiah), and Ethan (son of Kushaiah) from the clan of Merari were the heads of the musicians.

New Revised Standard

up to Baal-perazim, and David defeated them there. David said, "God has burst outd against my enemies by my hand, like a bursting flood." Therefore that place is called Baal-perazim.e 12They abandoned their gods there, and at David's command they were burned.

13 Once again the Philistines made a raid in the valley. 14When David again inquired of God, God said to him, "You shall not go up after them; go around and come on them opposite the balsam trees. 15When you hear the sound of marching in the tops of the balsam trees, then go out to battle; for God has gone out before you to strike down the army of the Philistines." 16David did as God had commanded him, and they struck down the Philistine army from Gibeon to Gezer. 17The fame of David went out into all lands, and the LORD brought the fear of him on all nations.

The Ark Brought to Jerusalem

15 DAVIDf BUILT houses for himself in the city of David, and he prepared a place for the ark of God and pitched a tent for it. 2Then David commanded that no one but the Levites were to carry the ark of God, for the LORD had chosen them to carry the ark of the LORD and to minister to him forever. 3David assembled all Israel in Jerusalem to bring up the ark of the LORD to its place, which he had prepared for it. 4Then David gathered together the descendants of Aaron and the Levites: 5of the sons of Kohath, Uriel the chief, with one hundred twenty of his kindred; 6of the sons of Merari, Asaiah the chief, with two hundred twenty of his kindred; 7of the sons of Gershom, Joel the chief, with one hundred thirty of his kindred; 8of the sons of Elizaphan, Shemaiah the chief, with two hundred of his kindred; 9of the sons of Hebron, Eliel the chief, with eighty of his kindred; 10of the sons of Uzziel, Amminadab the chief, with one hundred twelve of his kindred.

11 David summoned the priests Zadok and Abiathar, and the Levites Uriel, Asaiah, Joel, Shemaiah, Eliel, and Amminadab. 12He said to them, "You are the heads of families of the Levites; sanctify yourselves, you and your kindred, so that you may bring up the ark of the LORD, the God of Israel, to the place that I have prepared for it. 13Because you did not carry it the first time,g the LORD our God burst out against us, because we did not give it proper care." 14So the priests and the Levites sanctified themselves to bring up the ark of the LORD, the God of Israel. 15And the Levites carried the ark of God on their shoulders with the poles, as Moses had commanded according to the word of the LORD.

16 David also commanded the chiefs of the Levites to appoint their kindred as the singers to play on musical instruments, on harps and lyres and cymbals, to raise loud sounds of joy. 17So the Levites appointed Heman son of Joel; and of his kindred Asaph son of Berechiah; and of the sons of Merari, their kindred, Ethan son of Kushaiah; 18and with them their kindred of the second

---

c 15:2 When we transfer the Ark to its new home, implied.

d Heb paraz e That is Lord of Bursting Out f Heb He g Meaning of Heb uncertain

King James

18And with them their brethren of the second *degree,* Zechariah, Ben, and Jaaziel, and Shemiramoth, and Jehiel, and Unni, Eliab, and Benaiah, and Maaseiah, and Mattithiah, and Elipheleh, and Mikneiah, and Obededom, and Jeiel, the porters.

19So the singers, Heman, Asaph, and Ethan, *were appointed* to sound with cymbals of brass;

20And Zechariah, and Aziel, and Shemiramoth, and Jehiel, and Unni, and Eliab, and Maaseiah, and Benaiah, with psalteries on Alamoth;

21And Mattithiah, and Elipheleh, and Mikneiah, and Obed-edom, and Jeiel, and Azaziah, with harps on the Sheminith to excel.

22And Chenaniah, chief of the Levites, *was* for song: he instructed about the song, because he *was* skilful.

23And Berechiah and Elkanah *were* doorkeepers for the ark.

24And Shebaniah, and Jehoshaphat, and Nethaneel, and Amasai, and Zechariah, and Benaiah, and Eliezer, the priests, did blow with the trumpets before the ark of God: and Obed-edom and Jehiah *were* doorkeepers for the ark.

25¶ So David, and the elders of Israel, and the captains over thousands, went to bring up the ark of the covenant of the LORD out of the house of Obed-edom with joy.

26And it came to pass, when God helped the Levites that bare the ark of the covenant of the LORD, that they offered seven bullocks and seven rams.

27And David *was* clothed with a robe of fine linen, and all the Levites that bare the ark, and the singers, and Chenaniah the master of the song with the singers: David also *had* upon him an ephod of linen.

28Thus all Israel brought up the ark of the covenant of the LORD with shouting, and with sound of the cornet, and with trumpets, and with cymbals, making a noise with psalteries and harps.

29¶ And it came to pass, *as* the ark of the covenant of the LORD came to the city of David, that Michal the daughter of Saul looking out at a window saw king David dancing and playing: and she despised him in her heart.

16 SO THEY brought the ark of God, and set it in the midst of the tent that David had pitched for it: and they offered burnt sacrifices and peace offerings before God.

2And when David had made an end of offering the burnt offerings and the peace offerings, he blessed the people in the name of the LORD.

3And he dealt to every one of Israel, both man and woman, to every one a loaf of bread, and a good piece of flesh, and a flagon *of wine*.

4¶ And he appointed *certain* of the Levites to minister before the ark of the LORD, and to record, and to thank and praise the LORD God of Israel:

5Asaph the chief, and next to him Zechariah, Jeiel, and Shemiramoth, and Jehiel, and Mattithiah, and Eliab, and Benaiah, and Obed-edom: and Jeiel with psalteries and with harps; but Asaph made a sound with cymbals;

6Benaiah also and Jahaziel the priests with trumpets continually before the ark of the covenant of God.

7¶ Then on that day David delivered first *this psalm* to thank the LORD into the hand of Asaph and his brethren.

New International

with them their brothers next in rank: Zechariah,[a] Jaaziel, Shemiramoth, Jehiel, Unni, Eliab, Benaiah, Maaseiah, Mattithiah, Eliphelehu, Mikneiah, Obed-Edom and Jeiel,[b] the gatekeepers.

19The musicians Heman, Asaph and Ethan were to sound the bronze cymbals; 20Zechariah, Aziel, Shemiramoth, Jehiel, Unni, Eliab, Maaseiah and Benaiah were to play the lyres according to *alamoth*,[c] 21and Mattithiah, Eliphelehu, Mikneiah, Obed-Edom, Jeiel and Azaziah were to play the harps, directing according to *sheminith*.[c] 22Kenaniah the head Levite was in charge of the singing; that was his responsibility because he was skillful at it.

23Berekiah and Elkanah were to be doorkeepers for the ark. 24Shebaniah, Joshaphat, Nethanel, Amasai, Zechariah, Benaiah and Eliezer the priests were to blow trumpets before the ark of God. Obed-Edom and Jehiah were also to be doorkeepers for the ark.

25So David and the elders of Israel and the commanders of units of a thousand went to bring up the ark of the covenant of the LORD from the house of Obed-Edom, with rejoicing. 26Because God had helped the Levites who were carrying the ark of the covenant of the LORD, seven bulls and seven rams were sacrificed. 27Now David was clothed in a robe of fine linen, as were all the Levites who were carrying the ark, and as were the singers, and Kenaniah, who was in charge of the singing of the choirs. David also wore a linen ephod. 28So all Israel brought up the ark of the covenant of the LORD with shouts, with the sounding of rams' horns and trumpets, and of cymbals, and the playing of lyres and harps.

29As the ark of the covenant of the LORD was entering the City of David, Michal daughter of Saul watched from a window. And when she saw King David dancing and celebrating, she despised him in her heart.

16 THEY BROUGHT the ark of God and set it inside the tent that David had pitched for it, and they presented burnt offerings and fellowship offerings[d] before God. 2After David had finished sacrificing the burnt offerings and fellowship offerings, he blessed the people in the name of the LORD. 3Then he gave a loaf of bread, a cake of dates and a cake of raisins to each Israelite man and woman.

4He appointed some of the Levites to minister before the ark of the LORD, to make petition, to give thanks, and to praise the LORD, the God of Israel: 5Asaph was the chief, Zechariah second, then Jeiel, Shemiramoth, Jehiel, Mattithiah, Eliab, Benaiah, Obed-Edom and Jeiel. They were to play the lyres and harps, Asaph was to sound the cymbals, 6and Benaiah and Jahaziel the priests were to blow the trumpets regularly before the ark of the covenant of God.

David's Psalm of Thanks

7That day David first committed to Asaph and his associates this psalm of thanks to the LORD:

---

a *18* Three Hebrew manuscripts and most Septuagint manuscripts (see also verse 20 and 1 Chron. 16:5); most Hebrew manuscripts *Zechariah son and or Zechariah, Ben and*   b *18* Hebrew; Septuagint (see also verse 21) *Jeiel and Azaziah*   c *20,21* Probably a musical term   d *1* Traditionally *peace offerings*; also in verse 2

Living Bible

18The following men were chosen as their assistants: Zechariah, Ja-aziel, Shemiramoth, Jehiel, Unni, Eliab, Benaiah, Ma-asseiah, Mattithiah, Eliphelehu, Mikneiah, Obed-edom and Je-iel, the doorkeepers.

19Heman, Asaph, and Ethan were chosen to sound the bronze cymbals; 20and Zechariah, Azi-el, Shemiramoth, Jehiel, Unni, Eliab, Ma-aseiah, and Benaiah comprised an octet accompanied by harps.e 21Mattithiah, Eliphelehu, Mikneiah, Obed-edom, Je-iel, and Azaziah were the harpists.f 22The song leader was Chenaniah, the chief of the Levites, who was selected for his skill. 23Berechiah and Elkanah were guards for the Ark. 24Shebaniah, Joshaphat, Nethanel, Amasai, Zechariah, Benaiah, and Eliezer—all of whom were priests—formed a bugle corps to march at the head of the procession. And Obed-edom and Jehiah guarded the Ark.

25Then David and the elders of Israel and the high officers of the army went with great joy to the home of Obed-edom to take the Ark to Jerusalem. 26And because God didn't destroy the Levites who were carrying the Ark, they sacrificed seven bulls and seven lambs. 27David, the Levites carrying the Ark, the singers, and Chenaniah the song leader were all dressed in linen robes. David also wore a linen ephod. 28So the leaders of Israel took the Ark to Jerusalem with shouts of joy, the blowing of horns and trumpets, the crashing of cymbals, and loud playing on the harps and zithers.

29(But as the Ark arrived in Jerusalem, David's wife Michal, the daughter of King Saul, felt a deep disgust for David as she watched from the window and saw him dancing like a madman.)

16 SO THEY brought the Ark of God into the special tent that David had prepared for it, and the leaders of Israel sacrificed burnt offerings and peace offerings before God. 2At the conclusion of these offerings David blessed the people in the name of the Lord; 3then he gave every person presentg (men and women alike) a loaf of bread, some wine, and a cake of raisins.

4He appointed certain of the Levites to minister before the Ark by giving constant praise and thanks to the Lord God of Israel and by asking for his blessings upon his people. These are the names of those given this assignment: 5Asaph, the leader of this detail, sounded the cymbals. His associates were Zechariah, Je-iel, Shemiramoth, Jehiel, Mattithiah, Eliab, Benaiah, Obededom, and Je-iel; they played the harps and zithers. 6The priests Benaiah and Jahaziel played their trumpets regularly before the Ark.

7At that time David began the custom of using choirs in the Tabernacle to sing thanksgiving to the Lord. Asaph was the director of this choral group of priests.

New Revised Standard

order, Zechariah, Jaaziel, Shemiramoth, Jehiel, Unni, Eliab, Benaiah, Maaseiah, Mattithiah, Eliphelehu, and Mikneiah, and the gatekeepers Obed-edom and Jeiel. 19The singers Heman, Asaph, and Ethan were to sound bronze cymbals; 20Zechariah, Aziel, Shemiramoth, Jehiel, Unni, Eliab, Maaseiah, and Benaiah were to play harps according to Alamoth; 21but Mattithiah, Eliphelehu, Mikneiah, Obed-edom, Jeiel, and Azaziah were to lead with lyres according to the Sheminith. 22Chenaniah, leader of the Levites in music, was to direct the music, for he understood it. 23Berechiah and Elkanah were to be gatekeepers for the ark. 24Shebaniah, Joshaphat, Nethanel, Amasai, Zechariah, Benaiah, and Eliezer, the priests, were to blow the trumpets before the ark of God. Obed-edom and Jehiah also were to be gatekeepers for the ark.

25 So David and the elders of Israel, and the commanders of the thousands, went to bring up the ark of the covenant of the LORD from the house of Obed-edom with rejoicing. 26And because God helped the Levites who were carrying the ark of the covenant of the LORD, they sacrificed seven bulls and seven rams. 27David was clothed with a robe of fine linen, as also were all the Levites who were carrying the ark, and the singers, and Chenaniah the leader of the music of the singers; and David wore a linen ephod. 28So all Israel brought up the ark of the covenant of the LORD with shouting, to the sound of the horn, trumpets, and cymbals, and made loud music on harps and lyres.

29 As the ark of the covenant of the LORD came to the city of David, Michal daughter of Saul looked out of the window, and saw King David leaping and dancing; and she despised him in her heart.

The Ark Placed in the Tent

16 THEY BROUGHT in the ark of God, and set it inside the tent that David had pitched for it; and they offered burnt offerings and offerings of well-being before God. 2When David had finished offering the burnt offerings and the offerings of well-being, he blessed the people in the name of the LORD; 3and he distributed to every person in Israel—man and woman alike—to each a loaf of bread, a portion of meat,h and a cake of raisins.

4 He appointed certain of the Levites as ministers before the ark of the LORD, to invoke, to thank, and to praise the LORD, the God of Israel. 5Asaph was the chief, and second to him Zechariah, Jeiel, Shemiramoth, Jehiel, Mattithiah, Eliab, Benaiah, Obed-edom, and Jeiel, with harps and lyres; Asaph was to sound the cymbals, 6and the priests Benaiah and Jahaziel were to blow trumpets regularly, before the ark of the covenant of God.

David's Psalm of Thanksgiving

7 Then on that day David first appointed the singing of praises to the LORD by Asaph and his kindred.

---

e 15:20 accompanied by harps, literally, "set to Alamoth." The meaning of the term is uncertain. f 15:21 were the harpists, literally, "were to lead with zithers (or harps) set to the Shiminith." The meaning is uncertain. g 16:3 every person present, literally, "to each Israelite."

h Compare Gk Syr Vg: Meaning of Heb uncertain

King James

8Give thanks unto the LORD, call upon his name, make known his deeds among the people.

9Sing unto him, sing psalms unto him, talk ye of all his wondrous works.

10Glory ye in his holy name: let the heart of them rejoice that seek the LORD.

11Seek the LORD and his strength, seek his face continually.

12Remember his marvellous works that he hath done, his wonders, and the judgments of his mouth;

13O ye seed of Israel his servant, ye children of Jacob, his chosen ones.

14He *is* the LORD our God; his judgments *are* in all the earth.

15Be ye mindful always of his covenant; the word *which* he commanded to a thousand generations;

16*Even of the covenant* which he made with Abraham, and of his oath unto Isaac;

17And hath confirmed the same to Jacob for a law, *and* to Israel *for* an everlasting covenant,

18Saying, Unto thee will I give the land of Canaan, the lot of your inheritance;

19When ye were but few, even a few, and strangers in it.

20And *when* they went from nation to nation, and from *one* kingdom to another people;

21He suffered no man to do them wrong: yea, he reproved kings for their sakes,

22*Saying*, Touch not mine anointed, and do my prophets no harm.

23Sing unto the LORD, all the earth; show forth from day to day his salvation.

24Declare his glory among the heathen; his marvellous works among all nations.

25For great *is* the LORD, and greatly to be praised: he also *is* to be feared above all gods.

26For all the gods of the people *are* idols: but the LORD made the heavens.

27Glory and honour *are* in his presence; strength and gladness *are* in his place.

28Give unto the LORD, ye kindreds of the people, give unto the LORD glory and strength.

29Give unto the LORD the glory *due* unto his name: bring an offering, and come before him: worship the LORD in the beauty of holiness.

30Fear before him, all the earth: the world also shall be stable, that it be not moved.

31Let the heavens be glad, and let the earth rejoice: and let *men* say among the nations, The LORD reigneth.

32Let the sea roar, and the fulness thereof: let the fields rejoice, and all that *is* therein.

33Then shall the trees of the wood sing out at the presence of the LORD, because he cometh to judge the earth.

34O give thanks unto the LORD; for *he is* good; for his mercy *endureth* for ever.

New International

8Give thanks to the LORD, call on his name;
　make known among the nations what he has
　done.

9Sing to him, sing praise to him;
　tell of all his wonderful acts.

10Glory in his holy name;
　let the hearts of those who seek the LORD
　rejoice.

11Look to the LORD and his strength;
　seek his face always.

12Remember the wonders he has done,
　his miracles, and the judgments he
　pronounced,

13O descendants of Israel his servant,
　O sons of Jacob, his chosen ones.

14He is the LORD our God;
　his judgments are in all the earth.

15He remembersa his covenant forever,
　the word he commanded, for a thousand
　generations,

16the covenant he made with Abraham,
　the oath he swore to Isaac.

17He confirmed it to Jacob as a decree,
　to Israel as an everlasting covenant:

18"To you I will give the land of Canaan
　as the portion you will inherit."

19When they were but few in number,
　few indeed, and strangers in it,

20theyb wandered from nation to nation,
　from one kingdom to another.

21He allowed no man to oppress them;
　for their sake he rebuked kings:

22"Do not touch my anointed ones;
　do my prophets no harm."

23Sing to the LORD, all the earth;
　proclaim his salvation day after day.

24Declare his glory among the nations,
　his marvelous deeds among all peoples.

25For great is the LORD and most worthy of
　　praise;
　he is to be feared above all gods.

26For all the gods of the nations are idols,
　but the LORD made the heavens.

27Splendor and majesty are before him;
　strength and joy in his dwelling place.

28Ascribe to the LORD, O families of nations,
　ascribe to the LORD glory and strength,

29　ascribe to the LORD the glory due his name.
　Bring an offering and come before him;
　worship the LORD in the splendor of hisc
　　holiness.

30Tremble before him, all the earth!
　The world is firmly established; it cannot be
　moved.

31Let the heavens rejoice, let the earth be glad;
　let them say among the nations, "The LORD
　reigns!"

32Let the sea resound, and all that is in it;
　let the fields be jubilant, and everything in
　them!

33Then the trees of the forest will sing,
　they will sing for joy before the LORD,
　for he comes to judge the earth.

34Give thanks to the LORD, for he is good;
　his love endures forever.

---

a *15* Some Septuagint manuscripts (see also Psalm 105:8); Hebrew *Remember*
b *18-20* One Hebrew manuscript, Septuagint and Vulgate (see also Psalm 105:12); most Hebrew manuscripts *inherit, / 19though you are but few in number, / few indeed, and strangers in it." / 20They*　　c *29* Or LORD *with the splendor of*

Living Bible

8"Oh, give thanks to the Lord and pray to him," they
sang.
"Tell the peoples of the world
About his mighty doings.
9Sing to him; yes, sing his praises
And tell of his marvelous works.
10Glory in his holy name;
Let all rejoice who seek the Lord.
11Seek the Lord; yes, seek his strength
And seek his face untiringly.
12, 13O descendants of his servant Abraham,
O chosen sons of Jacob,
Remember his mighty miracles
And his marvelous miracles
And his authority:
14He is the Lord our God!
His authority is seen throughout the earth.
15Remember his covenant forever—
The words he commanded
To a thousand generations:
16His agreement with Abraham,
And his oath to Isaac,
17And his confirmation to Jacob.
He promised Israel
With an everlasting promise:
18'I will give you the land of Canaan
As your inheritance.'
19When Israel was few in number—oh, so few—
And merely strangers in the Promised Land;
20When they wandered from country to country,
From one kingdom to another—
21God didn't let anyone harm them.
Even kings were killed who sought to hurt them.
22'Don't harm my chosen people,' he declared.
'These are my prophets—touch them not.'
23Sing to the Lord, O earth,
Declare each day that he is the one who saves!
24Show his glory to the nations!
Tell everyone about his miracles.
25For the Lord is great, and should be highly praised;
He is to be held in awe above all gods.
26The other so-called gods are demons,
But the Lord made the heavens.
27Majesty and honor march before him,
Strength and gladness walk beside him.
28O people of all nations of the earth,
Ascribe great strength and glory to his name!
29Yes, ascribe to the Lord
The glory due his name!
Bring an offering and come before him;
Worship the Lord when clothed with holiness!
30Tremble before him, all the earth!
The world stands unmoved.
31Let the heavens be glad, the earth rejoice;
Let all the nations say, 'It is the Lord who reigns.'
32Let the vast seas roar,
Let the countryside and everything in it rejoice!
33Let the trees in the woods sing for joy before the
Lord,
For he comes to judge the earth.
34Oh, give thanks to the Lord, for he is good;
His love and his kindness go on forever.

New Revised Standard

8 O give thanks to the LORD, call on his name,
    make known his deeds among the peoples.
9 Sing to him, sing praises to him,
    tell of all his wonderful works.
10 Glory in his holy name;
    let the hearts of those who seek the LORD
    rejoice.
11 Seek the LORD and his strength,
    seek his presence continually.
12 Remember the wonderful works he has done,
    his miracles, and the judgments he uttered,
13 O offspring of his servant Israel,d
    children of Jacob, his chosen ones.
14 He is the LORD our God;
    his judgments are in all the earth.
15 Remember his covenant forever,
    the word that he commanded, for a
    thousand generations,
16 the covenant that he made with Abraham,
    his sworn promise to Isaac,
17 which he confirmed to Jacob as a statute,
    to Israel as an everlasting covenant,
18 saying, "To you I will give the land of
    Canaan
    as your portion for an inheritance."
19 When they were few in number,
    of little account, and strangers in the land,e
20 wandering from nation to nation,
    from one kingdom to another people,
21 he allowed no one to oppress them;
    he rebuked kings on their account,
22 saying, "Do not touch my anointed ones;
    do my prophets no harm."
23 Sing to the LORD, all the earth.
    Tell of his salvation from day to day.
24 Declare his glory among the nations,
    his marvelous works among all the peoples.
25 For great is the LORD, and greatly to be
    praised;
    he is to be revered above all gods.
26 For all the gods of the peoples are idols,
    but the LORD made the heavens.
27 Honor and majesty are before him;
    strength and joy are in his place.
28 Ascribe to the LORD, O families of the
    peoples,
    ascribe to the LORD glory and strength.
29 Ascribe to the LORD the glory due his name;
    bring an offering, and come before him.
    Worship the LORD in holy splendor;
30   tremble before him, all the earth.
    The world is firmly established; it shall
    never be moved.
31 Let the heavens be glad, and let the earth
    rejoice,
    and let them say among the nations, "The
    LORD is king!"
32 Let the sea roar, and all that fills it;
    let the field exult, and everything in it.
33 Then shall the trees of the forest sing for joy
    before the LORD, for he comes to judge the
    earth.
34 O give thanks to the LORD, for he is good;
    for his steadfast love endures forever.

d Another reading is *Abraham* (compare Ps 105.6)   e Heb *in it*

King James

35And say ye, Save us, O God of our salvation, and gather us together, and deliver us from the heathen, that we may give thanks to thy holy name, *and* glory in thy praise.

36Blessed *be* the LORD God of Israel for ever and ever. And all the people said, Amen, and praised the LORD.

37¶ So he left there before the ark of the covenant of the LORD Asaph and his brethren, to minister before the ark continually, as every day's work required:

38And Obed-edom with their brethren, threescore and eight; Obed-edom also the son of Jeduthun and Hosah *to be* porters:

39And Zadok the priest, and his brethren the priests, before the tabernacle of the LORD in the high place that *was* at Gibeon,

40To offer burnt offerings unto the LORD upon the altar of the burnt offering continually morning and evening, and *to do* according to all that is written in the law of the LORD, which he commanded Israel;

41And with them Heman and Jeduthun, and the rest that were chosen, who were expressed by name, to give thanks to the LORD, because his mercy *endureth* for ever;

42And with them Heman and Jeduthun with trumpets and cymbals for those that should make a sound, and with musical instruments of God. And the sons of Jeduthun *were* porters.

43And all the people departed every man to his house: and David returned to bless his house.

17 NOW IT came to pass, as David sat in his house, that David said to Nathan the prophet, Lo, I dwell in an house of cedars, but the ark of the covenant of the LORD *remaineth* under curtains.

2Then Nathan said unto David, Do all that *is* in thine heart; for God *is* with thee.

3¶ And it came to pass the same night, that the word of God came to Nathan, saying,

4Go and tell David my servant, Thus saith the LORD, Thou shalt not build me an house to dwell in:

5For I have not dwelt in an house since the day that I brought up Israel unto this day; but have gone from tent to tent, and from *one* tabernacle *to another.*

6Wheresoever I have walked with all Israel, spake I a word to any of the judges of Israel, whom I commanded to feed my people, saying, Why have ye not built me an house of cedars?

7Now therefore thus shalt thou say unto my servant David, Thus saith the LORD of hosts, I took thee from the sheepcote, *even* from following the sheep, that thou shouldest be ruler over my people Israel:

8And I have been with thee whithersoever thou hast walked, and have cut off all thine enemies from before thee, and have made thee a name like the name of the great men that *are* in the earth.

9Also I will ordain a place for my people Israel, and will plant them, and they shall dwell in their place, and shall be moved no more; neither shall the children of wickedness waste them any more, as at the beginning,

10And since the time that I commanded judges *to be* over my people Israel. Moreover I will subdue all thine enemies. Furthermore I tell thee that the LORD will build thee an house.

11¶ And it shall come to pass, when thy days be expired that thou must go *to be* with thy fathers, that I will raise up thy seed after thee, which shall be of thy sons; and I will establish his kingdom.

12He shall build me an house, and I will establish his throne for ever.

New International

35Cry out, "Save us, O God our Savior;
　gather us and deliver us from the nations,
that we may give thanks to your holy name,
　that we may glory in your praise."

36Praise be to the LORD, the God of Israel,
　from everlasting to everlasting.

Then all the people said "Amen" and "Praise the LORD."

37David left Asaph and his associates before the ark of the covenant of the LORD to minister there regularly, according to each day's requirements. 38He also left Obed-Edom and his sixty-eight associates to minister with them. Obed-Edom son of Jeduthun, and also Hosah, were gatekeepers.

39David left Zadok the priest and his fellow priests before the tabernacle of the LORD at the high place in Gibeon 40to present burnt offerings to the LORD on the altar of burnt offering regularly, morning and evening, in accordance with everything written in the Law of the LORD, which he had given Israel. 41With them were Heman and Jeduthun and the rest of those chosen and designated by name to give thanks to the LORD, "for his love endures forever." 42Heman and Jeduthun were responsible for the sounding of the trumpets and cymbals and for the playing of the other instruments for sacred song. The sons of Jeduthun were stationed at the gate.

43Then all the people left, each for his own home, and David returned home to bless his family.

God's Promise to David

17 AFTER DAVID was settled in his palace, he said to Nathan the prophet, "Here I am, living in a palace of cedar, while the ark of the covenant of the LORD is under a tent."

2Nathan replied to David, "Whatever you have in mind, do it, for God is with you."

3That night the word of God came to Nathan, saying:

4"Go and tell my servant David, 'This is what the LORD says: You are not the one to build me a house to dwell in. 5I have not dwelt in a house from the day I brought Israel up out of Egypt to this day. I have moved from one tent site to another, from one dwelling place to another. 6Wherever I have moved with all the Israelites, did I ever say to any of their leadersa whom I commanded to shepherd my people, "Why have you not built me a house of cedar?" '

7"Now then, tell my servant David, 'This is what the LORD Almighty says: I took you from the pasture and from following the flock, to be ruler over my people Israel. 8I have been with you wherever you have gone, and I have cut off all your enemies from before you. Now I will make your name like the names of the greatest men of the earth. 9And I will provide a place for my people Israel and will plant them so that they can have a home of their own and no longer be disturbed. Wicked people will not oppress them anymore, as they did at the beginning 10and have done ever since the time I appointed leaders over my people Israel. I will also subdue all your enemies.

" 'I declare to you that the LORD will build a house for you: 11When your days are over and you go to be with your fathers, I will raise up your offspring to succeed you, one of your own sons, and I will establish his kingdom. 12He is the one who will build a house for me, and I will establish his throne forever. 13I will be his father, and he will

<hr>

a 6 Traditionally *judges*; also in verse 10

Living Bible

35Cry out to him, 'Oh, save us, God of our salvation;
Bring us safely back from among the nations.
Then we will thank your holy name,
And triumph in your praise.'
36Blessed be Jehovah, God of Israel,
Forever and forevermore."
And all the people shouted "Amen!" and praised the
Lord.

37David arranged for Asaph and his fellow Levites to
minister regularly at the Tabernacle,b doing each day
whatever needed to be done. 38This group included
Obed-edom (the son of Jeduthun), Hosah and sixty-eight
of their colleagues as guards.

39Meanwhile the old Tabernacle of the Lord on the
hill of Gibeon continued to be active. David left Zadok
the priest and his fellow-priests to minister to the Lord
there. 40They sacrificed burnt offerings to the Lord each
morning and evening upon the altar set aside for that
purpose, just as the Lord had commanded Israel. 41David also appointed Heman, Jeduthun, and several others
who were chosen by name to give thanks to the Lord for
his constant love and mercy. 42They used their trumpets
and cymbals to accompany the singers with loud praises
to God. And Jeduthun's sons were appointed as guards.

43At last the celebration ended and the people returned to their homes, and David returned to bless his
own household.

17 AFTER DAVID had been living in his new palace for some time he said to Nathan the prophet,
"Look! I'm living here in a cedar-paneled home while
the Ark of the Covenant of God is out there in a tent!"
2And Nathan replied, "Carry out your plan in every
detail, for it is the will of the Lord."

3But that same night God said to Nathan, 4"Go and
give my servant David this message: 'You are not to
build my temple! 5I've gone from tent to tent as my
home from the time I brought Israel out of Egypt. 6In
all that time I never suggested to any of the leaders of
Israel—the shepherds I appointed to care for my people—that they should build me a cedar-lined temple.'

7"Tell my servant David, 'The Lord of heaven says
to you, I took you from being a shepherd and made you
the king of my people. 8And I have been with you everywhere you've gone; I have destroyed your enemies, and
I will make your name as great as the greatest of the
earth. 9And I will give a permanent home to my people
Israel, and will plant them in their land. They will not
be disturbed again; the wicked nations won't conquer
them as they did before, 10when the judges ruled them.
I will subdue all of your enemies. And I now declare that
I will cause your descendants to be kings of Israel just
as you are.

11" 'When your time here on earth is over and you
die, I will place one of your sons upon your throne; and
I will make his kingdom strong. 12He is the one who
shall build me a temple, and I will establish his royal line
of descent forever. 13I will be his father, and he shall be

New Revised Standard

35Say also:
"Save us, O God of our salvation,
and gather and rescue us from among the
nations,
that we may give thanks to your holy name,
and glory in your praise.
36 Blessed be the Lord, the God of Israel,
from everlasting to everlasting."
Then all the people said "Amen!" and praised the Lord.

Regular Worship Maintained

37 David left Asaph and his kinsfolk there before
the ark of the covenant of the Lord to minister regularly
before the ark as each day required, 38and also Obed-edom and hisc sixty-eight kinsfolk; while Obed-edom
son of Jeduthun and Hosah were to be gatekeepers.
39And he left the priest Zadok and his kindred the priests
before the tabernacle of the Lord in the high place that
was at Gibeon, 40to offer burnt offerings to the Lord on
the altar of burnt offering regularly, morning and evening, according to all that is written in the law of the
Lord that he commanded Israel. 41With them were Heman and Jeduthun, and the rest of those chosen and
expressly named to render thanks to the Lord, for his
steadfast love endures forever. 42Heman and Jeduthun
had with them trumpets and cymbals for the music, and
instruments for sacred song. The sons of Jeduthun were
appointed to the gate.

43 Then all the people departed to their homes, and
David went home to bless his household.

God's Covenant with David

17 NOW WHEN David settled in his house, David
said to the prophet Nathan, "I am living in a
house of cedar, but the ark of the covenant of the Lord
is under a tent." 2Nathan said to David, "Do all that you
have in mind, for God is with you."

3 But that same night the word of the Lord came to
Nathan, saying: 4Go and tell my servant David: Thus
says the Lord: You shall not build me a house to live
in. 5For I have not lived in a house since the day I
brought out Israel to this very day, but I have lived in
a tent and a tabernacle.d 6Wherever I have moved about
among all Israel, did I ever speak a word with any of the
judges of Israel, whom I commanded to shepherd my
people, saying, Why have you not built me a house of
cedar? 7Now therefore thus you shall say to my servant
David: Thus says the Lord of hosts: I took you from the
pasture, from following the sheep, to be ruler over my
people Israel; 8and I have been with you wherever you
went, and have cut off all your enemies before you; and
I will make for you a name, like the name of the great
ones of the earth. 9I will appoint a place for my people
Israel, and will plant them, so that they may live in their
own place, and be disturbed no more; and evildoers shall
wear them down no more, as they did formerly, 10from
the time that I appointed judges over my people Israel;
and I will subdue all your enemies.

Moreover I declare to you that the Lord will build
you a house. 11When your days are fulfilled to go to be
with your ancestors, I will raise up your offspring after
you, one of your own sons, and I will establish his
kingdom. 12He shall build a house for me, and I will
establish his throne forever. 13I will be a father to him,

---

b *16:37 at the Tabernacle,* literally, "before the Ark of the Covenant of the
Lord."

c Gk Syr Vg: Heb *their*   d Gk 2 Sam 7.6: Heb *but I have been from tent
to tent and from tabernacle*

King James

13I will be his father, and he shall be my son: and I will not take my mercy away from him, as I took *it* from *him* that was before thee:

14But I will settle him in mine house and in my kingdom for ever: and his throne shall be established for evermore.

15According to all these words, and according to all this vision, so did Nathan speak unto David.

16¶ And David the king came and sat before the LORD, and said, Who *am* I, O LORD God, and what *is* mine house, that thou hast brought me hitherto?

17And *yet* this was a small thing in thine eyes, O God; for thou hast *also* spoken of thy servant's house for a great while to come, and hast regarded me according to the estate of a man of high degree, O LORD God.

18What can David *speak* more to thee for the honour of thy servant? for thou knowest thy servant.

19O LORD, for thy servant's sake, and according to thine own heart, hast thou done all this greatness, in making known all *these* great things.

20O LORD, *there is* none like thee, neither *is there any* God beside thee, according to all that we have heard with our ears.

21And what one nation in the earth *is* like thy people Israel, whom God went to redeem *to be* his own people, to make thee a name of greatness and terribleness, by driving out nations from before thy people, whom thou hast redeemed out of Egypt?

22For thy people Israel didst thou make thine own people for ever; and thou, LORD, becamest their God.

23Therefore now, LORD, let the thing that thou hast spoken concerning thy servant and concerning his house be established for ever, and do as thou hast said.

24Let it even be established, that thy name may be magnified for ever, saying, The LORD of hosts *is* the God of Israel, *even* a God to Israel: and *let* the house of David thy servant *be* established before thee.

25For thou, O my God, hast told thy servant that thou wilt build him an house: therefore thy servant hath found *in his heart* to pray before thee.

26And now, LORD, thou art God, and hast promised this goodness unto thy servant:

27Now therefore let it please thee to bless the house of thy servant, that it may be before thee for ever: for thou blessest, O LORD, and *it shall be* blessed for ever.

18 NOW AFTER this it came to pass, that David smote the Philistines, and subdued them, and took Gath and her towns out of the hand of the Philistines.

2And he smote Moab; and the Moabites became David's servants, *and* brought gifts.

3¶ And David smote Hadarezer king of Zobah unto Hamath, as he went to stablish his dominion by the river Euphrates.

4And David took from him a thousand chariots, and seven thousand horsemen, and twenty thousand footmen: David also houghed all the chariot *horses,* but reserved of them an hundred chariots.

5And when the Syrians of Damascus came to help Hadarezer king of Zobah, David slew of the Syrians two and twenty thousand men.

6Then David put *garrisons* in Syria-damascus; and the Syrians became David's servants, *and* brought gifts. Thus the LORD preserved David whithersoever he went.

7And David took the shields of gold that were on the servants of Hadarezer, and brought them to Jerusalem.

New International

be my son. I will never take my love away from him, as I took it away from your predecessor. 14I will set him over my house and my kingdom forever; his throne will be established forever.' "

15Nathan reported to David all the words of this entire revelation.

David's Prayer

16Then King David went in and sat before the LORD, and he said:

"Who am I, O LORD God, and what is my family, that you have brought me this far? 17And as if this were not enough in your sight, O God, you have spoken about the future of the house of your servant. You have looked on me as though I were the most exalted of men, O LORD God.

18"What more can David say to you for honoring your servant? For you know your servant, 19O LORD. For the sake of your servant and according to your will, you have done this great thing and made known all these great promises.

20"There is no one like you, O LORD, and there is no God but you, as we have heard with our own ears. 21And who is like your people Israel—the one nation on earth whose God went out to redeem a people for himself, and to make a name for yourself, and to perform great and awesome wonders by driving out nations from before your people, whom you redeemed from Egypt? 22You made your people Israel your very own forever, and you, O LORD, have become their God.

23"And now, LORD, let the promise you have made concerning your servant and his house be established forever. Do as you promised, 24so that it will be established and that your name will be great forever. Then men will say, 'The LORD Almighty, the God over Israel, is Israel's God!' And the house of your servant David will be established before you.

25"You, my God, have revealed to your servant that you will build a house for him. So your servant has found courage to pray to you. 26O LORD, you are God! You have promised these good things to your servant. 27Now you have been pleased to bless the house of your servant, that it may continue forever in your sight; for you, O LORD, have blessed it, and it will be blessed forever."

David's Victories

18 IN THE course of time, David defeated the Philistines and subdued them, and he took Gath and its surrounding villages from the control of the Philistines.

2David also defeated the Moabites, and they became subject to him and brought tribute.

3Moreover, David fought Hadadezer king of Zobah, as far as Hamath, when he went to establish his control along the Euphrates River. 4David captured a thousand of his chariots, seven thousand charioteers and twenty thousand foot soldiers. He hamstrung all but a hundred of the chariot horses.

5When the Arameans of Damascus came to help Hadadezer king of Zobah, David struck down twenty-two thousand of them. 6He put garrisons in the Aramean kingdom of Damascus, and the Arameans became subject to him and brought tribute. The LORD gave David victory everywhere he went.

7David took the gold shields carried by the officers of Hadadezer and brought them to Jerusalem. 8From

Living Bible

my son; I will never remove my mercy and love from him as I did from Saul. 14I will place him over my people and over the kingdom of Israel forever—and his descendants will always be kings.' "

15So Nathan told King David everything the Lord had said.

16Then King David went in and sat before the Lord and said, "Who am I, O Lord God, and what is my family that you have given me all this? 17For all the great things you have already done for me are nothing in comparison to what you have promised to do in the future! For now, O Lord God, you are speaking of future generations of my children being kings too! You speak as though I were someone very great. 18What else can I say? You know that I am but a dog, yet you have decided to honor me! 19O Lord, you have given me these wonderful promises just because you want to be kind to me, because of your own great heart. 20O Lord, there is no one like you—there is no other God. In fact, we have never even heard of another god like you!

21"And what other nation in all the earth is like Israel? You have made a unique nation and have redeemed it from Egypt so that the people could be your people. And you made a great name for yourself when you did glorious miracles in driving out the nations from before your people. 22You have declared that your people Israel belong to you forever, and you have become their God.

23"And now I accept your promise, Lord, that I and my children will always rule this nation. 24And may this bring eternal honor to your name as everyone realizes that you always do what you say. They will exclaim, 'The Lord of heaven is indeed the God of Israel!' And Israel shall always be ruled by my children and their posterity! 25Now I have the courage to pray to you, for you have revealed this to me. 26God himself has promised this good thing to me! 27May this blessing rest upon my children forever, for when you grant a blessing, Lord, it is an eternal blessing!"

New Revised Standard

and he shall be a son to me. I will not take my steadfast love from him, as I took it from him who was before you, 14but I will confirm him in my house and in my kingdom forever, and his throne shall be established forever. 15In accordance with all these words and all this vision, Nathan spoke to David.

David's Prayer

16 Then King David went in and sat before the LORD, and said, "Who am I, O LORD God, and what is my house, that you have brought me thus far? 17And even this was a small thing in your sight, O God; you have also spoken of your servant's house for a great while to come. You regard me as someone of high rank,a O LORD God! 18And what more can David say to you for honoring your servant? You know your servant. 19For your servant's sake, O LORD, and according to your own heart, you have done all these great deeds, making known all these great things. 20There is no one like you, O LORD, and there is no God besides you, according to all that we have heard with our ears. 21Who is like your people Israel, one nation on the earth whom God went to redeem to be his people, making for yourself a name for great and terrible things, in driving out nations before your people whom you redeemed from Egypt? 22And you made your people Israel to be your people forever; and you, O LORD, became their God.

23 "And now, O LORD, as for the word that you have spoken concerning your servant and concerning his house, let it be established forever, and do as you have promised. 24Thus your name will be established and magnified forever in the saying, 'The LORD of hosts, the God of Israel, is Israel's God'; and the house of your servant David will be established in your presence. 25For you, my God, have revealed to your servant that you will build a house for him; therefore your servant has found it possible to pray before you. 26And now, O LORD, you are God, and you have promised this good thing to your servant; 27therefore may it please you to bless the house of your servant, that it may continue forever before you. For you, O LORD, have blessed and are blessedb forever."

David's Kingdom Established and Extended

18 DAVID FINALLY subdued the Philistines and conquered Gath and its surrounding towns. 2He also conquered Moab and required its people to send him a large sum of money every year. 3He conquered the dominion of King Hadadezer of Zobah (as far as Hamath) at the time Hadadezer went to tighten his grip along the Euphrates River. 4David captured a thousand of his chariots, seven thousand cavalry, and twenty thousand troops. He crippled all the chariot teams except a hundred that he kept for his own use.

5When the Syrians arrived from Damascus to help King Hadadezer, David killed twenty-two thousand of them; 6then he placed a garrison of his troops in Damascus, the Syrian capital. So the Syrians, too, were forced to send him large amounts of money every year. And the Lord gave David victory everywhere he went. 7He brought the gold shields of King Hadadezer's officers to Jerusalem, 8as well as a great amount of bronze from

18 SOME TIME afterward, David attacked the Philistines and subdued them; he took Gath and its villages from the Philistines.

2 He defeated Moab, and the Moabites became subject to David and brought tribute.

3 David also struck down King Hadadezer of Zobah, toward Hamath,a as he went to set up a monument at the river Euphrates. 4David took from him one thousand chariots, seven thousand cavalry, and twenty thousand foot soldiers. David hamstrung all the chariot horses, but left one hundred of them. 5When the Arameans of Damascus came to help King Hadadezer of Zobah, David killed twenty-two thousand Arameans. 6Then David put garrisonsc in Aram of Damascus; and the Arameans became subject to David, and brought tribute. The LORD gave victory to David wherever he went. 7David took the gold shields that were carried by the servants of Hadadezer, and brought them to Jerusalem. 8From Tibhath and from Cun, cities of Hadadezer,

a Meaning of Heb uncertain   b Or and it is blessed   c Gk Vg 2 Sam 8.6
Compare Syr: Heb lacks garrisons

King James

8Likewise from Tibhath, and from Chun, cities of Hadarezer, brought David very much brass, wherewith Solomon made the brasen sea, and the pillars, and the vessels of brass.

9¶ Now when Tou king of Hamath heard how David had smitten all the host of Hadarezer king of Zobah;

10He sent Hadoram his son to king David, to inquire of his welfare, and to congratulate him, because he had fought against Hadarezer, and smitten him; (for Hadarezer had war with Tou;) and *with him* all manner of vessels of gold and silver and brass.

11¶ Them also king David dedicated unto the LORD, with the silver and the gold that he brought from all *these* nations; from Edom, and from Moab, and from the children of Ammon, and from the Philistines, and from Amalek.

12Moreover Abishai the son of Zeruiah slew of the Edomites in the valley of salt eighteen thousand.

13¶ And he put garrisons in Edom; and all the Edomites became David's servants. Thus the LORD preserved David whithersoever he went.

14¶ So David reigned over all Israel, and executed judgment and justice among all his people.

15And Joab the son of Zeruiah *was* over the host; and Jehoshaphat the son of Ahilud, recorder.

16And Zadok the son of Ahitub, and Abimelech the son of Abiathar, *were* the priests; and Shavsha was scribe;

17And Benaiah the son of Jehoiada *was* over the Cherethites and the Pelethites; and the sons of David *were* chief about the king.

19 NOW IT came to pass after this, that Nahash the king of the children of Ammon died, and his son reigned in his stead.

2And David said, I will show kindness unto Hanun the son of Nahash, because his father showed kindness to me. And David sent messengers to comfort him concerning his father. So the servants of David came into the land of the children of Ammon to Hanun, to comfort him.

3But the princes of the children of Ammon said to Hanun, Thinkest thou that David doth honour thy father, that he hath sent comforters unto thee? are not his servants come unto thee for to search, and to overthrow, and to spy out the land?

4Wherefore Hanun took David's servants, and shaved them, and cut off their garments in the midst hard by their buttocks, and sent them away.

5Then there went *certain*, and told David how the men were served. And he sent to meet them: for the men were greatly ashamed. And the king said, Tarry at Jericho until your beards be grown, and *then* return.

6¶ And when the children of Ammon saw that they had made themselves odious to David, Hanun and the children of Ammon sent a thousand talents of silver to hire them chariots and horsemen out of Mesopotamia, and out of Syria-maachah, and out of Zobah.

7So they hired thirty and two thousand chariots, and the king of Maachah and his people; who came and pitched before Medeba. And the children of Ammon gathered themselves together from their cities, and came to battle.

8And when David heard *of it*, he sent Joab, and all the host of the mighty men.

9And the children of Ammon came out, and put the battle in array before the gate of the city: and the kings that were come *were* by themselves in the field.

10Now when Joab saw that the battle was set against him before and behind, he chose out of all the choice of Israel, and put *them* in array against the Syrians.

New International

Tebah[a] and Cun, towns that belonged to Hadadezer, David took a great quantity of bronze, which Solomon used to make the bronze Sea, the pillars and various bronze articles.

9When Tou king of Hamath heard that David had defeated the entire army of Hadadezer king of Zobah, 10he sent his son Hadoram to King David to greet him and congratulate him on his victory in battle over Hadadezer, who had been at war with Tou. Hadoram brought all kinds of articles of gold and silver and bronze.

11King David dedicated these articles to the LORD, as he had done with the silver and gold he had taken from all these nations: Edom and Moab, the Ammonites and the Philistines, and Amalek.

12Abishai son of Zeruiah struck down eighteen thousand Edomites in the Valley of Salt. 13He put garrisons in Edom, and all the Edomites became subject to David. The LORD gave David victory everywhere he went.

David's Officials

14David reigned over all Israel, doing what was just and right for all his people. 15Joab son of Zeruiah was over the army; Jehoshaphat son of Ahilud was recorder; 16Zadok son of Ahitub and Ahimelech[b] son of Abiathar were priests; Shavsha was secretary; 17Benaiah son of Jehoiada was over the Kerethites and Pelethites; and David's sons were chief officials at the king's side.

The Battle Against the Ammonites

19 IN THE course of time, Nahash king of the Ammonites died, and his son succeeded him as king. 2David thought, "I will show kindness to Hanun son of Nahash, because his father showed kindness to me." So David sent a delegation to express his sympathy to Hanun concerning his father.

When David's men came to Hanun in the land of the Ammonites to express sympathy to him, 3the Ammonite nobles said to Hanun, "Do you think David is honoring your father by sending men to you to express sympathy? Haven't his men come to you to explore and spy out the country and overthrow it?" 4So Hanun seized David's men, shaved them, cut off their garments in the middle at the buttocks, and sent them away.

5When someone came and told David about the men, he sent messengers to meet them, for they were greatly humiliated. The king said, "Stay at Jericho till your beards have grown, and then come back."

6When the Ammonites realized that they had become a stench in David's nostrils, Hanun and the Ammonites sent a thousand talents[c] of silver to hire chariots and charioteers from Aram Naharaim,[d] Aram Maacah and Zobah. 7They hired thirty-two thousand chariots and charioteers, as well as the king of Maacah with his troops, who came and camped near Medeba, while the Ammonites were mustered from their towns and moved out for battle.

8On hearing this, David sent Joab out with the entire army of fighting men. 9The Ammonites came out and drew up in battle formation at the entrance to their city, while the kings who had come were by themselves in the open country.

10Joab saw that there were battle lines in front of him and behind him; so he selected some of the best troops in Israel and deployed them against the Arameans. 11He

---

a 8 Hebrew *Tibhath*, a variant of *Tebah*   b 16 Some Hebrew manuscripts, Vulgate and Syriac (see also 2 Samuel 8:17); most Hebrew manuscripts *Abimelech*   c 6 That is, about 37 tons (about 34 metric tons)   d 6 That is, Northwest Mesopotamia

Living Bible

Hadadezer's cities of Tibhath and Cun. (King Solomon later melted the bronze and used it for the Temple. He molded it into the bronze tank, the pillars, and the instruments used in offering sacrifices on the altar.)

9When King Tou of Hamath learned that King David had destroyed Hadadezer's army, 10he sent his son Hadoram to greet and congratulate King David on his success and to present him with many gifts of gold, silver, and bronze, seeking an alliance. For Hadadezer and Tou had been enemies and there had been many wars between them. 11King David dedicated these gifts to the Lord, as he did the silver and gold he took from the nations of Edom, Moab, Ammon, Amalek, and the Philistines.

12Abishai (son of Zeruiah) then destroyed eighteen thousand Edomites in the Valley of Salt. 13He put garrisons in Edom and forced the Edomites to pay large sums of money annually to David. This is just another example of how the Lord gave David victory after victory. 14David reigned over all of Israel and was a just ruler.

15Joab (son of Zeruiah) was commander-in-chief of the army; Jehoshaphat (son of Ahilud) was the historian; 16Zadok (son of Ahitub) and Ahimelech (son of Abiathar) were the head priests; Shavsha was the king's special assistant;e 17Benaiah (son of Jehoiada) was in charge of the king's bodyguard—the Cherethites and Pelethites—and David's sons were his chief aides.

19 WHEN KING Nahash of Ammon died, his son Hanun became the new king.

2, 3Then David declared, "I am going to show friendship to Hanun because of all the kind things his father did for me."

So David sent a message of sympathy to Hanun for the death of his father. But when David's ambassadors arrived, King Hanun's counselors warned him, "Don't fool yourself that David has sent these men to honor your father! They are here to spy out the land so that they can come in and conquer it!"

4So King Hanun insulted King David's ambassadors by shaving their beards and cutting their robes off at the middle to expose their buttocks; then he sent them back to David in shame. 5When David heard what had happened, he sent a message to his embarrassed emissaries, telling them to stay at Jericho until their beards had grown out again. 6When King Hanun realized his mistake he sent $2,000,000 to enlist mercenary troops, chariots, and cavalry from Mesopotamia, Aram-maacah, and Zobah. 7He hired thirty-two thousand chariots, as well as the support of the king of Maacah and his entire army. These forces camped at Medeba where they were joined by the troops King Hanun had recruited from his cities.

8When David learned of this, he sent Joab and the mightiest warriors of Israel. 9The army of Ammon went out to meet them and began the battle at the gates of the city of Medeba. Meanwhile, the mercenary forces were out in the field. 10When Joab realized that the enemy forces were both in front and behind him, he divided his army and sent one group to engage the Syrians. 11The

New Revised Standard

David took a vast quantity of bronze; with it Solomon made the bronze sea and the pillars and the vessels of bronze.

9 When King Tou of Hamath heard that David had defeated the whole army of King Hadadezer of Zobah, 10he sent his son Hadoram to King David, to greet him and to congratulate him, because he had fought against Hadadezer and defeated him. Now Hadadezer had often been at war with Tou. He sent all sorts of articles of gold, of silver, and of bronze; 11these also King David dedicated to the LORD, together with the silver and gold that he had carried off from all the nations, from Edom, Moab, the Ammonites, the Philistines, and Amalek.

12 Abishai son of Zeruiah killed eighteen thousand Edomites in the Valley of Salt. 13He put garrisons in Edom; and all the Edomites became subject to David. And the LORD gave victory to David wherever he went.

David's Administration

14 So David reigned over all Israel; and he administered justice and equity to all his people. 15Joab son of Zeruiah was over the army; Jehoshaphat son of Ahilud was recorder; 16Zadok son of Ahitub and Ahimelech son of Abiathar were priests; Shavsha was secretary; 17Benaiah son of Jehoiada was over the Cherethites and the Pelethites; and David's sons were the chief officials in the service of the king.

Defeat of the Ammonites and Arameans

19 SOME TIME afterward, King Nahash of the Ammonites died, and his son succeeded him. 2David said, "I will deal loyally with Hanun son of Nahash, for his father dealt loyally with me." So David sent messengers to console him concerning his father. When David's servants came to Hanun in the land of the Ammonites, to console him, 3the officials of the Ammonites said to Hanun, "Do you think, because David has sent consolers to you, that he is honoring your father? Have not his servants come to you to search and to overthrow and to spy out the land?" 4So Hanun seized David's servants, shaved them, cut off their garments in the middle at their hips, and sent them away; 5and they departed. When David was told about the men, he sent messengers to them, for they felt greatly humiliated. The king said, "Remain at Jericho until your beards have grown, and then return."

6 When the Ammonites saw that they had made themselves odious to David, Hanun and the Ammonites sent a thousand talents of silver to hire chariots and cavalry from Mesopotamia, from Aram-maacah and from Zobah. 7They hired thirty-two thousand chariots and the king of Maacah with his army, who came and camped before Medeba. And the Ammonites were mustered from their cities and came to battle. 8When David heard of it, he sent Joab and all the army of the warriors. 9The Ammonites came out and drew up in battle array at the entrance of the city, and the kings who had come were by themselves in the open country.

10 When Joab saw that the line of battle was set against him both in front and in the rear, he chose some of the picked men of Israel and arrayed them against the Arameans; 11the rest of his troops he put in the charge

e 18:16 special assistant, literally, "secretary," or "scribe."

King James

11And the rest of the people he delivered unto the hand of Abishai his brother, and they set *themselves* in array against the children of Ammon.

12And he said, If the Syrians be too strong for me, then thou shalt help me: but if the children of Ammon be too strong for thee, then I will help thee.

13Be of good courage, and let us behave ourselves valiantly for our people, and for the cities of our God: and let the LORD do *that which is* good in his sight.

14So Joab and the people that *were* with him drew nigh before the Syrians unto the battle; and they fled before him.

15And when the children of Ammon saw that the Syrians were fled, they likewise fled before Abishai his brother, and entered into the city. Then Joab came to Jerusalem.

16¶ And when the Syrians saw that they were put to the worse before Israel, they sent messengers, and drew forth the Syrians that *were* beyond the river: and Shophach the captain of the host of Hadarezer *went* before them.

17And it was told David; and he gathered all Israel, and passed over Jordan, and came upon them, and set *the battle* in array against them. So when David had put the battle in array against the Syrians, they fought with him.

18But the Syrians fled before Israel; and David slew of the Syrians seven thousand *men which fought in* chariots, and forty thousand footmen, and killed Shophach the captain of the host.

19And when the servants of Hadarezer saw that they were put to the worse before Israel, they made peace with David, and became his servants: neither would the Syrians help the children of Ammon any more.

20 AND IT came to pass, that after the year was expired, at the time that kings go out *to battle*, Joab led forth the power of the army, and wasted the country of the children of Ammon, and came and besieged Rabbah. But David tarried at Jerusalem. And Joab smote Rabbah, and destroyed it.

2And David took the crown of their king from off his head, and found it to weigh a talent of gold, and *there were* precious stones in it; and it was set upon David's head: and he brought also exceeding much spoil out of the city.

3And he brought out the people that *were* in it, and cut *them* with saws, and with harrows of iron, and with axes. Even so dealt David with all the cities of the children of Ammon. And David and all the people returned to Jerusalem.

4¶ And it came to pass after this, that there arose war at Gezer with the Philistines; at which time Sibbechai the Hushathite slew Sippai, *that was* of the children of the giant: and they were subdued.

5And there was war again with the Philistines; and Elhanan the son of Jair slew Lahmi the brother of Goliath the Gittite, whose spear staff *was* like a weaver's beam.

6And yet again there was war at Gath, where was a man of *great* stature, whose fingers and toes *were* four and twenty, six *on each hand,* and six *on each foot:* and he also was the son of the giant.

7But when he defied Israel, Jonathan the son of Shimea David's brother slew him.

8These were born unto the giant in Gath; and they fell by the hand of David, and by the hand of his servants.

New International

put the rest of the men under the command of Abishai his brother, and they were deployed against the Ammonites. 12Joab said, "If the Arameans are too strong for me, then you are to rescue me; but if the Ammonites are too strong for you, then I will rescue you. 13Be strong and let us fight bravely for our people and the cities of our God. The LORD will do what is good in his sight."

14Then Joab and the troops with him advanced to fight the Arameans, and they fled before him. 15When the Ammonites saw that the Arameans were fleeing, they too fled before his brother Abishai and went inside the city. So Joab went back to Jerusalem.

16After the Arameans saw that they had been routed by Israel, they sent messengers and had Arameans brought from beyond the River,a with Shophach the commander of Hadadezer's army leading them.

17When David was told of this, he gathered all Israel and crossed the Jordan; he advanced against them and formed his battle lines opposite them. David formed his lines to meet the Arameans in battle, and they fought against him. 18But they fled before Israel, and David killed seven thousand of their charioteers and forty thousand of their foot soldiers. He also killed Shophach the commander of their army.

19When the vassals of Hadadezer saw that they had been defeated by Israel, they made peace with David and became subject to him.

So the Arameans were not willing to help the Ammonites anymore.

The Capture of Rabbah

20 IN THE spring, at the time when kings go off to war, Joab led out the armed forces. He laid waste the land of the Ammonites and went to Rabbah and besieged it, but David remained in Jerusalem. Joab attacked Rabbah and left it in ruins. 2David took the crown from the head of their kingb—its weight was found to be a talentc of gold, and it was set with precious stones—and it was placed on David's head. He took a great quantity of plunder from the city 3and brought out the people who were there, consigning them to labor with saws and with iron picks and axes. David did this to all the Ammonite towns. Then David and his entire army returned to Jerusalem.

War With the Philistines

4In the course of time, war broke out with the Philistines, at Gezer. At that time Sibbecai the Hushathite killed Sippai, one of the descendants of the Rephaites, and the Philistines were subjugated.

5In another battle with the Philistines, Elhanan son of Jair killed Lahmi the brother of Goliath the Gittite, who had a spear with a shaft like a weaver's rod.

6In still another battle, which took place at Gath, there was a huge man with six fingers on each hand and six toes on each foot—twenty-four in all. He also was descended from Rapha. 7When he taunted Israel, Jonathan son of Shimea, David's brother, killed him.

8These were descendants of Rapha in Gath, and they fell at the hands of David and his men.

---

a *16* That is, the Euphrates　b *2* Or *of Milcom,* that is, Molech　c *2* That is, about 75 pounds (about 34 kilograms)

Living Bible

other group, under the command of his brother Abishai, moved against the Ammonites.

12"If the Syrians are too strong for me, come and help me," Joab told his brother; "and if the Ammonites are too strong for you, I'll come and help you. 13Be courageous and let us act like men to save our people and the cities of our God. And may the Lord do what is best."

14So Joab and his troops attacked the Syrians, and the Syrians turned and fled. 15When the Ammonites, under attack by Abishai's troops, saw that the Syrians were retreating, they fled into the city. Then Joab returned to Jerusalem.

16After their defeat, the Syrians summoned additional troops from east of the Euphrates River, led personally by Shophach, King Hadadezer's commander-in-chief. 17, 18When this news reached David, he mobilized all Israel, crossed the Jordan River, and engaged the enemy troops in battle. But the Syrians again fled from David, and he killed seven thousand charioteers and forty thousand of their troops. He also killed Shophach, the commander-in-chief of the Syrian army. 19Then King Hadadezer's troops surrendered to King David and became his subjects. And never again did the Syrians aid the Ammonites in their battles.

20 THE FOLLOWING spring (spring was the season when wars usually began) Joab led the Israeli army in successful attacks against the cities and villages of the people of Ammon. After destroying them, he laid siege to Rabbah and conquered it. Meanwhile, David had stayed in Jerusalem. 2When David arrived on the scene, he removed the crown from the head of King Milcom*d* of Rabbah and placed it upon his own head. It was made of gold inlaid with gems and weighed seventy-five pounds! David also took great amounts of plunder from the city. 3He drove the people from the city and set them to work with saws, iron picks, and axes,*e* as was his custom with all the conquered Ammonite peoples. Then David and all his army returned to Jerusalem.

4The next war was against the Philistines again, at Gezer. But Sibbecai, a man from Hushath, killed one of the sons of the giant, Sippai, and so the Philistines surrendered. 5During another war with the Philistines, Elhanan (the son of Jair) killed Lahmi, the brother of Goliath the giant; the handle of his spear was like a weaver's beam! 6, 7During another battle, at Gath, a giant with six fingers on each hand and six toes on each foot (his father was also a giant) defied and taunted Israel; but he was killed by David's nephew Jonathan, the son of David's brother Shimea. 8These giants were descendants of the giants of Gath, and they were killed by David and his soldiers.

New Revised Standard

of his brother Abishai, and they were arrayed against the Ammonites. 12He said, "If the Arameans are too strong for me, then you shall help me; but if the Ammonites are too strong for you, then I will help you. 13Be strong, and let us be courageous for our people and for the cities of our God; and may the LORD do what seems good to him." 14So Joab and the troops who were with him advanced toward the Arameans for battle; and they fled before him. 15When the Ammonites saw that the Arameans fled, they likewise fled before Abishai, Joab's brother, and entered the city. Then Joab came to Jerusalem.

16 But when the Arameans saw that they had been defeated by Israel, they sent messengers and brought out the Arameans who were beyond the Euphrates, with Shophach the commander of the army of Hadadezer at their head. 17When David was informed, he gathered all Israel together, crossed the Jordan, came to them, and drew up his forces against them. When David set the battle in array against the Arameans, they fought with him. 18The Arameans fled before Israel; and David killed seven thousand Aramean charioteers and forty thousand foot soldiers, and also killed Shophach the commander of their army. 19When the servants of Hadadezer saw that they had been defeated by Israel, they made peace with David, and became subject to him. So the Arameans were not willing to help the Ammonites any more.

Siege and Capture of Rabbah

20 IN THE spring of the year, the time when kings go out to battle, Joab led out the army, ravaged the country of the Ammonites, and came and besieged Rabbah. But David remained at Jerusalem. Joab attacked Rabbah, and overthrew it. 2David took the crown of Milcom*f* from his head; he found that it weighed a talent of gold, and in it was a precious stone; and it was placed on David's head. He also brought out the booty of the city, a very great amount. 3He brought out the people who were in it, and set them to work*g* with saws and iron picks and axes.*h* Thus David did to all the cities of the Ammonites. Then David and all the people returned to Jerusalem.

Exploits against the Philistines

4 After this, war broke out with the Philistines at Gezer; then Sibbecai the Hushathite killed Sippai, who was one of the descendants of the giants; and the Philistines were subdued. 5 Again there was war with the Philistines; and Elhanan son of Jair killed Lahmi the brother of Goliath the Gittite, the shaft of whose spear was like a weaver's beam. 6Again there was war at Gath, where there was a man of great size, who had six fingers on each hand, and six toes on each foot, twenty-four in number; he also was descended from the giants. 7When he taunted Israel, Jonathan son of Shimea, David's brother, killed him. 8These were descended from the giants in Gath; they fell by the hand of David and his servants.

---

d 20:2 Milcom, implied. See 1 Kgs 11:5.   *e 20:3 and axes,* literally "he conducted them to the saw." Whether this means that he made them labor with saws or that he sawed them to pieces is uncertain.

f Gk Vg See 1 Kings 11.5, 33: MT *of their king*   *g* Compare 2 Sam 12.31: Heb *and he sawed*   *h* Compare 2 Sam 12.31: Heb *saws*

King James

21 AND SATAN stood up against Israel, and provoked David to number Israel.

2And David said to Joab and to the rulers of the people, Go, number Israel from Beer-sheba even to Dan; and bring the number of them to me, that I may know *it.*

3And Joab answered, The LORD make his people an hundred times so many more as they *be:* but, my lord the king, *are* they not all my lord's servants? why then doth my lord require this thing? why will he be a cause of trespass to Israel?

4Nevertheless the king's word prevailed against Joab. Wherefore Joab departed, and went throughout all Israel, and came to Jerusalem.

5¶ And Joab gave the sum of the number of the people unto David. And all *they of* Israel were a thousand thousand and an hundred thousand men that drew sword: and Judah *was* four hundred threescore and ten thousand men that drew sword.

6But Levi and Benjamin counted he not among them: for the king's word was abominable to Joab.

7And God was displeased with this thing; therefore he smote Israel.

8And David said unto God, I have sinned greatly, because I have done this thing: but now, I beseech thee, do away the iniquity of thy servant; for I have done very foolishly.

9¶ And the LORD spake unto Gad, David's seer, saying,

10Go and tell David, saying, Thus saith the LORD, I offer thee three *things:* choose thee one of them, that I may do *it* unto thee.

11So Gad came to David, and said unto him, Thus saith the LORD, Choose thee

12Either three years' famine; or three months to be destroyed before thy foes, while that the sword of thine enemies overtaketh *thee;* or else three days the sword of the LORD, even the pestilence, in the land, and the angel of the LORD destroying throughout all the coasts of Israel. Now therefore advise thyself what word I shall bring again to him that sent me.

13And David said unto Gad, I am in a great strait: let me fall now into the hand of the LORD; for very great *are* his mercies: but let me not fall into the hand of man.

14¶ So the LORD sent pestilence upon Israel: and there fell of Israel seventy thousand men.

15And God sent an angel unto Jerusalem to destroy it: and as he was destroying, the LORD beheld, and he repented him of the evil, and said to the angel that destroyed, It is enough, stay now thine hand. And the angel of the LORD stood by the threshingfloor of Ornan the Jebusite.

16And David lifted up his eyes, and saw the angel of the LORD stand between the earth and the heaven, having a drawn sword in his hand stretched out over Jerusalem. Then David and the elders *of Israel, who were* clothed in sackcloth, fell upon their faces.

17And David said unto God, *Is it* not I *that* commanded the people to be numbered? even I it is that have sinned and done evil indeed; but *as for* these sheep, what have they done? let thine hand, I pray thee, O LORD my God, be on me, and on my father's house; but not on thy people, that they should be plagued.

18¶ Then the angel of the LORD commanded Gad to say to David, that David should go up, and set up an altar unto the LORD in the threshingfloor of Ornan the Jebusite.

New International

David Numbers the Fighting Men

21 SATAN ROSE up against Israel and incited David to take a census of Israel. 2So David said to Joab and the commanders of the troops, "Go and count the Israelites from Beersheba to Dan. Then report back to me so that I may know how many there are."

3But Joab replied, "May the LORD multiply his troops a hundred times over. My lord the king, are they not all my lord's subjects? Why does my lord want to do this? Why should he bring guilt on Israel?"

4The king's word, however, overruled Joab; so Joab left and went throughout Israel and then came back to Jerusalem. 5Joab reported the number of the fighting men to David: In all Israel there were one million one hundred thousand men who could handle a sword, including four hundred and seventy thousand in Judah.

6But Joab did not include Levi and Benjamin in the numbering, because the king's command was repulsive to him. 7This command was also evil in the sight of God; so he punished Israel.

8Then David said to God, "I have sinned greatly by doing this. Now, I beg you, take away the guilt of your servant. I have done a very foolish thing."

9The LORD said to Gad, David's seer, 10"Go and tell David, 'This is what the LORD says: I am giving you three options. Choose one of them for me to carry out against you.' "

11So Gad went to David and said to him, "This is what the LORD says: 'Take your choice: 12three years of famine, three months of being swept awaya before your enemies, with their swords overtaking you, or three days of the sword of the LORD—days of plague in the land, with the angel of the LORD ravaging every part of Israel.' Now then, decide how I should answer the one who sent me."

13David said to Gad, "I am in deep distress. Let me fall into the hands of the LORD, for his mercy is very great; but do not let me fall into the hands of men."

14So the LORD sent a plague on Israel, and seventy thousand men of Israel fell dead. 15And God sent an angel to destroy Jerusalem. But as the angel was doing so, the LORD saw it and was grieved because of the calamity and said to the angel who was destroying the people, "Enough! Withdraw your hand." The angel of the LORD was then standing at the threshing floor of Araunahb the Jebusite.

16David looked up and saw the angel of the LORD standing between heaven and earth, with a drawn sword in his hand extended over Jerusalem. Then David and the elders, clothed in sackcloth, fell facedown.

17David said to God, "Was it not I who ordered the fighting men to be counted? I am the one who has sinned and done wrong. These are but sheep. What have they done? O LORD my God, let your hand fall upon me and my family, but do not let this plague remain on your people."

18Then the angel of the LORD ordered Gad to tell David to go up and build an altar to the LORD on the threshing floor of Araunah the Jebusite. 19So David

---

a 12 Hebrew; Septuagint and Vulgate (see also 2 Samuel 24:13) *of fleeing*
b 15 Hebrew *Ornan,* a variant of *Araunah;* also in verses 18-28

Living Bible

21 THEN SATAN brought disaster upon Israel, for he made David decide to take a census.

2"Take a complete census throughout the land[c] and bring me the totals," he told Joab and the other leaders.

3But Joab objected. "If the Lord were to multiply his people a hundred times, would they not all be yours? So why are you asking us to do this? Why must you cause Israel to sin?"

4But the king won the argument, and Joab did as he was told; he traveled all through Israel and returned to Jerusalem. 5The total population figure which he gave came to 1,100,000 men of military age in Israel and 470,000 in Judah. 6But he didn't include the tribes of Levi and Benjamin in his figures because he was so distressed at what the king had made him do.

7And God, too, was displeased with the census and punished Israel for it.

8But David said to God, "I am the one who has sinned. Please forgive me, for I realize now how wrong I was to do this."

9Then the Lord said to Gad, David's personal prophet, 10, 11"Go and tell David, 'The Lord has offered you three choices. Which will you choose? 12You may have three years of famine, or three months of destruction by the enemies of Israel, or three days of deadly plague as the angel of the Lord brings destruction to the land. Think it over and let me know what answer to return to the one who sent me.'"

13"This is a terrible decision to make," David replied, "but let me fall into the hands of the Lord rather than into the power of men, for God's mercies are very great."

14So the Lord sent a plague upon Israel and 70,000 men died as a result. 15During the plague God sent an angel to destroy Jerusalem; but then he felt such compassion that he changed his mind and commanded the destroying angel, "Stop! It is enough!" (The angel of the Lord was standing at the time by the threshing-floor of Ornan the Jebusite.) 16When David saw the angel of the Lord standing between heaven and earth with his sword drawn, pointing toward Jerusalem, he and the elders of Israel clothed themselves in sackcloth and fell to the ground before the Lord.

17And David said to God, "I am the one who sinned by ordering the census. But what have these sheep done? O Lord my God, destroy me and my family, but do not destroy your people."

18Then the angel of the Lord told Gad to instruct David to build an altar to the Lord at the threshing-floor of Ornan the Jebusite. 19, 20So David went to see Ornan,

New Revised Standard

The Census and Plague

21 SATAN STOOD up against Israel, and incited David to count the people of Israel. 2So David said to Joab and the commanders of the army, "Go, number Israel, from Beer-sheba to Dan, and bring me a report, so that I may know their number." 3But Joab said, "May the LORD increase the number of his people a hundredfold! Are they not, my lord the king, all of them my lord's servants? Why then should my lord require this? Why should he bring guilt on Israel?" 4But the king's word prevailed against Joab. So Joab departed and went throughout all Israel, and came back to Jerusalem. 5Joab gave the total count of the people to David. In all Israel there were one million one hundred thousand men who drew the sword, and in Judah four hundred seventy thousand who drew the sword. 6But he did not include Levi and Benjamin in the numbering, for the king's command was abhorrent to Joab.

7 But God was displeased with this thing, and he struck Israel. 8David said to God, "I have sinned greatly in that I have done this thing. But now, I pray, take away the guilt of your servant; for I have done very foolishly." 9The LORD spoke to Gad, David's seer, saying, 10"Go and say to David, 'Thus says the LORD: Three things I offer you; choose one of them, so that I may do it to you.'" 11So Gad came to David and said to him, "Thus says the LORD, 'Take your choice: 12either three years of famine; or three months of devastation by your foes, while the sword of your enemies overtakes you; or three days of the sword of the LORD, pestilence on the land, and the angel of the LORD destroying throughout all the territory of Israel.' Now decide what answer I shall return to the one who sent me." 13Then David said to Gad, "I am in great distress; let me fall into the hand of the LORD, for his mercy is very great; but let me not fall into human hands."

14 So the LORD sent a pestilence on Israel; and seventy thousand persons fell in Israel. 15And God sent an angel to Jerusalem to destroy it; but when he was about to destroy it, the LORD took note and relented concerning the calamity; he said to the destroying angel, "Enough! Stay your hand." The angel of the LORD was then standing by the threshing floor of Ornan the Jebusite. 16David looked up and saw the angel of the LORD standing between earth and heaven, and in his hand a drawn sword stretched out over Jerusalem. Then David and the elders, clothed in sackcloth, fell on their faces. 17And David said to God, "Was it not I who gave the command to count the people? It is I who have sinned and done very wickedly. But these sheep, what have they done? Let your hand, I pray, O LORD my God, be against me and against my father's house; but do not let your people be plagued!"

David's Altar and Sacrifice

18 Then the angel of the LORD commanded Gad to tell David that he should go up and erect an altar to the LORD on the threshing floor of Ornan the Jebusite. 19So

King James

19And David went up at the saying of Gad, which he spake in the name of the LORD.

20And Ornan turned back, and saw the angel; and his four sons with him hid themselves. Now Ornan was threshing wheat.

21And as David came to Ornan, Ornan looked and saw David, and went out of the threshingfloor, and bowed himself to David with *his* face to the ground.

22Then David said to Ornan, Grant me the place of *this* threshingfloor, that I may build an altar therein unto the LORD: thou shalt grant it me for the full price: that the plague may be stayed from the people.

23And Ornan said unto David, Take *it* to thee, and let my lord the king do *that which is* good in his eyes: lo, I give *thee* the oxen *also* for burnt offerings, and the threshing instruments for wood, and the wheat for the meat offering; I give it all.

24And king David said to Ornan, Nay; but I will verily buy it for the full price: for I will not take *that* which *is* thine for the LORD, nor offer burnt offerings without cost.

25So David gave to Ornan for the place six hundred shekels of gold by weight.

26And David built there an altar unto the LORD, and offered burnt offerings and peace offerings, and called upon the LORD; and he answered him from heaven by fire upon the altar of burnt offering.

27And the LORD commanded the angel; and he put up his sword again into the sheath thereof.

28¶ At that time when David saw that the LORD had answered him in the threshingfloor of Ornan the Jebusite, then he sacrificed there.

29For the tabernacle of the LORD, which Moses made in the wilderness, and the altar of the burnt offering, *were* at that season in the high place at Gibeon.

30But David could not go before it to inquire of God: for he was afraid because of the sword of the angel of the LORD.

22 THEN DAVID said, This *is* the house of the LORD God, and this *is* the altar of the burnt offering for Israel.

2And David commanded to gather together the strangers that *were* in the land of Israel; and he set masons to hew wrought stones to build the house of God.

3And David prepared iron in abundance for the nails for the doors of the gates, and for the joinings; and brass in abundance without weight;

4Also cedar trees in abundance: for the Zidonians and they of Tyre brought much cedar wood to David.

5And David said, Solomon my son *is* young and tender, and the house *that is* to be builded for the LORD *must be* exceeding magnifical, of fame and of glory throughout all countries: I will *therefore* now make preparation for it. So David prepared abundantly before his death.

6¶ Then he called for Solomon his son, and charged him to build an house for the LORD God of Israel.

7And David said to Solomon, My son, as for me, it was in my mind to build an house unto the name of the LORD my God:

8But the word of the LORD came to me, saying, Thou hast shed blood abundantly, and hast made great wars: thou shalt not build an house unto my name, because thou hast shed much blood upon the earth in my sight.

New International

went up in obedience to the word that Gad had spoken in the name of the LORD.

20While Araunah was threshing wheat, he turned and saw the angel; his four sons who were with him hid themselves. 21Then David approached, and when Araunah looked and saw him, he left the threshing floor and bowed down before David with his face to the ground.

22David said to him, "Let me have the site of your threshing floor so I can build an altar to the LORD, that the plague on the people may be stopped. Sell it to me at the full price."

23Araunah said to David, "Take it! Let my lord the king do whatever pleases him. Look, I will give the oxen for the burnt offerings, the threshing sledges for the wood, and the wheat for the grain offering. I will give all this."

24But King David replied to Araunah, "No, I insist on paying the full price. I will not take for the LORD what is yours, or sacrifice a burnt offering that costs me nothing."

25So David paid Araunah six hundred shekelsa of gold for the site. 26David built an altar to the LORD there and sacrificed burnt offerings and fellowship offerings.b He called on the LORD, and the LORD answered him with fire from heaven on the altar of burnt offering.

27Then the LORD spoke to the angel, and he put his sword back into its sheath. 28At that time, when David saw that the LORD had answered him on the threshing floor of Araunah the Jebusite, he offered sacrifices there. 29The tabernacle of the LORD, which Moses had made in the desert, and the altar of burnt offering were at that time on the high place at Gibeon. 30But David could not go before it to inquire of God, because he was afraid of the sword of the angel of the LORD.

22 THEN DAVID said, "The house of the LORD God is to be here, and also the altar of burnt offering for Israel."

Preparations for the Temple

2So David gave orders to assemble the aliens living in Israel, and from among them he appointed stonecutters to prepare dressed stone for building the house of God. 3He provided a large amount of iron to make nails for the doors of the gateways and for the fittings, and more bronze than could be weighed. 4He also provided more cedar logs than could be counted, for the Sidonians and Tyrians had brought large numbers of them to David.

5David said, "My son Solomon is young and inexperienced, and the house to be built for the LORD should be of great magnificence and fame and splendor in the sight of all the nations. Therefore I will make preparations for it." So David made extensive preparations before his death.

6Then he called for his son Solomon and charged him to build a house for the LORD, the God of Israel. 7David said to Solomon: "My son, I had it in my heart to build a house for the Name of the LORD my God. 8But this word of the LORD came to me: 'You have shed much blood and have fought many wars. You are not to build a house for my Name, because you have shed much blood on the earth in my sight. 9But you will have a son

---

a 25 That is, about 15 pounds (about 7 kilograms)   b 26 Traditionally *peace offerings*

Living Bible

who was threshing wheat at the time. Ornan saw the angel as he turned, and his four sons ran and hid. 21Then Ornan saw the king approaching. So he left the threshing-floor and bowed to the ground before King David.

22David said to Ornan, "Let me buy this threshing-floor from you at its full price; then I will build an altar to the Lord and the plague will stop."

23"Take it, my lord, and use it as you wish," Ornan said to David. "Take the oxen, too, for burnt offerings; use the threshing instruments for wood for the fire and use the wheat for the grain offering. I give it all to you."

24"No," the king replied, "I will buy it for the full price; I cannot take what is yours and give it to the Lord. I will not offer a burnt offering that has cost me nothing!"

25So David paid Ornan $4,300 in gold,c 26and built an altar to the Lord there, and sacrificed burnt offerings and peace offerings upon it; and he called out to the Lord, who answered by sending down fire from heaven to burn up the offering on the altar. 27Then the Lord commanded the angel to put back his sword into its sheath; 28and when David saw that the Lord had answered his plea, he sacrificed to him again. 29The Tabernacle and altar made by Moses in the wilderness were on the hill of Gibeon, 30but David didn't have time to go there to plead before the Lord, for he was terrified by the drawn sword of the angel of Jehovah.

22 THEN DAVID said, "Right here at Ornan's threshing-floor is the place where I'll build the Temple of the Lord and construct the altar for Israel's burnt offering!"

2David now drafted all the resident aliens in Israel to prepare blocks of squared stone for the Temple. 3They also manufactured iron into the great quantity of nails needed for the doors in the gates and for the clamps; and they smelted so much bronze that it was too much to weigh. 4The men of Tyre and Sidon brought great rafts of cedar logs to David.

5"Solomon my son is young and tender," David said, "and the Temple of the Lord must be a marvelous structure, famous and glorious throughout the world; so I will begin the preparations for it now."

So David collected the construction materials before his death. 6He now commanded his son Solomon to build a temple for the Lord God of Israel.

7"I wanted to build it myself," David told him, 8"but the Lord said not to do it. 'You have killed too many men in great wars,' he told me. 'You have reddened the ground before me with blood: so you are not to build my Temple. 9But I will give you a son,' he told me, 'who

New Revised Standard

David went up following Gad's instructions, which he had spoken in the name of the LORD. 20Ornan turned and saw the angel; and while his four sons who were with him hid themselves, Ornan continued to thresh wheat. 21As David came to Ornan, Ornan looked and saw David; he went out from the threshing floor, and did obeisance to David with his face to the ground. 22David said to Ornan, "Give me the site of the threshing floor that I may build on it an altar to the LORD—give it to me at its full price—so that the plague may be averted from the people." 23Then Ornan said to David, "Take it; and let my lord the king do what seems good to him; see, I present the oxen for burnt offerings, and the threshing sledges for the wood, and the wheat for a grain offering. I give it all." 24But King David said to Ornan, "No; I will buy them for the full price. I will not take for the LORD what is yours, nor offer burnt offerings that cost me nothing." 25So David paid Ornan six hundred shekels of gold by weight for the site. 26David built there an altar to the LORD and presented burnt offerings and offerings of well-being. He called upon the LORD, and he answered him with fire from heaven on the altar of burnt offering. 27Then the LORD commanded the angel, and he put his sword back into its sheath.

The Place Chosen for the Temple

28 At that time, when David saw that the LORD had answered him at the threshing floor of Ornan the Jebusite, he made his sacrifices there. 29For the tabernacle of the LORD, which Moses had made in the wilderness, and the altar of burnt offering were at that time in the high place at Gibeon; 30but David could not go before it to inquire of God, for he was afraid of the sword of the angel of the LORD.

22 THEN DAVID said, "Here shall be the house of the LORD God and here the altar of burnt offering for Israel."

David Prepares to Build the Temple

2 David gave orders to gather together the aliens who were residing in the land of Israel, and he set stonecutters to prepare dressed stones for building the house of God. 3David also provided great stores of iron for nails for the doors of the gates and for clamps, as well as bronze in quantities beyond weighing, 4and cedar logs without number—for the Sidonians and Tyrians brought great quantities of cedar to David. 5For David said, "My son Solomon is young and inexperienced, and the house that is to be built for the LORD must be exceedingly magnificent, famous and glorified throughout all lands; I will therefore make preparation for it." So David provided materials in great quantity before his death.

David's Charge to Solomon and the Leaders

6 Then he called for his son Solomon and charged him to build a house for the LORD, the God of Israel. 7David said to Solomon, "My son, I had planned to build a house to the name of the LORD my God. 8But the word of the LORD came to me, saying, 'You have shed much blood and have waged great wars; you shall not build a house to my name, because you have shed so much blood in my sight on the earth. 9See, a son shall

---

c 21:25 $4,300 in gold, literally, "six hundred shekels of gold by weight."

King James

9Behold, a son shall be born to thee, who shall be a man of rest; and I will give him rest from all his enemies round about: for his name shall be Solomon, and I will give peace and quietness unto Israel in his days.

10He shall build an house for my name; and he shall be my son, and I *will be* his father; and I will establish the throne of his kingdom over Israel for ever.

11Now, my son, the LORD be with thee; and prosper thou, and build the house of the LORD thy God, as he hath said of thee.

12Only the LORD give thee wisdom and understanding, and give thee charge concerning Israel, that thou mayest keep the law of the LORD thy God.

13Then shalt thou prosper, if thou takest heed to fulfil the statutes and judgments which the LORD charged Moses with concerning Israel: be strong, and of good courage; dread not, nor be dismayed.

14Now, behold, in my trouble I have prepared for the house of the LORD an hundred thousand talents of gold, and a thousand thousand talents of silver; and of brass and iron without weight; for it is in abundance: timber also and stone have I prepared; and thou mayest add thereto.

15Moreover *there are* workmen with thee in abundance, hewers and workers of stone and timber, and all manner of cunning men for every manner of work.

16Of the gold, the silver, and the brass, and the iron, *there is* no number. Arise *therefore*, and be doing, and the LORD be with thee.

17¶ David also commanded all the princes of Israel to help Solomon his son, *saying,*

18*Is* not the LORD your God with you? and hath he *not* given you rest on every side? for he hath given the inhabitants of the land into mine hand; and the land is subdued before the LORD, and before his people.

19Now set your heart and your soul to seek the LORD your God; arise therefore, and build ye the sanctuary of the LORD God, to bring the ark of the covenant of the LORD, and the holy vessels of God, into the house that is to be built to the name of the LORD.

23 SO WHEN David was old and full of days, he made Solomon his son king over Israel.

2¶ And he gathered together all the princes of Israel, with the priests and the Levites.

3Now the Levites were numbered from the age of thirty years and upward: and their number by their polls, man by man, was thirty and eight thousand.

4Of which, twenty and four thousand *were* to set forward the work of the house of the LORD; and six thousand *were* officers and judges:

5Moreover four thousand *were* porters; and four thousand praised the LORD with the instruments which I made, *said David,* to praise *therewith.*

6And David divided them into courses among the sons of Levi, *namely,* Gershon, Kohath, and Merari.

7¶ Of the Gershonites *were,* Laadan, and Shimei.

8The sons of Laadan; the chief *was* Jehiel, and Zetham, and Joel, three.

9The sons of Shimei; Shelomith, and Haziel, and Haran, three. These *were* the chief of the fathers of Laadan.

New International

who will be a man of peace and rest, and I will give him rest from all his enemies on every side. His name will be Solomon,a and I will grant Israel peace and quiet during his reign. 10He is the one who will build a house for my Name. He will be my son, and I will be his father. And I will establish the throne of his kingdom over Israel forever.'

11"Now, my son, the LORD be with you, and may you have success and build the house of the LORD your God, as he said you would. 12May the LORD give you discretion and understanding when he puts you in command over Israel, so that you may keep the law of the LORD your God. 13Then you will have success if you are careful to observe the decrees and laws that the LORD gave Moses for Israel. Be strong and courageous. Do not be afraid or discouraged.

14"I have taken great pains to provide for the temple of the LORD a hundred thousand talentsb of gold, a million talentsc of silver, quantities of bronze and iron too great to be weighed, and wood and stone. And you may add to them. 15You have many workmen: stonecutters, masons and carpenters, as well as men skilled in every kind of work 16in gold and silver, bronze and iron—craftsmen beyond number. Now begin the work, and the LORD be with you."

17Then David ordered all the leaders of Israel to help his son Solomon. 18He said to them, "Is not the LORD your God with you? And has he not granted you rest on every side? For he has handed the inhabitants of the land over to me, and the land is subject to the LORD and to his people. 19Now devote your heart and soul to seeking the LORD your God. Begin to build the sanctuary of the LORD God, so that you may bring the ark of the covenant of the LORD and the sacred articles belonging to God into the temple that will be built for the Name of the LORD."

The Levites

23 WHEN DAVID was old and full of years, he made his son Solomon king over Israel.

2He also gathered together all the leaders of Israel, as well as the priests and Levites. 3The Levites thirty years old or more were counted, and the total number of men was thirty-eight thousand. 4David said, "Of these, twenty-four thousand are to supervise the work of the temple of the LORD and six thousand are to be officials and judges. 5Four thousand are to be gatekeepers and four thousand are to praise the LORD with the musical instruments I have provided for that purpose."

6David divided the Levites into groups corresponding to the sons of Levi: Gershon, Kohath and Merari.

Gershonites

7Belonging to the Gershonites:
   Ladan and Shimei.
8The sons of Ladan:
   Jehiel the first, Zetham and Joel—three in all.
9The sons of Shimei:
   Shelomoth, Haziel and Haran—three in all.
   These were the heads of the families of Ladan.

---

a 9 *Solomon* sounds like and may be derived from the Hebrew for *peace.*
b *14* That is, about 3,750 tons (about 3,450 metric tons)   c *14* That is, about 37,500 tons (about 34,500 metric tons)

Living Bible

will be a man of peace, for I will give him peace with his enemies in the surrounding lands. His name shall be Solomon (meaning "Peaceful"), and I will give peace and quietness to Israel during his reign. 10He shall build my temple, and he shall be as my own son and I will be his father; and I will cause his sons and his descendants to reign over every generation of Israel.'

11"So now, my son, may the Lord be with you and prosper you as you do what he told you to do and build the Temple of the Lord. 12And may the Lord give you the good judgment to follow all his laws when he makes you king of Israel. 13For if you carefully obey the rules and regulations which he gave to Israel through Moses, you will prosper. Be strong and courageous, fearless and enthusiastic!

14"By hard work I have collected several billion dollars worth of gold bullion, millions in silver,d and so much iron and bronze that I haven't even weighed it; I have also gathered timber and stone for the walls. This is at least a beginning, something with which to start. 15And you have many skilled stonemasons and carpenters and craftsmen of every kind. 16They are expert gold and silver smiths and bronze and iron workers. So get to work, and may the Lord be with you!"

17Then David ordered all the leaders of Israel to assist his son in this project.

18"The Lord your God is with you," he declared. "He has given you peace with the surrounding nations, for I have conquered them in the name of the Lord and for his people. 19Now try with every fiber of your being to obey the Lord your God, and you will soon be bringing the Ark and the other holy articles of worship into the Temple of the Lord!"

23 BY THIS time David was an old, old man, so he stepped down from the throne and appointed his son Solomon as the new king of Israel. 2He summoned all the political and religious leaders of Israel for the coronation ceremony. 3At this time a census was taken of the men of the tribe of Levi who were thirty years or older. The total came to 38,000.

4, 5"Twenty-four thousand of them will supervise the work at the Temple," David instructed, "six thousand are to be bailiffs and judges, four thousand will be temple guards, and four thousand will praise the Lord with the musical instruments I have made."

6Then David divided them into three main divisions named after the sons of Levi—the Gershom division, the Kohath division and the Merari division.

7Subdivisions of the *Gershom* corps were named after his sons Ladan and Shime-i. 8, 9These subdivisions were still further divided into six groups named after the sons of *Ladan:* Jehiel the leader, Zetham, Joel; and the sons of *Shime-i*e—Shelomoth, Haziel, and Haran.

New Revised Standard

be born to you; he shall be a man of peace. I will give him peace from all his enemies on every side; for his name shall be Solomon,f and I will give peaceg and quiet to Israel in his days. 10He shall build a house for my name. He shall be a son to me, and I will be a father to him, and I will establish his royal throne in Israel forever.' 11Now, my son, the LORD be with you, so that you may succeed in building the house of the LORD your God, as he has spoken concerning you. 12Only, may the LORD grant you discretion and understanding, so that when he gives you charge over Israel you may keep the law of the LORD your God. 13Then you will prosper if you are careful to observe the statutes and the ordinances that the LORD commanded Moses for Israel. Be strong and of good courage. Do not be afraid or dismayed. 14With great pains I have provided for the house of the LORD one hundred thousand talents of gold, one million talents of silver, and bronze and iron beyond weighing, for there is so much of it; timber and stone too I have provided. To these you must add more. 15You have an abundance of workers: stonecutters, masons, carpenters, and all kinds of artisans without number, skilled in working 16gold, silver, bronze, and iron. Now begin the work, and the LORD be with you."

17 David also commanded all the leaders of Israel to help his son Solomon, saying, 18"Is not the LORD your God with you? Has he not given you peace on every side? For he has delivered the inhabitants of the land into my hand; and the land is subdued before the LORD and his people. 19Now set your mind and heart to seek the LORD your God. Go and build the sanctuary of the LORD God so that the ark of the covenant of the LORD and the holy vessels of God may be brought into a house built for the name of the LORD."

Families of the Levites and Their Functions

23 WHEN DAVID was old and full of days, he made his son Solomon king over Israel.

2 David assembled all the leaders of Israel and the priests and the Levites. 3The Levites, thirty years old and upward, were counted, and the total was thirty-eight thousand. 4"Twenty-four thousand of these," David said, "shall have charge of the work in the house of the LORD, six thousand shall be officers and judges, 5four thousand gatekeepers, and four thousand shall offer praises to the LORD with the instruments that I have made for praise." 6And David organized them in divisions corresponding to the sons of Levi: Gershon,h Kohath, and Merari.

7 The sons of Gershoni were Ladan and Shimei. 8The sons of Ladan: Jehiel the chief, Zetham, and Joel, three. 9The sons of Shimei: Shelomoth, Haziel, and Haran, three. These were the heads of families of Ladan.

---

d 22:14 *several billion dollars worth of gold bullion, and millions in silver,* literally, "a hundred thousand talents of gold" and "a million talents of silver."
e 23:9 *Shime-i,* probably not the same Shime-i as in vs 7.

f Heb *Shelomoh*   g Heb *shalom*   h Or *Gershom;* See 1 Chr 6.1, note, and 23.15   i Vg Compare Gk Syr: Heb *to the Gershonite*

King James

10And the sons of Shimei *were,* Jahath, Zina, and Jeush, and Beriah. These four *were* the sons of Shimei.

11And Jahath was the chief, and Zizah the second: but Jeush and Beriah had not many sons; therefore they were in one reckoning, according to *their* father's house.

12¶ The sons of Kohath; Amram, Izhar, Hebron, and Uzziel, four.

13The sons of Amram; Aaron and Moses: and Aaron was separated, that he should sanctify the most holy things, he and his sons for ever, to burn incense before the LORD, to minister unto him, and to bless in his name for ever.

14Now *concerning* Moses the man of God, his sons were named of the tribe of Levi.

15The sons of Moses *were,* Gershom, and Eliezer.

16Of the sons of Gershom, Shebuel *was* the chief.

17And the sons of Eliezer *were,* Rehabiah the chief. And Eliezer had none other sons; but the sons of Rehabiah were very many.

18Of the sons of Izhar; Shelomith the chief.

19Of the sons of Hebron; Jeriah the first, Amariah the second, Jahaziel the third, and Jekameam the fourth.

20Of the sons of Uzziel; Michah the first, and Jesiah the second.

21¶ The sons of Merari; Mahli, and Mushi. The sons of Mahli; Eleazar, and Kish.

22And Eleazar died, and had no sons, but daughters: and their brethren the sons of Kish took them.

23The sons of Mushi; Mahli, and Eder, and Jeremoth, three.

24¶ These *were* the sons of Levi after the house of their fathers; *even* the chief of the fathers, as they were counted by number of names by their polls, that did the work for the service of the house of the LORD, from the age of twenty years and upward.

25For David said, The LORD God of Israel hath given rest unto his people, that they may dwell in Jerusalem for ever:

26And also unto the Levites; they shall no *more* carry the tabernacle, nor any vessels of it for the service thereof.

27For by the last words of David the Levites *were* numbered from twenty years old and above:

28Because their office *was* to wait on the sons of Aaron for the service of the house of the LORD, in the courts, and in the chambers, and in the purifying of all holy things, and the work of the service of the house of God;

29Both for the showbread, and for the fine flour for meat offering, and for the unleavened cakes, and for *that which is baked in* the pan, and for that which is fried, and for all manner of measure and size;

30And to stand every morning to thank and praise the LORD, and likewise at even;

31And to offer all burnt sacrifices unto the LORD in the sabbaths, in the new moons, and on the set feasts, by number, according to the order commanded unto them, continually before the LORD:

New International

10And the sons of Shimei:

Jahath, Ziza,[a] Jeush and Beriah.

These were the sons of Shimei—four in all.

11Jahath was the first and Ziza the second, but Jeush and Beriah did not have many sons; so they were counted as one family with one assignment.

Kohathites

12The sons of Kohath:

Amram, Izhar, Hebron and Uzziel—four in all.

13The sons of Amram:

Aaron and Moses.

Aaron was set apart, he and his descendants forever, to consecrate the most holy things, to offer sacrifices before the LORD, to minister before him and to pronounce blessings in his name forever. 14The sons of Moses the man of God were counted as part of the tribe of Levi.

15The sons of Moses:

Gershom and Eliezer.

16The descendants of Gershom:

Shubael was the first.

17The descendants of Eliezer:

Rehabiah was the first.

Eliezer had no other sons, but the sons of Rehabiah were very numerous.

18The sons of Izhar:

Shelomith was the first.

19The sons of Hebron:

Jeriah the first, Amariah the second, Jahaziel the third and Jekameam the fourth.

20The sons of Uzziel:

Micah the first and Isshiah the second.

Merarites

21The sons of Merari:

Mahli and Mushi.

The sons of Mahli:

Eleazar and Kish.

22Eleazar died without having sons: he had only daughters. Their cousins, the sons of Kish, married them.

23The sons of Mushi:

Mahli, Eder and Jerimoth—three in all.

24These were the descendants of Levi by their families—the heads of families as they were registered under their names and counted individually, that is, the workers twenty years old or more who served in the temple of the LORD. 25For David had said, "Since the LORD, the God of Israel, has granted rest to his people and has come to dwell in Jerusalem forever, 26the Levites no longer need to carry the tabernacle or any of the articles used in its service." 27According to the last instructions of David, the Levites were counted from those twenty years old or more.

28The duty of the Levites was to help Aaron's descendants in the service of the temple of the LORD: to be in charge of the courtyards, the side rooms, the purification of all sacred things and the performance of other duties at the house of God. 29They were in charge of the bread set out on the table, the flour for the grain offerings, the unleavened wafers, the baking and the mixing, and all measurements of quantity and size. 30They were also to stand every morning to thank and praise the LORD. They were to do the same in the evening 31and whenever burnt offerings were presented to the LORD on Sabbaths and at New Moon festivals and at appointed feasts. They were to serve before the LORD regularly in the proper number and in the way prescribed for them.

---

a *10* One Hebrew manuscript, Septuagint and Vulgate (see also verse 11); most Hebrew manuscripts *Zina*

Living Bible

10, 11The subclans of *Shime-i* were named after his four sons: Jahath was greatest, Zizah[b] was next, and Jeush and Beriah were combined into a single subclan because neither had many sons.

12The division of Kohath was subdivided into four groups named after his sons Amram, Izhar, Hebron, and Uzziel.

13*Amram* was the ancestor of Aaron and Moses.[c] Aaron and his sons were set apart for the holy service of sacrificing the people's offerings to the Lord. He served the Lord constantly and pronounced blessings in his name at all times.

14, 15As for Moses, the man of God, his sons Gershom and Eliezer were included with the tribe of Levi. 16*Gershom's* sons were led by Shebuel, 17and *Eliezer's* only son, Rehabiah, was the leader of his clan, for he had many children.

18The sons of *Izhar* were led by Shelomith.

19The sons of *Hebron* were led by Jeriah. Amariah was second in command, Jahaziel was third, and Jekameam was fourth.

20The sons of *Uzziel* were led by Micah, and Isshiah was the second in command.

21The sons of *Merari* were Mahli and Mushi. The sons of *Mahli* were Eleazar and Kish. 22*Eleazar* died without any sons, and his daughters were married to their cousins, the sons of *Kish*. 23*Mushi's* sons were Mahli, Eder, and Jeremoth.

24In the census, all the men of Levi who were twenty years old or older were classified under the names of these clans and subclans; and they were all assigned to the ministry at the Temple. 25For David said, "The Lord God of Israel has given us peace, and he will always live in Jerusalem. 26Now the Levites will no longer need to carry the Tabernacle and its instruments from place to place."

27(This census of the tribe of Levi was one of the last things David did before his death.) 28The work of the Levites was to assist the priests—the descendants of Aaron—in the sacrifices at the Temple; they also did the custodial work and helped perform the ceremonies of purification. 29They provided the Bread of the Presence, the flour for the grain offerings, and the wafers made without yeast (either fried or mixed with olive oil); they also checked all the weights and measures. 30Each morning and evening they stood before the Lord to sing thanks and praise to him. 31They assisted in the special sacrifices of burnt offerings, the Sabbath sacrifices, the new moon celebrations, and at all the festivals. There were always as many Levites present as were required for the occasion. 32And they took care of the Tabernacle

New Revised Standard

10And the sons of Shimei: Jahath, Zina, Jeush, and Beriah. These four were the sons of Shimei. 11Jahath was the chief, and Zizah the second; but Jeush and Beriah did not have many sons, so they were enrolled as a single family.

12 The sons of Kohath: Amram, Izhar, Hebron, and Uzziel, four. 13The sons of Amram: Aaron and Moses. Aaron was set apart to consecrate the most holy things, so that he and his sons forever should make offerings before the Lord, and minister to him and pronounce blessings in his name forever; 14but as for Moses the man of God, his sons were to be reckoned among the tribe of Levi. 15The sons of Moses: Gershom and Eliezer. 16The sons of Gershom: Shebuel the chief. 17The sons of Eliezer: Rehabiah the chief; Eliezer had no other sons, but the sons of Rehabiah were very numerous. 18The sons of Izhar: Shelomith the chief. 19The sons of Hebron: Jeriah the chief, Amariah the second, Jahaziel the third, and Jekameam the fourth. 20The sons of Uzziel: Micah the chief and Isshiah the second.

21 The sons of Merari: Mahli and Mushi. The sons of Mahli: Eleazar and Kish. 22Eleazar died having no sons, but only daughters; their kindred, the sons of Kish, married them. 23The sons of Mushi: Mahli, Eder, and Jeremoth, three.

24 These were the sons of Levi by their ancestral houses, the heads of families as they were enrolled according to the number of the names of the individuals from twenty years old and upward who were to do the work for the service of the house of the Lord. 25For David said, "The Lord, the God of Israel, has given rest to his people; and he resides in Jerusalem forever. 26And so the Levites no longer need to carry the tabernacle or any of the things for its service"— 27for according to the last words of David these were the number of the Levites from twenty years old and upward— 28"but their duty shall be to assist the descendants of Aaron for the service of the house of the Lord, having the care of the courts and the chambers, the cleansing of all that is holy, and any work for the service of the house of God; 29to assist also with the rows of bread, the choice flour for the grain offering, the wafers of unleavened bread, the baked offering, the offering mixed with oil, and all measures of quantity or size. 30And they shall stand every morning, thanking and praising the Lord, and likewise at evening, 31and whenever burnt offerings are offered to the Lord on sabbaths, new moons, and appointed festivals, according to the number required of them, regularly before the Lord. 32Thus they shall keep charge of the

b 23:10, 11 Zizah, or "Zina."   c 23:13 Aaron and Moses, literally, "the sons of Amram: Aaron and Moses."

King James

32And that they should keep the charge of the tabernacle of the congregation, and the charge of the holy *place*, and the charge of the sons of Aaron their brethren, in the service of the house of the LORD.

24 NOW *THESE are* the divisions of the sons of Aaron. The sons of Aaron; Nadab, and Abihu, Eleazar, and Ithamar.

2But Nadab and Abihu died before their father, and had no children: therefore Eleazar and Ithamar executed the priest's office.

3And David distributed them, both Zadok of the sons of Eleazar, and Ahimelech of the sons of Ithamar, according to their offices in their service.

4And there were more chief men found of the sons of Eleazar than of the sons of Ithamar; and *thus* were they divided. Among the sons of Eleazar *there were* sixteen chief men of the house of *their* fathers, and eight among the sons of Ithamar according to the house of their fathers.

5Thus were they divided by lot, one sort with another; for the governors of the sanctuary, and governors *of the house* of God, were of the sons of Eleazar, and of the sons of Ithamar.

6And Shemaiah the son of Nethaneel the scribe, *one* of the Levites, wrote them before the king, and the princes, and Zadok the priest, and Ahimelech the son of Abiathar, and *before* the chief of the fathers of the priests and Levites: one principal household being taken for Eleazar, and *one* taken for Ithamar.

7Now the first lot came forth to Jehoiarib, the second to Jedaiah,

8The third to Harim, the fourth to Seorim,

9The fifth to Malchijah, the sixth to Mijamin,

10The seventh to Hakkoz, the eighth to Abijah,

11The ninth to Jeshuah, the tenth to Shecaniah,

12The eleventh to Eliashib, the twelfth to Jakim,

13The thirteenth to Huppah, the fourteenth to Jeshebeab,

14The fifteenth to Bilgah, the sixteenth to Immer,

15The seventeenth to Hezir, the eighteenth to Aphses,

16The nineteenth to Pethahiah, the twentieth to Jehezekel,

17The one and twentieth to Jachin, the two and twentieth to Gamul,

18The three and twentieth to Delaiah, the four and twentieth to Maaziah.

19These *were* the orderings of them in their service to come into the house of the LORD, according to their manner, under Aaron their father, as the LORD God of Israel had commanded him.

20¶ And the rest of the sons of Levi *were these:* Of the sons of Amram; Shubael: of the sons of Shubael; Jehdeiah.

21Concerning Rehabiah: of the sons of Rehabiah, the first *was* Isshiah.

22Of the Izharites; Shelomoth: of the sons of Shelomoth; Jahath.

23And the sons *of Hebron;* Jeriah *the first,* Amariah the second, Jahaziel the third, Jekameam the fourth.

New International

32And so the Levites carried out their responsibilities for the Tent of Meeting, for the Holy Place and, under their brothers the descendants of Aaron, for the service of the temple of the LORD.

The Divisions of Priests

24 THESE WERE the divisions of the sons of Aaron:

The sons of Aaron were Nadab, Abihu, Eleazar and Ithamar. 2But Nadab and Abihu died before their father did, and they had no sons; so Eleazar and Ithamar served as the priests. 3With the help of Zadok a descendant of Eleazar and Ahimelech a descendant of Ithamar, David separated them into divisions for their appointed order of ministering. 4A larger number of leaders were found among Eleazar's descendants than among Ithamar's, and they were divided accordingly: sixteen heads of families from Eleazar's descendants and eight heads of families from Ithamar's descendants. 5They divided them impartially by drawing lots, for there were officials of the sanctuary and officials of God among the descendants of both Eleazar and Ithamar.

6The scribe Shemaiah son of Nethanel, a Levite, recorded their names in the presence of the king and of the officials: Zadok the priest, Ahimelech son of Abiathar and the heads of families of the priests and of the Levites—one family being taken from Eleazar and then one from Ithamar.

7The first lot fell to Jehoiarib, the second to Jedaiah,

8the third to Harim, the fourth to Seorim,

9the fifth to Malkijah, the sixth to Mijamin,

10the seventh to Hakkoz, the eighth to Abijah,

11the ninth to Jeshua, the tenth to Shecaniah,

12the eleventh to Eliashib, the twelfth to Jakim,

13the thirteenth to Huppah, the fourteenth to Jeshebeab,

14the fifteenth to Bilgah, the sixteenth to Immer,

15the seventeenth to Hezir, the eighteenth to Happizzez,

16the nineteenth to Pethahiah, the twentieth to Jehezkel,

17the twenty-first to Jakin, the twenty-second to Gamul,

18the twenty-third to Delaiah and the twenty-fourth to Maaziah.

19This was their appointed order of ministering when they entered the temple of the LORD, according to the regulations prescribed for them by their forefather Aaron, as the LORD, the God of Israel, had commanded him.

The Rest of the Levites

20As for the rest of the descendants of Levi:
from the sons of Amram: Shubael;
from the sons of Shubael: Jehdeiah.
21As for Rehabiah, from his sons:
Isshiah was the first.
22From the Izharites: Shelomoth;
from the sons of Shelomoth: Jahath.
23The sons of Hebron: Jeriah the first,[a] Amariah the second, Jahaziel the third and Jekameam the fourth.

---

a 23 Two Hebrew manuscripts and some Septuagint manuscripts (see also 1 Chron. 23:19); most Hebrew manuscripts *The sons of Jeriah:*

Living Bible

and the Temple and assisted the priests in whatever way they were needed.

24 THE PRIESTS (the descendants of Aaron) were placed into two divisions named after Aaron's sons, Eleazar and Ithamar.

Nadab and Abihu were also sons of Aaron, but they died before their father did and had no children; so only Eleazar and Ithamar were left to carry on. ³David consulted with Zadok, who represented the Eleazar clan, and with Ahimelech, who represented the Ithamar clan; then he divided Aaron's descendants into many groups to serve at various times. ⁴*Eleazar's* descendants were divided into sixteen groups and *Ithamar's* into eight (for there was more leadership ability among the descendants of Eleazar).

⁵All tasks were assigned to the various groups by coin-toss[b] so that there would be no preference, for there were many famous men and high officials of the Temple in each division. ⁶Shemaiah, a Levite and the son of Nethanel, acted as recording secretary and wrote down the names and assignments in the presence of the king and of these leaders: Zadok the priest, Ahimelech the son of Abiathar, and the heads of the priests and Levites. Two groups from the division of Eleazar and one from the division of Ithamar were assigned to each task.

⁷⁻¹⁸The work was assigned (by coin-toss) in this order:

First, the group led by Jehoiarib;
Second, the group led by Jedaiah;
Third, the group led by Harim;
Fourth, the group led by Se-orim;
Fifth, the group led by Malchijah;
Sixth, the group led by Mijamin;
Seventh, the group led by Hakkoz;
Eighth, the group led by Ahijah;
Ninth, the group led by Jeshua;
Tenth, the group led by Shecaniah;
Eleventh, the group led by Eliashib;
Twelfth, the group led by Jakim;
Thirteenth, the group led by Huppah;
Fourteenth, the group led by Jeshebe-ab;
Fifteenth, the group led by Bilgah;
Sixteenth, the group led by Immer;
Seventeenth, the group led by Hezir;
Eighteenth, the group led by Happizzez;
Nineteenth, the group led by Pethahiah;
Twentieth, the group led by Jehezkel;
Twenty-first, the group led by Jachin;
Twenty-second, the group led by Gamul;
Twenty-third, the group led by Delaiah;
Twenty-fourth, the group led by Maaziah.

¹⁹Each group carried out the Temple duties as originally assigned by God through their ancestor Aaron.

²⁰These were the other descendants of Levi: Amram; his descendant Shuba-el; and Shuba-el's descendant Jehdeiah; ²¹the Rehabiah group, led by his oldest son Isshiah; ²²the Izhar group, consisting of Shelamoth and his descendant Jahath.

²³The Hebron group:
Jeriah, Hebron's oldest son;
Amariah, his second son;
Jahaziel, his third son;
Jekameam, his fourth son.

New Revised Standard

tent of meeting and the sanctuary, and shall attend the descendants of Aaron, their kindred, for the service of the house of the LORD."

Divisions of the Priests

24 THE DIVISIONS of the descendants of Aaron were these. The sons of Aaron: Nadab, Abihu, Eleazar, and Ithamar. ²But Nadab and Abihu died before their father, and had no sons; so Eleazar and Ithamar became the priests. ³Along with Zadok of the sons of Eleazar, and Ahimelech of the sons of Ithamar, David organized them according to the appointed duties in their service. ⁴Since more chief men were found among the sons of Eleazar than among the sons of Ithamar, they organized them under sixteen heads of ancestral houses of the sons of Eleazar, and eight of the sons of Ithamar. ⁵They organized them by lot, all alike, for there were officers of the sanctuary and officers of God among both the sons of Eleazar and the sons of Ithamar. ⁶The scribe Shemaiah son of Nethanel, a Levite, recorded them in the presence of the king, and the officers, and Zadok the priest, and Ahimelech son of Abiathar, and the heads of ancestral houses of the priests and of the Levites; one ancestral house being chosen for Eleazar and one chosen for Ithamar.

7 The first lot fell to Jehoiarib, the second to Jedaiah, ⁸the third to Harim, the fourth to Seorim, ⁹the fifth to Malchijah, the sixth to Mijamin, ¹⁰the seventh to Hakkoz, the eighth to Abijah, ¹¹the ninth to Jeshua, the tenth to Shecaniah, ¹²the eleventh to Eliashib, the twelfth to Jakim, ¹³the thirteenth to Huppah, the fourteenth to Jeshebeab, ¹⁴the fifteenth to Bilgah, the sixteenth to Immer, ¹⁵the seventeenth to Hezir, the eighteenth to Happizzez, ¹⁶the nineteenth to Pethahiah, the twentieth to Jehezkel, ¹⁷the twenty-first to Jachin, the twenty-second to Gamul, ¹⁸the twenty-third to Delaiah, the twenty-fourth to Maaziah. ¹⁹These had as their appointed duty in their service to enter the house of the LORD according to the procedure established for them by their ancestor Aaron, as the LORD God of Israel had commanded him.

Other Levites

20 And of the rest of the sons of Levi: of the sons of Amram, Shubael; of the sons of Shubael, Jehdeiah. ²¹Of Rehabiah: of the sons of Rehabiah, Isshiah the chief. ²²Of the Izharites, Shelomoth; of the sons of Shelomoth, Jahath. ²³The sons of Hebron:[c] Jeriah the chief,[d] Amariah the second, Jahaziel the third, Jekameam the fourth. ²⁴The sons of Uzziel, Micah; of the sons

---

b *24:5 by coin-toss,* literally, "by lot."

c See 23:19: Heb lacks *Hebron*   d See 23:19: Heb lacks *the chief*

King James

24Of the sons of Uzziel; Michah: of the sons of Michah; Shamir.

25The brother of Michah was Isshiah: of the sons of Isshiah; Zechariah.

26The sons of Merari were Mahli and Mushi: the sons of Jaaziah; Beno.

27¶ The sons of Merari by Jaaziah; Beno, and Shoham, and Zaccur, and Ibri.

28Of Mahli came Eleazar, who had no sons.

29Concerning Kish: the son of Kish was Jerahmeel.

30The sons also of Mushi; Mahli, and Eder, and Jerimoth. These were the sons of the Levites after the house of their fathers.

31These likewise cast lots over against their brethren the sons of Aaron in the presence of David the king, and Zadok, and Ahimelech, and the chief of the fathers of the priests and Levites, even the principal fathers over against their younger brethren.

25 MOREOVER DAVID and the captains of the host separated to the service of the sons of Asaph, and of Heman, and of Jeduthun, who should prophesy with harps, with psalteries, and with cymbals: and the number of the workmen according to their service was:

2Of the sons of Asaph; Zaccur, and Joseph, and Nethaniah, and Asarelah, the sons of Asaph under the hands of Asaph, which prophesied according to the order of the king.

3Of Jeduthun: the sons of Jeduthun; Gedaliah, and Zeri, and Jeshaiah, Hashabiah, and Mattithiah, six, under the hands of their father Jeduthun, who prophesied with a harp, to give thanks and to praise the LORD.

4Of Heman: the sons of Heman; Bukkiah, Mattaniah, Uzziel, Shebuel, and Jerimoth, Hananiah, Hanani, Eliathah, Giddalti, and Romamti-ezer, Joshbekashah, Mallothi, Hothir, and Mahazioth:

5All these were the sons of Heman the king's seer in the words of God, to lift up the horn. And God gave to Heman fourteen sons and three daughters.

6All these were under the hands of their father for song in the house of the LORD, with cymbals, psalteries, and harps, for the service of the house of God, according to the king's order to Asaph, Jeduthun, and Heman.

7So the number of them, with their brethren that were instructed in the songs of the LORD, even all that were cunning, was two hundred fourscore and eight.

8¶ And they cast lots, ward against ward, as well the small as the great, the teacher as the scholar.

9Now the first lot came forth for Asaph to Joseph: the second to Gedaliah, who with his brethren and sons were twelve:

10The third to Zaccur, he, his sons, and his brethren, were twelve:

11The fourth to Izri, he, his sons, and his brethren, were twelve:

12The fifth to Nethaniah, he, his sons, and his brethren, were twelve:

13The sixth to Bukkiah, he, his sons, and his brethren, were twelve:

14The seventh to Jesharelah, he, his sons, and his brethren, were twelve:

New International

24The son of Uzziel: Micah;
  from the sons of Micah: Shamir.

25The brother of Micah: Isshiah;
  from the sons of Isshiah: Zechariah.

26The sons of Merari: Mahli and Mushi.
  The son of Jaaziah: Beno.

27The sons of Merari:
  from Jaaziah: Beno, Shoham, Zaccur and Ibri.

28From Mahli: Eleazar, who had no sons.

29From Kish: the son of Kish:
  Jerahmeel.

30And the sons of Mushi: Mahli, Eder and Jerimoth.

These were the Levites, according to their families.
31They also cast lots, just as their brothers the descendants of Aaron did, in the presence of King David and of Zadok, Ahimelech, and the heads of families of the priests and of the Levites. The families of the oldest brother were treated the same as those of the youngest.

The Singers

25 DAVID, TOGETHER with the commanders of the army, set apart some of the sons of Asaph, Heman and Jeduthun for the ministry of prophesying, accompanied by harps, lyres and cymbals. Here is the list of the men who performed this service:

2From the sons of Asaph:
  Zaccur, Joseph, Nethaniah and Asarelah. The sons of Asaph were under the supervision of Asaph, who prophesied under the king's supervision.

3As for Jeduthun, from his sons:
  Gedaliah, Zeri, Jeshaiah, Shimei,a Hashabiah and Mattithiah, six in all, under the supervision of their father Jeduthun, who prophesied, using the harp in thanking and praising the LORD.

4As for Heman, from his sons:
  Bukkiah, Mattaniah, Uzziel, Shubael and Jerimoth; Hananiah, Hanani, Eliathah, Giddalti and Romamti-Ezer; Joshbekashah, Mallothi, Hothir and Mahazioth. 5All these were sons of Heman the king's seer. They were given him through the promises of God to exalt him.b God gave Heman fourteen sons and three daughters.

6All these men were under the supervision of their fathers for the music of the temple of the LORD, with cymbals, lyres and harps, for the ministry at the house of God. Asaph, Jeduthun and Heman were under the supervision of the king. 7Along with their relatives—all of them trained and skilled in music for the LORD—they numbered 288. 8Young and old alike, teacher as well as student, cast lots for their duties.

9The first lot, which was for Asaph, fell to Joseph,
  his sons and relatives,c   12d
the second to Gedaliah,
  he and his relatives and sons,   12
10the third to Zaccur,
  his sons and relatives,   12
11the fourth to Izri,e
  his sons and relatives,   12
12the fifth to Nethaniah,
  his sons and relatives,   12
13the sixth to Bukkiah,
  his sons and relatives,   12
14the seventh to Jesarelah,f
  his sons and relatives,   12

Living Bible

24, 25The Uzziel group was led by his son Micah and his grandsons Shamir and Isshiah, and by Isshiah's son Zechariah.

26, 27The Merari group was led by his sons: Mahli and Mushi. (Ja-aziah's group, led by his son Beno, included his brothers Shoham, Zaccur, and Ibri.) 28Mahli's descendants were Eleazar, who had no sons, 29and Kish, among whose sons was Jerahmeel. 30The sons of *Mushi* were Mahli, Eder, and Jerimoth.

These were the descendants of Levi in their various clans. 31Like the descendants of Aaron, they were assigned to their duties by coin-toss without distinction as to age or rank. It was done in the presence of King David, Zadok, Ahimelech, and the leaders of the priests and the Levites.

25 DAVID AND the officials of the Tabernacle then appointed men to prophesy to the accompaniment of zithers, harps, and cymbals. These men were from the groups of Asaph, Heman, and Jeduthun. Here is a list of their names and their work:

2Under the leadership of Asaph, the king's private prophet, were his sons Zaccur, Joseph, Nethaniah, and Asharelah.

3Under Jeduthun, who led in giving thanks and praising the Lord (while accompanied by the zither), were his six sons: Gedaliah, Zeri, Jeshaiah, Shime-i, Hashabiah, and Mattithiah.

4, 5Under the direction of Heman, the king's private chaplain, were his sons: Bukkiah, Mattaniah, Uzziel, Shebuel, Jerimoth, Hananiah, Hanani, Eliathah, Geddalti, Romamti-ezer, Joshbekashah, Mallothi, Hothir, and Mahazi-oth. (For God had honored him with fourteen sons and three daughters.) 6, 7Their music ministry included the playing of cymbals, harps, and zithers; all were under the direction of their father as they performed this ministry in the Tabernacle.

Asaph, Jeduthun, and Heman reported directly to the king. They and their families were all trained in singing praises to the Lord; each one—288 of them in all—was a master musician. 8The singers were appointed to their particular term of service by coin-toss, without regard to age or reputation.

9-31The first toss indicated Joseph of the Asaph clan;
The second, Gedaliah, along with twelve of his sons and brothers;
The third, Zaccur and twelve of his sons and brothers;
The fourth, Izri and twelve of his sons and brothers;
Fifth, Nethaniah and twelve of his sons and brothers;
Sixth, Bukkiah and twelve of his sons and brothers;
Seventh, Jesharelah and twelve of his sons and brothers;
Eighth, Jeshaiah and twelve of his sons and brothers;
Ninth, Mattaniah and twelve of his sons and brothers;
Tenth, Shime-i and twelve of his sons and brothers;
Eleventh, Azarel and twelve of his sons and brothers;
Twelfth, Hashabiah and twelve of his sons and brothers;
Thirteenth, Shuba-el and twelve of his sons and brothers;
Fourteenth, Mattithiah and twelve of his sons and brothers;
Fifteenth, Jeremoth and twelve of his sons and brothers;

New Revised Standard

of Micah, Shamir. 25The brother of Micah, Isshiah; of the sons of Isshiah, Zechariah. 26The sons of Merari: Mahli and Mushi. The sons of Jaaziah: Beno.g 27The sons of Merari: of Jaaziah, Beno,g Shoham, Zaccur, and Ibri. 28Of Mahli: Eleazar, who had no sons. 29Of Kish, the sons of Kish: Jerahmeel. 30The sons of Mushi: Mahli, Eder, and Jerimoth. These were the sons of the Levites according to their ancestral houses. 31These also cast lots corresponding to their kindred, the descendants of Aaron, in the presence of King David, Zadok, Ahimelech, and the heads of ancestral houses of the priests and of the Levites, the chief as well as the youngest brother.

The Temple Musicians

25 DAVID AND the officers of the army also set apart for the service the sons of Asaph, and of Heman, and of Jeduthun, who should prophesy with lyres, harps, and cymbals. The list of those who did the work and of their duties was: 2Of the sons of Asaph: Zaccur, Joseph, Nethaniah, and Asarelah, sons of Asaph, under the direction of Asaph, who prophesied under the direction of the king. 3Of Jeduthun, the sons of Jeduthun: Gedaliah, Zeri, Jeshaiah, Shimei,h Hashabiah, and Mattithiah, six, under the direction of their father Jeduthun, who prophesied with the lyre in thanksgiving and praise to the Lord. 4Of Heman, the sons of Heman: Bukkiah, Mattaniah, Uzziel, Shebuel, and Jerimoth, Hananiah, Hanani, Eliathah, Giddalti, and Romamti-ezer, Joshbekashah, Mallothi, Hothir, Mahazioth. 5All these were the sons of Heman the king's seer, according to the promise of God to exalt him; for God had given Heman fourteen sons and three daughters. 6They were all under the direction of their father for the music in the house of the Lord with cymbals, harps, and lyres for the service of the house of God. Asaph, Jeduthun, and Heman were under the order of the king. 7They and their kindred, who were trained in singing to the Lord, all of whom were skillful, numbered two hundred eighty-eight. 8And they cast lots for their duties, small and great, teacher and pupil alike.

9 The first lot fell for Asaph to Joseph; the second to Gedaliah, to him and his brothers and his sons, twelve; 10the third to Zaccur, his sons and his brothers, twelve; 11the fourth to Izri, his sons and his brothers, twelve; 12the fifth to Nethaniah, his sons and his brothers, twelve; 13the sixth to Bukkiah, his sons and his brothers, twelve; 14the seventh to Jesarelah,i his sons and his brothers, twelve; 15the eighth to Jeshaiah, his

g Or *his son*: Meaning of Heb uncertain   h One Ms: Gk: MT lacks *Shimei*
i Or *Asarelah*; see 25.2

King James

15The eighth to Jeshaiah, *he,* his sons, and his brethren, *were* twelve:

16The ninth to Mattaniah, *he,* his sons, and his brethren, *were* twelve:

17The tenth to Shimei, *he,* his sons, and his brethren, *were* twelve:

18The eleventh to Azareel, *he,* his sons, and his brethren, *were* twelve:

19The twelfth to Hashabiah, *he,* his sons, and his brethren, *were* twelve:

20The thirteenth to Shubael, *he,* his sons, and his brethren, *were* twelve:

21The fourteenth to Mattithiah, *he,* his sons, and his brethren, *were* twelve:

22The fifteenth to Jeremoth, *he,* his sons, and his brethren, *were* twelve:

23The sixteenth to Hananiah, *he,* his sons, and his brethren, *were* twelve:

24The seventeenth to Joshbekashah, *he,* his sons, and his brethren, *were* twelve:

25The eighteenth to Hanani, *he,* his sons, and his brethren, *were* twelve:

26The nineteenth to Mallothi, *he,* his sons, and his brethren, *were* twelve:

27The twentieth to Eliathah, *he,* his sons, and his brethren, *were* twelve:

28The one and twentieth to Hothir, *he,* his sons, and his brethren, *were* twelve:

29The two and twentieth to Giddalti, *he,* his sons, and his brethren, *were* twelve:

30The three and twentieth to Mahazioth, *he,* his sons, and his brethren, *were* twelve:

31The four and twentieth to Romamti-ezer, *he,* his sons, and his brethren, *were* twelve.

26 CONCERNING THE divisions of the porters: Of the Korhites *was* Meshelemiah the son of Kore, of the sons of Asaph.

2And the sons of Meshelemiah *were,* Zechariah the firstborn, Jediael the second, Zebadiah the third, Jathniel the fourth,

3Elam the fifth, Jehohanan the sixth, Elioenai the seventh.

4Moreover the sons of Obed-edom *were,* Shemaiah the firstborn, Jehozabad the second, Joah the third, and Sacar the fourth, and Nethaneel the fifth,

5Ammiel the sixth, Issachar the seventh, Peulthai the eighth: for God blessed him.

6Also unto Shemaiah his son were sons born, that ruled throughout the house of their father: for they *were* mighty men of valour.

7The sons of Shemaiah; Othni, and Rephael, and Obed, Elzabad, whose brethren *were* strong men, Elihu, and Semachiah.

8All these of the sons of Obed-edom: they and their sons and their brethren, able men for strength for the service, *were* threescore and two of Obed-edom.

9And Meshelemiah had sons and brethren, strong men, eighteen.

New International

15the eighth to Jeshaiah,
　his sons and relatives,　　　　　　　12
16the ninth to Mattaniah,
　his sons and relatives,　　　　　　　12
17the tenth to Shimei,
　his sons and relatives,　　　　　　　12
18the eleventh to Azarel,a
　his sons and relatives,　　　　　　　12
19the twelfth to Hashabiah,
　his sons and relatives,　　　　　　　12
20the thirteenth to Shubael,
　his sons and relatives,　　　　　　　12
21the fourteenth to Mattithiah,
　his sons and relatives,　　　　　　　12
22the fifteenth to Jerimoth,
　his sons and relatives,　　　　　　　12
23the sixteenth to Hananiah,
　his sons and relatives,　　　　　　　12
24the seventeenth to Joshbekashah,
　his sons and relatives,　　　　　　　12
25the eighteenth to Hanani,
　his sons and relatives,　　　　　　　12
26the nineteenth to Mallothi,
　his sons and relatives,　　　　　　　12
27the twentieth to Eliathah,
　his sons and relatives,　　　　　　　12
28the twenty-first to Hothir,
　his sons and relatives,　　　　　　　12
29the twenty-second to Giddalti,
　his sons and relatives,　　　　　　　12
30the twenty-third to Mahazioth,
　his sons and relatives,　　　　　　　12
31the twenty-fourth to Romamti-Ezer,
　his sons and relatives,　　　　　　　12

The Gatekeepers

26 THE DIVISIONS of the gatekeepers:

From the Korahites: Meshelemiah son of Kore, one of the sons of Asaph.

2Meshelemiah had sons:
　Zechariah the firstborn,
　Jediael the second,
　Zebadiah the third,
　Jathniel the fourth,
3Elam the fifth,
　Jehohanan the sixth
　and Eliehoenai the seventh.
4Obed-Edom also had sons:
　Shemaiah the firstborn,
　Jehozabad the second,
　Joah the third,
　Sacar the fourth,
　Nethanel the fifth,
5Ammiel the sixth,
　Issachar the seventh
　and Peullethai the eighth.
　(For God had blessed Obed-Edom.)

6His son Shemaiah also had sons, who were leaders in their father's family because they were very capable men. 7The sons of Shemaiah: Othni, Rephael, Obed and Elzabad; his relatives Elihu and Semakiah were also able men. 8All these were descendants of Obed-Edom; they and their sons and their relatives were capable men with the strength to do the work—descendants of Obed-Edom, 62 in all.

9Meshelemiah had sons and relatives, who were able men—18 in all.

Living Bible

Sixteenth, Hananiah and twelve of his sons and
brothers;
Seventeenth, Joshbekasha and twelve of his sons and
brothers;
Eighteenth, Hanani and twelve of his sons and
brothers;
Nineteenth, Mallothi and twelve of his sons and
brothers;
Twentieth, Eliathah and twelve of his sons and
brothers;
Twenty-first, Hothir and twelve of his sons and
brothers;
Twenty-second, Giddalti and twelve of his sons and
brothers;
Twenty-third, Mahazi-oth and twelve of his sons and
brothers;
Twenty-fourth, Romamti-ezer and twelve of his sons
and brothers.

New Revised Standard

sons and his brothers, twelve; 16 the ninth to Mattaniah,
his sons and his brothers, twelve; 17 the tenth to Shimei,
his sons and his brothers, twelve; 18 the eleventh to Azarel, his sons and his brothers, twelve; 19 the twelfth to
Hashabiah, his sons and his brothers, twelve; 20 to the
thirteenth, Shubael, his sons and his brothers, twelve;
21 to the fourteenth, Mattithiah, his sons and his brothers, twelve; 22 to the fifteenth, to Jeremoth, his sons and
his brothers, twelve; 23 to the sixteenth, to Hananiah, his
sons and his brothers, twelve; 24 to the seventeenth, to
Joshbekashah, his sons and his brothers, twelve; 25 to the
eighteenth, to Hanani, his sons and his brothers, twelve;
26 to the nineteenth, to Mallothi, his sons and his brothers, twelve; 27 to the twentieth, to Eliathah, his sons and
his brothers, twelve; 28 to the twenty-first, to Hothir, his
sons and his brothers, twelve; 29 to the twenty-second,
to Giddalti, his sons and his brothers, twelve; 30 to the
twenty-third, to Mahazioth, his sons and his brothers,
twelve; 31 to the twenty-fourth, to Romamti-ezer, his
sons and his brothers, twelve.

The Gatekeepers

26 THE TEMPLE guards were from the Asaph
division of the Korah clan. The captain of the
guard was Meshelemiah, the son of Kore.

2, 3 His sergeants were his sons:
Zechariah (the oldest),
Jedia-el (the second),
Zebadiah (the third),
Jathni-el (the fourth),
Elam (the fifth),
Jeho-hanan (the sixth),
Elie-ho-enai (the seventh).

4, 5 The sons of Obed-edom were also appointed as
Temple guards:
Shemaiah (the oldest),
Jehozabad (the second),
Joah (the third),
Sacar (the fourth),
Nethanel (the fifth),
Ammi-el (the sixth),
Issachar (the seventh),
Pe-ullethai (the eighth).

What a blessing God gave him with all those sons!
6, 7 Shemaiah's sons were all outstanding men, and
had positions of great authority in their clan. Their
names were:
Othni, Repha-el, Obed, Elzabad.
Their brave brothers, Elihu and Semachiah, were
also very able men.

8 All of these sons and grandsons of Obed-edom—all
sixty-two of them—were outstanding men who were
particularly well qualified for their work. 9 Meshelemiah's eighteen sons and brothers, too, were real leaders.

26 AS FOR the divisions of the gatekeepers: of the
Korahites, Meshelemiah son of Kore, of the
sons of Asaph. 2 Meshelemiah had sons: Zechariah the
firstborn, Jediael the second, Zebadiah the third, Jathni-
el the fourth, 3 Elam the fifth, Jehohanan the sixth, Eliehoenai the seventh. 4 Obed-edom had sons: Shemaiah
the firstborn, Jehozabad the second, Joah the third, Sachar the fourth, Nethanel the fifth, 5 Ammiel the sixth,
Issachar the seventh, Peullethai the eighth; for God
blessed him. 6 Also to his son Shemaiah sons were born
who exercised authority in their ancestral houses, for
they were men of great ability. 7 The sons of Shemaiah:
Othni, Rephael, Obed, and Elzabad, whose brothers
were able men, Elihu and Semachiah. 8 All these, sons
of Obed-edom with their sons and brothers, were able
men qualified for the service; sixty-two of Obed-edom.
9 Meshelemiah had sons and brothers, able men, eighteen. 10 Hosah, of the sons of Merari, had sons: Shimri

King James

¹⁰Also Hosah, of the children of Merari, had sons; Simri the chief, (for *though* he was not the firstborn, yet his father made him the chief;)

¹¹Hilkiah the second, Tebaliah the third, Zechariah the fourth: all the sons and brethren of Hosah *were* thirteen.

¹²Among these *were* the divisions of the porters, *even* among the chief men, *having* wards one against another, to minister in the house of the LORD.

¹³¶ And they cast lots, as well the small as the great, according to the house of their fathers, for every gate.

¹⁴And the lot eastward fell to Shelemiah. Then for Zechariah his son, a wise counsellor, they cast lots; and his lot came out northward.

¹⁵To Obed-edom southward; and to his sons the house of Asuppim.

¹⁶To Shuppim and Hosah *the lot came forth* westward, with the gate Shallecheth, by the causeway of the going up, ward against ward.

¹⁷Eastward *were* six Levites, northward four a day, southward four a day, and toward Asuppim two *and* two.

¹⁸At Parbar westward, four at the causeway, *and* two at Parbar.

¹⁹These *are* the divisions of the porters among the sons of Kore, and among the sons of Merari.

²⁰¶ And of the Levites, Ahijah *was* over the treasures of the house of God, and over the treasures of the dedicated things.

²¹*As concerning* the sons of Laadan; the sons of the Gershonite Laadan, chief fathers, *even* of Laadan the Gershonite, *were* Jehieli.

²²The sons of Jehieli; Zetham, and Joel his brother, *which were* over the treasures of the house of the LORD.

²³Of the Amramites, *and* the Izharites, the Hebronites, *and* the Uzzielites:

²⁴And Shebuel the son of Gershom, the son of Moses, *was* ruler of the treasures.

²⁵And his brethren by Eliezer; Rehabiah his son, and Jeshaiah his son, and Joram his son, and Zichri his son, and Shelomith his son.

²⁶Which Shelomith and his brethren *were* over all the treasures of the dedicated things, which David the king, and the chief fathers, the captains over thousands and hundreds, and the captains of the host, had dedicated.

²⁷Out of the spoils won in battles did they dedicate to maintain the house of the LORD.

²⁸And all that Samuel the seer, and Saul the son of Kish, and Abner the son of Ner, and Joab the son of Zeruiah, had dedicated; *and* whosoever had dedicated *any thing, it was* under the hand of Shelomith, and of his brethren.

²⁹¶ Of the Izharites, Chenaniah and his sons *were* for the outward business over Israel, for officers and judges.

³⁰*And* of the Hebronites, Hashabiah and his brethren, men of valour, a thousand and seven hundred, *were* officers among them of Israel on this side Jordan westward in all the business of the LORD, and in the service of the king.

³¹Among the Hebronites *was* Jerijah the chief, *even* among the Hebronites, according to the generations of his fathers. In the fortieth year of the reign of David they were sought for, and there were found among them mighty men of valour at Jazer of Gilead.

³²And his brethren, men of valour, *were* two thousand and seven hundred chief fathers, whom king David made rulers over the Reubenites, the Gadites, and the half tribe of Manasseh, for every matter pertaining to God, and affairs of the king.

New International

¹⁰Hosah the Merarite had sons: Shimri the first (although he was not the firstborn, his father had appointed him the first), ¹¹Hilkiah the second, Tabaliah the third and Zechariah the fourth. The sons and relatives of Hosah were 13 in all.

¹²These divisions of the gatekeepers, through their chief men, had duties for ministering in the temple of the LORD, just as their relatives had. ¹³Lots were cast for each gate, according to their families, young and old alike.

¹⁴The lot for the East Gate fell to Shelemiah.[a] Then lots were cast for his son Zechariah, a wise counselor, and the lot for the North Gate fell to him. ¹⁵The lot for the South Gate fell to Obed-Edom, and the lot for the storehouse fell to his sons. ¹⁶The lots for the West Gate and the Shalleketh Gate on the upper road fell to Shuppim and Hosah.

Guard was alongside of guard: ¹⁷There were six Levites a day on the east, four a day on the north, four a day on the south and two at a time at the storehouse. ¹⁸As for the court to the west, there were four at the road and two at the court itself.

¹⁹These were the divisions of the gatekeepers who were descendants of Korah and Merari.

The Treasurers and Other Officials

²⁰Their fellow Levites were[b] in charge of the treasuries of the house of God and the treasuries for the dedicated things.

²¹The descendants of Ladan, who were Gershonites through Ladan and who were heads of families belonging to Ladan the Gershonite, were Jehieli, ²²the sons of Jehieli, Zetham and his brother Joel. They were in charge of the treasuries of the temple of the LORD.

²³From the Amramites, the Izharites, the Hebronites and the Uzzielites:

²⁴Shubael, a descendant of Gershom son of Moses, was the officer in charge of the treasuries. ²⁵His relatives through Eliezer: Rehabiah his son, Jeshaiah his son, Joram his son, Zicri his son and Shelomith his son. ²⁶Shelomith and his relatives were in charge of all the treasuries for the things dedicated by King David, by the heads of families who were the commanders of thousands and commanders of hundreds, and by the other army commanders. ²⁷Some of the plunder taken in battle they dedicated for the repair of the temple of the LORD. ²⁸And everything dedicated by Samuel the seer and by Saul son of Kish, Abner son of Ner and Joab son of Zeruiah, and all the other dedicated things were in the care of Shelomith and his relatives.

²⁹From the Izharites: Kenaniah and his sons were assigned duties away from the temple, as officials and judges over Israel.

³⁰From the Hebronites: Hashabiah and his relatives—seventeen hundred able men—were responsible in Israel west of the Jordan for all the work of the LORD and for the king's service. ³¹As for the Hebronites, Jeriah was their chief according to the genealogical records of their families. In the fortieth year of David's reign a search was made in the records, and capable men among the Hebronites were found at Jazer in Gilead. ³²Jeriah had twenty-seven hundred relatives, who were able men and heads of families, and King David put them in charge of the Reubenites, the Gadites and the half-tribe of Manasseh for every matter pertaining to God and for the affairs of the king.

---

[a] *14* A variant of *Meshelemiah*   [b] *20* Septuagint; Hebrew *As for the Levites, Ahijah was*

Living Bible

10Hosah, one of the Merari group, appointed Shimri as the leader among his sons, though he was not the oldest. 11The names of some of his other sons were:

Hilkiah, the second;
Tebaliah, the third;
Zechariah, the fourth.

Hosah's sons and brothers numbered thirteen in all. 12The divisions of the Temple guards were named after the leaders. Like the other Levites, they were responsible to minister at the Temple. 13They were assigned guard duty at the various gates without regard to the reputation of their families, for it was all done by coin-toss. 14, 15The responsibility of the east gate went to Shelemiah and his group; of the north gate to his son Zechariah, a man of unusual wisdom; of the south gate to Obed-edom and his group (his sons were given charge of the storehouses); 16of the west gate and the Shallecheth Gate on the upper road, to Shuppim and Hosah. 17Six guards were assigned daily to the east gate, four to the north gate, four to the south gate, and two to each of the storehouses. 18Six guards were assigned each day to the west gate, four to the upper road, and two to the nearby areas. 19The Temple guards were chosen from the clans of Korah and Merari.

20, 21, 22Other Levites, led by Ahijah, were given the care of the gifts brought to the Lord and placed in the Temple treasury. These men of the Ladan subclan from the clan of Gershom included Zetham and Joel, the sons of Jehieli. 23, 24Shebuel, son of Gershom and grandson of Moses, was the chief officer of the treasury. He was in charge of the divisions named after Amram, Izhar, Hebron, and Uzziel.

25The line of descendants from Eliezer went through Rehabiah, Jesha-iah, Joram, Zichri, and Shelomoth. 26Shelomoth and his brothers were appointed to care for the gifts given to the Lord by King David and the other leaders of the nation such as the officers and generals of the army. 27For these men dedicated their war loot to support the operating expenses of the Temple. 28Shelomoth and his brothers were also responsible for the care of the items dedicated to the Lord by Samuel the prophet, Saul the son of Kish, Abner the son of Ner, Joab the son of Zeruiah, and anyone else of distinctionc who brought gifts to the Lord.

29Chenaniah and his sons (from the subclan of Izhar) were appointed public administrators and judges. 30Hashabiah and 1,700 of his clansmen from Hebron, all outstanding men, were placed in charge of the territory of Israel west of the Jordan River; they were responsible for the religious affairs and public administration of that area. 31, 32Twenty-seven hundred outstanding men of the clan of the Hebronites, under the supervision of Jerijah, were appointed to control the religious and public affairs of the tribes of Reuben, Gad, and the half-tribe of Manasseh. These men, all of whom had excellent qualifications, were appointed on the basis of their ancestry and ability at Jazer in Gilead in the fortieth year of King David's reign.

New Revised Standard

the chief (for though he was not the firstborn, his father made him chief), 11Hilkiah the second, Tebaliah the third, Zechariah the fourth: all the sons and brothers of Hosah totaled thirteen.

12 These divisions of the gatekeepers, corresponding to their leaders, had duties, just as their kindred did, ministering in the house of the Lord; 13and they cast lots by ancestral houses, small and great alike, for their gates. 14The lot for the east fell to Shelemiah. They cast lots also for his son Zechariah, a prudent counselor, and his lot came out for the north. 15Obed-edom's came out for the south, and to his sons was allotted the storehouse. 16For Shuppim and Hosah it came out for the west, at the gate of Shallecheth on the ascending road. Guard corresponded to guard. 17On the east there were six Levites each day,d on the north four each day, on the south four each day, as well as two and two at the storehouse; 18and for the colonnadee on the west there were four at the road and two at the colonnade.e 19These were the divisions of the gatekeepers among the Korahites and the sons of Merari.

The Treasurers, Officers, and Judges

20 And of the Levites, Ahijah had charge of the treasuries of the house of God and the treasuries of the dedicated gifts. 21The sons of Ladan, the sons of the Gershonites belonging to Ladan, the heads of families belonging to Ladan the Gershonite: Jehieli.f

22 The sons of Jehieli, Zetham and his brother Joel, were in charge of the treasuries of the house of the Lord. 23Of the Amramites, the Izharites, the Hebronites, and the Uzzielites: 24Shebuel son of Gershom, son of Moses, was chief officer in charge of the treasuries. 25His brothers: from Eliezer were his son Rehabiah, his son Jeshaiah, his son Joram, his son Zichri, and his son Shelomoth. 26This Shelomoth and his brothers were in charge of all the treasuries of the dedicated gifts that King David, and the heads of families, and the officers of the thousands and the hundreds, and the commanders of the army, had dedicated. 27From booty won in battles they dedicated gifts for the maintenance of the house of the Lord. 28Also all that Samuel the seer, and Saul son of Kish, and Abner son of Ner, and Joab son of Zeruiah had dedicated—all dedicated gifts were in the care of Shelomothg and his brothers.

29 Of the Izharites, Chenaniah and his sons were appointed to outside duties for Israel, as officers and judges. 30Of the Hebronites, Hashabiah and his brothers, one thousand seven hundred men of ability, had the oversight of Israel west of the Jordan for all the work of the Lord and for the service of the king. 31Of the Hebronites, Jerijah was chief of the Hebronites. (In the fortieth year of David's reign search was made, of whatever genealogy or family, and men of great ability among them were found at Jazer in Gilead.) 32King David appointed him and his brothers, two thousand seven hundred men of ability, heads of families, to have the oversight of the Reubenites, the Gadites, and the half-tribe of the Manassites for everything pertaining to God and for the affairs of the king.

---

c 26:28 anyone else of distinction, implied.

d Gk: Heb lacks each day   e Heb parbar: meaning uncertain   f The Hebrew text of verse 21 is confused   g Gk Compare 26.28: Heb Shelomith

King James

27 NOW THE children of Israel after their number, *to wit,* the chief fathers and captains of thousands and hundreds, and their officers that served the king in any matter of the courses, which came in and went out month by month throughout all the months of the year, of every course *were* twenty and four thousand.

2Over the first course for the first month *was* Jashobeam the son of Zabdiel: and in his course *were* twenty and four thousand.

3Of the children of Perez *was* the chief of all the captains of the host for the first month.

4And over the course of the second month *was* Dodai an Ahohite, and of his course *was* Mikloth also the ruler: in his course likewise *were* twenty and four thousand.

5The third captain of the host for the third month *was* Benaiah the son of Jehoiada, a chief priest: and in his course *were* twenty and four thousand.

6This *is that* Benaiah, *who was* mighty *among* the thirty, and above the thirty: and in his course *was* Ammizabad his son.

7The fourth *captain* for the fourth month *was* Asahel the brother of Joab, and Zebadiah his son after him: and in his course *were* twenty and four thousand.

8The fifth captain for the fifth month *was* Shamhuth the Izrahite: and in his course *were* twenty and four thousand.

9The sixth *captain* for the sixth month *was* Ira the son of Ikkesh the Tekoite: and in his course *were* twenty and four thousand.

10The seventh *captain* for the seventh month *was* Helez the Pelonite, of the children of Ephraim: and in his course *were* twenty and four thousand.

11The eighth *captain* for the eighth month *was* Sibbecai the Hushathite, of the Zarhites: and in his course *were* twenty and four thousand.

12The ninth *captain* for the ninth month *was* Abiezer the Anetothite, of the Benjamites: and in his course *were* twenty and four thousand.

13The tenth *captain* for the tenth month *was* Maharai the Netophathite, of the Zarhites: and in his course *were* twenty and four thousand.

14The eleventh *captain* for the eleventh month *was* Benaiah the Pirathonite, of the children of Ephraim: and in his course *were* twenty and four thousand.

15The twelfth *captain* for the twelfth month *was* Heldai the Netophathite, of Othniel: and in his course *were* twenty and four thousand.

16¶ Furthermore over the tribes of Israel: the ruler of the Reubenites *was* Eliezer the son of Zichri: of the Simeonites, Shephatiah the son of Maachah:

17Of the Levites, Hashabiah the son of Kemuel: of the Aaronites, Zadok:

18Of Judah, Elihu, *one* of the brethren of David: of Issachar, Omri the son of Michael:

19Of Zebulun, Ishmaiah the son of Obadiah: of Naphtali, Jerimoth the son of Azriel:

20Of the children of Ephraim, Hoshea the son of Azaziah: of the half tribe of Manasseh, Joel the son of Pedaiah:

21Of the half *tribe* of Manasseh in Gilead, Iddo the son of Zechariah: of Benjamin, Jaasiel the son of Abner:

22Of Dan, Azareel the son of Jeroham. These *were* the princes of the tribes of Israel.

23¶ But David took not the number of them from twenty years old and under: because the LORD had said he would increase Israel like to the stars of the heavens.

New International

Army Divisions

27 THIS IS the list of the Israelites—heads of families, commanders of thousands and commanders of hundreds, and their officers, who served the king in all that concerned the army divisions that were on duty month by month throughout the year. Each division consisted of 24,000 men.

2In charge of the first division, for the first month, was Jashobeam son of Zabdiel. There were 24,000 men in his division. 3He was a descendant of Perez and chief of all the army officers for the first month.

4In charge of the division for the second month was Dodai the Ahohite; Mikloth was the leader of his division. There were 24,000 men in his division. 5The third army commander, for the third month, was Benaiah son of Jehoiada the priest. He was chief and there were 24,000 men in his division. 6This was the Benaiah who was a mighty man among the Thirty and was over the Thirty. His son Ammizabad was in charge of his division.

7The fourth, for the fourth month, was Asahel the brother of Joab; his son Zebadiah was his successor. There were 24,000 men in his division.

8The fifth, for the fifth month, was the commander Shamhuth the Izrahite. There were 24,000 men in his division.

9The sixth, for the sixth month, was Ira the son of Ikkesh the Tekoite. There were 24,000 men in his division.

10The seventh, for the seventh month, was Helez the Pelonite, an Ephraimite. There were 24,000 men in his division.

11The eighth, for the eighth month, was Sibbecai the Hushathite, a Zerahite. There were 24,000 men in his division.

12The ninth, for the ninth month, was Abiezer the Anathothite, a Benjamite. There were 24,000 men in his division.

13The tenth, for the tenth month, was Maharai the Netophathite, a Zerahite. There were 24,000 men in his division.

14The eleventh, for the eleventh month, was Benaiah the Pirathonite, an Ephraimite. There were 24,000 men in his division.

15The twelfth, for the twelfth month, was Heldai the Netophathite, from the family of Othniel. There were 24,000 men in his division.

Officers of the Tribes

16The officers over the tribes of Israel:

over the Reubenites: Eliezer son of Zicri;
over the Simeonites: Shephatiah son of Maacah;
17over Levi: Hashabiah son of Kemuel;
over Aaron: Zadok;
18over Judah: Elihu, a brother of David;
over Issachar: Omri son of Michael;
19over Zebulun: Ishmaiah son of Obadiah;
over Naphtali: Jerimoth son of Azriel;
20over the Ephraimites: Hoshea son of Azaziah;
over half the tribe of Manasseh: Joel son of Pedaiah;
21over the half-tribe of Manasseh in Gilead: Iddo son of Zechariah;
over Benjamin: Jaasiel son of Abner;
22over Dan: Azarel son of Jeroham.
These were the officers over the tribes of Israel.

23David did not take the number of the men twenty years old or less, because the LORD had promised to make Israel as numerous as the stars in the sky. 24Joab

Living Bible

27 THE ISRAELI army was divided into twelve regiments, each with 24,000 troops, including officers and administrative staff. These units were called up for active duty one month each year. Here is the list of the units and their regimental commanders:

2, 3The commander of the First Division was Jashobeam. He had charge of 24,000 troops who were on duty the first month of each year.

4The commander of the Second Division was Dodai (a descendant of Ahohi). He had charge of 24,000 troops who were on duty the second month of each year. Mikloth was his executive officer.

5, 6The commander of the Third Division was Benaiah. His 24,000 men were on duty the third month of each year. (He was the son of Jehoiada the High Priest, and was the chief of the thirty highest-ranking officers in David's army.) His son Ammizabad succeeded him as division commander.

7The commander of the Fourth Division was Asahel (the brother of Joab), who was later replaced by his son Zebadiah. He had 24,000 men on duty the fourth month of each year.

8The commander of the Fifth Division was Shamuth from Izrah, with 24,000 men on duty the fifth month of each year.

9The commander of the Sixth Division was Ira, the son of Ikkesh from Tekoa; he had 24,000 men on duty the sixth month of each year.

10The commander of the Seventh Division was Helez from Pelona in Ephraim, with 24,000 men on duty the seventh month of each year.

11The commander of the Eighth Division was Sibbecai of the Hushite subclan from Zerah, who had 24,000 men on duty the eighth month of each year.

12The commander of the Ninth Division was Abi-ezer (from Anathoth in the tribe of Benjamin), who commanded 24,000 troops during the ninth month of each year.

13The commander of the Tenth Division was Maharai from Netophah in Zerah, with 24,000 men on duty the tenth month of each year.

14The commander of the Eleventh Division was Benaiah from Pirathon in Ephraim, with 24,000 men on duty during the eleventh month of each year.

15The commander of the Twelfth Division was Heldai from Netophah in the area of Othni-el, who commanded 24,000 men on duty during the twelfth month of each year.

16-22The top political officers of the tribes of Israel were as follows:

Over Reuben, Eliezer (son of Zichri);
Over Simeon, Shephatiah (son of Maacah);
Over Levi, Hashabiah (son of Kemuel);
Over the descendants of Aaron, Zadok;
Over Judah, Elihu (a brother of King David);
Over Issachar, Omri (son of Michael);
Over Zebulun, Ishmaiah (son of Obadiah);
Over Naphtali, Jeremoth (son of Azriel);
Over Ephraim, Hoshea (son of Azaziah);
Over the half-tribe of Manasseh, Joel (son of Pedaiah);
Over the other half of Manasseh, in Gilead, Iddo (son of Zechariah);
Over Benjamin, Ja-asiel (son of Abner);
Over Dan, Azarel (son of Jeroham).

23When David took his census he didn't include the twenty-year-olds, or those younger, for the Lord had promised a population explosion for his people.a 24Joab

New Revised Standard

The Military Divisions

27 THIS IS the list of the people of Israel, the heads of families, the commanders of the thousands and the hundreds, and their officers who served the king in all matters concerning the divisions that came and went, month after month throughout the year, each division numbering twenty-four thousand:

2 Jashobeam son of Zabdiel was in charge of the first division in the first month; in his division were twenty-four thousand. 3He was a descendant of Perez, and was chief of all the commanders of the army for the first month. 4Dodai the Ahohite was in charge of the division of the second month; Mikloth was the chief officer of his division. In his division were twenty-four thousand. 5The third commander, for the third month, was Benaiah son of the priest Jehoiada, as chief; in his division were twenty-four thousand. 6This is the Benaiah who was a mighty man of the Thirty and in command of the Thirty; his son Ammizabad was in charge of his division.b 7Asahel brother of Joab was fourth, for the fourth month, and his son Zebadiah after him; in his division were twenty-four thousand. 8The fifth commander, for the fifth month, was Shamhuth, the Izrahite; in his division were twenty-four thousand. 9Sixth, for the sixth month, was Ira son of Ikkesh the Tekoite; in his division were twenty-four thousand. 10Seventh, for the seventh month, was Helez the Pelonite, of the Ephraimites; in his division were twenty-four thousand. 11Eighth, for the eighth month, was Sibbecai the Hushathite, of the Zerahites; in his division were twenty-four thousand. 12Ninth, for the ninth month, was Abiezer of Anathoth, a Benjaminite; in his division were twenty-four thousand. 13Tenth, for the tenth month, was Maharai of Netophah, of the Zerahites; in his division were twenty-four thousand. 14Eleventh, for the eleventh month, was Benaiah of Pirathon, of the Ephraimites; in his division were twenty-four thousand. 15Twelfth, for the twelfth month, was Heldai the Netophathite, of Othniel; in his division were twenty-four thousand.

Leaders of Tribes

16 Over the tribes of Israel, for the Reubenites, Eliezer son of Zichri was chief officer; for the Simeonites, Shephatiah son of Maacah; 17for Levi, Hashabiah son of Kemuel; for Aaron, Zadok; 18for Judah, Elihu, one of David's brothers; for Issachar, Omri son of Michael; 19for Zebulun, Ishmaiah son of Obadiah; for Naphtali, Jerimoth son of Azriel; 20for the Ephraimites, Hoshea son of Azaziah; for the half-tribe of Manasseh, Joel son of Pedaiah; 21for the half-tribe of Manasseh in Gilead, Iddo son of Zechariah; for Benjamin, Jaasiel son of Abner; 22for Dan, Azarel son of Jeroham. These were the leaders of the tribes of Israel. 23David did not count those below twenty years of age, for the LORD had promised to make Israel as numerous as the stars of heaven.

---

a 27:23 *The Lord had promised a population explosion for his people*, literally, "the Lord had said he would increase Israel like to the stars of heaven."

b Gk Vg: Heb *Ammizabad was his division*

King James

24Joab the son of Zeruiah began to number, but he finished not, because there fell wrath for it against Israel; neither was the number put in the account of the chronicles of king David.

25¶ And over the king's treasures *was* Azmaveth the son of Adiel: and over the storehouses in the fields, in the cities, and in the villages, and in the castles, *was* Jehonathan the son of Uzziah:

26And over them that did the work of the field for tillage of the ground *was* Ezri the son of Chelub:

27And over the vineyards *was* Shimei the Ramathite: over the increase of the vineyards for the wine cellars *was* Zabdi the Shiphmite:

28And over the olive trees and the sycamore trees that *were* in the low plains *was* Baal-hanan the Gederite: and over the cellars of oil *was* Joash:

29And over the herds that fed in Sharon *was* Shitrai the Sharonite: and over the herds *that were* in the valleys *was* Shaphat the son of Adlai:

30Over the camels also *was* Obil the Ishmaelite: and over the asses *was* Jehdeiah the Meronothite:

31And over the flocks *was* Jaziz the Hagerite. All these *were* the rulers of the substance which *was* king David's.

32Also Jonathan David's uncle was a counsellor, a wise man, and a scribe: and Jehiel the son of Hachmoni *was* with the king's sons:

33And Ahithophel *was* the king's counsellor: and Hushai the Archite *was* the king's companion:

34And after Ahithophel *was* Jehoiada the son of Benaiah, and Abiathar: and the general of the king's army *was* Joab.

28 AND DAVID assembled all the princes of Israel, the princes of the tribes, and the captains of the companies that ministered to the king by course, and the captains over the thousands, and captains over the hundreds, and the stewards over all the substance and possession of the king, and of his sons, with the officers, and with the mighty men, and with all the valiant men, unto Jerusalem.

2Then David the king stood up upon his feet, and said, Hear me, my brethren, and my people: *As for me, I had* in mine heart to build an house of rest for the ark of the covenant of the LORD, and for the footstool of our God, and had made ready for the building:

3But God said unto me, Thou shalt not build an house for my name, because thou *hast been* a man of war, and hast shed blood.

4Howbeit the LORD God of Israel chose me before all the house of my father to be king over Israel for ever: for he hath chosen Judah *to be* the ruler; and of the house of Judah, the house of my father; and among the sons of my father he liked me to make *me* king over all Israel:

5And of all my sons, (for the LORD hath given me many sons,) he hath chosen Solomon my son to sit upon the throne of the kingdom of the LORD over Israel.

6And he said unto me, Solomon thy son, he shall build my house and my courts: for I have chosen him *to be* my son, and I will be his father.

7Moreover I will establish his kingdom for ever, if he be constant to do my commandments and my judgments, as at this day.

New International

son of Zeruiah began to count the men but did not finish. Wrath came on Israel on account of this numbering, and the number was not entered in the book[a] of the annals of King David.

The King's Overseers

25Azmaveth son of Adiel was in charge of the royal storehouses.

Jonathan son of Uzziah was in charge of the storehouses in the outlying districts, in the towns, the villages and the watchtowers.

26Ezri son of Kelub was in charge of the field workers who farmed the land.

27Shimei the Ramathite was in charge of the vineyards.

Zabdi the Shiphmite was in charge of the produce of the vineyards for the wine vats.

28Baal-Hanan the Gederite was in charge of the olive and sycamore-fig trees in the western foothills.

Joash was in charge of the supplies of olive oil.

29Shitrai the Sharonite was in charge of the herds grazing in Sharon.

Shaphat son of Adlai was in charge of the herds in the valleys.

30Obil the Ishmaelite was in charge of the camels. Jehdeiah the Meronothite was in charge of the donkeys.

31Jaziz the Hagrite was in charge of the flocks.

All these were the officials in charge of King David's property.

32Jonathan, David's uncle, was a counselor, a man of insight and a scribe. Jehiel son of Hacmoni took care of the king's sons.

33Ahithophel was the king's counselor.

Hushai the Arkite was the king's friend. 34Ahithophel was succeeded by Jehoiada son of Benaiah and by Abiathar.

Joab was the commander of the royal army.

David's Plans for the Temple

28 DAVID SUMMONED all the officials of Israel to assemble at Jerusalem: the officers over the tribes, the commanders of the divisions in the service of the king, the commanders of thousands and commanders of hundreds, and the officials in charge of all the property and livestock belonging to the king and his sons, together with the palace officials, the mighty men and all the brave warriors.

2King David rose to his feet and said: "Listen to me, my brothers and my people. I had it in my heart to build a house as a place of rest for the ark of the covenant of the LORD, for the footstool of our God, and I made plans to build it. 3But God said to me, 'You are not to build a house for my Name, because you are a warrior and have shed blood.'

4"Yet the LORD, the God of Israel, chose me from my whole family to be king over Israel forever. He chose Judah as leader, and from the house of Judah he chose my family, and from my father's sons he was pleased to make me king over all Israel. 5Of all my sons—and the LORD has given me many—he has chosen my son Solomon to sit on the throne of the kingdom of the LORD over Israel. 6He said to me: 'Solomon your son is the one who will build my house and my courts, for I have chosen him to be my son, and I will be his father. 7I will establish his kingdom forever if he is unswerving in carrying out my commands and laws, as is being done at this time.'

Living Bible

began the census, but he never finished it, for the anger of God broke out upon Israel; the final total was never put into the annals of King David.

25Azmaveth (son of Adi-el) was the chief financial officer in charge of the palace treasuries, and Jonathan (son of Uzziah) was chief of the regional treasuries throughout the cities, villages, and fortresses of Israel.

26Ezri (son of Chelub) was manager of the laborers on the king's estates. 27And Shime-i from Ramath had the oversight of the king's vineyards; and Zabdi from Shiphma was responsible for his wine production and storage. 28Baal-hanan from Gedera was responsible for the king's olive yards and sycamore trees in the lowlands bordering Philistine territory, while Joash had charge of the supplies of olive oil.

29Shitrai from Sharon was in charge of the cattle on the Plains of Sharon, and Shaphat (son of Adlai) had charge of those in the valleys. 30Obil, from the territory of Ishmael, had charge of the camels, and Jehdeiah from Meronoth had charge of the donkeys. 31The sheep were under the care of Jaziz the Hagrite. These men were King David's overseers.

32The attendant to the king's sons was Jonathan, David's uncle, a wise counselor and an educated man.b Jehiel (the son of Hachmoni) was their tutor.

33Ahithophel was the king's official counselor and Hushai the Archite was his personal advisor. 34Ahithophel was assisted by Jehoiada (the son of Benaiah) and by Abiathar. Joab was commander-in-chief of the Israeli army.

28 DAVID NOW summoned all of his officials to Jerusalem—the political leaders, the commanders of the twelve army divisions, the other army officers, those in charge of his property and livestock and all the other men of authority in his kingdom. 2He rose and stood before them and addressed them as follows:

"My brothers and my people! It was my desire to build a temple in which the Ark of the Covenant of the Lord could rest—a place for our God to live in.c I have now collected everything that is necessary for the building, 3but God has told me, 'You are not to build my temple, for you are a warrior and have shed much blood.'

4"Nevertheless, the Lord God of Israel has chosen me from among all my father's family to begin a dynasty that will rule Israel forever; he has chosen the tribe of Judah, and from among the families of Judah, my father's family; and from among his sons, the Lord took pleasure in me and has made me king over all Israel. 5And from among my sons—the Lord has given me many children—he has chosen Solomon to succeed me on the throne of his Kingdom of Israel. 6He has told me, 'Your son Solomon shall build my temple; for I have chosen him as my son and I will be his father. 7And if he continues to obey my commandments and instructions as he has until now, I will make his kingdom last forever.' "

New Revised Standard

24Joab son of Zeruiah began to count them, but did not finish; yet wrath came upon Israel for this, and the number was not entered into the account of the Annals of King David.

Other Civic Officials

25 Over the king's treasuries was Azmaveth son of Adiel. Over the treasuries in the country, in the cities, in the villages and in the towers, was Jonathan son of Uzziah. 26Over those who did the work of the field, tilling the soil, was Ezri son of Chelub. 27Over the vineyards was Shimei the Ramathite. Over the produce of the vineyards for the wine cellars was Zabdi the Shiphmite. 28Over the olive and sycamore trees in the Shephelah was Baal-hanan the Gederite. Over the stores of oil was Joash. 29Over the herds that pastured in Sharon was Shitrai the Sharonite. Over the herds in the valleys was Shaphat son of Adlai. 30Over the camels was Obil the Ishmaelite. Over the donkeys was Jehdeiah the Meronothite. Over the flocks was Jaziz the Hagrite. 31All these were stewards of King David's property.

32 Jonathan, David's uncle, was a counselor, being a man of understanding and a scribe; Jehiel son of Hachmoni attended the king's sons. 33Ahithophel was the king's counselor, and Hushai the Archite was the king's friend. 34After Ahithophel came Jehoiada son of Benaiah, and Abiathar. Joab was commander of the king's army.

Solomon Instructed to Build the Temple

28 DAVID ASSEMBLED at Jerusalem all the officials of Israel, the officials of the tribes, the officers of the divisions that served the king, the commanders of the thousands, the commanders of the hundreds, the stewards of all the property and cattle of the king and his sons, together with the palace officials, the mighty warriors, and all the warriors. 2Then King David rose to his feet and said: "Hear me, my brothers and my people. I had planned to build a house of rest for the ark of the covenant of the LORD, for the footstool of our God; and I made preparations for building. 3But God said to me, 'You shall not build a house for my name, for you are a warrior and have shed blood.' 4Yet the LORD God of Israel chose me from all my ancestral house to be king over Israel forever; for he chose Judah as leader, and in the house of Judah my father's house, and among my father's sons he took delight in making me king over all Israel. 5And of all my sons, for the LORD has given me many, he has chosen my son Solomon to sit upon the throne of the kingdom of the LORD over Israel. 6He said to me, 'It is your son Solomon who shall build my house and my courts, for I have chosen him to be a son to me, and I will be a father to him. 7I will establish his kingdom forever if he continues resolute in keeping my commandments and my ordinances, as he is today.' 8Now therefore in the sight of all Israel,

---

b 27:32 an educated man, literally, "a scribe."   c 28:2 a place for our God to live in, literally, "a footstool."

King James

8Now therefore in the sight of all Israel the congregation of the LORD, and in the audience of our God, keep and seek for all the commandments of the LORD your God: that ye may possess this good land, and leave it for an inheritance for your children after you for ever.

9¶ And thou, Solomon my son, know thou the God of thy father, and serve him with a perfect heart and with a willing mind: for the LORD searcheth all hearts, and understandeth all the imaginations of the thoughts: if thou seek him, he will be found of thee; but if thou forsake him, he will cast thee off for ever.

10Take heed now; for the LORD hath chosen thee to build an house for the sanctuary: be strong, and do it.

11¶ Then David gave to Solomon his son the pattern of the porch, and of the houses thereof, and of the treasuries thereof, and of the upper chambers thereof, and of the inner parlours thereof, and of the place of the mercy seat,

12And the pattern of all that he had by the spirit, of the courts of the house of the LORD, and of all the chambers round about, of the treasuries of the house of God, and of the treasuries of the dedicated things:

13Also for the courses of the priests and the Levites, and for all the work of the service of the house of the LORD, and for all the vessels of service in the house of the LORD.

14He gave of gold by weight for things of gold, for all instruments of all manner of service; silver also for all instruments of silver by weight, for all instruments of every kind of service:

15Even the weight for the candlesticks of gold, and for their lamps of gold, by weight for every candlestick, and for the lamps thereof: and for the candlesticks of silver by weight, both for the candlestick, and also for the lamps thereof, according to the use of every candlestick.

16And by weight he gave gold for the tables of shewbread, for every table; and likewise silver for the tables of silver:

17Also pure gold for the fleshhooks, and the bowls, and the cups: and for the golden basins he gave gold by weight for every basin; and likewise silver by weight for every basin of silver:

18And for the altar of incense refined gold by weight; and gold for the pattern of the chariot of the cherubims, that spread out their wings, and covered the ark of the covenant of the LORD.

19All this, said David, the LORD made me understand in writing by his hand upon me, even all the works of this pattern.

20And David said to Solomon his son, Be strong and of good courage, and do it: fear not, nor be dismayed: for the LORD God, even my God, will be with thee; he will not fail thee, nor forsake thee, until thou hast finished all the work for the service of the house of the LORD.

21And, behold, the courses of the priests and the Levites, even they shall be with thee for all the service of the house of God: and there shall be with thee for all manner of workmanship every willing skilful man, for any manner of service: also the princes and all the people will be wholly at thy commandment.

29 FURTHERMORE DAVID the king said unto all the congregation, Solomon my son, whom alone God hath chosen, is yet young and tender, and the work is great: for the palace is not for man, but for the LORD God.

New International

8"So now I charge you in the sight of all Israel and of the assembly of the LORD, and in the hearing of our God: Be careful to follow all the commands of the LORD your God, that you may possess this good land and pass it on as an inheritance to your descendants forever.

9"And you, my son Solomon, acknowledge the God of your father, and serve him with wholehearted devotion and with a willing mind, for the LORD searches every heart and understands every motive behind the thoughts. If you seek him, he will be found by you; but if you forsake him, he will reject you forever. 10Consider now, for the LORD has chosen you to build a temple as a sanctuary. Be strong and do the work."

11Then David gave his son Solomon the plans for the portico of the temple, its buildings, its storerooms, its upper parts, its inner rooms and the place of atonement. 12He gave him the plans of all that the Spirit had put in his mind for the courts of the temple of the LORD and all the surrounding rooms, for the treasuries of the temple of God and for the treasuries for the dedicated things. 13He gave him instructions for the divisions of the priests and Levites, and for all the work of serving in the temple of the LORD, as well as for all the articles to be used in its service. 14He designated the weight of gold for all the gold articles to be used in various kinds of service, and the weight of silver for all the silver articles to be used in various kinds of service: 15the weight of gold for the gold lampstands and their lamps, with the weight for each lampstand and its lamps; and the weight of silver for each silver lampstand and its lamps, according to the use of each lampstand; 16the weight of gold for each table for consecrated bread; the weight of silver for the silver tables; 17the weight of pure gold for the forks, sprinkling bowls and pitchers; the weight of gold for each gold dish; the weight of silver for each silver dish; 18and the weight of the refined gold for the altar of incense. He also gave him the plan for the chariot, that is, the cherubim of gold that spread their wings and shelter the ark of the covenant of the LORD.

19"All this," David said, "I have in writing from the hand of the LORD upon me, and he gave me understanding in all the details of the plan."

20David also said to Solomon his son, "Be strong and courageous, and do the work. Do not be afraid or discouraged, for the LORD God, my God, is with you. He will not fail you or forsake you until all the work for the service of the temple of the LORD is finished. 21The divisions of the priests and Levites are ready for all the work on the temple of God, and every willing man skilled in any craft will help you in all the work. The officials and all the people will obey your every command."

Gifts for Building the Temple

29 THEN KING David said to the whole assembly: "My son Solomon, the one whom God has chosen, is young and inexperienced. The task is great, because this palatial structure is not for man but for the LORD God. 2With all my resources I have provided for

Living Bible

8Then David turned to Solomon and said:a

"Here before the leaders of Israel, the people of God, and in the sight of our God, I am instructing you to search out every commandment of the Lord so that you may continue to rule this good land and leave it to your children to rule forever. 9Solomon, my son, get to know the God of your fathers. Worship and serve him with a clean heart and a willing mind, for the Lord sees every heart and understands and knows every thought. If you seek him, you will find him; but if you forsake him, he will permanently throw you aside. 10So be very careful, for the Lord has chosen you to build his holy temple. Be strong and do as he commands."

11Then David gave Solomon the blueprint of the Temple and its surroundings—the treasuries, the upstairs rooms, the inside rooms, and the sanctuary for the place of mercy. 12He also gave Solomon his plans for the outer court, the outside rooms, the Temple storage areas, and the treasuries for the gifts dedicated by famous persons. For the Holy Spirit had given David all these plans. 13The king also passed on to Solomon the instructions concerning the work of the various groups of priests and Levites; and he gave specifications for each item in the Temple which was to be used for worship and sacrifice.

14David weighed out enough gold and silver to make these various items, 15as well as the specific amount of gold needed for the lampstands and lamps. He also weighed out enough silver for the silver candlesticks and lamps, each according to its use. 16He weighed out the gold for the table on which the Bread of the Presence would be placed and for the other gold tables, and he weighed the silver for the silver tables. 17Then he weighed out the gold for the solid gold hooks used in handling the sacrificial meat and for the basins, cups, and bowls of gold and silver. 18Finally, he weighed out the refined gold for the altar of incense and for the gold angels whose wings were stretched over the Ark of the Covenant of the Lord.

19"Every part of this blueprint," David told Solomon, "was given to me in writing from the hand of the Lord." 20Then he continued, "Be strong and courageous and get to work. Don't be frightened by the size of the task, for the Lord my God is with you; he will not forsake you. He will see to it that everything is finished correctly. 21And these various groups of priests and Levites will serve in the Temple. Others with skills of every kind will volunteer, and the army and the entire nation are at your command."

New Revised Standard

the assembly of the LORD, and in the hearing of our God, observe and search out all the commandments of the LORD your God; that you may possess this good land, and leave it for an inheritance to your children after you forever.

9 "And you, my son Solomon, know the God of your father, and serve him with single mind and willing heart; for the LORD searches every mind, and understands every plan and thought. If you seek him, he will be found by you; but if you forsake him, he will abandon you forever. 10Take heed now, for the LORD has chosen you to build a house as the sanctuary; be strong, and act."

11 Then David gave his son Solomon the plan of the vestibule of the temple, and of its houses, its treasuries, its upper rooms, and its inner chambers, and of the room for the mercy seat;b 12and the plan of all that he had in mind: for the courts of the house of the LORD, all the surrounding chambers, the treasuries of the house of God, and the treasuries for dedicated gifts; 13for the divisions of the priests and of the Levites, and all the work of the service in the house of the LORD; for all the vessels for the service in the house of the LORD, 14the weight of gold for all golden vessels for each service, the weight of silver vessels for each service, 15the weight of the golden lampstands and their lamps, the weight of gold for each lampstand and its lamps, the weight of silver for a lampstand and its lamps, according to the use of each in the service, 16the weight of gold for each table for the rows of bread, the silver for the silver tables, 17and pure gold for the forks, the basins, and the cups; for the golden bowls and the weight of each; for the silver bowls and the weight of each; 18for the altar of incense made of refined gold, and its weight; also his plan for the golden chariot of the cherubim that spread their wings and covered the ark of the covenant of the LORD.

19 "All this, in writing at the LORD's direction, he made clear to me—the plan of all the works."

20 David said further to his son Solomon, "Be strong and of good courage, and act. Do not be afraid or dismayed; for the LORD God, my God, is with you. He will not fail you or forsake you, until all the work for the service of the house of the LORD is finished. 21Here are the divisions of the priests and the Levites for all the service of the house of God; and with you in all the work will be every volunteer who has skill for any kind of service; also the officers and all the people will be wholly at your command."

Offerings for Building the Temple

29 KING DAVID said to the whole assembly, "My son Solomon, whom alone God has chosen, is young and inexperienced, and the work is great; for the templec will not be for mortals but for the LORD God. 2So I have provided for the house of my God, so

29 THEN KING David turned to the entire assembly and said: "My son Solomon, whom God has chosen to be the next king of Israel, is still young and inexperienced, and the work ahead of him is enormous; for the temple he will build is not just another building—it is for the Lord God himself! 2Using every resource at

---

a 28:8 *Then David turned to Solomon and said,* implied.

b Or *the cover*   c Heb *fortress*

King James

2Now I have prepared with all my might for the house of my God the gold for *things to be made* of gold, and the silver for *things* of silver, and the brass for *things* of brass, the iron for *things* of iron, and wood for *things* of wood; onyx stones, and *stones* to be set, glistering stones, and of divers colours, and all manner of precious stones, and marble stones in abundance.

3Moreover, because I have set my affection to the house of my God, I have of mine own proper good, of gold and silver, *which* I have given to the house of my God, over and above all that I have prepared for the holy house,

4*Even* three thousand talents of gold, of the gold of Ophir, and seven thousand talents of refined silver, to overlay the walls of the houses *withal:*

5The gold for *things* of gold, and the silver for *things* of silver, and for all manner of work *to be made* by the hands of artificers. And who *then* is willing to consecrate his service this day unto the LORD?

6¶ Then the chief of the fathers and princes of the tribes of Israel, and the captains of thousands and of hundreds, with the rulers of the king's work, offered willingly,

7And gave for the service of the house of God of gold five thousand talents and ten thousand drams, and of silver ten thousand talents, and of brass eighteen thousand talents, and one hundred thousand talents of iron.

8And they with whom *precious* stones were found gave *them* to the treasure of the house of the LORD, by the hand of Jehiel the Gershonite.

9Then the people rejoiced, for that they offered willingly, because with perfect heart they offered willingly to the LORD: and David the king also rejoiced with great joy.

10¶ Wherefore David blessed the LORD before all the congregation: and David said, Blessed *be* thou, LORD God of Israel our father, for ever and ever.

11Thine, O LORD, *is* the greatness, and the power, and the glory, and the victory, and the majesty: for all *that is* in the heaven and in the earth *is thine;* thine *is* the kingdom, O LORD, and thou art exalted as head above all.

12Both riches and honour *come* of thee, and thou reignest over all; and in thine hand *is* power and might; and in thine hand it is to make great, and to give strength unto all.

13Now therefore, our God, we thank thee, and praise thy glorious name.

14But who *am* I, and what *is* my people, that we should be able to offer so willingly after this sort? for all things *come* of thee, and of thine own have we given thee.

15For we *are* strangers before thee, and sojourners, as *were* all our fathers: our days on the earth *are* as a shadow, and *there is* none abiding.

16O LORD our God, all this store that we have prepared to build thee an house for thine holy name *cometh* of thine hand, and *is* all thine own.

17I know also, my God, that thou triest the heart, and hast pleasure in uprightness. As for me, in the uprightness of mine heart I have willingly offered all these things: and now have I seen with joy thy people, which are present here, to offer willingly unto thee.

18O LORD God of Abraham, Isaac, and of Israel, our fathers, keep this for ever in the imagination of the thoughts of the heart of thy people, and prepare their heart unto thee:

19And give unto Solomon my son a perfect heart, to keep thy commandments, thy testimonies, and thy statutes, and to do all *these things,* and to build the palace, *for* the which I have made provision.

New International

the temple of my God—gold for the gold work, silver for the silver, bronze for the bronze, iron for the iron and wood for the wood, as well as onyx for the settings, turquoise,[a] stones of various colors, and all kinds of fine stone and marble—all of these in large quantities. 3Besides, in my devotion to the temple of my God I now give my personal treasures of gold and silver for the temple of my God, over and above everything I have provided for this holy temple: 4three thousand talents[b] of gold (gold of Ophir) and seven thousand talents[c] of refined silver, for the overlaying of the walls of the buildings, 5for the gold work and the silver work, and for all the work to be done by the craftsmen. Now, who is willing to consecrate himself today to the LORD?"

6Then the leaders of families, the officers of the tribes of Israel, the commanders of thousands and commanders of hundreds, and the officials in charge of the king's work gave willingly. 7They gave toward the work on the temple of God five thousand talents[d] and ten thousand darics[e] of gold, ten thousand talents[f] of silver, eighteen thousand talents[g] of bronze and a hundred thousand talents[h] of iron. 8Any who had precious stones gave them to the treasury of the temple of the LORD in the custody of Jehiel the Gershonite. 9The people rejoiced at the willing response of their leaders, for they had given freely and wholeheartedly to the LORD. David the king also rejoiced greatly.

David's Prayer

10David praised the LORD in the presence of the whole assembly, saying,

"Praise be to you, O LORD,
    God of our father Israel,
    from everlasting to everlasting.
11Yours, O LORD, is the greatness and the power
    and the glory and the majesty and the
    splendor,
    for everything in heaven and earth is yours.
Yours, O LORD, is the kingdom;
    you are exalted as head over all.
12Wealth and honor come from you;
    you are the ruler of all things.
In your hands are strength and power
    to exalt and give strength to all.
13Now, our God, we give you thanks,
    and praise your glorious name.

14"But who am I, and who are my people, that we should be able to give as generously as this? Everything comes from you, and we have given you only what comes from your hand. 15We are aliens and strangers in your sight, as were all our forefathers. Our days on earth are like a shadow, without hope. 16O LORD our God, as for all this abundance that we have provided for building you a temple for your Holy Name, it comes from your hand, and all of it belongs to you. 17I know, my God, that you test the heart and are pleased with integrity. All these things have I given willingly and with honest intent. And now I have seen with joy how willingly your people who are here have given to you. 18O LORD, God of our fathers Abraham, Isaac and Israel, keep this desire in the hearts of your people forever, and keep their hearts loyal to you. 19And give my son Solomon the wholehearted devotion to keep your commands, requirements and decrees and to do everything to build the palatial structure for which I have provided."

---

a 2 The meaning of the Hebrew for this word is uncertain.   b 4 That is, about 110 tons (about 100 metric tons)   c 4 That is, about 260 tons (about 240 metric tons)   d 7 That is, about 190 tons (about 170 metric tons)   e 7 That is, about 185 pounds (about 84 kilograms)   f 7 That is, about 375 tons (about 345 metric tons)   g 7 That is, about 675 tons (about 610 metric tons)   h 7 That is, about 3,750 tons (about 3,450 metric tons)

Living Bible

my command, I have gathered as much as I could for building it—enough gold, silver, bronze, iron, wood, and great quantities of onyx, other precious stones, costly jewels, and marble. 3And now, because of my devotion to the Temple of God, I am giving all of my own private treasures to aid in the construction. This is in addition to the building materials I have already collected. 4, 5These personal contributions consist of millions of dollars of gold from Ophir and huge amounts of silver to be used for overlaying the walls of the buildings. It will also be used for the articles made of gold and silver and for the artistic decorations. Now then, who will follow my example? Who will give himself and all that he has to the Lord?"

6, 7Then the clan leaders, the heads of the tribes, the army officers, and the administrative officers of the king pledged huge sums of gold, silver and foreign currency, also 675 tons of bronze; and 3,750 tons of iron. 8They also contributed great amounts of jewelry, which were deposited at the Temple treasury with Jehiel (a descendant of Gershom). 9Everyone was excited and happy for this opportunity of service, and King David was moved with deep joy.

10While still in the presence of the whole assembly, David expressed his praises to the Lord: "O Lord God of our father Israel, praise your name for ever and ever! 11Yours is the mighty power and glory and victory and majesty. Everything in the heavens and earth is yours, O Lord, and this is your kingdom. We adore you as being in control of everything. 12Riches and honor come from you alone, and you are the Ruler of all mankind; your hand controls power and might, and it is at your discretion that men are made great and given strength. 13O our God, we thank you and praise your glorious name, 14but who am I and who are my people that we should be permitted to give anything to you? Everything we have has come from you, and we only give you what is yours already! 15For we are here for but a moment, strangers in the land as our fathers were before us; our days on earth are like a shadow, gone so soon, without a trace. 16O Lord our God, all of this material that we have gathered to build a temple for your holy name comes from you! It all belongs to you! 17I know, my God, that you test men to see if they are good; for you enjoy good men. I have done all this with good motives, and I have watched your people offer their gifts willingly and joyously.

18"O Lord God of our fathers: Abraham, Isaac, and Israel! Make your people always want to obey you, and see to it that their love for you never changes. 19Give my son Solomon a good heart toward God, so that he will want to obey you in the smallest detail, and will look forward eagerly to finishing the building of your temple, for which I have made all of these preparations."

New Revised Standard

far as I was able, the gold for the things of gold, the silver for the things of silver, and the bronze for the things of bronze, the iron for the things of iron, and wood for the things of wood, besides great quantities of onyx and stones for setting, antimony, colored stones, all sorts of precious stones, and marble in abundance. 3Moreover, in addition to all that I have provided for the holy house, I have a treasure of my own of gold and silver, and because of my devotion to the house of my God I give it to the house of my God: 4three thousand talents of gold, of the gold of Ophir, and seven thousand talents of refined silver, for overlaying the walls of the house, 5and for all the work to be done by artisans, gold for the things of gold and silver for the things of silver. Who then will offer willingly, consecrating themselves today to the Lord?"

6 Then the leaders of ancestral houses made their freewill offerings, as did also the leaders of the tribes, the commanders of the thousands and of the hundreds, and the officers over the king's work. 7They gave for the service of the house of God five thousand talents and ten thousand darics of gold, ten thousand talents of silver, eighteen thousand talents of bronze, and one hundred thousand talents of iron. 8Whoever had precious stones gave them to the treasury of the house of the Lord, into the care of Jehiel the Gershonite. 9Then the people rejoiced because these had given willingly, for with single mind they had offered freely to the Lord; King David also rejoiced greatly.

David's Praise to God

10 Then David blessed the Lord in the presence of all the assembly; David said: "Blessed are you, O Lord, the God of our ancestor Israel, forever and ever. 11Yours, O Lord, are the greatness, the power, the glory, the victory, and the majesty; for all that is in the heavens and on the earth is yours; yours is the kingdom, O Lord, and you are exalted as head above all. 12Riches and honor come from you, and you rule over all. In your hand are power and might; and it is in your hand to make great and to give strength to all. 13And now, our God, we give thanks to you and praise your glorious name.

14 "But who am I, and what is my people, that we should be able to make this freewill offering? For all things come from you, and of your own have we given you. 15For we are aliens and transients before you, as were all our ancestors; our days on the earth are like a shadow, and there is no hope. 16O Lord our God, all this abundance that we have provided for building you a house for your holy name comes from your hand and is all your own. 17I know, my God, that you search the heart, and take pleasure in uprightness; in the uprightness of my heart I have freely offered all these things, and now I have seen your people, who are present here, offering freely and joyously to you. 18O Lord, the God of Abraham, Isaac, and Israel, our ancestors, keep forever such purposes and thoughts in the hearts of your people, and direct their hearts toward you. 19Grant to my son Solomon that with single mind he may keep your commandments, your decrees, and your statutes, performing all of them, and that he may build the templei for which I have made provision."

---

i Heb *fortress*

King James

20¶ And David said to all the congregation, Now bless the LORD your God. And all the congregation blessed the LORD God of their fathers, and bowed down their heads, and worshipped the LORD, and the king.

21And they sacrificed sacrifices unto the LORD, and offered burnt offerings unto the LORD, on the morrow after that day, *even* a thousand bullocks, a thousand rams, *and* a thousand lambs, with their drink offerings, and sacrifices in abundance for all Israel:

22And did eat and drink before the LORD on that day with great gladness. And they made Solomon the son of David king the second time, and anointed *him* unto the LORD *to be* the chief governor, and Zadok *to be* priest.

23Then Solomon sat on the throne of the LORD as king instead of David his father, and prospered; and all Israel obeyed him.

24And all the princes, and the mighty men, and all the sons likewise of king David, submitted themselves unto Solomon the king.

25And the LORD magnified Solomon exceedingly in the sight of all Israel, and bestowed upon him *such* royal majesty as had not been on any king before him in Israel.

26¶ Thus David the son of Jesse reigned over all Israel.

27And the time that he reigned over Israel *was* forty years; seven years reigned he in Hebron, and thirty and three *years* reigned he in Jerusalem.

28And he died in a good old age, full of days, riches, and honour: and Solomon his son reigned in his stead.

29Now the acts of David the king, first and last, behold, they *are* written in the book of Samuel the seer, and in the book of Nathan the prophet, and in the book of Gad the seer,

30With all his reign and his might, and the times that went over him, and over Israel, and over all the kingdoms of the countries.

New International

20Then David said to the whole assembly, "Praise the LORD your God." So they all praised the LORD, the God of their fathers; they bowed low and fell prostrate before the LORD and the king.

Solomon Acknowledged as King

21The next day they made sacrifices to the LORD and presented burnt offerings to him: a thousand bulls, a thousand rams and a thousand male lambs, together with their drink offerings, and other sacrifices in abundance for all Israel. 22They ate and drank with great joy in the presence of the LORD that day.

Then they acknowledged Solomon son of David as king a second time, anointing him before the LORD to be ruler and Zadok to be priest. 23So Solomon sat on the throne of the LORD as king in place of his father David. He prospered and all Israel obeyed him. 24All the officers and mighty men, as well as all of King David's sons, pledged their submission to King Solomon.

25The LORD highly exalted Solomon in the sight of all Israel and bestowed on him royal splendor such as no king over Israel ever had before.

The Death of David

26David son of Jesse was king over all Israel. 27He ruled over Israel forty years—seven in Hebron and thirty-three in Jerusalem. 28He died at a good old age, having enjoyed long life, wealth and honor. His son Solomon succeeded him as king.

29As for the events of King David's reign, from beginning to end, they are written in the records of Samuel the seer, the records of Nathan the prophet and the records of Gad the seer, 30together with the details of his reign and power, and the circumstances that surrounded him and Israel and the kingdoms of all the other lands.

Living Bible

²⁰Then David said to all the people, "Give praise to the Lord your God!" And they did, bowing low before the Lord and the king.

²¹The next day they brought a thousand young bulls, a thousand rams, and a thousand lambs as burnt offerings to the Lord; they also offered drink offerings and many other sacrifices on behalf of all Israel. ²²Then they feasted and drank before the Lord with great joy.

And again^a they crowned King David's son Solomon as their king. They anointed him before the Lord as their leader, and they anointed Zadok as their priest. ²³So God appointed Solomon to take the throne of his father David; and he prospered greatly, and all Israel obeyed him. ²⁴The national leaders, the army officers, and his brothers all pledged their allegiance to King Solomon. ²⁵And the Lord gave him great popularity with all the people of Israel, and he amassed even greater wealth and honor than his father.

^{26, 27}David was king of the land of Israel for forty years; seven of them during his reign in Hebron and thirty-three in Jerusalem. ²⁸He died at an old age, wealthy and honored; and his son Solomon reigned in his place. ²⁹Detailed biographies of King David have been written in the history of Samuel the prophet, the history written by Nathan the prophet, and in the history written by the prophet Gad. ³⁰These accounts tell of his reign and of his might and all that happened to him and to Israel and to the kings of the nearby nations.

New Revised Standard

20 Then David said to the whole assembly, "Bless the LORD your God." And all the assembly blessed the LORD, the God of their ancestors, and bowed their heads and prostrated themselves before the LORD and the king. ²¹On the next day they offered sacrifices and burnt offerings to the LORD, a thousand bulls, a thousand rams, and a thousand lambs, with their libations, and sacrifices in abundance for all Israel; ²²and they ate and drank before the LORD on that day with great joy.

Solomon Anointed King

They made David's son Solomon king a second time; they anointed him as the LORD's prince, and Zadok as priest. ²³Then Solomon sat on the throne of the LORD, succeeding his father David as king; he prospered, and all Israel obeyed him. ²⁴All the leaders and the mighty warriors, and also all the sons of King David, pledged their allegiance to King Solomon. ²⁵The LORD highly exalted Solomon in the sight of all Israel, and bestowed upon him such royal majesty as had not been on any king before him in Israel.

Summary of David's Reign

26 Thus David son of Jesse reigned over all Israel. ²⁷The period that he reigned over Israel was forty years; he reigned seven years in Hebron, and thirty-three years in Jerusalem. ²⁸He died in a good old age, full of days, riches, and honor; and his son Solomon succeeded him. ²⁹Now the acts of King David, from first to last, are written in the records of the seer Samuel, and in the records of the prophet Nathan, and in the records of the seer Gad, ³⁰with accounts of all his rule and his might and of the events that befell him and Israel and all the kingdoms of the earth.

---

^a 29:22 and again, or "and they installed him as co-regent" (with King David).

THE SECOND BOOK OF THE

Chronicles

2 Chronicles

1 AND SOLOMON the son of David was strengthened in his kingdom, and the LORD his God *was* with him, and magnified him exceedingly.

2Then Solomon spake unto all Israel, to the captains of thousands and of hundreds, and to the judges, and to every governor in all Israel, the chief of the fathers.

3So Solomon, and all the congregation with him, went to the high place that *was* at Gibeon; for there was the tabernacle of the congregation of God, which Moses the servant of the LORD had made in the wilderness.

4But the ark of God had David brought up from Kirjath-jearim to *the place which* David had prepared for it: for he had pitched a tent for it at Jerusalem.

5Moreover the brasen altar, that Bezaleel the son of Uri, the son of Hur, had made, he put before the tabernacle of the LORD: and Solomon and the congregation sought unto it.

6And Solomon went up thither to the brasen altar before the LORD, which *was* at the tabernacle of the congregation, and offered a thousand burnt offerings upon it.

7¶ In that night did God appear unto Solomon, and said unto him, Ask what I shall give thee.

8And Solomon said unto God, Thou hast shown great mercy unto David my father, and hast made me to reign in his stead.

9Now, O LORD God, let thy promise unto David my father be established: for thou hast made me king over a people like the dust of the earth in multitude.

10Give me now wisdom and knowledge, that I may go out and come in before this people: for who can judge this thy people, *that is so* great?

11And God said to Solomon, Because this was in thine heart, and thou hast not asked riches, wealth, or honour, nor the life of thine enemies, neither yet hast asked long life; but hast asked wisdom and knowledge for thyself, that thou mayest judge my people, over whom I have made thee king:

12Wisdom and knowledge *is* granted unto thee; and I will give thee riches, and wealth, and honour, such as none of the kings have had that *have been* before thee, neither shall there any after thee have the like.

13¶ Then Solomon came *from his journey* to the high place that *was* at Gibeon to Jerusalem, from before the tabernacle of the congregation, and reigned over Israel.

14And Solomon gathered chariots and horsemen: and he had a thousand and four hundred chariots, and twelve thousand horsemen, which he placed in the chariot cities, and with the king at Jerusalem.

15And the king made silver and gold at Jerusalem *as plenteous* as stones, and cedar trees made he as the sycamore trees that *are* in the vale for abundance.

16And Solomon had horses brought out of Egypt, and linen yarn: the king's merchants received the linen yarn at a price.

Solomon Asks for Wisdom

1 SOLOMON SON of David established himself firmly over his kingdom, for the LORD his God was with him and made him exceedingly great.

2Then Solomon spoke to all Israel—to the commanders of thousands and commanders of hundreds, to the judges and to all the leaders in Israel, the heads of families— 3and Solomon and the whole assembly went to the high place at Gibeon, for God's Tent of Meeting was there, which Moses the LORD's servant had made in the desert. 4Now David had brought up the ark of God from Kiriath Jearim to the place he had prepared for it, because he had pitched a tent for it in Jerusalem. 5But the bronze altar that Bezalel son of Uri, the son of Hur, had made was in Gibeon in front of the tabernacle of the LORD; so Solomon and the assembly inquired of him there. 6Solomon went up to the bronze altar before the LORD in the Tent of Meeting and offered a thousand burnt offerings on it.

7That night God appeared to Solomon and said to him, "Ask for whatever you want me to give you."

8Solomon answered God, "You have shown great kindness to David my father and have made me king in his place. 9Now, LORD God, let your promise to my father David be confirmed, for you have made me king over a people who are as numerous as the dust of the earth. 10Give me wisdom and knowledge, that I may lead this people, for who is able to govern this great people of yours?"

11God said to Solomon, "Since this is your heart's desire and you have not asked for wealth, riches or honor, nor for the death of your enemies, and since you have not asked for a long life but for wisdom and knowledge to govern my people over whom I have made you king, 12therefore wisdom and knowledge will be given you. And I will also give you wealth, riches and honor, such as no king who was before you ever had and none after you will have."

13Then Solomon went to Jerusalem from the high place at Gibeon, from before the Tent of Meeting. And he reigned over Israel.

14Solomon accumulated chariots and horses; he had fourteen hundred chariots and twelve thousand horses,[a] which he kept in the chariot cities and also with him in Jerusalem. 15The king made silver and gold as common in Jerusalem as stones, and cedar as plentiful as sycamore-fig trees in the foothills. 16Solomon's horses were imported from Egypt[b] and from Kue[c]—the royal merchants purchased them from Kue. 17They imported a

---

[a] *14* Or *charioteers*   [b] *16* Or possibly *Muzur*, a region in Cilicia; also in verse 17   [c] *16* Probably Cilicia

2 Chronicles

2 Chronicles

1 KING DAVID'S son Solomon was now the undisputed ruler of Israel, for the Lord his God had made him a powerful monarch. 2, 3He summoned all the army officers and judges to Gibeond as well as all the political and religious leaders of Israel. He led them up to the hill to the olde Tabernacle constructed by Moses, the Lord's assistant, while he was in the wilderness. 4(There was a later Tabernacle in Jerusalem, built by King David for the Ark of God when he removed it from Kiriath-jearim.) 5, 6The bronze altar made by Bezalel (son of Uri, son of Hur) still stood in front of the old Tabernacle, and now Solomon and those he had invited assembled themselves before it, as he sacrificed upon it 1,000 burnt offerings to the Lord.

7That night God appeared to Solomon and told him, "Ask me for anything, and I will give it to you!"

8Solomon replied, "O God, you have been so kind and good to my father David, and now you have given me the kingdom— 9this is all I want! For you have fulfilled your promise to David my father and have made me king over a nation as full of people as the earth is full of dust! 10Now give me wisdom and knowledge to rule them properly, for who is able to govern by himself such a great nation as this one of yours?"

11God replied, "Because your greatest desire is to help your people, and you haven't asked for personal wealth and honor, and you haven't asked me to curse your enemies, and you haven't asked for a long life, but for wisdom and knowledge to properly guide my people— 12yes, I am giving you the wisdom and knowledge you asked for! And I am also giving you such riches, wealth, and honor as no other king has ever had before you! And there will never again be so great a king in all the world!"

13Solomon then left the Tabernacle, returned down the hill, and went back to Jerusalem to rule Israel. 14He built up a huge force of 1,400 chariots and recruited 12,000 cavalry to guard the cities where the chariots were garaged, though some, of course, were stationed at Jerusalem near the king. 15During Solomon's reign, silver and gold were as plentiful in Jerusalem as rocks on the road! And expensive cedar lumber was used like common sycamore! 16Solomon sent horse-traders to Egypt to purchase entire herds at wholesale prices. 17At

Solomon Requests Wisdom

1 SOLOMON SON of David established himself in his kingdom; the LORD his God was with him and made him exceedingly great.

2 Solomon summoned all Israel, the commanders of the thousands and of the hundreds, the judges, and all the leaders of all Israel, the heads of families. 3Then Solomon, and the whole assembly with him, went to the high place that was at Gibeon; for God's tent of meeting, which Moses the servant of the LORD had made in the wilderness, was there. 4(But David had brought the ark of God up from Kiriath-jearim to the place that David had prepared for it; for he had pitched a tent for it in Jerusalem.) 5Moreover the bronze altar that Bezalel son of Uri, son of Hur, had made, was there in front of the tabernacle of the LORD. And Solomon and the assembly inquired at it. 6Solomon went up there to the bronze altar before the LORD, which was at the tent of meeting, and offered a thousand burnt offerings on it.

7 That night God appeared to Solomon, and said to him, "Ask what I should give you." 8Solomon said to God, "You have shown great and steadfast love to my father David, and have made me succeed him as king. 9O LORD God, let your promise to my father David now be fulfilled, for you have made me king over a people as numerous as the dust of the earth. 10Give me now wisdom and knowledge to go out and come in before this people, for who can rule this great people of yours?" 11God answered Solomon, "Because this was in your heart, and you have not asked for possessions, wealth, honor, or the life of those who hate you, and have not even asked for long life, but have asked for wisdom and knowledge for yourself that you may rule my people over whom I have made you king, 12wisdom and knowledge are granted to you. I will also give you riches, possessions, and honor, such as none of the kings had who were before you, and none after you shall have the like." 13So Solomon came fromf the high place at Gibeon, from the tent of meeting, to Jerusalem. And he reigned over Israel.

Solomon's Military and Commercial Activity

14 Solomon gathered together chariots and horses; he had fourteen hundred chariots and twelve thousand horses, which he stationed in the chariot cities and with the king in Jerusalem. 15The king made silver and gold as common in Jerusalem as stone, and he made cedar as plentiful as the sycamore of the Shephelah. 16Solomon's horses were imported from Egypt and Kue; the king's traders received them from Kue at the prevailing price.

---

d 1:2 He summoned all the army officers and judges to Gibeon, implied.
e 1:3 He led them up the hill to the old Tabernacle. Moses had built the Tabernacle 500 years before the reign of King Solomon.

f Gk Vg: Heb to

King James

17And they fetched up, and brought forth out of Egypt a chariot for six hundred *shekels* of silver, and an horse for an hundred and fifty: and so brought they out *horses* for all the kings of the Hittites, and for the kings of Syria, by their means.

2 AND SOLOMON determined to build an house for the name of the LORD, and an house for his kingdom.

2And Solomon told out threescore and ten thousand men to bear burdens, and fourscore thousand to hew in the mountain, and three thousand and six hundred to oversee them.

3¶ And Solomon sent to Huram the king of Tyre, saying, As thou didst deal with David my father, and didst send him cedars to build him an house to dwell therein, *even so deal with me*.

4Behold, I build an house to the name of the LORD my God, to dedicate *it* to him, *and* to burn before him sweet incense, and for the continual showbread, and for the burnt offerings morning and evening, on the sabbaths, and on the new moons, and on the solemn feasts of the LORD our God. This *is an ordinance* for ever to Israel.

5And the house which I build *is* great: for great *is* our God above all gods.

6But who is able to build him an house, seeing the heaven and heaven of heavens cannot contain him? who *am* I then, that I should build him an house, save only to burn sacrifice before him?

7Send me now therefore a man cunning to work in gold, and in silver, and in brass, and in iron, and in purple, and crimson, and blue, and that can skill to grave with the cunning men that *are* with me in Judah and in Jerusalem, whom David my father did provide.

8Send me also cedar trees, fir trees, and algum trees, out of Lebanon: for I know that thy servants can skill to cut timber in Lebanon; and, behold, my servants *shall be* with thy servants,

9Even to prepare me timber in abundance: for the house which I am about to build *shall be* wonderful great.

10And, behold, I will give to thy servants, the hewers that cut timber, twenty thousand measures of beaten wheat, and twenty thousand measures of barley, and twenty thousand baths of wine, and twenty thousand baths of oil.

11¶ Then Huram the king of Tyre answered in writing, which he sent to Solomon, Because the LORD hath loved his people, he hath made thee king over them.

12Huram said moreover, Blessed *be* the LORD God of Israel, that made heaven and earth, who hath given to David the king a wise son, endued with prudence and understanding, that might build an house for the LORD, and an house for his kingdom.

13And now I have sent a cunning man, endued with understanding, of Huram my father's,

14The son of a woman of the daughters of Dan, and his father *was* a man of Tyre, skilful to work in gold, and in silver, in brass, in iron, in stone, and in timber, in purple, in blue, and in fine linen, and in crimson; also to grave any manner of graving, and to find out every device which shall be put to him, with thy cunning men, and with the cunning men of my lord David thy father.

New International

chariot from Egypt for six hundred shekels[a] of silver, and a horse for a hundred and fifty.[b] They also exported them to all the kings of the Hittites and of the Arameans.

Preparations for Building the Temple

2 SOLOMON GAVE orders to build a temple for the Name of the LORD and a royal palace for himself. 2He conscripted seventy thousand men as carriers and eighty thousand as stonecutters in the hills and thirty-six hundred as foremen over them.

3Solomon sent this message to Hiram[c] king of Tyre:

"Send me cedar logs as you did for my father David when you sent him cedar to build a palace to live in. 4Now I am about to build a temple for the Name of the LORD my God and to dedicate it to him for burning fragrant incense before him, for setting out the consecrated bread regularly, and for making burnt offerings every morning and evening and on Sabbaths and New Moons and at the appointed feasts of the LORD our God. This is a lasting ordinance for Israel.

5"The temple I am going to build will be great, because our God is greater than all other gods. 6But who is able to build a temple for him, since the heavens, even the highest heavens, cannot contain him? Who then am I to build a temple for him, except as a place to burn sacrifices before him?

7"Send me, therefore, a man skilled to work in gold and silver, bronze and iron, and in purple, crimson and blue yarn, and experienced in the art of engraving, to work in Judah and Jerusalem with my skilled craftsmen, whom my father David provided.

8"Send me also cedar, pine and algum[d] logs from Lebanon, for I know that your men are skilled in cutting timber there. My men will work with yours 9to provide me with plenty of lumber, because the temple I build must be large and magnificent. 10I will give your servants, the woodsmen who cut the timber, twenty thousand cors[e] of ground wheat, twenty thousand cors of barley, twenty thousand baths[f] of wine and twenty thousand baths of olive oil."

11Hiram king of Tyre replied by letter to Solomon:

"Because the LORD loves his people, he has made you their king."

12And Hiram added:

"Praise be to the LORD, the God of Israel, who made heaven and earth! He has given King David a wise son, endowed with intelligence and discernment, who will build a temple for the LORD and a palace for himself.

13"I am sending you Huram-Abi, a man of great skill, 14whose mother was from Dan and whose father was from Tyre. He is trained to work in gold and silver, bronze and iron, stone and wood, and with purple and blue and crimson yarn and fine linen. He is experienced in all kinds of engraving and can execute any design given to him. He will work with your craftsmen and with those of my lord, David your father.

---

[a] *17* That is, about 15 pounds (about 7 kilograms)   [b] *17* That is, about 3 3/4 pounds (about 1.7 kilograms)   [c] *3* Hebrew *Huram*, a variant of *Hiram*; also in verses 11 and 12   [d] *8* Probably a variant of *almug*; possibly juniper   [e] *10* That is, probably about 125,000 bushels (about 4,400 kiloliters)   [f] *10* That is, probably about 115,000 gallons (about 440 kiloliters)

Living Bible

that time Egyptian chariots sold for $400 each and horses for $100, delivered at Jerusalem. Many of these were then resold to the kings of the Hittites and Syria.

2 SOLOMON NOW decided that the time had come to build a temple for the Lord and a palace for himself. ²This required a force of 70,000 laborers, 80,000 stonecutters in the hills, and 3,600 foremen. ³Solomon sent an ambassador to King Hiram at Tyre, requesting shipments of cedar lumber such as Hiram had supplied to David when he was building his palace.

⁴"I am about to build a temple for the Lord my God," Solomon told Hiram. "It will be a place where I can burn incense and sweet spices before God, and display the special sacrificial bread, and sacrifice burnt offerings each morning and evening, and on the Sabbaths, and at the new moon celebration and other regular festivals of the Lord our God. For God wants Israel always to celebrate these special occasions. ⁵It is going to be a wonderful temple because he is a great God, greater than any other. ⁶But who can ever build him a worthy home? Not even the highest heaven would be beautiful enough! And who am I to be allowed to build a temple for God? But it will be a place to worship him.g

⁷"So send me skilled craftsmen—goldsmiths and silversmiths, brass and iron workers; and send me weavers to make purple, crimson, and blue cloth; and skilled engravers to work beside the craftsmen of Judah and Jerusalem who were selected by my father David. ⁸Also send me cedar trees, fir trees, and algum trees from the Forests of Lebanon, for your men are without equal as lumbermen, and I will send my men to help them. ⁹An immense amount of lumber will be needed, for the temple I am going to build will be large and incredibly beautiful. ¹⁰As to the financial arrangements, I will pay your men 20,000 sacks of crushed wheat, 20,000 barrels of barley, 20,000 barrels of wine, and 20,000 barrels of olive oil."

¹¹King Hiram replied to King Solomon: "It is because the Lord loves his people that he has made you their king! ¹²Blessed be the Lord God of Israel who made the heavens and the earth and who has given to David such a wise, intelligent, and understanding son to build God's Temple, and a royal palace for himself.

¹³"I am sending you a master craftsman—my famous Huramabi! He is a brilliant man, ¹⁴the son of a Jewish woman from Dan in Israel; his father is from here in Tyre. He is a skillful goldsmith and silversmith, and also does exquisite work with brass and iron, and knows all about stonework, carpentry, and weaving; and he is an expert in the dyeing of purple and blue linen and crimson cloth. He is an engraver besides, and an inventor! He will work with your craftsmen and those appointed by my lord David, your father. ¹⁵So send along the wheat,

New Revised Standard

¹⁷They imported from Egypt, and then exported, a chariot for six hundred shekels of silver, and a horse for one hundred fifty; so through them these were exported to all the kings of the Hittites and the kings of Aram.

Preparations for Building the Temple

2ʰ SOLOMON DECIDED to build a temple for the name of the LORD, and a royal palace for himself. 2ⁱ Solomon conscripted seventy thousand laborers and eighty thousand stonecutters in the hill country, with three thousand six hundred to oversee them.

Alliance with Huram of Tyre

3 Solomon sent word to King Huram of Tyre: "Once you dealt with my father David and sent him cedar to build himself a house to live in. ⁴I am now about to build a house for the name of the LORD my God and dedicate it to him for offering fragrant incense before him, and for the regular offering of the rows of bread, and for burnt offerings morning and evening, on the sabbaths and the new moons and the appointed festivals of the LORD our God, as ordained forever for Israel. ⁵The house that I am about to build will be great, for our God is greater than other gods. ⁶But who is able to build him a house, since heaven, even highest heaven, cannot contain him? Who am I to build a house for him, except as a place to make offerings before him? ⁷So now send me an artisan skilled to work in gold, silver, bronze, and iron, and in purple, crimson, and blue fabrics, trained also in engraving, to join the skilled workers who are with me in Judah and Jerusalem, whom my father David provided. ⁸Send me also cedar, cypress, and algum timber from Lebanon, for I know that your servants are skilled in cutting Lebanon timber. My servants will work with your servants ⁹to prepare timber for me in abundance, for the house I am about to build will be great and wonderful. ¹⁰I will provide for your servants, those who cut the timber, twenty thousand cors of crushed wheat, twenty thousand cors of barley, twenty thousand bathsj of wine, and twenty thousand baths of oil."

11 Then King Huram of Tyre answered in a letter that he sent to Solomon, "Because the LORD loves his people he has made you king over them." ¹²Huram also said, "Blessed be the LORD God of Israel, who made heaven and earth, who has given King David a wise son, endowed with discretion and understanding, who will build a temple for the LORD, and a royal palace for himself.

13 "I have dispatched Huram-abi, a skilled artisan, endowed with understanding, ¹⁴the son of one of the Danite women, his father a Tyrian. He is trained to work in gold, silver, bronze, iron, stone, and wood, and in purple, blue, and crimson fabrics and fine linen, and to do all sorts of engraving and execute any design that may be assigned him, with your artisans, the artisans of my lord, your father David. ¹⁵Now, as for the wheat, bar-

---

g 2:6 *it will be a place to worship him,* literally, "a place to burn incense before him."

ʰ Ch 1.18 in Heb   ⁱ Ch 2.1 in Heb   ʲ A Hebrew measure of volume

King James

15Now therefore the wheat, and the barley, the oil, and the wine, which my lord hath spoken of, let him send unto his servants:

16And we will cut wood out of Lebanon, as much as thou shalt need: and we will bring it to thee in floats by sea to Joppa; and thou shalt carry it up to Jerusalem.

17¶ And Solomon numbered all the strangers that *were* in the land of Israel, after the numbering wherewith David his father had numbered them; and they were found an hundred and fifty thousand and three thousand and six hundred.

18And he set threescore and ten thousand of them *to be* bearers of burdens, and fourscore thousand *to be* hewers in the mountain, and three thousand and six hundred overseers to set the people awork.

3 THEN SOLOMON began to build the house of the LORD at Jerusalem in mount Moriah, where *the* LORD appeared unto David his father, in the place that David had prepared in the threshingfloor of Ornan the Jebusite.

2And he began to build in the second *day* of the second month, in the fourth year of his reign.

3¶ Now these *are the things wherein* Solomon was instructed for the building of the house of God. The length by cubits after the first measure *was* threescore cubits, and the breadth twenty cubits.

4And the porch that *was* in the front *of the house*, the length *of it was* according to the breadth of the house, twenty cubits, and the height *was* an hundred and twenty: and he overlaid it within with pure gold.

5And the greater house he ceiled with fir tree, which he overlaid with fine gold, and set thereon palm trees and chains.

6And he garnished the house with precious stones for beauty: and the gold *was* gold of Parvaim.

7He overlaid also the house, the beams, the posts, and the walls thereof, and the doors thereof, with gold; and graved cherubims on the walls.

8And he made the most holy house, the length whereof *was* according to the breadth of the house, twenty cubits, and the breadth thereof twenty cubits: and he overlaid it with fine gold, *amounting* to six hundred talents.

9And the weight of the nails *was* fifty shekels of gold. And he overlaid the upper chambers with gold.

10And in the most holy house he made two cherubims of image work, and overlaid them with gold.

11¶ And the wings of the cherubims *were* twenty cubits long: one wing *of the one cherub was* five cubits, reaching to the wall of the house: and the other wing *was likewise* five cubits, reaching to the wing of the other cherub.

12And *one* wing of the other cherub *was* five cubits, reaching to the wall of the house: and the other wing *was* five cubits *also*, joining to the wing of the other cherub.

13The wings of these cherubims spread themselves forth twenty cubits: and they stood on their feet, and their faces *were* inward.

14¶ And he made the veil *of* blue, and purple, and crimson, and fine linen, and wrought cherubims thereon.

15Also he made before the house two pillars of thirty and five cubits high, and the chapiter that *was* on the top of each of them *was* five cubits.

16And he made chains, *as* in the oracle, and put *them* on the heads of the pillars; and made an hundred pomegranates, and put *them* on the chains.

17And he reared up the pillars before the temple, one on the right hand, and the other on the left; and called the name of that on the right hand Jachin, and the name of that on the left Boaz.

New International

15"Now let my lord send his servants the wheat and barley and the olive oil and wine he promised, 16and we will cut all the logs from Lebanon that you need and will float them in rafts by sea down to Joppa. You can then take them up to Jerusalem."

17Solomon took a census of all the aliens who were in Israel, after the census his father David had taken; and they were found to be 153,600. 18He assigned 70,000 of them to be carriers and 80,000 to be stonecutters in the hills, with 3,600 foremen over them to keep the people working.

Solomon Builds the Temple

3 THEN SOLOMON began to build the temple of the LORD in Jerusalem on Mount Moriah, where the LORD had appeared to his father David. It was on the threshing floor of Araunah[a] the Jebusite, the place provided by David. 2He began building on the second day of the second month in the fourth year of his reign.

3The foundation Solomon laid for building the temple of God was sixty cubits long and twenty cubits wide[b] (using the cubit of the old standard). 4The portico at the front of the temple was twenty cubits[c] long across the width of the building and twenty cubits[d] high.

He overlaid the inside with pure gold. 5He paneled the main hall with pine and covered it with fine gold and decorated it with palm tree and chain designs. 6He adorned the temple with precious stones. And the gold he used was gold of Parvaim. 7He overlaid the ceiling beams, doorframes, walls and doors of the temple with gold, and he carved cherubim on the walls.

8He built the Most Holy Place, its length corresponding to the width of the temple—twenty cubits long and twenty cubits wide. He overlaid the inside with six hundred talents[e] of fine gold. 9The gold nails weighed fifty shekels.[f] He also overlaid the upper parts with gold.

10In the Most Holy Place he made a pair of sculptured cherubim and overlaid them with gold. 11The total wingspan of the cherubim was twenty cubits. One wing of the first cherub was five cubits[g] long and touched the temple wall, while its other wing, also five cubits long, touched the wing of the other cherub. 12Similarly one wing of the second cherub was five cubits long and touched the other temple wall, and its other wing, also five cubits long, touched the wing of the first cherub. 13The wings of these cherubim extended twenty cubits. They stood on their feet, facing the main hall.[h]

14He made the curtain of blue, purple and crimson yarn and fine linen, with cherubim worked into it.

15In the front of the temple he made two pillars, which together, were thirty-five cubits[i] long, each with a capital on top measuring five cubits. 16He made interwoven chains[j] and put them on top of the pillars. He also made a hundred pomegranates and attached them to the chains. 17He erected the pillars in the front of the temple, one to the south and one to the north. The one to the south he named Jakin[k] and the one to the north Boaz.[l]

a *1* Hebrew *Ornan*, a variant of *Araunah*   b *3* That is, about 90 feet (about 27 meters) long and 30 feet (about 9 meters) wide   c *4* That is, about 30 feet (about 9 meters); also in verses 8, 11 and 13   d *4* Some Septuagint and Syriac manuscripts; Hebrew *and a hundred and twenty*   e *8* That is, about 23 tons (about 21 metric tons)   f *9* That is, about 1 1/4 pounds (about 0.6 kilogram)   g *11* That is, about 7 1/2 feet (about 2.3 meters); also in verse 15   h *13* Or *facing inward*   i *15* That is, about 52 feet (about 16 meters)   j *16* Or possibly *made chains in the inner sanctuary*; the meaning of the Hebrew for this phrase is uncertain.   k *17* *Jakin* probably means *he establishes*.   l *17* *Boaz* probably means *in him is strength*.

Living Bible

barley, olive oil, and wine you mentioned, 16and we will begin cutting wood from the Lebanon mountains, as much as you need, and bring it to you in log floats across the sea to Joppa, and from there you can take them inland to Jerusalem."

17Solomon now took a census of all foreigners in the country (just as his father David had done) and found that there were 153,600 of them. 18He indentured 70,000 as common laborers, 80,000 as loggers and 3,600 as foremen.

3 FINALLY THE actual construction of the Temple began. Its location was in Jerusalem at the top of Mount Moriah, where the Lord had appeared to Solomon's father, King David, and where the threshing-floor of Ornan the Jebusite had been. David had selected it as the site for the Temple. 2The actual construction began on the seventeenth day of April in the fourth year of King Solomon's reign.

3The foundation was ninety feet long and thirty feet wide. 4A covered porch ran along the entire thirty-foot width of the Temple, with the inner walls and ceiling overlaid with pure gold! The roof was 180 feet high.

5The main part of the Temple was paneled with cypress wood, plated with pure gold, and engraved with palm trees and chains. 6Beautiful jewels were inlaid into the walls to add to the beauty; the gold, by the way, was of the best, from Parvaim. 7All the walls, beams, doors, and thresholds throughout the Temple were plated with gold, with angels engraved on the walls.

8Within the Temple, at one end, was the most sacred room—the Holy of Holies—thirty feet square. This too was overlaid with the finest gold, valued at millions of dollars. 9Twenty-six-ounce gold nails were used. The upper rooms were also plated with pure gold.

10Within the innermost room, the Holy of Holies, Solomon placed two sculptured statues of angels, and plated them with gold. 11, 12, 13They stood on the floor facing the outer room, with wings stretched wingtip to wingtip across the room, from wall to wall.m 14Across the entrance to this room he placed a veil of blue and crimson finespun linen, decorated with angels.

15At the front of the Temple were two pillars 52½ feet high, topped by a 7½-foot capital flaring out to the roof. 16He made chainsn and placed them on top of the pillars, with 100 pomegranates attached to the chains. 17Then he set up the pillars at the front of the Temple, one on the right and the other on the left. And he gave them names: Jachin (the one on the right), and Boaz (the one on the left).

New Revised Standard

ley, oil, and wine, of which my lord has spoken, let him send them to his servants. 16We will cut whatever timber you need from Lebanon, and bring it to you as rafts by sea to Joppa; you will take it up to Jerusalem."

17 Then Solomon took a census of all the aliens who were residing in the land of Israel, after the census that his father David had taken; and there were found to be one hundred fifty-three thousand six hundred. 18Seventy thousand of them he assigned as laborers, eighty thousand as stonecutters in the hill country, and three thousand six hundred as overseers to make the people work.

Solomon Builds the Temple

3 SOLOMON BEGAN to build the house of the Lord in Jerusalem on Mount Moriah, where the Lord had appeared to his father David, at the place that David had designated, on the threshing floor of Ornan the Jebusite. 2He began to build on the second day of the second month of the fourth year of his reign. 3These are Solomon's measurementso for building the house of God: the length, in cubits of the old standard, was sixty cubits, and the width twenty cubits. 4The vestibule in front of the nave of the house was twenty cubits long, across the width of the house;p and its height was one hundred twenty cubits. He overlaid it on the inside with pure gold. 5The nave he lined with cypress, covered it with fine gold, and made palms and chains on it. 6He adorned the house with settings of precious stones. The gold was gold from Parvaim. 7So he lined the house with gold—its beams, its thresholds, its walls, and its doors; and he carved cherubim on the walls.

8 He made the most holy place; its length, corresponding to the width of the house, was twenty cubits, and its width was twenty cubits; he overlaid it with six hundred talents of fine gold. 9The weight of the nails was fifty shekels of gold. He overlaid the upper chambers with gold.

10 In the most holy place he made two carved cherubim and overlaidq them with gold. 11The wings of the cherubim together extended twenty cubits: one wing of the one, five cubits long, touched the wall of the house, and its other wing, five cubits long, touched the wing of the other cherub; 12and of this cherub, one wing, five cubits long, touched the wall of the house, and the other wing, also five cubits long, was joined to the wing of the first cherub. 13The wings of these cherubim extended twenty cubits; the cherubimr stood on their feet, facing the nave. 14And Solomons made the curtain of blue and purple and crimson fabrics and fine linen, and worked cherubim into it.

15 In front of the house he made two pillars thirty-five cubits high, with a capital of five cubits on the top of each. 16He made encirclingt chains and put them on the tops of the pillars; and he made one hundred pomegranates, and put them on the chains. 17He set up the pillars in front of the temple, one on the right, the other on the left; the one on the right he called Jachin, and the one on the left, Boaz.

---

m 3:11-13 with wings stretched . . . from wall to wall, literally, "one wing of a cherub, five cubits long." n 3:16 He made chains, literally, "chains in the Holy of Holies, and . . ."

o Syr: Heb foundations   p Compare 1 Kings 6.3: Meaning of Heb uncertain   q Heb they overlaid   r Heb they   s Heb he   t Cn: Heb in the inner sanctuary

King James

4 MOREOVER HE made an altar of brass, twenty cubits the length thereof, and twenty cubits the breadth thereof, and ten cubits the height thereof.

2¶ Also he made a molten sea of ten cubits from brim to brim, round in compass, and five cubits the height thereof; and a line of thirty cubits did compass it round about.

3And under it *was* the similitude of oxen, which did compass it round about: ten in a cubit, compassing the sea round about. Two rows of oxen *were* cast, when it was cast.

4It stood upon twelve oxen, three looking toward the north, and three looking toward the west, and three looking toward the south, and three looking toward the east: and the sea *was set* above upon them, and all their hinder parts *were* inward.

5And the thickness of it *was* an handbreadth, and the brim of it like the work of the brim of a cup, with flowers of lilies; *and* it received and held three thousand baths.

6¶ He made also ten lavers, and put five on the right hand, and five on the left, to wash in them: such things as they offered for the burnt offering they washed in them; but the sea *was* for the priests to wash in.

7And he made ten candlesticks of gold according to their form, and set *them* in the temple, five on the right hand, and five on the left.

8He made also ten tables, and placed *them* in the temple, five on the right side, and five on the left. And he made an hundred basins of gold.

9¶ Furthermore he made the court of the priests, and the great court, and doors for the court, and overlaid the doors of them with brass.

10And he set the sea on the right side of the east end, over against the south.

11And Huram made the pots, and the shovels, and the basins. And Huram finished the work that he was to make for king Solomon for the house of God;

12*To wit,* the two pillars, and the pommels, and the chapiters *which were* on the top of the two pillars, and the two wreaths to cover the two pommels of the chapiters which *were* on the top of the two pillars;

13And four hundred pomegranates on the two wreaths; two rows of pomegranates on each wreath, to cover the two pommels of the chapiters which *were* upon the pillars.

14He made also bases, and lavers made he upon the bases;

15One sea, and twelve oxen under it.

16The pots also, and the shovels, and the fleshhooks, and all their instruments, did Huram his father make to king Solomon for the house of the LORD of bright brass.

17In the plain of Jordan did the king cast them, in the clay ground between Succoth and Zeredathah.

18Thus Solomon made all these vessels in great abundance: for the weight of the brass could not be found out.

19¶ And Solomon made all the vessels that *were for* the house of God, the golden altar also, and the tables whereon the showbread *was set;*

20Moreover the candlesticks with their lamps, that they should burn after the manner before the oracle, of pure gold;

21And the flowers, and the lamps, and the tongs, *made he of* gold, *and* that perfect gold;

22And the snuffers, and the basins, and the spoons, and the censers, *of* pure gold: and the entry of the house, the inner doors thereof for the most holy *place,* and the doors of the house of the temple, *were of* gold.

New International

The Temple's Furnishings

4 HE MADE a bronze altar twenty cubits long, twenty cubits wide and ten cubits high.[a] 2He made the Sea of cast metal, circular in shape, measuring ten cubits from rim to rim and five cubits[b] high. It took a line of thirty cubits[c] to measure around it. 3Below the rim, figures of bulls encircled it—ten to a cubit.[d] The bulls were cast in two rows in one piece with the Sea.

4The Sea stood on twelve bulls, three facing north, three facing west, three facing south and three facing east. The Sea rested on top of them, and their hindquarters were toward the center. 5It was a handbreadth[e] in thickness, and its rim was like the rim of a cup, like a lily blossom. It held three thousand baths.[f]

6He then made ten basins for washing and placed five on the south side and five on the north. In them the things to be used for the burnt offerings were rinsed, but the Sea was to be used by the priests for washing.

7He made ten gold lampstands according to the specifications for them and placed them in the temple, five on the south side and five on the north.

8He made ten tables and placed them in the temple, five on the south side and five on the north. He also made a hundred gold sprinkling bowls.

9He made the courtyard of the priests, and the large court and the doors for the court, and overlaid the doors with bronze. 10He placed the Sea on the south side, at the southeast corner.

11He also made the pots and shovels and sprinkling bowls.

So Huram finished the work he had undertaken for King Solomon in the temple of God:

12the two pillars;

the two bowl-shaped capitals on top of the pillars;

the two sets of network decorating the two bowl-shaped capitals on top of the pillars;

13the four hundred pomegranates for the two sets of network (two rows of pomegranates for each network, decorating the bowl-shaped capitals on top of the pillars);

14the stands with their basins;

15the Sea and the twelve bulls under it;

16the pots, shovels, meat forks and all related articles.

All the objects that Huram-Abi made for King Solomon for the temple of the LORD were of polished bronze. 17The king had them cast in clay molds in the plain of the Jordan between Succoth and Zarethan.[g] 18All these things that Solomon made amounted to so much that the weight of the bronze was not determined.

19Solomon also made all the furnishings that were in God's temple:

the golden altar;

the tables on which was the bread of the Presence;

20the lampstands of pure gold with their lamps, to burn in front of the inner sanctuary as prescribed;

21the gold floral work and lamps and tongs (they were solid gold);

22the pure gold wick trimmers, sprinkling bowls, dishes and censers; and the gold doors of the temple: the inner doors to the Most Holy Place and the doors of the main hall.

---

[a] *1* That is, about 30 feet (about 9 meters) long and wide, and about 15 feet (about 4.5 meters) high   [b] *2* That is, about 7 1/2 feet (about 2.3 meters)   [c] *2* That is, about 45 feet (about 13.5 meters)   [d] *3* That is, about 1 1/2 feet (about 0.5 meter)   [e] *5* That is, about 3 inches (about 8 centimeters)   [f] *5* That is, about 17,500 gallons (about 66 kiloliters)   [g] *17* Hebrew *Zeredatha,* a variant of *Zarethan*

Living Bible

4 HE ALSO made a bronze altar thirty feet long, thirty feet wide, and fifteen feet high. 2Then he forged a huge round tank fifteen feet across from rim to rim. The rim stood 7½ feet above the floor, and was forty-five feet around. 3The tank was encircled at its base by two rows of gourd designs, cast as part of the tank. 4The tank stood on twelve metal oxen facing outward; three faced north, three faced west, three faced south, and three faced east. 5The walls of the tank were five inches thick, flaring out like the cup of a lily. It held 3,000 barrels of water.

6He also constructed ten vats for water to wash the offerings, five to the right of the huge tank and five to the left. The priests used the tank, and not the vats, for their own washing.

7Carefully following God's instructions, he then cast ten gold lampstands and placed them in the Temple, five against each wall; 8he also built ten tables and placed five against each wall on the right and left. And he molded 100 solid gold bowls. 9Then he constructed a court for the priests, also the public court, and overlaid the doors of these courts with bronze. 10The huge tank was in the southeast corner of the outer room of the Temple. 11Huramabi also made the necessary pots, shovels, and basins for use in connection with the sacrifices.

So at last he completed the work assigned to him by King Solomon:

12-16The construction of the two pillars,

The two flared capitals on the tops of the pillars,

The two sets of chains on the capitals,

The 400 pomegranates hanging from the two sets of chains on the capitals,

The bases for the vats, and the vats themselves,

The huge tank and the twelve oxen under it,

The pots, shovels, and fleshhooks.

This skillful craftsman, Huramabi, made all of the above-mentioned items for King Solomon, using polished bronze. 17, 18The king did the casting at the claybanks of the Jordan valley between Succoth and Zeredah. Great quantities of bronze were used, too heavy to weigh.

19Solomon commanded that all of the furnishings of the Temple—the utensils, the altar, and the table for the Bread of the Presence must be made of gold; 20also the lamps and lampstands, 21the floral decorations, tongs, 22lamp snuffers, basins, spoons, and firepans—all were made of solid gold. Even the doorway of the Temple, the main door, and the inner doors to the Holy of Holies were overlaid with gold.

New Revised Standard

Furnishings of the Temple

4 HE MADE an altar of bronze, twenty cubits long, twenty cubits wide, and ten cubits high. 2Then he made the molten sea; it was round, ten cubits from rim to rim, and five cubits high. A line of thirty cubits would encircle it completely. 3Under it were panels all around, each of ten cubits, surrounding the sea; there were two rows of panels, cast when it was cast. 4It stood on twelve oxen, three facing north, three facing west, three facing south, and three facing east; the sea was set on them. The hindquarters of each were toward the inside. 5Its thickness was a handbreadth; its rim was made like the rim of a cup, like the flower of a lily; it held three thousand baths.h 6He also made ten basins in which to wash, and set five on the right side, and five on the left. In these they were to rinse what was used for the burnt offering. The sea was for the priests to wash in.

7 He made ten golden lampstands as prescribed, and set them in the temple, five on the south side and five on the north. 8He also made ten tables and placed them in the temple, five on the right side and five on the left. And he made one hundred basins of gold. 9He made the court of the priests, and the great court, and doors for the court; he overlaid their doors with bronze. 10He set the sea at the southeast corner of the house.

11 And Huram made the pots, the shovels, and the basins. Thus Huram finished the work that he did for King Solomon on the house of God: 12the two pillars, the bowls, and the two capitals on the top of the pillars; and the two latticeworks to cover the two bowls of the capitals that were on the top of the pillars; 13the four hundred pomegranates for the two latticeworks, two rows of pomegranates for each latticework, to cover the two bowls of the capitals that were on the pillars. 14He made the stands, the basins on the stands, 15the one sea, and the twelve oxen underneath it. 16The pots, the shovels, the forks, and all the equipment for these Huram-abi made of burnished bronze for King Solomon for the house of the LORD. 17In the plain of the Jordan the king cast them, in the clay ground between Succoth and Zeredah. 18Solomon made all these things in great quantities, so that the weight of the bronze was not determined.

19 So Solomon made all the things that were in the house of God: the golden altar, the tables for the bread of the Presence, 20the lampstands and their lamps of pure gold to burn before the inner sanctuary, as prescribed; 21the flowers, the lamps, and the tongs, of purest gold; 22the snuffers, basins, ladles, and firepans, of pure gold. As for the entrance to the temple: the inner doors to the most holy place and the doors of the nave of the temple were of gold.

h A Hebrew measure of volume

King James

5 THUS ALL the work that Solomon made for the house of the LORD was finished: and Solomon brought in *all* the things that David his father had dedicated; and the silver, and the gold, and all the instruments, put he among the treasures of the house of God.

2¶ Then Solomon assembled the elders of Israel, and all the heads of the tribes, the chief of the fathers of the children of Israel, unto Jerusalem, to bring up the ark of the covenant of the LORD out of the city of David, which *is* Zion.

3Wherefore all the men of Israel assembled themselves unto the king in the feast which *was* in the seventh month.

4And all the elders of Israel came; and the Levites took up the ark.

5And they brought up the ark, and the tabernacle of the congregation, and all the holy vessels that *were* in the tabernacle, these did the priests *and* the Levites bring up.

6Also king Solomon, and all the congregation of Israel that were assembled unto him before the ark, sacrificed sheep and oxen, which could not be told nor numbered for multitude.

7And the priests brought in the ark of the covenant of the LORD unto his place, to the oracle of the house, into the most holy *place, even* under the wings of the cherubims:

8For the cherubims spread forth *their* wings over the place of the ark, and the cherubims covered the ark and the staves thereof above.

9And they drew out the staves *of the ark,* that the ends of the staves were seen from the ark before the oracle; but they were not seen without. And there it is unto this day.

10*There was* nothing in the ark save the two tables which Moses put *therein* at Horeb, when the LORD made *a covenant* with the children of Israel, when they came out of Egypt.

11¶ And it came to pass, when the priests were come out of the holy *place:* (for all the priests *that were* present were sanctified, *and* did not *then* wait by course:

12Also the Levites *which were* the singers, all of them of Asaph, of Heman, of Jeduthun, with their sons and their brethren, *being* arrayed in white linen, having cymbals and psalteries and harps, stood at the east end of the altar, and with them an hundred and twenty priests sounding with trumpets:)

13It came even to pass, as the trumpeters and singers *were* as one, to make one sound to be heard in praising and thanking the LORD; and when they lifted up *their* voice with the trumpets and cymbals and instruments of music, and praised the LORD, *saying,* For *he is* good; for his mercy *endureth* for ever: that *then* the house was filled with a cloud, *even* the house of the LORD;

14So that the priests could not stand to minister by reason of the cloud: for the glory of the LORD had filled the house of God.

6 THEN SAID Solomon, The LORD hath said that he would dwell in the thick darkness.

2But I have built an house of habitation for thee, and a place for thy dwelling for ever.

3And the king turned his face, and blessed the whole congregation of Israel: and all the congregation of Israel stood.

New International

5 WHEN ALL the work Solomon had done for the temple of the LORD was finished, he brought in the things his father David had dedicated—the silver and gold and all the furnishings—and he placed them in the treasuries of God's temple.

The Ark Brought to the Temple

2Then Solomon summoned to Jerusalem the elders of Israel, all the heads of the tribes and the chiefs of the Israelite families, to bring up the ark of the LORD's covenant from Zion, the City of David. 3And all the men of Israel came together to the king at the time of the festival in the seventh month.

4When all the elders of Israel had arrived, the Levites took up the ark, 5and they brought up the ark and the Tent of Meeting and all the sacred furnishings in it. The priests, who were Levites, carried them up; 6and King Solomon and the entire assembly of Israel that had gathered about him were before the ark, sacrificing so many sheep and cattle that they could not be recorded or counted.

7The priests then brought the ark of the LORD's covenant to its place in the inner sanctuary of the temple, the Most Holy Place, and put it beneath the wings of the cherubim. 8The cherubim spread their wings over the place of the ark and covered the ark and its carrying poles. 9These poles were so long that their ends, extending from the ark, could be seen from in front of the inner sanctuary, but not from outside the Holy Place; and they are still there today. 10There was nothing in the ark except the two tablets that Moses had placed in it at Horeb, where the LORD made a covenant with the Israelites after they came out of Egypt.

11The priests then withdrew from the Holy Place. All the priests who were there had consecrated themselves, regardless of their divisions. 12All the Levites who were musicians—Asaph, Heman, Jeduthun and their sons and relatives—stood on the east side of the altar, dressed in fine linen and playing cymbals, harps and lyres. They were accompanied by 120 priests sounding trumpets. 13The trumpeters and singers joined in unison, as with one voice, to give praise and thanks to the LORD. Accompanied by trumpets, cymbals and other instruments, they raised their voices in praise to the LORD and sang:

"He is good;
   his love endures forever."

Then the temple of the LORD was filled with a cloud, 14and the priests could not perform their service because of the cloud, for the glory of the LORD filled the temple of God.

6 THEN SOLOMON said, "The LORD has said that he would dwell in a dark cloud; 2I have built a magnificent temple for you, a place for you to dwell forever."

3While the whole assembly of Israel was standing

Living Bible

5 SO THE Temple was finally finished. Then Solomon brought in the gifts dedicated to the Lord by his father, King David. They were stored in the Temple treasuries.

2Solomon now summoned to Jerusalem all of the leaders of Israel—the heads of the tribes and clans—for the ceremony of transferring the Ark from the [Tabernacle in thea] City of David, also known as Zion, [to its new home in the Templeb]. 3This celebration took place in October at the annual Festival of Tabernacles. 4, 5As the leaders of Israel watched, the Levites lifted the Ark and carried it out of the Tabernacle, along with all the other sacred vessels. 6King Solomon and the others sacrificed sheep and oxen before the Ark in such numbers that no one tried to keep count!

7, 8Then the priests carried the Ark into the inner room of the Temple—the Holy of Holies—and placed it beneath the angels' wings; their wings spread over the Ark and its carrying poles. 9These carrying poles were so long that their ends could be seen from the outer room, but not from the outside doorway.

The Ark is still there at the time of this writing. 10Nothing was in the Ark except the two stone tablets which Moses had put there at Mount Horeb, when the Lord made a covenant with the people of Israel as they were leaving Egypt.

11, 12When the priests had undergone the purification rites for themselves, they all took part in the ceremonies without regard to their normal duties. And how the Levites were praising the Lord as the priests came out of the Holy of Holies! The singers were Asaph, Heman, Jeduthun and all their sons and brothers, dressed in finespun linen robes and standing at the east side of the altar. The choir was accompanied by 120 priests who were trumpeters, while others played the cymbals, lyres, and harps. 13, 14The band and chorus united as one to praise and thank the Lord; their selections were interspersed with trumpet obbligatos, the clashing of cymbals, and the loud playing of other musical instruments—all praising and thanking the Lord. Their theme was "He is so good! His lovingkindness lasts forever!"

And at that moment the glory of the Lord, coming as a bright cloud, filled the Temple so that the priests could not continue their work.

6 THIS IS the prayer prayed by Solomon on that occasion:

"The Lord has said that he would live in the thick darkness,

But I have made a Temple for you, O Lord, to live in forever!"

3Then the king turned around to the people and they stood to receive his blessing:

New Revised Standard

5 THUS ALL the work that Solomon did for the house of the LORD was finished. Solomon brought in the things that his father David had dedicated, and stored the silver, the gold, and all the vessels in the treasuries of the house of God.

The Ark Brought into the Temple

2 Then Solomon assembled the elders of Israel and all the heads of the tribes, the leaders of the ancestral houses of the people of Israel, in Jerusalem, to bring up the ark of the covenant of the LORD out of the city of David, which is Zion. 3 And all the Israelites assembled before the king at the festival that is in the seventh month. 4 And all the elders of Israel came, and the Levites carried the ark. 5 So they brought up the ark, the tent of meeting, and all the holy vessels that were in the tent; the priests and the Levites brought them up. 6 King Solomon and all the congregation of Israel, who had assembled before him, were before the ark, sacrificing so many sheep and oxen that they could not be numbered or counted. 7 Then the priests brought the ark of the covenant of the LORD to its place, in the inner sanctuary of the house, in the most holy place, underneath the wings of the cherubim. 8 For the cherubim spread out their wings over the place of the ark, so that the cherubim made a covering above the ark and its poles. 9 The poles were so long that the ends of the poles were seen from the holy place in front of the inner sanctuary; but they could not be seen from outside; they are there to this day. 10 There was nothing in the ark except the two tablets that Moses put there at Horeb, where the LORD made a covenantc with the people of Israel after they came out of Egypt.

11 Now when the priests came out of the holy place (for all the priests who were present had sanctified themselves, without regard to their divisions, 12and all the levitical singers, Asaph, Heman, and Jeduthun, their sons and kindred, arrayed in fine linen, with cymbals, harps, and lyres, stood east of the altar with one hundred twenty priests who were trumpeters). 13 It was the duty of the trumpeters and singers to make themselves heard in unison in praise and thanksgiving to the LORD, and when the song was raised, with trumpets and cymbals and other musical instruments, in praise to the LORD,

"For he is good,
    for his steadfast love endures forever,"

the house, the house of the LORD, was filled with a cloud, 14so that the priests could not stand to minister because of the cloud; for the glory of the LORD filled the house of God.

Dedication of the Temple

6 THEN SOLOMON said, "The LORD has said that he would reside in thick darkness. 2I have built you an exalted house, a place for you to reside in forever."

3 Then the king turned around and blessed all the assembly of Israel, while all the assembly of Israel stood. 4 And he said, "Blessed be the LORD, the God of

---

a 5:2 Tabernacle in the, and   b 5:2 to its new home in the Temple, implied.   c Heb lacks a covenant

King James

4And he said, Blessed be the Lord God of Israel, who hath with his hands fulfilled *that* which he spake with his mouth to my father David, saying,

5Since the day that I brought forth my people out of the land of Egypt I chose no city among all the tribes of Israel to build an house in, that my name might be there; neither chose I any man to be a ruler over my people Israel:

6But I have chosen Jerusalem, that my name might be there; and have chosen David to be over my people Israel.

7Now it was in the heart of David my father to build an house for the name of the Lord God of Israel.

8But the Lord said to David my father, Forasmuch as it was in thine heart to build an house for my name, thou didst well in that it was in thine heart:

9Notwithstanding thou shalt not build the house; but thy son which shall come forth out of thy loins, he shall build the house for my name.

10The Lord therefore hath performed his word that he hath spoken: for I am risen up in the room of David my father, and am set on the throne of Israel, as the Lord promised, and have built the house for the name of the Lord God of Israel.

11And in it have I put the ark, wherein *is* the covenant of the Lord, that he made with the children of Israel.

12¶ And he stood before the altar of the Lord in the presence of all the congregation of Israel, and spread forth his hands:

13For Solomon had made a brasen scaffold, of five cubits long, and five cubits broad, and three cubits high, and had set it in the midst of the court: and upon it he stood, and kneeled down upon his knees before all the congregation of Israel, and spread forth his hands toward heaven,

14And said, O Lord God of Israel, *there is* no God like thee in the heaven, nor in the earth; which keepest covenant, and *showest* mercy unto thy servants, that walk before thee with all their hearts:

15Thou which hast kept with thy servant David my father that which thou hast promised him; and spakest with thy mouth, and hast fulfilled *it* with thine hand, as *it is* this day.

16Now therefore, O Lord God of Israel, keep with thy servant David my father that which thou hast promised him, saying, There shall not fail thee a man in my sight to sit upon the throne of Israel; yet so that thy children take heed to their way to walk in my law, as thou hast walked before me.

17Now then, O Lord God of Israel, let thy word be verified, which thou hast spoken unto thy servant David.

18But will God in very deed dwell with men on the earth? behold, heaven and the heaven of heavens cannot contain thee; how much less this house which I have built!

19Have respect therefore to the prayer of thy servant, and to his supplication, O Lord my God, to hearken unto the cry and the prayer which thy servant prayeth before thee:

20That thine eyes may be open upon this house day and night, upon the place whereof thou hast said that thou wouldest put thy name there; to hearken unto the prayer which thy servant prayeth toward this place.

21Hearken therefore unto the supplications of thy servant, and of thy people Israel, which they shall make toward this place: hear thou from thy dwelling place, *even* from heaven; and when thou hearest, forgive.

22¶ If a man sin against his neighbour, and an oath be laid upon him to make him swear, and the oath come before thine altar in this house;

New International

there, the king turned around and blessed them. 4Then he said:

"Praise be to the Lord, the God of Israel, who with his hands has fulfilled what he promised with his mouth to my father David. For he said, 5'Since the day I brought my people out of Egypt, I have not chosen a city in any tribe of Israel to have a temple built for my Name to be there, nor have I chosen anyone to be the leader over my people Israel. 6But now I have chosen Jerusalem for my Name to be there, and I have chosen David to rule my people Israel.'

7"My father David had it in his heart to build a temple for the Name of the Lord, the God of Israel. 8But the Lord said to my father David, 'Because it was in your heart to build a temple for my Name, you did well to have this in your heart. 9Nevertheless, you are not the one to build the temple, but your son, who is your own flesh and blood—he is the one who will build the temple for my Name.'

10"The Lord has kept the promise he made. I have succeeded David my father and now I sit on the throne of Israel, just as the Lord promised, and I have built the temple for the Name of the Lord, the God of Israel. 11There I have placed the ark, in which is the covenant of the Lord that he made with the people of Israel."

Solomon's Prayer of Dedication

12Then Solomon stood before the altar of the Lord in front of the whole assembly of Israel and spread out his hands. 13Now he had made a bronze platform, five cubits[a] long, five cubits wide and three cubits[b] high, and had placed it in the center of the outer court. He stood on the platform and then knelt down before the whole assembly of Israel and spread out his hands toward heaven. 14He said:

"O Lord, God of Israel, there is no God like you in heaven or on earth—you who keep your covenant of love with your servants who continue wholeheartedly in your way. 15You have kept your promise to your servant David my father; with your mouth you have promised and with your hand you have fulfilled it—as it is today.

16"Now Lord, God of Israel, keep for your servant David my father the promises you made to him when you said, 'You shall never fail to have a man to sit before me on the throne of Israel, if only your sons are careful in all they do to walk before me according to my law, as you have done.' 17And now, O Lord, God of Israel, let your word that you promised your servant David come true.

18"But will God really dwell on earth with men? The heavens, even the highest heavens, cannot contain you. How much less this temple I have built! 19Yet give attention to your servant's prayer and his plea for mercy, O Lord my God. Hear the cry and the prayer that your servant is praying in your presence. 20May your eyes be open toward this temple day and night, this place of which you said you would put your Name there. May you hear the prayer your servant prays toward this place. 21Hear the supplications of your servant and of your people Israel when they pray toward this place. Hear from heaven, your dwelling place; and when you hear, forgive.

22"When a man wrongs his neighbor and is required to take an oath and he comes and swears the oath before your altar in this temple, 23then hear

---

a *13* That is, about 7 1/2 feet (about 2.3 meters)　　b *13* That is, about 4 1/2 feet (about 1.3 meters)

Living Bible

4"Blessed be the Lord God of Israel," he said to them, "—the God who talked personally to my father David and has now fulfilled the promise he made to him. For he told him, 5, 6'I have never before, since bringing my people from the land of Egypt, chosen a city anywhere in Israel as the location of my Temple where my name will be glorified; and never before have I chosen a king for my people Israel. But now I have chosen Jerusalem as that city, and David as that king.'

7"My father David wanted to build this Temple, 8but the Lord said not to. It was good to have the desire, the Lord told him, 9but he was not the one to build it: his son was chosen for that task. 10And now the Lord has done what he promised, for I have become king in my father's place, and I have built the Temple for the Name of the Lord God of Israel, 11and placed the Ark there. And in the Ark is the Covenant between the Lord and his people Israel."

12, 13As he spoke, Solomon was standing before the people on a platform in the center of the outer court, in front of the altar of the Lord. The platform was made of bronze, 7½ feet square and 4½ feet high. Now, as all the people watched, he knelt down, reached out his arms toward heaven, and prayed this prayer:

14"O Lord God of Israel, there is no God like you in all of heaven and earth. You are the God who keeps his kind promises to all those who obey you, and who are anxious to do your will. 15And you have kept your promise to my father David,c as is evident today. 16And now, O God of Israel, carry out your further promise to him that 'your descendants shall always reign over Israel if they will obey my laws as you have.' 17Yes, Lord God of Israel, please fulfill this promise too. 18But will God really live upon the earth with men? Why, even the heaven and the heaven of heavens cannot contain you—how much less this Temple which I have built!

19"How I pray that you will heed my prayers, O Lord my God! Listen to my prayer that I am praying to you now! 20, 21Look down with favor day and night upon this Temple—upon this place where you have said that you would put your name. May you always hear and answer the prayers I will pray to you as I face toward this place. Listen to my prayers and to those of your people Israel when they pray toward this Temple; yes, hear us from heaven, and when you hear, forgive.

22"Whenever someone commits a crime, and is required to swear to his innocence before this altar, 23then

New Revised Standard

Israel, who with his hand has fulfilled what he promised with his mouth to my father David, saying, 5'Since the day that I brought my people out of the land of Egypt, I have not chosen a city from any of the tribes of Israel in which to build a house, so that my name might be there, and I chose no one as ruler over my people Israel; 6but I have chosen Jerusalem in order that my name may be there, and I have chosen David to be over my people Israel.' 7My father David had it in mind to build a house for the name of the LORD, the God of Israel. 8But the LORD said to my father David, 'You did well to consider building a house for my name; 9nevertheless you shall not build the house, but your son who shall be born to you shall build the house for my name.' 10Now the LORD has fulfilled his promise that he made; for I have succeeded my father David, and sit on the throne of Israel, as the LORD promised, and have built the house for the name of the LORD, the God of Israel. 11There I have set the ark, in which is the covenant of the LORD that he made with the people of Israel."

Solomon's Prayer of Dedication

12 Then Solomond stood before the altar of the LORD in the presence of the whole assembly of Israel, and spread out his hands. 13Solomon had made a bronze platform five cubits long, five cubits wide, and three cubits high, and had set it in the court; and he stood on it. Then he knelt on his knees in the presence of the whole assembly of Israel, and spread out his hands toward heaven. 14He said, "O LORD, God of Israel, there is no God like you, in heaven or on earth, keeping covenant in steadfast love with your servants who walk before you with all their heart— 15you who have kept for your servant, my father David, what you promised to him. Indeed, you promised with your mouth and this day have fulfilled with your hand. 16Therefore, O LORD, God of Israel, keep for your servant, my father David, that which you promised him, saying, 'There shall never fail you a successor before me to sit on the throne of Israel, if only your children keep to their way, to walk in my law as you have walked before me.' 17Therefore, O LORD, God of Israel, let your word be confirmed, which you promised to your servant David.

18 "But will God indeed reside with mortals on earth? Even heaven and the highest heaven cannot contain you, how much less this house that I have built! 19Regard your servant's prayer and his plea, O LORD my God, heeding the cry and the prayer that your servant prays to you. 20May your eyes be open day and night toward this house, the place where you promised to set your name, and may you heed the prayer that your servant prays toward this place. 21And hear the plea of your servant and of your people Israel, when they pray toward this place; may you hear from heaven your dwelling place; hear and forgive.

22 "If someone sins against another and is required to take an oath and comes and swears before your altar in this house, 23may you hear from heaven, and act, and

c 6:15 to my father David, literally, "David your servant."   d Heb he

King James

23Then hear thou from heaven, and do, and judge thy servants, by requiting the wicked, by recompensing his way upon his own head; and by justifying the righteous, by giving him according to his righteousness.

24¶ And if thy people Israel be put to the worse before the enemy, because they have sinned against thee; and shall return and confess thy name, and pray and make supplication before thee in this house;

25Then hear thou from the heavens, and forgive the sin of thy people Israel, and bring them again unto the land which thou gavest to them and to their fathers.

26¶ When the heaven is shut up, and there is no rain, because they have sinned against thee; yet if they pray toward this place, and confess thy name, and turn from their sin, when thou dost afflict them;

27Then hear thou from heaven, and forgive the sin of thy servants, and of thy people Israel, when thou hast taught them the good way, wherein they should walk; and send rain upon thy land, which thou hast given unto thy people for an inheritance.

28¶ If there be dearth in the land, if there be pestilence, if there be blasting, or mildew, locusts, or caterpillars; if their enemies besiege them in the cities of their land; whatsoever sore or whatsoever sickness *there be:*

29*Then* what prayer *or* what supplication soever shall be made of any man, or of all thy people Israel, when every one shall know his own sore and his own grief, and shall spread forth his hands in this house:

30Then hear thou from heaven thy dwellingplace, and forgive, and render unto every man according unto all his ways, whose heart thou knowest; (for thou only knowest the hearts of the children of men:)

31That they may fear thee, to walk in thy ways, so long as they live in the land which thou gavest unto our fathers.

32¶ Moreover concerning the stranger, which is not of thy people Israel, but is come from a far country for thy great name's sake, and thy mighty hand, and thy stretched out arm; if they come and pray in this house;

33Then hear thou from the heavens, *even* from thy dwellingplace, and do according to all that the stranger calleth to thee for; that all people of the earth may know thy name, and fear thee, as *doth* thy people Israel, and may know that this house which I have built is called by thy name.

34If thy people go out to war against their enemies by the way that thou shalt send them, and they pray unto thee toward this city which thou hast chosen, and the house which I have built for thy name;

35Then hear thou from the heavens their prayer and their supplication, and maintain their cause.

36If they sin against thee, (for *there is* no man which sinneth not,) and thou be angry with them, and deliver them over before *their* enemies, and they carry them away captives unto a land far off or near;

37Yet *if* they bethink themselves in the land whither they are carried captive, and turn and pray unto thee in the land of their captivity, saying, We have sinned, we have done amiss, and have dealt wickedly;

38If they return to thee with all their heart and with all their soul in the land of their captivity, whither they have carried them captives, and pray toward their land, which thou gavest unto their fathers, and *toward* the city which thou hast chosen, and toward the house which I have built for thy name:

39Then hear thou from the heavens, *even* from thy dwellingplace, their prayer and their supplications, and maintain their cause, and forgive thy people which have sinned against thee.

40Now, my God, let, I beseech thee, thine eyes be open, and *let* thine ears *be* attent unto the prayer *that is made* in this place.

New International

from heaven and act. Judge between your servants, repaying the guilty by bringing down on his own head what he has done. Declare the innocent not guilty and so establish his innocence.

24"When your people Israel have been defeated by an enemy because they have sinned against you and when they turn back and confess your name, praying and making supplication before you in this temple, 25then hear from heaven and forgive the sin of your people Israel and bring them back to the land you gave to them and their fathers.

26"When the heavens are shut up and there is no rain because your people have sinned against you, and when they pray toward this place and confess your name and turn from their sin because you have afflicted them, 27then hear from heaven and forgive the sin of your servants, your people Israel. Teach them the right way to live, and send rain on the land you gave your people for an inheritance.

28"When famine or plague comes to the land, or blight or mildew, locusts or grasshoppers, or when enemies besiege them in any of their cities, whatever disaster or disease may come, 29and when a prayer or plea is made by any of your people Israel—each one aware of his afflictions and pains, and spreading out his hands toward this temple— 30then hear from heaven, your dwelling place. Forgive, and deal with each man according to all he does, since you know his heart (for you alone know the hearts of men), 31so that they will fear you and walk in your ways all the time they live in the land you gave our fathers.

32"As for the foreigner who does not belong to your people Israel but has come from a distant land because of your great name and your mighty hand and your outstretched arm—when he comes and prays toward this temple, 33then hear from heaven, your dwelling place, and do whatever the foreigner asks of you, so that all the peoples of the earth may know your name and fear you, as do your own people Israel, and may know that this house I have built bears your Name.

34"When your people go to war against their enemies, wherever you send them, and when they pray to you toward this city you have chosen and the temple I have built for your Name, 35then hear from heaven their prayer and their plea, and uphold their cause.

36"When they sin against you—for there is no one who does not sin—and you become angry with them and give them over to the enemy, who takes them captive to a land far away or near; 37and if they have a change of heart in the land where they are held captive, and repent and plead with you in the land of their captivity and say, 'We have sinned, we have done wrong and acted wickedly'; 38and if they turn back to you with all their heart and soul in the land of their captivity where they were taken, and pray toward the land you gave their fathers, toward the city you have chosen and toward the temple I have built for your Name; 39then from heaven, your dwelling place, hear their prayer and their pleas, and uphold their cause. And forgive your people, who have sinned against you.

40"Now, my God, may your eyes be open and your ears attentive to the prayers offered in this place.

Living Bible

hear from heaven and punish him if he is lying, or else declare him innocent.

24"If your people Israel are destroyed before their enemies because they have sinned against you, and if they turn to you and call themselves your people, and pray to you here in this Temple, 25then listen to them from heaven and forgive their sins and give them back this land you gave to their fathers.

26"When the skies are shut and there is no rain because of our sins, and then we pray toward this Temple and claim you as our God, and turn from our sins because you have punished us, 27then listen from heaven and forgive the sins of your people, and teach them what is right; and send rain upon this land which you have given to your people as their own property.

28"If there is a famine in the land, or plagues, or crop disease, or attacks of locusts or caterpillars, or if your people's enemies are in the land besieging our cities— whatever the trouble is— 29listen to every individual's prayer concerning his private sorrow, as well as all the public prayers. 30Hear from heaven where you live, and forgive, and give each one whatever he deserves, for you know the hearts of all mankind. 31Then they will reverence you forever, and will continually walk where you tell them to go.ᵃ

32"And when foreigners hear of your power, and come from distant lands to worship your great name, and to pray toward this Temple, 33hear them from heaven where you live, and do what they request of you. Then all the peoples of the earth will hear of your fame and will reverence you, just as your people Israel do; and they too will know that this Temple I have built is truly yours.

34"If your people go out at your command to fight their enemies, and they pray toward this city of Jerusalem which you have chosen, and this Temple which I have built for your name, 35then hear their prayers from heaven and give them success.

36"If they sin against you (and who has never sinned?) and you become angry with them, and you let their enemies defeat them and take them away as captives to some foreign nation near or far, 37, 38and if in that land of exile they turn to you again, and face toward this land you gave their fathers, and this city and your Temple I have built, and plead with you with all their hearts to forgive them, 39then hear from heaven where you live and help them and forgive your people who have sinned against you.

40"Yes, O my God, be wide awake and attentive to all the prayers made to you in this place. 41And now,

New Revised Standard

judge your servants, repaying the guilty by bringing their conduct on their own head, and vindicating those who are in the right by rewarding them in accordance with their righteousness.

24 "When your people Israel, having sinned against you, are defeated before an enemy but turn again to you, confess your name, pray and plead with you in this house, 25may you hear from heaven, and forgive the sin of your people Israel, and bring them again to the land that you gave to them and to their ancestors.

26 "When heaven is shut up and there is no rain because they have sinned against you, and then they pray toward this place, confess your name, and turn from their sin, because you punish them, 27may you hear in heaven, forgive the sin of your servants, your people Israel, when you teach them the good way in which they should walk; and send down rain upon your land, which you have given to your people as an inheritance.

28 "If there is famine in the land, if there is plague, blight, mildew, locust, or caterpillar; if their enemies besiege them in any of the settlements of the lands; whatever suffering, whatever sickness there is; 29whatever prayer, whatever plea from any individual or from all your people Israel, all knowing their own suffering and their own sorrows so that they stretch out their hands toward this house; 30may you hear from heaven, your dwelling place, forgive, and render to all whose heart you know, according to all their ways, for only you know the human heart. 31Thus may they fear you and walk in your ways all the days that they live in the land that you gave to our ancestors.

32 "Likewise when foreigners, who are not of your people Israel, come from a distant land because of your great name, and your mighty hand, and your outstretched arm, when they come and pray toward this house, 33may you hear from heaven your dwelling place, and do whatever the foreigners ask of you, in order that all the peoples of the earth may know your name and fear you, as do your people Israel, and that they may know that your name has been invoked on this house that I have built.

34 "If your people go out to battle against their enemies, by whatever way you shall send them, and they pray to you toward this city that you have chosen and the house that I have built for your name, 35then hear from heaven their prayer and their plea, and maintain their cause.

36 "If they sin against you—for there is no one who does not sin—and you are angry with them and give them to an enemy, so that they are carried away captive to a land far or near; 37then if they come to their senses in the land to which they have been taken captive, and repent, and plead with you in the land of their captivity, saying, 'We have sinned, and have done wrong; we have acted wickedly'; 38if they repent with all their heart and soul in the land of their captivity, to which they were taken captive, and pray toward their land, which you gave to their ancestors, the city that you have chosen, and the house that I have built for your name, 39then hear from heaven your dwelling place their prayer and their pleas, maintain their cause and forgive your people who have sinned against you. 40Now, O my God, let your eyes be open and your ears attentive to prayer from this place.

ᵃ 6:31 where you tell them to go, or, "as long as they are living in this land which you gave to our fathers."

King James

41Now therefore arise, O Lord God, into thy resting place, thou, and the ark of thy strength: let thy priests, O Lord God, be clothed with salvation, and let thy saints rejoice in goodness.

42O Lord God, turn not away the face of thine anointed: remember the mercies of David thy servant.

7 NOW WHEN Solomon had made an end of praying, the fire came down from heaven, and consumed the burnt offering and the sacrifices; and the glory of the Lord filled the house.

2And the priests could not enter into the house of the Lord, because the glory of the Lord had filled the Lord's house.

3And when all the children of Israel saw how the fire came down, and the glory of the Lord upon the house, they bowed themselves with their faces to the ground upon the pavement, and worshipped, and praised the Lord, saying, For he is good; for his mercy endureth for ever.

4¶ Then the king and all the people offered sacrifices before the Lord.

5And king Solomon offered a sacrifice of twenty and two thousand oxen, and an hundred and twenty thousand sheep: so the king and all the people dedicated the house of God.

6And the priests waited on their offices: the Levites also with instruments of music of the Lord, which David the king had made to praise the Lord, because his mercy endureth for ever, when David praised by their ministry; and the priests sounded trumpets before them, and all Israel stood.

7Moreover Solomon hallowed the middle of the court that was before the house of the Lord: for there he offered burnt offerings, and the fat of the peace offerings, because the brasen altar which Solomon had made was not able to receive the burnt offerings, and the meat offerings, and the fat.

8¶ Also at the same time Solomon kept the feast seven days, and all Israel with him, a very great congregation, from the entering in of Hamath unto the river of Egypt.

9And in the eighth day they made a solemn assembly: for they kept the dedication of the altar seven days, and the feast seven days.

10And on the three and twentieth day of the seventh month he sent the people away into their tents, glad and merry in heart for the goodness that the Lord had shown unto David, and to Solomon, and to Israel his people.

11Thus Solomon finished the house of the Lord, and the king's house: and all that came into Solomon's heart to make in the house of the Lord, and in his own house, he prosperously effected.

12¶ And the Lord appeared to Solomon by night, and said unto him, I have heard thy prayer, and have chosen this place to myself for an house of sacrifice.

13If I shut up heaven that there be no rain, or if I command the locusts to devour the land, or if I send pestilence among my people;

14If my people, which are called by my name, shall humble themselves, and pray, and seek my face, and turn from their wicked ways; then will I hear from heaven, and will forgive their sin, and will heal their land.

15Now mine eyes shall be open, and mine ears attent unto the prayer that is made in this place.

16For now have I chosen and sanctified this house, that my name may be there for ever: and mine eyes and mine heart shall be there perpetually.

New International

41"Now arise, O Lord God, and come to
　　your resting place,
　　you and the ark of your might.
May your priests, O Lord God, be clothed
　　with salvation,
　　may your saints rejoice in your goodness.
42O Lord God, do not reject your anointed
　　one.
Remember the great love promised to
　　David your servant."

The Dedication of the Temple

7 WHEN SOLOMON finished praying, fire came down from heaven and consumed the burnt offering and the sacrifices, and the glory of the Lord filled the temple. 2The priests could not enter the temple of the Lord because the glory of the Lord filled it. 3When all the Israelites saw the fire coming down and the glory of the Lord above the temple, they knelt on the pavement with their faces to the ground, and they worshiped and gave thanks to the Lord, saying,

"He is good;
　　his love endures forever."

4Then the king and all the people offered sacrifices before the Lord. 5And King Solomon offered a sacrifice of twenty-two thousand head of cattle and a hundred and twenty thousand sheep and goats. So the king and all the people dedicated the temple of God. 6The priests took their positions, as did the Levites with the Lord's musical instruments, which King David had made for praising the Lord and which were used when he gave thanks, saying, "His love endures forever." Opposite the Levites, the priests blew their trumpets, and all the Israelites were standing.

7Solomon consecrated the middle part of the courtyard in front of the temple of the Lord, and there he offered burnt offerings and the fat of the fellowship offerings,a because the bronze altar he had made could not hold the burnt offerings, the grain offerings and the fat portions.

8So Solomon observed the festival at that time for seven days, and all Israel with him—a vast assembly, people from Lebob Hamath to the Wadi of Egypt. 9On the eighth day they held an assembly, for they had celebrated the dedication of the altar for seven days and the festival for seven days more. 10On the twenty-third day of the seventh month he sent the people to their homes, joyful and glad in heart for the good things the Lord had done for David and Solomon and for his people Israel.

The Lord Appears to Solomon

11When Solomon had finished the temple of the Lord and the royal palace, and had succeeded in carrying out all he had in mind to do in the temple of the Lord and in his own palace, 12the Lord appeared to him at night and said:

"I have heard your prayer and have chosen this place for myself as a temple for sacrifices.

13"When I shut up the heavens so that there is no rain, or command locusts to devour the land or send a plague among my people, 14if my people, who are called by my name, will humble themselves and pray and seek my face and turn from their wicked ways, then will I hear from heaven and will forgive their sin and will heal their land. 15Now my eyes will be open and my ears attentive to the prayers offered in this place. 16I have chosen and consecrated this temple so that my Name may be there forever. My eyes and my heart will always be there.

---

a 7 Traditionally peace offerings　　b 8 Or from the entrance to

Living Bible

O Lord God, arise and enter this resting place of yours where the Ark of your strength has been placed. Let your priests, O Lord God, be clothed with salvation, and let your people rejoice in your kind deeds. 42O Lord God, do not ignore me—do not turn your face away from me, your anointed one. Oh, remember your love for David and your kindness to him."

7 AS SOLOMON finished praying, fire flashed down from heaven and burned up the sacrifices! And the glory of the Lord filled the Temple, so that the priests couldn't enter! 3All the people had been watching and now they fell flat on the pavement, and worshiped and thanked the Lord.

"How good he is!" they exclaimed. "He is always so loving and kind."

4, 5Then the king and all the people dedicated the Temple by sacrificing burnt offerings to the Lord. King Solomon's contribution for this purpose was 22,000 oxen and 120,000 sheep. 6The priests were standing at their posts of duty, and the Levites were playing their thanksgiving song, "His Lovingkindness Is Forever," using the musical instruments King David himself had made and had used to praise the Lord. Then, when the priests blew the trumpets, all the people stood again. 7Solomon consecrated the inner court of the Temple for use that day as a place of sacrifice, because there were too many sacrifices for the bronze altar to accommodate.

8For the next seven days, they celebrated the Tabernacle Festival, with large crowds coming in from all over Israel; they arrived from as far away as Hamath at one end of the country to the brook of Egypt at the other. 9A final religious service was held on the eighth day. 10Then, on October 7, he sent the people home, joyful and happy because the Lord had been so good to David and Solomon and to his people Israel.

11So Solomon finished building the Temple as well as his own palace. He completed what he had planned to do.

12One night the Lord appeared to Solomon and told him, "I have heard your prayer and have chosen this Temple as the place where I want you to sacrifice to me. 13If I shut up the heavens so that there is no rain, or if I command the locust swarms to eat up all of your crops, or if I send an epidemic among you, 14then if my people will humble themselves and pray, and search for me, and turn from their wicked ways, I will hear them from heaven and forgive their sins and heal their land. 15I will listen, wide awake, to every prayer made in this place. 16For I have chosen this Temple and sanctified it to be my home forever; my eyes and my heart shall always be here.

New Revised Standard

41 "Now rise up, O Lord God, and go to your
        resting place,
     you and the ark of your might.
   Let your priests, O Lord God, be clothed
        with salvation,
     and let your faithful rejoice in your
        goodness.
42 O Lord God, do not reject your anointed one.
     Remember your steadfast love for your
        servant David."

Solomon Dedicates the Temple

7 WHEN SOLOMON had ended his prayer, fire came down from heaven and consumed the burnt offering and the sacrifices; and the glory of the Lord filled the temple. 2The priests could not enter the house of the Lord, because the glory of the Lord filled the Lord's house. 3When all the people of Israel saw the fire come down and the glory of the Lord on the temple, they bowed down on the pavement with their faces to the ground, and worshiped and gave thanks to the Lord, saying,
   "For he is good,
     for his steadfast love endures forever."

4 Then the king and all the people offered sacrifice before the Lord. 5King Solomon offered as a sacrifice twenty-two thousand oxen and one hundred twenty thousand sheep. So the king and all the people dedicated the house of God. 6The priests stood at their posts; the Levites also, with the instruments for music to the Lord that King David had made for giving thanks to the Lord—for his steadfast love endures forever—whenever David offered praises by their ministry. Opposite them the priests sounded trumpets; and all Israel stood.

7 Solomon consecrated the middle of the court that was in front of the house of the Lord; for there he offered the burnt offerings and the fat of the offerings of well-being because the bronze altar Solomon had made could not hold the burnt offering and the grain offering and the fat parts.

8 At that time Solomon held the festival for seven days, and all Israel with him, a very great congregation, from Lebo-hamath to the Wadi of Egypt. 9On the eighth day they held a solemn assembly; for they had observed the dedication of the altar seven days and the festival seven days. 10On the twenty-third day of the seventh month he sent the people away to their homes, joyful and in good spirits because of the goodness that the Lord had shown to David and to Solomon and to his people Israel.

11 Thus Solomon finished the house of the Lord and the king's house; all that Solomon had planned to do in the house of the Lord and in his own house he successfully accomplished.

God's Second Appearance to Solomon

12 Then the Lord appeared to Solomon in the night and said to him: "I have heard your prayer, and have chosen this place for myself as a house of sacrifice. 13When I shut up the heavens so that there is no rain, or command the locust to devour the land, or send pestilence among my people, 14if my people who are called by my name humble themselves, pray, seek my face, and turn from their wicked ways, then I will hear from heaven, and will forgive their sin and heal their land. 15Now my eyes will be open and my ears attentive to the prayer that is made in this place. 16For now I have chosen and consecrated this house so that my name may be there forever; my eyes and my heart will be there for all time. 17As for you, if you walk before me, as your father

King James

17And as for thee, if thou wilt walk before me, as David thy father walked, and do according to all that I have commanded thee, and shalt observe my statutes and my judgments;

18Then will I stablish the throne of thy kingdom, according as I have covenanted with David thy father, saying, There shall not fail thee a man *to be* ruler in Israel.

19But if ye turn away, and forsake my statutes and my commandments, which I have set before you, and shall go and serve other gods, and worship them;

20Then will I pluck them up by the roots out of my land which I have given them; and this house, which I have sanctified for my name, will I cast out of my sight, and will make it *to be* a proverb and a byword among all nations.

21And this house, which is high, shall be an astonishment to every one that passeth by it; so that he shall say, Why hath the LORD done thus unto this land, and unto this house?

22And it shall be answered, Because they forsook the LORD God of their fathers, which brought them forth out of the land of Egypt, and laid hold on other gods, and worshipped them, and served them: therefore hath he brought all this evil upon them.

8 AND IT came to pass at the end of twenty years, wherein Solomon had built the house of the LORD, and his own house,

2That the cities which Huram had restored to Solomon, Solomon built them, and caused the children of Israel to dwell there.

3And Solomon went to Hamath-zobah, and prevailed against it.

4And he built Tadmor in the wilderness, and all the store cities, which he built in Hamath.

5Also he built Beth-horon the upper, and Beth-horon the nether, fenced cities, with walls, gates, and bars;

6And Baalath, and all the store cities that Solomon had, and all the chariot cities, and the cities of the horsemen, and all that Solomon desired to build in Jerusalem, and in Lebanon, and throughout all the land of his dominion.

7¶ *As for* all the people *that were* left of the Hittites, and the Amorites, and the Perizzites, and the Hivites, and the Jebusites, which *were* not of Israel,

8*But* of their children, who were left after them in the land, whom the children of Israel consumed not, them did Solomon make to pay tribute until this day.

9But of the children of Israel did Solomon make no servants for his work; but they *were* men of war, and chief of his captains, and captains of his chariots and horsemen.

10And these *were* the chief of king Solomon's officers, *even* two hundred and fifty, that bare rule over the people.

11¶ And Solomon brought up the daughter of Pharaoh out of the city of David unto the house that he had built for her: for he said, My wife shall not dwell in the house of David king of Israel, because *the places are* holy, whereunto the ark of the LORD hath come.

12¶ Then Solomon offered burnt offerings unto the LORD on the altar of the LORD, which he had built before the porch,

13Even after a certain rate every day, offering according to the commandment of Moses, on the sabbaths, and on the new moons, and on the solemn feasts, three times in the year, *even* in the feast of unleavened bread, and in the feast of weeks, and in the feast of tabernacles.

New International

17"As for you, if you walk before me as David your father did, and do all I command, and observe my decrees and laws, 18I will establish your royal throne, as I covenanted with David your father when I said, 'You shall never fail to have a man to rule over Israel.'

19"But if youa turn away and forsake the decrees and commands I have given youa and go off to serve other gods and worship them, 20then I will uproot Israel from my land, which I have given them, and will reject this temple I have consecrated for my Name. I will make it a byword and an object of ridicule among all peoples. 21And though this temple is now so imposing, all who pass by will be appalled and say, 'Why has the LORD done such a thing to this land and to this temple?' 22People will answer, 'Because they have forsaken the LORD, the God of their fathers, who brought them out of Egypt, and have embraced other gods, worshiping and serving them—that is why he brought all this disaster on them.' "

Solomon's Other Activities

8 AT THE end of twenty years, during which Solomon built the temple of the LORD and his own palace, 2Solomon rebuilt the villages that Hiramb had given him, and settled Israelites in them. 3Solomon then went to Hamath Zobah and captured it. 4He also built up Tadmor in the desert and all the store cities he had built in Hamath. 5He rebuilt Upper Beth Horon and Lower Beth Horon as fortified cities, with walls and with gates and bars, 6as well as Baalath and all his store cities, and all the cities for his chariots and for his horsesc—whatever he desired to build in Jerusalem, in Lebanon and throughout all the territory he ruled.

7All the people left from the Hittites, Amorites, Perizzites, Hivites and Jebusites (these peoples were not Israelites), 8that is, their descendants remaining in the land, whom the Israelites had not destroyed—these Solomon conscripted for his slave labor force, as it is to this day. 9But Solomon did not make slaves of the Israelites for his work; they were his fighting men, commanders of his captains, and commanders of his chariots and charioteers. 10They were also King Solomon's chief officials—two hundred and fifty officials supervising the men.

11Solomon brought Pharaoh's daughter up from the City of David to the palace he had built for her, for he said, "My wife must not live in the palace of David king of Israel, because the places the ark of the LORD has entered are holy."

12On the altar of the LORD that he had built in front of the portico, Solomon sacrificed burnt offerings to the LORD, 13according to the daily requirement for offerings commanded by Moses for Sabbaths, New Moons and the three annual feasts—the Feast of Unleavened Bread, the Feast of Weeks and the Feast of Tabernacles. 14In

---

a *19* The Hebrew is plural.   b *2* Hebrew *Huram*, a variant of *Hiram*; also in verse 18   c *6* Or *charioteers*

Living Bible

17"As for yourself, if you follow me as your father David did, 18then I will see to it that you and your descendants will always be the kings of Israel; 19but if you don't follow me, if you refuse the laws I have given you, and worship idols, 20then I will destroy my people from this land of mine which I have given them, and this Temple shall be destroyed even though I have sanctified it for myself. Instead, I will make it a public horror and disgrace. 21Instead of its being famous, all who pass by will be incredulous.

" 'Why has the Lord done such a terrible thing to this land and to this Temple?' they will ask.

22"And the answer will be, 'Because his people abandoned the Lord God of their fathers, the God who brought them out of the land of Egypt, and they worshiped other gods instead. That is why he has done all this to them.' "

8 IT WAS now twenty years since Solomon had become king, and the great building projects of the Lord's Temple and his own royal palace were completed. 2He now turned his energies to rebuilding the cities which King Hiram of Tyre had given to him, and he relocated some of the people of Israel into them. 3It was at this time, too, that Solomon fought against the city of Hamath-zobah and conquered it. 4He built Tadmor in the desert, and built cities in Hamath as supply centers. 5He fortified the cities of upper Beth-horon and lower Beth-horon, both being supply centers, building their walls and installing barred gates. 6He also built Baalath and other supply centers at this time, and constructed cities where his chariots and horses were kept. He built to his heart's desire in Jerusalem and Lebanon and throughout the entire realm.

7, 8He began the practice that still continues of conscripting as slave laborers the Hittites, Amorites, Perizzites, Hivites, and Jebusites—the descendants of those nations which the Israelis had not completely wiped out. 9However, he didn't make slaves of any of the Israeli citizens, but used them as soldiers, officers, charioteers, and cavalrymen; 10also, two hundred fifty of them were government officials who administered all public affairs.

11Solomon now moved his wife (she was Pharaoh's daughter) from the City of David sector of Jerusalem to the new palace he had built for her. For he said, "She must not live in King David's palace, for the Ark of the Lord was there and it is holy ground."

12Then Solomon sacrificed burnt offerings to the Lord on the altar he had built in front of the porch of the Temple. 13The number of sacrifices differed from day to day in accordance with the instructions Moses had given; there were extra sacrifices on the Sabbaths, on new moon festivals, and at the three annual festivals—the Passover celebration, the Festival of Weeks, and the Festival of Tabernacles. 14In assigning the priests to

New Revised Standard

David walked, doing according to all that I have commanded you and keeping my statutes and my ordinances, 18then I will establish your royal throne, as I made covenant with your father David saying, 'You shall never lack a successor to rule over Israel.'

19 "But if you[d] turn aside and forsake my statutes and my commandments that I have set before you, and go and serve other gods and worship them, 20then I will pluck you[e] up from the land that I have given you;[e] and this house, which I have consecrated for my name, I will cast out of my sight, and will make it a proverb and a byword among all peoples. 21And regarding this house, now exalted, everyone passing by will be astonished, and say, 'Why has the LORD done such a thing to this land and to this house?' 22Then they will say, 'Because they abandoned the LORD the God of their ancestors who brought them out of the land of Egypt, and they adopted other gods, and worshiped them and served them; therefore he has brought all this calamity upon them.' "

Various Activities of Solomon

8 AT THE end of twenty years, during which Solomon had built the house of the LORD and his own house, 2Solomon rebuilt the cities that Huram had given to him, and settled the people of Israel in them.

3 Solomon went to Hamath-zobah, and captured it. 4He built Tadmor in the wilderness and all the storage towns that he built in Hamath. 5He also built Upper Beth-horon and Lower Beth-horon, fortified cities, with walls, gates, and bars, 6and Baalath, as well as all Solomon's storage towns, and all the towns for his chariots, the towns for his cavalry, and whatever Solomon desired to build, in Jerusalem, in Lebanon, and in all the land of his dominion. 7All the people who were left of the Hittites, the Amorites, the Perizzites, the Hivites, and the Jebusites, who were not of Israel, 8from their descendants who were still left in the land, whom the people of Israel had not destroyed—these Solomon conscripted for forced labor, as is still the case today. 9But of the people of Israel Solomon made no slaves for his work; they were soldiers, and his officers, the commanders of his chariotry and cavalry. 10These were the chief officers of King Solomon, two hundred fifty of them, who exercised authority over the people.

11 Solomon brought Pharaoh's daughter from the city of David to the house that he had built for her, for he said, "My wife shall not live in the house of King David of Israel, for the places to which the ark of the LORD has come are holy."

12 Then Solomon offered up burnt offerings to the LORD on the altar of the LORD that he had built in front of the vestibule, 13as the duty of each day required, offering according to the commandment of Moses for the sabbaths, the new moons, and the three annual festivals—the festival of unleavened bread, the festival of weeks, and the festival of booths. 14According to the

King James

14¶ And he appointed, according to the order of David his father, the courses of the priests to their service, and the Levites to their charges, to praise and minister before the priests, as the duty of every day required: the porters also by their courses at every gate: for so had David the man of God commanded.

15And they departed not from the commandment of the king unto the priests and Levites concerning any matter, or concerning the treasures.

16Now all the work of Solomon was prepared unto the day of the foundation of the house of the LORD, and until it was finished. *So* the house of the LORD was perfected.

17¶ Then went Solomon to Ezion-geber, and to Eloth, at the sea side in the land of Edom.

18And Huram sent him by the hands of his servants ships, and servants that had knowledge of the sea; and they went with the servants of Solomon to Ophir, and took thence four hundred and fifty talents of gold, and brought *them* to king Solomon.

9 AND WHEN the queen of Sheba heard of the fame of Solomon, she came to prove Solomon with hard questions at Jerusalem, with a very great company, and camels that bare spices, and gold in abundance, and precious stones: and when she was come to Solomon, she communed with him of all that was in her heart.

2And Solomon told her all her questions: and there was nothing hid from Solomon which he told her not.

3And when the queen of Sheba had seen the wisdom of Solomon, and the house that he had built,

4And the meat of his table, and the sitting of his servants, and the attendance of his ministers, and their apparel; his cupbearers also, and their apparel; and his ascent by which he went up into the house of the LORD; there was no more spirit in her.

5And she said to the king, *It was* a true report which I heard in mine own land of thine acts, and of thy wisdom:

6Howbeit I believed not their words, until I came, and mine eyes had seen *it:* and, behold, the one half of the greatness of thy wisdom was not told me: *for* thou exceedest the fame that I heard.

7Happy *are* thy men, and happy *are* these thy servants, which stand continually before thee, and hear thy wisdom.

8Blessed be the LORD thy God, which delighted in thee to set thee on his throne, *to be* king for the LORD thy God: because thy God loved Israel, to establish them for ever, therefore made he thee king over them, to do judgment and justice.

9And she gave the king an hundred and twenty talents of gold, and of spices great abundance, and precious stones: neither was there any such spice as the queen of Sheba gave king Solomon.

10And the servants also of Huram, and the servants of Solomon, which brought gold from Ophir, brought algum trees and precious stones.

11And the king made *of* the algum trees terraces to the house of the LORD, and to the king's palace, and harps and psalteries for singers: and there were none such seen before in the land of Judah.

12And king Solomon gave to the queen of Sheba all her desire, whatsoever she asked, beside *that* which she had brought unto the king. So she turned, and went away to her own land, she and her servants.

New International

keeping with the ordinance of his father David, he appointed the divisions of the priests for their duties, and the Levites to lead the praise and to assist the priests according to each day's requirement. He also appointed the gatekeepers by divisions for the various gates, because this was what David the man of God had ordered.

15They did not deviate from the king's commands to the priests or to the Levites in any matter, including that of the treasures.

16All Solomon's work was carried out, from the day the foundation of the temple of the LORD was laid until its completion. So the temple of the LORD was finished.

17Then Solomon went to Ezion Geber and Elath on the coast of Edom. 18And Hiram sent him ships commanded by his own officers, men who knew the sea. These, with Solomon's men, sailed to Ophir and brought back four hundred and fifty talents[a] of gold, which they delivered to King Solomon.

The Queen of Sheba Visits Solomon

9 WHEN THE queen of Sheba heard of Solomon's fame, she came to Jerusalem to test him with hard questions. Arriving with a very great caravan—with camels carrying spices, large quantities of gold, and precious stones—she came to Solomon and talked with him about all she had on her mind. 2Solomon answered all her questions; nothing was too hard for him to explain to her. 3When the queen of Sheba saw the wisdom of Solomon, as well as the palace he had built, 4the food on his table, the seating of his officials, the attending servants in their robes, the cupbearers in their robes and the burnt offerings he made at[b] the temple of the LORD, she was overwhelmed.

5She said to the king, "The report I heard in my own country about your achievements and your wisdom is true. 6But I did not believe what they said until I came and saw with my own eyes. Indeed, not even half the greatness of your wisdom was told me; you have far exceeded the report I heard. 7How happy your men must be! How happy your officials, who continually stand before you and hear your wisdom! 8Praise be to the LORD your God, who has delighted in you and placed you on his throne as king to rule for the LORD your God. Because of the love of your God for Israel and his desire to uphold them forever, he has made you king over them, to maintain justice and righteousness."

9Then she gave the king 120 talents[c] of gold, large quantities of spices, and precious stones. There had never been such spices as those the queen of Sheba gave to King Solomon.

10(The men of Hiram and the men of Solomon brought gold from Ophir; they also brought algumwood[d] and precious stones. 11The king used the algumwood to make steps for the temple of the LORD and for the royal palace, and to make harps and lyres for the musicians. Nothing like them had ever been seen in Judah.)

12King Solomon gave the queen of Sheba all she desired and asked for; he gave her more than she had brought to him. Then she left and returned with her retinue to her own country.

---

a *18* That is, about 17 tons (about 16 metric tons)   b *4* Or *the ascent by which he went up to*   c *9* That is, about 4 1/2 tons (about 4 metric tons)   d *10* Probably a variant of *almugwood*

Living Bible

their posts of duty he followed the organizational chart prepared by his father David; he also assigned the Levites to their work of praise and of helping the priests in each day's duties; and he assigned the gatekeepers to their gates. 15Solomon did not deviate in any way from David's instructions concerning these matters and concerning the treasury personnel. 16Thus Solomon successfully completed the construction of the Temple.

17, 18Then he went to the seaport towns of Eziongeber and Eloth, in Edom, to launch a fleet presented to him by King Hiram. These ships, with King Hiram's experienced crews working alongside Solomon's men, went to Ophir and brought back to him several million dollars worth of gold on each trip!

9 WHEN THE Queen of Sheba heard of Solomon's fabled wisdom, she came to Jerusalem to test him with hard questions. A very great retinue of aides and servants accompanied her, including camel-loads of spices, gold, and jewels. 2And Solomon answered all her problems. Nothing was hidden from him; he could explain everything to her. 3When she discovered how wise he really was, and how breathtaking the beauty of his palace, 4and how wonderful the food at his tables, and how many servants and aides he had, and when she saw their spectacular uniforms and his stewards in full regalia, and saw the size of the men in his bodyguard, she could scarcely believe it!

5Finally she exclaimed to the king, "Everything I heard about you in my own country is true! 6I didn't believe it until I got here and saw it with my own eyes. Your wisdom is far greater than I could ever have imagined. 7What a privilege for these men of yours to stand here and listen to you talk! 8Blessed be the Lord your God! How he must love Israel to give them a just king like you! He wants them to be a great, strong nation forever."

9She gave the king a gift of over a million dollars in gold, and great quantities of spices of incomparable quality, and many, many jewels. 10King Hiram's and King Solomon's crews brought gold from Ophir, also sandalwood and jewels. 11The king used the sandalwood to make terraced steps for the Temple and the palace, and to construct harps and lyres for the choir. Never before had there been such beautiful instruments in all the land of Judah.

12King Solomon gave the Queen of Sheba gifts of the same value as she had brought to him, plus everything else she asked for! Then she and her retinue returned to their own land.

New Revised Standard

ordinance of his father David, he appointed the divisions of the priests for their service, and the Levites for their offices of praise and ministry alongside the priests as the duty of each day required, and the gatekeepers in their divisions for the several gates; for so David the man of God had commanded. 15They did not turn away from what the king had commanded the priests and Levites regarding anything at all, or regarding the treasuries.

16 Thus all the work of Solomon was accomplished frome the day the foundation of the house of the LORD was laid until the house of the LORD was finished completely.

17 Then Solomon went to Ezion-geber and Eloth on the shore of the sea, in the land of Edom. 18Huram sent him, in the care of his servants, ships and servants familiar with the sea. They went to Ophir, together with the servants of Solomon, and imported from there four hundred fifty talents of gold and brought it to King Solomon.

Visit of the Queen of Sheba

9 WHEN THE queen of Sheba heard of the fame of Solomon, she came to Jerusalem to test him with hard questions, having a very great retinue and camels bearing spices and very much gold and precious stones. When she came to Solomon, she discussed with him all that was on her mind. 2Solomon answered all her questions; there was nothing hidden from Solomon that he could not explain to her. 3When the queen of Sheba had observed the wisdom of Solomon, the house that he had built, 4the food of his table, the seating of his officials, and the attendance of his servants, and their clothing, his valets, and their clothing, and his burnt offeringsf that he offered at the house of the LORD, there was no more spirit left in her.

5 So she said to the king, "The report was true that I heard in my own land of your accomplishments and of your wisdom, 6but I did not believe theg reports until I came and my own eyes saw it. Not even half of the greatness of your wisdom had been told to me; you far surpass the report that I had heard. 7Happy are your people! Happy are these your servants, who continually attend you and hear your wisdom! 8Blessed be the LORD your God, who has delighted in you and set you on his throne as king for the LORD your God. Because your God loved Israel and would establish them forever, he has made you king over them, that you may execute justice and righteousness." 9Then she gave the king one hundred twenty talents of gold, a very great quantity of spices, and precious stones: there were no spices such as those that the queen of Sheba gave to King Solomon.

10 Moreover the servants of Huram and the servants of Solomon who brought gold from Ophir brought algum wood and precious stones. 11From the algum wood, the king made stepsh for the house of the LORD and for the king's house, lyres also and harps for the singers; there never was seen the like of them before in the land of Judah.

12 Meanwhile King Solomon granted the queen of Sheba every desire that she expressed, well beyond what she had brought to the king. Then she returned to her own land, with her servants.

---

e Gk Syr Vg: Heb to   f Gk Syr Vg 1 Kings 10.5: Heb ascent   g Heb their
h Gk Vg: Meaning of Heb uncertain

King James

13¶ Now the weight of gold that came to Solomon in one year was six hundred and threescore and six talents of gold;

14Beside *that which* chapmen and merchants brought. And all the kings of Arabia and governors of the country brought gold and silver to Solomon.

15¶ And king Solomon made two hundred targets *of* beaten gold: six hundred *shekels* of beaten gold went to one target.

16And three hundred shields *made he of* beaten gold: three hundred *shekels* of gold went to one shield. And the king put them in the house of the forest of Lebanon.

17Moreover the king made a great throne of ivory, and overlaid it with pure gold.

18And *there were* six steps to the throne, with a footstool of gold, *which were* fastened to the throne, and stays on each side of the sitting place, and two lions standing by the stays:

19And twelve lions stood there on the one side and on the other upon the six steps. There was not the like made in any kingdom.

20¶ And all the drinking vessels of king Solomon *were of* gold, and all the vessels of the house of the forest of Lebanon *were of* pure gold: none *were of* silver; it was *not* any thing accounted of in the days of Solomon.

21For the king's ships went to Tarshish with the servants of Huram: every three years once came the ships of Tarshish bringing gold, and silver, ivory, and apes, and peacocks.

22And king Solomon passed all the kings of the earth in riches and wisdom.

23¶ And all the kings of the earth sought the presence of Solomon, to hear his wisdom, that God had put in his heart.

24And they brought every man his present, vessels of silver, and vessels of gold, and raiment, harness, and spices, horses, and mules, a rate year by year.

25¶ And Solomon had four thousand stalls for horses and chariots, and twelve thousand horsemen; whom he bestowed in the chariot cities, and with the king at Jerusalem.

26¶ And he reigned over all the kings from the river even unto the land of the Philistines, and to the border of Egypt.

27And the king made silver in Jerusalem as stones, and cedar trees made he as the sycamore trees that *are* in the low plains in abundance.

28And they brought unto Solomon horses out of Egypt, and out of all lands.

29¶ Now the rest of the acts of Solomon, first and last, *are* they not written in the book of Nathan the prophet, and in the prophecy of Ahijah the Shilonite, and in the visions of Iddo the seer against Jeroboam the son of Nebat?

30And Solomon reigned in Jerusalem over all Israel forty years.

31And Solomon slept with his fathers, and he was buried in the city of David his father: and Rehoboam his son reigned in his stead.

10 AND REHOBOAM went to Shechem: for to Shechem were all Israel come to make him king.

2And it came to pass, when Jeroboam the son of Nebat, who *was* in Egypt, whither he had fled from the presence of Solomon the king, heard *it*, that Jeroboam returned out of Egypt.

3And they sent and called him. So Jeroboam and all Israel came and spake to Rehoboam, saying,

New International

Solomon's Splendor

13The weight of the gold that Solomon received yearly was 666 talents,[a] 14not including the revenues brought in by merchants and traders. Also all the kings of Arabia and the governors of the land brought gold and silver to Solomon.

15King Solomon made two hundred large shields of hammered gold; six hundred bekas[b] of hammered gold went into each shield. 16He also made three hundred small shields of hammered gold, with three hundred bekas[c] of gold in each shield. The king put them in the Palace of the Forest of Lebanon.

17Then the king made a great throne inlaid with ivory and overlaid with pure gold. 18The throne had six steps, and a footstool of gold was attached to it. On both sides of the seat were armrests, with a lion standing beside each of them. 19Twelve lions stood on the six steps, one at either end of each step. Nothing like it had ever been made for any other kingdom. 20All King Solomon's goblets were gold, and all the household articles in the Palace of the Forest of Lebanon were pure gold. Nothing was made of silver, because silver was considered of little value in Solomon's day. 21The king had a fleet of trading ships[d] manned by Hiram's[e] men. Once every three years it returned, carrying gold, silver and ivory, and apes and baboons.

22King Solomon was greater in riches and wisdom than all the other kings of the earth. 23All the kings of the earth sought audience with Solomon to hear the wisdom God had put in his heart. 24Year after year, everyone who came brought a gift—articles of silver and gold, and robes, weapons and spices, and horses and mules.

25Solomon had four thousand stalls for horses and chariots, and twelve thousand horses,[f] which he kept in the chariot cities and also with him in Jerusalem. 26He ruled over all the kings from the River[g] to the land of the Philistines, as far as the border of Egypt. 27The king made silver as common in Jerusalem as stones, and cedar as plentiful as sycamore-fig trees in the foothills. 28Solomon's horses were imported from Egypt[h] and from all other countries.

Solomon's Death

29As for the other events of Solomon's reign, from beginning to end, are they not written in the records of Nathan the prophet, in the prophecy of Ahijah the Shilonite and in the visions of Iddo the seer concerning Jeroboam son of Nebat? 30Solomon reigned in Jerusalem over all Israel forty years. 31Then he rested with his fathers and was buried in the city of David his father. And Rehoboam his son succeeded him as king.

Israel Rebels Against Rehoboam

10 REHOBOAM WENT to Shechem, for all the Israelites had gone there to make him king. 2When Jeroboam son of Nebat heard this (he was in Egypt, where he had fled from King Solomon), he returned from Egypt. 3So they sent for Jeroboam, and he and all Israel went to Rehoboam and said to him: 4"Your

---

a 13 That is, about 25 tons (about 23 metric tons)   b 15 That is, about 7 1/2 pounds (about 3.5 kilograms)   c 16 That is, about 3 3/4 pounds (about 1.7 kilograms)   d 21 Hebrew *of ships that could go to Tarshish*   e 21 Hebrew *Huram*, a variant of *Hiram*   f 25 Or *charioteers*   g 26 That is, the Euphrates   h 28 Or possibly *Muzur*, a region in Cilicia

Living Bible

13, 14Solomon received a quarter of a billion dollars worth of gold each year from the kings of Arabia and many other lands that paid annual tribute to him. In addition, there was a trade balance from the exports of his merchants. 15He used some of the gold to make 200 large shields, each worth $100,000, 16and 300 smaller shields, each worth $50,000. The king placed these in the Forest of Lebanon Room in his palace. 17He also made a huge ivory throne overlaid with pure gold. 18It had six gold steps and a footstool of gold; also gold armrests, each flanked by a gold lion. 19Gold lions also stood at each side of each step. No other throne in all the world could be compared with it! 20All of King Solomon's cups were solid gold, as were all the furnishings in the Forest of Lebanon Room. Silver was too cheap to count for much in those days!

21Every three years the king sent his ships to Tarshish, using sailors supplied by King Hiram, to bring back gold, silver, ivory, apes, and peacocks.

22So King Solomon was richer and wiser than any other king in all the earth. 23Kings from every nation came to visit him, and to hear the wisdom God had put into his heart. 24Each brought him annual tribute of silver and gold bowls, clothing, armor, spices, horses, and mules.

25In addition, Solomon had 4,000 stalls of horses and chariots, and 12,000 cavalrymen stationed in the chariot cities, as well as in Jerusalem to protect the king. 26He ruled over all kings and kingdoms from the Euphrates River to the land of the Philistines and as far away as the border of Egypt. 27He made silver become as plentiful in Jerusalem as stones in the road! And cedar was used as though it were common sycamore. 28Horses were brought to him from Egypt and other countries.

29The rest of Solomon's biography is written in the history of Nathan the prophet and in the prophecy of Ahijah the Shilonite, and also in the visions of Iddo the seer concerning Jeroboam the son of Nebat.

30So Solomon reigned in Jerusalem over all of Israel for forty years. 31Then he died and was buried in Jerusalem, and his son Rehoboam became the new king.

10 ALL THE leaders of Israel came to Shechem for Rehoboam's coronation. 2, 3Meanwhile, friends of Jeroboam (son of Nebat) sent word to him of Solomon's death. He was in Egypt at the time, where he had gone to escape from King Solomon. He now quickly returned, and was present at the coronation, and led the people's demands on Rehoboam:

New Revised Standard

Solomon's Great Wealth

13 The weight of gold that came to Solomon in one year was six hundred sixty-six talents of gold, 14besides that which the traders and merchants brought; and all the kings of Arabia and the governors of the land brought gold and silver to Solomon. 15King Solomon made two hundred large shields of beaten gold; six hundred shekels of beaten gold went into each large shield. 16He made three hundred shields of beaten gold; three hundred shekels of gold went into each shield; and the king put them in the House of the Forest of Lebanon. 17The king also made a great ivory throne, and overlaid it with pure gold. 18The throne had six steps and a footstool of gold, which were attached to the throne, and on each side of the seat were arm rests and two lions standing beside the arm rests, 19while twelve lions were standing, one on each end of a step on the six steps. The like of it was never made in any kingdom. 20All King Solomon's drinking vessels were of gold, and all the vessels of the House of the Forest of Lebanon were of pure gold; silver was not considered as anything in the days of Solomon. 21For the king's ships went to Tarshish with the servants of Huram; once every three years the ships of Tarshish used to come bringing gold, silver, ivory, apes, and peacocks.i

22 Thus King Solomon excelled all the kings of the earth in riches and in wisdom. 23All the kings of the earth sought the presence of Solomon to hear his wisdom, which God had put into his mind. 24Every one of them brought a present, objects of silver and gold, garments, weaponry, spices, horses, and mules, so much year by year. 25Solomon had four thousand stalls for horses and chariots, and twelve thousand horses, which he stationed in the chariot cities and with the king in Jerusalem. 26He ruled over all the kings from the Euphrates to the land of the Philistines, and to the border of Egypt. 27The king made silver as common in Jerusalem as stone, and cedar as plentiful as the sycamore of the Shephelah. 28Horses were imported for Solomon from Egypt and from all lands.

Death of Solomon

29 Now the rest of the acts of Solomon, from first to last, are they not written in the history of the prophet Nathan, and in the prophecy of Ahijah the Shilonite, and in the visions of the seer Iddo concerning Jeroboam son of Nebat? 30Solomon reigned in Jerusalem over all Israel forty years. 31Solomon slept with his ancestors and was buried in the city of his father David; and his son Rehoboam succeeded him.

The Revolt against Rehoboam

10 REHOBOAM WENT to Shechem, for all Israel had come to Shechem to make him king. 2When Jeroboam son of Nebat heard of it (for he was in Egypt, where he had fled from King Solomon), then Jeroboam returned from Egypt. 3They sent and called him; and Jeroboam and all Israel came and said to Rehoboam, 4"Your father made our yoke heavy. Now there-

i Or *baboons*

King James

⁴Thy father made our yoke grievous: now therefore ease thou somewhat the grievous servitude of thy father, and his heavy yoke that he put upon us, and we will serve thee.

⁵And he said unto them, Come again unto me after three days. And the people departed.

⁶¶ And king Rehoboam took counsel with the old men that had stood before Solomon his father while he yet lived, saying, What counsel give ye *me* to return answer to this people?

⁷And they spake unto him, saying, If thou be kind to this people, and please them, and speak good words to them, they will be thy servants for ever.

⁸But he forsook the counsel which the old men gave him, and took counsel with the young men that were brought up with him, that stood before him.

⁹And he said unto them, What advice give ye that we may return answer to this people, which have spoken to me, saying, Ease somewhat the yoke that thy father did put upon us?

¹⁰And the young men that were brought up with him spake unto him, saying, Thus shalt thou answer the people that spake unto thee, saying, Thy father made our yoke heavy, but make thou *it* somewhat lighter for us; thus shalt thou say unto them, My little *finger* shall be thicker than my father's loins.

¹¹For whereas my father put a heavy yoke upon you, I will put more to your yoke: my father chastised you with whips, but I *will chastise you* with scorpions.

¹²So Jeroboam and all the people came to Rehoboam on the third day, as the king bade, saying, Come again to me on the third day.

¹³And the king answered them roughly; and king Rehoboam forsook the counsel of the old men,

¹⁴And answered them after the advice of the young men, saying, My father made your yoke heavy, but I will add thereto: my father chastised you with whips, but I *will chastise you* with scorpions.

¹⁵So the king hearkened not unto the people: for the cause was of God, that the LORD might perform his word, which he spake by the hand of Ahijah the Shilonite to Jeroboam the son of Nebat.

¹⁶¶ And when all Israel *saw* that the king would not hearken unto them, the people answered the king, saying, What portion have we in David? and *we have* none inheritance in the son of Jesse: every man to your tents, O Israel: *and* now, David, see to thine own house. So all Israel went to their tents.

¹⁷But *as for* the children of Israel that dwelt in the cities of Judah, Rehoboam reigned over them.

¹⁸Then king Rehoboam sent Hadoram that *was* over the tribute; and the children of Israel stoned him with stones, that he died. But king Rehoboam made speed to get him up to *his* chariot, to flee to Jerusalem.

¹⁹And Israel rebelled against the house of David unto this day.

11 AND WHEN Rehoboam was come to Jerusalem, he gathered of the house of Judah and Benjamin an hundred and fourscore thousand chosen *men*, which were warriors, to fight against Israel, that he might bring the kingdom again to Rehoboam.

²But the word of the LORD came to Shemaiah the man of God, saying,

³Speak unto Rehoboam the son of Solomon, king of Judah, and to all Israel in Judah and Benjamin, saying,

⁴Thus saith the LORD, Ye shall not go up, nor fight against your brethren: return every man to his house: for this thing is done of me. And they obeyed the words of the LORD, and returned from going against Jeroboam.

New International

father put a heavy yoke on us, but now lighten the harsh labor and the heavy yoke he put on us, and we will serve you."

⁵Rehoboam answered, "Come back to me in three days." So the people went away.

⁶Then King Rehoboam consulted the elders who had served his father Solomon during his lifetime. "How would you advise me to answer these people?" he asked.

⁷They replied, "If you will be kind to these people and please them and give them a favorable answer, they will always be your servants."

⁸But Rehoboam rejected the advice the elders gave him and consulted the young men who had grown up with him and were serving him. ⁹He asked them, "What is your advice? How should we answer these people who say to me, 'Lighten the yoke your father put on us'?"

¹⁰The young men who had grown up with him replied, "Tell the people who have said to you, 'Your father put a heavy yoke on us, but make our yoke lighter'—tell them, 'My little finger is thicker than my father's waist. ¹¹My father laid on you a heavy yoke; I will make it even heavier. My father scourged you with whips; I will scourge you with scorpions.'"

¹²Three days later Jeroboam and all the people returned to Rehoboam, as the king had said, "Come back to me in three days." ¹³The king answered them harshly. Rejecting the advice of the elders, ¹⁴he followed the advice of the young men and said, "My father made your yoke heavy; I will make it even heavier. My father scourged you with whips; I will scourge you with scorpions." ¹⁵So the king did not listen to the people, for this turn of events was from God, to fulfill the word the LORD had spoken to Jeroboam son of Nebat through Ahijah the Shilonite.

¹⁶When all Israel saw that the king refused to listen to them, they answered the king:

"What share do we have in David,
    what part in Jesse's son?
To your tents, O Israel!
    Look after your own house, O David!"

So all the Israelites went home. ¹⁷But as for the Israelites who were living in the towns of Judah, Rehoboam still ruled over them.

¹⁸King Rehoboam sent out Adoniram,ᵃ who was in charge of forced labor, but the Israelites stoned him to death. King Rehoboam, however, managed to get into his chariot and escape to Jerusalem. ¹⁹So Israel has been in rebellion against the house of David to this day.

11 WHEN REHOBOAM arrived in Jerusalem, he mustered the house of Judah and Benjamin—a hundred and eighty thousand fighting men—to make war against Israel and to regain the kingdom for Rehoboam.

²But this word of the LORD came to Shemaiah the man of God: ³"Say to Rehoboam son of Solomon king of Judah and to all the Israelites in Judah and Benjamin, ⁴'This is what the LORD says: Do not go up to fight against your brothers. Go home, every one of you, for this is my doing.'" So they obeyed the words of the LORD and turned back from marching against Jeroboam.

ᵃ *18* Hebrew *Hadoram*, a variant of *Adoniram*

Living Bible

4"Your father was a hard master," they said. "Be easier on us than he was, and we will let you be our king!"

5Rehoboam told them to return in three days for his decision. 6He discussed their demand with the old men who had counseled his father Solomon.

"What shall I tell them?" he asked.

7"If you want to be their king," they replied, "you will have to give them a favorable reply and treat them with kindness."

8, 9But he rejected their advice and asked the opinion of the young men who had grown up with him. "What do you fellows think I should do?" he asked. "Shall I be easier on them than my father was?"

10"No!" they replied. "Tell them, 'If you think my father was hard on you, just wait and see what I'll be like!' Tell them, 'My little finger is thicker than my father's loins! 11I am going to be tougher on you, not easier! My father used whips on you, but I'll use scorpions!' "

12So when Jeroboam and the people returned in three days to hear King Rehoboam's decision, 13he spoke roughly to them; for he refused the advice of the old men, 14and followed the counsel of the younger ones.

"My father gave you heavy burdens but I will give you heavier!" he told them. "My father punished you with whips, but I will punish you with scorpions!"

15So the king turned over the people's demands. (God caused him to do it in order to fulfill his predictionb spoken to Jeroboam by Ahijah, the Shilonite.) 16When the people realized what the king was saying they turned their backs and deserted him.

"Forget David and his dynasty!" they shouted angrily. "We'll get someone else to be our king. Let Rehoboam rule his own tribe of Judah! Let's go home!" So they did.

17The people of the tribe of Judah, however, remained loyal to Rehoboam. 18Afterwards, when King Rehoboam sent Hadoram to draft forced labor from the other tribes of Israel, the people stoned him to death. When this news reached King Rehoboam he jumped into his chariot and fled to Jerusalem. 19And Israel has refused to be ruled by a descendant of David to this day.

New Revised Standard

fore lighten the hard service of your father and his heavy yoke that he placed on us, and we will serve you." 5He said to them, "Come to me again in three days." So the people went away.

6 Then King Rehoboam took counsel with the older men who had attended his father Solomon while he was still alive, saying, "How do you advise me to answer this people?" 7They answered him, "If you will be kind to this people and please them, and speak good words to them, then they will be your servants forever." 8But he rejected the advice that the older men gave him, and consulted the young men who had grown up with him and now attended him. 9He said to them, "What do you advise that we answer this people who have said to me, 'Lighten the yoke that your father put on us'?" 10The young men who had grown up with him said to him, "Thus should you speak to the people who said to you, 'Your father made our yoke heavy, but you must lighten it for us'; tell them, 'My little finger is thicker than my father's loins. 11Now, whereas my father laid on you a heavy yoke, I will add to your yoke. My father disciplined you with whips, but I will discipline you with scorpions.' "

12 So Jeroboam and all the people came to Rehoboam the third day, as the king had said, "Come to me again the third day." 13The king answered them harshly. King Rehoboam rejected the advice of the older men; 14he spoke to them in accordance with the advice of the young men, "My father made your yoke heavy, but I will add to it; my father disciplined you with whips, but I will discipline you with scorpions." 15So the king did not listen to the people, because it was a turn of affairs brought about by God so that the LORD might fulfill his word, which he had spoken by Ahijah the Shilonite to Jeroboam son of Nebat.

16 When all Israel saw that the king would not listen to them, the people answered the king,

"What share do we have in David?
    We have no inheritance in the son of Jesse.
Each of you to your tents, O Israel!
    Look now to your own house, O David."

So all Israel departed to their tents. 17But Rehoboam reigned over the people of Israel who were living in the cities of Judah. 18When King Rehoboam sent Hadoram, who was taskmaster over the forced labor, the people of Israel stoned him to death. King Rehoboam hurriedly mounted his chariot to flee to Jerusalem. 19So Israel has been in rebellion against the house of David to this day.

Judah and Benjamin Fortified

11 UPON ARRIVAL at Jerusalem, Rehoboam mobilized the armies of Judah and Benjamin, 180,000 strong, and declared war against the rest of Israel in an attempt to reunite the kingdom.

2But the Lord told Shemaiah the prophet, 3"Go and say to King Rehoboam of Judah, Solomon's son, and to the people of Judah and of Benjamin: 4" 'The Lord says, Do not fight against your brothers. Go home, for I am behind their rebellion.' " So they obeyed the Lord and refused to fight against Jeroboam.

11 WHEN REHOBOAM came to Jerusalem, he assembled one hundred eighty thousand chosen troops of the house of Judah and Benjamin to fight against Israel, to restore the kingdom to Rehoboam. 2But the word of the LORD came to Shemaiah the man of God: 3Say to King Rehoboam of Judah, son of Solomon, and to all Israel in Judah and Benjamin, 4"Thus says the LORD: You shall not go up or fight against your kindred. Let everyone return home, for this thing is from me." So they heeded the word of the LORD and turned back from the expedition against Jeroboam.

b *10:15 to fulfill his prediction*, see 1 Kgs 11:30, 31.

King James

5¶ And Rehoboam dwelt in Jerusalem, and built cities for defence in Judah.

6He built even Bethlehem, and Etam, and Tekoa,

7And Beth-zur, and Shoco, and Adullam,

8And Gath, and Mareshah, and Ziph,

9And Adoraim, and Lachish, and Azekah,

10And Zorah, and Aijalon, and Hebron, which *are* in Judah and in Benjamin fenced cities.

11And he fortified the strong holds, and put captains in them, and store of victual, and of oil and wine.

12And in every several city *he put* shields and spears, and made them exceeding strong, having Judah and Benjamin on his side.

13¶ And the priests and the Levites that *were* in all Israel resorted to him out of all their coasts.

14For the Levites left their suburbs and their possession, and came to Judah and Jerusalem: for Jeroboam and his sons had cast them off from executing the priest's office unto the LORD:

15And he ordained him priests for the high places, and for the devils, and for the calves which he had made.

16And after them out of all the tribes of Israel such as set their hearts to seek the LORD God of Israel came to Jerusalem, to sacrifice unto the LORD God of their fathers.

17So they strengthened the kingdom of Judah, and made Rehoboam the son of Solomon strong, three years: for three years they walked in the way of David and Solomon.

18¶ And Rehoboam took him Mahalath the daughter of Jerimoth the son of David to wife, *and* Abihail the daughter of Eliab the son of Jesse;

19Which bare him children; Jeush, and Shamariah, and Zaham.

20And after her he took Maachah the daughter of Absalom; which bare him Abijah, and Attai, and Ziza, and Shelomith.

21And Rehoboam loved Maachah the daughter of Absalom above all his wives and his concubines: (for he took eighteen wives, and threescore concubines; and begat twenty and eight sons, and threescore daughters.)

22And Rehoboam made Abijah the son of Maachah the chief, *to be* ruler among his brethren: for *he thought* to make him king.

23And he dealt wisely, and dispersed of all his children throughout all the countries of Judah and Benjamin, unto every fenced city: and he gave them victual in abundance. And he desired many wives.

12 AND IT came to pass, when Rehoboam had established the kingdom, and had strengthened himself, he forsook the law of the LORD, and all Israel with him.

2And it came to pass, *that* in the fifth year of king Rehoboam Shishak king of Egypt came up against Jerusalem, because they had transgressed against the LORD,

3With twelve hundred chariots, and threescore thousand horsemen: and the people *were* without number that came with him out of Egypt; the Lubims, the Sukkiims, and the Ethiopians.

4And he took the fenced cities which *pertained* to Judah, and came to Jerusalem.

5¶ Then came Shemaiah the prophet to Rehoboam, and *to* the princes of Judah, that were gathered together to Jerusalem because of Shishak, and said unto them, Thus saith the LORD, Ye have forsaken me, and therefore have I also left you in the hand of Shishak.

6Whereupon the princes of Israel and the king humbled themselves; and they said, The LORD *is* righteous.

New International

Rehoboam Fortifies Judah

5Rehoboam lived in Jerusalem and built up towns for defense in Judah: 6Bethlehem, Etam, Tekoa, 7Beth Zur, Soco, Adullam, 8Gath, Mareshah, Ziph, 9Adoraim, Lachish, Azekah, 10Zorah, Aijalon and Hebron. These were fortified cities in Judah and Benjamin. 11He strengthened their defenses and put commanders in them, with supplies of food, olive oil and wine. 12He put shields and spears in all the cities, and made them very strong. So Judah and Benjamin were his.

13The priests and Levites from all their districts throughout Israel sided with him. 14The Levites even abandoned their pasturelands and property, and came to Judah and Jerusalem because Jeroboam and his sons had rejected them as priests of the LORD. 15And he appointed his own priests for the high places and for the goat and calf idols he had made. 16Those from every tribe of Israel who set their hearts on seeking the LORD, the God of Israel, followed the Levites to Jerusalem to offer sacrifices to the LORD, the God of their fathers. 17They strengthened the kingdom of Judah and supported Rehoboam son of Solomon three years, walking in the ways of David and Solomon during this time.

Rehoboam's Family

18Rehoboam married Mahalath, who was the daughter of David's son Jerimoth and of Abihail, the daughter of Jesse's son Eliab. 19She bore him sons: Jeush, Shemariah and Zaham. 20Then he married Maacah daughter of Absalom, who bore him Abijah, Attai, Ziza and Shelomith. 21Rehoboam loved Maacah daughter of Absalom more than any of his other wives and concubines. In all, he had eighteen wives and sixty concubines, twenty-eight sons and sixty daughters.

22Rehoboam appointed Abijah son of Maacah to be the chief prince among his brothers, in order to make him king. 23He acted wisely, dispersing some of his sons throughout the districts of Judah and Benjamin, and to all the fortified cities. He gave them abundant provisions and took many wives for them.

Shishak Attacks Jerusalem

12 AFTER REHOBOAM'S position as king was established and he had become strong, he and all Israel[a] with him abandoned the law of the LORD. 2Because they had been unfaithful to the LORD, Shishak king of Egypt attacked Jerusalem in the fifth year of King Rehoboam. 3With twelve hundred chariots and sixty thousand horsemen and the innumerable troops of Libyans, Sukkites and Cushites[b] that came with him from Egypt, 4he captured the fortified cities of Judah and came as far as Jerusalem.

5Then the prophet Shemaiah came to Rehoboam and to the leaders of Judah who had assembled in Jerusalem for fear of Shishak, and he said to them, "This is what the LORD says, 'You have abandoned me; therefore, I now abandon you to Shishak.'"

6The leaders of Israel and the king humbled themselves and said, "The LORD is just."

---

a *1* That is, Judah, as frequently in 2 Chronicles   b *3* That is, people from the upper Nile region

Living Bible

5-10Rehoboam stayed in Jerusalem and fortified these cities of Judah with walls and gates to protect himself: Bethlehem, Etam, Tekoa, Beth-zur, Soco, Adullam, Gath, Mareshah, Ziph, Adoraim, Lachish, Azekah, Zorah, Aijalon, and Hebron.

11He also rebuilt and strengthened the forts, and manned them with companies of soldiers under their officers, and stored them with food, olive oil, and wine. 12Shields and spears were placed in armories in every city as a further safety measure. For only Judah and Benjamin remained loyal to him.

13, 14However, the priests and Levites from the other tribes now abandoned their homes and moved to Judah and Jerusalem, for King Jeroboam had fired them, telling them to stop being priests of the Lord. 15He had appointed other priests instead who encouraged the people to worship idols instead of God, and to sacrifice to carved statues of goats and calves which he placed on the hills. 16Laymen, too, from all over Israel began moving to Jerusalem where they could freely worship the Lord God of their fathers, and sacrifice to him. 17This strengthened the kingdom of Judah, so King Rehoboam survived for three years without difficulty; for during those years there was an earnest effort to obey the Lord as King David and King Solomon had done.c

18Rehoboam married his cousind Mahalath. She was the daughter of David's son Jerimoth and of Abihail, the daughter of David's brother Eliab. 19Three sons were born from this marriage—Jeush, Shemariah, and Zaham.

20Later he married Maacah, the daughter of Absalom. The children she bore him were Abijah, Attai, Ziza, and Shelomith. 21He loved Maacah more than any of his other wives and concubines (he had eighteen wives and sixty concubines—with twenty-eight sons and sixty daughters). 22Maacah's son Abijah was his favorite, and he intended to make him the next king. 23He very wisely scattered his other sons in the fortified cities throughout the land of Judah and Benjamin, and gave them large allowances and arranged for them to have several wives apiece.

12 BUT JUST when Rehoboam was at the height of his popularity and power he abandoned the Lord, and the people followed him in this sin. 2As a result, King Shishak of Egypt attacked Jerusalem in the fifth year of King Rehoboam's reign, 3with twelve hundred chariots, sixty thousand cavalrymen and an unnumbered host of infantrymen—Egyptians, Libyans, Sukkiim, and Ethiopians. 4He quickly conquered Judah's fortified cities and soon arrived at Jerusalem.

5The prophet Shemaiah now met with Rehoboam and the Judean leaders from every part of the nation (they had fled to Jerusalem for safety), and told them, "The Lord says, 'You have forsaken me, so I have forsaken you and abandoned you to Shishak.' "

6Then the king and the leaders of Israel confessed their sins and exclaimed, "The Lord is right in doing this to us!"

New Revised Standard

5 Rehoboam resided in Jerusalem, and he built cities for defense in Judah. 6He built up Bethlehem, Etam, Tekoa, 7Beth-zur, Soco, Adullam, 8Gath, Mareshah, Ziph, 9Adoraim, Lachish, Azekah, 10Zorah, Aijalon, and Hebron, fortified cities that are in Judah and in Benjamin. 11He made the fortresses strong, and put commanders in them, and stores of food, oil, and wine. 12He also put large shields and spears in all the cities, and made them very strong. So he held Judah and Benjamin.

Priests and Levites Support Rehoboam

13 The priests and the Levites who were in all Israel presented themselves to him from all their territories. 14The Levites had left their common lands and their holdings and had come to Judah and Jerusalem, because Jeroboam and his sons had prevented them from serving as priests of the LORD, 15and had appointed his own priests for the high places, and for the goat-demons, and for the calves that he had made. 16Those who had set their hearts to seek the LORD God of Israel came after them from all the tribes of Israel to Jerusalem to sacrifice to the LORD, the God of their ancestors. 17They strengthened the kingdom of Judah, and for three years they made Rehoboam son of Solomon secure, for they walked for three years in the way of David and Solomon.

Rehoboam's Marriages

18 Rehoboam took as his wife Mahalath daughter of Jerimoth son of David, and of Abihail daughter of Eliab son of Jesse. 19She bore him sons: Jeush, Shemariah, and Zaham. 20After her he took Maacah daughter of Absalom, who bore him Abijah, Attai, Ziza, and Shelomith. 21Rehoboam loved Maacah daughter of Absalom more than all his other wives and concubines (he took eighteen wives and sixty concubines, and became the father of twenty-eight sons and sixty daughters). 22Rehoboam appointed Abijah son of Maacah as chief prince among his brothers, for he intended to make him king. 23He dealt wisely, and distributed some of his sons through all the districts of Judah and Benjamin, in all the fortified cities; he gave them abundant provisions, and found many wives for them.

Egypt Attacks Judah

12 WHEN THE rule of Rehoboam was established and he grew strong, he abandoned the law of the LORD, he and all Israel with him. 2In the fifth year of King Rehoboam, because they had been unfaithful to the LORD, King Shishak of Egypt came up against Jerusalem 3with twelve hundred chariots and sixty thousand cavalry. A countless army came with him from Egypt—Libyans, Sukkiim, and Ethiopians.e 4He took the fortified cities of Judah and came as far as Jerusalem. 5Then the prophet Shemaiah came to Rehoboam and to the officers of Judah, who had gathered at Jerusalem because of Shishak, and said to them, "Thus says the LORD: You abandoned me, so I have abandoned you to the hand of Shishak." 6Then the officers of Israel and the king humbled themselves and said, "The LORD is in the right." 7When the LORD saw that they humbled

---

c 11:17 as King David and King Solomon had done, literally, "they walked in the way of David and Solomon." d 11:18 Rehoboam married his cousin, implied.

e Or Nubians; Heb Cushites

King James

7And when the LORD saw that they humbled themselves, the word of the LORD came to Shemaiah, saying, They have humbled themselves; *therefore* I will not destroy them, but I will grant them some deliverance; and my wrath shall not be poured out upon Jerusalem by the hand of Shishak.

8Nevertheless they shall be his servants; that they may know my service, and the service of the kingdoms of the countries.

9So Shishak king of Egypt came up against Jerusalem, and took away the treasures of the house of the LORD, and the treasures of the king's house; he took all: he carried away also the shields of gold which Solomon had made.

10Instead of which king Rehoboam made shields of brass, and committed *them* to the hands of the chief of the guard, that kept the entrance of the king's house.

11And when the king entered into the house of the LORD, the guard came and fetched them, and brought them again into the guard chamber.

12And when he humbled himself, the wrath of the LORD turned from him, that he would not destroy *him* altogether: and also in Judah things went well.

13¶ So king Rehoboam strengthened himself in Jerusalem, and reigned: for Rehoboam *was* one and forty years old when he began to reign, and he reigned seventeen years in Jerusalem, the city which the LORD had chosen out of all the tribes of Israel, to put his name there. And his mother's name *was* Naamah an Ammonitess.

14And he did evil, because he prepared not his heart to seek the LORD.

15Now the acts of Rehoboam, first and last, *are* they not written in the book of Shemaiah the prophet, and of Iddo the seer concerning genealogies? And *there were* wars between Rehoboam and Jeroboam continually.

16And Rehoboam slept with his fathers, and was buried in the city of David: and Abijah his son reigned in his stead.

13 NOW IN the eighteenth year of king Jeroboam began Abijah to reign over Judah.

2He reigned three years in Jerusalem. His mother's name also *was* Michaiah the daughter of Uriel of Gibeah. And there was war between Abijah and Jeroboam.

3And Abijah set the battle in array with an army of valiant men of war, *even* four hundred thousand chosen men: Jeroboam also set the battle in array against him with eight hundred thousand chosen men, *being* mighty men of valour.

4¶ And Abijah stood up upon mount Zemaraim, which *is* in mount Ephraim, and said, Hear me, thou Jeroboam, and all Israel;

5Ought ye not to know that the LORD God of Israel gave the kingdom over Israel to David for ever, *even* to him and to his sons by a covenant of salt?

6Yet Jeroboam the son of Nebat, the servant of Solomon the son of David, is risen up, and hath rebelled against his lord.

7And there are gathered unto him vain men, the children of Belial, and have strengthened themselves against Rehoboam the son of Solomon, when Rehoboam was young and tender-hearted, and could not withstand them.

8And now ye think to withstand the kingdom of the LORD in the hand of the sons of David; and ye *be* a great multitude, and *there are* with you golden calves, which Jeroboam made you for gods.

New International

7When the LORD saw that they humbled themselves, this word of the LORD came to Shemaiah: "Since they have humbled themselves, I will not destroy them but will soon give them deliverance. My wrath will not be poured out on Jerusalem through Shishak. 8They will, however, become subject to him, so that they may learn the difference between serving me and serving the kings of other lands."

9When Shishak king of Egypt attacked Jerusalem, he carried off the treasures of the temple of the LORD and the treasures of the royal palace. He took everything, including the gold shields Solomon had made. 10So King Rehoboam made bronze shields to replace them and assigned these to the commanders of the guard on duty at the entrance to the royal palace. 11Whenever the king went to the LORD's temple, the guards went with him, bearing the shields, and afterward they returned them to the guardroom.

12Because Rehoboam humbled himself, the LORD's anger turned from him, and he was not totally destroyed. Indeed, there was some good in Judah.

13King Rehoboam established himself firmly in Jerusalem and continued as king. He was forty-one years old when he became king, and he reigned seventeen years in Jerusalem, the city the LORD had chosen out of all the tribes of Israel in which to put his Name. His mother's name was Naamah; she was an Ammonite. 14He did evil because he had not set his heart on seeking the LORD.

15As for the events of Rehoboam's reign, from beginning to end, are they not written in the records of Shemaiah the prophet and of Iddo the seer that deal with genealogies? There was continual warfare between Rehoboam and Jeroboam. 16Rehoboam rested with his fathers and was buried in the City of David. And Abijah his son succeeded him as king.

Abijah King of Judah

13 IN THE eighteenth year of the reign of Jeroboam, Abijah became king of Judah, 2and he reigned in Jerusalem three years. His mother's name was Maacah,[a] a daughter[b] of Uriel of Gibeah.

There was war between Abijah and Jeroboam. 3Abijah went into battle with a force of four hundred thousand able fighting men, and Jeroboam drew up a battle line against him with eight hundred thousand able troops.

4Abijah stood on Mount Zemaraim, in the hill country of Ephraim, and said, "Jeroboam and all Israel, listen to me! 5Don't you know that the LORD, the God of Israel, has given the kingship of Israel to David and his descendants forever by a covenant of salt? 6Yet Jeroboam son of Nebat, an official of Solomon son of David, rebelled against his master. 7Some worthless scoundrels gathered around him and opposed Rehoboam son of Solomon when he was young and indecisive and not strong enough to resist them.

8"And now you plan to resist the kingdom of the LORD, which is in the hands of David's descendants. You are indeed a vast army and have with you the golden calves that Jeroboam made to be your gods. 9But didn't

---

a 2 Most Septuagint manuscripts and Syriac (see also 2 Chron. 11:20 and 1 Kings 15:2); Hebrew *Micaiah*　　b 2 Or *granddaughter*

Living Bible

7And when the Lord saw them humble themselves he sent Shemaiah to tell them, "Because you have humbled yourselves, I will not completely destroy you; some will escape. I will not use Shishak to pour out my anger upon Jerusalem. 8But you must pay annual tribute to him. Then you will realize how much better it is to serve me than to serve him!"

9So King Shishak of Egypt conquered Jerusalem and took away all the treasures of the Temple and of the palace, also all of Solomon's gold shields. 10King Rehoboam replaced them with bronze shields and committed them to the care of the captain of his bodyguard. 11Whenever the king went to the Temple, the guards would carry them, and afterwards return them to the armory. 12When the king humbled himself, the Lord's anger was turned aside and he didn't send total destruction; in fact, even after Shishak's invasion, the economy of Judah remained strong.

13King Rehoboam reigned seventeen years in Jerusalem, the city God had chosen as his residence after considering all the other cities of Israel. He had become king at the age of forty-one, and his mother's name was Naamah the Ammonitess. 14But he was an evil king, for he never did decide really to please the Lord. 15The complete biography of Rehoboam is recorded in the histories written by Shemaiah the prophet and by Iddo the seer, and in *The Genealogical Register*.

There were continual wars between Rehoboam and Jeroboam. 16When Rehoboam died he was buried in Jerusalem, and his son Abijah became the new king.

13 ABIJAH BECAME the new king of Judah, in Jerusalem, in the eighteenth year of the reign of King Jeroboam of Israel. He lasted three years. His mother's name was Micaiah (daughter of Uriel of Gibeah).

Early in his reign war broke out between Judah and Israel. 3Judah, led by King Abijah, fielded 400,000 seasoned warriors against twice as many Israeli troops—strong, courageous men led by King Jeroboam. 4When the army of Judah arrived at Mount Zemaraim, in the hill country of Ephraim, King Abijah shouted to King Jeroboam and the Israeli army:

5"Listen! Don't you realize that the Lord God of Israel swore that David's descendants would always be the kings of Israel? 6Your King Jeroboam is a mere servant of David's son, and was a traitor to his master. 7Then a whole gang of worthless rebels joined him, defying Solomon's son Rehoboam, for he was young and frightened and couldn't stand up to them. 8Do you really think you can defeat the kingdom of the Lord that is led by a descendant of David? Your army is twice as large as mine, but you are cursed with those gold calves you have with you, that Jeroboam made for you—he calls them your gods! 9And you have driven away the priests of the

New Revised Standard

themselves, the word of the LORD came to Shemaiah, saying: "They have humbled themselves; I will not destroy them, but I will grant them some deliverance, and my wrath shall not be poured out on Jerusalem by the hand of Shishak. 8Nevertheless they shall be his servants, so that they may know the difference between serving me and serving the kingdoms of other lands."

9 So King Shishak of Egypt came up against Jerusalem; he took away the treasures of the house of the LORD and the treasures of the king's house; he took everything. He also took away the shields of gold that Solomon had made; 10but King Rehoboam made in place of them shields of bronze, and committed them to the hands of the officers of the guard, who kept the door of the king's house. 11Whenever the king went into the house of the LORD, the guard would come along bearing them, and would then bring them back to the guardroom. 12Because he humbled himself the wrath of the LORD turned from him, so as not to destroy them completely; moreover, conditions were good in Judah.

Death of Rehoboam

13 So King Rehoboam established himself in Jerusalem and reigned. Rehoboam was forty-one years old when he began to reign; he reigned seventeen years in Jerusalem, the city that the LORD had chosen out of all the tribes of Israel to put his name there. His mother's name was Naamah the Ammonite. 14He did evil, for he did not set his heart to seek the LORD.

15 Now the acts of Rehoboam, from first to last, are they not written in the records of the prophet Shemaiah and of the seer Iddo, recorded by genealogy? There were continual wars between Rehoboam and Jeroboam. 16Rehoboam slept with his ancestors and was buried in the city of David; and his son Abijah succeeded him.

Abijah Reigns over Judah

13 IN THE eighteenth year of King Jeroboam, Abijah began to reign over Judah. 2He reigned for three years in Jerusalem. His mother's name was Micaiah daughter of Uriel of Gibeah.

Now there was war between Abijah and Jeroboam. 3Abijah engaged in battle, having an army of valiant warriors, four hundred thousand picked men; and Jeroboam drew up his line of battle against him with eight hundred thousand picked mighty warriors. 4Then Abijah stood on the slope of Mount Zemaraim that is in the hill country of Ephraim, and said, "Listen to me, Jeroboam and all Israel! 5Do you not know that the LORD God of Israel gave the kingship over Israel forever to David and his sons by a covenant of salt? 6Yet Jeroboam son of Nebat, a servant of Solomon son of David, rose up and rebelled against his lord; 7and certain worthless scoundrels gathered around him and defied Rehoboam son of Solomon, when Rehoboam was young and irresolute and could not withstand them.

8 "And now you think that you can withstand the kingdom of the LORD in the hand of the sons of David, because you are a great multitude and have with you the golden calves that Jeroboam made as gods for you.

King James

9Have ye not cast out the priests of the LORD, the sons of Aaron, and the Levites, and have made you priests after the manner of the nations of *other* lands? so that whosoever cometh to consecrate himself with a young bullock and seven rams, *the same* may be a priest of *them that are* no gods.

10But as for us, the LORD *is* our God, and we have not forsaken him; and the priests, which minister unto the LORD, *are* the sons of Aaron, and the Levites *wait* upon *their* business:

11And they burn unto the LORD every morning and every evening burnt sacrifices and sweet incense: the showbread also *set they in order* upon the pure table; and the candlestick of gold with the lamps thereof, to burn every evening: for we keep the charge of the LORD our God; but ye have forsaken him.

12And, behold, God himself *is* with us for *our* captain, and his priests with sounding trumpets to cry alarm against you. O children of Israel, fight ye not against the LORD God of your fathers; for ye shall not prosper.

13¶ But Jeroboam caused an ambushment to come about behind them: so they were before Judah, and the ambushment *was* behind them.

14And when Judah looked back, behold, the battle *was* before and behind: and they cried unto the LORD, and the priests sounded with the trumpets.

15Then the men of Judah gave a shout: and as the men of Judah shouted, it came to pass, that God smote Jeroboam and all Israel before Abijah and Judah.

16And the children of Israel fled before Judah: and God delivered them into their hand.

17And Abijah and his people slew them with a great slaughter: so there fell down slain of Israel five hundred thousand chosen men.

18Thus the children of Israel were brought under at that time, and the children of Judah prevailed, because they relied upon the LORD God of their fathers.

19And Abijah pursued after Jeroboam, and took cities from him, Beth-el with the towns thereof, and Jeshanah with the towns thereof, and Ephrain with the towns thereof.

20Neither did Jeroboam recover strength again in the days of Abijah: and the LORD struck him, and he died.

21¶ But Abijah waxed mighty, and married fourteen wives, and begat twenty and two sons, and sixteen daughters.

22And the rest of the acts of Abijah, and his ways, and his sayings, *are* written in the story of the prophet Iddo.

14 SO ABIJAH slept with his fathers, and they buried him in the city of David: and Asa his son reigned in his stead. In his days the land was quiet ten years.

2And Asa did *that which was* good and right in the eyes of the LORD his God:

3For he took away the altars of the strange *gods*, and the high places, and brake down the images, and cut down the groves:

4And commanded Judah to seek the LORD God of their fathers, and to do the law and the commandment.

5Also he took away out of all the cities of Judah the high places and the images: and the kingdom was quiet before him.

6¶ And he built fenced cities in Judah: for the land had rest, and he had no war in those years; because the LORD had given him rest.

New International

you drive out the priests of the LORD, the sons of Aaron, and the Levites, and make priests of your own as the peoples of other lands do? Whoever comes to consecrate himself with a young bull and seven rams may become a priest of what are not gods.

10"As for us, the LORD is our God, and we have not forsaken him. The priests who serve the LORD are sons of Aaron, and the Levites assist them. 11Every morning and evening they present burnt offerings and fragrant incense to the LORD. They set out the bread on the ceremonially clean table and light the lamps on the gold lampstand every evening. We are observing the requirements of the LORD our God. But you have forsaken him. 12God is with us; he is our leader. His priests with their trumpets will sound the battle cry against you. Men of Israel, do not fight against the LORD, the God of your fathers, for you will not succeed."

13Now Jeroboam had sent troops around to the rear, so that while he was in front of Judah the ambush was behind them. 14Judah turned and saw that they were being attacked at both front and rear. Then they cried out to the LORD. The priests blew their trumpets 15and the men of Judah raised the battle cry. At the sound of their battle cry, God routed Jeroboam and all Israel before Abijah and Judah. 16The Israelites fled before Judah, and God delivered them into their hands. 17Abijah and his men inflicted heavy losses on them, so that there were five hundred thousand casualties among Israel's able men. 18The men of Israel were subdued on that occasion, and the men of Judah were victorious because they relied on the LORD, the God of their fathers.

19Abijah pursued Jeroboam and took from him the towns of Bethel, Jeshanah and Ephron, with their surrounding villages. 20Jeroboam did not regain power during the time of Abijah. And the LORD struck him down and he died.

21But Abijah grew in strength. He married fourteen wives and had twenty-two sons and sixteen daughters.

22The other events of Abijah's reign, what he did and what he said, are written in the annotations of the prophet Iddo.

14 AND ABIJAH rested with his fathers and was buried in the City of David. Asa his son succeeded him as king, and in his days the country was at peace for ten years.

Asa King of Judah

2Asa did what was good and right in the eyes of the LORD his God. 3He removed the foreign altars and the high places, smashed the sacred stones and cut down the Asherah poles.a 4He commanded Judah to seek the LORD, the God of their fathers, and to obey his laws and commands. 5He removed the high places and incense altars in every town in Judah, and the kingdom was at peace under him. 6He built up the fortified cities of Judah, since the land was at peace. No one was at war with him during those years, for the LORD gave him rest.

a 3 That is, symbols of the goddess Asherah; here and elsewhere in 2 Chronicles

Living Bible

Lord and the Levites, and have appointed heathen priests instead. Just like the people of other lands, you accept as priests anybody who comes along with a young bullock and seven rams for consecration. Anyone at all can be a priest of these no-gods of yours!

10"But as for us, the Lord is our God and we have not forsaken him. Only the descendants of Aaron are our priests, and the Levites alone may help them in their work. 11They burn sacrifices to the Lord every morning and evening—burnt offerings and sweet incense; and they place the Bread of the Presence upon the holy table. The gold lampstand is lighted every night, for we are careful to follow the instructions of the Lord our God; but you have forsaken him. 12So you see, God is with us; he is our Leader. His priests, trumpeting as they go, will lead us into battle against you. O people of Israel, do not fight against the Lord God of your fathers, for you will not succeed!"

13, 14Meanwhile, Jeroboam had secretly sent part of his army around behind the men of Judah to ambush them; so Judah was surrounded, with the enemy before and behind them. Then they cried out to the Lord for mercy, and the priests blew the trumpets. 15, 16The men of Judah began to shout. And as they shouted, God used King Abijah and the men of Judah to turn the tide of battle against King Jeroboam and the army of Israel, 17and they slaughtered 500,000 elite troops of Israel that day.

18, 19So Judah, depending upon the Lord God of their fathers, defeated Israel, and chased King Jeroboam's troops, and captured some of his cities—Bethel, Jeshanah, Ephron, and their suburbs. 20King Jeroboam of Israel never regained his power during Abijah's lifetime, and eventually the Lord struck him and he died.

21Meanwhile, King Abijah of Judah became very strong. He married fourteen wives and had twenty-two sons and sixteen daughters. 22His complete biography and speeches are recorded in the prophet Iddo's *History of Judah.*

14 KING ABIJAH was buried in Jerusalem. Then his son Asa became the new king of Judah, and there was peace in the land for the first ten years of his reign, 2for Asa was careful to obey the Lord his God. 3He demolished the heathen altars on the hills, and broke down the obelisks, and chopped down the shameful Asherim-idols, 4and demanded that the entire nation obey the commandments of the Lord God of their ancestors. 5Also, he removed the sun-images from the hills, and the incense altars from every one of Judah's cities. That is why God gave his kingdom peace. 6This made it possible for him to build walled cities throughout Judah.

New Revised Standard

9Have you not driven out the priests of the LORD, the descendants of Aaron, and the Levites, and made priests for yourselves like the peoples of other lands? Whoever comes to be consecrated with a young bull or seven rams becomes a priest of what are no gods. 10But as for us, the LORD is our God, and we have not abandoned him. We have priests ministering to the LORD who are descendants of Aaron, and Levites for their service. 11They offer to the LORD every morning and every evening burnt offerings and fragrant incense, set out the rows of bread on the table of pure gold, and care for the golden lampstand so that its lamps may burn every evening; for we keep the charge of the LORD our God, but you have abandoned him. 12See, God is with us at our head, and his priests have their battle trumpets to sound the call to battle against you. O Israelites, do not fight against the LORD, the God of your ancestors; for you cannot succeed."

13 Jeroboam had sent an ambush around to come on them from behind; thus his troops[b] were in front of Judah, and the ambush was behind them. 14When Judah turned, the battle was in front of them and behind them. They cried out to the LORD, and the priests blew the trumpets. 15Then the people of Judah raised the battle shout. And when the people of Judah shouted, God defeated Jeroboam and all Israel before Abijah and Judah. 16The Israelites fled before Judah, and God gave them into their hands. 17Abijah and his army defeated them with great slaughter; five hundred thousand picked men of Israel fell slain. 18Thus the Israelites were subdued at that time, and the people of Judah prevailed, because they relied on the LORD, the God of their ancestors. 19Abijah pursued Jeroboam, and took cities from him: Bethel with its villages and Jeshanah with its villages and Ephron[c] with its villages. 20Jeroboam did not recover his power in the days of Abijah; the LORD struck him down, and he died. 21But Abijah grew strong. He took fourteen wives, and became the father of twenty-two sons and sixteen daughters. 22The rest of the acts of Abijah, his behavior and his deeds, are written in the story of the prophet Iddo.

Asa Reigns

14[d] SO ABIJAH slept with his ancestors, and they buried him in the city of David. His son Asa succeeded him. In his days the land had rest for ten years. 2[e] Asa did what was good and right in the sight of the LORD his God. 3He took away the foreign altars and the high places, broke down the pillars, hewed down the sacred poles,[f] 4and commanded Judah to seek the LORD, the God of their ancestors, and to keep the law and the commandment. 5He also removed from all the cities of Judah the high places and the incense altars. And the kingdom had rest under him. 6He built fortified cities in Judah while the land had rest. He had no war in those years, for the LORD gave him peace. 7He said

---

b Heb *they*   c Another reading is *Ephrain*   d Ch 13.23 in Heb   e Ch 14.1 in Heb   f Heb *Asherim*

King James

7Therefore he said unto Judah, Let us build these cities, and make about *them* walls, and towers, gates, and bars, *while* the land *is* yet before us; because we have sought the LORD our God, we have sought *him,* and he hath given us rest on every side. So they built and prospered.

8And Asa had an army *of men* that bare targets and spears, out of Judah three hundred thousand; and out of Benjamin, that bare shields and drew bows, two hundred and fourscore thousand: all these *were* mighty men of valour.

9¶ And there came out against them Zerah the Ethiopian with an host of a thousand thousand, and three hundred chariots; and came unto Mareshah.

10Then Asa went out against him, and they set the battle in array in the valley of Zephathah at Mareshah.

11And Asa cried unto the LORD his God, and said, LORD, *it is* nothing with thee to help, whether with many, or with them that have no power: help us, O LORD our God; for we rest on thee, and in thy name we go against this multitude. O LORD, thou *art* our God; let not man prevail against thee.

12So the LORD smote the Ethiopians before Asa, and before Judah; and the Ethiopians fled.

13And Asa and the people that *were* with him pursued them unto Gerar: and the Ethiopians were overthrown, that they could not recover themselves; for they were destroyed before the LORD, and before his host; and they carried away very much spoil.

14And they smote all the cities round about Gerar; for the fear of the LORD came upon them: and they spoiled all the cities; for there was exceeding much spoil in them.

15They smote also the tents of cattle, and carried away sheep and camels in abundance, and returned to Jerusalem.

15 AND THE spirit of God came upon Azariah the son of Oded:

2And he went out to meet Asa, and said unto him, Hear ye me, Asa, and all Judah and Benjamin; The LORD *is* with you, while ye be with him; and if ye seek him, he will be found of you; but if ye forsake him, he will forsake you.

3Now for a long season Israel *hath been* without the true God, and without a teaching priest, and without law.

4But when they in their trouble did turn unto the LORD God of Israel, and sought him, he was found of them.

5And in those times *there was* no peace to him that went out, nor to him that came in, but great vexations *were* upon all the inhabitants of the countries.

6And nation was destroyed of nation, and city of city: for God did vex them with all adversity.

7Be ye strong therefore, and let not your hands be weak: for your work shall be rewarded.

8And when Asa heard these words, and the prophecy of Oded the prophet, he took courage, and put away the abominable idols out of all the land of Judah and Benjamin, and out of the cities which he had taken from mount Ephraim, and renewed the altar of the LORD, that *was* before the porch of the LORD.

9And he gathered all Judah and Benjamin, and the strangers with them out of Ephraim and Manasseh, and out of Simeon: for they fell to him out of Israel in abundance, when they saw that the LORD his God *was* with him.

10So they gathered themselves together at Jerusalem in the third month, in the fifteenth year of the reign of Asa.

New International

7"Let us build up these towns," he said to Judah, "and put walls around them, with towers, gates and bars. The land is still ours, because we have sought the LORD our God; we sought him and he has given us rest on every side." So they built and prospered.

8Asa had an army of three hundred thousand men from Judah, equipped with large shields and with spears, and two hundred and eighty thousand from Benjamin, armed with small shields and with bows. All these were brave fighting men.

9Zerah the Cushite marched out against them with a vast army[a] and three hundred chariots, and came as far as Mareshah. 10Asa went out to meet him, and they took up battle positions in the Valley of Zephathah near Mareshah.

11Then Asa called to the LORD his God and said, "LORD, there is no one like you to help the powerless against the mighty. Help us, O LORD our God, for we rely on you, and in your name we have come against this vast army. O LORD, you are our God; do not let man prevail against you."

12The LORD struck down the Cushites before Asa and Judah. The Cushites fled, 13and Asa and his army pursued them as far as Gerar. Such a great number of Cushites fell that they could not recover; they were crushed before the LORD and his forces. The men of Judah carried off a large amount of plunder. 14They destroyed all the villages around Gerar, for the terror of the LORD had fallen upon them. They plundered all these villages, since there was much booty there. 15They also attacked the camps of the herdsmen and carried off droves of sheep and goats and camels. Then they returned to Jerusalem.

Asa's Reform

15 THE SPIRIT of God came upon Azariah son of Oded. 2He went out to meet Asa and said to him, "Listen to me, Asa and all Judah and Benjamin. The LORD is with you when you are with him. If you seek him, he will be found by you, but if you forsake him, he will forsake you. 3For a long time Israel was without the true God, without a priest to teach and without the law. 4But in their distress they turned to the LORD, the God of Israel, and sought him, and he was found by them. 5In those days it was not safe to travel about, for all the inhabitants of the lands were in great turmoil. 6One nation was being crushed by another and one city by another, because God was troubling them with every kind of distress. 7But as for you, be strong and do not give up, for your work will be rewarded."

8When Asa heard these words and the prophecy of Azariah son of[b] Oded the prophet, he took courage. He removed the detestable idols from the whole land of Judah and Benjamin and from the towns he had captured in the hills of Ephraim. He repaired the altar of the LORD that was in front of the portico of the LORD's temple.

9Then he assembled all Judah and Benjamin and the people from Ephraim, Manasseh and Simeon who had settled among them, for large numbers had come over to him from Israel when they saw that the LORD his God was with him.

10They assembled at Jerusalem in the third month of the fifteenth year of Asa's reign. 11At that time they

---

a 9 Hebrew *with an army of a thousand thousands* or *with an army of thousands upon thousands*   b 8 Vulgate and Syriac (see also Septuagint and verse 1); Hebrew does not have *Azariah son of.*

Living Bible

7"Now is the time to do it, while the Lord is blessing us with peace because of our obedience to him," he told his people. "Let us build and fortify cities now, with walls, towers, gates, and bars." So they went ahead with these projects very successfully.

8King Asa's Judean army was 300,000 strong, equipped with light shields and spears. His army of Benjaminites numbered 280,000, armed with large shields and bows. Both armies were composed of well-trained, brave men.

9, 10But now he was attacked by an army of 1,000,000 troops from Ethiopia with 300 chariots, under the leadership of General Zerah. They advanced to the city of Mareshah, in the valley of Zephathah, and King Asa sent his troops to battle with them there.

11"O Lord," he cried out to God, "no one else can help us! Here we are, powerless against this mighty army. Oh, help us, Lord our God! For we trust in you alone to rescue us, and in your name we attack this vast horde. Don't let mere men defeat you!"

12Then the Lord defeated the Ethiopians, and Asa and the army of Judah triumphed as the Ethiopians fled. 13They chased them as far as Gerar, and the entire Ethiopian army was wiped out so that not one man remained; for the Lord and his army destroyed them all. Then the army of Judah carried off vast quantities of plunder. 14While they were at Gerar they attacked all the cities in that area, and terror from the Lord came upon the residents. As a result, additional vast quantities of plunder were collected from these cities too. 15They not only plundered the cities, but destroyed the cattle tents and captured great herds of sheep and camels before finally returning to Jerusalem.

15 THEN THE Spirit of God came upon Azariah (son of Oded), 2and he went out to meet King Asa as he was returning from the battle.

"Listen to me, Asa! Listen, armies of Judah and Benjamin!" he shouted. "The Lord will stay with you as long as you stay with him! Whenever you look for him, you will find him. But if you forsake him, he will forsake you. 3For a long time now, over in Israel, the people haven't worshiped the true God, and have not had a true priest to teach them. They have lived without God's laws. 4But whenever they have turned again to the Lord God of Israel in their distress, and searched for him, he has helped them. 5In their times of rebellion against God there was no peace. Problems troubled the nation on every hand. Crime was on the increase everywhere. 6There were external wars, and internal fighting of city against city, for God was plaguing them with all sorts of trouble. 7But you men of Judah, keep up the good work and don't get discouraged, for you will be rewarded."

8When King Asa heard this message from God, he took courage and destroyed all the idols in the land of Judah and Benjamin, and in the cities he had captured in the hill country of Ephraim, and he rebuilt the altar of the Lord in front of the Temple.

9Then he summoned all the people of Judah and Benjamin, and the immigrants from Israel (for many had come from the territories of Ephraim, Manasseh, and Simeon, in Israel, when they saw that the Lord God was with King Asa). 10They all came to Jerusalem in June of the fifteenth year of King Asa's reign, 11and sacri-

New Revised Standard

to Judah, "Let us build these cities, and surround them with walls and towers, gates and bars; the land is still ours because we have sought the LORD our God; we have sought him, and he has given us peace on every side." So they built and prospered. 8Asa had an army of three hundred thousand from Judah, armed with large shields and spears, and two hundred eighty thousand troops from Benjamin who carried shields and drew bows; all these were mighty warriors.

Ethiopian Invasion Repulsed

9 Zerah the Ethiopianc came out against them with an army of a million men and three hundred chariots, and came as far as Mareshah. 10Asa went out to meet him, and they drew up their lines of battle in the valley of Zephathah at Mareshah. 11Asa cried to the LORD his God, "O LORD, there is no difference for you between helping the mighty and the weak. Help us, O LORD our God, for we rely on you, and in your name we have come against this multitude. O LORD, you are our God; let no mortal prevail against you." 12So the LORD defeated the Ethiopiansd before Asa and before Judah, and the Ethiopiansd fled. 13Asa and the army with him pursued them as far as Gerar, and the Ethiopiansd fell until no one remained alive; for they were broken before the LORD and his army. The people of Judahe carried away a great quantity of booty. 14They defeated all the cities around Gerar, for the fear of the LORD was on them. They plundered all the cities; for there was much plunder in them. 15They also attacked the tents of those who had livestock,f and carried away sheep and goats in abundance, and camels. Then they returned to Jerusalem.

15 THE SPIRIT of God came upon Azariah son of Oded. 2He went out to meet Asa and said to him, "Hear me, Asa, and all Judah and Benjamin: The LORD is with you, while you are with him. If you seek him, he will be found by you, but if you abandon him, he will abandon you. 3For a long time Israel was without the true God, and without a teaching priest, and without law; 4but when in their distress they turned to the LORD, the God of Israel, and sought him, he was found by them. 5In those times it was not safe for anyone to go or come, for great disturbances afflicted all the inhabitants of the lands. 6They were broken in pieces, nation against nation and city against city, for God troubled them with every sort of distress. 7But you, take courage! Do not let your hands be weak, for your work shall be rewarded."

8 When Asa heard these words, the prophecy of Azariah son of Oded,g he took courage, and put away the abominable idols from all the land of Judah and Benjamin and from the towns that he had taken in the hill country of Ephraim. He repaired the altar of the LORD that was in front of the vestibule of the house of the LORD.h 9He gathered all Judah and Benjamin, and those from Ephraim, Manasseh, and Simeon who were residing as aliens with them, for great numbers had deserted to him from Israel when they saw that the LORD his God was with him. 10They were gathered at Jerusalem in the third month of the fifteenth year of the reign of Asa. 11They sacrificed to the LORD on that day, from

---

King James

11And they offered unto the LORD the same time, of the spoil *which* they had brought, seven hundred oxen and seven thousand sheep.

12And they entered into a covenant to seek the LORD God of their fathers with all their heart and with all their soul;

13That whosoever would not seek the LORD God of Israel should be put to death, whether small or great, whether man or woman.

14And they sware unto the LORD with a loud voice, and with shouting, and with trumpets, and with cornets.

15And all Judah rejoiced at the oath: for they had sworn with all their heart, and sought him with their whole desire; and he was found of them: and the LORD gave them rest round about.

16¶ And also *concerning* Maachah the mother of Asa the king, he removed her from *being* queen, because she had made an idol in a grove: and Asa cut down her idol, and stamped *it,* and burnt *it* at the brook Kidron.

17But the high places were not taken away out of Israel: nevertheless the heart of Asa was perfect all his days.

18¶ And he brought into the house of God the things that his father had dedicated, and that he himself had dedicated, silver, and gold, and vessels.

19And there was no *more* war unto the five and thirtieth year of the reign of Asa.

16 IN THE six and thirtieth year of the reign of Asa Baasha king of Israel came up against Judah, and built Ramah, to the intent that he might let none go out or come in to Asa king of Judah.

2Then Asa brought out silver and gold out of the treasures of the house of the LORD and of the king's house, and sent to Ben-hadad king of Syria, that dwelt at Damascus, saying,

3*There is* a league between me and thee, as *there was* between my father and thy father: behold, I have sent thee silver and gold; go, break thy league with Baasha king of Israel, that he may depart from me.

4And Ben-hadad hearkened unto king Asa, and sent the captains of his armies against the cities of Israel; and they smote Ijon, and Dan, and Abel-maim, and all the store cities of Naphtali.

5And it came to pass, when Baasha heard *it,* that he left off building of Ramah, and let his work cease.

6Then Asa the king took all Judah; and they carried away the stones of Ramah, and the timber thereof, wherewith Baasha was building; and he built therewith Geba and Mizpah.

7¶ And at that time Hanani the seer came to Asa king of Judah, and said unto him, Because thou hast relied on the king of Syria, and not relied on the LORD thy God, therefore is the host of the king of Syria escaped out of thine hand.

8Were not the Ethiopians and the Lubims a huge host, with very many chariots and horsemen? yet, because thou didst rely on the LORD, he delivered them into thine hand.

9For the eyes of the LORD run to and fro throughout the whole earth, to show himself strong in the behalf of *them* whose heart *is* perfect toward him. Herein thou hast done foolishly: therefore from henceforth thou shalt have wars.

10Then Asa was wroth with the seer, and put him in a prison house; for *he was* in a rage with him because of this *thing.* And Asa oppressed *some* of the people the same time.

11¶ And, behold, the acts of Asa, first and last, lo, they *are* written in the book of the kings of Judah and Israel.

New International

sacrificed to the LORD seven hundred head of cattle and seven thousand sheep and goats from the plunder they had brought back. 12They entered into a covenant to seek the LORD, the God of their fathers, with all their heart and soul. 13All who would not seek the LORD, the God of Israel, were to be put to death, whether small or great, man or woman. 14They took an oath to the LORD with loud acclamation, with shouting and with trumpets and horns. 15All Judah rejoiced about the oath because they had sworn it wholeheartedly. They sought God eagerly, and he was found by them. So the LORD gave them rest on every side.

16King Asa also deposed his grandmother Maacah from her position as queen mother, because she had made a repulsive Asherah pole. Asa cut the pole down, broke it up and burned it in the Kidron Valley. 17Although he did not remove the high places from Israel, Asa's heart was fully committed to the LORD all his life. 18He brought into the temple of God the silver and gold and the articles that he and his father had dedicated.

19There was no more war until the thirty-fifth year of Asa's reign.

Asa's Last Years

16 IN THE thirty-sixth year of Asa's reign Baasha king of Israel went up against Judah and fortified Ramah to prevent anyone from leaving or entering the territory of Asa king of Judah.

2Asa then took the silver and gold out of the treasuries of the LORD's temple and of his own palace and sent it to Ben-Hadad king of Aram, who was ruling in Damascus. 3"Let there be a treaty between me and you," he said, "as there was between my father and your father. See, I am sending you silver and gold. Now break your treaty with Baasha king of Israel so he will withdraw from me."

4Ben-Hadad agreed with King Asa and sent the commanders of his forces against the towns of Israel. They conquered Ijon, Dan, Abel Maima and all the store cities of Naphtali. 5When Baasha heard this, he stopped building Ramah and abandoned his work. 6Then King Asa brought all the men of Judah, and they carried away from Ramah the stones and timber Baasha had been using. With them he built up Geba and Mizpah.

7At that time Hanani the seer came to Asa king of Judah and said to him: "Because you relied on the king of Aram and not on the LORD your God, the army of the king of Aram has escaped from your hand. 8Were not the Cushitesb and Libyans a mighty army with great numbers of chariots and horsemenc? Yet when you relied on the LORD, he delivered them into your hand. 9For the eyes of the LORD range throughout the earth to strengthen those whose hearts are fully committed to him. You have done a foolish thing, and from now on you will be at war."

10Asa was angry with the seer because of this; he was so enraged that he put him in prison. At the same time Asa brutally oppressed some of the people.

11The events of Asa's reign, from beginning to end, are written in the book of the kings of Judah and Israel.

---

a 4 Also known as *Abel Beth Maacah*   b 8 That is, people from the upper Nile region   c 8 Or *charioteers*

Living Bible

ficed to the Lord seven hundred oxen and seven thousand sheep—it was part of the plunder they had captured in the battle. 12Then they entered into a contract to worship only the Lord God of their fathers, 13and agreed that anyone who refused to do this must die—whether old or young, man or woman. 14They shouted out their oath of loyalty to God with trumpets blaring and horns sounding. 15All were happy for this covenant with God, for they had entered into it with all their hearts and wills, and wanted him above everything else, and they found him! And he gave them peace throughout the nation.

16King Asa even removed his mother Maacah from being the queen mother because she made an Asherah-idol; he cut down the idol and crushed and burned it at Kidron Brook. 17Over in Israel the idol-temples were not removed. But here in Judah and Benjamin the heart of King Asa was perfect before God throughout his lifetime. 18He brought back into the Temple the silver and gold bowls which he and his father had dedicated to the Lord. 19So there was no more war until the thirty-fifth year of King Asa's reign.

16 IN THE thirty-sixth year of King Asa's reign, King Baasha of Israel declared war on him and built the fortressd of Ramah in order to control the road to Judah. 2Asa's response was to take the silver and gold from the Temple and from the palace, and to send it to King Ben-hadad of Syria, at Damascus, with this message:

3"Let us renew the mutual security pact that there was between your father and my father. See, here is silver and gold to induce you to break your alliance with King Baasha of Israel, so that he will leave me alone." 4Ben-hadad agreed to King Asa's request and mobilized his armies to attack Israel. They destroyed the cities of Ijon, Dan, Abel-maim and all of the supply centers in Naphtali. 5As soon as King Baasha of Israel heard what was happening, he discontinued building Ramah and gave up his plan to attack Judah. 6Then King Asa and the people of Judah went out to Ramah and carried away the building stones and timbers and used them to build Geba and Mizpah instead.

7About that time the prophet Hanani came to King Asa and told him, "Because you have put your trust in the king of Syria instead of in the Lord your God, the army of the king of Syria has escaped from you. 8Don't you remember what happened to the Ethiopians and Libyans and their vast army, with all of their chariots and cavalrymen? But you relied then on the Lord, and he delivered them all into your hand. 9For the eyes of the Lord search back and forth across the whole earth, looking for people whose hearts are perfect toward him, so that he can show his great power in helping them. What a fool you have been! From now on you shall have wars."

10Asa was so angry with the prophet for saying this that he threw him into jail. And Asa oppressed all the people at that time.

11The rest of the biography of Asa is written in *The Annals of the Kings of Israel and Judah*. 12In the thirty-

New Revised Standard

the booty that they had brought, seven hundred oxen and seven thousand sheep. 12They entered into a covenant to seek the LORD, the God of their ancestors, with all their heart and with all their soul. 13Whoever would not seek the LORD, the God of Israel, should be put to death, whether young or old, man or woman. 14They took an oath to the LORD with a loud voice, and with shouting, and with trumpets, and with horns. 15All Judah rejoiced over the oath; for they had sworn with all their heart, and had sought him with their whole desire, and he was found by them, and the LORD gave them rest all around.

16 King Asa even removed his mother Maacah from being queen mother because she had made an abominable image for Asherah. Asa cut down her image, crushed it, and burned it at the Wadi Kidron. 17But the high places were not taken out of Israel. Nevertheless the heart of Asa was true all his days. 18He brought into the house of God the votive gifts of his father and his own votive gifts—silver, gold, and utensils. 19And there was no more war until the thirty-fifth year of the reign of Asa.

Alliance with Aram Condemned

16 IN THE thirty-sixth year of the reign of Asa, King Baasha of Israel went up against Judah, and built Ramah, to prevent anyone from going out or coming into the territory ofe King Asa of Judah. 2Then Asa took silver and gold from the treasures of the house of the LORD and the king's house, and sent them to King Ben-hadad of Aram, who resided in Damascus, saying, 3"Let there be an alliance between me and you, like that between my father and your father; I am sending to you silver and gold; go, break your alliance with King Baasha of Israel, so that he may withdraw from me." 4Ben-hadad listened to King Asa, and sent the commanders of his armies against the cities of Israel. They conquered Ijon, Dan, Abel-maim, and all the store-cities of Naphtali. 5When Baasha heard of it, he stopped building Ramah, and let his work cease. 6Then King Asa brought all Judah, and they carried away the stones of Ramah and its timber, with which Baasha had been building, and with them he built up Geba and Mizpah.

7 At that time the seer Hanani came to King Asa of Judah, and said to him, "Because you relied on the king of Aram, and did not rely on the LORD your God, the army of the king of Aram has escaped you. 8Were not the Ethiopiansf and the Libyans a huge army with exceedingly many chariots and cavalry? Yet because you relied on the LORD, he gave them into your hand. 9For the eyes of the LORD range throughout the entire earth, to strengthen those whose heart is true to him. You have done foolishly in this; for from now on you will have wars." 10Then Asa was angry with the seer, and put him in the stocks, in prison, for he was in a rage with him because of this. And Asa inflicted cruelties on some of the people at the same time.

Asa's Disease and Death

11 The acts of Asa, from first to last, are written in the Book of the Kings of Judah and Israel. 12In the

---

d 16:1 built the fortress, literally, "high places."

e Heb lacks *the territory of*   f Or Nubians; Heb Cushites

King James

12And Asa in the thirty and ninth year of his reign was diseased in his feet, until his disease *was* exceeding *great:* yet in his disease he sought not to the LORD, but to the physicians.

13¶ And Asa slept with his fathers, and died in the one and fortieth year of his reign.

14And they buried him in his own sepulchres, which he had made for himself in the city of David, and laid him in the bed which was filled with sweet odours and divers kinds *of spices* prepared by the apothecaries' art: and they made a very great burning for him.

17 AND JEHOSHAPHAT his son reigned in his stead, and strengthened himself against Israel.

2And he placed forces in all the fenced cities of Judah, and set garrisons in the land of Judah, and in the cities of Ephraim, which Asa his father had taken.

3And the LORD was with Jehoshaphat, because he walked in the first ways of his father David, and sought not unto Baalim;

4But sought to the *Lord* God of his father, and walked in his commandments, and not after the doings of Israel.

5Therefore the LORD stablished the kingdom in his hand; and all Judah brought to Jehoshaphat presents; and he had riches and honour in abundance.

6And his heart was lifted up in the ways of the LORD: moreover he took away the high places and groves out of Judah.

7¶ Also in the third year of his reign he sent to his princes, *even* to Ben-hail, and to Obadiah, and to Zechariah, and to Nethaneel, and to Michaiah, to teach in the cities of Judah.

8And with them *he sent* Levites, *even* Shemaiah, and Nethaniah, and Zebadiah, and Asahel, and Shemiramoth, and Jehonathan, and Adonijah, and Tobijah, and Tob-adonijah, Levites; and with them Elishama and Jehoram, priests.

9And they taught in Judah, and *had* the book of the law of the LORD with them, and went about throughout all the cities of Judah, and taught the people.

10¶ And the fear of the LORD fell upon all the kingdoms of the lands that *were* round about Judah, so that they made no war against Jehoshaphat.

11Also *some* of the Philistines brought Jehoshaphat presents, and tribute silver; and the Arabians brought him flocks, seven thousand and seven hundred rams, and seven thousand and seven hundred he goats.

12¶ And Jehoshaphat waxed great exceedingly; and he built in Judah castles, and cities of store.

13And he had much business in the cities of Judah: and the men of war, mighty men of valour, *were* in Jerusalem.

14And these *are* the numbers of them according to the house of their fathers: Of Judah, the captains of thousands; Adnah the chief, and with him mighty men of valour three hundred thousand.

15And next to him *was* Jehohanan the captain, and with him two hundred and fourscore thousand.

16And next him *was* Amasiah the son of Zichri, who willingly offered himself unto the LORD; and with him two hundred thousand mighty men of valour.

17And of Benjamin; Eliada a mighty man of valour, and with him armed men with bow and shield two hundred thousand.

18And next him *was* Jehozabad, and with him an hundred and fourscore thousand ready prepared for the war.

19These waited on the king, beside *those* whom the king put in the fenced cities throughout all Judah.

New International

12In the thirty-ninth year of his reign Asa was afflicted with a disease in his feet. Though his disease was severe, even in his illness he did not seek help from the LORD, but only from the physicians. 13Then in the forty-first year of his reign Asa died and rested with his fathers. 14They buried him in the tomb that he had cut out for himself in the City of David. They laid him on a bier covered with spices and various blended perfumes, and they made a huge fire in his honor.

Jehoshaphat King of Judah

17 JEHOSHAPHAT HIS son succeeded him as king and strengthened himself against Israel. 2He stationed troops in all the fortified cities of Judah and put garrisons in Judah and in the towns of Ephraim that his father Asa had captured.

3The LORD was with Jehoshaphat because in his early years he walked in the ways his father David had followed. He did not consult the Baals 4but sought the God of his father and followed his commands rather than the practices of Israel. 5The LORD established the kingdom under his control; and all Judah brought gifts to Jehoshaphat, so that he had great wealth and honor. 6His heart was devoted to the ways of the LORD; furthermore, he removed the high places and the Asherah poles from Judah.

7In the third year of his reign he sent his officials Ben-Hail, Obadiah, Zechariah, Nethanel and Micaiah to teach in the towns of Judah. 8With them were certain Levites—Shemaiah, Nethaniah, Zebadiah, Asahel, Shemiramoth, Jehonathan, Adonijah, Tobijah and Tob-Adonijah—and the priests Elishama and Jehoram. 9They taught throughout Judah, taking with them the Book of the Law of the LORD; they went around to all the towns of Judah and taught the people.

10The fear of the LORD fell on all the kingdoms of the lands surrounding Judah, so that they did not make war with Jehoshaphat. 11Some Philistines brought Jehoshaphat gifts and silver as tribute, and the Arabs brought him flocks: seven thousand seven hundred rams and seven thousand seven hundred goats.

12Jehoshaphat became more and more powerful; he built forts and store cities in Judah 13and had large supplies in the towns of Judah. He also kept experienced fighting men in Jerusalem. 14Their enrollment by families was as follows:

From Judah, commanders of units of 1,000:
　Adnah the commander, with 300,000 fighting men;
15next, Jehohanan the commander, with 280,000;
16next, Amasiah son of Zicri, who volunteered himself for the service of the LORD, with 200,000.
17From Benjamin:
　Eliada, a valiant soldier, with 200,000 men armed with bows and shields;
18next, Jehozabad, with 180,000 men armed for battle.

19These were the men who served the king, besides those he stationed in the fortified cities throughout Judah.

Living Bible

ninth year of his reign, Asa became seriously diseased in his feet but he didn't go to the Lord with the problem, but to the doctors. 13, 14So he died in the forty-first year of his reign, and was buried in his own vault that he had hewn out for himself in Jerusalem. He was laid on a bed perfumed with sweet spices and ointments, and his people made a very great burning of incense for him at his funeral.

17 THEN HIS son Jehoshaphat became the king and mobilized for war against Israel. 2He placed garrisons in all of the fortified cities of Judah, in various other places throughout the country, and in the cities of Ephraim that his father had conquered.

3The Lord was with Jehoshaphat because he followed in the good footsteps of his father's early years, and did not worship idols. 4He obeyed the commandments of his father's God—quite unlike the people across the border in the land of Israel. 5So the Lord strengthened his position as king of Judah. All the people of Judah cooperated by paying their taxes, so he became very wealthy as well as being very popular. 6He boldly followed the paths of God—even knocking down the heathen altars on the hills, and destroying the Asherim idols.

7, 8, 9In the third year of his reign he began a nation-wide religious education program. He sent out top government officials as teachers in all the cities of Judah. These men included Ben-hail, Obadiah, Zechariah, Nethanel, and Micaiah. He also used the Levites for this purpose, including Shemaiah, Nethaniah, Zebadiah, Asahel, Shemiramoth, Jehonathan, Adonijah, Tobijah, and Tobadonijah; also the priests, Elishama and Jehoram. They took copies of *The Book of the Law of the Lord* to all the cities of Judah, to teach the Scriptures to the people.

10Then the fear of the Lord fell upon all the surrounding kingdoms so that none of them declared war on King Jehoshaphat.

11Even some of the Philistines brought him presents and annual tribute, and the Arabs donated 7,700 rams and 7,700 male goats. 12So Jehoshaphat became very strong, and built fortresses and supply cities throughout Judah.

13His public works program was also extensive, and he had a huge army stationed at Jerusalem, his capital. 14, 15Three hundred thousand Judean troops were there under General Adnah. Next in command was Jeho-ha-nan with an army of 280,000 men. 16Next was Amasiah (son of Zichri), a man of unusual piety, with 200,000 troops. 17Benjamin supplied 200,000 men equipped with bows and shields under the command of Eliada, a great general. 18His second in command was Jehozabad, with 180,000 trained men. 19These were the troops in Jerusalem in addition to those placed by the king in the fortified cities throughout the nation.

New Revised Standard

thirty-ninth year of his reign Asa was diseased in his feet, and his disease became severe; yet even in his disease he did not seek the LORD, but sought help from physicians. 13Then Asa slept with his ancestors, dying in the forty-first year of his reign. 14They buried him in the tomb that he had hewn out for himself in the city of David. They laid him on a bier that had been filled with various kinds of spices prepared by the perfumer's art; and they made a very great fire in his honor.

Jehoshaphat's Reign

17 HIS SON Jehoshaphat succeeded him, and strengthened himself against Israel. 2He placed forces in all the fortified cities of Judah, and set garrisons in the land of Judah, and in the cities of Ephraim that his father Asa had taken. 3The LORD was with Jehoshaphat, because he walked in the earlier ways of his father;a he did not seek the Baals, 4but sought the God of his father and walked in his commandments, and not according to the ways of Israel. 5Therefore the LORD established the kingdom in his hand. All Judah brought tribute to Jehoshaphat, and he had great riches and honor. 6His heart was courageous in the ways of the LORD; and furthermore he removed the high places and the sacred polesb from Judah.

7 In the third year of his reign he sent his officials, Ben-hail, Obadiah, Zechariah, Nethanel, and Micaiah, to teach in the cities of Judah. 8With them were the Levites, Shemaiah, Nethaniah, Zebadiah, Asahel, Shemiramoth, Jehonathan, Adonijah, Tobijah, and Tobadonijah; and with these Levites, the priests Elishama and Jehoram. 9They taught in Judah, having the book of the law of the LORD with them; they went around through all the cities of Judah and taught among the people.

10 The fear of the LORD fell on all the kingdoms of the lands around Judah, and they did not make war against Jehoshaphat. 11Some of the Philistines brought Jehoshaphat presents, and silver for tribute; and the Arabs also brought him seven thousand seven hundred rams and seven thousand seven hundred male goats. 12Jehoshaphat grew steadily greater. He built fortresses and storage cities in Judah. 13He carried out great works in the cities of Judah. He had soldiers, mighty warriors, in Jerusalem. 14This was the muster of them by ancestral houses: Of Judah, the commanders of the thousands: Adnah the commander, with three hundred thousand mighty warriors, 15and next to him Jehohanan the commander, with two hundred eighty thousand, 16and next to him Amasiah son of Zichri, a volunteer for the service of the LORD, with two hundred thousand mighty warriors. 17Of Benjamin: Eliada, a mighty warrior, with two hundred thousand armed with bow and shield, 18and next to him Jehozabad with one hundred eighty thousand armed for war. 19These were in the service of the king, besides those whom the king had placed in the fortified cities throughout all Judah.

King James

18 NOW JEHOSHAPHAT had riches and honour in abundance, and joined affinity with Ahab.

2And after *certain* years he went down to Ahab to Samaria. And Ahab killed sheep and oxen for him in abundance, and for the people that *he had* with him, and persuaded him to go up *with him* to Ramoth-gilead.

3And Ahab king of Israel said unto Jehoshaphat king of Judah, Wilt thou go with me to Ramoth-gilead? And he answered him, I *am* as thou *art,* and my people as thy people; and *we will be* with thee in the war.

4¶ And Jehoshaphat said unto the king of Israel, Inquire, I pray thee, at the word of the LORD today.

5Therefore the king of Israel gathered together of prophets four hundred men, and said unto them, Shall we go to Ramoth-gilead to battle, or shall I forbear? And they said, Go up; for God will deliver *it* into the king's hand.

6But Jehoshaphat said, *Is there* not here a prophet of the LORD besides, that we might inquire of him?

7And the king of Israel said unto Jehoshaphat, *There is* yet one man, by whom we may inquire of the LORD: but I hate him; for he never prophesied good unto me, but always evil: the same *is* Micaiah the son of Imla. And Jehoshaphat said, Let not the king say so.

8And the king of Israel called for one *of his* officers, and said, Fetch quickly Micaiah the son of Imla.

9And the king of Israel and Jehoshaphat king of Judah sat either of them on his throne, clothed in *their* robes, and they sat in a void place at the entering in of the gate of Samaria; and all the prophets prophesied before them.

10And Zedekiah the son of Chenaanah had made him horns of iron, and said, Thus saith the LORD, With these thou shalt push Syria until they be consumed.

11And all the prophets prophesied so, saying, Go up to Ramoth-gilead, and prosper: for the LORD shall deliver *it* into the hand of the king.

12And the messenger that went to call Micaiah spake to him, saying, Behold, the words of the prophets *declare* good to the king with one assent; let thy word therefore, I pray thee, be like one of theirs, and speak thou good.

13And Micaiah said, *As* the LORD liveth, even what my God saith, that will I speak.

14And when he was come to the king, the king said unto him, Micaiah, shall we go to Ramoth-gilead to battle, or shall I forbear? And he said, Go ye up, and prosper, and they shall be delivered into your hand.

15And the king said to him, How many times shall I adjure thee that thou say nothing but the truth to me in the name of the LORD?

16Then he said, I did see all Israel scattered upon the mountains, as sheep that have no shepherd: and the LORD said, These have no master; let them return *therefore* every man to his house in peace.

17And the king of Israel said to Jehoshaphat, Did I not tell thee *that* he would not prophesy good unto me, but evil?

18Again he said, Therefore hear the word of the LORD; I saw the LORD sitting upon his throne, and all the host of heaven standing on his right hand and *on* his left.

19And the LORD said, Who shall entice Ahab king of Israel, that he may go up and fall at Ramoth-gilead? And one spake saying after this manner, and another saying after that manner.

20Then there came out a spirit, and stood before the LORD, and said, I will entice him. And the LORD said unto him, Wherewith?

21And he said, I will go out, and be a lying spirit in the mouth of all his prophets. And *the LORD* said, Thou shalt entice *him,* and thou shalt also prevail: go out, and do *even* so.

New International

Micaiah Prophesies Against Ahab

18 NOW JEHOSHAPHAT had great wealth and honor, and he allied himself with Ahab by marriage. 2Some years later he went down to visit Ahab in Samaria. Ahab slaughtered many sheep and cattle for him and the people with him and urged him to attack Ramoth Gilead. 3Ahab king of Israel asked Jehoshaphat king of Judah, "Will you go with me against Ramoth Gilead?"

Jehoshaphat replied, "I am as you are, and my people as your people; we will join you in the war." 4But Jehoshaphat also said to the king of Israel, "First seek the counsel of the LORD."

5So the king of Israel brought together the prophets— four hundred men—and asked them, "Shall we go to war against Ramoth Gilead, or shall I refrain?"

"Go," they answered, "for God will give it into the king's hand."

6But Jehoshaphat asked, "Is there not a prophet of the LORD here whom we can inquire of?"

7The king of Israel answered Jehoshaphat, "There is still one man through whom we can inquire of the LORD, but I hate him because he never prophesies anything good about me, but always bad. He is Micaiah son of Imlah."

"The king should not say that," Jehoshaphat replied.

8So the king of Israel called one of his officials and said, "Bring Micaiah son of Imlah at once."

9Dressed in their royal robes, the king of Israel and Jehoshaphat king of Judah were sitting on their thrones at the threshing floor by the entrance to the gate of Samaria, with all the prophets prophesying before them. 10Now Zedekiah son of Kenaanah had made iron horns, and he declared, "This is what the LORD says: 'With these you will gore the Arameans until they are destroyed.'"

11All the other prophets were prophesying the same thing. "Attack Ramoth Gilead and be victorious," they said, "for the LORD will give it into the king's hand."

12The messenger who had gone to summon Micaiah said to him, "Look, as one man the other prophets are predicting success for the king. Let your word agree with theirs, and speak favorably."

13But Micaiah said, "As surely as the LORD lives, I can tell him only what my God says."

14When he arrived, the king asked him, "Micaiah, shall we go to war against Ramoth Gilead, or shall I refrain?"

"Attack and be victorious," he answered, "for they will be given into your hand."

15The king said to him, "How many times must I make you swear to tell me nothing but the truth in the name of the LORD?"

16Then Micaiah answered, "I saw all Israel scattered on the hills like sheep without a shepherd, and the LORD said, 'These people have no master. Let each one go home in peace.'"

17The king of Israel said to Jehoshaphat, "Didn't I tell you that he never prophesies anything good about me, but only bad?"

18Micaiah continued, "Therefore hear the word of the LORD: I saw the LORD sitting on his throne with all the host of heaven standing on his right and on his left. 19And the LORD said, 'Who will entice Ahab king of Israel into attacking Ramoth Gilead and going to his death there?'

"One suggested this, and another that. 20Finally, a spirit came forward, stood before the LORD and said, 'I will entice him.'

"'By what means?' the LORD asked.

21"'I will go and be a lying spirit in the mouths of all his prophets,' he said.

"'You will succeed in enticing him,' said the LORD. 'Go and do it.'

Living Bible

18 BUT RICH, popular King Jehoshaphat of Judah made a marriage alliance [for his son[a]] with [the daughter of[b]] King Ahab of Israel. [2]A few years later he went down to Samaria to visit King Ahab, and King Ahab gave a great party for him and his aides, butchering great numbers of sheep and oxen for the feast. Then he asked King Jehoshaphat to join forces with him against Ramoth-gilead.

[3, 4, 5]"Why, of course!" King Jehoshaphat replied. "I'm with you all the way. My troops are at your command! However, let's check with the Lord first."

So King Ahab summoned 400 of his heathen prophets and asked them, "Shall we go to war with Ramoth-gilead or not?"

And they replied, "Go ahead, for God will give you a great victory!"

[6, 7]But Jehoshaphat wasn't satisfied. "Isn't there some prophet of the Lord around here too?" he asked. "I'd like to ask him the same question."

"Well," Ahab told him, "there is one, but I hate him, for he never prophesies anything but evil! His name is Micaiah (son of Imlah)."

"Oh, come now, don't talk like that!" Jehoshaphat exclaimed. "Let's hear what he has to say."

[8]So the king of Israel called one of his aides. "Quick! Go and get Micaiah (son of Imlah)," he ordered.

[9]The two kings were sitting on thrones in full regalia at an open place near the Samaria gate, and all the "prophets" were prophesying before them. [10]One of them, Zedekiah (son of Chenaanah), made some iron horns for the occasion and proclaimed, "The Lord says you will gore the Syrians to death with these!"

[11]And all the others agreed. "Yes," they chorused, "go up to Ramoth-gilead and prosper, for the Lord will cause you to conquer."

[12]The man who went to get Micaiah told him what was happening, and what all the prophets were saying—that the war would end in triumph for the king.

"I hope you will agree with them and give the king a favorable reading," the man ventured.

[13]But Micaiah replied, "I vow by God that whatever God says is what I will say."

[14]When he arrived before the king, the king asked him, "Micaiah, shall we go to war against Ramoth-gilead or not?"

And Micaiah replied, "Sure, go ahead! It will be a glorious victory!"

[15]"Look here," the king said sharply, "how many times must I tell you to speak nothing except what the Lord tells you to?"

[16]Then Micaiah told him, "In my vision I saw all Israel scattered upon the mountain as sheep without a shepherd. And the Lord said, 'Their master has been killed. Send them home.' "

[17]"Didn't I tell you?" the king of Israel exclaimed to Jehoshaphat. "He does it every time. He *never* prophesies *anything* but evil against me."

[18]"Listen to what else the Lord has told me," Micaiah continued. "I saw him upon his throne surrounded by vast throngs of angels.

[19, 20]"And the Lord said, 'Who can get King Ahab to go to battle against Ramoth-gilead and be killed there?'

"There were many suggestions, but finally a spirit stepped forward before the Lord and said, 'I can do it!'

" 'How?' the Lord asked him.

[21]"He replied, 'I will be a lying spirit in the mouths of all of the king's prophets!'

" 'It will work,' the Lord said; 'go and do it.'

New Revised Standard

Micaiah Predicts Failure

18 NOW JEHOSHAPHAT had great riches and honor; and he made a marriage alliance with Ahab. [2]After some years he went down to Ahab in Samaria. Ahab slaughtered an abundance of sheep and oxen for him and for the people who were with him, and induced him to go up against Ramoth-gilead. [3]King Ahab of Israel said to King Jehoshaphat of Judah, "Will you go with me to Ramoth-gilead?" He answered him, "I am with you, my people are your people. We will be with you in the war."

4　But Jehoshaphat also said to the king of Israel, "Inquire first for the word of the LORD." [5]Then the king of Israel gathered the prophets together, four hundred of them, and said to them, "Shall we go to battle against Ramoth-gilead, or shall I refrain?" They said, "Go up; for God will give it into the hand of the king." [6]But Jehoshaphat said, "Is there no other prophet of the LORD here of whom we may inquire?" [7]The king of Israel said to Jehoshaphat, "There is still one other by whom we may inquire of the LORD, Micaiah son of Imlah; but I hate him, for he never prophesies anything favorable about me, but only disaster." Jehoshaphat said, "Let the king not say such a thing." [8]Then the king of Israel summoned an officer and said, "Bring quickly Micaiah son of Imlah." [9]Now the king of Israel and King Jehoshaphat of Judah were sitting on their thrones, arrayed in their robes; and they were sitting at the threshing floor at the entrance of the gate of Samaria; and all the prophets were prophesying before them. [10]Zedekiah son of Chenaanah made for himself horns of iron, and he said, "Thus says the LORD: With these you shall gore the Arameans until they are destroyed." [11]All the prophets were prophesying the same and saying, "Go up to Ramoth-gilead and triumph; the LORD will give it into the hand of the king."

12　The messenger who had gone to summon Micaiah said to him, "Look, the words of the prophets with one accord are favorable to the king; let your word be like the word of one of them, and speak favorably." [13]But Micaiah said, "As the LORD lives, whatever my God says, that I will speak."

14　When he had come to the king, the king said to him, "Micaiah, shall we go to Ramoth-gilead to battle, or shall I refrain?" He answered, "Go up and triumph; they will be given into your hand." [15]But the king said to him, "How many times must I make you swear to tell me nothing but the truth in the name of the LORD?" [16]Then Micaiah[c] said, "I saw all Israel scattered on the mountains, like sheep without a shepherd; and the LORD said, 'These have no master; let each one go home in peace.' " [17]The king of Israel said to Jehoshaphat, "Did I not tell you that he would not prophesy anything favorable about me, but only disaster?"

18　Then Micaiah[c] said, "Therefore hear the word of the LORD: I saw the LORD sitting on his throne, with all the host of heaven standing to the right and to the left of him. [19]And the LORD said, 'Who will entice King Ahab of Israel, so that he may go up and fall at Ramoth-gilead?' Then one said one thing, and another said another, [20]until a spirit came forward and stood before the LORD, saying, 'I will entice him.' The LORD asked him, 'How?' [21]He replied, 'I will go out and be a lying spirit in the mouth of all his prophets.' Then the LORD[c] said, 'You are to entice him, and you shall succeed; go out and do it.' [22]So you see, the LORD has put a lying spirit

---

[a] *18:1 for his son,* implied.　[b] *18:1 the daughter of,* implied in 21:6.　　[c] Heb *he*

King James

22Now therefore, behold, the LORD hath put a lying spirit in the mouth of these thy prophets, and the LORD hath spoken evil against thee.

23Then Zedekiah the son of Chenaanah came near, and smote Micaiah upon the cheek, and said, Which way went the spirit of the LORD from me to speak unto thee?

24And Micaiah said, Behold, thou shalt see on that day when thou shalt go into an inner chamber to hide thyself.

25Then the king of Israel said, Take ye Micaiah, and carry him back to Amon the governor of the city, and to Joash the king's son;

26And say, Thus saith the king, Put this *fellow* in the prison, and feed him with bread of affliction and with water of affliction, until I return in peace.

27And Micaiah said, If thou certainly return in peace, *then* hath not the LORD spoken by me. And he said, Hearken, all ye people.

28So the king of Israel and Jehoshaphat the king of Judah went up to Ramoth-gilead.

29And the king of Israel said unto Jehoshaphat, I will disguise myself, and will go to the battle; but put thou on thy robes. So the king of Israel disguised himself; and they went to the battle.

30Now the king of Syria had commanded the captains of the chariots that *were* with him, saying, Fight ye not with small or great, save only with the king of Israel.

31And it came to pass, when the captains of the chariots saw Jehoshaphat, that they said, It *is* the king of Israel. Therefore they compassed about him to fight: but Jehoshaphat cried out, and the LORD helped him; and God moved them *to depart* from him.

32For it came to pass, that, when the captains of the chariots perceived that it was not the king of Israel, they turned back again from pursuing him.

33And a *certain* man drew a bow at a venture, and smote the king of Israel between the joints of the harness: therefore he said to his chariot man, Turn thine hand, that thou mayest carry me out of the host; for I am wounded.

34And the battle increased that day: howbeit the king of Israel stayed *himself* up in *his* chariot against the Syrians until the even: and about the time of the sun going down he died.

19 AND JEHOSHAPHAT the king of Judah returned to his house in peace to Jerusalem.

2And Jehu the son of Hanani the seer went out to meet him, and said to king Jehoshaphat, Shouldest thou help the ungodly, and love them that hate the LORD? therefore *is* wrath upon thee from before the LORD.

3Nevertheless there are good things found in thee, in that thou hast taken away the groves out of the land, and hast prepared thine heart to seek God.

4And Jehoshaphat dwelt at Jerusalem: and he went out again through the people from Beer-sheba to mount Ephraim, and brought them back unto the LORD God of their fathers.

5¶ And he set judges in the land throughout all the fenced cities of Judah, city by city,

6And said to the judges, Take heed what ye do: for ye judge not for man, but for the LORD, who *is* with you in the judgment.

7Wherefore now let the fear of the LORD be upon you; take heed and do *it:* for *there is* no iniquity with the LORD our God, nor respect of persons, nor taking of gifts.

New International

22"So now the LORD has put a lying spirit in the mouths of these prophets of yours. The LORD has decreed disaster for you."

23Then Zedekiah son of Kenaanah went up and slapped Micaiah in the face. "Which way did the spirit froma the LORD go when he went from me to speak to you?" he asked.

24Micaiah replied, "You will find out on the day you go to hide in an inner room."

25The king of Israel then ordered, "Take Micaiah and send him back to Amon the ruler of the city and to Joash the king's son, 26and say, 'This is what the king says: Put this fellow in prison and give him nothing but bread and water until I return safely.' "

27Micaiah declared, "If you ever return safely, the LORD has not spoken through me." Then he added, "Mark my words, all you people!"

Ahab Killed at Ramoth Gilead

28So the king of Israel and Jehoshaphat king of Judah went up to Ramoth Gilead. 29The king of Israel said to Jehoshaphat, "I will enter the battle in disguise, but you wear your royal robes." So the king of Israel disguised himself and went into battle.

30Now the king of Aram had ordered his chariot commanders, "Do not fight with anyone, small or great, except the king of Israel." 31When the chariot commanders saw Jehoshaphat, they thought, "This is the king of Israel." So they turned to attack him, but Jehoshaphat cried out, and the LORD helped him. God drew them away from him, 32for when the chariot commanders saw that he was not the king of Israel, they stopped pursuing him.

33But someone drew his bow at random and hit the king of Israel between the sections of his armor. The king told the chariot driver, "Wheel around and get me out of the fighting. I've been wounded." 34All day long the battle raged, and the king of Israel propped himself up in his chariot facing the Arameans until evening. Then at sunset he died.

19 WHEN JEHOSHAPHAT king of Judah returned safely to his palace in Jerusalem, 2Jehu the seer, the son of Hanani, went out to meet him and said to the king, "Should you help the wicked and loveb those who hate the LORD? Because of this, the wrath of the LORD is upon you. 3There is, however, some good in you, for you have rid the land of the Asherah poles and have set your heart on seeking God."

Jehoshaphat Appoints Judges

4Jehoshaphat lived in Jerusalem, and he went out again among the people from Beersheba to the hill country of Ephraim and turned them back to the LORD, the God of their fathers. 5He appointed judges in the land, in each of the fortified cities of Judah. 6He told them, "Consider carefully what you do, because you are not judging for man but for the LORD, who is with you whenever you give a verdict. 7Now let the fear of the LORD be upon you. Judge carefully, for with the LORD our God there is no injustice or partiality or bribery."

---

a 23 Or *Spirit of*   b 2 Or *and make alliances with*

Living Bible

22"So you see, the Lord has put a lying spirit in the mouths of these prophets of yours, when actually he has determined just the opposite of what they are telling you!"

23Then Zedekiah (son of Chenaanah) walked up to Micaiah and slapped him across the face. "You liar!" he yelled. "When did the Spirit of the Lord leave me and enter you?"

24"You'll find out soon enough," Micaiah replied, "—when you are hiding in an inner room!"

25"Arrest this man and take him back to Governor Amon and to my son Joash," the king of Israel ordered. 26"Tell them, 'The king says to put this fellow in prison and feed him with bread and water until I return safely from the battle!' "

27Micaiah replied, "If you return safely, the Lord has not spoken through me." Then, turning to those around them, he remarked, "Take note of what I have said."

28So the king of Israel and the king of Judah led their armies to Ramoth-gilead.

29The king of Israel said to Jehoshaphat, "I'll disguise myself so that no one will recognize me, but you put on your royal robes!" So that is what they did.

30Now the king of Syria had issued these instructions to his charioteers: "Ignore everyone but the king of Israel!"

31So when the Syrian charioteers saw King Jehoshaphat of Judah in his royal robes, they went for him, supposing that he was the man they were after. But Jehoshaphat cried out to the Lord to save him, and the Lord made the charioteers see their mistake and leave him. 32For as soon as they realized he was not the king of Israel, they stopped chasing him. 33But one of the Syrian soldiers shot an arrow haphazardly at the Israeli troops, and it struck the king of Israel at the opening where the lower armor and the breastplate meet. "Get me out of here," he groaned to the driver of his chariot, "for I am badly wounded." 34The battle grew hotter and hotter all that day, and King Ahab went back in, propped up in his chariot, to fight the Syrians, but just as the sun sank into the western skies, he died.

19 AS KING Jehoshaphat of Judah returned home, uninjured, 2the prophet Jehu (son of Hanani) went out to meet him.

"Should you be helping the wicked, and loving those who hate the Lord?" he asked him. "Because of what you have done, God's wrath is upon you. 3But there are some good things about you, in that you got rid of the shame-idols throughout the land, and you have tried to be faithful to God."

4So Jehoshaphat made no more trips to Israel after that, but remained quietly at Jerusalem. Later he went out again among the people, traveling from Beer-sheba to the hill country of Ephraim to encourage them to worship the God of their ancestors. 5He appointed judges throughout the nation in all the larger cities, 6and instructed them:

"Watch your step—I have not appointed you—God has; and he will stand beside you and help you give justice in each case that comes before you. 7Be very much afraid to give any other decision than what God tells you to. For there must be no injustice among God's judges, no partiality, no taking of bribes."

New Revised Standard

in the mouth of these your prophets; the LORD has decreed disaster for you."

23 Then Zedekiah son of Chenaanah came up to Micaiah, slapped him on the cheek, and said, "Which way did the spirit of the LORD pass from me to speak to you?" 24Micaiah replied, "You will find out on that day when you go in to hide in an inner chamber." 25The king of Israel then ordered, "Take Micaiah, and return him to Amon the governor of the city and to Joash the king's son; 26and say, 'Thus says the king: Put this fellow in prison, and feed him on reduced rations of bread and water until I return in peace.' " 27Micaiah said, "If you return in peace, the LORD has not spoken by me." And he said, "Hear, you peoples, all of you!"

Defeat and Death of Ahab

28 So the king of Israel and King Jehoshaphat of Judah went up to Ramoth-gilead. 29The king of Israel said to Jehoshaphat, "I will disguise myself and go into battle, but you wear your robes." So the king of Israel disguised himself, and they went into battle. 30Now the king of Aram had commanded the captains of his chariots, "Fight with no one small or great, but only with the king of Israel." 31When the captains of the chariots saw Jehoshaphat, they said, "It is the king of Israel." So they turned to fight against him; and Jehoshaphat cried out, and the LORD helped him. God drew them away from him, 32for when the captains of the chariots saw that it was not the king of Israel, they turned back from pursuing him. 33But a certain man drew his bow and unknowingly struck the king of Israel between the scale armor and the breastplate; so he said to the driver of his chariot, "Turn around, and carry me out of the battle, for I am wounded." 34The battle grew hot that day, and the king of Israel propped himself up in his chariot facing the Arameans until evening; then at sunset he died.

19 KING JEHOSHAPHAT of Judah returned in safety to his house in Jerusalem. 2Jehu son of Hanani the seer went out to meet him and said to King Jehoshaphat, "Should you help the wicked and love those who hate the LORD? Because of this, wrath has gone out against you from the LORD. 3Nevertheless, some good is found in you, for you destroyed the sacred poles[c] out of the land, and have set your heart to seek God."

The Reforms of Jehoshaphat

4 Jehoshaphat resided at Jerusalem; then he went out again among the people, from Beer-sheba to the hill country of Ephraim, and brought them back to the LORD, the God of their ancestors. 5He appointed judges in the land in all the fortified cities of Judah, city by city, 6and said to the judges, "Consider what you are doing, for you judge not on behalf of human beings but on the LORD's behalf; he is with you in giving judgment. 7Now, let the fear of the LORD be upon you; take care what you do, for there is no perversion of justice with the LORD our God, or partiality, or taking of bribes."

c Heb *Asheroth*

King James

8¶ Moreover in Jerusalem did Jehoshaphat set of the Levites, and *of* the priests, and of the chief of the fathers of Israel, for the judgment of the LORD, and for controversies, when they returned to Jerusalem.

9And he charged them, saying, Thus shall ye do in the fear of the LORD, faithfully, and with a perfect heart.

10And what cause soever shall come to you of your brethren that dwell in their cities, between blood and blood, between law and commandment, statutes and judgments, ye shall even warn them that they trespass not against the LORD, and *so* wrath come upon you, and upon your brethren: this do, and ye shall not trespass.

11And, behold, Amariah the chief priest *is* over you in all matters of the LORD; and Zebadiah the son of Ishmael, the ruler of the house of Judah, for all the king's matters: also the Levites *shall be* officers before you. Deal courageously, and the LORD shall be with the good.

20 IT CAME to pass after this also, *that* the children of Moab, and the children of Ammon, and with them *other* beside the Ammonites, came against Jehoshaphat to battle.

2Then there came some that told Jehoshaphat, saying, There cometh a great multitude against thee from beyond the sea on this side Syria; and, behold, they *be* in Hazazon-tamar, which *is* En-gedi.

3And Jehoshaphat feared, and set himself to seek the LORD, and proclaimed a fast throughout all Judah.

4And Judah gathered themselves together, to ask *help* of the LORD: even out of all the cities of Judah they came to seek the LORD.

5¶ And Jehoshaphat stood in the congregation of Judah and Jerusalem, in the house of the LORD, before the new court,

6And said, O LORD God of our fathers, *art* not thou God in heaven? and rulest *not* thou over all the kingdoms of the heathen? and in thine hand *is there not* power and might, so that none is able to withstand thee?

7*Art* not thou our God, *who* didst drive out the inhabitants of this land before thy people Israel, and gavest it to the seed of Abraham thy friend for ever?

8And they dwelt therein, and have built thee a sanctuary therein for thy name, saying,

9If, *when* evil cometh upon us, *as* the sword, judgment, or pestilence, or famine, we stand before this house, and in thy presence, (for thy name *is* in this house,) and cry unto thee in our affliction, then thou wilt hear and help.

10And now, behold, the children of Ammon and Moab and mount Seir, whom thou wouldest not let Israel invade, when they came out of the land of Egypt, but they turned from them, and destroyed them not;

11Behold, *I say, how* they reward us, to come to cast us out of thy possession, which thou hast given us to inherit.

12O our God, wilt thou not judge them? for we have no might against this great company that cometh against us; neither know we what to do: but our eyes *are* upon thee.

13And all Judah stood before the LORD, with their little ones, their wives, and their children.

14¶ Then upon Jahaziel the son of Zechariah, the son of Benaiah, the son of Jeiel, the son of Mattaniah, a Levite of the sons of Asaph, came the spirit of the LORD in the midst of the congregation;

15And he said, Hearken ye, all Judah, and ye inhabitants of Jerusalem, and thou king Jehoshaphat, Thus saith the LORD unto you, Be not afraid nor dismayed by reason of this great multitude; for the battle *is* not yours, but God's.

New International

8In Jerusalem also, Jehoshaphat appointed some of the Levites, priests and heads of Israelite families to administer the law of the LORD and to settle disputes. And they lived in Jerusalem. 9He gave them these orders: "You must serve faithfully and wholeheartedly in the fear of the LORD. 10In every case that comes before you from your fellow countrymen who live in the cities—whether bloodshed or other concerns of the law, commands, decrees or ordinances—you are to warn them not to sin against the LORD; otherwise his wrath will come on you and your brothers. Do this, and you will not sin.

11"Amariah the chief priest will be over you in any matter concerning the LORD, and Zebadiah son of Ishmael, the leader of the tribe of Judah, will be over you in any matter concerning the king, and the Levites will serve as officials before you. Act with courage, and may the LORD be with those who do well."

Jehoshaphat Defeats Moab and Ammon

20 AFTER THIS, the Moabites and Ammonites with some of the Meunites[a] came to make war on Jehoshaphat.

2Some men came and told Jehoshaphat, "A vast army is coming against you from Edom,[b] from the other side of the Sea.[c] It is already in Hazazon Tamar" (that is, En Gedi). 3Alarmed, Jehoshaphat resolved to inquire of the LORD, and he proclaimed a fast for all Judah. 4The people of Judah came together to seek help from the LORD; indeed, they came from every town in Judah to seek him.

5Then Jehoshaphat stood up in the assembly of Judah and Jerusalem at the temple of the LORD in the front of the new courtyard 6and said:

"O LORD, God of our fathers, are you not the God who is in heaven? You rule over all the kingdoms of the nations. Power and might are in your hand, and no one can withstand you. 7O our God, did you not drive out the inhabitants of this land before your people Israel and give it forever to the descendants of Abraham your friend? 8They have lived in it and have built in it a sanctuary for your Name, saying, 9'If calamity comes upon us, whether the sword of judgment, or plague or famine, we will stand in your presence before this temple that bears your Name and will cry out to you in our distress, and you will hear us and save us.'

10"But now here are men from Ammon, Moab and Mount Seir, whose territory you would not allow Israel to invade when they came from Egypt; so they turned away from them and did not destroy them. 11See how they are repaying us by coming to drive us out of the possession you gave us as an inheritance. 12O our God, will you not judge them? For we have no power to face this vast army that is attacking us. We do not know what to do, but our eyes are upon you."

13All the men of Judah, with their wives and children and little ones, stood there before the LORD.

14Then the Spirit of the LORD came upon Jahaziel son of Zechariah, the son of Benaiah, the son of Jeiel, the son of Mattaniah, a Levite and descendant of Asaph, as he stood in the assembly.

15He said: "Listen, King Jehoshaphat and all who live in Judah and Jerusalem! This is what the LORD says to you: 'Do not be afraid or discouraged because of this vast army. For the battle is not yours, but God's. 16To-

a *1* Some Septuagint manuscripts; Hebrew *Ammonites*   b *2* One Hebrew manuscript; most Hebrew manuscripts, Septuagint and Vulgate *Aram*   c *2* That is, the Dead Sea

Living Bible

8Jehoshaphat set up courts in Jerusalem, too, with the Levites and priests and clan leaders and judges. 9These were his instructions to them: "You are to act always in the fear of God, with honest hearts. 10Whenever a case is referred to you by the judges out in the provinces, whether murder cases or other violations of the laws and ordinances of God, you are to clarify the evidence for them and help them to decide justly, lest the wrath of God come down upon you and them; if you do this, you will discharge your responsibility."

11Then he appointed Amariah, the High Priest, to be the court of final appeal in cases involving violation of sacred affairs; and Zebadiah (son of Ishmael), a ruler in Judah, as the court of final appeal in all civil cases; with the Levites as their assistants. "Be fearless in your stand for truth and honesty. And may God use you to defend the innocent," was his final word to them.

20 LATER ON, the armies of the kings of Moab, Ammon, and of the Meunites declared war on Jehoshaphat and the people of Judah. 2Word reached Jehoshaphat that "a vast army is marching against you from beyond the Dead Sea, from Syria. It is already at Hazazon-tamar" (also called Engedi). 3Jehoshaphat was badly shaken by this news and determined to beg for help from the Lord; so he announced that all the people of Judah should go without food for a time, in penitence and intercession before God. 4People from all across the nation came to Jerusalem to plead unitedly with him. 5Jehoshaphat stood among them as they gathered at the new court of the Temple, and prayed this prayer:

6"O Lord God of our fathers—the only God in all the heavens, the Ruler of all the kingdoms of the earth—you are so powerful, so mighty. Who can stand against you? 7O our God, didn't you drive out the heathen who lived in this land when your people arrived? And didn't you give this land forever to the descendants of your friend Abraham? 8Your people settled here and built this Temple for you, 9truly believing that in a time like this—whenever we are faced with any calamity such as war, disease, or famine—we can stand here before this Temple and before you—for you are here in this Temple—and cry out to you to save us; and that you will hear us and rescue us.

10"And now see what the armies of Ammon, Moab, and Mount Seir are doing. You wouldn't let our ancestors invade those nations when Israel left Egypt, so we went around and didn't destroy them. 11Now see how they reward us! For they have come to throw us out of your land which you have given us. 12O our God, won't you stop them? We have no way to protect ourselves against this mighty army. We don't know what to do, but we are looking to you."

13As the people from every part of Judah stood before the Lord with their little ones, wives, and children, 14the Spirit of the Lord came upon one of the men standing there—Jahaziel (son of Zechariah, son of Benaiah, son of Je-iel, son of Mattaniah the Levite, who was one of the sons of Asaph).

15"Listen to me, all you people of Judah and Jerusalem, and you, O king Jehoshaphat!" he exclaimed. "The Lord says, 'Don't be afraid! Don't be paralyzed by this mighty army! For the battle is not yours, but God's!

New Revised Standard

8 Moreover in Jerusalem Jehoshaphat appointed certain Levites and priests and heads of families of Israel, to give judgment for the LORD and to decide disputed cases. They had their seat at Jerusalem. 9He charged them: "This is how you shall act: in the fear of the LORD, in faithfulness, and with your whole heart; 10whenever a case comes to you from your kindred who live in their cities, concerning bloodshed, law or commandment, statutes or ordinances, then you shall instruct them, so that they may not incur guilt before the LORD and wrath may not come on you and your kindred. Do so, and you will not incur guilt. 11See, Amariah the chief priest is over you in all matters of the LORD; and Zebadiah son of Ishmael, the governor of the house of Judah, in all the king's matters; and the Levites will serve you as officers. Deal courageously, and may the LORD be with the good!"

Invasion from the East

20 AFTER THIS the Moabites and Ammonites, and with them some of the Meunites,d came against Jehoshaphat for battle. 2Messengerse came and told Jehoshaphat, "A great multitude is coming against you from Edom,f from beyond the sea; already they are at Hazazon-tamar" (that is, En-gedi). 3Jehoshaphat was afraid; he set himself to seek the LORD, and proclaimed a fast throughout all Judah. 4Judah assembled to seek help from the LORD; from all the towns of Judah they came to seek the LORD.

Jehoshaphat's Prayer and Victory

5 Jehoshaphat stood in the assembly of Judah and Jerusalem, in the house of the LORD, before the new court, 6and said, "O LORD, God of our ancestors, are you not God in heaven? Do you not rule over all the kingdoms of the nations? In your hand are power and might, so that no one is able to withstand you. 7Did you not, O our God, drive out the inhabitants of this land before your people Israel, and give it forever to the descendants of your friend Abraham? 8They have lived in it, and in it have built you a sanctuary for your name, saying, 9'If disaster comes upon us, the sword, judgment,g or pestilence, or famine, we will stand before this house, and before you, for your name is in this house, and cry to you in our distress, and you will hear and save.' 10See now, the people of Ammon, Moab, and Mount Seir, whom you would not let Israel invade when they came from the land of Egypt, and whom they avoided and did not destroy— 11they reward us by coming to drive us out of your possession that you have given us to inherit. 12O our God, will you not execute judgment upon them? For we are powerless against this great multitude that is coming against us. We do not know what to do, but our eyes are on you."

13 Meanwhile all Judah stood before the LORD, with their little ones, their wives, and their children. 14Then the spirit of the LORD came upon Jahaziel son of Zechariah, son of Benaiah, son of Jeiel, son of Mattaniah, a Levite of the sons of Asaph, in the middle of the assembly. 15He said, "Listen, all Judah and inhabitants of Jerusalem, and King Jehoshaphat: Thus says the LORD to you: 'Do not fear or be dismayed at this great multitude; for the battle is not yours but God's. 16Tomorrow

d Compare 26.7: Heb Ammonites   e Heb They   f One Ms: MT Aram   g Or the sword of judgment

King James

16Tomorrow go ye down against them: behold, they come up by the cliff of Ziz; and ye shall find them at the end of the brook, before the wilderness of Jeruel.

17Ye shall not *need* to fight in this *battle:* set yourselves, stand ye *still,* and see the salvation of the LORD with you, O Judah and Jerusalem: fear not, nor be dismayed; tomorrow go out against them: for the LORD *will be* with you.

18And Jehoshaphat bowed his head with *his* face to the ground: and all Judah and the inhabitants of Jerusalem fell before the LORD, worshipping the LORD.

19And the Levites, of the children of the Kohathites, and of the children of the Korhites, stood up to praise the LORD God of Israel with a loud voice on high.

20¶ And they rose early in the morning, and went forth into the wilderness of Tekoa: and as they went forth, Jehoshaphat stood and said, Hear me, O Judah, and ye inhabitants of Jerusalem; Believe in the LORD your God, so shall ye be established; believe his prophets, so shall ye prosper.

21And when he had consulted with the people, he appointed singers unto the LORD, and that should praise the beauty of holiness, as they went out before the army, and to say, Praise the LORD; for his mercy *endureth* for ever.

22¶ And when they began to sing and to praise, the LORD set ambushments against the children of Ammon, Moab, and mount Seir, which were come against Judah; and they were smitten.

23For the children of Ammon and Moab stood up against the inhabitants of mount Seir, utterly to slay and destroy *them:* and when they had made an end of the inhabitants of Seir, every one helped to destroy another.

24And when Judah came toward the watchtower in the wilderness, they looked unto the multitude, and, behold, they *were* dead bodies fallen to the earth, and none escaped.

25And when Jehoshaphat and his people came to take away the spoil of them, they found among them in abundance both riches with the dead bodies, and precious jewels, which they stripped off for themselves, more than they could carry away: and they were three days in gathering of the spoil, it was so much.

26¶ And on the fourth day they assembled themselves in the valley of Berachah; for there they blessed the LORD: therefore the name of the same place was called, The valley of Berachah, unto this day.

27Then they returned, every man of Judah and Jerusalem, and Jehoshaphat in the forefront of them, to go again to Jerusalem with joy; for the LORD had made them to rejoice over their enemies.

28And they came to Jerusalem with psalteries and harps and trumpets unto the house of the LORD.

29And the fear of God was on all the kingdoms of *those* countries, when they had heard that the LORD fought against the enemies of Israel.

30So the realm of Jehoshaphat was quiet: for his God gave him rest round about.

31¶ And Jehoshaphat reigned over Judah: *he was* thirty and four years old when he began to reign, and he reigned twenty and five years in Jerusalem. And his mother's name *was* Azubah the daughter of Shilhi.

32And he walked in the way of Asa his father, and departed not from it, doing *that which was* right in the sight of the LORD.

33Howbeit the high places were not taken away: for as yet the people had not prepared their hearts unto the God of their fathers.

34Now the rest of the acts of Jehoshaphat, first and last, behold, they *are* written in the book of Jehu the son of Hanani, who *is* mentioned in the book of the kings of Israel.

35¶ And after this did Jehoshaphat king of Judah join himself with Ahaziah king of Israel, who did very wickedly:

New International

morrow march down against them. They will be climbing up by the Pass of Ziz, and you will find them at the end of the gorge in the Desert of Jeruel. 17You will not have to fight this battle. Take up your positions; stand firm and see the deliverance the LORD will give you, O Judah and Jerusalem. Do not be afraid; do not be discouraged. Go out to face them tomorrow, and the LORD will be with you.' "

18Jehoshaphat bowed with his face to the ground, and all the people of Judah and Jerusalem fell down in worship before the LORD. 19Then some Levites from the Kohathites and Korahites stood up and praised the LORD, the God of Israel, with very loud voice.

20Early in the morning they left for the Desert of Tekoa. As they set out, Jehoshaphat stood and said, "Listen to me, Judah and people of Jerusalem! Have faith in the LORD your God and you will be upheld; have faith in his prophets and you will be successful." 21After consulting the people, Jehoshaphat appointed men to sing to the LORD and to praise him for the splendor of hisa holiness as they went out at the head of the army, saying:

"Give thanks to the LORD,
　for his love endures forever."

22As they began to sing and praise, the LORD set ambushes against the men of Ammon and Moab and Mount Seir who were invading Judah, and they were defeated. 23The men of Ammon and Moab rose up against the men from Mount Seir to destroy and annihilate them. After they finished slaughtering the men from Seir, they helped to destroy one another.

24When the men of Judah came to the place that overlooks the desert and looked toward the vast army, they saw only dead bodies lying on the ground; no one had escaped. 25So Jehoshaphat and his men went to carry off their plunder, and they found among them a great amount of equipment and clothingb and also articles of value—more than they could take away. There was so much plunder that it took three days to collect it. 26On the fourth day they assembled in the Valley of Beracah, where they praised the LORD. This is why it is called the Valley of Beracahc to this day.

27Then, led by Jehoshaphat, all the men of Judah and Jerusalem returned joyfully to Jerusalem, for the LORD had given them cause to rejoice over their enemies. 28They entered Jerusalem and went to the temple of the LORD with harps and lutes and trumpets.

29The fear of God came upon all the kingdoms of the countries when they heard how the LORD had fought against the enemies of Israel. 30And the kingdom of Jehoshaphat was at peace, for his God had given him rest on every side.

The End of Jehoshaphat's Reign

31So Jehoshaphat reigned over Judah. He was thirty-five years old when he became king of Judah, and he reigned in Jerusalem twenty-five years. His mother's name was Azubah daughter of Shilhi. 32He walked in the ways of his father Asa and did not stray from them; he did what was right in the eyes of the LORD. 33The high places, however, were not removed, and the people still had not set their hearts on the God of their fathers.

34The other events of Jehoshaphat's reign, from beginning to end, are written in the annals of Jehu son of Hanani, which are recorded in the book of the kings of Israel.

35Later, Jehoshaphat king of Judah made an alliance with Ahaziah king of Israel, who was guilty of wickedness. 36He agreed with him to construct a fleet of trading

---

a *21 Or* him with the splendor of　b *25 Some Hebrew manuscripts and Vulgate; most Hebrew manuscripts* corpses　c *26 Beracah means* praise.

Living Bible

16Tomorrow, go down and attack them! You will find them coming up the slopes of Ziz at the end of the valley that opens into the wilderness of Jeruel. 17But you will not need to fight! Take your places; stand quietly and see the incredible rescue operation God will perform for you, O people of Judah and Jerusalem! Don't be afraid or discouraged! Go out there tomorrow, for the Lord is with you!'"

18Then King Jehoshaphat fell to the ground with his face to the earth, and all the people of Judah and the people of Jerusalem did the same, worshiping the Lord. 19Then the Levites of the Kohath clan and the Korah clan stood to praise the Lord God of Israel with songs of praise that rang out strong and clear.

20Early the next morning the army of Judah went out into the wilderness of Tekoa. On the way Jehoshaphat stopped and called them to attention. "Listen to me, O people of Judah and Jerusalem," he said. "Believe in the Lord your God, and you shall have success! Believe his prophets, and everything will be all right!"

21After consultation with the leaders of the people, he determined that there should be a choir leading the march, clothed in sanctified garments and singing the song "His Lovingkindness Is Forever" as they walked along praising and thanking the Lord! 22And at the moment they began to sing and to praise, the Lord caused the armies of Ammon, Moab, and Mount Seir to begin fighting among themselves, and they destroyed each other! 23For the Ammonites and Moabites turned against their allies from Mount Seir and killed every one of them. And when they had finished that job, they turned against each other! 24So, when the army of Judah arrived at the watchtower that looks out over the wilderness, as far as they could look there were dead bodies lying on the ground—not a single one of the enemy had escaped. 25King Jehoshaphat and his people went out to plunder the bodies and came away loaded with money, garments, and jewels stripped from the corpses—so much that it took them three days to cart it all away! 26On the fourth day they gathered in the Valley of Blessing, as it is called today, and how they praised the Lord!

27Then they returned to Jerusalem, with Jehoshaphat leading them, full of joy that the Lord had given them this marvelous rescue from their enemies. 28They marched into Jerusalem accompanied by a band of harps, lyres, and trumpets and proceeded to the Temple. 29And as had happened before, when the surrounding kingdoms heard that the Lord himself had fought against the enemies of Israel, the fear of God fell upon them. 30So Jehoshaphat's kingdom was quiet, for his God had given him rest.

31A thumbnail sketch of King Jehoshaphat: He became king of Judah when he was thirty-five years old, and reigned twenty-five years, in Jerusalem. His mother's name was Azubah, the daughter of Shilhi. 32He was a good king, just as his father Asa was. He continually tried to follow the Lord, 33with the exception that he did not destroy the idol shrines on the hills, nor had the people as yet really decided to follow the God of their ancestors.

34The details of Jehoshaphat's reign from first to last are written in the history of Jehu the son of Hanani, which is inserted in *The Annals of the Kings of Israel.*

35But at the close of his life, Jehoshaphat, king of Judah, went into partnership with Ahaziah, king of Israel, who was a very wicked man. 36They made ships in

New Revised Standard

go down against them; they will come up by the ascent of Ziz; you will find them at the end of the valley, before the wilderness of Jeruel. 17This battle is not for you to fight; take your position, stand still, and see the victory of the Lord on your behalf, O Judah and Jerusalem.' Do not fear or be dismayed; tomorrow go out against them, and the Lord will be with you."

18 Then Jehoshaphat bowed down with his face to the ground, and all Judah and the inhabitants of Jerusalem fell down before the Lord, worshiping the Lord. 19And the Levites, of the Kohathites and the Korahites, stood up to praise the Lord, the God of Israel, with a very loud voice.

20 They rose early in the morning and went out into the wilderness of Tekoa; and as they went out, Jehoshaphat stood and said, "Listen to me, O Judah and inhabitants of Jerusalem! Believe in the Lord your God and you will be established; believe his prophets." 21When he had taken counsel with the people, he appointed those who were to sing to the Lord and praise him in holy splendor, as they went before the army, saying,

"Give thanks to the Lord,
    for his steadfast love endures forever."

22As they began to sing and praise, the Lord set an ambush against the Ammonites, Moab, and Mount Seir, who had come against Judah, so that they were routed. 23For the Ammonites and Moab attacked the inhabitants of Mount Seir, destroying them utterly; and when they had made an end of the inhabitants of Seir, they all helped to destroy one another.

24 When Judah came to the watchtower of the wilderness, they looked toward the multitude; they were corpses lying on the ground; no one had escaped. 25When Jehoshaphat and his people came to take the booty from them, they found livestockd in great numbers, goods, clothing, and precious things, which they took for themselves until they could carry no more. They spent three days taking the booty, because of its abundance. 26On the fourth day they assembled in the Valley of Beracah, for there they blessed the Lord; therefore that place has been called the Valley of Beracahe to this day. 27Then all the people of Judah and Jerusalem, with Jehoshaphat at their head, returned to Jerusalem with joy, for the Lord had enabled them to rejoice over their enemies. 28They came to Jerusalem, with harps and lyres and trumpets, to the house of the Lord. 29The fear of God came on all the kingdoms of the countries when they heard that the Lord had fought against the enemies of Israel. 30And the realm of Jehoshaphat was quiet, for his God gave him rest all around.

The End of Jehoshaphat's Reign

31 So Jehoshaphat reigned over Judah. He was thirty-five years old when he began to reign; he reigned twenty-five years in Jerusalem. His mother's name was Azubah daughter of Shilhi. 32He walked in the way of his father Asa and did not turn aside from it, doing what was right in the sight of the Lord. 33Yet the high places were not removed; the people had not yet set their hearts upon the God of their ancestors.

34 Now the rest of the acts of Jehoshaphat, from first to last, are written in the Annals of Jehu son of Hanani, which are recorded in the Book of the Kings of Israel.

35 After this King Jehoshaphat of Judah joined with King Ahaziah of Israel, who did wickedly. 36He joined

King James

36And he joined himself with him to make ships to go to Tarshish: and they made the ships in Ezion-geber.

37Then Eliezer the son of Dodavah of Mareshah prophesied against Jehoshaphat, saying, Because thou hast joined thyself with Ahaziah, the LORD hath broken thy works. And the ships were broken, that they were not able to go to Tarshish.

21 NOW JEHOSHAPHAT slept with his fathers, and was buried with his fathers in the city of David. And Jehoram his son reigned in his stead.

2And he had brethren the sons of Jehoshaphat, Azariah, and Jehiel, and Zechariah, and Azariah, and Michael, and Shephatiah: all these were the sons of Jehoshaphat king of Israel.

3And their father gave them great gifts of silver, and of gold, and of precious things, with fenced cities in Judah: but the kingdom gave he to Jehoram; because he was the firstborn.

4Now when Jehoram was risen up to the kingdom of his father, he strengthened himself, and slew all his brethren with the sword, and divers also of the princes of Israel.

5¶ Jehoram was thirty and two years old when he began to reign, and he reigned eight years in Jerusalem.

6And he walked in the way of the kings of Israel, like as did the house of Ahab: for he had the daughter of Ahab to wife: and he wrought that which was evil in the eyes of the LORD.

7Howbeit the LORD would not destroy the house of David, because of the covenant that he had made with David, and as he promised to give a light to him and to his sons for ever.

8¶ In his days the Edomites revolted from under the dominion of Judah, and made themselves a king.

9Then Jehoram went forth with his princes, and all his chariots with him: and he rose up by night, and smote the Edomites which compassed him in, and the captains of the chariots.

10So the Edomites revolted from under the hand of Judah unto this day. The same time also did Libnah revolt from under his hand; because he had forsaken the LORD God of his fathers.

11Moreover he made high places in the mountains of Judah, and caused the inhabitants of Jerusalem to commit fornication, and compelled Judah thereto.

12¶ And there came a writing to him from Elijah the prophet, saying, Thus saith the LORD God of David thy father, Because thou hast not walked in the ways of Jehoshaphat thy father, nor in the ways of Asa king of Judah,

13But hast walked in the way of the kings of Israel, and hast made Judah and the inhabitants of Jerusalem to go a-whoring, like to the whoredoms of the house of Ahab, and also hast slain thy brethren of thy father's house, which were better than thyself:

14Behold, with a great plague will the LORD smite thy people, and thy children, and thy wives, and all thy goods:

15And thou shalt have great sickness by disease of thy bowels, until thy bowels fall out by reason of the sickness day by day.

16¶ Moreover the LORD stirred up against Jehoram the spirit of the Philistines, and of the Arabians, that were near the Ethiopians:

17And they came up into Judah, and brake into it, and carried away all the substance that was found in the king's house, and his sons also, and his wives; so that there was never a son left him, save Jehoahaz, the youngest of his sons.

18¶ And after all this the LORD smote him in his bowels with an incurable disease.

New International

ships.a After these were built at Ezion Geber, 37Eliezer son of Dodavahu of Mareshah prophesied against Jehoshaphat, saying, "Because you have made an alliance with Ahaziah, the LORD will destroy what you have made." The ships were wrecked and were not able to set sail to trade.b

21 THEN JEHOSHAPHAT rested with his fathers and was buried with them in the City of David. And Jehoram his son succeeded him as king. 2Jehoram's brothers, the sons of Jehoshaphat, were Azariah, Jehiel, Zechariah, Azariahu, Michael and Shephatiah. All these were sons of Jehoshaphat king of Israel.c 3Their father had given them many gifts of silver and gold and articles of value, as well as fortified cities in Judah, but he had given the kingdom to Jehoram because he was his firstborn son.

Jehoram King of Judah

4When Jehoram established himself firmly over his father's kingdom, he put all his brothers to the sword along with some of the princes of Israel. 5Jehoram was thirty-two years old when he became king, and he reigned in Jerusalem eight years. 6He walked in the ways of the kings of Israel, as the house of Ahab had done, for he married a daughter of Ahab. He did evil in the eyes of the LORD. 7Nevertheless, because of the covenant the LORD had made with David, the LORD was not willing to destroy the house of David. He had promised to maintain a lamp for him and his descendants forever.

8In the time of Jehoram, Edom rebelled against Judah and set up its own king. 9So Jehoram went there with his officers and all his chariots. The Edomites surrounded him and his chariot commanders, but he rose up and broke through by night. 10To this day Edom has been in rebellion against Judah.

Libnah revolted at the same time, because Jehoram had forsaken the LORD, the God of his fathers. 11He had also built high places on the hills of Judah and had caused the people of Jerusalem to prostitute themselves and had led Judah astray.

12Jehoram received a letter from Elijah the prophet, which said:

"This is what the LORD, the God of your father David, says: 'You have not walked in the ways of your father Jehoshaphat or of Asa king of Judah. 13But you have walked in the ways of the kings of Israel, and you have led Judah and the people of Jerusalem to prostitute themselves, just as the house of Ahab did. You have also murdered your own brothers, members of your father's house, men who were better than you. 14So now the LORD is about to strike your people, your sons, your wives and everything that is yours, with a heavy blow. 15You yourself will be very ill with a lingering disease of the bowels, until the disease causes your bowels to come out.' "

16The LORD aroused against Jehoram the hostility of the Philistines and of the Arabs who lived near the Cushites. 17They attacked Judah, invaded it and carried off all the goods found in the king's palace, together with his sons and wives. Not a son was left to him except Ahaziah,d the youngest.

18After all this, the LORD afflicted Jehoram with an incurable disease of the bowels. 19In the course of time,

---

a 36 Hebrew of ships that could go to Tarshish   b 37 Hebrew sail for Tarshish   c 2 That is, Judah, as frequently in 2 Chronicles   d 17 Hebrew Jehoahaz, a variant of Ahaziah

Living Bible

Ezion-geber to sail to Tarshish. 37Then Eliezer, son of Dodavahu from Mareshah, prophesied against Jehoshaphat, telling him, "Because you have allied yourself with King Ahaziah, the Lord has destroyed your work." So the ships met disaster and never arrived at Tarshish.

21 WHEN JEHOSHAPHAT died, he was buried in the cemetery of the kings in Jerusalem, and his son Jehoram became the new ruler of Judah. 2His brothers—other sons of Jehoshaphat—were Azariah, Jehiel, Zechariah, Azariah, Michael, and Shephatiah. 3, 4Their father had given each of them valuable gifts of money and jewels, also the ownership of some of the fortified cities of Judah. However, he gave the kingship to Jehoram because he was the oldest. But when Jehoram had become solidly established as king, he killed all of his brothers and many other leaders of Israel. 5He was thirty-two years old when he began to reign, and he reigned eight years, in Jerusalem. 6But he was as wicked as the kings who were over in Israel. Yes, as wicked as Ahab, for Jehoram had married one of the daughters of Ahab, and his whole life was one constant binge of doing evil. 7However, the Lord was unwilling to end the dynasty of David, for he had made a covenant with David always to have one of his descendants upon the throne.

8At that time the king of Edom revolted, declaring his independence of Judah. 9Jehoram attacked him with his full army and with all of his chariots, marching by night, and almoste managed to subdue him. 10But to this day Edom has been successful in throwing off the yoke of Judah. Libnah revolted too, because Jehoram had turned away from the Lord God of his fathers. 11What's more, Jehoram constructed idol shrines in the mountains of Judah, and led the people of Jerusalem in worshiping idols; in fact, he compelled his people to worship them.

12Then Elijah the prophet wrote him this letter: "The Lord God of your ancestor David says that because you have not followed in the good ways of your father Jehoshaphat, nor the good ways of King Asa, 13but you have been as evil as the kings over in Israel, and have made the people of Jerusalem and Judah worship idols just as in the times of King Ahab, and because you have killed your brothers who were better than you, 14now the Lord will destroy your nation with a great plague. You, your children, your wives, and all that you have will be struck down. 15You will be stricken with an intestinal disease and your bowels will rot away."

16Then the Lord stirred up the Philistines and the Arabs living next to the Ethiopians to attack Jehoram. 17They marched against Judah, broke across the border, and carried away everything of value in the king's palace, including his sons and his wives; only his youngest son, Jehoahaz, escaped.

18It was after this that Jehovah struck him down with the incurable bowel disease. 19In the process of time, at

New Revised Standard

him in building ships to go to Tarshish; they built the ships in Ezion-geber. 37Then Eliezer son of Dodavahu of Mareshah prophesied against Jehoshaphat, saying, "Because you have joined with Ahaziah, the LORD will destroy what you have made." And the ships were wrecked and were not able to go to Tarshish.

Jehoram's Reign

21 JEHOSHAPHAT SLEPT with his ancestors and was buried with his ancestors in the city of David; his son Jehoram succeeded him. 2He had brothers, the sons of Jehoshaphat: Azariah, Jehiel, Zechariah, Azariah, Michael, and Shephatiah; all these were the sons of King Jehoshaphat of Judah.f 3Their father gave them many gifts, of silver, gold, and valuable possessions, together with fortified cities in Judah; but he gave the kingdom to Jehoram, because he was the firstborn. 4When Jehoram had ascended the throne of his father and was established, he put all his brothers to the sword, and also some of the officials of Israel. 5Jehoram was thirty-two years old when he began to reign; he reigned eight years in Jerusalem. 6He walked in the way of the kings of Israel, as the house of Ahab had done; for the daughter of Ahab was his wife. He did what was evil in the sight of the LORD. 7Yet the LORD would not destroy the house of David because of the covenant that he had made with David, and since he had promised to give a lamp to him and to his descendants forever.

Revolt of Edom

8 In his days Edom revolted against the rule of Judah and set up a king of their own. 9Then Jehoram crossed over with his commanders and all his chariots. He set out by night and attacked the Edomites, who had surrounded him and his chariot commanders. 10So Edom has been in revolt against the rule of Judah to this day. At that time Libnah also revolted against his rule, because he had forsaken the LORD, the God of his ancestors.

Elijah's Letter

11 Moreover he made high places in the hill country of Judah, and led the inhabitants of Jerusalem into unfaithfulness, and made Judah go astray. 12A letter came to him from the prophet Elijah, saying: "Thus says the LORD, the God of your father David: Because you have not walked in the ways of your father Jehoshaphat or in the ways of King Asa of Judah, 13but have walked in the way of the kings of Israel, and have led Judah and the inhabitants of Jerusalem into unfaithfulness, as the house of Ahab led Israel into unfaithfulness, and because you also have killed your brothers, members of your father's house, who were better than yourself, 14see, the LORD will bring a great plague on your people, your children, your wives, and all your possessions, 15and you yourself will have a severe sickness with a disease of your bowels, until your bowels come out, day after day, because of the disease."

16 The LORD aroused against Jehoram the anger of the Philistines and of the Arabs who are near the Ethiopians.g 17They came up against Judah, invaded it, and carried away all the possessions they found that belonged to the king's house, along with his sons and his wives, so that no son was left to him except Jehoahaz, his youngest son.

Disease and Death of Jehoram

18 After all this the LORD struck him in his bowels with an incurable disease. 19In course of time, at the end

---

e 21:9 *Jehoram attacked him . . . and almost,* literally, "Jehoram . . . struck down the Edomites . . . Nevertheless Edom . . . revolted. . . ."

f Gk Syr: Heb *Israel*   g Or *Nubians;* Heb *Cushites*

King James

19And it came to pass, that in process of time, after the end of two years, his bowels fell out by reason of his sickness: so he died of sore diseases. And his people made no burning for him, like the burning of his fathers.
20Thirty and two years old was he when he began to reign, and he reigned in Jerusalem eight years, and departed without being desired. Howbeit they buried him in the city of David, but not in the sepulchres of the kings.

22 AND THE inhabitants of Jerusalem made Ahaziah his youngest son king in his stead: for the band of men that came with the Arabians to the camp had slain all the eldest. So Ahaziah the son of Jehoram king of Judah reigned.

2Forty and two years old was Ahaziah when he began to reign, and he reigned one year in Jerusalem. His mother's name also was Athaliah the daughter of Omri.

3He also walked in the ways of the house of Ahab: for his mother was his counsellor to do wickedly.

4Wherefore he did evil in the sight of the LORD like the house of Ahab: for they were his counsellors after the death of his father to his destruction.

5¶ He walked also after their counsel, and went with Jehoram the son of Ahab king of Israel to war against Hazael king of Syria at Ramoth-gilead: and the Syrians smote Joram.

6And he returned to be healed in Jezreel because of the wounds which were given him at Ramah, when he fought with Hazael king of Syria. And Azariah the son of Jehoram king of Judah went down to see Jehoram the son of Ahab at Jezreel, because he was sick.

7And the destruction of Ahaziah was of God by coming to Joram: for when he was come, he went out with Jehoram against Jehu the son of Nimshi, whom the LORD had anointed to cut off the house of Ahab.

8And it came to pass, that, when Jehu was executing judgment upon the house of Ahab, and found the princes of Judah, and the sons of the brethren of Ahaziah, that ministered to Ahaziah, he slew them.

9And he sought Ahaziah: and they caught him, (for he was hid in Samaria,) and brought him to Jehu: and when they had slain him, they buried him: Because, said they, he is the son of Jehoshaphat, who sought the LORD with all his heart. So the house of Ahaziah had no power to keep still the kingdom.

10¶ But when Athaliah the mother of Ahaziah saw that her son was dead, she arose and destroyed all the seed royal of the house of Judah.

11But Jehoshabeath, the daughter of the king, took Joash the son of Ahaziah, and stole him from among the king's sons that were slain, and put him and his nurse in a bedchamber. So Jehoshabeath, the daughter of king Jehoram, the wife of Jehoiada the priest, (for she was the sister of Ahaziah,) hid him from Athaliah, so that she slew him not.

12And he was with them hid in the house of God six years: and Athaliah reigned over the land.

New International

at the end of the second year, his bowels came out because of the disease, and he died in great pain. His people made no fire in his honor, as they had for his fathers.
20Jehoram was thirty-two years old when he became king, and he reigned in Jerusalem eight years. He passed away, to no one's regret, and was buried in the City of David, but not in the tombs of the kings.

Ahaziah King of Judah

22 THE PEOPLE of Jerusalem made Ahaziah, Jehoram's youngest son, king in his place, since the raiders, who came with the Arabs into the camp, had killed all the older sons. So Ahaziah son of Jehoram king of Judah began to reign.

2Ahaziah was twenty-twoa years old when he became king, and he reigned in Jerusalem one year. His mother's name was Athaliah, a granddaughter of Omri.

3He too walked in the ways of the house of Ahab, for his mother encouraged him in doing wrong. 4He did evil in the eyes of the LORD, as the house of Ahab had done, for after his father's death they became his advisers, to his undoing. 5He also followed their counsel when he went with Joramb son of Ahab king of Israel to war against Hazael king of Aram at Ramoth Gilead. The Arameans wounded Joram; 6so he returned to Jezreel to recover from the wounds they had inflicted on him at Ramothc in his battle with Hazael king of Aram.

Then Ahaziahd son of Jehoram king of Judah went down to Jezreel to see Joram son of Ahab because he had been wounded.

7Through Ahaziah's visit to Joram, God brought about Ahaziah's downfall. When Ahaziah arrived, he went out with Joram to meet Jehu son of Nimshi, whom the LORD had anointed to destroy the house of Ahab. 8While Jehu was executing judgment on the house of Ahab, he found the princes of Judah and the sons of Ahaziah's relatives, who had been attending Ahaziah, and he killed them. 9He then went in search of Ahaziah, and his men captured him while he was hiding in Samaria. He was brought to Jehu and put to death. They buried him, for they said, "He was a son of Jehoshaphat, who sought the LORD with all his heart." So there was no one in the house of Ahaziah powerful enough to retain the kingdom.

Athaliah and Joash

10When Athaliah the mother of Ahaziah saw that her son was dead, she proceeded to destroy the whole royal family of the house of Judah. 11But Jehosheba,e the daughter of King Jehoram, took Joash son of Ahaziah and stole him away from among the royal princes who were about to be murdered and put him and his nurse in a bedroom. Because Jehosheba,e the daughter of King Jehoram and wife of the priest Jehoiada, was Ahaziah's sister, she hid the child from Athaliah so she could not kill him. 12He remained hidden with them at the temple of God for six years while Athaliah ruled the land.

---

a 2 Some Septuagint manuscripts and Syriac (see also 2 Kings 8:26); Hebrew forty-two   b 5 Hebrew Jehoram, a variant of Joram; also in verses 6 and 7   c 6 Hebrew Ramah, a variant of Ramoth   d 6 Some Hebrew manuscripts, Septuagint, Vulgate and Syriac (see also 2 Kings 8:29); most Hebrew manuscripts Azariah   e 11 Hebrew Jehoshabeath, a variant of Jehosheba

Living Bible

the end of two years, his intestines came out and he died in terrible suffering. (The customary pomp and ceremony was omitted at his funeral.) 20He was thirty-two years old when he began to reign and he reigned in Jerusalem eight years, and died unmourned. He was buried in Jerusalem, but not in the royal cemetery.

22 THEN THE people of Jerusalem chose Ahaziah,f his youngest son, as their new king (for the marauding bands of Arabs had killed his older sons). 2Ahaziah was twenty-two years oldg when he began to reign, and he reigned one year, in Jerusalem. His mother's name was Athaliah, granddaughter of Omri. 3He, too, walked in the evil ways of Ahab, for his mother encouraged him in doing wrong. 4Yes, he was as evil as Ahab, for Ahab's family became his advisors after his father's death, and they led him on to ruin.

5Following their evil advice, Ahaziah made an alliance with King Joram of Israel (the son of Ahab), who was at war with King Hazael of Syria at Ramoth-gilead. Ahaziah led his army there to join the battle. King Joram of Israel was wounded, 6and returned to Jezreel to recover. Ahaziah went to visit him, 7but this turned out to be a fatal mistake; for God had decided to punish Ahaziah for his alliance with Jehoram. It was during this visit that Ahaziah went out with Joram to challenge Jehu (son of Nimshi), whom the Lord had appointed to end the dynasty of Ahab.

8While Jehu was hunting down and killing the family and friends of Ahab, he met King Ahaziah's nephews, the princes of Judah, and killed them. 9As he and his men were searching for Ahaziah, they found him hiding in the city of Samaria, and brought him to Jehu, who killed him. Even so, Ahaziah was given a royal burial because he was the grandson of King Jehoshaphat—a man who enthusiastically served the Lord. None of his sons, however, except for Joash, lived to succeed him as king, 10for their grandmother Athaliah killed them when she heard the news of her son Ahaziah's death.

11Joash was rescued by his Aunt Jehoshabeath, who was King Ahaziah's sister,h and was hidden away in a storage room in the Temple. She was a daughter of King Jehoram, and the wife of Jehoiada the priest. 12Joash remained hidden in the Temple for six years while Athaliah reigned as queen. He was cared for by his nurse and by his aunt and uncle.

New Revised Standard

of two years, his bowels came out because of the disease, and he died in great agony. His people made no fire in his honor, like the fires made for his ancestors. 20He was thirty-two years old when he began to reign; he reigned eight years in Jerusalem. He departed with no one's regret. They buried him in the city of David, but not in the tombs of the kings.

Ahaziah's Reign

22 THE INHABITANTS of Jerusalem made his youngest son Ahaziah king as his successor; for the troops who came with the Arabs to the camp had killed all the older sons. So Ahaziah son of Jehoram reigned as king of Judah. 2Ahaziah was forty-two years old when he began to reign; he reigned one year in Jerusalem. His mother's name was Athaliah, a granddaughter of Omri. 3He also walked in the ways of the house of Ahab, for his mother was his counselor in doing wickedly. 4He did what was evil in the sight of the Lord, as the house of Ahab had done; for after the death of his father they were his counselors, to his ruin. 5He even followed their advice, and went with Jehoram son of King Ahab of Israel to make war against King Hazael of Aram at Ramoth-gilead. The Arameans wounded Joram, 6and he returned to be healed in Jezreel of the wounds that he had received at Ramah, when he fought King Hazael of Aram. And Ahaziah son of King Jehoram of Judah went down to see Joram son of Ahab in Jezreel, because he was sick.

7 But it was ordained by God that the downfall of Ahaziah should come about through his going to visit Joram. For when he came there he went out with Jehoram to meet Jehu son of Nimshi, whom the Lord had anointed to destroy the house of Ahab. 8When Jehu was executing judgment on the house of Ahab, he met the officials of Judah and the sons of Ahaziah's brothers, who attended Ahaziah, and he killed them. 9He searched for Ahaziah, who was captured while hiding in Samaria and was brought to Jehu, and put to death. They buried him, for they said, "He is the grandson of Jehoshaphat, who sought the Lord with all his heart." And the house of Ahaziah had no one able to rule the kingdom.

Athaliah Seizes the Throne

10 Now when Athaliah, Ahaziah's mother, saw that her son was dead, she set about to destroy all the royal family of the house of Judah. 11But Jehoshabeath, the king's daughter, took Joash son of Ahaziah, and stole him away from among the king's children who were about to be killed; she put him and his nurse in a bedroom. Thus Jehoshabeath, daughter of King Jehoram and wife of the priest Jehoiada—because she was a sister of Ahaziah—hid him from Athaliah, so that she did not kill him; 12he remained with them six years, hidden in the house of God, while Athaliah reigned over the land.

---

f 22:1 Ahaziah, also called "Jehoahaz." g 22:2 was twenty-two years old, some manuscripts read "forty-two years old"; but see 2 Kgs 8:26. h 22:11 who was King Ahaziah's sister, literally, "the king's daughter," i.e., King Jehoram's daughter, vs 11.

King James

23 AND IN the seventh year Jehoiada strength-ened himself, and took the captains of hun-dreds, Azariah the son of Jeroham, and Ishmael the son of Jehohanan, and Azariah the son of Obed, and Maase-iah the son of Adaiah, and Elishaphat the son of Zichri, into covenant with him.

2And they went about in Judah, and gathered the Levites out of all the cities of Judah, and the chief of the fathers of Israel, and they came to Jerusalem.

3And all the congregation made a covenant with the king in the house of God. And he said unto them, Be-hold, the king's son shall reign, as the LORD hath said of the sons of David.

4This *is* the thing that ye shall do; A third part of you entering on the sabbath, of the priests and of the Levites, *shall be* porters of the doors;

5And a third part *shall be* at the king's house; and a third part at the gate of the foundation: and all the people *shall be* in the courts of the house of the LORD.

6But let none come into the house of the LORD, save the priests, and they that minister of the Levites; they shall go in, for they *are* holy: but all the people shall keep the watch of the LORD.

7And the Levites shall compass the king round about, every man with his weapons in his hand; and whosoever *else* cometh into the house, he shall be put to death: but be ye with the king when he cometh in, and when he goeth out.

8So the Levites and all Judah did according to all things that Jehoiada the priest had commanded, and took every man his men that were to come in on the sabbath, with them that were to go *out* on the sabbath: for Jehoia-da the priest dismissed not the courses.

9Moreover Jehoiada the priest delivered to the cap-tains of hundreds spears, and bucklers, and shields, that *had been* king David's, which *were* in the house of God.

10And he set all the people, every man having his weapon in his hand, from the right side of the temple to the left side of the temple, along by the altar and the temple, by the king round about.

11Then they brought out the king's son, and put upon him the crown, and *gave him* the testimony, and made him king. And Jehoiada and his sons anointed him, and said, God save the king.

12¶ Now when Athaliah heard the noise of the people running and praising the king, she came to the people into the house of the LORD:

13And she looked, and, behold, the king stood at his pillar at the entering in, and the princes and the trumpets by the king: and all the people of the land rejoiced, and sounded with trumpets, also the singers with instruments of music, and such as taught to sing praise. Then Athali-ah rent her clothes, and said, Treason, Treason.

14Then Jehoiada the priest brought out the captains of hundreds that were set over the host, and said unto them, Have her forth of the ranges: and whoso followeth her, let him be slain with the sword. For the priest said, Slay her not in the house of the LORD.

15So they laid hands on her; and when she was come to the entering of the horse gate by the king's house, they slew her there.

16¶ And Jehoiada made a covenant between him, and between all the people, and between the king, that they should be the LORD's people.

17Then all the people went to the house of Baal, and brake it down, and brake his altars and his images in pieces, and slew Mattan the priest of Baal before the altars.

18Also Jehoiada appointed the offices of the house of the LORD by the hand of the priests the Levites, whom David had distributed in the house of the LORD, to offer the burnt offerings of the LORD, as *it is* written in the law of Moses, with rejoicing and with singing, *as it was ordained* by David.

New International

23 IN THE seventh year Jehoiada showed his strength. He made a covenant with the com-manders of units of a hundred: Azariah son of Jeroham, Ishmael son of Jehohanan, Azariah son of Obed, Maase-iah son of Adaiah, and Elishaphat son of Zicri. 2They went throughout Judah and gathered the Levites and the heads of Israelite families from all the towns. When they came to Jerusalem, 3the whole assembly made a cov-enant with the king at the temple of God.

Jehoiada said to them, "The king's son shall reign, as the LORD promised concerning the descendants of David. 4Now this is what you are to do: A third of you priests and Levites who are going on duty on the Sabbath are to keep watch at the doors, 5a third of you at the royal palace and a third at the Foundation Gate, and all the other men are to be in the courtyards of the temple of the LORD. 6No one is to enter the temple of the LORD except the priests and Levites on duty; they may enter because they are consecrated, but all the other men are to guard what the LORD has assigned to them.a 7The Levites are to station themselves around the king, each man with his weapons in his hand. Anyone who enters the temple must be put to death. Stay close to the king wherever he goes."

8The Levites and all the men of Judah did just as Jehoiada the priest ordered. Each one took his men—those who were going on duty on the Sabbath and those who were going off duty—for Jehoiada the priest had not released any of the divisions. 9Then he gave the commanders of units of a hundred the spears and the large and small shields that had belonged to King David and that were in the temple of God. 10He stationed all the men, each with his weapon in his hand, around the king—near the altar and the temple, from the south side to the north side of the temple.

11Jehoiada and his sons brought out the king's son and put the crown on him; they presented him with a copy of the covenant and proclaimed him king. They anointed him and shouted, "Long live the king!"

12When Athaliah heard the noise of the people run-ning and cheering the king, she went to them at the temple of the LORD. 13She looked, and there was the king, standing by his pillar at the entrance. The officers and the trumpeters were beside the king, and all the people of the land were rejoicing and blowing trumpets, and singers with musical instruments were leading the praises. Then Athaliah tore her robes and shouted, "Treason! Treason!"

14Jehoiada the priest sent out the commanders of units of a hundred, who were in charge of the troops, and said to them: "Bring her out between the ranksb and put to the sword anyone who follows her." For the priest had said, "Do not put her to death at the temple of the LORD." 15So they seized her as she reached the entrance of the Horse Gate on the palace grounds, and there they put her to death.

16Jehoiada then made a covenant that he and the peo-ple and the kingc would be the LORD's people. 17All the people went to the temple of Baal and tore it down. They smashed the altars and idols and killed Mattan the priest of Baal in front of the altars.

18Then Jehoiada placed the oversight of the temple of the LORD in the hands of the priests, who were Levites, to whom David had made assignments in the temple, to present the burnt offerings of the LORD as written in the Law of Moses, with rejoicing and singing, as David had ordered. 19He also stationed doorkeepers at the gates of

---

a 6 Or *to observe the LORD's command not to enter;*   b 14 Or *out from the precincts*   c 16 Or *covenant between the LORD, and the people and the king that they* (see 2 Kings 11:17)

Living Bible

23 IN THE seventh year of the reign of Queen Athaliah, Jehoiada the priest got up his courage and took some of the army officers into his confidence: Azariah (son of Jeroham), Ishmael (son of Jehohanan), Azariah (son of Obed), Maaseiah (son of Adaiah), and Elishaphat (son of Zichri). 2, 3These men traveled out across the nation secretly, to tell the Levites and clan leaders about his plans and to summon them to Jerusalem. On arrival they swore allegiance to the young king, who was still in hiding at the Temple.

"At last the time has come for the king's son to reign!" Jehoiada exclaimed. "The Lord's promise—that a descendant of King David shall be our king—will be true again. 4This is how we'll proceed: A third of you priests and Levites who come off duty on the Sabbath will stay at the entrance as guards. 5, 6Another third will go over to the palace, and a third will be at the Lower Gate. Everyone else must stay in the outer courts of the Temple, as required by God's laws. For only the priests and Levites on duty may enter the Temple itself, for they are sanctified. 7You Levites, form a bodyguard for the king, weapons in hand, and kill any unauthorized person entering the Temple. Stay right beside the king."

8So all the arrangements were made. Each of the three leaders led a third of the priests arriving for duty that Sabbath, and a third of those whose week's work was done and were going off duty—for Jehoiada the chief priest didn't release them to go home. 9Then Jehoiada issued spears and shields to all the army officers. These had once belonged to King David and were stored in the Temple. 10These officers, fully armed, formed a line from one side to the other in front of the Temple and around the altar in the outer court. 11Then they brought out the little prince and placed the crown upon his head and handed him a copy of the law of God, and proclaimed him king.

A great shout went up, "Long live the king!" as Jehoiada and his sons anointed him.

12When Queen Athaliah heard all the noise and commotion, and the shouts of praise to the king, she rushed over to the Temple to see what was going on—and there stood the king by his pillar at the entrance, with the army officers and the trumpeters surrounding him, and people from all over the land rejoicing and blowing trumpets, and the singers singing, accompanied by an orchestra leading the people in a great psalm of praise.

Athaliah ripped her clothes and screamed, "Treason! Treason!"

13, 14"Take her out and kill her," Jehoiada the priest shouted to the army officers. "Don't do it here at the Temple. And kill anyone who tries to help her."

15, 16, 17So the crowd opened up for them to take her out and they killed her at the palace stables.

Then Jehoiada made a solemn contract that he and the king and the people would be the Lord's. And all the people rushed over to the temple of Baal and knocked it down, and broke up the altars and knocked down the idols, and killed Mattan the priest of Baal before his altar. 18Jehoiada now appointed the Levite priests as guards, and to sacrifice the burnt offering to the Lord as prescribed in the law of Moses. He made the identical assignments of the Levite clans that King David had. They sang with joy as they worked. 19The guards at the

New Revised Standard

23 BUT IN the seventh year Jehoiada took courage, and entered into a compact with the commanders of the hundreds, Azariah son of Jeroham, Ishmael son of Jehohanan, Azariah son of Obed, Maaseiah son of Adaiah, and Elishaphat son of Zichri. 2They went around through Judah and gathered the Levites from all the towns of Judah, and the heads of families of Israel, and they came to Jerusalem. 3Then the whole assembly made a covenant with the king in the house of God. Jehoiadad said to them, "Here is the king's son! Let him reign, as the LORD promised concerning the sons of David. 4This is what you are to do: one third of you, priests and Levites, who come on duty on the sabbath, shall be gatekeepers, 5one third shall be at the king's house, and one third at the Gate of the Foundation; and all the people shall be in the courts of the house of the LORD. 6Do not let anyone enter the house of the LORD except the priests and ministering Levites; they may enter, for they are holy, but all the othere people shall observe the instructions of the LORD. 7The Levites shall surround the king, each with his weapons in his hand; and whoever enters the house shall be killed. Stay with the king in his comings and goings."

Joash Crowned King

8 The Levites and all Judah did according to all that the priest Jehoiada commanded; each brought his men, who were to come on duty on the sabbath, with those who were to go off duty on the sabbath; for the priest Jehoiada did not dismiss the divisions. 9The priest Jehoiada delivered to the captains the spears and the large and small shields that had been King David's, which were in the house of God; 10and he set all the people as a guard for the king, everyone with weapon in hand, from the south side of the house to the north side of the house, around the altar and the house. 11Then he brought out the king's son, put the crown on him, and gave him the covenant;f they proclaimed him king, and Jehoiada and his sons anointed him; and they shouted, "Long live the king!"

Athaliah Murdered

12 When Athaliah heard the noise of the people running and praising the king, she went into the house of the LORD to the people; 13and when she looked, there was the king standing by his pillar at the entrance, and the captains and the trumpeters beside the king, and all the people of the land rejoicing and blowing trumpets, and the singers with their musical instruments leading in the celebration. Athaliah tore her clothes, and cried, "Treason! Treason!" 14Then the priest Jehoiada brought out the captains who were set over the army, saying to them, "Bring her out between the ranks; anyone who follows her is to be put to the sword." For the priest said, "Do not put her to death in the house of the LORD." 15So they laid hands on her; she went into the entrance of the Horse Gate of the king's house, and there they put her to death.

16 Jehoiada made a covenant between himself and all the people and the king that they should be the LORD's people. 17Then all the people went to the house of Baal, and tore it down; his altars and his images they broke in pieces, and they killed Mattan, the priest of Baal, in front of the altars. 18Jehoiada assigned the care of the house of the LORD to the levitical priests whom David had organized to be in charge of the house of the LORD, to offer burnt offerings to the LORD, as it is written in the law of Moses, with rejoicing and with singing, according to the order of David. 19He stationed the gate-

King James

19And he set the porters at the gates of the house of the LORD, that none *which was* unclean in any thing should enter in.

20And he took the captains of hundreds, and the nobles, and the governors of the people, and all the people of the land, and brought down the king from the house of the LORD: and they came through the high gate into the king's house, and set the king upon the throne of the kingdom.

21And all the people of the land rejoiced: and the city was quiet, after that they had slain Athaliah with the sword.

24 JOASH *WAS* seven years old when he began to reign, and he reigned forty years in Jerusalem. His mother's name also *was* Zibiah of Beer-sheba.

2And Joash did *that which was* right in the sight of the LORD all the days of Jehoiada the priest.

3And Jehoiada took for him two wives; and he begat sons and daughters.

4¶ And it came to pass after this, *that* Joash was minded to repair the house of the LORD.

5And he gathered together the priest and the Levites, and said to them, Go out unto the cities of Judah, and gather of all Israel money to repair the house of your God from year to year, and see that ye hasten the matter. Howbeit the Levites hastened *it* not.

6And the king called for Jehoiada the chief, and said unto him, Why hast thou not required of the Levites to bring in out of Judah and out of Jerusalem the collection, *according to the commandment* of Moses the servant of the LORD, and of the congregation of Israel, for the tabernacle of witness?

7For the sons of Athaliah, that wicked woman, had broken up the house of God; and also all the dedicated things of the house of the LORD did they bestow upon Baalim.

8And at the king's commandment they made a chest, and set it without at the gate of the house of the LORD.

9And they made a proclamation through Judah and Jerusalem, to bring in to the LORD the collection *that* Moses the servant of God *laid* upon Israel in the wilderness.

10And all the princes and all the people rejoiced, and brought in, and cast into the chest, until they had made an end.

11Now it came to pass, that at what time the chest was brought unto the king's office by the hand of the Levites, and when they saw that *there was* much money, the king's scribe and the high priest's officer came and emptied the chest, and took it, and carried it to his place again. Thus they did day by day, and gathered money in abundance.

12And the king and Jehoiada gave it to such as did the work of the service of the house of the LORD, and hired masons and carpenters to repair the house of the LORD, and also such as wrought iron and brass to mend the house of the LORD.

13So the workmen wrought, and the work was perfected by them, and they set the house of God in his state, and strengthened it.

14And when they had finished *it*, they brought the rest of the money before the king and Jehoiada, whereof were made vessels for the house of the LORD, *even* vessels to minister, and to offer *withal*, and spoons, and vessels of gold and silver. And they offered burnt offerings in the house of the LORD continually all the days of Jehoiada.

15¶ But Jehoiada waxed old, and was full of days when he died; an hundred and thirty years old *was he* when he died.

New International

the LORD's temple so that no one who was in any way unclean might enter.

20He took with him the commanders of hundreds, the nobles, the rulers of the people and all the people of the land and brought the king down from the temple of the LORD. They went into the palace through the Upper Gate and seated the king on the royal throne, 21and all the people of the land rejoiced. And the city was quiet, because Athaliah had been slain with the sword.

Joash Repairs the Temple

24 JOASH WAS seven years old when he became king, and he reigned in Jerusalem forty years. His mother's name was Zibiah; she was from Beersheba. 2Joash did what was right in the eyes of the LORD all the years of Jehoiada the priest. 3Jehoiada chose two wives for him, and he had sons and daughters.

4Some time later Joash decided to restore the temple of the LORD. 5He called together the priests and Levites and said to them, "Go to the towns of Judah and collect the money due annually from all Israel, to repair the temple of your God. Do it now." But the Levites did not act at once.

6Therefore the king summoned Jehoiada the chief priest and said to him, "Why haven't you required the Levites to bring in from Judah and Jerusalem the tax imposed by Moses the servant of the LORD and by the assembly of Israel for the Tent of the Testimony?"

7Now the sons of that wicked woman Athaliah had broken into the temple of God and had used even its sacred objects for the Baals.

8At the king's command, a chest was made and placed outside, at the gate of the temple of the LORD. 9A proclamation was then issued in Judah and Jerusalem that they should bring to the LORD the tax that Moses the servant of God had required of Israel in the desert. 10All the officials and all the people brought their contributions gladly, dropping them into the chest until it was full. 11Whenever the chest was brought in by the Levites to the king's officials and they saw that there was a large amount of money, the royal secretary and the officer of the chief priest would come and empty the chest and carry it back to its place. They did this regularly and collected a great amount of money. 12The king and Jehoiada gave it to the men who carried out the work required for the temple of the LORD. They hired masons and carpenters to restore the LORD's temple, and also workers in iron and bronze to repair the temple.

13The men in charge of the work were diligent, and the repairs progressed under them. They rebuilt the temple of God according to its original design and reinforced it. 14When they had finished, they brought the rest of the money to the king and Jehoiada, and with it were made articles for the LORD's temple: articles for the service and for the burnt offerings, and also dishes and other objects of gold and silver. As long as Jehoiada lived, burnt offerings were presented continually in the temple of the LORD.

15Now Jehoiada was old and full of years, and he died at the age of a hundred and thirty. 16He was buried with

Living Bible

Temple gates kept out everything that was not consecrated and all unauthorized personnel.

20Then the army officers, nobles, governors, and all the people escorted the king from the Temple, wending their way from the Upper Gate to the palace, and seated the king upon his throne. 21So all the people of the land rejoiced, and the city was quiet and peaceful because Queen Athaliah was dead.

24 JOASH WAS seven years old when he became king, and he reigned forty years, in Jerusalem. His mother's name was Zibiah, from Beer-sheba. 2Joash tried hard to please the Lord all during the lifetime of Jehoiada the priest. 3Jehoiada arranged two marriages for him, and he had sons and daughters.

4Later on, Joash decided to repair and recondition the Temple. 5He summoned the priests and Levites and gave them these instructions:

"Go to all the cities of Judah and collect offerings for the building fund, so that we can maintain the Temple in good repair. Get at it right away. Don't delay." But the Levites took their time.

6So the king called for Jehoiada, the High Priest, and asked him, "Why haven't you demanded that the Levites go out and collect the Temple taxes from the cities of Judah, and from Jerusalem? The tax law enacted by Moses the servant of the Lord must be enforced so that the Temple can be repaired."

7, 8(The followers of wicked Athaliah had ravaged the Temple, and everything dedicated to the worship of God had been removed to the temple of Baalim.) So now the king instructed that a chest be made and set outside the Temple gate. 9Then a proclamation was sent to all the cities of Judah and throughout Jerusalem telling the people to bring to the Lord the tax that Moses the servant of God had assessed upon Israel. 10And all the leaders and the people were glad, and brought the money and placed it in the chest until it was full.

11Then the Levites carried the chest to the king's accounting office where the recording secretary and the representative of the High Priest counted the money, and took the chest back to the Temple again. This went on day after day, and money continued to pour in. 12The king and Jehoiada gave the money to the building superintendents, who hired masons and carpenters to restore the Temple; and to foundrymen who made articles of iron and brass. 13So the work went forward, and finally the Temple was in much better condition than before. 14When all was finished, the remaining money was brought to the king and Jehoiada, and it was agreed to use it for making the gold and silver spoons and bowls used for incense, and for making the instruments used in the sacrifices and offerings.

Burnt offerings were sacrificed continually during the lifetime of Jehoiada the priest. 15He lived to a very old age, finally dying at 130. 16He was buried in the City

New Revised Standard

keepers at the gates of the house of the LORD so that no one should enter who was in any way unclean. 20And he took the captains, the nobles, the governors of the people, and all the people of the land, and they brought the king down from the house of the LORD, marching through the upper gate to the king's house. They set the king on the royal throne. 21So all the people of the land rejoiced, and the city was quiet after Athaliah had been killed with the sword.

Joash Repairs the Temple

24 JOASH WAS seven years old when he began to reign; he reigned forty years in Jerusalem; his mother's name was Zibiah of Beer-sheba. 2Joash did what was right in the sight of the LORD all the days of the priest Jehoiada. 3Jehoiada got two wives for him, and he became the father of sons and daughters.

4 Some time afterward Joash decided to restore the house of the LORD. 5He assembled the priests and the Levites and said to them, "Go out to the cities of Judah and gather money from all Israel to repair the house of your God, year by year; and see that you act quickly." But the Levites did not act quickly. 6So the king summoned Jehoiada the chief, and said to him, "Why have you not required the Levites to bring in from Judah and Jerusalem the tax levied by Moses, the servant of the LORD, ona the congregation of Israel for the tent of the covenant?"b 7For the children of Athaliah, that wicked woman, had broken into the house of God, and had even used all the dedicated things of the house of the LORD for the Baals.

8 So the king gave command, and they made a chest, and set it outside the gate of the house of the LORD. 9A proclamation was made throughout Judah and Jerusalem to bring in for the LORD the tax that Moses the servant of God laid on Israel in the wilderness. 10All the leaders and all the people rejoiced and brought their tax and dropped it into the chest until it was full. 11Whenever the chest was brought to the king's officers by the Levites, when they saw that there was a large amount of money in it, the king's secretary and the officer of the chief priest would come and empty the chest and take it and return it to its place. So they did day after day, and collected money in abundance. 12The king and Jehoiada gave it to those who had charge of the work of the house of the LORD, and they hired masons and carpenters to restore the house of the LORD, and also workers in iron and bronze to repair the house of the LORD. 13So those who were engaged in the work labored, and the repairing went forward at their hands, and they restored the house of God to its proper condition and strengthened it. 14When they had finished, they brought the rest of the money to the king and Jehoiada, and with it were made utensils for the house of the LORD, utensils for the service and for the burnt offerings, and ladles, and vessels of gold and silver. They offered burnt offerings in the house of the LORD regularly all the days of Jehoiada.

Apostasy of Joash

15 But Jehoiada grew old and full of days, and died; he was one hundred thirty years old at his death. 16And

a Compare Vg: Heb and   b Or treaty, or testimony; Heb eduth

King James

16And they buried him in the city of David among the kings, because he had done good in Israel, both toward God, and toward his house.

17Now after the death of Jehoiada came the princes of Judah, and made obeisance to the king. Then the king hearkened unto them.

18And they left the house of the LORD God of their fathers, and served groves and idols: and wrath came upon Judah and Jerusalem for this their trespass.

19Yet he sent prophets to them, to bring them again unto the LORD; and they testified against them: but they would not give ear.

20And the spirit of God came upon Zechariah the son of Jehoiada the priest, which stood above the people, and said unto them, Thus saith God, Why transgress ye the commandments of the LORD, that ye cannot prosper? because ye have forsaken the LORD, he hath also forsaken you.

21And they conspired against him, and stoned him with stones at the commandment of the king in the court of the house of the LORD.

22Thus Joash the king remembered not the kindness which Jehoiada his father had done to him, but slew his son. And when he died, he said, The LORD look upon *it*, and require *it*.

23¶ And it came to pass at the end of the year, *that* the host of Syria came up against him: and they came to Judah and Jerusalem, and destroyed all the princes of the people from among the people, and sent all the spoil of them unto the king of Damascus.

24For the army of the Syrians came with a small company of men, and the LORD delivered a very great host into their hand, because they had forsaken the LORD God of their fathers. So they executed judgment against Joash.

25And when they were departed from him, (for they left him in great diseases,) his own servants conspired against him for the blood of the sons of Jehoiada the priest, and slew him on his bed, and he died: and they buried him in the city of David, but they buried him not in the sepulchres of the kings.

26And these are they that conspired against him; Zabad the son of Shimeath an Ammonitess, and Jehozabad the son of Shimrith a Moabitess.

27¶ Now *concerning* his sons, and the greatness of the burdens *laid* upon him, and the repairing of the house of God, behold, they *are* written in the story of the book of the kings. And Amaziah his son reigned in his stead.

25 AMAZIAH *WAS* twenty and five years old *when* he began to reign, and he reigned twenty and nine years in Jerusalem. And his mother's name *was* Jehoaddan of Jerusalem.

2And he did *that which was* right in the sight of the LORD, but not with a perfect heart.

3¶ Now it came to pass, when the kingdom was established to him, that he slew his servants that had killed the king his father.

4But he slew not their children, but *did* as *it is* written in the law in the book of Moses, where the LORD commanded, saying, The fathers shall not die for the children, neither shall the children die for the fathers, but every man shall die for his own sin.

New International

the kings in the City of David, because of the good he had done in Israel for God and his temple.

The Wickedness of Joash

17After the death of Jehoiada, the officials of Judah came and paid homage to the king, and he listened to them. 18They abandoned the temple of the LORD, the God of their fathers, and worshiped Asherah poles and idols. Because of their guilt, God's anger came upon Judah and Jerusalem. 19Although the LORD sent prophets to the people to bring them back to him, and though they testified against them, they would not listen.

20Then the Spirit of God came upon Zechariah son of Jehoiada the priest. He stood before the people and said, "This is what God says: 'Why do you disobey the LORD's commands? You will not prosper. Because you have forsaken the LORD, he has forsaken you.' "

21But they plotted against him, and by order of the king they stoned him to death in the courtyard of the LORD's temple. 22King Joash did not remember the kindness Zechariah's father Jehoiada had shown him but killed his son, who said as he lay dying, "May the LORD see this and call you to account."

23At the turn of the year,a the army of Aram marched against Joash; it invaded Judah and Jerusalem and killed all the leaders of the people. They sent all the plunder to their king in Damascus. 24Although the Aramean army had come with only a few men, the LORD delivered into their hands a much larger army. Because Judah had forsaken the LORD, the God of their fathers, judgment was executed on Joash. 25When the Arameans withdrew, they left Joash severely wounded. His officials conspired against him for murdering the son of Jehoiada the priest, and they killed him in his bed. So he died and was buried in the City of David, but not in the tombs of the kings.

26Those who conspired against him were Zabad,b son of Shimeath an Ammonite woman, and Jehozabad, son of Shimrithc a Moabite woman. 27The account of his sons, the many prophecies about him, and the record of the restoration of the temple of God are written in the annotations on the book of the kings. And Amaziah his son succeeded him as king.

Amaziah King of Judah

25 AMAZIAH WAS twenty-five years old when he became king, and he reigned in Jerusalem twenty-nine years. His mother's name was Jehoaddind; she was from Jerusalem. 2He did what was right in the eyes of the LORD, but not wholeheartedly. 3After the kingdom was firmly in his control, he executed the officials who had murdered his father the king. 4Yet he did not put their sons to death, but acted in accordance with what is written in the Law, in the Book of Moses, where the LORD commanded: "Fathers shall not be put to death for their children, nor children put to death for their fathers; each is to die for his own sins."e

---

a 23 Probably in the spring   b 26 A variant of *Jozabad*   c 26 A variant of *Shomer*   d 1 Hebrew *Jehoaddan*, a variant of *Jehoaddin*   e 4 Deut. 24:16

Living Bible

of David among the kings, because he had done so much good for Israel, for God, and for the Temple.

17, 18But after his death the leaders of Judah came to King Joash and induced him to abandon the Temple of the God of their ancestors, and to worship shame-idols instead! So the wrath of God came down upon Judah and Jerusalem again. 19God sent prophets to bring them back to the Lord, but the people wouldn't listen.

20Then the Spirit of God came upon Zechariah, Jehoiada's son. He called a meeting of all the people. Standing before them upon a platform, he said to them, "God wants to know why you are disobeying his commandments. For when you do, everything you try fails. You have forsaken the Lord, and now he has forsaken you."

21Then the leaders plotted to kill Zechariah, and finally King Joash himself ordered him executed in the court of the Temple. 22That was how King Joash repaid Jehoiada for his love and loyalty—by killing his son. Zechariah's last words as he died were, "Lord, see what they are doing and pay them back."

23A few months later the Syrian army arrived and conquered Judah and Jerusalem, killing all the leaders of the nation and sending back great quantities of booty to the king of Damascus. 24It was a great triumph for the tiny Syrian army, but the Lord let the great army of Judah be conquered by them because they had forsaken the Lord God of their ancestors. In that way God executed judgment upon Joash. 25When the Syrians left—leaving Joash severely wounded—his own officials decided to kill him for murdering the son of Jehoiada the priest. They assassinated him as he lay in bed, and buried him in the City of David, but not in the cemetery of the kings. 26The conspirators were Zabad, whose mother was Shime-ath, a woman from Ammon; and Jehozabad, whose mother was Shimrith, a woman from Moab. 27If you want to read about the sons of Joash, and the curses laid upon Joash, and about the restoration of the Temple, see *The Annals of the Kings.*

When Joash died, his son Amaziah became the new king.

25 AMAZIAH WAS twenty-five years old when he became king, and he reigned twenty-nine years, in Jerusalem. His mother's name was Jeho-addan, a native of Jerusalem. 2He did what was right, but sometimes resented it! 3When he was well established as the new king, he executed the men who had assassinated his father. 4However, he didn't kill their children but followed the command of the Lord written in the law of Moses, that the fathers shall not die for the children's sins, nor the children for the father's sins. No, everyone must pay for his own sins.

New Revised Standard

they buried him in the city of David among the kings, because he had done good in Israel, and for God and his house.

17 Now after the death of Jehoiada the officials of Judah came and did obeisance to the king; then the king listened to them. 18They abandoned the house of the LORD, the God of their ancestors, and served the sacred polesf and the idols. And wrath came upon Judah and Jerusalem for this guilt of theirs. 19Yet he sent prophets among them to bring them back to the LORD; they testified against them, but they would not listen.

20 Then the spirit of God took possession ofg Zechariah son of the priest Jehoiada; he stood above the people and said to them, "Thus says God: Why do you transgress the commandments of the LORD, so that you cannot prosper? Because you have forsaken the LORD, he has also forsaken you." 21But they conspired against him, and by command of the king they stoned him to death in the court of the house of the LORD. 22King Joash did not remember the kindness that Jehoiada, Zechariah's father, had shown him, but killed his son. As he was dying, he said, "May the LORD see and avenge!"

Death of Joash

23 At the end of the year the army of Aram came up against Joash. They came to Judah and Jerusalem, and destroyed all the officials of the people from among them, and sent all the booty they took to the king of Damascus. 24Although the army of Aram had come with few men, the LORD delivered into their hand a very great army, because they had abandoned the LORD, the God of their ancestors. Thus they executed judgment on Joash.

25 When they had withdrawn, leaving him severely wounded, his servants conspired against him because of the blood of the sonh of the priest Jehoiada, and they killed him on his bed. So he died; and they buried him in the city of David, but they did not bury him in the tombs of the kings. 26Those who conspired against him were Zabad son of Shimeath the Ammonite, and Jehozabad son of Shimrith the Moabite. 27Accounts of his sons, and of the many oracles against him, and of the rebuildingi of the house of God are written in the Commentary on the Book of the Kings. And his son Amaziah succeeded him.

Reign of Amaziah

25 AMAZIAH WAS twenty-five years old when he began to reign, and he reigned twenty-nine years in Jerusalem. His mother's name was Jehoaddan of Jerusalem. 2He did what was right in the sight of the LORD, yet not with a true heart. 3As soon as the royal power was firmly in his hand he killed his servants who had murdered his father the king. 4But he did not put their children to death, according to what is written in the law, in the book of Moses, where the LORD commanded, "The parents shall not be put to death for the children, or the children be put to death for the parents; but all shall be put to death for their own sins."

---

f Heb *Asherim*   g Heb *clothed itself with*   h Gk Vg: Heb *sons*   i Heb *founding*

King James

5¶ Moreover Amaziah gathered Judah together, and made them captains over thousands, and captains over hundreds, according to the houses of *their* fathers, throughout all Judah and Benjamin: and he numbered them from twenty years old and above, and found them three hundred thousand choice *men, able* to go forth to war, that could handle spear and shield.

6He hired also an hundred thousand mighty men of valour out of Israel for an hundred talents of silver.

7But there came a man of God to him, saying, O king, let not the army of Israel go with thee; for the LORD *is* not with Israel, *to wit, with* all the children of Ephraim.

8But if thou wilt go, do *it,* be strong for the battle: God shall make thee fall before the enemy: for God hath power to help, and to cast down.

9And Amaziah said to the man of God, But what shall we do for the hundred talents which I have given to the army of Israel? And the man of God answered, The LORD is able to give thee much more than this.

10Then Amaziah separated them, *to wit,* the army that was come to him out of Ephraim, to go home again: wherefore their anger was greatly kindled against Judah, and they returned home in great anger.

11And Amaziah strengthened himself, and led forth his people, and went to the valley of salt, and smote of the children of Seir ten thousand.

12And *other* ten thousand *left* alive did the children of Judah carry away captive, and brought them unto the top of the rock, and cast them down from the top of the rock, that they all were broken in pieces.

13¶ But the soldiers of the army which Amaziah sent back, that they should not go with him to battle, fell upon the cities of Judah, from Samaria even unto Beth-horon, and smote three thousand of them, and took much spoil.

14¶ Now it came to pass, after that Amaziah was come from the slaughter of the Edomites, that he brought the gods of the children of Seir, and set them up *to be his* gods, and bowed down himself before them, and burned incense unto them.

15Wherefore the anger of the LORD was kindled against Amaziah, and he sent unto him a prophet, which said unto him, Why hast thou sought after the gods of the people, which could not deliver their own people out of thine hand?

16And it came to pass, as he talked with him, that *the king* said unto him, Art thou made of the king's counsel? forbear; why shouldest thou be smitten? Then the prophet forbare, and said, I know that God hath determined to destroy thee, because thou hast done this, and hast not hearkened unto my counsel.

17¶ Then Amaziah king of Judah took advice, and sent to Joash, the son of Jehoahaz, the son of Jehu, king of Israel, saying, Come, let us see one another in the face.

18And Joash king of Israel sent to Amaziah king of Judah, saying, The thistle that *was* in Lebanon sent to the cedar that *was* in Lebanon, saying, Give thy daughter to my son to wife: and there passed by a wild beast that *was* in Lebanon, and trode down the thistle.

19Thou sayest, Lo, thou hast smitten the Edomites; and thine heart lifteth thee up to boast: abide now at home; why shouldest thou meddle to *thine* hurt, that thou shouldest fall, *even* thou, and Judah with thee?

20But Amaziah would not hear; for it *came* of God, that he might deliver them into the hand *of their enemies,* because they sought after the gods of Edom.

21So Joash the king of Israel went up; and they saw one another in the face, *both* he and Amaziah king of Judah, at Beth-shemesh, which *belongeth* to Judah.

22And Judah was put to the worse before Israel, and they fled every man to his tent.

New International

5Amaziah called the people of Judah together and assigned them according to their families to commanders of thousands and commanders of hundreds for all Judah and Benjamin. He then mustered those twenty years old or more and found that there were three hundred thousand men ready for military service, able to handle the spear and shield. 6He also hired a hundred thousand fighting men from Israel for a hundred talents[a] of silver.

7But a man of God came to him and said, "O king, these troops from Israel must not march with you, for the LORD is not with Israel—not with any of the people of Ephraim. 8Even if you go and fight courageously in battle, God will overthrow you before the enemy, for God has the power to help or to overthrow."

9Amaziah asked the man of God, "But what about the hundred talents I paid for these Israelite troops?"

The man of God replied, "The LORD can give you much more than that."

10So Amaziah dismissed the troops who had come to him from Ephraim and sent them home. They were furious with Judah and left for home in a great rage.

11Amaziah then marshaled his strength and led his army to the Valley of Salt, where he killed ten thousand men of Seir. 12The army of Judah also captured ten thousand men alive, took them to the top of a cliff and threw them down so that all were dashed to pieces.

13Meanwhile the troops that Amaziah had sent back and had not allowed to take part in the war raided Judean towns from Samaria to Beth Horon. They killed three thousand people and carried off great quantities of plunder.

14When Amaziah returned from slaughtering the Edomites, he brought back the gods of the people of Seir. He set them up as his own gods, bowed down to them and burned sacrifices to them. 15The anger of the LORD burned against Amaziah, and he sent a prophet to him, who said, "Why do you consult this people's gods, which could not save their own people from your hand?"

16While he was still speaking, the king said to him, "Have we appointed you an adviser to the king? Stop! Why be struck down?"

So the prophet stopped but said, "I know that God has determined to destroy you, because you have done this and have not listened to my counsel."

17After Amaziah king of Judah consulted his advisers, he sent this challenge to Jehoash[b] son of Jehoahaz, the son of Jehu, king of Israel: "Come, meet me face to face."

18But Jehoash king of Israel replied to Amaziah king of Judah: "A thistle in Lebanon sent a message to a cedar in Lebanon, 'Give your daughter to my son in marriage.' Then a wild beast in Lebanon came along and trampled the thistle underfoot. 19You say to yourself that you have defeated Edom, and now you are arrogant and proud. But stay at home! Why ask for trouble and cause your own downfall and that of Judah also?"

20Amaziah, however, would not listen, for God so worked that he might hand them over to ₁Jehoash₁, because they sought the gods of Edom. 21So Jehoash king of Israel attacked. He and Amaziah king of Judah faced each other at Beth Shemesh in Judah. 22Judah was routed by Israel, and every man fled to his home. 23Jehoash

a 6 That is, about 3 3/4 tons (about 3.4 metric tons); also in verse 9
b 17 Hebrew *Joash,* a variant of *Jehoash;* also in verses 18, 21, 23 and 25

Living Bible

5, 6Another thing Amaziah did was to organize the army, assigning leaders to each clan from Judah and Benjamin. Then he took a census and found that he had an army of 300,000 men twenty years old and older, all trained and highly skilled in the use of spear and sword. He also paid $200,000 to hire 100,000 experienced mercenaries from Israel.

7But a prophet arrived with this message from the Lord: "Sir, do not hire troops from Israel, for the Lord is not with them. 8If you let them go with your troops to battle, you will be defeated no matter how well you fight; for God has power to help or to frustrate."

9"But the money!" Amaziah whined. "What shall I do about that?"

And the prophet replied, "The Lord is able to give you much more than this!"

10So Amaziah sent them home again to Ephraim, which made them very angry and insulted. 11Then Amaziah took courage and led his army to the Valley of Salt, and there killed 10,000 men from Seir. 12Another 10,000 were taken alive to the top of a cliff and thrown over, so that they were crushed upon the rocks below.

13Meanwhile, the army of Israel that had been sent home raided several of the cities of Judah in the vicinity of Beth-horon, toward Samaria, killing 3,000 people and carrying off great quantities of booty.

14When King Amaziah returned from this slaughter of the Edomites, he brought with him idols taken from the people of Seir, and set them up as gods, and bowed before them, and burned incense to them! 15This made the Lord very angry and he sent a prophet to demand, "Why have you worshiped gods who couldn't even save their own people from you?"

16"Since when have I asked your advice?" the king retorted. "Be quiet now, before I have you killed."

The prophet left with this parting warning: "I know that God has determined to destroy you because you have worshiped these idols, and have not accepted my counsel."

17King Amaziah of Judah now took the advice of his counselors and declared war on King Joash of Israel (son of Jehoahaz, grandson of Jehu).

18King Joash replied with this parable: "Out in the Lebanon mountains a thistle demanded of a cedar tree, 'Give your daughter in marriage to my son.' Just then a wild animal came by and stepped on the thistle, crushing it! 19You are very proud about your conquest of Edom, but my advice is to stay home and don't meddle with me, lest you and all Judah get badly hurt."

20But Amaziah wouldn't listen, for God was arranging to destroy him for worshiping the gods of Edom. 21The armies met at Beth-shemesh, in Judah, 22and Judah was defeated, and its army fled home. 23King Joash

New Revised Standard

Slaughter of the Edomites

5 Amaziah assembled the people of Judah, and set them by ancestral houses under commanders of the thousands and of the hundreds for all Judah and Benjamin. He mustered those twenty years old and upward, and found that they were three hundred thousand picked troops fit for war, able to handle spear and shield. 6He also hired one hundred thousand mighty warriors from Israel for one hundred talents of silver. 7But a man of God came to him and said, "O king, do not let the army of Israel go with you, for the LORD is not with Israel—all these Ephraimites. 8Rather, go by yourself and act; be strong in battle, or God will fling you down before the enemy; for God has power to help or to overthrow." 9Amaziah said to the man of God, "But what shall we do about the hundred talents that I have given to the army of Israel?" The man of God answered, "The LORD is able to give you much more than this." 10Then Amaziah discharged the army that had come to him from Ephraim, letting them go home again. But they became very angry with Judah, and returned home in fierce anger.

11 Amaziah took courage, and led out his people; he went to the Valley of Salt, and struck down ten thousand men of Seir. 12The people of Judah captured another ten thousand alive, took them to the top of Sela, and threw them down from the top of Sela, so that all of them were dashed to pieces. 13But the men of the army whom Amaziah sent back, not letting them go with him to battle, fell on the cities of Judah from Samaria to Beth-horon; they killed three thousand people in them, and took much booty.

14 Now after Amaziah came from the slaughter of the Edomites, he brought the gods of the people of Seir, set them up as his gods, and worshiped them, making offerings to them. 15The LORD was angry with Amaziah and sent to him a prophet, who said to him, "Why have you resorted to a people's gods who could not deliver their own people from your hand?" 16But as he was speaking the king[c] said to him, "Have we made you a royal counselor? Stop! Why should you be put to death?" So the prophet stopped, but said, "I know that God has determined to destroy you, because you have done this and have not listened to my advice."

Israel Defeats Judah

17 Then King Amaziah of Judah took counsel and sent to King Joash son of Jehoahaz son of Jehu of Israel, saying, "Come, let us look one another in the face." 18King Joash of Israel sent word to King Amaziah of Judah, "A thornbush on Lebanon sent to a cedar on Lebanon, saying, 'Give your daughter to my son for a wife'; and a wild animal of Lebanon passed by and trampled down the thornbush. 19You say, 'See, I have defeated Edom,' and your heart has lifted you up in boastfulness. Now stay at home; why should you provoke trouble so that you fall, you and Judah with you?"

20 But Amaziah would not listen—it was God's doing, in order to hand them over, because they had sought the gods of Edom. 21So King Joash of Israel went up; he and King Amaziah of Judah faced one another in battle at Beth-shemesh, which belongs to Judah. 22Judah was defeated by Israel; everyone fled home. 23King

c Heb he

King James

23And Joash the king of Israel took Amaziah king of Judah, the son of Joash, the son of Jehoahaz, at Beth-shemesh, and brought him to Jerusalem, and brake down the wall of Jerusalem from the gate of Ephraim to the corner gate, four hundred cubits.

24And *he took* all the gold and the silver, and all the vessels that were found in the house of God with Obed-edom, and the treasures of the king's house, the hostages also, and returned to Samaria.

25¶ And Amaziah the son of Joash king of Judah lived after the death of Joash son of Jehoahaz king of Israel fifteen years.

26Now the rest of the acts of Amaziah, first and last, behold, *are* they not written in the book of the kings of Judah and Israel?

27¶ Now after the time that Amaziah did turn away from following the LORD they made a conspiracy against him in Jerusalem; and he fled to Lachish: but they sent to Lachish after him, and slew him there.

28And they brought him upon horses, and buried him with his fathers in the city of Judah.

26 THEN ALL the people of Judah took Uzziah, who *was* sixteen years old, and made him king in the room of his father Amaziah.

2He built Eloth, and restored it to Judah, after that the king slept with his fathers.

3Sixteen years old *was* Uzziah when he began to reign, and he reigned fifty and two years in Jerusalem. His mother's name also *was* Jecoliah of Jerusalem.

4And he did *that which was* right in the sight of the LORD, according to all that his father Amaziah did.

5And he sought God in the days of Zechariah, who had understanding in the visions of God: and as long as he sought the LORD, God made him to prosper.

6And he went forth and warred against the Philistines, and brake down the wall of Gath, and the wall of Jabneh, and the wall of Ashdod, and built cities about Ashdod, and among the Philistines.

7And God helped him against the Philistines, and against the Arabians that dwelt in Gur-baal, and the Mehunims.

8And the Ammonites gave gifts to Uzziah: and his name spread abroad *even* to the entering in of Egypt; for he strengthened *himself* exceedingly.

9Moreover Uzziah built towers in Jerusalem at the corner gate, and at the valley gate, and at the turning *of the wall,* and fortified them.

10Also he built towers in the desert, and digged many wells: for he had much cattle, both in the low country, and in the plains: husbandmen *also,* and vine dressers in the mountains, and in Carmel: for he loved husbandry.

11Moreover Uzziah had an host of fighting men, that went out to war by bands, according to the number of their account by the hand of Jeiel the scribe and Maaseiah the ruler, under the hand of Hananiah, *one* of the king's captains.

12The whole number of the chief of the fathers of the mighty men of valour *were* two thousand and six hundred.

13And under their hand *was* an army, three hundred thousand and seven thousand and five hundred, that made war with mighty power, to help the king against the enemy.

14And Uzziah prepared for them throughout all the host shields, and spears, and helmets, and habergeons, and bows, and slings *to cast* stones.

New International

king of Israel captured Amaziah king of Judah, the son of Joash, the son of Ahaziah,[a] at Beth Shemesh. Then Jehoash brought him to Jerusalem and broke down the wall of Jerusalem from the Ephraim Gate to the Corner Gate—a section about six hundred feet[b] long. 24He took all the gold and silver and all the articles found in the temple of God that had been in the care of Obed-Edom, together with the palace treasures and the hostages, and returned to Samaria.

25Amaziah son of Joash king of Judah lived for fifteen years after the death of Jehoash son of Jehoahaz king of Israel. 26As for the other events of Amaziah's reign, from beginning to end, are they not written in the book of the kings of Judah and Israel? 27From the time that Amaziah turned away from following the LORD, they conspired against him in Jerusalem and he fled to Lachish, but they sent men after him to Lachish and killed him there. 28He was brought back by horse and was buried with his fathers in the City of Judah.

Uzziah King of Judah

26 THEN ALL the people of Judah took Uzziah,[c] who was sixteen years old, and made him king in place of his father Amaziah. 2He was the one who rebuilt Elath and restored it to Judah after Amaziah rested with his fathers.

3Uzziah was sixteen years old when he became king, and he reigned in Jerusalem fifty-two years. His mother's name was Jecoliah; she was from Jerusalem. 4He did what was right in the eyes of the LORD, just as his father Amaziah had done. 5He sought God during the days of Zechariah, who instructed him in the fear[d] of God. As long as he sought the LORD, God gave him success.

6He went to war against the Philistines and broke down the walls of Gath, Jabneh and Ashdod. He then rebuilt towns near Ashdod and elsewhere among the Philistines. 7God helped him against the Philistines and against the Arabs who lived in Gur Baal and against the Meunites. 8The Ammonites brought tribute to Uzziah, and his fame spread as far as the border of Egypt, because he had become very powerful.

9Uzziah built towers in Jerusalem at the Corner Gate, at the Valley Gate and at the angle of the wall, and he fortified them. 10He also built towers in the desert and dug many cisterns, because he had much livestock in the foothills and in the plain. He had people working his fields and vineyards in the hills and in the fertile lands, for he loved the soil.

11Uzziah had a well-trained army, ready to go out by divisions according to their numbers as mustered by Jeiel the secretary and Maaseiah the officer under the direction of Hananiah, one of the royal officials. 12The total number of family leaders over the fighting men was 2,600. 13Under their command was an army of 307,500 men trained for war, a powerful force to support the king against his enemies. 14Uzziah provided shields, spears, helmets, coats of armor, bows and slingstones for the entire army. 15In Jerusalem he made ma-

---

a *23 Hebrew Jehoahaz, a variant of Ahaziah*   b *23 Hebrew four hundred cubits (about 180 meters)*   c *1 Also called Azariah*   d *5 Many Hebrew manuscripts, Septuagint and Syriac; other Hebrew manuscripts vision*

Living Bible

of Israel captured the defeated King Amaziah of Judah and took him as a prisoner to Jerusalem. Then King Joash ordered two hundred yards of the walls of Jerusalem dismantled, from the gate of Ephraim to the Corner Gate. 24He carried off all the treasures and gold bowls from the Temple, as well as the treasures from the palace; and he took hostages, including Obed-edom, and returned to Samaria.

25However, King Amaziah of Judah lived on for fifteen years after the death of King Joash of Israel. 26The complete biography of King Amaziah is written in *The Annals of the Kings of Judah and Israel*. 27This account includes a report of Amaziah's turning away from God, and how his people conspired against him in Jerusalem, and how he fled to Lachish—but they went after him and killed him there. 28And they brought him back on horses to Jerusalem and buried him in the royal cemetery.

26 THE PEOPLE of Judah now crowned sixteen-year-old Uzziah as their new king. 2After his father's death, he rebuilt the city of Eloth and restored it to Judah. 3In all, he reigned fifty-two years, in Jerusalem. His mother's name was Jecoliah, from Jerusalem. 4He followed in the footsteps of his father Amaziah, and was, in general, a good king in the Lord's sight.

5While Zechariah was alive Uzziah was always eager to please God. Zechariah was a man who had special revelations from God. And as long as the king followed the paths of God, he prospered, for God blessed him.

6He declared war on the Philistines and captured the city of Gath and broke down its walls, also those of Jabneh and Ashdod. Then he built new cities in the Ashdod area and in other parts of the Philistine country. 7God helped him not only with his wars against the Philistines but also in his battles with the Arabs of Gurbaal and in his wars with the Meunites. 8The Ammonites paid annual tribute to him, and his fame spread even to Egypt, for he was very powerful.

9He built fortified towers in Jerusalem at the Corner Gate, and the Valley Gate, and at the turning of the wall. 10He also constructed forts in the Negeb, and made many water reservoirs, for he had great herds of cattle out in the valleys and on the plains. He was a man who loved the soil and had many farms and vineyards, both on the hillsides and in the fertile valleys.

11He organized his army into regiments to which men were drafted under quotas set by Je-iel, the secretary of the army, and his assistant, Ma-aseiah. The commander-in-chief was General Hananiah. 12Twenty-six hundred brave clan leaders commanded these regiments. 13The army consisted of 307,500 men, all elite troops. 14Uzziah issued to them shields, spears, helmets, coats of mail, bows, and slingstones. 15And he produced engines of

New Revised Standard

Joash of Israel captured King Amaziah of Judah, son of Joash, son of Ahaziah, at Beth-shemesh; he brought him to Jerusalem, and broke down the wall of Jerusalem from the Ephraim Gate to the Corner Gate, a distance of four hundred cubits. 24He seized all the gold and silver, and all the vessels that were found in the house of God, and Obed-edom with them; he seized also the treasuries of the king's house, also hostages; then he returned to Samaria.

Death of Amaziah

25 King Amaziah son of Joash of Judah, lived fifteen years after the death of King Joash son of Jehoahaz of Israel. 26Now the rest of the deeds of Amaziah, from first to last, are they not written in the Book of the Kings of Judah and Israel? 27From the time that Amaziah turned away from the LORD they made a conspiracy against him in Jerusalem, and he fled to Lachish. But they sent after him to Lachish, and killed him there. 28They brought him back on horses; he was buried with his ancestors in the city of David.

Reign of Uzziah

26 THEN ALL the people of Judah took Uzziah, who was sixteen years old, and made him king to succeed his father Amaziah. 2He rebuilt Eloth and restored it to Judah, after the king slept with his ancestors. 3Uzziah was sixteen years old when he began to reign, and he reigned fifty-two years in Jerusalem. His mother's name was Jecoliah of Jerusalem. 4He did what was right in the sight of the LORD, just as his father Amaziah had done. 5He set himself to seek God in the days of Zechariah, who instructed him in the fear of God; and as long as he sought the LORD, God made him prosper.

6 He went out and made war against the Philistines, and broke down the wall of Gath and the wall of Jabneh and the wall of Ashdod; he built cities in the territory of Ashdod and elsewhere among the Philistines. 7God helped him against the Philistines, against the Arabs who lived in Gur-baal, and against the Meunites. 8The Ammonites paid tribute to Uzziah, and his fame spread even to the border of Egypt, for he became very strong. 9Moreover Uzziah built towers in Jerusalem at the Corner Gate, at the Valley Gate, and at the Angle, and fortified them. 10He built towers in the wilderness and hewed out many cisterns, for he had large herds, both in the Shephelah and in the plain, and he had farmers and vinedressers in the hills and in the fertile lands, for he loved the soil. 11Moreover Uzziah had an army of soldiers, fit for war, in divisions according to the numbers in the muster made by the secretary Jeiel and the officer Maaseiah, under the direction of Hananiah, one of the king's commanders. 12The whole number of the heads of ancestral houses of mighty warriors was two thousand six hundred. 13Under their command was an army of three hundred seven thousand five hundred, who could make war with mighty power, to help the king against the enemy. 14Uzziah provided for all the army the shields, spears, helmets, coats of mail, bows, and stones for slinging. 15In Jerusalem he set up machines, invent-

King James

New International

¹⁵And he made in Jerusalem engines, invented by cunning men, to be on the towers and upon the bulwarks, to shoot arrows and great stones withal. And his name spread far abroad; for he was marvellously helped, till he was strong.

¹⁶¶ But when he was strong, his heart was lifted up to *his* destruction: for he transgressed against the LORD his God, and went into the temple of the LORD to burn incense upon the altar of incense.

¹⁷And Azariah the priest went in after him, and with him fourscore priests of the LORD, *that were* valiant men:

¹⁸And they withstood Uzziah the king, and said unto him, *It appertaineth* not unto thee, Uzziah, to burn incense unto the LORD, but to the priests the sons of Aaron, that are consecrated to burn incense: go out of the sanctuary; for thou hast trespassed; neither *shall it be* for thine honour from the LORD God.

¹⁹Then Uzziah was wroth, and *had* a censer in his hand to burn incense: and while he was wroth with the priests, the leprosy even rose up in his forehead before the priests in the house of the LORD, from beside the incense altar.

²⁰And Azariah the chief priest, and all the priests, looked upon him, and, behold, he *was* leprous in his forehead, and they thrust him out from thence; yea, himself hasted also to go out, because the LORD had smitten him.

²¹And Uzziah the king was a leper unto the day of his death, and dwelt in a several house, *being* a leper; for he was cut off from the house of the LORD: and Jotham his son *was* over the king's house, judging the people of the land.

²²¶ Now the rest of the acts of Uzziah, first and last, did Isaiah the prophet, the son of Amoz, write.

²³So Uzziah slept with his fathers, and they buried him with his fathers in the field of the burial which *belonged* to the kings; for they said, He *is* a leper: and Jotham his son reigned in his stead.

27 JOTHAM *WAS* twenty and five years old when he began to reign, and he reigned sixteen years in Jerusalem. His mother's name also *was* Jerushah, the daughter of Zadok.

²And he did *that which was* right in the sight of the LORD, according to all that his father Uzziah did: howbeit he entered not into the temple of the LORD. And the people did yet corruptly.

³He built the high gate of the house of the LORD, and on the wall of Ophel he built much.

⁴Moreover he built cities in the mountains of Judah, and in the forests he built castles and towers.

⁵¶ He fought also with the king of the Ammonites, and prevailed against them. And the children of Ammon gave him the same year an hundred talents of silver, and ten thousand measures of wheat, and ten thousand of barley. So much did the children of Ammon pay unto him, both the second year, and the third.

⁶So Jotham became mighty, because he prepared his ways before the LORD his God.

⁷¶ Now the rest of the acts of Jotham, and all his wars, and his ways, lo, they *are* written in the book of the kings of Israel and Judah.

⁸He was five and twenty years old when he began to reign, and reigned sixteen years in Jerusalem.

⁹¶ And Jotham slept with his fathers, and they buried him in the city of David: and Ahaz his son reigned in his stead.

chines designed by skillful men for use on the towers and on the corner defenses to shoot arrows and hurl large stones. His fame spread far and wide, for he was greatly helped until he became powerful.

¹⁶But after Uzziah became powerful, his pride led to his downfall. He was unfaithful to the LORD his God, and entered the temple of the LORD to burn incense on the altar of incense. ¹⁷Azariah the priest with eighty other courageous priests of the LORD followed him in. ¹⁸They confronted him and said, "It is not right for you, Uzziah, to burn incense to the LORD. That is for the priests, the descendants of Aaron, who have been consecrated to burn incense. Leave the sanctuary, for you have been unfaithful; and you will not be honored by the LORD God."

¹⁹Uzziah, who had a censer in his hand ready to burn incense, became angry. While he was raging at the priests in their presence before the incense altar in the LORD's temple, leprosy^a broke out on his forehead. ²⁰When Azariah the chief priest and all the other priests looked at him, they saw that he had leprosy on his forehead, so they hurried him out. Indeed, he himself was eager to leave, because the LORD had afflicted him.

²¹King Uzziah had leprosy until the day he died. He lived in a separate house^b —leprous, and excluded from the temple of the LORD. Jotham his son had charge of the palace and governed the people of the land.

²²The other events of Uzziah's reign, from beginning to end, are recorded by the prophet Isaiah son of Amoz. ²³Uzziah rested with his fathers and was buried near them in a field for burial that belonged to the kings, for people said, "He had leprosy." And Jotham his son succeeded him as king.

Jotham King of Judah

27 JOTHAM WAS twenty-five years old when he became king, and he reigned in Jerusalem sixteen years. His mother's name was Jerusha daughter of Zadok. ²He did what was right in the eyes of the LORD, just as his father Uzziah had done, but unlike him he did not enter the temple of the LORD. The people, however, continued their corrupt practices. ³Jotham rebuilt the Upper Gate of the temple of the LORD and did extensive work on the wall at the hill of Ophel. ⁴He built towns in the Judean hills and forts and towers in the wooded areas.

⁵Jotham made war on the king of the Ammonites and conquered them. That year the Ammonites paid him a hundred talents^c of silver, ten thousand cors^d of wheat and ten thousand cors of barley. The Ammonites brought him the same amount also in the second and third years.

⁶Jotham grew powerful because he walked steadfastly before the LORD his God.

⁷The other events in Jotham's reign, including all his wars and the other things he did, are written in the book of the kings of Israel and Judah. ⁸He was twenty-five years old when he became king, and he reigned in Jerusalem sixteen years. ⁹Jotham rested with his fathers and was buried in the City of David. And Ahaz his son succeeded him as king.

---

^a *19* The Hebrew word was used for various diseases affecting the skin—not necessarily leprosy; also in verses 20, 21 and 23.   ^b *21* Or *in a house where he was relieved of responsibilities*   ^c *5* That is, about 3 3/4 tons (about 3.4 metric tons)   ^d *5* That is, probably about 62,000 bushels (about 2,200 kiloliters)

Living Bible

war manufactured in Jerusalem, invented by brilliant men to shoot arrows and huge stones from the towers and battlements. So he became very famous, for the Lord helped him wonderfully until he was very powerful.

16But at that point he became proud—and corrupt. He sinned against the Lord his God by entering the forbidden sanctuary of the Temple and personally burning incense upon the altar. 17, 18Azariah the High Priest went in after him with eighty other priests, all brave men, and demanded that he get out.

"It is not for you, Uzziah, to burn incense," they declared. "That is the work of the priests alone, the sons of Aaron who are consecrated to this work. Get out, for you have trespassed, and the Lord is not going to honor you for this!"

19Uzziah was furious, and refused to set down the incense burner he was holding. But look! Suddenly—leprosy appeared in his forehead! 20When Azariah and the others saw it, they rushed him out; in fact, he himself was as anxious to get out as they were to get him out, because the Lord had struck him.

21So King Uzziah was a leper until the day of his death and lived in isolation, cut off from his people and from the Temple. His son Jotham became vice-regent, in charge of the king's affairs and of the judging of the people of the land.

22The other details of Uzziah's reign from first to last are recorded by the prophet Isaiah (son of Amoz). 23When Uzziah died, he was buried in the royal cemetery even though he was a leper, and his son Jotham became the new king.

27 JOTHAM WAS twenty-five years old at the time he became king, and he reigned sixteen years, in Jerusalem. His mother was Jerushah, daughter of Zadok. 2He followed the generally good example of his father Uzziah—who had, however, sinned by invading the Temple—but even so his people became very corrupt.

3He built the Upper Gate of the Temple, and also did extensive rebuilding of the walls on the hill where the Temple was situated. 4And he built cities in the hill country of Judah, and erected fortresses and towers on the wooded hills.

5His war against the Ammonites was successful, so that for the next three years he received from them an annual tribute of $200,000 in silver, 10,000 sacks of wheat, and 10,000 sacks of barley. 6King Jotham became powerful because he was careful to follow the path of the Lord his God.

7The remainder of his history, including his wars and other activities, is written in *The Annals of the Kings of Israel and Judah.* 8In summary, then, he was twenty-five years old when he began to reign and he reigned sixteen years, in Jerusalem. 9When he died, he was buried in Jerusalem, and his son Ahaz became the new king.

New Revised Standard

ed by skilled workers, on the towers and the corners for shooting arrows and large stones. And his fame spread far, for he was marvelously helped until he became strong.

Pride and Apostasy

16 But when he had become strong he grew proud, to his destruction. For he was false to the LORD his God, and entered the temple of the LORD to make offering on the altar of incense. 17But the priest Azariah went in after him, with eighty priests of the LORD who were men of valor; 18they withstood King Uzziah, and said to him, "It is not for you, Uzziah, to make offering to the LORD, but for the priests the descendants of Aaron, who are consecrated to make offering. Go out of the sanctuary; for you have done wrong, and it will bring you no honor from the LORD God." 19Then Uzziah was angry. Now he had a censer in his hand to make offering, and when he became angry with the priests a leprous disease broke out on his forehead, in the presence of the priests in the house of the LORD, by the altar of incense. 20When the chief priest Azariah, and all the priests, looked at him, he was leprous in his forehead. They hurried him out, and he himself hurried to get out, because the LORD had struck him. 21King Uzziah was leprous to the day of his death, and being leprous lived in a separate house, for he was excluded from the house of the LORD. His son Jotham was in charge of the palace of the king, governing the people of the land.

22 Now the rest of the acts of Uzziah, from first to last, the prophet Isaiah son of Amoz wrote. 23Uzziah slept with his ancestors; they buried him near his ancestors in the burial field that belonged to the kings, for they said, "He is leprous."e His son Jotham succeeded him.

Reign of Jotham

27 JOTHAM WAS twenty-five years old when he began to reign; he reigned sixteen years in Jerusalem. His mother's name was Jerushah daughter of Zadok. 2He did what was right in the sight of the LORD just as his father Uzziah had done—only he did not invade the temple of the LORD. But the people still followed corrupt practices. 3He built the upper gate of the house of the LORD, and did extensive building on the wall of Ophel. 4Moreover he built cities in the hill country of Judah, and forts and towers on the wooded hills. 5He fought with the king of the Ammonites and prevailed against them. The Ammonites gave him that year one hundred talents of silver, ten thousand cors of wheat and ten thousand of barley. The Ammonites paid him the same amount in the second and the third years. 6So Jotham became strong because he ordered his ways before the LORD his God. 7Now the rest of the acts of Jotham, and all his wars and his ways, are written in the Book of the Kings of Israel and Judah. 8He was twenty-five years old when he began to reign; he reigned sixteen years in Jerusalem. 9Jotham slept with his ancestors, and they buried him in the city of David; and his son Ahaz succeeded him.

---

e A term for several skin diseases; precise meaning uncertain

King James

28 AHAZ *WAS* twenty years old when he began to reign, and he reigned sixteen years in Jerusalem: but he did not *that which was* right in the sight of the LORD, like David his father:

2For he walked in the ways of the kings of Israel, and made also molten images for Baalim.

3Moreover he burnt incense in the valley of the son of Hinnom, and burnt his children in the fire, after the abominations of the heathen whom the LORD had cast out before the children of Israel.

4He sacrificed also and burnt incense in the high places, and on the hills, and under every green tree.

5Wherefore the LORD his God delivered him into the hand of the king of Syria; and they smote him, and carried away a great multitude of them captives, and brought *them* to Damascus. And he was also delivered into the hand of the king of Israel, who smote him with a great slaughter.

6¶ For Pekah the son of Remaliah slew in Judah an hundred and twenty thousand in one day, *which were* all valiant men; because they had forsaken the LORD God of their fathers.

7And Zichri, a mighty man of Ephraim, slew Maaseiah the king's son, and Azrikam the governor of the house, and Elkanah *that was* next to the king.

8And the children of Israel carried away captive of their brethren two hundred thousand, women, sons, and daughters, and took also away much spoil from them, and brought the spoil to Samaria.

9But a prophet of the LORD was there, whose name *was* Oded: and he went out before the host that came to Samaria, and said unto them, Behold, because the LORD God of your fathers was wroth with Judah, he hath delivered them into your hand, and ye have slain them in a rage *that* reacheth up unto heaven.

10And now ye purpose to keep under the children of Judah and Jerusalem for bondmen and bondwomen unto you: *but are there* not with you, even with you, sins against the LORD your God?

11Now hear me therefore, and deliver the captives again, which ye have taken captive of your brethren: for the fierce wrath of the LORD *is* upon you.

12Then certain of the heads of the children of Ephraim, Azariah the son of Johanan, Berechiah the son of Meshillemoth, and Jehizkiah the son of Shallum, and Amasa the son of Hadlai, stood up against them that came from the war,

13And said unto them, Ye shall not bring in the captives hither: for whereas we have offended against the LORD *already,* ye intend to add *more* to our sins and to our trespass: for our trespass is great, and *there is* fierce wrath against Israel.

14So the armed men left the captives and the spoil before the princes and all the congregation.

15And the men which were expressed by name rose up, and took the captives, and with the spoil clothed all that were naked among them, and arrayed them, and shod them, and gave them to eat and to drink, and anointed them, and carried all the feeble of them upon asses, and brought them to Jericho, the city of palm trees, to their brethren: then they returned to Samaria.

16¶ At that time did king Ahaz send unto the kings of Assyria to help him.

New International

Ahaz King of Judah

28 AHAZ WAS twenty years old when he became king, and he reigned in Jerusalem sixteen years. Unlike David his father, he did not do what was right in the eyes of the LORD. 2He walked in the ways of the kings of Israel and also made cast idols for worshiping the Baals. 3He burned sacrifices in the Valley of Ben Hinnom and sacrificed his sons in the fire, following the detestable ways of the nations the LORD had driven out before the Israelites. 4He offered sacrifices and burned incense at the high places, on the hilltops and under every spreading tree.

5Therefore the LORD his God handed him over to the king of Aram. The Arameans defeated him and took many of his people as prisoners and brought them to Damascus.

He was also given into the hands of the king of Israel, who inflicted heavy casualties on him. 6In one day Pekah son of Remaliah killed a hundred and twenty thousand soldiers in Judah—because Judah had forsaken the LORD, the God of their fathers. 7Zicri, an Ephraimite warrior, killed Maaseiah the king's son, Azrikam the officer in charge of the palace, and Elkanah, second to the king. 8The Israelites took captive from their kinsmen two hundred thousand wives, sons and daughters. They also took a great deal of plunder, which they carried back to Samaria.

9But a prophet of the LORD named Oded was there, and he went out to meet the army when it returned to Samaria. He said to them, "Because the LORD, the God of your fathers, was angry with Judah, he gave them into your hand. But you have slaughtered them in a rage that reaches to heaven. 10And now you intend to make the men and women of Judah and Jerusalem your slaves. But aren't you also guilty of sins against the LORD your God? 11Now listen to me! Send back your fellow countrymen you have taken as prisoners, for the LORD's fierce anger rests on you."

12Then some of the leaders in Ephraim—Azariah son of Jehohanan, Berekiah son of Meshillemoth, Jehizkiah son of Shallum, and Amasa son of Hadlai—confronted those who were arriving from the war. 13"You must not bring those prisoners here," they said, "or we will be guilty before the LORD. Do you intend to add to our sin and guilt? For our guilt is already great, and his fierce anger rests on Israel."

14So the soldiers gave up the prisoners and plunder in the presence of the officials and all the assembly. 15The men designated by name took the prisoners, and from the plunder they clothed all who were naked. They provided them with clothes and sandals, food and drink, and healing balm. All those who were weak they put on donkeys. So they took them back to their fellow countrymen at Jericho, the City of Palms, and returned to Samaria.

16At that time King Ahaz sent to the king[a] of Assyria for help. 17The Edomites had again come and attacked

---

a *16* One Hebrew manuscript, Septuagint and Vulgate (see also 2 Kings 16:7); most Hebrew manuscripts *kings*

Living Bible

28 AHAZ WAS twenty years old when he became king and he reigned sixteen years, in Jerusalem. But he was an evil king, unlike his ancestor King David. ²For he followed the example of the kings over in Israel and worshiped the idols of Baal. ³He even went out to the Valley of Hinnom, and it was not just to burn incense to the idols, for he even sacrificed his own children in the fire, just like the heathen nations that were thrown out of the land by the Lord to make room for Israel. ⁴Yes, he sacrificed and burned incense at the idol shrines on the hills and under every green tree.

⁵That is why the Lord God allowed the king of Syria to defeat him and deport large numbers of his people to Damascus. The armies from Israel also slaughtered great numbers of his troops. ⁶On a single day, Pekah, the son of Remaliah, killed 120,000 of his bravest soldiers because they had turned away from the Lord God of their fathers. ⁷Then Zichri, a great warrior from Ephraim, killed the king's son Ma-aseiah, and the king's administrator Azrikam, and the king's second-in-command El-kanah. ⁸The armies from Israel also captured 200,000 Judean women and children, and tremendous amounts of booty which they took to Samaria.

⁹But Oded, a prophet of the Lord, was there in Samaria and he went out to meet the returning army.

"Look!" he exclaimed. "The Lord God of your fathers was angry with Judah and let you capture them, but you have butchered them without mercy, and all heaven is disturbed. ¹⁰And now are you going to make slaves of these people from Judah and Jerusalem? What about your own sins against the Lord your God? ¹¹Listen to me and return these relatives of yours to their homes, for now the fierce anger of the Lord is upon *you.*"

¹²Some of the top leaders of Ephraim also added their opposition. These men were Azariah the son of Johanan, Berechiah the son of Meshillemoth, Jehizkiah the son of Shallum, and Amasa the son of Hadlai.

¹³"You must not bring the captives here!" they declared. "If you do, the Lord will be angry, and this sin will be added to our many others. We are in enough trouble with God as it is."

¹⁴So the army officers turned over the captives and booty to the political leaders to decide what to do. ¹⁵Then the four men already mentioned distributed captured stores of clothing to the women and children who needed it, and gave them shoes, food, and wine, and put those who were sick and old on donkeys, and took them back to their families in Jericho, the City of Palm Trees. Then their escorts returned to Samaria.

¹⁶About that time King Ahaz of Judah asked the king of Assyria to be his ally in his war against the armies of Edom. For Edom was invading Judah and capturing many people as slaves. ¹⁷, ¹⁸Meanwhile, the Philistines

New Revised Standard

Reign of Ahaz

28 AHAZ WAS twenty years old when he began to reign; he reigned sixteen years in Jerusalem. He did not do what was right in the sight of the LORD, as his ancestor David had done, ²but he walked in the ways of the kings of Israel. He even made cast images for the Baals; ³and he made offerings in the valley of the son of Hinnom, and made his sons pass through fire, according to the abominable practices of the nations whom the LORD drove out before the people of Israel. ⁴He sacrificed and made offerings on the high places, on the hills, and under every green tree.

Aram and Israel Defeat Judah

5 Therefore the LORD his God gave him into the hand of the king of Aram, who defeated him and took captive a great number of his people and brought them to Damascus. He was also given into the hand of the king of Israel, who defeated him with great slaughter. ⁶Pekah son of Remaliah killed one hundred twenty thousand in Judah in one day, all of them valiant warriors, because they had abandoned the LORD, the God of their ancestors. ⁷And Zichri, a mighty warrior of Ephraim, killed the king's son Maaseiah, Azrikam the commander of the palace, and Elkanah the next in authority to the king.

Intervention of Oded

8 The people of Israel took captive two hundred thousand of their kin, women, sons, and daughters; they also took much booty from them and brought the booty to Samaria. ⁹But a prophet of the LORD was there, whose name was Oded; he went out to meet the army that came to Samaria, and said to them, "Because the LORD, the God of your ancestors, was angry with Judah, he gave them into your hand, but you have killed them in a rage that has reached up to heaven. ¹⁰Now you intend to subjugate the people of Judah and Jerusalem, male and female, as your slaves. But what have you except sins against the LORD your God? ¹¹Now hear me, and send back the captives whom you have taken from your kindred, for the fierce wrath of the LORD is upon you." ¹²Moreover, certain chiefs of the Ephraimites, Azariah son of Johanan, Berechiah son of Meshille-moth, Jehizkiah son of Shallum, and Amasa son of Hadlai, stood up against those who were coming from the war, ¹³and said to them, "You shall not bring the captives in here, for you propose to bring on us guilt against the LORD in addition to our present sins and guilt. For our guilt is already great, and there is fierce wrath against Israel." ¹⁴So the warriors left the captives and the booty before the officials and all the assembly. ¹⁵Then those who were mentioned by name got up and took the captives, and with the booty they clothed all that were naked among them; they clothed them, gave them sandals, provided them with food and drink, and anointed them; and carrying all the feeble among them on donkeys, they brought them to their kindred at Jericho, the city of palm trees. Then they returned to Samaria.

Assyria Refuses to Help Judah

16 At that time King Ahaz sent to the king[b] of Assyria for help. ¹⁷For the Edomites had again invaded and

---

b Gk Syr Vg Compare 2 Kings 16.7: Heb kings

King James

17For again the Edomites had come and smitten Judah, and carried away captives.

18The Philistines also had invaded the cities of the low country, and of the south of Judah, and had taken Beth-shemesh, and Ajalon, and Gederoth, and Shocho with the villages thereof, and Timnah with the villages thereof, Gimzo also and the villages thereof: and they dwelt there.

19For the LORD brought Judah low because of Ahaz king of Israel; for he made Judah naked, and transgressed sore against the LORD.

20And Tilgath-pilneser king of Assyria came unto him, and distressed him, but strengthened him not.

21For Ahaz took away a portion out of the house of the LORD, and out of the house of the king, and of the princes, and gave it unto the king of Assyria: but he helped him not.

22¶ And in the time of his distress did he trespass yet more against the LORD: this is that king Ahaz.

23For he sacrificed unto the gods of Damascus, which smote him: and he said, Because the gods of the kings of Syria help them, therefore will I sacrifice to them, that they may help me. But they were the ruin of him, and of all Israel.

24And Ahaz gathered together the vessels of the house of God, and cut in pieces the vessels of the house of God, and shut up the doors of the house of the LORD, and he made him altars in every corner of Jerusalem.

25And in every several city of Judah he made high places to burn incense unto other gods, and provoked to anger the LORD God of his fathers.

26¶ Now the rest of his acts and of all his ways, first and last, behold, they are written in the book of the kings of Judah and Israel.

27And Ahaz slept with his fathers, and they buried him in the city, even in Jerusalem: but they brought him not into the sepulchres of the kings of Israel: and Hezekiah his son reigned in his stead.

29 HEZEKIAH BEGAN to reign when he was five and twenty years old, and he reigned nine and twenty years in Jerusalem. And his mother's name was Abijah, the daughter of Zechariah.

2And he did that which was right in the sight of the LORD, according to all that David his father had done.

3¶ He in the first year of his reign, in the first month, opened the doors of the house of the LORD, and repaired them.

4And he brought in the priests and the Levites, and gathered them together into the east street,

5And said unto them, Hear me, ye Levites, sanctify now yourselves, and sanctify the house of the LORD God of your fathers, and carry forth the filthiness out of the holy place.

6For our fathers have trespassed, and done that which was evil in the eyes of the LORD our God, and have forsaken him, and have turned away their faces from the habitation of the LORD, and turned their backs.

7Also they have shut up the doors of the porch, and put out the lamps, and have not burned incense nor offered burnt offerings in the holy place unto the God of Israel.

8Wherefore the wrath of the LORD was upon Judah and Jerusalem, and he hath delivered them to trouble, to astonishment, and to hissing, as ye see with your eyes.

9For, lo, our fathers have fallen by the sword, and our sons and our daughters and our wives are in captivity for this.

10Now it is in mine heart to make a covenant with the LORD God of Israel, that his fierce wrath may turn away from us.

New International

Judah and carried away prisoners, 18while the Philistines had raided towns in the foothills and in the Negev of Judah. They captured and occupied Beth Shemesh, Aijalon and Gederoth, as well as Soco, Timnah and Gimzo, with their surrounding villages. 19The LORD had humbled Judah because of Ahaz king of Israel,[a] for he had promoted wickedness in Judah and had been most unfaithful to the LORD. 20Tiglath-Pileser[b] king of Assyria came to him, but he gave him trouble instead of help. 21Ahaz took some of the things from the temple of the LORD and from the royal palace and from the princes and presented them to the king of Assyria, but that did not help him.

22In his time of trouble King Ahaz became even more unfaithful to the LORD. 23He offered sacrifices to the gods of Damascus, who had defeated him; for he thought, "Since the gods of the kings of Aram have helped them, I will sacrifice to them so they will help me." But they were his downfall and the downfall of all Israel.

24Ahaz gathered together the furnishings from the temple of God and took them away.[c] He shut the doors of the LORD's temple and set up altars at every street corner in Jerusalem. 25In every town in Judah he built high places to burn sacrifices to other gods and provoked the LORD, the God of his fathers, to anger.

26The other events of his reign and all his ways, from beginning to end, are written in the book of the kings of Judah and Israel. 27Ahaz rested with his fathers and was buried in the city of Jerusalem, but he was not placed in the tombs of the kings of Israel. And Hezekiah his son succeeded him as king.

Hezekiah Purifies the Temple

29 HEZEKIAH WAS twenty-five years old when he became king, and he reigned in Jerusalem twenty-nine years. His mother's name was Abijah daughter of Zechariah. 2He did what was right in the eyes of the LORD, just as his father David had done.

3In the first month of the first year of his reign, he opened the doors of the temple of the LORD and repaired them. 4He brought in the priests and the Levites, assembled them in the square on the east side 5and said: "Listen to me, Levites! Consecrate yourselves now and consecrate the temple of the LORD, the God of your fathers. Remove all defilement from the sanctuary. 6Our fathers were unfaithful; they did evil in the eyes of the LORD our God and forsook him. They turned their faces away from the LORD's dwelling place and turned their backs on him. 7They also shut the doors of the portico and put out the lamps. They did not burn incense or present any burnt offerings at the sanctuary to the God of Israel. 8Therefore, the anger of the LORD has fallen on Judah and Jerusalem; he has made them an object of dread and horror and scorn, as you can see with your own eyes. 9This is why our fathers have fallen by the sword and why our sons and daughters and our wives are in captivity. 10Now I intend to make a covenant with the LORD, the God of Israel, so that his fierce anger will turn away from us. 11My sons, do not be negligent now, for the

a 19 That is, Judah, as frequently in 2 Chronicles   b 20 Hebrew Tilgath-Pilneser, a variant of Tiglath-Pileser   c 24 Or and cut them up

Living Bible

had invaded the lowland cities and the Negeb and had already captured Beth-shemesh, Aijalon, Gederoth, Soco, Timnah, and Gimzo with their surrounding villages, and were living there. 19For the Lord brought Judah very low on account of the evil deeds of King Ahaz of Israel,d for he had destroyed the spiritual fiber of Judah and had been faithless to the Lord. 20But when Tilgath-pilneser, king of Assyria, arrived, he caused trouble for King Ahaz instead of helping him. 21So even though Ahaz had given him the Temple gold and the palace treasures, it did no good.

22In this time of deep trial, King Ahaz collapsed spiritually. 23He sacrificed to the gods of the people of Damascus who had defeated him, for he felt that since these gods had helped the kings of Syria, they would help him too if he sacrificed to them. But instead, they were his ruin, and that of all his people. 24The king took the gold bowls from the Temple and slashed them to pieces, and nailed the door of the Temple shut so that no one could worship there, and made altars to the heathen gods in every corner of Jerusalem. 25And he did the same in every city of Judah, thus angering the Lord God of his fathers.

26The other details of his life and activities are recorded in *The Annals of the Kings of Judah and Israel*. 27When King Ahaz died, he was buried in Jerusalem but not in the royal tombs, and his son Hezekiah became the new king.

29 HEZEKIAH WAS twenty-five years old when he became the king of Judah, and he reigned twenty-nine years, in Jerusalem. His mother's name was Abijah, the daughter of Zechariah. 2His reign was generally good in the Lord's sight, just as his ancestor David's had been.

3In the very first month of the first year of his reign, he reopened the doors of the Temple and repaired them. 4, 5He summoned the priests and Levites to meet him at the open space east of the Temple, and addressed them thus:

"Listen to me, you Levites. Sanctify yourselves and sanctify the Temple of the Lord God of your ancestors— clean all the debris from the holy place. 6For our fathers have committed a deep sin before the Lord our God; they abandoned the Lord and his Temple and turned their backs on it. 7The doors have been shut tight, the perpetual flame has been put out, and the incense and burnt offerings have not been offered. 8Therefore the wrath of the Lord has been upon Judah and Jerusalem. He has caused us to be objects of horror, amazement, and contempt, as you see us today. 9Our fathers have been killed in war, and our sons and daughters and wives are in captivity because of this.

10"But now I want to make a covenant with the Lord God of Israel so that his fierce anger will turn away from us. 11My children, don't neglect your duties any longer,

New Revised Standard

defeated Judah, and carried away captives. 18And the Philistines had made raids on the cities in the Shephelah and the Negeb of Judah, and had taken Beth-shemesh, Aijalon, Gederoth, Soco with its villages, Timnah with its villages, and Gimzo with its villages; and they settled there. 19For the LORD brought Judah low because of King Ahaz of Israel, for he had behaved without restraint in Judah and had been faithless to the LORD. 20So King Tilgath-pilneser of Assyria came against him, and oppressed him instead of strengthening him. 21For Ahaz plundered the house of the LORD and the houses of the king and of the officials, and gave tribute to the king of Assyria; but it did not help him.

Apostasy and Death of Ahaz

22 In the time of his distress he became yet more faithless to the LORD—this same King Ahaz. 23For he sacrificed to the gods of Damascus, which had defeated him, and said, "Because the gods of the kings of Aram helped them, I will sacrifice to them so that they may help me." But they were the ruin of him, and of all Israel. 24Ahaz gathered together the utensils of the house of God, and cut in pieces the utensils of the house of God. He shut up the doors of the house of the LORD and made himself altars in every corner of Jerusalem. 25In every city of Judah he made high places to make offerings to other gods, provoking to anger the LORD, the God of his ancestors. 26Now the rest of his acts and all his ways, from first to last, are written in the Book of the Kings of Judah and Israel. 27Ahaz slept with his ancestors, and they buried him in the city, in Jerusalem; but they did not bring him into the tombs of the kings of Israel. His son Hezekiah succeeded him.

Reign of Hezekiah

29 HEZEKIAH BEGAN to reign when he was twenty-five years old; he reigned twenty-nine years in Jerusalem. His mother's name was Abijah daughter of Zechariah. 2He did what was right in the sight of the LORD, just as his ancestor David had done.

The Temple Cleansed

3 In the first year of his reign, in the first month, he opened the doors of the house of the LORD and repaired them. 4He brought in the priests and the Levites and assembled them in the square on the east. 5He said to them, "Listen to me, Levites! Sanctify yourselves, and sanctify the house of the LORD, the God of your ancestors, and carry out the filth from the holy place. 6For our ancestors have been unfaithful and have done what was evil in the sight of the LORD our God; they have forsaken him, and have turned away their faces from the dwelling of the LORD, and turned their backs. 7They also shut the doors of the vestibule and put out the lamps, and have not offered incense or made burnt offerings in the holy place to the God of Israel. 8Therefore the wrath of the LORD came upon Judah and Jerusalem, and he has made them an object of horror, of astonishment, and of hissing, as you see with your own eyes. 9Our fathers have fallen by the sword and our sons and our daughters and our wives are in captivity for this. 10Now it is in my heart to make a covenant with the LORD, the God of Israel, so that his fierce anger may turn away from us.

---

d 28:19 *of the evil deeds of King Ahaz of Israel*. King Ahaz ruled two tribes of Israel—Judah and Benjamin—and so is referred to here in this unusual way as a king of Israel.

King James

11My sons, be not now negligent: for the LORD hath chosen you to stand before him, to serve him, and that ye should minister unto him, and burn incense.

12¶ Then the Levites arose, Mahath the son of Amasai, and Joel the son of Azariah, of the sons of the Kohathites: and of the sons of Merari, Kish the son of Abdi, and Azariah the son of Jehalelel: and of the Gershonites; Joah the son of Zimmah, and Eden the son of Joah:

13And of the sons of Elizaphan; Shimri, and Jeiel: and of the sons of Asaph; Zechariah, and Mattaniah:

14And of the sons of Heman; Jehiel, and Shimei: and of the sons of Jeduthun; Shemaiah, and Uzziel.

15And they gathered their brethren, and sanctified themselves, and came, according to the commandment of the king, by the words of the LORD, to cleanse the house of the LORD.

16And the priests went into the inner part of the house of the LORD, to cleanse it, and brought out all the uncleanness that they found in the temple of the LORD into the court of the house of the LORD. And the Levites took it, to carry it out abroad into the brook Kidron.

17Now they began on the first day of the first month to sanctify, and on the eighth day of the month came they to the porch of the LORD: so they sanctified the house of the LORD in eight days; and in the sixteenth day of the first month they made an end.

18Then they went in to Hezekiah the king, and said, We have cleansed all the house of the LORD, and the altar of burnt offering, with all the vessels thereof, and the showbread table, with all the vessels thereof.

19Moreover all the vessels, which king Ahaz in his reign did cast away in his transgression, have we prepared and sanctified, and, behold, they are before the altar of the LORD.

20¶ Then Hezekiah the king rose early, and gathered the rulers of the city, and went up to the house of the LORD.

21And they brought seven bullocks, and seven rams, and seven lambs, and seven he goats, for a sin offering for the kingdom, and for the sanctuary, and for Judah. And he commanded the priests the sons of Aaron to offer them on the altar of the LORD.

22So they killed the bullocks, and the priests received the blood, and sprinkled it on the altar: likewise, when they had killed the rams, they sprinkled the blood upon the altar: they killed also the lambs, and they sprinkled the blood upon the altar.

23And they brought forth the he goats for the sin offering before the king and the congregation; and they laid their hands upon them:

24And the priests killed them, and they made reconciliation with their blood upon the altar, to make an atonement for all Israel: for the king commanded that the burnt offering and the sin offering should be made for all Israel.

25And he set the Levites in the house of the LORD with cymbals, with psalteries, and with harps, according to the commandment of David, and of Gad the king's seer, and Nathan the prophet: for so was the commandment of the LORD by his prophets.

26And the Levites stood with the instruments of David, and the priests with the trumpets.

27And Hezekiah commanded to offer the burnt offering upon the altar. And when the burnt offering began, the song of the LORD began also with the trumpets, and with the instruments ordained by David king of Israel.

28And all the congregation worshipped, and the singers sang, and the trumpeters sounded: and all this continued until the burnt offering was finished.

29And when they had made an end of offering, the king and all that were present with him bowed themselves, and worshipped.

New International

LORD has chosen you to stand before him and serve him, to minister before him and to burn incense."

12Then these Levites set to work:
from the Kohathites,
    Mahath son of Amasai and Joel son of Azariah;
from the Merarites,
    Kish son of Abdi and Azariah son of Jehallelel;
from the Gershonites,
    Joah son of Zimmah and Eden son of Joah;
13from the descendants of Elizaphan,
    Shimri and Jeiel;
from the descendants of Asaph,
    Zechariah and Mattaniah;
14from the descendants of Heman,
    Jehiel and Shimei;
from the descendants of Jeduthun,
    Shemaiah and Uzziel.

15When they had assembled their brothers and consecrated themselves, they went in to purify the temple of the LORD, as the king had ordered, following the word of the LORD. 16The priests went into the sanctuary of the LORD to purify it. They brought out to the courtyard of the LORD's temple everything unclean that they found in the temple of the LORD. The Levites took it and carried it out to the Kidron Valley. 17They began the consecration on the first day of the first month, and by the eighth day of the month they reached the portico of the LORD. For eight more days they consecrated the temple of the LORD itself, finishing on the sixteenth day of the first month.

18Then they went in to King Hezekiah and reported: "We have purified the entire temple of the LORD, the altar of burnt offering with all its utensils, and the table for setting out the consecrated bread, with all its articles. 19We have prepared and consecrated all the articles that King Ahaz removed in his unfaithfulness while he was king. They are now in front of the LORD's altar."

20Early the next morning King Hezekiah gathered the city officials together and went up to the temple of the LORD. 21They brought seven bulls, seven rams, seven male lambs and seven male goats as a sin offering for the kingdom, for the sanctuary and for Judah. The king commanded the priests, the descendants of Aaron, to offer these on the altar of the LORD. 22So they slaughtered the bulls, and the priests took the blood and sprinkled it on the altar; next they slaughtered the rams and sprinkled their blood on the altar; then they slaughtered the lambs and sprinkled their blood on the altar. 23The goats for the sin offering were brought before the king and the assembly, and they laid their hands on them. 24The priests then slaughtered the goats and presented their blood on the altar for a sin offering to atone for all Israel, because the king had ordered the burnt offering and the sin offering for all Israel.

25He stationed the Levites in the temple of the LORD with cymbals, harps and lyres in the way prescribed by David and Gad the king's seer and Nathan the prophet; this was commanded by the LORD through his prophets. 26So the Levites stood ready with David's instruments, and the priests with their trumpets.

27Hezekiah gave the order to sacrifice the burnt offering on the altar. As the offering began, singing to the LORD began also, accompanied by trumpets and the instruments of David king of Israel. 28The whole assembly bowed in worship, while the singers sang and the trumpeters played. All this continued until the sacrifice of the burnt offering was completed.

29When the offerings were finished, the king and everyone present with him knelt down and worshiped.

Living Bible

for the Lord has chosen you to minister to him and to burn incense."

12, 13, 14Then the Levites went into action:

From the Kohath clan, Mahath (son of Amasai) and Joel (son of Azariah);

From the Merari clan, Kish (son of Abdi) and Azariah (son of Jehallelel);

From the Gershon clan, Joah (son of Zimmah) and Eden (son of Joah).

From the Elizaphan clan, Shimri and Jeuel;

From the Asaph clan, Zechariah and Mattaniah;

From the Hemanite clan, Jehuel and Shime-i;

From the Jeduthun clan, Shemaiah and Uzziel.

15They in turn summoned their fellow Levites and sanctified themselves, and began to clean up and sanctify the Temple, as the king (who was speaking for the Lord) had commanded them. 16The priests cleaned up the inner room of the Temple, and brought out into the court all the filth and decay they found there. The Levites then carted it out to the brook Kidron. 17This all began on the first day of April, and by the eighth day they had reached the outer court, which took eight days to clean up, so the entire job was completed in sixteen days.

18Then they went back to the palace and reported to King Hezekiah, "We have completed the cleansing of the Temple and of the altar of burnt offerings and of its accessories, also the table of the Bread of the Presence and its equipment. 19What's more, we have recovered and sanctified all the utensils thrown away by King Ahaz when he closed the Temple. They are beside the altar of the Lord."

20Early the next morning, King Hezekiah went to the Temple with the city officials, 21taking seven young bulls, seven rams, seven lambs, and seven male goats for a sin offering for the nation and for the Temple. He instructed the priests, the sons of Aaron, to sacrifice them on the altar of the Lord. 22So they killed the young bulls, and the priests took the blood and sprinkled it on the altar, and they killed the rams and sprinkled their blood upon the altar, and did the same with the lambs. 23The male goats for the sin offering were then brought before the king and his officials, who laid their hands upon them. 24Then the priests killed the animals and made a sin offering with their blood upon the altar, to make atonement for all Israel as the king had commanded—for the king had specified that the burnt offering and sin offering must be sacrificed for the entire nation.

25, 26He organized Levites at the Temple into an orchestral group, using cymbals, psalteries, and harps. This was in accordance with the directions of David and the prophets Gad and Nathan—who had received their instructions from the Lord. The priests formed a trumpet corps. 27Then Hezekiah ordered the burnt offering to be placed upon the altar, and as the sacrifice began, the instruments of music began to play the songs of the Lord, accompanied by the trumpets. 28Throughout the entire ceremony everyone worshiped the Lord as the singers sang and the trumpets blew. 29Afterwards the king and his aides bowed low before the Lord in worship. 30Then King Hezekiah ordered the Levites to sing

New Revised Standard

11My sons, do not now be negligent, for the LORD has chosen you to stand in his presence to minister to him, and to be his ministers and make offerings to him."

12 Then the Levites arose, Mahath son of Amasai, and Joel son of Azariah, of the sons of the Kohathites; and of the sons of Merari, Kish son of Abdi, and Azariah son of Jehallelel; and of the Gershonites, Joah son of Zimmah, and Eden son of Joah; 13and of the sons of Elizaphan, Shimri and Jeuel; and of the sons of Asaph, Zechariah and Mattaniah; 14and of the sons of Heman, Jehuel and Shimei; and of the sons of Jeduthun, Shemaiah and Uzziel. 15They gathered their brothers, sanctified themselves, and went in as the king had commanded, by the words of the LORD, to cleanse the house of the LORD. 16The priests went into the inner part of the house of the LORD to cleanse it, and they brought out all the unclean things that they found in the temple of the LORD into the court of the house of the LORD; and the Levites took them and carried them out to the Wadi Kidron. 17They began to sanctify on the first day of the first month, and on the eighth day of the month they came to the vestibule of the LORD; then for eight days they sanctified the house of the LORD, and on the sixteenth day of the first month they finished. 18Then they went inside to King Hezekiah and said, "We have cleansed all the house of the LORD, the altar of burnt offering and all its utensils, and the table for the rows of bread and all its utensils. 19All the utensils that King Ahaz repudiated during his reign when he was faithless, we have made ready and sanctified; see, they are in front of the altar of the LORD."

Temple Worship Restored

20 Then King Hezekiah rose early, assembled the officials of the city, and went up to the house of the LORD. 21They brought seven bulls, seven rams, seven lambs, and seven male goats for a sin offering for the kingdom and for the sanctuary and for Judah. He commanded the priests the descendants of Aaron to offer them on the altar of the LORD. 22So they slaughtered the bulls, and the priests received the blood and dashed it against the altar; they slaughtered the rams and their blood was dashed against the altar; they also slaughtered the lambs and their blood was dashed against the altar. 23Then the male goats for the sin offering were brought to the king and the assembly; they laid their hands on them, 24and the priests slaughtered them and made a sin offering with their blood at the altar, to make atonement for all Israel. For the king commanded that the burnt offering and the sin offering should be made for all Israel.

25 He stationed the Levites in the house of the LORD with cymbals, harps, and lyres, according to the commandment of David and of Gad the king's seer and of the prophet Nathan, for the commandment was from the LORD through his prophets. 26The Levites stood with the instruments of David, and the priests with the trumpets. 27Then Hezekiah commanded that the burnt offering be offered on the altar. When the burnt offering began, the song to the LORD began also, and the trumpets, accompanied by the instruments of King David of Israel. 28The whole assembly worshiped, the singers sang, and the trumpeters sounded; all this continued until the burnt offering was finished. 29When the offering was finished, the king and all who were present with him bowed down and worshiped. 30King Hezekiah and the officials

King James

30Moreover Hezekiah the king and the princes commanded the Levites to sing praise unto the LORD with the words of David, and of Asaph the seer. And they sang praises with gladness, and they bowed their heads and worshipped.

31Then Hezekiah answered and said, Now ye have consecrated yourselves unto the LORD, come near and bring sacrifices and thank offerings into the house of the LORD. And the congregation brought in sacrifices and thank offerings; and as many as were of a free heart burnt offerings.

32And the number of the burnt offerings, which the congregation brought, was threescore and ten bullocks, an hundred rams, *and* two hundred lambs: all these *were* for a burnt offering to the LORD.

33And the consecrated things *were* six hundred oxen and three thousand sheep.

34But the priests were too few, so that they could not flay all the burnt offerings: wherefore their brethren the Levites did help them, till the work was ended, and until the *other* priests had sanctified themselves: for the Levites *were* more upright in heart to sanctify themselves than the priests.

35And also the burnt offerings *were* in abundance, with the fat of the peace offerings, and the drink offerings for *every* burnt offering. So the service of the house of the LORD was set in order.

36And Hezekiah rejoiced, and all the people, that God had prepared the people: for the thing was *done* suddenly.

30 AND HEZEKIAH sent to all Israel and Judah, and wrote letters also to Ephraim and Manasseh, that they should come to the house of the LORD at Jerusalem, to keep the passover unto the LORD God of Israel.

2For the king had taken counsel, and his princes, and all the congregation in Jerusalem, to keep the passover in the second month.

3For they could not keep it at that time, because the priests had not sanctified themselves sufficiently, neither had the people gathered themselves together to Jerusalem.

4And the thing pleased the king and all the congregation.

5So they established a decree to make proclamation throughout all Israel, from Beer-sheba even to Dan, that they should come to keep the passover unto the LORD God of Israel at Jerusalem: for they had not done *it* of a long *time in such sort* as it was written.

6So the posts went with the letters from the king and his princes throughout all Israel and Judah, and according to the commandment of the king, saying, Ye children of Israel, turn again unto the LORD God of Abraham, Isaac, and Israel, and he will return to the remnant of you, that are escaped out of the hand of the kings of Assyria.

7And be not ye like your fathers, and like your brethren, which trespassed against the LORD God of their fathers, *who* therefore gave them up to desolation, as ye see.

8Now be ye not stiffnecked, as your fathers *were, but* yield yourselves unto the LORD, and enter into his sanctuary, which he hath sanctified for ever: and serve the LORD your God, that the fierceness of his wrath may turn away from you.

9For if ye turn again unto the LORD, your brethren and your children *shall find* compassion before them that lead them captive, so that they shall come again into this land: for the LORD your God *is* gracious and merciful, and will not turn away *his* face from you, if ye return unto him.

New International

30King Hezekiah and his officials ordered the Levites to praise the LORD with the words of David and of Asaph the seer. So they sang praises with gladness and bowed their heads and worshiped.

31Then Hezekiah said, "You have now dedicated yourselves to the LORD. Come and bring sacrifices and thank offerings to the temple of the LORD." So the assembly brought sacrifices and thank offerings, and all whose hearts were willing brought burnt offerings.

32The number of burnt offerings the assembly brought was seventy bulls, a hundred rams and two hundred male lambs—all of them for burnt offerings to the LORD. 33The animals consecrated as sacrifices amounted to six hundred bulls and three thousand sheep and goats. 34The priests, however, were too few to skin all the burnt offerings; so their kinsmen the Levites helped them until the task was finished and until other priests had been consecrated, for the Levites had been more conscientious in consecrating themselves than the priests had been. 35There were burnt offerings in abundance, together with the fat of the fellowship offeringsa and the drink offerings that accompanied the burnt offerings.

So the service of the temple of the LORD was reestablished. 36Hezekiah and all the people rejoiced at what God had brought about for his people, because it was done so quickly.

Hezekiah Celebrates the Passover

30 HEZEKIAH SENT word to all Israel and Judah and also wrote letters to Ephraim and Manasseh, inviting them to come to the temple of the LORD in Jerusalem and celebrate the Passover to the LORD, the God of Israel. 2The king and his officials and the whole assembly in Jerusalem decided to celebrate the Passover in the second month. 3They had not been able to celebrate it at the regular time because not enough priests had consecrated themselves and the people had not assembled in Jerusalem. 4The plan seemed right both to the king and to the whole assembly. 5They decided to send a proclamation throughout Israel, from Beersheba to Dan, calling the people to come to Jerusalem and celebrate the Passover to the LORD, the God of Israel. It had not been celebrated in large numbers according to what was written.

6At the king's command, couriers went throughout Israel and Judah with letters from the king and from his officials, which read:

"People of Israel, return to the LORD, the God of Abraham, Isaac and Israel, that he may return to you who are left, who have escaped from the hand of the kings of Assyria. 7Do not be like your fathers and brothers, who were unfaithful to the LORD, the God of their fathers, so that he made them an object of horror, as you see. 8Do not be stiff-necked, as your fathers were; submit to the LORD. Come to the sanctuary, which he has consecrated forever. Serve the LORD your God, so that his fierce anger will turn away from you. 9If you return to the LORD, then your brothers and your children will be shown compassion by their captors and will come back to this land, for the LORD your God is gracious and compassionate. He will not turn his face from you if you return to him."

---

a *35* Traditionally *peace offerings*

Living Bible

before the Lord some of the psalms of David and of the prophet Asaph, which they gladly did, and bowed their heads and worshiped.

31"The consecration ceremony is now ended," Hezekiah said. "Now bring your sacrifices and thank offerings." So the people from every part of the nation brought their sacrifices and thank offerings, and those who wished to, brought burnt offerings too. 32, 33In all, there were 70 young bulls for burnt offerings, 100 rams, and 200 lambs. In addition, 600 oxen and 3,000 sheep were brought as holy gifts. 34But there were too few priests to prepare the burnt offerings, so their brothers the Levites helped them until the work was finished—and until more priests had reported to work—for the Levites were much more ready to sanctify themselves than the priests were. 35There was an abundance of burnt offerings, and the usual drink offering with each, and many peace offerings. So it was that the Temple was restored to service, and the sacrifices offered again. 36And Hezekiah and all the people were very happy because of what God had accomplished so quickly.

30 KING HEZEKIAH now sent letters throughout all of Israel, Judah, Ephraim, and Manasseh, inviting everyone to come to the Temple at Jerusalem for the annual Passover celebration. 2, 3The king, his aides, and all the assembly of Jerusalem had voted to celebrate the Passover in May this time, rather than at the normal time in April, because not enough priests were sanctified at the earlier date, and there wasn't enough time to get notices out. 4The king and his advisors were in complete agreement in this matter, 5so they sent a Passover proclamation throughout Israel, from Dan to Beer-sheba, inviting everyone. They had not kept it in great numbers as prescribed.b

6"Come back to the Lord God of Abraham, Isaac, and Israel," the king's letter said, "so that he will return to us who have escaped from the power of the kings of Assyria. 7Do not be like your fathers and brothers who sinned against the Lord God of their fathers and were destroyed. 8Do not be stubborn, as they were, but yield yourselves to the Lord and come to his Temple which he has sanctified forever, and worship the Lord your God so that his fierce anger will turn away from you. 9For if you turn to the Lord again, your brothers and your children will be treated mercifully by their captors, and they will be able to return to this land. For the Lord your God is full of kindness and mercy and will not continue to turn away his face from you if you return to him."

New Revised Standard

commanded the Levites to sing praises to the LORD with the words of David and of the seer Asaph. They sang praises with gladness, and they bowed down and worshiped.

31 Then Hezekiah said, "You have now consecrated yourselves to the LORD; come near, bring sacrifices and thank offerings to the house of the LORD." The assembly brought sacrifices and thank offerings; and all who were of a willing heart brought burnt offerings. 32 The number of the burnt offerings that the assembly brought was seventy bulls, one hundred rams, and two hundred lambs; all these were for a burnt offering to the LORD. 33 The consecrated offerings were six hundred bulls and three thousand sheep. 34 But the priests were too few and could not skin all the burnt offerings, so, until other priests had sanctified themselves, their kindred, the Levites, helped them until the work was finished—for the Levites were more conscientiousc than the priests in sanctifying themselves. 35 Besides the great number of burnt offerings there was the fat of the offerings of well-being, and there were the drink offerings for the burnt offerings. Thus the service of the house of the LORD was restored. 36 And Hezekiah and all the people rejoiced because of what God had done for the people; for the thing had come about suddenly.

The Great Passover

30 HEZEKIAH SENT word to all Israel and Judah, and wrote letters also to Ephraim and Manasseh, that they should come to the house of the LORD at Jerusalem, to keep the passover to the LORD the God of Israel. 2 For the king and his officials and all the assembly in Jerusalem had taken counsel to keep the passover in the second month 3 (for they could not keep it at its proper time because the priests had not sanctified themselves in sufficient number, nor had the people assembled in Jerusalem). 4 The plan seemed right to the king and all the assembly. 5 So they decreed to make a proclamation throughout all Israel, from Beer-sheba to Dan, that the people should come and keep the passover to the LORD the God of Israel, at Jerusalem; for they had not kept it in great numbers as prescribed. 6 So couriers went throughout all Israel and Judah with letters from the king and his officials, as the king had commanded, saying, "O people of Israel, return to the LORD, the God of Abraham, Isaac, and Israel, so that he may turn again to the remnant of you who have escaped from the hand of the kings of Assyria. 7 Do not be like your ancestors and your kindred, who were faithless to the LORD God of their ancestors, so that he made them a desolation, as you see. 8 Do not now be stiff-necked as your ancestors were, but yield yourselves to the LORD and come to his sanctuary, which he has sanctified forever, and serve the LORD your God, so that his fierce anger may turn away from you. 9 For as you return to the LORD, your kindred and your children will find compassion with their captors, and return to this land. For the LORD your God is gracious and merciful, and will not turn away his face from you, if you return to him."

---

b 30:5 They had not kept it in great numbers as prescribed, or, "The Passover had not been celebrated by the northern tribes of Israel for a long time; only a faithful few had been doing it in the proper way."

c Heb upright in heart

King James

10So the posts passed from city to city through the country of Ephraim and Manasseh even unto Zebulun: but they laughed them to scorn, and mocked them. 11Nevertheless divers of Asher and Manasseh and of Zebulun humbled themselves, and came to Jerusalem. 12Also in Judah the hand of God was to give them one heart to do the commandment of the king and of the princes, by the word of the LORD. 13¶ And there assembled at Jerusalem much people to keep the feast of unleavened bread in the second month, a very great congregation. 14And they arose and took away the altars that *were* in Jerusalem, and all the altars for incense took they away, and cast *them* into the brook Kidron.

15Then they killed the passover on the fourteenth *day* of the second month: and the priests and the Levites were ashamed, and sanctified themselves, and brought in the burnt offerings into the house of the LORD. 16And they stood in their place after their manner, according to the law of Moses the man of God: the priests sprinkled the blood, *which they received* of the hand of the Levites. 17For *there were* many in the congregation that were not sanctified: therefore the Levites had the charge of the killing of the passovers for every one *that was* not clean, to sanctify *them* unto the LORD. 18For a multitude of the people, *even* many of Ephraim, and Manasseh, Issachar, and Zebulun, had not cleansed themselves, yet did they eat the passover otherwise than it was written. But Hezekiah prayed for them, saying, The good LORD pardon every one 19That prepareth his heart to seek God, the LORD God of his fathers, though *he be* not *cleansed* according to the purification of the sanctuary. 20And the LORD hearkened to Hezekiah, and healed the people.

21And the children of Israel that were present at Jerusalem kept the feast of unleavened bread seven days with great gladness: and the Levites and the priests praised the LORD day by day, *singing* with loud instruments unto the LORD. 22And Hezekiah spake comfortably unto all the Levites that taught the good knowledge of the LORD: and they did eat throughout the feast seven days, offering peace offerings, and making confession to the LORD God of their fathers. 23And the whole assembly took counsel to keep other seven days: and they kept *other* seven days with gladness. 24For Hezekiah king of Judah did give to the congregation a thousand bullocks and seven thousand sheep; and the princes gave to the congregation a thousand bullocks and ten thousand sheep: and a great number of priests sanctified themselves. 25And all the congregation of Judah, with the priests and the Levites, and all the congregation that came out of Israel, and the strangers that came out of the land of Israel, and that dwelt in Judah, rejoiced. 26So there was great joy in Jerusalem: for since the time of Solomon the son of David king of Israel *there was* not the like in Jerusalem. 27¶ Then the priests the Levites arose and blessed the people: and their voice was heard, and their prayer came *up* to his holy dwellingplace, *even* unto heaven.

New International

10The couriers went from town to town in Ephraim and Manasseh, as far as Zebulun, but the people scorned and ridiculed them. 11Nevertheless, some men of Asher, Manasseh and Zebulun humbled themselves and went to Jerusalem. 12Also in Judah the hand of God was on the people to give them unity of mind to carry out what the king and his officials had ordered, following the word of the LORD.

13A very large crowd of people assembled in Jerusalem to celebrate the Feast of Unleavened Bread in the second month. 14They removed the altars in Jerusalem and cleared away the incense altars and threw them into the Kidron Valley.

15They slaughtered the Passover lamb on the fourteenth day of the second month. The priests and the Levites were ashamed and consecrated themselves and brought burnt offerings to the temple of the LORD. 16Then they took up their regular positions as prescribed in the Law of Moses the man of God. The priests sprinkled the blood handed to them by the Levites. 17Since many in the crowd had not consecrated themselves, the Levites had to kill the Passover lambs for all those who were not ceremonially clean and could not consecrate their lambs to the LORD. 18Although most of the many people who came from Ephraim, Manasseh, Issachar and Zebulun had not purified themselves, yet they ate the Passover, contrary to what was written. But Hezekiah prayed for them, saying, "May the LORD, who is good, pardon everyone 19who sets his heart on seeking God—the LORD, the God of his fathers—even if he is not clean according to the rules of the sanctuary." 20And the LORD heard Hezekiah and healed the people.

21The Israelites who were present in Jerusalem celebrated the Feast of Unleavened Bread for seven days with great rejoicing, while the Levites and priests sang to the LORD every day, accompanied by the LORD's instruments of praise.[a]

22Hezekiah spoke encouragingly to all the Levites, who showed good understanding of the service of the LORD. For the seven days they ate their assigned portion and offered fellowship offerings[b] and praised the LORD, the God of their fathers.

23The whole assembly then agreed to celebrate the festival seven more days; so for another seven days they celebrated joyfully. 24Hezekiah king of Judah provided a thousand bulls and seven thousand sheep and goats for the assembly, and the officials provided them with a thousand bulls and ten thousand sheep and goats. A great number of priests consecrated themselves. 25The entire assembly of Judah rejoiced, along with the priests and Levites and all who had assembled from Israel, including the aliens who had come from Israel and those who lived in Judah. 26There was great joy in Jerusalem, for since the days of Solomon son of David king of Israel there had been nothing like this in Jerusalem. 27The priests and the Levites stood to bless the people, and God heard them, for their prayer reached heaven, his holy dwelling place.

Living Bible

10So the messengers went from city to city throughout Ephraim and Manasseh and as far as Zebulun. But for the most part they were received with laughter and scorn! 11However, some from the tribes of Asher, Manasseh, and Zebulun turned to God and came to Jerusalem. 12But in Judah the entire nation felt a strong, God-given desire to obey the Lord's direction as commanded by the king and his officers. 13And so it was that a very large crowd assembled at Jerusalem in the month of May for the Passover celebration. 14They set to work and destroyed the heathen altars in Jerusalem, and knocked down all the incense altars, and threw them into Kidron Brook.

15On the first day of May the people killed their Passover lambs. Then the priests and Levites became ashamed of themselves for not taking a more active part, so they sanctified themselves and brought burnt offerings into the Temple. 16They stood at their posts as instructed by the law of Moses the man of God; and the priests sprinkled the blood received from the Levites.

17, 18, 19Since many of the people arriving from Ephraim, Manasseh, Issachar, and Zebulun were ceremonially impure because they had not undergone the purification rites, the Levites killed their Passover lambs for them, to sanctify them. Then King Hezekiah prayed for them and they were permitted to eat the Passover anyway, even though this was contrary to God's rules. But Hezekiah said, "May the good Lord pardon everyone who determines to follow the Lord God of his fathers, even though he is not properly sanctified for the ceremony." 20And the Lord listened to Hezekiah's prayer and did not destroy them.

21So the people of Israel celebrated the Passover at Jerusalem for seven days with great joy.

Meanwhile the Levites and priests praised the Lord with music and cymbals day after day. 22(King Hezekiah spoke very appreciatively to the Levites of their excellent music.)

So, for seven days the observance continued, and peace offerings were sacrificed, and the people confessed their sins to the Lord God of their fathers. 23The enthusiasm continued, so it was unanimously decided to continue the observance for another seven days. 24King Hezekiah gave the people 1,000 young bulls for offerings, and 7,000 sheep; and the princes donated 1,000 young bulls and 10,000 sheep. And at this time another large group of priests stepped forward and sanctified themselves.

25Then the people of Judah, together with the priests, the Levites, the foreign residents, and the visitors from Israel, were filled with deep joy. 26For Jerusalem hadn't seen a celebration like this one since the days of King David's son Solomon. 27Then the priests and Levites stood and blessed the people, and the Lord heard their prayers from his holy temple in heaven.

New Revised Standard

10   So the couriers went from city to city through the country of Ephraim and Manasseh, and as far as Zebulun; but they laughed them to scorn, and mocked them. 11Only a few from Asher, Manasseh, and Zebulun humbled themselves and came to Jerusalem. 12The hand of God was also on Judah to give them one heart to do what the king and the officials commanded by the word of the LORD.

13   Many people came together in Jerusalem to keep the festival of unleavened bread in the second month, a very large assembly. 14They set to work and removed the altars that were in Jerusalem, and all the altars for offering incense they took away and threw into the Wadi Kidron. 15They slaughtered the passover lamb on the fourteenth day of the second month. The priests and the Levites were ashamed, and they sanctified themselves and brought burnt offerings into the house of the LORD. 16They took their accustomed posts according to the law of Moses the man of God; the priests dashed the blood that they receivedᶜ from the hands of the Levites. 17For there were many in the assembly who had not sanctified themselves; therefore the Levites had to slaughter the passover lamb for everyone who was not clean, to make it holy to the LORD. 18For a multitude of the people, many of them from Ephraim, Manasseh, Issachar, and Zebulun, had not cleansed themselves, yet they ate the passover otherwise than as prescribed. But Hezekiah prayed for them, saying, "The good LORD pardon all 19who set their hearts to seek God, the LORD the God of their ancestors, even though not in accordance with the sanctuary's rules of cleanness." 20The LORD heard Hezekiah, and healed the people. 21The people of Israel who were present at Jerusalem kept the festival of unleavened bread seven days with great gladness; and the Levites and the priests praised the LORD day by day, accompanied by loud instruments for the LORD. 22Hezekiah spoke encouragingly to all the Levites who showed good skill in the service of the LORD. So the people ate the food of the festival for seven days, sacrificing offerings of well-being and giving thanks to the LORD the God of their ancestors.

23   Then the whole assembly agreed together to keep the festival for another seven days; so they kept it for another seven days with gladness. 24For King Hezekiah of Judah gave the assembly a thousand bulls and seven thousand sheep for offerings, and the officials gave the assembly a thousand bulls and ten thousand sheep. The priests sanctified themselves in great numbers. 25The whole assembly of Judah, the priests and the Levites, and the whole assembly that came out of Israel, and the resident aliens who came out of the land of Israel, and the resident aliens who lived in Judah, rejoiced. 26There was great joy in Jerusalem, for since the time of Solomon son of King David of Israel there had been nothing like this in Jerusalem. 27Then the priests and the Levites stood up and blessed the people, and their voice was heard; their prayer came to his holy dwelling in heaven.

ᶜ Heb lacks *that they received*

King James

31 NOW WHEN all this was finished, all Israel that were present went out to the cities of Judah, and brake the images in pieces, and cut down the groves, and threw down the high places and the altars out of all Judah and Benjamin, in Ephraim also and Manasseh, until they had utterly destroyed them all. Then all the children of Israel returned, every man to his possession, into their own cities.

2¶ And Hezekiah appointed the courses of the priests and the Levites after their courses, every man according to his service, the priests and Levites for burnt offerings and for peace offerings, to minister, and to give thanks, and to praise in the gates of the tents of the LORD.

3*He appointed* also the king's portion of his substance for the burnt offerings, *to wit,* for the morning and evening burnt offerings, and the burnt offerings for the sabbaths, and for the new moons, and for the set feasts, as *it is* written in the law of the LORD.

4Moreover he commanded the people that dwelt in Jerusalem to give the portion of the priests and the Levites, that they might be encouraged in the law of the LORD.

5¶ And as soon as the commandment came abroad, the children of Israel brought in abundance the firstfruits of corn, wine, and oil, and honey, and of all the increase of the field; and the tithe of all *things* brought they in abundantly.

6And *concerning* the children of Israel and Judah, that dwelt in the cities of Judah, they also brought in the tithe of oxen and sheep, and the tithe of holy things which were consecrated unto the LORD their God, and laid *them* by heaps.

7In the third month they began to lay the foundation of the heaps, and finished *them* in the seventh month.

8And when Hezekiah and the princes came and saw the heaps, they blessed the LORD, and his people Israel.

9Then Hezekiah questioned with the priests and the Levites concerning the heaps.

10And Azariah the chief priest of the house of Zadok answered him, and said, Since *the people* began to bring the offerings into the house of the LORD, we have had enough to eat, and have left plenty: for the LORD hath blessed his people; and that which is left *is* this great store.

11¶ Then Hezekiah commanded to prepare chambers in the house of the LORD; and they prepared *them,*

12And brought in the offerings and the tithes and the dedicated *things* faithfully: over which Cononiah the Levite *was* ruler, and Shimei his brother *was* the next.

13And Jehiel, and Azaziah, and Nahath, and Asahel, and Jerimoth, and Jozabad, and Eliel, and Ismachiah, and Mahath, and Benaiah, *were* overseers under the hand of Cononiah and Shimei his brother, at the commandment of Hezekiah the king, and Azariah the ruler of the house of God.

14And Kore the son of Imnah the Levite, the porter toward the east, *was* over the freewill offerings of God, to distribute the oblations of the LORD, and the most holy things.

15And next him *were* Eden, and Miniamin, and Jeshua, and Shemaiah, Amariah, and Shecaniah, in the cities of the priests, in *their* set office, to give to their brethren by courses, as well to the great as to the small:

16Beside their genealogy of males, from three years old and upward, *even* unto every one that entereth into the house of the LORD, his daily portion for their service in their charges according to their courses;

17Both to the genealogy of the priests by the house of their fathers, and the Levites from twenty years old and upward, in their charges by their courses;

New International

31 WHEN ALL this had ended, the Israelites who were there went out to the towns of Judah, smashed the sacred stones and cut down the Asherah poles. They destroyed the high places and the altars throughout Judah and Benjamin and in Ephraim and Manasseh. After they had destroyed all of them, the Israelites returned to their own towns and to their own property.

Contributions for Worship

2Hezekiah assigned the priests and Levites to divisions—each of them according to their duties as priests or Levites—to offer burnt offerings and fellowship offerings,[a] to minister, to give thanks and to sing praises at the gates of the LORD's dwelling. 3The king contributed from his own possessions for the morning and evening burnt offerings and for the burnt offerings on the Sabbaths, New Moons and appointed feasts as written in the Law of the LORD. 4He ordered the people living in Jerusalem to give the portion due the priests and Levites so they could devote themselves to the Law of the LORD. 5As soon as the order went out, the Israelites generously gave the firstfruits of their grain, new wine, oil and honey and all that the fields produced. They brought a great amount, a tithe of everything. 6The men of Israel and Judah who lived in the towns of Judah also brought a tithe of their herds and flocks and a tithe of the holy things dedicated to the LORD their God, and they piled them in heaps. 7They began doing this in the third month and finished in the seventh month. 8When Hezekiah and his officials came and saw the heaps, they praised the LORD and blessed his people Israel.

9Hezekiah asked the priests and Levites about the heaps; 10and Azariah the chief priest, from the family of Zadok, answered, "Since the people began to bring their contributions to the temple of the LORD, we have had enough to eat and plenty to spare, because the LORD has blessed his people, and this great amount is left over."

11Hezekiah gave orders to prepare storerooms in the temple of the LORD, and this was done. 12Then they faithfully brought in the contributions, tithes and dedicated gifts. Conaniah, a Levite, was in charge of these things, and his brother Shimei was next in rank. 13Jehiel, Azaziah, Nahath, Asahel, Jerimoth, Jozabad, Eliel, Ismakiah, Mahath and Benaiah were supervisors under Conaniah and Shimei his brother, by appointment of King Hezekiah and Azariah the official in charge of the temple of God.

14Kore son of Imnah the Levite, keeper of the East Gate, was in charge of the freewill offerings given to God, distributing the contributions made to the LORD and also the consecrated gifts. 15Eden, Miniamin, Jeshua, Shemaiah, Amariah and Shecaniah assisted him faithfully in the towns of the priests, distributing to their fellow priests according to their divisions, old and young alike.

16In addition, they distributed to the males three years old or more whose names were in the genealogical records—all who would enter the temple of the LORD to perform the daily duties of their various tasks, according to their responsibilities and their divisions. 17And they distributed to the priests enrolled by their families in the genealogical records and likewise to the Levites twenty years old or more, according to their responsibilities and their divisions. 18They included all the little ones, the

---

[a] *2 Traditionally peace offerings*

Living Bible

31 AFTERWARDS A massive campaign against idol worship was begun. Those who were at Jerusalem for the Passover went out to the cities of Judah, Benjamin, Ephraim, and Manasseh and tore down the idol altars, the obelisks, shameimages, and other heathen centers of worship. Then the people who had come to the Passover from the northern tribes returned again to their own homes.

²Hezekiah now organized the priests and Levites into service corps to offer the burnt offerings and peace offerings, and to worship and give thanks and praise to the Lord. ³He also made a personal contribution of animals for the daily morning and evening burnt offerings, as well as for the weekly Sabbath and monthly new moon festivals, and for the other annual feasts as required in the law of God.

⁴In addition, he required the people in Jerusalem to bring their tithes to the priests and Levites, so that they wouldn't need other employment but could apply themselves fully to their duties as required in the law of God. 5, ⁶The people responded immediately and generously with the first of their crops and grain, new wine, olive oil, money, and everything else—a tithe of all they owned, as required by law to be given to the Lord their God. Everything was laid out in great piles. The people who had moved to Judah from the northern tribes and the people of Judah living in the provinces also brought in the tithes of their cattle and sheep, and brought a tithe of the dedicated things to give to the Lord and piled them up in great heaps. 7, ⁸The first of these tithes arrived in June, and the piles continued to grow until October. When Hezekiah and his officials came and saw these huge piles, how they blessed the Lord and praised his people!

⁹"Where did all this come from?" Hezekiah asked the priests and Levites.

¹⁰And Azariah the High Priest from the clan of Zadok replied, "These are tithes! We have been eating from these stores of food for many weeks, but all this is left over, for the Lord has blessed his people."

¹¹Hezekiah decided to prepare storerooms in the Temple. 12, ¹³All the dedicated supplies were brought into the Lord's house. Conaniah, the Levite, was put in charge, assisted by his brother Shime-i and the following aides:

    Jehiel, Azaziah, Nahath, Asahel, Jerimoth, Jozabad, Eliel, Ismachiah, Mahath, Benaiah.

These appointments were made by King Hezekiah and Azariah the High Priest.

14, ¹⁵Kore (son of Imnah, the Levite), who was the gatekeeper at the East Gate, was put in charge of distributing the offerings to the priests. His faithful assistants were Eden, Miniamin, Jeshua, Shemaiah, Amariah, and Sheconiah. They distributed the gifts to the clans of priests in their cities, dividing it to young and old alike. ¹⁶However, the priests on duty at the Temple and their familiesᵇ were supplied directly from there, so they were not included in this distribution. 17, ¹⁸The priests were listed in the genealogical register by clans, and the Levites twenty years old and older were listed under the names of their work corps. A regular food allotment was given to all families of properly registered priests, for they had no other source of income because their time and energies were devoted to the service of the Temple.

New Revised Standard

Pagan Shrines Destroyed

31 NOW WHEN all this was finished, all Israel who were present went out to the cities of Judah and broke down the pillars, hewed down the sacred poles,ᶜ and pulled down the high places and the altars throughout all Judah and Benjamin, and in Ephraim and Manasseh, until they had destroyed them all. Then all the people of Israel returned to their cities, all to their individual properties.

2 Hezekiah appointed the divisions of the priests and of the Levites, division by division, everyone according to his service, the priests and the Levites, for burnt offerings and offerings of well-being, to minister in the gates of the camp of the LORD and to give thanks and praise. ³The contribution of the king from his own possessions was for the burnt offerings: the burnt offerings of morning and evening, and the burnt offerings for the sabbaths, the new moons, and the appointed festivals, as it is written in the law of the LORD. ⁴He commanded the people who lived in Jerusalem to give the portion due to the priests and the Levites, so that they might devote themselves to the law of the LORD. ⁵As soon as the word spread, the people of Israel gave in abundance the first fruits of grain, wine, oil, honey, and of all the produce of the field; and they brought in abundantly the tithe of everything. ⁶The people of Israel and Judah who lived in the cities of Judah also brought in the tithe of cattle and sheep, and the tithe of the dedicated things that had been consecrated to the LORD their God, and laid them in heaps. ⁷In the third month they began to pile up the heaps, and finished them in the seventh month. ⁸When Hezekiah and the officials came and saw the heaps, they blessed the LORD and his people Israel. ⁹Hezekiah questioned the priests and the Levites about the heaps. ¹⁰The chief priest Azariah, who was of the house of Zadok, answered him, "Since they began to bring the contributions into the house of the LORD, we have had enough to eat and have plenty to spare; for the LORD has blessed his people, so that we have this great supply left over."

Reorganization of Priests and Levites

11 Then Hezekiah commanded them to prepare store-chambers in the house of the LORD; and they prepared them. ¹²Faithfully they brought in the contributions, the tithes and the dedicated things. The chief officer in charge of them was Conaniah the Levite, with his brother Shimei as second; ¹³while Jehiel, Azaziah, Nahath, Asahel, Jerimoth, Jozabad, Eliel, Ismachiah, Mahath, and Benaiah were overseers assisting Conaniah and his brother Shimei, by the appointment of King Hezekiah and of Azariah the chief officer of the house of God. ¹⁴Kore son of Imnah the Levite, keeper of the east gate, was in charge of the freewill offerings to God, to apportion the contribution reserved for the LORD and the most holy offerings. ¹⁵Eden, Miniamin, Jeshua, Shemaiah, Amariah, and Shecaniah were faithfully assisting him in the cities of the priests, to distribute the portions to their kindred, old and young alike, by divisions, ¹⁶except those enrolled by genealogy, males from three years old and upwards, all who entered the house of the LORD as the duty of each day required, for their service according to their offices, by their divisions. ¹⁷The enrollment of the priests was according to their ancestral houses; that of the Levites from twenty years old and upwards was according to their offices, by their divisions. ¹⁸The priests were enrolled with all their little

---

ᵇ *31:16 and their families,* literally, "males from three years old and upward."   ᶜ Heb *Asherim*

King James

18And to the genealogy of all their little ones, their wives, and their sons, and their daughters, through all the congregation: for in their set office they sanctified themselves in holiness:

19Also of the sons of Aaron the priests, *which were* in the fields of the suburbs of their cities, in every several city, the men that were expressed by name, to give portions to all the males among the priests, and to all that were reckoned by genealogies among the Levites.

20¶ And thus did Hezekiah throughout all Judah, and wrought *that which was* good and right and truth before the LORD his God.

21And in every work that he began in the service of the house of God, and in the law, and in the commandments, to seek his God, he did *it* with all his heart, and prospered.

32 AFTER THESE things, and the establishment thereof, Sennacherib king of Assyria came, and entered into Judah, and encamped against the fenced cities, and thought to win them for himself.

2And when Hezekiah saw that Sennacherib was come, and that he was purposed to fight against Jerusalem,

3He took counsel with his princes and his mighty men to stop the waters of the fountains which *were* without the city: and they did help him.

4So there was gathered much people together, who stopped all the fountains, and the brook that ran through the midst of the land, saying, Why should the kings of Assyria come, and find much water?

5Also he strengthened himself, and built up all the wall that was broken, and raised *it* up to the towers, and another wall without, and repaired Millo *in* the city of David, and made darts and shields in abundance.

6And he set captains of war over the people, and gathered them together to him in the street of the gate of the city, and spake comfortably to them, saying,

7Be strong and courageous, be not afraid nor dismayed for the king of Assyria, nor for all the multitude that *is* with him: for *there be* more with us than with him:

8With him *is* an arm of flesh; but with us *is* the LORD our God to help us, and to fight our battles. And the people rested themselves upon the words of Hezekiah king of Judah.

9¶ After this did Sennacherib king of Assyria send his servants to Jerusalem, (but he *himself laid siege* against Lachish, and all his power with him,) unto Hezekiah king of Judah, and unto all Judah that *were* at Jerusalem, saying,

10Thus saith Sennacherib king of Assyria, Whereon do ye trust, that ye abide in the siege in Jerusalem?

11Doth not Hezekiah persuade you to give over yourselves to die by famine and by thirst, saying, The LORD our God shall deliver us out of the hand of the king of Assyria?

12Hath not the same Hezekiah taken away his high places and his altars, and commanded Judah and Jerusalem, saying, Ye shall worship before one altar, and burn incense upon it?

13Know ye not what I and my fathers have done unto all the people of *other* lands? were the gods of the nations of those lands any ways able to deliver their lands out of mine hand?

14Who *was there* among all the gods of those nations that my fathers utterly destroyed, that could deliver his people out of mine hand, that your God should be able to deliver you out of mine hand?

New International

wives, and the sons and daughters of the whole community listed in these genealogical records. For they were faithful in consecrating themselves.

19As for the priests, the descendants of Aaron, who lived on the farm lands around their towns or in any other towns, men were designated by name to distribute portions to every male among them and to all who were recorded in the genealogies of the Levites.

20This is what Hezekiah did throughout Judah, doing what was good and right and faithful before the LORD his God. 21In everything that he undertook in the service of God's temple and in obedience to the law and the commands, he sought his God and worked wholeheartedly. And so he prospered.

Sennacherib Threatens Jerusalem

32 AFTER ALL that Hezekiah had so faithfully done, Sennacherib king of Assyria came and invaded Judah. He laid siege to the fortified cities, thinking to conquer them for himself. 2When Hezekiah saw that Sennacherib had come and that he intended to make war on Jerusalem, 3he consulted with his officials and military staff about blocking off the water from the springs outside the city, and they helped him. 4A large force of men assembled, and they blocked all the springs and the stream that flowed through the land. "Why should the kingsa of Assyria come and find plenty of water?" they said. 5Then he worked hard repairing all the broken sections of the wall and building towers on it. He built another wall outside that one and reinforced the supporting terracesb of the City of David. He also made large numbers of weapons and shields.

6He appointed military officers over the people and assembled them before him in the square at the city gate and encouraged them with these words: 7"Be strong and courageous. Do not be afraid or discouraged because of the king of Assyria and the vast army with him, for there is a greater power with us than with him. 8With him is only the arm of flesh, but with us is the LORD our God to help us and to fight our battles." And the people gained confidence from what Hezekiah the king of Judah said.

9Later, when Sennacherib king of Assyria and all his forces were laying siege to Lachish, he sent his officers to Jerusalem with this message for Hezekiah king of Judah and for all the people of Judah who were there:

10"This is what Sennacherib king of Assyria says: On what are you basing your confidence, that you remain in Jerusalem under siege? 11When Hezekiah says, 'The LORD our God will save us from the hand of the king of Assyria,' he is misleading you, to let you die of hunger and thirst. 12Did not Hezekiah himself remove this god's high places and altars, saying to Judah and Jerusalem, 'You must worship before one altar and burn sacrifices on it'?

13"Do you not know what I and my fathers have done to all the peoples of the other lands? Were the gods of those nations ever able to deliver their land from my hand? 14Who of all the gods of these nations that my fathers destroyed has been able to save his people from me? How then can your god deliver you from my hand? 15Now do not let Hezekiah

Living Bible

19One of the priests was appointed in each of the cities of the priests to issue food and other supplies to all priests in the area, and to all registered Levites.

20In this way King Hezekiah handled the distribution throughout all Judah, doing what was just and fair in the sight of the Lord his God. 21He worked very hard to encourage respect for the Temple, the law, and godly living, and was very successful.

32 SOME TIME later, after this good work of King Hezekiah, King Sennacherib of Assyria invaded Judah and laid siege to the fortified cities, planning to place them under tribute. 2When it was clear that Sennacherib was intending to attack Jerusalem, 3Hezekiah summoned his princes and officers for a council of war, and it was decided to plug the springs outside the city. 4They organized a huge work crew to block them, and to cut off the brook running through the fields.

"Why should the king of Assyria come and find water?" they asked.

5Then Hezekiah further strengthened his defenses by repairing the wall wherever it was broken down and by adding to the fortifications, and constructing a second wall outside it. He also reinforced Fort Millo in the City of David, and manufactured large numbers of weapons and shields. 6He recruited an army and appointed officers and summoned them to the plains before the city, and encouraged them with this address:

7"Be strong, be brave, and do not be afraid of the king of Assyria or his mighty army, for there is someone with us who is far greater than he is! 8He has a great army, but they are all mere men, while we have the Lord our God to fight our battles for us!" This greatly encouraged them.

9Then King Sennacherib of Assyria, while still besieging the city of Lachish, sent ambassadors with this message to King Hezekiah and the citizens of Jerusalem:

10"King Sennacherib of Assyria asks, 'Do you think you can survive my siege of Jerusalem? 11King Hezekiah is trying to persuade you to commit suicide by staying there—to die by famine and thirst—while he promises that "the Lord our God will deliver us from the king of Assyria"! 12Don't you realize that Hezekiah is the very person who destroyed all the idols, and commanded Judah and Jerusalem to use only the one altar at the Temple, and to burn incense upon it alone? 13Don't you realize that I and the other kings of Assyria before me have never yet failed to conquer a nation we attacked? The gods of those nations weren't able to do a thing to save their lands! 14Name just one time when anyone, anywhere, was able to resist us successfully. What makes you think your God can do any better? 15Don't

New Revised Standard

children, their wives, their sons, and their daughters, the whole multitude; for they were faithful in keeping themselves holy. 19And for the descendants of Aaron, the priests, who were in the fields of common land belonging to their towns, town by town, the people designated by name were to distribute portions to every male among the priests and to everyone among the Levites who was enrolled.

20 Hezekiah did this throughout all Judah; he did what was good and right and faithful before the LORD his God. 21And every work that he undertook in the service of the house of God, and in accordance with the law and the commandments, to seek his God, he did with all his heart; and he prospered.

Sennacherib's Invasion

32 AFTER THESE things and these acts of faithfulness, King Sennacherib of Assyria came and invaded Judah and encamped against the fortified cities, thinking to win them for himself. 2When Hezekiah saw that Sennacherib had come and intended to fight against Jerusalem, 3he planned with his officers and his warriors to stop the flow of the springs that were outside the city; and they helped him. 4A great many people were gathered, and they stopped all the springs and the wadi that flowed through the land, saying, "Why should the Assyrian kings come and find water in abundance?" 5Hezekiahc set to work resolutely and built up the entire wall that was broken down, and raised towers on it,d and outside it he built another wall; he also strengthened the Millo in the city of David, and made weapons and shields in abundance. 6He appointed combat commanders over the people, and gathered them together to him in the square at the gate of the city and spoke encouragingly to them, saying, 7"Be strong and of good courage. Do not be afraid or dismayed before the king of Assyria and all the horde that is with him; for there is one greater with us than with him. 8With him is an arm of flesh; but with us is the LORD our God, to help us and to fight our battles." The people were encouraged by the words of King Hezekiah of Judah.

9 After this, while King Sennacherib of Assyria was at Lachish with all his forces, he sent his servants to Jerusalem to King Hezekiah of Judah and to all the people of Judah that were in Jerusalem, saying, 10"Thus says King Sennacherib of Assyria: On what are you relying, that you undergo the siege of Jerusalem? 11Is not Hezekiah misleading you, handing you over to die by famine and by thirst, when he tells you, 'The LORD our God will save us from the hand of the king of Assyria'? 12Was it not this same Hezekiah who took away his high places and his altars and commanded Judah and Jerusalem, saying, 'Before one altar you shall worship, and upon it you shall make your offerings'? 13Do you not know what I and my ancestors have done to all the peoples of other lands? Were the gods of the nations of those lands at all able to save their lands out of my hand? 14Who among all the gods of those nations that my ancestors utterly destroyed was able to save his people from my hand, that your God should be able to save you from my hand? 15Now therefore do not let Hezekiah

---

c Heb He   d Vg: Heb and raised on the towers

King James

15Now therefore let not Hezekiah deceive you, nor persuade you on this manner, neither yet believe him: for no god of any nation or kingdom was able to deliver his people out of mine hand, and out of the hand of my fathers: how much less shall your God deliver you out of mine hand?

16And his servants spake yet *more* against the LORD God, and against his servant Hezekiah.

17He wrote also letters to rail on the LORD God of Israel, and to speak against him, saying, As the gods of the nations of *other* lands have not delivered their people out of mine hand, so shall not the God of Hezekiah deliver his people out of mine hand.

18Then they cried with a loud voice in the Jews' speech unto the people of Jerusalem that *were* on the wall, to affright them, and to trouble them; that they might take the city.

19And they spake against the God of Jerusalem, as against the gods of the people of the earth, *which were* the work of the hands of man.

20And for this *cause* Hezekiah the king, and the prophet Isaiah the son of Amoz, prayed and cried to heaven.

21¶ And the LORD sent an angel, which cut off all the mighty men of valour, and the leaders and captains in the camp of the king of Assyria. So he returned with shame of face to his own land. And when he was come into the house of his god, they that came forth of his own bowels slew him there with the sword.

22Thus the LORD saved Hezekiah and the inhabitants of Jerusalem from the hand of Sennacherib the king of Assyria, and from the hand of all *other*, and guided them on every side.

23And many brought gifts unto the LORD to Jerusalem, and presents to Hezekiah king of Judah: so that he was magnified in the sight of all nations from thenceforth.

24¶ In those days Hezekiah was sick to the death, and prayed unto the LORD: and he spake unto him, and he gave him a sign.

25But Hezekiah rendered not again according to the benefit *done* unto him; for his heart was lifted up: therefore there was wrath upon him, and upon Judah and Jerusalem.

26Notwithstanding Hezekiah humbled himself for the pride of his heart, *both* he and the inhabitants of Jerusalem, so that the wrath of the LORD came not upon them in the days of Hezekiah.

27¶ And Hezekiah had exceeding much riches and honour: and he made himself treasuries for silver, and for gold, and for precious stones, and for spices, and for shields, and for all manner of pleasant jewels;

28Storehouses also for the increase of corn, and wine, and oil; and stalls for all manner of beasts, and cotes for flocks.

29Moreover he provided him cities, and possessions of flocks and herds in abundance: for God had given him substance very much.

30This same Hezekiah also stopped the upper watercourse of Gihon, and brought it straight down to the west side of the city of David. And Hezekiah prospered in all his works.

31¶ Howbeit in *the business of* the ambassadors of the princes of Babylon, who sent unto him to inquire of the wonder that was *done* in the land, God left him, to try him, that he might know all *that was* in his heart.

32¶ Now the rest of the acts of Hezekiah, and his goodness, behold, they *are* written in the vision of Isaiah the prophet, the son of Amoz, *and* in the book of the kings of Judah and Israel.

33And Hezekiah slept with his fathers, and they buried him in the chiefest of the sepulchres of the sons of David: and all Judah and the inhabitants of Jerusalem did him honour at his death. And Manasseh his son reigned in his stead.

New International

deceive you and mislead you like this. Do not believe him, for no god of any nation or kingdom has been able to deliver his people from my hand or the hand of my fathers. How much less will your god deliver you from my hand!"

16Sennacherib's officers spoke further against the LORD God and against his servant Hezekiah. 17The king also wrote letters insulting the LORD, the God of Israel, and saying this against him: "Just as the gods of the peoples of the other lands did not rescue their people from my hand, so the god of Hezekiah will not rescue his people from my hand." 18Then they called out in Hebrew to the people of Jerusalem who were on the wall, to terrify them and make them afraid in order to capture the city. 19They spoke about the God of Jerusalem as they did about the gods of the other peoples of the world—the work of men's hands.

20King Hezekiah and the prophet Isaiah son of Amoz cried out in prayer to heaven about this. 21And the LORD sent an angel, who annihilated all the fighting men and the leaders and officers in the camp of the Assyrian king. So he withdrew to his own land in disgrace. And when he went into the temple of his god, some of his sons cut him down with the sword.

22So the LORD saved Hezekiah and the people of Jerusalem from the hand of Sennacherib king of Assyria and from the hand of all others. He took care of thema on every side. 23Many brought offerings to Jerusalem for the LORD and valuable gifts for Hezekiah king of Judah. From then on he was highly regarded by all the nations.

Hezekiah's Pride, Success and Death

24In those days Hezekiah became ill and was at the point of death. He prayed to the LORD, who answered him and gave him a miraculous sign. 25But Hezekiah's heart was proud and he did not respond to the kindness shown him; therefore the LORD's wrath was on him and on Judah and Jerusalem. 26Then Hezekiah repented of the pride of his heart, as did the people of Jerusalem; therefore the LORD's wrath did not come upon them during the days of Hezekiah.

27Hezekiah had very great riches and honor, and he made treasuries for his silver and gold and for his precious stones, spices, shields and all kinds of valuables. 28He also made buildings to store the harvest of grain, new wine and oil; and he made stalls for various kinds of cattle, and pens for the flocks. 29He built villages and acquired great numbers of flocks and herds, for God had given him very great riches.

30It was Hezekiah who blocked the upper outlet of the Gihon spring and channeled the water down to the west side of the City of David. He succeeded in everything he undertook. 31But when envoys were sent by the rulers of Babylon to ask him about the miraculous sign that had occurred in the land, God left him to test him and to know everything that was in his heart.

32The other events of Hezekiah's reign and his acts of devotion are written in the vision of the prophet Isaiah son of Amoz in the book of the kings of Judah and Israel. 33Hezekiah rested with his fathers and was buried on the hill where the tombs of David's descendants are. All Judah and the people of Jerusalem honored him when he died. And Manasseh his son succeeded him as king.

---

a 22 Hebrew; Septuagint and Vulgate *He gave them rest*

Living Bible

let Hezekiah fool you! Don't believe him. I say it again—no god of any nation has ever yet been able to rescue his people from me or my ancestors; how much less your God!' " 16Thus the ambassador mocked the Lord God and God's servant Hezekiah, heaping up insults.

17King Sennacherib also sent letters scorning the Lord God of Israel.

"The gods of all the other nations failed to save their people from my hand, and the God of Hezekiah will fail, too," he wrote.

18The messengers who brought the letters shouted threats in the Jewish language to the people gathered on the walls of the city, trying to frighten and dishearten them. 19These messengers talked about the God of Jerusalem just as though he were one of the heathen gods—a handmade idol!

20Then King Hezekiah and Isaiah the prophet (son of Amoz) cried out in prayer to God in heaven, 21and the Lord sent an angel who destroyed the Assyrian army with all its officers and generals! So Sennacherib returned home in deep shame to his own land. And when he arrived at the temple of his god, some of his own sons killed him there. 22That is how the Lord saved Hezekiah and the people of Jerusalem. And now there was peace at last throughout his realm.

23From then on King Hezekiah became immensely respected among the surrounding nations, and many gifts for the Lord arrived at Jerusalem, with valuable presents for King Hezekiah, too.

24But about that time Hezekiah became deathly sick, and he prayed to the Lord, and the Lord replied with a miracle. 25However, Hezekiah didn't respond with true thanksgiving and praise, for he had become proud, and so the anger of God was upon him and upon Judah and Jerusalem. 26But finally Hezekiah and the residents of Jerusalem humbled themselves, so the wrath of the Lord did not fall upon them during Hezekiah's lifetime.

27So Hezekiah became very wealthy and was highly honored. He had to construct special treasury buildings for his silver, gold, precious stones, and spices, and for his shields and gold bowls. 28, 29He also built many storehouses for his grain, new wine, and olive oil, with many stalls for his animals, and folds for the great flocks of sheep and goats he purchased; and he acquired many towns, for God had given him great wealth. 30He dammed up the Upper Spring of Gihon and brought the water down through an aqueduct to the west side of the City of David sector in Jerusalem. He prospered in everything he did.

31However, when ambassadors arrived from Babylon to find out about the miracle of his being healed, God left him to himself in order to test him and to see what he was really like.

32The rest of the story of Hezekiah and all of the good things he did are written in *The Book of Isaiah* (the prophet, the son of Amoz), and in *The Annals of the Kings of Judah and Israel.* 33When Hezekiah died he was buried in the royal hillside cemetery among the other kings, and all Judah and Jerusalem honored him at his death. Then his son Manasseh became the new king.

New Revised Standard

deceive you or mislead you in this fashion, and do not believe him, for no god of any nation or kingdom has been able to save his people from my hand or from the hand of my ancestors. How much less will your God save you out of my hand!"

16 His servants said still more against the Lord God and against his servant Hezekiah. 17He also wrote letters to throw contempt on the Lord the God of Israel and to speak against him, saying, "Just as the gods of the nations in other lands did not rescue their people from my hands, so the God of Hezekiah will not rescue his people from my hand." 18They shouted it with a loud voice in the language of Judah to the people of Jerusalem who were on the wall, to frighten and terrify them, in order that they might take the city. 19They spoke of the God of Jerusalem as if he were like the gods of the peoples of the earth, which are the work of human hands.

Sennacherib's Defeat and Death

20 Then King Hezekiah and the prophet Isaiah son of Amoz prayed because of this and cried to heaven. 21 And the Lord sent an angel who cut off all the mighty warriors and commanders and officers in the camp of the king of Assyria. So he returned in disgrace to his own land. When he came into the house of his god, some of his own sons struck him down there with the sword. 22 So the Lord saved Hezekiah and the inhabitants of Jerusalem from the hand of King Sennacherib of Assyria and from the hand of all his enemies; he gave them rest[b] on every side. 23 Many brought gifts to the Lord in Jerusalem and precious things to King Hezekiah of Judah, so that he was exalted in the sight of all nations from that time onward.

Hezekiah's Sickness

24 In those days Hezekiah became sick and was at the point of death. He prayed to the Lord, and he answered him and gave him a sign. 25 But Hezekiah did not respond according to the benefit done to him, for his heart was proud. Therefore wrath came upon him and upon Judah and Jerusalem. 26 Then Hezekiah humbled himself for the pride of his heart, both he and the inhabitants of Jerusalem, so that the wrath of the Lord did not come upon them in the days of Hezekiah.

Hezekiah's Prosperity and Achievements

27 Hezekiah had very great riches and honor; and he made for himself treasuries for silver, for gold, for precious stones, for spices, for shields, and for all kinds of costly objects; 28storehouses also for the yield of grain, wine, and oil; and stalls for all kinds of cattle, and sheepfolds.[c] 29He likewise provided cities for himself, and flocks and herds in abundance; for God had given him very great possessions. 30This same Hezekiah closed the upper outlet of the waters of Gihon and directed them down to the west side of the city of David. Hezekiah prospered in all his works. 31So also in the matter of the envoys of the officials of Babylon, who had been sent to him to inquire about the sign that had been done in the land, God left him to himself, in order to test him and to know all that was in his heart.

32 Now the rest of the acts of Hezekiah, and his good deeds, are written in the vision of the prophet Isaiah son of Amoz in the Book of the Kings of Judah and Israel. 33Hezekiah slept with his ancestors, and they buried him on the ascent to the tombs of the descendants of David; and all Judah and the inhabitants of Jerusalem did him honor at his death. His son Manasseh succeeded him.

---

[b] Gk Vg: Heb *guided them*   [c] Gk Vg: Heb *flocks for folds*

King James

33 MANASSEH *WAS* twelve years old when he began to reign, and he reigned fifty and five years in Jerusalem:

2But did *that which was* evil in the sight of the LORD, like unto the abominations of the heathen, whom the LORD had cast out before the children of Israel.

3¶ For he built again the high places which Hezekiah his father had broken down, and he reared up altars for Baalim, and made groves, and worshipped all the host of heaven, and served them.

4Also he built altars in the house of the LORD, whereof the LORD had said, In Jerusalem shall my name be for ever.

5And he built altars for all the host of heaven in the two courts of the house of the LORD.

6And he caused his children to pass through the fire in the valley of the son of Hinnom: also he observed times, and used enchantments, and used witchcraft, and dealt with a familiar spirit, and with wizards: he wrought much evil in the sight of the LORD, to provoke him to anger.

7And he set a carved image, the idol which he had made, in the house of God, of which God had said to David and to Solomon his son, In this house, and in Jerusalem, which I have chosen before all the tribes of Israel, will I put my name for ever:

8Neither will I any more remove the foot of Israel from out of the land which I have appointed for your fathers; so that they will take heed to do all that I have commanded them, according to the whole law and the statutes and the ordinances by the hand of Moses.

9So Manasseh made Judah and the inhabitants of Jerusalem to err, *and* to do worse than the heathen, whom the LORD had destroyed before the children of Israel.

10And the LORD spake to Manasseh, and to his people: but they would not hearken.

11¶ Wherefore the LORD brought upon them the captains of the host of the king of Assyria, which took Manasseh among the thorns, and bound him with fetters, and carried him to Babylon.

12And when he was in affliction, he besought the LORD his God, and humbled himself greatly before the God of his fathers,

13And prayed unto him: and he was entreated of him, and heard his supplication, and brought him again to Jerusalem into his kingdom. Then Manasseh knew that the LORD he *was* God.

14Now after this he built a wall without the city of David, on the west side of Gihon, in the valley, even to the entering in at the fish gate, and compassed about Ophel, and raised it up a very great height, and put captains of war in all the fenced cities of Judah.

15And he took away the strange gods, and the idol out of the house of the LORD, and all the altars that he had built in the mount of the house of the LORD, and in Jerusalem, and cast *them* out of the city.

16And he repaired the altar of the LORD, and sacrificed thereon peace offerings and thank offerings, and commanded Judah to serve the LORD God of Israel.

17Nevertheless the people did sacrifice still in the high places, *yet* unto the LORD their God only.

18¶ Now the rest of the acts of Manasseh, and his prayer unto his God, and the words of the seers that spake to him in the name of the LORD God of Israel, behold, they *are written* in the book of the kings of Israel.

19His prayer also, and *how God* was entreated of him, and all his sins, and his trespass, and the places wherein he built high places, and set up groves and graven images, before he was humbled: behold, they *are* written among the sayings of the seers.

New International

Manasseh King of Judah

33 MANASSEH WAS twelve years old when he became king, and he reigned in Jerusalem fifty-five years. 2He did evil in the eyes of the LORD, following the detestable practices of the nations the LORD had driven out before the Israelites. 3He rebuilt the high places his father Hezekiah had demolished; he also erected altars to the Baals and made Asherah poles. He bowed down to all the starry hosts and worshiped them. 4He built altars in the temple of the LORD, of which the LORD had said, "My Name will remain in Jerusalem forever." 5In both courts of the temple of the LORD, he built altars to all the starry hosts. 6He sacrificed his sons in[a] the fire in the Valley of Ben Hinnom, practiced sorcery, divination and witchcraft, and consulted mediums and spiritists. He did much evil in the eyes of the LORD, provoking him to anger.

7He took the carved image he had made and put it in God's temple, of which God had said to David and to his son Solomon, "In this temple and in Jerusalem, which I have chosen out of all the tribes of Israel, I will put my Name forever. 8I will not again make the feet of the Israelites leave the land I assigned to your forefathers, if only they will be careful to do everything I commanded them concerning all the laws, decrees and ordinances given through Moses." 9But Manasseh led Judah and the people of Jerusalem astray, so that they did more evil than the nations the LORD had destroyed before the Israelites.

10The LORD spoke to Manasseh and his people, but they paid no attention. 11So the LORD brought against them the army commanders of the king of Assyria, who took Manasseh prisoner, put a hook in his nose, bound him with bronze shackles and took him to Babylon. 12In his distress he sought the favor of the LORD his God and humbled himself greatly before the God of his fathers. 13And when he prayed to him, the LORD was moved by his entreaty and listened to his plea; so he brought him back to Jerusalem and to his kingdom. Then Manasseh knew that the LORD is God.

14Afterward he rebuilt the outer wall of the City of David, west of the Gihon spring in the valley, as far as the entrance of the Fish Gate and encircling the hill of Ophel; he also made it much higher. He stationed military commanders in all the fortified cities in Judah.

15He got rid of the foreign gods and removed the image from the temple of the LORD, as well as all the altars he had built on the temple hill and in Jerusalem; and he threw them out of the city. 16Then he restored the altar of the LORD and sacrificed fellowship offerings[b] and thank offerings on it, and told Judah to serve the LORD, the God of Israel. 17The people, however, continued to sacrifice at the high places, but only to the LORD their God.

18The other events of Manasseh's reign, including his prayer to his God and the words the seers spoke to him in the name of the LORD, the God of Israel, are written in the annals of the kings of Israel.[c] 19His prayer and how God was moved by his entreaty, as well as all his sins and unfaithfulness, and the sites where he built high places and set up Asherah poles and idols before he humbled himself—all are written in the records of the seers.[d] 20Manasseh rested with his fathers and was bur-

---

a 6 Or *He made his sons pass through*　　*b 16* Traditionally *peace offerings*　　*c 18* That is, Judah, as frequently in 2 Chronicles　　*d 19* One Hebrew manuscript and Septuagint; most Hebrew manuscripts *of Hozai*

Living Bible

New Revised Standard

Reign of Manasseh

33 MANASSEH WAS only twelve years old when he became king, and he reigned fifty-five years, in Jerusalem. 2But it was an evil reign, for he encouraged his people to worship the idols of the heathen nations destroyed by the Lord when the people of Israel entered the land. 3He rebuilt the heathen altars his father Hezekiah had destroyed—the altars of Baal, and of the shame-images, and of the sun, moon, and stars. 4, 5He even constructed heathen altars in both courts of the Temple of the Lord, for worshiping the sun, moon and stars—in the very place where the Lord had said that he would be honored forever. 6And Manasseh sacrificed his own children as burnt offerings in the Valley of Hinnom. He consulted spirit-mediums, too, and fortune-tellers and sorcerers, and encouraged every sort of evil, making the Lord very angry.

7Think of it! He placed an idol in the very Temple of God, where God had told David and his son Solomon, "I will be honored here in this Temple, and in Jerusalem—the city I have chosen to be honored forever above all the other cities of Israel. 8And if you will only obey my commands—all the laws and instructions given to you by Moses—I won't ever again exile Israel from this land which I gave your ancestors."

9But Manasseh encouraged the people of Judah and Jerusalem to do even more evil than the nations the Lord destroyed when Israel entered the land. 10Warnings from the Lord were ignored by both Manasseh and his people. 11So God sent the Assyrian armies, and they seized him with hooks and bound him with bronze chains and carted him away to Babylon. 12Then at last he came to his senses and cried out humbly to God for help. 13And the Lord listened, and answered his plea by returning him to Jerusalem and to his kingdom! At that point Manasseh finally realized that the Lord was really God!

14It was after this that he rebuilt the outer wall of the City of David and the wall from west of the Spring of Gihon in the Kidron Valley, and then to the Fish Gate, and around Citadel Hill, where it was built very high. And he stationed his army generals in all of the fortified cities of Judah. 15He also removed the foreign gods from the hills and took his idol from the Temple and tore down the altars he had built on the mountain where the Temple stood, and the altars that were in Jerusalem, and dumped them outside the city. 16Then he rebuilt the altar of the Lord and offered sacrifices upon it—peace offerings and thanksgiving offerings—and demanded that the people of Judah worship the Lord God of Israel. 17However, the people still sacrificed upon the altars on the hills, but only to the Lord their God.

18The rest of Manasseh's deeds, and his prayer to God, and God's reply through the prophets—this is all written in *The Annals of the Kings of Israel.* 19His prayer, and the way God answered, and a frank account of his sins and errors, including a list of the locations where he built idols on the hills and set up shame-idols and graven images (this of course was before the great change in his attitude) is recorded in *The Annals of the Prophets.*

Reign of Manasseh

33 MANASSEH WAS twelve years old when he began to reign; he reigned fifty-five years in Jerusalem. 2He did what was evil in the sight of the LORD, according to the abominable practices of the nations whom the LORD drove out before the people of Israel. 3For he rebuilt the high places that his father Hezekiah had pulled down, and erected altars to the Baals, made sacred poles,e worshiped all the host of heaven, and served them. 4He built altars in the house of the LORD, of which the LORD had said, "In Jerusalem shall my name be forever." 5He built altars for all the host of heaven in the two courts of the house of the LORD. 6He made his son pass through fire in the valley of the son of Hinnom, practiced soothsaying and augury and sorcery, and dealt with mediums and with wizards. He did much evil in the sight of the LORD, provoking him to anger. 7The carved image of the idol that he had made he set in the house of God, of which God said to David and to his son Solomon, "In this house, and in Jerusalem, which I have chosen out of all the tribes of Israel, I will put my name forever; 8I will never again remove the feet of Israel from the land that I appointed for your ancestors, if only they will be careful to do all that I have commanded them, all the law, the statutes, and the ordinances given through Moses." 9Manasseh misled Judah and the inhabitants of Jerusalem, so that they did more evil than the nations whom the LORD had destroyed before the people of Israel.

Manasseh Restored after Repentance

10 The LORD spoke to Manasseh and to his people, but they gave no heed. 11Therefore the LORD brought against them the commanders of the army of the king of Assyria, who took Manasseh captive in manacles, bound him with fetters, and brought him to Babylon. 12While he was in distress he entreated the favor of the LORD his God and humbled himself greatly before the God of his ancestors. 13He prayed to him, and God received his entreaty, heard his plea, and restored him again to Jerusalem and to his kingdom. Then Manasseh knew that the LORD indeed was God.

14 Afterward he built an outer wall for the city of David west of Gihon, in the valley, reaching the entrance at the Fish Gate; he carried it around Ophel and raised it to a very great height. He also put commanders of the army in all the fortified cities in Judah. 15He took away the foreign gods and the idol from the house of the LORD, and all the altars that he had built on the mountain of the house of the LORD and in Jerusalem, and he threw them out of the city. 16He also restored the altar of the LORD and offered on it sacrifices of well-being and of thanksgiving; and he commanded Judah to serve the LORD the God of Israel. 17The people, however, still sacrificed at the high places, but only to the LORD their God.

Death of Manasseh

18 Now the rest of the acts of Manasseh, his prayer to his God, and the words of the seers who spoke to him in the name of the LORD God of Israel, these are in the Annals of the Kings of Israel. 19His prayer, and how God received his entreaty, all his sin and his faithlessness, the sites on which he built high places and set up the sacred polesf and the images, before he humbled himself, these are written in the records of the seers.g

---

e Heb *Asheroth*   f Heb *Asherim*   g One Ms Gk: MT *of Hozai*

King James

20¶ So Manasseh slept with his fathers, and they buried him in his own house: and Amon his son reigned in his stead.

21¶ Amon *was* two and twenty years old when he began to reign, and reigned two years in Jerusalem.

22But he did *that which was* evil in the sight of the LORD, as did Manasseh his father: for Amon sacrificed unto all the carved images which Manasseh his father had made, and served them;

23And humbled not himself before the LORD, as Manasseh his father had humbled himself; but Amon trespassed more and more.

24And his servants conspired against him, and slew him in his own house.

25¶ But the people of the land slew all them that had conspired against king Amon; and the people of the land made Josiah his son king in his stead.

34 JOSIAH *WAS* eight years old when he began to reign, and he reigned in Jerusalem one and thirty years.

2And he did *that which was* right in the sight of the LORD, and walked in the ways of David his father, and declined *neither* to the right hand, nor to the left.

3¶ For in the eighth year of his reign, while he was yet young, he began to seek after the God of David his father: and in the twelfth year he began to purge Judah and Jerusalem from the high places, and the groves, and the carved images, and the molten images.

4And they brake down the altars of Baalim in his presence; and the images, that *were* on high above them, he cut down; and the groves, and the carved images, and the molten images, he brake in pieces, and made dust *of them,* and strewed *it* upon the graves of them that had sacrificed unto them.

5And he burnt the bones of the priests upon their altars, and cleansed Judah and Jerusalem.

6And *so did he* in the cities of Manasseh, and Ephraim, and Simeon, even unto Naphtali, with their mattocks round about.

7And when he had broken down the altars and the groves, and had beaten the graven images into powder, and cut down all the idols throughout all the land of Israel, he returned to Jerusalem.

8¶ Now in the eighteenth year of his reign, when he had purged the land, and the house, he sent Shaphan the son of Azaliah, and Maaseiah the governor of the city, and Joah the son of Joahaz the recorder, to repair the house of the LORD his God.

9And when they came to Hilkiah the high priest, they delivered the money that was brought into the house of God, which the Levites that kept the doors had gathered of the hand of Manasseh and Ephraim, and of all the remnant of Israel, and of all Judah and Benjamin; and they returned to Jerusalem.

10And they put *it* in the hand of the workmen that had the oversight of the house of the LORD, and they gave it to the workmen that wrought in the house of the LORD, to repair and amend the house:

11Even to the artificers and builders gave they *it,* to buy hewn stone, and timber for couplings, and to floor the houses which the kings of Judah had destroyed.

12And the men did the work faithfully: and the overseers of them *were* Jahath and Obadiah, the Levites, of the sons of Merari; and Zechariah and Meshullam, of the sons of the Kohathites, to set *it* forward; and *other of* the Levites, all that could skill of instruments of music.

13Also *they were* over the bearers of burdens, and *were* overseers of all that wrought the work in any manner of service: and of the Levites *there were* scribes, and officers, and porters.

New International

ied in his palace. And Amon his son succeeded him as king.

Amon King of Judah

21Amon was twenty-two years old when he became king, and he reigned in Jerusalem two years. 22He did evil in the eyes of the LORD, as his father Manasseh had done. Amon worshiped and offered sacrifices to all the idols Manasseh had made. 23But unlike his father Manasseh, he did not humble himself before the LORD; Amon increased his guilt.

24Amon's officials conspired against him and assassinated him in his palace. 25Then the people of the land killed all who had plotted against King Amon, and they made Josiah his son king in his place.

Josiah's Reforms

34 JOSIAH WAS eight years old when he became king, and he reigned in Jerusalem thirty-one years. 2He did what was right in the eyes of the LORD and walked in the ways of his father David, not turning aside to the right or to the left.

3In the eighth year of his reign, while he was still young, he began to seek the God of his father David. In his twelfth year he began to purge Judah and Jerusalem of high places, Asherah poles, carved idols and cast images. 4Under his direction the altars of the Baals were torn down; he cut to pieces the incense altars that were above them, and smashed the Asherah poles, the idols and the images. These he broke to pieces and scattered over the graves of those who had sacrificed to them. 5He burned the bones of the priests on their altars, and so he purged Judah and Jerusalem. 6In the towns of Manasseh, Ephraim and Simeon, as far as Naphtali, and in the ruins around them, 7he tore down the altars and the Asherah poles and crushed the idols to powder and cut to pieces all the incense altars throughout Israel. Then he went back to Jerusalem.

8In the eighteenth year of Josiah's reign, to purify the land and the temple, he sent Shaphan son of Azaliah and Maaseiah the ruler of the city, with Joah son of Joahaz, the recorder, to repair the temple of the LORD his God.

9They went to Hilkiah the high priest and gave him the money that had been brought into the temple of God, which the Levites who were the doorkeepers had collected from the people of Manasseh, Ephraim and the entire remnant of Israel and from all the people of Judah and Benjamin and the inhabitants of Jerusalem. 10Then they entrusted it to the men appointed to supervise the work on the LORD's temple. These men paid the workers who repaired and restored the temple. 11They also gave money to the carpenters and builders to purchase dressed stone, and timber for joists and beams for the buildings that the kings of Judah had allowed to fall into ruin.

12The men did the work faithfully. Over them to direct them were Jahath and Obadiah, Levites descended from Merari, and Zechariah and Meshullam, descended from Kohath. The Levites—all who were skilled in playing musical instruments— 13had charge of the laborers and supervised all the workers from job to job. Some of the Levites were secretaries, scribes and doorkeepers.

Living Bible

20, 21When Manasseh died he was buried beneath his own palace, and his son Amon became the new king. Amon was twenty-two years old when he began to reign in Jerusalem, but he lasted for only two years. 22It was an evil reign like the early years of his father Manasseh; for Amon sacrificed to all the idols just as his father had. 23But he didn't change as his father did; instead he sinned more and more. 24At last his own officers assassinated him in his palace. 25But some public-spirited citizens killed all of those who assassinated him, and declared his son Josiah to be the new king.

34 JOSIAH WAS only eight years old when he became king. He reigned thirty-one years, in Jerusalem. 2His was a good reign, as he carefully followed the good example of his ancestor King David. 3For when he was sixteen years old, in the eighth year of his reign, he began to search for the God of his ancestor David; and four years later he began to clean up Judah and Jerusalem, destroying the heathen altars and the shame-idols on the hills. 4He went out personally to watch as the altars of Baal were knocked apart, the obelisks above the altars chopped down, and the shame-idols ground into dust and scattered over the graves of those who had sacrificed to them. 5Then he burned the bones of the heathen priests upon their own altars, feeling that this action would clear the people of Judah and Jerusalem from the guilt of their sin of idol-worship.

6Then he went to the cities of Manasseh, Ephraim, and Simeon, even to distant Naphtali, and did the same thing there. 7He broke down the heathen altars, ground to powder the shame-idols, and chopped down the obelisks. He did this everywhere throughout the whole land of Israel before returning to Jerusalem.

8During the eighteenth year of his reign, after he had purged the land and cleaned up the situation at the Temple, he appointed Shaphan (son of Azaliah) and Maaseiah, governor of Jerusalem, and Joah (son of Joahaz), the city treasurer, to repair the Temple. 9They set up a collection system for gifts for the Temple. The money was collected at the Temple gates by the Levites on guard duty there. Gifts were brought by the people coming from Manasseh, Ephraim, and other parts of the remnant of Israel, as well as from the people of Jerusalem. The money was taken to Hilkiah the High Priest for accounting, 10, 11and then used by the Levites to pay the carpenters and stonemasons, and to purchase building materials—stone building blocks, timber, lumber, and beams. He now rebuilt what earlier kings of Judah had torn down.

12The workmen were energetic under the leadership of Jahath and Obadiah, Levites of the subclan of Merari. Zechariah and Meshullam, of the subclan of Kohath, were the building superintendents. The Levites who were skilled musicians played background music while the work progressed. 13Other Levites superintended the unskilled laborers who carried in the materials to the workmen. Still others assisted as accountants, supervisors, and carriers.

New Revised Standard

20So Manasseh slept with his ancestors, and they buried him in his house. His son Amon succeeded him.

Amon's Reign and Death

21 Amon was twenty-two years old when he began to reign; he reigned two years in Jerusalem. 22He did what was evil in the sight of the LORD, as his father Manasseh had done. Amon sacrificed to all the images that his father Manasseh had made, and served them. 23He did not humble himself before the LORD, as his father Manasseh had humbled himself, but this Amon incurred more and more guilt. 24His servants conspired against him and killed him in his house. 25But the people of the land killed all those who had conspired against King Amon; and the people of the land made his son Josiah king to succeed him.

Reign of Josiah

34 JOSIAH WAS eight years old when he began to reign; he reigned thirty-one years in Jerusalem. 2He did what was right in the sight of the LORD, and walked in the ways of his ancestor David; he did not turn aside to the right or to the left. 3For in the eighth year of his reign, while he was still a boy, he began to seek the God of his ancestor David, and in the twelfth year he began to purge Judah and Jerusalem of the high places, the sacred poles,a and the carved and the cast images. 4In his presence they pulled down the altars of the Baals; he demolished the incense altars that stood above them. He broke down the sacred polesa and the carved and the cast images; he made dust of them and scattered it over the graves of those who had sacrificed to them. 5He also burned the bones of the priests on their altars, and purged Judah and Jerusalem. 6In the towns of Manasseh, Ephraim, and Simeon, and as far as Naphtali, in their ruinsb all around, 7he broke down the altars, beat the sacred polesa and the images into powder, and demolished all the incense altars throughout all the land of Israel. Then he returned to Jerusalem.

Discovery of the Book of the Law

8 In the eighteenth year of his reign, when he had purged the land and the house, he sent Shaphan son of Azaliah, Maaseiah the governor of the city, and Joah son of Joahaz, the recorder, to repair the house of the LORD his God. 9They came to the high priest Hilkiah and delivered the money that had been brought into the house of God, which the Levites, the keepers of the threshold, had collected from Manasseh and Ephraim and from all the remnant of Israel and from all Judah and Benjamin and from the inhabitants of Jerusalem. 10They delivered it to the workers who had the oversight of the house of the LORD, and the workers who were working in the house of the LORD gave it for repairing and restoring the house. 11They gave it to the carpenters and the builders to buy quarried stone, and timber for binders, and beams for the buildings that the kings of Judah had let go to ruin. 12The people did the work faithfully. Over them were appointed the Levites Jahath and Obadiah, of the sons of Merari, along with Zechariah and Meshullam, of the sons of the Kohathites, to have oversight. Other Levites, all skillful with instruments of music, 13were over the burden bearers and directed all who did work in every kind of service; and some of the Levites were scribes, and officials, and gatekeepers.

a Heb Asherim   b Meaning of Heb uncertain

King James

14¶ And when they brought out the money that was brought into the house of the LORD, Hilkiah the priest found a book of the law of the LORD *given* by Moses.

15And Hilkiah answered and said to Shaphan the scribe, I have found the book of the law in the house of the LORD. And Hilkiah delivered the book to Shaphan.

16And Shaphan carried the book to the king, and brought the king word back again, saying, All that was committed to thy servants, they do *it.*

17And they have gathered together the money that was found in the house of the LORD, and have delivered it into the hand of the overseers, and to the hand of the workmen.

18Then Shaphan the scribe told the king, saying, Hilkiah the priest hath given me a book. And Shaphan read it before the king.

19And it came to pass, when the king had heard the words of the law, that he rent his clothes.

20And the king commanded Hilkiah, and Ahikam the son of Shaphan, and Abdon the son of Micah, and Shaphan the scribe, and Asaiah a servant of the king's, saying,

21Go, inquire of the LORD for me, and for them that are left in Israel and in Judah, concerning the words of the book that is found: for great *is* the wrath of the LORD that is poured out upon us, because our fathers have not kept the word of the LORD, to do after all that is written in this book.

22And Hilkiah, and *they* that the king *had appointed,* went to Huldah the prophetess, the wife of Shallum the son of Tikvath, the son of Hasrah, keeper of the wardrobe; (now she dwelt in Jerusalem in the college:) and they spake to her to that *effect.*

23¶ And she answered them, Thus saith the LORD God of Israel, Tell ye the man that sent you to me,

24Thus saith the LORD, Behold, I will bring evil upon this place, and upon the inhabitants thereof, *even* all the curses that are written in the book which they have read before the king of Judah:

25Because they have forsaken me, and have burned incense unto other gods, that they might provoke me to anger with all the works of their hands; therefore my wrath shall be poured out upon this place, and shall not be quenched.

26And as for the king of Judah, who sent you to inquire of the LORD, so shall ye say unto him, Thus saith the LORD God of Israel *concerning* the words which thou hast heard;

27Because thine heart was tender, and thou didst humble thyself before God, when thou heardest his words against this place, and against the inhabitants thereof, and humbledst thyself before me, and didst rend thy clothes, and weep before me; I have even heard *thee* also, saith the LORD.

28Behold, I will gather thee to thy fathers, and thou shalt be gathered to thy grave in peace, neither shall thine eyes see all the evil that I will bring upon this place, and upon the inhabitants of the same. So they brought the king word again.

29¶ Then the king sent and gathered together all the elders of Judah and Jerusalem.

30And the king went up into the house of the LORD, and all the men of Judah, and the inhabitants of Jerusalem, and the priests, and the Levites, and all the people, great and small: and he read in their ears all the words of the book of the covenant that was found in the house of the LORD.

31And the king stood in his place, and made a covenant before the LORD, to walk after the LORD, and to keep his commandments, and his testimonies, and his statutes, with all his heart, and with all his soul, to perform the words of the covenant which are written in this book.

New International

The Book of the Law Found

14While they were bringing out the money that had been taken into the temple of the LORD, Hilkiah the priest found the Book of the Law of the LORD that had been given through Moses. 15Hilkiah said to Shaphan the secretary, "I have found the Book of the Law in the temple of the LORD." He gave it to Shaphan.

16Then Shaphan took the book to the king and reported to him: "Your officials are doing everything that has been committed to them. 17They have paid out the money that was in the temple of the LORD and have entrusted it to the supervisors and workers." 18Then Shaphan the secretary informed the king, "Hilkiah the priest has given me a book." And Shaphan read from it in the presence of the king.

19When the king heard the words of the Law, he tore his robes. 20He gave these orders to Hilkiah, Ahikam son of Shaphan, Abdon son of Micah,[a] Shaphan the secretary and Asaiah the king's attendant: 21"Go and inquire of the LORD for me and for the remnant in Israel and Judah about what is written in this book that has been found. Great is the LORD's anger that is poured out on us because our fathers have not kept the word of the LORD; they have not acted in accordance with all that is written in this book."

22Hilkiah and those the king had sent with him[b] went to speak to the prophetess Huldah, who was the wife of Shallum son of Tokhath,[c] the son of Hasrah,[d] keeper of the wardrobe. She lived in Jerusalem, in the Second District.

23She said to them, "This is what the LORD, the God of Israel, says: Tell the man who sent you to me, 24'This is what the LORD says: I am going to bring disaster on this place and its people—all the curses written in the book that has been read in the presence of the king of Judah. 25Because they have forsaken me and burned incense to other gods and provoked me to anger by all that their hands have made,[e] my anger will be poured out on this place and will not be quenched.' 26Tell the king of Judah, who sent you to inquire of the LORD, 'This is what the LORD, the God of Israel, says concerning the words you heard: 27Because your heart was responsive and you humbled yourself before God when you heard what he spoke against this place and its people, and because you humbled yourself before me and tore your robes and wept in my presence, I have heard you, declares the LORD. 28Now I will gather you to your fathers, and you will be buried in peace. Your eyes will not see all the disaster I am going to bring on this place and on those who live here.' "

So they took her answer back to the king.

29Then the king called together all the elders of Judah and Jerusalem. 30He went up to the temple of the LORD with the men of Judah, the people of Jerusalem, the priests and the Levites—all the people from the least to the greatest. He read in their hearing all the words of the Book of the Covenant, which had been found in the temple of the LORD. 31The king stood by his pillar and renewed the covenant in the presence of the LORD—to follow the LORD and keep his commands, regulations and decrees with all his heart and all his soul, and to obey the words of the covenant written in this book.

---

[a] 20 Also called *Acbor son of Micaiah*   [b] 22 One Hebrew manuscript, Vulgate and Syriac; most Hebrew manuscripts do not have *had sent with him.*   [c] 22 Also called *Tikvah*   [d] 22 Also called *Harhas*   [e] 25 Or *by everything they have done*

Living Bible

14One day when Hilkiah, the High Priest, was at the Temple recording the money collected at the gates, he found an old scroll which turned out to be the laws of God as given to Moses!

15, 16"Look!" Hilkiah exclaimed to Shaphan, the king's secretary. "See what I have found in the Temple! These are the laws of God!" Hilkiah gave the scroll to Shaphan, and Shaphan took it to the king, along with his report that there was good progress being made in the reconstruction of the Temple.

17"The money chests have been opened and counted, and the money has been put into the hand of the overseers and workmen," he said to the king.

18Then he mentioned the scroll, and how Hilkiah had discovered it. So he read it to the king. 19When the king heard what these laws required of God's people, he ripped his clothing in despair, 20and summoned Hilkiah, Ahikam (son of Shaphan), Abdon (son of Micah), Shaphan the treasurer, and Asaiah, the king's personal aide.

21"Go to the Temple and plead with the Lord for me!" the king told them. "Pray for all the remnant of Israel and Judah! For this scroll says that the reason the Lord's great anger has been poured out upon us is that our ancestors have not obeyed these laws that are written here."

22So the men went to Huldah the prophetess, the wife of Shallum (son of Tokhath, son of Hasrah). (Shallum was the king's tailor, living in the second ward.) When they told her of the king's trouble, 23she replied, "The Lord God of Israel says, Tell the man who sent you, 24" 'Yes, the Lord will destroy this city and its people. All the curses written in the scroll will come true. 25For my people have forsaken me and have worshiped heathen gods, and I am very angry with them for their deeds. Therefore, my unquenchable wrath is poured out upon this place.'

26"But the Lord also says this to the king of Judah who sent you to ask me about this: Tell him, the Lord God of Israel says, 27'Because you are sorry and have humbled yourself before God when you heard my words against this city and its people, and have ripped your clothing in despair and wept before me—I have heard you, says the Lord, 28and I will not send the promised evil upon this city and its people until after your death.' " So they brought back to the king this word from the Lord. 29Then the king summoned all the elders of Judah and Jerusalem, 30and the priests and Levites and all the people great and small, to accompany him to the Temple. There the king read the scroll to them—the covenant of God that was found in the Temple. 31As the king stood before them, he made a pledge to the Lord to follow his commandments with all his heart and soul, and to do what was written in the scroll. 32And he re-

New Revised Standard

14 While they were bringing out the money that had been brought into the house of the LORD, the priest Hilkiah found the book of the law of the LORD given through Moses. 15Hilkiah said to the secretary Shaphan, "I have found the book of the law in the house of the LORD"; and Hilkiah gave the book to Shaphan. 16Shaphan brought the book to the king, and further reported to the king, "All that was committed to your servants they are doing. 17They have emptied out the money that was found in the house of the LORD and have delivered it into the hand of the overseers and the workers." 18The secretary Shaphan informed the king, "The priest Hilkiah has given me a book." Shaphan then read it aloud to the king.

19 When the king heard the words of the law he tore his clothes. 20Then the king commanded Hilkiah, Ahikam son of Shaphan, Abdon son of Micah, the secretary Shaphan, and the king's servant Asaiah: 21"Go, inquire of the LORD for me and for those who are left in Israel and in Judah, concerning the words of the book that has been found; for the wrath of the LORD that is poured out on us is great, because our ancestors did not keep the word of the LORD, to act in accordance with all that is written in this book."

The Prophet Huldah Consulted

22 So Hilkiah and those whom the king had sent went to the prophet Huldah, the wife of Shallum son of Tokhath son of Hasrah, keeper of the wardrobe (who lived in Jerusalem in the Second Quarter) and spoke to her to that effect. 23 She declared to them, "Thus says the LORD, the God of Israel: Tell the man who sent you to me, 24Thus says the LORD: I will indeed bring disaster upon this place and upon its inhabitants, all the curses that are written in the book that was read before the king of Judah. 25Because they have forsaken me and have made offerings to other gods, so that they have provoked me to anger with all the works of their hands, my wrath will be poured out on this place and will not be quenched. 26But as to the king of Judah, who sent you to inquire of the LORD, thus shall you say to him: Thus says the LORD, the God of Israel: Regarding the words that you have heard, 27because your heart was penitent and you humbled yourself before God when you heard his words against this place and its inhabitants, and you have humbled yourself before me, and have torn your clothes and wept before me, I also have heard you, says the LORD. 28I will gather you to your ancestors and you shall be gathered to your grave in peace; your eyes shall not see all the disaster that I will bring on this place and its inhabitants." They took the message back to the king.

The Covenant Renewed

29 Then the king sent word and gathered together all the elders of Judah and Jerusalem. 30The king went up to the house of the LORD, with all the people of Judah, the inhabitants of Jerusalem, the priests and the Levites, all the people both great and small; he read in their hearing all the words of the book of the covenant that had been found in the house of the LORD. 31The king stood in his place and made a covenant before the LORD, to follow the LORD, keeping his commandments, his decrees, and his statutes, with all his heart and all his soul, to perform the words of the covenant that were written in this book. 32Then he made all who were

King James

32And he caused all that were present in Jerusalem and Benjamin to stand *to it*. And the inhabitants of Jerusalem did according to the covenant of God, the God of their fathers.

33And Josiah took away all the abominations out of all the countries that *pertained* to the children of Israel, and made all that *were* present in Israel to serve, *even* to serve the LORD their God. *And* all his days they departed not from following the LORD, the God of their fathers.

35 MOREOVER JOSIAH kept a passover unto the LORD in Jerusalem: and they killed the passover on the fourteenth *day* of the first month.

2And he set the priests in their charges, and encouraged them to the service of the house of the LORD,

3And said unto the Levites that taught all Israel, which were holy unto the LORD, Put the holy ark in the house which Solomon the son of David king of Israel did build; *it shall* not *be* a burden upon *your* shoulders: serve now the LORD your God, and his people Israel,

4And prepare *yourselves* by the houses of your fathers, after your courses, according to the writing of David king of Israel, and according to the writing of Solomon his son.

5And stand in the holy *place* according to the divisions of the families of the fathers of your brethren the people, and *after* the division of the families of the Levites.

6So kill the passover, and sanctify yourselves, and prepare your brethren, that *they* may do according to the word of the LORD by the hand of Moses.

7And Josiah gave to the people, of the flock, lambs and kids, all for the passover offerings, for all that were present, to the number of thirty thousand, and three thousand bullocks: these *were* of the king's substance.

8And his princes gave willingly unto the people, to the priests, and to the Levites: Hilkiah and Zechariah and Jehiel, rulers of the house of God, gave unto the priests for the passover offerings two thousand and six hundred *small cattle*, and three hundred oxen.

9Conaniah also, and Shemaiah and Nethaneel, his brethren, and Hashabiah and Jeiel and Jozabad, chief of the Levites, gave unto the Levites for passover offerings five thousand *small cattle*, and five hundred oxen.

10So the service was prepared, and the priests stood in their place, and the Levites in their courses, according to the king's commandment.

11And they killed the passover, and the priests sprinkled *the blood* from their hands, and the Levites flayed *them*.

12And they removed the burnt offerings, that they might give according to the divisions of the families of the people, to offer unto the LORD, as *it is* written in the book of Moses. And so *did they* with the oxen.

13And they roasted the passover with fire according to the ordinance: but the *other* holy *offerings* sod they in pots, and in caldrons, and in pans, and divided *them* speedily among all the people.

14And afterward they made ready for themselves, and for the priests: because the priests the sons of Aaron *were busied* in offering of burnt offerings and the fat until night; therefore the Levites prepared for themselves, and for the priests the sons of Aaron.

15And the singers the sons of Asaph *were* in their place, according to the commandment of David, and Asaph, and Heman, and Jeduthun the king's seer; and the porters *waited* at every gate; they might not depart from their service; for their brethren the Levites prepared for them.

New International

32Then he had everyone in Jerusalem and Benjamin pledge themselves to it; the people of Jerusalem did this in accordance with the covenant of God, the God of their fathers.

33Josiah removed all the detestable idols from all the territory belonging to the Israelites, and he had all who were present in Israel serve the LORD their God. As long as he lived, they did not fail to follow the LORD, the God of their fathers.

Josiah Celebrates the Passover

35 JOSIAH CELEBRATED the Passover to the LORD in Jerusalem, and the Passover lamb was slaughtered on the fourteenth day of the first month. 2He appointed the priests to their duties and encouraged them in the service of the LORD's temple. 3He said to the Levites, who instructed all Israel and who had been consecrated to the LORD: "Put the sacred ark in the temple that Solomon son of David king of Israel built. It is not to be carried about on your shoulders. Now serve the LORD your God and his people Israel. 4Prepare yourselves by families in your divisions, according to the directions written by David king of Israel and by his son Solomon.

5"Stand in the holy place with a group of Levites for each subdivision of the families of your fellow countrymen, the lay people. 6Slaughter the Passover lambs, consecrate yourselves and prepare the lambs for your fellow countrymen, doing what the LORD commanded through Moses."

7Josiah provided for all the lay people who were there a total of thirty thousand sheep and goats for the Passover offerings, and also three thousand cattle—all from the king's own possessions.

8His officials also contributed voluntarily to the people and the priests and Levites. Hilkiah, Zechariah and Jehiel, the administrators of God's temple, gave the priests twenty-six hundred Passover offerings and three hundred cattle. 9Also Conaniah along with Shemaiah and Nethanel, his brothers, and Hashabiah, Jeiel and Jozabad, the leaders of the Levites, provided five thousand Passover offerings and five hundred head of cattle for the Levites.

10The service was arranged and the priests stood in their places with the Levites in their divisions as the king had ordered. 11The Passover lambs were slaughtered, and the priests sprinkled the blood handed to them, while the Levites skinned the animals. 12They set aside the burnt offerings to give them to the subdivisions of the families of the people to offer to the LORD, as is written in the Book of Moses. They did the same with the cattle. 13They roasted the Passover animals over the fire as prescribed, and boiled the holy offerings in pots, caldrons and pans and served them quickly to all the people. 14After this, they made preparations for themselves and for the priests, because the priests, the descendants of Aaron, were sacrificing the burnt offerings and the fat portions until nightfall. So the Levites made preparations for themselves and for the Aaronic priests.

15The musicians, the descendants of Asaph, were in the places prescribed by David, Asaph, Heman and Jeduthun the king's seer. The gatekeepers at each gate did not need to leave their posts, because their fellow Levites made the preparations for them.

Living Bible

quired everyone in Jerusalem and Benjamin to subscribe to this pact with God, and all of them did.

33So Josiah removed all idols from the areas occupied by the Jews, and required all of them to worship Jehovah their God. And throughout the remainder of his lifetime they continued serving Jehovah, the God of their ancestors.

35 THEN JOSIAH announced that the Passover would be celebrated on the first day of April, in Jerusalem. The Passover lambs were slain that evening. 2He also reestablished the priests in their duties, and encouraged them to begin their work at the Temple again. 3He issued this order to the sanctified Levites, the religious teachers in Israel:

"Since the Ark is now in Solomon's Temple and you don't need to carry it back and forth upon your shoulders, spend your time ministering to the Lord and to his people. 4, 5Form yourselves into the traditional service corps of your ancestors, as first organized by King David of Israel and by his son Solomon. Each corps will assist particular clans of the people who bring in their offerings to the Temple. 6Kill the Passover lambs and sanctify yourselves and prepare to assist the people who come. Follow all of the instructions of the Lord through Moses."

7Then the king contributed 30,000 lambs and young goats for the people's Passover offerings, and 3,000 young bulls. 8The king's officials made willing contributions to the priests and Levites. Hilkiah, Zechariah, and Jehiel, the overseers of the Temple, gave the priests 2,600 sheep and goats, and 300 oxen as Passover offerings. 9The Levite leaders—Conaniah, Shemaiah, and Nethanel, and his brothers Hashabiah, Je-iel, and Jozabad—gave 5,000 sheep and goats and 500 oxen to the Levites for their Passover offerings.

10When everything was organized, and the priests were standing in their places, and the Levites were formed into service corps as the king had instructed, 11then the Levites killed the Passover lambs and presented the blood to the priests, who sprinkled it upon the altar as the Levites removed the skins. 12They piled up the carcasses for each tribe to present its own burnt sacrifices to the Lord, as it is written in the law of Moses. They did the same with the oxen. 13Then, as directed by the laws of Moses, they roasted the Passover lambs and boiled the holy offerings in pots, kettles, and pans, and hurried them out to the people to eat. 14Afterwards the Levites prepared a meal for themselves and for the priests, for they had been busy from morning till night offering the fat of the burnt offerings.

15The singers (the sons of Asaph) were in their places, following directions issued centuries earlier by King David, Asaph, Heman, and Jeduthun the king's prophet. The gatekeepers guarded the gates, and didn't need to leave their posts of duty, for their meals were brought to them by their Levite brothers. 16The entire

New Revised Standard

present in Jerusalem and in Benjamin pledge themselves to it. And the inhabitants of Jerusalem acted according to the covenant of God, the God of their ancestors. 33Josiah took away all the abominations from all the territory that belonged to the people of Israel, and made all who were in Israel worship the LORD their God. All his days they did not turn away from following the LORD the God of their ancestors.

Celebration of the Passover

35 JOSIAH KEPT a passover to the LORD in Jerusalem; they slaughtered the passover lamb on the fourteenth day of the first month. 2He appointed the priests to their offices and encouraged them in the service of the house of the LORD. 3He said to the Levites who taught all Israel and who were holy to the LORD, "Put the holy ark in the house that Solomon son of David, king of Israel, built; you need no longer carry it on your shoulders. Now serve the LORD your God and his people Israel. 4Make preparations by your ancestral houses by your divisions, following the written directions of King David of Israel and the written directions of his son Solomon. 5Take position in the holy place according to the groupings of the ancestral houses of your kindred the people, and let there be Levites for each division of an ancestral house.a 6Slaughter the passover lamb, sanctify yourselves, and on behalf of your kindred make preparations, acting according to the word of the LORD by Moses."

7 Then Josiah contributed to the people, as passover offerings for all that were present, lambs and kids from the flock to the number of thirty thousand, and three thousand bulls; these were from the king's possessions. 8His officials contributed willingly to the people, to the priests, and to the Levites. Hilkiah, Zechariah, and Jehiel, the chief officers of the house of God, gave to the priests for the passover offerings two thousand six hundred lambs and kids and three hundred bulls. 9Conaniah also, and his brothers Shemaiah and Nethanel, and Hashabiah and Jeiel and Jozabad, the chiefs of the Levites, gave to the Levites for the passover offerings five thousand lambs and kids and five hundred bulls.

10 When the service had been prepared for, the priests stood in their place, and the Levites in their divisions according to the king's command. 11They slaughtered the passover lamb, and the priests dashed the blood that they receivedb from them, while the Levites did the skinning. 12They set aside the burnt offerings so that they might distribute them according to the groupings of the ancestral houses of the people, to offer to the LORD, as it is written in the book of Moses. And they did the same with the bulls. 13They roasted the passover lamb with fire according to the ordinance; and they boiled the holy offerings in pots, in caldrons, and in pans, and carried them quickly to all the people. 14Afterward they made preparations for themselves and for the priests, because the priests the descendants of Aaron were occupied in offering the burnt offerings and the fat parts until night; so the Levites made preparations for themselves and for the priests, the descendants of Aaron. 15The singers, the descendants of Asaph, were in their place according to the command of David, and Asaph, and Heman, and the king's seer Jeduthun. The gatekeepers were at each gate; they did not need to interrupt their service, for their kindred the Levites made preparations for them.

a Meaning of Heb uncertain   b Heb lacks *that they received*

King James

16So all the service of the LORD was prepared the same day, to keep the passover, and to offer burnt offerings upon the altar of the LORD, according to the commandment of king Josiah.

17And the children of Israel that were present kept the passover at that time, and the feast of unleavened bread seven days.

18And there was no passover like to that kept in Israel from the days of Samuel the prophet; neither did all the kings of Israel keep such a passover as Josiah kept, and the priests, and the Levites, and all Judah and Israel that were present, and the inhabitants of Jerusalem.

19In the eighteenth year of the reign of Josiah was this passover kept.

20¶ After all this, when Josiah had prepared the temple, Necho king of Egypt came up to fight against Carchemish by Euphrates: and Josiah went out against him.

21But he sent ambassadors to him, saying, What have I to do with thee, thou king of Judah? I come not against thee this day, but against the house wherewith I have war: for God commanded me to make haste: forbear thee from meddling with God, who is with me, that he destroy thee not.

22Nevertheless Josiah would not turn his face from him, but disguised himself, that he might fight with him, and hearkened not unto the words of Necho from the mouth of God, and came to fight in the valley of Megiddo.

23And the archers shot at king Josiah; and the king said to his servants, Have me away; for I am sore wounded.

24His servants therefore took him out of that chariot, and put him in the second chariot that he had; and they brought him to Jerusalem, and he died, and was buried in one of the sepulchres of his fathers. And all Judah and Jerusalem mourned for Josiah.

25¶ And Jeremiah lamented for Josiah: and all the singing men and the singing women spake of Josiah in their lamentations to this day, and made them an ordinance in Israel: and, behold, they are written in the lamentations.

26Now the rest of the acts of Josiah, and his goodness, according to that which was written in the law of the LORD,

27And his deeds, first and last, behold, they are written in the book of the kings of Israel and Judah.

36 THEN THE people of the land took Jehoahaz the son of Josiah, and made him king in his father's stead in Jerusalem.

2Jehoahaz was twenty and three years old when he began to reign, and he reigned three months in Jerusalem.

3And the king of Egypt put him down at Jerusalem, and condemned the land in an hundred talents of silver and a talent of gold.

4And the king of Egypt made Eliakim his brother king over Judah and Jerusalem, and turned his name to Jehoiakim. And Necho took Jehoahaz his brother, and carried him to Egypt.

5¶ Jehoiakim was twenty and five years old when he began to reign, and he reigned eleven years in Jerusalem: and he did that which was evil in the sight of the LORD his God.

6Against him came up Nebuchadnezzar king of Babylon, and bound him in fetters, to carry him to Babylon.

New International

16So at that time the entire service of the LORD was carried out for the celebration of the Passover and the offering of burnt offerings on the altar of the LORD, as King Josiah had ordered. 17The Israelites who were present celebrated the Passover at that time and observed the Feast of Unleavened Bread for seven days. 18The Passover had not been observed like this in Israel since the days of the prophet Samuel; and none of the kings of Israel had ever celebrated such a Passover as did Josiah, with the priests, the Levites and all Judah and Israel who were there with the people of Jerusalem. 19This Passover was celebrated in the eighteenth year of Josiah's reign.

The Death of Josiah

20After all this, when Josiah had set the temple in order, Neco king of Egypt went up to fight at Carchemish on the Euphrates, and Josiah marched out to meet him in battle. 21But Neco sent messengers to him, saying, "What quarrel is there between you and me, O king of Judah? It is not you I am attacking at this time, but the house with which I am at war. God has told me to hurry; so stop opposing God, who is with me, or he will destroy you."

22Josiah, however, would not turn away from him, but disguised himself to engage him in battle. He would not listen to what Neco had said at God's command but went to fight him on the plain of Megiddo.

23Archers shot King Josiah, and he told his officers, "Take me away; I am badly wounded." 24So they took him out of his chariot, put him in the other chariot he had and brought him to Jerusalem, where he died. He was buried in the tombs of his fathers, and all Judah and Jerusalem mourned for him.

25Jeremiah composed laments for Josiah, and to this day all the men and women singers commemorate Josiah in the laments. These became a tradition in Israel and are written in the Laments.

26The other events of Josiah's reign and his acts of devotion, according to what is written in the Law of the LORD— 27all the events, from beginning to end, are written in the book of the kings of Israel and Judah.

36 AND THE people of the land took Jehoahaz son of Josiah and made him king in Jerusalem in place of his father.

Jehoahaz King of Judah

2Jehoahaz[a] was twenty-three years old when he became king, and he reigned in Jerusalem three months. 3The king of Egypt dethroned him in Jerusalem and imposed on Judah a levy of a hundred talents[b] of silver and a talent[c] of gold. 4The king of Egypt made Eliakim, a brother of Jehoahaz, king over Judah and Jerusalem and changed Eliakim's name to Jehoiakim. But Neco took Eliakim's brother Jehoahaz and carried him off to Egypt.

Jehoiakim King of Judah

5Jehoiakim was twenty-five years old when he became king, and he reigned in Jerusalem eleven years. He did evil in the eyes of the LORD his God. 6Nebuchadnezzar king of Babylon attacked him and bound him with bronze shackles to take him to Babylon. 7Nebuchadnez-

---

a 2 Hebrew Joahaz, a variant of Jehoahaz; also in verse 4   b 3 That is, about 3 3/4 tons (about 3.4 metric tons)   c 3 That is, about 75 pounds (about 34 kilograms)

Living Bible

Passover ceremony was completed in that one day. All the burnt offerings were sacrificed upon the altar of the Lord, as Josiah had instructed.

17Everyone present in Jerusalem took part in the Passover observance, and this was followed by the Feast of Unleavened Bread for the next seven days. 18Never since the time of Samuel the prophet had there been such a Passover—not one of the kings of Israel could vie with King Josiah in this respect, involving so many of the priests, Levites, and people from Jerusalem and from all parts of Judah, and from over in Israel. 19This all happened in the eighteenth year of the reign of Josiah.

20Afterwards King Neco of Egypt led his army at Carchemish on the Euphrates River, and Josiah declared war on him.

21But King Neco sent ambassadors to Josiah with this message: "I don't want a fight with you, O king of Judah! I have come only to fight the king of Assyria! Leave me alone! God has told me to hurry! Don't meddle with God or he will destroy you, for he is with me."

22But Josiah refused to turn back. Instead he led his army into the battle at the Valley of Megiddo. (He laid aside his royal robes so that the enemy wouldn't recognize him.) Josiah refused to believe that Neco's message was from God. 23The enemy archers struck King Josiah with their arrows and fatally wounded him.

"Take me out of the battle," he exclaimed to his aides.

24, 25So they lifted him out of his chariot and placed him in his second chariot and brought him back to Jerusalem where he died. He was buried there, in the royal cemetery. And all Judah and Jerusalem, including even Jeremiah the prophet, mourned for him, as did the Temple choirs. To this day they still sing sad songs about his death, for these songs of sorrow were recorded among the official lamentations.

26The other activities of Josiah, and his good deeds, and how he followed the laws of the Lord, 27all are written in *The Annals of the Kings of Israel and Judah*.

36 JOSIAH'S SON Jehoahaz was selected as the new king. 2He was twenty-three years old when he began to reign, but lasted only three months. 3Then he was deposed by the king of Egypt, who demanded an annual tribute from Judah of $230,000.

4The king of Egypt now appointed Eliakim, the brother of Jehoahaz, as the new king of Judah. (Eliakim's name was changed to Jehoiakim.) Jehoahaz was taken to Egypt as a prisoner. 5Jehoiakim was twenty-five years old when he became king, and he reigned eleven years, in Jerusalem; but his reign was an evil one. 6Finally Nebuchadnezzar king of Babylon conquered Jerusalem, and took away the king in chains to Babylon.

New Revised Standard

16 So all the service of the LORD was prepared that day, to keep the passover and to offer burnt offerings on the altar of the LORD, according to the command of King Josiah. 17The people of Israel who were present kept the passover at that time, and the festival of unleavened bread seven days. 18No passover like it had been kept in Israel since the days of the prophet Samuel; none of the kings of Israel had kept such a passover as was kept by Josiah, by the priests and the Levites, by all Judah and Israel who were present, and by the inhabitants of Jerusalem. 19In the eighteenth year of the reign of Josiah this passover was kept.

Defeat by Pharaoh Neco and Death of Josiah

20 After all this, when Josiah had set the temple in order, King Neco of Egypt went up to fight at Carchemish on the Euphrates, and Josiah went out against him. 21But Necod sent envoys to him, saying, "What have I to do with you, king of Judah? I am not coming against you today, but against the house with which I am at war; and God has commanded me to hurry. Cease opposing God, who is with me, so that he will not destroy you." 22But Josiah would not turn away from him, but disguised himself in order to fight with him. He did not listen to the words of Neco from the mouth of God, but joined battle in the plain of Megiddo. 23The archers shot King Josiah; and the king said to his servants, "Take me away, for I am badly wounded." 24So his servants took him out of the chariot and carried him in his second chariote and brought him to Jerusalem. There he died, and was buried in the tombs of his ancestors. All Judah and Jerusalem mourned for Josiah. 25Jeremiah also uttered a lament for Josiah, and all the singing men and singing women have spoken of Josiah in their laments to this day. They made these a custom in Israel; they are recorded in the Laments. 26Now the rest of the acts of Josiah and his faithful deeds in accordance with what is written in the law of the LORD, 27and his acts, first and last, are written in the Book of the Kings of Israel and Judah.

Reign of Jehoahaz

36 THE PEOPLE of the land took Jehoahaz son of Josiah and made him king to succeed his father in Jerusalem. 2Jehoahaz was twenty-three years old when he began to reign; he reigned three months in Jerusalem. 3Then the king of Egypt deposed him in Jerusalem and laid on the land a tribute of one hundred talents of silver and one talent of gold. 4The king of Egypt made his brother Eliakim king over Judah and Jerusalem, and changed his name to Jehoiakim; but Neco took his brother Jehoahaz and carried him to Egypt.

Reign and Captivity of Jehoiakim

5 Jehoiakim was twenty-five years old when he began to reign; he reigned eleven years in Jerusalem. He did what was evil in the sight of the LORD his God. 6Against him King Nebuchadnezzar of Babylon came up, and bound him with fetters to take him to Babylon.

---

d Heb *he*   e Or *the chariot of his deputy*

King James

7Nebuchadnezzar also carried of the vessels of the house of the LORD to Babylon, and put them in his temple at Babylon.

8Now the rest of the acts of Jehoiakim, and his abominations which he did, and that which was found in him, behold, they *are* written in the book of the kings of Israel and Judah: and Jehoiachin his son reigned in his stead.

9¶ Jehoiachin *was* eight years old when he began to reign, and he reigned three months and ten days in Jerusalem: and he did *that which was* evil in the sight of the LORD.

10And when the year was expired, king Nebuchadnezzar sent, and brought him to Babylon, with the goodly vessels of the house of the LORD, and made Zedekiah his brother king over Judah and Jerusalem.

11¶ Zedekiah *was* one and twenty years old when he began to reign, and reigned eleven years in Jerusalem.

12And he did *that which was* evil in the sight of the LORD his God, *and* humbled not himself before Jeremiah the prophet *speaking* from the mouth of the LORD.

13And he also rebelled against king Nebuchadnezzar, who had made him swear by God: but he stiffened his neck, and hardened his heart from turning unto the LORD God of Israel.

14¶ Moreover all the chief of the priests, and the people, transgressed very much after all the abominations of the heathen; and polluted the house of the LORD which he had hallowed in Jerusalem.

15And the LORD God of their fathers sent to them by his messengers, rising up betimes, and sending; because he had compassion on his people, and on his dwelling place:

16But they mocked the messengers of God, and despised his words, and misused his prophets, until the wrath of the LORD arose against his people, till *there was* no remedy.

17Therefore he brought upon them the king of the Chaldees, who slew their young men with the sword in the house of their sanctuary, and had no compassion upon young man or maiden, old man, or him that stooped for age: he gave *them* all into his hand.

18And all the vessels of the house of God, great and small, and the treasures of the house of the LORD, and the treasures of the king, and of his princes; all *these* he brought to Babylon.

19And they burnt the house of God, and brake down the wall of Jerusalem, and burnt all the palaces thereof with fire, and destroyed all the goodly vessels thereof.

20And them that had escaped from the sword carried he away to Babylon; where they were servants to him and his sons until the reign of the kingdom of Persia:

21To fulfil the word of the LORD by the mouth of Jeremiah, until the land had enjoyed her sabbaths: *for* as long as she lay desolate she kept sabbath, to fulfil threescore and ten years.

22¶ Now in the first year of Cyrus king of Persia, that the word of the LORD *spoken* by the mouth of Jeremiah might be accomplished, the LORD stirred up the spirit of Cyrus king of Persia, that he made a proclamation throughout all his kingdom, and *put it* also in writing, saying,

23Thus saith Cyrus king of Persia, All the kingdoms of the earth hath the LORD God of heaven given me; and he hath charged me to build him an house in Jerusalem, which *is* in Judah. Who *is there* among you of all his people? The LORD his God *be* with him, and let him go up.

New International

zar also took to Babylon articles from the temple of the LORD and put them in his temple[a] there.

8The other events of Jehoiakim's reign, the detestable things he did and all that was found against him, are written in the book of the kings of Israel and Judah. And Jehoiachin his son succeeded him as king.

Jehoiachin King of Judah

9Jehoiachin was eighteen[b] years old when he became king, and he reigned in Jerusalem three months and ten days. He did evil in the eyes of the LORD. 10In the spring, King Nebuchadnezzar sent for him and brought him to Babylon, together with articles of value from the temple of the LORD, and he made Jehoiachin's uncle,[c] Zedekiah, king over Judah and Jerusalem.

Zedekiah King of Judah

11Zedekiah was twenty-one years old when he became king, and he reigned in Jerusalem eleven years. 12He did evil in the eyes of the LORD his God and did not humble himself before Jeremiah the prophet, who spoke the word of the LORD. 13He also rebelled against King Nebuchadnezzar, who had made him take an oath in God's name. He became stiff-necked and hardened his heart and would not turn to the LORD, the God of Israel. 14Furthermore, all the leaders of the priests and the people became more and more unfaithful, following all the detestable practices of the nations and defiling the temple of the LORD, which he had consecrated in Jerusalem.

The Fall of Jerusalem

15The LORD, the God of their fathers, sent word to them through his messengers again and again, because he had pity on his people and on his dwelling place. 16But they mocked God's messengers, despised his words and scoffed at his prophets until the wrath of the LORD was aroused against his people and there was no remedy. 17He brought up against them the king of the Babylonians,[d] who killed their young men with the sword in the sanctuary, and spared neither young man nor young woman, old man or aged. God handed all of them over to Nebuchadnezzar. 18He carried to Babylon all the articles from the temple of God, both large and small, and the treasures of the LORD's temple and the treasures of the king and his officials. 19They set fire to God's temple and broke down the wall of Jerusalem; they burned all the palaces and destroyed everything of value there.

20He carried into exile to Babylon the remnant, who escaped from the sword, and they became servants to him and his sons until the kingdom of Persia came to power. 21The land enjoyed its sabbath rests; all the time of its desolation it rested, until the seventy years were completed in fulfillment of the word of the LORD spoken by Jeremiah.

22In the first year of Cyrus king of Persia, in order to fulfill the word of the LORD spoken by Jeremiah, the LORD moved the heart of Cyrus king of Persia to make a proclamation throughout his realm and to put it in writing:

23"This is what Cyrus king of Persia says:

" 'The LORD, the God of heaven, has given me all the kingdoms of the earth and he has appointed me to build a temple for him at Jerusalem in Judah. Anyone of his people among you—may the LORD his God be with him, and let him go up.' "

---

a 7 Or *palace*　　b 9 One Hebrew manuscript, some Septuagint manuscripts and Syriac (see also 2 Kings 24:8); most Hebrew manuscripts *eight*　　c 10 Hebrew *brother*, that is, relative (see 2 Kings 24:17)　　d 17 Or *Chaldeans*

Living Bible

7Nebuchadnezzar also took some of the gold bowls and other items from the Temple, placing them in his own temple in Babylon. 8The rest of the deeds of Jehoiakim, and all the evil he did, are written in *The Annals of the Kings of Judah;* and his son Jehoiachin became the new king.

9Jehoiachin was eighteenᵉ years old when he ascended the throne. But he lasted only three months and ten days, and it was an evil reign as far as the Lord was concerned. 10The following spring he was summoned to Babylon by King Nebuchadnezzar. Many treasures from the Temple were taken away to Babylon at that time, and King Nebuchadnezzar appointed Jehoiachin's brother Zedekiah as the new king of Judah and Jerusalem.

11Zedekiah was twenty-one years old when he became king and he reigned eleven years, in Jerusalem. 12His reign, too, was evil so far as the Lord was concerned, for he refused to take the counsel of Jeremiah the prophet, who gave him messages from the Lord. 13He rebelled against King Nebuchadnezzar, even though he had taken an oath of loyalty. Zedekiah was a hard and stubborn man so far as obeying the Lord God of Israel was concerned, for he refused to follow him.

14All the important people of the nation, including the High Priests, worshiped the heathen idols of the surrounding nations, thus polluting the Temple of the Lord in Jerusalem. 15Jehovah the God of their fathers sent his prophets again and again to warn them, for he had compassion on his people and on his Temple. 16But the people mocked these messengers of God and despised their words, scoffing at the prophets until the anger of the Lord could no longer be restrained, and there was no longer any remedy.

17Then the Lord brought the king of Babylon against them and killed their young men, even going after them right into the Temple, and had no pity upon them, killing even young girls and old men. The Lord used the king of Babylon to destroy them completely. 18He also took home with him all the items, great and small, used in the Temple, and treasures from both the Temple and the palace, and took with him all the royal princes. 19Then his army burned the Temple and broke down the walls of Jerusalem and burned all the palaces and destroyed all the valuable Temple utensils. 20Those who survived were taken away to Babylon as slaves to the king and his sons until the kingdom of Persia conquered Babylon.

21Thus the word of the Lord spoken through Jeremiah came true, that the land must rest for seventy years to make up for the years when the people refused to observe the Sabbath.

22,23But in the first year of King Cyrus of Persia, the Lord stirred up the spirit of Cyrus to make this proclamation throughout his kingdom, putting it into writing:

"All the kingdoms of the earth have been given to me by the Lord God of heaven, and he has instructed me to build him a Temple in Jerusalem, in the land of Judah. All among you who are the Lord's people, return to Israel for this task, and the Lord be with you."

This also fulfilled the prediction of Jeremiah the prophet.

New Revised Standard

7Nebuchadnezzar also carried some of the vessels of the house of the LORD to Babylon and put them in his palace in Babylon. 8Now the rest of the acts of Jehoiakim, and the abominations that he did, and what was found against him, are written in the Book of the Kings of Israel and Judah; and his son Jehoiachin succeeded him.

Reign and Captivity of Jehoiachin

9 Jehoiachin was eight years old when he began to reign; he reigned three months and ten days in Jerusalem. He did what was evil in the sight of the LORD. 10In the spring of the year King Nebuchadnezzar sent and brought him to Babylon, along with the precious vessels of the house of the LORD, and made his brother Zedekiah king over Judah and Jerusalem.

Reign of Zedekiah

11 Zedekiah was twenty-one years old when he began to reign; he reigned eleven years in Jerusalem. 12He did what was evil in the sight of the LORD his God. He did not humble himself before the prophet Jeremiah who spoke from the mouth of the LORD. 13He also rebelled against King Nebuchadnezzar, who had made him swear by God; he stiffened his neck and hardened his heart against turning to the LORD, the God of Israel. 14All the leading priests and the people also were exceedingly unfaithful, following all the abominations of the nations; and they polluted the house of the LORD that he had consecrated in Jerusalem.

The Fall of Jerusalem

15 The LORD, the God of their ancestors, sent persistently to them by his messengers, because he had compassion on his people and on his dwelling place; 16but they kept mocking the messengers of God, despising his words, and scoffing at his prophets, until the wrath of the LORD against his people became so great that there was no remedy.

17 Therefore he brought up against them the king of the Chaldeans, who killed their youths with the sword in the house of their sanctuary, and had no compassion on young man or young woman, the aged or the feeble; he gave them all into his hand. 18All the vessels of the house of God, large and small, and the treasures of the house of the LORD, and the treasures of the king and of his officials, all these he brought to Babylon. 19They burned the house of God, broke down the wall of Jerusalem, burned all its palaces with fire, and destroyed all its precious vessels. 20He took into exile in Babylon those who had escaped from the sword, and they became servants to him and to his sons until the establishment of the kingdom of Persia, 21to fulfill the word of the LORD by the mouth of Jeremiah, until the land had made up for its sabbaths. All the days that it lay desolate it kept sabbath, to fulfill seventy years.

Cyrus Proclaims Liberty for the Exiles

22 In the first year of King Cyrus of Persia, in fulfillment of the word of the LORD spoken by Jeremiah, the LORD stirred up the spirit of King Cyrus of Persia so that he sent a herald throughout all his kingdom and also declared in a written edict: 23"Thus says King Cyrus of Persia: The LORD, the God of heaven, has given me all the kingdoms of the earth, and he has charged me to build him a house at Jerusalem, which is in Judah. Whoever is among you of all his people, may the LORD his God be with him! Let him go up."

ᵉ *36:9 eighteen.* Some manuscripts read "eight years old."

Ezra

Ezra

Cyrus Helps the Exiles to Return

1 NOW IN the first year of Cyrus king of Persia, that the word of the LORD by the mouth of Jeremiah might be fulfilled, the LORD stirred up the spirit of Cyrus king of Persia, that he made a proclamation throughout all his kingdom, and *put it* also in writing, saying,

2Thus saith Cyrus king of Persia, The LORD God of heaven hath given me all the kingdoms of the earth; and he hath charged me to build him an house at Jerusalem, which *is* in Judah.

3Who *is there* among you of all his people? his God be with him, and let him go up to Jerusalem, which *is* in Judah, and build the house of the LORD God of Israel, (he *is* the God,) which *is* in Jerusalem.

4And whosoever remaineth in any place where he sojourneth, let the men of his place help him with silver, and with gold, and with goods, and with beasts, beside the freewill offering for the house of God that *is* in Jerusalem.

5¶ Then rose up the chief of the fathers of Judah and Benjamin, and the priests, and the Levites, with all *them* whose spirit God had raised, to go up to build the house of the LORD which *is* in Jerusalem.

6And all they that *were* about them strengthened their hands with vessels of silver, with gold, with goods, and with beasts, and with precious things, beside all *that* was willingly offered.

7¶ Also Cyrus the king brought forth the vessels of the house of the LORD, which Nebuchadnezzar had brought forth out of Jerusalem, and had put them in the house of his gods;

8Even those did Cyrus king of Persia bring forth by the hand of Mithredath the treasurer, and numbered them unto Sheshbazzar, the prince of Judah.

9And this *is* the number of them: thirty chargers of gold, a thousand chargers of silver, nine and twenty knives,

10Thirty basins of gold, silver basins of a second *sort* four hundred and ten, *and* other vessels a thousand.

11All the vessels of gold and of silver *were* five thousand and four hundred. All *these* did Sheshbazzar bring up with *them of* the captivity that were brought up from Babylon unto Jerusalem.

2 NOW THESE *are* the children of the province that went up out of the captivity, of those which had been carried away, whom Nebuchadnezzar the king of Babylon had carried away unto Babylon, and came again unto Jerusalem and Judah, every one unto his city;

1 IN THE first year of Cyrus king of Persia, in order to fulfill the word of the LORD spoken by Jeremiah, the LORD moved the heart of Cyrus king of Persia to make a proclamation throughout his realm and to put it in writing:

2"This is what Cyrus king of Persia says:

" 'The LORD, the God of heaven, has given me all the kingdoms of the earth and he has appointed me to build a temple for him at Jerusalem in Judah. 3Anyone of his people among you—may his God be with him, and let him go up to Jerusalem in Judah and build the temple of the LORD, the God of Israel, the God who is in Jerusalem. 4And the people of any place where survivors may now be living are to provide him with silver and gold, with goods and livestock, and with freewill offerings for the temple of God in Jerusalem.' "

5Then the family heads of Judah and Benjamin, and the priests and Levites—everyone whose heart God had moved—prepared to go up and build the house of the LORD in Jerusalem. 6All their neighbors assisted them with articles of silver and gold, with goods and livestock, and with valuable gifts, in addition to all the freewill offerings. 7Moreover, King Cyrus brought out the articles belonging to the temple of the LORD, which Nebuchadnezzar had carried away from Jerusalem and had placed in the temple of his god.a 8Cyrus king of Persia had them brought by Mithredath the treasurer, who counted them out to Sheshbazzar the prince of Judah.

9This was the inventory:

gold dishes	30
silver dishes	1,000
silver pansb	29
10gold bowls	30
matching silver bowls	410
other articles	1,000

11In all, there were 5,400 articles of gold and of silver. Sheshbazzar brought all these along when the exiles came up from Babylon to Jerusalem.

The List of the Exiles Who Returned

2 NOW THESE are the people of the province who came up from the captivity of the exiles, whom Nebuchadnezzar king of Babylon had taken captive to Babylon (they returned to Jerusalem and Judah, each to his own town, 2in company with Zerubbabel, Jeshua,

Ezra   Ezra

Living Bible

1 DURING THE first year of the reign of King Cyrus of Persia, the Lord fulfilled Jeremiah's prophecy[c] by giving King Cyrus the desire to send this proclamation throughout his empire (he also put it into the permanent records of the realm):

2"Cyrus, king of Persia, hereby announces that Jehovah, the God of heaven who gave me my vast empire, has now given me the responsibility of building him a Temple in Jerusalem, in the land of Judah. 3All Jews throughout the kingdom may now return to Jerusalem to rebuild this Temple of Jehovah, who is the God of Israel and of Jerusalem. May his blessings rest upon you. 4Those Jews[d] who do not go should contribute toward the expenses of those who do, and also supply them with clothing, transportation, supplies for the journey, and a freewill offering for the Temple."

5Then God gave a great desire to the leaders of the tribes of Judah and Benjamin, and to the priests and Levites, to return to Jerusalem at once to rebuild the Temple. 6And all the Jewish exiles who chose to remain in Persia gave them whatever assistance they could, as well as gifts for the Temple.

7King Cyrus himself donated the gold bowls and other valuable items which King Nebuchadnezzar had taken from the Temple at Jerusalem and had placed in the temple of his own gods. 8He instructed Mithredath, the treasurer of Persia, to present these gifts to Shesh-bazzar, the leader of the exiles returning to Judah.

9, 10The items Cyrus donated included:
1,000 gold trays,
1,000 silver trays,
29 censers,
30 bowls of solid gold,
2,410 silver bowls (of various designs),
1,000 miscellaneous items.

11In all there were 5,469 gold and silver items turned over to Shesh-bazzar to take back to Jerusalem.

2 HERE IS the list of the Jewish exiles who now returned to Jerusalem and to the other cities of Judah, from which their parents[e] had been deported to Babylon by King Nebuchadnezzar.

New Revised Standard

End of the Babylonian Captivity

1 IN THE first year of King Cyrus of Persia, in order that the word of the LORD by the mouth of Jeremiah might be accomplished, the LORD stirred up the spirit of King Cyrus of Persia so that he sent a herald throughout all his kingdom, and also in a written edict declared:

2 "Thus says King Cyrus of Persia: The LORD, the God of heaven, has given me all the kingdoms of the earth, and he has charged me to build him a house at Jerusalem in Judah. 3Any of those among you who are of his people—may their God be with them!—are now permitted to go up to Jerusalem in Judah, and rebuild the house of the LORD, the God of Israel—he is the God who is in Jerusalem; 4and let all survivors, in whatever place they reside, be assisted by the people of their place with silver and gold, with goods and with animals, besides freewill offerings for the house of God in Jerusalem."

5 The heads of the families of Judah and Benjamin, and the priests and the Levites—everyone whose spirit God had stirred—got ready to go up and rebuild the house of the LORD in Jerusalem. 6All their neighbors aided them with silver vessels, with gold, with goods, with animals, and with valuable gifts, besides all that was freely offered. 7King Cyrus himself brought out the vessels of the house of the LORD that Nebuchadnezzar had carried away from Jerusalem and placed in the house of his gods. 8King Cyrus of Persia had them released into the charge of Mithredath the treasurer, who counted them out to Sheshbazzar the prince of Judah. 9And this was the inventory: gold basins, thirty; silver basins, one thousand; knives,[f] twenty-nine; 10gold bowls, thirty; other silver bowls, four hundred ten; other vessels, one thousand; 11the total of the gold and silver vessels was five thousand four hundred. All these Sheshbazzar brought up, when the exiles were brought up from Babylonia to Jerusalem.

List of the Returned Exiles

2 NOW THESE were the people of the province who came from those captive exiles whom King Nebuchadnezzar of Babylon had carried captive to Babylonia; they returned to Jerusalem and Judah, all to their own towns. 2They came with Zerubbabel, Jeshua, Nehemi-

---

c 1:1 the Lord fulfilled Jeremiah's prophecy (see Jer 25:12; 29:10), i.e., the prediction that the Jews would remain in captivity in Babylon for seventy years. d 1:4 Those Jews, implied. Also in vs 6. e 2:1 their parents, implied.

f Vg: Meaning of Heb uncertain

King James

²Which came with Zerubbabel: Jeshua, Nehemiah, Seraiah, Reelaiah, Mordecai, Bilshan, Mizpar, Bigvai, Rehum, Baanah. The number of the men of the people of Israel:

³The children of Parosh, two thousand an hundred seventy and two.

⁴The children of Shephatiah, three hundred seventy and two.

⁵The children of Arah, seven hundred seventy and five.

⁶The children of Pahath-moab, of the children of Jeshua *and* Joab, two thousand eight hundred and twelve.

⁷The children of Elam, a thousand two hundred fifty and four.

⁸The children of Zattu, nine hundred forty and five.

⁹The children of Zaccai, seven hundred and three-score.

¹⁰The children of Bani, six hundred forty and two.

¹¹The children of Bebai, six hundred twenty and three.

¹²The children of Azgad, a thousand two hundred twenty and two.

¹³The children of Adonikam, six hundred sixty and six.

¹⁴The children of Bigvai, two thousand fifty and six.

¹⁵The children of Adin, four hundred fifty and four.

¹⁶The children of Ater of Hezekiah, ninety and eight.

¹⁷The children of Bezai, three hundred twenty and three.

¹⁸The children of Jorah, an hundred and twelve.

¹⁹The children of Hashum, two hundred twenty and three.

²⁰The children of Gibbar, ninety and five.

²¹The children of Bethlehem, an hundred twenty and three.

²²The men of Netophah, fifty and six.

²³The men of Anathoth, an hundred twenty and eight.

²⁴The children of Azmaveth, forty and two.

²⁵The children of Kirjath-arim, Chephirah, and Beeroth, seven hundred and forty and three.

²⁶The children of Ramah and Gaba, six hundred twenty and one.

²⁷The men of Michmas, an hundred twenty and two.

²⁸The men of Beth-el and Ai, two hundred twenty and three.

²⁹The children of Nebo, fifty and two.

³⁰The children of Magbish, an hundred fifty and six.

³¹The children of the other Elam, a thousand two hundred fifty and four.

³²The children of Harim, three hundred and twenty.

³³The children of Lod, Hadid, and Ono, seven hundred twenty and five.

³⁴The children of Jericho, three hundred forty and five.

³⁵The children of Senaah, three thousand and six hundred and thirty.

³⁶¶ The priests: the children of Jedaiah, of the house of Jeshua, nine hundred seventy and three.

³⁷The children of Immer, a thousand fifty and two.

³⁸The children of Pashur, a thousand two hundred forty and seven.

³⁹The children of Harim, a thousand and seventeen.

⁴⁰¶ The Levites: the children of Jeshua and Kadmiel, of the children of Hodaviah, seventy and four.

⁴¹¶ The singers: the children of Asaph, an hundred twenty and eight.

⁴²¶ The children of the porters: the children of Shallum, the children of Ater, the children of Talmon, the children of Akkub, the children of Hatita, the children of Shobai, *in* all an hundred thirty and nine.

New International

Nehemiah, Seraiah, Reelaiah, Mordecai, Bilshan, Mispar, Bigvai, Rehum and Baanah):

The list of the men of the people of Israel:

³the descendants of Parosh	2,172
⁴of Shephatiah	372
⁵of Arah	775
⁶of Pahath-Moab (through the line of Jeshua and Joab)	2,812
⁷of Elam	1,254
⁸of Zattu	945
⁹of Zaccai	760
¹⁰of Bani	642
¹¹of Bebai	623
¹²of Azgad	1,222
¹³of Adonikam	666
¹⁴of Bigvai	2,056
¹⁵of Adin	454
¹⁶of Ater (through Hezekiah)	98
¹⁷of Bezai	323
¹⁸of Jorah	112
¹⁹of Hashum	223
²⁰of Gibbar	95
²¹the men of Bethlehem	123
²²of Netophah	56
²³of Anathoth	128
²⁴of Azmaveth	42
²⁵of Kiriath Jearim,ᵃ Kephirah and Beeroth	743
²⁶of Ramah and Geba	621
²⁷of Micmash	122
²⁸of Bethel and Ai	223
²⁹of Nebo	52
³⁰of Magbish	156
³¹of the other Elam	1,254
³²of Harim	320
³³of Lod, Hadid and Ono	725
³⁴of Jericho	345
³⁵of Senaah	3,630

³⁶The priests:

the descendants of Jedaiah (through the family of Jeshua)	973
³⁷of Immer	1,052
³⁸of Pashhur	1,247
³⁹of Harim	1,017

⁴⁰The Levites:

the descendants of Jeshua and Kadmiel (through the line of Hodaviah)	74

⁴¹The singers:

the descendants of Asaph	128

⁴²The gatekeepers of the temple:

the descendants of Shallum, Ater, Talmon, Akkub, Hatita and Shobai	139

ᵃ *25* See Septuagint (see also Neh. 7:29); Hebrew *Kiriath Arim.*

Living Bible

2The leaders were:
Zerubbabel, Jeshua, Nehemiah, Seraiah, Re-el-aiah, Mordecai, Bilshan, Mispar, Bigvai, Rehum, Baanah.
Here is a census of those who returned (listed by subclans):
3-35From the subclan of Parosh, 2,172;
From the subclan of Shephatiah, 372;
From the subclan of Arah, 775;
From the subclan of Pahath-moab (the descendants of Jeshua and Joab), 2,812;
From the subclan of Elam, 1,254;
From the subclan of Zattu, 945;
From the subclan of Zaccai, 760;
From the subclan of Bani, 642;
From the subclan of Bebai, 623;
From the subclan of Azgad, 1,222;
From the subclan of Adonikam, 666;
From the subclan of Bigvai, 2,056;
From the subclan of Adin, 454;
From the subclan of Ater (the descendants of Hezekiah), 98;
From the subclan of Bezai, 323;
From the subclan of Jorah, 112;
From the subclan of Hashum, 223;
From the subclan of Gibbar, 95;
From the subclan of Bethlehem, 123;
From the subclan of Netophah, 56;
From the subclan of Anathoth, 128;
From the subclan of Azmaveth, 42;
From the subclans of Kiriatharim, Chephirah, and Be-eroth, 743;
From the subclans of Ramah and Geba, 621;
From the subclans of Michmas, 122;
From the subclans of Bethel and Ai, 223;
From the subclan of Nebo, 52;
From the subclan of Magbish, 156;
From the subclan of Elam, 1,254;
From the subclan of Harim, 320;
From the subclans of Lod, Hadid, and Ono, 725;
From the subclan of Jericho, 345;
From the subclan of Senaah, 3,630.
36-39Here are the statistics concerning the returning priests:
From the families of Jedaiah of the subclan of Jeshua, 973;
From the subclan of Immer, 1,052;
From the subclan of Pashhur, 1,247;
From the subclan of Harim, 1,017.
40, 41, 42Here are the statistics concerning the Levites who returned:
From the families of Jeshua and Kedmi-el of the subclan of Hodaviah, 74;
The choir members from the clan of Asaph, 128;
From the descendants of the gatekeepers (the families of Shallum, Ater, Talmon, Akkub, Hatita, and Shobai), 139.

New Revised Standard

ah, Seraiah, Reelaiah, Mordecai, Bilshan, Mispar, Bigvai, Rehum, and Baanah.
The number of the Israelite people: 3the descendants of Parosh, two thousand one hundred seventy-two. 4Of Shephatiah, three hundred seventy-two. 5Of Arah, seven hundred seventy-five. 6Of Pahath-moab, namely the descendants of Jeshua and Joab, two thousand eight hundred twelve. 7Of Elam, one thousand two hundred fifty-four. 8Of Zattu, nine hundred forty-five. 9Of Zaccai, seven hundred sixty. 10Of Bani, six hundred forty-two. 11Of Bebai, six hundred twenty-three. 12Of Azgad, one thousand two hundred twenty-two. 13Of Adonikam, six hundred sixty-six. 14Of Bigvai, two thousand fifty-six. 15Of Adin, four hundred fifty-four. 16Of Ater, namely of Hezekiah, ninety-eight. 17Of Bezai, three hundred twenty-three. 18Of Jorah, one hundred twelve. 19Of Hashum, two hundred twenty-three. 20Of Gibbar, ninety-five. 21Of Bethlehem, one hundred twenty-three. 22The people of Netophah, fifty-six. 23Of Anathoth, one hundred twenty-eight. 24The descendants of Azmaveth, forty-two. 25Of Kiriatharim, Chephirah, and Beeroth, seven hundred forty-three. 26Of Ramah and Geba, six hundred twenty-one. 27The people of Michmas, one hundred twenty-two. 28Of Bethel and Ai, two hundred twenty-three. 29The descendants of Nebo, fifty-two. 30Of Magbish, one hundred fifty-six. 31Of the other Elam, one thousand two hundred fifty-four. 32Of Harim, three hundred twenty. 33Of Lod, Hadid, and Ono, seven hundred twenty-five. 34Of Jericho, three hundred forty-five. 35Of Senaah, three thousand six hundred thirty.
36. The priests: the descendants of Jedaiah, of the house of Jeshua, nine hundred seventy-three. 37Of Immer, one thousand fifty-two. 38Of Pashhur, one thousand two hundred forty-seven. 39Of Harim, one thousand seventeen.
40. The Levites: the descendants of Jeshua and Kadmiel, of the descendants of Hodaviah, seventy-four. 41The singers: the descendants of Asaph, one hundred twenty-eight. 42The descendants of the gatekeepers: of Shallum, of Ater, of Talmon, of Akkub, of Hatita, and of Shobai, in all one hundred thirty-nine.

King James

43¶ The Nethinims: the children of Ziha, the children of Hasupha, the children of Tabbaoth,

44The children of Keros, the children of Siaha, the children of Padon,

45The children of Lebanah, the children of Hagabah, the children of Akkub,

46The children of Hagab, the children of Shalmai, the children of Hanan,

47The children of Giddel, the children of Gahar, the children of Reaiah,

48The children of Rezin, the children of Nekoda, the children of Gazzam,

49The children of Uzza, the children of Paseah, the children of Besai,

50the children of Asnah, the children of Mehunim, the children of Nephusim,

51The children of Bakbuk, the children of Hakupha, the children of Harhur,

52The children of Bazluth, the children of Mehida, the children of Harsha,

53The children of Barkos, the children of Sisera, the children of Thamah,

54The children of Neziah, the children of Hatipha.

55¶ The children of Solomon's servants: the children of Sotai, the children of Sophereth, the children of Peruda,

56The children of Jaalah, the children of Darkon, the children of Giddel,

57The children of Shephatiah, the children of Hattil, the children of Pochereth of Zebaim, the children of Ami.

58All the Nethinims, and the children of Solomon's servants, *were* three hundred ninety and two.

59And these *were* they which went up from Tel-melah, Tel-harsa, Cherub, Addan, *and* Immer: but they could not show their father's house, and their seed, whether they *were* of Israel:

60The children of Delaiah, the children of Tobiah, the children of Nekoda, six hundred fifty and two.

61¶ And of the children of the priests: the children of Habaiah, the children of Koz, the children of Barzillai; which took a wife of the daughters of Barzillai the Gileadite, and was called after their name:

62These sought their register *among* those that were reckoned by genealogy, but they were not found: therefore were they, as polluted, put from the priesthood.

63And the Tirshatha said unto them, that they should not eat of the most holy things, till there stood up a priest with Urim and with Thummim.

64¶ The whole congregation together *was* forty and two thousand three hundred *and* threescore,

65Beside their servants and their maids, of whom *there were* seven thousand three hundred thirty and seven: and *there were* among them two hundred singing men and singing women.

66Their horses *were* seven hundred thirty and six; their mules, two hundred forty and five;

67Their camels, four hundred thirty and five; *their* asses, six thousand seven hundred and twenty.

68¶ And *some* of the chief of the fathers, when they came to the house of the LORD which *is* at Jerusalem, offered freely for the house of God to set it up in his place:

69They gave after their ability unto the treasure of the work threescore and one thousand drams of gold, and five thousand pound of silver, and one hundred priests' garments.

70So the priests, and the Levites, and *some* of the people, and the singers, and the porters, and the Nethinims, dwelt in their cities, and all Israel in their cities.

New International

43The temple servants:

the descendants of
Ziha, Hasupha, Tabbaoth,
44Keros, Siaha, Padon,
45Lebanah, Hagabah, Akkub,
46Hagab, Shalmai, Hanan,
47Giddel, Gahar, Reaiah,
48Rezin, Nekoda, Gazzam,
49Uzza, Paseah, Besai,
50Asnah, Meunim, Nephussim,
51Bakbuk, Hakupha, Harhur,
52Bazluth, Mehida, Harsha,
53Barkos, Sisera, Temah,
54Neziah and Hatipha

55The descendants of the servants of Solomon:

the descendants of
Sotai, Hassophereth, Peruda,
56Jaala, Darkon, Giddel,
57Shephatiah, Hattil,
Pokereth-Hazzebaim and Ami

58The temple servants and the descendants of the servants of Solomon   392

59The following came up from the towns of Tel Melah, Tel Harsha, Kerub, Addon and Immer, but they could not show that their families were descended from Israel:

60The descendants of
Delaiah, Tobiah and Nekoda   652

61And from among the priests:

The descendants of
Hobaiah, Hakkoz and Barzillai (a man who had married a daughter of Barzillai the Gileadite and was called by that name).

62These searched for their family records, but they could not find them and so were excluded from the priesthood as unclean. 63The governor ordered them not to eat any of the most sacred food until there was a priest ministering with the Urim and Thummim.

64The whole company numbered 42,360, 65besides their 7,337 menservants and maidservants; and they also had 200 men and women singers. 66They had 736 horses, 245 mules, 67435 camels and 6,720 donkeys.

68When they arrived at the house of the LORD in Jerusalem, some of the heads of the families gave freewill offerings toward the rebuilding of the house of God on its site. 69According to their ability they gave to the treasury for this work 61,000 drachmasa of gold, 5,000 minasb of silver and 100 priestly garments. 70The priests, the Levites, the singers, the gatekeepers and the temple servants settled in their own towns, along with some of the other people, and the rest of the Israelites settled in their towns.

---

a 69 That is, about 1,100 pounds (about 500 kilograms)   b 69 That is, about 3 tons (about 2.9 metric tons)

Living Bible

43-54The following families of the Temple assistants were represented:

Ziha, Hasupha, Tabbaoth, Keros, Siaha, Padon, Lebanah, Hagabah, Akkub, Hagab, Shamlai, Hanan, Giddel, Gahar, Re-aiah, Rezin, Nekoda, Gazzam, Uzza, Paseah, Besai, Asnah, Me-unim, Nephisim, Bakbuk, Hakupha, Harhur, Bazluth, Mehida, Harsha, Barkos, Sisera, Temah, Neziah, Hatipha.

55, 56, 57Those who made the trip also included the descendants of King Solomon's officials:

Sotai, Hassophereth, Peruda, Jaalah, Darkon, Giddel, Shephatiah, Hattil, Pochereth-hazzebaim, Ami.

58The Temple assistants and the descendants of Solomon's officers numbered 392.

59Another group returned to Jerusalem at this time from the Persian cities of Telmelah, Tel-harsha, Cherub, Addan, and Immer. However, they had lost their genealogies and could not prove that they were really Israelites. 60This group included the subclans of Delaiah, Tobiah, and Nekoda—a total of 652.

61Three subclans of priests—Habaiah, Hakkoz, and Barzillai (he married one of the daughters of Barzillai the Gileadite and took her family name)—also returned to Jerusalem. 62, 63But they too had lost their genealogies, so the leaders refused to allow them to continue as priests; they would not even allow them to eat the priests' share of food from the sacrifices until the Urim and Thummim could be consulted, to find out from God whether they actually were descendants of priests or not.

64, 65So a total of 42,360 persons returned to Judah; in addition to 7,337 slaves and 200 choir members, both men and women. 66, 67They took with them 736 horses, 245 mules, 435 camels, and 6,720 donkeys.

68Some of the leaders were able to give generously toward the rebuilding of the Temple, 69and each gave as much as he could. The total value of their gifts amounted to $300,000 of gold, $170,000 of silver, and 100 robes for the priests.

70So the priests and Levites and some of the common people settled in Jerusalem and its nearby villages; and the singers, the gatekeepers, the Temple workers, and the rest of the people returned to the other cities of Judah from which they had come.

New Revised Standard

43 The temple servants: the descendants of Ziha, Hasupha, Tabbaoth, 44Keros, Siaha, Padon, 45Lebanah, Hagabah, Akkub, 46Hagab, Shamlai, Hanan, 47Giddel, Gahar, Reaiah, 48Rezin, Nekoda, Gazzam, 49Uzza, Paseah, Besai, 50Asnah, Meunim, Nephisim, 51Bakbuk, Hakupha, Harhur, 52Bazluth, Mehida, Harsha, 53Barkos, Sisera, Temah, 54Neziah, and Hatipha.

55 The descendants of Solomon's servants: Sotai, Hassophereth, Peruda, 56Jaalah, Darkon, Giddel, 57Shephatiah, Hattil, Pochereth-hazzebaim, and Ami.

58 All the temple servants and the descendants of Solomon's servants were three hundred ninety-two.

59 The following were those who came up from Tel-melah, Tel-harsha, Cherub, Addan, and Immer, though they could not prove their families or their descent, whether they belonged to Israel: 60the descendants of Delaiah, Tobiah, and Nekoda, six hundred fifty-two. 61Also, of the descendants of the priests: the descendants of Habaiah, Hakkoz, and Barzillai (who had married one of the daughters of Barzillai the Gileadite, and was called by their name). 62These looked for their entries in the genealogical records, but they were not found there, and so they were excluded from the priesthood as unclean; 63the governor told them that they were not to partake of the most holy food, until there should be a priest to consult Urim and Thummim.

64 The whole assembly together was forty-two thousand three hundred sixty, 65besides their male and female servants, of whom there were seven thousand three hundred thirty-seven; and they had two hundred male and female singers. 66They had seven hundred thirty-six horses, two hundred forty-five mules, 67four hundred thirty-five camels, and six thousand seven hundred twenty donkeys.

68 As soon as they came to the house of the LORD in Jerusalem, some of the heads of families made freewill offerings for the house of God, to erect it on its site. 69According to their resources they gave to the building fund sixty-one thousand darics of gold, five thousand minas of silver, and one hundred priestly robes.

70 The priests, the Levites, and some of the people lived in Jerusalem and its vicinity;c and the singers, the gatekeepers, and the temple servants lived in their towns, and all Israel in their towns.

---

c 1 Esdras 5.46: Heb lacks *lived in Jerusalem and its vicinity*

King James

3 AND WHEN the seventh month was come, and the children of Israel *were* in the cities, the people gathered themselves together as one man to Jerusalem.

²Then stood up Jeshua the son of Jozadak, and his brethren the priests, and Zerubbabel the son of Shealtiel, and his brethren, and builded the altar of the God of Israel, to offer burnt offerings thereon, as *it is* written in the law of Moses the man of God.

³And they set the altar upon his bases; for fear *was* upon them because of the people of those countries: and they offered burnt offerings thereon unto the LORD, *even* burnt offerings morning and evening.

⁴They kept also the feast of tabernacles, as *it is* written, and *offered* the daily burnt offerings by number, according to the custom, as the duty of every day required;

⁵And afterward *offered* the continual burnt offering, both of the new moons, and of all the set feasts of the LORD that were consecrated, and of every one that willingly offered a freewill offering unto the LORD.

⁶From the first day of the seventh month began they to offer burnt offerings unto the LORD. But the foundation of the temple of the LORD was not *yet* laid.

⁷They gave money also unto the masons, and to the carpenters; and meat, and drink, and oil, unto them of Zidon, and to them of Tyre, to bring cedar trees from Lebanon to the sea of Joppa, according to the grant that they had of Cyrus king of Persia.

⁸¶ Now in the second year of their coming unto the house of God at Jerusalem, in the second month, began Zerubbabel the son of Shealtiel, and Jeshua the son of Jozadak, and the remnant of their brethren the priests and the Levites, and all they that were come out of the captivity unto Jerusalem; and appointed the Levites, from twenty years old and upward, to set forward the work of the house of the LORD.

⁹Then stood Jeshua *with* his sons and his brethren, Kadmiel and his sons, the sons of Judah, together, to set forward the workmen in the house of God: the sons of Henadad, *with* their sons and their brethren the Levites.

¹⁰And when the builders laid the foundation of the temple of the LORD, they set the priests in their apparel with trumpets, and the Levites the sons of Asaph with cymbals, to praise the LORD, after the ordinance of David king of Israel.

¹¹And they sang together by course in praising and giving thanks unto the LORD; because *he is* good, for his mercy *endureth* for ever toward Israel. And all the people shouted with a great shout, when they praised the LORD, because the foundation of the house of the LORD was laid.

¹²But many of the priests and Levites and chief of the fathers, *who were* ancient men, that had seen the first house, when the foundation of this house was laid before their eyes, wept with a loud voice; and many shouted aloud for joy:

¹³So that the people could not discern the noise of the shout of joy from the noise of the weeping of the people: for the people shouted with a loud shout, and the noise was heard afar off.

4 NOW WHEN the adversaries of Judah and Benjamin heard that the children of the captivity builded the temple unto the LORD God of Israel;

New International

Rebuilding the Altar

3 WHEN THE seventh month came and the Israelites had settled in their towns, the people assembled as one man in Jerusalem. ²Then Jeshua son of Jozadak and his fellow priests and Zerubbabel son of Shealtiel and his associates began to build the altar of the God of Israel to sacrifice burnt offerings on it, in accordance with what is written in the Law of Moses the man of God. ³Despite their fear of the peoples around them, they built the altar on its foundation and sacrificed burnt offerings on it to the LORD, both the morning and evening sacrifices. ⁴Then in accordance with what is written, they celebrated the Feast of Tabernacles with the required number of burnt offerings prescribed for each day. ⁵After that, they presented the regular burnt offerings, the New Moon sacrifices and the sacrifices for all the appointed sacred feasts of the LORD, as well as those brought as freewill offerings to the LORD. ⁶On the first day of the seventh month they began to offer burnt offerings to the LORD, though the foundation of the LORD's temple had not yet been laid.

Rebuilding the Temple

⁷Then they gave money to the masons and carpenters, and gave food and drink and oil to the people of Sidon and Tyre, so that they would bring cedar logs by sea from Lebanon to Joppa, as authorized by Cyrus king of Persia.

⁸In the second month of the second year after their arrival at the house of God in Jerusalem, Zerubbabel son of Shealtiel, Jeshua son of Jozadak and the rest of their brothers (the priests and the Levites and all who had returned from the captivity to Jerusalem) began the work, appointing Levites twenty years of age and older to supervise the building of the house of the LORD. ⁹Jeshua and his sons and brothers and Kadmiel and his sons (descendants of Hodaviah[a]) and the sons of Henadad and their sons and brothers—all Levites—joined together in supervising those working on the house of God.

¹⁰When the builders laid the foundation of the temple of the LORD, the priests in their vestments and with trumpets, and the Levites (the sons of Asaph) with cymbals, took their places to praise the LORD, as prescribed by David king of Israel. ¹¹With praise and thanksgiving they sang to the LORD:

"He is good;
    his love to Israel endures forever."

And all the people gave a great shout of praise to the LORD, because the foundation of the house of the LORD was laid. ¹²But many of the older priests and Levites and family heads, who had seen the former temple, wept aloud when they saw the foundation of this temple being laid, while many others shouted for joy. ¹³No one could distinguish the sound of the shouts of joy from the sound of weeping, because the people made so much noise. And the sound was heard far away.

Opposition to the Rebuilding

4 WHEN THE enemies of Judah and Benjamin heard that the exiles were building a temple for the LORD, the God of Israel, ²they came to Zerubbabel and

ᵃ 9 Hebrew *Yehudah*, probably a variant of *Hodaviah*

Living Bible

3 DURING THE month of September everyone who had returned to Judah came to Jerusalem from their homes in the other towns. Then Jeshua (son of Jozadak) with his fellow priests, and Zerubbabel (son of Shealtiel) and his clan, rebuilt the altar of the God of Israel; and sacrificed burnt offerings upon it, as instructed in the laws of Moses, the man of God. 3The altar was rebuilt on its old site, and it was used immediately to sacrifice morning and evening burnt offerings to the Lord; for the people were fearful of attack.

4And they celebrated the Feast of Tabernacles as prescribed in the laws of Moses, sacrificing the burnt offerings specified for each day of the feast. 5They also offered the special sacrifices required for the Sabbaths, the new moon celebrations, and the other regular annual feasts of the Lord. Voluntary offerings of the people were also sacrificed. 6It was on the fifteenth day of Septemberᵇ that the priests began sacrificing the burnt offerings to the Lord. (This was before they began building the foundation of the Temple.)

7Then they hired masons and carpenters, and bought cedar logs from the people of Tyre and Sidon, paying for them with food, wine, and olive oil. The logs were brought down from the Lebanon mountains and floated along the coast of the Mediterranean Sea to Joppa, for King Cyrus had included this provision in his grant.

8The actual construction of the Temple began in June of the second year of their arrival at Jerusalem. The work force was made up of all those who had returned, and they were under the direction of Zerubbabel (son of Shealtiel), Jeshua (son of Jozadak), and their fellow priests and the Levites. The Levites who were twenty years old or older were appointed to supervise the workmen. 9The supervision of the entire project was given to Jeshua, Kadmi-el, Henadad, and their sons and relatives, all of whom were Levites.

10When the builders completed the foundation of the Temple, the priests put on their official robes and blew their trumpets; and the descendants of Asaph crashed their cymbals to praise the Lord in the manner ordained by King David. 11They sang rounds of praise and thanks to God, singing this song: "He is good, and his love and mercy toward Israel will last forever." Then all the people gave a great shout, praising God because the foundation of the Temple had been laid.

12But many of the priests and Levites and other leaders—the old men who remembered Solomon's beautiful Temple—wept aloud, while others were shouting for joy! 13So the shouting and the weeping mingled together in a loud commotion that could be heard from far away!

4 WHEN THE enemies of Judah and Benjamin heard that the exiles had returned and were rebuilding the Temple, 2they approached Zerubbabel and the

New Revised Standard

Worship Restored at Jerusalem

3 WHEN THE seventh month came, and the Israelites were in the towns, the people gathered together in Jerusalem. 2Then Jeshua son of Jozadak, with his fellow priests, and Zerubbabel son of Shealtiel with his kin set out to build the altar of the God of Israel, to offer burnt offerings on it, as prescribed in the law of Moses the man of God. 3They set up the altar on its foundation, because they were in dread of the neighboring peoples, and they offered burnt offerings upon it to the LORD, morning and evening. 4And they kept the festival of booths,ᶜ as prescribed, and offered the daily burnt offerings by number according to the ordinance, as required for each day, 5and after that the regular burnt offerings, the offerings at the new moon and at all the sacred festivals of the LORD, and the offerings of everyone who made a freewill offering to the LORD. 6From the first day of the seventh month they began to offer burnt offerings to the LORD. But the foundation of the temple of the LORD was not yet laid. 7So they gave money to the masons and the carpenters, and food, drink, and oil to the Sidonians and the Tyrians to bring cedar trees from Lebanon to the sea, to Joppa, according to the grant that they had from King Cyrus of Persia.

Foundation Laid for the Temple

8 In the second year after their arrival at the house of God at Jerusalem, in the second month, Zerubbabel son of Shealtiel and Jeshua son of Jozadak made a beginning, together with the rest of their people, the priests and the Levites and all who had come to Jerusalem from the captivity. They appointed the Levites, from twenty years old and upward, to have the oversight of the work on the house of the LORD. 9And Jeshua with his sons and his kin, and Kadmiel and his sons, Binnui and Hodaviahᵈ along with the sons of Henadad, the Levites, their sons and kin, together took charge of the workers in the house of God.

10 When the builders laid the foundation of the temple of the LORD, the priests in their vestments were stationed to praise the LORD with trumpets, and the Levites, the sons of Asaph, with cymbals, according to the directions of King David of Israel; 11and they sang responsively, praising and giving thanks to the LORD,

"For he is good,
    for his steadfast love endures forever toward
        Israel."

And all the people responded with a great shout when they praised the LORD, because the foundation of the house of the LORD was laid. 12But many of the priests and Levites and heads of families, old people who had seen the first house on its foundations, wept with a loud voice when they saw this house, though many shouted aloud for joy, 13so that the people could not distinguish the sound of the joyful shout from the sound of the people's weeping, for the people shouted so loudly that the sound was heard far away.

Resistance to Rebuilding the Temple

4 WHEN THE adversaries of Judah and Benjamin heard that the returned exiles were building a temple to the LORD, the God of Israel, 2they approached

---

ᵇ *3:6 fifteenth day of September,* literally, "the first day of the seventh month" of the Hebrew calender.

ᶜ Or *tabernacles;* Heb *succoth*   ᵈ Compare 2.40; Neh 7.43; 1 Esdras 5.58: Heb *sons of Judah*

King James

2Then they came to Zerubbabel, and to the chief of the fathers, and said unto them, Let us build with you: for we seek your God, as ye *do;* and we do sacrifice unto him since the days of Esar-haddon king of Assur, which brought us up hither.

3But Zerubbabel, and Jeshua, and the rest of the chief of the fathers of Israel, said unto them, Ye have nothing to do with us to build an house unto our God; but we ourselves together will build unto the LORD God of Israel, as king Cyrus the king of Persia hath commanded us.

4Then the people of the land weakened the hands of the people of Judah, and troubled them in building,

5And hired counsellors against them, to frustrate their purpose, all the days of Cyrus king of Persia, even until the reign of Darius king of Persia.

6And in the reign of Ahasuerus, in the beginning of his reign, wrote they *unto him* an accusation against the inhabitants of Judah and Jerusalem.

7¶ And in the days of Artaxerxes wrote Bishlam, Mithredath, Tabeel, and the rest of their companions, unto Artaxerxes king of Persia; and the writing of the letter *was* written in the Syrian tongue, and interpreted in the Syrian tongue.

8Rehum the chancellor and Shimshai the scribe wrote a letter against Jerusalem to Artaxerxes the king in this sort:

9Then *wrote* Rehum the chancellor, and Shimshai the scribe, and the rest of their companions; the Dinaites, the Apharsathchites, the Tarpelites, the Apharsites, the Archevites, the Babylonians, the Susanchites, the Dehavites, *and* the Elamites,

10And the rest of the nations whom the great and noble Asnapper brought over, and set in the cities of Samaria, and the rest *that are* on this side the river, and at such a time.

11¶ This *is* the copy of the letter that they sent unto him, *even* unto Artaxerxes the king; Thy servants the men on this side the river, and at such a time.

12Be it known unto the king, that the Jews which came up from thee to us are come unto Jerusalem, building the rebellious and the bad city, and have set up the walls *thereof,* and joined the foundations.

13Be it known now unto the king, that, if this city be builded, and the walls set up *again, then* will they not pay toll, tribute, and custom, and *so* thou shalt endamage the revenue of the kings.

14Now because we have maintenance from *the king's* palace, and it was not meet for us to see the king's dishonour, therefore have we sent and certified the king;

15That search may be made in the book of the records of thy fathers: so shalt thou find in the book of the records, and know that this city *is* a rebellious city, and hurtful unto kings and provinces, and that they have moved sedition within the same of old time: for which cause was this city destroyed.

16We certify the king that, if this city be builded *again,* and the walls thereof set up, by this means thou shalt have no portion on this side the river.

17¶ *Then* sent the king an answer unto Rehum the chancellor, and *to* Shimshai the scribe, and *to* the rest of their companions that dwell in Samaria, and *unto* the rest beyond the river, Peace, and at such a time.

18The letter which ye sent unto us hath been plainly read before me.

New International

to the heads of the families and said, "Let us help you build because, like you, we seek your God and have been sacrificing to him since the time of Esarhaddon king of Assyria, who brought us here."

3But Zerubbabel, Jeshua and the rest of the heads of the families of Israel answered, "You have no part with us in building a temple to our God. We alone will build it for the LORD, the God of Israel, as King Cyrus, the king of Persia, commanded us."

4Then the peoples around them set out to discourage the people of Judah and make them afraid to go on building.a 5They hired counselors to work against them and frustrate their plans during the entire reign of Cyrus king of Persia and down to the reign of Darius king of Persia.

Later Opposition Under Xerxes and Artaxerxes

6At the beginning of the reign of Xerxes,b they lodged an accusation against the people of Judah and Jerusalem.

7And in the days of Artaxerxes king of Persia, Bishlam, Mithredath, Tabeel and the rest of his associates wrote a letter to Artaxerxes. The letter was written in Aramaic script and in the Aramaic language.c,d

8Rehum the commanding officer and Shimshai the secretary wrote a letter against Jerusalem to Artaxerxes the king as follows:

9Rehum the commanding officer and Shimshai the secretary, together with the rest of their associates—the judges and officials over the men from Tripolis, Persia,e Erech and Babylon, the Elamites of Susa, 10and the other people whom the great and honorable Ashurbanipalf deported and settled in the city of Samaria and elsewhere in Trans-Euphrates.

11(This is a copy of the letter they sent him.)

To King Artaxerxes,

From your servants, the men of Trans-Euphrates:

12The king should know that the Jews who came up to us from you have gone to Jerusalem and are rebuilding that rebellious and wicked city. They are restoring the walls and repairing the foundations.

13Furthermore, the king should know that if this city is built and its walls are restored, no more taxes, tribute or duty will be paid, and the royal revenues will suffer. 14Now since we are under obligation to the palace and it is not proper for us to see the king dishonored, we are sending this message to inform the king, 15so that a search may be made in the archives of your predecessors. In these records you will find that this city is a rebellious city, troublesome to kings and provinces, a place of rebellion from ancient times. That is why this city was destroyed. 16We inform the king that if this city is built and its walls are restored, you will be left with nothing in Trans-Euphrates.

17The king sent this reply:

To Rehum the commanding officer, Shimshai the secretary and the rest of their associates living in Samaria and elsewhere in Trans-Euphrates:

Greetings.

18The letter you sent us has been read and translated in my presence. 19I issued an order and a

---

a 4 Or *and troubled them as they built*   b 6 Hebrew *Ahasuerus,* a variant of Xerxes' Persian name   c 7 Or *written in Aramaic and translated*   d 7 The text of Ezra 4:8—6:18 is in Aramaic.   e 9 Or *officials, magistrates and governors over the men from*   f 10 Aramaic *Osnappar,* a variant of Ashurbanipal

Living Bible

other leaders and suggested, "Let us work with you, for we are just as interested in your God as you are; we have sacrificed to him ever since King Esar-haddon of Assyria brought us here."

3But Zerubbabel and Jeshua and the other Jewish leaders replied, "No, you may have no part in this work. The Temple of the God of Israel must be built by the Israelis, just as King Cyrus has commanded."

4,5Then the local residents tried to discourage and frighten them by sending agents to tell lies about them to King Cyrus. This went on during his entire reign and lasted until King Darius took the throne.

6And afterwards, when King Ahasuerus began to reign, they wrote him a letter of accusation against the people of Judah and Jerusalem, 7and did the same thing during the reign of Artaxerxes. Bishlam, Mithredath, and Tabe-el and their associates wrote a letter to him in the Aramaic language, and it was translated to him. 8, 9Others who participated were Governor Rehum, Shimshai (a scribe), several judges and other local leaders, the Persians, the Babylonians, the men of Erech and Susa, 10and men from several other nations. (They had been taken from their own lands by the great and noble Osnappar and relocated in Jerusalem, Samaria, and throughout the neighboring lands west of the Euphrates River.)

11Here is the text of the letter they sent to King Artaxerxes:

"Sir: Greetings from your loyal subjects west of the Euphrates River. 12Please be informed that the Jews sent to Jerusalem from Babylon are rebuilding this historically rebellious and evil city; they have already rebuilt its walls and have repaired the foundations of the Temple. 13But we wish you to know that if this city is rebuilt, it will be much to your disadvantage, for the Jews will then refuse to pay their taxes to you.

14"Since we are grateful to you as our patron, and we do not want to see you taken advantage of and dishonored in this way, we have decided to send you this information. 15We suggest that you search the ancient records to discover what a rebellious city this has been in the past; in fact, it was destroyed because of its long history of sedition against the kings and countries who attempted to control it. 16We wish to declare that if this city is rebuilt and the walls finished, you might as well forget about this part of your empire beyond the Euphrates, for it will be lost to you."

17Then the king made this reply to Governor Rehum and Shimshai the scribe, and to their companions living in Samaria and throughout the area west of the Euphrates River:

18"Gentlemen: Greetings! The letter you sent has been translated and read to me. 19I have ordered a search

New Revised Standard

Zerubbabel and the heads of families and said to them, "Let us build with you, for we worship your God as you do, and we have been sacrificing to him ever since the days of King Esar-haddon of Assyria who brought us here." 3But Zerubbabel, Jeshua, and the rest of the heads of families in Israel said to them, "You shall have no part with us in building a house to our God; but we alone will build to the LORD, the God of Israel, as King Cyrus of Persia has commanded us."

4 Then the people of the land discouraged the people of Judah, and made them afraid to build, 5and they bribed officials to frustrate their plan throughout the reign of King Cyrus of Persia and until the reign of King Darius of Persia.

Rebuilding of Jerusalem Opposed

6 In the reign of Ahasuerus, in his accession year, they wrote an accusation against the inhabitants of Judah and Jerusalem.

7 And in the days of Artaxerxes, Bishlam and Mithredath and Tabeel and the rest of their associates wrote to King Artaxerxes of Persia; the letter was written in Aramaic and translated.g 8Rehum the royal deputy and Shimshai the scribe wrote a letter against Jerusalem to King Artaxerxes as follows 9(then Rehum the royal deputy, Shimshai the scribe, and the rest of their associates, the judges, the envoys, the officials, the Persians, the people of Erech, the Babylonians, the people of Susa, that is, the Elamites, 10and the rest of the nations whom the great and noble Osnappar deported and settled in the cities of Samaria and in the rest of the province Beyond the River wrote—and now 11this is a copy of the letter that they sent):

"To King Artaxerxes: Your servants, the people of the province Beyond the River, send greeting. And now 12may it be known to the king that the Jews who came up from you to us have gone to Jerusalem. They are rebuilding that rebellious and wicked city; they are finishing the walls and repairing the foundations. 13Now may it be known to the king that, if this city is rebuilt and the walls finished, they will not pay tribute, custom, or toll, and the royal revenue will be reduced. 14Now because we share the salt of the palace and it is not fitting for us to witness the king's dishonor, therefore we send and inform the king, 15so that a search may be made in the annals of your ancestors. You will discover in the annals that this is a rebellious city, hurtful to kings and provinces, and that sedition was stirred up in it from long ago. On that account this city was laid waste. 16We make known to the king that, if this city is rebuilt and its walls finished, you will then have no possession in the province Beyond the River."

17 The king sent an answer: "To Rehum the royal deputy and Shimshai the scribe and the rest of their associates who live in Samaria and in the rest of the province Beyond the River, greeting. And now 18the letter that you sent to us has been read in translation before me. 19So I made a decree, and someone searched

---

g Heb adds in Aramaic, indicating that 4.8-6.18 is in Aramaic. Another interpretation is The letter was written in the Aramaic script and set forth in the Aramaic language

King James

19And I commanded, and search hath been made, and it is found that this city of old time hath made insurrection against kings, and *that* rebellion and sedition have been made therein.

20There have been mighty kings also over Jerusalem, which have ruled over all *countries* beyond the river; and toll, tribute, and custom, was paid unto them.

21Give ye now commandment to cause these men to cease, and that this city be not builded, until *another* commandment shall be given from me.

22Take heed now that ye fail not to do this: why should damage grow to the hurt of the kings?

23¶ Now when the copy of king Artaxerxes' letter *was* read before Rehum, and Shimshai the scribe, and their companions, they went up in haste to Jerusalem unto the Jews, and made them to cease by force and power.

24Then ceased the work of the house of God which *is* at Jerusalem. So it ceased unto the second year of the reign of Darius king of Persia.

5 THEN THE prophets, Haggai the prophet, and Zechariah the son of Iddo, prophesied unto the Jews that *were* in Judah and Jerusalem in the name of the God of Israel, *even* unto them.

2Then rose up Zerubbabel the son of Shealtiel, and Jeshua the son of Jozadak, and began to build the house of God which *is* at Jerusalem: and with them *were* the prophets of God helping them.

3¶ At the same time came to them Tatnai, governor on this side the river, and Shethar-boznai, and their companions, and said thus unto them, Who hath commanded you to build this house, and to make up this wall?

4Then said we unto them after this manner, What are the names of the men that make this building?

5But the eye of their God was upon the elders of the Jews, that they could not cause them to cease, till the matter came to Darius: and then they returned answer by letter concerning this *matter*.

6¶ The copy of the letter that Tatnai, governor on this side the river, and Shethar-boznai, and his companions the Apharsachites, which *were* on this side the river, sent unto Darius the king:

7They sent a letter unto him, wherein was written thus; Unto Darius the king, all peace.

8Be it known unto the king, that we went into the province of Judea, to the house of the great God, which is builded with great stones, and timber is laid in the walls, and this work goeth fast on, and prospereth in their hands.

9Then asked we those elders, *and* said unto them thus, Who commanded you to build this house, and to make up these walls?

10We asked their names also, to certify thee, that we might write the names of the men that *were* the chief of them.

11And thus they returned us answer, saying, We are the servants of the God of heaven and earth, and build the house that was builded these many years ago, which a great king of Israel builded and set up.

12But after that our fathers had provoked the God of heaven unto wrath, he gave them into the hand of Nebuchadnezzar the king of Babylon, the Chaldean, who destroyed this house, and carried the people away into Babylon.

13But in the first year of Cyrus the king of Babylon *the same* king Cyrus made a decree to build this house of God.

New International

search was made, and it was found that this city has a long history of revolt against kings and has been a place of rebellion and sedition. 20Jerusalem has had powerful kings ruling over the whole of Trans-Euphrates, and taxes, tribute and duty were paid to them. 21Now issue an order to these men to stop work, so that this city will not be rebuilt until I so order. 22Be careful not to neglect this matter. Why let this threat grow, to the detriment of the royal interests?

23As soon as the copy of the letter of King Artaxerxes was read to Rehum and Shimshai the secretary and their associates, they went immediately to the Jews in Jerusalem and compelled them by force to stop.

24Thus the work on the house of God in Jerusalem came to a standstill until the second year of the reign of Darius king of Persia.

Tattenai's Letter to Darius

5 NOW HAGGAI the prophet and Zechariah the prophet, a descendant of Iddo, prophesied to the Jews in Judah and Jerusalem in the name of the God of Israel, who was over them. 2Then Zerubbabel son of Shealtiel and Jeshua son of Jozadak set to work to rebuild the house of God in Jerusalem. And the prophets of God were with them, helping them.

3At that time Tattenai, governor of Trans-Euphrates, and Shethar-Bozenai and their associates went to them and asked, "Who authorized you to rebuild this temple and restore this structure?" 4They also asked, "What are the names of the men constructing this building?"[a] 5But the eye of their God was watching over the elders of the Jews, and they were not stopped until a report could go to Darius and his written reply be received.

6This is a copy of the letter that Tattenai, governor of Trans-Euphrates, and Shethar-Bozenai and their associates, the officials of Trans-Euphrates, sent to King Darius. 7The report they sent him read as follows:

To King Darius:

Cordial greetings.

8The king should know that we went to the district of Judah, to the temple of the great God. The people are building it with large stones and placing the timbers in the walls. The work is being carried on with diligence and is making rapid progress under their direction.

9We questioned the elders and asked them, "Who authorized you to rebuild this temple and restore this structure?" 10We also asked them their names, so that we could write down the names of their leaders for your information.

11This is the answer they gave us:

"We are the servants of the God of heaven and earth, and we are rebuilding the temple that was built many years ago, one that a great king of Israel built and finished. 12But because our fathers angered the God of heaven, he handed them over to Nebuchadnezzar the Chaldean, king of Babylon, who destroyed this temple and deported the people to Babylon.

13"However, in the first year of Cyrus king of Babylon, King Cyrus issued a decree to rebuild this house of God. 14He even removed from the temple[b]

a 4 See Septuagint; Aramaic 4*We told them the names of the men constructing this building.*   b 14 Or *palace*

Living Bible

made of the records and have indeed found that Jerusalem has in times past been a hotbed of insurrection against many kings; in fact, rebellion and sedition are normal there! 20I find, moreover, that there have been some very great kings in Jerusalem who have ruled the entire land beyond the Euphrates River and have received vast tribute, custom, and toll. 21Therefore, I command that these men must stop their work until I have investigated the matter more thoroughly. 22Do not delay, for we must not permit the situation to get out of control!"

23When this letter from King Artaxerxes was read to Rehum and Shimshai, they hurried to Jerusalem and forced the Jews to stop building. 24So the work ended until the second year of the reign of King Darius of Persia.

5 BUT THERE were prophets in Jerusalem and Judah at that time—Haggai, and Zechariah (the son of Iddo)—who brought messages from the God of Israel to Zerubbabel (son of Shealtiel) and Jeshua (son of Jozadak), encouraging them to begin building again! So they did and the prophets helped them.

3But Tattenai, the governor of the lands west of the Euphrates, and Shethar-bozenai, and their companions soon arrived in Jerusalem and demanded, "Who gave you permission to rebuild this Temple and finish these walls?"

4They also asked for a list of the names of all the men who were working on the Temple. 5But because the Lord was overseeing the entire situation, our enemies did not force us to stop building, but let us continue while King Darius looked into the matter and returned his decision.

6Following is the letter which Governors Tattenai and Shethar-bozenai, and the other officials sent to King Darius:

7"To King Darius:

"Greetings!

8"We wish to inform you that we went to the construction site of the Temple of the great God of Judah. It is being built with huge stones, and timber is being laid in the city walls. The work is going forward with great energy and success. 9We asked the leaders, 'Who has given you permission to do this?' 10And we demanded their names so that we could notify you. 11Their answer was, 'We are the servants of the God of heaven and earth and we are rebuilding the Temple that was constructed here many centuries ago by a great king of Israel. 12But afterwards our ancestors angered the God of heaven, and he abandoned them and let King Nebuchadnezzar destroy this Temple and exile the people to Babylonia.'

13"But they insist that King Cyrus of Babylon, during the first year of his reign, issued a decree that the Temple should be rebuilt, 14and they say King Cyrus returned

New Revised Standard

and discovered that this city has risen against kings from long ago, and that rebellion and sedition have been made in it. 20Jerusalem has had mighty kings who ruled over the whole province Beyond the River, to whom tribute, custom, and toll were paid. 21Therefore issue an order that these people be made to cease, and that this city not be rebuilt, until I make a decree. 22Moreover, take care not to be slack in this matter; why should damage grow to the hurt of the king?"

23 Then when the copy of King Artaxerxes' letter was read before Rehum and the scribe Shimshai and their associates, they hurried to the Jews in Jerusalem and by force and power made them cease. 24At that time the work on the house of God in Jerusalem stopped and was discontinued until the second year of the reign of King Darius of Persia.

Restoration of the Temple Resumed

5 NOW THE prophets, Haggai[c] and Zechariah son of Iddo, prophesied to the Jews who were in Judah and Jerusalem, in the name of the God of Israel who was over them. 2Then Zerubbabel son of Shealtiel and Jeshua son of Jozadak set out to rebuild the house of God in Jerusalem; and with them were the prophets of God, helping them.

3 At the same time Tattenai the governor of the province Beyond the River and Shethar-bozenai and their associates came to them and spoke to them thus, "Who gave you a decree to build this house and to finish this structure?" 4They[d] also asked them this, "What are the names of the men who are building this building?" 5But the eye of their God was upon the elders of the Jews, and they did not stop them until a report reached Darius and then answer was returned by letter in reply to it.

6 The copy of the letter that Tattenai the governor of the province Beyond the River and Shethar-bozenai and his associates the envoys who were in the province Beyond the River sent to King Darius; 7they sent him a report, in which was written as follows: "To Darius the king, all peace! 8May it be known to the king that we went to the province of Judah, to the house of the great God. It is being built of hewn stone, and timber is laid in the walls; this work is being done diligently and prospers in their hands. 9Then we spoke to those elders and asked them, 'Who gave you a decree to build this house and to finish this structure?' 10We also asked them their names, for your information, so that we might write down the names of the men at their head. 11This was their reply to us: 'We are the servants of the God of heaven and earth, and we are rebuilding the house that was built many years ago, which a great king of Israel built and finished. 12But because our ancestors had angered the God of heaven, he gave them into the hand of King Nebuchadnezzar of Babylon, the Chaldean, who destroyed this house and carried away the people to Babylonia. 13However, King Cyrus of Babylon, in the first year of his reign, made a decree that this house of God should be rebuilt. 14Moreover, the gold and silver

c Aram adds the prophet   d Gk Syr: Aram We

King James

14And the vessels also of gold and silver of the house of God, which Nebuchadnezzar took out of the temple that *was* in Jerusalem, and brought them into the temple of Babylon, those did Cyrus the king take out of the temple of Babylon, and they were delivered unto *one,* whose name *was* Sheshbazzar, whom he had made governor;

15And said unto him, Take these vessels, go, carry them into the temple that *is* in Jerusalem, and let the house of God be builded in his place.

16Then came the same Sheshbazzar, *and* laid the foundation of the house of God which *is* in Jerusalem: and since that time even until now hath it been in building, and *yet* it is not finished.

17Now therefore, if *it seem* good to the king, let there be search made in the king's treasure house, which *is* there at Babylon, whether it be *so,* that a decree was made of Cyrus the king to build this house of God at Jerusalem, and let the king send his pleasure to us concerning this matter.

6 THEN DARIUS the king made a decree, and search was made in the house of the rolls, where the treasures were laid up in Babylon.

2And there was found at Achmetha, in the palace that *is* in the province of the Medes, a roll, and therein *was* a record thus written:

3In the first year of Cyrus the king *the same* Cyrus the king made a decree *concerning* the house of God at Jerusalem, Let the house be builded, the place where they offered sacrifices, and let the foundations thereof be strongly laid; the height thereof threescore cubits, *and* the breadth thereof threescore cubits;

4*With* three rows of great stones, and a row of new timber: and let the expenses be given out of the king's house:

5And also let the golden and silver vessels of the house of God, which Nebuchadnezzar took forth out of the temple which *is* at Jerusalem, and brought unto Babylon, be restored, and brought again unto the temple which *is* at Jerusalem, *every one* to his place, and place *them* in the house of God.

6Now *therefore,* Tatnai, governor beyond the river, Shethar-boznai, and your companions the Apharsachites, which *are* beyond the river, be ye far from thence:

7Let the work of this house of God alone; let the governor of the Jews and the elders of the Jews build this house of God in his place.

8Moreover I make a decree what ye shall do to the elders of these Jews for the building of this house of God: that of the king's goods, *even* of the tribute beyond the river, forthwith expenses be given unto these men, that they be not hindered.

9And that which they have need of, both young bullocks, and rams, and lambs, for the burnt offerings of the God of heaven, wheat, salt, wine, and oil, according to the appointment of the priests which *are* at Jerusalem, let it be given them day by day without fail:

10That they may offer sacrifices of sweet savours unto the God of heaven, and pray for the life of the king, and of his sons.

11Also I have made a decree, that whosoever shall alter this word, let timber be pulled down from his house, and being set up, let him be hanged thereon; and let his house be made a dunghill for this.

New International

of Babylon the gold and silver articles of the house of God, which Nebuchadnezzar had taken from the temple in Jerusalem and brought to the temple[a] in Babylon.

"Then King Cyrus gave them to a man named Sheshbazzar, whom he had appointed governor, 15and he told him, 'Take these articles and go and deposit them in the temple in Jerusalem. And rebuild the house of God on its site.' 16So this Sheshbazzar came and laid the foundations of the house of God in Jerusalem. From that day to the present it has been under construction but is not yet finished."

17Now if it pleases the king, let a search be made in the royal archives of Babylon to see if King Cyrus did in fact issue a decree to rebuild this house of God in Jerusalem. Then let the king send us his decision in this matter.

The Decree of Darius

6 KING DARIUS then issued an order, and they searched in the archives stored in the treasury at Babylon. 2A scroll was found in the citadel of Ecbatana in the province of Media, and this was written on it:

Memorandum:

3In the first year of King Cyrus, the king issued a decree concerning the temple of God in Jerusalem:

Let the temple be rebuilt as a place to present sacrifices, and let its foundations be laid. It is to be ninety feet[b] high and ninety feet wide, 4with three courses of large stones and one of timbers. The costs are to be paid by the royal treasury. 5Also, the gold and silver articles of the house of God, which Nebuchadnezzar took from the temple in Jerusalem and brought to Babylon, are to be returned to their places in the temple in Jerusalem; they are to be deposited in the house of God.

6Now then, Tattenai, governor of Trans-Euphrates, and Shethar-Bozenai and you, their fellow officials of that province, stay away from there. 7Do not interfere with the work on this temple of God. Let the governor of the Jews and the Jewish elders rebuild this house of God on its site.

8Moreover, I hereby decree what you are to do for these elders of the Jews in the construction of this house of God:

The expenses of these men are to be fully paid out of the royal treasury, from the revenues of Trans-Euphrates, so that the work will not stop. 9Whatever is needed—young bulls, rams, male lambs for burnt offerings to the God of heaven, and wheat, salt, wine and oil, as requested by the priests in Jerusalem—must be given them daily without fail, 10so that they may offer sacrifices pleasing to the God of heaven and pray for the well-being of the king and his sons.

11Furthermore, I decree that if anyone changes this edict, a beam is to be pulled from his house and he is to be lifted up and impaled on it. And for this crime his house is to be made a pile of rubble.

---

a *14* Or *palace*   b *3* Aramaic *sixty cubits* (about 27 meters)

Living Bible

the gold and silver bowls which Nebuchadnezzar had taken from the Temple in Jerusalem and had placed in the temple of Babylon. They say these items were delivered into the safekeeping of a man named Shesh-bazzar, whom King Cyrus appointed as governor of Judah. 15The king instructed him to return the bowls to Jerusalem and to let the Temple of God be built there as before. 16So Shesh-bazzar came and laid the foundations of the Temple at Jerusalem; and the people have been working on it ever since, though it is not yet completed. 17We request that you search in the royal library of Babylon to discover whether King Cyrus ever made such a decree; and then let us know your pleasure in this matter."

6 SO KING Darius issued orders that a search be made in the Babylonian archives, where documents were stored. 2Eventually the record was found in the palace at Ecbatana, in the province of Media. This is what it said: 3"In this first year of the reign of King Cyrus, a decree has been sent out concerning the Temple of God at Jerusalem where the Jews offer sacrifices. It is to be rebuilt, and the foundations are to be strongly laid. The height will be ninety feet and the width will be ninety feet. 4There will be three layers of huge stones in the foundation, topped with a layer of new timber. All expenses will be paid by the king. 5And the gold and silver bowls which were taken from the Temple of God by Nebuchadnezzar shall be taken back to Jerusalem and put into the Temple as they were before."

6So King Darius II sent this messagec to Governor Shethar-bozenai, and the other officials west of the Euphrates:

"Do not disturb the construction of the Temple. Let it be rebuilt on its former site, 7and don't molest the governor of Judah and the other leaders in their work. 8Moreover, I decree that you are to pay the full construction costs without delay from my taxes collected in your territory. 9Give the priests in Jerusalem young bulls, rams, and lambs for burnt offerings to the God of heaven; and give them wheat, wine, salt, and olive oil each day without fail. 10Then they will be able to offer acceptable sacrifices to the God of heaven, and to pray for me and my sons. 11Anyone who attempts to change this message in any way shall have the beams pulled from his house and built into a gallows on which he will be hanged;d and his house shall be reduced to a pile of rubble. 12The God who has chosen the city of Jerusalem

New Revised Standard

vessels of the house of God, which Nebuchadnezzar had taken out of the temple in Jerusalem and had brought into the temple of Babylon, these King Cyrus took out of the temple of Babylon, and they were delivered to a man named Sheshbazzar, whom he had made governor. 15He said to him, "Take these vessels; go and put them in the temple in Jerusalem, and let the house of God be rebuilt on its site." 16Then this Sheshbazzar came and laid the foundations of the house of God in Jerusalem; and from that time until now it has been under construction, and it is not yet finished.' 17And now, if it seems good to the king, have a search made in the royal archives there in Babylon, to see whether a decree was issued by King Cyrus for the rebuilding of this house of God in Jerusalem. Let the king send us his pleasure in this matter."

The Decree of Darius

6 THEN KING Darius made a decree, and they searched the archives where the documents were stored in Babylon. 2But it was in Ecbatana, the capital in the province of Media, that a scroll was found on which this was written: "A record. 3In the first year of his reign, King Cyrus issued a decree: Concerning the house of God at Jerusalem, let the house be rebuilt, the place where sacrifices are offered and burnt offerings are brought;e its height shall be sixty cubits and its width sixty cubits, 4with three courses of hewn stones and one course of timber; let the cost be paid from the royal treasury. 5Moreover, let the gold and silver vessels of the house of God, which Nebuchadnezzar took out of the temple in Jerusalem and brought to Babylon, be restored and brought back to the temple in Jerusalem, each to its place; you shall put them in the house of God."

6 "Now you, Tattenai, governor of the province Beyond the River, Shethar-bozenai, and you, their associates, the envoys in the province Beyond the River, keep away; 7let the work on this house of God alone; let the governor of the Jews and the elders of the Jews rebuild this house of God on its site. 8Moreover I make a decree regarding what you shall do for these elders of the Jews for the rebuilding of this house of God: the cost is to be paid to these people, in full and without delay, from the royal revenue, the tribute of the province Beyond the River. 9Whatever is needed—young bulls, rams, or sheep for burnt offerings to the God of heaven, wheat, salt, wine, or oil, as the priests in Jerusalem require—let that be given to them day by day without fail, 10so that they may offer pleasing sacrifices to the God of heaven, and pray for the life of the king and his children. 11Furthermore I decree that if anyone alters this edict, a beam shall be pulled out of the house of the perpetrator, who then shall be impaled on it. The house shall be made a dunghill. 12May the God who has established his name

---

c 6:6 King Darius sent this message, implied.   d 6:11 hanged, literally, impaled.   e Meaning of Aram uncertain

King James

12And the God that hath caused his name to dwell there destroy all kings and people, that shall put to their hand to alter *and* to destroy this house of God which *is* at Jerusalem. I Darius have made a decree; let it be done with speed.

13¶ Then Tatnai, governor on this side the river, She-thar-boznai, and their companions, according to that which Darius the king had sent, so they did speedily.

14And the elders of the Jews builded, and they prospered through the prophesying of Haggai the prophet and Zechariah the son of Iddo. And they builded, and finished *it,* according to the commandment of the God of Israel, and according to the commandment of Cyrus, and Darius, and Artaxerxes king of Persia.

15And this house was finished on the third day of the month Adar, which was in the sixth year of the reign of Darius the king.

16¶ And the children of Israel, the priests, and the Levites, and the rest of the children of the captivity, kept the dedication of this house of God with joy,

17And offered at the dedication of this house of God an hundred bullocks, two hundred rams, four hundred lambs; and for a sin offering for all Israel, twelve he goats, according to the number of the tribes of Israel.

18And they set the priests in their divisions, and the Levites in their courses, for the service of God, which *is* at Jerusalem; as it is written in the book of Moses.

19And the children of the captivity kept the passover upon the fourteenth *day* of the first month.

20For the priests and the Levites were purified together, all of them *were* pure, and killed the passover for all the children of the captivity, and for their brethren the priests, and for themselves.

21And the children of Israel, which were come again out of captivity, and all such as had separated themselves unto them from the filthiness of the heathen of the land, to seek the LORD God of Israel, did eat,

22And kept the feast of unleavened bread seven days with joy: for the LORD had made them joyful, and turned the heart of the king of Assyria unto them, to strengthen their hands in the work of the house of God, the God of Israel.

7 NOW AFTER these things, in the reign of Artaxerxes king of Persia, Ezra the son of Seraiah, the son of Azariah, the son of Hilkiah,

2The son of Shallum, the son of Zadok, the son of Ahitub,

3The son of Amariah, the son of Azariah, the son of Meraioth,

4The son of Zerahiah, the son of Uzzi, the son of Bukki,

5The son of Abishua, the son of Phinehas, the son of Eleazar, the son of Aaron the chief priest:

6This Ezra went up from Babylon; and he *was* a ready scribe in the law of Moses, which the LORD God of Israel had given: and the king granted him all his request, according to the hand of the LORD his God upon him.

New International

12May God, who has caused his Name to dwell there, overthrow any king or people who lifts a hand to change this decree or to destroy this temple in Jerusalem.

I Darius have decreed it. Let it be carried out with diligence.

Completion and Dedication of the Temple

13Then, because of the decree King Darius had sent, Tattenai, governor of Trans-Euphrates, and Shethar-Bozenai and their associates carried it out with diligence. 14So the elders of the Jews continued to build and prosper under the preaching of Haggai the prophet and Zechariah, a descendant of Iddo. They finished building the temple according to the command of the God of Israel and the decrees of Cyrus, Darius and Artaxerxes, kings of Persia. 15The temple was completed on the third day of the month Adar, in the sixth year of the reign of King Darius.

16Then the people of Israel—the priests, the Levites and the rest of the exiles—celebrated the dedication of the house of God with joy. 17For the dedication of this house of God they offered a hundred bulls, two hundred rams, four hundred male lambs and, as a sin offering for all Israel, twelve male goats, one for each of the tribes of Israel. 18And they installed the priests in their divisions and the Levites in their groups for the service of God at Jerusalem, according to what is written in the Book of Moses.

The Passover

19On the fourteenth day of the first month, the exiles celebrated the Passover. 20The priests and Levites had purified themselves and were all ceremonially clean. The Levites slaughtered the Passover lamb for all the exiles, for their brothers the priests and for themselves. 21So the Israelites who had returned from the exile ate it, together with all who had separated themselves from the unclean practices of their Gentile neighbors in order to seek the LORD, the God of Israel. 22For seven days they celebrated with joy the Feast of Unleavened Bread, because the LORD had filled them with joy by changing the attitude of the king of Assyria, so that he assisted them in the work on the house of God, the God of Israel.

Ezra Comes to Jerusalem

7 AFTER THESE things, during the reign of Artaxerxes king of Persia, Ezra son of Seraiah, the son of Azariah, the son of Hilkiah, 2the son of Shallum, the son of Zadok, the son of Ahitub, 3the son of Amariah, the son of Meraioth, the son of Azariah, the son of Meraioth, 4the son of Zerahiah, the son of Uzzi, the son of Bukki, 5the son of Abishua, the son of Phinehas, the son of Eleazar, the son of Aaron the chief priest— 6this Ezra came up from Babylon. He was a teacher well versed in the Law of Moses, which the LORD, the God of Israel, had given. The king had granted him everything he asked, for the hand of the LORD his God was on him. 7Some of the

Living Bible

will destroy any king and any nation that alters this commandment and destroys this Temple. I, Darius, have issued this decree; let it be obeyed with all diligence."

13Governors Tattenai and Shethar-bozenai, and their companions complied at once with the command of King Darius.

14So the Jewish leaders continued in their work, and they were greatly encouraged by the preaching of the prophets Haggai and Zechariah (son of Iddo).

The Temple was finally finished, as had been commanded by God and decreed by Cyrus, Darius, and Artaxerxes, the kings of Persia. 15The completion date was February 18ᵃ in the sixth year of the reign of King Darius II.

16The Temple was then dedicated with great joy by the priests, the Levites, and all the people. 17During the dedication celebration 100 young bulls, 200 rams, and 400 lambs were sacrificed; and twelve male goats were presented as a sin offering for the twelve tribes of Israel. 18Then the priests and Levites were divided into their various service corps, to do the work of God as instructed in the laws of Moses.

19The Passover was celebrated on the first day of April.ᵇ 20For by that time many of the priests and Levites had consecrated themselves. 21, 22And some of the heathen people who had been relocated in Judah turned from their immoral customs and joined the Israelis in worshiping the Lord God. They, with the entire nation, ate the Passover feast and celebrated the Feast of Unleavened Bread for seven days. There was great joy throughout the land because the Lord had caused the king of Assyria to be generous to Israel and to assist in the construction of the Temple.

7 HERE IS the genealogy of Ezra, who traveled from Babylon to Jerusalemᶜ during the reign of King Artaxerxes of Persia:
Ezra was the son of Seriah;
Seriah was the son of Azariah;
Azariah was the son of Hilkiah;
Hilkiah was the son of Shallum;
Shallum was the son of Zadok;
Zadok was the son of Ahitub;
Ahitub was the son of Amariah;
Amariah was the son of Meraioth;
Meraioth was the son of Zerahiah;
Zerahiah was the son of Uzzi;
Uzzi was the son of Bukki;
Bukki was the son of Abishu-a;
Abishu-a was the son of Phinehas;
Phinehas was the son of Eleazar;
Eleazar was the son of Aaron, the chief priest.
6As a Jewish religious leader, Ezra was well versed in Jehovah's laws which Moses had given to the people of Israel. He asked to be allowed to return to Jerusalem, and the king granted his request; for the Lord his God was blessing him. 7, 8, 9Many ordinary people as well

New Revised Standard

there overthrow any king or people that shall put forth a hand to alter this, or to destroy this house of God in Jerusalem. I, Darius, make a decree; let it be done with all diligence."

Completion and Dedication of the Temple

13 Then, according to the word sent by King Darius, Tattenai, the governor of the province Beyond the River, Shethar-bozenai, and their associates did with all diligence what King Darius had ordered. 14So the elders of the Jews built and prospered, through the prophesying of the prophet Haggai and Zechariah son of Iddo. They finished their building by command of the God of Israel and by decree of Cyrus, Darius, and King Artaxerxes of Persia; 15and this house was finished on the third day of the month of Adar, in the sixth year of the reign of King Darius.

16 The people of Israel, the priests and the Levites, and the rest of the returned exiles, celebrated the dedication of this house of God with joy. 17They offered at the dedication of this house of God one hundred bulls, two hundred rams, four hundred lambs, and as a sin offering for all Israel, twelve male goats, according to the number of the tribes of Israel. 18Then they set the priests in their divisions and the Levites in their courses for the service of God at Jerusalem, as it is written in the book of Moses.

The Passover Celebrated

19 On the fourteenth day of the first month the returned exiles kept the passover. 20For both the priests and the Levites had purified themselves; all of them were clean. So they killed the passover lamb for all the returned exiles, for their fellow priests, and for themselves. 21It was eaten by the people of Israel who had returned from exile, and also by all who had joined them and separated themselves from the pollutions of the nations of the land to worship the LORD, the God of Israel. 22With joy they celebrated the festival of unleavened bread seven days; for the LORD had made them joyful, and had turned the heart of the king of Assyria to them, so that he aided them in the work on the house of God, the God of Israel.

The Coming and Work of Ezra

7 AFTER THIS, in the reign of King Artaxerxes of Persia, Ezra son of Seraiah, son of Azariah, son of Hilkiah, 2son of Shallum, son of Zadok, son of Ahitub, 3son of Amariah, son of Azariah, son of Meraioth, 4son of Zerahiah, son of Uzzi, son of Bukki, 5son of Abishua, son of Phinehas, son of Eleazar, son of the chief priest Aaron— 6this Ezra went up from Babylonia. He was a scribe skilled in the law of Moses that the LORD the God of Israel had given; and the king granted him all that he asked, for the hand of the LORD his God was upon him.

ᵃ 6:15 *February 18*, literally "the third day of the month of Adar."
ᵇ 6:19 *first day of April*, literally, "the fourteenth day of the first month" of the Hebrew calendar.   ᶜ 7:1 *to Jerusalem*, implied.

King James

7And there went up *some* of the children of Israel, and of the priests, and the Levites, and the singers, and the porters, and the Nethinims, unto Jerusalem, in the seventh year of Artaxerxes the king.

8And he came to Jerusalem in the fifth month, which *was* in the seventh year of the king.

9For upon the first *day* of the first month began he to go up from Babylon, and on the first *day* of the fifth month came he to Jerusalem, according to the good hand of his God upon him.

10For Ezra had prepared his heart to seek the law of the LORD, and to do *it,* and to teach in Israel statutes and judgments.

11¶ Now this *is* the copy of the letter that the king Artaxerxes gave unto Ezra the priest, the scribe, *even* a scribe of the words of the commandments of the LORD, and of his statutes to Israel.

12Artaxerxes, king of kings, unto Ezra the priest, a scribe of the law of the God of heaven, perfect *peace,* and at such a time.

13I make a decree, that all they of the people of Israel, and *of* his priests and Levites, in my realm, which are minded of their own freewill to go up to Jerusalem, go with thee.

14Forasmuch as thou art sent of the king, and of his seven counsellors, to inquire concerning Judah and Jerusalem, according to the law of thy God which *is* in thine hand;

15And to carry the silver and gold, which the king and his counsellors have freely offered unto the God of Israel, whose habitation *is* in Jerusalem,

16And all the silver and gold that thou canst find in all the province of Babylon, with the freewill offering of the people, and of the priests, offering willingly for the house of their God which *is* in Jerusalem:

17That thou mayest buy speedily with this money bullocks, rams, lambs, with their meat offerings and their drink offerings, and offer them upon the altar of the house of your God which *is* in Jerusalem.

18And whatsoever shall seem good to thee, and to thy brethren, to do with the rest of the silver and the gold, that do after the will of your God.

19The vessels also that are given thee for the service of the house of thy God, *those* deliver thou before the God of Jerusalem.

20And whatsoever more shall be needful for the house of thy God, which thou shalt have occasion to bestow, bestow *it* out of the king's treasure house.

21And I, *even* I Artaxerxes the king, do make a decree to all the treasurers which *are* beyond the river, that whatsoever Ezra the priest, the scribe of the law of the God of heaven, shall require of you, it be done speedily,

22Unto an hundred talents of silver, and to an hundred measures of wheat, and to an hundred baths of wine, and to an hundred baths of oil, and salt without prescribing *how much.*

23Whatsoever is commanded by the God of heaven, let it be diligently done for the house of the God of heaven: for why should there be wrath against the realm of the king and his sons?

24Also we certify you, that touching any of the priests and Levites, singers, porters, Nethinims, or ministers of this house of God, it shall not be lawful to impose toll, tribute, or custom, upon them.

25And thou, Ezra, after the wisdom of thy God, that *is* in thine hand, set magistrates and judges, which may judge all the people that *are* beyond the river, all such as know the laws of thy God; and teach ye them that know *them* not.

26And whosoever will not do the law of thy God, and the law of the king, let judgment be executed speedily upon him, whether *it be* unto death, or to banishment, or to confiscation of goods, or to imprisonment.

New International

Israelites, including priests, Levites, singers, gatekeepers and temple servants, also came up to Jerusalem in the seventh year of King Artaxerxes.

8Ezra arrived in Jerusalem in the fifth month of the seventh year of the king. 9He had begun his journey from Babylon on the first day of the first month, and he arrived in Jerusalem on the first day of the fifth month, for the gracious hand of his God was on him. 10For Ezra had devoted himself to the study and observance of the Law of the LORD, and to teaching its decrees and laws in Israel.

King Artaxerxes' Letter to Ezra

11This is a copy of the letter King Artaxerxes had given to Ezra the priest and teacher, a man learned in matters concerning the commands and decrees of the LORD for Israel:

12aArtaxerxes, king of kings,

To Ezra the priest, a teacher of the Law of the God of heaven:

Greetings.

13Now I decree that any of the Israelites in my kingdom, including priests and Levites, who wish to go to Jerusalem with you, may go. 14You are sent by the king and his seven advisers to inquire about Judah and Jerusalem with regard to the Law of your God, which is in your hand. 15Moreover, you are to take with you the silver and gold that the king and his advisers have freely given to the God of Israel, whose dwelling is in Jerusalem, 16together with all the silver and gold you may obtain from the province of Babylon, as well as the freewill offerings of the people and priests for the temple of their God in Jerusalem. 17With this money be sure to buy bulls, rams and male lambs, together with their grain offerings and drink offerings, and sacrifice them on the altar of the temple of your God in Jerusalem.

18You and your brother Jews may then do whatever seems best with the rest of the silver and gold, in accordance with the will of your God. 19Deliver to the God of Jerusalem all the articles entrusted to you for worship in the temple of your God. 20And anything else needed for the temple of your God that you may have occasion to supply, you may provide from the royal treasury.

21Now I, King Artaxerxes, order all the treasurers of Trans-Euphrates to provide with diligence whatever Ezra the priest, a teacher of the Law of the God of heaven, may ask of you— 22up to a hundred talents[b] of silver, a hundred cors[c] of wheat, a hundred baths[d] of wine, a hundred baths[d] of olive oil, and salt without limit. 23Whatever the God of heaven has prescribed, let it be done with diligence for the temple of the God of heaven. Why should there be wrath against the realm of the king and of his sons? 24You are also to know that you have no authority to impose taxes, tribute or duty on any of the priests, Levites, singers, gatekeepers, temple servants or other workers at this house of God.

25And you, Ezra, in accordance with the wisdom of your God, which you possess, appoint magistrates and judges to administer justice to all the people of Trans-Euphrates—all who know the laws of your God. And you are to teach any who do not know them. 26Whoever does not obey the law of your God and the law of the king must surely be punished by death, banishment, confiscation of property, or imprisonment.

---

a *12* The text of Ezra 7:12-26 is in Aramaic.   b *22* That is, about 3 3/4 tons (about 3.4 metric tons)   c *22* That is, probably about 600 bushels (about 22 kiloliters)   d *22* That is, probably about 600 gallons (about 2.2 kiloliters)

Living Bible

as priests, Levites, singers, gatekeepers, and Temple workers traveled with him. They left Babylon in the middle of March in the seventh year of the reign of Artaxerxes and arrived at Jerusalem in the month of August; for the Lord gave them a good trip. ¹⁰This was because Ezra had determined to study and obey the laws of the Lord and to become a Bible teacher, teaching those laws to the people of Israel.

¹¹King Artaxerxes presented this letter to Ezra the priest, the student of God's commands:

¹²"From: Artaxerxes, the king of kings.

"To: Ezra, the priest, the teacher of the laws of the God of heaven.

¹³"I decree that any Jew in my realm, including the priests and Levites, may return to Jerusalem with you. ¹⁴I and my Council of Seven hereby instruct you to take a copy of God's laws to Judah and Jerusalem and to send back a report of the religious progress being made there. ¹⁵We also commission you to take with you to Jerusalem the silver and gold which we are presenting as an offering to the God of Israel.

¹⁶"Moreover, you are to collect voluntary Temple offerings of silver and gold from the Jews and their priests in all of the provinces of Babylon. ¹⁷These funds are to be used primarily for the purchase of oxen, rams, lambs, grain offerings, and drink offerings, all of which will be offered upon the altar of your Temple when you arrive in Jerusalem. ¹⁸The money that is left over may be used in whatever way you and your brothers feel is the will of your God. ¹⁹And take with you the gold bowls and other items we are giving you for the Temple of your God at Jerusalem. ²⁰If you run short of money for the construction of the Temple or for any similar needs, you may requisition funds from the royal treasury.

²¹"I, Artaxerxes the king, send this decree to all the treasurers in the provinces west of the Euphrates River: 'You are to give Ezra whatever he requests of you (for he is a priest and teacher of the laws of the God of heaven), ²²up to $200,000 in silver; 1,225 bushels of wheat; 990 gallons of wine; any amount of salt; ²³and whatever else the God of heaven demands for his Temple; for why should we risk God's wrath against the king and his sons? ²⁴I also decree that no priest, Levite, choir member, gatekeeper, Temple attendant, or other worker in the Temple shall be required to pay taxes of any kind.'

²⁵"And you, Ezra, are to use the wisdom God has given you to select and appoint judges and other officials to govern all the people west of the Euphrates River; if they are not familiar with the laws of your God, you are to teach them. ²⁶Anyone refusing to obey the law of your God and the law of the king shall be punished immediately by death, banishment, confiscation of goods, or imprisonment."

New Revised Standard

7 Some of the people of Israel, and some of the priests and Levites, the singers and gatekeepers, and the temple servants also went up to Jerusalem, in the seventh year of King Artaxerxes. ⁸They came to Jerusalem in the fifth month, which was in the seventh year of the king. ⁹On the first day of the first month the journey up from Babylon was begun, and on the first day of the fifth month he came to Jerusalem, for the gracious hand of his God was upon him. ¹⁰For Ezra had set his heart to study the law of the Lᴏʀᴅ, and to do it, and to teach the statutes and ordinances in Israel.

The Letter of Artaxerxes to Ezra

11 This is a copy of the letter that King Artaxerxes gave to the priest Ezra, the scribe, a scholar of the text of the commandments of the Lᴏʀᴅ and his statutes for Israel: ¹²"Artaxerxes, king of kings, to the priest Ezra, the scribe of the law of the God of heaven: Peace.ᵉ And now ¹³I decree that any of the people of Israel or their priests or Levites in my kingdom who freely offers to go to Jerusalem may go with you. ¹⁴For you are sent by the king and his seven counselors to make inquiries about Judah and Jerusalem according to the law of your God, which is in your hand, ¹⁵and also to convey the silver and gold that the king and his counselors have freely offered to the God of Israel, whose dwelling is in Jerusalem, ¹⁶with all the silver and gold that you shall find in the whole province of Babylonia, and with the freewill offerings of the people and the priests, given willingly for the house of their God in Jerusalem. ¹⁷With this money, then, you shall with all diligence buy bulls, rams, and lambs, and their grain offerings and their drink offerings, and you shall offer them on the altar of the house of your God in Jerusalem. ¹⁸Whatever seems good to you and your colleagues to do with the rest of the silver and gold, you may do, according to the will of your God. ¹⁹The vessels that have been given you for the service of the house of your God, you shall deliver before the God of Jerusalem. ²⁰And whatever else is required for the house of your God, which you are responsible for providing, you may provide out of the king's treasury.

21 "I, King Artaxerxes, decree to all the treasurers in the province Beyond the River: Whatever the priest Ezra, the scribe of the law of the God of heaven, requires of you, let it be done with all diligence, ²²up to one hundred talents of silver, one hundred cors of wheat, one hundred bathsᶠ of wine, one hundred bathsᶠ of oil, and unlimited salt. ²³Whatever is commanded by the God of heaven, let it be done with zeal for the house of the God of heaven, or wrath will come upon the realm of the king and his heirs. ²⁴We also notify you that it shall not be lawful to impose tribute, custom, or toll on any of the priests, the Levites, the singers, the doorkeepers, the temple servants, or other servants of this house of God.

25 "And you, Ezra, according to the God-given wisdom you possess, appoint magistrates and judges who may judge all the people in the province Beyond the River who know the laws of your God; and you shall teach those who do not know them. ²⁶All who will not obey the law of your God and the law of the king, let judgment be strictly executed on them, whether for death or for banishment or for confiscation of their goods or for imprisonment."

ᵉ Syr Vg 1 Esdras 8.9: Aram *Perfect*   ᶠ A Heb measure of volume

King James

27¶ Blessed *be* the LORD God of our fathers, which hath put *such a thing* as this in the king's heart, to beautify the house of the LORD which *is* in Jerusalem:

28And hath extended mercy unto me before the king, and his counsellors, and before all the king's mighty princes. And I was strengthened as the hand of the LORD my God *was* upon me, and I gathered together out of Israel chief men to go up with me.

8 THESE *ARE* now the chief of their fathers, and *this is* the genealogy of them that went up with me from Babylon, in the reign of Artaxerxes the king.

2Of the sons of Phinehas; Gershom: of the sons of Ithamar; Daniel: of the sons of David; Hattush.

3Of the sons of Shechaniah, of the sons of Pharosh; Zechariah: and with him were reckoned by genealogy of the males an hundred and fifty.

4Of the sons of Pahath-moab; Elihoenai the son of Zerahiah, and with him two hundred males.

5Of the sons of Shechaniah; the son of Jahaziel, and with him three hundred males.

6Of the sons also of Adin; Ebed the son of Jonathan, and with him fifty males.

7And of the sons of Elam; Jeshaiah the son of Athaliah, and with him seventy males.

8And of the sons of Shephatiah; Zebadiah the son of Michael, and with him fourscore males.

9Of the sons of Joab; Obadiah the son of Jehiel, and with him two hundred and eighteen males.

10And of the sons of Shelomith; the son of Josiphiah, and with him an hundred and threescore males.

11And of the sons of Bebai; Zechariah the son of Bebai, and with him twenty and eight males.

12And of the sons of Azgad; Johanan the son of Hakkatan, and with him an hundred and ten males.

13And of the last sons of Adonikam, whose names *are* these, Eliphelet, Jeiel, and Shemaiah, and with them threescore males.

14Of the sons also of Bigvai; Uthai, and Zabbud, and with them seventy males.

15¶ And I gathered them together to the river that runneth to Ahava; and there abode we in tents three days: and I viewed the people, and the priests, and found there none of the sons of Levi.

16Then sent I for Eliezer, for Ariel, for Shemaiah, and for Elnathan, and for Jarib, and for Elnathan, and for Nathan, and for Zechariah, and for Meshullam, chief men; also for Joiarib, and for Elnathan, men of understanding.

17And I sent them with commandment unto Iddo the chief at the place Casiphia, and I told them what they should say unto Iddo, *and* to his brethren the Nethinims, at the place Casiphia, that they should bring unto us ministers for the house of our God.

18And by the good hand of our God upon us they brought us a man of understanding, of the sons of Mahli, the son of Levi, the son of Israel; and Sherebiah, with his sons and his brethren, eighteen;

19And Hashabiah, and with him Jeshaiah of the sons of Merari, his brethren and their sons, twenty;

20Also of the Nethinims, whom David and the princes had appointed for the service of the Levites, two hundred and twenty Nethinims: all of them were expressed by name.

21¶ Then I proclaimed a fast there, at the river of Ahava, that we might afflict ourselves before our God, to seek of him a right way for us, and for our little ones, and for all our substance.

New International

27Praise be to the LORD, the God of our fathers, who has put it into the king's heart to bring honor to the house of the LORD in Jerusalem in this way 28and who has extended his good favor to me before the king and his advisers and all the king's powerful officials. Because the hand of the LORD my God was on me, I took courage and gathered leading men from Israel to go up with me.

List of the Family Heads Returning With Ezra

8 THESE ARE the family heads and those registered with them who came up with me from Babylon during the reign of King Artaxerxes:

2of the descendants of Phinehas, Gershom;
of the descendants of Ithamar, Daniel;
of the descendants of David, Hattush 3of the descendants of Shecaniah;

of the descendants of Parosh, Zechariah, and with him were registered 150 men;

4of the descendants of Pahath-Moab, Eliehoenai son of Zerahiah, and with him 200 men;

5of the descendants of Zattu,[a] Shecaniah son of Jahaziel, and with him 300 men;

6of the descendants of Adin, Ebed son of Jonathan, and with him 50 men;

7of the descendants of Elam, Jeshaiah son of Athaliah, and with him 70 men;

8of the descendants of Shephatiah, Zebadiah son of Michael, and with him 80 men;

9of the descendants of Joab, Obadiah son of Jehiel, and with him 218 men;

10of the descendants of Bani,[b] Shelomith son of Josiphiah, and with him 160 men;

11of the descendants of Bebai, Zechariah son of Bebai, and with him 28 men;

12of the descendants of Azgad, Johanan son of Hakkatan, and with him 110 men;

13of the descendants of Adonikam, the last ones, whose names were Eliphelet, Jeuel and Shemaiah, and with them 60 men;

14of the descendants of Bigvai, Uthai and Zaccur, and with them 70 men.

The Return to Jerusalem

15I assembled them at the canal that flows toward Ahava, and we camped there three days. When I checked among the people and the priests, I found no Levites there. 16So I summoned Eliezer, Ariel, Shemaiah, Elnathan, Jarib, Elnathan, Nathan, Zechariah and Meshullam, who were leaders, and Joiarib and Elnathan, who were men of learning, 17and I sent them to Iddo, the leader in Casiphia. I told them what to say to Iddo and his kinsmen, the temple servants in Casiphia, so that they might bring attendants to us for the house of our God. 18Because the gracious hand of our God was on us, they brought us Sherebiah, a capable man, from the descendants of Mahli son of Levi, the son of Israel, and Sherebiah's sons and brothers, 18 men; 19and Hashabiah, together with Jeshaiah from the descendants of Merari, and his brothers and nephews, 20 men. 20They also brought 220 of the temple servants—a body that David and the officials had established to assist the Levites. All were registered by name.

21There, by the Ahava Canal, I proclaimed a fast, so that we might humble ourselves before our God and ask him for a safe journey for us and our children, with all our possessions. 22I was ashamed to ask the king for

---

a 5 Some Septuagint manuscripts (also 1 Esdras 8:32); Hebrew does not have *Zattu*.   b 10 Some Septuagint manuscripts (also 1 Esdras 8:36); Hebrew does not have *Bani*.

Living Bible

27Well, praise the Lord God of our ancestors, who made the king want to beautify the Temple of the Lord in Jerusalem! 28And praise God for demonstrating such lovingkindness to mec by honoring me before the king and his Council of Seven and before all of his mighty princes! I was given great status because the Lord my God was with me; and I persuaded some of the leaders of Israel to return with me to Jerusalem.

8 THESE ARE the names and genealogies of the leaders who accompanied me from Babylon during the reign of King Artaxerxes:

2-14From the clan of Phinehas—Gershom;
From the clan of Ithamar—Daniel;
From the subclan of David of the clan of Shecaniah—Hattush;
From the clan of Parosh—Zechariah, and 150 other men;
From the clan of Pahath-moab—Eli-e-ho-enai (son of Zerahiah), and 200 other men;
From the clan of Shecaniah—the son of Jahaziel, and 300 other men;
From the clan of Adin—Ebed (son of Jonathan), and 50 other men;
From the clan of Elam—Jeshaiah (son of Athaliah), and 70 other men;
From the clan of Shephatiah—Zebadiah (son of Michael), and 80 other men;
From the clan of Joab—Obadiah (son of Jehiel), and 218 other men;
From the clan of Bani—Shelomith (son of Josiphiah), and 160 other men;
From the clan of Bebai—Zechariah (son of Bebai), and 28 other men;
From the clan of Azgad—Johanan (son of Hakkatan), and 110 other men;
From the clan of Adonikam—Eliphelet, Jeuel, Shemaiah, and 60 other men (they arrived at a later time);
From the clan of Bigvai—Uthai, Zaccur, and 70 other men.

15We assembled at the Ahava River and camped there for three days while I went over the lists of the people and the priests who had arrived; and I found that not one Levite had volunteered! 16So I sent for Eliezer, Ari-el, Shemaiah, Elnathan, Jarib, Elnathan, Nathan, Zechariah, and Meshullam, the Levite leaders; I also sent for Joiarib and Elnathan, who were very wise men. 17I sent them to Iddo, the leader of the Jews at Casiphia, to ask him and his brothers and the Temple attendants to send us priests for the Temple of God at Jerusalem. 18And God was good! He sent us an outstanding man named Sherebiah, along with eighteen of his sons and brothers; he was a very astute man and a descendant of Mahli, the son of Levi and grandson of Israel. 19God also sent Hashabiah; and Jeshaiah (the son of Merari), with twenty of his sons and brothers; 20and 220 Temple attendants. (The Temple attendants were assistants to the Levites—a job classification of Temple employees first instituted by King David.) These 220 men were all listed by name.

21Then I declared a fast while we were at the Ahava River so that we would humble ourselves before our God; and we prayed that he would give us a good journey and protect us, our children, and our goods as we traveled. 22For I was ashamed to ask the king for soldiers

New Revised Standard

27 Blessed be the LORD, the God of our ancestors, who put such a thing as this into the heart of the king to glorify the house of the LORD in Jerusalem, 28 and who extended to me steadfast love before the king and his counselors, and before all the king's mighty officers. I took courage, for the hand of the LORD my God was upon me, and I gathered leaders from Israel to go up with me.

Heads of Families Who Returned with Ezra

8 THESE ARE their family heads, and this is the genealogy of those who went up with me from Babylonia, in the reign of King Artaxerxes: 2Of the descendants of Phinehas, Gershom. Of Ithamar, Daniel. Of David, Hattush, 3of the descendants of Shecaniah. Of Parosh, Zechariah, with whom were registered one hundred fifty males. 4Of the descendants of Pahath-moab, Eliehoenai son of Zerahiah, and with him two hundred males. 5Of the descendants of Zattu,d Shecaniah son of Jahaziel, and with him three hundred males. 6Of the descendants of Adin, Ebed son of Jonathan, and with him fifty males. 7Of the descendants of Elam, Jeshaiah son of Athaliah, and with him seventy males. 8Of the descendants of Shephatiah, Zebadiah son of Michael, and with him eighty males. 9Of the descendants of Joab, Obadiah son of Jehiel, and with him two hundred eighteen males. 10Of the descendants of Bani,e Shelomith son of Josiphiah, and with him one hundred sixty males. 11Of the descendants of Bebai, Zechariah son of Bebai, and with him twenty-eight males. 12Of the descendants of Azgad, Johanan son of Hakkatan, and with him one hundred ten males. 13Of the descendants of Adonikam, those who came later, their names being Eliphelet, Jeuel, and Shemaiah, and with them sixty males. 14Of the descendants of Bigvai, Uthai and Zaccur, and with them seventy males.

Servants for the Temple

15 I gathered them by the river that runs to Ahava, and there we camped three days. As I reviewed the people and the priests, I found there none of the descendants of Levi. 16Then I sent for Eliezer, Ariel, Shemaiah, Elnathan, Jarib, Elnathan, Nathan, Zechariah, and Meshullam, who were leaders, and for Joiarib and Elnathan, who were wise, 17and sent them to Iddo, the leader at the place called Casiphia, telling them what to say to Iddo and his colleagues the temple servants at Casiphia, namely, to send us ministers for the house of our God. 18Since the gracious hand of our God was upon us, they brought us a man of discretion, of the descendants of Mahli son of Levi son of Israel, namely Sherebiah, with his sons and kin, eighteen; 19also Hashabiah and with him Jeshaiah of the descendants of Merari, with his kin and their sons, twenty; 20besides two hundred twenty of the temple servants, whom David and his officials had set apart to attend the Levites. These were all mentioned by name.

Fasting and Prayer for Protection

21 Then I proclaimed a fast there, at the river Ahava, that we might deny ourselvesf before our God, to seek from him a safe journey for ourselves, our children, and all our possessions. 22For I was ashamed to ask the

c 7:28 to me, i.e., Ezra, who is the speaker in the remainder of the book.

d Gk 1 Esdras 8.32: Heb lacks of Zattu   e Gk 1 Esdras 8.36: Heb lacks Bani
f Or might fast

King James

22For I was ashamed to require of the king a band of soldiers and horsemen to help us against the enemy in the way: because we had spoken unto the king, saying, The hand of our God *is* upon all them for good that seek him; but his power and his wrath *is* against all them that forsake him.

23So we fasted and besought our God for this: and he was entreated of us.

24¶ Then I separated twelve of the chief of the priests, Sherebiah, Hashabiah, and ten of their brethren with them,

25And weighed unto them the silver, and the gold, and the vessels, *even* the offering of the house of our God, which the king, and his counsellors, and his lords, and all Israel *there* present, had offered:

26I even weighed unto their hand six hundred and fifty talents of silver, and silver vessels an hundred talents, *and* of gold an hundred talents;

27Also twenty basins of gold, of a thousand drams; and two vessels of fine copper, precious as gold.

28And I said unto them, Ye *are* holy unto the LORD; the vessels *are* holy also; and the silver and the gold *are* a freewill offering unto the LORD God of your fathers.

29Watch ye, and keep *them*, until ye weigh *them* before the chief of the priests and the Levites, and chief of the fathers of Israel, at Jerusalem, in the chambers of the house of the LORD.

30So took the priests and the Levites the weight of the silver, and the gold, and the vessels, to bring *them* to Jerusalem unto the house of our God.

31¶ Then we departed from the river of Ahava on the twelfth *day* of the first month, to go unto Jerusalem: and the hand of our God was upon us, and he delivered us from the hand of the enemy, and of such as lay in wait by the way.

32And we came to Jerusalem, and abode there three days.

33¶ Now on the fourth day was the silver and the gold and the vessels weighed in the house of our God by the hand of Meremoth the son of Uriah the priest; and with him *was* Eleazar the son of Phinehas; and with them *was* Jozabad the son of Jeshua, and Noadiah the son of Binnui, Levites;

34By number *and* by weight of every one: and all the weight was written at that time.

35*Also* the children of those that had been carried away, which were come out of the captivity, offered burnt offerings unto the God of Israel, twelve bullocks for all Israel, ninety and six rams, seventy and seven lambs, twelve he goats *for* a sin offering: all *this was* a burnt offering unto the LORD.

36¶ And they delivered the king's commissions unto the king's lieutenants, and to the governors on this side the river: and they furthered the people, and the house of God.

9 NOW WHEN these things were done, the princes came to me, saying, The people of Israel, and the priests, and the Levites, have not separated themselves from the people of the lands, *doing* according to their abominations, *even* of the Canaanites, the Hittites, the Perizzites, the Jebusites, the Ammonites, the Moabites, the Egyptians, and the Amorites.

2For they have taken of their daughters for themselves, and for their sons: so that the holy seed have mingled themselves with the people of *those* lands: yea, the hand of the princes and rulers hath been chief in this trespass.

New International

soldiers and horsemen to protect us from enemies on the road, because we had told the king, "The gracious hand of our God is on everyone who looks to him, but his great anger is against all who forsake him." 23So we fasted and petitioned our God about this, and he answered our prayer.

24Then I set apart twelve of the leading priests, together with Sherebiah, Hashabiah and ten of their brothers, 25and I weighed out to them the offering of silver and gold and the articles that the king, his advisers, his officials and all Israel present there had donated for the house of our God. 26I weighed out to them 650 talents[a] of silver, silver articles weighing 100 talents,[b] 100 talents[b] of gold, 27720 bowls of gold valued at 1,000 darics,[c] and two fine articles of polished bronze, as precious as gold.

28I said to them, "You as well as these articles are consecrated to the LORD. The silver and gold are a freewill offering to the LORD, the God of your fathers. 29Guard them carefully until you weigh them out in the chambers of the house of the LORD in Jerusalem before the leading priests and the Levites and the family heads of Israel." 30Then the priests and Levites received the silver and gold and sacred articles that had been weighed out to be taken to the house of our God in Jerusalem.

31On the twelfth day of the first month we set out from the Ahava Canal to go to Jerusalem. The hand of our God was on us, and he protected us from enemies and bandits along the way. 32So we arrived in Jerusalem, where we rested three days.

33On the fourth day, in the house of our God, we weighed out the silver and gold and the sacred articles into the hands of Meremoth son of Uriah, the priest. Eleazar son of Phinehas was with him, and so were the Levites Jozabad son of Jeshua and Noadiah son of Binnui. 34Everything was accounted for by number and weight, and the entire weight was recorded at that time.

35Then the exiles who had returned from captivity sacrificed burnt offerings to the God of Israel: twelve bulls for all Israel, ninety-six rams, seventy-seven male lambs and, as a sin offering, twelve male goats. All this was a burnt offering to the LORD. 36They also delivered the king's orders to the royal satraps and to the governors of Trans-Euphrates, who then gave assistance to the people and to the house of God.

Ezra's Prayer About Intermarriage

9 AFTER THESE things had been done, the leaders came to me and said, "The people of Israel, including the priests and the Levites, have not kept themselves separate from the neighboring peoples with their detestable practices, like those of the Canaanites, Hittites, Perizzites, Jebusites, Ammonites, Moabites, Egyptians and Amorites. 2They have taken some of their daughters as wives for themselves and their sons, and have mingled the holy race with the peoples around them. And the leaders and officials have led the way in this unfaithfulness."

[a] *26 That is, about 25 tons (about 22 metric tons)* [b] *26 That is, about 3 3/4 tons (about 3.4 metric tons)* [c] *27 That is, about 19 pounds (about 8.5 kilograms)*

Living Bible

and cavalry to accompany us and protect us from the enemies along the way. After all, we had told the king that our God would protect all those who worshiped him, and that disaster could come only to those who had forsaken him! 23So we fasted and begged God to take care of us. And he did.

24I appointed twelve leaders of the priests—Sherebiah, Hashabiah, and ten other priests—25 to be in charge of transporting the silver, gold, the gold bowls, and the other items which the king and his council and the leaders and people of Israel had presented to the Temple of God. 26, 27I weighed the money as I gave it to them and found it to total $1,300,000 in silver; $200,000 in silver utensils; many millions in gold; and twenty gold bowls worth a total of $100,000. There were also two beautiful pieces of brass which were as precious as gold. 28I consecrated these men to the Lord, and then consecrated the treasures—the equipment and money and bowls which had been given as free-will offerings to the Lord God of our fathers.

29"Guard these treasures well!" I told them; "present them without a penny lost to the priests and the Levite leaders and the elders of Israel at Jerusalem, where they are to be placed in the treasury of the Temple."

30So the priests and the Levites accepted the responsibility of taking it to God's Temple in Jerusalem. 31We broke camp at the Ahava River at the end of March[d] and started off to Jerusalem; and God protected us and saved us from enemies and bandits along the way. 32So at last we arrived safely at Jerusalem.

33On the fourth day after our arrival the silver, gold, and other valuables were weighed in the Temple by Meremoth (the son of Uriah the priest), Eleazar (son of Phinehas), Jozabad (son of Jeshua), and Noadiah (son of Binnui)—all of whom were Levites. 34A receipt was given for each item, and the weight of the gold and silver was noted.

35Then everyone in our party sacrificed burnt offerings to the God of Israel—twelve oxen for the nation of Israel; ninety-six rams; seventy-seven lambs; and twelve goats as a sin offering. 36The king's decrees were delivered to his lieutenants and the governors of all the provinces west of the Euphrates River, and of course they then cooperated in the rebuilding of the Temple of God.

9 BUT THEN the Jewish leaders came to tell me that many of the Jewish people and even some of the priests and Levites had taken up the horrible customs of the heathen people who lived in the land—the Canaanites, Hittites, Perizzites, Jebusites, Ammonites, Moabites, Egyptians, and Amorites. 2The men of Israel had married girls from these heathen nations, and had taken them as wives for their sons. So the holy people of God were being polluted by these mixed marriages, and the political leaders were some of the worst offenders.

New Revised Standard

king for a band of soldiers and cavalry to protect us against the enemy on our way, since we had told the king that the hand of our God is gracious to all who seek him, but his power and his wrath are against all who forsake him. 23 So we fasted and petitioned our God for this, and he listened to our entreaty.

Gifts for the Temple

24 Then I set apart twelve of the leading priests: Sherebiah, Hashabiah, and ten of their kin with them. 25 And I weighed out to them the silver and the gold and the vessels, the offering for the house of our God that the king, his counselors, his lords, and all Israel there present had offered; 26 I weighed out into their hand six hundred fifty talents of silver, and one hundred silver vessels worth . . . talents,[e] and one hundred talents of gold, 27 twenty gold bowls worth a thousand darics, and two vessels of fine polished bronze as precious as gold. 28 And I said to them, "You are holy to the LORD, and the vessels are holy; and the silver and the gold are a freewill offering to the LORD, the God of your ancestors. 29 Guard them and keep them until you weigh them before the chief priests and the Levites and the heads of families in Israel at Jerusalem, within the chambers of the house of the LORD." 30 So the priests and the Levites took over the silver, the gold, and the vessels as they were weighed out, to bring them to Jerusalem, to the house of our God.

The Return to Jerusalem

31 Then we left the river Ahava on the twelfth day of the first month, to go to Jerusalem; the hand of our God was upon us, and he delivered us from the hand of the enemy and from ambushes along the way. 32 We came to Jerusalem and remained there three days. 33 On the fourth day, within the house of our God, the silver, the gold, and the vessels were weighed into the hands of the priest Meremoth son of Uriah, and with him was Eleazar son of Phinehas, and with them were the Levites, Jozabad son of Jeshua and Noadiah son of Binnui. 34 The total was counted and weighed, and the weight of everything was recorded.

35 At that time those who had come from captivity, the returned exiles, offered burnt offerings to the God of Israel, twelve bulls for all Israel, ninety-six rams, seventy-seven lambs, and as a sin offering twelve male goats; all this was a burnt offering to the LORD. 36 They also delivered the king's commissions to the king's satraps and to the governors of the province Beyond the River; and they supported the people and the house of God.

Denunciation of Mixed Marriages

9 AFTER THESE things had been done, the officials approached me and said, "The people of Israel, the priests, and the Levites have not separated themselves from the peoples of the lands with their abominations, from the Canaanites, the Hittites, the Perizzites, the Jebusites, the Ammonites, the Moabites, the Egyptians, and the Amorites. 2 For they have taken some of their daughters as wives for themselves and for their sons. Thus the holy seed has mixed itself with the peoples of the lands, and in this faithlessness the officials and leaders have led the way." 3 When I heard this, I tore

---

[d] 8:31 end of March, or, "the twelfth day of the first month" of the Hebrew calendar.

[e] The number of talents is lacking

King James

3And when I heard this thing, I rent my garment and my mantle, and plucked off the hair of my head and of my beard, and sat down astonied.

4Then were assembled unto me every one that trembled at the words of the God of Israel, because of the transgression of those that had been carried away; and I sat astonied until the evening sacrifice.

5¶ And at the evening sacrifice I arose up from my heaviness; and having rent my garment and my mantle, I fell upon my knees, and spread out my hands unto the LORD my God,

6And said, O my God, I am ashamed and blush to lift up my face to thee, my God: for our iniquities are increased over our head, and our trespass is grown up unto the heavens.

7Since the days of our fathers have we been in a great trespass unto this day; and for our iniquities have we, our kings, and our priests, been delivered into the hand of the kings of the lands, to the sword, to captivity, and to a spoil, and to confusion of face, as it is this day.

8And now for a little space grace hath been shown from the LORD our God, to leave us a remnant to escape, and to give us a nail in his holy place, that our God may lighten our eyes, and give us a little reviving in our bondage.

9For we were bondmen; yet our God hath not forsaken us in our bondage, but hath extended mercy unto us in the sight of the kings of Persia, to give us a reviving, to set up the house of our God, and to repair the desolations thereof, and to give us a wall in Judah and in Jerusalem.

10And now, O our God, what shall we say after this? for we have forsaken thy commandments,

11Which thou hast commanded by thy servants the prophets, saying, The land, unto which ye go to possess it, is an unclean land with the filthiness of the people of the lands, with their abominations, which have filled it from one end to another with their uncleanness.

12Now therefore give not your daughters unto their sons, neither take their daughters unto your sons, nor seek their peace or their wealth for ever: that ye may be strong, and eat the good of the land, and leave it for an inheritance to your children for ever.

13And after all that is come upon us for our evil deeds, and for our great trespass, seeing that thou our God hast punished us less than our iniquities deserve, and hast given us such deliverance as this;

14Should we again break thy commandments, and join in affinity with the people of these abominations? wouldest not thou be angry with us till thou hadst consumed us, so that there should be no remnant nor escaping?

15O LORD God of Israel, thou art righteous: for we remain yet escaped, as it is this day: behold, we are before thee in our trespasses: for we cannot stand before thee because of this.

10 NOW WHEN Ezra had prayed, and when he had confessed, weeping and casting himself down before the house of God, there assembled unto him out of Israel a very great congregation of men and women and children: for the people wept very sore.

2And Shechaniah the son of Jehiel, one of the sons of Elam, answered and said unto Ezra, We have trespassed against our God, and have taken strange wives of the people of the land: yet now there is hope in Israel concerning this thing.

New International

3When I heard this, I tore my tunic and cloak, pulled hair from my head and beard and sat down appalled. 4Then everyone who trembled at the words of the God of Israel gathered around me because of this unfaithfulness of the exiles. And I sat there appalled until the evening sacrifice.

5Then, at the evening sacrifice, I rose from my self-abasement, with my tunic and cloak torn, and fell on my knees with my hands spread out to the LORD my God 6and prayed:

"O my God, I am too ashamed and disgraced to lift up my face to you, my God, because our sins are higher than our heads and our guilt has reached to the heavens. 7From the days of our forefathers until now, our guilt has been great. Because of our sins, we and our kings and our priests have been subjected to the sword and captivity, to pillage and humiliation at the hand of foreign kings, as it is today.

8"But now, for a brief moment, the LORD our God has been gracious in leaving us a remnant and giving us a firm place in his sanctuary, and so our God gives light to our eyes and a little relief in our bondage. 9Though we are slaves, our God has not deserted us in our bondage. He has shown us kindness in the sight of the kings of Persia: He has granted us new life to rebuild the house of our God and repair its ruins, and he has given us a wall of protection in Judah and Jerusalem.

10"But now, O our God, what can we say after this? For we have disregarded the commands 11you gave through your servants the prophets when you said: 'The land you are entering to possess is a land polluted by the corruption of its peoples. By their detestable practices they have filled it with their impurity from one end to the other. 12Therefore, do not give your daughters in marriage to their sons or take their daughters for your sons. Do not seek a treaty of friendship with them at any time, that you may be strong and eat the good things of the land and leave it to your children as an everlasting inheritance.'

13"What has happened to us is a result of our evil deeds and our great guilt, and yet, our God, you have punished us less than our sins have deserved and have given us a remnant like this. 14Shall we again break your commands and intermarry with the peoples who commit such detestable practices? Would you not be angry enough with us to destroy us, leaving us no remnant or survivor? 15O LORD, God of Israel, you are righteous! We are left this day as a remnant. Here we are before you in our guilt, though because of it not one of us can stand in your presence."

The People's Confession of Sin

10 WHILE EZRA was praying and confessing, weeping and throwing himself down before the house of God, a large crowd of Israelites—men, women and children—gathered around him. They too wept bitterly. 2Then Shecaniah son of Jehiel, one of the descendants of Elam, said to Ezra, "We have been unfaithful to our God by marrying foreign women from the peoples around us. But in spite of this, there is still hope for Israel. 3Now let us make a covenant before our God to

Living Bible

3When I heard this, I tore my clothing and pulled hair from my head and beard and sat down utterly baffled. 4Then many who feared the God of Israel because of this sin of his people came and sat with me until the time of the evening burnt offering.

5Finally I stood before the Lord in great embarrassment; then I fell to my knees and lifted my hands to the Lord, 6and cried out, "O my God, I am ashamed; I blush to lift up my face to you, for our sins are piled higher than our heads and our guilt is as boundless as the heavens. 7Our whole history has been one of sin; that is why we and our kings and our priests were slain by the heathen kings—we were captured, robbed, and disgraced, just as we are today. 8But now we have been given a moment of peace, for you have permitted a few of us to return to Jerusalem from our exile. You have given us a moment of joy and new life in our slavery. 9For we were slaves, but in your love and mercy you did not abandon us to slavery; instead you caused the kings of Persia to be favorable to us. They have even given us their assistance in rebuilding the Temple of our God and in giving us Jerusalem as a walled city in Judah.

10"And now, O God, what can we say after all of this? For once again we have abandoned you and broken your laws! 11The prophets warned us that the land we would possess was totally defiled by the horrible practices of the people living there. From one end to the other it is filled with corruption. 12You told us not to let our daughters marry their sons, and not to let our sons marry their daughters, and not to help those nations in any way. You warned us that only if we followed this rule could we become a prosperous nation and forever leave that prosperity to our children as an inheritance. 13And now, even after our punishment in exile because of our wickedness (and we have been punished far less than we deserved), and even though you have let some of us return, 14we have broken your commandments again and intermarried with people who do these awful things. Surely your anger will destroy us now until not even this little remnant escapes. 15O Lord God of Israel, you are a just God; what hope can we have if you give us justice as we stand here before you in our wickedness?"

10 AS I lay on the ground in front of the Temple, weeping and praying and making this confession, a large crowd of men, women, and children gathered around and cried with me.

2Then Shecaniah (the son of Jehiel of the clan of Elam) said to me, "We acknowledge our sin against our God, for we have married these heathen women. But there is hope for Israel in spite of this. 3For we agree

New Revised Standard

my garment and my mantle, and pulled hair from my head and beard, and sat appalled. 4Then all who trembled at the words of the God of Israel, because of the faithlessness of the returned exiles, gathered around me while I sat appalled until the evening sacrifice.

Ezra's Prayer

5 At the evening sacrifice I got up from my fasting, with my garments and my mantle torn, and fell on my knees, spread out my hands to the LORD my God, 6and said,

"O my God, I am too ashamed and embarrassed to lift my face to you, my God, for our iniquities have risen higher than our heads, and our guilt has mounted up to the heavens. 7From the days of our ancestors to this day we have been deep in guilt, and for our iniquities we, our kings, and our priests have been handed over to the kings of the lands, to the sword, to captivity, to plundering, and to utter shame, as is now the case. 8But now for a brief moment favor has been shown by the LORD our God, who has left us a remnant, and given us a stake in his holy place, in order that hea may brighten our eyes and grant us a little sustenance in our slavery. 9For we are slaves; yet our God has not forsaken us in our slavery, but has extended to us his steadfast love before the kings of Persia, to give us new life to set up the house of our God, to repair its ruins, and to give us a wall in Judea and Jerusalem.

10 "And now, our God, what shall we say after this? For we have forsaken your commandments, 11which you commanded by your servants the prophets, saying, 'The land that you are entering to possess is a land unclean with the pollutions of the peoples of the lands, with their abominations. They have filled it from end to end with their uncleanness. 12Therefore do not give your daughters to their sons, neither take their daughters for your sons, and never seek their peace or prosperity, so that you may be strong and eat the good of the land and leave it for an inheritance to your children forever.' 13After all that has come upon us for our evil deeds and for our great guilt, seeing that you, our God, have punished us less than our iniquities deserved and have given us such a remnant as this, 14shall we break your commandments again and intermarry with the peoples who practice these abominations? Would you not be angry with us until you destroy us without remnant or survivor? 15O LORD, God of Israel, you are just, but we have escaped as a remnant, as is now the case. Here we are before you in our guilt, though no one can face you because of this."

The People's Response

10 WHILE EZRA prayed and made confession, weeping and throwing himself down before the house of God, a very great assembly of men, women, and children gathered to him out of Israel; the people also wept bitterly. 2Shecaniah son of Jehiel, of the descendants of Elam, addressed Ezra, saying, "We have broken faith with our God and have married foreign women from the peoples of the land, but even now there is hope for Israel in spite of this. 3So now let us make

a Heb our God

King James

3Now therefore let us make a covenant with our God to put away all the wives, and such as are born of them, according to the counsel of my lord, and of those that tremble at the commandment of our God; and let it be done according to the law.

4Arise; for *this* matter *belongeth* unto thee: we also *will be* with thee: be of good courage, and do *it*.

5Then arose Ezra, and made the chief priests, the Levites, and all Israel, to swear that they should do according to this word. And they sware.

6¶ Then Ezra rose up from before the house of God, and went into the chamber of Johanan the son of Eliashib: and *when* he came thither, he did eat no bread, nor drink water: for he mourned because of the transgression of them that had been carried away.

7And they made proclamation throughout Judah and Jerusalem unto all the children of the captivity, that they should gather themselves together unto Jerusalem;

8And that whosoever would not come within three days, according to the counsel of the princes and the elders, all his substance should be forfeited, and himself separated from the congregation of those that had been carried away.

9¶ Then all the men of Judah and Benjamin gathered themselves together unto Jerusalem within three days. It *was* the ninth month, on the twentieth *day* of the month; and all the people sat in the street of the house of God, trembling because of *this* matter, and for the great rain.

10And Ezra the priest stood up, and said unto them, Ye have transgressed, and have taken strange wives, to increase the trespass of Israel.

11Now therefore make confession unto the Lord God of your fathers, and do his pleasure: and separate yourselves from the people of the land, and from the strange wives.

12Then all the congregation answered and said with a loud voice, As thou hast said, so must we do.

13But the people *are* many, and *it is* a time of much rain, and we are not able to stand without, neither *is this* a work of one day or two: for we are many that have transgressed in this thing.

14Let now our rulers of all the congregation stand, and let all them which have taken strange wives in our cities come at appointed times, and with them the elders of every city, and the judges thereof, until the fierce wrath of our God for this matter be turned from us.

15¶ Only Jonathan the son of Asahel and Jahaziah the son of Tikvah were employed about this *matter:* and Meshullam and Shabbethai the Levite helped them.

16And the children of the captivity did so. And Ezra the priest, *with* certain chief of the fathers, after the house of their fathers, and all of them by *their* names, were separated, and sat down in the first day of the tenth month to examine the matter.

17And they made an end with all the men that had taken strange wives by the first day of the first month.

18¶ And among the sons of the priests there were found that had taken strange wives: *namely,* of the sons of Jeshua the son of Jozadak, and his brethren; Maaseiah, and Eliezer, and Jarib, and Gedaliah.

19And they gave their hands that they would put away their wives; and *being* guilty, *they offered* a ram of the flock for their trespass.

20And of the sons of Immer; Hanani, and Zebadiah.

21And of the sons of Harim; Maaseiah, and Elijah, and Shemaiah, and Jehiel, and Uzziah.

22And of the sons of Pashur; Elioenai, Maaseiah, Ishmael, Nethaneel, Jozabad, and Elasah.

23Also of the Levites; Jozabad, and Shimei, and Kelaiah, (the same *is* Kelita,) Pethahiah, Judah, and Eliezer.

24Of the singers also; Eliashib: and of the porters; Shallum, and Telem, and Uri.

New International

send away all these women and their children, in accordance with the counsel of my lord and of those who fear the commands of our God. Let it be done according to the Law. 4Rise up; this matter is in your hands. We will support you, so take courage and do it."

5So Ezra rose up and put the leading priests and Levites and all Israel under oath to do what had been suggested. And they took the oath. 6Then Ezra withdrew from before the house of God and went to the room of Jehohanan son of Eliashib. While he was there, he ate no food and drank no water, because he continued to mourn over the unfaithfulness of the exiles.

7A proclamation was then issued throughout Judah and Jerusalem for all the exiles to assemble in Jerusalem. 8Anyone who failed to appear within three days would forfeit all his property, in accordance with the decision of the officials and elders, and would himself be expelled from the assembly of the exiles.

9Within the three days, all the men of Judah and Benjamin had gathered in Jerusalem. And on the twentieth day of the ninth month, all the people were sitting in the square before the house of God, greatly distressed by the occasion and because of the rain. 10Then Ezra the priest stood up and said to them, "You have been unfaithful; you have married foreign women, adding to Israel's guilt. 11Now make confession to the Lord, the God of your fathers, and do his will. Separate yourselves from the peoples around you and from your foreign wives."

12The whole assembly responded with a loud voice: "You are right! We must do as you say. 13But there are many people here and it is the rainy season; so we cannot stand outside. Besides, this matter cannot be taken care of in a day or two, because we have sinned greatly in this thing. 14Let our officials act for the whole assembly. Then let everyone in our towns who has married a foreign woman come at a set time, along with the elders and judges of each town, until the fierce anger of our God in this matter is turned away from us." 15Only Jonathan son of Asahel and Jahzeiah son of Tikvah, supported by Meshullam and Shabbethai the Levite, opposed this.

16So the exiles did as was proposed. Ezra the priest selected men who were family heads, one from each family division, and all of them designated by name. On the first day of the tenth month they sat down to investigate the cases, 17and by the first day of the first month they finished dealing with all the men who had married foreign women.

Those Guilty of Intermarriage

18Among the descendants of the priests, the following had married foreign women:

From the descendants of Jeshua son of Jozadak, and his brothers: Maaseiah, Eliezer, Jarib and Gedaliah. 19(They all gave their hands in pledge to put away their wives, and for their guilt they each presented a ram from the flock as a guilt offering.)

20From the descendants of Immer:
Hanani and Zebadiah.

21From the descendants of Harim:
Maaseiah, Elijah, Shemaiah, Jehiel and Uzziah.

22From the descendants of Pashhur:
Elioenai, Maaseiah, Ishmael, Nethanel, Jozabad and Elasah.

23Among the Levites:

Jozabad, Shimei, Kelaiah (that is, Kelita), Pethahiah, Judah and Eliezer.

24From the singers:
Eliashib.

From the gatekeepers:
Shallum, Telem and Uri.

Living Bible

before our God to divorce our heathen wives and to send them away with our children; we will follow your commands, and the commands of the others who fear our God. We will obey the laws of God. 4Take courage and tell us how to proceed in setting things straight, and we will fully cooperate."

5So I stood up and demanded that the leaders of the priests and the Levites and all the people of Israel swear that they would do as Shecaniah had said; and they all agreed. 6Then I went into the room of Jehohanan in the Temple and refused all food and drink; for I was mourning because of the sin of the returned exiles.

7, 8Then a proclamation was made throughout Judah and Jerusalem that everyone should appear at Jerusalem within three days and that the leaders and elders had decided that anyone who refused to come would be disinherited and excommunicated from Israel. 9Within three days, on the fifth day of December,a all the men of Judah and Benjamin had arrived and were sitting in the open space before the Temple; and they were trembling because of the seriousness of the matter and because of the heavy rainfall. 10Then I, Ezra the priest, arose and addressed them:

"You have sinned, for you have married heathen women; now we are even more deeply under God's condemnation than we were before. 11Confess your sin to the Lord God of your fathers and do what he demands: separate yourselves from the heathen people about you and from these women."

12Then all the men spoke up and said, "We will do what you have said. 13But this isn't something that can be done in a day or two, for there are many of us involved in this sinful affair. And it is raining so hard that we can't stay out here much longer. 14Let our leaders arrange trials for us. Everyone who has a heathen wife will come at the scheduled time with the elders and judges of his city; then each case will be decided and the situation will be cleared up and the fierce wrath of our God will be turned away from us."

15Only Jonathan (son of Asahel), Jahzeiah (son of Tikvah), Meshullam, and Shabbethai the Levite opposed this course of action.

16-19So this was the plan that was followed: Some of the clan leaders and I were designated as judges; we began our work on December 15, and finished by March 15.

Following is the list of priests who had married heathen wives (they vowed to divorce their wives and acknowledged their guilt by offering rams as sacrifices):

Ma-aseiah, Eliezer, Jarib, Gedaliah.
20The sons of Immer:
Hanani, Zebadiah.
21The sons of Harim:
Ma-aseiah, Elijah, Shemaiah, Jehiel, Uzziah.
22The sons of Pashhur:
Eli-o-enai, Ma-aseiah, Ishmael, Nethanel, Jozabad, Elasah.
23The Levites who were guilty:
Jozabad, Shime-i, Kelaiah (also called Kelita), Petha-haiah, Judah, Eliezer.
24Of the singers, there was Eliashib.
Of the gatekeepers, Shallum, Telem, and Uri.

New Revised Standard

a covenant with our God to send away all these wives and their children, according to the counsel of my lord and of those who tremble at the commandment of our God; and let it be done according to the law. 4Take action, for it is your duty, and we are with you; be strong, and do it." 5Then Ezra stood up and made the leading priests, the Levites, and all Israel swear that they would do as had been said. So they swore.

Foreign Wives and Their Children Rejected

6 Then Ezra withdrew from before the house of God, and went to the chamber of Jehohanan son of Eliashib, where he spent the night.b He did not eat bread or drink water, for he was mourning over the faithlessness of the exiles. 7They made a proclamation throughout Judah and Jerusalem to all the returned exiles that they should assemble at Jerusalem, 8and that if any did not come within three days, by order of the officials and the elders all their property should be forfeited, and they themselves banned from the congregation of the exiles.

9 Then all the people of Judah and Benjamin assembled at Jerusalem within the three days; it was the ninth month, on the twentieth day of the month. All the people sat in the open square before the house of God, trembling because of this matter and because of the heavy rain. 10Then Ezra the priest stood up and said to them, "You have trespassed and married foreign women, and so increased the guilt of Israel. 11Now make confession to the LORD the God of your ancestors, and do his will; separate yourselves from the peoples of the land and from the foreign wives." 12Then all the assembly answered with a loud voice, "It is so; we must do as you have said. 13But the people are many, and it is a time of heavy rain; we cannot stand in the open. Nor is this a task for one day or for two, for many of us have transgressed in this matter. 14Let our officials represent the whole assembly, and let all in our towns who have taken foreign wives come at appointed times, and with them the elders and judges of every town, until the fierce wrath of our God on this account is averted from us." 15Only Jonathan son of Asahel and Jahzeiah son of Tikvah opposed this, and Meshullam and Shabbethai the Levites supported them.

16 Then the returned exiles did so. Ezra the priest selected men,c heads of families, according to their families, each of them designated by name. On the first day of the tenth month they sat down to examine the matter. 17By the first day of the first month they had come to the end of all the men who had married foreign women.

18 There were found of the descendants of the priests who had married foreign women, of the descendants of Jeshua son of Jozadak and his brothers: Maaseiah, Eliezer, Jarib, and Gedaliah. 19They pledged themselves to send away their wives, and their guilt offering was a ram of the flock for their guilt. 20Of the descendants of Immer: Hanani and Zebadiah. 21Of the descendants of Harim: Maaseiah, Elijah, Shemaiah, Jehiel, and Uzziah. 22Of the descendants of Pashhur: Elioenai, Maaseiah, Ishmael, Nethanel, Jozabad, and Elasah.

23 Of the Levites: Jozabad, Shimei, Kelaiah (that is, Kelita), Pethahiah, Judah, and Eliezer. 24Of the singers: Eliashib. Of the gatekeepers: Shallum, Telem, and Uri.

---

a *10:9 fifth day of December*, literally, "the twentieth day of the ninth month" of the Hebrew calendar.

b 1 Esdras 9.2: Heb *where he went*   c 1 Esdra 9.16: Syr: Heb *And there were selected Ezra,*

King James

25Moreover of Israel: of the sons of Parosh; Ramiah, and Jeziah, and Malchiah, and Miamin, and Eleazar, and Malchijah, and Benaiah.

26And of the sons of Elam; Mattaniah, Zechariah, and Jehiel, and Abdi, and Jeremoth, and Eliah.

27And of the sons of Zattu; Elioenai, Eliashib, Mattaniah, and Jeremoth, and Zabad, and Aziza.

28Of the sons also of Bebai; Jehohanan, Hananiah, Zabbai, and Athlai.

29And of the sons of Bani; Meshullam, Malluch, and Adaiah, Jashub, and Sheal, and Ramoth.

30And of the sons of Pahath-moab; Adna, and Chelal, Benaiah, Maaseiah, Mattaniah, Bezaleel, and Binnui, and Manasseh.

31And of the sons of Harim; Eliezer, Ishijah, Malchiah, Shemaiah, Shimeon,

32Benjamin, Malluch, and Shemariah.

33Of the sons of Hashum; Mattenai, Mattathah, Zabad, Eliphelet, Jeremai, Manasseh, and Shimei.

34Of the sons of Bani; Maadai, Amram, and Uel,

35Benaiah, Bedeiah, Chelluh,

36Vaniah, Meremoth, Eliashib,

37Mattaniah, Mattenai, and Jaasau,

38And Bani, and Binnui, Shimei,

39And Shelemiah, and Nathan, and Adaiah,

40Machnadebai, Shashai, Sharai,

41Azareel, and Shelemiah, Shemariah,

42Shallum, Amariah, and Joseph.

43Of the sons of Nebo; Jeiel, Mattithiah, Zabad, Zebina, Jadau, and Joel, Benaiah.

44All these had taken strange wives: and some of them had wives by whom they had children.

New International

25And among the other Israelites:

From the descendants of Parosh:
Ramiah, Izziah, Malkijah, Mijamin, Eleazar, Malkijah and Benaiah.

26From the descendants of Elam:
Mattaniah, Zechariah, Jehiel, Abdi, Jeremoth and Elijah.

27From the descendants of Zattu:
Elioenai, Eliashib, Mattaniah, Jeremoth, Zabad and Aziza.

28From the descendants of Bebai:
Jehohanan, Hananiah, Zabbai and Athlai.

29From the descendants of Bani:
Meshullam, Malluch, Adaiah, Jashub, Sheal and Jeremoth.

30From the descendants of Pahath-Moab:
Adna, Kelal, Benaiah, Maaseiah, Mattaniah, Bezalel, Binnui and Manasseh.

31From the descendants of Harim:
Eliezer, Ishijah, Malkijah, Shemaiah, Shimeon, 32Benjamin, Malluch and Shemariah.

33From the descendants of Hashum:
Mattenai, Mattattah, Zabad, Eliphelet, Jeremai, Manasseh and Shimei.

34From the descendants of Bani:
Maadai, Amram, Uel, 35Benaiah, Bedeiah, Keluhi, 36Vaniah, Meremoth, Eliashib, 37Mattaniah, Mattenai and Jaasu.

38From the descendants of Binnui:a
Shimei, 39Shelemiah, Nathan, Adaiah, 40Macnadebai, Shashai, Sharai, 41Azarel, Shelemiah, Shemariah, 42Shallum, Amariah and Joseph.

43From the descendants of Nebo:
Jeiel, Mattithiah, Zabad, Zebina, Jaddai, Joel and Benaiah.

44All these had married foreign women, and some of them had children by these wives.b

a 37,38 See Septuagint (also 1 Esdras 9:34); Hebrew Jaasu 38and Bani and Binnui.   b 44 Or and they sent them away with their children

Living Bible

25Here is the list of ordinary citizens who were declared guilty:

From the clan of Parosh:

Ramiah, Izziah, Malchijah, Mijamin, Eleazar, Hashabiah, Benaiah.

26From the clan of Elam:

Mattaniah, Zechariah, Jehiel, Abdi, Jeremoth, Elijah.

27From the clan of Zattu:

Eli-o-enai, Eliashib, Mattaniah, Jeremoth, Zabad, Aziza.

28From the clan of Bebai:

Jeho-hanan, Hananiah, Zabbai, Athlai.

29From the clan of Bani:

Meshullam, Malluch, Adaiah, Jashub, Sheal, Jeremoth.

30From the clan of Pahath-moab:

Adna, Chelal, Benaiah, Ma-aseiah, Mattaniah, Bezalel, Binnui, Manasseh.

31, 32From the clan of Harim:

Eliezer, Isshijah, Malchijah, Shemaiah, Shime-on, Benjamin, Malluch, Shemariah.

33From the clan of Hashum:

Mattenai, Mattattah, Zabad, Eliphelet, Jeremai, Manasseh, Shime-i.

34-42From the clan of Bani:

Ma-adai, Amram, Uel, Banaiah, Bedeiah, Cheluhi, Vaniah, Meremoth, Eliashib, Mattaniah, Mattenai, Jaasu, Bani, Binnui, Shime-i, Shelemiah, Nathan, Adaiah, Machnadebai, Shashai, Sharai, Azarel, Shelemiah, Shemariah, Shallum, Amariah, Joseph.

43From the clan of Nebo:

Je-iel, Mattithiah, Zabad, Zebina, Jaddai, Joel, Benaiah.

44Each of these men had heathen wives, and many had children by these wives.

New Revised Standard

25 And of Israel: of the descendants of Parosh: Ramiah, Izziah, Malchijah, Mijamin, Eleazar, Hashabiah,c and Benaiah. 26Of the descendants of Elam: Mattaniah, Zechariah, Jehiel, Abdi, Jeremoth, and Elijah. 27Of the descendants of Zattu: Elioenai, Eliashib, Mattaniah, Jeremoth, Zabad, and Aziza. 28Of the descendants of Bebai: Jehohanan, Hananiah, Zabbai, and Athlai. 29Of the descendants of Bani: Meshullam, Malluch, Adaiah, Jashub, Sheal, and Jeremoth. 30Of the descendants of Pahath-moab: Adna, Chelal, Benaiah, Maaseiah, Mattaniah, Bezalel, Binnui, and Manasseh. 31Of the descendants of Harim: Eliezer, Isshijah, Malchijah, Shemaiah, Shimeon, 32Benjamin, Malluch, and Shemariah. 33Of the descendants of Hashum: Mattenai, Mattattah, Zabad, Eliphelet, Jeremai, Manasseh, and Shimei. 34Of the descendants of Bani: Maadai, Amram, Uel, 35Benaiah, Bedeiah, Cheluhi, 36Vaniah, Meremoth, Eliashib, 37Mattaniah, Mattenai, and Jaasu. 38Of the descendants of Binnui:d Shimei, 39Shelemiah, Nathan, Adaiah, 40Machnadebai, Shashai, Sharai, 41Azarel, Shelemiah, Shemariah, 42Shallum, Amariah, and Joseph. 43Of the descendants of Nebo: Jeiel, Mattithiah, Zabad, Zebina, Jaddai, Joel, and Benaiah. 44All these had married foreign women, and they sent them away with their children.e

c 1 Esdras 9.26   Gk: Heb *Malchijah*   d Gk: Heb *Bani, Binnui*
e 1 Esdras 9.36; Meaning of Heb uncertain

THE BOOK OF

Nehemiah

Nehemiah

King James

1 THE WORDS of Nehemiah the son of Hachaliah. And it came to pass in the month Chisleu, in the twentieth year, as I was in Shushan the palace,

2That Hanani, one of my brethren, came, he and *certain* men of Judah; and I asked them concerning the Jews that had escaped, which were left of the captivity, and concerning Jerusalem.

3And they said unto me, The remnant that are left of the captivity there in the province *are* in great affliction and reproach: the wall of Jerusalem also *is* broken down, and the gates thereof are burned with fire.

4¶ And it came to pass, when I heard these words, that I sat down and wept, and mourned *certain* days, and fasted, and prayed before the God of heaven,

5And said, I beseech thee, O LORD God of heaven, the great and terrible God, that keepeth covenant and mercy for them that love him and observe his commandments:

6Let thine ear now be attentive, and thine eyes open, that thou mayest hear the prayer of thy servant, which I pray before thee now, day and night, for the children of Israel thy servants, and confess the sins of the children of Israel, which we have sinned against thee: both I and my father's house have sinned.

7We have dealt very corruptly against thee, and have not kept the commandments, nor the statutes, nor the judgments, which thou commandest thy servant Moses.

8Remember, I beseech thee, the word that thou commandedst thy servant Moses, saying, *If* ye transgress, I will scatter you abroad among the nations:

9But *if* ye turn unto me, and keep my commandments, and do them; though there were of you cast out unto the uttermost part of the heaven, *yet* will I gather them from thence, and will bring them unto the place that I have chosen to set my name there.

10Now these *are* thy servants and thy people, whom thou hast redeemed by thy great power, and by thy strong hand.

11O Lord, I beseech thee, let now thine ear be attentive to the prayer of thy servant, and to the prayer of thy servants, who desire to fear thy name: and prosper, I pray thee, thy servant this day, and grant him mercy in the sight of this man. For I was the king's cupbearer.

2 AND IT came to pass in the month Nisan, in the twentieth year of Artaxerxes the king, *that* wine *was* before him: and I took up the wine, and gave *it* unto the king. Now I had not been *beforetime* sad in his presence.

2Wherefore the king said unto me, Why *is* thy countenance sad, seeing thou *art* not sick? this *is* nothing *else* but sorrow of heart. Then I was very sore afraid,

New International

Nehemiah's Prayer

1 THE WORDS of Nehemiah son of Hacaliah:

In the month of Kislev in the twentieth year, while I was in the citadel of Susa, 2Hanani, one of my brothers, came from Judah with some other men, and I questioned them about the Jewish remnant that survived the exile, and also about Jerusalem.

3They said to me, "Those who survived the exile and are back in the province are in great trouble and disgrace. The wall of Jerusalem is broken down, and its gates have been burned with fire."

4When I heard these things, I sat down and wept. For some days I mourned and fasted and prayed before the God of heaven. 5Then I said:

"O LORD, God of heaven, the great and awesome God, who keeps his covenant of love with those who love him and obey his commands, 6let your ear be attentive and your eyes open to hear the prayer your servant is praying before you day and night for your servants, the people of Israel. I confess the sins we Israelites, including myself and my father's house, have committed against you. 7We have acted very wickedly toward you. We have not obeyed the commands, decrees and laws you gave your servant Moses.

8"Remember the instruction you gave your servant Moses, saying, 'If you are unfaithful, I will scatter you among the nations, 9but if you return to me and obey my commands, then even if your exiled people are at the farthest horizon, I will gather them from there and bring them to the place I have chosen as a dwelling for my Name.'

10"They are your servants and your people, whom you redeemed by your great strength and your mighty hand. 11O Lord, let your ear be attentive to the prayer of this your servant and to the prayer of your servants who delight in revering your name. Give your servant success today by granting him favor in the presence of this man."

I was cupbearer to the king.

Artaxerxes Sends Nehemiah to Jerusalem

2 IN THE month of Nisan in the twentieth year of King Artaxerxes, when wine was brought for him, I took the wine and gave it to the king. I had not been sad in his presence before; 2so the king asked me, "Why does your face look so sad when you are not ill? This can be nothing but sadness of heart."

I was very much afraid, 3but I said to the king, "May

Nehemiah　　　Nehemiah

1 THE AUTOBIOGRAPHY of *Nehemiah, the son of Hecaliah:*

In December of the twentieth year of the reign of King Artaxerxes of Persia,ᵃ when I was at the palace at Shushan, ²one of my fellow Jews named Hanani came to visit me with some men who had arrived from Judah. I took the opportunity to inquire about how things were going in Jerusalem.

"How are they getting along?" I asked. "—the Jews who returned to Jerusalem from their exile here?"

³"Well," they replied, "things are not good; the wall of Jerusalem is still torn down, and the gates are burned."

⁴When I heard this, I sat down and cried. In fact, I refused to eat for several days, for I spent the time in prayer to the God of heaven.

⁵"O Lord God," I cried out; "O great and awesome God who keeps his promises and is so loving and kind to those who love and obey him! Hear my prayer! ⁶, ⁷Listen carefully to what I say! Look down and see me praying night and day for your people Israel. I confess that we have sinned against you; yes, I and my people have committed the horrible sin of not obeying the commandments you gave us through your servant Moses. ⁸Oh, please remember what you told Moses! You said,

" *'If you sin, I will scatter you among the nations; ⁹but if you return to me and obey my laws, even though you are exiled to the farthest corners of the universe, I will bring you back to Jerusalem. For Jerusalem is the place in which I have chosen to live.'*

¹⁰"We are your servants, the people you rescued by your great power. ¹¹O Lord, please hear my prayer! Heed the prayers of those of us who delight to honor you. Please help me now as I go in and ask the king for a great favor—put it into his heart to be kind to me." (I was the king's cupbearer.)

2 ONE DAY in April, four months later, as I was serving the king his wine he asked me, "Why so sad? You aren't sick, are you? You look like a man with deep troubles." (For until then I had always been cheerful when I was with him.) I was badly frightened, ³but

Nehemiah Prays for His People

1 THE WORDS of Nehemiah son of Hacaliah. In the month of Chislev, in the twentieth year, while I was in Susa the capital, ²one of my brothers, Hanani, came with certain men from Judah; and I asked them about the Jews that survived, those who had escaped the captivity, and about Jerusalem. ³They replied, "The survivors there in the province who escaped captivity are in great trouble and shame; the wall of Jerusalem is broken down, and its gates have been destroyed by fire."

4 When I heard these words I sat down and wept, and mourned for days, fasting and praying before the God of heaven. ⁵I said, "O LORD God of heaven, the great and awesome God who keeps covenant and steadfast love with those who love him and keep his commandments; ⁶let your ear be attentive and your eyes open to hear the prayer of your servant that I now pray before you day and night for your servants, the people of Israel, confessing the sins of the people of Israel, which we have sinned against you. Both I and my family have sinned. ⁷We have offended you deeply, failing to keep the commandments, the statutes, and the ordinances that you commanded your servant Moses. ⁸Remember the word that you commanded your servant Moses, 'If you are unfaithful, I will scatter you among the peoples; ⁹but if you return to me and keep my commandments and do them, though your outcasts are under the farthest skies, I will gather them from there and bring them to the place at which I have chosen to establish my name.' ¹⁰They are your servants and your people, whom you redeemed by your great power and your strong hand. ¹¹O Lord, let your ear be attentive to the prayer of your servant, and to the prayer of your servants who delight in revering your name. Give success to your servant today, and grant him mercy in the sight of this man!"

At the time, I was cupbearer to the king.

Nehemiah Sent to Judah

2 IN THE month of Nisan, in the twentieth year of King Artaxerxes, when wine was served him, I carried the wine and gave it to the king. Now, I had never been sad in his presence before. ²So the king said to me, "Why is your face sad, since you are not sick? This can only be sadness of the heart." Then I was very much afraid. ³I said to the king, "May the king live

---

ᵃ *1:1 King Artaxerxes of Persia,* implied.

King James

3And said unto the king, Let the king live for ever: why should not my countenance be sad, when the city, the place of my fathers' sepulchres, *lieth* waste, and the gates thereof are consumed with fire?

4Then the king said unto me, For what dost thou make request? So I prayed to the God of heaven.

5And I said unto the king, If it please the king, and if thy servant have found favour in thy sight, that thou wouldest send me unto Judah, unto the city of my fathers' sepulchres, that I may build it.

6And the king said unto me, (the queen also sitting by him,) For how long shall thy journey be? and when wilt thou return? So it pleased the king to send me; and I set him a time.

7Moreover I said unto the king, If it please the king, let letters be given me to the governors beyond the river, that they may convey me over till I come into Judah;

8And a letter unto Asaph the keeper of the king's forest, that he may give me timber to make beams for the gates of the palace which *appertained* to the house, and for the wall of the city, and for the house that I shall enter into. And the king granted me, according to the good hand of my God upon me.

9¶ Then I came to the governors beyond the river, and gave them the king's letters. Now the king had sent captains of the army and horsemen with me.

10When Sanballat the Horonite, and Tobiah the servant, the Ammonite, heard *of it,* it grieved them exceedingly that there was come a man to seek the welfare of the children of Israel.

11So I came to Jerusalem, and was there three days.

12¶ And I arose in the night, I and some few men with me; neither told I *any* man what my God had put in my heart to do at Jerusalem: neither *was there any* beast with me, save the beast that I rode upon.

13And I went out by night by the gate of the valley, even before the dragon well, and to the dung port, and viewed the walls of Jerusalem, which were broken down, and the gates thereof were consumed with fire.

14Then I went on to the gate of the fountain, and to the king's pool: but *there was* no place for the beast *that was* under me to pass.

15Then went I up in the night by the brook, and viewed the wall, and turned back, and entered by the gate of the valley, and *so* returned.

16And the rulers knew not whither I went, or what I did; neither had I as yet told *it* to the Jews, nor to the priests, nor to the nobles, nor to the rulers, nor to the rest that did the work.

17¶ Then said I unto them, Ye see the distress that we *are* in, how Jerusalem *lieth* waste, and the gates therof are burned with fire: come, and let us build up the wall of Jerusalem, that we be no more a reproach.

18Then I told them of the hand of my God which was good upon me; as also the king's words that he had spoken unto me. And they said, Let us rise up and build. So they strengthened their hands for *this* good *work.*

19But when Sanballat the Horonite, and Tobiah the servant, the Ammonite, and Geshem the Arabian, heard *it,* they laughed us to scorn, and despised us, and said, What *is* this thing that ye do? will ye rebel against the king?

20Then answered I them, and said unto them, The God of heaven, he will prosper us; therefore we his servants will arise and build: but ye have no portion, nor right, nor memorial, in Jerusalem.

New International

the king live forever! Why should my face not look sad when the city where my fathers are buried lies in ruins, and its gates have been destroyed by fire?"

4The king said to me, "What is it you want?"

Then I prayed to the God of heaven, 5and I answered the king, "If it pleases the king and if your servant has found favor in his sight, let him send me to the city in Judah where my fathers are buried so that I can rebuild it."

6Then the king, with the queen sitting beside him, asked me, "How long will your journey take, and when will you get back?" It pleased the king to send me; so I set a time.

7I also said to him, "If it pleases the king, may I have letters to the governors of Trans-Euphrates, so that they will provide me safe-conduct until I arrive in Judah? 8And may I have a letter to Asaph, keeper of the king's forest, so he will give me timber to make beams for the gates of the citadel by the temple and for the city wall and for the residence I will occupy?" And because the gracious hand of my God was upon me, the king granted my requests. 9So I went to the governors of Trans-Euphrates and gave them the king's letters. The king had also sent army officers and cavalry with me.

10When Sanballat the Horonite and Tobiah the Ammonite official heard about this, they were very much disturbed that someone had come to promote the welfare of the Israelites.

Nehemiah Inspects Jerusalem's Walls

11I went to Jerusalem, and after staying there three days 12I set out during the night with a few men. I had not told anyone what my God had put in my heart to do for Jerusalem. There were no mounts with me except the one I was riding on.

13By night I went out through the Valley Gate toward the Jackala Well and the Dung Gate, examining the walls of Jerusalem, which had been broken down, and its gates, which had been destroyed by fire. 14Then I moved on toward the Fountain Gate and the King's Pool, but there was not enough room for my mount to get through; 15so I went up the valley by night, examining the wall. Finally, I turned back and reentered through the Valley Gate. 16The officials did not know where I had gone or what I was doing, because as yet I had said nothing to the Jews or the priests or nobles or officials or any others who would be doing the work.

17Then I said to them, "You see the trouble we are in: Jerusalem lies in ruins, and its gates have been burned with fire. Come, let us rebuild the wall of Jerusalem, and we will no longer be in disgrace." 18I also told them about the gracious hand of my God upon me and what the king had said to me.

They replied, "Let us start rebuilding." So they began this good work.

19But when Sanballat the Horonite, Tobiah the Ammonite official and Geshem the Arab heard about it, they mocked and ridiculed us. "What is this you are doing?" they asked. "Are you rebelling against the king?"

20I answered them by saying, "The God of heaven will give us success. We his servants will start rebuilding, but as for you, you have no share in Jerusalem or any claim or historic right to it."

---

a 13 Or *Serpent* or *Fig*

Living Bible

I replied, "Sir,[b] why shouldn't I be sad? For the city where my ancestors are buried is in ruins, and the gates have been burned down."

4"Well, what should be done?" the king asked.

With a quick prayer to the God of heaven, I replied, "If it please Your Majesty and if you look upon me with your royal favor, send me to Judah to rebuild the city of my fathers!"

5,6The king replied, with the queen sitting beside him, "How long will you be gone? When will you return?"

So it was agreed! And I set a time for my departure! 7Then I added this to my request: "If it please the king, give me letters to the governors west of the Euphrates River instructing them to let me travel through their countries on my way to Judah; 8also a letter to Asaph, the manager of the king's forest, instructing him to give me timber for the beams and for the gates of the fortress near the Temple, and for the city walls, and for a house for myself."

And the king granted these requests, for God was being gracious to me.

9When I arrived in the provinces west of the Euphrates River, I delivered the king's letters to the governors there. (The king, I should add, had sent along army officers and troops to protect me!) 10But when Sanballat (the Horonite) and Tobiah (an Ammonite who was a government official) heard of my arrival, they were very angry that anyone was interested in helping Israel.

11,12Three days after my arrival at Jerusalem I stole out during the night, taking only a few men with me; for I hadn't told a soul about the plans for Jerusalem which God had put into my heart. I was mounted on my donkey and the others were on foot, 13and we went out through the Valley Gate toward the Jackal's Well and over to the Dung Gate to see the broken walls and burned gates. 14,15Then we went to the Fountain Gate and to the King's Pool, but my donkey couldn't get through the rubble. So we circled the city, and I followed the brook, inspecting the wall, and entered again at the Valley Gate.

16The city officials did not know I had been out there, or why, for as yet I had said nothing to anyone about my plans—not to the political or religious leaders, or even to those who would be doing the work.

17But now I told them, "You know full well the tragedy of our city; it lies in ruins and its gates are burned. Let us rebuild the wall of Jerusalem and rid ourselves of this disgrace!"

18Then I told them about the desire God had put into my heart, and of my conversation with the king, and the plan to which he had agreed.

They replied at once, "Good! Let's rebuild the wall!" And so the work began.

19But when Sanballat and Tobiah and Geshem the Arab heard of our plan, they scoffed and said, "What are you doing, rebelling against the king like this?"

20But I replied, "The God of heaven will help us, and we, his servants, will rebuild this wall; but you may have no part in this affair."

New Revised Standard

forever! Why should my face not be sad, when the city, the place of my ancestors' graves, lies waste, and its gates have been destroyed by fire?" 4Then the king said to me, "What do you request?" So I prayed to the God of heaven. 5Then I said to the king, "If it pleases the king, and if your servant has found favor with you, I ask that you send me to Judah, to the city of my ancestors' graves, so that I may rebuild it." 6The king said to me (the queen also was sitting beside him), "How long will you be gone, and when will you return?" So it pleased the king to send me, and I set him a date. 7Then I said to the king, "If it pleases the king, let letters be given me to the governors of the province Beyond the River, that they may grant me passage until I arrive in Judah; 8and a letter to Asaph, the keeper of the king's forest, directing him to give me timber to make beams for the gates of the temple fortress, and for the wall of the city, and for the house that I shall occupy." And the king granted me what I asked, for the gracious hand of my God was upon me.

9 Then I came to the governors of the province Beyond the River, and gave them the king's letters. Now the king had sent officers of the army and cavalry with me. 10When Sanballat the Horonite and Tobiah the Ammonite official heard this, it displeased them greatly that someone had come to seek the welfare of the people of Israel.

Nehemiah's Inspection of the Walls

11 So I came to Jerusalem and was there for three days. 12Then I got up during the night, I and a few men with me; I told no one what my God had put into my heart to do for Jerusalem. The only animal I took was the animal I rode. 13I went out by night by the Valley Gate past the Dragon's Spring and to the Dung Gate, and I inspected the walls of Jerusalem that had been broken down and its gates that had been destroyed by fire. 14Then I went on to the Fountain Gate and to the King's Pool; but there was no place for the animal I was riding to continue. 15So I went up by way of the valley by night and inspected the wall. Then I turned back and entered by the Valley Gate, and so returned. 16The officials did not know where I had gone or what I was doing; I had not yet told the Jews, the priests, the nobles, the officials, and the rest that were to do the work.

Decision to Restore the Walls

17 Then I said to them, "You see the trouble we are in, how Jerusalem lies in ruins with its gates burned. Come, let us rebuild the wall of Jerusalem, so that we may no longer suffer disgrace." 18I told them that the hand of my God had been gracious upon me, and also the words that the king had spoken to me. Then they said, "Let us start building!" So they committed themselves to the common good. 19But when Sanballat the Horonite and Tobiah the Ammonite official, and Geshem the Arab heard of it, they mocked and ridiculed us, saying, "What is this that you are doing? Are you rebelling against the king?" 20Then I replied to them, "The God of heaven is the one who will give us success, and we his servants are going to start building; but you have no share or claim or historic right in Jerusalem."

b 2:3 *Sir*, literally, "Let the king live forever."

King James

3 THEN ELIASHIB the high priest rose up with his brethren the priests, and they builded the sheep gate; they sanctified it, and set up the doors of it; even unto the tower of Meah they sanctified it, unto the tower of Hananeel.

2And next unto him builded the men of Jericho. And next to them builded Zaccur the son of Imri.

3But the fish gate did the sons of Hassenaah build, who also laid the beams thereof, and set up the doors thereof, the locks thereof, and the bars thereof.

4And next unto them repaired Meremoth the son of Urijah, the son of Koz. And next unto them repaired Meshullam the son of Berechiah, the son of Meshezabeel. And next unto them repaired Zadok the son of Baana.

5And next unto them the Tekoites repaired; but their nobles put not their necks to the work of their Lord.

6Moreover the old gate repaired Jehoiada the son of Paseah, and Meshullam the son of Besodeiah; they laid the beams thereof, and set up the doors thereof, and the locks thereof, and the bars thereof.

7And next unto them repaired Melatiah the Gibeonite, and Jadon the Meronothite, the men of Gibeon, and of Mizpah, unto the throne of the governor on this side the river.

8Next unto him repaired Uzziel the son of Harhaiah, of the goldsmiths. Next unto him also repaired Hananiah the son of one of the apothecaries, and they fortified Jerusalem unto the broad wall.

9And next unto them repaired Rephaiah the son of Hur, the ruler of the half part of Jerusalem.

10And next unto them repaired Jedaiah the son of Harumaph, even over against his house. And next unto him repaired Hattush the son of Hashabniah.

11Malchijah the son of Harim, and Hashub the son of Pahath-moab, repaired the other piece, and the tower of the furnaces.

12And next unto him repaired Shallum the son of Halohesh, the ruler of the half part of Jerusalem, he and his daughters.

13The valley gate repaired Hanun, and the inhabitants of Zanoah; they built it, and set up the doors thereof, the locks thereof, and the bars thereof, and a thousand cubits on the wall unto the dung gate.

14But the dung gate repaired Malchiah the son of Rechab, the ruler of part of Beth-haccerem; he built it, and set up the doors thereof, the locks thereof, and the bars thereof.

15But the gate of the fountain repaired Shallun the son of Col-hozeh, the ruler of part of Mizpah; he built it, and covered it, and set up the doors thereof, the locks thereof, and the bars thereof, and the wall of the pool of Siloah by the king's garden, and unto the stairs that go down from the city of David.

16After him repaired Nehemiah the son of Azbuk, the ruler of the half part of Beth-zur, unto the place over against the sepulchres of David, and to the pool that was made, and unto the house of the mighty.

17After him repaired the Levites, Rehum the son of Bani. Next unto him repaired Hashabiah, the ruler of the half part of Keilah, in his part.

18After him repaired their brethren, Bavai the son of Henadad, the ruler of the half part of Keilah.

19And next to him repaired Ezer the son of Jeshua, the ruler of Mizpah, another piece over against the going up to the armoury at the turning of the wall.

20After him Baruch the son of Zabbai earnestly repaired the other piece, from the turning of the wall unto the door of the house of Eliashib the high priest.

21After him repaired Meremoth the son of Urijah the son of Koz another piece, from the door of the house of Eliashib even to the end of the house of Eliashib.

New International

Builders of the Wall

3 ELIASHIB THE high priest and his fellow priests went to work and rebuilt the Sheep Gate. They dedicated it and set its doors in place, building as far as the Tower of the Hundred, which they dedicated, and as far as the Tower of Hananel. 2The men of Jericho built the adjoining section, and Zaccur son of Imri built next to them.

3The Fish Gate was rebuilt by the sons of Hassenaah. They laid its beams and put its doors and bolts and bars in place. 4Meremoth son of Uriah, the son of Hakkoz, repaired the next section. Next to him Meshullam son of Berekiah, the son of Meshezabel, made repairs, and next to him Zadok son of Baana also made repairs. 5The next section was repaired by the men of Tekoa, but their nobles would not put their shoulders to the work under their supervisors.a

6The Jeshanahb Gate was repaired by Joiada son of Paseah and Meshullam son of Besodeiah. They laid its beams and put its doors and bolts and bars in place. 7Next to them, repairs were made by men from Gibeon and Mizpah—Melatiah of Gibeon and Jadon of Meronoth—places under the authority of the governor of Trans-Euphrates. 8Uzziel son of Harhaiah, one of the goldsmiths, repaired the next section; and Hananiah, one of the perfume-makers, made repairs next to that. They restoredc Jerusalem as far as the Broad Wall. 9Rephaiah son of Hur, ruler of a half-district of Jerusalem, repaired the next section. 10Adjoining this, Jedaiah son of Harumaph made repairs opposite his house, and Hattush son of Hashabneiah made repairs next to him. 11Malkijah son of Harim and Hasshub son of Pahath-Moab repaired another section and the Tower of the Ovens. 12Shallum son of Hallohesh, ruler of a half-district of Jerusalem, repaired the next section with the help of his daughters.

13The Valley Gate was repaired by Hanun and the residents of Zanoah. They rebuilt it and put its doors and bolts and bars in place. They also repaired five hundred yardsd of the wall as far as the Dung Gate.

14The Dung Gate was repaired by Malkijah son of Recab, ruler of the district of Beth Hakkerem. He rebuilt it and put its doors and bolts and bars in place.

15The Fountain Gate was repaired by Shallun son of Col-Hozeh, ruler of the district of Mizpah. He rebuilt it, roofing it over and putting its doors and bolts and bars in place. He also repaired the wall of the Pool of Siloam,e by the King's Garden, as far as the steps going down from the City of David. 16Beyond him, Nehemiah son of Azbuk, ruler of a half-district of Beth Zur, made repairs up to a point opposite the tombsf of David, as far as the artificial pool and the House of the Heroes.

17Next to him, the repairs were made by the Levites under Rehum son of Bani. Beside him, Hashabiah, ruler of half the district of Keilah, carried out repairs for his district. 18Next to him, the repairs were made by their countrymen under Binnuig son of Henadad, ruler of the other half-district of Keilah. 19Next to him, Ezer son of Jeshua, ruler of Mizpah, repaired another section, from a point facing the ascent to the armory as far as the angle. 20Next to him, Baruch son of Zabbai zealously repaired another section, from the angle to the entrance of the house of Eliashib the high priest. 21Next to him, Meremoth son of Uriah, the son of Hakkoz, repaired another section, from the entrance of Eliashib's house to the end of it.

---

a 5 Or their Lord or the governor   b 6 Or Old   c 8 Or They left out part of   d 13 Hebrew a thousand cubits (about 450 meters)   e 15 Hebrew Shelah, a variant of Shiloah, that is, Siloam   f 16 Hebrew; Septuagint, some Vulgate manuscripts and Syriac tomb   g 18 Two Hebrew manuscripts and Syriac (see also Septuagint and verse 24); most Hebrew manuscripts Bavvai

Living Bible

3 THEN ELIASHIB the High Priest and the other priests rebuilt the wall as far as the Tower of the Hundred and the Tower of Hananel; then they rebuilt the Sheep Gate, hung its doors, and dedicated it. 2Men from the city of Jericho worked next to them, and beyond them was the work crew led by Zaccur (son of Imri).

3The Fish Gate was built by the sons of Hassenaah; they did the whole thing—cut the beams, hung the doors, and made the bolts and bars. 4Meremoth (son of Uriah, son of Hakkoz) repaired the next section of wall, and beyond him were Meshullam (son of Berechiah, son of Meshezabel) and Zadok (son of Baana). 5Next were the men from Tekoa, but their leaders were lazy and didn't help.

6The Old Gate was repaired by Joiada (son of Paseah) and Meshullam (son of Besodeiah). They laid the beams, set up the doors, and installed the bolts and bars. 7Next to them were Melatiah from Gibeon; Jadon from Meronoth; and men from Gibeon and Mizpah, who were citizens of the province. 8Uzziel (son of Harhaiah) was a goldsmith by trade, but he too worked on the wall. Beyond him was Hananiah, a manufacturer of perfumes. Repairs were not needed from there to the Broad Wall.

9Rephaiah (son of Hur), the mayor of half of Jerusalem, was next down the wall from them. 10Jedaiah (son of Harumaph) repaired the wall beside his own house, and next to him was Hattush (son of Hashabneiah). 11Then came Malchijah (son of Harim) and Hasshub (son of Pahath-moab), who repaired the Furnace Tower in addition to a section of the wall. 12Shallum (son of Hallohesh) and his daughters repaired the next section. He was the mayor of the other half of Jerusalem.

13The people from Zanoah, led by Hanun, built the Valley Gate, hung the doors, and installed the bolts and bars; then they repaired the 1,500 feet of wall to the Dung Gate.

14The Dung Gate was repaired by Malchijah (son of Rechab), the mayor of the Beth-haccerem area; and after building it, he hung the doors and installed the bolts and bars.

15Shallum (son of Colhozeh), the mayor of the Mizpah district, repaired the Fountain Gate. He rebuilt it, roofed it, hung its doors, and installed its locks and bars. Then he repaired the wall from the Pool of Siloam to the king's garden and the stairs that descend from the City of David section of Jerusalem. 16Next to him was Nehemiah (son of Azbuk), the mayor of half the Bethzur district; he built as far as the royal cemetery, the water reservoir, and the old Officers' Club building.h 17Next was a group of Levites working under the supervision of Rehum (son of Bani). Then came Hashabiah, the mayor of half the Keilah district, who supervised the building of the wall in his own district. 18Next down the line were his clan brothers led by Bavvai (son of Henadad), the mayor of the other half of the Keilah district.

19Next to them the workers were led by Ezer (son of Jeshua), the mayor of another part of Mizpah; they also worked on the section of wall across from the Armory, where the wall turns. 20Next to him was Baruch (son of Zabbai), who built from the turn in the wall to the home of Eliashib the High Priest. 21Meremoth (son of Uriah, son of Hakkoz) built a section of the wall extending from a point opposite the door of Eliashib's house to the side of the house.

New Revised Standard

Organization of the Work

3 THEN THE high priest Eliashib set to work with his fellow priests and rebuilt the Sheep Gate. They consecrated it and set up its doors; they consecrated it as far as the Tower of the Hundred and as far as the Tower of Hananel. 2And the men of Jericho built next to him. And next to themi Zaccur son of Imri built.

3 The sons of Hassenaah built the Fish Gate; they laid its beams and set up its doors, its bolts, and its bars. 4Next to them Meremoth son of Uriah son of Hakkoz made repairs. Next to them Meshullam son of Berechiah son of Meshezabel made repairs. Next to them Zadok son of Baana made repairs. 5Next to them the Tekoites made repairs; but their nobles would not put their shoulders to the work of their Lord.j

6 Joiada son of Paseah and Meshullam son of Besodeiah repaired the Old Gate; they laid its beams and set up its doors, its bolts, and its bars. 7Next to them repairs were made by Melatiah the Gibeonite and Jadon the Meronothite—the men of Gibeon and of Mizpah—who were under the jurisdiction ofk the governor of the province Beyond the River. 8Next to them Uzziel son of Harhaiah, one of the goldsmiths, made repairs. Next to him Hananiah, one of the perfumers, made repairs; and they restored Jerusalem as far as the Broad Wall. 9Next to them Rephaiah son of Hur, ruler of half the district ofl Jerusalem, made repairs. 10Next to them Jedaiah son of Harumaph made repairs opposite his house; and next to him Hattush son of Hashabneiah made repairs. 11Malchijah son of Harim and Hasshub son of Pahath-moab repaired another section and the Tower of the Ovens. 12Next to him Shallum son of Hallohesh, ruler of half the district ofl Jerusalem, made repairs, he and his daughters.

13 Hanun and the inhabitants of Zanoah repaired the Valley Gate; they rebuilt it and set up its doors, its bolts, and its bars, and repaired a thousand cubits of the wall, as far as the Dung Gate.

14 Malchijah son of Rechab, ruler of the district ofm Beth-haccherem, repaired the Dung Gate; he rebuilt it and set up its doors, its bolts, and its bars.

15 And Shallum son of Col-hozeh, ruler of the district ofm Mizpah, repaired the Fountain Gate; he rebuilt it and covered it and set up its doors, its bolts, and its bars; and he built the wall of the Pool of Shelah of the king's garden, as far as the stairs that go down from the City of David. 16After him Nehemiah son of Azbuk, ruler of half the district ofl Beth-zur, repaired from a point opposite the graves of David, as far as the artificial pool and the house of the warriors. 17After him the Levites made repairs: Rehum son of Bani; next to him Hashabiah, ruler of half the district ofl Keilah, made repairs for his district. 18After him their kin made repairs: Binnui,n son of Henadad, ruler of half the district ofl Keilah; 19next to him Ezer son of Jeshua, rulero of half the district ofl Mizpah, repaired another section opposite the ascent to the armory at the Angle. 20After him Baruch son of Zabbai repaired another section from the Angle to the door of the house of the high priest Eliashib. 21After him Meremoth son of Uriah son of Hakkoz repaired another section from the door of the house of Eliashib to the end of the house of Eliashib. 22After him the priests, the men

i Heb him   j Or lords   k Meaning of Heb uncertain   l Or supervisor of half the portion assigned to   m Or supervisor of the portion assigned to   n Gk Syr Compare verse 24, 10.9: Heb Bavvai   o Or supervisor

King James

²²And after him repaired the priests, the men of the plain.

²³After him repaired Benjamin and Hashub over against their house. After him repaired Azariah the son of Maaseiah the son of Ananiah by his house.

²⁴After him repaired Binnui the son of Henadad another piece, from the house of Azariah unto the turning *of the wall*, even unto the corner.

²⁵Palal the son of Uzai, over against the turning *of the wall*, and the tower which lieth out from the king's high house, that *was* by the court of the prison. After him Pedaiah the son of Parosh.

²⁶Moreover the Nethinims dwelt in Ophel, unto *the place* over against the water gate toward the east, and the tower that lieth out.

²⁷After them the Tekoites repaired another piece, over against the great tower that lieth out, even unto the wall of Ophel.

²⁸From above the horse gate repaired the priests, every one over against his house.

²⁹After them repaired Zadok the son of Immer over against his house. After him repaired also Shemaiah the son of Shechaniah, the keeper of the east gate.

³⁰After him repaired Hananiah the son of Shelemiah, and Hanun the sixth son of Zalaph, another piece. After him repaired Meshullam the son of Berechiah over against his chamber.

³¹After him repaired Malchiah the goldsmith's son unto the place of the Nethinims, and of the merchants, over against the gate Miphkad, and to the going up of the corner.

³²And between the going up of the corner unto the sheep gate repaired the goldsmiths and the merchants.

4 BUT IT came to pass, that when Sanballat heard that we builded the wall, he was wroth, and took great indignation, and mocked the Jews.

²And he spake before his brethren and the army of Samaria, and said, What do these feeble Jews? will they fortify themselves? will they sacrifice? will they make an end in a day? will they revive the stones out of the heaps of the rubbish which are burned?

³Now Tobiah the Ammonite *was* by him, and he said, Even that which they build, if a fox go up, he shall even break down their stone wall.

⁴Hear, O our God; for we are despised: and turn their reproach upon their own head, and give them for a prey in the land of captivity:

⁵And cover not their iniquity, and let not their sin be blotted out from before thee: for they have provoked *thee* to anger before the builders.

⁶So built we the wall; and all the wall was joined together unto the half thereof: for the people had a mind to work.

⁷¶ But it came to pass, *that* when Sanballat, and Tobiah, and the Arabians, and the Ammonites, and the Ashdodites, heard that the walls of Jerusalem were made up, *and* that the breaches began to be stopped, then they were very wroth,

⁸And conspired all of them together to come *and* to fight against Jerusalem, and to hinder it.

⁹Nevertheless we made our prayer unto our God, and set a watch against them day and night, because of them.

¹⁰And Judah said, The strength of the bearers of burdens is decayed, and *there is* much rubbish; so that we are not able to build the wall.

¹¹And our adversaries said, They shall not know, neither see, till we come in the midst among them, and slay them, and cause the work to cease.

New International

²²The repairs next to him were made by the priests from the surrounding region. ²³Beyond them, Benjamin and Hasshub made repairs in front of their house; and next to them, Azariah son of Maaseiah, the son of Ananiah, made repairs beside his house. ²⁴Next to him, Binnui son of Henadad repaired another section, from Azariah's house to the angle and the corner, ²⁵and Palal son of Uzai worked opposite the angle and the tower projecting from the upper palace near the court of the guard. Next to him, Pedaiah son of Parosh ²⁶and the temple servants living on the hill of Ophel made repairs up to a point opposite the Water Gate toward the east and the projecting tower. ²⁷Next to them, the men of Tekoa repaired another section, from the great projecting tower to the wall of Ophel.

²⁸Above the Horse Gate, the priests made repairs, each in front of his own house. ²⁹Next to them, Zadok son of Immer made repairs opposite his house. Next to him, Shemaiah son of Shecaniah, the guard at the East Gate, made repairs. ³⁰Next to him, Hananiah son of Shelemiah, and Hanun, the sixth son of Zalaph, repaired another section. Next to them, Meshullam son of Berekiah made repairs opposite his living quarters. ³¹Next to him, Malkijah, one of the goldsmiths, made repairs as far as the house of the temple servants and the merchants, opposite the Inspection Gate, and as far as the room above the corner; ³²and between the room above the corner and the Sheep Gate the goldsmiths and merchants made repairs.

Opposition to the Rebuilding

4 WHEN SANBALLAT heard that we were rebuilding the wall, he became angry and was greatly incensed. He ridiculed the Jews, ²and in the presence of his associates and the army of Samaria, he said, "What are those feeble Jews doing? Will they restore their wall? Will they offer sacrifices? Will they finish in a day? Can they bring the stones back to life from those heaps of rubble—burned as they are?"

³Tobiah the Ammonite, who was at his side, said, "What they are building—if even a fox climbed up on it, he would break down their wall of stones!"

⁴Hear us, O our God, for we are despised. Turn their insults back on their own heads. Give them over as plunder in a land of captivity. ⁵Do not cover up their guilt or blot out their sins from your sight, for they have thrown insults in the face ofª the builders.

⁶So we rebuilt the wall till all of it reached half its height, for the people worked with all their heart.

⁷But when Sanballat, Tobiah, the Arabs, the Ammonites and the men of Ashdod heard that the repairs to Jerusalem's walls had gone ahead and that the gaps were being closed, they were very angry. ⁸They all plotted together to come and fight against Jerusalem and stir up trouble against it. ⁹But we prayed to our God and posted a guard day and night to meet this threat.

¹⁰Meanwhile, the people in Judah said, "The strength of the laborers is giving out, and there is so much rubble that we cannot rebuild the wall."

¹¹Also our enemies said, "Before they know it or see us, we will be right there among them and will kill them and put an end to the work."

ª 5 Or *have provoked you to anger before*

Living Bible

22Then came the priests from the plains outside the city.b 23Benjamin, Hasshub, and Azariah (son of Maaseiah, son of Ananiah) repaired the sections next to their own houses. 24Next was Binnui (son of Henadad), who built the portion of the wall from Azariah's house to the corner. 25Palal (son of Uzai) carried on the work from the corner to the foundations of the upper tower of the king's castle beside the prison yard. Next was Pedaiah (son of Parosh).

26The Temple attendants living in Ophel repaired the wall as far as the East Water Gate and the Projecting Tower. 27Then came the Tekoites, who repaired the section opposite the Castle Tower and over to the wall of Ophel. 28The priests repaired the wall beyond the Horse Gate, each one doing the section immediately opposite his own house.

29Zadok (son of Immer) also rebuilt the wall next to his own house, and beyond him was Shemaiah (son of Shecaniah), the gatekeeper of the East Gate. 30Next was Hananiah (son of Shelemiah); Hanun (the sixth son of Zalaph); and Meshullam (son of Berechiah), who built next to his own house. 31Malchijah, one of the goldsmiths, repaired as far as the Temple attendants' and merchants' Guild Hall, opposite the Muster Gate; then to the upper room at the corner. 32The other goldsmiths and merchants completed the wall from that corner to the Sheep Gate.

4 SANBALLAT WAS very angry when he learned that we were rebuilding the wall. He flew into a rage, and insulted and mocked us and laughed at us, and so did his friends and the Samaritan army officers. "What does this bunch of poor, feeble Jews think they are doing?" he scoffed. "Do they think they can build the wall in a day if they offer enough sacrifices? And look at those charred stones they are pulling out of the rubbish and using again!"

3Tobiah, who was standing beside him, remarked, "If even a fox walked along the top of their wall, it would collapse!

4Then I prayed, "Hear us, O Lord God, for we are being mocked. May their scoffing fall back upon their own heads, and may they themselves become captives in a foreign land! 5Do not ignore their sin. Do not blot it out, for they have despised you in despising us who are building your wall."

6At last the wall was completed to half its original height around the entire city—for the workers worked hard.

7But when Sanballat and Tobiah and the Arabians, Ammonites, and Ashdodites heard that the work was going right ahead and that the breaks in the wall were being repaired, they became furious. 8They plotted to lead an army against Jerusalem to bring about riots and confusion. 9But we prayed to our God and guarded the city day and night to protect ourselves.

10Then some of the leaders began complaining that the workmen were becoming tired; and there was so much rubble to be removed that we could never get it done by ourselves. 11Meanwhile, our enemies were planning to swoop down upon us and kill us, thus ending our work. 12And whenever the workers who lived in the

New Revised Standard

of the surrounding area, made repairs. 23After them Benjamin and Hasshub made repairs opposite their house. After them Azariah son of Maaseiah son of Ananiah made repairs beside his own house. 24After him Binnui son of Henadad repaired another section, from the house of Azariah to the Angle and to the corner. 25Palal son of Uzai repaired opposite the Angle and the tower projecting from the upper house of the king at the court of the guard. After him Pedaiah son of Parosh 26and the temple servants livingc on Ophel made repairs up to a point opposite the Water Gate on the east and the projecting tower. 27After him the Tekoites repaired another section opposite the great projecting tower as far as the wall of Ophel.

28 Above the Horse Gate the priests made repairs, each one opposite his own house. 29After them Zadok son of Immer made repairs opposite his own house. After him Shemaiah son of Shecaniah, the keeper of the East Gate, made repairs. 30After him Hananiah son of Shelemiah and Hanun son of Zalaph repaired another section. After him Meshullam son of Berechiah made repairs opposite his living quarters. 31After him Malchijah, one of the goldsmiths, made repairs as far as the house of the temple servants and of the merchants, opposite the Muster Gate,d and to the upper room of the corner. 32 And between the upper room of the corner and the Sheep Gate the goldsmiths and the merchants made repairs.

Hostile Plots Thwarted

4e NOW WHEN Sanballat heard that we were building the wall, he was angry and greatly enraged, and he mocked the Jews. 2He said in the presence of his associates and of the army of Samaria, "What are these feeble Jews doing? Will they restore things? Will they sacrifice? Will they finish it in a day? Will they revive the stones out of the heaps of rubbish—and burned ones at that?" 3Tobiah the Ammonite was beside him, and he said, "That stone wall they are building—any fox going up on it would break it down!" 4Hear, O our God, for we are despised; turn their taunt back on their own heads, and give them over as plunder in a land of captivity. 5Do not cover their guilt, and do not let their sin be blotted out from your sight; for they have hurled insults in the face of the builders.

6 So we rebuilt the wall, and all the wall was joined together to half its height; for the people had a mind to work.

7f But when Sanballat and Tobiah and the Arabs and the Ammonites and the Ashdodites heard that the repairing of the walls of Jerusalem was going forward and the gaps were beginning to be closed, they were very angry, 8and all plotted together to come and fight against Jerusalem and to cause confusion in it. 9So we prayed to our God, and set a guard as a protection against them day and night.

10 But Judah said, "The strength of the burden bearers is failing, and there is too much rubbish so that we are unable to work on the wall." 11And our enemies said, "They will not know or see anything before we come upon them and kill them and stop the work."

---

b 3:22 from the plains outside the city, implied.

c Cn: Heb were living   d Or Hammiphkad Gate   e Ch 3.33 in Heb
f Ch 4.1 in Heb

King James

12And it came to pass, that when the Jews which dwelt by them came, they said unto us ten times, From all places whence ye shall return unto us *they will be upon you.*

13¶ Therefore set I in the lower places behind the wall, *and* on the higher places, I even set the people after their families with their swords, their spears, and their bows.

14And I looked, and rose up, and said unto the nobles, and to the rulers, and to the rest of the people, Be not ye afraid of them: remember the Lord, *which is* great and terrible, and fight for your brethren, your sons, and your daughters, your wives, and your houses.

15And it came to pass, when our enemies heard that it was known unto us, and God had brought their counsel to nought, that we returned all of us to the wall, every one unto his work.

16And it came to pass from that time forth, *that* the half of my servants wrought in the work, and the other half of them held both the spears, the shields, and the bows, and the habergeons; and the rulers *were* behind all the house of Judah.

17They which builded on the wall, and they that bare burdens, with those that laded, *every* one with one of his hands wrought in the work, and with the other *hand* held a weapon.

18For the builders, every one had his sword girded by his side, and *so* builded. And he that sounded the trumpet *was* by me.

19¶ And I said unto the nobles, and to the rulers, and to the rest of the people, The work *is* great and large, and we are separated upon the wall, one far from another.

20In what place *therefore* ye hear the sound of the trumpet, resort ye thither unto us: our God shall fight for us.

21So we laboured in the work: and half of them held the spears from the rising of the morning till the stars appeared.

22Likewise at the same time said I unto the people, Let every one with his servant lodge within Jerusalem, that in the night they may be a guard to us, and labour on the day.

23So neither I, nor my brethren, nor my servants, nor the men of the guard which followed me, none of us put off our clothes, *saving that* every one put them off for washing.

5 AND THERE was a great cry of the people and of their wives against their brethren the Jews.

2For there were that said, We, our sons, and our daughters, *are* many: therefore we take up corn *for them,* that we may eat, and live.

3*Some* also there were that said, We have mortgaged our lands, vineyards, and houses, that we might buy corn, because of the dearth.

4There were also that said, We have borrowed money for the king's tribute, *and that upon* our lands and vineyards.

5Yet now our flesh *is* as the flesh of our brethren, our children as their children: and, lo, we bring into bondage our sons and our daughters to be servants, and *some* of our daughters are brought unto bondage *already:* neither *is it* in our power *to redeem them;* for other men have our lands and vineyards.

6¶ And I was very angry when I heard their cry and these words.

New International

12Then the Jews who lived near them came and told us ten times over, "Wherever you turn, they will attack us."

13Therefore I stationed some of the people behind the lowest points of the wall at the exposed places, posting them by families, with their swords, spears and bows. 14After I looked things over, I stood up and said to the nobles, the officials and the rest of the people, "Don't be afraid of them. Remember the Lord, who is great and awesome, and fight for your brothers, your sons and your daughters, your wives and your homes."

15When our enemies heard that we were aware of their plot and that God had frustrated it, we all returned to the wall, each to his own work.

16From that day on, half of my men did the work, while the other half were equipped with spears, shields, bows and armor. The officers posted themselves behind all the people of Judah 17who were building the wall. Those who carried materials did their work with one hand and held a weapon in the other, 18and each of the builders wore his sword at his side as he worked. But the man who sounded the trumpet stayed with me.

19Then I said to the nobles, the officials and the rest of the people, "The work is extensive and spread out, and we are widely separated from each other along the wall. 20Wherever you hear the sound of the trumpet, join us there. Our God will fight for us!"

21So we continued the work with half the men holding spears, from the first light of dawn till the stars came out. 22At that time I also said to the people, "Have every man and his helper stay inside Jerusalem at night, so they can serve us as guards by night and workmen by day." 23Neither I nor my brothers nor my men nor the guards with me took off our clothes; each had his weapon, even when he went for water.[a]

Nehemiah Helps the Poor

5 NOW THE men and their wives raised a great outcry against their Jewish brothers. 2Some were saying, "We and our sons and daughters are numerous; in order for us to eat and stay alive, we must get grain."

3Others were saying, "We are mortgaging our fields, our vineyards and our homes to get grain during the famine."

4Still others were saying, "We have had to borrow money to pay the king's tax on our fields and vineyards. 5Although we are of the same flesh and blood as our countrymen and though our sons are as good as theirs, yet we have to subject our sons and daughters to slavery. Some of our daughters have already been enslaved, but we are powerless, because our fields and our vineyards belong to others."

6When I heard their outcry and these charges, I was very angry. 7I pondered them in my mind and then ac-

---

a 23 The meaning of the Hebrew for this clause is uncertain.

Living Bible

nearby cities went home for a visit, our enemies tried to talk them out of returning to Jerusalem. 13So I placed armed guards from each family in the cleared spaces behind the walls.

14Then as I looked over the situation, I called together the leaders and the people and said to them, "Don't be afraid! Remember the Lord who is great and glorious; fight for your friends, your families, and your homes!"

15Our enemies learned that we knew of their plot, and that God had exposed and frustrated their plan. Now we all returned to our work on the wall; 16but from then on, only half worked while the other half stood guard behind them. 17And the masons and laborers worked with weapons within easy reach beside them, 18or with swords belted to their sides. The trumpeter stayed with me to sound the alarm.

19"The work is so spread out," I explained to them, "and we are separated so widely from each other, that when you hear the trumpet blow you must rush to where I am; and God will fight for us."

20, 21We worked early and late, from sunrise to sunset; and half the men were always on guard. 22I told everyone living outside the walls to move into Jerusalem so that their servants could go on guard duty as well as work during the day. 23During this period none of us—I, nor my brothers, nor the servants, nor the guards who were with me—ever took off our clothes except for washing.b And we carried our weapons with us at all times.

5 ABOUT THIS time there was a great outcry of protest from parents against some of the rich Jews who were profiteering on them. 2, 3, 4What was happening was that families who ran out of money for food had to sell their children or mortgage their fields, vineyards, and homes to these rich men; and some couldn't even do that, for they already had borrowed to the limit to pay their taxes.

5"We are their brothers, and our children are just like theirs," the people protested. "Yet we must sell our children into slavery to get enough money to live. We have already sold some of our daughters, and we are helpless to redeem them, for our fields, too, are mortgaged to these men."

6I was very angry when I heard this; 7so after thinking

New Revised Standard

12When the Jews who lived near them came, they said to us ten times, "From all the places where they livec they will come up against us."d 13So in the lowest parts of the space behind the wall, in open places, I stationed the people according to their families,e with their swords, their spears, and their bows. 14After I looked these things over, I stood up and said to the nobles and the officials and the rest of the people, "Do not be afraid of them. Remember the LORD, who is great and awesome, and fight for your kin, your sons, your daughters, your wives, and your homes."

15 When our enemies heard that their plot was known to us, and that God had frustrated it, we all returned to the wall, each to his work. 16From that day on, half of my servants worked on construction, and half held the spears, shields, bows, and body-armor; and the leaders posted themselves behind the whole house of Judah, 17who were building the wall. The burden bearers carried their loads in such a way that each labored on the work with one hand and with the other held a weapon. 18And each of the builders had his sword strapped at his side while he built. The man who sounded the trumpet was beside me. 19And I said to the nobles, the officials, and the rest of the people, "The work is great and widely spread out, and we are separated far from one another on the wall. 20Rally to us wherever you hear the sound of the trumpet. Our God will fight for us."

21 So we labored at the work, and half of them held the spears from break of dawn until the stars came out. 22I also said to the people at that time, "Let every man and his servant pass the night inside Jerusalem, so that they may be a guard for us by night and may labor by day." 23So neither I nor my brothers nor my servants nor the men of the guard who followed me ever took off our clothes; each kept his weapon in his right hand.f

Nehemiah Deals with Oppression

5 NOW THERE was a great outcry of the people and of their wives against their Jewish kin. 2For there were those who said, "With our sons and our daughters, we are many; we must get grain, so that we may eat and stay alive." 3There were also those who said, "We are having to pledge our fields, our vineyards, and our houses in order to get grain during the famine." 4And there were those who said, "We are having to borrow money on our fields and vineyards to pay the king's tax. 5Now our flesh is the same as that of our kindred; our children are the same as their children; and yet we are forcing our sons and daughters to be slaves, and some of our daughters have been ravished; we are powerless, and our fields and vineyards now belong to others."

6 I was very angry when I heard their outcry and these complaints. 7After thinking it over, I brought

---

b 4:23 except for washing, or "even when we went for water," or "not even at night." The meaning of the Hebrew text is uncertain.

c Cn: Heb you return   d Compare Gk Syr: Meaning of Heb uncertain
e Meaning of Heb uncertain   f Cn: Heb each his weapon the water

King James

7Then I consulted with myself, and I rebuked the nobles, and the rulers, and said unto them, Ye exact usury, every one of his brother. And I set a great assembly against them.

8And I said unto them, We after our ability have redeemed our brethren the Jews, which were sold unto the heathen; and will ye even sell your brethren? or shall they be sold unto us? Then held they their peace, and found nothing *to answer*.

9Also I said, It *is* not good that ye do: ought ye not to walk in the fear of our God because of the reproach of the heathen our enemies?

10I likewise, *and* my brethren, and my servants, might exact of them money and corn: I pray you, let us leave off this usury.

11Restore, I pray you, to them, even this day, their lands, their vineyards, their oliveyards, and their houses, also the hundredth *part* of the money, and of the corn, the wine, and the oil, that ye exact of them.

12Then said they, We will restore *them,* and will require nothing of them; so will we do as thou sayest. Then I called the priests, and took an oath of them, that they should do according to this promise.

13Also I shook my lap, and said, So God shake out every man from his house, and from his labour, that performeth not this promise, even thus be he shaken out, and emptied. And all the congregation said, Amen, and praised the LORD. And the people did according to this promise.

14¶ Moreover from the time that I was appointed to be their governor in the land of Judah, from the twentieth year even unto the two and thirtieth year of Artaxerxes the king, *that is,* twelve years, I and my brethren have not eaten the bread of the governor.

15But the former governors that *had been* before me were chargeable unto the people, and had taken of them bread and wine, beside forty shekels of silver; yea, even their servants bare rule over the people: but so did not I, because of the fear of God.

16Yea, also I continued in the work of this wall, neither bought we any land: and all my servants *were* gathered thither unto the work.

17Moreover *there were* at my table an hundred and fifty of the Jews and rulers, beside those that came unto us from among the heathen that *are* about us.

18Now *that* which was prepared *for me* daily *was* one ox *and* six choice sheep; also fowls were prepared for me, and once in ten days store of all sorts of wine: yet for all this required not I the bread of the governor, because the bondage was heavy upon this people.

19Think upon me, my God, for good, *according* to all that I have done for this people.

6 NOW IT came to pass, when Sanballat, and Tobiah, and Geshem the Arabian, and the rest of our enemies, heard that I had builded the wall, and *that* there was no breach left therein; (though at that time I had not set up the doors upon the gates;)

2That Sanballat and Geshem sent unto me, saying, Come, let us meet together in *some one of* the villages in the plain of Ono. But they thought to do me mischief.

3And I sent messengers unto them, saying, I *am* doing a great work, so that I cannot come down: why should the work cease, whilst I leave it, and come down to you?

4Yet they sent unto me four times after this sort; and I answered them after the same manner.

New International

cused the nobles and officials. I told them, "You are exacting usury from your own countrymen!" So I called together a large meeting to deal with them 8and said: "As far as possible, we have bought back our Jewish brothers who were sold to the Gentiles. Now you are selling your brothers, only for them to be sold back to us!" They kept quiet, because they could find nothing to say.

9So I continued, "What you are doing is not right. Shouldn't you walk in the fear of our God to avoid the reproach of our Gentile enemies? 10I and my brothers and my men are also lending the people money and grain. But let the exacting of usury stop! 11Give back to them immediately their fields, vineyards, olive groves and houses, and also the usury you are charging them— the hundredth part of the money, grain, new wine and oil."

12"We will give it back," they said. "And we will not demand anything more from them. We will do as you say."

Then I summoned the priests and made the nobles and officials take an oath to do what they had promised. 13I also shook out the folds of my robe and said, "In this way may God shake out of his house and possessions every man who does not keep this promise. So may such a man be shaken out and emptied!"

At this the whole assembly said, "Amen," and praised the LORD. And the people did as they had promised.

14Moreover, from the twentieth year of King Artaxerxes, when I was appointed to be their governor in the land of Judah, until his thirty-second year—twelve years—neither I nor my brothers ate the food allotted to the governor. 15But the earlier governors—those preceding me—placed a heavy burden on the people and took forty shekelsa of silver from them in addition to food and wine. Their assistants also lorded it over the people. But out of reverence for God I did not act like that. 16Instead, I devoted myself to the work on this wall. All my men were assembled there for the work; web did not acquire any land.

17Furthermore, a hundred and fifty Jews and officials ate at my table, as well as those who came to us from the surrounding nations. 18Each day one ox, six choice sheep and some poultry were prepared for me, and every ten days an abundant supply of wine of all kinds. In spite of all this, I never demanded the food allotted to the governor, because the demands were heavy on these people.

19Remember me with favor, O my God, for all I have done for these people.

Further Opposition to the Rebuilding

6 WHEN WORD came to Sanballat, Tobiah, Geshem the Arab and the rest of our enemies that I had rebuilt the wall and not a gap was left in it—though up to that time I had not set the doors in the gates— 2Sanballat and Geshem sent me this message: "Come, let us meet together in one of the villagesc on the plain of Ono."

But they were scheming to harm me; 3so I sent messengers to them with this reply: "I am carrying on a great project and cannot go down. Why should the work stop while I leave it and go down to you?" 4Four times they sent me the same message, and each time I gave them the same answer.

---

a *15* That is, about 1 pound (about 0.5 kilogram)   b *16* Most Hebrew manuscripts; some Hebrew manuscripts, Septuagint, Vulgate and Syriac *I*   c *2* Or *in Kephirim*

Living Bible

about it I spoke out against these rich government officials.

"What is this you are doing?" I demanded. "How dare you demand a mortgage as a condition for helping another Israelite?"

Then I called a public trial to deal with them.

8At the trial I shouted at them, "The rest of us are doing all we can to *help* our Jewish brothers who have returned from exile as slaves in distant lands, but you are forcing them right back into slavery again. How often must we redeem them?"

And they had nothing to say in their own defense. 9Then I pressed further. "What you are doing is very evil," I exclaimed. "Should you not walk in the fear of our God? Don't we have enough enemies among the nations around us who are trying to destroy us? 10The rest of us are lending money and grain to our fellow-Jews without any interest. I beg you, gentlemen, stop this business of usury. 11Restore their fields, vineyards, oliveyards, and homes to them this very day and drop your claims against them."

12So they agreed to do it and said that they would assist their brothers without requiring them to mortgage their lands and sell their children. Then I summoned the priests and made these men formally vow to carry out their promises. 13And I invoked the curse of God upon any of them who refused.d

"May God destroy your homes and livelihood if you fail to keep this promise," I declared.

And all the people shouted, "Amen," and praised the Lord. And the rich men did as they had promised.

14I would like to mention that for the entire twelve years that I was governor of Judah—from the twentieth until the thirty-second year of the reign of King Artaxerxes—my aides and I accepted no salaries or other assistance from the people of Israel. 15This was quite a contrast to the former governors who had demanded food and wine and $100 a day in cash, and had put the population at the mercy of their aides, who tyrannized them; but I obeyed God and did not act that way. 16I stayed at work on the wall and refused to speculate in land; I also required my officials to spend time on the wall. 17All this despite the fact that I regularly fed 150 Jewish officials at my table, besides visitors from other countries! 18The provisions required for each day were one ox, six fat sheep, and a large number of domestic fowls; and we needed a huge supply of all kinds of wines every ten days. Yet I refused to make a special levy against the people, for they were already having a difficult time. 19O my God, please keep in mind all that I've done for these people and bless me for it.

6 WHEN SANBALLAT, Tobiah, Geshem the Arab, and the rest of our enemies found out that we had almost completed the rebuilding of the wall—though we had not yet hung all the doors of the gates—2they sent me a message asking me to meet them in one of the villages in the Plain of Ono. But I realized they were plotting to kill me, 3so I replied by sending back this message to them:

"I am doing a great work! Why should I stop to come and visit with you?"

4Four times they sent the same message, and each time I gave the same reply. 5, 6The fifth time, Sanbal-

New Revised Standard

charges against the nobles and the officials; I said to them, "You are all taking interest from your own people." And I called a great assembly to deal with them, 8and said to them, "As far as we were able, we have bought back our Jewish kindred who had been sold to other nations; but now you are selling your own kin, who must then be bought back by us!" They were silent, and could not find a word to say. 9So I said, "The thing that you are doing is not good. Should you not walk in the fear of our God, to prevent the taunts of the nations our enemies? 10Moreover I and my brothers and my servants are lending them money and grain. Let us stop this taking of interest. 11Restore to them, this very day, their fields, their vineyards, their olive orchards, and their houses, and the interest on money, grain, wine, and oil that you have been exacting from them." 12Then they said, "We will restore everything and demand nothing more from them. We will do as you say." And I called the priests, and made them take an oath to do as they had promised. 13I also shook out the fold of my garment and said, "So may God shake out everyone from house and from property who does not perform this promise. Thus may they be shaken out and emptied." And all the assembly said, "Amen," and praised the Lord. And the people did as they had promised.

The Generosity of Nehemiah

14 Moreover from the time that I was appointed to be their governor in the land of Judah, from the twentieth year to the thirty-second year of King Artaxerxes, twelve years, neither I nor my brothers ate the food allowance of the governor. 15The former governors who were before me laid heavy burdens on the people, and took food and wine from them, besides forty shekels of silver. Even their servants lorded it over the people. But I did not do so, because of the fear of God. 16Indeed, I devoted myself to the work on this wall, and acquired no land; and all my servants were gathered there for the work. 17Moreover there were at my table one hundred fifty people, Jews and officials, besides those who came to us from the nations around us. 18Now that which was prepared for one day was one ox and six choice sheep; also fowls were prepared for me, and every ten days skins of wine in abundance; yet with all this I did not demand the food allowance of the governor, because of the heavy burden of labor on the people. 19Remember for my good, O my God, all that I have done for this people.

Intrigues of Enemies Foiled

6 NOW WHEN it was reported to Sanballat and Tobiah and to Geshem the Arab and to the rest of our enemies that I had built the wall and that there was no gap left in it (though up to that time I had not set up the doors in the gates), 2Sanballat and Geshem sent to me, saying, "Come and let us meet together in one of the villages in the plain of Ono." But they intended to do me harm. 3So I sent messengers to them, saying, "I am doing a great work and I cannot come down. Why should the work stop while I leave it to come down to you?" 4They sent to me four times in this way, and I answered them in the same manner. 5In the same way

---

d *5:13 I invoked the curse of God upon any of them who refused*, literally, "then I shook out the lap of my gown. . . ."

King James

5Then sent Sanballat his servant unto me in like manner the fifth time with an open letter in his hand;

6Wherein *was* written, It is reported among the heathen, and Gashmu saith *it, that* thou and the Jews think to rebel: for which cause thou buildest the wall, that thou mayest be their king, according to these words.

7And thou hast also appointed prophets to preach of thee at Jerusalem, saying, *There is* a king in Judah: and now shall it be reported to the king according to these words. Come now therefore, and let us take counsel together.

8Then I sent unto him, saying, There are no such things done as thou sayest, but thou feignest them out of thine own heart.

9For they all made us afraid, saying, Their hands shall be weakened from the work, that it be not done. Now therefore, *O God*, strengthen my hands.

10Afterward I came unto the house of Shemaiah the son of Delaiah the son of Mehetabeel, who *was* shut up; and he said, Let us meet together in the house of God, within the temple, and let us shut the doors of the temple: for they will come to slay thee; yea, in the night will they come to slay thee.

11And I said, Should such a man as I flee? and who *is there*, that, *being* as I *am*, would go into the temple to save his life? I will not go in.

12And, lo, I perceived that God had not sent him; but that he pronounced this prophecy against me: for Tobiah and Sanballat had hired him.

13Therefore *was* he hired, that I should be afraid, and do so, and sin, and *that* they might have *matter* for an evil report, that they might reproach me.

14My God, think thou upon Tobiah and Sanballat according to these their works, and on the prophetess Noadiah, and the rest of the prophets, that would have put me in fear.

15¶ So the wall was finished in the twenty and fifth *day* of *the month* Elul, in fifty and two days.

16And it came to pass, that when all our enemies heard *thereof*, and all the heathen that *were* about us saw *these things*, they were much cast down in their own eyes: for they perceived that this work was wrought of our God.

17¶ Moreover in those days the nobles of Judah sent many letters unto Tobiah, and *the letters* of Tobiah came unto them.

18For *there were* many in Judah sworn unto him, because he *was* the son-in-law of Shechaniah the son of Arah; and his son Johanan had taken the daughter of Meshullam the son of Berechiah.

19Also they reported his good deeds before me, and uttered my words to him. *And* Tobiah sent letters to put me in fear.

7 NOW IT came to pass, when the wall was built, and I had set up the doors, and the porters and the singers and the Levites were appointed,

2That I gave my brother Hanani, and Hananiah the ruler of the palace, charge over Jerusalem: for he *was* a faithful man, and feared God above many.

3And I said unto them, Let not the gates of Jerusalem be opened until the sun be hot; and while they stand by, let them shut the doors, and bar *them*: and appoint watches of the inhabitants of Jerusalem, every one in his watch, and every one *to be* over against his house.

4Now the city *was* large and great: but the people *were* few therein, and the houses *were* not builded.

New International

5Then, the fifth time, Sanballat sent his aide to me with the same message, and in his hand was an unsealed letter 6in which was written:

"It is reported among the nations—and Geshem[a] says it is true—that you and the Jews are plotting to revolt, and therefore you are building the wall. Moreover, according to these reports you are about to become their king 7and have even appointed prophets to make this proclamation about you in Jerusalem: 'There is a king in Judah!' Now this report will get back to the king; so come, let us confer together."

8I sent him this reply: "Nothing like what you are saying is happening; you are just making it up out of your head."

9They were all trying to frighten us, thinking, "Their hands will get too weak for the work, and it will not be completed."

But I prayed, "Now strengthen my hands."

10One day I went to the house of Shemaiah son of Delaiah, the son of Mehetabel, who was shut in at his home. He said, "Let us meet in the house of God, inside the temple, and let us close the temple doors, because men are coming to kill you—by night they are coming to kill you."

11But I said, "Should a man like me run away? Or should one like me go into the temple to save his life? I will not go!" 12I realized that God had not sent him, but that he had prophesied against me because Tobiah and Sanballat had hired him. 13He had been hired to intimidate me so that I would commit a sin by doing this, and then they would give me a bad name to discredit me.

14Remember Tobiah and Sanballat, O my God, because of what they have done; remember also the prophetess Noadiah and the rest of the prophets who have been trying to intimidate me.

The Completion of the Wall

15So the wall was completed on the twenty-fifth of Elul, in fifty-two days. 16When all our enemies heard about this, all the surrounding nations were afraid and lost their self-confidence, because they realized that this work had been done with the help of our God.

17Also, in those days the nobles of Judah were sending many letters to Tobiah, and replies from Tobiah kept coming to them. 18For many in Judah were under oath to him, since he was son-in-law to Shecaniah son of Arah, and his son Jehohanan had married the daughter of Meshullam son of Berekiah. 19Moreover, they kept reporting to me his good deeds and then telling him what I said. And Tobiah sent letters to intimidate me.

7 AFTER THE wall had been rebuilt and I had set the doors in place, the gatekeepers and the singers and the Levites were appointed. 2I put in charge of Jerusalem my brother Hanani, along with[b] Hananiah the commander of the citadel, because he was a man of integrity and feared God more than most men do. 3I said to them, "The gates of Jerusalem are not to be opened until the sun is hot. While the gatekeepers are still on duty, have them shut the doors and bar them. Also appoint residents of Jerusalem as guards, some at their posts and some near their own houses."

The List of the Exiles Who Returned

4Now the city was large and spacious, but there were few people in it, and the houses had not yet been rebuilt.

---

a 6 Hebrew *Gashmu*, a variant of *Geshem*   b 2 Or *Hanani, that is,*

Living Bible

lat's servant came with an open letter in his hand and this is what it said:

"Geshem tells me that everywhere he goes he hears that the Jews are planning to rebel, and that is why you are building the wall. He claims you plan to be their king—that is what is being said. 7He also reports that you have appointed prophets to campaign for you at Jerusalem by saying, 'Look! Nehemiah is just the man we need!'

"You can be very sure that I am going to pass along these interesting comments to King Artaxerxes! I suggest that you come and talk it over with me—for that is the only way you can save yourself!"

8My reply was, "You know you are lying. There isn't one bit of truth to the whole story. 9You're just trying to scare us into stopping our work." (O Lord God, please strengthen me!)

10A few days later I went to visit Shemaiah (son of Delaiah, who was the son of Mehetabel), for he said he was receiving a message from God.

"Let us hide in the Temple and bolt the door," he exclaimed, "for they are coming tonight to kill you."

11But I replied, "Should I, the governor, run away from danger? And if I go into the Temple, not being a priest, I would forfeit my life. No, I won't do it!"

12, 13Then I realized that God had not spoken to him, but Tobiah and Sanballat had hired him to scare me and make me sin by fleeing to the Temple; and then they would be able to accuse me.

14"O my God," I prayed, "don't forget all the evil of Tobiah, Sanballat, No-adiah the prophetess, and all the other prophets who have tried to discourage me."

15The wall was finally finished in early September—just fifty-two days after we had begun!

16When our enemies and the surrounding nations heard about it, they were frightened and humiliated, and they realized that the work had been done with the help of our God. 17During those fifty-two days many letters went back and forth between Tobiah and the wealthy politicians of Judah. 18For many in Judah had sworn allegiance to him because his father-in-law was Shecaniah (son of Arah) and because his son Jehohanan was married to the daughter of Meshullam (son of Berechiah). 19They all told me what a wonderful man Tobiah was, and then they told him everything I had said; and Tobiah sent many threatening letters to frighten me.

7 AFTER THE wall was finished and we had hung the doors in the gates and had appointed the gatekeepers, singers, and Levites, 2I gave the responsibility of governing Jerusalem to my brother Hanani and to Hananiah, the commander of the fortress—a very faithful man who revered God more than most people do. 3I issued instructions to them not to open the Jerusalem gates until well after sunrise, and to close and lock them while the guards were still on duty. I also directed that the guards be residents of Jerusalem, and that they must be on duty at regular times, and that each homeowner who lived near the wall must guard the section of wall next to his own home. 4For the city was large, but the population was small; and only a few houses were scattered throughout the city.

c 6:15 September, or, "twenty-fifth day of the month Elul."

New Revised Standard

Sanballat for the fifth time sent his servant to me with an open letter in his hand. 6In it was written, "It is reported among the nations—and Geshemd also says it—that you and the Jews intend to rebel; that is why you are building the wall; and according to this report you wish to become their king. 7You have also set up prophets to proclaim in Jerusalem concerning you, 'There is a king in Judah!' And now it will be reported to the king according to these words. So come, therefore, and let us confer together." 8Then I sent to him, saying, "No such things as you say have been done; you are inventing them out of your own mind" 9—for they all wanted to frighten us, thinking, "Their hands will drop from the work, and it will not be done." But now, O God, strengthen my hands.

10 One day when I went into the house of Shemaiah son of Delaiah son of Mehetabel, who was confined to his house, he said, "Let us meet together in the house of God, within the temple, and let us close the doors of the temple, for they are coming to kill you; indeed, tonight they are coming to kill you." 11But I said, "Should a man like me run away? Would a man like me go into the temple to save his life? I will not go in!" 12Then I perceived and saw that God had not sent him at all, but he had pronounced the prophecy against me because Tobiah and Sanballat had hired him. 13He was hired for this purpose, to intimidate me and make me sin by acting in this way, and so they could give me a bad name, in order to taunt me. 14Remember Tobiah and Sanballat, O my God, according to these things that they did, and also the prophetess Noadiah and the rest of the prophets who wanted to make me afraid.

The Wall Completed

15 So the wall was finished on the twenty-fifth day of the month Elul, in fifty-two days. 16And when all our enemies heard of it, all the nations around us were afraide and fell greatly in their own esteem; for they perceived that this work had been accomplished with the help of our God. 17Moreover in those days the nobles of Judah sent many letters to Tobiah, and Tobiah's letters came to them. 18For many in Judah were bound by oath to him, because he was the son-in-law of Shecaniah son of Arah: and his son Jehohanan had married the daughter of Meshullam son of Berechiah. 19Also they spoke of his good deeds in my presence, and reported my words to him. And Tobiah sent letters to intimidate me.

7 NOW WHEN the wall had been built and I had set up the doors, and the gatekeepers, the singers, and the Levites had been appointed, 2I gave my brother Hanani charge over Jerusalem, along with Hananiah the commander of the citadel—for he was a faithful man and feared God more than many. 3And I said to them, "The gates of Jerusalem are not to be opened until the sun is hot; while the gatekeepersf are still standing guard, let them shut and bar the doors. Appoint guards from among the inhabitants of Jerusalem, some at their watch posts, and others before their own houses." 4The city was wide and large, but the people within it were few and no houses had been built.

d Heb Gashmu   e Another reading is saw   f Heb while they

King James

5¶ And my God put into mine heart to gather together the nobles, and the rulers, and the people, that they might be reckoned by genealogy. And I found a register of the genealogy of them which came up at the first, and found written therein,

6These *are* the children of the province, that went up out of the captivity, of those that had been carried away, whom Nebuchadnezzar the king of Babylon had carried away, and came again to Jerusalem and to Judah, every one unto his city;

7Who came with Zerubbabel, Jeshua, Nehemiah, Azariah, Raamiah, Nahamani, Mordecai, Bilshan, Mispereth, Bigvai, Nehum, Baanah. The number, *I say,* of the men of the people of Israel *was this;*

8The children of Parosh, two thousand an hundred seventy and two.

9The children of Shephatiah, three hundred seventy and two.

10The children of Arah, six hundred fifty and two.

11The children of Pahath-moab, of the children of Jeshua and Joab, two thousand and eight hundred *and* eighteen.

12The children of Elam, a thousand two hundred fifty and four.

13The children of Zattu, eight hundred forty and five.

14The children of Zaccai, seven hundred and three-score.

15The children of Binnui, six hundred forty and eight.

16The children of Bebai, six hundred twenty and eight.

17The children of Azgad, two thousand three hundred twenty and two.

18The children of Adonikam, six hundred threescore and seven.

19The children of Bigvai, two thousand threescore and seven.

20The children of Adin, six hundred fifty and five.

21The children of Ater of Hezekiah, ninety and eight.

22The children of Hashum, three hundred twenty and eight.

23The children of Bezai, three hundred twenty and four.

24The children of Hariph, an hundred and twelve.

25The children of Gibeon, ninety and five.

26The men of Bethlehem and Netophah, an hundred fourscore and eight.

27The men of Anathoth, an hundred twenty and eight.

28The men of Beth-azmaveth, forty and two.

29The men of Kirjath-jearim, Chephirah, and Beeroth, seven hundred forty and three.

30The men of Ramah and Gaba, six hundred twenty and one.

31The men of Michmas, an hundred and twenty and two.

32The men of Beth-el and Ai, an hundred twenty and three.

33The men of the other Nebo, fifty and two.

34The children of the other Elam, a thousand two hundred fifty and four.

35The children of Harim, three hundred and twenty.

36The children of Jericho, three hundred forty and five.

37The children of Lod, Hadid, and Ono, seven hundred twenty and one.

38The children of Senaah, three thousand nine hundred and thirty.

39¶ The priests: the children of Jedaiah, of the house of Jeshua, nine hundred seventy and three.

40The children of Immer, a thousand fifty and two.

41The children of Pashur, a thousand two hundred forty and seven.

42The children of Harim, a thousand and seventeen.

New International

5So my God put it into my heart to assemble the nobles, the officials and the common people for registration by families. I found the genealogical record of those who had been the first to return. This is what I found written there:

6These are the people of the province who came up from the captivity of the exiles whom Nebuchadnezzar king of Babylon had taken captive (they returned to Jerusalem and Judah, each to his own town, 7in company with Zerubbabel, Jeshua, Nehemiah, Azariah, Raamiah, Nahamani, Mordecai, Bilshan, Mispereth, Bigvai, Nehum and Baanah):

The list of the men of Israel:

8the descendants of Parosh	2,172
9of Shephatiah	372
10of Arah	652
11of Pahath-Moab (through the line of Jeshua and Joab)	2,818
12of Elam	1,254
13of Zattu	845
14of Zaccai	760
15of Binnui	648
16of Bebai	628
17of Azgad	2,322
18of Adonikam	667
19of Bigvai	2,067
20of Adin	655
21of Ater (through Hezekiah)	98
22of Hashum	328
23of Bezai	324
24of Hariph	112
25of Gibeon	95
26the men of Bethlehem and Netophah	188
27of Anathoth	128
28of Beth Azmaveth	42
29of Kiriath Jearim, Kephirah and Beeroth	743
30of Ramah and Geba	621
31of Micmash	122
32of Bethel and Ai	123
33of the other Nebo	52
34of the other Elam	1,254
35of Harim	320
36of Jericho	345
37of Lod, Hadid and Ono	721
38of Senaah	3,930

39The priests:

the descendants of Jedaiah (through the family of Jeshua)	973
40of Immer	1,052
41of Pashhur	1,247
42of Harim	1,017

Living Bible

5Then the Lord told me to call together all the leaders of the city, along with the ordinary citizens, for registration. For I had found the record of the genealogies of those who had returned to Judah before, and this is what was written in it:

6"The following is a list of the names of the Jews who returned to Judah after being exiled by King Nebuchadnezzar of Babylon.

7"Their leaders were:

Zerubbabel, Jeshua, Nehemiah, Azariah, Raamiah, Nahamani, Mordecai, Bilshan, Mispereth, Bigvai, Nehum, Baanah.

"The others who returned at that time were:

8-38From the subclan of Parosh, 2,172;
From the subclan of Shephatiah, 372;
From the subclan of Arah, 652;
From the families of Jeshua and Joab of the subclan of Pahath-moab, 2,818;
From the subclan of Elam, 1,254;
From the subclan of Zattu, 845;
From the subclan of Zaccai, 760;
From the subclan of Binnui, 648;
From the subclan of Bebai, 628;
From the subclan of Azgad, 2,322;
From the subclan of Adonikam, 667;
From the subclan of Bigvai, 2,067;
From the subclan of Adin, 655;
From the family of Hezekiah of the subclan of Ater, 98;
From the subclan of Hashum, 328;
From the subclan of Bezai, 324;
From the subclan of Hariph, 112;
From the subclan of Gibeon, 95;
From the subclans of Bethlehem and Netophah, 188;
From the subclan of Anathoth, 128;
From the subclan of Beth-azmaveth, 42;
From the subclans of Kiriath-jearim, Chephirah, and Be-eroth, 743;
From the subclans of Ramah and Geba, 621;
From the subclans of Michmas, 122;
From the subclans of Bethel and Ai, 123;
From the subclan of Nebo, 52;
From the subclan of Elam, 1,254;
From the subclan of Harim, 320;
From the subclan of Jericho, 345;
From the subclans of Lod, Hadid, and Ono, 721;
From the subclan of Senaah, 3,930.

39-42"Here are the statistics concerning the returning priests:

From the family of Jeshua of the subclan of Jedaiah, 973;
From the subclan of Immer, 1,052;
From the subclan of Pashhur, 1,247;
From the subclan of Harim, 1,017.

New Revised Standard

Lists of the Returned Exiles

5 Then my God put it into my mind to assemble the nobles and the officials and the people to be enrolled by genealogy. And I found the book of the genealogy of those who were the first to come back, and I found the following written in it:

6 These are the people of the province who came up out of the captivity of those exiles whom King Nebuchadnezzar of Babylon had carried into exile; they returned to Jerusalem and Judah, each to his town. 7They came with Zerubbabel, Jeshua, Nehemiah, Azariah, Raamiah, Nahamani, Mordecai, Bilshan, Mispereth, Bigvai, Nehum, Baanah.

The number of the Israelite people: 8the descendants of Parosh, two thousand one hundred seventy-two. 9Of Shephatiah, three hundred seventy-two. 10Of Arah, six hundred fifty-two. 11Of Pahath-moab, namely the descendants of Jeshua and Joab, two thousand eight hundred eighteen. 12Of Elam, one thousand two hundred fifty-four. 13Of Zattu, eight hundred forty-five. 14Of Zaccai, seven hundred sixty. 15Of Binnui, six hundred forty-eight. 16Of Bebai, six hundred twenty-eight. 17Of Azgad, two thousand three hundred twenty-two. 18Of Adonikam, six hundred sixty-seven. 19Of Bigvai, two thousand sixty-seven. 20Of Adin, six hundred fifty-five. 21Of Ater, namely of Hezekiah, ninety-eight. 22Of Hashum, three hundred twenty-eight. 23Of Bezai, three hundred twenty-four. 24Of Hariph, one hundred twelve. 25Of Gibeon, ninety-five. 26The people of Bethlehem and Netophah, one hundred eighty-eight. 27Of Anathoth, one hundred twenty-eight. 28Of Beth-azmaveth, forty-two. 29Of Kiriath-jearim, Chephirah, and Beeroth, seven hundred forty-three. 30Of Ramah and Geba, six hundred twenty-one. 31Of Michmas, one hundred twenty-two. 32Of Bethel and Ai, one hundred twenty-three. 33Of the other Nebo, fifty-two. 34The descendants of the other Elam, one thousand two hundred fifty-four. 35Of Harim, three hundred twenty. 36Of Jericho, three hundred forty-five. 37Of Lod, Hadid, and Ono, seven hundred twenty-one. 38Of Senaah, three thousand nine hundred thirty.

39 The priests: the descendants of Jedaiah, namely the house of Jeshua, nine hundred seventy-three. 40Of Immer, one thousand fifty-two. 41Of Pashhur, one thousand two hundred forty-seven. 42Of Harim, one thousand seventeen.

King James

43¶ The Levites: the children of Jeshua, of Kadmiel, *and* of the children of Hodevah, seventy and four.

44¶ The singers: the children of Asaph, an hundred forty and eight.

45¶ The porters: the children of Shallum, the children of Ater, the children of Talmon, the children of Akkub, the children of Hatita, the children of Shobai, an hundred thirty and eight.

46¶ The Nethinims: the children of Ziha, the children of Hashupha, the children of Tabbaoth,

47The children of Keros, the children of Sia, the children of Padon,

48The children of Lebana, the children of Hagaba, the children of Shalmai,

49The children of Hanan, the children of Giddel, the children of Gahar,

50The children of Reaiah, the children of Rezin, the children of Nekoda,

51The children of Gazzam, the children of Uzza, the children of Phaseah,

52The children of Besai, the children of Meunim, the children of Nephishesim,

53The children of Bakbuk, the children of Hakupha, the children of Harhur,

54The children of Bazlith, the children of Mehida, the children of Harsha,

55The children of Barkos, the children of Sisera, the children of Tamah,

56The children of Neziah, the children of Hatipha.

57¶ The children of Solomon's servants: the children of Sotai, the children of Sophereth, the children of Perida,

58The children of Jaala, the children of Darkon, the children of Giddel,

59The children of Shephatiah, the children of Hattil, the children of Pochereth of Zebaim, the children of Amon.

60All the Nethinims, and the children of Solomon's servants, *were* three hundred ninety and two.

61And these *were* they which went up *also* from Telmelah, Tel-haresha, Cherub, Addon, and Immer: but they could not show their father's house, nor their seed, whether they *were* of Israel.

62The children of Delaiah, the children of Tobiah, the children of Nekoda, six hundred forty and two.

63¶ And of the priests: the children of Habaiah, the children of Koz, the children of Barzillai, which took *one* of the daughters of Barzillai the Gileadite to wife, and was called after their name.

64These sought their register *among* those that were reckoned by genealogy, but it was not found: therefore were they, as polluted, put from the priesthood.

65And the Tirshatha said unto them, that they should not eat of the most holy things, till there stood *up* a priest with Urim and Thummim.

66¶ The whole congregation together *was* forty and two thousand three hundred and threescore,

67Beside their manservants and their maidservants, of whom *there were* seven thousand three hundred thirty and seven: and they had two hundred forty and five singing men and singing women.

68Their horses, seven hundred thirty and six: their mules, two hundred forty and five:

69*Their* camels, four hundred thirty and five: six thousand seven hundred and twenty asses.

70¶ And some of the chief of the fathers gave unto the work. The Tirshatha gave to the treasure a thousand drams of gold, fifty basins, five hundred and thirty priests' garments.

71And *some* of the chief of the fathers gave to the treasure of the work twenty thousand drams of gold, and two thousand and two hundred pound of silver.

72And *that* which the rest of the people gave *was* twenty thousand drams of gold, and two thousand pound of silver, and threescore and seven priests' garments.

New International

43The Levites:

the descendants of Jeshua (through Kadmiel through the line of Hodaviah)   74

44The singers:

the descendants of Asaph   148

45The gatekeepers:

the descendants of
  Shallum, Ater, Talmon, Akkub, Hatita
  and Shobai   138

46The temple servants:

the descendants of
  Ziha, Hasupha, Tabbaoth,
47Keros, Sia, Padon,
48Lebana, Hagaba, Shalmai,
49Hanan, Giddel, Gahar,
50Reaiah, Rezin, Nekoda,
51Gazzam, Uzza, Paseah,
52Besai, Meunim, Nephussim,
53Bakbuk, Hakupha, Harhur,
54Bazluth, Mehida, Harsha,
55Barkos, Sisera, Temah,
56Neziah and Hatipha

57The descendants of the servants of Solomon:

the descendants of
  Sotai, Sophereth, Perida,
58Jaala, Darkon, Giddel,
59Shephatiah, Hattil,
  Pokereth-Hazzebaim and Amon

60The temple servants and the descendants of the servants of Solomon   392

61The following came up from the towns of Tel Melah, Tel Harsha, Kerub, Addon and Immer, but they could not show that their families were descended from Israel:

62the descendants of
  Delaiah, Tobiah and Nekoda   642

63And from among the priests:

the descendants of
  Hobaiah, Hakkoz and Barzillai (a man who had married a daughter of Barzillai the Gileadite and was called by that name).

64These searched for their family records, but they could not find them and so were excluded from the priesthood as unclean. 65The governor, therefore, ordered them not to eat any of the most sacred food until there should be a priest ministering with the Urim and Thummim.

66The whole company numbered 42,360, 67besides their 7,337 menservants and maidservants; and they also had 245 men and women singers. 68There were 736 horses, 245 mules,[a] 69435 camels and 6,720 donkeys.

70Some of the heads of the families contributed to the work. The governor gave to the treasury 1,000 drachmas[b] of gold, 50 bowls and 530 garments for priests. 71Some of the heads of the families gave to the treasury for the work 20,000 drachmas[c] of gold and 2,200 minas[d] of silver. 72The total given by the rest of the people was 20,000 drachmas of gold, 2,000 minas[e] of silver and 67 garments for priests.

---

a *68* Some Hebrew manuscripts (see also Ezra 2:66); most Hebrew manuscripts do not have this verse.   b *70* That is, about 19 pounds (about 8.5 kilograms)   c *71* That is, about 375 pounds (about 170 kilograms); also in verse 72   d *71* That is, about 1 1/3 tons (about 1.2 metric tons)   e *72* That is, about 1 1/4 tons (about 1.1 metric tons)

Living Bible

43, 44, 45"Here are the statistics concerning the Levites:

From the family of Kadmi-el of the subclan of Hodevah of the clan of Jeshua, 74;
The choir members from the clan of Asaph, 148;
From the clans of Shallum, (all of whom were gatekeepers), 138.

46-56"Of the Temple assistants, the following subclans were represented:

Ziha, Hasupha, Tabbaoth, Keros, Sia, Padon, Lebana, Hagaba, Shalmai, Hanan, Giddel, Gahar, Reaiah, Rezin, Nekoda, Gazzam, Uzza, Paseah, Besai, Asnah, Me-unim, Nephushesim, Bakbuk, Hakupha, Harhur, Bazlith, Mehida, Harsha, Barkos, Sisera, Temah, Neziah, Hatipha.

57, 58, 59"Following is a list of the descendants of Solomon's officials who returned to Judah:

Sotai, Sophereth, Perida, Jaala, Darkon, Giddel, Shephatiah, Hattil, Pochereth-hazzebaim, Amon.

60"In all, the Temple assistants and the descendants of Solomon's officers numbered 392."

61Another group returned to Jerusalem at that time from the Persian cities of Telmelah, Tel-harsha, Cherub, Addon, and Immer. But they had lost their genealogies and could not prove their Jewish ancestry; 62these were the subclans of Delaiah, Tobiah, and Nekoda—a total of 642.

63There were also several subclans of priests named after Habaiah, Hakkoz, and Barzillai (he married one of the daughters of Barzillai the Gileadite and took her family name), 64, 65whose genealogies had been lost. So they were not allowed to continue as priests or even to receive the priests' share of food from the sacrifices until the Urim and Thummim had been consulted to find out from God whether or not they actually were descendants of priests.

66There was a total of 42,360 citizens who returned to Judah at that time; 67also, 7,337 slaves and 245 choir members, both men and women. 68, 69They took with them 736 horses, 245 mules, 435 camels, and 6,720 donkeys.

70Some of their leaders gave gifts for the work. The governor gave $5,000 in gold, 50 gold bowls, and 530 sets of clothing for the priests. 71The other leaders gave a total of $100,000 in gold and $77,000 in silver; 72and the common people gave $100,000 in gold, $70,000 in silver, and sixty-seven sets of clothing for the priests.

New Revised Standard

43 The Levites: the descendants of Jeshua, namely of Kadmiel of the descendants of Hodevah, seventy-four. 44The singers: the descendants of Asaph, one hundred forty-eight. 45The gatekeepers: the descendants of Shallum, of Ater, of Talmon, of Akkub, of Hatita, of Shobai, one hundred thirty-eight.

46 The temple servants: the descendants of Ziha, of Hasupha, of Tabbaoth, 47of Keros, of Sia, of Padon, 48of Lebana, of Hagaba, of Shalmai, 49of Hanan, of Giddel, of Gahar, 50of Reaiah, of Rezin, of Nekoda, 51of Gazzam, of Uzza, of Paseah, 52of Besai, of Meunim, of Nephushesim, 53of Bakbuk, of Hakupha, of Harhur, 54of Bazlith, of Mehida, of Harsha, 55of Barkos, of Sisera, of Temah, 56of Neziah, of Hatipha.

57 The descendants of Solomon's servants: of Sotai, of Sophereth, of Perida, 58of Jaala, of Darkon, of Giddel, 59of Shephatiah, of Hattil, of Pochereth-hazzebaim, of Amon.

60 All the temple servants and the descendants of Solomon's servants were three hundred ninety-two.

61 The following were those who came up from Tel-melah, Tel-harsha, Cherub, Addon, and Immer, but they could not prove their ancestral houses or their descent, whether they belonged to Israel: 62the descendants of Delaiah, of Tobiah, of Nekoda, six hundred forty-two. 63Also, of the priests: the descendants of Hobaiah, of Hakkoz, of Barzillai (who had married one of the daughters of Barzillai the Gileadite and was called by their name). 64These sought their registration among those enrolled in the genealogies, but it was not found there, so they were excluded from the priesthood as unclean; 65the governor told them that they were not to partake of the most holy food, until a priest with Urim and Thummim should come.

66 The whole assembly together was forty-two thousand three hundred sixty, 67besides their male and female slaves, of whom there were seven thousand three hundred thirty-seven; and they had two hundred forty-five singers, male and female. 68They had seven hundred thirty-six horses, two hundred forty-five mules,f 69four hundred thirty-five camels, and six thousand seven hundred twenty donkeys.

70 Now some of the heads of ancestral houses contributed to the work. The governor gave to the treasury one thousand darics of gold, fifty basins, and five hundred thirty priestly robes. 71And some of the heads of ancestral houses gave into the building fund twenty thousand darics of gold and two thousand two hundred minas of silver. 72And what the rest of the people gave was twenty thousand darics of gold, two thousand minas of silver, and sixty-seven priestly robes.

---

f Ezra 2.66 and the margins of some Hebrew Mss: MT lacks *They had . . . forty-five mules*

King James

73So the priests, and the Levites, and the porters, and the singers, and *some* of the people, and the Nethinims, and all Israel, dwelt in their cities; and when the seventh month came, the children of Israel *were* in their cities.

8 AND ALL the people gathered themselves together as one man into the street that *was* before the water gate; and they spake unto Ezra the scribe to bring the book of the law of Moses, which the Lord had commanded to Israel.

2And Ezra the priest brought the law before the congregation both of men and women, and all that could hear with understanding, upon the first day of the seventh month.

3And he read therein before the street that *was* before the water gate from the morning until midday, before the men and the women, and those that could understand; and the ears of all the people *were attentive* unto the book of the law.

4And Ezra the scribe stood upon a pulpit of wood, which they had made for the purpose; and beside him stood Mattithiah, and Shema, and Anaiah, and Urijah, and Hilkiah, and Maaseiah, on his right hand; and on his left hand, Pedaiah, and Mishael, and Malchiah, and Hashum, and Hashbadana, Zechariah, *and* Meshullam.

5And Ezra opened the book in the sight of all the people; (for he was above all the people;) and when he opened it, all the people stood up:

6And Ezra blessed the Lord, the great God. And all the people answered, Amen, Amen, with lifting up their hands: and they bowed their heads, and worshipped the Lord with *their* faces to the ground.

7Also Jeshua, and Bani, and Sherebiah, Jamin, Akkub, Shabbethai, Hodijah, Maaseiah, Kelita, Azariah, Jozabad, Hanan, Pelaiah, and the Levites, caused the people to understand the law: and the people *stood* in their place.

8So they read in the book in the law of God distinctly, and gave the sense, and caused *them* to understand the reading.

9¶ And Nehemiah, which *is* the Tirshatha, and Ezra the priest the scribe, and the Levites that taught the people, said unto all the people, This day *is* holy unto the Lord your God; mourn not, nor weep. For all the people wept, when they heard the words of the law.

10Then he said unto them, Go your way, eat the fat, and drink the sweet, and send portions unto them for whom nothing is prepared: for *this* day *is* holy unto our Lord: neither be ye sorry; for the joy of the Lord is your strength.

11So the Levites stilled all the people, saying, Hold your peace, for the day *is* holy; neither be ye grieved.

12And all the people went their way to eat, and to drink, and to send portions, and to make great mirth, because they had understood the words that were declared unto them.

13¶ And on the second day were gathered together the chief of the fathers of all the people, the priests, and the Levites, unto Ezra the scribe, even to understand the words of the law.

14And they found written in the law which the Lord had commanded by Moses, that the children of Israel should dwell in booths in the feast of the seventh month:

15And that they should publish and proclaim in all their cities, and in Jerusalem, saying, Go forth unto the mount, and fetch olive branches, and pine branches, and myrtle branches, and palm branches, and branches of thick trees, to make booths, as *it is* written.

New International

73The priests, the Levites, the gatekeepers, the singers and the temple servants, along with certain of the people and the rest of the Israelites, settled in their own towns.

Ezra Reads the Law

When the seventh month came and the Israelites had settled in their towns,

8 ALL THE people assembled as one man in the square before the Water Gate. They told Ezra the scribe to bring out the Book of the Law of Moses, which the Lord had commanded for Israel.

2So on the first day of the seventh month Ezra the priest brought the Law before the assembly, which was made up of men and women and all who were able to understand. 3He read it aloud from daybreak till noon as he faced the square before the Water Gate in the presence of the men, women and others who could understand. And all the people listened attentively to the Book of the Law.

4Ezra the scribe stood on a high wooden platform built for the occasion. Beside him on his right stood Mattithiah, Shema, Anaiah, Uriah, Hilkiah and Maaseiah; and on his left were Pedaiah, Mishael, Malkijah, Hashum, Hashbaddanah, Zechariah and Meshullam.

5Ezra opened the book. All the people could see him because he was standing above them; and as he opened it, the people all stood up. 6Ezra praised the Lord, the great God; and all the people lifted their hands and responded, "Amen! Amen!" Then they bowed down and worshiped the Lord with their faces to the ground.

7The Levites—Jeshua, Bani, Sherebiah, Jamin, Akkub, Shabbethai, Hodiah, Maaseiah, Kelita, Azariah, Jozabad, Hanan and Pelaiah—instructed the people in the Law while the people were standing there. 8They read from the Book of the Law of God, making it clear[a] and giving the meaning so that the people could understand what was being read.

9Then Nehemiah the governor, Ezra the priest and scribe, and the Levites who were instructing the people said to them all, "This day is sacred to the Lord your God. Do not mourn or weep." For all the people had been weeping as they listened to the words of the Law.

10Nehemiah said, "Go and enjoy choice food and sweet drinks, and send some to those who have nothing prepared. This day is sacred to our Lord. Do not grieve, for the joy of the Lord is your strength."

11The Levites calmed all the people, saying, "Be still, for this is a sacred day. Do not grieve."

12Then all the people went away to eat and drink, to send portions of food and to celebrate with great joy, because they now understood the words that had been made known to them.

13On the second day of the month, the heads of all the families, along with the priests and the Levites, gathered around Ezra the scribe to give attention to the words of the Law. 14They found written in the Law, which the Lord had commanded through Moses, that the Israelites were to live in booths during the feast of the seventh month 15and that they should proclaim this word and spread it throughout their towns and in Jerusalem: "Go out into the hill country and bring back branches from olive and wild olive trees, and from myrtles, palms and shade trees, to make booths"—as it is written.[b]

---

a 8 Or God, translating it   b 15 See Lev. 23:37-40.

Living Bible

73The priests, the Levites, the gatekeepers, the choir members, the Temple attendants, and the rest of the people now returned home to their own towns and villages throughout Judah. But during the month of September, they came back to Jerusalem.

8 NOW, IN mid-September, all the people assembled at the plaza in front of the Water Gate and requested Ezra, their religious leader, to read to them the law of God which he had given to Moses.

So Ezra the priest brought out to them the scroll of Moses' laws. He stood on a wooden stand made especially for the occasion so that everyone could see him as he read. He faced the square in front of the Water Gate, and read from early morning until noon. Everyone stood up as he opened the scroll. And all who were old enough to understand paid close attention. To his right stood Mattithiah, Shema, Anaiah, Uriah, Hilkiah, and Ma-aseiah. To his left were Pedaiah, Misha-el, Malchijah, Hashum, Hash-baddenah, Zechariah, and Meshullam.

6Then Ezra blessed the Lord, the great God, and all the people said, "Amen," and lifted their hands toward heaven; then they bowed and worshiped the Lord with their faces toward the ground.

7, 8As Ezra read from the scroll, Jeshua, Bani, Sherebiah, Jamin, Akkub, Shabbethai, Hodiah, Ma-aseiah, Kelita, Azariah, Jozabad, Hanan, Pelaiah, and the Levites went among the peoplec and explained the meaning of the passage that was being read. 9All the people began sobbing when they heard the commands of the law.

Then Ezra the priest, and I as governor, and the Levites who were assisting me, said to them, "Don't cry on such a day as this! For today is a sacred day before the Lord your God— 10it is a time to celebrate with a hearty meal, and to send presents to those in need, for the joy of the Lord is your strength. You must not be dejected and sad!"

11And the Levites, too, quieted the people, telling them, "That's right! Don't weep! For this is a day of holy joy, not of sadness."

12So the people went away to eat a festive meal and to send presents; it was a time of great and joyful celebration because they could hear and understand God's words.

13The next day the clan leaders and the priests and Levites met with Ezra to go over the law in greater detail. 14As they studied it, they noted that Jehovah had told Moses that the people of Israel should live in tents during the Festival of Tabernacles to be held that month. 15He had said also that a proclamation should be made throughout the cities of the land, especially in Jerusalem, telling the people to go to the hills to get branches from olive, myrtle, palm, and fig trees and to make huts in which to live for the duration of the feast.

New Revised Standard

73 So the priests, the Levites, the gatekeepers, the singers, some of the people, the temple servants, and all Israel settled in their towns.

Ezra Summons the People to Obey the Law

When the seventh month came—the people of Israel being settled in their towns—

8 ALL THE people gathered together into the square before the Water Gate. They told the scribe Ezra to bring the book of the law of Moses, which the LORD had given to Israel. 2Accordingly, the priest Ezra brought the law before the assembly, both men and women and all who could hear with understanding. This was on the first day of the seventh month. 3He read from it facing the square before the Water Gate from early morning until midday, in the presence of the men and the women and those who could understand; and the ears of all the people were attentive to the book of the law. 4The scribe Ezra stood on a wooden platform that had been made for the purpose; and beside him stood Mattithiah, Shema, Anaiah, Uriah, Hilkiah, and Maaseiah on his right hand; and Pedaiah, Mishael, Malchijah, Hashum, Hash-baddanah, Zechariah, and Meshullam on his left hand. 5And Ezra opened the book in the sight of all the people, for he was standing above all the people; and when he opened it, all the people stood up. 6Then Ezra blessed the LORD, the great God, and all the people answered, "Amen, Amen," lifting up their hands. Then they bowed their heads and worshiped the LORD with their faces to the ground. 7Also Jeshua, Bani, Sherebiah, Jamin, Akkub, Shabbethai, Hodiah, Maaseiah, Kelita, Azariah, Jozabad, Hanan, Pelaiah, the Levites,d helped the people to understand the law, while the people remained in their places. 8So they read from the book, from the law of God, with interpretation. They gave the sense, so that the people understood the reading.

9 And Nehemiah, who was the governor, and Ezra the priest and scribe, and the Levites who taught the people said to all the people, "This day is holy to the LORD your God; do not mourn or weep." For all the people wept when they heard the words of the law. 10Then he said to them, "Go your way, eat the fat and drink sweet wine and send portions of them to those for whom nothing is prepared, for this day is holy to our LORD; and do not be grieved, for the joy of the LORD is your strength." 11So the Levites stilled all the people, saying, "Be quiet, for this day is holy; do not be grieved." 12And all the people went their way to eat and drink and to send portions and to make great rejoicing, because they had understood the words that were declared to them.

The Festival of Booths Celebrated

13 On the second day the heads of ancestral houses of all the people, with the priests and the Levites, came together to the scribe Ezra in order to study the words of the law. 14And they found it written in the law, which the LORD had commanded by Moses, that the people of Israel should live in boothse during the festival of the seventh month, 15and that they should publish and proclaim in all their towns and in Jerusalem as follows, "Go out to the hills and bring branches of olive, wild olive, myrtle, palm, and other leafy trees to make booths,e as it is written." 16So the people went out and brought

---

c 8:7, 8 the Levites went among the people, literally, "while the people remained in their places."

d 1 Esdras 9.48 Vg: Heb and the Levites   e Or tabernacles; Heb succoth

King James

16¶ So the people went forth, and brought *them*, and made themselves booths, every one upon the roof of his house, and in their courts, and in the courts of the house of God, and in the street of the water gate, and in the street of the gate of Ephraim.

17And all the congregation of them that were come again out of the captivity made booths, and sat under the booths: for since the days of Jeshua the son of Nun unto that day had not the children of Israel done so. And there was very great gladness.

18Also day by day, from the first day unto the last day, he read in the book of the law of God. And they kept the feast seven days; and on the eighth day *was* a solemn assembly, according unto the manner.

9 NOW IN the twenty and fourth day of this month the children of Israel were assembled with fasting, and with sackclothes, and earth upon them.

2And the seed of Israel separated themselves from all strangers, and stood and confessed their sins, and the iniquities of their fathers.

3And they stood up in their place, and read in the book of the law of the LORD their God *one* fourth part of the day; and *another* fourth part they confessed, and worshipped the LORD their God.

4¶ Then stood up upon the stairs, of the Levites, Jeshua, and Bani, Kadmiel, Shebaniah, Bunni, Sherebiah, Bani, *and* Chenani, and cried with a loud voice unto the LORD their God.

5Then the Levites, Jeshua, and Kadmiel, Bani, Hashabniah, Sherebiah, Hodijah, Shebaniah, *and* Pethahiah, said, Stand up *and* bless the LORD your God for ever and ever: and blessed be thy glorious name, which is exalted above all blessing and praise.

6Thou, *even* thou, *art* LORD alone; thou hast made heaven, the heaven of heavens, with all their host, the earth, and all *things* that *are* therein, the seas, and all that *is* therein, and thou preservest them all; and the host of heaven worshippeth thee.

7Thou *art* the LORD the God, who didst choose Abram, and broughtest him forth out of Ur of the Chaldees, and gavest him the name of Abraham;

8And foundest his heart faithful before thee, and madest a covenant with him to give the land of the Canaanites, the Hittites, the Amorites, and the Perizzites, and the Jebusites, and the Girgashites, to give *it, I say*, to his seed, and hast performed thy words; for thou *art* righteous:

9And didst see the affliction of our fathers in Egypt, and heardest their cry by the Red sea;

10And showedst signs and wonders upon Pharaoh, and on all his servants, and on all the people of his land: for thou knewest that they dealt proudly against them. So didst thou get thee a name, as *it is* this day.

11And thou didst divide the sea before them, so that they went through the midst of the sea on the dry land; and their persecutors thou threwest into the deeps, as a stone into the mighty waters.

12Moreover thou leddest them in the day by a cloudy pillar; and in the night by a pillar of fire, to give them light in the way wherein they should go.

13Thou camest down also upon mount Sinai, and spakest with them from heaven, and gavest them right judgments, and true laws, good statutes and commandments:

14And madest known unto them thy holy sabbath, and commandedst them precepts, statutes, and laws, by the hand of Moses thy servant:

New International

16So the people went out and brought back branches and built themselves booths on their own roofs, in their courtyards, in the courts of the house of God and in the square by the Water Gate and the one by the Gate of Ephraim. 17The whole company that had returned from exile built booths and lived in them. From the days of Joshua son of Nun until that day, the Israelites had not celebrated it like this. And their joy was very great.

18Day after day, from the first day to the last, Ezra read from the Book of the Law of God. They celebrated the feast for seven days, and on the eighth day, in accordance with the regulation, there was an assembly.

The Israelites Confess Their Sins

9 ON THE twenty-fourth day of the same month, the Israelites gathered together, fasting and wearing sackcloth and having dust on their heads. 2Those of Israelite descent had separated themselves from all foreigners. They stood in their places and confessed their sins and the wickedness of their fathers. 3They stood where they were and read from the Book of the Law of the LORD their God for a quarter of the day, and spent another quarter in confession and in worshiping the LORD their God. 4Standing on the stairs were the Levites—Jeshua, Bani, Kadmiel, Shebaniah, Bunni, Sherebiah, Bani and Kenani—who called with loud voices to the LORD their God. 5And the Levites—Jeshua, Kadmiel, Bani, Hashabneiah, Sherebiah, Hodiah, Shebaniah and Pethahiah—said: "Stand up and praise the LORD your God, who is from everlasting to everlasting.ᵃ"

"Blessed be your glorious name, and may it be exalted above all blessing and praise. 6You alone are the LORD. You made the heavens, even the highest heavens, and all their starry host, the earth and all that is on it, the seas and all that is in them. You give life to everything, and the multitudes of heaven worship you.

7"You are the LORD God, who chose Abram and brought him out of Ur of the Chaldeans and named him Abraham. 8You found his heart faithful to you, and you made a covenant with him to give to his descendants the land of the Canaanites, Hittites, Amorites, Perizzites, Jebusites and Girgashites. You have kept your promise because you are righteous.

9"You saw the suffering of our forefathers in Egypt; you heard their cry at the Red Sea.ᵇ 10You sent miraculous signs and wonders against Pharaoh, against all his officials and all the people of his land, for you knew how arrogantly the Egyptians treated them. You made a name for yourself, which remains to this day. 11You divided the sea before them, so that they passed through it on dry ground, but you hurled their pursuers into the depths, like a stone into mighty waters. 12By day you led them with a pillar of cloud, and by night with a pillar of fire to give them light on the way they were to take.

13"You came down on Mount Sinai; you spoke to them from heaven. You gave them regulations and laws that are just and right, and decrees and commands that are good. 14You made known to them your holy Sabbath and gave them commands, decrees and laws through your servant Moses. 15In

---

ᵃ 5 Or *God for ever and ever*   ᵇ 9 Hebrew *Yam Suph*; that is, Sea of Reeds

Living Bible

16So the people went out and cut branches and used them to build huts on the roofs of their houses, or in their courtyards, or in the court of the Temple, or on the plaza beside the Water Gate, or at the Ephraim Gate Plaza. 17They lived in these huts for the seven days of the feast, and everyone was filled with joy! (This procedure had not been carried out since the days of Joshua.) 18Ezra read from the scroll on each of the seven days of the feast, and on the eighth day there was a solemn closing service as required by the laws of Moses.

9 ON OCTOBER 10c the people returned for another observance; this time they fasted and clothed themselves with sackcloth and sprinkled dirt in their hair. And the Israelis separated themselves from all foreigners. 3The laws of God were read aloud to them for two or three hours, and for several more hours they took turns confessing their own sins and those of their ancestors. And everyone worshiped the Lord their God. 4Some of the Levites were on the platform praising the Lord God with songs of joy. These men were Jeshua, Kadmi-el, Bani, Shebaniah, Bunni, Sherebiah, Bani, and Chenani.

5Then the Levite leaders called out to the people, "Stand up and praise the Lord your God, for he lives from everlasting to everlasting. Praise his glorious name! It is far greater than we can think or say."

The leaders in this part of the service were Jeshua, Kadmi-el, Bani, Hashabneiah, Sherebiah, Hodiah, Shebaniah, and Pethahiah.

6Then Ezra prayed, "You alone are God. You have made the skies and the heavens, the earth and the seas, and everything in them. You preserve it all; and all the angels of heaven worship you.

7"You are the Lord God who chose Abram and brought him from Ur of the Chaldeans and renamed him Abraham. 8When he was faithful to you, you made a contract with him to forever give him and his descendants the land of the Canaanites, Hittites, Amorites, Perizzites, Jebusites, and Girgashites; and now you have done what you promised, for you are always true to your word.

9"You saw the troubles and sorrows of our ancestors in Egypt, and you heard their cries from beside the Red Sea. 10You displayed great miracles against Pharaoh and his people, for you knew how brutally the Egyptians were treating them; you have a glorious reputation because of those never-to-be-forgotten deeds. 11You divided the sea for your people so they could go through on dry land! And then you destroyed their enemies in the depths of the sea; they sank like stones beneath the mighty waters. 12You led our ancestors by a pillar of cloud during the day and a pillar of fire at night so that they could find their way.

13"You came down upon Mount Sinai and spoke with them from heaven and gave them good laws and true commandments, 14including the laws about the holy Sabbath; and you commanded them, through Moses your servant, to obey them all.

New Revised Standard

them, and made boothsd for themselves, each on the roofs of their houses, and in their courts and in the courts of the house of God, and in the square at the Water Gate and in the square at the Gate of Ephraim. 17And all the assembly of those who had returned from the captivity made boothsd and lived in them; for from the days of Jeshua son of Nun to that day the people of Israel had not done so. And there was very great rejoicing. 18And day by day, from the first day to the last day, he read from the book of the law of God. They kept the festival seven days; and on the eighth day there was a solemn assembly, according to the ordinance.

National Confession

9 NOW ON the twenty-fourth day of this month the people of Israel were assembled with fasting and in sackcloth, and with earth on their heads.e 2Then those of Israelite descent separated themselves from all foreigners, and stood and confessed their sins and the iniquities of their ancestors. 3They stood up in their place and read from the book of the law of the LORD their God for a fourth part of the day, and for another fourth they made confession and worshiped the LORD their God. 4Then Jeshua, Bani, Kadmiel, Shebaniah, Bunni, Sherebiah, Bani, and Chenani stood on the stairs of the Levites and cried out with a loud voice to the LORD their God. 5Then the Levites, Jeshua, Kadmiel, Bani, Hashabneiah, Sherebiah, Hodiah, Shebaniah, and Pethahiah, said, "Stand up and bless the LORD your God from everlasting to everlasting. Blessed be your glorious name, which is exalted above all blessing and praise."

6 And Ezra said:f "You are the LORD, you alone; you have made heaven, the heaven of heavens, with all their host, the earth and all that is on it, the seas and all that is in them. To all of them you give life, and the host of heaven worships you. 7You are the LORD, the God who chose Abram and brought him out of Ur of the Chaldeans and gave him the name Abraham; 8and you found his heart faithful before you, and made with him a covenant to give to his descendants the land of the Canaanite, the Hittite, the Amorite, the Perizzite, the Jebusite, and the Girgashite; and you have fulfilled your promise, for you are righteous.

9 "And you saw the distress of our ancestors in Egypt and heard their cry at the Red Sea.g 10You performed signs and wonders against Pharaoh and all his servants and all the people of his land, for you knew that they acted insolently against our ancestors. You made a name for yourself, which remains to this day. 11And you divided the sea before them, so that they passed through the sea on dry land, but you threw their pursuers into the depths, like a stone into mighty waters. 12Moreover, you led them by day with a pillar of cloud, and by night with a pillar of fire, to give them light on the way in which they should go. 13You came down also upon Mount Sinai, and spoke with them from heaven, and gave them right ordinances and true laws, good statutes and commandments, 14and you made known your holy sabbath to them and gave them commandments and statutes and a law through your servant Moses. 15For their

c 9:1 On October 10, literally, "the twenty-fourth day" of the Hebrew month.

d Or tabernacles; Heb succoth   e Heb on them   f Gk: Heb lacks And Ezra said   g Or Sea of Reeds

King James

15And gavest them bread from heaven for their hunger, and broughtest forth water for them out of the rock for their thirst, and promisedst them that they should go in to possess the land which thou hadst sworn to give them.

16But they and our fathers dealt proudly, and hardened their necks, and hearkened not to thy commandments,

17And refused to obey, neither were mindful of thy wonders that thou didst among them; but hardened their necks, and in their rebellion appointed a captain to return to their bondage: but thou *art* a God ready to pardon, gracious and merciful, slow to anger, and of great kindness, and forsookest them not.

18Yea, when they had made them a molten calf, and said, This *is* thy God that brought thee up out of Egypt, and had wrought great provocations;

19Yet thou in thy manifold mercies forsookest them not in the wilderness: the pillar of the cloud departed not from them by day, to lead them in the way; neither the pillar of fire by night, to show them light, and the way wherein they should go.

20Thou gavest also thy good spirit to instruct them, and withheldest not thy manna from their mouth, and gavest them water for their thirst.

21Yea, forty years didst thou sustain them in the wilderness, *so that* they lacked nothing; their clothes waxed not old, and their feet swelled not.

22Moreover thou gavest them kingdoms and nations, and didst divide them into corners: so they possessed the land of Sihon, and the land of the king of Heshbon, and the land of Og king of Bashan.

23Their children also multipliedst thou as the stars of heaven, and broughtest them into the land, concerning which thou hadst promised to their fathers, that they should go in to possess *it*.

24So the children went in and possessed the land, and thou subduedst before them the inhabitants of the land, the Canaanites, and gavest them into their hands, with their kings, and the people of the land, that they might do with them as they would.

25And they took strong cities, and a fat land, and possessed houses full of all goods, wells digged, vineyards, and oliveyards, and fruit trees in abundance: so they did eat, and were filled, and became fat, and delighted themselves in thy great goodness.

26Nevertheless they were disobedient, and rebelled against thee, and cast thy law behind their backs, and slew thy prophets which testified against them to turn them to thee, and they wrought great provocations.

27Therefore thou deliveredst them into the hand of their enemies, who vexed them: and in the time of their trouble, when they cried unto thee, thou heardest *them* from heaven; and according to thy manifold mercies thou gavest them saviours, who saved them out of the hand of their enemies.

28But after they had rest, they did evil again before thee: therefore leftest thou them in the hand of their enemies, so that they had the dominion over them: yet when they returned, and cried unto thee, thou heardest *them* from heaven; and many times didst thou deliver them according to thy mercies;

29And testifiedst against them, that thou mightest bring them again unto thy law: yet they dealt proudly, and hearkened not unto thy commandments, but sinned against thy judgments, (which if a man do, he shall live in them;) and withdrew the shoulder, and hardened their neck, and would not hear.

30Yet many years didst thou forbear them, and testifiedst against them by thy spirit in thy prophets: yet would they not give ear: therefore gavest thou them into the hand of the people of the lands.

31Nevertheless for thy great mercies' sake thou didst not utterly consume them, nor forsake them; for thou *art* a gracious and merciful God.

New International

their hunger you gave them bread from heaven and in their thirst you brought them water from the rock; you told them to go in and take possession of the land you had sworn with uplifted hand to give them.

16"But they, our forefathers, became arrogant and stiff-necked, and did not obey your commands. 17They refused to listen and failed to remember the miracles you performed among them. They became stiff-necked and in their rebellion appointed a leader in order to return to their slavery. But you are a forgiving God, gracious and compassionate, slow to anger and abounding in love. Therefore you did not desert them, 18even when they cast for themselves an image of a calf and said, 'This is your god, who brought you up out of Egypt,' or when they committed awful blasphemies.

19"Because of your great compassion you did not abandon them in the desert. By day the pillar of cloud did not cease to guide them on their path, nor the pillar of fire by night to shine on the way they were to take. 20You gave your good Spirit to instruct them. You did not withhold your manna from their mouths, and you gave them water for their thirst. 21For forty years you sustained them in the desert; they lacked nothing, their clothes did not wear out nor did their feet become swollen.

22"You gave them kingdoms and nations, allotting to them even the remotest frontiers. They took over the country of Sihon[a] king of Heshbon and the country of Og king of Bashan. 23You made their sons as numerous as the stars in the sky, and you brought them into the land that you told their fathers to enter and possess. 24Their sons went in and took possession of the land. You subdued before them the Canaanites, who lived in the land; you handed the Canaanites over to them, along with their kings and the peoples of the land, to deal with them as they pleased. 25They captured fortified cities and fertile land; they took possession of houses filled with all kinds of good things, wells already dug, vineyards, olive groves and fruit trees in abundance. They ate to the full and were well-nourished; they reveled in your great goodness.

26"But they were disobedient and rebelled against you; they put your law behind their backs. They killed your prophets, who had admonished them in order to turn them back to you; they committed awful blasphemies. 27So you handed them over to their enemies, who oppressed them. But when they were oppressed they cried out to you. From heaven you heard them, and in your great compassion you gave them deliverers, who rescued them from the hand of their enemies.

28"But as soon as they were at rest, they again did what was evil in your sight. Then you abandoned them to the hand of their enemies so that they ruled over them. And when they cried out to you again, you heard from heaven, and in your compassion you delivered them time after time.

29"You warned them to return to your law, but they became arrogant and disobeyed your commands. They sinned against your ordinances, by which a man will live if he obeys them. Stubbornly they turned their backs on you, became stiff-necked and refused to listen. 30For many years you were patient with them. By your Spirit you admonished them through your prophets. Yet they paid no attention, so you handed them over to the neighboring peoples. 31But in your great mercy you did not put an end to them or abandon them, for you are a gracious and merciful God.

[a] 22 One Hebrew manuscript and Septuagint; most Hebrew manuscripts *Sihon, that is, the country of the*

Living Bible

15"You gave them bread from heaven when they were hungry and water from the rock when they were thirsty. You commanded them to go in and conquer the land you had sworn to give them; 16but our ancestors were a proud and stubborn lot, and they refused to listen to your commandments.

17"They refused to obey and didn't pay any attention to the miracles you did for them; instead, they rebelled and appointed a leader to take them back into slavery in Egypt! But you are a God of forgiveness, always ready to pardon, gracious and merciful, slow to become angry, and full of love and mercy; you didn't abandon them, 18even though they made a calf-idol and proclaimed, 'This is our God! He brought us out of Egypt!' They sinned in so many ways, 19but in your great mercy you didn't abandon them to die in the wilderness! The pillar of cloud led them forward day by day, and the pillar of fire showed them the way through the night. 20You sent your good Spirit to instruct them, and you did not stop giving them bread from heaven or water for their thirst. 21For forty years you sustained them in the wilderness; they lacked nothing in all that time. Their clothes didn't wear out and their feet didn't swell!

22"Then you helped them conquer great kingdoms and many nations, and you placed your people in every corner of the land; they completely took over the land of King Sihon of Heshbon and King Og of Bashan. 23You caused a population explosion among the Israelis and brought them into the land you had promised to their ancestors. 24You subdued whole nations before them— even the kings and the people of the Canaanites were powerless! 25Your people captured fortified cities and fertile land; they took over houses full of good things, with cisterns and vineyards and oliveyards and many, many fruit trees; so they ate and were full and enjoyed themselves in all your blessings.

26"But despite all this they were disobedient and rebelled against you. They threw away your law, killed the prophets who told them to return to you, and they did many other terrible things. 27So you gave them to their enemies. But in their time of trouble they cried to you and you heard them from heaven, and in great mercy you sent them saviors who delivered them from their enemies. 28But when all was going well, your people turned to sin again, and once more you let their enemies conquer them. Yet whenever your people returned to you and cried to you for help, once more you listened from heaven, and in your wonderful mercy delivered them! 29You punished them in order to turn them toward your laws; but even though they should have obeyed them,b they were proud and wouldn't listen, and continued to sin. 30You were patient with them for many years. You sent your prophets to warn them about their sins, but still they wouldn't listen. So once again you allowed the heathen nations to conquer them. 31But in your great mercy you did not destroy them completely or abandon them forever. What a gracious and merciful God you are!

New Revised Standard

hunger you gave them bread from heaven, and for their thirst you brought water for them out of the rock, and you told them to go in to possess the land that you swore to give them.

16 "But they and our ancestors acted presumptuously and stiffened their necks and did not obey your commandments; 17they refused to obey, and were not mindful of the wonders that you performed among them; but they stiffened their necks and determined to return to their slavery in Egypt. But you are a God ready to forgive, gracious and merciful, slow to anger and abounding in steadfast love, and you did not forsake them. 18Even when they had cast an image of a calf for themselves and said, 'This is your God who brought you up out of Egypt,' and had committed great blasphemies, 19you in your great mercies did not forsake them in the wilderness; the pillar of cloud that led them in the way did not leave them by day, nor the pillar of fire by night that gave them light on the way by which they should go. 20You gave your good spirit to instruct them, and did not withhold your manna from their mouths, and gave them water for their thirst. 21Forty years you sustained them in the wilderness so that they lacked nothing; their clothes did not wear out and their feet did not swell. 22And you gave them kingdoms and peoples, and allotted to them every corner,c so they took possession of the land of King Sihon of Heshbon and the land of King Og of Bashan. 23You multiplied their descendants like the stars of heaven, and brought them into the land that you had told their ancestors to enter and possess. 24So the descendants went in and possessed the land, and you subdued before them the inhabitants of the land, the Canaanites, and gave them into their hands, with their kings and the peoples of the land, to do with them as they pleased. 25And they captured fortress cities and a rich land, and took possession of houses filled with all sorts of goods, hewn cisterns, vineyards, olive orchards, and fruit trees in abundance; so they ate, and were filled and became fat, and delighted themselves in your great goodness.

26 "Nevertheless they were disobedient and rebelled against you and cast your law behind their backs and killed your prophets, who had warned them in order to turn them back to you, and they committed great blasphemies. 27Therefore you gave them into the hands of their enemies, who made them suffer. Then in the time of their suffering they cried out to you and you heard them from heaven, and according to your great mercies you gave them saviors who saved them from the hands of their enemies. 28But after they had rest, they again did evil before you, and you abandoned them to the hands of their enemies, so that they had dominion over them; yet when they turned and cried to you, you heard from heaven, and many times you rescued them according to your mercies. 29And you warned them in order to turn them back to your law. Yet they acted presumptuously and did not obey your commandments, but sinned against your ordinances, by the observance of which a person shall live. They turned a stubborn shoulder and stiffened their neck and would not obey. 30Many years you were patient with them, and warned them by your spirit through your prophets; yet they would not listen. Therefore you handed them over to the peoples of the lands. 31Nevertheless, in your great mercies you did not make an end of them or forsake them, for you are a gracious and merciful God.

b 9:29 *even though they should have obeyed them*, literally, "by the observance of which a man shall live."

c Meaning of Heb uncertain

King James

32Now therefore, our God, the great, the mighty, and the terrible God, who keepest covenant and mercy, let not all the trouble seem little before thee, that hath come upon us, on our kings, on our princes, and on our priests, and on our prophets, and on our fathers, and on all thy people, since the time of the kings of Assyria unto this day.

33Howbeit thou *art* just in all that is brought upon us; for thou hast done right, but we have done wickedly:

34Neither have our kings, our princes, our priests, nor our fathers, kept thy law, nor hearkened unto thy commandments and thy testimonies, wherewith thou didst testify against them.

35For they have not served thee in their kingdom, and in thy great goodness that thou gavest them, and in the large and fat land which thou gavest before them, neither turned they from their wicked works.

36Behold, we *are* servants this day, and *for* the land that thou gavest unto our fathers to eat the fruit thereof and the good thereof, behold, we *are* servants in it:

37And it yieldeth much increase unto the kings whom thou hast set over us because of our sins: also they have dominion over our bodies, and over our cattle, at their pleasure, and we *are* in great distress.

38And because of all this we make a sure *covenant,* and write *it;* and our princes, Levites, *and* priests, seal *unto it.*

10 NOW THOSE that sealed *were,* Nehemiah, the Tirshatha, the son of Hachaliah, and Zidkijah,

2Seraiah, Azariah, Jeremiah,

3Pashur, Amariah, Malchijah,

4Hattush, Shebaniah, Malluch,

5Harim, Meremoth, Obadiah,

6Daniel, Ginnethon, Baruch,

7Meshullam, Abijah, Mijamin,

8Maaziah, Bilgai, Shemaiah: these *were* the priests.

9And the Levites: both Jeshua the son of Azaniah, Binnui of the sons of Henadad, Kadmiel;

10And their brethren, Shebaniah, Hodijah, Kelita, Pelaiah, Hanan,

11Micha, Rehob, Hashabiah,

12Zaccur, Sherebiah, Shebaniah,

13Hodijah, Bani, Beninu.

14The chief of the people; Parosh, Pahath-moab, Elam, Zatthu, Bani,

15Bunni, Azgad, Bebai,

16Adonijah, Bigvai, Adin,

17Ater, Hizkijah, Azzur,

18Hodijah, Hashum, Bezai,

19Hariph, Anathoth, Nebai,

20Magpiash, Meshullam, Hezir,

21Meshezabeel, Zadok, Jaddua,

22Pelatiah, Hanan, Anaiah,

23Hoshea, Hananiah, Hashub,

24Hallohesh, Pileha, Shobek,

25Rehum, Hashabnah, Maaseiah,

26And Ahijah, Hanan, Anan,

27Malluch, Harim, Baanah.

28¶ And the rest of the people, the priests, the Levites, the porters, the singers, the Nethinims, and all they that had separated themselves from the people of the lands unto the law of God, their wives, their sons, and their daughters, every one having knowledge, and having understanding;

New International

32"Now therefore, O our God, the great, mighty and awesome God, who keeps his covenant of love, do not let all this hardship seem trifling in your eyes—the hardship that has come upon us, upon our kings and leaders, upon our priests and prophets, upon our fathers and all your people, from the days of the kings of Assyria until today. 33In all that has happened to us, you have been just; you have acted faithfully, while we did wrong. 34Our kings, our leaders, our priests and our fathers did not follow your law; they did not pay attention to your commands or the warnings you gave them. 35Even while they were in their kingdom, enjoying your great goodness to them in the spacious and fertile land you gave them, they did not serve you or turn from their evil ways.

36"But see, we are slaves today, slaves in the land you gave our forefathers so they could eat its fruit and the other good things it produces. 37Because of our sins, its abundant harvest goes to the kings you have placed over us. They rule over our bodies and our cattle as they please. We are in great distress.

The Agreement of the People

38"In view of all this, we are making a binding agreement, putting it in writing, and our leaders, our Levites and our priests are affixing their seals to it."

10 THOSE WHO sealed it were:

Nehemiah the governor, the son of Hacaliah.

Zedekiah, 2Seraiah, Azariah, Jeremiah,

3Pashhur, Amariah, Malkijah,

4Hattush, Shebaniah, Malluch,

5Harim, Meremoth, Obadiah,

6Daniel, Ginnethon, Baruch,

7Meshullam, Abijah, Mijamin,

8Maaziah, Bilgai and Shemaiah.

These were the priests.

9The Levites:

Jeshua son of Azaniah, Binnui of the sons of Henadad, Kadmiel,

10and their associates: Shebaniah,

Hodiah, Kelita, Pelaiah, Hanan,

11Mica, Rehob, Hashabiah,

12Zaccur, Sherebiah, Shebaniah,

13Hodiah, Bani and Beninu.

14The leaders of the people:

Parosh, Pahath-Moab, Elam, Zattu, Bani,

15Bunni, Azgad, Bebai,

16Adonijah, Bigvai, Adin,

17Ater, Hezekiah, Azzur,

18Hodiah, Hashum, Bezai,

19Hariph, Anathoth, Nebai,

20Magpiash, Meshullam, Hezir,

21Meshezabel, Zadok, Jaddua,

22Pelatiah, Hanan, Anaiah,

23Hoshea, Hananiah, Hasshub,

24Hallohesh, Pilha, Shobek,

25Rehum, Hashabnah, Maaseiah,

26Ahiah, Hanan, Anan,

27Malluch, Harim and Baanah.

28"The rest of the people—priests, Levites, gatekeepers, singers, temple servants and all who separated themselves from the neighboring peoples for the sake of the Law of God, together with their wives and all their sons and daughters who are able to understand— 29all these now join their brothers

Living Bible

32"And now, O great and awesome God, you who keep your promises of love and kindness—do not let all the hardships we have gone through become as nothing to you. Great trouble has come upon us and upon our kings and princes and priests and prophets and ancestors from the days when the kings of Assyria first triumphed over us until now. 33Every time you punished us you were being perfectly fair; we have sinned so greatly that you gave us only what we deserved. 34Our kings, princes, priests, and ancestors didn't obey your laws or listen to your warnings. 35They did not worship you despite the wonderful things you did for them and the great goodness you showered upon them. You gave them a large, fat land, but they refused to turn from their wickedness.

36"So now we are slaves here in the land of plenty which you gave to our ancestors! Slaves among all this abundance! 37The lush yield of this land passes into the hands of the kings whom you have allowed to conquer us because of our sins. They have power over our bodies and our cattle, and we serve them at their pleasure and are in great misery. 38Because of all this, we again promise to serve the Lord! And we and our princes and Levites and priests put our names to this covenant."

10 I, NEHEMIAH the governor, signed the covenant. The others who signed it were: Zedekiah, Seraiah, Azariah, Jeremiah, Pashhur, Amariah, Malchijah, Hattush, Shebaniah, Malluch, Harim, Meremoth, Obadiah, Daniel, Ginnethon, Baruch, Meshullam, Abijah, Mija-min, Ma-aziah, Bilgai, Shemaiah. (All those listed above were priests.) 9-13These were the Levites who signed: Jeshua (son of Azaniah), Binnui (son of Henadad), Kadmi-el, Shebaniah, Hodiah, Kelita, Pelaiah, Ha-nan, Mica, Rehob, Hashabiah, Zaccur, Sherebiah, Shebaniah, Hodiah, Bani, Beninu. 14-27The political leaders who signed: Parosh, Pahath-moab, Elam, Zattu, Bani, Bunni, Azgad, Bebai, Adonijah, Bigvai, Adin, Ater, Heze-kiah, Azzur, Hodiah, Hashum, Bezai, Hariph, Ana-thoth, Nebai, Magpiash, Meshullam, Hezir, Me-shezabel, Zadok, Jaddu-a, Pelatiah, Hanan, Anaiah, Hoshea, Hananiah, Hasshub, Hallohesh, Pilha, Shobek, Rehum, Hashabnah, Ma-aseiah, Ahiah, Hanan, Anan, Malluch, Harim, Baanah. 28These men signed on behalf of the entire nation— for the common people; the priests; the Levites; the gatekeepers; the choir members; the Temple servants; and all the rest who, with their wives and sons and daughters who were old enough to understand, had separated themselves from the heathen people of the land in order to serve God. 29For we all heartily agreed to this oath

New Revised Standard

32 "Now therefore, our God—the great and mighty and awesome God, keeping covenant and steadfast love—do not treat lightly all the hardship that has come upon us, upon our kings, our officials, our priests, our prophets, our ancestors, and all your people, since the time of the kings of Assyria until today. 33 You have been just in all that has come upon us, for you have dealt faithfully and we have acted wickedly; 34 our kings, our officials, our priests, and our ancestors have not kept your law or heeded the commandments and the warnings that you gave them. 35 Even in their own kingdom, and in the great goodness that you bestowed on them, and in the large and rich land that you set before them, they did not serve you and did not turn from their wicked works. 36 Here we are, slaves to this day—slaves in the land that you gave to our ancestors to enjoy its fruit and its good gifts. 37 Its rich yield goes to the kings whom you have set over us because of our sins; they have power also over our bodies and over our livestock at their pleasure, and we are in great distress."

Those Who Signed the Covenant

38a Because of all this we make a firm agreement in writing, and on that sealed document are inscribed the names of our officials, our Levites, and our priests.

10b UPON THE sealed document are the names of Nehemiah the governor, son of Hacaliah, and Zedekiah; 2 Seraiah, Azariah, Jeremiah, 3 Pashhur, Am-ariah, Malchijah, 4 Hattush, Shebaniah, Malluch, 5 Ha-rim, Meremoth, Obadiah, 6 Daniel, Ginnethon, Baruch, 7 Meshullam, Abijah, Mijamin, 8 Maaziah, Bilgai, She-maiah; these are the priests. 9 And the Levites: Jeshua son of Azaniah, Binnui of the sons of Henadad, Kadmi-el; 10 and their associates, Shebaniah, Hodiah, Kelita, Pelaiah, Hanan, 11 Mica, Rehob, Hashabiah, 12 Zaccur, Sherebiah, Shebaniah, 13 Hodiah, Bani, Beninu. 14 The leaders of the people: Parosh, Pahath-moab, Elam, Zat-tu, Bani, 15 Bunni, Azgad, Bebai, 16 Adonijah, Bigvai, Adin, 17 Ater, Hezekiah, Azzur, 18 Hodiah, Hashum, Bezai, 19 Hariph, Anathoth, Nebai, 20 Magpiash, Me-shullam, Hezir, 21 Meshezabel, Zadok, Jaddua, 22 Pelati-ah, Hanan, Anaiah, 23 Hoshea, Hananiah, Hasshub, 24 Hallohesh, Pilha, Shobek, 25 Rehum, Hashabnah, Ma-aseiah, 26 Ahiah, Hanan, Anan, 27 Malluch, Harim, and Baanah.

Summary of the Covenant

28 The rest of the people, the priests, the Levites, the gatekeepers, the singers, the temple servants, and all who have separated themselves from the peoples of the lands to adhere to the law of God, their wives, their sons, their daughters, all who have knowledge and un-derstanding, 29 join with their kin, their nobles, and enter

King James

29They clave to their brethren, their nobles, and entered into a curse, and into an oath, to walk in God's law, which was given by Moses the servant of God, and to observe and do all the commandments of the LORD our Lord, and his judgments and his statutes;

30And that we would not give our daughters unto the people of the land, nor take their daughters for our sons:

31And *if* the people of the land bring ware or any victuals on the sabbath day to sell, *that* we would not buy it of them on the sabbath, or on the holy day: and *that* we would leave the seventh year, and the exaction of every debt.

32Also we made ordinances for us, to charge ourselves yearly with the third part of a shekel for the service of the house of our God;

33For the showbread, and for the continual meat offering, and for the continual burnt offering, of the sabbaths, of the new moons, for the set feasts, and for the holy *things,* and for the sin offerings to make an atonement for Israel, and *for* all the work of the house of our God.

34And we cast the lots among the priests, the Levites, and the people, for the wood offering, to bring *it* into the house of our God, after the houses of our fathers, at times appointed year by year, to burn upon the altar of the LORD our God, as *it is* written in the law:

35And to bring the firstfruits of our ground, and the firstfruits of all fruit of all trees, year by year, unto the house of the LORD:

36Also the firstborn of our sons, and of our cattle, as *it is* written in the law, and the firstlings of our herds and of our flocks, to bring to the house of our God, unto the priests that minister in the house of our God:

37And *that* we should bring the firstfruits of our dough, and our offerings, and the fruit of all manner of trees, of wine and of oil, unto the priests, to the chambers of the house of our God; and the tithes of our ground unto the Levites, that the same Levites might have the tithes in all the cities of our tillage.

38And the priest the son of Aaron shall be with the Levites, when the Levites take tithes: and the Levites shall bring up the tithe of the tithes unto the house of our God, to the chambers, into the treasure house.

39For the children of Israel and the children of Levi shall bring the offering of the corn, of the new wine, and the oil, unto the chambers, where *are* the vessels of the sanctuary, and the priests that minister, and the porters, and the singers: and we will not forsake the house of our God.

11 AND THE rulers of the people dwelt at Jerusalem: the rest of the people also cast lots, to bring one of ten to dwell in Jerusalem the holy city, and nine parts *to dwell in other* cities.

2And the people blessed all the men, that willingly offered themselves to dwell at Jerusalem.

3¶ Now these *are* the chief of the province that dwelt in Jerusalem: but in the cities of Judah dwelt every one in his possession in their cities, *to wit,* Israel, the priests, and the Levites, and the Nethinims, and the children of Solomon's servants.

New International

the nobles, and bind themselves with a curse and an oath to follow the Law of God given through Moses the servant of God and to obey carefully all the commands, regulations and decrees of the LORD our Lord.

30"We promise not to give our daughters in marriage to the peoples around us or take their daughters for our sons.

31"When the neighboring peoples bring merchandise or grain to sell on the Sabbath, we will not buy from them on the Sabbath or on any holy day. Every seventh year we will forgo working the land and will cancel all debts.

32"We assume the responsibility for carrying out the commands to give a third of a shekela each year for the service of the house of our God: 33for the bread set out on the table; for the regular grain offerings and burnt offerings; for the offerings on the Sabbaths, New Moon festivals and appointed feasts; for the holy offerings; for sin offerings to make atonement for Israel; and for all the duties of the house of our God.

34"We—the priests, the Levites and the people—have cast lots to determine when each of our families is to bring to the house of our God at set times each year a contribution of wood to burn on the altar of the LORD our God, as it is written in the Law.

35"We also assume responsibility for bringing to the house of the LORD each year the firstfruits of our crops and of every fruit tree.

36"As it is also written in the Law, we will bring the firstborn of our sons and of our cattle, of our herds and of our flocks to the house of our God, to the priests ministering there.

37"Moreover, we will bring to the storerooms of the house of our God, to the priests, the first of our ground meal, of our grain, offerings, of the fruit of all our trees and of our new wine and oil. And we will bring a tithe of our crops to the Levites, for it is the Levites who collect the tithes in all the towns where we work. 38A priest descended from Aaron is to accompany the Levites when they receive the tithes, and the Levites are to bring a tenth of the tithes up to the house of our God, to the storerooms of the treasury. 39The people of Israel, including the Levites, are to bring their contributions of grain, new wine and oil to the storerooms where the articles for the sanctuary are kept and where the ministering priests, the gatekeepers and the singers stay.

"We will not neglect the house of our God."

The New Residents of Jerusalem

11 NOW THE leaders of the people settled in Jerusalem, and the rest of the people cast lots to bring one out of every ten to live in Jerusalem, the holy city, while the remaining nine were to stay in their own towns. 2The people commended all the men who volunteered to live in Jerusalem.

3These are the provincial leaders who settled in Jerusalem (now some Israelites, priests, Levites, temple servants and descendants of Solomon's servants lived in the towns of Judah, each on his own property in the various

a 32 That is, about 1/8 ounce (about 4 grams)

Living Bible

and vowed to accept the curse of God unless we obeyed God's laws as issued by his servant Moses.

30 We also agreed not to let our daughters marry non-Jewish men and not to let our sons marry non-Jewish girls.

31 We further agreed that if the heathen people in the land should bring any grain or other produce to be sold on the Sabbath or on any other holy day, we would refuse to buy it. And we agreed not to do any work every seventh year and to forgive and cancel the debts of our brother Jews.

32 We also agreed to charge ourselves annually with a Temple tax so that there would be enough money to care for the Temple of our God; 33 for we needed supplies of the special Bread of the Presence, as well as grain offerings and burnt offerings for the Sabbaths, the new moon feasts, and the annual feasts. We also needed to purchase the other items necessary for the work of the Temple and for the atonement of Israel.

34 Then we tossed a coin[b] to determine when—at regular times each year—the families of the priests, Levites, and leaders should supply the wood for the burnt offerings at the Temple as required in the law.

35 We also agreed always to bring the first part of every crop to the Temple—whether it be a ground crop or from our fruit and olive trees.

36 We agreed to give to God our oldest sons and the firstborn of all our cattle, herds, and flocks, just as the law requires; we presented them to the priests who minister in the Temple of our God. 37 They stored the produce in the Temple of our God—the best of our grain crops, and other contributions, the first of our fruit, and the first of the new wine and olive oil. And we promised to bring to the Levites a tenth of everything our land produced, for the Levites were responsible to collect the tithes in all our rural towns. 38 A priest—a descendant of Aaron—would be with the Levites as they received these tithes, and a tenth of all that was collected as tithes was delivered to the Temple and placed in the storage areas. 39 The people and the Levites were required by law to bring these offerings of grain, new wine, and olive oil to the Temple and place them in the sacred containers for use by the ministering priests, the gatekeepers, and the choir singers.

So we agreed together not to neglect the Temple of our God.

11 THE ISRAELI officials were living in Jerusalem, the Holy City, at this time; but now a tenth of the people from the other cities and towns of Judah and Benjamin were selected by lot to live there too. 2 Some who moved to Jerusalem at this time were volunteers, and they were highly honored.

3 Following is a list of the names of the provincial officials who came to Jerusalem (though most of the leaders, the priests, the Levites, the Temple assistants, and the descendants of Solomon's servants continued to live in their own homes in the various cities of Judah).

New Revised Standard

into a curse and an oath to walk in God's law, which was given by Moses the servant of God, and to observe and do all the commandments of the LORD our Lord and his ordinances and his statutes. 30 We will not give our daughters to the peoples of the land or take their daughters for our sons; 31 and if the peoples of the land bring in merchandise or any grain on the sabbath day to sell, we will not buy it from them on the sabbath or on a holy day; and we will forego the crops of the seventh year and the exaction of every debt.

32 We also lay on ourselves the obligation to charge ourselves yearly one-third of a shekel for the service of the house of our God: 33 for the rows of bread, the regular grain offering, the regular burnt offering, the sabbaths, the new moons, the appointed festivals, the sacred donations, and the sin offerings to make atonement for Israel, and for all the work of the house of our God. 34 We have also cast lots among the priests, the Levites, and the people, for the wood offering, to bring it into the house of our God, by ancestral houses, at appointed times, year by year, to burn on the altar of the LORD our God, as it is written in the law. 35 We obligate ourselves to bring the first fruits of our soil and the first fruits of all fruit of every tree, year by year, to the house of the LORD; 36 also to bring to the house of our God, to the priests who minister in the house of our God, the firstborn of our sons and of our livestock, as it is written in the law, and the firstlings of our herds and of our flocks; 37 and to bring the first of our dough, and our contributions, the fruit of every tree, the wine and the oil, to the priests, to the chambers of the house of our God; and to bring to the Levites the tithes from our soil, for it is the Levites who collect the tithes in all our rural towns. 38 And the priest, the descendant of Aaron, shall be with the Levites when the Levites receive the tithes; and the Levites shall bring up a tithe of the tithes to the house of our God, to the chambers of the storehouse. 39 For the people of Israel and the sons of Levi shall bring the contribution of grain, wine, and oil to the storerooms where the vessels of the sanctuary are, and where the priests that minister, and the gatekeepers and the singers are. We will not neglect the house of our God.

Population of the City Increased

11 NOW THE leaders of the people lived in Jerusalem; and the rest of the people cast lots to bring one out of ten to live in the holy city Jerusalem, while nine-tenths remained in the other towns. 2 And the people blessed all those who willingly offered to live in Jerusalem.

3 These are the leaders of the province who lived in Jerusalem; but in the towns of Judah all lived on their property in their towns: Israel, the priests, the Levites, the temple servants, and the descendants of Solomon's servants. 4 And in Jerusalem lived some of the Judahites

---

b 10:34 *Then we tossed a coin,* literally, "cast lots," a form of dice.

King James

4And at Jerusalem dwelt *certain* of the children of Judah, and of the children of Benjamin. Of the children of Judah; Athaiah the son of Uzziah, the son of Zechariah, the son of Amariah, the son of Shephatiah, the son of Mahalaleel, of the children of Perez;

5And Maaseiah the son of Baruch, the son of Col-hozeh, the son of Hazaiah, the son of Adaiah, the son of Joiarib, the son of Zechariah, the son of Shiloni.

6All the sons of Perez that dwelt at Jerusalem *were* four hundred threescore and eight valiant men.

7And these *are* the sons of Benjamin; Sallu the son of Meshullam, the son of Joed, the son of Pedaiah, the son of Kolaiah, the son of Maaseiah, the son of Ithiel, the son of Jesaiah.

8And after him Gabbai, Sallai, nine hundred twenty and eight.

9And Joel the son of Zichri *was* their overseer: and Judah the son of Senuah *was* second over the city.

10Of the priests: Jedaiah the son of Joiarib, Jachin.

11Seraiah the son of Hilkiah, the son of Meshullam, the son of Zadok, the son of Meraioth, the son of Ahitub, *was* the ruler of the house of God.

12And their brethren that did the work of the house *were* eight hundred twenty and two: and Adaiah the son of Jeroham, the son of Pelaliah, the son of Amzi, the son of Zechariah, the son of Pashur, the son of Malchiah,

13And his brethren, chief of the fathers, two hundred forty and two: and Amashai the son of Azareel, the son of Ahasai, the son of Meshillemoth, the son of Immer.

14And their brethren, mighty men of valour, an hundred twenty and eight: and their overseer *was* Zabdiel, the son of *one of* the great men.

15Also of the Levites: Shemaiah the son of Hashub, the son of Azrikam, the son of Hashabiah, the son of Bunni;

16And Shabbethai and Jozabad, of the chief of the Levites, *had* the oversight of the outward business of the house of God.

17And Mattaniah the son of Micha, the son of Zabdi, the son of Asaph, *was* the principal to begin the thanksgiving in prayer: and Bakbukiah the second among his brethren, and Abda the son of Shammua, the son of Galal, the son of Jeduthun.

18All the Levites in the holy city *were* two hundred fourscore and four.

19Moreover the porters, Akkub, Talmon, and their brethren that kept the gates, *were* an hundred seventy and two.

20¶ And the residue of Israel, of the priests, *and* the Levites, *were* in all the cities of Judah, every one in his inheritance.

21But the Nethinims dwelt in Ophel: and Ziha and Gispa *were* over the Nethinims.

22The overseer also of the Levites at Jerusalem *was* Uzzi the son of Bani, the son of Hashabiah, the son of Mattaniah, the son of Micha. Of the sons of Asaph, the singers *were* over the business of the house of God.

23For *it was* the king's commandment concerning them, that a certain portion should be for the singers, due for every day.

24And Pethahiah the son of Meshezabeel, of the children of Zerah the son of Judah, *was* at the king's hand in all matters concerning the people.

New International

towns, 4while other people from both Judah and Benjamin lived in Jerusalem):

From the descendants of Judah:

Athaiah son of Uzziah, the son of Zechariah, the son of Amariah, the son of Shephatiah, the son of Mahalalel, a descendant of Perez; 5and Maaseiah son of Baruch, the son of Col-Hozeh, the son of Hazaiah, the son of Adaiah, the son of Joiarib, the son of Zechariah, a descendant of Shelah. 6The descendants of Perez who lived in Jerusalem totaled 468 able men.

7From the descendants of Benjamin:

Sallu son of Meshullam, the son of Joed, the son of Pedaiah, the son of Kolaiah, the son of Maaseiah, the son of Ithiel, the son of Jeshaiah, 8and his followers, Gabbai and Sallai—928 men. 9Joel son of Zicri was their chief officer, and Judah son of Hassenuah was over the Second District of the city.

10From the priests:

Jedaiah; the son of Joiarib; Jakin; 11Seraiah son of Hilkiah, the son of Meshullam, the son of Zadok, the son of Meraioth, the son of Ahitub, supervisor in the house of God, 12and their associates, who carried on work for the temple—822 men; Adaiah son of Jeroham, the son of Pelaliah, the son of Amzi, the son of Zechariah, the son of Pashhur, the son of Malkijah, 13and his associates, who were heads of families—242 men; Amashsai son of Azarel, the son of Ahzai, the son of Meshillemoth, the son of Immer, 14and his[a] associates, who were able men—128. Their chief officer was Zabdiel son of Haggedolim.

15From the Levites:

Shemaiah son of Hasshub, the son of Azrikam, the son of Hashabiah, the son of Bunni; 16Shabbethai and Jozabad, two of the heads of the Levites, who had charge of the outside work of the house of God; 17Mattaniah son of Mica, the son of Zabdi, the son of Asaph, the director who led in thanksgiving and prayer; Bakbukiah, second among his associates; and Abda son of Shammua, the son of Galal, the son of Jeduthun. 18The Levites in the holy city totaled 284.

19The gatekeepers:

Akkub, Talmon and their associates, who kept watch at the gates—172 men.

20The rest of the Israelites, with the priests and Levites, were in all the towns of Judah, each on his ancestral property.

21The temple servants lived on the hill of Ophel, and Ziha and Gishpa were in charge of them.

22The chief officer of the Levites in Jerusalem was Uzzi son of Bani, the son of Hashabiah, the son of Mattaniah, the son of Mica. Uzzi was one of Asaph's descendants, who were the singers responsible for the service of the house of God. 23The singers were under the king's orders, which regulated their daily activity.

24Pethahiah son of Meshezabel, one of the descendants of Zerah son of Judah, was the king's agent in all affairs relating to the people.

---

a *14* Most Septuagint manuscripts; Hebrew *their*

Living Bible

4, 5, 6Leaders from the tribe of Judah:

Athaiah (son of Uzziah, son of Zechariah, son of Amariah, son of Shephatiah, son of Mahalalel, a descendant of Perez);

Ma-aseiah (son of Baruch, son of Col-hozeh, son of Hazaiah, son of Adaiah, son of Joiarib, son of Zechariah, son of the Shilonite).

These were the 468 stalwart descendants of Perez who lived in Jerusalem.

7, 8, 9Leaders from the tribe of Benjamin:

Sallu (son of Meshullam, son of Joed, son of Pedaiah, son of Kolaiah, son of Ma-aseiah, son of Ithi-el, son of Jeshaiah).

The 968 descendants of Gabbai and Sallai. Their chief was Joel, son of Zichri, who was assisted by Judah, son of Hassenu-ah.

10-14Leaders from among the priests:

Jedaiah (son of Joiarib);

Jachin;

Seraiah (son of Hilkiah, son of Meshullam, son of Zadok, son of Meraioth, son of Ahitub the chief priest).

In all, there were 822 priests doing the work at the Temple under the leadership of these men. And there were 242 priests under the leadership of Adaiah (son of Jeroham, son of Pelaliah, son of Amzi, son of Zechariah, son of Pashhur, son of Malchijah).

There were also 128 stalwart men under the leadership of Amashsai (son of Azarel, son of Ahzai, son of Meshillemoth, son of Immer); who was assisted by Zabdiel (son of Haggedolim).

15, 16, 17Levite leaders:

Shemaiah (son of Hasshub, son of Azrikam, son of Hashabiah, son of Bunni);

Shabbethai and Jozabad, who were in charge of the work outside the Temple;

Mattaniah (son of Mica, son of Zabdi, son of Asaph) was the one who began the thanksgiving services with prayer;

Bakbukiah and Abda (son of Shammua, son of Galal, son of Jeduthun) were his assistants.

18In all, there were 284 Levites in Jerusalem.

19There were also 172 gatekeepers, led by Akkub, Talmon, and others of their clan. 20The other priests, Levites, and people lived wherever their family inheritance was located. 21However, the Temple workers (whose leaders were Ziha and Gishpa) all lived in Ophel.

22, 23The supervisor of the Levites in Jerusalem and of those serving at the Temple was Uzzi (son of Bani, son of Hashabiah, son of Mattaniah, son of Mica), a descendant of Asaph, whose clan became the Tabernacle singers. He was appointed by King David,b who also set the pay scale of the singers.

24Pethahiah (son of Meshezabel, a descendant of Zerah, a son of Judah) assisted in all matters of public administration.

New Revised Standard

and of the Benjaminites. Of the Judahites: Athaiah son of Uzziah son of Zechariah son of Amariah son of Shephatiah son of Mahalalel, of the descendants of Perez; 5and Maaseiah son of Baruch son of Col-hozeh son of Hazaiah son of Adaiah son of Joiarib son of Zechariah son of the Shilonite. 6All the descendants of Perez who lived in Jerusalem were four hundred sixty-eight valiant warriors.

7 And these are the Benjaminites: Sallu son of Meshullam son of Joed son of Pedaiah son of Kolaiah son of Maaseiah son of Ithiel son of Jeshaiah. 8And his brothersc Gabbai, Sallai: nine hundred twenty-eight. 9Joel son of Zichri was their overseer; and Judah son of Hassenuah was second in charge of the city.

10 Of the priests: Jedaiah son of Joiarib, Jachin, 11Seraiah son of Hilkiah son of Meshullam son of Zadok son of Meraioth son of Ahitub, officer of the house of God, 12and their associates who did the work of the house, eight hundred twenty-two; and Adaiah son of Jeroham son of Pelaliah son of Amzi son of Zechariah son of Pashhur son of Malchijah, 13and his associates, heads of ancestral houses, two hundred forty-two; and Amashsai son of Azarel son of Ahzai son of Meshillemoth son of Immer, 14and their associates, valiant warriors, one hundred twenty-eight; their overseer was Zabdiel son of Haggedolim.

15 And of the Levites: Shemaiah son of Hasshub son of Azrikam son of Hashabiah son of Bunni; 16and Shabbethai and Jozabad, of the leaders of the Levites, who were over the outside work of the house of God; 17and Mattaniah son of Mica son of Zabdi son of Asaph, who was the leader to begin the thanksgiving in prayer, and Bakbukiah, the second among his associates; and Abda son of Shammua son of Galal son of Jeduthun. 18All the Levites in the holy city were two hundred eighty-four.

19 The gatekeepers, Akkub, Talmon and their associates, who kept watch at the gates, were one hundred seventy-two. 20And the rest of Israel, and of the priests and the Levites, were in all the towns of Judah, all of them in their inheritance. 21But the temple servants lived on Ophel; and Ziha and Gishpa were over the temple servants.

22 The overseer of the Levites in Jerusalem was Uzzi son of Bani son of Hashabiah son of Mattaniah son of Mica, of the descendants of Asaph, the singers, in charge of the work of the house of God. 23For there was a command from the king concerning them, and a settled provision for the singers, as was required every day. 24And Pethahiah son of Meshezabel, of the descendants of Zerah son of Judah, was at the king's hand in all matters concerning the people.

---

b 11:22, 23 He was appointed by King David, literally, "There was a commandment from the king concerning them."

c Gk Mss: Heb And after him

King James

25And for the villages, with their fields, *some* of the children of Judah dwelt at Kirjath-arba, and *in* the villages thereof, and at Dibon, and *in* the villages thereof, and at Jekabzeel, and *in* the villages thereof,
26And at Jeshua, and at Moladah, and at Beth-phelet,
27And at Hazar-shual, and at Beer-sheba, and *in* the villages thereof,
28And at Ziklag, and at Mekonah, and in the villages thereof,
29And at En-rimmon, and at Zareah, and at Jarmuth,
30Zanoah, Adullam, and *in* their villages, at Lachish, and the fields thereof, at Azekah, and *in* the villages thereof. And they dwelt from Beer-sheba unto the valley of Hinnom.
31The children also of Benjamin from Geba *dwelt* at Michmash, and Aija, and Beth-el, and *in* their villages,
32*And* at Anathoth, Nob, Ananiah,
33Hazor, Ramah, Gittaim,
34Hadid, Zeboim, Neballat,
35Lod, and Ono, the valley of craftsmen.
36And of the Levites *were* divisions *in* Judah, *and* in Benjamin.

12 NOW THESE *are* the priests and the Levites that went up with Zerubbabel the son of Shealtiel, and Jeshua: Seraiah, Jeremiah, Ezra,
2Amariah, Malluch, Hattush,
3Shechaniah, Rehum, Meremoth,
4Iddo, Ginnetho, Abijah,
5Miamin, Maadiah, Bilgah,
6Shemaiah, and Joiarib, Jedaiah,
7Sallu, Amok, Hilkiah, Jedaiah. These *were* the chief of the priests and of their brethren in the days of Jeshua.
8Moreover the Levites: Jeshua, Binnui, Kadmiel, Sherebiah, Judah, *and* Mattaniah, *which was* over the thanksgiving, he and his brethren.
9Also Bakbukiah and Unni, their brethren, *were* over against them in the watches.
10¶ And Jeshua begat Joiakim, Joiakim also begat Eliashib, and Eliashib begat Joiada,
11And Joiada begat Jonathan, and Jonathan begat Jaddua.
12And in the days of Joiakim were priests, the chief of the fathers: of Seraiah, Meraiah; of Jeremiah, Hananiah;
13Of Ezra, Meshullam; of Amariah, Jehohanan;
14Of Melicu, Jonathan; of Shebaniah, Joseph;
15Of Harim, Adna; of Meraioth, Helkai;
16Of Iddo, Zechariah; of Ginnethon, Meshullam;
17Of Abijah, Zichri; of Miniamin, of Moadiah, Piltai;
18Of Bilgah, Shammua; of Shemaiah, Jehonathan;
19And of Joiarib, Mattenai; of Jedaiah, Uzzi;
20Of Sallai, Kallai; of Amok, Eber;
21Of Hilkiah, Hashabiah; of Jedaiah, Nethaneel.

New International

25As for the villages with their fields, some of the people of Judah lived in Kiriath Arba and its surrounding settlements, in Dibon and its settlements, in Jekabzeel and its villages, 26in Jeshua, in Moladah, in Beth Pelet, 27in Hazar Shual, in Beersheba and its settlements, 28in Ziklag, in Meconah and its settlements, 29in En Rimmon, in Zorah, in Jarmuth, 30Zanoah, Adullam and their villages, in Lachish and its fields, and in Azekah and its settlements. So they were living all the way from Beersheba to the Valley of Hinnom.
31The descendants of the Benjamites from Geba lived in Micmash, Aija, Bethel and its settlements, 32in Anathoth, Nob and Ananiah, 33in Hazor, Ramah and Gittaim, 34in Hadid, Zeboim and Neballat, 35in Lod and Ono, and in the Valley of the Craftsmen.
36Some of the divisions of the Levites of Judah settled in Benjamin.

Priests and Levites

12 THESE WERE the priests and Levites who returned with Zerubbabel son of Shealtiel and with Jeshua:
Seraiah, Jeremiah, Ezra,
2Amariah, Malluch, Hattush,
3Shecaniah, Rehum, Meremoth,
4Iddo, Ginnethon,a Abijah,
5Mijamin,b Moadiah, Bilgah,
6Shemaiah, Joiarib, Jedaiah,
7Sallu, Amok, Hilkiah and Jedaiah.
These were the leaders of the priests and their associates in the days of Jeshua.
8The Levites were Jeshua, Binnui, Kadmiel, Sherebiah, Judah, and also Mattaniah, who, together with his associates, was in charge of the songs of thanksgiving.
9Bakbukiah and Unni, their associates, stood opposite them in the services.
10Jeshua was the father of Joiakim, Joiakim the father of Eliashib, Eliashib the father of Joiada, 11Joiada the father of Jonathan, and Jonathan the father of Jaddua.
12In the days of Joiakim, these were the heads of the priestly families:
of Seraiah's family, Meraiah;
of Jeremiah's, Hananiah;
13of Ezra's, Meshullam;
of Amariah's, Jehohanan;
14of Malluch's, Jonathan;
of Shecaniah's,c Joseph;
15of Harim's, Adna;
of Meremoth's,d Helkai;
16of Iddo's, Zechariah;
of Ginnethon's, Meshullam;
17of Abijah's, Zicri;
of Miniamin's and of Moadiah's, Piltai;
18of Bilgah's, Shammua;
of Shemaiah's, Jehonathan;
19of Joiarib's, Mattenai;
of Jedaiah's, Uzzi;
20of Sallu's, Kallai;
of Amok's, Eber;
21of Hilkiah's, Hashabiah;
of Jedaiah's, Nethanel.

---

a 4 Many Hebrew manuscripts and Vulgate (see also Neh. 12:16); most Hebrew manuscripts *Ginnethoi*   b 5 A variant of *Miniamin*   c 14 Very many Hebrew manuscripts, some Septuagint manuscripts and Syriac (see also Neh. 12:3); most Hebrew manuscripts *Shebaniah's*   d 15 Some Septuagint manuscripts (see also Neh. 12:3); Hebrew *Meraioth's*

Living Bible

25-30Some of the towns where the people of Judah lived were:

Kiriath-arba, Dibon, Jekabzeel (and their surrounding villages), Jeshua, Moladah, Beth-pelet, Hazar-shual, Beer-sheba (and its surrounding villages), Ziklag, Meconah and its villages, En-rimmon, Zorah, Jarmuth, Zanoah, Adullam (and their surrounding villages), Lachish and its nearby fields, Azekah and its towns.

So the people spread from Beer-sheba to the valley of Hinnom.

31-35The people of the tribe of Benjamin lived at:

Geba, Michmash, Aija, Bethel (and its surrounding villages), Anathoth, Nob, Ananiah, Hazor, Ramah, Gittaim, Hadid, Zeboim, Neballat, Lod, Ono (the Valley of the Craftsmen).

36Some of the Levites who lived in Judah were sent to live with the tribe of Benjamin.

12 HERE IS a list of the priests who accompanied Zerubbabel (son of Shealtiel) and Jeshua: Seraiah, Jeremiah, Ezra, Amariah, Malluch, Hattush, Shecaniah, Rehum, Meremoth, Iddo, Ginnethoi, Abijah, Mijamin, Ma-adiah, Bilgah, Shemaiah, Joiarib, Jedaiah, Sallu, Amok, Hilkiah, Jedaiah.

8The Levites who went with them were: Jeshua, Binnui, Kadmi-el, Sherebiah, Judah, Mattaniah—who was the one in charge of the thanksgiving service.

9Bakbukiah and Unno, their fellow clansmen, helped them during the service.

10, 11Jeshua was the father of Joiakim;
Joiakim was the father of Eliashib;
Eliashib was the father of Joiada;
Joiada was the father of Jonathan;
Jonathan was the father of Jaddu-a.

12-21The following were the clan leaders of the priests who served under the High Priest Joiakim:
Meraiah, leader of the Seraiah clan;
Hananiah, leader of the Jeremiah clan;
Meshullam, leader of the Ezra clan;
Jehohanan, leader of the Amariah clan;
Jonathan, leader of the Malluchi clan;
Joseph, leader of the Shebaniah clan;
Adna, leader of the Harim clan;
Helkai, leader of the Meraioth clan;
Zechariah, leader of the Iddo clan;
Meshullam, leader of the Ginnethon clan;
Zichri, leader of the Abijah clan;
Piltai, leader of the Moadiah and Miniamin clans;
Shammu-a, leader of the Bilgah clan;
Jehonathan, leader of the Shemaiah clan;
Mattenai, leader of the Joiarib clan;
Uzzi, leader of the Jedaiah clan;
Kallai, leader of the Sallai clan;
Eber, leader of the Amok clan;
Hashabiah, leader of the Hilkiah clan;
Nethanel, leader of the Jedaiah clan.

New Revised Standard

Villages outside Jerusalem

25 And as for the villages, with their fields, some of the people of Judah lived in Kiriath-arba and its villages, and in Dibon and its villages, and in Jekabzeel and its villages, 26and in Jeshua and in Moladah and Beth-pelet, 27in Hazar-shual, in Beer-sheba and its villages, 28in Ziklag, in Meconah and its villages, 29in En-rimmon, in Zorah, in Jarmuth, 30Zanoah, Adullam, and their villages, Lachish and its fields, and Azekah and its villages. So they camped from Beer-sheba to the valley of Hinnom. 31The people of Benjamin also lived from Geba onward, at Michmash, Aija, Bethel and its villages, 32Anathoth, Nob, Ananiah, 33Hazor, Ramah, Gittaim, 34Hadid, Zeboim, Neballat, 35Lod, and Ono, the valley of artisans. 36And certain divisions of the Levites in Judah were joined to Benjamin.

A List of Priests and Levites

12 THESE ARE the priests and the Levites who came up with Zerubbabel son of Shealtiel, and Jeshua: Seraiah, Jeremiah, Ezra, 2Amariah, Malluch, Hattush, 3Shecaniah, Rehum, Meremoth, 4Iddo, Ginnethoi, Abijah, 5Mijamin, Maadiah, Bilgah, 6Shemaiah, Joiarib, Jedaiah, 7Sallu, Amok, Hilkiah, Jedaiah. These were the leaders of the priests and of their associates in the days of Jeshua.

8 And the Levites: Jeshua, Binnui, Kadmiel, Sherebiah, Judah, and Mattaniah, who with his associates was in charge of the songs of thanksgiving. 9And Bakbukiah and Unno their associates stood opposite them in the service. 10Jeshua was the father of Joiakim, Joiakim the father of Eliashib, Eliashib the father of Joiada, 11Joiada the father of Jonathan, and Jonathan the father of Jaddua.

12 In the days of Joiakim the priests, heads of ancestral houses, were: of Seraiah, Meraiah; of Jeremiah, Hananiah; 13of Ezra, Meshullam; of Amariah, Jehohanan; 14of Malluchi, Jonathan; of Shebaniah, Joseph; 15of Harim, Adna; of Meraioth, Helkai; 16of Iddo, Zechariah; of Ginnethon, Meshullam; 17of Abijah, Zichri; of Miniamin, of Moadiah, Piltai; 18of Bilgah, Shammua; of Shemaiah, Jehonathan; 19of Joiarib, Mattenai; of Jedaiah, Uzzi; 20of Sallai, Kallai; of Amok, Eber; 21of Hilkiah, Hashabiah; of Jedaiah, Nethanel.

King James

22¶ The Levites in the days of Eliashib, Joiada, and Johanan, and Jaddua, *were* recorded chief of the fathers: also the priests, to the reign of Darius the Persian.

23The sons of Levi, the chief of the fathers, *were* written in the book of the chronicles, even until the days of Johanan the son of Eliashib.

24And the chief of the Levites: Hashabiah, Sherebiah, and Jeshua the son of Kadmiel, with their brethren over against them, to praise *and* to give thanks, according to the commandment of David the man of God, ward over against ward.

25Mattaniah, and Bakbukiah, Obadiah, Meshullam, Talmon, Akkub, *were* porters keeping the ward at the thresholds of the gates.

26These *were* in the days of Joiakim the son of Jeshua, the son of Jozadak, and in the days of Nehemiah the governor, and of Ezra the priest, the scribe.

27¶ And at the dedication of the wall of Jerusalem they sought the Levites out of all their places, to bring them to Jerusalem, to keep the dedication with gladness, both with thanksgivings, and with singing, *with* cymbals, psalteries, and with harps.

28And the sons of the singers gathered themselves together, both out of the plain country round about Jerusalem, and from the villages of Netophathi;

29Also from the house of Gilgal, and out of the fields of Geba and Azmaveth: for the singers had builded them villages round about Jerusalem.

30And the priests and the Levites purified themselves, and purified the people, and the gates, and the wall.

31Then I brought up the princes of Judah upon the wall, and appointed two great *companies of them that gave* thanks, *whereof one* went on the right hand upon the wall toward the dung gate:

32And after them went Hoshaiah, and half of the princes of Judah,

33And Azariah, Ezra, and Meshullam,

34Judah, and Benjamin, and Shemaiah, and Jeremiah,

35And *certain* of the priests' sons with trumpets; *namely,* Zechariah the son of Jonathan, the son of Shemaiah, the son of Mattaniah, the son of Michaiah, the son of Zaccur, the son of Asaph:

36And his brethren, Shemaiah, and Azarael, Milalai, Gilalai, Maai, Nethaneel, and Judah, Hanani, with the musical instruments of David the man of God, and Ezra the scribe before them.

37And at the fountain gate, which was over against them, they went up by the stairs of the city of David, at the going up of the wall, above the house of David, even unto the water gate eastward.

38And the other *company of them that gave* thanks went over against *them,* and I after them, and the half of the people upon the wall, from beyond the tower of the furnaces even unto the broad wall;

39And from above the gate of Ephraim, and above the old gate, and above the fish gate, and the tower of Hananeel, and the tower of Meah, even unto the sheep gate: and they stood still in the prison gate.

40So stood the two *companies of them that gave* thanks in the house of God, and I, and the half of the rulers with me:

41And the priests; Eliakim, Maaseiah, Miniamin, Michaiah, Elioenai, Zechariah, *and* Hananiah, with trumpets;

42And Maaseiah, and Shemaiah, and Eleazar, and Uzzi, and Jehohanan, and Malchijah, and Elam, and Ezer. And the singers sang loud, with Jezrahiah *their* overseer.

43Also that day they offered great sacrifices, and rejoiced: for God had made them rejoice with great joy: the wives also and the children rejoiced: so that the joy of Jerusalem was heard even afar off.

New International

22The family heads of the Levites in the days of Eliashib, Joiada, Johanan and Jaddua, as well as those of the priests, were recorded in the reign of Darius the Persian. 23The family heads among the descendants of Levi up to the time of Johanan son of Eliashib were recorded in the book of the annals. 24And the leaders of the Levites were Hashabiah, Sherebiah, Jeshua son of Kadmiel, and their associates, who stood opposite them to give praise and thanksgiving, one section responding to the other, as prescribed by David the man of God.

25Mattaniah, Bakbukiah, Obadiah, Meshullam, Talmon and Akkub were gatekeepers who guarded the storerooms at the gates. 26They served in the days of Joiakim son of Jeshua, the son of Jozadak, and in the days of Nehemiah the governor and of Ezra the priest and scribe.

Dedication of the Wall of Jerusalem

27At the dedication of the wall of Jerusalem, the Levites were sought out from where they lived and were brought to Jerusalem to celebrate joyfully the dedication with songs of thanksgiving and with the music of cymbals, harps and lyres. 28The singers also were brought together from the region around Jerusalem—from the villages of the Netophathites, 29from Beth Gilgal, and from the area of Geba and Azmaveth, for the singers had built villages for themselves around Jerusalem. 30When the priests and Levites had purified themselves ceremonially, they purified the people, the gates and the wall.

31I had the leaders of Judah go up on top[a] of the wall. I also assigned two large choirs to give thanks. One was to proceed on top[b] of the wall to the right, toward the Dung Gate. 32Hoshaiah and half the leaders of Judah followed them, 33along with Azariah, Ezra, Meshullam, 34Judah, Benjamin, Shemaiah, Jeremiah, 35as well as some priests with trumpets, and also Zechariah son of Jonathan, the son of Shemaiah, the son of Mattaniah, the son of Micaiah, the son of Zaccur, the son of Asaph, 36and his associates—Shemaiah, Azarel, Milalai, Gilalai, Maai, Nethanel, Judah and Hanani—with musical instruments prescribed by David the man of God. Ezra the scribe led the procession. 37At the Fountain Gate they continued directly up the steps of the City of David on the ascent to the wall and passed above the house of David to the Water Gate on the east.

38The second choir proceeded in the opposite direction. I followed them on top[c] of the wall, together with half the people—past the Tower of the Ovens to the Broad Wall, 39over the Gate of Ephraim, the Jeshanah[d] Gate, the Fish Gate, the Tower of Hananel and the Tower of the Hundred, as far as the Sheep Gate. At the Gate of the Guard they stopped.

40The two choirs that gave thanks then took their places in the house of God; so did I, together with half the officials, 41as well as the priests—Eliakim, Maaseiah, Miniamin, Micaiah, Elioenai, Zechariah and Hananiah with their trumpets— 42and also Maaseiah, Shemaiah, Eleazar, Uzzi, Jehohanan, Malkijah, Elam and Ezer. The choirs sang under the direction of Jezrahiah. 43And on that day they offered great sacrifices, rejoicing because God had given them great joy. The women and children also rejoiced. The sound of rejoicing in Jerusalem could be heard far away.

a 31 Or go alongside   b 31 Or proceed alongside   c 38 Or them alongside
d 39 Or Old

Living Bible

22A genealogical record of the heads of the clans of the priests and Levites was compiled during the reign of King Darius of Persia, in the days of Eliashib, Joiada, Johanan, and Jaddu-a—all of whom were Levites. 23In *The Book of the Chronicles* the Levite names were recorded down to the days of Johanan, the son of Eliashib.

24These were the chiefs of the Levites at that time: Hashabiah, Sherebiah, and Jeshua (son of Kadmi-el). Their fellow-clansmen helped them during the ceremonies of praise and thanksgiving, just as commanded by David, the man of God. 25The gatekeepers who had charge of the collection centers at the gates were: Mattaniah, Bakbukiah, Obadiah, Meshullam, Talmon, Akkub.

26These were the men who were active in the time of Joiakim (son of Jeshua, son of Jozadak), and when I was the governor, and when Ezra was the priest and teacher of religion.

27During the dedication of the new Jerusalem wall, all the Levites throughout the land came to Jerusalem to assist in the ceremonies and to take part in the joyous occasion with their thanksgiving, cymbals, psaltries, and harps. 28The choir members also came to Jerusalem from the surrounding villages and from the villages of the Netophathites; 29they also came from Bethgilgal and the area of Geba and Azmaveth, for the singers had built their own villages as suburbs of Jerusalem. 30The priests and Levites first dedicated themselves, then the people, the gates, and the wall.

31, 32I led the Judean leaders to the top of the wall and divided them into two long lines to walk in opposite directions along the top of the wall, giving thanks as they went. The group which went to the right toward the Dung Gate consisted of half of the leaders of Judah, 33including Hoshaiah, Azariah, Ezra, Meshullam, 34Judah, Benjamin, Shemaiah, and Jeremiah.

35, 36The priests who played the trumpets were Zechariah (son of Jonathan, son of Shemaiah, son of Mattaniah, son of Micaiah, son of Zaccur, son of Asaph), Shemaiah, Azarel, Milalai, Gilalai, Maai, Nethanel, Judah, and Hanani. (They used the original musical instruments of King David.) Ezra the priest led this procession. 37When they arrived at the Fountain Gate they went straight ahead and climbed the stairs which go up beside the castle to the old City of David; then they went to the Water Gate on the east.

38The other group, of which I was a member, went around the other way to meet them. We walked from the Tower of Furnaces to the Broad Wall, 39then from the Ephraim Gate to the Old Gate, passed the Fish Gate and the Tower of Hananel, and went on to the gate of the Tower of the Hundred; then we continued on to the Sheep Gate and stopped at the Prison Gate.

40, 41Both choirs then proceeded to the Temple. Those with me were joined by the trumpet-playing priests— Eliakim, Ma-aseiah, Miniamin, Micaiah, Eli-o-enai, Zechariah, and Hananiah, 42and by the singers—Ma-aseiah, Shemaiah, Eleazar, Uzzi, Jehohanan, Malchijah, Elam and Ezer.

They sang loudly and clearly under the direction of Jezrahiah the choirmaster.

43Many sacrifices were offered on that joyous day, for God had given us cause for great joy. The women and children rejoiced too, and the joy of the people of Jerusalem was heard far away!

New Revised Standard

22 As for the Levites, in the days of Eliashib, Joiada, Johanan, and Jaddua, there were recorded the heads of ancestral houses; also the priests until the reign of Darius the Persian. 23The Levites, heads of ancestral houses, were recorded in the Book of the Annals until the days of Johanan son of Eliashib. 24And the leaders of the Levites: Hashabiah, Sherebiah, and Jeshua son of Kadmiel, with their associates over against them, to praise and to give thanks, according to the commandment of David the man of God, section opposite to section. 25Mattaniah, Bakbukiah, Obadiah, Meshullam, Talmon, and Akkub were gatekeepers standing guard at the storehouses of the gates. 26These were in the days of Joiakim son of Jeshua son of Jozadak, and in the days of the governor Nehemiah and of the priest Ezra, the scribe.

Dedication of the City Wall

27 Now at the dedication of the wall of Jerusalem they sought out the Levites in all their places, to bring them to Jerusalem to celebrate the dedication with rejoicing, with thanksgivings and with singing, with cymbals, harps, and lyres. 28The companies of the singers gathered together from the circuit around Jerusalem and from the villages of the Netophathites; 29also from Bethgilgal and from the region of Geba and Azmaveth; for the singers had built for themselves villages around Jerusalem. 30And the priests and the Levites purified themselves; and they purified the people and the gates and the wall.

31 Then I brought the leaders of Judah up onto the wall, and appointed two great companies that gave thanks and went in procession. One went to the right on the wall to the Dung Gate; 32and after them went Hoshaiah and half the officials of Judah, 33and Azariah, Ezra, Meshullam, 34Judah, Benjamin, Shemaiah, and Jeremiah, 35and some of the young priests with trumpets: Zechariah son of Jonathan son of Shemaiah son of Mattaniah son of Micaiah son of Zaccur son of Asaph; 36and his kindred, Shemaiah, Azarel, Milalai, Gilalai, Maai, Nethanel, Judah, and Hanani, with the musical instruments of David the man of God; and the scribe Ezra went in front of them. 37At the Fountain Gate, in front of them, they went straight up by the stairs of the city of David, at the ascent of the wall, above the house of David, to the Water Gate on the east.

38 The other company of those who gave thanks went to the left,e and I followed them with half of the people on the wall, above the Tower of the Ovens, to the Broad Wall, 39and above the Gate of Ephraim, and by the Old Gate, and by the Fish Gate and the Tower of Hananel and the Tower of the Hundred, to the Sheep Gate; and they came to a halt at the Gate of the Guard. 40So both companies of those who gave thanks stood in the house of God, and I and half of the officials with me; 41and the priests Eliakim, Maaseiah, Miniamin, Micaiah, Elioenai, Zechariah, and Hananiah, with trumpets; 42and Maaseiah, Shemaiah, Eleazar, Uzzi, Jehohanan, Malchijah, Elam, and Ezer. And the singers sang with Jezrahiah as their leader. 43They offered great sacrifices that day and rejoiced, for God had made them rejoice with great joy; the women and children also rejoiced. The joy of Jerusalem was heard far away.

e Cn: Heb *opposite*

King James

44¶ And at that time were some appointed over the chambers for the treasures, for the offerings, for the firstfruits, and for the tithes, to gather into them out of the fields of the cities the portions of the law for the priests and Levites: for Judah rejoiced for the priests and for the Levites that waited.

45And both the singers and the porters kept the ward of their God, and the ward of the purification, according to the commandment of David, *and* of Solomon his son.

46For in the days of David and Asaph of old *there were* chief of the singers, and songs of praise and thanksgiving unto God.

47And all Israel in the days of Zerubbabel, and in the days of Nehemiah, gave the portions of the singers and the porters, every day his portion: and they sanctified *holy things* unto the Levites; and the Levites sanctified *them* unto the children of Aaron.

13 ON THAT day they read in the book of Moses in the audience of the people; and therein was found written, that the Ammonite and the Moabite should not come into the congregation of God for ever;

2Because they met not the children of Israel with bread and with water, but hired Balaam against them, that he should curse them: howbeit our God turned the curse into a blessing.

3Now it came to pass, when they had heard the law, that they separated from Israel all the mixed multitude.

4¶ And before this, Eliashib the priest, having the oversight of the chamber of the house of our God, *was* allied unto Tobiah:

5And he had prepared for him a great chamber, where aforetime they laid the meat offerings, the frankincense, and the vessels, and the tithes of the corn, the new wine, and the oil, which was commanded *to be given* to the Levites, and the singers, and the porters; and the offerings of the priests.

6But in all this *time* was not I at Jerusalem: for in the two and thirtieth year of Artaxerxes king of Babylon came I unto the king, and after certain days obtained I leave of the king:

7And I came to Jerusalem, and understood of the evil that Eliashib did for Tobiah, in preparing him a chamber in the courts of the house of God.

8And it grieved me sore: therefore I cast forth all the household stuff of Tobiah out of the chamber.

9Then I commanded, and they cleansed the chambers: and thither brought I again the vessels of the house of God, with the meat offering and the frankincense.

10¶ And I perceived that the portions of the Levites had not been given *them:* for the Levites and the singers, that did the work, were fled every one to his field.

11Then contended I with the rulers, and said, Why is the house of God forsaken? And I gathered them together, and set them in their place.

12Then brought all Judah the tithe of the corn and the new wine and the oil unto the treasuries.

13And I made treasurers over the treasuries, Shelemiah the priest, and Zadok the scribe, and of the Levites, Pedaiah: and next to them *was* Hanan the son of Zaccur, the son of Mattaniah: for they were counted faithful, and their office *was* to distribute unto their brethren.

14Remember me, O my God, concerning this, and wipe not out my good deeds that I have done for the house of my God, and for the offices thereof.

15¶ In those days saw I in Judah *some* treading wine presses on the sabbath, and bringing in sheaves, and lading asses; as also wine, grapes, and figs, and all *manner of* burdens, which they brought into Jerusalem on the sabbath day: and I testified *against them* in the day wherein they sold victuals.

New International

44At that time men were appointed to be in charge of the storerooms for the contributions, firstfruits and tithes. From the fields around the towns they were to bring into the storerooms the portions required by the Law for the priests and the Levites, for Judah was pleased with the ministering priests and Levites. 45They performed the service of their God and the service of purification, as did also the singers and gatekeepers, according to the commands of David and his son Solomon. 46For long ago, in the days of David and Asaph, there had been directors for the singers and for the songs of praise and thanksgiving to God. 47So in the days of Zerubbabel and of Nehemiah, all Israel contributed the daily portions for the singers and gatekeepers. They also set aside the portion for the other Levites, and the Levites set aside the portion for the descendants of Aaron.

Nehemiah's Final Reforms

13 ON THAT day the Book of Moses was read aloud in the hearing of the people and there it was found written that no Ammonite or Moabite should ever be admitted into the assembly of God, 2because they had not met the Israelites with food and water but had hired Balaam to call a curse down on them. (Our God, however, turned the curse into a blessing.) 3When the people heard this law, they excluded from Israel all who were of foreign descent.

4Before this, Eliashib the priest had been put in charge of the storerooms of the house of our God. He was closely associated with Tobiah, 5and he had provided him with a large room formerly used to store the grain offerings and incense and temple articles, and also the tithes of grain, new wine and oil prescribed for the Levites, singers and gatekeepers, as well as the contributions for the priests.

6But while all this was going on, I was not in Jerusalem, for in the thirty-second year of Artaxerxes king of Babylon I had returned to the king. Some time later I asked his permission 7and came back to Jerusalem. Here I learned about the evil thing Eliashib had done in providing Tobiah a room in the courts of the house of God. 8I was greatly displeased and threw all Tobiah's household goods out of the room. 9I gave orders to purify the rooms, and then I put back into them the equipment of the house of God, with the grain offerings and the incense.

10I also learned that the portions assigned to the Levites had not been given to them, and that all the Levites and singers responsible for the service had gone back to their own fields. 11So I rebuked the officials and asked them, "Why is the house of God neglected?" Then I called them together and stationed them at their posts.

12All Judah brought the tithes of grain, new wine and oil into the storerooms. 13I put Shelemiah the priest, Zadok the scribe, and a Levite named Pedaiah in charge of the storerooms and made Hanan son of Zaccur, the son of Mattaniah, their assistant, because these men were considered trustworthy. They were made responsible for distributing the supplies to their brothers.

14Remember me for this, O my God, and do not blot out what I have so faithfully done for the house of my God and its services.

15In those days I saw men in Judah treading winepresses on the Sabbath and bringing in grain and loading it on donkeys, together with wine, grapes, figs and all other kinds of loads. And they were bringing all this into Jerusalem on the Sabbath. Therefore I warned them against selling food on that day. 16Men from Tyre who

Living Bible

44On that day men were appointed to be in charge of the treasuries, the wave offerings, the tithes, and first-of-the-harvest offerings, and to collect these from the farms as decreed by the laws of Moses. These offerings were assigned to the priests and Levites, for the people of Judah appreciated the priests and Levites and their ministry. 45They also appreciated the work of the singers and gatekeepers, who assisted them in worshiping God and performing the purification ceremonies as required by the laws of David and his son Solomon. 46(It was in the days of David and Asaph that the custom began of having choir directors to lead the choirs in hymns of praise and thanks to God.) 47So now, in the days of Zerubbabel and Nehemiah, the people brought a daily supply of food for the members of the choir, the gatekeepers, and the Levites. The Levites, in turn, gave a portion of what they received to the priests.a

13 ON THAT same day, as the laws of Moses were being read, the people found a statement which said that the Ammonites and Moabites should never be permitted to worship at the Temple.b 2For they had not been friendly to the people of Israel. Instead, they had hired Balaam to curse them—although God turned the curse into a blessing. 3When this rule was read, all the foreigners were immediately expelled from the assembly.

4Before this had happened, Eliashib the priest, who had been appointed as custodian of the Temple store-rooms and who was also a good friend of Tobiah, 5had converted a storage room into a beautiful guest room for Tobiah. The room had previously been used for storing the grain offerings, frankincense, bowls, and tithes of grain, new wine, and olive oil. Moses had decreed that these offerings belonged to the priests, Levites, the members of the choir, and the gatekeepers.

6I was not in Jerusalem at the time, for I had returned to Babylon in the thirty-second year of the reign of King Artaxerxes (though I later received his permission to go back again to Jerusalem). 7When I arrived back in Jerusalem and learned of this evil deed of Eliashib—that he had prepared a guest room in the Temple for Tobiah— 8I was very upset and threw out all of his belongings from the room. 9Then I demanded that the room be thoroughly cleaned, and I brought back the Temple bowls, the grain offerings, and frankincense.

10I also learned that the Levites had not been given what was due them, so they and the choir singers who were supposed to conduct the worship services had returned to their farms. 11I immediately confronted the leaders and demanded, "Why has the Temple been forsaken?" Then I called all the Levites back again and restored them to their proper duties. 12And once more all the people of Judah began bringing their tithes of grain, new wine, and olive oil to the Temple treasury.

13I put Shelemiah the priest, Zadok the scribe, and Pedaiah the Levite in charge of the administration of the storehouses; and I appointed Hanan (son of Zaccur, son of Mattaniah) as their assistant. These men had an excellent reputation, and their job was to make an honest distribution to their fellow-Levites.

14O my God, remember this good deed and do not forget all that I have done for the Temple.

15One day I was on a farm and saw some men treading winepresses on the Sabbath, hauling in sheaves, and loading their donkeys with wine, grapes, figs, and all sorts of produce which they took that day into Jerusalem. So I opposed them publicly. 16There were also

New Revised Standard

Temple Responsibilities

44 On that day men were appointed over the chambers for the stores, the contributions, the first fruits, and the tithes, to gather into them the portions required by the law for the priests and for the Levites from the fields belonging to the towns; for Judah rejoiced over the priests and the Levites who ministered. 45They performed the service of their God and the service of purification, as did the singers and the gatekeepers, according to the command of David and his son Solomon. 46For in the days of David and Asaph long ago there was a leader of the singers, and there were songs of praise and thanksgiving to God. 47In the days of Zerubbabel and in the days of Nehemiah all Israel gave the daily portions for the singers and the gatekeepers. They set apart that which was for the Levites; and the Levites set apart that which was for the descendants of Aaron.

Foreigners Separated from Israel

13 ON THAT day they read from the book of Moses in the hearing of the people; and in it was found written that no Ammonite or Moabite should ever enter the assembly of God, 2because they did not meet the Israelites with bread and water, but hired Balaam against them to curse them—yet our God turned the curse into a blessing. 3When the people heard the law, they separated from Israel all those of foreign descent.

The Reforms of Nehemiah

4 Now before this, the priest Eliashib, who was appointed over the chambers of the house of our God, and who was related to Tobiah, 5prepared for Tobiah a large room where they had previously put the grain offering, the frankincense, the vessels, and the tithes of grain, wine, and oil, which were given by commandment to the Levites, singers, and gatekeepers, and the contributions for the priests. 6While this was taking place I was not in Jerusalem, for in the thirty-second year of King Artaxerxes of Babylon I went to the king. After some time I asked leave of the king 7and returned to Jerusalem. I then discovered the wrong that Eliashib had done on behalf of Tobiah, preparing a room for him in the courts of the house of God. 8And I was very angry, and I threw all the household furniture of Tobiah out of the room. 9Then I gave orders and they cleansed the chambers, and I brought back the vessels of the house of God, with the grain offering and the frankincense.

10 I also found out that the portions of the Levites had not been given to them; so that the Levites and the singers, who had conducted the service, had gone back to their fields. 11So I remonstrated with the officials and said, "Why is the house of God forsaken?" And I gathered them together and set them in their stations. 12Then all Judah brought the tithe of the grain, wine, and oil into the storehouses. 13And I appointed as treasurers over the storehouses the priest Shelemiah, the scribe Zadok, and Pedaiah of the Levites, and as their assistant Hanan son of Zaccur son of Mattaniah, for they were considered faithful; and their duty was to distribute to their associates. 14Remember me, O my God, concerning this, and do not wipe out my good deeds that I have done for the house of my God and for his service.

Sabbath Reforms Begun

15 In those days I saw in Judah people treading wine presses on the sabbath, and bringing in heaps of grain and loading them on donkeys; and also wine, grapes, figs, and all kinds of burdens, which they brought into Jerusalem on the sabbath day; and I warned them at that time against selling food. 16Tyrians also, who lived in

---

a 12:47 to the priests, literally, "to the descendants of Aaron the priest."
b 13:1 See Deut 23:3-5.

King James

16There dwelt men of Tyre also therein, which brought fish, and all manner of ware, and sold on the sabbath unto the children of Judah, and in Jerusalem.

17Then I contended with the nobles of Judah, and said unto them, What evil thing is this that ye do, and profane the sabbath day?

18Did not your fathers thus, and did not our God bring all this evil upon us, and upon this city? yet ye bring more wrath upon Israel by profaning the sabbath.

19And it came to pass, that when the gates of Jerusalem began to be dark before the sabbath, I commanded that the gates should be shut, and charged that they should not be opened till after the sabbath: and some of my servants set I at the gates, that there should no burden be brought in on the sabbath day.

20So the merchants and sellers of all kind of ware lodged without Jerusalem once or twice.

21Then I testified against them, and said unto them, Why lodge ye about the wall? if ye do so again, I will lay hands on you. From that time forth came they no more on the sabbath.

22And I commanded the Levites that they should cleanse themselves, and that they should come and keep the gates, to sanctify the sabbath day. Remember me, O my God, concerning this also, and spare me according to the greatness of thy mercy.

23¶ In those days also saw I Jews that had married wives of Ashdod, of Ammon, and of Moab:

24And their children spake half in the speech of Ashdod, and could not speak in the Jews' language, but according to the language of each people.

25And I contended with them, and cursed them, and smote certain of them, and plucked off their hair, and made them swear by God, saying, Ye shall not give your daughters unto their sons, nor take their daughters unto your sons, or for yourselves.

26Did not Solomon king of Israel sin by these things? yet among many nations was there no king like him, who was beloved of his God, and God made him king over all Israel: nevertheless even him did outlandish women cause to sin.

27Shall we then hearken unto you to do all this great evil, to transgress against our God in marrying strange wives?

28And one of the sons of Joiada, the son of Eliashib the high priest, was son-in-law to Sanballat the Horonite: therefore I chased him from me.

29Remember them, O my God, because they have defiled the priesthood, and the covenant of the priesthood, and of the Levites.

30Thus cleansed I them from all strangers, and appointed the wards of the priests and the Levites, every one in his business;

31And for the wood offering, at times appointed, and for the firstfruits. Remember me, O my God, for good.

New International

lived in Jerusalem were bringing in fish and all kinds of merchandise and selling them in Jerusalem on the Sabbath to the people of Judah. 17I rebuked the nobles of Judah and said to them, "What is this wicked thing you are doing—desecrating the Sabbath day? 18Didn't your forefathers do the same things, so that our God brought all this calamity upon us and upon this city? Now you are stirring up more wrath against Israel by desecrating the Sabbath."

19When evening shadows fell on the gates of Jerusalem before the Sabbath, I ordered the doors to be shut and not opened until the Sabbath was over. I stationed some of my own men at the gates so that no load could be brought in on the Sabbath day. 20Once or twice the merchants and sellers of all kinds of goods spent the night outside Jerusalem. 21But I warned them and said, "Why do you spend the night by the wall? If you do this again, I will lay hands on you." From that time on they no longer came on the Sabbath. 22Then I commanded the Levites to purify themselves and go and guard the gates in order to keep the Sabbath day holy.

Remember me for this also, O my God, and show mercy to me according to your great love.

23Moreover, in those days I saw men of Judah who had married women from Ashdod, Ammon and Moab. 24Half of their children spoke the language of Ashdod or the language of one of the other peoples, and did not know how to speak the language of Judah. 25I rebuked them and called curses down on them. I beat some of the men and pulled out their hair. I made them take an oath in God's name and said: "You are not to give your daughters in marriage to their sons, nor are you to take their daughters in marriage for your sons or for yourselves. 26Was it not because of marriages like these that Solomon king of Israel sinned? Among the many nations there was no king like him. He was loved by his God, and God made him king over all Israel, but even he was led into sin by foreign women. 27Must we hear now that you too are doing all this terrible wickedness and are being unfaithful to our God by marrying foreign women?"

28One of the sons of Joiada son of Eliashib the high priest was son-in-law to Sanballat the Horonite. And I drove him away from me.

29Remember them, O my God, because they defiled the priestly office and the covenant of the priesthood and of the Levites.

30So I purified the priests and the Levites of everything foreign, and assigned them duties, each to his own task. 31I also made provision for contributions of wood at designated times, and for the firstfruits.

Remember me with favor, O my God.

Living Bible

some men from Tyre bringing in fish and all sorts of wares and selling them on the Sabbath to the people of Jerusalem.

17Then I asked the leaders of Judah, "Why are you profaning the Sabbath? 18Wasn't it enough that your fathers did this sort of thing and brought the present evil days upon us and upon our city? And now you are bringing more wrath upon the people of Israel by permitting the Sabbath to be desecrated in this way."

19So from then on I commanded that the gates of the city be shut as darkness fell on Friday evenings and not be opened until the Sabbath had ended; and I sent some of my servants to guard the gates so that no merchandise could be brought in on the Sabbath day. 20The merchants and tradesmen camped outside Jerusalem once or twice, 21but I spoke sharply to them and said, "What are you doing out here, camping around the wall? If you do this again, I will arrest you." And that was the last time they came on the Sabbath.

22Then I commanded the Levites to purify themselves and to guard the gates in order to preserve the sanctity of the Sabbath. Remember this good deed, O my God! Have compassion upon me in accordance with your great goodness.

23About the same time I realized that some of the Jews had married women from Ashdod, Ammon, and Moab, 24and that many of their children spoke in the language of Ashdod and couldn't speak the language of Judah at all. 25So I confronted these parents and cursed them and punched a few of them and knocked them around and pulled out their hair; and they vowed before God that they would not let their children intermarry with non-Jews.

26"Wasn't this exactly King Solomon's problem?" I demanded. "There was no king who could compare with him, and God loved him and made him the king over all Israel; but even so he was led into idolatry by foreign women. 27Do you think that we will let you get away with this sinful deed?"

28One of the sons of Jehoiada (the son of Eliashib the High Priest) was a son-in-law of Sanballat the Horonite, so I chased him out of the Temple. 29Remember them, O my God, for they have defiled the priesthood and the promises and vows of the priests and Levites. 30So I purged out the foreigners, and assigned tasks to the priests and Levites, making certain that each knew his work. 31They supplied wood for the altar at the proper times and cared for the sacrifices and the first offerings of every harvest. Remember me, my God, with your kindness.

New Revised Standard

the city, brought in fish and all kinds of merchandise and sold them on the sabbath to the people of Judah, and in Jerusalem. 17Then I remonstrated with the nobles of Judah and said to them, "What is this evil thing that you are doing, profaning the sabbath day? 18Did not your ancestors act in this way, and did not our God bring all this disaster on us and on this city? Yet you bring more wrath on Israel by profaning the sabbath."

19 When it began to be dark at the gates of Jerusalem before the sabbath, I commanded that the doors should be shut and gave orders that they should not be opened until after the sabbath. And I set some of my servants over the gates, to prevent any burden from being brought in on the sabbath day. 20Then the merchants and sellers of all kinds of merchandise spent the night outside Jerusalem once or twice. 21But I warned them and said to them, "Why do you spend the night in front of the wall? If you do so again, I will lay hands on you." From that time on they did not come on the sabbath. 22And I commanded the Levites that they should purify themselves and come and guard the gates, to keep the sabbath day holy. Remember this also in my favor, O my God, and spare me according to the greatness of your steadfast love.

Mixed Marriages Condemned

23 In those days also I saw Jews who had married women of Ashdod, Ammon, and Moab; 24and half of their children spoke the language of Ashdod, and they could not speak the language of Judah, but spoke the language of various peoples. 25And I contended with them and cursed them and beat some of them and pulled out their hair; and I made them take an oath in the name of God, saying, "You shall not give your daughters to their sons, or take their daughters for your sons or for yourselves. 26Did not King Solomon of Israel sin on account of such women? Among the many nations there was no king like him, and he was beloved by his God, and God made him king over all Israel; nevertheless, foreign women made even him to sin. 27Shall we then listen to you and do all this great evil and act treacherously against our God by marrying foreign women?"

28 And one of the sons of Jehoiada, son of the high priest Eliashib, was the son-in-law of Sanballat the Horonite; I chased him away from me. 29Remember them, O my God, because they have defiled the priesthood, the covenant of the priests and the Levites.

30 Thus I cleansed them from everything foreign, and I established the duties of the priests and Levites, each in his work; 31and I provided for the wood offering, at appointed times, and for the first fruits. Remember me, O my God, for good.

THE BOOK OF

Esther

Esther

1 NOW IT came to pass in the days of Ahasuerus, (this *is* Ahasuerus which reigned, from India even unto Ethiopia, *over* an hundred and seven and twenty provinces:)

²*That* in those days, when the king Ahasuerus sat on the throne of his kingdom, which *was* in Shushan the palace,

³In the third year of his reign, he made a feast unto all his princes and his servants; the power of Persia and Media, the nobles and princes of the provinces, *being* before him:

⁴When he showed the riches of his glorious kingdom and the honour of his excellent majesty many days, *even* an hundred and fourscore days.

⁵And when these days were expired, the king made a feast unto all the people that were present in Shushan the palace, both unto great and small, seven days, in the court of the garden of the king's palace;

⁶*Where were* white, green, and blue, *hangings*, fastened with cords of fine linen and purple to silver rings and pillars of marble: the beds *were of* gold and silver, upon a pavement of red, and blue, and white, and black, marble.

⁷And they gave *them* drink in vessels of gold, (the vessels being diverse one from another,) and royal wine in abundance, according to the state of the king.

⁸And the drinking *was* according to the law; none did compel: for so the king had appointed to all the officers of his house, that they should do according to every man's pleasure.

⁹Also Vashti the queen made a feast for the women *in* the royal house which *belonged* to king Ahasuerus.

¹⁰¶ On the seventh day, when the heart of the king was merry with wine, he commanded Mehuman, Biztha, Harbona, Bigtha, and Abagtha, Zethar, and Carcas, the seven chamberlains that served in the presence of Ahasuerus the king,

¹¹To bring Vashti the queen before the king with the crown royal, to show the people and the princes her beauty: for she *was* fair to look on.

¹²But the queen Vashti refused to come at the king's commandment by *his* chamberlains: therefore was the king very wroth, and his anger burned in him.

¹³¶ Then the king said to the wise men, which knew the times, (for so *was* the king's manner toward all that knew law and judgment:

¹⁴And the next unto him *was* Carshena, Shethar, Admatha, Tarshish, Meres, Marsena, *and* Memucan, the seven princes of Persia and Media, which saw the king's face, *and* which sat the first in the kingdom;)

¹⁵What shall we do unto the queen Vashti according to law, because she hath not performed the commandment of the king Ahasuerus by the chamberlains?

¹⁶And Memucan answered before the king and the princes, Vashti the queen hath not done wrong to the king only, but also to all the princes, and to all the people that *are* in all the provinces of the king Ahasuerus.

1 THIS IS what happened during the time of Xerxes,[a] the Xerxes who ruled over 127 provinces stretching from India to Cush[b]: ²At that time King Xerxes reigned from his royal throne in the citadel of Susa, ³and in the third year of his reign he gave a banquet for all his nobles and officials. The military leaders of Persia and Media, the princes, and the nobles of the provinces were present.

⁴For a full 180 days he displayed the vast wealth of his kingdom and the splendor and glory of his majesty. ⁵When these days were over, the king gave a banquet, lasting seven days, in the enclosed garden of the king's palace, for all the people from the least to the greatest, who were in the citadel of Susa. ⁶The garden had hangings of white and blue linen, fastened with cords of white linen and purple material to silver rings on marble pillars. There were couches of gold and silver on a mosaic pavement of porphyry, marble, mother-of-pearl and other costly stones. ⁷Wine was served in goblets of gold, each one different from the other, and the royal wine was abundant, in keeping with the king's liberality. ⁸By the king's command each guest was allowed to drink in his own way, for the king instructed all the wine stewards to serve each man what he wished.

⁹Queen Vashti also gave a banquet for the women in the royal palace of King Xerxes.

¹⁰On the seventh day, when King Xerxes was in high spirits from wine, he commanded the seven eunuchs who served him—Mehuman, Biztha, Harbona, Bigtha, Abagtha, Zethar and Carcas— ¹¹to bring before him Queen Vashti, wearing her royal crown, in order to display her beauty to the people and nobles, for she was lovely to look at. ¹²But when the attendants delivered the king's command, Queen Vashti refused to come. Then the king became furious and burned with anger.

¹³Since it was customary for the king to consult experts in matters of law and justice, he spoke with the wise men who understood the times ¹⁴and were closest to the king—Carshena, Shethar, Admatha, Tarshish, Meres, Marsena and Memucan, the seven nobles of Persia and Media who had special access to the king and were highest in the kingdom.

¹⁵"According to law, what must be done to Queen Vashti?" he asked. "She has not obeyed the command of King Xerxes that the eunuchs have taken to her."

¹⁶Then Memucan replied in the presence of the king and the nobles, "Queen Vashti has done wrong, not only against the king but also against all the nobles and the peoples of all the provinces of King Xerxes. ¹⁷For the

ª *1* Hebrew *Ahasuerus*, a variant of Xerxes' Persian name; here and throughout Esther   ᵇ *1* That is, the upper Nile region

Esther   # Esther

King Ahasuerus Deposes Queen Vashti

1 IT WAS the third year of the reign of King Ahasuerus, emperor of vast Media-Persia, with its 127 provinces stretching from India to Ethiopia. This was the year of the great celebration at Shushan Palace, to which the emperor invited all his governors, aides, and army officers, bringing them in from every part of Media-Persia for the occasion. 4The celebration lasted six months, a tremendous display of the wealth and glory of his empire.

5When it was all over, the king gave a special party for the palace servants and officials—janitors and cabinet officials alike—for seven days of revelry, held in the courtyard of the palace garden. 6The decorations were green, white, and blue, fastened with purple ribbonsᶜ tied to silver rings imbedded in marble pillars. Gold and silver benches stood on pavements of black, red, white, and yellow marble. 7Drinks were served in gold goblets of many designs, and there was an abundance of royal wine, for the king was feeling very generous. 8The only restriction on the drinking was that no one should be compelled to take more than he wanted, but those who wished could have as much as they pleased. For the king had instructed his officers to let everyone decide this matter for himself.

9Queen Vashti gave a party for the women of the palace at the same time.

10On the final day, when the king was feeling high, half drunk from wine, he told the seven eunuchs who were his personal aides—Mehuman, Biztha, Harbona, Bigtha, Abagtha, Zethar, and Carkas— 11to bring Queen Vashti to him with the royal crown upon her head so that all the men could gaze upon her beauty—for she was a very beautiful woman. 12But when they conveyed the emperor's order to Queen Vashti, she refused to come. The king was furious 13, 14, 15but first consulted his lawyers, for he did nothing without their advice. They were men of wisdom who knew the temper of the times as well as Persian law and justice, and the king trusted their judgment. These men were Carshena, Shethar, Admatha, Tarshish, Meres, Marsena, and Memucan—seven high officials of Media-Persia. They were his personal friends as well as being the chief officers of the government.

"What shall we do about this situation?" he asked them. "What penalty does the law provide for a queen who refuses to obey the king's orders, properly sent through his aides?"

16Memucan answered for the others, "Queen Vashti has wronged not only the king but every official and citizen of your empire. 17For women everywhere will

1 THIS HAPPENED in the days of Ahasuerus, the same Ahasuerus who ruled over one hundred twenty-seven provinces from India to Ethiopia.ᵈ 2In those days when King Ahasuerus sat on his royal throne in the citadel of Susa, 3in the third year of his reign, he gave a banquet for all his officials and ministers. The army of Persia and Media and the nobles and governors of the provinces were present, 4while he displayed the great wealth of his kingdom and the splendor and pomp of his majesty for many days, one hundred eighty days in all.

5 When these days were completed, the king gave for all the people present in the citadel of Susa, both great and small, a banquet lasting for seven days, in the court of the garden of the king's palace. 6There were white cotton curtains and blue hangings tied with cords of fine linen and purple to silver ringsᵉ and marble pillars. There were couches of gold and silver on a mosaic pavement of porphyry, marble, mother-of-pearl, and colored stones. 7Drinks were served in golden goblets, goblets of different kinds, and the royal wine was lavished according to the bounty of the king. 8Drinking was by flagons, without restraint; for the king had given orders to all the officials of his palace to do as each one desired. 9Furthermore, Queen Vashti gave a banquet for the women in the palace of King Ahasuerus.

10 On the seventh day, when the king was merry with wine, he commanded Mehuman, Biztha, Harbona, Bigtha and Abagtha, Zethar and Carkas, the seven eunuchs who attended him, 11to bring Queen Vashti before the king, wearing the royal crown, in order to show the peoples and the officials her beauty; for she was fair to behold. 12But Queen Vashti refused to come at the king's command conveyed by the eunuchs. At this the king was enraged, and his anger burned within him.

13 Then the king consulted the sages who knew the lawsᶠ (for this was the king's procedure toward all who were versed in law and custom, 14and those next to him were Carshena, Shethar, Admatha, Tarshish, Meres, Marsena, and Memucan, the seven officials of Persia and Media, who had access to the king, and sat first in the kingdom): 15"According to the law, what is to be done to Queen Vashti because she has not performed the command of King Ahasuerus conveyed by the eunuchs?" 16Then Memucan said in the presence of the king and the officials, "Not only has Queen Vashti done wrong to the king, but also to all the officials and all the peoples who are in all the provinces of King Ahasuerus.

ᶜ *1:6 fastened with purple ribbons,* literally, "fastened with cords of fine linen and purple thread."

ᵈ Or *Nubia;* Heb *Cush*   ᵉ Or *rods*   ᶠ Cn: Heb *times*

King James

17For *this* deed of the queen shall come abroad unto all women, so that they shall despise their husbands in their eyes, when it shall be reported, The king Ahasuerus commanded Vashti the queen to be brought in before him, but she came not.

18*Likewise* shall the ladies of Persia and Media say this day unto all the king's princes, which have heard of the deed of the queen. Thus *shall there arise* too much contempt and wrath.

19If it please the king, let there go a royal commandment from him, and let it be written among the laws of the Persians and the Medes, that it be not altered, That Vashti come no more before king Ahasuerus; and let the king give her royal estate unto another that is better than she.

20And when the king's decree which he shall make shall be published throughout all his empire, (for it is great,) all the wives shall give to their husbands honour, both to great and small.

21And the saying pleased the king and the princes; and the king did according to the word of Memucan:

22For he sent letters into all the king's provinces, into every province according to the writing thereof, and to every people after their language, that every man should bear rule in his own house, and that *it* should be published according to the language of every people.

2 AFTER THESE things, when the wrath of king Ahasuerus was appeased, he remembered Vashti, and what she had done, and what was decreed against her.

2Then said the king's servants that ministered unto him, Let there be fair young virgins sought for the king:

3And let the king appoint officers in all the provinces of his kingdom, that they may gather together all the fair young virgins unto Shushan the palace, to the house of the women, unto the custody of Hege the king's chamberlain, keeper of the women; and let their things for purification be given *them:*

4And let the maiden which pleaseth the king be queen instead of Vashti. And the thing pleased the king; and he did so.

5¶ *Now* in Shushan the palace there was a certain Jew, whose name *was* Mordecai, the son of Jair, the son of Shimei, the son of Kish, a Benjamite;

6Who had been carried away from Jerusalem with the captivity which had been carried away with Jeconiah king of Judah, whom Nebuchadnezzar the king of Babylon had carried away.

7And he brought up Hadassah, that *is,* Esther, his uncle's daughter: for she had neither father nor mother, and the maid *was* fair and beautiful; whom Mordecai, when her father and mother were dead, took for his own daughter.

8¶ So it came to pass, when the king's commandment and his decree was heard, and when many maidens were gathered together unto Shushan the palace, to the custody of Hegai, that Esther was brought also unto the king's house, to the custody of Hegai, keeper of the women.

9And the maiden pleased him, and she obtained kindness of him; and he speedily gave her her things for purification, with such things as belonged to her, and seven maidens, *which were* meet to be given her, out of the king's house: and he preferred her and her maids unto the best *place* of the house of the women.

10Esther had not shown her people nor her kindred: for Mordecai had charged her that she should not show *it.*

11And Mordecai walked every day before the court of the women's house, to know how Esther did, and what should become of her.

New International

queen's conduct will become known to all the women, and so they will despise their husbands and say, 'King Xerxes commanded Queen Vashti to be brought before him, but she would not come.' 18This very day the Persian and Median women of the nobility who have heard about the queen's conduct will respond to all the king's nobles in the same way. There will be no end of disrespect and discord.

19"Therefore, if it pleases the king, let him issue a royal decree and let it be written in the laws of Persia and Media, which cannot be repealed, that Vashti is never again to enter the presence of King Xerxes. Also let the king give her royal position to someone else who is better than she. 20Then when the king's edict is proclaimed throughout all his vast realm, all the women will respect their husbands, from the least to the greatest."

21The king and his nobles were pleased with this advice, so the king did as Memucan proposed. 22He sent dispatches to all parts of the kingdom, to each province in its own script and to each people in its own language, proclaiming in each people's tongue that every man should be ruler over his own household.

Esther Made Queen

2 LATER WHEN the anger of King Xerxes had subsided, he remembered Vashti and what she had done and what he had decreed about her. 2Then the king's personal attendants proposed, "Let a search be made for beautiful young virgins for the king. 3Let the king appoint commissioners in every province of his realm to bring all these beautiful girls into the harem at the citadel of Susa. Let them be placed under the care of Hegai, the king's eunuch, who is in charge of the women; and let beauty treatments be given to them. 4Then let the girl who pleases the king be queen instead of Vashti." This advice appealed to the king, and he followed it.

5Now there was in the citadel of Susa a Jew of the tribe of Benjamin, named Mordecai son of Jair, the son of Shimei, the son of Kish, 6who had been carried into exile from Jerusalem by Nebuchadnezzar king of Babylon, among those taken captive with Jehoiachin[a] king of Judah. 7Mordecai had a cousin named Hadassah, whom he had brought up because she had neither father nor mother. This girl, who was also known as Esther, was lovely in form and features, and Mordecai had taken her as his own daughter when her father and mother died.

8When the king's order and edict had been proclaimed, many girls were brought to the citadel of Susa and put under the care of Hegai. Esther also was taken to the king's palace and entrusted to Hegai, who had charge of the harem. 9The girl pleased him and won his favor. Immediately he provided her with her beauty treatments and special food. He assigned to her seven maids selected from the king's palace and moved her and her maids into the best place in the harem.

10Esther had not revealed her nationality and family background, because Mordecai had forbidden her to do so. 11Every day he walked back and forth near the courtyard of the harem to find out how Esther was and what was happening to her.

a 6 Hebrew *Jeconiah,* a variant of *Jehoiachin*

Living Bible

begin to disobey their husbands when they learn what Queen Vashti has done. 18And before this day is out, the wife of every one of us officials throughout your empire will hear what the queen did and will start talking to us husbands the same way, and there will be contempt and anger throughout your realm. 19We suggest that, subject to your agreement, you issue a royal edict, a law of the Medes and Persians that can never be changed, that Queen Vashti be forever banished from your presence and that you choose another queen more worthy than she. 20When this decree is published throughout your great kingdom, husbands everywhere, whatever their rank, will be respected by their wives!"

21The king and all his aides thought this made good sense, so he followed Memucan's counsel, 22and sent letters to all of his provinces, in all the local languages, stressing that every man should rule his home, and should assert his authority.

2 BUT AFTER King Ahasuerus' anger had cooled, he began brooding over the loss of Vashti, realizing that he would never see her again.

2So his aides suggested, "Let us go and find the most beautiful girls in the empire and bring them to the king for his pleasure. 3We will appoint agents in each province to select young lovelies for the royal harem. Hegai, the eunuch in charge, will see that they are given beauty treatments, 4and after that, the girl who pleases you most shall be the queen instead of Vashti."

This suggestion naturally pleased the king very much, and he put the plan into immediate effect.

5Now there was a certain Jew at the palace named Mordecai (son of Jair, son of Shime-i, son of Kish, a Benjaminite). 6He had been captured when Jerusalem was destroyed by King Nebuchadnezzar, and had been exiled to Babylon along with King Jeconiah of Judah and many others. 7This man had a beautiful and lovely young cousin, Hadassah (also called Esther), whose father and mother were dead, and whom he had adopted into his family and raised as his own daughter.b 8So now, as a result of the king's decree, Esther was brought to the king's harem at Shushan Palace, along with many other young girls. 9Hegai, who was responsible for the harem, was very much impressed with her, and did his best to make her happy; he ordered a special menu for her, favored her for the beauty treatments, gave her seven girls from the palace as her maids, and gave her the most luxurious apartment in the harem. 10Esther hadn't told anyone that she was a Jewess, for Mordecai had said not to. 11He came daily to the court of the harem to ask about Esther and to find out what was happening to her.

New Revised Standard

17For this deed of the queen will be made known to all women, causing them to look with contempt on their husbands, since they will say, 'King Ahasuerus commanded Queen Vashti to be brought before him, and she did not come.' 18This very day the noble ladies of Persia and Media who have heard of the queen's behavior will rebel againstc the king's officials, and there will be no end of contempt and wrath! 19If it pleases the king, let a royal order go out from him, and let it be written among the laws of the Persians and the Medes so that it may not be altered, that Vashti is never again to come before King Ahasuerus; and let the king give her royal position to another who is better than she. 20So when the decree made by the king is proclaimed throughout all his kingdom, vast as it is, all women will give honor to their husbands, high and low alike."

21 This advice pleased the king and the officials, and the king did as Memucan proposed; 22he sent letters to all the royal provinces, to every province in its own script and to every people in its own language, declaring that every man should be master in his own house.d

Esther Becomes Queen

2 AFTER THESE things, when the anger of King Ahasuerus had abated, he remembered Vashti and what she had done and what had been decreed against her. 2Then the king's servants who attended him said, "Let beautiful young virgins be sought out for the king. 3And let the king appoint commissioners in all the provinces of his kingdom to gather all the beautiful young virgins to the harem in the citadel of Susa under custody of Hegai, the king's eunuch, who is in charge of the women; let their cosmetic treatments be given them. 4And let the girl who pleases the king be queen instead of Vashti." This pleased the king, and he did so.

5 Now there was a Jew in the citadel of Susa whose name was Mordecai son of Jair son of Shimei son of Kish, a Benjaminite. 6Kishe had been carried away from Jerusalem among the captives carried away with King Jeconiah of Judah, whom King Nebuchadnezzar of Babylon had carried away. 7Mordecaif had brought up Hadassah, that is Esther, his cousin, for she had neither father nor mother; the girl was fair and beautiful, and when her father and her mother died, Mordecai adopted her as his own daughter. 8So when the king's order and his edict were proclaimed, and when many young women were gathered in the citadel of Susa in custody of Hegai, Esther also was taken into the king's palace and put in custody of Hegai, who had charge of the women. 9The girl pleased him and won his favor, and he quickly provided her with her cosmetic treatments and her portion of food, and with seven chosen maids from the king's palace, and advanced her and her maids to the best place in the harem. 10Esther did not reveal her people or kindred, for Mordecai had charged her not to tell. 11Every day Mordecai would walk around in front of the court of the harem, to learn how Esther was and how she fared.

---

b 2:7 his own daughter, showing that Mordecai had adopted his cousin as his daughter.

c Cn: Heb will tell d Heb adds and speak according to the language of his people e Heb a Benjamite f who f Heb He

King James

12¶ Now when every maid's turn was come to go in to king Ahasuerus, after that she had been twelve months, according to the manner of the women, (for so were the days of their purifications accomplished, *to wit,* six months with oil of myrrh, and six months with sweet odours, and with *other* things for the purifying of the women;)

13Then thus came *every* maiden unto the king; whatsoever she desired was given her to go with her out of the house of the women unto the king's house.

14In the evening she went, and on the morrow she returned into the second house of the women, to the custody of Shaashgaz, the king's chamberlain, which kept the concubines: she came in unto the king no more, except the king delighted in her, and that she were called by name.

15¶ Now when the turn of Esther, the daughter of Abihail the uncle of Mordecai, who had taken her for his daughter, was come to go in unto the king, she required nothing but what Hegai the king's chamberlain, the keeper of the women, appointed. And Esther obtained favour in the sight of all them that looked upon her.

16So Esther was taken unto king Ahasuerus into his house royal in the tenth month, which *is* the month Tebeth, in the seventh year of his reign.

17And the king loved Esther above all the women, and she obtained grace and favour in his sight more than all the virgins; so that he set the royal crown upon her head, and made her queen instead of Vashti.

18Then the king made a great feast unto all his princes and his servants, *even* Esther's feast; and he made a release to the provinces, and gave gifts, according to the state of the king.

19And when the virgins were gathered together the second time, then Mordecai sat in the king's gate.

20Esther had not *yet* shown her kindred nor her people; as Mordecai had charged her: for Esther did the commandment of Mordecai, like as when she was brought up with him.

21¶ In those days, while Mordecai sat in the king's gate, two of the king's chamberlains, Bigthan and Teresh, of those which kept the door, were wroth, and sought to lay hand on the king Ahasuerus.

22And the thing was known to Mordecai, who told *it* unto Esther the queen; and Esther certified the king *thereof* in Mordecai's name.

23And when inquisition was made of the matter, it was found out; therefore they were both hanged on a tree: and it was written in the book of the chronicles before the king.

3 AFTER THESE things did king Ahasuerus promote Haman the son of Hammedatha the Agagite, and advanced him, and set his seat above all the princes that *were* with him.

2And all the king's servants, that *were* in the king's gate, bowed, and reverenced Haman: for the king had so commanded concerning him. But Mordecai bowed not, nor did *him* reverence.

3Then the king's servants, which *were* in the king's gate, said unto Mordecai, Why transgressest thou the king's commandment?

4Now it came to pass, when they spake daily unto him, and he hearkened not unto them, that they told Haman, to see whether Mordecai's matters would stand: for he had told them that he *was* a Jew.

New International

12Before a girl's turn came to go in to King Xerxes, she had to complete twelve months of beauty treatments prescribed for the women, six months with oil of myrrh and six with perfumes and cosmetics. 13And this is how she would go to the king: Anything she wanted was given her to take with her from the harem to the king's palace. 14In the evening she would go there and in the morning return to another part of the harem to the care of Shaashgaz, the king's eunuch who was in charge of the concubines. She would not return to the king unless he was pleased with her and summoned her by name.

15When the turn came for Esther (the girl Mordecai had adopted, the daughter of his uncle Abihail) to go to the king, she asked for nothing other than what Hegai, the king's eunuch who was in charge of the harem, suggested. And Esther won the favor of everyone who saw her. 16She was taken to King Xerxes in the royal residence in the tenth month, the month of Tebeth, in the seventh year of his reign.

17Now the king was attracted to Esther more than to any of the other women, and she won his favor and approval more than any of the other virgins. So he set a royal crown on her head and made her queen instead of Vashti. 18And the king gave a great banquet, Esther's banquet, for all his nobles and officials. He proclaimed a holiday throughout the provinces and distributed gifts with royal liberality.

Mordecai Uncovers a Conspiracy

19When the virgins were assembled a second time, Mordecai was sitting at the king's gate. 20But Esther had kept secret her family background and nationality just as Mordecai had told her to do, for she continued to follow Mordecai's instructions as she had done when he was bringing her up.

21During the time Mordecai was sitting at the king's gate, Bigthanaa and Teresh, two of the king's officers who guarded the doorway, became angry and conspired to assassinate King Xerxes. 22But Mordecai found out about the plot and told Queen Esther, who in turn reported it to the king, giving credit to Mordecai. 23And when the report was investigated and found to be true, the two officials were hanged on a gallows.b All this was recorded in the book of the annals in the presence of the king.

Haman's Plot to Destroy the Jews

3 AFTER THESE events, King Xerxes honored Haman son of Hammedatha, the Agagite, elevating him and giving him a seat of honor higher than that of all the other nobles. 2All the royal officials at the king's gate knelt down and paid honor to Haman, for the king had commanded this concerning him. But Mordecai would not kneel down or pay him honor.

3Then the royal officials at the king's gate asked Mordecai, "Why do you disobey the king's command?" 4Day after day they spoke to him but he refused to comply. Therefore they told Haman about it to see whether Mordecai's behavior would be tolerated, for he had told them he was a Jew.

---

a 21 Hebrew *Bigthan,* a variant of *Bigthana*   b 23 Or *were hung* (or *impaled*) *on poles;* similarly elsewhere in Esther

Living Bible

12, 13, 14The instructions concerning these girls were that before being taken to the king's bed, each would be given six months of beauty treatments with oil of myrrh, followed by six months with special perfumes and ointments. Then, as each girl's turn came for spending the night with King Ahasuerus, she was given her choice of clothing or jewelry she wished, to enhance her beauty. She was taken to the king's apartment in the evening and the next morning returned to the second harem where the king's wives lived. There she was under the care of Shaashgaz, another of the king's eunuchs, and lived there the rest of her life, never seeing the king again unless he had especially enjoyed her, and called for her by name.

15When it was Esther'sᶜ turn to go to the king, she accepted the advice of Hegai, the eunuch in charge of the harem, dressing according to his instructions. And all the other girls exclaimed with delight when they saw her. 16So Esther was taken to the palace of the king in January of the seventh year of his reign. 17Well, the king loved Esther more than any of the other girls. He was so delighted with her that he set the royal crown on her head and declared her queen instead of Vashti. 18To celebrate the occasion, he threw another big party for all his officials and servants, giving generous gifts to everyone and making grants to the provinces in the form of remission of taxes.

19Later, the king demanded a second bevy of beautiful girls.ᵈ By that time Mordecai had become a government official.

20Esther still hadn't told anyone she was a Jewess, for she was still following Mordecai's orders, just as she had in his home.

21One day, as Mordecai was on duty at the palace, two of the king's eunuchs, Bigthan and Teresh—who were guards at the palace gate—became angry at the king and plotted to assassinate him. 22Mordecai heard about it and passed on the information to Queen Esther, who told the king, crediting Mordecai with the information. 23An investigation was made, the two men found guilty, and impaled alive.ᵉ This was all duly recorded in the book of the history of King Ahasuerus' reign.

3 SOON AFTERWARDS King Ahasuerus appointed Haman (son of Hammedatha the Agagite), as prime minister. He was the most powerful official in the empire next to the king himself. 2Now all the king's officials bowed before him in deep reverence whenever he passed by, for so the king had commanded. But Mordecai refused to bow.

3, 4"Why are you disobeying the king's commandment?" the others demanded day after day, but he still refused. Finally they spoke to Haman about it, to see whether Mordecai could get away with it because of his being a Jew, which was the excuse he had given them.

New Revised Standard

12 The turn came for each girl to go in to King Ahasuerus, after being twelve months under the regulations for the women, since this was the regular period of their cosmetic treatment, six months with oil of myrrh and six months with perfumes and cosmetics for women. 13When the girl went in to the king she was given whatever she asked for to take with her from the harem to the king's palace. 14In the evening she went in; then in the morning she came back to the second harem in custody of Shaashgaz, the king's eunuch, who was in charge of the concubines; she did not go in to the king again, unless the king delighted in her and she was summoned by name.

15 When the turn came for Esther daughter of Abihail the uncle of Mordecai, who had adopted her as his own daughter, to go in to the king, she asked for nothing except what Hegai the king's eunuch, who had charge of the women, advised. Now Esther was admired by all who saw her. 16When Esther was taken to King Ahasuerus in his royal palace in the tenth month, which is the month of Tebeth, in the seventh year of his reign, 17the king loved Esther more than all the other women; of all the virgins she won his favor and devotion, so that he set the royal crown on her head and made her queen instead of Vashti. 18Then the king gave a great banquet to all his officials and ministers—"Esther's banquet." He also granted a holidayᶠ to the provinces, and gave gifts with royal liberality.

Mordecai Discovers a Plot

19 When the virgins were being gathered together,ᵍ Mordecai was sitting at the king's gate. 20Now Esther had not revealed her kindred or her people, as Mordecai had charged her; for Esther obeyed Mordecai just as when she was brought up by him. 21In those days, while Mordecai was sitting at the king's gate, Bigthan and Teresh, two of the king's eunuchs, who guarded the threshold, became angry and conspired to assassinateʰ King Ahasuerus. 22But the matter came to the knowledge of Mordecai, and he told it to Queen Esther, and Esther told the king in the name of Mordecai. 23When the affair was investigated and found to be so, both the men were hanged on the gallows. It was recorded in the book of the annals in the presence of the king.

Haman Undertakes to Destroy the Jews

3 AFTER THESE things King Ahasuerus promoted Haman son of Hammedatha the Agagite, and advanced him and set his seat above all the officials who were with him. 2And all the king's servants who were at the king's gate bowed down and did obeisance to Haman; for the king had so commanded concerning him. But Mordecai did not bow down or do obeisance. 3Then the king's servants who were at the king's gate said to Mordecai, "Why do you disobey the king's command?" 4When they spoke to him day after day and he would not listen to them, they told Haman, in order to see whether Mordecai's words would avail; for he had told them that he was a Jew. 5When Haman saw that

---

ᶜ *2:15 Esther's,* literally, "Esther, the daughter of Abihail, who was Mordecai's uncle, who had adopted her." ᵈ *2:19 a second bevy of beautiful girls,* or "When Esther and the other girls had been transferred to the second harem." ᵉ *2:23 impaled alive,* literally, "hanged on a tree." Possibly the meaning is that they were crucified.

ᶠ Or *an amnesty* ᵍ Heb adds *a second time* ʰ Heb *to lay hands on*

King James

5And when Haman saw that Mordecai bowed not, nor did him reverence, then was Haman full of wrath.

6And he thought scorn to lay hands on Mordecai alone; for they had shown him the people of Mordecai: wherefore Haman sought to destroy all the Jews that *were* throughout the whole kingdom of Ahasuerus, *even* the people of Mordecai.

7¶ In the first month, that *is,* the month Nisan, in the twelfth year of king Ahasuerus, they cast Pur, that *is,* the lot, before Haman from day to day, and from month to month, *to* the twelfth *month,* that *is,* the month Adar.

8¶ And Haman said unto king Ahasuerus, There is a certain people scattered abroad and dispersed among the people in all the provinces of thy kingdom; and their laws *are* diverse from all people; neither keep they the king's laws: therefore it *is* not for the king's profit to suffer them.

9If it please the king, let it be written that they may be destroyed: and I will pay ten thousand talents of silver to the hands of those that have the charge of the business, to bring *it* into the king's treasuries.

10And the king took his ring from his hand, and gave it unto Haman the son of Hammedatha the Agagite, the Jews' enemy.

11And the king said unto Haman, The silver *is* given to thee, the people also, to do with them as it seemeth good to thee.

12Then were the king's scribes called on the thirteenth day of the first month, and there was written according to all that Haman had commanded unto the king's lieutenants, and to the governors that *were* over every province, and to the rulers of every people of every province according to the writing thereof, and *to* every people after their language; in the name of king Ahasuerus was it written, and sealed with the king's ring.

13And the letters were sent by posts into all the king's provinces, to destroy, to kill, and to cause to perish, all Jews, both young and old, little children and women, in one day, *even* upon the thirteenth *day* of the twelfth month, which *is* the month Adar, and *to* take the spoil of them for a prey.

14The copy of the writing for a commandment to be given in every province was published unto all people, that they should be ready against that day.

15The posts went out, being hastened by the king's commandment, and the decree was given in Shushan the palace. And the king and Haman sat down to drink; but the city Shushan was perplexed.

4 WHEN MORDECAI perceived all that was done, Mordecai rent his clothes, and put on sackcloth with ashes, and went out into the midst of the city, and cried with a loud and a bitter cry;

2And came even before the king's gate: for none *might* enter into the king's gate clothed with sackcloth.

3And in every province, whithersoever the king's commandment and his decree came, *there was* great mourning among the Jews, and fasting, and weeping, and wailing; and many lay in sackcloth and ashes.

4¶ So Esther's maids and her chamberlains came and told *it* her. Then was the queen exceedingly grieved; and she sent raiment to clothe Mordecai, and to take away his sackcloth from him: but he received *it* not.

5Then called Esther for Hatach, *one* of the king's chamberlains, whom he had appointed to attend upon her, and gave him a commandment to Mordecai, to know what it *was,* and why it *was.*

6So Hatach went forth to Mordecai unto the street of the city, which *was* before the king's gate.

New International

5When Haman saw that Mordecai would not kneel down or pay him honor, he was enraged. 6Yet having learned who Mordecai's people were, he scorned the idea of killing only Mordecai. Instead Haman looked for a way to destroy all Mordecai's people, the Jews, throughout the whole kingdom of Xerxes.

7In the twelfth year of King Xerxes, in the first month, the month of Nisan, they cast the *pur* (that is, the lot) in the presence of Haman to select a day and month. And the lot fell on[a] the twelfth month, the month of Adar.

8Then Haman said to King Xerxes, "There is a certain people dispersed and scattered among the peoples in all the provinces of your kingdom whose customs are different from those of all other people and who do not obey the king's laws; it is not in the king's best interest to tolerate them. 9If it pleases the king, let a decree be issued to destroy them, and I will put ten thousand talents[b] of silver into the royal treasury for the men who carry out this business."

10So the king took his signet ring from his finger and gave it to Haman son of Hammedatha, the Agagite, the enemy of the Jews. 11"Keep the money," the king said to Haman, "and do with the people as you please."

12Then on the thirteenth day of the first month the royal secretaries were summoned. They wrote out in the script of each province and in the language of each people all Haman's orders to the king's satraps, the governors of the various provinces and the nobles of the various peoples. These were written in the name of King Xerxes himself and sealed with his own ring. 13Dispatches were sent by couriers to all the king's provinces with the order to destroy, kill and annihilate all the Jews—young and old, women and little children—on a single day, the thirteenth day of the twelfth month, the month of Adar, and to plunder their goods. 14A copy of the text of the edict was to be issued as law in every province and made known to the people of every nationality so they would be ready for that day.

15Spurred on by the king's command, the couriers went out, and the edict was issued in the citadel of Susa. The king and Haman sat down to drink, but the city of Susa was bewildered.

Mordecai Persuades Esther to Help

4 WHEN MORDECAI learned of all that had been done, he tore his clothes, put on sackcloth and ashes, and went out into the city, wailing loudly and bitterly. 2But he went only as far as the king's gate, because no one clothed in sackcloth was allowed to enter it. 3In every province to which the edict and order of the king came, there was great mourning among the Jews, with fasting, weeping and wailing. Many lay in sackcloth and ashes.

4When Esther's maids and eunuchs came and told her about Mordecai, she was in great distress. She sent clothes for him to put on instead of his sackcloth, but he would not accept them. 5Then Esther summoned Hathach, one of the king's eunuchs assigned to attend her, and ordered him to find out what was troubling Mordecai and why.

6So Hathach went out to Mordecai in the open square of the city in front of the king's gate. 7Mordecai told him

---

a 7 Septuagint; Hebrew does not have *And the lot fell on.*　　b 9 That is, about 375 tons (about 345 metric tons)

Living Bible

5, 6Haman was furious, but decided not to lay hands on Mordecai alone, but to move against all of Mordecai's people, the Jews, and destroy all of them throughout the whole kingdom of Ahasuerus.

7The most propitious time for this action was determined by throwing dice. This was done in April of the twelfth year of the reign of Ahasuerus, and February of the following year was the date indicated.

8Haman now approached the king about the matter. "There is a certain race of people scattered through all the provinces of your kingdom," he began, "and their laws are different from those of any other nation, and they refuse to obey the king's laws; therefore, it is not in the king's interest to let them live. 9If it please the king, issue a decree that they be destroyed, and I will pay $20,000,000 into the royal treasury for the expenses involved in this purge."

10The king agreed, confirming his decision by removing his ring from his finger and giving it to Haman,c telling him, 11"Keep the money, but go ahead and do as you like with these people—whatever you think best."

12Two or three weeks later,d Haman called in the king's secretaries and dictated letters to the governors and officials throughout the empire, to each province in its own languages and dialects; these letters were signed in the name of King Ahasuerus and sealed with his ring.

13They were then sent by messengers into all the provinces of the empire, decreeing that the Jews—young and old, women and children—must all be killed on the 28th day of February of the following year, and their property given to those who killed them. 14"A copy of this edict," the letter stated, "must be proclaimed as law in every province, and made known to all your people, so that they will be ready to do their duty on the appointed day." 15The edict went out by the king's speediest couriers, after being first proclaimed in the city of Shushan. Then the king and Haman sat down for a drinking spree as the city fell into confusion and panic.

4 WHEN MORDECAI learned what had been done, he tore his clothes and put on sackcloth and ashes, and went out into the city, crying with a loud and bitter wail. 2Then he stood outside the gate of the palace, for no one was permitted to enter in mourning clothes. 3And throughout all the provinces there was great mourning among the Jews, fasting, weeping, and despair at the king's decree; and many lay in sackcloth and ashes.

4When Esther's maids and eunuchs came and told her about Mordecai, she was deeply distressed and sent clothing to him to replace the sackcloth, but he refused it. 5Then Esther sent for Hathach, one of the king's eunuchs who had been appointed as her attendant, and told him to go out to Mordecai and find out what the trouble was, and why he was acting like that. 6So Hathach went out to the city square, and found Mordecai just outside the palace gates, 7and heard the whole story

New Revised Standard

Mordecai did not bow down or do obeisance to him, Haman was infuriated. 6But he thought it beneath him to lay hands on Mordecai alone. So, having been told who Mordecai's people were, Haman plotted to destroy all the Jews, the people of Mordecai, throughout the whole kingdom of Ahasuerus.

7 In the first month, which is the month of Nisan, in the twelfth year of King Ahasuerus, they cast Pur—which means "the lot"—before Haman for the day and for the month, and the lot fell on the thirteenth daye of the twelfth month, which is the month of Adar. 8Then Haman said to King Ahasuerus, "There is a certain people scattered and separated among the peoples in all the provinces of your kingdom; their laws are different from those of every other people, and they do not keep the king's laws, so that it is not appropriate for the king to tolerate them. 9If it pleases the king, let a decree be issued for their destruction, and I will pay ten thousand talents of silver into the hands of those who have charge of the king's business, so that they may put it into the king's treasuries." 10So the king took his signet ring from his hand and gave it to Haman son of Hammedatha the Agagite, the enemy of the Jews. 11The king said to Haman, "The money is given to you, and the people as well, to do with them as it seems good to you."

12 Then the king's secretaries were summoned on the thirteenth day of the first month, and an edict, according to all that Haman commanded, was written to the king's satraps and to the governors over all the provinces and to the officials of all the peoples, to every province in its own script and every people in its own language; it was written in the name of King Ahasuerus and sealed with the king's ring. 13Letters were sent by couriers to all the king's provinces, giving orders to destroy, to kill, and to annihilate all Jews, young and old, women and children, in one day, the thirteenth day of the twelfth month, which is the month of Adar, and to plunder their goods. 14A copy of the document was to be issued as a decree in every province by proclamation, calling on all the peoples to be ready for that day. 15The couriers went quickly by order of the king, and the decree was issued in the citadel of Susa. The king and Haman sat down to drink; but the city of Susa was thrown into confusion.

Esther Agrees to Help the Jews

4 WHEN MORDECAI learned all that had been done, Mordecai tore his clothes and put on sackcloth and ashes, and went through the city, wailing with a loud and bitter cry; 2he went up to the entrance of the king's gate, for no one might enter the king's gate clothed with sackcloth. 3In every province, wherever the king's command and his decree came, there was great mourning among the Jews, with fasting and weeping and lamenting, and most of them lay in sackcloth and ashes.

4 When Esther's maids and her eunuchs came and told her, the queen was deeply distressed; she sent garments to clothe Mordecai, so that he might take off his sackcloth; but he would not accept them. 5Then Esther called for Hathach, one of the king's eunuchs, who had been appointed to attend her, and ordered him to go to Mordecai to learn what was happening and why. 6Hathach went out to Mordecai in the open square of the city in front of the king's gate, 7and Mordecai told him all

c 3:10 to Haman, literally, "Haman, son of Hammedatha the Agagite."
d 3:12 two or three weeks later, literally, "Then, on the thirteenth day of the first month."

e Cn Compare Gk and verse 13 below: Heb the twelfth month

King James

7And Mordecai told him of all that had happened unto him, and of the sum of the money that Haman had promised to pay to the king's treasuries for the Jews, to destroy them.

8Also he gave him the copy of the writing of the decree that was given at Shushan to destroy them, to show it unto Esther, and to declare it unto her, and to charge her that she should go in unto the king, to make supplication unto him, and to make request before him for her people.

9And Hatach came and told Esther the words of Mordecai.

10¶ Again Esther spake unto Hatach, and gave him commandment unto Mordecai;

11All the king's servants, and the people of the king's provinces, do know, that whosoever, whether man or woman, shall come unto the king into the inner court, who is not called, there is one law of his to put him to death, except such to whom the king shall hold out the golden sceptre, that he may live: but I have not been called to come in unto the king these thirty days.

12And they told to Mordecai Esther's words.

13Then Mordecai commanded to answer Esther, Think not with thyself that thou shalt escape in the king's house, more than all the Jews.

14For if thou altogether holdest thy peace at this time, then shall there enlargement and deliverance arise to the Jews from another place; but thou and thy father's house shall be destroyed: and who knoweth whether thou art come to the kingdom for such a time as this?

15¶ Then Esther bade them return Mordecai this answer,

16Go, gather together all the Jews that are present in Shushan, and fast ye for me, and neither eat nor drink three days, night or day: I also and my maidens will fast likewise; and so will I go in unto the king, which is not according to the law: and if I perish, I perish.

17So Mordecai went his way, and did according to all that Esther had commanded him.

5 NOW IT came to pass on the third day, that Esther put on her royal apparel, and stood in the inner court of the king's house, over against the king's house: and the king sat upon his royal throne in the royal house, over against the gate of the house.

2And it was so, when the king saw Esther the queen standing in the court, that she obtained favour in his sight: and the king held out to Esther the golden sceptre that was in his hand. So Esther drew near, and touched the top of the sceptre.

3Then said the king unto her, What wilt thou, queen Esther? and what is thy request? it shall be even given thee to the half of the kingdom.

4And Esther answered, If it seem good unto the king, let the king and Haman come this day unto the banquet that I have prepared for him.

5Then the king said, Cause Haman to make haste, that he may do as Esther hath said. So the king and Haman came to the banquet that Esther had prepared.

6¶ And the king said unto Esther at the banquet of wine, What is thy petition? and it shall be granted thee: and what is thy request? even to the half of the kingdom it shall be performed.

7Then answered Esther, and said, My petition and my request is:

8If I have found favour in the sight of the king, and if it please the king to grant my petition, and to perform my request, let the king and Haman come to the banquet that I shall prepare for them, and I will do tomorrow as the king hath said.

New International

everything that had happened to him, including the exact amount of money Haman had promised to pay into the royal treasury for the destruction of the Jews. 8He also gave him a copy of the text of the edict for their annihilation, which had been published in Susa, to show to Esther and explain it to her, and he told him to urge her to go into the king's presence to beg for mercy and plead with him for her people.

9Hathach went back and reported to Esther what Mordecai had said. 10Then she instructed him to say to Mordecai, 11"All the king's officials and the people of the royal provinces know that for any man or woman who approaches the king in the inner court without being summoned the king has but one law: that he be put to death. The only exception to this is for the king to extend the gold scepter to him and spare his life. But thirty days have passed since I was called to go to the king."

12When Esther's words were reported to Mordecai, 13he sent back this answer: "Do not think that because you are in the king's house you alone of all the Jews will escape. 14For if you remain silent at this time, relief and deliverance for the Jews will arise from another place, but you and your father's family will perish. And who knows but that you have come to royal position for such a time as this?"

15Then Esther sent this reply to Mordecai: 16"Go, gather together all the Jews who are in Susa, and fast for me. Do not eat or drink for three days, night or day. I and my maids will fast as you do. When this is done, I will go to the king, even though it is against the law. And if I perish, I perish."

17So Mordecai went away and carried out all of Esther's instructions.

Esther's Request to the King

5 ON THE third day Esther put on her royal robes and stood in the inner court of the palace, in front of the king's hall. The king was sitting on his royal throne in the hall, facing the entrance. 2When he saw Queen Esther standing in the court, he was pleased with her and held out to her the gold scepter that was in his hand. So Esther approached and touched the tip of the scepter.

3Then the king asked, "What is it, Queen Esther? What is your request? Even up to half the kingdom, it will be given you."

4"If it pleases the king," replied Esther, "let the king, together with Haman, come today to a banquet I have prepared for him."

5"Bring Haman at once," the king said, "so that we may do what Esther asks."

So the king and Haman went to the banquet Esther had prepared. 6As they were drinking wine, the king again asked Esther, "Now what is your petition? It will be given you. And what is your request? Even up to half the kingdom, it will be granted."

7Esther replied, "My petition and my request is this: 8If the king regards me with favor and if it pleases the king to grant my petition and fulfill my request, let the king and Haman come tomorrow to the banquet I will prepare for them. Then I will answer the king's question."

Living Bible

from him; and about the $20,000,000 Haman had promised to pay into the king's treasury for the destruction of the Jews. 8Mordecai also gave Hathach a copy of the king's decree dooming all Jews, and told him to show it to Esther and to tell her what was happening, and that she should go to the king to plead for her people. 9So Hathach returned to Esther with Mordecai's message. 10Esther told Hathach to go back and say to Mordecai,

11"All the world knows that anyone, whether man or woman, who goes into the king's inner court without his summons is doomed to die unless the king holds out his gold scepter; and the king has not called for me to come to him in more than a month."

12So Hathach gave Esther's message to Mordecai.

13This was Mordecai's reply to Esther: "Do you think you will escape there in the palace, when all other Jews are killed? 14If you keep quiet at a time like this, God will deliver the Jews from some other source, but you and your relatives will die; what's more, who can say but that God has brought you into the palace for just such a time as this?"

15Then Esther said to tell Mordecai:

16"Go and gather together all the Jews of Shushan and fast for me; do not eat or drink for three days, night or day; and I and my maids will do the same; and then, though it is strictly forbidden, I will go in to see the king; and if I perish, I perish."

17So Mordecai did as Esther told him to.

5 THREE DAYS later Esther put on her royal robes and entered the inner court just beyond the royal hall of the palace, where the king was sitting upon his royal throne. 2And when he saw Queen Esther standing there in the inner court, he welcomed her, holding out the golden scepter to her. So Esther approached and touched its tip.

3Then the king asked her, "What do you wish, Queen Esther? What is your request? I will give it to you, even if it is half the kingdom!"

4And Esther replied, "If it please Your Majesty, I want you and Haman to come to a banquet I have prepared for you today."

5The king turned to his aides. "Tell Haman to hurry!" he said. So the king and Haman came to Esther's banquet.

6During the wine course the king said to Esther, "Now tell me what you really want, and I will give it to you, even if it is half of the kingdom!"

7, 8Esther replied, "My request, my deepest wish, is that if Your Majesty loves me, and wants to grant my request, that you come again with Haman tomorrow to the banquet I shall prepare for you. And tomorrow I will explain what this is all about."

New Revised Standard

that had happened to him, and the exact sum of money that Haman had promised to pay into the king's treasuries for the destruction of the Jews. 8Mordecai also gave him a copy of the written decree issued in Susa for their destruction, that he might show it to Esther, explain it to her, and charge her to go to the king to make supplication to him and entreat him for her people.

9 Hathach went and told Esther what Mordecai had said. 10Then Esther spoke to Hathach and gave him a message for Mordecai, saying, 11"All the king's servants and the people of the king's provinces know that if any man or woman goes to the king inside the inner court without being called, there is but one law—all alike are to be put to death. Only if the king holds out the golden scepter to someone, may that person live. I myself have not been called to come in to the king for thirty days." 12When they told Mordecai what Esther had said, 13Mordecai told them to reply to Esther, "Do not think that in the king's palace you will escape any more than all the other Jews. 14For if you keep silence at such a time as this, relief and deliverance will rise for the Jews from another quarter, but you and your father's family will perish. Who knows? Perhaps you have come to royal dignity for just such a time as this." 15Then Esther said in reply to Mordecai, 16"Go, gather all the Jews to be found in Susa, and hold a fast on my behalf, and neither eat nor drink for three days, night or day. I and my maids will also fast as you do. After that I will go to the king, though it is against the law; and if I perish, I perish." 17Mordecai then went away and did everything as Esther had ordered him.

Esther's Banquet

5 ON THE third day Esther put on her royal robes and stood in the inner court of the king's palace, opposite the king's hall. The king was sitting on his royal throne inside the palace opposite the entrance to the palace. 2As soon as the king saw Queen Esther standing in the court, she won his favor and he held out to her the golden scepter that was in his hand. Then Esther approached and touched the top of the scepter. 3The king said to her, "What is it, Queen Esther? What is your request? It shall be given you, even to the half of my kingdom." 4Then Esther said, "If it pleases the king, let the king and Haman come today to a banquet that I have prepared for the king." 5Then the king said, "Bring Haman quickly, so that we may do as Esther desires." So the king and Haman came to the banquet that Esther had prepared. 6While they were drinking wine, the king said to Esther, "What is your petition? It shall be granted you. And what is your request? Even to the half of my kingdom, it shall be fulfilled." 7Then Esther said, "This is my petition and request: 8If I have won the king's favor, and if it pleases the king to grant my petition and fulfill my request, let the king and Haman come tomorrow to the banquet that I will prepare for them, and then I will do as the king has said."

King James

9¶ Then went Haman forth that day joyful and with a glad heart: but when Haman saw Mordecai in the king's gate, that he stood not up, nor moved for him, he was full of indignation against Mordecai.

10Nevertheless Haman refrained himself: and when he came home, he sent and called for his friends, and Zeresh his wife.

11And Haman told them of the glory of his riches, and the multitude of his children, and all *the things* wherein the king had promoted him, and how he had advanced him above the princes and servants of the king.

12Haman said moreover, Yea, Esther the queen did let no man come in with the king unto the banquet that she had prepared but myself; and tomorrow am I invited unto her also with the king.

13Yet all this availeth me nothing, so long as I see Mordecai the Jew sitting at the king's gate.

14¶ Then said Zeresh his wife and all his friends unto him, Let a gallows be made of fifty cubits high, and tomorrow speak thou unto the king that Mordecai may be hanged thereon: then go thou in merrily with the king unto the banquet. And the thing pleased Haman; and he caused the gallows to be made.

6 ON THAT night could not the king sleep, and he commanded to bring the book of records of the chronicles; and they were read before the king.

2And it was found written, that Mordecai had told of Bigthana and Teresh, two of the king's chamberlains, the keepers of the door, who sought to lay hand on the king Ahasuerus.

3And the king said, What honour and dignity hath been done to Mordecai for this? Then said the king's servants that ministered unto him, There is nothing done for him.

4¶ And the king said, Who *is* in the court? Now Haman was come into the outward court of the king's house, to speak unto the king to hang Mordecai on the gallows that he had prepared for him.

5And the king's servants said unto him, Behold, Haman standeth in the court. And the king said, Let him come in.

6So Haman came in. And the king said unto him, What shall be done unto the man whom the king delighteth to honour? Now Haman thought in his heart, To whom would the king delight to do honour more than to myself?

7And Haman answered the king, For the man whom the king delighteth to honour,

8Let the royal apparel be brought which the king *useth* to wear, and the horse that the king rideth upon, and the crown royal which is set upon his head:

9And let this apparel and horse be delivered to the hand of one of the king's most noble princes, that they may array the man *withal* whom the king delighteth to honour, and bring him on horseback through the street of the city, and proclaim before him, Thus shall it be done to the man whom the king delighteth to honour.

10Then the king said to Haman, Make haste, *and* take the apparel and the horse, as thou hast said, and do even so to Mordecai the Jew, that sitteth at the king's gate: let nothing fail of all that thou hast spoken.

11Then took Haman the apparel and the horse, and arrayed Mordecai, and brought him on horseback through the street of the city, and proclaimed before him, Thus shall it be done unto the man whom the king delighteth to honour.

12¶ And Mordecai came again to the king's gate. But Haman hasted to his house mourning, and having his head covered.

New International

Haman's Rage Against Mordecai

9Haman went out that day happy and in high spirits. But when he saw Mordecai at the king's gate and observed that he neither rose nor showed fear in his presence, he was filled with rage against Mordecai. 10Nevertheless, Haman restrained himself and went home.

Calling together his friends and Zeresh, his wife, 11Haman boasted to them about his vast wealth, his many sons, and all the ways the king had honored him and how he had elevated him above the other nobles and officials. 12"And that's not all," Haman added. "I'm the only person Queen Esther invited to accompany the king to the banquet she gave. And she has invited me along with the king tomorrow. 13But all this gives me no satisfaction as long as I see that Jew Mordecai sitting at the king's gate."

14His wife Zeresh and all his friends said to him, "Have a gallows built, seventy-five feet[a] high, and ask the king in the morning to have Mordecai hanged on it. Then go with the king to the dinner and be happy." This suggestion delighted Haman, and he had the gallows built.

Mordecai Honored

6 THAT NIGHT the king could not sleep; so he ordered the book of the chronicles, the record of his reign, to be brought in and read to him. 2It was found recorded there that Mordecai had exposed Bigthana and Teresh, two of the king's officers who guarded the doorway, who had conspired to assassinate King Xerxes.

3"What honor and recognition has Mordecai received for this?" the king asked.

"Nothing has been done for him," his attendants answered.

4The king said, "Who is in the court?" Now Haman had just entered the outer court of the palace to speak to the king about hanging Mordecai on the gallows he had erected for him.

5His attendants answered, "Haman is standing in the court."

"Bring him in," the king ordered.

6When Haman entered, the king asked him, "What should be done for the man the king delights to honor?"

Now Haman thought to himself, "Who is there that the king would rather honor than me?" 7So he answered the king, "For the man the king delights to honor, 8have them bring a royal robe the king has worn and a horse the king has ridden, one with a royal crest placed on its head. 9Then let the robe and horse be entrusted to one of the king's most noble princes. Let them robe the man the king delights to honor, and lead him on the horse through the city streets, proclaiming before him, 'This is what is done for the man the king delights to honor!' "

10"Go at once," the king commanded Haman. "Get the robe and the horse and do just as you have suggested for Mordecai the Jew, who sits at the king's gate. Do not neglect anything you have recommended."

11So Haman got the robe and the horse. He robed Mordecai, and led him on horseback through the city streets, proclaiming before him, "This is what is done for the man the king delights to honor!"

12Afterward Mordecai returned to the king's gate. But Haman rushed home, with his head covered in grief,

---

a 14 Hebrew *fifty cubits* (about 23 meters)

Living Bible

9What a happy man was Haman as he left the banquet! But when he saw Mordecai there at the gate, not standing up or trembling before him, he was furious. 10However, he restrained himself and went on home and gathered together his friends and Zeresh his wife, 11and boasted to them about his wealth, and his many children, and promotions the king had given him, and how he had become the greatest man in the kingdom next to the king himself.

12Then he delivered his punch line: "Yes, and Esther the queen invited only me and the king himself to the banquet she prepared for us; and tomorrow we are invited again! 13But yet," he added, "all this is nothing when I see Mordecai the Jew just sitting there in front of the king's gate, refusing to bow to me."

14"Well," suggested Zeresh his wife and all his friends, "get ready a 75-foot-high gallows, and in the morning ask the king to let you hang Mordecai on it; and when this is done you can go on your merry way with the king to the banquet." This pleased Haman immensely and he ordered the gallows built.

6 THAT NIGHT the king had trouble sleeping and decided to read awhile. He ordered the historical records of his kingdom from the library, and in them he came across the item telling how Mordecai had exposed the plot of Bigthana and Teresh, two of the king's eunuchs, watchmen at the palace gates, who had plotted to assassinate him.

3"What reward did we ever give Mordecai for this?" the king asked.

His courtiers replied, "Nothing!"

4"Who is on duty in the outer court?" the king inquired. Now, as it happened, Haman had just arrived in the outer court of the palace to ask the king to hang Mordecai from the gallows he was building.

5So the courtiers replied to the king, "Haman is out there."

"Bring him in," the king ordered. 6So Haman came in and the king said to him, "What should I do to honor a man who truly pleases me?"

Haman thought to himself, "Whom would he want to honor more than me?" 7, 8So he replied, "Bring out some of the royal robes the king himself has worn, and the king's own horse, and the royal crown, 9and instruct one of the king's most noble princes to robe the man and to lead him through the streets on the king's own horse, shouting before him, 'This is the way the king honors those who truly please him!'"

10"Excellent!" the king said to Haman. "Hurry and take these robes and my horse, and do just as you have said—to Mordecai the Jew, who works at the Chancellery. Follow every detail you have suggested."

11So Haman took the robes and put them on Mordecai and mounted him on the king's own steed, and led him through the streets of the city, shouting, "This is the way the king honors those he delights in."

12Afterwards Mordecai returned to his job, but Haman hurried home utterly humiliated. 13When Haman

New Revised Standard

Haman Plans to Have Mordecai Hanged

9 Haman went out that day happy and in good spirits. But when Haman saw Mordecai in the king's gate, and observed that he neither rose nor trembled before him, he was infuriated with Mordecai; 10 nevertheless Haman restrained himself and went home. Then he sent and called for his friends and his wife Zeresh, 11 and Haman recounted to them the splendor of his riches, the number of his sons, all the promotions with which the king had honored him, and how he had advanced him above the officials and the ministers of the king. 12 Haman added, "Even Queen Esther let no one but myself come with the king to the banquet that she prepared. Tomorrow also I am invited by her, together with the king. 13 Yet all this does me no good so long as I see the Jew Mordecai sitting at the king's gate." 14 Then his wife Zeresh and all his friends said to him, "Let a gallows fifty cubits high be made, and in the morning tell the king to have Mordecai hanged on it; then go with the king to the banquet in good spirits." This advice pleased Haman, and he had the gallows made.

The King Honors Mordecai

6 ON THAT night the king could not sleep, and he gave orders to bring the book of records, the annals, and they were read to the king. 2 It was found written how Mordecai had told about Bigthana and Teresh, two of the king's eunuchs, who guarded the threshold, and who had conspired to assassinate[b] King Ahasuerus. 3 Then the king said, "What honor or distinction has been bestowed on Mordecai for this?" The king's servants who attended him said, "Nothing has been done for him." 4 The king said, "Who is in the court?" Now Haman had just entered the outer court of the king's palace to speak to the king about having Mordecai hanged on the gallows that he had prepared for him. 5 So the king's servants told him, "Haman is there, standing in the court." The king said, "Let him come in." 6 So Haman came in, and the king said to him, "What shall be done for the man whom the king wishes to honor?" Haman said to himself, "Whom would the king wish to honor more than me?" 7 So Haman said to the king, "For the man whom the king wishes to honor, 8 let royal robes be brought, which the king has worn, and a horse that the king has ridden, with a royal crown on its head. 9 Let the robes and the horse be handed over to one of the king's most noble officials; let him[c] robe the man whom the king wishes to honor, and let him[c] conduct the man on horseback through the open square of the city, proclaiming before him: 'Thus shall it be done for the man whom the king wishes to honor.' " 10 Then the king said to Haman, "Quickly, take the robes and the horse, as you have said, and do so to the Jew Mordecai who sits at the king's gate. Leave out nothing that you have mentioned." 11 So Haman took the robes and the horse and robed Mordecai and led him riding through the open square of the city, proclaiming, "Thus shall it be done for the man whom the king wishes to honor."

12 Then Mordecai returned to the king's gate, but Haman hurried to his house, mourning and with his head covered. 13 When Haman told his wife Zeresh and all his

---

b Heb *to lay hands on*   c Heb *them*

King James

13And Haman told Zeresh his wife and all his friends every *thing* that had befallen him. Then said his wise men and Zeresh his wife unto him, If Mordecai *be* of the seed of the Jews, before whom thou hast begun to fall, thou shalt not prevail against him, but shalt surely fall before him.

14And while they *were* yet talking with him, came the king's chamberlains, and hasted to bring Haman unto the banquet that Esther had prepared.

7 SO THE king and Haman came to banquet with Esther the queen.

2And the king said again unto Esther on the second day at the banquet of wine, What *is* thy petition, queen Esther? and it shall be granted thee: and what *is* thy request? and it shall be performed, *even* to the half of the kingdom.

3Then Esther the queen answered and said, If I have found favour in thy sight, O king, and if it please the king, let my life be given me at my petition, and my people at my request:

4For we are sold, I and my people, to be destroyed, to be slain, and to perish. But if we had been sold for bondmen and bondwomen, I had held my tongue, although the enemy could not countervail the king's damage.

5¶ Then the king Ahasuerus answered and said unto Esther the queen, Who is he, and where is he, that durst presume in his heart to do so?

6And Esther said, The adversary and enemy *is* this wicked Haman. Then Haman was afraid before the king and the queen.

7¶ And the king arising from the banquet of wine in his wrath *went* into the palace garden: and Haman stood up to make request for his life to Esther the queen; for he saw that there was evil determined against him by the king.

8Then the king returned out of the palace garden into the place of the banquet of wine; and Haman was fallen upon the bed whereon Esther *was*. Then said the king, Will he force the queen also before me in the house? As the word went out of the king's mouth, they covered Haman's face.

9And Harbonah, one of the chamberlains, said before the king, Behold also, the gallows fifty cubits high, which Haman had made for Mordecai, who had spoken good for the king, standeth in the house of Haman. Then the king said, Hang him thereon.

10So they hanged Haman on the gallows that he had prepared for Mordecai. Then was the king's wrath pacified.

8 ON THAT day did the king Ahasuerus give the house of Haman the Jew's enemy unto Esther the queen. And Mordecai came before the king; for Esther had told what he *was* unto her.

2And the king took off his ring, which he had taken from Haman, and gave it unto Mordecai. And Esther set Mordecai over the house of Haman.

3¶ And Esther spake yet again before the king, and fell down at his feet, and besought him with tears to put away the mischief of Haman the Agagite, and his device that he had devised against the Jews.

New International

13and told Zeresh his wife and all his friends everything that had happened to him.

His advisers and his wife Zeresh said to him, "Since Mordecai, before whom your downfall has started, is of Jewish origin, you cannot stand against him—you will surely come to ruin!" 14While they were still talking with him, the king's eunuchs arrived and hurried Haman away to the banquet Esther had prepared.

Haman Hanged

7 SO THE king and Haman went to dine with Queen Esther, 2and as they were drinking wine on that second day, the king again asked, "Queen Esther, what is your petition? It will be given you. What is your request? Even up to half the kingdom, it will be granted."

3Then Queen Esther answered, "If I have found favor with you, O king, and if it pleases your majesty, grant me my life—this is my petition. And spare my people— this is my request. 4For I and my people have been sold for destruction and slaughter and annihilation. If we had merely been sold as male and female slaves, I would have kept quiet, because no such distress would justify disturbing the king.a"

5King Xerxes asked Queen Esther, "Who is he? Where is the man who has dared to do such a thing?"

6Esther said, "The adversary and enemy is this vile Haman."

Then Haman was terrified before the king and queen. 7The king got up in a rage, left his wine and went out into the palace garden. But Haman, realizing that the king had already decided his fate, stayed behind to beg Queen Esther for his life.

8Just as the king returned from the palace garden to the banquet hall, Haman was falling on the couch where Esther was reclining.

The king exclaimed, "Will he even molest the queen while she is with me in the house?"

As soon as the word left the king's mouth, they covered Haman's face. 9Then Harbona, one of the eunuchs attending the king, said, "A gallows seventy-five feetb high stands by Haman's house. He had it made for Mordecai, who spoke up to help the king."

The king said, "Hang him on it!" 10So they hanged Haman on the gallows he had prepared for Mordecai. Then the king's fury subsided.

The King's Edict in Behalf of the Jews

8 THAT SAME day King Xerxes gave Queen Esther the estate of Haman, the enemy of the Jews. And Mordecai came into the presence of the king, for Esther had told how he was related to her. 2The king took off his signet ring, which he had reclaimed from Haman, and presented it to Mordecai. And Esther appointed him over Haman's estate.

3Esther again pleaded with the king, falling at his feet and weeping. She begged him to put an end to the evil plan of Haman the Agagite, which he had devised

---

a 4 Or *quiet, but the compensation our adversary offers cannot be compared with the loss the king would suffer*   b 9 Hebrew *fifty cubits* (about 23 meters)

Living Bible

told Zereh his wife and all his friends what had happened, they said, "If Mordecai is a Jew, you will never succeed in your plans against him; to continue to oppose him will be fatal."

14While they were still discussing it with him, the king's messengers arrived to conduct Haman quickly to the banquet Esther had prepared.

7 SO THE king and Haman came to Esther's banquet. 2Again, during the wine course, the king asked her, "What is your petition, Queen Esther? What do you wish? Whatever it is, I will give it to you, even if it is half of my kingdom!"

3And at last Queen Esther replied, "If I have won your favor, O king, and if it please Your Majesty, save my life and the lives of my people. 4For I and my people have been sold to those who will destroy us. We are doomed to destruction and slaughter. If we were only to be sold as slaves, perhaps I could remain quiet, though even then there would be incalculable damage to the king that no amount of money could begin to cover."

5"What are you talking about?" King Ahasuerus demanded. "Who would dare touch you?"

6Esther replied, "This wicked Haman is our enemy."

Then Haman grew pale with fright before the king and queen. 7The king jumped to his feet and went out into the palace garden as Haman stood up to plead for his life to Queen Esther, for he knew that he was doomed. 8In despair he fell upon the couch where Queen Esther was reclining, just as the king returned from the palace garden.

"Will he even rape the queen right here in the palace, before my very eyes?" the king roared. Instantly the death veil was placed over Haman's face.

9Then Harbona, one of the king's aides, said, "Sir, Haman has just ordered a 75-foot gallows constructed, to hang Mordecai, the man who saved the king from assassination! It stands in Haman's courtyard."

"Hang Haman on it," the king ordered.

10So they did, and the king's wrath was pacified.

8 ON THAT same day King Ahasuerus gave the estate of Haman, the Jews' enemy, to Queen Esther. Then Mordecai was brought before the king, for Esther had told the king that he was her cousin and foster father.c 2The king took off his ring—which he had taken back from Haman—and gave it to Mordecai [appointing him Prime Ministerd]; and Esther appointed Mordecai to be in charge of Haman's estate.

3And now once more Esther came before the king, falling down at his feet and begging him with tears to stop Haman's plot against the Jews. 4And again the king

New Revised Standard

friends everything that had happened to him, his advisers and his wife Zeresh said to him, "If Mordecai, before whom your downfall has begun, is of the Jewish people, you will not prevail against him, but will surely fall before him."

Haman's Downfall and Mordecai's Advancement

14 While they were still talking with him, the king's eunuchs arrived and hurried Haman off to the banquet that Esther had prepared.

7 SO THE king and Haman went in to feast with Queen Esther. 2On the second day, as they were drinking wine, the king again said to Esther, "What is your petition, Queen Esther? It shall be granted you. And what is your request? Even to the half of my kingdom, it shall be fulfilled." 3Then Queen Esther answered, "If I have won your favor, O king, and if it pleases the king, let my life be given me—that is my petition—and the lives of my people—that is my request. 4For we have been sold, I and my people, to be destroyed, to be killed, and to be annihilated. If we had been sold merely as slaves, men and women, I would have held my peace; but no enemy can compensate for this damage to the king."e 5Then King Ahasuerus said to Queen Esther, "Who is he, and where is he, who has presumed to do this?" 6Esther said, "A foe and enemy, this wicked Haman!" Then Haman was terrified before the king and the queen. 7The king rose from the feast in wrath and went into the palace garden, but Haman stayed to beg his life from Queen Esther, for he saw that the king had determined to destroy him. 8When the king returned from the palace garden to the banquet hall, Haman had thrown himself on the couch where Esther was reclining; and the king said, "Will he even assault the queen in my presence, in my own house?" As the words left the mouth of the king, they covered Haman's face. 9Then Harbona, one of the eunuchs in attendance on the king, said, "Look, the very gallows that Haman has prepared for Mordecai, whose word saved the king, stands at Haman's house, fifty cubits high." And the king said, "Hang him on that." 10So they hanged Haman on the gallows that he had prepared for Mordecai. Then the anger of the king abated.

Esther Saves the Jews

8 ON THAT day King Ahasuerus gave to Queen Esther the house of Haman, the enemy of the Jews; and Mordecai came before the king, for Esther had told what he was to her. 2Then the king took off his signet ring, which he had taken from Haman, and gave it to Mordecai. So Esther set Mordecai over the house of Haman.

3 Then Esther spoke again to the king; she fell at his feet, weeping and pleading with him to avert the evil design of Haman the Agagite and the plot that he had devised against the Jews. 4The king held out the golden

---

c 8:1 he was her cousin and foster father, literally, "had made known how they were related."   d 8:2 appointing him Prime Minister, implied.

e Meaning of Heb uncertain

King James

4Then the king held out the golden sceptre toward Esther. So Esther arose, and stood before the king,

5And said, If it please the king, and if I have found favour in his sight, and the thing *seem* right before the king, and I *be* pleasing in his eyes, let it be written to reverse the letters devised by Haman the son of Hammedatha the Agagite, which he wrote to destroy the Jews which *are* in all the king's provinces:

6For how can I endure to see the evil that shall come unto my people? or how can I endure to see the destruction of my kindred?

7¶ Then the king Ahasuerus said unto Esther the queen and to Mordecai the Jew, Behold, I have given Esther the house of Haman, and him they have hanged upon the gallows, because he laid his hand upon the Jews.

8Write ye also for the Jews, as it liketh you, in the king's name, and seal *it* with the king's ring: for the writing which is written in the king's name, and sealed with the king's ring, may no man reverse.

9Then were the king's scribes called at that time in the third month, that *is*, the month Sivan, on the three and twentieth *day* thereof; and it was written according to all that Mordecai commanded unto the Jews, and to the lieutenants, and the deputies and rulers of the provinces which *are* from India unto Ethiopia, an hundred twenty and seven provinces, unto every province according to the writing thereof, and unto every people after their language, and to the Jews according to their writing, and according to their language.

10And he wrote in the king Ahasuerus' name, and sealed *it* with the king's ring, and sent letters by posts on horseback, *and* riders on mules, camels, *and* young dromedaries:

11Wherein the king granted the Jews which *were* in every city to gather themselves together, and to stand for their life, to destroy, to slay, and to cause to perish, all the power of the people and province that would assault them, *both* little ones and women, and *to take* the spoil of them for a prey,

12Upon one day in all the provinces of king Ahasuerus, *namely,* upon the thirteenth *day* of the twelfth month, which *is* the month Adar.

13The copy of the writing for a commandment to be given in every province *was* published unto all people, and that the Jews should be ready against that day to avenge themselves on their enemies.

14*So* the posts that rode upon mules *and* camels went out, being hastened and pressed on by the king's commandment. And the decree was given at Shushan the palace.

15¶ And Mordecai went out from the presence of the king in royal apparel of blue and white, and with a great crown of gold, and with a garment of fine linen and purple: and the city of Shushan rejoiced and was glad.

16The Jews had light, and gladness, and joy, and honour.

17And in every province, and in every city, whithersoever the king's commandment and his decree came, the Jews had joy and gladness, a feast and a good day. And many of the people of the land became Jews; for the fear of the Jews fell upon them.

New International

against the Jews. 4Then the king extended the gold scepter to Esther and she arose and stood before him.

5"If it pleases the king," she said, "and if he regards me with favor and thinks it the right thing to do, and if he is pleased with me, let an order be written overruling the dispatches that Haman son of Hammedatha, the Agagite, devised and wrote to destroy the Jews in all the king's provinces. 6For how can I bear to see disaster fall on my people? How can I bear to see the destruction of my family?"

7King Xerxes replied to Queen Esther and to Mordecai the Jew, "Because Haman attacked the Jews, I have given his estate to Esther, and they have hanged him on the gallows. 8Now write another decree in the king's name in behalf of the Jews as seems best to you, and seal it with the king's signet ring—for no document written in the king's name and sealed with his ring can be revoked."

9At once the royal secretaries were summoned—on the twenty-third day of the third month, the month of Sivan. They wrote out all Mordecai's orders to the Jews, and to the satraps, governors and nobles of the 127 provinces stretching from India to Cush.[a] These orders were written in the script of each province and the language of each people and also to the Jews in their own script and language. 10Mordecai wrote in the name of King Xerxes, sealed the dispatches with the king's signet ring, and sent them by mounted couriers, who rode fast horses especially bred for the king.

11The king's edict granted the Jews in every city the right to assemble and protect themselves; to destroy, kill and annihilate any armed force of any nationality or province that might attack them and their women and children; and to plunder the property of their enemies. 12The day appointed for the Jews to do this in all the provinces of King Xerxes was the thirteenth day of the twelfth month, the month of Adar. 13A copy of the text of the edict was to be issued as law in every province and made known to the people of every nationality so that the Jews would be ready on that day to avenge themselves on their enemies.

14The couriers, riding the royal horses, raced out, spurred on by the king's command. And the edict was also issued in the citadel of Susa.

15Mordecai left the king's presence wearing royal garments of blue and white, a large crown of gold and a purple robe of fine linen. And the city of Susa held a joyous celebration. 16For the Jews it was a time of happiness and joy, gladness and honor. 17In every province and in every city, wherever the edict of the king went, there was joy and gladness among the Jews, with feasting and celebrating. And many people of other nationalities became Jews because fear of the Jews had seized them.

---

[a] 9 That is, the upper Nile region

Living Bible

held out the golden scepter to Esther. So she arose and stood before him, 5and said, "If it please Your Majesty, and if you love me, send out a decree reversing Haman's order to destroy the Jews throughout the king's provinces. 6For how can I endure it, to see my people butchered and destroyed?"

7Then King Ahasuerus said to Queen Esther and Mordecai the Jew, "I have given Esther the palace of Haman and he has been hanged upon the gallows because he tried to destroy you. 8Now go ahead and send a message to the Jews, telling them whatever you want to in the king's name, and seal it with the king's ring, so that it can never be reversed."b

9, 10Immediately the king's secretaries were called in—it was now the 23rd day of the month of July—and they wrote as Mordecai dictated—a decree to the Jews and to the officials, governors, and princes of all the provinces from India to Ethiopia, 127 in all: the decree was translated into the languages and dialects of all the people of the kingdom. Mordecai wrote in the name of King Ahasuerus and sealed the message with the king's ring and sent the letters by swift carriers—riders on camels, mules, and young dromedaries used in the king's service. 11This decree gave the Jews everywhere permission to unite in the defense of their lives and their families, to destroy all the forces opposed to them, and to take their property. 12The day chosen for this throughout all the provinces of King Ahasuerus was the 28th day of February!c 13It further stated that a copy of this decree, which must be recognized everywhere as law, must be broadcast to all the people so that the Jews would be ready and prepared to overcome their enemies. 14So the mail went out swiftly, carried by the king's couriers and speeded by the king's commandment. The same decree was also issued at Shushan Palace.

15Then Mordecai put on the royal robes of blue and white and the great crown of gold, with an outer cloak of fine linen and purple, and went out from the presence of the king through the city streets filled with shouting people. 16And the Jews had joy and gladness, and were honored everywhere. 17And in every city and province, as the king's decree arrived, the Jews were filled with joy and had a great celebration and declared a holiday. And many of the people of the land pretended to be Jews, for they feared what the Jews might do to them.

New Revised Standard

scepter to Esther, 5and Esther rose and stood before the king. She said, "If it pleases the king, and if I have won his favor, and if the thing seems right before the king, and I have his approval, let an order be written to revoke the letters devised by Haman son of Hammedatha the Agagite, which he wrote giving orders to destroy the Jews who are in all the provinces of the king. 6For how can I bear to see the calamity that is coming on my people? Or how can I bear to see the destruction of my kindred?" 7Then King Ahasuerus said to Queen Esther and to the Jew Mordecai, "See, I have given Esther the house of Haman, and they have hanged him on the gallows, because he plotted to lay hands on the Jews. 8You may write as you please with regard to the Jews, in the name of the king, and seal it with the king's ring; for an edict written in the name of the king and sealed with the king's ring cannot be revoked."

9 The king's secretaries were summoned at that time, in the third month, which is the month of Sivan, on the twenty-third day; and an edict was written, according to all that Mordecai commanded, to the Jews and to the satraps and the governors and the officials of the provinces from India to Ethiopia,d one hundred twenty-seven provinces, to every province in its own script and to every people in its own language, and also to the Jews in their script and their language. 10He wrote letters in the name of King Ahasuerus, sealed them with the king's ring, and sent them by mounted couriers riding on fast steeds bred from the royal herd.e 11By these letters the king allowed the Jews who were in every city to assemble and defend their lives, to destroy, to kill, and to annihilate any armed force of any people or province that might attack them, with their children and women, and to plunder their goods 12on a single day throughout all the provinces of King Ahasuerus, on the thirteenth day of the twelfth month, which is the month of Adar. 13A copy of the writ was to be issued as a decree in every province and published to all peoples, and the Jews were to be ready on that day to take revenge on their enemies. 14So the couriers, mounted on their swift royal steeds, hurried out, urged by the king's command. The decree was issued in the citadel of Susa.

15 Then Mordecai went out from the presence of the king, wearing royal robes of blue and white, with a great golden crown and a mantle of fine linen and purple, while the city of Susa shouted and rejoiced. 16For the Jews there was light and gladness, joy and honor. 17In every province and in every city, wherever the king's command and his edict came, there was gladness and joy among the Jews, a festival and a holiday. Furthermore, many of the peoples of the country professed to be Jews, because the fear of the Jews had fallen upon them.

---

b 8:8 *so that it can never be reversed.* Haman's message, too, had been sealed with the king's ring and could not be reversed, even by the king. This was part of the famed "law of the Medes and Persians." Now the king is giving permission for whatever other decree Mordecai can devise that will offset the first, without actually canceling it.   c 8:12 *the 28th day of February.* This was the same day set by Haman for the extermination of the Jews.

d Or *Nubia;* Heb *Cush*   e Meaning of Heb uncertain

King James

9 NOW IN the twelfth month, that *is,* the month Adar, on the thirteenth day of the same, when the king's commandment and his decree drew near to be put in execution, in the day that the enemies of the Jews hoped to have power over them, (though it was turned to the contrary, that the Jews had rule over them that hated them;)

²The Jews gathered themselves together in their cities throughout all the provinces of the king Ahasuerus, to lay hand on such as sought their hurt: and no man could withstand them; for the fear of them fell upon all people.

³And all the rulers of the provinces, and the lieutenants, and the deputies, and officers of the king, helped the Jews; because the fear of Mordecai fell upon them.

⁴For Mordecai *was* great in the king's house, and his fame went out throughout all the provinces: for this man Mordecai waxed greater and greater.

⁵Thus the Jews smote all their enemies with the stroke of the sword, and slaughter, and destruction, and did what they would unto those that hated them.

⁶And in Shushan the palace the Jews slew and destroyed five hundred men.

⁷And Parshandatha, and Dalphon, and Aspatha,

⁸And Poratha, and Adalia, and Aridatha,

⁹And Parmashta, and Arisai, and Aridai, and Vajezatha,

¹⁰The ten sons of Haman the sons of Hammedatha, the enemy of the Jews, slew they; but on the spoil laid they not their hand.

¹¹On that day the number of those that were slain in Shushan the palace was brought before the king.

¹²¶ And the king said unto Esther the queen, The Jews have slain and destroyed five hundred men in Shushan the palace, and the ten sons of Haman; what have they done in the rest of the king's provinces? now what *is* thy petition? and it shall be granted thee: or what *is* thy request further? and it shall be done.

¹³Then said Esther, If it please the king, let it be granted to the Jews which *are* in Shushan to do tomorrow also according unto this day's decree, and let Haman's ten sons be hanged upon the gallows.

¹⁴And the king commanded it so to be done: and the decree was given at Shushan; and they hanged Haman's ten sons.

¹⁵For the Jews that *were* in Shushan gathered themselves together on the fourteenth day also of the month Adar, and slew three hundred men at Shushan; but on the prey they laid not their hand.

¹⁶But the other Jews that *were* in the king's provinces gathered themselves together, and stood for their lives, and had rest from their enemies, and slew of their foes seventy and five thousand, but they laid not their hands on the prey,

¹⁷On the thirteenth day of the month Adar; and on the fourteenth day of the same rested they, and made it a day of feasting and gladness.

¹⁸But the Jews that *were* at Shushan assembled together on the thirteenth *day* thereof, and on the fourteenth thereof; and on the fifteenth *day* of the same they rested, and made it a day of feasting and gladness.

¹⁹Therefore the Jews of the villages, that dwelt in the unwalled towns, made the fourteenth day of the month Adar *a day of* gladness and feasting, and a good day, and of sending portions one to another.

²⁰¶ And Mordecai wrote these things, and sent letters unto all the Jews that *were* in all the provinces of the king Ahasuerus, *both* nigh and far,

²¹To stablish *this* among them, that they should keep the fourteenth day of the month Adar, and the fifteenth day of the same, yearly,

New International

Triumph of the Jews

9 ON THE thirteenth day of the twelfth month, the month of Adar, the edict commanded by the king was to be carried out. On this day the enemies of the Jews had hoped to overpower them, but now the tables were turned and the Jews got the upper hand over those who hated them. ²The Jews assembled in their cities in all the provinces of King Xerxes to attack those seeking their destruction. No one could stand against them, because the people of all the other nationalities were afraid of them. ³And all the nobles of the provinces, the satraps, the governors and the king's administrators helped the Jews, because fear of Mordecai had seized them. ⁴Mordecai was prominent in the palace; his reputation spread throughout the provinces, and he became more and more powerful.

⁵The Jews struck down all their enemies with the sword, killing and destroying them, and they did what they pleased to those who hated them. ⁶In the citadel of Susa, the Jews killed and destroyed five hundred men. ⁷They also killed Parshandatha, Dalphon, Aspatha, ⁸Poratha, Adalia, Aridatha, ⁹Parmashta, Arisai, Aridai and Vaizatha, ¹⁰the ten sons of Haman son of Hammedatha, the enemy of the Jews. But they did not lay their hands on the plunder.

¹¹The number of those slain in the citadel of Susa was reported to the king that same day. ¹²The king said to Queen Esther, "The Jews have killed and destroyed five hundred men and the ten sons of Haman in the citadel of Susa. What have they done in the rest of the king's provinces? Now what is your petition? It will be given you. What is your request? It will also be granted."

¹³"If it pleases the king," Esther answered, "give the Jews in Susa permission to carry out this day's edict tomorrow also, and let Haman's ten sons be hanged on gallows."

¹⁴So the king commanded that this be done. An edict was issued in Susa, and they hanged the ten sons of Haman. ¹⁵The Jews in Susa came together on the fourteenth day of the month of Adar, and they put to death in Susa three hundred men, but they did not lay their hands on the plunder.

¹⁶Meanwhile, the remainder of the Jews who were in the king's provinces also assembled to protect themselves and get relief from their enemies. They killed seventy-five thousand of them but did not lay their hands on the plunder. ¹⁷This happened on the thirteenth day of the month of Adar, and on the fourteenth they rested and made it a day of feasting and joy.

Purim Celebrated

¹⁸The Jews in Susa, however, had assembled on the thirteenth and fourteenth, and then on the fifteenth they rested and made it a day of feasting and joy.

¹⁹That is why rural Jews—those living in villages—observe the fourteenth of the month of Adar as a day of joy and feasting, a day for giving presents to each other.

²⁰Mordecai recorded these events, and he sent letters to all the Jews throughout the provinces of King Xerxes, near and far, ²¹to have them celebrate annually the fourteenth and fifteenth days of the month of Adar ²²as the

Living Bible

9 SO ON the 28th day of February, the day the two decrees of the king were to be put into effect—the day the Jews' enemies had hoped to vanquish them, though it turned out quite to the contrary—the Jews gathered in their cities throughout all the king's provinces to defend themselves against any who might try to harm them; but no one tried, for they were greatly feared. 3And all the rulers of the provinces—the governors, officials, and aides—helped the Jews for fear of Mordecai; 4for Mordecai was a mighty name in the king's palace and his fame was known throughout all the provinces, for he had become more and more powerful.

5But the Jews went ahead on that appointed day and slaughtered their enemies. 6They even killed 500 men in Shushan. 7-10They also killed the ten sons of Haman (son of Hammedatha), the Jews' enemy—

Parshandatha, Dalphon, Aspatha, Poratha, Adalia, Aridatha, Parmashta, Arisai, Aridai, and Vaizatha. But they did not try to take Haman's property.

11Late that evening, when the king was informed of the number of those slain in Shushan, 12he called for Queen Esther. "The Jews have killed 500 men in Shushan alone," he exclaimed, "and also Haman's ten sons. If they have done that here, I wonder what has happened in the rest of the provinces! But now, what more do you want? It will be granted to you. Tell me and I will do it."

13And Esther said, "If it please Your Majesty, let the Jews who are here at Shushan do again tomorrow as they have done today, and let Haman's ten sons be hanged upon the gallows."

14So the king agreed, and the decree was announced at Shushan, and they hung up the bodies of Haman's ten sons. 15Then the Jews at Shushan gathered together the next day also and killed 300 more men, though again they took no property.

16Meanwhile, the other Jews throughout the king's provinces had gathered together and stood for their lives and destroyed all their enemies, killing 75,000 of those who hated them; but they did not take their goods. 17Throughout the provinces this was done on the 28th day of February, and the next day they rested, celebrating their victory with feasting and gladness. 18But the Jews at Shushan went on killing their enemies the second day also, and rested the next day, with feasting and gladness. 19And so it is that the Jews in the unwalled villages throughout Israel to this day have an annual celebration on the second day, when they rejoice and send gifts to each other.

20Mordecai wrote a history of all these events, and sent letters to the Jews near and far, throughout all the king's provinces, 21encouraging them to declare an annual holiday on the last two days of the month, 22to

New Revised Standard

Destruction of the Enemies of the Jews

9 NOW IN the twelfth month, which is the month of Adar, on the thirteenth day, when the king's command and edict were about to be executed, on the very day when the enemies of the Jews hoped to gain power over them, but which had been changed to a day when the Jews would gain power over their foes, 2the Jews gathered in their cities throughout all the provinces of King Ahasuerus to lay hands on those who had sought their ruin; and no one could withstand them, because the fear of them had fallen upon all peoples. 3All the officials of the provinces, the satraps and the governors, and the royal officials were supporting the Jews, because the fear of Mordecai had fallen upon them. 4For Mordecai was powerful in the king's house, and his fame spread throughout all the provinces as the man Mordecai grew more and more powerful. 5So the Jews struck down all their enemies with the sword, slaughtering, and destroying them, and did as they pleased to those who hated them. 6In the citadel of Susa the Jews killed and destroyed five hundred people. 7They killed Parshandatha, Dalphon, Aspatha, 8Poratha, Adalia, Aridatha, 9Parmashta, Arisai, Aridai, Vaizatha, 10the ten sons of Haman son of Hammedatha, the enemy of the Jews; but they did not touch the plunder.

11 That very day the number of those killed in the citadel of Susa was reported to the king. 12The king said to Queen Esther, "In the citadel of Susa the Jews have killed five hundred people and also the ten sons of Haman. What have they done in the rest of the king's provinces? Now what is your petition? It shall be granted you. And what further is your request? It shall be fulfilled." 13Esther said, "If it pleases the king, let the Jews who are in Susa be allowed tomorrow also to do according to this day's edict, and let the ten sons of Haman be hanged on the gallows." 14So the king commanded this to be done; a decree was issued in Susa, and the ten sons of Haman were hanged. 15The Jews who were in Susa gathered also on the fourteenth day of the month of Adar and they killed three hundred persons in Susa; but they did not touch the plunder.

16 Now the other Jews who were in the king's provinces also gathered to defend their lives, and gained relief from their enemies, and killed seventy-five thousand of those who hated them; but they laid no hands on the plunder. 17This was on the thirteenth day of the month of Adar, and on the fourteenth day they rested and made that a day of feasting and gladness.

The Feast of Purim Inaugurated

18 But the Jews who were in Susa gathered on the thirteenth day and on the fourteenth, and rested on the fifteenth day, making that a day of feasting and gladness. 19Therefore the Jews of the villages, who live in the open towns, hold the fourteenth day of the month of Adar as a day for gladness and feasting, a holiday on which they send gifts of food to one another.

20 Mordecai recorded these things, and sent letters to all the Jews who were in all the provinces of King Ahasuerus, both near and far, 21enjoining them that they should keep the fourteenth day of the month Adar and also the fifteenth day of the same month, year by year,

King James

22As the days wherein the Jews rested from their enemies, and the month which was turned unto them from sorrow to joy, and from mourning into a good day: that they should make them days of feasting and joy, and of sending portions one to another, and gifts to the poor.

23And the Jews undertook to do as they had begun, and as Mordecai had written unto them;

24Because Haman the son of Hammedatha, the Agagite, the enemy of all the Jews, had devised against the Jews to destroy them, and had cast Pur, that *is,* the lot, to consume them, and to destroy them;

25But when *Esther* came before the king, he commanded by letters that his wicked device, which he devised against the Jews, should return upon his own head, and that he and his sons should be hanged on the gallows.

26Wherefore they called these days Purim after the name of Pur. Therefore for all the words of this letter, and *of that* which they had seen concerning this matter, and which had come unto them,

27The Jews ordained, and took upon them, and upon their seed, and upon all such as joined themselves unto them, so as it should not fail, that they would keep these two days according to their writing, and according to their *appointed* time every year;

28And *that* these days *should be* remembered and kept throughout every generation, every family, every province, and every city; and *that* these days of Purim should not fail from among the Jews, nor the memorial of them perish from their seed.

29Then Esther the queen, the daughter of Abihail, and Mordecai the Jew, wrote with all authority, to confirm this second letter of Purim.

30And he sent the letters unto all the Jews, to the hundred twenty and seven provinces of the kingdom of Ahasuerus, *with* words of peace and truth,

31To confirm these days of Purim in their times *appointed,* according as Mordecai the Jew and Esther the queen had enjoined them, and as they had decreed for themselves and for their seed, the matters of the fastings and their cry.

32And the decree of Esther confirmed these matters of Purim; and it was written in the book.

10 AND THE king Ahasuerus laid a tribute upon the land, and *upon* the isles of the sea. 2And all the acts of his power and of his might, and the declaration of the greatness of Mordecai, whereunto the king advanced him, *are* they not written in the book of the chronicles of the kings of Media and Persia?

3For Mordecai the Jew *was* next unto king Ahasuerus, and great among the Jews, and accepted of the multitude of his brethren, seeking the wealth of his people, and speaking peace to all his seed.

New International

time when the Jews got relief from their enemies, and as the month when their sorrow was turned into joy and their mourning into a day of celebration. He wrote them to observe the days as days of feasting and joy and giving presents of food to one another and gifts to the poor.

23So the Jews agreed to continue the celebration they had begun, doing what Mordecai had written to them. 24For Haman son of Hammedatha, the Agagite, the enemy of all the Jews, had plotted against the Jews to destroy them and had cast the *pur* (that is, the lot) for their ruin and destruction. 25But when the plot came to the king's attention,[a] he issued written orders that the evil scheme Haman had devised against the Jews should come back onto his own head, and that he and his sons should be hanged on the gallows. 26(Therefore these days were called Purim, from the word *pur.*) Because of everything written in this letter and because of what they had seen and what had happened to them, 27the Jews took it upon themselves to establish the custom that they and their descendants and all who join them should without fail observe these two days every year, in the way prescribed and at the time appointed. 28These days should be remembered and observed in every generation by every family, and in every province and in every city. And these days of Purim should never cease to be celebrated by the Jews, nor should the memory of them die out among their descendants.

29So Queen Esther, daughter of Abihail, along with Mordecai the Jew, wrote with full authority to confirm this second letter concerning Purim. 30And Mordecai sent letters to all the Jews in the 127 provinces of the kingdom of Xerxes—words of goodwill and assurance— 31to establish these days of Purim at their designated times, as Mordecai the Jew and Queen Esther had decreed for them, and as they had established for themselves and their descendants in regard to their times of fasting and lamentation. 32Esther's decree confirmed these regulations about Purim, and it was written down in the records.

The Greatness of Mordecai

10 KING XERXES imposed tribute throughout the empire, to its distant shores. 2And all his acts of power and might, together with a full account of the greatness of Mordecai to which the king had raised him, are they not written in the book of the annals of the kings of Media and Persia? 3Mordecai the Jew was second in rank to King Xerxes, preeminent among the Jews, and held in high esteem by his many fellow Jews, because he worked for the good of his people and spoke up for the welfare of all the Jews.

---

a 25 Or *when Esther came before the king*

Living Bible

celebrate with feasting, gladness, and the giving of gifts these historic days when the Jews were saved from their enemies, when their sorrow was turned to gladness and their mourning into happiness.

23So the Jews adopted Mordecai's suggestion and began this annual custom, 24, 25as a reminder of the time when Haman (son of Hammedatha the Agagite), the enemy of all the Jews, had plotted to destroy them at the time determined by a throw of the dice; and to remind them that when the matter came before the king, he issued a decree causing Haman's plot to boomerang, and he and his sons were hanged on the gallows. 26That is why this celebration is called "Purim," because the word for "throwing dice" in Persian is "pur." 27All the Jews throughout the realm agreed to inaugurate this tradition and to pass it on to their descendants and to all who became Jews; they declared they would never fail to celebrate these two days at the appointed time each year. 28It would be an annual event from generation to generation, celebrated by every family throughout the countryside and cities of the empire, so that the memory of what had happened would never perish from the Jewish race.

29, 30, 31Meanwhile, Queen Esther (daughter of Abihail and later adopted by Mordecai the Jew) had written a letter throwing her full support behind Mordecai's letter inaugurating his annual Feast of Purim. In addition, letters were sent to all the Jews throughout the 127 provinces of the kingdom of Ahasuerus with messages of good will, and encouragement to confirm these two days annually as the Feast of Purim, decreed by both Mordecai the Jew and by Queen Esther; indeed, the Jews themselves had decided upon this tradition as a remembrance of the time of their national fasting and prayer. 32So the commandment of Esther confirmed these dates and it was recorded as law.

10 KING AHASUERUS not only laid tribute upon the mainland, but even on the islands of the sea. 2His great deeds, and also the full account of the greatness of Mordecai and the honors given him by the king, are written in *The Book of the Chronicles of the Kings of Media and Persia*. 3Mordecai the Jew was the Prime Minister, with authority next to that of King Ahasuerus himself. He was, of course, very great among the Jews, and respected by all his countrymen because he did his best for his people, and was a friend at court for all of them.

New Revised Standard

22as the days on which the Jews gained relief from their enemies, and as the month that had been turned for them from sorrow into gladness and from mourning into a holiday; that they should make them days of feasting and gladness, days for sending gifts of food to one another and presents to the poor. 23So the Jews adopted as a custom what they had begun to do, as Mordecai had written to them.

24 Haman son of Hammedatha the Agagite, the enemy of all the Jews, had plotted against the Jews to destroy them, and had cast Pur—that is "the lot"—to crush and destroy them; 25but when Esther came before the king, he gave orders in writing that the wicked plot that he had devised against the Jews should come upon his own head, and that he and his sons should be hanged on the gallows. 26Therefore these days are called Purim, from the word Pur. Thus because of all that was written in this letter, and of what they had faced in this matter, and of what had happened to them, 27the Jews established and accepted as a custom for themselves and their descendants and all who joined them, that without fail they would continue to observe these two days every year, as it was written and at the time appointed. 28These days should be remembered and kept throughout every generation, in every family, province, and city; and these days of Purim should never fall into disuse among the Jews, nor should the commemoration of these days cease among their descendants.

29 Queen Esther daughter of Abihail, along with the Jew Mordecai, gave full written authority, confirming this second letter about Purim. 30Letters were sent wishing peace and security to all the Jews, to the one hundred twenty-seven provinces of the kingdom of Ahasuerus, 31and giving orders that these days of Purim should be observed at their appointed seasons, as the Jew Mordecai and Queen Esther enjoined on the Jews, just as they had laid down for themselves and for their descendants regulations concerning their fasts and their lamentations. 32The command of Queen Esther fixed these practices of Purim, and it was recorded in writing.

10 KING AHASUERUS laid tribute on the land and on the islands of the sea. 2All the acts of his power and might, and the full account of the high honor of Mordecai, to which the king advanced him, are they not written in the annals of the kings of Media and Persia? 3For Mordecai the Jew was next in rank to King Ahasuerus, and he was powerful among the Jews and popular with his many kindred, for he sought the good of his people and interceded for the welfare of all his descendants.

THE BOOK OF

Job

Job

1 THERE WAS a man in the land of Uz, whose name *was* Job; and that man was perfect and upright, and one that feared God, and eschewed evil.

2And there were born unto him seven sons and three daughters.

3His substance also was seven thousand sheep, and three thousand camels, and five hundred yoke of oxen, and five hundred she asses, and a very great household; so that this man was the greatest of all the men of the east.

4And his sons went and feasted *in their* houses, every one his day; and sent and called for their three sisters to eat and to drink with them.

5And it was so, when the days of *their* feasting were gone about, that Job sent and sanctified them, and rose up early in the morning, and offered burnt offerings *according* to the number of them all: for Job said, It may be that my sons have sinned, and cursed God in their hearts. Thus did Job continually.

6¶ Now there was a day when the sons of God came to present themselves before the LORD, and Satan came also among them.

7And the LORD said unto Satan, Whence comest thou? Then Satan answered the LORD, and said, From going to and fro in the earth, and from walking up and down in it.

8And the LORD said unto Satan, Hast thou considered my servant Job, that *there is* none like him in the earth, a perfect and an upright man, one that feareth God, and escheweth evil?

9Then Satan answered the LORD, and said, Doth Job fear God for nought?

10Hast not thou made an hedge about him, and about his house, and about all that he hath on every side? thou hast blessed the work of his hands, and his substance is increased in the land.

11But put forth thine hand now, and touch all that he hath, and he will curse thee to thy face.

12And the LORD said unto Satan, Behold, all that he hath *is* in thy power; only upon himself put not forth thine hand. So Satan went forth from the presence of the LORD.

13¶ And there was a day when his sons and his daughters *were* eating and drinking wine in their eldest brother's house:

14And there came a messenger unto Job, and said, The oxen were plowing, and the asses feeding beside them:

15And the Sabeans fell *upon them,* and took them away; yea, they have slain the servants with the edge of the sword; and I only am escaped alone to tell thee.

16While he *was* yet speaking, there came also another, and said, The fire of God is fallen from heaven, and hath burned up the sheep, and the servants, and consumed them; and I only am escaped alone to tell thee.

Prologue

1 IN THE land of Uz there lived a man whose name was Job. This man was blameless and upright; he feared God and shunned evil. 2He had seven sons and three daughters, 3and he owned seven thousand sheep, three thousand camels, five hundred yoke of oxen and five hundred donkeys, and had a large number of servants. He was the greatest man among all the people of the East.

4His sons used to take turns holding feasts in their homes, and they would invite their three sisters to eat and drink with them. 5When a period of feasting had run its course, Job would send and have them purified. Early in the morning he would sacrifice a burnt offering for each of them, thinking, "Perhaps my children have sinned and cursed God in their hearts." This was Job's regular custom.

Job's First Test

6One day the angels[a] came to present themselves before the LORD, and Satan[b] also came with them. 7The LORD said to Satan, "Where have you come from?"

Satan answered the LORD, "From roaming through the earth and going back and forth in it."

8Then the LORD said to Satan, "Have you considered my servant Job? There is no one on earth like him; he is blameless and upright, a man who fears God and shuns evil."

9"Does Job fear God for nothing?" Satan replied. 10"Have you not put a hedge around him and his household and everything he has? You have blessed the work of his hands, so that his flocks and herds are spread throughout the land. 11But stretch out your hand and strike everything he has, and he will surely curse you to your face."

12The LORD said to Satan, "Very well, then, everything he has is in your hands, but on the man himself do not lay a finger."

Then Satan went out from the presence of the LORD.

13One day when Job's sons and daughters were feasting and drinking wine at the oldest brother's house, 14a messenger came to Job and said, "The oxen were plowing and the donkeys were grazing nearby, 15and the Sabeans attacked and carried them off. They put the servants to the sword, and I am the only one who has escaped to tell you!"

16While he was still speaking, another messenger came and said, "The fire of God fell from the sky and burned up the sheep and the servants, and I am the only one who has escaped to tell you!"

a 6 Hebrew *the sons of God*   b 6 *Satan* means *accuser.*

Living Bible	New Revised Standard

Job

Job

Job and His Family

1 THERE LIVED in the land of Uz a man named Job—a good[c] man who feared God and stayed away from evil. 2, 3He had a large family of seven sons and three daughters, and was immensely wealthy,[d] for he owned 7,000 sheep, 3,000 camels, 500 teams of oxen, 500 female donkeys, and employed many servants. He was, in fact, the richest cattleman in that entire area.

4Every year when Job's sons had birthdays, they invited their brothers and sisters to their homes for a celebration. On these occasions they would eat and drink with great merriment. 5When these birthday parties ended—and sometimes they lasted several days—Job would summon his children to him and sanctify them, getting up early in the morning and offering a burnt offering for each of them. For Job said, "Perhaps my sons have sinned and turned away from God[e] in their hearts." This was Job's regular practice.

6One day as the angels[f] came to present themselves before the Lord, Satan, the Accuser, came with them.

7"Where have you come from?" the Lord asked Satan.

And Satan replied, "From Earth, where I've been watching everything that's going on."

8Then the Lord asked Satan, "Have you noticed my servant Job? He is the finest man in all the earth—a good[g] man who fears God and will have nothing to do with evil."

9"Why shouldn't he, when you pay him so well?" Satan scoffed. 10"You have always protected him and his home and his property from all harm. You have prospered everything he does—look how rich he is! No wonder he 'worships' you! 11But just take away his wealth, and you'll see him curse you to your face!"

12, 13And the Lord replied to Satan, "You may do anything you like with his wealth, but don't harm him physically."

So Satan went away; and sure enough, not long afterwards when Job's sons and daughters were dining at the oldest brother's house, tragedy struck.

14, 15A messenger rushed to Job's home with this news: "Your oxen were plowing, with the donkeys feeding beside them, when the Sabeans raided us, drove away the animals and killed all the farmhands except me. I am the only one left."

16While this messenger was still speaking, another arrived with more bad news: "The fire of God has fallen from heaven and burned up your sheep and all the herdsmen, and I alone have escaped to tell you."

1 THERE WAS once a man in the land of Uz whose name was Job. That man was blameless and upright, one who feared God and turned away from evil. 2There were born to him seven sons and three daughters. 3He had seven thousand sheep, three thousand camels, five hundred yoke of oxen, five hundred donkeys, and very many servants; so that this man was the greatest of all the people of the east. 4His sons used to go and hold feasts in one another's houses in turn; and they would send and invite their three sisters to eat and drink with them. 5And when the feast days had run their course, Job would send and sanctify them, and he would rise early in the morning and offer burnt offerings according to the number of them all; for Job said, "It may be that my children have sinned, and cursed God in their hearts." This is what Job always did.

Attack on Job's Character

6 One day the heavenly beings[h] came to present themselves before the LORD, and Satan[i] also came among them. 7The LORD said to Satan,[i] "Where have you come from?" Satan[i] answered the LORD, "From going to and fro on the earth, and from walking up and down on it." 8The LORD said to Satan,[i] "Have you considered my servant Job? There is no one like him on the earth, a blameless and upright man who fears God and turns away from evil." 9Then Satan[i] answered the LORD, "Does Job fear God for nothing? 10Have you not put a fence around him and his house and all that he has, on every side? You have blessed the work of his hands, and his possessions have increased in the land. 11But stretch out your hand now, and touch all that he has, and he will curse you to your face." 12The LORD said to Satan,[i] "Very well, all that he has is in your power; only do not stretch out your hand against him!" So Satan[i] went out from the presence of the LORD.

Job Loses Property and Children

13 One day when his sons and daughters were eating and drinking wine in the eldest brother's house, 14a messenger came to Job and said, "The oxen were plowing and the donkeys were feeding beside them, 15and the Sabeans fell on them and carried them off, and killed the servants with the edge of the sword; I alone have escaped to tell you." 16While he was still speaking, another came and said, "The fire of God fell from heaven and burned up the sheep and the servants, and consumed them; I alone have escaped to tell you." 17While he was still

King James

17While he *was* yet speaking, there came also another, and said, The Chaldeans made out three bands, and fell upon the camels, and have carried them away, yea, and slain the servants with the edge of the sword; and I only am escaped alone to tell thee.

18While he *was* yet speaking, there came also another, and said, Thy sons and thy daughters *were* eating and drinking wine in their eldest brother's house:

19And, behold, there came a great wind from the wilderness, and smote the four corners of the house, and it fell upon the young men, and they are dead; and I only am escaped alone to tell thee.

20Then Job arose, and rent his mantle, and shaved his head, and fell down upon the ground, and worshipped,

21And said, Naked came I out of my mother's womb, and naked shall I return thither: the LORD gave, and the LORD hath taken away; blessed be the name of the LORD.

22In all this Job sinned not, nor charged God foolishly.

2 AGAIN THERE was a day when the sons of God came to present themselves before the LORD, and Satan came also among them to present himself before the LORD.

2And the LORD said unto Satan, From whence comest thou? And Satan answered the LORD, and said, From going to and fro in the earth, and from walking up and down in it.

3And the LORD said unto Satan, Hast thou considered my servant Job, that *there is* none like him in the earth, a perfect and an upright man, one that feareth God, and escheweth evil? and still he holdeth fast his integrity, although thou movedst me against him, to destroy him without cause.

4And Satan answered the LORD, and said, Skin for skin, yea, all that a man hath will he give for his life.

5But put forth thine hand now, and touch his bone and his flesh, and he will curse thee to thy face.

6And the LORD said unto Satan, Behold, he *is* in thine hand; but save his life.

7¶ So went Satan forth from the presence of the LORD, and smote Job with sore boils from the sole of his foot unto his crown.

8And he took him a potsherd to scrape himself withal; and he sat down among the ashes.

9¶ Then said his wife unto him, Dost thou still retain thine integrity? curse God, and die.

10But he said unto her, Thou speakest as one of the foolish women speaketh. What? shall we receive good at the hand of God, and shall we not receive evil? In all this did not Job sin with his lips.

11¶ Now when Job's three friends heard of all this evil that was come upon him, they came every one from his own place; Eliphaz the Temanite, and Bildad the Shuhite, and Zophar the Naamathite: for they had made an appointment together to come to mourn with him and to comfort him.

12And when they lifted up their eyes afar off, and knew him not, they lifted up their voice, and wept; and they rent every one his mantle, and sprinkled dust upon their heads toward heaven.

13So they sat down with him upon the ground seven days and seven nights, and none spake a word unto him: for they saw that *his* grief was very great.

New International

17While he was still speaking, another messenger came and said, "The Chaldeans formed three raiding parties and swept down on your camels and carried them off. They put the servants to the sword, and I am the only one who has escaped to tell you!"

18While he was still speaking, yet another messenger came and said, "Your sons and daughters were feasting and drinking wine at the oldest brother's house, 19when suddenly a mighty wind swept in from the desert and struck the four corners of the house. It collapsed on them and they are dead, and I am the only one who has escaped to tell you!"

20At this, Job got up and tore his robe and shaved his head. Then he fell to the ground in worship 21and said:

> "Naked I came from my mother's womb,
>   and naked I will depart.[a]
> The LORD gave and the LORD has taken away;
>   may the name of the LORD be praised."

22In all this, Job did not sin by charging God with wrongdoing.

Job's Second Test

2 ON ANOTHER day the angels[b] came to present themselves before the LORD, and Satan also came with them to present himself before him. 2And the LORD said to Satan, "Where have you come from?"

Satan answered the LORD, "From roaming through the earth and going back and forth in it."

3Then the LORD said to Satan, "Have you considered my servant Job? There is no one on earth like him; he is blameless and upright, a man who fears God and shuns evil. And he still maintains his integrity, though you incited me against him to ruin him without any reason."

4"Skin for skin!" Satan replied. "A man will give all he has for his own life. 5But stretch out your hand and strike his flesh and bones, and he will surely curse you to your face."

6The LORD said to Satan, "Very well, then, he is in your hands; but you must spare his life."

7So Satan went out from the presence of the LORD and afflicted Job with painful sores from the soles of his feet to the top of his head. 8Then Job took a piece of broken pottery and scraped himself with it as he sat among the ashes.

9His wife said to him, "Are you still holding on to your integrity? Curse God and die!"

10He replied, "You are talking like a foolish[c] woman. Shall we accept good from God, and not trouble?"

In all this, Job did not sin in what he said.

Job's Three Friends

11When Job's three friends, Eliphaz the Temanite, Bildad the Shuhite and Zophar the Naamathite, heard about all the troubles that had come upon him, they set out from their homes and met together by agreement to go and sympathize with him and comfort him. 12When they saw him from a distance, they could hardly recognize him; they began to weep aloud, and they tore their robes and sprinkled dust on their heads. 13Then they sat on the ground with him for seven days and seven nights. No one said a word to him, because they saw how great his suffering was.

a 21 Or *will return there*   b 1 Hebrew *the sons of God*   c 10 The Hebrew word rendered *foolish* denotes moral deficiency.

Living Bible

17Before this man finished, still another messenger rushed in: "Three bands of Chaldeans have driven off your camels and killed your servants, and I alone have escaped to tell you."

18As he was still speaking, another arrived to say, "Your sons and daughters were feasting in their oldest brother's home, 19when suddenly a mighty wind swept in from the desert, and engulfed the house so that the roof fell in on them and all are dead; and I alone escaped to tell you."

20Then Job stood up and tore his robe in griefd and fell down upon the ground before God. 21"I came naked from my mother's womb," he said, "and I shall have nothing when I die. The Lord gave me everything I had, and they were his to take away. Blessed be the name of the Lord."

22In all of this, Job did not sin or revile God.

2 NOW THE angelse came again to present themselves before the Lord, and Satan with them.

2"Where have you come from?" the Lord asked Satan.

"From Earth, where I've been watching everything that's going on," Satan replied.

3"Well, have you noticed my servant Job?" the Lord asked. "He is the finest man in all the earth—a good man who fears God and turns away from all evil. And he has kept his faith in me despite the fact that you persuaded me to let you harm him without any cause."

4, 5"Skin for skin," Satan replied. "A man will give anything to save his life. Touch his body with sickness and he will curse you to your face!"

6"Do with him as you please," the Lord replied; "only spare his life."

7So Satan went out from the presence of the Lord and struck Job with a terrible case of boils from head to foot. 8Then Job took a broken piece of pottery to scrape himself, and sat among the ashes.

9His wife said to him, "Are you still trying to be godly when God has done all this to you? Curse him and die."

10But he replied, "You talk like some heathen woman. What? Shall we receive only pleasant things from the hand of God and never anything unpleasant?" So in all this Job said nothing wrong.

11When three of Job's friends heard of all the tragedy that had befallen him, they got in touch with each other and traveled from their homes to comfort and console him. Their names were Eliphaz the Temanite, Bildad the Shuhite, and Zophar the Naamathite. 12Job was so changed that they could scarcely recognize him. Wailing loudly in despair, they tore their robes and threw dust into the air and put earth on their heads to demonstrate their sorrow. 13Then they sat upon the ground with him silently for seven days and nights, no one speaking a word; for they saw that his suffering was too great for words.

New Revised Standard

speaking, another came and said, "The Chaldeans formed three columns, made a raid on the camels and carried them off, and killed the servants with the edge of the sword; I alone have escaped to tell you." 18While he was still speaking, another came and said, "Your sons and daughters were eating and drinking wine in their eldest brother's house, 19and suddenly a great wind came across the desert, struck the four corners of the house, and it fell on the young people, and they are dead; I alone have escaped to tell you."

20 Then Job arose, tore his robe, shaved his head, and fell on the ground and worshiped. 21He said, "Naked I came from my mother's womb, and naked shall I return there; the LORD gave, and the LORD has taken away; blessed be the name of the LORD."

22 In all this Job did not sin or charge God with wrongdoing.

Attack on Job's Health

2 ONE DAY the heavenly beingsf came to present themselves before the LORD, and Satang also came among them to present himself before the LORD. 2The LORD said to Satan,g "Where have you come from?" Satanh answered the LORD, "From going to and fro on the earth, and from walking up and down on it." 3The LORD said to Satan,g "Have you considered my servant Job? There is no one like him on the earth, a blameless and upright man who fears God and turns away from evil. He still persists in his integrity, although you incited me against him, to destroy him for no reason." 4Then Satang answered the LORD, "Skin for skin! All that people have they will give to save their lives.i 5But stretch out your hand now and touch his bone and his flesh, and he will curse you to your face." 6The LORD said to Satan,g "Very well, he is in your power; only spare his life."

7 So Satang went out from the presence of the LORD, and inflicted loathsome sores on Job from the sole of his foot to the crown of his head. 8Jobi took a potsherd with which to scrape himself, and sat among the ashes.

9 Then his wife said to him, "Do you still persist in your integrity? Cursek God, and die." 10But he said to her, "You speak as any foolish woman would speak. Shall we receive the good at the hand of God, and not receive the bad?" In all this Job did not sin with his lips.

Job's Three Friends

11 Now when Job's three friends heard of all these troubles that had come upon him, each of them set out from his home—Eliphaz the Temanite, Bildad the Shuhite, and Zophar the Naamathite. They met together to go and console and comfort him. 12When they saw him from a distance, they did not recognize him, and they raised their voices and wept aloud; they tore their robes and threw dust in the air upon their heads. 13They sat with him on the ground seven days and seven nights, and no one spoke a word to him, for they saw that his suffering was very great.

---

d 1:20 tore his robe in grief, literally, "tore his robe and shaved his head." e 2:1 the angels, literally, "the sons of God."

f Heb sons of God   g Or the Accuser; Heb ha-satan   h Or The Accuser; Heb ha-satan   i Or All that the man has he will give for his life   j Heb He   k Heb Bless

King James

3 AFTER THIS opened Job his mouth, and cursed his day.

2And Job spake, and said,

3Let the day perish wherein I was born, and the night *in which* it was said, There is a man child conceived.

4Let that day be darkness; let not God regard it from above, neither let the light shine upon it.

5Let darkness and the shadow of death stain it; let a cloud dwell upon it; let the blackness of the day terrify it.

6*As for* that night, let darkness seize upon it; let it not be joined unto the days of the year, let it not come into the number of the months.

7Lo, let that night be solitary, let no joyful voice come therein.

8Let them curse it that curse the day, who are ready to raise up their mourning.

9Let the stars of the twilight thereof be dark; let it look for light, but *have* none; neither let it see the dawning of the day:

10Because it shut not up the doors of my *mother's* womb, nor hid sorrow from mine eyes.

11Why died I not from the womb? *why* did I *not* give up the ghost when I came out of the belly?

12Why did the knees prevent me? or why the breasts that I should suck?

13For now should I have lain still and been quiet, I should have slept: then had I been at rest,

14With kings and counsellors of the earth, which built desolate places for themselves;

15Or with princes that had gold, who filled their houses with silver:

16Or as an hidden untimely birth I had not been; as infants *which* never saw light.

17There the wicked cease *from* troubling; and there the weary be at rest.

18*There* the prisoners rest together; they hear not the voice of the oppressor.

19The small and great are there; and the servant *is* free from his master.

20Wherefore is light given to him that is in misery, and life unto the bitter *in* soul;

21Which long for death, but it *cometh* not; and dig for it more than for hid treasures;

22Which rejoice exceedingly, *and* are glad, when they can find the grave?

23*Why is light given* to a man whose way is hid, and whom God hath hedged in?

24For my sighing cometh before I eat, and my roarings are poured out like the waters.

25For the thing which I greatly feared is come upon me, and that which I was afraid of is come unto me.

26I was not in safety, neither had I rest, neither was I quiet; yet trouble came.

4 THEN ELIPHAZ the Temanite answered and said, 2*If* we assay to commune with thee, wilt thou be grieved? but who can withhold himself from speaking?

New International

Job Speaks

3 AFTER THIS, Job opened his mouth and cursed the day of his birth. 2He said:

3"May the day of my birth perish,
  and the night it was said, 'A boy is born!'

4That day—may it turn to darkness;
  may God above not care about it;
  may no light shine upon it.

5May darkness and deep shadowa claim it once more;
  may a cloud settle over it;
  may blackness overwhelm its light.

6That night—may thick darkness seize it;
  may it not be included among the days of the year
  nor be entered in any of the months.

7May that night be barren;
  may no shout of joy be heard in it.

8May those who curse daysb curse that day,
  those who are ready to rouse Leviathan.

9May its morning stars become dark;
  may it wait for daylight in vain
  and not see the first rays of dawn,

10for it did not shut the doors of the womb on me
  to hide trouble from my eyes.

11"Why did I not perish at birth,
  and die as I came from the womb?

12Why were there knees to receive me
  and breasts that I might be nursed?

13For now I would be lying down in peace;
  I would be asleep and at rest

14with kings and counselors of the earth,
  who built for themselves places now lying in ruins,

15with rulers who had gold,
  who filled their houses with silver.

16Or why was I not hidden in the ground like a stillborn child,
  like an infant who never saw the light of day?

17There the wicked cease from turmoil,
  and there the weary are at rest.

18Captives also enjoy their ease;
  they no longer hear the slave driver's shout.

19The small and the great are there,
  and the slave is freed from his master.

20"Why is light given to those in misery,
  and life to the bitter of soul,

21to those who long for death that does not come,
  who search for it more than for hidden treasure,

22who are filled with gladness
  and rejoice when they reach the grave?

23Why is life given to a man
  whose way is hidden,
  whom God has hedged in?

24For sighing comes to me instead of food;
  my groans pour out like water.

25What I feared has come upon me;
  what I dreaded has happened to me.

26I have no peace, no quietness;
  I have no rest, but only turmoil."

Eliphaz

4 THEN ELIPHAZ the Temanite replied:

2"If someone ventures a word with you, will you be impatient?
  But who can keep from speaking?

Living Bible

3 AT LAST Job spoke, and cursed the day of his birth.

2, 3"Let the day of my birth be cursed," he said, "and the night when I was conceived. 4Let that day be forever forgotten.c Let it be lost even to God, shrouded in eternal darkness. 5Yes, let the darkness claim it for its own, and may a black cloud overshadow it. 6May it be blotted off the calendar, never again to be counted among the days of the month of that year. 7Let that night be bleak and joyless. 8Let those who are experts at cursing curse it.d 9Let the stars of the night disappear. Let it long for light, but never see it, never see the morning light. 10Curse it for its failure to shut my mother's womb, for letting me be born to come to all this trouble.

11"Why didn't I die at birth? 12Why did the midwife let me live? Why did she nurse me at her breasts? 13For if only I had died at birth, then I would be quiet now, asleep and at rest, 14, 15along with prime ministers and kings with all their pomp, and wealthy princes whose castles are full of rich treasures. 16Oh, to have been still-born!—to have never breathed or seen the light. 17For there in death the wicked cease from troubling, and there the weary are at rest. 18There even prisoners are at ease, with no brutal jailer to curse them. 19Both rich and poor alike are there, and the slave is free at last from his master.

20, 21"Oh, why should light and life be given to those in misery and bitterness, who long for death, and it won't come; who search for death as others search for food or money? 22What blessed relief when at last they die? 23Why is a man allowed to be born if God is only going to give him a hopeless life of uselessness and frustration? 24I cannot eat for sighing; my groans pour out like water. 25What I always feared has happened to me. 26I was not fat and lazy, yet trouble struck me down."

4 A REPLY to Job from Eliphaz the Temanite:
2"Will you let me say a word? For who could keep from speaking out? 3, 4In the paste you have told many

New Revised Standard

Job Curses the Day He Was Born

3 AFTER THIS Job opened his mouth and cursed the day of his birth. 2Job said:

3 "Let the day perish in which I was born,
   and the night that said,
   'A man-child is conceived.'
4 Let that day be darkness!
   May God above not seek it,
   or light shine on it.
5 Let gloom and deep darkness claim it.
   Let clouds settle upon it;
   let the blackness of the day terrify it.
6 That night—let thick darkness seize it!
   let it not rejoice among the days of the year;
   let it not come into the number of the
       months.
7 Yes, let that night be barren;
   let no joyful cry be heardf in it.
8 Let those curse it who curse the Sea,g
   those who are skilled to rouse up Leviathan.
9 Let the stars of its dawn be dark;
   let it hope for light, but have none;
   may it not see the eyelids of the morning—
10 because it did not shut the doors of my
       mother's womb,
   and hide trouble from my eyes.

11 "Why did I not die at birth,
   come forth from the womb and expire?
12 Why were there knees to receive me,
   or breasts for me to suck?
13 Now I would be lying down and quiet;
   I would be asleep; then I would be at rest
14 with kings and counselors of the earth
   who rebuild ruins for themselves,
15 or with princes who have gold,
   who fill their houses with silver.
16 Or why was I not buried like a stillborn child,
   like an infant that never sees the light?
17 There the wicked cease from troubling,
   and there the weary are at rest.
18 There the prisoners are at ease together;
   they do not hear the voice of the
       taskmaster.
19 The small and the great are there,
   and the slaves are free from their masters.

20 "Why is light given to one in misery,
   and life to the bitter in soul,
21 who long for death, but it does not come,
   and dig for it more than for hidden
       treasures;
22 who rejoice exceedingly,
   and are glad when they find the grave?
23 Why is light given to one who cannot see the
       way,
   whom God has fenced in?
24 For my sighing comes likeh my bread,
   and my groanings are poured out like water.
25 Truly the thing that I fear comes upon me,
   and what I dread befalls me.
26 I am not at ease, nor am I quiet;
   I have no rest; but trouble comes."

Eliphaz Speaks: Job Has Sinned

4 THEN ELIPHAZ the Temanite answered:
2 "If one ventures a word with you, will you
       be offended?
   But who can keep from speaking?

---

c 3:4 day be forever forgotten, literally, "a day of darkness."   d 3:8 Let those who are experts at cursing curse it, literally, "Let them who can curse the sea, who know how to rouse the sea monster, curse it."   e 4:3, 4 in the past, implied.

f Heb come   g Cn: Heb day   h Heb before

King James

3Behold, thou hast instructed many, and thou hast strengthened the weak hands.

4Thy words have upholden him that was falling, and thou hast strengthened the feeble knees.

5But now it is come upon thee, and thou faintest; it toucheth thee, and thou art troubled.

6*Is* not *this* thy fear, thy confidence, thy hope, and the uprightness of thy ways?

7Remember, I pray thee, who *ever* perished, being innocent? or where were the righteous cut off?

8Even as I have seen, they that plow iniquity, and sow wickedness, reap the same.

9By the blast of God they perish, and by the breath of his nostrils are they consumed.

10The roaring of the lion, and the voice of the fierce lion, and the teeth of the young lions, are broken.

11The old lion perisheth for lack of prey, and the stout lion's whelps are scattered abroad.

12Now a thing was secretly brought to me, and mine ear received a little thereof.

13In thoughts from the visions of the night, when deep sleep falleth on men,

14Fear came upon me, and trembling, which made all my bones to shake.

15Then a spirit passed before my face; the hair of my flesh stood up:

16It stood still, but I could not discern the form thereof: an image *was* before mine eyes, *there was* silence, and I heard a voice, *saying,*

17Shall mortal man be more just than God? shall a man be more pure than his maker?

18Behold, he put no trust in his servants; and his angels he charged with folly:

19How much less *in* them that dwell in houses of clay, whose foundation *is* in the dust, *which* are crushed before the moth?

20They are destroyed from morning to evening: they perish for ever without any regarding *it*.

21Doth not their excellency *which is* in them go away? they die, even without wisdom.

5 CALL NOW, if there be any that will answer thee; and to which of the saints wilt thou turn?

2For wrath killeth the foolish man, and envy slayeth the silly one.

3I have seen the foolish taking root: but suddenly I cursed his habitation.

4His children are far from safety, and they are crushed in the gate, neither *is there* any to deliver *them*.

5Whose harvest the hungry eateth up, and taketh it even out of the thorns, and the robber swalloweth up their substance.

6Although affliction cometh not forth of the dust, neither doth trouble spring out of the ground;

New International

3Think how you have instructed many,
    how you have strengthened feeble hands.

4Your words have supported those who stumbled;
    you have strengthened faltering knees.

5But now trouble comes to you, and you are
        discouraged;
    it strikes you, and you are dismayed.

6Should not your piety be your confidence
    and your blameless ways your hope?

7"Consider now: Who, being innocent, has ever
        perished?
    Where were the upright ever destroyed?

8As I have observed, those who plow evil
    and those who sow trouble reap it.

9At the breath of God they are destroyed;
    at the blast of his anger they perish.

10The lions may roar and growl,
    yet the teeth of the great lions are broken.

11The lion perishes for lack of prey,
    and the cubs of the lioness are scattered.

12"A word was secretly brought to me,
    my ears caught a whisper of it.

13Amid disquieting dreams in the night,
    when deep sleep falls on men,

14fear and trembling seized me
    and made all my bones shake.

15A spirit glided past my face,
    and the hair on my body stood on end.

16It stopped,
    but I could not tell what it was.
A form stood before my eyes,
    and I heard a hushed voice:

17'Can a mortal be more righteous than God?
    Can a man be more pure than his Maker?

18If God places no trust in his servants,
    if he charges his angels with error,

19how much more those who live in houses of
        clay,
    whose foundations are in the dust,
    who are crushed more readily than a moth!

20Between dawn and dusk they are broken to
        pieces;
    unnoticed, they perish forever.

21Are not the cords of their tent pulled up,
    so that they die without wisdom?'[a]

5 "CALL IF you will, but who will answer you?
    To which of the holy ones will you turn?

2Resentment kills a fool,
    and envy slays the simple.

3I myself have seen a fool taking root,
    but suddenly his house was cursed.

4His children are far from safety,
    crushed in court without a defender.

5The hungry consume his harvest,
    taking it even from among thorns,
    and the thirsty pant after his wealth.

6For hardship does not spring from the soil,
    nor does trouble sprout from the ground.

---

a 21 Some interpreters end the quotation after verse 17.

Living Bible

a troubled soul to trust in God[b] and have encouraged those who are weak or falling, or lie crushed upon the ground or are tempted to despair. 5But now, when trouble strikes, you faint and are broken.

6"At such a time as this should not trust in God still be your confidence? Shouldn't you believe that God will care for those who are good?[c] 7, 8Stop and think! Have you ever known a truly good and innocent person who was punished? Experience teaches that it is those who sow sin and trouble who harvest the same. 9They die beneath the hand of God. 10Though they are fierce as young lions, they shall all be broken and destroyed. 11Like aged, helpless lions they shall starve, and all their children shall be scattered.

12"This truth was given me in secret, as though whispered in my ear. 13It came in a nighttime vision as others slept. 14Suddenly, fear gripped me; I trembled and shook with terror, 15as a spirit passed before my face—my hair stood up on end. 16I felt the spirit's presence, but couldn't see it standing there. Then out of the dreadful silence came this voice:

17" 'Is mere man more just than God? More pure than his Creator?'

18, 19"If God cannot trust his own messengers (for even angels make mistakes), how much less men made of dust, who are crushed to death as easily as moths! 20They are alive in the morning, but by evening they are dead, gone forever with hardly a thought from anyone. 21Their candle of life is snuffed out. They die and no one cares.

New Revised Standard

3 See, you have instructed many;
   you have strengthened the weak hands.
4 Your words have supported those who were
    stumbling,
   and you have made firm the feeble knees.
5 But now it has come to you, and you are
    impatient;
   it touches you, and you are dismayed.
6 Is not your fear of God your confidence,
   and the integrity of your ways your hope?

7 "Think now, who that was innocent ever
    perished?
   Or where were the upright cut off?
8 As I have seen, those who plow iniquity
   and sow trouble reap the same.
9 By the breath of God they perish,
   and by the blast of his anger they are
    consumed.
10 The roar of the lion, the voice of the fierce
    lion,
   and the teeth of the young lions are broken.
11 The strong lion perishes for lack of prey,
   and the whelps of the lioness are scattered.

12 "Now a word came stealing to me,
   my ear received the whisper of it.
13 Amid thoughts from visions of the night,
   when deep sleep falls on mortals,
14 dread came upon me, and trembling,
   which made all my bones shake.
15 A spirit glided past my face;
   the hair of my flesh bristled.
16 It stood still,
   but I could not discern its appearance.
   A form was before my eyes;
   there was silence, then I heard a voice:
17 'Can mortals be righteous before[d] God?
   Can human beings be pure before[d] their
    Maker?
18 Even in his servants he puts no trust,
   and his angels he charges with error;
19 how much more those who live in houses of
    clay,
   whose foundation is in the dust,
   who are crushed like a moth.
20 Between morning and evening they are
    destroyed;
   they perish forever without any regarding it.
21 Their tent-cord is plucked up within them,
   and they die devoid of wisdom.'

Job Is Corrected by God

5 "THEY CRY for help but no one listens; they turn to their gods, but none gives them aid. 2They die in helpless frustration, overcome by their own anger. 3Those who turn from God may be successful for the moment, but then comes sudden disaster. 4Their children are cheated, with no one to defend them. 5Their harvests are stolen and their wealth slakes the thirst of many others, not themselves! 6Misery comes upon them to punish them for sowing seeds of sin. 7Mankind heads

5 "CALL NOW; is there anyone who will answer
    you?
   To which of the holy ones will you turn?
2 Surely vexation kills the fool,
   and jealousy slays the simple.
3 I have seen fools taking root,
   but suddenly I cursed their dwelling.
4 Their children are far from safety,
   they are crushed in the gate,
   and there is no one to deliver them.
5 The hungry eat their harvest,
   and they take it even out of the thorns;[e]
   and the thirsty[f] pant after their wealth.
6 For misery does not come from the earth,
   nor does trouble sprout from the ground;

---

b *4:3, 4 you have told many a troubled soul to trust in God*, literally, "you have instructed many." c *4:6 God will care for those who are good?* Literally, "the integrity of your ways, your hope."

d Or *more than* e Meaning of Heb uncertain f Aquila Symmachus Syr Vg: Heb *snare*

King James

7Yet man is born unto trouble, as the sparks fly upward.

8I would seek unto God, and unto God would I commit my cause:

9Which doeth great things and unsearchable; marvellous things without number:

10Who giveth rain upon the earth, and sendeth waters upon the fields:

11To set up on high those that be low; that those which mourn may be exalted to safety.

12He disappointeth the devices of the crafty, so that their hands cannot perform *their* enterprise.

13He taketh the wise in their own craftiness: and the counsel of the froward is carried headlong.

14They meet with darkness in the daytime, and grope in the noonday as in the night.

15But he saveth the poor from the sword, from their mouth, and from the hand of the mighty.

16So the poor hath hope, and iniquity stoppeth her mouth.

17Behold, happy *is* the man whom God correcteth: therefore despise not thou the chastening of the Almighty:

18For he maketh sore, and bindeth up: he woundeth, and his hands make whole.

19He shall deliver thee in six troubles: yea, in seven there shall no evil touch thee.

20In famine he shall redeem thee from death: and in war from the power of the sword.

21Thou shalt be hid from the scourge of the tongue: neither shalt thou be afraid of destruction when it cometh.

22At destruction and famine thou shalt laugh: neither shalt thou be afraid of the beasts of the earth.

23For thou shalt be in league with the stones of the field: and the beasts of the field shall be at peace with thee.

24And thou shalt know that thy tabernacle *shall be* in peace; and thou shalt visit thy habitation, and shalt not sin.

25Thou shalt know also that thy seed *shall be* great, and thine offspring as the grass of the earth.

26Thou shalt come to *thy* grave in a full age, like as a shock of corn cometh in in his season.

27Lo this, we have searched it, so it *is;* hear it, and know thou *it* for thy good.

6 BUT JOB answered and said,
2Oh that my grief were thoroughly weighed, and my calamity laid in the balances together!

3For now it would be heavier than the sand of the sea: therefore my words are swallowed up.

4For the arrows of the Almighty *are* within me, the poison whereof drinketh up my spirit: the terrors of God do set themselves in array against me.

New International

7Yet man is born to trouble
  as surely as sparks fly upward.

8"But if it were I, I would appeal to God;
  I would lay my cause before him.

9He performs wonders that cannot be fathomed,
  miracles that cannot be counted.

10He bestows rain on the earth;
  he sends water upon the countryside.

11The lowly he sets on high,
  and those who mourn are lifted to safety.

12He thwarts the plans of the crafty,
  so that their hands achieve no success.

13He catches the wise in their craftiness,
  and the schemes of the wily are swept away.

14Darkness comes upon them in the daytime;
  at noon they grope as in the night.

15He saves the needy from the sword in their mouth;
  he saves them from the clutches of the powerful.

16So the poor have hope,
  and injustice shuts its mouth.

17"Blessed is the man whom God corrects;
  so do not despise the discipline of the Almighty.[a]

18For he wounds, but he also binds up;
  he injures, but his hands also heal.

19From six calamities he will rescue you;
  in seven no harm will befall you.

20In famine he will ransom you from death,
  and in battle from the stroke of the sword.

21You will be protected from the lash of the tongue,
  and need not fear when destruction comes.

22You will laugh at destruction and famine,
  and need not fear the beasts of the earth.

23For you will have a covenant with the stones of the field,
  and the wild animals will be at peace with you.

24You will know that your tent is secure;
  you will take stock of your property and find nothing missing.

25You will know that your children will be many,
  and your descendants like the grass of the earth.

26You will come to the grave in full vigor,
  like sheaves gathered in season.

27"We have examined this, and it is true.
  So hear it and apply it to yourself."

Job

6 THEN JOB replied:

2"If only my anguish could be weighed
  and all my misery be placed on the scales!

3It would surely outweigh the sand of the seas—
  no wonder my words have been impetuous.

4The arrows of the Almighty are in me,
  my spirit drinks in their poison;
  God's terrors are marshaled against me.

---

a 17 Hebrew *Shaddai*; here and throughout Job

Living Bible

for sin and misery as predictably as flames shoot upwards from a fire.

8"My advice to you is this: Go to God and confess your sins to him.b 9For he does wonderful miracles, marvels without number. 10He sends the rain upon the earth to water the fields, 11and gives prosperity to the poor and humble, and takes sufferers to safety.

12"He frustrates the plans of crafty men. 13They are caught in their own traps; he thwarts their schemes. 14They grope like blind men in the daylight; they see no better in the daytime than at night.

15"God saves the fatherless and the poor from the grasp of these oppressors. 16And so at last the poor have hope, and the fangs of the wicked are broken.

17"How enviable the man whom God corrects! Oh, do not despise the chastening of the Lord when you sin. 18For though he wounds, he binds and heals again. 19He will deliver you again and again, so that no evil can touch you.

20"He will keep you from death in famine, and from the power of the sword in time of war.

21"You will be safe from slander; no need to fear the future.

22"You shall laugh at war and famine; wild animals will leave you alone. 23Dangerous animals will be at peace with you.

24"You need not worry about your home while you are gone; nothing shall be stolen from your barns.

25"Your sons shall become important men; your descendants shall be as numerous as grass! 26You shall live a long, good life; like standing grain, you'll not be harvested until it's time! 27I have found from experience that all of this is true. For your own good, listen to my counsel."

New Revised Standard

7 but human beings are born to trouble
  just as sparksc fly upward.

8 "As for me, I would seek God,
  and to God I would commit my cause.
9 He does great things and unsearchable,
  marvelous things without number.
10 He gives rain on the earth
  and sends waters on the fields;
11 he sets on high those who are lowly,
  and those who mourn are lifted to safety.
12 He frustrates the devices of the crafty,
  so that their hands achieve no success.
13 He takes the wise in their own craftiness;
  and the schemes of the wily are brought to
    a quick end.
14 They meet with darkness in the daytime,
  and grope at noonday as in the night.
15 But he saves the needy from the sword of
    their mouth,
  from the hand of the mighty.
16 So the poor have hope,
  and injustice shuts its mouth.

17 "How happy is the one whom God reproves;
  therefore do not despise the discipline of the
    Almighty.d
18 For he wounds, but he binds up;
  he strikes, but his hands heal.
19 He will deliver you from six troubles;
  in seven no harm shall touch you.
20 In famine he will redeem you from death,
  and in war from the power of the sword.
21 You shall be hidden from the scourge of the
    tongue,
  and shall not fear destruction when it
    comes.
22 At destruction and famine you shall laugh,
  and shall not fear the wild animals of the
    earth.
23 For you shall be in league with the stones of
    the field,
  and the wild animals shall be at peace with
    you.
24 You shall know that your tent is safe,
  you shall inspect your fold and miss
    nothing.
25 You shall know that your descendants will be
    many,
  and your offspring like the grass of the
    earth.
26 You shall come to your grave in ripe old age,
  as a shock of grain comes up to the
    threshing floor in its season.
27 See, we have searched this out; it is true.
  Hear, and know it for yourself."

Job Replies: My Complaint Is Just

6 THEN JOB answered:
2 "O that my vexation were weighed,
  and all my calamity laid in the balances!
3 For then it would be heavier than the sand of
    the sea;
  therefore my words have been rash.
4 For the arrows of the Almightyd are in me;
  my spirit drinks their poison;
  the terrors of God are arrayed against me.

6 JOB'S REPLY:
2"Oh, that my sadness and troubles were weighed. 3For they are heavier than the sand of a thousand seashores. That is why I spoke so rashly. 4For the Lord has struck me down with his arrows; he has sent his poisoned arrows deep within my heart. All God's terrors are arrayed against me. 5, 6, 7When wild donkeys bray, it is

b 5:8 Go to God and confess your sins to him, literally, "I would seek God, and to God would I commit my cause."

c Or birds; Heb sons of Resheph   d Traditional rendering of Heb Shaddai

King James

5Doth the wild ass bray when he hath grass? or loweth the ox over his fodder?

6Can that which is unsavoury be eaten without salt? or is there *any* taste in the white of an egg?

7The things *that* my soul refused to touch *are* as my sorrowful meat.

8Oh that I might have my request; and that God would grant *me* the thing that I long for!

9Even that it would please God to destroy me; that he would let loose his hand, and cut me off!

10Then should I yet have comfort; yea, I would harden myself in sorrow: let him not spare; for I have not concealed the words of the Holy One.

11What *is* my strength, that I should hope? and what *is* mine end, that I should prolong my life?

12*Is* my strength the strength of stones? or *is* my flesh of brass?

13*Is* not my help in me? and is wisdom driven quite from me?

14To him that is afflicted pity *should be shown* from his friend; but he forsaketh the fear of the Almighty.

15My brethren have dealt deceitfully as a brook, *and* as the stream of brooks they pass away;

16Which are blackish by reason of the ice, *and* wherein the snow is hid:

17What time they wax warm, they vanish: when it is hot, they are consumed out of their place.

18The paths of their way are turned aside; they go to nothing, and perish.

19The troops of Tema looked, the companies of Sheba waited for them.

20They were confounded because they had hoped; they came thither, and were ashamed.

21For now ye are nothing; ye see *my* casting down, and are afraid.

22Did I say, Bring unto me? or, Give a reward for me of your substance?

23Or, Deliver me from the enemy's hand? or, Redeem me from the hand of the mighty?

24Teach me, and I will hold my tongue: and cause me to understand wherein I have erred.

25How forcible are right words! but what doth your arguing reprove?

26Do ye imagine to reprove words, and the speeches of one that is desperate, *which are* as wind?

27Yea, ye overwhelm the fatherless, and ye dig *a pit* for your friend.

28Now therefore be content, look upon me; for *it is* evident unto you if I lie.

29Return, I pray you, let it not be iniquity; yea, return again, my righteousness *is* in it.

30Is there iniquity in my tongue? cannot my taste discern perverse things?

New International

5Does a wild donkey bray when it has grass,
    or an ox bellow when it has fodder?
6Is tasteless food eaten without salt,
    or is there flavor in the white of an egg[a]?
7I refuse to touch it;
    such food makes me ill.

8"Oh, that I might have my request,
    that God would grant what I hope for,
9that God would be willing to crush me,
    to let loose his hand and cut me off!
10Then I would still have this consolation—
    my joy in unrelenting pain—
    that I had not denied the words of the Holy
      One.

11"What strength do I have, that I should still
      hope?
    What prospects, that I should be patient?
12Do I have the strength of stone?
    Is my flesh bronze?
13Do I have any power to help myself,
    now that success has been driven from me?

14"A despairing man should have the devotion of
      his friends,
    even though he forsakes the fear of the
      Almighty.
15But my brothers are as undependable as
      intermittent streams,
    as the streams that overflow
16when darkened by thawing ice
    and swollen with melting snow,
17but that cease to flow in the dry season,
    and in the heat vanish from their channels.
18Caravans turn aside from their routes;
    they go up into the wasteland and perish.
19The caravans of Tema look for water,
    the traveling merchants of Sheba look in
      hope.
20They are distressed, because they had been
      confident;
    they arrive there, only to be disappointed.
21Now you too have proved to be of no help;
    you see something dreadful and are afraid.
22Have I ever said, 'Give something on my
      behalf,
    pay a ransom for me from your wealth,
23deliver me from the hand of the enemy,
    ransom me from the clutches of the ruthless'?

24"Teach me, and I will be quiet;
    show me where I have been wrong.
25How painful are honest words!
    But what do your arguments prove?
26Do you mean to correct what I say,
    and treat the words of a despairing man as
      wind?
27You would even cast lots for the fatherless
    and barter away your friend.

28"But now be so kind as to look at me.
    Would I lie to your face?
29Relent, do not be unjust;
    reconsider, for my integrity is at stake.[b]
30Is there any wickedness on my lips?
    Can my mouth not discern malice?

[a] 6 The meaning of the Hebrew for this phrase is uncertain.   [b] 29 Or *my righteousness still stands*

Living Bible

because their grass is gone; oxen do not low when they
have food; a man complains when there is no salt in his
food. And how tasteless is the uncooked white of an
egg—my appetite is gone when I look at it; I gag at the
thought of eating it!

8, 9"Oh, that God would grant the thing I long for
most—to die beneath his hand, and be freed from his
painful grip. 10This, at least, gives me comfort despite
all the pain—that I have not denied the words of the holy
God. 11Oh, why does my strength sustain me? How can
I be patient till I die? 12Am I unfeeling, like stone? Is
my flesh made of brass? 13For I am utterly helpless,
without any hope.

14"One should be kind to a fainting friend, but you
have accused me without the slightest fear of God.
15–18My brother, you have proved as unreliable as a
brook; it floods when there is ice and snow, but in hot
weather, disappears. The caravans turn aside to be refreshed, but there is nothing there to drink, and so they
perish. 19, 20, 21When caravans from Tema and from
Sheba stop for water there, their hopes are dashed. And
so my hopes in you are dashed—you turn away from me
in terror and refuse to help. 22But why? Have I ever
asked you for one slightest thing? Have I begged you for
a present? 23Have I ever asked your help? 24All I want
is a reasonable answer—then I will keep quiet. Tell me,
what have I done wrong?

25, 26"It is wonderful to speak the truth, but your criticisms are not based on fact. Are you going to condemn
me just because I impulsively cried out in desperation?
27That would be like injuring a helpless orphan, or selling a friend. 28Look at me! Would I lie to your face?
29Stop assuming my guilt, for I am righteous. Don't be
so unjust. 30Don't I know the difference between right
and wrong? Would I not admit it if I had sinned?

New Revised Standard

5 Does the wild ass bray over its grass,
      or the ox low over its fodder?
6 Can that which is tasteless be eaten without
      salt,
      or is there any flavor in the juice of
      mallows?c
7 My appetite refuses to touch them;
      they are like food that is loathsome to me.c
8 "O that I might have my request,
      and that God would grant my desire;
9 that it would please God to crush me,
      that he would let loose his hand and cut me
      off!
10 This would be my consolation;
      I would even exulte in unrelenting pain;
      for I have not denied the words of the Holy
      One.
11 What is my strength, that I should wait?
      And what is my end, that I should be
      patient?
12 Is my strength the strength of stones,
      or is my flesh bronze?
13 In truth I have no help in me,
      and any resource is driven from me.

14 "Those who withholdd kindness from a friend
      forsake the fear of the Almighty.e
15 My companions are treacherous like a
      torrent-bed,
      like freshets that pass away,
16 that run dark with ice,
      turbid with melting snow.
17 In time of heat they disappear;
      when it is hot, they vanish from their place.
18 The caravans turn aside from their course;
      they go up into the waste, and perish.
19 The caravans of Tema look,
      the travelers of Sheba hope.
20 They are disappointed because they were
      confident;
      they come there and are confounded.
21 Such you have now become to me;f
      you see my calamity, and are afraid.
22 Have I said, 'Make me a gift'?
      Or, 'From your wealth offer a bribe for
      me'?
23 Or, 'Save me from an opponent's hand'?
      Or, 'Ransom me from the hand of
      oppressors'?

24 "Teach me, and I will be silent;
      make me understand how I have gone
      wrong.
25 How forceful are honest words!
      But your reproof, what does it reprove?
26 Do you think that you can reprove words,
      as if the speech of the desperate were wind?
27 You would even cast lots over the orphan,
      and bargain over your friend.

28 "But now, be pleased to look at me;
      for I will not lie to your face.
29 Turn, I pray, let no wrong be done.
      Turn now, my vindication is at stake.
30 Is there any wrong on my tongue?
      Cannot my taste discern calamity?

---

c Meaning of Heb uncertain   d Syr Vg Compare Tg: Meaning of Heb
uncertain   e Traditional rendering of Heb *Shaddai*   f Cn Compare Gk Syr:
Meaning of Heb uncertain

<table>
<tr><td>

King James

</td><td>

New International

</td></tr>
</table>

King James

7 IS THERE not an appointed time to man upon earth? *are not* his days also like the days of an hireling?

2As a servant earnestly desireth the shadow, and as an hireling looketh for *the reward of* his work:

3So am I made to possess months of vanity, and wearisome nights are appointed to me.

4When I lie down, I say, When shall I arise, and the night be gone? and I am full of tossings to and fro unto the dawning of the day.

5My flesh is clothed with worms and clods of dust; my skin is broken, and become loathsome.

6My days are swifter than a weaver's shuttle, and are spent without hope.

7O remember that my life *is* wind: mine eye shall no more see good.

8The eye of him that hath seen me shall see me no *more:* thine eyes *are* upon me, and I *am* not.

9*As* the cloud is consumed and vanisheth away: so he that goeth down to the grave shall come up no *more.*

10He shall return no more to his house, neither shall his place know him any more.

11Therefore I will not refrain my mouth; I will speak in the anguish of my spirit; I will complain in the bitterness of my soul.

12*Am* I a sea, or a whale, that thou settest a watch over me?

13When I say, My bed shall comfort me, my couch shall ease my complaint;

14Then thou scarest me with dreams, and terrifiest me through visions:

15So that my soul chooseth strangling, *and* death rather than my life.

16I loathe *it;* I would not live always: let me alone; for my days *are* vanity.

17What *is* man, that thou shouldest magnify him? and that thou shouldest set thine heart upon him?

18And *that* thou shouldest visit him every morning, *and* try him every moment?

19How long wilt thou not depart from me, nor let me alone till I swallow down my spittle?

20I have sinned; what shall I do unto thee, O thou preserver of men? why hast thou set me as a mark against thee, so that I am a burden to myself?

21And why dost thou not pardon my transgression, and take away mine iniquity? for now shall I sleep in the dust; and thou shalt seek me in the morning, but I *shall* not *be.*

8 THEN ANSWERED Bildad the Shuhite, and said, 2How long wilt thou speak these *things?* and *how long shall* the words of thy mouth *be like* a strong wind?

3Doth God pervert judgment? or doth the Almighty pervert justice?

4If thy children have sinned against him, and he have cast them away for their transgression;

5If thou wouldest seek unto God betimes, and make thy supplication to the Almighty;

New International

7 "DOES NOT man have hard service on earth? Are not his days like those of a hired man?
2Like a slave longing for the evening shadows, or a hired man waiting eagerly for his wages,
3so I have been allotted months of futility, and nights of misery have been assigned to me.
4When I lie down I think, 'How long before I get up?'
The night drags on, and I toss till dawn.
5My body is clothed with worms and scabs, my skin is broken and festering.

6"My days are swifter than a weaver's shuttle, and they come to an end without hope.
7Remember, O God, that my life is but a breath; my eyes will never see happiness again.
8The eye that now sees me will see me no longer;
you will look for me, but I will be no more.
9As a cloud vanishes and is gone, so he who goes down to the grave[a] does not return.
10He will never come to his house again; his place will know him no more.

11"Therefore I will not keep silent; I will speak out in the anguish of my spirit, I will complain in the bitterness of my soul.
12Am I the sea, or the monster of the deep, that you put me under guard?
13When I think my bed will comfort me and my couch will ease my complaint,
14even then you frighten me with dreams and terrify me with visions,
15so that I prefer strangling and death, rather than this body of mine.
16I despise my life; I would not live forever.
Let me alone; my days have no meaning.

17"What is man that you make so much of him, that you give him so much attention,
18that you examine him every morning and test him every moment?
19Will you never look away from me, or let me alone even for an instant?
20If I have sinned, what have I done to you, O watcher of men?
Why have you made me your target?
Have I become a burden to you?[b]
21Why do you not pardon my offenses and forgive my sins?
For I will soon lie down in the dust; you will search for me, but I will be no more."

Bildad

8 THEN BILDAD the Shuhite replied:

2"How long will you say such things?
Your words are a blustering wind.
3Does God pervert justice?
Does the Almighty pervert what is right?
4When your children sinned against him, he gave them over to the penalty of their sin.
5But if you will look to God and plead with the Almighty,

a 9 Hebrew *Sheol*   b 20 A few manuscripts of the Masoretic Text, an ancient Hebrew scribal tradition and Septuagint; most manuscripts of the Masoretic Text *I have become a burden to myself.*

Living Bible

7 "HOW MANKIND must struggle. A man's life is long and hard, like that of a slave. 2How he longs for the day to end. How he grinds on to the end of the week and his wages. 3And so to me also have been allotted months of frustration, these long and weary nights. 4When I go to bed I think, 'Oh, that it were morning,' and then I toss till dawn.

5"My skin is filled with worms and blackness. My flesh breaks open, full of pus. 6My life drags by—day after hopeless day. 7My life is but a breath, and nothing good is left. 8You see me now, but not for long. Soon you'll look upon me dead. 9As a cloud disperses and vanishes, so those who die shall go away forever—10gone forever from their family and their home—never to be seen again. 11Ah, let me express my anguish. Let me be free to speak out of the bitterness of my soul.

12"O God, am I some monster, that you never let me alone? 13, 14Even when I try to forget my misery in sleep, you terrify me with nightmares. 15I would rather die of strangulation than go on and on like this. 16I hate my life. Oh, let me alone for these few remaining days. 17What is mere man that you should spend your time persecuting him? 18Must you be his inquisitor every morning, and test him every moment of the day? 19Why won't you let me alone—even long enough to spit?

20"Has my sin harmed you, O God, Watcher of mankind? Why have you made me your target, and made my life so heavy a burden to me? 21Why not just pardon my sin and take it all away? For all too soon I'll lie down in the dust and die, and when you look for me, I shall be gone."

8 *BILDAD THE Shuhite replies to Job:*
2"How long will you go on like this, Job, blowing words around like wind? 3Does God twist justice? 4If your children sinned against him, and he punished them, 5and you begged Almighty God for them— 6if you were

New Revised Standard

Job: My Suffering Is without End

7 "DO NOT human beings have a hard service on earth,
   and are not their days like the days of a laborer?

2 Like a slave who longs for the shadow,
   and like laborers who look for their wages,

3 so I am allotted months of emptiness,
   and nights of misery are apportioned to me.

4 When I lie down I say, 'When shall I rise?'
   But the night is long,
   and I am full of tossing until dawn.

5 My flesh is clothed with worms and dirt;
   my skin hardens, then breaks out again.

6 My days are swifter than a weaver's shuttle,
   and come to their end without hope.[c]

7 "Remember that my life is a breath;
   my eye will never again see good.

8 The eye that beholds me will see me no more;
   while your eyes are upon me, I shall be gone.

9 As the cloud fades and vanishes,
   so those who go down to Sheol do not come up;

10 they return no more to their houses,
   nor do their places know them any more.

11 "Therefore I will not restrain my mouth;
   I will speak in the anguish of my spirit;
   I will complain in the bitterness of my soul.

12 Am I the Sea, or the Dragon,
   that you set a guard over me?

13 When I say, 'My bed will comfort me,
   my couch will ease my complaint,'

14 then you scare me with dreams
   and terrify me with visions,

15 so that I would choose strangling
   and death rather than this body.

16 I loathe my life; I would not live forever.
   Let me alone, for my days are a breath.

17 What are human beings, that you make so much of them,
   that you set your mind on them,

18 visit them every morning,
   test them every moment?

19 Will you not look away from me for a while,
   let me alone until I swallow my spittle?

20 If I sin, what do I do to you, you watcher of humanity?
   Why have you made me your target?
   Why have I become a burden to you?

21 Why do you not pardon my transgression
   and take away my iniquity?
   For now I shall lie in the earth;
   you will seek me, but I shall not be."

Bildad Speaks: Job Should Repent

8 THEN BILDAD the Shuhite answered:
2 "How long will you say these things,
   and the words of your mouth be a great wind?

3 Does God pervert justice?
   Or does the Almighty[d] pervert the right?

4 If your children sinned against him,
   he delivered them into the power of their transgression.

5 If you will seek God
   and make supplication to the Almighty,[d]

---

[c] Or *as the thread runs out*   [d] Traditional rendering of Heb *Shaddai*

King James

6If thou *wert* pure and upright; surely now he would awake for thee, and make the habitation of thy righteousness prosperous.

7Though thy beginning was small, yet thy latter end should greatly increase.

8For inquire, I pray thee, of the former age, and prepare thyself to the search of their fathers:

9(For we *are but of* yesterday, and know nothing, because our days upon earth *are* a shadow:)

10Shall not they teach thee, *and* tell thee, and utter words out of their heart?

11Can the rush grow up without mire? can the flag grow without water?

12Whilst it *is* yet in his greenness, *and* not cut down, it withereth before any *other* herb.

13So *are* the paths of all that forget God; and the hypocrite's hope shall perish:

14Whose hope shall be cut off, and whose trust *shall be* a spider's web.

15He shall lean upon his house, but it shall not stand: he shall hold it fast, but it shall not endure.

16He *is* green before the sun, and his branch shooteth forth in his garden.

17His roots are wrapped about the heap, *and* seeth the place of stones.

18If he destroy him from his place, then *it* shall deny him, *saying,* I have not seen thee.

19Behold, this *is* the joy of his way, and out of the earth shall others grow.

20Behold, God will not cast away a perfect *man,* neither will he help the evil doers:

21Till he fill thy mouth with laughing, and thy lips with rejoicing.

22They that hate thee shall be clothed with shame; and the dwellingplace of the wicked shall come to nought.

9 THEN JOB answered and said,
2I know *it is* so of a truth: but how should man be just with God?

3If he will contend with him, he cannot answer him one of a thousand.

4*He is* wise in heart, and mighty in strength: who hath hardened *himself* against him, and hath prospered?

5Which removeth the mountains, and they know not: which overturneth them in his anger.

6Which shaketh the earth out of her place, and the pillars thereof tremble.

7Which commandeth the sun, and it riseth not; and sealeth up the stars.

8Which alone spreadeth out the heavens, and treadeth upon the waves of the sea.

9Which maketh Arcturus, Orion, and Pleiades, and the chambers of the south.

10Which doeth great things past finding out; yea, and wonders without number.

New International

6if you are pure and upright,
    even now he will rouse himself on your
        behalf
    and restore you to your rightful place.
7Your beginnings will seem humble,
    so prosperous will your future be.

8"Ask the former generations
    and find out what their fathers learned,
9for we were born only yesterday and know
        nothing,
    and our days on earth are but a shadow.
10Will they not instruct you and tell you?
    Will they not bring forth words from their
        understanding?
11Can papyrus grow tall where there is no marsh?
    Can reeds thrive without water?
12While still growing and uncut,
    they wither more quickly than grass.
13Such is the destiny of all who forget God;
    so perishes the hope of the godless.
14What he trusts in is fragilea;
    what he relies on is a spider's web.
15He leans on his web, but it gives way;
    he clings to it, but it does not hold.
16He is like a well-watered plant in the sunshine,
    spreading its shoots over the garden;
17it entwines its roots around a pile of rocks
    and looks for a place among the stones.
18But when it is torn from its spot,
    that place disowns it and says, 'I never saw
        you.'
19Surely its life withers away,
    andb from the soil other plants grow.

20"Surely God does not reject a blameless man
    or strengthen the hands of evildoers.
21He will yet fill your mouth with laughter
    and your lips with shouts of joy.
22Your enemies will be clothed in shame,
    and the tents of the wicked will be no more."

Job
9 THEN JOB replied:

2"Indeed, I know that this is true.
    But how can a mortal be righteous before
        God?
3Though one wished to dispute with him,
    he could not answer him one time out of a
        thousand.
4His wisdom is profound, his power is vast.
    Who has resisted him and come out
        unscathed?
5He moves mountains without their knowing it
    and overturns them in his anger.
6He shakes the earth from its place
    and makes its pillars tremble.
7He speaks to the sun and it does not shine;
    he seals off the light of the stars.
8He alone stretches out the heavens
    and treads on the waves of the sea.
9He is the Maker of the Bear and Orion,
    the Pleiades and the constellations of the
        south.
10He performs wonders that cannot be fathomed,
    miracles that cannot be counted.

---

a *14* The meaning of the Hebrew for this word is uncertain.   b *19* Or *Surely all the joy it has / is that*

Living Bible

pure and good, he would hear your prayer, and answer you, and bless you with a happy home. 7And though you started with little, you would end with much.

8"Read the history books and see— 9for we were born but yesterday and know so little; our days here on earth are as transient as shadows. 10But the wisdom of the past will teach you. The experience of others will speak to you, reminding you that 11, 12, 13those who forget God have no hope. They are like rushes without any mire to grow in; or grass without water to keep it alive. Suddenly it begins to wither, even before it is cut. 14A man without God is trusting in a spider's web. Everything he counts on will collapse. 15If he counts on his home for security, it won't last. 16At dawn he seems so strong and virile, like a green plant; his branches spread across the garden. 17His roots are in the stream, down among the stones. 18But when he disappears, he isn't even missed! 19That is all he can look forward to! And others spring up from the earth to replace him!

20"But look! God will not cast away a good man, nor prosper evildoers. 21He will yet fill your mouth with laughter and your lips with shouts of joy. 22Those who hate you shall be clothed with shame, and the wicked destroyed."

9 *JOB'S REPLY:*
2"Yes, I know all that. You're not telling me anything new. But how can a man be truly good in the eyes of God? 3If God decides to argue with him, can a man answer even one question of a thousand he asks? 4For God is so wise and so mighty. Who has ever opposed him successfully?

5"Suddenly he moves the mountains, overturning them in his anger. 6He shakes the earth to its foundations. 7The sun won't rise, the stars won't shine, if he commands it so! 8Only he has stretched the heavens out and stalked along the seas. 9He made the Bear, Orion and the Pleiades, and the constellations of the southern Zodiac.

10"He does incredible miracles, too many to count.

New Revised Standard

6 if you are pure and upright,
  surely then he will rouse himself for you
  and restore to you your rightful place.
7 Though your beginning was small,
  your latter days will be very great.

8 "For inquire now of bygone generations,
  and consider what their ancestors have
    found;
9 for we are but of yesterday, and we know
    nothing,
  for our days on earth are but a shadow.
10 Will they not teach you and tell you
  and utter words out of their understanding?

11 "Can papyrus grow where there is no marsh?
  Can reeds flourish where there is no water?
12 While yet in flower and not cut down,
  they wither before any other plant.
13 Such are the paths of all who forget God;
  the hope of the godless shall perish.
14 Their confidence is gossamer,
  a spider's house their trust.
15 If one leans against its house, it will not
    stand;
  if one lays hold of it, it will not endure.
16 The wicked thrive[c] before the sun,
  and their shoots spread over the garden.
17 Their roots twine around the stoneheap;
  they live among the rocks.[d]
18 If they are destroyed from their place,
  then it will deny them, saying, 'I have
      never seen you.'
19 See, these are their happy ways,[e]
  and out of the earth still others will spring.

20 "See, God will not reject a blameless person,
  nor take the hand of evildoers.
21 He will yet fill your mouth with laughter,
  and your lips with shouts of joy.
22 Those who hate you will be clothed with
    shame,
  and the tent of the wicked will be no
      more."

Job Replies: There Is No Mediator

9 THEN JOB answered:
2 "Indeed I know that this is so;
  but how can a mortal be just before God?
3 If one wished to contend with him,
  one could not answer him once in a
      thousand.
4 He is wise in heart, and mighty in strength
  —who has resisted him, and succeeded?—
5 he who removes mountains, and they do not
    know it,
  when he overturns them in his anger;
6 who shakes the earth out of its place,
  and its pillars tremble;
7 who commands the sun, and it does not rise;
  who seals up the stars;
8 who alone stretched out the heavens
  and trampled the waves of the Sea;[f]
9 who made the Bear and Orion,
  the Pleiades and the chambers of the south;
10 who does great things beyond understanding,
  and marvelous things without number.

---

c Heb *He thrives*   d Gk Vg: Meaning of Heb uncertain   e Meaning of Heb uncertain   f Or *trampled the back of the sea dragon*

King James

11Lo, he goeth by me, and I see *him* not: he passeth on also, but I perceive him not.

12Behold, he taketh away, who can hinder him? who will say unto him, What doest thou?

13*If* God will not withdraw his anger, the proud helpers do stoop under him.

14How much less shall I answer him, *and* choose out my words *to reason* with him?

15Whom, though I were righteous, *yet* would I not answer, *but* I would make supplication to my judge.

16If I had called, and he had answered me; *yet* would I not believe that he had hearkened unto my voice.

17For he breaketh me with a tempest, and multiplieth my wounds without cause.

18He will not suffer me to take my breath, but filleth me with bitterness.

19If *I speak* of strength, lo, *he is* strong: and if of judgment, who shall set me a time *to plead?*

20If I justify myself, mine own mouth shall condemn me: *if I say,* I *am* perfect, it shall also prove me perverse.

21*Though* I *were* perfect, *yet* would I not know my soul: I would despise my life.

22This *is* one *thing,* therefore I said *it,* He destroyeth the perfect and the wicked.

23If the scourge slay suddenly, he will laugh at the trial of the innocent.

24The earth is given into the hand of the wicked: he covereth the faces of the judges thereof; if not, where, *and* who *is* he?

25Now my days are swifter than a post: they flee away, they see no good.

26They are passed away as the swift ships: as the eagle *that* hasteth to the prey.

27If I say, I will forget my complaint, I will leave off my heaviness, and comfort *myself:*

28I am afraid of all my sorrows, I know that thou wilt not hold me innocent.

29*If* I be wicked, why then labour I in vain?

30If I wash myself with snow water, and make my hands never so clean;

31Yet shalt thou plunge me in the ditch, and mine own clothes shall abhor me.

32For *he is* not a man, as I *am, that* I should answer him, *and* we should come together in judgment.

33Neither is there any daysman betwixt us, *that* might lay his hand upon us both.

34Let him take his rod away from me, and let not his fear terrify me:

35*Then* would I speak, and not fear him; but *it is* not so with me.

10 MY SOUL is weary of my life; I will leave my complaint upon myself; I will speak in the bitterness of my soul.

New International

11When he passes me, I cannot see him;
    when he goes by, I cannot perceive him.
12If he snatches away, who can stop him?
    Who can say to him, 'What are you doing?'
13God does not restrain his anger;
    even the cohorts of Rahab cowered at his
        feet.

14"How then can I dispute with him?
    How can I find words to argue with him?
15Though I were innocent, I could not answer
        him;
    I could only plead with my Judge for mercy.
16Even if I summoned him and he responded,
    I do not believe he would give me a hearing.
17He would crush me with a storm
    and multiply my wounds for no reason.
18He would not let me regain my breath
    but would overwhelm me with misery.
19If it is a matter of strength, he is mighty!
    And if it is a matter of justice, who will
        summon him[a]?
20Even if I were innocent, my mouth would
        condemn me;
    if I were blameless, it would pronounce me
        guilty.

21"Although I am blameless,
    I have no concern for myself;
    I despise my own life.
22It is all the same; that is why I say,
    'He destroys both the blameless and the
        wicked.'
23When a scourge brings sudden death,
    he mocks the despair of the innocent.
24When a land falls into the hands of the wicked,
    he blindfolds its judges.
    If it is not he, then who is it?

25"My days are swifter than a runner;
    they fly away without a glimpse of joy.
26They skim past like boats of papyrus,
    like eagles swooping down on their prey.
27If I say, 'I will forget my complaint,
    I will change my expression, and smile,'
28I still dread all my sufferings,
    for I know you will not hold me innocent.
29Since I am already found guilty,
    why should I struggle in vain?
30Even if I washed myself with soap[b]
    and my hands with washing soda,
31you would plunge me into a slime pit
    so that even my clothes would detest me.

32"He is not a man like me that I might answer
        him,
    that we might confront each other in court.
33If only there were someone to arbitrate between
        us,
    to lay his hand upon us both,
34someone to remove God's rod from me,
    so that his terror would frighten me no more.
35Then I would speak up without fear of him,
    but as it now stands with me, I cannot.

10 "I LOATHE my very life;
    therefore I will give free rein to my
        complaint
    and speak out in the bitterness of my soul.

---

a *19* See Septuagint; Hebrew *me.*   b *30* Or *snow*

Living Bible

11He passes by, invisible; he moves along, but I don't see him go. 12When he sends death to snatch a man away,c who can stop him? Who dares to ask him, 'What are you doing?'

13"And God does not abate his anger. The pride of mand collapses before him. 14And who am I that I should try to argue with Almighty God, or even reason with him? 15Even if I were sinless I wouldn't say a word. I would only plead for mercy. 16And even if my prayers were answered I could scarce believe that he had heard my cry. 17For he is the one who destroys, and multiplies my wounds without a cause. 18He will not let me breathe, but fills me with bitter sorrows. 19He alone is strong and just.

20"But I? Am I righteous? My own mouth says no. Even if I were perfect, God would prove me wicked. 21And even if I am utterly innocent, I dare not think of it. I despise what I am. 22Innocent or evil, it is all the same to him, for he destroys both kinds. 23He will laugh when calamity crushes the innocent. 24The whole earth is in the hands of the wicked. God blinds the eyes of the judges and lets them be unfair. If not he, then who?

25"My life passes swiftly away, filled with tragedy. 26My years disappear like swift ships, like the eagle that swoops upon its prey.

27"If I decided to forget my complaints against God, to end my sadness and be cheerful, 28then he would pour even greater sorrows upon me. For I know that you will not hold me innocent, 29but will condemn me. So what's the use of trying? 30Even if I were to wash myself with purest water and cleanse my hands with lye to make them utterly clean, 31even so you would plunge me into the ditch and mud; and even my clothing would be less filthy than you consider me to be!

32, 33"And I cannot defend myself, for you are no mere man as I am. If you were, then we could discuss it fairly, but there is no umpire between us, no middle man, no mediator to bring us together. 34Oh, let him stop beating me, so that I need no longer live in terror of his punishment. 35Then I could speak without fear to him, and tell him boldly that I am not guilty.

New Revised Standard

11 Look, he passes by me, and I do not see him;
       he moves on, but I do not perceive him.
12 He snatches away; who can stop him?
       Who will say to him, 'What are you
           doing?'

13 "God will not turn back his anger;
       the helpers of Rahab bowed beneath him.
14 How then can I answer him,
       choosing my words with him?
15 Though I am innocent, I cannot answer him;
       I must appeal for mercy to my accuser.e
16 If I summoned him and he answered me,
       I do not believe that he would listen to my
           voice.
17 For he crushes me with a tempest,
       and multiplies my wounds without cause;
18 he will not let me get my breath,
       but fills me with bitterness.
19 If it is a contest of strength, he is the strong
           one!
       If it is a matter of justice, who can summon
           him?f
20 Though I am innocent, my own mouth would
           condemn me;
       though I am blameless, he would prove me
           perverse.
21 I am blameless; I do not know myself;
       I loathe my life.
22 It is all one; therefore I say,
       he destroys both the blameless and the
           wicked.
23 When disaster brings sudden death,
       he mocks at the calamityg of the innocent.
24 The earth is given into the hand of the
           wicked;
       he covers the eyes of its judges—
       if it is not he, who then is it?

25 "My days are swifter than a runner;
       they flee away, they see no good.
26 They go by like skiffs of reed,
       like an eagle swooping on the prey.
27 If I say, 'I will forget my complaint;
       I will put off my sad countenance and be of
           good cheer,'
28 I become afraid of all my suffering,
       for I know you will not hold me innocent.
29 I shall be condemned;
       why then do I labor in vain?
30 If I wash myself with soap
       and cleanse my hands with lye,
31 yet you will plunge me into filth,
       and my own clothes will abhor me.
32 For he is not a mortal, as I am, that I might
           answer him,
       that we should come to trial together.
33 There is no umpireh between us,
       who might lay his hand on us both.
34 If he would take his rod away from me,
       and not let dread of him terrify me,
35 then I would speak without fear of him,
       for I know I am not what I am thought to
           be.i

Job: I Loathe My Life

10 "I AM weary of living. Let me complain freely. I will speak in my sorrow and bitterness. 2I will

10 "I LOATHE my life;
       I will give free utterance to my complaint;
       I will speak in the bitterness of my soul.

c 9:12 *to snatch a man away,* literally, "he seizes." d 9:13 *The pride of man,* or, "the helpers of Rahab."

e Or *for my right* f Compare Gk: Heb *me* g Meaning of Heb uncertain h Another reading is *Would that there were an umpire* i Cn: Heb *for I am not so in myself*

King James

2I will say unto God, Do not condemn me; show me wherefore thou contendest with me.

3*Is it* good unto thee that thou shouldest oppress, that thou shouldest despise the work of thine hands, and shine upon the counsel of the wicked?

4Hast thou eyes of flesh? or seest thou as man seeth?

5*Are* thy days as the days of man? *are* thy years as man's days,

6That thou inquirest after mine iniquity, and searchest after my sin?

7Thou knowest that I am not wicked; and *there is* none that can deliver out of thine hand.

8Thine hands have made me and fashioned me together round about; yet thou dost destroy me.

9Remember, I beseech thee, that thou hast made me as the clay; and wilt thou bring me into dust again?

10Hast thou not poured me out as milk, and curdled me like cheese?

11Thou hast clothed me with skin and flesh, and hast fenced me with bones and sinews.

12Thou hast granted me life and favour, and thy visitation hath preserved my spirit.

13And these *things* hast thou hid in thine heart: I know that this *is* with thee.

14If I sin, then thou markest me, and thou wilt not acquit me from mine iniquity.

15If I be wicked, woe unto me; and *if* I be righteous, *yet* will I not lift up my head. *I am* full of confusion; therefore see thou mine affliction.

16For it increaseth. Thou huntest me as a fierce lion: and again thou showest thyself marvellous upon me.

17Thou renewest thy witnesses against me, and increasest thine indignation upon me; changes and war *are* against me.

18Wherefore then hast thou brought me forth out of the womb? Oh that I had given up the ghost, and no eye had seen me!

19I should have been as though I had not been; I should have been carried from the womb to the grave.

20*Are* not my days few? cease *then, and* let me alone, that I may take comfort a little,

21Before I go *whence* I shall not return, *even* to the land of darkness and the shadow of death;

22A land of darkness, as darkness *itself; and* of the shadow of death, without any order, and *where* the light *is* as darkness.

11 THEN ANSWERED Zophar the Naamathite, and said,

2Should not the multitude of words be answered? and should a man full of talk be justified?

3Should thy lies make men hold their peace? and when thou mockest, shall no man make thee ashamed?

New International

2I will say to God: Do not condemn me,
   but tell me what charges you have against
    me.
3Does it please you to oppress me,
   to spurn the work of your hands,
   while you smile on the schemes of the
    wicked?
4Do you have eyes of flesh?
   Do you see as a mortal sees?
5Are your days like those of a mortal
   or your years like those of a man,
6that you must search out my faults
   and probe after my sin—
7though you know that I am not guilty
   and that no one can rescue me from your
    hand?

8"Your hands shaped me and made me.
   Will you now turn and destroy me?
9Remember that you molded me like clay.
   Will you now turn me to dust again?
10Did you not pour me out like milk
   and curdle me like cheese,
11clothe me with skin and flesh
   and knit me together with bones and sinews?
12You gave me life and showed me kindness,
   and in your providence watched over my
    spirit.

13"But this is what you concealed in your heart,
   and I know that this was in your mind:
14If I sinned, you would be watching me
   and would not let my offense go unpunished.
15If I am guilty—woe to me!
   Even if I am innocent, I cannot lift my head,
   for I am full of shame
   and drowned in[a] my affliction.
16If I hold my head high, you stalk me like a lion
   and again display your awesome power
    against me.
17You bring new witnesses against me
   and increase your anger toward me;
   your forces come against me wave upon
    wave.

18"Why then did you bring me out of the womb?
   I wish I had died before any eye saw me.
19If only I had never come into being,
   or had been carried straight from the womb to
    the grave!
20Are not my few days almost over?
   Turn away from me so I can have a
    moment's joy
21before I go to the place of no return,
   to the land of gloom and deep shadow,[b]
22to the land of deepest night,
   of deep shadow and disorder,
   where even the light is like darkness."

Zophar

11 THEN ZOPHAR the Naamathite replied:

2"Are all these words to go unanswered?
   Is this talker to be vindicated?
3Will your idle talk reduce men to silence?
   Will no one rebuke you when you mock?

---

a 15 Or *and aware of*   b 21 Or *and the shadow of death*; also in verse 22

Living Bible

say to God, 'Don't just condemn me—tell me *why* you are doing it. ³Does it really seem right to you to oppress and despise me, a man you have made; and to send joy and prosperity to the wicked? ⁴⁻⁷Are you unjust[c] like men? Is your life so short that you must hound me for sins you know full well I've not committed? Is it because you know no one can save me from your hand?

⁸"'You have made me, and yet you destroy me. ⁹Oh, please remember that I'm made of dust—will you change me back again to dust so soon? ¹⁰You have already poured me from bottle to bottle like milk, and curdled me like cheese. ¹¹You gave me skin and flesh and knit together bones and sinews. ¹²You gave me life and were so kind and loving to me, and I was preserved by your care.

¹³, ¹⁴'Yet all the time your real motive in making me was to destroy me if I sinned; and to refuse to forgive my iniquity. ¹⁵Just the slightest wickedness, and I am done for. And if I'm good, that doesn't count. I am filled with frustration. ¹⁶If I start to get up off the ground, you leap upon me like a lion and quickly finish me off. ¹⁷Again and again you witness against me and pour out an ever-increasing volume of wrath upon me and bring fresh armies against me.

¹⁸"'Why then did you even let me be born? Why didn't you let me die at birth? ¹⁹Then I would have been spared this miserable existence. I would have gone directly from the womb to the grave. ²⁰, ²¹Can't you see how little time I have left? Oh, let me alone that I may have a little moment of comfort before I leave for the land of darkness and the shadow of death, never to return— ²²a land as dark as midnight, a land of the shadow of death where only confusion reigns, and where the brightest light is dark as midnight.'"

11 ZOPHAR THE Naamathite replies to Job: ²"Shouldn't someone stem this torrent of words? Is a man proved right by all this talk? ³Should I remain silent while you boast? When you mock God, shouldn't someone make you ashamed? ⁴You claim you

New Revised Standard

2 I will say to God, Do not condemn me;
　　let me know why you contend against me.
3 Does it seem good to you to oppress,
　　to despise the work of your hands
　　and favor the schemes of the wicked?
4 Do you have eyes of flesh?
　　Do you see as humans see?
5 Are your days like the days of mortals,
　　or your years like human years,
6 that you seek out my iniquity
　　and search for my sin,
7 although you know that I am not guilty,
　　and there is no one to deliver out of your
　　hand?
8 Your hands fashioned and made me;
　　and now you turn and destroy me.[d]
9 Remember that you fashioned me like clay;
　　and will you turn me to dust again?
10 Did you not pour me out like milk
　　and curdle me like cheese?
11 You clothed me with skin and flesh,
　　and knit me together with bones and sinews.
12 You have granted me life and steadfast love,
　　and your care has preserved my spirit.
13 Yet these things you hid in your heart;
　　I know that this was your purpose.
14 If I sin, you watch me,
　　and do not acquit me of my iniquity.
15 If I am wicked, woe to me!
　　If I am righteous, I cannot lift up my head,
　　for I am filled with disgrace
　　and look upon my affliction.
16 Bold as a lion you hunt me;
　　you repeat your exploits against me.
17 You renew your witnesses against me,
　　and increase your vexation toward me;
　　you bring fresh troops against me.[e]

18 "Why did you bring me forth from the womb?
　　Would that I had died before any eye had
　　seen me,
19 and were as though I had not been,
　　carried from the womb to the grave.
20 Are not the days of my life few?[f]
　　Let me alone, that I may find a little
　　comfort[g]
21 before I go, never to return,
　　to the land of gloom and deep darkness,
22 the land of gloom[h] and chaos,
　　where light is like darkness."

Zophar Speaks: Job's Guilt Deserves Punishment

11 THEN ZOPHAR the Naamathite answered:
2 "Should a multitude of words go
　　unanswered,
　　and should one full of talk be vindicated?
3 Should your babble put others to silence,
　　and when you mock, shall no one shame
　　you?

---

d Cn Compare Gk Syr: Heb *made me together all around, and you destroy me* 　e Cn Compare Gk: Heb *toward me; changes and a troop are with me*　f Cn Compare Gk Syr: Heb *Are not my days few? Let him cease!*　g Heb *that I may brighten up a little*　h Heb *gloom as darkness, deep darkness*

King James

4For thou hast said, My doctrine *is* pure, and I am clean in thine eyes.

5But oh that God would speak, and open his lips against thee;

6And that he would show thee the secrets of wisdom, that *they are* double to that which is! Know therefore that God exacteth of thee *less* than thine iniquity *deserveth.*

7Canst thou by searching find out God? canst thou find out the Almighty unto perfection?

8*It is* as high as heaven; what canst thou do? deeper than hell; what canst thou know?

9The measure thereof *is* longer than the earth, and broader than the sea.

10If he cut off, and shut up, or gather together, then who can hinder him?

11For he knoweth vain men: he seeth wickedness also; will he not then consider *it?*

12For vain man would be wise, though man be born *like* a wild ass's colt.

13If thou prepare thine heart, and stretch out thine hands toward him;

14If iniquity *be* in thine hand, put it far away, and let not wickedness dwell in thy tabernacles.

15For then shalt thou lift up thy face without spot; yea, thou shalt be stedfast, and shalt not fear:

16Because thou shalt forget *thy* misery, *and* remember *it* as waters *that* pass away:

17And *thine* age shall be clearer than the noonday; thou shalt shine forth, thou shalt be as the morning.

18And thou shalt be secure, because there is hope; yea, thou shalt dig *about thee, and* thou shalt take thy rest in safety.

19Also thou shalt lie down, and none shall make *thee* afraid; yea, many shall make suit unto thee.

20But the eyes of the wicked shall fail, and they shall not escape, and their hope *shall be as* the giving up of the ghost.

New International

4You say to God, 'My beliefs are flawless
    and I am pure in your sight.'
5Oh, how I wish that God would speak,
    that he would open his lips against you
6and disclose to you the secrets of wisdom,
    for true wisdom has two sides.
    Know this: God has even forgotten some of
        your sin.

7"Can you fathom the mysteries of God?
    Can you probe the limits of the Almighty?
8They are higher than the heavens—what can
        you do?
    They are deeper than the depths of the
        grave[a]—what can you know?
9Their measure is longer than the earth
    and wider than the sea.

10"If he comes along and confines you in prison
    and convenes a court, who can oppose him?
11Surely he recognizes deceitful men;
    and when he sees evil, does he not take note?
12But a witless man can no more become wise
    than a wild donkey's colt can be born a
        man.[b]

13"Yet if you devote your heart to him
    and stretch out your hands to him,
14if you put away the sin that is in your hand
    and allow no evil to dwell in your tent,
15then you will lift up your face without shame;
    you will stand firm and without fear.
16You will surely forget your trouble,
    recalling it only as waters gone by.
17Life will be brighter than noonday,
    and darkness will become like morning.
18You will be secure, because there is hope;
    you will look about you and take your rest in
        safety.
19You will lie down, with no one to make you
        afraid,
    and many will court your favor.
20But the eyes of the wicked will fail,
    and escape will elude them;
    their hope will become a dying gasp."

12 AND JOB answered and said,

2No doubt but ye *are* the people, and wisdom shall die with you.

3But I have understanding as well as you; I *am* not inferior to you: yea, who knoweth not such things as these?

4I am *as* one mocked of his neighbour, who calleth upon God, and he answereth him: the just upright *man is* laughed to scorn.

5He that is ready to slip with *his* feet *is as* a lamp despised in the thought of him that is at ease.

Job

12 THEN JOB replied:

2"Doubtless you are the people,
    and wisdom will die with you!
3But I have a mind as well as you;
    I am not inferior to you.
    Who does not know all these things?

4"I have become a laughingstock to my friends,
    though I called upon God and he answered—
    a mere laughingstock, though righteous and
        blameless!
5Men at ease have contempt for misfortune
    as the fate of those whose feet are slipping.

---

a 8 Hebrew *than Sheol*   b 12 Or *wild donkey can be born tame*

Living Bible

are pure in the eyes of God! 5Oh, that God would speak and tell you what he thinks! 6Oh, that he would make you truly see yourself, for he knows everything you've done. Listen! God is doubtless punishing you far less than you deserve!

7"Do you know the mind and purposes of God? Will long searching make them known to you? Are you qualified to judge the Almighty? 8He is as faultless as heaven is high—but who are you? His mind is fathomless—what can you know in comparison? 9His Spirit is broader than the earth and wider than the sea. 10If he rushes in and makes an arrest, and calls the court to order, who is going to stop him? 11For he knows perfectly all the faults and sins of mankind; he sees all sin without searching.

12"Mere man is as likely to be wise, as a wild donkey's colt is likely to be born a man!

13, 14"Before you turn to God and stretch out your hands to him, get rid of your sins and leave all iniquity behind you. 15Only then, without the spots of sin to defile you, can you walk steadily forward to God without fear. 16Only then can you forget your misery. It will all be in the past. 17And your life will be cloudless; any darkness will be as bright as morning!

18"You will have courage because you will have hope. You will take your time, and rest in safety. 19You will lie down unafraid and many will look to you for help. 20But the wicked shall find no way to escape; their only hope is death."

12 *JOB'S REPLY:*
2"Yes, I realize you know everything! All wisdom will die with you! 3Well, I know a few things myself—you are no better than I am. And who doesn't know these things you've been saying? 4I, the man who begged God for help, and God answered him, have become a laughingstock to my neighbors. Yes, I, a righteous man, am now the man they scoff at. 5Meanwhile, the rich mock those in trouble and are quick to despise all those in need. 6For robbers prosper. Go ahead and

New Revised Standard

4 For you say, 'My conduct[c] is pure,
      and I am clean in God's[d] sight.'
5 But oh, that God would speak,
      and open his lips to you,
6 and that he would tell you the secrets of
         wisdom!
   For wisdom is many-sided.[e]
   Know then that God exacts of you less than
         your guilt deserves.

7 "Can you find out the deep things of God?
   Can you find out the limit of the
         Almighty?[f]
8 It is higher than heaven[g]—what can you do?
   Deeper than Sheol—what can you know?
9 Its measure is longer than the earth,
      and broader than the sea.
10 If he passes through, and imprisons,
      and assembles for judgment, who can hinder
         him?
11 For he knows those who are worthless;
      when he sees iniquity, will he not consider
         it?
12 But a stupid person will get understanding,
      when a wild ass is born human.[e]

13 "If you direct your heart rightly,
      you will stretch out your hands toward him.
14 If iniquity is in your hand, put it far away,
      and do not let wickedness reside in your
         tents.
15 Surely then you will lift up your face without
         blemish;
      you will be secure, and will not fear.
16 You will forget your misery;
      you will remember it as waters that have
         passed away.
17 And your life will be brighter than the
         noonday;
      its darkness will be like the morning.
18 And you will have confidence, because there
         is hope;
      you will be protected[h] and take your rest in
         safety.
19 You will lie down, and no one will make you
         afraid;
      many will entreat your favor.
20 But the eyes of the wicked will fail;
      all way of escape will be lost to them,
      and their hope is to breathe their last."

Job Replies: I Am a Laughingstock

12 THEN JOB answered:
2 "No doubt you are the people,
      and wisdom will die with you.
3 But I have understanding as well as you;
      I am not inferior to you.
   Who does not know such things as these?
4 I am a laughingstock to my friends;
   I, who called upon God and he answered
         me,
   a just and blameless man, I am a
         laughingstock.
5 Those at ease have contempt for misfortune,[e]
   but it is ready for those whose feet are
         unstable.

---

c Gk: Heb *teaching*   d Heb *your*   e Meaning of Heb uncertain
f Traditional rendering of Heb *Shaddai*   g Heb *The heights of heaven*   h Or
you will look around

King James

6The tabernacles of robbers prosper, and they that provoke God are secure; into whose hand God bringeth *abundantly*.

7But ask now the beasts, and they shall teach thee; and the fowls of the air, and they shall tell thee:

8Or speak to the earth, and it shall teach thee: and the fishes of the sea shall declare unto thee.

9Who knoweth not in all these that the hand of the LORD hath wrought this?

10In whose hand *is* the soul of every living thing, and the breath of all mankind.

11Doth not the ear try words? and the mouth taste his meat?

12With the ancient *is* wisdom; and in length of days understanding.

13With him *is* wisdom and strength, he hath counsel and understanding.

14Behold, he breaketh down, and it cannot be built again: he shutteth up a man, and there can be no opening.

15Behold, he withholdeth the waters, and they dry up: also he sendeth them out, and they overturn the earth.

16With him *is* strength and wisdom: the deceived and the deceiver *are* his.

17He leadeth counsellors away spoiled, and maketh the judges fools.

18He looseth the bond of kings, and girdeth their loins with a girdle.

19He leadeth princes away spoiled, and overthroweth the mighty.

20He removeth away the speech of the trusty, and taketh away the understanding of the aged.

21He poureth contempt upon princes, and weakeneth the strength of the mighty.

22He discovereth deep things out of darkness, and bringeth out to light the shadow of death.

23He increaseth the nations, and destroyeth them: he enlargeth the nations, and straiteneth them *again*.

24He taketh away the heart of the chief of the people of the earth, and causeth them to wander in a wilderness *where there is* no way.

25They grope in the dark without light, and he maketh them to stagger like *a* drunken *man*.

13 LO, MINE eye hath seen all *this*, mine ear hath heard and understood it.

2What ye know, *the same* do I know also: I *am* not inferior unto you.

3Surely I would speak to the Almighty, and I desire to reason with God.

4But ye *are* forgers of lies, ye *are* all physicians of no value.

5O that ye would altogether hold your peace! and it should be your wisdom.

6Hear now my reasoning, and hearken to the pleadings of my lips.

7Will ye speak wickedly for God? and talk deceitfully for him?

8Will ye accept his person? will ye contend for God?

9Is it good that he should search you out? or as one man mocketh another, do ye *so* mock him?

New International

6The tents of marauders are undisturbed,
　and those who provoke God are secure—
　those who carry their god in their hands.[a]

7"But ask the animals, and they will teach you,
　or the birds of the air, and they will tell you;

8or speak to the earth, and it will teach you,
　or let the fish of the sea inform you.

9Which of all these does not know
　that the hand of the LORD has done this?

10In his hand is the life of every creature
　and the breath of all mankind.

11Does not the ear test words
　as the tongue tastes food?

12Is not wisdom found among the aged?
　Does not long life bring understanding?

13"To God belong wisdom and power;
　counsel and understanding are his.

14What he tears down cannot be rebuilt;
　the man he imprisons cannot be released.

15If he holds back the waters, there is drought;
　if he lets them loose, they devastate the land.

16To him belong strength and victory;
　both deceived and deceiver are his.

17He leads counselors away stripped
　and makes fools of judges.

18He takes off the shackles put on by kings
　and ties a loincloth[b] around their waist.

19He leads priests away stripped
　and overthrows men long established.

20He silences the lips of trusted advisers
　and takes away the discernment of elders.

21He pours contempt on nobles
　and disarms the mighty.

22He reveals the deep things of darkness
　and brings deep shadows into the light.

23He makes nations great, and destroys them;
　he enlarges nations, and disperses them.

24He deprives the leaders of the earth of their reason;
　he sends them wandering through a trackless waste.

25They grope in darkness with no light;
　he makes them stagger like drunkards.

13 "MY EYES have seen all this,
　my ears have heard and understood it.

2What you know, I also know;
　I am not inferior to you.

3But I desire to speak to the Almighty
　and to argue my case with God.

4You, however, smear me with lies;
　you are worthless physicians, all of you!

5If only you would be altogether silent!
　For you, that would be wisdom.

6Hear now my argument;
　listen to the plea of my lips.

7Will you speak wickedly on God's behalf?
　Will you speak deceitfully for him?

8Will you show him partiality?
　Will you argue the case for God?

9Would it turn out well if he examined you?
　Could you deceive him as you might deceive men?

Living Bible

provoke God—it makes no difference! He will supply your every need anyway!

7, 8, 9 "Who doesn't know that the Lord does things like that? Ask the dumbest beast—he knows that it is so; ask the birds—they will tell you; or let the earth teach you, or the fish of the sea. 10For the soul of every living thing is in the hand of God, and the breath of all mankind. 11Just as my mouth can taste good food, so my mind tastes truth when I hear it. 12And as you say, older men like me[c] are wise. They understand. 13But true wisdom and power are God's. He alone knows what we should do; he understands.

14"And how great is his might! What he destroys can't be rebuilt. When he closes in on a man, there is no escape. 15He withholds the rain, and the earth becomes a desert; he sends the storms, and floods the ground. 16Yes, with him is strength and wisdom. Deceivers and deceived are both his slaves.

17"He makes fools of counselors and judges. 18He reduces kings to slaves and frees their servants. 19Priests are led away as slaves. He overthrows the mighty. 20He takes away the voice of orators, and the insight of the elders. 21He pours contempt upon princes, and weakens the strong. 22He floods the darkness with light, even the dark shadow of death. 23He raises up a nation and then destroys it. He makes it great, and then reduces it to nothing. 24, 25He takes away the understanding of presidents and kings, and leaves them wandering, lost and groping, without a guiding light.

13 "LOOK, I have seen many instances such as you describe. I understand what you are saying. 2I know as much as you do. I'm not stupid. 3Oh, how I long to speak directly to the Almighty. I want to talk this over with God himself. 4For you are misinterpreting the whole thing. You are doctors who don't know what they are doing. 5Oh, please be quiet! That would be your highest wisdom.

6"Listen to me now, to my reasons for what I think, and to my pleadings.

7"Must you go on 'speaking for God' when he never once has said the things that you are putting in his mouth? 8Does God want your help if you are going to twist the truth for him? 9Be careful that he doesn't find out what you are doing! Or do you think you can fool God as well as men? 10No, you will be in serious trouble

New Revised Standard

6   The tents of robbers are at peace,
       and those who provoke God are secure,
       who bring their god in their hands.[d]

7   "But ask the animals, and they will teach you;
       the birds of the air, and they will tell you;
8   ask the plants of the earth,[e] and they will
           teach you;
       and the fish of the sea will declare to you.
9   Who among all these does not know
       that the hand of the LORD has done this?
10 In his hand is the life of every living thing
       and the breath of every human being.
11 Does not the ear test words
       as the palate tastes food?
12 Is wisdom with the aged,
       and understanding in length of days?

13 "With God[f] are wisdom and strength;
       he has counsel and understanding.
14 If he tears down, no one can rebuild;
       if he shuts someone in, no one can open up.
15 If he withholds the waters, they dry up;
       if he sends them out, they overwhelm the
           land.
16 With him are strength and wisdom;
       the deceived and the deceiver are his.
17 He leads counselors away stripped,
       and makes fools of judges.
18 He looses the sash of kings,
       and binds a waistcloth on their loins.
19 He leads priests away stripped,
       and overthrows the mighty.
20 He deprives of speech those who are trusted,
       and takes away the discernment of the
           elders.
21 He pours contempt on princes,
       and looses the belt of the strong.
22 He uncovers the deeps out of darkness,
       and brings deep darkness to light.
23 He makes nations great, then destroys them;
       he enlarges nations, then leads them away.
24 He strips understanding from the leaders[g] of
           the earth,
       and makes them wander in a pathless waste.
25 They grope in the dark without light;
       he makes them stagger like a drunkard.

13 "LOOK, MY eye has seen all this,
       my ear has heard and understood it.
2   What you know, I also know;
       I am not inferior to you.
3   But I would speak to the Almighty,[h]
       and I desire to argue my case with God.
4   As for you, you whitewash with lies;
       all of you are worthless physicians.
5   If you would only keep silent,
       that would be your wisdom!
6   Hear now my reasoning,
       and listen to the pleadings of my lips.
7   Will you speak falsely for God,
       and speak deceitfully for him?
8   Will you show partiality toward him,
       will you plead the case for God?
9   Will it be well with you when he searches you
           out?
       Or can you deceive him, as one person
           deceives another?

---

c 12:12 older men like me, implied.

d Or whom God brought forth by his hand; Meaning of Heb uncertain   e Or speak to the earth   f Heb him   g Heb adds of the people   h Traditional rendering of Heb Shaddai

King James

10He will surely reprove you, if ye do secretly accept persons.

11Shall not his excellency make you afraid? and his dread fall upon you?

12Your remembrances *are* like unto ashes, your bodies to bodies of clay.

13Hold your peace, let me alone, that I may speak, and let come on me what *will*.

14Wherefore do I take my flesh in my teeth, and put my life in mine hand?

15Though he slay me, yet will I trust in him: but I will maintain mine own ways before him.

16He also *shall be* my salvation: for an hypocrite shall not come before him.

17Hear diligently my speech, and my declaration with your ears.

18Behold now, I have ordered *my* cause; I know that I shall be justified.

19Who *is* he *that* will plead with me? for now, if I hold my tongue, I shall give up the ghost.

20Only do not two *things* unto me: then will I not hide myself from thee.

21Withdraw thine hand far from me: and let not thy dread make me afraid.

22Then call thou, and I will answer: or let me speak, and answer thou me.

23How many *are* mine iniquities and sins? make me to know my transgression and my sin.

24Wherefore hidest thou thy face, and holdest me for thine enemy?

25Wilt thou break a leaf driven to and fro? and wilt thou pursue the dry stubble?

26For thou writest bitter things against me, and makest me to possess the iniquities of my youth.

27Thou puttest my feet also in the stocks, and lookest narrowly unto all my paths; thou settest a print upon the heels of my feet.

28And he, as a rotten thing, consumeth, as a garment that is motheaten.

14 MAN *THAT* is born of a woman *is* of few days, and full of trouble.

2He cometh forth like a flower, and is cut down: he fleeth also as a shadow, and continueth not.

3And dost thou open thine eyes upon such an one, and bringest me into judgment with thee?

4Who can bring a clean *thing* out of an unclean? not one.

5Seeing his days *are* determined, the number of his months *are* with thee, thou hast appointed his bounds that he cannot pass;

6Turn from him, that he may rest, till he shall accomplish, as an hireling, his day.

7For there is hope of a tree, if it be cut down, that it will sprout again, and that the tender branch thereof will not cease.

New International

10He would surely rebuke you
    if you secretly showed partiality.

11Would not his splendor terrify you?
    Would not the dread of him fall on you?

12Your maxims are proverbs of ashes;
    your defenses are defenses of clay.

13"Keep silent and let me speak;
    then let come to me what may.

14Why do I put myself in jeopardy
    and take my life in my hands?

15Though he slay me, yet will I hope in him;
    I will surely[a] defend my ways to his face.

16Indeed, this will turn out for my deliverance,
    for no godless man would dare come before
        him!

17Listen carefully to my words;
    let your ears take in what I say.

18Now that I have prepared my case,
    I know I will be vindicated.

19Can anyone bring charges against me?
    If so, I will be silent and die.

20"Only grant me these two things, O God,
    and then I will not hide from you:

21Withdraw your hand far from me,
    and stop frightening me with your terrors.

22Then summon me and I will answer,
    or let me speak, and you reply.

23How many wrongs and sins have I committed?
    Show me my offense and my sin.

24Why do you hide your face
    and consider me your enemy?

25Will you torment a windblown leaf?
    Will you chase after dry chaff?

26For you write down bitter things against me
    and make me inherit the sins of my youth.

27You fasten my feet in shackles;
    you keep close watch on all my paths
    by putting marks on the soles of my feet.

28"So man wastes away like something rotten,
    like a garment eaten by moths.

14 "MAN BORN of woman
    is of few days and full of trouble.

2He springs up like a flower and withers away;
    like a fleeting shadow, he does not endure.

3Do you fix your eye on such a one?
    Will you bring him[b] before you for
        judgment?

4Who can bring what is pure from the impure?
    No one!

5Man's days are determined;
    you have decreed the number of his months
    and have set limits he cannot exceed.

6So look away from him and let him alone,
    till he has put in his time like a hired man.

7"At least there is hope for a tree:
    If it is cut down, it will sprout again,
    and its new shoots will not fail.

Living Bible

with him if you use lies to try to help him out. ¹¹Doesn't his majesty strike terror to your heart? How can you do this thing? ¹²These tremendous statements you have made have about as much value as ashes. Your defense of God is as fragile as a clay vase!

¹³Be silent now and let me alone, that I may speak— and I am willing to face the consequences. ¹⁴Yes, I will take my life in my hand and say what I really think. ¹⁵God may kill me for saying this—in fact, I expect him to. Nevertheless I am going to argue my case with him.ᶜ ¹⁶This at least will be in my favor, that I am not godless, to be rejected instantly from his presence. ¹⁷Listen closely to what I am about to say. Hear me out.

¹⁸This is my case: *I know that I am righteous.* ¹⁹Who can argue with me over this? If you could prove me wrong I would stop defending myself and die.

²⁰O God, there are two things I beg you not to do to me; only then will I be able to face you. ²¹Don't abandon me. And don't terrify me with your awesome presence. ²²Call to me to come—how quickly I will answer! Or let me speak to you, and you reply. ²³Tell me, what have I done wrong? Help me! Point out my sin to me. ²⁴Why do you turn away from me? Why hand me over to my enemy? ²⁵Would you blame a leaf that is blown about by the wind? Will you chase dry, useless straws?

²⁶You write bitter things against me and bring up all the follies of my youth. ²⁷, ²⁸You send me to prison and shut me in on every side. I am like a fallen, rotten tree, like a moth-eaten coat.

14 "HOW FRAIL is man, how few his days, how full of trouble! ²He blossoms for a moment like a flower—and withers; as the shadow of a passing cloud, he quickly disappears. ³Must you be so harsh with frail men, and demand an accounting from them? ⁴How can you demand purity in one born impure? ⁵You have set mankind so brief a span of life—months is all you give him! Not one bit longer may he live. ⁶So give him a little rest, won't you? Turn away your angry gaze and let him have a few moments of relief before he dies.

⁷For there is hope for a tree—if it's cut down it sprouts again, and grows tender, new branches.

New Revised Standard

10 He will surely rebuke you
    if in secret you show partiality.
11 Will not his majesty terrify you,
    and the dread of him fall upon you?
12 Your maxims are proverbs of ashes,
    your defenses are defenses of clay.

13 "Let me have silence, and I will speak,
    and let come on me what may.
14 I will take my flesh in my teeth,
    and put my life in my hand.ᵈ
15 See, he will kill me; I have no hope;ᵉ
    but I will defend my ways to his face.
16 This will be my salvation,
    that the godless shall not come before him.
17 Listen carefully to my words,
    and let my declaration be in your ears.
18 I have indeed prepared my case;
    I know that I shall be vindicated.
19 Who is there that will contend with me?
    For then I would be silent and die.

Job's Despondent Prayer

20 Only grant two things to me,
    then I will not hide myself from your face:
21 withdraw your hand far from me,
    and do not let dread of you terrify me.
22 Then call, and I will answer;
    or let me speak, and you reply to me.
23 How many are my iniquities and my sins?
    Make me know my transgression and my
      sin.
24 Why do you hide your face,
    and count me as your enemy?
25 Will you frighten a windblown leaf
    and pursue dry chaff?
26 For you write bitter things against me,
    and make me reapᶠ the iniquities of my
      youth.
27 You put my feet in the stocks,
    and watch all my paths;
    you set a bound to the soles of my feet.
28 One wastes away like a rotten thing,
    like a garment that is moth-eaten.

14 "A MORTAL, born of woman, few of days
    and full of trouble,
2 comes up like a flower and withers,
    flees like a shadow and does not last.
3 Do you fix your eyes on such a one?
    Do you bring me into judgment with you?
4 Who can bring a clean thing out of an
      unclean?
    No one can.
5 Since their days are determined,
    and the number of their months is known to
      you,
    and you have appointed the bounds that they
      cannot pass,
6 look away from them, and desist,ᵍ
    that they may enjoy, like laborers, their
      days.

7 "For there is hope for a tree,
    if it is cut down, that it will sprout again,
    and that its shoots will not cease.

ᶜ *13:15* Or, "Though he slay me, yet will I trust in him. I will argue my case before him."

ᵈ Gk: Heb *Why should I take . . . in my hand?* ᵉ Or *Though he kill me, yet I will trust in him* ᶠ Heb *inherit* ᵍ Cn: Heb *that they may desist*

King James

8Though the root thereof wax old in the earth, and the stock thereof die in the ground;

9*Yet* through the scent of water it will bud, and bring forth boughs like a plant.

10But man dieth, and wasteth away: yea, man giveth up the ghost, and where *is* he?

11*As* the waters fail from the sea, and the flood decayeth and drieth up:

12So man lieth down, and riseth not: till the heavens *be* no more, they shall not awake, nor be raised out of their sleep.

13O that thou wouldest hide me in the grave, that thou wouldest keep me secret, until thy wrath be past, that thou wouldest appoint me a set time, and remember me!

14If a man die, shall he live *again?* all the days of my appointed time will I wait, till my change come.

15Thou shalt call, and I will answer thee: thou wilt have a desire to the work of thine hands.

16For now thou numberest my steps: dost thou not watch over my sin?

17My transgression *is* sealed up in a bag, and thou sewest up mine iniquity.

18And surely the mountain falling cometh to nought, and the rock is removed out of his place.

19The waters wear the stones: thou washest away the things which grow *out* of the dust of the earth; and thou destroyest the hope of man.

20Thou prevailest for ever against him, and he passeth: thou changest his countenance, and sendest him away.

21His sons come to honour, and he knoweth *it* not; and they are brought low, but he perceiveth *it* not of them.

22But his flesh upon him shall have pain, and his soul within him shall mourn.

15 THEN ANSWERED Eliphaz the Temanite, and said,

2Should a wise man utter vain knowledge, and fill his belly with the east wind?

3Should he reason with unprofitable talk? or with speeches wherewith he can do no good?

4Yea, thou castest off fear, and restrainest prayer before God.

5For thy mouth uttereth thine iniquity, and thou choosest the tongue of the crafty.

6Thine own mouth condemneth thee, and not I: yea, thine own lips testify against thee.

7*Art* thou the first man *that* was born? or wast thou made before the hills?

8Hast thou heard the secret of God? and dost thou restrain wisdom to thyself ?

9What knowest thou, that we know not? *what* understandest thou, which *is* not in us?

10With us *are* both the grayheaded and very aged men, much elder than thy father.

11*Are* the consolations of God small with thee? is there any secret thing with thee?

New International

8Its roots may grow old in the ground
　　and its stump die in the soil,
9yet at the scent of water it will bud
　　and put forth shoots like a plant.
10But man dies and is laid low;
　　he breathes his last and is no more.
11As water disappears from the sea
　　or a riverbed becomes parched and dry,
12so man lies down and does not rise;
　　till the heavens are no more, men will not awake
　　or be roused from their sleep.

13"If only you would hide me in the grave[a]
　　and conceal me till your anger has passed!
　If only you would set me a time
　　and then remember me!
14If a man dies, will he live again?
　　All the days of my hard service
　　I will wait for my renewal[b] to come.
15You will call and I will answer you;
　　you will long for the creature your hands
　　　have made.
16Surely then you will count my steps
　　but not keep track of my sin.
17My offenses will be sealed up in a bag;
　　you will cover over my sin.

18"But as a mountain erodes and crumbles
　　and as a rock is moved from its place,
19as water wears away stones
　　and torrents wash away the soil,
　　so you destroy man's hope.
20You overpower him once for all, and he is gone;
　　you change his countenance and send him away.
21If his sons are honored, he does not know it;
　　if they are brought low, he does not see it.
22He feels but the pain of his own body
　　and mourns only for himself."

Eliphaz

15 THEN ELIPHAZ the Temanite replied:

2"Would a wise man answer with empty notions
　　or fill his belly with the hot east wind?
3Would he argue with useless words,
　　with speeches that have no value?
4But you even undermine piety
　　and hinder devotion to God.
5Your sin prompts your mouth;
　　you adopt the tongue of the crafty.
6Your own mouth condemns you, not mine;
　　your own lips testify against you.

7"Are you the first man ever born?
　　Were you brought forth before the hills?
8Do you listen in on God's council?
　　Do you limit wisdom to yourself?
9What do you know that we do not know?
　　What insights do you have that we do not have?
10The gray-haired and the aged are on our side,
　　men even older than your father.
11Are God's consolations not enough for you,
　　words spoken gently to you?

Living Bible

8, 9Though its roots have grown old in the earth, and its stump decays, it may sprout and bud again at the touch of water, like a new seedling. 10But when a man dies and is buried, where does his spirit go? 11, 12As water evaporates from a lake, as a river disappears in drought, so a man lies down for the last time, and does not rise again until the heavens are no more; he shall not awaken, nor be roused from his sleep. 13Oh, that you would hide me with the dead, and forget me there until your anger ends; but mark your calendar to think of me again!

14"If a man dies, shall he live again? This thought gives me hope, so that in all my anguish I eagerly await sweet death! 15You would call and I would come, and you would reward all I do. 16But now, instead, you give me so few steps upon the stage of life, and notice every mistake I make. 17You bundle them all together as evidence against me.

18, 19"Mountains wear away and disappear. Water grinds the stones to sand. Torrents tear away the soil. So every hope of man is worn away. 20, 21Always you are against him, and then he passes off the scene. You make him old and wrinkled, then send him away. He never knows it if his sons are honored; or they may fail and face disaster, but he knows it not. 22For him there is only sorrow and pain."

15 THE ANSWER of Eliphaz the Temanite:
2"You are supposed to be a wise man, and yet you give us all this foolish talk. You are nothing but a windbag. 3It isn't right to speak so foolishly. What good do such words do? 4, 5Have you no fear of God? No reverence for him? Your sins are telling your mouth what to say! Your words are based on clever deception, 6but why should I condemn you? Your own mouth does! 7, 8"Are you the wisest man alive? Were you born before the hills were made? Have you heard the secret counsel of God? Are you called into his counsel room? Do you have a monopoly on wisdom? 9What do you know more than we do? What do you understand that we don't? 10On our side are aged men much older than your father! 11Is God's comfort too little for you? Is his gentleness too rough?

New Revised Standard

8 Though its root grows old in the earth,
    and its stump dies in the ground,
9 yet at the scent of water it will bud
    and put forth branches like a young plant.
10 But mortals die, and are laid low;
    humans expire, and where are they?
11 As waters fail from a lake,
    and a river wastes away and dries up,
12 so mortals lie down and do not rise again;
    until the heavens are no more, they will not awake
    or be roused out of their sleep.
13 Oh that you would hide me in Sheol,
    that you would conceal me until your wrath is past,
    that you would appoint me a set time, and remember me!
14 If mortals die, will they live again?
    All the days of my service I would wait
    until my release should come.
15 You would call, and I would answer you;
    you would long for the work of your hands.
16 For then you would note number my steps,
    you would not keep watch over my sin;
17 my transgression would be sealed up in a bag,
    and you would cover over my iniquity.

18 "But the mountain falls and crumbles away,
    and the rock is removed from its place;
19 the waters wear away the stones;
    the torrents wash away the soil of the earth;
    so you destroy the hope of mortals.
20 You prevail forever against them, and they pass away;
    you change their countenance, and send them away.
21 Their children come to honor, and they do not know it;
    they are brought low, and it goes unnoticed.
22 They feel only the pain of their own bodies,
    and mourn only for themselves."

Eliphaz Speaks: Job Undermines Religion

15 THEN ELIPHAZ the Temanite answered:
2 "Should the wise answer with windy knowledge,
    and fill themselves with the east wind?
3 Should they argue in unprofitable talk,
    or in words with which they can do no good?
4 But you are doing away with the fear of God,
    and hindering meditation before God.
5 For your iniquity teaches your mouth,
    and you choose the tongue of the crafty.
6 Your own mouth condemns you, and not I;
    your own lips testify against you.

7 "Are you the firstborn of the human race?
    Were you brought forth before the hills?
8 Have you listened in the council of God?
    And do you limit wisdom to yourself?
9 What do you know that we do not know?
    What do you understand that is not clear to us?
10 The gray-haired and the aged are on our side,
    those older than your father.
11 Are the consolations of God too small for you,
    or the word that deals gently with you?

---

c Syr: Heb lacks *not*

King James

12Why doth thine heart carry thee away? and what do thy eyes wink at,

13That thou turnest thy spirit against God, and lettest *such* words go out of thy mouth?

14What *is* man, that he should be clean? and *he which is* born of a woman, that he should be righteous?

15Behold, he putteth no trust in his saints; yea, the heavens are not clean in his sight.

16How much more abominable and filthy *is* man, which drinketh iniquity like water?

17I will show thee, hear me; and that *which* I have seen I will declare;

18Which wise men have told from their fathers, and have not hid *it:*

19Unto whom alone the earth was given, and no stranger passed among them.

20The wicked man travaileth with pain all *his* days, and the number of years is hidden to the oppressor.

21A dreadful sound *is* in his ears: in prosperity the destroyer shall come upon him.

22He believeth not that he shall return out of darkness, and he is waited for of the sword.

23He wandereth abroad for bread, *saying,* Where *is it?* he knoweth that the day of darkness is ready at his hand.

24Trouble and anguish shall make him afraid; they shall prevail against him, as a king ready to the battle.

25For he stretcheth out his hand against God, and strengtheneth himself against the Almighty.

26He runneth upon him, *even* on *his* neck, upon the thick bosses of his bucklers:

27Because he covereth his face with his fatness, and maketh collops of fat on *his* flanks.

28And he dwelleth in desolate cities, *and* in houses which no man inhabiteth, which are ready to become heaps.

29He shall not be rich, neither shall his substance continue, neither shall he prolong the perfection thereof upon the earth.

30He shall not depart out of darkness; the flame shall dry up his branches, and by the breath of his mouth shall he go away.

31Let not him that is deceived trust in vanity: for vanity shall be his recompence.

32It shall be accomplished before his time, and his branch shall not be green.

33He shall shake off his unripe grape as the vine, and shall cast off his flower as the olive.

34For the congregation of hypocrites *shall be* desolate, and fire shall consume the tabernacles of bribery.

35They conceive mischief, and bring forth vanity, and their belly prepareth deceit.

New International

12Why has your heart carried you away,
    and why do your eyes flash,
13so that you vent your rage against God
    and pour out such words from your mouth?

14"What is man, that he could be pure,
    or one born of woman, that he could be
        righteous?
15If God places no trust in his holy ones,
    if even the heavens are not pure in his eyes,
16how much less man, who is vile and corrupt,
    who drinks up evil like water!

17"Listen to me and I will explain to you;
    let me tell you what I have seen,
18what wise men have declared,
    hiding nothing received from their fathers
19(to whom alone the land was given
    when no alien passed among them):
20All his days the wicked man suffers torment,
    the ruthless through all the years stored up for
        him.
21Terrifying sounds fill his ears;
    when all seems well, marauders attack him.
22He despairs of escaping the darkness;
    he is marked for the sword.
23He wanders about—food for vultures[a];
    he knows the day of darkness is at hand.
24Distress and anguish fill him with terror;
    they overwhelm him, like a king poised to
        attack,
25because he shakes his fist at God
    and vaunts himself against the Almighty,
26defiantly charging against him
    with a thick, strong shield.

27"Though his face is covered with fat
    and his waist bulges with flesh,
28he will inhabit ruined towns
    and houses where no one lives,
    houses crumbling to rubble.
29He will no longer be rich and his wealth will
        not endure,
    nor will his possessions spread over the land.
30He will not escape the darkness;
    a flame will wither his shoots,
    and the breath of God's mouth will carry him
        away.
31Let him not deceive himself by trusting what is
        worthless,
    for he will get nothing in return.
32Before his time he will be paid in full,
    and his branches will not flourish.
33He will be like a vine stripped of its unripe
        grapes,
    like an olive tree shedding its blossoms.
34For the company of the godless will be barren,
    and fire will consume the tents of those who
        love bribes.
35They conceive trouble and give birth to evil;
    their womb fashions deceit."

[a] 23 Or *about, looking for food*

Living Bible

12"What is this you are doing, getting carried away by your anger, with flashing eyes? 13And you turn against God and say all these evil things against him. 14What man in all the earth can be as pure and righteous as you claim to be? 15Why, God doesn't even trust the angels! Even the heavens can't be absolutely pure compared with him! 16How much less someone like you, who is corrupt and sinful, drinking in sin as a sponge soaks up water!

17, 18, 19"Listen, and I will answer you from my own experience, confirmed by the experience of wise men who have been told this same thing from their fathers— our ancestors to whom alone the land was given—and they have passed this wisdom to us:

20"A wicked man is always in trouble throughout his life. 21He is surrounded by terrors, and if there are good days they will soon be gone. 22He dares not go out into the darkness, lest he be murdered. 23, 24He wanders around begging for food. He lives in fear, distress, and anguish. His enemies conquer him as a king defeats his foes. 25, 26Armed with his tin shield, he clenches his fist against God, defying the Almighty, stubbornly assaulting him.

27, 28"This wicked man is fat and rich, and has lived in conquered cities after killing off its citizens. 29But he will not continue to be rich, or to extend his possessions. 30No, darkness shall overtake him forever; the breath of God shall destroy him; the flames shall burn up all he has.

31"Let him no longer trust in foolish riches;b let him no longer deceive himself, for the money he trusts in will be his only reward. 32Before he dies, all this futility will become evident to him. For all he counted on will disappear, 33and fall to the ground like a withered grape.c How little will come of his hopes! 34For the godless are barren: they can produce nothing truly good. God's fire consumes them with all their possessions. 35The only thing they can 'conceive' is sin, and their hearts give birth only to wickedness."

New Revised Standard

12 Why does your heart carry you away,
    and why do your eyes flash,d
13 so that you turn your spirit against God,
    and let such words go out of your mouth?
14 What are mortals, that they can be clean?
    Or those born of woman, that they can be
        righteous?
15 God puts no trust even in his holy ones,
    and the heavens are not clean in his sight;
16 how much less one who is abominable and
        corrupt,
    one who drinks iniquity like water!

17 "I will show you; listen to me;
    what I have seen I will declare—
18 what sages have told,
    and their ancestors have not hidden,
19 to whom alone the land was given,
    and no stranger passed among them.
20 The wicked writhe in pain all their days,
    through all the years that are laid up for the
        ruthless.
21 Terrifying sounds are in their ears;
    in prosperity the destroyer will come upon
        them.
22 They despair of returning from darkness,
    and they are destined for the sword.
23 They wander abroad for bread, saying, 'Where
        is it?'
    They know that a day of darkness is ready
        at hand;
24 distress and anguish terrify them;
    they prevail against them, like a king
        prepared for battle.
25 Because they stretched out their hands against
        God,
    and bid defiance to the Almighty,e
26 running stubbornly against him
    with a thick-bossed shield;
27 because they have covered their faces with
        their fat,
    and gathered fat upon their loins,
28 they will live in desolate cities,
    in houses that no one should inhabit,
    houses destined to become heaps of ruins;
29 they will not be rich, and their wealth will not
        endure,
    nor will they strike root in the earth;f
30 they will not escape from darkness;
    the flame will dry up their shoots,
    and their blossomg will be swept awayh by
        the wind.
31 Let them not trust in emptiness, deceiving
        themselves;
    for emptiness will be their recompense.
32 It will be paid in full before their time,
    and their branch will not be green.
33 They will shake off their unripe grape, like
        the vine,
    and cast off their blossoms, like the olive
        tree.
34 For the company of the godless is barren,
    and fire consumes the tents of bribery.
35 They conceive mischief and bring forth evil
    and their heart prepares deceit."

---

b 15:31 trust in foolish riches, literally, "trust in vanity."   c 15:33 fall to the ground like a withered grape, literally, "shall cast off his flower as the olive tree."

d Meaning of Heb uncertain   e Traditional rendering of Heb Shaddai   f Vg: Meaning of Heb uncertain   g Gk: Heb mouth   h Cn: Heb will depart

King James

16 THEN JOB answered and said,
2I have heard many such things: miserable comforters *are* ye all.

3Shall vain words have an end? or what emboldeneth thee that thou answerest?

4I also could speak as ye *do:* if your soul were in my soul's stead, I could heap up words against you, and shake mine head at you.

5*But* I would strengthen you with my mouth, and the moving of my lips should assuage *your grief.*

6Though I speak, my grief is not assuaged: and *though* I forbear, what am I eased?

7But now he hath made me weary: thou hast made desolate all my company.

8And thou hast filled me with wrinkles, *which* is a witness *against me:* and my leanness rising up in me beareth witness to my face.

9He teareth *me* in his wrath, who hateth me: he gnasheth upon me with his teeth; mine enemy sharpeneth his eyes upon me.

10They have gaped upon me with their mouth; they have smitten me upon the cheek reproachfully; they have gathered themselves together against me.

11God hath delivered me to the ungodly, and turned me over into the hands of the wicked.

12I was at ease, but he hath broken me asunder: he hath also taken *me* by my neck, and shaken me to pieces, and set me up for his mark.

13His archers compass me round about, he cleaveth my reins asunder, and doth not spare; he poureth out my gall upon the ground.

14He breaketh me with breach upon breach, he runneth upon me like a giant.

15I have sewed sackcloth upon my skin, and defiled my horn in the dust.

16My face is foul with weeping, and on my eyelids *is* the shadow of death;

17Not for *any* injustice in mine hands: also my prayer *is* pure.

18O earth, cover not thou my blood, and let my cry have no place.

19Also now, behold, my witness *is* in heaven, and my record *is* on high.

20My friends scorn me: *but* mine eye poureth out *tears* unto God.

21O that one might plead for a man with God, as a man *pleadeth* for his neighbour!

22When a few years are come, then I shall go the way *whence* I shall not return.

17 MY BREATH is corrupt, my days are extinct, the graves *are ready* for me.
2*Are there* not mockers with me? and doth not mine eye continue in their provocation?

3Lay down now, put me in a surety with thee; who *is* he *that* will strike hands with me?

New International

Job

16 THEN JOB replied:
2"I have heard many things like these;
miserable comforters are you all!

3Will your long-winded speeches never end?
What ails you that you keep on arguing?

4I also could speak like you,
if you were in my place;
I could make fine speeches against you
and shake my head at you.

5But my mouth would encourage you;
comfort from my lips would bring you relief.

6"Yet if I speak, my pain is not relieved;
and if I refrain, it does not go away.

7Surely, O God, you have worn me out;
you have devastated my entire household.

8You have bound me—and it has become a
witness;
my gauntness rises up and testifies against
me.

9God assails me and tears me in his anger
and gnashes his teeth at me;
my opponent fastens on me his piercing eyes.

10Men open their mouths to jeer at me;
they strike my cheek in scorn
and unite together against me.

11God has turned me over to evil men
and thrown me into the clutches of the
wicked.

12All was well with me, but he shattered me;
he seized me by the neck and crushed me.
He has made me his target;
13 his archers surround me.
Without pity, he pierces my kidneys
and spills my gall on the ground.

14Again and again he bursts upon me;
he rushes at me like a warrior.

15"I have sewed sackcloth over my skin
and buried my brow in the dust.

16My face is red with weeping,
deep shadows ring my eyes;

17yet my hands have been free of violence
and my prayer is pure.

18"O earth, do not cover my blood;
may my cry never be laid to rest!

19Even now my witness is in heaven;
my advocate is on high.

20My intercessor is my frienda
as my eyes pour out tears to God;

21on behalf of a man he pleads with God
as a man pleads for his friend.

22"Only a few years will pass
before I go on the journey of no return.

17 MY SPIRIT is broken,
my days are cut short,
the grave awaits me.

2Surely mockers surround me;
my eyes must dwell on their hostility.

3"Give me, O God, the pledge you demand.
Who else will put up security for me?

---

a 20 Or *My friends treat me with scorn*

Living Bible

16

JOB'S REPLY:

2"I have heard all this before. What miserable comforters all of you are. 3Won't you ever stop your flow of foolish words? What have I said that makes you speak so endlessly? 4But perhaps I'd sermonize the same as you—if you were I and I were you. I would spout off my criticisms against you and shake my head at you. 5But no! I would speak in such a way that it would help you. I would try to take away your grief.

6"But now my grief remains no matter how I defend myself; nor does it help if I refuse to speak. 7For God has ground me down, and taken away my family. 8O God, you have turned me to skin and bones—as a proof, they say, of my sins. 9God hates me and angrily tears at my flesh; he has gnashed upon me with his teeth, and watched to snuff out any sign of life. 10These 'comforters' have gaping jaws to swallow me; they slap my cheek. My enemies gather themselves against me. 11And God has delivered me over to sinners, into the hands of the wicked.

12"I was living quietly until he broke me apart. He has taken me by the neck and dashed me to pieces, then hung me up as his target. 13His archers surround me, letting fly their arrows, so that the ground is wet from my blood. 14Again and again he attacks me, running upon me like a giant. 15Here I sit in sackcloth; and have laid all hope in the dust. 16My eyes are red with weeping, and on my eyelids is the shadow of death.

17"Yet I am innocent, and my prayer is pure. 18O earth, do not conceal my blood. Let it protest on my behalf.

19"Yet even now the Witness to my innocence is there in heaven; my Advocate is there on high. 20My friends scoff at me, but I pour out my tears to God, 21pleading that he will listen as a man would listen to his neighbor. 22For all too soon I must go down that road from which I shall never return.

17

"I AM sick and near to death; the grave is ready to receive me. 2I am surrounded by mockers. I see them everywhere. 3, 4Will no one anywhere confirm my innocence? But you, O God, have kept them back from understanding this. Oh, do not let them triumph.

New Revised Standard

Job Reaffirms His Innocence

16

THEN JOB answered:
2 "I have heard many such things;
   miserable comforters are you all.
3 Have windy words no limit?
   Or what provokes you that you keep on
      talking?
4 I also could talk as you do,
   if you were in my place;
   I could join words together against you,
      and shake my head at you.
5 I could encourage you with my mouth,
   and the solace of my lips would assuage
      your pain.

6 "If I speak, my pain is not assuaged,
   and if I forbear, how much of it leaves me?
7 Surely now God has worn me out;
   he has[b] made desolate all my company.
8 And he has[b] shriveled me up,
   which is a witness against me;
   my leanness has risen up against me,
      and it testifies to my face.
9 He has torn me in his wrath, and hated me;
   he has gnashed his teeth at me;
   my adversary sharpens his eyes against me.
10 They have gaped at me with their mouths;
   they have struck me insolently on the cheek;
   they mass themselves together against me.
11 God gives me up to the ungodly,
   and casts me into the hands of the wicked.
12 I was at ease, and he broke me in two;
   he seized me by the neck and dashed me to
      pieces;
   he set me up as his target;
13   his archers surround me.
He slashes open my kidneys, and shows no
      mercy;
   he pours out my gall on the ground.
14 He bursts upon me again and again;
   he rushes at me like a warrior.
15 I have sewed sackcloth upon my skin,
   and have laid my strength in the dust.
16 My face is red with weeping,
   and deep darkness is on my eyelids,
17 though there is no violence in my hands,
   and my prayer is pure.

18 "O earth, do not cover my blood;
   let my outcry find no resting place.
19 Even now, in fact, my witness is in heaven,
   and he that vouches for me is on high.
20 My friends scorn me;
   my eye pours out tears to God,
21 that he would maintain the right of a mortal
      with God,
   as[c] one does for a neighbor.
22 For when a few years have come,
   I shall go the way from which I shall not
      return.

Job Prays for Relief

17

MY SPIRIT is broken, my days are extinct,
   the grave is ready for me.
2 Surely there are mockers around me,
   and my eye dwells on their provocation.

3 "Lay down a pledge for me with yourself;
   who is there that will give surety for me?

b Heb *you have*   c Syr Vg Tg: Heb *and*

King James

4For thou hast hid their heart from understanding: therefore shalt thou not exalt *them*.

5He that speaketh flattery to *his* friends, even the eyes of his children shall fail.

6He hath made me also a byword of the people; and aforetime I was as a tabret.

7Mine eye also is dim by reason of sorrow, and all my members *are* as a shadow.

8Upright *men* shall be astonied at this, and the innocent shall stir up himself against the hypocrite.

9The righteous also shall hold on his way, and he that hath clean hands shall be stronger and stronger.

10But as for you all, do ye return, and come now: for I cannot find *one* wise *man* among you.

11My days are past, my purposes are broken off, *even* the thoughts of my heart.

12They change the night into day: the light *is* short because of darkness.

13If I wait, the grave *is* mine house: I have made my bed in the darkness.

14I have said to corruption, Thou *art* my father: to the worm, *Thou art* my mother, and my sister.

15And where *is* now my hope? as for my hope, who shall see it?

16They shall go down to the bars of the pit, when *our* rest together *is* in the dust.

18 THEN ANSWERED Bildad the Shuhite, and said,

2How long *will it be ere* ye make an end of words? mark, and afterwards we will speak.

3Wherefore are we counted as beasts, *and* reputed vile in your sight?

4He teareth himself in his anger: shall the earth be forsaken for thee? and shall the rock be removed out of his place?

5Yea, the light of the wicked shall be put out, and the spark of his fire shall not shine.

6The light shall be dark in his tabernacle, and his candle shall be put out with him.

7The steps of his strength shall be straitened, and his own counsel shall cast him down.

8For he is cast into a net by his own feet, and he walketh upon a snare.

9The gin shall take *him* by the heel, *and* the robber shall prevail against him.

10The snare *is* laid for him in the ground, and a trap for him in the way.

11Terrors shall make him afraid on every side, and shall drive him to his feet.

12His strength shall be hungerbitten, and destruction *shall be* ready at his side.

13It shall devour the strength of his skin: *even* the firstborn of death shall devour his strength.

14His confidence shall be rooted out of his tabernacle, and it shall bring him to the king of terrors.

15It shall dwell in his tabernacle, because *it is* none of his: brimstone shall be scattered upon his habitation.

New International

4You have closed their minds to understanding; therefore you will not let them triumph.

5If a man denounces his friends for reward, the eyes of his children will fail.

6"God has made me a byword to everyone, a man in whose face people spit.

7My eyes have grown dim with grief; my whole frame is but a shadow.

8Upright men are appalled at this; the innocent are aroused against the ungodly.

9Nevertheless, the righteous will hold to their ways, and those with clean hands will grow stronger.

10"But come on, all of you, try again! I will not find a wise man among you.

11My days have passed, my plans are shattered, and so are the desires of my heart.

12These men turn night into day; in the face of darkness they say, 'Light is near.'

13If the only home I hope for is the grave,a if I spread out my bed in darkness,

14if I say to corruption, 'You are my father,' and to the worm, 'My mother' or 'My sister,'

15where then is my hope? Who can see any hope for me?

16Will it go down to the gates of deatha? Will we descend together into the dust?"

Bildad

18 THEN BILDAD the Shuhite replied:

2"When will you end these speeches? Be sensible, and then we can talk.

3Why are we regarded as cattle and considered stupid in your sight?

4You who tear yourself to pieces in your anger, is the earth to be abandoned for your sake? Or must the rocks be moved from their place?

5"The lamp of the wicked is snuffed out; the flame of his fire stops burning.

6The light in his tent becomes dark; the lamp beside him goes out.

7The vigor of his step is weakened; his own schemes throw him down.

8His feet thrust him into a net and he wanders into its mesh.

9A trap seizes him by the heel; a snare holds him fast.

10A noose is hidden for him on the ground; a trap lies in his path.

11Terrors startle him on every side and dog his every step.

12Calamity is hungry for him; disaster is ready for him when he falls.

13It eats away parts of his skin; death's firstborn devours his limbs.

14He is torn from the security of his tent and marched off to the king of terrors.

15Fire residesb in his tent; burning sulfur is scattered over his dwelling.

Living Bible

5If they accept bribes to denounce their friends, their children shall go blind.

6"He has made me a mockery among the people; they spit in my face. 7My eyes are dim with weeping and I am but a shadow of my former self. 8Fair-minded men are astonished when they see me.

"Yet, finally, the innocent shall come out on top, above the godless; 9the righteous shall move onward and forward; those with pure hearts shall become stronger and stronger.

10"As for you—all of you please go away; for I do not find a wise man among you. 11My good days are in the past. My hopes have disappeared. My heart's desires are broken. 12They say that night is day and day is night; how they pervert the truth!

13, 14"If I die, I go out into darkness, and call the grave my father, and the worm my mother and my sister. 15Where then is my hope? Can anyone find any? 16No, my hope will go down with me to the grave. We shall rest together in the dust!"

18 THE FURTHER reply of Bildad the Shuhite: 2"Who are you trying to fool? Speak some sense if you want us to answer! 3Have we become like animals to you, stupid and dumb? 4Just because you tear your clothes in anger, is this going to start an earthquake? Shall we all go and hide?

5"The truth remains that if you do not prosper, it is because you are wicked. And your bright flame shall be put out. 6There will be darkness in every home where there is wickedness.

7"The confident stride of the wicked man will be shortened; he will realize his failing strength. 8, 9He walks into traps, and robbers will ambush him. 10There is a booby-trap in every path he takes. 11He has good cause for fear—his enemy is close behind him!

12"His vigor is depleted by hunger; calamity stands ready to pounce upon him. 13His skin is eaten by disease. Death shall devour him. 14The wealth he trusted in shall reject him, and he shall be brought down to the King of Terrors. 15His home shall disappear beneath a

New Revised Standard

4 Since you have closed their minds to
    understanding,
  therefore you will not let them triumph.
5 Those who denounce friends for reward—
    the eyes of their children will fail.

6 "He has made me a byword of the peoples,
    and I am one before whom people spit.
7 My eye has grown dim from grief,
    and all my members are like a shadow.
8 The upright are appalled at this,
    and the innocent stir themselves up against
      the godless.
9 Yet the righteous hold to their way,
    and they that have clean hands grow
      stronger and stronger.
10 But you, come back now, all of you,
    and I shall not find a sensible person among
      you.
11 My days are past, my plans are broken off,
    the desires of my heart.
12 They make night into day;
    'The light,' they say, 'is near to the
      darkness.'c
13 If I look for Sheol as my house,
    if I spread my couch in darkness,
14 if I say to the Pit, 'You are my father,'
    and to the worm, 'My mother,' or 'My
      sister,'
15 where then is my hope?
    Who will see my hope?
16 Will it go down to the bars of Sheol?
    Shall we descend together into the dust?"

Bildad Speaks: God Punishes the Wicked

18 THEN BILDAD the Shuhite answered:
2 "How long will you hunt for words?
    Consider, and then we shall speak.
3 Why are we counted as cattle?
    Why are we stupid in your sight?
4 You who tear yourself in your anger—
    shall the earth be forsaken because of you,
    or the rock be removed out of its place?

5 "Surely the light of the wicked is put out,
    and the flame of their fire does not shine.
6 The light is dark in their tent,
    and the lamp above them is put out.
7 Their strong steps are shortened,
    and their own schemes throw them down.
8 For they are thrust into a net by their own
      feet,
    and they walk into a pitfall.
9 A trap seizes them by the heel;
    a snare lays hold of them.
10 A rope is hid for them in the ground,
    a trap for them in the path.
11 Terrors frighten them on every side,
    and chase them at their heels.
12 Their strength is consumed by hunger,d
    and calamity is ready for their stumbling.
13 By disease their skin is consumed,e
    the firstborn of Death consumes their limbs.
14 They are torn from the tent in which they
      trusted,
    and are brought to the king of terrors.
15 In their tents nothing remains;
    sulfur is scattered upon their habitations.

c Meaning of Heb uncertain   d Or *Disaster is hungry for them*   e Cn: Heb
It consumes the limbs of his skin

King James

16His roots shall be dried up beneath, and above shall his branch be cut off.

17His remembrance shall perish from the earth, and he shall have no name in the street.

18He shall be driven from light into darkness, and chased out of the world.

19He shall neither have son nor nephew among his people, nor any remaining in his dwellings.

20They that come after *him* shall be astonied at his day, as they that went before were affrighted.

21Surely such *are* the dwellings of the wicked, and this *is* the place *of him that* knoweth not God.

19 THEN JOB answered and said,
2How long will ye vex my soul, and break me in pieces with words?

3These ten times have ye reproached me: ye are not ashamed *that* ye make yourselves strange to me.

4And be it indeed *that* I have erred, mine error remaineth with myself.

5If indeed ye will magnify *yourselves* against me, and plead against me my reproach:

6Know now that God hath overthrown me, and hath compassed me with his net.

7Behold, I cry out of wrong, but I am not heard: I cry aloud, but *there is* no judgment.

8He hath fenced up my way that I cannot pass, and he hath set darkness in my paths.

9He hath stripped me of my glory, and taken the crown *from* my head.

10He hath destroyed me on every side, and I am gone: and mine hope hath he removed like a tree.

11He hath also kindled his wrath against me, and he counteth me unto him as *one of* his enemies.

12His troops come together, and raise up their way against me, and encamp round about my tabernacle.

13He hath put my brethren far from me, and mine acquaintance are verily estranged from me.

14My kinsfolk have failed, and my familiar friends have forgotten me.

15They that dwell in mine house, and my maids, count me for a stranger: I am an alien in their sight.

16I called my servant, and he gave *me* no answer; I entreated him with my mouth.

17My breath is strange to my wife, though I entreated for the children's *sake* of mine own body.

18Yea, young children despised me; I arose, and they spake against me.

19All my inward friends abhorred me: and they whom I loved are turned against me.

20My bone cleaveth to my skin and to my flesh, and I am escaped with the skin of my teeth.

21Have pity upon me, have pity upon me, O ye my friends; for the hand of God hath touched me.

New International

16His roots dry up below
and his branches wither above.

17The memory of him perishes from the earth;
he has no name in the land.

18He is driven from light into darkness
and is banished from the world.

19He has no offspring or descendants among his people,
no survivor where once he lived.

20Men of the west are appalled at his fate;
men of the east are seized with horror.

21Surely such is the dwelling of an evil man;
such is the place of one who knows not God."

Job

19 THEN JOB replied:

2"How long will you torment me
and crush me with words?

3Ten times now you have reproached me;
shamelessly you attack me.

4If it is true that I have gone astray,
my error remains my concern alone.

5If indeed you would exalt yourselves above me
and use my humiliation against me,

6then know that God has wronged me
and drawn his net around me.

7"Though I cry, 'I've been wronged!' I get no response;
though I call for help, there is no justice.

8He has blocked my way so I cannot pass;
he has shrouded my paths in darkness.

9He has stripped me of my honor
and removed the crown from my head.

10He tears me down on every side till I am gone;
he uproots my hope like a tree.

11His anger burns against me;
he counts me among his enemies.

12His troops advance in force;
they build a siege ramp against me
and encamp around my tent.

13"He has alienated my brothers from me;
my acquaintances are completely estranged from me.

14My kinsmen have gone away;
my friends have forgotten me.

15My guests and my maidservants count me a stranger;
they look upon me as an alien.

16I summon my servant, but he does not answer,
though I beg him with my own mouth.

17My breath is offensive to my wife;
I am loathsome to my own brothers.

18Even the little boys scorn me;
when I appear, they ridicule me.

19All my intimate friends detest me;
those I love have turned against me.

20I am nothing but skin and bones;
I have escaped with only the skin of my teeth.[a]

21"Have pity on me, my friends, have pity,
for the hand of God has struck me.

---

[a] *20 Or only my gums*

Living Bible

fiery barrage of brimstone. 16He shall die from the roots up, and all his branches will be lopped off.

17"All memory of his existence will perish from the earth; no one will remember him. 18He will be driven out from the kingdom of light into darkness, and chased out of the world. 19He will have neither son nor grandson left, nor any other relatives. 20Old and young alike will be horrified by his fate. 21Yes, that is what happens to sinners, to those rejecting God."

19 THE REPLY of Job:
2"How long are you going to trouble me, and try to break me with your words? 3Ten times now you have declared I am a sinner. Why aren't you ashamed to deal with me so harshly? 4And if indeed I was wrong, you have yet to prove it. 5You think yourselves so great? Then prove my guilt!

6"The fact of the matter is that God has overthrown me and caught me in his net. 7I scream for help and no one hears me. I shriek, but get no justice. 8God has blocked my path and turned my light to darkness. 9He has stripped me of my glory and removed the crown from my head. 10He has broken me down on every side, and I am done for. He has destroyed all hope. 11His fury burns against me; he counts me as an enemy. 12He sends his troops to surround my tent.

13"He has sent away my brothers, and my friends. 14My relatives have failed me; my friends have all forsaken me. 15Those living in my home, even my servants, regard me as a stranger. I am like a foreigner to them. 16I call my servant, but he doesn't come; I even beg him! 17My own wife and brothers refuse to recognize me. 18Even young children despise me. When I stand to speak, they mock.

19"My best friends abhor me. Those I loved have turned against me. 20I am skin and bones and have escaped death by the skin of my teeth.

21"Oh, my friends, pity me, for the angry hand of God has touched me. 22Why must you persecute me as

New Revised Standard

16 Their roots dry up beneath,
   and their branches wither above.
17 Their memory perishes from the earth,
   and they have no name in the street.
18 They are thrust from light into darkness,
   and driven out of the world.
19 They have no offspring or descendant among
      their people,
   and no survivor where they used to live.
20 They of the west are appalled at their fate,
   and horror seizes those of the east.
21 Surely such are the dwellings of the ungodly,
   such is the place of those who do not know
      God."

Job Replies: I Know That My Redeemer Lives

19 THEN JOB answered:
2 "How long will you torment me,
   and break me in pieces with words?
3 These ten times you have cast reproach upon
      me;
   are you not ashamed to wrong me?
4 And even if it is true that I have erred,
   my error remains with me.
5 If indeed you magnify yourselves against me,
   and make my humiliation an argument
      against me,
6 know then that God has put me in the wrong,
   and closed his net around me.
7 Even when I cry out, 'Violence!' I am not
      answered;
   I call aloud, but there is no justice.
8 He has walled up my way so that I cannot
      pass,
   and he has set darkness upon my paths.
9 He has stripped my glory from me,
   and taken the crown from my head.
10 He breaks me down on every side, and I am
      gone,
   he has uprooted my hope like a tree.
11 He has kindled his wrath against me,
   and counts me as his adversary.
12 His troops come on together;
   they have thrown up siegeworksb against
      me,
   and encamp around my tent.

13 "He has put my family far from me,
   and my acquaintances are wholly estranged
      from me.
14 My relatives and my close friends have failed
      me;
15 the guests in my house have forgotten me;
   my serving girls count me as a stranger;
   I have become an alien in their eyes.
16 I call to my servant, but he gives me no
      answer;
   I must myself plead with him.
17 My breath is repulsive to my wife;
   I am loathsome to my own family.
18 Even young children despise me;
   when I rise, they talk against me.
19 All my intimate friends abhor me,
   and those whom I loved have turned against
      me.
20 My bones cling to my skin and to my flesh,
   and I have escaped by the skin of my teeth.
21 Have pity on me, have pity on me, O you my
      friends,
   for the hand of God has touched me!

b Cn: Heb *their way*

King James

22Why do ye persecute me as God, and are not satis-fied with my flesh?

23Oh that my words were now written! oh that they were printed in a book!

24That they were graven with an iron pen and lead in the rock for ever!

25For I know *that* my redeemer liveth, and *that* he shall stand at the latter *day* upon the earth:

26And *though* after my skin *worms* destroy this *body*, yet in my flesh shall I see God:

27Whom I shall see for myself, and mine eyes shall behold, and not another; *though* my reins be consumed within me.

28But ye should say, Why persecute we him, seeing the root of the matter is found in me?

29Be ye afraid of the sword: for wrath *bringeth* the punishments of the sword, that ye may know *there is* a judgment.

20 THEN ANSWERED Zophar the Naamathite, and said,

2Therefore do my thoughts cause me to answer, and for *this* I make haste.

3I have heard the check of my reproach, and the spirit of my understanding causeth me to answer.

4Knowest thou *not* this of old, since man was placed upon earth,

5That the triumphing of the wicked *is* short, and the joy of the hypocrite *but* for a moment?

6Though his excellency mount up to the heavens, and his head reach unto the clouds;

7Yet he shall perish for ever like his own dung: they which have seen him shall say, Where *is* he?

8He shall fly away as a dream, and shall not be found: yea, he shall be chased away as a vision of the night.

9The eye also *which* saw him shall *see him* no more; neither shall his place any more behold him.

10His children shall seek to please the poor, and his hands shall restore their goods.

11His bones are full *of the sin* of his youth, which shall lie down with him in the dust.

12Though wickedness be sweet in his mouth, *though* he hide it under his tongue;

13Though he spare it, and forsake it not; but keep it still within his mouth:

14Yet his meat in his bowels is turned, *it is* the gall of asps within him.

15He hath swallowed down riches, and he shall vomit them up again: God shall cast them out of his belly.

16He shall suck the poison of asps: the viper's tongue shall slay him.

17He shall not see the rivers, the floods, the brooks of honey and butter.

New International

22Why do you pursue me as God does?
Will you never get enough of my flesh?

23"Oh, that my words were recorded,
that they were written on a scroll,

24that they were inscribed with an iron tool ona
lead,
or engraved in rock forever!

25I know that my Redeemerb lives,
and that in the end he will stand upon the
earth.c

26And after my skin has been destroyed,
yetd ine my flesh I will see God;

27I myself will see him
with my own eyes—I, and not another.
How my heart yearns within me!

28"If you say, 'How we will hound him,
since the root of the trouble lies in him,f'

29you should fear the sword yourselves;
for wrath will bring punishment by the sword,
and then you will know that there is
judgment.g"

Zophar

20 THEN ZOPHAR the Naamathite replied:

2"My troubled thoughts prompt me to answer
because I am greatly disturbed.

3I hear a rebuke that dishonors me,
and my understanding inspires me to reply.

4"Surely you know how it has been from of old,
ever since manh was placed on the earth,

5that the mirth of the wicked is brief,
the joy of the godless lasts but a moment.

6Though his pride reaches to the heavens
and his head touches the clouds,

7he will perish forever, like his own dung;
those who have seen him will say, 'Where is
he?'

8Like a dream he flies away, no more to be
found,
banished like a vision of the night.

9The eye that saw him will not see him again;
his place will look on him no more.

10His children must make amends to the poor;
his own hands must give back his wealth.

11The youthful vigor that fills his bones
will lie with him in the dust.

12"Though evil is sweet in his mouth
and he hides it under his tongue,

13though he cannot bear to let it go
and keeps it in his mouth,

14yet his food will turn sour in his stomach;
it will become the venom of serpents within
him.

15He will spit out the riches he swallowed;
God will make his stomach vomit them up.

16He will suck the poison of serpents;
the fangs of an adder will kill him.

17He will not enjoy the streams,
the rivers flowing with honey and cream.

a 24 Or *and*   b 25 Or *defender*   c 25 Or *upon my grave*   d 26 Or *And after I awake, / though this body, has been destroyed, / then*   e 26 Or / *apart from*   f 28 Many Hebrew manuscripts, Septuagint and Vulgate; most Hebrew manuscripts *me*   g 29 Or / *that you may come to know the Almighty*   h 4 Or *Adam*

Living Bible

God does? Why aren't you satisfied with my anguish?
23, 24Oh, that I could write my plea with an iron pen in the rock forever.

25"But as for me, I know that my Redeemer lives, and that he will stand upon the earth at last. 26And I know that after this body has decayed, this body shall see God!i 27Then he will be on *my* side! Yes, I shall see him, not as a stranger, but as a friend! What a glorious hope!

28"How dare you go on persecuting me, as though I were proven guilty? 29I warn you, you yourselves are in danger of punishment for your attitude."

20 THE SPEECH of Zophar the Naamathite:
2"I hasten to reply, for I have the answer for you. 3You have tried to make me feel ashamed of myself for calling you a sinner, but my spirit won't let me stop.

4"Don't you realize that ever since man was first placed upon the earth, 5the triumph of the wicked has been short-lived, and the joy of the godless but for a moment? 6Though the godless be proud as the heavens, and walk with his nose in the air, 7yet he shall perish forever, cast away like his own dung. Those who knew him will wonder where he is gone. 8He will fade like a dream. 9Neither his friends nor his family will ever see him again.

10"His children shall beg from the poor, their hard labor shall repay his debts. 11Though still a young man, his bones shall lie in the dust.

12"He enjoyed the taste of his wickedness, letting it melt in his mouth, 13sipping it slowly, lest it disappear.

14"But suddenly the food he has eaten turns sour within him. 15He will vomit the plunder he gorged. God won't let him keep it down. 16It is like poison and death to him. 17He shall not enjoy the goods he stole; they will not be butter and honey to him after all. 18His labors

New Revised Standard

22   Why do you, like God, pursue me,
         never satisfied with my flesh?
23   "O that my words were written down!
         O that they were inscribed in a book!
24   O that with an iron pen and with lead
         they were engraved on a rock forever!
25   For I know that my Redeemerj lives,
         and that at the last hek will stand upon the
         earth;l
26   and after my skin has been thus destroyed,
         then inm my flesh I shall see God,n
27   whom I shall see on my side,o
         and my eyes shall behold, and not another.
         My heart faints within me!
28   If you say, 'How we will persecute him!'
         and, 'The root of the matter is found in
         him';
29   be afraid of the sword,
         for wrath brings the punishment of the
         sword,
         so that you may know there is a judgment."

Zophar Speaks: Wickedness Receives Just Retribution

20 THEN ZOPHAR the Naamathite answered:
2   "Pay attention! My thoughts urge me to
         answer,
         because of the agitation within me.
3   I hear censure that insults me,
         and a spirit beyond my understanding
         answers me.
4   Do you not know this from of old,
         ever since mortals were placed on earth,
5   that the exulting of the wicked is short,
         and the joy of the godless is but for a
         moment?
6   Even though they mount up high as the
         heavens,
         and their head reaches to the clouds,
7   they will perish forever like their own dung;
         those who have seen them will say, 'Where
         are they?'
8   They will fly away like a dream, and not be
         found;
         they will be chased away like a vision of
         the night.
9   The eye that saw them will see them no more,
         nor will their place behold them any longer.
10   Their children will seek the favor of the poor,
         and their hands will give back their wealth.
11   Their bodies, once full of youth,
         will lie down in the dust with them.

12   "Though wickedness is sweet in their mouth,
         though they hide it under their tongues,
13   though they are loath to let it go,
         and hold it in their mouths,
14   yet their food is turned in their stomachs;
         it is the venom of asps within them.
15   They swallow down riches and vomit them up
         again;
         God casts them out of their bellies.
16   They will suck the poison of asps;
         the tongue of a viper will kill them.
17   They will not look on the rivers,
         the streams flowing with honey and curds.

---

i 19:26 *this body shall see God*, or, "then even without my flesh I shall see God."

j Or *Vindicator*   k Or *that he the Last*   l Heb *dust*   m Or *without*
n Meaning of Heb of this verse uncertain   o Or *for myself*

King James

18That which he laboured for shall he restore, and shall not swallow *it* down: according to *his* substance *shall* the restitution *be,* and he shall not rejoice *therein.*

19Because he hath oppressed *and* hath forsaken the poor; *because* he hath violently taken away an house which he builded not;

20Surely he shall not feel quietness in his belly, he shall not save of that which he desired.

21There shall none of his meat be left; therefore shall no man look for his goods.

22In the fulness of his sufficiency he shall be in straits: every hand of the wicked shall come upon him.

23*When* he is about to fill his belly, *God* shall cast the fury of his wrath upon him, and shall rain *it* upon him while he is eating.

24He shall flee from the iron weapon, *and* the bow of steel shall strike him through.

25It is drawn, and cometh out of the body; yea, the glittering sword cometh out of his gall: terrors *are* upon him.

26All darkness *shall be* hid in his secret places: a fire not blown shall consume him; it shall go ill with him that is left in his tabernacle.

27The heaven shall reveal his iniquity; and the earth shall rise up against him.

28The increase of his house shall depart, *and his goods* shall flow away in the day of his wrath.

29This *is* the portion of a wicked man from God, and the heritage appointed unto him by God.

21 BUT JOB answered and said, 2Hear diligently my speech, and let this be your consolations.

3Suffer me that I may speak; and after that I have spoken, mock on.

4As for me, *is* my complaint to man? and if *it were so,* why should not my spirit be troubled?

5Mark me, and be astonished, and lay *your* hand upon *your* mouth.

6Even when I remember I am afraid, and trembling taketh hold on my flesh.

7Wherefore do the wicked live, become old, yea, are mighty in power?

8Their seed is established in their sight with them, and their offspring before their eyes.

9Their houses *are* safe from fear, neither *is* the rod of God upon them.

10Their bull gendereth, and faileth not; their cow calveth, and casteth not her calf.

11They send forth their little ones like a flock, and their children dance.

12They take the timbrel and harp, and rejoice at the sound of the organ.

13They spend their days in wealth, and in a moment go down to the grave.

14Therefore they say unto God, Depart from us; for we desire not the knowledge of thy ways.

New International

18What he toiled for he must give back uneaten;
  he will not enjoy the profit from his trading.
19For he has oppressed the poor and left them destitute;
  he has seized houses he did not build.

20"Surely he will have no respite from his craving;
  he cannot save himself by his treasure.
21Nothing is left for him to devour;
  his prosperity will not endure.
22In the midst of his plenty, distress will overtake him;
  the full force of misery will come upon him.
23When he has filled his belly,
  God will vent his burning anger against him
  and rain down his blows upon him.
24Though he flees from an iron weapon,
  a bronze-tipped arrow pierces him.
25He pulls it out of his back,
  the gleaming point out of his liver.
  Terrors will come over him;
26 total darkness lies in wait for his treasures.
  A fire unfanned will consume him
  and devour what is left in his tent.
27The heavens will expose his guilt;
  the earth will rise up against him.
28A flood will carry off his house,
  rushing watersa on the day of God's wrath.
29Such is the fate God allots the wicked,
  the heritage appointed for them by God."

Job

21 THEN JOB replied:

2"Listen carefully to my words;
  let this be the consolation you give me.
3Bear with me while I speak,
  and after I have spoken, mock on.

4"Is my complaint directed to man?
  Why should I not be impatient?
5Look at me and be astonished;
  clap your hand over your mouth.
6When I think about this, I am terrified;
  trembling seizes my body.
7Why do the wicked live on,
  growing old and increasing in power?
8They see their children established around them,
  their offspring before their eyes.
9Their homes are safe and free from fear;
  the rod of God is not upon them.
10Their bulls never fail to breed;
  their cows calve and do not miscarry.
11They send forth their children as a flock;
  their little ones dance about.
12They sing to the music of tambourine and harp;
  they make merry to the sound of the flute.
13They spend their years in prosperity
  and go down to the graveb in peace.c
14Yet they say to God, 'Leave us alone!
  We have no desire to know your ways.

a 28 Or *The possessions in his house will be carried off,* / *washed away*
b 13 Hebrew *Sheol*   c 13 Or *in an instant*

Living Bible

shall not be rewarded; wealth will give him no joy. ¹⁹For he has oppressed the poor and foreclosed their homes; he will never recover. ²⁰Though he was always greedy, now he has nothing; of all the things he dreamed of— none remain. ²¹Because he stole at every opportunity, his prosperity shall not continue.

²²"He shall run into trouble at the peak of his powers; all the wicked shall destroy him. ²³Just as he is about to fill his belly, God will rain down wrath upon him. ²⁴He will be chased and struck down. ²⁵The arrow is pulled from his body—and the glittering point comes out from his gall. The terrors of death are upon him.

²⁶"His treasures will be lost in deepest darkness. A raging fire will devour his goods, consuming all he has left. ²⁷The heavens will reveal his sins, and the earth will give testimony against him. ²⁸His wealth will disappear beneath the wrath of God. ²⁹This is what awaits the wicked man, for God prepares it for him."

21 *JOB'S REPLY:*
², ³"Listen to me; let me speak, and afterwards, mock on.

⁴"I am complaining about God,ᵈ not man; no wonder my spirit is so troubled. ⁵Look at me in horror, and lay your hand upon your mouth. ⁶Even I am frightened when I see myself. Horror takes hold upon me and I shudder.

⁷"The truth is that the wicked live on to a good old age, and become great and powerful. ⁸They live to see their children grow to maturity around them, and their grandchildren, too. ⁹Their homes are safe from every fear, and God does not punish them. ¹⁰Their cattle are productive, ¹¹they have many happy children, ¹², ¹³they spend their time singing and dancing. They are wealthy and need deny themselves nothing; they are prosperous to the end. ¹⁴All this despite the fact that they ordered God away and wanted no part of him and his ways.

New Revised Standard

18 They will give back the fruit of their toil,
      and will not swallow it down;
    from the profit of their trading
      they will get no enjoyment.
19 For they have crushed and abandoned the
        poor,
      they have seized a house that they did not
        build.
20 "They knew no quiet in their bellies;
      in their greed they let nothing escape.
21 There was nothing left after they had eaten;
      therefore their prosperity will not endure.
22 In full sufficiency they will be in distress;
      all the force of misery will come upon
        them.
23 To fill their belly to the full
      Godᵉ will send his fierce anger into them,
      and rain it upon them as their food.ᶠ
24 They will flee from an iron weapon;
      a bronze arrow will strike them through.
25 It is drawn forth and comes out of their body,
      and the glittering point comes out of their
        gall;
      terrors come upon them.
26 Utter darkness is laid up for their treasures;
      a fire fanned by no one will devour them;
      what is left in their tent will be consumed.
27 The heavens will reveal their iniquity,
      and the earth will rise up against them.
28 The possessions of their house will be carried
        away,
      dragged off in the day of God'sᵍ wrath.
29 This is the portion of the wicked from God,
      the heritage decreed for them by God."

Job Replies: The Wicked Often Go Unpunished

21 THEN JOB answered:
2 "Listen carefully to my words,
      and let this be your consolation.
3 Bear with me, and I will speak;
      then after I have spoken, mock on.
4 As for me, is my complaint addressed to
        mortals?
      Why should I not be impatient?
5 Look at me, and be appalled,
      and lay your hand upon your mouth.
6 When I think of it I am dismayed,
      and shuddering seizes my flesh.
7 Why do the wicked live on,
      reach old age, and grow mighty in power?
8 Their children are established in their
        presence,
      and their offspring before their eyes.
9 Their houses are safe from fear,
      and no rod of God is upon them.
10 Their bull breeds without fail;
      their cow calves and never miscarries.
11 They send out their little ones like a flock,
      and their children dance around.
12 They sing to the tambourine and the lyre,
      and rejoice to the sound of the pipe.
13 They spend their days in prosperity,
      and in peace they go down to Sheol.
14 They say to God, 'Leave us alone!
      We do not desire to know your ways.

ᵈ 21:4 *I am complaining about God*, implied.

ᵉ Heb *he*   ᶠ Cn: Meaning of Heb uncertain   ᵍ Heb *his*

King James

15What *is* the Almighty, that we should serve him? and what profit should we have, if we pray unto him?

16Lo, their good *is* not in their hand: the counsel of the wicked is far from me.

17How oft is the candle of the wicked put out! and *how oft* cometh their destruction upon them! *God* distributeth sorrows in his anger.

18They are as stubble before the wind, and as chaff that the storm carrieth away.

19God layeth up his iniquity for his children: he rewardeth him, and he shall know *it*.

20His eyes shall see his destruction, and he shall drink of the wrath of the Almighty.

21For what pleasure *hath* he in his house after him, when the number of his months is cut off in the midst?

22Shall *any* teach God knowledge? seeing he judgeth those that are high.

23One dieth in his full strength, being wholly at ease and quiet.

24His breasts are full of milk, and his bones are moistened with marrow.

25And another dieth in the bitterness of his soul, and never eateth with pleasure.

26They shall lie down alike in the dust, and the worms shall cover them.

27Behold, I know your thoughts, and the devices *which* ye wrongfully imagine against me.

28For ye say, Where *is* the house of the prince? and where *are* the dwelling places of the wicked?

29Have ye not asked them that go by the way? and do ye not know their tokens,

30That the wicked is reserved to the day of destruction? they shall be brought forth to the day of wrath.

31Who shall declare his way to his face? and who shall repay him *what* he hath done?

32Yet shall he be brought to the grave, and shall remain in the tomb.

33The clods of the valley shall be sweet unto him, and every man shall draw after him, as *there are* innumerable before him.

34How then comfort ye me in vain, seeing in your answers there remaineth falsehood?

22 THEN ELIPHAZ the Temanite answered and said,

2Can a man be profitable unto God, as he that is wise may be profitable unto himself?

New International

15Who is the Almighty, that we should serve him?
  What would we gain by praying to him?'
16But their prosperity is not in their own hands,
  so I stand aloof from the counsel of the wicked.

17"Yet how often is the lamp of the wicked snuffed out?
  How often does calamity come upon them,
  the fate God allots in his anger?
18How often are they like straw before the wind,
  like chaff swept away by a gale?
19It is said,ₐ 'God stores up a man's punishment for his sons.'
  Let him repay the man himself, so that he will know it!
20Let his own eyes see his destruction;
  let him drink of the wrath of the Almighty.ᵃ
21For what does he care about the family he leaves behind
  when his allotted months come to an end?

22"Can anyone teach knowledge to God,
  since he judges even the highest?
23One man dies in full vigor,
  completely secure and at ease,
24his bodyᵇ well nourished,
  his bones rich with marrow.
25Another man dies in bitterness of soul,
  never having enjoyed anything good.
26Side by side they lie in the dust,
  and worms cover them both.

27"I know full well what you are thinking,
  the schemes by which you would wrong me.
28You say, 'Where now is the great man's house,
  the tents where wicked men lived?'
29Have you never questioned those who travel?
  Have you paid no regard to their accounts—
30that the evil man is spared from the day of calamity,
  that he is delivered fromᶜ the day of wrath?
31Who denounces his conduct to his face?
  Who repays him for what he has done?
32He is carried to the grave,
  and watch is kept over his tomb.
33The soil in the valley is sweet to him;
  all men follow after him,
  and a countless throng goesᵈ before him.

34"So how can you console me with your nonsense?
  Nothing is left of your answers but falsehood!"

Eliphaz

22 THEN ELIPHAZ the Temanite replied:

2"Can a man be of benefit to God?
  Can even a wise man benefit him?

ᵃ *17-20 Verses 17 and 18 may be taken as exclamations and 19 and 20 as declarations.*   ᵇ *24 The meaning of the Hebrew for this word is uncertain.*   ᶜ *30 Or man is reserved for the day of calamity, / that he is brought forth to*   ᵈ *33 Or / as a countless throng went*

Living Bible

15" 'Who is Almighty God?' they scoff. 'Why should we obey him? What good will it do us?'

16"Look, everything the wicked touch has turned to gold! But I refuse even to deal with people like that. 17Yet the wicked get away with it every time. They never have trouble, and God skips them when he distributes his sorrows and anger. 18Are they driven before the wind like straw? Are they carried away by the storm? Not at all!

19" 'Well,' you say, 'at least God will punish their children!' But I say that God should punish the man who sins, not his children! Let him feel the penalty himself. 20Yes, let him be destroyed for his iniquity. Let him drink deeply of the anger of the Almighty. 21For when he is dead, then he will never again be able to enjoy his family.

22"But who can rebuke God, the supreme Judge? 23, 24He destroys those who are healthy, wealthy, fat, and prosperous; 25God also destroys those in deep and grinding poverty who have never known anything good. 26Both alike are buried in the same dust, both eaten by the same worms.

27"I know what you are going to say— 28you will tell me of rich and wicked men who came to disaster because of their sins. 29But I reply, Ask anyone who has been around and he can tell you the truth, 30, 31, 32that the evil man is usually spared in the day of calamity, and allowed to escape. No one rebukes him openly. No one repays him for what he has done. And an honor guard keeps watch at his grave. 33A great funeral procession precedes and follows him as the soft earth covers him. 34How can you comfort me when your whole premise is so wrong?"

New Revised Standard

15   What is the Almighty,e that we should serve
        him?
     And what profit do we get if we pray to
        him?'
16   Is not their prosperity indeed their own
        achievement?f
     The plans of the wicked are repugnant to
        me.

17   "How often is the lamp of the wicked put out?
     How often does calamity come upon them?
     How often does Godg distribute pains in his
        anger?
18   How often are they like straw before the
        wind,
     and like chaff that the storm carries away?
19   You say, 'God stores up their iniquity for
        their children.'
     Let it be paid back to them, so that they
        may know it.
20   Let their own eyes see their destruction,
     and let them drink of the wrath of the
        Almighty.e
21   For what do they care for their household after
        them,
     when the number of their months is cut off?
22   Will any teach God knowledge,
     seeing that he judges those that are on high?
23   One dies in full prosperity,
     being wholly at ease and secure,
24   his loins full of milk
     and the marrow of his bones moist.
25   Another dies in bitterness of soul,
     never having tasted of good.
26   They lie down alike in the dust,
     and the worms cover them.

27   "Oh, I know your thoughts,
     and your schemes to wrong me.
28   For you say, 'Where is the house of the
        prince?
     Where is the tent in which the wicked
        lived?'
29   Have you not asked those who travel the
        roads,
     and do you not accept their testimony,
30   that the wicked are spared in the day of
        calamity,
     and are rescued in the day of wrath?
31   Who declares their way to their face,
     and who repays them for what they have
        done?
32   When they are carried to the grave,
     a watch is kept over their tomb.
33   The clods of the valley are sweet to them;
     everyone will follow after,
     and those who went before are innumerable.
34   How then will you comfort me with empty
        nothings?
     There is nothing left of your answers but
        falsehood."

Eliphaz Speaks: Job's Wickedness Is Great

22 ANOTHER ADDRESS from Eliphaz:
2"Is mere man of any worth to God? Even the wisest is of value only to himself! 3Is it any pleasure to

22 THEN ELIPHAZ the Temanite answered:
2   "Can a mortal be of use to God?
     Can even the wisest be of service to him?

e Traditional rendering of Heb Shaddai   f Heb in their hand   g Heb he

King James

3*Is it* any pleasure to the Almighty, that thou art righteous? or *is it* gain *to him,* that thou makest thy ways perfect?

4Will he reprove thee for fear of thee? will he enter with thee into judgment?

5*Is* not thy wickedness great? and thine iniquities infinite?

6For thou hast taken a pledge from thy brother for nought, and stripped the naked of their clothing.

7Thou hast not given water to the weary to drink, and thou hast withholden bread from the hungry.

8But *as for* the mighty man, he had the earth; and the honourable man dwelt in it.

9Thou hast sent widows away empty, and the arms of the fatherless have been broken.

10Therefore snares *are* round about thee, and sudden fear troubleth thee;

11Or darkness, *that* thou canst not see; and abundance of waters cover thee.

12*Is* not God in the height of heaven? and behold the height of the stars, how high they are!

13And thou sayest, How doth God know? can he judge through the dark cloud?

14Thick clouds *are* a covering to him, that he seeth not; and he walketh in the circuit of heaven.

15Hast thou marked the old way which wicked men have trodden?

16Which were cut down out of time, whose foundation was overflown with a flood:

17Which said unto God, Depart from us: and what can the Almighty do for them?

18Yet he filled their houses with good *things:* but the counsel of the wicked is far from me.

19The righteous see *it,* and are glad: and the innocent laugh them to scorn.

20Whereas our substance is not cut down, but the remnant of them the fire consumeth.

21Acquaint now thyself with him, and be at peace: thereby good shall come unto thee.

22Receive, I pray thee, the law from his mouth, and lay up his words in thine heart.

23If thou return to the Almighty, thou shalt be built up, thou shalt put away iniquity far from thy tabernacles.

24Then shalt thou lay up gold as dust, and the *gold* of Ophir as the stones of the brooks.

25Yea, the Almighty shall be thy defence, and thou shalt have plenty of silver.

26For then shalt thou have thy delight in the Almighty, and shalt lift up thy face unto God.

27Thou shalt make thy prayer unto him, and he shall hear thee, and thou shalt pay thy vows.

28Thou shalt also decree a thing, and it shall be established unto thee: and the light shall shine upon thy ways.

29When *men* are cast down, then thou shalt say, *There is* lifting up; and he shall save the humble person.

New International

3What pleasure would it give the Almighty if you were righteous?
What would he gain if your ways were blameless?

4"Is it for your piety that he rebukes you and brings charges against you?

5Is not your wickedness great?
Are not your sins endless?

6You demanded security from your brothers for no reason;
you stripped men of their clothing, leaving them naked.

7You gave no water to the weary and you withheld food from the hungry,

8though you were a powerful man, owning land—
an honored man, living on it.

9And you sent widows away empty-handed and broke the strength of the fatherless.

10That is why snares are all around you, why sudden peril terrifies you,

11why it is so dark you cannot see, and why a flood of water covers you.

12"Is not God in the heights of heaven?
And see how lofty are the highest stars!

13Yet you say, 'What does God know?
Does he judge through such darkness?

14Thick clouds veil him, so he does not see us as he goes about in the vaulted heavens.'

15Will you keep to the old path that evil men have trod?

16They were carried off before their time, their foundations washed away by a flood.

17They said to God, 'Leave us alone!
What can the Almighty do to us?'

18Yet it was he who filled their houses with good things,
so I stand aloof from the counsel of the wicked.

19"The righteous see their ruin and rejoice; the innocent mock them, saying,

20'Surely our foes are destroyed, and fire devours their wealth.'

21"Submit to God and be at peace with him; in this way prosperity will come to you.

22Accept instruction from his mouth and lay up his words in your heart.

23If you return to the Almighty, you will be restored:
If you remove wickedness far from your tent

24and assign your nuggets to the dust, your gold of Ophir to the rocks in the ravines,

25then the Almighty will be your gold, the choicest silver for you.

26Surely then you will find delight in the Almighty
and will lift up your face to God.

27You will pray to him, and he will hear you, and you will fulfill your vows.

28What you decide on will be done, and light will shine on your ways.

29When men are brought low and you say, 'Lift them up!'
then he will save the downcast.

Living Bible

the Almighty if you are righteous? Would it be any gain to him if you were perfect? 4Is it because you are good that he is punishing you? 5Not at all! It is because of your wickedness! Your sins are endless!

6"For instance, you must have refused to loan money to needy friends unless they gave you all their clothing as a pledge—yes, you must have stripped them to the bone. 7You must have refused water to the thirsty, and bread to the starving. 8But no doubt you gave men of importance anything they wanted, and let the wealthy live wherever they chose. 9You sent widows away without helping them, and broke the arms of orphans. 10, 11That is why you are now surrounded by traps and sudden fears, and darkness and waves of horror.

12"God is so great—higher than the heavens, higher than the stars. 13But you reply, 'That is why he can't see what I am doing! How can he judge through the thick darkness? 14For thick clouds swirl about him so that he cannot see us. He is way up there, walking on the vault of heaven.'

15, 16"Don't you realize that those treading the ancient paths of sin are snatched away in youth, and the foundations of their lives washed out forever? 17For they said to God, 'Go away, God! What can you do for us?' 18(God forbid that I should say a thing like that.) Yet they forgot that he had filled their homes with good things. 19And now the righteous shall see them destroyed; the innocent shall laugh the wicked to scorn. 20'See,' they will say, 'the last of our enemies have been destroyed in the fire.'

21"Quit quarreling with God! Agree with him and you will have peace at last! His favor will surround you if you will only admit that you were wrong. 22Listen to his instructions and store them in your heart. 23If you return to God and put right all the wrong in your home, then you will be restored. 24If you give up your lust for money, and throw your gold away, 25then the Almighty himself shall be your treasure; he will be your precious silver!

26"Then you will delight yourself in the Lord, and look up to God. 27You will pray to him, and he will hear you, and you will fulfill all your promises to him. 28Whatever you wish will happen! And the light of heaven will shine upon the road ahead of you. 29If you are attacked and knocked down, you will know that there is

New Revised Standard

3 Is it any pleasure to the Almighty[a] if you are righteous,
   or is it gain to him if you make your ways blameless?
4 Is it for your piety that he reproves you,
   and enters into judgment with you?
5 Is not your wickedness great?
   There is no end to your iniquities.
6 For you have exacted pledges from your family for no reason,
   and stripped the naked of their clothing.
7 You have given no water to the weary to drink,
   and you have withheld bread from the hungry.
8 The powerful possess the land,
   and the favored live in it.
9 You have sent widows away empty-handed,
   and the arms of the orphans you have crushed.[b]
10 Therefore snares are around you,
   and sudden terror overwhelms you,
11 or darkness so that you cannot see;
   a flood of water covers you.

12 "Is not God high in the heavens?
   See the highest stars, how lofty they are!
13 Therefore you say, 'What does God know?
   Can he judge through the deep darkness?
14 Thick clouds enwrap him, so that he does not see,
   and he walks on the dome of heaven.'
15 Will you keep to the old way
   that the wicked have trod?
16 They were snatched away before their time;
   their foundation was washed away by a flood.
17 They said to God, 'Leave us alone,'
   and 'What can the Almighty[a] do to us?'[c]
18 Yet he filled their houses with good things—
   but the plans of the wicked are repugnant to me.
19 The righteous see it and are glad;
   the innocent laugh them to scorn,
20 saying, 'Surely our adversaries are cut off,
   and what they left, the fire has consumed.'

21 "Agree with God,[d] and be at peace;
   in this way good will come to you.
22 Receive instruction from his mouth,
   and lay up his words in your heart.
23 If you return to the Almighty,[a] you will be restored,
   if you remove unrighteousness from your tents,
24 if you treat gold like dust,
   and gold of Ophir like the stones of the torrent-bed,
25 and if the Almighty[a] is your gold
   and your precious silver,
26 then you will delight yourself in the Almighty,[a]
   and lift up your face to God.
27 You will pray to him, and he will hear you,
   and you will pay your vows.
28 You will decide on a matter, and it will be established for you,
   and light will shine on your ways.
29 When others are humiliated, you say it is pride;
   for he saves the humble.

a Traditional rendering of Heb Shaddai   b Gk Syr Tg Vg: Heb were crushed
c Gk Syr: Heb them   d Heb him

King James

30He shall deliver the island of the innocent: and it is delivered by the pureness of thine hands.

23 THEN JOB answered and said,
2Even today *is* my complaint bitter: my stroke is heavier than my groaning.

3Oh that I knew where I might find him! *that* I might come *even* to his seat!

4I would order *my* cause before him, and fill my mouth with arguments.

5I would know the words *which* he would answer me, and understand what he would say unto me.

6Will he plead against me with *his* great power? No; but he would put *strength* in me.

7There the righteous might dispute with him; so should I be delivered for ever from my judge.

8Behold, I go forward, but he *is not there;* and backward, but I cannot perceive him:

9On the left hand, where he doth work, but I cannot behold *him:* he hideth himself on the right hand, that I cannot see *him:*

10But he knoweth the way that I take: *when* he hath tried me, I shall come forth as gold.

11My foot hath held his steps, his way have I kept, and not declined.

12Neither have I gone back from the commandment of his lips; I have esteemed the words of his mouth more than my necessary *food.*

13But he *is* in one *mind,* and who can turn him? and *what* his soul desireth, even *that* he doeth.

14For he performeth *the thing that is* appointed for me: and many such *things are* with him.

15Therefore am I troubled at his presence: when I consider, I am afraid of him.

16For God maketh my heart soft, and the Almighty troubleth me:

17Because I was not cut off before the darkness, *neither* hath he covered the darkness from my face.

24 WHY, SEEING times are not hidden from the Almighty, do they that know him not see his days?

2*Some* remove the landmarks; they violently take away flocks, and feed *thereof.*

3They drive away the ass of the fatherless, they take the widow's ox for a pledge.

4They turn the needy out of the way: the poor of the earth hide themselves together.

5Behold, *as* wild asses in the desert, go they forth to their work; rising betimes for a prey: the wilderness *yieldeth* food for them *and* for *their* children.

6They reap *every one* his corn in the field: and they gather the vintage of the wicked.

New International

30He will deliver even one who is not innocent, who will be delivered through the cleanness of your hands."

Job
23 THEN JOB replied:

2"Even today my complaint is bitter;
    his hand[a] is heavy in spite of[b] my groaning.
3If only I knew where to find him;
    if only I could go to his dwelling!
4I would state my case before him
    and fill my mouth with arguments.
5I would find out what he would answer me,
    and consider what he would say.
6Would he oppose me with great power?
    No, he would not press charges against me.
7There an upright man could present his case
        before him,
    and I would be delivered forever from my
        judge.
8"But if I go to the east, he is not there;
    if I go to the west, I do not find him.
9When he is at work in the north, I do not see
        him;
    when he turns to the south, I catch no
        glimpse of him.
10But he knows the way that I take;
    when he has tested me, I will come forth as
        gold.
11My feet have closely followed his steps;
    I have kept to his way without turning aside.
12I have not departed from the commands of his
        lips;
    I have treasured the words of his mouth more
        than my daily bread.
13"But he stands alone, and who can oppose him?
    He does whatever he pleases.
14He carries out his decree against me,
    and many such plans he still has in store.
15That is why I am terrified before him;
    when I think of all this, I fear him.
16God has made my heart faint;
    the Almighty has terrified me.
17Yet I am not silenced by the darkness,
    by the thick darkness that covers my face.

24 "WHY DOES the Almighty not set times for
        judgment?
    Why must those who know him look in vain
        for such days?
2Men move boundary stones;
    they pasture flocks they have stolen.
3They drive away the orphan's donkey
    and take the widow's ox in pledge.
4They thrust the needy from the path
    and force all the poor of the land into hiding.
5Like wild donkeys in the desert,
    the poor go about their labor of foraging
        food;
    the wasteland provides food for their children.
6They gather fodder in the fields
    and glean in the vineyards of the wicked.

---

[a] 2 Septuagint and Syriac; Hebrew *I the hand on me*   [b] 2 Or *heavy on me in*

Living Bible

someone who will lift you up again. Yes, he will save the humble, 30and help even sinners by your pure hands."

23 THE REPLY of Job:

2"My complaint today is still a bitter one, and my punishment far more severe than my fault deserves. 3Oh, that I knew where to find God—that I could go to his throne and talk with him there. 4, 5I would tell him all about my side of this argument, and listen to his reply, and understand what he wants. 6Would he merely overpower me with his greatness? No, he would listen with sympathy. 7Fair and honest men could reason with him, and be acquitted by my Judge.

8"But I search in vain. I seek him here, I seek him there, and cannot find him. 9I seek him in his workshop in the North, but cannot find him there; nor can I find him in the South; there, too, he hides himself. 10But he knows every detail of what is happening to me; and when he has examined me, he will pronounce me completely innocent—as pure as solid gold!

11"I have stayed in God's paths, following his steps. I have not turned aside. 12I have not refused his commandments but have enjoyed them more than my daily food. 13Nevertheless, his mind concerning me remains unchanged, and who can turn him from his purposes? Whatever he wants to do, he does. 14So he will do to me all he has planned, and there is more ahead.c

15"No wonder I am so terrified in his presence. When I think of it, terror grips me. 16, 17God has given me a fainting heart; he, the Almighty, has terrified me with darkness all around me, thick, impenetrable darkness everywhere.

24 "WHY DOESN'T God open the court and listen to my case? Why must the godly wait for him in vain? 2For a crime wave has engulfed us—landmarks are moved, flocks of sheep are stolen, 3and even the donkeys of the poor and fatherless are taken. Poor widows must surrender the little they have as a pledge to get a loan. 4The needy are kicked aside; they must get out of the way. 5Like the wild donkeys in the desert, the poor must spend all their time just getting barely enough to keep soul and body together. They are sent into the desert to search for food for their children. 6They eat what they find that grows wild, and must even glean the vineyards of the wicked. 7All night they lie naked in the

New Revised Standard

30 He will deliver even those who are guilty;
   they will escape because of the cleanness of
    your hands."d

Job Replies: My Complaint Is Bitter

23 THEN JOB answered:

2 "Today also my complaint is bitter;e
   hisf hand is heavy despite my groaning.
3 Oh, that I knew where I might find him,
   that I might come even to his dwelling!
4 I would lay my case before him,
   and fill my mouth with arguments.
5 I would learn what he would answer me,
   and understand what he would say to me.
6 Would he contend with me in the greatness of
    his power?
   No; but he would give heed to me.
7 There an upright person could reason with
    him,
   and I should be acquitted forever by my
    judge.

8 "If I go forward, he is not there;
   or backward, I cannot perceive him;
9 on the left he hides, and I cannot behold him;
   I turng to the right, but I cannot see him.
10 But he knows the way that I take;
   when he has tested me, I shall come out
    like gold.
11 My foot has held fast to his steps;
   I have kept his way and have not turned
    aside.
12 I have not departed from the commandment of
    his lips;
   I have treasured inh my bosom the words of
    his mouth.
13 But he stands alone and who can dissuade
    him?
   What he desires, that he does.
14 For he will complete what he appoints for me;
   and many such things are in his mind.
15 Therefore I am terrified at his presence;
   when I consider, I am in dread of him.
16 God has made my heart faint;
   the Almightyi has terrified me;
17 If only I could vanish in darkness,
   and thick darkness would cover my face!j

Job Complains of Violence on the Earth

24 "WHY ARE times not kept by the
    Almighty,i
   and why do those who know him never see
    his days?
2 The wickedk remove landmarks;
   they seize flocks and pasture them.
3 They drive away the donkey of the orphan;
   they take the widow's ox for a pledge.
4 They thrust the needy off the road;
   the poor of the earth all hide themselves.
5 Like wild asses in the desert
   they go out to their toil,
   scavenging in the wasteland
    food for their young.
6 They reap in a field not their own
   and they glean in the vineyard of the
    wicked.

---

c 23:14 and there is more ahead, literally, "and many such things are with him."

d Meaning of Heb uncertain   e Syr Vg Tg: Heb rebellious   f Gk Syr: Heb my   g Syr Vg: Heb he turns   h Gk Vg: Heb from   i Traditional rendering of Heb Shaddai   j Or But I am not destroyed by the darkness; he has concealed the thick darkness from me   k Gk: Heb they

King James

7They cause the naked to lodge without clothing, that *they have* no covering in the cold.

8They are wet with the showers of the mountains, and embrace the rock for want of a shelter.

9They pluck the fatherless from the breast, and take a pledge of the poor.

10They cause *him* to go naked without clothing, and they take away the sheaf *from* the hungry;

11*Which* make oil within their walls, *and* tread *their* winepresses, and suffer thirst.

12Men groan from out of the city, and the soul of the wounded crieth out: yet God layeth not folly *to them.*

13They are of those that rebel against the light; they know not the ways thereof, nor abide in the paths thereof.

14The murderer rising with the light killeth the poor and needy, and in the night is as a thief.

15The eye also of the adulterer waiteth for the twilight, saying, No eye shall see me: and disguiseth *his* face.

16In the dark they dig through houses, *which* they had marked for themselves in the daytime: they know not the light.

17For the morning *is* to them even as the shadow of death: if *one* know *them, they are in* the terrors of the shadow of death.

18He *is* swift as the waters; their portion is cursed in the earth: he beholdeth not the way of the vineyards.

19Drought and heat consume the snow waters: *so doth* the grave *those which* have sinned.

20The womb shall forget him; the worm shall feed sweetly on him; he shall be no more remembered; and wickedness shall be broken as a tree.

21He evil entreateth the barren *that* beareth not: and doeth not good to the widow.

22He draweth also the mighty with his power: he riseth up, and no *man* is sure of life.

23*Though* it be given him *to be* in safety, whereon he resteth; yet his eyes *are* upon their ways.

24They are exalted for a little while, but are gone and brought low; they are taken out of the way as all *other,* and cut off as the tops of the ears of corn.

25And if *it be* not *so* now, who will make me a liar, and make my speech nothing worth?

25 THEN ANSWERED Bildad the Shuhite, and said,

2Dominion and fear *are* with him, he maketh peace in his high places.

3Is there any number of his armies? and upon whom doth not his light arise?

New International

7Lacking clothes, they spend the night naked;
　　they have nothing to cover themselves in the
　　cold.

8They are drenched by mountain rains
　　and hug the rocks for lack of shelter.

9The fatherless child is snatched from the breast;
　　the infant of the poor is seized for a debt.

10Lacking clothes, they go about naked;
　　they carry the sheaves, but still go hungry.

11They crush olives among the terracesa;
　　they tread the winepresses, yet suffer thirst.

12The groans of the dying rise from the city,
　　and the souls of the wounded cry out for
　　help.
　　But God charges no one with wrongdoing.

13"There are those who rebel against the light,
　　who do not know its ways
　　or stay in its paths.

14When daylight is gone, the murderer rises up
　　and kills the poor and needy;
　　in the night he steals forth like a thief.

15The eye of the adulterer watches for dusk;
　　he thinks, 'No eye will see me,'
　　and he keeps his face concealed.

16In the dark, men break into houses,
　　but by day they shut themselves in;
　　they want nothing to do with the light.

17For all of them, deep darkness is their
　　morningb;
　　they make friends with the terrors of
　　darkness.c

18"Yet they are foam on the surface of the water;
　　their portion of the land is cursed,
　　so that no one goes to the vineyards.

19As heat and drought snatch away the melted
　　snow,
　　so the graved snatches away those who have
　　sinned.

20The womb forgets them,
　　the worm feasts on them;
　　evil men are no longer remembered
　　but are broken like a tree.

21They prey on the barren and childless woman,
　　and to the widow show no kindness.

22But God drags away the mighty by his power;
　　though they become established, they have no
　　assurance of life.

23He may let them rest in a feeling of security,
　　but his eyes are on their ways.

24For a little while they are exalted, and then they
　　are gone;
　　they are brought low and gathered up like all
　　others;
　　they are cut off like heads of grain.

25"If this is not so, who can prove me false
　　and reduce my words to nothing?"

Bildad

25 THEN BILDAD the Shuhite replied:

2"Dominion and awe belong to God;
　　he establishes order in the heights of heaven.

3Can his forces be numbered?
　　Upon whom does his light not rise?

---

a *11* Or *olives between the millstones;* the meaning of the Hebrew for this word is uncertain.　b *17* Or *them, their morning is like the shadow of death*　c *17* Or *of the shadow of death*　d *19* Hebrew *Sheol*

Living Bible

cold, without clothing or covering. 8They are wet with the showers of the mountains and live in caves for want of a home.

9"The wicked snatch fatherless children from their mother's breasts, and take a poor man's baby as a pledge before they will loan him any money or grain. 10That is why they must go about naked, without clothing, and are forced to carry food while they are starving. 11They are forced to press out the olive oil without tasting it, and to tread out the grape juice as they suffer from thirst. 12The bones of the dying cry from the city; the wounded cry for help; yet God does not respond to their moaning.

13"The wicked rebel against the light and are not acquainted with the right and the good. 14, 15They are murderers who rise in the early dawn to kill the poor and needy; at night they are thieves and adulterers, waiting for the twilight 'when no one will see me,' they say. They mask their faces so no one will know them. 16They break into houses at night and sleep in the daytime—they are not acquainted with the light. 17The black night is their morning; they ally themselves with the terrors of the darkness.

18"But how quickly they disappear from the face of the earth. Everything they own is cursed. They leave no property for their children. 19Death consumes sinners as drought and heat consume snow. 20Even the sinner's own mother shall forget him. Worms shall feed sweetly on him. No one will remember him any more. For wicked men are broken like a tree in the storm. 21For they have taken advantage of the childless who have no protecting sons. They refuse to help the needy widows.

22, 23"Yet sometimese it seems as though God preserves the rich by his power, and restores them to life when anyone else would die. God gives them confidence and strength, and helps them in many ways. 24But though they are very great now, yet in a moment they shall be gone like all others, cut off like heads of grain. 25Can anyone claim otherwise? Who can prove me a liar and claim that I am wrong?"

25 THE FURTHER reply of Bildad the Shuhite: 2"God is powerful and dreadful. He enforces peace in heaven. 3Who is able to number his hosts of angels? And his light shines down on all the earth. 4How

New Revised Standard

7 They lie all night naked, without clothing,
      and have no covering in the cold.
8 They are wet with the rain of the mountains,
      and cling to the rock for want of shelter.

9 "There are those who snatch the orphan child
         from the breast,
      and take as a pledge the infant of the poor.
10 They go about naked, without clothing;
      though hungry, they carry the sheaves;
11 between their terracesf they press out oil;
      they tread the wine presses, but suffer thirst.
12 From the city the dying groan,
      and the throat of the wounded cries for
         help;
      yet God pays no attention to their prayer.

13 "There are those who rebel against the light,
      who are not acquainted with its ways,
      and do not stay in its paths.
14 The murderer rises at dusk
      to kill the poor and needy,
      and in the night is like a thief.
15 The eye of the adulterer also waits for the
         twilight,
      saying, 'No eye will see me';
      and he disguises his face.
16 In the dark they dig through houses;
      by day they shut themselves up;
      they do not know the light.
17 For deep darkness is morning to all of them;
      for they are friends with the terrors of deep
         darkness.

18 "Swift are they on the face of the waters;
      their portion in the land is cursed;
      no treader turns toward their vineyards.
19 Drought and heat snatch away the snow
         waters;
      so does Sheol those who have sinned.
20 The womb forgets them;
      the worm finds them sweet;
      they are no longer remembered;
      so wickedness is broken like a tree.

21 "They harmg the childless woman,
      and do no good to the widow.
22 Yet Godh prolongs the life of the mighty by
         his power;
      they rise up when they despair of life.
23 He gives them security, and they are
         supported;
      his eyes are upon their ways.
24 They are exalted a little while, and then are
         gone;
      they wither and fade like the mallow;i
      they are cut off like the heads of grain.
25 If it is not so, who will prove me a liar,
      and show that there is nothing in what I
         say?"

Bildad Speaks: How Can a Mortal Be Righteous Before God?

25   THEN BILDAD the Shuhite answered:
2 "Dominion and fear are with God;j
      he makes peace in his high heaven.
3 Is there any number to his armies?
      Upon whom does his light not arise?

---

e 24:22, 23 *Yet sometimes,* implied.

f Meaning of Heb uncertain   g Gk Tg: Heb *feed on* or *associate with*   h Heb *he*   i Gk: Heb *like all others*   j Heb *him*

King James

4How then can man be justified with God? or how can he be clean *that is* born of a woman?

5Behold even to the moon, and it shineth not; yea, the stars are not pure in his sight.

6How much less man, *that is* a worm? and the son of man, *which is* a worm?

26 BUT JOB answered and said,
2How hast thou helped *him that is* without power? *how* savest thou the arm *that hath* no strength?

3How hast thou counselled *him that hath* no wisdom? and *how* hast thou plentifully declared the thing as it is?

4To whom hast thou uttered words? and whose spirit came from thee?

5Dead *things* are formed from under the waters, and the inhabitants thereof.

6Hell *is* naked before him, and destruction hath no covering.

7He stretcheth out the north over the empty place, *and* hangeth the earth upon nothing.

8He bindeth up the waters in his thick clouds; and the cloud is not rent under them.

9He holdeth back the face of his throne, *and* spreadeth his cloud upon it.

10He hath compassed the waters with bounds, until the day and night come to an end.

11The pillars of heaven tremble and are astonished at his reproof.

12He divideth the sea with his power, and by his understanding he smiteth through the proud.

13By his spirit he hath garnished the heavens; his hand hath formed the crooked serpent.

14Lo, these *are* parts of his ways: but how little a portion is heard of him? but the thunder of his power who can understand?

27 MOREOVER JOB continued his parable, and said,
2As God liveth, *who* hath taken away my judgment; and the Almighty, *who* hath vexed my soul;

3All the while my breath *is* in me, and the spirit of God *is* in my nostrils;

4My lips shall not speak wickedness, nor my tongue utter deceit.

5God forbid that I should justify you: till I die I will not remove mine integrity from me.

6My righteousness I hold fast, and will not let it go: my heart shall not reproach *me* so long as I live.

7Let mine enemy be as the wicked, and he that riseth up against me as the unrighteous.

8For what *is* the hope of the hypocrite, though he hath gained, when God taketh away his soul?

New International

4How then can a man be righteous before God?
How can one born of woman be pure?

5If even the moon is not bright
and the stars are not pure in his eyes,

6how much less man, who is but a maggot—
a son of man, who is only a worm!"

26 *Job* THEN JOB replied:

2"How you have helped the powerless!
How you have saved the arm that is feeble!

3What advice you have offered to one without
wisdom!
And what great insight you have displayed!

4Who has helped you utter these words?
And whose spirit spoke from your mouth?

5"The dead are in deep anguish,
those beneath the waters and all that live in
them.

6Death[a] is naked before God;
Destruction[b] lies uncovered.

7He spreads out the northern ₁skies₁ over empty
space;
he suspends the earth over nothing.

8He wraps up the waters in his clouds,
yet the clouds do not burst under their
weight.

9He covers the face of the full moon,
spreading his clouds over it.

10He marks out the horizon on the face of the
waters
for a boundary between light and darkness.

11The pillars of the heavens quake,
aghast at his rebuke.

12By his power he churned up the sea;
by his wisdom he cut Rahab to pieces.

13By his breath the skies became fair;
his hand pierced the gliding serpent.

14And these are but the outer fringe of his works;
how faint the whisper we hear of him!
Who then can understand the thunder of his
power?"

27 AND JOB continued his discourse:

2"As surely as God lives, who has denied me
justice,
the Almighty, who has made me taste
bitterness of soul,

3as long as I have life within me,
the breath of God in my nostrils,

4my lips will not speak wickedness,
and my tongue will utter no deceit.

5I will never admit you are in the right;
till I die, I will not deny my integrity.

6I will maintain my righteousness and never let
go of it;
my conscience will not reproach me as long
as I live.

7"May my enemies be like the wicked,
my adversaries like the unjust!

8For what hope has the godless when he is cut
off,
when God takes away his life?

Living Bible

can mere man stand before God and claim to be righteous? Who in all the earth can boast that he is clean? ⁵God is so glorious that even the moon and stars are less than nothing as compared to him. ⁶How much less is man, who is but a worm in his sight?"

26 JOB'S REPLY:
²"What wonderful helpers you all are! And how you have encouraged me in my great need! ³How you have enlightened my stupidity! What wise things you have said! ⁴How did you ever think of all these brilliant comments?

⁵,⁶"The dead stand naked, trembling before God in the place where they go. ⁷God stretches out heaven over empty space, and hangs the earth upon nothing. ⁸He wraps the rain in his thick clouds and the clouds are not split by the weight. ⁹He shrouds his throne with his clouds. ¹⁰He sets a boundary for the ocean, yes, and a boundary for the day and for the night. ¹¹The pillars of heaven tremble at his rebuke. ¹²And by his power the sea grows calm; he is skilled at crushing its pride! ¹³The heavens are made beautiful by his Spirit;ᶜ he pierces the swiftly gliding serpent.

¹⁴"These are some of the minor things he does, merely a whisper of his power. Who then can withstand his thunder?"

27 JOB'S FINAL defense:
²"I vow by the living God, who has taken away my rights, even the Almighty God who has embittered my soul, ³that as long as I live, while I have breath from God, ⁴my lips shall speak no evil, my tongue shall speak no lies. ⁵I will never, never agree that you are right; until I die I will vow my innocence. ⁶I am not a sinner—I repeat it again and again. My conscience is clear for as long as I live. ⁷Those who declare otherwise are my wicked enemies. They are evil men.

⁸"But what hope has the godless when God cuts him off and takes away his life? ⁹Will God listen to his cry

New Revised Standard

⁴ How then can a mortal be righteous before God?
How can one born of woman be pure?
⁵ If even the moon is not bright
and the stars are not pure in his sight,
⁶ how much less a mortal, who is a maggot,
and a human being, who is a worm!"

Job Replies: God's Majesty Is Unsearchable

26 THEN JOB answered:
² "How you have helped one who has no power!
How you have assisted the arm that has no strength!
³ How you have counseled one who has no wisdom,
and given much good advice!
⁴ With whose help have you uttered words,
and whose spirit has come forth from you?
⁵ The shades below tremble,
the waters and their inhabitants.
⁶ Sheol is naked before God,
and Abaddon has no covering.
⁷ He stretches out Zaphonᵈ over the void,
and hangs the earth upon nothing.
⁸ He binds up the waters in his thick clouds,
and the cloud is not torn open by them.
⁹ He covers the face of the full moon,
and spreads over it his cloud.
¹⁰ He has described a circle on the face of the waters,
at the boundary between light and darkness.
¹¹ The pillars of heaven tremble,
and are astounded at his rebuke.
¹² By his power he stilled the Sea;
by his understanding he struck down Rahab.
¹³ By his wind the heavens were made fair;
his hand pierced the fleeing serpent.
¹⁴ These are indeed but the outskirts of his ways;
and how small a whisper do we hear of him!
But the thunder of his power who can understand?"

Job Maintains His Integrity

27 JOB AGAIN took up his discourse and said:
² "As God lives, who has taken away my right,
and the Almighty,ᵉ who has made my soul bitter,
³ as long as my breath is in me
and the spirit of God is in my nostrils,
⁴ my lips will not speak falsehood,
and my tongue will not utter deceit.
⁵ Far be it from me to say that you are right;
until I die I will not put away my integrity from me.
⁶ I hold fast my righteousness, and will not let it go;
my heart does not reproach me for any of my days.

⁷ "May my enemy be like the wicked,
and may my opponent be like the unrighteous.
⁸ For what is the hope of the godless when God cuts them off,
when God takes away their lives?

ᶜ *26:13 The heavens are made beautiful by his Spirit,* or "the bars of heaven are afraid of him." See vs 11.

ᵈ Or *the North*   ᵉ Traditional rendering of Heb *Shaddai*

King James

9Will God hear his cry when trouble cometh upon him?

10Will he delight himself in the Almighty? will he always call upon God?

11I will teach you by the hand of God: *that* which *is* with the Almighty will I not conceal.

12Behold, all ye yourselves have seen *it;* why then are ye thus altogether vain?

13This *is* the portion of a wicked man with God, and the heritage of oppressors, *which* they shall receive of the Almighty.

14If his children be multiplied, *it is* for the sword: and his offspring shall not be satisfied with bread.

15Those that remain of him shall be buried in death: and his widows shall not weep.

16Though he heap up silver as the dust, and prepare raiment as the clay;

17He may prepare *it,* but the just shall put *it* on, and the innocent shall divide the silver.

18He buildeth his house as a moth, and as a booth *that* the keeper maketh.

19The rich man shall lie down, but he shall not be gathered: he openeth his eyes, and he *is* not.

20Terrors take hold on him as waters, a tempest stealeth him away in the night.

21The east wind carrieth him away, and he departeth: and as a storm hurleth him out of his place.

22For *God* shall cast upon him, and not spare: he would fain flee out of his hand.

23Men shall clap their hands at him, and shall hiss him out of his place.

28 SURELY THERE is a vein for the silver, and a place for gold *where* they refine *it.*

2Iron is taken out of the earth, and brass *is* molten *out of* the stone.

3He setteth an end to darkness, and searcheth out all perfection: the stones of darkness, and the shadow of death.

4The flood breaketh out from the inhabitant; *even the waters* forgotten of the foot: they are dried up, they are gone away from men.

5As for the earth, out of it cometh bread: and under it is turned up as it were fire.

6The stones of it *are* the place of sapphires: and it hath dust of gold.

7There *is* a path which no fowl knoweth, and which the vulture's eye hath not seen:

8The lion's whelps have not trodden it, nor the fierce lion passed by it.

9He putteth forth his hand upon the rock; he overturneth the mountains by the roots.

10He cutteth out rivers among the rocks; and his eye seeth every precious thing.

11He bindeth the floods from overflowing; and *the thing that is* hid bringeth he forth to light.

12But where shall wisdom be found? and where *is* the place of understanding?

New International

9Does God listen to his cry
  when distress comes upon him?

10Will he find delight in the Almighty?
  Will he call upon God at all times?

11"I will teach you about the power of God;
  the ways of the Almighty I will not conceal.

12You have all seen this yourselves.
  Why then this meaningless talk?

13"Here is the fate God allots to the wicked,
  the heritage a ruthless man receives from the
    Almighty:

14However many his children, their fate is the
    sword;
  his offspring will never have enough to eat.

15The plague will bury those who survive him,
  and their widows will not weep for them.

16Though he heaps up silver like dust
  and clothes like piles of clay,

17what he lays up the righteous will wear,
  and the innocent will divide his silver.

18The house he builds is like a moth's cocoon,
  like a hut made by a watchman.

19He lies down wealthy, but will do so no more;
  when he opens his eyes, all is gone.

20Terrors overtake him like a flood;
  a tempest snatches him away in the night.

21The east wind carries him off, and he is gone;
  it sweeps him out of his place.

22It hurls itself against him without mercy
  as he flees headlong from its power.

23It claps its hands in derision
  and hisses him out of his place.

28 "THERE IS a mine for silver
  and a place where gold is refined.

2Iron is taken from the earth,
  and copper is smelted from ore.

3Man puts an end to the darkness;
  he searches the farthest recesses
  for ore in the blackest darkness.

4Far from where people dwell he cuts a shaft,
  in places forgotten by the foot of man;
  far from men he dangles and sways.

5The earth, from which food comes,
  is transformed below as by fire;

6sapphiresa come from its rocks,
  and its dust contains nuggets of gold.

7No bird of prey knows that hidden path,
  no falcon's eye has seen it.

8Proud beasts do not set foot on it,
  and no lion prowls there.

9Man's hand assaults the flinty rock
  and lays bare the roots of the mountains.

10He tunnels through the rock;
  his eyes see all its treasures.

11He searchesb the sources of the rivers
  and brings hidden things to light.

12"But where can wisdom be found?
  Where does understanding dwell?

a 6 Or *lapis lazuli;* also in verse 16   b 11 Septuagint, Aquila and Vulgate; Hebrew *He dams up*

Living Bible

when trouble comes upon him? 10For he does not delight himself in the Almighty or pay any attention to God except in times of crisis.

11"I will teach you about God— 12but really, I don't need to, for you yourselves know as much about him as I do; yet you are saying all these useless things to me.

13"This is the fate awaiting the wicked from the hand of the Almighty: 14If he has a multitude of children, it is so that they will die in war, or starve to death. 15Those who survive shall be brought down to the grave by disease and plague, with no one to mourn them, not even their wives.

16"The evil man may accumulate money like dust, with closets jammed full of clothing— 17yes, he may order them made by his tailor, but the innocent shall wear that clothing, and shall divide his silver among them. 18Every house built by the wicked is as fragile as a spider web, as full of cracks as a leafy booth!

19"He goes to bed rich, but wakes up to find that all his wealth is gone. 20Terror overwhelms him, and he is blown away in the storms of the night. 21The east wind carries him away, and he is gone. It sweeps him into eternity. 22For God shall hurl at him unsparingly. He longs to flee from God. 23Everyone will cheer at his death, and boo him into eternity.

28

"MEN KNOW how to mine silver and refine gold, 2to dig iron from the earth and melt copper from stone. 3, 4Men know how to put light into darkness so that a mine shaft can be sunk into the earth, and the earth searched and its deep secrets explored. Into the black rock, shadowed by death, men descend on ropes, swinging back and forth.

5"Men know how to obtain food from the surface of the earth, while underneath there is fire.

6"They know how to find sapphires and gold dust— 7treasures that no bird of prey can see, no eagle's eye observe— 8for they are deep within the mines. No wild animal has ever walked upon those treasures; no lion has set his paw there. 9Men know how to tear apart flinty rocks and how to overturn the roots of mountains. 10They drill tunnels in the rocks and lay bare precious stones. 11They dam up streams of water and pan the gold.c

12"But though men can do all these things, they don't know where to find wisdom and understanding. 13They

New Revised Standard

9 Will God hear their cry
   when trouble comes upon them?
10 Will they take delight in the Almighty?d
   Will they call upon God at all times?
11 I will teach you concerning the hand of God;
   that which is with the Almightyd I will not
      conceal.
12 All of you have seen it yourselves;
   why then have you become altogether vain?

13 "This is the portion of the wicked with God,
   and the heritage that oppressors receive
      from the Almighty:d
14 If their children are multiplied, it is for the
      sword;
   and their offspring have not enough to eat.
15 Those who survive them the pestilence buries,
   and their widows make no lamentation.
16 Though they heap up silver like dust,
   and pile up clothing like clay—
17 they may pile it up, but the just will wear it,
   and the innocent will divide the silver.
18 They build their houses like nests,
   like booths made by sentinels of the
      vineyard.
19 They go to bed with wealth, but will do so no
      more;
   they open their eyes, and it is gone.
20 Terrors overtake them like a flood;
   in the night a whirlwind carries them off.
21 The east wind lifts them up and they are gone;
   it sweeps them out of their place.
22 Ite hurls at them without pity;
   they flee from itsf power in headlong flight.
23 Ite claps itsf hands at them,
   and hisses at them from itsf place.

Interlude: Where Wisdom Is Found

28

"SURELY THERE is a mine for silver,
   and a place for gold to be refined.
2 Iron is taken out of the earth,
   and copper is smelted from ore.
3 Miners put an end to darkness,
   and search out to the farthest bound
   the ore in gloom and deep darkness.
4 They open shafts in a valley away from
      human habitation;
   they are forgotten by travelers,
   they sway suspended, remote from people.
5 As for the earth, out of it comes bread;
   but underneath it is turned up as by fire.
6 Its stones are the place of sapphires,h
   and its dust contains gold.

7 "That path no bird of prey knows,
   and the falcon's eye has not seen it.
8 The proud wild animals have not trodden it;
   the lion has not passed over it.

9 "They put their hand to the flinty rock,
   and overturn mountains by the roots.
10 They cut out channels in the rocks,
   and their eyes see every precious thing.
11 The sources of the rivers they probe;i
   hidden things they bring to light.

12 "But where shall wisdom be found?
   And where is the place of understanding?

---

c 28:11 *They dam up streams of waters and pan the gold,* literally, "He brings forth to the light things that are hidden."

d Traditional rendering of Heb *Shaddai*   e Or *He* (that is God)   f Or *his*   g Heb *He puts*   h Or *lapis lazuli*   i Gk Vg: Heb *bind*

King James

13Man knoweth not the price thereof; neither is it found in the land of the living.

14The depth saith, It *is* not in me: and the sea saith, *It is* not with me.

15It cannot be gotten for gold, neither shall silver be weighed *for* the price thereof.

16It cannot be valued with the gold of Ophir, with the precious onyx, or the sapphire.

17The gold and the crystal cannot equal it: and the exchange of it *shall not be for* jewels of fine gold.

18No mention shall be made of coral, or of pearls: for the price of wisdom *is* above rubies.

19The topaz of Ethiopia shall not equal it, neither shall it be valued with pure gold.

20Whence then cometh wisdom? and where *is* the place of understanding?

21Seeing it is hid from the eyes of all living, and kept close from the fowls of the air.

22Destruction and death say, We have heard the fame thereof with our ears.

23God understandeth the way thereof, and he knoweth the place thereof.

24For he looketh to the ends of the earth, *and* seeth under the whole heaven;

25To make the weight for the winds; and he weigheth the waters by measure.

26When he made a decree for the rain, and a way for the lightning of the thunder:

27Then did he see it, and declare it; he prepared it, yea, and searched it out.

28And unto man he said, Behold, the fear of the Lord, that *is* wisdom; and to depart from evil *is* understanding.

29 MOREOVER JOB continued his parable, and said,

2Oh that I were as *in* months past, as *in* the days *when* God preserved me;

3When his candle shined upon my head, *and when* by his light I walked *through* darkness;

4As I was in the days of my youth, when the secret of God *was* upon my tabernacle;

5When the Almighty *was* yet with me, *when* my children *were* about me;

6When I washed my steps with butter, and the rock poured me out rivers of oil;

7When I went out to the gate through the city, *when* I prepared my seat in the street!

8The young men saw me, and hid themselves: and the aged arose, *and* stood up.

9The princes refrained talking, and laid *their* hand on their mouth.

10The nobles held their peace, and their tongue cleaved to the roof of their mouth.

11When the ear heard *me*, then it blessed me; and when the eye saw *me*, it gave witness to me:

12Because I delivered the poor that cried, and the fatherless, and *him that had* none to help him.

New International

13Man does not comprehend its worth;
    it cannot be found in the land of the living.

14The deep says, 'It is not in me';
    the sea says, 'It is not with me.'

15It cannot be bought with the finest gold,
    nor can its price be weighed in silver.

16It cannot be bought with the gold of Ophir,
    with precious onyx or sapphires.

17Neither gold nor crystal can compare with it,
    nor can it be had for jewels of gold.

18Coral and jasper are not worthy of mention;
    the price of wisdom is beyond rubies.

19The topaz of Cush cannot compare with it;
    it cannot be bought with pure gold.

20"Where then does wisdom come from?
    Where does understanding dwell?

21It is hidden from the eyes of every living thing,
    concealed even from the birds of the air.

22Destruction[a] and Death say,
    'Only a rumor of it has reached our ears.'

23God understands the way to it
    and he alone knows where it dwells,

24for he views the ends of the earth
    and sees everything under the heavens.

25When he established the force of the wind
    and measured out the waters,

26when he made a decree for the rain
    and a path for the thunderstorm,

27then he looked at wisdom and appraised it;
    he confirmed it and tested it.

28And he said to man,
    'The fear of the Lord—that is wisdom,
    and to shun evil is understanding.' "

29 JOB CONTINUED his discourse:

2"How I long for the months gone by,
    for the days when God watched over me,

3when his lamp shone upon my head
    and by his light I walked through darkness!

4Oh, for the days when I was in my prime,
    when God's intimate friendship blessed my house,

5when the Almighty was still with me
    and my children were around me,

6when my path was drenched with cream
    and the rock poured out for me streams of olive oil.

7"When I went to the gate of the city
    and took my seat in the public square,

8the young men saw me and stepped aside
    and the old men rose to their feet;

9the chief men refrained from speaking
    and covered their mouths with their hands;

10the voices of the nobles were hushed,
    and their tongues stuck to the roof of their mouths.

11Whoever heard me spoke well of me,
    and those who saw me commended me,

12because I rescued the poor who cried for help,
    and the fatherless who had none to assist him.

Living Bible

not only don't know how to get it, but, in fact, it is not to be found among the living.

14" 'It's not here,' the oceans say; and the seas reply, 'Nor is it here.'

15"It cannot be bought for gold or silver, 16nor for all the gold of Ophir or precious onyx stones or sapphires. 17Wisdom is far more valuable than gold and glass. It cannot be bought for jewels mounted in fine gold. 18Coral or crystal is worthless in trying to get it; its price is far above rubies. 19Topaz from Ethiopia cannot purchase it, nor even the purest gold.

20"Then where can we get it? Where can it be found? 21For it is hid from the eyes of all mankind; even the sharp-eyed birds in the sky cannot discover it.

22"But Destruction and Death speak of knowing something about it! 23, 24And God surely knows where it is to be found, for he looks throughout the whole earth, under all the heavens. 25He makes the winds blow and sets the boundaries of the oceans. 26He makes the laws of the rain and a path for the lightning. 27He knows where wisdom is and declares it to all who will listen. He established it and examined it thoroughly. 28And this is what he says to all mankind: 'Look, to fear the Lord is true wisdom; to forsake evil is real understanding.' "

29 *JOB CONTINUES:*
2"Oh, for the years gone by when God took care of me, 3when he lighted the way before me and I walked safely through the darkness; 4yes, in my early years, when the friendship of God was felt in my home; 5when the Almighty was still with me and my children were around me; 6when my projects prospered, and even the rock poured out streams of olive oil to me!

7"Those were the days when I went out to the city gate and took my place among the honored elders. 8The young saw me and stepped aside, and even the aged rose and stood up in respect at my coming. 9The princes stood in silence and laid their hands upon their mouths. 10The highest officials of the city stood in quietness. 11All rejoiced in what I said. All who saw me spoke well of me.

12"For I, as an honest judge,b helped the poor in their need, and the fatherless who had no one to help them.

New Revised Standard

13 Mortals do not know the way to it,c
   and it is not found in the land of the living.
14 The deep says, 'It is not in me,'
   and the sea says, 'It is not with me.'
15 It cannot be gotten for gold,
   and silver cannot be weighed out as its price.
16 It cannot be valued in the gold of Ophir,
   in precious onyx or sapphire.d
17 Gold and glass cannot equal it,
   nor can it be exchanged for jewels of fine gold.
18 No mention shall be made of coral or of crystal;
   the price of wisdom is above pearls.
19 The chrysolite of Ethiopiae cannot compare with it,
   nor can it be valued in pure gold.

20 "Where then does wisdom come from?
   And where is the place of understanding?
21 It is hidden from the eyes of all living,
   and concealed from the birds of the air.
22 Abaddon and Death say,
   'We have heard a rumor of it with our ears.'

23 "God understands the way to it,
   and he knows its place.
24 For he looks to the ends of the earth,
   and sees everything under the heavens.
25 When he gave to the wind its weight,
   and apportioned out the waters by measure;
26 when he made a decree for the rain,
   and a way for the thunderbolt;
27 then he saw it and declared it;
   he established it, and searched it out.
28 And he said to humankind,
   'Truly, the fear of the Lord, that is wisdom;
   and to depart from evil is understanding.' "

Job Finishes His Defense

29 JOB AGAIN took up his discourse and said:
2 "Oh, that I were as in the months of old,
   as in the days when God watched over me;
3 when his lamp shone over my head,
   and by his light I walked through darkness;
4 when I was in my prime,
   when the friendship of God was upon my tent;
5 when the Almightyf was still with me,
   when my children were around me;
6 when my steps were washed with milk,
   and the rock poured out for me streams of oil!
7 When I went out to the gate of the city,
   when I took my seat in the square,
8 the young men saw me and withdrew,
   and the aged rose up and stood;
9 the nobles refrained from talking,
   and laid their hands on their mouths;
10 the voices of princes were hushed,
   and their tongues stuck to the roof of their mouths.
11 When the ear heard, it commended me,
   and when the eye saw, it approved;
12 because I delivered the poor who cried,
   and the orphan who had no helper.

b *29:12 For I, as an honest judge,* implied in vs 7.

c Gk: Heb *its price*   d Or *lapis lazuli*   e Or *Nubia*; Heb *Cush*   f Traditional rendering of Heb *Shaddai*

King James

13The blessing of him that was ready to perish came upon me: and I caused the widow's heart to sing for joy.

14I put on righteousness, and it clothed me: my judgment *was* as a robe and a diadem.

15I was eyes to the blind, and feet *was* I to the lame.

16I *was* a father to the poor: and the cause *which* I knew not I searched out.

17And I brake the jaws of the wicked, and plucked the spoil out of his teeth.

18Then I said, I shall die in my nest, and I shall multiply *my* days as the sand.

19My root *was* spread out by the waters, and the dew lay all night upon my branch.

20My glory *was* fresh in me, and my bow was renewed in my hand.

21Unto me *men* gave ear, and waited, and kept silence at my counsel.

22After my words they spake not again; and my speech dropped upon them.

23And they waited for me as for the rain; and they opened their mouth wide *as* for the latter rain.

24*If* I laughed on them, they believed *it* not; and the light of my countenance they cast not down.

25I chose out their way, and sat chief, and dwelt as a king in the army, as one *that* comforteth the mourners.

30 BUT NOW *they that are* younger than I have me in derision, whose fathers I would have disdained to have set with the dogs of my flock.

2Yea, whereto *might* the strength of their hands *profit* me, in whom old age was perished?

3For want and famine *they were* solitary; fleeing into the wilderness in former time desolate and waste.

4Who cut up mallows by the bushes, and juniper roots *for* their meat.

5They were driven forth from among *men*, (they cried after them as *after* a thief;)

6To dwell in the cliffs of the valleys, *in* caves of the earth, and *in* the rocks.

7Among the bushes they brayed; under the nettles they were gathered together.

8*They were* children of fools, yea, children of base men: they were viler than the earth.

9And now am I their song, yea, I am their byword.

10They abhor me, they flee far from me, and spare not to spit in my face.

11Because he hath loosed my cord, and afflicted me, they have also let loose the bridle before me.

12Upon *my* right *hand* rise the youth; they push away my feet, and they raise up against me the ways of their destruction.

New International

13The man who was dying blessed me;
  I made the widow's heart sing.
14I put on righteousness as my clothing;
  justice was my robe and my turban.
15I was eyes to the blind
  and feet to the lame.
16I was a father to the needy;
  I took up the case of the stranger.
17I broke the fangs of the wicked
  and snatched the victims from their teeth.

18"I thought, 'I will die in my own house,
  my days as numerous as the grains of sand.
19My roots will reach to the water,
  and the dew will lie all night on my branches.
20My glory will remain fresh in me,
  the bow ever new in my hand.'

21"Men listened to me expectantly,
  waiting in silence for my counsel.
22After I had spoken, they spoke no more;
  my words fell gently on their ears.
23They waited for me as for showers
  and drank in my words as the spring rain.
24When I smiled at them, they scarcely believed it;
  the light of my face was precious to them.[a]
25I chose the way for them and sat as their chief;
  I dwelt as a king among his troops;
  I was like one who comforts mourners.

30 "BUT NOW they mock me,
  men younger than I,
whose fathers I would have disdained
  to put with my sheep dogs.
2Of what use was the strength of their hands to me,
  since their vigor had gone from them?
3Haggard from want and hunger,
  they roamed[b] the parched land
  in desolate wastelands at night.
4In the brush they gathered salt herbs,
  and their food[c] was the root of the broom tree.
5They were banished from their fellow men,
  shouted at as if they were thieves.
6They were forced to live in the dry stream beds,
  among the rocks and in holes in the ground.
7They brayed among the bushes
  and huddled in the undergrowth.
8A base and nameless brood,
  they were driven out of the land.

9"And now their sons mock me in song;
  I have become a byword among them.
10They detest me and keep their distance;
  they do not hesitate to spit in my face.
11Now that God has unstrung my bow and afflicted me,
  they throw off restraint in my presence.
12On my right the tribe[d] attacks;
  they lay snares for my feet,
  they build their siege ramps against me.

---

[a] 24 The meaning of the Hebrew for this clause is uncertain.   [b] 3 Or *gnawed*
[c] 4 Or *fuel*   [d] 12 The meaning of the Hebrew for this word is uncertain.

Living Bible

13I helped those who were ready to perish and they blessed me. And I caused the widows' hearts to sing for joy. 14All I did was just and honest, for righteousness was my clothing! 15I served as eyes for the blind and feet for the lame. 16I was as a father to the poor, and saw to it that even strangers received a fair trial. 17I knocked out the fangs of the godless oppressors and made them drop their victims.

18"I thought, 'Surely I shall die quietly in my nest after a long, good life.' 19For everything I did prospered; the dew lay all night upon my fields and watered them. 20Fresh honors were constantly given me, and my abilities were constantly refreshed and renewed. 21Everyone listened to me and valued my advice, and were silent until I spoke. 22And after I spoke, they spoke no more, for my counsel satisfied them. 23They longed for me to speak as those in drought-time long for rain. They waited eagerly with open mouths. 24When they were discouraged, I smiled and that encouraged them, and lightened their spirits. 25I told them what they should do, and corrected them as their chief, or as a king instructs his army, and as one who comforts those who mourn.

30 "BUT NOW those younger than I deride me—young men whose fathers are less than my dogs. 2Oh, they have strong backs all right, but they are useless, stupid fools. 3They are gaunt with famine and have been cast out into deserts and the wastelands, desolate and gloomy. 4They eat roots and leaves, 5having been driven from civilization. Men shouted after them as after thieves. 6So now they live in frightening ravines, and in caves, and among the rocks. 7They sound like animals among the bushes, huddling together for shelter beneath the nettles. 8These sons of theirs have also turned out to be fools, yes, children of no name, outcasts of civilization.

9"And now I have become the subject of their ribald song! I am a joke among *them!* 10*They* despise me and won't come near me, and don't mind spitting in my face. 11For God has placed my life in jeopardy. These young men, having humbled me, now cast off all restraint before me. 12This rabble trip me and lay traps in my path.

New Revised Standard

13 The blessing of the wretched came upon me,
   and I caused the widow's heart to sing for
      joy.
14 I put on righteousness, and it clothed me;
   my justice was like a robe and a turban.
15 I was eyes to the blind,
   and feet to the lame.
16 I was a father to the needy,
   and I championed the cause of the stranger.
17 I broke the fangs of the unrighteous,
   and made them drop their prey from their
      teeth.
18 Then I thought, 'I shall die in my nest,
   and I shall multiply my days like the
      phoenix;e
19 my roots spread out to the waters,
   with the dew all night on my branches;
20 my glory was fresh with me,
   and my bow ever new in my hand.'

21 "They listened to me, and waited,
   and kept silence for my counsel.
22 After I spoke they did not speak again,
   and my word dropped upon them like dew.f
23 They waited for me as for the rain;
   they opened their mouths as for the spring
      rain.
24 I smiled on them when they had no
      confidence;
   and the light of my countenance they did
      not extinguish.g
25 I chose their way, and sat as chief,
   and I lived like a king among his troops,
   like one who comforts mourners.

30 "BUT NOW they make sport of me,
   those who are younger than I,
whose fathers I would have disdained
   to set with the dogs of my flock.
2 What could I gain from the strength of their
      hands?
   All their vigor is gone.
3 Through want and hard hunger
   they gnaw the dry and desolate ground,
4 they pick mallow and the leaves of bushes,
   and to warm themselves the roots of broom.
5 They are driven out from society;
   people shout after them as after a thief.
6 In the gullies of wadis they must live,
   in holes in the ground, and in the rocks.
7 Among the bushes they bray;
   under the nettles they huddle together.
8 A senseless, disreputable brood,
   they have been whipped out of the land.

9 "And now they mock me in song;
   I am a byword to them.
10 They abhor me, they keep aloof from me;
   they do not hesitate to spit at the sight of
      me.
11 Because God has loosed my bowstring and
      humbled me,
   they have cast off restraint in my presence.
12 On my right hand the rabble rise up;
   they send me sprawling,
   and build roads for my ruin.

---

e Or *like sand*   f Heb lacks *like dew*   g Meaning of Heb uncertain

King James

13They mar my path, they set forward my calamity, they have no helper.

14They came *upon me* as a wide breaking in *of waters:* in the desolation they rolled themselves *upon me.*

15Terrors are turned upon me: they pursue my soul as the wind: and my welfare passeth away as a cloud.

16And now my soul is poured out upon me; the days of affliction have taken hold upon me.

17My bones are pierced in me in the night season: and my sinews take no rest.

18By the great force *of my disease* is my garment changed: it bindeth me about as the collar of my coat.

19He hath cast me into the mire, and I am become like dust and ashes.

20I cry unto thee, and thou dost not hear me: I stand up, and thou regardest me *not.*

21Thou art become cruel to me: with thy strong hand thou opposest thyself against me.

22Thou liftest me up to the wind; thou causest me to ride *upon it,* and dissolvest my substance.

23For I know *that* thou wilt bring me *to* death, and *to* the house appointed for all living.

24Howbeit he will not stretch out *his* hand to the grave, though they cry in his destruction.

25Did not I weep for him that was in trouble? was *not* my soul grieved for the poor?

26When I looked for good, then evil came *unto me:* and when I waited for light, there came darkness.

27My bowels boiled, and rested not: the days of affliction prevented me.

28I went mourning without the sun: I stood up, *and* I cried in the congregation.

29I am a brother to dragons, and a companion to owls.

30My skin is black upon me, and my bones are burned with heat.

31My harp also is *turned* to mourning, and my organ into the voice of them that weep.

31 I MADE a covenant with mine eyes; why then should I think upon a maid?

2For what portion of God *is there* from above? and *what* inheritance of the Almighty from on high?

3*Is* not destruction to the wicked? and a strange *punishment* to the workers of iniquity?

4Doth not he see my ways, and count all my steps?

5If I have walked with vanity, or if my foot hath hasted to deceit;

6Let me be weighed in an even balance, that God may know mine integrity.

7If my step hath turned out of the way, and mine heart walked after mine eyes, and if any blot hath cleaved to mine hands;

8*Then* let me sow, and let another eat; yea, let my offspring be rooted out.

New International

13They break up my road;
   they succeed in destroying me—
   without anyone's helping them.a
14They advance as through a gaping breach;
   amid the ruins they come rolling in.
15Terrors overwhelm me;
   my dignity is driven away as by the wind,
   my safety vanishes like a cloud.
16"And now my life ebbs away;
   days of suffering grip me.
17Night pierces my bones;
   my gnawing pains never rest.
18In his great power ⌊God⌋ becomes like clothing
   to meb;
   he binds me like the neck of my garment.
19He throws me into the mud,
   and I am reduced to dust and ashes.
20"I cry out to you, O God, but you do not
      answer;
   I stand up, but you merely look at me.
21You turn on me ruthlessly;
   with the might of your hand you attack me.
22You snatch me up and drive me before the
      wind;
   you toss me about in the storm.
23I know you will bring me down to death,
   to the place appointed for all the living.
24"Surely no one lays a hand on a broken man
   when he cries for help in his distress.
25Have I not wept for those in trouble?
   Has not my soul grieved for the poor?
26Yet when I hoped for good, evil came;
   when I looked for light, then came darkness.
27The churning inside me never stops;
   days of suffering confront me.
28I go about blackened, but not by the sun;
   I stand up in the assembly and cry for help.
29I have become a brother of jackals,
   a companion of owls.
30My skin grows black and peels;
   my body burns with fever.
31My harp is tuned to mourning,
   and my flute to the sound of wailing.

31 "I MADE a covenant with my eyes
   not to look lustfully at a girl.
2For what is man's lot from God above,
   his heritage from the Almighty on high?
3Is it not ruin for the wicked,
   disaster for those who do wrong?
4Does he not see my ways
   and count my every step?

5"If I have walked in falsehood
   or my foot has hurried after deceit—
6let God weigh me in honest scales
   and he will know that I am blameless—
7if my steps have turned from the path,
   if my heart has been led by my eyes,
   or if my hands have been defiled,
8then may others eat what I have sown,
   and may my crops be uprooted.

---

a *13* Or me. / 'No one can help him,' ⌊they say⌋.   b *18* Hebrew; Septuagint ⌊God⌋ grasps my clothing

Living Bible

13They block my road and do everything they can to hasten my calamity, knowing full well that I have no one to help me. **14**They come at me from all directions. They rush upon me when I am down.

15"I live in terror now. They hold me in contempt and my prosperity has vanished as a cloud before a strong wind. **16**My heart is broken. Depression haunts my days. **17**My weary nights are filled with pain as though something were relentlessly gnawing at my bones. **18**All night long I toss and turn, and my garments bind about me. **19**God has thrown me into the mud. I have become as dust and ashes.

20"I cry to you, O God, but you don't answer me. I stand before you and you don't bother to look. **21**You have become cruel toward me, and persecute me with great power and effect. **22**You throw me into the whirlwind and dissolve me in the storm. **23**And I know that your purpose for me is death. **24**I expected my fall to be broken, just as one who falls stretches out his hand or cries for help in his calamity.

25"And did I not weep for those in trouble? Wasn't I deeply grieved for the needy? **26**I therefore looked for good to come. Evil came instead. I waited for the light. Darkness came. **27**My heart is troubled and restless. Waves of affliction have come upon me. **28, 29**I am black, but not from sunburn. I stand up and cry to the assembly for help. [But I might as well save my breath,c] for I am considered a brother to jackals and a companion to ostriches. **30**My skin is black and peeling. My bones burn with fever. **31**The voice of joy and gladness has turned to mourning.

31 "I MADE a covenant with my eyes not to look with lust upon a girl. **2, 3**I know full well that Almighty God above sends calamity on those who do. **4**He sees everything I do, and every step I take.

5"If I have lied and deceived— **6**but God knows that I am innocent— **7, 8**or if I have stepped off God's pathway, or if my heart has lusted for what my eyes have seen, or if I am guilty of any other sin, then let someone else reap the crops I have sown and let all that I have planted be rooted out.

New Revised Standard

13   They break up my path,
    they promote my calamity;
    no one restrainsd them.
14 As through a wide breach they come;
    amid the crash they roll on.
15 Terrors are turned upon me;
    my honor is pursued as by the wind,
    and my prosperity has passed away like a
     cloud.

16 "And now my soul is poured out within me;
    days of affliction have taken hold of me.
17 The night racks my bones,
    and the pain that gnaws me takes no rest.
18 With violence he seizes my garment;e
    he grasps me byf the collar of my tunic.
19 He has cast me into the mire,
    and I have become like dust and ashes.
20 I cry to you and you do not answer me;
    I stand, and you merely look at me.
21 You have turned cruel to me;
    with the might of your hand you persecute
     me.
22 You lift me up on the wind, you make me
     ride on it,
    and you toss me about in the roar of the
     storm.
23 I know that you will bring me to death,
    and to the house appointed for all living.

24 "Surely one does not turn against the needy,g
    when in disaster they cry for help.h
25 Did I not weep for those whose day was hard?
    Was not my soul grieved for the poor?
26 But when I looked for good, evil came;
    and when I waited for light, darkness came.
27 My inward parts are in turmoil, and are never
     still;
    days of affliction come to meet me.
28 I go about in sunless gloom;
    I stand up in the assembly and cry for help.
29 I am a brother of jackals,
    and a companion of ostriches.
30 My skin turns black and falls from me,
    and my bones burn with heat.
31 My lyre is turned to mourning,
    and my pipe to the voice of those who
     weep.

31 "I HAVE made a covenant with my eyes;
    how then could I look upon a virgin?
2 What would be my portion from God above,
    and my heritage from the Almightyi on
     high?
3 Does not calamity befall the unrighteous,
    and disaster the workers of iniquity?
4 Does he not see my ways,
    and number all my steps?

5 "If I have walked with falsehood,
    and my foot has hurried to deceit—
6 let me be weighed in a just balance,
    and let God know my integrity!—
7 if my step has turned aside from the way,
    and my heart has followed my eyes,
    and if any spot has clung to my hands;
8 then let me sow, and another eat;
    and let what grows for me be rooted out.

---

c 30:28, 29 *But I might as well save my breath,* implied.

d Cn: Heb *helps*   e Gk: Heb *my garment is disfigured*   f Heb *like*   g Heb *ruin*   h Cn: Meaning of Heb uncertain   i Traditional rendering of Heb *Shaddai*

King James

9If mine heart have been deceived by a woman, or *if* I have laid wait at my neighbour's door;

10*Then* let my wife grind unto another, and let others bow down upon her.

11For this *is* an heinous crime; yea, it *is* an iniquity *to be punished by* the judges.

12For it *is* a fire *that* consumeth to destruction, and would root out all mine increase.

13If I did despise the cause of my manservant or of my maidservant, when they contended with me;

14What then shall I do when God riseth up? and when he visiteth, what shall I answer him?

15Did not he that made me in the womb make him? and did not one fashion us in the womb?

16If I have withheld the poor from *their* desire, or have caused the eyes of the widow to fail;

17Or have eaten my morsel myself alone, and the fatherless hath not eaten thereof;

18(For from my youth he was brought up with me, as *with* a father, and I have guided her from my mother's womb;)

19If I have seen any perish for want of clothing, or any poor without covering;

20If his loins have not blessed me, and *if* he were *not* warmed with the fleece of my sheep;

21If I have lifted up my hand against the fatherless, when I saw my help in the gate:

22*Then* let mine arm fall from my shoulder blade, and mine arm be broken from the bone.

23For destruction *from* God *was* a terror to me, and by reason of his highness I could not endure.

24If I have made gold my hope, or have said to the fine gold, *Thou art* my confidence;

25If I rejoiced because my wealth *was* great, and because mine hand had gotten much;

26If I beheld the sun when it shined, or the moon walking *in* brightness;

27And my heart hath been secretly enticed, or my mouth hath kissed my hand:

28This also *were* an iniquity *to be punished by* the judge: for I should have denied the God *that is* above.

29If I rejoiced at the destruction of him that hated me, or lifted up myself when evil found him:

30Neither have I suffered my mouth to sin by wishing a curse to his soul.

31If the men of my tabernacle said not, Oh that we had of his flesh! we cannot be satisfied.

32The stranger did not lodge in the street: *but* I opened my doors to the traveller.

New International

9"If my heart has been enticed by a woman,
　　or if I have lurked at my neighbor's door,
10then may my wife grind another man's grain,
　　and may other men sleep with her.
11For that would have been shameful,
　　a sin to be judged.
12It is a fire that burns to Destruction[a];
　　it would have uprooted my harvest.

13"If I have denied justice to my menservants and maidservants
　　when they had a grievance against me,
14what will I do when God confronts me?
　　What will I answer when called to account?
15Did not he who made me in the womb make them?
　　Did not the same one form us both within our mothers?

16"If I have denied the desires of the poor
　　or let the eyes of the widow grow weary,
17if I have kept my bread to myself,
　　not sharing it with the fatherless—
18but from my youth I reared him as would a father,
　　and from my birth I guided the widow—
19if I have seen anyone perishing for lack of clothing,
　　or a needy man without a garment,
20and his heart did not bless me
　　for warming him with the fleece from my sheep,
21if I have raised my hand against the fatherless,
　　knowing that I had influence in court,
22then let my arm fall from the shoulder,
　　let it be broken off at the joint.
23For I dreaded destruction from God,
　　and for fear of his splendor I could not do such things.

24"If I have put my trust in gold
　　or said to pure gold, 'You are my security,'
25if I have rejoiced over my great wealth,
　　the fortune my hands had gained,
26if I have regarded the sun in its radiance
　　or the moon moving in splendor,
27so that my heart was secretly enticed
　　and my hand offered them a kiss of homage,
28then these also would be sins to be judged,
　　for I would have been unfaithful to God on high.

29"If I have rejoiced at my enemy's misfortune
　　or gloated over the trouble that came to him—
30I have not allowed my mouth to sin
　　by invoking a curse against his life—
31if the men of my household have never said,
　　'Who has not had his fill of Job's meat?'—
32but no stranger had to spend the night in the street,
　　for my door was always open to the traveler—

a 12 Hebrew *Abaddon*

Living Bible

⁹"Or if I have longed for another man's wife, ¹⁰then may I die, and may my wife be in another man's home, and someone else become her husband. ¹¹For lust is a shameful sin, a crime that should be punished. ¹²It is a devastating fire that destroys to hell, and would root out all I have planted.

¹³"If I have been unfair to my servants, ¹⁴how could I face God? What could I say when he questioned me about it? ¹⁵For God made me, and made my servant too. He created us both.

¹⁶"If I have hurt the poor or caused widows to weep, ¹⁷or refused food to hungry orphans— ¹⁸(but we have always cared for orphans in our home, treating them as our own children)— ¹⁹, ²⁰or if I have seen anyone freezing and not given him clothing, or fleece from my sheep to keep him warm, ²¹or if I have taken advantage of an orphan because I thought I could get away with it— ²²if I have done any of these things, then let my arm be torn from its socket! Let my shoulder be wrenched out of place! ²³Rather that than face the judgment sent by God; that I dread more than anything else. For if the majesty of God opposes me, what hope is there?

²⁴"If I have put my trust in money, ²⁵if my happiness depends on wealth, ²⁶or if I have looked at the sun shining in the skies, or the moon walking down her silver pathway, ²⁷and my heart has been secretly enticed, and I have worshiped them by kissing my hand to them, ²⁸this, too, must be punished by the judges. For if I had done such things, it would mean that I denied the God of heaven.

²⁹"If I have rejoiced at harm to an enemy— ³⁰(but actually I have never cursed anyone nor asked for revenge)— ³¹or if any of my servants have ever gone hungry— ³²(actually I have never turned away even a stranger but have opened my doors to all)— ³³or if, like

New Revised Standard

9 "If my heart has been enticed by a woman,
    and I have lain in wait at my neighbor's door;
10 then let my wife grind for another,
    and let other men kneel over her.
11 For that would be a heinous crime;
    that would be a criminal offense;
12 for that would be a fire consuming down to Abaddon,
    and it would burn to the root all my harvest.

13 "If I have rejected the cause of my male or female slaves,
    when they brought a complaint against me;
14 what then shall I do when God rises up?
    When he makes inquiry, what shall I answer him?
15 Did not he who made me in the womb make them?
    And did not one fashion us in the womb?

16 "If I have withheld anything that the poor desired,
    or have caused the eyes of the widow to fail,
17 or have eaten my morsel alone,
    and the orphan has not eaten from it—
18 for from my youth I reared the orphan[b] like a father,
    and from my mother's womb I guided the widow[c]—
19 if I have seen anyone perish for lack of clothing,
    or a poor person without covering,
20 whose loins have not blessed me,
    and who was not warmed with the fleece of my sheep;
21 if I have raised my hand against the orphan,
    because I saw I had supporters at the gate;
22 then let my shoulder blade fall from my shoulder,
    and let my arm be broken from its socket.
23 For I was in terror of calamity from God,
    and I could not have faced his majesty.

24 "If I have made gold my trust,
    or called fine gold my confidence;
25 if I have rejoiced because my wealth was great,
    or because my hand had gotten much;
26 if I have looked at the sun[d] when it shone,
    or the moon moving in splendor,
27 and my heart has been secretly enticed,
    and my mouth has kissed my hand;
28 this also would be an iniquity to be punished by the judges,
    for I should have been false to God above.

29 "If I have rejoiced at the ruin of those who hated me,
    or exulted when evil overtook them—
30 I have not let my mouth sin
    by asking for their lives with a curse—
31 if those of my tent ever said,
    'O that we might be sated with his flesh!'[e]—
32 the stranger has not lodged in the street;
    I have opened my doors to the traveler—

King James

33If I covered my transgressions as Adam, by hiding mine iniquity in my bosom:

34Did I fear a great multitude, or did the contempt of families terrify me, that I kept silence, *and* went not out of the door?

35Oh that one would hear me! behold, my desire *is*, *that* the Almighty would answer me, and *that* mine adversary had written a book.

36Surely I would take it upon my shoulder, *and* bind it *as* a crown to me.

37I would declare unto him the number of my steps; as a prince would I go near unto him.

38If my land cry against me, or that the furrows likewise thereof complain;

39If I have eaten the fruits thereof without money, or have caused the owners thereof to lose their life:

40Let thistles grow instead of wheat, and cockle instead of barley. The words of Job are ended.

32 SO THESE three men ceased to answer Job, because he *was* righteous in his own eyes.

2Then was kindled the wrath of Elihu the son of Barachel the Buzite, of the kindred of Ram: against Job was his wrath kindled, because he justified himself rather than God.

3Also against his three friends was his wrath kindled, because they had found no answer, and *yet* had condemned Job.

4Now Elihu had waited till Job had spoken, because they *were* elder than he.

5When Elihu saw that *there was* no answer in the mouth of *these* three men, then his wrath was kindled.

6And Elihu the son of Barachel the Buzite answered and said, I *am* young, and ye *are* very old; wherefore I was afraid, and durst not show you mine opinion.

7I said, Days should speak, and multitude of years should teach wisdom.

8But *there is* a spirit in man: and the inspiration of the Almighty giveth them understanding.

9Great men are not *always* wise: neither do the aged understand judgment.

10Therefore I said, Hearken to me; I also will show mine opinion.

11Behold, I waited for your words; I gave ear to your reasons, whilst ye searched out what to say.

12Yea, I attended unto you, and, behold, *there was* none of you that convinced Job, *or* that answered his words:

13Lest ye should say, We have found out wisdom: God thrusteth him down, not man.

14Now he hath not directed *his* words against me: neither will I answer him with your speeches.

15They were amazed, they answered no more: they left off speaking.

New International

33if I have concealed my sin as men do,[a]
　by hiding my guilt in my heart
34because I so feared the crowd
　and so dreaded the contempt of the clans
　that I kept silent and would not go outside

35("Oh, that I had someone to hear me!
　I sign now my defense—let the Almighty
　　answer me;
　let my accuser put his indictment in writing.
36Surely I would wear it on my shoulder,
　I would put it on like a crown.
37I would give him an account of my every step;
　like a prince I would approach him.)—

38"if my land cries out against me
　and all its furrows are wet with tears,
39if I have devoured its yield without payment
　or broken the spirit of its tenants,
40then let briers come up instead of wheat
　and weeds instead of barley."

The words of Job are ended.

Elihu

32 SO THESE three men stopped answering Job, because he was righteous in his own eyes. 2But Elihu son of Barakel the Buzite, of the family of Ram, became very angry with Job for justifying himself rather than God. 3He was also angry with the three friends, because they had found no way to refute Job, and yet had condemned him.[b] 4Now Elihu had waited before speaking to Job because they were older than he. 5But when he saw that the three men had nothing more to say, his anger was aroused.

6So Elihu son of Barakel the Buzite said:

"I am young in years,
　and you are old;
that is why I was fearful,
　not daring to tell you what I know.
7I thought, 'Age should speak;
　advanced years should teach wisdom.'
8But it is the spirit[c] in a man,
　the breath of the Almighty, that gives him
　　understanding.
9It is not only the old[d] who are wise,
　not only the aged who understand what is
　　right.

10"Therefore I say: Listen to me;
　I too will tell you what I know.
11I waited while you spoke,
　I listened to your reasoning;
　while you were searching for words,
12 I gave you my full attention.
But not one of you has proved Job wrong;
　none of you has answered his arguments.
13Do not say, 'We have found wisdom;
　let God refute him, not man.'
14But Job has not marshaled his words against
　　me,
　and I will not answer him with your
　　arguments.

15"They are dismayed and have no more to say;
　words have failed them.

---

a 33 Or *as Adam did*   b 3 Masoretic Text; an ancient Hebrew scribal tradition *Job, and so had condemned God*   c 8 Or *Spirit*; also in verse 18   d 9 Or *many*; or *great*

Living Bible

New Revised Standard

Adam, I have tried to hide my sins, ³⁴fearing the crowd and its contempt, so that I refused to acknowledge my sin and do not go out of my way to help others— ³⁵(oh, that there were someone who would listen to me and try to see my side of this argument. Look, I will sign my signature to my defense; now let the Almighty show me that I am wrong; let *him* approve the indictments made against me by my enemies. ³⁶I would treasure it like a crown. ³⁷Then I would tell him exactly what I have done and why, presenting my defense as one he listens to).

^{38, 39}"Or if my land accuses me because I stole the fruit it bears, or if I have murdered its owners to get their land for myself, ⁴⁰then let thistles grow on that land instead of wheat, and weeds instead of barley."

Job's words are ended.

33 if I have concealed my transgressions as others do,[e]
   by hiding my iniquity in my bosom,
34 because I stood in great fear of the multitude,
   and the contempt of families terrified me,
   so that I kept silence, and did not go out of doors—
35 Oh, that I had one to hear me!
   (Here is my signature! let the Almighty[f] answer me!)
   Oh, that I had the indictment written by my adversary!
36 Surely I would carry it on my shoulder;
   I would bind it on me like a crown;
37 I would give him an account of all my steps;
   like a prince I would approach him.

38 "If my land has cried out against me,
   and its furrows have wept together;
39 if I have eaten its yield without payment,
   and caused the death of its owners;
40 let thorns grow instead of wheat,
   and foul weeds instead of barley."

The words of Job are ended.

Elihu Rebukes Job's Friends

32 THE THREE men refused to reply further to Job because he kept insisting on his innocence. ²Then Elihu (son of Barachel, the Buzite, of the Clan of Ram) became angry because Job refused to admit he had sinned and to acknowledge that God had just cause for punishing him. ³But he was also angry with Job's three friends because they had been unable to answer Job's arguments and yet had condemned him. ⁴Elihu had waited until now to speak because the others were older than he.

⁵But when he saw that they had no further reply, he spoke out angrily, ⁶and said, "I am young and you are old, so I held back and did not dare to tell you what I think, ⁷for those who are older are said to be wiser; ^{8, 9}but it is not mere age that makes men wise. Rather, it is the spirit in a man, the breath of the Almighty which makes him intelligent. ¹⁰So listen to me awhile and let me express my opinion.

^{11, 12}"I have waited all this time, listening very carefully to your arguments, but not one of them has convinced Job that he is a sinner, or has proved that he is. ¹³And don't give me that line about 'only God can convince the sinner of his sin.' ¹⁴If Job had been arguing with me, I would not answer with that kind of logic! ¹⁵"You sit there baffled, with no further replies.

32 SO THESE three men ceased to answer Job, because he was righteous in his own eyes. ²Then Elihu son of Barachel the Buzite, of the family of Ram, became angry. He was angry at Job because he justified himself rather than God; ³he was angry also at Job's three friends because they had found no answer, though they had declared Job to be in the wrong.[g] ⁴Now Elihu had waited to speak to Job, because they were older than he. ⁵But when Elihu saw that there was no answer in the mouths of these three men, he became angry.

6 Elihu son of Barachel the Buzite answered:
   "I am young in years,
   and you are aged;
   therefore I was timid and afraid
   to declare my opinion to you.
7 I said, 'Let days speak,
   and many years teach wisdom.'
8 But truly it is the spirit in a mortal,
   the breath of the Almighty,[f] that makes for understanding.
9 It is not the old[h] that are wise,
   nor the aged that understand what is right.
10 Therefore I say, 'Listen to me;
   let me also declare my opinion.'

11 "See, I waited for your words,
   I listened for your wise sayings,
   while you searched out what to say.
12 I gave you my attention,
   but there was in fact no one that confuted Job,
   no one among you that answered his words.
13 Yet do not say, 'We have found wisdom;
   God may vanquish him, not a human.'
14 He has not directed his words against me,
   and I will not answer him with your speeches.

15 "They are dismayed, they answer no more;
   they have not a word to say.

---

^e Or *as Adam did*   ^f Traditional rendering of Heb *Shaddai*   ^g Another ancient tradition reads *answer, and had put God in the wrong*   ^h Gk Syr Vg: Heb *many*

King James

16When I had waited, (for they spake not, but stood still, *and* answered no more;)

17*I said,* I will answer also my part, I also will show mine opinion.

18For I am full of matter, the spirit within me constraineth me.

19Behold, my belly *is* as wine *which* hath no vent; it is ready to burst like new bottles.

20I will speak, that I may be refreshed: I will open my lips and answer.

21Let me not, I pray you, accept any man's person, neither let me give flattering titles unto man.

22For I know not to give flattering titles; *in so doing* my maker would soon take me away.

33 WHEREFORE, JOB, I pray thee, hear my speeches, and hearken to all my words.

2Behold, now I have opened my mouth, my tongue hath spoken in my mouth.

3My words *shall be of* the uprightness of my heart: and my lips shall utter knowledge clearly.

4The spirit of God hath made me, and the breath of the Almighty hath given me life.

5If thou canst answer me, set *thy words* in order before me, stand up.

6Behold, I *am* according to thy wish in God's stead: I also am formed out of the clay.

7Behold, my terror shall not make thee afraid, neither shall my hand be heavy upon thee.

8Surely thou hast spoken in mine hearing, and I have heard the voice of *thy* words, *saying,*

9I am clean without transgression, I *am* innocent; neither *is there* iniquity in me.

10Behold, he findeth occasions against me, he counteth me for his enemy,

11He putteth my feet in the stocks, he marketh all my paths.

12Behold, *in* this thou art not just: I will answer thee, that God is greater than man.

13Why dost thou strive against him? for he giveth not account of any of his matters.

14For God speaketh once, yea twice, *yet man* perceiveth it not.

15In a dream, in a vision of the night, when deep sleep falleth upon men, in slumberings upon the bed;

16Then he openeth the ears of men, and sealeth their instruction,

17That he may withdraw man *from his* purpose, and hide pride from man.

18He keepeth back his soul from the pit, and his life from perishing by the sword.

19He is chastened also with pain upon his bed, and the multitude of his bones with strong *pain:*

New International

16Must I wait, now that they are silent,
now that they stand there with no reply?

17I too will have my say;
I too will tell what I know.

18For I am full of words,
and the spirit within me compels me;

19inside I am like bottled-up wine,
like new wineskins ready to burst.

20I must speak and find relief;
I must open my lips and reply.

21I will show partiality to no one,
nor will I flatter any man;

22for if I were skilled in flattery,
my Maker would soon take me away.

33 "BUT NOW, Job, listen to my words;
pay attention to everything I say.

2I am about to open my mouth;
my words are on the tip of my tongue.

3My words come from an upright heart;
my lips sincerely speak what I know.

4The Spirit of God has made me;
the breath of the Almighty gives me life.

5Answer me then, if you can;
prepare yourself and confront me.

6I am just like you before God;
I too have been taken from clay.

7No fear of me should alarm you,
nor should my hand be heavy upon you.

8"But you have said in my hearing—
I heard the very words—

9'I am pure and without sin;
I am clean and free from guilt.

10Yet God has found fault with me;
he considers me his enemy.

11He fastens my feet in shackles;
he keeps close watch on all my paths.'

12"But I tell you, in this you are not right,
for God is greater than man.

13Why do you complain to him
that he answers none of man's words[a]?

14For God does speak—now one way, now
another—
though man may not perceive it.

15In a dream, in a vision of the night,
when deep sleep falls on men
as they slumber in their beds,

16he may speak in their ears
and terrify them with warnings,

17to turn man from wrongdoing
and keep him from pride,

18to preserve his soul from the pit,[b]
his life from perishing by the sword.[c]

19Or a man may be chastened on a bed of pain
with constant distress in his bones,

---

a 13 Or *that he does not answer for any of his actions*   b 18 Or *preserve him from the grave*   c 18 Or *from crossing the River*

Living Bible

16Shall I then continue to wait when you are silent? 17No, I will give my answer too. 18For I am pent up and full of words, and the spirit within me urges me on. 19I am like a wine cask without a vent! My words are ready to burst out! 20I must speak to find relief, so let me give my answers. 21, 22Don't insist that I be cautious lest I insult someone, and don't make me flatter anyone. Let me be frank, lest God should strike me dead.

33 "PLEASE LISTEN, Job, to what I have to say. 2I have begun to speak; now let me continue. 3I will speak the truth with all sincerity. 4For the Spirit of God has made me, and the breath of the Almighty gives me life. 5Don't hesitate to answer me if you can.

6"Look, I am the one you were wishing for, someone to stand between you and God and to be both his representative and yours. 7You need not be frightened of me. I am not some person of renown to make you nervous and afraid. I, too, am made of common clay.

8"You have said it in my hearing, yes, you've said it again and again— 9'I am pure, I am innocent; I have not sinned.' 10You say God is using a fine-toothed comb to try to find a single fault, and so to count you as his enemy. 11'And he puts my feet in the stocks,' you say, 'and watches every move I make.'

12"All right, here is my reply: In this very thing, you have sinned by speaking of God that way. For God is greater than man. 13Why should you fight against him just because he does not give account to you of what he does?

14"For God speaks again and again, 15in dreams, in visions of the night when deep sleep falls on men as they lie on their beds. 16He opens their ears in times like that, and gives them wisdom and instruction, 17, 18causing them to change their minds, and keeping them from pride, and warning them of the penalties of sin, and keeping them from falling into some trap.

19"Or, God sends sickness and pain, even though no bone is broken, 20so that a man loses all taste and appe-

New Revised Standard

16 And am I to wait, because they do not speak,
    because they stand there, and answer no
      more?
17 I also will give my answer;
    I also will declare my opinion.
18 For I am full of words;
    the spirit within me constrains me.
19 My heart is indeed like wine that has no vent;
    like new wineskins, it is ready to burst.
20 I must speak, so that I may find relief;
    I must open my lips and answer.
21 I will not show partiality to any person
    or use flattery toward anyone.
22 For I do not know how to flatter—
    or my Maker would soon put an end to me!

Elihu Rebukes Job

33 "BUT NOW, hear my speech, O Job,
    and listen to all my words.
2 See, I open my mouth;
    the tongue in my mouth speaks.
3 My words declare the uprightness of my heart,
    and what my lips know they speak
      sincerely.
4 The spirit of God has made me,
    and the breath of the Almighty[d] gives me
      life.
5 Answer me, if you can;
    set your words in order before me; take
      your stand.
6 See, before God I am as you are;
    I too was formed from a piece of clay.
7 No fear of me need terrify you;
    my pressure will not be heavy on you.

8 "Surely, you have spoken in my hearing,
    and I have heard the sound of your words.
9 You say, 'I am clean, without transgression;
    I am pure, and there is no iniquity in me.
10 Look, he finds occasions against me,
    he counts me as his enemy;
11 he puts my feet in the stocks,
    and watches all my paths.'

12 "But in this you are not right. I will answer
    you:
    God is greater than any mortal.
13 Why do you contend against him,
    saying, 'He will answer none of my[e]
      words'?
14 For God speaks in one way,
    and in two, though people do not perceive
      it.
15 In a dream, in a vision of the night,
    when deep sleep falls on mortals,
    while they slumber on their beds,
16 then he opens their ears,
    and terrifies them with warnings,
17 that he may turn them aside from their deeds,
    and keep them from pride,
18 to spare their souls from the Pit,
    their lives from traversing the River.
19 They are also chastened with pain upon their
      beds,
    and with continual strife in their bones,

---

[d] Traditional rendering of Heb *Shaddai*   [e] Compare Gk: Heb *his*

King James

²⁰So that his life abhorreth bread, and his soul dainty meat.

²¹His flesh is consumed away, that it cannot be seen; and his bones *that* were not seen stick out.

²²Yea, his soul draweth near unto the grave, and his life to the destroyers.

²³If there be a messenger with him, an interpreter, one among a thousand, to show unto man his uprightness:

²⁴Then he is gracious unto him, and saith, Deliver him from going down to the pit: I have found a ransom.

²⁵His flesh shall be fresher than a child's: he shall return to the days of his youth:

²⁶He shall pray unto God, and he will be favourable unto him: and he shall see his face with joy: for he will render unto man his righteousness.

²⁷He looketh upon men, and *if any* say, I have sinned, and perverted *that which was* right, and it profited me not;

²⁸He will deliver his soul from going into the pit, and his life shall see the light.

²⁹Lo, all these *things* worketh God oftentimes with man,

³⁰To bring back his soul from the pit, to be enlightened with the light of the living.

³¹Mark well, O Job, hearken unto me: hold thy peace, and I will speak.

³²If thou hast any thing to say, answer me: speak, for I desire to justify thee.

³³If not, hearken unto me: hold thy peace, and I shall teach thee wisdom.

34 FURTHERMORE ELIHU answered and said, ²Hear my words, O ye wise *men;* and give ear unto me, ye that have knowledge.

³For the ear trieth words, as the mouth tasteth meat.

⁴Let us choose to us judgment: let us know among ourselves what *is* good.

⁵For Job hath said, I am righteous: and God hath taken away my judgment.

⁶Should I lie against my right? my wound *is* incurable without transgression.

⁷What man *is* like Job, *who* drinketh up scorning like water?

⁸Which goeth in company with the workers of iniquity, and walketh with wicked men.

⁹For he hath said, It profiteth a man nothing that he should delight himself with God.

¹⁰Therefore hearken unto me, ye men of understanding: far be it from God, *that he should do* wickedness; and *from* the Almighty, *that he should commit* iniquity.

New International

²⁰so that his very being finds food repulsive
    and his soul loathes the choicest meal.
²¹His flesh wastes away to nothing,
    and his bones, once hidden, now stick out.
²²His soul draws near to the pit,^a
    and his life to the messengers of death.^b

²³"Yet if there is an angel on his side
    as a mediator, one out of a thousand,
    to tell a man what is right for him,
²⁴to be gracious to him and say,
    'Spare him from going down to the pit^c;
    I have found a ransom for him'—
²⁵then his flesh is renewed like a child's;
    it is restored as in the days of his youth.
²⁶He prays to God and finds favor with him,
    he sees God's face and shouts for joy;
    he is restored by God to his righteous state.
²⁷Then he comes to men and says,
    'I sinned, and perverted what was right,
    but I did not get what I deserved.
²⁸He redeemed my soul from going down to the
        pit,^d
    and I will live to enjoy the light.'

²⁹"God does all these things to a man—
    twice, even three times—
³⁰to turn back his soul from the pit,^e
    that the light of life may shine on him.

³¹"Pay attention, Job, and listen to me;
    be silent, and I will speak.
³²If you have anything to say, answer me;
    speak up, for I want you to be cleared.
³³But if not, then listen to me;
    be silent, and I will teach you wisdom."

34 THEN ELIHU said:

²"Hear my words, you wise men;
    listen to me, you men of learning.
³For the ear tests words
    as the tongue tastes food.
⁴Let us discern for ourselves what is right;
    let us learn together what is good.

⁵"Job says, 'I am innocent,
    but God denies me justice.
⁶Although I am right,
    I am considered a liar;
    although I am guiltless,
    his arrow inflicts an incurable wound.'
⁷What man is like Job,
    who drinks scorn like water?
⁸He keeps company with evildoers;
    he associates with wicked men.
⁹For he says, 'It profits a man nothing
    when he tries to please God.'

¹⁰"So listen to me, you men of understanding.
    Far be it from God to do evil,
    from the Almighty to do wrong.

---

^a 22 Or *He draws near to the grave*   ^b 22 Or *to the dead*   ^c 24 Or *grave*
^d 28 Or *redeemed me from going down to the grave*   ^e 30 Or *turn him back
from the grave*

Living Bible

tite for food and doesn't care for even the daintiest dessert. 21He becomes thin, mere skin and bones, 22and draws near to death.

23, 24"But if a messenger from heaven is there to intercede for him as a friend, to show him what is right, then God pities him and says,f 'Set him free. Do not make him die, for I have found a substitute.' 25Then his body will become as healthy as a child's, firm and youthful again. 26And when he prays to God, God will hear and answer and receive him with joy, and return him to his duties. 27And he will declare to his friends, 'I sinned, but God let me go. 28He did not let me die. I will go on living in the realm of light.'

29"Yes, God often does these things for man—30brings back his soul from the pit, so that he may live in the light of the living. 31Mark this well, O Job. Listen to me, and let me say more. 32But if you have anything to say at this point, go ahead. I want to hear it, for I am anxious to justify you. 33But if not, then listen to me. Keep silence and I will teach you wisdom!"

New Revised Standard

20 so that their lives loathe bread,
      and their appetites dainty food.
21 Their flesh is so wasted away that it cannot be
      seen;
      and their bones, once invisible, now stick
      out.
22 Their souls draw near the Pit,
      and their lives to those who bring death.
23 Then, if there should be for one of them an
      angel,
      a mediator, one of a thousand,
      one who declares a person upright,
24 and he is gracious to that person, and says,
      'Deliver him from going down into the Pit;
      I have found a ransom;
25 let his flesh become fresh with youth;
      let him return to the days of his youthful
      vigor.'
26 Then he prays to God, and is accepted by
      him,
      he comes into his presence with joy,
      and Godg repays him for his righteousness.
27 That person sings to others and says,
      'I sinned, and perverted what was right,
      and it was not paid back to me.
28 He has redeemed my soul from going down to
      the Pit,
      and my life shall see the light.'

29 "God indeed does all these things,
      twice, three times, with mortals,
30 to bring back their souls from the Pit,
      so that they may see the light of life.h
31 Pay heed, Job, listen to me;
      be silent, and I will speak.
32 If you have anything to say, answer me;
      speak, for I desire to justify you.
33 If not, listen to me;
      be silent, and I will teach you wisdom."

34

ELIHU CONTINUED:

2"Listen to me, you wise men. 3We can choose the sounds we want to listen to; we can choose the taste we want in food, 4and we should choose to follow what is right. But first of all we must define among ourselves what is good. 5For Job has said, 'I am innocent, but God says I'm not. 6I am called a liar, even though I am innocent. I am horribly punished, even though I have not sinned.'

7, 8"Who else is as arrogant as Job? He must have spent much time with evil men, 9for he said, 'Why waste time trying to please God?'

10"Listen to me, you with understanding. Surely everyone knows that God doesn't sin! 11Rather, he pun-

Elihu Proclaims God's Justice

34

THEN ELIHU continued and said:

2   "Hear my words, you wise men,
      and give ear to me, you who know;
3   for the ear tests words
      as the palate tastes food.
4   Let us choose what is right;
      let us determine among ourselves what is
      good.
5   For Job has said, 'I am innocent,
      and God has taken away my right;
6   in spite of being right I am counted a liar;
      my wound is incurable, though I am without
      transgression.'
7   Who is there like Job,
      who drinks up scoffing like water,
8   who goes in company with evildoers
      and walks with the wicked?
9   For he has said, 'It profits one nothing
      to take delight in God.'

10 "Therefore, hear me, you who have sense,
      far be it from God that he should do
      wickedness,
      and from the Almightyi that he should do
      wrong.

---

f 33:23, 24 then God pities him and says, or, "and if the Angel says."

g Heb he   h Syr: Heb to be lighted with the light of life   i Traditional rendering of Heb Shaddai

King James

11For the work of a man shall he render unto him, and cause every man to find according to *his* ways.

12Yea, surely God will not do wickedly, neither will the Almighty pervert judgment.

13Who hath given him a charge over the earth? or who hath disposed the whole world?

14If he set his heart upon man, *if* he gather unto himself his spirit and his breath;

15All flesh shall perish together, and man shall turn again unto dust.

16If now *thou hast* understanding, hear this: hearken to the voice of my words.

17Shall even he that hateth right govern? and wilt thou condemn him that is most just?

18*Is it fit* to say to a king, *Thou art* wicked? *and* to princes, *Ye are* ungodly?

19*How much less to him* that accepteth not the persons of princes, nor regardeth the rich more than the poor? for they all *are* the work of his hands.

20In a moment shall they die, and the people shall be troubled at midnight, and pass away: and the mighty shall be taken away without hand.

21For his eyes *are* upon the ways of man, and he seeth all his goings.

22*There is* no darkness, nor shadow of death, where the workers of iniquity may hide themselves.

23For he will not lay upon man more *than right;* that he should enter into judgment with God.

24He shall break in pieces mighty men without number, and set others in their stead.

25Therefore he knoweth their works, and he overturneth *them* in the night, so that they are destroyed.

26He striketh them as wicked men in the open sight of others;

27Because they turned back from him, and would not consider any of his ways:

28So that they cause the cry of the poor to come unto him, and he heareth the cry of the afflicted.

29When he giveth quietness, who then can make trouble? and when he hideth *his* face, who then can behold him? whether *it be done* against a nation, or against a man only:

30That the hypocrite reign not, lest the people be ensnared.

31Surely it is meet to be said unto God, I have borne *chastisement,* I will not offend *any more:*

32*That which* I see not teach thou me: if I have done iniquity, I will do no more.

33*Should it be* according to thy mind? he will recompense it, whether thou refuse, or whether thou choose; and not I: therefore speak what thou knowest.

34Let men of understanding tell me, and let a wise man hearken unto me.

35Job hath spoken without knowledge, and his words *were* without wisdom.

36My desire *is that* Job may be tried unto the end because of *his* answers for wicked men.

New International

11He repays a man for what he has done;
  he brings upon him what his conduct
    deserves.

12It is unthinkable that God would do wrong,
  that the Almighty would pervert justice.

13Who appointed him over the earth?
  Who put him in charge of the whole world?

14If it were his intention
  and he withdrew his spirit[a] and breath,

15all mankind would perish together
  and man would return to the dust.

16"If you have understanding, hear this;
  listen to what I say.

17Can he who hates justice govern?
  Will you condemn the just and mighty One?

18Is he not the One who says to kings, 'You are
    worthless,'
  and to nobles, 'You are wicked,'

19who shows no partiality to princes
  and does not favor the rich over the poor,
    for they are all the work of his hands?

20They die in an instant, in the middle of the
    night;
  the people are shaken and they pass away;
  the mighty are removed without human hand.

21"His eyes are on the ways of men;
  he sees their every step.

22There is no dark place, no deep shadow,
  where evildoers can hide.

23God has no need to examine men further,
  that they should come before him for
    judgment.

24Without inquiry he shatters the mighty
  and sets up others in their place.

25Because he takes note of their deeds,
  he overthrows them in the night and they are
    crushed.

26He punishes them for their wickedness
  where everyone can see them,

27because they turned from following him
  and had no regard for any of his ways.

28They caused the cry of the poor to come before
    him,
  so that he heard the cry of the needy.

29But if he remains silent, who can condemn
    him?
  If he hides his face, who can see him?
  Yet he is over man and nation alike,

30 to keep a godless man from ruling,
  from laying snares for the people.

31"Suppose a man says to God,
  'I am guilty but will offend no more.

32Teach me what I cannot see;
  if I have done wrong, I will not do so again.'

33Should God then reward you on your terms,
  when you refuse to repent?
You must decide, not I;
  so tell me what you know.

34"Men of understanding declare,
  wise men who hear me say to me,

35'Job speaks without knowledge;
  his words lack insight.'

36Oh, that Job might be tested to the utmost
  for answering like a wicked man!

---

[a] *14 Or Spirit*

Living Bible

ishes the sinners. ¹²There is no truer statement than this: *God is never wicked or unjust.* ¹³He alone has authority over the earth and dispenses justice for the world. ¹⁴If God were to withdraw his Spirit, ¹⁵all life would disappear and mankind would turn again to dust.

¹⁶"Listen now and try to understand. ¹⁷Could God govern if he hated justice? Are you going to condemn the Almighty Judge? ¹⁸Are you going to condemn this God who says to kings and nobles, 'You are wicked and unjust'? ¹⁹For he doesn't care how great a man may be, and doesn't pay any more attention to the rich than to the poor. He made them all. ²⁰In a moment they die, and at midnight great and small shall suddenly pass away, removed by no human hand.

²¹"For God carefully watches the goings on of all mankind; he sees them all. ²²No darkness is thick enough to hide evil men from his eyes, ²³so there is no need to wait for some great crime before a man is called before God in judgment. ²⁴Without making a big issue over it, God simply shatters the greatest of men, and puts others in their places. ²⁵He watches what they do and in a single night he overturns them, destroying them, ²⁶or openly strikes them down as wicked men. ²⁷For they turned aside from following him, ²⁸causing the cry of the poor to come to the attention of God. Yes, he hears the cries of those being oppressed. ²⁹, ³⁰Yet when he chooses not to speak, who can criticize? Again, he may prevent a vile man from ruling, thus saving a nation from ruin, and he can depose an entire nation just as easily.

³¹"Why don't people exclaim to their God, 'We have sinned, but we will stop'? ³²Or, 'We know not what evil we have done; only tell us, and we will cease at once.'

³³"Must God tailor his justice to your demands? Must he change the order of the universe to suit your whims? The answer must be obvious even to you! ³⁴, ³⁵Anyone even half bright will agree with me that you, Job, are speaking like a fool. ³⁶You should be given the maximum penalty for the wicked way you have talked about

New Revised Standard

11 For according to their deeds he will repay
      them,
         and according to their ways he will make it
         befall them.
12 Of a truth, God will not do wickedly,
         and the Almighty[b] will not pervert justice.
13 Who gave him charge over the earth
         and who laid on him[c] the whole world?
14 If he should take back his spirit[d] to himself,
         and gather to himself his breath,
15 all flesh would perish together,
         and all mortals return to dust.

16 "If you have understanding, hear this;
         listen to what I say.
17 Shall one who hates justice govern?
         Will you condemn one who is righteous and
         mighty,
18 who says to a king, 'You scoundrel!'[ ]
         and to princes, 'You wicked men!';
19 who shows no partiality to nobles,
         nor regards the rich more than the poor,
         for they are all the work of his hands?
20 In a moment they die;
         at midnight the people are shaken and pass
         away,
         and the mighty are taken away by no human
         hand.

21 "For his eyes are upon the ways of mortals,
         and he sees all their steps.
22 There is no gloom or deep darkness
         where evildoers may hide themselves.
23 For he has not appointed a time[e] for anyone
         to go before God in judgment.
24 He shatters the mighty without investigation,
         and sets others in their place.
25 Thus, knowing their works,
         he overturns them in the night, and they are
         crushed.
26 He strikes them for their wickedness
         while others look on,
27 because they turned aside from following him,
         and had no regard for any of his ways,
28 so that they caused the cry of the poor to
         come to him,
         and he heard the cry of the afflicted—
29 When he is quiet, who can condemn?
         When he hides his face, who can behold
         him,
         whether it be a nation or an individual?—
30 so that the godless should not reign,
         or those who ensnare the people.

31 "For has anyone said to God,
         'I have endured punishment; I will not
         offend any more;
32 teach me what I do not see;
         if I have done iniquity, I will do it no
         more'?
33 Will he then pay back to suit you,
         because you reject it?
      For you must choose, and not I;
         therefore declare what you know.[f]
34 Those who have sense will say to me,
         and the wise who hear me will say,
35 'Job speaks without knowledge,
         his words are without insight.'
36 Would that Job were tried to the limit,
         because his answers are those of the
         wicked.

---

b Traditional rendering of Heb *Shaddai*   c Heb lacks *on him*   d Heb *his heart his spirit*   e Cn: Heb *yet*   f Meaning of Heb of verses 29-33 uncertain

King James

37For he addeth rebellion unto his sin, he clappeth *his hands* among us, and multiplieth his words against God.

35 ELIHU SPAKE moreover, and said, 2Thinkest thou this to be right, *that* thou saidst, My righteousness *is* more than God's?

3For thou saidst, What advantage will it be unto thee? *and,* What profit shall I have, *if I be cleansed* from my sin?

4I will answer thee, and thy companions with thee.

5Look unto the heavens, and see; and behold the clouds *which* are higher than thou.

6If thou sinnest, what doest thou against him? or *if* thy transgressions be multiplied, what doest thou unto him?

7If thou be righteous, what givest thou him? or what receiveth he of thine hand?

8Thy wickedness *may hurt* a man as thou *art;* and thy righteousness *may profit* the son of man.

9By reason of the multitude of oppressions they make *the oppressed* to cry: they cry out by reason of the arm of the mighty.

10But none saith, Where *is* God my maker, who giveth songs in the night;

11Who teacheth us more than the beasts of the earth, and maketh us wiser than the fowls of heaven?

12There they cry, but none giveth answer, because of the pride of evil men.

13Surely God will not hear vanity, neither will the Almighty regard it.

14Although thou sayest thou shalt not see him, *yet* judgment *is* before him; therefore trust thou in him.

15But now, because *it is* not *so,* he hath visited in his anger; yet he knoweth *it* not in great extremity:

16Therefore doth Job open his mouth in vain; he multiplieth words without knowledge.

36 ELIHU ALSO proceeded, and said, 2Suffer me a little, and I will show thee that *I have* yet to speak on God's behalf.

3I will fetch my knowledge from afar, and will ascribe righteousness to my Maker.

4For truly my words *shall* not *be* false: he that is perfect in knowledge *is* with thee.

5Behold, God *is* mighty, and despiseth not *any: he is* mighty in strength *and* wisdom.

6He preserveth not the life of the wicked: but giveth right to the poor.

New International

37To his sin he adds rebellion;
     scornfully he claps his hands among us
     and multiplies his words against God."

35 THEN ELIHU said:

2"Do you think this is just?
     You say, 'I will be cleared by God.a'
3Yet you ask him, 'What profit is it to me,b
     and what do I gain by not sinning?'

4"I would like to reply to you
     and to your friends with you.
5Look up at the heavens and see;
     gaze at the clouds so high above you.
6If you sin, how does that affect him?
     If your sins are many, what does that do to
       him?
7If you are righteous, what do you give to him,
     or what does he receive from your hand?
8Your wickedness affects only a man like
       yourself,
     and your righteousness only the sons of men.

9"Men cry out under a load of oppression;
     they plead for relief from the arm of the
       powerful.
10But no one says, 'Where is God my Maker,
     who gives songs in the night,
11who teaches more to us than toc the beasts of
       the earth
     and makes us wiser thand the birds of the
       air?'
12He does not answer when men cry out
     because of the arrogance of the wicked.
13Indeed, God does not listen to their empty plea;
     the Almighty pays no attention to it.
14How much less, then, will he listen
     when you say that you do not see him,
     that your case is before him
     and you must wait for him,
15and further, that his anger never punishes
     and he does not take the least notice of
       wickedness.e
16So Job opens his mouth with empty talk;
     without knowledge he multiplies words."

36 ELIHU CONTINUED:

2"Bear with me a little longer and I will
       show you
     that there is more to be said in God's behalf.
3I get my knowledge from afar;
     I will ascribe justice to my Maker.
4Be assured that my words are not false;
     one perfect in knowledge is with you.

5"God is mighty, but does not despise men;
     he is mighty, and firm in his purpose.
6He does not keep the wicked alive
     but gives the afflicted their rights.

a *2* Or *My righteousness is more than God's*   b *3* Or *you*   c *11* Or *teaches us by*   d *11* Or *us wise by*   e *15* Symmachus, Theodotion and Vulgate; the meaning of the Hebrew for this word is uncertain.

Living Bible

God. 37For now you have added rebellion, arrogance and blasphemy to your other sins."

35 ELIHU CONTINUED:

2, 3"Do you think it is right for you to claim, 'I haven't sinned, but I'm no better off before God than if I had'?

4"I will answer you, and all your friends too. 5Look up there into the sky, high above you. 6If you sin, does that shake the heavens and knock God from his throne? Even if you sin again and again, what effect will it have upon him? 7Or if you are good, is this some great gift to him? 8Your sins may hurt another man, or your good deeds may profit him. 9, 10The oppressed may shriek beneath their wrongs and groan beneath the power of the rich; yet none of them cry to God, asking, 'Where is God my Maker who gives songs in the night, 11and makes us a little wiser than the animals and birds?'

12"But when anyone does cry out this question to him, he never replies by instant punishment of the tyrants.f 13But it is false to say he doesn't hear those cries; 14, 15and it is even more false to say that he doesn't see what is going on. He *does* bring about justice at last, if you will only wait. But do you cry out against him because he does not instantly respond in anger? 16Job, you have spoken like a fool."

36 ELIHU CONTINUED:

2"Let me go on and I will show you the truth of what I am saying. For I have not finished defending God! 3I will give you many illustrations of the righteousness of my Maker. 4I am telling you the honest truth, for I am a man of well-rounded knowledge.

5"God is almighty and yet does not despise anyone! And he is perfect in his understanding. 6He does not reward the wicked with his blessings, but gives them their full share of punishment. 7He does not ignore the

New Revised Standard

37 For he adds rebellion to his sin;
    he claps his hands among us,
    and multiplies his words against God."

Elihu Condemns Self-Righteousness

35 ELIHU CONTINUED and said:

2 "Do you think this to be just?
   You say, 'I am in the right before God.'
3 If you ask, 'What advantage have I?
   How am I better off than if I had sinned?'
4 I will answer you
   and your friends with you.
5 Look at the heavens and see;
   observe the clouds, which are higher than
     you.
6 If you have sinned, what do you accomplish
     against him?
   And if your transgressions are multiplied,
     what do you do to him?
7 If you are righteous, what do you give to him;
   or what does he receive from your hand?
8 Your wickedness affects others like you,
   and your righteousness, other human beings.

9 "Because of the multitude of oppressions
     people cry out;
   they call for help because of the arm of the
     mighty.
10 But no one says, 'Where is God my Maker,
     who gives strength in the night,
11 who teaches us more than the animals of the
     earth,
   and makes us wiser than the birds of the
     air?'
12 There they cry out, but he does not answer,
     because of the pride of evildoers.
13 Surely God does not hear an empty cry,
     nor does the Almightyg regard it.
14 How much less when you say that you do not
     see him,
   that the case is before him, and you are
     waiting for him!
15 And now, because his anger does not punish,
     and he does not greatly heed transgression,h
16 Job opens his mouth in empty talk,
   he multiplies words without knowledge."

Elihu Exalts God's Goodness

36 ELIHU CONTINUED and said:

2 "Bear with me a little, and I will show
     you,
   for I have yet something to say on God's
     behalf.
3 I will bring my knowledge from far away,
   and ascribe righteousness to my Maker.
4 For truly my words are not false;
   one who is perfect in knowledge is with
     you.

5 "Surely God is mighty and does not despise
     any;
   he is mighty in strength of understanding.
6 He does not keep the wicked alive,
   but gives the afflicted their right.

---

f 35:12 *instant punishment of the tyrants,* or, "because of man's base pride."

g Traditional rendering of Heb *Shaddai*   h Theodotion Symmachus Compare Vg: Meaning of Heb uncertain

King James

7He withdraweth not his eyes from the righteous: but with kings *are they* on the throne; yea, he doth establish them for ever, and they are exalted.

8And if *they be* bound in fetters, *and* be holden in cords of affliction;

9Then he showeth them their work, and their transgressions that they have exceeded.

10He openeth also their ear to discipline, and commandeth that they return from iniquity.

11If they obey and serve *him*, they shall spend their days in prosperity, and their years in pleasures.

12But if they obey not, they shall perish by the sword, and they shall die without knowledge.

13But the hypocrites in heart heap up wrath: they cry not when he bindeth them.

14They die in youth, and their life *is* among the unclean.

15He delivereth the poor in his affliction, and openeth their ears in oppression.

16Even so would he have removed thee out of the strait *into* a broad place, where *there is* no straitness; and that which should be set on thy table *should be* full of fatness.

17But thou hast fulfilled the judgment of the wicked: judgment and justice take hold *on thee*.

18Because *there is* wrath, *beware* lest he take thee away with *his* stroke: then a great ransom cannot deliver thee.

19Will he esteem thy riches? *no*, not gold, nor all the forces of strength.

20Desire not the night, when people are cut off in their place.

21Take heed, regard not iniquity: for this hast thou chosen rather than affliction.

22Behold, God exalteth by his power: who teacheth like him?

23Who hath enjoined him his way? or who can say, Thou hast wrought iniquity?

24Remember that thou magnify his work, which men behold.

25Every man may see it; man may behold *it* afar off.

26Behold, God *is* great, and we know *him* not, neither can the number of his years be searched out.

27For he maketh small the drops of water: they pour down rain according to the vapour thereof:

28Which the clouds do drop *and* distil upon man abundantly.

29Also can *any* understand the spreadings of the clouds, *or* the noise of his tabernacle?

30Behold, he spreadeth his light upon it, and covereth the bottom of the sea.

31For by them judgeth he the people; he giveth meat in abundance.

New International

7He does not take his eyes off the righteous;
he enthrones them with kings
and exalts them forever.

8But if men are bound in chains,
held fast by cords of affliction,

9he tells them what they have done—
that they have sinned arrogantly.

10He makes them listen to correction
and commands them to repent of their evil.

11If they obey and serve him,
they will spend the rest of their days in
prosperity
and their years in contentment.

12But if they do not listen,
they will perish by the sword[a]
and die without knowledge.

13"The godless in heart harbor resentment;
even when he fetters them, they do not cry
for help.

14They die in their youth,
among male prostitutes of the shrines.

15But those who suffer he delivers in their
suffering;
he speaks to them in their affliction.

16"He is wooing you from the jaws of distress
to a spacious place free from restriction,
to the comfort of your table laden with choice
food.

17But now you are laden with the judgment due
the wicked;
judgment and justice have taken hold of you.

18Be careful that no one entices you by riches;
do not let a large bribe turn you aside.

19Would your wealth
or even all your mighty efforts
sustain you so you would not be in distress?

20Do not long for the night,
to drag people away from their homes.[b]

21Beware of turning to evil,
which you seem to prefer to affliction.

22"God is exalted in his power.
Who is a teacher like him?

23Who has prescribed his ways for him,
or said to him, 'You have done wrong'?

24Remember to extol his work,
which men have praised in song.

25All mankind has seen it;
men gaze on it from afar.

26How great is God—beyond our understanding!
The number of his years is past finding out.

27"He draws up the drops of water,
which distill as rain to the streams[c];

28the clouds pour down their moisture
and abundant showers fall on mankind.

29Who can understand how he spreads out the
clouds,
how he thunders from his pavilion?

30See how he scatters his lightning about him,
bathing the depths of the sea.

31This is the way he governs[d] the nations
and provides food in abundance.

ª *12* Or *will cross the River*   ᵇ *20* The meaning of the Hebrew for verses 18-20 is uncertain.   ᶜ *27* Or *distill from the mist as rain*   ᵈ *31* Or *nourishes*

Living Bible

good men but honors them by placing them upon eternal, kingly thrones. 8If troubles come upon them, and they are enslaved and afflicted, 9then he takes the trouble to point out to them the reason, what they have done that is wrong, or how they have behaved proudly. 10He helps them hear his instruction to turn away from their sin.

11"If they listen and obey him, then they will be blessed with prosperity throughout their lives. 12If they won't listen to him, they shall perish in battle and die because of their lack of good sense. 13But the godless reap his anger. They do not even return to him when he punishes them. 14They die young after lives of dissipation and depravity. 15He delivers by distress! This makes them listen to him!

16"How he wanted to lure you away from danger into a wide and pleasant valley and to prosper you there. 17But you are too preoccupied with your imagined grievances against others. 18Watch out! Don't let your anger at others lead you into scoffing at God! Don't let your suffering embitter you at the only one who can deliver you. 19Do you really think that if you shout loudly enough against God, he will be ashamed and repent? Will this put an end to your chastisement?

20"Do not desire the nighttime, with its opportunities for crime. 21Turn back from evil, for it was to prevent you from getting into a life of evil that God sent this suffering.

22"Look, God is all-powerful. Who is a teacher like him? 23Who can say that what he does is absurd or evil? 24Instead, glorify him for his mighty works for which he is so famous. 25Everyone has seen these things from a distance.

26"God is so great that we cannot begin to know him. No one can begin to understand eternity. 27He draws up the water vapor and then distills it into rain, 28which the skies pour down. 29Can anyone really understand the spreading of the clouds, and the thunders within? 30See how he spreads the lightning around him, and blankets the tops of the mountains. 31By his fantastic powers in nature he punishes or blesses the people, giving them

New Revised Standard

7 He does not withdraw his eyes from the
   righteous,
   but with kings on the throne
   he sets them forever, and they are exalted.
8 And if they are bound in fetters
   and caught in the cords of affliction,
9 then he declares to them their work
   and their transgressions, that they are
   behaving arrogantly.
10 He opens their ears to instruction,
   and commands that they return from
   iniquity.
11 If they listen, and serve him,
   they complete their days in prosperity,
   and their years in pleasantness.
12 But if they do not listen, they shall perish by
   the sword,
   and die without knowledge.

13 "The godless in heart cherish anger;
   they do not cry for help when he binds
   them.
14 They die in their youth,
   and their life ends in shame.e
15 He delivers the afflicted by their affliction,
   and opens their ear by adversity.
16 He also allured you out of distress
   into a broad place where there was no
   constraint,
   and what was set on your table was full of
   fatness.

17 "But you are obsessed with the case of the
   wicked;
   judgment and justice seize you.
18 Beware that wrath does not entice you into
   scoffing,
   and do not let the greatness of the ransom
   turn you aside.
19 Will your cry avail to keep you from distress,
   or will all the force of your strength?
20 Do not long for the night,
   when peoples are cut off in their place.
21 Beware! Do not turn to iniquity;
   because of that you have been tried by
   affliction.
22 See, God is exalted in his power;
   who is a teacher like him?
23 Who has prescribed for him his way,
   or who can say, 'You have done wrong'?

Elihu Proclaims God's Majesty

24 "Remember to extol his work,
   of which mortals have sung.
25 All people have looked on it;
   everyone watches it from far away.
26 Surely God is great, and we do not know him;
   the number of his years is unsearchable.
27 For he draws up the drops of water;
   he distillsf his mist in rain,
28 which the skies pour down
   and drop upon mortals abundantly.
29 Can anyone understand the spreading of the
   clouds,
   the thunderings of his pavilion?
30 See, he scatters his lightning around him
   and covers the roots of the sea.
31 For by these he governs peoples;
   he gives food in abundance.

e Heb ends among the temple prostitutes   f Cn: Heb they distill

King James

32With clouds he covereth the light; and commandeth it *not to shine* by *the cloud* that cometh betwixt.

33The noise thereof showeth concerning it, the cattle also concerning the vapour.

37 AT THIS also my heart trembleth, and is moved out of his place.

2Hear attentively the noise of his voice, and the sound *that* goeth out of his mouth.

3He directeth it under the whole heaven, and his lightning unto the ends of the earth.

4After it a voice roareth: he thundereth with the voice of his excellency; and he will not stay them when his voice is heard.

5God thundereth marvellously with his voice; great things doeth he, which we cannot comprehend.

6For he saith to the snow, Be thou *on* the earth; likewise to the small rain, and to the great rain of his strength.

7He sealeth up the hand of every man; that all men may know his work.

8Then the beasts go into dens, and remain in their places.

9Out of the south cometh the whirlwind: and cold out of the north.

10By the breath of God frost is given: and the breadth of the waters is straitened.

11Also by watering he wearieth the thick cloud: he scattereth his bright cloud:

12And it is turned round about by his counsels: that they may do whatsoever he commandeth them upon the face of the world in the earth.

13He causeth it to come, whether for correction, or for his land, or for mercy.

14Hearken unto this, O Job: stand still, and consider the wondrous works of God.

15Dost thou know when God disposed them, and caused the light of his cloud to shine?

16Dost thou know the balancings of the clouds, the wondrous works of him which is perfect in knowledge?

17How thy garments *are* warm, when he quieteth the earth by the south *wind?*

18Hast thou with him spread out the sky, *which is* strong, *and* as a molten lookingglass?

19Teach us what we shall say unto him; *for* we cannot order *our speech* by reason of darkness.

20Shall it be told him that I speak? if a man speak, surely he shall be swallowed up.

21And now *men* see not the bright light which *is* in the clouds: but the wind passeth, and cleanseth them.

22Fair weather cometh out of the north: with God *is* terrible majesty.

New International

32He fills his hands with lightning
and commands it to strike its mark.

33His thunder announces the coming storm;
even the cattle make known its approach.[a]

37 "AT THIS my heart pounds
and leaps from its place.

2Listen! Listen to the roar of his voice,
to the rumbling that comes from his mouth.

3He unleashes his lightning beneath the whole heaven
and sends it to the ends of the earth.

4After that comes the sound of his roar;
he thunders with his majestic voice.
When his voice resounds,
he holds nothing back.

5God's voice thunders in marvelous ways;
he does great things beyond our understanding.

6He says to the snow, 'Fall on the earth,'
and to the rain shower, 'Be a mighty downpour.'

7So that all men he has made may know his work,
he stops every man from his labor.[b]

8The animals take cover;
they remain in their dens.

9The tempest comes out from its chamber,
the cold from the driving winds.

10The breath of God produces ice,
and the broad waters become frozen.

11He loads the clouds with moisture;
he scatters his lightning through them.

12At his direction they swirl around
over the face of the whole earth
to do whatever he commands them.

13He brings the clouds to punish men,
or to water his earth[c] and show his love.

14"Listen to this, Job;
stop and consider God's wonders.

15Do you know how God controls the clouds
and makes his lightning flash?

16Do you know how the clouds hang poised,
those wonders of him who is perfect in knowledge?

17You who swelter in your clothes
when the land lies hushed under the south wind,

18can you join him in spreading out the skies,
hard as a mirror of cast bronze?

19"Tell us what we should say to him;
we cannot draw up our case because of our darkness.

20Should he be told that I want to speak?
Would any man ask to be swallowed up?

21Now no one can look at the sun,
bright as it is in the skies
after the wind has swept them clean.

22Out of the north he comes in golden splendor;
God comes in awesome majesty.

---

a 33 Or *announces his coming— l the One zealous against evil*   b 7 Or l *he fills all men with fear by his power*   c 13 Or *to favor them*

Living Bible

food in abundance. 32He fills his hands with lightning bolts. He hurls each at its target. 33We feel his presence in the thunder. Even the cattle know when a storm is coming.

37 "MY HEART trembles at this. 2Listen, listen to the thunder of his voice. 3It rolls across the heavens and his lightning flashes out in every direction. 4Afterwards comes the roaring of the thunder—the tremendous voice of his majesty. 5His voice is glorious in the thunder. We cannot comprehend the greatness of his power. 6For he directs the snow, the showers, and storm to fall upon the earth. 7Man's work stops at such a time, so that all men everywhere may recognize his power. 8The wild animals hide in the rocks or in their dens.

9"From the south comes the rain; from the north, the cold. 10God blows upon the rivers, and even the widest torrents freeze. 11He loads the clouds with moisture and they send forth his lightning. 12The lightning bolts are directed by his hand, and do whatever he commands throughout the earth. 13He sends the stormsd as punishment, or, in his lovingkindness, to encourage.

14"Listen, O Job, stop and consider the wonderful miracles of God. 15Do you know how God controls all nature, and causes the lightning to flash forth from the clouds? 16, 17Do you understand the balancing of the clouds with wonderful perfection and skill? Do you know why you become warm when the south wind is blowing and everything is still? 18Can you spread out the gigantic mirror of the skies as he does?

19, 20"You who think you know so much,e teach the rest of us how we should approach God. For we are too dull to know! With your wisdom, would we then dare to approach him? Well, does a man wish to be swallowed alive? 21For as we cannot look at the sun for its brightness when the winds have cleared away the clouds, 22neither can we gaze at the terrible majesty of God breaking forth upon us from heaven, clothed in

New Revised Standard

32 He covers his hands with the lightning,
        and commands it to strike the mark.
33 Its crashingf tells about him;
        he is jealousf with anger against iniquity.

37 "AT THIS also my heart trembles,
        and leaps out of its place.
2 Listen, listen to the thunder of his voice
        and the rumbling that comes from his
        mouth.
3 Under the whole heaven he lets it loose,
        and his lightning to the corners of the earth.
4 After it his voice roars;
        he thunders with his majestic voice
        and he does not restrain the lightningsg
        when his voice is heard.
5 God thunders wondrously with his voice;
        he does great things that we cannot
        comprehend.
6 For to the snow he says, 'Fall on the earth';
        and the shower of rain, his heavy shower of
        rain,
7 serves as a sign on everyone's hand,
        so that all whom he has made may know
        it.h
8 Then the animals go into their lairs
        and remain in their dens.
9 From its chamber comes the whirlwind,
        and cold from the scattering winds.
10 By the breath of God ice is given,
        and the broad waters are frozen fast.
11 He loads the thick cloud with moisture;
        the clouds scatter his lightning.
12 They turn round and round by his guidance,
        to accomplish all that he commands them
        on the face of the habitable world.
13 Whether for correction, or for his land,
        or for love, he causes it to happen.

14 "Hear this, O Job;
        stop and consider the wondrous works of
        God.
15 Do you know how God lays his command
        upon them,
        and causes the lightning of his cloud to
        shine?
16 Do you know the balancings of the clouds,
        the wondrous works of the one whose
        knowledge is perfect,
17 you whose garments are hot
        when the earth is still because of the south
        wind?
18 Can you, like him, spread out the skies,
        hard as a molten mirror?
19 Teach us what we shall say to him;
        we cannot draw up our case because of
        darkness.
20 Should he be told that I want to speak?
        Did anyone ever wish to be swallowed up?
21 Now, no one can look on the light
        when it is bright in the skies,
        when the wind has passed and cleared them.
22 Out of the north comes golden splendor;
        around God is awesome majesty.

---

d 37:13 He sends the storms, implied.   e 37:19, 20 You who think you know so much, implied.

f Meaning of Heb uncertain   g Heb them   h Meaning of Heb of verse 7 uncertain

King James

23*Touching* the Almighty, we cannot find him out: *he is* excellent in power, and in judgment, and in plenty of justice: he will not afflict.

24Men do therefore fear him: he respecteth not any *that are* wise of heart.

38 THEN THE LORD answered Job out of the whirlwind, and said,

2Who *is* this that darkeneth counsel by words without knowledge?

3Gird up now thy loins like a man; for I will demand of thee, and answer thou me.

4Where wast thou when I laid the foundations of the earth? declare, if thou hast understanding.

5Who hath laid the measures thereof, if thou knowest? or who hath stretched the line upon it?

6Whereupon are the foundations thereof fastened? or who laid the corner stone thereof;

7When the morning stars sang together, and all the sons of God shouted for joy?

8Or *who* shut up the sea with doors, when it brake forth, *as if* it had issued out of the womb?

9When I made the cloud the garment thereof, and thick darkness a swaddlingband for it,

10And brake up for it my decreed *place*, and set bars and doors,

11And said, Hitherto shalt thou come, but no further: and here shall thy proud waves be stayed?

12Hast thou commanded the morning since thy days; *and* caused the dayspring to know his place;

13That it might take hold of the ends of the earth, that the wicked might be shaken out of it?

14It is turned as clay *to* the seal; and they stand as a garment.

15And from the wicked their light is withholden, and the high arm shall be broken.

16Hast thou entered into the springs of the sea? or hast thou walked in the search of the depth?

17Have the gates of death been opened unto thee? or hast thou seen the doors of the shadow of death?

18Hast thou perceived the breadth of the earth? declare if thou knowest it all.

19Where *is* the way *where* light dwelleth? and *as for* darkness, where *is* the place thereof,

20That thou shouldest take it to the bound thereof, and that thou shouldest know the paths *to* the house thereof?

21Knowest thou *it*, because thou wast then born? or *because* the number of thy days *is* great?

New International

23The Almighty is beyond our reach and exalted in power;
  in his justice and great righteousness, he does not oppress.
24Therefore, men revere him,
  for does he not have regard for all the wise in heart?a"

The LORD Speaks

38 THEN THE LORD answered Job out of the storm. He said:

2"Who is this that darkens my counsel
  with words without knowledge?
3Brace yourself like a man;
  I will question you,
  and you shall answer me.

4"Where were you when I laid the earth's foundation?
  Tell me, if you understand.
5Who marked off its dimensions? Surely you know!
  Who stretched a measuring line across it?
6On what were its footings set,
  or who laid its cornerstone—
7while the morning stars sang together
  and all the angelsb shouted for joy?

8"Who shut up the sea behind doors
  when it burst forth from the womb,
9when I made the clouds its garment
  and wrapped it in thick darkness,
10when I fixed limits for it
  and set its doors and bars in place,
11when I said, 'This far you may come and no farther;
  here is where your proud waves halt'?

12"Have you ever given orders to the morning,
  or shown the dawn its place,
13that it might take the earth by the edges
  and shake the wicked out of it?
14The earth takes shape like clay under a seal;
  its features stand out like those of a garment.
15The wicked are denied their light,
  and their upraised arm is broken.

16"Have you journeyed to the springs of the sea
  or walked in the recesses of the deep?
17Have the gates of death been shown to you?
  Have you seen the gates of the shadow of deathc?
18Have you comprehended the vast expanses of the earth?
  Tell me, if you know all this.

19"What is the way to the abode of light?
  And where does darkness reside?
20Can you take them to their places?
  Do you know the paths to their dwellings?
21Surely you know, for you were already born!
  You have lived so many years!

---

a 24 Or *for he does not have regard for any who think they are wise.*
b 7 Hebrew *the sons of God*   c 17 Or *gates of deep shadows*

Living Bible

dazzling splendor. 23We cannot imagine the power of the Almighty, and yet he is so just and merciful that he does not destroy us. 24No wonder men everywhere fear him! For he is not impressed by the world's wisest men!"

38 THEN THE Lord answered Job from the whirlwind:

2"Why are you using your ignorance to deny my providence? 3Now get ready to fight, for I am going to demand some answers from you, and you must reply.

4"Where were you when I laid the foundations of the earth? Tell me, if you know so much. 5Do you know how its dimensions were determined, and who did the surveying? 6, 7What supports its foundations, and who laid its cornerstone, as the morning stars sang together and all the angels shouted for joy?

8, 9"Who decreed the boundaries of the seas when they gushed from the depths? Who clothed them with clouds and thick darkness, 10and barred them by limiting their shores, 11and said, 'Thus far and no farther shall you come, and here shall your proud waves stop!'?

12"Have you ever once commanded the morning to appear, and caused the dawn to rise in the east? 13Have you ever told the daylight to spread to the ends of the earth, to end the night's wickedness? 14Have you ever robed the dawn in red, 15and disturbed the haunts of wicked men and stopped the arm raised to strike?

16"Have you explored the springs from which the seas come, or walked in the sources of their depths? 17, 18Has the location of the gates of Death been revealed to you? Do you realize the extent of the earth? Tell me about it if you know! 19Where does the light come from, and how do you get there? Or tell me about the darkness. Where does it come from? 20Can you find its boundaries, or go to its source? 21But of course you know all this! For you were born before it was all created, and you are so very experienced!

New Revised Standard

23 The Almighty[d]—we cannot find him;
    he is great in power and justice,
    and abundant righteousness he will not
        violate.
24 Therefore mortals fear him;
    he does not regard any who are wise in
        their own conceit."

The LORD Answers Job

38 THEN THE LORD answered Job out of the whirlwind:

2 "Who is this that darkens counsel by words
    without knowledge?
3 Gird up your loins like a man,
    I will question you, and you shall declare to
        me.

4 "Where were you when I laid the foundation
        of the earth?
    Tell me, if you have understanding.
5 Who determined its measurements—surely
        you know!
    Or who stretched the line upon it?
6 On what were its bases sunk,
    or who laid its cornerstone
7 when the morning stars sang together
    and all the heavenly beings[e] shouted for
        joy?

8 "Or who shut in the sea with doors
    when it burst out from the womb?—
9 when I made the clouds its garment,
    and thick darkness its swaddling band,
10 and prescribed bounds for it,
    and set bars and doors,
11 and said, 'Thus far shall you come, and no
        farther,
    and here shall your proud waves be
        stopped'?

12 "Have you commanded the morning since
        your days began,
    and caused the dawn to know its place,
13 so that it might take hold of the skirts of the
        earth,
    and the wicked be shaken out of it?
14 It is changed like clay under the seal,
    and it is dyed[f] like a garment.
15 Light is withheld from the wicked,
    and their uplifted arm is broken.

16 "Have you entered into the springs of the sea,
    or walked in the recesses of the deep?
17 Have the gates of death been revealed to you,
    or have you seen the gates of deep
        darkness?
18 Have you comprehended the expanse of the
        earth?
    Declare, if you know all this.

19 "Where is the way to the dwelling of light,
    and where is the place of darkness,
20 that you may take it to its territory
    and that you may discern the paths to its
        home?
21 Surely you know, for you were born then,
    and the number of your days is great!

d Traditional rendering of Heb Shaddai   e Heb sons of God   f Cn: Heb and they stand forth

King James

22Hast thou entered into the treasures of the snow? or hast thou seen the treasures of the hail,

23Which I have reserved against the time of trouble, against the day of battle and war?

24By what way is the light parted, *which* scattereth the east wind upon the earth?

25Who hath divided a watercourse for the overflowing of waters, or a way for the lightning of thunder;

26To cause it to rain on the earth, *where* no man *is; on* the wilderness, wherein *there is* no man;

27To satisfy the desolate and waste *ground;* and to cause the bud of the tender herb to spring forth?

28Hath the rain a father? or who hath begotten the drops of dew?

29Out of whose womb came the ice? and the hoary frost of heaven, who hath gendered it?

30The waters are hid as *with* a stone, and the face of the deep is frozen.

31Canst thou bind the sweet influences of Pleiades, or loose the bands of Orion?

32Canst thou bring forth Mazzaroth in his season? or canst thou guide Arcturus with his sons?

33Knowest thou the ordinances of heaven? canst thou set the dominion thereof in the earth?

34Canst thou lift up thy voice to the clouds, that abundance of waters may cover thee?

35Canst thou send lightnings, that they may go, and say unto thee, Here we *are?*

36Who hath put wisdom in the inward parts? or who hath given understanding to the heart?

37Who can number the clouds in wisdom? or who can stay the bottles of heaven,

38When the dust groweth into hardness, and the clods cleave fast together?

39Wilt thou hunt the prey for the lion? or fill the appetite of the young lions,

40When they couch in *their* dens, *and* abide in the covert to lie in wait?

41Who provideth for the raven his food? when his young ones cry unto God, they wander for lack of meat.

New International

22"Have you entered the storehouses of the snow
    or seen the storehouses of the hail,
23which I reserve for times of trouble,
    for days of war and battle?
24What is the way to the place where the
        lightning is dispersed,
    or the place where the east winds are
        scattered over the earth?
25Who cuts a channel for the torrents of rain,
    and a path for the thunderstorm,
26to water a land where no man lives,
    a desert with no one in it,
27to satisfy a desolate wasteland
    and make it sprout with grass?
28Does the rain have a father?
    Who fathers the drops of dew?
29From whose womb comes the ice?
    Who gives birth to the frost from the heavens
30when the waters become hard as stone,
    when the surface of the deep is frozen?
31"Can you bind the beautiful[a] Pleiades?
    Can you loose the cords of Orion?
32Can you bring forth the constellations in their
        seasons[b]
    or lead out the Bear[c] with its cubs?
33Do you know the laws of the heavens?
    Can you set up [God's][d] dominion over the
        earth?
34"Can you raise your voice to the clouds
    and cover yourself with a flood of water?
35Do you send the lightning bolts on their way?
    Do they report to you, 'Here we are'?
36Who endowed the heart[e] with wisdom
    or gave understanding to the mind[e]?
37Who has the wisdom to count the clouds?
    Who can tip over the water jars of the
        heavens
38when the dust becomes hard
    and the clods of earth stick together?
39"Do you hunt the prey for the lioness
    and satisfy the hunger of the lions
40when they crouch in their dens
    or lie in wait in a thicket?
41Who provides food for the raven
    when its young cry out to God
    and wander about for lack of food?

39 KNOWEST THOU the time when the wild goats of the rock bring forth? *or* canst thou mark when the hinds do calve?

2Canst thou number the months *that* they fulfil? or knowest thou the time when they bring forth?

3They bow themselves, they bring forth their young ones, they cast out their sorrows.

4Their young ones are in good liking, they grow up with corn; they go forth, and return not unto them.

39 "DO YOU know when the mountain goats
        give birth?
    Do you watch when the doe bears her fawn?
2Do you count the months till they bear?
    Do you know the time they give birth?
3They crouch down and bring forth their young;
    their labor pains are ended.
4Their young thrive and grow strong in the
        wilds;
    they leave and do not return.

---

a 31 Or *the twinkling;* or *the chains of the*   b 32 Or *the morning star in its season*   c 32 Or *out Leo*   d 33 Or *his;* or *their*   e 36 The meaning of the Hebrew for this word is uncertain.

Living Bible

22, 23"Have you visited the treasuries of the snow, or seen where hail is made and stored? For I have reserved it for the time when I will need it in war. 24Where is the path to the distribution point of light? Where is the home of the east wind? 25, 26, 27Who dug the valleys for the torrents of rain? Who laid out the path for the lightning, causing the rain to fall upon the barren deserts, so that the parched and barren ground is satisfied with water, and tender grass springs up?

28"Has the rain a father? Where does dew come from? 29Who is the mother of the ice and frost? 30For the water changes and turns to ice, as hard as rock.

31"Can you hold back the stars? Can you restrain Orion or Pleiades? 32Can you ensure the proper sequence of the seasons, or guide the constellation of the Bear with her satellites across the heavens? 33Do you know the laws of the universe and how the heavens influence the earth? 34Can you shout to the clouds and make it rain? 35Can you make lightning appear and cause it to strike as you direct it?

36"Who gives intuition and instinct?f 37, 38Who is wise enough to number all the clouds? Who can tilt the water jars of heaven, when everything is dust and clods? 39, 40Can you stalk prey like a lioness, to satisfy the young lions' appetites as they lie in their dens, or lie in wait in the jungle? 41Who provides for the ravens when their young cry out to God as they try to struggle up from their nest in hunger?

39 "DO YOU know how mountain goats give birth? Have you ever seen them giving birth to their young? 2, 3Do you know how many months of pregnancy they have before they bow themselves to give birth to their young, and carry their burden no longer? 4Their young grow up in the open field, then leave their parents and return to them no more.

New Revised Standard

22 "Have you entered the storehouses of the
    snow,
    or have you seen the storehouses of the
    hail,
23 which I have reserved for the time of trouble,
    for the day of battle and war?
24 What is the way to the place where the light is
    distributed,
    or where the east wind is scattered upon the
    earth?

25 "Who has cut a channel for the torrents of
    rain,
    and a way for the thunderbolt,
26 to bring rain on a land where no one lives,
    on the desert, which is empty of human
    life,
27 to satisfy the waste and desolate land,
    and to make the ground put forth grass?

28 "Has the rain a father,
    or who has begotten the drops of dew?
29 From whose womb did the ice come forth,
    and who has given birth to the hoarfrost of
    heaven?
30 The waters become hard like stone,
    and the face of the deep is frozen.

31 "Can you bind the chains of the Pleiades,
    or loose the cords of Orion?
32 Can you lead forth the Mazzaroth in their
    season,
    or can you guide the Bear with its children?
33 Do you know the ordinances of the heavens?
    Can you establish their rule on the earth?

34 "Can you lift up your voice to the clouds,
    so that a flood of waters may cover you?
35 Can you send forth lightnings, so that they
    may go
    and say to you, 'Here we are'?
36 Who has put wisdom in the inward parts,g
    or given understanding to the mind?g
37 Who has the wisdom to number the clouds?
    Or who can tilt the waterskins of the
    heavens,
38 when the dust runs into a mass
    and the clods cling together?

39 "Can you hunt the prey for the lion,
    or satisfy the appetite of the young lions,
40 when they crouch in their dens,
    or lie in wait in their covert?
41 Who provides for the raven its prey,
    when its young ones cry to God,
    and wander about for lack of food?

39 "DO YOU know when the mountain goats
    give birth?
    Do you observe the calving of the deer?
2 Can you number the months that they fulfill,
    and do you know the time when they give
    birth,
3 when they crouch to give birth to their
    offspring,
    and are delivered of their young?
4 Their young ones become strong, they grow
    up in the open;
    they go forth, and do not return to them.

f 38:36 *Who gives intuition and instinct?* Or, "Who has put wisdom in the inward parts, and given understanding to the mind?"

g Meaning of Heb uncertain

King James

5Who hath sent out the wild ass free? or who hath loosed the bands of the wild ass?

6Whose house I have made the wilderness, and the barren land his dwellings.

7He scorneth the multitude of the city, neither regardeth he the crying of the driver.

8The range of the mountains *is* his pasture, and he searcheth after every green thing.

9Will the unicorn be willing to serve thee, or abide by thy crib?

10Canst thou bind the unicorn with his band in the furrow? or will he harrow the valleys after thee?

11Wilt thou trust him, because his strength *is* great? or wilt thou leave thy labour to him?

12Wilt thou believe him, that he will bring home thy seed, and gather *it into* thy barn?

13*Gavest thou* the goodly wings unto the peacocks? or wings and feathers unto the ostrich?

14Which leaveth her eggs in the earth, and warmeth them in dust,

15And forgetteth that the foot may crush them, or that the wild beast may break them.

16She is hardened against her young ones, as though *they were* not hers: her labour is in vain without fear;

17Because God hath deprived her of wisdom, neither hath he imparted to her understanding.

18What time she lifteth up herself on high, she scorneth the horse and his rider.

19Hast thou given the horse strength? hast thou clothed his neck with thunder?

20Canst thou make him afraid as a grasshopper? the glory of his nostrils *is* terrible.

21He paweth in the valley, and rejoiceth in *his* strength: he goeth on to meet the armed men.

22He mocketh at fear, and is not affrighted; neither turneth he back from the sword.

23The quiver rattleth against him, the glittering spear and the shield.

24He swalloweth the ground with fierceness and rage: neither believeth he that *it is* the sound of the trumpet.

25He saith among the trumpets, Ha, ha; and he smelleth the battle afar off, the thunder of the captains, and the shouting.

26Doth the hawk fly by thy wisdom, *and* stretch her wings toward the south?

27Doth the eagle mount up at thy command, and make her nest on high?

28She dwelleth and abideth on the rock, upon the crag of the rock, and the strong place.

29From thence she seeketh the prey, *and* her eyes behold afar off.

30Her young ones also suck up blood: and where the slain *are*, there *is* she.

New International

5"Who let the wild donkey go free?
  Who untied his ropes?
6I gave him the wasteland as his home,
  the salt flats as his habitat.
7He laughs at the commotion in the town;
  he does not hear a driver's shout.
8He ranges the hills for his pasture
  and searches for any green thing.

9"Will the wild ox consent to serve you?
  Will he stay by your manger at night?
10Can you hold him to the furrow with a harness?
  Will he till the valleys behind you?
11Will you rely on him for his great strength?
  Will you leave your heavy work to him?
12Can you trust him to bring in your grain
  and gather it to your threshing floor?

13"The wings of the ostrich flap joyfully,
  but they cannot compare with the pinions and
  feathers of the stork.
14She lays her eggs on the ground
  and lets them warm in the sand,
15unmindful that a foot may crush them,
  that some wild animal may trample them.
16She treats her young harshly, as if they were
  not hers;
  she cares not that her labor was in vain,
17for God did not endow her with wisdom
  or give her a share of good sense.
18Yet when she spreads her feathers to run,
  she laughs at horse and rider.

19"Do you give the horse his strength
  or clothe his neck with a flowing mane?
20Do you make him leap like a locust,
  striking terror with his proud snorting?
21He paws fiercely, rejoicing in his strength,
  and charges into the fray.
22He laughs at fear, afraid of nothing;
  he does not shy away from the sword.
23The quiver rattles against his side,
  along with the flashing spear and lance.
24In frenzied excitement he eats up the ground;
  he cannot stand still when the trumpet
  sounds.
25At the blast of the trumpet he snorts, 'Aha!'
  He catches the scent of battle from afar,
  the shout of commanders and the battle cry.

26"Does the hawk take flight by your wisdom
  and spread his wings toward the south?
27Does the eagle soar at your command
  and build his nest on high?
28He dwells on a cliff and stays there at night;
  a rocky crag is his stronghold.
29From there he seeks out his food;
  his eyes detect it from afar.
30His young ones feast on blood,
  and where the slain are, there is he."

Living Bible

5"Who makes the wild donkeys wild? 6I have placed them in the wilderness and given them salt plains to live in. 7For they hate the noise of the city and want no drivers shouting at them! 8The mountain ranges are their pastureland; there they search for every blade of grass.

9"Will the wild ox be your happy servant? Will he stay beside your feeding crib? 10Can you use a wild ox to plow with? Will he pull the harrow for you? 11Because he is so strong, will you trust him? Will you let him decide where to work? 12Can you send him out to bring in the grain from the threshing-floor?

13"The ostrich flaps her wings grandly, but has no true motherly love. 14She lays her eggs on top of the earth, to warm them in the dust. 15She forgets that someone may step on them and crush them, or the wild animals destroy them. 16She ignores her young as though they weren't her own, and is unconcerned though they die, 17for God has deprived her of wisdom. 18But whenever she jumps up to run, she passes the swiftest horse with its rider.

19"Have you given the horse strength, or clothed his neck with a quivering mane? 20Have you made him able to leap forward like a locust? His majestic snorting is something to hear! 21, 22, 23He paws the earth and rejoices in his strength, and when he goes to war, he is unafraid and does not run away though the arrows rattle against him, or the flashing spear and javelin. 24Fiercely he paws the ground and rushes forward into battle when the trumpet blows. 25At the sound of the bugle he shouts, 'Aha!' He smells the battle when far away. He rejoices at the shouts of battle and the roar of the captain's commands.

26"Do you know how a hawk soars and spreads her wings to the south? 27Is it at your command that the eagle rises high upon the cliffs to make her nest? 28She lives upon the cliffs, making her home in her mountain fortress. 29From there she spies her prey, from a very great distance. 30Her nestlings gulp down blood, for she goes wherever the slain are."

New Revised Standard

5 "Who has let the wild ass go free?
Who has loosed the bonds of the swift ass,
6 to which I have given the steppe for its home,
the salt land for its dwelling place?
7 It scorns the tumult of the city;
it does not hear the shouts of the driver.
8 It ranges the mountains as its pasture,
and it searches after every green thing.

9 "Is the wild ox willing to serve you?
Will it spend the night at your crib?
10 Can you tie it in the furrow with ropes,
or will it harrow the valleys after you?
11 Will you depend on it because its strength is
great,
and will you hand over your labor to it?
12 Do you have faith in it that it will return,
and bring your grain to your threshing
floor?a

13 "The ostrich's wings flap wildly,
though its pinions lack plumage.b
14 For it leaves its eggs to the earth,
and lets them be warmed on the ground,
15 forgetting that a foot may crush them,
and that a wild animal may trample them.
16 It deals cruelly with its young, as if they were
not its own;
though its labor should be in vain, yet it has
no fear;
17 because God has made it forget wisdom,
and given it no share in understanding.
18 When it spreads its plumes aloft,b
it laughs at the horse and its rider.

19 "Do you give the horse its might?
Do you clothe its neck with mane?
20 Do you make it leap like the locust?
Its majestic snorting is terrible.
21 It pawsc violently, exults mightily;
it goes out to meet the weapons.
22 It laughs at fear, and is not dismayed;
it does not turn back from the sword.
23 Upon it rattle the quiver,
the flashing spear, and the javelin.
24 With fierceness and rage it swallows the
ground;
it cannot stand still at the sound of the
trumpet.
25 When the trumpet sounds, it says 'Aha!'
From a distance it smells the battle,
the thunder of the captains, and the
shouting.

26 "Is it by your wisdom that the hawk soars,
and spreads its wings toward the south?
27 Is it at your command that the eagle mounts
up
and makes its nest on high?
28 It lives on the rock and makes its home
in the fastness of the rocky crag.
29 From there it spies the prey;
its eyes see it from far away.
30 Its young ones suck up blood;
and where the slain are, there it is."

---

a Heb *your grain and your threshing floor*   b Meaning of Heb uncertain
c Gk Syr Vg: Heb *they dig*

King James

40 MOREOVER THE Lord answered Job, and said,

2Shall he that contendeth with the Almighty instruct *him?* he that reproveth God, let him answer it.

3¶ Then Job answered the Lord, and said,

4Behold, I am vile; what shall I answer thee? I will lay mine hand upon my mouth.

5Once have I spoken; but I will not answer: yea, twice; but I will proceed no further.

6¶ Then answered the Lord unto Job out of the whirlwind, and said,

7Gird up thy loins now like a man: I will demand of thee, and declare thou unto me.

8Wilt thou also disannul my judgment? wilt thou condemn me, that thou mayest be righteous?

9Hast thou an arm like God? or canst thou thunder with a voice like him?

10Deck thyself now *with* majesty and excellency; and array thyself with glory and beauty.

11Cast abroad the rage of thy wrath: and behold every one *that is* proud, and abase him.

12Look on every one *that is* proud, *and* bring him low; and tread down the wicked in their place.

13Hide them in the dust together; *and* bind their faces in secret.

14Then will I also confess unto thee that thine own right hand can save thee.

15¶ Behold now behemoth, which I made with thee; he eateth grass as an ox.

16Lo now, his strength *is* in his loins, and his force *is* in the navel of his belly.

17He moveth his tail like a cedar: the sinews of his stones are wrapped together.

18His bones *are as* strong pieces of brass; his bones *are* like bars of iron.

19He *is* the chief of the ways of God: he that made him can make his sword to approach *unto him.*

20Surely the mountains bring him forth food, where all the beasts of the field play.

21He lieth under the shady trees, in the covert of the reed, and fens.

22The shady trees cover him *with* their shadow; the willows of the brook compass him about.

23Behold, he drinketh up a river, *and* hasteth not: he trusteth that he can draw up Jordan into his mouth.

24He taketh it with his eyes: *his* nose pierceth through snares.

New International

40 THE LORD said to Job:

2"Will the one who contends with the
    Almighty correct him?
Let him who accuses God answer him!"

3Then Job answered the Lord:

4"I am unworthy—how can I reply to you?
    I put my hand over my mouth.
5I spoke once, but I have no answer—
    twice, but I will say no more."

6Then the Lord spoke to Job out of the storm:

7"Brace yourself like a man;
    I will question you,
    and you shall answer me.

8"Would you discredit my justice?
    Would you condemn me to justify yourself?
9Do you have an arm like God's,
    and can your voice thunder like his?
10Then adorn yourself with glory and splendor,
    and clothe yourself in honor and majesty.
11Unleash the fury of your wrath,
    look at every proud man and bring him low,
12look at every proud man and humble him,
    crush the wicked where they stand.
13Bury them all in the dust together;
    shroud their faces in the grave.
14Then I myself will admit to you
    that your own right hand can save you.

15"Look at the behemoth,[a]
    which I made along with you
    and which feeds on grass like an ox.
16What strength he has in his loins,
    what power in the muscles of his belly!
17His tail[b] sways like a cedar;
    the sinews of his thighs are close-knit.
18His bones are tubes of bronze,
    his limbs like rods of iron.
19He ranks first among the works of God,
    yet his Maker can approach him with his
        sword.
20The hills bring him their produce,
    and all the wild animals play nearby.
21Under the lotus plants he lies,
    hidden among the reeds in the marsh.
22The lotuses conceal him in their shadow;
    the poplars by the stream surround him.
23When the river rages, he is not alarmed;
    he is secure, though the Jordan should surge
        against his mouth.
24Can anyone capture him by the eyes,[c]
    or trap him and pierce his nose?

41 CANST THOU draw out leviathan with an hook? or his tongue with a cord *which* thou lettest down?

41 "CAN YOU pull in the leviathan[d] with a
    fishhook
    or tie down his tongue with a rope?

---

a 15 Possibly the hippopotamus or the elephant   b 17 Possibly trunk
c 24 Or *by a water hole*   d 1 Possibly the crocodile

Living Bible

40 *THE LORD went on:*
2"Do you still want to argue with the Almighty? Or will you yield? Do you—God's critic—have the answers?"

3*Then Job replied to God:*

4"I am nothing—how could I ever find the answers? I lay my hand upon my mouth in silence. 5I have said too much already."

6*Then the Lord spoke to Job again from the whirlwind:*

7"Stand up like a man and brace yourself for battle. Let me ask you a question, and give me the answer. 8Are you going to discredit my justice and condemn me, so that you can say you are right? 9Are you as strong as God, and can you shout as loudly as he? 10All right then, put on your robes of state, your majesty and splendor. 11Give vent to your anger. Let it overflow against the proud. 12Humiliate the haughty with a glance; tread down the wicked where they stand. 13Knock them into the dust, stone-faced in death. 14If you can do that, then I'll agree with you that your own strength can save you.

15"Take a look at the hippopotamus!e I made him, too, just as I made you! He eats grass like an ox. 16See his powerful loins and the muscles of his belly. 17His tail is as straight as a cedar. The sinews of his thighs are tightly knit together. 18His vertebrae lie straight as a tube of brass. His ribs are like iron bars. 19How ferocious he is among all of God's creation, so let whoever hopes to master him bring a sharp sword! 20The mountains offer their best food to him—the other wild animals on which he preys. 21He lies down under the lotus plants, hidden by the reeds, 22covered by their shade among the willows there beside the stream. 23He is not disturbed by raging rivers, not even when the swelling Jordan rushes down upon him. 24No one can catch him off guard or put a ring in his nose and lead him away.

41 "CAN YOU catch a crocodilef with a hook and line? Or put a noose around his tongue? 2Can

New Revised Standard

40 AND THE LORD said to Job:
2 "Shall a faultfinder contend with the Almighty?g
Anyone who argues with God must respond."

Job's Response to God

3 Then Job answered the LORD:
4 "See, I am of small account; what shall I answer you?
I lay my hand on my mouth.
5 I have spoken once, and I will not answer;
twice, but will proceed no further."

God's Challenge to Job

6 Then the LORD answered Job out of the whirlwind:
7 "Gird up your loins like a man;
I will question you, and you declare to me.
8 Will you even put me in the wrong?
Will you condemn me that you may be justified?
9 Have you an arm like God,
and can you thunder with a voice like his?

10 "Deck yourself with majesty and dignity;
clothe yourself with glory and splendor.
11 Pour out the overflowings of your anger,
and look on all who are proud, and abase them.
12 Look on all who are proud, and bring them low;
tread down the wicked where they stand.
13 Hide them all in the dust together;
bind their faces in the world below.h
14 Then I will also acknowledge to you
that your own right hand can give you victory.

15 "Look at Behemoth,
which I made just as I made you;
it eats grass like an ox.
16 Its strength is in its loins,
and its power in the muscles of its belly.
17 It makes its tail stiff like a cedar;
the sinews of its thighs are knit together.
18 Its bones are tubes of bronze,
its limbs like bars of iron.

19 "It is the first of the great acts of God—
only its Maker can approach it with the sword.
20 For the mountains yield food for it
where all the wild animals play.
21 Under the lotus plants it lies,
in the covert of the reeds and in the marsh.
22 The lotus trees cover it for shade;
the willows of the wadi surround it.
23 Even if the river is turbulent, it is not frightened;
it is confident though Jordan rushes against its mouth.
24 Can one take it with hooksi
or pierce its nose with a snare?

41 j "CAN YOU draw out Leviathank with a fishhook,
or press down its tongue with a cord?

---

e 40:15 *the hippopotamus,* literally, "behemoth." f 41:1 *a crocodile,* literally, "leviathan."

g Traditional rendering of Heb *Shaddai* h Heb *the hidden place* i Cn: Heb *in his eyes* j Ch 40.25 in Heb k Or *the crocodile*

King James

2Canst thou put an hook into his nose? or bore his jaw through with a thorn?

3Will he make many supplications unto thee? will he speak soft *words* unto thee?

4Will he make a covenant with thee? wilt thou take him for a servant for ever?

5Wilt thou play with him as *with* a bird? or wilt thou bind him for thy maidens?

6Shall the companions make a banquet of him? shall they part him among the merchants?

7Canst thou fill his skin with barbed irons? or his head with fish spears?

8Lay thine hand upon him, remember the battle, do no more.

9Behold, the hope of him is in vain: shall not *one* be cast down even at the sight of him?

10None *is so* fierce that dare stir him up: who then is able to stand before me?

11Who hath prevented me, that I should repay *him?* *whatsoever is* under the whole heaven is mine.

12I will not conceal his parts, nor his power, nor his comely proportion.

13Who can discover the face of his garment? *or* who can come *to him* with his double bridle?

14Who can open the doors of his face? his teeth *are* terrible round about.

15*His* scales *are his* pride, shut up together *as with* a close seal.

16One is so near to another, that no air can come between them.

17They are joined one to another, they stick together, that they cannot be sundered.

18By his sneezings a light doth shine, and his eyes *are* like the eyelids of the morning.

19Out of his mouth go burning lamps, *and* sparks of fire leap out.

20Out of his nostrils goeth smoke, as *out* of a seething pot or caldron.

21His breath kindleth coals, and a flame goeth out of his mouth.

22In his neck remaineth strength, and sorrow is turned into joy before him.

23The flakes of his flesh are joined together: they are firm in themselves; they cannot be moved.

24His heart is as firm as a stone; yea, as hard as a piece of the nether *millstone.*

25When he raiseth up himself, the mighty are afraid: by reason of breakings they purify themselves.

26The sword of him that layeth at him cannot hold: the spear, the dart, nor the habergeon.

27He esteemeth iron as straw, *and* brass as rotten wood.

28The arrow cannot make him flee: slingstones are turned with him into stubble.

29Darts are counted as stubble: he laugheth at the shaking of a spear.

30Sharp stones *are* under him: he spreadeth sharp pointed things upon the mire.

31He maketh the deep to boil like a pot: he maketh the sea like a pot of ointment.

32He maketh a path to shine after him; *one* would think the deep *to be* hoary.

33Upon earth there is not his like, who is made without fear.

New International

2Can you put a cord through his nose
    or pierce his jaw with a hook?
3Will he keep begging you for mercy?
    Will he speak to you with gentle words?
4Will he make an agreement with you
    for you to take him as your slave for life?
5Can you make a pet of him like a bird
    or put him on a leash for your girls?
6Will traders barter for him?
    Will they divide him up among the
      merchants?
7Can you fill his hide with harpoons
    or his head with fishing spears?
8If you lay a hand on him,
    you will remember the struggle and never do
      it again!
9Any hope of subduing him is false;
    the mere sight of him is overpowering.
10No one is fierce enough to rouse him.
    Who then is able to stand against me?
11Who has a claim against me that I must pay?
    Everything under heaven belongs to me.

12"I will not fail to speak of his limbs,
    his strength and his graceful form.
13Who can strip off his outer coat?
    Who would approach him with a bridle?
14Who dares open the doors of his mouth,
    ringed about with his fearsome teeth?
15His back hasa rows of shields
    tightly sealed together;
16each is so close to the next
    that no air can pass between.
17They are joined fast to one another;
    they cling together and cannot be parted.
18His snorting throws out flashes of light;
    his eyes are like the rays of dawn.
19Firebrands stream from his mouth;
    sparks of fire shoot out.
20Smoke pours from his nostrils
    as from a boiling pot over a fire of reeds.
21His breath sets coals ablaze,
    and flames dart from his mouth.
22Strength resides in his neck;
    dismay goes before him.
23The folds of his flesh are tightly joined;
    they are firm and immovable.
24His chest is hard as rock,
    hard as a lower millstone.
25When he rises up, the mighty are terrified;
    they retreat before his thrashing.
26The sword that reaches him has no effect,
    nor does the spear or the dart or the javelin.
27Iron he treats like straw
    and bronze like rotten wood.
28Arrows do not make him flee;
    slingstones are like chaff to him.
29A club seems to him but a piece of straw;
    he laughs at the rattling of the lance.
30His undersides are jagged potsherds,
    leaving a trail in the mud like a threshing
      sledge.
31He makes the depths churn like a boiling
      caldron
    and stirs up the sea like a pot of ointment.
32Behind him he leaves a glistening wake;
    one would think the deep had white hair.
33Nothing on earth is his equal—
    a creature without fear.

a 15 Or *His pride is his*

Living Bible

you tie him with a rope through the nose, or pierce his jaw with a spike? 3Will he beg you to desist or try to flatter you from your intentions? 4Will he agree to let you make him your slave for life? 5Can you make a pet of him like a bird, or give him to your little girls to play with? 6Do fishing partners sell him to the fishmongers? 7Will his hide be hurt by darts, or his head with a harpoon?

8"If you lay your hands upon him, you will long remember the battle that ensues, and you will never try it again! 9No, it's useless to try to capture him. It is frightening even to think about it! 10No one dares to stir *him* up, let alone try to conquer him. And if no one can stand before *him,* who can stand before *me?* 11I owe no one anything. Everything under the heaven is mine.

12"I should mention, too, the tremendous strength in his limbs, and throughout his enormous frame. 13Who can penetrate his hide, or who dares come within reach of his jaws? 14For his teeth are terrible. 15, 16, 17His overlapping scales are his pride, making a tight seal, so no air can get between them, and nothing can penetrate.

18"When he sneezes, the sunlight sparkles like lightning across the vapor droplets. His eyes glow like sparks. 19Fire leaps from his mouth. 20Smoke flows from his nostrils, like steam from a boiling pot that is fired by dry rushes. 21Yes, his breath would kindle coals—flames leap from his mouth.

22"The tremendous strength in his neck strikes terror wherever he goes. 23His flesh is hard and firm, not soft and fat. 24His heart is hard as rock, just like a millstone. 25When he stands up, the strongest are afraid. Terror grips them. 26No sword can stop him, nor spear nor dart nor pointed shaft. 27, 28Iron is nothing but straw to him, and brass is rotten wood. Arrows cannot make him flee. Slingstones are as ineffective as straw. 29Clubs do no good, and he laughs at the javelins hurled at him. 30His belly is covered with scales as sharp as shards; they tear up the ground as he drags through the mud.

31, 32"He makes the water boil with his commotion. He churns the depths. He leaves a shining wake of froth behind him. One would think the sea was made of frost! 33There is nothing else so fearless anywhere on earth.

New Revised Standard

2 Can you put a rope in its nose,
    or pierce its jaw with a hook?
3 Will it make many supplications to you?
    Will it speak soft words to you?
4 Will it make a covenant with you
    to be taken as your servant forever?
5 Will you play with it as with a bird,
    or will you put it on leash for your girls?
6 Will traders bargain over it?
    Will they divide it up among the merchants?
7 Can you fill its skin with harpoons,
    or its head with fishing spears?
8 Lay hands on it;
    think of the battle; you will not do it again!
9b Any hope of capturing itc will be
      disappointed;
    were not even the godsd overwhelmed at
      the sight of it?
10 No one is so fierce as to dare to stir it up.
    Who can stand before it?
11 Who can confront ite and be safe?f
    —under the whole heaven, who?g
12 "I will not keep silence concerning its limbs,
    or its mighty strength, or its splendid frame.
13 Who can strip off its outer garment?
    Who can penetrate its double coat of mail?h
14 Who can open the doors of its face?
    There is terror all around its teeth.
15 Its backi is made of shields in rows,
    shut up closely as with a seal.
16 One is so near to another
    that no air can come between them.
17 They are joined one to another;
    they clasp each other and cannot be
      separated.
18 Its sneezes flash forth light,
    and its eyes are like the eyelids of the
      dawn.
19 From its mouth go flaming torches;
    sparks of fire leap out.
20 Out of its nostrils comes smoke,
    as from a boiling pot and burning rushes.
21 Its breath kindles coals,
    and a flame comes out of its mouth.
22 In its neck abides strength,
    and terror dances before it.
23 The folds of its flesh cling together;
    it is firmly cast and immovable.
24 Its heart is as hard as stone,
    as hard as the lower millstone.
25 When it raises itself up the gods are afraid;
    at the crashing they are beside themselves.
26 Though the sword reaches it, it does not avail,
    nor does the spear, the dart, or the javelin.
27 It counts iron as straw,
    and bronze as rotten wood.
28 The arrow cannot make it flee;
    slingstones, for it, are turned to chaff.
29 Clubs are counted as chaff;
    it laughs at the rattle of javelins.
30 Its underparts are like sharp potsherds;
    it spreads itself like a threshing sledge on
      the mire.
31 It makes the deep boil like a pot;
    it makes the sea like a pot of ointment.
32 It leaves a shining wake behind it;
    one would think the deep to be
      white-haired.
33 On earth it has no equal,
    a creature without fear.

b Ch 41.1 in Heb   c Heb *of it*   d Cn Compare Symmachus Syr: Heb *one is*   e Heb *me*   f Gk: Heb *that I shall repay*   g Heb *to me*   h Gk: Heb *bridle*   i Cn Compare Gk Vg: Heb *pride*

King James

34He beholdeth all high *things:* he *is* a king over all the children of pride.

42 THEN JOB answered the Lord, and said,
2I know that thou canst do every *thing,* and *that* no thought can be withholden from thee.

3Who *is* he that hideth counsel without knowledge? therefore have I uttered that I understood not; things too wonderful for me, which I knew not.

4Hear, I beseech thee, and I will speak: I will demand of thee, and declare thou unto me.

5I have heard of thee by the hearing of the ear: but now mine eye seeth thee.

6Wherefore I abhor *myself,* and repent in dust and ashes.

7¶ And it was *so,* that after the Lord had spoken these words unto Job, the Lord said to Eliphaz the Temanite, My wrath is kindled against thee, and against thy two friends: for ye have not spoken of me *the thing that is* right, as my servant Job *hath.*

8Therefore take unto you now seven bullocks and seven rams, and go to my servant Job, and offer up for yourselves a burnt offering; and my servant Job shall pray for you: for him will I accept: lest I deal with you *after your* folly, in that ye have not spoken of me *the thing which is* right, like my servant Job.

9So Eliphaz the Temanite and Bildad the Shuhite *and* Zophar the Naamathite went, and did according as the Lord commanded them: the Lord also accepted Job.

10And the Lord turned the captivity of Job, when he prayed for his friends: also the Lord gave Job twice as much as he had before.

11Then came there unto him all his brethren, and all his sisters, and all they that had been of his acquaintance before, and did eat bread with him in his house: and they bemoaned him, and comforted him over all the evil that the Lord had brought upon him: every man also gave him a piece of money, and every one an earring of gold.

12So the Lord blessed the latter end of Job more than his beginning: for he had fourteen thousand sheep, and six thousand camels, and a thousand yoke of oxen, and a thousand she asses.

13He had also seven sons and three daughters.

14And he called the name of the first, Jemima; and the name of the second, Kezia; and the name of the third, Keren-happuch.

15And in all the land were no women found *so* fair as the daughters of Job: and their father gave them inheritance among their brethren.

16After this lived Job an hundred and forty years, and saw his sons, and his sons' sons, *even* four generations.

17So Job died, *being* old and full of days.

New International

34He looks down on all that are haughty;
    he is king over all that are proud."

Job

42 THEN JOB replied to the Lord:

2"I know that you can do all things;
    no plan of yours can be thwarted.
3You asked, 'Who is this that obscures my
        counsel without knowledge?'
    Surely I spoke of things I did not understand,
    things too wonderful for me to know.

4"You said, 'Listen now, and I will speak;
    I will question you,
    and you shall answer me.'
5My ears had heard of you
    but now my eyes have seen you.
6Therefore I despise myself
    and repent in dust and ashes."

Epilogue

7After the Lord had said these things to Job, he said to Eliphaz the Temanite, "I am angry with you and your two friends, because you have not spoken of me what is right, as my servant Job has. 8So now take seven bulls and seven rams and go to my servant Job and sacrifice a burnt offering for yourselves. My servant Job will pray for you, and I will accept his prayer and not deal with you according to your folly. You have not spoken of me what is right, as my servant Job has." 9So Eliphaz the Temanite, Bildad the Shuhite and Zophar the Naamathite did what the Lord told them; and the Lord accepted Job's prayer.

10After Job had prayed for his friends, the Lord made him prosperous again and gave him twice as much as he had before. 11All his brothers and sisters and everyone who had known him before came and ate with him in his house. They comforted and consoled him over all the trouble the Lord had brought upon him, and each one gave him a piece of silver[a] and a gold ring.

12The Lord blessed the latter part of Job's life more than the first. He had fourteen thousand sheep, six thousand camels, a thousand yoke of oxen and a thousand donkeys. 13And he also had seven sons and three daughters. 14The first daughter he named Jemimah, the second Keziah and the third Keren-Happuch. 15Nowhere in all the land were there found women as beautiful as Job's daughters, and their father granted them an inheritance along with their brothers.

16After this, Job lived a hundred and forty years; he saw his children and their children to the fourth generation. 17And so he died, old and full of years.

---

a *11* Hebrew *him a kesitah;* a kesitah was a unit of money of unknown weight and value.

Living Bible

34Of all the beasts, he is the proudest—monarch of all that he sees."

42 THEN JOB replied to God:
2"I know that you can do anything and that no one can stop you. 3You ask who it is who has so foolishly denied your providence. It is I. I was talking about things I knew nothing about and did not understand, things far too wonderful for me.

4"[You said,b] 'Listen and I will speak! Let me put the questions to you! See if you can answer them!'

5"[But now I say,c] 'I had heard about you before, but now I have seen you, 6and I loathe myself and repent in dust and ashes.' "

7After the Lord had finished speaking with Job, he said to Eliphaz the Temanite:

"I am angry with you and with your two friends, for you have not been right in what you have said about me, as my servant Job was. 8Now take seven young bulls and seven rams and go to my servant Job and offer a burnt offering for yourselves; and my servant Job will pray for you, and I will accept his prayer on your behalf, and won't destroy you as I should because of your sin, your failure to speak rightly concerning my servant Job."

9So Eliphaz the Temanite, and Bildad the Shuhite, and Zophar the Naamathite did as the Lord commanded them, and the Lord accepted Job's prayer on their behalf. 10Then, when Job prayed for his friends, the Lord restored his wealth and happiness! In fact, the Lord gave him twice as much as before! 11Then all of his brothers, sisters, and former friends arrived and feasted with him in his home, consoling him for all his sorrow, and comforting him because of all the trials the Lord had brought upon him. And each of them brought him a gift of money, and a gold ring.

12So the Lord blessed Job at the end of his life more than at the beginning. For now he had 14,000 sheep, 6,000 camels, 1,000 teams of oxen, and 1,000 female donkeys.

13, 14God also gave him seven more sons and three more daughters.

These were the names of his daughters: Jemima, Kezia, Keren.d

15And in all the land there were no other girls as lovely as the daughters of Job; and their father put them into his will along with their brothers.

16Job lived 140 years after that, living to see his grandchildren and great-grandchildren too. 17Then at last he died, an old, old man, after living a long, good life.

New Revised Standard

34 It surveys everything that is lofty;
      it is king over all that are proud."

Job Is Humbled and Satisfied

42 THEN JOB answered the Lord:
2 "I know that you can do all things,
      and that no purpose of yours can be thwarted.
3 'Who is this that hides counsel without knowledge?'
   Therefore I have uttered what I did not understand,
      things too wonderful for me, which I did not know.
4 'Hear, and I will speak;
      I will question you, and you declare to me.'
5 I had heard of you by the hearing of the ear,
      but now my eye sees you;
6 therefore I despise myself,
      and repent in dust and ashes."

Job's Friends Are Humiliated

7 After the Lord had spoken these words to Job, the Lord said to Eliphaz the Temanite: "My wrath is kindled against you and against your two friends; for you have not spoken of me what is right, as my servant Job has. 8Now therefore take seven bulls and seven rams, and go to my servant Job, and offer up for yourselves a burnt offering; and my servant Job shall pray for you, for I will accept his prayer not to deal with you according to your folly; for you have not spoken of me what is right, as my servant Job has done." 9So Eliphaz the Temanite and Bildad the Shuhite and Zophar the Naamathite went and did what the Lord had told them; and the Lord accepted Job's prayer.

Job's Fortunes Are Restored Twofold

10 And the Lord restored the fortunes of Job when he had prayed for his friends; and the Lord gave Job twice as much as he had before. 11Then there came to him all his brothers and sisters and all who had known him before, and they ate bread with him in his house; they showed him sympathy and comforted him for all the evil that the Lord had brought upon him; and each of them gave him a piece of moneye and a gold ring. 12The Lord blessed the latter days of Job more than his beginning; and he had fourteen thousand sheep, six thousand camels, a thousand yoke of oxen, and a thousand donkeys. 13He also had seven sons and three daughters. 14He named the first Jemimah, the second Keziah, and the third Keren-happuch. 15In all the land there were no women so beautiful as Job's daughters; and their father gave them an inheritance along with their brothers. 16After this Job lived one hundred and forty years, and saw his children, and his children's children, four generations. 17And Job died, old and full of days.

---

b 42:4 You said, implied.   c 42:5 But now I say, Implied.
d 42:13, 14 gave him seven more sons and three more daughters, making a total of twenty children, ten of whom were in heaven. Keren, literally "Keren-happuch."

e Heb a qesitah

THE BOOK OF

Psalms

Psalms

Book I

1 BLESSED *IS* the man that walketh not in the counsel of the ungodly, nor standeth in the way of sinners, nor sitteth in the seat of the scornful.

2But his delight *is* in the law of the LORD; and in his law doth he meditate day and night.

3And he shall be like a tree planted by the rivers of water, that bringeth forth his fruit in his season; his leaf also shall not wither; and whatsoever he doeth shall prosper.

4The ungodly *are* not so: but *are* like the chaff which the wind driveth away.

5Therefore the ungodly shall not stand in the judgment, nor sinners in the congregation of the righteous.

6For the LORD knoweth the way of the righteous: but the way of the ungodly shall perish.

2 WHY DO the heathen rage, and the people imagine a vain thing?

2The kings of the earth set themselves, and the rulers take counsel together, against the LORD, and against his anointed, *saying,*

3Let us break their bands asunder, and cast away their cords from us.

4He that sitteth in the heavens shall laugh: the Lord shall have them in derision.

5Then shall he speak unto them in his wrath, and vex them in his sore displeasure.

6Yet have I set my king upon my holy hill of Zion.

7I will declare the decree: the LORD hath said unto me, Thou *art* my Son; this day have I begotten thee.

8Ask of me, and I shall give *thee* the heathen *for* thine inheritance, and the uttermost parts of the earth *for* thy possession.

9Thou shalt break them with a rod of iron; thou shalt dash them in pieces like a potter's vessel.

10Be wise now therefore, O ye kings: be instructed, ye judges of the earth.

11Serve the LORD with fear, and rejoice with trembling.

BOOK I

Psalms 1–41

1 BLESSED IS the man
who does not walk in the counsel of the
    wicked
or stand in the way of sinners
    or sit in the seat of mockers.
2But his delight is in the law of the LORD,
    and on his law he meditates day and night.
3He is like a tree planted by streams of water,
    which yields its fruit in season
and whose leaf does not wither.
    Whatever he does prospers.

4Not so the wicked!
    They are like chaff
    that the wind blows away.
5Therefore the wicked will not stand in the
    judgment,
    nor sinners in the assembly of the righteous.

6For the LORD watches over the way of the
    righteous,
    but the way of the wicked will perish.

2 WHY DO the nations conspire[a]
    and the peoples plot in vain?
2The kings of the earth take their stand
    and the rulers gather together
against the LORD
    and against his Anointed One.[b]
3"Let us break their chains," they say,
    "and throw off their fetters."

4The One enthroned in heaven laughs;
    the Lord scoffs at them.
5Then he rebukes them in his anger
    and terrifies them in his wrath, saying,
6"I have installed my King[c]
    on Zion, my holy hill."

7I will proclaim the decree of the LORD:

He said to me, "You are my Son[d];
    today I have become your Father.[e]
8Ask of me,
    and I will make the nations your inheritance,
    the ends of the earth your possession.
9You will rule them with an iron scepter[f];
    you will dash them to pieces like pottery."

10Therefore, you kings, be wise;
    be warned, you rulers of the earth.
11Serve the LORD with fear
    and rejoice with trembling.

---

a *1* Hebrew; Septuagint *rage*   b *2* Or *anointed one*   c *6* Or *king*   d *7* Or *son*; also in verse 12   e *7* Or *have begotten you*   f *9* Or *will break them with a rod of iron*

Psalms

The Psalms

BOOK I

(Psalms 1–41)

The Two Ways

1 OH, THE joys of those who do not follow evil men's advice, who do not hang around with sinners, scoffing at the things of God: 2But they delight in doing everything God wants them to, and day and night are always meditating on his laws and thinking about ways to follow him more closely.

3They are like trees along a river bank bearing luscious fruit each season without fail. Their leaves shall never wither, and all they do shall prosper.

4But for sinners, what a different story! They blow away like chaff before the wind. 5They are not safe on Judgment Day; they shall not stand among the godly.

6For the Lord watches over all the plans and paths of godly men, but the paths of the godless lead to doom.

1 HAPPY ARE those
who do not follow the advice of the wicked,
or take the path that sinners tread,
or sit in the seat of scoffers;
2 but their delight is in the law of the Lord,
and on his law they meditate day and night.
3 They are like trees
planted by streams of water,
which yield their fruit in its season,
and their leaves do not wither.
In all that they do, they prosper.

4 The wicked are not so,
but are like chaff that the wind drives away.
5 Therefore the wicked will not stand in the
judgment,
nor sinners in the congregation of the
righteous;
6 for the Lord watches over the way of the
righteous,
but the way of the wicked will perish.

God's Promise to His Anointed

2 WHAT FOOLS the nations areg to rage against the Lord! How strange that men should try to outwit God!h 2For a summit conference of the nations has been called to plot against the Lord and his Messiah, Christ the King.i 3"Come, let us break his chains," they say, "and free ourselves from all this slavery to God."

4But God in heaven merely laughs! He is amused by all their puny plans. 5And then in fierce fury he rebukes them and fills them with fear.

6For the Lord declares,j "This is the King of my choice, and I have enthroned him in Jerusalem, my holy city."k

7His chosen one replies,l "I will reveal the everlasting purposes of God, for the Lord has said to me, 'You are my Son. This is your Coronation Day.m Today I am giving you your glory.' " 8"Only ask, and I will give you all the nations of the world. 9Rule them with an iron rod; smash them like clay pots!"

10O kings and rulers of the earth, listen while there is time. 11Serve the Lord with reverent fear; rejoice with trembling. 12Fall down before his Son and kiss his feetn

2 WHY DO the nations conspire,
and the peoples plot in vain?
2 The kings of the earth set themselves,
and the rulers take counsel together,
against the Lord and his anointed, saying,
3 "Let us burst their bonds asunder,
and cast their cords from us."

4 He who sits in the heavens laughs;
the Lord has them in derision.
5 Then he will speak to them in his wrath,
and terrify them in his fury, saying,
6 "I have set my king on Zion, my holy hill."

7 I will tell of the decree of the Lord:
He said to me, "You are my son;
today I have begotten you.
8 Ask of me, and I will make the nations your
heritage,
and the ends of the earth your possession.
9 You shall break them with a rod of iron,
and dash them in pieces like a potter's
vessel."

10 Now therefore, O kings, be wise;
be warned, O rulers of the earth.
11 Serve the Lord with fear,
with trembling 12kiss his feet,o

---

g *2:1 What fools the nations are*, literally, "Why do the heathen rage?" h *2:1 How strange that men should try to outwit God*, literally, "meditate a vain thing." i *2:2 his Messiah, Christ the King*, literally, "his anointed." j *2:6 for the Lord declares*, implied. k *2:6 Jerusalem, my holy city*, literally, "Upon Zion, my holy mountain." l *2:7 His chosen one replies*, implied. m *2:7 This is your Coronation Day*, literally, "this day have I begotten you." n *2:12 Fall down before his Son and kiss his feet*, implied.

o Cn: Meaning of Heb of verses 11b and 12a is uncertain

King James

¹²Kiss the Son, lest he be angry, and ye perish *from* the way, when his wrath is kindled but a little. Blessed *are* all they that put their trust in him.

A Psalm of David, when he fled from Absalom his son.

3 LORD, HOW are they increased that trouble me! many *are* they that rise up against me.

²Many *there be* which say of my soul, *There is* no help for him in God. Selah.

³But thou, O LORD, *art* a shield for me; my glory, and the lifter up of mine head.

⁴I cried unto the LORD with my voice, and he heard me out of his holy hill. Selah.

⁵I laid me down and slept; I awaked; for the LORD sustained me.

⁶I will not be afraid of ten thousands of people, that have set *themselves* against me round about.

⁷Arise, O LORD; save me, O my God: for thou hast smitten all mine enemies *upon* the cheek bone; thou hast broken the teeth of the ungodly.

⁸Salvation *belongeth* unto the LORD: thy blessing *is* upon thy people. Selah.

To the chief Musician on Neginoth, A Psalm of David.

4 HEAR ME when I call, O God of my righteousness: thou hast enlarged me *when I was* in distress; have mercy upon me, and hear my prayer.

²O ye sons of men, how long *will ye turn* my glory into shame? *how long* will ye love vanity, *and* seek after leasing? Selah.

³But know that the LORD hath set apart him that is godly for himself: the LORD will hear when I call unto him.

⁴Stand in awe, and sin not: commune with your own heart upon your bed, and be still. Selah.

⁵Offer the sacrifices of righteousness, and put your trust in the LORD.

⁶*There be* many that say, Who will show us *any* good? LORD, lift thou up the light of thy countenance upon us.

⁷Thou hast put gladness in my heart, more than in the time *that* their corn and their wine increased.

⁸I will both lay me down in peace, and sleep: for thou, LORD, only makest me dwell in safety.

New International

¹²Kiss the Son, lest he be angry
    and you be destroyed in your way,
  for his wrath can flare up in a moment.
    Blessed are all who take refuge in him.

A psalm of David. When he fled from his son Absalom.

3 O LORD, how many are my foes!
    How many rise up against me!
²Many are saying of me,
    "God will not deliver him."   *Selah*ᵃ

³But you are a shield around me, O LORD;
    you bestow glory on me and liftᵇ up my
      head.
⁴To the LORD I cry aloud,
    and he answers me from his holy hill.   *Selah*

⁵I lie down and sleep;
    I wake again, because the LORD sustains me.
⁶I will not fear the tens of thousands
    drawn up against me on every side.

⁷Arise, O LORD!
    Deliver me, O my God!
  Strike all my enemies on the jaw;
    break the teeth of the wicked.

⁸From the LORD comes deliverance.
    May your blessing be on your people.   *Selah*

For the director of music. With stringed instruments.
A psalm of David.

4 ANSWER ME when I call to you,
    O my righteous God.
  Give me relief from my distress;
    be merciful to me and hear my prayer.

²How long, O men, will you turn my glory into
      shameᶜ?
    How long will you love delusions and seek
      false godsᵈ?   *Selah*
³Know that the LORD has set apart the godly for
      himself;
    the LORD will hear when I call to him.

⁴In your anger do not sin;
    when you are on your beds,
    search your hearts and be silent.   *Selah*
⁵Offer right sacrifices
    and trust in the LORD.

⁶Many are asking, "Who can show us any
      good?"
    Let the light of your face shine upon us,
      O LORD.
⁷You have filled my heart with greater joy
    than when their grain and new wine abound.
⁸I will lie down and sleep in peace,
    for you alone, O LORD,
    make me dwell in safety.

ᵃ 2 A word of uncertain meaning, occurring frequently in the Psalms; possibly
a musical term   ᵇ 3 Or LORD, / my Glorious One, who lifts   ᶜ 2 Or you
dishonor my Glorious One   ᵈ 2 Or seek lies

Living Bible

before his anger is roused and you perish. I am warning you—his wrath will soon begin. But oh, the joys of those who put their trust in him!

3 A Psalm of David, when he fled from Absalom his son. O LORD, so many are against me. So many seek to harm me. I have so many enemies. 2So many say that God will never help me. 3But Lord, you are my shield, my glory, and my only hope. You alone can lift my head, now bowed in shame.e 4I cried out to the Lord, and he heard me from his Temple in Jerusalem.f 5Then I lay down and slept in peace and woke up safely, for the Lord was watching over me. 6And now, although ten thousand enemies surround me on every side, I am not afraid. 7I will cry to him, "Arise, O Lord! Save me, O my God!" And he will slap them in the face, insulting them and breaking off their teeth.g

8For salvation comes from God. What joys he gives to all his people.

4 O GOD, you have declared me perfect in your eyes;h you have always cared for me in my distress; now hear me as I call again. Have mercy on me. Hear my prayer.

2The Lord God asks, "Sons of men, will you forever turn my glory into shame by worshiping these silly idols, when every claim that's made for them is false?"

3Mark this well: The Lord has set apart the redeemed for himself. Therefore he will listen to me and answer when I call to him.

4Stand before the Lord in awe,i and do not sin against him. Lie quietly upon your bed in silent meditation. 5Put your trust in the Lord, and offer him pleasing sacrifices.

6Many say that God will never help us. Prove them wrong,j O Lord, by letting the light of your face shine down upon us. 7Yes, the gladness you have given me is far greater than their joys at harvest time as they gaze at their bountiful crops. 8I will lie down in peace and sleep, for though I am alone, O Lord, you will keep me safe.

New Revised Standard

or he will be angry, and you will perish in the way;
  for his wrath is quickly kindled.

Happy are all who take refuge in him.

Trust in God under Adversity

A Psalm of David, when he fled from his son Absalom.

3 O LORD, how many are my foes!
  Many are rising against me;
2 many are saying to me,
  "There is no help for youk in God." *Selah*

3 But you, O LORD, are a shield around me,
  my glory, and the one who lifts up my head.
4 I cry aloud to the LORD,
  and he answers me from his holy hill. *Selah*

5 I lie down and sleep;
  I wake again, for the LORD sustains me.
6 I am not afraid of ten thousands of people
  who have set themselves against me all around.

7 Rise up, O LORD!
  Deliver me, O my God!
For you strike all my enemies on the cheek;
  you break the teeth of the wicked.

8 Deliverance belongs to the LORD;
  may your blessing be on your people! *Selah*

Confident Plea for Deliverance from Enemies

To the leader: with stringed instruments. A Psalm of David.

4 ANSWER ME when I call, O God of my right!
  You gave me room when I was in distress.
  Be gracious to me, and hear my prayer.

2 How long, you people, shall my honor suffer shame?
  How long will you love vain words, and seek after lies? *Selah*
3 But know that the LORD has set apart the faithful for himself;
  the LORD hears when I call to him.

4 When you are disturbed,l do not sin;
  ponder it on your beds, and be silent. *Selah*
5 Offer right sacrifices,
  and put your trust in the LORD.

6 There are many who say, "O that we might see some good!
  Let the light of your face shine on us, O LORD!"
7 You have put gladness in my heart
  more than when their grain and wine abound.

8 I will both lie down and sleep in peace;
  for you alone, O LORD, make me lie down in safety.

---

e 3:3 now bowed in shame, implied.   f 3:4 from his Temple in Jerusalem, literally, "from his holy mountain."   g 3:7 insulting them and breaking off their teeth, implied.   h 4:1 O God, you have declared me perfect in your eyes, literally, "God of my righteousness."   i 4:4 Stand before the Lord in awe, literally, "Be ye angry."   j 4:6 Prove them wrong, implied.

k Syr: Heb him   l Or are angry

King James

To the chief Musician upon Nehiloth, A Psalm of David.

5 GIVE EAR to my words, O LORD, consider my meditation.

²Hearken unto the voice of my cry, my King, and my God: for unto thee will I pray.

³My voice shalt thou hear in the morning, O LORD; in the morning will I direct *my prayer* unto thee, and will look up.

⁴For thou *art* not a God that hath pleasure in wickedness: neither shall evil dwell with thee.

⁵The foolish shall not stand in thy sight: thou hatest all workers of iniquity.

⁶Thou shalt destroy them that speak leasing: the LORD will abhor the bloody and deceitful man.

⁷But as for me, I will come *into* thy house in the multitude of thy mercy: *and* in thy fear will I worship toward thy holy temple.

⁸Lead me, O LORD, in thy righteousness because of mine enemies; make thy way straight before my face.

⁹For *there is* no faithfulness in their mouth; their inward part *is* very wickedness; their throat *is* an open sepulchre; they flatter with their tongue.

¹⁰Destroy thou them, O God; let them fall by their own counsels; cast them out in the multitude of their transgressions; for they have rebelled against thee.

¹¹But let all those that put their trust in thee rejoice: let them ever shout for joy, because thou defendest them: let them also that love thy name be joyful in thee.

¹²For thou, LORD, wilt bless the righteous; with favour wilt thou compass him as *with* a shield.

To the chief Musician on Neginoth upon Sheminith, A Psalm of David.

6 O LORD, rebuke me not in thine anger, neither chasten me in thy hot displeasure.

²Have mercy upon me, O LORD; for I *am* weak: O LORD, heal me; for my bones are vexed.

³My soul is also sore vexed: but thou, O LORD, how long?

⁴Return, O LORD, deliver my soul: oh save me for thy mercies' sake.

⁵For in death *there is* no remembrance of thee: in the grave who shall give thee thanks?

⁶I am weary with my groaning; all the night make I my bed to swim; I water my couch with my tears.

⁷Mine eye is consumed because of grief; it waxeth old because of all mine enemies.

New International

For the director of music. For flutes. A psalm of David.

5 GIVE EAR to my words, O LORD,
consider my sighing.

²Listen to my cry for help,
my King and my God,
for to you I pray.

³In the morning, O LORD, you hear my voice;
in the morning I lay my requests before you
and wait in expectation.

⁴You are not a God who takes pleasure in evil;
with you the wicked cannot dwell.

⁵The arrogant cannot stand in your presence;
you hate all who do wrong.

⁶You destroy those who tell lies;
bloodthirsty and deceitful men
the LORD abhors.

⁷But I, by your great mercy,
will come into your house;
in reverence will I bow down
toward your holy temple.

⁸Lead me, O LORD, in your righteousness
because of my enemies—
make straight your way before me.

⁹Not a word from their mouth can be trusted;
their heart is filled with destruction.
Their throat is an open grave;
with their tongue they speak deceit.

¹⁰Declare them guilty, O God!
Let their intrigues be their downfall.
Banish them for their many sins,
for they have rebelled against you.

¹¹But let all who take refuge in you be glad;
let them ever sing for joy.
Spread your protection over them,
that those who love your name may rejoice in
you.

¹²For surely, O LORD, you bless the righteous;
you surround them with your favor as with a
shield.

For the director of music. With stringed instruments.
According to *sheminith*.ª A psalm of David.

6 O LORD, do not rebuke me in your anger
or discipline me in your wrath.

²Be merciful to me, LORD, for I am faint;
O LORD, heal me, for my bones are in agony.

³My soul is in anguish.
How long, O LORD, how long?

⁴Turn, O LORD, and deliver me;
save me because of your unfailing love.

⁵No one remembers you when he is dead.
Who praises you from the graveᵇ?

⁶I am worn out from groaning;
all night long I flood my bed with weeping
and drench my couch with tears.

⁷My eyes grow weak with sorrow;
they fail because of all my foes.

ª Title: Probably a musical term   ᵇ 5 Hebrew *Sheol*

Living Bible

5 O LORD, hear me praying; listen to my plea, O God my King, for I will never pray to anyone but you. ³Each morning I will look to you in heaven and lay my requests before you, praying earnestly.

⁴I know you get no pleasure from wickedness and cannot tolerate the slightest sin. ⁵Therefore proud sinners will not survive your searching gaze, for how you hate their evil deeds. ⁶You will destroy them for their lies; how you abhor all murder and deception.

⁷But as for me, I will come into your Temple protected by your mercy and your love; I will worship you with deepest awe.

⁸Lord, lead me as you promised me you would; otherwise my enemies will conquer me. Tell me clearly what to do, which way to turn. ⁹For they cannot speak one truthful word. Their hearts are filled to the brim with wickedness. Their suggestions are full of the stench of sin and death. Their tongues are filled with flatteries to gain their wicked ends. ¹⁰O God, hold them responsible. Catch them in their own traps; let them fall beneath the weight of their own transgressions, for they rebel against you.

¹¹But make everyone rejoice who puts his trust in you. Keep them shouting for joy because you are defending them. Fill all who love you with your happiness. ¹²For you bless the godly man, O Lord; you protect him with your shield of love.

6 NO, LORD! Don't punish me in the heat of your anger. ²Pity me, O Lord, for I am weak. Heal me, for my body is sick, ³and I am upset and disturbed. My mind is filled with apprehension and with gloom. Oh, restore me soon.

⁴Come, O Lord, and make me well. In your kindness save me. ⁵For if I die I cannot give you glory by praising you before my friends.ᶜ ⁶I am worn out with pain; every night my pillow is wet with tears. ⁷My eyes are growing old and dim with grief because of all my enemies.

ᶜ *6:5 For if I die I cannot give you glory by praising you before my friends,* literally, "In the grave, who shall give you thanks?" Isaiah 57:1, 2 may indicate that Old Testament saints believed in a conscious and pleasant hereafter for those who love God.

New Revised Standard

Trust in God for Deliverance from Enemies

To the leader: for the flutes. A Psalm of David.

5 GIVE EAR to my words, O LORD;
   give heed to my sighing.
2 Listen to the sound of my cry,
      my King and my God,
      for to you I pray.
3 O LORD, in the morning you hear my voice;
      in the morning I plead my case to you, and
      watch.

4 For you are not a God who delights in
         wickedness;
      evil will not sojourn with you.
5 The boastful will not stand before your eyes;
      you hate all evildoers.
6 You destroy those who speak lies;
      the LORD abhors the bloodthirsty and
         deceitful.

7 But I, through the abundance of your steadfast
         love,
      will enter your house,
   I will bow down toward your holy temple
      in awe of you.
8 Lead me, O LORD, in your righteousness
      because of my enemies;
      make your way straight before me.

9 For there is no truth in their mouths;
      their hearts are destruction;
   their throats are open graves;
      they flatter with their tongues.
10 Make them bear their guilt, O God;
      let them fall by their own counsels;
   because of their many transgressions cast them
         out,
      for they have rebelled against you.

11 But let all who take refuge in you rejoice;
      let them ever sing for joy.
   Spread your protection over them,
      so that those who love your name may exult
         in you.
12 For you bless the righteous, O LORD;
      you cover them with favor as with a shield.

Prayer for Recovery from Grave Illness

To the leader: with stringed instruments; according to The Sheminith. A Psalm of David.

6 O LORD, do not rebuke me in your anger,
   or discipline me in your wrath.
2 Be gracious to me, O LORD, for I am
         languishing;
   O LORD, heal me, for my bones are shaking
      with terror.
3 My soul also is struck with terror,
      while you, O LORD—how long?

4 Turn, O LORD, save my life;
      deliver me for the sake of your steadfast
         love.
5 For in death there is no remembrance of you;
      in Sheol who can give you praise?

6 I am weary with my moaning;
      every night I flood my bed with tears;
      I drench my couch with my weeping.
7 My eyes waste away because of grief;
      they grow weak because of all my foes.

King James

8Depart from me, all ye workers of iniquity; for the LORD hath heard the voice of my weeping.

9The LORD hath heard my supplication; the LORD will receive my prayer.

10Let all mine enemies be ashamed and sore vexed: let them return *and* be ashamed suddenly.

Shiggaion of David, which he sang unto the LORD, concerning the words of Cush the Benjamite.

7 O LORD my God, in thee do I put my trust: save me from all them that persecute me, and deliver me:

2Lest he tear my soul like a lion, rending *it* in pieces, while *there is* none to deliver.

3O LORD my God, if I have done this; if there be iniquity in my hands;

4If I have rewarded evil unto him that was at peace with me; (yea, I have delivered him that without cause is mine enemy:)

5Let the enemy persecute my soul, and take *it;* yea, let him tread down my life upon the earth, and lay mine honour in the dust. Selah.

6Arise, O LORD, in thine anger, lift up thyself because of the rage of mine enemies: and awake for me *to* the judgment *that* thou hast commanded.

7So shall the congregation of the people compass thee about: for their sakes therefore return thou on high.

8The LORD shall judge the people: judge me, O LORD, according to my righteousness, and according to mine integrity *that is* in me.

9Oh let the wickedness of the wicked come to an end; but establish the just: for the righteous God trieth the hearts and reins.

10My defence *is* of God, which saveth the upright in heart.

11God judgeth the righteous, and God is angry *with the wicked* every day.

12If he turn not, he will whet his sword; he hath bent his bow, and made it ready.

13He hath also prepared for him the instruments of death; he ordaineth his arrows against the persecutors.

14Behold, he travaileth with iniquity, and hath conceived mischief, and brought forth falsehood.

15He made a pit, and digged it, and is fallen into the ditch *which* he made.

16His mischief shall return upon his own head, and his violent dealing shall come down upon his own pate.

17I will praise the LORD according to his righteousness: and will sing praise to the name of the LORD most high.

New International

8Away from me, all you who do evil,
    for the LORD has heard my weeping.
9The LORD has heard my cry for mercy;
    the LORD accepts my prayer.
10All my enemies will be ashamed and dismayed;
    they will turn back in sudden disgrace.

A *shiggaion*[a] of David, which he sang to the LORD concerning Cush, a Benjamite.

7 O LORD my God, I take refuge in you;
    save and deliver me from all who pursue me,
2or they will tear me like a lion
    and rip me to pieces with no one to rescue
    me.

3O LORD my God, if I have done this
    and there is guilt on my hands—
4if I have done evil to him who is at peace with
    me
    or without cause have robbed my foe—
5then let my enemy pursue and overtake me;
    let him trample my life to the ground
    and make me sleep in the dust.   Selah

6Arise, O LORD, in your anger;
    rise up against the rage of my enemies.
    Awake, my God; decree justice.
7Let the assembled peoples gather around you.
    Rule over them from on high;
8   let the LORD judge the peoples.
  Judge me, O LORD, according to my
        righteousness,
    according to my integrity, O Most High.
9O righteous God,
    who searches minds and hearts,
  bring to an end the violence of the wicked
    and make the righteous secure.

10My shield[b] is God Most High,
    who saves the upright in heart.
11God is a righteous judge,
    a God who expresses his wrath every day.
12If he does not relent,
    he[c] will sharpen his sword;
    he will bend and string his bow.
13He has prepared his deadly weapons;
    he makes ready his flaming arrows.

14He who is pregnant with evil
    and conceives trouble gives birth to
        disillusionment.
15He who digs a hole and scoops it out
    falls into the pit he has made.
16The trouble he causes recoils on himself;
    his violence comes down on his own head.

17I will give thanks to the LORD because of his
        righteousness
    and will sing praise to the name of the LORD
    Most High.

---

a Title: Probably a literary or musical term   b *10* Or *sovereign*   c *12* Or
If a man does not repent, / God

Living Bible

8Go, leave me now, you men of evil deeds, for the Lord has heard my weeping 9and my pleading. He will answer all my prayers. 10All my enemies shall be suddenly dishonored, terror-stricken, and disgraced. God will turn them back in shame.

7 I AM depending on you, O Lord my God, to save me from my persecutors. 2Don't let them pounce upon me as a lion would and maul me and drag me away with no one to rescue me. 3It would be different, Lord, if I were doing evil things— 4if I were paying back evil for good or unjustly attacking those I dislike. 5Then it would be right for you to let my enemies destroy me, crush me to the ground, and trample my life in the dust.
6But Lord! Arise in anger against the anger of my enemies. Awake! Demand justice for me, Lord! 7, 8Gather all peoples before you; sit high above them, judging their sins. But justify me publicly; establish my honor and truth before them all. 9End all wickedness, O Lord, and bless all who truly worship God;d for you, the righteous God, look deep within the hearts of men and examine all their motives and their thoughts.
10God is my shield; he will defend me. He saves those whose hearts and lives are true and right.e
11God is a judge who is perfectly fair, and he is angry with the wicked every day. 12Unless they repent, he will sharpen his sword and slay them.
He has bent and strung his bow 13and fitted it with deadly arrows made from shafts of fire.
14The wicked man conceives an evil plot, labors with its dark details, and brings to birth his treachery and lies; 15let him fall into his own trap. 16May the violence he plans for others boomerang upon himself; let him die.
17Oh, how grateful and thankful I am to the Lord because he is so good. I will sing praise to the name of the Lord who is above all lords.

New Revised Standard

8 Depart from me, all you workers of evil,
      for the LORD has heard the sound of my
      weeping.
9 The LORD has heard my supplication;
      the LORD accepts my prayer.
10 All my enemies shall be ashamed and struck
      with terror;
      they shall turn back, and in a moment be
      put to shame.

Plea for Help against Persecutors
  A Shiggaion of David, which he sang to the LORD
      concerning Cush, a Benjaminite.

7 O LORD my God, in you I take refuge;
      save me from all my pursuers, and deliver
      me,
2 or like a lion they will tear me apart;
      they will drag me away, with no one to
      rescue.

3 O LORD my God, if I have done this,
      if there is wrong in my hands,
4 if I have repaid my ally with harm
      or plundered my foe without cause,
5 then let the enemy pursue and overtake me,
      trample my life to the ground,
      and lay my soul in the dust.   *Selah*

6 Rise up, O LORD, in your anger;
      lift yourself up against the fury of my
      enemies;
      awake, O my God;f you have appointed a
      judgment.
7 Let the assembly of the peoples be gathered
      around you,
      and over it take your seatg on high.
8 The LORD judges the peoples;
      judge me, O LORD, according to my
      righteousness
      and according to the integrity that is in me.

9 O let the evil of the wicked come to an end,
      but establish the righteous,
   you who test the minds and hearts,
      O righteous God.
10 God is my shield,
      who saves the upright in heart.
11 God is a righteous judge,
      and a God who has indignation every day.

12 If one does not repent, Godh will whet his
      sword;
      he has bent and strung his bow;
13 he has prepared his deadly weapons,
      making his arrows fiery shafts.
14 See how they conceive evil,
      and are pregnant with mischief,
      and bring forth lies.
15 They make a pit, digging it out,
      and fall into the hole that they have made.
16 Their mischief returns upon their own heads,
      and on their own heads their violence
      descends.

17 I will give to the LORD the thanks due to his
      righteousness,
      and sing praise to the name of the LORD,
      the Most High.

d 7:9 *God,* literally, "the just."   e 7:10 *He saves those whose hearts and lives are true and right,* literally, "the upright in heart."

f Or *awake for me*   g Cn: Heb *return*   h Heb *he*

King James

To the chief Musician upon Gittith, A Psalm of David.

8 O LORD our Lord, how excellent *is* thy name in all the earth! who hast set thy glory above the heavens.

2Out of the mouth of babes and sucklings hast thou ordained strength because of thine enemies, that thou mightest still the enemy and the avenger.

3When I consider thy heavens, the work of thy fingers, the moon and the stars, which thou hast ordained;

4What is man, that thou art mindful of him? and the son of man, that thou visitest him?

5For thou hast made him a little lower than the angels, and hast crowned him with glory and honour.

6Thou madest him to have dominion over the works of thy hands; thou hast put all *things* under his feet:

7All sheep and oxen, yea, and the beasts of the field;

8The fowl of the air, and the fish of the sea, *and* whatsoever passeth through the paths of the seas.

9O LORD our Lord, how excellent *is* thy name in all the earth!

To the chief Musician upon Muth-labben, A Psalm of David.

9 I WILL praise *thee*, O LORD, with my whole heart; I will show forth all thy marvellous works.

2I will be glad and rejoice in thee: I will sing praise to thy name, O thou most High.

3When mine enemies are turned back, they shall fall and perish at thy presence.

4For thou hast maintained my right and my cause; thou satest in the throne judging right.

5Thou hast rebuked the heathen, thou hast destroyed the wicked, thou hast put out their name for ever and ever.

6O thou enemy, destructions are come to a perpetual end: and thou hast destroyed cities; their memorial is perished with them.

7But the LORD shall endure for ever: he hath prepared his throne for judgment.

8And he shall judge the world in righteousness, he shall minister judgment to the people in uprightness.

9The LORD also will be a refuge for the oppressed, a refuge in times of trouble.

10And they that know thy name will put their trust in thee: for thou, LORD, hast not forsaken them that seek thee.

New International

For the director of music. According to *gittith*.[a] A psalm of David.

8 O LORD, our Lord, how majestic is your name in all the earth!

You have set your glory above the heavens.

2From the lips of children and infants you have ordained praise[b] because of your enemies, to silence the foe and the avenger.

3When I consider your heavens, the work of your fingers, the moon and the stars, which you have set in place,

4what is man that you are mindful of him, the son of man that you care for him?

5You made him a little lower than the heavenly beings[c] and crowned him with glory and honor.

6You made him ruler over the works of your hands; you put everything under his feet:

7all flocks and herds, and the beasts of the field,

8the birds of the air, and the fish of the sea, all that swim the paths of the seas.

9O LORD, our Lord, how majestic is your name in all the earth!

For the director of music. To the tune of, "The Death of the Son." A psalm of David.

9[d] I WILL praise you, O LORD, with all my heart; I will tell of all your wonders.

2I will be glad and rejoice in you; I will sing praise to your name, O Most High.

3My enemies turn back; they stumble and perish before you.

4For you have upheld my right and my cause; you have sat on your throne, judging righteously.

5You have rebuked the nations and destroyed the wicked; you have blotted out their name for ever and ever.

6Endless ruin has overtaken the enemy, you have uprooted their cities; even the memory of them has perished.

7The LORD reigns forever; he has established his throne for judgment.

8He will judge the world in righteousness; he will govern the peoples with justice.

9The LORD is a refuge for the oppressed, a stronghold in times of trouble.

10Those who know your name will trust in you, for you, LORD, have never forsaken those who seek you.

a Title: Probably a musical term   b 2 Or *strength*   c 5 Or *than God*
d Psalms 9 and 10 may have been originally a single acrostic poem, the stanzas of which begin with the successive letters of the Hebrew alphabet. In the Septuagint they constitute one psalm.

Living Bible

8 O LORD our God, the majesty and glory of your name fills all the earth and overflows the heavens. 2You have taught the little children to praise you perfectly. May their example shame and silence your enemies!

3When I look up into the night skies and see the work of your fingers—the moon and the stars you have made— 4I cannot understand how you can bother with mere puny man, to pay any attention to him!

5And yet you have made him only a little lower than the angels,e and placed a crown of glory and honor upon his head.

6You have put him in charge of everything you made; everything is put under his authority: 7all sheep and oxen, and wild animals too, 8the birds and fish, and all the life in the sea. 9O Jehovah, our Lord, the majesty and glory of your name fills the earth.

9 O LORD, I will praise you with all my heart, and tell everyone about the marvelous things you do. 2I will be glad, yes, filled with joy because of you. I will sing your praises, O Lord God above all gods.f

3My enemies will fall back and perish in your presence; 4you have vindicated me; you have endorsed my work, declaring from your throne that it is good.g 5You have rebuked the nations and destroyed the wicked, blotting out their names forever and ever. 6O enemies of mine, you are doomed forever. The Lord will destroy your cities; even the memory of them will disappear.

7,8But the Lord lives on forever; he sits upon his throne to judge justly the nations of the world. 9All who are oppressed may come to him. He is a refuge for them in their times of trouble. 10All those who know your mercy, Lord, will count on you for help. For you have never yet forsaken those who trust in you.

New Revised Standard

Divine Majesty and Human Dignity

To the leader: according to The Gittith. A Psalm of David.

8 O LORD, our Sovereign,
how majestic is your name in all the earth!

You have set your glory above the heavens.
2 Out of the mouths of babes and infants
you have founded a bulwark because of your foes,
to silence the enemy and the avenger.

3 When I look at your heavens, the work of your fingers,
the moon and the stars that you have established;
4 what are human beings that you are mindful of them,
mortalsh that you care for them?

5 Yet you have made them a little lower than God,i
and crowned them with glory and honor.
6 You have given them dominion over the works of your hands;
you have put all things under their feet,
7 all sheep and oxen,
and also the beasts of the field,
8 the birds of the air, and the fish of the sea,
whatever passes along the paths of the seas.

9 O LORD, our Sovereign,
how majestic is your name in all the earth!

God's Power and Justice

To the leader: according to Muth-labben. A Psalm of David.

9 I WILL give thanks to the LORD with my whole heart;
I will tell of all your wonderful deeds.
2 I will be glad and exult in you;
I will sing praise to your name, O Most High.

3 When my enemies turned back,
they stumbled and perished before you.
4 For you have maintained my just cause;
you have sat on the throne giving righteous judgment.

5 You have rebuked the nations, you have destroyed the wicked;
you have blotted out their name forever and ever.
6 The enemies have vanished in everlasting ruins;
their cities you have rooted out;
the very memory of them has perished.

7 But the LORD sits enthroned forever,
he has established his throne for judgment.
8 He judges the world with righteousness;
he judges the peoples with equity.

9 The LORD is a stronghold for the oppressed,
a stronghold in times of trouble.
10 And those who know your name put their trust in you,
for you, O LORD, have not forsaken those who seek you.

---

e 8:5 only a little lower than the angels, or, "only a little lower than God!"
f 9:2 O Lord God above all gods, literally, "O Most High." g 9:4 you have endorsed my work, declaring from your throne that it is good, literally, "You sit on the throne, judging righteously."

h Heb ben adam, lit. son of man i Or than the divine beings or angels; Heb elohim

King James

11Sing praises to the LORD, which dwelleth in Zion: declare among the people his doings.

12When he maketh inquisition for blood, he remembereth them: he forgetteth not the cry of the humble.

13Have mercy upon me, O LORD; consider my trouble *which I suffer* of them that hate me, thou that liftest me up from the gates of death:

14That I may show forth all thy praise in the gates of the daughter of Zion: I will rejoice in thy salvation.

15The heathen are sunk down in the pit *that* they made: in the net which they hid is their own foot taken.

16The LORD is known *by* the judgment *which* he executeth: the wicked is snared in the work of his own hands. Higgaion. Selah.

17The wicked shall be turned into hell, *and* all the nations that forget God.

18For the needy shall not always be forgotten: the expectation of the poor shall *not* perish for ever.

19Arise, O LORD; let not man prevail: let the heathen be judged in thy sight.

20Put them in fear, O LORD: *that* the nations may know themselves *to be but* men. Selah.

New International

11Sing praises to the LORD, enthroned in Zion;
 proclaim among the nations what he has
  done.
12For he who avenges blood remembers;
 he does not ignore the cry of the afflicted.

13O LORD, see how my enemies persecute me!
 Have mercy and lift me up from the gates of
  death,
14that I may declare your praises
 in the gates of the Daughter of Zion
 and there rejoice in your salvation.
15The nations have fallen into the pit they have
  dug;
 their feet are caught in the net they have
  hidden.
16The LORD is known by his justice;
 the wicked are ensnared by the work of their
  hands.   *Higgaion.*a *Selah*
17The wicked return to the grave,b
 all the nations that forget God.
18But the needy will not always be forgotten,
 nor the hope of the afflicted ever perish.

19Arise, O LORD, let not man triumph;
 let the nations be judged in your presence.
20Strike them with terror, O LORD;
 let the nations know they are but men.   *Selah*

10 WHY STANDEST thou afar off, O LORD? *why* hidest thou *thyself* in times of trouble?

2The wicked in *his* pride doth persecute the poor: let them be taken in the devices that they have imagined.

3For the wicked boasteth of his heart's desire, and blesseth the covetous, *whom* the LORD abhorreth.

4The wicked, through the pride of his countenance, will not seek *after God: God is* not in all his thoughts.

5His ways are always grievous; thy judgments *are* far above out of his sight: *as for* all his enemies, he puffeth at them.

6He hath said in his heart, I shall not be moved: for *I shall* never *be* in adversity.

7His mouth is full of cursing and deceit and fraud: under his tongue *is* mischief and vanity.

8He sitteth in the lurking places of the villages: in the secret places doth he murder the innocent: his eyes are privily set against the poor.

9He lieth in wait secretly as a lion in his den: he lieth in wait to catch the poor: he doth catch the poor, when he draweth him into his net.

10c WHY, O LORD, do you stand far off?
 Why do you hide yourself in times of
  trouble?

2In his arrogance the wicked man hunts down the
  weak,
 who are caught in the schemes he devises.
3He boasts of the cravings of his heart;
 he blesses the greedy and reviles the LORD.
4In his pride the wicked does not seek him;
 in all his thoughts there is no room for God.
5His ways are always prosperous;
 he is haughty and your laws are far from him;
 he sneers at all his enemies.
6He says to himself, "Nothing will shake me;
 I'll always be happy and never have trouble."
7His mouth is full of curses and lies and threats;
 trouble and evil are under his tongue.
8He lies in wait near the villages;
 from ambush he murders the innocent,
 watching in secret for his victims.
9He lies in wait like a lion in cover;
 he lies in wait to catch the helpless;
 he catches the helpless and drags them off in
  his net.

a *16* Or *Meditation*; possibly a musical notation   b *17* Hebrew *Sheol*
c Psalms 9 and 10 may have been originally a single acrostic poem, the stanzas
of which begin with the successive letters of the Hebrew alphabet. In the
Septuagint they constitute one psalm.

Living Bible

11Oh, sing out your praises to the God who lives in Jerusalem.d Tell the world about his unforgettable deeds. 12He who avenges murder has an open ear to those who cry to him for justice. He does not ignore the prayers of men in trouble when they call to him for help.

13And now, O Lord, have mercy on me; see how I suffer at the hands of those who hate me. Lord, snatch me back from the jaws of death. 14Save me, so that I can praise you publicly before all the people at Jerusalem's gatese and rejoice that you have rescued me.

15The nations fall into the pitfalls they have dug for others; the trap they set has snapped on them. 16The Lord is famous for the way he punishes the wicked in their own snares!f

17The wicked shall be sent away to hell; this is the fate of all the nations forgetting the Lord. 18For the needs of the needy shall not be ignored forever; the hopes of the poor shall not always be crushed.

19O Lord, arise and judge and punish the nations; don't let them defy you! 20Make them tremble in fear; put the nations in their place until at last they know they are but puny men.

10 LORD, WHY are you standing aloof and far away? Why do you hide when I need you the most?

2Come and deal with all these proud and wicked men who viciously persecute the poor. Pour upon these men the evil they planned for others! 3For these men brag of all their evil lusts; they revile God and congratulate those the Lord abhors, whose only goal in life is money.

4These wicked men, so proud and haughty, seem to think that God is dead.g They wouldn't think of looking for him! 5Yet there is success in everything they do, and their enemies fall before them. They do not see your punishment awaiting them. 6They boast that neither God nor man can ever keep them down—somehow they'll find a way!

7Their mouths are full of profanity and lies and fraud. They are always boasting of their evil plans. 8They lurk in dark alleys of the city and murder passersby. 9Like lions they crouch silently, waiting to pounce upon the poor. Like hunters they catch their victims in their traps.

New Revised Standard

11 Sing praises to the LORD, who dwells in Zion.
   Declare his deeds among the peoples.
12 For he who avenges blood is mindful of them;
   he does not forget the cry of the afflicted.

13 Be gracious to me, O LORD.
   See what I suffer from those who hate me;
   you are the one who lifts me up from the gates of death,
14 so that I may recount all your praises,
   and, in the gates of daughter Zion,
   rejoice in your deliverance.

15 The nations have sunk in the pit that they made;
   in the net that they hid has their own foot been caught.
16 The LORD has made himself known, he has executed judgment;
   the wicked are snared in the work of their own hands. *Higgaion. Selah*

17 The wicked shall depart to Sheol,
   all the nations that forget God.

18 For the needy shall not always be forgotten,
   nor the hope of the poor perish forever.

19 Rise up, O LORD! Do not let mortals prevail;
   let the nations be judged before you.
20 Put them in fear, O LORD;
   let the nations know that they are only human. *Selah*

Prayer for Deliverance from Enemies

10 WHY, O LORD, do you stand far off?
   Why do you hide yourself in times of trouble?
2 In arrogance the wicked persecute the poor—
   let them be caught in the schemes they have devised.

3 For the wicked boast of the desires of their heart,
   those greedy for gain curse and renounce the LORD.
4 In the pride of their countenance the wicked say, "God will not seek it out";
   all their thoughts are, "There is no God."

5 Their ways prosper at all times;
   your judgments are on high, out of their sight;
   as for their foes, they scoff at them.
6 They think in their heart, "We shall not be moved;
   throughout all generations we shall not meet adversity."

7 Their mouths are filled with cursing and deceit and oppression;
   under their tongues are mischief and iniquity.
8 They sit in ambush in the villages;
   in hiding places they murder the innocent.

Their eyes stealthily watch for the helpless;
9 they lurk in secret like a lion in its covert;
   they lurk that they may seize the poor;
   they seize the poor and drag them off in their net.

---

d 9:11 *in Jerusalem*, literally, "in Zion." e 9:14 *at Jerusalem's gates*, literally, "in the gates of the daughter of Zion." f 9:16 The Hebrew text adds at the end of the verse: "Higgaion. Selah." The meanings of these words are not known. g 10:4 *that God is dead*, literally, "that there is no God."

King James

10He croucheth, *and* humbleth himself, that the poor may fall by his strong ones.

11He hath said in his heart, God hath forgotten: he hideth his face; he will never see *it*.

12Arise, O LORD; O God, lift up thine hand: forget not the humble.

13Wherefore doth the wicked contemn God? he hath said in his heart, Thou wilt not require *it*.

14Thou hast seen *it;* for thou beholdest mischief and spite, to requite *it* with thy hand: the poor committeth himself unto thee; thou art the helper of the fatherless.

15Break thou the arm of the wicked and the evil *man:* seek out his wickedness *till* thou find none.

16The LORD *is* King for ever and ever: the heathen are perished out of his land.

17LORD, thou hast heard the desire of the humble: thou wilt prepare their heart, thou wilt cause thine ear to hear:

18To judge the fatherless and the oppressed, that the man of the earth may no more oppress.

To the chief Musician, *A Psalm* of David.

11 IN THE LORD put I my trust: how say ye to my soul, Flee *as* a bird to your mountain?

2For, lo, the wicked bend *their* bow, they make ready their arrow upon the string, that they may privily shoot at the upright in heart.

3If the foundations be destroyed, what can the righteous do?

4The LORD *is* in his holy temple, the LORD's throne *is* in heaven: his eyes behold, his eyelids try, the children of men.

5The LORD trieth the righteous: but the wicked and him that loveth violence his soul hateth.

6Upon the wicked he shall rain snares, fire and brimstone, and an horrible tempest: *this shall be* the portion of their cup.

7For the righteous LORD loveth righteousness; his countenance doth behold the upright.

To the chief Musician upon Sheminith, A Psalm of David.

12 HELP, LORD; for the godly man ceaseth; for the faithful fail from among the children of men.

2They speak vanity every one with his neighbour: *with* flattering lips *and* with a double heart do they speak.

New International

10His victims are crushed, they collapse; they fall under his strength.

11He says to himself, "God has forgotten; he covers his face and never sees."

12Arise, LORD! Lift up your hand, O God. Do not forget the helpless.

13Why does the wicked man revile God? Why does he say to himself, "He won't call me to account"?

14But you, O God, do see trouble and grief; you consider it to take it in hand. The victim commits himself to you; you are the helper of the fatherless.

15Break the arm of the wicked and evil man; call him to account for his wickedness that would not be found out.

16The LORD is King for ever and ever; the nations will perish from his land.

17You hear, O LORD, the desire of the afflicted; you encourage them, and you listen to their cry,

18defending the fatherless and the oppressed, in order that man, who is of the earth, may terrify no more.

For the director of music. Of David.

11 IN THE LORD I take refuge. How then can you say to me: "Flee like a bird to your mountain.

2For look, the wicked bend their bows; they set their arrows against the strings to shoot from the shadows at the upright in heart.

3When the foundations are being destroyed, what can the righteous do[a]?"

4The LORD is in his holy temple; the LORD is on his heavenly throne. He observes the sons of men; his eyes examine them.

5The LORD examines the righteous, but the wicked[b] and those who love violence his soul hates.

6On the wicked he will rain fiery coals and burning sulfur; a scorching wind will be their lot.

7For the LORD is righteous, he loves justice; upright men will see his face.

For the director of music. According to *sheminith.*[c] A psalm of David.

12 HELP, LORD, for the godly are no more; the faithful have vanished from among men.

2Everyone lies to his neighbor; their flattering lips speak with deception.

---

[a] 3 Or *what is the Righteous One doing*   [b] 5 Or *The LORD, the Righteous One, examines the wicked, /*   [c] Title: Probably a musical term

Living Bible

¹⁰The unfortunate are overwhelmed by their superior strength and fall beneath their blows. ¹¹"God isn't watching," they say to themselves; "he'll never know!"

¹²O Lord, arise! O God, crush them! Don't forget the poor or anyone else in need. ¹³Why do you let the wicked get away with this contempt for God? For they think that God will never call them to account. ¹⁴Lord, you see what they are doing. You have noted each evil act. You know what trouble and grief they have caused. Now punish them. O Lord, the poor man trusts himself to you; you are known as the helper of the helpless. ¹⁵Break the arms of these wicked men. Go after them until the last of them is destroyed.

¹⁶The Lord is King forever and forever. Those who follow other gods shall be swept from his land.

¹⁷Lord, you know the hopes of humble people. Surely you will hear their cries and comfort their hearts by helping them. ¹⁸You will be with the orphans and all who are oppressed, so that mere earthly man will terrify them no longer.

11 HOW DARE you tell me, "Flee[d] to the mountains for safety," when I am trusting in the Lord?

²For the wicked have strung their bows, drawn their arrows tight against the bowstrings, and aimed from ambush at the people of God. ³"Law and order have collapsed,"[e] we are told. "What can the righteous do but flee?"

⁴But the Lord is still in his holy temple; he still rules from heaven. He closely watches everything that happens here on earth. ⁵He puts the righteous and the wicked to the test; he hates those loving violence. ⁶He will rain down fire and brimstone on the wicked and scorch them with his burning wind.

⁷For God is good, and he loves goodness; the godly shall see his face.[f]

12 LORD! HELP! Godly men are fast disappearing. Where in all the world can dependable men be found? ²Everyone deceives and flatters and lies. There is no sincerity left.

New Revised Standard

¹⁰ They stoop, they crouch,
and the helpless fall by their might.
¹¹ They think in their heart, "God has forgotten,
he has hidden his face, he will never see it."

¹² Rise up, O LORD; O God, lift up your hand;
do not forget the oppressed.
¹³ Why do the wicked renounce God,
and say in their hearts, "You will not call us to account"?

¹⁴ But you do see! Indeed you note trouble and grief,
that you may take it into your hands;
the helpless commit themselves to you;
you have been the helper of the orphan.

¹⁵ Break the arm of the wicked and evildoers;
seek out their wickedness until you find none.
¹⁶ The LORD is king forever and ever;
the nations shall perish from his land.

¹⁷ O LORD, you will hear the desire of the meek;
you will strengthen their heart, you will incline your ear
¹⁸ to do justice for the orphan and the oppressed,
so that those from earth may strike terror no more.[g]

Song of Trust in God

To the leader. Of David.

11 IN THE LORD I take refuge; how can you say to me,
"Flee like a bird to the mountains;[h]
² for look, the wicked bend the bow,
they have fitted their arrow to the string,
to shoot in the dark at the upright in heart.
³ If the foundations are destroyed,
what can the righteous do?"

⁴ The LORD is in his holy temple;
the LORD's throne is in heaven.
His eyes behold, his gaze examines humankind.
⁵ The LORD tests the righteous and the wicked,
and his soul hates the lover of violence.
⁶ On the wicked he will rain coals of fire and sulfur;
a scorching wind shall be the portion of their cup.
⁷ For the LORD is righteous;
he loves righteous deeds;
the upright shall behold his face.

Plea for Help in Evil Times

To the leader: according to The Sheminith. A Psalm of David.

12 HELP, O LORD, for there is no longer anyone who is godly;
the faithful have disappeared from humankind.
² They utter lies to each other;
with flattering lips and a double heart they speak.

---

[d] *11:1 Flee,* literally, "Flee as a bird."   [e] *11:3 Law and order have collapsed,* literally, "If the foundations have been torn down."   [f] *11:7 For God is good, and he loves goodness; the godly shall see his face* or, "His face shines down in mercy and joy upon the good."

[g] Meaning of Heb uncertain   [h] Gk Syr Jerome Tg: Heb *flee to your mountain, O bird*

King James

3The LORD shall cut off all flattering lips, *and* the tongue that speaketh proud things:

4Who have said, With our tongue will we prevail; our lips *are* our own: who *is* lord over us?

5For the oppression of the poor, for the sighing of the needy, now will I arise, saith the LORD; I will set *him* in safety *from him that* puffeth at him.

6The words of the LORD *are* pure words: *as* silver tried in a furnace of earth, purified seven times.

7Thou shalt keep them, O LORD, thou shalt preserve them from this generation for ever.

8The wicked walk on every side, when the vilest men are exalted.

To the chief Musician, A Psalm of David.

13 HOW LONG wilt thou forget me, O LORD? for ever? how long wilt thou hide thy face from me?

2How long shall I take counsel in my soul, *having* sorrow in my heart daily? how long shall mine enemy be exalted over me?

3Consider *and* hear me, O LORD my God: lighten mine eyes, lest I sleep the *sleep of* death;

4Lest mine enemy say, I have prevailed against him; *and* those that trouble me rejoice when I am moved.

5But I have trusted in thy mercy; my heart shall rejoice in thy salvation.

6I will sing unto the LORD, because he hath dealt bountifully with me.

To the chief Musician, *A Psalm* of David.

14 THE FOOL hath said in his heart, *There is* no God. They are corrupt, they have done abominable works, *there is* none that doeth good.

2The LORD looked down from heaven upon the children of men, to see if there were any that did understand, *and* seek God.

3They are all gone aside, they are *all* together become filthy: *there is* none that doeth good, no, not one.

4Have all the workers of iniquity no knowledge? who eat up my people *as* they eat bread, and call not upon the LORD.

5There were they in great fear: for God *is* in the generation of the righteous.

6Ye have shamed the counsel of the poor, because the LORD *is* his refuge.

New International

3May the LORD cut off all flattering lips
    and every boastful tongue
4that says, "We will triumph with our tongues;
    we own our lips[a]—who is our master?"

5"Because of the oppression of the weak
    and the groaning of the needy,
I will now arise," says the LORD.
    "I will protect them from those who malign
        them."
6And the words of the LORD are flawless,
    like silver refined in a furnace of clay,
    purified seven times.

7O LORD, you will keep us safe
    and protect us from such people forever.
8The wicked freely strut about
    when what is vile is honored among men.

For the director of music. A psalm of David.

13 HOW LONG, O LORD? Will you forget me
    forever?
    How long will you hide your face from me?
2How long must I wrestle with my thoughts
    and every day have sorrow in my heart?
    How long will my enemy triumph over me?

3Look on me and answer, O LORD my God.
    Give light to my eyes, or I will sleep in
        death;
4my enemy will say, "I have overcome him,"
    and my foes will rejoice when I fall.

5But I trust in your unfailing love;
    my heart rejoices in your salvation.
6I will sing to the LORD,
    for he has been good to me.

For the director of music. Of David.

14 THE FOOL[b] says in his heart,
    "There is no God."
They are corrupt, their deeds are vile;
    there is no one who does good.

2The LORD looks down from heaven
    on the sons of men
to see if there are any who understand,
    any who seek God.
3All have turned aside,
    they have together become corrupt;
there is no one who does good,
    not even one.

4Will evildoers never learn—
    those who devour my people as men eat
        bread
    and who do not call on the LORD?
5There they are, overwhelmed with dread,
    for God is present in the company of the
        righteous.
6You evildoers frustrate the plans of the poor,
    but the LORD is their refuge.

---

a 4 Or / our lips are our plowshares   *b 1 The Hebrew words rendered fool in Psalms denote one who is morally deficient.*

Living Bible

3, 4But the Lord will not deal gently with people who act like that; he will destroy those proud liars who say, "We will lie to our hearts' content. Our lips are our own; who can stop us?"

5The Lord replies, "I will arise and defend the oppressed, the poor, the needy. I will rescue them as they have longed for me to do." 6The Lord's promise is sure. He speaks no careless word; all he says is purest truth, like silver seven times refined. 7O Lord, we know that you will forever preserve your own from the reach of evil men, 8although they prowl on every side and vileness is praised throughout the land.

13 HOW LONG will you forget me, Lord? Forever? How long will you look the other way when I am in need? 2How long must I be hiding daily anguish in my heart? How long shall my enemy have the upper hand?

3Answer me, O Lord my God; give me light in my darkness lest I die. 4Don't let my enemies say, "We have conquered him!" Don't let them gloat that I am down.

5But I will always trust in you and in your mercy and shall rejoice in your salvation. 6I will sing to the Lord because he has blessed me so richly.

14 THAT MAN is a fool who says to himself, "There is no God!" Anyone who talks like that is warped and evil and cannot really be a good person at all.

2The Lord looks down from heaven on all mankind to see if there are any who are wise, who want to please God. 3But no, all have strayed away; all are rotten with sin. Not one is good, not one! 4They eat my people like bread and wouldn't think of praying! Don't they really know any better?

5Terror shall grip them, for God is with those who love him. 6He is the refuge of the poor and humble when evildoers are oppressing them. 7Oh, that the time of their

New Revised Standard

3 May the LORD cut off all flattering lips,
  the tongue that makes great boasts,
4 those who say, "With our tongues we will prevail;
  our lips are our own—who is our master?"

5 "Because the poor are despoiled, because the needy groan,
  I will now rise up," says the LORD;
  "I will place them in the safety for which they long."
6 The promises of the LORD are promises that are pure,
  silver refined in a furnace on the ground,
  purified seven times.

7 You, O LORD, will protect us;
  you will guard us from this generation forever.
8 On every side the wicked prowl,
  as vileness is exalted among humankind.

Prayer for Deliverance from Enemies

To the leader. A Psalm of David.

13 HOW LONG, O LORD? Will you forget me forever?
  How long will you hide your face from me?
2 How long must I bear pain[c] in my soul,
  and have sorrow in my heart all day long?
  How long shall my enemy be exalted over me?

3 Consider and answer me, O LORD my God!
  Give light to my eyes, or I will sleep the sleep of death,
4 and my enemy will say, "I have prevailed";
  my foes will rejoice because I am shaken.

5 But I trusted in your steadfast love;
  my heart shall rejoice in your salvation.
6 I will sing to the LORD,
  because he has dealt bountifully with me.

Denunciation of Godlessness

To the leader. Of David.

14 FOOLS SAY in their hearts, "There is no God."
  They are corrupt, they do abominable deeds;
  there is no one who does good.

2 The LORD looks down from heaven on humankind
  to see if there are any who are wise,
  who seek after God.

3 They have all gone astray, they are all alike perverse;
  there is no one who does good,
  no, not one.

4 Have they no knowledge, all the evildoers
  who eat up my people as they eat bread,
  and do not call upon the LORD?

5 There they shall be in great terror,
  for God is with the company of the righteous.
6 You would confound the plans of the poor,
  but the LORD is their refuge.

---

c Syr: Heb *hold counsels*

King James

7Oh that the salvation of Israel *were come* out of Zion! when the LORD bringeth back the captivity of his people, Jacob shall rejoice, *and* Israel shall be glad.

A Psalm of David.

15 LORD, WHO shall abide in thy tabernacle? who shall dwell in thy holy hill?

2He that walketh uprightly, and worketh righteousness, and speaketh the truth in his heart.

3*He that* backbiteth not with his tongue, nor doeth evil to his neighbour, nor taketh up a reproach against his neighbour.

4In whose eyes a vile person is contemned; but he honoureth them that fear the LORD. *He that* sweareth to *his own* hurt, and changeth not.

5*He that* putteth not out his money to usury, nor taketh reward against the innocent. He that doeth these *things* shall never be moved.

Michtam of David.

16 PRESERVE ME, O God: for in thee do I put my trust.

2*O my soul,* thou hast said unto the LORD, Thou *art* my Lord: my goodness *extendeth* not to thee;

3*But* to the saints that *are* in the earth, and *to* the excellent, in whom *is* all my delight.

4Their sorrows shall be multiplied *that* hasten *after* another *god:* their drink offerings of blood will I not offer, nor take up their names into my lips.

5The LORD *is* the portion of mine inheritance and of my cup: thou maintainest my lot.

6The lines are fallen unto me in pleasant *places;* yea, I have a goodly heritage.

7I will bless the LORD, who hath given me counsel: my reins also instruct me in the night seasons.

8I have set the LORD always before me: because *he is* at my right hand, I shall not be moved.

9Therefore my heart is glad, and my glory rejoiceth: my flesh also shall rest in hope.

10For thou wilt not leave my soul in hell; neither wilt thou suffer thine Holy One to see corruption.

11Thou wilt show me the path of life: in thy presence *is* fulness of joy; at thy right hand *there are* pleasures for evermore.

New International

7Oh, that salvation for Israel would come out of Zion!
When the LORD restores the fortunes of his people,
  let Jacob rejoice and Israel be glad!

A psalm of David.

15 LORD, WHO may dwell in your sanctuary?
Who may live on your holy hill?

2He whose walk is blameless
  and who does what is righteous,
who speaks the truth from his heart
3 and has no slander on his tongue,
who does his neighbor no wrong
  and casts no slur on his fellowman,
4who despises a vile man
  but honors those who fear the LORD,
who keeps his oath
  even when it hurts,
5who lends his money without usury
  and does not accept a bribe against the innocent.

He who does these things
  will never be shaken.

A *miktam*[a] of David.

16 KEEP ME safe, O God,
  for in you I take refuge.

2I said to the LORD, "You are my Lord;
  apart from you I have no good thing."
3As for the saints who are in the land,
  they are the glorious ones in whom is all my delight.[b]
4The sorrows of those will increase
  who run after other gods.
I will not pour out their libations of blood
  or take up their names on my lips.

5LORD, you have assigned me my portion and my cup;
  you have made my lot secure.
6The boundary lines have fallen for me in pleasant places;
  surely I have a delightful inheritance.

7I will praise the LORD, who counsels me;
  even at night my heart instructs me.
8I have set the LORD always before me.
Because he is at my right hand,
  I will not be shaken.

9Therefore my heart is glad and my tongue rejoices;
  my body also will rest secure,
10because you will not abandon me to the grave,[c]
  nor will you let your Holy One[d] see decay.
11You have made[e] known to me the path of life;
  you will fill me with joy in your presence,
  with eternal pleasures at your right hand.

a Title: Probably a literary or musical term   b 3 Or *As for the pagan priests who are in the land / and the nobles in whom all delight, I said:*   c 10 Hebrew *Sheol*   d 10 Or *your faithful one*   e 11 Or *You will make*

Living Bible

rescue were already here, that God would come from Zion now to save his people. What gladness when the Lord has rescued Israel!

15 LORD, WHO may go and find refuge and shelter in your tabernacle up on your holy hill? ²Anyone who leads a blameless life and is truly sincere. ³Anyone who refuses to slander others, does not listen to gossip, never harms his neighbor, ⁴speaks out against sin, criticizes those committing it, commends the faithful followers of the Lord, keeps a promise even if it ruins him, ⁵does not crush his debtors with high interest rates, and refuses to testify against the innocent despite the bribes offered him—such a man shall stand firm forever.

16 SAVE ME, O God, because I have come to you for refuge. ²I said to him, "You are my Lord; I have no other help but yours." ³I want the company of the godly men and women in the land; they are the true nobility. ⁴Those choosing other gods shall all be filled with sorrow; I will not offer the sacrifices they do or even speak the names of their gods.

⁵The Lord himself is my inheritance, my prize. He is my food and drink, my highest joy! He guards all that is mine. ⁶He sees that I am given pleasant brooks and meadows as my share!ᶠ What a wonderful inheritance! ⁷I will bless the Lord who counsels me; he gives me wisdom in the night. He tells me what to do.

⁸I am always thinking of the Lord; and because he is so near, I never need to stumble or to fall.

⁹Heart, body, and soul are filled with joy. ¹⁰For you will not leave me among the dead; you will not allow your beloved one to rot in the grave. ¹¹You have let me experience the joys of life and the exquisite pleasures of your own eternal presence.

New Revised Standard

⁷ O that deliverance for Israel would come from Zion!
  When the LORD restores the fortunes of his people,
  Jacob will rejoice; Israel will be glad.

Who Shall Abide in God's Sanctuary?
A Psalm of David.

15 O LORD, who may abide in your tent? Who may dwell on your holy hill?

² Those who walk blamelessly, and do what is right,
  and speak the truth from their heart;
³ who do not slander with their tongue,
  and do no evil to their friends,
  nor take up a reproach against their neighbors;
⁴ in whose eyes the wicked are despised,
  but who honor those who fear the LORD;
  who stand by their oath even to their hurt;
⁵ who do not lend money at interest,
  and do not take a bribe against the innocent.

  Those who do these things shall never be moved.

Song of Trust and Security in God
A Miktam of David.

16 PROTECT ME, O God, for in you I take refuge.
² I say to the LORD, "You are my Lord;
  I have no good apart from you."ᵍ

³ As for the holy ones in the land, they are the noble,
  in whom is all my delight.

⁴ Those who choose another god multiply their sorrows;ʰ
  their drink offerings of blood I will not pour out
  or take their names upon my lips.

⁵ The LORD is my chosen portion and my cup;
  you hold my lot.
⁶ The boundary lines have fallen for me in pleasant places;
  I have a goodly heritage.

⁷ I bless the LORD who gives me counsel;
  in the night also my heart instructs me.
⁸ I keep the LORD always before me;
  because he is at my right hand, I shall not be moved.

⁹ Therefore my heart is glad, and my soul rejoices;
  my body also rests secure.
¹⁰ For you do not give me up to Sheol,
  or let your faithful one see the Pit.

¹¹ You show me the path of life.
  In your presence there is fullness of joy;
  in your right hand are pleasures forevermore.

ᶠ *16:6 He sees that I am given pleasant brooks and meadows as my share,*
literally, "The boundary lines are fallen unto me in pleasant places."

ᵍ Jerome Tg: Meaning of Heb uncertain   ʰ Cn: Meaning of Heb uncertain

King James

New International

A Prayer of David.

17 HEAR THE right, O LORD, attend unto my cry, give ear unto my prayer, *that goeth* not out of feigned lips.

2Let my sentence come forth from thy presence; let thine eyes behold the things that are equal.

3Thou hast proved mine heart; thou hast visited *me* in the night; thou hast tried me, *and* shalt find nothing; I am purposed *that* my mouth shall not transgress.

4Concerning the works of men, by the word of thy lips I have kept *me from* the paths of the destroyer.

5Hold up my goings in thy paths, *that* my footsteps slip not.

6I have called upon thee, for thou wilt hear me, O God: incline thine ear unto me, *and hear* my speech.

7Show thy marvellous lovingkindness, O thou that savest by thy right hand them which put their trust *in thee* from those that rise up *against them.*

8Keep me as the apple of the eye, hide me under the shadow of thy wings,

9From the wicked that oppress me, *from* my deadly enemies, *who* compass me about.

10They are inclosed in their own fat: with their mouth they speak proudly.

11They have now compassed us in our steps: they have set their eyes bowing down to the earth;

12Like as a lion *that* is greedy of his prey, and as it were a young lion lurking in secret places.

13Arise, O LORD, disappoint him, cast him down: deliver my soul from the wicked, *which is* thy sword:

14From men *which are* thy hand, O LORD, from men of the world, *which have* their portion in *this* life, and whose belly thou fillest with thy hid *treasure:* they are full of children, and leave the rest of their *substance* to their babes.

15As for me, I will behold thy face in righteousness: I shall be satisfied, when I awake, with thy likeness.

A prayer of David.

17 HEAR, O LORD, my righteous plea;
　　listen to my cry.
Give ear to my prayer—
　　it does not rise from deceitful lips.
2May my vindication come from you;
　　may your eyes see what is right.

3Though you probe my heart and examine me at
　　night,
　　though you test me, you will find nothing;
　　I have resolved that my mouth will not sin.
4As for the deeds of men—
　　by the word of your lips
I have kept myself
　　from the ways of the violent.
5My steps have held to your paths;
　　my feet have not slipped.

6I call on you, O God, for you will answer me;
　　give ear to me and hear my prayer.
7Show the wonder of your great love,
　　you who save by your right hand
　　those who take refuge in you from their foes.
8Keep me as the apple of your eye;
　　hide me in the shadow of your wings
9from the wicked who assail me,
　　from my mortal enemies who surround me.

10They close up their callous hearts,
　　and their mouths speak with arrogance.
11They have tracked me down, they now surround
　　me,
　　with eyes alert, to throw me to the ground.
12They are like a lion hungry for prey,
　　like a great lion crouching in cover.

13Rise up, O LORD, confront them, bring them
　　down;
　　rescue me from the wicked by your sword.
14O LORD, by your hand save me from such men,
　　from men of this world whose reward is in
　　　this life.

You still the hunger of those you cherish;
　　their sons have plenty,
　　and they store up wealth for their children.
15And I—in righteousness I will see your face;
　　when I awake, I will be satisfied with seeing
　　　your likeness.

To the chief Musician, *A Psalm* of David, the servant of the LORD, who spake unto the LORD the words of this song in the day *that* the LORD delivered him from the hand of all his enemies, and from the hand of Saul: And he said,

18 I WILL love thee, O LORD, my strength.
2The LORD *is* my rock, and my fortress, and my deliverer; my God, my strength, in whom I will trust; my buckler, and the horn of my salvation, *and* my high tower.

3I will call upon the LORD, *who is worthy* to be praised: so shall I be saved from mine enemies.

For the director of music. Of David the servant of the LORD. He sang to the LORD the words of this song when the LORD delivered him from the hand of all his enemies and from the hand of Saul. He said:

18 I LOVE you, O LORD, my strength.

2The LORD is my rock, my fortress and my
　　deliverer;
　　my God is my rock, in whom I take refuge.
He is my shield and the horn[a] of my
　　salvation, my stronghold.
3I call to the LORD, who is worthy of praise,
　　and I am saved from my enemies.

Living Bible

17 I AM pleading for your help, O Lord; for I have been honest and have done what is right, and you must listen to my earnest cry! ²Publicly acquit me, Lord, for you are always fair. ³You have tested me and seen that I am good. You have come even in the night and found nothing amiss and know that I have told the truth. ⁴I have followed your commands and have not gone along with cruel and evil men. ⁵My feet have not slipped from your paths.

⁶Why am I praying like this? Because I know you will answer me, O God! Yes, listen as I pray. ⁷Show me your strong love in wonderful ways, O Savior of all those seeking your help against their foes. ⁸Protect me as you would the pupil of your eye; hide me in the shadow of your wings as you hover over me.

⁹My enemies encircle me with murder in their eyes. ¹⁰They are pitiless and arrogant. Listen to their boasting. ¹¹They close in upon me and are ready to throw me to the ground. ¹²They are like lions eager to tear me apart, like young lions hiding and waiting their chance.

¹³, ¹⁴Lord, arise and stand against them. Push them back! Come and save me from these men of the world whose only concern is earthly gain—these men whom you have filled with your treasures so that their children and grandchildren are rich and prosperous.

¹⁵But as for me, my contentment is not in wealth but in seeing you and knowing all is well between us. And when I awake in heaven, I will be fully satisfied, for I will see you face to face.

This song of David was written at a time when the Lord had delivered him from his many enemies, including Saul.

18 LORD, HOW I love you! For you have done such tremendous things for me.

²The Lord is my fort where I can enter and be safe; no one can follow me in and slay me. He is a rugged mountain where I hide; he is my Savior, a rock where none can reach me, and a tower of safety. He is my shield. He is the strong horn of a mighty fighting bull. ³All I need to do is cry to him—oh, praise the Lord—and I am saved from all my enemies!

New Revised Standard

Prayer for Deliverance from Persecutors
A Prayer of David.

17 HEAR A just cause, O LORD; attend to my cry;
   give ear to my prayer from lips free of deceit.
² From you let my vindication come;
   let your eyes see the right.

³ If you try my heart, if you visit me by night,
   if you test me, you will find no wickedness in me;
   my mouth does not transgress.
⁴ As for what others do, by the word of your lips
   I have avoided the ways of the violent.
⁵ My steps have held fast to your paths;
   my feet have not slipped.

⁶ I call upon you, for you will answer me, O God;
   incline your ear to me, hear my words.
⁷ Wondrously show your steadfast love,
   O savior of those who seek refuge
   from their adversaries at your right hand.

⁸ Guard me as the apple of the eye;
   hide me in the shadow of your wings,
⁹ from the wicked who despoil me,
   my deadly enemies who surround me.
¹⁰ They close their hearts to pity;
   with their mouths they speak arrogantly.
¹¹ They track me down;ᵇ now they surround me;
   they set their eyes to cast me to the ground.
¹² They are like a lion eager to tear,
   like a young lion lurking in ambush.

¹³ Rise up, O LORD, confront them, overthrow them!
   By your sword deliver my life from the wicked,
¹⁴ from mortals—by your hand, O LORD—
   from mortals whose portion in life is in this world.
May their bellies be filled with what you have stored up for them;
   may their children have more than enough;
   may they leave something over to their little ones.

¹⁵ As for me, I shall behold your face in righteousness;
   when I awake I shall be satisfied, beholding your likeness.

Royal Thanksgiving for Victory

To the leader. A Psalm of David the servant of the LORD, who addressed the words of this song to the LORD on the day when the LORD delivered him from the hand of all his enemies, and from the hand of Saul. He said:

18 I LOVE you, O LORD, my strength.
² The LORD is my rock, my fortress, and my deliverer,
   my God, my rock in whom I take refuge,
   my shield, and the horn of my salvation,
   my stronghold.
³ I call upon the LORD, who is worthy to be praised,
   so I shall be saved from my enemies.

ᵇ One Ms Compare Syr: MT *Our steps*

King James

4The sorrows of death compassed me, and the floods of ungodly men made me afraid.

5The sorrows of hell compassed me about: the snares of death prevented me.

6In my distress I called upon the LORD, and cried unto my God: he heard my voice out of his temple, and my cry came before him, *even* into his ears.

7Then the earth shook and trembled; the foundations also of the hills moved and were shaken, because he was wroth.

8There went up a smoke out of his nostrils, and fire out of his mouth devoured: coals were kindled by it.

9He bowed the heavens also, and came down: and darkness *was* under his feet.

10And he rode upon a cherub, and did fly: yea, he did fly upon the wings of the wind.

11He made darkness his secret place; his pavilion round about him *were* dark waters *and* thick clouds of the skies.

12At the brightness *that was* before him his thick clouds passed, hail *stones* and coals of fire.

13The LORD also thundered in the heavens, and the Highest gave his voice; hail *stones* and coals of fire.

14Yea, he sent out his arrows, and scattered them; and he shot out lightnings, and discomfited them.

15Then the channels of waters were seen, and the foundations of the world were discovered at thy rebuke, O LORD, at the blast of the breath of thy nostrils.

16He sent from above, he took me, he drew me out of many waters.

17He delivered me from my strong enemy, and from them which hated me: for they were too strong for me.

18They prevented me in the day of my calamity: but the LORD was my stay.

19He brought me forth also into a large place; he delivered me, because he delighted in me.

20The LORD rewarded me according to my righteousness; according to the cleanness of my hands hath he recompensed me.

21For I have kept the ways of the LORD, and have not wickedly departed from my God.

22For all his judgments *were* before me, and I did not put away his statutes from me.

23I was also upright before him, and I kept myself from mine iniquity.

24Therefore hath the LORD recompensed me according to my righteousness, according to the cleanness of my hands in his eyesight.

25With the merciful thou wilt show thyself merciful; with an upright man thou wilt show thyself upright;

26With the pure thou wilt show thyself pure; and with the froward thou wilt show thyself froward.

New International

4The cords of death entangled me;
    the torrents of destruction overwhelmed me.
5The cords of the grave[a] coiled around me;
    the snares of death confronted me.
6In my distress I called to the LORD;
    I cried to my God for help.
 From his temple he heard my voice;
    my cry came before him, into his ears.
7The earth trembled and quaked,
    and the foundations of the mountains shook;
    they trembled because he was angry.
8Smoke rose from his nostrils;
    consuming fire came from his mouth,
    burning coals blazed out of it.
9He parted the heavens and came down;
    dark clouds were under his feet.
10He mounted the cherubim and flew;
    he soared on the wings of the wind.
11He made darkness his covering, his canopy
        around him—
    the dark rain clouds of the sky.
12Out of the brightness of his presence clouds
        advanced,
    with hailstones and bolts of lightning.
13The LORD thundered from heaven;
    the voice of the Most High resounded.[b]
14He shot his arrows and scattered the enemies,,
    great bolts of lightning and routed them.
15The valleys of the sea were exposed
    and the foundations of the earth laid bare
 at your rebuke, O LORD,
    at the blast of breath from your nostrils.

16He reached down from on high and took hold of
        me;
    he drew me out of deep waters.
17He rescued me from my powerful enemy,
    from my foes, who were too strong for me.
18They confronted me in the day of my disaster,
    but the LORD was my support.
19He brought me out into a spacious place;
    he rescued me because he delighted in me.

20The LORD has dealt with me according to my
        righteousness;
    according to the cleanness of my hands he
        has rewarded me.
21For I have kept the ways of the LORD;
    I have not done evil by turning from my God.
22All his laws are before me;
    I have not turned away from his decrees.
23I have been blameless before him
    and have kept myself from sin.
24The LORD has rewarded me according to my
        righteousness,
    according to the cleanness of my hands in his
        sight.

25To the faithful you show yourself faithful,
    to the blameless you show yourself blameless,
26to the pure you show yourself pure,
    but to the crooked you show yourself shrewd.

---

a 5 Hebrew *Sheol*   b 13 Some Hebrew manuscripts and Septuagint (see also 2 Samuel 22:14); most Hebrew manuscripts *resounded, / amid hailstones and bolts of lightning*

Living Bible

4Death bound me with chains, and the floods of ungodliness mounted a massive attack against me. 5Trapped and helpless, I struggled against the ropes that drew me on to death.

6In my distress I screamed to the Lord for his help. And he heard me from heaven;c my cry reached his ears. 7Then the earth rocked and reeled, and mountains shook and trembled. How they quaked! For he was angry. 8Fierce flames leaped from his mouth, setting fire to the earth;d smoke blew from his nostrils. 9He bent the heavens down and came to my defense;e thick darkness was beneath his feet. 10Mounted on a mighty angel,f he sped swiftly to my aid with wings of wind. 11He enshrouded himself with darkness, veiling his approach with dense clouds dark as murky waters. 12Suddenly the brilliance of his presence broke through the clouds with lightningg and a mighty storm of hail.

13The Lord thundered in the heavens; the God above all gods has spoken—oh, the hailstones; oh, the fire! 14He flashed his fearful arrows of lightning and routed all my enemies. See how they run! 15Then at your command, O Lord, the sea receded from the shore. At the blast of your breath the depths were laid bare.

16He reached down from heaven and took me and drew me out of my great trials. He rescued me from deep waters. 17He delivered me from my strong enemy, from those who hated me—I who was helpless in their hands. 18On the day when I was weakest, they attacked. But the Lord held me steady. 19He led me to a place of safety, for he delights in me.

20The Lord rewarded me for doing right and being pure. 21For I have followed his commands and have not sinned by turning back from following him. 22I kept close watch on all his laws; I did not refuse a single one. 23I did my best to keep them all, holding myself back from doing wrong. 24And so the Lord has paid me with his blessings, for I have done what is right, and I am pure of heart. This he knows, for he watches my every step.

25Lord, how merciful you are to those who are merciful. And you do not punish those who run from evil.h 26You give blessings to the pure but pain to those who leave your paths. 27You deliver the humble but condemn

New Revised Standard

4 The cords of death encompassed me;
   the torrents of perdition assailed me;
5 the cords of Sheol entangled me;
   the snares of death confronted me.

6 In my distress I called upon the LORD;
   to my God I cried for help.
From his temple he heard my voice,
   and my cry to him reached his ears.

7 Then the earth reeled and rocked;
   the foundations also of the mountains trembled
   and quaked, because he was angry.
8 Smoke went up from his nostrils,
   and devouring fire from his mouth;
   glowing coals flamed forth from him.
9 He bowed the heavens, and came down;
   thick darkness was under his feet.
10 He rode on a cherub, and flew;
   he came swiftly upon the wings of the wind.
11 He made darkness his covering around him,
   his canopy thick clouds dark with water.
12 Out of the brightness before him
   there broke through his clouds
   hailstones and coals of fire.
13 The LORD also thundered in the heavens,
   and the Most High uttered his voice.i
14 And he sent out his arrows, and scattered them;
   he flashed forth lightnings, and routed them.
15 Then the channels of the sea were seen,
   and the foundations of the world were laid bare
at your rebuke, O LORD,
   at the blast of the breath of your nostrils.

16 He reached down from on high, he took me;
   he drew me out of mighty waters.
17 He delivered me from my strong enemy,
   and from those who hated me;
   for they were too mighty for me.
18 They confronted me in the day of my calamity;
   but the LORD was my support.
19 He brought me out into a broad place;
   he delivered me, because he delighted in me.

20 The LORD rewarded me according to my righteousness;
   according to the cleanness of my hands he recompensed me.
21 For I have kept the ways of the LORD,
   and have not wickedly departed from my God.
22 For all his ordinances were before me,
   and his statutes I did not put away from me.
23 I was blameless before him,
   and I kept myself from guilt.
24 Therefore the LORD has recompensed me
   according to my righteousness,
   according to the cleanness of my hands in his sight.

25 With the loyal you show yourself loyal;
   with the blameless you show yourself blameless;
26 with the pure you show yourself pure;
   and with the crooked you show yourself perverse.

---

c 18:6 from heaven, literally, "out of his temple." d 18:8 setting fire to the earth, literally, "coals were kindled by it." e 18:9 He bent the heavens down and came to my defense, implied. f 18:10 a mighty angel, literally, "a cherub." g 18:12 lightning, literally, "coals of fire." h 18:25 And you do not punish those who run from evil, literally, "with the upright you show yourself upright."

i Gk See 2 Sam 22.14: Heb adds hailstones and coals of fire

King James

27For thou wilt save the afflicted people; but wilt bring down high looks.

28For thou wilt light my candle: the LORD my God will enlighten my darkness.

29For by thee I have run through a troop; and by my God have I leaped over a wall.

30*As for* God, his way *is* perfect: the word of the LORD is tried: he *is* a buckler to all those that trust in him.

31For who *is* God save the LORD? or who *is* a rock save our God?

32*It is* God that girdeth me with strength, and maketh my way perfect.

33He maketh my feet like hinds' *feet,* and setteth me upon my high places.

34He teacheth my hands to war, so that a bow of steel is broken by mine arms.

35Thou hast also given me the shield of thy salvation: and thy right hand hath holden me up, and thy gentleness hath made me great.

36Thou hast enlarged my steps under me, that my feet did not slip.

37I have pursued mine enemies, and overtaken them: neither did I turn again till they were consumed.

38I have wounded them that they were not able to rise: they are fallen under my feet.

39For thou hast girded me with strength unto the battle: thou hast subdued under me those that rose up against me.

40Thou hast also given me the necks of mine enemies; that I might destroy them that hate me.

41They cried, but *there was* none to save *them: even* unto the LORD, but he answered them not.

42Then did I beat them small as the dust before the wind: I did cast them out as the dirt in the streets.

43Thou hast delivered me from the strivings of the people; *and* thou hast made me the head of the heathen: a people *whom* I have not known shall serve me.

44As soon as they hear of me, they shall obey me: the strangers shall submit themselves unto me.

45The strangers shall fade away, and be afraid out of their close places.

46The LORD liveth; and blessed *be* my rock; and let the God of my salvation be exalted.

47*It is* God that avengeth me, and subdueth the people under me.

48He delivereth me from mine enemies: yea, thou liftest me up above those that rise up against me: thou hast delivered me from the violent man.

49Therefore will I give thanks unto thee, O LORD, among the heathen, and sing praises unto thy name.

50Great deliverance giveth he to his king; and showeth mercy to his anointed, to David, and to his seed for evermore.

New International

27You save the humble
　　but bring low those whose eyes are haughty.

28You, O LORD, keep my lamp burning;
　　my God turns my darkness into light.

29With your help I can advance against a troopa;
　　with my God I can scale a wall.

30As for God, his way is perfect;
　　the word of the LORD is flawless.
　He is a shield
　　for all who take refuge in him.

31For who is God besides the LORD?
　　And who is the Rock except our God?

32It is God who arms me with strength
　　and makes my way perfect.

33He makes my feet like the feet of a deer;
　　he enables me to stand on the heights.

34He trains my hands for battle;
　　my arms can bend a bow of bronze.

35You give me your shield of victory,
　　and your right hand sustains me;
　　you stoop down to make me great.

36You broaden the path beneath me,
　　so that my ankles do not turn.

37I pursued my enemies and overtook them;
　　I did not turn back till they were destroyed.

38I crushed them so that they could not rise;
　　they fell beneath my feet.

39You armed me with strength for battle;
　　you made my adversaries bow at my feet.

40You made my enemies turn their backs in
　　　flight,
　　and I destroyed my foes.

41They cried for help, but there was no one to
　　　save them—
　　to the LORD, but he did not answer.

42I beat them as fine as dust borne on the wind;
　　I poured them out like mud in the streets.

43You have delivered me from the attacks of the
　　　people;
　　you have made me the head of nations;
　　people I did not know are subject to me.

44As soon as they hear me, they obey me;
　　foreigners cringe before me.

45They all lose heart;
　　they come trembling from their strongholds.

46The LORD lives! Praise be to my Rock!
　　Exalted be God my Savior!

47He is the God who avenges me,
　　who subdues nations under me,

48　who saves me from my enemies.
　You exalted me above my foes;
　　from violent men you rescued me.

49Therefore I will praise you among the nations,
　　O LORD;
　　I will sing praises to your name.

50He gives his king great victories;
　　he shows unfailing kindness to his anointed,
　　to David and his descendants forever.

Living Bible

the proud and haughty ones. 28You have turned on my light! The Lord my God has made my darkness turn to light. 29Now in your strength I can scale any wall, attack any troop.

30What a God he is! How perfect in every way! All his promises prove true. He is a shield for everyone who hides behind him. 31For who is God except our Lord? Who but he is as a rock?

32He fills me with strength and protects me wherever I go. 33He gives me the surefootedness of a mountain goat upon the crags. He leads me safely along the top of the cliffs. 34He prepares me for battle and gives me strength to draw an ironb bow!

35You have given me your salvation as my shield. Your right hand, O Lord, supports me; your gentleness has made me great. 36You have made wide steps beneath my feet so that I need never slip. 37I chased my enemies; I caught up with them and did not turn back until all were conquered. 38I pinned them to the ground; all were helpless before me. I placed my feet upon their necks. 39For you have armed me with strong armor for the battle. My enemies quail before me and fall defeated at my feet. 40You made them turn and run; I destroyed all who hated me. 41They shouted for help but no one dared to rescue them; they cried to the Lord, but he refused to answer them. 42So I crushed them fine as dust and cast them to the wind. I threw them away like sweepings from the floor. 43, 44, 45You gave me victory in every battle. The nations came and served me. Even those I didn't know before come now and bow before me. Foreigners who have never seen me submit instantly. They come trembling from their strongholds.

46God is alive! Praise him who is the great rock of protection. 47He is the God who pays back those who harm me and subdues the nations before me.

48He rescues me from my enemies; he holds me safely out of their reach and saves me from these powerful opponents. 49For this, O Lord, I will praise you among the nations. 50Many times you have miraculously rescued me, the king you appointed. You have been loving and kind to me and will be to my descendants.

New Revised Standard

27 For you deliver a humble people,
    but the haughty eyes you bring down.
28 It is you who light my lamp;
    the LORD, my God, lights up my darkness.
29 By you I can crush a troop,
    and by my God I can leap over a wall.
30 This God—his way is perfect;
    the promise of the LORD proves true;
    he is a shield for all who take refuge in
        him.

31 For who is God except the LORD?
    And who is a rock besides our God?—
32 the God who girded me with strength,
    and made my way safe.
33 He made my feet like the feet of a deer,
    and set me secure on the heights.
34 He trains my hands for war,
    so that my arms can bend a bow of bronze.
35 You have given me the shield of your
        salvation,
    and your right hand has supported me;
    your helpc has made me great.
36 You gave me a wide place for my steps under
        me,
    and my feet did not slip.
37 I pursued my enemies and overtook them;
    and did not turn back until they were
        consumed.
38 I struck them down, so that they were not able
        to rise;
    they fell under my feet.
39 For you girded me with strength for the battle;
    you made my assailants sink under me.
40 You made my enemies turn their backs to me,
    and those who hated me I destroyed.
41 They cried for help, but there was no one to
        save them;
    they cried to the LORD, but he did not
        answer them.
42 I beat them fine, like dust before the wind;
    I cast them out like the mire of the streets.

43 You delivered me from strife with the
        peoples;d
    you made me head of the nations;
    people whom I had not known served me.
44 As soon as they heard of me they obeyed me;
    foreigners came cringing to me.
45 Foreigners lost heart,
    and came trembling out of their strongholds.

46 The LORD lives! Blessed be my rock,
    and exalted be the God of my salvation,
47 the God who gave me vengeance
    and subdued peoples under me;
48 who delivered me from my enemies;
    indeed, you exalted me above my
        adversaries;
    you delivered me from the violent.

49 For this I will extol you, O LORD, among the
        nations,
    and sing praises to your name.
50 Great triumphs he gives to his king,
    and shows steadfast love to his anointed,
    to David and his descendants forever.

---

b 18:34 an iron bow, literally, "a bow of bronze."   c Or gentleness   d Gk Tg: Heb people

King James

To the chief Musician, A Psalm of David.

19 THE HEAVENS declare the glory of God; and the firmament showeth his handiwork.

2Day unto day uttereth speech, and night unto night showeth knowledge.

3*There is* no speech nor language, *where* their voice is not heard.

4Their line is gone out through all the earth, and their words to the end of the world. In them hath he set a tabernacle for the sun,

5Which *is* as a bridegroom coming out of his chamber, *and* rejoiceth as a strong man to run a race.

6His going forth *is* from the end of the heaven, and his circuit unto the ends of it: and there is nothing hid from the heat thereof.

7The law of the LORD *is* perfect, converting the soul: the testimony of the LORD *is* sure, making wise the simple.

8The statutes of the LORD *are* right, rejoicing the heart: the commandment of the LORD *is* pure, enlightening the eyes.

9The fear of the LORD *is* clean, enduring for ever: the judgments of the LORD *are* true *and* righteous altogether.

10More to be desired *are they* than gold, yea, than much fine gold: sweeter also than honey and the honeycomb.

11Moreover by them is thy servant warned: *and* in keeping of them *there is* great reward.

12Who can understand *his* errors? cleanse thou me from secret *faults*.

13Keep back thy servant also from presumptuous *sins;* let them not have dominion over me: then shall I be upright, and I shall be innocent from the great transgression.

14Let the words of my mouth, and the meditation of my heart, be acceptable in thy sight, O LORD, my strength, and my redeemer.

To the chief Musician, A Psalm of David.

20 THE LORD hear thee in the day of trouble; the name of the God of Jacob defend thee;

2Send thee help from the sanctuary, and strengthen thee out of Zion;

3Remember all thy offerings, and accept thy burnt sacrifice; Selah.

4Grant thee according to thine own heart, and fulfil all thy counsel.

New International

For the director of music. A psalm of David.

19 THE HEAVENS declare the glory of God; the skies proclaim the work of his hands.

2Day after day they pour forth speech; night after night they display knowledge.

3There is no speech or language where their voice is not heard.[a]

4Their voice[b] goes out into all the earth, their words to the ends of the world.

In the heavens he has pitched a tent for the sun,
5 which is like a bridegroom coming forth from his pavilion,
like a champion rejoicing to run his course.

6It rises at one end of the heavens and makes its circuit to the other; nothing is hidden from its heat.

7The law of the LORD is perfect, reviving the soul.
The statutes of the LORD are trustworthy, making wise the simple.

8The precepts of the LORD are right, giving joy to the heart.
The commands of the LORD are radiant, giving light to the eyes.

9The fear of the LORD is pure, enduring forever.
The ordinances of the LORD are sure and altogether righteous.

10They are more precious than gold, than much pure gold;
they are sweeter than honey, than honey from the comb.

11By them is your servant warned; in keeping them there is great reward.

12Who can discern his errors? Forgive my hidden faults.

13Keep your servant also from willful sins; may they not rule over me.
Then will I be blameless, innocent of great transgression.

14May the words of my mouth and the meditation of my heart
be pleasing in your sight,
O LORD, my Rock and my Redeemer.

For the director of music. A psalm of David.

20 MAY THE LORD answer you when you are in distress;
may the name of the God of Jacob protect you.

2May he send you help from the sanctuary and grant you support from Zion.

3May he remember all your sacrifices and accept your burnt offerings.   *Selah*

4May he give you the desire of your heart and make all your plans succeed.

---

a 3 Or *They have no speech, there are no words; / no sound is heard from them*   b 4 Septuagint, Jerome and Syriac; Hebrew *line*

Living Bible

19 THE HEAVENS are telling the glory of God;
they are a marvelous display of his craftsmanship. ²Day and night they keep on telling about God. ³,⁴Without a sound or word, silent in the skies, their message reaches out to all the world. The sun lives in the heavens where God placed it ⁵and moves out across the skies as radiant as a bridegroomᶜ going to his wedding,ᵈ or as joyous as an athlete looking forward to a race! ⁶The sun crosses the heavens from end to end, and nothing can hide from its heat.

⁷,⁸God's laws are perfect. They protect us, make us wise, and give us joy and light. ⁹God's laws are pure, eternal, just.ᵉ ¹⁰They are more desirable than gold. They are sweeter than honey dripping from a honeycomb. ¹¹For they warn us away from harm and give success to those who obey them.

¹²But how can I ever know what sins are lurking in my heart? Cleanse me from these hidden faults. ¹³And keep me from deliberate wrongs; help me to stop doing them. Only then can I be free of guilt and innocent of some great crime.

¹⁴May my spoken words and unspoken thoughts be pleasing even to you, O Lord my Rock and my Redeemer.

20 IN YOUR day of trouble, may the Lord be with you! May the God of Jacob keep you from all harm. ²May he send you aid from his sanctuary in Zion. ³May he remember with pleasure the gifts you have given him, your sacrifices and burnt offerings. ⁴May he grant you your heart's desire and fulfill all your plans.

New Revised Standard

God's Glory in Creation and the Law
To the leader. A Psalm of David.

19 THE HEAVENS are telling the glory of
God;
and the firmamentᶠ proclaims his
handiwork.
² Day to day pours forth speech,
and night to night declares knowledge.
³ There is no speech, nor are there words;
their voice is not heard;
⁴ yet their voiceᵍ goes out through all the earth,
and their words to the end of the world.

In the heavensʰ he has set a tent for the sun,
⁵ which comes out like a bridegroom from his
wedding canopy,
and like a strong man runs its course with
joy.
⁶ Its rising is from the end of the heavens,
and its circuit to the end of them;
and nothing is hid from its heat.

⁷ The law of the LORD is perfect,
reviving the soul;
the decrees of the LORD are sure,
making wise the simple;
⁸ the precepts of the LORD are right,
rejoicing the heart;
the commandment of the LORD is clear,
enlightening the eyes;
⁹ the fear of the LORD is pure,
enduring forever;
the ordinances of the LORD are true
and righteous altogether.
¹⁰ More to be desired are they than gold,
even much fine gold;
sweeter also than honey,
and drippings of the honeycomb.

¹¹ Moreover by them is your servant warned;
in keeping them there is great reward.
¹² But who can detect their errors?
Clear me from hidden faults.
¹³ Keep back your servant also from the
insolent;ⁱ
do not let them have dominion over me.
Then I shall be blameless,
and innocent of great transgression.

¹⁴ Let the words of my mouth and the meditation
of my heart
be acceptable to you,
O LORD, my rock and my redeemer.

Prayer for Victory
To the leader. A Psalm of David.

20 THE LORD answer you in the day of
trouble!
The name of the God of Jacob protect you!
² May he send you help from the sanctuary,
and give you support from Zion.
³ May he remember all your offerings,
and regard with favor your burnt sacrifices.
Selah

⁴ May he grant you your heart's desire,
and fulfill all your plans.

ᶜ *19:5 as radiant as a bridegroom,* literally, "is like a bridegroom."
ᵈ *19:5 going to his wedding,* implied. Literally, "going forth from his chamber." ᵉ *19:9 God's laws are pure, eternal, just,* or, "The rules governing the worship of the Lord are pure and need never be changed."

ᶠ Or *dome* ᵍ Gk Jerome Compare Syr: Heb *line* ʰ Heb *In them* ⁱ Or *from proud thoughts*

King James

5We will rejoice in thy salvation, and in the name of our God we will set up *our* banners: the LORD fulfil all thy petitions.

6Now know I that the LORD saveth his anointed; he will hear him from his holy heaven with the saving strength of his right hand.

7Some *trust* in chariots, and some in horses: but we will remember the name of the LORD our God.

8They are brought down and fallen: but we are risen, and stand upright.

9Save, LORD: let the king hear us when we call.

To the chief Musician, A Psalm of David.

21 THE KING shall joy in thy strength, O LORD; and in thy salvation how greatly shall he rejoice!

2Thou hast given him his heart's desire, and hast not withholden the request of his lips. Selah.

3For thou preventest him with the blessings of goodness: thou settest a crown of pure gold on his head.

4He asked life of thee, *and* thou gavest *it* him, *even* length of days for ever and ever.

5His glory *is* great in thy salvation: honour and majesty hast thou laid upon him.

6For thou hast made him most blessed for ever: thou hast made him exceeding glad with thy countenance.

7For the king trusteth in the LORD, and through the mercy of the most High he shall not be moved.

8Thine hand shall find out all thine enemies: thy right hand shall find out those that hate thee.

9Thou shalt make them as a fiery oven in the time of thine anger: the LORD shall swallow them up in his wrath, and the fire shall devour them.

10Their fruit shalt thou destroy from the earth, and their seed from among the children of men.

11For they intended evil against thee: they imagined a mischievous device, *which* they are not able *to perform*.

12Therefore shalt thou make them turn their back, *when* thou shalt make ready *thine arrows* upon thy strings against the face of them.

13Be thou exalted, LORD, in thine own strength: *so* will we sing and praise thy power.

To the chief Musician upon Aijeleth Shahar,
A Psalm of David.

22 MY GOD, my God, why hast thou forsaken me? *why art thou so* far from helping me, *and from* the words of my roaring?

2O my God, I cry in the daytime, but thou hearest not; and in the night season, and am not silent.

New International

5We will shout for joy when you are victorious
and will lift up our banners in the name of
our God.

May the LORD grant all your requests.

6Now I know that the LORD saves his anointed;
he answers him from his holy heaven
with the saving power of his right hand.
7Some trust in chariots and some in horses,
but we trust in the name of the LORD our
God.
8They are brought to their knees and fall,
but we rise up and stand firm.

9O LORD, save the king!
Answer[a] us when we call!

For the director of music. A psalm of David.

21 O LORD, the king rejoices in your strength.
How great is his joy in the victories you
give!
2You have granted him the desire of his heart
and have not withheld the request of his lips.
Selah

3You welcomed him with rich blessings
and placed a crown of pure gold on his head.
4He asked you for life, and you gave it to him—
length of days, for ever and ever.
5Through the victories you gave, his glory is
great;
you have bestowed on him splendor and
majesty.
6Surely you have granted him eternal blessings
and made him glad with the joy of your
presence.
7For the king trusts in the LORD;
through the unfailing love of the Most High
he will not be shaken.

8Your hand will lay hold on all your enemies;
your right hand will seize your foes.
9At the time of your appearing
you will make them like a fiery furnace.
In his wrath the LORD will swallow them up,
and his fire will consume them.
10You will destroy their descendants from the
earth,
their posterity from mankind.
11Though they plot evil against you
and devise wicked schemes, they cannot
succeed;
12for you will make them turn their backs
when you aim at them with drawn bow.

13Be exalted, O LORD, in your strength;
we will sing and praise your might.

For the director of music. To the tune of, "The Doe of the
Morning." A psalm of David.

22 MY GOD, my God, why have you forsaken
me?
Why are you so far from saving me,
so far from the words of my groaning?
2O my God, I cry out by day, but you do not
answer,
by night, and am not silent.

Living Bible

5May there be shouts of joy when we hear the news of your victory, flags flying with praise to God for all that he has done for you. May he answer all your prayers!

6"God save the king"—I know he does! He hears me from highest heaven and sends great victories. 7Some nations boast of armies and of weaponry, but our boast is in the Lord our God. 8Those nations will collapse and perish; we will arise to stand firm and sure!

9Give victory to our king, O Lord; oh, hear our prayer.

21 HOW THE king rejoices in your strength, O Lord! How he exults in your salvation. 2For you have given him his heart's desire, everything he asks you for!

3You welcomed him to the throne with success and prosperity. You set a royal crown of solid gold upon his head. 4He asked for a long, good life, and you have granted his request; the days of his life stretch on and on forever. 5You have given him fame and honor. You have clothed him with splendor and majesty. 6You have endowed him with eternal happiness. You have given him the unquenchable joy of your presence. 7And because the king trusts in the Lord, he will never stumble, never fall; for he depends upon the steadfast love of the God who is above all gods.

8Your hand, O Lord, will find your enemies, all who hate you. 9, 10When you appear, they will be destroyed in the fierce fire of your presence. The Lord will destroy them and their children. 11For these men plot against you, Lord, but they cannot possibly succeed. 12They will turn and flee when they see your arrows aimed straight at them.

13Accept our praise, O Lord, for all your glorious power. We will write songs to celebrate your mighty acts!

22 MY GOD, my God, why have you forsaken me? Why do you refuse to help me or even to listen to my groans? 2Day and night I keep on weeping,

New Revised Standard

5 May we shout for joy over your victory,
    and in the name of our God set up our
    banners.
May the LORD fulfill all your petitions.

6 Now I know that the LORD will help his
    anointed;
  he will answer him from his holy heaven
    with mighty victories by his right hand.
7 Some take pride in chariots, and some in
    horses,
  but our pride is in the name of the LORD
    our God.
8 They will collapse and fall,
    but we shall rise and stand upright.

9 Give victory to the king, O LORD;
    answer us when we call.b

Thanksgiving for Victory

To the leader. A Psalm of David.

21 IN YOUR strength the king rejoices,
    O LORD,
  and in your help how greatly he exults!
2 You have given him his heart's desire,
    and have not withheld the request of his
    lips.   *Selah*
3 For you meet him with rich blessings;
    you set a crown of fine gold on his head.
4 He asked you for life; you gave it to him—
    length of days forever and ever.
5 His glory is great through your help;
    splendor and majesty you bestow on him.
6 You bestow on him blessings forever;
    you make him glad with the joy of your
    presence.
7 For the king trusts in the LORD,
    and through the steadfast love of the Most
    High he shall not be moved.

8 Your hand will find out all your enemies;
    your right hand will find out those who hate
    you.
9 You will make them like a fiery furnace
    when you appear.
  The LORD will swallow them up in his wrath,
    and fire will consume them.
10 You will destroy their offspring from the
    earth,
    and their children from among humankind.
11 If they plan evil against you,
    if they devise mischief, they will not
    succeed.
12 For you will put them to flight;
    you will aim at their faces with your bows.

13 Be exalted, O LORD, in your strength!
    We will sing and praise your power.

Plea for Deliverance from Suffering and Hostility

To the leader: according to The Deer of the Dawn. A Psalm
of David.

22 MY GOD, my God, why have you forsaken
    me?
  Why are you so far from helping me, from
    the words of my groaning?
2 O my God, I cry by day, but you do not
    answer;
    and by night, but find no rest.

b Gk: Heb *give victory, O LORD; let the King answer us when we call*

King James

3But thou *art* holy, *O thou* that inhabitest the praises of Israel.

4Our fathers trusted in thee: they trusted, and thou didst deliver them.

5They cried unto thee, and were delivered: they trusted in thee, and were not confounded.

6But I *am* a worm, and no man; a reproach of men, and despised of the people.

7All they that see me laugh me to scorn: they shoot out the lip, they shake the head, *saying,*

8He trusted on the LORD *that* he would deliver him: let him deliver him, seeing he delighted in him.

9But thou *art* he that took me out of the womb: thou didst make me hope *when I was* upon my mother's breasts.

10I was cast upon thee from the womb: thou *art* my God from my mother's belly.

11Be not far from me; for trouble *is* near; for *there is* none to help.

12Many bulls have compassed me: strong *bulls* of Bashan have beset me round.

13They gaped upon me *with* their mouths, *as* a ravening and a roaring lion.

14I am poured out like water, and all my bones are out of joint: my heart is like wax; it is melted in the midst of my bowels.

15My strength is dried up like a potsherd; and my tongue cleaveth to my jaws; and thou hast brought me into the dust of death.

16For dogs have compassed me: the assembly of the wicked have inclosed me: they pierced my hands and my feet.

17I may tell all my bones: they look *and* stare upon me.

18They part my garments among them, and cast lots upon my vesture.

19But be not thou far from me, O LORD: O my strength, haste thee to help me.

20Deliver my soul from the sword; my darling from the power of the dog.

21Save me from the lion's mouth: for thou hast heard me from the horns of the unicorns.

22I will declare thy name unto my brethren: in the midst of the congregation will I praise thee.

23Ye that fear the LORD, praise him; all ye the seed of Jacob, glorify him; and fear him, all ye the seed of Israel.

24For he hath not despised nor abhorred the affliction of the afflicted; neither hath he hid his face from him; but when he cried unto him, he heard.

New International

3Yet you are enthroned as the Holy One; you are the praise of Israel.[a]

4In you our fathers put their trust; they trusted and you delivered them.

5They cried to you and were saved; in you they trusted and were not disappointed.

6But I am a worm and not a man, scorned by men and despised by the people.

7All who see me mock me; they hurl insults, shaking their heads:

8"He trusts in the LORD; let the LORD rescue him. Let him deliver him, since he delights in him."

9Yet you brought me out of the womb; you made me trust in you even at my mother's breast.

10From birth I was cast upon you; from my mother's womb you have been my God.

11Do not be far from me, for trouble is near and there is no one to help.

12Many bulls surround me; strong bulls of Bashan encircle me.

13Roaring lions tearing their prey open their mouths wide against me.

14I am poured out like water, and all my bones are out of joint. My heart has turned to wax; it has melted away within me.

15My strength is dried up like a potsherd, and my tongue sticks to the roof of my mouth; you lay me[b] in the dust of death.

16Dogs have surrounded me; a band of evil men has encircled me, they have pierced[c] my hands and my feet.

17I can count all my bones; people stare and gloat over me.

18They divide my garments among them and cast lots for my clothing.

19But you, O LORD, be not far off; O my Strength, come quickly to help me.

20Deliver my life from the sword, my precious life from the power of the dogs.

21Rescue me from the mouth of the lions; save[d] me from the horns of the wild oxen.

22I will declare your name to my brothers; in the congregation I will praise you.

23You who fear the LORD, praise him! All you descendants of Jacob, honor him! Revere him, all you descendants of Israel!

24For he has not despised or disdained the suffering of the afflicted one; he has not hidden his face from him but has listened to his cry for help.

a 3 Or *Yet you are holy, / enthroned on the praises of Israel*   b 15 Or / *I am laid*   c 16 Some Hebrew manuscripts, Septuagint and Syriac; most Hebrew manuscripts / *like the lion,*   d 21 Or / *you have heard*

Living Bible

crying for your help, but there is no reply— 3, 4for *you are holy*.

The praises of our fathers surrounded your throne; they trusted you and you delivered them. 5You heard their cries for help and saved them; they were never disappointed when they sought your aid.

6But I am a worm, not a man, scorned and despised by my own people and by all mankind. 7Everyone who sees me mocks and sneers and shrugs. 8"Is this the one who rolled his burden on the Lord?" they laugh. "Is this the one who claims the Lord delights in him? We'll believe it when we see God rescue him!"

9, 10, 11Lord, how you have helped me before!e You took me safely from my mother's womb and brought me through the years of infancy. I have depended upon you since birth; you have always been my God. Don't leave me now, for trouble is near and no one else can possibly help.

12I am surrounded by fearsome enemies, strong as the giant bulls from Bashan. 13They come at me with open jaws, like roaring lions attacking their prey. 14My strength has drained away like water, and all my bones are out of joint. My heart melts like wax; 15my strength has dried up like sun-baked clay; my tongue sticks to my mouth, for you have laid me in the dust of death. 16The enemy, this gang of evil men, circles me like a pack of dogs; they have pierced my hands and feet. 17I can count every bone in my body. See these men of evil gloat and stare; 18they divide my clothes among themselves by a toss of the dice.

19O Lord, don't stay away. O God my Strength, hurry to my aid. 20Rescue me from death; spare my precious life from all these evil men.f 21Save me from these lions' jaws and from the horns of these wild oxen. Yes, God will answer me and rescue me.

22I will praise you to all my brothers; I will stand up before the congregation and testify of the wonderful things you have done. 23"Praise the Lord, each one of you who fears him," I will say. "Each of youg must fear and reverence his name. Let all Israel sing his praises, 24for he has not despised my cries of deep despair; he has not turned and walked away. When I cried to him, he heard and came."

New Revised Standard

3   Yet you are holy,
        enthroned on the praises of Israel.
4   In you our ancestors trusted;
        they trusted, and you delivered them.
5   To you they cried, and were saved;
        in you they trusted, and were not put to
            shame.

6   But I am a worm, and not human;
        scorned by others, and despised by the
            people.
7   All who see me mock at me;
        they make mouths at me, they shake their
            heads;
8   "Commit your cause to the LORD; let him
            deliver—
        let him rescue the one in whom he
            delights!"

9   Yet it was you who took me from the womb;
        you kept me safe on my mother's breast.
10 On you I was cast from my birth,
        and since my mother bore me you have
            been my God.
11 Do not be far from me,
        for trouble is near
        and there is no one to help.

12 Many bulls encircle me,
        strong bulls of Bashan surround me;
13 they open wide their mouths at me,
        like a ravening and roaring lion.

14 I am poured out like water,
        and all my bones are out of joint;
    my heart is like wax;
        it is melted within my breast;
15 my mouthh is dried up like a potsherd,
        and my tongue sticks to my jaws;
        you lay me in the dust of death.

16 For dogs are all around me;
        a company of evildoers encircles me.
    My hands and feet have shriveled;i
17 I can count all my bones.
    They stare and gloat over me;
18 they divide my clothes among themselves,
        and for my clothing they cast lots.

19 But you, O LORD, do not be far away!
        O my help, come quickly to my aid!
20 Deliver my soul from the sword,
        my lifej from the power of the dog!
21 Save me from the mouth of the lion!

    From the horns of the wild oxen you have
            rescuedk me.
22 I will tell of your name to my brothers and
            sisters;l
        in the midst of the congregation I will
            praise you:
23 You who fear the LORD, praise him!
        All you offspring of Jacob, glorify him;
        stand in awe of him, all you offspring of
            Israel!
24 For he did not despise or abhor
        the affliction of the afflicted;
    he did not hide his face from me,m
        but heard when In cried to him.

---

e 22:9-11 *Lord, how you have helped me before*, implied.   f 22:20 *Rescue me from death; spare my precious life from all these evil men*, literally, "Deliver my soul from the sword, my only one from the power of the dog!"
g 22:23 *Each of you*, literally, "all you sons of Jacob."

h Cn: Heb *strength*   i Meaning of Heb uncertain   j Heb *my only one*
k Heb *answered*   l Or *kindred*   m Heb *him*   n Heb *he*

King James

25My praise *shall be* of thee in the great congregation: I will pay my vows before them that fear him.

26The meek shall eat and be satisfied: they shall praise the LORD that seek him: your heart shall live for ever.

27All the ends of the world shall remember and turn unto the LORD: and all the kindreds of the nations shall worship before thee.

28For the kingdom *is* the LORD's: and he *is* the governor among the nations.

29All *they that be* fat upon earth shall eat and worship: all they that go down to the dust shall bow before him: and none can keep alive his own soul.

30A seed shall serve him; it shall be accounted to the Lord for a generation.

31They shall come, and shall declare his righteousness unto a people that shall be born, that he hath done *this*.

A Psalm of David.

23 THE LORD *is* my shepherd; I shall not want. 2He maketh me to lie down in green pastures: he leadeth me beside the still waters.

3He restoreth my soul: he leadeth me in the paths of righteousness for his name's sake.

4Yea, though I walk through the valley of the shadow of death, I will fear no evil: for thou *art* with me; thy rod and thy staff they comfort me.

5Thou preparest a table before me in the presence of mine enemies: thou anointest my head with oil; my cup runneth over.

6Surely goodness and mercy shall follow me all the days of my life: and I will dwell in the house of the LORD for ever.

A Psalm of David.

24 THE EARTH *is* the LORD's, and the fulness thereof; the world, and they that dwell therein. 2For he hath founded it upon the seas, and established it upon the floods.

3Who shall ascend into the hill of the LORD? or who shall stand in his holy place?

New International

25From you comes the theme of my praise in the great assembly; before those who fear you[a] will I fulfill my vows.

26The poor will eat and be satisfied; they who seek the LORD will praise him— may your hearts live forever!

27All the ends of the earth will remember and turn to the LORD, and all the families of the nations will bow down before him,

28for dominion belongs to the LORD and he rules over the nations.

29All the rich of the earth will feast and worship; all who go down to the dust will kneel before him— those who cannot keep themselves alive.

30Posterity will serve him; future generations will be told about the Lord.

31They will proclaim his righteousness to a people yet unborn— for he has done it.

A psalm of David.

23 THE LORD is my shepherd, I shall not be in want.
2 He makes me lie down in green pastures, he leads me beside quiet waters,
3 he restores my soul.
He guides me in paths of righteousness for his name's sake.
4Even though I walk through the valley of the shadow of death,[b] I will fear no evil, for you are with me; your rod and your staff, they comfort me.

5You prepare a table before me in the presence of my enemies.
You anoint my head with oil; my cup overflows.
6Surely goodness and love will follow me all the days of my life, and I will dwell in the house of the LORD forever.

Of David. A psalm.

24 THE EARTH is the LORD's, and everything in it,
the world, and all who live in it;
2for he founded it upon the seas and established it upon the waters.

3Who may ascend the hill of the LORD? Who may stand in his holy place?

---

a 25 Hebrew *him*   b 4 Or *through the darkest valley*

Living Bible

25Yes, I will stand and praise you[c] before all the people. I will publicly fulfill my vows in the presence of all who reverence your name.

26The poor[d] shall eat and be satisfied; all who seek the Lord shall find him and shall praise his name. Their hearts shall rejoice with everlasting joy. 27The whole earth shall see it and return to the Lord; the people of every nation shall worship him.

28For the Lord is King and rules the nations. 29Both proud and humble together, all who are mortal—born to die—shall worship him. 30Our children too shall serve him, for they shall hear from us about the wonders of the Lord; 31generations yet unborn shall hear of all the miracles he did for us.

23 BECAUSE THE Lord is my Shepherd, I have everything I need!

2, 3He lets me rest in the meadow grass and leads me beside the quiet streams. He gives me new strength. He helps me do what honors him the most.

4Even when walking through the dark valley of death I will not be afraid, for you are close beside me, guarding, guiding all the way.[e]

5You provide delicious food for me in the presence of my enemies. You have welcomed me as your guest;[f] blessings overflow!

6Your goodness and unfailing kindness shall be with me all of my life, and afterwards I will live with you forever in your home.

24 THE EARTH belongs to God! Everything in all the world is his! 2He is the one who pushed the oceans back to let dry land appear.[g]

3Who may climb the mountain of the Lord and enter where he lives? Who may stand before the Lord? 4Only

New Revised Standard

25 From you comes my praise in the great
        congregation;
    my vows I will pay before those who fear
        him.
26 The poor[h] shall eat and be satisfied;
    those who seek him shall praise the LORD.
    May your hearts live forever!
27 All the ends of the earth shall remember
        and turn to the LORD;
    and all the families of the nations
        shall worship before him.[i]
28 For dominion belongs to the LORD,
    and he rules over the nations.

29 To him,[j] indeed, shall all who sleep in[k] the
        earth bow down;
    before him shall bow all who go down to
        the dust,
    and I shall live for him.[l]
30 Posterity will serve him;
    future generations will be told about the
        Lord,
31 and[m] proclaim his deliverance to a people yet
        unborn,
    saying that he has done it.

The Divine Shepherd

A Psalm of David.

23 THE LORD is my shepherd, I shall not
        want.
2   He makes me lie down in green pastures;
    he leads me beside still waters;[n]
3   he restores my soul.[o]
    He leads me in right paths[p]
        for his name's sake.

4 Even though I walk through the darkest
        valley,[q]
    I fear no evil;
    for you are with me;
    your rod and your staff—
        they comfort me.

5 You prepare a table before me
        in the presence of my enemies;
    you anoint my head with oil;
        my cup overflows.
6 Surely[r] goodness and mercy[s] shall follow me
        all the days of my life,
    and I shall dwell in the house of the LORD
        my whole life long.[t]

Entrance into the Temple

Of David. A Psalm.

24 THE EARTH is the LORD's and all that is in
        it,
    the world, and those who live in it;
2 for he has founded it on the seas,
    and established it on the rivers.

3 Who shall ascend the hill of the LORD?
    And who shall stand in his holy place?

---

c 22:25 *praise you,* literally, "praise from you."   d 22:26 *The poor,* literally, "the afflicted."   e 23:4 *for you are close beside me, guarding, guiding all the way,* literally, "Your rod and your staff comfort me."   f 23:5 *You have welcomed me as your guest,* literally, "You have anointed my head with oil, my cup runs over."   g 24:2 *He is the one who pushed the oceans back to let dry land appear,* literally, "He has founded it upon the seas."

h Or *afflicted*   i Gk Syr Jerome: Heb *you*   j Cn: Heb *They have eaten and*   k Cn: Heb *all the fat ones*   l Compare Gk Syr Vg: Heb *and he who cannot keep himself alive*   m Compare Gk: Heb *it will be told about the Lord to the generation,* 31*they will come and*   n Heb *waters of rest*   o Or *life*   p Or *paths of righteousness*   q Or *the valley of the shadow of death*   r Or *Only*   s Or *kindness*   t Heb *for length of days*

King James

4He that hath clean hands, and a pure heart; who hath not lifted up his soul unto vanity, nor sworn deceitfully. 5He shall receive the blessing from the LORD, and righteousness from the God of his salvation. 6This *is* the generation of them that seek him, that seek thy face, O Jacob. Selah.

7Lift up your heads, O ye gates; and be ye lift up, ye everlasting doors; and the King of glory shall come in. 8Who *is* this King of glory? The LORD strong and mighty, the LORD mighty in battle. 9Lift up your heads, O ye gates; even lift *them* up, ye everlasting doors; and the King of glory shall come in. 10Who *is* this King of glory? The LORD of hosts, he *is* the King of glory. Selah.

A Psalm of David.

25 UNTO THEE, O LORD, do I lift up my soul. 2O my God, I trust in thee: let me not be ashamed, let not mine enemies triumph over me. 3Yea, let none that wait on thee be ashamed: let them be ashamed which transgress without cause. 4Show me thy ways, O LORD; teach me thy paths. 5Lead me in thy truth, and teach me: for thou *art* the God of my salvation; on thee do I wait all the day. 6Remember, O LORD, thy tender mercies and thy lovingkindnesses; for they *have been* ever of old. 7Remember not the sins of my youth, nor my transgressions: according to thy mercy remember thou me for thy goodness' sake, O LORD. 8Good and upright *is* the LORD: therefore will he teach sinners in the way. 9The meek will he guide in judgment: and the meek will he teach his way. 10All the paths of the LORD *are* mercy and truth unto such as keep his covenant and his testimonies. 11For thy name's sake, O LORD, pardon mine iniquity; for it *is* great. 12What man *is* he that feareth the LORD? him shall he teach in the way *that* he shall choose. 13His soul shall dwell at ease; and his seed shall inherit the earth. 14The secret of the LORD *is* with them that fear him; and he will show them his covenant.

New International

4He who has clean hands and a pure heart,
　who does not lift up his soul to an idol
　or swear by what is false.[a]
5He will receive blessing from the LORD
　and vindication from God his Savior.
6Such is the generation of those who seek him,
　who seek your face, O God of Jacob.[b]　*Selah*

7Lift up your heads, O you gates;
　be lifted up, you ancient doors,
　that the King of glory may come in.
8Who is this King of glory?
　The LORD strong and mighty,
　the LORD mighty in battle.
9Lift up your heads, O you gates;
　lift them up, you ancient doors,
　that the King of glory may come in.
10Who is he, this King of glory?
　The LORD Almighty—
　he is the King of glory.　　　　　*Selah*

Of David.

25[c] TO YOU, O LORD, I lift up my soul;
　2　in you I trust, O my God.
Do not let me be put to shame,
　nor let my enemies triumph over me.
3No one whose hope is in you
　will ever be put to shame,
but they will be put to shame
　who are treacherous without excuse.

4Show me your ways, O LORD,
　teach me your paths;
5guide me in your truth and teach me,
　for you are God my Savior,
　and my hope is in you all day long.
6Remember, O LORD, your great mercy and
　　　love,
　for they are from of old.
7Remember not the sins of my youth
　and my rebellious ways;
according to your love remember me,
　for you are good, O LORD.

8Good and upright is the LORD;
　therefore he instructs sinners in his ways.
9He guides the humble in what is right
　and teaches them his way.
10All the ways of the LORD are loving and faithful
　for those who keep the demands of his
　　　covenant.
11For the sake of your name, O LORD,
　forgive my iniquity, though it is great.
12Who, then, is the man that fears the LORD?
　He will instruct him in the way chosen for
　　　him.
13He will spend his days in prosperity,
　and his descendants will inherit the land.
14The LORD confides in those who fear him;
　he makes his covenant known to them.

a 4 Or *swear falsely*　b 6 Two Hebrew manuscripts and Syriac (see also Septuagint); most Hebrew manuscripts *face, Jacob*　c This psalm is an acrostic poem, the verses of which begin with the successive letters of the Hebrew alphabet.

Living Bible

those with pure hands and hearts, who do not practice dishonesty and lying. 5They will receive God's own goodness[d] as their blessing from him, planted in their lives by God himself, their Savior. 6These are the ones who are allowed to stand before the Lord and worship the God of Jacob.

7Open up, O ancient gates, and let the King of Glory in. 8Who is this King of Glory? The Lord, strong and mighty, invincible in battle. 9Yes, open wide the gates and let the King of Glory in.

10Who is this King of Glory? The Commander of all of heaven's armies!

25 TO YOU, O Lord, I pray. 2Don't fail me, Lord, for I am trusting you. Don't let my enemies succeed. Don't give them victory over me. 3None of those who have faith in God will ever be disgraced for trusting him. But all who harm the innocent shall be defeated.

4Show me the path where I should go, O Lord; point out the right road for me to walk. 5Lead me; teach me; for you are the God who gives me salvation. I have no hope except in you. 6, 7Overlook my youthful sins, O Lord! Look at me instead through eyes of mercy and forgiveness, through eyes of everlasting love and kindness.

8The Lord is good and glad to teach the proper path to all who go astray; 9he will teach the ways that are right and best to those who humbly turn to him. 10And when we obey him, every path he guides us on is fragrant with his lovingkindness and his truth.

11But Lord, my sins! How many they are. Oh, pardon them for the honor of your name.

12Where is the man who fears the Lord? God will teach him how to choose the best.

13He shall live within God's circle of blessing, and his children shall inherit the earth.

14Friendship with God is reserved for those who reverence him. With them alone he shares the secrets of his promises.

New Revised Standard

4 Those who have clean hands and pure hearts,
  who do not lift up their souls to what is
    false,
  and do not swear deceitfully.
5 They will receive blessing from the LORD,
  and vindication from the God of their
    salvation.
6 Such is the company of those who seek him,
  who seek the face of the God of Jacob.[e]
  Selah

7 Lift up your heads, O gates!
  and be lifted up, O ancient doors!
  that the King of glory may come in.
8 Who is the King of glory?
  The LORD, strong and mighty,
  the LORD, mighty in battle.
9 Lift up your heads, O gates!
  and be lifted up, O ancient doors!
  that the King of glory may come in.
10 Who is this King of glory?
  The LORD of hosts,
  he is the King of glory. *Selah*

Prayer for Guidance and for Deliverance
Of David.

25 TO YOU, O LORD, I lift up my soul.
2 O my God, in you I trust;
  do not let me be put to shame;
  do not let my enemies exult over me.
3 Do not let those who wait for you be put to
    shame;
  let them be ashamed who are wantonly
    treacherous.

4 Make me to know your ways, O LORD;
  teach me your paths.
5 Lead me in your truth, and teach me,
  for you are the God of my salvation;
  for you I wait all day long.

6 Be mindful of your mercy, O LORD, and of
    your steadfast love,
  for they have been from of old.
7 Do not remember the sins of my youth or my
    transgressions;
  according to your steadfast love remember
    me,
  for your goodness' sake, O LORD!

8 Good and upright is the LORD;
  therefore he instructs sinners in the way.
9 He leads the humble in what is right,
  and teaches the humble his way.
10 All the paths of the LORD are steadfast love
    and faithfulness,
  for those who keep his covenant and his
    decrees.

11 For your name's sake, O LORD,
  pardon my guilt, for it is great.
12 Who are they that fear the LORD?
  He will teach them the way that they should
    choose.

13 They will abide in prosperity,
  and their children shall possess the land.
14 The friendship of the LORD is for those who
    fear him,
  and he makes his covenant known to them.

---

[d] 24:5 *God's own goodness,* literally, "righteousness," right standing with God.

[e] Gk Syr: Heb *your face, O Jacob*

King James

15Mine eyes *are* ever toward the LORD; for he shall pluck my feet out of the net.

16Turn thee unto me, and have mercy upon me; for I *am* desolate and afflicted.

17The troubles of my heart are enlarged: *O* bring thou me out of my distresses.

18Look upon mine affliction and my pain; and forgive all my sins.

19Consider mine enemies; for they are many; and they hate me with cruel hatred.

20O keep my soul, and deliver me: let me not be ashamed; for I put my trust in thee.

21Let integrity and uprightness preserve me; for I wait on thee.

22Redeem Israel, O God, out of all his troubles.

A Psalm of David.

26 JUDGE ME, O LORD; for I have walked in mine integrity: I have trusted also in the LORD; *therefore* I shall not slide.

2Examine me, O LORD, and prove me; try my reins and my heart.

3For thy lovingkindness *is* before mine eyes: and I have walked in thy truth.

4I have not sat with vain persons, neither will I go in with dissemblers.

5I have hated the congregation of evildoers; and will not sit with the wicked.

6I will wash mine hands in innocency: so will I compass thine altar, O LORD:

7That I may publish with the voice of thanksgiving, and tell of all thy wondrous works.

8LORD, I have loved the habitation of thy house, and the place where thine honour dwelleth.

9Gather not my soul with sinners, nor my life with bloody men:

10In whose hands *is* mischief, and their right hand is full of bribes.

11But as for me, I will walk in mine integrity: redeem me, and be merciful unto me.

12My foot standeth in an even place: in the congregations will I bless the LORD.

A Psalm of David.

27 THE LORD *is* my light and my salvation; whom shall I fear? the LORD *is* the strength of my life; of whom shall I be afraid?

2When the wicked, *even* mine enemies and my foes, came upon me to eat up my flesh, they stumbled and fell.

New International

15My eyes are ever on the LORD,
    for only he will release my feet from the
    snare.

16Turn to me and be gracious to me,
    for I am lonely and afflicted.

17The troubles of my heart have multiplied;
    free me from my anguish.

18Look upon my affliction and my distress
    and take away all my sins.

19See how my enemies have increased
    and how fiercely they hate me!

20Guard my life and rescue me;
    let me not be put to shame,
    for I take refuge in you.

21May integrity and uprightness protect me,
    because my hope is in you.

22Redeem Israel, O God,
    from all their troubles!

Of David.

26 VINDICATE ME, O LORD,
    for I have led a blameless life;
I have trusted in the LORD
    without wavering.

2Test me, O LORD, and try me,
    examine my heart and my mind;

3for your love is ever before me,
    and I walk continually in your truth.

4I do not sit with deceitful men,
    nor do I consort with hypocrites;

5I abhor the assembly of evildoers
    and refuse to sit with the wicked.

6I wash my hands in innocence,
    and go about your altar, O LORD,

7proclaiming aloud your praise
    and telling of all your wonderful deeds.

8I love the house where you live, O LORD,
    the place where your glory dwells.

9Do not take away my soul along with sinners,
    my life with bloodthirsty men,

10in whose hands are wicked schemes,
    whose right hands are full of bribes.

11But I lead a blameless life;
    redeem me and be merciful to me.

12My feet stand on level ground;
    in the great assembly I will praise the LORD.

Of David.

27 THE LORD is my light and my salvation—
    whom shall I fear?
The LORD is the stronghold of my life—
    of whom shall I be afraid?

2When evil men advance against me
    to devour my flesh,a
when my enemies and my foes attack me,
    they will stumble and fall.

---

a 2 Or *to slander me*

Living Bible

¹⁵My eyes are ever looking to the Lord for help, for he alone can rescue me. ¹⁶Come, Lord, and show me your mercy, for I am helpless, overwhelmed, in deep distress; ¹⁷my problems go from bad to worse. Oh, save me from them all! ¹⁸See my sorrows; feel my pain; forgive my sins. ¹⁹See how many enemies I have and how viciously they hate me! ²⁰Save me from them! Deliver my life from their power! Oh, let it never be said that I trusted you in vain!

²¹Assign me Godliness and Integrity as my bodyguards, for I expect you to protect me ²²and to ransom Israel from all her troubles.

26 DISMISS ALL the charges against me, Lord, for I have tried to keep your laws and have trusted you without wavering. ²Cross-examine me, O Lord, and see that this is so; test my motives and affections too. ³For I have taken your lovingkindness and your truth as my ideals. ⁴I do not have fellowship with tricky, two-faced men; they are false and hypocritical. ⁵I hate the sinners' hangouts and refuse to enter them. ⁶I wash my hands to prove my innocence and come before your altar, ⁷singing a song of thanksgiving and telling about your miracles.

⁸Lord, I love your home, this shrine where the brilliant, dazzling splendor of your presence lives.

^{9, 10}Don't treat me as a common sinner or murderer who plots against the innocent and demands bribes.

¹¹No, I am not like that, O Lord; I try to walk a straight and narrow path of doing what is right; therefore in mercy save me.

¹²I publicly praise the Lord for keeping me from slipping and falling.

27 THE LORD is my light and my salvation; he protects me from danger—whom shall I fear? ²When evil men come to destroy me, they will stumble and fall! ³Yes, though a mighty army marches against

New Revised Standard

15 My eyes are ever toward the LORD,
    for he will pluck my feet out of the net.

16 Turn to me and be gracious to me,
    for I am lonely and afflicted.
17 Relieve the troubles of my heart,
    and bring me^b out of my distress.
18 Consider my affliction and my trouble,
    and forgive all my sins.

19 Consider how many are my foes,
    and with what violent hatred they hate me.
20 O guard my life, and deliver me;
    do not let me be put to shame, for I take
        refuge in you.
21 May integrity and uprightness preserve me,
    for I wait for you.

22 Redeem Israel, O God,
    out of all its troubles.

Plea for Justice and Declaration of Righteousness
Of David.

26 VINDICATE ME, O LORD,
    for I have walked in my integrity,
    and I have trusted in the LORD without
        wavering.
2 Prove me, O LORD, and try me;
    test my heart and mind.
3 For your steadfast love is before my eyes,
    and I walk in faithfulness to you.^c

4 I do not sit with the worthless,
    nor do I consort with hypocrites;
5 I hate the company of evildoers,
    and will not sit with the wicked.

6 I wash my hands in innocence,
    and go around your altar, O LORD,
7 singing aloud a song of thanksgiving,
    and telling all your wondrous deeds.

8 O LORD, I love the house in which you dwell,
    and the place where your glory abides.
9 Do not sweep me away with sinners,
    nor my life with the bloodthirsty,
10 those in whose hands are evil devices,
    and whose right hands are full of bribes.

11 But as for me, I walk in my integrity;
    redeem me, and be gracious to me.
12 My foot stands on level ground;
    in the great congregation I will bless the
        LORD.

Triumphant Song of Confidence
Of David.

27 THE LORD is my light and my salvation;
    whom shall I fear?
    The LORD is the stronghold^d of my life;
    of whom shall I be afraid?

2 When evildoers assail me
    to devour my flesh—
    my adversaries and foes—
    they shall stumble and fall.

^b Or *The troubles of my heart are enlarged; bring me*   ^c Or *in your faithfulness*
^d Or *refuge*

King James

3Though an host should encamp against me, my heart shall not fear: though war should rise against me, in this *will* I *be* confident.

4One *thing* have I desired of the LORD, that will I seek after; that I may dwell in the house of the LORD all the days of my life, to behold the beauty of the LORD, and to inquire in his temple.

5For in the time of trouble he shall hide me in his pavilion: in the secret of his tabernacle shall he hide me; he shall set me up upon a rock.

6And now shall mine head be lifted up above mine enemies round about me: therefore will I offer in his tabernacle sacrifices of joy; I will sing, yea, I will sing praises unto the LORD.

7Hear, O LORD, *when* I cry with my voice: have mercy also upon me, and answer me.

8*When thou saidst,* Seek ye my face; my heart said unto thee, Thy face, LORD, will I seek.

9Hide not thy face *far* from me; put not thy servant away in anger: thou hast been my help; leave me not, neither forsake me, O God of my salvation.

10When my father and my mother forsake me, then the LORD will take me up.

11Teach me thy way, O LORD, and lead me in a plain path, because of mine enemies.

12Deliver me not over unto the will of mine enemies: for false witnesses are risen up against me, and such as breathe out cruelty.

13*I had fainted,* unless I had believed to see the goodness of the LORD in the land of the living.

14Wait on the LORD: be of good courage, and he shall strengthen thine heart: wait, I say, on the LORD.

New International

3Though an army besiege me,
 my heart will not fear;
though war break out against me,
 even then will I be confident.

4One thing I ask of the LORD,
 this is what I seek:
that I may dwell in the house of the LORD
 all the days of my life,
to gaze upon the beauty of the LORD
 and to seek him in his temple.

5For in the day of trouble
 he will keep me safe in his dwelling;
he will hide me in the shelter of his tabernacle
 and set me high upon a rock.

6Then my head will be exalted
 above the enemies who surround me;
at his tabernacle will I sacrifice with shouts of joy;
 I will sing and make music to the LORD.

7Hear my voice when I call, O LORD;
 be merciful to me and answer me.

8My heart says of you, "Seek his[a] face!"
 Your face, LORD, I will seek.

9Do not hide your face from me,
 do not turn your servant away in anger;
 you have been my helper.
Do not reject me or forsake me,
 O God my Savior.

10Though my father and mother forsake me,
 the LORD will receive me.

11Teach me your way, O LORD;
 lead me in a straight path
 because of my oppressors.

12Do not turn me over to the desire of my foes,
 for false witnesses rise up against me,
 breathing out violence.

13I am still confident of this:
 I will see the goodness of the LORD
 in the land of the living.

14Wait for the LORD;
 be strong and take heart
 and wait for the LORD.

A Psalm of David.

28 UNTO THEE will I cry, O LORD my rock; be not silent to me: lest, *if* thou be silent to me, I become like them that go down into the pit.

2Hear the voice of my supplications, when I cry unto thee, when I lift up my hands toward thy holy oracle.

3Draw me not away with the wicked, and with the workers of iniquity, which speak peace to their neighbours, but mischief *is* in their hearts.

Of David.

28 TO YOU I call, O LORD my Rock;
 do not turn a deaf ear to me.
For if you remain silent,
 I will be like those who have gone down to the pit.

2Hear my cry for mercy
 as I call to you for help,
as I lift up my hands
 toward your Most Holy Place.

3Do not drag me away with the wicked,
 with those who do evil,
who speak cordially with their neighbors
 but harbor malice in their hearts.

a 8 Or *To you, O my heart, he has said,* "Seek my

Living Bible

me, my heart shall know no fear! I am confident that God will save me.

⁴The one thing I want from God, the thing I seek most of all, is the privilege of meditating in his Temple, living in his presence every day of my life, delighting in his incomparable perfections and glory. ⁵There I'll be when troubles come. He will hide me. He will set me on a high rock ⁶out of reach of all my enemies. Then I will bring him sacrifices and sing his praises with much joy.

⁷Listen to my pleading, Lord! Be merciful and send the help I need.

⁸My heart has heard you say, "Come and talk with me, O my people." And my heart responds, "Lord, I am coming."

⁹Oh, do not hide yourself when I am trying to find you. Do not angrily reject your servant. You have been my help in all my trials before; don't leave me now. Don't forsake me, O God of my salvation. ¹⁰For if my father and mother should abandon me, you would welcome and comfort me.

¹¹Tell me what to do, O Lord, and make it plain because I am surrounded by waiting enemies. ¹²Don't let them get me, Lord! Don't let me fall into their hands! For they accuse me of things I never did, and all the while are plotting cruelty. ¹³I am expecting the Lord to rescue me again, so that once again I will see his goodness to me here in the land of the living.

¹⁴Don't be impatient. Wait for the Lord, and he will come and save you! Be brave, stouthearted and courageous. Yes, wait and he will help you.

28 I PLEAD with you to help me, Lord, for you are my Rock of safety. If you refuse to answer me, I might as well give up and die. ²Lord, I lift my hands to heaven[b] and implore your help. Oh, listen to my cry.

³Don't punish me with all the wicked ones who speak so sweetly to their neighbors while planning to murder them. ⁴Give them the punishment they so richly deserve!

New Revised Standard

³ Though an army encamp against me,
  my heart shall not fear;
though war rise up against me,
  yet I will be confident.

⁴ One thing I asked of the Lord,
  that will I seek after:
to live in the house of the Lord
  all the days of my life,
to behold the beauty of the Lord,
  and to inquire in his temple.

⁵ For he will hide me in his shelter
  in the day of trouble;
he will conceal me under the cover of his tent;
  he will set me high on a rock.

⁶ Now my head is lifted up
  above my enemies all around me,
and I will offer in his tent
  sacrifices with shouts of joy;
I will sing and make melody to the Lord.

⁷ Hear, O Lord, when I cry aloud,
  be gracious to me and answer me!
⁸ "Come," my heart says, "seek his face!"
  Your face, Lord, do I seek.
⁹   Do not hide your face from me.

Do not turn your servant away in anger,
  you who have been my help.
Do not cast me off, do not forsake me,
  O God of my salvation!
¹⁰ If my father and mother forsake me,
  the Lord will take me up.

¹¹ Teach me your way, O Lord,
  and lead me on a level path
  because of my enemies.
¹² Do not give me up to the will of
    my adversaries,
  for false witnesses have risen against me,
  and they are breathing out violence.

¹³ I believe that I shall see the goodness of the
    Lord
  in the land of the living.
¹⁴ Wait for the Lord;
  be strong, and let your heart take courage;
  wait for the Lord!

Prayer for Help and Thanksgiving for It
Of David.

28 TO YOU, O Lord, I call;
  my rock, do not refuse to hear me,
for if you are silent to me,
  I shall be like those who go down to the
    Pit.
² Hear the voice of my supplication,
  as I cry to you for help,
as I lift up my hands
  toward your most holy sanctuary.[c]

³ Do not drag me away with the wicked,
  with those who are workers of evil,
who speak peace with their neighbors,
  while mischief is in their hearts.

---

[b] 28:2 *to heaven*, literally, "Your innermost shrine," i.e., the Holy of Holies within the Tabernacle.

[c] Heb *your innermost sanctuary*

King James

4Give them according to their deeds, and according to the wickedness of their endeavours: give them after the work of their hands; render to them their desert.

5Because they regard not the works of the LORD, nor the operation of his hands, he shall destroy them, and not build them up.

6Blessed *be* the LORD, because he hath heard the voice of my supplications.

7The LORD *is* my strength and my shield; my heart trusted in him, and I am helped: therefore my heart greatly rejoiceth; and with my song will I praise him.

8The LORD *is* their strength, and he *is* the saving strength of his anointed.

9Save thy people, and bless thine inheritance: feed them also, and lift them up for ever.

A Psalm of David.

29 GIVE UNTO the LORD, O ye mighty, give unto the LORD glory and strength.

2Give unto the LORD the glory due unto his name; worship the LORD in the beauty of holiness.

3The voice of the LORD *is* upon the waters: the God of glory thundereth: the LORD *is* upon many waters.

4The voice of the LORD *is* powerful; the voice of the LORD *is* full of majesty.

5The voice of the LORD breaketh the cedars; yea, the LORD breaketh the cedars of Lebanon.

6He maketh them also to skip like a calf; Lebanon and Sirion like a young unicorn.

7The voice of the LORD divideth the flames of fire.

8The voice of the LORD shaketh the wilderness; the LORD shaketh the wilderness of Kadesh.

9The voice of the LORD maketh the hinds to calve, and discovereth the forests: and in his temple doth every one speak of *his* glory.

10The LORD sitteth upon the flood; yea, the LORD sitteth King for ever.

11The LORD will give strength unto his people; the LORD will bless his people with peace.

A Psalm *and* Song *at* the dedication of the house of David.

30 I WILL extol thee, O LORD; for thou hast lifted me up, and hast not made my foes to rejoice over me.

2O LORD my God, I cried unto thee, and thou hast healed me.

3O LORD, thou hast brought up my soul from the grave: thou hast kept me alive, that I should not go down to the pit.

New International

4Repay them for their deeds
    and for their evil work;
repay them for what their hands have done
    and bring back upon them what they deserve.
5Since they show no regard for the works of the
    LORD
    and what his hands have done,
he will tear them down
    and never build them up again.

6Praise be to the LORD,
    for he has heard my cry for mercy.
7The LORD is my strength and my shield;
    my heart trusts in him, and I am helped.
My heart leaps for joy
    and I will give thanks to him in song.

8The LORD is the strength of his people,
    a fortress of salvation for his anointed one.
9Save your people and bless your inheritance;
    be their shepherd and carry them forever.

A psalm of David.

29 ASCRIBE TO the LORD, O mighty ones,
    ascribe to the LORD glory and strength.
2Ascribe to the LORD the glory due his name;
    worship the LORD in the splendor of his[a]
        holiness.

3The voice of the LORD is over the waters;
    the God of glory thunders,
    the LORD thunders over the mighty waters.
4The voice of the LORD is powerful;
    the voice of the LORD is majestic.
5The voice of the LORD breaks the cedars;
    the LORD breaks in pieces the cedars of
        Lebanon.
6He makes Lebanon skip like a calf,
    Sirion[b] like a young wild ox.
7The voice of the LORD strikes
    with flashes of lightning.
8The voice of the LORD shakes the desert;
    the LORD shakes the Desert of Kadesh.
9The voice of the LORD twists the oaks[c]
    and strips the forests bare.
And in his temple all cry, "Glory!"

10The LORD sits[d] enthroned over the flood;
    the LORD is enthroned as King forever.
11The LORD gives strength to his people;
    the LORD blesses his people with peace.

A psalm. A song. For the dedication of the temple.[e] Of David.

30 I WILL exalt you, O LORD,
    for you lifted me out of the depths
    and did not let my enemies gloat over me.
2O LORD my God, I called to you for help
    and you healed me.
3O LORD, you brought me up from the grave[f];
    you spared me from going down into the pit.

---

[a] 2 Or LORD *with the splendor of*   [b] 6 That is, Mount Hermon   [c] 9 Or LORD *makes the deer give birth*   [d] 10 Or *sat*   [e] Title: Or *palace*   [f] 3 Hebrew *Sheol*

Living Bible

Measure it out to them in proportion to their wickedness; pay them back for all their evil deeds. 5They care nothing for God or what he has done or what he has made; therefore God will dismantle them like old buildings, never to be rebuilt again.

6Oh, praise the Lord, for he has listened to my pleadings! 7He is my strength, my shield from every danger. I trusted in him, and he helped me. Joy rises in my heart until I burst out in songs of praise to him. 8The Lord protects his people and gives victory to his anointed king.

9Defend your people, Lord; defend and bless your chosen ones. Lead them like a shepherd and carry them forever in your arms.

29 PRAISE THE Lord, you angels of his; praise his glory and his strength. 2Praise him for his majestic glory, the glory of his name. Come before him clothed in sacred garments.

3The voice of the Lord echoes from the clouds. The God of glory thunders through the skies. 4So powerful is his voice; so full of majesty. 5, 6It breaks down the cedars. It splits the giant trees of Lebanon. It shakes Mount Lebanon and Mount Sirion. They leap and skip before him like young calves! 7The voice of the Lord thunders through the lightning. 8It resounds through the deserts and shakes the wilderness of Kadesh. 9The voice of the Lord spins and topples the mighty oaks.g It strips the forests bare. They whirl and sway beneath the blast. But in his temple all are praising, "Glory, glory to the Lord."

10At the Flood, the Lord showed his control of all creation. Now he continues to unveil his power. 11He will give his people strength. He will bless them with peace.

30 I WILL praise you, Lord, for you have saved me from my enemies. You refuse to let them triumph over me. 2O Lord my God, I pleaded with you, and you gave me my health again. 3You brought me back from the brink of the grave, from death itself, and here I am alive!

New Revised Standard

4 Repay them according to their work,
    and according to the evil of their deeds;
repay them according to the work of their
    hands;
    render them their due reward.
5 Because they do not regard the works of the
    LORD,
    or the work of his hands,
he will break them down and build them up
    no more.

6 Blessed be the LORD,
    for he has heard the sound of my pleadings.
7 The LORD is my strength and my shield;
    in him my heart trusts;
so I am helped, and my heart exults,
    and with my song I give thanks to him.

8 The LORD is the strength of his people;
    he is the saving refuge of his anointed.
9 O save your people, and bless your heritage;
    be their shepherd, and carry them forever.

The Voice of God in a Great Storm

A Psalm of David.

29 ASCRIBE TO the LORD, O heavenly
    beings,h
ascribe to the LORD glory and strength.
2 Ascribe to the LORD the glory of his name;
    worship the LORD in holy splendor.

3 The voice of the LORD is over the waters;
    the God of glory thunders,
    the LORD, over mighty waters.
4 The voice of the LORD is powerful;
    the voice of the LORD is full of majesty.

5 The voice of the LORD breaks the cedars;
    the LORD breaks the cedars of Lebanon.
6 He makes Lebanon skip like a calf,
    and Sirion like a young wild ox.

7 The voice of the LORD flashes forth flames of
    fire.
8 The voice of the LORD shakes the wilderness;
    the LORD shakes the wilderness of Kadesh.

9 The voice of the LORD causes the oaks to
    whirl,i
    and strips the forest bare;
    and in his temple all say, "Glory!"

10 The LORD sits enthroned over the flood;
    the LORD sits enthroned as king forever.
11 May the LORD give strength to his people!
    May the LORD bless his people with peace!

Thanksgiving for Recovery from Grave Illness

A Psalm. A Song at the dedication of the temple. Of David.

30 I WILL extol you, O LORD, for you have
    drawn me up,
    and did not let my foes rejoice over me.
2 O LORD my God, I cried to you for help,
    and you have healed me.
3 O LORD, you brought up my soul from Sheol,
    restored me to life from among those gone
        down to the Pit.j

---

g 29:9 spins and topples the mighty oaks, or, "makes the hinds to calve."

h Heb sons of gods   i Or causes the deer to calve   j Or that I should not go down to the Pit

King James

4Sing unto the LORD, O ye saints of his, and give thanks at the remembrance of his holiness.

5For his anger *endureth but* a moment; in his favour *is* life: weeping may endure for a night, but joy *cometh* in the morning.

6And in my prosperity I said, I shall never be moved.

7LORD, by thy favour thou hast made my mountain to stand strong: thou didst hide thy face, *and* I was troubled.

8I cried to thee, O LORD; and unto the LORD I made supplication.

9What profit *is there* in my blood, when I go down to the pit? Shall the dust praise thee? shall it declare thy truth?

10Hear, O LORD, and have mercy upon me: LORD, be thou my helper.

11Thou hast turned for me my mourning into dancing: thou hast put off my sackcloth, and girded me with gladness;

12To the end that *my* glory may sing praise to thee, and not be silent. O LORD my God, I will give thanks unto thee for ever.

To the chief Musician, A Psalm of David.

31 IN THEE, O LORD, do I put my trust; let me never be ashamed: deliver me in thy righteousness.

2Bow down thine ear to me; deliver me speedily: be thou my strong rock, for an house of defence to save me.

3For thou *art* my rock and my fortress; therefore for thy name's sake lead me, and guide me.

4Pull me out of the net that they have laid privily for me: for thou *art* my strength.

5Into thine hand I commit my spirit: thou hast redeemed me, O LORD God of truth.

6I have hated them that regard lying vanities: but I trust in the LORD.

7I will be glad and rejoice in thy mercy: for thou hast considered my trouble; thou hast known my soul in adversities;

8And hast not shut me up into the hand of the enemy: thou hast set my feet in a large room.

New International

4Sing to the LORD, you saints of his;
  praise his holy name.

5For his anger lasts only a moment,
  but his favor lasts a lifetime;
weeping may remain for a night,
  but rejoicing comes in the morning.

6When I felt secure, I said,
  "I will never be shaken."

7O LORD, when you favored me,
  you made my mountaina stand firm;
but when you hid your face,
  I was dismayed.

8To you, O LORD, I called;
  to the Lord I cried for mercy:

9"What gain is there in my destruction,b
  in my going down into the pit?
Will the dust praise you?
  Will it proclaim your faithfulness?

10Hear, O LORD, and be merciful to me;
  O LORD, be my help."

11You turned my wailing into dancing;
  you removed my sackcloth and clothed me
    with joy,

12that my heart may sing to you and not be silent.
  O LORD my God, I will give you thanks
    forever.

For the director of music. A psalm of David.

31 IN YOU, O LORD, I have taken refuge;
  let me never be put to shame;
  deliver me in your righteousness.

2Turn your ear to me,
  come quickly to my rescue;
  be my rock of refuge,
  a strong fortress to save me.

3Since you are my rock and my fortress,
  for the sake of your name lead and guide me.

4Free me from the trap that is set for me,
  for you are my refuge.

5Into your hands I commit my spirit;
  redeem me, O LORD, the God of truth.

6I hate those who cling to worthless idols;
  I trust in the LORD.

7I will be glad and rejoice in your love,
  for you saw my affliction
  and knew the anguish of my soul.

8You have not handed me over to the enemy
  but have set my feet in a spacious place.

a 7 Or *hill country*   b 9 Or *there if I am silenced*

Living Bible

4Oh, sing to him, you saints of his; give thanks to his holy name. 5His anger lasts a moment; his favor lasts for life! Weeping may go on all night, but in the morning there is joy.

6, 7In my prosperity I said, "This is forever; nothing can stop me now! The Lord has shown his favor. He has made me steady as a mountain." Then, Lord, you turned your face away from me and cut off your river of blessings.c Suddenly my courage was gone; I was terrified and panic-stricken. 8I cried to you, O Lord; oh, how I pled: 9"What will you gain, O Lord, from killing me? How can I praise you then to all my friends? How can my dust in the grave speak out and tell the world about your faithfulness? 10Hear me, Lord; oh, have pity and help me." 11Then he turned my sorrow into joy! He took away my clothes of mourning and clothed me with joy 12so that I might sing glad praises to the Lord instead of lying in silence in the grave. O Lord my God, I will keep on thanking you forever!

31 LORD, I trust in you alone. Don't let my enemies defeat me. Rescue me because you are the God who always does what is right. 2Answer quickly when I cry to you; bend low and hear my whispered plea.d Be for me a great Rock of safety from my foes. 3Yes, you are my Rock and my fortress; honor your name by leading me out of this peril. 4Pull me from the trap my enemies have set for me. For you alone are strong enough.e 5, 6Into your hand I commit my spirit.

You have rescued me, O God who keeps his promises. I worship only you; how you hate all those who worship idols, those imitation gods. 7I am radiant with joy because of your mercy, for you have listened to my troubles and have seen the crisis in my soul. 8You have not handed me over to my enemy, but have given me open ground in which to maneuver.

New Revised Standard

4 Sing praises to the LORD, O you his faithful
    ones,
    and give thanks to his holy name.
5 For his anger is but for a moment;
    his favor is for a lifetime.
Weeping may linger for the night,
    but joy comes with the morning.

6 As for me, I said in my prosperity,
    "I shall never be moved."
7 By your favor, O LORD,
    you had established me as a strong
        mountain;
you hid your face;
    I was dismayed.

8 To you, O LORD, I cried,
    and to the LORD I made supplication:
9 "What profit is there in my death,
    if I go down to the Pit?
Will the dust praise you?
    Will it tell of your faithfulness?
10 Hear, O LORD, and be gracious to me!
    O LORD, be my helper!"

11 You have turned my mourning into dancing;
    you have taken off my sackcloth
    and clothed me with joy,
12 so that my soulf may praise you and not be
        silent.
    O LORD my God, I will give thanks to you
        forever.

Prayer and Praise for Deliverance from Enemies
To the leader. A Psalm of David.

31 IN YOU, O LORD, I seek refuge;
    do not let me ever be put to shame;
    in your righteousness deliver me.
2 Incline your ear to me;
    rescue me speedily.
Be a rock of refuge for me,
    a strong fortress to save me.

3 You are indeed my rock and my fortress;
    for your name's sake lead me and guide
        me,
4 take me out of the net that is hidden for me,
    for you are my refuge.
5 Into your hand I commit my spirit;
    you have redeemed me, O LORD, faithful
        God.

6 You hateg those who pay regard to worthless
        idols,
    but I trust in the LORD.
7 I will exult and rejoice in your steadfast love,
    because you have seen my affliction;
    you have taken heed of my adversities,
8 and have not delivered me into the hand of the
        enemy;
    you have set my feet in a broad place.

---

c 30:6, 7 cut off your river of blessings, implied.   d 31:2 hear my whispered plea, implied.   e 31:4 For you alone are strong enough, literally, "For you are my refuge."

f Heb that glory   g One Heb Ms Gk Syr Jerome: MT I hate

King James

9Have mercy upon me, O LORD, for I am in trouble: mine eye is consumed with grief, *yea,* my soul and my belly.

10For my life is spent with grief, and my years with sighing: my strength faileth because of mine iniquity, and my bones are consumed.

11I was a reproach among all mine enemies, but especially among my neighbours, and a fear to mine acquaintance: they that did see me without fled from me.

12I am forgotten as a dead man out of mind: I am like a broken vessel.

13For I have heard the slander of many: fear *was* on every side: while they took counsel together against me, they devised to take away my life.

14But I trusted in thee, O LORD: I said, Thou *art* my God.

15My times *are* in thy hand: deliver me from the hand of mine enemies, and from them that persecute me.

16Make thy face to shine upon thy servant: save me for thy mercies' sake.

17Let me not be ashamed, O LORD; for I have called upon thee: let the wicked be ashamed, *and* let them be silent in the grave.

18Let the lying lips be put to silence; which speak grievous things proudly and contemptuously against the righteous.

19*Oh* how great *is* thy goodness, which thou hast laid up for them that fear thee; *which* thou hast wrought for them that trust in thee before the sons of men!

20Thou shalt hide them in the secret of thy presence from the pride of man: thou shalt keep them secretly in a pavilion from the strife of tongues.

21Blessed *be* the LORD: for he hath shown me his marvellous kindness in a strong city.

22For I said in my haste, I am cut off from before thine eyes: nevertheless thou heardest the voice of my supplications when I cried unto thee.

23O love the LORD, all ye his saints: *for* the LORD preserveth the faithful, and plentifully rewardeth the proud doer.

24Be of good courage, and he shall strengthen your heart, all ye that hope in the LORD.

A Psalm of David, Maschil.

32 BLESSED *IS* he *whose* transgression *is* forgiven, *whose* sin *is* covered.

New International

9Be merciful to me, O LORD, for I am in distress;
my eyes grow weak with sorrow,
my soul and my body with grief.

10My life is consumed by anguish
and my years by groaning;
my strength fails because of my affliction,[a]
and my bones grow weak.

11Because of all my enemies,
I am the utter contempt of my neighbors;
I am a dread to my friends—
those who see me on the street flee from me.

12I am forgotten by them as though I were dead;
I have become like broken pottery.

13For I hear the slander of many;
there is terror on every side;
they conspire against me
and plot to take my life.

14But I trust in you, O LORD;
I say, "You are my God."

15My times are in your hands;
deliver me from my enemies
and from those who pursue me.

16Let your face shine on your servant;
save me in your unfailing love.

17Let me not be put to shame, O LORD,
for I have cried out to you;
but let the wicked be put to shame
and lie silent in the grave.[b]

18Let their lying lips be silenced,
for with pride and contempt
they speak arrogantly against the righteous.

19How great is your goodness,
which you have stored up for those who fear you,
which you bestow in the sight of men
on those who take refuge in you.

20In the shelter of your presence you hide them
from the intrigues of men;
in your dwelling you keep them safe
from accusing tongues.

21Praise be to the LORD,
for he showed his wonderful love to me
when I was in a besieged city.

22In my alarm I said,
"I am cut off from your sight!"
Yet you heard my cry for mercy
when I called to you for help.

23Love the LORD, all his saints!
The LORD preserves the faithful,
but the proud he pays back in full.

24Be strong and take heart,
all you who hope in the LORD.

Of David. A *maskil.*[c]

32 BLESSED IS he
whose transgressions are forgiven,
whose sins are covered.

---

a *10* Or *guilt*   b *17* Hebrew *Sheol*   c Title: Probably a literary or musical term

Living Bible

9, 10O Lord, have mercy on me in my anguish. My eyes are red from weeping; my health is broken from sorrow. I am pining away with grief; my years are shortened, drained away because of sadness. My sins have sapped my strength; I stoop with sorrow and with shame.d 11I am scorned by all my enemies and even more by my neighbors and friends. They dread meeting me and look the other way when I go by. 12I am forgotten like a dead man, like a broken and discarded pot. 13I heard the lies about me, the slanders of my enemies. Everywhere I looked I was afraid, for they were plotting against my life.

14, 15But I am trusting you, O Lord, I said, "You alone are my God; my times are in your hands. Rescue me from those who hunt me down relentlessly. 16Let your favor shine again upon your servant; save me just because you are so kind! 17Don't disgrace me, Lord, by not replying when I call to you for aid. But let the wicked be shamed by what they trust in; let them lie silently in their graves, 18their lying lips quieted at last—the lips of these arrogant men who are accusing honest men of evil deeds."

19Oh, how great is your goodness to those who publicly declare that you will rescue them. For you have stored up great blessings for those who trust and reverence you.

20Hide your loved ones in the shelter of your presence, safe beneath your hand, safe from all conspiring men. 21Blessed is the Lord, for he has shown me that his never-failing love protects me like the walls of a fort! 22I spoke too hastily when I said, "The Lord has deserted me," for you listened to my plea and answered me.

23Oh, love the Lord, all of you who are his people; for the Lord protects those who are loyal to him, but harshly punishes all who haughtily reject him. 24So cheer up! Take courage if you are depending on the Lord.

New Revised Standard

9 Be gracious to me, O Lord, for I am in
       distress;
   my eye wastes away from grief,
       my soul and body also.
10 For my life is spent with sorrow,
       and my years with sighing;
   my strength fails because of my misery,e
       and my bones waste away.
11 I am the scorn of all my adversaries,
       a horrorf to my neighbors,
   an object of dread to my acquaintances;
       those who see me in the street flee from
           me.
12 I have passed out of mind like one who is
           dead;
       I have become like a broken vessel.
13 For I hear the whispering of many—
           terror all around!—
   as they scheme together against me,
       as they plot to take my life.
14 But I trust in you, O Lord;
       I say, "You are my God."
15 My times are in your hand;
       deliver me from the hand of my enemies
           and persecutors.
16 Let your face shine upon your servant;
       save me in your steadfast love.
17 Do not let me be put to shame, O Lord,
       for I call on you;
   let the wicked be put to shame;
       let them go dumbfounded to Sheol.
18 Let the lying lips be stilled
       that speak insolently against the righteous
           with pride and contempt.

19 O how abundant is your goodness
       that you have laid up for those who fear
           you,
   and accomplished for those who take refuge in
           you,
       in the sight of everyone!
20 In the shelter of your presence you hide them
       from human plots;
   you hold them safe under your shelter
       from contentious tongues.
21 Blessed be the Lord,
       for he has wondrously shown his steadfast
           love to me
   when I was beset as a city under siege.
22 I had said in my alarm,
       "I am driven farg from your sight."
   But you heard my supplications
       when I cried out to you for help.
23 Love the Lord, all you his saints.
       The Lord preserves the faithful,
   but abundantly repays the one who acts
           haughtily.
24 Be strong, and let your heart take courage,
       all you who wait for the Lord.

The Joy of Forgiveness

Of David. A Maskil.

32 WHAT HAPPINESS for those whose guilt has been forgiven! What joys when sins are covered over! What relief for those who have confessed their sins and God has cleared their record.

32 HAPPY ARE those whose transgression is
       forgiven,
   whose sin is covered.

---

d 31:9, 10 *My sins have sapped my strength; I stoop with sorrow and shame,* literally, "Even my bones are rotting away."

e Gk Syr: Heb *my iniquity*   f Cn: Heb *exceedingly*   g Another reading is *cut off*

King James

2Blessed *is* the man unto whom the LORD imputeth not iniquity, and in whose spirit *there is* no guile.

3When I kept silence, my bones waxed old through my roaring all the day long.

4For day and night thy hand was heavy upon me: my moisture is turned into the drought of summer. Selah.

5I acknowledged my sin unto thee, and mine iniquity have I not hid. I said, I will confess my transgressions unto the LORD; and thou forgavest the iniquity of my sin. Selah.

6For this shall every one that is godly pray unto thee in a time when thou mayest be found: surely in the floods of great waters they shall not come nigh unto him.

7Thou *art* my hiding place; thou shalt preserve me from trouble; thou shalt compass me about with songs of deliverance. Selah.

8I will instruct thee and teach thee in the way which thou shalt go: I will guide thee with mine eye.

9Be ye not as the horse, *or* as the mule, *which* have no understanding: whose mouth must be held in with bit and bridle, lest they come near unto thee.

10Many sorrows *shall be* to the wicked: but he that trusteth in the LORD, mercy shall compass him about.

11Be glad in the LORD, and rejoice, ye righteous: and shout for joy, all *ye that are* upright in heart.

33 REJOICE IN the LORD, O ye righteous: *for* praise is comely for the upright.

2Praise the LORD with harp: sing unto him with the psaltery *and* an instrument of ten strings.

3Sing unto him a new song; play skilfully with a loud noise.

4For the word of the LORD *is* right; and all his works *are done* in truth.

5He loveth righteousness and judgment: the earth is full of the goodness of the LORD.

6By the word of the LORD were the heavens made; and all the host of them by the breath of his mouth.

7He gathereth the waters of the sea together as an heap: he layeth up the depth in storehouses.

8Let all the earth fear the LORD: let all the inhabitants of the world stand in awe of him.

New International

2Blessed is the man
  whose sin the LORD does not count against
    him
  and in whose spirit is no deceit.

3When I kept silent,
  my bones wasted away
  through my groaning all day long.
4For day and night
  your hand was heavy upon me;
  my strength was sapped
  as in the heat of summer.   *Selah*
5Then I acknowledged my sin to you
  and did not cover up my iniquity.
I said, "I will confess
  my transgressions to the LORD"—
and you forgave
  the guilt of my sin.   *Selah*

6Therefore let everyone who is godly pray to you
  while you may be found;
surely when the mighty waters rise,
  they will not reach him.
7You are my hiding place;
  you will protect me from trouble
  and surround me with songs of deliverance.
                                        Selah

8I will instruct you and teach you in the way you
    should go;
  I will counsel you and watch over you.
9Do not be like the horse or the mule,
  which have no understanding
but must be controlled by bit and bridle
  or they will not come to you.
10Many are the woes of the wicked,
  but the LORD's unfailing love
  surrounds the man who trusts in him.

11Rejoice in the LORD and be glad, you righteous;
  sing, all you who are upright in heart!

33 SING JOYFULLY to the LORD, you
    righteous;
  it is fitting for the upright to praise him.
2Praise the LORD with the harp;
  make music to him on the ten-stringed lyre.
3Sing to him a new song;
  play skillfully, and shout for joy.

4For the word of the LORD is right and true;
  he is faithful in all he does.
5The LORD loves righteousness and justice;
  the earth is full of his unfailing love.

6By the word of the LORD were the heavens
    made,
  their starry host by the breath of his mouth.
7He gathers the waters of the sea into jars[a];
  he puts the deep into storehouses.
8Let all the earth fear the LORD;
  let all the people of the world revere him.

---

a 7 Or *sea as into a heap*

Living Bible

³There was a time when I wouldn't admit what a sinner I was.ᵇ But my dishonesty made me miserable and filled my days with frustration. ⁴All day and all night your hand was heavy on me. My strength evaporated like water on a sunny day ⁵until I finally admitted all my sins to you and stopped trying to hide them. I said to myself, "I will confess them to the Lord." And you forgave me! All my guilt is gone.

⁶Now I say that each believer should confess his sins to God when he is aware of them, while there is time to be forgiven. Judgment will not touch himᶜ if he does.

⁷You are my hiding place from every storm of life; you even keep me from getting into trouble! You surround me with songs of victory. ⁸I will instruct you (says the Lord) and guide you along the best pathway for your life; I will advise you and watch your progress. ⁹Don't be like a senseless horse or mule that has to have a bit in its mouth to keep it in line!

¹⁰Many sorrows come to the wicked, but abiding love surrounds those who trust in the Lord. ¹¹So rejoice in him, all those who are his,ᵈ and shout for joy, all those who try to obey him.ᵉ

33 LET ALL the joys of the godly well up in praise to the Lord, for it is right to praise him. ²Play joyous melodies of praise upon the lyre and on the harp. ³Compose new songs of praise to him, accompanied skillfully on the harp; sing joyfully.

⁴For all God's words are right, and everything he does is worthy of our trust. ⁵He loves whatever is just and good; the earth is filled with his tender love. ⁶He merely spoke, and the heavens were formed, and all the galaxies of stars. ⁷He made the oceans, pouring them into his vast reservoirs.

⁸Let everyone in all the world—men, women and children—fear the Lord and stand in awe of him. ⁹For

---

New Revised Standard

² Happy are those to whom the LORD imputes no iniquity,
  and in whose spirit there is no deceit.

³ While I kept silence, my body wasted away
  through my groaning all day long.

⁴ For day and night your hand was heavy upon me;
  my strength was dried upᶠ as by the heat of summer.   *Selah*

⁵ Then I acknowledged my sin to you,
  and I did not hide my iniquity;
  I said, "I will confess my transgressions to the LORD,"
  and you forgave the guilt of my sin.   *Selah*

⁶ Therefore let all who are faithful
  offer prayer to you;
  at a time of distress,ᵍ the rush of mighty waters
  shall not reach them.

⁷ You are a hiding place for me;
  you preserve me from trouble;
  you surround me with glad cries of deliverance.   *Selah*

⁸ I will instruct you and teach you the way you should go;
  I will counsel you with my eye upon you.

⁹ Do not be like a horse or a mule, without understanding,
  whose temper must be curbed with bit and bridle,
  else it will not stay near you.

¹⁰ Many are the torments of the wicked,
  but steadfast love surrounds those who trust in the LORD.

¹¹ Be glad in the LORD and rejoice, O righteous,
  and shout for joy, all you upright in heart.

The Greatness and Goodness of God

33 REJOICE IN the LORD, O you righteous.
  Praise befits the upright.

² Praise the LORD with the lyre;
  make melody to him with the harp of ten strings.

³ Sing to him a new song;
  play skillfully on the strings, with loud shouts.

⁴ For the word of the LORD is upright,
  and all his work is done in faithfulness.

⁵ He loves righteousness and justice;
  the earth is full of the steadfast love of the LORD.

⁶ By the word of the LORD the heavens were made,
  and all their host by the breath of his mouth.

⁷ He gathered the waters of the sea as in a bottle;
  he put the deeps in storehouses.

⁸ Let all the earth fear the LORD;
  let all the inhabitants of the world stand in awe of him.

ᵇ *32:3 when I wouldn't admit what a sinner I was,* literally, "when I kept silence." ᶜ *32:6 Judgment will not touch him,* literally, "When the great waters overflow they shall not reach him." ᵈ *32:11 all those who are his,* literally, "you righteous." ᵉ *32:11 all those who try to obey him,* literally, "all who are upright in heart."

ᶠ Meaning of Heb uncertain ᵍ Cn: Heb *at a time of finding only*

King James

9For he spake, and it was *done;* he commanded, and it stood fast.

10The LORD bringeth the counsel of the heathen to nought: he maketh the devices of the people of none effect.

11The counsel of the LORD standeth for ever, the thoughts of his heart to all generations.

12Blessed *is* the nation whose God *is* the LORD; *and* the people *whom* he hath chosen for his own inheritance.

13The LORD looketh from heaven; he beholdeth all the sons of men.

14From the place of his habitation he looketh upon all the inhabitants of the earth.

15He fashioneth their hearts alike; he considereth all their works.

16There is no king saved by the multitude of an host: a mighty man is not delivered by much strength.

17An horse *is* a vain thing for safety: neither shall he deliver *any* by his great strength.

18Behold, the eye of the LORD *is* upon them that fear him, upon them that hope in his mercy;

19To deliver their soul from death, and to keep them alive in famine.

20Our soul waiteth for the LORD: he *is* our help and our shield.

21For our heart shall rejoice in him, because we have trusted in his holy name.

22Let thy mercy, O LORD, be upon us, according as we hope in thee.

A Psalm of David, when he changed his behaviour before Abimelech; who drove him away, and he departed.

34 I WILL bless the LORD at all times: his praise *shall* continually *be* in my mouth.

2My soul shall make her boast in the LORD: the humble shall hear *thereof,* and be glad.

3O magnify the LORD with me, and let us exalt his name together.

4I sought the LORD, and he heard me, and delivered me from all my fears.

5They looked unto him, and were lightened: and their faces were not ashamed.

6This poor man cried, and the LORD heard *him,* and saved him out of all his troubles.

7The angel of the LORD encampeth round about them that fear him, and delivereth them.

8O taste and see that the LORD *is* good: blessed *is* the man *that* trusteth in him.

9O fear the LORD, ye his saints: for *there is* no want to them that fear him.

10The young lions do lack, and suffer hunger: but they that seek the LORD shall not want any good *thing.*

New International

9For he spoke, and it came to be;
  he commanded, and it stood firm.

10The LORD foils the plans of the nations;
  he thwarts the purposes of the peoples.

11But the plans of the LORD stand firm forever,
  the purposes of his heart through all
    generations.

12Blessed is the nation whose God is the LORD,
  the people he chose for his inheritance.

13From heaven the LORD looks down
  and sees all mankind;

14from his dwelling place he watches
  all who live on earth—

15he who forms the hearts of all,
  who considers everything they do.

16No king is saved by the size of his army;
  no warrior escapes by his great strength.

17A horse is a vain hope for deliverance;
  despite all its great strength it cannot save.

18But the eyes of the LORD are on those who fear
    him,
  on those whose hope is in his unfailing love,

19to deliver them from death
  and keep them alive in famine.

20We wait in hope for the LORD;
  he is our help and our shield.

21In him our hearts rejoice,
  for we trust in his holy name.

22May your unfailing love rest upon us, O LORD,
  even as we put our hope in you.

Of David. When he pretended to be insane before Abimelech, who drove him away, and he left.

34[a] I WILL extol the LORD at all times;
  his praise will always be on my lips.

2My soul will boast in the LORD;
  let the afflicted hear and rejoice.

3Glorify the LORD with me;
  let us exalt his name together.

4I sought the LORD, and he answered me;
  he delivered me from all my fears.

5Those who look to him are radiant;
  their faces are never covered with shame.

6This poor man called, and the LORD heard him;
  he saved him out of all his troubles.

7The angel of the LORD encamps around those
      who fear him,
  and he delivers them.

8Taste and see that the LORD is good;
  blessed is the man who takes refuge in him.

9Fear the LORD, you his saints,
  for those who fear him lack nothing.

10The lions may grow weak and hungry,
  but those who seek the LORD lack no good
    thing.

[a] This psalm is an acrostic poem, the verses of which begin with the successive letters of the Hebrew alphabet.

Living Bible

when he but spoke, the world began! It appeared at his command! ¹⁰And with a breath he can scatter the plans of all the nations who oppose him, ¹¹but his own plan stands forever. His intentions are the same for every generation.

¹²Blessed is the nation whose God is the Lord, whose people he has chosen as his own. ¹³, ¹⁴, ¹⁵The Lord gazes down upon mankind from heaven where he lives. He has made their hearts and closely watches everything they do.

¹⁶, ¹⁷The best-equipped army cannot save a king—for great strength is not enough to save anyone. A war horse is a poor risk for winning victories—it is strong but it cannot save.

¹⁸, ¹⁹But the eyes of the Lord are watching over those who fear him, who rely upon his steady love. He will keep them from death even in times of famine! ²⁰We depend upon the Lord alone to save us. Only he can help us; he protects us like a shield. ²¹No wonder we are happy in the Lord! For we are trusting him. We trust his holy name. ²²Yes, Lord, let your constant love surround us, for our hopes are in you alone.

34 I WILL praise the Lord no matter what happens. I will constantly speak of his glories and grace.ᵇ ²I will boast of all his kindness to me. Let all who are discouraged take heart. ³Let us praise the Lord together, and exalt his name.

⁴For I cried to him and he answered me! He freed me from all my fears. ⁵Others too were radiant at what he did for them. Theirs was no downcast look of rejection! ⁶This poor man cried to the Lord—and the Lord heard him and saved him out of his troubles. ⁷For the Angel of the Lord guards and rescues all who reverence him.

⁸Oh, put God to the test and see how kind he is! See for yourself the way his mercies shower down on all who trust in him. ⁹If you belong to the Lord, reverence him; for everyone who does this has everything he needs. ¹⁰Even strong young lions sometimes go hungry, but those of us who reverence the Lord will never lack any good thing.

New Revised Standard

9 For he spoke, and it came to be;
   he commanded, and it stood firm.

10 The LORD brings the counsel of the nations to
      nothing;
   he frustrates the plans of the peoples.

11 The counsel of the LORD stands forever,
   the thoughts of his heart to all generations.

12 Happy is the nation whose God is the LORD,
   the people whom he has chosen as his
      heritage.

13 The LORD looks down from heaven;
   he sees all humankind.

14 From where he sits enthroned he watches
   all the inhabitants of the earth—

15 he who fashions the hearts of them all,
   and observes all their deeds.

16 A king is not saved by his great army;
   a warrior is not delivered by his great
      strength.

17 The war horse is a vain hope for victory,
   and by its great might it cannot save.

18 Truly the eye of the LORD is on those who
      fear him,
   on those who hope in his steadfast love,

19 to deliver their soul from death,
   and to keep them alive in famine.

20 Our soul waits for the LORD;
   he is our help and shield.

21 Our heart is glad in him,
   because we trust in his holy name.

22 Let your steadfast love, O LORD, be upon us,
   even as we hope in you.

Praise for Deliverance from Trouble

Of David, when he feigned madness before Abimelech, so
that he drove him out, and he went away.

34 I WILL bless the LORD at all times;
   his praise shall continually be in my
      mouth.

2 My soul makes its boast in the LORD;
   let the humble hear and be glad.

3 O magnify the LORD with me,
   and let us exalt his name together.

4 I sought the LORD, and he answered me,
   and delivered me from all my fears.

5 Look to him, and be radiant;
   so yourᶜ faces shall never be ashamed.

6 This poor soul cried, and was heard by the
      LORD,
   and was saved from every trouble.

7 The angel of the LORD encamps
   around those who fear him, and delivers
      them.

8 O taste and see that the LORD is good;
   happy are those who take refuge in him.

9 O fear the LORD, you his holy ones,
   for those who fear him have no want.

10 The young lions suffer want and hunger,
   but those who seek the LORD lack no good
      thing.

ᵇ *34:1 I will constantly speak of his glories and grace,* literally, "His praise shall continually be in my mouth."

ᶜ Gk Syr Jerome: Heb *their*

King James

11Come, ye children, hearken unto me: I will teach you the fear of the LORD.

12What man *is he that* desireth life, *and* loveth *many* days, that he may see good?

13Keep thy tongue from evil, and thy lips from speaking guile.

14Depart from evil, and do good; seek peace, and pursue it.

15The eyes of the LORD *are* upon the righteous, and his ears *are open* unto their cry.

16The face of the LORD *is* against them that do evil, to cut off the remembrance of them from the earth.

17*The righteous* cry, and the LORD heareth, and delivereth them out of all their troubles.

18The LORD *is* nigh unto them that are of a broken heart; and saveth such as be of a contrite spirit.

19Many *are* the afflictions of the righteous: but the LORD delivereth him out of them all.

20He keepeth all his bones: not one of them is broken.

21Evil shall slay the wicked: and they that hate the righteous shall be desolate.

22The LORD redeemeth the soul of his servants: and none of them that trust in him shall be desolate.

A Psalm of David.

35 PLEAD *MY cause*, O LORD, with them that strive with me: fight against them that fight against me.

2Take hold of shield and buckler, and stand up for mine help.

3Draw out also the spear, and stop *the way* against them that persecute me: say unto my soul, I *am* thy salvation.

4Let them be confounded and put to shame that seek after my soul: let them be turned back and brought to confusion that devise my hurt.

5Let them be as chaff before the wind: and let the angel of the LORD chase *them*.

6Let their way be dark and slippery: and let the angel of the LORD persecute them.

7For without cause have they hid for me their net *in* a pit, *which* without cause they have digged for my soul.

8Let destruction come upon him at unawares; and let his net that he hath hid catch himself: into that very destruction let him fall.

9And my soul shall be joyful in the LORD: it shall rejoice in his salvation.

10All my bones shall say, LORD, who *is* like unto thee, which deliverest the poor from him that is too strong for him, yea, the poor and the needy from him that spoileth him?

11False witnesses did rise up; they laid to my charge *things* that I knew not.

12They rewarded me evil for good *to* the spoiling of my soul.

New International

11Come, my children, listen to me;
   I will teach you the fear of the LORD.

12Whoever of you loves life
   and desires to see many good days,

13keep your tongue from evil
   and your lips from speaking lies.

14Turn from evil and do good;
   seek peace and pursue it.

15The eyes of the LORD are on the righteous
   and his ears are attentive to their cry;

16the face of the LORD is against those who do evil,
   to cut off the memory of them from the earth.

17The righteous cry out, and the LORD hears them;
   he delivers them from all their troubles.

18The LORD is close to the brokenhearted
   and saves those who are crushed in spirit.

19A righteous man may have many troubles,
   but the LORD delivers him from them all;

20he protects all his bones,
   not one of them will be broken.

21Evil will slay the wicked;
   the foes of the righteous will be condemned.

22The LORD redeems his servants;
   no one will be condemned who takes refuge in him.

Of David.

35 CONTEND, O LORD, with those who contend with me;
   fight against those who fight against me.

2Take up shield and buckler;
   arise and come to my aid.

3Brandish spear and javelin[a]
   against those who pursue me.
Say to my soul,
   "I am your salvation."

4May those who seek my life
   be disgraced and put to shame;
may those who plot my ruin
   be turned back in dismay.

5May they be like chaff before the wind,
   with the angel of the LORD driving them away;

6may their path be dark and slippery,
   with the angel of the LORD pursuing them.

7Since they hid their net for me without cause
   and without cause dug a pit for me,

8may ruin overtake them by surprise—
   may the net they hid entangle them,
   may they fall into the pit, to their ruin.

9Then my soul will rejoice in the LORD
   and delight in his salvation.

10My whole being will exclaim,
   "Who is like you, O LORD?
You rescue the poor from those too strong for them,
   the poor and needy from those who rob them."

11Ruthless witnesses come forward;
   they question me on things I know nothing about.

12They repay me evil for good
   and leave my soul forlorn.

---

[a] *3 Or and block the way*

Living Bible

11Sons and daughters, come and listen and let me teach you the importance of trusting and fearing the Lord. 12Do you want a long, good life? 13Then watch your tongue! Keep your lips from lying. 14Turn from all known sin and spend your time in doing good. Try to live in peace with everyone; work hard at it.

15For the eyes of the Lord are intently watching all who live good lives, and he gives attention when they cry to him. 16But the Lord has made up his mind to wipe out even the memory of evil men from the earth. 17Yes, the Lord hears the good man when he calls to him for help, and saves him out of all his troubles.

18The Lord is close to those whose hearts are breaking; he rescues those who are humbly sorry for their sins. 19The good man does not escape all troubles—he has them too. But the Lord helps him in each and every one. 20Not one of his bones is broken.

21Calamity will surely overtake the wicked; heavy penalties are meted out to those who hate the good. 22But as for those who serve the Lord, he will redeem them; everyone who takes refuge in him will be freely pardoned.

35 O LORD, fight those fighting me; declare war on them for their attacks on me. 2Put on your armor, take your shield and protect me by standing in front. 3Lift your spear in my defense, for my pursuers are getting very close. Let me hear you say that you will save me from them. 4Dishonor those who are trying to kill me. Turn them back and confuse them. 5Blow them away like chaff in the wind—wind sent by the Angel of the Lord. 6Make their path dark and slippery before them, with the Angel of the Lord pursuing them. 7For though I did them no wrong, yet they laid a trap for me and dug a pitfall in my path. 8Let them be overtaken by sudden ruin, caught in their own net, and destroyed.

9But I will rejoice in the Lord. He shall rescue me! 10From the bottom of my heart praise rises to him. Where is his equal in all of heaven and earth? Who else protects the weak and helpless from the strong, and the poor and needy from those who would rob them?

11These evil men swear to a lie. They accuse me of things I have never even heard about. 12I do them good, but they return me harm. I am sinking down to death.

New Revised Standard

11 Come, O children, listen to me;
      I will teach you the fear of the LORD.
12 Which of you desires life,
      and covets many days to enjoy good?
13 Keep your tongue from evil,
      and your lips from speaking deceit.
14 Depart from evil, and do good;
      seek peace, and pursue it.

15 The eyes of the LORD are on the righteous,
      and his ears are open to their cry.
16 The face of the LORD is against evildoers,
      to cut off the remembrance of them from
        the earth.
17 When the righteous cry for help, the LORD
        hears,
      and rescues them from all their troubles.
18 The LORD is near to the brokenhearted,
      and saves the crushed in spirit.

19 Many are the afflictions of the righteous,
      but the LORD rescues them from them all.
20 He keeps all their bones;
      not one of them will be broken.
21 Evil brings death to the wicked,
      and those who hate the righteous will be
        condemned.
22 The LORD redeems the life of his servants;
      none of those who take refuge in him will
        be condemned.

Prayer for Deliverance from Enemies
Of David.

35 CONTEND, O LORD, with those who contend with me;
      fight against those who fight against me!
2 Take hold of shield and buckler,
      and rise up to help me!
3 Draw the spear and javelin
      against my pursuers;
   say to my soul,
      "I am your salvation."

4 Let them be put to shame and dishonor
      who seek after my life.
   Let them be turned back and confounded
      who devise evil against me.
5 Let them be like chaff before the wind,
      with the angel of the LORD driving them on.
6 Let their way be dark and slippery,
      with the angel of the LORD pursuing them.

7 For without cause they hid their net[b] for me;
      without cause they dug a pit[c] for my life.
8 Let ruin come on them unawares.
   And let the net that they hid ensnare them;
      let them fall in it—to their ruin.

9 Then my soul shall rejoice in the LORD,
      exulting in his deliverance.
10 All my bones shall say,
      "O LORD, who is like you?
   You deliver the weak
      from those too strong for them,
      the weak and needy from those who despoil
        them."

11 Malicious witnesses rise up;
      they ask me about things I do not know.
12 They repay me evil for good;
      my soul is forlorn.

King James

13But as for me, when they were sick, my clothing *was* sackcloth: I humbled my soul with fasting; and my prayer returned into mine own bosom.

14I behaved myself as though *he had been* my friend or brother: I bowed down heavily, as one that mourneth *for his* mother.

15But in mine adversity they rejoiced, and gathered themselves together: *yea,* the abjects gathered themselves together against me, and I knew *it* not; they did tear *me,* and ceased not:

16With hypocritical mockers in feasts, they gnashed upon me with their teeth.

17Lord, how long wilt thou look on? rescue my soul from their destructions, my darling from the lions.

18I will give thee thanks in the great congregation: I will praise thee among much people.

19Let not them that are mine enemies wrongfully rejoice over me: *neither* let them wink with the eye that hate me without a cause.

20For they speak not peace: but they devise deceitful matters against *them that are* quiet in the land.

21Yea, they opened their mouth wide against me, *and* said, Aha, aha, our eye hath seen *it.*

22*This* thou hast seen, O LORD: keep not silence: O Lord, be not far from me.

23Stir up thyself, and awake to my judgment, *even* unto my cause, my God and my Lord.

24Judge me, O LORD my God, according to thy righteousness; and let them not rejoice over me.

25Let them not say in their hearts, Ah, so would we have it: let them not say, We have swallowed him up.

26Let them be ashamed and brought to confusion together that rejoice at mine hurt: let them be clothed with shame and dishonour that magnify *themselves* against me.

27Let them shout for joy, and be glad, that favour my righteous cause: yea, let them say continually, Let the LORD be magnified, which hath pleasure in the prosperity of his servant.

28And my tongue shall speak of thy righteousness *and* of thy praise all the day long.

To the chief Musician, *A Psalm* of David the servant of the LORD.

36 THE TRANSGRESSION of the wicked saith within my heart, *that there is* no fear of God before his eyes.

2For he flattereth himself in his own eyes, until his iniquity be found to be hateful.

New International

13Yet when they were ill, I put on sackcloth
    and humbled myself with fasting.
When my prayers returned to me unanswered,
14 I went about mourning
    as though for my friend or brother.
I bowed my head in grief
    as though weeping for my mother.
15But when I stumbled, they gathered in glee;
    attackers gathered against me when I was
      unaware.
They slandered me without ceasing.
16Like the ungodly they maliciously mocked[a];
    they gnashed their teeth at me.
17O Lord, how long will you look on?
    Rescue my life from their ravages,
    my precious life from these lions.
18I will give you thanks in the great assembly;
    among throngs of people I will praise you.

19Let not those gloat over me
    who are my enemies without cause;
    let not those who hate me without reason
      maliciously wink the eye.
20They do not speak peaceably,
    but devise false accusations
    against those who live quietly in the land.
21They gape at me and say, "Aha! Aha!
    With our own eyes we have seen it."

22O LORD, you have seen this; be not silent.
    Do not be far from me, O Lord.
23Awake, and rise to my defense!
    Contend for me, my God and Lord.
24Vindicate me in your righteousness, O LORD my
      God;
    do not let them gloat over me.
25Do not let them think, "Aha, just what we
      wanted!"
    or say, "We have swallowed him up."

26May all who gloat over my distress
    be put to shame and confusion;
    may all who exalt themselves over me
    be clothed with shame and disgrace.
27May those who delight in my vindication
    shout for joy and gladness;
    may they always say, "The LORD be exalted,
    who delights in the well-being of his
      servant."
28My tongue will speak of your righteousness
    and of your praises all day long.

For the director of music. Of David the servant of the LORD.

36 AN ORACLE is within my heart
    concerning the sinfulness of the wicked:[b]
There is no fear of God
    before his eyes.
2For in his own eyes he flatters himself
    too much to detect or hate his sin.

---

a 16 Septuagint; Hebrew may mean *ungodly circle of mockers.*   b *1* Or *heart: 1 Sin proceeds from the wicked.*

Living Bible

13When they were ill, I mourned before the Lord in sackcloth, asking him to make them well; I refused to eat; I prayed for them with utmost earnestness, but God did not listen. 14I went about sadly as though it were my mother, friend or brother who was sick and nearing death. 15But now that I am in trouble they are glad; they come together in meetings filled with slander against me—I didn't even know some of those who were there. 16For they gather with the worthless fellows of the town and spend their time cursing me.

17Lord, how long will you stand there, doing nothing? Act now and rescue me, for I have but one life and these young lions are out to get it. 18Save me, and I will thank you publicly before the entire congregation, before the largest crowd I can find.

19Don't give victory to those who fight me without any reason! Don't let them rejoicec at my fall—let them die. 20They don't talk of peace and doing good, but of plots against innocent men who are minding their own business. 21They shout that they have seen *me* doing wrong! "Aha!" they say. "With our own eyes we saw him do it." 22Lord, you know all about it. Don't stay silent! Don't desert me now!

23Rise up, O Lord my God; vindicate me. 24Declare me "not guilty," for you are just.d Don't let my enemies rejoice over me in my troubles. 25Don't let them say, "Aha! Our dearest wish against him will soon be fulfilled!" and, "At last we have him!" 26Shame them; let these who boast against me and who rejoice at my troubles be themselves overcome by misfortune that strips them bare of everything they own. Bare them to dishonor. 27But give great joy to all who wish me well. Let them shout with delight, "Great is the Lord who enjoys helping his child!"e 28And I will tell everyone how great and good you are; I will praise you all day long.

New Revised Standard

13 But as for me, when they were sick,
      I wore sackcloth;
      I afflicted myself with fasting.
   I prayed with head bowedf on my bosom,
14   as though I grieved for a friend or a brother;
   I went about as one who laments for a
      mother,
      bowed down and in mourning.

15 But at my stumbling they gathered in glee,
      they gathered together against me;
   ruffians whom I did not know
      tore at me without ceasing;
16 they impiously mocked more and more,g
      gnashing at me with their teeth.

17 How long, O LORD, will you look on?
      Rescue me from their ravages,
      my life from the lions!
18 Then I will thank you in the great
      congregation;
      in the mighty throng I will praise you.

19 Do not let my treacherous enemies rejoice
      over me,
      or those who hate me without cause wink
      the eye.
20 For they do not speak peace,
      but they conceive deceitful words
      against those who are quiet in the land.
21 They open wide their mouths against me;
      they say, "Aha, Aha,
      our eyes have seen it."

22 You have seen, O LORD; do not be silent!
      O Lord, do not be far from me!
23 Wake up! Bestir yourself for my defense,
      for my cause, my God and my Lord!
24 Vindicate me, O LORD, my God,
      according to your righteousness,
      and do not let them rejoice over me.
25 Do not let them say to themselves,
      "Aha, we have our heart's desire."
   Do not let them say, "We have swallowed
      youh up."

26 Let all those who rejoice at my calamity
      be put to shame and confusion;
   let those who exalt themselves against me
      be clothed with shame and dishonor.

27 Let those who desire my vindication
      shout for joy and be glad,
      and say evermore,
   "Great is the LORD,
      who delights in the welfare of his servant."
28 Then my tongue shall tell of your
      righteousness
      and of your praise all day long.

Human Wickedness and Divine Goodness

To the leader. Of David, the servant of the LORD.

36 SIN LURKS deep in the hearts of the wicked, forever urging them on to evil deeds. They have no fear of God to hold them back. 2Instead, in their conceit, they think they can hide their evil deeds and not get caught. 3Everything they say is crooked and deceit-

36 TRANSGRESSION SPEAKS to the wicked
   deep in their hearts;
      there is no fear of God
      before their eyes.
 2 For they flatter themselves in their own eyes
      that their iniquity cannot be found out and
      hated.

---

c 35:19 *Don't let them rejoice,* literally, "wink with the eye."
d 35:24 *Declare me "not guilty," for you are just,* literally, "Judge me according to your righteousness." e 35:27 *child,* literally, "servant."

f Or *My prayer turned back* g Cn Compare Gk: Heb *like the profanest of mockers of a cake* h Heb *him*

King James

3The words of his mouth *are* iniquity and deceit: he hath left off to be wise, *and* to do good.

4He deviseth mischief upon his bed; he setteth himself in a way *that is* not good; he abhorreth not evil.

5Thy mercy, O Lord, *is* in the heavens; *and* thy faithfulness *reacheth* unto the clouds.

6Thy righteousness *is* like the great mountains; thy judgments *are* a great deep: O Lord, thou preservest man and beast.

7How excellent *is* thy lovingkindness, O God! therefore the children of men put their trust under the shadow of thy wings.

8They shall be abundantly satisfied with the fatness of thy house; and thou shalt make them drink of the river of thy pleasures.

9For with thee *is* the fountain of life: in thy light shall we see light.

10O continue thy lovingkindness unto them that know thee; and thy righteousness to the upright in heart.

11Let not the foot of pride come against me, and let not the hand of the wicked remove me.

12There are the workers of iniquity fallen: they are cast down, and shall not be able to rise.

A Psalm of David.

37 FRET NOT thyself because of evildoers, neither be thou envious against the workers of iniquity.

2For they shall soon be cut down like the grass, and wither as the green herb.

3Trust in the Lord, and do good; *so* shalt thou dwell in the land, and verily thou shalt be fed.

4Delight thyself also in the Lord; and he shall give thee the desires of thine heart.

5Commit thy way unto the Lord; trust also in him; and he shall bring *it* to pass.

6And he shall bring forth thy righteousness as the light, and thy judgment as the noonday.

7Rest in the Lord, and wait patiently for him: fret not thyself because of him who prospereth in his way, because of the man who bringeth wicked devices to pass.

8Cease from anger, and forsake wrath: fret not thyself in any wise to do evil.

9For evildoers shall be cut off: but those that wait upon the Lord, they shall inherit the earth.

10For yet for a little while, and the wicked *shall* not *be:* yea, thou shalt diligently consider his place, and it *shall* not *be.*

11But the meek shall inherit the earth; and shall delight themselves in the abundance of peace.

New International

3The words of his mouth are wicked and deceitful;
  he has ceased to be wise and to do good.
4Even on his bed he plots evil;
  he commits himself to a sinful course
  and does not reject what is wrong.

5Your love, O Lord, reaches to the heavens,
  your faithfulness to the skies.
6Your righteousness is like the mighty mountains,
  your justice like the great deep.
O Lord, you preserve both man and beast.
7 How priceless is your unfailing love!
Both high and low among men
  finda refuge in the shadow of your wings.
8They feast on the abundance of your house;
  you give them drink from your river of delights.
9For with you is the fountain of life;
  in your light we see light.

10Continue your love to those who know you,
  your righteousness to the upright in heart.
11May the foot of the proud not come against me,
  nor the hand of the wicked drive me away.
12See how the evildoers lie fallen—
  thrown down, not able to rise!

Of David.

37b DO NOT fret because of evil men
  or be envious of those who do wrong;
2for like the grass they will soon wither,
  like green plants they will soon die away.

3Trust in the Lord and do good;
  dwell in the land and enjoy safe pasture.
4Delight yourself in the Lord
  and he will give you the desires of your heart.

5Commit your way to the Lord;
  trust in him and he will do this:
6He will make your righteousness shine like the dawn,
  the justice of your cause like the noonday sun.

7Be still before the Lord and wait patiently for him;
  do not fret when men succeed in their ways,
  when they carry out their wicked schemes.

8Refrain from anger and turn from wrath;
  do not fret—it leads only to evil.
9For evil men will be cut off,
  but those who hope in the Lord will inherit the land.

10A little while, and the wicked will be no more;
  though you look for them, they will not be found.
11But the meek will inherit the land
  and enjoy great peace.

---

a 7 Or *love, O God! | Men find*; or *love! | Both heavenly beings and men / find*   b This psalm is an acrostic poem, the stanzas of which begin with the successive letters of the Hebrew alphabet.

Living Bible

ful; they are no longer wise and good. 4They lie awake at night to hatch their evil plots, instead of planning how to keep away from wrong.

5Your steadfast love, O Lord, is as great as all the heavens. Your faithfulness reaches beyond the clouds. 6Your justice is as solid as God's mountains. Your decisions are as full of wisdom as the oceans are with water. You are concernedᶜ for men and animals alike. 7How precious is your constant love, O God! All humanity takes refuge in the shadow of your wings. 8You feed them with blessings from your own table and let them drink from your rivers of delight.

9For you are the Fountain of life; our light is from your Light. 10Pour out your unfailing love on those who know you! Never stop giving your blessingsᵈ to those who long to do your will.

11Don't let these proud men trample me. Don't let their wicked hands push me around. 12Look! They have fallen. They are thrown down and will not rise again.

37 NEVER ENVY the wicked! 2Soon they fade away like grass and disappear. 3Trust in the Lord instead. Be kind and good to others; then you will live safely here in the land and prosper, feeding in safety.

4Be delighted with the Lord. Then he will give you all your heart's desires. 5Commit everything you do to the Lord. Trust him to help you do it and he will. 6Your innocence will be clear to everyone. He will vindicate you with the blazing light of justice shining down as from the noonday sun.

7Rest in the Lord; wait patiently for him to act. Don't be envious of evil men who prosper.

8Stop your anger! Turn off your wrath. Don't fret and worry—it only leads to harm. 9For the wicked shall be destroyed, but those who trust the Lord shall be given every blessing. 10Only a little while and the wicked shall disappear. You will look for them in vain. 11But all who humble themselves before the Lord shall be given every blessing, and shall have wonderful peace.

New Revised Standard

3 The words of their mouths are mischief and
        deceit;
    they have ceased to act wisely and do good.
4 They plot mischief while on their beds;
    they are set on a way that is not good;
    they do not reject evil.
5 Your steadfast love, O LORD, extends to the
        heavens,
    your faithfulness to the clouds.
6 Your righteousness is like the mighty
        mountains,
    your judgments are like the great deep;
    you save humans and animals alike,
        O LORD.

7 How precious is your steadfast love, O God!
    All people may take refuge in the shadow
        of your wings.
8 They feast on the abundance of your house,
    and you give them drink from the river of
        your delights.
9 For with you is the fountain of life;
    in your light we see light.

10 O continue your steadfast love to those who
        know you,
    and your salvation to the upright of heart!
11 Do not let the foot of the arrogant tread on
        me,
    or the hand of the wicked drive me away.
12 There the evildoers lie prostrate;
    they are thrust down, unable to rise.

Exhortation to Patience and Trust
Of David.

37 DO NOT fret because of the wicked;
        do not be envious of wrongdoers,
2 for they will soon fade like the grass,
    and wither like the green herb.

3 Trust in the LORD, and do good;
    so you will live in the land, and enjoy
        security.
4 Take delight in the LORD,
    and he will give you the desires of your
        heart.

5 Commit your way to the LORD;
    trust in him, and he will act.
6 He will make your vindication shine like the
        light,
    and the justice of your cause like the
        noonday.

7 Be still before the LORD, and wait patiently
        for him;
    do not fret over those who prosper in their
        way,
    over those who carry out evil devices.

8 Refrain from anger, and forsake wrath.
    Do not fret—it leads only to evil.
9 For the wicked shall be cut off,
    but those who wait for the LORD shall
        inherit the land.

10 Yet a little while, and the wicked will be no
        more;
    though you look diligently for their place,
    they will not be there.
11 But the meek shall inherit the land,
    and delight themselves in abundant
        prosperity.

ᶜ 36:6 *You are concerned*, literally, "You preserve." ᵈ 36:10 *your blessings*, literally, "your righteousness."

King James

12The wicked plotteth against the just, and gnasheth upon him with his teeth.

13The Lord shall laugh at him: for he seeth that his day is coming.

14The wicked have drawn out the sword, and have bent their bow, to cast down the poor and needy, *and* to slay such as be of upright conversation.

15Their sword shall enter into their own heart, and their bows shall be broken.

16A little that a righteous man hath *is* better than the riches of many wicked.

17For the arms of the wicked shall be broken: but the LORD upholdeth the righteous.

18The LORD knoweth the days of the upright: and their inheritance shall be for ever.

19They shall not be ashamed in the evil time: and in the days of famine they shall be satisfied.

20But the wicked shall perish, and the enemies of the LORD *shall be* as the fat of lambs: they shall consume; into smoke shall they consume away.

21The wicked borroweth, and payeth not again: but the righteous showeth mercy, and giveth.

22For *such as be* blessed of him shall inherit the earth; and *they that be* cursed of him shall be cut off.

23The steps of a *good* man are ordered by the LORD: and he delighteth in his way.

24Though he fall, he shall not be utterly cast down: for the LORD upholdeth *him with* his hand.

25I have been young, and *now* am old; yet have I not seen the righteous forsaken, nor his seed begging bread.

26*He is* ever merciful, and lendeth; and his seed *is* blessed.

27Depart from evil, and do good; and dwell for evermore.

28For the LORD loveth judgment, and forsaketh not his saints; they are preserved for ever: but the seed of the wicked shall be cut off.

29The righteous shall inherit the land, and dwell therein for ever.

30The mouth of the righteous speaketh wisdom, and his tongue talketh of judgment.

31The law of his God *is* in his heart; none of his steps shall slide.

32The wicked watcheth the righteous, and seeketh to slay him.

33The LORD will not leave him in his hand, nor condemn him when he is judged.

New International

12The wicked plot against the righteous
and gnash their teeth at them;
13but the Lord laughs at the wicked,
for he knows their day is coming.

14The wicked draw the sword
and bend the bow
to bring down the poor and needy,
to slay those whose ways are upright.
15But their swords will pierce their own hearts,
and their bows will be broken.

16Better the little that the righteous have
than the wealth of many wicked;
17for the power of the wicked will be broken,
but the LORD upholds the righteous.

18The days of the blameless are known to the
LORD,
and their inheritance will endure forever.
19In times of disaster they will not wither;
in days of famine they will enjoy plenty.

20But the wicked will perish:
The LORD's enemies will be like the beauty
of the fields,
they will vanish—vanish like smoke.

21The wicked borrow and do not repay,
but the righteous give generously;
22those the LORD blesses will inherit the land,
but those he curses will be cut off.

23If the LORD delights in a man's way,
he makes his steps firm;
24though he stumble, he will not fall,
for the LORD upholds him with his hand.

25I was young and now I am old,
yet I have never seen the righteous forsaken
or their children begging bread.
26They are always generous and lend freely;
their children will be blessed.

27Turn from evil and do good;
then you will dwell in the land forever.
28For the LORD loves the just
and will not forsake his faithful ones.

They will be protected forever,
but the offspring of the wicked will be cut
off;
29the righteous will inherit the land
and dwell in it forever.

30The mouth of the righteous man utters wisdom,
and his tongue speaks what is just.
31The law of his God is in his heart;
his feet do not slip.

32The wicked lie in wait for the righteous,
seeking their very lives;
33but the LORD will not leave them in their power
or let them be condemned when brought to
trial.

Living Bible

12, 13The Lord is laughing at those who plot against the godly, for he knows their judgment day is coming. 14Evil men take aim to slay the poor; they are ready to butcher those who do right. 15But their swords will be plunged into their own hearts and all their weapons will be broken.

16It is better to have little and be godly than to own an evil man's wealth; 17for the strength of evil men shall be broken, but the Lord takes care of those he has forgiven.a

18Day by day the Lord observes the good deeds done by godly men,b and gives them eternal rewards. 19He cares for them when times are hard; even in famine, they will have enough. 20But evil men shall perish. These enemies of God will wither like grass, and disappear like smoke. 21Evil men borrow and "cannot pay it back"! But the good man returns what he owes with some extra besides. 22Those blessed by the Lord shall inherit the earth, but those cursed by him shall die.

23The steps of good men are directed by the Lord. He delights in each step they take. 24If they fall it isn't fatal, for the Lord holds them with his hand.

25I have been young and now I am old. And in all my years I have never seen the Lord forsake a man who loves him; nor have I seen the children of the godly go hungry. 26Instead, the godly are able to be generous with their gifts and loans to others, and their children are a blessing.

27So if you want an eternal home, leave your evil, low-down ways and live good lives. 28For the Lord loves justice and fairness; he will never abandon his people. They will be kept safe forever; but all who love wickedness shall perish.

29The godly shall be firmly planted in the land, and live there forever. 30, 31The godly man is a good counselor because he is just and fair and knows right from wrong.

32Evil men spy on the godly, waiting for an excuse to accuse them and then demanding their death. 33But the Lord will not let these evil men succeed, nor let the godly be condemned when they are brought before the judge.

New Revised Standard

12 The wicked plot against the righteous,
       and gnash their teeth at them;
13 but the LORD laughs at the wicked,
       for he sees that their day is coming.

14 The wicked draw the sword and bend their
           bows
       to bring down the poor and needy,
       to kill those who walk uprightly;
15 their sword shall enter their own heart,
       and their bows shall be broken.

16 Better is a little that the righteous person has
       than the abundance of many wicked.
17 For the arms of the wicked shall be broken,
       but the LORD upholds the righteous.

18 The LORD knows the days of the blameless,
       and their heritage will abide forever;
19 they are not put to shame in evil times,
       in the days of famine they have abundance.

20 But the wicked perish,
       and the enemies of the LORD are like the
           glory of the pastures;
       they vanish—like smoke they vanish away.

21 The wicked borrow, and do not pay back,
       but the righteous are generous and keep
           giving;
22 for those blessed by the LORD shall inherit the
           land,
       but those cursed by him shall be cut off.

23 Our stepsc are made firm by the LORD,
       when he delights in ourd way;
24 though we stumble,e wef shall not fall
           headlong,
       for the LORD holds usg by the hand.

25 I have been young, and now am old,
       yet I have not seen the righteous forsaken
       or their children begging bread.
26 They are ever giving liberally and lending,
       and their children become a blessing.

27 Depart from evil, and do good;
       so you shall abide forever.
28 For the LORD loves justice;
       he will not forsake his faithful ones.

       The righteous shall be kept safe forever,
       but the children of the wicked shall be cut
           off.
29 The righteous shall inherit the land,
       and live in it forever.

30 The mouths of the righteous utter wisdom,
       and their tongues speak justice.
31 The law of their God is in their hearts;
       their steps do not slip.

32 The wicked watch for the righteous,
       and seek to kill them.
33 The LORD will not abandon them to their
           power,
       or let them be condemned when they are
           brought to trial.

---

a 37:17 those he has forgiven, literally, "the righteous." b 37:18 Day by day the Lord observes the good deeds done by godly men, literally, "knows the days of the upright."

c Heb a man's steps d Heb his e Heb he stumbles f Heb he g Heb him

King James

34Wait on the LORD, and keep his way, and he shall exalt thee to inherit the land: when the wicked are cut off, thou shalt see *it*.

35I have seen the wicked in great power, and spreading himself like a green bay tree.

36Yet he passed away, and, lo, he *was* not: yea, I sought him, but he could not be found.

37Mark the perfect *man*, and behold the upright: for the end of *that* man *is* peace.

38But the transgressors shall be destroyed together: the end of the wicked shall be cut off.

39But the salvation of the righteous *is* of the LORD: *he is* their strength in the time of trouble.

40And the LORD shall help them, and deliver them: he shall deliver them from the wicked, and save them, because they trust in him.

A Psalm of David, to bring to remembrance.

38 O LORD, rebuke me not in thy wrath: neither chasten me in thy hot displeasure.

2For thine arrows stick fast in me, and thy hand presseth me sore.

3*There is* no soundness in my flesh because of thine anger; neither *is there any* rest in my bones because of my sin.

4For mine iniquities are gone over mine head: as an heavy burden they are too heavy for me.

5My wounds stink *and* are corrupt because of my foolishness.

6I am troubled; I am bowed down greatly; I go mourning all the day long.

7For my loins are filled with a loathsome *disease:* and *there is* no soundness in my flesh.

8I am feeble and sore broken: I have roared by reason of the disquietness of my heart.

9Lord, all my desire *is* before thee; and my groaning is not hid from thee.

10My heart panteth, my strength faileth me: as for the light of mine eyes, it also is gone from me.

11My lovers and my friends stand aloof from my sore; and my kinsmen stand afar off.

12They also that seek after my life lay snares *for me:* and they that seek my hurt speak mischievous things, and imagine deceits all the day long.

13But I, as a deaf *man,* heard not; and *I was* as a dumb man *that* openeth not his mouth.

14Thus I was as a man that heareth not, and in whose mouth *are* no reproofs.

15For in thee, O LORD, do I hope: thou wilt hear, O Lord my God.

New International

34Wait for the LORD
  and keep his way.
He will exalt you to inherit the land;
  when the wicked are cut off, you will see it.

35I have seen a wicked and ruthless man
  flourishing like a green tree in its native soil,
36but he soon passed away and was no more;
  though I looked for him, he could not be
    found.

37Consider the blameless, observe the upright;
  there is a futurea for the man of peace.
38But all sinners will be destroyed;
  the futureb of the wicked will be cut off.

39The salvation of the righteous comes from the
  LORD;
  he is their stronghold in time of trouble.
40The LORD helps them and delivers them;
  he delivers them from the wicked and saves
    them,
  because they take refuge in him.

A psalm of David. A petition.

38 O LORD, do not rebuke me in your anger
  or discipline me in your wrath.
2For your arrows have pierced me,
  and your hand has come down upon me.
3Because of your wrath there is no health in my
  body;
  my bones have no soundness because of my
    sin.
4My guilt has overwhelmed me
  like a burden too heavy to bear.

5My wounds fester and are loathsome
  because of my sinful folly.
6I am bowed down and brought very low;
  all day long I go about mourning.
7My back is filled with searing pain;
  there is no health in my body.
8I am feeble and utterly crushed;
  I groan in anguish of heart.

9All my longings lie open before you, O Lord;
  my sighing is not hidden from you.
10My heart pounds, my strength fails me;
  even the light has gone from my eyes.
11My friends and companions avoid me because
  of my wounds;
  my neighbors stay far away.
12Those who seek my life set their traps,
  those who would harm me talk of my ruin;
  all day long they plot deception.

13I am like a deaf man, who cannot hear,
  like a mute, who cannot open his mouth;
14I have become like a man who does not hear,
  whose mouth can offer no reply.
15I wait for you, O LORD;
  you will answer, O Lord my God.

---

a *37 Or there will be posterity*   b *38 Or posterity*

Living Bible

New Revised Standard

| Living Bible | New Revised Standard |

³⁴Don't be impatient for the Lord to act! Keep traveling steadily along his pathway and in due season he will honor you with every blessing,ᶜ and you will see the wicked destroyed. ³⁵, ³⁶I myself have seen it happen: a proud and evil man, towering like a cedar of Lebanon, but when I looked again, he was gone! I searched but could not find him! ³⁷But the good man—what a different story! For the good man—the blameless, the upright, the man of peace—he has a wonderful future ahead of him. For him there is a happy ending. ³⁸But evil men shall be destroyed, and their posterity shall be cut off.

³⁹The Lord saves the godly! He is their salvation and their refuge when trouble comes. ⁴⁰Because they trust in him, he helps them and delivers them from the plots of evil men.

38 O LORD, don't punish me while you are angry! ²Your arrows have struck deep; your blows are crushing me. ³, ⁴Because of your anger my body is sick, my health is broken beneath my sins. They are like a flood, higher than my head; they are a burden too heavy to bear. ⁵, ⁶My wounds are festering and full of pus. Because of my sins I am bent and racked with pain. My days are filled with anguish. ⁷My loins burn with inflammationᵈ and my whole body is diseased. ⁸I am exhausted and crushed; I groan in despair.ᵉ

⁹Lord, you know how I long for my health once more. You hear my every sigh. ¹⁰My heart beats wildly, my strength fails, and I am going blind. ¹¹My loved ones and friends stay away, fearing my disease. Even my own family stands at a distance.

¹²Meanwhile my enemies are trying to kill me. They plot my ruin and spend all their waking hours planning treachery. ¹³, ¹⁴But I am deaf to all their threats; I am silent before them as a man who cannot speak. I have nothing to say. ¹⁵For I am waiting for you, O Lord my

34 Wait for the LORD, and keep to his way,
and he will exalt you to inherit the land;
you will look on the destruction of the
wicked.

35 I have seen the wicked oppressing,
and towering like a cedar of Lebanon.ᶠ
36 Again I⁸ passed by, and they were no more;
though I sought them, they could not be
found.

37 Mark the blameless, and behold the upright,
for there is posterity for the peaceable.
38 But transgressors shall be altogether destroyed;
the posterity of the wicked shall be cut off.

39 The salvation of the righteous is from the
LORD;
he is their refuge in the time of trouble.
40 The LORD helps them and rescues them;
he rescues them from the wicked, and saves
them,
because they take refuge in him.

A Penitent Sufferer's Plea for Healing

A Psalm of David, for the memorial offering.

38 O LORD, do not rebuke me in your anger,
or discipline me in your wrath.
2 For your arrows have sunk into me,
and your hand has come down on me.

3 There is no soundness in my flesh
because of your indignation;
there is no health in my bones
because of my sin.
4 For my iniquities have gone over my head;
they weigh like a burden too heavy for me.

5 My wounds grow foul and fester
because of my foolishness;
6 I am utterly bowed down and prostrate;
all day long I go around mourning.
7 For my loins are filled with burning,
and there is no soundness in my flesh.
8 I am utterly spent and crushed;
I groan because of the tumult of my heart.

9 O Lord, all my longing is known to you;
my sighing is not hidden from you.
10 My heart throbs, my strength fails me;
as for the light of my eyes—it also has
gone from me.
11 My friends and companions stand aloof from
my affliction,
and my neighbors stand far off.

12 Those who seek my life lay their snares;
those who seek to hurt me speak of ruin,
and meditate treachery all day long.

13 But I am like the deaf, I do not hear;
like the mute, who cannot speak.
14 Truly, I am like one who does not hear,
and in whose mouth is no retort.

15 But it is for you, O LORD, that I wait;
it is you, O LORD my God, who will
answer.

ᶜ *37:34 with every blessing,* literally, "to possess the land."   ᵈ *38:7 My loins burn with inflammation,* implied.   ᵉ *38:8 in despair,* or, "because of the pains in my heart."

ᶠ Gk: Meaning of Heb uncertain   ⁸ Gk Syr Jerome: Heb *he*

King James

16For I said, *Hear me,* lest *otherwise* they should rejoice over me: when my foot slippeth, they magnify *themselves* against me.

17For I *am* ready to halt, and my sorrow *is* continually before me.

18For I will declare mine iniquity; I will be sorry for my sin.

19But mine enemies *are* lively, *and* they are strong: and they that hate me wrongfully are multiplied.

20They also that render evil for good are mine adversaries; because I follow *the thing that* good *is.*

21Forsake me not, O LORD: O my God, be not far from me.

22Make haste to help me, O Lord my salvation.

To the chief Musician, *even to* Jeduthun, A Psalm of David.

39 I SAID, I will take heed to my ways, that I sin not with my tongue: I will keep my mouth with a bridle, while the wicked is before me.

2I was dumb with silence, I held my peace, *even* from good; and my sorrow was stirred.

3My heart was hot within me, while I was musing the fire burned: *then* spake I with my tongue,

4LORD, make me to know mine end, and the measure of my days, what it *is;* that I may know how frail I *am.*

5Behold, thou hast made my days *as* an handbreadth; and mine age *is* as nothing before thee: verily every man at his best state *is* altogether vanity. Selah.

6Surely every man walketh in a vain show: surely they are disquieted in vain: he heapeth up *riches,* and knoweth not who shall gather them.

7And now, Lord, what wait I for? my hope *is* in thee.

8Deliver me from all my transgressions: make me not the reproach of the foolish.

9I was dumb, I opened not my mouth; because thou didst *it.*

10Remove thy stroke away from me: I am consumed by the blow of thine hand.

11When thou with rebukes dost correct man for iniquity, thou makest his beauty to consume away like a moth: surely every man *is* vanity. Selah.

12Hear my prayer, O LORD, and give ear unto my cry; hold not thy peace at my tears: for I *am* a stranger with thee, *and* a sojourner, as all my fathers *were.*

13O spare me, that I may recover strength, before I go hence, and be no more.

New International

16For I said, "Do not let them gloat
    or exalt themselves over me when my foot
    slips."
17For I am about to fall,
    and my pain is ever with me.
18I confess my iniquity;
    I am troubled by my sin.
19Many are those who are my vigorous enemies;
    those who hate me without reason are
        numerous.
20Those who repay my good with evil
    slander me when I pursue what is good.
21O LORD, do not forsake me;
    be not far from me, O my God.
22Come quickly to help me,
    O Lord my Savior.

For the director of music. For Jeduthun. A psalm of David.

39 I SAID, "I will watch my ways
    and keep my tongue from sin;
I will put a muzzle on my mouth
    as long as the wicked are in my presence."
2But when I was silent and still,
    not even saying anything good,
    my anguish increased.
3My heart grew hot within me,
    and as I meditated, the fire burned;
    then I spoke with my tongue:
4"Show me, O LORD, my life's end
    and the number of my days;
    let me know how fleeting is my life.
5You have made my days a mere handbreadth;
    the span of my years is as nothing before
        you.
Each man's life is but a breath.   *Selah*
6Man is a mere phantom as he goes to and fro:
    He bustles about, but only in vain;
    he heaps up wealth, not knowing who will
        get it.
7"But now, Lord, what do I look for?
    My hope is in you.
8Save me from all my transgressions;
    do not make me the scorn of fools.
9I was silent; I would not open my mouth,
    for you are the one who has done this.
10Remove your scourge from me;
    I am overcome by the blow of your hand.
11You rebuke and discipline men for their sin;
    you consume their wealth like a moth—
    each man is but a breath.   *Selah*

12"Hear my prayer, O LORD,
    listen to my cry for help;
    be not deaf to my weeping.
For I dwell with you as an alien,
    a stranger, as all my fathers were.
13Look away from me, that I may rejoice again
    before I depart and am no more."

Living Bible

God. Come and protect me. 16Put an end to their arrogance, these who gloat when I am cast down!

17How constantly I find myself upon the verge of sin;a this source of sorrow always stares me in the face. 18I confess my sins; I am sorry for what I have done. 19But my enemies persecute with vigor, and continue to hate me—though I have done nothing against them to deserve it. 20They repay me evil for good and hate me for standing for the right.

21Don't leave me, Lord; don't go away! 22Come quickly! Help me, O my Savior.

39 I SAID to myself, I'm going to quit complaining! I'll keep quiet, especially when the ungodly are around me. 2, 3But as I stood there silently the turmoil within me grew to the bursting point. The more I mused, the hotter the fires inside. Then at last I spoke, and pled with God: 4Lord, help me to realize how brief my time on earth will be. Help me to know that I am here for but a moment more. 5, 6My life is no longer than my hand! My whole lifetime is but a moment to you. Proud man! Frail as breath! A shadow! And all his busy rushing ends in nothing. He heaps up riches for someone else to spend. 7And so, Lord, my only hope is in you.

8Save me from being overpowered by my sins, for even fools will mock me then.

9Lord, I am speechless before you. I will not open my mouth to speak one word of complaint, for my punishment is from you.b

10Lord, don't hit me anymore—I am exhausted beneath your hand. 11When you punish a man for his sins, he is destroyed, for he is as fragile as a moth-infested cloth; yes, man is frail as breath.

12Hear my prayer, O Lord; listen to my cry! Don't sit back, unmindful of my tears. For I am your guest. I am a traveler passing through the earth, as all my fathers were.

13Spare me, Lord! Let me recover and be filled with happiness again before my death.

New Revised Standard

16 For I pray, "Only do not let them rejoice over
     me,
       those who boast against me when my foot
         slips."

17 For I am ready to fall,
     and my pain is ever with me.
18 I confess my iniquity;
     I am sorry for my sin.
19 Those who are my foes without causec are
     mighty,
       and many are those who hate me
         wrongfully.
20 Those who render me evil for good
     are my adversaries because I follow after
       good.

21 Do not forsake me, O LORD;
     O my God, do not be far from me;
22 make haste to help me,
     O Lord, my salvation.

Prayer for Wisdom and Forgiveness
   To the leader: to Jeduthun. A Psalm of David.

39 I SAID, "I will guard my ways
     that I may not sin with my tongue;
   I will keep a muzzle on my mouth
     as long as the wicked are in my presence."
2 I was silent and still;
     I held my peace to no avail;
   my distress grew worse,
3   my heart became hot within me.
   While I mused, the fire burned;
     then I spoke with my tongue:

4 "LORD, let me know my end,
     and what is the measure of my days;
     let me know how fleeting my life is.
5 You have made my days a few handbreadths,
     and my lifetime is as nothing in your sight.
   Surely everyone stands as a mere breath.
                                        Selah
6   Surely everyone goes about like a shadow.
   Surely for nothing they are in turmoil;
     they heap up, and do not know who will
       gather.

7 "And now, O Lord, what do I wait for?
     My hope is in you.
8 Deliver me from all my transgressions.
     Do not make me the scorn of the fool.
9 I am silent; I do not open my mouth,
     for it is you who have done it.
10 Remove your stroke from me;
     I am worn down by the blowsd of your
       hand.

11 "You chastise mortals
     in punishment for sin,
   consuming like a moth what is dear to them;
     surely everyone is a mere breath.   *Selah*

12 "Hear my prayer, O LORD,
     and give ear to my cry;
     do not hold your peace at my tears.
   For I am your passing guest,
     an alien, like all my forebears.
13 Turn your gaze away from me, that I may
       smile again,
     before I depart and am no more."

---

a 38:17 *How constantly I find myself upon the verge of sin,* literally, "I am ready to fall." b 39:9 *for my punishment is from you,* literally, "for you have done it."

c Q Ms: MT *my living foes*   d Heb *hostility*

King James

To the chief Musician, A Psalm of David.

40 I WAITED patiently for the LORD; and he inclined unto me, and heard my cry.

2He brought me up also out of an horrible pit, out of the miry clay, and set my feet upon a rock, *and* established my goings.

3And he hath put a new song in my mouth, *even* praise unto our God: many shall see *it,* and fear, and shall trust in the LORD.

4Blessed *is* that man that maketh the LORD his trust, and respecteth not the proud, nor such as turn aside to lies.

5Many, O LORD my God, *are* thy wonderful works *which* thou hast done, and thy thoughts *which are* to us-ward: they cannot be reckoned up in order unto thee: *if* I would declare and speak *of them,* they are more than can be numbered.

6Sacrifice and offering thou didst not desire; mine ears hast thou opened: burnt offering and sin offering hast thou not required.

7Then said I, Lo, I come: in the volume of the book *it is* written of me,

8I delight to do thy will, O my God: yea, thy law *is* within my heart.

9I have preached righteousness in the great congregation: lo, I have not refrained my lips, O LORD, thou knowest.

10I have not hid thy righteousness within my heart; I have declared thy faithfulness and thy salvation: I have not concealed thy lovingkindness and thy truth from the great congregation.

11Withhold not thou thy tender mercies from me, O LORD: let thy lovingkindness and thy truth continually preserve me.

12For innumerable evils have compassed me about: mine iniquities have taken hold upon me, so that I am not able to look up; they are more than the hairs of mine head: therefore my heart faileth me.

13Be pleased, O LORD, to deliver me: O LORD, make haste to help me.

14Let them be ashamed and confounded together that seek after my soul to destroy it; let them be driven backward and put to shame that wish me evil.

15Let them be desolate for a reward of their shame that say unto me, Aha, aha.

New International

For the director of music. Of David. A psalm.

40 I WAITED patiently for the LORD;
he turned to me and heard my cry.
2He lifted me out of the slimy pit,
out of the mud and mire;
he set my feet on a rock
and gave me a firm place to stand.
3He put a new song in my mouth,
a hymn of praise to our God.
Many will see and fear
and put their trust in the LORD.

4Blessed is the man
who makes the LORD his trust,
who does not look to the proud,
to those who turn aside to false gods.[a]
5Many, O LORD my God,
are the wonders you have done.
The things you planned for us
no one can recount to you;
were I to speak and tell of them,
they would be too many to declare.

6Sacrifice and offering you did not desire,
but my ears you have pierced[b,c];
burnt offerings and sin offerings
you did not require.
7Then I said, "Here I am, I have come—
it is written about me in the scroll.[d]
8I desire to do your will, O my God;
your law is within my heart."

9I proclaim righteousness in the great assembly;
I do not seal my lips,
as you know, O LORD.
10I do not hide your righteousness in my heart;
I speak of your faithfulness and salvation.
I do not conceal your love and your truth
from the great assembly.

11Do not withhold your mercy from me, O LORD;
may your love and your truth always protect
me.
12For troubles without number surround me;
my sins have overtaken me, and I cannot see.
They are more than the hairs of my head,
and my heart fails within me.

13Be pleased, O LORD, to save me;
O LORD, come quickly to help me.
14May all who seek to take my life
be put to shame and confusion;
may all who desire my ruin
be turned back in disgrace.
15May those who say to me, "Aha! Aha!"
be appalled at their own shame.

a 4 Or *to falsehood*   b 6 Hebrew; Septuagint *but a body you have prepared for me* (see also Symmachus and Theodotion)   c 6 Or *opened*   d 7 Or *come / with the scroll written for me*

Living Bible

40 I WAITED patiently for God to help me; then he listened and heard my cry. ²He lifted me out of the pit of despair, out from the bog and the mire, and set my feet on a hard, firm path and steadied me as I walked along. ³He has given me a new song to sing, of praises to our God. Now many will hear of the glorious things he did for me, and stand in awe before the Lord, and put their trust in him. ⁴Many blessings are given to those who trust the Lord, and have no confidence in those who are proud, or who trust in idols.

⁵O Lord my God, many and many a time you have done great miracles for us and we are ever in your thoughts. Who else can do such glorious things? No one else can be compared with you. There isn't time to tell of all your wonderful deeds.

⁶It isn't sacrifices and offerings which you really want from your people. Burnt animals bring no special joy to your heart. But you have accepted the offer of my life-long service.ᵉ ⁷Then Iᶠ said, "See, I have come, just as all the prophets foretold. ⁸And I delight to do your will, my God, for your law is written upon my heart!"

⁹I have told everyone the Good News that you forgive people's sins.ᵍ I have not been timid about it, as you well know, O Lord. ¹⁰I have not kept this Good News hidden in my heart, but have proclaimed your loving-kindness and truth to all the congregation.

¹¹O Lord, don't hold back your tender mercies from me! My only hope is in your love and faithfulness. ¹²Otherwise I perish, for problems far too big for me to solve are piled higher than my head. Meanwhile my sins, too many to count, have all caught up with me and I am ashamed to look up. My heart quails within me.

¹³Please, Lord, rescue me! Quick! Come and help me! ¹⁴, ¹⁵Confuse them! Turn them around and send them sprawling—all these who are trying to destroy me. Disgrace these scoffers with their utter failure!

New Revised Standard

Thanksgiving for Deliverance and Prayer for Help

To the leader. Of David. A Psalm.

40 I WAITED patiently for the LORD;
    he inclined to me and heard my cry.
² He drew me up from the desolate pit,ʰ
    out of the miry bog,
and set my feet upon a rock,
    making my steps secure.
³ He put a new song in my mouth,
    a song of praise to our God.
Many will see and fear,
    and put their trust in the LORD.

⁴ Happy are those who make
    the LORD their trust,
who do not turn to the proud,
    to those who go astray after false gods.
⁵ You have multiplied, O LORD my God,
    your wondrous deeds and your thoughts
        toward us;
    none can compare with you.
Were I to proclaim and tell of them,
    they would be more than can be counted.

⁶ Sacrifice and offering you do not desire,
    but you have given me an open ear.ⁱ
Burnt offering and sin offering
    you have not required.
⁷ Then I said, "Here I am;
    in the scroll of the book it is written of
        me.ʲ
⁸ I delight to do your will, O my God;
    your law is within my heart."

⁹ I have told the glad news of deliverance
    in the great congregation;
see, I have not restrained my lips,
    as you know, O LORD.
¹⁰ I have not hidden your saving help within my
        heart,
    I have spoken of your faithfulness and your
        salvation;
I have not concealed your steadfast love and
        your faithfulness
    from the great congregation.

¹¹ Do not, O LORD, withhold
    your mercy from me;
let your steadfast love and your faithfulness
    keep me safe forever.
¹² For evils have encompassed me
    without number;
my iniquities have overtaken me,
    until I cannot see;
they are more than the hairs of my head,
    and my heart fails me.

¹³ Be pleased, O LORD, to deliver me;
    O LORD, make haste to help me.
¹⁴ Let all those be put to shame and confusion
    who seek to snatch away my life;
let those be turned back and brought to
        dishonor
    who desire my hurt.
¹⁵ Let those be appalled because of their shame
    who say to me, "Aha, Aha!"

ᵉ *40:6 But you have accepted the offer of my lifelong service,* literally, "my ears you have dug." ᶠ *40:7 This verse was quoted by Christ as applying to himself. See Jn 4:34.* ᵍ *40:9 the Good News that you forgive people's sins,* literally, "your righteousness." Also in vs 10.

ʰ Cn: Heb *pit of tumult* ⁱ Heb *ears you have dug for me* ʲ Meaning of Heb uncertain

King James

16Let all those that seek thee rejoice and be glad in thee: let such as love thy salvation say continually, The LORD be magnified.

17But I *am* poor and needy; *yet* the Lord thinketh upon me: thou *art* my help and my deliverer; make no tarrying, O my God.

To the chief Musician, A Psalm of David.

41 BLESSED *IS* he that considereth the poor: the LORD will deliver him in time of trouble.

2The LORD will preserve him, and keep him alive; *and* he shall be blessed upon the earth: and thou wilt not deliver him unto the will of his enemies.

3The LORD will strengthen him upon the bed of languishing: thou wilt make all his bed in his sickness.

4I said, LORD, be merciful unto me: heal my soul; for I have sinned against thee.

5Mine enemies speak evil of me, When shall he die, and his name perish?

6And if he come to see *me*, he speaketh vanity: his heart gathereth iniquity to itself; *when* he goeth abroad, he telleth *it*.

7All that hate me whisper together against me: against me do they devise my hurt.

8An evil disease, *say they*, cleaveth fast unto him: and *now* that he lieth he shall rise up no more.

9Yea, mine own familiar friend, in whom I trusted, which did eat of my bread, hath lifted up *his* heel against me.

10But thou, O LORD, be merciful unto me, and raise me up, that I may requite them.

11By this I know that thou favourest me, because mine enemy doth not triumph over me.

12And as for me, thou upholdest me in mine integrity, and settest me before thy face for ever.

13Blessed *be* the LORD God of Israel from everlasting, and to everlasting. Amen, and Amen.

Book II
To the chief Musician, Maschil, for the sons of Korah.

42 AS THE hart panteth after the water brooks, so panteth my soul after thee, O God.

2My soul thirsteth for God, for the living God: when shall I come and appear before God?

3My tears have been my meat day and night, while they continually say unto me, Where *is* thy God?

New International

16But may all who seek you
  rejoice and be glad in you;
may those who love your salvation always say,
  "The LORD be exalted!"

17Yet I am poor and needy;
  may the Lord think of me.
You are my help and my deliverer;
  O my God, do not delay.

For the director of music. A psalm of David.

41 BLESSED IS he who has regard for the weak;
  the LORD delivers him in times of trouble.

2The LORD will protect him and preserve his life;
  he will bless him in the land
  and not surrender him to the desire of his foes.

3The LORD will sustain him on his sickbed
  and restore him from his bed of illness.

4I said, "O LORD, have mercy on me;
  heal me, for I have sinned against you."

5My enemies say of me in malice,
  "When will he die and his name perish?"

6Whenever one comes to see me,
  he speaks falsely, while his heart gathers slander;
  then he goes out and spreads it abroad.

7All my enemies whisper together against me;
  they imagine the worst for me, saying,

8"A vile disease has beset him;
  he will never get up from the place where he lies."

9Even my close friend, whom I trusted,
  he who shared my bread,
  has lifted up his heel against me.

10But you, O LORD, have mercy on me;
  raise me up, that I may repay them.

11I know that you are pleased with me,
  for my enemy does not triumph over me.

12In my integrity you uphold me
  and set me in your presence forever.

13Praise be to the LORD, the God of Israel,
  from everlasting to everlasting.
      Amen and Amen.

BOOK II

Psalms 42–72

For the director of music. A *maskil*[a] of the Sons of Korah.

42[b] AS THE deer pants for streams of water,
  so my soul pants for you, O God.

2My soul thirsts for God, for the living God.
  When can I go and meet with God?

3My tears have been my food
  day and night,
while men say to me all day long,
  "Where is your God?"

---

[a] Title: Probably a literary or musical term   [b] In many Hebrew manuscripts Psalms 42 and 43 constitute one psalm.

Living Bible

16But may the joy of the Lord be given to everyone who loves him and his salvation. May they constantly exclaim, "How great God is!"

17I am poor and weak, yet the Lord is thinking about me right now! O my God, you are my helper. You are my Savior; come quickly, and save me. Please don't delay!

41 GOD BLESSES those who are kind to the poor. He helps them out of their troubles. 2He protects them and keeps them alive; he publicly honors them and destroys the power of their enemies. 3He nurses them when they are sick, and soothes their pains and worries.c

4"O Lord," I prayed, "be kind and heal me, for I have confessed my sins." 5But my enemies say, "May he soon die and be forgotten!" 6They act so friendly when they come to visit me while I am sick; but all the time they hate me and are glad that I am lying there upon my bed of pain. And when they leave, they laugh and mock. 7They whisper together about what they will do when I am dead. 8"It's fatal, whatever it is," they say. "He'll never get out of that bed!"

9Even my best friend has turned against me—a man I completely trusted; how often we ate together. 10Lord, don't you desert me! Be gracious, Lord, and make me well again so I can pay them back! 11I know you are pleased with me because you haven't let my enemies triumph over me. 12You have preserved me because I was honest; you have admitted me forever to your presence.

13Bless the Lord, the God of Israel, who exists from everlasting ages past—and on into everlasting eternity ahead. Amen and amen!

42 AS THE deer pants for water, so I long for you, O God. 2I thirst for God, the living God. Where can I find him to come and stand before him? 3Day and night I weep for his help, and all the while my enemies taunt me. "Where is this God of yours?" they scoff.

New Revised Standard

16 But may all who seek you
    rejoice and be glad in you;
may those who love your salvation
    say continually, "Great is the LORD!"
17 As for me, I am poor and needy,
    but the Lord takes thought for me.
You are my help and my deliverer;
    do not delay, O my God.

Assurance of God's Help and a Plea for Healing

To the leader. A Psalm of David.

41 HAPPY ARE those who consider the poor;d
    the LORD delivers them in the day of
       trouble.
2 The LORD protects them and keeps them alive;
    they are called happy in the land.
You do not give them up to the will of their
    enemies.
3 The LORD sustains them on their sickbed;
    in their illness you heal all their
       infirmities.e

4 As for me, I said, "O LORD, be gracious to
       me;
    heal me, for I have sinned against you."
5 My enemies wonder in malice
    when I will die, and my name perish.
6 And when they come to see me, they utter
       empty words,
    while their hearts gather mischief;
    when they go out, they tell it abroad.
7 All who hate me whisper together about me;
    they imagine the worst for me.

8 They think that a deadly thing has fastened on
       me,
    that I will not rise again from where I lie.
9 Even my bosom friend in whom I trusted,
    who ate of my bread, has lifted the heel
       against me.
10 But you, O LORD, be gracious to me,
    and raise me up, that I may repay them.

11 By this I know that you are pleased with me;
    because my enemy has not triumphed over
       me.
12 But you have upheld me because of my
       integrity,
    and set me in your presence forever.

13 Blessed be the LORD, the God of Israel,
    from everlasting to everlasting.
       Amen and Amen.

BOOK II

(Psalms 42–72)

Longing for God and His Help in Distress

To the leader. A Maskil of the Korahites.

42 AS A deer longs for flowing streams,
    so my soul longs for you, O God.
2 My soul thirsts for God,
    for the living God.
When shall I come and behold
    the face of God?
3 My tears have been my food
    day and night,
while people say to me continually,
    "Where is your God?"

---

c *41:3 He nurses them when they are sick, and soothes their pains and worries,* literally, "You make all his bed in his sickness."

d Or *weak*   e Heb *you change all his bed*

King James

4When I remember these *things*, I pour out my soul in me: for I had gone with the multitude, I went with them to the house of God, with the voice of joy and praise, with a multitude that kept holyday.

5Why art thou cast down, O my soul? and *why* art thou disquieted in me? hope thou in God: for I shall yet praise him *for* the help of his countenance.

6O my God, my soul is cast down within me: therefore will I remember thee from the land of Jordan, and of the Hermonites, from the hill Mizar.

7Deep calleth unto deep at the noise of thy waterspouts: all thy waves and thy billows are gone over me.

8*Yet* the LORD will command his lovingkindness in the daytime, and in the night his song *shall be* with me, *and* my prayer unto the God of my life.

9I will say unto God my rock, Why hast thou forgotten me? why go I mourning because of the oppression of the enemy?

10*As* with a sword in my bones, mine enemies reproach me; while they say daily unto me, Where *is* thy God?

11Why art thou cast down, O my soul? and why art thou disquieted within me? hope thou in God: for I shall yet praise him, *who is* the health of my countenance, and my God.

43 JUDGE ME, O God, and plead my cause against an ungodly nation: O deliver me from the deceitful and unjust man.

2For thou *art* the God of my strength: why dost thou cast me off? why go I mourning because of the oppression of the enemy?

3O send out thy light and thy truth: let them lead me; let them bring me unto thy holy hill, and to thy tabernacles.

4Then will I go unto the altar of God, unto God my exceeding joy: yea, upon the harp will I praise thee, O God my God.

5Why art thou cast down, O my soul? and why art thou disquieted within me? hope in God: for I shall yet praise him, *who is* the health of my countenance, and my God.

New International

4These things I remember
  as I pour out my soul:
how I used to go with the multitude,
  leading the procession to the house of God,
with shouts of joy and thanksgiving
  among the festive throng.

5Why are you downcast, O my soul?
  Why so disturbed within me?
Put your hope in God,
  for I will yet praise him,
  my Savior and 6my God.

My[a] soul is downcast within me;
  therefore I will remember you
from the land of the Jordan,
  the heights of Hermon—from Mount Mizar.

7Deep calls to deep
  in the roar of your waterfalls;
all your waves and breakers
  have swept over me.

8By day the LORD directs his love,
  at night his song is with me—
  a prayer to the God of my life.

9I say to God my Rock,
  "Why have you forgotten me?
Why must I go about mourning,
  oppressed by the enemy?"

10My bones suffer mortal agony
  as my foes taunt me,
saying to me all day long,
  "Where is your God?"

11Why are you downcast, O my soul?
  Why so disturbed within me?
Put your hope in God,
  for I will yet praise him,
  my Savior and my God.

43[b] VINDICATE ME, O God,
  and plead my cause against an ungodly
    nation;
  rescue me from deceitful and wicked men.

2You are God my stronghold.
  Why have you rejected me?
Why must I go about mourning,
  oppressed by the enemy?

3Send forth your light and your truth,
  let them guide me;
let them bring me to your holy mountain,
  to the place where you dwell.

4Then will I go to the altar of God,
  to God, my joy and my delight.
I will praise you with the harp,
  O God, my God.

5Why are you downcast, O my soul?
  Why so disturbed within me?
Put your hope in God,
  for I will yet praise him,
  my Savior and my God.

a 5,6 A few Hebrew manuscripts, Septuagint and Syriac; most Hebrew manuscripts *praise him for his saving help.* / 6*O my God, my*   b In many Hebrew manuscripts Psalms 42 and 43 constitute one psalm.

Living Bible

4, 5Take courage, my soul! Do you remember those times (but how could you ever forget them!) when you led a great procession to the Temple on festival days, singing with joy, praising the Lord? Why then be downcast? Why be discouraged and sad? Hope in God! I shall yet praise him again. Yes, I shall again praise him for his help.c

6Yet I am standing here depressed and gloomy, but I will meditate upon your kindness to this lovely land where the Jordan River flows and where Mount Hermon and Mount Mizar stand. 7All your waves and billows have gone over me, and floods of sorrow pour upon me like a thundering cataract.d

8Yet day by day the Lord also pours out his steadfast love upon me, and through the night I sing his songs and pray to God who gives me life.

9"O God my Rock," I cry, "why have you forsaken me? Why must I suffer these attacks from my enemies?" 10Their taunts pierce me like a fatal wound; again and again they scoff, "Where is that God of yours?" 11But O my soul, don't be discouraged. Don't be upset. Expect God to act! For I know that I shall again have plenty of reason to praise him for all that he will do. He is my help! He is my God!

43 O GOD, defend me from the charges of these merciless, deceitful men. 2For you are God, my only place of refuge. Why have you tossed me aside? Why must I mourn at the oppression of my enemies?

3Oh, send out your light and your truth—let them lead me. Let them lead me to your Temple on your holy mountain, Zion. 4There I will go to the altar of God my exceeding joy, and praise him with my harp. O God—my God! 5O my soul, why be so gloomy and discouraged? Trust in God! I shall again praise him for his wondrous help; he will make me smile again,e for he is my God!

New Revised Standard

4   These things I remember,
      as I pour out my soul:
    how I went with the throng,f
      and led them in procession to the house of
         God,
    with glad shouts and songs of thanksgiving,
      a multitude keeping festival.
5   Why are you cast down, O my soul,
      and why are you disquieted within me?
    Hope in God; for I shall again praise him,
      my help 6and my God.

    My soul is cast down within me;
      therefore I remember you
    from the land of Jordan and of Hermon,
      from Mount Mizar.
7   Deep calls to deep
      at the thunder of your cataracts;
    all your waves and your billows
      have gone over me.
8   By day the LORD commands his steadfast
         love,
      and at night his song is with me,
      a prayer to the God of my life.

9   I say to God, my rock,
      "Why have you forgotten me?
    Why must I walk about mournfully
      because the enemy oppresses me?"
10 As with a deadly wound in my body,
      my adversaries taunt me,
    while they say to me continually,
      "Where is your God?"

11 Why are you cast down, O my soul,
      and why are you disquieted within me?
    Hope in God; for I shall again praise him,
      my help and my God.

Prayer to God in Time of Trouble

43 VINDICATE ME, O God, and defend my
         cause
      against an ungodly people;
    from those who are deceitful and unjust
      deliver me!
2   For you are the God in whom I take refuge;
      why have you cast me off?
    Why must I walk about mournfully
      because of the oppression of the enemy?

3   O send out your light and your truth;
      let them lead me;
    let them bring me to your holy hill
      and to your dwelling.
4   Then I will go to the altar of God,
      to God my exceeding joy;
    and I will praise you with the harp,
      O God, my God.

5   Why are you cast down, O my soul,
      and why are you disquieted within me?
    Hope in God; for I shall again praise him,
      my help and my God.

---

c 42:5 for his help, literally, "for the help of his countenance."   d 42:7 floods of sorrow pour upon me like a thundering cataract, literally, "deep calls to deep at the noise of your waterfalls."   e 43:5 he will make me smile again, literally, "he is the help of my countenance."

f Meaning of Heb uncertain

King James

New International

To the chief Musician for the sons of Korah, Maschil.

44 WE HAVE heard with our ears, O God, our fathers have told us, *what* work thou didst in their days, in the times of old.

2*How* thou didst drive out the heathen with thy hand, and plantedst them; *how* thou didst afflict the people, and cast them out.

3For they got not the land in possession by their own sword, neither did their own arm save them: but thy right hand, and thine arm, and the light of thy countenance, because thou hadst a favour unto them.

4Thou art my King, O God: command deliverances for Jacob.

5Through thee will we push down our enemies: through thy name will we tread them under that rise up against us.

6For I will not trust in my bow, neither shall my sword save me.

7But thou hast saved us from our enemies, and hast put them to shame that hated us.

8In God we boast all the day long, and praise thy name for ever. Selah.

9But thou hast cast off, and put us to shame; and goest not forth with our armies.

10Thou makest us to turn back from the enemy: and they which hate us spoil for themselves.

11Thou hast given us like sheep *appointed* for meat; and hast scattered us among the heathen.

12Thou sellest thy people for nought, and dost not increase *thy wealth* by their price.

13Thou makest us a reproach to our neighbours, a scorn and a derision to them that are round about us.

14Thou makest us a byword among the heathen, a shaking of the head among the people.

15My confusion *is* continually before me, and the shame of my face hath covered me,

16For the voice of him that reproacheth and blasphemeth; by reason of the enemy and avenger.

17All this is come upon us; yet have we not forgotten thee, neither have we dealt falsely in thy covenant.

18Our heart is not turned back, neither have our steps declined from thy way;

19Though thou hast sore broken us in the place of dragons, and covered us with the shadow of death.

20If we have forgotten the name of our God, or stretched out our hands to a strange god;

21Shall not God search this out? for he knoweth the secrets of the heart.

22Yea, for thy sake are we killed all the day long; we are counted as sheep for the slaughter.

23Awake, why sleepest thou, O Lord? arise, cast *us* not off for ever.

For the director of music. Of the Sons of Korah. A *maskil*.[a]

44 WE HAVE heard with our ears, O God;
  our fathers have told us
what you did in their days,
  in days long ago.
2With your hand you drove out the nations
  and planted our fathers;
you crushed the peoples
  and made our fathers flourish.
3It was not by their sword that they won the
    land,
  nor did their arm bring them victory;
it was your right hand, your arm,
  and the light of your face, for you loved
    them.

4You are my King and my God,
  who decrees[b] victories for Jacob.
5Through you we push back our enemies;
  through your name we trample our foes.
6I do not trust in my bow,
  my sword does not bring me victory;
7but you give us victory over our enemies,
  you put our adversaries to shame.
8In God we make our boast all day long,
  and we will praise your name forever.   *Selah*

9But now you have rejected and humbled us;
  you no longer go out with our armies.
10You made us retreat before the enemy,
  and our adversaries have plundered us.
11You gave us up to be devoured like sheep
  and have scattered us among the nations.
12You sold your people for a pittance,
  gaining nothing from their sale.

13You have made us a reproach to our neighbors,
  the scorn and derision of those around us.
14You have made us a byword among the nations;
  the peoples shake their heads at us.
15My disgrace is before me all day long,
  and my face is covered with shame
16at the taunts of those who reproach and revile
    me,
  because of the enemy, who is bent on
    revenge.

17All this happened to us,
  though we had not forgotten you
  or been false to your covenant.
18Our hearts had not turned back;
  our feet had not strayed from your path.
19But you crushed us and made us a haunt for
    jackals
  and covered us over with deep darkness.

20If we had forgotten the name of our God
  or spread out our hands to a foreign god,
21would not God have discovered it,
  since he knows the secrets of the heart?
22Yet for your sake we face death all day long;
  we are considered as sheep to be slaughtered.

23Awake, O Lord! Why do you sleep?
  Rouse yourself! Do not reject us forever.

---

a Title: Probably a literary or musical term   b 4 Septuagint, Aquila and Syriac; Hebrew *King, O God; I* command

Living Bible

44 O GOD, we have heard of the glorious miracles
you did in the days of long ago. Our forefathers
have told us how you drove the heathen nations from this
land and gave it all to us, spreading Israel from one end
of the country to the other. ³They did not conquer by
their own strength and skill, but by your mighty power
and because you smiled upon them and favored them.

⁴You are my King and my God. Decree victories for
your people. ⁵For it is only by your power and through
your name that we tread down our enemies; ⁶I do not
trust my weapons. They could never save me. ⁷Only you
can give us the victory over those who hate us.

⁸My constant boast is God. I can never thank you
enough! ⁹And yet for a time, O Lord, you have tossed
us aside in dishonor, and have not helped us in our
battles. ¹⁰You have actually fought against us and defeated us before our foes. Our enemies have invaded our
land and pillaged the countryside. ¹¹You have treated us
like sheep in a slaughter pen, and scattered us among the
nations. ¹²You sold us for a pittance. You valued us at
nothing at all. ¹³The neighboring nations laugh and
mock at us because of all the evil you have sent. ¹⁴You
have made the word "Jew" a byword of contempt and
shame among the nations, disliked by all. 15, 16I am
constantly despised, mocked, taunted and cursed by my
vengeful enemies.

¹⁷And all this has happened, Lord, despite our loyalty
to you. We have not violated your covenant. ¹⁸Our
hearts have not deserted you! We have not left your path
by a single step. ¹⁹If we had, we could understand your
punishing us in the barren wilderness and sending us into
darkness and death. ²⁰If we had turned away from worshiping our God, and were worshiping idols, ²¹would
God not know it? Yes, he knows the secrets of every
heart. ²²But that is not our case. For we are facing death
threats constantly because of serving you! We are like
sheep awaiting slaughter.

²³Waken! Rouse yourself! Don't sleep, O Lord! Are
we cast off forever? ²⁴Why do you look the other way?

New Revised Standard

National Lament and Prayer for Help

To the leader. Of the Korahites. A Maskil.

44 WE HAVE heard with our ears, O God,
  our ancestors have told us,
what deeds you performed in their days,
  in the days of old:
2 you with your own hand drove out the
    nations,
  but them you planted;
  you afflicted the peoples,
  but them you set free;
3 for not by their own sword did they win the
    land,
  nor did their own arm give them victory;
but your right hand, and your arm,
  and the light of your countenance,
  for you delighted in them.

4 You are my King and my God;
    you command[c] victories for Jacob.
5 Through you we push down our foes;
    through your name we tread down our
      assailants.
6 For not in my bow do I trust,
    nor can my sword save me.
7 But you have saved us from our foes,
    and have put to confusion those who hate
      us.
8 In God we have boasted continually,
    and we will give thanks to your name
      forever.   *Selah*

9 Yet you have rejected us and abased us,
    and have not gone out with our armies.
10 You made us turn back from the foe,
    and our enemies have gotten spoil.
11 You have made us like sheep for slaughter,
    and have scattered us among the nations.
12 You have sold your people for a trifle,
    demanding no high price for them.

13 You have made us the taunt of our neighbors,
    the derision and scorn of those around us.
14 You have made us a byword among the
      nations,
    a laughingstock[d] among the peoples.
15 All day long my disgrace is before me,
    and shame has covered my face
16 at the words of the taunters and revilers,
    at the sight of the enemy and the avenger.

17 All this has come upon us,
    yet we have not forgotten you,
    or been false to your covenant.
18 Our heart has not turned back,
    nor have our steps departed from your way,
19 yet you have broken us in the haunt of
      jackals,
    and covered us with deep darkness.

20 If we had forgotten the name of our God,
    or spread out our hands to a strange god,
21 would not God discover this?
    For he knows the secrets of the heart.
22 Because of you we are being killed all day
      long,
    and accounted as sheep for the slaughter.

23 Rouse yourself! Why do you sleep, O Lord?
    Awake, do not cast us off forever!

---

c Gk Syr: Heb *You are my King, O God; command*   d Heb *a shaking of the head*

King James

24Wherefore hidest thou thy face, *and* forgettest our affliction and our oppression?

25For our soul is bowed down to the dust: our belly cleaveth unto the earth.

26Arise for our help, and redeem us for thy mercies' sake.

To the chief Musician upon Shoshannim, for the sons of Korah, Maschil, A Song of loves.

45 MY HEART is inditing a good matter: I speak of the things which I have made touching the king: my tongue *is* the pen of a ready writer.

2Thou art fairer than the children of men: grace is poured into thy lips: therefore God hath blessed thee for ever.

3Gird thy sword upon *thy* thigh, O *most* mighty, with thy glory and thy majesty.

4And in thy majesty ride prosperously because of truth and meekness *and* righteousness; and thy right hand shall teach thee terrible things.

5Thine arrows *are* sharp in the heart of the king's enemies; *whereby* the people fall under thee.

6Thy throne, O God, *is* for ever and ever: the sceptre of thy kingdom *is* a right sceptre.

7Thou lovest righteousness, and hatest wickedness: therefore God, thy God, hath anointed thee with the oil of gladness above thy fellows.

8All thy garments *smell* of myrrh, and aloes, *and* cassia, out of the ivory palaces, whereby they have made thee glad.

9Kings' daughters *were* among thy honourable women: upon thy right hand did stand the queen in gold of Ophir.

10Hearken, O daughter, and consider, and incline thine ear; forget also thine own people, and thy father's house;

11So shall the king greatly desire thy beauty: for he *is* thy Lord; and worship thou him.

12And the daughter of Tyre *shall be there* with a gift; *even* the rich among the people shall entreat thy favour.

13The king's daughter *is* all glorious within: her clothing *is* of wrought gold.

14She shall be brought unto the king in raiment of needlework: the virgins her companions that follow her shall be brought unto thee.

15With gladness and rejoicing shall they be brought: they shall enter into the king's palace.

16Instead of thy fathers shall be thy children, whom thou mayest make princes in all the earth.

New International

24Why do you hide your face
  and forget our misery and oppression?

25We are brought down to the dust;
  our bodies cling to the ground.

26Rise up and help us;
  redeem us because of your unfailing love.

For the director of music. To the tune of, "Lilies." Of the Sons of Korah. A *maskil.*[a] A wedding song.

45 MY HEART is stirred by a noble theme
  as I recite my verses for the king;
  my tongue is the pen of a skillful writer.

2You are the most excellent of men
  and your lips have been anointed with grace,
  since God has blessed you forever.

3Gird your sword upon your side, O mighty one;
  clothe yourself with splendor and majesty.

4In your majesty ride forth victoriously
  in behalf of truth, humility and righteousness;
  let your right hand display awesome deeds.

5Let your sharp arrows pierce the hearts of the
    king's enemies;
  let the nations fall beneath your feet.

6Your throne, O God, will last for ever and ever;
  a scepter of justice will be the scepter of your
    kingdom.

7You love righteousness and hate wickedness;
  therefore God, your God, has set you above
    your companions
  by anointing you with the oil of joy.

8All your robes are fragrant with myrrh and aloes
    and cassia;
  from palaces adorned with ivory
  the music of the strings makes you glad.

9Daughters of kings are among your honored
    women;
  at your right hand is the royal bride in gold
    of Ophir.

10Listen, O daughter, consider and give ear:
  Forget your people and your father's house.

11The king is enthralled by your beauty;
  honor him, for he is your lord.

12The Daughter of Tyre will come with a gift,[b]
  men of wealth will seek your favor.

13All glorious is the princess within her chamber;
  her gown is interwoven with gold.

14In embroidered garments she is led to the king;
  her virgin companions follow her
  and are brought to you.

15They are led in with joy and gladness;
  they enter the palace of the king.

16Your sons will take the place of your fathers;
  you will make them princes throughout the
    land.

a Title: Probably a literary or musical term   b 12 Or A Tyrian robe is among the gifts

Living Bible

Why do you ignore our sorrows and oppression? 25We lie face downward in the dust. 26Rise up, O Lord, and come and help us. Save us by your constant love.

45 MY HEART is overflowing with a beautiful thought! I will write a lovely poem to the King, for I am as full of words as the speediest writer pouring out his story.
2You are the fairest of all;
Your words are filled with grace;
God himself is blessing you forever.
3Arm yourself, O Mighty One,
So glorious, so majestic!
4And in your majesty
Go on to victory,
Defending truth, humility, and justice.
Go forth to awe-inspiring deeds!
5Your arrows are sharp
In your enemies' hearts;
They fall before you.
6Your throne, O God, endures forever.
Justice is your royal scepter.
7You love what is good
And hate what is wrong.
Therefore God, your God,
Has given you more gladness
Than anyone else.
8Your robes are perfumed with myrrh, aloes and cassia. In your palaces of inlaid ivory, lovely music is being played for your enjoyment. 9Kings' daughters are among your concubines.c Standing beside you is the queen, wearing jewelry of finest gold from Ophir.

10, 11"I advise you, O daughter, not to fret about your parents in your homeland far away. Your royal husband delights in your beauty. Reverence him, for he is your lord. 12The people of Tyre, the richest people of our day, will shower you with gifts and entreat your favors."

13The bride,d a princess, waits within her chamber, robed in beautiful clothing woven with gold. 14Lovelye she is, led beside her maids of honor to the king! 15What a joyful, glad procession as they enter in the palace gates! 16"Your sons will some day be kings like their father. They shall sit on thrones around the world!

New Revised Standard

24 Why do you hide your face?
   Why do you forget our affliction and
      oppression?
25 For we sink down to the dust;
   our bodies cling to the ground.
26 Rise up, come to our help.
   Redeem us for the sake of your steadfast
      love.

Ode for a Royal Wedding

To the leader: according to Lilies. Of the Korahites. A
   Maskil. A love song.

45 MY HEART overflows with a goodly theme;
   I address my verses to the king;
   my tongue is like the pen of a ready scribe.

2 You are the most handsome of men;
   grace is poured upon your lips;
   therefore God has blessed you forever.
3 Gird your sword on your thigh, O mighty one,
   in your glory and majesty.

4 In your majesty ride on victoriously
   for the cause of truth and to defendf the
      right;
   let your right hand teach you dread deeds.
5 Your arrows are sharp
   in the heart of the king's enemies;
   the peoples fall under you.

6 Your throne, O God,g endures forever and
      ever.
   Your royal scepter is a scepter of equity;
7 you love righteousness and hate wickedness.
   Therefore God, your God, has anointed you
      with the oil of gladness beyond your
      companions;
8 your robes are all fragrant with myrrh and
      aloes and cassia.
   From ivory palaces stringed instruments make
      you glad;
9 daughters of kings are among your ladies of
      honor;
   at your right hand stands the queen in gold
      of Ophir.

10 Hear, O daughter, consider and incline your
      ear;
   forget your people and your father's house,
11 and the king will desire your beauty.
   Since he is your lord, bow to him;
12 the peopleh of Tyre will seek your favor
      with gifts,
   the richest of the people 13with all kinds of
      wealth.

   The princess is decked in her chamber with
      gold-woven robes;i
14 in many-colored robes she is led to the
      king;
   behind her the virgins, her companions,
      follow.
15 With joy and gladness they are led along
   as they enter the palace of the king.

16 In the place of ancestors you, O king,j shall
      have sons;
   you will make them princes in all the earth.

---

c 45:9 concubines, literally, "honorable women." d 45:13 The bride, literally, "The king's daughter." e 45:14 Lovely, literally, "embroidered work."

f Cn: Heb and the meekness of g Or Your throne is a throne of God, it h Heb daughter i Or people. 13All glorious is the princess within, gold embroidery is her clothing j Heb lacks O king

King James

17I will make thy name to be remembered in all generations: therefore shall the people praise thee for ever and ever.

To the chief Musician for the sons of Korah,
A Song upon Alamoth.

46 GOD *IS* our refuge and strength, a very present help in trouble.

2Therefore will not we fear, though the earth be removed, and though the mountains be carried into the midst of the sea;

3*Though* the waters thereof roar *and* be troubled, *though* the mountains shake with the swelling thereof. Selah.

4*There is* a river, the streams whereof shall make glad the city of God, the holy *place* of the tabernacles of the most High.

5God *is* in the midst of her; she shall not be moved: God shall help her, *and that* right early.

6The heathen raged, the kingdoms were moved: he uttered his voice, the earth melted.

7The LORD of hosts *is* with us; the God of Jacob *is* our refuge. Selah.

8Come, behold the works of the LORD, what desolations he hath made in the earth.

9He maketh wars to cease unto the end of the earth; he breaketh the bow, and cutteth the spear in sunder; he burneth the chariot in the fire.

10Be still, and know that I *am* God: I will be exalted among the heathen, I will be exalted in the earth.

11The LORD of hosts *is* with us; the God of Jacob *is* our refuge. Selah.

To the chief Musician, A Psalm for the sons of Korah.

47 O CLAP your hands, all ye people; shout unto God with the voice of triumph.

2For the LORD most high *is* terrible; *he is* a great King over all the earth.

3He shall subdue the people under us, and the nations under our feet.

4He shall choose our inheritance for us, the excellency of Jacob whom he loved. Selah.

5God is gone up with a shout, the LORD with the sound of a trumpet.

6Sing praises to God, sing praises: sing praises unto our King, sing praises.

7For God *is* the King of all the earth: sing ye praises with understanding.

8God reigneth over the heathen: God sitteth upon the throne of his holiness.

9The princes of the people are gathered together, *even* the people of the God of Abraham: for the shields of the earth *belong* unto God: he is greatly exalted.

New International

17I will perpetuate your memory through all generations;
   therefore the nations will praise you for ever and ever.

For the director of music. Of the Sons of Korah. According to *alamoth.*[a] A song.

46 GOD IS our refuge and strength,
   an ever-present help in trouble.
2Therefore we will not fear, though the earth give way
   and the mountains fall into the heart of the sea,
3though its waters roar and foam
   and the mountains quake with their surging.
                                                    Selah

4There is a river whose streams make glad the city of God,
   the holy place where the Most High dwells.
5God is within her, she will not fall;
   God will help her at break of day.
6Nations are in uproar, kingdoms fall;
   he lifts his voice, the earth melts.

7The LORD Almighty is with us;
   the God of Jacob is our fortress.   *Selah*

8Come and see the works of the LORD,
   the desolations he has brought on the earth.
9He makes wars cease to the ends of the earth;
   he breaks the bow and shatters the spear,
   he burns the shields[b] with fire.
10"Be still, and know that I am God;
   I will be exalted among the nations,
   I will be exalted in the earth."

11The LORD Almighty is with us;
   the God of Jacob is our fortress.   *Selah*

For the director of music. Of the Sons of Korah. A psalm.

47 CLAP YOUR hands, all you nations;
   shout to God with cries of joy.
2How awesome is the LORD Most High,
   the great King over all the earth!
3He subdued nations under us,
   peoples under our feet.
4He chose our inheritance for us,
   the pride of Jacob, whom he loved.   *Selah*

5God has ascended amid shouts of joy,
   the LORD amid the sounding of trumpets.
6Sing praises to God, sing praises;
   sing praises to our King, sing praises.
7For God is the King of all the earth;
   sing to him a psalm[c] of praise.
8God reigns over the nations;
   God is seated on his holy throne.
9The nobles of the nations assemble
   as the people of the God of Abraham,
for the kings[d] of the earth belong to God;
   he is greatly exalted.

---

[a] Title: Probably a musical term   [b] 9 Or *chariots*   [c] 7 Or *a maskil*
(probably a literary or musical term)   [d] 9 Or *shields*

Living Bible

17"I will cause your name to be honored in all generations; the nations of the earth will praise you forever."

46 GOD IS our refuge and strength, a tested help
in times of trouble. 2And so we need not fear
even if the world blows up, and the mountains crumble
into the sea. 3Let the oceans roar and foam; let the mountains tremble!

4There is a river of joy flowing through the City of
our God—the sacred home of the God above all gods.
5God himself is living in that City; therefore it stands
unmoved despite the turmoil everywhere. He will not
delay his help. 6The nations rant and rave in anger—but
when God speaks, the earth melts in submission and
kingdoms totter into ruin.

7The Commander of the armies of heaven is here
among us. He, the God of Jacob, has come to rescue us.

8Come, see the glorious things that our God does,
how he brings ruin upon the world, 9and causes wars to
end throughout the earth, breaking and burning every
weapon. 10"Stand silent! Know that I am God! I will be
honored by every nation in the world!

11The Commander of the heavenly armies is here
among *us!* He, the God of Jacob, has come to rescue *us!*

47 COME, EVERYONE, and clap for joy! Shout
triumphant praises to the Lord! 2For the Lord,
the God above all gods, is awesome beyond words; he
is the great King of all the earth. 3He subdues the nations
before us, 4and will personally select his choicest blessings for his Jewish peoplee—the very best for those he
loves.

5God has ascended with a mighty shout, with trumpets blaring. 6, 7Sing out your praises to our God, our
King. Yes, sing your highest praises to our King, the
King of all the earth. Sing thoughtful praises! 8He reigns
above the nations, sitting on his holy throne. 9The Gentile rulers of the world have joined with us in praisingf
him—praisingf the God of Abraham—for the battle
shields of all the armies of the world are his trophies. He
is highly honored everywhere.

New Revised Standard

17 I will cause your name to be celebrated in all
generations;
therefore the peoples will praise you forever
and ever.

God's Defense of His City and People

To the leader. Of the Korahites. According to Alamoth.
A Song.

46 GOD IS our refuge and strength,
a very presentg help in trouble.
2 Therefore we will not fear, though the earth
should change,
though the mountains shake in the heart of
the sea;
3 though its waters roar and foam,
though the mountains tremble with its
tumult.   *Selah*

4 There is a river whose streams make glad the
city of God,
the holy habitation of the Most High.
5 God is in the midst of the city;h it shall not
be moved;
God will help it when the morning dawns.
6 The nations are in an uproar, the kingdoms
totter;
he utters his voice, the earth melts.
7 The LORD of hosts is with us;
the God of Jacob is our refuge.i   *Selah*

8 Come, behold the works of the LORD;
see what desolations he has brought on the
earth.
9 He makes wars cease to the end of the earth;
he breaks the bow, and shatters the spear;
he burns the shields with fire.
10 "Be still, and know that I am God!
I am exalted among the nations,
I am exalted in the earth."
11 The LORD of hosts is with us;
the God of Jacob is our refuge.i   *Selah*

God's Rule over the Nations

To the leader. Of the Korahites. A Psalm.

47 CLAP YOUR hands, all you peoples;
shout to God with loud songs of joy.
2 For the LORD, the Most High, is awesome,
a great king over all the earth.
3 He subdued peoples under us,
and nations under our feet.
4 He chose our heritage for us,
the pride of Jacob whom he loves.   *Selah*

5 God has gone up with a shout,
the LORD with the sound of a trumpet.
6 Sing praises to God, sing praises;
sing praises to our King, sing praises.
7 For God is the king of all the earth;
sing praises with a psalm.j

8 God is king over the nations;
God sits on his holy throne.
9 The princes of the peoples gather
as the people of the God of Abraham.
For the shields of the earth belong to God;
he is highly exalted.

---

e 47:4 *his Jewish people,* literally, "the pride of Jacob."   f 47:9 *praising
. . . praising,* implied.

g Or *well proved*   h Heb *of it*   i Or *fortress*   j Heb *Maskil*

King James

A Song *and* Psalm for the sons of Korah.

48 GREAT *IS* the LORD, and greatly to be praised in the city of our God, *in* the mountain of his holiness.

2Beautiful for situation, the joy of the whole earth, *is* mount Zion, *on* the sides of the north, the city of the great King.

3God is known in her palaces for a refuge.

4For, lo, the kings were assembled, they passed by together.

5They saw *it, and* so they marvelled; they were troubled, *and* hasted away.

6Fear took hold upon them there, *and* pain, as of a woman in travail.

7Thou breakest the ships of Tarshish with an east wind.

8As we have heard, so have we seen in the city of the LORD of hosts, in the city of our God: God will establish it for ever. Selah.

9We have thought of thy lovingkindness, O God, in the midst of thy temple.

10According to thy name, O God, so *is* thy praise unto the ends of the earth: thy right hand is full of righteousness.

11Let mount Zion rejoice, let the daughters of Judah be glad, because of thy judgments.

12Walk about Zion, and go round about her: tell the towers thereof.

13Mark ye well her bulwarks, consider her palaces; that ye may tell *it* to the generation following.

14For this God *is* our God for ever and ever: he will be our guide *even* unto death.

To the chief Musician, A Psalm for the sons of Korah.

49 HEAR THIS, all *ye* people; give ear, all *ye* inhabitants of the world:

2Both low and high, rich and poor, together.

3My mouth shall speak of wisdom; and the meditation of my heart *shall be* of understanding.

4I will incline mine ear to a parable: I will open my dark saying upon the harp.

5Wherefore should I fear in the days of evil, *when* the iniquity of my heels shall compass me about?

6They that trust in their wealth, and boast themselves in the multitude of their riches;

7None *of them* can by any means redeem his brother, nor give to God a ransom for him:

8(For the redemption of their soul *is* precious, and it ceaseth for ever:)

9That he should still live for ever, *and* not see corruption.

New International

A song. A psalm of the Sons of Korah.

48 GREAT IS the LORD, and most worthy of praise,
  in the city of our God, his holy mountain.
2It is beautiful in its loftiness,
  the joy of the whole earth.
Like the utmost heights of Zaphon[a] is Mount Zion,
  the[b] city of the Great King.
3God is in her citadels;
  he has shown himself to be her fortress.

4When the kings joined forces,
  when they advanced together,
5they saw her, and were astounded;
  they fled in terror.
6Trembling seized them there,
  pain like that of a woman in labor.
7You destroyed them like ships of Tarshish
  shattered by an east wind.

8As we have heard,
  so have we seen
in the city of the LORD Almighty,
  in the city of our God:
God makes her secure forever.   *Selah*

9Within your temple, O God,
  we meditate on your unfailing love.
10Like your name, O God,
  your praise reaches to the ends of the earth;
  your right hand is filled with righteousness.
11Mount Zion rejoices,
  the villages of Judah are glad
  because of your judgments.

12Walk about Zion, go around her,
  count her towers,
13consider well her ramparts,
  view her citadels,
  that you may tell of them to the next generation.

14For this God is our God for ever and ever;
  he will be our guide even to the end.

For the director of music. Of the Sons of Korah. A psalm.

49 HEAR THIS, all you peoples;
  listen, all who live in this world,
2both low and high,
  rich and poor alike:
3My mouth will speak words of wisdom;
  the utterance from my heart will give understanding.
4I will turn my ear to a proverb;
  with the harp I will expound my riddle:

5Why should I fear when evil days come,
  when wicked deceivers surround me—
6those who trust in their wealth
  and boast of their great riches?
7No man can redeem the life of another
  or give to God a ransom for him—
8the ransom for a life is costly,
  no payment is ever enough—
9that he should live on forever
  and not see decay.

---

a 2 *Zaphon* can refer to a sacred mountain or the direction north.   b 2 Or *earth, / Mount Zion, on the northern side / of the*

Living Bible

48 HOW GREAT is the Lord! How much we should praise him. He lives upon Mount Zion in Jerusalem. ²What a glorious sight! See Mount Zion rising north of the cityᶜ high above the plains for all to see—Mount Zion, joy of all the earth, the residence of the great King.

³God himself is the defender of Jerusalem.ᵈ ⁴The kings of the earth have arrived together to inspect the city. ⁵They marvel at the sight and hurry home again, ⁶afraid of what they have seen; they are filled with panic like a woman in travail! ⁷For God destroys the mightiest warships with a breath of wind. ⁸We have heard of the city's glory—the city of our God, the Commander of the armies of heaven. And now we see it for ourselves! God has established Jerusalem forever.

⁹Lord, here in your Temple we meditate upon your kindness and your love. ¹⁰Your name is known throughout the earth, O God. You are praised everywhere for the salvationᵉ you have scattered throughout the world. ¹¹O Jerusalem,ᶠ rejoice! O people of Judah, rejoice! For God will see to it that you are finally treated fairly. ¹²Go, inspect the city! Walk around and count her many towers! ¹³Note her walls and tour her palaces, so that you can tell your children.

¹⁴For this great God is our God forever and ever. He will be our guide until we die.

49 LISTEN, EVERYONE! High and low, rich and poor, all around the world—listen to my words, ³for they are wise and filled with insight.

⁴I will tell in song accompanied by harps the answer to one of life's most perplexing problems: ⁵*There is no need to fear when times of trouble come,* even though surrounded by enemies! ⁶They trust in their wealth and boast about how rich they are, ⁷yet not one of them, though rich as kings, can ransom his own brother from the penalty of sin! For God's forgiveness does not come that way.ᵍ ⁸, ⁹For a soul is far too precious to be ransomed by mere earthly wealth. There is not enough of it in all the earth to buy eternal life for just one soul, to keep it out of hell.ʰ

ᶜ *48:2 north of the city,* literally, "on the sides of the north." ᵈ *48:3 God himself is the defender of Jerusalem,* literally, "God has made himself known in her palaces for a high tower." ᵉ *48:10 You are praised everywhere for the salvation,* literally, "Your right hand is filled with righteousness." ᶠ *48:11 O Jerusalem,* literally, "Mount Zion." ᵍ *49:7 For God's forgiveness does not come that way,* implied in text. ʰ *49:8, 9 to keep it out of hell,* literally, "so that he should not see the Pit."

New Revised Standard

The Glory and Strength of Zion
A Song. A Psalm of the Korahites.

48 GREAT IS the Lᴏʀᴅ and greatly to be praised
in the city of our God.
His holy mountain, ²beautiful in elevation,
is the joy of all the earth,
Mount Zion, in the far north,
the city of the great King.
³ Within its citadels God
has shown himself a sure defense.

⁴ Then the kings assembled,
they came on together.
⁵ As soon as they saw it, they were astounded;
they were in panic, they took to flight;
⁶ trembling took hold of them there,
pains as of a woman in labor,
⁷ as when an east wind shatters
the ships of Tarshish.
⁸ As we have heard, so have we seen
in the city of the Lᴏʀᴅ of hosts,
in the city of our God,
which God establishes forever.   *Selah*

⁹ We ponder your steadfast love, O God,
in the midst of your temple.
¹⁰ Your name, O God, like your praise,
reaches to the ends of the earth.
Your right hand is filled with victory.
¹¹ Let Mount Zion be glad,
let the townsⁱ of Judah rejoice
because of your judgments.

¹² Walk about Zion, go all around it,
count its towers,
¹³ consider well its ramparts;
go through its citadels,
that you may tell the next generation
¹⁴ that this is God,
our God forever and ever.
He will be our guide forever.

The Folly of Trust in Riches
To the leader. Of the Korahites. A Psalm.

49 HEAR THIS, all you peoples;
give ear, all inhabitants of the world,
² both low and high,
rich and poor together.
³ My mouth shall speak wisdom;
the meditation of my heart shall be
understanding.
⁴ I will incline my ear to a proverb;
I will solve my riddle to the music of the
harp.

⁵ Why should I fear in times of trouble,
when the iniquity of my persecutors
surrounds me,
⁶ those who trust in their wealth
and boast of the abundance of their riches?
⁷ Truly, no ransom avails for one's life,ʲ
there is no price one can give to God for it.
⁸ For the ransom of life is costly,
and can never suffice
⁹ that one should live on forever
and never see the grave.ᵏ

ⁱ Heb *daughters*   ʲ Another reading is *no one can ransom a brother*   ᵏ Heb *the pit*

King James

10For he seeth *that* wise men die, likewise the fool and the brutish person perish, and leave their wealth to others.

11Their inward thought *is, that* their houses *shall continue* for ever, *and* their dwelling places to all generations; they call *their* lands after their own names.

12Nevertheless man *being* in honour abideth not: he is like the beasts *that* perish.

13This their way *is* their folly: yet their posterity approve their sayings. Selah.

14Like sheep they are laid in the grave; death shall feed on them; and the upright shall have dominion over them in the morning; and their beauty shall consume in the grave from their dwelling.

15But God will redeem my soul from the power of the grave: for he shall receive me. Selah.

16Be not thou afraid when one is made rich, when the glory of his house is increased;

17For when he dieth he shall carry nothing away: his glory shall not descend after him.

18Though while he lived he blessed his soul: and *men* will praise thee, when thou doest well to thyself.

19He shall go to the generation of his fathers; they shall never see light.

20Man *that is* in honour, and understandeth not, is like the beasts *that* perish.

A Psalm of Asaph.

50 THE MIGHTY God, *even* the LORD, hath spoken, and called the earth from the rising of the sun unto the going down thereof.

2Out of Zion, the perfection of beauty, God hath shined.

3Our God shall come, and shall not keep silence: a fire shall devour before him, and it shall be very tempestuous round about him.

4He shall call to the heavens from above, and to the earth, that he may judge his people.

5Gather my saints together unto me; those that have made a covenant with me by sacrifice.

6And the heavens shall declare his righteousness: for God *is* judge himself. Selah.

7Hear, O my people, and I will speak; O Israel, and I will testify against thee: I *am* God, *even* thy God.

8I will not reprove thee for thy sacrifices or thy burnt offerings, *to have been* continually before me.

9I will take no bullock out of thy house, *nor* he goats out of thy folds.

10For every beast of the forest *is* mine, *and* the cattle upon a thousand hills.

11I know all the fowls of the mountains: and the wild beasts of the field *are* mine.

12If I were hungry, I would not tell thee: for the world *is* mine, and the fulness thereof.

New International

10For all can see that wise men die;
     the foolish and the senseless alike perish
     and leave their wealth to others.
11Their tombs will remain their housesa forever,
     their dwellings for endless generations,
     though they hadb named lands after
     themselves.

12But man, despite his riches, does not endure;
     he isc like the beasts that perish.

13This is the fate of those who trust in
     themselves,
     and of their followers, who approve their
     sayings.   *Selah*
14Like sheep they are destined for the grave,d
     and death will feed on them.
The upright will rule over them in the morning;
     their forms will decay in the grave,d
     far from their princely mansions.
15But God will redeem my lifee from the grave;
     he will surely take me to himself.   *Selah*

16Do not be overawed when a man grows rich,
     when the splendor of his house increases;
17for he will take nothing with him when he dies,
     his splendor will not descend with him.
18Though while he lived he counted himself
     blessed—
     and men praise you when you prosper—
19he will join the generation of his fathers,
     who will never see the light of lifej.

20A man who has riches without understanding
     is like the beasts that perish.

A psalm of Asaph.

50 THE MIGHTY One, God, the LORD,
     speaks and summons the earth
     from the rising of the sun to the place where
     it sets.
2From Zion, perfect in beauty,
     God shines forth.
3Our God comes and will not be silent;
     a fire devours before him,
     and around him a tempest rages.
4He summons the heavens above,
     and the earth, that he may judge his people:
5"Gather to me my consecrated ones,
     who made a covenant with me by sacrifice."
6And the heavens proclaim his righteousness,
     for God himself is judge.   *Selah*

7"Hear, O my people, and I will speak,
     O Israel, and I will testify against you:
     I am God, your God.
8I do not rebuke you for your sacrifices
     or your burnt offerings, which are ever before
     me.
9I have no need of a bull from your stall
     or of goats from your pens,
10for every animal of the forest is mine,
     and the cattle on a thousand hills.
11I know every bird in the mountains,
     and the creatures of the field are mine.
12If I were hungry I would not tell you,
     for the world is mine, and all that is in it.

a *11* Septuagint and Syriac; Hebrew *In their thoughts their houses will remain*   b *11* Or *I for they have*   c *12* Hebrew; Septuagint and Syriac read verse 12 the same as verse 20.   d *14* Hebrew *Sheol*; also in verse 15   e *15* Or *soul*

Living Bible

10Rich man! Proud man! Wise man! You must die like all the rest! You have no greater lease on life than foolish, stupid men. You must leave your wealth to others. 11You name your estates after yourselves as though your lands could be forever yours, and you could live on them eternally. 12But man with all his pomp must die like any animal. 13Such is the folly of these men, though after they die they will be quoted as having great wisdom.

14Death is the shepherd of all mankind. And "in the morning" those who are evil will be the slaves of those who are good. For the power of their wealth is gone when they die;f they cannot take it with them.

15But as for me, God will redeem my soul from the power of death, for he will receive me. 16So do not be dismayed when evil men grow rich and build their lovely homes. 17For when they die they carry nothing with them! Their honors will not follow them. 18Though a man calls himself happy all through his life—and the world loudly applauds success— 19yet in the end he dies like everyone else, and enters eternal darkness.

20For man with all his pompg must die like any animal.

50 THE MIGHTY God, the Lord, has summoned all mankind from east to west! 2God's glory-light shines from the beautiful Templeh on Mount Zion. 3He comes with the noise of thunder,i surrounded by devastating fire; a great storm rages round about him. 4He has come to judge his people. To heaven and earth he shouts, 5"Gather together my own people who by their sacrifice upon my altar have promised to obeyj me." 6God will judge them with complete fairness, for all heaven declares that he is just.

7O my people, listen! For I am your God. Listen! Here are my charges against you: 8I have no complaint about the sacrifices you bring to my altar, for you bring them regularly. 9But it isn't sacrificial bullocks and goats that I really want from you. 10, 11For all the animals of field and forest are mine! The cattle on a thousand hills! And all the birds upon the mountains! 12If I were hungry, I would not mention it to you—for all the world is mine, and everything in it. 13No, I don't need

New Revised Standard

10 When we look at the wise, they die;
   fool and dolt perish together
   and leave their wealth to others.
11 Their gravesk are their homes forever,
   their dwelling places to all generations,
   though they named lands their own.
12 Mortals cannot abide in their pomp;
   they are like the animals that perish.

13 Such is the fate of the foolhardy,
   the end of thosel who are pleased with their
   lot.   Selah
14 Like sheep they are appointed for Sheol;
   Death shall be their shepherd;
   straight to the grave they descend,m
   and their form shall waste away;
   Sheol shall be their home.n
15 But God will ransom my soul from the power
   of Sheol,
   for he will receive me.   Selah

16 Do not be afraid when some become rich,
   when the wealth of their houses increases.
17 For when they die they will carry nothing
   away;
   their wealth will not go down after them.
18 Though in their lifetime they count themselves
   happy
   —for you are praised when you do well for
   yourself—
19 theyo will go to the company of their
   ancestors,
   who will never again see the light.
20 Mortals cannot abide in their pomp;
   they are like the animals that perish.

The Acceptable Sacrifice

A Psalm of Asaph.

50 THE MIGHTY one, God the LORD,
   speaks and summons the earth
   from the rising of the sun to its setting.
2 Out of Zion, the perfection of beauty,
   God shines forth.

3 Our God comes and does not keep silence,
   before him is a devouring fire,
   and a mighty tempest all around him.
4 He calls to the heavens above
   and to the earth, that he may judge his
   people:
5 "Gather to me my faithful ones,
   who made a covenant with me by sacrifice!"
6 The heavens declare his righteousness,
   for God himself is judge.   Selah

7 "Hear, O my people, and I will speak,
   O Israel, I will testify against you.
   I am God, your God.
8 Not for your sacrifices do I rebuke you;
   your burnt offerings are continually before
   me.
9 I will not accept a bull from your house,
   or goats from your folds.
10 For every wild animal of the forest is mine,
   the cattle on a thousand hills.
11 I know all the birds of the air,p
   and all that moves in the field is mine.

12 "If I were hungry, I would not tell you,
   for the world and all that is in it is mine.

---

f 49:14 For the power of their wealth is gone when they die, literally, "Their beauty shall be for Sheol to consume." g 49:20 with all his pomp, literally, "but without insight." It is uncertain whether this phrase was part of the original text. h 50:2 from the beautiful Temple, literally, "Out of Zion, the perfection of beauty." i 50:3 comes with the noise of thunder, literally, "comes, and does not keep silence." j 50:5 who by their sacrifice upon my altar have promised to obey, literally, "who made a covenant with me by sacrifice."

k Gk Syr Compare Tg: Heb their inward (thought) l Tg: Heb after them
m Cn: Heb the upright shall have dominion over them in the morning
n Meaning of Heb uncertain o Cn: Heb you p Gk Syr Tg: Heb mountains

King James

13Will I eat the flesh of bulls, or drink the blood of goats?

14Offer unto God thanksgiving; and pay thy vows unto the most High:

15And call upon me in the day of trouble: I will deliver thee, and thou shalt glorify me.

16But unto the wicked God saith, What hast thou to do to declare my statutes, or *that* thou shouldest take my covenant in thy mouth?

17Seeing thou hatest instruction, and castest my words behind thee.

18When thou sawest a thief, then thou consentedst with him, and hast been partaker with adulterers.

19Thou givest thy mouth to evil, and thy tongue frameth deceit.

20Thou sittest *and* speakest against thy brother; thou slanderest thine own mother's son.

21These *things* hast thou done, and I kept silence; thou thoughtest that I was altogether *such an one* as thyself: *but* I will reprove thee, and set *them* in order before thine eyes.

22Now consider this, ye that forget God, lest I tear *you* in pieces, and *there be* none to deliver.

23Whoso offereth praise glorifieth me: and to him that ordereth *his* conversation *aright* will I show the salvation of God.

New International

13Do I eat the flesh of bulls
    or drink the blood of goats?
14Sacrifice thank offerings to God,
    fulfill your vows to the Most High,
15and call upon me in the day of trouble;
    I will deliver you, and you will honor me."

16But to the wicked, God says:

"What right have you to recite my laws
    or take my covenant on your lips?
17You hate my instruction
    and cast my words behind you.
18When you see a thief, you join with him;
    you throw in your lot with adulterers.
19You use your mouth for evil
    and harness your tongue to deceit.
20You speak continually against your brother
    and slander your own mother's son.
21These things you have done and I kept silent;
    you thought I was altogethera like you.
But I will rebuke you
    and accuse you to your face.

22"Consider this, you who forget God,
    or I will tear you to pieces, with none to
        rescue:
23He who sacrifices thank offerings honors me,
    and he prepares the way
        so that I may show himb the salvation of
            God."

To the chief Musician, A Psalm of David, when Nathan the prophet came unto him, after he had gone in to Bath-sheba.

51 HAVE MERCY upon me, O God, according to thy lovingkindness: according unto the multitude of thy tender mercies blot out my transgressions.

2Wash me thoroughly from mine iniquity, and cleanse me from my sin.

3For I acknowledge my transgressions: and my sin *is* ever before me.

4Against thee, thee only, have I sinned, and done *this* evil in thy sight: that thou mightest be justified when thou speakest, *and* be clear when thou judgest.

5Behold, I was shapen in iniquity; and in sin did my mother conceive me.

6Behold, thou desirest truth in the inward parts: and in the hidden *part* thou shalt make me to know wisdom.

7Purge me with hyssop, and I shall be clean: wash me, and I shall be whiter than snow.

8Make me to hear joy and gladness; *that* the bones *which* thou hast broken may rejoice.

9Hide thy face from my sins, and blot out all mine iniquities.

10Create in me a clean heart, O God; and renew a right spirit within me.

11Cast me not away from thy presence; and take not thy holy spirit from me.

12Restore unto me the joy of thy salvation; and uphold me *with thy* free spirit.

For the director of music. A psalm of David. When the prophet Nathan came to him after David had committed adultery with Bathsheba.

51 HAVE MERCY on me, O God,
    according to your unfailing love;
according to your great compassion
    blot out my transgressions.
2Wash away all my iniquity
    and cleanse me from my sin.

3For I know my transgressions,
    and my sin is always before me.
4Against you, you only, have I sinned
    and done what is evil in your sight,
so that you are proved right when you speak
    and justified when you judge.
5Surely I was sinful at birth,
    sinful from the time my mother conceived
        me.
6Surely you desire truth in the inner partsc;
    you teachd me wisdom in the inmost place.

7Cleanse me with hyssop, and I will be clean;
    wash me, and I will be whiter than snow.
8Let me hear joy and gladness;
    let the bones you have crushed rejoice.
9Hide your face from my sins
    and blot out all my iniquity.

10Create in me a pure heart, O God,
    and renew a steadfast spirit within me.
11Do not cast me from your presence
    or take your Holy Spirit from me.
12Restore to me the joy of your salvation
    and grant me a willing spirit, to sustain me.

---

a 21 Or thought the 'I AM' was   b 23 Or and to him who considers his way
/ I will show   c 6 The meaning of the Hebrew for this phrase is uncertain.
d 6 Or you desired . . . ; / you taught

Living Bible

your sacrifices of flesh and blood. 14, 15What I want from you is your true thanks; I want your promises fulfilled. *I want you to trust me in your times of trouble, so I can rescue you, and you can give me glory.*

16But God says to evil men: Recite my laws no longer, and stop claiming my promises, 17for you have refused my discipline, disregarding my laws. 18You see a thief and help him, and spend your time with evil and immoral men. 19You curse and lie, and vile language streams from your mouths. 20You slander your own brother. 21I remained silent—you thought I didn't care—but now your time of punishment has come, and I list all the above charges against you. 22This is the last chance for all of you who have forgotten God, before I tear you apart—and no one can help you then.

23But true praise is a worthy sacrifice; this really honors me. Those who walk my paths will receive salvation from the Lord.

Written after Nathan the prophet had come to inform David of God's judgment against him because of his adultery with Bath-sheba, and his murder of Uriah, her husband.

51 O LOVING and kind God, have mercy. Have pity upon me and take away the awful stain of my transgressions. 2Oh, wash me, cleanse me from this guilt. Let me be pure again. 3For I admit my shameful deed—it haunts me day and night. 4It is against you and you alone I sinned, and did this terrible thing. You saw it all, and your sentence against me is just. 5But I was born a sinner, yes, from the moment my mother conceived me. 6You deserve honesty from the heart; yes, utter sincerity and truthfulness. Oh, give me this wisdom.

7Sprinkle me with the cleansing blood[e] and I shall be clean again. Wash me and I shall be whiter than snow. 8And after you have punished me, give me back my joy again. 9Don't keep looking at my sins—erase them from your sight. 10Create in me a new, clean heart, O God, filled with clean thoughts and right desires. 11Don't toss me aside, banished forever from your presence. Don't take your Holy Spirit from me. 12Restore to me again the joy of your salvation, and make me willing to obey you.

New Revised Standard

13 Do I eat the flesh of bulls,
    or drink the blood of goats?
14 Offer to God a sacrifice of thanksgiving,[f]
    and pay your vows to the Most High.
15 Call on me in the day of trouble;
    I will deliver you, and you shall glorify
    me."

16 But to the wicked God says:
    "What right have you to recite my statutes,
    or take my covenant on your lips?
17 For you hate discipline,
    and you cast my words behind you.
18 You make friends with a thief when you see
    one,
    and you keep company with adulterers.

19 "You give your mouth free rein for evil,
    and your tongue frames deceit.
20 You sit and speak against your kin;
    you slander your own mother's child.
21 These things you have done and I have been
    silent;
    you thought that I was one just like
    yourself.
But now I rebuke you, and lay the charge
    before you.

22 "Mark this, then, you who forget God,
    or I will tear you apart, and there will be no
    one to deliver.
23 Those who bring thanksgiving as their
    sacrifice honor me;
    to those who go the right way[g]
I will show the salvation of God."

Prayer for Cleansing and Pardon

To the leader. A Psalm of David, when the prophet Nathan came to him, after he had gone in to Bathsheba.

51 HAVE MERCY on me, O God,
    according to your steadfast love;
according to your abundant mercy
    blot out my transgressions.
2 Wash me thoroughly from my iniquity,
    and cleanse me from my sin.

3 For I know my transgressions,
    and my sin is ever before me.
4 Against you, you alone, have I sinned,
    and done what is evil in your sight,
so that you are justified in your sentence
    and blameless when you pass judgment.
5 Indeed, I was born guilty,
    a sinner when my mother conceived me.

6 You desire truth in the inward being;[h]
    therefore teach me wisdom in my secret
    heart.
7 Purge me with hyssop, and I shall be clean;
    wash me, and I shall be whiter than snow.
8 Let me hear joy and gladness;
    let the bones that you have crushed rejoice.
9 Hide your face from my sins,
    and blot out all my iniquities.

10 Create in me a clean heart, O God,
    and put a new and right[i] spirit within me.
11 Do not cast me away from your presence,
    and do not take your holy spirit from me.
12 Restore to me the joy of your salvation,
    and sustain in me a willing[j] spirit.

King James

13Then will I teach transgressors thy ways; and sinners shall be converted unto thee.

14Deliver me from bloodguiltiness, O God, thou God of my salvation: *and* my tongue shall sing aloud of thy righteousness.

15O Lord, open thou my lips: and my mouth shall show forth thy praise.

16For thou desirest not sacrifice; else would I give *it*: thou delightest not in burnt offering.

17The sacrifices of God *are* a broken spirit: a broken and a contrite heart, O God, thou wilt not despise.

18Do good in thy good pleasure unto Zion: build thou the walls of Jerusalem.

19Then shalt thou be pleased with the sacrifices of righteousness, with burnt offering and whole burnt offering: then shall they offer bullocks upon thine altar.

To the chief Musician, Maschil, *A Psalm* of David, when Doeg the Edomite came and told Saul, and said unto him, David is come to the house of Ahimelech.

52 WHY BOASTEST thou thyself in mischief, O mighty man? the goodness of God *endureth* continually.

2Thy tongue deviseth mischiefs; like a sharp razor, working deceitfully.

3Thou lovest evil more than good; *and* lying rather than to speak righteousness. Selah.

4Thou lovest all devouring words, O *thou* deceitful tongue.

5God shall likewise destroy thee for ever, he shall take thee away, and pluck thee out of *thy* dwellingplace, and root thee out of the land of the living. Selah.

6The righteous also shall see, and fear, and shall laugh at him:

7Lo, *this is* the man *that* made not God his strength; but trusted in the abundance of his riches, *and* strengthened himself in his wickedness.

8But I *am* like a green olive tree in the house of God: I trust in the mercy of God for ever and ever.

9I will praise thee for ever, because thou hast done *it*: and I will wait on thy name; for *it is* good before thy saints.

New International

13Then I will teach transgressors your ways,
    and sinners will turn back to you.
14Save me from bloodguilt, O God,
    the God who saves me,
    and my tongue will sing of your
        righteousness.
15O Lord, open my lips,
    and my mouth will declare your praise.
16You do not delight in sacrifice, or I would bring
        it;
    you do not take pleasure in burnt offerings.
17The sacrifices of God are[a] a broken spirit;
    a broken and contrite heart,
    O God, you will not despise.

18In your good pleasure make Zion prosper;
    build up the walls of Jerusalem.
19Then there will be righteous sacrifices,
    whole burnt offerings to delight you;
    then bulls will be offered on your altar.

For the director of music. A *maskil*[b] of David. When Doeg the Edomite had gone to Saul and told him: "David has gone to the house of Ahimelech."

52 WHY DO you boast of evil, you mighty
        man?
    Why do you boast all day long,
    you who are a disgrace in the eyes of God?
2Your tongue plots destruction;
    it is like a sharpened razor,
    you who practice deceit.
3You love evil rather than good,
    falsehood rather than speaking the truth. *Selah*
4You love every harmful word,
    O you deceitful tongue!

5Surely God will bring you down to everlasting
        ruin:
    He will snatch you up and tear you from your
        tent;
    he will uproot you from the land of the
        living.   *Selah*
6The righteous will see and fear;
    they will laugh at him, saying,
7"Here now is the man
    who did not make God his stronghold
    but trusted in his great wealth
    and grew strong by destroying others!"

8But I am like an olive tree
    flourishing in the house of God;
    I trust in God's unfailing love
    for ever and ever.
9I will praise you forever for what you have
        done;
    in your name I will hope, for your name is
        good.
    I will praise you in the presence of your
        saints.

---

a 17 Or My sacrifice, O God, is   b Title: Probably a literary or musical term

Living Bible

13Then I will teach your ways to other sinners, and they—guilty like me—will repent and return to you. 14, 15Don't sentence me to death. O my God, you alone can rescue me. Then I will sing of your forgiveness,c for my lips will be unsealed—oh, how I will praise you.

16You don't want penance;d if you did, how gladly I would do it! You aren't interested in offerings burned before you on the altar. 17It is a broken spirit you want— remorse and penitence. A broken and a contrite heart, O God, you will not ignore.

18And Lord, don't punish Israel for my sins—help your people and protect Jerusalem.e

19And when my heart is right,f then you will rejoice in the good that I dog and in the bullocks I bring to sacrifice upon your altar.

Written by David to protest against his enemy Doeg (1 Samuel 22), who later slaughtered eighty-five priests and their families.

52 YOU CALL yourself a *hero*, do you? You boast about this evil deed of yours against God's people. 2You are sharp as a tack in plotting your evil tricks. 3How you love wickedness—far more than good! And lying more than truth! 4You love to slander— you love to say anything that will do harm, O man with the lying tongue.

5But God will strike you down and pull you from your home, and drag you away from the land of the living. 6The followers of God will see it happen. They will watch in awe. Then they will laugh and say, 7"See what happens to those who despise God and trust in their wealth, and become ever more bold in their wickedness."h

8But I am like a sheltered olive tree protected by the Lord himself. I trust in the mercy of God forever and ever. 9O Lord, I will praise you forever and ever for your punishment.i And I will wait for your mercies— for everyone knows what a merciful God you are.

New Revised Standard

13 Then I will teach transgressors your ways,
  and sinners will return to you.
14 Deliver me from bloodshed, O God,
  O God of my salvation,
  and my tongue will sing aloud of your
  deliverance.

15 O Lord, open my lips,
  and my mouth will declare your praise.
16 For you have no delight in sacrifice;
  if I were to give a burnt offering, you
  would not be pleased.
17 The sacrifice acceptable to Godj is a broken
  spirit;
  a broken and contrite heart, O God, you
  will not despise.

18 Do good to Zion in your good pleasure;
  rebuild the walls of Jerusalem,
19 then you will delight in right sacrifices,
  in burnt offerings and whole burnt offerings;
  then bulls will be offered on your altar.

Judgment on the Deceitful

To the leader. A Maskil of David, when Doeg the Edomite came to Saul and said to him, "David has come to the house of Ahimelech."

52 WHY DO you boast, O mighty one,
  of mischief done against the godly?k
  All day long 2you are plotting destruction.
  Your tongue is like a sharp razor,
  you worker of treachery.
3 You love evil more than good,
  and lying more than speaking the truth.
                                              Selah
4 You love all words that devour,
  O deceitful tongue.

5 But God will break you down forever;
  he will snatch and tear you from your tent;
  he will uproot you from the land of the
  living.   Selah
6 The righteous will see, and fear,
  and will laugh at the evildoer,l saying,
7 "See the one who would not take
  refuge in God,
  but trusted in abundant riches,
  and sought refuge in wealth!"m

8 But I am like a green olive tree
  in the house of God.
  I trust in the steadfast love of God
  forever and ever.
9 I will thank you forever,
  because of what you have done.
  In the presence of the faithful
  I will proclaimn your name, for it is good.

---

c 51:14, 15 *forgiveness*, literally, "righteousness." d 51:16 *penance*, literally, "a sacrifice." e 51:18 *and protect Jerusalem*, literally, "Do good in your good pleasure unto Zion; build the walls of Jerusalem." f 51:19 *And when my heart is right*, implied. g 51:19 *then you will rejoice in the good that I do*, literally, "then you will delight in the sacrifice of righteousness." h 52:7 *become ever more bold in their wickedness*, literally, "strengthened himself in his wickedness." i 52:9 *for your punishment*, literally, "because you have done it."

j Or *My sacrifice, O God*, k Cn Compare Syr: Heb *the kindness of God* l Heb *him* m Syr Tg: Heb *in his destruction* n Cn: Heb *wait for*

King James

53 THE FOOL hath said in his heart, *There is* no God. Corrupt are they, and have done abominable iniquity: *there is* none that doeth good.

²God looked down from heaven upon the children of men, to see if there were *any* that did understand, that did seek God.

³Every one of them is gone back: they are altogether become filthy; *there is* none that doeth good, no, not one.

⁴Have the workers of iniquity no knowledge? who eat up my people *as* they eat bread: they have not called upon God.

⁵There were they in great fear, *where* no fear was: for God hath scattered the bones of him that encampeth *against* thee: thou hast put *them* to shame, because God hath despised them.

⁶Oh that the salvation of Israel *were come* out of Zion! When God bringeth back the captivity of his people, Jacob shall rejoice, *and* Israel shall be glad.

54 SAVE ME, O God, by thy name, and judge me by thy strength.

²Hear my prayer, O God; give ear to the words of my mouth.

³For strangers are risen up against me, and oppressors seek after my soul: they have not set God before them. Selah.

⁴Behold, God *is* mine helper: the Lord *is* with them that uphold my soul.

⁵He shall reward evil unto mine enemies: cut them off in thy truth.

⁶I will freely sacrifice unto thee: I will praise thy name, O LORD; for *it is* good.

⁷For he hath delivered me out of all trouble: and mine eye hath seen *his desire* upon mine enemies.

55 GIVE EAR to my prayer, O God; and hide not thyself from my supplication.

²Attend unto me, and hear me: I mourn in my complaint, and make a noise;

New International

53 THE FOOL says in his heart,
    "There is no God."
They are corrupt, and their ways are vile;
    there is no one who does good.

²God looks down from heaven
    on the sons of men
to see if there are any who understand,
    any who seek God.
³Everyone has turned away,
    they have together become corrupt;
there is no one who does good,
    not even one.

⁴Will the evildoers never learn—
    those who devour my people as men eat
        bread
and who do not call on God?
⁵There they were, overwhelmed with dread,
    where there was nothing to dread.
God scattered the bones of those who attacked
        you;
    you put them to shame, for God despised
        them.

⁶Oh, that salvation for Israel would come out of
        Zion!
    When God restores the fortunes of his people,
    let Jacob rejoice and Israel be glad!

54 SAVE ME, O God, by your name;
    vindicate me by your might.
²Hear my prayer, O God;
    listen to the words of my mouth.

³Strangers are attacking me;
    ruthless men seek my life—
    men without regard for God.   *Selah*

⁴Surely God is my help;
    the Lord is the one who sustains me.

⁵Let evil recoil on those who slander me;
    in your faithfulness destroy them.

⁶I will sacrifice a freewill offering to you;
    I will praise your name, O LORD,
    for it is good.
⁷For he has delivered me from all my troubles,
    and my eyes have looked in triumph on my
        foes.

55 LISTEN TO my prayer, O God,
    do not ignore my plea;
²   hear me and answer me.
My thoughts trouble me and I am distraught

ᵃ Title: Probably a musical term   ᵇ Title: Probably a literary or musical term

Living Bible

New Revised Standard

Denunciation of Godlessness

To the leader: according to Mahalath. A Maskil of David.

53 ONLY A fool would say to himself, "There is no God." And why does he say it?c Because of his wicked heart, his dark and evil deeds. His life is corroded with sin.

2God looks down from heaven, searching among all mankind to see if there is a single one who does right and really seeks for God. 3But all have turned their backs on him; they are filthy with sin—corrupt and rotten through and through. Not one is good, not one! 4How can this be? Can't they understand anything? For they devour my people like bread and refuse to come to God. 5But soon unheard-of terror will fall on them. God will scatter the bones of these, your enemies. They are doomed, for God has rejected them.

6Oh, that God would come from Zion now and save Israel! Only when the Lord himself restores them can they ever be really happy again.

53 FOOLS SAY in their hearts, "There is no God."
   They are corrupt, they commit abominable acts;
      there is no one who does good.

2 God looks down from heaven on humankind
      to see if there are any who are wise,
      who seek after God.

3 They have all fallen away, they are all alike perverse;
      there is no one who does good,
      no, not one.

4 Have they no knowledge, those evildoers,
      who eat up my people as they eat bread,
      and do not call upon God?

5 There they shall be in great terror,
      in terror such as has not been.
   For God will scatter the bones of the ungodly;f
      they will be put to shame,g for God has rejected them.

6 O that deliverance for Israel would come from Zion!
   When God restores the fortunes of his people,
      Jacob will rejoice; Israel will be glad.

Prayer for Vindication

To the leader: with stringed instruments. A Maskil of David, when the Ziphites went and told Saul, "David is in hiding among us."

Written by David at the time the men of Ziph tried to betray him to Saul.

54 COME WITH great power,d O God, and save me! Defend me with your might! 2Oh, listen to my prayer. 3For violent men have risen against me—ruthless men who care nothing for God are seeking my life.

4But God is my helper. He is a friend of mine!e 5He will cause the evil deeds of my enemies to boomerang upon them. Do as you promised and put an end to these wicked men, O God. 6Gladly I bring my sacrifices to you; I will praise your name, O Lord, for it is good.

7God has rescued me from all my trouble, and triumphed over my enemies.

54 SAVE ME, O God, by your name,
      and vindicate me by your might.
2 Hear my prayer, O God;
      give ear to the words of my mouth.

3 For the insolent have risen against me,
      the ruthless seek my life;
      they do not set God before them.   *Selah*

4 But surely, God is my helper;
      the Lord is the upholder ofh my life.
5 He will repay my enemies for their evil.
      In your faithfulness, put an end to them.

6 With a freewill offering I will sacrifice to you;
      I will give thanks to your name, O LORD,
      for it is good.
7 For he has delivered me from every trouble,
      and my eye has looked in triumph on my enemies.

Complaint about a Friend's Treachery

To the leader: with stringed instruments. A Maskil of David.

55 LISTEN TO my prayer, O God; don't hide yourself when I cry to you. 2Hear me, Lord! Listen to me! For I groan and weep beneath my burden of woe.

55 GIVE EAR to my prayer, O God;
      do not hide yourself from my supplication.
2 Attend to me, and answer me;
      I am troubled in my complaint.
   I am distraught 3by the noise of the enemy,

---

c *53:1 And why does he say it?* Implied.   d *54:1 great power,* literally, "your name."   e *54:4 He is a friend of mine,* literally, "The Lord is of them that uphold my soul."

f Cn Compare Gk Syr: Heb *him who encamps against you*   g Gk: Heb *you will put to shame*   h Gk Syr Jerome: Heb *is of those who uphold* or *is with those who uphold*

King James

3Because of the voice of the enemy, because of the oppression of the wicked: for they cast iniquity upon me, and in wrath they hate me.

4My heart is sore pained within me: and the terrors of death are fallen upon me.

5Fearfulness and trembling are come upon me, and horror hath overwhelmed me.

6And I said, Oh that I had wings like a dove! *for then* would I fly away, and be at rest.

7Lo, *then* would I wander far off, *and* remain in the wilderness. Selah.

8I would hasten my escape from the windy storm *and* tempest.

9Destroy, O Lord, *and* divide their tongues: for I have seen violence and strife in the city.

10Day and night they go about it upon the walls thereof: mischief also and sorrow *are* in the midst of it.

11Wickedness *is* in the midst thereof: deceit and guile depart not from her streets.

12For *it was* not an enemy *that* reproached me; then I could have borne *it:* neither *was it* he that hated me *that* did magnify *himself* against me; then I would have hid myself from him:

13But *it was* thou, a man mine equal, my guide, and mine acquaintance.

14We took sweet counsel together, *and* walked unto the house of God in company.

15Let death seize upon them, *and* let them go down quick into hell: for wickedness *is* in their dwellings, *and* among them.

16As for me, I will call upon God; and the LORD shall save me.

17Evening, and morning, and at noon, will I pray, and cry aloud: and he shall hear my voice.

18He hath delivered my soul in peace from the battle *that was* against me: for there were many with me.

19God shall hear, and afflict them, even he that abideth of old. Selah. Because they have no changes, therefore they fear not God.

20He hath put forth his hands against such as be at peace with him: he hath broken his covenant.

21*The words* of his mouth were smoother than butter, but war *was* in his heart: his words were softer than oil, yet *were* they drawn swords.

22Cast thy burden upon the LORD, and he shall sustain thee: he shall never suffer the righteous to be moved.

23But thou, O God, shalt bring them down into the pit of destruction: bloody and deceitful men shall not live out half their days; but I will trust in thee.

New International

3   at the voice of the enemy,
    at the stares of the wicked;
  for they bring down suffering upon me
    and revile me in their anger.

4My heart is in anguish within me;
    the terrors of death assail me.
5Fear and trembling have beset me;
    horror has overwhelmed me.
6I said, "Oh, that I had the wings of a dove!
    I would fly away and be at rest—
7I would flee far away
    and stay in the desert;   *Selah*
8I would hurry to my place of shelter,
    far from the tempest and storm."

9Confuse the wicked, O Lord, confound their
    speech,
  for I see violence and strife in the city.
10Day and night they prowl about on its walls;
    malice and abuse are within it.
11Destructive forces are at work in the city;
    threats and lies never leave its streets.

12If an enemy were insulting me,
    I could endure it;
  if a foe were raising himself against me,
    I could hide from him.
13But it is you, a man like myself,
    my companion, my close friend,
14with whom I once enjoyed sweet fellowship
    as we walked with the throng at the house of
      God.

15Let death take my enemies by surprise;
    let them go down alive to the grave,[a]
  for evil finds lodging among them.

16But I call to God,
    and the LORD saves me.
17Evening, morning and noon
    I cry out in distress,
    and he hears my voice.
18He ransoms me unharmed
    from the battle waged against me,
    even though many oppose me.
19God, who is enthroned forever,
    will hear them and afflict them—   *Selah*
  men who never change their ways
    and have no fear of God.

20My companion attacks his friends;
    he violates his covenant.
21His speech is smooth as butter,
    yet war is in his heart;
  his words are more soothing than oil,
    yet they are drawn swords.

22Cast your cares on the LORD
    and he will sustain you;
  he will never let the righteous fall.
23But you, O God, will bring down the wicked
    into the pit of corruption;
  bloodthirsty and deceitful men
    will not live out half their days.

But as for me, I trust in you.

a *15* Hebrew *Sheol*

Living Bible

3My enemies shout against me and threaten me with death. They surround me with terror and plot to kill me. Their fury and hatred rise to engulf me. 4My heart is in anguish within me. Stark fear overpowers me. 5Trembling and horror overwhelm me. 6Oh, for wings like a dove, to fly away and rest! 7I would fly to the far-off deserts and stay there. 8I would flee to some refuge from all this storm.

9O Lord, make these enemies begin to quarrel among themselves—destroy them with their own violence and strife.b 10Though they patrol their walls night and day against invaders, their real problem is internal—wickedness and dishonesty are entrenched in the heart of the city. 11There is murder and robbery there, and cheating in the markets and wherever you look.

12It was not an enemy who taunted me—then I could have borne it; I could have hidden and escaped. 13But it was you, a man like myself, my companion and my friend. 14What fellowship we had, what wonderful discussions as we walked together to the Temple of the Lord on holy days.

15Let death seize them and cut them down in their prime, for there is sin in their homes, and they are polluted to the depths of their souls.

16But I will call upon the Lord to save me—and he will. 17I will pray morning, noon, and night, pleading aloud with God; and he will hear and answer. 18Though the tide of battle runs strongly against me, for so many are fighting me, yet he will rescue me. 19God himself—God from everlasting ages past—will answer them! For they refuse to fear him or even honor his commands.

20This friend of mine betrayed me—I who was at peace with him. He broke his promises. 21His words were oily smooth, but in his heart was war. His words were sweet, but underneath were daggers.

22Give your burdens to the Lord. He will carry them. He will not permit the godly to slip or fall. 23He will send my enemies to the pit of destruction. Murderers and liars will not live out half their days. But I am trusting you to save me.

New Revised Standard

    because of the clamor of the wicked.
For they bringc trouble upon me,
    and in anger they cherish enmity against
      me.

4 My heart is in anguish within me,
    the terrors of death have fallen upon me.
5 Fear and trembling come upon me,
    and horror overwhelms me.
6 And I say, "O that I had wings like a dove!
    I would fly away and be at rest;
7 truly, I would flee far away;
    I would lodge in the wilderness;   *Selah*
8 I would hurry to find a shelter for myself
    from the raging wind and tempest."

9 Confuse, O Lord, confound their speech;
    for I see violence and strife in the city.
10 Day and night they go around it
    on its walls,
and iniquity and trouble are within it;
11 ruin is in its midst;
oppression and fraud
    do not depart from its marketplace.

12 It is not enemies who taunt me—
    I could bear that;
it is not adversaries who deal insolently with
    me—
    I could hide from them.
13 But it is you, my equal,
    my companion, my familiar friend,
14 with whom I kept pleasant company;
    we walked in the house of God with the
      throng.
15 Let death come upon them;
    let them go down alive to Sheol;
    for evil is in their homes and in their hearts.

16 But I call upon God,
    and the LORD will save me.
17 Evening and morning and at noon
    I utter my complaint and moan,
    and he will hear my voice.
18 He will redeem me unharmed
    from the battle that I wage,
    for many are arrayed against me.
19 God, who is enthroned from of old,   *Selah*
    will hear, and will humble them—
because they do not change,
    and do not fear God.

20 My companion laid hands on a friend
    and violated a covenant with med
21 with speech smoother than butter,
    but with a heart set on war;
with words that were softer than oil,
    but in fact were drawn swords.

22 Cast your burdene on the LORD,
    and he will sustain you;
he will never permit
    the righteous to be moved.

23 But you, O God, will cast them down
    into the lowest pit;
the bloodthirsty and treacherous
    shall not live out half their days.
But I will trust in you.

---

b 55:9 *destroy them with their own violence and strife,* literally, "for I have seen violence and strife in the city."

c Cn Compare Gk: Heb *they cause to totter*   d Heb lacks *with me*   e Or *Cast what he has given you*

King James

To the chief Musician upon Jonath-elem-rechokim, Michtam of David, when the Philistines took him in Gath.

56 BE MERCIFUL unto me, O God: for man would swallow me up; he fighting daily oppresseth me.

2Mine enemies would daily swallow *me* up: for *they be* many that fight against me, O thou most High.

3What time I am afraid, I will trust in thee.

4In God I will praise his word, in God I have put my trust; I will not fear what flesh can do unto me.

5Every day they wrest my words: all their thoughts *are* against me for evil.

6They gather themselves together, they hide themselves, they mark my steps, when they wait for my soul.

7Shall they escape by iniquity? in *thine* anger cast down the people, O God.

8Thou tellest my wanderings: put thou my tears into thy bottle: *are they* not in thy book?

9When I cry *unto thee*, then shall mine enemies turn back: this I know; for God *is* for me.

10In God will I praise *his* word: in the LORD will I praise *his* word.

11In God have I put my trust: I will not be afraid what man can do unto me.

12Thy vows *are* upon me, O God: I will render praises unto thee.

13For thou hast delivered my soul from death: *wilt* not *thou deliver* my feet from falling, that I may walk before God in the light of the living?

To the chief Musician, Al-taschith, Michtam of David, when he fled from Saul in the cave.

57 BE MERCIFUL unto me, O God, be merciful unto me: for my soul trusteth in thee: yea, in the shadow of thy wings will I make my refuge, until *these* calamities be overpast.

2I will cry unto God most high; unto God that performeth *all things* for me.

3He shall send from heaven, and save me *from* the reproach of him that would swallow me up. Selah. God shall send forth his mercy and his truth.

4My soul *is* among lions: *and* I lie *even among* them that are set on fire, *even* the sons of men, whose teeth *are* spears and arrows, and their tongue a sharp sword.

5Be thou exalted, O God, above the heavens; *let* thy glory *be* above all the earth.

For the director of music. To the tune of, "A Dove on Distant Oaks." Of David. A *miktam*.[a] When the Philistines had seized him in Gath.

56 BE MERCIFUL to me, O God, for men hotly pursue me;
    all day long they press their attack.
2My slanderers pursue me all day long;
    many are attacking me in their pride.

3When I am afraid,
    I will trust in you.
4In God, whose word I praise,
    in God I trust; I will not be afraid.
    What can mortal man do to me?

5All day long they twist my words;
    they are always plotting to harm me.
6They conspire, they lurk,
    they watch my steps,
    eager to take my life.

7On no account let them escape;
    in your anger, O God, bring down the
        nations.
8Record my lament;
    list my tears on your scroll[b]—
    are they not in your record?

9Then my enemies will turn back
    when I call for help.
    By this I will know that God is for me.
10In God, whose word I praise,
    in the LORD, whose word I praise—
11in God I trust; I will not be afraid.
    What can man do to me?

12I am under vows to you, O God;
    I will present my thank offerings to you.
13For you have delivered me[c] from death
    and my feet from stumbling,
   that I may walk before God
    in the light of life.[d]

For the director of music. To the tune of, "Do Not Destroy." Of David. A *miktam*.[a] When he had fled from Saul into the cave.

57 HAVE MERCY on me, O God, have mercy on me,
    for in you my soul takes refuge.
I will take refuge in the shadow of your wings
    until the disaster has passed.

2I cry out to God Most High,
    to God, who fulfills his purpose for me.
3He sends from heaven and saves me,
    rebuking those who hotly pursue me;   *Selah*
    God sends his love and his faithfulness.

4I am in the midst of lions;
    I lie among ravenous beasts—
men whose teeth are spears and arrows,
    whose tongues are sharp swords.

5Be exalted, O God, above the heavens;
    let your glory be over all the earth.

---

a Title: Probably a literary or musical term   b 8 Or / *put my tears in your wineskin*   c 13 Or *my soul*   d 13 Or *the land of the living*

Living Bible

New Revised Standard

Trust in God under Persecution

To the leader: according to The Dove on Far-off Terebinths.
Of David. A Miktam, when the Philistines seized him in
Gath.

56 LORD, HAVE mercy on me; all day long the
enemy troops press in. So many are proud to
fight against me; how they long to conquer me.
3, 4But when I am afraid, I will put my confidence in
you. Yes, I will trust the promises of God. And since
I am trusting him, what can mere man do to me? 5They
are always twisting what I say. All their thoughts are
how to harm me. 6They meet together to perfect their
plans; they hide beside the trail, listening for my steps,
waiting to kill me. 7They expect to get away with it.
Don't let them, Lord. In anger cast them to the ground.

8You have seen me tossing and turning through the
night. You have collected all my tears and preserved
them in your bottle! You have recorded every one in
your book.

9The very day I call for help, the tide of battle turns.
My enemies flee! This one thing I *know: God is for me!*
10, 11I am trusting God—oh, praise his promises! I am
not afraid of anything mere man can do to me! Yes,
praise his promises. 12I will surely do what I have promised, Lord, and thank you for your help. 13For you have
saved me from death and my feet from slipping, so that
I can walk before the Lord in the land of the living.

56 BE GRACIOUS to me, O God, for people
trample on me;
all day long foes oppress me;
2 my enemies trample on me all day long,
for many fight against me.
O Most High, 3 when I am afraid,
I put my trust in you.
4 In God, whose word I praise,
in God I trust; I am not afraid;
what can flesh do to me?

5 All day long they seek to injure my cause;
all their thoughts are against me for evil.
6 They stir up strife, they lurk,
they watch my steps.
As they hoped to have my life,
7 so repaye them for their crime;
in wrath cast down the peoples, O God!

8 You have kept count of my tossings;
put my tears in your bottle.
Are they not in your record?
9 Then my enemies will retreat
in the day when I call.
This I know, thatf God is for me.
10 In God, whose word I praise,
in the LORD, whose word I praise,
11 in God I trust; I am not afraid.
What can a mere mortal do to me?

12 My vows to you I must perform, O God;
I will render thank offerings to you.
13 For you have delivered my soul from death,
and my feet from falling,
so that I may walk before God
in the light of life.

Praise and Assurance under Persecution

To the leader: Do Not Destroy. Of David. A Miktam, when
he fled from Saul, in the cave.

57 O GOD, have pity, for I am trusting you! I will
hide beneath the shadow of your wings until this
storm is past. 2I will cry to the God of heaven who does
such wonders for me. 3He will send down help from
heaven to save me, because of his love and his faithfulness. He will rescue me from these liars who are so
intent upon destroying me. 4I am surrounded by fierce
lions—hotheads whose teeth are sharp as spears and
arrows. Their tongues are like swords. 5Lord, be exalted
above the highest heavens! Show your glory high above
the earth. 6My enemies have set a trap for me. Frantic

57 BE MERCIFUL to me, O God, be merciful
to me,
for in you my soul takes refuge;
in the shadow of your wings I will take
refuge,
until the destroying storms pass by.
2 I cry to God Most High,
to God who fulfills his purpose for me.
3 He will send from heaven and save me,
he will put to shame those who trample on
me.   *Selah*
God will send forth his steadfast love and his
faithfulness.

4 I lie down among lions
that greedily devourg human prey;
their teeth are spears and arrows,
their tongues sharp swords.

5 Be exalted, O God, above the heavens.
Let your glory be over all the earth.

e Cn: Heb *rescue*   f Or *because*   g Cn: Heb *are aflame for*

King James

6They have prepared a net for my steps; my soul is bowed down: they have digged a pit before me, into the midst whereof they are fallen *themselves*. Selah.

7My heart is fixed, O God, my heart is fixed: I will sing and give praise.

8Awake up, my glory; awake, psaltery and harp: I *myself* will awake early.

9I will praise thee, O Lord, among the people: I will sing unto thee among the nations.

10For thy mercy *is* great unto the heavens, and thy truth unto the clouds.

11Be thou exalted, O God, above the heavens: *let* thy glory *be* above all the earth.

To the chief Musician, Al-taschith, Michtam of David.

58 DO YE indeed speak righteousness, O congregation? do ye judge uprightly, O ye sons of men?

2Yea, in heart ye work wickedness; ye weigh the violence of your hands in the earth.

3The wicked are estranged from the womb: they go astray as soon as they be born, speaking lies.

4Their poison *is* like the poison of a serpent: *they are* like the deaf adder *that* stoppeth her ear;

5Which will not hearken to the voice of charmers, charming never so wisely.

6Break their teeth, O God, in their mouth: break out the great teeth of the young lions, O LORD.

7Let them melt away as waters *which* run continually: *when* he bendeth *his* bow to shoot his arrows, let them be as cut in pieces.

8As a snail *which* melteth, let *every one of them* pass away: *like* the untimely birth of a woman, *that* they may not see the sun.

9Before your pots can feel the thorns, he shall take them away as with a whirlwind, both living, and in *his* wrath.

10The righteous shall rejoice when he seeth the vengeance: he shall wash his feet in the blood of the wicked.

11So that a man shall say, Verily *there is* a reward for the righteous: verily he is a God that judgeth in the earth.

To the chief Musician, Al-taschith, Michtam of David; when Saul sent, and they watched the house to kill him.

59 DELIVER ME from mine enemies, O my God: defend me from them that rise up against me.

2Deliver me from the workers of iniquity, and save me from bloody men.

New International

6They spread a net for my feet—
  I was bowed down in distress.
 They dug a pit in my path—
  but they have fallen into it themselves. *Selah*

7My heart is steadfast, O God,
  my heart is steadfast;
 I will sing and make music.
8Awake, my soul!
  Awake, harp and lyre!
 I will awaken the dawn.

9I will praise you, O Lord, among the nations;
  I will sing of you among the peoples.
10For great is your love, reaching to the heavens;
  your faithfulness reaches to the skies.

11Be exalted, O God, above the heavens;
  let your glory be over all the earth.

For the director of music. ⌊To the tune of⌋ "Do Not Destroy." Of David. A *miktam*.a

58 DO YOU rulers indeed speak justly?
  Do you judge uprightly among men?
2No, in your heart you devise injustice,
  and your hands mete out violence on the earth.

3Even from birth the wicked go astray;
  from the womb they are wayward and speak lies.
4Their venom is like the venom of a snake,
  like that of a cobra that has stopped its ears,
5that will not heed the tune of the charmer,
  however skillful the enchanter may be.

6Break the teeth in their mouths, O God;
  tear out, O LORD, the fangs of the lions!
7Let them vanish like water that flows away;
  when they draw the bow, let their arrows be blunted.
8Like a slug melting away as it moves along,
  like a stillborn child, may they not see the sun.

9Before your pots can feel ⌊the heat of⌋ the thorns—
  whether they be green or dry—the wicked will be swept away.b
10The righteous will be glad when they are avenged,
  when they bathe their feet in the blood of the wicked.
11Then men will say,
  "Surely the righteous still are rewarded;
  surely there is a God who judges the earth."

For the director of music. ⌊To the tune of⌋ "Do Not Destroy." Of David. A *miktam*.a When Saul had sent men to watch David's house in order to kill him.

59 DELIVER ME from my enemies, O God;
  protect me from those who rise up against me.
2Deliver me from evildoers
  and save me from bloodthirsty men.

---

a Title: Probably a literary or musical term   b 9 The meaning of the Hebrew for this verse is uncertain.

Living Bible

fear grips me. They have dug a pitfall in my path. But look! They themselves have fallen into it!

7O God, my heart is quiet and confident. No wonder I can sing your praises! 8Rouse yourself, my soul! Arise, O harp and lyre! Let us greet the dawn with song! 9I will thank you publicly throughout the land. I will sing your praises among the nations. 10Your kindness and love are as vast as the heavens. Your faithfulness is higher than the skies.

11Yes, be exalted, O God, above the heavens. May your glory shine throughout the earth.

58 JUSTICE? YOU high and mighty politicians don't even know the meaning of the word! Fairness? Which of you has any left? Not one! All your dealings are crooked: you give "justice" in exchange for bribes.c 3These men are born sinners, lying from their earliest words! 4, 5They are poisonous as deadly snakes, cobras that close their ears to the most expert of charmers.

6O God, break off their fangs. Tear out the teeth of these young lions, Lord. 7Let them disappear like water into thirsty ground. Make their weapons useless in their hands.d 8Let them be as snails that dissolve into slime; and as those who die at birth, who never see the sun. 9God will sweep away both old and young. He will destroy them more quickly than a cooking pot can feel the blazing fire of thorns beneath it.

10The godly shall rejoice in the triumph of right;e they shall walk the blood-stained fields of slaughtered, wicked men. 11Then at last everyone will know that good is rewarded, and that there is a God who judges justly here on earth.

Written by David at the time King Saul set guards at his home to capture and kill him. (1 Samuel 19:11)

59 O MY God, save me from my enemies. Protect me from these who have come to destroy me. 2Preserve me from these criminals, these murderers.

---

c *58:1, 2 All your dealings are crooked: you give "justice" in exchange for bribes,* literally, "you deal out the violence of your hands in the land." d *58:7 Make their weapons useless in their hands,* or, "Let them be trodden down and wither like grass." e *58:10 in the triumph of right,* literally, "when he sees the vengeance."

New Revised Standard

6 They set a net for my steps;
    my soul was bowed down.
  They dug a pit in my path,
    but they have fallen into it themselves.
                                              Selah
7 My heart is steadfast, O God,
    my heart is steadfast.
  I will sing and make melody.
8   Awake, my soul!
  Awake, O harp and lyre!
    I will awake the dawn.
9 I will give thanks to you, O Lord, among the peoples;
    I will sing praises to you among the nations.
10 For your steadfast love is as high as the heavens;
    your faithfulness extends to the clouds.
11 Be exalted, O God, above the heavens.
    Let your glory be over all the earth.

Prayer for Vengeance

To the leader: Do Not Destroy. Of David. A Miktam.

58 DO YOU indeed decree what is right, you gods?f
  Do you judge people fairly?
2 No, in your hearts you devise wrongs;
    your hands deal out violence on earth.

3 The wicked go astray from the womb;
    they err from their birth, speaking lies.
4 They have venom like the venom of a serpent,
    like the deaf adder that stops its ear,
5 so that it does not hear the voice of charmers
    or of the cunning enchanter.

6 O God, break the teeth in their mouths;
    tear out the fangs of the young lions,
    O LORD!
7 Let them vanish like water that runs away;
    like grass let them be trodden downg and wither.
8 Let them be like the snail that dissolves into slime;
    like the untimely birth that never sees the sun.
9 Sooner than your pots can feel the heat of thorns,
    whether green or ablaze, may he sweep them away!

10 The righteous will rejoice when they see vengeance done;
    they will bathe their feet in the blood of the wicked.
11 People will say, "Surely there is a reward for the righteous;
    surely there is a God who judges on earth."

Prayer for Deliverance from Enemies

To the leader: Do Not Destroy. Of David. A Miktam, when Saul ordered his house to be watched in order to kill him.

59 DELIVER ME from my enemies, O my God;
    protect me from those who rise up against me.
2 Deliver me from those who work evil;
    from the bloodthirsty save me.

---

f Or *mighty lords*   g Cn: Meaning of Heb uncertain

King James

3For, lo, they lie in wait for my soul: the mighty are gathered against me; not *for* my transgression, nor *for* my sin, O LORD.

4They run and prepare themselves without *my* fault: awake to help me, and behold.

5Thou therefore, O LORD God of hosts, the God of Israel, awake to visit all the heathen: be not merciful to any wicked transgressors. Selah.

6They return at evening: they make a noise like a dog, and go round about the city.

7Behold, they belch out with their mouth: swords *are* in their lips: for who, *say they,* doth hear?

8But thou, O LORD, shalt laugh at them; thou shalt have all the heathen in derision.

9*Because of* his strength will I wait upon thee: for God *is* my defence.

10The God of my mercy shall prevent me: God shall let me see *my desire* upon mine enemies.

11Slay them not, lest my people forget: scatter them by thy power; and bring them down, O Lord our shield.

12*For* the sin of their mouth *and* the words of their lips let them even be taken in their pride: and for cursing and lying *which* they speak.

13Consume *them* in wrath, consume *them,* that they *may* not *be:* and let them know that God ruleth in Jacob unto the ends of the earth. Selah.

14And at evening let them return; *and* let them make a noise like a dog, and go round about the city.

15Let them wander up and down for meat, and grudge if they be not satisfied.

16But I will sing of thy power; yea, I will sing aloud of thy mercy in the morning: for thou hast been my defence and refuge in the day of my trouble.

17Unto thee, O my strength, will I sing: for God *is* my defence, *and* the God of my mercy.

To the chief Musician upon Shushan-eduth, Michtam of David, to teach; when he strove with Aram-naharaim and with Aram-zobah, when Joab returned, and smote of Edom in the valley of salt twelve thousand.

60

O GOD, thou hast cast us off, thou hast scattered us, thou hast been displeased; O turn thyself to us again.

2Thou hast made the earth to tremble; thou hast broken it: heal the breaches thereof; for it shaketh.

3Thou hast shown thy people hard things: thou hast made us to drink the wine of astonishment.

New International

3See how they lie in wait for me!
Fierce men conspire against me
for no offense or sin of mine, O LORD.
4I have done no wrong, yet they are ready to
attack me.
Arise to help me; look on my plight!
5O LORD God Almighty, the God of Israel,
rouse yourself to punish all the nations;
show no mercy to wicked traitors.   *Selah*

6They return at evening,
snarling like dogs,
and prowl about the city.
7See what they spew from their mouths—
they spew out swords from their lips,
and they say, "Who can hear us?"
8But you, O LORD, laugh at them;
you scoff at all those nations.

9O my Strength, I watch for you;
you, O God, are my fortress, 10my loving
God.

God will go before me
and will let me gloat over those who slander
me.
11But do not kill them, O Lord our shield,[a]
or my people will forget.
In your might make them wander about,
and bring them down.
12For the sins of their mouths,
for the words of their lips,
let them be caught in their pride.
For the curses and lies they utter,
13   consume them in wrath,
consume them till they are no more.
Then it will be known to the ends of the earth
that God rules over Jacob.   *Selah*

14They return at evening,
snarling like dogs,
and prowl about the city.
15They wander about for food
and howl if not satisfied.
16But I will sing of your strength,
in the morning I will sing of your love;
for you are my fortress,
my refuge in times of trouble.

17O my Strength, I sing praise to you;
you, O God, are my fortress, my loving God.

For the director of music. To the tune of "The Lily of the Covenant." A *miktam*[b] of David. For teaching. When he fought Aram Naharaim[c] and Aram Zobah,[d] and when Joab returned and struck down twelve thousand Edomites in the Valley of Salt.

60

YOU HAVE rejected us, O God, and burst forth upon us;
you have been angry—now restore us!
2You have shaken the land and torn it open;
mend its fractures, for it is quaking.
3You have shown your people desperate times;
you have given us wine that makes us
stagger.

a *11* Or *sovereign*   b Title: Probably a literary or musical term   c Title: That is, Arameans of Northwest Mesopotamia   d Title: That is, Arameans of central Syria

Living Bible

³They lurk in ambush for my life. Strong men are out there waiting. And not, O Lord, because I've done them wrong. ⁴Yet they prepare to kill me. Lord, waken! See what is happening! Help me! ⁵(And O Jehovah, God of heaven's armies, God of Israel, arise and punish the heathen nations surrounding us.) Do not spare these evil, treacherous men. ⁶At evening they come to spy, slinking around like dogs that prowl the city. ⁷I hear them shouting insults and cursing God, for "No one will hear us," they think. ⁸Lord, laugh at them! (And scoff at these surrounding nations too.)

⁹O God my Strength! I will sing your praises, for you are my place of safety. ¹⁰My God is changeless in his love for me and he will come and help me. He will let me see my wish come true upon my enemies. ¹¹Don't kill them—for my people soon forget such lessons—but stagger them with your power and bring them to their knees. Bring them to the dust, O Lord our shield. ¹², ¹³They are proud, cursing liars. Angrily destroy them. Wipe them out. (And let the nations find out too that God rules in Israel and will reign throughout the world.) ¹⁴, ¹⁵Let these evil men slink back at evening, and prowl the city all night before they are satisfied, howling like dogs and searching for food.

¹⁶But as for me, I will sing each morning about your power and mercy. For you have been my high tower of refuge, a place of safety in the day of my distress. ¹⁷O my Strength, to you I sing my praises; for you are my high tower of safety, my God of mercy.

Written by David at the time he was at war with Syria, with the outcome still uncertain; this was when Joab, captain of his forces, slaughtered 12,000 men of Edom in the Valley of Salt.

60 O GOD, you have rejected us and broken our defenses; you have become angry and deserted us. Lord, restore us again to your favor. ²You have caused this nation to tremble in fear; you have torn it apart. Lord, heal it now, for it is shaken to its depths. ³You have been very hard on us and made us reel beneath your blows.

New Revised Standard

3 Even now they lie in wait for my life;
    the mighty stir up strife against me.
For no transgression or sin of mine, O LORD,
4   for no fault of mine, they run and make
     ready.

Rouse yourself, come to my help and see!
5   You, LORD God of hosts, are God of Israel.
Awake to punish all the nations;
    spare none of those who treacherously plot
    evil.   *Selah*

6 Each evening they come back,
    howling like dogs
    and prowling about the city.
7 There they are, bellowing with their mouths,
    with sharp words^e on their lips—
    for "Who," they think,^f "will hear us?"

8 But you laugh at them, O LORD;
    you hold all the nations in derision.
9 O my strength, I will watch for you;
    for you, O God, are my fortress.
10 My God in his steadfast love will meet me;
    my God will let me look in triumph on my
    enemies.

11 Do not kill them, or my people may forget;
    make them totter by your power, and bring
        them down,
    O Lord, our shield.
12 For the sin of their mouths, the words of their
        lips,
    let them be trapped in their pride.
For the cursing and lies that they utter,
13   consume them in wrath;
    consume them until they are no more.
Then it will be known to the ends of the earth
    that God rules over Jacob.   *Selah*

14 Each evening they come back,
    howling like dogs
    and prowling about the city.
15 They roam about for food,
    and growl if they do not get their fill.

16 But I will sing of your might;
    I will sing aloud of your steadfast love in
        the morning.
For you have been a fortress for me
    and a refuge in the day of my distress.
17 O my strength, I will sing praises to you,
    for you, O God, are my fortress,
    the God who shows me steadfast love.

Prayer for National Victory after Defeat

To the leader: according to the Lily of the Covenant. A Miktam of David; for instruction; when he struggled with Aram-naharaim and with Aram-zobah, and when Joab on his return killed twelve thousand Edomites in the Valley of Salt.

60 O GOD, you have rejected us, broken our defenses;
    you have been angry; now restore us!
2 You have caused the land to quake; you have
        torn it open;
    repair the cracks in it, for it is tottering.
3 You have made your people suffer hard
        things;
    you have given us wine to drink that made
        us reel.

King James

4Thou hast given a banner to them that fear thee, that it may be displayed because of the truth. Selah.

5That thy beloved may be delivered; save *with* thy right hand, and hear me.

6God hath spoken in his holiness; I will rejoice, I will divide Shechem, and mete out the valley of Succoth.

7Gilead *is* mine, and Manasseh *is* mine; Ephraim also *is* the strength of mine head; Judah *is* my lawgiver;

8Moab *is* my washpot; over Edom will I cast out my shoe: Philistia, triumph thou because of me.

9Who will bring me *into* the strong city? who will lead me into Edom?

10*Wilt* not thou, O God, *which* hadst cast us off? and *thou,* O God, *which* didst not go out with our armies?

11Give us help from trouble: for vain *is* the help of man.

12Through God we shall do valiantly: for he *it is that* shall tread down our enemies.

To the chief Musician upon Neginah, *A Psalm* of David.

61 HEAR MY cry, O God; attend unto my prayer. 2From the end of the earth will I cry unto thee, when my heart is overwhelmed: lead me to the rock *that* is higher than I.

3For thou hast been a shelter for me, *and* a strong tower from the enemy.

4I will abide in thy tabernacle for ever: I will trust in the covert of thy wings. Selah.

5For thou, O God, hast heard my vows: thou hast given *me* the heritage of those that fear thy name.

6Thou wilt prolong the king's life: *and* his years as many generations.

7He shall abide before God for ever: O prepare mercy and truth, *which* may preserve him.

8So will I sing praise unto thy name for ever, that I may daily perform my vows.

To the chief Musician, to Jeduthun, A Psalm of David.

62 TRULY MY soul waiteth upon God: from him *cometh* my salvation.

2He only *is* my rock and my salvation; *he is* my defence; I shall not be greatly moved.

New International

4But for those who fear you, you have raised a banner
to be unfurled against the bow.   *Selah*

5Save us and help us with your right hand,
that those you love may be delivered.
6God has spoken from his sanctuary:
"In triumph I will parcel out Shechem
and measure off the Valley of Succoth.
7Gilead is mine, and Manasseh is mine;
Ephraim is my helmet,
Judah my scepter.
8Moab is my washbasin,
upon Edom I toss my sandal;
over Philistia I shout in triumph."

9Who will bring me to the fortified city?
Who will lead me to Edom?
10Is it not you, O God, you who have rejected us
and no longer go out with our armies?
11Give us aid against the enemy,
for the help of man is worthless.
12With God we will gain the victory,
and he will trample down our enemies.

For the director of music. With stringed instruments.
Of David.

61 HEAR MY cry, O God;
listen to my prayer.

2From the ends of the earth I call to you,
I call as my heart grows faint;
lead me to the rock that is higher than I.
3For you have been my refuge,
a strong tower against the foe.

4I long to dwell in your tent forever
and take refuge in the shelter of your wings.
                                                   Selah
5For you have heard my vows, O God;
you have given me the heritage of those who
fear your name.

6Increase the days of the king's life,
his years for many generations.
7May he be enthroned in God's presence forever;
appoint your love and faithfulness to protect
him.

8Then will I ever sing praise to your name
and fulfill my vows day after day.

For the director of music. For Jeduthun. A psalm of David.

62 MY SOUL finds rest in God alone;
my salvation comes from him.
2He alone is my rock and my salvation;
he is my fortress, I will never be shaken.

Living Bible

4, 5But you have given us a banner to rally to; all who love truth will rally to it;a then you can deliver your beloved people. Use your strong right arm to rescue us. 6, 7God has promised to help us. He has vowed it by his holiness! No wonder I exult! "Shechem, Succoth, Gilead, Manasseh—still are mine!" he says. "Judah shall continue to produce kings, and Ephraim great warriors. 8Moab shall become my lowly servant, and Edom my slave. And I will shout in triumph over the Philistines."

9, 10Who will bring me into Edom's strong cities? God will! He who cast us off! He who abandoned us to our foes! 11Yes, Lord, help us against our enemies, for man's help is useless.

12With God's help we shall do mighty things, for he will trample down our foes.

61 O GOD, listen to me! Hear my prayer! 2For wherever I am, though far away at the ends of the earth, I will cry to you for help. When my heart is faint and overwhelmed, lead me to the mighty, towering Rock of safety. 3For you are my refuge, a high tower where my enemies can never reach me. 4I shall live forever in your tabernacle; oh, to be safe beneath the shelter of your wings! 5For you have heard my vows, O God, to praiseb you every day, and you have given me the blessings you reserve for those who reverence your name.

6You will give mec added years of life, as rich and full as those of many generations, all packed into one. 7And I shall live before the Lord forever. Oh, send your lovingkindness and truth to guard and watch over me, 8and I will praise your name continually, fulfilling my vow of praising you each day.

62 I STAND silently before the Lord, waiting for him to rescue me. For salvation comes from him alone. 2Yes, he alone is my Rock, my rescuer, defense and fortress. Why then should I be tense with fear when troubles come?

New Revised Standard

4 You have set up a banner for those who fear
      you,
    to rally to it out of bowshot.d   Selah
5 Give victory with your right hand, and answer
      us,e
    so that those whom you love may be
      rescued.

6 God has promised in his sanctuary:f
    "With exultation I will divide up Shechem,
      and portion out the Vale of Succoth.
7 Gilead is mine, and Manasseh is mine;
    Ephraim is my helmet;
      Judah is my scepter.
8 Moab is my washbasin;
    on Edom I hurl my shoe;
      over Philistia I shout in triumph."

9 Who will bring me to the fortified city?
    Who will lead me to Edom?
10 Have you not rejected us, O God?
    You do not go out, O God, with our
      armies.
11 O grant us help against the foe,
    for human help is worthless.
12 With God we shall do valiantly;
    it is he who will tread down our foes.

Assurance of God's Protection

To the leader: with stringed instruments. Of David.

61 HEAR MY cry, O God;
      listen to my prayer.
2 From the end of the earth I call to you,
    when my heart is faint.

    Lead me to the rock
      that is higher than I;
3 for you are my refuge,
      a strong tower against the enemy.

4 Let me abide in your tent forever,
    find refuge under the shelter of your wings.
                                          Selah
5 For you, O God, have heard my vows;
    you have given me the heritage of those
      who fear your name.

6 Prolong the life of the king;
    may his years endure to all generations!
7 May he be enthroned forever before God;
    appoint steadfast love and faithfulness to
      watch over him!

8 So I will always sing praises to your name,
    as I pay my vows day after day.

Song of Trust in God Alone

To the leader: according to Jeduthun. A Psalm of David.

62 FOR GOD alone my soul waits in silence;
      from him comes my salvation.
2 He alone is my rock and my salvation,
    my fortress; I shall never be shaken.

---

a 60:4, 5 *all who love truth will rally to it*, literally, "that it may be displayed because of the truth." b 61:5 *to praise*, implied in vs 8. c 61:6 *me*, literally, "to the days of the king."

d Gk Syr Jerome: Heb *because of the truth* e Another reading is *me* f Or *by his holiness*

King James

³How long will ye imagine mischief against a man? ye shall be slain all of you: as a bowing wall *shall ye be, and as* a tottering fence.

⁴They only consult to cast *him* down from his excellency: they delight in lies: they bless with their mouth, but they curse inwardly. Selah.

⁵My soul, wait thou only upon God; for my expectation *is* from him.

⁶He only *is* my rock and my salvation: *he is* my defence; I shall not be moved.

⁷In God *is* my salvation and my glory: the rock of my strength, *and* my refuge, *is* in God.

⁸Trust in him at all times; ye people, pour out your heart before him: God *is* a refuge for us. Selah.

⁹Surely men of low degree *are* vanity, *and* men of high degree *are* a lie: to be laid in the balance, they *are* altogether *lighter* than vanity.

¹⁰Trust not in oppression, and become not vain in robbery: if riches increase, set not your heart *upon them*.

¹¹God hath spoken once; twice have I heard this; that power *belongeth* unto God.

¹²Also unto thee, O Lord, *belongeth* mercy: for thou renderest to every man according to his work.

New International

³How long will you assault a man?
    Would all of you throw him down—
    this leaning wall, this tottering fence?
⁴They fully intend to topple him
    from his lofty place;
    they take delight in lies.
  With their mouths they bless,
    but in their hearts they curse.   Selah

⁵Find rest, O my soul, in God alone;
    my hope comes from him.
⁶He alone is my rock and my salvation;
    he is my fortress, I will not be shaken.
⁷My salvation and my honor depend on God[a];
    he is my mighty rock, my refuge.
⁸Trust in him at all times, O people;
    pour out your hearts to him,
    for God is our refuge.   Selah

⁹Lowborn men are but a breath,
    the highborn are but a lie;
  if weighed on a balance, they are nothing;
    together they are only a breath.
¹⁰Do not trust in extortion
    or take pride in stolen goods;
  though your riches increase,
    do not set your heart on them.

¹¹One thing God has spoken,
    two things have I heard:
  that you, O God, are strong,
¹² and that you, O Lord, are loving.
  Surely you will reward each person
    according to what he has done.

A Psalm of David, when he was in the wilderness of Judah.

63 O GOD, thou *art* my God; early will I seek thee: my soul thirsteth for thee, my flesh longeth for thee in a dry and thirsty land, where no water is;

²To see thy power and thy glory, so *as* I have seen thee in the sanctuary.

³Because thy lovingkindness *is* better than life, my lips shall praise thee.

⁴Thus will I bless thee while I live: I will lift up my hands in thy name.

⁵My soul shall be satisfied as *with* marrow and fatness; and my mouth shall praise *thee* with joyful lips:

⁶When I remember thee upon my bed, *and* meditate on thee in the *night* watches.

⁷Because thou hast been my help, therefore in the shadow of thy wings will I rejoice.

⁸My soul followeth hard after thee: thy right hand upholdeth me.

⁹But those *that* seek my soul, to destroy *it*, shall go into the lower parts of the earth.

¹⁰They shall fall by the sword: they shall be a portion for foxes.

¹¹But the king shall rejoice in God; every one that sweareth by him shall glory: but the mouth of them that speak lies shall be stopped.

A psalm of David. When he was in the Desert of Judah.

63 O GOD, you are my God,
    earnestly I seek you;
  my soul thirsts for you,
    my body longs for you,
  in a dry and weary land
    where there is no water.

²I have seen you in the sanctuary
    and beheld your power and your glory.
³Because your love is better than life,
    my lips will glorify you.
⁴I will praise you as long as I live,
    and in your name I will lift up my hands.
⁵My soul will be satisfied as with the richest of
        foods;
    with singing lips my mouth will praise you.

⁶On my bed I remember you;
    I think of you through the watches of the
        night.
⁷Because you are my help,
    I sing in the shadow of your wings.
⁸My soul clings to you;
    your right hand upholds me.

⁹They who seek my life will be destroyed;
    they will go down to the depths of the earth.
¹⁰They will be given over to the sword
    and become food for jackals.
¹¹But the king will rejoice in God;
    all who swear by God's name will praise
        him,
    while the mouths of liars will be silenced.

ᵃ 7 Or / *God Most High is my salvation and my honor*

Living Bible

3, 4But what is this? They pick on me at a time when my throneb is tottering; they plot my death and use lies and deceit to try to force me from the throne.b They are so friendly to my face while cursing in their hearts! 5But I stand silently before the Lord, waiting for him to rescue me. For salvation comes from him alone. 6Yes, he alone is my Rock, my rescuer, defense and fortress— why then should I be tense with fear when troubles come?

7My protection and successc come from God alone. He is my refuge, a Rock where no enemy can reach me. 8O my people, trust him all the time. Pour out your longings before him, for he can help! 9The greatest of men, or the lowest—both alike are nothing in his sight. They weigh less than air on scales.

10, 11Don't become rich by extortion and robbery; if your riches increase, don't be proud. 12God has said it many times, that power belongs to him; (and also, O Lord, steadfast love belongs to you). He rewards each one of us according to what our works deserve.

A Psalm of David when he was hiding in the wilderness of Judea.

63 O GOD, my God! How I search for you! How I thirst for you in this parched and weary land where there is no water. How I long to find you! 2How I wish I could go into your sanctuary to see your strength and glory, 3for your love and kindness are better to me than life itself. How I praise you! 4I will bless you as long as I live, lifting up my hands to you in prayer. 5At last I shall be fully satisfied; I will praise you with great joy.

6I lie awake at night thinking of you— 7of how much you have helped me—and how I rejoice through the night beneath the protecting shadow of your wings. 8I follow close behind you, protected by your strong right arm. 9But those plotting to destroy me shall go down to the depths of hell. 10They are doomed to die by the sword, to become the food of jackals. 11But Id will rejoice in God. All who trust in him exult, while liars shall be silenced.

New Revised Standard

3 How long will you assail a person,
    will you batter your victim, all of you,
    as you would a leaning wall, a tottering
        fence?
4 Their only plan is to bring down a person of
        prominence.
    They take pleasure in falsehood;
  they bless with their mouths,
    but inwardly they curse.   *Selah*

5 For God alone my soul waits in silence,
    for my hope is from him.
6 He alone is my rock and my salvation,
    my fortress; I shall not be shaken.
7 On God rests my deliverance and my honor;
    my mighty rock, my refuge is in God.

8 Trust in him at all times, O people;
    pour out your heart before him;
    God is a refuge for us.   *Selah*

9 Those of low estate are but a breath,
    those of high estate are a delusion;
    in the balances they go up;
    they are together lighter than a breath.
10 Put no confidence in extortion,
    and set no vain hopes on robbery;
    if riches increase, do not set your heart on
        them.

11 Once God has spoken;
    twice have I heard this:
    that power belongs to God,
12   and steadfast love belongs to you, O Lord.
    For you repay to all
        according to their work.

Comfort and Assurance in God's Presence

A Psalm of David, when he was in the Wilderness of Judah.

63 O GOD, you are my God, I seek you,
    my soul thirsts for you;
  my flesh faints for you,
    as in a dry and weary land where there is
        no water.
2 So I have looked upon you in the sanctuary,
    beholding your power and glory.
3 Because your steadfast love is better than life,
    my lips will praise you.
4 So I will bless you as long as I live;
    I will lift up my hands and call on your
        name.

5 My soul is satisfied as with a rich feast,e
    and my mouth praises you with joyful lips
6 when I think of you on my bed,
    and meditate on you in the watches of the
        night;
7 for you have been my help,
    and in the shadow of your wings I sing for
        joy.
8 My soul clings to you;
    your right hand upholds me.

9 But those who seek to destroy my life
    shall go down into the depths of the earth;
10 they shall be given over to the power of the
        sword,
    they shall be prey for jackals.
11 But the king shall rejoice in God;
    all who swear by him shall exult,
    for the mouths of liars will be stopped.

---

b 62:3, 4 *when my throne,* implied. c 62:7 *success,* literally, "glory."
d 63:11 *I,* literally, "the king."

e Heb *with fat and fatness*

King James

To the chief Musician, A Psalm of David.

64 HEAR MY voice, O God, in my prayer: preserve my life from fear of the enemy.

2Hide me from the secret counsel of the wicked; from the insurrection of the workers of iniquity:

3Who whet their tongue like a sword, *and* bend *their bows to shoot* their arrows, *even* bitter words:

4That they may shoot in secret at the perfect: suddenly do they shoot at him, and fear not.

5They encourage themselves *in* an evil matter: they commune of laying snares privily; they say, Who shall see them?

6They search out iniquities; they accomplish a diligent search: both the inward *thought* of every one *of them*, and the heart, *is* deep.

7But God shall shoot at them *with* an arrow; suddenly shall they be wounded.

8So they shall make their own tongue to fall upon themselves: all that see them shall flee away.

9And all men shall fear, and shall declare the work of God; for they shall wisely consider of his doing.

10The righteous shall be glad in the LORD, and shall trust in him; and all the upright in heart shall glory.

To the chief Musician, A Psalm *and* Song of David.

65 PRAISE WAITETH for thee, O God, in Sion: and unto thee shall the vow be performed.

2O thou that hearest prayer, unto thee shall all flesh come.

3Iniquities prevail against me: *as for* our transgressions, thou shalt purge them away.

4Blessed *is the man whom* thou choosest, and causest to approach *unto thee, that* he may dwell in thy courts: we shall be satisfied with the goodness of thy house, *even* of thy holy temple.

5*By* terrible things in righteousness wilt thou answer us, O God of our salvation; *who art* the confidence of all the ends of the earth, and of them that are afar off *upon* the sea:

6Which by his strength setteth fast the mountains; *being* girded with power:

7Which stilleth the noise of the seas, the noise of their waves, and the tumult of the people.

8They also that dwell in the uttermost parts are afraid at thy tokens: thou makest the outgoings of the morning and evening to rejoice.

New International

For the director of music. A psalm of David.

64 HEAR ME, O God, as I voice my complaint;
  protect my life from the threat of the enemy.
2Hide me from the conspiracy of the wicked,
  from that noisy crowd of evildoers.

3They sharpen their tongues like swords
  and aim their words like deadly arrows.
4They shoot from ambush at the innocent man;
  they shoot at him suddenly, without fear.

5They encourage each other in evil plans,
  they talk about hiding their snares;
  they say, "Who will see them[a]?"
6They plot injustice and say,
  "We have devised a perfect plan!"
  Surely the mind and heart of man are
  cunning.

7But God will shoot them with arrows;
  suddenly they will be struck down.
8He will turn their own tongues against them
  and bring them to ruin;
  all who see them will shake their heads in
  scorn.

9All mankind will fear;
  they will proclaim the works of God
  and ponder what he has done.
10Let the righteous rejoice in the LORD
  and take refuge in him;
  let all the upright in heart praise him!

For the director of music. A psalm of David. A song.

65 PRAISE AWAITS[b] you, O God, in Zion;
  to you our vows will be fulfilled.
2O you who hear prayer,
  to you all men will come.
3When we were overwhelmed by sins,
  you forgave[c] our transgressions.
4Blessed are those you choose
  and bring near to live in your courts!
We are filled with the good things of your
  house,
  of your holy temple.

5You answer us with awesome deeds of
  righteousness,
  O God our Savior,
  the hope of all the ends of the earth
  and of the farthest seas,
6who formed the mountains by your power,
  having armed yourself with strength,
7who stilled the roaring of the seas,
  the roaring of their waves,
  and the turmoil of the nations.
8Those living far away fear your wonders;
  where morning dawns and evening fades
  you call forth songs of joy.

---

a 5 Or *us*   b 1 Or *befits*; the meaning of the Hebrew for this word is uncertain.
c 3 Or *made atonement for*

Living Bible

64 LORD, LISTEN to my complaint: Oh, preserve
my life from the conspiracy of these wicked
men, these gangs of criminals. 3They cut me down with
sharpened tongues; they aim their bitter words like arrows straight at my heart. 4They shoot from ambush at
the innocent. Suddenly the deed is done, yet they are not
afraid. 5They encourage each other to do evil. They meet
in secret to set their traps. "He will never notice them
here," they say. 6They keep a sharp lookout for opportunities of crime. They spend long hours with all their
endless evil thoughts and plans.[d]
7But God himself will shoot them down. Suddenly
his arrow will pierce them. 8They will stagger backward, destroyed by those they spoke against. All who
see it happening will scoff at them. 9Then everyone shall
stand in awe and confess the greatness of the miracles
of God; at last they will realize what amazing things he
does. 10And the godly shall rejoice in the Lord, and trust
and praise him.

65 O GOD in Zion, we wait before you in silent
praise, and thus fulfill our vow. And because
you answer prayer, all mankind will come to you with
their requests. 3Though sins fill our hearts, you forgive
them all. 4How greatly to be envied are those you have
chosen to come and live with you within the holy tabernacle courts! What joys await us among all the good
things there. 5With dread deeds and awesome power you
will defend us from our enemies,[e] O God who saves us.
You are the only hope of all mankind throughout the
world and far away upon the sea.
6He formed the mountains by his mighty strength.
7He quiets the raging oceans and all the world's clamor.
8In the farthest corners of the earth the glorious acts of
God shall startle everyone. The dawn and sunset shout
for joy! 9He waters the earth to make it fertile. The rivers

[d] *64:6 They spend long hours with all their endless evil thoughts and plans,* literally, "And the inward thought and the heart of everyone is deep." [e] *65:5 will defend us from our enemies,* literally, "will answer in righteousness."

New Revised Standard

Prayer for Protection from Enemies

To the leader. A Psalm of David.

64 HEAR MY voice, O God, in my complaint;
preserve my life from the dread enemy.
2 Hide me from the secret plots of the wicked,
from the scheming of evildoers,
3 who whet their tongues like swords,
who aim bitter words like arrows,
4 shooting from ambush at the blameless;
they shoot suddenly and without fear.
5 They hold fast to their evil purpose;
they talk of laying snares secretly,
thinking, "Who can see us?[f]
6 Who can search out our crimes?[g]
We have thought out a cunningly conceived
plot."
For the human heart and mind are deep.

7 But God will shoot his arrow at them;
they will be wounded suddenly.
8 Because of their tongue he will bring them to
ruin;[h]
all who see them will shake with horror.
9 Then everyone will fear;
they will tell what God has brought about,
and ponder what he has done.

10 Let the righteous rejoice in the LORD
and take refuge in him.
Let all the upright in heart glory.

Thanksgiving for Earth's Bounty

To the leader. A Psalm of David. A Song.

65 PRAISE IS due to you,
O God, in Zion;
and to you shall vows be performed,
2 O you who answer prayer!
To you all flesh shall come.
3 When deeds of iniquity overwhelm us,
you forgive our transgressions.
4 Happy are those whom you choose and bring
near
to live in your courts.
We shall be satisfied with the goodness of
your house,
your holy temple.

5 By awesome deeds you answer us with
deliverance,
O God of our salvation;
you are the hope of all the ends of the earth
and of the farthest seas.
6 By your[i] strength you established the
mountains;
you are girded with might.
7 You silence the roaring of the seas,
the roaring of their waves,
the tumult of the peoples.
8 Those who live at earth's farthest bounds are
awed by your signs;
you make the gateways of the morning and
the evening shout for joy.

[f] Syr: Heb *them* [g] Cn: Heb *They search out crimes* [h] Cn: Heb *They will bring him to ruin, their tongue being against them* [i] Gk Jerome: Heb *his*

King James

9Thou visitest the earth, and waterest it: thou greatly enrichest it with the river of God, *which* is full of water: thou preparest them corn, when thou hast so provided for it.

10Thou waterest the ridges thereof abundantly: thou settlest the furrows thereof: thou makest it soft with showers: thou blessest the springing thereof.

11Thou crownest the year with thy goodness; and thy paths drop fatness.

12They drop *upon* the pastures of the wilderness: and the little hills rejoice on every side.

13The pastures are clothed with flocks; the valleys also are covered over with corn; they shout for joy, they also sing.

To the chief Musician, A Song *or* Psalm.

66 MAKE A joyful noise unto God, all ye lands: 2Sing forth the honour of his name: make his praise glorious.

3Say unto God, How terrible *art thou in* thy works! through the greatness of thy power shall thine enemies submit themselves unto thee.

4All the earth shall worship thee, and shall sing unto thee; they shall sing *to* thy name. Selah.

5Come and see the works of God: *he is* terrible *in his* doing toward the children of men.

6He turned the sea into dry *land:* they went through the flood on foot: there did we rejoice in him.

7He ruleth by his power for ever; his eyes behold the nations: let not the rebellious exalt themselves. Selah.

8O bless our God, ye people, and make the voice of his praise to be heard:

9Which holdeth our soul in life, and suffereth not our feet to be moved.

10For thou, O God, hast proved us: thou hast tried us, as silver is tried.

11Thou broughtest us into the net; thou laidst affliction upon our loins.

12Thou hast caused men to ride over our heads; we went through fire and through water: but thou broughtest us out into a wealthy *place.*

13I will go into thy house with burnt offerings: I will pay thee my vows,

14Which my lips have uttered, and my mouth hath spoken, when I was in trouble.

15I will offer unto thee burnt sacrifices of fatlings, with the incense of rams; I will offer bullocks with goats. Selah.

16Come *and* hear, all ye that fear God, and I will declare what he hath done for my soul.

17I cried unto him with my mouth, and he was extolled with my tongue.

18If I regard iniquity in my heart, the Lord will not hear *me:*

19*But* verily God hath heard *me;* he hath attended to the voice of my prayer.

New International

9You care for the land and water it;
    you enrich it abundantly.
The streams of God are filled with water
    to provide the people with grain,
    for so you have ordained it.a
10You drench its furrows
    and level its ridges;
you soften it with showers
    and bless its crops.
11You crown the year with your bounty,
    and your carts overflow with abundance.
12The grasslands of the desert overflow;
    the hills are clothed with gladness.
13The meadows are covered with flocks
    and the valleys are mantled with grain;
    they shout for joy and sing.

For the director of music. A song. A psalm.

66 SHOUT WITH joy to God, all the earth!
2   Sing the glory of his name;
    make his praise glorious!
3Say to God, "How awesome are your deeds!
    So great is your power
    that your enemies cringe before you.
4All the earth bows down to you;
    they sing praise to you,
    they sing praise to your name."   *Selah*

5Come and see what God has done,
    how awesome his works in man's behalf!
6He turned the sea into dry land,
    they passed through the waters on foot—
    come, let us rejoice in him.
7He rules forever by his power,
    his eyes watch the nations—
    let not the rebellious rise up against him.
                                        Selah

8Praise our God, O peoples,
    let the sound of his praise be heard;
9he has preserved our lives
    and kept our feet from slipping.
10For you, O God, tested us;
    you refined us like silver.
11You brought us into prison
    and laid burdens on our backs.
12You let men ride over our heads;
    we went through fire and water,
    but you brought us to a place of abundance.

13I will come to your temple with burnt offerings
    and fulfill my vows to you—
14vows my lips promised and my mouth spoke
    when I was in trouble.
15I will sacrifice fat animals to you
    and an offering of rams;
    I will offer bulls and goats.   *Selah*

16Come and listen, all you who fear God;
    let me tell you what he has done for me.
17I cried out to him with my mouth;
    his praise was on my tongue.
18If I had cherished sin in my heart,
    the Lord would not have listened;
19but God has surely listened
    and heard my voice in prayer.

a 9 Or *for that is how you prepare the land*

Living Bible

of God will not run dry! He prepares the earth for his people and sends them rich harvests of grain. 10He waters the furrows with abundant rain. Showers soften the earth, melting the clods and causing seeds to sprout across the land. 11, 12Then he crowns it all with green, lush pastures in the wilderness; hillsides blossom with joy. 13The pastures are filled with flocks of sheep, and the valleys are carpeted with grain. All the world shouts with joy, and sings.

66 SING TO the Lord, all the earth! 2Sing of his glorious name! Tell the world how wonderful he is.

3How awe-inspiring are your deeds, O God! How great your power! No wonder your enemies surrender! 4All the earth shall worship you and sing of your glories. 5Come, see the glorious things God has done. What marvelous miracles happen to his people! 6He made a dry road through the sea for them. They went across on foot. What excitement and joy there was that day!

7Because of his great power he rules forever. He watches every movement of the nations. O rebel lands, he will deflate your pride.

8Let everyone bless God and sing his praises, 9for he holds our lives in his hands. And he holds our feet to the path. 10You have purified us with fire,b O Lord, like silver in a crucible. 11You captured us in your net and laid great burdens on our backs. 12You sent troops to ride across our broken bodies.c We went through fire and flood. But in the end, you brought us into wealth and great abundance.

13Now I have come to your Temple with burnt offerings to pay my vows. 14For when I was in trouble I promised you many offerings. 15That is why I am bringing you these fat male goats, rams and calves. The smoke of their sacrifice shall rise before you.

16Come and hear, all of you who reverence the Lord, and I will tell you what he did for me: 17For I cried to him for help, with praises ready on my tongue. 18He would not have listened if I had not confessed my sins. 19But he listened! He heard my prayer! He paid attention to it!

New Revised Standard

9 You visit the earth and water it,
      you greatly enrich it;
   the river of God is full of water;
      you provide the people with grain,
      for so you have prepared it.
10 You water its furrows abundantly,
      settling its ridges,
   softening it with showers,
      and blessing its growth.
11 You crown the year with your bounty;
      your wagon tracks overflow with richness.
12 The pastures of the wilderness overflow,
      the hills gird themselves with joy,
13 the meadows clothe themselves with flocks,
      the valleys deck themselves with grain,
      they shout and sing together for joy.

Praise for God's Goodness to Israel

To the leader. A Song. A Psalm.

66 MAKE A joyful noise to God, all the earth;
2   sing the glory of his name;
      give to him glorious praise.
3 Say to God, "How awesome are your deeds!
      Because of your great power, your enemies
         cringe before you.
4 All the earth worships you;
      they sing praises to you,
      sing praises to your name."   *Selah*

5 Come and see what God has done:
      he is awesome in his deeds among mortals.
6 He turned the sea into dry land;
      they passed through the river on foot.
   There we rejoiced in him,
7 who rules by his might forever,
   whose eyes keep watch on the nations—
      let the rebellious not exalt themselves. *Selah*

8 Bless our God, O peoples,
      let the sound of his praise be heard,
9 who has kept us among the living,
      and has not let our feet slip.
10 For you, O God, have tested us;
      you have tried us as silver is tried.
11 You brought us into the net;
      you laid burdens on our backs;
12 you let people ride over our heads;
      we went through fire and through water;
   yet you have brought us out to a spacious
         place.d

13 I will come into your house with burnt
            offerings;
      I will pay you my vows,
14 those that my lips uttered
      and my mouth promised when I was in
            trouble.
15 I will offer to you burnt offerings of fatlings,
      with the smoke of the sacrifice of rams;
   I will make an offering of bulls and goats.
                                              Selah

16 Come and hear, all you who fear God,
      and I will tell what he has done for me.
17 I cried aloud to him,
      and he was extolled with my tongue.
18 If I had cherished iniquity in my heart,
      the Lord would not have listened.
19 But truly God has listened;
      he has given heed to the words of my
            prayer.

---

b 66:10 *You have purified us with fire,* implied.   c 66:12 *You sent troops to ride across our broken bodies,* literally, "You caused men to ride over our heads."

d Cn Compare Gk Syr Jerome Tg: Heb *to a saturation*

King James

20Blessed *be* God, which hath not turned away my prayer, nor his mercy from me.

To the chief Musician on Neginoth, A Psalm *or* Song.

67 GOD BE merciful unto us, and bless us; *and* cause his face to shine upon us; Selah.

2That thy way may be known upon earth, thy saving health among all nations.

3Let the people praise thee, O God; let all the people praise thee.

4O let the nations be glad and sing for joy: for thou shalt judge the people righteously, and govern the nations upon earth. Selah.

5Let the people praise thee, O God; let all the people praise thee.

6Then shall the earth yield her increase; *and* God, *even* our own God, shall bless us.

7God shall bless us; and all the ends of the earth shall fear him.

To the chief Musician, A Psalm *or* Song of David.

68 LET GOD arise, let his enemies be scattered: let them also that hate him flee before him.

2As smoke is driven away, *so* drive *them* away: as wax melteth before the fire, *so* let the wicked perish at the presence of God.

3But let the righteous be glad; let them rejoice before God: yea, let them exceedingly rejoice.

4Sing unto God, sing praises to his name: extol him that rideth upon the heavens by his name JAH, and rejoice before him.

5A father of the fatherless, and a judge of the widows, *is* God in his holy habitation.

6God setteth the solitary in families: he bringeth out those which are bound with chains: but the rebellious dwell in a dry *land*.

7O God, when thou wentest forth before thy people, when thou didst march through the wilderness; Selah:

8The earth shook, the heavens also dropped at the presence of God: *even* Sinai itself *was moved* at the presence of God, the God of Israel.

9Thou, O God, didst send a plentiful rain, whereby thou didst confirm thine inheritance, when it was weary.

10Thy congregation hath dwelt therein: thou, O God, hast prepared of thy goodness for the poor.

New International

20Praise be to God,
    who has not rejected my prayer
    or withheld his love from me!

For the director of music. With stringed instruments.
A psalm. A song.

67 MAY GOD be gracious to us and bless us
    and make his face shine upon us,   *Selah*
2that your ways may be known on earth,
    your salvation among all nations.

3May the peoples praise you, O God;
    may all the peoples praise you.
4May the nations be glad and sing for joy,
    for you rule the peoples justly
    and guide the nations of the earth.   *Selah*
5May the peoples praise you, O God;
    may all the peoples praise you.

6Then the land will yield its harvest,
    and God, our God, will bless us.
7God will bless us,
    and all the ends of the earth will fear him.

For the director of music. Of David. A psalm. A song.

68 MAY GOD arise, may his enemies be
    scattered;
    may his foes flee before him.
2As smoke is blown away by the wind,
    may you blow them away;
as wax melts before the fire,
    may the wicked perish before God.
3But may the righteous be glad
    and rejoice before God;
    may they be happy and joyful.

4Sing to God, sing praise to his name,
    extol him who rides on the clouds[a]—
his name is the LORD—
    and rejoice before him.
5A father to the fatherless, a defender of
    widows,
    is God in his holy dwelling.
6God sets the lonely in families,[b]
    he leads forth the prisoners with singing;
    but the rebellious live in a sun-scorched land.

7When you went out before your people, O God,
    when you marched through the wasteland,
                                        Selah
8the earth shook,
    the heavens poured down rain,
    before God, the One of Sinai,
    before God, the God of Israel.
9You gave abundant showers, O God;
    you refreshed your weary inheritance.
10Your people settled in it,
    and from your bounty, O God, you provided
    for the poor.

---

a 4 Or / *prepare the way for him who rides through the deserts*   b 6 Or *the desolate in a homeland*

Living Bible

20Blessed be God who didn't turn away when I was praying, and didn't refuse me his kindness and love.

67 O GOD, in mercy bless us; let your face beam with joy as you look down at us. 2Send us around the world with the news of your saving power and your eternal plan for all mankind. 3How everyone throughout the earth will praise the Lord! 4How glad the nations will be, singing for joy because you are their Kingᶜ and will give true justice to their people! 5Praise God, O world! May all the peoples of the earth give thanks to you. 6, 7For the earth has yielded abundant harvests. God, even our own God, will bless us. And peoples from remotest lands will worship him.

68 ARISE, O God, and scatter all your enemies! Chase them away! 2Drive them off like smoke before the wind; melt them like wax in fire! So let the wicked perish at the presence of God.

3But may the godly man exult. May he rejoice and be merry. 4Sing praises to the Lord! Raise your voice in song to him who rides upon the clouds!ᵈ Jehovah is his name—oh, rejoice in his presence. 5He is a father to the fatherless; he gives justice to the widows, for he is holy.ᵉ 6He gives families to the lonely, and releases prisoners from jail, singing with joy! But for rebels there is famine and distress.

7O God, when you led your people through the wilderness, 8the earth trembled and the heavens shook. Mount Sinai quailed before you—the God of Israel. 9, 10You sent abundant rain upon your land, O God, to refresh it in its weariness! There your people lived, for you gave them this home when they were destitute.

New Revised Standard

20 Blessed be God,
    because he has not rejected my prayer
    or removed his steadfast love from me.

The Nations Called to Praise God

To the leader: with stringed instruments. A Psalm. A Song.

67 MAY GOD be gracious to us and bless us
    and make his face to shine upon us, *Selah*
2 that your way may be known upon earth,
    your saving power among all nations.
3 Let the peoples praise you, O God;
    let all the peoples praise you.

4 Let the nations be glad and sing for joy,
    for you judge the peoples with equity
    and guide the nations upon earth. *Selah*
5 Let the peoples praise you, O God;
    let all the peoples praise you.

6 The earth has yielded its increase;
    God, our God, has blessed us.
7 May God continue to bless us;
    let all the ends of the earth revere him.

Praise and Thanksgiving

To the leader. Of David. A Psalm. A Song.

68 LET GOD rise up, let his enemies be
    scattered;
    let those who hate him flee before him.
2 As smoke is driven away, so drive them
        away;
    as wax melts before the fire,
    let the wicked perish before God.
3 But let the righteous be joyful;
    let them exult before God;
    let them be jubilant with joy.

4 Sing to God, sing praises to his name;
    lift up a song to him who rides upon the
        cloudsᶠ—
his name is the LORD—
    be exultant before him.

5 Father of orphans and protector of widows
    is God in his holy habitation.
6 God gives the desolate a home to live in;
    he leads out the prisoners to prosperity,
    but the rebellious live in a parched land.

7 O God, when you went out before your
        people,
    when you marched through the wilderness,
                                                Selah
8 the earth quaked, the heavens poured down
        rain
    at the presence of God, the God of Sinai,
    at the presence of God, the God of Israel.
9 Rain in abundance, O God, you showered
        abroad;
    you restored your heritage when it
        languished;
10 your flock found a dwelling in it;
    in your goodness, O God, you provided for
        the needy.

King James

11The Lord gave the word: great *was* the company of those that published *it*.

12Kings of armies did flee apace: and she that tarried at home divided the spoil.

13Though ye have lain among the pots, *yet shall ye be as* the wings of a dove covered with silver, and her feathers with yellow gold.

14When the Almighty scattered kings in it, it was *white* as snow in Salmon.

15The hill of God *is as* the hill of Bashan; an high hill *as* the hill of Bashan.

16Why leap ye, ye high hills? *this is* the hill *which* God desireth to dwell in; yea, the LORD will dwell *in it* for ever.

17The chariots of God *are* twenty thousand, *even* thousands of angels: the Lord *is* among them, *as in* Sinai, in the holy *place*.

18Thou hast ascended on high, thou hast led captivity captive: thou hast received gifts for men; yea, *for* the rebellious also, that the LORD God might dwell *among them*.

19Blessed *be* the Lord, *who* daily loadeth us *with benefits, even* the God of our salvation. Selah.

20*He that is* our God *is* the God of salvation; and unto GOD the Lord *belong* the issues from death.

21But God shall wound the head of his enemies, *and* the hairy scalp of such an one as goeth on still in his trespasses.

22The Lord said, I will bring again from Bashan, I will bring *my people* again from the depths of the sea:

23That thy foot may be dipped in the blood of *thine* enemies, *and* the tongue of thy dogs in the same.

24They have seen thy goings, O God; *even* the goings of my God, my King, in the sanctuary.

25The singers went before, the players on instruments *followed* after; among *them were* the damsels playing with timbrels.

26Bless ye God in the congregations, *even* the Lord, from the fountain of Israel.

27There *is* little Benjamin *with* their ruler, the princes of Judah *and* their council, the princes of Zebulun, *and* the princes of Naphtali.

28Thy God hath commanded thy strength: strengthen, O God, that which thou hast wrought for us.

29Because of thy temple at Jerusalem shall kings bring presents unto thee.

New International

11The Lord announced the word,
  and great was the company of those who
    proclaimed it:
12"Kings and armies flee in haste;
  in the camps men divide the plunder.
13Even while you sleep among the campfires,[a]
  the wings of ˌmyˌ dove are sheathed with
    silver,
  its feathers with shining gold."
14When the Almighty[b] scattered the kings in the
    land,
  it was like snow fallen on Zalmon.

15The mountains of Bashan are majestic
    mountains;
  rugged are the mountains of Bashan.
16Why gaze in envy, O rugged mountains,
  at the mountain where God chooses to reign,
  where the LORD himself will dwell forever?
17The chariots of God are tens of thousands
  and thousands of thousands;
  the Lord ˌhas comeˌ from Sinai into his
    sanctuary.
18When you ascended on high,
  you led captives in your train;
  you received gifts from men,
even from[c] the rebellious—
  that you,[d] O LORD God, might dwell there.

19Praise be to the Lord, to God our Savior,
  who daily bears our burdens.   *Selah*
20Our God is a God who saves;
  from the Sovereign LORD comes escape from
    death.

21Surely God will crush the heads of his enemies,
  the hairy crowns of those who go on in their
    sins.
22The Lord says, "I will bring them from Bashan;
  I will bring them from the depths of the sea,
23that you may plunge your feet in the blood of
    your foes,
  while the tongues of your dogs have their
    share."

24Your procession has come into view, O God,
  the procession of my God and King into the
    sanctuary.
25In front are the singers, after them the
    musicians;
  with them are the maidens playing
    tambourines.
26Praise God in the great congregation;
  praise the LORD in the assembly of Israel.
27There is the little tribe of Benjamin, leading
    them,
  there the great throng of Judah's princes,
  and there the princes of Zebulun and of
    Naphtali.

28Summon your power, O God[e];
  show us your strength, O God, as you have
    done before.
29Because of your temple at Jerusalem
  kings will bring you gifts.

---

a *13* Or *saddlebags*   b *14* Hebrew *Shaddai*   c *18* Or *gifts for men, / even*
d *18* Or *they*   e *28* Many Hebrew manuscripts, Septuagint and Syriac; most
Hebrew manuscripts *Your God has summoned power for you*

Living Bible

11, 12, 13The Lord speaks. The enemy flees. The women at home[f] cry out the happy news: "The armies that came to destroy us have fled!" Now all the women of Israel are dividing the booty. See them sparkle with jewels of silver and gold, covered all over as wings cover doves! 14God scattered their enemies like snowflakes melting in the forests of Zalmon.

15, 16O mighty mountains in Bashan! O splendid many-peaked ranges! Well may you look with envy at Mount Zion, the mount where God has chosen to live forever. 17Surrounded by unnumbered chariots, the Lord moves on from Mount Sinai and comes to his holy temple high upon Mount Zion. 18He ascends the heights, leading many captives in his train. He receives gifts for men,[g] even those who once were rebels. God will live among us here.

19What a glorious Lord! He who daily bears our burdens also gives us our salvation.

20He frees us! He rescues us from death. 21But he will crush his enemies, for they refuse to leave their guilty, stubborn ways. 22The Lord says, "Come," to all his people's enemies;[h] they are hiding on Mount Hermon's highest slopes and deep within the sea! 23His people must destroy them. Cover your feet with their blood; dogs will eat them.

24The procession of God my King moves onward to the sanctuary— 25singers in front, musicians behind, girls playing the timbrels in between. 26Let all the people of Israel praise the Lord, who is Israel's fountain. 27The little tribe of Benjamin leads the way. The princes and elders of Judah, and the princes of Zebulun and Naphtali are right behind.[i] 28Summon your might; display your strength, O God, for you have done such mighty things for us.

29The kings of the earth are bringing their gifts to your temple in Jerusalem. 30Rebuke our enemies, O Lord.

New Revised Standard

11 The Lord gives the command;
      great is the company of those[j] who bore the tidings:
12 "The kings of the armies, they flee, they flee!"
    The women at home divide the spoil,
13 though they stay among the sheepfolds—
    the wings of a dove covered with silver,
      its pinions with green gold.
14 When the Almighty[k] scattered kings there,
      snow fell on Zalmon.

15 O mighty mountain, mountain of Bashan;
      O many-peaked mountain, mountain of Bashan!
16 Why do you look with envy, O many-peaked mountain,
      at the mount that God desired for his abode,
    where the LORD will reside forever?

17 With mighty chariotry, twice ten thousand,
      thousands upon thousands,
    the Lord came from Sinai into the holy place.[l]
18 You ascended the high mount,
      leading captives in your train
    and receiving gifts from people,
    even from those who rebel against the LORD God's abiding there.
19 Blessed be the Lord,
      who daily bears us up;
      God is our salvation.   Selah
20 Our God is a God of salvation,
      and to GOD, the Lord, belongs escape from death.

21 But God will shatter the heads of his enemies,
      the hairy crown of those who walk in their guilty ways.
22 The Lord said,
      "I will bring them back from Bashan,
    I will bring them back from the depths of the sea,
23 so that you may bathe[m] your feet in blood,
      so that the tongues of your dogs may have their share from the foe."

24 Your solemn processions are seen,[n] O God,
      the processions of my God, my King, into the sanctuary—
25 the singers in front, the musicians last,
      between them girls playing tambourines:
26 "Bless God in the great congregation,
      the LORD, O you who are of Israel's fountain!"
27 There is Benjamin, the least of them, in the lead,
      the princes of Judah in a body,
      the princes of Zebulun, the princes of Naphtali.

28 Summon your might, O God;
      show your strength, O God, as you have done for us before.
29 Because of your temple at Jerusalem
      kings bear gifts to you.

---

f 68:11-13 at home, literally, "among the sheepfolds." g 68:18 he receives gifts for men, implied in Ephesians 4:8. h 68:22 to all his people's enemies, literally, "I will bring back from Bashan." i 68:27 are right behind, implied.

j Or company of the women k Traditional rendering of Heb Shaddai l Cn: Heb The Lord among them Sinai in the holy (place) m Gk Syr Tg: Heb shatter n Or have been seen

King James

30Rebuke the company of spearmen, the multitude of the bulls, with the calves of the people, *till every one* submit himself with pieces of silver: scatter thou the people *that* delight in war.

31Princes shall come out of Egypt; Ethiopia shall soon stretch out her hands unto God.

32Sing unto God, ye kingdoms of the earth; O sing praises unto the Lord; Selah:

33To him that rideth upon the heavens of heavens, *which were* of old; lo, he doth send out his voice, *and that* a mighty voice.

34Ascribe ye strength unto God: his excellency *is* over Israel, and his strength *is* in the clouds.

35O God, *thou art* terrible out of thy holy places: the God of Israel *is* he that giveth strength and power unto *his* people. Blessed *be* God.

To the chief Musician upon Shoshannim, *A Psalm* of David.

69 SAVE ME, O God; for the waters are come in unto *my* soul.

2I sink in deep mire, where *there is* no standing: I am come into deep waters, where the floods overflow me.

3I am weary of my crying: my throat is dried: mine eyes fail while I wait for my God.

4They that hate me without a cause are more than the hairs of mine head: they that would destroy me, *being* mine enemies wrongfully, are mighty: then I restored *that* which I took not away.

5O God, thou knowest my foolishness; and my sins are not hid from thee.

6Let not them that wait on thee, O Lord GOD of hosts, be ashamed for my sake: let not those that seek thee be confounded for my sake, O God of Israel.

7Because for thy sake I have borne reproach; shame hath covered my face.

8I am become a stranger unto my brethren, and an alien unto my mother's children.

9For the zeal of thine house hath eaten me up; and the reproaches of them that reproached thee are fallen upon me.

10When I wept, *and chastened* my soul with fasting, that was to my reproach.

11I made sackcloth also my garment; and I became a proverb to them.

12They that sit in the gate speak against me; and I *was* the song of the drunkards.

New International

30Rebuke the beast among the reeds,
   the herd of bulls among the calves of the nations.
Humbled, may it bring bars of silver.
   Scatter the nations who delight in war.
31Envoys will come from Egypt;
   Cush[a] will submit herself to God.
32Sing to God, O kingdoms of the earth,
   sing praise to the Lord,   *Selah*
33to him who rides the ancient skies above,
   who thunders with mighty voice.
34Proclaim the power of God,
   whose majesty is over Israel,
   whose power is in the skies.
35You are awesome, O God, in your sanctuary;
   the God of Israel gives power and strength to
      his people.

Praise be to God!

For the director of music. To the tune of, "Lilies."
   Of David.

69 SAVE ME, O God,
   for the waters have come up to my neck.
2I sink in the miry depths,
   where there is no foothold.
I have come into the deep waters;
   the floods engulf me.
3I am worn out calling for help;
   my throat is parched.
My eyes fail,
   looking for my God.
4Those who hate me without reason
   outnumber the hairs of my head;
many are my enemies without cause,
   those who seek to destroy me.
I am forced to restore
   what I did not steal.

5You know my folly, O God;
   my guilt is not hidden from you.

6May those who hope in you
   not be disgraced because of me,
   O Lord, the LORD Almighty;
may those who seek you
   not be put to shame because of me,
   O God of Israel.
7For I endure scorn for your sake,
   and shame covers my face.
8I am a stranger to my brothers,
   an alien to my own mother's sons;
9for zeal for your house consumes me,
   and the insults of those who insult you fall on
      me.
10When I weep and fast,
   I must endure scorn;
11when I put on sackcloth,
   people make sport of me.
12Those who sit at the gate mock me,
   and I am the song of the drunkards.

a 31 That is, the upper Nile region

Living Bible

Bring them—submissive, tax in hand.[b] Scatter all who delight in war. [31]Egypt will send gifts of precious metals. Ethiopia will stretch out her hands to God in adoration. [32]Sing to the Lord, O kingdoms of the earth—sing praises to the Lord, [33]to him who rides upon the ancient heavens, whose mighty voice thunders from the sky.

[34]Power belongs to God! His majesty shines down on Israel; his strength is mighty in the heavens. [35]What awe we feel, kneeling here before him in the sanctuary. The God of Israel gives strength and mighty power to his people. Blessed be God!

69 SAVE ME, O my God. The floods have risen. Deeper and deeper I sink in the mire; the waters rise around me. [3]I have wept until I am exhausted; my throat is dry and hoarse; my eyes are swollen with weeping, waiting for my God to act. [4]I cannot even count all those who hate me without cause. They are influential men, these who plot to kill me though I am innocent. They demand that I be punished for what I didn't do.

[5]O God, you know so well how stupid I am, and you know all my sins. [6]O Lord God of the armies of heaven, don't let me be a stumbling block to those who trust in you. O God of Israel, don't let me cause them to be confused, [7]though I am mocked and cursed and shamed for your sake. [8]Even my own brothers pretend they don't know me! [9]My zeal for God and his work[c] burns hot within me. And because I advocate your cause, your enemies insult me even as they insult you. [10]How they scoff and mock me when I mourn and fast before the Lord! [11]How they talk about me when I wear sackcloth to show my humiliation and sorrow for my sins! [12]I am the talk of the town and the song of the drunkards. [13]But

New Revised Standard

30 Rebuke the wild animals that live among the
  reeds,
  the herd of bulls with the calves of the
  peoples.
  Trample[d] under foot those who lust after
  tribute;
  scatter the peoples who delight in war.[e]
31 Let bronze be brought from Egypt;
  let Ethiopia[f] hasten to stretch out its hands
  to God.
32 Sing to God, O kingdoms of the earth;
  sing praises to the Lord,   *Selah*
33 O rider in the heavens, the ancient heavens;
  listen, he sends out his voice, his mighty
  voice.
34 Ascribe power to God,
  whose majesty is over Israel;
  and whose power is in the skies.
35 Awesome is God in his[g] sanctuary,
  the God of Israel;
  he gives power and strength to his people.

  Blessed be God!

Prayer for Deliverance from Persecution

To the leader: according to Lilies. Of David.

69 SAVE ME, O God,
  for the waters have come up to my neck.
2 I sink in deep mire,
  where there is no foothold;
  I have come into deep waters,
  and the flood sweeps over me.
3 I am weary with my crying;
  my throat is parched.
  My eyes grow dim
  with waiting for my God.

4 More in number than the hairs of my head
  are those who hate me without cause;
  many are those who would destroy me,
  my enemies who accuse me falsely.
  What I did not steal
  must I now restore?
5 O God, you know my folly;
  the wrongs I have done are not hidden from
  you.

6 Do not let those who hope in you be put to
  shame because of me,
  O Lord GOD of hosts;
  do not let those who seek you be dishonored
  because of me,
  O God of Israel.
7 It is for your sake that I have borne reproach,
  that shame has covered my face.
8 I have become a stranger to my kindred,
  an alien to my mother's children.

9 It is zeal for your house that has consumed
  me;
  the insults of those who insult you have
  fallen on me.
10 When I humbled my soul with fasting,[h]
  they insulted me for doing so.
11 When I made sackcloth my clothing,
  I became a byword to them.
12 I am the subject of gossip for those who sit in
  the gate,
  and the drunkards make songs about me.

---

[b] 68:30 *submissive, tax in hand,* literally, "everyone submitting himself with pieces of silver." An alternate rendering of vs 30 could be, "Trample upon those who lust after the tribute of smaller nations, and who delight in aggressive wars."   [c] 69:9 *his work,* literally, "for your house."

[d] Cn: Heb *Trampling*   [e] Meaning of Heb of verse 30 is uncertain   [f] Or *Nubia;* Heb *Cush*   [g] Gk: Heb *from your*   [h] Gk Syr: Heb *I wept, with fasting my soul,* or *I made my soul mourn with fasting*

King James

13But as for me, my prayer *is* unto thee, O LORD, *in* an acceptable time: O God, in the multitude of thy mercy hear me, in the truth of thy salvation.

14Deliver me out of the mire, and let me not sink: let me be delivered from them that hate me, and out of the deep waters.

15Let not the waterflood overflow me, neither let the deep swallow me up, and let not the pit shut her mouth upon me.

16Hear me, O LORD; for thy lovingkindness *is* good: turn unto me according to the multitude of thy tender mercies.

17And hide not thy face from thy servant; for I am in trouble: hear me speedily.

18Draw nigh unto my soul, *and* redeem it: deliver me because of mine enemies.

19Thou hast known my reproach, and my shame, and my dishonour: mine adversaries *are* all before thee.

20Reproach hath broken my heart; and I am full of heaviness: and I looked *for some* to take pity, but *there was* none; and for comforters, but I found none.

21They gave me also gall for my meat; and in my thirst they gave me vinegar to drink.

22Let their table become a snare before them: and *that which should have been* for *their* welfare, *let it become* a trap.

23Let their eyes be darkened, that they see not; and make their loins continually to shake.

24Pour out thine indignation upon them, and let thy wrathful anger take hold of them.

25Let their habitation be desolate; *and* let none dwell in their tents.

26For they persecute *him* whom thou hast smitten; and they talk to the grief of those whom thou hast wounded.

27Add iniquity unto their iniquity: and let them not come into thy righteousness.

28Let them be blotted out of the book of the living, and not be written with the righteous.

29But I *am* poor and sorrowful: let thy salvation, O God, set me up on high.

30I will praise the name of God with a song, and will magnify him with thanksgiving.

31*This* also shall please the LORD better than an ox *or* bullock that hath horns and hoofs.

32The humble shall see *this, and* be glad: and your heart shall live that seek God.

33For the LORD heareth the poor, and despiseth not his prisoners.

34Let the heaven and earth praise him, the seas, and every thing that moveth therein.

35For God will save Zion, and will build the cities of Judah: that they may dwell there, and have it in possession.

New International

13But I pray to you, O LORD,
   in the time of your favor;
in your great love, O God,
   answer me with your sure salvation.

14Rescue me from the mire,
   do not let me sink;
deliver me from those who hate me,
   from the deep waters.

15Do not let the floodwaters engulf me
   or the depths swallow me up
   or the pit close its mouth over me.

16Answer me, O LORD, out of the goodness of
      your love;
   in your great mercy turn to me.

17Do not hide your face from your servant;
   answer me quickly, for I am in trouble.

18Come near and rescue me;
   redeem me because of my foes.

19You know how I am scorned, disgraced and
      shamed;
   all my enemies are before you.

20Scorn has broken my heart
   and has left me helpless;
I looked for sympathy, but there was none,
   for comforters, but I found none.

21They put gall in my food
   and gave me vinegar for my thirst.

22May the table set before them become a snare;
   may it become retribution anda a trap.

23May their eyes be darkened so they cannot see,
   and their backs be bent forever.

24Pour out your wrath on them;
   let your fierce anger overtake them.

25May their place be deserted;
   let there be no one to dwell in their tents.

26For they persecute those you wound
   and talk about the pain of those you hurt.

27Charge them with crime upon crime;
   do not let them share in your salvation.

28May they be blotted out of the book of life
   and not be listed with the righteous.

29I am in pain and distress;
   may your salvation, O God, protect me.

30I will praise God's name in song
   and glorify him with thanksgiving.

31This will please the LORD more than an ox,
   more than a bull with its horns and hoofs.

32The poor will see and be glad—
   you who seek God, may your hearts live!

33The LORD hears the needy
   and does not despise his captive people.

34Let heaven and earth praise him,
   the seas and all that move in them,

35for God will save Zion
   and rebuild the cities of Judah.
   Then people will settle there and possess it;

---

a 22 Or *snare / and their fellowship become*

Living Bible

I keep right on praying to you, Lord. For now is the time—you are bending down to hear! You are ready with a plentiful supply of love and kindness. Now answer my prayer and rescue me as you promised.b 14Pull me out of this mire. Don't let me sink in. Rescue me from those who hate me, and from these deep waters I am in.

15Don't let the floods overwhelm me, or the ocean swallow me; save me from the pit that threatens me. 16O Jehovah, answer my prayers, for your lovingkindness is wonderful; your mercy is so plentiful, so tender and so kind. 17Don't hide from me,c for I am in deep trouble. Quick! Come and save me. 18Come, Lord, and rescue me. Ransom me from all my enemies. 19You know how they talk about me, and how they so shamefully dishonor me. You see them all and know what each has said.

20Their contempt has broken my heart; my spirit is heavy within me. If even one would show some pity, if even one would comfort me! 21For food they gave me gall; for my awful thirst they offered vinegar. 22Let their joysd turn to ashes and their peace disappear; 23let darkness, blindness and great feebleness be theirs. 24Pour out your fury upon them; consume them with the fierceness of your anger. 25Let their homes be desolate and abandoned. 26For they persecute the one you have smitten, and scoff at the pain of the one you have pierced. 27Pile their sins high and do not overlook them. 28Let these men be blotted from the list of the living;e do not give them the joys of life with the righteous.

29But rescue me, O God, from my poverty and pain. 30Then I will praise God with my singing! My thanks will be his praise— 31that will please him more than sacrificing a bullock or an ox. 32The humble shall see their God at work for them. No wonder they will be so glad! All who seek for God shall live in joy. 33For Jehovah hears the cries of his needy ones, and does not look the other way.

34Praise him, all heaven and earth! Praise him, all the seas and everything in them! 35For God will save Jerusalem;f he rebuilds the cities of Judah. His people shall live in them and not be dispossessed. 36Their children

New Revised Standard

13 But as for me, my prayer is to you, O LORD.
    At an acceptable time, O God,
    in the abundance of your steadfast love,
        answer me.
With your faithful help 14rescue me
    from sinking in the mire;
let me be delivered from my enemies
    and from the deep waters.
15 Do not let the flood sweep over me,
    or the deep swallow me up,
    or the Pit close its mouth over me.

16 Answer me, O LORD, for your steadfast love
        is good;
    according to your abundant mercy, turn to
        me.
17 Do not hide your face from your servant,
    for I am in distress—make haste to answer
        me.
18 Draw near to me, redeem me,
    set me free because of my enemies.

19 You know the insults I receive,
    and my shame and dishonor;
    my foes are all known to you.
20 Insults have broken my heart,
    so that I am in despair.
I looked for pity, but there was none;
    and for comforters, but I found none.
21 They gave me poison for food,
    and for my thirst they gave me vinegar to
        drink.

22 Let their table be a trap for them,
    a snare for their allies.
23 Let their eyes be darkened so that they cannot
        see,
    and make their loins tremble continually.
24 Pour out your indignation upon them,
    and let your burning anger overtake them.
25 May their camp be a desolation;
    let no one live in their tents.
26 For they persecute those whom you have
        struck down,
    and those whom you have wounded, they
        attack still more.g
27 Add guilt to their guilt;
    may they have no acquittal from you.
28 Let them be blotted out of the book of the
        living;
    let them not be enrolled among the
        righteous.
29 But I am lowly and in pain;
    let your salvation, O God, protect me.

30 I will praise the name of God with a song;
    I will magnify him with thanksgiving.
31 This will please the LORD more than an ox
    or a bull with horns and hoofs.
32 Let the oppressed see it and be glad;
    you who seek God, let your hearts revive.
33 For the LORD hears the needy,
    and does not despise his own that are in
        bonds.

34 Let heaven and earth praise him,
    the seas and everything that moves in them.
35 For God will save Zion
    and rebuild the cities of Judah;
and his servants shall liveh there and possess
        it;

b 69:13 and rescue me as you promised, literally, "in the truth of your salvation."   c 69:17 me, literally, "your servant."   d 69:22 their joys, literally, "their table."   e 69:28 Let these men be blotted from the list of the living, or, "Let them be blotted out of the book of life."   f 69:35 Jerusalem, literally, "Zion."

g Gk Syr: Heb recount the pain of   h Syr: Heb and they shall live

King James

36The seed also of his servants shall inherit it: and they that love his name shall dwell therein.

To the chief Musician, *A Psalm* of David, to bring to remembrance.

70 *MAKE HASTE,* O God, to deliver me; make haste to help me, O LORD.

2Let them be ashamed and confounded that seek after my soul: let them be turned backward, and put to confusion, that desire my hurt.

3Let them be turned back for a reward of their shame that say, Aha, aha.

4Let all those that seek thee rejoice and be glad in thee: and let such as love thy salvation say continually, Let God be magnified.

5But I *am* poor and needy: make haste unto me, O God: thou *art* my help and my deliverer; O LORD, make no tarrying.

71 IN THEE, O LORD, do I put my trust: let me never be put to confusion.

2Deliver me in thy righteousness, and cause me to escape: incline thine ear unto me, and save me.

3Be thou my strong habitation, whereunto I may continually resort: thou hast given commandment to save me; for thou *art* my rock and my fortress.

4Deliver me, O my God, out of the hand of the wicked, out of the hand of the unrighteous and cruel man.

5For thou *art* my hope, O Lord GOD: *thou art* my trust from my youth.

6By thee have I been holden up from the womb: thou art he that took me out of my mother's bowels: my praise *shall be* continually of thee.

7I am as a wonder unto many; but thou *art* my strong refuge.

8Let my mouth be filled *with* thy praise *and with* thy honour all the day.

9Cast me not off in the time of old age; forsake me not when my strength faileth.

10For mine enemies speak against me; and they that lay wait for my soul take counsel together.

11Saying, God hath forsaken him: persecute and take him; for *there is* none to deliver *him.*

12O God, be not far from me: O my God, make haste for my help.

13Let them be confounded *and* consumed that are adversaries to my soul; let them be covered *with* reproach and dishonour that seek my hurt.

14But I will hope continually, and will yet praise thee more and more.

15My mouth shall show forth thy righteousness *and* thy salvation all the day; for I know not the numbers *thereof.*

New International

36   the children of his servants will inherit it,
  and those who love his name will dwell there.

For the director of music. Of David. A petition.

70 HASTEN, O God, to save me;
  O LORD, come quickly to help me.
2May those who seek my life
  be put to shame and confusion;
may all who desire my ruin
  be turned back in disgrace.
3May those who say to me, "Aha! Aha!"
  turn back because of their shame.
4But may all who seek you
  rejoice and be glad in you;
may those who love your salvation always say,
  "Let God be exalted!"

5Yet I am poor and needy;
  come quickly to me, O God.
You are my help and my deliverer;
  O LORD, do not delay.

71 IN YOU, O LORD, I have taken refuge;
  let me never be put to shame.
2Rescue me and deliver me in your
    righteousness;
  turn your ear to me and save me.
3Be my rock of refuge,
  to which I can always go;
give the command to save me,
  for you are my rock and my fortress.
4Deliver me, O my God, from the hand of the
    wicked,
  from the grasp of evil and cruel men.

5For you have been my hope, O Sovereign
    LORD,
  my confidence since my youth.
6From birth I have relied on you;
  you brought me forth from my mother's
    womb.
  I will ever praise you.
7I have become like a portent to many,
  but you are my strong refuge.
8My mouth is filled with your praise,
  declaring your splendor all day long.

9Do not cast me away when I am old;
  do not forsake me when my strength is gone.
10For my enemies speak against me;
  those who wait to kill me conspire together.
11They say, "God has forsaken him;
  pursue him and seize him,
  for no one will rescue him."
12Be not far from me, O God;
  come quickly, O my God, to help me.
13May my accusers perish in shame;
  may those who want to harm me
  be covered with scorn and disgrace.

14But as for me, I will always have hope;
  I will praise you more and more.
15My mouth will tell of your righteousness,
  of your salvation all day long,
  though I know not its measure.

Living Bible

shall inherit the land; all who love his name shall live there safely.

70 RESCUE ME, O God! Lord, hurry to my aid! 2, 3They are after my life, and delight in hurting me. Confuse them! Shame them! Stop them! Don't let them keep on mocking me! 4But fill the followers of God with joy. Let those who love your salvation exclaim, "What a wonderful God he is!" 5But I am in deep trouble. Rush to my aid, for only you can help and save me. O Lord, don't delay.

71 LORD, YOU are my refuge! Don't let me down! 2Save me from my enemies, for you are just! Rescue me! Bend down your ear and listen to my plea and save me. 3Be to me a great protecting Rock, where I am always welcome, safe from all attacks. For you have issued the order to save me. 4Rescue me, O God, from these unjust and cruel men. 5O Lord, you alone are my hope; I've trusted you from childhood. 6Yes, you have been with me from birth and have helped me constantly—no wonder I am always praising you! 7My success—at which so many stand amazed—is because you are my mighty protector. 8All day long I'll praise and honor you, O God, for all that you have done for me.

9And now, in my old age, don't set me aside. Don't forsake me now when my strength is failing. 10My enemies are whispering, 11"God has forsaken him! Now we can get him. There is no one to help him now!" 12O God, don't stay away! Come quickly! Help! 13Destroy them! Cover them with failure and disgrace—these enemies of mine.

14I will keep on expecting you to help me. I praise you more and more. 15I cannot count the times when you have faithfully rescued me from danger. I will tell everyone how good you are, and of your constant, daily care.

New Revised Standard

36   the children of his servants shall inherit it,
     and those who love his name shall live in it.

Prayer for Deliverance from Enemies

To the leader. Of David, for the memorial offering.

70 BE PLEASED, O God, to deliver me.
     O LORD, make haste to help me!
2   Let those be put to shame and confusion
     who seek my life.
     Let those be turned back and brought to
          dishonor
     who desire to hurt me.
3   Let those who say, "Aha, Aha!"
     turn back because of their shame.

4   Let all who seek you
     rejoice and be glad in you.
     Let those who love your salvation
     say evermore, "God is great!"
5   But I am poor and needy;
     hasten to me, O God!
     You are my help and my deliverer;
     O LORD, do not delay!

Prayer for Lifelong Protection and Help

71 IN YOU, O LORD, I take refuge;
     let me never be put to shame.
2   In your righteousness deliver me and rescue
          me;
     incline your ear to me and save me.
3   Be to me a rock of refuge,
     a strong fortress,a to save me,
     for you are my rock and my fortress.

4   Rescue me, O my God, from the hand of the
          wicked,
     from the grasp of the unjust and cruel.
5   For you, O Lord, are my hope,
     my trust, O LORD, from my youth.
6   Upon you I have leaned from my birth;
     it was you who took me from my mother's
          womb.
     My praise is continually of you.

7   I have been like a portent to many,
     but you are my strong refuge.
8   My mouth is filled with your praise,
     and with your glory all day long.
9   Do not cast me off in the time of old age;
     do not forsake me when my strength is
          spent.
10 For my enemies speak concerning me,
     and those who watch for my life consult
          together.
11 They say, "Pursue and seize that person
     whom God has forsaken,
     for there is no one to deliver."

12 O God, do not be far from me;
     O my God, make haste to help me!
13 Let my accusers be put to shame and
          consumed;
     let those who seek to hurt me
     be covered with scorn and disgrace.
14 But I will hope continually,
     and will praise you yet more and more.
15 My mouth will tell of your righteous acts,
     of your deeds of salvation all day long,
     though their number is past my knowledge.

a Gk Compare 31.3: Heb *to come continually you have commanded*

King James

16I will go in the strength of the Lord GOD: I will make mention of thy righteousness, *even* of thine only.

17O God, thou hast taught me from my youth: and hitherto have I declared thy wondrous works.

18Now also when I am old and grayheaded, O God, forsake me not; until I have shown thy strength unto *this* generation, *and* thy power to every one *that* is to come.

19Thy righteousness also, O God, *is* very high, who hast done great things: O God, who *is* like unto thee!

20*Thou,* which hast shown me great and sore troubles, shalt quicken me again, and shalt bring me up again from the depths of the earth.

21Thou shalt increase my greatness, and comfort me on every side.

22I will also praise thee with the psaltery, *even* thy truth, O my God: unto thee will I sing with the harp, O thou Holy One of Israel.

23My lips shall greatly rejoice when I sing unto thee; and my soul, which thou hast redeemed.

24My tongue also shall talk of thy righteousness all the day long: for they are confounded, for they are brought unto shame, that seek my hurt.

A Psalm for Solomon.

72 GIVE THE king thy judgments, O God, and thy righteousness unto the king's son.

2He shall judge thy people with righteousness, and thy poor with judgment.

3The mountains shall bring peace to the people, and the little hills, by righteousness.

4He shall judge the poor of the people, he shall save the children of the needy, and shall break in pieces the oppressor.

5They shall fear thee as long as the sun and moon endure, throughout all generations.

6He shall come down like rain upon the mown grass: as showers *that* water the earth.

7In his days shall the righteous flourish; and abundance of peace so long as the moon endureth.

8He shall have dominion also from sea to sea, and from the river unto the ends of the earth.

9They that dwell in the wilderness shall bow before him; and his enemies shall lick the dust.

10The kings of Tarshish and of the isles shall bring presents: the kings of Sheba and Seba shall offer gifts.

11Yea, all kings shall fall down before him: all nations shall serve him.

New International

16I will come and proclaim your mighty acts,
    O Sovereign LORD;
  I will proclaim your righteousness, yours
    alone.
17Since my youth, O God, you have taught me,
    and to this day I declare your marvelous
    deeds.
18Even when I am old and gray,
    do not forsake me, O God,
  till I declare your power to the next generation,
    your might to all who are to come.

19Your righteousness reaches to the skies, O God,
    you who have done great things.
  Who, O God, is like you?
20Though you have made me see troubles, many
    and bitter,
    you will restore my life again;
  from the depths of the earth
    you will again bring me up.
21You will increase my honor
    and comfort me once again.

22I will praise you with the harp
    for your faithfulness, O my God;
  I will sing praise to you with the lyre,
    O Holy One of Israel.
23My lips will shout for joy
    when I sing praise to you—
    I, whom you have redeemed.
24My tongue will tell of your righteous acts
    all day long,
  for those who wanted to harm me
    have been put to shame and confusion.

Of Solomon.

72 ENDOW THE king with your justice,
    O God,
  the royal son with your righteousness.
2He willa judge your people in righteousness,
    your afflicted ones with justice.
3The mountains will bring prosperity to the
    people,
    the hills the fruit of righteousness.
4He will defend the afflicted among the people
    and save the children of the needy;
    he will crush the oppressor.

5He will endureb as long as the sun,
    as long as the moon, through all generations.
6He will be like rain falling on a mown field,
    like showers watering the earth.
7In his days the righteous will flourish;
    prosperity will abound till the moon is no
    more.

8He will rule from sea to sea
    and from the Riverc to the ends of the
    earth.d
9The desert tribes will bow before him
    and his enemies will lick the dust.
10The kings of Tarshish and of distant shores
    will bring tribute to him;
  the kings of Sheba and Seba
    will present him gifts.
11All kings will bow down to him
    and all nations will serve him.

a 2 Or *May he*; similarly in verses 3-11 and 17   b 5 Septuagint; Hebrew *You will be feared*   c 8 That is, the Euphrates   d 8 Or *the end of the land*

Living Bible

16I walk in the strength of the Lord God. I tell everyone that you alone are just and good. 17O God, you have helped me from my earliest childhood—and I have constantly testified to others of the wonderful things you do. 18And now that I am old and gray, don't forsake me. Give me time to tell this new generation (and their children too) about all your mighty miracles. 19Your power and goodness, Lord, reach to the highest heavens. You have done such wonderful things. Where is there another God like you? 20You have let me sink down deep in desperate problems. But you will bring me back to life again, up from the depths of the earth. 21You will give me greater honor than before, and turn again and comfort me.

22I will praise you with music, telling of your faithfulness to all your promises, O Holy One of Israel. 23I will shout and sing your praises for redeeming me. 24I will talk to others all day long about your justice and your goodness. For all who tried to hurt me have been disgraced and dishonored.

72 O GOD, help the king to judge as you would, and help his son to walk in godliness. 2Help him to give justice to your people, even to the poor. 3May the mountains and hills flourish in prosperity because of his good reign. 4Help him to defend the poor and needy and to crush their oppressors. 5May the poor and needy revere you constantly, as long as sun and moon continue in the skies! Yes, forever!

6May the reign of this son of mine*e* be as gentle and fruitful as the springtime rains upon the grass—like showers that water the earth! 7May all good men flourish in his reign, with abundance of peace to the end of time.

8Let him reign from sea to sea, and from the Euphrates River to the ends of the earth. 9The desert nomads shall bow before him; his enemies shall fall face downward in the dust. 10Kings along the Mediterranean coast—the kings of Tarshish and the islands—and those from Sheba and from Seba—all will bring their gifts. 11Yes, kings from everywhere! All will bow before him! All will serve him!

New Revised Standard

16 I will come praising the mighty deeds of the
        Lord GOD,
    I will praise your righteousness, yours
        alone.

17 O God, from my youth you have taught me,
        and I still proclaim your wondrous deeds.
18 So even to old age and gray hairs,
        O God, do not forsake me,
    until I proclaim your might
        to all the generations to come.*f*
    Your power 19and your righteousness, O God,
        reach the high heavens.

    You who have done great things,
        O God, who is like you?
20 You who have made me see many troubles
            and calamities
    will revive me again;
    from the depths of the earth
        you will bring me up again.
21 You will increase my honor,
        and comfort me once again.

22 I will also praise you with the harp
        for your faithfulness, O my God;
    I will sing praises to you with the lyre,
        O Holy One of Israel.
23 My lips will shout for joy
        when I sing praises to you;
    my soul also, which you have rescued.
24 All day long my tongue will talk of your
            righteous help,
    for those who tried to do me harm
        have been put to shame, and disgraced.

Prayer for Guidance and Support for the King
                    Of Solomon.

72 GIVE THE king your justice, O God,
        and your righteousness to a king's son.
2 May he judge your people with righteousness,
        and your poor with justice.
3 May the mountains yield prosperity for the
            people,
        and the hills, in righteousness.
4 May he defend the cause of the poor of the
            people,
        give deliverance to the needy,
        and crush the oppressor.

5 May he live*g* while the sun endures,
        and as long as the moon, throughout all
            generations.
6 May he be like rain that falls on the mown
            grass,
        like showers that water the earth.
7 In his days may righteousness flourish
        and peace abound, until the moon is no
            more.

8 May he have dominion from sea to sea,
        and from the River to the ends of the earth.
9 May his foes*h* bow down before him,
        and his enemies lick the dust.
10 May the kings of Tarshish and of the isles
            render him tribute,
        may the kings of Sheba and Seba
            bring gifts.
11 May all kings fall down before him,
        all nations give him service.

---

e 72:6 *this son of mine*. The reference seems to look beyond Solomon's son to Jesus the Messiah.

f Gk Compare Syr: Heb *to a generation, to all that come*   *g* Gk: Heb *may they fear you*   *h* Cn: Heb *those who live in the wilderness*

King James

12For he shall deliver the needy when he crieth; the poor also, and *him* that hath no helper.

13He shall spare the poor and needy, and shall save the souls of the needy.

14He shall redeem their soul from deceit and violence: and precious shall their blood be in his sight.

15And he shall live, and to him shall be given of the gold of Sheba: prayer also shall be made for him continually; *and* daily shall he be praised.

16There shall be an handful of corn in the earth upon the top of the mountains; the fruit thereof shall shake like Lebanon: and *they* of the city shall flourish like grass of the earth.

17His name shall endure for ever: his name shall be continued as long as the sun: and *men* shall be blessed in him: all nations shall call him blessed.

18Blessed *be* the LORD God, the God of Israel, who only doeth wondrous things.

19And blessed *be* his glorious name for ever: and let the whole earth be filled *with* his glory; Amen, and Amen.

20The prayers of David the son of Jesse are ended.

Book III
A Psalm of Asaph.

73 TRULY GOD *is* good to Israel, *even* to such as are of a clean heart.

2But as for me, my feet were almost gone; my steps had well nigh slipped.

3For I was envious at the foolish, *when* I saw the prosperity of the wicked.

4For *there are* no bands in their death: but their strength *is* firm.

5They *are* not in trouble *as other* men; neither are they plagued like *other* men.

6Therefore pride compasseth them about as a chain; violence covereth them *as a* garment.

7Their eyes stand out with fatness: they have more than heart could wish.

8They are corrupt, and speak wickedly *concerning* oppression: they speak loftily.

9They set their mouth against the heavens, and their tongue walketh through the earth.

10Therefore his people return hither: and waters of a full *cup* are wrung out to them.

11And they say, How doth God know? and is there knowledge in the most High?

12Behold, these *are* the ungodly, who prosper in the world; they increase in riches.

13Verily I have cleansed my heart *in* vain, and washed my hands in innocency.

14For all the day long have I been plagued, and chastened every morning.

New International

12For he will deliver the needy who cry out,
    the afflicted who have no one to help.
13He will take pity on the weak and the needy
    and save the needy from death.
14He will rescue them from oppression and
    violence,
    for precious is their blood in his sight.

15Long may he live!
    May gold from Sheba be given him.
May people ever pray for him
    and bless him all day long.
16Let grain abound throughout the land;
    on the tops of the hills may it sway.
Let its fruit flourish like Lebanon;
    let it thrive like the grass of the field.
17May his name endure forever;
    may it continue as long as the sun.

All nations will be blessed through him,
    and they will call him blessed.

18Praise be to the LORD God, the God of Israel,
    who alone does marvelous deeds.
19Praise be to his glorious name forever;
    may the whole earth be filled with his glory.
        Amen and Amen.

20This concludes the prayers of David son of
    Jesse.

BOOK III

Psalms 73–89
A psalm of Asaph.

73 SURELY GOD is good to Israel,
    to those who are pure in heart.

2But as for me, my feet had almost slipped;
    I had nearly lost my foothold.
3For I envied the arrogant
    when I saw the prosperity of the wicked.

4They have no struggles;
    their bodies are healthy and strong.[a]
5They are free from the burdens common to
    man;
    they are not plagued by human ills.
6Therefore pride is their necklace;
    they clothe themselves with violence.
7From their callous hearts comes iniquity[b];
    the evil conceits of their minds know no
    limits.
8They scoff, and speak with malice;
    in their arrogance they threaten oppression.
9Their mouths lay claim to heaven,
    and their tongues take possession of the earth.
10Therefore their people turn to them
    and drink up waters in abundance.[c]
11They say, "How can God know?
    Does the Most High have knowledge?"

12This is what the wicked are like—
    always carefree, they increase in wealth.

13Surely in vain have I kept my heart pure;
    in vain have I washed my hands in
    innocence.
14All day long I have been plagued;
    I have been punished every morning.

---

a 4 With a different word division of the Hebrew; Masoretic Text *struggles at their death; / their bodies are healthy* b 7 Syriac (see also Septuagint); Hebrew *Their eyes bulge with fat* c 10 The meaning of the Hebrew for this verse is uncertain.

Living Bible

12He will take care of the helpless and poor when they cry to him; for they have no one else to defend them. 13He feels pity for the weak and needy, and will rescue them. 14He will save them from oppression and from violence, for their lives are precious to him.

15And he shall live; and to him will be given the gold of Sheba, and there will be constant praise for him.d His peoplee will bless him all day long. 16Bless us with abundant crops throughout the land, even on the highland plains; may there be fruit like that of Lebanon; may the cities be as full of people as the fields are of grass. 17His name will be honored forever; it will continue as the sun; and all will be blessed in him; all nations will praise him.

18Blessed be Jehovah God, the God of Israel, who only does wonderful things! 19Blessed be his glorious name forever! Let the whole earth be filled with his glory. Amen, and amen!

20(This ends the psalms of David, son of Jesse.)

73 HOW GOOD God is to Israel—to those whose hearts are pure. 2But as for me, I came *so* close to the edge of the cliff! My feet were slipping and I was almost gone. 3For I was envious of the prosperity of the proud and wicked. 4Yes, all through life their road is smooth!f They grow sleek and fat. 5They aren't always in trouble and plagued with problems like everyone else, 6so their pride sparkles like a jeweled necklace, and their clothing is woven of cruelty! 7These fat cats have everything their hearts could ever wish for! 8They scoff at God and threaten his people. How proudly they speak! 9They boast against the very heavens, and their words strut through the earth.

10And so God's people are dismayed and confused, and drink it all in. 11"Does God realize what is going on?" they ask. 12"Look at these men of arrogance; they never have to lift a finger—theirs is a life of ease; and all the time their riches multiply."

13Have I been wasting my time? Why take the trouble to be pure? 14All I get out of it is trouble and woe—every day and all day long! 15If I had really said that, I would

New Revised Standard

12 For he delivers the needy when they call,
        the poor and those who have no helper.
13 He has pity on the weak and the needy,
        and saves the lives of the needy.
14 From oppression and violence he redeems
            their life;
        and precious is their blood in his sight.

15 Long may he live!
        May gold of Sheba be given to him.
    May prayer be made for him continually,
        and blessings invoked for him all day long.
16 May there be abundance of grain in the land;
        may it wave on the tops of the mountains;
        may its fruit be like Lebanon;
    and may people blossom in the cities
        like the grass of the field.
17 May his name endure forever,
        his fame continue as long as the sun.
    May all nations be blessed in him;g
        may they pronounce him happy.

18 Blessed be the LORD, the God of Israel,
        who alone does wondrous things.
19 Blessed be his glorious name forever;
        may his glory fill the whole earth.
                    Amen and Amen.

20 The prayers of David son of Jesse are ended.

BOOK III

(Psalms 73–89)

Plea for Relief from Oppressors

A Psalm of Asaph.

73 TRULY GOD is good to the upright,h
        to those who are pure in heart.
2   But as for me, my feet had almost stumbled;
        my steps had nearly slipped.
3   For I was envious of the arrogant;
        I saw the prosperity of the wicked.

4   For they have no pain;
        their bodies are sound and sleek.
5   They are not in trouble as others are;
        they are not plagued like other people.
6   Therefore pride is their necklace;
        violence covers them like a garment.
7   Their eyes swell out with fatness;
        their hearts overflow with follies.
8   They scoff and speak with malice;
        loftily they threaten oppression.
9   They set their mouths against heaven,
        and their tongues range over the earth.

10 Therefore the people turn and praise them,i
        and find no fault in them.j
11 And they say, "How can God know?
        Is there knowledge in the Most High?"
12 Such are the wicked;
        always at ease, they increase in riches.
13 All in vain I have kept my heart clean
        and washed my hands in innocence.
14 For all day long I have been plagued,
        and am punished every morning.

---

d 72:15 *there will be constant praise for him*, literally, "men shall pray for him continually." e 72:15 *His people*, implied. Literally, "they" or "he." f 73:4 *all through life their road is smooth*, or, "they never have any pains."

g Or *bless themselves by him* h Or *good to Israel* i Cn: Heb *his people return here* j Cn: Heb *abundant waters are drained by them*

King James

15If I say, I will speak thus; behold, I should offend *against* the generation of thy children.

16When I thought to know this, it *was* too painful for me;

17Until I went into the sanctuary of God; *then* understood I their end.

18Surely thou didst set them in slippery places: thou castedst them down into destruction.

19How are they *brought* into desolation, as in a moment! they are utterly consumed with terrors.

20As a dream when *one* awaketh; *so,* O Lord, when thou awakest, thou shalt despise their image.

21Thus my heart was grieved, and I was pricked in my reins.

22So foolish *was* I, and ignorant: I was *as* a beast before thee.

23Nevertheless I *am* continually with thee: thou hast holden *me* by my right hand.

24Thou shalt guide me with thy counsel, and afterward receive me *to* glory.

25Whom have I in heaven *but thee?* and *there is* none upon earth *that* I desire beside thee.

26My flesh and my heart faileth: *but* God *is* the strength of my heart, and my portion for ever.

27For, lo, they that are far from thee shall perish: thou hast destroyed all them that go a-whoring from thee.

28But *it is* good for me to draw near to God: I have put my trust in the Lord GOD, that I may declare all thy works.

Maschil of Asaph.

74 O GOD, why hast thou cast *us* off for ever? *why* doth thine anger smoke against the sheep of thy pasture?

2Remember thy congregation, *which* thou hast purchased of old; the rod of thine inheritance, *which* thou hast redeemed; this mount Zion, wherein thou hast dwelt.

3Lift up thy feet unto the perpetual desolations; *even* all *that* the enemy hath done wickedly in the sanctuary.

4Thine enemies roar in the midst of thy congregations; they set up their ensigns *for* signs.

5*A man* was famous according as he had lifted up axes upon the thick trees.

6But now they break down the carved work thereof at once with axes and hammers.

7They have cast fire into thy sanctuary, they have defiled *by casting down* the dwellingplace of thy name to the ground.

8They said in their hearts, Let us destroy them together: they have burned up all the synagogues of God in the land.

New International

15If I had said, "I will speak thus,"
    I would have betrayed your children.
16When I tried to understand all this,
    it was oppressive to me
17till I entered the sanctuary of God;
    then I understood their final destiny.

18Surely you place them on slippery ground;
    you cast them down to ruin.
19How suddenly are they destroyed,
    completely swept away by terrors!
20As a dream when one awakes,
    so when you arise, O Lord,
    you will despise them as fantasies.

21When my heart was grieved
    and my spirit embittered,
22I was senseless and ignorant;
    I was a brute beast before you.

23Yet I am always with you;
    you hold me by my right hand.
24You guide me with your counsel,
    and afterward you will take me into glory.
25Whom have I in heaven but you?
    And earth has nothing I desire besides you.
26My flesh and my heart may fail,
    but God is the strength of my heart
    and my portion forever.

27Those who are far from you will perish;
    you destroy all who are unfaithful to you.
28But as for me, it is good to be near God.
    I have made the Sovereign LORD my refuge;
    I will tell of all your deeds.

A *maskil*[a] of Asaph.

74 WHY HAVE you rejected us forever,
        O God?
Why does your anger smolder against the
    sheep of your pasture?
2Remember the people you purchased of old,
    the tribe of your inheritance, whom you
        redeemed—
Mount Zion, where you dwelt.
3Turn your steps toward these everlasting ruins,
    all this destruction the enemy has brought on
        the sanctuary.

4Your foes roared in the place where you met
        with us;
    they set up their standards as signs.
5They behaved like men wielding axes
    to cut through a thicket of trees.
6They smashed all the carved paneling
    with their axes and hatchets.
7They burned your sanctuary to the ground;
    they defiled the dwelling place of your Name.
8They said in their hearts, "We will crush them
        completely!"
    They burned every place where God was
        worshiped in the land.

---

a Title: Probably a literary or musical term

Living Bible

have been a traitor to your people. 16Yet it is so hard to explain it—this prosperity of those who hate the Lord. 17Then one day I went into God's sanctuary to meditate, and thought about the future of these evil men. 18What a slippery path they are on—suddenly God will send them sliding over the edge of the cliff and down to their destruction: 19an instant end to all their happiness, an eternity of terror. 20Their present life is only a dream! They will awaken to the truth as one awakens from a dream of things that never really were!

21When I saw this, what turmoil filled my heart! 22I saw myself so stupid and so ignorant; I must seem like an animal to you, O God. 23But even so, you love me! You are holding my right hand! 24You will keep on guiding me all my life with your wisdom and counsel; and afterwards receive me into the glories of heaven!b 25Whom have I in heaven but you? And I desire no one on earth as much as you! 26My health fails; my spirits droop, yet God remains! He is the strength of my heart; he is mine forever!

27But those refusing to worship God will perish, for he destroys those serving other gods.

28But as for me, I get as close to him as I can! I have chosen him and I will tell everyone about the wonderful ways he rescues me.

74 O GOD, why have you cast us away forever? Why is your anger hot against us—the sheep of your own pasture? 2Remember that we are your people—the ones you chose in ancient times from slavery and made the choicest of your possessions. You chose Jerusalemc as your home on earth!

3Walk through the awful ruins of the city, and see what the enemy has done to your sanctuary. 4There they shouted their battle cry and erected their idols to flaunt their victory. 5, 6Everything lies in shambles like a forest chopped to the ground. They came with their axes and sledgehammers and smashed and chopped the carved paneling, 7and set the sanctuary on fire, and razed it to the ground—your sanctuary, Lord. 8"Let's wipe out every trace of God," they said, and went through the entire country burning down the assembly places where we worshiped you.

New Revised Standard

15 If I had said, "I will talk on in this way,"
    I would have been untrue to the circle of
        your children.
16 But when I thought how to understand this,
    it seemed to me a wearisome task,
17 until I went into the sanctuary of God;
    then I perceived their end.
18 Truly you set them in slippery places;
    you make them fall to ruin.
19 How they are destroyed in a moment,
    swept away utterly by terrors!
20 They ared like a dream when one awakes;
    on awaking you despise their phantoms.
21 When my soul was embittered,
    when I was pricked in heart,
22 I was stupid and ignorant;
    I was like a brute beast toward you.
23 Nevertheless I am continually with you;
    you hold my right hand.
24 You guide me with your counsel,
    and afterward you will receive me with
        honor.e
25 Whom have I in heaven but you?
    And there is nothing on earth that I desire
        other than you.
26 My flesh and my heart may fail,
    but God is the strength of my heart and
        my portion forever.
27 Indeed, those who are far from you will
        perish;
    you put an end to those who are false to
        you.
28 But for me it is good to be near God;
    I have made the Lord GOD my refuge,
    to tell of all your works.

Plea for Help in Time of National Humiliation

A Maskil of Asaph.

74 O GOD, why do you cast us off forever?
    Why does your anger smoke against the
        sheep of your pasture?
2 Remember your congregation, which you
        acquired long ago,
    which you redeemed to be the tribe of your
        heritage.
    Remember Mount Zion, where you came to
        dwell.
3 Direct your steps to the perpetual ruins;
    the enemy has destroyed everything in the
        sanctuary.
4 Your foes have roared within your holy place;
    they set up their emblems there.
5 At the upper entrance they hacked
    the wooden trellis with axes.g
6 And then, with hatchets and hammers,
    they smashed all its carved work.
7 They set your sanctuary on fire;
    they desecrated the dwelling place of your
        name,
    bringing it to the ground.
8 They said to themselves, "We will utterly
        subdue them";
    they burned all the meeting places of God
        in the land.

---

b 73:24 *receive me into the glories of heaven,* or, "you will bring me unto honor." c 74:2 *Jerusalem,* literally, "Mount Zion."

d Cn: Heb *Lord* e Or *to glory* f Heb *rock* g Cn Compare Gk Syr: Meaning of Heb uncertain

King James

9We see not our signs: *there is* no more any prophet: neither *is there* among us any that knoweth how long.

10O God, how long shall the adversary reproach? shall the enemy blaspheme thy name for ever?

11Why withdrawest thou thy hand, even thy right hand? pluck *it* out of thy bosom.

12For God *is* my King of old, working salvation in the midst of the earth.

13Thou didst divide the sea by thy strength; thou brakest the heads of the dragons in the waters.

14Thou brakest the heads of leviathan in pieces, *and* gavest him *to be* meat to the people inhabiting the wilderness.

15Thou didst cleave the fountain and the flood: thou driedst up mighty rivers.

16The day *is* thine, the night also *is* thine: thou hast prepared the light and the sun.

17Thou hast set all the borders of the earth: thou hast made summer and winter.

18Remember this, *that* the enemy hath reproached, O LORD, and *that* the foolish people have blasphemed thy name.

19O deliver not the soul of thy turtledove unto the multitude *of the wicked:* forget not the congregation of thy poor for ever.

20Have respect unto the covenant: for the dark places of the earth are full of the habitations of cruelty.

21O let not the oppressed return ashamed: let the poor and needy praise thy name.

22Arise, O God, plead thine own cause: remember how the foolish man reproacheth thee daily.

23Forget not the voice of thine enemies: the tumult of those that rise up against thee increaseth continually.

To the chief Musician, Al-taschith, A Psalm *or* Song of Asaph.

75 UNTO THEE, O God, do we give thanks, *unto thee* do we give thanks: for *that* thy name is near thy wondrous works declare.

2When I shall receive the congregation I will judge uprightly.

3The earth and all the inhabitants thereof are dissolved: I bear up the pillars of it. Selah.

4I said unto the fools, Deal not foolishly: and to the wicked, Lift not up the horn:

5Lift not up your horn on high: speak *not with* a stiff neck.

New International

9We are given no miraculous signs;
no prophets are left,
and none of us knows how long this will be.

10How long will the enemy mock you, O God?
Will the foe revile your name forever?

11Why do you hold back your hand, your right hand?
Take it from the folds of your garment and destroy them!

12But you, O God, are my king from of old;
you bring salvation upon the earth.

13It was you who split open the sea by your power;
you broke the heads of the monster in the waters.

14It was you who crushed the heads of Leviathan
and gave him as food to the creatures of the desert.

15It was you who opened up springs and streams;
you dried up the ever flowing rivers.

16The day is yours, and yours also the night;
you established the sun and moon.

17It was you who set all the boundaries of the earth;
you made both summer and winter.

18Remember how the enemy has mocked you,
O LORD,
how foolish people have reviled your name.

19Do not hand over the life of your dove to wild beasts;
do not forget the lives of your afflicted people forever.

20Have regard for your covenant,
because haunts of violence fill the dark places of the land.

21Do not let the oppressed retreat in disgrace;
may the poor and needy praise your name.

22Rise up, O God, and defend your cause;
remember how fools mock you all day long.

23Do not ignore the clamor of your adversaries,
the uproar of your enemies, which rises continually.

For the director of music. To the tune of, "Do Not Destroy." A psalm of Asaph. A song.

75 WE GIVE thanks to you, O God,
we give thanks, for your Name is near;
men tell of your wonderful deeds.

2You say, "I choose the appointed time;
it is I who judge uprightly.

3When the earth and all its people quake,
it is I who hold its pillars firm.   *Selah*

4To the arrogant I say, 'Boast no more,'
and to the wicked, 'Do not lift up your horns.

5Do not lift your horns against heaven;
do not speak with outstretched neck.'"

Living Bible

9, 10There is nothing left to show that we are your people. The prophets are gone, and who can say when it all will end? How long, O God, will you allow our enemies to dishonor your name? Will you let them get away with this forever? 11Why do you delay? Why hold back your power? Unleash your fist and give them a final blow.

12God is my King from ages past; you have been actively helping me everywhere throughout the land. 13, 14You divided the Red Sea with your strength; you crushed the sea-god's heads! You gave him to the desert tribes to eat! 15At your command the springs burst forth to give your people water; and then you dried a path for them across the ever-flowing Jordan. 16Day and night alike belong to you; you made the starlight and the sun. 17All nature is within your hands; you make the summer and the winter too. 18Lord, see how these enemies scoff at you. O Jehovah, an arrogant nation has blasphemed your name.

19O Lord, save me! Protect your turtledove from the hawks.a Save your beloved people from these beasts. 20Remember your promise! For the land is full of darkness and cruel men. 21O Lord, don't let your downtrodden people be constantly insulted. Give cause for these poor and needy ones to praise your name! 22Arise, O God, and state your case against our enemies. Remember the insults these rebels have hurled against you all day long. 23Don't overlook the cursing of these enemies of yours; it grows louder and louder.

75 HOW WE thank you, Lord! Your mighty miracles give proof that you care.

2"Yes," the Lord replies, "and when I am ready, I will punish the wicked! 3Though the earth shakes and all its people live in turmoil, yet its pillars are firm, for I have set them in place!"

4I warned the proud to cease their arrogance! I told the wicked to lower their insolent gaze,b 5and to stop being stubborn and proud. 6, 7For promotion and power

New Revised Standard

9 We do not see our emblems;
   there is no longer any prophet,
   and there is no one among us who knows
      how long.
10 How long, O God, is the foe to scoff?
   Is the enemy to revile your name forever?
11 Why do you hold back your hand;
   why do you keep your hand inc your
      bosom?

12 Yet God my King is from of old,
   working salvation in the earth.
13 You divided the sea by your might;
   you broke the heads of the dragons in the
      waters.
14 You crushed the heads of Leviathan;
   you gave him as foodd for the creatures of
      the wilderness.
15 You cut openings for springs and torrents;
   you dried up ever-flowing streams.
16 Yours is the day, yours also the night;
   you established the luminariese and the sun.
17 You have fixed all the bounds of the earth;
   you made summer and winter.

18 Remember this, O LORD, how the enemy
      scoffs,
   and an impious people reviles your name.
19 Do not deliver the soul of your dove to the
      wild animals;
   do not forget the life of your poor forever.

20 Have regard for yourf covenant,
   for the dark places of the land are full of
      the haunts of violence.
21 Do not let the downtrodden be put to shame;
   let the poor and needy praise your name.
22 Rise up, O God, plead your cause;
   remember how the impious scoff at you all
      day long.
23 Do not forget the clamor of your foes,
   the uproar of your adversaries that goes up
      continually.

Thanksgiving for God's Wondrous Deeds
To the leader: Do Not Destroy. A Psalm of Asaph. A Song.

75 WE GIVE thanks to you, O God;
   we give thanks; your name is near.
People tell of your wondrous deeds.

2 At the set time that I appoint
   I will judge with equity.
3 When the earth totters, with all its inhabitants,
   it is I who keep its pillars steady.   Selah
4 I say to the boastful, "Do not boast,"
   and to the wicked, "Do not lift up your
      horn;
5 do not lift up your horn on high,
   or speak with insolent neck."

---

a 74:19 the hawks, literally, "the wild beasts."   b 75:4 lower their insolent gaze, literally, "lift not up the horn."

c Cn: Heb do you consume your right hand from   d Heb food for the people
e Or moon; Heb light   f Gk Syr: Heb the

King James

6For promotion *cometh* neither from the east, nor from the west, nor from the south.

7But God *is* the judge: he putteth down one, and setteth up another.

8For in the hand of the LORD *there is* a cup, and the wine is red; it is full of mixture; and he poureth out of the same: but the dregs thereof, all the wicked of the earth shall wring *them* out, *and* drink *them*.

9But I will declare for ever; I will sing praises to the God of Jacob.

10All the horns of the wicked also will I cut off; *but* the horns of the righteous shall be exalted.

To the chief Musician on Neginoth,
A Psalm *or* Song of Asaph.

76 IN JUDAH *is* God known: his name *is* great in Israel.

2In Salem also is his tabernacle, and his dwelling-place in Zion.

3There brake he the arrows of the bow, the shield, and the sword, and the battle. Selah.

4Thou *art* more glorious *and* excellent than the mountains of prey.

5The stout-hearted are spoiled, they have slept their sleep: and none of the men of might have found their hands.

6At thy rebuke, O God of Jacob, both the chariot and horse are cast into a dead sleep.

7Thou, *even* thou, *art* to be feared: and who may stand in thy sight when once thou art angry?

8Thou didst cause judgment to be heard from heaven; the earth feared, and was still,

9When God arose to judgment, to save all the meek of the earth. Selah.

10Surely the wrath of man shall praise thee: the remainder of wrath shalt thou restrain.

11Vow, and pay unto the LORD your God: let all that be round about him bring presents unto him that ought to be feared.

12He shall cut off the spirit of princes: *he is* terrible to the kings of the earth.

To the chief Musician, to Jeduthun, A Psalm of Asaph.

77 I CRIED unto God with my voice, *even* unto God with my voice; and he gave ear unto me.

2In the day of my trouble I sought the Lord: my sore ran in the night, and ceased not: my soul refused to be comforted.

3I remembered God, and was troubled: I complained, and my spirit was overwhelmed. Selah.

4Thou holdest mine eyes waking: I am so troubled that I cannot speak.

5I have considered the days of old, the years of ancient times.

New International

6No one from the east or the west
  or from the desert can exalt a man.
7But it is God who judges:
  He brings one down, he exalts another.
8In the hand of the LORD is a cup
  full of foaming wine mixed with spices;
he pours it out, and all the wicked of the earth
  drink it down to its very dregs.

9As for me, I will declare this forever;
  I will sing praise to the God of Jacob.
10I will cut off the horns of all the wicked,
  but the horns of the righteous will be lifted up.

For the director of music. With stringed instruments.
A psalm of Asaph. A song.

76 IN JUDAH God is known;
  his name is great in Israel.
2His tent is in Salem,
  his dwelling place in Zion.
3There he broke the flashing arrows,
  the shields and the swords, the weapons of war.   *Selah*

4You are resplendent with light,
  more majestic than mountains rich with game.
5Valiant men lie plundered,
  they sleep their last sleep;
not one of the warriors
  can lift his hands.
6At your rebuke, O God of Jacob,
  both horse and chariot lie still.
7You alone are to be feared.
  Who can stand before you when you are angry?
8From heaven you pronounced judgment,
  and the land feared and was quiet—
9when you, O God, rose up to judge,
  to save all the afflicted of the land.   *Selah*
10Surely your wrath against men brings you praise,
  and the survivors of your wrath are restrained.[a]

11Make vows to the LORD your God and fulfill them;
  let all the neighboring lands
  bring gifts to the One to be feared.
12He breaks the spirit of rulers;
  he is feared by the kings of the earth.

For the director of music. For Jeduthun. Of Asaph.
A psalm.

77 I CRIED out to God for help;
  I cried out to God to hear me.
2When I was in distress, I sought the Lord;
  at night I stretched out untiring hands
  and my soul refused to be comforted.

3I remembered you, O God, and I groaned;
  I mused, and my spirit grew faint.   *Selah*
4You kept my eyes from closing;
  I was too troubled to speak.
5I thought about the former days,
  the years of long ago;

Living Bible

come from nowhere on earth, but only from God. He promotes one and deposes another. 8In Jehovah's hand there is a cup of pale and sparkling wine. It is his judgment, poured out upon the wicked of the earth. They must drain that cup to the dregs.

9But as for me, I shall forever declare the praises of the God of Jacob. 10"I will cut off the strength of evil men," says the Lord,b "and increase the power of good men in their place."

76 GOD'S REPUTATION is very great in Judah and in Israel. 2His home is in Jerusalem. He lives upon Mount Zion. 3There he breaks the weapons of our enemies.

4The everlasting mountains cannot compare with you in glory! 5The mightiest of our enemies are conquered. They lie before us in the sleep of death; not one can lift a hand against us. 6When you rebuked them, God of Jacob, steeds and riders fell. 7No wonder you are greatly feared! Who can stand before an angry God? 8You pronounce sentence on them from heaven; the earth trembles and stands silently before you. 9You stand up to punish the evil-doers and to defend the meek of the earth. 10Man's futile wrath will bring you glory. You will use it as an ornament!

11Fulfill all your vows that you have made to Jehovah your God. Let everyone bring him presents. He should be reverenced and feared, 12for he cuts down princes and does awesome things to the kings of the earth.

77 I CRY to the Lord; I call and call to him. Oh, that he would listen. 2I am in deep trouble and I need his help so much. All night long I pray, lifting my hands to heaven, pleading. There can be no joy for me until he acts. 3I think of God and moan, overwhelmed with longing for his help. 4I cannot sleep until you act. I am too distressed even to pray!

5I keep thinking of the good old days of the past, long since ended. 6Then my nights were filled with joyous

New Revised Standard

6 For not from the east or from the west
      and not from the wilderness comes lifting
      up;
7 but it is God who executes judgment,
      putting down one and lifting up another.
8 For in the hand of the LORD there is a cup
      with foaming wine, well mixed;
he will pour a draught from it,
      and all the wicked of the earth
      shall drain it down to the dregs.
9 But I will rejoicec forever;
      I will sing praises to the God of Jacob.

10 All the horns of the wicked I will cut off,
      but the horns of the righteous shall be
      exalted.

Israel's God—Judge of All the Earth

To the leader: with stringed instruments. A Psalm of Asaph.
A Song.

76 IN JUDAH God is known,
      his name is great in Israel.
2 His abode has been established in Salem,
      his dwelling place in Zion.
3 There he broke the flashing arrows,
      the shield, the sword, and the weapons of
      war.   Selah

4 Glorious are you, more majestic
      than the everlasting mountains.d
5 The stouthearted were stripped of their spoil;
      they sank into sleep;
none of the troops
      was able to lift a hand.
6 At your rebuke, O God of Jacob,
      both rider and horse lay stunned.

7 But you indeed are awesome!
      Who can stand before you
      when once your anger is roused?
8 From the heavens you uttered judgment;
      the earth feared and was still
9 when God rose up to establish judgment,
      to save all the oppressed of the earth. Selah

10 Human wrath serves only to praise you,
      when you bind the last bit of youre wrath
      around you.
11 Make vows to the LORD your God, and
      perform them;
      let all who are around him bring gifts
      to the one who is awesome,
12 who cuts off the spirit of princes,
      who inspires fear in the kings of the earth.

God's Mighty Deeds Recalled

To the leader: according to Jeduthun. Of Asaph. A Psalm.

77 I CRY aloud to God,
      aloud to God, that he may hear me.
2 In the day of my trouble I seek the Lord;
      in the night my hand is stretched out
      without wearying;
      my soul refuses to be comforted.
3 I think of God, and I moan;
      I meditate, and my spirit faints.   Selah

4 You keep my eyelids from closing;
      I am so troubled that I cannot speak.
5 I consider the days of old,
      and remember the years of long ago.

---

b 75:10 says the Lord, implied.   c Gk: Heb declare   d Gk: Heb the mountains of prey   e Heb lacks your

King James

6I call to remembrance my song in the night: I commune with mine own heart: and my spirit made diligent search.

7Will the Lord cast off for ever? and will he be favourable no more?

8Is his mercy clean gone for ever? doth *his* promise fail for evermore?

9Hath God forgotten to be gracious? hath he in anger shut up his tender mercies? Selah.

10And I said, This *is* my infirmity: *but I will remember* the years of the right hand of the most High.

11I will remember the works of the LORD: surely I will remember thy wonders of old.

12I will meditate also of all thy work, and talk of thy doings.

13Thy way, O God, *is* in the sanctuary: who *is so* great a God as *our* God?

14Thou *art* the God that doest wonders: thou hast declared thy strength among the people.

15Thou hast with *thine* arm redeemed thy people, the sons of Jacob and Joseph. Selah.

16The waters saw thee, O God, the waters saw thee; they were afraid: the depths also were troubled.

17The clouds poured out water: the skies sent out a sound: thine arrows also went abroad.

18The voice of thy thunder *was* in the heaven: the lightnings lightened the world: the earth trembled and shook.

19Thy way *is* in the sea, and thy path in the great waters, and thy footsteps are not known.

20Thou leddest thy people like a flock by the hand of Moses and Aaron.

Maschil of Asaph.

78 GIVE EAR, O my people, *to* my law: incline your ears to the words of my mouth.

2I will open my mouth in a parable: I will utter dark sayings of old:

3Which we have heard and known, and our fathers have told us.

4We will not hide *them* from their children, showing to the generation to come the praises of the LORD, and his strength, and his wonderful works that he hath done.

5For he established a testimony in Jacob, and appointed a law in Israel, which he commanded our fathers, that they should make them known to their children:

6That the generation to come might know *them, even* the children *which* should be born; *who* should arise and declare *them* to their children:

7That they might set their hope in God, and not forget the works of God, but keep his commandments:

8And might not be as their fathers, a stubborn and rebellious generation; a generation *that* set not their heart aright, and whose spirit was not stedfast with God.

New International

6I remembered my songs in the night.
My heart mused and my spirit inquired:

7"Will the Lord reject forever?
Will he never show his favor again?
8Has his unfailing love vanished forever?
Has his promise failed for all time?
9Has God forgotten to be merciful?
Has he in anger withheld his compassion?"
Selah

10Then I thought, "To this I will appeal:
the years of the right hand of the Most High."
11I will remember the deeds of the LORD;
yes, I will remember your miracles of long ago.
12I will meditate on all your works
and consider all your mighty deeds.

13Your ways, O God, are holy.
What god is so great as our God?
14You are the God who performs miracles;
you display your power among the peoples.
15With your mighty arm you redeemed your people,
the descendants of Jacob and Joseph.   *Selah*

16The waters saw you, O God,
the waters saw you and writhed;
the very depths were convulsed.
17The clouds poured down water,
the skies resounded with thunder;
your arrows flashed back and forth.
18Your thunder was heard in the whirlwind,
your lightning lit up the world;
the earth trembled and quaked.
19Your path led through the sea,
your way through the mighty waters,
though your footprints were not seen.

20You led your people like a flock
by the hand of Moses and Aaron.

A *maskil*[a] of Asaph.

78 O MY people, hear my teaching;
listen to the words of my mouth.
2I will open my mouth in parables,
I will utter hidden things, things from of old—
3what we have heard and known,
what our fathers have told us.
4We will not hide them from their children;
we will tell the next generation
the praiseworthy deeds of the LORD,
his power, and the wonders he has done.
5He decreed statutes for Jacob
and established the law in Israel,
which he commanded our forefathers
to teach their children,
6so the next generation would know them,
even the children yet to be born,
and they in turn would tell their children.
7Then they would put their trust in God
and would not forget his deeds
but would keep his commands.
8They would not be like their forefathers—
a stubborn and rebellious generation,
whose hearts were not loyal to God,
whose spirits were not faithful to him.

---

a Title: Probably a literary or musical term

Living Bible

songs. I search my soul and meditate upon the difference now. 7Has the Lord rejected me forever? Will he never again be favorable? 8Is his lovingkindness gone forever? Has his promise failed? 9Has he forgotten to be kind to one so undeserving? Has he slammed the door in anger on his love? 10And I said: This is my fate, that the blessings of God have changed to hate.b 11I recall the many miracles he did for me so long ago. 12Those wonderful deeds are constantly in my thoughts. I cannot stop thinking about them.

13O God, your ways are holy. Where is there any other as mighty as you? 14You are the God of miracles and wonders! You still demonstrate your awesome power.

15You have redeemed us who are the sons of Jacob and of Joseph by your might. 16When the Red Sea saw you, how it feared! It trembled to its depths! 17The clouds poured down their rain, the thunder rolled and crackled in the sky. Your lightning flashed. 18There was thunder in the whirlwind; the lightning lighted up the world! The earth trembled and shook.

19Your road led by a pathway through the sea—a pathway no one knew was there! 20You led your people along that road like a flock of sheep, with Moses and Aaron as their shepherds.

78 O MY people, listen to my teaching. Open your ears to what I am saying. 2, 3For I will show you lessons from our history, stories handed down to us from former generations. 4I will reveal these truths to you so that you can describe these glorious deeds of Jehovah to your children, and tell them about the mighty miracles he did. 5For he gave his laws to Israel, and commanded our fathers to teach them to their children, 6so that they in turn could teach their children too. Thus his laws pass down from generation to generation. 7In this way each generation has been able to obey his laws and to set its hope anew on God and not forget his glorious miracles. 8Thus they did not need to be as their fathers were—stubborn, rebellious, unfaithful, refusing to give their hearts to God.

New Revised Standard

6 I communec with my heart in the night;
   I meditate and search my spirit:d
7 "Will the Lord spurn forever,
   and never again be favorable?
8 Has his steadfast love ceased forever?
   Are his promises at an end for all time?
9 Has God forgotten to be gracious?
   Has he in anger shut up his compassion?"
                                          Selah
10 And I say, "It is my grief
   that the right hand of the Most High has
      changed."

11 I will call to mind the deeds of the LORD;
   I will remember your wonders of old.
12 I will meditate on all your work,
   and muse on your mighty deeds.
13 Your way, O God, is holy.
   What god is so great as our God?
14 You are the God who works wonders;
   you have displayed your might among the
      peoples.
15 With your strong arm you redeemed your
      people,
   the descendants of Jacob and Joseph. *Selah*

16 When the waters saw you, O God,
   when the waters saw you, they were afraid;
   the very deep trembled.
17 The clouds poured out water;
   the skies thundered;
   your arrows flashed on every side.
18 The crash of your thunder was in the
      whirlwind;
   your lightnings lit up the world;
   the earth trembled and shook.
19 Your way was through the sea,
   your path, through the mighty waters;
   yet your footprints were unseen.
20 You led your people like a flock
   by the hand of Moses and Aaron.

God's Goodness and Israel's Ingratitude

A Maskil of Asaph.

78 GIVE EAR, O my people, to my teaching;
   incline your ears to the words of my
      mouth.
2 I will open my mouth in a parable;
   I will utter dark sayings from of old,
3 things that we have heard and known,
   that our ancestors have told us.
4 We will not hide them from their children;
   we will tell to the coming generation
   the glorious deeds of the LORD, and his might,
   and the wonders that he has done.

5 He established a decree in Jacob,
   and appointed a law in Israel,
   which he commanded our ancestors
      to teach to their children;
6 that the next generation might know them,
   the children yet unborn,
   and rise up and tell them to their children,
7   so that they should set their hope in God,
   and not forget the works of God,
      but keep his commandments;
8 and that they should not be like their
      ancestors,
   a stubborn and rebellious generation,
   a generation whose heart was not steadfast,
   whose spirit was not faithful to God.

b 77:10 that the blessings of God have changed to hate, literally, "that the right hand of the Most High has changed."

c Gk Syr: Heb My music   d Syr Jerome: Heb my spirit searches

King James

9The children of Ephraim, *being* armed, *and* carrying bows, turned back in the day of battle.

10They kept not the covenant of God, and refused to walk in his law;

11And forgat his works, and his wonders that he had shown them.

12Marvellous things did he in the sight of their fathers, in the land of Egypt, *in* the field of Zoan.

13He divided the sea, and caused them to pass through; and he made the waters to stand as an heap.

14In the daytime also he led them with a cloud, and all the night with a light of fire.

15He clave the rocks in the wilderness, and gave *them* drink as *out of* the great depths.

16He brought streams also out of the rock, and caused waters to run down like rivers.

17And they sinned yet more against him by provoking the most High in the wilderness.

18And they tempted God in their heart by asking meat for their lust.

19Yea, they spake against God; they said, Can God furnish a table in the wilderness?

20Behold, he smote the rock, that the waters gushed out, and the streams overflowed; can he give bread also? can he provide flesh for his people?

21Therefore the LORD heard *this,* and was wroth: so a fire was kindled against Jacob, and anger also came up against Israel;

22Because they believed not in God, and trusted not in his salvation:

23Though he had commanded the clouds from above, and opened the doors of heaven,

24And had rained down manna upon them to eat, and had given them of the corn of heaven.

25Man did eat angels' food: he sent them meat to the full.

26He caused an east wind to blow in the heaven: and by his power he brought in the south wind.

27He rained flesh also upon them as dust, and feathered fowls like as the sand of the sea:

28And he let *it* fall in the midst of their camp, round about their habitations.

29So they did eat, and were well filled: for he gave them their own desire;

30They were not estranged from their lust. But while their meat *was* yet in their mouths,

31The wrath of God came upon them, and slew the fattest of them, and smote down the chosen *men* of Israel.

32For all this they sinned still, and believed not for his wondrous works.

33Therefore their days did he consume in vanity, and their years in trouble.

34When he slew them, then they sought him: and they returned and inquired early after God.

35And they remembered that God *was* their rock, and the high God their redeemer.

36Nevertheless they did flatter him with their mouth, and they lied unto him with their tongues.

37For their heart was not right with him, neither were they stedfast in his covenant.

New International

9The men of Ephraim, though armed with bows, turned back on the day of battle;

10they did not keep God's covenant and refused to live by his law.

11They forgot what he had done, the wonders he had shown them.

12He did miracles in the sight of their fathers in the land of Egypt, in the region of Zoan.

13He divided the sea and led them through; he made the water stand firm like a wall.

14He guided them with the cloud by day and with light from the fire all night.

15He split the rocks in the desert and gave them water as abundant as the seas;

16he brought streams out of a rocky crag and made water flow down like rivers.

17But they continued to sin against him, rebelling in the desert against the Most High.

18They willfully put God to the test by demanding the food they craved.

19They spoke against God, saying, "Can God spread a table in the desert?

20When he struck the rock, water gushed out, and streams flowed abundantly. But can he also give us food? Can he supply meat for his people?"

21When the LORD heard them, he was very angry; his fire broke out against Jacob, and his wrath rose against Israel,

22for they did not believe in God or trust in his deliverance.

23Yet he gave a command to the skies above and opened the doors of the heavens;

24he rained down manna for the people to eat, he gave them the grain of heaven.

25Men ate the bread of angels; he sent them all the food they could eat.

26He let loose the east wind from the heavens and led forth the south wind by his power.

27He rained meat down on them like dust, flying birds like sand on the seashore.

28He made them come down inside their camp, all around their tents.

29They ate till they had more than enough, for he had given them what they craved.

30But before they turned from the food they craved, even while it was still in their mouths,

31God's anger rose against them; he put to death the sturdiest among them, cutting down the young men of Israel.

32In spite of all this, they kept on sinning; in spite of his wonders, they did not believe.

33So he ended their days in futility and their years in terror.

34Whenever God slew them, they would seek him; they eagerly turned to him again.

35They remembered that God was their Rock, that God Most High was their Redeemer.

36But then they would flatter him with their mouths, lying to him with their tongues;

37their hearts were not loyal to him, they were not faithful to his covenant.

Living Bible

9The people of Ephraim, though fully armed, turned their backs and fled when the day of battle came, 10because they didn't obey his laws. They refused to follow his ways. 11, 12And they forgot about the wonderful miracles God had done for them, and for their fathers in Egypt. 13For he divided the sea before them and led them through! The water stood banked up along both sides of them! 14In the daytime he led them by a cloud, and at night by a pillar of fire. 15He split open the rocks in the wilderness to give them plenty of water, as though gushing from a spring. 16Streams poured from the rock, flowing like a river!

17Yet they kept on with their rebellion, sinning against the God who is above all gods. 18They murmured and complained, demanding other food than God was giving them. 19, 20They even spoke against God himself. "Why can't he give us decent food as well as water?" they grumbled. 21Jehovah heard them and was angry; the fire of his wrath burned against Israel, 22because they didn't believe in God or trust in him to care for them, 23even though he commanded the skies to open—he opened the windows of heaven— 24and rained down manna for their food. He gave them bread from heaven! 25They ate angels' food! He gave them all they could hold.

26And he led forth the east wind and guided the south wind by his mighty power. 27He rained down birds as thick as dust, clouds of them like sands along the shore! 28He caused the birds to fall to the ground among the tents. 29The people ate their fill. He gave them what they asked for. 30But they had hardly finished eating, and the meat was yet in their mouths, 31when the anger of the Lord rose against them and killed the finest of Israel's young men. 32Yet even so the people kept on sinning and refused to believe in miracles. 33So he cut their lives short and gave them years of terror and disaster.

34Then at last, when he had ruined them, they walked awhile behind him; how earnestly they turned around and followed him! 35Then they remembered that God was their Rock—that their Savior was the God above all gods. 36But it was only with their words they followed him, not with their hearts; 37their hearts were far away. They did not keep their promises. 38Yet he was merciful

New Revised Standard

9 The Ephraimites, armed with[a] the bow,
   turned back on the day of battle.
10 They did not keep God's covenant,
   but refused to walk according to his law.
11 They forgot what he had done,
   and the miracles that he had shown them.
12 In the sight of their ancestors he worked
      marvels
   in the land of Egypt, in the fields of Zoan.
13 He divided the sea and let them pass through
      it,
   and made the waters stand like a heap.
14 In the daytime he led them with a cloud,
   and all night long with a fiery light.
15 He split rocks open in the wilderness,
   and gave them drink abundantly as from the
      deep.
16 He made streams come out of the rock,
   and caused waters to flow down like rivers.

17 Yet they sinned still more against him,
   rebelling against the Most High in the
      desert.
18 They tested God in their heart
   by demanding the food they craved.
19 They spoke against God, saying,
   "Can God spread a table in the wilderness?
20 Even though he struck the rock so that water
      gushed out
   and torrents overflowed,
can he also give bread,
   or provide meat for his people?"

21 Therefore, when the LORD heard, he was full
      of rage;
   a fire was kindled against Jacob,
   his anger mounted against Israel,
22 because they had no faith in God,
   and did not trust his saving power.
23 Yet he commanded the skies above,
   and opened the doors of heaven;
24 he rained down on them manna to eat,
   and gave them the grain of heaven.
25 Mortals ate of the bread of angels;
   he sent them food in abundance.
26 He caused the east wind to blow in the
      heavens,
   and by his power he led out the south wind;
27 he rained flesh upon them like dust,
   winged birds like the sand of the seas;
28 he let them fall within their camp,
   all around their dwellings.
29 And they ate and were well filled,
   for he gave them what they craved.
30 But before they had satisfied their craving,
   while the food was still in their mouths,
31 the anger of God rose against them
   and he killed the strongest of them,
   and laid low the flower of Israel.

32 In spite of all this they still sinned;
   they did not believe in his wonders.
33 So he made their days vanish like a breath,
   and their years in terror.
34 When he killed them, they sought for him;
   they repented and sought God earnestly.
35 They remembered that God was their rock,
   the Most High God their redeemer.
36 But they flattered him with their mouths;
   they lied to him with their tongues.
37 Their heart was not steadfast toward him;
   they were not true to his covenant.

a Heb *armed with shooting*

King James

38But he, *being* full of compassion, forgave *their* iniquity, and destroyed *them* not: yea, many a time turned he his anger away, and did not stir up all his wrath.

39For he remembered that they *were but* flesh; a wind that passeth away, and cometh not again.

40How oft did they provoke him in the wilderness, *and* grieve him in the desert!

41Yea, they turned back and tempted God, and limited the Holy One of Israel.

42They remembered not his hand, *nor* the day when he delivered them from the enemy.

43How he had wrought his signs in Egypt, and his wonders in the field of Zoan:

44And had turned their rivers into blood; and their floods, that they could not drink.

45He sent divers sorts of flies among them, which devoured them; and frogs, which destroyed them.

46He gave also their increase unto the caterpillar, and their labour unto the locust.

47He destroyed their vines with hail, and their sycamore trees with frost.

48He gave up their cattle also to the hail, and their flocks to hot thunderbolts.

49He cast upon them the fierceness of his anger, wrath, and indignation, and trouble, by sending evil angels *among them*.

50He made a way to his anger; he spared not their soul from death, but gave their life over to the pestilence;

51And smote all the firstborn in Egypt; the chief of *their* strength in the tabernacles of Ham:

52But made his own people to go forth like sheep, and guided them in the wilderness like a flock.

53And he led them on safely, so that they feared not: but the sea overwhelmed their enemies.

54And he brought them to the border of his sanctuary, *even to* this mountain, *which* his right hand had purchased.

55He cast out the heathen also before them, and divided them an inheritance by line, and made the tribes of Israel to dwell in their tents.

56Yet they tempted and provoked the most high God, and kept not his testimonies:

57But turned back, and dealt unfaithfully like their fathers: they were turned aside like a deceitful bow.

58For they provoked him to anger with their high places, and moved him to jealousy with their graven images.

59When God heard *this*, he was wroth, and greatly abhorred Israel:

60So that he forsook the tabernacle of Shiloh, the tent *which* he placed among men;

61And delivered his strength into captivity, and his glory into the enemy's hand.

62He gave his people over also unto the sword; and was wroth with his inheritance.

63The fire consumed their young men; and their maidens were not given to marriage.

64Their priests fell by the sword; and their widows made no lamentation.

65Then the Lord awaked as one out of sleep, *and* like a mighty man that shouteth by reason of wine.

New International

38Yet he was merciful;
    he forgave their iniquities
    and did not destroy them.
Time after time he restrained his anger
    and did not stir up his full wrath.
39He remembered that they were but flesh,
    a passing breeze that does not return.
40How often they rebelled against him in the
        desert
    and grieved him in the wasteland!
41Again and again they put God to the test;
    they vexed the Holy One of Israel.
42They did not remember his power—
    the day he redeemed them from the
        oppressor,
43the day he displayed his miraculous signs in
        Egypt,
    his wonders in the region of Zoan.
44He turned their rivers to blood;
    they could not drink from their streams.
45He sent swarms of flies that devoured them,
    and frogs that devastated them.
46He gave their crops to the grasshopper,
    their produce to the locust.
47He destroyed their vines with hail
    and their sycamore-figs with sleet.
48He gave over their cattle to the hail,
    their livestock to bolts of lightning.
49He unleashed against them his hot anger,
    his wrath, indignation and hostility—
    a band of destroying angels.
50He prepared a path for his anger;
    he did not spare them from death
    but gave them over to the plague.
51He struck down all the firstborn of Egypt,
    the firstfruits of manhood in the tents of
        Ham.
52But he brought his people out like a flock;
    he led them like sheep through the desert.
53He guided them safely, so they were unafraid;
    but the sea engulfed their enemies.
54Thus he brought them to the border of his holy
        land,
    to the hill country his right hand had taken.
55He drove out nations before them
    and allotted their lands to them as an
        inheritance;
    he settled the tribes of Israel in their homes.

56But they put God to the test
    and rebelled against the Most High;
    they did not keep his statutes.
57Like their fathers they were disloyal and
        faithless,
    as unreliable as a faulty bow.
58They angered him with their high places;
    they aroused his jealousy with their idols.
59When God heard them, he was very angry;
    he rejected Israel completely.
60He abandoned the tabernacle of Shiloh,
    the tent he had set up among men.
61He sent the ark of his might into captivity,
    his splendor into the hands of the enemy.
62He gave his people over to the sword;
    he was very angry with his inheritance.
63Fire consumed their young men,
    and their maidens had no wedding songs;
64their priests were put to the sword,
    and their widows could not weep.

65Then the Lord awoke as from sleep,
    as a man wakes from the stupor of wine.

Living Bible

and forgave their sins and didn't destroy them all. Many and many a time he held back his anger. 39For he remembered that they were merely mortal men, gone in a moment like a breath of wind.

40Oh, how often they rebelled against him in those desert years and grieved his heart. 41Again and again they turned away and tempted God to kill them, and limited the Holy One of Israel from giving them his blessings. 42They forgot his power and love, and how he had rescued them from their enemies; 43they forgot the plagues he sent upon the Egyptians in Tanisa— 44how he turned their rivers into blood, so that no one could drink, 45and how he sent vast swarms of flies to fill the land, and how the frogs had covered all of Egypt! 46He gave their crops to caterpillars. Their harvest was consumed by locusts. 47He destroyed their grapevines and their sycamores with hail. 48Their cattle died in the fields, mortally wounded by huge hailstones from heaven. Their sheep were killed by lightning. 49He loosed on them the fierceness of his anger, sending sorrow and trouble. He dispatched against them a band of destroying angels. 50He gave free course to his anger and did not spare the Egyptians' lives, but handed them over to plagues and sickness. 51Then he killed the eldest sonb in each Egyptian family—he who was the beginning of its strength and joy.

52But he led forth his own people like a flock, guiding them safely through the wilderness. 53He kept them safe, so they were not afraid. But the Sea closed in upon their enemies and overwhelmed them. 54He brought them to the border of his land of blessing, to this land of hills he made for them. 55He drove out the nations occupying the land, and gave each tribe of Israel its apportioned place as its home.

56Yet though he did all this for them, they still rebelled against the God above all gods, and refused to follow his commands. 57They turned back from entering the Promised Land and disobeyed as their fathers had. Like a crooked arrow, they missed the target of God's will. 58They made him angry by erecting idols and altars to other gods.

59When God saw their deeds, his wrath was strong and he despised his people. 60Then he abandoned his Tabernacle at Shiloh, where he had lived among mankind, 61and allowed his Ark to be captured; he surrendered his glory into enemy hands. 62He caused his people to be butchered because his anger was intense. 63Their young men were killed by fire and their girls died before they were old enough to sing their wedding songs. 64The priests were slaughtered and their widows died before they could even begin their lament. 65Then the Lord rose up as though awakening from sleep, and like a mighty man aroused by wine, 66he routed his

New Revised Standard

38 Yet he, being compassionate,
     forgave their iniquity,
     and did not destroy them;
   often he restrained his anger,
     and did not stir up all his wrath.
39 He remembered that they were but flesh,
     a wind that passes and does not come again.
40 How often they rebelled against him in the
       wilderness
     and grieved him in the desert!
41 They tested God again and again,
     and provoked the Holy One of Israel.
42 They did not keep in mind his power,
     or the day when he redeemed them from the
       foe;
43 when he displayed his signs in Egypt,
     and his miracles in the fields of Zoan.
44 He turned their rivers to blood,
     so that they could not drink of their
       streams.
45 He sent among them swarms of flies, which
       devoured them,
     and frogs, which destroyed them.
46 He gave their crops to the caterpillar,
     and the fruit of their labor to the locust.
47 He destroyed their vines with hail,
     and their sycamores with frost.
48 He gave over their cattle to the hail,
     and their flocks to thunderbolts.
49 He let loose on them his fierce anger,
     wrath, indignation, and distress,
     a company of destroying angels.
50 He made a path for his anger;
     he did not spare them from death,
     but gave their lives over to the plague.
51 He struck all the firstborn in Egypt,
     the first issue of their strength in the tents
       of Ham.
52 Then he led out his people like sheep,
     and guided them in the wilderness like a
       flock.
53 He led them in safety, so that they were not
       afraid;
     but the sea overwhelmed their enemies.
54 And he brought them to his holy hill,
     to the mountain that his right hand had
       won.
55 He drove out nations before them;
     he apportioned them for a possession
     and settled the tribes of Israel in their tents.

56 Yet they tested the Most High God,
     and rebelled against him.
     They did not observe his decrees,
57 but turned away and were faithless like their
       ancestors;
     they twisted like a treacherous bow.
58 For they provoked him to anger with their
       high places;
     they moved him to jealousy with their idols.
59 When God heard, he was full of wrath,
     and he utterly rejected Israel.
60 He abandoned his dwelling at Shiloh,
     the tent where he dwelt among mortals,
61 and delivered his power to captivity,
     his glory to the hand of the foe.
62 He gave his people to the sword,
     and vented his wrath on his heritage.
63 Fire devoured their young men,
     and their girls had no marriage song.
64 Their priests fell by the sword,
     and their widows made no lamentation.
65 Then the Lord awoke as from sleep,
     like a warrior shouting because of wine.

---

a 78:43 Tanis, literally, "the plains of Zoan." b 78:51, the eldest son, literally, "all the firstborn."

King James

66And he smote his enemies in the hinder parts: he put them to a perpetual reproach.

67Moreover he refused the tabernacle of Joseph, and chose not the tribe of Ephraim:

68But chose the tribe of Judah, the mount Zion which he loved.

69And he built his sanctuary like high *palaces,* like the earth which he hath established for ever.

70He chose David also his servant, and took him from the sheepfolds:

71From following the ewes great with young he brought him to feed Jacob his people, and Israel his inheritance.

72So he fed them according to the integrity of his heart; and guided them by the skilfulness of his hands.

A Psalm of Asaph.

79 O GOD, the heathen are come into thine inheritance; thy holy temple have they defiled; they have laid Jerusalem on heaps.

2The dead bodies of thy servants have they given *to be* meat unto the fowls of the heaven, the flesh of thy saints unto the beasts of the earth.

3Their blood have they shed like water round about Jerusalem; and *there was* none to bury *them.*

4We are become a reproach to our neighbours, a scorn and derision to them that are round about us.

5How long, LORD? wilt thou be angry for ever? shall thy jealousy burn like fire?

6Pour out thy wrath upon the heathen that have not known thee, and upon the kingdoms that have not called upon thy name.

7For they have devoured Jacob, and laid waste his dwellingplace.

8O remember not against us former iniquities: let thy tender mercies speedily prevent us: for we are brought very low.

9Help us, O God of our salvation, for the glory of thy name: and deliver us, and purge away our sins, for thy name's sake.

10Wherefore should the heathen say, Where *is* their God? let him be known among the heathen in our sight *by* the revenging of the blood of thy servants *which is* shed.

11Let the sighing of the prisoner come before thee; according to the greatness of thy power preserve thou those that are appointed to die;

12And render unto our neighbours sevenfold into their bosom their reproach, wherewith they have reproached thee, O Lord.

13So we thy people and sheep of thy pasture will give thee thanks for ever: we will show forth thy praise to all generations.

New International

66He beat back his enemies;
　　he put them to everlasting shame.
67Then he rejected the tents of Joseph,
　　he did not choose the tribe of Ephraim;
68but he chose the tribe of Judah,
　　Mount Zion, which he loved.
69He built his sanctuary like the heights,
　　like the earth that he established forever.
70He chose David his servant
　　and took him from the sheep pens;
71from tending the sheep he brought him
　　to be the shepherd of his people Jacob,
　　of Israel his inheritance.
72And David shepherded them with integrity of heart;
　　with skillful hands he led them.

A psalm of Asaph.

79 O GOD, the nations have invaded your
　　inheritance;
　　they have defiled your holy temple,
　　they have reduced Jerusalem to rubble.
2They have given the dead bodies of your
　　servants
　　as food to the birds of the air,
　　the flesh of your saints to the beasts of the
　　earth.
3They have poured out blood like water
　　all around Jerusalem,
　　and there is no one to bury the dead.
4We are objects of reproach to our neighbors,
　　of scorn and derision to those around us.

5How long, O LORD? Will you be angry forever?
　　How long will your jealousy burn like fire?
6Pour out your wrath on the nations
　　that do not acknowledge you,
　　on the kingdoms
　　that do not call on your name;
7for they have devoured Jacob
　　and destroyed his homeland.
8Do not hold against us the sins of the fathers;
　　may your mercy come quickly to meet us,
　　for we are in desperate need.

9Help us, O God our Savior,
　　for the glory of your name;
　　deliver us and forgive our sins
　　for your name's sake.
10Why should the nations say,
　　"Where is their God?"
　　Before our eyes, make known among the
　　nations
　　that you avenge the outpoured blood of your
　　servants.
11May the groans of the prisoners come before
　　you;
　　by the strength of your arm
　　preserve those condemned to die.
12Pay back into the laps of our neighbors seven
　　times
　　the reproach they have hurled at you, O Lord.
13Then we your people, the sheep of your
　　pasture,
　　will praise you forever;
　　from generation to generation
　　we will recount your praise.

Living Bible

enemies and drove them back and sent them to eternal shame. 67But he rejected Joseph's family, the tribe of Ephraim, 68and chose the tribe of Judah—and Mount Zion which he loved. 69There he built his towering temple, solid and enduring as the heavens and the earth. 70He chose his servant David, taking him from feeding sheep, 71, 72and from following the ewes with lambs; God presented David to his people as their shepherd and he cared for them with a true heart and skillful hands.

79 O GOD, your land has been conquered by the heathen nations. Your Temple is defiled and Jerusalem is a heap of ruins. 2The bodies of your people lie exposed—food for birds and animals. 3The enemy has butchered the entire population of Jerusalem; blood has flowed like water. No one is left even to bury them. 4The nations all around us scoff. They heap contempt on us.

5O Jehovah, how long will you be angry with us? Forever? Will your jealousy burn till every hope is gone? 6Pour out your wrath upon the godless nations, not on us! And on kingdoms that refuse to pray, that will not call upon your name! 7For they have destroyed your people Israel, invading every home. 8Oh, do not hold us guilty for our former sins! Let your tenderhearted mercies meet our needs, for we are brought low to the dust. 9Help us, God of our salvation! Help us for the honor of your name. Oh, save us and forgive our sins. 10Why should the heathen nations be allowed to scoff, "Where is their God?" Publicly avenge this slaughter of your people! 11Listen to the sighing of the prisoners and those condemned to die. Demonstrate the greatness of your power by saving them. 12O Lord, take sevenfold vengeance on these nations scorning you.

13Then we your people, the sheep of your pasture, will thank you forever and forever, praising your greatness from generation to generation.

New Revised Standard

66 He put his adversaries to rout;
   he put them to everlasting disgrace.

67 He rejected the tent of Joseph,
   he did not choose the tribe of Ephraim;
68 but he chose the tribe of Judah,
   Mount Zion, which he loves.
69 He built his sanctuary like the high heavens,
   like the earth, which he has founded
     forever.
70 He chose his servant David,
   and took him from the sheepfolds;
71 from tending the nursing ewes he brought him
   to be the shepherd of his people Jacob,
   of Israel, his inheritance.
72 With upright heart he tended them,
   and guided them with skillful hand.

Plea for Mercy for Jerusalem

A Psalm of Asaph.

79 O GOD, the nations have come into your inheritance;
   they have defiled your holy temple;
   they have laid Jerusalem in ruins.
2 They have given the bodies of your servants
   to the birds of the air for food,
   the flesh of your faithful to the wild animals
     of the earth.
3 They have poured out their blood like water
   all around Jerusalem,
   and there was no one to bury them.
4 We have become a taunt to our neighbors,
   mocked and derided by those around us.

5 How long, O LORD? Will you be angry
     forever?
   Will your jealous wrath burn like fire?
6 Pour out your anger on the nations
   that do not know you,
   and on the kingdoms
   that do not call on your name.
7 For they have devoured Jacob
   and laid waste his habitation.

8 Do not remember against us the iniquities of
     our ancestors;
   let your compassion come speedily to meet
     us,
   for we are brought very low.
9 Help us, O God of our salvation,
   for the glory of your name;
   deliver us, and forgive our sins,
   for your name's sake.
10 Why should the nations say,
   "Where is their God?"
   Let the avenging of the outpoured blood of
     your servants
   be known among the nations before our
     eyes.

11 Let the groans of the prisoners come before
     you;
   according to your great power preserve
     those doomed to die.
12 Return sevenfold into the bosom of our
     neighbors
   the taunts with which they taunted you,
     O Lord!
13 Then we your people, the flock of your
     pasture,
   will give thanks to you forever;
   from generation to generation we will
     recount your praise.

King James

To the chief Musician upon Shoshannim-Eduth,
A Psalm of Asaph.

80 GIVE EAR, O Shepherd of Israel, thou that leadest Joseph like a flock; thou that dwellest *between* the cherubims, shine forth.

2Before Ephraim and Benjamin and Manasseh stir up thy strength, and come *and* save us.

3Turn us again, O God, and cause thy face to shine; and we shall be saved.

4O Lord God of hosts, how long wilt thou be angry against the prayer of thy people?

5Thou feedest them with the bread of tears; and givest them tears to drink in great measure.

6Thou makest us a strife unto our neighbours: and our enemies laugh among themselves.

7Turn us again, O God of hosts, and cause thy face to shine; and we shall be saved.

8Thou hast brought a vine out of Egypt: thou hast cast out the heathen, and planted it.

9Thou preparedst *room* before it, and didst cause it to take deep root, and it filled the land.

10The hills were covered with the shadow of it, and the boughs thereof *were like* the goodly cedars.

11She sent out her boughs unto the sea, and her branches unto the river.

12Why hast thou *then* broken down her hedges, so that all they which pass by the way do pluck her?

13The boar out of the wood doth waste it, and the wild beast of the field doth devour it.

14Return, we beseech thee, O God of hosts: look down from heaven, and behold, and visit this vine;

15And the vineyard which thy right hand hath planted, and the branch *that* thou madest strong for thyself.

16*It is* burned with fire, *it is* cut down: they perish at the rebuke of thy countenance.

17Let thy hand be upon the man of thy right hand, upon the son of man *whom* thou madest strong for thyself.

18So will not we go back from thee: quicken us, and we will call upon thy name.

19Turn us again, O Lord God of hosts, cause thy face to shine; and we shall be saved.

To the chief Musician upon Gittith, *A Psalm* of Asaph.

81 SING ALOUD unto God our strength: make a joyful noise unto the God of Jacob.

2Take a psalm, and bring hither the timbrel, the pleasant harp with the psaltery.

3Blow up the trumpet in the new moon, in the time appointed, on our solemn feast day.

4For this *was* a statute for Israel, *and* a law of the God of Jacob.

New International

For the director of music. To the tune of, "The Lilies of the Covenant." Of Asaph. A psalm.

80 HEAR US, O Shepherd of Israel,
   you who lead Joseph like a flock;
you who sit enthroned between the cherubim,
   shine forth
2 before Ephraim, Benjamin and Manasseh.
Awaken your might;
   come and save us.

3Restore us, O God;
   make your face shine upon us,
   that we may be saved.

4O Lord God Almighty,
   how long will your anger smolder
   against the prayers of your people?
5You have fed them with the bread of tears;
   you have made them drink tears by the
     bowlful.
6You have made us a source of contention to our
   neighbors,
   and our enemies mock us.

7Restore us, O God Almighty;
   make your face shine upon us,
   that we may be saved.

8You brought a vine out of Egypt;
   you drove out the nations and planted it.
9You cleared the ground for it,
   and it took root and filled the land.
10The mountains were covered with its shade,
   the mighty cedars with its branches.
11It sent out its boughs to the Sea,[a]
   its shoots as far as the River.[b]

12Why have you broken down its walls
   so that all who pass by pick its grapes?
13Boars from the forest ravage it
   and the creatures of the field feed on it.
14Return to us, O God Almighty!
   Look down from heaven and see!
Watch over this vine,
15 the root your right hand has planted,
   the son[c] you have raised up for yourself.

16Your vine is cut down, it is burned with fire;
   at your rebuke your people perish.
17Let your hand rest on the man at your right
   hand,
   the son of man you have raised up for
     yourself.
18Then we will not turn away from you;
   revive us, and we will call on your name.

19Restore us, O Lord God Almighty;
   make your face shine upon us,
   that we may be saved.

For the director of music. According to *gittith*.[d] Of Asaph.

81 SING FOR joy to God our strength;
   shout aloud to the God of Jacob!
2Begin the music, strike the tambourine,
   play the melodious harp and lyre.

3Sound the ram's horn at the New Moon,
   and when the moon is full, on the day of our
     Feast;
4this is a decree for Israel,
   an ordinance of the God of Jacob.

---

^a *11* Probably the Mediterranean   ^b *11* That is, the Euphrates   ^c *15* Or branch   ^d Title: Probably a musical term

Living Bible

80 O SHEPHERD of Israel who leads Israel like a flock; O God enthroned above the Guardian Angels, bend down your ear and listen as I plead. Display your power and radiant glory. 2Let Ephraim, Benjamin and Manasseh see you rouse yourself and use your mighty power to rescue us.

3Turn us again to yourself, O God. Look down on us in joy and love;e only then shall we be saved.

4O Jehovah, God of heaven's armies, how long will you be angry and reject our prayers? 5You have fed us with sorrow and tears, 6and have made us the scorn of the neighboring nations. They laugh among themselves.

7Turn us again to yourself, O God of Hosts. Look down on us in joy and love;f only then shall we be saved. 8You brought us from Egypt as though we were a tender vine and drove away the heathen from your land and planted us. 9You cleared the ground and tilled the soil and we took root and filled the land. 10The mountains were covered with our shadow; we were like the mighty cedar trees,g 11covering the entire land from the Mediterranean Sea to the Euphrates River. 12But now you have broken down our walls, leaving us without protection. 13The boar from the forest roots around us, and the wild animals feed on us.

14Come back, we beg of you, O God of the armies of heaven, and bless us. Look down from heaven and see our plight and care for this your vine! 15Protect what you yourself have planted, this son you have raised for yourself. 16For we are chopped and burned by our enemies. May they perish at your frown. 17Strengthen the man you love,h the son of your choice,i 18and we will never forsake you again. Revive us to trust in you.

19Turn us again to yourself, O God of the armies of heaven. Look down on us, your face aglow with joy and love—only then shall we be saved.

81 THE LORD makes us strong! Sing praises! Sing to Israel's God!

2Sing, accompanied by drums; pluck the sweet lyre and harp. 3Sound the trumpet! Come to the joyous celebrations at full moon, new moon and all the other holidays. 4For God has given us these times of joy; they are scheduled in the laws of Israel. 5He gave them as re-

e 80:3 *Look down on us in joy and love*, literally, "Cause your face to shine upon us."   f 80:7 *in joy and love*, literally, "Cause your face to shine upon us."   g 80:10 *the mighty cedar trees*, literally, "the cedars of God."   h 80:17 *the man you love*, literally, "the man of your right hand."   i 80:17 *the son of your choice*, literally, "the son of man you made strong for yourself."

New Revised Standard

Prayer for Israel's Restoration

To the leader: on Lilies, a Covenant. Of Asaph. A Psalm.

80 GIVE EAR, O Shepherd of Israel,
    you who lead Joseph like a flock!
You who are enthroned upon the cherubim,
    shine forth
2   before Ephraim and Benjamin and
        Manasseh.
Stir up your might,
    and come to save us!

3   Restore us, O God;
        let your face shine, that we may be saved.

4   O LORD God of hosts,
        how long will you be angry with your
        people's prayers?
5   You have fed them with the bread of tears,
        and given them tears to drink in full
        measure.
6   You make us the scorn of our neighbors;
        our enemies laugh among themselves.

7   Restore us, O God of hosts;
        let your face shine, that we may be saved.

8   You brought a vine out of Egypt;
        you drove out the nations and planted it.
9   You cleared the ground for it;
        it took deep root and filled the land.
10   The mountains were covered with its shade,
        the mighty cedars with its branches;
11   it sent out its branches to the sea,
        and its shoots to the River.
12   Why then have you broken down its walls,
        so that all who pass along the way pluck its
        fruit?
13   The boar from the forest ravages it,
        and all that move in the field feed on it.

14   Turn again, O God of hosts;
        look down from heaven, and see;
        have regard for this vine,
15   the stock that your right hand planted.k
16   They have burned it with fire, they have cut it
        down;l
        may they perish at the rebuke of your
        countenance.
17   But let your hand be upon the one at your
        right hand,
        the one whom you made strong for yourself.
18   Then we will never turn back from you;
        give us life, and we will call on your name.

19   Restore us, O LORD God of hosts;
        let your face shine, that we may be saved.

God's Appeal to Stubborn Israel

To the leader: according to The Gittith. Of Asaph.

81 SING ALOUD to God our strength;
    shout for joy to the God of Jacob.
2   Raise a song, sound the tambourine,
        the sweet lyre with the harp.
3   Blow the trumpet at the new moon,
        at the full moon, on our festal day.
4   For it is a statute for Israel,
        an ordinance of the God of Jacob.

j Syr: Heb *strife*   k Heb adds *from verse 17 and upon the one whom you made strong for yourself*   l Cn: Heb *it is cut down*

King James

5This he ordained in Joseph *for* a testimony, when he went out through the land of Egypt: *where* I heard a language *that* I understood not.

6I removed his shoulder from the burden: his hands were delivered from the pots.

7Thou calledst in trouble, and I delivered thee; I answered thee in the secret place of thunder: I proved thee at the waters of Meribah. Selah.

8Hear, O my people, and I will testify unto thee: O Israel, if thou wilt hearken unto me;

9There shall no strange god be in thee; neither shalt thou worship any strange god.

10I *am* the LORD thy God, which brought thee out of the land of Egypt: open thy mouth wide, and I will fill it.

11But my people would not hearken to my voice; and Israel would none of me.

12So I gave them up unto their own hearts' lust: *and* they walked in their own counsels.

13Oh that my people had hearkened unto me, *and* Israel had walked in my ways!

14I should soon have subdued their enemies, and turned my hand against their adversaries.

15The haters of the LORD should have submitted themselves unto him: but their time should have endured for ever.

16He should have fed them also with the finest of the wheat: and with honey out of the rock should I have satisfied thee.

A Psalm of Asaph.

82 GOD STANDETH in the congregation of the mighty; he judgeth among the gods.

2How long will ye judge unjustly, and accept the persons of the wicked? Selah.

3Defend the poor and fatherless: do justice to the afflicted and needy.

4Deliver the poor and needy: rid *them* out of the hand of the wicked.

5They know not, neither will they understand; they walk on in darkness: all the foundations of the earth are out of course.

6I have said, Ye *are* gods; and all of you *are* children of the most High.

7But ye shall die like men, and fall like one of the princes.

8Arise, O God, judge the earth: for thou shalt inherit all nations.

A Song *or* Psalm of Asaph.

83 KEEP NOT thou silence, O God: hold not thy peace, and be not still, O God.

New International

5He established it as a statute for Joseph
  when he went out against Egypt,
  where we heard a language we did not
    understand.a

6He says, "I removed the burden from their
    shoulders;
  their hands were set free from the basket.

7In your distress you called and I rescued you,
  I answered you out of a thundercloud;
  I tested you at the waters of Meribah.   *Selah*

8"Hear, O my people, and I will warn you—
  if you would but listen to me, O Israel!

9You shall have no foreign god among you;
  you shall not bow down to an alien god.

10I am the LORD your God,
  who brought you up out of Egypt.
  Open wide your mouth and I will fill it.

11"But my people would not listen to me;
  Israel would not submit to me.

12So I gave them over to their stubborn hearts
  to follow their own devices.

13"If my people would but listen to me,
  if Israel would follow my ways,

14how quickly would I subdue their enemies
  and turn my hand against their foes!

15Those who hate the LORD would cringe before
    him,
  and their punishment would last forever.

16But you would be fed with the finest of wheat;
  with honey from the rock I would satisfy
    you."

A psalm of Asaph.

82 GOD PRESIDES in the great assembly;
  he gives judgment among the "gods":

2"How long will youb defend the unjust
  and show partiality to the wicked?   *Selah*

3Defend the cause of the weak and fatherless;
  maintain the rights of the poor and oppressed.

4Rescue the weak and needy;
  deliver them from the hand of the wicked.

5"They know nothing, they understand nothing.
  They walk about in darkness;
  all the foundations of the earth are shaken.

6"I said, 'You are "gods";
  you are all sons of the Most High.'

7But you will die like mere men;
  you will fall like every other ruler."

8Rise up, O God, judge the earth,
  for all the nations are your inheritance.

A song. A psalm of Asaph.

83 O GOD, do not keep silent;
  be not quiet, O God, be not still.

a 5 Or / *and we heard a voice we had not known*   b 2 The Hebrew is plural.

Living Bible

minders of his war against Egypt where we were slaves on foreign soil.

I heard an unknown voice that said, 6"Now I will relieve your shoulder of its burden; I will free your hands from their heavy tasks." 7He said, "You cried to me in trouble and I saved you; I answered from Mount Sinai[c] where the thunder hides. I tested your faith at Meribah, when you complained there was no water. 8Listen to me, O my people, while I give you stern warnings. O Israel, if you will only listen! 9*You must never worship any other god,* nor ever have an idol in your home.[d] 10For it was I, Jehovah your God, who brought you out of the land of Egypt. Only test me![e] Open your mouth wide and see if I won't fill it. You will receive every blessing you can use!

11"But no, my people won't listen. Israel doesn't want me around. 12So I am letting them go their blind and stubborn way, living according to their own desires.

13"But oh, that my people would listen to me! Oh, that Israel would follow me, walking in my paths! 14How quickly then I would subdue her enemies! How soon my hands would be upon her foes! 15Those who hate the Lord would cringe before him; their desolation would last forever. 16But he would feed you with the choicest foods. He would satisfy you with honey for the taking."[f]

82 GOD STANDS up to open heaven's court. He pronounces judgment on the judges.[g] 2How long will you judges refuse to listen to the evidence? How long will you shower special favors on the wicked? 3Give fair judgment to the poor man, the afflicted, the fatherless, the destitute. 4Rescue the poor and helpless from the grasp of evil men. 5But you are so foolish and so ignorant! Because you are in darkness, all the foundations of society[h] are shaken to the core. 6I have called you all "gods" and "sons of the Most High." 7But in death you are mere men. You will fall as any prince—for all must die.

8Stand up, O God, and judge the earth. For all of it belongs to you. All nations are in your hands.

83 O GOD, don't sit idly by, silent and inactive when we pray. Answer us! Deliver us!

New Revised Standard

5 He made it a decree in Joseph,
    when he went out over[i] the land of Egypt.

I hear a voice I had not known:
6 "I relieved your[j] shoulder of the burden;
    your[j] hands were freed from the basket.
7 In distress you called, and I rescued you;
    I answered you in the secret place of
        thunder;
    I tested you at the waters of Meribah. *Selah*
8 Hear, O my people, while I admonish you;
    O Israel, if you would but listen to me!
9 There shall be no strange god among you;
    you shall not bow down to a foreign god.
10 I am the LORD your God,
    who brought you up out of the land of
        Egypt.
    Open your mouth wide and I will fill it.

11 "But my people did not listen to my voice;
    Israel would not submit to me.
12 So I gave them over to their stubborn hearts,
    to follow their own counsels.
13 O that my people would listen to me,
    that Israel would walk in my ways!
14 Then I would quickly subdue their enemies,
    and turn my hand against their foes.
15 Those who hate the LORD would cringe before
        him,
    and their doom would last forever.
16 I would feed you[k] with the finest of the
        wheat,
    and with honey from the rock I would
        satisfy you."

A Plea for Justice

A Psalm of Asaph.

82 GOD HAS taken his place in the divine
    council;
    in the midst of the gods he holds judgment:
2 "How long will you judge unjustly
    and show partiality to the wicked? *Selah*
3 Give justice to the weak and the orphan;
    maintain the right of the lowly and the
        destitute.
4 Rescue the weak and the needy;
    deliver them from the hand of the wicked."

5 They have neither knowledge nor
        understanding,
    they walk around in darkness;
    all the foundations of the earth are shaken.

6 I say, "You are gods,
    children of the Most High, all of you;
7 nevertheless, you shall die like mortals,
    and fall like any prince."[l]

8 Rise up, O God, judge the earth;
    for all the nations belong to you!

Prayer for Judgment on Israel's Foes

A Song. A Psalm of Asaph.

83 O GOD, do not keep silence;
    do not hold your peace or be still, O God!

c *81:7 from Mount Sinai,* implied. Literally, "in the hiding place of thunder."
d *81:9 nor ever have an idol in your home,* literally, "There shall no foreign god be in you." e *81:10 Only test me,* implied. f *81:16 honey for the taking,* literally, "honey out of the rock." g *82:1 He pronounces judgment on the judges,* implied in vss 2-4, 6. Literally, "He judges among the gods."
h *82:5 of society,* literally, "of the earth."

i Or *against* j Heb *his* k Cn Compare verse 16b: Heb *he would feed him*
l Or *fall as one man, O princes*

King James

2For, lo, thine enemies make a tumult: and they that hate thee have lifted up the head.

3They have taken crafty counsel against thy people, and consulted against thy hidden ones.

4They have said, Come, and let us cut them off from *being* a nation; that the name of Israel may be no more in remembrance.

5For they have consulted together with one consent: they are confederate against thee:

6The tabernacles of Edom, and the Ishmaelites; of Moab, and the Hagarenes;

7Gebal, and Ammon, and Amalek; the Philistines with the inhabitants of Tyre;

8Assur also is joined with them: they have helped the children of Lot. Selah.

9Do unto them as *unto* the Midianites; as *to* Sisera, as *to* Jabin, at the brook of Kison:

10*Which* perished at En-dor: they became *as* dung for the earth.

11Make their nobles like Oreb, and like Zeeb: yea, all their princes as Zebah, and as Zalmunna:

12Who said, Let us take to ourselves the houses of God in possession.

13O my God, make them like a wheel; as the stubble before the wind.

14As the fire burneth a wood, and as the flame setteth the mountains on fire;

15So persecute them with thy tempest, and make them afraid with thy storm.

16Fill their faces with shame; that they may seek thy name, O LORD.

17Let them be confounded and troubled for ever; yea, let them be put to shame, and perish:

18That *men* may know that thou, whose name alone *is* JEHOVAH, *art* the most high over all the earth.

To the chief Musician upon Gittith, A Psalm for the sons of Korah.

84 HOW AMIABLE *are* thy tabernacles, O LORD of hosts!

2My soul longeth, yea, even fainteth for the courts of the LORD: my heart and my flesh crieth out for the living God.

3Yea, the sparrow hath found an house, and the swallow a nest for herself, where she may lay her young, *even* thine altars, O LORD of hosts, my King, and my God.

4Blessed *are* they that dwell in thy house: they will be still praising thee. Selah.

5Blessed *is* the man whose strength *is* in thee; in whose heart *are* the ways *of them*.

6*Who* passing through the valley of Baca make it a well; the rain also filleth the pools.

7They go from strength to strength, *every one of them* in Zion appeareth before God.

8O LORD God of hosts, hear my prayer: give ear, O God of Jacob. Selah.

New International

2See how your enemies are astir,
  how your foes rear their heads.
3With cunning they conspire against your people;
  they plot against those you cherish.
4"Come," they say, "let us destroy them as a nation,
  that the name of Israel be remembered no more."

5With one mind they plot together;
  they form an alliance against you—
6the tents of Edom and the Ishmaelites,
  of Moab and the Hagrites,
7Gebal,[a] Ammon and Amalek,
  Philistia, with the people of Tyre.
8Even Assyria has joined them
  to lend strength to the descendants of Lot.
                                            Selah

9Do to them as you did to Midian,
  as you did to Sisera and Jabin at the river Kishon,
10who perished at Endor
  and became like refuse on the ground.
11Make their nobles like Oreb and Zeeb,
  all their princes like Zebah and Zalmunna,
12who said, "Let us take possession
  of the pasturelands of God."

13Make them like tumbleweed, O my God,
  like chaff before the wind.
14As fire consumes the forest
  or a flame sets the mountains ablaze,
15so pursue them with your tempest
  and terrify them with your storm.
16Cover their faces with shame
  so that men will seek your name, O LORD.

17May they ever be ashamed and dismayed;
  may they perish in disgrace.
18Let them know that you, whose name is the LORD—
  that you alone are the Most High over all the earth.

For the director of music. According to *gittith*.[b] Of the Sons of Korah. A psalm.

84 HOW LOVELY is your dwelling place,
O LORD Almighty!
2My soul yearns, even faints,
  for the courts of the LORD;
my heart and my flesh cry out
  for the living God.

3Even the sparrow has found a home,
  and the swallow a nest for herself,
  where she may have her young—
a place near your altar,
  O LORD Almighty, my King and my God.
4Blessed are those who dwell in your house;
  they are ever praising you.   *Selah*

5Blessed are those whose strength is in you,
  who have set their hearts on pilgrimage.
6As they pass through the Valley of Baca,
  they make it a place of springs;
  the autumn rains also cover it with pools.[c]
7They go from strength to strength,
  till each appears before God in Zion.

8Hear my prayer, O LORD God Almighty;
  listen to me, O God of Jacob.   *Selah*

a 7 That is, Byblos   b Title: Probably a musical term   c 6 Or *blessings*

Living Bible

2Don't you hear the tumult and commotion of your enemies? Don't you see what they are doing, these proud men who hate the Lord? 3They are full of craftiness and plot against your people, laying plans to slay your precious ones. 4"Come," they say, "and let us wipe out Israel as a nation—we will destroy the very memory of her existence." 5This was their unanimous decision at their summit conference—they signed a treaty to ally themselves against Almighty God— 6these Ishmaelites and Edomites and Moabites and Hagrites; 7people from the lands of Gebal, Ammon, Amalek, Philistia and Tyre; 8Assyria has joined them too, and is allied with the descendants of Lot.d

9Do to them as once you did to Midian, or as you did to Sisera and Jabin at the river Kishon, 10and as you did to your enemies at Endor, whose decaying corpses fertilized the soil. 11Make their mighty nobles die as Oreb did,e and Zeeb;e let all their princes die like Zebahf and Zalmunna,f 12who said, "Let us seize for our own use these pasturelands of God!"

13O my God, blow them away like dust; like chaff before the wind— 14as a forest fire that roars across a mountain. 15Chase them with your fiery storms, tempests and tornados. 16Utterly disgrace them until they recognize your power and name, O Lord. 17Make them failures in everything they do; let them be ashamed and terrified 18until they learn that you alone, Jehovah, are the God above all gods in supreme charge of all the earth.

New Revised Standard

2 Even now your enemies are in tumult;
    those who hate you have raised their heads.
3 They lay crafty plans against your people;
    they consult together against those you
        protect.
4 They say, "Come, let us wipe them out as a
        nation;
    let the name of Israel be remembered no
        more."
5 They conspire with one accord;
    against you they make a covenant—
6 the tents of Edom and the Ishmaelites,
    Moab and the Hagrites,
7 Gebal and Ammon and Amalek,
    Philistia with the inhabitants of Tyre;
8 Assyria also has joined them;
    they are the strong arm of the children of
        Lot.   Selah

9 Do to them as you did to Midian,
    as to Sisera and Jabin at the Wadi Kishon,
10 who were destroyed at En-dor,
    who became dung for the ground.
11 Make their nobles like Oreb and Zeeb,
    all their princes like Zebah and Zalmunna,
12 who said, "Let us take the pastures of God
    for our own possession."

13 O my God, make them like whirling dust,g
    like chaff before the wind.
14 As fire consumes the forest,
    as the flame sets the mountains ablaze,
15 so pursue them with your tempest
    and terrify them with your hurricane.
16 Fill their faces with shame,
    so that they may seek your name, O LORD.
17 Let them be put to shame and dismayed
        forever;
    let them perish in disgrace.
18 Let them know that you alone,
    whose name is the LORD,
    are the Most High over all the earth.

The Joy of Worship in the Temple

To the leader: according to The Gittith. Of the Korahites.
A Psalm.

84 HOW LOVELY is your Temple, O Lord of the armies of heaven.

2I long, yes, faint with longing to be able to enter your courtyard and come near to the Living God. 3Even the sparrows and swallows are welcome to come and nest among your altars and there have their young, O Lord of heaven's armies, my King and my God! 4How happy are those who can live in your Temple, singing your praises.

5Happy are those who are strong in the Lord, who want above all else to follow your steps. 6When they walk through the Valley of Weeping it will become a place of springs where pools of blessing and refreshment collect after rains! 7They will grow constantly in strength and each of them is invited to meet with the Lord in Zion.

8O Jehovah, God of the heavenly armies, hear my prayer! Listen, God of Israel. 9O God, our Defender and

84 HOW LOVELY is your dwelling place,
        O LORD of hosts!
2 My soul longs, indeed it faints
    for the courts of the LORD;
my heart and my flesh sing for joy
    to the living God.

3 Even the sparrow finds a home,
    and the swallow a nest for herself,
    where she may lay her young,
at your altars, O LORD of hosts,
    my King and my God.
4 Happy are those who live in your house,
    ever singing your praise.   Selah

5 Happy are those whose strength is in you,
    in whose heart are the highways to Zion.h
6 As they go through the valley of Baca
    they make it a place of springs;
    the early rain also covers it with pools.
7 They go from strength to strength;
    the God of gods will be seen in Zion.

8 O LORD God of hosts, hear my prayer;
    give ear, O God of Jacob!   Selah

---

d 83:8 *the descendants of Lot*. The Moabites and Ammonites were among Lot's descendants.   e 83:11 *as Oreb did, and Zeeb*, see Judges 7:25.
f 83:11 *like Zebah and Zalmunna*, see Judges 8:21.   g Or *a tumbleweed*   h Heb lacks *to Zion*

King James

9Behold, O God our shield, and look upon the face of thine anointed.

10For a day in thy courts is better than a thousand. I had rather be a doorkeeper in the house of my God, than to dwell in the tents of wickedness.

11For the LORD God is a sun and shield: the LORD will give grace and glory: no good thing will he withhold from them that walk uprightly.

12O LORD of hosts, blessed is the man that trusteth in thee.

To the chief Musician, A Psalm for the sons of Korah.

85 LORD, THOU hast been favourable unto thy land: thou hast brought back the captivity of Jacob.

2Thou hast forgiven the iniquity of thy people, thou hast covered all their sin. Selah.

3Thou hast taken away all thy wrath: thou hast turned thyself from the fierceness of thine anger.

4Turn us, O God of our salvation, and cause thine anger toward us to cease.

5Wilt thou be angry with us for ever? wilt thou draw out thine anger to all generations?

6Wilt thou not revive us again: that thy people may rejoice in thee?

7Show us thy mercy, O LORD, and grant us thy salvation.

8I will hear what God the LORD will speak: for he will speak peace unto his people, and to his saints: but let them not turn again to folly.

9Surely his salvation is nigh them that fear him; that glory may dwell in our land.

10Mercy and truth are met together; righteousness and peace have kissed each other.

11Truth shall spring out of the earth; and righteousness shall look down from heaven.

12Yea, the LORD shall give that which is good; and our land shall yield her increase.

13Righteousness shall go before him; and shall set us in the way of his steps.

A Prayer of David.

86 BOW DOWN thine ear, O LORD, hear me: for I am poor and needy.

2Preserve my soul; for I am holy: O thou my God, save thy servant that trusteth in thee.

3Be merciful unto me, O Lord: for I cry unto thee daily.

4Rejoice the soul of thy servant: for unto thee, O Lord, do I lift up my soul.

5For thou, Lord, art good, and ready to forgive; and plenteous in mercy unto all them that call upon thee.

6Give ear, O LORD, unto my prayer; and attend to the voice of my supplications.

New International

9Look upon our shield,a O God;
  look with favor on your anointed one.

10Better is one day in your courts
  than a thousand elsewhere;
I would rather be a doorkeeper in the house of
    my God
  than dwell in the tents of the wicked.

11For the LORD God is a sun and shield;
  the LORD bestows favor and honor;
no good thing does he withhold
  from those whose walk is blameless.

12O LORD Almighty,
  blessed is the man who trusts in you.

For the director of music. Of the Sons of Korah. A psalm.

85 YOU SHOWED favor to your land, O LORD;
  you restored the fortunes of Jacob.
2You forgave the iniquity of your people
  and covered all their sins.   Selah
3You set aside all your wrath
  and turned from your fierce anger.

4Restore us again, O God our Savior,
  and put away your displeasure toward us.
5Will you be angry with us forever?
  Will you prolong your anger through all
    generations?
6Will you not revive us again,
  that your people may rejoice in you?
7Show us your unfailing love, O LORD,
  and grant us your salvation.

8I will listen to what God the LORD will say;
  he promises peace to his people, his saints—
  but let them not return to folly.
9Surely his salvation is near those who fear him,
  that his glory may dwell in our land.

10Love and faithfulness meet together;
  righteousness and peace kiss each other.
11Faithfulness springs forth from the earth,
  and righteousness looks down from heaven.
12The LORD will indeed give what is good,
  and our land will yield its harvest.
13Righteousness goes before him
  and prepares the way for his steps.

A prayer of David.

86 HEAR, O LORD, and answer me,
  for I am poor and needy.
2Guard my life, for I am devoted to you.
  You are my God; save your servant
  who trusts in you.
3Have mercy on me, O Lord,
  for I call to you all day long.
4Bring joy to your servant,
  for to you, O Lord,
  I lift up my soul.

5You are forgiving and good, O Lord,
  abounding in love to all who call to you.
6Hear my prayer, O LORD;
  listen to my cry for mercy.

a 9 Or sovereign

Living Bible

our Shield, have mercy on the one you have anointed as your king.[b]

10A single day spent in your Temple is better than a thousand anywhere else! I would rather be a doorman of the Temple of my God than live in palaces[c] of wickedness. 11For Jehovah God is our Light and our Protector. He gives us grace and glory. No good thing will he withhold from those who walk along his paths.[d]

12O Lord of the armies of heaven, blessed are those who trust in you.

85 LORD, YOU have poured out amazing blessings on this land! You have restored the fortunes of Israel,[e] 2and forgiven the sins of your people— yes, covered over each one, 3so that all your wrath, your blazing anger, is now ended.

4Now bring us back to loving you,[f] O Lord, so that your anger will never need rise against us again. 5(Or will you be always angry—on and on to distant generations?) 6Oh, revive us! Then your people can rejoice in you again. 7Pour out your love and kindness on us, Lord, and grant us your salvation.

8I am listening carefully to all the Lord is saying—for he speaks peace to his people, his saints, if they will only stop their sinning. 9Surely his salvation is near to those who reverence him; our land will be filled with his glory.

10Mercy and truth have met together. Grim justice[g] and peace have kissed! 11Truth rises from the earth and righteousness smiles down from heaven.

12Yes, the Lord pours down his blessings on the land and it yields its bountiful crops. 13Justice goes before him to make a pathway for his steps.[h]

86 BEND DOWN and hear my prayer, O Lord, and answer me, for I am deep in trouble.

2Protect me from death, for I try to follow all your laws. Save me, for I am serving you and trusting you. 3Be merciful, O Lord, for I am looking up to you in constant hope. 4Give me happiness, O Lord, for I worship only you. 5O Lord, you are so good and kind, so ready to forgive; so full of mercy for all who ask your aid.

6Listen closely to my prayer, O God. Hear my urgent

New Revised Standard

9 Behold our shield, O God;
    look on the face of your anointed.

10 For a day in your courts is better
    than a thousand elsewhere.
I would rather be a doorkeeper in the house of
    my God
    than live in the tents of wickedness.

11 For the LORD God is a sun and shield;
    he bestows favor and honor.
No good thing does the LORD withhold
    from those who walk uprightly.

12 O LORD of hosts,
    happy is everyone who trusts in you.

Prayer for the Restoration of God's Favor
To the leader. Of the Korahites. A Psalm.

85 LORD, YOU were favorable to your land;
    you restored the fortunes of Jacob.
2 You forgave the iniquity of your people;
    you pardoned all their sin.   Selah
3 You withdrew all your wrath;
    you turned from your hot anger.

4 Restore us again, O God of our salvation,
    and put away your indignation toward us.
5 Will you be angry with us forever?
    Will you prolong your anger to all
    generations?
6 Will you not revive us again,
    so that your people may rejoice in you?
7 Show us your steadfast love, O LORD,
    and grant us your salvation.

8 Let me hear what God the LORD will speak,
    for he will speak peace to his people,
    to his faithful, to those who turn to him in
    their hearts.[i]
9 Surely his salvation is at hand for those who
    fear him,
    that his glory may dwell in our land.

10 Steadfast love and faithfulness will meet;
    righteousness and peace will kiss each
    other.
11 Faithfulness will spring up from the ground,
    and righteousness will look down from the
    sky.
12 The LORD will give what is good,
    and our land will yield its increase.
13 Righteousness will go before him,
    and will make a path for his steps.

Supplication for Help against Enemies
A Prayer of David.

86 INCLINE YOUR ear, O LORD, and answer
    me,
    for I am poor and needy.
2 Preserve my life, for I am devoted to you;
    save your servant who trusts in you.
You are my God; 3be gracious to me, O Lord,
    for to you do I cry all day long.
4 Gladden the soul of your servant,
    for to you, O Lord, I lift up my soul.
5 For you, O Lord, are good and forgiving,
    abounding in steadfast love to all who call
    on you.
6 Give ear, O LORD, to my prayer;
    listen to my cry of supplication.

---

b 84:9 your king, literally, "your anointed."   c 84:10 palaces, literally, "tents."   d 84:11 walk along his paths, literally, "walk uprightly." e 85:1 restored the fortunes of Israel, literally, "brought back the captivity." f 85:4 Now bring us back to loving you, or, "Turn to us."   g 85:10 justice, literally, "righteousness."   h 85:13 make a pathway for his steps, or, "set us in the way of his steps."

i Gk: Heb but let them not turn back to folly

King James

7In the day of my trouble I will call upon thee: for thou wilt answer me.

8Among the gods *there is* none like unto thee, O Lord; neither *are there any works* like unto thy works.

9All nations whom thou hast made shall come and worship before thee, O Lord; and shall glorify thy name.

10For thou *art* great, and doest wondrous things: thou *art* God alone.

11Teach me thy way, O LORD; I will walk in thy truth: unite my heart to fear thy name.

12I will praise thee, O Lord my God, with all my heart: and I will glorify thy name for evermore.

13For great *is* thy mercy toward me: and thou hast delivered my soul from the lowest hell.

14O God, the proud are risen against me, and the assemblies of violent *men* have sought after my soul; and have not set thee before them.

15But thou, O Lord, *art* a God full of compassion, and gracious, longsuffering, and plenteous in mercy and truth.

16O turn unto me, and have mercy upon me; give thy strength unto thy servant, and save the son of thine handmaid.

17Show me a token for good; that they which hate me may see *it,* and be ashamed: because thou, LORD, hast helped me, and comforted me.

A Psalm *or* Song for the sons of Korah.

87 HIS FOUNDATION *is* in the holy mountains.
2The LORD loveth the gates of Zion more than all the dwellings of Jacob.

3Glorious things are spoken of thee, O city of God. Selah.

4I will make mention of Rahab and Babylon to them that know me: behold Philistia, and Tyre, with Ethiopia; this *man* was born there.

5And of Zion it shall be said, This and that man was born in her: and the highest himself shall establish her.

6The LORD shall count, when he writeth up the people, *that* this *man* was born there. Selah.

7As well the singers as the players on instruments *shall be there:* all my springs *are* in thee.

A Song *or* Psalm for the sons of Korah, to the chief Musician upon Mahalath Leannoth, Maschil of Heman the Ezrahite.

88 O LORD God of my salvation, I have cried day *and* night before thee:

New International

7In the day of my trouble I will call to you, for you will answer me.

8Among the gods there is none like you, O Lord; no deeds can compare with yours.

9All the nations you have made will come and worship before you, O Lord; they will bring glory to your name.

10For you are great and do marvelous deeds; you alone are God.

11Teach me your way, O LORD, and I will walk in your truth; give me an undivided heart, that I may fear your name.

12I will praise you, O Lord my God, with all my heart; I will glorify your name forever.

13For great is your love toward me; you have delivered me from the depths of the grave.a

14The arrogant are attacking me, O God; a band of ruthless men seeks my life— men without regard for you.

15But you, O Lord, are a compassionate and gracious God, slow to anger, abounding in love and faithfulness.

16Turn to me and have mercy on me; grant your strength to your servant and save the son of your maidservant.b

17Give me a sign of your goodness, that my enemies may see it and be put to shame, for you, O LORD, have helped me and comforted me.

Of the Sons of Korah. A psalm. A song.

87 HE HAS set his foundation on the holy mountain;
2 the LORD loves the gates of Zion more than all the dwellings of Jacob.

3Glorious things are said of you,
O city of God: Selah

4"I will record Rahabc and Babylon among those who acknowledge me— Philistia too, and Tyre, along with Cushd— and will say, 'Thise one was born in Zion.' "

5Indeed, of Zion it will be said,
"This one and that one were born in her, and the Most High himself will establish her."

6The LORD will write in the register of the peoples:
"This one was born in Zion." Selah

7As they make music they will sing,
"All my fountains are in you."

A song. A psalm of the Sons of Korah. For the director of music. According to *mahalath leannoth.*f A *maskil*g of Heman the Ezrahite.

88 O LORD, the God who saves me, day and night I cry out before you.

---

a *13* Hebrew *Sheol*　b *16* Or *save your faithful son*　c *4* A poetic name for Egypt　d *4* That is, the upper Nile region　e *4* Or *"O Rahab and Babylon, / Philistia, Tyre and Cush, / I will record concerning those who acknowledge me: / 'This*　f Title: Possibly a tune, "The Suffering of Affliction"　g Title: Probably a literary or musical term

Living Bible

cry. 7I will call to you whenever trouble strikes, and you will help me.

8Where among the heathen gods is there a god like you? Where are their miracles? 9All the nations—and you made each one—will come and bow before you, Lord, and praise your great and holy name. 10For you are great, and do great miracles. You alone are God.

11Tell me where you want me to go and I will go there. May every fiber of my being unite in reverence to your name. 12With all my heart I will praise you. I will give glory to your name forever, 13for you love me so much! You are constantly so kind! You have rescued me from deepest hell.

14O God, proud and insolent men defy me; violent, godless men are trying to kill me. 15But you are merciful and gentle, Lord, slow in getting angry, full of constant lovingkindness and of truth; 16so look down in pity and grant strength to your servant and save me. 17Send me a sign of your favor. When those who hate me see it they will lose face because you help and comfort me.

87 HIGH ON his holy mountain stands Jerusalem,h the city of God, the city he loves more than any other!

3O city of God, what wondrous tales are told of you! 4Nowadays when I mention among my friends the names of Egypt and Babylonia, Philistia and Tyre, or even distant Ethiopia, someone boasts that he was born in one or another of those countries. 5But someday the highest honor will be to be a native of Jerusalem! For the God above all gods will personally bless this city. 6When he registers her citizens he will place a checkmark beside the names of those who were born here. 7And in the festivals they'll sing, "All my heart is in Jerusalem."

88 O JEHOVAH, God of my salvation, I have wept before you day and night. 2Now hear my

New Revised Standard

7 In the day of my trouble I call on you,
      for you will answer me.

8 There is none like you among the gods,
         O Lord,
      nor are there any works like yours.
9 All the nations you have made shall come
         and bow down before you, O Lord,
      and shall glorify your name.
10 For you are great and do wondrous things;
      you alone are God.
11 Teach me your way, O LORD,
      that I may walk in your truth;
      give me an undivided heart to revere your
         name.
12 I give thanks to you, O Lord my God, with
         my whole heart,
      and I will glorify your name forever.
13 For great is your steadfast love toward me;
      you have delivered my soul from the depths
         of Sheol.

14 O God, the insolent rise up against me;
      a band of ruffians seeks my life,
      and they do not set you before them.
15 But you, O Lord, are a God merciful and
         gracious,
      slow to anger and abounding in steadfast
         love and faithfulness.
16 Turn to me and be gracious to me;
      give your strength to your servant;
      save the child of your serving girl.
17 Show me a sign of your favor,
      so that those who hate me may see it and be
         put to shame,
      because you, LORD, have helped me and
         comforted me.

The Joy of Living in Zion

Of the Korahites. A Psalm. A Song.

87 ON THE holy mount stands the city he founded;
2   the LORD loves the gates of Zion
      more than all the dwellings of Jacob.
3 Glorious things are spoken of you,
      O city of God.   *Selah*

4 Among those who know me I mention Rahab
         and Babylon;
      Philistia too, and Tyre, with Ethiopiai—
      "This one was born there," they say.

5 And of Zion it shall be said,
      "This one and that one were born in it";
      for the Most High himself will establish it.
6 The LORD records, as he registers the peoples,
      "This one was born there."   *Selah*

7 Singers and dancers alike say,
      "All my springs are in you."

Prayer for Help in Despondency

A Song. A Psalm of the Korahites. To the leader: according to Mahalath Leannoth. A Maskil of Heman the Ezrahite.

88 O LORD, God of my salvation,
      when, at night, I cry out in your presence,

---

h *87:1 Jerusalem*, literally, "Zion."   i Or *Nubia*; Heb *Cush*

King James

2Let my prayer come before thee: incline thine ear unto my cry;

3For my soul is full of troubles: and my life draweth nigh unto the grave.

4I am counted with them that go down into the pit: I am as a man *that hath* no strength:

5Free among the dead, like the slain that lie in the grave, whom thou rememberest no more: and they are cut off from thy hand.

6Thou hast laid me in the lowest pit, in darkness, in the deeps.

7Thy wrath lieth hard upon me, and thou hast afflicted *me* with all thy waves. Selah.

8Thou hast put away mine acquaintance far from me; thou hast made me an abomination unto them: *I am* shut up, and I cannot come forth.

9Mine eye mourneth by reason of affliction: LORD, I have called daily upon thee, I have stretched out my hands unto thee.

10Wilt thou show wonders to the dead? shall the dead arise *and* praise thee? Selah.

11Shall thy lovingkindness be declared in the grave? *or* thy faithfulness in destruction?

12Shall thy wonders be known in the dark? and thy righteousness in the land of forgetfulness?

13But unto thee have I cried, O LORD; and in the morning shall my prayer prevent thee.

14LORD, why castest thou off my soul? *why* hidest thou thy face from me?

15I *am* afflicted and ready to die from *my* youth up: *while* I suffer thy terrors I am distracted.

16Thy fierce wrath goeth over me; thy terrors have cut me off.

17They came round about me daily like water; they compassed me about together.

18Lover and friend hast thou put far from me, *and* mine acquaintance into darkness.

Maschil of Ethan the Ezrahite.

89 I WILL sing of the mercies of the LORD for ever: with my mouth will I make known thy faithfulness to all generations.

2For I have said, Mercy shall be built up for ever: thy faithfulness shalt thou establish in the very heavens.

3I have made a covenant with my chosen, I have sworn unto David my servant,

4Thy seed will I establish for ever, and build up thy throne to all generations. Selah.

5And the heavens shall praise thy wonders, O LORD: thy faithfulness also in the congregation of the saints.

New International

2May my prayer come before you;
   turn your ear to my cry.

3For my soul is full of trouble
   and my life draws near the grave.[a]

4I am counted among those who go down to the pit;
   I am like a man without strength.

5I am set apart with the dead,
   like the slain who lie in the grave,
whom you remember no more,
   who are cut off from your care.

6You have put me in the lowest pit,
   in the darkest depths.

7Your wrath lies heavily upon me;
   you have overwhelmed me with all your waves.   Selah

8You have taken from me my closest friends
   and have made me repulsive to them.
I am confined and cannot escape;
9   my eyes are dim with grief.

I call to you, O LORD, every day;
   I spread out my hands to you.

10Do you show your wonders to the dead?
   Do those who are dead rise up and praise you?   Selah

11Is your love declared in the grave,
   your faithfulness in Destruction[b]?

12Are your wonders known in the place of darkness,
   or your righteous deeds in the land of oblivion?

13But I cry to you for help, O LORD;
   in the morning my prayer comes before you.

14Why, O LORD, do you reject me
   and hide your face from me?

15From my youth I have been afflicted and close to death;
   I have suffered your terrors and am in despair.

16Your wrath has swept over me;
   your terrors have destroyed me.

17All day long they surround me like a flood;
   they have completely engulfed me.

18You have taken my companions and loved ones from me;
   the darkness is my closest friend.

A *maskil*[c] of Ethan the Ezrahite.

89 I WILL sing of the LORD's great love forever;
   with my mouth I will make your faithfulness known through all generations.

2I will declare that your love stands firm forever,
   that you established your faithfulness in heaven itself.

3You said, "I have made a covenant with my chosen one,
   I have sworn to David my servant,

4'I will establish your line forever
   and make your throne firm through all generations.' "   Selah

5The heavens praise your wonders, O LORD,
   your faithfulness too, in the assembly of the holy ones.

a 3 Hebrew *Sheol*   b 11 Hebrew *Abaddon*   c Title: Probably a literary or musical term

Living Bible

prayers; oh, listen to my cry, 3for my life is full of troubles, and death draws near. 4They say my life is ebbing out—a hopeless case. 5They have left me here to die, like those slain on battlefields, from whom your mercies are removed.

6You have thrust me down to the darkest depths. 7Your wrath lies heavy on me; wave after wave engulfs me. 8You have made my friends to loathe me, and they have gone away. I am in a trap with no way out. 9My eyes grow dim with weeping. Each day I beg your help; O Lord, I reach my pleading hands to you for mercy.

10Soon it will be too late! Of what use are your miracles when I am in the grave? How can I praise you then? 11Can those in the grave declare your lovingkindness? Can they proclaim your faithfulness? 12Can the darkness speak of your miracles? Can anyone in the Land of Forgetfulness talk about your help?

13O Lord, I plead for my life and will keep on pleading day by day. 14O Jehovah, why have you thrown my life away? Why are you turning your face from me, and looking the other way?

15From my youth I have been sickly and ready to die. I stand helpless before your terrors. 16Your fierce wrath has overwhelmed me. Your terrors have cut me off. 17They flow around me all day long. 18Lover, friend, acquaintance—all are gone. There is only darkness everywhere.

89

FOREVER AND ever I will sing about the tender kindness of the Lord! Young and old shall hear about your blessings. 2Your love and kindness are forever; your truth is as enduring as the heavens.

3,4The Lord God says,d "I have made a solemn agreement with my chosen servant David. I have taken an oath to establish his descendants as kings forever on his throne, from now until eternity!"

5All heaven shall praise your miracles, O Lord; myriads of angelse will praise you for your faithfulness. 6For

New Revised Standard

2 let my prayer come before you;
    incline your ear to my cry.

3 For my soul is full of troubles,
    and my life draws near to Sheol.
4 I am counted among those who go down to
        the Pit;
    I am like those who have no help,
5 like those forsaken among the dead,
    like the slain that lie in the grave,
like those whom you remember no more,
    for they are cut off from your hand.
6 You have put me in the depths of the Pit,
    in the regions dark and deep.
7 Your wrath lies heavy upon me,
    and you overwhelm me with all your waves.
                                                        Selah

8 You have caused my companions to shun me;
    you have made me a thing of horror to
        them.
    I am shut in so that I cannot escape;
9   my eye grows dim through sorrow.
Every day I call on you, O Lord;
    I spread out my hands to you.
10 Do you work wonders for the dead?
    Do the shades rise up to praise you? Selah
11 Is your steadfast love declared in the grave,
    or your faithfulness in Abaddon?
12 Are your wonders known in the darkness,
    or your saving help in the land of
        forgetfulness?

13 But I, O Lord, cry out to you;
    in the morning my prayer comes before
        you.
14 O Lord, why do you cast me off?
    Why do you hide your face from me?
15 Wretched and close to death from my youth
        up,
    I suffer your terrors; I am desperate.f
16 Your wrath has swept over me;
    your dread assaults destroy me.
17 They surround me like a flood all day long;
    from all sides they close in on me.
18 You have caused friend and neighbor to shun
        me;
    my companions are in darkness.

God's Covenant with David

A Maskil of Ethan the Ezrahite.

89

I WILL sing of your steadfast love,
    O Lord,g forever;
with my mouth I will proclaim your
    faithfulness to all generations.
2 I declare that your steadfast love is established
        forever;
    your faithfulness is as firm as the heavens.

3 You said, "I have made a covenant with my
        chosen one,
    I have sworn to my servant David:
4 'I will establish your descendants forever,
    and build your throne for all generations.' "
                                                        Selah

5 Let the heavens praise your wonders, O Lord,
    your faithfulness in the assembly of the holy
        ones.

---

d 89:3, 4 The Lord says, implied.   e 89:5 myriads of angels, literally, "the assembly of the holy ones."

f Meaning of Heb uncertain   g Gk: Heb the steadfast love of the Lord

King James

6For who in the heaven can be compared unto the LORD? *who* among the sons of the mighty can be likened unto the LORD?

7God is greatly to be feared in the assembly of the saints, and to be had in reverence of all *them that are* about him.

8O LORD God of hosts, who *is* a strong LORD like unto thee? or to thy faithfulness round about thee?

9Thou rulest the raging of the sea: when the waves thereof arise, thou stillest them.

10Thou hast broken Rahab in pieces, as one that is slain; thou hast scattered thine enemies with thy strong arm.

11The heavens *are* thine, the earth also *is* thine: *as for* the world and the fulness thereof, thou hast founded them.

12The north and the south thou hast created them: Tabor and Hermon shall rejoice in thy name.

13Thou hast a mighty arm: strong is thy hand, *and* high is thy right hand.

14Justice and judgment *are* the habitation of thy throne: mercy and truth shall go before thy face.

15Blessed *is* the people that know the joyful sound: they shall walk, O LORD, in the light of thy countenance.

16In thy name shall they rejoice all the day: and in thy righteousness shall they be exalted.

17For thou *art* the glory of their strength: and in thy favour our horn shall be exalted.

18For the LORD *is* our defence; and the Holy One of Israel *is* our king.

19Then thou spakest in vision to thy holy one, and saidst, I have laid help upon *one that is* mighty; I have exalted *one* chosen out of the people.

20I have found David my servant; with my holy oil have I anointed him:

21With whom my hand shall be established: mine arm also shall strengthen him.

22The enemy shall not exact upon him; nor the son of wickedness afflict him.

23And I will beat down his foes before his face, and plague them that hate him.

24But my faithfulness and my mercy *shall be* with him: and in my name shall his horn be exalted.

25I will set his hand also in the sea, and his right hand in the rivers.

26He shall cry unto me, Thou *art* my father, my God, and the rock of my salvation.

27Also I will make him *my* firstborn, higher than the kings of the earth.

28My mercy will I keep for him for evermore, and my covenant shall stand fast with him.

29His seed also will I make *to endure* for ever, and his throne as the days of heaven.

New International

6For who in the skies above can compare with the LORD?
Who is like the LORD among the heavenly beings?

7In the council of the holy ones God is greatly feared;
he is more awesome than all who surround him.

8O LORD God Almighty, who is like you?
You are mighty, O LORD, and your faithfulness surrounds you.

9You rule over the surging sea;
when its waves mount up, you still them.

10You crushed Rahab like one of the slain;
with your strong arm you scattered your enemies.

11The heavens are yours, and yours also the earth;
you founded the world and all that is in it.

12You created the north and the south;
Tabor and Hermon sing for joy at your name.

13Your arm is endued with power;
your hand is strong, your right hand exalted.

14Righteousness and justice are the foundation of your throne;
love and faithfulness go before you.

15Blessed are those who have learned to acclaim you,
who walk in the light of your presence, O LORD.

16They rejoice in your name all day long;
they exult in your righteousness.

17For you are their glory and strength,
and by your favor you exalt our horn.[a]

18Indeed, our shield[b] belongs to the LORD,
our king to the Holy One of Israel.

19Once you spoke in a vision,
to your faithful people you said:
"I have bestowed strength on a warrior;
I have exalted a young man from among the people.

20I have found David my servant;
with my sacred oil I have anointed him.

21My hand will sustain him;
surely my arm will strengthen him.

22No enemy will subject him to tribute;
no wicked man will oppress him.

23I will crush his foes before him
and strike down his adversaries.

24My faithful love will be with him,
and through my name his horn[c] will be exalted.

25I will set his hand over the sea,
his right hand over the rivers.

26He will call out to me, 'You are my Father,
my God, the Rock my Savior.'

27I will also appoint him my firstborn,
the most exalted of the kings of the earth.

28I will maintain my love to him forever,
and my covenant with him will never fail.

29I will establish his line forever,
his throne as long as the heavens endure.

---

a *17 Horn* here symbolizes strong one.   b *18* Or *sovereign*   c *24 Horn* here symbolizes strength.

Living Bible

who in all of heaven can be compared with God? What mightiest angel[d] is anything like him? 7The highest of angelic powers[e] stand in dread and awe of him. Who is as revered as he by those surrounding him? 8O Jehovah, Commander of the heavenly armies, where is there any other Mighty One like you? Faithfulness is your very character.

9You rule the oceans when their waves arise in fearful storms; you speak, and they lie still. 10You have cut haughty Egypt[f] to pieces. Your enemies are scattered by your awesome power. 11The heavens are yours, the world, everything—for you created them all. 12You created north and south! Mount Tabor and Mount Hermon rejoice to be signed by your name as their maker! 13Strong is your arm! Strong is your hand! Your right hand is lifted high in glorious strength.

14, 15Your throne is founded on two strong pillars—the one is Justice and the other Righteousness. Mercy and Truth walk before you as your attendants. Blessed are those who hear the joyful blast of the trumpet, for they shall walk in the light of your presence. 16They rejoice all day long in your wonderful reputation and in your perfect righteousness. 17You are their strength. What glory! Our power is based on your favor! 18Yes, our protection is from the Lord himself and he, the Holy One of Israel, has given us our king.

19In a vision you spoke to your prophet[g] and said, "I have chosen a splendid young man from the common people to be the king— 20he is my servant David! I have anointed him with my holy oil. 21I will steady him and make him strong. 22His enemies shall not outwit him, nor shall the wicked overpower him. 23I will beat down his adversaries before him, and destroy those who hate him. 24I will protect and bless him constantly and surround him with my love; he will be great because of me. 25He will hold sway from the Euphrates River to the Mediterranean Sea. 26And he will cry to me, 'You are my Father, my God, and my Rock of Salvation.'

27"I will treat him as my firstborn son, and make him the mightiest king in all the earth. 28I will love him forever, and be kind to him always; my covenant with him will never end. 29He will always have an heir; his throne will be as endless as the days of heaven.

New Revised Standard

6 For who in the skies can be compared to the
      LORD?
   Who among the heavenly beings is like the
      LORD,
7 a God feared in the council of the holy ones,
      great and awesome[h] above all that are
      around him?
8 O LORD God of hosts,
      who is as mighty as you, O LORD?
   Your faithfulness surrounds you.
9 You rule the raging of the sea;
      when its waves rise, you still them.
10 You crushed Rahab like a carcass;
      you scattered your enemies with your
      mighty arm.
11 The heavens are yours, the earth also is yours;
      the world and all that is in it—you have
      founded them.
12 The north and the south[i]—you created them;
      Tabor and Hermon joyously praise your
      name.
13 You have a mighty arm;
      strong is your hand, high your right hand.
14 Righteousness and justice are the foundation
      of your throne;
      steadfast love and faithfulness go before
      you.
15 Happy are the people who know the festal
      shout,
   who walk, O LORD, in the light of your
      countenance;
16 they exult in your name all day long,
      and extol your righteousness.
17 For you are the glory of their strength;
      by your favor our horn is exalted.
18 For our shield belongs to the LORD,
      our king to the Holy One of Israel.

19 Then you spoke in a vision to your faithful
      one, and said:
   "I have set the crown[k] on one who is
      mighty,
   I have exalted one chosen from the people.
20 I have found my servant David;
      with my holy oil I have anointed him;
21 my hand shall always remain with him;
      my arm also shall strengthen him.
22 The enemy shall not outwit him,
      the wicked shall not humble him.
23 I will crush his foes before him
      and strike down those who hate him.
24 My faithfulness and steadfast love shall be
      with him;
      and in my name his horn shall be exalted.
25 I will set his hand on the sea
      and his right hand on the rivers.
26 He shall cry to me, 'You are my Father,
      my God, and the Rock of my salvation!'
27 I will make him the firstborn,
      the highest of the kings of the earth.
28 Forever I will keep my steadfast love for him,
      and my covenant with him will stand firm.
29 I will establish his line forever,
      and his throne as long as the heavens
      endure.

---

d 89:6 *mightiest angel*, literally, "the sons of the mighty."   e 89:7 *angelic powers*, literally, "the assembly of the holy ones."   f 89:10 *Egypt*, literally, "Rahab."   g 89:19 *your prophet*, literally, "your saint," apparently a reference to Samuel, who was sent to anoint David as king.

h Gk Syr: Heb *greatly awesome*   i Or *Zaphon and Yamin*   j Cn: Heb *are exalted in*   k Cn: Heb *help*

King James

30If his children forsake my law, and walk not in my judgments;

31If they break my statutes, and keep not my commandments;

32Then will I visit their transgression with the rod, and their iniquity with stripes.

33Nevertheless my lovingkindness will I not utterly take from him, nor suffer my faithfulness to fail.

34My covenant will I not break, nor alter the thing that is gone out of my lips.

35Once have I sworn by my holiness that I will not lie unto David.

36His seed shall endure for ever, and his throne as the sun before me.

37It shall be established for ever as the moon, and *as* a faithful witness in heaven. Selah.

38But thou hast cast off and abhorred, thou hast been wroth with thine anointed.

39Thou hast made void the covenant of thy servant: thou hast profaned his crown *by casting it* to the ground.

40Thou hast broken down all his hedges; thou hast brought his strong holds to ruin.

41All that pass by the way spoil him: he is a reproach to his neighbours.

42Thou hast set up the right hand of his adversaries; thou hast made all his enemies to rejoice.

43Thou hast also turned the edge of his sword, and hast not made him to stand in the battle.

44Thou hast made his glory to cease, and cast his throne down to the ground.

45The days of his youth hast thou shortened: thou hast covered him with shame. Selah.

46How long, LORD? wilt thou hide thyself for ever? shall thy wrath burn like fire?

47Remember how short my time is: wherefore hast thou made all men in vain?

48What man *is he that* liveth, and shall not see death? shall he deliver his soul from the hand of the grave? Selah.

49Lord, where *are* thy former lovingkindnesses, *which* thou swarest unto David in thy truth?

50Remember, Lord, the reproach of thy servants; *how* I do bear in my bosom *the reproach of* all the mighty people;

51Wherewith thine enemies have reproached, O LORD; wherewith they have reproached the footsteps of thine anointed.

52Blessed *be* the LORD for evermore. Amen, and Amen.

New International

30"If his sons forsake my law
    and do not follow my statutes,
31if they violate my decrees
    and fail to keep my commands,
32I will punish their sin with the rod,
    their iniquity with flogging;
33but I will not take my love from him,
    nor will I ever betray my faithfulness.
34I will not violate my covenant
    or alter what my lips have uttered.
35Once for all, I have sworn by my holiness—
    and I will not lie to David—
36that his line will continue forever
    and his throne endure before me like the sun;
37it will be established forever like the moon,
    the faithful witness in the sky."   *Selah*

38But you have rejected, you have spurned,
    you have been very angry with your anointed
        one.
39You have renounced the covenant with your
        servant
    and have defiled his crown in the dust.
40You have broken through all his walls
    and reduced his strongholds to ruins.
41All who pass by have plundered him;
    he has become the scorn of his neighbors.
42You have exalted the right hand of his foes;
    you have made all his enemies rejoice.
43You have turned back the edge of his sword
    and have not supported him in battle.
44You have put an end to his splendor
    and cast his throne to the ground.
45You have cut short the days of his youth;
    you have covered him with a mantle of
        shame.   *Selah*

46How long, O LORD? Will you hide yourself
        forever?
    How long will your wrath burn like fire?
47Remember how fleeting is my life.
    For what futility you have created all men!
48What man can live and not see death,
    or save himself from the power of the
        grave[a]?   *Selah*
49O Lord, where is your former great love,
    which in your faithfulness you swore to
        David?
50Remember, Lord, how your servant has[b] been
        mocked,
    how I bear in my heart the taunts of all the
        nations,
51the taunts with which your enemies have
        mocked, O LORD,
    with which they have mocked every step of
        your anointed one.

52Praise be to the LORD forever!
    Amen and Amen.

---

a 48 Hebrew *Sheol*   b 50 Or *your servants have*

Living Bible

30, 31, 32If his children forsake my laws and don't obey them, then I will punish them, 33but I will never completely take away my lovingkindness from them, nor let my promise fail. 34No, I will not break my covenant; I will not take back one word of what I said. 35, 36For I have sworn to David (and a holy God can never lie), that his dynasty will go on forever, and his throne will continue to the end of time.c 37It shall be eternal as the moon, my faithful witness in the sky!"

38Then why cast me off, rejected? Why be so angry with the one you chose as king? 39Have you renounced your covenant with him? For you have thrown his crown in the dust. 40You have broken down the walls protecting him and laid in ruins every fort defending him. 41Everyone who comes along has robbed him while his neighbors mock. 42You have strengthened his enemies against him and made them rejoice. 43You have struck down his sword and refused to help him in battle. 44You have ended his splendor and overturned his throne. 45You have made him old before his time and publicly disgraced him.

46O Jehovah, how long will this go on? Will you hide yourself from me forever? How long will your wrath burn like fire? 47Oh, remember how short you have made man's lifespan. Is it an empty, futile life you give the sons of men? 48No man can live forever. All will die. Who can rescue his life from the power of the grave?

49Lord, where is the love you used to have for me? Where is your kindness that you promised to David with a faithful pledge? 50Lord, see how all the people are despising me. 51Your enemies joke about me, the one you anointed as their king.

52And yet—blessed be the Lord forever! Amen and amen!

New Revised Standard

30 If his children forsake my law
  and do not walk according to my
    ordinances,
31 if they violate my statutes
  and do not keep my commandments,
32 then I will punish their transgression with the
    rod
  and their iniquity with scourges;
33 but I will not remove from him my steadfast
    love,
  or be false to my faithfulness.
34 I will not violate my covenant,
  or alter the word that went forth from my
    lips.
35 Once and for all I have sworn by my holiness;
  I will not lie to David.
36 His line shall continue forever,
  and his throne endure before me like the
    sun.
37 It shall be established forever like the moon,
  an enduring witness in the skies."   Selah

38 But now you have spurned and rejected him;
  you are full of wrath against your anointed.
39 You have renounced the covenant with your
    servant;
  you have defiled his crown in the dust.
40 You have broken through all his walls;
  you have laid his strongholds in ruins.
41 All who pass by plunder him;
  he has become the scorn of his neighbors.
42 You have exalted the right hand of his foes;
  you have made all his enemies rejoice.
43 Moreover, you have turned back the edge of
    his sword,
  and you have not supported him in battle.
44 You have removed the scepter from his
    hand,d
  and hurled his throne to the ground.
45 You have cut short the days of his youth;
  you have covered him with shame.   Selah

46 How long, O Lord? Will you hide yourself
    forever?
  How long will your wrath burn like fire?
47 Remember how short my time is—e
  for what vanity you have created all
    mortals!
48 Who can live and never see death?
  Who can escape the power of Sheol?   Selah

49 Lord, where is your steadfast love of old,
  which by your faithfulness you swore to
    David?
50 Remember, O Lord, how your servant is
    taunted;
  how I bear in my bosom the insults of the
    peoples,f
51 with which your enemies taunt, O Lord,
  with which they taunted the footsteps of
    your anointed.

52 Blessed be the Lord forever.
  Amen and Amen.

---

c 89:35, 36 his throne will continue to the end of time, literally, "his throne as the sun before me."

d Cn: Heb removed his cleanness   e Meaning of Heb uncertain   f Cn: Heb bosom all of many peoples

King James

New International

Book IV
A Prayer of Moses the man of God.

90 LORD, THOU hast been our dwellingplace in all generations.

2Before the mountains were brought forth, or ever thou hadst formed the earth and the world, even from everlasting to everlasting, thou *art* God.

3Thou turnest man to destruction; and sayest, Return, ye children of men.

4For a thousand years in thy sight *are but* as yesterday when it is past, and *as* a watch in the night.

5Thou carriest them away as with a flood; they are *as* a sleep: in the morning *they are* like grass *which* groweth up.

6In the morning it flourisheth, and groweth up; in the evening it is cut down, and withereth.

7For we are consumed by thine anger, and by thy wrath are we troubled.

8Thou hast set our iniquities before thee, our secret *sins* in the light of thy countenance.

9For all our days are passed away in thy wrath: we spend our years as a tale *that is told*.

10The days of our years *are* threescore years and ten; and if by reason of strength *they be* fourscore years, yet *is* their strength labour and sorrow; for it is soon cut off, and we fly away.

11Who knoweth the power of thine anger? even according to thy fear, *so is* thy wrath.

12So teach *us* to number our days, that we may apply *our* hearts unto wisdom.

13Return, O LORD, how long? and let it repent thee concerning thy servants.

14O satisfy us early with thy mercy; that we may rejoice and be glad all our days.

15Make us glad according to the days *wherein* thou hast afflicted us, *and* the years *wherein* we have seen evil.

16Let thy work appear unto thy servants, and thy glory unto their children.

17And let the beauty of the LORD our God be upon us: and establish thou the work of our hands upon us; yea, the work of our hands establish thou it.

Psalms 90–106
A prayer of Moses the man of God.

90 LORD, YOU have been our dwelling place throughout all generations.

2Before the mountains were born
or you brought forth the earth and the world,
from everlasting to everlasting you are God.

3You turn men back to dust,
saying, "Return to dust, O sons of men."
4For a thousand years in your sight
are like a day that has just gone by,
or like a watch in the night.
5You sweep men away in the sleep of death;
they are like the new grass of the morning—
6though in the morning it springs up new,
by evening it is dry and withered.

7We are consumed by your anger
and terrified by your indignation.
8You have set our iniquities before you,
our secret sins in the light of your presence.
9All our days pass away under your wrath;
we finish our years with a moan.
10The length of our days is seventy years—
or eighty, if we have the strength;
yet their span[a] is but trouble and sorrow,
for they quickly pass, and we fly away.

11Who knows the power of your anger?
For your wrath is as great as the fear that is
due you.
12Teach us to number our days aright,
that we may gain a heart of wisdom.

13Relent, O LORD! How long will it be?
Have compassion on your servants.
14Satisfy us in the morning with your unfailing
love,
that we may sing for joy and be glad all our
days.
15Make us glad for as many days as you have
afflicted us,
for as many years as we have seen trouble.
16May your deeds be shown to your servants,
your splendor to their children.

17May the favor[b] of the Lord our God rest upon
us;
establish the work of our hands for us—
yes, establish the work of our hands.

91 HE THAT dwelleth in the secret place of the most High shall abide under the shadow of the Almighty.

2I will say of the LORD, *He is* my refuge and my fortress: my God; in him will I trust.

3Surely he shall deliver thee from the snare of the fowler, *and* from the noisome pestilence. .

91 HE WHO dwells in the shelter of the Most High
will rest in the shadow of the Almighty.[c]
2I will say[d] of the LORD, "He is my refuge and
my fortress,
my God, in whom I trust."

3Surely he will save you from the fowler's snare
and from the deadly pestilence.

Living Bible

New Revised Standard

BOOK IV

(Psalms 90–106)

God's Eternity and Human Frailty

A Prayer of Moses, the man of God.

A prayer of Moses, the man of God.

90 LORD, THROUGH all the generations you have been our home! ²Before the mountains were created, before the earth was formed, you are God without beginning or end.

³You speak, and man turns back to dust. ⁴A thousand years are but as yesterday to you! They are like a single hour!ᵉ ⁵, ⁶We glide along the tides of time as swiftly as a racing river, and vanish as quickly as a dream. We are like grass that is green in the morning but mowed down and withered before the evening shadows fall. ⁷We die beneath your anger; we are overwhelmed by your wrath. ⁸You spread out our sins before you—our secret sins—and see them all. ⁹No wonder the years are long and heavy here beneath your wrath. All our days are filled with sighing.

¹⁰Seventy years are given us! And some may even live to eighty. But even the best of these years are often emptiness and pain; soon they disappear, and we are gone. ¹¹Who can realize the terrors of your anger? Which of us can fear you as he should?

¹²Teach us to number our days and recognize how few they are; help us to spend them as we should.

¹³O Jehovah, come and bless us! How long will you delay? Turn away your anger from us. ¹⁴Satisfy us in our earliestᶠ youth with your lovingkindness, giving us constant joy to the end of our lives. ¹⁵Give us gladness in proportion to our former misery! Replace the evil years with good. ¹⁶Let us see your miracles again; let our children see glorious things, the kind you used to do, ¹⁷and let the Lord our God favor us and give us success. May he give permanence to all we do.

90 LORD, YOU have been our dwelling placeᵍ in all generations.
² Before the mountains were brought forth,
    or ever you had formed the earth and the
       world,
    from everlasting to everlasting you are God.

³ You turn usʰ back to dust,
    and say, "Turn back, you mortals."
⁴ For a thousand years in your sight
    are like yesterday when it is past,
    or like a watch in the night.

⁵ You sweep them away; they are like a dream,
    like grass that is renewed in the morning;
⁶ in the morning it flourishes and is renewed;
    in the evening it fades and withers.

⁷ For we are consumed by your anger;
    by your wrath we are overwhelmed.
⁸ You have set our iniquities before you,
    our secret sins in the light of your
       countenance.

⁹ For all our days pass away under your wrath;
    our years come to an endⁱ like a sigh.
¹⁰ The days of our life are seventy years,
    or perhaps eighty, if we are strong;
    even then their spanʲ is only toil and trouble;
    they are soon gone, and we fly away.

¹¹ Who considers the power of your anger?
    Your wrath is as great as the fear that is due
       you.
¹² So teach us to count our days
    that we may gain a wise heart.

¹³ Turn, O LORD! How long?
    Have compassion on your servants!
¹⁴ Satisfy us in the morning with your steadfast
       love,
    so that we may rejoice and be glad all our
       days.
¹⁵ Make us glad as many days as you have
       afflicted us,
    and as many years as we have seen evil.
¹⁶ Let your work be manifest to your servants,
    and your glorious power to their children.
¹⁷ Let the favor of the Lord our God be upon us,
    and prosper for us the work of our hands—
    O prosper the work of our hands!

Assurance of God's Protection

91 WE LIVE within the shadow of the Almighty, sheltered by the God who is above all gods. ²This I declare, that he alone is my refuge, my place of safety; he is my God, and I am trusting him. ³For he rescues you from every trap, and protects you from the fatal plague. ⁴He will shield you with his wings! They

91 YOU WHO live in the shelter of the Most
       High,
    who abide in the shadow of the Almighty,ᵏ
² will say to the LORD, "My refuge and my
       fortress;
    my God, in whom I trust."
³ For he will deliver you from the snare of the
       fowler
    and from the deadly pestilence;

ᵉ *90:4 They are like a single hour*, literally, "as a watch in the night."
ᶠ *90:14 earliest*, literally, "early."

ᵍ Another reading is *our refuge*   ʰ Heb *humankind*   ⁱ Syr: Heb *we bring our years to an end*   ʲ Cn Compare Gk Syr Jerome Tg: Heb *pride*   ᵏ Traditional rendering of Heb *Shaddai*

King James

⁴He shall cover thee with his feathers, and under his wings shalt thou trust: his truth *shall be thy* shield and buckler.

⁵Thou shalt not be afraid for the terror by night; *nor* for the arrow *that* flieth by day;

⁶*Nor* for the pestilence *that* walketh in darkness; *nor* for the destruction *that* wasteth at noonday.

⁷A thousand shall fall at thy side, and ten thousand at thy right hand; *but* it shall not come nigh thee.

⁸Only with thine eyes shalt thou behold and see the reward of the wicked.

⁹Because thou hast made the LORD, *which is* my refuge, *even* the most High, thy habitation;

¹⁰There shall no evil befall thee, neither shall any plague come nigh thy dwelling.

¹¹For he shall give his angels charge over thee, to keep thee in all thy ways.

¹²They shall bear thee up in *their* hands, lest thou dash thy foot against a stone.

¹³Thou shalt tread upon the lion and adder: the young lion and the dragon shalt thou trample under feet.

¹⁴Because he hath set his love upon me, therefore will I deliver him: I will set him on high, because he hath known my name.

¹⁵He shall call upon me, and I will answer him: I *will be* with him in trouble; I will deliver him, and honour him.

¹⁶With long life will I satisfy him, and show him my salvation.

A Psalm *or* Song for the sabbath day.

92 IT IS a good *thing* to give thanks unto the LORD, and to sing praises unto thy name, O most High:

²To show forth thy lovingkindness in the morning, and thy faithfulness every night,

³Upon an instrument of ten strings, and upon the psaltery; upon the harp with a solemn sound.

⁴For thou, LORD, hast made me glad through thy work: I will triumph in the works of thy hands.

⁵O LORD, how great are thy works! *and* thy thoughts are very deep.

⁶A brutish man knoweth not; neither doth a fool understand this.

⁷When the wicked spring as the grass, and when all the workers of iniquity do flourish; *it is* that they shall be destroyed for ever:

⁸But thou, LORD, *art most* high for evermore.

⁹For, lo, thine enemies, O LORD, for, lo, thine enemies shall perish; all the workers of iniquity shall be scattered.

¹⁰But my horn shalt thou exalt like *the horn of* an unicorn: I shall be anointed with fresh oil.

¹¹Mine eye also shall see *my desire* on mine enemies, *and* mine ears shall hear *my desire* of the wicked that rise up against me.

New International

⁴He will cover you with his feathers,
  and under his wings you will find refuge;
  his faithfulness will be your shield and
    rampart.
⁵You will not fear the terror of night,
  nor the arrow that flies by day,
⁶nor the pestilence that stalks in the darkness,
  nor the plague that destroys at midday.
⁷A thousand may fall at your side,
  ten thousand at your right hand,
  but it will not come near you.
⁸You will only observe with your eyes
  and see the punishment of the wicked.

⁹If you make the Most High your dwelling—
  even the LORD, who is my refuge—
¹⁰then no harm will befall you,
  no disaster will come near your tent.
¹¹For he will command his angels concerning you
  to guard you in all your ways;
¹²they will lift you up in their hands,
  so that you will not strike your foot against a
    stone.
¹³You will tread upon the lion and the cobra;
  you will trample the great lion and the
    serpent.

¹⁴"Because he loves me," says the LORD, "I will
    rescue him;
  I will protect him, for he acknowledges my
    name.
¹⁵He will call upon me, and I will answer him;
  I will be with him in trouble,
  I will deliver him and honor him.
¹⁶With long life will I satisfy him
  and show him my salvation."

A psalm. A song. For the Sabbath day.

92 IT IS good to praise the LORD
  and make music to your name, O Most
    High,
²to proclaim your love in the morning
  and your faithfulness at night,
³to the music of the ten-stringed lyre
  and the melody of the harp.

⁴For you make me glad by your deeds, O LORD;
  I sing for joy at the works of your hands.
⁵How great are your works, O LORD,
  how profound your thoughts!
⁶The senseless man does not know,
  fools do not understand,
⁷that though the wicked spring up like grass
  and all evildoers flourish,
  they will be forever destroyed.

⁸But you, O LORD, are exalted forever.

⁹For surely your enemies, O LORD,
  surely your enemies will perish;
  all evildoers will be scattered.
¹⁰You have exalted my hornª like that of a wild
    ox;
  fine oils have been poured upon me.
¹¹My eyes have seen the defeat of my adversaries;
  my ears have heard the rout of my wicked
    foes.

ª *10 Horn* here symbolizes strength.

Living Bible

will shelter you. His faithful promises are your armor. 5Now you don't need to be afraid of the dark any more, nor fear the dangers of the day; 6nor dread the plagues of darkness, nor disasters in the morning.b

7Though a thousand fall at my side, though ten thousand are dying around me, the evil will not touch me. 8I will see how the wicked are punished but I will not share it. 9For Jehovah is my refuge! I choose the God above all gods to shelter me. 10How then can evil overtake me or any plague come near? 11For he orders his angels to protect you wherever you go. 12They will steady you with their hands to keep you from stumbling against the rocks on the trail. 13You can safely meet a lion or step on poisonous snakes, yes, even trample them beneath your feet!

14For the Lord says, "Because he loves me, I will rescue him; I will make him great because he trusts in my name. 15When he calls on me I will answer; I will be with him in trouble, and rescue him and honor him. 16I will satisfy him with a full lifec and give him my salvation."

*A song to sing on the Lord's Day.*d

92 IT IS good to say, "Thank you" to the Lord, to sing praises to the God who is above all gods. 2Every morning tell him, "Thank you for your kindness," and every evening rejoice in all his faithfulness. 3Sing his praises, accompanied by music from the harp and lute and lyre. 4You have done so much for me, O Lord. No wonder I am glad! I sing for joy.

5O Lord, what miracles you do! And how deep are your thoughts! 6Unthinking people do not understand them! No fool can comprehend this: 7that although the wicked flourish like weeds, there is only eternal destruction ahead of them. 8But the Lord continues forever, exalted in the heavens, 9while his enemies—all evil-doers—shall be scattered.

10But you have made me as strong as a wild bull. How refreshed I am by your blessings!e 11I have heard the doom of my enemies announced and seen them destroyed. 12But the godly shall flourish like palm trees,

New Revised Standard

4 he will cover you with his pinions,
      and under his wings you will find refuge;
      his faithfulness is a shield and buckler.
5 You will not fear the terror of the night,
      or the arrow that flies by day,
6 or the pestilence that stalks in darkness,
      or the destruction that wastes at noonday.

7 A thousand may fall at your side,
      ten thousand at your right hand,
      but it will not come near you.
8 You will only look with your eyes
      and see the punishment of the wicked.

9 Because you have made the LORD your refuge,f
      the Most High your dwelling place,
10 no evil shall befall you,
      no scourge come near your tent.

11 For he will command his angels concerning
         you
      to guard you in all your ways.
12 On their hands they will bear you up,
      so that you will not dash your foot against a stone.
13 You will tread on the lion and the adder,
      the young lion and the serpent you will trample under foot.

14 Those who love me, I will deliver;
      I will protect those who know my name.
15 When they call to me, I will answer them;
      I will be with them in trouble,
      I will rescue them and honor them.
16 With long life I will satisfy them,
      and show them my salvation.

Thanksgiving for Vindication

A Psalm. A Song for the Sabbath Day.

92 IT IS good to give thanks to the LORD,
      to sing praises to your name, O Most High;
2 to declare your steadfast love in the morning,
      and your faithfulness by night,
3 to the music of the lute and the harp,
      to the melody of the lyre.
4 For you, O LORD, have made me glad by your work;
      at the works of your hands I sing for joy.

5 How great are your works, O LORD!
      Your thoughts are very deep!
6 The dullard cannot know,
      the stupid cannot understand this:
7 though the wicked sprout like grass
      and all evildoers flourish,
      they are doomed to destruction forever,
8 but you, O LORD, are on high forever.
9 For your enemies, O LORD,
      for your enemies shall perish;
      all evildoers shall be scattered.

10 But you have exalted my horn like that of the wild ox;
      you have poured over meg fresh oil.
11 My eyes have seen the downfall of my enemies;
      my ears have heard the doom of my evil assailants.

---

b *91:6 in the morning,* literally, "at noonday."   c *91:16 with a full life,* literally, "with long life."   d *92:1 on the Lord's Day,* literally, "for the Sabbath day."   e *92:10 by your blessings,* literally, "anointed with fresh oil."

f Cn: Heb *Because you, LORD, are my refuge; you have made*   g Syr: Meaning of Heb uncertain

King James

12The righteous shall flourish like the palm tree: he shall grow like a cedar in Lebanon.

13Those that be planted in the house of the LORD shall flourish in the courts of our God.

14They shall still bring forth fruit in old age; they shall be fat and flourishing;

15To show that the LORD *is* upright: *he is* my rock, and *there is* no unrighteousness in him.

93 THE LORD reigneth, he is clothed with majesty; the LORD is clothed with strength, *wherewith* he hath girded himself: the world also is stablished, that it cannot be moved.

2Thy throne *is* established of old: thou *art* from everlasting.

3The floods have lifted up, O LORD, the floods have lifted up their voice; the floods lift up their waves.

4The LORD on high *is* mightier than the noise of many waters, *yea, than* the mighty waves of the sea.

5Thy testimonies are very sure: holiness becometh thine house, O LORD, for ever.

94 O LORD God, to whom vengeance belongeth; O God, to whom vengeance belongeth, show thyself.

2Lift up thyself, thou judge of the earth: render a reward to the proud.

3LORD, how long shall the wicked, how long shall the wicked triumph?

4*How long* shall they utter *and* speak hard things? *and* all the workers of iniquity boast themselves?

5They break in pieces thy people, O LORD, and afflict thine heritage.

6They slay the widow and the stranger, and murder the fatherless.

7Yet they say, The LORD shall not see, neither shall the God of Jacob regard *it*.

8Understand, ye brutish among the people: and *ye* fools, when will ye be wise?

9He that planted the ear, shall he not hear? he that formed the eye, shall he not see?

10He that chastiseth the heathen, shall not he correct? he that teacheth man knowledge, *shall not he know?*

11The LORD knoweth the thoughts of man, that they *are* vanity.

12Blessed *is* the man whom thou chastenest, O LORD, and teachest him out of thy law;

13That thou mayest give him rest from the days of adversity, until the pit be digged for the wicked.

14For the LORD will not cast off his people, neither will he forsake his inheritance.

15But judgment shall return unto righteousness: and all the upright in heart shall follow it.

New International

12The righteous will flourish like a palm tree,
  they will grow like a cedar of Lebanon;
13planted in the house of the LORD,
  they will flourish in the courts of our God.
14They will still bear fruit in old age,
  they will stay fresh and green,
15proclaiming, "The LORD is upright;
  he is my Rock, and there is no wickedness in
    him."

93 THE LORD reigns, he is robed in majesty;
  the LORD is robed in majesty
  and is armed with strength.
The world is firmly established;
  it cannot be moved.
2Your throne was established long ago;
  you are from all eternity.

3The seas have lifted up, O LORD,
  the seas have lifted up their voice;
  the seas have lifted up their pounding waves.
4Mightier than the thunder of the great waters,
  mightier than the breakers of the sea—
  the LORD on high is mighty.

5Your statutes stand firm;
  holiness adorns your house
  for endless days, O LORD.

94 O LORD, the God who avenges,
  O God who avenges, shine forth.
2Rise up, O Judge of the earth;
  pay back to the proud what they deserve.
3How long will the wicked, O LORD,
  how long will the wicked be jubilant?

4They pour out arrogant words;
  all the evildoers are full of boasting.
5They crush your people, O LORD;
  they oppress your inheritance.
6They slay the widow and the alien;
  they murder the fatherless.
7They say, "The LORD does not see;
  the God of Jacob pays no heed."

8Take heed, you senseless ones among the
    people;
  you fools, when will you become wise?
9Does he who implanted the ear not hear?
  Does he who formed the eye not see?
10Does he who disciplines nations not punish?
  Does he who teaches man lack knowledge?
11The LORD knows the thoughts of man;
  he knows that they are futile.

12Blessed is the man you discipline, O LORD,
  the man you teach from your law;
13you grant him relief from days of trouble,
  till a pit is dug for the wicked.
14For the LORD will not reject his people;
  he will never forsake his inheritance.
15Judgment will again be founded on
    righteousness,
  and all the upright in heart will follow it.

Living Bible

and grow tall as the cedars of Lebanon. ¹³For they are transplanted into the Lord's own garden, and are under his personal care. ¹⁴Even in old age they will still produce fruit and be vital and green. ¹⁵This honors the Lord, and exhibits his faithful care. He is my shelter. There is nothing but goodness in him!

93 JEHOVAH IS King! He is robed in majesty and strength. The world is his throne.ᵃ
²O Lord, you have reigned from prehistoric times, from the everlasting past. ³The mighty oceans thunder your praise. ⁴You are mightier than all the breakers pounding on the seashores of the world! ⁵Your royal decrees cannot be changed. Holiness is forever the keynote of your reign.

94 LORD GOD, to whom vengeance belongs, let your glory shine out. Arise and judge the earth; sentence the proud to the penalties they deserve. ³Lord, how long shall the wicked be allowed to triumph and exult? ⁴Hear their insolence! See their arrogance! How these men of evil boast! ⁵See them oppressing your people, O Lord, afflicting those you love. 6. ⁷They murder widows, immigrants, and orphans, for "The Lord isn't looking," they say, "and besides, heᵇ doesn't care."
⁸Fools! ⁹Is God deaf and blind—he who makes ears and eyes? ¹⁰He punishes the nations—won't he also punish you? He knows everything—doesn't he also know what you are doing?
¹¹The Lord is fully aware of how limited and futile the thoughts of mankind are, 12. 13so he helps us by punishing them. This makes us follow his paths, and gives us respite from our enemies while God traps them and destroys them. ¹⁴The Lord will not forsake his people, for they are his prize. ¹⁵Judgment will again be just and all the upright will rejoice.

New Revised Standard

12 The righteous flourish like the palm tree,
        and grow like a cedar in Lebanon.
13 They are planted in the house of the LORD;
        they flourish in the courts of our God.
14 In old age they still produce fruit;
        they are always green and full of sap,
15 showing that the LORD is upright;
        he is my rock, and there is no
            unrighteousness in him.

The Majesty of God's Rule

93 THE LORD is king, he is robed in majesty;
        the LORD is robed, he is girded with
            strength.
    He has established the world; it shall never be
        moved;
2   your throne is established from of old;
        you are from everlasting.

3   The floods have lifted up, O LORD,
        the floods have lifted up their voice;
        the floods lift up their roaring.
4   More majestic than the thunders of mighty
            waters,
        more majestic than the wavesᶜ of the sea,
        majestic on high is the LORD!

5   Your decrees are very sure;
        holiness befits your house,
        O LORD, forevermore.

God the Avenger of the Righteous

94 O LORD, you God of vengeance,
        you God of vengeance, shine forth!
2   Rise up, O judge of the earth;
        give to the proud what they deserve!
3   O LORD, how long shall the wicked,
        how long shall the wicked exult?

4   They pour out their arrogant words;
        all the evildoers boast.
5   They crush your people, O LORD,
        and afflict your heritage.
6   They kill the widow and the stranger,
        they murder the orphan,
7   and they say, "The LORD does not see;
        the God of Jacob does not perceive."

8   Understand, O dullest of the people;
        fools, when will you be wise?
9   He who planted the ear, does he not hear?
    He who formed the eye, does he not see?
10 He who disciplines the nations,
        he who teaches knowledge to humankind,
        does he not chastise?
11 The LORD knows our thoughts,ᵈ
        that they are but an empty breath.

12 Happy are those whom you discipline,
            O LORD,
        and whom you teach out of your law,
13 giving them respite from days of trouble,
        until a pit is dug for the wicked.
14 For the LORD will not forsake his people;
        he will not abandon his heritage;
15 for justice will return to the righteous,
        and all the upright in heart will follow it.

ᵃ 93:1 The world is his throne, literally, "The world is established . . . your throne is established." ᵇ 94:6, 7 he, literally, "the God of Jacob." 　　ᶜ Cn: Heb majestic are the waves 　ᵈ Heb the thoughts of humankind

King James

16Who will rise up for me against the evildoers? *or* who will stand up for me against the workers of iniquity?

17Unless the LORD *had been* my help, my soul had almost dwelt in silence.

18When I said, My foot slippeth; thy mercy, O LORD, held me up.

19In the multitude of my thoughts within me thy comforts delight my soul.

20Shall the throne of iniquity have fellowship with thee, which frameth mischief by a law?

21They gather themselves together against the soul of the righteous, and condemn the innocent blood.

22But the LORD is my defence; and my God *is* the rock of my refuge.

23And he shall bring upon them their own iniquity, and shall cut them off in their own wickedness; *yea,* the LORD our God shall cut them off.

95 O COME, let us sing unto the LORD: let us make a joyful noise to the rock of our salvation.

2Let us come before his presence with thanksgiving, and make a joyful noise unto him with psalms.

3For the LORD *is* a great God, and a great King above all gods.

4In his hand *are* the deep places of the earth: the strength of the hills *is* his also.

5The sea *is* his, and he made it: and his hands formed the dry *land*.

6O come, let us worship and bow down: let us kneel before the LORD our maker.

7For he *is* our God; and we *are* the people of his pasture, and the sheep of his hand. Today if ye will hear his voice,

8Harden not your heart, as in the provocation, *and* as *in* the day of temptation in the wilderness:

9When your fathers tempted me, proved me, and saw my work.

10Forty years long was I grieved with *this* generation, and said, It *is* a people that do err in their heart, and they have not known my ways:

11Unto whom I sware in my wrath that they should not enter into my rest.

96 O SING unto the LORD a new song: sing unto the LORD, all the earth.

2Sing unto the LORD, bless his name; show forth his salvation from day to day.

3Declare his glory among the heathen, his wonders among all people.

4For the LORD *is* great, and greatly to be praised: he *is* to be feared above all gods.

5For all the gods of the nations *are* idols: but the LORD made the heavens.

New International

16Who will rise up for me against the wicked?
  Who will take a stand for me against
    evildoers?
17Unless the LORD had given me help,
  I would soon have dwelt in the silence of
    death.
18When I said, "My foot is slipping,"
  your love, O LORD, supported me.
19When anxiety was great within me,
  your consolation brought joy to my soul.

20Can a corrupt throne be allied with you—
  one that brings on misery by its decrees?
21They band together against the righteous
  and condemn the innocent to death.
22But the LORD has become my fortress,
  and my God the rock in whom I take refuge.
23He will repay them for their sins
  and destroy them for their wickedness;
  the LORD our God will destroy them.

95 COME, LET us sing for joy to the LORD;
  let us shout aloud to the Rock of our
    salvation.
2Let us come before him with thanksgiving
  and extol him with music and song.

3For the LORD is the great God,
  the great King above all gods.
4In his hand are the depths of the earth,
  and the mountain peaks belong to him.
5The sea is his, for he made it,
  and his hands formed the dry land.

6Come, let us bow down in worship,
  let us kneel before the LORD our Maker;
7for he is our God
  and we are the people of his pasture,
  the flock under his care.

  Today, if you hear his voice,
8 do not harden your hearts as you did at
      Meribah,a
    as you did that day at Massahb in the desert,
9where your fathers tested and tried me,
  though they had seen what I did.
10For forty years I was angry with that generation;
  I said, "They are a people whose hearts go
      astray,
  and they have not known my ways."
11So I declared on oath in my anger,
  "They shall never enter my rest."

96 SING TO the LORD a new song;
  sing to the LORD, all the earth.
2Sing to the LORD, praise his name;
  proclaim his salvation day after day.
3Declare his glory among the nations,
  his marvelous deeds among all peoples.

4For great is the LORD and most worthy of
      praise;
  he is to be feared above all gods.
5For all the gods of the nations are idols,
  but the LORD made the heavens.

a 8 *Meribah* means *quarreling.*   b 8 *Massah* means *testing.*

Living Bible

16Who will protect me from the wicked? Who will be my shield? 17I would have died unless the Lord had helped me. 18I screamed, "I'm slipping, Lord!" and he was kind and saved me.

19Lord, when doubts fill my mind, when my heart is in turmoil, quiet me and give me renewed hope and cheer. 20Will you permit a corrupt government to rule under your protection—a government permitting wrong to defeat right? 21, 22Do you approve of those who condemn the innocent to death? No! The Lord my God is my fortress—the mighty Rock where I can hide. 23God has made the sins of evil men to boomerang upon them! He will destroy them by their own plans. Jehovah our God will cut them off.

95 OH, COME, let us sing to the Lord! Give a joyous shout in honor of the Rock of our salvation!

2Come before him with thankful hearts. Let us sing him psalms of praise. 3For the Lord is a great God, the great King ofc all gods. 4He controls the formation of the depths of the earth and the mightiest mountains; all are his. 5He made the sea and formed the land; they too are his. 6Come, kneel before the Lord our Maker, 7for he is our God. We are his sheep and he is our Shepherd. Oh, that you would hear him calling you today and come to him!

8Don't harden your hearts as Israel did in the wildernessd at Meribah and Massah. 9For there your fathers doubted me, though they had seen so many of my miracles before. My patience was severely tried by their complaints. 10"For forty years I watched them in disgust," the Lord God says. "They were a nation whose thoughts and heart were far away from me. They refused to accept my laws. 11Therefore in mighty wrath I swore that they would never enter the Promised Land, the place of rest I planned for them."

96 SING A new song to the Lord! Sing it everywhere around the world! 2Sing out his praises! Bless his name. Each day tell someone that he saves.

3Publish his glorious acts throughout the earth. Tell everyone about the amazing things he does. 4For the Lord is great beyond description, and greatly to be praised. Worship only him among the gods! 5For the gods of other nations are merely idols, but our God made

New Revised Standard

16 Who rises up for me against the wicked?
    Who stands up for me against evildoers?
17 If the LORD had not been my help,
    my soul would soon have lived in the land
      of silence.
18 When I thought, "My foot is slipping,"
    your steadfast love, O LORD, held me up.
19 When the cares of my heart are many,
    your consolations cheer my soul.
20 Can wicked rulers be allied with you,
    those who contrive mischief by statute?
21 They band together against the life of the
      righteous,
    and condemn the innocent to death.
22 But the LORD has become my stronghold,
    and my God the rock of my refuge.
23 He will repay them for their iniquity
    and wipe them out for their wickedness;
    the LORD our God will wipe them out.

A Call to Worship and Obedience

95 O COME, let us sing to the LORD;
    let us make a joyful noise to the rock of
      our salvation!
2 Let us come into his presence with
      thanksgiving;
    let us make a joyful noise to him with songs
      of praise!
3 For the LORD is a great God,
    and a great King above all gods.
4 In his hand are the depths of the earth;
    the heights of the mountains are his also.
5 The sea is his, for he made it,
    and the dry land, which his hands have
      formed.

6 O come, let us worship and bow down,
    let us kneel before the LORD, our Maker!
7 For he is our God,
    and we are the people of his pasture,
    and the sheep of his hand.

O that today you would listen to his voice!
8 Do not harden your hearts, as at Meribah,
    as on the day at Massah in the wilderness,
9 when your ancestors tested me,
    and put me to the proof, though they had
      seen my work.
10 For forty years I loathed that generation
    and said, "They are a people whose hearts
      go astray,
    and they do not regard my ways."
11 Therefore in my anger I swore,
    "They shall not enter my rest."

Praise to God Who Comes in Judgment

96 O SING to the LORD a new song;
    sing to the LORD, all the earth.
2 Sing to the LORD, bless his name;
    tell of his salvation from day to day.
3 Declare his glory among the nations,
    his marvelous works among all the peoples.
4 For great is the LORD, and greatly to be
      praised;
    he is to be revered above all gods.
5 For all the gods of the peoples are idols,
    but the LORD made the heavens.

---

c 95:3 *King of*, literally, "King above."   d 95:8 *in the wilderness*, see Exodus 17:7.

King James	New International

King James

6Honour and majesty *are* before him: strength and beauty *are* in his sanctuary.

7Give unto the LORD, O ye kindreds of the people, give unto the LORD glory and strength.

8Give unto the LORD the glory *due unto* his name: bring an offering, and come into his courts.

9O worship the LORD in the beauty of holiness: fear before him, all the earth.

10Say among the heathen *that* the LORD reigneth: the world also shall be established that it shall not be moved: he shall judge the people righteously.

11Let the heavens rejoice, and let the earth be glad; let the sea roar, and the fulness thereof.

12Let the field be joyful, and all that *is* therein: then shall all the trees of the wood rejoice

13Before the LORD: for he cometh, for he cometh to judge the earth: he shall judge the world with righteousness, and the people with his truth.

New International

6Splendor and majesty are before him;
strength and glory are in his sanctuary.

7Ascribe to the LORD, O families of nations,
ascribe to the LORD glory and strength.

8Ascribe to the LORD the glory due his name;
bring an offering and come into his courts.

9Worship the LORD in the splendor of his[a]
holiness;
tremble before him, all the earth.

10Say among the nations, "The LORD reigns."
The world is firmly established, it cannot be moved;
he will judge the peoples with equity.

11Let the heavens rejoice, let the earth be glad;
let the sea resound, and all that is in it;
12 let the fields be jubilant, and everything in them.
Then all the trees of the forest will sing for joy;
13 they will sing before the LORD, for he comes,
he comes to judge the earth.
He will judge the world in righteousness
and the peoples in his truth.

---

97 THE LORD reigneth; let the earth rejoice; let the multitude of isles be glad *thereof.*

2Clouds and darkness *are* round about him: righteousness and judgment *are* the habitation of his throne.

3A fire goeth before him, and burneth up his enemies round about.

4His lightnings enlightened the world: the earth saw, and trembled.

5The hills melted like wax at the presence of the LORD, at the presence of the Lord of the whole earth.

6The heavens declare his righteousness, and all the people see his glory.

7Confounded be all they that serve graven images, that boast themselves of idols: worship him, all *ye* gods.

8Zion heard, and was glad; and the daughters of Judah rejoiced because of thy judgments, O LORD.

9For thou, LORD, *art* high above all the earth: thou art exalted far above all gods.

10Ye that love the LORD, hate evil: he preserveth the souls of his saints; he delivereth them out of the hand of the wicked.

11Light is sown for the righteous, and gladness for the upright in heart.

12Rejoice in the LORD, ye righteous; and give thanks at the remembrance of his holiness.

97 THE LORD reigns, let the earth be glad;
let the distant shores rejoice.

2Clouds and thick darkness surround him;
righteousness and justice are the foundation of his throne.

3Fire goes before him
and consumes his foes on every side.

4His lightning lights up the world;
the earth sees and trembles.

5The mountains melt like wax before the LORD,
before the Lord of all the earth.

6The heavens proclaim his righteousness,
and all the peoples see his glory.

7All who worship images are put to shame,
those who boast in idols—
worship him, all you gods!

8Zion hears and rejoices
and the villages of Judah are glad
because of your judgments, O LORD.

9For you, O LORD, are the Most High over all the earth;
you are exalted far above all gods.

10Let those who love the LORD hate evil,
for he guards the lives of his faithful ones
and delivers them from the hand of the wicked.

11Light is shed upon the righteous
and joy on the upright in heart.

12Rejoice in the LORD, you who are righteous,
and praise his holy name.

A Psalm.

98 O SING unto the LORD a new song; for he hath done marvellous things: his right hand, and his holy arm, hath gotten him the victory.

A psalm.

98 SING TO the LORD a new song,
for he has done marvelous things;
his right hand and his holy arm
have worked salvation for him.

a 9 Or LORD with the splendor of

Living Bible

the heavens! 6Honor and majesty surround him; strength and beauty are in his Temple.

7O nations of the world, confess that God alone is glorious and strong. 8Give him the glory he deserves! Bring your offering and come to worship him.b 9Worship the Lord with the beauty of holy lives.c Let the earth tremble before him. 10Tell the nations that Jehovah reigns! He rules the world. His power can never be overthrown. He will judge all nations fairly.

11Let the heavens be glad, the earth rejoice; let the vastness of the roaring seas demonstrate his glory. 12Praise him for the growing fields, for they display his greatness. Let the trees of the forest rustle with praise. 13For the Lord is coming to judge the earth; he will judge the nations fairly and with truth!

97 JEHOVAH IS King! Let all the earth rejoice! Tell the farthest islands to be glad.

2Clouds and darkness surround him. Righteousness and justice are the foundation of his throne. 3Fire goes forth before him and burns up all his foes. 4His lightning flashes out across the world. The earth sees and trembles. 5The mountains melt like wax before the Lord of all the earth. 6The heavens declare his perfect righteousness; every nation sees his glory.

7Let those who worship idols be disgraced—all who brag about their worthless gods—for every god must bow to him! 8, 9Jerusalem and all the cities of Judah have heard of your justice, Lord, and are glad that you reign in majesty over the entire earth and are far greater than these other gods.

10The Lord loves those who hate evil; he protects the lives of his people, and rescues them from the wicked. 11Light is sown for the godly and joy for the good. 12May all who are godly be happy in the Lord and crown him,d our holy God.

98 SING A new song to the Lord telling about his mighty deeds! For he has won a mighty victory by his power and holiness. 2, 3He has announced this

New Revised Standard

6 Honor and majesty are before him;
     strength and beauty are in his sanctuary.

7 Ascribe to the Lord, O families of the
         peoples,
     ascribe to the Lord glory and strength.
8 Ascribe to the Lord the glory due his name;
     bring an offering, and come into his courts.
9 Worship the Lord in holy splendor;
     tremble before him, all the earth.

10 Say among the nations, "The Lord is king!
     The world is firmly established; it shall
         never be moved.
     He will judge the peoples with equity."
11 Let the heavens be glad, and let the earth
         rejoice;
     let the sea roar, and all that fills it;
12   let the field exult, and everything in it.
     Then shall all the trees of the forest sing for
         joy
13   before the Lord; for he is coming,
     for he is coming to judge the earth.
     He will judge the world with righteousness,
         and the peoples with his truth.

The Glory of God's Reign

97 THE LORD is king! Let the earth rejoice;
     let the many coastlands be glad!
2 Clouds and thick darkness are all around him;
     righteousness and justice are the foundation
         of his throne.
3 Fire goes before him,
     and consumes his adversaries on every side.
4 His lightnings light up the world;
     the earth sees and trembles.
5 The mountains melt like wax before the Lord,
     before the Lord of all the earth.

6 The heavens proclaim his righteousness;
     and all the peoples behold his glory.
7 All worshipers of images are put to shame,
     those who make their boast in worthless
         idols;
     all gods bow down before him.
8 Zion hears and is glad,
     and the townse of Judah rejoice,
     because of your judgments, O God.
9 For you, O Lord, are most high over all the
         earth;
     you are exalted far above all gods.

10 The Lord loves those who hatef evil;
     he guards the lives of his faithful;
     he rescues them from the hand of the
         wicked.
11 Light dawnsg for the righteous,
     and joy for the upright in heart.
12 Rejoice in the Lord, O you righteous,
     and give thanks to his holy name!

Praise the Judge of the World

A Psalm.

98 O SING to the Lord a new song,
     for he has done marvelous things.
     His right hand and his holy arm
         have gotten him victory.

e Heb daughters   f Cn: Heb You who love the Lord hate   g Gk Syr Jerome: Heb is sown

King James

2The LORD hath made known his salvation: his righteousness hath he openly shown in the sight of the heathen.

3He hath remembered his mercy and his truth toward the house of Israel: all the ends of the earth have seen the salvation of our God.

4Make a joyful noise unto the LORD, all the earth: make a loud noise, and rejoice, and sing praise.

5Sing unto the LORD with the harp; with the harp, and the voice of a psalm.

6With trumpets and sound of cornet make a joyful noise before the LORD, the King.

7Let the sea roar, and the fulness thereof; the world, and they that dwell therein.

8Let the floods clap *their* hands: let the hills be joyful together

9Before the LORD; for he cometh to judge the earth: with righteousness shall he judge the world, and the people with equity.

New International

2The LORD has made his salvation known
    and revealed his righteousness to the nations.
3He has remembered his love
    and his faithfulness to the house of Israel;
all the ends of the earth have seen
    the salvation of our God.

4Shout for joy to the LORD, all the earth,
    burst into jubilant song with music;
5make music to the LORD with the harp,
    with the harp and the sound of singing,
6with trumpets and the blast of the ram's horn—
    shout for joy before the LORD, the King.

7Let the sea resound, and everything in it,
    the world, and all who live in it.
8Let the rivers clap their hands,
    let the mountains sing together for joy;
9let them sing before the LORD,
    for he comes to judge the earth.
He will judge the world in righteousness
    and the peoples with equity.

99 THE LORD reigneth; let the people tremble: he sitteth *between* the cherubims; let the earth be moved.

2The LORD *is* great in Zion; and he *is* high above all the people.

3Let them praise thy great and terrible name; *for it is* holy.

4The king's strength also loveth judgment; thou dost establish equity, thou executest judgment and righteousness in Jacob.

5Exalt ye the LORD our God, and worship at his footstool; *for he is* holy.

6Moses and Aaron among his priests, and Samuel among them that call upon his name; they called upon the LORD, and he answered them.

7He spake unto them in the cloudy pillar: they kept his testimonies, and the ordinance *that* he gave them.

8Thou answeredst them, O LORD our God: thou wast a God that forgavest them, though thou tookest vengeance of their inventions.

9Exalt the LORD our God, and worship at his holy hill; for the LORD our God *is* holy.

99 THE LORD reigns,
    let the nations tremble;
he sits enthroned between the cherubim,
    let the earth shake.
2Great is the LORD in Zion;
    he is exalted over all the nations.
3Let them praise your great and awesome
        name—
    he is holy.

4The King is mighty, he loves justice—
    you have established equity;
in Jacob you have done
    what is just and right.
5Exalt the LORD our God
    and worship at his footstool;
    he is holy.

6Moses and Aaron were among his priests,
    Samuel was among those who called on his
        name;
    they called on the LORD
    and he answered them.
7He spoke to them from the pillar of cloud;
    they kept his statutes and the decrees he gave
        them.

8O LORD our God,
    you answered them;
you were to Israela a forgiving God,
    though you punished their misdeeds.b
9Exalt the LORD our God
    and worship at his holy mountain,
    for the LORD our God is holy.

A Psalm of praise.

100 MAKE A joyful noise unto the LORD, all ye lands.

2Serve the LORD with gladness: come before his presence with singing.

A psalm. For giving thanks.

100 SHOUT FOR joy to the LORD, all the earth.
2   Worship the LORD with gladness;
    come before him with joyful songs.

a 8 Hebrew them   b 8 Or / an avenger of the wrongs done to them

Living Bible

victory and revealed it to every nation by fulfilling his promise to be kind to Israel. The whole earth has seen God's salvation of his people. 4That is why the earth breaks out in praise to God, and sings for utter joy!

5Sing your praise accompanied by music from the harp. 6Let the cornets and trumpets shout! Make a joyful symphony before the Lord, the King! 7Let the sea in all its vastness roar with praise! Let the earth and all those living on it shout, "Glory to the Lord."

8, 9Let the waves clap their hands in glee, and the hills sing out their songs of joy before the Lord, for he is coming to judge the world with perfect justice.

99 JEHOVAH IS King! Let the nations tremble! He is enthroned between the Guardian Angels. Let the whole earth shake.

2Jehovah sits in majesty in Zion, supreme above all rulers of the earth. 3Let them reverence your great and holy name.

4This mighty King is determined to give justice. Fairness is the touchstone of everything he does. He gives justice throughout Israel. 5Exalt the Lord our holy God! Bow low before his feet.

6When Moses and Aaron and Samuel, his prophet, cried to him for help, he answered them. 7He spoke to them from the pillar of cloud and they followed his instructions. 8O Jehovah our God! You answered them and forgave their sins, yet punished them when they went wrong.

9Exalt the Lord our God, and worship at his holy mountain in Jerusalem, for he is holy.

100 SHOUT WITH joy before the Lord, O earth! 2Obey him gladly; come before him, singing with joy.

New Revised Standard

2 The LORD has made known his victory;
    he has revealed his vindication in the sight
        of the nations.
3 He has remembered his steadfast love and
        faithfulness
    to the house of Israel.
All the ends of the earth have seen
    the victory of our God.

4 Make a joyful noise to the LORD, all the earth;
    break forth into joyous song and sing
        praises.
5 Sing praises to the LORD with the lyre,
    with the lyre and the sound of melody.
6 With trumpets and the sound of the horn
    make a joyful noise before the King, the
        LORD.

7 Let the sea roar, and all that fills it;
    the world and those who live in it.
8 Let the floods clap their hands;
    let the hills sing together for joy
9 at the presence of the LORD, for he is coming
    to judge the earth.
He will judge the world with righteousness,
    and the peoples with equity.

Praise to God for His Holiness

99 THE LORD is king; let the peoples tremble!
    He sits enthroned upon the cherubim; let
        the earth quake!
2 The LORD is great in Zion;
    he is exalted over all the peoples.
3 Let them praise your great and awesome
        name.
    Holy is he!
4 Mighty King,c lover of justice,
    you have established equity;
you have executed justice
    and righteousness in Jacob.
5 Extol the LORD our God;
    worship at his footstool.
    Holy is he!

6 Moses and Aaron were among his priests,
    Samuel also was among those who called on
        his name.
    They cried to the LORD, and he answered
        them.
7 He spoke to them in the pillar of cloud;
    they kept his decrees,
    and the statutes that he gave them.

8 O LORD our God, you answered them;
    you were a forgiving God to them,
    but an avenger of their wrongdoings.
9 Extol the LORD our God,
    and worship at his holy mountain;
    for the LORD our God is holy.

All Lands Summoned to Praise God

A Psalm of thanksgiving.

100 MAKE A joyful noise to the LORD, all the
    earth.
2 Worship the LORD with gladness;
    come into his presence with singing.

---

c Cn: Heb And a king's strength

King James

3Know ye that the LORD he *is* God: *it is* he *that* hath made us, and not we ourselves; *we are* his people, and the sheep of his pasture.

4Enter into his gates with thanksgiving, *and* into his courts with praise: be thankful unto him, *and* bless his name.

5For the LORD *is* good; his mercy *is* everlasting; and his truth *endureth* to all generations.

A Psalm of David.

101 I WILL sing of mercy and judgment: unto thee, O LORD, will I sing.

2I will behave myself wisely in a perfect way. O when wilt thou come unto me? I will walk within my house with a perfect heart.

3I will set no wicked thing before mine eyes: I hate the work of them that turn aside; *it* shall not cleave to me.

4A froward heart shall depart from me: I will not know a wicked *person*.

5Whoso privily slandereth his neighbour, him will I cut off: him that hath an high look and a proud heart will not I suffer.

6Mine eyes *shall be* upon the faithful of the land, that they may dwell with me: he that walketh in a perfect way, he shall serve me.

7He that worketh deceit shall not dwell within my house: he that telleth lies shall not tarry in my sight.

8I will early destroy all the wicked of the land; that I may cut off all wicked doers from the city of the LORD.

A Prayer of the afflicted, when he is overwhelmed, and poureth out his complaint before the LORD.

102 HEAR MY prayer, O LORD, and let my cry come unto thee.

2Hide not thy face from me in the day *when* I am in trouble; incline thine ear unto me: in the day *when* I call answer me speedily.

3For my days are consumed like smoke, and my bones are burned as an hearth.

4My heart is smitten, and withered like grass; so that I forget to eat my bread.

5By reason of the voice of my groaning my bones cleave to my skin.

6I am like a pelican of the wilderness: I am like an owl of the desert.

New International

3Know that the LORD is God.
    It is he who made us, and we are his[a];
    we are his people, the sheep of his pasture.

4Enter his gates with thanksgiving
    and his courts with praise;
    give thanks to him and praise his name.

5For the LORD is good and his love endures
        forever;
    his faithfulness continues through all
        generations.

Of David. A psalm.

101 I WILL sing of your love and justice;
        to you, O LORD, I will sing praise.

2I will be careful to lead a blameless life—
    when will you come to me?

I will walk in my house
    with blameless heart.

3I will set before my eyes
    no vile thing.

The deeds of faithless men I hate;
    they will not cling to me.

4Men of perverse heart shall be far from me;
    I will have nothing to do with evil.

5Whoever slanders his neighbor in secret,
    him will I put to silence;
whoever has haughty eyes and a proud heart,
    him will I not endure.

6My eyes will be on the faithful in the land,
    that they may dwell with me;
he whose walk is blameless
    will minister to me.

7No one who practices deceit
    will dwell in my house;
no one who speaks falsely
    will stand in my presence.

8Every morning I will put to silence
    all the wicked in the land;
I will cut off every evildoer
    from the city of the LORD.

A prayer of an afflicted man. When he is faint and pours out his lament before the LORD.

102 HEAR MY prayer, O LORD;
        let my cry for help come to you.

2Do not hide your face from me
    when I am in distress.
Turn your ear to me;
    when I call, answer me quickly.

3For my days vanish like smoke;
    my bones burn like glowing embers.

4My heart is blighted and withered like grass;
    I forget to eat my food.

5Because of my loud groaning
    I am reduced to skin and bones.

6I am like a desert owl,
    like an owl among the ruins.

Living Bible

³Try to realize what this means—the Lord is God! He made us—we are his people, the sheep of his pasture. ⁴Go through his open gates with great thanksgiving; enter his courts with praise. Give thanks to him and bless his name. ⁵For the Lord is always good. He is always loving and kind, and his faithfulness goes on and on to each succeeding generation.

101 I WILL sing about your lovingkindness and your justice, Lord. I will sing your praises! ²I will try to walk a blameless path, but how I need your help, especially in my own home, where I long to act as I should. ³Help me to refuse the low and vulgar things; help me to abhor all crooked deals of every kind, to have no part in them. ⁴I will reject all selfishness and stay away from every evil. ⁵I will not tolerate anyone who secretly slanders his neighbors; I will not permit conceit and pride. ⁶I will make the godly of the land my heroes, and invite them to my home. Only those who are truly good shall be my servants. ⁷But I will not allow those who deceive and lie to stay in my house. ⁸My daily task will be to ferret out criminals and free the city of God from their grip.

A prayer when overwhelmed with trouble.

102 LORD, HEAR my prayer! Listen to my plea! ²Don't turn away from me in this time of my distress. Bend down your ear and give me speedy answers, ³, ⁴for my days disappear like smoke. My health is broken and my heart is sick; it is trampled like grass and is withered. My food is tasteless, and I have lost my appetite. ⁵I am reduced to skin and bones because of all my groaning and despair. ⁶I am like a vulture in a far-off wilderness,

New Revised Standard

3 Know that the LORD is God.
  It is he that made us, and we are his;[b]
  we are his people, and the sheep of his
    pasture.

4 Enter his gates with thanksgiving,
  and his courts with praise.
  Give thanks to him, bless his name.

5 For the LORD is good;
  his steadfast love endures forever,
  and his faithfulness to all generations.

A Sovereign's Pledge of Integrity and Justice
Of David. A Psalm.

101 I WILL sing of loyalty and of justice;
    to you, O LORD, I will sing.
2 I will study the way that is blameless.
  When shall I attain it?

  I will walk with integrity of heart
    within my house;
3 I will not set before my eyes
  anything that is base.

  I hate the work of those who fall away;
    it shall not cling to me.
4 Perverseness of heart shall be far from me;
  I will know nothing of evil.

5 One who secretly slanders a neighbor
  I will destroy.
  A haughty look and an arrogant heart
  I will not tolerate.

6 I will look with favor on the faithful in the
    land,
  so that they may live with me;
  whoever walks in the way that is blameless
    shall minister to me.

7 No one who practices deceit
  shall remain in my house;
  no one who utters lies
    shall continue in my presence.

8 Morning by morning I will destroy
  all the wicked in the land,
  cutting off all evildoers
  from the city of the LORD.

Prayer to the Eternal King for Help
A prayer of one afflicted, when faint and pleading before
the LORD.

102 HEAR MY prayer, O LORD;
    let my cry come to you.
2 Do not hide your face from me
  in the day of my distress.
  Incline your ear to me;
    answer me speedily in the day when I call.

3 For my days pass away like smoke,
  and my bones burn like a furnace.
4 My heart is stricken and withered like grass;
  I am too wasted to eat my bread.
5 Because of my loud groaning
  my bones cling to my skin.
6 I am like an owl of the wilderness,
  like a little owl of the waste places.

---

b Another reading is *and not we ourselves*

King James

7I watch, and am as a sparrow alone upon the house top.

8Mine enemies reproach me all the day; *and* they that are mad against me are sworn against me.

9For I have eaten ashes like bread, and mingled my drink with weeping,

10Because of thine indignation and thy wrath: for thou hast lifted me up, and cast me down.

11My days *are* like a shadow that declineth; and I am withered like grass.

12But thou, O LORD, shalt endure for ever; and thy remembrance unto all generations.

13Thou shalt arise, *and* have mercy upon Zion: for the time to favour her, yea, the set time, is come.

14For thy servants take pleasure in her stones, and favour the dust thereof.

15So the heathen shall fear the name of the LORD, and all the kings of the earth thy glory.

16When the LORD shall build up Zion, he shall appear in his glory.

17He will regard the prayer of the destitute, and not despise their prayer.

18This shall be written for the generation to come: and the people which shall be created shall praise the LORD.

19For he hath looked down from the height of his sanctuary; from heaven did the LORD behold the earth;

20To hear the groaning of the prisoner; to loose those that are appointed to death;

21To declare the name of the LORD in Zion, and his praise in Jerusalem;

22When the people are gathered together, and the kingdoms, to serve the LORD.

23He weakened my strength in the way; he shortened my days.

24I said, O my God, take me not away in the midst of my days: thy years *are* throughout all generations.

25Of old hast thou laid the foundation of the earth: and the heavens *are* the work of thy hands.

26They shall perish, but thou shalt endure: yea, all of them shall wax old like a garment; as a vesture shalt thou change them, and they shall be changed:

27But thou *art* the same, and thy years shall have no end.

28The children of thy servants shall continue, and their seed shall be established before thee.

A Psalm of David.

103 BLESS THE LORD, O my soul: and all that is within me, *bless* his holy name.

2Bless the LORD, O my soul, and forget not all his benefits:

3Who forgiveth all thine iniquities; who healeth all thy diseases;

4Who redeemeth thy life from destruction; who crowneth thee with lovingkindness and tender mercies;

New International

7I lie awake; I have become
    like a bird alone on a roof.
8All day long my enemies taunt me;
    those who rail against me use my name as a
        curse.
9For I eat ashes as my food
    and mingle my drink with tears
10because of your great wrath,
    for you have taken me up and thrown me
        aside.
11My days are like the evening shadow;
    I wither away like grass.

12But you, O LORD, sit enthroned forever;
    your renown endures through all generations.
13You will arise and have compassion on Zion,
    for it is time to show favor to her;
    the appointed time has come.
14For her stones are dear to your servants;
    her very dust moves them to pity.
15The nations will fear the name of the LORD,
    all the kings of the earth will revere your
        glory.
16For the LORD will rebuild Zion
    and appear in his glory.
17He will respond to the prayer of the destitute;
    he will not despise their plea.

18Let this be written for a future generation,
    that a people not yet created may praise the
        LORD:
19"The LORD looked down from his sanctuary on
        high,
    from heaven he viewed the earth,
20to hear the groans of the prisoners
    and release those condemned to death."
21So the name of the LORD will be declared in
        Zion
    and his praise in Jerusalem
22when the peoples and the kingdoms
    assemble to worship the LORD.

23In the course of my life[a] he broke my strength;
    he cut short my days.
24So I said:
    "Do not take me away, O my God, in the
        midst of my days;
    your years go on through all generations.
25In the beginning you laid the foundations of the
        earth,
    and the heavens are the work of your hands.
26They will perish, but you remain;
    they will all wear out like a garment.
    Like clothing you will change them
    and they will be discarded.
27But you remain the same,
    and your years will never end.
28The children of your servants will live in your
        presence;
    their descendants will be established before
        you."

Of David.

103 PRAISE THE LORD, O my soul;
    all my inmost being, praise his holy
        name.
2Praise the LORD, O my soul,
    and forget not all his benefits—
3who forgives all your sins
    and heals all your diseases,
4who redeems your life from the pit
    and crowns you with love and compassion,

Living Bible

or like an owl alone in the desert. 7I lie awake, lonely as a solitary sparrow on the roof.

8My enemies taunt me day after day and curse at me. 9, 10I eat ashes instead of bread. My tears run down into my drink because of your anger against me, because of your wrath. For you have rejected me and thrown me out. 11My life is passing swiftly as the evening shadows. I am withering like grass, 12while you, Lord, are a famous King forever. Your fame will endure to every generation.

13I know that you will come and have mercy on Jerusalem—and now is the time to pity her—the time you promised help. 14For your people love every stone in her walls and feel sympathy for every grain of dust in her streets. 15Now let the nations and their rulers tremble before the Lord, before his glory. 16For Jehovah will rebuild Jerusalem! He will appear in his glory!

17He will listen to the prayers of the destitute, for he is never too busy to heed their requests. 18I am recording this so that future generations will also praise the Lord for all that he has done. And a people that shall be created shall praise the Lord. 19Tell them that God looked down from his temple in heaven, 20and heard the groans of his people in slavery—they were children of death—and released them, 21, 22so that multitudes would stream to the Temple in Jerusalem to praise him, and his praises were sung throughout the city; and many rulers throughout the earth came to worship him.

23He has cut me down in middle life, shortening my days. 24But I cried to him, "O God, you live forever and forever! Don't let me die half through my years! 25In ages past you laid the foundations of the earth, and made the heavens with your hands! 26They shall perish, but you go on forever. They will grow old, like worn-out clothing, and you will change them like a man putting on a new shirt and throwing away the old one! 27But you yourself never grow old. You are forever, and your years never end.

28"But our families will continue; generation after generation will be preserved by your protection."

103 I BLESS the holy name of God with all my heart. 2Yes, I will bless the Lord and not forget the glorious things he does for me.

3He forgives all my sins. He heals me. 4He ransoms me from hell. He surrounds me with lovingkindness and tender mercies. 5He fills my life with good things! My

New Revised Standard

7 I lie awake;
   I am like a lonely bird on the housetop.
8 All day long my enemies taunt me;
   those who deride me use my name for a curse.
9 For I eat ashes like bread,
   and mingle tears with my drink,
10 because of your indignation and anger;
   for you have lifted me up and thrown me aside.
11 My days are like an evening shadow;
   I wither away like grass.

12 But you, O Lord, are enthroned forever;
   your name endures to all generations.
13 You will rise up and have compassion on Zion,
   for it is time to favor it;
   the appointed time has come.
14 For your servants hold its stones dear,
   and have pity on its dust.
15 The nations will fear the name of the Lord,
   and all the kings of the earth your glory.
16 For the Lord will build up Zion;
   he will appear in his glory.
17 He will regard the prayer of the destitute,
   and will not despise their prayer.

18 Let this be recorded for a generation to come,
   so that a people yet unborn may praise the Lord:
19 that he looked down from his holy height,
   from heaven the Lord looked at the earth,
20 to hear the groans of the prisoners,
   to set free those who were doomed to die;
21 so that the name of the Lord may be declared in Zion,
   and his praise in Jerusalem,
22 when peoples gather together,
   and kingdoms, to worship the Lord.

23 He has broken my strength in midcourse;
   he has shortened my days.
24 "O my God," I say, "do not take me away
   at the mid-point of my life,
you whose years endure
   throughout all generations."

25 Long ago you laid the foundation of the earth,
   and the heavens are the work of your hands.
26 They will perish, but you endure;
   they will all wear out like a garment.
You change them like clothing, and they pass away;
27 but you are the same, and your years have no end.
28 The children of your servants shall live secure;
   their offspring shall be established in your presence.

Thanksgiving for God's Goodness
Of David.

103 BLESS THE Lord, O my soul,
   and all that is within me,
   bless his holy name.
2 Bless the Lord, O my soul,
   and do not forget all his benefits—
3 who forgives all your iniquity,
   who heals all your diseases,
4 who redeems your life from the Pit,
   who crowns you with steadfast love and mercy,

King James

5Who satisfieth thy mouth with good *things; so that* thy youth is renewed like the eagle's.

6The LORD executeth righteousness and judgment for all that are oppressed.

7He made known his ways unto Moses, his acts unto the children of Israel.

8The LORD *is* merciful and gracious, slow to anger, and plenteous in mercy.

9He will not always chide: neither will he keep *his* anger for ever.

10He hath not dealt with us after our sins; nor rewarded us according to our iniquities.

11For as the heaven is high above the earth, *so* great is his mercy toward them that fear him.

12As far as the east is from the west, *so* far hath he removed our transgressions from us.

13Like as a father pitieth *his* children, *so* the LORD pitieth them that fear him.

14For he knoweth our frame; he remembereth that we *are* dust.

15*As for* man, his days *are* as grass: as a flower of the field, so he flourisheth.

16For the wind passeth over it, and it is gone; and the place thereof shall know it no more.

17But the mercy of the LORD *is* from everlasting to everlasting upon them that fear him, and his righteousness unto children's children;

18To such as keep his covenant, and to those that remember his commandments to do them.

19The LORD hath prepared his throne in the heavens; and his kingdom ruleth over all.

20Bless the LORD, ye his angels, that excel in strength, that do his commandments, hearkening unto the voice of his word.

21Bless ye the LORD, all *ye* his hosts; ye ministers of his, that do his pleasure.

22Bless the LORD, all his works in all places of his dominion: bless the LORD, O my soul.

New International

5who satisfies your desires with good things
　so that your youth is renewed like the eagle's.

6The LORD works righteousness
　and justice for all the oppressed.

7He made known his ways to Moses,
　his deeds to the people of Israel:

8The LORD is compassionate and gracious,
　slow to anger, abounding in love.

9He will not always accuse,
　nor will he harbor his anger forever;

10he does not treat us as our sins deserve
　or repay us according to our iniquities.

11For as high as the heavens are above the earth,
　so great is his love for those who fear him;

12as far as the east is from the west,
　so far has he removed our transgressions from
　us.

13As a father has compassion on his children,
　so the LORD has compassion on those who
　fear him;

14for he knows how we are formed,
　he remembers that we are dust.

15As for man, his days are like grass,
　he flourishes like a flower of the field;

16the wind blows over it and it is gone,
　and its place remembers it no more.

17But from everlasting to everlasting
　the LORD's love is with those who fear him,
　and his righteousness with their children's
　children—

18with those who keep his covenant
　and remember to obey his precepts.

19The LORD has established his throne in heaven,
　and his kingdom rules over all.

20Praise the LORD, you his angels,
　you mighty ones who do his bidding,
　who obey his word.

21Praise the LORD, all his heavenly hosts,
　you his servants who do his will.

22Praise the LORD, all his works
　everywhere in his dominion.

Praise the LORD, O my soul.

104

BLESS THE LORD, O my soul. O LORD my God, thou art very great; thou art clothed with honour and majesty.

2Who coverest *thyself* with light as *with* a garment: who stretchest out the heavens like a curtain:

3Who layeth the beams of his chambers in the waters: who maketh the clouds his chariot: who walketh upon the wings of the wind:

4Who maketh his angels spirits; his ministers a flaming fire:

5*Who* laid the foundations of the earth, *that* it should not be removed for ever.

6Thou coveredst it with the deep as *with* a garment: the waters stood above the mountains.

104

PRAISE THE LORD, O my soul.

O LORD my God, you are very great;
　you are clothed with splendor and majesty.

2He wraps himself in light as with a garment;
　he stretches out the heavens like a tent

3 and lays the beams of his upper chambers on
　their waters.

He makes the clouds his chariot
　and rides on the wings of the wind.

4He makes winds his messengers,a
　flames of fire his servants.

5He set the earth on its foundations;
　it can never be moved.

6You covered it with the deep as with a garment;
　the waters stood above the mountains.

Living Bible

youth is renewed like the eagle's! 6He gives justice to all who are treated unfairly. 7He revealed his will and nature to Moses and the people of Israel.

8He is merciful and tender toward those who don't deserve it; he is slow to get angry and full of kindness and love. 9He never bears a grudge, nor remains angry forever. 10He has not punished us as we deserve for all our sins, 11for his mercy toward those who fear and honor him is as great as the height of the heavens above the earth. 12He has removed our sins as far away from us as the east is from the west. 13He is like a father to us, tender and sympathetic to those who reverence him. 14For he knows we are but dust, 15and that our days are few and brief, like grass, like flowers, 16blown by the wind and gone forever.

17, 18But the lovingkindness of the Lord is from everlasting to everlasting, to those who reverence him; his salvation is to children's children of those who are faithful to his covenant and remember to obey him!

19The Lord has made the heavens his throne; from there he rules over everything there is. 20Bless the Lord, you mighty angels of his who carry out his orders, listening for each of his commands. 21Yes, bless the Lord, you armies of his angels who serve him constantly.

22Let everything everywhere bless the Lord. And how I bless him too!

104 I BLESS the Lord: O Lord my God, how great you are! You are robed with honor and with majesty and light! You stretched out the starry curtain of the heavens, 3and hollowed out the surface of the earth to form the seas. The clouds are his chariots. He rides upon the wings of the wind. 4The angels[b] are his messengers—his servants of fire!

5You bound the world together so that it would never fall apart. 6You clothed the earth with floods of waters covering up the mountains. 7, 8You spoke, and at the

New Revised Standard

5 who satisfies you with good as long as you live[c]
so that your youth is renewed like the eagle's.

6 The LORD works vindication
and justice for all who are oppressed.
7 He made known his ways to Moses,
his acts to the people of Israel.
8 The LORD is merciful and gracious,
slow to anger and abounding in steadfast love.
9 He will not always accuse,
nor will he keep his anger forever.
10 He does not deal with us according to our sins,
nor repay us according to our iniquities.
11 For as the heavens are high above the earth,
so great is his steadfast love toward those who fear him;
12 as far as the east is from the west,
so far he removes our transgressions from us.
13 As a father has compassion for his children,
so the LORD has compassion for those who fear him.
14 For he knows how we were made;
he remembers that we are dust.

15 As for mortals, their days are like grass;
they flourish like a flower of the field;
16 for the wind passes over it, and it is gone,
and its place knows it no more.
17 But the steadfast love of the LORD is from everlasting to everlasting
on those who fear him,
and his righteousness to children's children,
18 to those who keep his covenant
and remember to do his commandments.

19 The LORD has established his throne in the heavens,
and his kingdom rules over all.
20 Bless the LORD, O you his angels,
you mighty ones who do his bidding,
obedient to his spoken word.
21 Bless the LORD, all his hosts,
his ministers that do his will.
22 Bless the LORD, all his works,
in all places of his dominion.
Bless the LORD, O my soul.

God the Creator and Provider

104 BLESS THE LORD, O my soul.
O LORD my God, you are very great.
You are clothed with honor and majesty,
2 wrapped in light as with a garment.
You stretch out the heavens like a tent,
3 you set the beams of your[d] chambers on the waters,
you make the clouds your[d] chariot,
you ride on the wings of the wind,
4 you make the winds your[d] messengers,
fire and flame your[d] ministers.

5 You set the earth on its foundations,
so that it shall never be shaken.
6 You cover it with the deep as with a garment;
the waters stood above the mountains.

---

b *104:4* angels, literally, "spirits."   c Meaning of Heb uncertain   d Heb *his*

King James

7At thy rebuke they fled; at the voice of thy thunder they hasted away.

8They go up by the mountains; they go down by the valleys unto the place which thou hast founded for them.

9Thou hast set a bound that they may not pass over; that they turn not again to cover the earth.

10He sendeth the springs into the valleys, *which* run among the hills.

11They give drink to every beast of the field: the wild asses quench their thirst.

12By them shall the fowls of the heaven have their habitation, *which* sing among the branches.

13He watereth the hills from his chambers: the earth is satisfied with the fruit of thy works.

14He causeth the grass to grow for the cattle, and herb for the service of man: that he may bring forth food out of the earth;

15And wine *that* maketh glad the heart of man, *and* oil to make *his* face to shine, and bread *which* strengtheneth man's heart.

16The trees of the LORD are full *of sap;* the cedars of Lebanon, which he hath planted.

17Where the birds make their nests: *as for* the stork, the fir trees *are* her house.

18The high hills *are* a refuge for the wild goats; *and* the rocks for the conies.

19He appointed the moon for seasons: the sun knoweth his going down.

20Thou makest darkness, and it is night: wherein all the beasts of the forest do creep *forth.*

21The young lions roar after their prey, and seek their meat from God.

22The sun ariseth, they gather themselves together, and lay them down in their dens.

23Man goeth forth unto his work and to his labour until the evening.

24O LORD, how manifold are thy works! in wisdom hast thou made them all: the earth is full of thy riches.

25So *is* this great and wide sea, wherein *are* things creeping innumerable, both small and great beasts.

26There go the ships: *there is* that leviathan, *whom* thou hast made to play therein.

27These wait all upon thee; that thou mayest give *them* their meat in due season.

28*That* thou givest them they gather: thou openest thine hand, they are filled with good.

29Thou hidest thy face, they are troubled: thou takest away their breath, they die, and return to their dust.

30Thou sendest forth thy spirit, they are created: and thou renewest the face of the earth.

31The glory of the LORD shall endure for ever: the LORD shall rejoice in his works.

32He looketh on the earth, and it trembleth: he toucheth the hills, and they smoke.

New International

7But at your rebuke the waters fled,
  at the sound of your thunder they took to
    flight;
8they flowed over the mountains,
  they went down into the valleys,
  to the place you assigned for them.
9You set a boundary they cannot cross;
  never again will they cover the earth.

10He makes springs pour water into the ravines;
  it flows between the mountains.
11They give water to all the beasts of the field;
  the wild donkeys quench their thirst.
12The birds of the air nest by the waters;
  they sing among the branches.
13He waters the mountains from his upper
    chambers;
  the earth is satisfied by the fruit of his work.
14He makes grass grow for the cattle,
  and plants for man to cultivate—
  bringing forth food from the earth:
15wine that gladdens the heart of man,
  oil to make his face shine,
  and bread that sustains his heart.
16The trees of the LORD are well watered,
  the cedars of Lebanon that he planted.
17There the birds make their nests;
  the stork has its home in the pine trees.
18The high mountains belong to the wild goats;
  the crags are a refuge for the coneys.[a]

19The moon marks off the seasons,
  and the sun knows when to go down.
20You bring darkness, it becomes night,
  and all the beasts of the forest prowl.
21The lions roar for their prey
  and seek their food from God.
22The sun rises, and they steal away;
  they return and lie down in their dens.
23Then man goes out to his work,
  to his labor until evening.

24How many are your works, O LORD!
  In wisdom you made them all;
  the earth is full of your creatures.
25There is the sea, vast and spacious,
  teeming with creatures beyond number—
  living things both large and small.
26There the ships go to and fro,
  and the leviathan, which you formed to frolic
    there.

27These all look to you
  to give them their food at the proper time.
28When you give it to them,
  they gather it up;
when you open your hand,
  they are satisfied with good things.
29When you hide your face,
  they are terrified;
when you take away their breath,
  they die and return to the dust.
30When you send your Spirit,
  they are created,
  and you renew the face of the earth.

31May the glory of the LORD endure forever;
  may the LORD rejoice in his works—
32he who looks at the earth, and it trembles,
  who touches the mountains, and they smoke.

[a] *18* That is, the hyrax or rock badger

Living Bible

sound of your shout the water collected into its vast ocean beds, and mountains rose and valleys sank to the levels you decreed. 9And then you set a boundary for the seas, so that they would never again cover the earth.

10He placed springs in the valleys, and streams that gush from the mountains. 11They give water for all the animals to drink. There the wild donkeys quench their thirst, 12and the birds nest beside the streams and sing among the branches of the trees. 13He sends rain upon the mountains and fills the earth with fruit. 14The tender grass grows up at his command to feed the cattle, and there are fruit trees, vegetables and grain for man to cultivate, 15and wine to make him glad, and olive oil as lotion for his skin, and bread to give him strength. 16The Lord planted the cedars of Lebanon. They are tall and flourishing. 17There the birds make their nests, the storks in the firs. 18High in the mountains are pastures for the wild goats, and rock-badgers burrow in among the rocks and find protection there.

19He assigned the moon to mark the months, and the sun to mark the days. 20He sends the night and darkness, when all the forest folk come out. 21Then the young lions roar for their food, but they are dependent on the Lord. 22At dawn they slink back into their dens to rest, 23and men go off to work until the evening shadows fall again. 24O Lord, what a variety you have made! And in wisdom you have made them all! The earth is full of your riches.

25There before me lies the mighty ocean, teeming with life of every kind, both great and small. 26And look! See the ships! And over there, the whale you made to play in the sea. 27Every one of these depends on you to give them daily food. 28You supply it, and they gather it. You open wide your hand to feed them and they are satisfied with all your bountiful provision.

29But if you turn away from them, then all is lost. And when you gather up their breath, they die and turn again to dust.

30Then you send your Spirit, and new life is bornb to replenish all the living of the earth. 31Praise God forever! How he must rejoice in all his work! 32The earth trembles at his glance; the mountains burst into flame at his touch.

New Revised Standard

7   At your rebuke they flee;
       at the sound of your thunder they take to
         flight.
8   They rose up to the mountains, ran down to
         the valleys
       to the place that you appointed for them.
9   You set a boundary that they may not pass,
       so that they might not again cover the earth.

10   You make springs gush forth in the valleys;
       they flow between the hills,
11   giving drink to every wild animal;
       the wild asses quench their thirst.
12   By the streamsc the birds of the air have their
         habitation;
       they sing among the branches.
13   From your lofty abode you water the
         mountains;
       the earth is satisfied with the fruit of your
         work.

14   You cause the grass to grow for the cattle,
       and plants for people to use,d
     to bring forth food from the earth,
15   and wine to gladden the human heart,
       oil to make the face shine,
       and bread to strengthen the human heart.
16   The trees of the LORD are watered abundantly,
       the cedars of Lebanon that he planted.
17   In them the birds build their nests;
       the stork has its home in the fir trees.
18   The high mountains are for the wild goats;
       the rocks are a refuge for the coneys.
19   You have made the moon to mark the seasons;
       the sun knows its time for setting.
20   You make darkness, and it is night,
       when all the animals of the forest come
         creeping out.
21   The young lions roar for their prey,
       seeking their food from God.
22   When the sun rises, they withdraw
       and lie down in their dens.
23   People go out to their work
       and to their labor until the evening.

24   O LORD, how manifold are your works!
       In wisdom you have made them all;
       the earth is full of your creatures.
25   Yonder is the sea, great and wide,
       creeping things innumerable are there,
       living things both small and great.
26   There go the ships,
       and Leviathan that you formed to sport in
         it.

27   These all look to you
       to give them their food in due season;
28   when you give to them, they gather it up;
       when you open your hand, they are filled
         with good things.
29   When you hide your face, they are dismayed;
       when you take away their breath, they die
       and return to their dust.
30   When you send forth your spirit,e they are
         created;
       and you renew the face of the ground.

31   May the glory of the LORD endure forever;
       may the LORD rejoice in his works—
32   who looks on the earth and it trembles,
       who touches the mountains and they smoke.

b 104:30 born, literally, "created."   c Heb By them   d Or to cultivate   e Or your breath

King James

³³I will sing unto the Lord as long as I live: I will sing praise to my God while I have my being.
³⁴My meditation of him shall be sweet: I will be glad in the Lord.
³⁵Let the sinners be consumed out of the earth, and let the wicked be no more. Bless thou the Lord, O my soul. Praise ye the Lord.

105 O GIVE thanks unto the Lord; call upon his name: make known his deeds among the people.
²Sing unto him, sing psalms unto him: talk ye of all his wondrous works.
³Glory ye in his holy name: let the heart of them rejoice that seek the Lord.
⁴Seek the Lord, and his strength: seek his face evermore.
⁵Remember his marvellous works that he hath done; his wonders, and the judgments of his mouth;
⁶O ye seed of Abraham his servant, ye children of Jacob his chosen.
⁷He *is* the Lord our God: his judgments *are* in all the earth.
⁸He hath remembered his covenant for ever, the word *which* he commanded to a thousand generations.
⁹Which *covenant* he made with Abraham, and his oath unto Isaac;
¹⁰And confirmed the same unto Jacob for a law, *and* to Israel *for* an everlasting covenant:
¹¹Saying, Unto thee will I give the land of Canaan, the lot of your inheritance:
¹²When they were *but* a few men in number; yea, very few, and strangers in it.
¹³When they went from one nation to another, from *one* kingdom to another people;
¹⁴He suffered no man to do them wrong: yea, he reproved kings for their sakes;
¹⁵*Saying,* Touch not mine anointed, and do my prophets no harm.
¹⁶Moreover he called for a famine upon the land: he brake the whole staff of bread.
¹⁷He sent a man before them, *even* Joseph, *who* was sold for a servant:
¹⁸Whose feet they hurt with fetters: he was laid in iron:
¹⁹Until the time that his word came: the word of the Lord tried him.
²⁰The king sent and loosed him; *even* the ruler of the people, and let him go free.
²¹He made him lord of his house, and ruler of all his substance:
²²To bind his princes at his pleasure; and teach his senators wisdom.
²³Israel also came into Egypt; and Jacob sojourned in the land of Ham.
²⁴And he increased his people greatly; and made them stronger than their enemies.

New International

³³I will sing to the Lord all my life;
  I will sing praise to my God as long as I live.
³⁴May my meditation be pleasing to him,
  as I rejoice in the Lord.
³⁵But may sinners vanish from the earth
  and the wicked be no more.

Praise the Lord, O my soul.

Praise the Lord.ᵃ

105 GIVE THANKS to the Lord, call on his name;
  make known among the nations what he has done.
²Sing to him, sing praise to him;
  tell of all his wonderful acts.
³Glory in his holy name;
  let the hearts of those who seek the Lord rejoice.
⁴Look to the Lord and his strength;
  seek his face always.

⁵Remember the wonders he has done,
  his miracles, and the judgments he pronounced,
⁶O descendants of Abraham his servant,
  O sons of Jacob, his chosen ones.
⁷He is the Lord our God;
  his judgments are in all the earth.

⁸He remembers his covenant forever,
  the word he commanded, for a thousand generations,
⁹the covenant he made with Abraham,
  the oath he swore to Isaac.
¹⁰He confirmed it to Jacob as a decree,
  to Israel as an everlasting covenant:
¹¹"To you I will give the land of Canaan
  as the portion you will inherit."

¹²When they were but few in number,
  few indeed, and strangers in it,
¹³they wandered from nation to nation,
  from one kingdom to another.
¹⁴He allowed no one to oppress them;
  for their sake he rebuked kings:
¹⁵"Do not touch my anointed ones;
  do my prophets no harm."

¹⁶He called down famine on the land
  and destroyed all their supplies of food;
¹⁷and he sent a man before them—
  Joseph, sold as a slave.
¹⁸They bruised his feet with shackles,
  his neck was put in irons,
¹⁹till what he foretold came to pass,
  till the word of the Lord proved him true.
²⁰The king sent and released him,
  the ruler of peoples set him free.
²¹He made him master of his household,
  ruler over all he possessed,
²²to instruct his princes as he pleased
  and teach his elders wisdom.

²³Then Israel entered Egypt;
  Jacob lived as an alien in the land of Ham.
²⁴The Lord made his people very fruitful;
  he made them too numerous for their foes,

Living Bible

33I will sing to the Lord as long as I live. I will praise God to my last breath! 34May he be pleased by all these thoughts about him, for he is the source of all my joy. 35Let all sinners perish—all who refuse to praise him. But I will praise him. Hallelujah!

105 THANK THE Lord for all the glorious things he does; proclaim them to the nations. 2Sing his praises and tell everyone about his miracles. 3Glory in the Lord; O worshipers of God, rejoice.

4Search for him and for his strength, and keep on searching!

5, 6Think of the mighty deeds he did for us, his chosen ones—descendants of God's servant Abraham, and of Jacob. Remember how he destroyed our enemies. 7He is the Lord our God. His goodnessᵇ is seen everywhere throughout the land. 8, 9Though a thousand generations pass he never forgets his promise, his covenant with Abraham and Isaac, 10, 11and confirmed with Jacob. This is his never-ending treaty with the people of Israel: *"I will give you the land of Canaan as your inheritance."* 12He said this when they were but few in number, very few, and were only visitors in Canaan. 13Later they were dispersed among the nations, and were driven from one kingdom to another; 14but through it all he would not let one thing be done to them apart from his decision.ᶜ He destroyed many a king who tried! 15"Touch not these chosen ones of mine," he warned, "and do not hurt my prophets."

16He called for a famine on the land of Canaan, cutting off its food supply. 17Then he sent Joseph as a slave to Egypt to save his people from starvation. 18There in prison they hurt his feet with fetters, and placed his neck in an iron collar, 19until God's time finally came—how God tested his patience! 20Then the king sent for him and set him free. 21He was put in charge of all the king's possessions. 22At his pleasure he could imprison the king's aides and teach the king's advisors.

23Then Jacob (Israel) arrived in Egypt and lived there with his sons. 24In the years that followed, the people of Israel multiplied explosively, until they were a greater nation than their rulers. 25At that point God turned the

New Revised Standard

33 I will sing to the LORD as long as I live;
    I will sing praise to my God while I have
      being.
34 May my meditation be pleasing to him,
    for I rejoice in the LORD.
35 Let sinners be consumed from the earth,
    and let the wicked be no more.
Bless the LORD, O my soul.
Praise the LORD!

God's Faithfulness to Israel

105 O GIVE thanks to the LORD, call on his name,
    make known his deeds among the peoples.
2 Sing to him, sing praises to him;
    tell of all his wonderful works.
3 Glory in his holy name;
    let the hearts of those who seek the LORD
      rejoice.
4 Seek the LORD and his strength;
    seek his presence continually.
5 Remember the wonderful works he has done,
    his miracles, and the judgments he uttered,
6 O offspring of his servant Abraham,ᵈ
    children of Jacob, his chosen ones.

7 He is the LORD our God;
    his judgments are in all the earth.
8 He is mindful of his covenant forever,
    of the word that he commanded, for a
      thousand generations,
9 the covenant that he made with Abraham,
    his sworn promise to Isaac,
10 which he confirmed to Jacob as a statute,
    to Israel as an everlasting covenant,
11 saying, "To you I will give the land of
     Canaan
    as your portion for an inheritance."

12 When they were few in number,
    of little account, and strangers in it,
13 wandering from nation to nation,
    from one kingdom to another people,
14 he allowed no one to oppress them;
    he rebuked kings on their account,
15 saying, "Do not touch my anointed ones;
    do my prophets no harm."

16 When he summoned famine against the land,
    and broke every staff of bread,
17 he had sent a man ahead of them,
    Joseph, who was sold as a slave.
18 His feet were hurt with fetters,
    his neck was put in a collar of iron;
19 until what he had said came to pass,
    the word of the LORD kept testing him.
20 The king sent and released him;
    the ruler of the peoples set him free.
21 He made him lord of his house,
    and ruler of all his possessions,
22 to instructᵉ his officials at his pleasure,
    and to teach his elders wisdom.

23 Then Israel came to Egypt;
    Jacob lived as an alien in the land of Ham.
24 And the LORD made his people very fruitful,
    and made them stronger than their foes,

ᵇ *105:7 His goodness*, literally, "His judgments."   ᶜ *105:14 he would not let one thing be done to them apart from his decision*, literally, "He suffered no man to do them wrong."

ᵈ Another reading is *Israel* (compare 1 Chr 16.13)   ᵉ Gk Syr Jerome: Heb *to bind*

King James

²⁵He turned their heart to hate his people, to deal subtly with his servants.

²⁶He sent Moses his servant; *and* Aaron whom he had chosen.

²⁷They showed his signs among them, and wonders in the land of Ham.

²⁸He sent darkness, and made it dark; and they rebelled not against his word.

²⁹He turned their waters into blood, and slew their fish.

³⁰Their land brought forth frogs in abundance, in the chambers of their kings.

³¹He spake, and there came divers sorts of flies, *and* lice in all their coasts.

³²He gave them hail for rain, *and* flaming fire in their land.

³³He smote their vines also and their fig trees; and brake the trees of their coasts.

³⁴He spake, and the locusts came, and caterpillars, and that without number,

³⁵And did eat up all the herbs in their land, and devoured the fruit of their ground.

³⁶He smote also all the firstborn in their land, the chief of all their strength.

³⁷He brought them forth also with silver and gold: and *there was* not one feeble *person* among their tribes.

³⁸Egypt was glad when they departed: for the fear of them fell upon them.

³⁹He spread a cloud for a covering; and fire to give light in the night.

⁴⁰*The people* asked, and he brought quails, and satisfied them with the bread of heaven.

⁴¹He opened the rock, and the waters gushed out; they ran in the dry places *like* a river.

⁴²For he remembered his holy promise, *and* Abraham his servant.

⁴³And he brought forth his people with joy, *and* his chosen with gladness:

⁴⁴And gave them the lands of the heathen: and they inherited the labour of the people:

⁴⁵That they might observe his statutes, and keep his laws. Praise ye the LORD.

New International

²⁵whose hearts he turned to hate his people,
    to conspire against his servants.

²⁶He sent Moses his servant,
    and Aaron, whom he had chosen.

²⁷They performed his miraculous signs among them,
    his wonders in the land of Ham.

²⁸He sent darkness and made the land dark—
    for had they not rebelled against his words?

²⁹He turned their waters into blood,
    causing their fish to die.

³⁰Their land teemed with frogs,
    which went up into the bedrooms of their rulers.

³¹He spoke, and there came swarms of flies,
    and gnats throughout their country.

³²He turned their rain into hail,
    with lightning throughout their land;

³³he struck down their vines and fig trees
    and shattered the trees of their country.

³⁴He spoke, and the locusts came,
    grasshoppers without number;

³⁵they ate up every green thing in their land,
    ate up the produce of their soil.

³⁶Then he struck down all the firstborn in their land,
    the firstfruits of all their manhood.

³⁷He brought out Israel, laden with silver and gold,
    and from among their tribes no one faltered.

³⁸Egypt was glad when they left,
    because dread of Israel had fallen on them.

³⁹He spread out a cloud as a covering,
    and a fire to give light at night.

⁴⁰They asked, and he brought them quail
    and satisfied them with the bread of heaven.

⁴¹He opened the rock, and water gushed out;
    like a river it flowed in the desert.

⁴²For he remembered his holy promise
    given to his servant Abraham.

⁴³He brought out his people with rejoicing,
    his chosen ones with shouts of joy;

⁴⁴he gave them the lands of the nations,
    and they fell heir to what others had toiled for—

⁴⁵that they might keep his precepts
    and observe his laws.

Praise the LORD.^a

---

106 PRAISE YE the LORD. O give thanks unto the LORD; for *he is* good: for his mercy *endureth* for ever.

²Who can utter the mighty acts of the LORD? *who* can show forth all his praise?

³Blessed *are* they that keep judgment, *and* he that doeth righteousness at all times.

⁴Remember me, O LORD, with the favour *that thou bearest unto* thy people: O visit me with thy salvation;

⁵That I may see the good of thy chosen, that I may rejoice in the gladness of thy nation, that I may glory with thine inheritance.

106 PRAISE THE LORD.^b

Give thanks to the LORD, for he is good;
    his love endures forever.

²Who can proclaim the mighty acts of the LORD
    or fully declare his praise?

³Blessed are they who maintain justice,
    who constantly do what is right.

⁴Remember me, O LORD, when you show favor to your people,
    come to my aid when you save them,

⁵that I may enjoy the prosperity of your chosen ones,
    that I may share in the joy of your nation
    and join your inheritance in giving praise.

ª 45 Hebrew *Hallelu Yah*   ^b *1* Hebrew *Hallelu Yah*; also in verse 48

Living Bible

Egyptians against the Israelis; they hated and enslaved them.

26But God sent Moses as his representative, and Aaron with him, 27to call down miracles of terror upon the land of Egypt. 28Theyc followed his instructions and he sent thick darkness through the land, 29and turned the nation's water into blood, poisoning the fish. 30Then frogs invaded in enormous numbers; they were found even in the king's private rooms. 31When Moses spoke, the flies and other insects swarmed in vast clouds from one end of Egypt to the other. 32Instead of rain he sent down murderous hail, and lightning flashes overwhelmed the nation. 33Their grape vines and fig trees were ruined; all the trees lay broken on the ground. 34He spoke, and hordes of locusts came, 35and ate up everything green, destroying all the crops. 36Then he killed the oldest child in each Egyptian home, their pride and joy— 37and brought his people safely out from Egypt, loaded with silver and gold; there were no sick and feeble folk among them then. 38Egypt was glad when they were gone, for the dread of them was great.

39He spread out a cloud above them to shield them from the burning sun, and gave them a pillar of flame at night to give them light. 40They asked for meat and he sent them quail, and gave them manna—bread from heaven. 41He opened up a rock, and water gushed out to form a river through the dry and barren land; 42for he remembered his sacred promises to Abraham his servant.

43So he brought his chosen ones singing into the Promised Land. 44He gave them the lands of the Gentiles, complete with their growing crops; they ate what others planted. 45This was done to make them faithful and obedient to his laws. Hallelujah!

106 HALLELUJAH! THANK you, Lord! How good you are! Your love for us continues on forever. 2Who can ever list the glorious miracles of God? Who can ever praise him half enough?

3Happiness comes to those who are fair to others and are always just and good.

4Remember me too, O Lord, while you are blessing and saving your people. 5Let me share in your chosen ones' prosperity and rejoice in all their joys, and receive the glory you give to them.

New Revised Standard

25 whose hearts he then turned to hate his
        people,
      to deal craftily with his servants.

26 He sent his servant Moses,
      and Aaron whom he had chosen.
27 They performed his signs among them,
      and miracles in the land of Ham.
28 He sent darkness, and made the land dark;
      they rebelledd against his words.
29 He turned their waters into blood,
      and caused their fish to die.
30 Their land swarmed with frogs,
      even in the chambers of their kings.
31 He spoke, and there came swarms of flies,
      and gnats throughout their country.
32 He gave them hail for rain,
      and lightning that flashed through their land.
33 He struck their vines and fig trees,
      and shattered the trees of their country.
34 He spoke, and the locusts came,
      and young locusts without number;
35 they devoured all the vegetation in their land,
      and ate up the fruit of their ground.
36 He struck down all the firstborn in their land,
      the first issue of all their strength.

37 Then he brought Israele out with silver and
        gold,
      and there was no one among their tribes
        who stumbled.
38 Egypt was glad when they departed,
      for dread of them had fallen upon it.
39 He spread a cloud for a covering,
      and fire to give light by night.
40 They asked, and he brought quails,
      and gave them food from heaven in
        abundance.
41 He opened the rock, and water gushed out;
      it flowed through the desert like a river.
42 For he remembered his holy promise,
      and Abraham, his servant.

43 So he brought his people out with joy,
      his chosen ones with singing.
44 He gave them the lands of the nations,
      and they took possession of the wealth of
        the peoples,
45 that they might keep his statutes
      and observe his laws.
    Praise the LORD!

A Confession of Israel's Sins

106 PRAISE THE LORD!
      O give thanks to the LORD, for he is
        good;
      for his steadfast love endures forever.
2 Who can utter the mighty doings of the LORD,
      or declare all his praise?
3 Happy are those who observe justice,
      who do righteousness at all times.

4 Remember me, O LORD, when you show
        favor to your people;
      help me when you deliver them;
5 that I may see the prosperity of your chosen
        ones,
      that I may rejoice in the gladness of your
        nation,
      that I may glory in your heritage.

---

c 105:28 they, implied.   d Cn Compare Gk Syr: Heb they did not rebel   e Heb them

King James

6We have sinned with our fathers, we have committed iniquity, we have done wickedly.

7Our fathers understood not thy wonders in Egypt; they remembered not the multitude of thy mercies; but provoked *him* at the sea, *even* at the Red sea.

8Nevertheless he saved them for his name's sake, that he might make his mighty power to be known.

9He rebuked the Red sea also, and it was dried up: so he led them through the depths, as through the wilderness.

10And he saved them from the hand of him that hated *them*, and redeemed them from the hand of the enemy.

11And the waters covered their enemies: there was not one of them left.

12Then believed they his words; they sang his praise.

13They soon forgat his works; they waited not for his counsel:

14But lusted exceedingly in the wilderness, and tempted God in the desert.

15And he gave them their request; but sent leanness into their soul.

16They envied Moses also in the camp, *and* Aaron the saint of the LORD.

17The earth opened and swallowed up Dathan, and covered the company of Abiram.

18And a fire was kindled in their company; the flame burned up the wicked.

19They made a calf in Horeb, and worshipped the molten image.

20Thus they changed their glory into the similitude of an ox that eateth grass.

21They forgat God their saviour, which had done great things in Egypt;

22Wondrous works in the land of Ham, *and* terrible things by the Red sea.

23Therefore he said that he would destroy them, had not Moses his chosen stood before him in the breach, to turn away his wrath, lest he should destroy *them*.

24Yea, they despised the pleasant land, they believed not his word:

25But murmured in their tents, *and* hearkened not unto the voice of the LORD.

26Therefore he lifted up his hand against them, to overthrow them in the wilderness:

27To overthrow their seed also among the nations, and to scatter them in the lands.

28They joined themselves also unto Baal-peor, and ate the sacrifices of the dead.

29Thus they provoked *him* to anger with their inventions: and the plague brake in upon them.

New International

6We have sinned, even as our fathers did;
  we have done wrong and acted wickedly.
7When our fathers were in Egypt,
  they gave no thought to your miracles;
they did not remember your many kindnesses,
  and they rebelled by the sea, the Red Sea.a
8Yet he saved them for his name's sake,
  to make his mighty power known.
9He rebuked the Red Sea, and it dried up;
  he led them through the depths as through a
    desert.
10He saved them from the hand of the foe;
  from the hand of the enemy he redeemed
    them.
11The waters covered their adversaries;
  not one of them survived.
12Then they believed his promises
  and sang his praise.

13But they soon forgot what he had done
  and did not wait for his counsel.
14In the desert they gave in to their craving;
  in the wasteland they put God to the test.
15So he gave them what they asked for,
  but sent a wasting disease upon them.

16In the camp they grew envious of Moses
  and of Aaron, who was consecrated to the
    LORD.
17The earth opened up and swallowed Dathan;
  it buried the company of Abiram.
18Fire blazed among their followers;
  a flame consumed the wicked.

19At Horeb they made a calf
  and worshiped an idol cast from metal.
20They exchanged their Glory
  for an image of a bull, which eats grass.
21They forgot the God who saved them,
  who had done great things in Egypt,
22miracles in the land of Ham
  and awesome deeds by the Red Sea.
23So he said he would destroy them—
  had not Moses, his chosen one,
stood in the breach before him
  to keep his wrath from destroying them.

24Then they despised the pleasant land;
  they did not believe his promise.
25They grumbled in their tents
  and did not obey the LORD.
26So he swore to them with uplifted hand
  that he would make them fall in the desert,
27make their descendants fall among the nations
  and scatter them throughout the lands.

28They yoked themselves to the Baal of Peor
  and ate sacrifices offered to lifeless gods;
29they provoked the LORD to anger by their
    wicked deeds,
  and a plague broke out among them.

---

a 7 Hebrew *Yam Suph*; that is, Sea of Reeds; also in verses 9 and 22

Living Bible

6Both we and our fathers have sinned so much. 7They weren't impressed by the wonder of your miracles in Egypt, and soon forgot your many acts of kindness to them. Instead they rebelled against you at the Red Sea. 8Even so you saved them—to defend the honor of your name and demonstrate your power to all the world. 9You commanded the Red Sea to divide, forming a dry road across its bottom. Yes, as dry as any desert! 10Thus you rescued them from their enemies. 11Then the water returned and covered the road and drowned their foes; not one survived.

12Then at last his people believed him. Then they finally sang his praise.

13Yet how quickly they forgot again! They wouldn't wait for him to act, 14but demanded better food,b testing God's patience to the breaking point. 15So he gave them their demands, but sent them leanness in their souls.c 16They were envious of Moses; yes, and Aaron, too, the man anointedd by God as his priest. 17Because of this the earth opened and swallowed Dathan, Abiram and his friends; 18and fire fell from heaven to consume these wicked men. 19, 20For they preferred a statue of an ox that eats grass, to the glorious presence of God himself. 21, 22Thus they despised their Savior who had done such mighty miracles in Egypt and at the Sea. 23So the Lord declared he would destroy them. But Moses, his chosen one, stepped into the breach between the people and their God and begged him to turn from his wrath, and not destroy them.

24They refused to enter the Promised Land, for they wouldn't believe his solemn oath to care for them. 25Instead, they pouted in their tents and mourned and despised his command. 26Therefore he swore that he would kill them in the wilderness 27and send their children away to distant lands as exiles. 28Then our fathers joined the worshipers of Baal at Peor and even offered sacrifices to the dead!e 29With all these things they angered him—and so a plague broke out upon them 30and

New Revised Standard

6 Both we and our ancestors have sinned;
     we have committed iniquity, have done
       wickedly.
7 Our ancestors, when they were in Egypt,
     did not consider your wonderful works;
   they did not remember the abundance of your
       steadfast love,
     but rebelled against the Most Highf at the
       Red Sea.g
8 Yet he saved them for his name's sake,
     so that he might make known his mighty
       power.
9 He rebuked the Red Sea,g and it became dry;
     he led them through the deep as through a
       desert.
10 So he saved them from the hand of the foe,
     and delivered them from the hand of the
       enemy.
11 The waters covered their adversaries;
     not one of them was left.
12 Then they believed his words;
     they sang his praise.

13 But they soon forgot his works;
     they did not wait for his counsel.
14 But they had a wanton craving in the
       wilderness,
     and put God to the test in the desert;
15 he gave them what they asked,
     but sent a wasting disease among them.

16 They were jealous of Moses in the camp,
     and of Aaron, the holy one of the LORD.
17 The earth opened and swallowed up Dathan,
     and covered the faction of Abiram.
18 Fire also broke out in their company;
     the flame burned up the wicked.

19 They made a calf at Horeb
     and worshiped a cast image.
20 They exchanged the glory of Godh
     for the image of an ox that eats grass.
21 They forgot God, their Savior,
     who had done great things in Egypt,
22 wondrous works in the land of Ham,
     and awesome deeds by the Red Sea.g
23 Therefore he said he would destroy them—
     had not Moses, his chosen one,
   stood in the breach before him,
     to turn away his wrath from destroying
       them.

24 Then they despised the pleasant land,
     having no faith in his promise.
25 They grumbled in their tents,
     and did not obey the voice of the LORD.
26 Therefore he raised his hand and swore to
       them
     that he would make them fall in the
       wilderness,
27 and would dispersei their descendants among
       the nations,
     scattering them over the lands.

28 Then they attached themselves to the Baal of
       Peor,
     and ate sacrifices offered to the dead;
29 they provoked the LORD to anger with their
       deeds,
     and a plague broke out among them.

---

b 106:14 demanded better food, literally, "lusted exceedingly."
c 106:15 God sent them leanness in their souls, or, "but sent a plague to punish them." d 106:16 the man anointed, literally, "the holy one of Jehovah." e 106:28 to the dead, or, "to lifeless idols."

f Cn Compare 78.17, 56: Heb rebelled at the sea   g Or Sea of Reeds
h Compare Gk Mss: Heb exchanged their glory   i Syr Compare Ezek 20.23: Heb cause to fall

King James

30Then stood up Phinehas, and executed judgment: and *so* the plague was stayed.

31And that was counted unto him for righteousness unto all generations for evermore.

32They angered *him* also at the waters of strife, so that it went ill with Moses for their sakes:

33Because they provoked his spirit, so that he spake unadvisedly with his lips.

34They did not destroy the nations, concerning whom the LORD commanded them:

35But were mingled among the heathen, and learned their works.

36And they served their idols: which were a snare unto them.

37Yea, they sacrificed their sons and their daughters unto devils,

38And shed innocent blood, *even* the blood of their sons and of their daughters, whom they sacrificed unto the idols of Canaan: and the land was polluted with blood.

39Thus were they defiled with their own works, and went a-whoring with their own inventions.

40Therefore was the wrath of the LORD kindled against his people, insomuch that he abhorred his own inheritance.

41And he gave them into the hand of the heathen; and they that hated them ruled over them.

42Their enemies also oppressed them, and they were brought into subjection under their hand.

43Many times did he deliver them; but they provoked *him* with their counsel, and were brought low for their iniquity.

44Nevertheless he regarded their affliction, when he heard their cry:

45And he remembered for them his covenant, and repented according to the multitude of his mercies.

46He made them also to be pitied of all those that carried them captives.

47Save us, O LORD our God, and gather us from among the heathen, to give thanks unto thy holy name, *and* to triumph in thy praise.

48Blessed *be* the LORD God of Israel from everlasting to everlasting: and let all the people say, Amen. Praise ye the LORD.

New International

30But Phinehas stood up and intervened,
  and the plague was checked.
31This was credited to him as righteousness
  for endless generations to come.
32By the waters of Meribah they angered the
    LORD,
  and trouble came to Moses because of them;
33for they rebelled against the Spirit of God,
  and rash words came from Moses' lips.[a]

34They did not destroy the peoples
  as the LORD had commanded them,
35but they mingled with the nations
  and adopted their customs.
36They worshiped their idols,
  which became a snare to them.
37They sacrificed their sons
  and their daughters to demons.
38They shed innocent blood,
  the blood of their sons and daughters,
  whom they sacrificed to the idols of Canaan,
  and the land was desecrated by their blood.
39They defiled themselves by what they did;
  by their deeds they prostituted themselves.

40Therefore the LORD was angry with his people
  and abhorred his inheritance.
41He handed them over to the nations,
  and their foes ruled over them.
42Their enemies oppressed them
  and subjected them to their power.
43Many times he delivered them,
  but they were bent on rebellion
  and they wasted away in their sin.

44But he took note of their distress
  when he heard their cry;
45for their sake he remembered his covenant
  and out of his great love he relented.
46He caused them to be pitied
  by all who held them captive.

47Save us, O LORD our God,
  and gather us from the nations,
  that we may give thanks to your holy name
  and glory in your praise.

48Praise be to the LORD, the God of Israel,
  from everlasting to everlasting.
Let all the people say, "Amen!"

Praise the LORD.

BOOK V

Psalms 107–150

Book V

107 O GIVE thanks unto the LORD, for *he is* good: for his mercy *endureth* for ever.

2Let the redeemed of the LORD say *so*, whom he hath redeemed from the hand of the enemy;

3And gathered them out of the lands, from the east, and from the west, from the north, and from the south.

107 GIVE THANKS to the LORD, for he is good;
  his love endures forever.
2Let the redeemed of the LORD say this—
  those he redeemed from the hand of the foe,
3those he gathered from the lands,
  from east and west, from north and south.[b]

a 33 Or *against his spirit,* / *and rash words came from his lips*   b 3 Hebrew *north and the sea*

Living Bible

continued until Phineas executed those whose sins had caused the plague to start. 31(For this good deed Phineas will be remembered forever.)

32At Meribah, too, Israel angered God, causing Moses serious trouble, 33for he became angry and spoke foolishly.

34Nor did Israel destroy the nations in the land as God had told them to, 35but mingled in among the heathen and learned their evil ways, 36sacrificing to their idols, and were led away from God. 37, 38They even sacrificed their little children to the demons—the idols of Canaan—shedding innocent blood and polluting the land with murder. 39Their evil deeds defiled them, for their love of idols was adultery in the sight of God. 40That is why Jehovah's anger burned against his people, and he abhorred them. 41, 42That is why he let the heathen nations crush them. They were ruled by those who hated them and oppressed by their enemies.

43Again and again he delivered them from their slavery, but they continued to rebel against him, and were finally destroyed by their sin. 44Yet, even so, he listened to their cries and heeded their distress; 45he remembered his promises to them and relented because of his great love, 46and caused even their enemies who captured them to pity them.

47O Lord God, save us! Regather us from the nations so we can thank your holy name and rejoice and praise you.

48Blessed be the Lord, the God of Israel, from everlasting to everlasting. Let all the people say, "Amen!" Hallelujah!

107 SAY "THANK you" to the Lord for being so good, for always being so loving and kind. 2Has the Lord redeemed you? Then speak out! Tell others he has saved you from your enemies.

3He brought the exiles back from the farthest corners of the earth. 4They were wandering homeless in the

New Revised Standard

30 Then Phinehas stood up and interceded,
     and the plague was stopped.
31 And that has been reckoned to him as
         righteousness
     from generation to generation forever.

32 They angered the LORDᶜ at the waters of
         Meribah,
     and it went ill with Moses on their account;
33 for they made his spirit bitter,
     and he spoke words that were rash.

34 They did not destroy the peoples,
     as the LORD commanded them,
35 but they mingled with the nations
     and learned to do as they did.
36 They served their idols,
     which became a snare to them.
37 They sacrificed their sons
     and their daughters to the demons;
38 they poured out innocent blood,
     the blood of their sons and daughters,
   whom they sacrificed to the idols of Canaan;
     and the land was polluted with blood.
39 Thus they became unclean by their acts,
     and prostituted themselves in their doings.

40 Then the anger of the LORD was kindled
         against his people,
     and he abhorred his heritage;
41 he gave them into the hand of the nations,
     so that those who hated them ruled over
         them.
42 Their enemies oppressed them,
     and they were brought into subjection under
         their power.
43 Many times he delivered them,
     but they were rebellious in their purposes,
     and were brought low through their iniquity.
44 Nevertheless he regarded their distress
     when he heard their cry.
45 For their sake he remembered his covenant,
     and showed compassion according to the
         abundance of his steadfast love.
46 He caused them to be pitied
     by all who held them captive.

47 Save us, O LORD our God,
     and gather us from among the nations,
   that we may give thanks to your holy name
     and glory in your praise.

48 Blessed be the LORD, the God of Israel,
     from everlasting to everlasting.
   And let all the people say, "Amen."
   Praise the LORD!

BOOK V

(Psalms 107–150)

Thanksgiving for Deliverance from Many Troubles

107 O GIVE thanks to the LORD, for he is good;
     for his steadfast love endures forever.
2 Let the redeemed of the LORD say so,
     those he redeemed from trouble
3 and gathered in from the lands,
     from the east and from the west,
     from the north and from the south.ᵈ

ᶜ Heb *him*   ᵈ Cn: Heb *sea*

King James

4They wandered in the wilderness in a solitary way; they found no city to dwell in.

5Hungry and thirsty, their soul fainted in them.

6Then they cried unto the LORD in their trouble, *and* he delivered them out of their distresses.

7And he led them forth by the right way, that they might go to a city of habitation.

8Oh that *men* would praise the LORD *for* his goodness, and *for* his wonderful works to the children of men!

9For he satisfieth the longing soul, and filleth the hungry soul with goodness.

10Such as sit in darkness and the shadow of death, *being* bound in affliction and iron;

11Because they rebelled against the words of God, and contemned the counsel of the most High:

12Therefore he brought down their heart with labour; they fell down, and *there was* none to help.

13Then they cried unto the LORD in their trouble, *and* he saved them out of their distresses.

14He brought them out of darkness and the shadow of death, and brake their bands in sunder.

15Oh that *men* would praise the LORD *for* his goodness, and *for* his wonderful works to the children of men!

16For he hath broken the gates of brass, and cut the bars of iron in sunder.

17Fools because of their transgression, and because of their iniquities, are afflicted.

18Their soul abhorreth all manner of meat; and they draw near unto the gates of death.

19Then they cry unto the LORD in their trouble, *and* he saveth them out of their distresses.

20He sent his word, and healed them, and delivered *them* from their destructions.

21Oh that *men* would praise the LORD *for* his goodness, and *for* his wonderful works to the children of men!

22And let them sacrifice the sacrifices of thanksgiving, and declare his works with rejoicing.

23They that go down to the sea in ships, that do business in great waters;

24These see the works of the LORD, and his wonders in the deep.

25For he commandeth, and raiseth the stormy wind, which lifteth up the waves thereof.

26They mount up to the heaven, they go down again to the depths: their soul is melted because of trouble.

27They reel to and fro, and stagger like a drunken man, and are at their wit's end.

28Then they cry unto the LORD in their trouble, and he bringeth them out of their distresses.

29He maketh the storm a calm, so that the waves thereof are still.

30Then are they glad because they be quiet; so he bringeth them unto their desired haven.

31Oh that *men* would praise the LORD *for* his goodness, and *for* his wonderful works to the children of men!

32Let them exalt him also in the congregation of the people, and praise him in the assembly of the elders.

New International

4Some wandered in desert wastelands, finding no way to a city where they could settle.

5They were hungry and thirsty, and their lives ebbed away.

6Then they cried out to the LORD in their trouble, and he delivered them from their distress.

7He led them by a straight way to a city where they could settle.

8Let them give thanks to the LORD for his unfailing love and his wonderful deeds for men,

9for he satisfies the thirsty and fills the hungry with good things.

10Some sat in darkness and the deepest gloom, prisoners suffering in iron chains,

11for they had rebelled against the words of God and despised the counsel of the Most High.

12So he subjected them to bitter labor; they stumbled, and there was no one to help.

13Then they cried to the LORD in their trouble, and he saved them from their distress.

14He brought them out of darkness and the deepest gloom and broke away their chains.

15Let them give thanks to the LORD for his unfailing love and his wonderful deeds for men,

16for he breaks down gates of bronze and cuts through bars of iron.

17Some became fools through their rebellious ways and suffered affliction because of their iniquities.

18They loathed all food and drew near the gates of death.

19Then they cried to the LORD in their trouble, and he saved them from their distress.

20He sent forth his word and healed them; he rescued them from the grave.

21Let them give thanks to the LORD for his unfailing love and his wonderful deeds for men.

22Let them sacrifice thank offerings and tell of his works with songs of joy.

23Others went out on the sea in ships; they were merchants on the mighty waters.

24They saw the works of the LORD, his wonderful deeds in the deep.

25For he spoke and stirred up a tempest that lifted high the waves.

26They mounted up to the heavens and went down to the depths; in their peril their courage melted away.

27They reeled and staggered like drunken men; they were at their wits' end.

28Then they cried out to the LORD in their trouble, and he brought them out of their distress.

29He stilled the storm to a whisper; the waves of the sea were hushed.

30They were glad when it grew calm, and he guided them to their desired haven.

31Let them give thanks to the LORD for his unfailing love and his wonderful deeds for men.

32Let them exalt him in the assembly of the people and praise him in the council of the elders.

Living Bible

desert, 5hungry and thirsty and faint. 6"Lord, help!" they cried, and he did! 7He led them straight to safety and a place to live. 8Oh, that these men would praise the Lord for his loving-kindness, and for all of his wonderful deeds! 9For he satisfies the thirsty soul and fills the hungry soul with good.

10Who are these who sit in darkness, in the shadow of death, crushed by misery and slavery? 11They rebelled against the Lord, scorning him who is the God above all gods. 12That is why he broke them with hard labor; they fell and none could help them rise again. 13Then they cried to the Lord in their troubles, and he rescued them! 14He led them from the darkness and shadow of death and snapped their chains. 15Oh, that these men would praise the Lord for his lovingkindness and for all of his wonderful deeds! 16For he broke down their prison gates of brass and cut apart their iron bars.

17Others, the fools, were ill because of their sinful ways. 18Their appetites were gone and death was near. 19Then they cried to the Lord in their troubles, and he helped them and delivered them. 20He spoke, and they were healed—snatched from the door of death. 21Oh, that these men would praise the Lord for his lovingkindness and for all of his wonderful deeds! 22Let them tell him "Thank you" as their sacrifice, and sing about his glorious deeds.

23And then there are the sailors sailing the seven seas, plying the trade routes of the world. 24They, too, observe the power of God in action. 25He calls to the storm winds; the waves rise high. 26Their ships are tossed to the heavens and sink again to the depths; the sailors cringe in terror. 27They reel and stagger like drunkards and are at their wit's end. 28Then they cry to the Lord in their trouble, and he saves them. 29He calms the storm and stills the waves. 30What a blessing is that stillness, as he brings them safely into harbor! 31Oh, that these men would praise the Lord for his lovingkindness and for all of his wonderful deeds! 32Let them praise him publicly before the congregation, and before the leaders of the nation.

New Revised Standard

4 Some wandered in desert wastes,
   finding no way to an inhabited town;
5 hungry and thirsty,
   their soul fainted within them.
6 Then they cried to the LORD in their trouble,
   and he delivered them from their distress;
7 he led them by a straight way,
   until they reached an inhabited town.
8 Let them thank the LORD for his steadfast love,
   for his wonderful works to humankind.
9 For he satisfies the thirsty,
   and the hungry he fills with good things.

10 Some sat in darkness and in gloom,
   prisoners in misery and in irons,
11 for they had rebelled against the words of God,
   and spurned the counsel of the Most High.
12 Their hearts were bowed down with hard labor;
   they fell down, with no one to help.
13 Then they cried to the LORD in their trouble,
   and he saved them from their distress;
14 he brought them out of darkness and gloom,
   and broke their bonds asunder.
15 Let them thank the LORD for his steadfast love,
   for his wonderful works to humankind.
16 For he shatters the doors of bronze,
   and cuts in two the bars of iron.

17 Some were sick[a] through their sinful ways,
   and because of their iniquities endured affliction;
18 they loathed any kind of food,
   and they drew near to the gates of death.
19 Then they cried to the LORD in their trouble,
   and he saved them from their distress;
20 he sent out his word and healed them,
   and delivered them from destruction.
21 Let them thank the LORD for his steadfast love,
   for his wonderful works to humankind.
22 And let them offer thanksgiving sacrifices,
   and tell of his deeds with songs of joy.

23 Some went down to the sea in ships,
   doing business on the mighty waters;
24 they saw the deeds of the LORD,
   his wondrous works in the deep.
25 For he commanded and raised the stormy wind,
   which lifted up the waves of the sea.
26 They mounted up to heaven, they went down to the depths;
   their courage melted away in their calamity;
27 they reeled and staggered like drunkards,
   and were at their wits' end.
28 Then they cried to the LORD in their trouble,
   and he brought them out from their distress;
29 he made the storm be still,
   and the waves of the sea were hushed.
30 Then they were glad because they had quiet,
   and he brought them to their desired haven.
31 Let them thank the LORD for his steadfast love,
   for his wonderful works to humankind.
32 Let them extol him in the congregation of the people,
   and praise him in the assembly of the elders.

a Cn: Heb *fools*

King James

33He turneth rivers into a wilderness, and the water-springs into dry ground;

34A fruitful land into barrenness, for the wickedness of them that dwell therein.

35He turneth the wilderness into a standing water, and dry ground into watersprings.

36And there he maketh the hungry to dwell, that they may prepare a city for habitation;

37And sow the fields, and plant vineyards, which may yield fruits of increase.

38He blesseth them also, so that they are multiplied greatly; and suffereth not their cattle to decrease.

39Again, they are minished and brought low through oppression, affliction, and sorrow.

40He poureth contempt upon princes, and causeth them to wander in the wilderness, *where there is* no way.

41Yet setteth he the poor on high from affliction, and maketh *him* families like a flock.

42The righteous shall see *it,* and rejoice: and all iniquity shall stop her mouth.

43Whoso *is* wise, and will observe these *things,* even they shall understand the lovingkindness of the LORD.

A Song *or* Psalm of David.

108 O GOD, my heart is fixed; I will sing and give praise, even with my glory.

2Awake, psaltery and harp: I *myself* will awake early.

3I will praise thee, O LORD, among the people: and I will sing praises unto thee among the nations.

4For thy mercy *is* great above the heavens: and thy truth *reacheth* unto the clouds.

5Be thou exalted, O God, above the heavens: and thy glory above all the earth;

6That thy beloved may be delivered: save *with* thy right hand, and answer me.

7God hath spoken in his holiness; I will rejoice, I will divide Shechem, and mete out the valley of Succoth.

8Gilead *is* mine; Manasseh *is* mine; Ephraim also *is* the strength of mine head; Judah *is* my lawgiver;

9Moab *is* my washpot; over Edom will I cast out my shoe; over Philistia will I triumph.

10Who will bring me into the strong city? who will lead me into Edom?

11*Wilt* not *thou,* O God, *who* hast cast us off? and wilt not thou, O God, go forth with our hosts?

12Give us help from trouble: for vain *is* the help of man.

13Through God we shall do valiantly: for he *it is that* shall tread down our enemies.

New International

33He turned rivers into a desert,
    flowing springs into thirsty ground,
34and fruitful land into a salt waste,
    because of the wickedness of those who lived
        there.
35He turned the desert into pools of water
    and the parched ground into flowing springs;
36there he brought the hungry to live,
    and they founded a city where they could
        settle.
37They sowed fields and planted vineyards
    that yielded a fruitful harvest;
38he blessed them, and their numbers greatly
        increased,
    and he did not let their herds diminish.

39Then their numbers decreased, and they were
        humbled
    by oppression, calamity and sorrow;
40he who pours contempt on nobles
    made them wander in a trackless waste.
41But he lifted the needy out of their affliction
    and increased their families like flocks.
42The upright see and rejoice,
    but all the wicked shut their mouths.

43Whoever is wise, let him heed these things
    and consider the great love of the LORD.

A song. A psalm of David.

108 MY HEART is steadfast, O God;
    I will sing and make music with all my
        soul.
2Awake, harp and lyre!
    I will awaken the dawn.
3I will praise you, O LORD, among the nations;
    I will sing of you among the peoples.
4For great is your love, higher than the heavens;
    your faithfulness reaches to the skies.
5Be exalted, O God, above the heavens,
    and let your glory be over all the earth.

6Save us and help us with your right hand,
    that those you love may be delivered.
7God has spoken from his sanctuary:
    "In triumph I will parcel out Shechem
    and measure off the Valley of Succoth.
8Gilead is mine, Manasseh is mine;
    Ephraim is my helmet,
    Judah my scepter.
9Moab is my washbasin,
    upon Edom I toss my sandal;
    over Philistia I shout in triumph."

10Who will bring me to the fortified city?
    Who will lead me to Edom?
11Is it not you, O God, you who have rejected us
    and no longer go out with our armies?
12Give us aid against the enemy,
    for the help of man is worthless.
13With God we will gain the victory,
    and he will trample down our enemies.

Living Bible

33He dries up rivers, 34and turns the good land of the wicked into deserts of salt. 35Again, he turns deserts into fertile, watered valleys. 36He brings the hungry to settle there and build their cities, 37to sow their fields and plant their vineyards, and reap their bumper crops! 38How he blesses them! They raise big families there, and many cattle.

39But others become poor through oppression, trouble and sorrow. 40For God pours contempt upon the haughty and causes princes to wander among ruins; 41but he rescues the poor who are godly and gives them many children and much prosperity. 42Good men everywhere will see it and be glad, while evil men are stricken silent.

43Listen, if you are wise, to what I am saying. Think about the lovingkindness of the Lord!

108 O GOD, my heart is ready to praise you! I will sing and rejoice before you.
2Wake up, O harp and lyre! We will meet the dawn with song. 3I will praise you everywhere around the world, in every nation. 4For your lovingkindness is great beyond measure, high as the heavens. Your faithfulness reaches the skies. 5His glory is far more vast than the heavens. It towers above the earth. 6Hear the cry of your beloved child—come with mighty power and rescue me.

7God has given sacred promises; no wonder I exult! He has promised to give us all the land of Shechem, and also Succoth Valley. 8"Gilead is mine to give to you," he says, "and Manasseh as well; the land of Ephraim is the helmet on my head. Judah is my scepter. 9But Moab and Edom are despised;a and I will shout in triumph over the Philistines."

10Who but God can give me strength to conquer these fortified cities? Who else can lead me into Edom? 11Lord, have you thrown us away? Have you deserted our army? 12Oh, help us fight against our enemies, for men are useless allies. 13But with the help of God we shall do mighty acts of valor. For he treads down our foes.

New Revised Standard

33 He turns rivers into a desert,
    springs of water into thirsty ground,
34 a fruitful land into a salty waste,
    because of the wickedness of its inhabitants.
35 He turns a desert into pools of water,
    a parched land into springs of water.
36 And there he lets the hungry live,
    and they establish a town to live in;
37 they sow fields, and plant vineyards,
    and get a fruitful yield.
38 By his blessing they multiply greatly,
    and he does not let their cattle decrease.

39 When they are diminished and brought low
    through oppression, trouble, and sorrow,
40 he pours contempt on princes
    and makes them wander in trackless wastes;
41 but he raises up the needy out of distress,
    and makes their families like flocks.
42 The upright see it and are glad;
    and all wickedness stops its mouth.
43 Let those who are wise give heed to these things,
    and consider the steadfast love of the LORD.

Praise and Prayer for Victory

A Song. A Psalm of David.

108 MY HEART is steadfast, O God, my heart is steadfast;b
    I will sing and make melody.
    Awake, my soul!c
2 Awake, O harp and lyre!
    I will awake the dawn.
3 I will give thanks to you, O LORD, among the peoples,
    and I will sing praises to you among the nations.
4 For your steadfast love is higher than the heavens,
    and your faithfulness reaches to the clouds.

5 Be exalted, O God, above the heavens,
    and let your glory be over all the earth.
6 Give victory with your right hand, and answer me,
    so that those whom you love may be rescued.

7 God has promised in his sanctuary:d
    "With exultation I will divide up Shechem,
    and portion out the Vale of Succoth.
8 Gilead is mine; Manasseh is mine;
    Ephraim is my helmet;
    Judah is my scepter.
9 Moab is my washbasin;
    on Edom I hurl my shoe;
    over Philistia I shout in triumph."

10 Who will bring me to the fortified city?
    Who will lead me to Edom?
11 Have you not rejected us, O God?
    You do not go out, O God, with our armies.
12 O grant us help against the foe,
    for human help is worthless.
13 With God we shall do valiantly;
    it is he who will tread down our foes.

---

a 108:9 *But Moab and Edom are despised*, literally, "Moab is my washbasin; upon Edom I cast my shoe."

b Heb Mss Gk Syr: MT lacks *my heart is steadfast*   c Compare 57.8: Heb *also my soul*   d Or *by his holiness*

King James

To the chief Musician, A Psalm of David.

109 HOLD NOT thy peace, O God of my praise;
2For the mouth of the wicked and the mouth of the deceitful are opened against me: they have spoken against me with a lying tongue.

3They compassed me about also with words of hatred; and fought against me without a cause.

4For my love they are my adversaries: but I *give myself unto* prayer.

5And they have rewarded me evil for good, and hatred for my love.

6Set thou a wicked man over him: and let Satan stand at his right hand.

7When he shall be judged, let him be condemned: and let his prayer become sin.

8Let his days be few; *and* let another take his office.

9Let his children be fatherless, and his wife a widow.

10Let his children be continually vagabonds, and beg: let them seek *their bread* also out of their desolate places.

11Let the extortioner catch all that he hath; and let the strangers spoil his labour.

12Let there be none to extend mercy unto him: neither let there be any to favour his fatherless children.

13Let his posterity be cut off; *and* in the generation following let their name be blotted out.

14Let the iniquity of his fathers be remembered with the Lord; and let not the sin of his mother be blotted out.

15Let them be before the Lord continually, that he may cut off the memory of them from the earth.

16Because that he remembered not to show mercy, but persecuted the poor and needy man, that he might even slay the broken in heart.

17As he loved cursing, so let it come unto him: as he delighted not in blessing, so let it be far from him.

18As he clothed himself with cursing like as with his garment, so let it come into his bowels like water, and like oil into his bones.

19Let it be unto him as the garment *which* covereth him, and for a girdle wherewith he is girded continually.

20*Let* this *be* the reward of mine adversaries from the Lord, and of them that speak evil against my soul.

21But do thou for me, O God the Lord, for thy name's sake: because thy mercy *is* good, deliver thou me.

22For I *am* poor and needy, and my heart is wounded within me.

23I am gone like the shadow when it declineth: I am tossed up and down as the locust.

24My knees are weak through fasting; and my flesh faileth of fatness.

25I became also a reproach unto them: *when* they looked upon me they shaked their heads.

26Help me, O Lord my God: O save me according to thy mercy:

New International

For the director of music. Of David. A psalm.

109 O GOD, whom I praise,
do not remain silent,
2for wicked and deceitful men
have opened their mouths against me;
they have spoken against me with lying
tongues.
3With words of hatred they surround me;
they attack me without cause.
4In return for my friendship they accuse me,
but I am a man of prayer.
5They repay me evil for good,
and hatred for my friendship.

6Appoint[a] an evil man[b] to oppose him;
let an accuser[c] stand at his right hand.
7When he is tried, let him be found guilty,
and may his prayers condemn him.
8May his days be few;
may another take his place of leadership.
9May his children be fatherless
and his wife a widow.
10May his children be wandering beggars;
may they be driven[d] from their ruined homes.
11May a creditor seize all he has;
may strangers plunder the fruits of his labor.
12May no one extend kindness to him
or take pity on his fatherless children.
13May his descendants be cut off,
their names blotted out from the next
generation.
14May the iniquity of his fathers be remembered
before the Lord;
may the sin of his mother never be blotted
out.
15May their sins always remain before the Lord,
that he may cut off the memory of them from
the earth.

16For he never thought of doing a kindness,
but hounded to death the poor
and the needy and the brokenhearted.
17He loved to pronounce a curse—
may it[e] come on him;
he found no pleasure in blessing—
may it be[f] far from him.
18He wore cursing as his garment;
it entered into his body like water,
into his bones like oil.
19May it be like a cloak wrapped about him,
like a belt tied forever around him.
20May this be the Lord's payment to my
accusers,
to those who speak evil of me.

21But you, O Sovereign Lord,
deal well with me for your name's sake;
out of the goodness of your love, deliver me.
22For I am poor and needy,
and my heart is wounded within me.
23I fade away like an evening shadow;
I am shaken off like a locust.
24My knees give way from fasting;
my body is thin and gaunt.
25I am an object of scorn to my accusers;
when they see me, they shake their heads.

26Help me, O Lord my God;
save me in accordance with your love.

a 6 Or *They say:*, "Appoint (with quotation marks at the end of verse 19)
b 6 Or *the Evil One* c 6 Or *let Satan* d 10 Septuagint; Hebrew *sought*
e 17 Or *curse, / and it has* f 17 Or *blessing, / and it is*

Living Bible

109 O GOD of my praise, don't stand silent and aloof ²while the wicked slander me and tell their lies. ³They have no reason to hate and fight me, yet they do! ⁴I love them, but even while I am praying for them, they are trying to destroy me. ⁵They return evil for good, and hatred for love.

⁶Show him how it feels!ᵍ Let lies be told about him, and bring him to court before an unfair judge. ⁷When his case is called for judgment, let him be pronounced guilty. Count his prayers as sins. ⁸Let his years be few and brief; let others step forward to replace him. ⁹, ¹⁰May his children become fatherless and his wife a widow; may they be evicted from the ruins of their home. ¹¹May creditors seize his entire estate and strangers take all he has earned. ¹², ¹³Let no one be kind to him; let no one pity his fatherless children. May they die. May his family name be blotted out in a single generation. ¹⁴Punish the sins of his father and mother. Don't overlook them. ¹⁵Think constantly about the evil things he has done, and cut off his name from the memory of man.

¹⁶For he refused all kindness to others, and persecuted those in need, and hounded brokenhearted ones to death. ¹⁷He loved to curse others; now you curse him. He never blessed others; now don't you bless him. ¹⁸Cursing is as much a part of him as his clothing, or as the water he drinks, or the rich food he eats. ¹⁹Now may those curses return and cling to him like his clothing or his belt. ²⁰This is the Lord's punishment upon my enemies who tell lies about me and threaten me with death.

²¹But as for me, O Lord, deal with me as your child, as one who bears your name! Because you are so kind, O Lord, deliver me.

²², ²³I am slipping down the hill to death; I am shaken off from life as easily as a man brushes a grasshopper from his arm. ²⁴My knees are weak from fasting and I am skin and bones. ²⁵I am a symbol of failure to all mankind; when they see me they shake their heads. ²⁶Help me, O Lord my God! Save me because you are loving and kind. ²⁷Do it publicly, so all will see that

New Revised Standard

Prayer for Vindication and Vengeance

To the leader. Of David. A Psalm.

109 DO NOT be silent, O God of my praise.
² For wicked and deceitful mouths are
    opened against me,
    speaking against me with lying tongues.
³ They beset me with words of hate,
    and attack me without cause.
⁴ In return for my love they accuse me,
    even while I make prayer for them.ʰ
⁵ So they reward me evil for good,
    and hatred for my love.

⁶ They say,ⁱ "Appoint a wicked man against
    him;
    let an accuser stand on his right.
⁷ When he is tried, let him be found guilty;
    let his prayer be counted as sin.
⁸ May his days be few;
    may another seize his position.
⁹ May his children be orphans,
    and his wife a widow.
¹⁰ May his children wander about and beg;
    may they be driven out ofʲ the ruins they
    inhabit.
¹¹ May the creditor seize all that he has;
    may strangers plunder the fruits of his toil.
¹² May there be no one to do him a kindness,
    nor anyone to pity his orphaned children.
¹³ May his posterity be cut off;
    may his name be blotted out in the second
    generation.
¹⁴ May the iniquity of his fatherᵏ be remembered
    before the LORD,
    and do not let the sin of his mother be
    blotted out.
¹⁵ Let them be before the LORD continually,
    and may hisˡ memory be cut off from the
    earth.
¹⁶ For he did not remember to show kindness,
    but pursued the poor and needy
    and the brokenhearted to their death.
¹⁷ He loved to curse; let curses come on him.
    He did not like blessing; may it be far from
    him.
¹⁸ He clothed himself with cursing as his coat,
    may it soak into his body like water,
    like oil into his bones.
¹⁹ May it be like a garment that he wraps around
    himself,
    like a belt that he wears every day."

²⁰ May that be the reward of my accusers from
    the LORD,
    of those who speak evil against my life.
²¹ But you, O LORD my Lord,
    act on my behalf for your name's sake;
    because your steadfast love is good, deliver
    me.
²² For I am poor and needy,
    and my heart is pierced within me.
²³ I am gone like a shadow at evening;
    I am shaken off like a locust.
²⁴ My knees are weak through fasting;
    my body has become gaunt.
²⁵ I am an object of scorn to my accusers;
    when they see me, they shake their heads.

²⁶ Help me, O LORD my God!
    Save me according to your steadfast love.

ᵍ *109:6 Show him how it feels,* implied.

ʰ Syr: Heb *I prayer* ⁱ Heb lacks *They say* ʲ Gk: Heb *and seek* ᵏ Cn: Heb *fathers* ˡ Gk: Heb *their*

King James

27That they may know that this *is* thy hand; *that* thou, LORD, hast done it.

28Let them curse, but bless thou: when they arise, let them be ashamed; but let thy servant rejoice.

29Let mine adversaries be clothed with shame, and let them cover themselves with their own confusion, as with a mantle.

30I will greatly praise the LORD with my mouth; yea, I will praise him among the multitude.

31For he shall stand at the right hand of the poor, to save *him* from those that condemn his soul.

A Psalm of David.

110 THE LORD said unto my Lord, Sit thou at my right hand, until I make thine enemies thy footstool.

2The LORD shall send the rod of thy strength out of Zion: rule thou in the midst of thine enemies.

3Thy people *shall be* willing in the day of thy power, in the beauties of holiness from the womb of the morning: thou hast the dew of thy youth.

4The LORD hath sworn, and will not repent, Thou *art* a priest for ever after the order of Melchizedek.

5The Lord at thy right hand shall strike through kings in the day of his wrath.

6He shall judge among the heathen, he shall fill *the places* with the dead bodies; he shall wound the heads over many countries.

7He shall drink of the brook in the way: therefore shall he lift up the head.

111 PRAISE YE the LORD. I will praise the LORD with *my* whole heart, in the assembly of the upright, and *in* the congregation.

2The works of the LORD *are* great, sought out of all them that have pleasure therein.

3His work *is* honourable and glorious: and his righteousness endureth for ever.

4He hath made his wonderful works to be remembered: the LORD *is* gracious and full of compassion.

5He hath given meat unto them that fear him: he will ever be mindful of his covenant.

6He hath shown his people the power of his works, that he may give them the heritage of the heathen.

7The works of his hands *are* verity and judgment; all his commandments *are* sure.

8They stand fast for ever and ever, *and are* done in truth and uprightness.

New International

27Let them know that it is your hand,
that you, O LORD, have done it.

28They may curse, but you will bless;
when they attack they will be put to shame,
but your servant will rejoice.

29My accusers will be clothed with disgrace
and wrapped in shame as in a cloak.

30With my mouth I will greatly extol the LORD;
in the great throng I will praise him.

31For he stands at the right hand of the needy one,
to save his life from those who condemn him.

Of David. A psalm.

110 THE LORD says to my Lord:
"Sit at my right hand
until I make your enemies
a footstool for your feet."

2The LORD will extend your mighty scepter from Zion;
you will rule in the midst of your enemies.

3Your troops will be willing
on your day of battle.
Arrayed in holy majesty,
from the womb of the dawn
you will receive the dew of your youth.[a]

4The LORD has sworn
and will not change his mind:
"You are a priest forever,
in the order of Melchizedek."

5The Lord is at your right hand;
he will crush kings on the day of his wrath.

6He will judge the nations, heaping up the dead
and crushing the rulers of the whole earth.

7He will drink from a brook beside the way[b];
therefore he will lift up his head.

111[c] PRAISE THE LORD.[d]

I will extol the LORD with all my heart
in the council of the upright and in the assembly.

2Great are the works of the LORD;
they are pondered by all who delight in them.

3Glorious and majestic are his deeds,
and his righteousness endures forever.

4He has caused his wonders to be remembered;
the LORD is gracious and compassionate.

5He provides food for those who fear him;
he remembers his covenant forever.

6He has shown his people the power of his works,
giving them the lands of other nations.

7The works of his hands are faithful and just;
all his precepts are trustworthy.

8They are steadfast for ever and ever,
done in faithfulness and uprightness.

a 3 Or / *your young men will come to you like the dew*   b 7 Or / *The One who grants succession will set him in authority*   c This psalm is an acrostic poem, the lines of which begin with the successive letters of the Hebrew alphabet.   d 1 Hebrew *Hallelu Yah*

Living Bible

you yourself have done it. 28Then let them curse me if they like—I won't mind that if you are blessing me! For then all their efforts to destroy me will fail, and I shall go right on rejoicing!

29Make them fail in everything they do. Clothe them with disgrace. 30But I will give repeated thanks to the Lord, praising him to everyone. 31For he stands beside the poor and hungry to save them from their enemies.

110 JEHOVAH SAID to my Lord the Messiah,ᵉ "Rule as my regent—I will subdue your enemies and make them bow low before you."

2Jehovah has established your throneᶠ in Jerusalemᵍ to rule over your enemies. 3In that day of your power your people shall come to you willingly, dressed in holy altar robes.ʰ And your strength shall be renewed day by day like morning dew. 4Jehovah has taken oath, and will not rescind his vow, that you are a priest forever likeⁱ Melchizedek. 5God stands beside you to protect you. He will strike down many kings in the day of his anger. 6He will punish the nations, and fill them with their dead. He will crush many heads. 7But he himself shall be refreshed from springs along the way.

111 HALLELUJAH! I want to express publicly before his people my heartfelt thanks to God for his mighty miracles. All who are thankful should ponder them with me. 3For his miracles demonstrate his honor, majesty, and eternal goodness.

4Who can forget the wonders he performs—deeds of mercy and of grace? 5He gives food to those who trust him; he never forgets his promises. 6He has shown his great power to his people by giving them the land of Israel, though it was the home of many nations living there. 7All he does is just and good, and all his laws are right, 8for they are formed from truth and goodness, and stand firm forever. 9He has paid a full ransom for his

New Revised Standard

27 Let them know that this is your hand;
   you, O LORD, have done it.
28 Let them curse, but you will bless.
   Let my assailants be put to shame;ʲ may
   your servant be glad.
29 May my accusers be clothed with dishonor;
   may they be wrapped in their own shame as
   in a mantle.
30 With my mouth I will give great thanks to the
   LORD;
   I will praise him in the midst of the throng.
31 For he stands at the right hand of the needy,
   to save them from those who would
   condemn them to death.

Assurance of Victory for God's Priest-King
Of David. A Psalm.

110 THE LORD says to my lord,
   "Sit at my right hand
until I make your enemies your footstool."

2 The LORD sends out from Zion
   your mighty scepter.
   Rule in the midst of your foes.
3 Your people will offer themselves willingly
   on the day you lead your forces
   on the holy mountains.ᵏ
From the womb of the morning,
   like dew, your youthˡ will come to you.
4 The LORD has sworn and will not change his
   mind,
   "You are a priest forever according to the
   order of Melchizedek."ᵐ

5 The Lord is at your right hand;
   he will shatter kings on the day of his
   wrath.
6 He will execute judgment among the nations,
   filling them with corpses;
he will shatter heads
   over the wide earth.
7 He will drink from the stream by the path;
   therefore he will lift up his head.

Praise for God's Wonderful Works

111 PRAISE THE LORD!
   I will give thanks to the LORD with my
   whole heart,
   in the company of the upright, in the
   congregation.
2 Great are the works of the LORD,
   studied by all who delight in them.
3 Full of honor and majesty is his work,
   and his righteousness endures forever.
4 He has gained renown by his wonderful deeds;
   the LORD is gracious and merciful.
5 He provides food for those who fear him;
   he is ever mindful of his covenant.
6 He has shown his people the power of his
   works,
   in giving them the heritage of the nations.
7 The works of his hands are faithful and just;
   all his precepts are trustworthy.
8 They are established forever and ever,
   to be performed with faithfulness and
   uprightness.

ᵉ *110:1 the Messiah,* implied. In Matthew 22:41-45, Jesus applies these words to himself. ᶠ *110:2 Jehovah has established your throne,* literally, "The Lord will send forth the rod of your strength out of Zion." ᵍ *110:2 in Jerusalem,* literally, "from Zion." ʰ *110:3 holy altar robes,* literally, "in holy array." ⁱ *110:4 like,* literally, "after the manner of."

ʲ Gk: Heb *They have risen up and have been put to shame* ᵏ Another reading is *in holy splendor* ˡ Cn: Heb *the dew of your youth* ᵐ Or *forever, a rightful king by my edict*

King James

9He sent redemption unto his people: he hath commanded his covenant for ever: holy and reverend *is* his name.

10The fear of the LORD *is* the beginning of wisdom: a good understanding have all they that do *his commandments:* his praise endureth for ever.

112 PRAISE YE the LORD. Blessed *is* the man *that* feareth the LORD, *that* delighteth greatly in his commandments.

2His seed shall be mighty upon earth: the generation of the upright shall be blessed.

3Wealth and riches *shall be* in his house: and his righteousness endureth for ever.

4Unto the upright there ariseth light in the darkness: *he is* gracious, and full of compassion, and righteous.

5A good man showeth favour, and lendeth: he will guide his affairs with discretion.

6Surely he shall not be moved for ever: the righteous shall be in everlasting remembrance.

7He shall not be afraid of evil tidings: his heart is fixed, trusting in the LORD.

8His heart *is* established, he shall not be afraid, until he see *his desire* upon his enemies.

9He hath dispersed, he hath given to the poor; his righteousness endureth for ever; his horn shall be exalted with honour.

10The wicked shall see *it,* and be grieved; he shall gnash with his teeth, and melt away: the desire of the wicked shall perish.

113 PRAISE YE the LORD. Praise, O ye servants of the LORD, praise the name of the LORD.

2Blessed be the name of the LORD from this time forth and for evermore.

3From the rising of the sun unto the going down of the same the LORD's name *is* to be praised.

4The LORD *is* high above all nations, *and* his glory above the heavens.

5Who *is* like unto the LORD our God, who dwelleth on high,

6Who humbleth *himself* to behold *the things that are* in heaven, and in the earth!

7He raiseth up the poor out of the dust, *and* lifteth the needy out of the dunghill;

8That he may set *him* with princes, *even* with the princes of his people.

9He maketh the barren woman to keep house, *and to* be a joyful mother of children. Praise ye the LORD.

New International

9He provided redemption for his people;
  he ordained his covenant forever—
  holy and awesome is his name.

10The fear of the LORD is the beginning of
    wisdom;
  all who follow his precepts have good
    understanding.
  To him belongs eternal praise.

112 a PRAISE THE LORD.b

  Blessed is the man who fears the LORD,
  who finds great delight in his commands.

2His children will be mighty in the land;
  the generation of the upright will be blessed.
3Wealth and riches are in his house,
  and his righteousness endures forever.
4Even in darkness light dawns for the upright,
  for the gracious and compassionate and
    righteous man.c
5Good will come to him who is generous and
    lends freely,
  who conducts his affairs with justice.
6Surely he will never be shaken;
  a righteous man will be remembered forever.
7He will have no fear of bad news;
  his heart is steadfast, trusting in the LORD.
8His heart is secure, he will have no fear;
  in the end he will look in triumph on his
    foes.
9He has scattered abroad his gifts to the poor,
  his righteousness endures forever;
  his hornd will be lifted high in honor.

10The wicked man will see and be vexed,
  he will gnash his teeth and waste away;
  the longings of the wicked will come to
    nothing.

113 PRAISE THE LORD.e

  Praise, O servants of the LORD,
  praise the name of the LORD.
2Let the name of the LORD be praised,
  both now and forevermore.
3From the rising of the sun to the place where it
    sets,
  the name of the LORD is to be praised.

4The LORD is exalted over all the nations,
  his glory above the heavens.
5Who is like the LORD our God,
  the One who sits enthroned on high,
6who stoops down to look
  on the heavens and the earth?

7He raises the poor from the dust
  and lifts the needy from the ash heap;
8he seats them with princes,
  with the princes of their people.
9He settles the barren woman in her home
  as a happy mother of children.

  Praise the LORD.

a This psalm is an acrostic poem, the lines of which begin with the successive letters of the Hebrew alphabet. b *1* Hebrew *Hallelu Yah* c *4* Or *1 for the LORD, is gracious and compassionate and righteous* d *9 Horn* here symbolizes dignity. e *1* Hebrew *Hallelu Yah;* also in verse 9

Living Bible

people; now they are always free to come to Jehovah (what a holy, awe-inspiring name that is).

¹⁰How can men be wise? The only way to begin is by reverence for God. For growth in wisdom comes from obeying his laws. Praise his name forever.

112 PRAISE THE Lord! For all who fear God and trust in him are blessed beyond expression. Yes, happy is the man who delights in doing his commands.

²His children shall be honored everywhere, for good men's sons have a special heritage. ³He himself shall be wealthy, and his good deeds will never be forgotten. ⁴When darkness overtakes him, light will come bursting in. He is kind and merciful— ⁵and all goes well for the generous man who conducts his business fairly.

⁶Such a man will not be overthrown by evil circumstances. God's constant care of him will make a deep impression on all who see it. ⁷He does not fear bad news, nor live in dread of what may happen. For he is settled in his mind that Jehovah will take care of him. ⁸That is why he is not afraid, but can calmly face his foes. ⁹He gives generously to those in need. His deeds will never be forgotten.ᶠ He shall have influence and honor.

¹⁰Evil-minded men will be infuriated when they see all this; they will gnash their teeth in anger and slink away, their hopes thwarted.

113 HALLELUJAH! O servants of Jehovah, praise his name. ²Blessed is his name forever and forever. ³Praise him from sunrise to sunset! ⁴For he is high above the nations; his glory is far greater than the heavens.

⁵Who can be compared with God enthroned on high? ⁶Far below him are the heavens and the earth; he stoops to look, ⁷and lifts the poor from the dirt, and the hungry from the garbage dump, ⁸and sets them among princes! ⁹He gives children to the childless wife, so that she becomes a happy mother.

Hallelujah! Praise the Lord.

New Revised Standard

9 He sent redemption to his people;
   he has commanded his covenant forever.
   Holy and awesome is his name.
10 The fear of the LORD is the beginning of
   wisdom;
     all those who practice it₂ have a good
     understanding.
   His praise endures forever.

Blessings of the Righteous

112 PRAISE THE LORD!
   Happy are those who fear the LORD,
   who greatly delight in his commandments.
2 Their descendants will be mighty in the land;
   the generation of the upright will be
   blessed.
3 Wealth and riches are in their houses,
   and their righteousness endures forever.
4 They rise in the darkness as a light for the
   upright;
   they are gracious, merciful, and righteous.
5 It is well with those who deal generously and
   lend,
   who conduct their affairs with justice.
6 For the righteous will never be moved;
   they will be remembered forever.
7 They are not afraid of evil tidings;
   their hearts are firm, secure in the LORD.
8 Their hearts are steady, they will not be
   afraid;
   in the end they will look in triumph on their
   foes.
9 They have distributed freely, they have given
   to the poor;
   their righteousness endures forever;
   their horn is exalted in honor.
10 The wicked see it and are angry;
   they gnash their teeth and melt away;
   the desire of the wicked comes to nothing.

God the Helper of the Needy

113 PRAISE THE LORD!
   Praise, O servants of the LORD;
   praise the name of the LORD.

2 Blessed be the name of the LORD
   from this time on and forevermore.
3 From the rising of the sun to its setting
   the name of the LORD is to be praised.
4 The LORD is high above all nations,
   and his glory above the heavens.

5 Who is like the LORD our God,
   who is seated on high,
6 who looks far down
   on the heavens and the earth?
7 He raises the poor from the dust,
   and lifts the needy from the ash heap,
8 to make them sit with princes,
   with the princes of his people.
9 He gives the barren woman a home,
   making her the joyous mother of children.
   Praise the LORD!

ᶠ *112:9 His deeds will never be forgotten,* literally, "his righteousness endures forever."

ᵍ Gk Syr: Heb *them*

King James

New International

114 WHEN ISRAEL went out of Egypt, the house of Jacob from a people of strange language;

2Judah was his sanctuary, *and* Israel his dominion.

3The sea saw *it*, and fled: Jordan was driven back.

4The mountains skipped like rams, *and* the little hills like lambs.

5What *ailed* thee, O thou sea, that thou fleddest? thou Jordan, *that* thou wast driven back?

6Ye mountains, *that* ye skipped like rams; *and* ye little hills, like lambs?

7Tremble, thou earth, at the presence of the Lord, at the presence of the God of Jacob;

8Which turned the rock *into* a standing water, the flint into a fountain of waters.

115 NOT UNTO us, O LORD, not unto us, but unto thy name give glory, for thy mercy, *and* for thy truth's sake.

2Wherefore should the heathen say, Where *is* now their God?

3But our God *is* in the heavens: he hath done whatsoever he hath pleased.

4Their idols *are* silver and gold, the work of men's hands.

5They have mouths, but they speak not: eyes have they, but they see not:

6They have ears, but they hear not: noses have they, but they smell not:

7They have hands, but they handle not: feet have they, but they walk not: neither speak they through their throat.

8They that make them are like unto them; *so is* every one that trusteth in them.

9O Israel, trust thou in the LORD: he *is* their help and their shield.

10O house of Aaron, trust in the LORD: he *is* their help and their shield.

11Ye that fear the LORD, trust in the LORD: he *is* their help and their shield.

12The LORD hath been mindful of us: he will bless *us;* he will bless the house of Israel; he will bless the house of Aaron.

13He will bless them that fear the LORD, *both* small and great.

14The LORD shall increase you more and more, you and your children.

15Ye *are* blessed of the LORD which made heaven and earth.

16The heaven, *even* the heavens, *are* the LORD'S: but the earth hath he given to the children of men.

114 WHEN ISRAEL came out of Egypt, the house of Jacob from a people of foreign tongue,

2Judah became God's sanctuary,
　Israel his dominion.

3The sea looked and fled,
　the Jordan turned back;

4the mountains skipped like rams,
　the hills like lambs.

5Why was it, O sea, that you fled,
　O Jordan, that you turned back,

6you mountains, that you skipped like rams,
　you hills, like lambs?

7Tremble, O earth, at the presence of the Lord,
　at the presence of the God of Jacob,

8who turned the rock into a pool,
　the hard rock into springs of water.

115 NOT TO us, O LORD, not to us
　but to your name be the glory,
　because of your love and faithfulness.

2Why do the nations say,
　"Where is their God?"

3Our God is in heaven;
　he does whatever pleases him.

4But their idols are silver and gold,
　made by the hands of men.

5They have mouths, but cannot speak,
　eyes, but they cannot see;

6they have ears, but cannot hear,
　noses, but they cannot smell;

7they have hands, but cannot feel,
　feet, but they cannot walk;
　nor can they utter a sound with their throats.

8Those who make them will be like them,
　and so will all who trust in them.

9O house of Israel, trust in the LORD—
　he is their help and shield.

10O house of Aaron, trust in the LORD—
　he is their help and shield.

11You who fear him, trust in the LORD—
　he is their help and shield.

12The LORD remembers us and will bless us:
　He will bless the house of Israel,
　he will bless the house of Aaron,

13he will bless those who fear the LORD—
　small and great alike.

14May the LORD make you increase,
　both you and your children.

15May you be blessed by the LORD,
　the Maker of heaven and earth.

16The highest heavens belong to the LORD,
　but the earth he has given to man.

Living Bible

114
LONG AGO when the Israelis escaped from Egypt, from that land of foreign tongue, ²then the lands of Judah and of Israel became God's new home and kingdom.

³The Red Sea saw them coming and quickly broke apart before them. The Jordan River opened up a path for them to cross. ⁴The mountains skipped like rams, the little hills like lambs! ⁵What's wrong, Red Sea, that made you cut yourself in two? What happened, Jordan River, to your waters? Why were they held back? ⁶Why, mountains, did you skip like rams? Why, little hills, like lambs?

⁷Tremble, O earth, at the presence of the Lord, the God of Jacob. ⁸For he caused gushing streams to burst from flinty rock.

115
GLORIFY YOUR name, not ours, O Lord! Cause everyone to praise your lovingkindness and your truth. ²Why let the nations say, "Their God is dead!"ᵃ

³For he is in the heavens, and does as he wishes. ⁴Their gods are merely manmade things of silver and of gold. ⁵They can't talk or see, despite their eyes and mouths! ⁶Nor can they hear, nor smell, ⁷nor use their hands or feet! Nor speak! ⁸And those who make and worship them are just as foolish as their idols are.

⁹O Israel, trust the Lord! He is your helper. He is your shield. ¹⁰O priests of Aaron, trust the Lord! He is your helper; he is your shield. ¹¹All of you, his people, trust in him. He is your helper; he is your shield.

¹²Jehovah is constantly thinking about us and he will surely bless us. He will bless the people of Israel and the priests of Aaron, ¹³and all, both great and small, who reverence him.

¹⁴May the Lord richly bless both you and your children. ¹⁵Yes, Jehovah who made heaven and earth will personally bless you! ¹⁶The heavens belong to the Lord, but he has given the earth to all mankind.

New Revised Standard

God's Wonders at the Exodus

114
WHEN ISRAEL went out from Egypt, the house of Jacob from a people of strange language,
2 Judah became God'sᵇ sanctuary,
   Israel his dominion.

3 The sea looked and fled;
   Jordan turned back.
4 The mountains skipped like rams,
   the hills like lambs.

5 Why is it, O sea, that you flee?
   O Jordan, that you turn back?
6 O mountains, that you skip like rams?
   O hills, like lambs?

7 Tremble, O earth, at the presence of the
   LORD,
   at the presence of the God of Jacob,
8 who turns the rock into a pool of water,
   the flint into a spring of water.

The Impotence of Idols and the Greatness of God

115
NOT TO us, O LORD, not to us, but to your name give glory,
   for the sake of your steadfast love and your faithfulness.
2 Why should the nations say,
   "Where is their God?"

3 Our God is in the heavens;
   he does whatever he pleases.
4 Their idols are silver and gold,
   the work of human hands.
5 They have mouths, but do not speak;
   eyes, but do not see.
6 They have ears, but do not hear;
   noses, but do not smell.
7 They have hands, but do not feel;
   feet, but do not walk;
   they make no sound in their throats.
8 Those who make them are like them;
   so are all who trust in them.

9 O Israel, trust in the LORD!
   He is their help and their shield.
10 O house of Aaron, trust in the LORD!
   He is their help and their shield.
11 You who fear the LORD, trust in the LORD!
   He is their help and their shield.

12 The LORD has been mindful of us; he will bless us;
   he will bless the house of Israel;
   he will bless the house of Aaron;
13 he will bless those who fear the LORD,
   both small and great.

14 May the LORD give you increase,
   both you and your children.
15 May you be blessed by the LORD,
   who made heaven and earth.

16 The heavens are the LORD's heavens,
   but the earth he has given to human beings.

ᵃ 115:2 *Their God is dead,* literally, "Where is their God?"   ᵇHeb *his*

King James

17The dead praise not the LORD, neither any that go down into silence.

18But we will bless the LORD from this time forth and for evermore. Praise the LORD.

116 I LOVE the LORD, because he hath heard my voice *and* my supplications.

2Because he hath inclined his ear unto me, therefore will I call upon *him* as long as I live.

3The sorrows of death compassed me, and the pains of hell gat hold upon me: I found trouble and sorrow.

4Then called I upon the name of the LORD; O LORD, I beseech thee, deliver my soul.

5Gracious *is* the LORD, and righteous; yea, our God *is* merciful.

6The LORD preserveth the simple: I was brought low, and he helped me.

7Return unto thy rest, O my soul; for the LORD hath dealt bountifully with thee.

8For thou hast delivered my soul from death, mine eyes from tears, *and* my feet from falling.

9I will walk before the LORD in the land of the living.

10I believed, therefore have I spoken: I was greatly afflicted:

11I said in my haste, All men *are* liars.

12What shall I render unto the LORD *for* all his benefits toward me?

13I will take the cup of salvation, and call upon the name of the LORD.

14I will pay my vows unto the LORD now in the presence of all his people.

15Precious in the sight of the LORD *is* the death of his saints.

16O LORD, truly I *am* thy servant; I *am* thy servant, *and* the son of thine handmaid: thou hast loosed my bonds.

17I will offer to thee the sacrifice of thanksgiving, and will call upon the name of the LORD.

18I will pay my vows unto the LORD now in the presence of all his people,

19In the courts of the LORD's house, in the midst of thee, O Jerusalem. Praise ye the LORD.

117 O PRAISE the LORD, all ye nations: praise him, all ye people.

2For his merciful kindness is great toward us: and the truth of the LORD *endureth* for ever. Praise ye the LORD.

New International

17It is not the dead who praise the LORD, those who go down to silence;

18it is we who extol the LORD, both now and forevermore.

Praise the LORD.[a]

116 I LOVE the LORD, for he heard my voice; he heard my cry for mercy.

2Because he turned his ear to me, I will call on him as long as I live.

3The cords of death entangled me, the anguish of the grave[b] came upon me; I was overcome by trouble and sorrow.

4Then I called on the name of the LORD: "O LORD, save me!"

5The LORD is gracious and righteous; our God is full of compassion.

6The LORD protects the simplehearted; when I was in great need, he saved me.

7Be at rest once more, O my soul, for the LORD has been good to you.

8For you, O LORD, have delivered my soul from death, my eyes from tears, my feet from stumbling,

9that I may walk before the LORD in the land of the living.

10I believed; therefore[c] I said, "I am greatly afflicted."

11And in my dismay I said, "All men are liars."

12How can I repay the LORD for all his goodness to me?

13I will lift up the cup of salvation and call on the name of the LORD.

14I will fulfill my vows to the LORD in the presence of all his people.

15Precious in the sight of the LORD is the death of his saints.

16O LORD, truly I am your servant; I am your servant, the son of your maidservant[d]; you have freed me from my chains.

17I will sacrifice a thank offering to you and call on the name of the LORD.

18I will fulfill my vows to the LORD in the presence of all his people,

19in the courts of the house of the LORD— in your midst, O Jerusalem.

Praise the LORD.[a]

117 PRAISE THE LORD, all you nations; extol him, all you peoples.

2For great is his love toward us, and the faithfulness of the LORD endures forever.

Praise the LORD.[a]

---

a 18,19,2 Hebrew Hallelu Yah   *b 3 Hebrew Sheol*   *c 10 Or believed even when*   *d 16 Or servant, your faithful son*

Living Bible

17The dead cannot sing praises to Jehovah here on earth,e 18but we can! We praise him forever! Hallelujah! Praise the Lord!

116 I LOVE the Lord because he hears my prayers and answers them. 2Because he bends down and listens, I will pray as long as I breathe! 3Death stared me in the face—I was frightened and sad. 4Then I cried, "Lord, save me!" 5How kind he is! How good he is! So merciful, this God of ours! 6The Lord protects the simple and the childlike; I was facing death and then he saved me. 7Now I can relax. For the Lord has done this wonderful miracle for me. 8He has saved me from death, my eyes from tears, my feet from stumbling. 9I shall live! Yes, in his presence—here on earth!

10, 11In my discouragement I thought, "They are lying when they say I will recover."f 12But now what can I offer Jehovah for all he has done for me? 13I will bring him an offering of wineg and praise his name for saving me. 14I will publicly bring him the sacrifice I vowed I would. 15His loved ones are very precious to him and he does not lightly let them die.h

16O Lord, you have freed me from my bonds and I will serve you forever. 17I will worship you and offer you a sacrifice of thanksgiving. 18, 19Here in the courts of the Temple in Jerusalem, before all the people, I will pay everything I vowed to the Lord. Praise the Lord.

117 PRAISE THE Lord, all nations everywhere. Praise him, all the peoples of the earth. 2For he loves us very dearly, and his truth endures. Praise the Lord.

New Revised Standard

17 The dead do not praise the LORD,
      nor do any that go down into silence.
18 But we will bless the LORD
      from this time on and forevermore.
    Praise the LORD!

Thanksgiving for Recovery from Illness

116 I LOVE the LORD, because he has heard
      my voice and my supplications.
2 Because he inclined his ear to me,
      therefore I will call on him as long as I
      live.
3 The snares of death encompassed me;
      the pangs of Sheol laid hold on me;
      I suffered distress and anguish.
4 Then I called on the name of the LORD:
      "O LORD, I pray, save my life!"

5 Gracious is the LORD, and righteous;
      our God is merciful.
6 The LORD protects the simple;
      when I was brought low, he saved me.
7 Return, O my soul, to your rest,
      for the LORD has dealt bountifully with you.

8 For you have delivered my soul from death,
      my eyes from tears,
      my feet from stumbling.
9 I walk before the LORD
      in the land of the living.
10 I kept my faith, even when I said,
      "I am greatly afflicted";
11 I said in my consternation,
      "Everyone is a liar."

12 What shall I return to the LORD
      for all his bounty to me?
13 I will lift up the cup of salvation
      and call on the name of the LORD,
14 I will pay my vows to the LORD
      in the presence of all his people.
15 Precious in the sight of the LORD
      is the death of his faithful ones.
16 O LORD, I am your servant;
      I am your servant, the child of your serving
      girl.
      You have loosed my bonds.
17 I will offer to you a thanksgiving sacrifice
      and call on the name of the LORD.
18 I will pay my vows to the LORD
      in the presence of all his people,
19 in the courts of the house of the LORD,
      in your midst, O Jerusalem.
    Praise the LORD!

Universal Call to Worship

117 PRAISE THE LORD, all you nations!
      Extol him, all you peoples!
2 For great is his steadfast love toward us,
      and the faithfulness of the LORD endures
      forever.
    Praise the LORD!

---

e 115:17 The dead cannot sing praises to Jehovah here on earth, implied.
f 116:10, 11 In my discouragement I thought, "They are lying when they say I will recover." Literally, "I said in my alarm, all men are liars."   g 116:13 an offering of wine, literally, "the cup of salvation," i.e., the thank offering of wine for saving me.   h 116:15 His loved ones are very precious to him and he does not lightly let them die, literally, "Precious in the sight of the Lord is the death of his saints." See context for the validity of the paraphrase.

King James

118 O GIVE thanks unto the LORD; for *he is* good: because his mercy *endureth* for ever.

2Let Israel now say, that his mercy *endureth* for ever.

3Let the house of Aaron now say, that his mercy *endureth* for ever.

4Let them now that fear the LORD say, that his mercy *endureth* for ever.

5I called upon the LORD in distress: the LORD answered me, *and set me* in a large place.

6The LORD *is* on my side; I will not fear: what can man do unto me?

7The LORD taketh my part with them that help me: therefore shall I see *my desire* upon them that hate me.

8*It is* better to trust in the LORD than to put confidence in man.

9*It is* better to trust in the LORD than to put confidence in princes.

10All nations compassed me about: but in the name of the LORD will I destroy them.

11They compassed me about; yea, they compassed me about: but in the name of the LORD I will destroy them.

12They compassed me about like bees; they are quenched as the fire of thorns: for in the name of the LORD I will destroy them.

13Thou hast thrust sore at me that I might fall: but the LORD helped me.

14The LORD *is* my strength and song, and is become my salvation.

15The voice of rejoicing and salvation *is* in the tabernacles of the righteous: the right hand of the LORD doeth valiantly.

16The right hand of the LORD is exalted: the right hand of the LORD doeth valiantly.

17I shall not die, but live, and declare the works of the LORD.

18The LORD hath chastened me sore: but he hath not given me over unto death.

19Open to me the gates of righteousness: I will go into them, *and* I will praise the LORD:

20This gate of the LORD, into which the righteous shall enter.

21I will praise thee: for thou hast heard me, and art become my salvation.

22The stone *which* the builders refused is become the head *stone* of the corner.

23This is the LORD's doing; it *is* marvellous in our eyes.

24This *is* the day *which* the LORD hath made; we will rejoice and be glad in it.

25Save now, I beseech thee, O LORD: O LORD, I beseech thee, send now prosperity.

26Blessed *be* he that cometh in the name of the LORD: we have blessed you out of the house of the LORD.

New International

118 GIVE THANKS to the LORD, for he is good;
  his love endures forever.

2Let Israel say:
  "His love endures forever."
3Let the house of Aaron say:
  "His love endures forever."
4Let those who fear the LORD say:
  "His love endures forever."

5In my anguish I cried to the LORD,
  and he answered by setting me free.
6The LORD is with me; I will not be afraid.
  What can man do to me?
7The LORD is with me; he is my helper.
  I will look in triumph on my enemies.

8It is better to take refuge in the LORD
  than to trust in man.
9It is better to take refuge in the LORD
  than to trust in princes.

10All the nations surrounded me,
  but in the name of the LORD I cut them off.
11They surrounded me on every side,
  but in the name of the LORD I cut them off.
12They swarmed around me like bees,
  but they died out as quickly as burning thorns;
  in the name of the LORD I cut them off.

13I was pushed back and about to fall,
  but the LORD helped me.
14The LORD is my strength and my song;
  he has become my salvation.

15Shouts of joy and victory
  resound in the tents of the righteous:
  "The LORD's right hand has done mighty things!
16 The LORD's right hand is lifted high;
  the LORD's right hand has done mighty things!"

17I will not die but live,
  and will proclaim what the LORD has done.
18The LORD has chastened me severely,
  but he has not given me over to death.

19Open for me the gates of righteousness;
  I will enter and give thanks to the LORD.
20This is the gate of the LORD
  through which the righteous may enter.
21I will give you thanks, for you answered me;
  you have become my salvation.

22The stone the builders rejected
  has become the capstone;
23the LORD has done this,
  and it is marvelous in our eyes.
24This is the day the LORD has made;
  let us rejoice and be glad in it.

25O LORD, save us;
  O LORD, grant us success.
26Blessed is he who comes in the name of the LORD.
  From the house of the LORD we bless you.[a]

---

a 26 The Hebrew is plural.

Living Bible

118 OH, THANK the Lord, for he's so good! His lovingkindness is forever.

2Let the congregation of Israel praise him with these same words: "His lovingkindness is forever." 3And let the priests of Aaron chant, "His lovingkindness is forever." 4Let the Gentile converts chant, "His lovingkindness is forever."

5In my distress I prayed to the Lord and he answered me and rescued me. 6He is for me! How can I be afraid? What can mere man do to me? 7The Lord is on my side, he will help me. Let those who hate me beware.

8It is better to trust the Lord than to put confidence in men. 9It is better to take refuge in him than in the mightiest king!

10Though all the nations of the world attack me, I will march out behind his banner and destroy them. 11Yes, they surround and attack me; but with his flag flying above me I will cut them off. 12They swarm around me like bees; they blaze against me like a roaring flame. Yet beneath his flag I shall destroy them. 13You did your best to kill me, O my enemy, but the Lord helped me. 14He is my strength and song in the heat of battle, and now he has given me the victory. 15, 16Songs of joy at the news of our rescue are sung in the homes of the godly. The strong arm of the Lord has done glorious things! 17I shall not die, but live to tell of all his deeds. 18The Lord has punished me, but not handed me over to death.

19Open the gates of the Temple[b]—I will go in and give him my thanks. 20Those gates are the way into the presence of the Lord, and the godly enter there. 21O Lord, thank you so much for answering my prayer and saving me.

22The stone rejected by the builders has now become the capstone of the arch![c] 23This is the Lord's doing, and it is marvelous to see! 24This is the day the Lord has made. We will rejoice and be glad in it. 25O Lord, please help us. Save us. Give us success. 26Blessed is the one who is coming, the one sent by the Lord.[d] We bless you from the Temple.

New Revised Standard

A Song of Victory

118 O GIVE thanks to the LORD, for he is good;
his steadfast love endures forever!

2 Let Israel say,
"His steadfast love endures forever."
3 Let the house of Aaron say,
"His steadfast love endures forever."
4 Let those who fear the LORD say,
"His steadfast love endures forever."

5 Out of my distress I called on the LORD;
the LORD answered me and set me in a broad place.
6 With the LORD on my side I do not fear.
What can mortals do to me?
7 The LORD is on my side to help me;
I shall look in triumph on those who hate me.
8 It is better to take refuge in the LORD
than to put confidence in mortals.
9 It is better to take refuge in the LORD
than to put confidence in princes.

10 All nations surrounded me;
in the name of the LORD I cut them off!
11 They surrounded me, surrounded me on every side;
in the name of the LORD I cut them off!
12 They surrounded me like bees;
they blazed[e] like a fire of thorns;
in the name of the LORD I cut them off!
13 I was pushed hard,[f] so that I was falling,
but the LORD helped me.
14 The LORD is my strength and my might;
he has become my salvation.

15 There are glad songs of victory in the tents of the righteous:
"The right hand of the LORD does valiantly;
16 the right hand of the LORD is exalted;
the right hand of the LORD does valiantly."
17 I shall not die, but I shall live,
and recount the deeds of the LORD.
18 The LORD has punished me severely,
but he did not give me over to death.

19 Open to me the gates of righteousness,
that I may enter through them
and give thanks to the LORD.
20 This is the gate of the LORD;
the righteous shall enter through it.

21 I thank you that you have answered me
and have become my salvation.
22 The stone that the builders rejected
has become the chief cornerstone.
23 This is the LORD's doing;
it is marvelous in our eyes.
24 This is the day that the LORD has made;
let us rejoice and be glad in it.[g]
25 Save us, we beseech you, O LORD!
O LORD, we beseech you, give us success!

26 Blessed is the one who comes in the name of the LORD.[h]
We bless you from the house of the LORD.

---

b 118:19 *the gates of the Temple,* literally, "the gates of righteousness."
c 118:22 *the capstone of the arch,* literally, "the head of the corner."
d 118:26 *the one sent by the Lord,* literally, "in the name of the Lord."

e Gk: Heb *were extinguished*   f Gk Syr Jerome: Heb *You pushed me hard*
g Or *in him*   h Or *Blessed in the name of the LORD is the one who comes*

King James

27God *is* the LORD, which hath shown us light: bind the sacrifice with cords, *even* unto the horns of the altar.

28Thou *art* my God, and I will praise thee: *thou art* my God, I will exalt thee.

29O give thanks unto the LORD; for *he is* good: for his mercy *endureth* for ever.

ALEPH.

119 BLESSED *ARE* the undefiled in the way, who walk in the law of the LORD.

2Blessed *are* they that keep his testimonies, *and that* seek him with the whole heart.

3They also do no iniquity: they walk in his ways.

4Thou hast commanded *us* to keep thy precepts diligently.

5O that my ways were directed to keep thy statutes!

6Then shall I not be ashamed, when I have respect unto all thy commandments.

7I will praise thee with uprightness of heart, when I shall have learned thy righteous judgments.

8I will keep thy statutes: O forsake me not utterly.

BETH.

9Wherewithal shall a young man cleanse his way? by taking heed *thereto* according to thy word.

10With my whole heart have I sought thee: O let me not wander from thy commandments.

11Thy word have I hid in mine heart, that I might not sin against thee.

12Blessed *art* thou, O LORD: teach me thy statutes.

13With my lips have I declared all the judgments of thy mouth.

14I have rejoiced in the way of thy testimonies, as *much as* in all riches.

15I will meditate in thy precepts, and have respect unto thy ways.

16I will delight myself in thy statutes: I will not forget thy word.

GIMEL.

17Deal bountifully with thy servant, *that* I may live, and keep thy word.

18Open thou mine eyes, that I may behold wondrous things out of thy law.

19I *am* a stranger in the earth: hide not thy commandments from me.

20My soul breaketh for the longing *that it hath* unto thy judgments at all times.

21Thou hast rebuked the proud *that are* cursed, which do err from thy commandments.

22Remove from me reproach and contempt; for I have kept thy testimonies.

23Princes also did sit *and* speak against me: *but* thy servant did meditate in thy statutes.

24Thy testimonies also *are* my delight *and* my counsellors.

New International

27The LORD is God,
  and he has made his light shine upon us.
With boughs in hand, join in the festal
    procession
  up[a] to the horns of the altar.

28You are my God, and I will give you thanks;
  you are my God, and I will exalt you.

29Give thanks to the LORD, for he is good;
  his love endures forever.

א Aleph

119[b] BLESSED ARE they whose ways are blameless,
  who walk according to the law of the LORD.

2Blessed are they who keep his statutes
  and seek him with all their heart.

3They do nothing wrong;
  they walk in his ways.

4You have laid down precepts
  that are to be fully obeyed.

5Oh, that my ways were steadfast
  in obeying your decrees!

6Then I would not be put to shame
  when I consider all your commands.

7I will praise you with an upright heart
  as I learn your righteous laws.

8I will obey your decrees;
  do not utterly forsake me.

ב Beth

9How can a young man keep his way pure?
  By living according to your word.

10I seek you with all my heart;
  do not let me stray from your commands.

11I have hidden your word in my heart
  that I might not sin against you.

12Praise be to you, O LORD;
  teach me your decrees.

13With my lips I recount
  all the laws that come from your mouth.

14I rejoice in following your statutes
  as one rejoices in great riches.

15I meditate on your precepts
  and consider your ways.

16I delight in your decrees;
  I will not neglect your word.

ג Gimel

17Do good to your servant, and I will live;
  I will obey your word.

18Open my eyes that I may see
  wonderful things in your law.

19I am a stranger on earth;
  do not hide your commands from me.

20My soul is consumed with longing
  for your laws at all times.

21You rebuke the arrogant, who are cursed
  and who stray from your commands.

22Remove from me scorn and contempt,
  for I keep your statutes.

23Though rulers sit together and slander me,
  your servant will meditate on your decrees.

24Your statutes are my delight;
  they are my counselors.

---

[a] 27 Or *Bind the festal sacrifice with ropes / and take it*   [b] This psalm is an acrostic poem; the verses of each stanza begin with the same letter of the Hebrew alphabet.

Living Bible

27, 28Jehovah God is our light. I present to him my sacrifice upon the altar, for you are my God, and I shall give you this thanks and this praise. 29Oh, give thanks to the Lord, for he is so good! For his lovingkindness is forever.

119 HAPPY ARE all who perfectly follow the laws of God. 2Happy are all who search for God, and always do his will, 3rejecting compromise with evil, and walking only in his paths. 4You have given us your laws to obey— 5oh, how I want to follow them consistently. 6Then I will not be disgraced, for I will have a clean record.

7After you have corrected mec I will thank you by living as I should! 8I *will* obey! Oh, don't forsake me and let me slip back into sin again.d

9How can a young man stay pure? By reading your Word and following its rules. 10I have tried my best to find you—don't let me wander off from your instructions. 11I have thought much about your words, and stored them in my heart so that they would hold me back from sin.

12Blessed Lord, teach me your rules. 13I have recited your laws, 14and rejoiced in them more than in riches. 15I will meditate upon them and give them my full respect. 16I will delight in them and not forget them.

17Bless me with lifee so that I can continue to obey you. 18Open my eyes to see wonderful things in your Word. 19I am but a pilgrim here on earth: how I need a map—and your commands are my chart and guide. 20I long for your instructions more than I can tell.

21You rebuke those cursed proud ones who refuse your commands— 22don't let them scorn me for obeying you. 23For even princes sit and talk against me, but I will continue in your plans. 24Your laws are both my light and my counselors.

New Revised Standard

27 The Lord is God,
      and he has given us light.
    Bind the festal procession with branches,
      up to the horns of the altar.f

28 You are my God, and I will give thanks to
        you;
      you are my God, I will extol you.

29 O give thanks to the Lord, for he is good,
      for his steadfast love endures forever.

The Glories of God's Law

119 HAPPY ARE those whose way is
          blameless,
      who walk in the law of the Lord.
 2 Happy are those who keep his decrees,
      who seek him with their whole heart,
 3 who also do no wrong,
      but walk in his ways.
 4 You have commanded your precepts
      to be kept diligently.
 5 O that my ways may be steadfast
      in keeping your statutes!
 6 Then I shall not be put to shame,
      having my eyes fixed on all your
        commandments.
 7 I will praise you with an upright heart,
      when I learn your righteous ordinances.
 8 I will observe your statutes;
      do not utterly forsake me.

 9 How can young people keep their way pure?
      By guarding it according to your word.
10 With my whole heart I seek you;
      do not let me stray from your
        commandments.
11 I treasure your word in my heart,
      so that I may not sin against you.
12 Blessed are you, O Lord;
      teach me your statutes.
13 With my lips I declare
      all the ordinances of your mouth.
14 I delight in the way of your decrees
      as much as in all riches.
15 I will meditate on your precepts,
      and fix my eyes on your ways.
16 I will delight in your statutes;
      I will not forget your word.

17 Deal bountifully with your servant,
      so that I may live and observe your word.
18 Open my eyes, so that I may behold
      wondrous things out of your law.
19 I live as an alien in the land;
      do not hide your commandments from me.
20 My soul is consumed with longing
      for your ordinances at all times.
21 You rebuke the insolent, accursed ones,
      who wander from your commandments;
22 take away from me their scorn and contempt,
      for I have kept your decrees.
23 Even though princes sit plotting against me,
      your servant will meditate on your statutes.
24 Your decrees are my delight,
      they are my counselors.

---

c 119:7 *After you have corrected me*, literally, "when I learn [have experienced] your righteous judgments." d 119:8 *Oh, don't forsake me and let me slip back into sin again*, literally, "Oh, forsake me not utterly." e 119:17 *Bless me with life*, literally, "deal bountifully that I may live."

f Meaning of Heb uncertain

King James

DALETH.

25My soul cleaveth unto the dust: quicken thou me according to thy word.

26I have declared my ways, and thou heardest me: teach me thy statutes.

27Make me to understand the way of thy precepts: so shall I talk of thy wondrous works.

28My soul melteth for heaviness: strengthen thou me according unto thy word.

29Remove from me the way of lying: and grant me thy law graciously.

30I have chosen the way of truth: thy judgments have I laid *before me*.

31I have stuck unto thy testimonies: O LORD, put me not to shame.

32I will run the way of thy commandments, when thou shalt enlarge my heart.

HE.

33Teach me, O LORD, the way of thy statutes; and I shall keep it *unto* the end.

34Give me understanding, and I shall keep thy law; yea, I shall observe it with *my* whole heart.

35Make me to go in the path of thy commandments; for therein do I delight.

36Incline my heart unto thy testimonies, and not to covetousness.

37Turn away mine eyes from beholding vanity; *and* quicken thou me in thy way.

38Stablish thy word unto thy servant, who *is devoted* to thy fear.

39Turn away my reproach which I fear: for thy judgments *are* good.

40Behold, I have longed after thy precepts: quicken me in thy righteousness.

VAU.

41Let thy mercies come also unto me, O LORD, *even* thy salvation, according to thy word.

42So shall I have wherewith to answer him that reproacheth me: for I trust in thy word.

43And take not the word of truth utterly out of my mouth; for I have hoped in thy judgments.

44So shall I keep thy law continually for ever and ever.

45And I will walk at liberty: for I seek thy precepts.

46I will speak of thy testimonies also before kings, and will not be ashamed.

47And I will delight myself in thy commandments, which I have loved.

48My hands also will I lift up unto thy commandments, which I have loved; and I will meditate in thy statutes.

ZAIN.

49Remember the word unto thy servant, upon which thou hast caused me to hope.

50This *is* my comfort in my affliction: for thy word hath quickened me.

51The proud have had me greatly in derision: *yet* have I not declined from thy law.

52I remembered thy judgments of old, O LORD; and have comforted myself.

53Horror hath taken hold upon me because of the wicked that forsake thy law.

New International

ד Daleth

25I am laid low in the dust;
 preserve my life according to your word.

26I recounted my ways and you answered me;
 teach me your decrees.

27Let me understand the teaching of your precepts;
 then I will meditate on your wonders.

28My soul is weary with sorrow;
 strengthen me according to your word.

29Keep me from deceitful ways;
 be gracious to me through your law.

30I have chosen the way of truth;
 I have set my heart on your laws.

31I hold fast to your statutes, O LORD;
 do not let me be put to shame.

32I run in the path of your commands,
 for you have set my heart free.

ה He

33Teach me, O LORD, to follow your decrees;
 then I will keep them to the end.

34Give me understanding, and I will keep your law
 and obey it with all my heart.

35Direct me in the path of your commands,
 for there I find delight.

36Turn my heart toward your statutes
 and not toward selfish gain.

37Turn my eyes away from worthless things;
 preserve my life according to your word.[a]

38Fulfill your promise to your servant,
 so that you may be feared.

39Take away the disgrace I dread,
 for your laws are good.

40How I long for your precepts!
 Preserve my life in your righteousness.

ו Waw

41May your unfailing love come to me, O LORD,
 your salvation according to your promise;

42then I will answer the one who taunts me,
 for I trust in your word.

43Do not snatch the word of truth from my mouth,
 for I have put my hope in your laws.

44I will always obey your law,
 for ever and ever.

45I will walk about in freedom,
 for I have sought out your precepts.

46I will speak of your statutes before kings
 and will not be put to shame,

47for I delight in your commands
 because I love them.

48I lift up my hands to[b] your commands, which I love,
 and I meditate on your decrees.

ז Zayin

49Remember your word to your servant,
 for you have given me hope.

50My comfort in my suffering is this:
 Your promise preserves my life.

51The arrogant mock me without restraint,
 but I do not turn from your law.

52I remember your ancient laws, O LORD,
 and I find comfort in them.

53Indignation grips me because of the wicked,
 who have forsaken your law.

---

[a] 37 Two manuscripts of the Masoretic Text and Dead Sea Scrolls; most manuscripts of the Masoretic Text *life in your way*   [b] 48 Or *for*

Living Bible

25I am completely discouraged—I lie in the dust. Revive me by your Word. 26I told you my plans and you replied. Now give me your instructions. 27Make me understand what you want; for then I shall see your miracles.

28I weep with grief; my heart is heavy with sorrow; encourage and cheer me with your words. 29, 30Keep me far from every wrong; help me, undeserving as I am, to obey your laws, for I have chosen to do right. 31I cling to your commands and follow them as closely as I can. Lord, don't let me make a mess of things. 32If you will only help me to want your will, then I will follow your laws even more closely.

33, 34Just tell me what to do and I will do it, Lord. As long as I live I'll wholeheartedly obey. 35Make me walk along the right paths for I know how delightful they really are.

36Help me to prefer obedience to making money! 37Turn me away from wanting any other plan than yours.c Revive my heart toward you. 38Reassure me that your promises are for me, for I trust and revere you.

39How I dread being mocked for obeying, for your laws are right and good. 40, 41, 42I long to obey them! Therefore in fairness renew my life, for this was your promise—yes, Lord, to save me! Now spare me by your kindness and your love. Then I will have an answer for those who taunt me, for I trust your promises.

43May I never forget your words; for they are my only hope. 44, 45, 46Therefore I will keep on obeying you forever and forever, free within the limits of your laws. I will speak to kings about their value, and they will listen with interest and respect.

47How I love your laws! How I enjoy your commands! 48"Come, come to me," I call to them, for I love them and will let them fill my life.

49, 50Never forget your promises to me your servant, for they are my only hope. They give me strength in all my troubles; how they refresh and revive me! 51Proud men hold me in contempt for obedience to God, but I stand unmoved. 52From my earliest youth I have tried to obey you; your Word has been my comfort.

53I am very angry with those who spurn your commands. 54For these laws of yours have been my source

New Revised Standard

25 My soul clings to the dust;
    revive me according to your word.
26 When I told of my ways, you answered me;
    teach me your statutes.
27 Make me understand the way of your
      precepts,
    and I will meditate on your wondrous
      works.
28 My soul melts away for sorrow;
    strengthen me according to your word.
29 Put false ways far from me;
    and graciously teach me your law.
30 I have chosen the way of faithfulness;
    I set your ordinances before me.
31 I cling to your decrees, O LORD;
    let me not be put to shame.
32 I run the way of your commandments,
    for you enlarge my understanding.

33 Teach me, O LORD, the way of your statutes,
    and I will observe it to the end.
34 Give me understanding, that I may keep your
      law
    and observe it with my whole heart.
35 Lead me in the path of your commandments,
    for I delight in it.
36 Turn my heart to your decrees,
    and not to selfish gain.
37 Turn my eyes from looking at vanities;
    give me life in your ways.
38 Confirm to your servant your promise,
    which is for those who fear you.
39 Turn away the disgrace that I dread,
    for your ordinances are good.
40 See, I have longed for your precepts;
    in your righteousness give me life.

41 Let your steadfast love come to me, O LORD,
    your salvation according to your promise.
42 Then I shall have an answer for those who
      taunt me,
    for I trust in your word.
43 Do not take the word of truth utterly out of
      my mouth,
    for my hope is in your ordinances.
44 I will keep your law continually,
    forever and ever.
45 I shall walk at liberty,
    for I have sought your precepts.
46 I will also speak of your decrees before kings,
    and shall not be put to shame;
47 I find my delight in your commandments,
    because I love them.
48 I revere your commandments, which I love,
    and I will meditate on your statutes.

49 Remember your word to your servant,
    in which you have made me hope.
50 This is my comfort in my distress,
    that your promise gives me life.
51 The arrogant utterly deride me,
    but I do not turn away from your law.
52 When I think of your ordinances from of old,
    I take comfort, O LORD.
53 Hot indignation seizes me because of the
      wicked,
    those who forsake your law.

---

c 119:37 from wanting any other plan than yours, literally, "from beholding vanity."

King James

54Thy statutes have been my songs in the house of my pilgrimage.

55I have remembered thy name, O LORD, in the night, and have kept thy law.

56This I had, because I kept thy precepts.

CHETH.

57*Thou art* my portion, O LORD: I have said that I would keep thy words.

58I entreated thy favour with *my* whole heart: be merciful unto me according to thy word.

59I thought on my ways, and turned my feet unto thy testimonies.

60I made haste, and delayed not to keep thy commandments.

61The bands of the wicked have robbed me: *but* I have not forgotten thy law.

62At midnight I will rise to give thanks unto thee because of thy righteous judgments.

63I *am* a companion of all *them* that fear thee, and of them that keep thy precepts.

64The earth, O LORD, is full of thy mercy: teach me thy statutes.

TETH.

65Thou hast dealt well with thy servant, O LORD, according unto thy word.

66Teach me good judgment and knowledge: for I have believed thy commandments.

67Before I was afflicted I went astray: but now have I kept thy word.

68Thou *art* good, and doest good; teach me thy statutes.

69The proud have forged a lie against me: *but* I will keep thy precepts with *my* whole heart.

70Their heart is as fat as grease; *but* I delight in thy law.

71*It is* good for me that I have been afflicted; that I might learn thy statutes.

72The law of thy mouth *is* better unto me than thousands of gold and silver.

JOD.

73Thy hands have made me and fashioned me: give me understanding, that I may learn thy commandments.

74They that fear thee will be glad when they see me; because I have hoped in thy word.

75I know, O LORD, that thy judgments *are* right, and *that* thou in faithfulness hast afflicted me.

76Let, I pray thee, thy merciful kindness be for my comfort, according to thy word unto thy servant.

77Let thy tender mercies come unto me, that I may live: for thy law *is* my delight.

78Let the proud be ashamed; for they dealt perversely with me without a cause: *but* I will meditate in thy precepts.

79Let those that fear thee turn unto me, and those that have known thy testimonies.

80Let my heart be sound in thy statutes; that I be not ashamed.

CAPH.

81My soul fainteth for thy salvation: *but* I hope in thy word.

82Mine eyes fail for thy word, saying, When wilt thou comfort me?

New International

54Your decrees are the theme of my song
  wherever I lodge.

55In the night I remember your name, O LORD,
  and I will keep your law.

56This has been my practice:
  I obey your precepts.

ח Heth

57You are my portion, O LORD;
  I have promised to obey your words.

58I have sought your face with all my heart;
  be gracious to me according to your promise.

59I have considered my ways
  and have turned my steps to your statutes.

60I will hasten and not delay
  to obey your commands.

61Though the wicked bind me with ropes,
  I will not forget your law.

62At midnight I rise to give you thanks
  for your righteous laws.

63I am a friend to all who fear you,
  to all who follow your precepts.

64The earth is filled with your love, O LORD;
  teach me your decrees.

ט Teth

65Do good to your servant
  according to your word, O LORD.

66Teach me knowledge and good judgment,
  for I believe in your commands.

67Before I was afflicted I went astray,
  but now I obey your word.

68You are good, and what you do is good;
  teach me your decrees.

69Though the arrogant have smeared me with lies,
  I keep your precepts with all my heart.

70Their hearts are callous and unfeeling,
  but I delight in your law.

71It was good for me to be afflicted
  so that I might learn your decrees.

72The law from your mouth is more precious to
    me
  than thousands of pieces of silver and gold.

י Yodh

73Your hands made me and formed me;
  give me understanding to learn your
    commands.

74May those who fear you rejoice when they see
    me,
  for I have put my hope in your word.

75I know, O LORD, that your laws are righteous,
  and in faithfulness you have afflicted me.

76May your unfailing love be my comfort,
  according to your promise to your servant.

77Let your compassion come to me that I may
    live,
  for your law is my delight.

78May the arrogant be put to shame for wronging
    me without cause;
  but I will meditate on your precepts.

79May those who fear you turn to me,
  those who understand your statutes.

80May my heart be blameless toward your
    decrees,
  that I may not be put to shame.

כ Kaph

81My soul faints with longing for your salvation,
  but I have put my hope in your word.

82My eyes fail, looking for your promise;
  I say, "When will you comfort me?"

Living Bible

of joy and singing through all these years of my earthly pilgrimage. ⁵⁵I obey them even at night and keep my thoughts, O Lord, on you. ⁵⁶What a blessing this has been to me—to constantly obey.

⁵⁷Jehovah is mine! And I promise to obey! ⁵⁸With all my heart I want your blessings. Be merciful just as you promised. ⁵⁹, ⁶⁰I thought about the wrong direction in which I was headed, and turned around and came running back to you. ⁶¹Evil men have tried to drag me into sin, but I am firmly anchored to your laws.

⁶²At midnight I will rise to give my thanks to you for your good laws. ⁶³Anyone is my brother who fears and trusts the Lord and obeys him. ⁶⁴O Lord, the earth is full of your lovingkindness! Teach me your good paths.

⁶⁵Lord, I am overflowing with your blessings, just as you promised. ⁶⁶Now teach me good judgment as well as knowledge. For your laws are my guide. ⁶⁷I used to wander off until you punished me; now I closely follow all you say. ⁶⁸You are good and do only good; make me follow your lead.

⁶⁹Proud men have made up lies about me, but the truth is that I obey your laws with all my heart. ⁷⁰Their minds are dull and stupid, but I have sense enough to follow you.

⁷¹, ⁷²The punishment you gave me was the best thing that could have happened to me, for it taught me to pay attention to your laws. They are more valuable to me than millions in silver and gold!

⁷³You made my body, Lord; now give me sense to heed your laws. ⁷⁴All those who fear and trust in you will welcome me because I too am trusting in your Word.

⁷⁵, ⁷⁶, ⁷⁷I know, O Lord, that your decisions are right and that your punishment was right and did me good. Now let your lovingkindness comfort me, just as you promised. Surround me with your tender mercies, that I may live. For your law is my delight.

⁷⁸Let the proud be disgraced, for they have cut me down with all their lies. But I will concentrate my thoughts upon your laws.

⁷⁹Let all others join me, who trust and fear you, and we will discuss your laws. ⁸⁰Help me to love your every wish; then I will never have to be ashamed of myself.

⁸¹I faint for your salvation; but I expect your help, for you have promised it. ⁸²My eyes are straining to see your promises come true. When will you comfort me with your help? ⁸³I am shriveled like a wineskin in the smoke,

New Revised Standard

54 Your statutes have been my songs
    wherever I make my home.
55 I remember your name in the night, O Lord,
    and keep your law.
56 This blessing has fallen to me,
    for I have kept your precepts.

57 The Lord is my portion;
    I promise to keep your words.
58 I implore your favor with all my heart;
    be gracious to me according to your
        promise.
59 When I think of your ways,
    I turn my feet to your decrees;
60 I hurry and do not delay
    to keep your commandments.
61 Though the cords of the wicked ensnare me,
    I do not forget your law.
62 At midnight I rise to praise you,
    because of your righteous ordinances.
63 I am a companion of all who fear you,
    of those who keep your precepts.
64 The earth, O Lord, is full of your steadfast
        love;
    teach me your statutes.

65 You have dealt well with your servant,
    O Lord, according to your word.
66 Teach me good judgment and knowledge,
    for I believe in your commandments.
67 Before I was humbled I went astray,
    but now I keep your word.
68 You are good and do good;
    teach me your statutes.
69 The arrogant smear me with lies,
    but with my whole heart I keep your
        precepts.
70 Their hearts are fat and gross,
    but I delight in your law.
71 It is good for me that I was humbled,
    so that I might learn your statutes.
72 The law of your mouth is better to me
    than thousands of gold and silver pieces.

73 Your hands have made and fashioned me;
    give me understanding that I may learn your
        commandments.
74 Those who fear you shall see me and rejoice,
    because I have hoped in your word.
75 I know, O Lord, that your judgments are
        right,
    and that in faithfulness you have humbled
        me.
76 Let your steadfast love become my comfort
    according to your promise to your servant.
77 Let your mercy come to me, that I may live;
    for your law is my delight.
78 Let the arrogant be put to shame,
    because they have subverted me with guile;
    as for me, I will meditate on your precepts.
79 Let those who fear you turn to me,
    so that they may know your decrees.
80 May my heart be blameless in your statutes,
    so that I may not be put to shame.

81 My soul languishes for your salvation;
    I hope in your word.
82 My eyes fail with watching for your promise;
    I ask, "When will you comfort me?"

King James

83For I am become like a bottle in the smoke; *yet* do I not forget thy statutes.

84How many *are* the days of thy servant? when wilt thou execute judgment on them that persecute me?

85The proud have digged pits for me, which *are* not after thy law.

86All thy commandments *are* faithful: they persecute me wrongfully; help thou me.

87They had almost consumed me upon earth; but I forsook not thy precepts.

88Quicken me after thy lovingkindness; so shall I keep the testimony of thy mouth.

LAMED.

89For ever, O LORD, thy word is settled in heaven.

90Thy faithfulness *is* unto all generations: thou hast established the earth, and it abideth.

91They continue this day according to thine ordinances: for all *are* thy servants.

92Unless thy law *had been* my delights, I should then have perished in mine affliction.

93I will never forget thy precepts: for with them thou hast quickened me.

94I *am* thine, save me; for I have sought thy precepts.

95The wicked have waited for me to destroy me: *but* I will consider thy testimonies.

96I have seen an end of all perfection: *but* thy commandment *is* exceeding broad.

MEM.

97O how love I thy law! it *is* my meditation all the day.

98Thou through thy commandments hast made me wiser than mine enemies: for they *are* ever with me.

99I have more understanding than all my teachers: for thy testimonies *are* my meditation.

100I understand more than the ancients, because I keep thy precepts.

101I have refrained my feet from every evil way, that I might keep thy word.

102I have not departed from thy judgments: for thou hast taught me.

103How sweet are thy words unto my taste! *yea, sweeter* than honey to my mouth!

104Through thy precepts I get understanding: therefore I hate every false way.

NUN.

105Thy word *is* a lamp unto my feet, and a light unto my path.

106I have sworn, and I will perform *it*, that I will keep thy righteous judgments.

107I am afflicted very much: quicken me, O LORD, according unto thy word.

108Accept, I beseech thee, the freewill offerings of my mouth, O LORD, and teach me thy judgments.

109My soul *is* continually in my hand: yet do I not forget thy law.

110The wicked have laid a snare for me: yet I erred not from thy precepts.

111Thy testimonies have I taken as an heritage for ever: for they *are* the rejoicing of my heart.

112I have inclined mine heart to perform thy statutes always, *even unto* the end.

New International

83Though I am like a wineskin in the smoke, I do not forget your decrees.

84How long must your servant wait? When will you punish my persecutors?

85The arrogant dig pitfalls for me, contrary to your law.

86All your commands are trustworthy; help me, for men persecute me without cause.

87They almost wiped me from the earth, but I have not forsaken your precepts.

88Preserve my life according to your love, and I will obey the statutes of your mouth.

ל Lamedh

89Your word, O LORD, is eternal; it stands firm in the heavens.

90Your faithfulness continues through all generations; you established the earth, and it endures.

91Your laws endure to this day, for all things serve you.

92If your law had not been my delight, I would have perished in my affliction.

93I will never forget your precepts, for by them you have preserved my life.

94Save me, for I am yours; I have sought out your precepts.

95The wicked are waiting to destroy me, but I will ponder your statutes.

96To all perfection I see a limit; but your commands are boundless.

מ Mem

97Oh, how I love your law! I meditate on it all day long.

98Your commands make me wiser than my enemies, for they are ever with me.

99I have more insight than all my teachers, for I meditate on your statutes.

100I have more understanding than the elders, for I obey your precepts.

101I have kept my feet from every evil path so that I might obey your word.

102I have not departed from your laws, for you yourself have taught me.

103How sweet are your words to my taste, sweeter than honey to my mouth!

104I gain understanding from your precepts; therefore I hate every wrong path.

נ Nun

105Your word is a lamp to my feet and a light for my path.

106I have taken an oath and confirmed it, that I will follow your righteous laws.

107I have suffered much; preserve my life, O LORD, according to your word.

108Accept, O LORD, the willing praise of my mouth, and teach me your laws.

109Though I constantly take my life in my hands, I will not forget your law.

110The wicked have set a snare for me, but I have not strayed from your precepts.

111Your statutes are my heritage forever; they are the joy of my heart.

112My heart is set on keeping your decrees to the very end.

Living Bible

exhausted with waiting. But still I cling to your laws and obey them. 84How long must I wait before you punish those who persecute me? 85, 86These proud men who hate your truth and laws have dug deep pits for me to fall in. Their lies have brought me into deep trouble. Help me, for you love only truth. 87They had almost finished me off, yet I refused to yield and disobey your laws. 88In your kindness, spare my life; then I can continue to obey you.

89Forever, O Lord, your Word stands firm in heaven. 90, 91Your faithfulness extends to every generation, like the earth you created; it endures by your decree, for everything serves your plans.

92I would have despaired and perished unless your laws had been my deepest delight. 93I will never lay aside your laws, for you have used them to restore my joy and health. 94I am yours! Save me! For I have tried to live according to your desires. 95Though the wicked hide along the way to kill me, I will quietly keep my mind upon your promises.

96Nothing is perfect except your words. 97Oh, how I love them. I think about them all day long. 98They make me wiser than my enemies, because they are my constant guide. 99Yes, wiser than my teachers, for I am ever thinking of your rules. 100They make me even wiser than the aged.

101I have refused to walk the paths of evil for I will remain obedient to your Word. 102, 103No, I haven't turned away from what you taught me; your words are sweeter than honey. 104And since only your rules can give me wisdom and understanding, no wonder I hate every false teaching.

105Your words are a flashlight to light the path ahead of me, and keep me from stumbling. 106I've said it once and I'll say it again and again: I will obey these wonderful laws of yours.

107I am close to death at the hands of my enemies; oh, give me back my life again, just as you promised me. 108Accept my grateful thanks and teach me your desires. 109My life hangs in the balance, but I will not give up obedience to your laws. 110The wicked have set their traps for me along your path, but I will not turn aside. 111Your laws are my joyous treasure forever. 112I am determined to obey you until I die.

New Revised Standard

83 For I have become like a wineskin in the
    smoke,
    yet I have not forgotten your statutes.
84 How long must your servant endure?
    When will you judge those who persecute
    me?
85 The arrogant have dug pitfalls for me;
    they flout your law.
86 All your commandments are enduring;
    I am persecuted without cause; help me!
87 They have almost made an end of me on
    earth;
    but I have not forsaken your precepts.
88 In your steadfast love spare my life,
    so that I may keep the decrees of your
    mouth.

89 The Lord exists forever;
    your word is firmly fixed in heaven.
90 Your faithfulness endures to all generations;
    you have established the earth, and it stands
    fast.
91 By your appointment they stand today,
    for all things are your servants.
92 If your law had not been my delight,
    I would have perished in my misery.
93 I will never forget your precepts,
    for by them you have given me life.
94 I am yours; save me,
    for I have sought your precepts.
95 The wicked lie in wait to destroy me,
    but I consider your decrees.
96 I have seen a limit to all perfection,
    but your commandment is exceedingly
    broad.

97 Oh, how I love your law!
    It is my meditation all day long.
98 Your commandment makes me wiser than my
    enemies,
    for it is always with me.
99 I have more understanding than all my
    teachers,
    for your decrees are my meditation.
100 I understand more than the aged,
    for I keep your precepts.
101 I hold back my feet from every evil way,
    in order to keep your word.
102 I do not turn away from your ordinances,
    for you have taught me.
103 How sweet are your words to my taste,
    sweeter than honey to my mouth!
104 Through your precepts I get understanding;
    therefore I hate every false way.

105 Your word is a lamp to my feet
    and a light to my path.
106 I have sworn an oath and confirmed it,
    to observe your righteous ordinances.
107 I am severely afflicted;
    give me life, O Lord, according to your
    word.
108 Accept my offerings of praise, O Lord,
    and teach me your ordinances.
109 I hold my life in my hand continually,
    but I do not forget your law.
110 The wicked have laid a snare for me,
    but I do not stray from your precepts.
111 Your decrees are my heritage forever;
    they are the joy of my heart.
112 I incline my heart to perform your statutes
    forever, to the end.

King James

SAMECH.

113I hate *vain* thoughts: but thy law do I love.

114Thou *art* my hiding place and my shield: I hope in thy word.

115Depart from me, ye evildoers: for I will keep the commandments of my God.

116Uphold me according unto thy word, that I may live: and let me not be ashamed of my hope.

117Hold thou me up, and I shall be safe: and I will have respect unto thy statutes continually.

118Thou hast trodden down all them that err from thy statutes: for their deceit *is* falsehood.

119Thou puttest away all the wicked of the earth *like* dross: therefore I love thy testimonies.

120My flesh trembleth for fear of thee; and I am afraid of thy judgments.

AIN.

121I have done judgment and justice: leave me not to mine oppressors.

122Be surety for thy servant for good: let not the proud oppress me.

123Mine eyes fail for thy salvation, and for the word of thy righteousness.

124Deal with thy servant according unto thy mercy, and teach me thy statutes.

125I *am* thy servant; give me understanding, that I may know thy testimonies.

126*It is* time for *thee*, LORD, to work: *for* they have made void thy law.

127Therefore I love thy commandments above gold; yea, above fine gold.

128Therefore I esteem all *thy* precepts *concerning* all *things to be* right; *and* I hate every false way.

PE.

129Thy testimonies *are* wonderful: therefore doth my soul keep them.

130The entrance of thy words giveth light; it giveth understanding unto the simple.

131I opened my mouth, and panted: for I longed for thy commandments.

132Look thou upon me, and be merciful unto me, as thou usest to do unto those that love thy name.

133Order my steps in thy word: and let not any iniquity have dominion over me.

134Deliver me from the oppression of man: so will I keep thy precepts.

135Make thy face to shine upon thy servant; and teach me thy statutes.

136Rivers of waters run down mine eyes, because they keep not thy law.

TZADDI.

137Righteous *art* thou, O LORD, and upright *are* thy judgments.

138Thy testimonies *that* thou hast commanded *are* righteous and very faithful.

139My zeal hath consumed me, because mine enemies have forgotten thy words.

140Thy word *is* very pure: therefore thy servant loveth it.

141I *am* small and despised: *yet* do not I forget thy precepts.

New International

ס Samekh

113I hate double-minded men,
   but I love your law.

114You are my refuge and my shield;
   I have put my hope in your word.

115Away from me, you evildoers,
   that I may keep the commands of my God!

116Sustain me according to your promise, and I
      will live;
   do not let my hopes be dashed.

117Uphold me, and I will be delivered;
   I will always have regard for your decrees.

118You reject all who stray from your decrees,
   for their deceitfulness is in vain.

119All the wicked of the earth you discard like
      dross;
   therefore I love your statutes.

120My flesh trembles in fear of you;
   I stand in awe of your laws.

ע Ayin

121I have done what is righteous and just;
   do not leave me to my oppressors.

122Ensure your servant's well-being;
   let not the arrogant oppress me.

123My eyes fail, looking for your salvation,
   looking for your righteous promise.

124Deal with your servant according to your love
   and teach me your decrees.

125I am your servant; give me discernment
   that I may understand your statutes.

126It is time for you to act, O LORD;
   your law is being broken.

127Because I love your commands
   more than gold, more than pure gold,

128and because I consider all your precepts right,
   I hate every wrong path.

פ Pe

129Your statutes are wonderful;
   therefore I obey them.

130The unfolding of your words gives light;
   it gives understanding to the simple.

131I open my mouth and pant,
   longing for your commands.

132Turn to me and have mercy on me,
   as you always do to those who love your
      name.

133Direct my footsteps according to your word;
   let no sin rule over me.

134Redeem me from the oppression of men,
   that I may obey your precepts.

135Make your face shine upon your servant
   and teach me your decrees.

136Streams of tears flow from my eyes,
   for your law is not obeyed.

צ Tsadhe

137Righteous are you, O LORD,
   and your laws are right.

138The statutes you have laid down are righteous;
   they are fully trustworthy.

139My zeal wears me out,
   for my enemies ignore your words.

140Your promises have been thoroughly tested,
   and your servant loves them.

141Though I am lowly and despised,
   I do not forget your precepts.

Living Bible

113I hate those who are undecided whether or not to obey you; but my choice is clear—I love your law. 114You are my refuge and my shield, and your promises are my only source of hope. 115Begone, you evil-minded men. Don't try to stop me from obeying God's commands. 116Lord, you promised to let me live! Never let it be said that God failed me. 117Hold me safe above the heads of all my enemies; then I can continue to obey your laws.

118But you have rejected all who reject your laws. They are only fooling themselves. 119The wicked are the scum you skim off and throw away; no wonder I love to obey your laws! 120I tremble in fear of you; I fear your punishments.

121Don't leave me to the mercy of my enemies, for I have done what is right; I've been perfectly fair. 122Commit yourself to bless me! Don't let the proud oppress me! 123My eyes grow dim with longing for you to fulfill your wonderful promise to rescue me. 124Lord, deal with me in lovingkindness, and teach me, your servant, to obey; 125for I am your servant; therefore give me common sense to apply your rules to everything I do.

126Lord, it is time for you to act. For these evil men have violated your laws, 127while I love your commandments more than the finest gold. 128Every law of God is right, whatever it concerns. I hate every other way.

129Your laws are wonderful; no wonder I obey them. 130As your plan unfolds, even the simple can understand it. 131No wonder I wait expectantly for each of your commands.

132Come and have mercy on me as is your way with those who love you. 133Guide me with your laws so that I will not be overcome by evil. 134Rescue me from the oppression of evil men; then I can obey you. 135Look down in love upon me and teach me all your laws. 136I weep because your laws are disobeyed.

137O Lord, you are just and your punishments are fair. 138Your demands are just and right. 139I am indignant and angry because of the way my enemies have disregarded your laws. 140I have thoroughly tested your promises and that is why I love them so much. 141I am worthless and despised, but I don't despise your laws.

New Revised Standard

113 I hate the double-minded,
        but I love your law.
114 You are my hiding place and my shield;
        I hope in your word.
115 Go away from me, you evildoers,
        that I may keep the commandments of my
            God.
116 Uphold me according to your promise, that I
            may live,
        and let me not be put to shame in my hope.
117 Hold me up, that I may be safe
        and have regard for your statutes
            continually.
118 You spurn all who go astray from your
            statutes;
        for their cunning is in vain.
119 All the wicked of the earth you count as
            dross;
        therefore I love your decrees.
120 My flesh trembles for fear of you,
        and I am afraid of your judgments.

121 I have done what is just and right;
        do not leave me to my oppressors.
122 Guarantee your servant's well-being;
        do not let the godless oppress me.
123 My eyes fail from watching for your salvation,
        and for the fulfillment of your righteous
            promise.
124 Deal with your servant according to your
            steadfast love,
        and teach me your statutes.
125 I am your servant; give me understanding,
        so that I may know your decrees.
126 It is time for the LORD to act,
        for your law has been broken.
127 Truly I love your commandments
        more than gold, more than fine gold.
128 Truly I direct my steps by all your precepts;a
        I hate every false way.

129 Your decrees are wonderful;
        therefore my soul keeps them.
130 The unfolding of your words gives light;
        it imparts understanding to the simple.
131 With open mouth I pant,
        because I long for your commandments.
132 Turn to me and be gracious to me,
        as is your custom toward those who love
            your name.
133 Keep my steps steady according to your
            promise,
        and never let iniquity have dominion over
            me.
134 Redeem me from human oppression,
        that I may keep your precepts.
135 Make your face shine upon your servant,
        and teach me your statutes.
136 My eyes shed streams of tears
        because your law is not kept.

137 You are righteous, O LORD,
        and your judgments are right.
138 You have appointed your decrees in
            righteousness
        and in all faithfulness.
139 My zeal consumes me
        because my foes forget your words.
140 Your promise is well tried,
        and your servant loves it.
141 I am small and despised,
        yet I do not forget your precepts.

a Gk Jerome: Meaning of Heb uncertain

King James

142Thy righteousness *is* an everlasting righteousness, and thy law *is* the truth.

143Trouble and anguish have taken hold on me: *yet* thy commandments *are* my delights.

144The righteousness of thy testimonies *is* everlasting: give me understanding, and I shall live.

KOPH.

145I cried with *my* whole heart; hear me, O LORD: I will keep thy statutes.

146I cried unto thee; save me, and I shall keep thy testimonies.

147I prevented the dawning of the morning, and cried: I hoped in thy word.

148Mine eyes prevent the *night* watches, that I might meditate in thy word.

149Hear my voice according unto thy lovingkindness: O LORD, quicken me according to thy judgment.

150They draw nigh that follow after mischief: they are far from thy law.

151Thou *art* near, O LORD; and all thy commandments *are* truth.

152Concerning thy testimonies, I have known of old that thou hast founded them for ever.

RESH.

153Consider mine affliction, and deliver me: for I do not forget thy law.

154Plead my cause, and deliver me: quicken me according to thy word.

155Salvation *is* far from the wicked: for they seek not thy statutes.

156Great *are* thy tender mercies, O LORD: quicken me according to thy judgments.

157Many *are* my persecutors and mine enemies; *yet* do I not decline from thy testimonies.

158I beheld the transgressors, and was grieved; because they kept not thy word.

159Consider how I love thy precepts: quicken me, O LORD, according to thy lovingkindness.

160Thy word *is* true *from* the beginning: and every one of thy righteous judgments *endureth* for ever.

SCHIN.

161Princes have persecuted me without a cause: but my heart standeth in awe of thy word.

162I rejoice at thy word, as one that findeth great spoil.

163I hate and abhor lying: *but* thy law do I love.

164Seven times a day do I praise thee because of thy righteous judgments.

165Great peace have they which love thy law: and nothing shall offend them.

166LORD, I have hoped for thy salvation, and done thy commandments.

167My soul hath kept thy testimonies; and I love them exceedingly.

168I have kept thy precepts and thy testimonies: for all my ways *are* before thee.

TAU

169Let my cry come near before thee, O LORD: give me understanding according to thy word.

170Let my supplication come before thee: deliver me according to thy word.

171My lips shall utter praise, when thou hast taught me thy statutes.

New International

142Your righteousness is everlasting
    and your law is true.

143Trouble and distress have come upon me,
    but your commands are my delight.

144Your statutes are forever right;
    give me understanding that I may live.

ק Qoph

145I call with all my heart; answer me, O LORD,
    and I will obey your decrees.

146I call out to you; save me
    and I will keep your statutes.

147I rise before dawn and cry for help;
    I have put my hope in your word.

148My eyes stay open through the watches of the
        night,
    that I may meditate on your promises.

149Hear my voice in accordance with your love;
    preserve my life, O LORD, according to your
        laws.

150Those who devise wicked schemes are near,
    but they are far from your law.

151Yet you are near, O LORD,
    and all your commands are true.

152Long ago I learned from your statutes
    that you established them to last forever.

ר Resh

153Look upon my suffering and deliver me,
    for I have not forgotten your law.

154Defend my cause and redeem me;
    preserve my life according to your promise.

155Salvation is far from the wicked,
    for they do not seek out your decrees.

156Your compassion is great, O LORD;
    preserve my life according to your laws.

157Many are the foes who persecute me,
    but I have not turned from your statutes.

158I look on the faithless with loathing,
    for they do not obey your word.

159See how I love your precepts;
    preserve my life, O LORD, according to your
        love.

160All your words are true;
    all your righteous laws are eternal.

ש Sin and Shin

161Rulers persecute me without cause,
    but my heart trembles at your word.

162I rejoice in your promise
    like one who finds great spoil.

163I hate and abhor falsehood
    but I love your law.

164Seven times a day I praise you
    for your righteous laws.

165Great peace have they who love your law,
    and nothing can make them stumble.

166I wait for your salvation, O LORD,
    and I follow your commands.

167I obey your statutes,
    for I love them greatly.

168I obey your precepts and your statutes,
    for all my ways are known to you.

ת Taw

169May my cry come before you, O LORD;
    give me understanding according to your
        word.

170May my supplication come before you;
    deliver me according to your promise.

171May my lips overflow with praise,
    for you teach me your decrees.

Living Bible

142Your justice is eternal for your laws are perfectly fair. 143In my distress and anguish, your commandments comfort me. 144Your laws are always fair; help me to understand them and I shall live.

145I am praying with great earnestness; answer me, O Lord, and I will obey your laws. 146"Save me," I cry, "for I am obeying." 147Early in the morning, before the sun is up, I am praying and pointing out how much I trust in you. 148I stay awake through the night to think about your promises. 149Because you are so loving and kind, listen to me and make me well again.

150Here come these lawless men to attack me; 151but you are near, O Lord; all your commandments are based on truth. 152I have known from earliest days that your will never changes.

153Look down upon my sorrows and rescue me, for I am obeying your commands. 154Yes, rescue me and give me back my life again just as you have promised. 155The wicked are far from salvation for they do not care for your laws. 156Lord, how great is your mercy; oh, give me back my life again.

157My enemies are so many. They try to make me disobey, but I have not swerved from your will. 158I loathed these traitors because they care nothing for your laws. 159Lord, see how much I really love your demands. Now give me back my life and health because you are so kind. 160There is utter truth in all your laws; your decrees are eternal.

161Great men have persecuted me, though they have no reason to, but I stand in awe of only your words. 162I rejoice in your laws like one who finds a great treasure. 163How I hate all falsehood but how I love your laws. 164I will praise you seven times a day because of your wonderful laws.

165Those who love your laws have great peace of heart and mind and do not stumble. 166I long for your salvation, Lord, and so I have obeyed your laws. 167I have looked for your commandments and I love them very much; 168yes, I have searched for them. You know this because everything I do is known to you.

169O Lord, listen to my prayers; give me the common sense you promised. 170Hear my prayers; rescue me as you said you would. 171I praise you for letting me learn your laws. 172I will sing about their wonder, for each of

New Revised Standard

142 Your righteousness is an everlasting
    righteousness,
  and your law is the truth.
143 Trouble and anguish have come upon me,
  but your commandments are my delight.
144 Your decrees are righteous forever;
  give me understanding that I may live.

145 With my whole heart I cry; answer me,
    O Lord.
  I will keep your statutes.
146 I cry to you; save me,
  that I may observe your decrees.
147 I rise before dawn and cry for help;
  I put my hope in your words.
148 My eyes are awake before each watch of the
    night,
  that I may meditate on your promise.
149 In your steadfast love hear my voice;
  O Lord, in your justice preserve my life.
150 Those who persecute me with evil purpose
    draw near;
  they are far from your law.
151 Yet you are near, O Lord,
  and all your commandments are true.
152 Long ago I learned from your decrees
  that you have established them forever.

153 Look on my misery and rescue me,
  for I do not forget your law.
154 Plead my cause and redeem me;
  give me life according to your promise.
155 Salvation is far from the wicked,
  for they do not seek your statutes.
156 Great is your mercy, O Lord;
  give me life according to your justice.
157 Many are my persecutors and my adversaries,
  yet I do not swerve from your decrees.
158 I look at the faithless with disgust,
  because they do not keep your commands.
159 Consider how I love your precepts;
  preserve my life according to your steadfast
    love.
160 The sum of your word is truth;
  and every one of your righteous ordinances
    endures forever.

161 Princes persecute me without cause,
  but my heart stands in awe of your words.
162 I rejoice at your word
  like one who finds great spoil.
163 I hate and abhor falsehood,
  but I love your law.
164 Seven times a day I praise you
  for your righteous ordinances.
165 Great peace have those who love your law;
  nothing can make them stumble.
166 I hope for your salvation, O Lord,
  and I fulfill your commandments.
167 My soul keeps your decrees;
  I love them exceedingly.
168 I keep your precepts and decrees,
  for all my ways are before you.

169 Let my cry come before you, O Lord;
  give me understanding according to your
    word.
170 Let my supplication come before you;
  deliver me according to your promise.
171 My lips will pour forth praise,
  because you teach me your statutes.

King James

172My tongue shall speak of thy word: for all thy commandments *are* righteousness.

173Let thine hand help me; for I have chosen thy precepts.

174I have longed for thy salvation, O LORD; and thy law *is* my delight.

175Let my soul live, and it shall praise thee; and let thy judgments help me.

176I have gone astray like a lost sheep; seek thy servant; for I do not forget thy commandments.

A Song of degrees.

120 IN MY distress I cried unto the LORD, and he heard me.

2Deliver my soul, O LORD, from lying lips, *and* from a deceitful tongue.

3What shall be given unto thee? or what shall be done unto thee, thou false tongue?

4Sharp arrows of the mighty, with coals of juniper.

5Woe is me, that I sojourn in Mesech, *that* I dwell in the tents of Kedar!

6My soul hath long dwelt with him that hateth peace.

7I *am for* peace: but when I speak, they *are* for war.

A Song of degrees.

121 I WILL lift up mine eyes unto the hills, from whence cometh my help.

2My help *cometh* from the LORD, which made heaven and earth.

3He will not suffer thy foot to be moved: he that keepeth thee will not slumber.

4Behold, he that keepeth Israel shall neither slumber nor sleep.

5The LORD *is* thy keeper: the LORD *is* thy shade upon thy right hand.

6The sun shall not smite thee by day, nor the moon by night.

7The LORD shall preserve thee from all evil: he shall preserve thy soul.

8The LORD shall preserve thy going out and thy coming in from this time forth, and even for evermore.

A Song of degrees of David.

122 I WAS glad when they said unto me, Let us go into the house of the LORD.

2Our feet shall stand within thy gates, O Jerusalem.

3Jerusalem is builded as a city that is compact together:

4Whither the tribes go up, the tribes of the LORD, unto the testimony of Israel, to give thanks unto the name of the LORD.

New International

172May my tongue sing of your word,
    for all your commands are righteous.

173May your hand be ready to help me,
    for I have chosen your precepts.

174I long for your salvation, O LORD,
    and your law is my delight.

175Let me live that I may praise you,
    and may your laws sustain me.

176I have strayed like a lost sheep.
    Seek your servant,
    for I have not forgotten your commands.

A song of ascents.

120 I CALL on the LORD in my distress,
        and he answers me.

2Save me, O LORD, from lying lips
    and from deceitful tongues.

3What will he do to you,
    and what more besides, O deceitful tongue?

4He will punish you with a warrior's sharp
        arrows,
    with burning coals of the broom tree.

5Woe to me that I dwell in Meshech,
    that I live among the tents of Kedar!

6Too long have I lived
    among those who hate peace.

7I am a man of peace;
    but when I speak, they are for war.

A song of ascents.

121 I LIFT up my eyes to the hills—
        where does my help come from?

2My help comes from the LORD,
    the Maker of heaven and earth.

3He will not let your foot slip—
    he who watches over you will not slumber;

4indeed, he who watches over Israel
    will neither slumber nor sleep.

5The LORD watches over you—
    the LORD is your shade at your right hand;

6the sun will not harm you by day,
    nor the moon by night.

7The LORD will keep you from all harm—
    he will watch over your life;

8the LORD will watch over your coming and
        going
    both now and forevermore.

A song of ascents. Of David.

122 I REJOICED with those who said to me,
        "Let us go to the house of the LORD."

2Our feet are standing
    in your gates, O Jerusalem.

3Jerusalem is built like a city
    that is closely compacted together.

4That is where the tribes go up,
    the tribes of the LORD,
    to praise the name of the LORD
    according to the statute given to Israel.

Living Bible

them is just. 173Stand ready to help me because I have chosen to follow your will. 174O Lord, I have longed for your salvation, and your law is my delight. 175If you will let me live, I will praise you; let your laws assist me.

176I have wandered away like a lost sheep; come and find me for I have not turned away from your commandments.

120 IN MY troubles I pled with God to help me and he did!
2Deliver me, O Lord, from liars. 3O lying tongue, what shall be your fate? 4You shall be pierced with sharp arrows and burned with glowing coals.a

5, 6My troubles pile high among these haters of the Lord, these men of Meshech and Kedar. I am tired of being here among these men who hate peace. 7I am for peace, but they are for war, and my voice goes unheeded in their councils.

121 SHALL I look to the mountain gods for help? 2No! My help is from Jehovah who made the mountains! And the heavens too! 3, 4He will never let me stumble, slip or fall. For he is always watching, never sleeping.

5Jehovah himself is caring for you! He is your defender.b 6He protects you day and night. 7He keeps you from all evil, and preserves your life. 8He keeps his eye upon you as you come and go, and always guards you.

122 I WAS glad for the suggestion of going to Jerusalem, to the Temple of the Lord. 2, 3Now we are standing here inside the crowded city. 4All Israel—Jehovah's people—have come to worship as the law requires, to thank and praise the Lord. 5Look!

New Revised Standard

172 My tongue will sing of your promise,
   for all your commandments are right.
173 Let your hand be ready to help me,
   for I have chosen your precepts.
174 I long for your salvation, O LORD,
   and your law is my delight.
175 Let me live that I may praise you,
   and let your ordinances help me.
176 I have gone astray like a lost sheep; seek out
   your servant,
   for I do not forget your commandments.

Prayer for Deliverance from Slanderers

A Song of Ascents.

120 IN MY distress I cry to the LORD,
   that he may answer me:
2 "Deliver me, O LORD,
   from lying lips,
   from a deceitful tongue."

3 What shall be given to you?
   And what more shall be done to you,
   you deceitful tongue?
4 A warrior's sharp arrows,
   with glowing coals of the broom tree!

5 Woe is me, that I am an alien in Meshech,
   that I must live among the tents of Kedar.
6 Too long have I had my dwelling
   among those who hate peace.
7 I am for peace;
   but when I speak,
   they are for war.

Assurance of God's Protection

A Song of Ascents.

121 I LIFT up my eyes to the hills—
   from where will my help come?
2 My help comes from the LORD,
   who made heaven and earth.

3 He will not let your foot be moved;
   he who keeps you will not slumber.
4 He who keeps Israel
   will neither slumber nor sleep.

5 The LORD is your keeper;
   the LORD is your shade at your right hand.
6 The sun shall not strike you by day,
   nor the moon by night.

7 The LORD will keep you from all evil;
   he will keep your life.
8 The LORD will keep
   your going out and your coming in
   from this time on and forevermore.

Song of Praise and Prayer for Jerusalem

A Song of Ascents. Of David.

122 I WAS glad when they said to me,
   "Let us go to the house of the LORD!"
2 Our feet are standing
   within your gates, O Jerusalem.

3 Jerusalem—built as a city
   that is bound firmly together.
4 To it the tribes go up,
   the tribes of the LORD,
   as was decreed for Israel,
   to give thanks to the name of the LORD.

a 120:4 *with glowing coals,* literally, "with coals of the broom tree."
b 121:5 *He is your defender,* literally, "your shade at your right hand."

King James

5For there are set thrones of judgment, the thrones of the house of David.

6Pray for the peace of Jerusalem: they shall prosper that love thee.

7Peace be within thy walls, *and* prosperity within thy palaces.

8For my brethren and companions' sakes, I will now say, Peace *be* within thee.

9Because of the house of the LORD our God I will seek thy good.

A Song of degrees.

123 UNTO THEE lift I up mine eyes, O thou that dwellest in the heavens.

2Behold, as the eyes of servants *look* unto the hand of their masters, *and* as the eyes of a maiden unto the hand of her mistress; so our eyes *wait* upon the LORD our God, until that he have mercy upon us.

3Have mercy upon us, O LORD, have mercy upon us: for we are exceedingly filled with contempt.

4Our soul is exceedingly filled with the scorning of those that are at ease, *and* with the contempt of the proud.

A Song of degrees of David.

124 IF *IT had not been* the LORD who was on our side, now may Israel say;

2If *it had not been* the LORD who was on our side, when men rose up against us:

3Then they had swallowed us up quick, when their wrath was kindled against us:

4Then the waters had overwhelmed us, the stream had gone over our soul:

5Then the proud waters had gone over our soul.

6Blessed *be* the LORD, who hath not given us *as* a prey to their teeth.

7Our soul is escaped as a bird out of the snare of the fowlers: the snare is broken, and we are escaped.

8Our help *is* in the name of the LORD, who made heaven and earth.

A Song of degrees.

125 THEY THAT trust in the LORD *shall be* as mount Zion, *which* cannot be removed, *but* abideth for ever.

2As the mountains *are* round about Jerusalem, so the LORD *is* round about his people from henceforth even for ever.

New International

5There the thrones for judgment stand,
  the thrones of the house of David.

6Pray for the peace of Jerusalem:
  "May those who love you be secure.
7May there be peace within your walls
  and security within your citadels."
8For the sake of my brothers and friends,
  I will say, "Peace be within you."
9For the sake of the house of the LORD our God,
  I will seek your prosperity.

A song of ascents.

123 I LIFT up my eyes to you,
  to you whose throne is in heaven.
2As the eyes of slaves look to the hand of their
  master,
  as the eyes of a maid look to the hand of her
  mistress,
  so our eyes look to the LORD our God,
  till he shows us his mercy.

3Have mercy on us, O LORD, have mercy on us,
  for we have endured much contempt.
4We have endured much ridicule from the proud,
  much contempt from the arrogant.

A song of ascents. Of David.

124 IF THE LORD had not been on our side—
  let Israel say—
2if the LORD had not been on our side
  when men attacked us,
3when their anger flared against us,
  they would have swallowed us alive;
4the flood would have engulfed us,
  the torrent would have swept over us,
5the raging waters
  would have swept us away.

6Praise be to the LORD,
  who has not let us be torn by their teeth.
7We have escaped like a bird
  out of the fowler's snare;
  the snare has been broken,
  and we have escaped.
8Our help is in the name of the LORD,
  the Maker of heaven and earth.

A song of ascents.

125 THOSE WHO trust in the LORD are like
  Mount Zion,
  which cannot be shaken but endures forever.
2As the mountains surround Jerusalem,
  so the LORD surrounds his people
  both now and forevermore.

Living Bible

There are the judges holding court beside the city gates, deciding all the people's arguments.

6Pray for the peace of Jerusalem. May all who love this city prosper. 7O Jerusalem, may there be peace within your walls and prosperity in your palaces. 8This I ask for the sake of all my brothers and my friends who live here; 9and may there be peace as a protection to the Temple of the Lord.

123 O GOD enthroned in heaven, I lift my eyes to you. 2We look to Jehovah our God for his mercy and kindness just as a servant keeps his eyes upon his master or a slave girl watches her mistress for the slightest signal. 3, 4Have mercy on us, Lord, have mercy. For we have had our fill of contempt and of the scoffing of the rich and proud.

124 IF THE Lord had not been on our side (let all Israel admit it), if the Lord had not been on our side, 2, 3we would have been swallowed alive by our enemies, destroyed by their anger. 4, 5We would have drowned beneath the flood of these men's fury and pride.

6Blessed be Jehovah who has not let them devour us. 7We have escaped with our lives as a bird from a hunter's snare. The snare is broken and we are free! 8Our help is from the Lord who made heaven and earth.

125 THOSE WHO trust in the Lord are steady as Mount Zion, unmoved by any circumstance. 2Just as the mountains surround and protect Jerusalem, so the Lord surrounds and protects his people. 3For

New Revised Standard

5 For there the thrones for judgment were set up,
  the thrones of the house of David.

6 Pray for the peace of Jerusalem:
  "May they prosper who love you.
7 Peace be within your walls,
  and security within your towers."
8 For the sake of my relatives and friends
  I will say, "Peace be within you."
9 For the sake of the house of the LORD our God,
  I will seek your good.

Supplication for Mercy
  A Song of Ascents.

123 TO YOU I lift up my eyes,
  O you who are enthroned in the heavens!
2 As the eyes of servants
  look to the hand of their master,
  as the eyes of a maid
  to the hand of her mistress,
  so our eyes look to the LORD our God,
  until he has mercy upon us.

3 Have mercy upon us, O LORD, have mercy upon us,
  for we have had more than enough of contempt.
4 Our soul has had more than its fill
  of the scorn of those who are at ease,
  of the contempt of the proud.

Thanksgiving for Israel's Deliverance
  A Song of Ascents. Of David.

124 IF IT had not been the LORD who was on our side
  —let Israel now say—
2 if it had not been the LORD who was on our side,
  when our enemies attacked us,
3 then they would have swallowed us up alive,
  when their anger was kindled against us;
4 then the flood would have swept us away,
  the torrent would have gone over us;
5 then over us would have gone
  the raging waters.

6 Blessed be the LORD,
  who has not given us
  as prey to their teeth.
7 We have escaped like a bird
  from the snare of the fowlers;
  the snare is broken,
  and we have escaped.

8 Our help is in the name of the LORD,
  who made heaven and earth.

The Security of God's People
  A Song of Ascents.

125 THOSE WHO trust in the LORD are like Mount Zion,
  which cannot be moved, but abides forever.
2 As the mountains surround Jerusalem,
  so the LORD surrounds his people,
  from this time on and forevermore.

King James

3For the rod of the wicked shall not rest upon the lot of the righteous; lest the righteous put forth their hands unto iniquity.

4Do good, O LORD, unto *those that be* good, and to *them that are* upright in their hearts.

5As for such as turn aside unto their crooked ways, the LORD shall lead them forth with the workers of iniquity: *but* peace *shall be* upon Israel.

A Song of degrees.

126 WHEN THE LORD turned again the captivity of Zion, we were like them that dream.

2Then was our mouth filled with laughter, and our tongue with singing: then said they among the heathen, The LORD hath done great things for them.

3The LORD hath done great things for us; *whereof* we are glad.

4Turn again our captivity, O LORD, as the streams in the south.

5They that sow in tears shall reap in joy.

6He that goeth forth and weepeth, bearing precious seed, shall doubtless come again with rejoicing, bringing his sheaves *with him.*

A Song of degrees for Solomon.

127 EXCEPT THE LORD build the house, they labour in vain that build it: except the LORD keep the city, the watchman waketh *but* in vain.

2It is vain for you to rise up early, to sit up late, to eat the bread of sorrows: *for* so he giveth his beloved sleep.

3Lo, children *are* an heritage of the LORD *and* the fruit of the womb *is* his reward.

4As arrows *are* in the hand of a mighty man; so *are* children of the youth.

5Happy *is* the man that hath his quiver full of them: they shall not be ashamed, but they shall speak with the enemies in the gate.

A Song of degrees.

128 BLESSED IS every one that feareth the LORD; that walketh in his ways.

2For thou shalt eat the labour of thine hands: happy *shalt* thou *be*, and *it shall be* well with thee.

3Thy wife *shall be* as a fruitful vine by the sides of thine house: thy children like olive plants round about thy table.

4Behold, that thus shall the man be blessed that feareth the LORD.

New International

3The scepter of the wicked will not remain
  over the land allotted to the righteous,
for then the righteous might use
  their hands to do evil.

4Do good, O LORD, to those who are good,
  to those who are upright in heart.
5But those who turn to crooked ways
  the LORD will banish with the evildoers.

Peace be upon Israel.

A song of ascents.

126 WHEN THE LORD brought back the
  captives toa Zion,
we were like men who dreamed.b
2Our mouths were filled with laughter,
  our tongues with songs of joy.
Then it was said among the nations,
  "The LORD has done great things for them."
3The LORD has done great things for us,
  and we are filled with joy.

4Restore our fortunes,c O LORD,
  like streams in the Negev.
5Those who sow in tears
  will reap with songs of joy.
6He who goes out weeping,
  carrying seed to sow,
will return with songs of joy,
  carrying sheaves with him.

A song of ascents. Of Solomon.

127 UNLESS THE LORD builds the house,
  its builders labor in vain.
Unless the LORD watches over the city,
  the watchmen stand guard in vain.
2In vain you rise early
  and stay up late,
toiling for food to eat—
  for he grants sleep tod those he loves.

3Sons are a heritage from the LORD,
  children a reward from him.
4Like arrows in the hands of a warrior
  are sons born in one's youth.
5Blessed is the man
  whose quiver is full of them.
They will not be put to shame
  when they contend with their enemies in the
    gate.

A song of ascents.

128 BLESSED ARE all who fear the LORD,
  who walk in his ways.
2You will eat the fruit of your labor;
  blessings and prosperity will be yours.
3Your wife will be like a fruitful vine
  within your house;
your sons will be like olive shoots
  around your table.
4Thus is the man blessed
  who fears the LORD.

---

a 1 Or LORD *restored the fortunes of*   b 1 Or *men restored to health*   c 4 Or *Bring back our captives*   d 2 Or *eat— / for while they sleep he provides for*

Living Bible

the wicked shall not rule the godly, lest the godly be forced to do wrong. 4O Lord, do good to those who are good, whose hearts are right with the Lord; 5but lead evil men to execution. And let Israel have quietness and peace.

126 WHEN JEHOVAH brought back his exiles to Jerusalem, it was like a dream! 2How we laughed and sang for joy. And the other nations said, "What amazing things the Lord has done for them."

3Yes, glorious things! What wonder! What joy! 4May we be refreshed*e* as by streams in the desert.

5Those who sow tears shall reap joy. 6Yes, they go out weeping, carrying seed for sowing, and return singing, carrying their sheaves.

127 UNLESS THE Lord builds a house, the builders' work is useless. Unless the Lord protects a city, sentries do no good. 2It is senseless for you to work so hard from early morning until late at night, fearing you will starve to death; for God wants his loved ones to get their proper rest.

3Children are a gift from God; they are his reward. 4Children born to a young man are like sharp arrows to defend him.

5Happy is the man who has his quiver full of them. That man shall have the help he needs when arguing with his enemies.*f*

128 BLESSINGS ON all who reverence and trust the Lord—on all who obey him! 2Their reward shall be prosperity and happiness. 3Your wife shall be contented in your home. And look at all those children! There they sit around the dinner table as vigorous and healthy as young olive trees. 4That is God's reward to those who reverence and trust him.

New Revised Standard

3 For the scepter of wickedness shall not rest
   on the land allotted to the righteous,
 so that the righteous might not stretch out
   their hands to do wrong.
4 Do good, O LORD, to those who are good,
   and to those who are upright in their hearts.
5 But those who turn aside to their own crooked
   ways
 the LORD will lead away with evildoers.
 Peace be upon Israel!

A Harvest of Joy

A Song of Ascents.

126 WHEN THE LORD restored the fortunes of Zion,g
 we were like those who dream.
2 Then our mouth was filled with laughter,
   and our tongue with shouts of joy;
 then it was said among the nations,
   "The LORD has done great things for them."
3 The LORD has done great things for us,
   and we rejoiced.

4 Restore our fortunes, O LORD,
   like the watercourses in the Negeb.
5 May those who sow in tears
   reap with shouts of joy.
6 Those who go out weeping,
   bearing the seed for sowing,
 shall come home with shouts of joy,
   carrying their sheaves.

God's Blessings in the Home

A Song of Ascents. Of Solomon.

127 UNLESS THE LORD builds the house,
 those who build it labor in vain.
 Unless the LORD guards the city,
   the guard keeps watch in vain.
2 It is in vain that you rise up early
   and go late to rest,
 eating the bread of anxious toil;
   for he gives sleep to his beloved.h
3 Sons are indeed a heritage from the LORD,
   the fruit of the womb a reward.
4 Like arrows in the hand of a warrior
   are the sons of one's youth.
5 Happy is the man who has
   his quiver full of them.
 He shall not be put to shame
   when he speaks with his enemies in the
   gate.

The Happy Home of the Faithful

A Song of Ascents.

128 HAPPY IS everyone who fears the LORD,
 who walks in his ways.
2 You shall eat the fruit of the labor of your
   hands;
   you shall be happy, and it shall go well
   with you.

3 Your wife will be like a fruitful vine
   within your house;
 your children will be like olive shoots
   around your table.
4 Thus shall the man be blessed
   who fears the LORD.

---

e 126:4 May we be refreshed, literally, "Restore our fortunes, Lord."
f 127:5 when arguing with his enemies, literally, "when they speak with their enemies in the gate."

g Or *brought back those who returned to Zion* h Or *for he provides for his beloved during sleep*

King James

5The LORD shall bless thee out of Zion: and thou shalt see the good of Jerusalem all the days of thy life.

6Yea, thou shalt see thy children's children, *and* peace upon Israel.

A Song of degrees.

129 MANY A time have they afflicted me from my youth, may Israel now say:

2Many a time have they afflicted me from my youth: yet they have not prevailed against me.

3The plowers plowed upon my back: they made long their furrows.

4The LORD *is* righteous: he hath cut asunder the cords of the wicked.

5Let them all be confounded and turned back that hate Zion.

6Let them be as the grass *upon* the housetops, which withereth afore it groweth up:

7Wherewith the mower filleth not his hand; nor he that bindeth sheaves his bosom.

8Neither do they which go by say, The blessing of the LORD *be* upon you: we bless you in the name of the LORD.

A Song of degrees.

130 OUT OF the depths have I cried unto thee, O LORD.

2Lord, hear my voice: let thine ears be attentive to the voice of my supplications.

3If thou, LORD, shouldest mark iniquities, O Lord, who shall stand?

4But *there is* forgiveness with thee, that thou mayest be feared.

5I wait for the LORD, my soul doth wait, and in his word do I hope.

6My soul *waiteth* for the Lord more than they that watch for the morning: *I say, more than* they that watch for the morning.

7Let Israel hope in the LORD: for with the LORD *there is* mercy, and with him *is* plenteous redemption.

8And he shall redeem Israel from all his iniquities.

A Song of degrees of David.

131 LORD, MY heart is not haughty, nor mine eyes lofty: neither do I exercise myself in great matters, or in things too high for me.

2Surely I have behaved and quieted myself, as a child that is weaned of his mother: my soul *is* even as a weaned child.

3Let Israel hope in the LORD from henceforth and for ever.

New International

5May the LORD bless you from Zion
  all the days of your life;
may you see the prosperity of Jerusalem,
6 and may you live to see your children's
    children.

Peace be upon Israel.

A song of ascents.

129 THEY HAVE greatly oppressed me from my youth—
  let Israel say—
2they have greatly oppressed me from my youth,
  but they have not gained the victory over me.
3Plowmen have plowed my back
  and made their furrows long.
4But the LORD is righteous;
  he has cut me free from the cords of the
    wicked.

5May all who hate Zion
  be turned back in shame.
6May they be like grass on the roof,
  which withers before it can grow;
7with it the reaper cannot fill his hands,
  nor the one who gathers fill his arms.
8May those who pass by not say,
  "The blessing of the LORD be upon you;
  we bless you in the name of the LORD."

A song of ascents.

130 OUT OF the depths I cry to you, O LORD;
2 O Lord, hear my voice.
Let your ears be attentive
  to my cry for mercy.

3If you, O LORD, kept a record of sins,
  O Lord, who could stand?
4But with you there is forgiveness;
  therefore you are feared.

5I wait for the LORD, my soul waits,
  and in his word I put my hope.
6My soul waits for the Lord
  more than watchmen wait for the morning,
  more than watchmen wait for the morning.

7O Israel, put your hope in the LORD,
  for with the LORD is unfailing love
  and with him is full redemption.
8He himself will redeem Israel
  from all their sins.

A song of ascents. Of David.

131 MY HEART is not proud, O LORD, my eyes are not haughty;
I do not concern myself with great matters
  or things too wonderful for me.
2But I have stilled and quieted my soul;
  like a weaned child with its mother,
  like a weaned child is my soul within me.

3O Israel, put your hope in the LORD
  both now and forevermore.

Living Bible

5May the Lord continually bless you with heaven's blessingsa as well as with human joys.b 6May you live to enjoy your grandchildren! And may God bless Israel!

129 PERSECUTED FROM my earliest youth (Israel is speaking), 2and faced with never-ending discrimination—but not destroyed! My enemies have never been able to finish me off!

3, 4Though my back is cut to ribbons with their whips, the Lord is good. For he has snapped the chains that evil men had bound me with.

5May all who hate the Jews be brought to ignomini-ous defeat. 6, 7May they be as grass in shallow soil, turning sere and yellow when half grown, ignored by the reaper, despised by the binder. 8And may those passing by refuse to bless them by saying, "Jehovah's blessings be upon you; we bless you in Jehovah's name."

130 O LORD, from the depths of despair I cry for your help: 2"Hear me! Answer! Help me!"

3, 4Lord, if you keep in mind our sins then who can ever get an answer to his prayers? But you forgive! What an awesome thing this is! 5That is why I wait expectant-ly, trusting God to help, for he has promised. 6I long for him more than sentinels long for the dawn.

7O Israel, hope in the Lord; for he is loving and kind, and comes to us with armloads of salvation. 8He himself shall ransom Israel from her slavery to sin.

131 LORD, I am not proud and haughty. I don't think myself better than others. I don't pre-tend to "know it all." 2I am quiet now before the Lord, just as a child who is weaned from the breast. Yes, my begging has been stilled.

3O Israel, you too should quietly trust in the Lord—now, and always.

New Revised Standard

5 The LORD bless you from Zion.
      May you see the prosperity of Jerusalem
         all the days of your life.
6 May you see your children's children.
      Peace be upon Israel!

Prayer for the Downfall of Israel's Enemies
A Song of Ascents.

129 "OFTEN HAVE they attacked me from
         my youth"
      —let Israel now say—
2 "often have they attacked me from my youth,
      yet they have not prevailed against me.
3 The plowers plowed on my back;
      they made their furrows long."
4 The LORD is righteous;
      he has cut the cords of the wicked.
5 May all who hate Zion
      be put to shame and turned backward.
6 Let them be like the grass on the housetops
      that withers before it grows up,
7 with which reapers do not fill their hands
      or binders of sheaves their arms,
8 while those who pass by do not say,
      "The blessing of the LORD be upon you!
      We bless you in the name of the LORD!"

Waiting for Divine Redemption
A Song of Ascents.

130 OUT OF the depths I cry to you,
         O LORD.
2   Lord, hear my voice!
   Let your ears be attentive
      to the voice of my supplications!

3 If you, O LORD, should mark iniquities,
      Lord, who could stand?
4 But there is forgiveness with you,
      so that you may be revered.

5 I wait for the LORD, my soul waits,
      and in his word I hope;
6 my soul waits for the Lord
      more than those who watch for the morning,
      more than those who watch for the morning.

7 O Israel, hope in the LORD!
      For with the LORD there is steadfast love,
      and with him is great power to redeem.
8 It is he who will redeem Israel
      from all its iniquities.

Song of Quiet Trust
A Song of Ascents. Of David.

131 O LORD, my heart is not lifted up,
         my eyes are not raised too high;
   I do not occupy myself with things
      too great and too marvelous for me.
2 But I have calmed and quieted my soul,
      like a weaned child with its mother;
      my soul is like the weaned child that is with
         me.c

3 O Israel, hope in the LORD
      from this time on and forevermore.

---

a 128:5 with heaven's blessings, literally, "from Zion." b 128:5 as well as with human joys, literally, "of Jerusalem."

c Or my soul within me is like a weaned child

King James

A Song of degrees.

132 LORD, REMEMBER David, *and* all his afflictions:

2How he sware unto the LORD, *and* vowed unto the
mighty *God* of Jacob;

3Surely I will not come into the tabernacle of my
house, nor go up into my bed;

4I will not give sleep to mine eyes, *or* slumber to mine
eyelids,

5Until I find out a place for the LORD, an habitation
for the mighty *God* of Jacob.

6Lo, we heard of it at Ephratah: we found it in the
fields of the wood.

7We will go into his tabernacles: we will worship at
his footstool.

8Arise, O LORD, into thy rest; thou, and the ark of thy
strength.

9Let thy priests be clothed with righteousness; and let
thy saints shout for joy.

10For thy servant David's sake turn not away the face
of thine anointed.

11The LORD hath sworn *in* truth unto David; he will
not turn from it; Of the fruit of thy body will I set upon
thy throne.

12If thy children will keep my covenant and my testimony that I shall teach them, their children shall also sit
upon thy throne for evermore.

13For the LORD hath chosen Zion; he hath desired *it*
for his habitation.

14This *is* my rest for ever: here will I dwell; for I have
desired it.

15I will abundantly bless her provision: I will satisfy
her poor with bread.

16I will also clothe her priests with salvation: and her
saints shall shout aloud for joy.

17There will I make the horn of David to bud: I have
ordained a lamp for mine anointed.

18His enemies will I clothe with shame: but upon
himself shall his crown flourish.

A Song of degrees of David.

133 BEHOLD, HOW good and how pleasant *it
is* for brethren to dwell together in unity!

2*It is* like the precious ointment upon the head, that
ran down upon the beard, *even* Aaron's beard: that went
down to the skirts of his garments;

3As the dew of Hermon, *and as the dew* that descended upon the mountains of Zion: for there the LORD commanded the blessing, *even* life for evermore.

New International

A song of ascents.

132 O LORD, remember David
and all the hardships he endured.

2He swore an oath to the LORD
and made a vow to the Mighty One of Jacob:
3"I will not enter my house
or go to my bed;
4I will allow no sleep to my eyes,
no slumber to my eyelids,
5till I find a place for the LORD,
a dwelling for the Mighty One of Jacob."

6We heard it in Ephrathah,
we came upon it in the fields of Jaar[a;b]
7"Let us go to his dwelling place;
let us worship at his footstool—
8arise, O LORD, and come to your resting place,
you and the ark of your might.
9May your priests be clothed with righteousness;
may your saints sing for joy."

10For the sake of David your servant,
do not reject your anointed one.

11The LORD swore an oath to David,
a sure oath that he will not revoke:
"One of your own descendants
I will place on your throne—
12if your sons keep my covenant
and the statutes I teach them,
then their sons will sit
on your throne for ever and ever."

13For the LORD has chosen Zion,
he has desired it for his dwelling:
14"This is my resting place for ever and ever;
here I will sit enthroned, for I have desired
it—
15I will bless her with abundant provisions;
her poor will I satisfy with food.
16I will clothe her priests with salvation,
and her saints will ever sing for joy.

17"Here I will make a horn[c] grow for David
and set up a lamp for my anointed one.
18I will clothe his enemies with shame,
but the crown on his head will be
resplendent."

A song of ascents. Of David.

133 HOW GOOD and pleasant it is
when brothers live together in unity!

2It is like precious oil poured on the head,
running down on the beard,
running down on Aaron's beard,
down upon the collar of his robes.
3It is as if the dew of Hermon
were falling on Mount Zion.
For there the LORD bestows his blessing,
even life forevermore.

[a] 6 That is, Kiriath Jearim [b] 6 Or *heard of it in Ephrathah, / we found
it in the fields of Jaar.* (And no quotes around verses 7-9) [c] *17 Horn* here
symbolizes strong one, that is, king.

Living Bible

132 LORD, DO you remember that time when my heart[d] was so filled with turmoil? 2–5I couldn't rest, I couldn't sleep, thinking how I ought to build a permanent home for the Ark of the Lord,[e] a Temple for the mighty one of Israel. Then I vowed that I would do it; I made a solemn promise to the Lord.

6First the Ark was in Ephrathah,[f] then in the distant countryside of Jaar. 7But now it will be settled in the Temple, in God's permanent home here on earth. That is where we will go to worship him.[g] 8Arise, O Lord, and enter your Temple with the Ark, the symbol of your power.

9We will clothe the priests in white, the symbol of all purity. May our nation shout for joy.

10Do not reject your servant David—the king you chose for your people. 11For you promised me that my son would sit on my throne and succeed me. And surely you will never go back on a promise! 12You also promised that if my descendants will obey the terms of your contract with me, then the dynasty of David shall never end.

13O Lord, you have chosen Jerusalem[h] as your home: 14"This is my permanent home where I shall live," you said, "for I have always wanted it this way. 15I will make this city prosperous and satisfy her poor with food. 16I will clothe her priests with salvation; her saints shall shout for joy. 17David's power shall grow, for I have decreed for him a mighty Son.[i] 18I'll clothe his enemies with shame, but he shall be a glorious King."

133 HOW WONDERFUL it is, how pleasant, when brothers live in harmony! 2For harmony is as precious as the fragrant anointing oil that was poured over Aaron's head, and ran down onto his beard, and onto the border of his robe. 3Harmony is as refreshing as the dew on Mount Hermon, on the mountains of Israel. And God has pronounced this eternal blessing on Jerusalem,[h] even life forevermore.

New Revised Standard

The Eternal Dwelling of God in Zion
A Song of Ascents.

132 O LORD, remember in David's favor all the hardships he endured;
2 how he swore to the LORD
   and vowed to the Mighty One of Jacob,
3 "I will not enter my house
   or get into my bed;
4 I will not give sleep to my eyes
   or slumber to my eyelids,
5 until I find a place for the LORD,
   a dwelling place for the Mighty One of Jacob."

6 We heard of it in Ephrathah;
   we found it in the fields of Jaar.
7 "Let us go to his dwelling place;
   let us worship at his footstool."

8 Rise up, O LORD, and go to your resting place,
   you and the ark of your might.
9 Let your priests be clothed with righteousness,
   and let your faithful shout for joy.
10 For your servant David's sake
   do not turn away the face of your anointed one.

11 The LORD swore to David a sure oath
   from which he will not turn back:
   "One of the sons of your body
   I will set on your throne.
12 If your sons keep my covenant
   and my decrees that I shall teach them,
   their sons also, forevermore,
   shall sit on your throne."

13 For the LORD has chosen Zion;
   he has desired it for his habitation:
14 "This is my resting place forever;
   here I will reside, for I have desired it.
15 I will abundantly bless its provisions;
   I will satisfy its poor with bread.
16 Its priests I will clothe with salvation,
   and its faithful will shout for joy.
17 There I will cause a horn to sprout up for David;
   I have prepared a lamp for my anointed one.
18 His enemies I will clothe with disgrace,
   but on him, his crown will gleam."

The Blessedness of Unity
A Song of Ascents.

133 HOW VERY good and pleasant it is when kindred live together in unity!
2 It is like the precious oil on the head,
   running down upon the beard,
on the beard of Aaron,
   running down over the collar of his robes.
3 It is like the dew of Hermon,
   which falls on the mountains of Zion.
For there the LORD ordained his blessing,
   life forevermore.

---

d 132:1 *my heart*, literally, "David's soul."   e 132:2-5 *the Ark of the Lord*, implied.   f 132:6 *First the Ark was in Ephrathah*, literally, "Lo, we heard of it in Ephrathah."   g 132:7 *That is where we will go to worship him*, literally, "We will go into his tabernacles; we will worship at his footstool."
h 132:13,133:3 *Jerusalem*, literally, "Zion."   i 132:17 *a mighty Son*, literally, "a progeny."

King James

A Song of degrees.

134 BEHOLD, BLESS ye the LORD, all *ye* servants of the LORD, which by night stand in the house of the LORD.

2Lift up your hands *in* the sanctuary, and bless the LORD.

3The LORD that made heaven and earth bless thee out of Zion.

135 PRAISE YE the LORD. Praise ye the name of the LORD; praise *him*, O ye servants of the LORD.

2Ye that stand in the house of the LORD, in the courts of the house of our God,

3Praise the LORD; for the LORD *is* good: sing praises unto his name; for *it is* pleasant.

4For the LORD hath chosen Jacob unto himself, *and* Israel for his peculiar treasure.

5For I know that the LORD *is* great, and *that* our Lord *is* above all gods.

6Whatsoever the LORD pleased, *that* did he in heaven, and in earth, in the seas, and all deep places.

7He causeth the vapours to ascend from the ends of the earth; he maketh lightnings for the rain; he bringeth the wind out of his treasuries.

8Who smote the firstborn of Egypt, both of man and beast.

9*Who* sent tokens and wonders into the midst of thee, O Egypt, upon Pharaoh, and upon all his servants.

10Who smote great nations, and slew mighty kings;

11Sihon king of the Amorites, and Og king of Bashan, and all the kingdoms of Canaan:

12And gave their land *for* an heritage, an heritage unto Israel his people.

13Thy name, O LORD, *endureth* for ever; *and* thy memorial, O LORD, throughout all generations.

14For the LORD will judge his people, and he will repent himself concerning his servants.

15The idols of the heathen *are* silver and gold, the work of men's hands.

16They have mouths, but they speak not; eyes have they, but they see not;

17They have ears, but they hear not; neither is there *any* breath in their mouths.

18They that make them are like unto them: *so is* every one that trusteth in them.

19Bless the LORD, O house of Israel: bless the LORD, O house of Aaron:

20Bless the LORD, O house of Levi: ye that fear the LORD, bless the LORD.

21Blessed be the LORD out of Zion, which dwelleth at Jerusalem. Praise ye the LORD.

New International

A song of ascents.

134 PRAISE THE LORD, all you servants of the LORD
who minister by night in the house of the LORD.

2Lift up your hands in the sanctuary
and praise the LORD.

3May the LORD, the Maker of heaven and earth,
bless you from Zion.

135 PRAISE THE LORD.[a]
Praise the name of the LORD;
praise him, you servants of the LORD,
2you who minister in the house of the LORD,
in the courts of the house of our God.

3Praise the LORD, for the LORD is good;
sing praise to his name, for that is pleasant.

4For the LORD has chosen Jacob to be his own,
Israel to be his treasured possession.

5I know that the LORD is great,
that our Lord is greater than all gods.

6The LORD does whatever pleases him,
in the heavens and on the earth,
in the seas and all their depths.

7He makes clouds rise from the ends of the
earth;
he sends lightning with the rain
and brings out the wind from his storehouses.

8He struck down the firstborn of Egypt,
the firstborn of men and animals.

9He sent his signs and wonders into your midst,
O Egypt,
against Pharaoh and all his servants.

10He struck down many nations
and killed mighty kings—

11Sihon king of the Amorites,
Og king of Bashan
and all the kings of Canaan—

12and he gave their land as an inheritance,
an inheritance to his people Israel.

13Your name, O LORD, endures forever,
your renown, O LORD, through all
generations.

14For the LORD will vindicate his people
and have compassion on his servants.

15The idols of the nations are silver and gold,
made by the hands of men.

16They have mouths, but cannot speak,
eyes, but they cannot see;

17they have ears, but cannot hear,
nor is there breath in their mouths.

18Those who make them will be like them,
and so will all who trust in them.

19O house of Israel, praise the LORD;
O house of Aaron, praise the LORD;

20O house of Levi, praise the LORD;
you who fear him, praise the LORD.

21Praise be to the LORD from Zion,
to him who dwells in Jerusalem.

Praise the LORD.

---

a *1* Hebrew *Hallelu Yah*; also in verses 3 and 21

Living Bible

134

OH, BLESS the Lord, you who serve him as watchmen in the Temple every night. 2Lift your hands in holiness and bless the Lord.

3The Lord bless you from Zion—the Lord who made heaven and earth.

135

HALLELUJAH! 2Yes, let his people praise him as they stand in his Temple courts. 3Praise the Lord because he is so good; sing to his wonderful name. 4For the Lord has chosen Israel as his personal possession.

5I know the greatness of the Lord—that he is greater far than any other god. 6He does whatever pleases him throughout all of heaven and earth, and in the deepest seas. 7He makes mists rise throughout the earth and sends the lightning to bring down the rain; and sends the winds from his treasuries. 8He destroyed the eldest child in each Egyptian home, along with the firstborn of the flocks. 9He did great miracles in Egypt before Pharaoh and all his people. 10He smote great nations, slaying mighty kings— 11Sihon, king of Amorites; and Og, the king of Bashan; and the kings of Canaan— 12and gave their land as an eternal gift to his people Israel.

13O Jehovah, your name endures forever; your fame is known to every generation. 14For Jehovah will vindicate his people, and have compassion on his servants.

15The heathen worship idols of gold and silver, made by men— 16idols with speechless mouths and sightless eyes 17and ears that cannot hear; they cannot even breathe. 18Those who make them become like them! And so do all who trust in them!

19O Israel, bless Jehovah! High priests of Aaron, bless his name. 20O Levite priests, bless the Lord Jehovah! Oh, bless his name, all of you who trust and reverence him. 21All people of Jerusalem, praise the Lord,b for he lives here in Jerusalem. Hallelujah!

New Revised Standard

Praise in the Night

A Song of Ascents.

134

COME, BLESS the LORD, all you servants of the LORD, who stand by night in the house of the LORD!

2 Lift up your hands to the holy place, and bless the LORD.

3 May the LORD, maker of heaven and earth, bless you from Zion.

Praise for God's Goodness and Might

135

PRAISE THE LORD!
Praise the name of the LORD;
give praise, O servants of the LORD,
2 you that stand in the house of the LORD,
in the courts of the house of our God.
3 Praise the LORD, for the LORD is good;
sing to his name, for he is gracious.
4 For the LORD has chosen Jacob for himself,
Israel as his own possession.

5 For I know that the LORD is great;
our Lord is above all gods.
6 Whatever the LORD pleases he does,
in heaven and on earth,
in the seas and all deeps.
7 He it is who makes the clouds rise at the end
of the earth;
he makes lightnings for the rain
and brings out the wind from his
storehouses.

8 He it was who struck down the firstborn of
Egypt,
both human beings and animals;
9 he sent signs and wonders
into your midst, O Egypt,
against Pharaoh and all his servants.
10 He struck down many nations
and killed mighty kings—
11 Sihon, king of the Amorites,
and Og, king of Bashan,
and all the kingdoms of Canaan—
12 and gave their land as a heritage,
a heritage to his people Israel.

13 Your name, O LORD, endures forever,
your renown, O LORD, throughout all ages.
14 For the LORD will vindicate his people,
and have compassion on his servants.

15 The idols of the nations are silver and gold,
the work of human hands.
16 They have mouths, but they do not speak;
they have eyes, but they do not see;
17 they have ears, but they do not hear,
and there is no breath in their mouths.
18 Those who make them
and all who trust them
shall become like them.

19 O house of Israel, bless the LORD!
O house of Aaron, bless the LORD!
20 O house of Levi, bless the LORD!
You that fear the LORD, bless the LORD!
21 Blessed be the LORD from Zion,
he who resides in Jerusalem.
Praise the LORD!

b *135:21 All people of Jerusalem, praise the Lord,* literally, "the Lord be blessed from Zion."

King James

136 O GIVE thanks unto the LORD; for *he is* good: for his mercy *endureth* for ever.

2O give thanks unto the God of gods: for his mercy *endureth* for ever.

3O give thanks to the Lord of lords: for his mercy *endureth* for ever.

4To him who alone doeth great wonders: for his mercy *endureth* for ever.

5To him that by wisdom made the heavens: for his mercy *endureth* for ever.

6To him that stretched out the earth above the waters: for his mercy *endureth* for ever.

7To him that made great lights: for his mercy *endureth* for ever:

8The sun to rule by day: for his mercy *endureth* for ever:

9The moon and stars to rule by night: for his mercy *endureth* for ever.

10To him that smote Egypt in their firstborn: for his mercy *endureth* for ever:

11And brought out Israel from among them: for his mercy *endureth* for ever:

12With a strong hand, and with a stretched out arm: for his mercy *endureth* for ever.

13To him which divided the Red sea into parts: for his mercy *endureth* for ever:

14And made Israel to pass through the midst of it: for his mercy *endureth* for ever:

15But overthrew Pharaoh and his host in the Red sea: for his mercy *endureth* for ever.

16To him which led his people through the wilderness: for his mercy *endureth* for ever.

17To him which smote great kings: for his mercy *endureth* for ever:

18And slew famous kings: for his mercy *endureth* for ever:

19Sihon king of the Amorites: for his mercy *endureth* for ever:

20And Og the king of Bashan: for his mercy *endureth* for ever:

21And gave their land for an heritage: for his mercy *endureth* for ever:

22*Even* an heritage unto Israel his servant: for his mercy *endureth* for ever.

23Who remembered us in our low estate: for his mercy *endureth* for ever:

24And hath redeemed us from our enemies: for his mercy *endureth* for ever.

25Who giveth food to all flesh: for his mercy *endureth* for ever.

26O give thanks unto the God of heaven: for his mercy *endureth* for ever.

137 BY THE rivers of Babylon, there we sat down, yea, we wept, when we remembered Zion.

2We hanged our harps upon the willows in the midst thereof.

New International

136 GIVE THANKS to the LORD, for he is good.
His love endures forever.
2Give thanks to the God of gods.
His love endures forever.
3Give thanks to the Lord of lords:
His love endures forever.

4to him who alone does great wonders,
His love endures forever.
5who by his understanding made the heavens,
His love endures forever.
6who spread out the earth upon the waters,
His love endures forever.
7who made the great lights—
His love endures forever.
8the sun to govern the day,
His love endures forever.
9the moon and stars to govern the night;
His love endures forever.

10to him who struck down the firstborn of Egypt
His love endures forever.
11and brought Israel out from among them
His love endures forever.
12with a mighty hand and outstretched arm;
His love endures forever.

13to him who divided the Red Sea[a] asunder
His love endures forever.
14and brought Israel through the midst of it,
His love endures forever.
15but swept Pharaoh and his army into the Red Sea;
His love endures forever.

16to him who led his people through the desert,
His love endures forever.
17who struck down great kings,
His love endures forever.
18and killed mighty kings—
His love endures forever.
19Sihon king of the Amorites
His love endures forever.
20and Og king of Bashan—
His love endures forever.
21and gave their land as an inheritance,
His love endures forever.
22an inheritance to his servant Israel;
His love endures forever.

23to the One who remembered us in our low estate
His love endures forever.
24and freed us from our enemies,
His love endures forever.
25and who gives food to every creature.
His love endures forever.

26Give thanks to the God of heaven.
His love endures forever.

137 BY THE rivers of Babylon we sat and wept
when we remembered Zion.
2There on the poplars
we hung our harps,

---

a 13 Hebrew *Yam Suph*; that is, Sea of Reeds; also in verse 15

Living Bible

136 OH, GIVE thanks to the Lord, for he is good; his lovingkindness continues forever. ²Give thanks to the God of gods, for his lovingkindness continues forever. ³Give thanks to the Lord of lords, for his lovingkindness continues forever. ⁴Praise him who alone does mighty miracles, for his lovingkindness continues forever. ⁵Praise him who made the heavens, for his lovingkindness continues forever. ⁶Praise him who planted the water within the earth,ᵇ for his lovingkindness continues forever. ⁷Praise him who made the heavenly lights, for his lovingkindness continues forever: ⁸the sun to rule the day, for his lovingkindness continues forever; ⁹and the moon and stars at night, for his lovingkindness continues forever. ¹⁰Praise the God who smote the firstborn of Egypt, for his lovingkindness to Israelᶜ continues forever.

¹¹, ¹²He brought them out with mighty power and upraised fist to strike their enemies, for his lovingkindness to Israel continues forever. ¹³Praise the Lord who opened the Red Sea to make a path before them, for his lovingkindness continues forever, ¹⁴and led them safely through, for his lovingkindness continues forever— ¹⁵but drowned Pharaoh's army in the sea, for his lovingkindness to Israel continues forever.

¹⁶Praise him who led his people through the wilderness, for his lovingkindness continues forever. ¹⁷Praise him who saved his people from the power of mighty kings, for his lovingkindness continues forever, ¹⁸and killed famous kings who were their enemies, for his lovingkindness to Israel continues forever: ¹⁹Sihon, king of Amorites—for God's lovingkindness to Israel continues forever— ²⁰and Og, king of Bashan—for his lovingkindness to Israel continues forever. ²¹God gave the land of these kings to Israel as a gift forever, for his lovingkindness to Israel continues forever; ²²yes, a permanent gift to his servant Israel, for his lovingkindness continues forever.

²³He remembered our utter weakness, for his lovingkindness continues forever. ²⁴And saved us from our foes, for his lovingkindness continues forever.

²⁵He gives food to every living thing, for his lovingkindness continues forever. ²⁶Oh, give thanks to the God of heaven, for his lovingkindness continues forever.

137 WEEPING, WE sat beside the rivers of Babylon thinking of Jerusalem. ²We have put away our lyres, hanging them upon the branches of the willow trees, ³, ⁴for how can we sing? Yet our captors,

New Revised Standard

God's Work in Creation and in History

136 O GIVE thanks to the LORD, for he is good,
    for his steadfast love endures forever.
2 O give thanks to the God of gods,
    for his steadfast love endures forever.
3 O give thanks to the Lord of lords,
    for his steadfast love endures forever;

4 who alone does great wonders,
    for his steadfast love endures forever;
5 who by understanding made the heavens,
    for his steadfast love endures forever;
6 who spread out the earth on the waters,
    for his steadfast love endures forever;
7 who made the great lights,
    for his steadfast love endures forever;
8 the sun to rule over the day,
    for his steadfast love endures forever;
9 the moon and stars to rule over the night,
    for his steadfast love endures forever;

10 who struck Egypt through their firstborn,
    for his steadfast love endures forever;
11 and brought Israel out from among them,
    for his steadfast love endures forever;
12 with a strong hand and an outstretched arm,
    for his steadfast love endures forever;
13 who divided the Red Seaᵈ in two,
    for his steadfast love endures forever;
14 and made Israel pass through the midst of it,
    for his steadfast love endures forever;
15 but overthrew Pharaoh and his army in the
    Red Sea,ᵈ
    for his steadfast love endures forever;
16 who led his people through the wilderness,
    for his steadfast love endures forever;
17 who struck down great kings,
    for his steadfast love endures forever;
18 and killed famous kings,
    for his steadfast love endures forever;
19 Sihon, king of the Amorites,
    for his steadfast love endures forever;
20 and Og, king of Bashan,
    for his steadfast love endures forever;
21 and gave their land as a heritage,
    for his steadfast love endures forever;
22 a heritage to his servant Israel,
    for his steadfast love endures forever.

23 It is he who remembered us in our low estate,
    for his steadfast love endures forever;
24 and rescued us from our foes,
    for his steadfast love endures forever;
25 who gives food to all flesh,
    for his steadfast love endures forever.

26 O give thanks to the God of heaven,
    for his steadfast love endures forever.

Lament over the Destruction of Jerusalem

137 BY THE rivers of Babylon—
    there we sat down and there we wept
    when we remembered Zion.
2 On the willowsᵉ there
    we hung up our harps.

ᵇ *136:6 who planted the water within the earth,* or, "who separated the earth from the oceans." ᶜ *136:10 to Israel,* implied here and in verses 12, 15, 18, 19, 20, 21.

ᵈ Or *Sea of Reeds* ᵉ Or *poplars*

King James

3For there they that carried us away captive required of us a song; and they that wasted us *required of us* mirth, *saying,* Sing us *one* of the songs of Zion.

4How shall we sing the LORD's song in a strange land?

5If I forget thee, O Jerusalem, let my right hand forget *her cunning*.

6If I do not remember thee, let my tongue cleave to the roof of my mouth; if I prefer not Jerusalem above my chief joy.

7Remember, O LORD, the children of Edom in the day of Jerusalem; who said, Rase *it,* rase *it, even* to the foundation thereof.

8O daughter of Babylon, who art to be destroyed; happy *shall he be,* that rewardeth thee as thou hast served us.

9Happy *shall he be,* that taketh and dasheth thy little ones against the stones.

A *Psalm* of David.

138 I WILL praise thee with my whole heart: before the gods will I sing praise unto thee.

2I will worship toward thy holy temple, and praise thy name for thy lovingkindness and for thy truth: for thou hast magnified thy word above all thy name.

3In the day when I cried thou answeredst me, *and* strengthenedst me *with* strength in my soul.

4All the kings of the earth shall praise thee, O LORD, when they hear the words of thy mouth.

5Yea, they shall sing in the ways of the LORD: for great *is* the glory of the LORD.

6Though the LORD *be* high, yet hath he respect unto the lowly: but the proud he knoweth afar off.

7Though I walk in the midst of trouble, thou wilt revive me: thou shalt stretch forth thine hand against the wrath of mine enemies, and thy right hand shall save me.

8The LORD will perfect *that which* concerneth me: thy mercy, O LORD, *endureth* for ever: forsake not the works of thine own hands.

To the chief Musician, A Psalm of David.

139 O LORD, thou hast searched me, and known *me.*

2Thou knowest my downsitting and mine uprising, thou understandest my thought afar off.

3Thou compassest my path and my lying down, and art acquainted *with* all my ways.

New International

3for there our captors asked us for songs,
our tormentors demanded songs of joy;
they said, "Sing us one of the songs of Zion!"

4How can we sing the songs of the LORD
while in a foreign land?

5If I forget you, O Jerusalem,
may my right hand forget its skill.

6May my tongue cling to the roof of my mouth
if I do not remember you,
if I do not consider Jerusalem
my highest joy.

7Remember, O LORD, what the Edomites did
on the day Jerusalem fell.
"Tear it down," they cried,
"tear it down to its foundations!"

8O Daughter of Babylon, doomed to destruction,
happy is he who repays you
for what you have done to us—
9he who seizes your infants
and dashes them against the rocks.

Of David.

138 I WILL praise you, O LORD, with all my heart;
before the "gods" I will sing your praise.

2I will bow down toward your holy temple
and will praise your name
for your love and your faithfulness,
for you have exalted above all things
your name and your word.

3When I called, you answered me;
you made me bold and stouthearted.

4May all the kings of the earth praise you,
O LORD,
when they hear the words of your mouth.

5May they sing of the ways of the LORD,
for the glory of the LORD is great.

6Though the LORD is on high, he looks upon the lowly,
but the proud he knows from afar.

7Though I walk in the midst of trouble,
you preserve my life;
you stretch out your hand against the anger of
my foes,
with your right hand you save me.

8The LORD will fulfill his purpose for me;
your love, O LORD, endures forever—
do not abandon the works of your hands.

For the director of music. Of David. A psalm.

139 O LORD, you have searched me
and you know me.

2You know when I sit and when I rise;
you perceive my thoughts from afar.

3You discern my going out and my lying down;
you are familiar with all my ways.

Living Bible

our tormentors, demand that we sing for them the happy songs of Zion! 5, 6If I forget you, O Jerusalem, let my right hand forget its skill upon the harp. If I fail to love her more than my highest joy, let me never sing again.

7O Jehovah, do not forget what these Edomites did on that day when the armies of Babylon captured Jerusalem. "Raze her to the ground!" they yelled. 8O Babylon, evil beast, you shall be destroyed. Blessed is the man who destroys you as you have destroyed us. 9Blessed is the man who takes your babies and smashes them against the rocks!a

138 LORD, WITH all my heart I thank you. I will sing your praises before the armies of angels.b 2I face your Temple as I worship, giving thanks to you for all your lovingkindness and your faithfulness, for your promises are backed by all the honor of your name.c 3When I pray, you answer me, and encourage me by giving me the strength I need.

4Every king in all the earth shall give you thanks, O Lord, for all of them shall hear your voice. 5Yes, they shall sing about Jehovah's glorious ways, for his glory is very great. 6Yet though he is so great, he respects the humble, but proud men must keep their distance. 7Though I am surrounded by troubles, you will bring me safely through them. You will clench your fist against my angry enemies! Your power will save me. 8The Lord will work out his plans for my life—for your lovingkindness, Lord, continues forever. Don't abandon me— for you made me.

139 O LORD, you have examined my heart and know everything about me. 2You know when I sit or stand. When far away you know my every thought. 3You chart the path ahead of me, and tell me where to stop and rest. Every moment, you know where I am. 4You know what I am going to say before I even

New Revised Standard

3   For there our captors
        asked us for songs,
    and our tormentors asked for mirth, saying,
        "Sing us one of the songs of Zion!"

4   How could we sing the LORD's song
        in a foreign land?
5   If I forget you, O Jerusalem,
        let my right hand wither!
6   Let my tongue cling to the roof of my mouth,
        if I do not remember you,
    if I do not set Jerusalem
        above my highest joy.

7   Remember, O LORD, against the Edomites
        the day of Jerusalem's fall,
    how they said, "Tear it down! Tear it down!
        Down to its foundations!"
8   O daughter Babylon, you devastator!d
        Happy shall they be who pay you back
        what you have done to us!
9   Happy shall they be who take your little ones
        and dash them against the rock!

Thanksgiving and Praise
Of David.

138 I GIVE you thanks, O LORD, with my whole heart;
        before the gods I sing your praise;
2   I bow down toward your holy temple
        and give thanks to your name for your
            steadfast love and your faithfulness;
    for you have exalted your name and your
            word
        above everything.e
3   On the day I called, you answered me,
        you increased my strength of soul.f

4   All the kings of the earth shall praise you,
        O LORD,
    for they have heard the words of your
        mouth.
5   They shall sing of the ways of the LORD,
        for great is the glory of the LORD.
6   For though the LORD is high, he regards the
            lowly;
    but the haughty he perceives from far away.

7   Though I walk in the midst of trouble,
        you preserve me against the wrath of my
            enemies;
    you stretch out your hand,
        and your right hand delivers me.
8   The LORD will fulfill his purpose for me;
        your steadfast love, O LORD, endures
            forever.
    Do not forsake the work of your hands.

The Inescapable God
To the leader. Of David. A Psalm.

139 O LORD, you have searched me and known me.
2   You know when I sit down and when I rise
            up;
        you discern my thoughts from far away.
3   You search out my path and my lying down,
        and are acquainted with all my ways.

---

a 137:9 *Blessed is the man who takes your babies and smashes them against the rocks!* Perhaps this could be paraphrased, "Blessed is he who invades and sacks your city."   b 138:1 *before the armies of angels,* or, "before the gods." The same Hebrew word is used here as in Ps 8:5.   c 138:2 *for your promises are backed by all the honor of your name,* literally, "You have exalted your Word above all your name."

d Or *you who are devastated*   e Cn: Heb *you have exalted your word above all your name*   f Syr Compare Gk Tg: Heb *you made me arrogant in my soul with strength*

King James

4For *there is* not a word in my tongue, *but,* lo, O Lord, thou knowest it altogether.

5Thou hast beset me behind and before, and laid thine hand upon me.

6*Such* knowledge *is* too wonderful for me; it is high, I cannot *attain* unto it.

7Whither shall I go from thy spirit? or whither shall I flee from thy presence?

8If I ascend up into heaven, thou *art* there: if I make my bed in hell, behold, thou *art there.*

9*If* I take the wings of the morning, *and* dwell in the uttermost parts of the sea;

10Even there shall thy hand lead me, and thy right hand shall hold me.

11If I say, Surely the darkness shall cover me; even the night shall be light about me.

12Yea, the darkness hideth not from thee; but the night shineth as the day: the darkness and the light *are* both alike *to thee.*

13For thou hast possessed my reins: thou hast covered me in my mother's womb.

14I will praise thee; for I am fearfully *and* wonderfully made: marvellous *are* thy works; and *that* my soul knoweth right well.

15My substance was not hid from thee, when I was made in secret, *and* curiously wrought in the lowest parts of the earth.

16Thine eyes did see my substance, yet being unperfect; and in thy book all *my members* were written, *which* in continuance were fashioned, when *as yet there was* none of them.

17How precious also are thy thoughts unto me, O God! how great is the sum of them!

18*If* I should count them, they are more in number than the sand: when I awake, I am still with thee.

19Surely thou wilt slay the wicked, O God: depart from me therefore, ye bloody men.

20For they speak against thee wickedly, *and* thine enemies take *thy name* in vain.

21Do not I hate them, O Lord, that hate thee? and am not I grieved with those that rise up against thee?

22I hate them with perfect hatred: I count them mine enemies.

23Search me, O God, and know my heart: try me, and know my thoughts:

24And see if *there be any* wicked way in me, and lead me in the way everlasting.

To the chief Musician, A Psalm of David.

140 DELIVER ME, O Lord, from the evil man: preserve me from the violent man;

2Which imagine mischiefs in *their* heart; continually are they gathered together *for* war.

3They have sharpened their tongues like a serpent; adders' poison *is* under their lips. Selah.

New International

4Before a word is on my tongue
  you know it completely, O Lord.

5You hem me in—behind and before;
  you have laid your hand upon me.
6Such knowledge is too wonderful for me,
  too lofty for me to attain.

7Where can I go from your Spirit?
  Where can I flee from your presence?
8If I go up to the heavens, you are there;
  if I make my bed in the depths,[a] you are
    there.
9If I rise on the wings of the dawn,
  if I settle on the far side of the sea,
10even there your hand will guide me,
  your right hand will hold me fast.

11If I say, "Surely the darkness will hide me
  and the light become night around me,"
12even the darkness will not be dark to you;
  the night will shine like the day,
  for darkness is as light to you.

13For you created my inmost being;
  you knit me together in my mother's womb.
14I praise you because I am fearfully and
    wonderfully made;
  your works are wonderful,
  I know that full well.
15My frame was not hidden from you
  when I was made in the secret place.
  When I was woven together in the depths of the
    earth,
16 your eyes saw my unformed body.
All the days ordained for me
  were written in your book
  before one of them came to be.

17How precious to[b] me are your thoughts,
    O God!
  How vast is the sum of them!
18Were I to count them,
  they would outnumber the grains of sand.
  When I awake,
  I am still with you.

19If only you would slay the wicked, O God!
  Away from me, you bloodthirsty men!
20They speak of you with evil intent;
  your adversaries misuse your name.
21Do I not hate those who hate you, O Lord,
  and abhor those who rise up against you?
22I have nothing but hatred for them;
  I count them my enemies.

23Search me, O God, and know my heart;
  test me and know my anxious thoughts.
24See if there is any offensive way in me,
  and lead me in the way everlasting.

For the director of music. A psalm of David.

140 RESCUE ME, O Lord, from evil men;
  protect me from men of violence,
2who devise evil plans in their hearts
  and stir up war every day.
3They make their tongues as sharp as a serpent's;
  the poison of vipers is on their lips.   *Selah*

Living Bible

say it. 5You both precede and follow me, and place your hand of blessing on my head.

6This is too glorious, too wonderful to believe! 7I can *never* be lost to your Spirit! I can *never* get away from my God! 8If I go up to heaven, you are there; if I go down to the place of the dead, you are there. 9If I ride the morning winds to the farthest oceans, 10even there your hand will guide me, your strength will support me. 11If I try to hide in the darkness, the night becomes light around me. 12For even darkness cannot hide from God; to you the night shines as bright as day. Darkness and light are both alike to you.

13You made all the delicate, inner parts of my body, and knit them together in my mother's womb. 14Thank you for making me so wonderfully complex! It is amazing to think about. Your workmanship is marvelous—and how well I know it. 15You were there while I was being formed in utter seclusion! 16You saw me before I was born and scheduled each day of my life before I began to breathe. Every day was recorded in your Book!

17, 18How precious it is, Lord, to realize that you are thinking about me constantly! I can't even count how many times a day your thoughts turn towards me.c And when I waken in the morning, you are still thinking of me!

19Surely you will slay the wicked, Lord! Away, bloodthirsty men! Begone! 20They blaspheme your name and stand in arrogance against you—how silly can they be? 21O Lord, shouldn't I hate those who hate you? Shouldn't I be grieved with them? 22Yes, I hate them, for your enemies are my enemies too.

23Search me, O God, and know my heart; test my thoughts. 24Point out anything you find in me that makes you sad, and lead me along the path of everlasting life.

140 O LORD, deliver me from evil men. Preserve me from the violent, 2who plot and stir up trouble all day long. 3Their words sting like poisonous snakes. 4Keep me out of their power. Preserve me

New Revised Standard

4 Even before a word is on my tongue,
      O LORD, you know it completely.
5 You hem me in, behind and before,
      and lay your hand upon me.
6 Such knowledge is too wonderful for me;
      it is so high that I cannot attain it.

7 Where can I go from your spirit?
      Or where can I flee from your presence?
8 If I ascend to heaven, you are there;
      if I make my bed in Sheol, you are there.
9 If I take the wings of the morning
      and settle at the farthest limits of the sea,
10 even there your hand shall lead me,
      and your right hand shall hold me fast.
11 If I say, "Surely the darkness shall cover me,
      and the light around me become night,"
12 even the darkness is not dark to you;
      the night is as bright as the day,
      for darkness is as light to you.

13 For it was you who formed my inward parts;
      you knit me together in my mother's womb.
14 I praise you, for I am fearfully and
        wonderfully made.
      Wonderful are your works;
      that I know very well.
15 My frame was not hidden from you,
      when I was being made in secret,
      intricately woven in the depths of the earth.
16 Your eyes beheld my unformed substance.
      In your book were written
      all the days that were formed for me,
      when none of them as yet existed.
17 How weighty to me are your thoughts,
        O God!
      How vast is the sum of them!
18 I try to count them—they are more than the
        sand;
      I come to the endd—I am still with you.

19 O that you would kill the wicked, O God,
      and that the bloodthirsty would depart from
        me—
20 those who speak of you maliciously,
      and lift themselves up against you for evil!e
21 Do I not hate those who hate you, O LORD?
      And do I not loathe those who rise up
        against you?
22 I hate them with perfect hatred;
      I count them my enemies.
23 Search me, O God, and know my heart;
      test me and know my thoughts.
24 See if there is any wickedf way in me,
      and lead me in the way everlasting.g

Prayer for Deliverance from Enemies
To the leader. A Psalm of David.

140 DELIVER ME, O LORD, from evildoers;
      protect me from those who are violent,
2 who plan evil things in their minds
      and stir up wars continually.
3 They make their tongue sharp as a snake's,
      and under their lips is the venom of vipers.
                                          Selah

---

c 139:17, 18 *I can't even count how many times a day your thoughts turn towards me,* literally, "how precious are your thoughts to me."

d Or *I awake*   e Cn: Meaning of Heb uncertain   f Heb *hurtful*   g Or *the ancient way.* Compare Jer 6.16

King James

4Keep me, O LORD, from the hands of the wicked; preserve me from the violent man; who have purposed to overthrow my goings.

5The proud have hid a snare for me, and cords; they have spread a net by the wayside; they have set gins for me. Selah.

6I said unto the LORD, Thou *art* my God: hear the voice of my supplications, O LORD.

7O GOD the Lord, the strength of my salvation, thou hast covered my head in the day of battle.

8Grant not, O LORD, the desires of the wicked: further not his wicked device; *lest* they exalt themselves. Selah.

9*As for* the head of those that compass me about, let the mischief of their own lips cover them.

10Let burning coals fall upon them: let them be cast into the fire; into deep pits, that they rise not up again.

11Let not an evil speaker be established in the earth: evil shall hunt the violent man to overthrow *him*.

12I know that the LORD will maintain the cause of the afflicted, *and* the right of the poor.

13Surely the righteous shall give thanks unto thy name: the upright shall dwell in thy presence.

New International

4Keep me, O LORD, from the hands of the
  wicked;
protect me from men of violence
  who plan to trip my feet.
5Proud men have hidden a snare for me;
  they have spread out the cords of their net
  and have set traps for me along my path.
                                          Selah

6O LORD, I say to you, "You are my God."
  Hear, O LORD, my cry for mercy.
7O Sovereign LORD, my strong deliverer,
  who shields my head in the day of battle—
8do not grant the wicked their desires, O LORD;
  do not let their plans succeed,
  or they will become proud.   *Selah*

9Let the heads of those who surround me
  be covered with the trouble their lips have
    caused.
10Let burning coals fall upon them;
  may they be thrown into the fire,
  into miry pits, never to rise.
11Let slanderers not be established in the land;
  may disaster hunt down men of violence.

12I know that the LORD secures justice for the
    poor
  and upholds the cause of the needy.
13Surely the righteous will praise your name
  and the upright will live before you.

A Psalm of David.

141 LORD, I cry unto thee: make haste unto me; give ear unto my voice, when I cry unto thee.

2Let my prayer be set forth before thee *as* incense; *and* the lifting up of my hands *as* the evening sacrifice.

3Set a watch, O LORD, before my mouth; keep the door of my lips.

4Incline not my heart to *any* evil thing, to practise wicked works with men that work iniquity: and let me not eat of their dainties.

5Let the righteous smite me; *it shall be* a kindness; and let him reprove me; *it shall be* an excellent oil, *which* shall not break my head: for yet my prayer also *shall be* in their calamities.

6When their judges are overthrown in stony places, they shall hear my words; for they are sweet.

7Our bones are scattered at the grave's mouth, as when one cutteth and cleaveth *wood* upon the earth.

A psalm of David.

141 O LORD, I call to you; come quickly to me.
Hear my voice when I call to you.
2May my prayer be set before you like incense;
  may the lifting up of my hands be like the
    evening sacrifice.

3Set a guard over my mouth, O LORD;
  keep watch over the door of my lips.
4Let not my heart be drawn to what is evil,
  to take part in wicked deeds
with men who are evildoers;
  let me not eat of their delicacies.

5Let a righteous mana strike me—it is a
    kindness;
  let him rebuke me—it is oil on my head.
  My head will not refuse it.

Yet my prayer is ever against the deeds of
    evildoers;
6 their rulers will be thrown down from the
      cliffs,
  and the wicked will learn that my words were
    well spoken.
7They will say, "As one plows and breaks up
    the earth,
  so our bones have been scattered at the mouth
    of the grave.b"

Living Bible

from their violence, for they are plotting against me. [5]These proud men have set a trap to catch me, a noose to yank me up and leave me dangling in the air; they wait in ambush with a net to throw over and hold me helpless in its meshes.

[6, 7, 8]O Jehovah, my Lord and Savior, my God and my shield—hear me as I pray! Don't let these wicked men succeed; don't let them prosper and be proud. [9]Let their plots boomerang! Let them be destroyed by the very evil they have planned for me. [10]Let burning coals fall down upon their heads, or throw them into the fire, or into deep pits from which they can't escape.

[11]Don't let liars prosper here in our land; quickly punish them. [12]But the Lord will surely help those they persecute; he will maintain the rights of the poor. [13]Surely the godly are thanking you, for they shall live in your presence.

141 QUICK, LORD, answer me—for I have prayed. Listen when I cry to you for help! [2]Regard my prayer as my evening sacrifice and as incense wafting up to you.

[3]Help me, Lord, to keep my mouth shut and my lips sealed. [4]Take away my lust for evil things; don't let me want to be with sinners, doing what they do, sharing their delicacies. [5]Let the godly smite me! It will be a kindness! If they reprove me, it is medicine! Don't let me refuse it. But I am in constant prayer against the wicked and their deeds. [6, 7]When their leaders are condemned, and their bones are strewn across the ground,[c] then these men will finally listen to me and know that I am trying to help them.

New Revised Standard

[4] Guard me, O LORD, from the hands of the wicked;
   protect me from the violent
      who have planned my downfall.
[5] The arrogant have hidden a trap for me,
   and with cords they have spread a net,[d]
      along the road they have set snares for me.
                                        Selah

[6] I say to the LORD, "You are my God;
   give ear, O LORD, to the voice of my
      supplications."
[7] O LORD, my Lord, my strong deliverer,
   you have covered my head in the day
      of battle.
[8] Do not grant, O LORD, the desires of the
      wicked;
   do not further their evil plot.[e]   *Selah*

[9] Those who surround me lift up their heads;[f]
   let the mischief of their lips overwhelm
      them!
[10] Let burning coals fall on them!
   Let them be flung into pits, no more to rise!
[11] Do not let the slanderer be established in the
      land;
   let evil speedily hunt down the violent!

[12] I know that the LORD maintains the cause of
      the needy,
   and executes justice for the poor.
[13] Surely the righteous shall give thanks to your
      name;
   the upright shall live in your presence.

Prayer for Preservation from Evil
A Psalm of David.

141 I CALL upon you, O LORD; come quickly
      to me;
   give ear to my voice when I call to you.
[2] Let my prayer be counted as incense before
      you,
   and the lifting up of my hands as an
      evening sacrifice.

[3] Set a guard over my mouth, O LORD;
   keep watch over the door of my lips.
[4] Do not turn my heart to any evil,
   to busy myself with wicked deeds
in company with those who work iniquity;
   do not let me eat of their delicacies.

[5] Let the righteous strike me;
   let the faithful correct me.
Never let the oil of the wicked anoint my
      head,[g]
   for my prayer is continually[h] against their
      wicked deeds.
[6] When they are given over to those who shall
      condemn them,
   then they shall learn that my words were
      pleasant.
[7] Like a rock that one breaks apart and shatters
      on the land,
   so shall their bones be strewn at the mouth
      of Sheol.[i]

---

[c] 141:6, 7 *When their leaders are condemned, and their bones are strewn across the ground,* literally, "As when one plows and cleaves the earth, our bones are scattered at the mouth of Sheol."

[d] Or *they have spread cords as a net*   [e] Heb adds *they are exalted*   [f] Cn Compare Gk: Heb *those who surround me are uplifted in head;* Heb divides verses 8 and 9 differently   [g] Gk: Meaning of Heb uncertain   [h] Cn: Heb *for continually and my prayer*   [i] Meaning of Heb of verses 5-7 is uncertain

King James

8But mine eyes *are* unto thee, O GOD the Lord: in thee is my trust; leave not my soul destitute.

9Keep me from the snares *which* they have laid for me, and the gins of the workers of iniquity.

10Let the wicked fall into their own nets, whilst that I withal escape.

Maschil of David; A Prayer when he was in the cave.

142 I CRIED unto the LORD with my voice; with my voice unto the LORD did I make my supplication.

2I poured out my complaint before him; I showed before him my trouble.

3When my spirit was overwhelmed within me, then thou knewest my path. In the way wherein I walked have they privily laid a snare for me.

4I looked on *my* right hand, and beheld, but *there was* no man that would know me: refuge failed me; no man cared for my soul.

5I cried unto thee, O LORD: I said, Thou *art* my refuge *and* my portion in the land of the living.

6Attend unto my cry; for I am brought very low: deliver me from my persecutors; for they are stronger than I.

7Bring my soul out of prison, that I may praise thy name: the righteous shall compass me about; for thou shalt deal bountifully with me.

A Psalm of David.

143 HEAR MY prayer, O LORD, give ear to my supplications: in thy faithfulness answer me, *and* in thy righteousness.

2And enter not into judgment with thy servant: for in thy sight shall no man living be justified.

3For the enemy hath persecuted my soul; he hath smitten my life down to the ground; he hath made me to dwell in darkness, as those that have been long dead.

4Therefore is my spirit overwhelmed within me; my heart within me is desolate.

5I remember the days of old; I meditate on all thy works; I muse on the work of thy hands.

6I stretch forth my hands unto thee: my soul *thirsteth* after thee, as a thirsty land. Selah.

7Hear me speedily, O LORD: my spirit faileth: hide not thy face from me, lest I be like unto them that go down into the pit.

New International

8But my eyes are fixed on you, O Sovereign LORD;
    in you I take refuge—do not give me over to death.

9Keep me from the snares they have laid for me,
    from the traps set by evildoers.

10Let the wicked fall into their own nets,
    while I pass by in safety.

A *maskil*[a] of David. When he was in the cave. A prayer.

142 I CRY aloud to the LORD;
    I lift up my voice to the LORD for mercy.

2I pour out my complaint before him;
    before him I tell my trouble.

3When my spirit grows faint within me,
    it is you who know my way.
In the path where I walk
    men have hidden a snare for me.

4Look to my right and see;
    no one is concerned for me.
I have no refuge;
    no one cares for my life.

5I cry to you, O LORD;
    I say, "You are my refuge,
    my portion in the land of the living."

6Listen to my cry,
    for I am in desperate need;
rescue me from those who pursue me,
    for they are too strong for me.

7Set me free from my prison,
    that I may praise your name.

Then the righteous will gather about me
    because of your goodness to me.

A psalm of David.

143 O LORD, hear my prayer,
    listen to my cry for mercy;
in your faithfulness and righteousness
    come to my relief.

2Do not bring your servant into judgment,
    for no one living is righteous before you.

3The enemy pursues me,
    he crushes me to the ground;
he makes me dwell in darkness
    like those long dead.

4So my spirit grows faint within me;
    my heart within me is dismayed.

5I remember the days of long ago;
    I meditate on all your works
    and consider what your hands have done.

6I spread out my hands to you;
    my soul thirsts for you like a parched land.
           Selah

7Answer me quickly, O LORD;
    my spirit fails.
Do not hide your face from me
    or I will be like those who go down to the pit.

---

a Title: Probably a literary or musical term

Living Bible

8I look to you for help, O Lord God. You are my refuge. Don't let them slay me. 9Keep me out of their traps. 10Let them fall into their own snares, while I escape.

142 HOW I plead with God, how I implore his mercy, pouring out my troubles before him. 3For I am overwhelmed and desperate, and you alone know which way I ought to turn to miss the traps my enemies have set for me. 4(There's one—just over there to the right!) No one gives me a passing thought. No one will help me; no one cares a bit what happens to me. 5Then I prayed to Jehovah. "Lord," I pled, "you are my only place of refuge. Only you can keep me safe.

6"Hear my cry, for I am very low. Rescue me from my persecutors, for they are too strong for me. 7Bring me out of prison, so that I can thank you. The godly will rejoice with me for all your help."

143 HEAR MY prayer, O Lord; answer my plea, because you are faithful to your promises.b 2Don't bring me to trial! For as compared with you, no one is perfect.

3My enemies chased and caught me. They have knocked me to the ground. They force me to live in the darkness like those in the grave. 4I am losing all hope; I am paralyzed with fear.

5I remember the glorious miracles you did in days of long ago. 6I reach out for you. I thirst for you as parched land thirsts for rain. 7Come quickly, Lord, and answer me, for my depression deepens; don't turn away from me or I shall die. 8Let me see your kindness to me in the

New Revised Standard

8 But my eyes are turned toward you, O GOD,
my Lord;
   in you I seek refuge; do not leave me
   defenseless.
9 Keep me from the trap that they have laid for
me,
   and from the snares of evildoers.
10 Let the wicked fall into their own nets,
   while I alone escape.

Prayer for Deliverance from Persecutors
A Maskil of David. When he was in the cave. A Prayer.

142 WITH MY voice I cry to the LORD;
with my voice I make supplication to
the LORD.
2 I pour out my complaint before him;
   I tell my trouble before him.
3 When my spirit is faint,
   you know my way.

In the path where I walk
   they have hidden a trap for me.
4 Look on my right hand and see—
   there is no one who takes notice of me;
no refuge remains to me;
   no one cares for me.

5 I cry to you, O LORD;
   I say, "You are my refuge,
   my portion in the land of the living."
6 Give heed to my cry,
   for I am brought very low.

Save me from my persecutors,
   for they are too strong for me.
7 Bring me out of prison,
   so that I may give thanks to your name.
The righteous will surround me,
   for you will deal bountifully with me.

Prayer for Deliverance from Enemies
A Psalm of David.

143 HEAR MY prayer, O LORD;
give ear to my supplications in your
faithfulness;
   answer me in your righteousness.
2 Do not enter into judgment with your servant,
   for no one living is righteous before you.

3 For the enemy has pursued me,
   crushing my life to the ground,
   making me sit in darkness like those long
   dead.
4 Therefore my spirit faints within me;
   my heart within me is appalled.

5 I remember the days of old,
   I think about all your deeds,
   I meditate on the works of your hands.
6 I stretch out my hands to you;
   my soul thirsts for you like a parched land.
               Selah

7 Answer me quickly, O LORD;
   my spirit fails.
Do not hide your face from me,
   or I shall be like those who go down to the
   Pit.

---

b *143:1 answer my plea, because you are faithful to your promises*, literally, "answer me in faithfulness and righteousness."

King James

8Cause me to hear thy lovingkindness in the morning; for in thee do I trust: cause me to know the way wherein I should walk; for I lift up my soul unto thee.

9Deliver me, O LORD, from mine enemies: I flee unto thee to hide me.

10Teach me to do thy will; for thou *art* my God: thy spirit *is* good; lead me into the land of uprightness.

11Quicken me, O LORD, for thy name's sake: for thy righteousness' sake bring my soul out of trouble.

12And of thy mercy cut off mine enemies, and destroy all them that afflict my soul: for I *am* thy servant.

A Psalm of David.

144 BLESSED *BE* the LORD my strength, which teacheth my hands to war, *and* my fingers to fight:

2My goodness, and my fortress; my high tower, and my deliverer; my shield, and *he* in whom I trust; who subdueth my people under me.

3LORD, what *is* man, that thou takest knowledge of him! *or* the son of man, that thou makest account of him!

4Man is like to vanity: his days *are* as a shadow that passeth away.

5Bow thy heavens, O LORD, and come down: touch the mountains, and they shall smoke.

6Cast forth lightning, and scatter them: shoot out thine arrows, and destroy them.

7Send thine hand from above; rid me, and deliver me out of great waters, from the hand of strange children;

8Whose mouth speaketh vanity, and their right hand *is* a right hand of falsehood.

9I will sing a new song unto thee, O God: upon a psaltery *and* an instrument of ten strings will I sing praises unto thee.

10*It is he* that giveth salvation unto kings: who delivereth David his servant from the hurtful sword.

11Rid me, and deliver me from the hand of strange children, whose mouth speaketh vanity, and their right hand *is* a right hand of falsehood:

New International

8Let the morning bring me word of your
　　unfailing love,
　for I have put my trust in you.
Show me the way I should go,
　for to you I lift up my soul.
9Rescue me from my enemies, O LORD,
　for I hide myself in you.
10Teach me to do your will,
　for you are my God;
may your good Spirit
　lead me on level ground.

11For your name's sake, O LORD, preserve my
　　life;
　in your righteousness, bring me out of
　　trouble.
12In your unfailing love, silence my enemies;
　destroy all my foes,
　for I am your servant.

Of David.

144 PRAISE BE to the LORD my Rock,
who trains my hands for war,
my fingers for battle.

2He is my loving God and my fortress,
　my stronghold and my deliverer,
my shield, in whom I take refuge,
　who subdues peoplesa under me.

3O LORD, what is man that you care for him,
　the son of man that you think of him?
4Man is like a breath;
　his days are like a fleeting shadow.

5Part your heavens, O LORD, and come down;
　touch the mountains, so that they smoke.
6Send forth lightning and scatter the enemies;
　shoot your arrows and rout them.
7Reach down your hand from on high;
　deliver me and rescue me
from the mighty waters,
　from the hands of foreigners
8whose mouths are full of lies,
　whose right hands are deceitful.

9I will sing a new song to you, O God;
　on the ten-stringed lyre I will make music to
　　you,
10to the One who gives victory to kings,
　who delivers his servant David from the
　　deadly sword.

11Deliver me and rescue me
　from the hands of foreigners
whose mouths are full of lies,
　whose right hands are deceitful.

Living Bible

morning, for I am trusting you. Show me where to walk, for my prayer is sincere. 9Save me from my enemies. O Lord, I run to you to hide me. 10Help me to do your will, for you are my God. Lead me in good paths, for your Spirit is good.

11Lord, saving me will bring glory to your name. Bring me out of all this trouble because you are true to your promises. 12And because you are loving and kind to me, cut off all my enemies and destroy those who are trying to harm me; for I am your servant.

144 BLESS THE Lord who is my immovable Rock. He gives me strength and skill in battle. 2He is always kind and loving to me; he is my fortress, my tower of strength and safety, my deliverer. He stands before me as a shield. He subdues my people under me.

3O Lord, what is man that you even notice him? Why bother at all with the human race?[b] 4For man is but a breath; his days are like a passing shadow.

5Bend down the heavens, Lord, and come. The mountains smoke beneath your touch.

6Let loose your lightning bolts, your arrows, Lord, upon your enemies, and scatter them.

7Reach down from heaven and rescue me; deliver me from deep waters, from the power of my enemies. 8Their mouths are filled with lies; they swear to the truth of what is false.

9I will sing you a new song, O God, with a ten-stringed harp. 10For you grant victory to kings! You are the one who will rescue your servant David from the fatal sword. 11Save me! Deliver me from these enemies, these liars, these treacherous men.

New Revised Standard

8 Let me hear of your steadfast love in the
    morning,
  for in you I put my trust.
Teach me the way I should go,
  for to you I lift up my soul.

9 Save me, O LORD, from my enemies;
  I have fled to you for refuge.[c]
10 Teach me to do your will,
  for you are my God.
Let your good spirit lead me
  on a level path.

11 For your name's sake, O LORD, preserve my
    life.
  In your righteousness bring me out of
    trouble.
12 In your steadfast love cut off my enemies,
  and destroy all my adversaries,
  for I am your servant.

Prayer for National Deliverance and Security
Of David.

144 BLESSED BE the LORD, my rock,
  who trains my hands for war, and my
    fingers for battle;
2 my rock[d] and my fortress,
  my stronghold and my deliverer,
  my shield, in whom I take refuge,
  who subdues the peoples[e] under me.

3 O LORD, what are human beings that you
    regard them,
  or mortals that you think of them?
4 They are like a breath;
  their days are like a passing shadow.

5 Bow your heavens, O LORD, and come down;
  touch the mountains so that they smoke.
6 Make the lightning flash and scatter them;
  send out your arrows and rout them.
7 Stretch out your hand from on high;
  set me free and rescue me from the mighty
    waters,
  from the hand of aliens,
8 whose mouths speak lies,
  and whose right hands are false.

9 I will sing a new song to you, O God;
  upon a ten-stringed harp I will play to you,
10 the one who gives victory to kings,
  who rescues his servant David.
11 Rescue me from the cruel sword,
  and deliver me from the hand of aliens,
  whose mouths speak lies,
  and whose right hands are false.

b *144:3 Why bother at all with the human race?* literally, "or the son of man that you take account of him?"

c One Heb Ms Gk: MT *to you I have hidden*   d With 18.2 and 2 Sam 22.2: Heb *my steadfast love*   e Heb Mss Syr Aquila Jerome: MT *my people*

King James

12That our sons *may be* as plants grown up in their youth; *that* our daughters *may be* as corner stones, polished *after* the similitude of a palace:

13*That* our garners *may be* full, affording all manner of store: *that* our sheep may bring forth thousands and ten thousands in our streets:

14*That* our oxen *may be* strong to labour; *that there be* no breaking in, nor going out; that *there be* no complaining in our streets.

15Happy *is that* people, that is in such a case: *yea,* happy *is that* people, whose God *is* the LORD.

David's *Psalm* of praise.

145 I WILL extol thee, my God, O king; and I will bless thy name for ever and ever.

2Every day will I bless thee; and I will praise thy name for ever and ever.

3Great *is* the LORD, and greatly to be praised; and his greatness *is* unsearchable.

4One generation shall praise thy works to another, and shall declare thy mighty acts.

5I will speak of the glorious honour of thy majesty, and of thy wondrous works.

6And *men* shall speak of the might of thy terrible acts: and I will declare thy greatness.

7They shall abundantly utter the memory of thy great goodness, and shall sing of thy righteousness.

8The LORD *is* gracious, and full of compassion; slow to anger, and of great mercy.

9The LORD *is* good to all: and his tender mercies *are* over all his works.

10All thy works shall praise thee, O LORD; and thy saints shall bless thee.

11They shall speak of the glory of thy kingdom, and talk of thy power;

12To make known to the sons of men his mighty acts, and the glorious majesty of his kingdom.

13Thy kingdom *is* an everlasting kingdom, and thy dominion *endureth* throughout all generations.

14The LORD upholdeth all that fall, and raiseth up all *those that be* bowed down.

15The eyes of all wait upon thee; and thou givest them their meat in due season.

16Thou openest thine hand, and satisfiest the desire of every living thing.

New International

12Then our sons in their youth
   will be like well-nurtured plants,
and our daughters will be like pillars
   carved to adorn a palace.
13Our barns will be filled
   with every kind of provision.
Our sheep will increase by thousands,
   by tens of thousands in our fields;
14   our oxen will draw heavy loads.[a]
There will be no breaching of walls,
   no going into captivity,
   no cry of distress in our streets.

15Blessed are the people of whom this is true;
   blessed are the people whose God is the
   LORD.

A psalm of praise. Of David.

145[b] I WILL exalt you, my God the King;
   I will praise your name for ever and ever.
2Every day I will praise you
   and extol your name for ever and ever.

3Great is the LORD and most worthy of praise;
   his greatness no one can fathom.
4One generation will commend your works to
      another;
   they will tell of your mighty acts.
5They will speak of the glorious splendor of your
      majesty,
   and I will meditate on your wonderful
      works.[c]
6They will tell of the power of your awesome
      works,
   and I will proclaim your great deeds.
7They will celebrate your abundant goodness
   and joyfully sing of your righteousness.

8The LORD is gracious and compassionate,
   slow to anger and rich in love.
9The LORD is good to all;
   he has compassion on all he has made.
10All you have made will praise you, O LORD;
   your saints will extol you.
11They will tell of the glory of your kingdom
   and speak of your might,
12so that all men may know of your mighty acts
   and the glorious splendor of your kingdom.
13Your kingdom is an everlasting kingdom,
   and your dominion endures through all
      generations.

The LORD is faithful to all his promises
   and loving toward all he has made.[d]
14The LORD upholds all those who fall
   and lifts up all who are bowed down.
15The eyes of all look to you,
   and you give them their food at the proper
      time.
16You open your hand
   and satisfy the desires of every living thing.

---

a *14* Or *our chieftains will be firmly established*   b This psalm is an acrostic poem, the verses of which (including verse 13b) begin with the successive letters of the Hebrew alphabet.   c *5* Dead Sea Scrolls and Syriac (see also Septuagint); Masoretic Text *On the glorious splendor of your majesty / and on your wonderful works I will meditate*   d *13* One manuscript of the Masoretic Text, Dead Sea Scrolls and Syriac (see also Septuagint); most manuscripts of the Masoretic Text do not have the last two lines of verse 13.

Living Bible

12-15Here is my description ofe a truly happy land where Jehovah is God:

Sons vigorous and tall as growing plants.
Daughters of graceful beauty like the pillars of a palace wall.
Barns full to the brim with crops of every kind.
Sheep by the thousands out in our fields.
Oxen loaded down with produce.
No enemy attacking the walls, but peace everywhere.
No crime in our streets.
Yes, happy are those whose God is Jehovah.

145 I WILL praise you, my God and King, and bless your name each day and forever.

3Great is Jehovah! Greatly praise him! His greatness is beyond discovery! 4Let each generation tell its children what glorious things he does. 5I will meditate about your glory, splendor, majesty and miracles. 6Your awe-inspiring deeds shall be on every tongue; I will proclaim your greatness. 7Everyone will tell about how good you are, and sing about your righteousness.

8Jehovah is kind and merciful, slow to get angry, full of love. 9He is good to everyone, and his compassion is intertwined with everything he does. 10All living things shall thank you, Lord, and your people will bless you. 11They will talk together about the glory of your kingdom and mention examples of your power. 12They will tell about your miracles and about the majesty and glory of your reign. 13For your kingdom never ends. You rule generation after generation.

14The Lord lifts the fallen and those bent beneath their loads. 15The eyes of all mankind look up to you for help; you give them their food as they need it. 16You constantly satisfy the hunger and thirst of every living thing.

New Revised Standard

12 May our sons in their youth
be like plants full grown,
our daughters like corner pillars,
cut for the building of a palace.
13 May our barns be filled,
with produce of every kind;
may our sheep increase by thousands,
by tens of thousands in our fields,
14 and may our cattle be heavy with young.
May there be no breach in the walls,f no exile,
and no cry of distress in our streets.

15 Happy are the people to whom such blessings fall;
happy are the people whose God is the LORD.

The Greatness and the Goodness of God

Praise. Of David.

145 I WILL extol you, my God and King,
and bless your name forever and ever.
2 Every day I will bless you,
and praise your name forever and ever.
3 Great is the LORD, and greatly to be praised;
his greatness is unsearchable.

4 One generation shall laud your works to another,
and shall declare your mighty acts.
5 On the glorious splendor of your majesty,
and on your wondrous works, I will meditate.
6 The might of your awesome deeds shall be proclaimed,
and I will declare your greatness.
7 They shall celebrate the fame of your abundant goodness,
and shall sing aloud of your righteousness.

8 The LORD is gracious and merciful,
slow to anger and abounding in steadfast love.
9 The LORD is good to all,
and his compassion is over all that he has made.

10 All your works shall give thanks to you, O LORD,
and all your faithful shall bless you.
11 They shall speak of the glory of your kingdom,
and tell of your power,
12 to make known to all people yourg mighty deeds,
and the glorious splendor of yourh kingdom.
13 Your kingdom is an everlasting kingdom,
and your dominion endures throughout all generations.

The LORD is faithful in all his words,
and gracious in all his deeds.i
14 The LORD upholds all who are falling,
and raises up all who are bowed down.
15 The eyes of all look to you,
and you give them their food in due season.
16 You open your hand,
satisfying the desire of every living thing.

---

e 144:12-15 Here is my description of, implied.

f Heb lacks in the walls   g Gk Jerome Syr: Heb his   h Heb his   i These two lines supplied by Q Ms Gk Syr

King James

17The LORD *is* righteous in all his ways, and holy in all his works.

18The LORD *is* nigh unto all them that call upon him, to all that call upon him in truth.

19He will fulfil the desire of them that fear him: he also will hear their cry, and will save them.

20The LORD preserveth all them that love him: but all the wicked will he destroy.

21My mouth shall speak the praise of the LORD: and let all flesh bless his holy name for ever and ever.

146 PRAISE YE the LORD. Praise the LORD, O my soul.

2While I live will I praise the LORD: I will sing praises unto my God while I have any being.

3Put not your trust in princes, *nor* in the son of man, in whom *there is* no help.

4His breath goeth forth, he returneth to his earth; in that very day his thoughts perish.

5Happy *is* he that *hath* the God of Jacob for his help, whose hope *is* in the LORD his God:

6Which made heaven, and earth, the sea, and all that therein *is:* which keepeth truth for ever:

7Which executeth judgment for the oppressed: which giveth food to the hungry. The LORD looseth the prisoners:

8The LORD openeth *the eyes of* the blind: the LORD raiseth them that are bowed down: the LORD loveth the righteous:

9The LORD preserveth the strangers; he relieveth the fatherless and widow: but the way of the wicked he turneth upside down.

10The LORD shall reign for ever, *even* thy God, O Zion, unto all generations. Praise ye the LORD.

147 PRAISE YE the LORD: for *it is* good to sing praises unto our God; for *it is* pleasant; *and* praise is comely.

2The LORD doth build up Jerusalem: he gathereth together the outcasts of Israel.

3He healeth the broken in heart, and bindeth up their wounds.

4He telleth the number of the stars; he calleth them all by *their* names.

5Great *is* our Lord, and of great power: his understanding *is* infinite.

6The LORD lifteth up the meek: he casteth the wicked down to the ground.

7Sing unto the LORD with thanksgiving; sing praise upon the harp unto our God:

8Who covereth the heaven with clouds, who prepareth rain for the earth, who maketh grass to grow upon the mountains.

New International

17The LORD is righteous in all his ways
   and loving toward all he has made.

18The LORD is near to all who call on him,
   to all who call on him in truth.

19He fulfills the desires of those who fear him;
   he hears their cry and saves them.

20The LORD watches over all who love him,
   but all the wicked he will destroy.

21My mouth will speak in praise of the LORD.
   Let every creature praise his holy name
   for ever and ever.

146 PRAISE THE LORD.ᵃ

   Praise the LORD, O my soul.
2   I will praise the LORD all my life;
   I will sing praise to my God as long as I live.

3Do not put your trust in princes,
   in mortal men, who cannot save.
4When their spirit departs, they return to the
      ground;
   on that very day their plans come to nothing.
5Blessed is he whose help is the God of Jacob,
   whose hope is in the LORD his God,
6the Maker of heaven and earth,
   the sea, and everything in them—
   the LORD, who remains faithful forever.
7He upholds the cause of the oppressed
   and gives food to the hungry.
   The LORD sets prisoners free,
8   the LORD gives sight to the blind,
   the LORD lifts up those who are bowed down,
   the LORD loves the righteous.
9The LORD watches over the alien
   and sustains the fatherless and the widow,
   but he frustrates the ways of the wicked.

10The LORD reigns forever,
   your God, O Zion, for all generations.

   Praise the LORD.

147 PRAISE THE LORD.ᵇ

   How good it is to sing praises to our God,
   how pleasant and fitting to praise him!

2The LORD builds up Jerusalem;
   he gathers the exiles of Israel.
3He heals the brokenhearted
   and binds up their wounds.

4He determines the number of the stars
   and calls them each by name.
5Great is our Lord and mighty in power;
   his understanding has no limit.
6The LORD sustains the humble
   but casts the wicked to the ground.

7Sing to the LORD with thanksgiving;
   make music to our God on the harp.
8He covers the sky with clouds;
   he supplies the earth with rain
   and makes grass grow on the hills.

ᵃ *l* Hebrew *Hallelu Yah*; also in verse 10   ᵇ *l* Hebrew *Hallelu Yah*; also
in verse 20

Living Bible

17The Lord is fair in everything he does, and full of kindness. 18He is close to all who call on him sincerely. 19He fulfills the desires of those who reverence and trust him; he hears their cries for help and rescues them. 20He protects all those who love him, but destroys the wicked.

21I will praise the Lord and call on all men everywhere to bless his holy name forever and forever.

146 PRAISE THE Lord! Yes, really praise him! 2I will praise him as long as I live, yes, even with my dying breath.

3Don't look to men for help; their greatest leaders fail; 4for every man must die. His breathing stops, life ends, and in a moment all he planned for himself is ended. 5But happy is the man who has the God of Jacob as his helper, whose hope is in the Lord his God— 6the God who made both earth and heaven, the seas and everything in them. He is the God who keeps every promise, 7and gives justice to the poor and oppressed, and food to the hungry. He frees the prisoners, 8and opens the eyes of the blind; he lifts the burdens from those bent down beneath their loads. For the Lord loves good men. 9He protects the immigrants, and cares for the orphans and widows. But he turns topsy-turvy the plans of the wicked.

10The Lord will reign forever. O Jerusalem,c your God is King in every generation! Hallelujah! Praise the Lord!

147 HALLELUJAH! YES, praise the Lord! How good it is to sing his praises! How delightful, and how right!

2He is rebuilding Jerusalem and bringing back the exiles. 3He heals the brokenhearted, binding up their wounds. 4He counts the stars and calls them all by name. 5How great he is! His power is absolute! His understanding is unlimited. 6The Lord supports the humble, but brings the wicked into the dust.

7Sing out your thanks to him; sing praises to our God, accompanied by harps. 8He covers the heavens with clouds, sends down the showers and makes the green grass grow in mountain pastures. 9He feeds the wild

New Revised Standard

17 The LORD is just in all his ways,
        and kind in all his doings.
18 The LORD is near to all who call on him,
        to all who call on him in truth.
19 He fulfills the desire of all who fear him;
        he also hears their cry, and saves them.
20 The LORD watches over all who love him,
        but all the wicked he will destroy.

21 My mouth will speak the praise of the LORD,
        and all flesh will bless his holy name
            forever and ever.

Praise for God's Help

146 PRAISE THE LORD!
        Praise the LORD, O my soul!
2 I will praise the LORD as long as I live;
        I will sing praises to my God all my life
            long.

3 Do not put your trust in princes,
        in mortals, in whom there is no help.
4 When their breath departs, they return to the
            earth;
        on that very day their plans perish.

5 Happy are those whose help is the God of
            Jacob,
        whose hope is in the LORD their God,
6 who made heaven and earth,
        the sea, and all that is in them;
    who keeps faith forever;
7   who executes justice for the oppressed;
        who gives food to the hungry.

    The LORD sets the prisoners free;
8   the LORD opens the eyes of the blind.
    The LORD lifts up those who are bowed down;
        the LORD loves the righteous.
9 The LORD watches over the strangers;
        he upholds the orphan and the widow,
        but the way of the wicked he brings to ruin.

10 The LORD will reign forever,
        your God, O Zion, for all generations.
    Praise the LORD!

Praise for God's Care for Jerusalem

147 PRAISE THE LORD!
        How good it is to sing praises to our
            God;
        for he is gracious, and a song of praise is
            fitting.
2 The LORD builds up Jerusalem;
        he gathers the outcasts of Israel.
3 He heals the brokenhearted,
        and binds up their wounds.
4 He determines the number of the stars;
        he gives to all of them their names.
5 Great is our Lord, and abundant in power;
        his understanding is beyond measure.
6 The LORD lifts up the downtrodden;
        he casts the wicked to the ground.

7 Sing to the LORD with thanksgiving;
        make melody to our God on the lyre.
8 He covers the heavens with clouds,
        prepares rain for the earth,
        makes grass grow on the hills.

c 146:10 O Jerusalem, literally, "Zion."

King James

9He giveth to the beast his food, *and* to the young ravens which cry.

10He delighteth not in the strength of the horse: he taketh not pleasure in the legs of a man.

11The Lord taketh pleasure in them that fear him, in those that hope in his mercy.

12Praise the Lord, O Jerusalem; praise thy God, O Zion.

13For he hath strengthened the bars of thy gates; he hath blessed thy children within thee.

14He maketh peace *in* thy borders, *and* filleth thee with the finest of the wheat.

15He sendeth forth his commandment *upon* earth: his word runneth very swiftly.

16He giveth snow like wool: he scattereth the hoarfrost like ashes.

17He casteth forth his ice like morsels: who can stand before his cold?

18He sendeth out his word, and melteth them: he causeth his wind to blow, *and* the waters flow.

19He showeth his word unto Jacob, his statutes and his judgments unto Israel.

20He hath not dealt so with any nation: and *as for his* judgments, they have not known them. Praise ye the Lord.

New International

9He provides food for the cattle
    and for the young ravens when they call.

10His pleasure is not in the strength of the horse,
    nor his delight in the legs of a man;

11the Lord delights in those who fear him,
    who put their hope in his unfailing love.

12Extol the Lord, O Jerusalem;
    praise your God, O Zion,

13for he strengthens the bars of your gates
    and blesses your people within you.

14He grants peace to your borders
    and satisfies you with the finest of wheat.

15He sends his command to the earth;
    his word runs swiftly.

16He spreads the snow like wool
    and scatters the frost like ashes.

17He hurls down his hail like pebbles.
    Who can withstand his icy blast?

18He sends his word and melts them;
    he stirs up his breezes, and the waters flow.

19He has revealed his word to Jacob,
    his laws and decrees to Israel.

20He has done this for no other nation;
    they do not know his laws.

Praise the Lord.

---

148 PRAISE YE the Lord. Praise ye the Lord from the heavens: praise him in the heights.

2Praise ye him, all his angels: praise ye him, all his hosts.

3Praise ye him, sun and moon: praise him, all ye stars of light.

4Praise him, ye heavens of heavens, and ye waters that *be* above the heavens.

5Let them praise the name of the Lord: for he commanded, and they were created.

6He hath also stablished them for ever and ever; he hath made a decree which shall not pass.

7Praise the Lord from the earth, ye dragons, and all deeps:

8Fire, and hail; snow, and vapour; stormy wind fulfilling his word:

9Mountains, and all hills; fruitful trees, and all cedars:

10Beasts, and all cattle; creeping things, and flying fowl:

11Kings of the earth, and all people; princes, and all judges of the earth:

12Both young men, and maidens; old men, and children:

13Let them praise the name of the Lord: for his name alone is excellent; his glory *is* above the earth and heaven.

148 PRAISE THE Lord.[a]

Praise the Lord from the heavens,
    praise him in the heights above.

2Praise him, all his angels,
    praise him, all his heavenly hosts.

3Praise him, sun and moon,
    praise him, all you shining stars.

4Praise him, you highest heavens
    and you waters above the skies.

5Let them praise the name of the Lord,
    for he commanded and they were created.

6He set them in place for ever and ever;
    he gave a decree that will never pass away.

7Praise the Lord from the earth,
    you great sea creatures and all ocean depths,

8lightning and hail, snow and clouds,
    stormy winds that do his bidding,

9you mountains and all hills,
    fruit trees and all cedars,

10wild animals and all cattle,
    small creatures and flying birds,

11kings of the earth and all nations,
    you princes and all rulers on earth,

12young men and maidens,
    old men and children.

13Let them praise the name of the Lord,
    for his name alone is exalted;
    his splendor is above the earth and the
        heavens.

[a] *1* Hebrew *Hallelu Yah; also in verse 14*

Living Bible

animals and the young ravens cry to him for food. 10The speed of a horse is nothing to him. How puny in his sight is the strength of a man. 11But his joy is in those who reverence him, those who expect him to be loving and kind.

12Praise him, O Jerusalem! Praise your God, O Zion! 13For he has fortified your gates against all enemies, and blessed your children. 14He sends peace across your nation, and fills your barns with plenty of the finest wheat. 15He sends his orders to the world. How swiftly his word flies. 16He sends the snow in all its lovely whiteness, and scatters the frost upon the ground, 17and hurls the hail upon the earth. Who can stand before his freezing cold? 18But then he calls for warmer weather, and the spring winds blow and all the river ice is broken. 19He has made known his laws and ceremonies of worship to Israel— 20something he has not done with any other nation; they have not known his commands.

Hallelujah! Yes, praise the Lord!

148 PRAISE THE Lord, O heavens! Praise him from the skies! 2Praise him, all his angels, all the armies of heaven. 3Praise him, sun and moon, and all you twinkling stars. 4Praise him, skies above. Praise him, vapors high above the clouds.

5Let everything he has made give praise to him. For he issued his command, and they came into being; 6he established them forever and forever. His orders will never be revoked.

7And praise him down here on earth, you creatures of the ocean depths. 8Let fire and hail, snow, rain, wind and weather, all obey. 9Let the mountains and hills, the fruit trees and cedars, 10the wild animals and cattle, the snakes and birds, 11the kings and all the people with their rulers and their judges, 12young men and maidens, old men and children— 13all praise the Lord together. For he alone is worthy. His glory is far greater than all of earth and heaven. 14He has made his people strong,

New Revised Standard

9 He gives to the animals their food,
   and to the young ravens when they cry.
10 His delight is not in the strength of the horse,
   nor his pleasure in the speed of a runner;b
11 but the LORD takes pleasure in those who fear him,
   in those who hope in his steadfast love.

12 Praise the LORD, O Jerusalem!
   Praise your God, O Zion!
13 For he strengthens the bars of your gates;
   he blesses your children within you.
14 He grants peacec within your borders;
   he fills you with the finest of wheat.
15 He sends out his command to the earth;
   his word runs swiftly.
16 He gives snow like wool;
   he scatters frost like ashes.
17 He hurls down hail like crumbs—
   who can stand before his cold?
18 He sends out his word, and melts them;
   he makes his wind blow, and the waters flow.
19 He declares his word to Jacob,
   his statutes and ordinances to Israel.
20 He has not dealt thus with any other nation;
   they do not know his ordinances.
   Praise the LORD!

Praise for God's Universal Glory

148 PRAISE THE LORD!
   Praise the LORD from the heavens;
   praise him in the heights!
2 Praise him, all his angels;
   praise him, all his host!

3 Praise him, sun and moon;
   praise him, all you shining stars!
4 Praise him, you highest heavens,
   and you waters above the heavens!

5 Let them praise the name of the LORD,
   for he commanded and they were created.
6 He established them forever and ever;
   he fixed their bounds, which cannot be passed.d

7 Praise the LORD from the earth,
   you sea monsters and all deeps,
8 fire and hail, snow and frost,
   stormy wind fulfilling his command!

9 Mountains and all hills,
   fruit trees and all cedars!
10 Wild animals and all cattle,
   creeping things and flying birds!

11 Kings of the earth and all peoples,
   princes and all rulers of the earth!
12 Young men and women alike,
   old and young together!

13 Let them praise the name of the LORD,
   for his name alone is exalted;
   his glory is above earth and heaven.

b Heb *legs of a person*   c Or *prosperity*   d Or *he set a law that cannot pass away*

King James

14He also exalteth the horn of his people, the praise of all his saints; *even* of the children of Israel, a people near unto him. Praise ye the LORD.

149 PRAISE YE the LORD. Sing unto the LORD a new song, *and* his praise in the congregation of saints.

2Let Israel rejoice in him that made him: let the children of Zion be joyful in their King.

3Let them praise his name in the dance: let them sing praises unto him with the timbrel and harp.

4For the LORD taketh pleasure in his people: he will beautify the meek with salvation.

5Let the saints be joyful in glory: let them sing aloud upon their beds.

6*Let* the high *praises* of God *be* in their mouth, and a twoedged sword in their hand;

7To execute vengeance upon the heathen, *and* punishments upon the people;

8To bind their kings with chains, and their nobles with fetters of iron;

9To execute upon them the judgment written: this honour have all his saints. Praise ye the LORD.

150 PRAISE YE the LORD. Praise God in his sanctuary: praise him in the firmament of his power.

2Praise him for his mighty acts; praise him according to his excellent greatness.

3Praise him with the sound of the trumpet: praise him with the psaltery and harp.

4Praise him with the timbrel and dance: praise him with stringed instruments and organs.

5Praise him upon the loud cymbals: praise him upon the high sounding cymbals.

6Let every thing that hath breath praise the LORD. Praise ye the LORD.

New International

14He has raised up for his people a horn,[a]
the praise of all his saints,
of Israel, the people close to his heart.

Praise the LORD.

149 PRAISE THE LORD.[b]
Sing to the LORD a new song,
his praise in the assembly of the saints.

2Let Israel rejoice in their Maker;
let the people of Zion be glad in their King.
3Let them praise his name with dancing
and make music to him with tambourine and
harp.
4For the LORD takes delight in his people;
he crowns the humble with salvation.
5Let the saints rejoice in this honor
and sing for joy on their beds.

6May the praise of God be in their mouths
and a double-edged sword in their hands,
7to inflict vengeance on the nations
and punishment on the peoples,
8to bind their kings with fetters,
their nobles with shackles of iron,
9to carry out the sentence written against them.
This is the glory of all his saints.

Praise the LORD.

150 PRAISE THE LORD.[c]
Praise God in his sanctuary;
praise him in his mighty heavens.
2Praise him for his acts of power;
praise him for his surpassing greatness.
3Praise him with the sounding of the trumpet,
praise him with the harp and lyre,
4praise him with tambourine and dancing,
praise him with the strings and flute,
5praise him with the clash of cymbals,
praise him with resounding cymbals.

6Let everything that has breath praise the LORD.

Praise the LORD.

---

[a] *14 Horn* here symbolizes strong one, that is, king.   [b] *1* Hebrew *Hallelu Yah*; also in verse 9   [c] *1* Hebrew *Hallelu Yah*; also in verse 6

Living Bible

honoring his godly ones—the people of Israel, the people closest to him.

Hallelujah! Yes, praise the Lord!

149 HALLELUJAH! YES, praise the Lord! Sing him a new song. Sing his praises, all his people.

2O Israel, rejoice in your Maker. O people of Jerusalem, exult in your King. 3Praise his name with dancing, accompanied by drums and lyre.

4, 5For Jehovah enjoys his people; he will save the humble. Let his people rejoice in this honor. Let them sing for joy as they lie upon their beds.

6, 7Adore him, O his people! And take a double-edged sword to execute his punishment upon the nations. 8Bind their kings and leaders with iron chains, 9and execute their sentences.

He is the glory of his people. Hallelujah! Praise him!

150 HALLELUJAH! YES, praise the Lord! Praise him in his Temple, and in the heavens he made with mighty power.d 2Praise him for his mighty works. Praise his unequaled greatness. 3Praise him with the trumpet and with lute and harp. 4Praise him with the drums and dancing. Praise him with stringed instruments and horns. 5Praise him with the cymbals, yes, loud clanging cymbals.

6Let everything alive give praises to the Lord! *You* praise him!

Hallelujah!

New Revised Standard

14 He has raised up a horn for his people,
    praise for all his faithful,
        for the people of Israel who are close to
        him.
    Praise the LORD!

Praise for God's Goodness to Israel

149 PRAISE THE LORD!
    Sing to the LORD a new song,
        his praise in the assembly of the faithful.
2 Let Israel be glad in its Maker;
        let the children of Zion rejoice in their
        King.
3 Let them praise his name with dancing,
        making melody to him with tambourine and
        lyre.
4 For the LORD takes pleasure in his people;
        he adorns the humble with victory.
5 Let the faithful exult in glory;
        let them sing for joy on their couches.
6 Let the high praises of God be in their throats
        and two-edged swords in their hands,
7 to execute vengeance on the nations
        and punishment on the peoples,
8 to bind their kings with fetters
        and their nobles with chains of iron,
9 to execute on them the judgment decreed.
        This is glory for all his faithful ones.
    Praise the LORD!

Praise for God's Surpassing Greatness

150 PRAISE THE LORD!
    Praise God in his sanctuary;
        praise him in his mighty firmament!e
2 Praise him for his mighty deeds;
        praise him according to his surpassing
        greatness!

3 Praise him with trumpet sound;
        praise him with lute and harp!
4 Praise him with tambourine and dance;
        praise him with strings and pipe!
5 Praise him with clanging cymbals;
        praise him with loud clashing cymbals!
6 Let everything that breathes praise the LORD!
    Praise the LORD!

---

d *150:1 in the heavens he made with mighty power,* literally, "in the firmament of his power."

e Or *dome*

THE

Proverbs

Proverbs

King James

1 THE PROVERBS of Solomon the son of David, king of Israel;

2To know wisdom and instruction; to perceive the words of understanding;

3To receive the instruction of wisdom, justice, and judgment, and equity;

4To give subtlety to the simple, to the young man knowledge and discretion.

5A wise *man* will hear, and will increase learning; and a man of understanding shall attain unto wise counsels:

6To understand a proverb, and the interpretation; the words of the wise, and their dark sayings.

7¶ The fear of the LORD *is* the beginning of knowledge: *but* fools despise wisdom and instruction.

8My son, hear the instruction of thy father, and forsake not the law of thy mother:

9For they *shall be* an ornament of grace unto thy head, and chains about thy neck.

10¶ My son, if sinners entice thee, consent thou not.

11If they say, Come with us, let us lay wait for blood, let us lurk privily for the innocent without cause:

12Let us swallow them up alive as the grave; and whole, as those that go down into the pit:

13We shall find all precious substance, we shall fill our houses with spoil:

14Cast in thy lot among us; let us all have one purse:

15My son, walk not thou in the way with them; refrain thy foot from their path:

16For their feet run to evil, and make haste to shed blood.

17Surely in vain the net is spread in the sight of any bird.

18And they lay wait for their *own* blood; they lurk privily for their *own* lives.

19So *are* the ways of every one that is greedy of gain; *which* taketh away the life of the owners thereof.

20¶ Wisdom crieth without; she uttereth her voice in the streets:

21She crieth in the chief place of concourse, in the openings of the gates: in the city she uttereth her words, *saying,*

New International

Prologue: Purpose and Theme

1 THE PROVERBS of Solomon son of David, king of Israel:

2for attaining wisdom and discipline;
 for understanding words of insight;
3for acquiring a disciplined and prudent life,
 doing what is right and just and fair;
4for giving prudence to the simple,
 knowledge and discretion to the young—
5let the wise listen and add to their learning,
 and let the discerning get guidance—
6for understanding proverbs and parables,
 the sayings and riddles of the wise.

7The fear of the LORD is the beginning of
 knowledge,
 but foolsa despise wisdom and discipline.

Exhortations to Embrace Wisdom

Warning Against Enticement

8Listen, my son, to your father's instruction
 and do not forsake your mother's teaching.
9They will be a garland to grace your head
 and a chain to adorn your neck.

10My son, if sinners entice you,
 do not give in to them.
11If they say, "Come along with us;
 let's lie in wait for someone's blood,
 let's waylay some harmless soul;
12let's swallow them alive, like the grave,b
 and whole, like those who go down to the pit;
13we will get all sorts of valuable things
 and fill our houses with plunder;
14throw in your lot with us,
 and we will share a common purse"—
15my son, do not go along with them,
 do not set foot on their paths;
16for their feet rush into sin,
 they are swift to shed blood.
17How useless to spread a net
 in full view of all the birds!
18These men lie in wait for their own blood;
 they waylay only themselves!
19Such is the end of all who go after ill-gotten
 gain;
 it takes away the lives of those who get it.

Warning Against Rejecting Wisdom

20Wisdom calls aloud in the street,
 she raises her voice in the public squares;
21at the head of the noisy streetsc she cries out,
 in the gateways of the city she makes her
 speech:

---

a 7 The Hebrew words rendered *fool* in Proverbs, and often elsewhere in the Old Testament, denote one who is morally deficient.   b 12 Hebrew *Sheol*
c 21 Hebrew; Septuagint / *on the tops of the walls*

Living Bible

Proverbs

1 THESE ARE the proverbs of King Solomon of Israel, David's son:

²He wrote them to teach his people how to live—how to act in every circumstance, ³for he wanted them to be understanding, just and fair in everything they did. ⁴"I want to make the simple-minded wise!" he said. "I want to warn young men about some problems they will face. ⁵, ⁶I want those already wise to become the wiser and become leaders by exploring the depths of meaning in these nuggets of truth."

⁷, ⁸, ⁹How does a man become wise? The first step is to trust and reverence the Lord!

Only fools refuse to be taught. Listen to your father and mother. What you learn from them will stand you in good stead; it will gain you many honors.ᵈ

¹⁰If young toughs tell you, "Come and join us"—turn your back on them! ¹¹"We'll hide and rob and kill," they say. ¹²"Good or bad, we'll treat them all alike. ¹³And the loot we'll get! All kinds of stuff! ¹⁴Come on, throw in your lot with us; we'll split with you in equal shares."

¹⁵Don't do it, son! Stay far from men like that, ¹⁶for crime is their way of life, and murder is their specialty. ¹⁷When a bird sees a trap being set, it stays away, ¹⁸but not these men; they trap themselves! They lay a booby trap for their own lives. ¹⁹Such is the fate of all who live by violence and murder.ᵉ They will die a violent death.

²⁰Wisdom shouts in the streets for a hearing. ²¹She calls out to the crowds along Main Street, and to the judges in their courts, and to everyone in all the land:

New Revised Standard

Proverbs

1 THE PROVERBS of Solomon son of David, king of Israel:

Prologue

2 For learning about wisdom and instruction,
      for understanding words of insight,
3 for gaining instruction in wise dealing,
      righteousness, justice, and equity;
4 to teach shrewdness to the simple,
      knowledge and prudence to the young—
5 Let the wise also hear and gain in learning,
      and the discerning acquire skill,
6 to understand a proverb and a figure,
      the words of the wise and their riddles.

7 The fear of the LORD is the beginning of
         knowledge;
      fools despise wisdom and instruction.

Warnings against Evil Companions

8 Hear, my child, your father's instruction,
      and do not reject your mother's teaching;
9 for they are a fair garland for your head,
      and pendants for your neck.
10 My child, if sinners entice you,
      do not consent.
11 If they say, "Come with us, let us lie in wait
         for blood;
      let us wantonly ambush the innocent;
12 like Sheol let us swallow them alive
      and whole, like those who go down to the
         Pit.
13 We shall find all kinds of costly things;
      we shall fill our houses with booty.
14 Throw in your lot among us;
      we will all have one purse"—
15 my child, do not walk in their way,
      keep your foot from their paths;
16 for their feet run to evil,
      and they hurry to shed blood.
17 For in vain is the net baited
      while the bird is looking on;
18 yet they lie in wait—to kill themselves!
      and set an ambush—for their own lives!
19 Such is the endᶠ of all who are greedy for
         gain;
      it takes away the life of its possessors.

The Call of Wisdom

20 Wisdom cries out in the street;
      in the squares she raises her voice.
21 At the busiest corner she cries out;
      at the entrance of the city gates she speaks:

ᵈ 1:7-9 *many honors*, literally, "a fair garland and adornment."   ᵉ *1:19 all who live by violence and murder*, literally, "all who are greedy of gain."   ᶠ Gk: Heb *ways*

King James

22How long, ye simple ones, will ye love simplicity? and the scorners delight in their scorning, and fools hate knowledge?

23Turn you at my reproof: behold, I will pour out my spirit unto you, I will make known my words unto you.

24¶ Because I have called, and ye refused; I have stretched out my hand, and no man regarded;

25But ye have set at nought all my counsel, and would none of my reproof:

26I also will laugh at your calamity; I will mock when your fear cometh;

27When your fear cometh as desolation, and your destruction cometh as a whirlwind; when distress and anguish cometh upon you.

28Then shall they call upon me, but I will not answer; they shall seek me early, but they shall not find me:

29For that they hated knowledge, and did not choose the fear of the LORD:

30They would none of my counsel: they despised all my reproof.

31Therefore shall they eat of the fruit of their own way, and be filled with their own devices.

32For the turning away of the simple shall slay them, and the prosperity of fools shall destroy them.

33But whoso hearkeneth unto me shall dwell safely, and shall be quiet from fear of evil.

2 MY SON, if thou wilt receive my words, and hide my commandments with thee;

2So that thou incline thine ear unto wisdom, *and* apply thine heart to understanding;

3Yea, if thou criest after knowledge, *and* liftest up thy voice for understanding;

4If thou seekest her as silver, and searchest for her as *for* hid treasures;

5Then shalt thou understand the fear of the LORD, and find the knowledge of God.

6For the LORD giveth wisdom: out of his mouth *cometh* knowledge and understanding.

7He layeth up sound wisdom for the righteous: *he is* a buckler to them that walk uprightly.

8He keepeth the paths of judgment, and preserveth the way of his saints.

9Then shalt thou understand righteousness, and judgment, and equity; *yea,* every good path.

10¶ When wisdom entereth into thine heart, and knowledge is pleasant unto thy soul;

11Discretion shall preserve thee, understanding shall keep thee:

12To deliver thee from the way of the evil *man,* from the man that speaketh froward things;

13Who leave the paths of uprightness, to walk in the ways of darkness;

14Who rejoice to do evil, *and* delight in the frowardness of the wicked;

15Whose ways *are* crooked, and *they* froward in their paths:

New International

22"How long will you simple ones[a] love your simple ways?

How long will mockers delight in mockery and fools hate knowledge?

23If you had responded to my rebuke, I would have poured out my heart to you and made my thoughts known to you.

24But since you rejected me when I called and no one gave heed when I stretched out my hand,

25since you ignored all my advice and would not accept my rebuke,

26I in turn will laugh at your disaster; I will mock when calamity overtakes you—

27when calamity overtakes you like a storm, when disaster sweeps over you like a whirlwind, when distress and trouble overwhelm you.

28"Then they will call to me but I will not answer; they will look for me but will not find me.

29Since they hated knowledge and did not choose to fear the LORD,

30since they would not accept my advice and spurned my rebuke,

31they will eat the fruit of their ways and be filled with the fruit of their schemes.

32For the waywardness of the simple will kill them, and the complacency of fools will destroy them;

33but whoever listens to me will live in safety and be at ease, without fear of harm."

Moral Benefits of Wisdom

2 MY SON, if you accept my words and store up my commands within you,

2turning your ear to wisdom and applying your heart to understanding,

3and if you call out for insight and cry aloud for understanding,

4and if you look for it as for silver and search for it as for hidden treasure,

5then you will understand the fear of the LORD and find the knowledge of God.

6For the LORD gives wisdom, and from his mouth come knowledge and understanding.

7He holds victory in store for the upright, he is a shield to those whose walk is blameless,

8for he guards the course of the just and protects the way of his faithful ones.

9Then you will understand what is right and just and fair—every good path.

10For wisdom will enter your heart, and knowledge will be pleasant to your soul.

11Discretion will protect you, and understanding will guard you.

12Wisdom will save you from the ways of wicked men, from men whose words are perverse,

13who leave the straight paths to walk in dark ways,

14who delight in doing wrong and rejoice in the perverseness of evil,

15whose paths are crooked and who are devious in their ways.

---

[a] 22 The Hebrew word rendered *simple* in Proverbs generally denotes one without moral direction and inclined to evil.

Living Bible

22"You simpletons!" she cries. "How long will you go on being fools? How long will you scoff at wisdom and fight the facts? 23Come here and listen to me! I'll pour out the spirit of wisdom upon you, and make you wise. 24I have called you so often but still you won't come. I have pleaded, but all in vain. 25For you have spurned my counsel and reproof. 26Some day you'll be in trouble, and I'll laugh! Mock me, will you?—I'll mock you! 27When a storm of terror surrounds you, and when you are engulfed by anguish and distress, 28then I will not answer your cry for help. It will be too late though you search for me ever so anxiously.

29"For you closed your eyes to the facts and did not choose to reverence and trust the Lord, 30and you turned your back on me, spurning my advice. 31That is why you must eat the bitter fruit of having your own way, and experience the full terrors of the pathway you have chosen. 32For you turned away from me—to death; your own complacency will kill you. Fools! 33But all who listen to me shall live in peace and safety, unafraid."

2 EVERY YOUNG man who listens to me and obeys my instructions will be given wisdom and good sense. 3, 4, 5Yes, if you want better insight and discernment, and are searching for them as you would for lost money or hidden treasure, then wisdom will be given you, and knowledge of God himself; you will soon learn the importance of reverence for the Lord and of trusting him.

6For the Lord grants wisdom! His every word is a treasure of knowledge and understanding. 7, 8He grants good sense to the godly—his saints. He is their shield, protecting them and guarding their pathway. 9He shows how to distinguish right from wrong, how to find the right decision every time. 10For wisdom and truth will enter the very center of your being, filling your life with joy. 11, 12, 13You will be given the sense to stay away from evil men who want you to be their partners in crime—men who turn from God's ways to walk down dark and evil paths, 14and exult in doing wrong, for they thoroughly enjoy their sins. 15Everything they do is crooked and wrong.

New Revised Standard

22 "How long, O simple ones, will you love
        being simple?
    How long will scoffers delight in their
        scoffing
    and fools hate knowledge?
23 Give heed to my reproof;
    I will pour out my thoughts to you;
    I will make my words known to you.
24 Because I have called and you refused,
        have stretched out my hand and no one
        heeded,
25 and because you have ignored all my counsel
        and would have none of my reproof,
26 I also will laugh at your calamity;
        I will mock when panic strikes you,
27 when panic strikes you like a storm,
        and your calamity comes like a whirlwind,
        when distress and anguish come upon you.
28 Then they will call upon me, but I will not
        answer;
    they will seek me diligently, but will not
        find me.
29 Because they hated knowledge
        and did not choose the fear of the LORD,
30 would have none of my counsel,
        and despised all my reproof,
31 therefore they shall eat the fruit of their way
        and be sated with their own devices.
32 For waywardness kills the simple,
        and the complacency of fools destroys them;
33 but those who listen to me will be secure
        and will live at ease, without dread of
        disaster."

The Value of Wisdom

2 MY CHILD, if you accept my words
        and treasure up my commandments within
        you,
2 making your ear attentive to wisdom
        and inclining your heart to understanding;
3 if you indeed cry out for insight,
        and raise your voice for understanding;
4 if you seek it like silver,
        and search for it as for hidden treasures—
5 then you will understand the fear of the LORD
        and find the knowledge of God.
6 For the LORD gives wisdom;
        from his mouth come knowledge and
        understanding;
7 he stores up sound wisdom for the upright;
        he is a shield to those who walk
        blamelessly,
8 guarding the paths of justice
        and preserving the way of his faithful ones.
9 Then you will understand righteousness and
        justice
    and equity, every good path;
10 for wisdom will come into your heart,
        and knowledge will be pleasant to your
        soul;
11 prudence will watch over you;
        and understanding will guard you.
12 It will save you from the way of evil,
        from those who speak perversely,
13 who forsake the paths of uprightness
        to walk in the ways of darkness,
14 who rejoice in doing evil
        and delight in the perverseness of evil;
15 those whose paths are crooked,
        and who are devious in their ways.

King James

16To deliver thee from the strange woman, *even* from the stranger *which* flattereth with her words;

17Which forsaketh the guide of her youth, and forgetteth the covenant of her God.

18For her house inclineth unto death, and her paths unto the dead.

19None that go unto her return again, neither take they hold of the paths of life.

20That thou mayest walk in the way of good *men,* and keep the paths of the righteous.

21For the upright shall dwell in the land, and the perfect shall remain in it,

22But the wicked shall be cut off from the earth, and the transgressors shall be rooted out of it.

3 MY SON, forget not my law; but let thine heart keep my commandments:

2For length of days, and long life, and peace, shall they add to thee.

3Let not mercy and truth forsake thee: bind them about thy neck; write them upon the table of thine heart:

4So shalt thou find favour and good understanding in the sight of God and man.

5¶ Trust in the LORD with all thine heart; and lean not unto thine own understanding.

6In all thy ways acknowledge him, and he shall direct thy paths.

7¶ Be not wise in thine own eyes: fear the LORD, and depart from evil.

8It shall be health to thy navel, and marrow to thy bones.

9Honour the LORD with thy substance, and with the firstfruits of all thine increase:

10So shall thy barns be filled with plenty, and thy presses shall burst out with new wine.

11¶ My son, despise not the chastening of the LORD; neither be weary of his correction:

12For whom the LORD loveth he correcteth; even as a father the son *in whom* he delighteth.

13¶ Happy *is* the man *that* findeth wisdom, and the man *that* getteth understanding.

14For the merchandise of it *is* better than the merchandise of silver, and the gain thereof than fine gold.

15She *is* more precious than rubies: and all the things thou canst desire are not to be compared unto her.

16Length of days *is* in her right hand; *and* in her left hand riches and honour.

17Her ways *are* ways of pleasantness, and all her paths *are* peace.

18She *is* a tree of life to them that lay hold upon her: and happy *is every* one that retaineth her.

19The LORD by wisdom hath founded the earth; by understanding hath he established the heavens.

New International

16It will save you also from the adulteress,
　　from the wayward wife with her seductive
　　words,
17who has left the partner of her youth
　　and ignored the covenant she made before
　　God.a
18For her house leads down to death
　　and her paths to the spirits of the dead.
19None who go to her return
　　or attain the paths of life.

20Thus you will walk in the ways of good men
　　and keep to the paths of the righteous.
21For the upright will live in the land,
　　and the blameless will remain in it;
22but the wicked will be cut off from the land,
　　and the unfaithful will be torn from it.

Further Benefits of Wisdom

3 MY SON, do not forget my teaching,
　　but keep my commands in your heart,
2for they will prolong your life many years
　　and bring you prosperity.

3Let love and faithfulness never leave you;
　　bind them around your neck,
　　write them on the tablet of your heart.
4Then you will win favor and a good name
　　in the sight of God and man.

5Trust in the LORD with all your heart
　　and lean not on your own understanding;
6in all your ways acknowledge him,
　　and he will make your paths straight.b

7Do not be wise in your own eyes;
　　fear the LORD and shun evil.
8This will bring health to your body
　　and nourishment to your bones.

9Honor the LORD with your wealth,
　　with the firstfruits of all your crops;
10then your barns will be filled to overflowing,
　　and your vats will brim over with new wine.

11My son, do not despise the LORD's discipline
　　and do not resent his rebuke,
12because the LORD disciplines those he loves,
　　as a fatherc the son he delights in.

13Blessed is the man who finds wisdom,
　　the man who gains understanding,
14for she is more profitable than silver
　　and yields better returns than gold.
15She is more precious than rubies;
　　nothing you desire can compare with her.
16Long life is in her right hand;
　　in her left hand are riches and honor.
17Her ways are pleasant ways,
　　and all her paths are peace.
18She is a tree of life to those who embrace her;
　　those who lay hold of her will be blessed.

19By wisdom the LORD laid the earth's
　　foundations,
　　by understanding he set the heavens in place;

a 17 Or covenant of her God　　b 6 Or will direct your paths　　c 12 Hebrew; Septuagint / and he punishes

Living Bible

16, 17Only wisdom from the Lord can save a man from the flattery of prostitutes; these girls have abandoned their husbands and flouted the laws of God. 18Their houses lie along the road to death and hell. 19The men who enter them are doomed. None of these men will ever be the same again.d

20Follow the steps of the godly instead, and stay on the right path, 21for only good men enjoy life to the full;e 22evil men lose the good things they might have had,f and they themselves shall be destroyed.

3 MY SON, never forget the things I've taught you. If you want a long and satisfying life, closely follow my instructions. 3Never tire of loyalty and kindness. Hold these virtues tightly. Write them deep within your heart. 4, 5If you want favor with both God and man, and a reputation for good judgment and common sense, then trust the Lord completely; don't ever trust yourself. 6In everything you do, put God first, and he will direct you and crown your efforts with success.

7, 8Don't be conceited, sure of your own wisdom. Instead, trust and reverence the Lord, and turn your back on evil; when you do that, then you will be given renewed health and vitality.

9, 10Honor the Lord by giving him the first part of all your income, and he will fill your barns with wheat and barley and overflow your wine vats with the finest wines.

11, 12Young man, do not resent it when God chastens and corrects you, for his punishment is proof of his love. Just as a father punishes a son he delights in to make him better, so the Lord corrects you.

13, 14, 15The man who knows right from wrongg and has good judgment and common sense is happier than the man who is immensely rich! For such wisdom is far more valuable than precious jewels. Nothing else compares with it. 16, 17Wisdom gives:

A long, good life
Riches
Honor
Pleasure
Peace

18Wisdom is a tree of life to those who eat her fruit; happy is the man who keeps on eating it.

19The Lord's wisdom founded the earth; his understanding established all the universe and space. 20The

New Revised Standard

16 You will be saved from the looseh woman,
  from the adulteress with her smooth words,
17 who forsakes the partner of her youth
  and forgets her sacred covenant;
18 for her wayi leads down to death,
  and her paths to the shades;
19 those who go to her never come back,
  nor do they regain the paths of life.

20 Therefore walk in the way of the good,
  and keep to the paths of the just.
21 For the upright will abide in the land,
  and the innocent will remain in it;
22 but the wicked will be cut off from the land,
  and the treacherous will be rooted out of it.

Admonition to Trust and Honor God

3 MY CHILD, do not forget my teaching,
  but let your heart keep my commandments;
2 for length of days and years of life
  and abundant welfare they will give you.

3 Do not let loyalty and faithfulness forsake
    you;
  bind them around your neck,
  write them on the tablet of your heart.
4 So you will find favor and good repute
  in the sight of God and of people.

5 Trust in the LORD with all your heart,
  and do not rely on your own insight.
6 In all your ways acknowledge him,
  and he will make straight your paths.
7 Do not be wise in your own eyes;
  fear the LORD, and turn away from evil.
8 It will be a healing for your flesh
  and a refreshment for your body.

9 Honor the LORD with your substance
  and with the first fruits of all your produce;
10 then your barns will be filled with plenty,
  and your vats will be bursting with wine.

11 My child, do not despise the LORD's discipline
  or be weary of his reproof,
12 for the LORD reproves the one he loves,
  as a father the son in whom he delights.

The True Wealth

13 Happy are those who find wisdom,
  and those who get understanding,
14 for her income is better than silver,
  and her revenue better than gold.
15 She is more precious than jewels,
  and nothing you desire can compare with
    her.
16 Long life is in her right hand;
  in her left hand are riches and honor.
17 Her ways are ways of pleasantness,
  and all her paths are peace.
18 She is a tree of life to those who lay hold of
    her;
  those who hold her fast are called happy.

God's Wisdom in Creation

19 The LORD by wisdom founded the earth;
  by understanding he established the heavens;

---

d 2:19 None of these men will ever be the same again, literally, "never return to the ways of life." e 2:21 enjoy life to the full, literally, "shall dwell in the land." f 2:22 lose the good things they might have had, literally, "shall be cut off from the land." g 3:13-15 The man who knows right from wrong, literally, "The man that finds wisdom."

h Heb strange   i Cn: Heb house

King James

20By his knowledge the depths are broken up, and the clouds drop down the dew.

21¶ My son, let not them depart from thine eyes: keep sound wisdom and discretion:

22So shall they be life unto thy soul, and grace to thy neck.

23Then shalt thou walk in thy way safely, and thy foot shall not stumble.

24When thou liest down, thou shalt not be afraid: yea, thou shalt lie down, and thy sleep shall be sweet.

25Be not afraid of sudden fear, neither of the desolation of the wicked, when it cometh.

26For the LORD shall be thy confidence, and shall keep thy foot from being taken.

27¶ Withhold not good from them to whom it is due, when it is in the power of thine hand to do *it*.

28Say not unto thy neighbour, Go, and come again, and tomorrow I will give; when thou hast it by thee.

29Devise not evil against thy neighbour, seeing he dwelleth securely by thee.

30¶ Strive not with a man without cause, if he have done thee no harm.

31¶ Envy thou not the oppressor, and choose none of his ways.

32For the froward *is* abomination to the LORD: but his secret *is* with the righteous.

33¶ The curse of the LORD *is* in the house of the wicked: but he blesseth the habitation of the just.

34Surely he scorneth the scorners: but he giveth grace unto the lowly.

35The wise shall inherit glory: but shame shall be the promotion of fools.

4 HEAR, YE children, the instruction of a father, and attend to know understanding.

2For I give you good doctrine, forsake ye not my law.

3For I was my father's son, tender and only *beloved* in the sight of my mother.

4He taught me also, and said unto me, Let thine heart retain my words: keep my commandments, and live.

5Get wisdom, get understanding: forget *it* not; neither decline from the words of my mouth.

6Forsake her not, and she shall preserve thee: love her, and she shall keep thee.

7Wisdom *is* the principal thing; *therefore* get wisdom: and with all thy getting get understanding.

8Exalt her, and she shall promote thee: she shall bring thee to honour, when thou dost embrace her.

9She shall give to thine head an ornament of grace: a crown of glory shall she deliver to thee.

10Hear, O my son, and receive my sayings; and the years of thy life shall be many.

New International

20by his knowledge the deeps were divided,
    and the clouds let drop the dew.

21My son, preserve sound judgment and
      discernment,
    do not let them out of your sight;

22they will be life for you,
    an ornament to grace your neck.

23Then you will go on your way in safety,
    and your foot will not stumble;

24when you lie down, you will not be afraid;
    when you lie down, your sleep will be sweet.

25Have no fear of sudden disaster
    or of the ruin that overtakes the wicked,

26for the LORD will be your confidence
    and will keep your foot from being snared.

27Do not withhold good from those who deserve
      it,
    when it is in your power to act.

28Do not say to your neighbor,
    "Come back later; I'll give it tomorrow"—
    when you now have it with you.

29Do not plot harm against your neighbor,
    who lives trustfully near you.

30Do not accuse a man for no reason—
    when he has done you no harm.

31Do not envy a violent man
    or choose any of his ways,

32for the LORD detests a perverse man
    but takes the upright into his confidence.

33The LORD's curse is on the house of the
      wicked,
    but he blesses the home of the righteous.

34He mocks proud mockers
    but gives grace to the humble.

35The wise inherit honor,
    but fools he holds up to shame.

Wisdom Is Supreme

4 LISTEN, MY sons, to a father's instruction;
    pay attention and gain understanding.

2I give you sound learning,
    so do not forsake my teaching.

3When I was a boy in my father's house,
    still tender, and an only child of my mother,

4he taught me and said,
    "Lay hold of my words with all your heart;
    keep my commands and you will live.

5Get wisdom, get understanding;
    do not forget my words or swerve from them.

6Do not forsake wisdom, and she will protect
      you;
    love her, and she will watch over you.

7Wisdom is supreme; therefore get wisdom.
    Though it cost all you have,a get
      understanding.

8Esteem her, and she will exalt you;
    embrace her, and she will honor you.

9She will set a garland of grace on your head
    and present you with a crown of splendor."

10Listen, my son, accept what I say,
    and the years of your life will be many.

---

a 7 Or *Whatever else you get*

Living Bible

deep fountains of the earth were broken open by his knowledge, and the skies poured down rain.

21Have two goals: wisdom—that is, knowing and doing right—and common sense. Don't let them slip away, 22for they fill you with living energy, and bring you honor and respect.b 23They keep you safe from defeat and disaster and from stumbling off the trail. 24, 25, 26With them on guard you can sleep without fear; you need not be afraid of disaster or the plots of wicked men, for the Lord is with you; he protects you.

27, 28Don't withhold repayment of your debts. Don't say "some other time," if you can pay now. 29Don't plot against your neighbor; he is trusting you. 30Don't get into needless fights. 31Don't envy violent men. Don't copy their ways. 32For such men are an abomination to the Lord, but he gives his friendship to the godly. 33The curse of God is on the wicked, but his blessing is on the upright. 34The Lord mocks at mockers, but helps the humble. 35The wise are promoted to honor, but fools are promoted to shame!

4 YOUNG MEN, listen to me as you would to your father. Listen, and grow wise, for I speak the truth—don't turn away. 3For I, too, was once a son, tenderly loved by my mother as an only child, and the companion of my father. 4He told me never to forget his words. "If you follow them," he said, "you will have a long and happy life. 5Learn to be wise," he said, "and develop good judgment and common sense! I cannot overemphasize this point."c 6Cling to wisdom—she will protect you. Love her—she will guard you.

7Getting wisdom is the most important thing you can do! And with your wisdom, develop common sense and good judgment. 8, 9If you exalt wisdom, she will exalt you. Hold her fast and she will lead you to great honor; she will place a beautiful crown upon your head. 10My son, listen to me and do as I say, and you will have a long, good life.

New Revised Standard

20 by his knowledge the deeps broke open,
    and the clouds drop down the dew.

The True Security

21 My child, do not let these escape from your
        sight:
    keep sound wisdom and prudence,
22 and they will be life for your soul
    and adornment for your neck.
23 Then you will walk on your way securely
    and your foot will not stumble.
24 If you sit down,d you will not be afraid;
    when you lie down, your sleep will be
        sweet.
25 Do not be afraid of sudden panic,
    or of the storm that strikes the wicked;
26 for the LORD will be your confidence
    and will keep your foot from being caught.

27 Do not withhold good from those to whom it
        is due,e
    when it is in your power to do it.
28 Do not say to your neighbor, "Go, and come
        again,
    tomorrow I will give it"—when you have it
        with you.
29 Do not plan harm against your neighbor
    who lives trustingly beside you.
30 Do not quarrel with anyone without cause,
    when no harm has been done to you.
31 Do not envy the violent
    and do not choose any of their ways;
32 for the perverse are an abomination to the
        LORD,
    but the upright are in his confidence.
33 The LORD's curse is on the house of the
        wicked,
    but he blesses the abode of the righteous.
34 Toward the scorners he is scornful,
    but to the humble he shows favor.
35 The wise will inherit honor,
    but stubborn fools, disgrace.

Parental Advice

4 LISTEN, CHILDREN, to a father's instruction,
    and be attentive, that you may gainf
        insight;
 2 for I give you good precepts:
    do not forsake my teaching.
 3 When I was a son with my father,
    tender, and my mother's favorite,
 4 he taught me, and said to me,
    "Let your heart hold fast my words;
    keep my commandments, and live.
 5 Get wisdom; get insight: do not forget, nor
        turn away
    from the words of my mouth.
 6 Do not forsake her, and she will keep you;
    love her, and she will guard you.
 7 The beginning of wisdom is this: Get wisdom,
    and whatever else you get, get insight.
 8 Prize her highly, and she will exalt you;
    she will honor you if you embrace her.
 9 She will place on your head a fair garland;
    she will bestow on you a beautiful crown."

Admonition to Keep to the Right Path

10 Hear, my child, and accept my words,
    that the years of your life may be many.

---

b 3:22 *bring you honor and respect*, literally, "be an ornament to your neck."
c 4:5 *I cannot overemphasize this point*, literally, "Forget not nor turn from the words of my mouth."

d Gk: Heb *lie down*   e Heb *from its owners*   f Heb *know*

King James

11I have taught thee in the way of wisdom; I have led thee in right paths.

12When thou goest, thy steps shall not be straitened; and when thou runnest, thou shalt not stumble.

13Take fast hold of instruction; let *her* not go: keep her; for she *is* thy life.

14¶ Enter not into the path of the wicked, and go not in the way of evil *men*.

15Avoid it, pass not by it, turn from it, and pass away.

16For they sleep not, except they have done mischief; and their sleep is taken away, unless they cause *some* to fall.

17For they eat the bread of wickedness, and drink the wine of violence.

18But the path of the just *is* as the shining light, that shineth more and more unto the perfect day.

19The way of the wicked *is* as darkness: they know not at what they stumble.

20¶ My son, attend to my words; incline thine ear unto my sayings.

21Let them not depart from thine eyes; keep them in the midst of thine heart.

22For they *are* life unto those that find them, and health to all their flesh.

23¶ Keep thy heart with all diligence; for out of it *are* the issues of life.

24Put away from thee a froward mouth, and perverse lips put far from thee.

25Let thine eyes look right on, and let thine eyelids look straight before thee.

26Ponder the path of thy feet, and let all thy ways be established.

27Turn not to the right hand nor to the left: remove thy foot from evil.

5 MY SON, attend unto my wisdom, *and* bow thine ear to my understanding:

2That thou mayest regard discretion, and *that* thy lips may keep knowledge.

3¶ For the lips of a strange woman drop *as* an honeycomb, and her mouth *is* smoother than oil:

4But her end is bitter as wormwood, sharp as a two-edged sword.

5Her feet go down to death; her steps take hold on hell.

6Lest thou shouldest ponder the path of life, her ways are moveable, *that* thou canst not know *them*.

7Hear me now therefore, O ye children, and depart not from the words of my mouth.

8Remove thy way far from her, and come not nigh the door of her house:

9Lest thou give thine honour unto others, and thy years unto the cruel:

10Lest strangers be filled with thy wealth; and thy labours *be* in the house of a stranger;

11And thou mourn at the last, when thy flesh and thy body are consumed,

12And say, How have I hated instruction, and my heart despised reproof;

New International

11I guide you in the way of wisdom
and lead you along straight paths.

12When you walk, your steps will not be hampered;
when you run, you will not stumble.

13Hold on to instruction, do not let it go;
guard it well, for it is your life.

14Do not set foot on the path of the wicked
or walk in the way of evil men.

15Avoid it, do not travel on it;
turn from it and go on your way.

16For they cannot sleep till they do evil;
they are robbed of slumber till they make
someone fall.

17They eat the bread of wickedness
and drink the wine of violence.

18The path of the righteous is like the first gleam
of dawn,
shining ever brighter till the full light of day.

19But the way of the wicked is like deep
darkness;
they do not know what makes them stumble.

20My son, pay attention to what I say;
listen closely to my words.

21Do not let them out of your sight,
keep them within your heart;

22for they are life to those who find them
and health to a man's whole body.

23Above all else, guard your heart,
for it is the wellspring of life.

24Put away perversity from your mouth;
keep corrupt talk far from your lips.

25Let your eyes look straight ahead,
fix your gaze directly before you.

26Make levela paths for your feet
and take only ways that are firm.

27Do not swerve to the right or the left;
keep your foot from evil.

Warning Against Adultery

5 MY SON, pay attention to my wisdom,
listen well to my words of insight,

2that you may maintain discretion
and your lips may preserve knowledge.

3For the lips of an adulteress drip honey,
and her speech is smoother than oil;

4but in the end she is bitter as gall,
sharp as a double-edged sword.

5Her feet go down to death;
her steps lead straight to the grave.b

6She gives no thought to the way of life;
her paths are crooked, but she knows it not.

7Now then, my sons, listen to me;
do not turn aside from what I say.

8Keep to a path far from her,
do not go near the door of her house,

9lest you give your best strength to others
and your years to one who is cruel,

10lest strangers feast on your wealth
and your toil enrich another man's house.

11At the end of your life you will groan,
when your flesh and body are spent.

12You will say, "How I hated discipline!
How my heart spurned correction!

Living Bible

11I would have you learn this great fact: that a life of doing right is the wisest life there is. 12If you live that kind of life, you'll not limp or stumble as you run. 13Carry out my instructions; don't forget them, for they will lead you to real living.

14Don't do as the wicked do. 15Avoid their haunts—turn away, go somewhere else, 16for evil men can't sleep until they've done their evil deed for the day. They can't rest unless they cause someone to stumble and fall. 17They eat and drink wickedness and violence!

18But the good man walks along in the ever-brightening light of God's favor; the dawn gives way to morning splendor, 19while the evil man gropes and stumbles in the dark.

20Listen, son of mine, to what I say. Listen carefully. 21Keep these thoughts ever in mind; let them penetrate deep within your heart, 22for they will mean real life for you, and radiant health.

23*Above all else, guard your affections*. For they influence everything else in your life. 24Spurn the careless kiss of a prostitute.c Stay far from her. 25Look straight ahead; don't even turn your head to look. 26Watch your step. Stick to the path and be safe. 27Don't sidetrack; pull back your foot from danger.

5 LISTEN TO me, my son! I know what I am saying; *listen!* 2Watch yourself, lest you be indiscreet and betray some vital information. 3For the lips of a prostituted are as sweet as honey, and smooth flattery is her stock in trade. 4But afterwards only a bitter conscience is left to you,e sharp as a double-edged sword. 5She leads you down to death and hell. 6For she does not know the path to life. She staggers down a crooked trail, and doesn't even realize where it leads.

7Young men, listen to me, and never forget what I'm about to say: 8*Run from her! Don't go near her house,* 9lest you fall to her temptation and lose your honor, and give the remainder of your life to the cruel and merciless;f 10lest strangers obtain your wealth, and you become a slave of foreigners. 11Lest afterwards you groan in anguish and in shame, when syphilisg consumes your body, 12and you say, "Oh, if only I had listened! If only I had not demanded my own way! 13Oh, why wouldn't

New Revised Standard

11 I have taught you the way of wisdom;
    I have led you in the paths of uprightness.
12 When you walk, your step will not be
       hampered;
    and if you run, you will not stumble.
13 Keep hold of instruction; do not let go;
    guard her, for she is your life.
14 Do not enter the path of the wicked,
    and do not walk in the way of evildoers.
15 Avoid it; do not go on it;
    turn away from it and pass on.
16 For they cannot sleep unless they have done
       wrong;
    they are robbed of sleep unless they have
       made someone stumble.
17 For they eat the bread of wickedness
    and drink the wine of violence.
18 But the path of the righteous is like the light
       of dawn,
    which shines brighter and brighter until full
       day.
19 The way of the wicked is like deep darkness;
    they do not know what they stumble over.
20 My child, be attentive to my words;
    incline your ear to my sayings.
21 Do not let them escape from your sight;
    keep them within your heart.
22 For they are life to those who find them,
    and healing to all their flesh.
23 Keep your heart with all vigilance,
    for from it flow the springs of life.
24 Put away from you crooked speech,
    and put devious talk far from you.
25 Let your eyes look directly forward,
    and your gaze be straight before you.
26 Keep straight the path of your feet,
    and all your ways will be sure.
27 Do not swerve to the right or to the left;
    turn your foot away from evil.

Warning against Impurity and Infidelity

5 MY CHILD, be attentive to my wisdom;
    incline your ear to my understanding,
2   so that you may hold on to prudence,
    and your lips may guard knowledge.
3   For the lips of a looseh woman drip honey,
    and her speech is smoother than oil;
4   but in the end she is bitter as wormwood,
    sharp as a two-edged sword.
5   Her feet go down to death;
    her steps follow the path to Sheol.
6   She does not keep straight to the path of life;
    her ways wander, and she does not know it.

7   And now, my child,i listen to me,
    and do not depart from the words of my
       mouth.
8   Keep your way far from her,
    and do not go near the door of her house;
9   or you will give your honor to others,
    and your years to the merciless;
10 and strangers will take their fill of your
       wealth,
    and your labors will go to the house of an
       alien;
11 and at the end of your life you will groan,
    when your flesh and body are consumed,
12 and you say, "Oh, how I hated discipline,
    and my heart despised reproof!

c 4:24 *Spurn the careless kiss of a prostitute,* implied; literally, "Put away from you a wayward mouth." d 5:3 *of a prostitute,* or "of another man's wife." e 5:4 *But afterwards only a bitter conscience is left you,* literally, "But in the end she is bitter as wormwood." f 5:9 *and give the remainder of your life to the cruel and merciless.* Perhaps the reference is to blackmail, or to fear of vengeance from the wronged husband. g 5:11 syphilis, literally, "disease."

h Heb *strange*   i Gk Vg: Heb *children*

King James

13And have not obeyed the voice of my teachers, nor inclined mine ear to them that instructed me!

14I was almost in all evil in the midst of the congregation and assembly.

15¶ Drink waters out of thine own cistern, and running waters out of thine own well.

16Let thy fountains be dispersed abroad, *and* rivers of waters in the streets.

17Let them be only thine own, and not strangers' with thee.

18Let thy fountain be blessed: and rejoice with the wife of thy youth.

19*Let her be as* the loving hind and pleasant roe; let her breasts satisfy thee at all times; and be thou ravished always with her love.

20And why wilt thou, my son, be ravished with a strange woman, and embrace the bosom of a stranger?

21For the ways of man *are* before the eyes of the LORD, and he pondereth all his goings.

22¶ His own iniquities shall take the wicked himself, and he shall be holden with the cords of his sins.

23He shall die without instruction; and in the greatness of his folly he shall go astray.

6 MY SON, if thou be surety for thy friend, *if* thou hast stricken thy hand with a stranger,

2Thou art snared with the words of thy mouth, thou art taken with the words of thy mouth.

3Do this now, my son, and deliver thyself, when thou art come into the hand of thy friend; go, humble thyself, and make sure thy friend.

4Give not sleep to thine eyes, nor slumber to thine eyelids.

5Deliver thyself as a roe from the hand *of the hunter,* and as a bird from the hand of the fowler.

6¶ Go to the ant, thou sluggard; consider her ways, and be wise:

7Which having no guide, overseer, or ruler,

8Provideth her meat in the summer, *and* gathereth her food in the harvest.

9How long wilt thou sleep, O sluggard? when wilt thou arise out of thy sleep?

10*Yet* a little sleep, a little slumber, a little folding of the hands to sleep:

11So shall thy poverty come as one that travelleth, and thy want as an armed man.

12¶ A naughty person, a wicked man, walketh with a froward mouth.

13He winketh with his eyes, he speaketh with his feet, he teacheth with his fingers;

14Frowardness *is* in his heart, he deviseth mischief continually; he soweth discord.

15Therefore shall his calamity come suddenly; suddenly shall he be broken without remedy.

New International

13I would not obey my teachers
  or listen to my instructors.
14I have come to the brink of utter ruin
  in the midst of the whole assembly."

15Drink water from your own cistern,
  running water from your own well.
16Should your springs overflow in the streets,
  your streams of water in the public squares?
17Let them be yours alone,
  never to be shared with strangers.
18May your fountain be blessed,
  and may you rejoice in the wife of your
    youth.
19A loving doe, a graceful deer—
  may her breasts satisfy you always,
  may you ever be captivated by her love.
20Why be captivated, my son, by an adulteress?
  Why embrace the bosom of another man's
    wife?
21For a man's ways are in full view of the LORD,
  and he examines all his paths.
22The evil deeds of a wicked man ensnare him;
  the cords of his sin hold him fast.
23He will die for lack of discipline,
  led astray by his own great folly.

Warnings Against Folly

6 MY SON, if you have put up security for your
  neighbor,
  if you have struck hands in pledge for
    another,
2if you have been trapped by what you said,
  ensnared by the words of your mouth,
3then do this, my son, to free yourself,
  since you have fallen into your neighbor's
    hands:
Go and humble yourself;
  press your plea with your neighbor!
4Allow no sleep to your eyes,
  no slumber to your eyelids.
5Free yourself, like a gazelle from the hand of
    the hunter,
  like a bird from the snare of the fowler.

6Go to the ant, you sluggard;
  consider its ways and be wise!
7It has no commander,
  no overseer or ruler,
8yet it stores its provisions in summer
  and gathers its food at harvest.

9How long will you lie there, you sluggard?
  When will you get up from your sleep?
10A little sleep, a little slumber,
  a little folding of the hands to rest—
11and poverty will come on you like a bandit
  and scarcity like an armed man.[a]

12A scoundrel and villain,
  who goes about with a corrupt mouth,
13 who winks with his eye,
  signals with his feet
  and motions with his fingers,
14 who plots evil with deceit in his heart—
  he always stirs up dissension.
15Therefore disaster will overtake him in an
    instant;
  he will suddenly be destroyed—without
    remedy.

---

a 11 Or like a vagrant / and scarcity like a beggar

Living Bible

I take advice? Why was I so stupid? [14]For now I must face public disgrace."

[15]Drink from your own well, my son—be faithful and true to your wife. [16]Why should you beget children with women of the street? [17]Why share your children with those outside your home? [18]Be happy, yes, rejoice in the wife of your youth. [19]Let her breasts and tender embrace[b] satisfy you. Let her love alone fill you with delight. [20]Why delight yourself with prostitutes, embracing what isn't yours? [21]*For God is closely watching you,* and he weighs carefully everything you do.

[22]The wicked man is doomed by his own sins; they are ropes that catch and hold him. [23]He shall die because he will not listen to the truth; he has let himself be led away into incredible folly.

6 SON, IF you endorse a note for someone you hardly know, guaranteeing his debt, you are in serious trouble. [2]You may have trapped yourself by your agreement. [3]Quick! Get out of it if you possibly can! Swallow your pride; don't let embarrassment stand in the way. Go and beg to have your name erased. [4]Don't put it off. Do it now. Don't rest until you do. [5]If you can get out of this trap you have saved yourself like a deer that escapes from a hunter, or a bird from the net.

[6]Take a lesson from the ants, you lazy fellow. Learn from their ways and be wise! [7]For though they have no king to make them work, [8]yet they labor hard all summer, gathering food for the winter. [9]But you—all you do is sleep. When will you wake up? [10]"Let me sleep a little longer!" Sure, just a little more! [11]And as you sleep, poverty creeps upon you like a robber and destroys you; want attacks you in full armor.

[12, 13]Let me describe for you a worthless and a wicked man; first, he is a constant liar; he signals his true intentions to his friends with eyes and feet and fingers. [14]He is always thinking up new schemes to swindle people. He stirs up trouble everywhere. [15]But he will be destroyed suddenly, broken beyond hope of healing.

New Revised Standard

13 I did not listen to the voice of my teachers
   or incline my ear to my instructors.
14 Now I am at the point of utter ruin
   in the public assembly."

15 Drink water from your own cistern,
   flowing water from your own well.
16 Should your springs be scattered abroad,
   streams of water in the streets?
17 Let them be for yourself alone,
   and not for sharing with strangers.
18 Let your fountain be blessed,
   and rejoice in the wife of your youth,
19   a lovely deer, a graceful doe.
   May her breasts satisfy you at all times;
   may you be intoxicated always by her love.
20 Why should you be intoxicated, my son, by
      another woman
   and embrace the bosom of an adulteress?
21 For human ways are under the eyes of the
      LORD,
   and he examines all their paths.
22 The iniquities of the wicked ensnare them,
   and they are caught in the toils of their sin.
23 They die for lack of discipline,
   and because of their great folly they are
      lost.

Practical Admonitions

6 MY CHILD, if you have given your pledge to
      your neighbor,
   if you have bound yourself to another,[c]
2 you are snared by the utterance of your lips,[d]
   caught by the words of your mouth.
3 So do this, my child, and save yourself,
   for you have come into your neighbor's
      power:
   go, hurry,[e] and plead with your neighbor.
4 Give your eyes no sleep
   and your eyelids no slumber;
5 save yourself like a gazelle from the hunter,[f]
   like a bird from the hand of the fowler.

6 Go to the ant, you lazybones;
   consider its ways, and be wise.
7 Without having any chief
   or officer or ruler,
8 it prepares its food in summer,
   and gathers its sustenance in harvest.
9 How long will you lie there, O lazybones?
   When will you rise from your sleep?
10 A little sleep, a little slumber,
   a little folding of the hands to rest,
11 and poverty will come upon you like a robber,
   and want, like an armed warrior.

12 A scoundrel and a villain
   goes around with crooked speech,
13 winking the eyes, shuffling the feet,
   pointing the fingers,
14 with perverted mind devising evil,
   continually sowing discord;
15 on such a one calamity will descend suddenly;
   in a moment, damage beyond repair.

---

[b] *5:19 Let her breasts and tender embrace,* literally, "as a loving hind and a pleasant doe."

[c] Or *a stranger* [d] Cn Compare Gk Syr: Heb *the words of you*
humble yourself [f] Cn: Heb *from the hand*

King James

16¶ These six *things* doth the LORD hate: yea, seven *are* an abomination unto him:

17A proud look, a lying tongue, and hands that shed innocent blood,

18An heart that deviseth wicked imaginations, feet that be swift in running to mischief,

19A false witness *that* speaketh lies, and he that soweth discord among brethren.

20¶ My son, keep thy father's commandment, and forsake not the law of thy mother:

21Bind them continually upon thine heart, *and* tie them about thy neck.

22When thou goest, it shall lead thee; when thou sleepest, it shall keep thee; and *when* thou awakest, it shall talk with thee.

23For the commandment *is* a lamp; and the law *is* light; and reproofs of instruction *are* the way of life:

24To keep thee from the evil woman, from the flattery of the tongue of a strange woman.

25Lust not after her beauty in thine heart; neither let her take thee with her eyelids.

26For by means of a whorish woman *a man is brought* to a piece of bread: and the adulteress will hunt for the precious life.

27Can a man take fire in his bosom, and his clothes not be burned?

28Can one go upon hot coals, and his feet not be burned?

29So he that goeth in to his neighbour's wife; whosoever toucheth her shall not be innocent.

30*Men* do not despise a thief, if he steal to satisfy his soul when he is hungry;

31But *if* he be found, he shall restore sevenfold; he shall give all the substance of his house.

32*But* whoso committeth adultery with a woman lacketh understanding: he *that* doeth it destroyeth his own soul.

33A wound and dishonour shall he get; and his reproach shall not be wiped away.

34For jealousy *is* the rage of a man: therefore he will not spare in the day of vengeance.

35He will not regard any ransom; neither will he rest content, though thou givest many gifts.

7 MY SON, keep my words, and lay up my commandments with thee.

2Keep my commandments, and live; and my law as the apple of thine eye.

3Bind them upon thy fingers, write upon the table of thine heart.

4Say unto wisdom, Thou *art* my sister; and call understanding *thy* kinswoman:

5That they may keep thee from the strange woman, from the stranger *which* flattereth with her words.

6¶ For at the window of my house I looked through my casement,

New International

16There are six things the LORD hates,
  seven that are detestable to him:
17   haughty eyes,
    a lying tongue,
    hands that shed innocent blood,
18   a heart that devises wicked schemes,
    feet that are quick to rush into evil,
19   a false witness who pours out lies
    and a man who stirs up dissension among
     brothers.

Warning Against Adultery

20My son, keep your father's commands
  and do not forsake your mother's teaching.
21Bind them upon your heart forever;
  fasten them around your neck.
22When you walk, they will guide you;
  when you sleep, they will watch over you;
  when you awake, they will speak to you.
23For these commands are a lamp,
  this teaching is a light,
  and the corrections of discipline
  are the way to life,
24keeping you from the immoral woman,
  from the smooth tongue of the wayward wife.
25Do not lust in your heart after her beauty
  or let her captivate you with her eyes,
26for the prostitute reduces you to a loaf of bread,
  and the adulteress preys upon your very life.
27Can a man scoop fire into his lap
  without his clothes being burned?
28Can a man walk on hot coals
  without his feet being scorched?
29So is he who sleeps with another man's wife;
  no one who touches her will go unpunished.

30Men do not despise a thief if he steals
  to satisfy his hunger when he is starving.
31Yet if he is caught, he must pay sevenfold,
  though it costs him all the wealth of his
   house.
32But a man who commits adultery lacks
   judgment;
  whoever does so destroys himself.
33Blows and disgrace are his lot,
  and his shame will never be wiped away;
34for jealousy arouses a husband's fury,
  and he will show no mercy when he takes
   revenge.
35He will not accept any compensation;
  he will refuse the bribe, however great it is.

Warning Against the Adulteress

7 MY SON, keep my words
  and store up my commands within you.
2Keep my commands and you will live;
  guard my teachings as the apple of your eye.
3Bind them on your fingers;
  write them on the tablet of your heart.
4Say to wisdom, "You are my sister,"
  and call understanding your kinsman;
5they will keep you from the adulteress,
  from the wayward wife with her seductive
   words.

6At the window of my house
  I looked out through the lattice.

Living Bible

16-19For there are six things the Lord hates—no, seven:

Haughtiness
Lying
Murdering
Plotting evil
Eagerness to do wrong
A false witness
Sowing discord among brothers

20Young man, obey your father and your mother. 21Take to heart all of their advice; keep in mind everything they tell you. 22Every day and all night long their counsel will lead you and save you from harm; when you wake up in the morning, let their instructions guide you into the new day. 23For their advice is a beam of light directed into the dark corners of your mind to warn you of danger and to give you a good life. 24Their counsel will keep you far away from prostitutes with all their flatteries, and unfaithful wives of other men.

25Don't lust for their beauty. Don't let their coyness seduce you. 26For a prostitute will bring a man to poverty, and an adulteress may cost him his very life. 27Can a man hold fire against his chest and not be burned? 28Can he walk on hot coals and not blister his feet? 29So it is with the man who commits adultery with another's wife. He shall not go unpunished for this sin. 30Excuses might even be found for a thief, if he steals when he is starving! 31But even so, he is fined seven times as much as he stole, though it may mean selling everything in his house to pay it back.

32But the man who commits adultery is an utter fool, for he destroys his own soul. 33Wounds and constant disgrace are his lot, 34for the woman's husband will be furious in his jealousy, and he will have no mercy on you in his day of vengeance. 35You won't be able to buy him off no matter what you offer.

7 FOLLOW MY advice, my son; always keep it in mind and stick to it. 2Obey me and live! Guard my words as your most precious possession. 3Write them down,a and also keep them deep within your heart. 4Love wisdom like a sweetheart; make her a beloved member of your family. 5Let her hold you back from affairs with other women—from listening to their flattery.

6I was looking out the window of my house one day,

New Revised Standard

16 There are six things that the LORD hates,
     seven that are an abomination to him:
17 haughty eyes, a lying tongue,
     and hands that shed innocent blood,
18 a heart that devises wicked plans,
     feet that hurry to run to evil,
19 a lying witness who testifies falsely,
     and one who sows discord in a family.

20 My child, keep your father's commandment,
     and do not forsake your mother's teaching.
21 Bind them upon your heart always;
     tie them around your neck.
22 When you walk, theyb will lead you;
     when you lie down, theyb will watch over
        you;
     and when you awake, theyb will talk with
        you.
23 For the commandment is a lamp and the
        teaching a light,
     and the reproofs of discipline are the way of
        life,
24 to preserve you from the wife of another,c
     from the smooth tongue of the adulteress.
25 Do not desire her beauty in your heart,
     and do not let her capture you with her
        eyelashes;
26 for a prostitute's fee is only a loaf of bread,d
     but the wife of another stalks a man's very
        life.
27 Can fire be carried in the bosom
     without burning one's clothes?
28 Or can one walk on hot coals
     without scorching the feet?
29 So is he who sleeps with his neighbor's wife;
     no one who touches her will go unpunished.
30 Thieves are not despised who steal only
     to satisfy their appetite when they are
        hungry.
31 Yet if they are caught, they will pay
        sevenfold;
     they will forfeit all the goods of their house.
32 But he who commits adultery has no sense;
     he who does it destroys himself.
33 He will get wounds and dishonor,
     and his disgrace will not be wiped away.
34 For jealousy arouses a husband's fury,
     and he shows no restraint when he takes
        revenge.
35 He will accept no compensation,
     and refuses a bribe no matter how great.

The False Attractions of Adultery

7 MY CHILD, keep my words
     and store up my commandments with you;
2 keep my commandments and live,
     keep my teachings as the apple of your eye;
3 bind them on your fingers,
     write them on the tablet of your heart.
4 Say to wisdom, "You are my sister,"
     and call insight your intimate friend,
5 that they may keep you from the loosee
        woman,
     from the adulteress with her smooth words.

6 For at the window of my house
     I looked out through my lattice,

a *7:3 Write them down*, literally, "Bind them upon your fingers."

b Heb *it* c Gk: MT *the evil woman* d Cn Compare Gk Syr Vg Tg: Heb *for because of a harlot to a piece of bread* e Heb *strange*

King James

7And beheld among the simple ones, I discerned among the youths, a young man void of understanding,

8Passing through the street near her corner; and he went the way to her house,

9In the twilight, in the evening, in the black and dark night:

10And, behold, there met him a woman *with* the attire of an harlot, and subtle of heart.

11(She *is* loud and stubborn; her feet abide not in her house:

12Now *is she* without, now in the streets, and lieth in wait at every corner.)

13So she caught him, and kissed him, *and* with an impudent face said unto him,

14*I have* peace offerings with me; this day have I paid my vows.

15Therefore came I forth to meet thee, diligently to seek thy face, and I have found thee.

16I have decked my bed with coverings of tapestry, with carved *works*, with fine linen of Egypt.

17I have perfumed my bed with myrrh, aloes, and cinnamon.

18Come, let us take our fill of love until the morning: let us solace ourselves with loves.

19For the goodman *is* not at home, he is gone a long journey:

20He hath taken a bag of money with him, *and* will come home at the day appointed.

21With her much fair speech she caused him to yield, with the flattering of her lips she forced him.

22He goeth after her straightway, as an ox goeth to the slaughter, or as a fool to the correction of the stocks;

23Till a dart strike through his liver; as a bird hasteth to the snare, and knoweth not that it *is* for his life.

24¶ Hearken unto me now therefore, O ye children, and attend to the words of my mouth.

25Let not thine heart decline to her ways, go not astray in her paths.

26For she hath cast down many wounded: yea, many strong *men* have been slain by her.

27Her house *is* the way to hell, going down to the chambers of death.

8 DOTH NOT wisdom cry? and understanding put forth her voice?

2She standeth in the top of high places, by the way in the places of the paths.

3She crieth at the gates, at the entry of the city, at the coming in at the doors.

4Unto you, O men, I call; and my voice *is* to the sons of man.

5O ye simple, understand wisdom: and, ye fools, be ye of an understanding heart.

6Hear; for I will speak of excellent things; and the opening of my lips *shall be* right things.

7For my mouth shall speak truth; and wickedness *is* an abomination to my lips.

8All the words of my mouth *are* in righteousness; *there is* nothing froward or perverse in them.

New International

7I saw among the simple,
    I noticed among the young men,
    a youth who lacked judgment.

8He was going down the street near her corner,
    walking along in the direction of her house

9at twilight, as the day was fading,
    as the dark of night set in.

10Then out came a woman to meet him,
    dressed like a prostitute and with crafty
        intent.

11(She is loud and defiant,
    her feet never stay at home;

12now in the street, now in the squares,
    at every corner she lurks.)

13She took hold of him and kissed him
    and with a brazen face she said:

14"I have fellowship offeringsa at home;
    today I fulfilled my vows.

15So I came out to meet you;
    I looked for you and have found you!

16I have covered my bed
    with colored linens from Egypt.

17I have perfumed my bed
    with myrrh, aloes and cinnamon.

18Come, let's drink deep of love till morning;
    let's enjoy ourselves with love!

19My husband is not at home;
    he has gone on a long journey.

20He took his purse filled with money
    and will not be home till full moon."

21With persuasive words she led him astray;
    she seduced him with her smooth talk.

22All at once he followed her
    like an ox going to the slaughter,
    like a deerb stepping into a noosec

23   till an arrow pierces his liver,
    like a bird darting into a snare,
        little knowing it will cost him his life.

24Now then, my sons, listen to me;
    pay attention to what I say.

25Do not let your heart turn to her ways
    or stray into her paths.

26Many are the victims she has brought down;
    her slain are a mighty throng.

27Her house is a highway to the grave,d
    leading down to the chambers of death.

Wisdom's Call

8 DOES NOT wisdom call out?
    Does not understanding raise her voice?

2On the heights along the way,
    where the paths meet, she takes her stand;

3beside the gates leading into the city,
    at the entrances, she cries aloud:

4"To you, O men, I call out;
    I raise my voice to all mankind.

5You who are simple, gain prudence;
    you who are foolish, gain understanding.

6Listen, for I have worthy things to say;
    I open my lips to speak what is right.

7My mouth speaks what is true,
    for my lips detest wickedness.

8All the words of my mouth are just;
    none of them is crooked or perverse.

---

a *14* Traditionally *peace offerings*   b *22* Syriac (see also Septuagint); Hebrew *fool*   c *22* The meaning of the Hebrew for this line is uncertain.   d *27* Hebrew *Sheol*

Living Bible

7and saw a simple-minded lad, a young man lacking common sense, 8, 9walking at twilight down the street to the house of this wayward girl, a prostitute. 10She approached him, saucy and pert, and dressed seductively. 11, 12She was the brash, coarse type, seen often in the streets and markets, soliciting at every corner for men to be her lovers.

13She put her arms around him and kissed him, and with a saucy look she said, "I was just coming to look for you and here you are! 14–17Come home with me and I'll fix you a wonderful dinner,e and after that—well, my bed is spread with lovely, colored sheets of finest linen imported from Egypt, perfumed with myrrh, aloes and cinnamon. 18Come on, let's take our fill of love until morning, 19for my husband is away on a long trip. 20He has taken a wallet full of money with him, and won't return for several days."

21So she seduced him with her pretty speech, her coaxing and her wheedling, until he yielded to her. He couldn't resist her flattery. 22He followed her as an ox going to the butcher, or as a stag that is trapped, 23waiting to be killed with an arrow through its heart. He was as a bird flying into a snare, not knowing the fate awaiting it there.

24Listen to me, young men, and not only listen but obey; 25don't let your desires get out of hand; don't let yourself think about her. Don't go near her; stay away from where she walks, lest she tempt you and seduce you. 26For she has been the ruin of multitudes—a vast host of men have been her victims. 27If you want to find the road to hell, look for her house.

New Revised Standard

7 and I saw among the simple ones,
   I observed among the youths,
   a young man without sense,
8 passing along the street near her corner,
   taking the road to her house
9 in the twilight, in the evening,
   at the time of night and darkness.

10 Then a woman comes toward him,
   decked out like a prostitute, wily of heart.f
11 She is loud and wayward;
   her feet do not stay at home;
12 now in the street, now in the squares,
   and at every corner she lies in wait.
13 She seizes him and kisses him,
   and with impudent face she says to him:
14 "I had to offer sacrifices,
   and today I have paid my vows;
15 so now I have come out to meet you,
   to seek you eagerly, and I have found you!
16 I have decked my couch with coverings,
   colored spreads of Egyptian linen;
17 I have perfumed my bed with myrrh,
   aloes, and cinnamon.
18 Come, let us take our fill of love until
      morning;
   let us delight ourselves with love.
19 For my husband is not at home;
   he has gone on a long journey.
20 He took a bag of money with him;
   he will not come home until full moon."

21 With much seductive speech she persuades
      him;
   with her smooth talk she compels him.
22 Right away he follows her,
   and goes like an ox to the slaughter,
   or bounds like a stag toward the trapg
23 until an arrow pierces its entrails.
   He is like a bird rushing into a snare,
   not knowing that it will cost him his life.

24 And now, my children, listen to me,
   and be attentive to the words of my mouth.
25 Do not let your hearts turn aside to her ways;
   do not stray into her paths.
26 for many are those she has laid low,
   and numerous are her victims.
27 Her house is the way to Sheol,
   going down to the chambers of death.

The Gifts of Wisdom

8 CAN'T YOU hear the voice of wisdom? She is standing at the city gates and at every fork in the road, and at the door of every house. Listen to what she says: 4, 5"Listen, men!" she calls. "How foolish and naive you are! Let me give you understanding. O foolish ones, let me show you common sense! 6, 7Listen to me! For I have important information for you. Everything I say is right and true, for I hate lies and every kind of deception. 8My advice is wholesome and good. There is nothing of evil in it. 9My words are plain and clear

8 DOES NOT wisdom call,
   and does not understanding raise her voice?
2 On the heights, beside the way,
   at the crossroads she takes her stand;
3 beside the gates in front of the town,
   at the entrance of the portals she cries out:
4 "To you, O people, I call,
   and my cry is to all that live.
5 O simple ones, learn prudence;
   acquire intelligence, you who lack it.
6 Hear, for I will speak noble things,
   and from my lips will come what is right;
7 for my mouth will utter truth;
   wickedness is an abomination to my lips.
8 All the words of my mouth are righteous;
   there is nothing twisted or crooked in them.

---

e 7:14-17 I'll fix you a wonderful dinner, literally, "Sacrifices of peace offerings were due from me; this day have I paid my vows." If she meant this literally, she was telling him that she had plenty of food on hand, left from her sacrifice at the Temple.

f Meaning of Heb uncertain   g Cn Compare Gk: Meaning of Heb uncertain

King James

9They *are* all plain to him that understandeth, and right to them that find knowledge.

10Receive my instruction, and not silver; and knowledge rather than choice gold.

11For wisdom *is* better than rubies; and all the things that may be desired are not to be compared to it.

12I wisdom dwell with prudence, and find out knowledge of witty inventions.

13The fear of the LORD *is* to hate evil: pride, and arrogancy, and the evil way, and the froward mouth, do I hate.

14Counsel *is* mine, and sound wisdom: I *am* understanding; I have strength.

15By me kings reign, and princes decree justice.

16By me princes rule, and nobles, *even* all the judges of the earth.

17I love them that love me; and those that seek me early shall find me.

18Riches and honour *are* with me; *yea*, durable riches and righteousness.

19My fruit *is* better than gold, yea, than fine gold; and my revenue than choice silver.

20I lead in the way of righteousness, in the midst of the paths of judgment:

21That I may cause those that love me to inherit substance; and I will fill their treasures.

22The LORD possessed me in the beginning of his way, before his works of old.

23I was set up from everlasting, from the beginning, or ever the earth was.

24When *there were* no depths, I was brought forth; when *there were* no fountains abounding with water.

25Before the mountains were settled, before the hills was I brought forth:

26While as yet he had not made the earth, nor the fields, nor the highest part of the dust of the world.

27When he prepared the heavens, I *was* there: when he set a compass upon the face of the depth:

28When he established the clouds above: when he strengthened the fountains of the deep:

29When he gave to the sea his decree, that the waters should not pass his commandment: when he appointed the foundations of the earth:

30Then I was by him, *as* one brought up *with him:* and I was daily *his* delight, rejoicing always before him;

31Rejoicing in the habitable part of his earth; and my delights *were* with the sons of men.

32Now therefore hearken unto me, O ye children: for blessed *are they that* keep my ways.

33Hear instruction, and be wise, and refuse it not.

34Blessed *is* the man that heareth me, watching daily at my gates, waiting at the posts of my doors.

35For whoso findeth me findeth life, and shall obtain favour of the LORD.

New International

9To the discerning all of them are right;
they are faultless to those who have
knowledge.

10Choose my instruction instead of silver,
knowledge rather than choice gold,

11for wisdom is more precious than rubies,
and nothing you desire can compare with her.

12"I, wisdom, dwell together with prudence;
I possess knowledge and discretion.

13To fear the LORD is to hate evil;
I hate pride and arrogance,
evil behavior and perverse speech.

14Counsel and sound judgment are mine;
I have understanding and power.

15By me kings reign
and rulers make laws that are just;

16by me princes govern,
and all nobles who rule on earth.[a]

17I love those who love me,
and those who seek me find me.

18With me are riches and honor,
enduring wealth and prosperity.

19My fruit is better than fine gold;
what I yield surpasses choice silver.

20I walk in the way of righteousness,
along the paths of justice,

21bestowing wealth on those who love me
and making their treasuries full.

22"The LORD brought me forth as the first of his
works,[b,c]
before his deeds of old;

23I was appointed[d] from eternity,
from the beginning, before the world began.

24When there were no oceans, I was given birth,
when there were no springs abounding with
water;

25before the mountains were settled in place,
before the hills, I was given birth,

26before he made the earth or its fields
or any of the dust of the world.

27I was there when he set the heavens in place,
when he marked out the horizon on the face
of the deep,

28when he established the clouds above
and fixed securely the fountains of the deep,

29when he gave the sea its boundary
so the waters would not overstep his
command,
and when he marked out the foundations of the
earth.

30 Then I was the craftsman at his side.
I was filled with delight day after day,
rejoicing always in his presence,

31rejoicing in his whole world
and delighting in mankind.

32"Now then, my sons, listen to me;
blessed are those who keep my ways.

33Listen to my instruction and be wise;
do not ignore it.

34Blessed is the man who listens to me,
watching daily at my doors,
waiting at my doorway.

35For whoever finds me finds life
and receives favor from the LORD.

a 16 Many Hebrew manuscripts and Septuagint; most Hebrew manuscripts and nobles—all righteous rulers　b 22 Or way; or dominion　c 22 Or The LORD possessed me at the beginning of his work; or The LORD brought me forth at the beginning of his work　d 23 Or fashioned

Living Bible

to anyone with half a mind—if it is only open! 10My instruction is far more valuable than silver or gold."

11For the value of wisdom is far above rubies; nothing can be compared with it. 12Wisdom and good judgment live together, for wisdom knows where to discover knowledge and understanding. 13If anyone respects and fears God, he will hate evil. For wisdom hates pride, arrogance, corruption and deceit of every kind.

14, 15, 16"I, Wisdom, give good advice and common sense. Because of my strength, kings reign in power, and rulers make just laws. 17I love all who love me. Those who search for me shall surely find me. 18Unending riches, honor, justice and righteousness are mine to distribute. 19My gifts are better than the purest gold or sterling silver! 20My paths are those of justice and right. 21Those who love and follow me are indeed wealthy. I fill their treasuries. 22The Lord formed me in the beginning, before he created anything else.e 23From ages past, I am. I existed before the earth began. 24I lived before the oceans were created, before the springs bubbled forth their waters onto the earth; 25before the mountains and the hills were made. 26Yes, I was born before God made the earth and fields, and the first handfuls of soil.

27, 28, 29"I was there when he established the heavens and formed the great springs in the depths of the oceans. I was there when he set the limits of the seas and gave them his instructions not to spread beyond their boundaries. I was there when he made the blueprint for the earth and oceans. 30I was the craftsman at his side. I was his constant delight, rejoicing always in his presence. 31And how happy I was with what he created—his wide world and all his family of mankind! 32And so, young men, listen to me, for how happy are all who follow my instructions.

33"Listen to my counsel—oh, don't refuse it—and be wise. 34Happy is the man who is so anxious to be with me that he watches for me daily at my gates, or waits for me outside my home! 35For whoever finds me finds life and wins approval from the Lord. 36But the one who

New Revised Standard

9 They are all straight to one who understands
    and right to those who find knowledge.
10 Take my instruction instead of silver,
    and knowledge rather than choice gold;
11 for wisdom is better than jewels,
    and all that you may desire cannot compare
    with her.
12 I, wisdom, live with prudence,f
    and I attain knowledge and discretion.
13 The fear of the LORD is hatred of evil.
    Pride and arrogance and the way of evil
    and perverted speech I hate.
14 I have good advice and sound wisdom;
    I have insight, I have strength.
15 By me kings reign,
    and rulers decree what is just;
16 by me rulers rule,
    and nobles, all who govern rightly.
17 I love those who love me,
    and those who seek me diligently find me.
18 Riches and honor are with me,
    enduring wealth and prosperity.
19 My fruit is better than gold, even fine gold,
    and my yield than choice silver.
20 I walk in the way of righteousness,
    along the paths of justice,
21 endowing with wealth those who love me,
    and filling their treasuries.

Wisdom's Part in Creation

22 The LORD created me at the beginningg of his
        work,h
    the first of his acts of long ago.
23 Ages ago I was set up,
    at the first, before the beginning of the
        earth.
24 When there were no depths I was brought
        forth,
    when there were no springs abounding with
        water.
25 Before the mountains had been shaped,
    before the hills, I was brought forth—
26 when he had not yet made earth and fields,f
    or the world's first bits of soil.
27 When he established the heavens, I was there,
    when he drew a circle on the face of the
        deep,
28 when he made firm the skies above,
    when he established the fountains of the
        deep,
29 when he assigned to the sea its limit,
    so that the waters might not transgress his
        command,
    when he marked out the foundations of the
        earth,
30 then I was beside him, like a master
        worker;i
    and I was daily hisj delight,
    rejoicing before him always,
31 rejoicing in his inhabited world
    and delighting in the human race.

32 And now, my children, listen to me:
    happy are those who keep my ways.
33 Hear instruction and be wise,
    and do not neglect it.
34 Happy is the one who listens to me,
    watching daily at my gates,
    waiting beside my doors.
35 For whoever finds me finds life
    and obtains favor from the LORD;

---

e 8:22 The reference here is to Wisdom. If this verse refers to Christ, this alternate translation is possible from the Hebrew text: "The Lord possessed me at the beginning of his work."

f Meaning of Heb uncertain   g Or *me as the beginning*   h Heb *way*
i Another reading is *little child*   j Gk: Heb lacks *his*

King James

³⁶But he that sinneth against me wrongeth his own soul: all they that hate me love death.

9 WISDOM HATH builded her house, she hath hewn out her seven pillars:

²She hath killed her beasts; she hath mingled her wine; she hath also furnished her table.

³She hath sent forth her maidens; she crieth upon the highest places of the city,

⁴Whoso *is* simple, let him turn in hither: *as for* him that wanteth understanding, she saith to him,

⁵Come, eat of my bread, and drink of the wine *which* I have mingled.

⁶Forsake the foolish, and live; and go in the way of understanding.

⁷He that reproveth a scorner getteth to himself shame: and he that rebuketh a wicked *man getteth* himself a blot.

⁸Reprove not a scorner, lest he hate thee: rebuke a wise man, and he will love thee.

⁹Give *instruction* to a wise *man*, and he will be yet wiser: teach a just *man*, and he will increase in learning.

¹⁰The fear of the LORD *is* the beginning of wisdom: and the knowledge of the holy *is* understanding.

¹¹For by me thy days shall be multiplied, and the years of thy life shall be increased.

¹²If thou be wise, thou shalt be wise for thyself: but *if* thou scornest, thou alone shalt bear *it*.

¹³¶ A foolish woman *is* clamorous: *she is* simple, and knoweth nothing.

¹⁴For she sitteth at the door of her house, on a seat in the high places of the city,

¹⁵To call passengers who go right on their ways:

¹⁶Whoso *is* simple, let him turn in hither: and *as for* him that wanteth understanding, she saith to him,

¹⁷Stolen waters are sweet, and bread *eaten* in secret is pleasant.

¹⁸But he knoweth not that the dead *are* there; *and that* her guests *are* in the depths of hell.

10 THE PROVERBS of Solomon. A wise son maketh a glad father: but a foolish son *is* the heaviness of his mother.

²Treasures of wickedness profit nothing: but righteousness delivereth from death.

³The LORD will not suffer the soul of the righteous to famish: but he casteth away the substance of the wicked.

⁴He becometh poor that dealeth *with* a slack hand: but the hand of the diligent maketh rich.

⁵He that gathereth in summer *is* a wise son: *but* he that sleepeth in harvest *is* a son that causeth shame.

New International

³⁶But whoever fails to find me harms himself; all who hate me love death."

Invitations of Wisdom and of Folly

9 WISDOM HAS built her house; she has hewn out its seven pillars.

²She has prepared her meat and mixed her wine; she has also set her table.

³She has sent out her maids, and she calls from the highest point of the city.

⁴"Let all who are simple come in here!" she says to those who lack judgment.

⁵"Come, eat my food and drink the wine I have mixed.

⁶Leave your simple ways and you will live; walk in the way of understanding.

⁷"Whoever corrects a mocker invites insult; whoever rebukes a wicked man incurs abuse.

⁸Do not rebuke a mocker or he will hate you; rebuke a wise man and he will love you.

⁹Instruct a wise man and he will be wiser still; teach a righteous man and he will add to his learning.

¹⁰"The fear of the LORD is the beginning of wisdom, and knowledge of the Holy One is understanding.

¹¹For through me your days will be many, and years will be added to your life.

¹²If you are wise, your wisdom will reward you; if you are a mocker, you alone will suffer."

¹³The woman Folly is loud; she is undisciplined and without knowledge.

¹⁴She sits at the door of her house, on a seat at the highest point of the city,

¹⁵calling out to those who pass by, who go straight on their way.

¹⁶"Let all who are simple come in here!" she says to those who lack judgment.

¹⁷"Stolen water is sweet; food eaten in secret is delicious!"

¹⁸But little do they know that the dead are there, that her guests are in the depths of the grave.^a

Proverbs of Solomon

10 THE PROVERBS of Solomon:

A wise son brings joy to his father, but a foolish son grief to his mother.

²Ill-gotten treasures are of no value, but righteousness delivers from death.

³The LORD does not let the righteous go hungry but he thwarts the craving of the wicked.

⁴Lazy hands make a man poor, but diligent hands bring wealth.

⁵He who gathers crops in summer is a wise son, but he who sleeps during harvest is a disgraceful son.

^a *18 Hebrew Sheol*

Living Bible

misses me has injured himself irreparably. Those who refuse me show that they love death."

9 WISDOM HAS built a palace supported on seven pillars, 2and has prepared a great banquet, and mixed the wines, 3and sent out her maidens inviting all to come. She calls from the busiest intersections in the city, 4"Come, you simple ones without good judgment; 5come to wisdom's banquet and drink the wines that I have mixed. 6Leave behind your foolishness and begin to live; learn how to be wise."

7, 8If you rebuke a mocker, you will only get a smart retort; yes, he will snarl at you. So don't bother with him; he will only hate you for trying to help him. But a wise man, when rebuked, will love you all the more. 9Teach a wise man, and he will be the wiser; teach a good man, and he will learn more. 10*For the reverence and fear of God are basic to all wisdom. Knowing God results in every other kind of understanding.* 11"I, Wisdom, will make the hours of your day more profitable and the years of your life more fruitful." 12Wisdom is its own reward, and if you scorn her, you hurt only yourself.

13A prostitute is loud and brash, and never has enough of lust and shame. 14She sits at the door of her house or stands at the street corners of the city, 15whispering to men going by, and to those minding their own business. 16"Come home with me," she urges simpletons. 17"Stolen melonsb are the sweetest; stolen applesc taste the best!" 18But they don't realize that her former guests are now citizens of hell.

10 HAPPY IS the man with a level-headed son; sad the mother of a rebel.
2Ill-gotten gain brings no lasting happiness; right living does.
3The Lord will not let a good man starve to death, nor will he let the wicked man's riches continue forever.
4Lazy men are soon poor; hard workers get rich.
5A wise youth makes hay while the sun shines, but what a shame to see a lad who sleeps away his hour of opportunity.

New Revised Standard

36 but those who miss me injure themselves;
all who hate me love death."

Wisdom's Feast

9 WISDOM HAS built her house,
she has hewn her seven pillars.
2 She has slaughtered her animals, she has mixed her wine,
she has also set her table.
3 She has sent out her servant-girls, she calls from the highest places in the town,
4 "You that are simple, turn in here!"
To those without sense she says,
5 "Come, eat of my bread
and drink of the wine I have mixed.
6 Lay aside immaturity,d and live,
and walk in the way of insight."

General Maxims

7 Whoever corrects a scoffer wins abuse;
whoever rebukes the wicked gets hurt.
8 A scoffer who is rebuked will only hate you;
the wise, when rebuked, will love you.
9 Give instructione to the wise, and they will become wiser still;
teach the righteous and they will gain in learning.
10 The fear of the LORD is the beginning of wisdom,
and the knowledge of the Holy One is insight.
11 For by me your days will be multiplied,
and years will be added to your life.
12 If you are wise, you are wise for yourself;
if you scoff, you alone will bear it.

Folly's Invitation and Promise

13 The foolish woman is loud;
she is ignorant and knows nothing.
14 She sits at the door of her house,
on a seat at the high places of the town,
15 calling to those who pass by,
who are going straight on their way,
16 "You who are simple, turn in here!"
And to those without sense she says,
17 "Stolen water is sweet,
and bread eaten in secret is pleasant."
18 But they do not know that the deadf are there,
that her guests are in the depths of Sheol.

Wise Sayings of Solomon

10 THE PROVERBS of Solomon.

A wise child makes a glad father,
but a foolish child is a mother's grief.
2 Treasures gained by wickedness do not profit,
but righteousness delivers from death.
3 The LORD does not let the righteous go hungry,
but he thwarts the craving of the wicked.
4 A slack hand causes poverty,
but the hand of the diligent makes rich.
5 A child who gathers in summer is prudent,
but a child who sleeps in harvest brings shame.

---

b 9:17 *Stolen melons,* literally, "stolen water." c 9:17 *stolen apples,* literally, "stolen food."

d Or *simpleness* e Heb lacks *instruction* f Heb *shades*

King James

6Blessings *are* upon the head of the just: but violence covereth the mouth of the wicked.

7The memory of the just *is* blessed: but the name of the wicked shall rot.

8The wise in heart will receive commandments: but a prating fool shall fall.

9He that walketh uprightly walketh surely: but he that perverteth his ways shall be known.

10He that winketh with the eye causeth sorrow: but a prating fool shall fall.

11The mouth of a righteous *man is* a well of life: but violence covereth the mouth of the wicked.

12Hatred stirreth up strifes: but love covereth all sins.

13In the lips of him that hath understanding wisdom is found: but a rod *is* for the back of him that is void of understanding.

14Wise *men* lay up knowledge: but the mouth of the foolish *is* near destruction.

15The rich man's wealth *is* his strong city: the destruction of the poor *is* their poverty.

16The labour of the righteous *tendeth* to life: the fruit of the wicked to sin.

17He *is in* the way of life that keepeth instruction: but he that refuseth reproof erreth.

18He that hideth hatred *with* lying lips, and he that uttereth a slander, *is* a fool.

19In the multitude of words there wanteth not sin: but he that refraineth his lips *is* wise.

20The tongue of the just *is* as choice silver: the heart of the wicked *is* little worth.

21The lips of the righteous feed many: but fools die for want of wisdom.

22The blessing of the LORD, it maketh rich, and he addeth no sorrow with it.

23*It is* as sport to a fool to do mischief: but a man of understanding hath wisdom.

24The fear of the wicked, it shall come upon him: but the desire of the righteous shall be granted.

25As the whirlwind passeth, so *is* the wicked no *more:* but the righteous *is* an everlasting foundation.

26As vinegar to the teeth, and as smoke to the eyes, so *is* the sluggard to them that send him.

27The fear of the LORD prolongeth days: but the years of the wicked shall be shortened.

28The hope of the righteous *shall be* gladness: but the expectation of the wicked shall perish.

29The way of the LORD *is* strength to the upright: but destruction *shall be* to the workers of iniquity.

30The righteous shall never be removed: but the wicked shall not inhabit the earth.

New International

6Blessings crown the head of the righteous,
   but violence overwhelms the mouth of the
   wicked.[a]

7The memory of the righteous will be a blessing,
   but the name of the wicked will rot.

8The wise in heart accept commands,
   but a chattering fool comes to ruin.

9The man of integrity walks securely,
   but he who takes crooked paths will be found
   out.

10He who winks maliciously causes grief,
   and a chattering fool comes to ruin.

11The mouth of the righteous is a fountain of life,
   but violence overwhelms the mouth of the
   wicked.

12Hatred stirs up dissension,
   but love covers over all wrongs.

13Wisdom is found on the lips of the discerning,
   but a rod is for the back of him who lacks
   judgment.

14Wise men store up knowledge,
   but the mouth of a fool invites ruin.

15The wealth of the rich is their fortified city,
   but poverty is the ruin of the poor.

16The wages of the righteous bring them life,
   but the income of the wicked brings them
   punishment.

17He who heeds discipline shows the way to life,
   but whoever ignores correction leads others
   astray.

18He who conceals his hatred has lying lips,
   and whoever spreads slander is a fool.

19When words are many, sin is not absent,
   but he who holds his tongue is wise.

20The tongue of the righteous is choice silver,
   but the heart of the wicked is of little value.

21The lips of the righteous nourish many,
   but fools die for lack of judgment.

22The blessing of the LORD brings wealth,
   and he adds no trouble to it.

23A fool finds pleasure in evil conduct,
   but a man of understanding delights in
   wisdom.

24What the wicked dreads will overtake him;
   what the righteous desire will be granted.

25When the storm has swept by, the wicked are
   gone,
   but the righteous stand firm forever.

26As vinegar to the teeth and smoke to the eyes,
   so is a sluggard to those who send him.

27The fear of the LORD adds length to life,
   but the years of the wicked are cut short.

28The prospect of the righteous is joy,
   but the hopes of the wicked come to nothing.

29The way of the LORD is a refuge for the
   righteous,
   but it is the ruin of those who do evil.

30The righteous will never be uprooted,
   but the wicked will not remain in the land.

---

[a] 6 Or *but the mouth of the wicked conceals violence*; also in verse 11

Living Bible

6The good man is covered with blessings from head to foot, but an evil man inwardly curses his luck.b

7We all have happy memories of good men gone to their reward, but the names of wicked men stink after them.

8The wise man is glad to be instructed, but a self-sufficient fool falls flat on his face.

9A good man has firm footing, but a crook will slip and fall.

10Winking at sin leads to sorrow; bold reproof leads to peace.

11There is living truth in what a good man says, but the mouth of the evil man is filled with curses.

12Hatred stirs old quarrels, but love overlooks insults.

13Men with common sense are admiredc as counselors; those without it are beaten as servants.

14A wise man holds his tongue. Only a fool blurts out everything he knows; that only leads to sorrow and trouble.

15The rich man's wealth is his onlyd strength. The poor man's poverty is his onlyd curse.

16The good man's earnings advance the cause of righteousness. The evil man squanders his on sin.

17Anyone willing to be corrected is on the pathway to life. Anyone refusing has lost his chance.

18To hide hatred is to be a liar; to slander is to be a fool.

19Don't talk so much. You keep putting your foot in your mouth. Be sensible and turn off the flow!

20When a good man speaks, he is worth listening to, but the words of fools are a dime a dozen.

21A godly man gives good advice, but a rebel is destroyed by lack of common sense.

22The Lord's blessing is our greatest wealth. All our work adds nothing to it!e

23A fool's fun is being bad; a wise man's fun is being wise!

24The wicked man's fears will all come true, and so will the good man's hopes.

25Disaster strikes like a cyclone and the wicked are whirled away. But the good man has a strong anchor.

26A lazy fellow is a pain to his employers—like smoke in their eyes or vinegar that sets the teeth on edge.

27Reverence for God adds hours to each day;f so how can the wicked expect a long, good life?

28The hope of good men is eternal happiness; the hopes of evil men are all in vain.

29God protects the upright but destroys the wicked.

30The good shall never lose God's blessings, but the wicked shall lose everything.

New Revised Standard

6 Blessings are on the head of the righteous,
  but the mouth of the wicked conceals
    violence.

7 The memory of the righteous is a blessing,
  but the name of the wicked will rot.

8 The wise of heart will heed commandments,
  but a babbling fool will come to ruin.

9 Whoever walks in integrity walks securely,
  but whoever follows perverse ways will be
    found out.

10 Whoever winks the eye causes trouble,
   but the one who rebukes boldly makes
     peace.g

11 The mouth of the righteous is a fountain of
     life,
   but the mouth of the wicked conceals
     violence.

12 Hatred stirs up strife,
   but love covers all offenses.

13 On the lips of one who has understanding
     wisdom is found,
   but a rod is for the back of one who lacks
     sense.

14 The wise lay up knowledge,
   but the babbling of a fool brings ruin near.

15 The wealth of the rich is their fortress;
   the poverty of the poor is their ruin.

16 The wage of the righteous leads to life,
   the gain of the wicked to sin.

17 Whoever heeds instruction is on the path to
     life,
   but one who rejects a rebuke goes astray.

18 Lying lips conceal hatred,
   and whoever utters slander is a fool.

19 When words are many, transgression is not
     lacking,
   but the prudent are restrained in speech.

20 The tongue of the righteous is choice silver;
   the mind of the wicked is of little worth.

21 The lips of the righteous feed many,
   but fools die for lack of sense.

22 The blessing of the LORD makes rich,
   and he adds no sorrow with it.h

23 Doing wrong is like sport to a fool,
   but wise conduct is pleasure to a person of
     understanding.

24 What the wicked dread will come upon them,
   but the desire of the righteous will be
     granted.

25 When the tempest passes, the wicked are no
     more,
   but the righteous are established forever.

26 Like vinegar to the teeth, and smoke to the
     eyes,
   so are the lazy to their employers.

27 The fear of the LORD prolongs life,
   but the years of the wicked will be short.

28 The hope of the righteous ends in gladness,
   but the expectation of the wicked comes to
     nothing.

29 The way of the LORD is a stronghold for the
     upright,
   but destruction for evildoers.

30 The righteous will never be removed,
   but the wicked will not remain in the land.

---

b 10:6 an evil man inwardly curses his luck, literally, "but the mouth of the wicked conceals violence." c 10:13 admired, implied. d 10:15 only . . . only, implied. e 10:22 All our work adds nothing to it, or, "and he adds no sorrow therewith." f 10:27 adds hours to each day, literally, "prolongs days."

g Gk: Heb but a babbling fool will come · to it

King James

31The mouth of the just bringeth forth wisdom: but the froward tongue shall be cut out.

32The lips of the righteous know what is acceptable: but the mouth of the wicked *speaketh* frowardness.

11 A FALSE balance *is* abomination to the LORD: but a just weight *is* his delight.

2*When* pride cometh, then cometh shame: but with the lowly *is* wisdom.

3The integrity of the upright shall guide them: but the perverseness of transgressors shall destroy them.

4Riches profit not in the day of wrath: but righteousness delivereth from death.

5The righteousness of the perfect shall direct his way: but the wicked shall fall by his own wickedness.

6The righteousness of the upright shall deliver them: but transgressors shall be taken in *their own* naughtiness.

7When a wicked man dieth, *his* expectation shall perish: and the hope of unjust *men* perisheth.

8The righteous is delivered out of trouble, and the wicked cometh in his stead.

9An hypocrite with *his* mouth destroyeth his neighbour: but through knowledge shall the just be delivered.

10When it goeth well with the righteous, the city rejoiceth: and when the wicked perish, *there is* shouting.

11By the blessing of the upright the city is exalted: but it is overthrown by the mouth of the wicked.

12He that is void of wisdom despiseth his neighbour: but a man of understanding holdeth his peace.

13A talebearer revealeth secrets: but he that is of a faithful spirit concealeth the matter.

14Where no counsel *is*, the people fall: but in the multitude of counsellors *there is* safety.

15He that is surety for a stranger shall smart *for it:* and he that hateth suretyship is sure.

16A gracious woman retaineth honour: and strong *men* retain riches.

17The merciful man doeth good to his own soul: but *he that is* cruel troubleth his own flesh.

18The wicked worketh a deceitful work: but to him that soweth righteousness *shall be* a sure reward.

19As righteousness *tendeth* to life: so he that pursueth evil *pursueth it* to his own death.

New International

31The mouth of the righteous brings forth wisdom,
but a perverse tongue will be cut out.

32The lips of the righteous know what is fitting,
but the mouth of the wicked only what is perverse.

11 THE LORD abhors dishonest scales,
but accurate weights are his delight.

2When pride comes, then comes disgrace,
but with humility comes wisdom.

3The integrity of the upright guides them,
but the unfaithful are destroyed by their duplicity.

4Wealth is worthless in the day of wrath,
but righteousness delivers from death.

5The righteousness of the blameless makes a straight way for them,
but the wicked are brought down by their own wickedness.

6The righteousness of the upright delivers them,
but the unfaithful are trapped by evil desires.

7When a wicked man dies, his hope perishes;
all he expected from his power comes to nothing.

8The righteous man is rescued from trouble,
and it comes on the wicked instead.

9With his mouth the godless destroys his neighbor,
but through knowledge the righteous escape.

10When the righteous prosper, the city rejoices;
when the wicked perish, there are shouts of joy.

11Through the blessing of the upright a city is exalted,
but by the mouth of the wicked it is destroyed.

12A man who lacks judgment derides his neighbor,
but a man of understanding holds his tongue.

13A gossip betrays a confidence,
but a trustworthy man keeps a secret.

14For lack of guidance a nation falls,
but many advisers make victory sure.

15He who puts up security for another will surely suffer,
but whoever refuses to strike hands in pledge is safe.

16A kindhearted woman gains respect,
but ruthless men gain only wealth.

17A kind man benefits himself,
but a cruel man brings trouble on himself.

18The wicked man earns deceptive wages,
but he who sows righteousness reaps a sure reward.

19The truly righteous man attains life,
but he who pursues evil goes to his death.

Living Bible

31The good man gives wise advice, but the liar's counsel is shunned.

32The upright speak what is helpful; the wicked speak rebellion.

11 THE LORD hates cheating and delights in honesty.

2Proud men end in shame, but the meek become wise.

3A good man is guided by his honesty; the evil man is destroyed by his dishonesty.

4Your riches won't help you on Judgment Day; only righteousness counts then.

5Good people are directed by their honesty; the wicked shall fall beneath their load of sins.

6The good man's goodness delivers him; the evil man's treachery is his undoing.

7When an evil man dies, his hopes all perish, for they are based upon this earthly life.

8God rescues good men from danger while letting the wicked fall into it.

9Evil words destroy. Godly skill rebuilds.a

10The whole city celebrates a good man's success— and also the godless man's death.

11The good influence of godly citizens causes a city to prosper, but the moral decay of the wicked drives it downhill.

12To quarrel with a neighbor is foolish; a man with good sense holds his tongue.

13A gossip goes around spreading rumors, while a trustworthy man tries to quiet them.

14Without wise leadership, a nation is in trouble; but with good counselors there is safety.

15Be sure you know a person well before you vouch for his credit! Better refuse than suffer later.

16Honor goes to kind and gracious women, mereb money to cruel men.

17Your own soul is nourished when you are kind; it is destroyed when you are cruel.

18The evil man gets rich for the moment, but the good man's reward lasts forever.

19The good man finds life; the evil man, death.

New Revised Standard

31 The mouth of the righteous brings forth
    wisdom,
    but the perverse tongue will be cut off.
32 The lips of the righteous know what is
    acceptable,
    but the mouth of the wicked what is
    perverse.

11 A FALSE balance is an abomination to the
    LORD,
    but an accurate weight is his delight.
2 When pride comes, then comes disgrace;
    but wisdom is with the humble.
3 The integrity of the upright guides them,
    but the crookedness of the treacherous
    destroys them.
4 Riches do not profit in the day of wrath,
    but righteousness delivers from death.
5 The righteousness of the blameless keeps their
    ways straight,
    but the wicked fall by their own
    wickedness.
6 The righteousness of the upright saves them,
    but the treacherous are taken captive by
    their schemes.
7 When the wicked die, their hope perishes,
    and the expectation of the godless comes to
    nothing.
8 The righteous are delivered from trouble,
    and the wicked get into it instead.
9 With their mouths the godless would destroy
    their neighbors,
    but by knowledge the righteous are
    delivered.
10 When it goes well with the righteous, the city
    rejoices;
    and when the wicked perish, there is
    jubilation.
11 By the blessing of the upright a city is
    exalted,
    but it is overthrown by the mouth of the
    wicked.
12 Whoever belittles another lacks sense,
    but an intelligent person remains silent.
13 A gossip goes about telling secrets,
    but one who is trustworthy in spirit keeps a
    confidence.
14 Where there is no guidance, a nationc falls,
    but in an abundance of counselors there is
    safety.
15 To guarantee loans for a stranger brings
    trouble,
    but there is safety in refusing to do so.
16 A gracious woman gets honor,
    but she who hates virtue is covered with
    shame.d
    The timid become destitute,e
    but the aggressive gain riches.
17 Those who are kind reward themselves,
    but the cruel do themselves harm.
18 The wicked earn no real gain,
    but those who sow righteousness get a true
    reward.
19 Whoever is steadfast in righteousness will
    live,
    but whoever pursues evil will die.

---

a 11:9 Evil words destroy. Godly skill rebuilds, or, "When a godless man slanders his neighbor, the charges won't stick because everyone knows his reputation."   b 11:16 mere, implied.

c Or an army   d Compare Gk Syr: Heb lacks but she . . . shame   e Gk: Heb lacks The timid . . . destitute

King James

20They that are of a froward heart *are* abomination to the LORD: but *such as are* upright in *their* way *are* his delight.

21*Though* hand *join* in hand, the wicked shall not be unpunished: but the seed of the righteous shall be delivered.

22*As* a jewel of gold in a swine's snout, *so is* a fair woman which is without discretion.

23The desire of the righteous *is* only good: *but* the expectation of the wicked *is* wrath.

24There is that scattereth, and yet increaseth; and *there is* that withholdeth more than is meet, but *it tendeth* to poverty.

25The liberal soul shall be made fat: and he that watereth shall be watered also himself.

26He that withholdeth corn, the people shall curse him: but blessing *shall be* upon the head of him that selleth *it*.

27He that diligently seeketh good procureth favour: but he that seeketh mischief, it shall come unto him.

28He that trusteth in his riches shall fall: but the righteous shall flourish as a branch.

29He that troubleth his own house shall inherit the wind: and the fool *shall be* servant to the wise of heart.

30The fruit of the righteous *is* a tree of life; and he that winneth souls *is* wise.

31Behold, the righteous shall be recompensed in the earth: much more the wicked and the sinner.

12 WHOSO LOVETH instruction loveth knowledge: but he that hateth reproof *is* brutish.

2A good *man* obtaineth favour of the LORD: but a man of wicked devices will he condemn.

3A man shall not be established by wickedness: but the root of the righteous shall not be moved.

4A virtuous woman *is* a crown to her husband: but she that maketh ashamed *is* as rottenness in his bones.

5The thoughts of the righteous *are* right: *but* the counsels of the wicked *are* deceit.

6The words of the wicked *are* to lie in wait for blood: but the mouth of the upright shall deliver them.

7The wicked are overthrown, and *are* not: but the house of the righteous shall stand.

8A man shall be commended according to his wisdom: but he that is of a perverse heart shall be despised.

9*He that is* despised, and hath a servant, *is* better than he that honoureth himself, and lacketh bread.

10A righteous *man* regardeth the life of his beast: but the tender mercies of the wicked *are* cruel.

11He that tilleth his land shall be satisfied with bread: but he that followeth vain *persons is* void of understanding.

New International

20The LORD detests men of perverse heart
but he delights in those whose ways are
blameless.

21Be sure of this: The wicked will not go
unpunished,
but those who are righteous will go free.

22Like a gold ring in a pig's snout
is a beautiful woman who shows no
discretion.

23The desire of the righteous ends only in good,
but the hope of the wicked only in wrath.

24One man gives freely, yet gains even more;
another withholds unduly, but comes to
poverty.

25A generous man will prosper;
he who refreshes others will himself be
refreshed.

26People curse the man who hoards grain,
but blessing crowns him who is willing to
sell.

27He who seeks good finds goodwill,
but evil comes to him who searches for it.

28Whoever trusts in his riches will fall,
but the righteous will thrive like a green leaf.

29He who brings trouble on his family will inherit
only wind,
and the fool will be servant to the wise.

30The fruit of the righteous is a tree of life,
and he who wins souls is wise.

31If the righteous receive their due on earth,
how much more the ungodly and the sinner!

12 WHOEVER LOVES discipline loves
knowledge,
but he who hates correction is stupid.

2A good man obtains favor from the LORD,
but the LORD condemns a crafty man.

3A man cannot be established through
wickedness,
but the righteous cannot be uprooted.

4A wife of noble character is her husband's
crown,
but a disgraceful wife is like decay in his
bones.

5The plans of the righteous are just,
but the advice of the wicked is deceitful.

6The words of the wicked lie in wait for blood,
but the speech of the upright rescues them.

7Wicked men are overthrown and are no more,
but the house of the righteous stands firm.

8A man is praised according to his wisdom,
but men with warped minds are despised.

9Better to be a nobody and yet have a servant
than pretend to be somebody and have no
food.

10A righteous man cares for the needs of his
animal,
but the kindest acts of the wicked are cruel.

11He who works his land will have abundant
food,
but he who chases fantasies lacks judgment.

Living Bible

20The Lord hates the stubborn but delights in those who are good.

21You can be very sure the evil man will not go unpunished forever. And you can also be very sure God will rescue the children of the godly.

22A beautiful woman lacking discretion and modesty is like a fine gold ring in a pig's snout.

23The good man can look forward to happiness, while the wicked can expect only wrath.

24, 25It is possible to give away and become richer! It is also possible to hold on too tightly and lose everything. Yes, the liberal man shall be rich! By watering others, he waters himself.

26People curse the man who holds his grain for higher prices, but they bless the man who sells it to them in their time of need.

27If you search for good you will find God's favor; if you search for evil you will find his curse.

28Trust in your money and down you go! Trust in God and flourish as a tree!

29The fool who provokes his family to anger and resentment will finally have nothing worthwhile left. He shall be the servant of a wiser man.

30Godly men are growing a tree that bears life-giving fruit, and all who win souls are wise.a

31Even the godly shall be rewarded here on earth; how much more the wicked!

12 TO LEARN, you must want to be taught. To refuse reproof is stupid.

2The Lord blesses good men and condemns the wicked.

3Wickedness never brings real success; only the godly have that.

4A worthy wife is her husband's joy and crown; the other kind corrodes his strength and tears down everything he does.

5A good man's mind is filled with honest thoughts; an evil man's mind is crammed with lies.

6The wicked accuse; the godly defend.

7The wicked shall perish; the godly shall stand.

8Everyone admires a man with good sense, but a man with a warped mind is despised.

9It is better to get your hands dirty—and eat,b than to be too proud to work—and starve.

10A good man is concerned for the welfare of his animals, but even the kindness of godless men is cruel.

11Hard work means prosperity;c only a fool idles away his time.

New Revised Standard

20 Crooked minds are an abomination to the
        LORD,
      but those of blameless ways are his delight.
21 Be assured, the wicked will not go
        unpunished,
      but those who are righteous will escape.
22 Like a gold ring in a pig's snout
      is a beautiful woman without good sense.
23 The desire of the righteous ends only in good;
      the expectation of the wicked in wrath.
24 Some give freely, yet grow all the richer;
      others withhold what is due, and only suffer
        want.
25 A generous person will be enriched,
      and one who gives water will get water.
26 The people curse those who hold back grain,
      but a blessing is on the head of those who
        sell it.
27 Whoever diligently seeks good seeks favor,
      but evil comes to the one who searches for
        it.
28 Those who trust in their riches will wither,d
      but the righteous will flourish like green
        leaves.
29 Those who trouble their households will
        inherit wind,
      and the fool will be servant to the wise.
30 The fruit of the righteous is a tree of life,
      but violencee takes lives away.
31 If the righteous are repaid on earth,
      how much more the wicked and the sinner!

12 WHOEVER LOVES discipline loves
        knowledge,
      but those who hate to be rebuked are stupid.
2 The good obtain favor from the LORD,
      but those who devise evil he condemns.
3 No one finds security by wickedness,
      but the root of the righteous will never be
        moved.
4 A good wife is the crown of her husband,
      but she who brings shame is like rottenness
        in his bones.
5 The thoughts of the righteous are just;
      the advice of the wicked is treacherous.
6 The words of the wicked are a deadly
        ambush,
      but the speech of the upright delivers them.
7 The wicked are overthrown and are no more,
      but the house of the righteous will stand.
8 One is commended for good sense,
      but a perverse mind is despised.
9 Better to be despised and have a servant,
      than to be self-important and lack food.
10 The righteous know the needs of their
        animals,
      but the mercy of the wicked is cruel.
11 Those who till their land will have plenty of
        food,
      but those who follow worthless pursuits
        have no sense.

---

a 11:30 all who win souls are wise, or, "he that is wise wins souls."
b 12:9 and eat, implied.   c 12:11 Hard work means prosperity, literally,
"He who tills his ground shall have his fill of bread."

d Cn: Heb fall   e Cn Compare Gk Syr: Heb a wise man

King James

12The wicked desireth the net of evil *men:* but the root of the righteous yieldeth *fruit.*

13The wicked is snared by the transgression of *his* lips: but the just shall come out of trouble.

14A man shall be satisfied with good by the fruit of *his* mouth: and the recompence of a man's hands shall be rendered unto him.

15The way of a fool *is* right in his own eyes: but he that hearkeneth unto counsel *is* wise.

16A fool's wrath is presently known: but a prudent *man* covereth shame.

17*He that* speaketh truth showeth forth righteousness: but a false witness deceit.

18There is that speaketh like the piercings of a sword: but the tongue of the wise *is* health.

19The lip of truth shall be established for ever: but a lying tongue *is* but for a moment.

20Deceit *is* in the heart of them that imagine evil: but to the counsellors of peace *is* joy.

21There shall no evil happen to the just: but the wicked shall be filled with mischief.

22Lying lips *are* abomination to the LORD: but they that deal truly *are* his delight.

23A prudent man concealeth knowledge: but the heart of fools proclaimeth foolishness.

24The hand of the diligent shall bear rule: but the slothful shall be under tribute.

25Heaviness in the heart of man maketh it stoop: but a good word maketh it glad.

26The righteous *is* more excellent than his neighbour: but the way of the wicked seduceth them.

27The slothful *man* roasteth not that which he took in hunting: but the substance of a diligent man *is* precious.

28In the way of righteousness *is* life; and *in* the pathway *thereof there is* no death.

13 A WISE son *heareth* his father's instruction: but a scorner heareth not rebuke.

2A man shall eat good by the fruit of *his* mouth: but the soul of the transgressors *shall eat* violence.

3He that keepeth his mouth keepeth his life: *but* he that openeth wide his lips shall have destruction.

4The soul of the sluggard desireth, and *hath* nothing: but the soul of the diligent shall be made fat.

5A righteous *man* hateth lying: but a wicked *man* is loathsome, and cometh to shame.

6Righteousness keepeth *him that is* upright in the way: but wickedness overthroweth the sinner.

New International

12The wicked desire the plunder of evil men,
　but the root of the righteous flourishes.

13An evil man is trapped by his sinful talk,
　but a righteous man escapes trouble.

14From the fruit of his lips a man is filled with good things
　as surely as the work of his hands rewards him.

15The way of a fool seems right to him,
　but a wise man listens to advice.

16A fool shows his annoyance at once,
　but a prudent man overlooks an insult.

17A truthful witness gives honest testimony,
　but a false witness tells lies.

18Reckless words pierce like a sword,
　but the tongue of the wise brings healing.

19Truthful lips endure forever,
　but a lying tongue lasts only a moment.

20There is deceit in the hearts of those who plot evil,
　but joy for those who promote peace.

21No harm befalls the righteous,
　but the wicked have their fill of trouble.

22The LORD detests lying lips,
　but he delights in men who are truthful.

23A prudent man keeps his knowledge to himself,
　but the heart of fools blurts out folly.

24Diligent hands will rule,
　but laziness ends in slave labor.

25An anxious heart weighs a man down,
　but a kind word cheers him up.

26A righteous man is cautious in friendship,a
　but the way of the wicked leads them astray.

27The lazy man does not roastb his game,
　but the diligent man prizes his possessions.

28In the way of righteousness there is life;
　along that path is immortality.

13 A WISE son heeds his father's instruction,
but a mocker does not listen to rebuke.

2From the fruit of his lips a man enjoys good things,
　but the unfaithful have a craving for violence.

3He who guards his lips guards his life,
　but he who speaks rashly will come to ruin.

4The sluggard craves and gets nothing,
　but the desires of the diligent are fully satisfied.

5The righteous hate what is false,
　but the wicked bring shame and disgrace.

6Righteousness guards the man of integrity,
　but wickedness overthrows the sinner.

---

a *26 Or man is a guide to his neighbor* b *27 The meaning of the Hebrew for this word is uncertain.*

Living Bible

¹²Crooks are jealous of each other's loot, while good men long to help each other.

¹³Lies will get any man into trouble, but honesty is its own defense.

¹⁴Telling the truth gives a man great satisfaction, and hard work returns many blessings to him.

¹⁵A fool thinks he needs no advice, but a wise man listens to others.

¹⁶A fool is quick-tempered; a wise man stays cool when insulted.

¹⁷A good man is known by his truthfulness; a false man by deceit and lies.

¹⁸Some people like to make cutting remarks, but the words of the wise soothe and heal.

¹⁹Truth stands the test of time; lies are soon exposed.

²⁰Deceit fills hearts that are plotting for evil; joy fills hearts that are planning for good!

²¹No real harm befalls the good, but there is constant trouble for the wicked.

²²God delights in those who keep their promises, and abhors those who don't.

²³A wise man doesn't display his knowledge, but a fool displays his foolishness.

²⁴Work hard and become a leader; be lazy and never succeed.

²⁵Anxious hearts are very heavy but a word of encouragement does wonders!

²⁶The good man asks advice from friends; the wicked plunge ahead—and fall.

²⁷A lazy man won't even dress the game he gets while hunting, but the diligent man makes good use of everything he finds.

²⁸The path of the godly leads to life. So why fear death?

13 A WISE youth accepts his father's rebuke; a young mocker doesn't.

²The good man wins his case by careful argument; the evil-minded only wants to fight.

³Self-control means controlling the tongue! A quick retort can ruin everything.

⁴Lazy people want much but get little, while the diligent are prospering.

⁵A good man hates lies; wicked men lie constantly^c and come to shame.

⁶A man's goodness helps him all through life, while evil men are being destroyed by their wickedness.

New Revised Standard

¹² The wicked covet the proceeds of wickedness,^d
but the root of the righteous bears fruit.

¹³ The evil are ensnared by the transgression of their lips,
but the righteous escape from trouble.

¹⁴ From the fruit of the mouth one is filled with good things,
and manual labor has its reward.

¹⁵ Fools think their own way is right,
but the wise listen to advice.

¹⁶ Fools show their anger at once,
but the prudent ignore an insult.

¹⁷ Whoever speaks the truth gives honest evidence,
but a false witness speaks deceitfully.

¹⁸ Rash words are like sword thrusts,
but the tongue of the wise brings healing.

¹⁹ Truthful lips endure forever,
but a lying tongue lasts only a moment.

²⁰ Deceit is in the mind of those who plan evil,
but those who counsel peace have joy.

²¹ No harm happens to the righteous,
but the wicked are filled with trouble.

²² Lying lips are an abomination to the LORD,
but those who act faithfully are his delight.

²³ One who is clever conceals knowledge,
but the mind of a fool^e broadcasts folly.

²⁴ The hand of the diligent will rule,
while the lazy will be put to forced labor.

²⁵ Anxiety weighs down the human heart,
but a good word cheers it up.

²⁶ The righteous gives good advice to friends,^f
but the way of the wicked leads astray.

²⁷ The lazy do not roast^g their game,
but the diligent obtain precious wealth.^g

²⁸ In the path of righteousness there is life,
in walking its path there is no death.

13 A WISE child loves discipline,^h
but a scoffer does not listen to rebuke.

² From the fruit of their words good persons eat good things,
but the desire of the treacherous is for wrongdoing.

³ Those who guard their mouths preserve their lives;
those who open wide their lips come to ruin.

⁴ The appetite of the lazy craves, and gets nothing,
while the appetite of the diligent is richly supplied.

⁵ The righteous hate falsehood,
but the wicked act shamefully and disgracefully.

⁶ Righteousness guards one whose way is upright,
but sin overthrows the wicked.

^d Or *covet the catch of the wicked*   ^e Heb *the heart of fools*   ^f Syr: Meaning of Heb uncertain   ^g Meaning of Heb uncertain   ^h Cn: Heb *A wise child the discipline of his father*

^c *13:5 wicked men lie constantly,* implied.

King James

7There is that maketh himself rich, yet *hath* nothing: *there is* that maketh himself poor, yet *hath* great riches.

8The ransom of a man's life *are* his riches: but the poor heareth not rebuke.

9The light of the righteous rejoiceth: but the lamp of the wicked shall be put out.

10Only by pride cometh contention: but with the well advised *is* wisdom.

11Wealth *gotten* by vanity shall be diminished: but he that gathereth by labour shall increase.

12Hope deferred maketh the heart sick: but *when* the desire cometh, *it is* a tree of life.

13Whoso despiseth the word shall be destroyed: but he that feareth the commandment shall be rewarded.

14The law of the wise *is* a fountain of life, to depart from the snares of death.

15Good understanding giveth favour: but the way of transgressors *is* hard.

16Every prudent *man* dealeth with knowledge: but a fool layeth open *his* folly.

17A wicked messenger falleth into mischief: but a faithful ambassador *is* health.

18Poverty and shame *shall be to* him that refuseth instruction: but he that regardeth reproof shall be honoured.

19The desire accomplished is sweet to the soul: but *it is* abomination to fools to depart from evil.

20He that walketh with wise *men* shall be wise: but a companion of fools shall be destroyed.

21Evil pursueth sinners: but to the righteous good shall be repaid.

22A good *man* leaveth an inheritance to his children's children: and the wealth of the sinner *is* laid up for the just.

23Much food *is in* the tillage of the poor: but there is *that is* destroyed for want of judgment.

24He that spareth his rod hateth his son: but he that loveth him chasteneth him betimes.

25The righteous eateth to the satisfying of his soul: but the belly of the wicked shall want.

14 EVERY WISE woman buildeth her house: but the foolish plucketh it down with her hands.

2He that walketh in his uprightness feareth the LORD: but *he that is* perverse in his ways despiseth him.

3In the mouth of the foolish *is* a rod of pride: but the lips of the wise shall preserve them.

4Where no oxen *are*, the crib *is* clean: but much increase *is* by the strength of the ox.

5A faithful witness will not lie: but a false witness will utter lies.

New International

7One man pretends to be rich, yet has nothing; another pretends to be poor, yet has great wealth.

8A man's riches may ransom his life, but a poor man hears no threat.

9The light of the righteous shines brightly, but the lamp of the wicked is snuffed out.

10Pride only breeds quarrels, but wisdom is found in those who take advice.

11Dishonest money dwindles away, but he who gathers money little by little makes it grow.

12Hope deferred makes the heart sick, but a longing fulfilled is a tree of life.

13He who scorns instruction will pay for it, but he who respects a command is rewarded.

14The teaching of the wise is a fountain of life, turning a man from the snares of death.

15Good understanding wins favor, but the way of the unfaithful is hard.[a]

16Every prudent man acts out of knowledge, but a fool exposes his folly.

17A wicked messenger falls into trouble, but a trustworthy envoy brings healing.

18He who ignores discipline comes to poverty and shame, but whoever heeds correction is honored.

19A longing fulfilled is sweet to the soul, but fools detest turning from evil.

20He who walks with the wise grows wise, but a companion of fools suffers harm.

21Misfortune pursues the sinner, but prosperity is the reward of the righteous.

22A good man leaves an inheritance for his children's children, but a sinner's wealth is stored up for the righteous.

23A poor man's field may produce abundant food, but injustice sweeps it away.

24He who spares the rod hates his son, but he who loves him is careful to discipline him.

25The righteous eat to their hearts' content, but the stomach of the wicked goes hungry.

14 THE WISE woman builds her house, but with her own hands the foolish one tears hers down.

2He whose walk is upright fears the LORD, but he whose ways are devious despises him.

3A fool's talk brings a rod to his back, but the lips of the wise protect them.

4Where there are no oxen, the manger is empty, but from the strength of an ox comes an abundant harvest.

5A truthful witness does not deceive, but a false witness pours out lies.

a 15 Or *unfaithful does not endure*

Living Bible

7Some rich people are poor, and some poor people have great wealth!

8Being kidnapped and held for ransom never worries the poor man!

9The good man's life is full of light. The sinner's road is dark and gloomy.

10Pride leads to arguments; be humble, take advice and become wise.

11Wealth from gambling quickly disappears; wealth from hard work grows.

12Hope deferred makes the heart sick; but when dreams come true at last, there is life and joy.b

13Despise God's Word and find yourself in trouble. Obey it and succeed.

14The advice of a wise man refreshes like water from a mountain spring. Those accepting it become aware of the pitfalls on ahead.

15A man with good sense is appreciated. A treacherous man must walk a rocky road.

16A wise man thinks ahead; a fool doesn't, and even brags about it!

17An unreliable messenger can cause a lot of trouble. Reliable communication permits progress.

18If you refuse criticism you will end in poverty and disgrace; if you accept criticism you are on the road to fame.

19It is pleasant to see plans develop. That is why fools refuse to give them up even when they are wrong.

20Be with wise men and become wise. Be with evil men and become evil.

21Curses chase sinners, while blessings chase the righteous!

22When a good man dies, he leaves an inheritance to his grandchildren; but when a sinner dies, his wealth is stored up for the godly.

23A poor man's farm may have good soil, but injustice robs him of its riches.

24If you refuse to discipline your son, it proves you don't love him; for if you love him you will be prompt to punish him.

25The good man eats to live, while the evil man lives to eat.c

14 A WISE woman builds her house, while a foolish woman tears hers down by her own efforts.

2To do right honors God; to sin is to despise him.

3A rebel's foolish talk should prick his own pride! But the wise man's speech is respected.

4An empty stable stays clean—but there is no income from an empty stable.

5A truthful witness never lies; a false witness always lies.

New Revised Standard

7 Some pretend to be rich, yet have nothing;
　　others pretend to be poor, yet have great
　　wealth.

8 Wealth is a ransom for a person's life,
　　but the poor get no threats.

9 The light of the righteous rejoices,
　　but the lamp of the wicked goes out.

10 By insolence the heedless make strife,
　　but wisdom is with those who take advice.

11 Wealth hastily gottend will dwindle,
　　but those who gather little by little will
　　increase it.

12 Hope deferred makes the heart sick,
　　but a desire fulfilled is a tree of life.

13 Those who despise the word bring destruction
　　on themselves,
　　but those who respect the commandment
　　will be rewarded.

14 The teaching of the wise is a fountain of life,
　　so that one may avoid the snares of death.

15 Good sense wins favor,
　　but the way of the faithless is their ruin.e

16 The clever do all things intelligently,
　　but the fool displays folly.

17 A bad messenger brings trouble,
　　but a faithful envoy, healing.

18 Poverty and disgrace are for the one who
　　ignores instruction,
　　but one who heeds reproof is honored.

19 A desire realized is sweet to the soul,
　　but to turn away from evil is an
　　abomination to fools.

20 Whoever walks with the wise becomes wise,
　　but the companion of fools suffers harm.

21 Misfortune pursues sinners,
　　but prosperity rewards the righteous.

22 The good leave an inheritance to their
　　children's children,
　　but the sinner's wealth is laid up for the
　　righteous.

23 The field of the poor may yield much food,
　　but it is swept away through injustice.

24 Those who spare the rod hate their children,
　　but those who love them are diligent to
　　discipline them.

25 The righteous have enough to satisfy their
　　appetite,
　　but the belly of the wicked is empty.

14 THE WISE womanf builds her house,
　　but the foolish tears it down with her own
　　hands.

2 Those who walk uprightly fear the LORD,
　　but one who is devious in conduct despises
　　him.

3 The talk of fools is a rod for their backs,g
　　but the lips of the wise preserve them.

4 Where there are no oxen, there is no grain;
　　abundant crops come by the strength of the
　　ox.

5 A faithful witness does not lie,
　　but a false witness breathes out lies.

---

b 13:12 but when dreams come true at last, there is life and joy, literally, "it is a tree of life."　c 13:25 while the evil man lives to eat, literally, "but the wicked never get enough."

d Gk Vg: Heb from vanity　e Cn Compare Gk Syr Vg Tg: Heb is enduring
f Heb Wisdom of women　g Cn: Heb a rod of pride

King James

6A scorner seeketh wisdom, and *findeth it* not: but knowledge *is* easy unto him that understandeth.

7Go from the presence of a foolish man, when thou perceivest not *in him* the lips of knowledge.

8The wisdom of the prudent *is* to understand his way: but the folly of fools *is* deceit.

9Fools make a mock at sin: but among the righteous *there is* favour.

10The heart knoweth his own bitterness; and a stranger doth not intermeddle with his joy.

11The house of the wicked shall be overthrown: but the tabernacle of the upright shall flourish.

12There is a way which seemeth right unto a man, but the end thereof *are* the ways of death.

13Even in laughter the heart is sorrowful; and the end of that mirth *is* heaviness.

14The backslider in heart shall be filled with his own ways: and a good man *shall be satisfied* from himself.

15The simple believeth every word: but the prudent *man* looketh well to his going.

16A wise *man* feareth, and departeth from evil: but the fool rageth, and is confident.

17*He that is* soon angry dealeth foolishly: and a man of wicked devices is hated.

18The simple inherit folly: but the prudent are crowned with knowledge.

19The evil bow before the good; and the wicked at the gates of the righteous.

20The poor is hated even of his own neighbour: but the rich *hath* many friends.

21He that despiseth his neighbour sinneth: but he that hath mercy on the poor, happy *is* he.

22Do they not err that devise evil? but mercy and truth *shall be* to them that devise good.

23In all labour there is profit: but the talk of the lips *tendeth* only to penury.

24The crown of the wise *is* their riches: *but* the foolishness of fools *is* folly.

25A true witness delivereth souls: but a deceitful *witness* speaketh lies.

26In the fear of the Lord *is* strong confidence: and his children shall have a place of refuge.

27The fear of the Lord *is* a fountain of life, to depart from the snares of death.

28In the multitude of people *is* the king's honour: but in the want of people *is* the destruction of the prince.

29*He that is* slow to wrath *is* of great understanding: but *he that is* hasty of spirit exalteth folly.

30A sound heart *is* the life of the flesh: but envy the rottenness of the bones.

31He that oppresseth the poor reproacheth his Maker: but he that honoureth him hath mercy on the poor.

32The wicked is driven away in his wickedness: but the righteous hath hope in his death.

New International

6The mocker seeks wisdom and finds none,
    but knowledge comes easily to the discerning.

7Stay away from a foolish man,
    for you will not find knowledge on his lips.

8The wisdom of the prudent is to give thought to their ways,
    but the folly of fools is deception.

9Fools mock at making amends for sin,
    but goodwill is found among the upright.

10Each heart knows its own bitterness,
    and no one else can share its joy.

11The house of the wicked will be destroyed,
    but the tent of the upright will flourish.

12There is a way that seems right to a man,
    but in the end it leads to death.

13Even in laughter the heart may ache,
    and joy may end in grief.

14The faithless will be fully repaid for their ways,
    and the good man rewarded for his.

15A simple man believes anything,
    but a prudent man gives thought to his steps.

16A wise man fears the Lord and shuns evil,
    but a fool is hotheaded and reckless.

17A quick-tempered man does foolish things,
    and a crafty man is hated.

18The simple inherit folly,
    but the prudent are crowned with knowledge.

19Evil men will bow down in the presence of the good,
    and the wicked at the gates of the righteous.

20The poor are shunned even by their neighbors,
    but the rich have many friends.

21He who despises his neighbor sins,
    but blessed is he who is kind to the needy.

22Do not those who plot evil go astray?
    But those who plan what is good find[a] love and faithfulness.

23All hard work brings a profit,
    but mere talk leads only to poverty.

24The wealth of the wise is their crown,
    but the folly of fools yields folly.

25A truthful witness saves lives,
    but a false witness is deceitful.

26He who fears the Lord has a secure fortress,
    and for his children it will be a refuge.

27The fear of the Lord is a fountain of life,
    turning a man from the snares of death.

28A large population is a king's glory,
    but without subjects a prince is ruined.

29A patient man has great understanding,
    but a quick-tempered man displays folly.

30A heart at peace gives life to the body,
    but envy rots the bones.

31He who oppresses the poor shows contempt for their Maker,
    but whoever is kind to the needy honors God.

32When calamity comes, the wicked are brought down,
    but even in death the righteous have a refuge.

---

a 22 Or *show*

Living Bible

6A mocker never finds the wisdom he claims he is looking for, yet it comes easily to the man with common sense.

7If you are looking for advice, stay away from fools.

8The wise man looks ahead. The fool attempts to fool himself and won't face facts.

9The common bond of rebels is their guilt.b The common bond of godly people is good will.

10Only the person involved can know his own bitterness or joy—no one else can really share it.

11The work of the wicked will perish; the work of the godly will flourish.

12Before every man there lies a wide and pleasant road that seems right but ends in death.

13Laughter cannot mask a heavy heart. When the laughter ends, the grief remains.

14The backslider gets bored with himself; the godly man's life is exciting.

15Only a simpleton believes everything he's told! A prudent man understands the need for proof.

16A wise man is cautious and avoids danger; a fool plunges ahead with great confidence.

17A short-tempered man is a fool. He hates the man who is patient.

18The simpleton is crowned with folly; the wise man is crowned with knowledge.

19Evil men shall bow before the godly.

20, 21Even his own neighbors despise the poor man, while the rich have many "friends." But to despise the poor is to sin. Blessed are those who help them.

22Those who plot evil shall wander away and be lost, but those who plan good shall be granted mercy and quietness.

23Work brings profit; talk brings poverty!

24Wise men are praised for their wisdom; fools are despised for their folly.

25A witness who tells the truth saves good men from being sentenced to death, but a false witness is a traitor.

26Reverence for God gives a man strength; his children have a place of refuge and security.

27Reverence for the Lord is a fountain of life; its waters keep a man from death.

28A growing population is a king's glory; a dwindling nation is his doom.

29A wise man controls his temper. He knows that anger causes mistakes.

30A relaxed attitude lengthens a man's life; jealousy rots it away.

31Anyone who oppresses the poor is insulting God who made them. To help the poor is to honor God.

32The godly have a refuge when they die, but the wicked are crushed by their sins.

New Revised Standard

6 A scoffer seeks wisdom in vain,
  but knowledge is easy for one who
    understands.

7 Leave the presence of a fool,
  for there you do not find words of
    knowledge.

8 It is the wisdom of the clever to understand
    where they go,
  but the folly of fools misleads.

9 Fools mock at the guilt offering,c
  but the upright enjoy God's favor.

10 The heart knows its own bitterness,
  and no stranger shares its joy.

11 The house of the wicked is destroyed,
  but the tent of the upright flourishes.

12 There is a way that seems right to a person,
  but its end is the way to death.d

13 Even in laughter the heart is sad,
  and the end of joy is grief.

14 The perverse get what their ways deserve,
  and the good, what their deeds deserve.e

15 The simple believe everything,
  but the clever consider their steps.

16 The wise are cautious and turn away from
    evil,
  but the fool throws off restraint and is
    careless.

17 One who is quick-tempered acts foolishly,
  and the schemer is hated.

18 The simple are adorned withf folly,
  but the clever are crowned with knowledge.

19 The evil bow down before the good,
  the wicked at the gates of the righteous.

20 The poor are disliked even by their neighbors,
  but the rich have many friends.

21 Those who despise their neighbors are sinners,
  but happy are those who are kind to the
    poor.

22 Do they not err that plan evil?
  Those who plan good find loyalty and
    faithfulness.

23 In all toil there is profit,
  but mere talk leads only to poverty.

24 The crown of the wise is their wisdom,g
  but folly is the garlandh of fools.

25 A truthful witness saves lives,
  but one who utters lies is a betrayer.

26 In the fear of the LORD one has strong
    confidence,
  and one's children will have a refuge.

27 The fear of the LORD is a fountain of life,
  so that one may avoid the snares of death.

28 The glory of a king is a multitude of people;
  without people a prince is ruined.

29 Whoever is slow to anger has great
    understanding,
  but one who has a hasty temper exalts folly.

30 A tranquil mind gives life to the flesh,
  but passion makes the bones rot.

31 Those who oppress the poor insult their
    Maker,
  but those who are kind to the needy honor
    him.

32 The wicked are overthrown by their
    evildoing,
  but the righteous find a refuge in their
    integrity.i

---

b 14:9 The common bond of rebels is their guilt, or, "Fools make a mock at sin." The Hebrew is obscure.

c Meaning of Heb uncertain   d Heb ways of death   e Cn: Heb from upon him   f Or inherit   g Cn Compare Gk: Heb riches   h Cn: Heb is the folly   i Gk Syr: Heb in their death

King James

33Wisdom resteth in the heart of him that hath understanding: but *that which is* in the midst of fools is made known.

34Righteousness exalteth a nation: but sin *is* a reproach to any people.

35The king's favour *is* toward a wise servant: but his wrath is *against* him that causeth shame.

15 A SOFT answer turneth away wrath: but grievous words stir up anger.

2The tongue of the wise useth knowledge aright: but the mouth of fools poureth out foolishness.

3The eyes of the LORD *are* in every place, beholding the evil and the good.

4A wholesome tongue *is* a tree of life: but perverseness therein *is* a breach in the spirit.

5A fool despiseth his father's instruction: but he that regardeth reproof is prudent.

6In the house of the righteous *is* much treasure: but in the revenues of the wicked is trouble.

7The lips of the wise disperse knowledge: but the heart of the foolish *doeth* not so.

8The sacrifice of the wicked *is* an abomination to the LORD: but the prayer of the upright *is* his delight.

9The way of the wicked *is* an abomination unto the LORD: but he loveth him that followeth after righteousness.

10Correction *is* grievous unto him that forsaketh the way: *and* he that hateth reproof shall die.

11Hell and destruction *are* before the LORD: how much more then the hearts of the children of men?

12A scorner loveth not one that reproveth him: neither will he go unto the wise.

13A merry heart maketh a cheerful countenance: but by sorrow of the heart the spirit is broken.

14The heart of him that hath understanding seeketh knowledge: but the mouth of fools feedeth on foolishness.

15All the days of the afflicted *are* evil: but he that is of a merry heart *hath* a continual feast.

16Better *is* little with the fear of the LORD than great treasure and trouble therewith.

17Better *is* a dinner of herbs where love is, than a stalled ox and hatred therewith.

18A wrathful man stirreth up strife: but *he that is* slow to anger appeaseth strife.

19The way of the slothful *man is* as an hedge of thorns: but the way of the righteous *is* made plain.

20A wise son maketh a glad father: but a foolish man despiseth his mother.

21Folly *is* joy to *him that is* destitute of wisdom: but a man of understanding walketh uprightly.

New International

33Wisdom reposes in the heart of the discerning and even among fools she lets herself be known.[a]

34Righteousness exalts a nation,
    but sin is a disgrace to any people.

35A king delights in a wise servant,
    but a shameful servant incurs his wrath.

15 A GENTLE answer turns away wrath,
    but a harsh word stirs up anger.

2The tongue of the wise commends knowledge,
    but the mouth of the fool gushes folly.

3The eyes of the LORD are everywhere,
    keeping watch on the wicked and the good.

4The tongue that brings healing is a tree of life,
    but a deceitful tongue crushes the spirit.

5A fool spurns his father's discipline,
    but whoever heeds correction shows
        prudence.

6The house of the righteous contains great
        treasure,
    but the income of the wicked brings them
        trouble.

7The lips of the wise spread knowledge;
    not so the hearts of fools.

8The LORD detests the sacrifice of the wicked,
    but the prayer of the upright pleases him.

9The LORD detests the way of the wicked
    but he loves those who pursue righteousness.

10Stern discipline awaits him who leaves the path;
    he who hates correction will die.

11Death and Destruction[b] lie open before the
        LORD—
    how much more the hearts of men!

12A mocker resents correction;
    he will not consult the wise.

13A happy heart makes the face cheerful,
    but heartache crushes the spirit.

14The discerning heart seeks knowledge,
    but the mouth of a fool feeds on folly.

15All the days of the oppressed are wretched,
    but the cheerful heart has a continual feast.

16Better a little with the fear of the LORD
    than great wealth with turmoil.

17Better a meal of vegetables where there is love
    than a fattened calf with hatred.

18A hot-tempered man stirs up dissension,
    but a patient man calms a quarrel.

19The way of the sluggard is blocked with thorns,
    but the path of the upright is a highway.

20A wise son brings joy to his father,
    but a foolish man despises his mother.

21Folly delights a man who lacks judgment,
    but a man of understanding keeps a straight
        course.

---

a 33 Hebrew; Septuagint and Syriac / *but in the heart of fools she is not known*
b 11 Hebrew *Sheol and Abaddon*

Living Bible

33Wisdom is enshrined in the hearts of men of common sense, but it must shout loudly before fools will hear it.

34Godliness exalts a nation, but sin is a reproach to any people.

35A king rejoices in servants who know what they are doing; he is angry with those who cause trouble.

15 A GENTLE answer turns away wrath, but harsh words cause quarrels.

2A wise teacher makes learning a joy; a rebellious teacher spouts foolishness.

3The Lord is watching everywhere and keeps his eye on both the evil and the good.

4Gentle words cause life and health; griping brings discouragement.

5Only a fool despises his father's advice; a wise son considers each suggestion.

6There is treasure in being good, but trouble dogs the wicked.

7Only the good can give good advice. Rebels can't.

8The Lord hates the gifts of the wicked, but delights in the prayers of his people.

9, 10The Lord despises the deeds of the wicked, but loves those who try to be good. If they stop trying, the Lord will punish them; if they rebel against that punishment, they will die.

11The depths of hell are open to God's knowledge. How much more the hearts of all mankind!

12A mocker stays away from wise men because he hates to be scolded.

13A happy face means a glad heart; a sad face means a breaking heart.

14A wise man is hungry for truth, while the mocker feeds on trash.

15When a man is gloomy, everything seems to go wrong; when he is cheerful, everything seems right!

16Better a little with reverence for God, than great treasure and trouble with it.

17It is better to eat soup with someone you love than steak with someone you hate.

18A quick-tempered man starts fights; a cool-tempered man tries to stop them.

19A lazy fellow has trouble all through life; the good man's path is easy!

20A sensible son gladdens his father. A rebellious son saddens his mother.c

21If a man enjoys folly, something is wrong! The sensible stay on the pathways of right.

New Revised Standard

33 Wisdom is at home in the mind of one who
        has understanding,
    but it is notd known in the heart of fools.
34 Righteousness exalts a nation,
    but sin is a reproach to any people.
35 A servant who deals wisely has the king's
        favor,
    but his wrath falls on one who acts
        shamefully.

15 A SOFT answer turns away wrath,
    but a harsh word stirs up anger.
2 The tongue of the wise dispenses knowledge,e
    but the mouths of fools pour out folly.
3 The eyes of the LORD are in every place,
    keeping watch on the evil and the good.
4 A gentle tongue is a tree of life,
    but perverseness in it breaks the spirit.
5 A fool despises a parent's instruction,
    but the one who heeds admonition is
        prudent.
6 In the house of the righteous there is much
        treasure,
    but trouble befalls the income of the
        wicked.
7 The lips of the wise spread knowledge;
    not so the minds of fools.
8 The sacrifice of the wicked is an abomination
        to the LORD,
    but the prayer of the upright is his delight.
9 The way of the wicked is an abomination to
        the LORD,
    but he loves the one who pursues
        righteousness.
10 There is severe discipline for one who
        forsakes the way,
    but one who hates a rebuke will die.
11 Sheol and Abaddon lie open before the LORD,
    how much more human hearts!
12 Scoffers do not like to be rebuked;
    they will not go to the wise.
13 A glad heart makes a cheerful countenance,
    but by sorrow of heart the spirit is broken.
14 The mind of one who has understanding seeks
        knowledge,
    but the mouths of fools feed on folly.
15 All the days of the poor are hard,
    but a cheerful heart has a continual feast.
16 Better is a little with the fear of the LORD
    than great treasure and trouble with it.
17 Better is a dinner of vegetables where love is
    than a fatted ox and hatred with it.
18 Those who are hot-tempered stir up strife,
    but those who are slow to anger calm
        contention.
19 The way of the lazy is overgrown with thorns,
    but the path of the upright is a level
        highway.
20 A wise child makes a glad father,
    but the foolish despise their mothers.
21 Folly is a joy to one who has no sense,
    but a person of understanding walks straight
        ahead.

---

c 15:20 saddens his mother, literally, "despises his mother."   d Gk Syr: Heb lacks not   e Cn: Heb makes knowledge good

King James

22Without counsel purposes are disappointed: but in the multitude of counsellors they are established.

23A man hath joy by the answer of his mouth: and a word *spoken* in due season, how good *is it!*

24The way of life *is* above to the wise, that he may depart from hell beneath.

25The LORD will destroy the house of the proud: but he will establish the border of the widow.

26The thoughts of the wicked *are* an abomination to the LORD: but *the words* of the pure *are* pleasant words.

27He that is greedy of gain troubleth his own house; but he that hateth gifts shall live.

28The heart of the righteous studieth to answer: but the mouth of the wicked poureth out evil things.

29The LORD *is* far from the wicked: but he heareth the prayer of the righteous.

30The light of the eyes rejoiceth the heart: *and* a good report maketh the bones fat.

31The ear that heareth the reproof of life abideth among the wise.

32He that refuseth instruction despiseth his own soul: but he that heareth reproof getteth understanding.

33The fear of the LORD *is* the instruction of wisdom; and before honour *is* humility.

16 THE PREPARATIONS of the heart in man, and the answer of the tongue, *is* from the LORD.

2All the ways of a man *are* clean in his own eyes; but the LORD weigheth the spirits.

3Commit thy works unto the LORD, and thy thoughts shall be established.

4The LORD hath made all *things* for himself: yea, even the wicked for the day of evil.

5Every one *that is* proud in heart *is* an abomination to the LORD: *though* hand *join* in hand, he shall not be unpunished.

6By mercy and truth iniquity is purged: and by the fear of the LORD *men* depart from evil.

7When a man's ways please the LORD, he maketh even his enemies to be at peace with him.

8Better *is* a little with righteousness than great revenues without right.

9A man's heart deviseth his way: but the LORD directeth his steps.

10A divine sentence *is* in the lips of the king: his mouth transgresseth not in judgment.

11A just weight and balance *are* the LORD's: all the weights of the bag *are* his work.

12*It is* an abomination to kings to commit wickedness: for the throne is established by righteousness.

13Righteous lips *are* the delight of kings; and they love him that speaketh right.

New International

22Plans fail for lack of counsel, but with many advisers they succeed.

23A man finds joy in giving an apt reply— and how good is a timely word!

24The path of life leads upward for the wise to keep him from going down to the grave.[a]

25The LORD tears down the proud man's house but he keeps the widow's boundaries intact.

26The LORD detests the thoughts of the wicked, but those of the pure are pleasing to him.

27A greedy man brings trouble to his family, but he who hates bribes will live.

28The heart of the righteous weighs its answers, but the mouth of the wicked gushes evil.

29The LORD is far from the wicked but he hears the prayer of the righteous.

30A cheerful look brings joy to the heart, and good news gives health to the bones.

31He who listens to a life-giving rebuke will be at home among the wise.

32He who ignores discipline despises himself, but whoever heeds correction gains understanding.

33The fear of the LORD teaches a man wisdom,[b] and humility comes before honor.

16 TO MAN belong the plans of the heart, but from the LORD comes the reply of the tongue.

2All a man's ways seem innocent to him, but motives are weighed by the LORD.

3Commit to the LORD whatever you do, and your plans will succeed.

4The LORD works out everything for his own ends— even the wicked for a day of disaster.

5The LORD detests all the proud of heart. Be sure of this: They will not go unpunished.

6Through love and faithfulness sin is atoned for; through the fear of the LORD a man avoids evil.

7When a man's ways are pleasing to the LORD, he makes even his enemies live at peace with him.

8Better a little with righteousness than much gain with injustice.

9In his heart a man plans his course, but the LORD determines his steps.

10The lips of a king speak as an oracle, and his mouth should not betray justice.

11Honest scales and balances are from the LORD; all the weights in the bag are of his making.

12Kings detest wrongdoing, for a throne is established through righteousness.

13Kings take pleasure in honest lips; they value a man who speaks the truth.

a 24 Hebrew *Sheol*   b 33 Or *Wisdom teaches the fear of the* LORD

Living Bible

22Plans go wrong with too few counselors; many counselors bring success.

23Everyone enjoys giving good advice, and how wonderful it is to be able to say the right thing at the right time!

24The road of the godly leads upward, leaving hell behind.

25The Lord destroys the possessions of the proud but cares for widows.

26The Lord hates the thoughts of the wicked but delights in kind words.c

27Dishonest money brings grief to all the family, but hating bribes brings happiness.d

28A good man thinks before he speaks; the evil man pours out his evil words without a thought.

29The Lord is far from the wicked, but he hears the prayers of the righteous.

30Pleasant sights and good reports give happiness and health.

31, 32If you profit from constructive criticism you will be elected to the wise men's hall of fame. But to reject criticism is to harm yourself and your own best interests.

33Humility and reverence for the Lord will make you both wise and honored.

16 WE CAN make our plans, but the final outcome is in God's hands.

2We can always "prove" that we are right, but is the Lord convinced?

3Commit your work to the Lord, then it will succeed.

4The Lord has made everything for his own purposes—even the wicked, for punishment.

5Pride disgusts the Lord. Take my word for it— *proud men shall be punished.*

6Iniquity is atoned for by mercy and truth; evil is avoided by reverence for God.

7When a man is trying to please God, God makes even his worst enemies to be at peace with him.

8A little, gained honestly, is better than great wealth gotten by dishonest means.

9We should make plans—counting on God to direct us.

10God will help the king to judge the people fairly; there need be no mistakes.

11The Lord demands fairness in every business deal.e He established this principle.

12It is a horrible thing for a king to do evil. His right to rule depends upon his fairness.f

13The king rejoices when his people are truthful and fair.

New Revised Standard

22 Without counsel, plans go wrong,
　　but with many advisers they succeed.
23 To make an apt answer is a joy to anyone,
　　and a word in season, how good it is!
24 For the wise the path of life leads upward,
　　in order to avoid Sheol below.
25 The LORD tears down the house of the proud,
　　but maintains the widow's boundaries.
26 Evil plans are an abomination to the LORD,
　　but gracious words are pure.
27 Those who are greedy for unjust gain make
　　　　trouble for their households,
　　but those who hate bribes will live.
28 The mind of the righteous ponders how to
　　　　answer,
　　but the mouth of the wicked pours out evil.
29 The LORD is far from the wicked,
　　but he hears the prayer of the righteous.
30 The light of the eyes rejoices the heart,
　　and good news refreshes the body.
31 The ear that heeds wholesome admonition
　　will lodge among the wise.
32 Those who ignore instruction despise
　　　　themselves,
　　but those who heed admonition gain
　　　　understanding.
33 The fear of the LORD is instruction in wisdom,
　　and humility goes before honor.

16 THE PLANS of the mind belong to mortals,
　　but the answer of the tongue is from the
　　　　LORD.
2 All one's ways may be pure in one's own
　　　　eyes,
　　but the LORD weighs the spirit.
3 Commit your work to the LORD,
　　and your plans will be established.
4 The LORD has made everything for its
　　　　purpose,
　　even the wicked for the day of trouble.
5 All those who are arrogant are an abomination
　　　　to the LORD;
　　be assured, they will not go unpunished.
6 By loyalty and faithfulness iniquity is atoned
　　　　for,
　　and by the fear of the LORD one avoids evil.
7 When the ways of people please the LORD,
　　he causes even their enemies to be at peace
　　　　with them.
8 Better is a little with righteousness
　　than large income with injustice.
9 The human mind plans the way,
　　but the LORD directs the steps.
10 Inspired decisions are on the lips of a king;
　　his mouth does not sin in judgment.
11 Honest balances and scales are the LORD's;
　　all the weights in the bag are his work.
12 It is an abomination to kings to do evil,
　　for the throne is established by
　　　　righteousness.
13 Righteous lips are the delight of a king,
　　and he loves those who speak what is right.

---

c 15:26 *but delights in kind words,* literally, "but kind words are pure."
d 15:27 *brings happiness,* literally, "you will live." e 16:11 *The Lord demands fairness in every business deal,* literally, "A just balance and scales are the Lord's; all the weights in the bag are his work."　f 16:12 *His right to rule depends upon his fairness,* literally, "for the throne is established by righteousness."

King James

14The wrath of a king *is as* messengers of death: but a wise man will pacify it.

15In the light of the king's countenance *is* life; and his favour *is* as a cloud of the latter rain.

16How much better *is it* to get wisdom than gold! and to get understanding rather to be chosen than silver!

17The highway of the upright *is* to depart from evil: he that keepeth his way preserveth his soul.

18Pride *goeth* before destruction, and an haughty spirit before a fall.

19Better *it is to be* of an humble spirit with the lowly, than to divide the spoil with the proud.

20He that handleth a matter wisely shall find good: and whoso trusteth in the LORD, happy *is* he.

21The wise in heart shall be called prudent: and the sweetness of the lips increaseth learning.

22Understanding *is* a wellspring of life unto him that hath it: but the instruction of fools *is* folly.

23The heart of the wise teacheth his mouth, and addeth learning to his lips.

24Pleasant words *are as* an honeycomb, sweet to the soul, and health to the bones.

25There is a way that seemeth right unto a man, but the end thereof *are* the ways of death.

26He that laboureth laboureth for himself; for his mouth craveth it of him.

27An ungodly man diggeth up evil: and in his lips *there is* as a burning fire.

28A froward man soweth strife: and a whisperer separateth chief friends.

29A violent man enticeth his neighbour, and leadeth him into the way *that is* not good.

30He shutteth his eyes to devise froward things: moving his lips he bringeth evil to pass.

31The hoary head *is* a crown of glory, *if* it be found in the way of righteousness.

32*He that is* slow to anger *is* better than the mighty; and he that ruleth his spirit than he that taketh a city.

33The lot is cast into the lap; but the whole disposing thereof *is* of the LORD.

17 BETTER *IS* a dry morsel, and quietness therewith, than an house full of sacrifices *with* strife.

2A wise servant shall have rule over a son that causeth shame, and shall have part of the inheritance among the brethren.

3The refining pot *is* for silver, and the furnace for gold: but the LORD trieth the hearts.

4A wicked doer giveth heed to false lips; *and* a liar giveth ear to a naughty tongue.

New International

14A king's wrath is a messenger of death, but a wise man will appease it.

15When a king's face brightens, it means life; his favor is like a rain cloud in spring.

16How much better to get wisdom than gold, to choose understanding rather than silver!

17The highway of the upright avoids evil; he who guards his way guards his life.

18Pride goes before destruction, a haughty spirit before a fall.

19Better to be lowly in spirit and among the oppressed than to share plunder with the proud.

20Whoever gives heed to instruction prospers, and blessed is he who trusts in the LORD.

21The wise in heart are called discerning, and pleasant words promote instruction.a

22Understanding is a fountain of life to those who have it, but folly brings punishment to fools.

23A wise man's heart guides his mouth, and his lips promote instruction.b

24Pleasant words are a honeycomb, sweet to the soul and healing to the bones.

25There is a way that seems right to a man, but in the end it leads to death.

26The laborer's appetite works for him; his hunger drives him on.

27A scoundrel plots evil, and his speech is like a scorching fire.

28A perverse man stirs up dissension, and a gossip separates close friends.

29A violent man entices his neighbor and leads him down a path that is not good.

30He who winks with his eye is plotting perversity; he who purses his lips is bent on evil.

31Gray hair is a crown of splendor; it is attained by a righteous life.

32Better a patient man than a warrior, a man who controls his temper than one who takes a city.

33The lot is cast into the lap, but its every decision is from the LORD.

17 BETTER A dry crust with peace and quiet than a house full of feasting,c with strife.

2A wise servant will rule over a disgraceful son, and will share the inheritance as one of the brothers.

3The crucible for silver and the furnace for gold, but the LORD tests the heart.

4A wicked man listens to evil lips; a liar pays attention to a malicious tongue.

a 21 Or *words make a man persuasive*   b 23 Or *mouth / and makes his lips persuasive*   c 1 Hebrew *sacrifices*

Living Bible

14The anger of the king is a messenger of death and a wise man will appease it.

15Many favors are showered on those who please the king.

16How much better is wisdom than gold, and understanding than silver!

17The path of the godly leads away from evil; he who follows that path is safe.

18Pride goes before destruction and haughtiness before a fall.

19Better poor and humble than proud and rich.

20God blesses those who obey him; happy the man who puts his trust in the Lord.

21The wise man is known by his common sense, and a pleasant teacher is the best.

22Wisdom is a fountain of life to those possessing it, but a fool's burden is his folly.

23From a wise mind comes careful and persuasive speech.

24Kind words are like honey—enjoyable and healthful.

25Before every man there lies a wide and pleasant road he thinks is right, but it ends in death.

26Hunger is good—if it makes you work to satisfy it!

27Idle hands are the devil's workshop; idle lips are his mouthpiece.d

28An evil man sows strife; gossip separates the best of friends.

29Wickedness loves company—and leads others into sin.e

30The wicked man stares into space with pursed lips, deep in thought, planning his evil deeds.

31White hair is a crown of glory and is seen most among the godly.

32It is better to be slow-tempered than famous; it is better to have self-control than to control an army.

33We toss the coin,f but it is the Lord who controls its decision.

17 A DRY crust eaten in peace is better than steak every day along with argument and strife.

2A wise slave will rule his master's wicked sons and share their estate.

3Silver and gold are purified by fire, but God purifies hearts.

4The wicked enjoy fellowship with others who are wicked; liars enjoy liars.

New Revised Standard

14 A king's wrath is a messenger of death,
   and whoever is wise will appease it.

15 In the light of a king's face there is life,
   and his favor is like the clouds that bring
   the spring rain.

16 How much better to get wisdom than gold!
   To get understanding is to be chosen rather
   than silver.

17 The highway of the upright avoids evil;
   those who guard their way preserve their
   lives.

18 Pride goes before destruction,
   and a haughty spirit before a fall.

19 It is better to be of a lowly spirit among the
   poor
   than to divide the spoil with the proud.

20 Those who are attentive to a matter will
   prosper,
   and happy are those who trust in the Lord.

21 The wise of heart is called perceptive,
   and pleasant speech increases
   persuasiveness.

22 Wisdom is a fountain of life to one who has
   it,
   but folly is the punishment of fools.

23 The mind of the wise makes their speech
   judicious,
   and adds persuasiveness to their lips.

24 Pleasant words are like a honeycomb,
   sweetness to the soul and health to the
   body.

25 Sometimes there is a way that seems to be
   right,
   but in the end it is the way to death.

26 The appetite of workers works for them;
   their hunger urges them on.

27 Scoundrels concoct evil,
   and their speech is like a scorching fire.

28 A perverse person spreads strife,
   and a whisperer separates close friends.

29 The violent entice their neighbors,
   and lead them in a way that is not good.

30 One who winks the eyes plansg perverse
   things;
   one who compresses the lips brings evil to
   pass.

31 Gray hair is a crown of glory;
   it is gained in a righteous life.

32 One who is slow to anger is better than the
   mighty,
   and one whose temper is controlled than one
   who captures a city.

33 The lot is cast into the lap,
   but the decision is the Lord's alone.

17 BETTER IS a dry morsel with quiet
   than a house full of feasting with strife.

2 A slave who deals wisely will rule over a
   child who acts shamefully,
   and will share the inheritance as one of the
   family.

3 The crucible is for silver, and the furnace is
   for gold,
   but the Lord tests the heart.

4 An evildoer listens to wicked lips;
   and a liar gives heed to a mischievous
   tongue.

---

d 16:27 Idle hands are the devil's workshop; idle lips are his mouthpiece, literally, "A worthless man devises mischief; and in his lips there is a scorching fire."   e 16:29 Wickedness loves company—and leads others into sin, or, "An evil man deceives his neighbor and leads him into loss."   f 16:33 toss the coin, literally, "cast dice into the lap."

g Gk Syr Vg Tg: Heb to plan

King James

5Whoso mocketh the poor reproacheth his Maker: *and* he that is glad at calamities shall not be unpunished.

6Children's children *are* the crown of old men; and the glory of children *are* their fathers.

7Excellent speech becometh not a fool: much less do lying lips a prince.

8A gift *is as* a precious stone in the eyes of him that hath it: whithersoever it turneth, it prospereth.

9He that covereth a transgression seeketh love; but he that repeateth a matter separateth *very* friends.

10A reproof entereth more into a wise man than an hundred stripes into a fool.

11An evil *man* seeketh only rebellion: therefore a cruel messenger shall be sent against him.

12Let a bear robbed of her whelps meet a man, rather than a fool in his folly.

13Whoso rewardeth evil for good, evil shall not depart from his house.

14The beginning of strife *is as* when one letteth out water: therefore leave off contention, before it be meddled with.

15He that justifieth the wicked, and he that condemneth the just, even they both *are* abomination to the LORD.

16Wherefore *is there* a price in the hand of a fool to get wisdom, seeing *he hath* no heart *to it?*

17A friend loveth at all times, and a brother is born for adversity.

18A man void of understanding striketh hands, *and* becometh surety in the presence of his friend.

19He loveth transgression that loveth strife: *and* he that exalteth his gate seeketh destruction.

20He that hath a froward heart findeth no good: and he that hath a perverse tongue falleth into mischief.

21He that begetteth a fool *doeth it* to his sorrow: and the father of a fool hath no joy.

22A merry heart doeth good *like* a medicine: but a broken spirit drieth the bones.

23A wicked *man* taketh a gift out of the bosom to pervert the ways of judgment.

24Wisdom *is* before him that hath understanding; but the eyes of a fool *are* in the ends of the earth.

25A foolish son *is* a grief to his father, and bitterness to her that bare him.

26Also to punish the just *is* not good, *nor* to strike princes for equity.

27He that hath knowledge spareth his words: *and* a man of understanding is of an excellent spirit.

28Even a fool, when he holdeth his peace, is counted wise: *and* he that shutteth his lips *is esteemed* a man of understanding.

New International

5He who mocks the poor shows contempt for their Maker;
whoever gloats over disaster will not go unpunished.

6Children's children are a crown to the aged,
and parents are the pride of their children.

7Arrogant[a] lips are unsuited to a fool—
how much worse lying lips to a ruler!

8A bribe is a charm to the one who gives it;
wherever he turns, he succeeds.

9He who covers over an offense promotes love,
but whoever repeats the matter separates close friends.

10A rebuke impresses a man of discernment
more than a hundred lashes a fool.

11An evil man is bent only on rebellion;
a merciless official will be sent against him.

12Better to meet a bear robbed of her cubs
than a fool in his folly.

13If a man pays back evil for good,
evil will never leave his house.

14Starting a quarrel is like breaching a dam;
so drop the matter before a dispute breaks out.

15Acquitting the guilty and condemning the innocent—
the LORD detests them both.

16Of what use is money in the hand of a fool,
since he has no desire to get wisdom?

17A friend loves at all times,
and a brother is born for adversity.

18A man lacking in judgment strikes hands in pledge
and puts up security for his neighbor.

19He who loves a quarrel loves sin;
he who builds a high gate invites destruction.

20A man of perverse heart does not prosper;
he whose tongue is deceitful falls into trouble.

21To have a fool for a son brings grief;
there is no joy for the father of a fool.

22A cheerful heart is good medicine,
but a crushed spirit dries up the bones.

23A wicked man accepts a bribe in secret
to pervert the course of justice.

24A discerning man keeps wisdom in view,
but a fool's eyes wander to the ends of the earth.

25A foolish son brings grief to his father
and bitterness to the one who bore him.

26It is not good to punish an innocent man,
or to flog officials for their integrity.

27A man of knowledge uses words with restraint,
and a man of understanding is even-tempered.

28Even a fool is thought wise if he keeps silent,
and discerning if he holds his tongue.

a 7 Or *Eloquent*

Living Bible

5Mocking the poor is mocking the God who made them. He will punish those who rejoice at others' misfortunes.

6An old man's grandchildren are his crowning glory. A child's glory is his father.

7Truth from a rebel or lies from a king are both unexpected.

8A bribe works like magic. Whoever uses it will prosper!b

9Love forgets mistakes; nagging about them parts the best of friends.

10A rebuke to a man of common sense is more effective than a hundred lashes on the back of a rebel.

11The wicked live for rebellion; they shall be severely punished.c

12It is safer to meet a bear robbed of her cubs than a fool caught in his folly.

13If you repay evil for good, a curse is upon your home.

14It is hard to stop a quarrel once it starts,d so don't let it begin.

15The Lord despises those who say that bad is good, and good is bad.

16It is senseless to pay tuition to educate a rebel who has no heart for truth.e

17A true friend is always loyal, and a brother is born to help in time of need.

18It is poor judgment to countersign another's note, to become responsible for his debts.

19Sinners love to fight; boasting is looking for trouble.

20An evil man is suspicious of everyonef and tumbles into constant trouble.

21It's no fun to be a rebel's father.

22A cheerful heart does good like medicine, but a broken spirit makes one sick.

23It is wrong to accept a bribe to twist justice.

24Wisdom is the main pursuit of sensible men, but a fool's goals are at the ends of the earth!

25A rebellious son is a grief to his father and a bitter blow to his mother.

26How short-sighted to fine the godly for being good! And to punish nobles for being honest!

27, 28The man of few words and settled mind is wise; therefore, even a fool is thought to be wise when he is silent. It pays him to keep his mouth shut.

New Revised Standard

5 Those who mock the poor insult their Maker;
     those who are glad at calamity will not go
       unpunished.
6 Grandchildren are the crown of the aged,
     and the glory of children is their parents.
7 Fine speech is not becoming to a fool;
     still less is false speech to a ruler.g
8 A bribe is like a magic stone in the eyes of
       those who give it;
     wherever they turn they prosper.
9 One who forgives an affront fosters friendship,
     but one who dwells on disputes will alienate
       a friend.
10 A rebuke strikes deeper into a discerning
       person
     than a hundred blows into a fool.
11 Evil people seek only rebellion,
     but a cruel messenger will be sent against
       them.
12 Better to meet a she-bear robbed of its cubs
     than to confront a fool immersed in folly.
13 Evil will not depart from the house
     of one who returns evil for good.
14 The beginning of strife is like letting out
       water;
     so stop before the quarrel breaks out.
15 One who justifies the wicked and one who
       condemns the righteous
     are both alike an abomination to the LORD.
16 Why should fools have a price in hand
     to buy wisdom, when they have no mind to
       learn?
17 A friend loves at all times,
     and kinsfolk are born to share adversity.
18 It is senseless to give a pledge,
     to become surety for a neighbor.
19 One who loves transgression loves strife;
     one who builds a high threshold invites
       broken bones.
20 The crooked of mind do not prosper,
     and the perverse of tongue fall into
       calamity.
21 The one who begets a fool gets trouble;
     the parent of a fool has no joy.
22 A cheerful heart is a good medicine,
     but a downcast spirit dries up the bones.
23 The wicked accept a concealed bribe
     to pervert the ways of justice.
24 The discerning person looks to wisdom,
     but the eyes of a fool to the ends of the
       earth.
25 Foolish children are a grief to their father
     and bitterness to her who bore them.
26 To impose a fine on the innocent is not right,
     or to flog the noble for their integrity.
27 One who spares words is knowledgeable;
     one who is cool in spirit has understanding.
28 Even fools who keep silent are considered
       wise;
     when they close their lips, they are deemed
       intelligent.

King James

18 THROUGH DESIRE a man, having separated himself, seeketh *and* intermeddleth with all wisdom.

2A fool hath no delight in understanding, but that his heart may discover itself.

3When the wicked cometh, *then* cometh also contempt, and with ignominy reproach.

4The words of a man's mouth *are as* deep waters, *and* the wellspring of wisdom *as* a flowing brook.

5*It is* not good to accept the person of the wicked, to overthrow the righteous in judgment.

6A fool's lips enter into contention, and his mouth calleth for strokes.

7A fool's mouth *is* his destruction, and his lips *are* the snare of his soul.

8The words of a talebearer *are* as wounds, and they go down into the innermost parts of the belly.

9He also that is slothful in his work is brother to him that is a great waster.

10The name of the LORD *is* a strong tower: the righteous runneth into it, and is safe.

11The rich man's wealth *is* his strong city, and as an high wall in his own conceit.

12Before destruction the heart of man is haughty, and before honour *is* humility.

13He that answereth a matter before he heareth *it*, it *is* folly and shame unto him.

14The spirit of a man will sustain his infirmity; but a wounded spirit who can bear?

15The heart of the prudent getteth knowledge; and the ear of the wise seeketh knowledge.

16A man's gift maketh room for him, and bringeth him before great men.

17*He that is* first in his own cause *seemeth* just; but his neighbour cometh and searcheth him.

18The lot causeth contentions to cease, and parteth between the mighty.

19A brother offended *is harder to be won* than a strong city: and *their* contentions *are* like the bars of a castle.

20A man's belly shall be satisfied with the fruit of his mouth; *and* with the increase of his lips shall he be filled.

21Death and life *are* in the power of the tongue: and they that love it shall eat the fruit thereof.

22*Whoso* findeth a wife findeth a good *thing,* and obtaineth favour of the LORD.

23The poor useth entreaties; but the rich answereth roughly.

24A man *that hath* friends must show himself friendly: and there is a friend *that* sticketh closer than a brother.

New International

18 AN UNFRIENDLY man pursues selfish ends;
　　he defies all sound judgment.

2A fool finds no pleasure in understanding
　but delights in airing his own opinions.

3When wickedness comes, so does contempt,
　and with shame comes disgrace.

4The words of a man's mouth are deep waters,
　but the fountain of wisdom is a bubbling brook.

5It is not good to be partial to the wicked
　or to deprive the innocent of justice.

6A fool's lips bring him strife,
　and his mouth invites a beating.

7A fool's mouth is his undoing,
　and his lips are a snare to his soul.

8The words of a gossip are like choice morsels;
　they go down to a man's inmost parts.

9One who is slack in his work
　is brother to one who destroys.

10The name of the LORD is a strong tower;
　the righteous run to it and are safe.

11The wealth of the rich is their fortified city;
　they imagine it an unscalable wall.

12Before his downfall a man's heart is proud,
　but humility comes before honor.

13He who answers before listening—
　that is his folly and his shame.

14A man's spirit sustains him in sickness,
　but a crushed spirit who can bear?

15The heart of the discerning acquires knowledge;
　the ears of the wise seek it out.

16A gift opens the way for the giver
　and ushers him into the presence of the great.

17The first to present his case seems right,
　till another comes forward and questions him.

18Casting the lot settles disputes
　and keeps strong opponents apart.

19An offended brother is more unyielding than a fortified city,
　and disputes are like the barred gates of a citadel.

20From the fruit of his mouth a man's stomach is filled;
　with the harvest from his lips he is satisfied.

21The tongue has the power of life and death,
　and those who love it will eat its fruit.

22He who finds a wife finds what is good
　and receives favor from the LORD.

23A poor man pleads for mercy,
　but a rich man answers harshly.

24A man of many companions may come to ruin,
　but there is a friend who sticks closer than a brother.

Living Bible

18 THE SELFISH man quarrels against every sound principle of conduct by demanding his own way.

2A rebel doesn't care about the facts. All he wants to do is yell.a

3Sin brings disgrace.

4A wise man's words express deep streams of thought.

5It is wrong for a judge to favor the wicked and condemn the innocent.

6, 7A fool gets into constant fights. His mouth is his undoing! His words endanger him.

8What dainty morsels rumors are. They are eaten with great relish!

9A lazy man is brother to the saboteur.

10The Lordb is a strong fortress. The godly run to him and are safe.

11The rich man thinks of his wealth as an impregnable defense, a high wall of safety. What a dreamer!

12Pride ends in destruction; humility ends in honor.

13What a shame—yes, how stupid!—to decide before knowing the facts!

14A man's couragec can sustain his broken body, but when courage dies, what hope is left?

15The intelligent man is always open to new ideas. In fact, he looks for them.

16A gift does wonders; it will bring you before men of importance!

17Any story sounds true until someone tells the other side and sets the record straight.

18A coin tossd ends arguments and settles disputes between powerful opponents.

19It is harder to win back the friendship of an offended brother than to capture a fortified city.e His anger shuts you out like iron bars.

20Ability to give wise advice satisfies like a good meal!

21Those who love to talk will suffer the consequences. Men have died for saying the wrong thing!

22The man who finds a wife finds a good thing; she is a blessing to him from the Lord.

23The poor man pleads and the rich man answers with insults.

24There are "friends" who pretend to be friends, but there is a friend who sticks closer than a brother.

New Revised Standard

18 THE ONE who lives alone is self-indulgent, showing contempt for all who have sound judgment.f

2 A fool takes no pleasure in understanding,
but only in expressing personal opinion.

3 When wickedness comes, contempt comes also;
and with dishonor comes disgrace.

4 The words of the mouth are deep waters;
the fountain of wisdom is a gushing stream.

5 It is not right to be partial to the guilty,
or to subvert the innocent in judgment.

6 A fool's lips bring strife,
and a fool's mouth invites a flogging.

7 The mouths of fools are their ruin,
and their lips a snare to themselves.

8 The words of a whisperer are like delicious morsels;
they go down into the inner parts of the body.

9 One who is slack in work
is close kin to a vandal.

10 The name of the LORD is a strong tower;
the righteous run into it and are safe.

11 The wealth of the rich is their strong city;
in their imagination it is like a high wall.

12 Before destruction one's heart is haughty,
but humility goes before honor.

13 If one gives answer before hearing,
it is folly and shame.

14 The human spirit will endure sickness;
but a broken spirit—who can bear?

15 An intelligent mind acquires knowledge,
and the ear of the wise seeks knowledge.

16 A gift opens doors;
it gives access to the great.

17 The one who first states a case seems right,
until the other comes and cross-examines.

18 Casting the lot puts an end to disputes
and decides between powerful contenders.

19 An ally offended is stronger than a city;g
such quarreling is like the bars of a castle.

20 From the fruit of the mouth one's stomach is satisfied;
the yield of the lips brings satisfaction.

21 Death and life are in the power of the tongue,
and those who love it will eat its fruits.

22 He who finds a wife finds a good thing,
and obtains favor from the LORD.

23 The poor use entreaties,
but the rich answer roughly.

24 Someh friends play at friendshipi
but a true friend sticks closer than one's nearest kin.

King James

19 BETTER *IS* the poor that walketh in his integrity, than *he that is* perverse in his lips, and is a fool.

2Also, *that* the soul *be* without knowledge, *it is* not good; and he that hasteth with *his* feet sinneth.

3The foolishness of man perverteth his way: and his heart fretteth against the LORD.

4Wealth maketh many friends; but the poor is separated from his neighbour.

5A false witness shall not be unpunished, and *he that* speaketh lies shall not escape.

6Many will entreat the favour of the prince: and every man *is* a friend to him that giveth gifts.

7All the brethren of the poor do hate him: how much more do his friends go far from him? he pursueth *them with* words, *yet they are* wanting *to him.*

8He that getteth wisdom loveth his own soul: he that keepeth understanding shall find good.

9A false witness shall not be unpunished, and *he that* speaketh lies shall perish.

10Delight is not seemly for a fool; much less for a servant to have rule over princes.

11The discretion of a man deferreth his anger; and *it is* his glory to pass over a transgression.

12The king's wrath *is* as the roaring of a lion; but his favour *is* as dew upon the grass.

13A foolish son *is* the calamity of his father: and the contentions of a wife *are* a continual dropping.

14House and riches *are* the inheritance of fathers: and a prudent wife *is* from the LORD.

15Slothfulness casteth into a deep sleep; and an idle soul shall suffer hunger.

16He that keepeth the commandment keepeth his own soul; *but* he that despiseth his ways shall die.

17He that hath pity upon the poor lendeth unto the LORD; and that which he hath given will he pay him again.

18Chasten thy son while there is hope, and let not thy soul spare for his crying.

19A man of great wrath shall suffer punishment: for if thou deliver *him,* yet thou must do it again.

20Hear counsel, and receive instruction, that thou mayest be wise in thy latter end.

21*There are* many devices in a man's heart; nevertheless the counsel of the LORD, that shall stand.

22The desire of a man *is* his kindness: and a poor man *is* better than a liar.

23The fear of the LORD *tendeth* to life: and *he that* hath it shall abide satisfied; he shall not be visited with evil.

24A slothful *man* hideth his hand in *his* bosom, and will not so much as bring it to his mouth again.

New International

19 BETTER A poor man whose walk is blameless
than a fool whose lips are perverse.

2It is not good to have zeal without knowledge,
nor to be hasty and miss the way.

3A man's own folly ruins his life,
yet his heart rages against the LORD.

4Wealth brings many friends,
but a poor man's friend deserts him.

5A false witness will not go unpunished,
and he who pours out lies will not go free.

6Many curry favor with a ruler,
and everyone is the friend of a man who gives gifts.

7A poor man is shunned by all his relatives—
how much more do his friends avoid him!
Though he pursues them with pleading,
they are nowhere to be found.[a]

8He who gets wisdom loves his own soul;
he who cherishes understanding prospers.

9A false witness will not go unpunished,
and he who pours out lies will perish.

10It is not fitting for a fool to live in luxury—
how much worse for a slave to rule over princes!

11A man's wisdom gives him patience;
it is to his glory to overlook an offense.

12A king's rage is like the roar of a lion,
but his favor is like dew on the grass.

13A foolish son is his father's ruin,
and a quarrelsome wife is like a constant dripping.

14Houses and wealth are inherited from parents,
but a prudent wife is from the LORD.

15Laziness brings on deep sleep,
and the shiftless man goes hungry.

16He who obeys instructions guards his life,
but he who is contemptuous of his ways will die.

17He who is kind to the poor lends to the LORD,
and he will reward him for what he has done.

18Discipline your son, for in that there is hope;
do not be a willing party to his death.

19A hot-tempered man must pay the penalty;
if you rescue him, you will have to do it again.

20Listen to advice and accept instruction,
and in the end you will be wise.

21Many are the plans in a man's heart,
but it is the LORD's purpose that prevails.

22What a man desires is unfailing love[b];
better to be poor than a liar.

23The fear of the LORD leads to life:
Then one rests content, untouched by trouble.

24The sluggard buries his hand in the dish;
he will not even bring it back to his mouth!

---

[a] 7 The meaning of the Hebrew for this sentence is uncertain.   [b] 22 Or *A man's greed is his shame*

Living Bible

19 BETTER BE poor and honest than rich[c] and dishonest.

²It is dangerous and sinful to rush into the unknown.

³A man may ruin his chances by his own foolishness and then blame it on the Lord!

⁴A wealthy man has many "friends"; the poor man has none left.

⁵Punish false witnesses. Track down liars.

⁶Many beg favors from a man who is generous; everyone is his friend!

⁷A poor man's own brothers turn away from him in embarrassment;[d] how much more his friends! He calls after them, but they are gone.

⁸He who loves wisdom loves his own best interest and will be a success.

⁹A false witness shall be punished and a liar shall be caught.

¹⁰It doesn't seem right for a fool to succeed or for a slave to rule over princes!

¹¹A wise man restrains his anger and overlooks insults. This is to his credit.

¹²The king's anger is as dangerous as a lion's. But his approval is as refreshing as the dew on grass.

¹³A rebellious son is a calamity to his father, and a nagging wife annoys like constant dripping.

¹⁴A father can give his sons homes and riches, but only the Lord can give them understanding wives.

¹⁵A lazy man sleeps soundly—and he goes hungry!

¹⁶Keep the commandments and keep your life; despising them means death.

¹⁷When you help the poor you are lending to the Lord—and he pays wonderful interest on your loan!

¹⁸Discipline your son in his early years while there is hope. If you don't you will ruin his life.

¹⁹A short-tempered man must bear his own penalty; you can't do much to help him. If you try once you must try a dozen times!

²⁰Get all the advice you can and be wise the rest of your life.

²¹Man proposes, but God disposes.

²²Kindness makes a man attractive. And it is better to be poor than dishonest.

²³Reverence for God gives life, happiness, and protection from harm.

²⁴Some men are so lazy they won't even feed themselves!

New Revised Standard

19 BETTER THE poor walking in integrity
than one perverse of speech who is a fool.

2 Desire without knowledge is not good,
and one who moves too hurriedly misses the
way.

3 One's own folly leads to ruin,
yet the heart rages against the LORD.

4 Wealth brings many friends,
but the poor are left friendless.

5 A false witness will not go unpunished,
and a liar will not escape.

6 Many seek the favor of the generous,
and everyone is a friend to a giver of gifts.

7 If the poor are hated even by their kin,
how much more are they shunned by
their friends!
When they call after them, they are not
there.[e]

8 To get wisdom is to love oneself;
to keep understanding is to prosper.

9 A false witness will not go unpunished,
and the liar will perish.

10 It is not fitting for a fool to live in luxury,
much less for a slave to rule over princes.

11 Those with good sense are slow to anger,
and it is their glory to overlook an offense.

12 A king's anger is like the growling of a lion,
but his favor is like dew on the grass.

13 A stupid child is ruin to a father,
and a wife's quarreling is a continual
dripping of rain.

14 House and wealth are inherited from parents,
but a prudent wife is from the LORD.

15 Laziness brings on deep sleep;
an idle person will suffer hunger.

16 Those who keep the commandment will live;
those who are heedless of their ways will
die.

17 Whoever is kind to the poor lends to the
LORD,
and will be repaid in full.

18 Discipline your children while there is hope;
do not set your heart on their destruction.

19 A violent tempered person will pay the
penalty;
if you effect a rescue, you will only have to
do it again.[e]

20 Listen to advice and accept instruction,
that you may gain wisdom for the future.

21 The human mind may devise many plans,
but it is the purpose of the LORD that will
be established.

22 What is desirable in a person is loyalty,
and it is better to be poor than a liar.

23 The fear of the LORD is life indeed;
filled with it one rests secure
and suffers no harm.

24 The lazy person buries a hand in the dish,
and will not even bring it back to the
mouth.

King James

25Smite a scorner, and the simple will beware: and reprove one that hath understanding, *and* he will understand knowledge.

26He that wasteth *his* father, *and* chaseth away *his* mother, *is* a son that causeth shame, and bringeth reproach.

27Cease, my son, to hear the instruction *that causeth* to err from the words of knowledge.

28An ungodly witness scorneth judgment: and the mouth of the wicked devoureth iniquity.

29Judgments are prepared for scorners, and stripes for the back of fools.

20 WINE *IS* a mocker, strong drink *is* raging: and whosoever is deceived thereby is not wise.

2The fear of a king *is* as the roaring of a lion: *whoso* provoketh him to anger sinneth *against* his own soul.

3*It is* an honour for a man to cease from strife: but every fool will be meddling.

4The sluggard will not plow by reason of the cold; *therefore* shall he beg in harvest, and *have* nothing.

5Counsel in the heart of man *is like* deep water; but a man of understanding will draw it out.

6Most men will proclaim every one his own goodness: but a faithful man who can find?

7The just *man* walketh in his integrity: his children *are* blessed after him.

8A king that sitteth in the throne of judgment scattereth away all evil with his eyes.

9Who can say, I have made my heart clean, I am pure from my sin?

10Divers weights, *and* divers measures, both of them *are* alike abomination to the LORD.

11Even a child is known by his doings, whether his work *be* pure, and whether *it be* right.

12The hearing ear, and the seeing eye, the LORD hath made even both of them.

13Love not sleep, lest thou come to poverty; open thine eyes, *and* thou shalt be satisfied with bread.

14*It is* naught, *it is* naught, saith the buyer: but when he is gone his way, then he boasteth.

15There is gold, and a multitude of rubies: but the lips of knowledge *are* a precious jewel.

16Take his garment that is surety *for* a stranger: and take a pledge of him for a strange woman.

17Bread of deceit *is* sweet to a man; but afterwards his mouth shall be filled with gravel.

18*Every* purpose is established by counsel: and with good advice make war.

19He that goeth about *as* a talebearer revealeth secrets: therefore meddle not with him that flattereth with his lips.

20Whoso curseth his father or his mother, his lamp shall be put out in obscure darkness.

New International

25Flog a mocker, and the simple will learn prudence;
rebuke a discerning man, and he will gain knowledge.

26He who robs his father and drives out his mother
is a son who brings shame and disgrace.

27Stop listening to instruction, my son,
and you will stray from the words of knowledge.

28A corrupt witness mocks at justice,
and the mouth of the wicked gulps down evil.

29Penalties are prepared for mockers,
and beatings for the backs of fools.

20 WINE IS a mocker and beer a brawler;
whoever is led astray by them is not wise.

2A king's wrath is like the roar of a lion;
he who angers him forfeits his life.

3It is to a man's honor to avoid strife,
but every fool is quick to quarrel.

4A sluggard does not plow in season;
so at harvest time he looks but finds nothing.

5The purposes of a man's heart are deep waters,
but a man of understanding draws them out.

6Many a man claims to have unfailing love,
but a faithful man who can find?

7The righteous man leads a blameless life;
blessed are his children after him.

8When a king sits on his throne to judge,
he winnows out all evil with his eyes.

9Who can say, "I have kept my heart pure;
I am clean and without sin"?

10Differing weights and differing measures—
the LORD detests them both.

11Even a child is known by his actions,
by whether his conduct is pure and right.

12Ears that hear and eyes that see—
the LORD has made them both.

13Do not love sleep or you will grow poor;
stay awake and you will have food to spare.

14"It's no good, it's no good!" says the buyer;
then off he goes and boasts about his purchase.

15Gold there is, and rubies in abundance,
but lips that speak knowledge are a rare jewel.

16Take the garment of one who puts up security for a stranger;
hold it in pledge if he does it for a wayward woman.

17Food gained by fraud tastes sweet to a man,
but he ends up with a mouth full of gravel.

18Make plans by seeking advice;
if you wage war, obtain guidance.

19A gossip betrays a confidence;
so avoid a man who talks too much.

20If a man curses his father or mother,
his lamp will be snuffed out in pitch darkness.

Living Bible

25Punish a mocker and others will learn from his example. Reprove a wise man and he will be the wiser.

26A son who mistreats his father or mother is a public disgrace.

27Stop listening to teaching that contradicts what you know is right.

28A worthless witness cares nothing for truth—he enjoys his sinning too much.

29Mockers and rebels shall be severely punished.

20 WINE GIVES false courage; hard liquor leads to brawls; what fools men are to let it master them, making them reel drunkenly down the street!

2The king's fury is like that of a roaring lion; to rouse his anger is to risk your life.

3It is an honor for a man to stay out of a fight. Only fools insist on quarreling.

4If you won't plow in the cold, you won't eat at the harvest.

5Though good advice lies deep within a counselor's heart, the wise man will draw it out.

6Most people will tell you what loyal friends they are, but are they telling the truth?

7It is a wonderful heritage to have an honest father.

8A king sitting as judge weighs all the evidence carefully, distinguishing the true from false.

9Who can ever say, "I have cleansed my heart; I am sinless"?

10The Lord despises every kind of cheating.a

11The character of even a child can be known by the way he acts—whether what he does is pure and right.

12If you have good eyesight and good hearing, thankb God who gave them to you.

13If you love sleep, you will end in poverty. Stay awake, work hard, and there will be plenty to eat!

14"Utterly worthless!" says the buyer as he haggles over the price. But afterwards he brags about his bargain!

15Good sense is far more valuable than gold or precious jewels.

16It is risky to make loans to strangers!

17Some men enjoy cheating, but the cake they buy with such ill-gotten gain will turn to gravel in their mouths.

18Don't go ahead with your plans without the advice of others; don't go to war until they agree.

19Don't tell your secrets to a gossipc unless you want them broadcast to the world.

20God puts out the light of the man who curses his father or mother.

New Revised Standard

25 Strike a scoffer, and the simple will learn
    prudence;
      reprove the intelligent, and they will gain
        knowledge.
26 Those who do violence to their father and
        chase away their mother
      are children who cause shame and bring
        reproach.
27 Cease straying, my child, from the words of
        knowledge,
      in order that you may hear instruction.
28 A worthless witness mocks at justice,
      and the mouth of the wicked devours
        iniquity.
29 Condemnation is ready for scoffers,
      and flogging for the backs of fools.

20 WINE IS a mocker, strong drink a brawler,
      and whoever is led astray by it is not wise.
2 The dread anger of a king is like the growling
        of a lion;
      anyone who provokes him to anger forfeits
        life itself.
3 It is honorable to refrain from strife,
      but every fool is quick to quarrel.
4 The lazy person does not plow in season;
      harvest comes, and there is nothing to be
        found.
5 The purposes in the human mind are like deep
        water,
      but the intelligent will draw them out.
6 Many proclaim themselves loyal,
      but who can find one worthy of trust?
7 The righteous walk in integrity—
      happy are the children who follow them!
8 A king who sits on the throne of judgment
      winnows all evil with his eyes.
9 Who can say, "I have made my heart clean;
      I am pure from my sin"?
10 Diverse weights and diverse measures
      are both alike an abomination to the LORD.
11 Even children make themselves known by
        their acts,
      by whether what they do is pure and right.
12 The hearing ear and the seeing eye—
      the LORD has made them both.
13 Do not love sleep, or else you will come to
        poverty;
      open your eyes, and you will have plenty of
        bread.
14 "Bad, bad," says the buyer,
      then goes away and boasts.
15 There is gold, and abundance of costly stones;
      but the lips informed by knowledge are a
        precious jewel.
16 Take the garment of one who has given surety
        for a stranger;
      seize the pledge given as surety for
        foreigners.
17 Bread gained by deceit is sweet,
      but afterward the mouth will be full of
        gravel.
18 Plans are established by taking advice;
      wage war by following wise guidance.
19 A gossip reveals secrets;
      therefore do not associate with a babbler.
20 If you curse father or mother,
      your lamp will go out in utter darkness.

a 20:10 every kind of cheating, literally, "diverse weights and diverse measures."   b 20:12 thank, implied.   c 20:19 Don't tell your secrets to a gossip, literally, "company not with him."

King James

21An inheritance *may be* gotten hastily at the beginning; but the end thereof shall not be blessed.

22Say not thou, I will recompense evil; *but* wait on the LORD, and he shall save thee.

23Divers weights *are* an abomination unto the LORD; and a false balance *is* not good.

24Man's goings *are* of the LORD; how can a man then understand his own way?

25*It is* a snare to the man *who* devoureth *that which is* holy, and after vows to make inquiry.

26A wise king scattereth the wicked, and bringeth the wheel over them.

27The spirit of man *is* the candle of the LORD, searching all the inward parts of the belly.

28Mercy and truth preserve the king: and his throne is upholden by mercy.

29The glory of young men *is* their strength: and the beauty of old men *is* the gray head.

30The blueness of a wound cleanseth away evil: so *do* stripes the inward parts of the belly.

21 THE KING'S heart *is* in the hand of the LORD, *as* the rivers of water: he turneth it whithersoever he will.

2Every way of a man *is* right in his own eyes: but the LORD pondereth the hearts.

3To do justice and judgment *is* more acceptable to the LORD than sacrifice.

4An high look, and a proud heart, *and* the plowing of the wicked, *is* sin.

5The thoughts of the diligent *tend* only to plenteousness; but of every one *that is* hasty only to want.

6The getting of treasures by a lying tongue *is* a vanity tossed to and fro of them that seek death.

7The robbery of the wicked shall destroy them; because they refuse to do judgment.

8The way of man *is* froward and strange: but *as for* the pure, his work *is* right.

9*It is* better to dwell in a corner of the housetop, than with a brawling woman in a wide house.

10The soul of the wicked desireth evil: his neighbour findeth no favour in his eyes.

11When the scorner is punished, the simple is made wise: and when the wise is instructed, he receiveth knowledge.

12The righteous *man* wisely considereth the house of the wicked: *but God* overthroweth the wicked for *their* wickedness.

13Whoso stoppeth his ears at the cry of the poor, he also shall cry himself, but shall not be heard.

New International

21An inheritance quickly gained at the beginning will not be blessed at the end.

22Do not say, "I'll pay you back for this wrong!" Wait for the LORD, and he will deliver you.

23The LORD detests differing weights, and dishonest scales do not please him.

24A man's steps are directed by the LORD. How then can anyone understand his own way?

25It is a trap for a man to dedicate something rashly and only later to consider his vows.

26A wise king winnows out the wicked; he drives the threshing wheel over them.

27The lamp of the LORD searches the spirit of a man[a]; it searches out his inmost being.

28Love and faithfulness keep a king safe; through love his throne is made secure.

29The glory of young men is their strength, gray hair the splendor of the old.

30Blows and wounds cleanse away evil, and beatings purge the inmost being.

21 THE KING'S heart is in the hand of the LORD; he directs it like a watercourse wherever he pleases.

2All a man's ways seem right to him, but the LORD weighs the heart.

3To do what is right and just is more acceptable to the LORD than sacrifice.

4Haughty eyes and a proud heart, the lamp of the wicked, are sin!

5The plans of the diligent lead to profit as surely as haste leads to poverty.

6A fortune made by a lying tongue is a fleeting vapor and a deadly snare.[b]

7The violence of the wicked will drag them away, for they refuse to do what is right.

8The way of the guilty is devious, but the conduct of the innocent is upright.

9Better to live on a corner of the roof than share a house with a quarrelsome wife.

10The wicked man craves evil; his neighbor gets no mercy from him.

11When a mocker is punished, the simple gain wisdom; when a wise man is instructed, he gets knowledge.

12The Righteous One[c] takes note of the house of the wicked and brings the wicked to ruin.

13If a man shuts his ears to the cry of the poor, he too will cry out and not be answered.

---

a 27 Or *The spirit of man is the LORD's lamp*　b 6 Some Hebrew manuscripts, Septuagint and Vulgate; most Hebrew manuscripts *vapor for those who seek death*　c 12 Or *The righteous man*

Living Bible

21Quick wealth is not a blessing in the end.

22Don't repay evil for evil. Wait for the Lord to handle the matter.

23The Lord loathes all cheating and dishonesty.d

24Since the Lord is directing our steps, why try to understand everything that happens along the way?

25It is foolish and rash to make a promise to the Lord before counting the cost.

26A wise king stamps out crime by severe punishment.

27A man's consciencee is the Lord's searchlight exposing his hidden motives.

28If a king is kind, honest and fair, his kingdom stands secure.

29The glory of young men is their strength; of old men, their experience.f

30Punishment that hurts chases evil from the heart.

New Revised Standard

21 An estate quickly acquired in the beginning
    will not be blessed in the end.

22 Do not say, "I will repay evil";
    wait for the LORD, and he will help you.

23 Differing weights are an abomination to the
    LORD,
    and false scales are not good.

24 All our steps are ordered by the LORD;
    how then can we understand our own ways?

25 It is a snare for one to say rashly, "It is holy,"
    and begin to reflect only after making a
    vow.

26 A wise king winnows the wicked,
    and drives the wheel over them.

27 The human spirit is the lamp of the LORD,
    searching every inmost part.

28 Loyalty and faithfulness preserve the king,
    and his throne is upheld by righteousness.i

29 The glory of youths is their strength,
    but the beauty of the aged is their gray hair.

30 Blows that wound cleanse away evil;
    beatings make clean the innermost parts.

21

JUST AS water is turned into irrigation ditches, so the Lord directs the king's thoughts. He turns them wherever he wants to.

2We can justify our every deed but God looks at our motives.

3God is more pleased when we are just and fair than when we give him gifts.

4Pride, lust, and evil actionsg are all sin.

5Steady plodding brings prosperity; hasty speculation brings poverty.

6Dishonest gain will never last, so why take the risk?

7Because the wicked are unfair, their violence boomerangs and destroys them.

8A man is known by his actions.h An evil man lives an evil life; a good man lives a godly life.

9It is better to live in the corner of an attic than with a crabby woman in a lovely home.

10An evil man loves to harm others; being a good neighbor is out of his line.

11The wise man learns by listening; the simpleton can learn only by seeing scorners punished.

12God, the Righteous One, knows what is going on in the homes of the wicked, and will bring the wicked to judgment.

13He who shuts his ears to the cries of the poor will be ignored in his own time of need.

21

THE KING'S heart is a stream of water in the hand of the LORD;
    he turns it wherever he will.

2 All deeds are right in the sight of the doer,
    but the LORD weighs the heart.

3 To do righteousness and justice
    is more acceptable to the LORD than
    sacrifice.

4 Haughty eyes and a proud heart—
    the lamp of the wicked—are sin.

5 The plans of the diligent lead surely to
    abundance,
    but everyone who is hasty comes only to
    want.

6 The getting of treasures by a lying tongue
    is a fleeting vapor and a snarej of death.

7 The violence of the wicked will sweep them
    away,
    because they refuse to do what is just.

8 The way of the guilty is crooked,
    but the conduct of the pure is right.

9 It is better to live in a corner of the housetop
    than in a house shared with a contentious
    wife.

10 The souls of the wicked desire evil;
    their neighbors find no mercy in their eyes.

11 When a scoffer is punished, the simple
    become wiser;
    when the wise are instructed, they increase
    in knowledge.

12 The Righteous One observes the house of the
    wicked;
    he casts the wicked down to ruin.

13 If you close your ear to the cry of the poor,
    you will cry out and not be heard.

---

d 20:23 all cheating and dishonesty, literally, "diverse weights . . . false scales." e 20:27 conscience, literally, "spirit." f 20:29 their experience, literally, "the hoary head." g 21:4 evil actions, literally, "the tillage of the wicked." h 21:8 A man is known by his actions, implied.

i Gk: Heb loyalty   j Gk: Heb seekers

King James

14A gift in secret pacifieth anger: and a reward in the bosom strong wrath.

15*It is* joy to the just to do judgment: but destruction *shall be* to the workers of iniquity.

16The man that wandereth out of the way of understanding shall remain in the congregation of the dead.

17He that loveth pleasure *shall be* a poor man: he that loveth wine and oil shall not be rich.

18The wicked *shall be* a ransom for the righteous, and the transgressor for the upright.

19*It is* better to dwell in the wilderness, than with a contentious and an angry woman.

20*There is* treasure to be desired and oil in the dwelling of the wise; but a foolish man spendeth it up.

21He that followeth after righteousness and mercy findeth life, righteousness, and honour.

22A wise *man* scaleth the city of the mighty, and casteth down the strength of the confidence thereof.

23Whoso keepeth his mouth and his tongue keepeth his soul from troubles.

24Proud *and* haughty scorner *is* his name, who dealeth in proud wrath.

25The desire of the slothful killeth him; for his hands refuse to labour.

26He coveteth greedily all the day long: but the righteous giveth and spareth not.

27The sacrifice of the wicked *is* abomination: how much more, *when* he bringeth it with a wicked mind?

28A false witness shall perish: but the man that heareth speaketh constantly.

29A wicked man hardeneth his face: but *as for* the upright, he directeth his way.

30*There is* no wisdom nor understanding nor counsel against the LORD.

31The horse *is* prepared against the day of battle: but safety *is* of the LORD.

22 A *GOOD* name *is* rather to be chosen than great riches, *and* loving favour rather than silver and gold.

2The rich and poor meet together: the LORD *is* the maker of them all.

3A prudent *man* foreseeth the evil, and hideth himself: but the simple pass on, and are punished.

New International

14A gift given in secret soothes anger,
    and a bribe concealed in the cloak pacifies
        great wrath.

15When justice is done, it brings joy to the
        righteous
    but terror to evildoers.

16A man who strays from the path of
        understanding
    comes to rest in the company of the dead.

17He who loves pleasure will become poor;
    whoever loves wine and oil will never be
        rich.

18The wicked become a ransom for the righteous,
    and the unfaithful for the upright.

19Better to live in a desert
    than with a quarrelsome and ill-tempered
        wife.

20In the house of the wise are stores of choice
        food and oil,
    but a foolish man devours all he has.

21He who pursues righteousness and love
    finds life, prosperitya and honor.

22A wise man attacks the city of the mighty
    and pulls down the stronghold in which they
        trust.

23He who guards his mouth and his tongue
    keeps himself from calamity.

24The proud and arrogant man—"Mocker" is his
        name;
    he behaves with overweening pride.

25The sluggard's craving will be the death of him,
    because his hands refuse to work.

26All day long he craves for more,
    but the righteous give without sparing.

27The sacrifice of the wicked is detestable—
    how much more so when brought with evil
        intent!

28A false witness will perish,
    and whoever listens to him will be destroyed
        forever.b

29A wicked man puts up a bold front,
    but an upright man gives thought to his ways.

30There is no wisdom, no insight, no plan
    that can succeed against the LORD.

31The horse is made ready for the day of battle,
    but victory rests with the LORD.

22 A GOOD name is more desirable than great
        riches;
    to be esteemed is better than silver or gold.

2Rich and poor have this in common:
    The LORD is the Maker of them all.

3A prudent man sees danger and takes refuge,
    but the simple keep going and suffer for it.

a 21 Or *righteousness*   b 28 Or / *but the words of an obedient man will live
on*

Living Bible

14An angry man is silenced by giving him a gift!

15A good man loves justice, but it is a calamity to evil-doers.

16The man who strays away from common sense will end up dead!

17A man who loves pleasure becomes poor; wine and luxury are not the way to riches!

18The wicked will finally lose; the righteous will finally win.c

19Better to live in the desert than with a quarrelsome, complaining woman.

20The wise man saves for the future,d but the foolish man spends whatever he gets.

21The man who tries to be good, loving and kind finds life, righteousness and honor.

22The wise man conquers the strong man and levels his defenses.

23Keep your mouth closed and you'll stay out of trouble.

24Mockers are proud, haughty and arrogant.

25, 26The lazy man longs for many things but his hands refuse to work. He is greedy to get, while the godly love to give!

27God loathes the gifts of evil men, especially if they are trying to bribe him!

28No one believes a liar, but everyone respects the words of an honest man.

29An evil man is stubborn, but a godly man will reconsider.e

30No one, regardless of how shrewd or well-advised he is, can stand against the Lord.

31Go ahead and prepare for the conflict,f but victory comes from God.

22 IF YOU must choose, take a good name rather than great riches; for to be held in loving esteem is better than silver and gold.

2The rich and the poor are alike before the Lord who made them all.

3A prudent man foresees the difficulties ahead and prepares for them; the simpleton goes blindly on and suffers the consequences.

New Revised Standard

14 A gift in secret averts anger;
   and a concealed bribe in the bosom, strong wrath.

15 When justice is done, it is a joy to the righteous,
   but dismay to evildoers.

16 Whoever wanders from the way of understanding
   will rest in the assembly of the dead.

17 Whoever loves pleasure will suffer want;
   whoever loves wine and oil will not be rich.

18 The wicked is a ransom for the righteous,
   and the faithless for the upright.

19 It is better to live in a desert land
   than with a contentious and fretful wife.

20 Precious treasure remainsg in the house of the wise,
   but the fool devours it.

21 Whoever pursues righteousness and kindness
   will find lifeh and honor.

22 One wise person went up against a city of warriors
   and brought down the stronghold in which they trusted.

23 To watch over mouth and tongue
   is to keep out of trouble.

24 The proud, haughty person, named "Scoffer,"
   acts with arrogant pride.

25 The craving of the lazy person is fatal,
   for lazy hands refuse to labor.

26 All day long the wicked covet,i
   but the righteous give and do not hold back.

27 The sacrifice of the wicked is an abomination;
   how much more when brought with evil intent.

28 A false witness will perish,
   but a good listener will testify successfully.

29 The wicked put on a bold face,
   but the upright give thought toj their ways.

30 No wisdom, no understanding, no counsel,
   can avail against the LORD.

31 The horse is made ready for the day of battle,
   but the victory belongs to the LORD.

22 A GOOD name is to be chosen rather than great riches,
   and favor is better than silver or gold.

2 The rich and the poor have this in common:
   the LORD is the maker of them all.

3 The clever see danger and hide;
   but the simple go on, and suffer for it.

---

c *21:18 The wicked will finally lose; the righteous will finally win,* literally "the wicked is a ransom for the righteous." d *21:20 The wise man saves for the future,* literally, "There is precious treasure and oil in the dwelling of the wise." e *21:29 An evil man is stubborn, but a godly man will reconsider,* or "The wicked man is brazen; the godly man is thoughtful." f *21:31 Go ahead and prepare for the conflict,* literally, "The horse is prepared against the day of battle."

g Gk: Heb *and oil* h Gk: Heb *life and righteousness* i Gk: Heb *all day long one covets covetously* j Another reading is *establish*

King James

⁴By humility *and* the fear of the Lord *are* riches, and honour, and life.

⁵Thorns *and* snares *are* in the way of the froward: he that doth keep his soul shall be far from them.

⁶Train up a child in the way he should go: and when he is old, he will not depart from it.

⁷The rich ruleth over the poor, and the borrower *is* servant to the lender.

⁸He that soweth iniquity shall reap vanity: and the rod of his anger shall fail.

⁹He that hath a bountiful eye shall be blessed; for he giveth of his bread to the poor.

¹⁰Cast out the scorner, and contention shall go out; yea, strife and reproach shall cease.

¹¹He that loveth pureness of heart, *for* the grace of his lips the king *shall be* his friend.

¹²The eyes of the Lord preserve knowledge, and he overthroweth the words of the transgressor.

¹³The slothful *man* saith, *There is* a lion without, I shall be slain in the streets.

¹⁴The mouth of strange women *is* a deep pit: he that is abhorred of the Lord shall fall therein.

¹⁵Foolishness *is* bound in the heart of a child; *but* the rod of correction shall drive it far from him.

¹⁶He that oppresseth the poor to increase his *riches, and* he that giveth to the rich, *shall* surely *come* to want.

¹⁷Bow down thine ear, and hear the words of the wise, and apply thine heart unto my knowledge.

¹⁸For *it is* a pleasant thing if thou keep them within thee; they shall withal be fitted in thy lips.

¹⁹That thy trust may be in the Lord, I have made known to thee this day, even to thee.

²⁰Have not I written to thee excellent things in counsels and knowledge,

²¹That I might make thee know the certainty of the words of truth; that thou mightest answer the words of truth to them that send unto thee?

²²Rob not the poor, because he *is* poor: neither oppress the afflicted in the gate:

²³For the Lord will plead their cause, and spoil the soul of those that spoiled them.

²⁴Make no friendship with an angry man; and with a furious man thou shalt not go:

²⁵Lest thou learn his ways, and get a snare to thy soul.

²⁶Be not thou *one* of them that strike hands, *or* of them that are sureties for debts.

²⁷If thou hast nothing to pay, why should he take away thy bed from under thee?

²⁸Remove not the ancient landmark, which thy fathers have set.

New International

⁴Humility and the fear of the Lord
bring wealth and honor and life.

⁵In the paths of the wicked lie thorns and snares,
but he who guards his soul stays far from
them.

⁶Train[a] a child in the way he should go,
and when he is old he will not turn from it.

⁷The rich rule over the poor,
and the borrower is servant to the lender.

⁸He who sows wickedness reaps trouble,
and the rod of his fury will be destroyed.

⁹A generous man will himself be blessed,
for he shares his food with the poor.

¹⁰Drive out the mocker, and out goes strife;
quarrels and insults are ended.

¹¹He who loves a pure heart and whose speech is
gracious
will have the king for his friend.

¹²The eyes of the Lord keep watch over
knowledge,
but he frustrates the words of the unfaithful.

¹³The sluggard says, "There is a lion outside!"
or, "I will be murdered in the streets!"

¹⁴The mouth of an adulteress is a deep pit;
he who is under the Lord's wrath will fall
into it.

¹⁵Folly is bound up in the heart of a child,
but the rod of discipline will drive it far from
him.

¹⁶He who oppresses the poor to increase his
wealth
and he who gives gifts to the rich—both
come to poverty.

Sayings of the Wise

¹⁷Pay attention and listen to the sayings of the
wise;
apply your heart to what I teach,
¹⁸for it is pleasing when you keep them in your
heart
and have all of them ready on your lips.
¹⁹So that your trust may be in the Lord,
I teach you today, even you.
²⁰Have I not written thirty[b] sayings for you,
sayings of counsel and knowledge,
²¹teaching you true and reliable words,
so that you can give sound answers
to him who sent you?

²²Do not exploit the poor because they are poor
and do not crush the needy in court,
²³for the Lord will take up their case
and will plunder those who plunder them.

²⁴Do not make friends with a hot-tempered man,
do not associate with one easily angered,
²⁵or you may learn his ways
and get yourself ensnared.

²⁶Do not be a man who strikes hands in pledge
or puts up security for debts;
²⁷if you lack the means to pay,
your very bed will be snatched from under
you.

²⁸Do not move an ancient boundary stone
set up by your forefathers.

ᵃ *6 Or Start*   ᵇ *20 Or not formerly written; or not written excellent*

Living Bible

⁴True humility and respect for the Lord lead a man to riches, honor and long life.

⁵The rebel walks a thorny, treacherous road; the man who values his soul will stay away.

⁶Teach a child to choose the right path, and when he is older he will remain upon it.

⁷Just as the rich rule the poor, so the borrower is servant to the lender.

⁸The unjust tyrant will reap disaster and his reign of terror shall end.

⁹Happy is the generous man, the one who feeds the poor.

¹⁰Throw out the mocker, and you will be rid of tension, fighting and quarrels.

¹¹He who values grace and truth is the king's friend.

¹²The Lord preserves the upright but ruins the plansᶜ of the wicked.

¹³The lazy man is full of excuses. "I can't go to work!" he says. "If I go outside I might meet a lion in the street and be killed!"

¹⁴A prostitute is a dangerous trap; those cursed of God are caught in it.

¹⁵A youngster's heart is filled with rebellion, but punishment will drive it out of him.

¹⁶He who gains by oppressing the poor or by bribing the rich shall end in poverty.

¹⁷, ¹⁸, ¹⁹Listen to this wise advice; follow it closely, for it will do you good, and you can pass it on to others: *Trust in the Lord.*

²⁰, ²¹In the past, haven't I been right? Then believe what I am telling you now, and share it with others.

²², ²³Don't rob the poor and sick! For the Lord is their defender. If you injure them he will punish you.

²⁴, ²⁵Keep away from angry, short-tempered men, lest you learn to be like them and endanger your soul.

²⁶, ²⁷Unless you have the extra cash on hand, don't countersign a note. Why risk everything you own? They'll even take your bed!

²⁸Do not move the ancient boundary marks. That is stealing.ᵈ

New Revised Standard

⁴ The reward for humility and fear of the LORD
is riches and honor and life.
⁵ Thorns and snares are in the way of the
perverse;
the cautious will keep far from them.
⁶ Train children in the right way,
and when old, they will not stray.
⁷ The rich rules over the poor,
and the borrower is the slave of the lender.
⁸ Whoever sows injustice will reap calamity,
and the rod of anger will fail.
⁹ Those who are generous are blessed,
for they share their bread with the poor.
¹⁰ Drive out a scoffer, and strife goes out;
quarreling and abuse will cease.
¹¹ Those who love a pure heart and are gracious
in speech
will have the king as a friend.
¹² The eyes of the LORD keep watch over
knowledge,
but he overthrows the words of the faithless.
¹³ The lazy person says, "There is a lion outside!
I shall be killed in the streets!"
¹⁴ The mouth of a looseᵉ woman is a deep pit;
he with whom the LORD is angry falls into
it.
¹⁵ Folly is bound up in the heart of a boy,
but the rod of discipline drives it far away.
¹⁶ Oppressing the poor in order to enrich oneself,
and giving to the rich, will lead only to
loss.

Sayings of the Wise

¹⁷   The words of the wise:

Incline your ear and hear my words,ᶠ
and apply your mind to my teaching;
¹⁸ for it will be pleasant if you keep them within
you,
if all of them are ready on your lips.
¹⁹ So that your trust may be in the LORD,
I have made them known to you
today—yes, to you.
²⁰ Have I not written for you thirty sayings
of admonition and knowledge,
²¹ to show you what is right and true,
so that you may give a true answer to those
who sent you?

²² Do not rob the poor because they are poor,
or crush the afflicted at the gate;
²³ for the LORD pleads their cause
and despoils of life those who despoil them.
²⁴ Make no friends with those given to anger,
and do not associate with hotheads,
²⁵ or you may learn their ways
and entangle yourself in a snare.
²⁶ Do not be one of those who give pledges,
who become surety for debts.
²⁷ If you have nothing with which to pay,
why should your bed be taken from under
you?
²⁸ Do not remove the ancient landmark
that your ancestors set up.

ᶜ *22:12 the plans,* literally, "the words."   ᵈ *22:28 That is stealing,* implied, see 23:10, 11.

ᵉ Heb *strange*   ᶠ Cn Compare Gk: Heb *Incline your ear, and hear the words of the wise*

King James

29Seest thou a man diligent in his business? he shall stand before kings; he shall not stand before mean *men*.

23 WHEN THOU sittest to eat with a ruler, consider diligently what *is* before thee:

2And put a knife to thy throat, if thou *be* a man given to appetite.

3Be not desirous of his dainties: for they *are* deceitful meat.

4Labour not to be rich: cease from thine own wisdom.

5Wilt thou set thine eyes upon that which is not? for *riches* certainly make themselves wings; they fly away as an eagle toward heaven.

6Eat thou not the bread of *him that hath* an evil eye, neither desire thou his dainty meats:

7For as he thinketh in his heart, so *is* he: Eat and drink, saith he to thee; but his heart *is* not with thee.

8The morsel *which* thou hast eaten shalt thou vomit up, and lose thy sweet words.

9Speak not in the ears of a fool: for he will despise the wisdom of thy words.

10Remove not the old landmark; and enter not into the fields of the fatherless:

11For their redeemer *is* mighty; he shall plead their cause with thee.

12Apply thine heart unto instruction, and thine ears to the words of knowledge.

13Withhold not correction from the child: for *if* thou beatest him with the rod, he shall not die.

14Thou shalt beat him with the rod, and shalt deliver his soul from hell.

15My son, if thine heart be wise, my heart shall rejoice, even mine.

16Yea, my reins shall rejoice, when thy lips speak right things.

17Let not thine heart envy sinners: but *be thou* in the fear of the LORD all the day long.

18For surely there is an end; and thine expectation shall not be cut off.

19Hear thou, my son, and be wise, and guide thine heart in the way.

20Be not among winebibbers; among riotous eaters of flesh:

21For the drunkard and the glutton shall come to poverty: and drowsiness shall clothe *a man* with rags.

22Hearken unto thy father that begat thee, and despise not thy mother when she is old.

23Buy the truth, and sell *it* not; *also* wisdom, and instruction, and understanding.

24The father of the righteous shall greatly rejoice: and he that begetteth a wise *child* shall have joy of him.

25Thy father and thy mother shall be glad, and she that bare thee shall rejoice.

New International

29Do you see a man skilled in his work?
He will serve before kings;
he will not serve before obscure men.

23 WHEN YOU sit to dine with a ruler,
note well what[a] is before you,

2and put a knife to your throat
if you are given to gluttony.

3Do not crave his delicacies,
for that food is deceptive.

4Do not wear yourself out to get rich;
have the wisdom to show restraint.

5Cast but a glance at riches, and they are gone,
for they will surely sprout wings
and fly off to the sky like an eagle.

6Do not eat the food of a stingy man,
do not crave his delicacies;

7for he is the kind of man
who is always thinking about the cost.[b]
"Eat and drink," he says to you,
but his heart is not with you.

8You will vomit up the little you have eaten
and will have wasted your compliments.

9Do not speak to a fool,
for he will scorn the wisdom of your words.

10Do not move an ancient boundary stone
or encroach on the fields of the fatherless,

11for their Defender is strong;
he will take up their case against you.

12Apply your heart to instruction
and your ears to words of knowledge.

13Do not withhold discipline from a child;
if you punish him with the rod, he will not die.

14Punish him with the rod
and save his soul from death.[c]

15My son, if your heart is wise,
then my heart will be glad;

16my inmost being will rejoice
when your lips speak what is right.

17Do not let your heart envy sinners,
but always be zealous for the fear of the LORD.

18There is surely a future hope for you,
and your hope will not be cut off.

19Listen, my son, and be wise,
and keep your heart on the right path.

20Do not join those who drink too much wine
or gorge themselves on meat,

21for drunkards and gluttons become poor,
and drowsiness clothes them in rags.

22Listen to your father, who gave you life,
and do not despise your mother when she is old.

23Buy the truth and do not sell it;
get wisdom, discipline and understanding.

24The father of a righteous man has great joy;
he who has a wise son delights in him.

25May your father and mother be glad;
may she who gave you birth rejoice!

---

a 1 Or who   b 7 Or for as he thinks within himself, / so he is; or for as he puts on a feast, / so he is   c 14 Hebrew Sheol

Living Bible

29Do you know a hard-working man? He shall be successful and stand before kings!

23 WHEN DINING with a rich man,d be on your guard and don't stuff yourself, though it all tastes so good; for he is trying to bribe you, and no good is going to come of his invitation.

4, 5Don't weary yourself trying to get rich. Why waste your time? For riches can disappear as though they had the wings of a bird!

6, 7, 8Don't associate with evil men; don't long for their favors and gifts. Their kindness is a trick; they want to use you as their pawn. The delicious food they serve will turn sour in your stomach and you will vomit it, and have to take back your words of appreciation for their "kindness."

9Don't waste your breath on a rebel. He will despise the wisest advice.

10, 11Don't steal the land of defenseless orphans by moving their ancient boundary marks, for their Redeemer is strong; he himself will accuse you.

12Don't refuse to accept criticism; get all the helpe you can.

13, 14Don't fail to correct your children; discipline won't hurt them! They won't die if you use a stick on them! Punishment will keep them out of hell.

15, 16My son, how I will rejoice if you become a man of common sense. Yes, my heart will thrill to your thoughtful, wise words.

17, 18Don't envy evil men but continue to reverence the Lord all the time, for surely you have a wonderful future ahead of you. There is hope for you yet!

19, 20, 21O my son, be wise and stay in God's paths; don't carouse with drunkards and gluttons, for they are on their way to poverty. And remember that too much sleep clothes a man with rags. 22Listen to your father's advice and don't despise an old mother's experience. 23Get the facts at any price, and hold on tightly to all the good sense you can get. 24, 25The father of a godly man has cause for joy—what pleasure a wise son is! So give your parents joy!

New Revised Standard

29 Do you see those who are skillful in their
        work?
     they will serve kings;
     they will not serve common people.

23 WHEN YOU sit down to eat with a ruler,
        observe carefully whatf is before you,
2   and put a knife to your throat
        if you have a big appetite.
3   Do not desire the ruler'sg delicacies,
        for they are deceptive food.
4   Do not wear yourself out to get rich;
        be wise enough to desist.
5   When your eyes light upon it, it is gone;
        for suddenly it takes wings to itself,
        flying like an eagle toward heaven.
6   Do not eat the bread of the stingy;
        do not desire their delicacies;
7   for like a hair in the throat, so are they.h
     "Eat and drink!" they say to you;
        but they do not mean it.
8   You will vomit up the little you have eaten,
        and you will waste your pleasant words.
9   Do not speak in the hearing of a fool,
        who will only despise the wisdom of your
             words.
10 Do not remove an ancient landmark
        or encroach on the fields of orphans,
11 for their redeemer is strong;
        he will plead their cause against you.
12 Apply your mind to instruction
        and your ear to words of knowledge.
13 Do not withhold discipline from your children;
        if you beat them with a rod, they will not
             die.
14 If you beat them with the rod,
        you will save their lives from Sheol.
15 My child, if your heart is wise,
        my heart too will be glad.
16 My soul will rejoice
        when your lips speak what is right.
17 Do not let your heart envy sinners,
        but always continue in the fear of the LORD.
18 Surely there is a future,
        and your hope will not be cut off.

19 Hear, my child, and be wise,
        and direct your mind in the way.
20 Do not be among winebibbers,
        or among gluttonous eaters of meat;
21 for the drunkard and the glutton will come to
             poverty,
        and drowsiness will clothe them with rags.
22 Listen to your father who begot you,
        and do not despise your mother when she is
             old.
23 Buy truth, and do not sell it;
        buy wisdom, instruction, and understanding.
24 The father of the righteous will greatly rejoice;
        he who begets a wise son will be glad in
             him.
25 Let your father and mother be glad;
        let her who bore you rejoice.

d 23:1 a rich man, literally, "a ruler."   e 23:12 help, literally, "knowledge."   f Or who   g Heb his   h Meaning of Heb uncertain

King James

26My son, give me thine heart, and let thine eyes observe my ways.

27For a whore *is* a deep ditch; and a strange woman *is* a narrow pit.

28She also lieth in wait as *for* a prey, and increaseth the transgressors among men.

29Who hath woe? who hath sorrow? who hath contentions? who hath babbling? who hath wounds without cause? who hath redness of eyes?

30They that tarry long at the wine; they that go to seek mixed wine.

31Look not thou upon the wine when it is red, when it giveth his colour in the cup, *when* it moveth itself aright.

32At the last it biteth like a serpent, and stingeth like an adder.

33Thine eyes shall behold strange women, and thine heart shall utter perverse things.

34Yea, thou shalt be as he that lieth down in the midst of the sea, or as he that lieth upon the top of a mast.

35They have stricken me, *shalt thou say, and* I was not sick; they have beaten me, *and* I felt *it* not: when shall I awake? I will seek it yet again.

24 BE NOT thou envious against evil men, neither desire to be with them.

2For their heart studieth destruction, and their lips talk of mischief.

3Through wisdom is an house builded; and by understanding it is established:

4And by knowledge shall the chambers be filled with all precious and pleasant riches.

5A wise man *is* strong; yea, a man of knowledge increaseth strength.

6For by wise counsel thou shalt make thy war: and in multitude of counsellors *there is* safety.

7Wisdom *is* too high for a fool: he openeth not his mouth in the gate.

8He that deviseth to do evil shall be called a mischievous person.

9The thought of foolishness *is* sin: and the scorner *is* an abomination to men.

10*If* thou faint in the day of adversity, thy strength *is* small.

11If thou forbear to deliver *them that are* drawn unto death, and *those that are* ready to be slain;

12If thou sayest, Behold, we knew it not; doth not he that pondereth the heart consider *it?* and he that keepeth thy soul, doth *not* he know *it?* and shall *not* he render to *every* man according to his works?

New International

26My son, give me your heart
   and let your eyes keep to my ways,
27for a prostitute is a deep pit
   and a wayward wife is a narrow well.
28Like a bandit she lies in wait,
   and multiplies the unfaithful among men.

29Who has woe? Who has sorrow?
   Who has strife? Who has complaints?
   Who has needless bruises? Who has bloodshot
      eyes?
30Those who linger over wine,
   who go to sample bowls of mixed wine.
31Do not gaze at wine when it is red,
   when it sparkles in the cup,
   when it goes down smoothly!
32In the end it bites like a snake
   and poisons like a viper.
33Your eyes will see strange sights
   and your mind imagine confusing things.
34You will be like one sleeping on the high seas,
   lying on top of the rigging.
35"They hit me," you will say, "but I'm not hurt!
   They beat me, but I don't feel it!
   When will I wake up
   so I can find another drink?"

24 DO NOT envy wicked men,
   do not desire their company;
2for their hearts plot violence,
   and their lips talk about making trouble.

3By wisdom a house is built,
   and through understanding it is established;
4through knowledge its rooms are filled
   with rare and beautiful treasures.

5A wise man has great power,
   and a man of knowledge increases strength;
6for waging war you need guidance,
   and for victory many advisers.

7Wisdom is too high for a fool;
   in the assembly at the gate he has nothing to
      say.

8He who plots evil
   will be known as a schemer.
9The schemes of folly are sin,
   and men detest a mocker.

10If you falter in times of trouble,
   how small is your strength!
11Rescue those being led away to death;
   hold back those staggering toward slaughter.
12If you say, "But we knew nothing about this,"
   does not he who weighs the heart perceive it?
   Does not he who guards your life know it?
   Will he not repay each person according to
      what he has done?

Living Bible

26, 27, 28O my son, trust my advice—stay away from prostitutes. For a prostitute is a deep and narrow grave. Like a robber, she waits for her victims as one after another become unfaithful to their wives.

29, 30Whose heart is filled with anguish and sorrow? Who is always fighting and quarreling? Who is the man with bloodshot eyes and many wounds? It is the one who spends long hours in the taverns, trying out new mixtures. 31Don't let the sparkle and the smooth taste of strong wine deceive you. 32For in the end it bites like a poisonous serpent; it stings like an adder. 33You will see hallucinations and have delirium tremens, and you will say foolish, silly things that would embarrass you no end when sober. 34You will stagger like a sailor tossed at sea, clinging to a swaying mast. 35And afterwards you will say, "I didn't even know it when they beat me up. . . . Let's go and have another drink!"

24 DON'T ENVY godless men; don't even enjoy their company. 2For they spend their days plotting violence and cheating.

3, 4Any enterprise is built by wise planning, becomes strong through common sense, and profits wonderfully by keeping abreast of the facts.

5A wise man is mightier than a strong man. Wisdom is mightier than strength.

6Don't go to war without wise guidance; there is safety in many counselors.

7Wisdom is too much for a rebel. He'll not be chosen as a counselor!

8To plan evil is as wrong as doing it.

9The rebel's schemes are sinful, and the mocker is the scourge of all mankind.

10You are a poor specimen if you can't stand the pressure of adversity.

11, 12Rescue those who are unjustly sentenced to death; don't stand back and let them die. Don't try to disclaim responsibility by saying you didn't know about it. For God, who knows all hearts, knows yours, and he knows you knew! And he will reward everyone according to his deeds.

New Revised Standard

26 My child, give me your heart,
     and let your eyes observea my ways.
27 For a prostitute is a deep pit;
     an adulteressb is a narrow well.
28 She lies in wait like a robber
     and increases the number of the faithless.

29 Who has woe? Who has sorrow?
     Who has strife? Who has complaining?
  Who has wounds without cause?
     Who has redness of eyes?
30 Those who linger late over wine,
     those who keep trying mixed wines.
31 Do not look at wine when it is red,
     when it sparkles in the cup
     and goes down smoothly.
32 At the last it bites like a serpent,
     and stings like an adder.
33 Your eyes will see strange things,
     and your mind utter perverse things.
34 You will be like one who lies down in the
        midst of the sea,
     like one who lies on the top of a mast.c
35 "They struck me," you will say,d "but I was
        not hurt;
     they beat me, but I did not feel it.
  When shall I awake?
  I will seek another drink."

24 DO NOT envy the wicked,
     nor desire to be with them;
2 for their minds devise violence,
     and their lips talk of mischief.

3 By wisdom a house is built,
     and by understanding it is established;
4 by knowledge the rooms are filled
     with all precious and pleasant riches.
5 Wise warriors are mightier than strong ones,e
     and those who have knowledge than those
        who have strength;
6 for by wise guidance you can wage your war,
     and in abundance of counselors there is
        victory.
7 Wisdom is too high for fools;
     in the gate they do not open their mouths.

8 Whoever plans to do evil
     will be called a mischief-maker.
9 The devising of folly is sin,
     and the scoffer is an abomination to all.

10 If you faint in the day of adversity,
     your strength being small;
11 if you hold back from rescuing those taken
        away to death,
     those who go staggering to the slaughter;
12 if you say, "Look, we did not know this"—
     does not he who weighs the heart perceive
        it?
  Does not he who keeps watch over your soul
        know it?
  And will he not repay all according to their
        deeds?

---

a Another reading is *delight in*   b Heb *an alien woman*   c Meaning of Heb uncertain   d Gk Syr Vg Tg: Heb lacks *you will say*   e Gk Compare Syr Tg: Heb *A wise man is strength*

King James

13My son, eat thou honey, because *it is* good; and the honeycomb, *which is* sweet to thy taste:

14So *shall* the knowledge of wisdom *be* unto thy soul: when thou hast found *it*, then there shall be a reward, and thy expectation shall not be cut off.

15Lay not wait, O wicked *man*, against the dwelling of the righteous; spoil not his resting place:

16For a just *man* falleth seven times, and riseth up again: but the wicked shall fall into mischief.

17Rejoice not when thine enemy falleth, and let not thine heart be glad when he stumbleth:

18Lest the LORD see *it*, and it displease him, and he turn away his wrath from him.

19Fret not thyself because of evil *men*, neither be thou envious at the wicked;

20For there shall be no reward to the evil *man*; the candle of the wicked shall be put out.

21My son, fear thou the LORD and the king: *and* meddle not with them that are given to change:

22For their calamity shall rise suddenly; and who knoweth the ruin of them both?

23These *things* also *belong* to the wise. *It is* not good to have respect of persons in judgment.

24He that saith unto the wicked, Thou *art* righteous; him shall the people curse, nations shall abhor him:

25But to them that rebuke *him* shall be delight, and a good blessing shall come upon them.

26*Every man* shall kiss *his* lips that giveth a right answer.

27Prepare thy work without, and make it fit for thyself in the field; and afterwards build thine house.

28Be not a witness against thy neighbour without cause; and deceive *not* with thy lips.

29Say not, I will do so to him as he hath done to me: I will render to the man according to his work.

30I went by the field of the slothful, and by the vineyard of the man void of understanding;

31And, lo, it was all grown over with thorns, *and* nettles had covered the face thereof, and the stone wall thereof was broken down.

32Then I saw, *and* considered *it* well: I looked upon *it*, *and* received instruction.

33*Yet* a little sleep, a little slumber, a little folding of the hands to sleep:

34So shall thy poverty come *as* one that travelleth; and thy want as an armed man.

New International

13Eat honey, my son, for it is good;
    honey from the comb is sweet to your taste.
14Know also that wisdom is sweet to your soul;
    if you find it, there is a future hope for you,
    and your hope will not be cut off.

15Do not lie in wait like an outlaw against a
        righteous man's house,
    do not raid his dwelling place;
16for though a righteous man falls seven times, he
        rises again,
    but the wicked are brought down by calamity.

17Do not gloat when your enemy falls;
    when he stumbles, do not let your heart
        rejoice,
18or the LORD will see and disapprove
    and turn his wrath away from him.

19Do not fret because of evil men
    or be envious of the wicked,
20for the evil man has no future hope,
    and the lamp of the wicked will be snuffed
        out.

21Fear the LORD and the king, my son,
    and do not join with the rebellious,
22for those two will send sudden destruction upon
        them,
    and who knows what calamities they can
        bring?

Further Sayings of the Wise

23These also are sayings of the wise:

To show partiality in judging is not good:
24Whoever says to the guilty, "You are
        innocent"—
    peoples will curse him and nations denounce
        him.
25But it will go well with those who convict the
        guilty,
    and rich blessing will come upon them.

26An honest answer
    is like a kiss on the lips.

27Finish your outdoor work
    and get your fields ready;
    after that, build your house.

28Do not testify against your neighbor without
        cause,
    or use your lips to deceive.
29Do not say, "I'll do to him as he has done to
        me;
    I'll pay that man back for what he did."

30I went past the field of the sluggard,
    past the vineyard of the man who lacks
        judgment;
31thorns had come up everywhere,
    the ground was covered with weeds,
    and the stone wall was in ruins.
32I applied my heart to what I observed
    and learned a lesson from what I saw:
33A little sleep, a little slumber,
    a little folding of the hands to rest—
34and poverty will come on you like a bandit
    and scarcity like an armed man.[a]

---

a 34 Or *like a vagrant / and scarcity like a beggar*

Living Bible

13, 14My son, honey whets the appetite, and so does wisdom! When you enjoy becoming wise, there is hope for you! A bright future lies ahead!

15, 16O evil man, leave the upright man alone, and quit trying to cheat him out of his rights. Don't you know that this good man, though you trip him up seven times, will each time rise again? But one calamity is enough to lay you low.

17Do not rejoice when your enemy meets trouble. Let there be no gladness when he falls— 18for the Lord may be displeased with you and stop punishing him!

19, 20Don't envy the wicked. Don't covet his riches. For the evil man has no future; his light will be snuffed out.

21, 22My son, watch your step before the Lord and the king, and don't associate with radicals. For you will go down with them to sudden disaster, and who knows where it all will end?

23It is wrong to sentence the poor, and let the rich go free. 24He who says to the wicked, "You are innocent," shall be cursed by many people of many nations; 25but blessings shall be showered on those who rebuke sin fearlessly.

26It is an honor to receive a frank reply.

27Develop your business first before building your house.

28, 29Don't testify spitefully against an innocent neighbor. Why lie about him? Don't say, "Now I can pay him back for all his meanness to me!"

30, 31I walked by the field of a certain lazy fellow and saw that it was overgrown with thorns, and covered with weeds; and its walls were broken down. 32, 33Then, as I looked, I learned this lesson:

"A little extra sleep,
A little more slumber,
A little folding of the hands to rest"

34means that poverty will break in upon you suddenly like a robber, and violently like a bandit.

New Revised Standard

13 My child, eat honey, for it is good,
     and the drippings of the honeycomb are
         sweet to your taste.
14 Know that wisdom is such to your soul;
     if you find it, you will find a future,
     and your hope will not be cut off.

15 Do not lie in wait like an outlaw against the
         home of the righteous;
     do no violence to the place where the
         righteous live;
16 for though they fall seven times, they will rise
         again;
     but the wicked are overthrown by calamity.

17 Do not rejoice when your enemies fall,
     and do not let your heart be glad when they
         stumble,
18 or else the LORD will see it and be displeased,
     and turn away his anger from them.

19 Do not fret because of evildoers.
     Do not envy the wicked;
20 for the evil have no future;
     the lamp of the wicked will go out.

21 My child, fear the LORD and the king,
     and do not disobey either of them;b
22 for disaster comes from them suddenly,
     and who knows the ruin that both can
         bring?

Further Sayings of the Wise

23   These also are sayings of the wise:

     Partiality in judging is not good.
24 Whoever says to the wicked, "You are
         innocent,"
     will be cursed by peoples, abhorred by
         nations;
25 but those who rebuke the wicked will have
         delight,
     and a good blessing will come upon them.
26 One who gives an honest answer
     gives a kiss on the lips.

27 Prepare your work outside,
     get everything ready for you in the field;
     and after that build your house.

28 Do not be a witness against your neighbor
         without cause,
     and do not deceive with your lips.
29 Do not say, "I will do to others as they have
         done to me;
     I will pay them back for what they have
         done."

30 I passed by the field of one who was lazy,
     by the vineyard of a stupid person;
31 and see, it was all overgrown with thorns;
     the ground was covered with nettles,
     and its stone wall was broken down.
32 Then I saw and considered it;
     I looked and received instruction.
33 A little sleep, a little slumber,
     a little folding of the hands to rest,
34 and poverty will come upon you like a robber,
     and want, like an armed warrior.

b Gk: Heb *do not associate with those who change*

King James

25 THESE *ARE* also proverbs of Solomon, which the men of Hezekiah king of Judah copied out.

2*It is* the glory of God to conceal a thing: but the honour of kings *is* to search out a matter.

3The heaven for height, and the earth for depth, and the heart of kings *is* unsearchable.

4Take away the dross from the silver, and there shall come forth a vessel for the refiner.

5Take away the wicked *from* before the king, and his throne shall be established in righteousness.

6Put not forth thyself in the presence of the king, and stand not in the place of great *men:*

7For better *it is* that it be said unto thee, Come up hither; than that thou shouldest be put lower in the presence of the prince whom thine eyes have seen.

8Go not forth hastily to strive, lest *thou know not* what to do in the end thereof, when thy neighbour hath put thee to shame.

9Debate thy cause with thy neighbour *himself;* and discover not a secret to another:

10Lest he that heareth *it* put thee to shame, and thine infamy turn not away.

11A word fitly spoken *is like* apples of gold in pictures of silver.

12*As* an earring of gold, and an ornament of fine gold, *so is* a wise reprover upon an obedient ear.

13As the cold of snow in the time of harvest, *so is* a faithful messenger to them that send him: for he refresheth the soul of his masters.

14Whoso boasteth himself of a false gift *is like* clouds and wind without rain.

15By long forbearing is a prince persuaded, and a soft tongue breaketh the bone.

16Hast thou found honey? eat so much as is sufficient for thee, lest thou be filled therewith, and vomit it.

17Withdraw thy foot from thy neighbour's house; lest he be weary of thee, and *so* hate thee.

18A man that beareth false witness against his neighbour *is* a maul, and a sword, and a sharp arrow.

19Confidence in an unfaithful man in time of trouble *is like* a broken tooth, and a foot out of joint.

20*As* he that taketh away a garment in cold weather, *and as* vinegar upon nitre, so *is* he that singeth songs to an heavy heart.

21If thine enemy be hungry, give him bread to eat; and if he be thirsty, give him water to drink:

22For thou shalt heap coals of fire upon his head, and the LORD shall reward thee.

23The north wind driveth away rain: so *doth* an angry countenance a backbiting tongue.

New International

More Proverbs of Solomon

25 THESE ARE more proverbs of Solomon, copied by the men of Hezekiah king of Judah:

2It is the glory of God to conceal a matter;
  to search out a matter is the glory of kings.

3As the heavens are high and the earth is deep,
  so the hearts of kings are unsearchable.

4Remove the dross from the silver,
  and out comes material fora the silversmith;

5remove the wicked from the king's presence,
  and his throne will be established through righteousness.

6Do not exalt yourself in the king's presence,
  and do not claim a place among great men;

7it is better for him to say to you, "Come up here,"
  than for him to humiliate you before a nobleman.

What you have seen with your eyes
8 do not bringb hastily to court,
  for what will you do in the end
  if your neighbor puts you to shame?

9If you argue your case with a neighbor,
  do not betray another man's confidence,

10or he who hears it may shame you
  and you will never lose your bad reputation.

11A word aptly spoken
  is like apples of gold in settings of silver.

12Like an earring of gold or an ornament of fine gold
  is a wise man's rebuke to a listening ear.

13Like the coolness of snow at harvest time
  is a trustworthy messenger to those who send him;
  he refreshes the spirit of his masters.

14Like clouds and wind without rain
  is a man who boasts of gifts he does not give.

15Through patience a ruler can be persuaded,
  and a gentle tongue can break a bone.

16If you find honey, eat just enough—
  too much of it, and you will vomit.

17Seldom set foot in your neighbor's house—
  too much of you, and he will hate you.

18Like a club or a sword or a sharp arrow
  is the man who gives false testimony against his neighbor.

19Like a bad tooth or a lame foot
  is reliance on the unfaithful in times of trouble.

20Like one who takes away a garment on a cold day,
  or like vinegar poured on soda,
  is one who sings songs to a heavy heart.

21If your enemy is hungry, give him food to eat;
  if he is thirsty, give him water to drink.

22In doing this, you will heap burning coals on his head,
  and the LORD will reward you.

23As a north wind brings rain,
  so a sly tongue brings angry looks.

---

a 4 Or *comes a vessel from*   b 7,8 Or *nobleman / on whom you had set your eyes. / *8Do not go*

Living Bible

25 THESE PROVERBS of Solomon[c] were discovered and copied by the aides of King Hezekiah[d] of Judah:

2,3It is God's privilege to conceal things, and the king's privilege to discover and invent. You cannot understand the height of heaven, the size of the earth, or all that goes on in the king's mind!

4,5When you remove dross from silver, you have sterling ready for the silversmith. When you remove corrupt men from the king's court, his reign will be just and fair.

6,7Don't demand an audience with the king as though you were some powerful prince. It is better to wait for an invitation rather than to be sent back to the end of the line, publicly disgraced!

8,9,10Don't be hot-headed and rush to court! You may start something you can't finish and go down before your neighbor in shameful defeat. So discuss the matter with him privately. Don't tell anyone else, lest he accuse you of slander and you can't withdraw what you said.

11Timely advice is as lovely as gold apples in a silver basket.

12It is a badge of honor to accept valid criticism.

13A faithful employee is as refreshing as a cool day[e] in the hot summertime.

14One who doesn't give the gift he promised is like a cloud blowing over a desert without dropping any rain.

15Be patient and you will finally win, for a soft tongue can break hard bones.

16Do you like honey? Don't eat too much of it, or it will make you sick!

17Don't visit your neighbor too often, or you will outwear your welcome!

18Telling lies about someone is as harmful as hitting him with an axe, or wounding him with a sword, or shooting him with a sharp arrow.

19Putting confidence in an unreliable man is like chewing with a sore tooth, or trying to run on a broken foot.

20Being happy-go-lucky around a person whose heart is heavy is as bad as stealing his jacket in cold weather, or rubbing salt in his wounds.[f]

21,22If your enemy is hungry, give him food! If he is thirsty, give him something to drink! This will make him feel ashamed of himself, and God will reward you.

23As surely as a wind from the north brings cold,[g] just as surely a retort causes anger!

New Revised Standard

Further Wise Sayings of Solomon

25 THESE ARE other proverbs of Solomon that the officials of King Hezekiah of Judah copied.

2 It is the glory of God to conceal things,
   but the glory of kings is to search things
      out.

3 Like the heavens for height, like the earth for
      depth,
   so the mind of kings is unsearchable.

4 Take away the dross from the silver,
   and the smith has material for a vessel;

5 take away the wicked from the presence of the
      king,
   and his throne will be established in
      righteousness.

6 Do not put yourself forward in the king's
      presence
   or stand in the place of the great;

7 for it is better to be told, "Come up here,"
   than to be put lower in the presence of a
      noble.

What your eyes have seen
8   do not hastily bring into court;
   for[h] what will you do in the end,
      when your neighbor puts you to shame?

9 Argue your case with your neighbor directly,
   and do not disclose another's secret;

10 or else someone who hears you will bring
      shame upon you,
   and your ill repute will have no end.

11 A word fitly spoken
   is like apples of gold in a setting of silver.

12 Like a gold ring or an ornament of gold
   is a wise rebuke to a listening ear.

13 Like the cold of snow in the time of harvest
   are faithful messengers to those who send
      them;
   they refresh the spirit of their masters.

14 Like clouds and wind without rain
   is one who boasts of a gift never given.

15 With patience a ruler may be persuaded,
   and a soft tongue can break bones.

16 If you have found honey, eat only enough for
      you,
   or else, having too much, you will vomit it.

17 Let your foot be seldom in your neighbor's
      house,
   otherwise the neighbor will become weary
      of you and hate you.

18 Like a war club, a sword, or a sharp arrow
   is one who bears false witness against a
      neighbor.

19 Like a bad tooth or a lame foot
   is trust in a faithless person in time of
      trouble.

20 Like vinegar on a wound[i]
   is one who sings songs to a heavy heart.
   Like a moth in clothing or a worm in wood,
      sorrow gnaws at the human heart.[j]

21 If your enemies are hungry, give them bread
      to eat;
   and if they are thirsty, give them water to
      drink;

22 for you will heap coals of fire on their heads,
   and the LORD will reward you.

23 The north wind produces rain,
   and a backbiting tongue, angry looks.

---

c 25:1 *These proverbs of Solomon.* 1 Kgs 4:32.   d 25:1 *King Hezekiah.*
Hezekiah lived 200 years after Solomon.   e 25:13 *a cool day,* literally,
"snow."   f 25:20 *rubbing salt in his wounds,* literally, "like vinegar upon
soda."   g 25:23 *cold,* literally, "rain."

h Cn: Heb *or else*   i Gk: Heb *Like one who takes off a garment on a cold
day, like vinegar on lye*   j Gk Syr Tg: Heb lacks *Like a moth . . . human
heart*

King James

²⁴*It is* better to dwell in the corner of the housetop, than with a brawling woman and in a wide house.

²⁵*As* cold waters to a thirsty soul, so *is* good news from a far country.

²⁶A righteous man falling down before the wicked *is as* a troubled fountain, and a corrupt spring.

²⁷*It is* not good to eat much honey: so *for men* to search their own glory *is not* glory.

²⁸He that *hath* no rule over his own spirit *is like* a city *that is* broken down, *and* without walls.

26 AS SNOW in summer, and as rain in harvest, so honour is not seemly for a fool.

²As the bird by wandering, as the swallow by flying, so the curse causeless shall not come.

³A whip for the horse, a bridle for the ass, and a rod for the fool's back.

⁴Answer not a fool according to his folly, lest thou also be like unto him.

⁵Answer a fool according to his folly, lest he be wise in his own conceit.

⁶He that sendeth a message by the hand of a fool cutteth off the feet, *and* drinketh damage.

⁷The legs of the lame are not equal: so *is* a parable in the mouth of fools.

⁸As he that bindeth a stone in a sling, so *is* he that giveth honour to a fool.

⁹*As* a thorn goeth up into the hand of a drunkard, so *is* a parable in the mouth of fools.

¹⁰The great *God* that formed all *things* both rewardeth the fool, and rewardeth transgressors.

¹¹As a dog returneth to his vomit, *so* a fool returneth to his folly.

¹²Seest thou a man wise in his own conceit? *there is* more hope of a fool than of him.

¹³The slothful *man* saith, *There is* a lion in the way; a lion *is* in the streets.

¹⁴*As* the door turneth upon his hinges, so *doth* the slothful upon his bed.

¹⁵The slothful hideth his hand in *his* bosom; it grieveth him to bring it again to his mouth.

¹⁶The sluggard *is* wiser in his own conceit than seven men that can render a reason.

¹⁷He that passeth by, *and* meddleth with strife *belonging* not to him, *is like* one that taketh a dog by the ears.

¹⁸As a mad *man* who casteth firebrands, arrows, and death,

¹⁹So *is* the man *that* deceiveth his neighbour, and saith, Am not I in sport?

²⁰Where no wood is, *there* the fire goeth out: so where *there* is no talebearer, the strife ceaseth.

²¹*As* coals *are* to burning coals, and wood to fire; so *is* a contentious man to kindle strife.

New International

²⁴Better to live on a corner of the roof
   than share a house with a quarrelsome wife.

²⁵Like cold water to a weary soul
   is good news from a distant land.

²⁶Like a muddied spring or a polluted well
   is a righteous man who gives way to the
   wicked.

²⁷It is not good to eat too much honey,
   nor is it honorable to seek one's own honor.

²⁸Like a city whose walls are broken down
   is a man who lacks self-control.

26 LIKE SNOW in summer or rain in harvest, honor is not fitting for a fool.

²Like a fluttering sparrow or a darting swallow,
   an undeserved curse does not come to rest.

³A whip for the horse, a halter for the donkey,
   and a rod for the backs of fools!

⁴Do not answer a fool according to his folly,
   or you will be like him yourself.

⁵Answer a fool according to his folly,
   or he will be wise in his own eyes.

⁶Like cutting off one's feet or drinking violence
   is the sending of a message by the hand of a
   fool.

⁷Like a lame man's legs that hang limp
   is a proverb in the mouth of a fool.

⁸Like tying a stone in a sling
   is the giving of honor to a fool.

⁹Like a thornbush in a drunkard's hand
   is a proverb in the mouth of a fool.

¹⁰Like an archer who wounds at random
   is he who hires a fool or any passer-by.

¹¹As a dog returns to its vomit,
   so a fool repeats his folly.

¹²Do you see a man wise in his own eyes?
   There is more hope for a fool than for him.

¹³The sluggard says, "There is a lion in the road,
   a fierce lion roaming the streets!"

¹⁴As a door turns on its hinges,
   so a sluggard turns on his bed.

¹⁵The sluggard buries his hand in the dish;
   he is too lazy to bring it back to his mouth.

¹⁶The sluggard is wiser in his own eyes
   than seven men who answer discreetly.

¹⁷Like one who seizes a dog by the ears
   is a passer-by who meddles in a quarrel not
   his own.

¹⁸Like a madman shooting
   firebrands or deadly arrows

¹⁹is a man who deceives his neighbor
   and says, "I was only joking!"

²⁰Without wood a fire goes out;
   without gossip a quarrel dies down.

²¹As charcoal to embers and as wood to fire,
   so is a quarrelsome man for kindling strife.

Living Bible

24It is better to live in a corner of an attic than in a beautiful home with a cranky, quarrelsome woman.

25Good news from far away is like cold water to the thirsty.

26If a godly man compromises with the wicked, it is like polluting a fountain or muddying a spring.

27Just as it is harmful to eat too much honey, so also it is bad for men to think about all the honors they deserve!

28A man without self-control is as defenseless as a city with broken-down walls.

26 HONOR DOESN'T go with fools any more than snow with summertime or rain with harvest time!

2An undeserved curse has no effect. Its intended victim will be no more harmed by it than by a sparrow or swallow flitting through the sky.

3Guide a horse with a whip, a donkey with a bridle, and a rebel with a rod to his back!

4, 5When arguing with a rebel, don't use foolish arguments as he does, or you will become as foolish as he is! Prick his conceit with silly replies!a

6To trust a rebel to convey a message is as foolish as cutting off your feet and drinking poison!

7In the mouth of a fool a proverb becomes as useless as a paralyzed leg.

8Honoring a rebel will backfire like a stone tied to a slingshot!

9A rebel will misapply an illustration so that its point will no more be felt than a thorn in the hand of a drunkard.

10The master may get better work from an untrained apprentice than from a skilled rebel!

11As a dog returns to his vomit, so a fool repeats his folly.

12There is one thing worse than a fool, and that is a man who is conceited.

13The lazy man won't go out and work. "There might be a lion outside!" he says. 14He sticks to his bed like a door to its hinges! 15He is too tired even to lift his food from his dish to his mouth! 16Yet in his own opinion he is smarter than seven wise men.

17Yanking a dog's ears is no more foolish than interfering in an argument that isn't any of your business.

18, 19A man who is caught lying to his neighbor and says, "I was just fooling," is like a madman throwing around firebrands, arrows and death!

20Fire goes out for lack of fuel, and tensions disappear when gossip stops.

21A quarrelsome man starts fights as easily as a matchb sets fire to paper.

New Revised Standard

24 It is better to live in a corner of the housetop
   than in a house shared with a contentious
   wife.

25 Like cold water to a thirsty soul,
   so is good news from a far country.

26 Like a muddied spring or a polluted fountain
   are the righteous who give way before the
   wicked.

27 It is not good to eat much honey,
   or to seek honor on top of honor.

28 Like a city breached, without walls,
   is one who lacks self-control.

26 LIKE SNOW in summer or rain in harvest,
   so honor is not fitting for a fool.

2 Like a sparrow in its flitting, like a swallow in
   its flying,
   an undeserved curse goes nowhere.

3 A whip for the horse, a bridle for the donkey,
   and a rod for the back of fools.

4 Do not answer fools according to their folly,
   or you will be a fool yourself.

5 Answer fools according to their folly,
   or they will be wise in their own eyes.

6 It is like cutting off one's foot and drinking
   down violence,
   to send a message by a fool.

7 The legs of a disabled person hang limp;
   so does a proverb in the mouth of a fool.

8 It is like binding a stone in a sling
   to give honor to a fool.

9 Like a thornbush brandished by the hand of a
   drunkard
   is a proverb in the mouth of a fool.

10 Like an archer who wounds everybody
   is one who hires a passing fool or
   drunkard.c

11 Like a dog that returns to its vomit
   is a fool who reverts to his folly.

12 Do you see persons wise in their own eyes?
   There is more hope for fools than for them.

13 The lazy person says, "There is a lion in the
   road!
   There is a lion in the streets!"

14 As a door turns on its hinges,
   so does a lazy person in bed.

15 The lazy person buries a hand in the dish,
   and is too tired to bring it back to the
   mouth.

16 The lazy person is wiser in self-esteem
   than seven who can answer discreetly.

17 Like somebody who takes a passing dog by
   the ears
   is one who meddles in the quarrel of
   another.

18 Like a maniac who shoots deadly firebrands
   and arrows,

19 so is one who deceives a neighbor
   and says, "I am only joking!"

20 For lack of wood the fire goes out,
   and where there is no whisperer, quarreling
   ceases.

21 As charcoal is to hot embers and wood to fire,
   so is a quarrelsome person for kindling
   strife.

---

a 26:4, 5 *Prick his conceit with silly replies*, implied. Literally, "Reply to a fool as his folly requires."   b 26:21 *as easily as a match*, literally, "like hot embers to coals and wood to fire."

c Meaning of Heb uncertain

King James

22The words of a talebearer *are* as wounds, and they go down into the innermost parts of the belly.

23Burning lips and a wicked heart *are like* a potsherd covered with silver dross.

24He that hateth dissembleth with his lips, and layeth up deceit within him;

25When he speaketh fair, believe him not: for *there are* seven abominations in his heart.

26*Whose* hatred is covered by deceit, his wickedness shall be shown before the *whole* congregation.

27Whoso diggeth a pit shall fall therein: and he that rolleth a stone, it will return upon him.

28A lying tongue hateth *those that are* afflicted by it; and a flattering mouth worketh ruin.

27 BOAST NOT thyself of tomorrow; for thou knowest not what a day may bring forth.

2Let another man praise thee, and not thine own mouth; a stranger, and not thine own lips.

3A stone *is* heavy, and the sand weighty; but a fool's wrath *is* heavier than them both.

4Wrath *is* cruel, and anger *is* outrageous; but who *is* able to stand before envy?

5Open rebuke *is* better than secret love.

6Faithful *are* the wounds of a friend; but the kisses of an enemy *are* deceitful.

7The full soul loatheth an honeycomb; but to the hungry soul every bitter thing is sweet.

8As a bird that wandereth from her nest, so *is* a man that wandereth from his place.

9Ointment and perfume rejoice the heart: so *doth* the sweetness of a man's friend by hearty counsel.

10Thine own friend, and thy father's friend, forsake not; neither go into thy brother's house in the day of thy calamity: *for* better *is* a neighbour *that is* near than a brother far off.

11My son, be wise, and make my heart glad, that I may answer him that reproacheth me.

12A prudent *man* foreseeth the evil, *and* hideth himself; *but* the simple pass on, *and* are punished.

13Take his garment that is surety for a stranger, and take a pledge of him for a strange woman.

14He that blesseth his friend with a loud voice, rising early in the morning, it shall be counted a curse to him.

New International

22The words of a gossip are like choice morsels; they go down to a man's inmost parts.

23Like a coating of glaze[a] over earthenware are fervent lips with an evil heart.

24A malicious man disguises himself with his lips, but in his heart he harbors deceit.

25Though his speech is charming, do not believe him, for seven abominations fill his heart.

26His malice may be concealed by deception, but his wickedness will be exposed in the assembly.

27If a man digs a pit, he will fall into it; if a man rolls a stone, it will roll back on him.

28A lying tongue hates those it hurts, and a flattering mouth works ruin.

27 DO NOT boast about tomorrow, for you do not know what a day may bring forth.

2Let another praise you, and not your own mouth; someone else, and not your own lips.

3Stone is heavy and sand a burden, but provocation by a fool is heavier than both.

4Anger is cruel and fury overwhelming, but who can stand before jealousy?

5Better is open rebuke than hidden love.

6Wounds from a friend can be trusted, but an enemy multiplies kisses.

7He who is full loathes honey, but to the hungry even what is bitter tastes sweet.

8Like a bird that strays from its nest is a man who strays from his home.

9Perfume and incense bring joy to the heart, and the pleasantness of one's friend springs from his earnest counsel.

10Do not forsake your friend and the friend of your father, and do not go to your brother's house when disaster strikes you— better a neighbor nearby than a brother far away.

11Be wise, my son, and bring joy to my heart; then I can answer anyone who treats me with contempt.

12The prudent see danger and take refuge, but the simple keep going and suffer for it.

13Take the garment of one who puts up security for a stranger; hold it in pledge if he does it for a wayward woman.

14If a man loudly blesses his neighbor early in the morning, it will be taken as a curse.

---

a 23 With a different word division of the Hebrew; Masoretic Text *of silver dross*

Living Bible

22Gossip is a dainty morsel eaten with great relish. 23Pretty words may hide a wicked heart, just as a pretty glaze covers a common clay pot.

24, 25, 26A man with hate in his heart may sound pleasant enough, but don't believe him; for he is cursing you in his heart. Though he pretends to be so kind, his hatred will finally come to light for all to see.

27The man who sets a trap for others will get caught in it himself. Roll a boulder down on someone, and it will roll back and crush you.

28Flattery is a form of hatred and wounds cruelly.

27 DON'T BRAG about your plans for tomorrow—wait and see what happens.

2Don't praise yourself; let others do it!

3A rebel's frustrations are heavier than sand and rocks.

4Jealousy is more dangerous and cruel than anger.

5Open rebuke is better than hidden love!

6Wounds from a friend are better than kisses from an enemy!

7Even honey seems tasteless to a man who is full; but if he is hungry, he'll eat anything!

8A man who strays from home is like a bird that wanders from its nest.

9Friendly suggestions are as pleasant as perfume.

10Never abandon a friend—either yours or your father's. Then you won't need to go to a distant relative for help in your time of need.

11My son, how happy I will be if you turn out to be sensible! It will be a public honor to me.

12A sensible man watches for problems ahead and prepares to meet them. The simpleton never looks, and suffers the consequences.

13The world's poorest credit risk is the man who agrees to pay a stranger's debts.

14If you shout a pleasant greeting to a friend too early in the morning, he will count it as a curse!

New Revised Standard

22 The words of a whisperer are like delicious morsels;
   they go down into the inner parts of the body.
23 Like the glaze[b] covering an earthen vessel
   are smooth[c] lips with an evil heart.
24 An enemy dissembles in speaking
   while harboring deceit within;
25 when an enemy speaks graciously, do not believe it,
   for there are seven abominations concealed within;
26 though hatred is covered with guile,
   the enemy's wickedness will be exposed in the assembly.
27 Whoever digs a pit will fall into it,
   and a stone will come back on the one who starts it rolling.
28 A lying tongue hates its victims,
   and a flattering mouth works ruin.

27 DO NOT boast about tomorrow,
   for you do not know what a day may bring.
2 Let another praise you, and not your own mouth—
   a stranger, and not your own lips.
3 A stone is heavy, and sand is weighty,
   but a fool's provocation is heavier than both.
4 Wrath is cruel, anger is overwhelming,
   but who is able to stand before jealousy?
5 Better is open rebuke
   than hidden love.
6 Well meant are the wounds a friend inflicts,
   but profuse are the kisses of an enemy.
7 The sated appetite spurns honey,
   but to a ravenous appetite even the bitter is sweet.
8 Like a bird that strays from its nest
   is one who strays from home.
9 Perfume and incense make the heart glad,
   but the soul is torn by trouble.[d]
10 Do not forsake your friend or the friend of your parent;
   do not go to the house of your kindred in the day of your calamity.
   Better is a neighbor who is nearby
   than kindred who are far away.
11 Be wise, my child, and make my heart glad,
   so that I may answer whoever reproaches me.
12 The clever see danger and hide;
   but the simple go on, and suffer for it.
13 Take the garment of one who has given surety for a stranger;
   seize the pledge given as surety for foreigners.[e]
14 Whoever blesses a neighbor with a loud voice,
   rising early in the morning,
   will be counted as cursing.

b Cn: Heb silver of dross   c Gk: Heb burning   d Gk: Heb the sweetness of a friend is better than one's own counsel   e Vg and 20.16: Heb for a foreign woman

King James

15A continual dropping in a very rainy day and a contentious woman are alike.

16Whosoever hideth her hideth the wind, and the ointment of his right hand, *which* betrayeth *itself*.

17Iron sharpeneth iron; so a man sharpeneth the countenance of his friend.

18Whoso keepeth the fig tree shall eat the fruit thereof: so he that waiteth on his master shall be honoured.

19As in water face *answereth* to face, so the heart of man to man.

20Hell and destruction are never full; so the eyes of man are never satisfied.

21*As* the refining pot for silver, and the furnace for gold; so *is* a man to his praise.

22Though thou shouldest bray a fool in a mortar among wheat with a pestle, *yet* will not his foolishness depart from him.

23Be thou diligent to know the state of thy flocks, *and* look well to thy herds.

24For riches *are* not for ever: and doth the crown *endure* to every generation?

25The hay appeareth, and the tender grass showeth itself, and herbs of the mountains are gathered.

26The lambs *are* for thy clothing, and the goats *are* the price of the field.

27And *thou shalt have* goats' milk enough for thy food, for the food of thy household, and *for* the maintenance for thy maidens.

28 THE WICKED flee when no man pursueth: but the righteous are bold as a lion.

2For the transgression of a land many *are* the princes thereof: but by a man of understanding *and* knowledge the state *thereof* shall be prolonged.

3A poor man that oppresseth the poor *is like* a sweeping rain which leaveth no food.

4They that forsake the law praise the wicked: but such as keep the law contend with them.

5Evil men understand not judgment: but they that seek the LORD understand all *things*.

6Better *is* the poor that walketh in his uprightness, than *he that is* perverse *in his* ways, though he *be* rich.

7Whoso keepeth the law *is* a wise son: but he that is a companion of riotous *men* shameth his father.

8He that by usury and unjust gain increaseth his substance, he shall gather it for him that will pity the poor.

9He that turneth away his ear from hearing the law, even his prayer *shall be* abomination.

10Whoso causeth the righteous to go astray in an evil way, he shall fall himself into his own pit: but the upright shall have good *things* in possession.

New International

15A quarrelsome wife is like
    a constant dripping on a rainy day;
16restraining her is like restraining the wind
    or grasping oil with the hand.

17As iron sharpens iron,
    so one man sharpens another.

18He who tends a fig tree will eat its fruit,
    and he who looks after his master will be
        honored.

19As water reflects a face,
    so a man's heart reflects the man.

20Death and Destruction[a] are never satisfied,
    and neither are the eyes of man.

21The crucible for silver and the furnace for gold,
    but man is tested by the praise he receives.

22Though you grind a fool in a mortar,
    grinding him like grain with a pestle,
    you will not remove his folly from him.

23Be sure you know the condition of your flocks,
    give careful attention to your herds;
24for riches do not endure forever,
    and a crown is not secure for all generations.
25When the hay is removed and new growth
        appears
    and the grass from the hills is gathered in,
26the lambs will provide you with clothing,
    and the goats with the price of a field.
27You will have plenty of goats' milk
    to feed you and your family
    and to nourish your servant girls.

28 THE WICKED man flees though no one
        pursues,
    but the righteous are as bold as a lion.

2When a country is rebellious, it has many
        rulers,
    but a man of understanding and knowledge
        maintains order.

3A ruler[b] who oppresses the poor
    is like a driving rain that leaves no crops.

4Those who forsake the law praise the wicked,
    but those who keep the law resist them.

5Evil men do not understand justice,
    but those who seek the LORD understand it
        fully.

6Better a poor man whose walk is blameless
    than a rich man whose ways are perverse.

7He who keeps the law is a discerning son,
    but a companion of gluttons disgraces his
        father.

8He who increases his wealth by exorbitant
        interest
    amasses it for another, who will be kind to
        the poor.

9If anyone turns a deaf ear to the law,
    even his prayers are detestable.

10He who leads the upright along an evil path
    will fall into his own trap,
    but the blameless will receive a good
        inheritance.

a 20 Hebrew *Sheol and Abaddon*   b 3 Or *A poor man*

Living Bible

15A constant dripping on a rainy day and a cranky woman are much alike! 16You can no more stop her complaints than you can stop the wind or hold onto anything with oil-slick hands.

17A friendly discussion is as stimulating as the sparks that fly when iron strikes iron.

18A workman may eat from the orchard he tends; anyone should be rewarded who protects another's interests.

19A mirror reflects a man's face, but what he is really like is shown by the kind of friends he chooses.

20Ambitionᶜ and death are alike in this: neither is ever satisfied.

21The purity of silver and gold can be tested in a crucible, but a man is tested by his reaction to men's praise.

22You can't separate a rebel from his foolishness though you crush him to powder.

23, 24Riches can disappear fast. And the king's crown doesn't stay in his family forever—so watch your businessᵈ interests closely. Know the state of your flocks and your herds; 25, 26, 27then there will be lamb's wool enough for clothing, and goat's milk enough for food for all your household after the hay is harvested, and the new crop appears, and the mountain grasses are gathered in.

New Revised Standard

15 A continual dripping on a rainy day
      and a contentious wife are alike;
16 to restrain her is to restrain the wind
      or to grasp oil in the right hand.ᵉ
17 Iron sharpens iron,
      and one person sharpens the witsᶠ of
        another.
18 Anyone who tends a fig tree will eat its fruit,
      and anyone who takes care of a master will
        be honored.
19 Just as water reflects the face,
      so one human heart reflects another.
20 Sheol and Abaddon are never satisfied,
      and human eyes are never satisfied.
21 The crucible is for silver, and the furnace is
        for gold,
      so a person is testedᵍ by being praised.
22 Crush a fool in a mortar with a pestle
        along with crushed grain,
      but the folly will not be driven out.
23 Know well the condition of your flocks,
      and give attention to your herds;
24 for riches do not last forever,
      nor a crown for all generations.
25 When the grass is gone, and new growth
        appears,
      and the herbage of the mountains is
        gathered,
26 the lambs will provide your clothing,
      and the goats the price of a field;
27 there will be enough goats' milk for your
        food,
      for the food of your household
      and nourishment for your servant-girls.

28 THE WICKED flee when no one is chasing them! But the godly are bold as lions!

2When there is moral rot within a nation, its government topples easily; but with honest, sensible leaders there is stability.

3When a poor man oppresses those even poorer, he is like an unexpected flood sweeping away their last hope.

4To complain about the law is to praise wickedness. To obey the law is to fight evil.

5Evil men don't understand the importance of justice, but those who follow the Lord are much concerned about it.

6Better to be poor and honest than rich and a cheater.

7Young men who are wise obey the law; a son who is a member of a lawless gang is a shame to his father.

8Income from exploiting the poor will end up in the hands of someone who pities them.

9God doesn't listen to the prayers of those who flout the law.

10A curse on those who lead astray the godly. But men who encourage the upright to do good shall be given a worthwhile reward.

28 THE WICKED flee when no one pursues, but the righteous are as bold as a lion.

2 When a land rebels
      it has many rulers;
    but with an intelligent ruler
      there is lasting order.ᵉ
3 A rulerʰ who oppresses the poor
      is a beating rain that leaves no food.
4 Those who forsake the law praise the wicked,
      but those who keep the law struggle against
        them.
5 The evil do not understand justice,
      but those who seek the LORD understand it
        completely.
6 Better to be poor and walk in integrity
      than to be crooked in one's ways even
        though rich.
7 Those who keep the law are wise children,
      but companions of gluttons shame their
        parents.
8 One who augments wealth by exorbitant
        interest
      gathers it for another who is kind to the
        poor.
9 When one will not listen to the law,
      even one's prayers are an abomination.
10 Those who mislead the upright into evil ways
      will fall into pits of their own making,
      but the blameless will have a goodly
        inheritance.

ᶜ 27:20 Ambition, literally, "A man's eyes." Possibly the reference is to lust.
ᵈ 27:23, 24 business, implied.

ᵉ Meaning of Heb uncertain   ᶠ Heb face   ᵍ Heb lacks is tested   ʰ Cn: Heb A poor person

King James

11The rich man *is* wise in his own conceit; but the poor that hath understanding searcheth him out.

12When righteous *men* do rejoice, *there is* great glory: but when the wicked rise, a man is hidden.

13He that covereth his sins shall not prosper: but whoso confesseth and forsaketh *them* shall have mercy.

14Happy *is* the man that feareth always: but he that hardeneth his heart shall fall into mischief.

15*As* a roaring lion, and a ranging bear; *so is* a wicked ruler over the poor people.

16The prince that wanteth understanding *is* also a great oppressor: *but* he that hateth covetousness shall prolong *his* days.

17A man that doeth violence to the blood of *any* person shall flee to the pit; let no man stay him.

18Whoso walketh uprightly shall be saved: but *he that is* perverse *in his* ways shall fall at once.

19He that tilleth his land shall have plenty of bread: but he that followeth after vain *persons* shall have poverty enough.

20A faithful man shall abound with blessings: but he that maketh haste to be rich shall not be innocent.

21To have respect of persons *is* not good: for for a piece of bread *that* man will transgress.

22He that hasteth to be rich *hath* an evil eye, and considereth not that poverty shall come upon him.

23He that rebuketh a man afterwards shall find more favour than he that flattereth with the tongue.

24Whoso robbeth his father or his mother, and saith, *It is* no transgression; the same *is* the companion of a destroyer.

25He that is of a proud heart stirreth up strife: but he that putteth his trust in the LORD shall be made fat.

26He that trusteth in his own heart is a fool: but whoso walketh wisely, he shall be delivered.

27He that giveth unto the poor shall not lack: but he that hideth his eyes shall have many a curse.

28When the wicked rise, men hide themselves: but when they perish, the righteous increase.

29 HE, THAT being often reproved hardeneth *his* neck, shall suddenly be destroyed, and that without remedy.

2When the righteous are in authority, the people rejoice: but when the wicked beareth rule, the people mourn.

New International

11A rich man may be wise in his own eyes,
　　but a poor man who has discernment sees
　　　through him.

12When the righteous triumph, there is great
　　elation;
　　but when the wicked rise to power, men go
　　　into hiding.

13He who conceals his sins does not prosper,
　　but whoever confesses and renounces them
　　　finds mercy.

14Blessed is the man who always fears the LORD,
　　but he who hardens his heart falls into
　　　trouble.

15Like a roaring lion or a charging bear
　　is a wicked man ruling over a helpless
　　　people.

16A tyrannical ruler lacks judgment,
　　but he who hates ill-gotten gain will enjoy a
　　　long life.

17A man tormented by the guilt of murder
　　will be a fugitive till death;
　　let no one support him.

18He whose walk is blameless is kept safe,
　　but he whose ways are perverse will suddenly
　　　fall.

19He who works his land will have abundant
　　food,
　　but the one who chases fantasies will have his
　　　fill of poverty.

20A faithful man will be richly blessed,
　　but one eager to get rich will not go
　　　unpunished.

21To show partiality is not good—
　　yet a man will do wrong for a piece of bread.

22A stingy man is eager to get rich
　　and is unaware that poverty awaits him.

23He who rebukes a man will in the end gain
　　more favor
　　than he who has a flattering tongue.

24He who robs his father or mother
　　and says, "It's not wrong"—
　　he is partner to him who destroys.

25A greedy man stirs up dissension,
　　but he who trusts in the LORD will prosper.

26He who trusts in himself is a fool,
　　but he who walks in wisdom is kept safe.

27He who gives to the poor will lack nothing,
　　but he who closes his eyes to them receives
　　　many curses.

28When the wicked rise to power, people go into
　　hiding;
　　but when the wicked perish, the righteous
　　　thrive.

29 A MAN who remains stiff-necked after many
　　rebukes
　　will suddenly be destroyed—without remedy.

2When the righteous thrive, the people rejoice;
　　when the wicked rule, the people groan.

Living Bible

11Rich men are conceited, but their real poverty is evident to the poor.

12When the godly are successful, everyone is glad. When the wicked succeed, everyone is sad.

13A man who refuses to admit his mistakes can never be successful. But if he confesses and forsakes them, he gets another chance.

14Blessed is the man who reveres God, but the man who doesn't care is headed for serious trouble.

15A wicked ruler is as dangerous to the poor as a lion or bear attacking them.

16Only a stupid prince will oppress his people, but a king will have a long reign if he hates dishonesty and bribes.

17A murderer's conscience will drive him into hell. Don't stop him!

18Good men will be rescued from harm, but cheaters will be destroyed.

19Hard work brings prosperity; playing around brings poverty.

20The man who wants to do right will get a rich reward. But the man who wants to get rich quick will quickly fail.

21Giving preferred treatment to rich people is a clear case of selling one's soul for a piece of bread.

22Trying to get rich quick is evil and leads to poverty.

23In the end, people appreciate frankness more than flattery.

24A man who robs his parents and says, "What's wrong with that?" is no better than a murderer.

25Greed causes fighting; trusting God leads to prosperity.

26A man is a fool to trust himself! But those who use God's wisdom are safe.

27If you give to the poor, your needs will be supplied! But a curse upon those who close their eyes to poverty.

28When the wicked prosper, good men go away; when the wicked meet disaster, good men return.

New Revised Standard

11 The rich is wise in self-esteem,
      but an intelligent poor person sees through
         the pose.

12 When the righteous triumph, there is great
         glory,
      but when the wicked prevail, people go into
         hiding.

13 No one who conceals transgressions will
         prosper,
      but one who confesses and forsakes them
         will obtain mercy.

14 Happy is the one who is never without fear,
      but one who is hard-hearted will fall into
         calamity.

15 Like a roaring lion or a charging bear
      is a wicked ruler over a poor people.

16 A ruler who lacks understanding is a cruel
         oppressor;
      but one who hates unjust gain will enjoy a
         long life.

17 If someone is burdened with the blood of
         another,
      let that killer be a fugitive until death;
      let no one offer assistance.

18 One who walks in integrity will be safe,
      but whoever follows crooked ways will fall
         into the Pit.a

19 Anyone who tills the land will have plenty of
         bread,
      but one who follows worthless pursuits will
         have plenty of poverty.

20 The faithful will abound with blessings,
      but one who is in a hurry to be rich will not
         go unpunished.

21 To show partiality is not good—
      yet for a piece of bread a person may do
         wrong.

22 The miser is in a hurry to get rich
      and does not know that loss is sure to
         come.

23 Whoever rebukes a person will afterward find
         more favor
      than one who flatters with the tongue.

24 Anyone who robs father or mother
      and says, "That is no crime,"
      is partner to a thug.

25 The greedy person stirs up strife,
      but whoever trusts in the LORD will be
         enriched.

26 Those who trust in their own wits are fools;
      but those who walk in wisdom come
         through safely.

27 Whoever gives to the poor will lack nothing,
      but one who turns a blind eye will get many
         a curse.

28 When the wicked prevail, people go into
         hiding;
      but when they perish, the righteous
         increase.

29 THE MAN who is often reproved but refuses to accept criticism will suddenly be broken and never have another chance.

2With good men in authority, the people rejoice; but with the wicked in power, they groan.

29 ONE WHO is often reproved, yet remains
         stubborn,
      will suddenly be broken beyond healing.
2 When the righteous are in authority, the
         people rejoice;
      but when the wicked rule, the people groan.

a Syr: Heb *fall all at once*

King James

³Whoso loveth wisdom rejoiceth his father: but he that keepeth company with harlots spendeth *his* substance.

⁴The king by judgment establisheth the land: but he that receiveth gifts overthroweth it.

⁵A man that flattereth his neighbour spreadeth a net for his feet.

⁶In the transgression of an evil man *there is* a snare: but the righteous doth sing and rejoice.

⁷The righteous considereth the cause of the poor: *but* the wicked regardeth not to know *it.*

⁸Scornful men bring a city into a snare: but wise *men* turn away wrath.

⁹*If* a wise man contendeth with a foolish man, whether he rage or laugh, *there is* no rest.

¹⁰The bloodthirsty hate the upright: but the just seek his soul.

¹¹A fool uttereth all his mind: but a wise *man* keepeth it in till afterwards.

¹²If a ruler hearken to lies, all his servants *are* wicked.

¹³The poor and the deceitful man meet together: the LORD lighteneth both their eyes.

¹⁴The king that faithfully judgeth the poor, his throne shall be established for ever.

¹⁵The rod and reproof give wisdom: but a child left *to himself* bringeth his mother to shame.

¹⁶When the wicked are multiplied, transgression increaseth: but the righteous shall see their fall.

¹⁷Correct thy son, and he shall give thee rest; yea, he shall give delight unto thy soul.

¹⁸Where *there is* no vision, the people perish: but he that keepeth the law, happy *is* he.

¹⁹A servant will not be corrected by words: for though he understand he will not answer.

²⁰Seest thou a man *that is* hasty in his words? *there is* more hope of a fool than of him.

²¹He that delicately bringeth up his servant from a child shall have him become *his* son at the length.

²²An angry man stirreth up strife, and a furious man aboundeth in transgression.

²³A man's pride shall bring him low: but honour shall uphold the humble in spirit.

²⁴Whoso is partner with a thief hateth his own soul: he heareth cursing, and betrayeth *it* not.

²⁵The fear of man bringeth a snare: but whoso putteth his trust in the LORD shall be safe.

²⁶Many seek the ruler's favour; but *every* man's judgment *cometh* from the LORD.

²⁷An unjust man *is* an abomination to the just: and *he that is* upright in the way *is* abomination to the wicked.

New International

³A man who loves wisdom brings joy to his father,
but a companion of prostitutes squanders his wealth.

⁴By justice a king gives a country stability,
but one who is greedy for bribes tears it down.

⁵Whoever flatters his neighbor
is spreading a net for his feet.

⁶An evil man is snared by his own sin,
but a righteous one can sing and be glad.

⁷The righteous care about justice for the poor,
but the wicked have no such concern.

⁸Mockers stir up a city,
but wise men turn away anger.

⁹If a wise man goes to court with a fool,
the fool rages and scoffs, and there is no peace.

¹⁰Bloodthirsty men hate a man of integrity
and seek to kill the upright.

¹¹A fool gives full vent to his anger,
but a wise man keeps himself under control.

¹²If a ruler listens to lies,
all his officials become wicked.

¹³The poor man and the oppressor have this in common:
The LORD gives sight to the eyes of both.

¹⁴If a king judges the poor with fairness,
his throne will always be secure.

¹⁵The rod of correction imparts wisdom,
but a child left to himself disgraces his mother.

¹⁶When the wicked thrive, so does sin,
but the righteous will see their downfall.

¹⁷Discipline your son, and he will give you peace;
he will bring delight to your soul.

¹⁸Where there is no revelation, the people cast off restraint;
but blessed is he who keeps the law.

¹⁹A servant cannot be corrected by mere words;
though he understands, he will not respond.

²⁰Do you see a man who speaks in haste?
There is more hope for a fool than for him.

²¹If a man pampers his servant from youth,
he will bring grief[a] in the end.

²²An angry man stirs up dissension,
and a hot-tempered one commits many sins.

²³A man's pride brings him low,
but a man of lowly spirit gains honor.

²⁴The accomplice of a thief is his own enemy;
he is put under oath and dare not testify.

²⁵Fear of man will prove to be a snare,
but whoever trusts in the LORD is kept safe.

²⁶Many seek an audience with a ruler,
but it is from the LORD that man gets justice.

²⁷The righteous detest the dishonest;
the wicked detest the upright.

---

a 21 The meaning of the Hebrew for this word is uncertain.

Living Bible

3A wise son makes his father happy, but a lad who hangs around with prostitutes disgraces him.

4A just king gives stability to his nation, but one who demands bribes destroys it.

5, 6Flattery is a trap; evil men are caught in it, but good men stay away and sing for joy.

7The good man knows the poor man's rights; the godless don't care.

8Fools start fights everywhere while wise men try to keep peace.

9There's no use arguing with a fool. He only rages and scoffs, and tempers flare.

10The godly pray for those who long to kill them.

11A rebel shouts in anger; a wise man holds his temper in and cools it.

12A wicked ruler will have wicked aides on his staff.

13Rich and poor are alike in this: each depends on God for light.

14A king who is fair to the poor shall have a long reign.

15Scolding and spanking a child helps him to learn. Left to himself, he brings shame to his mother.

16When rulers are wicked, their people are too; but good men will live to see the tyrant's downfall.

17Discipline your son and he will give you happiness and peace of mind.

18Where there is ignorance of God, crime runs wild; but what a wonderful thing it is for a nation to know and keep his laws.

19Sometimesᵇ mere words are not enough—discipline is needed. For the words may not be heeded.

20There is more hope for a fool than for a man of quick temper.

21Pamper a servant from childhood, and he will expect you to treat him as a son!

22A hot-tempered man starts fights and gets into all kinds of trouble.

23Pride ends in a fall, while humility brings honor.

24A man who assists a thief must really hate himself! For he knows the consequence but does it anyway.

25Fear of man is a dangerous trap, but to trust in God means safety.

26Do you want justice? Don't fawn on the judge, but ask the Lord for it!

27The good hate the badness of the wicked. The wicked hate the goodness of the good.

New Revised Standard

3 A child who loves wisdom makes a parent glad,
but to keep company with prostitutes is to squander one's substance.

4 By justice a king gives stability to the land,
but one who makes heavy exactions ruins it.

5 Whoever flatters a neighbor
is spreading a net for the neighbor's feet.

6 In the transgression of the evil there is a snare,
but the righteous sing and rejoice.

7 The righteous know the rights of the poor;
the wicked have no such understanding.

8 Scoffers set a city aflame,
but the wise turn away wrath.

9 If the wise go to law with fools,
there is ranting and ridicule without relief.

10 The bloodthirsty hate the blameless,
and they seek the life of the upright.

11 A fool gives full vent to anger,
but the wise quietly holds it back.

12 If a ruler listens to falsehood,
all his officials will be wicked.

13 The poor and the oppressor have this in common:
the LORD gives light to the eyes of both.

14 If a king judges the poor with equity,
his throne will be established forever.

15 The rod and reproof give wisdom,
but a mother is disgraced by a neglected child.

16 When the wicked are in authority, transgression increases,
but the righteous will look upon their downfall.

17 Discipline your children, and they will give you rest;
they will give delight to your heart.

18 Where there is no prophecy, the people cast off restraint,
but happy are those who keep the law.

19 By mere words servants are not disciplined,
for though they understand, they will not give heed.

20 Do you see someone who is hasty in speech?
There is more hope for a fool than for anyone like that.

21 A slave pampered from childhood
will come to a bad end.ᶜ

22 One given to anger stirs up strife,
and the hothead causes much transgression.

23 A person's pride will bring humiliation,
but one who is lowly in spirit will obtain honor.

24 To be a partner of a thief is to hate one's own life;
one hears the victim's curse, but discloses nothing.ᵈ

25 The fear of othersᵉ lays a snare,
but one who trusts in the LORD is secure.

26 Many seek the favor of a ruler,
but it is from the LORD that one gets justice.

27 The unjust are an abomination to the righteous,
but the upright are an abomination to the wicked.

ᵇ 29:19 *Sometimes*, literally, "for a servant."

ᶜ Vg: Meaning of Heb uncertain   ᵈ Meaning of Heb uncertain   ᵉ Or *human fear*

King James

30 THE WORDS of Agur the son of Jakeh, *even* the prophecy: the man spake unto Ithiel, even unto Ithiel and Ucal,

2Surely I *am* more brutish than *any* man, and have not the understanding of a man.

3I neither learned wisdom, nor have the knowledge of the holy.

4Who hath ascended up into heaven, or descended? who hath gathered the wind in his fists? who hath bound the waters in a garment? who hath established all the ends of the earth? what *is* his name, and what *is* his son's name, if thou canst tell?

5Every word of God *is* pure: he *is* a shield unto them that put their trust in him.

6Add thou not unto his words, lest he reprove thee, and thou be found a liar.

7Two *things* have I required of thee; deny me *them* not before I die:

8Remove far from me vanity and lies: give me neither poverty nor riches; feed me with food convenient for me:

9Lest I be full, and deny *thee,* and say, Who *is* the LORD? or lest I be poor, and steal, and take the name of my God *in vain.*

10Accuse not a servant unto his master, lest he curse thee, and thou be found guilty.

11*There is* a generation *that* curseth their father, and doth not bless their mother.

12*There is* a generation *that are* pure in their own eyes, and *yet* is not washed from their filthiness.

13*There is* a generation, O how lofty are their eyes! and their eyelids are lifted up.

14*There is* a generation, whose teeth *are as* swords, and their jaw teeth *as* knives, to devour the poor from off the earth, and the needy from *among* men.

15The horseleach hath two daughters, *crying,* Give, give. There are three *things that* are never satisfied, *yea,* four *things* say not, *It is* enough:

16The grave; and the barren womb; the earth *that* is not filled with water; and the fire *that* saith not, *It is* enough.

17The eye *that* mocketh at *his* father, and despiseth to obey *his* mother, the ravens of the valley shall pick it out, and the young eagles shall eat it.

18There be three *things which* are too wonderful for me, yea, four which I know not:

19The way of an eagle in the air; the way of a serpent upon a rock; the way of a ship in the midst of the sea; and the way of a man with a maid.

New International

Sayings of Agur

30 THE SAYINGS of Agur son of Jakeh—an oracle:a

This man declared to Ithiel,
    to Ithiel and to Ucal:b

2"I am the most ignorant of men;
    I do not have a man's understanding.
3I have not learned wisdom,
    nor have I knowledge of the Holy One.
4Who has gone up to heaven and come down?
    Who has gathered up the wind in the hollow
        of his hands?
Who has wrapped up the waters in his cloak?
    Who has established all the ends of the earth?
What is his name, and the name of his son?
    Tell me if you know!

5"Every word of God is flawless;
    he is a shield to those who take refuge in
        him.
6Do not add to his words,
    or he will rebuke you and prove you a liar.

7"Two things I ask of you, O LORD;
    do not refuse me before I die:
8Keep falsehood and lies far from me;
    give me neither poverty nor riches,
    but give me only my daily bread.
9Otherwise, I may have too much and disown
        you
    and say, 'Who is the LORD?'
Or I may become poor and steal,
    and so dishonor the name of my God.

10"Do not slander a servant to his master,
    or he will curse you, and you will pay for it.

11"There are those who curse their fathers
    and do not bless their mothers;
12those who are pure in their own eyes
    and yet are not cleansed of their filth;
13those whose eyes are ever so haughty,
    whose glances are so disdainful;
14those whose teeth are swords
    and whose jaws are set with knives
to devour the poor from the earth,
    the needy from among mankind.

15"The leech has two daughters.
    'Give! Give!' they cry.

"There are three things that are never satisfied,
    four that never say, 'Enough!':
16the grave,c the barren womb,
    land, which is never satisfied with water,
    and fire, which never says, 'Enough!'

17"The eye that mocks a father,
    that scorns obedience to a mother,
will be pecked out by the ravens of the valley,
    will be eaten by the vultures.

18"There are three things that are too amazing for
        me,
    four that I do not understand:
19the way of an eagle in the sky,
    the way of a snake on a rock,
the way of a ship on the high seas,
    and the way of a man with a maiden.

---

a *1* Or *Jakeh of Massa* b *1* Masoretic Text; with a different word division of the Hebrew *declared,* "I am weary, O God; / I am weary, O God, and faint. c *16* Hebrew *Sheol*

Living Bible

New Revised Standard

30 THESE ARE the messages of Agur, son of Jakeh addressed to Ithiel and Ucal:

²I am tired out, O God, and ready to die. I am too stupid even to call myself a human being! ³I cannot understand man,ᵈ let alone God. ⁴Who else but God goes back and forth to heaven? Who else holds the wind in his fists, and wraps up the oceans in his cloak? Who but God has created the world? If there is any other, what is his name—and his Son's name—if you know it?

⁵Every word of God proves true. He defends all who come to him for protection. ⁶Do not add to his words, lest he rebuke you, and you be found a liar.

⁷O God, I beg two favors from you before I die: ⁸First, help me never to tell a lie. Second, give me neither poverty nor riches! Give me just enough to satisfy my needs! ⁹For if I grow rich, I may become content without God. And if I am too poor, I may steal, and thus insult God's holy name.

¹⁰Never falsely accuse a man to his employer, lest he curse you for your sin.

¹¹,¹²There are those who curse their father and mother, and feel themselves faultless despite their many sins. ¹³,¹⁴They are proud beyond description, arrogant, disdainful. They devour the poor with teeth as sharp as knives!

¹⁵,¹⁶There are two things never satisfied, like a leech forever craving more: no, three things! no, four!

Hell

The barren womb

A barren desert

Fire

¹⁷A man who mocks his father and despises his mother shall have his eye plucked out by ravens and eaten by vultures.

¹⁸,¹⁹There are three things too wonderful for me to understand—no, four!

How an eagle glides through the sky.

How a serpent crawls upon a rock.

How a ship finds its way across the heaving ocean.

The growth of love between a man and a girl.ᵉ

Sayings of Agur

30 THE WORDS of Agur son of Jakeh. An oracle.

Thus says the man: I am weary, O God,
 I am weary, O God. How can I prevail?ᶠ
2 Surely I am too stupid to be human;
 I do not have human understanding.
3 I have not learned wisdom,
 nor have I knowledge of the holy ones.ᵍ
4 Who has ascended to heaven and come down?
 Who has gathered the wind in the hollow of
   the hand?
 Who has wrapped up the waters in a garment?
 Who has established all the ends of the
   earth?
 What is the person's name?
 And what is the name of the person's child?
 Surely you know!

5 Every word of God proves true;
 he is a shield to those who take refuge in
   him.
6 Do not add to his words,
 or else he will rebuke you, and you will be
   found a liar.

7 Two things I ask of you;
 do not deny them to me before I die:
8 Remove far from me falsehood and lying;
 give me neither poverty nor riches;
 feed me with the food that I need,
9 or I shall be full, and deny you,
 and say, "Who is the LORD?"
 or I shall be poor, and steal,
 and profane the name of my God.

10 Do not slander a servant to a master,
 or the servant will curse you, and you will
   be held guilty.

11 There are those who curse their fathers
 and do not bless their mothers.
12 There are those who are pure in their own
   eyes
 yet are not cleansed of their filthiness.
13 There are those—how lofty are their eyes,
 how high their eyelids lift!
14 There are those whose teeth are swords,
 whose teeth are knives,
 to devour the poor from off the earth,
 the needy from among mortals.

15 The leechʰ has two daughters;
 "Give, give," they cry.
 Three things are never satisfied;
 four never say, "Enough":
16 Sheol, the barren womb,
 the earth ever thirsty for water,
 and the fire that never says, "Enough."ʰ

17 The eye that mocks a father
 and scorns to obey a mother
 will be pecked out by the ravens of the valley
 and eaten by the vultures.

18 Three things are too wonderful for me;
 four I do not understand:
19 the way of an eagle in the sky,
 the way of a snake on a rock,
 the way of a ship on the high seas,
 and the way of a man with a girl.

ᵈ 30:3 *I cannot understand man*, literally, "I have not learned wisdom."
ᵉ 30:18, 19 *The growth of love between a man and a girl*, literally, "the way of a man with a maid." Some linguists believe the meaning is, "why a girl will let herself be seduced."

ᶠ Or *I am spent*. Meaning of Heb uncertain   ᵍ Or *Holy One*   ʰ Meaning of Heb uncertain

King James

20Such *is* the way of an adulterous woman; she eateth, and wipeth her mouth, and saith, I have done no wickedness.

21For three *things* the earth is disquieted, and for four *which* it cannot bear:

22For a servant when he reigneth; and a fool when he is filled with meat;

23For an odious *woman* when she is married; and an handmaid that is heir to her mistress.

24There be four *things which are* little upon the earth, but they *are* exceeding wise:

25The ants *are* a people not strong, yet they prepare their meat in the summer;

26The conies *are but* a feeble folk, yet make they their houses in the rocks;

27The locusts have no king, yet go they forth all of them by bands;

28The spider taketh hold with her hands, and is in kings' palaces.

29There be three *things* which go well, yea, four are comely in going:

30A lion *which is* strongest among beasts, and turneth not away for any;

31A greyhound; an he goat also; and a king, against whom *there is* no rising up.

32If thou hast done foolishly in lifting up thyself, or if thou hast thought evil, *lay* thine hand upon thy mouth.

33Surely the churning of milk bringeth forth butter, and the wringing of the nose bringeth forth blood: so the forcing of wrath bringeth forth strife.

31 THE WORDS of king Lemuel, the prophecy that his mother taught him.

2What, my son? and what, the son of my womb? and what, the son of my vows?

3Give not thy strength unto women, nor thy ways to that which destroyeth kings.

4*It is* not for kings, O Lemuel, *it is* not for kings to drink wine; nor for princes strong drink:

5Lest they drink, and forget the law, and pervert the judgment of any of the afflicted.

6Give strong drink unto him that is ready to perish, and wine unto those that be of heavy hearts.

7Let him drink, and forget his poverty, and remember his misery no more.

8Open thy mouth for the dumb in the cause of all such as are appointed to destruction.

9Open thy mouth, judge righteously, and plead the cause of the poor and needy.

10¶ Who can find a virtuous woman? for her price *is* far above rubies.

11The heart of her husband doth safely trust in her, so that he shall have no need of spoil.

12She will do him good and not evil all the days of her life.

New International

20"This is the way of an adulteress:
  She eats and wipes her mouth
  and says, 'I've done nothing wrong.'

21"Under three things the earth trembles,
  under four it cannot bear up:

22a servant who becomes king,
  a fool who is full of food,

23an unloved woman who is married,
  and a maidservant who displaces her mistress.

24"Four things on earth are small,
  yet they are extremely wise:

25Ants are creatures of little strength,
  yet they store up their food in the summer;

26coneys[a] are creatures of little power,
  yet they make their home in the crags;

27locusts have no king,
  yet they advance together in ranks;

28a lizard can be caught with the hand,
  yet it is found in kings' palaces.

29"There are three things that are stately in their
      stride,
  four that move with stately bearing:

30a lion, mighty among beasts,
  who retreats before nothing;

31a strutting rooster, a he-goat,
  and a king with his army around him.[b]

32"If you have played the fool and exalted
      yourself,
  or if you have planned evil,
  clap your hand over your mouth!

33For as churning the milk produces butter,
  and as twisting the nose produces blood,
  so stirring up anger produces strife."

Sayings of King Lemuel

31 THE SAYINGS of King Lemuel—an oracle[c]
  his mother taught him:

2"O my son, O son of my womb,
  O son of my vows,[d]

3do not spend your strength on women,
  your vigor on those who ruin kings.

4"It is not for kings, O Lemuel—
  not for kings to drink wine,
  not for rulers to crave beer,

5lest they drink and forget what the law decrees,
  and deprive all the oppressed of their rights.

6Give beer to those who are perishing,
  wine to those who are in anguish;

7let them drink and forget their poverty
  and remember their misery no more.

8"Speak up for those who cannot speak for
      themselves,
  for the rights of all who are destitute.

9Speak up and judge fairly;
  defend the rights of the poor and needy."

Epilogue: The Wife of Noble Character

10[e]A wife of noble character who can find?
  She is worth far more than rubies.

11Her husband has full confidence in her
  and lacks nothing of value.

12She brings him good, not harm,
  all the days of her life.

---

a 26 That is, the hyrax or rock badger   b 31 Or *king secure against revolt*
c 1 Or *of Lemuel king of Massa, which*   d 2 Or / *the answer to my prayers*
e 10 Verses 10-31 are an acrostic, each verse beginning with a successive
letter of the Hebrew alphabet.

Living Bible

20There is another thing too: how a prostitute can sin and then say, "What's wrong with that?"

21, 22, 23There are three things that make the earth tremble—no, four it cannot stand:

A slave who becomes a king.

A rebel who prospers.

A bitter woman when she finally marries.

A servant girl who marries her mistress' husband.f

24-28There are four things that are small but unusually wise:

Ants: they aren't strong, but store up food for the winter.

Cliff badgers: delicate little animals who protect themselves by living among the rocks.

The locusts: though they have no leader, they stay together in swarms.

The lizards: they are easy to catch and kill, yet are found even in king's palaces!

29, 30, 31There are three stately monarchs in the earth—no, four:

The lion, king of the animals. He won't turn aside for anyone.

The peacock.

The male goat.

A king as he leads his army.

32If you have been a fool by being proud or plotting evil, don't brag about it—cover your mouth with your hand in shame.

33As the churning of cream yields butter, and a blow to the nose causes bleeding, so anger causes quarrels.

31 THESE ARE the wise sayings of King Lemuel of Massa,g taught to him at his mother's knee:

2O my son, whom I have dedicated to the Lord, 3do not spend your time with women—the royal pathway to destruction.

4And it is not for kings, O Lemuel, to drink wine and whiskey. 5For if they drink they may forget their duties and be unable to give justice to those who are oppressed. 6, 7Hard liquor is for sick men at the brink of death, and wine for those in deep depression. Let them drink to forget their poverty and misery.

8You should defend those who cannot help themselves. 9Yes, speak up for the poor and helpless, and see that they get justice.

10If you can find a truly good wife, she is worth more than precious gems! 11Her husband can trust her, and she will richly satisfy his needs. 12She will not hinder him, but help him all her life. 13She finds wool and flax and

New Revised Standard

20 This is the way of an adulteress:
   she eats, and wipes her mouth,
   and says, "I have done no wrong."

21 Under three things the earth trembles;
   under four it cannot bear up:
22 a slave when he becomes king,
   and a fool when glutted with food;
23 an unloved woman when she gets a husband,
   and a maid when she succeeds her mistress.

24 Four things on earth are small,
   yet they are exceedingly wise:
25 the ants are a people without strength,
   yet they provide their food in the summer;
26 the badgers are a people without power,
   yet they make their homes in the rocks;
27 the locusts have no king,
   yet all of them march in rank;
28 the lizardh can be grasped in the hand,
   yet it is found in kings' palaces.

29 Three things are stately in their stride;
   four are stately in their gait:
30 the lion, which is mightiest among wild animals
   and does not turn back before any;
31 the strutting rooster,i the he-goat,
   and a king striding beforej his people.

32 If you have been foolish, exalting yourself,
   or if you have been devising evil,
   put your hand on your mouth.
33 For as pressing milk produces curds,
   and pressing the nose produces blood,
   so pressing anger produces strife.

The Teaching of King Lemuel's Mother

31 THE WORDS of King Lemuel. An oracle tha his mother taught him:

2 No, my son! No, son of my womb!
   No, son of my vows!
3 Do not give your strength to women,
   your ways to those who destroy kings.
4 It is not for kings, O Lemuel,
   it is not for kings to drink wine,
   or for rulers to desirek strong drink;
5 or else they will drink and forget what has been decreed,
   and will pervert the rights of all the afflicted.
6 Give strong drink to one who is perishing,
   and wine to those in bitter distress;
7 let them drink and forget their poverty,
   and remember their misery no more.
8 Speak out for those who cannot speak,
   for the rights of all the destitute.l
9 Speak out, judge righteously,
   defend the rights of the poor and needy.

Ode to a Capable Wife

10 A capable wife who can find?
   She is far more precious than jewels.
11 The heart of her husband trusts in her,
   and he will have no lack of gain.
12 She does him good, and not harm,
   all the days of her life.

---

f 30:21-23 marries her mistress' husband, literally, "who succeeds her mistress." g 31:1 King Lemuel of Massa, or, "of King Lemuel the oracle."

h Or spider i Gk Syr Tg Compare Vg: Meaning of Heb uncertain j Meaning of Heb uncertain k Cn: Heb where l Heb all children of passing away

King James

13She seeketh wool, and flax, and worketh willingly with her hands.

14She is like the merchants' ships; she bringeth her food from afar.

15She riseth also while it is yet night, and giveth meat to her household, and a portion to her maidens.

16She considereth a field, and buyeth it: with the fruit of her hands she planteth a vineyard.

17She girdeth her loins with strength, and strengtheneth her arms.

18She perceiveth that her merchandise is good: her candle goeth not out by night.

19She layeth her hands to the spindle, and her hands hold the distaff.

20She stretcheth out her hand to the poor; yea, she reacheth forth her hands to the needy.

21She is not afraid of the snow for her household: for all her household are clothed with scarlet.

22She maketh herself coverings of tapestry; her clothing is silk and purple.

23Her husband is known in the gates, when he sitteth among the elders of the land.

24She maketh fine linen, and selleth it; and delivereth girdles unto the merchant.

25Strength and honour are her clothing; and she shall rejoice in time to come.

26She openeth her mouth with wisdom; and in her tongue is the law of kindness.

27She looketh well to the ways of her household, and eateth not the bread of idleness.

28Her children arise up, and call her blessed; her husband also, and he praiseth her.

29Many daughters have done virtuously, but thou excellest them all.

30Favour is deceitful, and beauty is vain: but a woman that feareth the LORD, she shall be praised.

31Give her of the fruit of her hands; and let her own works praise her in the gates.

New International

13She selects wool and flax
   and works with eager hands.

14She is like the merchant ships,
   bringing her food from afar.

15She gets up while it is still dark;
   she provides food for her family
   and portions for her servant girls.

16She considers a field and buys it;
   out of her earnings she plants a vineyard.

17She sets about her work vigorously;
   her arms are strong for her tasks.

18She sees that her trading is profitable,
   and her lamp does not go out at night.

19In her hand she holds the distaff
   and grasps the spindle with her fingers.

20She opens her arms to the poor
   and extends her hands to the needy.

21When it snows, she has no fear for her
   household;
   for all of them are clothed in scarlet.

22She makes coverings for her bed;
   she is clothed in fine linen and purple.

23Her husband is respected at the city gate,
   where he takes his seat among the elders of
   the land.

24She makes linen garments and sells them,
   and supplies the merchants with sashes.

25She is clothed with strength and dignity;
   she can laugh at the days to come.

26She speaks with wisdom,
   and faithful instruction is on her tongue.

27She watches over the affairs of her household
   and does not eat the bread of idleness.

28Her children arise and call her blessed;
   her husband also, and he praises her:

29"Many women do noble things,
   but you surpass them all."

30Charm is deceptive, and beauty is fleeting;
   but a woman who fears the LORD is to be
   praised.

31Give her the reward she has earned,
   and let her works bring her praise at the city
   gate.

Living Bible

busily spins it. 14She buys imported foods, brought by ship from distant ports. 15She gets up before dawn to prepare breakfast for her household, and plans the day's work for her servant girls. 16She goes out to inspect a field, and buys it; with her own hands she plants a vineyard. 17She is energetic, a hard worker, 18and watches for bargains. She works far into the night!

19, 20She sews for the poor, and generously helps those in need. 21She has no fear of winter for her household, for she has made warm clothes for all of them. 22She also upholsters with finest tapestry; her own clothing is beautifully made—a purple gown of pure linen. 23Her husband is well known, for he sits in the council chamber with the other civic leaders. 24She makes belted linen garments to sell to the merchants.

25She is a woman of strength and dignity, and has no fear of old age. 26When she speaks, her words are wise, and kindness is the rule for everything she says. 27She watches carefully all that goes on throughout her household, and is never lazy. 28Her children stand and bless her; so does her husband. He praises her with these words: 29"There are many fine women in the world, but you are the best of them all!"

30Charm can be deceptive and beauty doesn't last, but a woman who fears and reverences God shall be greatly praised. 31Praise her for the many fine things she does. These good deeds of hers shall bring her honor and recognition from people of importance.a

New Revised Standard

13 She seeks wool and flax,
and works with willing hands.
14 She is like the ships of the merchant,
she brings her food from far away.
15 She rises while it is still night
and provides food for her household
and tasks for her servant-girls.
16 She considers a field and buys it;
with the fruit of her hands she plants a vineyard.
17 She girds herself with strength,
and makes her arms strong.
18 She perceives that her merchandise is profitable.
Her lamp does not go out at night.
19 She puts her hands to the distaff,
and her hands hold the spindle.
20 She opens her hand to the poor,
and reaches out her hands to the needy.
21 She is not afraid for her household when it snows,
for all her household are clothed in crimson.
22 She makes herself coverings;
her clothing is fine linen and purple.
23 Her husband is known in the city gates,
taking his seat among the elders of the land.
24 She makes linen garments and sells them;
she supplies the merchant with sashes.
25 Strength and dignity are her clothing,
and she laughs at the time to come.
26 She opens her mouth with wisdom,
and the teaching of kindness is on her tongue.
27 She looks well to the ways of her household,
and does not eat the bread of idleness.
28 Her children rise up and call her happy;
her husband too, and he praises her:
29 "Many women have done excellently,
but you surpass them all."
30 Charm is deceitful, and beauty is vain,
but a woman who fears the LORD is to be praised.
31 Give her a share in the fruit of her hands,
and let her works praise her in the city gates.

---

a 31:31 *These good deeds of hers shall bring her honor and recognition from people of importance*, literally, "Give her the fruit of her hands; and let her works praise her in the gates."

Ecclesiastes

OR, THE PREACHER

1 THE WORDS of the Preacher, the son of David, king in Jerusalem.

2Vanity of vanities, saith the Preacher, vanity of vanities; all *is* vanity.

3What profit hath a man of all his labour which he taketh under the sun?

4*One* generation passeth away, and *another* generation cometh: but the earth abideth for ever.

5The sun also ariseth, and the sun goeth down, and hasteth to his place where he arose.

6The wind goeth toward the south, and turneth about unto the north; it whirleth about continually, and the wind returneth again according to his circuits.

7All the rivers run into the sea; yet the sea *is* not full; unto the place from whence the rivers come, thither they return again.

8All things *are* full of labour; man cannot utter *it:* the eye is not satisfied with seeing, nor the ear filled with hearing.

9The thing that hath been, it *is that* which shall be; and that which is done *is* that which shall be done: and *there is* no new *thing* under the sun.

10Is there *any* thing whereof it may be said, See, this *is* new? it hath been already of old time, which was before us.

11*There is* no remembrance of former *things;* neither shall there be *any* remembrance of *things* that are to come with *those* that shall come after.

12¶ I the Preacher was king over Israel in Jerusalem.

13And I gave my heart to seek and search out by wisdom concerning all *things* that are done under heaven: this sore travail hath God given to the sons of man to be exercised therewith.

14I have seen all the works that are done under the sun; and, behold, all *is* vanity and vexation of spirit.

15*That which is* crooked cannot be made straight: and that which is wanting cannot be numbered.

16I communed with mine own heart, saying, Lo, I am come to great estate, and have gotten more wisdom than all *they* that have been before me in Jerusalem: yea, my heart had great experience of wisdom and knowledge.

17And I gave my heart to know wisdom, and to know madness and folly: I perceived that this also is vexation of spirit.

18For in much wisdom *is* much grief: and he that increaseth knowledge increaseth sorrow.

Ecclesiastes

Everything Is Meaningless

1 THE WORDS of the Teacher,[a] son of David, king in Jerusalem:

2"Meaningless! Meaningless!"
    says the Teacher.
"Utterly meaningless!
    Everything is meaningless."

3What does man gain from all his labor
    at which he toils under the sun?
4Generations come and generations go,
    but the earth remains forever.
5The sun rises and the sun sets,
    and hurries back to where it rises.
6The wind blows to the south
    and turns to the north;
round and round it goes,
    ever returning on its course.
7All streams flow into the sea,
    yet the sea is never full.
To the place the streams come from,
    there they return again.
8All things are wearisome,
    more than one can say.
The eye never has enough of seeing,
    nor the ear its fill of hearing.
9What has been will be again,
    what has been done will be done again;
    there is nothing new under the sun.
10Is there anything of which one can say,
    "Look! This is something new"?
It was here already, long ago;
    it was here before our time.
11There is no remembrance of men of old,
    and even those who are yet to come
will not be remembered
    by those who follow.

Wisdom Is Meaningless

12I, the Teacher, was king over Israel in Jerusalem. 13I devoted myself to study and to explore by wisdom all that is done under heaven. What a heavy burden God has laid on men! 14I have seen all the things that are done under the sun; all of them are meaningless, a chasing after the wind.

15What is twisted cannot be straightened;
    what is lacking cannot be counted.

16I thought to myself, "Look, I have grown and increased in wisdom more than anyone who has ruled over Jerusalem before me; I have experienced much of wisdom and knowledge." 17Then I applied myself to the understanding of wisdom, and also of madness and folly, but I learned that this, too, is a chasing after the wind.

18For with much wisdom comes much sorrow;
    the more knowledge, the more grief.

a *1* Or *leader of the assembly*; also in verses 2 and 12

Ecclesiastes

Ecclesiastes

Living Bible:

1 THE AUTHOR: Solomon[b] of Jerusalem, King David's son, "The Preacher."

2In my opinion, nothing is worthwhile; everything is futile. 3-7For what does a man get for all his hard work? Generations come and go but it makes no difference.[c] The sun rises and sets and hurries around to rise again. The wind blows south and north, here and there, twisting back and forth, getting nowhere.[d] The rivers run into the sea but the sea is never full, and the water returns again to the rivers, and flows again to the sea . . . 8-11everything is unutterably weary and tiresome. No matter how much we see, we are never satisfied; no matter how much we hear, we are not content.

History merely repeats itself. Nothing is truly new; it has all been done or said before. What can you point to that is new? How do you know it didn't exist long ages ago? We don't remember what happened in those former times, and in the future generations no one will remember what we have done back here.

12-15I, the Preacher, was king of Israel, living in Jerusalem. And I applied myself to search for understanding about everything in the universe. I discovered that the lot of man, which God has dealt to him, is not a happy one. It is all foolishness, chasing the wind. What is wrong cannot be righted; it is water over the dam; and there is no use thinking of what might have been.

16, 17, 18I said to myself, "Look, I am better educated than any of the kings before me in Jerusalem. I have greater wisdom and knowledge." So I worked hard to be wise instead of foolish[e]—but now I realize that even this was like chasing the wind. For the more my wisdom, the more my grief; to increase knowledge only increases distress.

New Revised Standard:

Reflections of a Royal Philosopher

1 THE WORDS of the Teacher,[f] the son of David, king in Jerusalem.

2 Vanity of vanities, says the Teacher,[f]
   vanity of vanities! All is vanity.
3 What do people gain from all the toil
   at which they toil under the sun?
4 A generation goes, and a generation comes,
   but the earth remains forever.
5 The sun rises and the sun goes down,
   and hurries to the place where it rises.
6 The wind blows to the south,
   and goes around to the north;
round and round goes the wind,
   and on its circuits the wind returns.
7 All streams run to the sea,
   but the sea is not full;
to the place where the streams flow,
   there they continue to flow.
8 All things[g] are wearisome;
   more than one can express;
the eye is not satisfied with seeing,
   or the ear filled with hearing.
9 What has been is what will be,
   and what has been done is what will be
      done;
   there is nothing new under the sun.
10 Is there a thing of which it is said,
   "See, this is new"?
It has already been,
   in the ages before us.
11 The people of long ago are not remembered,
   nor will there be any remembrance
of people yet to come
   by those who come after them.

The Futility of Seeking Wisdom

12 I, the Teacher,[f] when king over Israel in Jerusalem, 13applied my mind to seek and to search out by wisdom all that is done under heaven; it is an unhappy business that God has given to human beings to be busy with. 14I saw all the deeds that are done under the sun; and see, all is vanity and a chasing after wind.[h]
15 What is crooked cannot be made straight,
   and what is lacking cannot be counted.

16 I said to myself, "I have acquired great wisdom, surpassing all who were over Jerusalem before me; and my mind has had great experience of wisdom and knowledge." 17And I applied my mind to know wisdom and to know madness and folly. I perceived that this also is but a chasing after wind.[h]
18 For in much wisdom is much vexation,
   and those who increase knowledge increase
      sorrow.

---

b *1:1 Solomon,* implied. Literally, "the words of the Preacher, the son (or descendant) of David, King of Jerusalem." c *1:3-7 it makes no difference,* literally, "but the earth remains forever." d *1:3-7 getting nowhere,* implied. e *1:16-18 So I worked hard to be wise instead of foolish,* or, "I sought to learn about composure and madness."

f Heb *Qoheleth,* traditionally rendered *Preacher* g Or *words* h Or *a feeding on wind.* See Hos 12.1

King James

2 I SAID in mine heart, Go to now, I will prove thee with mirth, therefore enjoy pleasure: and, behold, this also *is* vanity.

2I said of laughter, *It is* mad: and of mirth, What doeth it?

3I sought in mine heart to give myself unto wine, yet acquainting mine heart with wisdom; and to lay hold on folly, till I might see what *was* that good for the sons of men, which they should do under the heaven all the days of their life.

4I made me great works; I builded me houses; I planted me vineyards:

5I made me gardens and orchards, and I planted trees in them of all *kind of* fruits:

6I made me pools of water, to water therewith the wood that bringeth forth trees:

7I got *me* servants and maidens, and had servants born in my house; also I had great possessions of great and small cattle above all that were in Jerusalem before me:

8I gathered me also silver and gold, and the peculiar treasure of kings and of the provinces: I gat me men singers and women singers, and the delights of the sons of men, *as* musical instruments, and that of all sorts.

9So I was great, and increased more than all that were before me in Jerusalem: also my wisdom remained with me.

10And whatsoever mine eyes desired I kept not from them, I withheld not my heart from any joy; for my heart rejoiced in all my labour: and this was my portion of all my labour.

11Then I looked on all the works that my hands had wrought, and on the labour that I had laboured to do: and, behold, all *was* vanity and vexation of spirit, and *there was* no profit under the sun.

12¶ And I turned myself to behold wisdom, and madness, and folly: for what *can* the man *do* that cometh after the king? *even* that which hath been already done.

13Then I saw that wisdom excelleth folly, as far as light excelleth darkness.

14The wise man's eyes *are* in his head; but the fool walketh in darkness: and I myself perceived also that one event happeneth to them all.

15Then said I in my heart, As it happeneth to the fool, so it happeneth even to me; and why was I then more wise? Then I said in my heart, that this also *is* vanity.

16For *there is* no remembrance of the wise more than of the fool for ever; seeing that which now *is* in the days to come shall all be forgotten. And how dieth the wise *man?* as the fool.

17Therefore I hated life; because the work that is wrought under the sun *is* grievous unto me: for all *is* vanity and vexation of spirit.

18¶ Yea, I hated all my labour which I had taken under the sun: because I should leave it unto the man that shall be after me.

19And who knoweth whether he shall be a wise *man* or a fool? yet shall he have rule over all my labour wherein I have laboured, and wherein I have shown myself wise under the sun. This *is* also vanity.

20Therefore I went about to cause my heart to despair of all the labour which I took under the sun.

21For there is a man whose labour *is* in wisdom, and in knowledge, and in equity; yet to a man that hath not laboured therein shall he leave it *for* his portion. This also *is* vanity and a great evil.

22For what hath man of all his labour, and of the vexation of his heart, wherein he hath laboured under the sun?

23For all his days *are* sorrows, and his travail grief; yea, his heart taketh not rest in the night. This is also vanity.

New International

Pleasures Are Meaningless

2 I THOUGHT in my heart, "Come now, I will test you with pleasure to find out what is good." But that also proved to be meaningless. 2"Laughter," I said, "is foolish. And what does pleasure accomplish?" 3I tried cheering myself with wine, and embracing folly— my mind still guiding me with wisdom. I wanted to see what was worthwhile for men to do under heaven during the few days of their lives.

4I undertook great projects: I built houses for myself and planted vineyards. 5I made gardens and parks and planted all kinds of fruit trees in them. 6I made reservoirs to water groves of flourishing trees. 7I bought male and female slaves and had other slaves who were born in my house. I also owned more herds and flocks than anyone in Jerusalem before me. 8I amassed silver and gold for myself, and the treasure of kings and provinces. I acquired men and women singers, and a harem[a] as well— the delights of the heart of man. 9I became greater by far than anyone in Jerusalem before me. In all this my wisdom stayed with me.

10I denied myself nothing my eyes desired;
    I refused my heart no pleasure.
My heart took delight in all my work,
    and this was the reward for all my labor.
11Yet when I surveyed all that my hands had done
    and what I had toiled to achieve,
everything was meaningless, a chasing after the wind;
    nothing was gained under the sun.

Wisdom and Folly Are Meaningless

12Then I turned my thoughts to consider wisdom,
    and also madness and folly.
What more can the king's successor do
    than what has already been done?
13I saw that wisdom is better than folly,
    just as light is better than darkness.
14The wise man has eyes in his head,
    while the fool walks in the darkness;
but I came to realize
    that the same fate overtakes them both.

15Then I thought in my heart,

"The fate of the fool will overtake me also.
    What then do I gain by being wise?"
I said in my heart,
    "This too is meaningless."
16For the wise man, like the fool, will not be
    long remembered;
    in days to come both will be forgotten.
Like the fool, the wise man too must die!

Toil Is Meaningless

17So I hated life, because the work that is done under the sun was grievous to me. All of it is meaningless, a chasing after the wind. 18I hated all the things I had toiled for under the sun, because I must leave them to the one who comes after me. 19And who knows whether he will be a wise man or a fool? Yet he will have control over all the work into which I have poured my effort and skill under the sun. This too is meaningless. 20So my heart began to despair over all my toilsome labor under the sun. 21For a man may do his work with wisdom, knowledge and skill, and then he must leave all he owns to someone who has not worked for it. This too is meaningless and a great misfortune. 22What does a man get for all the toil and anxious striving with which he labors under the sun? 23All his days his work is pain and grief; even at night his mind does not rest. This too is meaningless.

---

a *8* The meaning of the Hebrew for this phrase is uncertain.

Living Bible

2 I SAID to myself, "Come now, be merry; enjoy yourself to the full." But I found that this, too, was futile. For it is silly to be laughing all the time; what good does it do?

3So, after a lot of thinking, I decided to try the road of drink, while still holding steadily to my course of seeking wisdom.

Next I changed my course again and followed the path of folly, so that I could experience the only happiness most men have throughout their lives.

4,5,6Then I tried to find fulfillment by inaugurating a great public works program: homes, vineyards, gardens, parks and orchards for myself, and reservoirs to hold the water to irrigate my plantations.

7,8Next I bought slaves, both men and women, and others were born within my household. I also bred great herds and flocks, more than any of the kings before me. I collected silver and gold as taxes from many kings and provinces.

In the cultural arts, I organized men's and women's choirs and orchestras.

And then there were my many beautiful concubines. 9So I became greater than any of the kings in Jerusalem before me, and with it all I remained clear-eyed, so that I could evaluate all these things. 10Anything I wanted, I took, and did not restrain myself from any joy. I even found great pleasure in hard work. This pleasure was, indeed, my only reward for all my labors.

11But as I looked at everything I had tried, it was all so useless, a chasing of the wind, and there was nothing really worthwhile anywhere.

12Now I began a study of the comparative virtues of wisdom and folly, and anyone else would come to the same conclusion I didb— 13,14that wisdom is of more value than foolishness, just as light is better than darkness; for the wise man sees, while the fool is blind. And yet I noticed that there was one thing that happened to wise and foolish alike— 15just as the fool will die, so will I. So of what value is all my wisdom? Then I realized that even wisdom is futile. 16For the wise and fool both die, and in the days to come both will be long forgotten. 17So now I hate life because it is all so irrational; all is foolishness, chasing the wind.

18And I am disgusted about this, that I must leave the fruits of all my hard work to others. 19And who can tell whether my son will be a wise man or a fool? And yet all I have will be given to him—how discouraging!

20-23So I turned in despair from hard work as the answer to my search for satisfaction. For though I spend my life searching for wisdom, knowledge, and skill, I must leave all of it to someone who hasn't done a day's work in his life; he inherits all my efforts, free of charge. This is not only foolish, but unfair. So what does a man get for all his hard work? Days full of sorrow and grief, and restless, bitter nights. It is all utterly ridiculous.

New Revised Standard

The Futility of Self-Indulgence

2 I SAID to myself, "Come now, I will make a test of pleasure; enjoy yourself." But again, this also was vanity. 2I said of laughter, "It is mad," and of pleasure, "What use is it?" 3I searched with my mind how to cheer my body with wine—my mind still guiding me with wisdom—and how to lay hold on folly, until I might see what was good for mortals to do under heaven during the few days of their life. 4I made great works; I built houses and planted vineyards for myself; 5I made myself gardens and parks, and planted in them all kinds of fruit trees. 6I made myself pools from which to water the forest of growing trees. 7I bought male and female slaves, and had slaves who were born in my house; I also had great possessions of herds and flocks, more than any who had been before me in Jerusalem. 8I also gathered for myself silver and gold and the treasure of kings and of the provinces; I got singers, both men and women, and delights of the flesh, and many concubines.c

9 So I became great and surpassed all who were before me in Jerusalem; also my wisdom remained with me. 10Whatever my eyes desired I did not keep from them; I kept my heart from no pleasure, for my heart found pleasure in all my toil, and this was my reward for all my toil. 11Then I considered all that my hands had done and the toil I had spent in doing it, and again, all was vanity and a chasing after wind,d and there was nothing to be gained under the sun.

Wisdom and Joy Given to One Who Pleases God

12 So I turned to consider wisdom and madness and folly; for what can the one do who comes after the king? Only what has already been done. 13Then I saw that wisdom excels folly as light excels darkness.

14 The wise have eyes in their head,
   but fools walk in darkness.

Yet I perceived that the same fate befalls all of them. 15Then I said to myself, "What happens to the fool will happen to me also; why then have I been so very wise?" And I said to myself that this also is vanity. 16For there is no enduring remembrance of the wise or of fools, seeing that in the days to come all will have been long forgotten. How can the wise die just like fools? 17So I hated life, because what is done under the sun was grievous to me; for all is vanity and a chasing after wind.e

18 I hated all my toil in which I had toiled under the sun, seeing that I must leave it to those who come after me 19—and who knows whether they will be wise or foolish? Yet they will be master of all for which I toiled and used my wisdom under the sun. This also is vanity. 20So I turned and gave my heart up to despair concerning all the toil of my labors under the sun, 21because sometimes one who has toiled with wisdom and knowledge and skill must leave all to be enjoyed by another who did not toil for it. This also is vanity and a great evil. 22What do mortals get from all the toil and strain with which they toil under the sun? 23For all their days are full of pain, and their work is a vexation; even at night their minds do not rest. This also is vanity.

---

b *2:12 anyone else would come to the same conclusion I did*, literally, "for what can the man do who comes after the king?"

c Meaning of Heb uncertain   d Or *a feeding on wind*. See Hos 12.1   e Or *a feeding on wind*. See Hos 12.1

King James

24¶ *There is* nothing better for a man, *than* that he should eat and drink, and *that* he should make his soul enjoy good in his labour. This also I saw, that it *was* from the hand of God.

25For who can eat, or who else can hasten *hereunto,* more than I?

26For *God* giveth to a man that *is* good in his sight wisdom, and knowledge, and joy: but to the sinner he giveth travail, to gather and to heap up, that he may give to *him that is* good before God. This also *is* vanity and vexation of spirit.

3 TO EVERY *thing there is* a season, and a time to every purpose under the heaven:

2A time to be born, and a time to die; a time to plant, and a time to pluck up *that which is* planted;

3A time to kill, and a time to heal; a time to break down, and a time to build up;

4A time to weep, and a time to laugh; a time to mourn, and a time to dance;

5A time to cast away stones, and a time to gather stones together; a time to embrace, and a time to refrain from embracing;

6A time to get, and a time to lose; a time to keep, and a time to cast away;

7A time to rend, and a time to sew; a time to keep silence, and a time to speak;

8A time to love, and a time to hate; a time of war, and a time of peace.

9What profit hath he that worketh in that wherein he laboureth?

10I have seen the travail, which God hath given to the sons of men to be exercised in it.

11He hath made every *thing* beautiful in his time: also he hath set the world in their heart, so that no man can find out the work that God maketh from the beginning to the end.

12I know that *there is* no good in them, but for *a man* to rejoice, and to do good in his life.

13And also that every man should eat and drink, and enjoy the good of all his labour, *it is* the gift of God.

14I know that, whatsoever God doeth, it shall be for ever: nothing can be put to it, nor anything taken from it: and God doeth *it,* that *men* should fear before him.

15That which hath been is now; and that which is to be hath already been; and God requireth that which is past.

16¶ And moreover I saw under the sun the place of judgment, *that* wickedness *was* there; and the place of righteousness, *that* iniquity *was* there.

17I said in mine heart, God shall judge the righteous and the wicked: for *there is* a time there for every purpose and for every work.

18I said in mine heart concerning the estate of the sons of men, that God might manifest them, and that they might see that they themselves are beasts.

19For that which befalleth the sons of men befalleth beasts; even one thing befalleth them: as the one dieth, so dieth the other; yea, they have all one breath; so that a man hath no preeminence above a beast: for all *is* vanity.

New International

24A man can do nothing better than to eat and drink and find satisfaction in his work. This too, I see, is from the hand of God, 25for without him, who can eat or find enjoyment? 26To the man who pleases him, God gives wisdom, knowledge and happiness, but to the sinner he gives the task of gathering and storing up wealth to hand it over to the one who pleases God. This too is meaningless, a chasing after the wind.

A Time for Everything

3 THERE IS a time for everything,
   and a season for every activity under heaven:

2   a time to be born and a time to die,
    a time to plant and a time to uproot,
3   a time to kill and a time to heal,
    a time to tear down and a time to build,
4   a time to weep and a time to laugh,
    a time to mourn and a time to dance,
5   a time to scatter stones and a time to gather
      them,
    a time to embrace and a time to refrain,
6   a time to search and a time to give up,
    a time to keep and a time to throw away,
7   a time to tear and a time to mend,
    a time to be silent and a time to speak,
8   a time to love and a time to hate,
    a time for war and a time for peace.

9What does the worker gain from his toil? 10I have seen the burden God has laid on men. 11He has made everything beautiful in its time. He has also set eternity in the hearts of men; yet they cannot fathom what God has done from beginning to end. 12I know that there is nothing better for men than to be happy and do good while they live. 13That everyone may eat and drink, and find satisfaction in all his toil—this is the gift of God. 14I know that everything God does will endure forever; nothing can be added to it and nothing taken from it. God does it so that men will revere him.

15Whatever is has already been,
   and what will be has been before;
   and God will call the past to account.[a]

16And I saw something else under the sun:

In the place of judgment—wickedness was
      there,
   in the place of justice—wickedness was there.

17I thought in my heart,

"God will bring to judgment
   both the righteous and the wicked,
for there will be a time for every activity,
   a time for every deed."

18I also thought, "As for men, God tests them so that they may see that they are like the animals. 19Man's fate is like that of the animals; the same fate awaits them both: As one dies, so dies the other. All have the same breath[b]; man has no advantage over the animal. Everything is meaningless. 20All go to the same place; all

---

a 15 Or *God calls back the past*   b 19 Or *spirit*

Living Bible

24, 25, 26So I decided that there was nothing better for a man to do than to enjoy his food and drink, and his job. Then I realized that even this pleasure is from the hand of God. For who can eat or enjoy apart from him? For God gives those who please him wisdom, knowledge, and joy; but if a sinner becomes wealthy, God takes the wealth away from him and gives it to those who please him. So here, too, we see an example of foolishly chasing the wind.

3 THERE IS a right time for everything:
2A time to be born;
A time to die;
A time to plant;
A time to harvest;
3A time to kill;
A time to heal;
A time to destroy;
A time to rebuild;
4A time to cry;
A time to laugh;
A time to grieve;
A time to dance;
5A time for scattering stones;
A time for gathering stones;
A time to hug;
A time not to hug;
6A time to find;
A time to lose;
A time for keeping;
A time for throwing away;
7A time to tear;
A time to repair;
A time to be quiet;
A time to speak up;
8A time for loving;
A time for hating;
A time for war;
A time for peace.
9What does one really get from hard work?
10I have thought about this in connection with all the various kinds of work God has given to mankind. 11Everything is appropriate in its own time. But though God has planted eternity in the hearts of men, even so, many cannot see the whole scope of God's work from beginning to end. 12So I conclude that, first, there is nothing better for a man than to be happy and enjoy himself as long as he can; 13and second, that he should eat and drink and enjoy the fruits of his labors, for these are gifts from God.

14And I know this, that whatever God does is final— nothing can be added or taken from it; God's purpose in this is that man should fear the all-powerful God.c

15Whatever is, has been long ago; and whatever is going to be has been before; God brings to pass again what was in the distant past and disappeared.d

16Moreover, I notice that throughout the earth justice is giving way to crime and even the police courts are corrupt. 17I said to myself, "In due season God will judge everything man does, both good and bad."

18And then I realized that God is letting the world go on its sinful way so that he can test mankind, and so that men themselves will see that they are no better than beasts. 19For men and animals both breathe the same air, and both die. So mankind has no real advantage over the beasts; what an absurdity! 20All go to one place—the

New Revised Standard

24 There is nothing better for mortals than to eat and drink, and find enjoyment in their toil. This also, I saw, is from the hand of God; 25for apart from hime who can eat or who can have enjoyment? 26For to the one who pleases him God gives wisdom and knowledge and joy; but to the sinner he gives the work of gathering and heaping, only to give to one who pleases God. This also is vanity and a chasing after wind.f

Everything Has Its Time

3 FOR EVERYTHING there is a season, and a time for every matter under heaven:
2 a time to be born, and a time to die;
a time to plant, and a time to pluck up what is planted;
3 a time to kill, and a time to heal;
a time to break down, and a time to build up;
4 a time to weep, and a time to laugh;
a time to mourn, and a time to dance;
5 a time to throw away stones, and a time to gather stones together;
a time to embrace, and a time to refrain from embracing;
6 a time to seek, and a time to lose;
a time to keep, and a time to throw away;
7 a time to tear, and a time to sew;
a time to keep silence, and a time to speak;
8 a time to love, and a time to hate;
a time for war, and a time for peace.

The God-Given Task

9 What gain have the workers from their toil? 10I have seen the business that God has given to everyone to be busy with. 11He has made everything suitable for its time; moreover he has put a sense of past and future into their minds, yet they cannot find out what God has done from the beginning to the end. 12I know that there is nothing better for them than to be happy and enjoy themselves as long as they live; 13moreover, it is God's gift that all should eat and drink and take pleasure in all their toil. 14I know that whatever God does endures forever; nothing can be added to it, nor anything taken from it; God has done this, so that all should stand in awe before him. 15That which is, already has been; that which is to be, already is; and God seeks out what has gone by.g

Judgment and the Future Belong to God

16 Moreover I saw under the sun that in the place of justice, wickedness was there, and in the place of righteousness, wickedness was there as well. 17I said in my heart, God will judge the righteous and the wicked, for he has appointed a time for every matter, and for every work. 18I said in my heart with regard to human beings that God is testing them to show that they are but animals. 19For the fate of humans and the fate of animals is the same; as one dies, so dies the other. They all have the same breath, and humans have no advantage over the animals; for all is vanity. 20All go to one place; all are

---

c 3:14 God's purpose in this is that man should fear the all-powerful God, implied. d 3:15 God brings to pass again what was in the distant past and disappeared, literally, "God seeks what has been driven away."

e Gk Syr: Heb apart from me f Or a feeding on wind. See Hos 12.1 g Heb what is pursued

King James

20All go unto one place; all are of the dust, and all turn to dust again.

21Who knoweth the spirit of man that goeth upward, and the spirit of the beast that goeth downward to the earth?

22Wherefore I perceive that *there is* nothing better, than that a man should rejoice in his own works; for that *is* his portion: for who shall bring him to see what shall be after him?

4 SO I returned, and considered all the oppressions that are done under the sun: and behold the tears of *such as were* oppressed, and they had no comforter; and on the side of their oppressors *there was* power; but they had no comforter.

2Wherefore I praised the dead which are already dead more than the living which are yet alive.

3Yea, better *is he* than both they, which hath not yet been, who hath not seen the evil work that is done under the sun.

4¶ Again, I considered all travail, and every right work, that for this a man is envied of his neighbour. This *is* also vanity and vexation of spirit.

5The fool foldeth his hands together, and eateth his own flesh.

6Better *is* an handful *with* quietness, than both the hands full *with* travail and vexation of spirit.

7¶ Then I returned, and I saw vanity under the sun.

8There is one *alone*, and *there is* not a second; yea, he hath neither child nor brother: yet *is there* no end of all his labour; neither is his eye satisfied with riches; neither *saith he,* For whom do I labour, and bereave my soul of good? This *is* also vanity, yea, it *is* a sore travail.

9¶ Two *are* better than one; because they have a good reward for their labour.

10For if they fall, the one will lift up his fellow: but woe to him *that is* alone when he falleth; for *he hath* not another to help him up.

11Again, if two lie together, then they have heat: but how can one be warm *alone?*

12And if one prevail against him, two shall withstand him; and a threefold cord is not quickly broken.

13¶ Better *is* a poor and a wise child than an old and foolish king, who will no more be admonished.

14For out of prison he cometh to reign; whereas also *he that is* born in his kingdom becometh poor.

15I considered all the living which walk under the sun, with the second child that shall stand up in his stead.

New International

come from dust, and to dust all return. 21Who knows if the spirit of man rises upward and if the spirit of the animal^a goes down into the earth?"

22So I saw that there is nothing better for a man than to enjoy his work, because that is his lot. For who can bring him to see what will happen after him?

Oppression, Toil, Friendlessness

4 AGAIN I looked and saw all the oppression that was taking place under the sun:

I saw the tears of the oppressed—
and they have no comforter;
power was on the side of their oppressors—
and they have no comforter.
2And I declared that the dead,
who had already died,
are happier than the living,
who are still alive.
3But better than both
is he who has not yet been,
who has not seen the evil
that is done under the sun.

4And I saw that all labor and all achievement spring from man's envy of his neighbor. This too is meaningless, a chasing after the wind.

5The fool folds his hands
and ruins himself.
6Better one handful with tranquillity
than two handfuls with toil
and chasing after the wind.

7Again I saw something meaningless under the sun:

8There was a man all alone;
he had neither son nor brother.
There was no end to his toil,
yet his eyes were not content with his wealth.
"For whom am I toiling," he asked,
"and why am I depriving myself of
enjoyment?"
This too is meaningless—
a miserable business!

9Two are better than one,
because they have a good return for their
work:
10If one falls down,
his friend can help him up.
But pity the man who falls
and has no one to help him up!
11Also, if two lie down together, they will keep
warm.
But how can one keep warm alone?
12Though one may be overpowered,
two can defend themselves.
A cord of three strands is not quickly broken.

Advancement Is Meaningless

13Better a poor but wise youth than an old but foolish king who no longer knows how to take warning. 14The youth may have come from prison to the kingship, or he may have been born in poverty within his kingdom. 15I saw that all who lived and walked under the sun followed the youth, the king's successor. 16There was no

---

^a *21 Or Who knows the spirit of man, which rises upward, or the spirit of the animal, which*

Living Bible

dust from which they came and to which they must return. 21For who can prove that the spirit of man goes upward and the spirit of animals goes downward into dust? 22So I saw that there is nothing better for men than that they should be happy in their work, for that is what they are here for, and no one can bring them back to life to enjoy what will be in the future, so let them enjoy it now.

4 NEXT I observed all the oppression and sadness throughout the earth—the tears of the oppressed, and no one helping them, while on the side of their oppressors were powerful allies. 2So I felt that the dead were better off than the living. 3And most fortunate of all are those who have never been born, and have never seen all the evil and crime throughout the earth.

4Then I observed that the basic motive for success is the driving force of envy and jealousy! But this, too, is foolishness, chasing the wind. 5, 6The fool won't work and almost starves, but feels that it is better to be lazy and barely get by, than to work hard when, in the long run, it is all so futile.

7I also observed another piece of foolishness around the earth. 8This is the case of a man who is quite alone, without a son or brother, yet he works hard to keep gaining more riches, and to whom will he leave it all? And why is he giving up so much now? It is all so pointless and depressing.

9Two can accomplish more than twice as much as one, for the results can be much better. 10If one falls, the other pulls him up; but if a man falls when he is alone, he's in trouble.

11Also, on a cold night, two under the same blanket gain warmth from each other, but how can one be warm alone? 12And one standing alone can be attacked and defeated, but two can stand back-to-back and conquer; three is even better, for a triple-braided cord is not easily broken.

13It is better to be a poor but wise youth than to be an old and foolish king who refuses all advice. 14Such a lad could come from prison and succeed. He might even become king, though born in poverty. 15Everyone is eager to help a youth like that, even to help him usurp the throne. 16He can become the leader of millions of

New Revised Standard

from the dust, and all turn to dust again. 21Who knows whether the human spirit goes upward and the spirit of animals goes downward to the earth? 22So I saw that there is nothing better than that all should enjoy their work, for that is their lot; who can bring them to see what will be after them?

4 AGAIN I saw all the oppressions that are practiced under the sun. Look, the tears of the oppressed—with no one to comfort them! On the side of their oppressors there was power—with no one to comfort them. 2And I thought the dead, who have already died, more fortunate than the living, who are still alive; 3but better than both is the one who has not yet been, and has not seen the evil deeds that are done under the sun.

4 Then I saw that all toil and all skill in work come from one person's envy of another. This also is vanity and a chasing after wind.b

5 Fools fold their hands
　　and consume their own flesh.
6 Better is a handful with quiet
　　than two handfuls with toil,
　　and a chasing after wind.b

7 Again, I saw vanity under the sun: 8the case of solitary individuals, without sons or brothers; yet there is no end to all their toil, and their eyes are never satisfied with riches. "For whom am I toiling," they ask, "and depriving myself of pleasure?" This also is vanity and an unhappy business.

The Value of a Friend

9 Two are better than one, because they have a good reward for their toil. 10For if they fall, one will lift up the other; but woe to one who is alone and falls and does not have another to help. 11Again, if two lie together, they keep warm; but how can one keep warm alone? 12And though one might prevail against another, two will withstand one. A threefold cord is not quickly broken.

13 Better is a poor but wise youth than an old but foolish king, who will no longer take advice. 14One can indeed come out of prison to reign, even though born poor in the kingdom. 15I saw all the living who, moving about under the sun, follow thatc youth who replaced the king;d 16there was no end to all those people whom

b Or a feeding on wind. See Hos 12.1　　c Heb the second　　d Heb him

King James

16There is no end of all the people, even of all that have been before them: they also that come after shall not rejoice in him. Surely this also is vanity and vexation of spirit.

5 KEEP THY foot when thou goest to the house of God, and be more ready to hear, than to give the sacrifice of fools: for they consider not that they do evil. 2Be not rash with thy mouth, and let not thine heart be hasty to utter any thing before God: for God is in heaven, and thou upon earth: therefore let thy words be few. 3For a dream cometh through the multitude of business; and a fool's voice is known by multitude of words. 4When thou vowest a vow unto God, defer not to pay it; for he hath no pleasure in fools: pay that which thou hast vowed. 5Better is it that thou shouldest not vow, than that thou shouldest vow and not pay. 6Suffer not thy mouth to cause thy flesh to sin; neither say thou before the angel, that it was an error: wherefore should God be angry at thy voice, and destroy the work of thine hands? 7For in the multitude of dreams and many words there are also divers vanities: but fear thou God. 8¶ If thou seest the oppression of the poor, and violent perverting of judgment and justice in a province, marvel not at the matter: for he that is higher than the highest regardeth; and there be higher than they. 9¶ Moreover the profit of the earth is for all: the king himself is served by the field. 10He that loveth silver shall not be satisfied with silver; nor he that loveth abundance with increase: this is also vanity. 11When goods increase, they are increased that eat them: and what good is there to the owners thereof, saving the beholding of them with their eyes? 12The sleep of a labouring man is sweet, whether he eat little or much: but the abundance of the rich will not suffer him to sleep. 13There is a sore evil which I have seen under the sun, namely, riches kept for the owners thereof to their hurt. 14But those riches perish by evil travail: and he begetteth a son, and there is nothing in his hand. 15As he came forth of his mother's womb, naked shall he return to go as he came, and shall take nothing of his labour, which he may carry away in his hand. 16And this also is a sore evil, that in all points as he came, so shall he go: and what profit hath he that hath laboured for the wind? 17All his days also he eateth in darkness, and he hath much sorrow and wrath with his sickness. 18¶ Behold that which I have seen: it is good and comely for one to eat and to drink, and to enjoy the good of all his labour that he taketh under the sun all the days of his life, which God giveth him: for it is his portion.

New International

end to all the people who were before them. But those who came later were not pleased with the successor. This too is meaningless, a chasing after the wind.

Stand in Awe of God

5 GUARD YOUR steps when you go to the house of God. Go near to listen rather than to offer the sacrifice of fools, who do not know that they do wrong.

2Do not be quick with your mouth,
  do not be hasty in your heart
  to utter anything before God.
God is in heaven
  and you are on earth,
  so let your words be few.
3As a dream comes when there are many cares,
  so the speech of a fool when there are many
    words.

4When you make a vow to God, do not delay in fulfilling it. He has no pleasure in fools; fulfill your vow. 5It is better not to vow than to make a vow and not fulfill it. 6Do not let your mouth lead you into sin. And do not protest to the temple messenger, "My vow was a mistake." Why should God be angry at what you say and destroy the work of your hands? 7Much dreaming and many words are meaningless. Therefore stand in awe of God.

Riches Are Meaningless

8If you see the poor oppressed in a district, and justice and rights denied, do not be surprised at such things; for one official is eyed by a higher one, and over them both are others higher still. 9The increase from the land is taken by all; the king himself profits from the fields.

10Whoever loves money never has money enough;
  whoever loves wealth is never satisfied with
    his income.
  This too is meaningless.

11As goods increase,
  so do those who consume them.
And what benefit are they to the owner
  except to feast his eyes on them?

12The sleep of a laborer is sweet,
  whether he eats little or much,
but the abundance of a rich man
  permits him no sleep.

13I have seen a grievous evil under the sun:

wealth hoarded to the harm of its owner,
14 or wealth lost through some misfortune,
so that when he has a son
  there is nothing left for him.
15Naked a man comes from his mother's womb,
  and as he comes, so he departs.
He takes nothing from his labor
  that he can carry in his hand.

16This too is a grievous evil:

As a man comes, so he departs,
  and what does he gain,
  since he toils for the wind?
17All his days he eats in darkness,
  with great frustration, affliction and anger.

18Then I realized that it is good and proper for a man to eat and drink, and to find satisfaction in his toilsome labor under the sun during the few days of life God has given him—for this is his lot. 19Moreover, when God

Living Bible

people, and be very popular. But, then, the younger generation grows up around him and rejects him! So again, it is all foolishness, chasing the wind.

5 AS YOU enter the Temple, keep your ears open and your mouth shut! Don't be a fool who doesn't even realize it is sinful to make rash promises to God, for he is in heaven and you are only here on earth, so let your words be few. Just as being too busy gives you nightmares, so being a fool makes you a blabbermouth. 4So when you talk to God and vow to him that you will do something, don't delay in doing it, for God has no pleasure in fools. Keep your promise to him. 5It is far better not to say you'll do something than to say you will and then not do it. 6, 7In that case, your mouth is making you sin. Don't try to defend yourself by telling the messenger from God that it was all a mistake [to make the vow[a]]. That would make God very angry; and he might[b] destroy your prosperity. Dreaming instead of doing is foolishness, and there is ruin in a flood of empty words; fear God instead.

8If you see some poor man being oppressed by the rich, with miscarriage of justice anywhere throughout the land, don't be surprised! For every official is under orders from higher up, and the higher officials look up to their superiors. And so the matter is lost in red tape and bureaucracy.[c] 9And over them all is the king. Oh, for a king who is devoted to his country! Only he can bring order from this chaos.

10He who loves money shall never have enough. The foolishness of thinking that wealth brings happiness! 11The more you have, the more you spend, right up to the limits of your income, so what is the advantage of wealth—except perhaps to watch it as it runs through your fingers! 12The man who works hard sleeps well whether he eats little or much, but the rich must worry and suffer insomnia.

13, 14There is another serious problem I have seen everywhere—savings are put into risky investments that turn sour, and soon there is nothing left to pass on to one's son. 15The man who speculates is soon back to where he began—with nothing. 16This, as I said, is a very serious problem, for all his hard work has been for nothing; he has been working for the wind. It is all swept away. 17All the rest of his life he is under a cloud—gloomy, discouraged, frustrated, and angry.

18Well, one thing, at least, is good: It is for a man to eat well, drink a good glass of wine, accept his position in life, and enjoy his work whatever his job may be, for however long the Lord may let him live. 19, 20And, of

New Revised Standard

he led. Yet those who come later will not rejoice in him. Surely this also is vanity and a chasing after wind.[d]

Reverence, Humility, and Contentment

5[e] GUARD YOUR steps when you go to the house of God; to draw near to listen is better than the sacrifice offered by fools; for they do not know how to keep from doing evil.[f] 2[g]Never be rash with your mouth, nor let your heart be quick to utter a word before God, for God is in heaven, and you upon earth; therefore let your words be few.

3 For dreams come with many cares, and a fool's voice with many words.

4 When you make a vow to God, do not delay fulfilling it; for he has no pleasure in fools. Fulfill what you vow. 5It is better that you should not vow than that you should vow and not fulfill it. 6Do not let your mouth lead you into sin, and do not say before the messenger that it was a mistake; why should God be angry at your words, and destroy the work of your hands?

7 With many dreams come vanities and a multitude of words;[h] but fear God.

8 If you see in a province the oppression of the poor and the violation of justice and right, do not be amazed at the matter; for the high official is watched by a higher, and there are yet higher ones over them. 9But all things considered, this is an advantage for a land: a king for a plowed field.[i]

10 The lover of money will not be satisfied with money; nor the lover of wealth, with gain. This also is vanity.

11 When goods increase, those who eat them increase; and what gain has their owner but to see them with his eyes?

12 Sweet is the sleep of laborers, whether they eat little or much; but the surfeit of the rich will not let them sleep.

13 There is a grievous ill that I have seen under the sun: riches were kept by their owners to their hurt, 14and those riches were lost in a bad venture; though they are parents of children, they have nothing in their hands. 15As they came from their mother's womb, so they shall go again, naked as they came; they shall take nothing for their toil, which they may carry away with their hands. 16This also is a grievous ill: just as they came, so shall they go; and what gain do they have from toiling for the wind? 17Besides, all their days they eat in darkness, in much vexation and sickness and resentment.

18 This is what I have seen to be good: it is fitting to eat and drink and find enjoyment in all the toil with which one toils under the sun the few days of the life God gives us; for this is our lot. 19Likewise all to whom

---

[a] 5:6, 7 to make the vow, implied. [b] 5:6, 7 he might, implied. [c] 5:8 the matter is lost in red tape and bureaucracy, literally, "and there are yet higher ones over them."

[d] Or a feeding on wind. See Hos 12.1 [e] Ch 4.17 in Heb [f] Cn: Heb they do not know how to do evil [g] Ch 5.1 in Heb [h] Meaning of Heb uncertain [i] Meaning of Heb uncertain

King James

19Every man also to whom God hath given riches and wealth, and hath given him power to eat thereof, and to take his portion, and to rejoice in his labour; this *is* the gift of God.

20For he shall not much remember the days of his life; because God answereth *him* in the joy of his heart.

6 THERE IS an evil which I have seen under the sun, and it *is* common among men:

2A man to whom God hath given riches, wealth, and honour, so that he wanteth nothing for his soul of all that he desireth, yet God giveth him not power to eat thereof, but a stranger eateth it: this *is* vanity, and it *is* an evil disease.

3¶ If a man beget an hundred *children,* and live many years, so that the days of his years be many, and his soul be not filled with good, and also *that* he have no burial; I say, *that* an untimely birth *is* better than he.

4For he cometh in with vanity, and departeth in darkness, and his name shall be covered with darkness.

5Moreover he hath not seen the sun, nor known *any thing:* this hath more rest than the other.

6¶ Yea, though he live a thousand years twice *told,* yet hath he seen no good: do not all go to one place?

7All the labour of man *is* for his mouth, and yet the appetite is not filled.

8For what hath the wise more than the fool? what hath the poor, that knoweth to walk before the living?

9¶ Better *is* the sight of the eyes than the wandering of the desire: this *is* also vanity and vexation of spirit.

10That which hath been is named already, and it is known that it *is* man: neither may he contend with him that is mightier than he.

11¶ Seeing there be many things that increase vanity, what *is* man the better?

12For who knoweth what *is* good for man in *this* life, all the days of his vain life which he spendeth as a shadow? for who can tell a man what shall be after him under the sun?

7 A GOOD name *is* better than precious ointment; and the day of death than the day of one's birth.

2¶ *It is* better to go to the house of mourning, than to go to the house of feasting: for that *is* the end of all men; and the living will lay *it* to his heart.

3Sorrow *is* better than laughter: for by the sadness of the countenance the heart is made better.

4The heart of the wise *is* in the house of mourning; but the heart of fools *is* in the house of mirth.

5*It is* better to hear the rebuke of the wise, than for a man to hear the song of fools.

6For as the crackling of thorns under a pot, so *is* the laughter of the fool: this also *is* vanity.

New International

gives any man wealth and possessions, and enables him to enjoy them, to accept his lot and be happy in his work—this is a gift of God. 20He seldom reflects on the days of his life, because God keeps him occupied with gladness of heart.

6 I HAVE seen another evil under the sun, and it weighs heavily on men: 2God gives a man wealth, possessions and honor, so that he lacks nothing his heart desires, but God does not enable him to enjoy them, and a stranger enjoys them instead. This is meaningless, a grievous evil.

3A man may have a hundred children and live many years; yet no matter how long he lives, if he cannot enjoy his prosperity and does not receive proper burial, I say that a stillborn child is better off than he. 4It comes without meaning, it departs in darkness, and in darkness its name is shrouded. 5Though it never saw the sun or knew anything, it has more rest than does that man— 6even if he lives a thousand years twice over but fails to enjoy his prosperity. Do not all go to the same place?

7All man's efforts are for his mouth,
    yet his appetite is never satisfied.
8What advantage has a wise man
    over a fool?
  What does a poor man gain
    by knowing how to conduct himself before
      others?
9Better what the eye sees
    than the roving of the appetite.
  This too is meaningless,
    a chasing after the wind.

10Whatever exists has already been named,
    and what man is has been known;
  no man can contend
    with one who is stronger than he.
11The more the words,
    the less the meaning,
    and how does that profit anyone?

12For who knows what is good for a man in life, during the few and meaningless days he passes through like a shadow? Who can tell him what will happen under the sun after he is gone?

Wisdom

7 A GOOD name is better than fine perfume, and the day of death better than the day of birth.
2It is better to go to a house of mourning
    than to go to a house of feasting,
  for death is the destiny of every man;
    the living should take this to heart.
3Sorrow is better than laughter,
    because a sad face is good for the heart.
4The heart of the wise is in the house of
      mourning,
    but the heart of fools is in the house of
      pleasure.
5It is better to heed a wise man's rebuke
    than to listen to the song of fools.
6Like the crackling of thorns under the pot,
    so is the laughter of fools.
    This too is meaningless.

Living Bible

course, it is very good if a man has received wealth from the Lord, and the good health to enjoy it. To enjoy your work and to accept your lot in life—that is indeed a gift from God. The person who does that will not need to look back with sorrow on his past, for God gives him joy.

6 YES, BUT there is a very serious evil which I have seen everywhere— 2God has given to some men very great wealth and honor, so that they can have everything they want but he doesn't give them the health to enjoy it, and they die and others get it all! This is absurd, a hollow mockery, and a serious fault.

3Even if a man has a hundred sons and as many daughters and lives to be very old, but leaves so little money at his death that his children can't even give him a decent burial—I say that he would be better off born dead. 4For though his birth would then be futile and end in darkness, without even a name, 5never seeing the sun or even knowing its existence, yet that is better than to be an old, unhappy man. 6Though a man lives a thousand years twice over, but doesn't find contentment—well, what's the use?

7, 8Wise men and fools alike spend their lives scratching for food, and never seem to get enough. Both have the same problem, yet the poor man who is wise lives a far better life. 9A bird in the hand is worth two in the bush; mere dreaming of nice things is foolish; it's chasing the wind.

10All things are decided by fate; it was known long ago what each man would be. So there's no use arguing with God about your destiny.

11The more words you speak, the less they mean, so why bother to speak at all?

12In these few days of our empty lifetimes, who can say how one's days can best be spent? Who can know what will prove best for the future after he is gone? For who knows the future?

7 A GOOD reputation is more valuable than the most expensive perfume.

The day one dies is better than the day he is born! 2It is better to spend your time at funerals than at festivals. For you are going to die and it is a good thing to think about it while there is still time. 3Sorrow is better than laughter, for sadness has a refining influence on us. 4Yes, a wise man thinks much of death, while the fool thinks only of having a good time now.

5It is better to be criticized by a wise man than to be praised by a fool! 6For a fool's compliment is as quickly gone as paper in fire, and it is silly to be impressed by it.

New Revised Standard

God gives wealth and possessions and whom he enables to enjoy them, and to accept their lot and find enjoyment in their toil—this is the gift of God. 20For they will scarcely brood over the days of their lives, because God keeps them occupied with the joy of their hearts.

The Frustration of Desires

6 THERE IS an evil that I have seen under the sun, and it lies heavy upon humankind: 2 those to whom God gives wealth, possessions, and honor, so that they lack nothing of all that they desire, yet God does not enable them to enjoy these things, but a stranger enjoys them. This is vanity; it is a grievous ill. 3A man may beget a hundred children, and live many years; but however many are the days of his years, if he does not enjoy life's good things, or has no burial, I say that a stillborn child is better off than he. 4For it comes into vanity and goes into darkness, and in darkness its name is covered; 5moreover it has not seen the sun or known anything; yet it finds rest rather than he. 6Even though he should live a thousand years twice over, yet enjoy no good—do not all go to one place?

7 All human toil is for the mouth, yet the appetite is not satisfied. 8For what advantage have the wise over fools? And what do the poor have who know how to conduct themselves before the living? 9Better is the sight of the eyes than the wandering of desire; this also is vanity and a chasing after wind.a

10 Whatever has come to be has already been named, and it is known what human beings are, and that they are not able to dispute with those who are stronger. 11The more words, the more vanity, so how is one the better? 12For who knows what is good for mortals while they live the few days of their vain life, which they pass like a shadow? For who can tell them what will be after them under the sun?

A Disillusioned View of Life

7 A GOOD name is better than precious
   ointment,
       and the day of death, than the day of birth.
2 It is better to go to the house of mourning
       than to go to the house of feasting;
   for this is the end of everyone,
       and the living will lay it to heart.
3 Sorrow is better than laughter,
       for by sadness of countenance the heart is
       made glad.
4 The heart of the wise is in the house of
       mourning;
       but the heart of fools is in the house of
       mirth.
5 It is better to hear the rebuke of the wise
       than to hear the song of fools.
6 For like the crackling of thorns under a pot,
       so is the laughter of fools;
       this also is vanity.

---

a Or a feeding on wind. See Hos 12.1

King James

7¶ Surely oppression maketh a wise man mad; and a gift destroyeth the heart.

8Better *is* the end of a thing than the beginning thereof: *and* the patient in spirit *is* better than the proud in spirit.

9Be not hasty in thy spirit to be angry: for anger resteth in the bosom of fools.

10Say not thou, What is *the cause* that the former days were better than these? for thou dost not inquire wisely concerning this.

11¶ Wisdom *is* good with an inheritance: and *by it there is* profit to them that see the sun.

12For wisdom *is* a defence, *and* money *is* a defence: but the excellency of knowledge *is, that* wisdom giveth life to them that have it.

13Consider the work of God: for who can make *that* straight, which he hath made crooked?

14In the day of prosperity be joyful, but in the day of adversity consider: God also hath set the one over against the other, to the end that man should find nothing after him.

15All *things* have I seen in the days of my vanity: there is a just *man* that perisheth in his righteousness, and there is a wicked *man* that prolongeth *his* life in his wickedness.

16Be not righteous over much; neither make thyself over wise: why shouldest thou destroy thyself?

17Be not over much wicked, neither be thou foolish: why shouldest thou die before thy time?

18*It is* good that thou shouldest take hold of this; yea, also from this withdraw not thine hand: for he that feareth God shall come forth of them all.

19Wisdom strengtheneth the wise more than ten mighty *men* which are in the city.

20For *there is* not a just man upon earth, that doeth good, and sinneth not.

21Also take no heed unto all words that are spoken; lest thou hear thy servant curse thee:

22For oftentimes also thine own heart knoweth that thou thyself likewise hast cursed others.

23¶ All this have I proved by wisdom: I said, I will be wise; but it *was* far from me.

24That which is far off, and exceeding deep, who can find it out?

25I applied mine heart to know, and to search, and to seek out wisdom, and the reason *of things,* and to know the wickedness of folly, even of foolishness *and* madness:

26And I find more bitter than death the woman, whose heart *is* snares and nets, *and* her hands *as* bands: whoso pleaseth God shall escape from her; but the sinner shall be taken by her.

New International

7Extortion turns a wise man into a fool,
   and a bribe corrupts the heart.

8The end of a matter is better than its beginning,
   and patience is better than pride.

9Do not be quickly provoked in your spirit,
   for anger resides in the lap of fools.

10Do not say, "Why were the old days better than
      these?"
   For it is not wise to ask such questions.

11Wisdom, like an inheritance, is a good thing
   and benefits those who see the sun.

12Wisdom is a shelter
   as money is a shelter,
but the advantage of knowledge is this:
   that wisdom preserves the life of its
      possessor.

13Consider what God has done:

Who can straighten
   what he has made crooked?

14When times are good, be happy;
   but when times are bad, consider:
God has made the one
   as well as the other.
Therefore, a man cannot discover
   anything about his future.

15In this meaningless life of mine I have seen both of these:

a righteous man perishing in his righteousness,
   and a wicked man living long in his
      wickedness.

16Do not be overrighteous,
   neither be overwise—
   why destroy yourself?

17Do not be overwicked,
   and do not be a fool—
   why die before your time?

18It is good to grasp the one
   and not let go of the other.
The man who fears God will avoid all
   extremes.ᵃ

19Wisdom makes one wise man more powerful
   than ten rulers in a city.

20There is not a righteous man on earth
   who does what is right and never sins.

21Do not pay attention to every word people say,
   or you may hear your servant cursing you—

22for you know in your heart
   that many times you yourself have cursed
      others.

23All this I tested by wisdom and I said,

"I am determined to be wise"—
   but this was beyond me.

24Whatever wisdom may be,
   it is far off and most profound—
   who can discover it?

25So I turned my mind to understand,
   to investigate and to search out wisdom and
      the scheme of things
and to understand the stupidity of wickedness
   and the madness of folly.

26I find more bitter than death
   the woman who is a snare,
whose heart is a trap
   and whose hands are chains.
The man who pleases God will escape her,
   but the sinner she will ensnare.

ᵃ *18 Or will follow them both*

Living Bible

7The wise man is turned into a fool by a bribe; it destroys his understanding.

8Finishing is better than starting! Patience is better than pride! 9Don't be quick-tempered—that is being a fool.

10Don't long for "the good old days," for you don't know whether they were any better than these!

11To be wise is as good as being rich; in fact, it is better. 12You can get anything by either wisdom or money, but being wise has many advantages.

13See the way God does things and fall into line. Don't fight the facts of nature.b Who can straighten what he has made crooked? 14Enjoy prosperity whenever you can, and when hard times strike, realize that God gives one as well as the other—so that everyone will realize that nothing is certain in this life.

15, 16, 17In this silly life I have seen everything, including the fact that some of the good die young and some of the wicked live on and on. So don't be too good or too wise! Why destroy yourself? On the other hand, don't be too wicked either—don't be a fool! Why should you die before your time?

18Tackle every task that comes along, and if you fear God you can expect his blessing.

19A wise man is stronger than the mayors of ten big cities! 20And there is not a single man in all the earth who is always good and never sins.

21, 22Don't eavesdrop! You may hear your servant cursing you! For you know how often you yourself curse others!

23I have tried my best to be wise. I declared, "I *will* be wise," but it didn't work. 24Wisdom is far away, and very difficult to find. 25I searched everywhere, determined to find wisdom and the reason for things, and to prove to myself the wickedness of folly, and that foolishness is madness.

26A prostitute is more bitter than death.c May it please God that you escape from her, but sinners don't evade her snares.

New Revised Standard

7   Surely oppression makes the wise foolish,
      and a bribe corrupts the heart.
8   Better is the end of a thing than its beginning;
      the patient in spirit are better than the proud
      in spirit.
9   Do not be quick to anger,
      for anger lodges in the bosom of fools.
10   Do not say, "Why were the former days better
      than these?"
      For it is not from wisdom that you ask this.
11   Wisdom is as good as an inheritance,
      an advantage to those who see the sun.
12   For the protection of wisdom is like the
      protection of money,
      and the advantage of knowledge is that
      wisdom gives life to the one who
      possesses it.
13   Consider the work of God;
      who can make straight what he has made
      crooked?

14   In the day of prosperity be joyful, and in the day of adversity consider; God has made the one as well as the other, so that mortals may not find out anything that will come after them.

The Riddles of Life

15   In my vain life I have seen everything; there are righteous people who perish in their righteousness, and there are wicked people who prolong their life in their evildoing. 16Do not be too righteous, and do not act too wise; why should you destroy yourself? 17Do not be too wicked, and do not be a fool; why should you die before your time? 18It is good that you should take hold of the one, without letting go of the other; for the one who fears God shall succeed with both.

19   Wisdom gives strength to the wise more than ten rulers that are in a city.

20   Surely there is no one on earth so righteous as to do good without ever sinning.

21   Do not give heed to everything that people say, or you may hear your servant cursing you; 22your heart knows that many times you have yourself cursed others.

23   All this I have tested by wisdom; I said, "I will be wise," but it was far from me. 24That which is, is far off, and deep, very deep; who can find it out? 25I turned my mind to know and to search out and to seek wisdom and the sum of things, and to know that wickedness is folly and that foolishness is madness. 26I found more bitter than death the woman who is a trap, whose heart is snares and nets, whose hands are fetters; one who pleases God escapes her, but the sinner is taken by her.

b 7:13 *Don't fight the facts of nature,* implied.   c 7:26 *A prostitute is more bitter than death,* literally, "the woman whose heart is snares and nets."

King James

27Behold, this have I found, saith the preacher, *counting* one by one, to find out the account:

28Which yet my soul seeketh, but I find not: one man among a thousand have I found; but a woman among all those have I not found.

29Lo, this only have I found, that God hath made man upright; but they have sought out many inventions.

8 WHO *IS* as the wise *man?* and who knoweth the interpretation of a thing? a man's wisdom maketh his face to shine, and the boldness of his face shall be changed.

2*I counsel thee* to keep the king's commandment, and *that* in regard of the oath of God.

3Be not hasty to go out of his sight: stand not in an evil thing; for he doeth whatsoever pleaseth him.

4Where the word of a king *is, there is* power: and who may say unto him, What doest thou?

5Whoso keepeth the commandment shall feel no evil thing: and a wise man's heart discerneth both time and judgment.

6¶ Because to every purpose there is time and judgment, therefore the misery of man *is* great upon him.

7For he knoweth not that which shall be: for who can tell him when it shall be?

8*There is* no man that hath power over the spirit to retain the spirit; neither *hath he* power in the day of death: and *there is* no discharge in *that* war; neither shall wickedness deliver those that are given to it.

9All this have I seen, and applied my heart unto every work that is done under the sun: *there is* a time wherein one man ruleth over another to his own hurt.

10And so I saw the wicked buried, who had come and gone from the place of the holy, and they were forgotten in the city where they had so done: this *is* also vanity.

11Because sentence against an evil work is not executed speedily, therefore the heart of the sons of men is fully set in them to do evil.

12¶ Though a sinner do evil an hundred times, and his *days* be prolonged, yet surely I know that it shall be well with them that fear God, which fear before him:

13But it shall not be well with the wicked, neither shall he prolong *his* days, *which are* as a shadow; because he feareth not before God.

14There is a vanity which is done upon the earth; that there be just *men,* unto whom it happeneth according to the work of the wicked; again, there be wicked *men,* to whom it happeneth according to the work of the righteous: I said that this also *is* vanity.

15Then I commended mirth, because a man hath no better thing under the sun, than to eat, and to drink, and to be merry: for that shall abide with him of his labour the days of his life, which God giveth him under the sun.

New International

27"Look," says the Teacher,[a] "this is what I have discovered:

"Adding one thing to another to discover the scheme of things—
28 while I was still searching but not finding—
I found one upright man among a thousand, but not one upright woman among them all.
29This only have I found:
God made mankind upright, but men have gone in search of many schemes."

8 WHO IS like the wise man?
Who knows the explanation of things?
Wisdom brightens a man's face and changes its hard appearance.

Obey the King

2Obey the king's command, I say, because you took an oath before God. 3Do not be in a hurry to leave the king's presence. Do not stand up for a bad cause, for he will do whatever he pleases. 4Since a king's word is supreme, who can say to him, "What are you doing?"

5Whoever obeys his command will come to no harm,
and the wise heart will know the proper time and procedure.
6For there is a proper time and procedure for every matter,
though a man's misery weighs heavily upon him.

7Since no man knows the future,
who can tell him what is to come?
8No man has power over the wind to contain it[b];
so no one has power over the day of his death.
As no one is discharged in time of war,
so wickedness will not release those who practice it.

9All this I saw, as I applied my mind to everything done under the sun. There is a time when a man lords it over others to his own[c] hurt. 10Then too, I saw the wicked buried—those who used to come and go from the holy place and receive praise[d] in the city where they did this. This too is meaningless.

11When the sentence for a crime is not quickly carried out, the hearts of the people are filled with schemes to do wrong. 12Although a wicked man commits a hundred crimes and still lives a long time, I know that it will go better with God-fearing men, who are reverent before God. 13Yet because the wicked do not fear God, it will not go well with them, and their days will not lengthen like a shadow.

14There is something else meaningless that occurs on earth: righteous men who get what the wicked deserve, and wicked men who get what the righteous deserve. This too, I say, is meaningless. 15So I commend the enjoyment of life, because nothing is better for a man under the sun than to eat and drink and be glad. Then joy will accompany him in his work all the days of the life God has given him under the sun.

Living Bible

27, 28This is my conclusion, says the Preacher. Step by step I came to this result after researching in every direction: One tenth of one percent of the men I interviewed could be said to be wise, but not one woman! 29And I found that though God has made men upright, each has turned away to follow his own downward road.

8 HOW WONDERFUL to be wise, to understand things, to be able to analyze them and interpret them. Wisdom lights up a man's face, softening its hardness.
2, 3Obey the king as you have vowed to do. Don't always be trying to get out of doing your duty, even when it's unpleasant. For the king punishes those who disobey. 4The king's command is backed by great power, and no one can withstand it or question it. 5Those who obey him will not be punished. The wise man will find a time and a way to do what he says. 6, 7Yes, there is a time and a way for everything, though man's trouble lies heavy upon him; for how can he avoid what he doesn't know is going to happen?
8No one can hold back his spirit from departing; no one has the power to prevent his day of death, for there is no discharge from that obligation and that dark battle. Certainly a man's wickedness is not going to help him then.
9, 10I have thought deeply about all that goes on here in the world, where people have the power of injuring each other. I have seen wicked men buried and as their friends returned from the cemetery, having forgotten all the dead man's evil deeds, these men were praised in the very city where they had committed their many crimes! How odd! 11Because God does not punish sinners instantly, people feel it is safe to do wrong. 12But though a man sins a hundred times and still lives, I know very well that those who fear God will be better off, 13unlike the wicked, who will not live long, good lives—their days shall pass away as quickly as shadows because they don't fear God.
14There is a strange thing happening here upon the earth: Providence seems to treat some good men as though they were wicked, and some wicked men as though they were good. This is all very vexing and troublesome!
15Then I decided to spend my time having fun, because I felt that there was nothing better in all the earth than that a man should eat, drink, and be merry, with the hope that this happiness would stick with him in all the hard work which God gives to mankind everywhere.

New Revised Standard

27See, this is what I found, says the Teacher,e adding one thing to another to find the sum, 28which my mind has sought repeatedly, but I have not found. One man among a thousand I found, but a woman among all these I have not found. 29See, this alone I found, that God made human beings straightforward, but they have devised many schemes.

Obey the King and Enjoy Yourself

8 WHO IS like the wise man?
  And who knows the interpretation of a
       thing?
  Wisdom makes one's face shine,
     and the hardness of one's countenance is
        changed.
2 Keepf the king's command because of your sacred oath. 3Do not be terrified; go from his presence, do not delay when the matter is unpleasant, for he does whatever he pleases. 4For the word of the king is powerful, and who can say to him, "What are you doing?" 5Whoever obeys a command will meet no harm, and the wise mind will know the time and way. 6For every matter has its time and way, although the troubles of mortals lie heavy upon them. 7Indeed, they do not know what is to be, for who can tell them how it will be? 8No one has power over the windg to restrain the wind,g or power over the day of death; there is no discharge from the battle, nor does wickedness deliver those who practice it. 9All this I observed, applying my mind to all that is done under the sun, while one person exercises authority over another to the other's hurt.

God's Ways Are Inscrutable

10 Then I saw the wicked buried; they used to go in and out of the holy place, and were praised in the city where they had done such things.h This also is vanity. 11Because sentence against an evil deed is not executed speedily, the human heart is fully set to do evil. 12Though sinners do evil a hundred times and prolong their lives, yet I know that it will be well with those who fear God, because they stand in fear before him, 13but it will not be well with the wicked, neither will they prolong their days like a shadow, because they do not stand in fear before God.
14 There is a vanity that takes place on earth, that there are righteous people who are treated according to the conduct of the wicked, and there are wicked people who are treated according to the conduct of the righteous. I said that this also is vanity. 15So I commend enjoyment, for there is nothing better for people under the sun than to eat, and drink, and enjoy themselves, for this will go with them in their toil through the days of life that God gives them under the sun.

---

e *Qoheleth*, traditionally rendered *Preacher*   f Heb *I keep*   g Or *breath*
h Meaning of Heb uncertain

King James

16¶ When I applied mine heart to know wisdom, and to see the business that is done upon the earth: (for also *there is that* neither day nor night seeth sleep with his eyes:)

17Then I beheld all the work of God, that a man cannot find out the work that is done under the sun: because though a man labour to seek *it* out, yet he shall not find *it;* yea further; though a wise *man* think to know *it,* yet shall he not be able to find *it.*

9 FOR ALL this I considered in my heart even to declare all this, that the righteous, and the wise, and their works, *are* in the hand of God: no man knoweth either love or hatred *by* all *that is* before them.

2All *things* come alike to all: *there is* one event to the righteous, and to the wicked; to the good and to the clean, and to the unclean; to him that sacrificeth, and to him that sacrificeth not: as *is* the good, so *is* the sinner; *and* he that sweareth, as *he* that feareth an oath.

3This *is* an evil among all *things* that are done under the sun, that *there is* one event unto all: yea, also the heart of the sons of men is full of evil, and madness *is* in their heart while they live, and after that *they* go to the dead.

4¶ For to him that is joined to all the living there is hope: for a living dog is better than a dead lion.

5For the living know that they shall die: but the dead know not any thing, neither have they any more a reward; for the memory of them is forgotten.

6Also their love, and their hatred, and their envy, is now perished; neither have they any more a portion for ever in any *thing* that is done under the sun.

7¶ Go thy way, eat thy bread with joy, and drink thy wine with a merry heart; for God now accepteth thy works.

8Let thy garments be always white; and let thy head lack no ointment.

9Live joyfully with the wife whom thou lovest all the days of the life of thy vanity, which he hath given thee under the sun, all the days of thy vanity: for that *is* thy portion in *this* life, and in thy labour which thou takest under the sun.

10Whatsoever thy hand findeth to do, do *it* with thy might; for *there is* no work, nor device, nor knowledge, nor wisdom, in the grave, whither thou goest.

11¶ I returned, and saw under the sun, that the race *is* not to the swift, nor the battle to the strong, neither yet bread to the wise, nor yet riches to men of understanding, nor yet favour to men of skill; but time and chance happeneth to them all.

12For man also knoweth not his time: as the fishes that are taken in an evil net, and as the birds that are caught in the snare; so *are* the sons of men snared in an evil time, when it falleth suddenly upon them.

13¶ This wisdom have I seen also under the sun, and it *seemed* great unto me:

New International

16When I applied my mind to know wisdom and to observe man's labor on earth—his eyes not seeing sleep day or night— 17then I saw all that God has done. No one can comprehend what goes on under the sun. Despite all his efforts to search it out, man cannot discover its meaning. Even if a wise man claims he knows, he cannot really comprehend it.

A Common Destiny for All

9 SO I reflected on all this and concluded that the righteous and the wise and what they do are in God's hands, but no man knows whether love or hate awaits him. 2All share a common destiny—the righteous and the wicked, the good and the bad,[a] the clean and the unclean, those who offer sacrifices and those who do not.

As it is with the good man,
    so with the sinner;
as it is with those who take oaths,
    so with those who are afraid to take them.

3This is the evil in everything that happens under the sun: The same destiny overtakes all. The hearts of men, moreover, are full of evil and there is madness in their hearts while they live, and afterward they join the dead. 4Anyone who is among the living has hope[b]—even a live dog is better off than a dead lion!

5For the living know that they will die,
    but the dead know nothing;
they have no further reward,
    and even the memory of them is forgotten.
6Their love, their hate
    and their jealousy have long since vanished;
never again will they have a part
    in anything that happens under the sun.

7Go, eat your food with gladness, and drink your wine with a joyful heart, for it is now that God favors what you do. 8Always be clothed in white, and always anoint your head with oil. 9Enjoy life with your wife, whom you love, all the days of this meaningless life that God has given you under the sun— all your meaningless days. For this is your lot in life and in your toilsome labor under the sun. 10Whatever your hand finds to do, do it with all your might, for in the grave,[c] where you are going, there is neither working nor planning nor knowledge nor wisdom.

11I have seen something else under the sun:

The race is not to the swift
    or the battle to the strong,
nor does food come to the wise
    or wealth to the brilliant
    or favor to the learned;
but time and chance happen to them all.

12Moreover, no man knows when his hour will come:

As fish are caught in a cruel net,
    or birds are taken in a snare,
so men are trapped by evil times
    that fall unexpectedly upon them.

Wisdom Better Than Folly

13I also saw under the sun this example of wisdom that greatly impressed me: 14There was once a small city

Living Bible

16, 17In my search for wisdom I observed all that was going on everywhere across the earth—ceaseless activity, day and night. (Of course, only God can see everything, and even the wisest man who says he knows everything, doesn't!)

9 THIS, TOO, I carefully explored—that godly and wise men are in God's will; no one knows whether he will favor them or not. All is chance! 2, 3The same providence confronts everyone, whether good or bad, religious or irreligious, profane or godly. It seems so unfair, that one fate comes to all. That is why men are not more careful to be good, but instead choose their own mad course, for they have no hope—there is nothing but death ahead anyway.

4There is hope only for the living. "It is better to be a live dog than a dead lion!" 5For the living at least know that they will die! But the dead know nothingd; they don't even have their memories.d 6Whatever they did in their lifetimes—loving, hating, envying—is long gone, and they have no part in anything here on earth any more. 7So go ahead, eat, drink, and be merry, for it makes no difference to God! 8Wear fine clothes—with a dash of cologne! 9Live happily with the woman you love through the fleeting days of life, for the wife God gives you is your best reward down here for all your earthly toil. 10Whatever you do, do well, for in death, where you are going, there is no working or planning, or knowing, or understanding.d

11Again I looked throughout the earth and saw that the swiftest person does not always win the race, nor the strongest man the battle, and that wise men are often poor, and skillful men are not necessarily famous; but it is all by chance, by happening to be at the right place at the right time. 12A man never knows when he is going to run into bad luck. He is like a fish caught in a net, or a bird caught in a snare.

13Here is another thing that has made a deep impression on me as I have watched human affairs: 14There was

New Revised Standard

16 When I applied my mind to know wisdom, and to see the business that is done on earth, how one's eyes see sleep neither day nor night, 17then I saw all the work of God, that no one can find out what is happening under the sun. However much they may toil in seeking, they will not find it out; even though those who are wise claim to know, they cannot find it out.

Take Life as It Comes

9 ALL THIS I laid to heart, examining it all, how the righteous and the wise and their deeds are in the hand of God; whether it is love or hate one does not know. Everything that confronts them 2is vanity,e since the same fate comes to all, to the righteous and the wicked, to the good and the evil,f to the clean and the unclean, to those who sacrifice and those who do not sacrifice. As are the good, so are the sinners; those who swear are like those who shun an oath. 3This is an evil in all that happens under the sun, that the same fate comes to everyone. Moreover, the hearts of all are full of evil; madness is in their hearts while they live, and after that they go to the dead. 4But whoever is joined with all the living has hope, for a living dog is better than a dead lion. 5The living know that they will die, but the dead know nothing; they have no more reward, and even the memory of them is lost. 6Their love and their hate and their envy have already perished; never again will they have any share in all that happens under the sun.

7 Go, eat your bread with enjoyment, and drink your wine with a merry heart; for God has long ago approved what you do. 8Let your garments always be white; do not let oil be lacking on your head. 9Enjoy life with the wife whom you love, all the days of your vain life that are given you under the sun, because that is your portion in life and in your toil at which you toil under the sun. 10Whatever your hand finds to do, do with your might; for there is no work or thought or knowledge or wisdom in Sheol, to which you are going.

11 Again I saw that under the sun the race is not to the swift, nor the battle to the strong, nor bread to the wise, nor riches to the intelligent, nor favor to the skillful; but time and chance happen to them all. 12For no one can anticipate the time of disaster. Like fish taken in a cruel net, and like birds caught in a snare, so mortals are snared at a time of calamity, when it suddenly falls upon them.

Wisdom Superior to Folly

13 I have also seen this example of wisdom under the sun, and it seemed great to me. 14There was a little

---

d 9:5,9:10 But the dead know nothing. These statements are Solomon's discouraged opinion, and do not reflect a knowledge of God's truth on these points.

e Syr Compare Gk: Heb Everything that confronts them 2is everything   f Gk Syr Vg: Heb lacks and the evil

King James

14*There was* a little city, and few men within it; and there came a great king against it, and besieged it, and built great bulwarks against it:

15Now there was found in it a poor wise man, and he by his wisdom delivered the city; yet no man remembered that same poor man.

16Then said I, Wisdom *is* better than strength: nevertheless the poor man's wisdom *is* despised, and his words are not heard.

17The words of wise *men are* heard in quiet more than the cry of him that ruleth among fools.

18Wisdom *is* better than weapons of war: but one sinner destroyeth much good.

10 DEAD FLIES cause the ointment of the apothecary to send forth a stinking savour: *so doth* a little folly him that is in reputation for wisdom *and* honour.

2A wise man's heart *is* at his right hand; but a fool's heart at his left.

3Yea also, when he that is a fool walketh by the way, his wisdom faileth *him,* and he saith to every one *that* he *is* a fool.

4If the spirit of the ruler rise up against thee, leave not thy place; for yielding pacifieth great offences.

5There is an evil *which* I have seen under the sun, as an error *which* proceedeth from the ruler:

6Folly is set in great dignity, and the rich sit in low place.

7I have seen servants upon horses, and princes walking as servants upon the earth.

8He that diggeth a pit shall fall into it; and whoso breaketh an hedge, a serpent shall bite him.

9Whoso removeth stones shall be hurt therewith; *and* he that cleaveth wood shall be endangered thereby.

10If the iron be blunt, and he do not whet the edge, then must he put to more strength: but wisdom *is* profitable to direct.

11Surely the serpent will bite without enchantment; and a babbler is no better.

12The words of a wise man's mouth *are* gracious; but the lips of a fool will swallow up himself.

13The beginning of the words of his mouth *is* foolishness: and the end of his talk *is* mischievous madness.

14A fool also is full of words: a man cannot tell what shall be; and what shall be after him, who can tell him?

15The labour of the foolish wearieth every one of them, because he knoweth not how to go to the city.

16¶ Woe to thee, O land, when thy king *is* a child, and thy princes eat in the morning!

17Blessed *art* thou, O land, when thy king *is* the son of nobles, and thy princes eat in due season, for strength, and not for drunkenness!

18¶ By much slothfulness the building decayeth; and through idleness of the hands the house droppeth through.

19¶ A feast is made for laughter, and wine maketh merry: but money answereth all *things.*

New International

with only a few people in it. And a powerful king came against it, surrounded it and built huge siegeworks against it. 15Now there lived in that city a man poor but wise, and he saved the city by his wisdom. But nobody remembered that poor man. 16So I said, "Wisdom is better than strength." But the poor man's wisdom is despised, and his words are no longer heeded.

17The quiet words of the wise are more to be heeded
  than the shouts of a ruler of fools.
18Wisdom is better than weapons of war,
  but one sinner destroys much good.

10 AS DEAD flies give perfume a bad smell,
  so a little folly outweighs wisdom and honor.
2The heart of the wise inclines to the right,
  but the heart of the fool to the left.
3Even as he walks along the road,
  the fool lacks sense
  and shows everyone how stupid he is.
4If a ruler's anger rises against you,
  do not leave your post;
  calmness can lay great errors to rest.

5There is an evil I have seen under the sun,
  the sort of error that arises from a ruler:
6Fools are put in many high positions,
  while the rich occupy the low ones.
7I have seen slaves on horseback,
  while princes go on foot like slaves.
8Whoever digs a pit may fall into it;
  whoever breaks through a wall may be bitten
  by a snake.
9Whoever quarries stones may be injured by
  them;
  whoever splits logs may be endangered by
  them.
10If the ax is dull
  and its edge unsharpened,
more strength is needed
  but skill will bring success.

11If a snake bites before it is charmed,
  there is no profit for the charmer.

12Words from a wise man's mouth are gracious,
  but a fool is consumed by his own lips.
13At the beginning his words are folly;
  at the end they are wicked madness—
14 and the fool multiplies words.

No one knows what is coming—
  who can tell him what will happen after him?

15A fool's work wearies him;
  he does not know the way to town.

16Woe to you, O land whose king was a servant[a]
  and whose princes feast in the morning.
17Blessed are you, O land whose king is of noble
  birth
  and whose princes eat at a proper time—
  for strength and not for drunkenness.

18If a man is lazy, the rafters sag;
  if his hands are idle, the house leaks.

19A feast is made for laughter,
  and wine makes life merry,
  but money is the answer for everything.

---

a *16 Or king is a child*

Living Bible

a small city with only a few people living in it, and a great king came with his army and besieged it. 15There was in the city a wise man, very poor, and he knew what to do to save the city, and so it was rescued. But afterwards no one thought any more about him. 16Then I realized that though wisdom is better than strength, nevertheless, if the wise man is poor, he will be despised, and what he says will not be appreciated. 17But even so, the quiet words of a wise man are better than the shout of a king of fools. 18Wisdom is better than weapons of war, but one rotten apple can spoil a barrelful.

10 DEAD FLIES will cause even a bottle of perfume to stink! Yes, a small mistake can outweigh much wisdom and honor. 2A wise man's heart leads him to do right, and a fool's heart leads him to do evil. 3You can identify a fool just by the way he walks down the street!

4If the boss is angry with you, don't quit! A quiet spirit will quiet his bad temper.

5There is another evil I have seen as I have watched the world go by, a sad situation concerning kings and rulers: 6For I have seen foolish men given great authority, and rich men not given their rightful place of dignity! 7I have even seen servants riding, while princes walk like servants!

8, 9Dig a well—and fall into it! Demolish an old wall—and be bitten by a snake! When working in a quarry, stones will fall and crush you! There is risk in each stroke of your axe!

10A dull axe requires great strength; be wise and sharpen the blade.

11When the horse is stolen, it is too late to lock the barn.b

12, 13It is pleasant to listen to wise words, but a fool's speech brings him to ruin. Since he begins with a foolish premise, his conclusion is sheer madness. 14A fool knows all about the future and tells everyone in detail! But who can really know what is going to happen? 15A fool is so upset by a little work that he has no strength for the simplest matter.c

16, 17Woe to the land whose king is a child and whose leaders are already drunk in the morning. Happy the land whose king is a nobleman, and whose leaders work hard before they feast and drink, and then only to strengthen themselves for the tasks ahead! 18Laziness lets the roof leak, and soon the rafters begin to rot. 19A party gives laughter, and wine gives happiness, and money gives everything! 20Never curse the king, not even in your

New Revised Standard

city with few people in it. A great king came against it and besieged it, building great siegeworks against it. 15Now there was found in it a poor wise man, and he by his wisdom delivered the city. Yet no one remembered that poor man. 16So I said, "Wisdom is better than might; yet the poor man's wisdom is despised, and his words are not heeded."

17 The quiet words of the wise are more to be
    heeded
       than the shouting of a ruler among fools.
18 Wisdom is better than weapons of war,
       but one bungler destroys much good.

Miscellaneous Observations

10 DEAD FLIES make the perfumer's ointment
       give off a foul odor;
    so a little folly outweighs wisdom and
       honor.
2 The heart of the wise inclines to the right,
       but the heart of a fool to the left.
3 Even when fools walk on the road, they lack
       sense,
       and show to everyone that they are fools.
4 If the anger of the ruler rises against you, do
       not leave your post,
       for calmness will undo great offenses.

5 There is an evil that I have seen under the sun, as great an error as if it proceeded from the ruler: 6folly is set in many high places, and the rich sit in a low place. 7I have seen slaves on horseback, and princes walking on foot like slaves.

8 Whoever digs a pit will fall into it;
       and whoever breaks through a wall will be
          bitten by a snake.
9 Whoever quarries stones will be hurt by them;
       and whoever splits logs will be endangered
          by them.
10 If the iron is blunt, and one does not whet the
       edge,
       then more strength must be exerted;
       but wisdom helps one to succeed.
11 If the snake bites before it is charmed,
       there is no advantage in a charmer.

12 Words spoken by the wise bring them favor,
       but the lips of fools consume them.
13 The words of their mouths begin in
       foolishness,
       and their talk ends in wicked madness;
14 yet fools talk on and on.
    No one knows what is to happen,
       and who can tell anyone what the future
          holds?
15 The toil of fools wears them out,
       for they do not even know the way to town.

16 Alas for you, O land, when your king is a
       servant,d
       and your princes feast in the morning!
17 Happy are you, O land, when your king is a
       nobleman,
       and your princes feast at the proper time—
       for strength, and not for drunkenness!
18 Through sloth the roof sinks in,
       and through indolence the house leaks.
19 Feasts are made for laughter;
       wine gladdens life,
       and money meets every need.

b 10:11 it is too late to lock the barn, literally, "If the serpent bites before it is charmed, there is no advantage to the charmer." c 10:15 for the simplest matter, literally, "for a trip to the city."

d Or a child

King James

20¶ Curse not the king, no not in thy thought; and curse not the rich in thy bedchamber: for a bird of the air shall carry the voice, and that which hath wings shall tell the matter.

11 CAST THY bread upon the waters: for thou shalt find it after many days.

2Give a portion to seven, and also to eight; for thou knowest not what evil shall be upon the earth.

3If the clouds be full of rain, they empty *themselves* upon the earth: and if the tree fall toward the south, or toward the north, in the place where the tree falleth, there it shall be.

4He that observeth the wind shall not sow; and he that regardeth the clouds shall not reap.

5As thou knowest not what *is* the way of the spirit, *nor* how the bones *do grow* in the womb of her that is with child: even so thou knowest not the works of God who maketh all.

6In the morning sow thy seed, and in the evening withhold not thine hand: for thou knowest not whether shall prosper, either this or that, or whether they both *shall be* alike good.

7¶ Truly the light *is* sweet, and a pleasant *thing it is* for the eyes to behold the sun:

8But if a man live many years, *and* rejoice in them all; yet let him remember the days of darkness; for they shall be many. All that cometh *is* vanity.

9¶ Rejoice, O young man, in thy youth; and let thy heart cheer thee in the days of thy youth, and walk in the ways of thine heart, and in the sight of thine eyes: but know thou, that for all these *things* God will bring thee into judgment.

10Therefore remove sorrow from thy heart, and put away evil from thy flesh: for childhood and youth *are* vanity.

12 REMEMBER NOW thy Creator in the days of thy youth, while the evil days come not, nor the years draw nigh, when thou shalt say, I have no pleasure in them;

2While the sun, or the light, or the moon, or the stars, be not darkened, nor the clouds return after the rain:

3In the day when the keepers of the house shall tremble, and the strong men shall bow themselves, and the grinders cease because they are few, and those that look out of the windows be darkened,

4And the doors shall be shut in the streets, when the sound of the grinding is low, and he shall rise up at the voice of the bird, and all the daughters of music shall be brought low;

New International

20Do not revile the king even in your thoughts,
  or curse the rich in your bedroom,
because a bird of the air may carry your words,
  and a bird on the wing may report what you
    say.

Bread Upon the Waters

11 CAST YOUR bread upon the waters,
  for after many days you will find it again.
2Give portions to seven, yes to eight;
  for you do not know what disaster may come
    upon the land.

3If clouds are full of water,
  they pour rain upon the earth.
Whether a tree falls to the south or to the north,
  in the place where it falls, there will it lie.
4Whoever watches the wind will not plant;
  whoever looks at the clouds will not reap.

5As you do not know the path of the wind,
  or how the body is formeda in a mother's
    womb,
so you cannot understand the work of God,
  the Maker of all things.

6Sow your seed in the morning,
  and at evening let not your hands be idle,
for you do not know which will succeed,
  whether this or that,
  or whether both will do equally well.

Remember Your Creator While Young

7Light is sweet,
  and it pleases the eyes to see the sun.
8However many years a man may live,
  let him enjoy them all.
But let him remember the days of darkness,
  for they will be many.
  Everything to come is meaningless.

9Be happy, young man, while you are young,
  and let your heart give you joy in the days of
    your youth.
Follow the ways of your heart
  and whatever your eyes see,
but know that for all these things
  God will bring you to judgment.
10So then, banish anxiety from your heart
  and cast off the troubles of your body,
  for youth and vigor are meaningless.

12 REMEMBER YOUR Creator
  in the days of your youth,
before the days of trouble come
  and the years approach when you will say,
    "I find no pleasure in them"—
2before the sun and the light
  and the moon and the stars grow dark,
  and the clouds return after the rain;
3when the keepers of the house tremble,
  and the strong men stoop,
when the grinders cease because they are few,
  and those looking through the windows grow
    dim;
4when the doors to the street are closed
  and the sound of grinding fades;
when men rise up at the sound of birds,
  but all their songs grow faint;

---

a 5 Or *know how life* (or *the spirit*) / *enters the body being formed*

Living Bible

thoughts; nor the rich man, either; for a little bird will tell them what you've said.

11 GIVE GENEROUSLY, for your gifts will return to you later. ²Divide your gifts among many,ᵇ for in the days ahead you yourself may need much help.

³When the clouds are heavy, the rains come down; when a tree falls, whether south or north, the die is cast, for there it lies. ⁴If you wait for perfect conditions, you will never get anything done.ᶜ ⁵God's ways are as mysterious as the pathway of the wind, and as the manner in which a human spirit is infused into the little body of a baby while it is yet in its mother's womb. ⁶Keep on sowing your seed, for you never know which will grow—perhaps it all will.

⁷It is a wonderful thing to be alive! ⁸If a person lives to be very old, let him rejoice in every day of life, but let him also remember that eternity is far longer, and that everything down here is futile in comparison.

⁹Young man, it's wonderful to be young! Enjoy every minute of it! Do all you want to; take in everything, but realize that you must account to God for everything you do. ¹⁰So banish grief and pain, but remember that youth, with a whole life before it, can make serious mistakes.

12 DON'T LET the excitement of being young cause you to forget about your Creator. Honor him in your youth before the evil years come—when you'll no longer enjoy living. ²It will be too late then to try to remember him, when the sun and light and moon and stars are dim to your old eyes, and there is no silver lining left among your clouds. ³For there will come a time when your limbs will tremble with age, and your strong legs will become weak, and your teeth will be too few to do their work, and there will be blindness, too. ⁴Then let your lips be tightly closed while eating, when your teeth are gone! And you will waken at dawn with the first note of the birds; but you yourself will be deaf and tuneless, with quavering voice. ⁵You will be afraid

ᵇ 11:2 Divide your gifts among many, literally, "Give a portion to seven, yes, even to eight." ᶜ 11:4 you will never get anything done, literally, "He that observeth the wind shall not sow and he that regardeth the clouds shall not reap."

New Revised Standard

²⁰ Do not curse the king, even in your thoughts,
    or curse the rich, even in your bedroom;
for a bird of the air may carry your voice,
    or some winged creature tell the matter.

The Value of Diligence

11 SEND OUT your bread upon the waters,
    for after many days you will get it back.
² Divide your means seven ways, or even eight,
    for you do not know what disaster may
        happen on earth.
³ When clouds are full,
    they empty rain on the earth;
whether a tree falls to the south or to the
        north,
    in the place where the tree falls, there it
        will lie.
⁴ Whoever observes the wind will not sow;
    and whoever regards the clouds will not
        reap.

5 Just as you do not know how the breath comes to the bones in the mother's womb, so you do not know the work of God, who makes everything.

6 In the morning sow your seed, and at evening do not let your hands be idle; for you do not know which will prosper, this or that, or whether both alike will be good.

Youth and Old Age

7 Light is sweet, and it is pleasant for the eyes to see the sun.

8 Even those who live many years should rejoice in them all; yet let them remember that the days of darkness will be many. All that comes is vanity.

9 Rejoice, young man, while you are young, and let your heart cheer you in the days of your youth. Follow the inclination of your heart and the desire of your eyes, but know that for all these things God will bring you into judgment.

10 Banish anxiety from your mind, and put away pain from your body; for youth and the dawn of life are vanity.

12 REMEMBER YOUR creator in the days of your youth, before the days of trouble come, and the years draw near when you will say, "I have no pleasure in them"; ²before the sun and the light and the moon and the stars are darkened and the clouds return withᵈ the rain; ³in the day when the guards of the house tremble, and the strong men are bent, and the women who grind cease working because they are few, and those who look through the windows see dimly; ⁴when the doors on the street are shut, and the sound of the grinding is low, and one rises up at the sound of a bird, and all the daughters of song are brought low; ⁵when one

ᵈ Or after; Heb 'ahar

King James

5Also *when* they shall be afraid of *that which is* high, and fears *shall be* in the way, and the almond tree shall flourish, and the grasshopper shall be a burden, and desire shall fail: because man goeth to his long home, and the mourners go about the streets:

6Or ever the silver cord be loosed, or the golden bowl be broken, or the pitcher be broken at the fountain, or the wheel broken at the cistern.

7Then shall the dust return to the earth as it was: and the spirit shall return unto God who gave it.

8¶ Vanity of vanities, saith the preacher; all *is* vanity.

9And moreover, because the preacher was wise, he still taught the people knowledge; yea, he gave good heed, and sought out, *and* set in order many proverbs.

10The preacher sought to find out acceptable words: and *that which was* written *was* upright, *even* words of truth.

11The words of the wise *are* as goads, and as nails fastened *by* the masters of assemblies, *which* are given from one shepherd.

12And further, by these, my son, be admonished: of making many books *there is* no end; and much study *is* a weariness of the flesh.

13¶ Let us hear the conclusion of the whole matter: Fear God, and keep his commandments: for this *is* the whole *duty* of man.

14For God shall bring every work into judgment, with every secret thing, whether *it be* good, or whether *it be* evil.

New International

5when men are afraid of heights
    and of dangers in the streets;
when the almond tree blossoms
    and the grasshopper drags himself along
    and desire no longer is stirred.
Then man goes to his eternal home
    and mourners go about the streets.

6Remember him—before the silver cord is
        severed,
    or the golden bowl is broken;
before the pitcher is shattered at the spring,
    or the wheel broken at the well,
7and the dust returns to the ground it came from,
    and the spirit returns to God who gave it.

8"Meaningless! Meaningless!" says the Teacher.[a]
    "Everything is meaningless!"

The Conclusion of the Matter

9Not only was the Teacher wise, but also he imparted knowledge to the people. He pondered and searched out and set in order many proverbs. 10The Teacher searched to find just the right words, and what he wrote was upright and true.

11The words of the wise are like goads, their collected sayings like firmly embedded nails—given by one Shepherd. 12Be warned, my son, of anything in addition to them.

Of making many books there is no end, and much study wearies the body.

13Now all has been heard;
        here is the conclusion of the matter:
Fear God and keep his commandments,
        for this is the whole duty of man.
14For God will bring every deed into judgment,
        including every hidden thing,
        whether it is good or evil.

Living Bible

of heights and of falling—a white-haired, withered old man, dragging himself along: without sexual desire, standing at death's door, and nearing his everlasting home as the mourners go along the streets.

6Yes, remember your Creator now while you are young, before the silver cord of life snaps, and the gold bowl is broken, and the pitcher is broken at the fountain, and the wheel is broken at the cistern; 7and the dust returns to the earth as it was, and the spirit returns to God who gave it. 8All is futile, says the Preacher; utterly futile.

9But then, because the Preacher was wise, he went on teaching the people all he knew; and he collected proverbs and classified them. 10For the Preacher was not only a wise man, but a good teacher; he not only taught what he knew to the people, but taught them in an interesting manner. 11The wise man's words are like goads that spur to action. They nail down important truths. Students are wise who master what their teachers tell them.

12But, my son, be warned: there is no end of opinions ready to be expressed. Studying them can go on forever, and become very exhausting!

13Here is my final conclusion: fear God and obey his commandments, for this is the entire duty of man. 14For God will judge us for everything we do, including every hidden thing, good or bad.

New Revised Standard

is afraid of heights, and terrors are in the road; the almond tree blossoms, the grasshopper drags itself alongb and desire fails; because all must go to their eternal home, and the mourners will go about the streets; 6before the silver cord is snapped,c and the golden bowl is broken, and the pitcher is broken at the fountain, and the wheel broken at the cistern, 7and the dust returns to the earth as it was, and the breathd returns to God who gave it. 8 Vanity of vanities, says the Teacher;e all is vanity.

Epilogue

9   Besides being wise, the Teachere also taught the people knowledge, weighing and studying and arranging many proverbs. 10The Teachere sought to find pleasing words, and he wrote words of truth plainly.

11   The sayings of the wise are like goads, and like nails firmly fixed are the collected sayings that are given by one shepherd.f 12Of anything beyond these, my child, beware. Of making many books there is no end, and much study is a weariness of the flesh.

13   The end of the matter; all has been heard. Fear God, and keep his commandments; for that is the whole duty of everyone. 14For God will bring every deed into judgment, includingg every secret thing, whether good or evil.

b Or is a burden   c Syr Vg Compare Gk: Heb is removed   d Or the spirit
e Qoheleth, traditionally rendered Preacher   f Meaning of Heb uncertain
g Or into the judgment on

THE

Song of Solomon

Song of Songs

1 THE SONG of songs, which *is* Solomon's.
²Let him kiss me with the kisses of his mouth: for thy love *is* better than wine.

³Because of the savour of thy good ointments thy name *is as* ointment poured forth, therefore do the virgins love thee.

⁴Draw me, we will run after thee: the king hath brought me into his chambers: we will be glad and rejoice in thee, we will remember thy love more than wine: the upright love thee.

⁵I *am* black, but comely, O ye daughters of Jerusalem, as the tents of Kedar, as the curtains of Solomon.

⁶Look not upon me, because I *am* black, because the sun hath looked upon me: my mother's children were angry with me; they made me the keeper of the vineyards; *but* mine own vineyard have I not kept.

⁷Tell me, O thou whom my soul loveth, where thou feedest, where thou makest *thy flock* to rest at noon: for why should I be as one that turneth aside by the flocks of thy companions?

⁸¶ If thou know not, O thou fairest among women, go thy way forth by the footsteps of the flock, and feed thy kids beside the shepherds' tents.

⁹I have compared thee, O my love, to a company of horses in Pharaoh's chariots.

¹⁰Thy cheeks are comely with rows *of jewels,* thy neck with chains *of gold.*

¹¹We will make thee borders of gold with studs of silver.

¹²¶ While the king *sitteth* at his table, my spikenard sendeth forth the smell thereof.

1 SOLOMON'S SONG of Songs.

Beloveda

²Let him kiss me with the kisses of his mouth—
    for your love is more delightful than wine.
³Pleasing is the fragrance of your perfumes;
    your name is like perfume poured out.
    No wonder the maidens love you!
⁴Take me away with you—let us hurry!
    Let the king bring me into his chambers.

Friends

    We rejoice and delight in youb;
    we will praise your love more than wine.

Beloved

    How right they are to adore you!

⁵Dark am I, yet lovely,
    O daughters of Jerusalem,
    dark like the tents of Kedar,
    like the tent curtains of Solomon.c
⁶Do not stare at me because I am dark,
    because I am darkened by the sun.
  My mother's sons were angry with me
    and made me take care of the vineyards;
    my own vineyard I have neglected.
⁷Tell me, you whom I love, where you graze
      your flock
    and where you rest your sheep at midday.
  Why should I be like a veiled woman
    beside the flocks of your friends?

Friends

⁸If you do not know, most beautiful of women,
    follow the tracks of the sheep
  and graze your young goats
    by the tents of the shepherds.

Lover

⁹I liken you, my darling, to a mare
    harnessed to one of the chariots of Pharaoh.
¹⁰Your cheeks are beautiful with earrings,
    your neck with strings of jewels.
¹¹We will make you earrings of gold,
    studded with silver.

Beloved

¹²While the king was at his table,
    my perfume spread its fragrance.

ᵃ Primarily on the basis of the gender of the Hebrew pronouns used, male and female speakers are indicated in the margins by the captions *Lover* and *Beloved* respectively. The words of others are marked *Friends*. In some instances the divisions and their captions are debatable.   ᵇ 4 The Hebrew is masculine singular.   ᶜ 5 Or *Salma*

THE

The Song of Solomon

Song of Solomon

1 *THIS SONG of songs, more wonderful than any other, was composed by King Solomon:*

*The Girl:*d 2"Kiss me again and again, for your love is sweeter than wine. 3How fragrant your cologne, and how great your name! No wonder all the young girls love you! 4Take me with you; come, let's run!"

The Girl: "The king has brought me into his palace. How happy we will be! Your love is better than wine. No wonder all the young girls love you!"

The Girl: 5"I am dark but beautiful, O girls of Jerusalem, tanned as the dark tents of Kedar."

King Solomon: "But lovely as the silken tents of Solomon!"

The Girl: 6"Don't look down on me, you city girls,e just because my complexion is so dark—the sun has tanned me. My brothers were angry with me and sent me out into the sunf to tend the vineyards, but see what it has done to me!"g

The Girl: 7"Tell me, O one I love, where are you leading your flock today? Where will you be at noon? For I will come and join you there instead of wandering like a vagabond among the flocks of your companions."

King Solomon: 8"If you don't know, O most beautiful woman in all the world, follow the trail of my flock to the shepherds' tents, and there feed your sheep and their lambs. 9What a lovely filly you are,h my love! 10How lovely your cheeks are, with your hairi falling down upon them! How stately your neck with that long string of jewels. 11We shall make you gold earrings and silver beads."

The Girl: 12"The king lies on his bed, enchanted by the

1 THE SONG of Songs, which is Solomon's.

Colloquy of Bride and Friends

2 Let him kiss me with the kisses of his mouth!
   For your love is better than wine,
3   your anointing oils are fragrant,
   your name is perfume poured out;
      therefore the maidens love you.
4 Draw me after you, let us make haste.
      The king has brought me into his chambers.
   We will exult and rejoice in you;
      we will extol your love more than wine;
      rightly do they love you.

5 I am black and beautiful,
      O daughters of Jerusalem,
   like the tents of Kedar,
      like the curtains of Solomon.
6 Do not gaze at me because I am dark,
      because the sun has gazed on me.
   My mother's sons were angry with me;
      they made me keeper of the vineyards,
      but my own vineyard I have not kept!
7 Tell me, you whom my soul loves,
      where you pasture your flock,
      where you make it lie down at noon;
   for why should I be like one who is veiled
      beside the flocks of your companions?

8 If you do not know,
      O fairest among women,
   follow the tracks of the flock,
      and pasture your kids
      beside the shepherds' tents.

Colloquy of Bridegroom, Friends, and Bride

9 I compare you, my love,
      to a mare among Pharaoh's chariots.
10 Your cheeks are comely with ornaments,
      your neck with strings of jewels.
11 We will make you ornaments of gold,
      studded with silver.

12 While the king was on his couch,
      my nard gave forth its fragrance.

---

d *1:2 The Girl.* The headings identifying the speakers are conjectures and are not in the original text.   e *1:6 you city girls,* implied in vs 5.   f *1:6 sent me out into the sun,* implied.   g *1:6 see what it has done to me,* literally, "but my own vineyards are neglected."   h *1:9 What a lovely filly you are,* literally, "I compare you to my mare harnessed to Pharaoh's chariot."   i *1:10 with your hair,* literally, "ornaments."

King James

13A bundle of myrrh *is* my wellbeloved unto me; he shall lie all night betwixt my breasts.

14My beloved *is* unto me *as* a cluster of camphire in the vineyards of En-gedi.

15Behold, thou *art* fair, my love; behold, thou *art* fair; thou *hast* doves' eyes.

16Behold, thou *art* fair, my beloved, yea, pleasant: also our bed *is* green.

17The beams of our house *are* cedar, *and* our rafters of fir.

2 I AM the rose of Sharon, *and* the lily of the valleys.

2As the lily among thorns, so *is* my love among the daughters.

3As the apple tree among the trees of the wood, so *is* my beloved among the sons. I sat down under his shadow with great delight, and his fruit *was* sweet to my taste.

4He brought me to the banqueting house, and his banner over me *was* love.

5Stay me with flagons, comfort me with apples: for I *am* sick of love.

6His left hand *is* under my head, and his right hand doth embrace me.

7I charge you, O ye daughters of Jerusalem, by the roes, and by the hinds of the field, that ye stir not up, nor awake *my* love, till he please.

8¶ The voice of my beloved! behold, he cometh leaping upon the mountains, skipping upon the hills.

9My beloved is like a roe or a young hart: behold, he standeth behind our wall, he looketh forth at the windows, showing himself through the lattice.

10My beloved spake, and said unto me, Rise up, my love, my fair one, and come away.

11For, lo, the winter is past, the rain is over *and* gone;

12The flowers appear on the earth; the time of the singing *of birds* is come, and the voice of the turtle is heard in our land;

13The fig tree putteth forth her green figs, and the vines *with* the tender grape give a *good* smell. Arise, my love, my fair one, and come away.

New International

13My lover is to me a sachet of myrrh
  resting between my breasts.

14My lover is to me a cluster of henna blossoms
  from the vineyards of En Gedi.

Lover

15How beautiful you are, my darling!
  Oh, how beautiful!
  Your eyes are doves.

Beloved

16How handsome you are, my lover!
  Oh, how charming!
  And our bed is verdant.

Lover

17The beams of our house are cedars;
  our rafters are firs.

Beloved[a]

2 I AM a rose[b] of Sharon,
  a lily of the valleys.

Lover

2Like a lily among thorns
  is my darling among the maidens.

Beloved

3Like an apple tree among the trees of the forest
  is my lover among the young men.
  I delight to sit in his shade,
  and his fruit is sweet to my taste.

4He has taken me to the banquet hall,
  and his banner over me is love.

5Strengthen me with raisins,
  refresh me with apples,
  for I am faint with love.

6His left arm is under my head,
  and his right arm embraces me.

7Daughters of Jerusalem, I charge you
  by the gazelles and by the does of the field:
  Do not arouse or awaken love
  until it so desires.

8Listen! My lover!
  Look! Here he comes,
  leaping across the mountains,
  bounding over the hills.

9My lover is like a gazelle or a young stag.
  Look! There he stands behind our wall,
  gazing through the windows,
  peering through the lattice.

10My lover spoke and said to me,
  "Arise, my darling,
  my beautiful one, and come with me.

11See! The winter is past;
  the rains are over and gone.

12Flowers appear on the earth;
  the season of singing has come,
  the cooing of doves
  is heard in our land.

13The fig tree forms its early fruit;
  the blossoming vines spread their fragrance.
  Arise, come, my darling;
  my beautiful one, come with me."

a *1* Or *Lover*   b *1* Possibly a member of the crocus family

Living Bible

fragrance of my perfume. 13My beloved one is a sachet of myrrh lying between my breasts."

King Solomon: 14"My beloved is a bouquet of flowers in the gardens of Engedi. 15How beautiful you are, my love, how beautiful! Your eyes are soft as doves'. 16What a lovely, pleasant thing you are, lying here upon the grass, 17shaded by the cedar trees and firs."

2 *THE GIRL:* "I am the rose of Sharon, the lily of the valley."

King Solomon: 2"Yes, a lily among thorns, so is my beloved as compared with any other girls."

The Girl: 3"My lover is an apple tree, the finest in the orchard as compared with any of the other youths. I am seated in his much-desired shade and his fruit is lovely to eat. 4He brings me to the banquet hall and everyone can see how much he loves me. 5Oh, feed me with your love—your 'raisins' and your 'apples'—for I am utterly lovesick. 6His left hand is under my head and with his right hand he embraces me. 7O girls of Jerusalem, I adjure you by the gazelles and deer in the park, that you do not awaken my lover.c Let him sleep!"

The Girl: 8"Ah, I hear him—my beloved! Here he comes, leaping upon the mountains and bounding over the hills. 9My beloved is like a gazelle or young deer. Look, there he is behind the wall, now looking in at the windows.

10"My beloved said to me, 'Rise up, my love, my fair one, and come away. 11For the winter is past, the rain is over and gone. 12The flowers are springing up and the time of the singing of birds has come. Yes, spring is here.d 13The leaves are coming oute and the grape vines are in blossom. How delicious they smell! Arise, my love, my fair one, and come away.'

New Revised Standard

13 My beloved is to me a bag of myrrh
       that lies between my breasts.
14 My beloved is to me a cluster of henna
       blossoms
    in the vineyards of En-gedi.

15 Ah, you are beautiful, my love;
       ah, you are beautiful;
       your eyes are doves.
16 Ah, you are beautiful, my beloved,
       truly lovely.
    Our couch is green;
17   the beams of our house are cedar,
       our raftersf are pine.

2 I AM a roseg of Sharon,
    a lily of the valleys.

2 As a lily among brambles,
       so is my love among maidens.

3 As an apple tree among the trees of the wood,
       so is my beloved among young men.
    With great delight I sat in his shadow,
       and his fruit was sweet to my taste.
4 He brought me to the banqueting house,
       and his intention toward me was love.
5 Sustain me with raisins,
       refresh me with apples;
    for I am faint with love.
6 O that his left hand were under my head,
       and that his right hand embraced me!
7 I adjure you, O daughters of Jerusalem,
       by the gazelles or the wild does:
    do not stir up or awaken love
       until it is ready!

Springtime Rhapsody

8 The voice of my beloved!
       Look, he comes,
    leaping upon the mountains,
       bounding over the hills.
9 My beloved is like a gazelle
       or a young stag.
    Look, there he stands
       behind our wall,
    gazing in at the windows,
       looking through the lattice.
10 My beloved speaks and says to me:
    "Arise, my love, my fair one,
       and come away;
11 for now the winter is past,
       the rain is over and gone.
12 The flowers appear on the earth;
       the time of singing has come,
    and the voice of the turtledove
       is heard in our land.
13 The fig tree puts forth its figs,
       and the vines are in blossom;
       they give forth fragrance.
    Arise, my love, my fair one,
       and come away.

c *2:7 do not awaken my lover,* literally, "that you stir not up nor awaken love until it please." d *2:12 spring is here,* literally, "the voice of the turtledove is heard in our land." e *2:13 the leaves are coming out,* literally, "The fig tree puts forth its figs."

f Meaning of Heb uncertain   g Heb *crocus*

King James

14¶ O my dove, *that art* in the clefts of the rock, in the secret *places* of the stairs, let me see thy countenance, let me hear thy voice; for sweet *is* thy voice, and thy countenance *is* comely.

15Take us the foxes, the little foxes, that spoil the vines: for our vines *have* tender grapes.

16¶ My beloved *is* mine, and I *am* his: he feedeth among the lilies.

17Until the day break, and the shadows flee away, turn, my beloved, and be thou like a roe or a young hart upon the mountains of Bether.

3 BY NIGHT on my bed I sought him whom my soul loveth: I sought him, but I found him not.

2I will rise now, and go about the city in the streets, and in the broad ways I will seek him whom my soul loveth: I sought him, but I found him not.

3The watchmen that go about the city found me: *to whom I said,* Saw ye him whom my soul loveth?

4*It was* but a little that I passed from them, but I found him whom my soul loveth: I held him, and would not let him go, until I had brought him into my mother's house, and into the chamber of her that conceived me.

5I charge you, O ye daughters of Jerusalem, by the roes, and by the hinds of the field, that ye stir not up, nor awake *my* love, till he please.

6¶ Who *is* this that cometh out of the wilderness like pillars of smoke, perfumed with myrrh and frankincense, with all powders of the merchant?

7Behold his bed, which *is* Solomon's; threescore valiant men *are* about it, of the valiant of Israel.

8They all hold swords, *being* expert in war: every man *hath* his sword upon his thigh because of fear in the night.

9King Solomon made himself a chariot of the wood of Lebanon.

10He made the pillars thereof *of* silver, the bottom thereof *of* gold, the covering of it *of* purple, the midst thereof being paved *with* love, for the daughters of Jerusalem.

New International

Lover

14My dove in the clefts of the rock,
    in the hiding places on the mountainside,
show me your face,
    let me hear your voice;
for your voice is sweet,
    and your face is lovely.
15Catch for us the foxes,
    the little foxes
that ruin the vineyards,
    our vineyards that are in bloom.

Beloved

16My lover is mine and I am his;
    he browses among the lilies.
17Until the day breaks
    and the shadows flee,
turn, my lover,
    and be like a gazelle
or like a young stag
    on the rugged hills.a

3 ALL NIGHT long on my bed
    I looked for the one my heart loves;
    I looked for him but did not find him.
2I will get up now and go about the city,
    through its streets and squares;
I will search for the one my heart loves.
    So I looked for him but did not find him.
3The watchmen found me
    as they made their rounds in the city.
    "Have you seen the one my heart loves?"
4Scarcely had I passed them
    when I found the one my heart loves.
I held him and would not let him go
    till I had brought him to my mother's house,
    to the room of the one who conceived me.
5Daughters of Jerusalem, I charge you
    by the gazelles and by the does of the field:
Do not arouse or awaken love
    until it so desires.

6Who is this coming up from the desert
    like a column of smoke,
perfumed with myrrh and incense
    made from all the spices of the merchant?
7Look! It is Solomon's carriage,
    escorted by sixty warriors,
    the noblest of Israel,
8all of them wearing the sword,
    all experienced in battle,
each with his sword at his side,
    prepared for the terrors of the night.
9King Solomon made for himself the carriage;
    he made it of wood from Lebanon.
10Its posts he made of silver,
    its base of gold.
Its seat was upholstered with purple,
    its interior lovingly inlaid
    byb the daughters of Jerusalem.

---

a 17 Or *the hills of Bether*   b 10 Or *its inlaid interior a gift of love / from*

Living Bible

14"My dove is hiding behind some rocks, behind an outcrop of the cliff. Call to me and let me hear your lovely voice and see your handsome face.
15"The little foxes are ruining the vineyards. Catch them, for the grapes are all in blossom.
16"My beloved is mine and I am his. He is feeding among the lilies! 17Before the dawn comes and the shadows flee away, come to me, my beloved, and be like a gazelle or a young stag on the mountains of spices."

3 THE GIRL: "One night my lover was missing from my bed. I got up to look for him but couldn't find him. 2I went out into the streets of the city and the roads to seek him, but I searched in vain. 3The police stopped me and I said to them, 'Have you seen him anywhere, this one I love so much?' 4It was only a little while afterwards that I found him and held him and would not let him go until I had brought him into my childhood home, into my mother's old bedroom. 5I adjure you, O women of Jerusalem, by the gazelles and deer of the park, not to awake my lover. Let him sleep."

The Young Women of Jerusalem: 6"Who is this sweeping in from the deserts like a cloud of smoke along the ground, smelling of myrrh and frankincense and every other spice that can be bought? 7Look, it is the chariot[c] of Solomon with sixty of the mightiest men of his army surrounding it. 8They are all skilled swordsmen and experienced bodyguards. Each one has his sword upon his thigh to defend his king against any onslaught in the night. 9For King Solomon made himself a chariot from the wood of Lebanon. 10Its posts are silver, its canopy gold, the seat is purple; and the back is inlaid with these words: 'With love from the girls of Jerusalem!' "
The Girl: 11"Go out and see King Solomon, O young

New Revised Standard

14 O my dove, in the clefts of the rock,
in the covert of the cliff,
let me see your face,
let me hear your voice;
for your voice is sweet,
and your face is lovely.
15 Catch us the foxes,
the little foxes,
that ruin the vineyards—
for our vineyards are in blossom."

16 My beloved is mine and I am his;
he pastures his flock among the lilies.
17 Until the day breathes
and the shadows flee,
turn, my beloved, be like a gazelle
or a young stag on the cleft mountains.[d]

Love's Dream

3 UPON MY bed at night
I sought him whom my soul loves;
I sought him, but found him not;
I called him, but he gave no answer.[e]
2 "I will rise now and go about the city,
in the streets and in the squares;
I will seek him whom my soul loves."
I sought him, but found him not.
3 The sentinels found me,
as they went about in the city.
"Have you seen him whom my soul loves?"
4 Scarcely had I passed them,
when I found him whom my soul loves.
I held him, and would not let him go
until I brought him into my mother's house,
and into the chamber of her that conceived me.
5 I adjure you, O daughters of Jerusalem,
by the gazelles or the wild does:
do not stir up or awaken love
until it is ready!

The Groom and His Party Approach

6 What is that coming up from the wilderness,
like a column of smoke,
perfumed with myrrh and frankincense,
with all the fragrant powders of the merchant?
7 Look, it is the litter of Solomon!
Around it are sixty mighty men
of the mighty men of Israel,
8 all equipped with swords
and expert in war,
each with his sword at his thigh
because of alarms by night.
9 King Solomon made himself a palanquin
from the wood of Lebanon.
10 He made its posts of silver,
its back of gold, its seat of purple;
its interior was inlaid with love.[f]

---

c 3:7 *it is the chariot,* literally, "litter."

d Or *on the mountains of Bether:* meaning of Heb uncertain   e Gk: Heb lacks this line   f Meaning of Heb uncertain

King James

11Go forth, O ye daughters of Zion, and behold king Solomon with the crown wherewith his mother crowned him in the day of his espousals, and in the day of the gladness of his heart.

4 BEHOLD, THOU *art* fair, my love; behold, thou *art* fair; thou *hast* doves' eyes within thy locks: thy hair *is* as a flock of goats, that appear from mount Gilead.

2Thy teeth *are* like a flock *of sheep that are even* shorn, which came up from the washing; whereof every one bear twins, and none *is* barren among them.

3Thy lips *are* like a thread of scarlet, and thy speech *is* comely: thy temples *are* like a piece of a pomegranate within thy locks.

4Thy neck *is* like the tower of David builded for an armoury, whereon there hang a thousand bucklers, all shields of mighty men.

5Thy two breasts *are* like two young roes that are twins, which feed among the lilies.

6Until the day break, and the shadows flee away, I will get me to the mountain of myrrh, and to the hill of frankincense.

7Thou *art* all fair, my love; *there is* no spot in thee.

8¶ Come with me from Lebanon, *my* spouse, with me from Lebanon: look from the top of Amana, from the top of Shenir and Hermon, from the lions' dens, from the mountains of the leopards.

9Thou hast ravished my heart, my sister, *my* spouse; thou hast ravished my heart with one of thine eyes, with one chain of thy neck.

10How fair is thy love, my sister, *my* spouse! how much better is thy love than wine! and the smell of thine ointments than all spices!

11Thy lips, O *my* spouse, drop *as* the honeycomb: honey and milk *are* under thy tongue; and the smell of thy garments *is* like the smell of Lebanon.

12A garden inclosed *is* my sister, *my* spouse; a spring shut up, a fountain sealed.

New International

11Come out, you daughters of Zion,
   and look at King Solomon wearing the
     crown,
   the crown with which his mother crowned
     him
on the day of his wedding,
   the day his heart rejoiced.

Lover

4 HOW BEAUTIFUL you are, my darling!
   Oh, how beautiful!
   Your eyes behind your veil are doves.
   Your hair is like a flock of goats
     descending from Mount Gilead.
2Your teeth are like a flock of sheep just shorn,
   coming up from the washing.
Each has its twin;
   not one of them is alone.
3Your lips are like a scarlet ribbon;
   your mouth is lovely.
Your temples behind your veil
   are like the halves of a pomegranate.
4Your neck is like the tower of David,
   built with elegancea;
on it hang a thousand shields,
   all of them shields of warriors.
5Your two breasts are like two fawns,
   like twin fawns of a gazelle
   that browse among the lilies.
6Until the day breaks
   and the shadows flee,
I will go to the mountain of myrrh
   and to the hill of incense.
7All beautiful you are, my darling;
   there is no flaw in you.

8Come with me from Lebanon, my bride,
   come with me from Lebanon.
Descend from the crest of Amana,
   from the top of Senir, the summit of Hermon,
from the lions' dens
   and the mountain haunts of the leopards.
9You have stolen my heart, my sister, my bride;
   you have stolen my heart
with one glance of your eyes,
   with one jewel of your necklace.
10How delightful is your love, my sister, my
   bride!
How much more pleasing is your love than
   wine,
   and the fragrance of your perfume than any
   spice!
11Your lips drop sweetness as the honeycomb, my
   bride;
milk and honey are under your tongue.
   The fragrance of your garments is like that of
   Lebanon.
12You are a garden locked up, my sister, my
   bride;
   you are a spring enclosed, a sealed fountain.

---

a 4 The meaning of the Hebrew for this word is uncertain.

Living Bible

women of Zion; see the crown with which his mother crowned him on his wedding day, his day of gladness."

4 KING SOLOMON: "How beautiful you are, my love, how beautiful! Your eyes are those of doves. Your hair falls across your face like flocks of goats that frisk across the slopes of Gilead. ²Your teeth are white as sheep's wool, newly shorn and washed; perfectly matched, without one missing. ³Your lips are like a thread of scarlet—and how beautiful your mouth. Your cheeks are matched lovelinessᵇ behind your locks.ᶜ ⁴Your neck is statelyᵈ as the tower of David, jeweled with a thousand heroes' shields. ⁵Your breasts are like twin fawns of a gazelle, feeding among the lilies. ⁶Until the morning dawns and the shadows flee away, I will go to the mountain of myrrh and to the hill of frankincense. ⁷You are so beautiful, my love, in every part of you.

⁸"Come with me from Lebanon, my bride. We will look down from the summit of the mountain, from the top of Mount Hermon,ᵉ where the lions have their dens, and panthers prowl. ⁹You have ravished my heart, my lovely one, my bride; I am overcome by one glance of your eyes, by a single bead of your necklace. ¹⁰How sweet is your love, my darling, my bride. How much better it is than mere wine. The perfume of your love is more fragrant than all the richest spices. ¹¹Your lips, my dear, are made of honey. Yes, honey and cream are under your tongue, and the scent of your garments is like the scent of the mountains and cedars of Lebanon.

¹²"My darling bride is like a private garden, a spring that no one else can have, a fountain of my own.

New Revised Standard

Daughters of Jerusalem,
11   come out.
Look, O daughters of Zion,
     at King Solomon,
at the crown with which his mother crowned
     him
     on the day of his wedding,
     on the day of the gladness of his heart.

The Bride's Beauty Extolled

4 HOW BEAUTIFUL you are, my love,
     how very beautiful!
Your eyes are doves
     behind your veil.
Your hair is like a flock of goats,
     moving down the slopes of Gilead.
2   Your teeth are like a flock of shorn ewes
        that have come up from the washing,
    all of which bear twins,
        and not one among them is bereaved.
3   Your lips are like a crimson thread,
        and your mouth is lovely.
    Your cheeks are like halves of a pomegranate
        behind your veil.
4   Your neck is like the tower of David,
        built in courses;
    on it hang a thousand bucklers,
        all of them shields of warriors.
5   Your two breasts are like two fawns,
        twins of a gazelle,
        that feed among the lilies.
6   Until the day breathes
        and the shadows flee,
    I will hasten to the mountain of myrrh
        and the hill of frankincense.
7   You are altogether beautiful, my love;
        there is no flaw in you.
8   Come with me from Lebanon, my bride;
        come with me from Lebanon.
    Departᶠ from the peak of Amana,
        from the peak of Senir and Hermon,
    from the dens of lions,
        from the mountains of leopards.

9   You have ravished my heart, my sister, my
            bride,
        you have ravished my heart with a glance of
            your eyes,
        with one jewel of your necklace.
10 How sweet is your love, my sister, my bride!
        how much better is your love than wine,
        and the fragrance of your oils than any
            spice!
11 Your lips distill nectar, my bride;
        honey and milk are under your tongue;
        the scent of your garments is like the scent
            of Lebanon.
12 A garden locked is my sister, my bride,
        a garden locked, a fountain sealed.

ᵇ 4:3 *matched loveliness*, literally, "like halves of a pomegranate."
ᶜ 4:3 *behind your locks*, literally, "behind your veil."   ᵈ 4:4 *your neck is stately*, implied.   ᵉ 4:8 *top of Mount Hermon*, literally, "Depart from the peak of Amana, from the peak of Senir and Hermon."

ᶠ Or *Look*

King James

13Thy plants *are* an orchard of pomegranates, with pleasant fruits; camphire, with spikenard,

14Spikenard and saffron; calamus and cinnamon, with all trees of frankincense; myrrh and aloes, with all the chief spices:

15A fountain of gardens, a well of living waters, and streams from Lebanon.

16¶ Awake, O north wind; and come, thou south; blow upon my garden, *that* the spices thereof may flow out. Let my beloved come into his garden, and eat his pleasant fruits.

5 I AM come into my garden, my sister, *my* spouse: I have gathered my myrrh with my spice; I have eaten my honeycomb with my honey; I have drunk my wine with my milk: eat, O friends; drink, yea, drink abundantly, O beloved.

2¶ I sleep, but my heart waketh: *it is* the voice of my beloved that knocketh, *saying*, Open to me, my sister, my love, my dove, my undefiled: for my head is filled with dew, *and* my locks with the drops of the night.

3I have put off my coat; how shall I put it on? I have washed my feet; how shall I defile them?

4My beloved put in his hand by the hole *of the door,* and my bowels were moved for him.

5I rose up to open to my beloved; and my hands dropped *with* myrrh, and my fingers *with* sweetsmelling myrrh, upon the handles of the lock.

6I opened to my beloved; but my beloved had withdrawn himself, *and* was gone: my soul failed when he spake: I sought him, but I could not find him; I called him, but he gave me no answer.

7The watchmen that went about the city found me, they smote me, they wounded me; the keepers of the walls took away my veil from me.

8I charge you, O daughters of Jerusalem, if ye find my beloved, that ye tell him, that I *am* sick of love.

New International

13Your plants are an orchard of pomegranates
    with choice fruits,
    with henna and nard,
14 nard and saffron,
    calamus and cinnamon,
    with every kind of incense tree,
    with myrrh and aloes
    and all the finest spices.
15You are[a] a garden fountain,
    a well of flowing water
    streaming down from Lebanon.

Beloved

16Awake, north wind,
    and come, south wind!
Blow on my garden,
    that its fragrance may spread abroad.
Let my lover come into his garden
    and taste its choice fruits.

Lover

5 I HAVE come into my garden, my sister, my bride;
    I have gathered my myrrh with my spice.
I have eaten my honeycomb and my honey;
    I have drunk my wine and my milk.

Friends

Eat, O friends, and drink;
    drink your fill, O lovers.

Beloved

2I slept but my heart was awake.
    Listen! My lover is knocking:
"Open to me, my sister, my darling,
    my dove, my flawless one.
My head is drenched with dew,
    my hair with the dampness of the night."
3I have taken off my robe—
    must I put it on again?
I have washed my feet—
    must I soil them again?
4My lover thrust his hand through the
      latch-opening;
    my heart began to pound for him.
5I arose to open for my lover,
    and my hands dripped with myrrh,
my fingers with flowing myrrh,
    on the handles of the lock.
6I opened for my lover,
    but my lover had left; he was gone.
    My heart sank at his departure.[b]
I looked for him but did not find him.
    I called him but he did not answer.
7The watchmen found me
    as they made their rounds in the city.
They beat me, they bruised me;
    they took away my cloak,
    those watchmen of the walls!
8O daughters of Jerusalem, I charge you—
    if you find my lover,
what will you tell him?
    Tell him I am faint with love.

---

[a] *15 Or I am* (spoken by the *Beloved*)   [b] *6 Or heart had gone out to him when he spoke*

Living Bible

13, 14You are like a lovely orchard bearing precious fruit,c with the rarest of perfumes; nard and saffron, calamus and cinnamon, and perfume from every other incense tree, as well as myrrh and aloes, and every other lovely spice. 15You are a garden fountain, a well of living water, refreshing as the streams from the Lebanon mountains."

The Girl: 16"Come, north wind, awaken; come, south wind, blow upon my garden and waft its lovely perfume to my beloved. Let him come into his garden and eat its choicest fruits."

5 *KING SOLOMON:* "I am here in my garden, my darling, my bride! I gather my myrrh with my spices and eat my honeycomb with my honey. I drink my wine with my milk."

The Young Women of Jerusalem: "Oh, lover and beloved, eat and drink! Yes, drink deeply!"

The Girl: 2"One night as I was sleeping, my heart awakened in a dream. I heard the voice of my beloved; he was knocking at my bedroom door. 'Open to me, my darling, my lover, my lovely dove,' he said, 'for I have been out in the night and am covered with dew.' 3"But I said, 'I have disrobed. Shall I get dressed again? I have washed my feet, and should I get them soiled?'

4"My beloved tried to unlatch the door and my heart was thrilled within me. 5I jumped up to open it and my hands dripped with perfume, my fingers with lovely myrrh as I pulled back the bolt. 6I opened to my beloved, but he was gone. My heart stopped. I searched for him but couldn't find him anywhere. I called to him, but there was no reply. 7The guards found me and struck and wounded me. The watchman on the wall tore off my veil. 8I adjure you, O women of Jerusalem, if you find my beloved one, tell him that I am sick with love."

The Young Women of Jerusalem: 9"O woman of rare

New Revised Standard

13 Your channeld is an orchard of pomegranates
     with all choicest fruits,
     henna with nard,
14 nard and saffron, calamus and cinnamon,
     with all trees of frankincense,
    myrrh and aloes,
     with all chief spices—
15 a garden fountain, a well of living water,
     and flowing streams from Lebanon.

16 Awake, O north wind,
     and come, O south wind!
    Blow upon my garden
     that its fragrance may be wafted abroad.
    Let my beloved come to his garden,
     and eat its choicest fruits.

5 I COME to my garden, my sister, my bride;
  I gather my myrrh with my spice,
   I eat my honeycomb with my honey,
   I drink my wine with my milk.

Eat, friends, drink,
  and be drunk with love.

Another Dream

2 I slept, but my heart was awake.
   Listen! my beloved is knocking.
   "Open to me, my sister, my love,
    my dove, my perfect one;
   for my head is wet with dew,
    my locks with the drops of the night."
3 I had put off my garment;
    how could I put it on again?
   I had bathed my feet;
    how could I soil them?
4 My beloved thrust his hand into the opening,
    and my inmost being yearned for him.
5 I arose to open to my beloved,
    and my hands dripped with myrrh,
   my fingers with liquid myrrh,
    upon the handles of the bolt.
6 I opened to my beloved,
    but my beloved had turned and was gone.
   My soul failed me when he spoke.
   I sought him, but did not find him;
    I called him, but he gave no answer.
7 Making their rounds in the city
    the sentinels found me;
   they beat me, they wounded me,
    they took away my mantle,
    those sentinels of the walls.
8 I adjure you, O daughters of Jerusalem,
    if you find my beloved,
   tell him this:
    I am faint with love.

---

c *4:13, 14 You are like a lovely orchard bearing precious fruit,* literally, "Your shoots are an orchard of pomegranates. . . ."

d Meaning of Heb uncertain

King James

9¶ What *is* thy beloved more than *another* beloved, O thou fairest among women? what *is* thy beloved more than *another* beloved, that thou dost so charge us?

10My beloved *is* white and ruddy, the chiefest among ten thousand.

11His head *is as* the most fine gold, his locks *are* bushy, *and* black as a raven.

12His eyes *are as the eyes* of doves by the rivers of waters, washed with milk, *and* fitly set.

13His cheeks *are* as a bed of spices, *as* sweet flowers: his lips *like* lilies, dropping sweetsmelling myrrh.

14His hands *are as* gold rings set with the beryl: his belly *is as* bright ivory overlaid *with* sapphires.

15His legs *are as* pillars of marble, set upon sockets of fine gold: his countenance *is* as Lebanon, excellent as the cedars.

16His mouth *is* most sweet: yea, he *is* altogether lovely. This *is* my beloved, and this *is* my friend, O daughters of Jerusalem.

6 WHITHER IS thy beloved gone, O thou fairest among women? whither is thy beloved turned aside? that we may seek him with thee.

2My beloved is gone down into his garden, to the beds of spices, to feed in the gardens, and to gather lilies.

3I *am* my beloved's, and my beloved *is* mine: he feedeth among the lilies.

4¶ Thou *art* beautiful, O my love, as Tirzah, comely as Jerusalem, terrible as *an army* with banners.

5Turn away thine eyes from me, for they have overcome me: thy hair is as a flock of goats that appear from Gilead.

6Thy teeth *are* as a flock of sheep which go up from the washing, whereof every one beareth twins, and *there is* not one barren among them.

7As a piece of a pomegranate *are* thy temples within thy locks.

8There are threescore queens, and fourscore concubines, and virgins without number.

New International

Friends

9How is your beloved better than others,
    most beautiful of women?
How is your beloved better than others,
    that you charge us so?

Beloved

10My lover is radiant and ruddy,
    outstanding among ten thousand.
11His head is purest gold;
    his hair is wavy
    and black as a raven.
12His eyes are like doves
    by the water streams,
    washed in milk,
    mounted like jewels.
13His cheeks are like beds of spice
    yielding perfume.
His lips are like lilies
    dripping with myrrh.
14His arms are rods of gold
    set with chrysolite.
His body is like polished ivory
    decorated with sapphires.[a]
15His legs are pillars of marble
    set on bases of pure gold.
His appearance is like Lebanon,
    choice as its cedars.
16His mouth is sweetness itself;
    he is altogether lovely.
This is my lover, this my friend,
    O daughters of Jerusalem.

Friends

6 WHERE HAS your lover gone,
    most beautiful of women?
Which way did your lover turn,
    that we may look for him with you?

Beloved

2My lover has gone down to his garden,
    to the beds of spices,
to browse in the gardens
    and to gather lilies.
3I am my lover's and my lover is mine;
    he browses among the lilies.

Lover

4You are beautiful, my darling, as Tirzah,
    lovely as Jerusalem,
    majestic as troops with banners.
5Turn your eyes from me;
    they overwhelm me.
Your hair is like a flock of goats
    descending from Gilead.
6Your teeth are like a flock of sheep
    coming up from the washing.
Each has its twin,
    not one of them is alone.
7Your temples behind your veil
    are like the halves of a pomegranate.
8Sixty queens there may be,
    and eighty concubines,
    and virgins beyond number;

---

a 14 Or *lapis lazuli*

Living Bible

beauty, what is it about your loved one that is better than any other, that you command us this?"

The Girl: 10"My beloved one is tanned and handsome, better than ten thousand others! 11His head is purest gold, and he has wavy, raven hair. 12His eyes are like doves beside the water brooks, deep and quiet. 13His cheeks are like sweetly scented beds of spices. His lips are perfumed lilies, his breath like myrrh. 14His arms are round bars of gold set with topaz; his body is bright ivory encrusted with jewels. 15His legs are as pillars of marble set in sockets of finest gold, like cedars of Lebanon; none can rival him. 16His mouth is altogether sweet, lovable in every way. Such, O women of Jerusalem, is my beloved, my friend."

6 THE YOUNG *Women of Jerusalem:* "O rarest of beautiful women, where has your loved one gone? We will help you find him."

The Girl: 2"He has gone down to his garden, to his spice beds, to pasture his flock and to gather the lilies. 3I am my beloved's and my beloved is mine. He pastures his flock among the lilies!"

King Solomon: 4"O my beloved, you are as beautiful as the lovely land of Tirzah, yes, beautiful as Jerusalem, and how you capture my heart.b 5Look the other way, for your eyes have overcome me! Your hair, as it falls across your face, is like a flock of goats frisking down the slopes of Gilead. 6Your teeth are white as freshly washed ewes, perfectly matched and not one missing. 7Your cheeks are matched lovelinessc behind your hair. 8I have sixty other wives, all queens, and eighty concubines, and unnumbered virgins available to me; 9but you, my dove, my perfect

New Revised Standard

Colloquy of Friends and Bride

9 What is your beloved more than another
   beloved,
   O fairest among women?
What is your beloved more than another
   beloved,
   that you thus adjure us?

10 My beloved is all radiant and ruddy,
   distinguished among ten thousand.
11 His head is the finest gold;
   his locks are wavy,
   black as a raven.
12 His eyes are like doves
   beside springs of water,
   bathed in milk,
   fitly set.d
13 His cheeks are like beds of spices,
   yielding fragrance.
   His lips are lilies,
   distilling liquid myrrh.
14 His arms are rounded gold,
   set with jewels.
   His body is ivory work,d
   encrusted with sapphires.e
15 His legs are alabaster columns,
   set upon bases of gold.
   His appearance is like Lebanon,
   choice as the cedars.
16 His speech is most sweet,
   and he is altogether desirable.
   This is my beloved and this is my friend,
   O daughters of Jerusalem.

6 WHERE HAS your beloved gone,
   O fairest among women?
Which way has your beloved turned,
   that we may seek him with you?

2 My beloved has gone down to his garden,
   to the beds of spices,
   to pasture his flock in the gardens,
   and to gather lilies.
3 I am my beloved's and my beloved is mine;
   he pastures his flock among the lilies.

The Bride's Matchless Beauty

4 You are beautiful as Tirzah, my love,
   comely as Jerusalem,
   terrible as an army with banners.
5 Turn away your eyes from me,
   for they overwhelm me!
   Your hair is like a flock of goats,
   moving down the slopes of Gilead.
6 Your teeth are like a flock of ewes,
   that have come up from the washing;
   all of them bear twins,
   and not one among them is bereaved.
7 Your cheeks are like halves of a pomegranate
   behind your veil.
8 There are sixty queens and eighty concubines,
   and maidens without number.

b 6:4 *how you capture my heart,* literally, "You are . . . terrible as an army with banners."   c 6:7 *Your cheeks are matched loveliness,* literally, "like the halves of a pomegranate."

d Meaning of Heb uncertain   e Heb *lapis lazuli*

King James

9My dove, my undefiled is *but* one; she *is* the *only* one of her mother, she *is* the choice *one* of her that bare her. The daughters saw her, and blessed her; *yea*, the queens and the concubines, and they praised her.

10¶ Who *is* she *that* looketh forth as the morning, fair as the moon, clear as the sun, *and* terrible as *an army* with banners?

11I went down into the garden of nuts to see the fruits of the valley, *and* to see whether the vine flourished, *and* the pomegranates budded.

12Or ever I was aware, my soul made me *like* the chariots of Amminadib.

13Return, return, O Shulamite; return, return, that we may look upon thee. What will ye see in the Shulamite? As it were the company of two armies.

7 HOW BEAUTIFUL are thy feet with shoes, O prince's daughter! the joints of thy thighs *are* like jewels, the work of the hands of a cunning workman.

2Thy navel *is like* a round goblet, *which* wanteth not liquor: thy belly *is like* an heap of wheat set about with lilies.

3Thy two breasts *are* like two young roes *that are* twins.

4Thy neck *is* as a tower of ivory; thine eyes *like* the fishpools in Heshbon, by the gate of Bath-rabbim: thy nose *is* as the tower of Lebanon which looketh toward Damascus.

5Thine head upon thee *is* like Carmel, and the hair of thine head like purple; the king *is* held in the galleries.

6How fair and how pleasant art thou, O love, for delights!

7This thy stature is like to a palm tree, and thy breasts to clusters *of grapes*.

8I said, I will go up to the palm tree, I will take hold of the boughs thereof: now also thy breasts shall be as clusters of the vine, and the smell of thy nose like apples;

9And the roof of thy mouth like the best wine for my beloved, that goeth *down* sweetly, causing the lips of those that are asleep to speak.

10¶ I *am* my beloved's, and his desire *is* toward me.

11Come, my beloved, let us go forth into the field; let us lodge in the villages.

New International

9but my dove, my perfect one, is unique,
  the only daughter of her mother,
  the favorite of the one who bore her.
The maidens saw her and called her blessed;
  the queens and concubines praised her.

Friends

10Who is this that appears like the dawn,
  fair as the moon, bright as the sun,
  majestic as the stars in procession?

Lover

11I went down to the grove of nut trees
  to look at the new growth in the valley,
to see if the vines had budded
  or the pomegranates were in bloom.
12Before I realized it,
  my desire set me among the royal chariots of
    my people.[a]

Friends

13Come back, come back, O Shulammite;
  come back, come back, that we may gaze on
    you!

Lover

Why would you gaze on the Shulammite
  as on the dance of Mahanaim?

7 HOW BEAUTIFUL your sandaled feet,
  O prince's daughter!
Your graceful legs are like jewels,
  the work of a craftsman's hands.
2Your navel is a rounded goblet
  that never lacks blended wine.
Your waist is a mound of wheat
  encircled by lilies.
3Your breasts are like two fawns,
  twins of a gazelle.
4Your neck is like an ivory tower.
Your eyes are the pools of Heshbon
  by the gate of Bath Rabbim.
Your nose is like the tower of Lebanon
  looking toward Damascus.
5Your head crowns you like Mount Carmel.
  Your hair is like royal tapestry;
  the king is held captive by its tresses.
6How beautiful you are and how pleasing,
  O love, with your delights!
7Your stature is like that of the palm,
  and your breasts like clusters of fruit.
8I said, "I will climb the palm tree;
  I will take hold of its fruit."
May your breasts be like the clusters of the
    vine,
  the fragrance of your breath like apples,
9 and your mouth like the best wine.

Beloved

May the wine go straight to my lover,
  flowing gently over lips and teeth.[b]
10I belong to my lover,
  and his desire is for me.
11Come, my lover, let us go to the countryside,
  let us spend the night in the villages.[c]

---

[a] 12 Or *among the chariots of Amminadab*; or *among the chariots of the people of the prince*   [b] 9 Septuagint, Aquila, Vulgate and Syriac; Hebrew *lips of sleepers*   [c] 11 Or *henna bushes*

Living Bible

one, are the only one among them all, without an
equal! The women of Jerusalem were delighted when
they saw you and even the queens and concubines
praise you. 10'Who is this,' they ask, 'arising as the
dawn, fair as the moon, pure as the sun, so utterly
captivating?' "d

The Girl: 11"I went down into the orchard of nuts and
out to the valley to see the springtime there, to see
whether the grape vines were budding or the pomegranates were blossoming yet. 12Before I realized it
I was stricken with terrible homesickness and wanted
to be back among my own people."e

The Young Women of Jerusalem: 13"Return, return to
us, O maid of Shulam. Come back, come back, that
we may see you once again."

The Girl: "Why should you seek a mere Shulammite?"
King Solomon: "Because you dance so beautifully."f

7 KING SOLOMON: "How beautiful your tripping
feet, O queenly maiden. Your rounded thighs are
like jewels, the work of the most skilled of craftsmen.
2Your navel is lovely as a goblet filled with wine.
Your waistg is like a heap of wheat set about with
lilies. 3Your two breasts are like two fawns, yes,
lovely twins.h 4Your neck is stately as an ivory tower, your eyes as limpid pools in Heshbon by the gate
of Bath-rabbim. Your nose is shapelyi like the tower
of Lebanon overlooking Damascus.
5"As Mount Carmel crowns the mountains, so your
hair is your crown. The king is held captive in your
queenly tresses.
6"Oh, how delightful you are; how pleasant, O love,
for utter delight! 7You are tall and slim like a palm
tree, and your breasts are like its clusters of dates. 8I
said, I will climb up into the palm tree and take hold
of its branches. Now may your breasts be like grape
clusters, and the scent of your breath like apples, 9and
your kisses as exciting as the best of wine, smooth
and sweet, causing the lips of those who are asleep
to speak."

The Girl: 10"I am my beloved's and I am the one he
desires. 11Come, my beloved, let us go out into the
fields and stay in the villages. 12Let us get up early

New Revised Standard

9 My dove, my perfect one, is the only one,
      the darling of her mother,
      flawless to her that bore her.
   The maidens saw her and called her happy;
      the queens and concubines also, and they
         praised her.

10 "Who is this that looks forth like the dawn,
      fair as the moon, bright as the sun,
      terrible as an army with banners?"

11 I went down to the nut orchard,
      to look at the blossoms of the valley,
   to see whether the vines had budded,
      whether the pomegranates were in bloom.

12 Before I was aware, my fancy set me
      in a chariot beside my prince.j

13k Return, return, O Shulammite!
      Return, return, that we may look upon you.

   Why should you look upon the Shulammite,
      as upon a dance before two armies?l

Expressions of Praise

7 HOW GRACEFUL are your feet in sandals,
      O queenly maiden!
   Your rounded thighs are like jewels,
      the work of a master hand.
2 Your navel is a rounded bowl
      that never lacks mixed wine.
   Your belly is a heap of wheat,
      encircled with lilies.
3 Your two breasts are like two fawns,
      twins of a gazelle.
4 Your neck is like an ivory tower.
   Your eyes are pools in Heshbon,
      by the gate of Bath-rabbim.
   Your nose is like a tower of Lebanon,
      overlooking Damascus.
5 Your head crowns you like Carmel,
      and your flowing locks are like purple;
      a king is held captive in the tresses.m

6 How fair and pleasant you are,
      O loved one, delectable maiden!n
7 You are statelyo as a palm tree,
      and your breasts are like its clusters.
8 I say I will climb the palm tree
      and lay hold of its branches.
   Oh, may your breasts be like clusters of the
         vine,
      and the scent of your breath like apples,
9 and your kissesp like the best wine
      that goes downq smoothly,
      gliding over lips and teeth.r

10 I am my beloved's,
      and his desire is for me.
11 Come, my beloved,
      let us go forth into the fields,
      and lodge in the villages;

---

d *6:10 so utterly captivating,* literally, "terrible as an army with banners."
e *6:12 among my own people,* literally, "the chariots of my princely people."
Another possible reading is, "terrible desire to sit beside my beloved in his
chariot." f *6:13 you dance so beautifully,* literally, "as upon a dance before
two armies." g *7:2 your waist,* literally, "belly." h *7:3 lovely twins,*
literally, "twins of a gazelle." i *7:4 Your nose is shapely,* implied.

j Cn: Meaning of Heb uncertain k Ch 7.1 in Heb l Or *dance of Mahanaim*
m Meaning of Heb uncertain n Syr: Heb *in delights* o Heb *This your
stature is* p Heb *palate* q Heb *down for my lover* r Gk Syr Vg: Heb
lips of sleepers

King James

12Let us get up early to the vineyards; let us see if the vine flourish, *whether* the tender grape appear, *and* the pomegranates bud forth: there will I give thee my loves.

13The mandrakes give a smell, and at our gates *are* all manner of pleasant *fruits*, new and old, *which* I have laid up for thee, O my beloved.

8 O THAT thou *wert* as my brother, that sucked the breasts of my mother! *when* I should find thee without, I would kiss thee; yea, I should not be despised.

2I would lead thee, *and* bring thee into my mother's house, *who* would instruct me: I would cause thee to drink of spiced wine of the juice of my pomegranate.

3His left hand *should be* under my head, and his right hand should embrace me.

4I charge you, O daughters of Jerusalem, that ye stir not up, nor awake *my* love, until he please.

5Who *is* this that cometh up from the wilderness, leaning upon her beloved? I raised thee up under the apple tree: there thy mother brought thee forth: there she brought thee forth *that* bare thee.

6¶ Set me as a seal upon thine heart, as a seal upon thine arm: for love *is* strong as death; jealousy *is* cruel as the grave: the coals thereof *are* coals of fire, *which hath* a most vehement flame.

7Many waters cannot quench love, neither can the floods drown it: if a man would give all the substance of his house for love, it would utterly be contemned.

8¶ We have a little sister, and she hath no breasts: what shall we do for our sister in the day when she shall be spoken for?

9If she *be* a wall, we will build upon her a palace of silver: and if she *be* a door, we will inclose her with boards of cedar.

10I *am* a wall, and my breasts like towers: then was I in his eyes as one that found favour.

11Solomon had a vineyard at Baal-hamon; he let out the vineyard unto keepers; every one for the fruit thereof was to bring a thousand *pieces* of silver.

New International

12Let us go early to the vineyards
  to see if the vines have budded,
 if their blossoms have opened,
  and if the pomegranates are in bloom—
  there I will give you my love.
13The mandrakes send out their fragrance,
  and at our door is every delicacy,
 both new and old,
  that I have stored up for you, my lover.

8 IF ONLY you were to me like a brother,
  who was nursed at my mother's breasts!
 Then, if I found you outside,
  I would kiss you,
  and no one would despise me.
2I would lead you
  and bring you to my mother's house—
  she who has taught me.
 I would give you spiced wine to drink,
  the nectar of my pomegranates.
3His left arm is under my head
  and his right arm embraces me.
4Daughters of Jerusalem, I charge you:
  Do not arouse or awaken love
  until it so desires.

Friends

5Who is this coming up from the desert
  leaning on her lover?

Beloved

 Under the apple tree I roused you;
  there your mother conceived you,
  there she who was in labor gave you birth.
6Place me like a seal over your heart,
  like a seal on your arm;
 for love is as strong as death,
  its jealousy[a] unyielding as the grave.[b]
 It burns like blazing fire,
  like a mighty flame.[c]
7Many waters cannot quench love;
  rivers cannot wash it away.
 If one were to give
  all the wealth of his house for love,
  it[d] would be utterly scorned.

Friends

8We have a young sister,
  and her breasts are not yet grown.
 What shall we do for our sister
  for the day she is spoken for?
9If she is a wall,
  we will build towers of silver on her.
 If she is a door,
  we will enclose her with panels of cedar.

Beloved

10I am a wall,
  and my breasts are like towers.
 Thus I have become in his eyes
  like one bringing contentment.
11Solomon had a vineyard in Baal Hamon;
  he let out his vineyard to tenants.
 Each was to bring for its fruit
  a thousand shekels[e] of silver.

---

a 6 Or *ardor*   b 6 Hebrew *Sheol*   c 6 Or / *like the very flame of the LORD*
d 7 Or *he*   e 11 That is, about 25 pounds (about 11.5 kilograms); also in verse 12

Living Bible

and go out to the vineyards and see whether the vines have budded and whether the blossoms have opened and whether the pomegranates are in flower. And there I will give you my love. ¹³There the mandrakes give forth their fragrance and the rarest fruits are at our doors, the new as well as old, for I have stored them up for my beloved."

8 *THE GIRL:* "Oh, if only you were my brother; then I could kiss you no matter who was watching, and no one would laugh at me. ²I would bring you to my childhood home,ᶠ and there you would teach me. I would give you spiced wine to drink, sweet pomegranate wine. ³His left hand would be under my head and his right hand would embrace me. ⁴I adjure you, O women of Jerusalem, not to awaken him until he please."

The Young Women of Jerusalem: ⁵"Who is this coming up from the desert, leaning on her beloved?"

King Solomon: "Under the apple tree where your mother gave birth to you in her travail, there I awakened your love."

The Girl: ⁶"Seal me in your heart with permanent betrothal, for love is strong as death and jealousy is as cruel as Sheol. It flashes fire, the very flame of Jehovah. ⁷Many waters cannot quench the flame of love, neither can the floods drown it. If a man tried to buy it with everything he owned, he couldn't do it."

The Girl's Brothers: ⁸"We have a little sister too young for breasts. What shall we do if someone asks to marry her?"

King Solomon: ⁹"If she has no breastsᵍ we will build upon her a battlement of silver,ʰ and if she is a door we will enclose her with cedar boards."ʰ

The Girl: ¹⁰"I am slim, tall,ⁱ and full-breastedʲ and I have found favor in my lover's eyes. ¹¹Solomon had a vineyard at Baal-hamon which he rented out to some farmers there, the rent being one thousand pieces of silver from each. ¹²But as for my own vine-

New Revised Standard

¹² let us go out early to the vineyards,
      and see whether the vines have budded,
   whether the grape blossoms have opened
      and the pomegranates are in bloom.
   There I will give you my love.
¹³ The mandrakes give forth fragrance,
      and over our doors are all choice fruits,
   new as well as old,
      which I have laid up for you, O my
         beloved.

8 O THAT you were like a brother to me,
   who nursed at my mother's breast!
   If I met you outside, I would kiss you,
      and no one would despise me.
² I would lead you and bring you
      into the house of my mother,
      and into the chamber of the one who bore
         me.ᵏ
   I would give you spiced wine to drink,
      the juice of my pomegranates.
³ O that his left hand were under my head,
      and that his right hand embraced me!
⁴ I adjure you, O daughters of Jerusalem,
      do not stir up or awaken love
      until it is ready!

Homecoming

⁵ Who is that coming up from the wilderness,
      leaning upon her beloved?

   Under the apple tree I awakened you.
   There your mother was in labor with you;
      there she who bore you was in labor.

⁶ Set me as a seal upon your heart,
      as a seal upon your arm;
   for love is strong as death,
      passion fierce as the grave.
   Its flashes are flashes of fire,
      a raging flame.
⁷ Many waters cannot quench love,
      neither can floods drown it.
   If one offered for love
      all the wealth of his house,
      it would be utterly scorned.

⁸ We have a little sister,
      and she has no breasts.
   What shall we do for our sister,
      on the day when she is spoken for?
⁹ If she is a wall,
      we will build upon her a battlement of
         silver;
   but if she is a door,
      we will enclose her with boards of cedar.
¹⁰ I was a wall,
      and my breasts were like towers;
   then I was in his eyes
      as one who bringsˡ peace.
¹¹ Solomon had a vineyard at Baal-hamon;
      he entrusted the vineyard to keepers;
      each one was to bring for its fruit a
         thousand pieces of silver.

ᶠ *8:2 my childhood home,* literally, "my mother's house."   ᵍ *8:9 if she has no breasts,*   ʰ *8:9 build upon her a battlement of silver . . . enclose her with cedar boards,* the meaning is obscure.   ⁱ *8:10 tall,* literally, "I am as a wall."   ʲ *8:10 full-breasted,* literally, "My breasts are as towers."

ᵏ Gk Syr: Heb *my mother; she* (or *you*) *will teach me*   ˡ Or *finds*

King James

12My vineyard, which *is* mine, *is* before me: thou, O Solomon, *must have* a thousand, and those that keep the fruit thereof two hundred.

13Thou that dwellest in the gardens, the companions hearken to thy voice: cause me to hear *it*.

14¶ Make haste, my beloved, and be thou like to a roe or to a young hart upon the mountains of spices.

New International

12But my own vineyard is mine to give;
    the thousand shekels are for you, O Solomon,
    and two hundreda are for those who tend its
      fruit.

Lover

13You who dwell in the gardens
    with friends in attendance,
    let me hear your voice!

Beloved

14Come away, my lover,
    and be like a gazelle
    or like a young stag
    on the spice-laden mountains.

Living Bible

yard, you, O Solomon, shall have my thousand pieces of silver and I will give two hundred pieces to those who care for it. 13O my beloved, living in the gardens, how wonderful that your companions may listen to your voice; let me hear it too. 14Come quickly, my beloved, and be like a gazelle or young deer upon the mountains of spices."

New Revised Standard

12 My vineyard, my very own, is for myself;
      you, O Solomon, may have the thousand,
      and the keepers of the fruit two hundred!

13 O you who dwell in the gardens,
      my companions are listening for your voice;
      let me hear it.

14 Make haste, my beloved,
      and be like a gazelle
    or a young stag
      upon the mountains of spices!

THE BOOK OF THE PROPHET

Isaiah

Isaiah

1 THE VISION of Isaiah the son of Amoz, which he saw concerning Judah and Jerusalem in the days of Uzziah, Jotham, Ahaz, *and* Hezekiah, kings of Judah.

²Hear, O heavens, and give ear, O earth: for the LORD hath spoken, I have nourished and brought up children, and they have rebelled against me.

³The ox knoweth his owner, and the ass his master's crib: *but* Israel doth not know, my people doth not consider.

⁴Ah sinful nation, a people laden with iniquity, a seed of evildoers, children that are corrupters: they have forsaken the LORD, they have provoked the Holy One of Israel unto anger, they are gone away backward.

⁵¶ Why should ye be stricken any more? ye will revolt more and more: the whole head is sick, and the whole heart faint.

⁶From the sole of the foot even unto the head *there is* no soundness in it; *but* wounds, and bruises, and putrifying sores: they have not been closed, neither bound up, neither mollified with ointment.

⁷Your country *is* desolate, your cities *are* burned with fire: your land, strangers devour it in your presence, and *it is* desolate, as overthrown by strangers.

⁸And the daughter of Zion is left as a cottage in a vineyard, as a lodge in a garden of cucumbers, as a besieged city.

⁹Except the LORD of hosts had left unto us a very small remnant, we should have been as Sodom, *and* we should have been like unto Gomorrah.

¹⁰¶ Hear the word of the LORD, ye rulers of Sodom; give ear unto the law of our God, ye people of Gomorrah.

¹¹To what purpose *is* the multitude of your sacrifices unto me? saith the LORD: I am full of the burnt offerings of rams, and the fat of fed beasts; and I delight not in the blood of bullocks, or of lambs, or of he goats.

1 THE VISION concerning Judah and Jerusalem that Isaiah son of Amoz saw during the reigns of Uzziah, Jotham, Ahaz and Hezekiah, kings of Judah.

A Rebellious Nation

²Hear, O heavens! Listen, O earth!
  For the LORD has spoken:
"I reared children and brought them up,
  but they have rebelled against me.
³The ox knows his master,
  the donkey his owner's manger,
but Israel does not know,
  my people do not understand."

⁴Ah, sinful nation,
  a people loaded with guilt,
a brood of evildoers,
  children given to corruption!
They have forsaken the LORD;
  they have spurned the Holy One of Israel
  and turned their backs on him.

⁵Why should you be beaten anymore?
  Why do you persist in rebellion?
Your whole head is injured,
  your whole heart afflicted.
⁶From the sole of your foot to the top of your
        head
  there is no soundness—
only wounds and welts
  and open sores,
not cleansed or bandaged
  or soothed with oil.

⁷Your country is desolate,
  your cities burned with fire;
your fields are being stripped by foreigners
  right before you,
  laid waste as when overthrown by strangers.
⁸The Daughter of Zion is left
  like a shelter in a vineyard,
like a hut in a field of melons,
  like a city under siege.
⁹Unless the LORD Almighty
  had left us some survivors,
we would have become like Sodom,
  we would have been like Gomorrah.

¹⁰Hear the word of the LORD,
  you rulers of Sodom;
listen to the law of our God,
  you people of Gomorrah!
¹¹"The multitude of your sacrifices—
  what are they to me?" says the LORD.
"I have more than enough of burnt offerings,
  of rams and the fat of fattened animals;
I have no pleasure
  in the blood of bulls and lambs and goats.

Isaiah

1 THESE ARE *the messages that came to Isaiah, son of Amoz, in the visions he saw during the reigns of King Uzziah, King Jotham, King Ahaz and King Hezekiah—all kings of Judah. In these messages God showed him what was going to happen to Judah and Jerusalem in the days ahead.*

2Listen, O heaven and earth, to what the Lord is saying:

The children I raised and cared for so long and tenderly have turned against me. 3Even the animals—the donkey and the ox—know their owner and appreciate his care for them, but not my people Israel. No matter what I do for them, they still don't care. 4Oh, what a sinful nation they are! They walk bent-backed beneath their load of guilt. Their fathers before them were evil too. Born to be bad, they have turned their backs upon the Lord, and have despised the Holy One of Israel. They have cut themselves off from my help.

5, 6Oh, my people, haven't you had enough of punishment? Why will you force me to whip you again and again? Must you forever rebel? From head to foot you are sick and weak and faint, covered with bruises and welts and infected wounds, unanointed and unbound. 7Your country lies in ruins; your cities are burned; while you watch, foreigners are destroying and plundering everything they see. 8You stand there helpless and abandoned like a watchman's shanty in the field when the harvest time is over—or when the crop is stripped and robbed.

9*If the Lord Almighty had not stepped in to save a few of us, we would have been wiped out as Sodom and Gomorrah were.* 10An apt comparison!a Listen, you leaders of Israel, you men of Sodom and Gomorrah, as I call you now. Listen to the Lord. Hear what he is telling you! 11I am sick of your sacrifices. Don't bring me any more of them. I don't want your fat rams; I don't want to see the blood from your offerings. 12, 13Who

---

Isaiah

1 THE VISION of Isaiah son of Amoz, which he saw concerning Judah and Jerusalem in the days of Uzziah, Jotham, Ahaz, and Hezekiah, kings of Judah.

The Wickedness of Judah

2 Hear, O heavens, and listen, O earth;
    for the LORD has spoken:
I reared children and brought them up,
    but they have rebelled against me.
3 The ox knows its owner,
    and the donkey its master's crib;
but Israel does not know,
    my people do not understand.

4 Ah, sinful nation,
    people laden with iniquity,
offspring who do evil,
    children who deal corruptly,
who have forsaken the LORD,
    who have despised the Holy One of Israel,
    who are utterly estranged!

5 Why do you seek further beatings?
    Why do you continue to rebel?
The whole head is sick,
    and the whole heart faint.
6 From the sole of the foot even to the head,
    there is no soundness in it,
but bruises and sores
    and bleeding wounds;
they have not been drained, or bound up,
    or softened with oil.

7 Your country lies desolate,
    your cities are burned with fire;
in your very presence
    aliens devour your land;
    it is desolate, as overthrown by foreigners.
8 And daughter Zion is left
    like a booth in a vineyard,
like a shelter in a cucumber field,
    like a besieged city.
9 If the LORD of hosts
    had not left us a few survivors,
we would have been like Sodom,
    and become like Gomorrah.

10 Hear the word of the LORD,
    you rulers of Sodom!
Listen to the teaching of our God,
    you people of Gomorrah!
11 What to me is the multitude of your
      sacrifices?
    says the LORD;
I have had enough of burnt offerings of rams
    and the fat of fed beasts;
I do not delight in the blood of bulls,
    or of lambs, or of goats.

---

a *1:10 An apt comparison,* implied.

King James

12When ye come to appear before me, who hath required this at your hand, to tread my courts?

13Bring no more vain oblations; incense is an abomination unto me; the new moons and sabbaths, the calling of assemblies, I cannot away with; *it is* iniquity, even the solemn meeting.

14Your new moons and your appointed feasts my soul hateth: they are a trouble unto me; I am weary to bear *them*.

15And when ye spread forth your hands, I will hide mine eyes from you: yea, when ye make many prayers, I will not hear: your hands are full of blood.

16¶ Wash you, make you clean; put away the evil of your doings from before mine eyes; cease to do evil;

17Learn to do well; seek judgment, relieve the oppressed, judge the fatherless, plead for the widow.

18Come now, and let us reason together, saith the LORD: though your sins be as scarlet, they shall be as white as snow; though they be red like crimson, they shall be as wool.

19If ye be willing and obedient, ye shall eat the good of the land:

20But if ye refuse and rebel, ye shall be devoured with the sword: for the mouth of the LORD hath spoken *it*.

21¶ How is the faithful city become an harlot! it was full of judgment; righteousness lodged in it; but now murderers.

22Thy silver is become dross, thy wine mixed with water:

23Thy princes *are* rebellious, and companions of thieves: every one loveth gifts, and followeth after rewards: they judge not the fatherless, neither doth the cause of the widow come unto them.

24Therefore saith the Lord, the LORD of hosts, the mighty One of Israel, Ah, I will ease me of mine adversaries, and avenge me of mine enemies:

25¶ And I will turn my hand upon thee, and purely purge away thy dross, and take away all thy tin:

26And I will restore thy judges as at the first, and thy counsellors as at the beginning: afterward thou shalt be called, The city of righteousness, the faithful city.

27Zion shall be redeemed with judgment, and her converts with righteousness.

New International

12When you come to appear before me,
     who has asked this of you,
     this trampling of my courts?
13Stop bringing meaningless offerings!
     Your incense is detestable to me.
   New Moons, Sabbaths and convocations—
     I cannot bear your evil assemblies.
14Your New Moon festivals and your appointed
        feasts
     my soul hates.
   They have become a burden to me;
     I am weary of bearing them.
15When you spread out your hands in prayer,
     I will hide my eyes from you;
   even if you offer many prayers,
     I will not listen.
   Your hands are full of blood;
16   wash and make yourselves clean.
   Take your evil deeds
     out of my sight!
   Stop doing wrong,
17   learn to do right!
   Seek justice,
     encourage the oppressed.[a]
   Defend the cause of the fatherless,
     plead the case of the widow.

18"Come now, let us reason together,"
     says the LORD.
   "Though your sins are like scarlet,
     they shall be as white as snow;
   though they are red as crimson,
     they shall be like wool.
19If you are willing and obedient,
     you will eat the best from the land;
20but if you resist and rebel,
     you will be devoured by the sword."
          For the mouth of the LORD has spoken.

21See how the faithful city
     has become a harlot!
   She once was full of justice;
     righteousness used to dwell in her—
     but now murderers!
22Your silver has become dross,
     your choice wine is diluted with water.
23Your rulers are rebels,
     companions of thieves;
   they all love bribes
     and chase after gifts.
   They do not defend the cause of the fatherless;
     the widow's case does not come before them.
24Therefore the Lord, the LORD Almighty,
     the Mighty One of Israel, declares:
   "Ah, I will get relief from my foes
     and avenge myself on my enemies.
25I will turn my hand against you;
     I will thoroughly purge away your dross
     and remove all your impurities.
26I will restore your judges as in days of old,
     your counselors as at the beginning.
   Afterward you will be called
     the City of Righteousness,
     the Faithful City."

27Zion will be redeemed with justice,
     her penitent ones with righteousness.

Living Bible

wants your sacrifices when you have no sorrow for your sins? The incense you bring me is a stench in my nostrils. Your holy celebrations of the new moon and the Sabbath, and your special days for fasting—even your most pious meetings—all are frauds! I want nothing more to do with them. 14I hate them all; I can't stand the sight of them. 15From now on, when you pray with your hands stretched out to heaven, I won't look or listen. Even though you make many prayers, I will not hear, for your hands are those of murderers; they are covered with the blood of your innocent victims.

16Oh, wash yourselves! Be clean! Let me no longer see you doing all these wicked things; quit your evil ways. 17Learn to do good, to be fair and to help the poor, the fatherless, and widows.

18Come, let's talk this over! says the Lord; no matter how deep the stain of your sins, I can take it out and make you as clean as freshly fallen snow. Even if you are stained as red as crimson, I can make you white as wool! 19If you will only let me help you, if you will only obey, then I will make you rich! 20But if you keep on turning your backs and refusing to listen to me, you will be killed by your enemies; I, the Lord, have spoken.

21Jerusalem, once my faithful wife! And now a prostitute! Running after other gods! Once "The City of Fair Play," but now a gang of murderers. 22Once like sterling silver; now mixed with worthless alloy! Once so pure, but now diluted like watered-down wine! 23Your leaders are rebels, companions of thieves; all of them take bribes and won't defend the widows and orphans. 24Therefore the Lord, the Mighty One of Israel, says: I will pour out my anger on you, my enemies! 25I myself will melt you in a smelting pot, and skim off your slag.

26And afterwards I will give you good judges and wise counselors like those you used to have. Then your city shall again be called "The City of Justice," and "The Faithful Town." 27Those who return to the Lord, who are just and good, shall be redeemed.

New Revised Standard

12 When you come to appear before me,b
   who asked this from your hand?
   Trample my courts no more;
13 bringing offerings is futile;
   incense is an abomination to me.
New moon and sabbath and calling of
      convocation—
   I cannot endure solemn assemblies with
      iniquity.
14 Your new moons and your appointed festivals
   my soul hates;
they have become a burden to me,
   I am weary of bearing them.
15 When you stretch out your hands,
   I will hide my eyes from you;
even though you make many prayers,
   I will not listen;
   your hands are full of blood.
16 Wash yourselves; make yourselves clean;
   remove the evil of your doings
   from before my eyes;
cease to do evil,
17   learn to do good;
seek justice,
   rescue the oppressed,
defend the orphan,
   plead for the widow.

18 Come now, let us argue it out,
   says the LORD:
though your sins are like scarlet,
   they shall be like snow;
though they are red like crimson,
   they shall become like wool.
19 If you are willing and obedient,
   you shall eat the good of the land;
20 but if you refuse and rebel,
   you shall be devoured by the sword;
   for the mouth of the LORD has spoken.

The Degenerate City
21 How the faithful city
   has become a whore!
   She that was full of justice,
righteousness lodged in her—
   but now murderers!
22 Your silver has become dross,
   your wine is mixed with water.
23 Your princes are rebels
   and companions of thieves.
Everyone loves a bribe
   and runs after gifts.
They do not defend the orphan,
   and the widow's cause does not come
      before them.

24 Therefore says the Sovereign, the LORD of
      hosts, the Mighty One of Israel:
Ah, I will pour out my wrath on my enemies,
   and avenge myself on my foes!
25 I will turn my hand against you;
   I will smelt away your dross as with lye
   and remove all your alloy.
26 And I will restore your judges as at the first,
   and your counselors as at the beginning.
Afterward you shall be called the city of
      righteousness,
   the faithful city.

27 Zion shall be redeemed by justice,
   and those in her who repent, by
      righteousness.

b Or see my face

King James

28¶ And the destruction of the transgressors and of the sinners *shall be* together, and they that forsake the LORD shall be consumed.

29For they shall be ashamed of the oaks which ye have desired, and ye shall be confounded for the gardens that ye have chosen.

30For ye shall be as an oak whose leaf fadeth, and as a garden that hath no water.

31And the strong shall be as tow, and the maker of it as a spark, and they shall both burn together, and none shall quench *them*.

2 THE WORD that Isaiah the son of Amoz saw concerning Judah and Jerusalem.

2And it shall come to pass in the last days, *that* the mountain of the LORD's house shall be established in the top of the mountains, and shall be exalted above the hills; and all nations shall flow unto it.

3And many people shall go and say, Come ye, and let us go up to the mountain of the LORD, to the house of the God of Jacob; and he will teach us of his ways, and we will walk in his paths: for out of Zion shall go forth the law, and the word of the LORD from Jerusalem.

4And he shall judge among the nations, and shall rebuke many people: and they shall beat their swords into plowshares, and their spears into pruninghooks: nation shall not lift up sword against nation, neither shall they learn war any more.

5O house of Jacob, come ye, and let us walk in the light of the LORD.

6¶ Therefore thou hast forsaken thy people the house of Jacob, because they be replenished from the east, and *are* soothsayers like the Philistines, and they please themselves in the children of strangers.

7Their land also is full of silver and gold, neither *is* there any end of their treasures; their land is also full of horses, neither *is there any* end of their chariots:

8Their land also is full of idols; they worship the work of their own hands, that which their own fingers have made:

9And the mean man boweth down, and the great man humbleth himself: therefore forgive them not.

10¶ Enter into the rock, and hide thee in the dust, for fear of the LORD, and for the glory of his majesty.

New International

28But rebels and sinners will both be broken,
    and those who forsake the LORD will perish.

29"You will be ashamed because of the sacred oaks
    in which you have delighted;
you will be disgraced because of the gardens
    that you have chosen.
30You will be like an oak with fading leaves,
    like a garden without water.
31The mighty man will become tinder
    and his work a spark;
both will burn together,
    with no one to quench the fire."

The Mountain of the LORD

2 THIS IS what Isaiah son of Amoz saw concerning Judah and Jerusalem:

2In the last days

the mountain of the LORD's temple will be
    established
    as chief among the mountains;
it will be raised above the hills,
    and all nations will stream to it.

3Many peoples will come and say,

"Come, let us go up to the mountain of the
    LORD,
    to the house of the God of Jacob.
He will teach us his ways,
    so that we may walk in his paths."
The law will go out from Zion,
    the word of the LORD from Jerusalem.
4He will judge between the nations
    and will settle disputes for many peoples.
They will beat their swords into plowshares
    and their spears into pruning hooks.
Nation will not take up sword against nation,
    nor will they train for war anymore.

5Come, O house of Jacob,
    let us walk in the light of the LORD.

The Day of the LORD

6You have abandoned your people,
    the house of Jacob.
They are full of superstitions from the East;
    they practice divination like the Philistines
    and clasp hands with pagans.
7Their land is full of silver and gold;
    there is no end to their treasures.
Their land is full of horses;
    there is no end to their chariots.
8Their land is full of idols;
    they bow down to the work of their hands,
    to what their fingers have made.
9So man will be brought low
    and mankind humbled—
    do not forgive them.a

10Go into the rocks,
    hide in the ground
from dread of the LORD
    and the splendor of his majesty!

---

a 9 Or *not raise them up*

Living Bible

28(But all sinners shall utterly perish, for they refuse to come to me.) 29Shame will cover you, and you will blush to think of all those times you sacrificed to idols in your groves of "sacred" oaks. 30You will perish like a withered tree or a garden without water. 31The strongest among you will disappear like burning straw; your evil deeds are the spark that sets the straw on fire, and no one will be able to put it out.

2 THIS IS another message to Isaiah from the Lord concerning Judah and Jerusalem:

2In the last days Jerusalem and the Temple of the Lord will become the world's greatest attraction,b and people from many lands will flow there to worship the Lord.

3"Come," everyone will say, "let us go up the mountain of the Lord, to the Temple of the God of Israel; there he will teach us his laws, and we will obey them." For in those days the world will be ruled from Jerusalem. 4The Lord will settle international disputes; all the nations will convert their weapons of war into implements of peace.c Then at the last all wars will stop and all military training will end. 5O Israel, come, let us walk in the light of the Lord, and be obedient to his laws!d

6The Lord has rejected you because you welcome foreigners from the East who practice magic and communicate with evil spirits, as the Philistines do.

7Israel has vast treasures of silver and gold, and great numbers of horses and chariots 8and idols—the land is full of them! They are man-made, and yet you worship them! 9Small and great, all bow before them; God will not forgive you for this sin.

10Crawl into the caves in the rocks and hide in terror from his glorious majesty, 11for the day is coming when

New Revised Standard

28 But rebels and sinners shall be destroyed
together,
and those who forsake the LORD shall be
consumed.
29 For you shall be ashamed of the oaks
in which you delighted;
and you shall blush for the gardens
that you have chosen.
30 For you shall be like an oak
whose leaf withers,
and like a garden without water.
31 The strong shall become like tinder,
and their worke like a spark;
they and their work shall burn together,
with no one to quench them.

The Future House of God

2 THE WORD that Isaiah son of Amoz saw concerning Judah and Jerusalem.

2 In days to come
the mountain of the LORD's house
shall be established as the highest of the
mountains,
and shall be raised above the hills;
all the nations shall stream to it.
3 Many peoples shall come and say,
"Come, let us go up to the mountain of the
LORD,
to the house of the God of Jacob;
that he may teach us his ways
and that we may walk in his paths."
For out of Zion shall go forth instruction,
and the word of the LORD from Jerusalem.
4 He shall judge between the nations,
and shall arbitrate for many peoples;
they shall beat their swords into plowshares,
and their spears into pruning hooks;
nation shall not lift up sword against nation,
neither shall they learn war any more.

Judgment Pronounced on Arrogance

5 O house of Jacob,
come, let us walk
in the light of the LORD!
6 For you have forsaken the ways off your
people,
O house of Jacob.
Indeed they are full of diviners from the east
and of soothsayers like the Philistines,
and they clasp hands with foreigners.
7 Their land is filled with silver and gold,
and there is no end to their treasures;
their land is filled with horses,
and there is no end to their chariots.
8 Their land is filled with idols;
they bow down to the work of their hands,
to what their own fingers have made.
9 And so people are humbled,
and everyone is brought low—
do not forgive them!
10 Enter into the rock,
and hide in the dust
from the terror of the LORD,
and from the glory of his majesty.

---

b 2:2 will become the world's greatest attraction, literally, "shall be established as the highest of the mountains." c 2:4 will convert their weapons of war into implements of peace, literally, "beat their swords into plowshares and their spears into pruning hooks." d 2:5 and be obedient to his laws, implied.

e Or its makers   f Heb lacks the ways of   g Cn: Heb lacks of diviners

King James

11The lofty looks of man shall be humbled, and the haughtiness of men shall be bowed down, and the LORD alone shall be exalted in that day.

12For the day of the LORD of hosts *shall be* upon every *one that is* proud and lofty, and upon every *one that is* lifted up; and he shall be brought low:

13And upon all the cedars of Lebanon, *that are* high and lifted up, and upon all the oaks of Bashan,

14And upon all the high mountains, and upon all the hills *that are* lifted up,

15And upon every high tower, and upon every fenced wall,

16And upon all the ships of Tarshish, and upon all pleasant pictures.

17And the loftiness of man shall be bowed down, and the haughtiness of men shall be made low: and the LORD alone shall be exalted in that day.

18And the idols he shall utterly abolish.

19And they shall go into the holes of the rocks, and into the caves of the earth, for fear of the LORD, and for the glory of his majesty, when he ariseth to shake terribly the earth.

20In that day a man shall cast his idols of silver, and his idols of gold, which they made *each one* for himself to worship, to the moles and to the bats;

21To go into the clefts of the rocks, and into the tops of the ragged rocks, for fear of the LORD, and for the glory of his majesty, when he ariseth to shake terribly the earth.

22Cease ye from man, whose breath *is* in his nostrils: for wherein is he to be accounted of?

3 FOR, BEHOLD, the Lord, the LORD of hosts, doth take away from Jerusalem and from Judah the stay and the staff, the whole stay of bread, and the whole stay of water,

2The mighty man, and the man of war, the judge, and the prophet, and the prudent, and the ancient,

3The captain of fifty, and the honourable man, and the counsellor, and the cunning artificer, and the eloquent orator.

4And I will give children *to be* their princes, and babes shall rule over them.

5And the people shall be oppressed, every one by another, and every one by his neighbour: the child shall behave himself proudly against the ancient, and the base against the honourable.

6When a man shall take hold of his brother of the house of his father, *saying*, Thou hast clothing, be thou our ruler, and *let* this ruin *be* under thy hand:

New International

11The eyes of the arrogant man will be humbled
    and the pride of men brought low;
  the LORD alone will be exalted in that day.

12The LORD Almighty has a day in store
    for all the proud and lofty,
    for all that is exalted
      (and they will be humbled),
13for all the cedars of Lebanon, tall and lofty,
    and all the oaks of Bashan,
14for all the towering mountains
    and all the high hills,
15for every lofty tower
    and every fortified wall,
16for every trading ship[a]
    and every stately vessel.
17The arrogance of man will be brought low
    and the pride of men humbled;
  the LORD alone will be exalted in that day,
18   and the idols will totally disappear.

19Men will flee to caves in the rocks
    and to holes in the ground
  from dread of the LORD
    and the splendor of his majesty,
    when he rises to shake the earth.
20In that day men will throw away
    to the rodents and bats
  their idols of silver and idols of gold,
    which they made to worship.
21They will flee to caverns in the rocks
    and to the overhanging crags
  from dread of the LORD
    and the splendor of his majesty,
    when he rises to shake the earth.

22Stop trusting in man,
    who has but a breath in his nostrils.
  Of what account is he?

Judgment on Jerusalem and Judah

3 SEE NOW, the Lord,
    the LORD Almighty,
  is about to take from Jerusalem and Judah
    both supply and support:
  all supplies of food and all supplies of water,
2   the hero and warrior,
    the judge and prophet,
    the soothsayer and elder,
3the captain of fifty and man of rank,
    the counselor, skilled craftsman and clever
      enchanter.

4I will make boys their officials;
    mere children will govern them.
5People will oppress each other—
    man against man, neighbor against neighbor.
  The young will rise up against the old,
    the base against the honorable.

6A man will seize one of his brothers
    at his father's home, and say,
  "You have a cloak, you be our leader;
    take charge of this heap of ruins!"

a 16 Hebrew *every ship of Tarshish*

Living Bible

your proud looks will be brought low; the Lord alone will be exalted. 12On that day the Lord Almighty will move against the proud and haughty and bring them to the dust. 13All the tall cedars of Lebanon and all the mighty oaks of Bashan shall bend low, 14and all the high mountains and hills, 15and every high tower and wall, 16and all the proud ocean ships and trim harbor craft— *all* shall be crushed before the Lord that day. 17All the glory of mankind will bow low; the pride of men will lie in the dust, and the Lord alone will be exalted. 18And all idols will be utterly abolished and destroyed.

19When the Lord stands up from his throne to shake up the earth, his enemies will crawl with fear into the holes in the rocks and into the caves because of the glory of his majesty. 20Then at last they will abandon their gold and silver idols to the moles and bats, 21and crawl into the caverns to hide among the jagged rocks at the tops of the cliffs to try to get away from the terror of the Lord and the glory of his majesty when he rises to terrify the earth. 22Puny man! Frail as his breath! Don't ever put your trust in him!

3 THE LORD will cut off Jerusalem's and Judah's food and water supplies 2and kill her leaders; he will destroy her armies, judges, prophets, elders, 3army officers, businessmen, lawyers, magicians and politicians. 4Israel's kings will be like babies, ruling childishly. 5And the worst sort of anarchy will prevail—everyone stepping on someone else, neighbors fighting neighbors, youths revolting against authority, criminals sneering at honorable men.

6In those days a man will say to his brother, "You have some extra clothing, so you be our king and take care of this mess."

New Revised Standard

11 The haughty eyes of people shall be brought
     low,
   and the pride of everyone shall be humbled;
   and the LORD alone will be exalted
     in that day.

12 For the LORD of hosts has a day
     against all that is proud and lofty,
     against all that is lifted up and high;[b]

13 against all the cedars of Lebanon,
     lofty and lifted up;
   and against all the oaks of Bashan;

14 against all the high mountains,
     and against all the lofty hills;

15 against every high tower,
     and against every fortified wall;

16 against all the ships of Tarshish,
     and against all the beautiful craft.[c]

17 The haughtiness of people shall be humbled,
     and the pride of everyone shall be brought
       low;
   and the LORD alone will be exalted on that
     day.

18 The idols shall utterly pass away.

19 Enter the caves of the rocks
     and the holes of the ground,
   from the terror of the LORD,
     and from the glory of his majesty,
     when he rises to terrify the earth.

20 On that day people will throw away
     to the moles and to the bats
   their idols of silver and their idols of gold,
     which they made for themselves to worship,

21 to enter the caverns of the rocks
     and the clefts in the crags,
   from the terror of the LORD,
     and from the glory of his majesty,
     when he rises to terrify the earth.

22 Turn away from mortals,
     who have only breath in their nostrils,
     for of what account are they?

3 FOR NOW the Sovereign, the LORD of hosts,
   is taking away from Jerusalem and from
     Judah

support and staff—
     all support of bread,
     and all support of water—

2 warrior and soldier,
     judge and prophet,
     diviner and elder,

3 captain of fifty
     and dignitary,
   counselor and skillful magician
     and expert enchanter.

4 And I will make boys their princes,
     and babes shall rule over them.

5 The people will be oppressed,
     everyone by another
     and everyone by a neighbor;
   the youth will be insolent to the elder,
     and the base to the honorable.

6 Someone will even seize a relative,
     a member of the clan, saying,
   "You have a cloak;
     you shall be our leader,
   and this heap of ruins
     shall be under your rule."

b Cn Compare Gk: Heb *low*   c Compare Gk: Meaning of Heb uncertain

King James

7In that day shall he swear, saying, I will not be an healer; for in my house *is* neither bread nor clothing: make me not a ruler of the people.

8For Jerusalem is ruined, and Judah is fallen: because their tongue and their doings *are* against the LORD, to provoke the eyes of his glory.

9¶ The show of their countenance doth witness against them; and they declare their sin as Sodom, they hide *it* not. Woe unto their soul! for they have rewarded evil unto themselves.

10Say ye to the righteous, that *it shall be* well *with him:* for they shall eat the fruit of their doings.

11Woe unto the wicked! *it shall be* ill *with him:* for the reward of his hands shall be given him.

12¶ *As for* my people, children *are* their oppressors, and women rule over them. O my people, they which lead thee cause *thee* to err, and destroy the way of thy paths.

13The LORD standeth up to plead, and standeth to judge the people.

14The LORD will enter into judgment with the ancients of his people, and the princes thereof: for ye have eaten up the vineyard; the spoil of the poor *is* in your houses.

15What mean ye *that* ye beat my people to pieces, and grind the faces of the poor? saith the Lord GOD of hosts.

16¶ Moreover the LORD saith, Because the daughters of Zion are haughty, and walk with stretched forth necks and wanton eyes, walking and mincing *as* they go, and making a tinkling with their feet:

17Therefore the Lord will smite with a scab the crown of the head of the daughters of Zion, and the LORD will discover their secret parts.

18In that day the Lord will take away the bravery of *their* tinkling ornaments *about their feet,* and *their* cauls, and *their* round tires like the moon,

19The chains, and the bracelets, and the mufflers,

20The bonnets, and the ornaments of the legs, and the headbands, and the tablets, and the earrings,

21The rings, and nose jewels,

22The changeable suits of apparel, and the mantles, and the wimples, and the crisping pins,

23The glasses, and the fine linen, and the hoods, and the veils.

24And it shall come to pass, *that* instead of sweet smell there shall be stink; and instead of a girdle a rent; and instead of well set hair baldness; and instead of a stomacher a girding of sackcloth; *and* burning instead of beauty.

25Thy men shall fall by the sword, and thy mighty in the war.

26And her gates shall lament and mourn; and she *being* desolate shall sit upon the ground.

New International

7But in that day he will cry out,
  "I have no remedy.
I have no food or clothing in my house;
  do not make me the leader of the people."

8Jerusalem staggers,
  Judah is falling;
their words and deeds are against the LORD,
  defying his glorious presence.
9The look on their faces testifies against them;
  they parade their sin like Sodom;
  they do not hide it.
Woe to them!
  They have brought disaster upon themselves.

10Tell the righteous it will be well with them,
  for they will enjoy the fruit of their deeds.
11Woe to the wicked! Disaster is upon them!
  They will be paid back for what their hands
    have done.

12Youths oppress my people,
  women rule over them.
O my people, your guides lead you astray;
  they turn you from the path.

13The LORD takes his place in court;
  he rises to judge the people.
14The LORD enters into judgment
  against the elders and leaders of his people:
"It is you who have ruined my vineyard;
  the plunder from the poor is in your houses.
15What do you mean by crushing my people
  and grinding the faces of the poor?"
          declares the Lord, the LORD Almighty.

16The LORD says,
  "The women of Zion are haughty,
walking along with outstretched necks,
  flirting with their eyes,
tripping along with mincing steps,
  with ornaments jingling on their ankles.
17Therefore the Lord will bring sores on the heads
  of the women of Zion;
  the LORD will make their scalps bald."

18In that day the Lord will snatch away their finery: the bangles and headbands and crescent necklaces, 19the earrings and bracelets and veils, 20the headdresses and ankle chains and sashes, the perfume bottles and charms, 21the signet rings and nose rings, 22the fine robes and the capes and cloaks, the purses 23and mirrors, and the linen garments and tiaras and shawls.

24Instead of fragrance there will be a stench;
    instead of a sash, a rope;
  instead of well-dressed hair, baldness;
    instead of fine clothing, sackcloth;
    instead of beauty, branding.
25Your men will fall by the sword,
    your warriors in battle.
26The gates of Zion will lament and mourn;
    destitute, she will sit on the ground.

Living Bible

7"No!" he will reply. "I cannot be of any help! I have no extra food or clothes. Don't get me involved!"

8Israel's civil government will be in utter ruin because the Jews have spoken out against their Lord and will not worship him; they offend his glory. 9The very look on their faces gives them away and shows their guilt. And they boast that their sin is equal to the sin of Sodom; they are not even ashamed. What a catastrophe! They have doomed themselves.

10But all is well for the godly man. Tell him, "What a reward you are going to get!" 11But say to the wicked, "Your doom is sure. You too shall get your just deserts. Your well-earned punishment is on the way."

12O my people! Can't you see what fools your rulers are? Weak as women! Foolish as little children playing king. True leaders? No, misleaders! Leading you down the garden path to destruction.

13The Lord stands up! He is the great Prosecuting Attorney presenting his case against his people! 14First to feel his wrath will be the elders and the princes, for they have defrauded the poor. They have filled their barns with grain extorted from the helpless peasants.

15"How dare you grind my people in the dust like that?" the Lord Almighty will demand of them.

16Next, he will judge the haughty Jewish women, who mince along, noses in the air, tinkling bracelets on their ankles, with wanton eyes that rove among the crowds to catch the glances of the men. 17The Lord will send a plague of scabs to ornament their heads! He will expose their nakedness for all to see. 18No longer shall they tinkle with self-assurance as they walk. For the Lord will strip away their artful beauty and their ornaments, 19their necklaces and bracelets and veils of shimmering gauze. 20Gone shall be their scarves and ankle chains, headbands, earrings, and perfumes; 21their rings and jewels, 22and party clothes and negligees and capes and ornate combs and purses; 23their mirrors, lovely lingerie, beautiful dresses and veils. 24Instead of smelling of sweet perfume, they'll stink; for sashes they'll use ropes; their well-set hair will all fall out; they'll wear sacks instead of robes.

All their beauty will be gone; all that will be left to them is shame and disgrace. 25, 26Their husbands shall die in battle; the women, ravaged, shall sit crying on the ground.

New Revised Standard

7 But the other will cry out on that day, saying,
　"I will not be a healer;
　in my house there is neither bread nor
　　　cloak;
　you shall not make me
　　　leader of the people."
8 For Jerusalem has stumbled
　　and Judah has fallen,
　because their speech and their deeds are
　　　against the LORD,
　defying his glorious presence.

9 The look on their faces bears witness against
　　them;
　they proclaim their sin like Sodom,
　　they do not hide it.
　Woe to them!
　For they have brought evil on themselves.
10 Tell the innocent how fortunate they are,
　　for they shall eat the fruit of their labors.
11 Woe to the guilty! How unfortunate they are,
　　for what their hands have done shall be
　　　done to them.
12 My people—children are their oppressors,
　　and women rule over them.
　O my people, your leaders mislead you,
　　and confuse the course of your paths.

13 The LORD rises to argue his case;
　　he stands to judge the peoples.
14 The LORD enters into judgment
　　with the elders and princes of his people:
　It is you who have devoured the vineyard;
　　the spoil of the poor is in your houses.
15 What do you mean by crushing my people,
　　by grinding the face of the poor? says the
　　　Lord GOD of hosts.

16 The LORD said:
　Because the daughters of Zion are haughty
　　and walk with outstretched necks,
　　glancing wantonly with their eyes,
　mincing along as they go,
　　tinkling with their feet;
17 the Lord will afflict with scabs
　　the heads of the daughters of Zion,
　　and the LORD will lay bare their secret
　　　parts.

18 In that day the Lord will take away the finery of the anklets, the headbands, and the crescents; 19the pendants, the bracelets, and the scarfs; 20the headdresses, the armlets, the sashes, the perfume boxes, and the amulets; 21the signet rings and nose rings; 22the festal robes, the mantles, the cloaks, and the handbags; 23the garments of gauze, the linen garments, the turbans, and the veils.

24　Instead of perfume there will be a stench;
　　　and instead of a sash, a rope;
　　and instead of well-set hair, baldness;
　　　and instead of a rich robe, a binding of
　　　　sackcloth;
　　　instead of beauty, shame.a
25　Your men shall fall by the sword
　　　and your warriors in battle.
26　And her gates shall lament and mourn;
　　　ravaged, she shall sit upon the ground.

a Q Ms: MT lacks *shame*

King James

4 AND IN that day seven women shall take hold of one man, saying, We will eat our own bread, and wear our own apparel: only let us be called by thy name, to take away our reproach.

2In that day shall the branch of the LORD be beautiful and glorious, and the fruit of the earth *shall be* excellent and comely for them that are escaped of Israel.

3And it shall come to pass, *that he that is* left in Zion, and *he that* remaineth in Jerusalem, shall be called holy, *even* every one that is written among the living in Jerusalem:

4When the Lord shall have washed away the filth of the daughters of Zion, and shall have purged the blood of Jerusalem from the midst thereof by the spirit of judgment, and by the spirit of burning.

5And the LORD will create upon every dwellingplace of mount Zion, and upon her assemblies, a cloud and smoke by day, and the shining of a flaming fire by night: for upon all the glory *shall be* a defence.

6And there shall be a tabernacle for a shadow in the daytime from the heat, and for a place of refuge, and for a covert from storm and from rain.

5 NOW WILL I sing to my wellbeloved a song of my beloved touching his vineyard. My wellbeloved hath a vineyard in a very fruitful hill:

2And he fenced it, and gathered out the stones thereof, and planted it with the choicest vine, and built a tower in the midst of it, and also made a winepress therein: and he looked that it should bring forth grapes, and it brought forth wild grapes.

3And now, O inhabitants of Jerusalem, and men of Judah, judge, I pray you, betwixt me and my vineyard.

4What could have been done more to my vineyard, that I have not done in it? wherefore, when I looked that it should bring forth grapes, brought it forth wild grapes?

5And now go to; I will tell you what I will do to my vineyard: I will take away the hedge thereof, and it shall be eaten up; *and* break down the wall thereof, and it shall be trodden down:

6And I will lay it waste: it shall not be pruned, nor digged; but there shall come up briers and thorns: I will also command the clouds that they rain no rain upon it.

7For the vineyard of the LORD of hosts *is* the house of Israel, and the men of Judah his pleasant plant: and he looked for judgment, but behold oppression; for righteousness, but behold a cry.

New International

4 IN THAT day seven women
will take hold of one man
and say, "We will eat our own food
and provide our own clothes;
only let us be called by your name.
Take away our disgrace!"

The Branch of the LORD

2In that day the Branch of the LORD will be beautiful and glorious, and the fruit of the land will be the pride and glory of the survivors in Israel. 3Those who are left in Zion, who remain in Jerusalem, will be called holy, all who are recorded among the living in Jerusalem. 4The Lord will wash away the filth of the women of Zion; he will cleanse the bloodstains from Jerusalem by a spirita of judgment and a spirita of fire. 5Then the LORD will create over all of Mount Zion and over those who assemble there a cloud of smoke by day and a glow of flaming fire by night; over all the glory will be a canopy. 6It will be a shelter and shade from the heat of the day, and a refuge and hiding place from the storm and rain.

The Song of the Vineyard

5 I WILL sing for the one I love
a song about his vineyard:
My loved one had a vineyard
on a fertile hillside.
2He dug it up and cleared it of stones
and planted it with the choicest vines.
He built a watchtower in it
and cut out a winepress as well.
Then he looked for a crop of good grapes,
but it yielded only bad fruit.

3"Now you dwellers in Jerusalem and men of
Judah,
judge between me and my vineyard.
4What more could have been done for my
vineyard
than I have done for it?
When I looked for good grapes,
why did it yield only bad?
5Now I will tell you
what I am going to do to my vineyard:
I will take away its hedge,
and it will be destroyed;
I will break down its wall,
and it will be trampled.
6I will make it a wasteland,
neither pruned nor cultivated,
and briers and thorns will grow there.
I will command the clouds
not to rain on it."

7The vineyard of the LORD Almighty
is the house of Israel,
and the men of Judah
are the garden of his delight.
And he looked for justice, but saw bloodshed;
for righteousness, but heard cries of distress.

a 4 Or *the Spirit*

Living Bible

4 AT THAT time so few men will be left alive that seven women will fight over each of them and say, "Let us all marry you! We will furnish our own food and clothing; only let us be called by your name so that we won't be mocked as old maids."

2, 3, 4Those whose names are written down to escape the destruction of Jerusalem will be washed and rinsed of all their moral filth by the horrors and the fire. They will be God's holy people. And the land will produce for them its lushest bounty and its richest fruit.b 5Then the Lord will provide shade on all Jerusalem—over every home and all its public grounds—a canopy of smoke and cloud throughout the day, and clouds of fire at night, covering the Glorious Land, 6protecting it from daytime heat and from rains and storms.

5 NOW I will sing a song about his vineyard to the one I love. *My Beloved has a vineyard on a very fertile hill. 2He plowed it and took out all the rocks and planted his vineyard with the choicest vines. He built a watchtower and cut a winepress in the rocks. Then he waited for the harvest, but the grapes that grew were wild and sour and not at all the sweet ones he expected.*

3Now, men of Jerusalem and Judah, you have heard the case! You be the judges! 4What more could I have done? Why did my vineyard give me wild grapes instead of sweet? 5I will tear down the fences and let my vineyard go to pasture to be trampled by cattle and sheep. 6I won't prune it or hoe it, but let it be overgrown with briars and thorns. I will command the clouds not to rain on it any more.

7I have given you the story of God's people. They are the vineyard that I spoke about. Israel and Judah are his pleasant acreage! He expected them to yield a crop of justice, but found bloodshed instead. He expected righteousness, but the cries of deep oppression met his ears.c 8You buy up property so others have no place to

New Revised Standard

4 SEVEN WOMEN shall take hold of one man in that day, saying,
"We will eat our own bread and wear our own clothes;
just let us be called by your name;
take away our disgrace."

The Future Glory of the Survivors in Zion

2 On that day the branch of the LORD shall be beautiful and glorious, and the fruit of the land shall be the pride and glory of the survivors of Israel. 3Whoever is left in Zion and remains in Jerusalem will be called holy, everyone who has been recorded for life in Jerusalem, 4once the Lord has washed away the filth of the daughters of Zion and cleansed the bloodstains of Jerusalem from its midst by a spirit of judgment and by a spirit of burning. 5Then the LORD will create over the whole site of Mount Zion and over its places of assembly a cloud by day and smoke and the shining of a flaming fire by night. Indeed over all the glory there will be a canopy. 6It will serve as a pavilion, a shade by day from the heat, and a refuge and a shelter from the storm and rain.

The Song of the Unfruitful Vineyard

5 LET ME sing for my beloved
my love-song concerning his vineyard:
My beloved had a vineyard
on a very fertile hill.
2 He dug it and cleared it of stones,
and planted it with choice vines;
he built a watchtower in the midst of it,
and hewed out a wine vat in it;
he expected it to yield grapes,
but it yielded wild grapes.

3 And now, inhabitants of Jerusalem
and people of Judah,
judge between me
and my vineyard.
4 What more was there to do for my vineyard
that I have not done in it?
When I expected it to yield grapes,
why did it yield wild grapes?

5 And now I will tell you
what I will do to my vineyard.
I will remove its hedge,
and it shall be devoured;
I will break down its wall,
and it shall be trampled down.
6 I will make it a waste;
it shall not be pruned or hoed,
and it shall be overgrown with briers and thorns;
I will also command the clouds
that they rain no rain upon it.

7 For the vineyard of the LORD of hosts
is the house of Israel,
and the people of Judah
are his pleasant planting;
he expected justice,
but saw bloodshed;
righteousness,
but heard a cry!

b 4:2-4 *its richest fruit.* Literally, "In that day the branch of the Lord will be beautiful and glorious." The phrase "branch of the Lord" refers to God's people, or it may be a prophecy of the coming Messiah.   c 5:7 *crop of justice, but found bloodshed instead. . . . expected righteousness, but the cries of deep oppression met his ears.* Here is an example of serious punning often used by the prophets: the Hebrew words for "justice" and "bloodshed" sound very much alike, as do those for "righteousness" and "cry."

King James

8¶ Woe unto them that join house to house, *that* lay field to field, till *there be* no place, that they may be placed alone in the midst of the earth!

9In mine ears *said* the LORD of hosts, Of a truth many houses shall be desolate, *even* great and fair, without inhabitant.

10Yea, ten acres of vineyard shall yield one bath, and the seed of an homer shall yield an ephah.

11¶ Woe unto them that rise up early in the morning, *that* they may follow strong drink; that continue until night, *till* wine inflame them!

12And the harp, and the viol, the tabret, and pipe, and wine, are in their feasts: but they regard not the work of the LORD, neither consider the operation of his hands.

13¶ Therefore my people are gone into captivity, because *they have* no knowledge: and their honourable men *are* famished, and their multitude dried up with thirst.

14Therefore hell hath enlarged herself, and opened her mouth without measure: and their glory, and their multitude, and their pomp, and he that rejoiceth, shall descend into it.

15And the mean man shall be brought down, and the mighty man shall be humbled, and the eyes of the lofty shall be humbled:

16But the LORD of hosts shall be exalted in judgment, and God that is holy shall be sanctified in righteousness.

17Then shall the lambs feed after their manner, and the waste places of the fat ones shall strangers eat.

18Woe unto them that draw iniquity with cords of vanity, and sin as it were with a cart rope:

19That say, Let him make speed, *and* hasten his work, that we may see *it:* and let the counsel of the Holy One of Israel draw nigh and come, that we may know *it!*

20¶ Woe unto them that call evil good, and good evil; that put darkness for light, and light for darkness; that put bitter for sweet, and sweet for bitter!

21Woe unto *them that are* wise in their own eyes, and prudent in their own sight!

22Woe unto *them that are* mighty to drink wine, and men of strength to mingle strong drink:

23Which justify the wicked for reward, and take away the righteousness of the righteous from him!

New International

Woes and Judgments

8Woe to you who add house to house
  and join field to field
till no space is left
  and you live alone in the land.

9The LORD Almighty has declared in my hearing:

"Surely the great houses will become desolate,
  the fine mansions left without occupants.
10A ten-acre[a] vineyard will produce only a bath[b]
    of wine,
  a homer[c] of seed only an ephah[d] of grain."

11Woe to those who rise early in the morning
  to run after their drinks,
who stay up late at night
  till they are inflamed with wine.
12They have harps and lyres at their banquets,
  tambourines and flutes and wine,
but they have no regard for the deeds of the
    LORD,
  no respect for the work of his hands.
13Therefore my people will go into exile
  for lack of understanding;
their men of rank will die of hunger
  and their masses will be parched with thirst.
14Therefore the grave[e] enlarges its appetite
  and opens its mouth without limit;
into it will descend their nobles and masses
  with all their brawlers and revelers.
15So man will be brought low
  and mankind humbled,
  the eyes of the arrogant humbled.
16But the LORD Almighty will be exalted by his
    justice,
  and the holy God will show himself holy by
    his righteousness.
17Then sheep will graze as in their own pasture;
  lambs will feed[f] among the ruins of the rich.

18Woe to those who draw sin along with cords of
    deceit,
  and wickedness as with cart ropes,
19to those who say, "Let God hurry,
  let him hasten his work
  so we may see it.
Let it approach,
  let the plan of the Holy One of Israel come,
  so we may know it."

20Woe to those who call evil good
    and good evil,
  who put darkness for light
    and light for darkness,
  who put bitter for sweet
    and sweet for bitter.

21Woe to those who are wise in their own eyes
  and clever in their own sight.

22Woe to those who are heroes at drinking wine
  and champions at mixing drinks,
23who acquit the guilty for a bribe,
  but deny justice to the innocent.

---

a *10* Hebrew *ten-yoke*, that is, the land plowed by 10 yoke of oxen in one day   b *10* That is, probably about 6 gallons (about 22 liters)   c *10* That is, probably about 6 bushels (about 220 liters)   d *10* That is, probably about 3/5 bushel (about 22 liters)   e *14* Hebrew *Sheol*   f *17* Septuagint; Hebrew / *strangers will eat*

Living Bible

live. Your homes are built on great estates so you can be alone in the midst of the earth! 9But the Lord Almighty has sworn your awful fate—with my own ears I heard him say, "Many a beautiful home will lie deserted, their owners killed or gone." 10An acre of vineyard will not produce a gallon of juice! Ten bushels of seed will yield a one-bushel crop!

11Woe to you who get up early in the morning to go on long drinking bouts that last till late at night—woe to you drunken bums. 12You furnish lovely music at your grand parties; the orchestras are superb! But for the Lord you have no thought or care. 13Therefore I will send you into exile far away because you neither know nor care that I have done so much for you. Your great and honored men will starve, and the common people will die of thirst.

14Hell is licking its chops in anticipation of this delicious morsel, Jerusalem. Her great and small shall be swallowed up, and all her drunken throngs. 15In that day the haughty shall be brought down to the dust; the proud shall be humbled; 16but the Lord Almighty is exalted above all, for he alone is holy, just and good. 17In those days flocks will feed among the ruins. Lambs and calves and kids will pasture there!

18Woe to those who drag their sins behind them like a bullockg on a rope. 19They even mock the Holy One of Israel and dare the Lord to punish them.h "Hurry up and punish us, O Lord," they say. "We want to see what you can do!" 20They say that what is right is wrong, and what is wrong is right; that black is white and white is black; bitter is sweet and sweet is bitter.

21Woe to those who are wise and shrewd in their own eyes! 22Woe to those who are "heroes" when it comes to drinking, and boast about the liquor they can hold. 23They take bribes to pervert justice, letting the wicked go free and putting innocent men in jail. 24Therefore

New Revised Standard

Social Injustice Denounced

8 Ah, you who join house to house,
    who add field to field,
until there is room for no one but you,
    and you are left to live alone
    in the midst of the land!
9 The LORD of hosts has sworn in my hearing:
    Surely many houses shall be desolate,
    large and beautiful houses, without
        inhabitant.
10 For ten acres of vineyard shall yield but one
        bath,
    and a homer of seed shall yield a mere
        ephah.i

11 Ah, you who rise early in the morning
    in pursuit of strong drink,
who linger in the evening
    to be inflamed by wine,
12 whose feasts consist of lyre and harp,
    tambourine and flute and wine,
but who do not regard the deeds of the LORD,
    or see the work of his hands!
13 Therefore my people go into exile without
        knowledge;
    their nobles are dying of hunger,
    and their multitude is parched with thirst.

14 Therefore Sheol has enlarged its appetite
    and opened its mouth beyond measure;
the nobility of Jerusalemj and her multitude
        go down,
    her throng and all who exult in her.
15 People are bowed down, everyone is brought
        low,
    and the eyes of the haughty are humbled.
16 But the LORD of hosts is exalted by justice,
    and the Holy God shows himself holy by
        righteousness.
17 Then the lambs shall graze as in their pasture,
    fatlings and kidsk shall feed among the
        ruins.

18 Ah, you who drag iniquity along with cords of
        falsehood,
    who drag sin along as with cart ropes,
19 who say, "Let him make haste,
    let him speed his work
        that we may see it;
let the plan of the Holy One of Israel hasten
        to fulfillment,
    that we may know it!"
20 Ah, you who call evil good
        and good evil,
who put darkness for light
        and light for darkness,
who put bitter for sweet
        and sweet for bitter!
21 Ah, you who are wise in your own eyes,
    and shrewd in your own sight!
22 Ah, you who are heroes in drinking wine
    and valiant at mixing drink,
23 who acquit the guilty for a bribe,
    and deprive the innocent of their rights!

---

g 5:18 like a bullock on a rope, or "with cords of falsehood."   h 5:19 and dare the Lord to punish them, implied.

i The Heb bath, homer, and ephah are measures of quantity   j Heb her nobility   k Cn Compare Gk: Heb aliens

King James

24Therefore as the fire devoureth the stubble, and the flame consumeth the chaff, *so* their root shall be as rottenness, and their blossom shall go up as dust: because they have cast away the law of the LORD of hosts, and despised the word of the Holy One of Israel.

25Therefore is the anger of the LORD kindled against his people, and he hath stretched forth his hand against them, and hath smitten them: and the hills did tremble, and their carcases *were* torn in the midst of the streets. For all this his anger is not turned away, but his hand *is* stretched out still.

26¶ And he will lift up an ensign to the nations from far, and will hiss unto them from the end of the earth: and, behold, they shall come with speed swiftly:

27None shall be weary nor stumble among them; none shall slumber nor sleep; neither shall the girdle of their loins be loosed, nor the latchet of their shoes be broken:

28Whose arrows *are* sharp, and all their bows bent, their horses' hoofs shall be counted like flint, and their wheels like a whirlwind:

29Their roaring *shall be* like a lion, they shall roar like young lions: yea, they shall roar, and lay hold of the prey, and shall carry *it* away safe, and none shall deliver *it*.

30And in that day they shall roar against them like the roaring of the sea: and if *one* look unto the land, behold darkness *and* sorrow, and the light is darkened in the heavens thereof.

6 IN THE year that king Uzziah died I saw also the Lord sitting upon a throne, high and lifted up, and his train filled the temple.

2Above it stood the seraphims: each one had six wings; with twain he covered his face, and with twain he covered his feet, and with twain he did fly.

3And one cried unto another, and said, Holy, holy, holy, *is* the LORD of hosts: the whole earth *is* full of his glory.

4And the posts of the door moved at the voice of him that cried, and the house was filled with smoke.

5¶ Then said I, Woe *is* me! for I am undone; because I *am* a man of unclean lips, and I dwell in the midst of a people of unclean lips: for mine eyes have seen the King, the LORD of hosts.

6Then flew one of the seraphims unto me, having a live coal in his hand, *which* he had taken with the tongs from off the altar:

7And he laid *it* upon my mouth, and said, Lo, this hath touched thy lips; and thine iniquity is taken away, and thy sin purged.

8Also I heard the voice of the Lord, saying, Whom shall I send, and who will go for us? Then said I, Here *am* I; send me.

9¶ And he said, Go, and tell this people, Hear ye indeed, but understand not; and see ye indeed, but perceive not.

New International

24Therefore, as tongues of fire lick up straw
　　and as dry grass sinks down in the flames,
　so their roots will decay
　　and their flowers blow away like dust;
　for they have rejected the law of the LORD
　　Almighty
　　and spurned the word of the Holy One of
　　　Israel.
25Therefore the LORD's anger burns against his
　　people;
　his hand is raised and he strikes them down.
　The mountains shake,
　　and the dead bodies are like refuse in the
　　　streets.

　Yet for all this, his anger is not turned away,
　　his hand is still upraised.

26He lifts up a banner for the distant nations,
　he whistles for those at the ends of the earth.
　Here they come,
　　swiftly and speedily!
27Not one of them grows tired or stumbles,
　not one slumbers or sleeps;
　not a belt is loosened at the waist,
　　not a sandal thong is broken.
28Their arrows are sharp,
　all their bows are strung;
　their horses' hoofs seem like flint,
　　their chariot wheels like a whirlwind.
29Their roar is like that of the lion,
　they roar like young lions;
　they growl as they seize their prey
　and carry it off with no one to rescue.
30In that day they will roar over it
　like the roaring of the sea.
　And if one looks at the land,
　he will see darkness and distress;
　　even the light will be darkened by the clouds.

Isaiah's Commission

6 IN THE year that King Uzziah died, I saw the Lord seated on a throne, high and exalted, and the train of his robe filled the temple. 2Above him were seraphs, each with six wings: With two wings they covered their faces, with two they covered their feet, and with two they were flying. 3And they were calling to one another:

　"Holy, holy, holy is the LORD Almighty;
　　the whole earth is full of his glory."

4At the sound of their voices the doorposts and thresholds shook and the temple was filled with smoke. 5"Woe to me!" I cried. "I am ruined! For I am a man of unclean lips, and I live among a people of unclean lips, and my eyes have seen the King, the LORD Almighty."

6Then one of the seraphs flew to me with a live coal in his hand, which he had taken with tongs from the altar. 7With it he touched my mouth and said, "See, this has touched your lips; your guilt is taken away and your sin atoned for."

8Then I heard the voice of the Lord saying, "Whom shall I send? And who will go for us?"

And I said, "Here am I. Send me!"

9He said, "Go and tell this people:

　" 'Be ever hearing, but never understanding;
　　be ever seeing, but never perceiving.'

Living Bible

God will deal with them and burn them. They will disappear like straw on fire. Their roots will rot and their flowers wither, for they have thrown away the laws of God and despised the Word of the Holy One of Israel. 25That is why the anger of the Lord is hot against his people; that is why he has reached out his hand to smash them. The hills will tremble, and the rotting bodies of his people will be thrown as refuse in the streets. But even so, his anger is not ended; his hand is heavy on them still.

26He will send a signal to the nations far away, whistling to those at the ends of the earth, and they will come racing toward Jerusalem. 27They never weary, never stumble, never stop; their belts are tight, their bootstraps strong; they run without stopping for rest or for sleep. 28Their arrows are sharp; their bows are bent; sparks fly from their horses' hoofs, and the wheels of their chariots spin like the wind. 29They roar like lions and pounce upon the prey. They seize my people and carry them off into captivity with none to rescue them. 30They growl over their victims like the roaring of the sea. Over all Israel lies a pall of darkness and sorrow and the heavens are black.

New Revised Standard

Foreign Invasion Predicted

24 Therefore, as the tongue of fire devours the
      stubble,
    and as dry grass sinks down in the flame,
so their root will become rotten,
    and their blossom go up like dust;
for they have rejected the instruction of the
      LORD of hosts,
    and have despised the word of the Holy
      One of Israel.

25 Therefore the anger of the LORD was kindled
      against his people,
    and he stretched out his hand against them
      and struck them;
    the mountains quaked,
and their corpses were like refuse
    in the streets.
For all this his anger has not turned away,
    and his hand is stretched out still.

26 He will raise a signal for a nation far away,
    and whistle for a people at the ends of the
      earth;
Here they come, swiftly, speedily!
27 None of them is weary, none stumbles,
    none slumbers or sleeps,
not a loincloth is loose,
    not a sandal-thong broken;
28 their arrows are sharp,
    all their bows bent,
their horses' hoofs seem like flint,
    and their wheels like the whirlwind.
29 Their roaring is like a lion,
    like young lions they roar;
they growl and seize their prey,
    they carry it off, and no one can rescue.
30 They will roar over it on that day,
    like the roaring of the sea.
And if one look to the land—
    only darkness and distress;
and the light grows dark with clouds.

A Vision of God in the Temple

6 THE YEAR King Uzziah died I saw the Lord! He was sitting on a lofty throne, and the Temple was filled with his glory. 2Hovering about him were mighty, six-winged angels of fire. With two of their wings they covered their faces; with two others they covered their feet, and with two they flew. 3In a great antiphonal chorus they sang, "Holy, holy, holy is the Lord Almighty; the whole earth is filled with his glory." 4Such singing it was! It shook the Temple to its foundations, and suddenly the entire sanctuary was filled with smoke.

5Then I said, "My doom is sealed, for I am a foul-mouthed sinner, a member of a sinful, foul-mouthed race; and I have looked upon the King, the Lord of heaven's armies."

6Then one of the mighty angels flew over to the altar and with a pair of tongs picked out a burning coal. 7He touched my lips with it and said, "Now you are pronounced 'Not guilty' because this coal has touched your lips. Your sins are all forgiven."

8Then I heard the Lord asking, "Whom shall I send as a messenger to my people? Who will go?"

And I said, "Lord, I'll go! Send *me*."

9And he said, "Yes, go. But tell my people this: 'Though you hear my words repeatedly, you won't understand them. Though you watch and watch as I perform my miracles, still you won't know what they mean.' 10Dull their understanding, close their ears and

6 IN THE year that King Uzziah died, I saw the Lord sitting on a throne, high and lofty; and the hem of his robe filled the temple. 2Seraphs were in attendance above him; each had six wings: with two they covered their faces, and with two they covered their feet,[a] and with two they flew. 3And one called to another and said:

"Holy, holy, holy is the LORD of hosts;
    the whole earth is full of his glory."

4The pivots[a] on the thresholds shook at the voices of those who called, and the house filled with smoke. 5And I said: "Woe is me! I am lost, for I am a man of unclean lips, and I live among a people of unclean lips; yet my eyes have seen the King, the LORD of hosts!"

6 Then one of the seraphs flew to me, holding a live coal that had been taken from the altar with a pair of tongs. 7The seraph[b] touched my mouth with it and said: "Now that this has touched your lips, your guilt has departed and your sin is blotted out." 8Then I heard the voice of the Lord saying, "Whom shall I send, and who will go for us?" And I said, "Here am I; send me!" 9And he said, "Go and say to this people:

'Keep listening, but do not comprehend;
keep looking, but do not understand.'

King James

10Make the heart of this people fat, and make their ears heavy, and shut their eyes; lest they see with their eyes, and hear with their ears, and understand with their heart, and convert, and be healed.

11Then said I, Lord, how long? And he answered, Until the cities be wasted without inhabitant, and the houses without man, and the land be utterly desolate,

12And the LORD have removed men far away, and *there be* a great forsaking in the midst of the land.

13¶ But yet in it *shall be* a tenth, and *it* shall return, and shall be eaten: as a teil tree, and as an oak, whose substance *is* in them, when they cast *their leaves: so* the holy seed *shall be* the substance thereof.

7 AND IT came to pass in the days of Ahaz the son of Jotham, the son of Uzziah, king of Judah, *that* Rezin the king of Syria, and Pekah the son of Remaliah, king of Israel, went up toward Jerusalem to war against it, but could not prevail against it.

2And it was told the house of David, saying, Syria is confederate with Ephraim. And his heart was moved, and the heart of his people, as the trees of the wood are moved with the wind.

3Then said the LORD unto Isaiah, Go forth now to meet Ahaz, thou, and Shear-jashub thy son, at the end of the conduit of the upper pool in the highway of the fuller's field;

4And say unto him, Take heed, and be quiet; fear not, neither be fainthearted for the two tails of these smoking firebrands, for the fierce anger of Rezin with Syria, and of the son of Remaliah.

5Because Syria, Ephraim, and the son of Remaliah, have taken evil counsel against thee, saying,

6Let us go up against Judah, and vex it, and let us make a breach therein for us, and set a king in the midst of it, *even* the son of Tabeal:

7Thus saith the Lord GOD, It shall not stand, neither shall it come to pass.

8For the head of Syria *is* Damascus, and the head of Damascus *is* Rezin; and within threescore and five years shall Ephraim be broken, that it be not a people.

9And the head of Ephraim *is* Samaria, and the head of Samaria *is* Remaliah's son. If ye will not believe, surely ye shall not be established.

10¶ Moreover the LORD spake again unto Ahaz, saying,

11Ask thee a sign of the LORD thy God; ask it either in the depth, or in the height above.

12But Ahaz said, I will not ask, neither will I tempt the LORD.

13And he said, Hear ye now, O house of David; *Is it* a small thing for you to weary men, but will ye weary my God also?

New International

10Make the heart of this people calloused;
    make their ears dull
    and close their eyes.[a]
Otherwise they might see with their eyes,
    hear with their ears,
    understand with their hearts,
and turn and be healed."

11Then I said, "For how long, O Lord?"
And he answered:

"Until the cities lie ruined
    and without inhabitant,
until the houses are left deserted
    and the fields ruined and ravaged,
12until the LORD has sent everyone far away
    and the land is utterly forsaken.
13And though a tenth remains in the land,
    it will again be laid waste.
But as the terebinth and oak
    leave stumps when they are cut down,
    so the holy seed will be the stump in the
        land."

The Sign of Immanuel

7 WHEN AHAZ son of Jotham, the son of Uzziah, was king of Judah, King Rezin of Aram and Pekah son of Remaliah king of Israel marched up to fight against Jerusalem, but they could not overpower it.

2Now the house of David was told, "Aram has allied itself with[b] Ephraim"; so the hearts of Ahaz and his people were shaken, as the trees of the forest are shaken by the wind.

3Then the LORD said to Isaiah, "Go out, you and your son Shear-Jashub,[c] to meet Ahaz at the end of the aqueduct of the Upper Pool, on the road to the Washerman's Field. 4Say to him, 'Be careful, keep calm and don't be afraid. Do not lose heart because of these two smoldering stubs of firewood—because of the fierce anger of Rezin and Aram and of the son of Remaliah. 5Aram, Ephraim and Remaliah's son have plotted your ruin, saying, 6"Let us invade Judah; let us tear it apart and divide it among ourselves, and make the son of Tabeel king over it." 7Yet this is what the Sovereign LORD says:

" 'It will not take place,
    it will not happen,
8for the head of Aram is Damascus,
    and the head of Damascus is only Rezin.
Within sixty-five years
    Ephraim will be too shattered to be a people.
9The head of Ephraim is Samaria,
    and the head of Samaria is only Remaliah's
        son.
If you do not stand firm in your faith,
    you will not stand at all.' "

10Again the LORD spoke to Ahaz, 11"Ask the LORD your God for a sign, whether in the deepest depths or in the highest heights."

12But Ahaz said, "I will not ask; I will not put the LORD to the test."

13Then Isaiah said, "Hear now, you house of David! Is it not enough to try the patience of men? Will you try the patience of my God also? 14Therefore the Lord him-

---

[a] 9,10 Hebrew; Septuagint *'You will be ever hearing, but never understanding; / you will be ever seeing, but never perceiving.' / *[10]*This people's heart has become calloused; / they hardly hear with their ears, / and they have closed their eyes*   [b] 2 Or *has set up camp in*   [c] 3 *Shear-Jashub* means *a remnant will return.*

Living Bible

shut their eyes. I don't want them to see or to hear or to understand, or to turn to me to heal them."d

11Then I said, "Lord, how long will it be before they are ready to listen?"

And he replied, "Not until their cities are destroyed— without a person left—and the whole country is an utter wasteland, 12and they are all taken away as slaves to other countries far away, and all the land of Israel lies deserted! 13Yet a tenth—a remnant—will survive; and though Israel is invaded again and again and destroyed, yet Israel will be like a tree cut down, whose stump still lives to grow again."

7 DURING THE reign of Ahaz (the son of Jotham and grandson of Uzziah), Jerusalem was attacked by King Rezin of Syria and King Pekah of Israel (the son of Remaliah).e But it was not taken; the city stood. 2However, when the news came to the royal court, "Syria is allied with Israel against us!" the hearts of the king and his people trembled with fear as the trees of a forest shake in a storm.

3Then the Lord said to Isaiah, "Go out to meet King Ahaz, you and Shear-jashub, your son. You will find him at the end of the aqueduct which leads from Gihon Spring to the upper reservoir, near the road that leads down to the bleaching field. 4Tell him to quit worrying. Tell him he needn't be frightened by the fierce anger of those two has-beens, Rezin and Pekah. 5Yes, the kings of Syria and Israel are coming against you.

"They say, 6'We will invade Judah and throw her people into panic. Then we'll fight our way into Jerusalem and install the son of Tabeel as their king.'

7"But the Lord God says, This plan will not succeed, 8for Damascus will remain the capital of Syria alone, and King Rezin's kingdom will not increase its boundaries. And within sixty-five years Ephraim, too, will be crushed and broken.f 9Samaria is the capital of Ephraim alone and King Pekah's power will not increase. You don't believe me? If you want me to protect you, you must learn to believe what I say."

10Not long after this, the Lord sent this further message to King Ahaz:

11"Ask me for a sign, Ahaz, to prove that I will indeed crush your enemies as I have said. Ask anything you like, in heaven or on earth."g

12But the king refused. "No," he said, "I'll not bother the Lord with anything like that." 13Then Isaiah said, O House of David, you aren't satisfied to exhaust *my* patience; you exhaust the Lord's as well! 14All right

New Revised Standard

10 Make the mind of this people dull,
        and stop their ears,
        and shut their eyes,
    so that they may not look with their eyes,
        and listen with their ears,
    and comprehend with their minds,
        and turn and be healed."
11 Then I said, "How long, O Lord?" And he
        said:
    "Until cities lie waste
        without inhabitant,
    and houses without people,
        and the land is utterly desolate;
12 until the LORD sends everyone far away,
        and vast is the emptiness in the midst of the
        land.
13 Even if a tenth part remain in it,
        it will be burned again,
    like a terebinth or an oak
        whose stump remains standing
        when it is felled."h
    The holy seed is its stump.

Isaiah Reassures King Ahaz

7 IN THE days of Ahaz son of Jotham son of Uzzi-ah, king of Judah, King Rezin of Aram and King Pekah son of Remaliah of Israel went up to attack Jerusalem, but could not mount an attack against it. 2When the house of David heard that Aram had allied itself with Ephraim, the heart of Ahazi and the heart of his people shook as the trees of the forest shake before the wind.

3 Then the LORD said to Isaiah, Go out to meet Ahaz, you and your son Shear-jashub,j at the end of the conduit of the upper pool on the highway to the Fuller's Field, 4and say to him, Take heed, be quiet, do not fear, and do not let your heart be faint because of these two smoldering stumps of firebrands, because of the fierce anger of Rezin and Aram and the son of Remaliah. 5Because Aram—with Ephraim and the son of Remaliah— has plotted evil against you, saying, 6Let us go up against Judah and cut off Jerusalemk and conquer it for ourselves and make the son of Tabeel king in it; 7therefore thus says the Lord GOD:
        It shall not stand,
            and it shall not come to pass.
8   For the head of Aram is Damascus,
            and the head of Damascus is Rezin.
    (Within sixty-five years Ephraim will be shattered,
    no longer a people.)
9   The head of Ephraim is Samaria,
            and the head of Samaria is the son of
            Remaliah.
    If you do not stand firm in faith,
        you shall not stand at all.

Isaiah Gives Ahaz the Sign of Immanuel

10 Again the LORD spoke to Ahaz, saying, 11Ask a sign of the LORD your God; let it be deep as Sheol or high as heaven. 12But Ahaz said, I will not ask, and I will not put the LORD to the test. 13Then Isaiahl said: "Hear then, O house of David! Is it too little for you to weary mortals, that you weary my God also? 14Therefore the

---

d *6:10* Apparently God's patience with their chronic rebellion was finally exhausted.   e *7:1 the son of Remaliah.* "The usurper, the son of Remaliah" is implied.   f *7:8 Ephraim will be crushed and broken.* Samaria, the capital of "Ephraim," fell to the Assyrian armies in 722 B.C., thirteen years after this oracle—ending the Northern Kingdom.   g *7:11 Ask anything you like, in heaven or on earth,* literally, "let it be deep as Sheol or high as heaven."

h Meaning of Heb uncertain   i Heb *his heart*   j That is *A remnant shall return*   k Heb *cut it off*   l Heb *he*

King James

14Therefore the Lord himself shall give you a sign; Behold, a virgin shall conceive, and bear a son, and shall call his name Immanuel.

15Butter and honey shall he eat, that he may know to refuse the evil, and choose the good.

16For before the child shall know to refuse the evil, and choose the good, the land that thou abhorrest shall be forsaken of both her kings.

17¶ The LORD shall bring upon thee, and upon thy people, and upon thy father's house, days that have not come, from the day that Ephraim departed from Judah; *even* the king of Assyria.

18And it shall come to pass in that day, *that* the LORD shall hiss for the fly that *is* in the uttermost part of the rivers of Egypt, and for the bee that *is* in the land of Assyria.

19And they shall come, and shall rest all of them in the desolate valleys, and in the holes of the rocks, and upon all thorns, and upon all bushes.

20In the same day shall the Lord shave with a razor that is hired, *namely*, by them beyond the river, by the king of Assyria, the head, and the hair of the feet: and it shall also consume the beard.

21And it shall come to pass in that day, *that* a man shall nourish a young cow, and two sheep;

22And it shall come to pass, for the abundance of milk *that* they shall give he shall eat butter: for butter and honey shall every one eat that is left in the land.

23And it shall come to pass in that day, *that* every place shall be, where there were a thousand vines at a thousand silverlings, it shall *even* be for briers and thorns.

24With arrows and with bows shall *men* come thither; because all the land shall become briers and thorns.

25And *on* all hills that shall be digged with the mattock, there shall not come thither the fear of briers and thorns: but it shall be for the sending forth of oxen, and for the treading of lesser cattle.

8 MOREOVER THE LORD said unto me, Take thee a great roll, and write in it with a man's pen concerning Maher-shalal-hash-baz.

2And I took unto me faithful witnesses to record, Uriah the priest, and Zechariah the son of Jeberechiah.

3And I went unto the prophetess; and she conceived, and bare a son. Then said the LORD to me, Call his name Maher-shalal-hash-baz.

New International

self will give you[a] a sign: The virgin will be with child and will give birth to a son, and[b] will call him Immanuel.[c] 15He will eat curds and honey when he knows enough to reject the wrong and choose the right. 16But before the boy knows enough to reject the wrong and choose the right, the land of the two kings you dread will be laid waste. 17The LORD will bring on you and on your people and on the house of your father a time unlike any since Ephraim broke away from Judah—he will bring the king of Assyria."

18In that day the LORD will whistle for flies from the distant streams of Egypt and for bees from the land of Assyria. 19They will all come and settle in the steep ravines and in the crevices in the rocks, on all the thornbushes and at all the water holes. 20In that day the Lord will use a razor hired from beyond the River[d]—the king of Assyria—to shave your head and the hair of your legs, and to take off your beards also. 21In that day, a man will keep alive a young cow and two goats. 22And because of the abundance of the milk they give, he will have curds to eat. All who remain in the land will eat curds and honey. 23In that day, in every place where there were a thousand vines worth a thousand silver shekels,[e] there will be only briers and thorns. 24Men will go there with bow and arrow, for the land will be covered with briers and thorns. 25As for all the hills once cultivated by the hoe, you will no longer go there for fear of the briers and thorns; they will become places where cattle are turned loose and where sheep run.

Assyria, the LORD's Instrument

8 THE LORD said to me, "Take a large scroll and write on it with an ordinary pen: Maher-Shalal-Hash-Baz.[f] 2And I will call in Uriah the priest and Zechariah son of Jeberekiah as reliable witnesses for me."

3Then I went to the prophetess, and she conceived and gave birth to a son. And the LORD said to me, "Name him Maher-Shalal-Hash-Baz. 4Before the boy knows

---

a *14* The Hebrew is plural.   b *14* Masoretic Text; Dead Sea Scrolls *and he* or *and they*   c *14* *Immanuel* means *God with us.*   d *20* That is, the Euphrates   e *23* That is, about 25 pounds (about 11.5 kilograms)   f *1* *Maher-Shalal-Hash-Baz* means *quick to the plunder, swift to the spoil;* also in verse 3.

Living Bible

then, the Lord himself will choose the sign—a child shall be born to a virgin![g] And she shall call him Immanuel (meaning, "God is with us"). 15, 16By the time this child is weaned[h] and knows right from wrong, the two kings you fear so much—the kings of Israel and Syria[i]—will both be dead.[j]

17But later on,[k] the Lord will bring a terrible curse on you and on your nation and your family. There will be terror, such as has not been known since the division of Solomon's empire into Israel and Judah—the mighty king of Assyria will come with his great army! 18At that time the Lord will whistle for the army of Upper Egypt,[l] and of Assyria too, to swarm down upon you like flies and destroy you, like bees to sting and to kill. 19They will come in vast hordes, spreading across the whole land, even into the desolate valleys and caves and thorny parts, as well as to all your fertile acres. 20In that day the Lord will take this "razor"—these Assyrians you have hired to save you[m]—and use it on you to shave off everything you have: your land, your crops, your people.[n]

21, 22When they finally stop plundering, the whole nation will be a pastureland; whole flocks and herds will be destroyed, and a farmer will be fortunate to have a cow and two sheep left. But the abundant pastureland will yield plenty of milk, and everyone left will live on curds and wild honey. 23At that time the lush vineyards will become patches of briars. 24All the land will be one vast thornfield, a hunting ground overrun by wildlife. 25No one will go to the fertile hillsides where once the gardens grew, for thorns will cover them; cattle, sheep and goats will graze there.

8   AGAIN THE Lord sent me a message: "Make a large signboard and write on it the birth announcement of the son I am going to give you. Use capital letters! His name will be Maher-shalal-hash-baz, which means 'Your enemies will soon be destroyed.'"[o] 2I asked Uriah the priest and Zechariah the son of Jeberechiah, both known as honest men, to watch me as I wrote so they could testify that I had written it [before the child was even on the way].[p] 3Then I had sexual intercourse with my wife and she conceived, and bore me a son, and the Lord said, "Call him Maher-shalal-hash-baz. 4This name prophesies that within a couple of

New Revised Standard

Lord himself will give you a sign. Look, the young woman[q] is with child and shall bear a son, and shall name him Immanuel.[r] 15He shall eat curds and honey by the time he knows how to refuse the evil and choose the good. 16For before the child knows how to refuse the evil and choose the good, the land before whose two kings you are in dread will be deserted. 17The LORD will bring on you and on your people and on your ancestral house such days as have not come since the day that Ephraim departed from Judah—the king of Assyria."

18 On that day the LORD will whistle for the fly that is at the sources of the streams of Egypt, and for the bee that is in the land of Assyria. 19And they will all come and settle in the steep ravines, and in the clefts of the rocks, and on all the thornbushes, and on all the pastures.

20 On that day the Lord will shave with a razor hired beyond the River—with the king of Assyria—the head and the hair of the feet; and it will take off the beard as well.

21 On that day one will keep alive a young cow and two sheep, 22and will eat curds because of the abundance of milk that they give; for everyone that is left in the land shall eat curds and honey.

23 On that day every place where there used to be a thousand vines, worth a thousand shekels of silver, will become briers and thorns. 24With bow and arrows one will go there, for all the land will be briers and thorns; 25and as for all the hills that used to be hoed with a hoe, you will not go there for fear of briers and thorns; but they will become a place where cattle are let loose and where sheep tread.

Isaiah's Son a Sign of the Assyrian Invasion

8   THEN THE LORD said to me, Take a large tablet and write on it in common characters, "Belonging to Maher-shalal-hash-baz,"[s] 2and have it attested[t] for me by reliable witnesses, the priest Uriah and Zechariah son of Jeberechiah. 3And I went to the prophetess, and she conceived and bore a son. Then the LORD said to me, Name him Maher-shalal-hash-baz; 4for before the child

g 7:14 a child shall be born to a virgin. The controversial Hebrew word used here sometimes means "virgin" and sometimes "young woman." Its immediate use here refers to Isaiah's young wife and her newborn son (8:1-4). This, of course, was not a virgin birth. God's sign was that before this child was old enough to talk (vs 4) the two invading kings would be destroyed. However, the Gospel of Matthew (1:23) tells us that there was a further fulfillment of this prophecy, in that a virgin (Mary) conceived and bore a son, Immanuel, the Christ. We have therefore properly used this higher meaning, "virgin," in vs 14, as otherwise the Matthew account loses its significance. h 7:15, 16 By the time this child is weaned, literally, "For before this child shall know (is old enough) to refuse evil and to choose the good . . . and (is old enough to) eat curds and honey." i 7:15, 16 the kings of Israel and Syria, implied. j 7:15, 16 [will both be dead, or, "the lands will be deserted (of their kings)." k 7:17 But later on, implied. l 7:18 will whistle for the army of Upper Egypt, literally, "sources of the streams of Egypt" refers to Upper Egypt where the powerful 25th Ethiopian Dynasty would soon arise. m 7:20 hired to save you, see 2 Kings 16:7, 8. n 7:20 your land, your crops, your people, literally, "head-hair, beard, body-hair." o 8:1 Your enemies will soon be destroyed, literally, "plundering and despoiling (will) come quickly." p 8:2 before the child was even on the way, implied.

q Gk the virgin   r That is God is with us   s That is The spoil speeds, the prey hastens   t Q Ms Gk Syr: MT and I caused to be attested

King James

4For before the child shall have knowledge to cry, My father, and my mother, the riches of Damascus and the spoil of Samaria shall be taken away before the king of Assyria.

5¶ The LORD spake also unto me again, saying,

6Forasmuch as this people refuseth the waters of Shiloah that go softly, and rejoice in Rezin and Remaliah's son;

7Now therefore, behold, the Lord bringeth up upon them the waters of the river, strong and many, *even* the king of Assyria, and all his glory: and he shall come up over all his channels, and go over all his banks:

8And he shall pass through Judah; he shall overflow and go over, he shall reach *even* to the neck; and the stretching out of his wings shall fill the breadth of thy land, O Immanuel.

9¶ Associate yourselves, O ye people, and ye shall be broken in pieces; and give ear, all ye of far countries: gird yourselves, and ye shall be broken in pieces; gird yourselves, and ye shall be broken in pieces.

10Take counsel together, and it shall come to nought; speak the word, and it shall not stand: for God *is* with us.

11¶ For the LORD spake thus to me with a strong hand, and instructed me that I should not walk in the way of this people, saying,

12Say ye not, A confederacy, to all *them to* whom this people shall say, A confederacy; neither fear ye their fear, nor be afraid.

13Sanctify the LORD of hosts himself; and *let* him *be* your fear, and *let* him *be* your dread.

14And he shall be for a sanctuary; but for a stone of stumbling and for a rock of offence to both the houses of Israel, for a gin and for a snare to the inhabitants of Jerusalem.

15And many among them shall stumble, and fall, and be broken, and be snared, and be taken.

16Bind up the testimony, seal the law among my disciples.

17And I will wait upon the LORD, that hideth his face from the house of Jacob, and I will look for him.

18Behold, I and the children whom the LORD hath given me *are* for signs and for wonders in Israel from the LORD of hosts, which dwelleth in mount Zion.

19¶ And when they shall say unto you, Seek unto them that have familiar spirits, and unto wizards that peep, and that mutter: should not a people seek unto their God? for the living to the dead?

20To the law and to the testimony: if they speak not according to this word, *it is* because *there is* no light in them.

21And they shall pass through it, hardly bestead and hungry: and it shall come to pass, that when they shall be hungry, they shall fret themselves, and curse their king and their God, and look upward.

New International

how to say 'My father' or 'My mother,' the wealth of Damascus and the plunder of Samaria will be carried off by the king of Assyria."

5The LORD spoke to me again:

6"Because this people has rejected
    the gently flowing waters of Shiloah
and rejoices over Rezin
    and the son of Remaliah,
7therefore the Lord is about to bring against them
    the mighty floodwaters of the River[a]—
    the king of Assyria with all his pomp.
It will overflow all its channels,
    run over all its banks
8and sweep on into Judah, swirling over it,
    passing through it and reaching up to the
        neck.
Its outspread wings will cover the breadth of
        your land,
    O Immanuel[b]!"

9Raise the war cry,[c] you nations, and be
        shattered!
    Listen, all you distant lands.
Prepare for battle, and be shattered!
Prepare for battle, and be shattered!
10Devise your strategy, but it will be thwarted;
    propose your plan, but it will not stand,
    for God is with us.[d]

Fear God

11The LORD spoke to me with his strong hand upon me, warning me not to follow the way of this people. He said:

12"Do not call conspiracy
    everything that these people call conspiracy[e];
do not fear what they fear,
    and do not dread it.
13The LORD Almighty is the one you are to regard
        as holy,
    he is the one you are to fear,
    he is the one you are to dread,
14and he will be a sanctuary;
    but for both houses of Israel he will be
a stone that causes men to stumble
    and a rock that makes them fall.
And for the people of Jerusalem he will be
    a trap and a snare.
15Many of them will stumble;
    they will fall and be broken,
    they will be snared and captured."

16Bind up the testimony
    and seal up the law among my disciples.
17I will wait for the LORD,
    who is hiding his face from the house of
        Jacob.
I will put my trust in him.

18Here am I, and the children the LORD has given me. We are signs and symbols in Israel from the LORD Almighty, who dwells on Mount Zion.

19When men tell you to consult mediums and spiritists, who whisper and mutter, should not a people inquire of their God? Why consult the dead on behalf of the living? 20To the law and to the testimony! If they do not speak according to this word, they have no light of dawn. 21Distressed and hungry, they will roam through the land; when they are famished, they will become enraged and, looking upward, will curse their king and their God. 22Then they will look toward the earth and see

a 7 That is, the Euphrates   b 8 *Immanuel* means *God with us.*   c 9 Or *Do your worst*   d 10 Hebrew *Immanuel*   e 12 Or *Do not call for a treaty / every time these people call for a treaty*

Living Bible

years, before this child is even old enough to say 'Daddy' or 'Mommy,' the king of Assyria will invade both Damascus and Samaria and carry away their riches."

5Then the Lord spoke to me again and said:

6"Since the people of Jerusalem are planning to refuse my gentle caref and are enthusiastic about asking King Rezin and King Pekah to come and aid them, 7, 8therefore I will overwhelm my people with Euphrates' mighty flood; the king of Assyria and all his mighty armies will rage against them. This flood will overflow all its channels and sweep into your land of Judah, O Immanuel, submerging it from end to end."

9, 10Do your worst, O Syria and Israel,g our enemies,h but you will not succeed—you will be shattered. Listen to me, all you enemies of ours: Prepare for war against us—and perish! Yes! Perish! Call your councils of war, develop your strategies, prepare your plans of attacking us, and perish! For God is with us.i

11The Lord has said in strongest terms: Do not under any circumstances go along with the plans of Judah to surrender to Syria and Israel. 12Don't let people call you a traitor for staying true to God. Don't you panic as so many of your neighbors are doing when they think of Syria and Israel attacking you. 13Don't fear anything except the Lord of the armies of heaven! If you fear him, you need fear nothing else. 14, 15He will be your safety; but Israel and Judah have refused his care and thereby stumbled against the Rock of their salvation and lie fallen and crushed beneath it: God's presence among them has endangered them! 16Write down all these things I am going to do, says the Lord, and seal it up for the future. Entrust it to some godly man to pass on down to godly men of future generations.

17I will wait for the Lord to help us, though he is hiding now. My only hope is in him. 18I and the children God has given me have symbolic names that reveal the plans of the Lord of heaven's armies for his people: Isaiah means "Jehovah will save (his people)," Shear-jashub means "A remnant shall return," and Maher-shalal-hash-baz means "Your enemies will soon be destroyed." 19So why are you trying to find out the future by consulting witches and mediums? Don't listen to their whisperings and mutterings. Can the living find out the future from the dead? Why not ask your God?

20"Check these witches' words against the Word of God!" he says. "If their messages are different than mine, it is because I have not sent them; for they have no light or truth in them. 21My people will be led away captive, stumbling, weary and hungry. And because they are hungry they will rave and shake their fists at heaven and curse their King and their God. 22Wherever

New Revised Standard

knows how to call "My father" or "My mother," the wealth of Damascus and the spoil of Samaria will be carried away by the king of Assyria.

5 The LORD spoke to me again: 6Because this people has refused the waters of Shiloah that flow gently, and melt in fear beforej Rezin and the son of Remaliah; 7therefore, the Lord is bringing up against it the mighty flood waters of the River, the king of Assyria and all his glory; it will rise above all its channels and overflow all its banks; 8it will sweep on into Judah as a flood, and, pouring over, it will reach up to the neck; and its outspread wings will fill the breadth of your land, O Immanuel.

9 Band together, you peoples, and be dismayed;
     listen, all you far countries;
   gird yourselves and be dismayed;
     gird yourselves and be dismayed!
10 Take counsel together, but it shall be brought
       to naught;
   speak a word, but it will not stand,
     for God is with us.k
11 For the LORD spoke thus to me while his hand was strong upon me, and warned me not to walk in the way of this people, saying: 12Do not call conspiracy all that this people calls conspiracy, and do not fear what it fears, or be in dread. 13But the LORD of hosts, him you shall regard as holy; let him be your fear, and let him be your dread. 14He will become a sanctuary, a stone one strikes against; for both houses of Israel he will become a rock one stumbles over—a trap and a snare for the inhabitants of Jerusalem. 15And many among them shall stumble; they shall fall and be broken; they shall be snared and taken.

Disciples of Isaiah

16 Bind up the testimony, seal the teaching among my disciples. 17I will wait for the LORD, who is hiding his face from the house of Jacob, and I will hope in him. 18See, I and the children whom the LORD has given me are signs and portents in Israel from the LORD of hosts, who dwells on Mount Zion. 19Now if people say to you, "Consult the ghosts and the familiar spirits that chirp and mutter; should not a people consult their gods, the dead on behalf of the living, 20for teaching and for instruction?" Surely, those who speak like this will have no dawn! 21They will pass through the land,l greatly distressed and hungry; when they are hungry, they will be enraged and will cursem their king and their gods. They will turn their faces upward, 22or they will look to the

---

f 8:6 are planning to refuse my gentle care, literally means "have refused the waters of Shiloah that go softly." g 8:9, 10 O Syria and Israel, literally, "O peoples." h 8:9, 10 our enemies, implied. i 8:9, 10 For God is with us, or, "Immanuel."

j Cn: Meaning of Heb uncertain   k Heb immanu el   l Heb it
m Or curse by

King James

22And they shall look unto the earth; and behold trouble and darkness, dimness of anguish; and *they shall be* driven to darkness.

9 NEVERTHELESS THE dimness *shall* not *be* such as *was* in her vexation, when at the first he lightly afflicted the land of Zebulun and the land of Naphtali, and afterward did more grievously afflict *her by* the way of the sea, beyond Jordan, in Galilee of the nations. 2The people that walked in darkness have seen a great light: they that dwell in the land of the shadow of death, upon them hath the light shined. 3Thou hast multiplied the nation, *and* not increased the joy: they joy before thee according to the joy in harvest, *and* as *men* rejoice when they divide the spoil. 4For thou hast broken the yoke of his burden, and the staff of his shoulder, the rod of his oppressor, as in the day of Midian. 5For every battle of the warrior *is* with confused noise, and garments rolled in blood; but *this* shall be with burning *and* fuel of fire. 6For unto us a child is born, unto us a son is given: and the government shall be upon his shoulder: and his name shall be called Wonderful, Counsellor, The mighty God, The everlasting Father, The Prince of Peace. 7Of the increase of *his* government and peace *there shall be* no end, upon the throne of David, and upon his kingdom, to order it, and to establish it with judgment and with justice from henceforth even for ever. The zeal of the LORD of hosts will perform this. 8¶ The Lord sent a word into Jacob, and it hath lighted upon Israel. 9And all the people shall know, *even* Ephraim and the inhabitant of Samaria, that say in the pride and stoutness of heart, 10The bricks are fallen down, but we will build with hewn stones: the sycamores are cut down, but we will change *them into* cedars.

New International

only distress and darkness and fearful gloom, and they will be thrust into utter darkness.

To Us a Child Is Born

9 NEVERTHELESS, THERE will be no more gloom for those who were in distress. In the past he humbled the land of Zebulun and the land of Naphtali, but in the future he will honor Galilee of the Gentiles, by the way of the sea, along the Jordan—

2The people walking in darkness
　　have seen a great light;
on those living in the land of the shadow of death[a]
　　a light has dawned.
3You have enlarged the nation
　　and increased their joy;
they rejoice before you
　　as people rejoice at the harvest,
as men rejoice
　　when dividing the plunder.
4For as in the day of Midian's defeat,
　　you have shattered
the yoke that burdens them,
　　the bar across their shoulders,
　　the rod of their oppressor.
5Every warrior's boot used in battle
　　and every garment rolled in blood
will be destined for burning,
　　will be fuel for the fire.
6For to us a child is born,
　　to us a son is given,
　　and the government will be on his shoulders.
And he will be called
　　Wonderful Counselor,[b] Mighty God,
　　Everlasting Father, Prince of Peace.
7Of the increase of his government and peace
　　there will be no end.
He will reign on David's throne
　　and over his kingdom,
establishing and upholding it
　　with justice and righteousness
　　from that time on and forever.
The zeal of the LORD Almighty
　　will accomplish this.

The LORD's Anger Against Israel

8The Lord has sent a message against Jacob;
　　it will fall on Israel.
9All the people will know it—
　　Ephraim and the inhabitants of Samaria—
who say with pride
　　and arrogance of heart,
10"The bricks have fallen down,
　　but we will rebuild with dressed stone;
the fig trees have been felled,
　　but we will replace them with cedars."

---

a 2 Or *land of darkness*　　b 6 Or *Wonderful, Counselor*

Living Bible

they look there will be trouble and anguish and dark despair. And they will be thrust out into the darkness."

9 NEVERTHELESS, THAT time of darkness and despair shall not go on forever. Though soon the land of Zebulun and Naphtali will be under God's contempt and judgment, yet in the future these very lands, Galilee and Northern Transjordan, where lies the road to the sea, will be filled with glory. 2The people who walk in darkness shall see a great Light—a Light that will shine on all those who live in the land of the shadow of death. 3For Israel will again be great, filled with joy like that of reapers when the harvest time has come, and like that of men dividing up the plunder they have won. 4For God will break the chains that bind his people and the whip that scourges them, just as he did when he destroyed the vast host of the Midianites by Gideon's little band. 5In that glorious day of peace there will no longer be the issuing of battle gear; no more the blood-stained uniforms of war; all such will be burned.

6For unto us a Child is born; unto us a Son is given; and the government shall be upon his shoulder. These will be his royal titles: "Wonderful," "Counselor," "The Mighty God," "The Everlasting Father," "The Prince of Peace." 7His ever-expanding, peaceful government will never end. He will rule with perfect fairness and justice from the throne of his father David. He will bring true justice and peace to all the nations of the world. This is going to happen because the Lord of heaven's armies has dedicated himself to do it!

8, 9, 10The Lord has spoken out against that braggart Israel who says that though our land lies in ruins now, we will rebuild it better than before. The sycamore trees are cut down, but we will replace them with cedars!

New Revised Standard

earth, but will see only distress and darkness, the gloom of anguish; and they will be thrust into thick darkness.c

The Righteous Reign of the Coming King

9d BUT THERE will be no gloom for those who were in anguish. In the former time he brought into contempt the land of Zebulun and the land of Naphtali, but in the latter time he will make glorious the way of the sea, the land beyond the Jordan, Galilee of the nations.
2e The people who walked in darkness
    have seen a great light;
  those who lived in a land of deep darkness—
    on them light has shined.
3 You have multiplied the nation,
    you have increased its joy;
  they rejoice before you
    as with joy at the harvest,
    as people exult when dividing plunder.
4 For the yoke of their burden,
    and the bar across their shoulders,
    the rod of their oppressor,
    you have broken as on the day of Midian.
5 For all the boots of the tramping warriors
    and all the garments rolled in blood
    shall be burned as fuel for the fire.
6 For a child has been born for us,
    a son given to us;
  authority rests upon his shoulders;
  and he is named
  Wonderful Counselor, Mighty God,
  Everlasting Father, Prince of Peace.
7 His authority shall grow continually,
    and there shall be endless peace
  for the throne of David and his kingdom.
  He will establish and uphold it
  with justice and with righteousness
    from this time onward and forevermore.
  The zeal of the LORD of hosts will do this.

Judgment on Arrogance and Oppression

8 The Lord sent a word against Jacob,
    and it fell on Israel;
9 and all the people knew it—
    Ephraim and the inhabitants of Samaria—
    but in pride and arrogance of heart they
      said:
10 "The bricks have fallen,
    but we will build with dressed stones;
  the sycamores have been cut down,
    but we will put cedars in their place."

c Meaning of Heb uncertain   d Ch 8.23 in Heb   e Ch 9.1 in Heb

King James

11Therefore the LORD shall set up the adversaries of Rezin against him, and join his enemies together;

12The Syrians before, and the Philistines behind; and they shall devour Israel with open mouth. For all this his anger is not turned away, but his hand *is* stretched out still.

13¶ For the people turneth not unto him that smiteth them, neither do they seek the LORD of hosts.

14Therefore the LORD will cut off from Israel head and tail, branch and rush, in one day.

15The ancient and honourable, he *is* the head; and the prophet that teacheth lies, he *is* the tail.

16For the leaders of this people cause *them* to err; and *they that are* led of them *are* destroyed.

17Therefore the Lord shall have no joy in their young men, neither shall have mercy on their fatherless and widows: for every one *is* an hypocrite and an evildoer, and every mouth speaketh folly. For all this his anger is not turned away, but his hand *is* stretched out still.

18¶ For wickedness burneth as the fire: it shall devour the briers and thorns, and shall kindle in the thickets of the forest, and they shall mount up *like* the lifting up of smoke.

19Through the wrath of the LORD of hosts is the land darkened, and the people shall be as the fuel of the fire: no man shall spare his brother.

20And he shall snatch on the right hand, and be hungry; and he shall eat on the left hand, and they shall not be satisfied: they shall eat every man the flesh of his own arm:

21Manasseh, Ephraim; and Ephraim, Manasseh: *and* they together *shall be* against Judah. For all this his anger is not turned away, but his hand *is* stretched out still.

10 WOE UNTO them that decree unrighteous decrees, and that write grievousness *which* they have prescribed;

2To turn aside the needy from judgment, and to take away the right from the poor of my people, that widows may be their prey, and *that* they may rob the fatherless!

3And what will ye do in the day of visitation, and in the desolation *which* shall come from far? to whom will ye flee for help? and where will ye leave your glory?

4Without me they shall bow down under the prisoners, and they shall fall under the slain. For all this his anger is not turned away, but his hand *is* stretched out still.

New International

11But the LORD has strengthened Rezin's foes against them
and has spurred their enemies on.
12Arameans from the east and Philistines from the west
have devoured Israel with open mouth.

Yet for all this, his anger is not turned away,
his hand is still upraised.

13But the people have not returned to him who struck them,
nor have they sought the LORD Almighty.
14So the LORD will cut off from Israel both head and tail,
both palm branch and reed in a single day;
15the elders and prominent men are the head,
the prophets who teach lies are the tail.
16Those who guide this people mislead them,
and those who are guided are led astray.
17Therefore the Lord will take no pleasure in the young men,
nor will he pity the fatherless and widows,
for everyone is ungodly and wicked,
every mouth speaks vileness.

Yet for all this, his anger is not turned away,
his hand is still upraised.

18Surely wickedness burns like a fire;
it consumes briers and thorns,
it sets the forest thickets ablaze,
so that it rolls upward in a column of smoke.
19By the wrath of the LORD Almighty
the land will be scorched
and the people will be fuel for the fire;
no one will spare his brother.
20On the right they will devour,
but still be hungry;
on the left they will eat,
but not be satisfied.
Each will feed on the flesh of his own offspring[a]:
21 Manasseh will feed on Ephraim, and Ephraim on Manasseh;
together they will turn against Judah.

Yet for all this, his anger is not turned away,
his hand is still upraised.

10 WOE TO those who make unjust laws,
to those who issue oppressive decrees,
2to deprive the poor of their rights
and withhold justice from the oppressed of my people,
making widows their prey
and robbing the fatherless.
3What will you do on the day of reckoning,
when disaster comes from afar?
To whom will you run for help?
Where will you leave your riches?
4Nothing will remain but to cringe among the captives
or fall among the slain.

Yet for all this, his anger is not turned away,
his hand is still upraised.

---

a *20 Or arm*

Living Bible

11, 12The Lord's reply to your bragging is to bring yourb enemies against you—the Syrians on the east and the Philistines on the west. With bared fangs they will devour Israel. And even then the Lord's anger against you will not be satisfied—his fist will still be poised to smash you. 13For after all this punishment you will not repent and turn to him, the Lord of heaven's armies. 14, 15Therefore the Lord, in one day, will destroy the leaders of Israel and the lying prophets. 16For the leaders of his people have led them down the paths of ruin.

17That is why the Lord has no joy in their young men, and no mercy upon even the widows and orphans, for they are all filthy-mouthed, wicked liars. That is why his anger is not yet satisfied, but his fist is still poised to smash them all. 18He will burn up all this wickedness, these thorns and briars; and the flames will consume the forests, too, and send a vast cloud of smoke billowing up from their burning. 19, 20The land is blackened by that fire, by the wrath of the Lord of heaven's armies. The people are fuel for the fire. Each fights against his brother to steal his food, but will never have enough. Finally they will even eat their own children! 21Manasseh against Ephraim and Ephraim against Manasseh— and both against Judah. Yet even after all of this, God's anger is not yet satisfied. His hand is still heavy upon them, to crush them.

10 WOE TO unjust judges and to those who issue unfair laws, says the Lord, 2so that there is no justice for the poor, the widows and orphans. Yes, it is true that they even rob the widows and fatherless children.

3Oh, what will you do when I visit you in that day when I send desolation upon you from a distant land? To whom will you turn then for your help? Where will your treasures be safe? 4I will not help you; you will stumble along as prisoners or lie among the slain. And even then my anger will not be satisfied, but my fist will still be poised to strike you. 5, 6Assyria is the whip of my anger;

New Revised Standard

11 So the LORD raised adversariesc against them,
    and stirred up their enemies,
12 the Arameans on the east and the Philistines
        on the west,
    and they devoured Israel with open mouth.
  For all this his anger has not turned away;
    his hand is stretched out still.

13 The people did not turn to him who struck
        them,
    or seek the LORD of hosts.
14 So the LORD cut off from Israel head and tail,
    palm branch and reed in one day—
15 elders and dignitaries are the head,
    and prophets who teach lies are the tail;
16 for those who led this people led them astray,
    and those who were led by them were left
        in confusion.
17 That is why the Lord did not have pity ond
        their young people,
    or compassion on their orphans and widows;
  for everyone was godless and an evildoer,
    and every mouth spoke folly.
  For all this his anger has not turned away,
    his hand is stretched out still.

18 For wickedness burned like a fire,
    consuming briers and thorns;
  it kindled the thickets of the forest,
    and they swirled upward in a column of
        smoke.
19 Through the wrath of the LORD of hosts
    the land was burned,
  and the people became like fuel for the fire;
    no one spared another.
20 They gorged on the right, but still were
        hungry,
    and they devoured on the left, but were not
        satisfied;
  they devoured the flesh of their own kindred;e
21 Manasseh devoured Ephraim, and Ephraim
        Manasseh,
    and together they were against Judah.
  For all this his anger has not turned away;
    his hand is stretched out still.

10 AH, YOU who make iniquitous decrees,
    who write oppressive statutes,
2 to turn aside the needy from justice
    and to rob the poor of my people of their
        right,
  that widows may be your spoil,
    and that you may make the orphans your
        prey!
3 What will you do on the day of punishment,
    in the calamity that will come from far
        away?
  To whom will you flee for help,
    and where will you leave your wealth,
4 so as not to crouch among the prisoners
    or fall among the slain?
  For all this his anger has not turned away;
    his hand is stretched out still.

---

b 9:11, 12 your enemies, or, "Rezin's enemies," in some ancient versions.   c Cn: Heb the adversaries of Rezin   d Q Ms: MT rejoice over   e Or arm

King James

5¶ O Assyrian, the rod of mine anger, and the staff in their hand is mine indignation.

6I will send him against an hypocritical nation, and against the people of my wrath will I give him a charge, to take the spoil, and to take the prey, and to tread them down like the mire of the streets.

7Howbeit he meaneth not so, neither doth his heart think so; but *it is* in his heart to destroy and cut off nations not a few.

8For he saith, *Are* not my princes altogether kings?

9*Is* not Calno as Carchemish? *is* not Hamath as Arpad? *is* not Samaria as Damascus?

10As my hand hath found the kingdoms of the idols, and whose graven images did excel them of Jerusalem and of Samaria;

11Shall I not, as I have done unto Samaria and her idols, so do to Jerusalem and her idols?

12Wherefore it shall come to pass, *that* when the Lord hath performed his whole work upon mount Zion and on Jerusalem, I will punish the fruit of the stout heart of the king of Assyria, and the glory of his high looks.

13For he saith, By the strength of my hand I have done *it,* and by my wisdom; for I am prudent: and I have removed the bounds of the people, and have robbed their treasures, and I have put down the inhabitants like a valiant *man:*

14And my hand hath found as a nest the riches of the people: and as one gathereth eggs *that are* left, have I gathered all the earth; and there was none that moved the wing, or opened the mouth, or peeped.

15Shall the axe boast itself against him that heweth therewith? *or* shall the saw magnify itself against him that shaketh it? as if the rod should shake *itself* against them that lift it up, *or* as if the staff should lift up *itself,* as if it were no wood.

16Therefore shall the Lord, the Lord of hosts, send among his fat ones leanness; and under his glory he shall kindle a burning like the burning of a fire.

17And the light of Israel shall be for a fire, and his Holy One for a flame: and it shall burn and devour his thorns and his briers in one day;

18And shall consume the glory of his forest, and of his fruitful field, both soul and body: and they shall be as when a standardbearer fainteth.

19And the rest of the trees of his forest shall be few, that a child may write them.

New International

God's Judgment on Assyria

5"Woe to the Assyrian, the rod of my anger,
    in whose hand is the club of my wrath!
6I send him against a godless nation,
    I dispatch him against a people who anger
      me,
to seize loot and snatch plunder,
    and to trample them down like mud in the
      streets.
7But this is not what he intends,
    this is not what he has in mind;
his purpose is to destroy,
    to put an end to many nations.
8'Are not my commanders all kings?' he says.
9 'Has not Calno fared like Carchemish?
Is not Hamath like Arpad,
    and Samaria like Damascus?
10As my hand seized the kingdoms of the idols,
    kingdoms whose images excelled those of
      Jerusalem and Samaria—
11shall I not deal with Jerusalem and her images
    as I dealt with Samaria and her idols?' "

12When the Lord has finished all his work against Mount Zion and Jerusalem, he will say, "I will punish the king of Assyria for the willful pride of his heart and the haughty look in his eyes. 13For he says:

" 'By the strength of my hand I have done this,
    and by my wisdom, because I have
      understanding.
I removed the boundaries of nations,
    I plundered their treasures;
like a mighty one I subdued[a] their kings.
14As one reaches into a nest,
    so my hand reached for the wealth of the
      nations;
as men gather abandoned eggs,
    so I gathered all the countries;
not one flapped a wing,
    or opened its mouth to chirp.' "

15Does the ax raise itself above him who swings
      it,
    or the saw boast against him who uses it?
As if a rod were to wield him who lifts it up,
    or a club brandish him who is not wood!
16Therefore, the Lord, the Lord Almighty,
    will send a wasting disease upon his sturdy
      warriors;
under his pomp a fire will be kindled
    like a blazing flame.
17The Light of Israel will become a fire,
    their Holy One a flame;
in a single day it will burn and consume
    his thorns and his briers.
18The splendor of his forests and fertile fields
    it will completely destroy,
    as when a sick man wastes away.
19And the remaining trees of his forests will be so
      few
    that a child could write them down.

Living Bible

his military strength is my weapon upon this godless nation, doomed and damned; he will enslave them and plunder them and trample them like dirt beneath his feet. 7But the king of Assyria will not know that it is I who sent him. He will merely think he is attacking my people as part of his plan to conquer the world. 8He will declare that every one of his princes will soon be a king, ruling a conquered land.

9"We will destroy Calno just as we did Carchemish," he will say, "and Hamath will go down before us as Arpad did; and we will destroy Samaria just as we did Damascus. 10Yes, we have finished off many a kingdom whose idols were far greater than those in Jerusalem and Samaria, 11so when we have defeated Samaria and her idols we will destroy Jerusalem with hers."

12After the Lord has used the king of Assyria to accomplish his purpose, then he will turn upon the Assyrians and punish them too—for they are proud and haughty men.

13They boast, "We in our own power and wisdom have won these wars. We are great and wise. By our own strength we broke down the walls and destroyed the people and carried off their treasures. 14In our greatness we have robbed their nests of riches and gathered up kingdoms as a farmer gathers eggs, and no one can move a finger or open his mouth to peep against us!"

15But the Lord says, "Shall the axe boast greater power than the man who uses it? Is the saw greater than the man who saws? Can a rod strike unless a hand is moving it? Can a cane walk by itself?"

16Because of all your evil boasting, O king of Assyria, the Lord of Hosts will send a plague among your proud troops, and strike them down. 17God, the Light and Holy One of Israel, will be the fire and flame that will destroy them. In a single night he will burn those thorns and briars, the Assyrians who destroyed the land of Israel.b 18Assyria's vast army is like a glorious forest, yet it will be destroyed. The Lord will destroy them, soul and body, as when a sick man wastes away. 19Only a few from all that mighty army will be left; so few a child could count them!

New Revised Standard

Arrogant Assyria Also Judged

5 Ah, Assyria, the rod of my anger—
  the club in their hands is my fury!
6 Against a godless nation I send him,
  and against the people of my wrath I
      command him,
  to take spoil and seize plunder,
  and to tread them down like the mire of the
      streets.
7 But this is not what he intends,
  nor does he have this in mind;
  but it is in his heart to destroy,
  and to cut off nations not a few.
8 For he says:
  "Are not my commanders all kings?
9 Is not Calno like Carchemish?
  Is not Hamath like Arpad?
  Is not Samaria like Damascus?
10 As my hand has reached to the kingdoms of
      the idols
  whose images were greater than those of
      Jerusalem and Samaria,
11 shall I not do to Jerusalem and her idols
  what I have done to Samaria and her
      images?"

12 When the Lord has finished all his work on Mount Zion and on Jerusalem, hec will punish the arrogant boasting of the king of Assyria and his haughty pride. 13For he says:
  "By the strength of my hand I have done it,
  and by my wisdom, for I have
      understanding;
  I have removed the boundaries of peoples,
  and have plundered their treasures;
  like a bull I have brought down those who
      sat on thrones.
14 My hand has found, like a nest,
  the wealth of the peoples;
  and as one gathers eggs that have been
      forsaken,
  so I have gathered all the earth;
  and there was none that moved a wing,
  or opened its mouth, or chirped."

15 Shall the ax vaunt itself over the one who
      wields it,
  or the saw magnify itself against the one
      who handles it?
  As if a rod should raise the one who lifts it
      up,
  or as if a staff should lift the one who is not
      wood!
16 Therefore the Sovereign, the LORD of hosts,
  will send wasting sickness among his stout
      warriors,
  and under his glory a burning will be kindled,
      like the burning of fire.
17 The light of Israel will become a fire,
  and his Holy One a flame;
  and it will burn and devour
  his thorns and briers in one day.
18 The glory of his forest and his fruitful land
  the LORD will destroy, both soul and body,
  and it will be as when an invalid wastes
      away.
19 The remnant of the trees of his forest will be
      so few
  that a child can write them down.

---

b *10:17 land of Israel*, see 2 Kings 19:35 and Isaiah 37:36.   c Heb *I*

King James

New International

20¶ And it shall come to pass in that day, *that* the remnant of Israel, and such as are escaped of the house of Jacob, shall no more again stay upon him that smote them; but shall stay upon the LORD, the Holy One of Israel, in truth.

21The remnant shall return, *even* the remnant of Jacob, unto the mighty God.

22For though thy people Israel be as the sand of the sea, *yet* a remnant of them shall return: the consumption decreed shall overflow with righteousness.

23For the Lord GOD of hosts shall make a consumption, even determined, in the midst of all the land.

24¶ Therefore thus saith the Lord GOD of hosts, O my people that dwellest in Zion, be not afraid of the Assyrian: he shall smite thee with a rod, and shall lift up his staff against thee, after the manner of Egypt.

25For yet a very little while, and the indignation shall cease, and mine anger in their destruction.

26And the LORD of hosts shall stir up a scourge for him according to the slaughter of Midian at the rock of Oreb: and *as* his rod *was* upon the sea, so shall he lift it up after the manner of Egypt.

27And it shall come to pass in that day, *that* his burden shall be taken away from off thy shoulder, and his yoke from off thy neck, and the yoke shall be destroyed because of the anointing.

28He is come to Aiath, he is passed to Migron; at Michmash he hath laid up his carriages:

29They are gone over the passage: they have taken up their lodging at Geba; Ramah is afraid; Gibeah of Saul is fled.

30Lift up thy voice, O daughter of Gallim: cause it to be heard unto Laish, O poor Anathoth.

31Madmenah is removed; the inhabitants of Gebim gather themselves to flee.

32As yet shall he remain at Nob that day: he shall shake his hand *against* the mount of the daughter of Zion, the hill of Jerusalem.

33Behold, the Lord, the LORD of hosts, shall lop the bough with terror: and the high ones of stature *shall be* hewn down, and the haughty shall be humbled.

34And he shall cut down the thickets of the forest with iron, and Lebanon shall fall by a mighty one.

The Remnant of Israel

20In that day the remnant of Israel,
　　the survivors of the house of Jacob,
will no longer rely on him
　　who struck them down
but will truly rely on the LORD,
　　the Holy One of Israel.
21A remnant will return,[a] a remnant of Jacob
　　will return to the Mighty God.
22Though your people, O Israel, be like the sand
　　by the sea,
　　only a remnant will return.
Destruction has been decreed,
　　overwhelming and righteous.
23The Lord, the LORD Almighty, will carry out
　　the destruction decreed upon the whole land.

24Therefore, this is what the Lord, the LORD Almighty, says:

"O my people who live in Zion,
　　do not be afraid of the Assyrians,
who beat you with a rod
　　and lift up a club against you, as Egypt did.
25Very soon my anger against you will end
　　and my wrath will be directed to their
　　　destruction."

26The LORD Almighty will lash them with a whip,
　　as when he struck down Midian at the rock of
　　　Oreb;
and he will raise his staff over the waters,
　　as he did in Egypt.
27In that day their burden will be lifted from your
　　　shoulders,
　　their yoke from your neck;
the yoke will be broken
　　because you have grown so fat.[b]

28They enter Aiath;
　　they pass through Migron;
　　they store supplies at Micmash.
29They go over the pass, and say,
　　"We will camp overnight at Geba."
Ramah trembles;
　　Gibeah of Saul flees.
30Cry out, O Daughter of Gallim!
　　Listen, O Laishah!
　　Poor Anathoth!
31Madmenah is in flight;
　　the people of Gebim take cover.
32This day they will halt at Nob;
　　they will shake their fist
at the mount of the Daughter of Zion,
　　at the hill of Jerusalem.

33See, the Lord, the LORD Almighty,
　　will lop off the boughs with great power.
The lofty trees will be felled,
　　the tall ones will be brought low.
34He will cut down the forest thickets with an ax;
　　Lebanon will fall before the Mighty One.

The Branch From Jesse

11 A SHOOT will come up from the stump of
　　　Jesse;
　　from his roots a Branch will bear fruit.

11 AND THERE shall come forth a rod out of the stem of Jesse, and a Branch shall grow out of his roots:

---

a 21 Hebrew *shear-jashub*; also in verse 22　　b 27 Hebrew; Septuagint *broken / from your shoulders*

Living Bible

20Then at last, those left in Israel and in Judah will trust the Lord, the Holy One of Israel, instead of fearing the Assyrians. 21A remnant of them will return to the mighty God. 22But though Israel be now as many as the sands along the shore, yet only a few of them will be left to return at that time; God has rightly decided to destroy his people. 23Yes, it has already been decided by the Lord God to consume them.

24Therefore the Lord God says, "O my people in Jerusalem, don't be afraid of the Assyrians when they oppress you just as the Egyptians did long ago. 25It will not last very long; in a little while my anger against you will end, and then it will rise against them to destroy them."

26The Lord Almighty will send his angel to slay them in a mighty slaughter like the time when Gideon triumphed over Midian at the rock of Oreb or the time God drowned the Egyptian armies in the sea. 27On that day God will end the bondage of his people. He will break the slave-yoke off their necks, and destroy it as decreed.c

28, 29Look, the mighty armies of Assyria are coming! Now they are at Aiath, now at Migron; they are storing some of their equipment at Michmash and crossing over the pass; they are staying overnight at Geba. Fear strikes the city of Ramah; all the people of Gibeah—the city of Saul—are running for their lives. 30Well may you scream in terror, O people of Gallim. Shout out a warning to Laish, for the mighty army comes. O poor Anathoth, what a fate is yours! 31There go the people of Madmenah, all fleeing, and the citizens of Gebim are preparing to run. 32But the enemy stops at Nob for the remainder of that day. He shakes his fist at Jerusalem on Mount Zion.

33Then, look, look! The Lord, the Lord of the armies of heaven, is chopping down the mighty tree! He is destroying all of that vast army, great and small alike, both officers and men. 34He, the Mighty One, will cut down the enemy as a woodsman's axe cuts down the forest trees in Lebanon.

11 THE ROYAL line of Davidd will be cut off, chopped down like a tree; but from the stump will grow a Shoote—yes, a new Branche from the old root. 2And the Spirit of the Lord shall rest upon him, the

New Revised Standard

The Repentant Remnant of Israel

20 On that day the remnant of Israel and the survivors of the house of Jacob will no more lean on the one who struck them, but will lean on the LORD, the Holy One of Israel, in truth. 21A remnant will return, the remnant of Jacob, to the mighty God. 22For though your people Israel were like the sand of the sea, only a remnant of them will return. Destruction is decreed, overflowing with righteousness. 23For the Lord GOD of hosts will make a full end, as decreed, in all the earth.f

24 Therefore thus says the Lord GOD of hosts: O my people, who live in Zion, do not be afraid of the Assyrians when they beat you with a rod and lift up their staff against you as the Egyptians did. 25For in a very little while my indignation will come to an end, and my anger will be directed to their destruction. 26The LORD of hosts will wield a whip against them, as when he struck Midian at the rock of Oreb; his staff will be over the sea, and he will lift it as he did in Egypt. 27On that day his burden will be removed from your shoulder, and his yoke will be destroyed from your neck.

28   He has gone up from Rimmon,g
    he has come to Aiath;
  he has passed through Migron,
    at Michmash he stores his baggage;
29 they have crossed over the pass,
    at Geba they lodge for the night;
  Ramah trembles,
    Gibeah of Saul has fled.
30 Cry aloud, O daughter Gallim!
    Listen, O Laishah!
    Answer her, O Anathoth!
31 Madmenah is in flight,
    the inhabitants of Gebim flee for safety.
32 This very day he will halt at Nob,
    he will shake his fist
    at the mount of daughter Zion,
    the hill of Jerusalem.

33 Look, the Sovereign, the LORD of hosts,
    will lop the boughs with terrifying power;
  the tallest trees will be cut down,
    and the lofty will be brought low.
34 He will hack down the thickets of the forest
    with an ax,
    and Lebanon with its majestic treesh will
    fall.

The Peaceful Kingdom

11 A SHOOT shall come out from the stump of Jesse,
and a branch shall grow out of his roots.

---

c 10:27 as decreed, literally, "because of ointment." Some see here a reference to the Messiah, the Anointed One. d 11:1 David, literally Jesse, and e 11:1 from the stump will grow a Shoot—yes, a new Branch, Christ, the Messiah.

f Or land g Cn: Heb and his yoke from your neck, and a yoke will be destroyed because of fatness h Cn Compare Gk Vg: Heb with a majestic one

King James

2And the spirit of the LORD shall rest upon him, the spirit of wisdom and understanding, the spirit of counsel and might, the spirit of knowledge and of the fear of the LORD;

3And shall make him of quick understanding in the fear of the LORD: and he shall not judge after the sight of his eyes, neither reprove after the hearing of his ears:

4But with righteousness shall he judge the poor, and reprove with equity for the meek of the earth: and he shall smite the earth with the rod of his mouth, and with the breath of his lips shall he slay the wicked.

5And righteousness shall be the girdle of his loins, and faithfulness the girdle of his reins.

6The wolf also shall dwell with the lamb, and the leopard shall lie down with the kid; and the calf and the young lion and the fatling together; and a little child shall lead them.

7And the cow and the bear shall feed; their young ones shall lie down together: and the lion shall eat straw like the ox.

8And the sucking child shall play on the hole of the asp, and the weaned child shall put his hand on the cockatrice' den.

9They shall not hurt nor destroy in all my holy mountain: for the earth shall be full of the knowledge of the LORD, as the waters cover the sea.

10¶ And in that day there shall be a root of Jesse, which shall stand for an ensign of the people; to it shall the Gentiles seek: and his rest shall be glorious.

11And it shall come to pass in that day, *that* the Lord shall set his hand again the second time to recover the remnant of his people, which shall be left, from Assyria, and from Egypt, and from Pathros, and from Cush, and from Elam, and from Shinar, and from Hamath, and from the islands of the sea.

12And he shall set up an ensign for the nations, and shall assemble the outcasts of Israel, and gather together the dispersed of Judah from the four corners of the earth.

13The envy also of Ephraim shall depart, and the adversaries of Judah shall be cut off: Ephraim shall not envy Judah, and Judah shall not vex Ephraim.

14But they shall fly upon the shoulders of the Philistines toward the west; they shall spoil them of the east together: they shall lay their hand upon Edom and Moab; and the children of Ammon shall obey them.

15And the LORD shall utterly destroy the tongue of the Egyptian sea; and with his mighty wind shall he shake his hand over the river, and shall smite it in the seven streams, and make *men* go over dryshod.

16And there shall be an highway for the remnant of his people, which shall be left, from Assyria; like as it was to Israel in the day that he came up out of the land of Egypt.

New International

2The Spirit of the LORD will rest on him—
    the Spirit of wisdom and of understanding,
    the Spirit of counsel and of power,
    the Spirit of knowledge and of the fear of the
        LORD—
3and he will delight in the fear of the LORD.

He will not judge by what he sees with his
        eyes,
    or decide by what he hears with his ears;
4but with righteousness he will judge the needy,
    with justice he will give decisions for the
        poor of the earth.
He will strike the earth with the rod of his
        mouth;
    with the breath of his lips he will slay the
        wicked.
5Righteousness will be his belt
    and faithfulness the sash around his waist.

6The wolf will live with the lamb,
    the leopard will lie down with the goat,
the calf and the lion and the yearlinga together;
    and a little child will lead them.
7The cow will feed with the bear,
    their young will lie down together,
    and the lion will eat straw like the ox.
8The infant will play near the hole of the cobra,
    and the young child put his hand into the
        viper's nest.
9They will neither harm nor destroy
    on all my holy mountain,
for the earth will be full of the knowledge of
        the LORD
    as the waters cover the sea.

10In that day the Root of Jesse will stand as a banner for the peoples; the nations will rally to him, and his place of rest will be glorious. 11In that day the Lord will reach out his hand a second time to reclaim the remnant that is left of his people from Assyria, from Lower Egypt, from Upper Egypt,b from Cush,c from Elam, from Babylonia,d from Hamath and from the islands of the sea.

12He will raise a banner for the nations
    and gather the exiles of Israel;
he will assemble the scattered people of Judah
    from the four quarters of the earth.
13Ephraim's jealousy will vanish,
    and Judah's enemiese will be cut off;
Ephraim will not be jealous of Judah,
    nor Judah hostile toward Ephraim.
14They will swoop down on the slopes of Philistia
        to the west;
    together they will plunder the people to the
        east.
They will lay hands on Edom and Moab,
    and the Ammonites will be subject to them.
15The LORD will dry up
    the gulf of the Egyptian sea;
with a scorching wind he will sweep his hand
    over the Euphrates River.f
He will break it up into seven streams
    so that men can cross over in sandals.
16There will be a highway for the remnant of his
        people
    that is left from Assyria,
as there was for Israel
    when they came up from Egypt.

---

a 6 Hebrew; Septuagint *lion will feed*   b 11 Hebrew *from Pathros*
c 11 That is, the upper Nile region   d 11 Hebrew *Shinar*   e 13 Or *hostility*
f 15 Hebrew *the River*

Living Bible

Spirit of wisdom, understanding, counsel and might; the Spirit of knowledge and of the fear of the Lord. ³His delight will be obedience to the Lord. He will not judge by appearance, false evidence, or hearsay, ⁴but will defend the poor and the exploited. He will rule against the wicked who oppress them. ⁵For he will be clothed with fairness and with truth.

⁶In that day the wolf and the lamb will lie down together, and the leopard and goats will be at peace. Calves and fat cattle will be safe among lions, and a little child shall lead them all. ⁷The cows will graze among bears; cubs and calves will lie down together, and lions will eat grass like the cows. ⁸Babies will crawl safely among poisonous snakes, and a little child who puts his hand in a nest of deadly adders will pull it out unharmed. ⁹Nothing will hurt or destroy in all my holy mountain, for as the waters fill the sea, so shall the earth be full of the knowledge of the Lord.

¹⁰In that day he who created the royal dynasty of David⁸ will be a banner of salvation to all the world. The nations will rally to him, for the land where he lives will be a glorious place. ¹¹At that time the Lord will bring back a remnant of his people for the second time, returning them to the land of Israel from Assyria, Upper and Lower Egypt, Ethiopia, Elam, Babylonia, Hamath and all the distant coastal lands. ¹²He will raise a flag among the nations for them to rally to; he will gather the scattered Israelites from the ends of the earth. ¹³Then, at last, the jealousy between Israel and Judah will end; they will not fight each other any more. ¹⁴Together they will fly against the nations possessing their land on the east and on the west, uniting forces to destroy them, and they will occupy the nations of Edom and Moab and Ammon.

¹⁵The Lord will dry a path through the Red Sea,ʰ and wave his hand over the Euphrates,ⁱ sending a mighty wind to divide it into seven streams that can easily be crossed. ¹⁶He will make a highway from Assyria for the remnant there, just as he did for all of Israel long ago when they returned from Egypt.

New Revised Standard

2   The spirit of the LORD shall rest on him,
      the spirit of wisdom and understanding,
      the spirit of counsel and might,
      the spirit of knowledge and the fear of the
         LORD.
3   His delight shall be in the fear of the LORD.

    He shall not judge by what his eyes see,
      or decide by what his ears hear;
4   but with righteousness he shall judge the poor,
      and decide with equity for the meek of the
         earth;
    he shall strike the earth with the rod of his
         mouth,
      and with the breath of his lips he shall kill
         the wicked.
5   Righteousness shall be the belt around his
         waist,
      and faithfulness the belt around his loins.

6   The wolf shall live with the lamb,
      the leopard shall lie down with the kid,
    the calf and the lion and the fatling together,
      and a little child shall lead them.
7   The cow and the bear shall graze,
      their young shall lie down together;
      and the lion shall eat straw like the ox.
8   The nursing child shall play over the hole of
         the asp,
      and the weaned child shall put its hand on
         the adder's den.
9   They will not hurt or destroy
      on all my holy mountain;
    for the earth will be full of the knowledge of
         the LORD
      as the waters cover the sea.

Return of the Remnant of Israel and Judah

10   On that day the root of Jesse shall stand as a signal to the peoples; the nations shall inquire of him, and his dwelling shall be glorious.

11   On that day the Lord will extend his hand yet a second time to recover the remnant that is left of his people, from Assyria, from Egypt, from Pathros, from Ethiopia,ʲ from Elam, from Shinar, from Hamath, and from the coastlands of the sea.

12   He will raise a signal for the nations,
      and will assemble the outcasts of Israel,
    and gather the dispersed of Judah
      from the four corners of the earth.
13   The jealousy of Ephraim shall depart,
      the hostility of Judah shall be cut off;
    Ephraim shall not be jealous of Judah,
      and Judah shall not be hostile towards
         Ephraim.
14   But they shall swoop down on the backs of
         the Philistines in the west,
      together they shall plunder the people of the
         east.
    They shall put forth their hand against Edom
         and Moab,
      and the Ammonites shall obey them.
15   And the LORD will utterly destroy
      the tongue of the sea of Egypt;
    and will wave his hand over the River
      with his scorching wind;
    and will split it into seven channels,
      and make a way to cross on foot;
16   so there shall be a highway from Assyria
      for the remnant that is left of his people,
    as there was for Israel
      when they came up from the land of Egypt.

ᵍ 11:10 *royal dynasty of David,* literally, "the Root of Jesse." Possibly the meaning is, "the Heir of David's royal line."   ʰ 11:15 *the Red Sea,* literally, "the Sea of Egypt."   ⁱ 11:15 *the Euphrates,* literally, "the River."

ʲ Or *Nubia;* Heb *Cush*

King James

New International

12 AND IN that day thou shalt say, O LORD, I will praise thee: though thou wast angry with me, thine anger is turned away, and thou comfortedst me.

²Behold, God *is* my salvation; I will trust, and not be afraid: for the LORD JEHOVAH *is* my strength and *my* song; he also is become my salvation.

³Therefore with joy shall ye draw water out of the wells of salvation.

⁴And in that day shall ye say, Praise the LORD, call upon his name, declare his doings among the people, make mention that his name is exalted.

⁵Sing unto the LORD; for he hath done excellent things: this *is* known in all the earth.

⁶Cry out and shout, thou inhabitant of Zion: for great *is* the Holy One of Israel in the midst of thee.

Songs of Praise

12 IN THAT day you will say:

"I will praise you, O LORD.
    Although you were angry with me,
your anger has turned away
    and you have comforted me.
²Surely God is my salvation;
    I will trust and not be afraid.
The LORD, the LORD, is my strength and my
        song;
    he has become my salvation."
³With joy you will draw water
    from the wells of salvation.

⁴In that day you will say:

"Give thanks to the LORD, call on his name;
    make known among the nations what he has
        done,
    and proclaim that his name is exalted.
⁵Sing to the LORD, for he has done glorious
        things;
    let this be known to all the world.
⁶Shout aloud and sing for joy, people of Zion,
    for great is the Holy One of Israel among
        you."

A Prophecy Against Babylon

13 THE BURDEN of Babylon, which Isaiah the son of Amoz did see.

²Lift ye up a banner upon the high mountain, exalt the voice unto them, shake the hand, that they may go into the gates of the nobles.

³I have commanded my sanctified ones, I have also called my mighty ones for mine anger, *even* them that rejoice in my highness.

⁴The noise of a multitude in the mountains, like as of a great people; a tumultuous noise of the kingdoms of nations gathered together: the LORD of hosts mustereth the host of the battle.

⁵They come from a far country, from the end of heaven, *even* the LORD, and the weapons of his indignation, to destroy the whole land.

⁶¶ Howl ye; for the day of the LORD *is* at hand; it shall come as a destruction from the Almighty.

⁷Therefore shall all hands be faint, and every man's heart shall melt:

⁸And they shall be afraid: pangs and sorrows shall take hold of them; they shall be in pain as a woman that travaileth: they shall be amazed one at another; their faces *shall be as* flames.

⁹Behold, the day of the LORD cometh, cruel both with wrath and fierce anger, to lay the land desolate: and he shall destroy the sinners thereof out of it.

13 AN ORACLE concerning Babylon that Isaiah son of Amoz saw:

²Raise a banner on a bare hilltop,
    shout to them;
beckon to them
    to enter the gates of the nobles.
³I have commanded my holy ones;
    I have summoned my warriors to carry out
        my wrath—
    those who rejoice in my triumph.

⁴Listen, a noise on the mountains,
    like that of a great multitude!
Listen, an uproar among the kingdoms,
    like nations massing together!
The LORD Almighty is mustering
    an army for war.
⁵They come from faraway lands,
    from the ends of the heavens—
the LORD and the weapons of his wrath—
    to destroy the whole country.

⁶Wail, for the day of the LORD is near;
    it will come like destruction from the
        Almighty.ᵃ
⁷Because of this, all hands will go limp,
    every man's heart will melt.
⁸Terror will seize them,
    pain and anguish will grip them;
    they will writhe like a woman in labor.
They will look aghast at each other,
    their faces aflame.

⁹See, the day of the LORD is coming
    —a cruel day, with wrath and fierce anger—
to make the land desolate
    and destroy the sinners within it.

ᵃ 6 Hebrew *Shaddai*

Living Bible

12 ON THAT day you will say, "Praise the Lord! He was angry with me, but now he comforts me. ²See, God has come to save me! I will trust and not be afraid, for the Lord is my strength and song; he is my salvation. ³Oh, the joy of drinking deeply from the Fountain of Salvation!"

⁴ In that wonderful day you will say, "Thank the Lord! Praise his name! Tell the world about his wondrous love.ᵇ How mighty he is!" ⁵Sing to the Lord, for he has done wonderful things. Make known his praise around the world. ⁶Let all the people of Jerusalem shout his praise with joy. For great and mighty is the Holy One of Israel, who lives among you.

13 THIS IS the vision God showed Isaiah (son of Amoz) concerning Babylon's doom.

²See the flags waving as their enemy attacks. Shout to them, O Israel, and wave them on as they march against Babylon to destroy the palaces of the rich and mighty. ³I, the Lord, have set apart these armies for this task; I have called those rejoicing in their strength to do this work, to satisfy my anger. ⁴Hear the tumult on the mountains! Listen as the armies march! It is the tumult and the shout of many nations. The Lord Almighty has brought them here, ⁵from countries far away. They are his weapons against you, O Babylon. They carry his anger with them and will destroy your whole land.

⁶Scream in terror, for the Lord's time has come, the time for the Almighty to crush you. ⁷Your arms lie paralyzed with fear; the strongest hearts melt, ⁸and are afraid. Fear grips you with terrible pangs, like those of a woman in labor. You look at one another, helpless, as the flames of the burning city reflect upon your pallid faces. ⁹For see, the day of the Lord is coming, the terrible day of his wrath and fierce anger. The land shall be destroyed, and all the sinners with it. ¹⁰The heavens will

New Revised Standard

Thanksgiving and Praise

12 YOU WILL say in that day:
I will give thanks to you, O LORD,
for though you were angry with me,
your anger turned away,
and you comforted me.

² Surely God is my salvation;
I will trust, and will not be afraid,
for the LORD GODᶜ is my strength and my
might;
he has become my salvation.

³ With joy you will draw water from the wells of
salvation. ⁴And you will say in that day:
Give thanks to the LORD,
call on his name;
make known his deeds among the nations;
proclaim that his name is exalted.

⁵ Sing praises to the LORD, for he has done
gloriously;
let this be knownᵈ in all the earth.

⁶ Shout aloud and sing for joy, O royalᵉ Zion,
for great in your midst is the Holy One of
Israel.

Proclamation against Babylon

13 THE ORACLE concerning Babylon that Isaiah son of Amoz saw.

² On a bare hill raise a signal,
cry aloud to them;
wave the hand for them to enter
the gates of the nobles.

³ I myself have commanded my consecrated
ones,
have summoned my warriors, my proudly
exulting ones,
to execute my anger.

⁴ Listen, a tumult on the mountains
as of a great multitude!
Listen, an uproar of kingdoms,
of nations gathering together!
The LORD of hosts is mustering
an army for battle.

⁵ They come from a distant land,
from the end of the heavens,
the LORD and the weapons of his indignation,
to destroy the whole earth.

⁶ Wail, for the day of the LORD is near;
it will come like destruction from the
Almighty!ᶠ

⁷ Therefore all hands will be feeble,
and every human heart will melt,

⁸ and they will be dismayed.
Pangs and agony will seize them;
they will be in anguish like a woman in
labor.
They will look aghast at one another;
their faces will be aflame.

⁹ See, the day of the LORD comes,
cruel, with wrath and fierce anger,
to make the earth a desolation,
and to destroy its sinners from it.

ᵇ *12:4 Tell the world about his wondrous love*, literally, "Proclaim his doings among the nations."

ᶜ Heb *for Yah, the* LORD   ᵈ Or *this is made known*   ᵉ Or *O inhabitant of*
ᶠ Traditional rendering of Heb *Shaddai*

King James

10For the stars of heaven and the constellations thereof shall not give their light: the sun shall be darkened in his going forth, and the moon shall not cause her light to shine.

11And I will punish the world for *their* evil, and the wicked for their iniquity; and I will cause the arrogancy of the proud to cease, and will lay low the haughtiness of the terrible.

12I will make a man more precious than fine gold; even a man than the golden wedge of Ophir.

13Therefore I will shake the heavens, and the earth shall remove out of her place, in the wrath of the LORD of hosts, and in the day of his fierce anger.

14And it shall be as the chased roe, and as a sheep that no man taketh up: they shall every man turn to his own people, and flee every one into his own land.

15Every one that is found shall be thrust through; and every one that is joined *unto them* shall fall by the sword.

16Their children also shall be dashed to pieces before their eyes; their houses shall be spoiled, and their wives ravished.

17Behold, I will stir up the Medes against them, which shall not regard silver; and *as for* gold, they shall not delight in it.

18*Their* bows also shall dash the young men to pieces; and they shall have no pity on the fruit of the womb; their eye shall not spare children.

19¶ And Babylon, the glory of kingdoms, the beauty of the Chaldees' excellency, shall be as when God overthrew Sodom and Gomorrah.

20It shall never be inhabited, neither shall it be dwelt in from generation to generation: neither shall the Arabian pitch tent there; neither shall the shepherds make their fold there.

21But wild beasts of the desert shall lie there; and their houses shall be full of doleful creatures; and owls shall dwell there, and satyrs shall dance there.

22And the wild beasts of the islands shall cry in their desolate houses, and dragons in *their* pleasant palaces: and her time *is* near to come, and her days shall not be prolonged.

14 FOR THE LORD will have mercy on Jacob, and will yet choose Israel, and set them in their own land: and the strangers shall be joined with them, and they shall cleave to the house of Jacob.

2And the people shall take them, and bring them to their place: and the house of Israel shall possess them in the land of the LORD for servants and handmaids: and they shall take them captives, whose captives they were; and they shall rule over their oppressors.

3And it shall come to pass in the day that the LORD shall give thee rest from thy sorrow, and from thy fear, and from the hard bondage wherein thou wast made to serve,

New International

10The stars of heaven and their constellations
  will not show their light.
The rising sun will be darkened
  and the moon will not give its light.
11I will punish the world for its evil,
  the wicked for their sins.
I will put an end to the arrogance of the
    haughty
  and will humble the pride of the ruthless.
12I will make man scarcer than pure gold,
  more rare than the gold of Ophir.
13Therefore I will make the heavens tremble;
  and the earth will shake from its place
at the wrath of the LORD Almighty,
  in the day of his burning anger.

14Like a hunted gazelle,
  like sheep without a shepherd,
each will return to his own people,
  each will flee to his native land.
15Whoever is captured will be thrust through;
  all who are caught will fall by the sword.
16Their infants will be dashed to pieces before
    their eyes;
  their houses will be looted and their wives
    ravished.
17See, I will stir up against them the Medes,
  who do not care for silver
  and have no delight in gold.
18Their bows will strike down the young men;
  they will have no mercy on infants
  nor will they look with compassion on
    children.
19Babylon, the jewel of kingdoms,
  the glory of the Babylonians'[a] pride,
will be overthrown by God
  like Sodom and Gomorrah.
20She will never be inhabited
  or lived in through all generations;
no Arab will pitch his tent there,
  no shepherd will rest his flocks there.
21But desert creatures will lie there,
  jackals will fill her houses;
there the owls will dwell,
  and there the wild goats will leap about.
22Hyenas will howl in her strongholds,
  jackals in her luxurious palaces.
Her time is at hand,
  and her days will not be prolonged.

14 THE LORD will have compassion on Jacob;
  once again he will choose Israel
and will settle them in their own land.
Aliens will join them
  and unite with the house of Jacob.
2Nations will take them
  and bring them to their own place.
And the house of Israel will possess the nations
  as menservants and maidservants in the
    LORD's land.
They will make captives of their captors
  and rule over their oppressors.

3On the day the LORD gives you relief from suffering

Living Bible

be black above them. No light will shine from stars or sun or moon.

11And I will punish the world for its evil, the wicked for their sin; I will crush the arrogance of the proud man and the haughtiness of the rich. 12Few will live when I have finished up my work.

Men will be as scarce as gold—of greater value than the gold of Ophir. 13For I will shake the heavens in my wrath and fierce anger, and the earth will move from its place in the skies.

14The armies of Babylon will run until exhausted, fleeing back to their own land like deer chased by dogs, wandering like sheep deserted by their shepherd. 15Those who don't run will be butchered. 16Their little children will be dashed to death against the pavement right before their eyes; their homes will be sacked, and their wives raped by the attacking hordes. 17For I will stir up the Medes against Babylon, and no amount of silver or gold will buy them off. 18The attacking armies will have no mercy on the young people of Babylon or the babies or the children.

19And so Babylon, the most glorious of kingdoms, the flower of Chaldean culture, will be as utterly destroyed as Sodom and Gomorrah were when God sent fire from heaven; 20Babylon will never rise again. Generation after generation will come and go, but the land will never again be lived in.b The nomads will not even camp there. The shepherds won't let their sheep stay overnight. 21The wild animals of the desert will make it their home. The houses will be haunted by howling creatures. Ostriches will live there, and the demons will come there to dance. 22Hyenas and jackals will den within the palaces. Babylon's days are numbered; her time of doom will soon be here.

14 BUT THE Lord will have mercy on the Israelis; they are still his special ones. He will bring them back to settle once again in the land of Israel. And many nationalities will come and join them there and be their loyal allies. 2The nations of the world will help them to return, and those coming to live in their land will serve them. Those enslaving Israel will be enslaved— Israel shall rule her enemies!

3In that wonderful day when the Lord gives his people rest from sorrow and fear, from slavery and chains,

New Revised Standard

10 For the stars of the heavens and their
        constellations
    will not give their light;
    the sun will be dark at its rising,
    and the moon will not shed its light.
11 I will punish the world for its evil,
    and the wicked for their iniquity;
    I will put an end to the pride of the arrogant,
    and lay low the insolence of tyrants.
12 I will make mortals more rare than fine gold,
    and humans than the gold of Ophir.
13 Therefore I will make the heavens tremble,
    and the earth will be shaken out of its
        place,
    at the wrath of the LORD of hosts
    in the day of his fierce anger.
14 Like a hunted gazelle,
    or like sheep with no one to gather them,
    all will turn to their own people,
    and all will flee to their own lands.
15 Whoever is found will be thrust through,
    and whoever is caught will fall by the
        sword.
16 Their infants will be dashed to pieces
        before their eyes;
    their houses will be plundered,
    and their wives ravished.
17 See, I am stirring up the Medes against them,
    who have no regard for silver
    and do not delight in gold.
18 Their bows will slaughter the young men;
    they will have no mercy on the fruit of the
        womb;
    their eyes will not pity children.
19 And Babylon, the glory of kingdoms,
    the splendor and pride of the Chaldeans,
    will be like Sodom and Gomorrah
    when God overthrew them.
20 It will never be inhabited
    or lived in for all generations;
    Arabs will not pitch their tents there,
    shepherds will not make their flocks lie
        down there.
21 But wild animals will lie down there,
    and its houses will be full of howling
        creatures;
    there ostriches will live,
    and there goat-demons will dance.
22 Hyenas will cry in its towers,
    and jackals in the pleasant palaces;
    its time is close at hand,
    and its days will not be prolonged.

Restoration of Judah

14 BUT THE LORD will have compassion on Jacob and will again choose Israel, and will set them in their own land; and aliens will join them and attach themselves to the house of Jacob. 2And the nations will take them and bring them to their place, and the house of Israel will possess the nationsc as male and female slaves in the LORD's land; they will take captive those who were their captors, and rule over those who oppressed them.

Downfall of the King of Babylon

3 When the LORD has given you rest from your pain and turmoil and the hard service with which you were

c Heb them

King James

4¶ That thou shalt take up this proverb against the king of Babylon, and say, How hath the oppressor ceased! the golden city ceased!

5The LORD hath broken the staff of the wicked, *and* the sceptre of the rulers.

6He who smote the people in wrath with a continual stroke, he that ruled the nations in anger, is persecuted, *and* none hindereth.

7The whole earth is at rest, *and* is quiet: they break forth into singing.

8Yea, the fir trees rejoice at thee, *and* the cedars of Lebanon, *saying,* Since thou art laid down, no feller is come up against us.

9Hell from beneath is moved for thee to meet *thee* at thy coming: it stirreth up the dead for thee, *even* all the chief ones of the earth; it hath raised up from their thrones all the kings of the nations.

10All they shall speak and say unto thee, Art thou also become weak as we? art thou become like unto us?

11Thy pomp is brought down to the grave, *and* the noise of thy viols: the worm is spread under thee, and the worms cover thee.

12How art thou fallen from heaven, O Lucifer, son of the morning! *how* art thou cut down to the ground, which didst weaken the nations!

13For thou hast said in thine heart, I will ascend into heaven, I will exalt my throne above the stars of God: I will sit also upon the mount of the congregation, in the sides of the north:

14I will ascend above the heights of the clouds: I will be like the most High.

15Yet thou shalt be brought down to hell, to the sides of the pit.

16They that see thee shall narrowly look upon thee, *and* consider thee, *saying, Is* this the man that made the earth to tremble, that did shake kingdoms;

17*That* made the world as a wilderness, and destroyed the cities thereof; *that* opened not the house of his prisoners?

18All the kings of the nations, *even* all of them, lie in glory, every one in his own house.

19But thou art cast out of thy grave like an abominable branch, *and as* the raiment of those that are slain, thrust through with a sword, that go down to the stones of the pit; as a carcase trodden under feet.

20Thou shalt not be joined with them in burial, because thou hast destroyed thy land, *and* slain thy people: the seed of evildoers shall never be renowned.

New International

and turmoil and cruel bondage, 4you will take up this taunt against the king of Babylon:

> How the oppressor has come to an end!
>   How his fury[a] has ended!
> 5The LORD has broken the rod of the wicked,
>   the scepter of the rulers,
> 6which in anger struck down peoples
>   with unceasing blows,
> and in fury subdued nations
>   with relentless aggression.
> 7All the lands are at rest and at peace;
>   they break into singing.
> 8Even the pine trees and the cedars of Lebanon
>   exult over you and say,
> "Now that you have been laid low,
>   no woodsman comes to cut us down."

> 9The grave[b] below is all astir
>   to meet you at your coming;
> it rouses the spirits of the departed to greet
>   you—
>   all those who were leaders in the world;
> it makes them rise from their thrones—
>   all those who were kings over the nations.
> 10They will all respond,
>   they will say to you,
> "You also have become weak, as we are;
>   you have become like us."
> 11All your pomp has been brought down to the
>   grave,
>   along with the noise of your harps;
> maggots are spread out beneath you
>   and worms cover you.

> 12How you have fallen from heaven,
>   O morning star, son of the dawn!
> You have been cast down to the earth,
>   you who once laid low the nations!
> 13You said in your heart,
>   "I will ascend to heaven;
> I will raise my throne
>   above the stars of God;
> I will sit enthroned on the mount of assembly,
>   on the utmost heights of the sacred
>   mountain.[c]
> 14I will ascend above the tops of the clouds;
>   I will make myself like the Most High."
> 15But you are brought down to the grave,
>   to the depths of the pit.

> 16Those who see you stare at you,
>   they ponder your fate:
> "Is this the man who shook the earth
>   and made kingdoms tremble,
> 17the man who made the world a desert,
>   who overthrew its cities
>   and would not let his captives go home?"

> 18All the kings of the nations lie in state,
>   each in his own tomb.
> 19But you are cast out of your tomb
>   like a rejected branch;
> you are covered with the slain,
>   with those pierced by the sword,
>   those who descend to the stones of the pit.
> Like a corpse trampled underfoot,
> 20   you will not join them in burial,
> for you have destroyed your land
>   and killed your people.

> The offspring of the wicked
>   will never be mentioned again.

---

a 4 Dead Sea Scrolls, Septuagint and Syriac; the meaning of the word in the Masoretic Text is uncertain.   b 9 Hebrew *Sheol*; also in verses 11 and 15
c 13 Or *the north*; Hebrew *Zaphon*

Living Bible

⁴you will jeer at the king of Babylon and say, "You bully, you! At last you have what was coming to you! ⁵For the Lord has crushed your wicked power, and broken your evil rule." ⁶You persecuted my people with unceasing blows of rage and held the nations in your angry grip. You were unrestrained in tyranny. ⁷But at last the whole earth is at rest and is quiet! All the world begins to sing! ⁸Even the trees of the woods—the fir trees and cedars of Lebanon—sing out this joyous song: "Your power is broken; no one will bother us now; at last we have peace."

⁹The denizens of hell crowd to meet you as you enter their domain. World leaders and earth's mightiest kings, long dead, are there to see you. ¹⁰With one voice they all cry out, "Now you are as weak as we are!" ¹¹Your might and power are gone; they are buried with you. All the pleasant music in your palace has ceased; now maggots are your sheet, worms your blanket!

¹²How you are fallen from heaven, O Lucifer, son of the morning! How you are cut down to the ground—mighty though you were against the nations of the world. ¹³For you said to yourself, "I will ascend to heaven and rule the angels.ᵈ I will take the highest throne. I will preside on the Mount of Assembly far away in the north.ᵉ ¹⁴I will climb to the highest heavens and be like the Most High." ¹⁵But instead, you will be brought down to the pit of hell, down to its lowest depths. ¹⁶Everyone there will stare at you and ask, "Can this be the one who shook the earth and the kingdoms of the world? ¹⁷Can this be the one who destroyed the world and made it into a shambles and demolished its greatest cities and had no mercy on his prisoners?"

¹⁸The kings of the nations lie in stately glory in their graves, ¹⁹but your body is thrown out like a broken branch; it lies in an open grave, covered with the dead bodies of those slain in battle. It lies as a carcass in the road, trampled and mangled by horses' hoofs. ²⁰No monument will be given you, for you have destroyed your nation and slain your people. Your son will not succeed you as the king. ²¹Slay the children of this sin-

New Revised Standard

made to serve, ⁴you will take up this taunt against the king of Babylon:

How the oppressor has ceased!
   How his insolenceᶠ has ceased!
⁵ The LORD has broken the staff of the wicked,
   the scepter of rulers,
⁶ that struck down the peoples in wrath
   with unceasing blows,
that ruled the nations in anger
   with unrelenting persecution.
⁷ The whole earth is at rest and quiet;
   they break forth into singing.
⁸ The cypresses exult over you,
   the cedars of Lebanon, saying,
"Since you were laid low,
   no one comes to cut us down."
⁹ Sheol beneath is stirred up
   to meet you when you come;
it rouses the shades to greet you,
   all who were leaders of the earth;
it raises from their thrones
   all who were kings of the nations.
¹⁰ All of them will speak
   and say to you:
"You too have become as weak as we!
   You have become like us!"
¹¹ Your pomp is brought down to Sheol,
   and the sound of your harps;
maggots are the bed beneath you,
   and worms are your covering.

¹² How you are fallen from heaven,
   O Day Star, son of Dawn!
How you are cut down to the ground,
   you who laid the nations low!
¹³ You said in your heart,
   "I will ascend to heaven;
I will raise my throne
   above the stars of God;
I will sit on the mount of assembly
   on the heights of Zaphon;ᵍ
¹⁴ I will ascend to the tops of the clouds,
   I will make myself like the Most High."
¹⁵ But you are brought down to Sheol,
   to the depths of the Pit.
¹⁶ Those who see you will stare at you,
   and ponder over you:
"Is this the man who made the earth tremble,
   who shook kingdoms,
¹⁷ who made the world like a desert
   and overthrew its cities,
   who would not let his prisoners go home?"
¹⁸ All the kings of the nations lie in glory,
   each in his own tomb;
¹⁹ but you are cast out, away from your grave,
   like loathsome carrion,ʰ
clothed with the dead, those pierced by the
   sword,
who go down to the stones of the Pit,
   like a corpse trampled underfoot.
²⁰ You will not be joined with them in burial,
   because you have destroyed your land,
   you have killed your people.

May the descendants of evildoers
   nevermore be named!

ᵈ 14:13 the angels, literally, "the stars of God."   ᵉ 14:13 I will preside on the Mount of Assembly far away in the north, literally, "I will sit upon the mount of the congregation in the sides of the north" (Ps 48:2); or, "on the slopes of Mount Saphon."

ᶠ Q Ms Compare Gk Syr Vg: Meaning of MT uncertain   ᵍ Or assembly in the far north   ʰ Cn Compare Gk: Heb like a loathed branch

King James

21Prepare slaughter for his children for the iniquity of their fathers; that they do not rise, nor possess the land, nor fill the face of the world with cities.

22For I will rise up against them, saith the LORD of hosts, and cut off from Babylon the name, and remnant, and son, and nephew, saith the LORD.

23I will also make it a possession for the bittern, and pools of water: and I will sweep it with the besom of destruction, saith the LORD of hosts.

24¶ The LORD of hosts hath sworn, saying, Surely as I have thought, so shall it come to pass; and as I have purposed, *so* shall it stand:

25That I will break the Assyrian in my land, and upon my mountains tread him under foot: then shall his yoke depart from off them, and his burden depart from off their shoulders.

26This *is* the purpose that is purposed upon the whole earth: and this *is* the hand that is stretched out upon all the nations.

27For the LORD of hosts hath purposed, and who shall disannul *it?* and his hand *is* stretched out, and who shall turn it back?

28In the year that king Ahaz died was this burden.

29¶ Rejoice not thou, whole Palestina, because the rod of him that smote thee is broken: for out of the serpent's root shall come forth a cockatrice, and his fruit *shall be* a fiery flying serpent.

30And the firstborn of the poor shall feed, and the needy shall lie down in safety: and I will kill thy root with famine, and he shall slay thy remnant.

31Howl, O gate; cry, O city; thou, whole Palestina, *art* dissolved: for there shall come from the north a smoke, and none *shall be* alone in his appointed times.

32What shall *one* then answer the messengers of the nation? That the LORD hath founded Zion, and the poor of his people shall trust in it.

New International

21Prepare a place to slaughter his sons
  for the sins of their forefathers;
they are not to rise to inherit the land
  and cover the earth with their cities.

22"I will rise up against them,"
  declares the LORD Almighty.
"I will cut off from Babylon her name and
    survivors,
  her offspring and descendants,"
                    declares the LORD.
23"I will turn her into a place for owls
  and into swampland;
I will sweep her with the broom of destruction,"
  declares the LORD Almighty.

A Prophecy Against Assyria

24The LORD Almighty has sworn,

"Surely, as I have planned, so it will be,
  and as I have purposed, so it will stand.
25I will crush the Assyrian in my land;
  on my mountains I will trample him down.
His yoke will be taken from my people,
  and his burden removed from their
    shoulders."

26This is the plan determined for the whole world;
  this is the hand stretched out over all nations.
27For the LORD Almighty has purposed, and who
    can thwart him?
His hand is stretched out, and who can turn it
    back?

A Prophecy Against the Philistines

28This oracle came in the year King Ahaz died:

29Do not rejoice, all you Philistines,
  that the rod that struck you is broken;
from the root of that snake will spring up a
    viper,
  its fruit will be a darting, venomous serpent.
30The poorest of the poor will find pasture,
  and the needy will lie down in safety.
But your root I will destroy by famine;
  it will slay your survivors.

31Wail, O gate! Howl, O city!
  Melt away, all you Philistines!
A cloud of smoke comes from the north,
  and there is not a straggler in its ranks.
32What answer shall be given
  to the envoys of that nation?
"The LORD has established Zion,
  and in her his afflicted people will find
    refuge."

A Prophecy Against Moab

15 THE BURDEN of Moab. Because in the night Ar of Moab is laid waste, *and* brought to silence; because in the night Kir of Moab is laid waste, *and* brought to silence;

2He is gone up to Bajith, and to Dibon, the high places, to weep: Moab shall howl over Nebo, and over Medeba: on all their heads *shall be* baldness, *and* every beard cut off.

15 AN ORACLE concerning Moab:

Ar in Moab is ruined,
  destroyed in a night!
Kir in Moab is ruined,
  destroyed in a night!
2Dibon goes up to its temple,
  to its high places to weep;
  Moab wails over Nebo and Medeba.
Every head is shaved
  and every beard cut off.

Living Bible

ner. Do not let them rise and conquer the land nor re-build the cities of the world.

22I, myself, have risen against him, says the Lord of heaven's armies, and will cut off his children and his children's children from ever sitting on his throne. 23I will make Babylon into a desolate land of porcupines, full of swamps and marshes. I will sweep the land with the broom of destruction, says the Lord of the armies of heaven. 24He has taken an oath to do it! For this is his purpose and plan. 25I have decided to break the Assyrian army when they are in Israel and to crush them on my mountains; my people shall no longer be their slaves. 26This is my plan for the whole earth—I will do it by my mighty power that reaches everywhere around the world. 27The Lord, the God of battle, has spoken—who can change his plans? When his hand moves, who can stop him?

28This is the message that came to me the year King Ahaz died:

29Don't rejoice, Philistines, that the king who smote you is dead.a That rod is broken, yes; but his son will be a greater scourge to you than his father ever was! From the snake will be born an adder, a fiery serpent to destroy you! 30I will shepherd the poor of my people; they shall graze in my pasture! The needy shall lie down in peace. But as for you—I will wipe you out with famine and the sword. 31Weep, Philistine cities—you are doomed. All your nation is doomed. For a perfectly trained armyb is coming down from the north against you. 32What then shall we tell the reporters? Tell them that the Lord has founded Jerusalem and is determined that the poor of his people will find a refuge within her walls.

15 HERE IS God's message to Moab: In one night your cities of Ar and Kir will be destroyed. 2Your people in Dibon go mourning to their temples to weep for the fate of Nebo and Medeba; they shave their heads in sorrow and cut off their beards. 3They wear

New Revised Standard

21 Prepare slaughter for his sons
    because of the guilt of their father.c
Let them never rise to possess the earth
    or cover the face of the world with cities.

22 I will rise up against them, says the Lord of hosts, and will cut off from Babylon name and remnant, offspring and posterity, says the Lord. 23And I will make it a possession of the hedgehog, and pools of water, and I will sweep it with the broom of destruction, says the Lord of hosts.

An Oracle concerning Assyria

24 The Lord of hosts has sworn:
    As I have designed,
        so shall it be;
    and as I have planned,
        so shall it come to pass:
25 I will break the Assyrian in my land,
    and on my mountains trample him under
        foot;
his yoke shall be removed from them,
    and his burden from their shoulders.
26 This is the plan that is planned
    concerning the whole earth;
and this is the hand that is stretched out
    over all the nations.
27 For the Lord of hosts has planned,
    and who will annul it?
His hand is stretched out,
    and who will turn it back?

An Oracle concerning Philistia

28 In the year that King Ahaz died this oracle came:

29 Do not rejoice, all you Philistines,
        that the rod that struck you is broken,
    for from the root of the snake will come forth
        an adder,
    and its fruit will be a flying fiery serpent.
30 The firstborn of the poor will graze,
        and the needy lie down in safety;
    but I will make your root die of famine,
        and your remnant Id will kill.
31 Wail, O gate; cry, O city;
        melt in fear, O Philistia, all of you!
    For smoke comes out of the north,
        and there is no straggler in its ranks.

32 What will one answer the messengers of the
            nation?
    "The Lord has founded Zion,
        and the needy among his people
        will find refuge in her."

An Oracle concerning Moab

15 AN ORACLE concerning Moab.

    Because Ar is laid waste in a night,
        Moab is undone;
    because Kir is laid waste in a night,
        Moab is undone.
2   Dibone has gone up to the temple,
        to the high places to weep;
    over Nebo and over Medeba
        Moab wails.
    On every head is baldness,
        every beard is shorn;

---

a 14:29 the king who smote you is dead. Shalmaneser V of Assyria.
b 14:31 a perfectly trained army is coming down. Sargon of Assyria.

c Syr Compare Gk: Heb fathers   d Q Ms Vg: MT he   e Cn: Heb the house and Dibon

King James

3In their streets they shall gird themselves with sackcloth: on the tops of their houses, and in their streets, every one shall howl, weeping abundantly.

4And Heshbon shall cry, and Elealeh: their voice shall be heard *even* unto Jahaz: therefore the armed soldiers of Moab shall cry out; his life shall be grievous unto him.

5My heart shall cry out for Moab; his fugitives *shall flee* unto Zoar, an heifer of three years old: for by the mounting up of Luhith with weeping shall they go it up; for in the way of Horonaim they shall raise up a cry of destruction.

6For the waters of Nimrim shall be desolate: for the hay is withered away, the grass faileth, there is no green thing.

7Therefore the abundance they have gotten, and that which they have laid up, shall they carry away to the brook of the willows.

8For the cry is gone round about the borders of Moab; the howling thereof unto Eglaim, and the howling thereof unto Beer-elim.

9For the waters of Dimon shall be full of blood: for I will bring more upon Dimon, lions upon him that escapeth of Moab, and upon the remnant of the land.

16 SEND YE the lamb to the ruler of the land from Sela to the wilderness, unto the mount of the daughter of Zion.

2For it shall be, *that,* as a wandering bird cast out of the nest, *so* the daughters of Moab shall be at the fords of Arnon.

3Take counsel, execute judgment; make thy shadow as the night in the midst of the noonday; hide the outcasts; betray not him that wandereth.

4Let mine outcasts dwell with thee, Moab; be thou a covert to them from the face of the spoiler: for the extortioner is at an end, the spoiler ceaseth, the oppressors are consumed out of the land.

5And in mercy shall the throne be established: and he shall sit upon it in truth in the tabernacle of David, judging, and seeking judgment, and hasting righteousness.

6¶ We have heard of the pride of Moab; *he is* very proud: *even* of his haughtiness, and his pride, and his wrath: *but* his lies *shall* not *be* so.

New International

3In the streets they wear sackcloth;
  on the roofs and in the public squares
they all wail,
  prostrate with weeping.
4Heshbon and Elealeh cry out,
  their voices are heard all the way to Jahaz.
Therefore the armed men of Moab cry out,
  and their hearts are faint.
5My heart cries out over Moab;
  her fugitives flee as far as Zoar,
  as far as Eglath Shelishiyah.
They go up the way to Luhith,
  weeping as they go;
on the road to Horonaim
  they lament their destruction.
6The waters of Nimrim are dried up
  and the grass is withered;
the vegetation is gone
  and nothing green is left.
7So the wealth they have acquired and stored up
  they carry away over the Ravine of the
    Poplars.
8Their outcry echoes along the border of Moab;
  their wailing reaches as far as Eglaim,
  their lamentation as far as Beer Elim.
9Dimon'sa waters are full of blood,
  but I will bring still more upon Dimona—
  a lion upon the fugitives of Moab
  and upon those who remain in the land.

16 SEND LAMBS as tribute
  to the ruler of the land,
from Sela, across the desert,
  to the mount of the Daughter of Zion.
2Like fluttering birds
  pushed from the nest,
so are the women of Moab
  at the fords of the Arnon.

3"Give us counsel,
  render a decision.
Make your shadow like night—
  at high noon.
Hide the fugitives,
  do not betray the refugees.
4Let the Moabite fugitives stay with you;
  be their shelter from the destroyer."

The oppressor will come to an end,
  and destruction will cease;
  the aggressor will vanish from the land.
5In love a throne will be established;
  in faithfulness a man will sit on it—
  one from the houseb of David—
one who in judging seeks justice
  and speeds the cause of righteousness.

6We have heard of Moab's pride—
  her overweening pride and conceit,
  her pride and her insolence—
  but her boasts are empty.

Living Bible

sackcloth through the streets, and from every home comes the sound of weeping. 4The cries from the cities of Heshbon and Elealeh are heard far away, even in Jahaz. The bravest warriors of Moab cry in utter terror.

5My heart weeps for Moab! His people flee to Zoar and Eglath. Weeping, they climb the upward road to Luhith, and their crying will be heard all along the road to Horonaim. 6Even Nimrim River is desolate! The grassy banks are dried up and the tender plants are gone. 7The desperate refugees take only the possessions they can carry, and flee across the Brook of Willows. 8The whole land of Moab is a land of weeping, from one end to the other. 9The stream near Dibon will run red with blood, but I am not through with Dibon yet! Lions will hunt down the survivors, both those who escape and those who remain.

16 MOAB'S REFUGEES at Sela send lambs as a token of alliance with the king of Judah. 2The women of Moab are left at the fords of the Arnon River like homeless birds. 3[The ambassadors, who accompany the gift to Jerusalemc] plead for advice and help. "Give us sanctuary. Protect us. Do not turn us over to our foes. 4, 5Let our outcasts stay among you; hide them from our enemies! God will reward you for your kindness to us. If you let Moab's fugitives settle among you, then, when the terror is past, God will establish David's throne forever, and on that throne he will place a just and righteous King."

6Is this proud Moab, concerning which we heard so much? His arrogance and insolence are all gone now!

New Revised Standard

3 in the streets they bind on sackcloth;
     on the housetops and in the squares
     everyone wails and melts in tears.
4 Heshbon and Elealeh cry out,
     their voices are heard as far as Jahaz;
   therefore the loins of Moab quiver;d
     his soul trembles.
5 My heart cries out for Moab;
     his fugitives flee to Zoar,
   to Eglath-shelishiyah.
   For at the ascent of Luhith
     they go up weeping;
   on the road to Horonaim
     they raise a cry of destruction;
6 the waters of Nimrim
     are a desolation;
   the grass is withered, the new growth fails,
     the verdure is no more.
7 Therefore the abundance they have gained
     and what they have laid up
   they carry away
     over the Wadi of the Willows.
8 For a cry has gone
     around the land of Moab;
   the wailing reaches to Eglaim,
     the wailing reaches to Beer-elim.
9 For the waters of Dibone are full of blood;
     yet I will bring upon Dibone even more—
   a lion for those of Moab who escape,
     for the remnant of the land.

16 SEND LAMBS
     to the ruler of the land,
   from Sela, by way of the desert,
     to the mount of daughter Zion.
2 Like fluttering birds,
     like scattered nestlings,
   so are the daughters of Moab
     at the fords of the Arnon.
3 "Give counsel,
     grant justice;
   make your shade like night
     at the height of noon;
   hide the outcasts,
     do not betray the fugitive;
4 let the outcasts of Moab
     settle among you;
   be a refuge to them
     from the destroyer."

   When the oppressor is no more,
     and destruction has ceased,
   and marauders have vanished from the land,
5 then a throne shall be established in steadfast
     love
   in the tent of David,
     and on it shall sit in faithfulness
   a ruler who seeks justice
     and is swift to do what is right.

6 We have heard of the pride of Moab
     —how proud he is!—
   of his arrogance, his pride, and his insolence;
     his boasts are false.

---

c 16:3 The ambassadors, who accompany the gift to Jerusalem, implied.

d Cn Compare Gk Syr: Heb the armed men of Moab cry aloud   e Q Ms Vg Compare Syr: MT Dimon

King James

7Therefore shall Moab howl for Moab, every one shall howl: for the foundations of Kir-hareseth shall ye mourn; surely *they are* stricken.

8For the fields of Heshbon languish, *and* the vine of Sibmah: the lords of the heathen have broken down the principal plants thereof, they are come *even* unto Jazer, they wandered *through* the wilderness: her branches are stretched out, they are gone over the sea.

9¶ Therefore I will bewail with the weeping of Jazer the vine of Sibmah: I will water thee with my tears, O Heshbon, and Elealeh: for the shouting for thy summer fruits and for thy harvest is fallen.

10And gladness is taken away, and joy out of the plentiful field; and in the vineyards there shall be no singing, neither shall there be shouting: the treaders shall tread out no wine in *their* presses; I have made *their* *vintage* shouting to cease.

11Wherefore my bowels shall sound like an harp for Moab, and mine inward parts for Kir-haresh.

12¶ And it shall come to pass, when it is seen that Moab is weary on the high place, that he shall come to his sanctuary to pray; but he shall not prevail.

13This *is* the word that the LORD hath spoken concerning Moab since that time.

14But now the LORD hath spoken, saying, Within three years, as the years of an hireling, and the glory of Moab shall be contemned, with all that great multitude; and the remnant *shall be* very small *and* feeble.

17 THE BURDEN of Damascus. Behold, Damascus is taken away from *being* a city, and it shall be a ruinous heap.

2The cities of Aroer *are* forsaken: they shall be for flocks, which shall lie down, and none shall make *them* afraid.

3The fortress also shall cease from Ephraim, and the kingdom from Damascus, and the remnant of Syria: they shall be as the glory of the children of Israel, saith the LORD of hosts.

4And in that day it shall come to pass, *that* the glory of Jacob shall be made thin, and the fatness of his flesh shall wax lean.

5And it shall be as when the harvestman gathereth the corn, and reapeth the ears with his arm; and it shall be as he that gathereth ears in the valley of Rephaim.

6¶ Yet gleaning grapes shall be left in it, as the shaking of an olive tree, two *or* three berries in the top of the uppermost bough, four *or* five in the outmost fruitful branches thereof, saith the LORD God of Israel.

New International

7Therefore the Moabites wail,
they wail together for Moab.
Lament and grieve
for the mena of Kir Hareseth.
8The fields of Heshbon wither,
the vines of Sibmah also.
The rulers of the nations
have trampled down the choicest vines,
which once reached Jazer
and spread toward the desert.
Their shoots spread out
and went as far as the sea.
9So I weep, as Jazer weeps,
for the vines of Sibmah.
O Heshbon, O Elealeh,
I drench you with tears!
The shouts of joy over your ripened fruit
and over your harvests have been stilled.
10Joy and gladness are taken away from the orchards;
no one sings or shouts in the vineyards;
no one treads out wine at the presses,
for I have put an end to the shouting.
11My heart laments for Moab like a harp,
my inmost being for Kir Hareseth.
12When Moab appears at her high place,
she only wears herself out;
when she goes to her shrine to pray,
it is to no avail.

13This is the word the LORD has already spoken concerning Moab. 14But now the LORD says: "Within three years, as a servant bound by contract would count them, Moab's splendor and all her many people will be despised, and her survivors will be very few and feeble."

An Oracle Against Damascus

17 AN ORACLE concerning Damascus:

"See, Damascus will no longer be a city
but will become a heap of ruins.
2The cities of Aroer will be deserted
and left to flocks, which will lie down,
with no one to make them afraid.
3The fortified city will disappear from Ephraim,
and royal power from Damascus;
the remnant of Aram will be
like the glory of the Israelites,"
declares the LORD Almighty.

4"In that day the glory of Jacob will fade;
the fat of his body will waste away.
5It will be as when a reaper gathers the standing grain
and harvests the grain with his arm—
as when a man gleans heads of grain
in the Valley of Rephaim.
6Yet some gleanings will remain,
as when an olive tree is beaten,
leaving two or three olives on the topmost branches,
four or five on the fruitful boughs,"
declares the LORD, the God of Israel.

Living Bible

7Therefore all Moab weeps. Yes, Moab, you will mourn for stricken Kir-hareseth, 8and for the abandoned farms of Heshbon and the vineyards at Sibmah. The enemy war-lords have cut down the best of the grape vines; their armies spread out as far as Jazer in the deserts, and even down to the sea. 9So I wail and lament for Jazer and the vineyards of Sibmah. My tears shall flow for Heshbon and Elealeh, for destruction has come upon their summer fruits and harvests. 10Gone now is the gladness, gone the joy of harvest. The happy singing in the vineyards will be heard no more; the treading out of the grapes in the wine presses has ceased forever. I have ended all their harvest joys.

11I will weep, weep, weep, for Moab; and my sorrow for Kir-haresh will be very great. 12The people of Moab will pray in anguish to their idols at the tops of the hills, but it will do no good; they will cry to their gods in their idol temples, but none will come to save them. 13, 14All this concerning Moab has been said before; but now the Lord says that within three years, without fail, the glory of Moab shall be ended, and few of all its people will be left alive.

17 THIS IS God's message to Damascus, capital of Syria:

Look, Damascus is gone! It is no longer a city—it has become a heap of ruins! 2The cities of Aroer are deserted. Sheep pasture there, lying quiet and unafraid, with no one to chase them away. 3The strength of Israel and the power of Damascus will end, and the remnant of Syria shall be destroyed. For as Israel's glory departed, so theirs, too, will disappear, declares the Lord Almighty. 4Yes, the glory of Israel will be very dim when poverty stalks the land. 5Israel will be as abandoned as the harvested grain fields in the Valley of Rephaim. 6Oh, a very few of her people will be left, just as a few stray olives are left on the trees when the harvest is ended, two or three in the highest branches, four or five out on the tips of the limbs. That is how it will be in Damascus and Israel—stripped bare of people except for a few of the poor who remain.

New Revised Standard

7   Therefore let Moab wail,
    let everyone wail for Moab.
Mourn, utterly stricken,
    for the raisin cakes of Kir-hareseth.

8   For the fields of Heshbon languish,
    and the vines of Sibmah,
whose clusters once made drunk
    the lords of the nations,
reached to Jazer
    and strayed to the desert;
their shoots once spread abroad
    and crossed over the sea.

9   Therefore I weep with the weeping of Jazer
    for the vines of Sibmah;
I drench you with my tears,
    O Heshbon and Elealeh;
for the shout over your fruit harvest
    and your grain harvest has ceased.

10   Joy and gladness are taken away
    from the fruitful field;
and in the vineyards no songs are sung,
    no shouts are raised;
no treader treads out wine in the presses;
    the vintage-shout is hushed.[b]

11   Therefore my heart throbs like a harp for Moab,
    and my very soul for Kir-heres.

12 When Moab presents himself, when he wearies himself upon the high place, when he comes to his sanctuary to pray, he will not prevail.

13 This was the word that the LORD spoke concerning Moab in the past. 14 But now the LORD says, In three years, like the years of a hired worker, the glory of Moab will be brought into contempt, in spite of all its great multitude; and those who survive will be very few and feeble.

An Oracle concerning Damascus

17 AN ORACLE concerning Damascus.

See, Damascus will cease to be a city,
    and will become a heap of ruins.

2   Her towns will be deserted forever;[c]
    they will be places for flocks,
which will lie down, and no one will make
    them afraid.

3   The fortress will disappear from Ephraim,
    and the kingdom from Damascus;
and the remnant of Aram will be
    like the glory of the children of Israel,
      says the LORD of hosts.

4   On that day
the glory of Jacob will be brought low,
    and the fat of his flesh will grow lean.

5   And it shall be as when reapers gather
      standing grain
    and their arms harvest the ears,
and as when one gleans the ears of grain
    in the Valley of Rephaim.

6   Gleanings will be left in it,
    as when an olive tree is beaten—
two or three berries
    in the top of the highest bough,
four or five
    on the branches of a fruit tree,
      says the LORD God of Israel.

b Gk: Heb *I have hushed*   c Cn Compare Gk: Heb *the cities of Aroer are deserted*

King James

7At that day shall a man look to his Maker, and his eyes shall have respect to the Holy One of Israel.

8And he shall not look to the altars, the work of his hands, neither shall respect *that* which his fingers have made, either the groves, or the images.

9¶ In that day shall his strong cities be as a forsaken bough, and an uppermost branch, which they left because of the children of Israel: and there shall be desolation.

10Because thou hast forgotten the God of thy salvation, and hast not been mindful of the rock of thy strength, therefore shalt thou plant pleasant plants, and shalt set it with strange slips:

11In the day shalt thou make thy plant to grow, and in the morning shalt thou make thy seed to flourish: *but* the harvest *shall be* a heap in the day of grief and of desperate sorrow.

12¶ Woe to the multitude of many people, *which* make a noise like the noise of the seas; and to the rushing of nations, *that* make a rushing like the rushing of mighty waters!

13The nations shall rush like the rushing of many waters: but *God* shall rebuke them, and they shall flee far off, and shall be chased as the chaff of the mountains before the wind, and like a rolling thing before the whirlwind.

14And behold at eveningtide trouble; *and* before the morning he *is* not. This *is* the portion of them that spoil us, and the lot of them that rob us.

New International

7In that day men will look to their Maker
and turn their eyes to the Holy One of Israel.
8They will not look to the altars,
the work of their hands,
and they will have no regard for the Asherah
poles[a]
and the incense altars their fingers have
made.

9In that day their strong cities, which they left because of the Israelites, will be like places abandoned to thickets and undergrowth. And all will be desolation.

10You have forgotten God your Savior;
you have not remembered the Rock, your
fortress.
Therefore, though you set out the finest plants
and plant imported vines,
11though on the day you set them out, you make
them grow,
and on the morning when you plant them,
you bring them to bud,
yet the harvest will be as nothing
in the day of disease and incurable pain.

12Oh, the raging of many nations—
they rage like the raging sea!
Oh, the uproar of the peoples—
they roar like the roaring of great waters!
13Although the peoples roar like the roar of
surging waters,
when he rebukes them they flee far away,
driven before the wind like chaff on the hills,
like tumbleweed before a gale.
14In the evening, sudden terror!
Before the morning, they are gone!
This is the portion of those who loot us,
the lot of those who plunder us.

A Prophecy Against Cush

18 WOE TO the land shadowing with wings, which *is* beyond the rivers of Ethiopia:

2That sendeth ambassadors by the sea, even in vessels of bulrushes upon the waters, *saying,* Go, ye swift messengers, to a nation scattered and peeled, to a people terrible from their beginning hitherto; a nation meted out and trodden down, whose land the rivers have spoiled!

3All ye inhabitants of the world, and dwellers on the earth, see ye, when he lifteth up an ensign on the mountains; and when he bloweth a trumpet, hear ye.

4For so the LORD said unto me, I will take my rest, and I will consider in my dwellingplace like a clear heat upon herbs, *and* like a cloud of dew in the heat of harvest.

5For afore the harvest, when the bud is perfect, and the sour grape is ripening in the flower, he shall both cut off the sprigs with pruning hooks, and take away *and* cut down the branches.

18 WOE TO the land of whirring wings[b]
along the rivers of Cush,[c]
2which sends envoys by sea
in papyrus boats over the water.

Go, swift messengers,
to a people tall and smooth-skinned,
to a people feared far and wide,
an aggressive nation of strange speech,
whose land is divided by rivers.

3All you people of the world,
you who live on the earth,
when a banner is raised on the mountains,
you will see it,
and when a trumpet sounds,
you will hear it.
4This is what the LORD says to me:
"I will remain quiet and will look on from my
dwelling place,
like shimmering heat in the sunshine,
like a cloud of dew in the heat of harvest."
5For, before the harvest, when the blossom is
gone
and the flower becomes a ripening grape,
he will cut off the shoots with pruning knives,
and cut down and take away the spreading
branches.

a 8 That is, symbols of the goddess Asherah   b 1 Or *of locusts*   c 1 That is, the upper Nile region

Living Bible

7Then at last they will think of God their Creator and have respect for the Holy One of Israel. 8They will no longer ask their idols for help in that day, neither will they worship what their hands have made! They will no longer have respect for the images of Ashtaroth and the sun-idols.

9Their largest cities will be as deserted as the distant wooded hills and mountain tops and become like the abandoned cities of the Amorites, deserted when the Israelites approached (so long agod). 10Why? Because you have turned from the God who can save you—the Rock who can hide you; therefore, even though you plant a wonderful, rare crop of greatest value, 11and though it grows so well that it will blossom on the very morning that you plant it, yet you will never harvest it—your only harvest will be a pile of grief and incurable pain.

12Look, see the armies thundering toward God's land. 13But though they roar like breakers rolling upon a beach, God will silence them. They will flee, scattered like chaff by the wind, like whirling dust before a storm. 14In the evening Israel waits in terror, but by dawn her enemies are dead. This is the just reward of those who plunder and destroy the people of God.

18 AH, LAND beyond the upper reaches of the Nile,e where winged sailboats glide along the river! 2Land that sends ambassadors in fast boats down the Nile! Let swift messengers return to you, O strong and supple nation feared far and wide, a conquering, destroying nation whose land the upper Nile divides.f And this is the message sent to you:

3When I raise my battle flag upon the mountain, let all the world take notice! When I blow the trumpet, listen! 4For the Lord has told me this: Let your mighty army now advance against the land of Israel.g God will watch quietly from his Temple in Jerusalem—serene as on a pleasant summer day or a lovely autumn morning during harvest time. 5But before you have begun the attack, and while your plans are ripening like grapes, he will cut you off as though with pruning shears. He will snip the spreading tendrils. 6Your mighty army will be

New Revised Standard

7 On that day people will regard their Maker, and their eyes will look to the Holy One of Israel; 8 they will not have regard for the altars, the work of their hands, and they will not look to what their own fingers have made, either the sacred polesh or the altars of incense.

9 On that day their strong cities will be like the deserted places of the Hivites and the Amorites,i which they deserted because of the children of Israel, and there will be desolation.

10 For you have forgotten the God of your
        salvation,
    and have not remembered the Rock of your
        refuge;
    therefore, though you plant pleasant plants
        and set out slips of an alien god,
11 though you make them grow on the day that
        you plant them,
    and make them blossom in the morning that
        you sow;
    yet the harvest will flee away
        in a day of grief and incurable pain.

12 Ah, the thunder of many peoples,
        they thunder like the thundering of the sea!
    Ah, the roar of nations,
        they roar like the roaring of mighty waters!
13 The nations roar like the roaring of many
        waters,
    but he will rebuke them, and they will flee
        far away,
    chased like chaff on the mountains before the
        wind
    and whirling dust before the storm.
14 At evening time, lo, terror!
        Before morning, they are no more.
    This is the fate of those who despoil us,
        and the lot of those who plunder us.

An Oracle concerning Ethiopia

18 AH, LAND of whirring wings
        beyond the rivers of Ethiopia,j
2 sending ambassadors by the Nile
        in vessels of papyrus on the waters!
    Go, you swift messengers,
        to a nation tall and smooth,
    to a people feared near and far,
        a nation mighty and conquering,
        whose land the rivers divide.

3 All you inhabitants of the world,
        you who live on the earth,
    when a signal is raised on the mountains,
        look!
    When a trumpet is blown, listen!
4 For thus the LORD said to me:
    I will quietly look from my dwelling
        like clear heat in sunshine,
        like a cloud of dew in the heat of harvest.
5 For before the harvest, when the blossom is
        over
    and the flower becomes a ripening grape,
    he will cut off the shoots with pruning hooks,
        and the spreading branches he will hew
        away.

---

d 17:9 so long ago, implied.   e 18:1 upper reaches of the Nile, literally, "land beyond the rivers of Ethiopia." Ethiopia was the seat of the powerful 25th Egyptian Dynasty (730-660 B.C.).   f 18:2 whose land the upper Nile divides, literally, "whose land the rivers divide."   g 18:4 of Israel, implied.

h Heb Asherim   i Cn Compare Gk: Heb places of the wood and the highest bough   j Or Nubia; Heb Cush

King James

6They shall be left together unto the fowls of the mountains, and to the beasts of the earth: and the fowls shall summer upon them, and all the beasts of the earth shall winter upon them.

7¶ In that time shall the present be brought unto the LORD of hosts of a people scattered and peeled, and from a people terrible from their beginning hitherto; a nation meted out and trodden under foot, whose land the rivers have spoiled, to the place of the name of the LORD of hosts, the mount Zion.

19 THE BURDEN of Egypt. Behold, the LORD rideth upon a swift cloud, and shall come into Egypt: and the idols of Egypt shall be moved at his presence, and the heart of Egypt shall melt in the midst of it.

2And I will set the Egyptians against the Egyptians: and they shall fight every one against his brother, and every one against his neighbour; city against city, *and* kingdom against kingdom.

3And the spirit of Egypt shall fail in the midst thereof; and I will destroy the counsel thereof: and they shall seek to the idols, and to the charmers, and to them that have familiar spirits, and to the wizards.

4And the Egyptians will I give over into the hand of a cruel lord; and a fierce king shall rule over them, saith the Lord, the LORD of hosts.

5And the waters shall fail from the sea, and the river shall be wasted and dried up.

6And they shall turn the rivers far away; *and* the brooks of defence shall be emptied and dried up: the reeds and flags shall wither.

7The paper reeds by the brooks, by the mouth of the brooks, and every thing sown by the brooks, shall wither, be driven away, and be no *more*.

8The fishers also shall mourn, and all they that cast angle into the brooks shall lament, and they that spread nets upon the waters shall languish.

9Moreover they that work in fine flax, and they that weave networks, shall be confounded.

10And they shall be broken in the purposes thereof, all that make sluices *and* ponds for fish.

11¶ Surely the princes of Zoan *are* fools, the counsel of the wise counsellors of Pharaoh is become brutish: how say ye unto Pharaoh, I *am* the son of the wise, the son of ancient kings?

12Where *are* they? where *are* thy wise *men?* and let them tell thee now, and let them know what the LORD of hosts hath purposed upon Egypt.

New International

6They will all be left to the mountain birds of prey
  and to the wild animals;
the birds will feed on them all summer,
  the wild animals all winter.

7At that time gifts will be brought to the LORD Almighty

from a people tall and smooth-skinned,
  from a people feared far and wide,
an aggressive nation of strange speech,
  whose land is divided by rivers—

the gifts will be brought to Mount Zion, the place of the Name of the LORD Almighty.

A Prophecy About Egypt

19 AN ORACLE concerning Egypt:

See, the LORD rides on a swift cloud
  and is coming to Egypt.
The idols of Egypt tremble before him,
  and the hearts of the Egyptians melt within
  them.

2"I will stir up Egyptian against Egyptian—
  brother will fight against brother,
  neighbor against neighbor,
  city against city,
  kingdom against kingdom.
3The Egyptians will lose heart,
  and I will bring their plans to nothing;
they will consult the idols and the spirits of the
  dead,
  the mediums and the spiritists.
4I will hand the Egyptians over
  to the power of a cruel master,
and a fierce king will rule over them,"
  declares the Lord, the LORD Almighty.

5The waters of the river will dry up,
  and the riverbed will be parched and dry.
6The canals will stink;
  the streams of Egypt will dwindle and dry up.
  The reeds and rushes will wither,
7   also the plants along the Nile,
  at the mouth of the river.
Every sown field along the Nile
  will become parched, will blow away and be
  no more.
8The fishermen will groan and lament,
  all who cast hooks into the Nile;
those who throw nets on the water
  will pine away.
9Those who work with combed flax will despair,
  the weavers of fine linen will lose hope.
10The workers in cloth will be dejected,
  and all the wage earners will be sick at heart.

11The officials of Zoan are nothing but fools;
  the wise counselors of Pharaoh give senseless
  advice.
How can you say to Pharaoh,
  "I am one of the wise men,
  a disciple of the ancient kings"?

12Where are your wise men now?
  Let them show you and make known
what the LORD Almighty
  has planned against Egypt.

Living Bible

left dead on the field for the mountain birds and wild animals to eat; the vultures will tear bodies all summer, and the wild animals will gnaw bones all winter. 7But the time will come when that strong and mighty nation, a terror to all both far and near, that conquering, destroying nation whose land the rivers divide, will bring gifts to the Lord Almighty in Jerusalem, where he has placed his name.

19 THIS IS God's message concerning Egypt: Look, the Lord is coming against Egypt, riding on a swift cloud; the idols of Egypt tremble; the hearts of the Egyptians melt with fear. 2I will set them to fighting against each other—brother against brother, neighbor against neighbor, city against city, province against province. 3Her wise counselors are all at their wits' ends to know what to do; they plead with their idols for wisdom, and call upon mediums, wizards and witches to show them what to do.

4I will hand over Egypt to a hard, cruel master, to a vicious king, says the Lord Almighty. 5And the waters of the Nile will fail to rise and flood the fields; the ditches will be parched and dry, 6their channels fouled with rotting reeds. 7All green things along the river bank will wither and blow away. All crops will perish; everything will die. 8The fishermen will weep for lack of work; those who fish with hooks and those who use the nets will all be unemployed. 9The weavers will have no flax or cotton, for the crops will fail. 10Great men and small—all will be crushed and broken.

11What fools the counselors of Zoan are! Their best counsel to the king of Egypt is utterly stupid and wrong. Will they still boast of their wisdom? Will they dare tell Pharaoh about the long line of wise men they have come from? 12What has happened to your "wise counselors," O Pharaoh? Where has their wisdom gone? If they are wise, let them tell you what the Lord is going to do to Egypt. 13The "wise men" from Zoan are also fools, and

New Revised Standard

6 They shall all be left
   to the birds of prey of the mountains
   and to the animals of the earth.
And the birds of prey will summer on them,
   and all the animals of the earth will winter
      on them.

7 At that time gifts will be brought to the LORD of hosts froma a people tall and smooth, from a people feared near and far, a nation mighty and conquering, whose land the rivers divide, to Mount Zion, the place of the name of the LORD of hosts.

An Oracle concerning Egypt

19 AN ORACLE concerning Egypt.

See, the LORD is riding on a swift cloud
   and comes to Egypt;
the idols of Egypt will tremble at his
      presence,
   and the heart of the Egyptians will melt
      within them.
2 I will stir up Egyptians against Egyptians,
   and they will fight, one against the other,
   neighbor against neighbor,
   city against city, kingdom against kingdom;
3 the spirit of the Egyptians within them will be
      emptied out,
   and I will confound their plans;
they will consult the idols and the spirits of
      the dead
   and the ghosts and the familiar spirits;
4 I will deliver the Egyptians
   into the hand of a hard master;
a fierce king will rule over them,
   says the Sovereign, the LORD of hosts.

5 The waters of the Nile will be dried up,
   and the river will be parched and dry;
6 its canals will become foul,
   and the branches of Egypt's Nile will
      diminish and dry up,
   reeds and rushes will rot away.
7 There will be bare places by the Nile,
   on the brink of the Nile;
and all that is sown by the Nile will dry up,
   be driven away, and be no more.
8 Those who fish will mourn;
   all who cast hooks in the Nile will lament,
   and those who spread nets on the water will
      languish.
9 The workers in flax will be in despair,
   and the carders and those at the loom will
      grow pale.
10 Its weavers will be dismayed,
   and all who work for wages will be grieved.

11 The princes of Zoan are utterly foolish;
   the wise counselors of Pharaoh give stupid
      counsel.
How can you say to Pharaoh,
   "I am one of the sages,
   a descendant of ancient kings"?
12 Where now are your sages?
   Let them tell you and make known
   what the LORD of hosts has planned against
      Egypt.

a Q Ms Gk Vg: MT *of*

King James

¹³The princes of Zoan are become fools, the princes of Noph are deceived; they have also seduced Egypt, *even they that are* the stay of the tribes thereof.

¹⁴The LORD hath mingled a perverse spirit in the midst thereof: and they have caused Egypt to err in every work thereof, as a drunken *man* staggereth in his vomit.

¹⁵Neither shall there be *any* work for Egypt, which the head or tail, branch or rush, may do.

¹⁶In that day shall Egypt be like unto women: and it shall be afraid and fear because of the shaking of the hand of the LORD of hosts, which he shaketh over it.

¹⁷And the land of Judah shall be a terror unto Egypt, every one that maketh mention thereof shall be afraid in himself, because of the counsel of the LORD of hosts, which he hath determined against it.

¹⁸¶ In that day shall five cities in the land of Egypt speak the language of Canaan, and swear to the LORD of hosts; one shall be called, The city of destruction.

¹⁹In that day shall there be an altar to the LORD in the midst of the land of Egypt, and a pillar at the border thereof to the LORD.

²⁰And it shall be for a sign and for a witness unto the LORD of hosts in the land of Egypt: for they shall cry unto the LORD because of the oppressors, and he shall send them a saviour, and a great one, and he shall deliver them.

²¹And the LORD shall be known to Egypt, and the Egyptians shall know the LORD in that day, and shall do sacrifice and oblation; yea, they shall vow a vow unto the LORD, and perform *it.*

²²And the LORD shall smite Egypt: he shall smite and heal *it:* and they shall return *even* to the LORD, and he shall be entreated of them, and shall heal them.

²³¶ In that day shall there be a highway out of Egypt to Assyria, and the Assyrian shall come into Egypt, and the Egyptian into Assyria, and the Egyptians shall serve with the Assyrians.

²⁴In that day shall Israel be the third with Egypt and with Assyria, *even* a blessing in the midst of the land:

²⁵Whom the LORD of hosts shall bless, saying, Blessed *be* Egypt my people, and Assyria the work of my hands, and Israel mine inheritance.

20 IN THE year that Tartan came unto Ashdod, (when Sargon the king of Assyria sent him,) and fought against Ashdod, and took it;

²At the same time spake the LORD by Isaiah the son of Amoz, saying, Go and loose the sackcloth from off thy loins, and put off thy shoe from thy foot. And he did so, walking naked and barefoot.

³And the LORD said, Like as my servant Isaiah hath walked naked and barefoot three years *for* a sign and wonder upon Egypt and upon Ethiopia;

⁴So shall the king of Assyria lead away the Egyptians prisoners, and the Ethiopians captives, young and old, naked and barefoot, even with *their* buttocks uncovered, to the shame of Egypt.

⁵And they shall be afraid and ashamed of Ethiopia their expectation, and of Egypt their glory.

⁶And the inhabitant of this isle shall say in that day, Behold, such *is* our expectation, whither we flee for help to be delivered from the king of Assyria: and how shall we escape?

New International

¹³The officials of Zoan have become fools,
   the leaders of Memphis[a] are deceived;
the cornerstones of her peoples
   have led Egypt astray.
¹⁴The LORD has poured into them
   a spirit of dizziness;
they make Egypt stagger in all that she does,
   as a drunkard staggers around in his vomit.
¹⁵There is nothing Egypt can do—
   head or tail, palm branch or reed.

¹⁶In that day the Egyptians will be like women. They will shudder with fear at the uplifted hand that the LORD Almighty raises against them. ¹⁷And the land of Judah will bring terror to the Egyptians; everyone to whom Judah is mentioned will be terrified, because of what the LORD Almighty is planning against them.

¹⁸In that day five cities in Egypt will speak the language of Canaan and swear allegiance to the LORD Almighty. One of them will be called the City of Destruction.[b]

¹⁹In that day there will be an altar to the LORD in the heart of Egypt, and a monument to the LORD at its border. ²⁰It will be a sign and witness to the LORD Almighty in the land of Egypt. When they cry out to the LORD because of their oppressors, he will send them a savior and defender, and he will rescue them. ²¹So the LORD will make himself known to the Egyptians, and in that day they will acknowledge the LORD. They will worship with sacrifices and grain offerings; they will make vows to the LORD and keep them. ²²The LORD will strike Egypt with a plague; he will strike them and heal them. They will turn to the LORD, and he will respond to their pleas and heal them.

²³In that day there will be a highway from Egypt to Assyria. The Assyrians will go to Egypt and the Egyptians to Assyria. The Egyptians and Assyrians will worship together. ²⁴In that day Israel will be the third, along with Egypt and Assyria, a blessing on the earth. ²⁵The LORD Almighty will bless them, saying, "Blessed be Egypt my people, Assyria my handiwork, and Israel my inheritance."

A Prophecy Against Egypt and Cush

20 IN THE year that the supreme commander, sent by Sargon king of Assyria, came to Ashdod and attacked and captured it— ²at that time the LORD spoke through Isaiah son of Amoz. He said to him, "Take off the sackcloth from your body and the sandals from your feet." And he did so, going around stripped and barefoot.

³Then the LORD said, "Just as my servant Isaiah has gone stripped and barefoot for three years, as a sign and portent against Egypt and Cush,[c] ⁴so the king of Assyria will lead away stripped and barefoot the Egyptian captives and Cushite exiles, young and old, with buttocks bared—to Egypt's shame. ⁵Those who trusted in Cush and boasted in Egypt will be afraid and put to shame. ⁶In that day the people who live on this coast will say, 'See what has happened to those we relied on, those we fled to for help and deliverance from the king of Assyria! How then can we escape?' "

---

^a *13* Hebrew *Noph*   ^b *18* Most manuscripts of the Masoretic Text; some manuscripts of the Masoretic Text, Dead Sea Scrolls and Vulgate *City of the Sun* (that is, Heliopolis)   ^c *3* That is, the upper Nile region; also in verse 5

Living Bible

those from Memphis are utterly deluded. They are the best you can find, but they have ruined Egypt with their foolish counsel. 14The Lord has sent a spirit of foolishness on them, so that all their suggestions are wrong; they make Egypt stagger like a sick drunkard. 15Egypt cannot be saved by anything or anybody—no one can show her the way.

16In that day the Egyptians will be as weak as women, cowering in fear beneath the upraised fist of God. 17Just to speak the name of Israel will strike deep terror in their hearts, for the Lord Almighty has laid his plans against them.

18At that time five of the cities of Egypt will follow the Lord Almighty and will begin to speak the Hebrew language.d One of these will be Heliopolis, "The City of the Sun." 19And there will be an altar to the Lord in the heart of Egypt in those days, and a monument to the Lord at its border. 20This will be for a sign of loyalty to the Lord Almighty; then when they cry to the Lord for help against those who oppress them, he will send them a Savior—and he shall deliver them.

21In that day the Lord will make himself known to the Egyptians. Yes, they will know the Lord and give their sacrifices and offerings to him; they will make promises to God and keep them. 22The Lord will smite Egypt and then restore her! For the Egyptians will turn to the Lord and he will listen to their plea and heal them.

23In that day Egypt and Iraqe will be connected by a highway, and the Egyptians and the Iraqi will move freely back and forth between their lands, and they shall worship the same God. 24And Israel will be their ally; the three will be together, and Israel will be a blessing to them. 25For the Lord will bless Egypt and Iraq because of their friendshipf with Israel. He will say, "Blessed be Egypt, my people; blessed be Iraq, the land I have made; blessed be Israel, my inheritance!"

20 IN THE year when Sargon, king of Assyria, sent the commander-in-chief of his army against the Philistine city of Ashdod and captured it, 2the Lord told Isaiah, the son of Amoz, to take off his clothing, including his shoes, and to walk around naked and barefoot. And Isaiah did as he was told.

3Then the Lord said, My servant Isaiah, who has been walking naked and barefoot for the last three years, is a symbol of the terrible troubles I will bring upon Egypt and Ethiopia. 4For the king of Assyria will take away the Egyptians and Ethiopians as prisoners, making them walk naked and barefoot, both young and old, their buttocks uncovered, to the shame of Egypt. 5, 6Then how dismayed the Philistinesg will be, who counted on "Ethiopia's power" and their "glorious ally," Egypt! And they will say, "If this can happen to Egypt, what chance have we?"

New Revised Standard

13 The princes of Zoan have become fools,
      and the princes of Memphis are deluded;
    those who are the cornerstones of its tribes
      have led Egypt astray.
14 The LORD has poured into themh
      a spirit of confusion;
    and they have made Egypt stagger in all its
      doings
    as a drunkard staggers around in vomit.
15 Neither head nor tail, palm branch or reed,
      will be able to do anything for Egypt.

16 On that day the Egyptians will be like women, and tremble with fear before the hand that the LORD of hosts raises against them. 17And the land of Judah will become a terror to the Egyptians; everyone to whom it is mentioned will fear because of the plan that the LORD of hosts is planning against them.

Egypt, Assyria, and Israel Blessed

18 On that day there will be five cities in the land of Egypt that speak the language of Canaan and swear allegiance to the LORD of hosts. One of these will be called the City of the Sun.

19 On that day there will be an altar to the LORD in the center of the land of Egypt, and a pillar to the LORD at its border. 20It will be a sign and a witness to the LORD of hosts in the land of Egypt; when they cry to the LORD because of oppressors, he will send them a savior, and will defend and deliver them. 21The LORD will make himself known to the Egyptians; and the Egyptians will know the LORD on that day, and will worship with sacrifice and burnt offering, and they will make vows to the LORD and perform them. 22The LORD will strike Egypt, striking and healing; they will return to the LORD, and he will listen to their supplications and heal them.

23 On that day there will be a highway from Egypt to Assyria, and the Assyrian will come into Egypt, and the Egyptian into Assyria, and the Egyptians will worship with the Assyrians.

24 On that day Israel will be the third with Egypt and Assyria, a blessing in the midst of the earth, 25whom the LORD of hosts has blessed, saying, "Blessed be Egypt my people, and Assyria the work of my hands, and Israel my heritage."

Isaiah Dramatizes the Conquest of Egypt and Ethiopia

20 IN THE year that the commander-in-chief, who was sent by King Sargon of Assyria, came to Ashdod and fought against it and took it— 2at that time the LORD had spoken to Isaiah son of Amoz, saying, "Go, and loose the sackcloth from your loins and take your sandals off your feet," and he had done so, walking naked and barefoot. 3Then the LORD said, "Just as my servant Isaiah has walked naked and barefoot for three years as a sign and a portent against Egypt and Ethiopia,i 4so shall the king of Assyria lead away the Egyptians as captives and the Ethiopiansj as exiles, both the young and the old, naked and barefoot, with buttocks uncovered, to the shame of Egypt. 5And they shall be dismayed and confounded because of Ethiopiai their hope and of Egypt their boast. 6In that day the inhabitants of this coastland will say, 'See, this is what has happened to those in whom we hoped and to whom we fled for help and deliverance from the king of Assyria! And we, how shall we escape?' "

---

d 19:18 the Hebrew language, literally, "the language of Canaan."
e 19:23 Iraq, literally, "Assyria."   f 19:25 because of their friendship, implied.   g 20:5, 6 Philistines, literally, "inhabitants of the coastland."

h Gk Compare Tg: Heb it   i Or Nubia; Heb Cush   j Or Nubians; Heb Cushites

King James

21 THE BURDEN of the desert of the sea. As whirlwinds in the south pass through; *so* it cometh from the desert, from a terrible land.

2A grievous vision is declared unto me; the treacherous dealer dealeth treacherously, and the spoiler spoileth. Go up, O Elam: besiege, O Media; all the sighing thereof have I made to cease.

3Therefore are my loins filled with pain: pangs have taken hold upon me, as the pangs of a woman that travaileth: I was bowed down at the hearing *of it;* I was dismayed at the seeing *of it.*

4My heart panted, fearfulness affrighted me: the night of my pleasure hath he turned into fear unto me.

5Prepare the table, watch in the watchtower, eat, drink: arise, ye princes, *and* anoint the shield.

6For thus hath the Lord said unto me, Go, set a watchman, let him declare what he seeth.

7And he saw a chariot *with* a couple of horsemen, a chariot of asses, *and* a chariot of camels; and he hearkened diligently with much heed:

8And he cried, A lion: My lord, I stand continually upon the watchtower in the daytime, and I am set in my ward whole nights:

9And, behold, here cometh a chariot of men, *with* a couple of horsemen. And he answered and said, Babylon is fallen, is fallen; and all the graven images of her gods he hath broken unto the ground.

10O my threshing, and the corn of my floor: that which I have heard of the LORD of hosts, the God of Israel, have I declared unto you.

11¶ The burden of Dumah. He calleth to me out of Seir, Watchman, what of the night? Watchman, what of the night?

12The watchman said, The morning cometh, and also the night: if ye will inquire, inquire ye: return, come.

13¶ The burden upon Arabia. In the forest in Arabia shall ye lodge, O ye travelling companies of Dedanim.

New International

A Prophecy Against Babylon

21 AN ORACLE concerning the Desert by the Sea:

Like whirlwinds sweeping through the
    southland,
an invader comes from the desert,
    from a land of terror.

2A dire vision has been shown to me:
    The traitor betrays, the looter takes loot.
Elam, attack! Media, lay siege!
    I will bring to an end all the groaning she
        caused.

3At this my body is racked with pain,
    pangs seize me, like those of a woman in
        labor;
I am staggered by what I hear,
    I am bewildered by what I see.
4My heart falters,
    fear makes me tremble;
the twilight I longed for
    has become a horror to me.

5They set the tables,
    they spread the rugs,
    they eat, they drink!
Get up, you officers,
    oil the shields!

6This is what the Lord says to me:

"Go, post a lookout
    and have him report what he sees.
7When he sees chariots
    with teams of horses,
riders on donkeys
    or riders on camels,
let him be alert,
    fully alert."

8And the lookout[a] shouted,

"Day after day, my lord, I stand on the
    watchtower;
every night I stay at my post.
9Look, here comes a man in a chariot
    with a team of horses.
And he gives back the answer:
    'Babylon has fallen, has fallen!
All the images of its gods
    lie shattered on the ground!' "

10O my people, crushed on the threshing floor,
    I tell you what I have heard
from the LORD Almighty,
    from the God of Israel.

A Prophecy Against Edom

11An oracle concerning Dumah[b]:

Someone calls to me from Seir,
    "Watchman, what is left of the night?
    Watchman, what is left of the night?"
12The watchman replies,
    "Morning is coming, but also the night.
If you would ask, then ask;
    and come back yet again."

A Prophecy Against Arabia

13An oracle concerning Arabia:

You caravans of Dedanites,
    who camp in the thickets of Arabia,

---

a 8 *Dead Sea Scrolls and Syriac; Masoretic Text* A lion   b 11 *Dumah means*
silence or stillness, a wordplay on *Edom.*

Living Bible

21 THIS IS God's message concerning Babylon:[c] Disaster is roaring down upon you from the terrible desert, like a whirlwind sweeping from the Negeb. 2I see an awesome vision: oh, the horror of it all! God is telling me what he is going to do. I see you plundered and destroyed. Elamites and Medes will take part in the siege. Babylon will fall, and the groaning of all the nations she enslaved will end. 3My stomach constricts and burns with pain; sharp pangs of horror are upon me, like the pangs of a woman giving birth to a child. I faint when I hear what God is planning; I am terrified, blinded with dismay. 4My mind reels; my heart races; I am gripped by awful fear. All rest at night—so pleasant once—is gone; I lie awake, trembling.

5Look! They are preparing a great banquet! They load the tables with food; they pull up their chairs[d] to eat. . . . Quick, quick, grab your shields and prepare for battle! You are being attacked![e]

6, 7Meanwhile (in my vision)[f] the Lord had told me, "Put a watchman on the city wall to shout out what he sees. When he sees riders in pairs on donkeys and camels,[g] tell him, 'This is it!'"

8, 9So I put the watchman on the wall, and at last he shouted, "Sir, day after day and night after night I have been here at my post. Now at last—look! Here come riders in pairs!"

Then I heard a Voice shout out, "Babylon is fallen, is fallen; and all the idols of Babylon lie broken on the ground."

10O my people, threshed and winnowed, I have told you all that the Lord Almighty, the God of Israel, has said.

11This is God's message to Edom:[h]

Someone from among you keeps calling, calling to me: "Watchman, what of the night? Watchman, what of the night? How much time is left?" 12The watchman replies, "Your judgment day is dawning now. Turn again to God, so that I can give you better news. Seek for him, then come and ask again!"

13This is God's message concerning Arabia:

O caravans from Dedan, you will hide in the deserts of Arabia. 14O people of Tema, bring food and water to

New Revised Standard

Oracles concerning Babylon, Edom, and Arabia

21 THE ORACLE concerning the wilderness of the sea.[i]

As whirlwinds in the Negeb sweep on,
　it comes from the desert,
　from a terrible land.
2 A stern vision is told to me;
　the betrayer betrays,
　and the destroyer destroys.
Go up, O Elam,
　lay siege, O Media;
all the sighing she has caused
　I bring to an end.
3 Therefore my loins are filled with anguish;
　pangs have seized me,
　like the pangs of a woman in labor;
I am bowed down so that I cannot hear,
　I am dismayed so that I cannot see.
4 My mind reels, horror has appalled me;
　the twilight I longed for
　has been turned for me into trembling.
5 They prepare the table,
　they spread the rugs,
　they eat, they drink.
Rise up, commanders,
　oil the shield!
6 For thus the Lord said to me:
"Go, post a lookout,
　let him announce what he sees.
7 When he sees riders, horsemen in pairs,
　riders on donkeys, riders on camels,
let him listen diligently,
　very diligently."
8 Then the watcher[j] called out:
"Upon a watchtower I stand, O Lord,
　continually by day,
and at my post I am stationed
　throughout the night.
9 Look, there they come, riders,
　horsemen in pairs!"
Then he responded,
　"Fallen, fallen is Babylon;
and all the images of her gods
　lie shattered on the ground."
10 O my threshed and winnowed one,
　what I have heard from the Lord of hosts,
　the God of Israel, I announce to you.

11 The oracle concerning Dumah.

One is calling to me from Seir,
"Sentinel, what of the night?
　Sentinel, what of the night?"
12 The sentinel says:
"Morning comes, and also the night.
　If you will inquire, inquire;
　come back again."

13 The oracle concerning the desert plain.

In the scrub of the desert plain you will lodge,
　O caravans of Dedanites.

---

c 21:1 *Babylon*, implied in v 9. 	d 21:5 *pull up their chairs*, literally, "spread out the rugs." 	e 21:5 *you are being attacked*. More details of the feast are seen in Daniel, ch 5, as this prophecy was fulfilled when Cyrus captured the city. 	f 21:6, 7 *in my vision*, implied. 	g 21:6, 7 *riders in pairs on donkeys and camels*, literally, "When he sees a troop, horsemen in pairs, riders on asses, riders on camels." Possibly the meaning is that the asses and camels were paired for the attack. The city fell to the Medes and Persians, perhaps represented by these paired riders. 	h 21:11 *Edom*, literally, "Dumah."

i Q Ms: MT *a lion*

King James

14The inhabitants of the land of Tema brought water to him that was thirsty, they prevented with their bread him that fled.

15For they fled from the swords, from the drawn sword, and from the bent bow, and from the grievousness of war.

16For thus hath the Lord said unto me, Within a year, according to the years of an hireling, and all the glory of Kedar shall fail:

17And the residue of the number of archers, the mighty men of the children of Kedar, shall be diminished: for the LORD God of Israel hath spoken *it*.

22 THE BURDEN of the valley of vision. What aileth thee now, that thou art wholly gone up to the housetops?

2Thou that art full of stirs, a tumultuous city, a joyous city: thy slain *men are* not slain with the sword, nor dead in battle.

3All thy rulers are fled together, they are bound by the archers: all that are found in thee are bound together, *which* have fled from far.

4Therefore said I, Look away from me; I will weep bitterly, labour not to comfort me, because of the spoiling of the daughter of my people.

5For *it is* a day of trouble, and of treading down, and of perplexity by the Lord GOD of hosts in the valley of vision, breaking down the walls, and of crying to the mountains.

6And Elam bare the quiver with chariots of men *and* horsemen, and Kir uncovered the shield.

7And it shall come to pass, *that* thy choicest valleys shall be full of chariots, and the horsemen shall set themselves in array at the gate.

8¶ And he discovered the covering of Judah, and thou didst look in that day to the armour of the house of the forest.

9Ye have seen also the breaches of the city of David, that they are many: and ye gathered together the waters of the lower pool.

10And ye have numbered the houses of Jerusalem, and the houses have ye broken down to fortify the wall.

11Ye made also a ditch between the two walls for the water of the old pool: but ye have not looked unto the maker thereof, neither had respect unto him that fashioned it long ago.

12And in that day did the Lord GOD of hosts call to weeping, and to mourning, and to baldness, and to girding with sackcloth:

13And behold joy and gladness, slaying oxen, and killing sheep, eating flesh, and drinking wine: let us eat and drink; for tomorrow we shall die.

14And it was revealed in mine ears by the LORD of hosts, Surely this iniquity shall not be purged from you till ye die, saith the Lord GOD of hosts.

New International

14　bring water for the thirsty;
　you who live in Tema,
　　bring food for the fugitives.
15They flee from the sword,
　from the drawn sword,
　from the bent bow
　and from the heat of battle.
16This is what the Lord says to me: "Within one year, as a servant bound by contract would count it, all the pomp of Kedar will come to an end. 17The survivors of the bowmen, the warriors of Kedar, will be few." The LORD, the God of Israel, has spoken.

A Prophecy About Jerusalem

22 AN ORACLE concerning the Valley of Vision:

　What troubles you now,
　　that you have all gone up on the roofs,
2O town full of commotion,
　O city of tumult and revelry?
　Your slain were not killed by the sword,
　　nor did they die in battle.
3All your leaders have fled together;
　they have been captured without using the
　　bow.
All you who were caught were taken prisoner
　　together,
　having fled while the enemy was still far
　　away.
4Therefore I said, "Turn away from me;
　let me weep bitterly.
Do not try to console me
　over the destruction of my people."

5The Lord, the LORD Almighty, has a day
　of tumult and trampling and terror
　in the Valley of Vision,
　a day of battering down walls
　and of crying out to the mountains.
6Elam takes up the quiver,
　with her charioteers and horses;
　Kir uncovers the shield.
7Your choicest valleys are full of chariots,
　and horsemen are posted at the city gates;
8　the defenses of Judah are stripped away.

And you looked in that day
　to the weapons in the Palace of the Forest;
9you saw that the City of David
　had many breaches in its defenses;
you stored up water
　in the Lower Pool.
10You counted the buildings in Jerusalem
　and tore down houses to strengthen the wall.
11You built a reservoir between the two walls
　for the water of the Old Pool,
but you did not look to the One who made it,
　or have regard for the One who planned it
　　long ago.

12The Lord, the LORD Almighty,
　called you on that day
to weep and to wail,
　to tear out your hair and put on sackcloth.
13But see, there is joy and revelry,
　slaughtering of cattle and killing of sheep,
　eating of meat and drinking of wine!
"Let us eat and drink," you say,
　"for tomorrow we die!"

14The LORD Almighty has revealed this in my hearing: "Till your dying day this sin will not be atoned for," says the Lord, the LORD Almighty.

Living Bible

these weary fugitives! 15They have fled from drawn swords and sharp arrows and the terrors of war! 16"But a long year from now,"a says the Lord, "the great power of their enemy,b the mighty tribe of Kedar, will end. 17Only a few of its stalwart archers will survive." The Lord, the God of Israel, has spoken.

22 THIS IS God's message concerning Jerusalem:c
What is happening? Where is everyone going? Why are they running to the rooftops? What are they looking at? 2The whole city is in terrible uproar. What's the trouble in this busy, happy city?d Bodies! Lying everywhere, slain by plaguee and not by sword. 3All your leaders flee; they surrender without resistance. The people slip away but they are captured, too. 4Let me alone to weep. Don't try to comfort me—let me cry for my people as I watch them being destroyed. 5Oh, what a day of crushing trouble! What a day of confusion and terror from the Lord God of heaven's armies! The walls of Jerusalem are breached and the cry of death echoes from the mountainsides. 6, 7Elamites are the archers; Syrians drive the chariots; the men of Kir hold up the shields. They fill your choicest valleys and crowd against your gates.

8God has removed his protecting care. You run to the armory for your weapons! 9, 10, 11You inspect the walls of Jerusalem to see what needs repair! You check over the houses and tear some down for stone for fixing walls. Between the city walls, you build a reservoir for water from the lower pool! But all your feverish plans will not avail, for you never ask for help from God, who lets this come upon you. He is the one who planned it long ago. 12The Lord God called you to repent, to weep and mourn and shave your heads in sorrow for your sins, and to wear clothes made of sackcloth to show your remorse. 13But instead, you sing and dance and play, and feast and drink. "Let us eat, drink, and be merry," you say: "What's the difference, for tomorrow we die." 14The Lord Almighty has revealed to me that this sin will never be forgiven you until the day you die.

New Revised Standard

14 Bring water to the thirsty,
     meet the fugitive with bread,
     O inhabitants of the land of Tema.
15 For they have fled from the swords,
     from the drawn sword,
     from the bent bow,
     and from the stress of battle.
16 For thus the Lord said to me: Within a year, according to the years of a hired worker, all the glory of Kedar will come to an end; 17and the remaining bows of Kedar's warriors will be few; for the LORD, the God of Israel, has spoken.

A Warning of Destruction of Jerusalem

22 THE ORACLE concerning the valley of vision.

What do you mean that you have gone up,
     all of you, to the housetops,
2 you that are full of shoutings,
     tumultuous city, exultant town?
Your slain are not slain by the sword,
     nor are they dead in battle.
3 Your rulers have all fled together;
     they were captured without the use of a
         bow.f
All of you who were found were captured,
     though they had fled far away.g
4 Therefore I said:
Look away from me,
     let me weep bitter tears;
do not try to comfort me
     for the destruction of my beloved people.

5 For the Lord GOD of hosts has a day
     of tumult and trampling and confusion
     in the valley of vision,
a battering down of walls
     and a cry for help to the mountains.
6 Elam bore the quiver
     with chariots and cavalry,h
     and Kir uncovered the shield.
7 Your choicest valleys were full of chariots,
     and the cavalry took their stand at the gates.
8 He has taken away the covering of Judah.

On that day you looked to the weapons of the House of the Forest, 9and you saw that there were many breaches in the city of David, and you collected the waters of the lower pool. 10You counted the houses of Jerusalem, and you broke down the houses to fortify the wall. 11You made a reservoir between the two walls for the water of the old pool. But you did not look to him who did it, or have regard for him who planned it long ago.

12 In that day the Lord GOD of hosts
     called to weeping and mourning,
     to baldness and putting on sackcloth;
13 but instead there was joy and festivity,
     killing oxen and slaughtering sheep,
     eating meat and drinking wine.
"Let us eat and drink,
     for tomorrow we die."
14 The LORD of hosts has revealed himself in my ears:
Surely this iniquity will not be forgiven you
     until you die,
     says the Lord GOD of hosts.

---

a 21:16 But a long year from now. The Dead Sea manuscript reads, "within three years, according to the year of a hireling," like 16:14.   b 21:16 the great power of their enemy, implied.   c 22:1 Jerusalem, literally, "The Valley of Vision."   d 22:2 happy city, implied.   e 22:2 slain by plague, implied.

f Or without their bows   g Gk Syr Vg: Heb fled from far away   h Meaning of Heb uncertain

King James

15¶ Thus saith the Lord GOD of hosts, Go, get thee unto this treasurer, *even* unto Shebna, which *is* over the house, *and say,*

16What hast thou here? and whom hast thou here, that thou hast hewed thee out a sepulchre here, *as* he that heweth him out a sepulchre on high, *and* that graveth an habitation for himself in a rock?

17Behold, the LORD will carry thee away with a mighty captivity, and will surely cover thee.

18He will surely violently turn and toss thee *like* a ball into a large country: there shalt thou die, and there the chariots of thy glory *shall be* the shame of thy lord's house.

19And I will drive thee from thy station, and from thy state shall he pull thee down.

20¶ And it shall come to pass in that day, that I will call my servant Eliakim the son of Hilkiah:

21And I will clothe him with thy robe, and strengthen him with thy girdle, and I will commit thy government into his hand: and he shall be a father to the inhabitants of Jerusalem, and to the house of Judah.

22And the key of the house of David will I lay upon his shoulder; so he shall open, and none shall shut; and he shall shut, and none shall open.

23And I will fasten him *as* a nail in a sure place; and he shall be for a glorious throne to his father's house.

24And they shall hang upon him all the glory of his father's house, the offspring and the issue, all vessels of small quantity, from the vessels of cups, even to all the vessels of flagons.

25In that day, saith the LORD of hosts, shall the nail that is fastened in the sure place be removed, and be cut down, and fall; and the burden that *was* upon it shall be cut off: for the LORD hath spoken *it.*

23 THE BURDEN of Tyre. Howl, ye ships of Tarshish; for it is laid waste, so that there is no house, no entering in: from the land of Chittim it is revealed to them.

2Be still, ye inhabitants of the isle; thou whom the merchants of Zidon, that pass over the sea, have replenished.

3And by great waters the seed of Sihor, the harvest of the river, *is* her revenue; and she is a mart of nations.

4Be thou ashamed, O Zidon: for the sea hath spoken, *even* the strength of the sea, saying, I travail not, nor bring forth children, neither do I nourish up young men, *nor* bring up virgins.

5As at the report concerning Egypt, *so* shall they be sorely pained at the report of Tyre.

6Pass ye over to Tarshish; howl, ye inhabitants of the isle.

New International

15This is what the Lord, the LORD Almighty, says:

"Go, say to this steward,
  to Shebna, who is in charge of the palace:
16What are you doing here and who gave you
    permission
  to cut out a grave for yourself here,
hewing your grave on the height
  and chiseling your resting place in the rock?

17"Beware, the LORD is about to take firm hold of
    you
  and hurl you away, O you mighty man.
18He will roll you up tightly like a ball
  and throw you into a large country.
There you will die
  and there your splendid chariots will
    remain—
  you disgrace to your master's house!
19I will depose you from your office,
  and you will be ousted from your position.

20"In that day I will summon my servant, Eliakim son of Hilkiah. 21I will clothe him with your robe and fasten your sash around him and hand your authority over to him. He will be a father to those who live in Jerusalem and to the house of Judah. 22I will place on his shoulder the key to the house of David; what he opens no one can shut, and what he shuts no one can open. 23I will drive him like a peg into a firm place; he will be a seat[a] of honor for the house of his father. 24All the glory of his family will hang on him: its offspring and offshoots—all its lesser vessels, from the bowls to all the jars.

25"In that day," declares the LORD Almighty, "the peg driven into the firm place will give way; it will be sheared off and will fall; and the load hanging on it will be cut down." The LORD has spoken.

A Prophecy About Tyre

23 AN ORACLE concerning Tyre:

Wail, O ships of Tarshish!
For Tyre is destroyed
  and left without house or harbor.
From the land of Cyprus[b]
  word has come to them.

2Be silent, you people of the island
  and you merchants of Sidon,
    whom the seafarers have enriched.
3On the great waters
  came the grain of the Shihor;
the harvest of the Nile[c] was the revenue of
    Tyre,
  and she became the marketplace of the
    nations.

4Be ashamed, O Sidon, and you, O fortress of
    the sea,
  for the sea has spoken:
"I have neither been in labor nor given birth;
  I have neither reared sons nor brought up
    daughters."
5When word comes to Egypt,
  they will be in anguish at the report from
    Tyre.

6Cross over to Tarshish;
  wail, you people of the island.

---

a 23 Or *throne*   b 1 Hebrew *Kittim*   c 2,3 Masoretic Text; one Dead Sea Scroll *Sidon, / who cross over the sea; / your envoys* ³*are on the great waters. / The grain of the Shihor, / the harvest of the Nile,*

Living Bible

15, 16Furthermore, the same Lord God of the armies of heaven has told me this: Go and say to Shebna, the palace administrator: "And who do you think you are, building this beautiful sepulchre in the rock for yourself? 17For the Lord who allowed you to be clothed so gorgeously will hurl you away, sending you into captivity, O strong man! 18He will wad you up in his hands like a ball and toss you away into a distant, barren land; there you will die, O glorious one—you who disgrace your nation!

19"Yes, I will drive you out of office," says the Lord, "and pull you down from your high position. 20And then I will call my servant Eliakim, the son of Hilkiah, to replace you. 21He shall have your uniform and title and authority, and he will be a father to the people of Jerusalem and all Judah. 22I will give him responsibility over all my people; whatever he says will be done; none will be able to stop him. 23, 24I will make of him a strong and steady peg to support my people; they will load him with responsibility, and he will be an honor to his family name." 25But the Lord will pull out that other peg that seems to be so firmly fastened to the wall! It will come out and fall to the ground, and everything it supports will fall with it, for the Lord has spoken.

23 THIS IS God's message to Tyre: Weep, O ships of Tyre, returning home from distant lands!d Weep for your harbor, for it is gone! The rumors that you heard in Cyprus are all true. 2, 3Deathly silence is everywhere. Stillness reigns where once your hustling port was full of ships from Sidon, bringing merchandise from far across the ocean, from Egypt and along the Nile. You were the merchandise mart of the world. 4Be ashamed, O Sidon, stronghold of the sea. For you are childless now! 5When Egypt hears the news, there will be great sorrow. 6Flee to Tarshish, men of Tyre, weeping as you go. 7This silent ruin is all that's

New Revised Standard

Denunciation of Self-Seeking Officials

15 Thus says the Lord GOD of hosts: Come, go to this steward, to Shebna, who is master of the household, and say to him: 16What right do you have here? Who are your relatives here, that you have cut out a tomb here for yourself, cutting a tomb on the height, and carving a habitation for yourself in the rock? 17The LORD is about to hurl you away violently, my fellow. He will seize firm hold on you, 18whirl you round and round, and throw you like a ball into a wide land; there you shall die, and there your splendid chariots shall lie, O you disgrace to your master's house! 19I will thrust you from your office, and you will be pulled down from your post.

20 On that day I will call my servant Eliakim son of Hilkiah, 21and will clothe him with your robe and bind your sash on him. I will commit your authority to his hand, and he shall be a father to the inhabitants of Jerusalem and to the house of Judah. 22I will place on his shoulder the key of the house of David; he shall open, and no one shall shut; he shall shut, and no one shall open. 23I will fasten him like a peg in a secure place, and he will become a throne of honor to his ancestral house. 24And they will hang on him the whole weight of his ancestral house, the offspring and issue, every small vessel, from the cups to all the flagons. 25On that day, says the LORD of hosts, the peg that was fastened in a secure place will give way; it will be cut down and fall, and the load that was on it will perish, for the LORD has spoken.

An Oracle concerning Tyre

23 THE ORACLE concerning Tyre.

Wail, O ships of Tarshish,
  for your fortress is destroyed.e
When they came in from Cyprus
  they learned of it.
2 Be still, O inhabitants of the coast,
  O merchants of Sidon,
your messengers crossed over the seaf
3   and were on the mighty waters;
your revenue was the grain of Shihor,
  the harvest of the Nile;
you were the merchant of the nations.
4 Be ashamed, O Sidon, for the sea has spoken,
  the fortress of the sea, saying:
"I have neither labored nor given birth,
  I have neither reared young men
  nor brought up young women."
5 When the report comes to Egypt,
  they will be in anguish over the report about
    Tyre.
6 Cross over to Tarshish—
  wail, O inhabitants of the coast!

---

d 23:1 *Tyre.* Tyre was originally a colony of the mother-city, Sidon. Also in vs 4.

e Cn Compare verse 14: Heb *for it is destroyed, without houses*   f Q Ms: MT *crossing over the sea, they replenished you*

King James

7Is this your joyous *city,* whose antiquity *is* of ancient days? her own feet shall carry her afar off to sojourn.

8Who hath taken this counsel against Tyre, the crowning *city,* whose merchants *are* princes, whose traffickers *are* the honourable of the earth?

9The LORD of hosts hath purposed it, to stain the pride of all glory, *and* to bring into contempt all the honourable of the earth.

10Pass through thy land as a river, O daughter of Tarshish: *there is* no more strength.

11He stretched out his hand over the sea, he shook the kingdoms: the LORD hath given a commandment against the merchant *city,* to destroy the strong holds thereof.

12And he said, Thou shalt no more rejoice, O thou oppressed virgin, daughter of Zidon: arise, pass over to Chittim; there also shalt thou have no rest.

13Behold the land of the Chaldeans; this people was not, *till* the Assyrian founded it for them that dwell in the wilderness: they set up the towers thereof, they raised up the palaces thereof; *and* he brought it to ruin.

14Howl, ye ships of Tarshish: for your strength is laid waste.

15And it shall come to pass in that day, that Tyre shall be forgotten seventy years, according to the days of one king: after the end of seventy years shall Tyre sing as an harlot.

16Take an harp, go about the city, thou harlot that hast been forgotten; make sweet melody, sing many songs, that thou mayest be remembered.

17¶ And it shall come to pass after the end of seventy years, that the LORD will visit Tyre, and she shall turn to her hire, and shall commit fornication with all the kingdoms of the world upon the face of the earth.

18And her merchandise and her hire shall be holiness to the LORD: it shall not be treasured nor laid up; for her merchandise shall be for them that dwell before the LORD, to eat sufficiently, and for durable clothing.

24 BEHOLD, THE LORD maketh the earth empty, and maketh it waste, and turneth it upside down, and scattereth abroad the inhabitants thereof.

2And it shall be, as with the people, so with the priest; as with the servant, so with his master; as with the maid, so with her mistress; as with the buyer, so with the seller; as with the lender, so with the borrower; as with the taker of usury, so with the giver of usury to him.

3The land shall be utterly emptied, and utterly spoiled: for the LORD hath spoken this word.

New International

7Is this your city of revelry,
    the old, old city,
  whose feet have taken her
    to settle in far-off lands?
8Who planned this against Tyre,
    the bestower of crowns,
  whose merchants are princes,
    whose traders are renowned in the earth?
9The LORD Almighty planned it,
    to bring low the pride of all glory
  and to humble all who are renowned on the
    earth.

10Tilla your land as along the Nile,
    O Daughter of Tarshish,
  for you no longer have a harbor.
11The LORD has stretched out his hand over the
    sea
    and made its kingdoms tremble.
  He has given an order concerning Phoeniciab
    that her fortresses be destroyed.
12He said, "No more of your reveling,
    O Virgin Daughter of Sidon, now crushed!

  "Up, cross over to Cyprusc;
    even there you will find no rest."
13Look at the land of the Babylonians,d
    this people that is now of no account!
  The Assyrians have made it
    a place for desert creatures;
  they raised up their siege towers,
    they stripped its fortresses bare
    and turned it into a ruin.

14Wail, you ships of Tarshish;
    your fortress is destroyed!

15At that time Tyre will be forgotten for seventy years, the span of a king's life. But at the end of these seventy years, it will happen to Tyre as in the song of the prostitute:

16"Take up a harp, walk through the city,
    O prostitute forgotten;
  play the harp well, sing many a song,
    so that you will be remembered."

17At the end of seventy years, the LORD will deal with Tyre. She will return to her hire as a prostitute and will ply her trade with all the kingdoms on the face of the earth. 18Yet her profit and her earnings will be set apart for the LORD; they will not be stored up or hoarded. Her profits will go to those who live before the LORD, for abundant food and fine clothes.

The LORD's Devastation of the Earth

24 SEE, THE LORD is going to lay waste the earth
    and devastate it;
  he will ruin its face
    and scatter its inhabitants—
2it will be the same
    for priest as for people,
    for master as for servant,
    for mistress as for maid,
    for seller as for buyer,
    for borrower as for lender,
    for debtor as for creditor.
3The earth will be completely laid waste
    and totally plundered.
          The LORD has spoken this word.

a *10* Dead Sea Scrolls and some Septuagint manuscripts; Masoretic Text *Go through*   b *11* Hebrew *Canaan*   c *12* Hebrew *Kittim*   d *13* Or *Chaldeans*

Living Bible

left of your once joyous land. What a history was yours! Think of all the colonists you sent to distant lands!

8Who has brought this disaster on Tyre, empire builder and top trader of the world? 9The Commander of the armies of heaven has done it to destroy your pride and show his contempt for all the greatness of mankind. 10Sail on, O ships of Tarshish, for your harbor is gone. 11The Lord holds out his hand over the seas; he shakes the kingdoms of the earth; he has spoken out against this great merchant city, to destroy its strength.

12He says, "Never again, O dishonored virgin, daughter of Sidon, will you rejoice, will you be strong. Even if you flee to Cyprus, you will find no rest."

13It will be the Babylonians, not the Assyrians, who consign Tyre to the wild beasts. They will lay siege to it, raze its palaces and make it a heap of ruins. 14Wail, you ships that ply the oceans, for your home port is destroyed!

15,16For seventy years Tyre will be forgotten. Then, in the days of another king, the city will come back to life again; she will sing sweet songs as a harlot sings who, long absent from her lovers, walks the streets to look for them again and is remembered. 17Yes, after seventy years, the Lord will revive Tyre, but she will be no different than she was before; she will return again to all her evil ways around the world. 18Yet [the distant time will come whene] her businesses will give their profits to the Lord! They will not be hoarded but used for good food and fine clothes for the priests of the Lord!

24 LOOK! THE Lord is overturning the land of Judah and making it a vast wasteland of destruction. See how he is emptying out all its people and scattering them over the face of the earth. 2Priests and people, servants and masters, slave girls and mistresses, buyers and sellers, lenders and borrowers, bankers and debtors—none will be spared. 3The land will be completely emptied and looted. The Lord has spoken.

New Revised Standard

7 Is this your exultant city
     whose origin is from days of old,
   whose feet carried her
     to settle far away?
8 Who has planned this
     against Tyre, the bestower of crowns,
   whose merchants were princes,
     whose traders were the honored of
       the earth?
9 The LORD of hosts has planned it—
     to defile the pride of all glory,
     to shame all the honored of the earth.
10 Cross over to your own land,
      O ships off Tarshish;
    this is a harborg no more.
11 He has stretched out his hand over the sea,
      he has shaken the kingdoms;
    the LORD has given command concerning
        Canaan
      to destroy its fortresses.
12 He said:
    You will exult no longer,
      O oppressed virgin daughter Sidon;
    rise, cross over to Cyprus—
      even there you will have no rest.

13 Look at the land of the Chaldeans! This is the people; it was not Assyria. They destined Tyre for wild animals. They erected their siege towers, they tore down her palaces, they made her a ruin.h

14 Wail, O ships of Tarshish,
      for your fortress is destroyed.

15From that day Tyre will be forgotten for seventy years, the lifetime of one king. At the end of seventy years, it will happen to Tyre as in the song about the prostitute:

16 Take a harp,
      go about the city,
      you forgotten prostitute!
    Make sweet melody,
      sing many songs,
      that you may be remembered.

17At the end of seventy years, the LORD will visit Tyre, and she will return to her trade, and will prostitute herself with all the kingdoms of the world on the face of the earth. 18Her merchandise and her wages will be dedicated to the LORD; her profitsi will not be stored or hoarded, but her merchandise will supply abundant food and fine clothing for those who live in the presence of the LORD.

Impending Judgment on the Earth

24 NOW THE LORD is about to lay waste the
     earth and make it desolate,
   and he will twist its surface and scatter its
       inhabitants.
2 And it shall be, as with the people, so with
       the priest;
     as with the slave, so with his master;
     as with the maid, so with her mistress;
   as with the buyer, so with the seller;
     as with the lender, so with the borrower;
     as with the creditor, so with the debtor.
3 The earth shall be utterly laid waste and
       utterly despoiled;
     for the LORD has spoken this word.

---

e 23:18 the distant time will come. implied.

f Cn Compare Gk: Heb like the Nile, daughter g Cn: Heb restraint
h Meaning of Heb uncertain i Heb it

King James

⁴The earth mourneth *and* fadeth away, the world languisheth *and* fadeth away, the haughty people of the earth do languish.

⁵The earth also is defiled under the inhabitants thereof; because they have transgressed the laws, changed the ordinance, broken the everlasting covenant.

⁶Therefore hath the curse devoured the earth, and they that dwell therein are desolate: therefore the inhabitants of the earth are burned, and few men left.

⁷The new wine mourneth, the vine languisheth, all the merryhearted do sigh.

⁸The mirth of tabrets ceaseth, the noise of them that rejoice endeth, the joy of the harp ceaseth.

⁹They shall not drink wine with a song; strong drink shall be bitter to them that drink it.

¹⁰The city of confusion is broken down: every house is shut up, that no man may come in.

¹¹*There is* a crying for wine in the streets; all joy is darkened, the mirth of the land is gone.

¹²In the city is left desolation, and the gate is smitten with destruction.

¹³¶ When thus it shall be in the midst of the land among the people, *there shall be* as the shaking of an olive tree, *and* as the gleaning grapes when the vintage is done.

¹⁴They shall lift up their voice, they shall sing for the majesty of the LORD, they shall cry aloud from the sea.

¹⁵Wherefore glorify ye the LORD in the fires, *even* the name of the LORD God of Israel in the isles of the sea.

¹⁶¶ From the uttermost part of the earth have we heard songs, *even* glory to the righteous. But I said, My leanness, my leanness, woe unto me! the treacherous dealers have dealt treacherously; yea, the treacherous dealers have dealt very treacherously.

¹⁷Fear, and the pit, and the snare, *are* upon thee, O inhabitant of the earth.

¹⁸And it shall come to pass, *that* he who fleeth from the noise of the fear shall fall into the pit; and he that cometh up out of the midst of the pit shall be taken in the snare: for the windows from on high are open, and the foundations of the earth do shake.

¹⁹The earth is utterly broken down, the earth is clean dissolved, the earth is moved exceedingly.

²⁰The earth shall reel to and fro like a drunkard, and shall be removed like a cottage; and the transgression thereof shall be heavy upon it; and it shall fall, and not rise again.

²¹And it shall come to pass in that day, *that* the LORD shall punish the host of the high ones *that are* on high, and the kings of the earth upon the earth.

²²And they shall be gathered together, *as* prisoners are gathered in the pit, and shall be shut up in the prison, and after many days shall they be visited.

New International

⁴The earth dries up and withers,
  the world languishes and withers,
  the exalted of the earth languish.
⁵The earth is defiled by its people;
  they have disobeyed the laws,
  violated the statutes
  and broken the everlasting covenant.
⁶Therefore a curse consumes the earth;
  its people must bear their guilt.
Therefore earth's inhabitants are burned up,
  and very few are left.
⁷The new wine dries up and the vine withers;
  all the merrymakers groan.
⁸The gaiety of the tambourines is stilled,
  the noise of the revelers has stopped,
  the joyful harp is silent.
⁹No longer do they drink wine with a song;
  the beer is bitter to its drinkers.
¹⁰The ruined city lies desolate;
  the entrance to every house is barred.
¹¹In the streets they cry out for wine;
  all joy turns to gloom,
  all gaiety is banished from the earth.
¹²The city is left in ruins,
  its gate is battered to pieces.
¹³So will it be on the earth
  and among the nations,
as when an olive tree is beaten,
  or as when gleanings are left after the grape
    harvest.

¹⁴They raise their voices, they shout for joy;
  from the west they acclaim the LORD's
    majesty.
¹⁵Therefore in the east give glory to the LORD;
  exalt the name of the LORD, the God of
    Israel,
  in the islands of the sea.
¹⁶From the ends of the earth we hear singing:
  "Glory to the Righteous One."

But I said, "I waste away, I waste away!
  Woe to me!
The treacherous betray!
  With treachery the treacherous betray!"
¹⁷Terror and pit and snare await you,
  O people of the earth.
¹⁸Whoever flees at the sound of terror
  will fall into a pit;
whoever climbs out of the pit
  will be caught in a snare.

The floodgates of the heavens are opened,
  the foundations of the earth shake.
¹⁹The earth is broken up,
  the earth is split asunder,
  the earth is thoroughly shaken.
²⁰The earth reels like a drunkard,
  it sways like a hut in the wind;
so heavy upon it is the guilt of its rebellion
  that it falls—never to rise again.

²¹In that day the LORD will punish
  the powers in the heavens above
  and the kings on the earth below.
²²They will be herded together
  like prisoners bound in a dungeon;
they will be shut up in prison
  and be punished[a] after many days.

Living Bible

4, 5The land suffers for the sins of its people. The earth languishes, the crops wither, the skies refuse their rain. The land is defiled by crime; the people have twisted the laws of God and broken his everlasting commands. 6Therefore the curse of God is upon them; they are left desolate, destroyed by the drought. Few will be left alive.

7All the joys of life will go: the grape harvest will fail, the wine will be gone, the merrymakers will sigh and mourn. 8The melodious chords of the harp and timbrel are heard no more; the happy days are ended. 9No more are the joys of wine and song; strong drink turns bitter in the mouth.

10The city lies in chaos; every home and shop is locked up tight to keep out looters. 11Mobs form in the streets, crying for wine; joy has reached its lowest ebb; gladness has been banished from the land. 12The city is left in ruins; its gates are battered down. 13Throughout the landb the story is the same—only a remnant is left.

14But all who are left will shout and sing for joy; those in the west will praise the majesty of God, 15, 16and those in the east will respond with praise. Hear them singing to the Lord from the ends of the earth, singing glory to the Righteous One!

But my heart is heavy with grief, for evil still prevails and treachery is everywhere. 17Terror and the captivity of hell are still your lot, O men of the world. 18When you flee in terror you will fall into a pit, and if you escape from the pit you will step into a trap, for destruction falls from the heavens upon you; the world is shaken beneath you. 19The earth has broken down in utter collapse; everything is lost, abandoned and confused. 20The world staggers like a drunkard; it shakes like a tent in a storm. It falls and will not rise again, for the sins of the earth are very great.

21On that day the Lord will punish the fallen angels in the heavens, and the proud rulers of the nations on earth. 22They will be rounded up like prisoners and imprisoned in a dungeon until they are tried and condemned. 23Then the Lord of heaven's armies will mount

New Revised Standard

4 The earth dries up and withers,
    the world languishes and withers;
    the heavens languish together with the earth.
5 The earth lies polluted
    under its inhabitants;
for they have transgressed laws,
    violated the statutes,
    broken the everlasting covenant.
6 Therefore a curse devours the earth,
    and its inhabitants suffer for their guilt;
therefore the inhabitants of the earth dwindled,
    and few people are left.
7 The wine dries up,
    the vine languishes,
    all the merry-hearted sigh.
8 The mirth of the timbrels is stilled,
    the noise of the jubilant has ceased,
    the mirth of the lyre is stilled.
9 No longer do they drink wine with singing;
    strong drink is bitter to those who drink it.
10 The city of chaos is broken down,
    every house is shut up so that no one can
      enter.
11 There is an outcry in the streets for lack of
      wine;
    all joy has reached its eventide;
    the gladness of the earth is banished.
12 Desolation is left in the city,
    the gates are battered into ruins.
13 For thus it shall be on the earth
    and among the nations,
as when an olive tree is beaten,
    as at the gleaning when the grape harvest is
      ended.

14 They lift up their voices, they sing for joy;
    they shout from the west over the majesty
      of the Lord.
15 Therefore in the east give glory to the Lord;
    in the coastlands of the sea glorify the name
      of the Lord, the God of Israel.
16 From the ends of the earth we hear songs of
      praise,
    of glory to the Righteous One.
But I say, I pine away,
    I pine away. Woe is me!
For the treacherous deal treacherously,
    the treacherous deal very treacherously.

17 Terror, and the pit, and the snare
    are upon you, O inhabitant of the earth!
18 Whoever flees at the sound of the terror
    shall fall into the pit;
and whoever climbs out of the pit
    shall be caught in the snare.
For the windows of heaven are opened,
    and the foundations of the earth tremble.
19 The earth is utterly broken,
    the earth is torn asunder,
    the earth is violently shaken.
20 The earth staggers like a drunkard,
    it sways like a hut;
its transgression lies heavy upon it,
    and it falls, and will not rise again.

21 On that day the Lord will punish
    the host of heaven in heaven,
    and on earth the kings of the earth.
22 They will be gathered together
    like prisoners in a pit;
they will be shut up in a prison,
    and after many days they will be punished.

b 24:13 throughout the land, or possibly, "throughout the nations of the world."

King James

23Then the moon shall be confounded, and the sun ashamed, when the LORD of hosts shall reign in mount Zion, and in Jerusalem, and before his ancients gloriously.

25 O LORD, thou *art* my God; I will exalt thee, I will praise thy name; for thou hast done wonderful *things; thy* counsels of old *are* faithfulness *and* truth.

2For thou hast made of a city an heap; *of* a defenced city a ruin: a palace of strangers to be no city; it shall never be built.

3Therefore shall the strong people glorify thee, the city of the terrible nations shall fear thee.

4For thou hast been a strength to the poor, a strength to the needy in his distress, a refuge from the storm, a shadow from the heat, when the blast of the terrible ones *is* as a storm *against* the wall.

5Thou shalt bring down the noise of strangers, as the heat in a dry place; *even* the heat with the shadow of a cloud: the branch of the terrible ones shall be brought low.

6¶ And in this mountain shall the LORD of hosts make unto all people a feast of fat things, a feast of wines on the lees, of fat things full of marrow, of wines on the lees well refined.

7And he will destroy in this mountain the face of the covering cast over all people, and the veil that is spread over all nations.

8He will swallow up death in victory; and the Lord GOD will wipe away tears from off all faces; and the rebuke of his people shall he take away from off all the earth: for the LORD hath spoken *it*.

9¶ And it shall be said in that day, Lo, this *is* our God; we have waited for him, and he will save us: this *is* the LORD; we have waited for him, we will be glad and rejoice in his salvation.

10For in this mountain shall the hand of the LORD rest, and Moab shall be trodden down under him, even as straw is trodden down for the dunghill.

11And he shall spread forth his hands in the midst of them, as he that swimmeth spreadeth forth *his hands* to swim: and he shall bring down their pride together with the spoils of their hands.

12And the fortress of the high fort of thy walls shall he bring down, lay low, *and* bring to the ground, *even* to the dust.

New International

23The moon will be abashed, the sun ashamed;
  for the LORD Almighty will reign
on Mount Zion and in Jerusalem,
  and before its elders, gloriously.

Praise to the LORD

25 O LORD, you are my God;
  I will exalt you and praise your name,
for in perfect faithfulness
  you have done marvelous things,
  things planned long ago.

2You have made the city a heap of rubble,
  the fortified town a ruin,
  the foreigners' stronghold a city no more;
  it will never be rebuilt.

3Therefore strong peoples will honor you;
  cities of ruthless nations will revere you.

4You have been a refuge for the poor,
  a refuge for the needy in his distress,
  a shelter from the storm
  and a shade from the heat.
For the breath of the ruthless
  is like a storm driving against a wall
5 and like the heat of the desert.
You silence the uproar of foreigners;
  as heat is reduced by the shadow of a cloud,
  so the song of the ruthless is stilled.

6On this mountain the LORD Almighty will
    prepare
  a feast of rich food for all peoples,
a banquet of aged wine—
  the best of meats and the finest of wines.
7On this mountain he will destroy
  the shroud that enfolds all peoples,
the sheet that covers all nations;
8 he will swallow up death forever.
The Sovereign LORD will wipe away the tears
  from all faces;
he will remove the disgrace of his people
  from all the earth.
                    The LORD has spoken.

9In that day they will say,

"Surely this is our God;
  we trusted in him, and he saved us.
This is the LORD, we trusted in him;
  let us rejoice and be glad in his salvation."

10The hand of the LORD will rest on this
    mountain;
  but Moab will be trampled under him
  as straw is trampled down in the manure.
11They will spread out their hands in it,
  as a swimmer spreads out his hands to swim.
God will bring down their pride
  despite the cleverness[a] of their hands.
12He will bring down your high fortified walls
  and lay them low;
he will bring them down to the ground,
  to the very dust.

---

a *11* The meaning of the Hebrew for this word is uncertain.

Living Bible

his throne in Zion and rule gloriously in Jerusalem, in the sight of all the elders of his people. Such glory there will be that all the brightness of the sun and moon will seem to fade away.

25 O LORD, I will honor and praise your name, for you are my God; you do such wonderful things! You planned them long ago, and now you have accomplished them, just as you said! ²You turn mighty cities into heaps of ruins. The strongest forts are turned to rubble. Beautiful palaces in distant lands disappear and will never be rebuilt. ³Therefore strong nations will shake with fear before you; ruthless nations will obey and glorify your name.

⁴But to the poor, O Lord, you are a refuge from the storm, a shadow from the heat, a shelter from merciless men who are like a driving rain that melts down an earthen wall. ⁵As a hot, dry land is cooled by clouds, you will cool the pride of ruthless nations. ⁶Here on Mount Zion in Jerusalem, the Lord Almighty will spread a wondrous feast for everyone around the world—a delicious feast of good food, with clear, well-aged wine and choice beef. ⁷At that time he will remove the cloud of gloom, the pall of death that hangs over the earth; ⁸he will swallow up death forever. The Lord God will wipe away all tears and take away forever all insults and mockery against his land and people. The Lord has spoken—he will surely do it!

⁹In that day the people will proclaim, "This is our God, in whom we trust, for whom we waited. Now at last he is here." What a day of rejoicing! ¹⁰For the Lord's good hand will rest upon Jerusalem, and Moab will be crushed as straw beneath his feet and left to rot. ¹¹God will push them down just as a swimmer pushes down the water with his hands. He will end their pride and all their evil works. ¹²The high walls of Moab will be demolished and brought to dust.

New Revised Standard

23 Then the moon will be abashed,
       and the sun ashamed;
   for the LORD of hosts will reign
       on Mount Zion and in Jerusalem,
   and before his elders he will manifest his
       glory.

Praise for Deliverance from Oppression

25 O LORD, you are my God;
       I will exalt you, I will praise your name;
   for you have done wonderful things,
       plans formed of old, faithful and sure.
2   For you have made the city a heap,
       the fortified city a ruin;
   the palace of aliens is a city no more,
       it will never be rebuilt.
3   Therefore strong peoples will glorify you;
       cities of ruthless nations will fear you.
4   For you have been a refuge to the poor,
       a refuge to the needy in their distress,
       a shelter from the rainstorm and a shade
           from the heat.
   When the blast of the ruthless was like a
           winter rainstorm,
5   the noise of aliens like heat in a dry place,
   you subdued the heat with the shade of
           clouds;
       the song of the ruthless was stilled.

6   On this mountain the LORD of hosts will make
           for all peoples
       a feast of rich food, a feast of well-aged
           wines,
       of rich food filled with marrow, of
           well-aged wines strained clear.
7   And he will destroy on this mountain
       the shroud that is cast over all peoples,
       the sheet that is spread over all nations;
   he will swallow up death forever.
8   Then the Lord GOD will wipe away the tears
           from all faces,
       and the disgrace of his people he will take
           away from all the earth,
   for the LORD has spoken.
9   It will be said on that day,
       Lo, this is our God; we have waited for
           him, so that he might save us.
   This is the LORD for whom we have waited;
       let us be glad and rejoice in his salvation.
10 For the hand of the LORD will rest on this
           mountain.

   The Moabites shall be trodden down in their
           place
       as straw is trodden down in a dung-pit.
11 Though they spread out their hands in the
           midst of it,
       as swimmers spread out their hands to
           swim,
       their pride will be laid low despite the
           struggleᵇ of their hands.
12 The high fortifications of his walls will be
           brought down,
       laid low, cast to the ground, even to the
           dust.

ᵇ Meaning of Heb uncertain

King James

26 IN THAT day shall this song be sung in the land of Judah; We have a strong city; salvation will *God* appoint *for* walls and bulwarks.

2Open ye the gates, that the righteous nation which keepeth the truth may enter in.

3Thou wilt keep *him* in perfect peace, *whose* mind *is* stayed *on thee:* because he trusteth in thee.

4Trust ye in the LORD for ever: for in the LORD JEHO-VAH *is* everlasting strength:

5¶ For he bringeth down them that dwell on high; the lofty city, he layeth it low; he layeth it low, *even* to the ground; he bringeth it *even* to the dust.

6The foot shall tread it down, *even* the feet of the poor, *and* the steps of the needy.

7The way of the just *is* uprightness: thou, most upright, dost weigh the path of the just.

8Yea, in the way of thy judgments, O LORD, have we waited for thee; the desire of *our* soul *is* to thy name, and to the remembrance of thee.

9With my soul have I desired thee in the night; yea, with my spirit within me will I seek thee early: for when thy judgments *are* in the earth, the inhabitants of the world will learn righteousness.

10Let favour be shown to the wicked, *yet* will he not learn righteousness: in the land of uprightness will he deal unjustly, and will not behold the majesty of the LORD.

11LORD, *when* thy hand is lifted up, they will not see: *but* they shall see, and be ashamed for *their* envy at the people; yea, the fire of thine enemies shall devour them.

12¶ LORD, thou wilt ordain peace for us: for thou also hast wrought all our works in us.

13O LORD our God, *other* lords beside thee have had dominion over us: *but* by thee only will we make mention of thy name.

14*They are* dead, they shall not live; *they are* deceased, they shall not rise: therefore hast thou visited and destroyed them, and made all their memory to perish.

15Thou hast increased the nation, O LORD, thou hast increased the nation: thou art glorified: thou hadst removed *it* far *unto* all the ends of the earth.

16LORD, in trouble have they visited thee, they poured out a prayer *when* thy chastening *was* upon them.

17Like as a woman with child, *that* draweth near the time of her delivery, is in pain, *and* crieth out in her pangs; so have we been in thy sight, O LORD.

New International

A Song of Praise

26 IN THAT day this song will be sung in the land of Judah:

We have a strong city;
    God makes salvation
    its walls and ramparts.
2Open the gates
    that the righteous nation may enter,
    the nation that keeps faith.
3You will keep in perfect peace
    him whose mind is steadfast,
    because he trusts in you.
4Trust in the LORD forever,
    for the LORD, the LORD, is the Rock eternal.
5He humbles those who dwell on high,
    he lays the lofty city low;
  he levels it to the ground
    and casts it down to the dust.
6Feet trample it down—
    the feet of the oppressed,
    the footsteps of the poor.

7The path of the righteous is level;
    O upright One, you make the way of the
        righteous smooth.
8Yes, LORD, walking in the way of your laws,[a]
    we wait for you;
  your name and renown
    are the desire of our hearts.
9My soul yearns for you in the night;
    in the morning my spirit longs for you.
When your judgments come upon the earth,
    the people of the world learn righteousness.
10Though grace is shown to the wicked,
    they do not learn righteousness;
  even in a land of uprightness they go on doing
        evil
    and regard not the majesty of the LORD.
11O LORD, your hand is lifted high,
    but they do not see it.
Let them see your zeal for your people and be
        put to shame;
    let the fire reserved for your enemies
        consume them.

12LORD, you establish peace for us;
    all that we have accomplished you have done
        for us.
13O LORD, our God, other lords besides you have
        ruled over us,
    but your name alone do we honor.
14They are now dead, they live no more;
    those departed spirits do not rise.
You punished them and brought them to ruin;
    you wiped out all memory of them.
15You have enlarged the nation, O LORD;
    you have enlarged the nation.
You have gained glory for yourself;
    you have extended all the borders of the land.

16LORD, they came to you in their distress;
    when you disciplined them,
    they could barely whisper a prayer.[b]
17As a woman with child and about to give birth
    writhes and cries out in her pain,
    so were we in your presence, O LORD.

---

a 8 Or *judgments*   b 16 The meaning of the Hebrew for this clause is uncertain.

Living Bible

26 LISTEN TO them singing! In that day the whole land of Judah will sing this song:
"Our city is strong! We are surrounded by the walls of his salvation!" ²Open the gates to everyone, for all may enter in who love the Lord. ³He will keep in perfect peace all those who trust in him, whose thoughts turn often to the Lord! ⁴Trust in the Lord God always, for in the Lord Jehovah is your everlasting strength. ⁵He humbles the proud and brings the haughty city to the dust; its walls come crashing down. ⁶He presents it to the poor and needy for their use.

⁷But for good men the path is not uphill and rough! God does not give them a rough and treacherous path, but smooths the road before them. ⁸O Lord, we love to do your will! Our hearts' desire is to glorify your name. ⁹All night long I search for you; earnestly I seek for God; for only when you come in judgment on the earth to punish it will people turn away from wickedness and do what is right.

¹⁰Your kindness to the wicked doesn't make them good; they keep on doing wrong and take no notice of your majesty. ¹¹They do not listen when you threaten; they will not look to see your upraised fist. Show them how much you love your people. Perhaps then they will be ashamed! Yes, let them be burned up by the fire reserved for your enemies.

¹²Lord, grant us peace; for all we have and are has come from you. ¹³O Lord our God, once we worshiped other gods; but now we worship you alone. ¹⁴Those we served before are dead and gone; never again will they return. You came against them and destroyed them, and they are long forgotten. ¹⁵O praise the Lord! He has made our nation very great. He has widened the boundaries of our land!

¹⁶Lord, in their distress they sought for you. When your punishment was on them, they poured forth a whispered prayer. ¹⁷How we missed your presence, Lord! We suffered as a woman giving birth, who cries and writhes in pain. ¹⁸We too have writhed in agony, but all

New Revised Standard

Judah's Song of Victory

26 ON THAT day this song will be sung in the land of Judah:
We have a strong city;
  he sets up victory
  like walls and bulwarks.
2 Open the gates,
  so that the righteous nation that keeps faith
  may enter in.
3 Those of steadfast mind you keep in peace—
  in peace because they trust in you.
4 Trust in the LORD forever,
  for in the LORD GOD[c]
  you have an everlasting rock.
5 For he has brought low
  the inhabitants of the height;
  the lofty city he lays low.
He lays it low to the ground,
  casts it to the dust.
6 The foot tramples it,
  the feet of the poor,
  the steps of the needy.

7 The way of the righteous is level;
  O Just One, you make smooth the path of
    the righteous.
8 In the path of your judgments,
  O LORD, we wait for you;
your name and your renown
  are the soul's desire.
9 My soul yearns for you in the night,
  my spirit within me earnestly seeks you.
For when your judgments are in the earth,
  the inhabitants of the world learn
    righteousness.
10 If favor is shown to the wicked,
  they do not learn righteousness;
in the land of uprightness they deal perversely
  and do not see the majesty of the LORD.
11 O LORD, your hand is lifted up,
  but they do not see it.
Let them see your zeal for your people, and
  be ashamed.
Let the fire for your adversaries consume
  them.
12 O LORD, you will ordain peace for us,
  for indeed, all that we have done, you have
    done for us.
13 O LORD our God,
  other lords besides you have ruled over us,
  but we acknowledge your name alone.
14 The dead do not live;
  shades do not rise—
because you have punished and destroyed
  them,
  and wiped out all memory of them.
15 But you have increased the nation, O LORD,
  you have increased the nation; you are
    glorified;
  you have enlarged all the borders of the
    land.

16 O LORD, in distress they sought you,
  they poured out a prayer[d]
  when your chastening was on them.
17 Like a woman with child,
  who writhes and cries out in her pangs
  when she is near her time,
so were we because of you, O LORD;

c Heb *in Yah, the LORD*   d Meaning of Heb uncertain

King James

¹⁸We have been with child, we have been in pain, we have as it were brought forth wind; we have not wrought any deliverance in the earth; neither have the inhabitants of the world fallen.

¹⁹Thy dead *men* shall live, *together with* my dead body shall they arise. Awake and sing, ye that dwell in dust: for thy dew *is as* the dew of herbs, and the earth shall cast out the dead.

²⁰¶ Come, my people, enter thou into thy chambers, and shut thy doors about thee: hide thyself as it were for a little moment, until the indignation be overpast.

²¹For, behold, the LORD cometh out of his place to punish the inhabitants of the earth for their iniquity: the earth also shall disclose her blood, and shall no more cover her slain.

27 IN THAT day the LORD with his sore and great and strong sword shall punish leviathan the piercing serpent, even leviathan that crooked serpent; and he shall slay the dragon that *is* in the sea.

²In that day sing ye unto her, A vineyard of red wine.

³I the LORD do keep it; I will water it every moment: lest *any* hurt it, I will keep it night and day.

⁴Fury *is* not in me: who would set the briers *and* thorns against me in battle? I would go through them, I would burn them together.

⁵Or let him take hold of my strength, *that* he may make peace with me; *and* he shall make peace with me.

⁶He shall cause them that come of Jacob to take root: Israel shall blossom and bud, and fill the face of the world with fruit.

⁷¶ Hath he smitten him, as he smote those that smote him? *or* is he slain according to the slaughter of them that are slain by him?

⁸In measure, when it shooteth forth, thou wilt debate with it: he stayeth his rough wind in the day of the east wind.

⁹By this therefore shall the iniquity of Jacob be purged; and this *is* all the fruit to take away his sin; when he maketh all the stones of the altar as chalkstones that are beaten in sunder, the groves and images shall not stand up.

¹⁰Yet the defenced city *shall be* desolate, *and* the habitation forsaken, and left like a wilderness: there shall the calf feed, and there shall he lie down, and consume the branches thereof.

New International

¹⁸We were with child, we writhed in pain,
  but we gave birth to wind.
We have not brought salvation to the earth;
  we have not given birth to people of the
    world.

¹⁹But your dead will live;
  their bodies will rise.
You who dwell in the dust,
  wake up and shout for joy.
Your dew is like the dew of the morning;
  the earth will give birth to her dead.

²⁰Go, my people, enter your rooms
  and shut the doors behind you;
hide yourselves for a little while
  until his wrath has passed by.
²¹See, the LORD is coming out of his dwelling
  to punish the people of the earth for their
    sins.
The earth will disclose the blood shed upon her;
  she will conceal her slain no longer.

Deliverance of Israel

27 IN THAT day,

  the LORD will punish with his sword,
    his fierce, great and powerful sword,
Leviathan the gliding serpent,
  Leviathan the coiling serpent;
he will slay the monster of the sea.

²In that day—

"Sing about a fruitful vineyard:
³ I, the LORD, watch over it;
    I water it continually.
I guard it day and night
  so that no one may harm it.
⁴ I am not angry.
If only there were briers and thorns confronting
    me!
I would march against them in battle;
  I would set them all on fire.
⁵Or else let them come to me for refuge;
  let them make peace with me,
  yes, let them make peace with me."

⁶In days to come Jacob will take root,
  Israel will bud and blossom
  and fill all the world with fruit.

⁷Has the LORD struck her
  as he struck down those who struck her?
Has she been killed
  as those were killed who killed her?
⁸By warfareᵃ and exile you contend with her—
  with his fierce blast he drives her out,
  as on a day the east wind blows.
⁹By this, then, will Jacob's guilt be atoned for,
  and this will be the full fruitage of the
    removal of his sin:
When he makes all the altar stones
  to be like chalk stones crushed to pieces,
no Asherah polesᵇ or incense altars
  will be left standing.
¹⁰The fortified city stands desolate,
  an abandoned settlement, forsaken like the
    desert;
there the calves graze,
  there they lie down;
  they strip its branches bare.

ᵃ 8 See Septuagint; the meaning of the Hebrew for this word is uncertain.
ᵇ 9 That is, symbols of the goddess Asherah

Living Bible

to no avail. No deliverance has come from all our efforts. 19Yet we have this assurance: Those who belong to God shall live again. Their bodies shall rise again! Those who dwell in the dust shall awake and sing for joy! For God's light of life will fall like dew upon them!

20Go home, my people, and lock the doors! Hide for a little while until the Lord's wrath against your enemies has passed. 21Look! The Lord is coming from the heavens to punish the people of the earth for their sins. The earth will no longer hide the murderers. The guilty will be found.

27 IN THAT day the Lord will take his terrible, swift sword and punish leviathan, the swiftly moving serpent, the coiling, writhing serpent, the dragon of the sea.

2In that day [of Israel's freedomc] let this anthem be their song:

3Israeld is my vineyard; I, the Lord, will tend the fruitful vines; every day I'll water them, and day and night I'll watch to keep all enemies away. 4, 5My anger against Israel is gone. If I find thorns and briars bothering her, I will burn them up, unless these enemies of mine surrender and beg for peace and my protection. 6The time will come when Israel will take root and bud and blossom and fill the whole earth with her fruit!

7, 8Has God punished Israel as much as he has punished her enemies? No, for he has devastated her enemies,e while he has punished Israel but a little, exiling her far from her own land as though blown away in a storm from the east. 9And why did God do it? It was to purge awayf her sins, to rid her of all her idol altars and her idols. They will never be worshiped again. 10Her walled cities will be silent and empty, houses abandoned, streets grown up with grass, cows grazing through the city munching on twigs and branches.

New Revised Standard

18   we were with child, we writhed,
      but we gave birth only to wind.
We have won no victories on earth,
    and no one is born to inhabit the world.
19   Your dead shall live, their corpsesg shall rise.
   O dwellers in the dust, awake and sing for
      joy!
For your dew is a radiant dew,
   and the earth will give birth to those long
      dead.h

20   Come, my people, enter your chambers,
      and shut your doors behind you;
hide yourselves for a little while
      until the wrath is past.
21   For the LORD comes out from his place
      to punish the inhabitants of the earth for
        their iniquity;
the earth will disclose the blood shed on it,
   and will no longer cover its slain.

Israel's Redemption

27 ON THAT day the LORD with his cruel and great and strong sword will punish Leviathan the fleeing serpent, Leviathan the twisting serpent, and he will kill the dragon that is in the sea.

2   On that day:
      A pleasant vineyard, sing about it!
3   I, the LORD, am its keeper;
      every moment I water it.
I guard it night and day
      so that no one can harm it;
4   I have no wrath.
If it gives me thorns and briers,
      I will march to battle against it.
      I will burn it up.
5   Or else let it cling to me for protection,
      let it make peace with me,
      let it make peace with me.

6   In days to comei Jacob shall take root,
      Israel shall blossom and put forth shoots,
      and fill the whole world with fruit.

7   Has he struck them down as he struck down
        those who struck them?
Or have they been killed as their killers
        were killed?
8   By expulsion,j by exile you struggled against
        them;
with his fierce blast he removed them in the
      day of the east wind.
9   Therefore by this the guilt of Jacob will be
        expiated,
   and this will be the full fruit of the removal
      of his sin:
when he makes all the stones of the altars
      like chalkstones crushed to pieces,
   no sacred polesk or incense altars will
      remain standing.
10   For the fortified city is solitary,
      a habitation deserted and forsaken, like the
        wilderness;
the calves graze there,
      there they lie down, and strip its branches.

---

c 27:2 *of Israel's freedom,* implied.   d 27:3 *Israel,* implied. Also in vs 4.
e 27:7 *devastated her enemies,* implied.   f 27:9 *purge away,* literally, "atone for."

g Cn Compare Syr Tg: Heb *my corpse*   h Heb *to the shades*   i Heb *Those to come*   j Meaning of Heb uncertain   k Heb *Asherim*

King James

11When the boughs thereof are withered, they shall be broken off: the women come, *and* set them on fire: for it *is* a people of no understanding: therefore he that made them will not have mercy on them, and he that formed them will show them no favour.

12¶ And it shall come to pass in that day, *that* the LORD shall beat off from the channel of the river unto the stream of Egypt, and ye shall be gathered one by one, O ye children of Israel.

13And it shall come to pass in that day, *that* the great trumpet shall be blown, and they shall come which were ready to perish in the land of Assyria, and the outcasts in the land of Egypt, and shall worship the LORD in the holy mount at Jerusalem.

28 WOE TO the crown of pride, to the drunkards of Ephraim, whose glorious beauty *is* a fading flower, which *are* on the head of the fat valleys of them that are overcome with wine!

2Behold, the Lord hath a mighty and strong one, *which* as a tempest of hail *and* a destroying storm, as a flood of mighty waters overflowing, shall cast down to the earth with the hand.

3The crown of pride, the drunkards of Ephraim, shall be trodden under feet:

4And the glorious beauty, which *is* on the head of the fat valley, shall be a fading flower, *and* as the hasty fruit before the summer; which *when* he that looketh upon it seeth, while it is yet in his hand he eateth it up.

5¶ In that day shall the LORD of hosts be for a crown of glory, and for a diadem of beauty, unto the residue of his people,

6And for a spirit of judgment to him that sitteth in judgment, and for strength to them that turn the battle to the gate.

7¶ But they also have erred through wine, and through strong drink are out of the way; the priest and the prophet have erred through strong drink, they are swallowed up of wine, they are out of the way through strong drink; they err in vision, they stumble *in* judgment.

8For all tables are full of vomit *and* filthiness, *so that there is* no place *clean*.

9¶ Whom shall he teach knowledge? and whom shall he make to understand doctrine? *them that are* weaned from the milk, *and* drawn from the breasts.

10For precept *must be* upon precept, precept upon precept; line upon line, line upon line; here a little, *and* there a little:

New International

11When its twigs are dry, they are broken off
  and women come and make fires with them.
For this is a people without understanding;
  so their Maker has no compassion on them,
  and their Creator shows them no favor.

12In that day the LORD will thresh from the flowing Euphrates[a] to the Wadi of Egypt, and you, O Israelites, will be gathered up one by one. 13And in that day a great trumpet will sound. Those who were perishing in Assyria and those who were exiled in Egypt will come and worship the LORD on the holy mountain in Jerusalem.

Woe to Ephraim

28 WOE TO that wreath, the pride of Ephraim's drunkards,
  to the fading flower, his glorious beauty,
set on the head of a fertile valley—
  to that city, the pride of those laid low by wine!

2See, the Lord has one who is powerful and strong.
Like a hailstorm and a destructive wind,
like a driving rain and a flooding downpour,
  he will throw it forcefully to the ground.

3That wreath, the pride of Ephraim's drunkards,
  will be trampled underfoot.

4That fading flower, his glorious beauty,
  set on the head of a fertile valley,
will be like a fig ripe before harvest—
  as soon as someone sees it and takes it in his hand,
  he swallows it.

5In that day the LORD Almighty
  will be a glorious crown,
a beautiful wreath
  for the remnant of his people.

6He will be a spirit of justice
  to him who sits in judgment,
a source of strength
  to those who turn back the battle at the gate.

7And these also stagger from wine
  and reel from beer:
Priests and prophets stagger from beer
  and are befuddled with wine;
they reel from beer,
  they stagger when seeing visions,
  they stumble when rendering decisions.

8All the tables are covered with vomit
  and there is not a spot without filth.

9"Who is it he is trying to teach?
  To whom is he explaining his message?
To children weaned from their milk,
  to those just taken from the breast?

10For it is:
  Do and do, do and do,
  rule on rule, rule on rule[b];
  a little here, a little there."

a *12* Hebrew *River*   b *10* Hebrew / *sav lasav sav lasav* / *kav lakav kav lakav* (possibly meaningless sounds; perhaps a mimicking of the prophet's words); also in verse 13

Living Bible

11My people are like the dead branches of a tree, broken off and used to burn beneath the pots. They are a foolish nation, a witless, stupid people, for they turn away from God. Therefore, he who made them will not have pity on them or show them his mercy. 12Yet the time will come when the Lord will gather them together one by one like handpicked grain, selecting them here and there from his great threshing floor that reaches all the way from the Euphrates River to the Egyptian boundary. 13In that day the great trumpet will be blown, and many about to perish among their enemies, Assyria and Egypt, will be rescued and brought back to Jerusalem to worship the Lord in his holy mountain.

28 WOE TO the city of Samaria, surrounded by her rich valley—Samaria, the pride and delight of the drunkards of Israel! Woe to her fading beauty, the crowning glory of a nation of men lying drunk in the streets! 2For the Lord will send a mighty army (the Assyrians) against you; like a mighty hailstorm he will burst upon you and dash you to the ground. 3The proud city of Samaria—yes, the joy and delight of the drunkards of Israel—will be hurled to the ground and trampled beneath the enemies' feet. 4Once glorious, her fading beauty surrounded by a fertile valley will suddenly be gone, greedily snatched away as an early fig is hungrily snatched and gobbled up!

5Then at last the Lord Almighty himself will be their crowning glory, the diadem of beauty to his people who are left. 6He will give a longing for justice to your judges and great courage to your soldiers who are battling to the last before your gates. 7But Jerusalem is now led by drunks! Her priests and prophets reel and stagger, making stupid errors and mistakes. 8Their tables are covered with vomit; filth is everywhere.

9"Who does Isaiah think he is," the people say, "to speak to us like this! Are we little children, barely old enough to talk? 10He tells us everything over and over again, a line at a time and in such simple words!"

New Revised Standard

11 When its boughs are dry, they are broken;
    women come and make a fire of them.
For this is a people without understanding;
    therefore he that made them will not have
        compassion on them,
    he that formed them will show them no
        favor.

12 On that day the LORD will thresh from the channel of the Euphrates to the Wadi of Egypt, and you will be gathered one by one, O people of Israel. 13And on that day a great trumpet will be blown, and those who were lost in the land of Assyria and those who were driven out to the land of Egypt will come and worship the LORD on the holy mountain at Jerusalem.

Judgment on Corrupt Rulers, Priests, and Prophets

28 AH, THE proud garland of the drunkards of Ephraim,
    and the fading flower of its glorious beauty,
    which is on the head of those bloated with
        rich food, of those overcome with
            wine!
2 See, the Lord has one who is mighty and
        strong;
    like a storm of hail, a destroying tempest,
    like a storm of mighty, overflowing waters;
    with his hand he will hurl them down to the
        earth.
3 Trampled under foot will be
    the proud garland of the drunkards of
        Ephraim.
4 And the fading flower of its glorious beauty,
    which is on the head of those bloated with
        rich food,
    will be like a first-ripe fig before the summer;
    whoever sees it, eats it up
        as soon as it comes to hand.

5 In that day the LORD of hosts will be a
        garland of glory,
    and a diadem of beauty, to the remnant of
        his people;
6 and a spirit of justice to the one who sits in
        judgment,
    and strength to those who turn back the
        battle at the gate.

7 These also reel with wine
    and stagger with strong drink;
the priest and the prophet reel with strong
        drink,
    they are confused with wine,
    they stagger with strong drink;
they err in vision,
    they stumble in giving judgment.
8 All tables are covered with filthy vomit;
    no place is clean.

9 "Whom will he teach knowledge,
    and to whom will he explain the message?
Those who are weaned from milk,
    those taken from the breast?
10 For it is precept upon precept, precept upon
        precept,
    line upon line, line upon line,
    here a little, there a little."c

c Meaning of Heb of this verse uncertain

King James

11For with stammering lips and another tongue will he speak to this people.

12To whom he said, This *is* the rest *wherewith* ye may cause the weary to rest; and this *is* the refreshing: yet they would not hear.

13But the word of the LORD was unto them precept upon precept, precept upon precept; line upon line, line upon line; here a little, *and* there a little; that they might go, and fall backward, and be broken, and snared, and taken.

14¶ Wherefore hear the word of the LORD, ye scornful men, that rule this people which *is* in Jerusalem.

15Because ye have said, We have made a covenant with death, and with hell are we at agreement; when the overflowing scourge shall pass through, it shall not come unto us: for we have made lies our refuge, and under falsehood have we hid ourselves:

16¶ Therefore thus saith the Lord GOD, Behold, I lay in Zion for a foundation a stone, a tried stone, a precious corner *stone,* a sure foundation: he that believeth shall not make haste.

17Judgment also will I lay to the line, and righteousness to the plummet: and the hail shall sweep away the refuge of lies, and the waters shall overflow the hiding place.

18¶ And your covenant with death shall be disannulled, and your agreement with hell shall not stand; when the overflowing scourge shall pass through, then ye shall be trodden down by it.

19From the time that it goeth forth it shall take you: for morning by morning shall it pass over, by day and by night: and it shall be a vexation only *to* understand the report.

20For the bed is shorter than that *a man* can stretch himself *on it:* and the covering narrower than that he can wrap himself *in it.*

21For the LORD shall rise up as *in* mount Perazim, he shall be wroth as *in* the valley of Gibeon, that he may do his work, his strange work; and bring to pass his act, his strange act.

22Now therefore be ye not mockers, lest your bands be made strong: for I have heard from the Lord GOD of hosts a consumption, even determined upon the whole earth.

New International

11Very well then, with foreign lips and strange
    tongues
God will speak to this people,
12to whom he said,
    "This is the resting place, let the weary rest";
and, "This is the place of repose"—
    but they would not listen.
13So then, the word of the LORD to them will
    become:
Do and do, do and do,
    rule on rule, rule on rule;
a little here, a little there—
so that they will go and fall backward,
    be injured and snared and captured.

14Therefore hear the word of the LORD, you
    scoffers
who rule this people in Jerusalem.
15You boast, "We have entered into a covenant
    with death,
with the grave[a] we have made an agreement.
When an overwhelming scourge sweeps by,
    it cannot touch us,
for we have made a lie our refuge
    and falsehood[b] our hiding place."

16So this is what the Sovereign LORD says:

"See, I lay a stone in Zion,
    a tested stone,
a precious cornerstone for a sure foundation;
    the one who trusts will never be dismayed.
17I will make justice the measuring line
    and righteousness the plumb line;
hail will sweep away your refuge, the lie,
    and water will overflow your hiding place.
18Your covenant with death will be annulled;
    your agreement with the grave will not stand.
When the overwhelming scourge sweeps by,
    you will be beaten down by it.
19As often as it comes it will carry you away;
    morning after morning, by day and by night,
    it will sweep through."

The understanding of this message
    will bring sheer terror.
20The bed is too short to stretch out on,
    the blanket too narrow to wrap around you.
21The LORD will rise up as he did at Mount
    Perazim,
he will rouse himself as in the Valley of
    Gibeon—
to do his work, his strange work,
    and perform his task, his alien task.
22Now stop your mocking,
    or your chains will become heavier;
the Lord, the LORD Almighty, has told me
    of the destruction decreed against the whole
    land.

---

a *15* Hebrew *Sheol*; also in verse 18   b *15* Or *false gods*

Living Bible

11But they won't listen; the only language they can understand is punishment! So God will punish them by sending against them foreigners who speak strange gibberish! Only then will they listen to him! 12They could have rest in their own land if they would obey him, if they were kind and good. He told them that, but they wouldn't listen to him. 13So the Lord will spell it out for them again, repeating it over and over in simple words whenever he can; yet over this simple, straightforward message they will stumble and fall and be broken, trapped and captured.

14Therefore hear the word of the Lord, you scoffing rulers in Jerusalem:

15You have struck a bargain with Death, you say, and sold yourselves to the devil[c] in exchange for his protection against the Assyrians. "They can never touch us," you say, "for we are under the care of one who will deceive and fool them."

16But the Lord God says, See, I am placing a Foundation Stone in Zion—a firm, tested, precious Cornerstone that is safe to build on. He who believes need never run away again. 17I will take the line and plummet of justice to check the foundation wall you built; it looks so fine, but it is so weak a storm of hail will knock it down! The enemy will come like a flood and sweep it away, and you will be drowned. 18I will cancel your agreement of compromise with Death and the devil, so when the terrible enemy floods in, you will be trampled into the ground. 19Again and again that flood will come and carry you off, until at last the unmixed horror of the truth of my warnings will finally dawn on you.

20The bed you have made is far too short to lie on; the blankets are too narrow to cover you. 21The Lord will come suddenly and in anger, as at Mount Perazim and Gibeon, to do a strange, unusual thing—to destroy his own people! 22So scoff no more, lest your punishment be made even greater, for the Lord God has plainly told me that he is determined to crush you.

New Revised Standard

11 Truly, with stammering lip
      and with alien tongue
   he will speak to this people,
12   to whom he has said,
   "This is rest;
      give rest to the weary;
   and this is repose";
      yet they would not hear.
13 Therefore the word of the LORD will be to
      them,
   "Precept upon precept, precept upon
      precept,
   line upon line, line upon line,
      here a little, there a little;"[d]
   in order that they may go, and fall backward,
      and be broken, and snared, and taken.

14 Therefore hear the word of the LORD, you
      scoffers
   who rule this people in Jerusalem.
15 Because you have said, "We have made a
      covenant with death,
   and with Sheol we have an agreement;
   when the overwhelming scourge passes
      through
   it will not come to us;
   for we have made lies our refuge,
      and in falsehood we have taken shelter";
16 therefore thus says the Lord GOD,
   See, I am laying in Zion a foundation stone,
      a tested stone,
   a precious cornerstone, a sure foundation:
      "One who trusts will not panic."
17 And I will make justice the line,
      and righteousness the plummet;
   hail will sweep away the refuge of lies,
      and waters will overwhelm the shelter.
18 Then your covenant with death will be
      annulled,
   and your agreement with Sheol will not
      stand;
   when the overwhelming scourge passes
      through
   you will be beaten down by it.
19 As often as it passes through, it will take you;
   for morning by morning it will pass
      through,
      by day and by night;
   and it will be sheer terror to understand the
      message.
20 For the bed is too short to stretch oneself on
      it,
   and the covering too narrow to wrap oneself
      in it.
21 For the LORD will rise up as on Mount
      Perazim,
   he will rage as in the valley of Gibeon;
   to do his deed—strange is his deed!
      and to work his work—alien is his work!
22 Now therefore do not scoff,
      or your bonds will be made stronger;
   for I have heard a decree of destruction
      from the Lord GOD of hosts upon the whole
      land.

---

c 28:15 *and sold yourselves to the devil,* literally, "Sheol," "the underworld."

d Meaning of Heb of this verse uncertain

King James

23¶ Give ye ear, and hear my voice; hearken, and hear my speech.

24Doth the plowman plow all day to sow? doth he open and break the clods of his ground?

25When he hath made plain the face thereof, doth he not cast abroad the fitches, and scatter the cummin, and cast in the principal wheat and the appointed barley and the rie in their place?

26For his God doth instruct him to discretion, *and* doth teach him.

27For the fitches are not threshed with a threshing instrument, neither is a cart wheel turned about upon the cummin; but the fitches are beaten out with a staff, and the cummin with a rod.

28Bread *corn* is bruised; because he will not ever be threshing it, nor break *it with* the wheel of his cart, nor bruise it *with* his horsemen.

29This also cometh forth from the LORD of hosts, *which* is wonderful in counsel, *and* excellent in working.

29 WOE TO Ariel, to Ariel, the city *where* David dwelt! add ye year to year; let them kill sacrifices.

2Yet I will distress Ariel, and there shall be heaviness and sorrow: and it shall be unto me as Ariel.

3And I will camp against thee round about, and will lay siege against thee with a mount, and I will raise forts against thee.

4And thou shalt be brought down, *and* shalt speak out of the ground, and thy speech shall be low out of the dust, and thy voice shall be, as of one that hath a familiar spirit, out of the ground, and thy speech shall whisper out of the dust.

5Moreover the multitude of thy strangers shall be like small dust, and the multitude of the terrible ones *shall be* as chaff that passeth away: yea, it shall be at an instant suddenly.

6Thou shalt be visited of the LORD of hosts with thunder, and with earthquake, and great noise, with storm and tempest, and the flame of devouring fire.

7¶ And the multitude of all the nations that fight against Ariel, even all that fight against her and her munition, and that distress her, shall be as a dream of a night vision.

8It shall even be as when an hungry *man* dreameth, and, behold, he eateth; but he awaketh, and his soul is empty: or as when a thirsty man dreameth, and, behold, he drinketh; but he awaketh, and, behold, *he is* faint, and his soul hath appetite: so shall the multitude of all the nations be, that fight against mount Zion.

New International

23Listen and hear my voice;
　pay attention and hear what I say.
24When a farmer plows for planting, does he
　　plow continually?
　Does he keep on breaking up and harrowing
　　the soil?
25When he has leveled the surface,
　does he not sow caraway and scatter cummin?
　Does he not plant wheat in its place,[a]
　barley in its plot,[a]
　and spelt in its field?
26His God instructs him
　and teaches him the right way.

27Caraway is not threshed with a sledge,
　nor is a cartwheel rolled over cummin;
caraway is beaten out with a rod,
　and cummin with a stick.
28Grain must be ground to make bread;
　so one does not go on threshing it forever.
Though he drives the wheels of his threshing
　　cart over it,
　his horses do not grind it.
29All this also comes from the LORD Almighty,
　wonderful in counsel and magnificent in
　　wisdom.

Woe to David's City

29 WOE TO you, Ariel, Ariel,
　　the city where David settled!
Add year to year
　and let your cycle of festivals go on.
2Yet I will besiege Ariel;
　she will mourn and lament,
　she will be to me like an altar hearth.[b]
3I will encamp against you all around;
　I will encircle you with towers
　and set up my siege works against you.
4Brought low, you will speak from the ground;
　your speech will mumble out of the dust.
Your voice will come ghostlike from the earth;
　out of the dust your speech will whisper.

5But your many enemies will become like fine
　　dust,
　the ruthless hordes like blown chaff.
Suddenly, in an instant,
6　the LORD Almighty will come
　with thunder and earthquake and great noise,
　　with windstorm and tempest and flames of a
　　devouring fire.
7Then the hordes of all the nations that fight
　　against Ariel,
　that attack her and her fortress and besiege
　　her,
　will be as it is with a dream,
　with a vision in the night—
8as when a hungry man dreams that he is eating,
　but he awakens, and his hunger remains;
as when a thirsty man dreams that he is
　　drinking,
　but he awakens faint, with his thirst
　　unquenched.
So will it be with the hordes of all the nations
　that fight against Mount Zion.

---

a 25 The meaning of the Hebrew for this word is uncertain.　b 2 The Hebrew for *altar hearth* sounds like the Hebrew for *Ariel.*

Living Bible

23, 24Listen to me, listen as I plead: Does a farmer always plow and never sow? Is he forever harrowing the soil and never planting it? 25Does he not finally plant his many kinds of grain, each in its own section of his land? 26He knows just what to do, for God has made him see and understand. 27He doesn't thresh all grains the same. A sledge is never used on dill, but it is beaten with a stick. A threshing wheel is never rolled on cummin, but it is beaten softly with a flail. 28Bread grain is easily crushed, so he doesn't keep on pounding it. 29The Lord Almighty is a wonderful teacher and gives the farmer wisdom.

29 WOE TO Jerusalem,c the city of David. Year after year you make your many offerings, 2but I will send heavy judgment upon you and there will be weeping and sorrow. For Jerusalem shall become as her name "Ariel" means—an altar covered with blood. 3I will be your enemy. I will surround Jerusalem and lay siege against it, and build forts around it to destroy it. 4Your voice will whisper like a ghost from the earth where you lie buried.

5But suddenly your ruthless enemies will be driven away like chaff before the wind. 6In an instant, I, the Lord of Hosts, will come upon them with thunder, earthquake, whirlwind and fire. 7And all the nations fighting Jerusalem will vanish like a dream! 8As a hungry man dreams of eating, but is still hungry, and as a thirsty man dreams of drinking, but is still faint from thirst when he wakes up, so your enemies will dream of victorious conquest, but all to no avail.

New Revised Standard

23 Listen, and hear my voice;
    Pay attention, and hear my speech.
24 Do those who plow for sowing plow
        continually?
    Do they continually open and harrow their
        ground?
25 When they have leveled its surface,
        do they not scatter dill, sow cummin,
    and plant wheat in rows
        and barley in its proper place,
        and spelt as the border?
26 For they are well instructed;
        their God teaches them.

27 Dill is not threshed with a threshing sledge,
        nor is a cart wheel rolled over cummin;
    but dill is beaten out with a stick,
        and cummin with a rod.
28 Grain is crushed for bread,
        but one does not thresh it forever;
    one drives the cart wheel and horses over it,
        but does not pulverize it.
29 This also comes from the LORD of hosts;
        he is wonderful in counsel,
        and excellent in wisdom.

The Siege of Jerusalem

29 AH, ARIEL, Ariel,
        the city where David encamped!
    Add year to year;
        let the festivals run their round.
2 Yet I will distress Ariel,
        and there shall be moaning and lamentation,
    and Jerusalemd shall be to me like an
        Ariel.e
3 And like Davidf I will encamp against you;
        I will besiege you with towers
        and raise siegeworks against you.
4 Then deep from the earth you shall speak,
        from low in the dust your words shall come;
    your voice shall come from the ground like
        the voice of a ghost,
    and your speech shall whisper out of the
        dust.

5 But the multitude of your foesg shall be like
        small dust,
    and the multitude of tyrants like flying
        chaff.
    And in an instant, suddenly,
6   you will be visited by the LORD of hosts
    with thunder and earthquake and great noise,
        with whirlwind and tempest, and the flame
        of a devouring fire.
7 And the multitude of all the nations that fight
        against Ariel,
    all that fight against her and her stronghold,
        and who distress her,
    shall be like a dream, a vision of the night.
8 Just as when a hungry person dreams of eating
        and wakes up still hungry,
    or a thirsty person dreams of drinking
        and wakes up faint, still thirsty,
    so shall the multitude of all the nations be
        that fight against Mount Zion.

---

c 29:1 to Jerusalem, literally, "to Ariel."

d Heb she   e Probable meaning, altar hearth; compare Ezek 43.15   f Gk:
Meaning of Heb uncertain   g Cn: Heb strangers

King James

9¶ Stay yourselves, and wonder; cry ye out, and cry: they are drunken, but not with wine; they stagger, but not with strong drink.

10For the LORD hath poured out upon you the spirit of deep sleep, and hath closed your eyes: the prophets and your rulers, the seers hath he covered.

11And the vision of all is become unto you as the words of a book that is sealed, which *men* deliver to one that is learned, saying, Read this, I pray thee: and he saith, I cannot; for it *is* sealed:

12And the book is delivered to him that is not learned, saying, Read this, I pray thee: and he saith, I am not learned.

13¶ Wherefore the Lord said, Forasmuch as this people draw near *me* with their mouth, and with their lips do honour me, but have removed their heart far from me, and their fear toward me is taught by the precept of men:

14Therefore, behold, I will proceed to do a marvellous work among this people, *even* a marvellous work and a wonder: for the wisdom of their wise *men* shall perish, and the understanding of their prudent *men* shall be hid.

15Woe unto them that seek deep to hide their counsel from the LORD, and their works are in the dark, and they say, Who seeth us? and who knoweth us?

16Surely your turning of things upside down shall be esteemed as the potter's clay: for shall the work say of him that made it, He made me not? or shall the thing framed say of him that framed it, He had no understanding?

17*Is* it not yet a very little while, and Lebanon shall be turned into a fruitful field, and the fruitful field shall be esteemed as a forest?

18¶ And in that day shall the deaf hear the words of the book, and the eyes of the blind shall see out of obscurity, and out of darkness.

19The meek also shall increase *their* joy in the LORD, and the poor among men shall rejoice in the Holy One of Israel.

20For the terrible one is brought to nought, and the scorner is consumed, and all that watch for iniquity are cut off:

21That make a man an offender for a word, and lay a snare for him that reproveth in the gate, and turn aside the just for a thing of nought.

22Therefore thus saith the LORD, who redeemed Abraham, concerning the house of Jacob, Jacob shall not now be ashamed, neither shall his face now wax pale.

23But when he seeth his children, the work of mine hands, in the midst of him, they shall sanctify my name, and sanctify the Holy One of Jacob, and shall fear the God of Israel.

New International

9Be stunned and amazed,
    blind yourselves and be sightless;
be drunk, but not from wine,
    stagger, but not from beer.
10The LORD has brought over you a deep sleep:
    He has sealed your eyes (the prophets);
    he has covered your heads (the seers).

11For you this whole vision is nothing but words sealed in a scroll. And if you give the scroll to someone who can read, and say to him, "Read this, please," he will answer, "I can't; it is sealed." 12Or if you give the scroll to someone who cannot read, and say, "Read this, please," he will answer, "I don't know how to read."

13The Lord says:

"These people come near to me with their
        mouth
    and honor me with their lips,
    but their hearts are far from me.
Their worship of me
    is made up only of rules taught by men.a
14Therefore once more I will astound these people
    with wonder upon wonder;
the wisdom of the wise will perish,
    the intelligence of the intelligent will vanish."
15Woe to those who go to great depths
    to hide their plans from the LORD,
who do their work in darkness and think,
    "Who sees us? Who will know?"
16You turn things upside down,
    as if the potter were thought to be like the
        clay!
Shall what is formed say to him who formed it,
    "He did not make me"?
Can the pot say of the potter,
    "He knows nothing"?

17In a very short time, will not Lebanon be turned
        into a fertile field
    and the fertile field seem like a forest?
18In that day the deaf will hear the words of the
        scroll,
    and out of gloom and darkness
    the eyes of the blind will see.
19Once more the humble will rejoice in the LORD;
    the needy will rejoice in the Holy One of
        Israel.
20The ruthless will vanish,
    the mockers will disappear,
    and all who have an eye for evil will be cut
        down—
21those who with a word make a man out to be
        guilty,
    who ensnare the defender in court
    and with false testimony deprive the innocent
        of justice.

22Therefore this is what the LORD, who redeemed Abraham, says to the house of Jacob:

"No longer will Jacob be ashamed;
    no longer will their faces grow pale.
23When they see among them their children,
    the work of my hands,
they will keep my name holy;
    they will acknowledge the holiness of the
        Holy One of Jacob,
    and will stand in awe of the God of Israel.

---

a *13 Hebrew; Septuagint* They worship me in vain; / their teachings are but rules taught by men

Living Bible

9You are amazed, incredulous? You don't believe it? Then go ahead and be blind if you must! You are stupid—and not from drinking, either! Stagger, and not from wine! 10For the Lord has poured out upon you a spirit of deep sleep. He has closed the eyes of your prophets and seers, 11so all of these future events are a sealed book to them. When you give it to one who can read, he says, "I can't, for it's sealed." 12When you give it to another, he says, "Sorry, I can't read."

13And so the Lord says, "Since these people say they are mine but they do not obey me, and since their worship amounts to mere words learned by rote, 14therefore I will take awesome vengeance on these hypocrites, and make their wisest counselors as fools."

15Woe to those who try to hide their plans from God, who try to keep him in the dark concerning what they do! "God can't see us," they say to themselves. "He doesn't know what is going on!" 16How stupid can they be! Isn't he, the Potter, greater than you, the jars he makes? Will you say to him, "He didn't make us"? Does a machine call its inventor dumb?

17Soon—and it will not be very long—the wilderness of Lebanon will be a fruitful field again, a lush and fertile forest. 18In that day the deaf will hear the words of a book, and out of their gloom and darkness the blind will see my plans. 19The meek will be filled with fresh joy from the Lord, and the poor shall exult in the Holy One of Israel. 20Bullies will vanish and scoffers will cease, and all those plotting evil will be killed— 21the violent man who fights at the drop of a hat, the man who waits in hiding to beat up the judge who sentenced him, and the men who use any excuse to be unfair.

22That is why the Lord who redeemed Abraham says: My people will no longer pale with fear, or be ashamed. 23For when they see the surging birth rate and the expanding economy,b then they will fear and rejoice in my name, and praise the Holy One of Israel, and stand in

New Revised Standard

9   Stupefy yourselves and be in a stupor,
       blind yourselves and be blind!
     Be drunk, but not from wine;
       stagger, but not from strong drink!
10 For the LORD has poured out upon you
       a spirit of deep sleep;
     he has closed your eyes, you prophets,
       and covered your heads, you seers.

11   The vision of all this has become for you like the words of a sealed document. If it is given to those who can read, with the command, "Read this," they say, "We cannot, for it is sealed." 12And if it is given to those who cannot read, saying, "Read this," they say, "We cannot read."

13 The Lord said:
     Because these people draw near with their
         mouths
       and honor me with their lips,
     while their hearts are far from me,
     and their worship of me is a human
         commandment learned by rote;
14 so I will again do
       amazing things with this people,
       shocking and amazing.
     The wisdom of their wise shall perish,
       and the discernment of the discerning shall
         be hidden.

15 Ha! You who hide a plan too deep for the
         LORD,
       whose deeds are in the dark,
     and who say, "Who sees us? Who knows
         us?"
16 You turn things upside down!
       Shall the potter be regarded as the clay?
     Shall the thing made say of its maker,
       "He did not make me";
     or the thing formed say of the one who
         formed it,
       "He has no understanding"?

Hope for the Future

17 Shall not Lebanon in a very little while
       become a fruitful field,
     and the fruitful field be regarded as a
         forest?
18 On that day the deaf shall hear
       the words of a scroll,
     and out of their gloom and darkness
       the eyes of the blind shall see.
19 The meek shall obtain fresh joy in the LORD,
       and the neediest people shall exult in the
         Holy One of Israel.
20 For the tyrant shall be no more,
       and the scoffer shall cease to be;
     all those alert to do evil shall be cut off—
21 those who cause a person to lose a lawsuit,
       who set a trap for the arbiter in the gate,
     and without grounds deny justice to the one
         in the right.

22 Therefore thus says the LORD, who redeemed Abraham, concerning the house of Jacob:
     No longer shall Jacob be ashamed,
       no longer shall his face grow pale.
23 For when he sees his children,
       the work of my hands, in his midst,
       they will sanctify my name;
     they will sanctify the Holy One of Jacob,
       and will stand in awe of the God of Israel.

b 29:23 *the surging birth rate and the expanding economy,* literally, "when he sees his children, the work of my hands, in his midst."

King James

New International

24They also that erred in spirit shall come to understanding, and they that murmured shall learn doctrine.

24Those who are wayward in spirit will gain
    understanding;
    those who complain will accept instruction."

Woe to the Obstinate Nation

30 WOE TO the rebellious children, saith the LORD, that take counsel, but not of me; and that cover with a covering, but not of my spirit, that they may add sin to sin:

30 "WOE TO the obstinate children,"
    declares the LORD,
"to those who carry out plans that are not mine,
    forming an alliance, but not by my Spirit,
    heaping sin upon sin;

2That walk to go down into Egypt, and have not asked at my mouth; to strengthen themselves in the strength of Pharaoh, and to trust in the shadow of Egypt!

2who go down to Egypt
    without consulting me;
who look for help to Pharaoh's protection,
    to Egypt's shade for refuge.

3Therefore shall the strength of Pharaoh be your shame, and the trust in the shadow of Egypt *your* confusion.

3But Pharaoh's protection will be to your shame,
    Egypt's shade will bring you disgrace.

4For his princes were at Zoan, and his ambassadors came to Hanes.

4Though they have officials in Zoan
    and their envoys have arrived in Hanes,

5They were all ashamed of a people *that* could not profit them, nor be an help nor profit, but a shame, and also a reproach.

5everyone will be put to shame
    because of a people useless to them,
who bring neither help nor advantage,
    but only shame and disgrace."

6The burden of the beasts of the south: into the land of trouble and anguish, from whence *come* the young and old lion, the viper and fiery flying serpent, they will carry their riches upon the shoulders of young asses, and their treasures upon the bunches of camels, to a people *that* shall not profit *them*.

6An oracle concerning the animals of the Negev:

Through a land of hardship and distress,
    of lions and lionesses,
    of adders and darting snakes,
the envoys carry their riches on donkeys' backs,
    their treasures on the humps of camels,
to that unprofitable nation,

7For the Egyptians shall help in vain, and to no purpose: therefore have I cried concerning this, Their strength *is* to sit still.

7   to Egypt, whose help is utterly useless.
Therefore I call her
    Rahab the Do-Nothing.

8¶ Now go, write it before them in a table, and note it in a book, that it may be for the time to come for ever and ever:

8Go now, write it on a tablet for them,
    inscribe it on a scroll,
that for the days to come
    it may be an everlasting witness.

9That this *is* a rebellious people, lying children, children *that* will not hear the law of the LORD:

9These are rebellious people, deceitful children,
    children unwilling to listen to the LORD's
        instruction.

10Which say to the seers, See not; and to the prophets, Prophesy not unto us right things, speak unto us smooth things, prophesy deceits:

10They say to the seers,
    "See no more visions!"
and to the prophets,
    "Give us no more visions of what is right!
Tell us pleasant things,
    prophesy illusions.

11Get you out of the way, turn aside out of the path, cause the Holy One of Israel to cease from before us.

11Leave this way,
    get off this path,
and stop confronting us
    with the Holy One of Israel!"

12Wherefore thus saith the Holy One of Israel, Because ye despise this word, and trust in oppression and perverseness, and stay thereon:

12Therefore, this is what the Holy One of Israel says:

"Because you have rejected this message,
    relied on oppression
    and depended on deceit,

13Therefore this iniquity shall be to you as a breach ready to fall, swelling out in a high wall, whose breaking cometh suddenly at an instant.

13this sin will become for you
    like a high wall, cracked and bulging,
    that collapses suddenly, in an instant.

14And he shall break it as the breaking of the potters' vessel that is broken in pieces; he shall not spare: so that there shall not be found in the bursting of it a sherd to take fire from the hearth, or to take water *withal* out of the pit.

14It will break in pieces like pottery,
    shattered so mercilessly
that among its pieces not a fragment will be
        found
for taking coals from a hearth
    or scooping water out of a cistern."

Living Bible

awe of him. 24Those in error will believe the truth, and complainers will be willing to be taught!

30 WOE TO my rebellious children, says the Lord; you ask advice from everyone but me, and decide to do what I don't want you to do. You yoke yourselves with unbelievers, thus piling up your sins. 2For without consulting me you have gone down to Egypt to find aid and have put your trust in Pharaoh for his protection.ᵃ 3But in trusting Pharaoh, you will be disappointed, humiliated and disgraced, for he can't deliver on his promises to save you. 4For though his power extends to Zoan and Hanes, 5yet it will all turn out to your shame—he won't help one little bit!

6See them moving slowly across the terrible desert to Egypt—donkeys and camels laden down with treasure to pay for Egypt's aid. On through the badlands they go, where lions and swift venomous snakes live—and Egypt will give you nothing in return! 7For Egypt's promises are worthless! "The Reluctant Dragon,"ᵇ I call her!

8Now go and write down this word of mine concerning Egypt, so that it will stand until the end of time, forever and forever, as an indictment of Israel's unbelief. 9For if you don't write it, they will claim I never warned them. "Oh, no," they'll say, "you never told us that!"

For they are stubborn rebels. 10, 11They tell my prophets, "Shut up—we don't want any more of your reports!" Or they say, "Don't tell us the truth; tell us nice things; tell us lies. Forget all this gloom; we've heard more than enough about your 'Holy One of Israel' and all he says."

12This is the reply of the Holy One of Israel:

Because you despise what I tell you and trust instead in frauds and lies and won't repent, 13therefore calamity will come upon you suddenly, as upon a bulging wall that bursts and falls; in one moment it comes crashing down. 14God will smash you like a broken dish; he will not act sparingly. Not a piece will be left large enough to use for carrying coals from the hearth, or a little water from the well. 15For the Lord God, the Holy One of

New Revised Standard

24 And those who err in spirit will come to
    understanding,
  and those who grumble will accept
    instruction.

The Futility of Reliance on Egypt

30 OH, REBELLIOUS children, says the LORD,
  who carry out a plan, but not mine;
who make an alliance, but against my will,
  adding sin to sin;
2 who set out to go down to Egypt
  without asking for my counsel,
to take refuge in the protection of Pharaoh,
  and to seek shelter in the shadow of Egypt;
3 Therefore the protection of Pharaoh shall
    become your shame,
  and the shelter in the shadow of Egypt your
    humiliation.
4 For though his officials are at Zoan
  and his envoys reach Hanes,
5 everyone comes to shame
  through a people that cannot profit them,
that brings neither help nor profit,
  but shame and disgrace.

6 An oracle concerning the animals of the Negeb.
Through a land of trouble and distress,
  of lioness and roaringᶜ lion,
  of viper and flying serpent,
they carry their riches on the backs of
    donkeys,
  and their treasures on the humps of camels,
to a people that cannot profit them.
7 For Egypt's help is worthless and empty,
  therefore I have called her,
  "Rahab who sits still."ᵈ

A Rebellious People

8 Go now, write it before them on a tablet,
  and inscribe it in a book,
so that it may be for the time to come
  as a witness forever.
9 For they are a rebellious people,
  faithless children,
children who will not hear
  the instruction of the LORD;
10 who say to the seers, "Do not see";
  and to the prophets, "Do not prophesy to us
    what is right;
speak to us smooth things,
  prophesy illusions,
11 leave the way, turn aside from the path,
  let us hear no more about the Holy One of
    Israel."
12 Therefore thus says the Holy One of Israel:
Because you reject this word,
  and put your trust in oppression and deceit,
  and rely on them;
13 therefore this iniquity shall become for you
  like a break in a high wall, bulging out, and
    about to collapse,
  whose crash comes suddenly, in an instant;
14 its breaking is like that of a potter's vessel
  that is smashed so ruthlessly
that among its fragments not a sherd is found
  for taking fire from the hearth,
  or dipping water out of the cistern.

ᵃ 30:2 Hezekiah was seeking a defensive alliance with Ethiopia's Egyptian dynasty against Sennacherib of Assyria.   ᵇ 30:7 The Reluctant Dragon, literally, "Rahab who sits still."

ᶜ Cn: Heb *from them*   ᵈ Meaning of Heb uncertain

King James

15For thus saith the Lord GOD, the Holy One of Israel; In returning and rest shall ye be saved; in quietness and in confidence shall be your strength: and ye would not.

16But ye said, No; for we will flee upon horses; therefore shall ye flee: and, We will ride upon the swift; therefore shall they that pursue you be swift.

17One thousand *shall flee* at the rebuke of one; at the rebuke of five shall ye flee: till ye be left as a beacon upon the top of a mountain, and as an ensign on an hill.

18¶ And therefore will the LORD wait, that he may be gracious unto you, and therefore will he be exalted, that he may have mercy upon you: for the LORD *is* a God of judgment: blessed *are* all they that wait for him.

19For the people shall dwell in Zion at Jerusalem: thou shalt weep no more: he will be very gracious unto thee at the voice of thy cry; when he shall hear it, he will answer thee.

20And *though* the Lord give you the bread of adversity, and the water of affliction, yet shall not thy teachers be removed into a corner any more, but thine eyes shall see thy teachers:

21And thine ears shall hear a word behind thee, saying, This *is* the way, walk ye in it, when ye turn to the right hand, and when ye turn to the left.

22Ye shall defile also the covering of thy graven images of silver, and the ornament of thy molten images of gold: thou shalt cast them away as a menstruous cloth; thou shalt say unto it, Get thee hence.

23Then shall he give the rain of thy seed, that thou shalt sow the ground withal; and bread of the increase of the earth, and it shall be fat and plenteous: in that day shall thy cattle feed in large pastures.

24The oxen likewise and the young asses that ear the ground shall eat clean provender, which hath been winnowed with the shovel and with the fan.

25And there shall be upon every high mountain, and upon every high hill, rivers *and* streams of waters in the day of the great slaughter, when the towers fall.

26Moreover the light of the moon shall be as the light of the sun, and the light of the sun shall be sevenfold, as the light of seven days, in the day that the LORD bindeth up the breach of his people, and healeth the stroke of their wound.

27¶ Behold, the name of the LORD cometh from far, burning *with* his anger, and the burden *thereof is* heavy: his lips are full of indignation, and his tongue as a devouring fire:

28And his breath, as an overflowing stream, shall reach to the midst of the neck, to sift the nations with the sieve of vanity: and *there shall be* a bridle in the jaws of the people, causing *them* to err.

29Ye shall have a song, as in the night *when* a holy solemnity is kept; and gladness of heart, as when one goeth with a pipe to come into the mountain of the LORD, to the mighty One of Israel.

30And the LORD shall cause his glorious voice to be heard, and shall show the lighting down of his arm, with the indignation of *his* anger, and *with* the flame of a devouring fire, *with* scattering, and tempest, and hailstones.

31For through the voice of the LORD shall the Assyrian be beaten down, *which* smote with a rod.

New International

15This is what the Sovereign LORD, the Holy One of Israel, says:

"In repentance and rest is your salvation,
    in quietness and trust is your strength,
    but you would have none of it.
16You said, 'No, we will flee on horses.'
    Therefore you will flee!
You said, 'We will ride off on swift horses.'
    Therefore your pursuers will be swift!
17A thousand will flee
    at the threat of one;
at the threat of five
    you will all flee away,
till you are left
    like a flagstaff on a mountaintop,
    like a banner on a hill."

18Yet the LORD longs to be gracious to you;
    he rises to show you compassion.
For the LORD is a God of justice.
    Blessed are all who wait for him!

19O people of Zion, who live in Jerusalem, you will weep no more. How gracious he will be when you cry for help! As soon as he hears, he will answer you. 20Although the Lord gives you the bread of adversity and the water of affliction, your teachers will be hidden no more; with your own eyes you will see them. 21Whether you turn to the right or to the left, your ears will hear a voice behind you, saying, "This is the way; walk in it." 22Then you will defile your idols overlaid with silver and your images covered with gold; you will throw them away like a menstrual cloth and say to them, "Away with you!"

23He will also send you rain for the seed you sow in the ground, and the food that comes from the land will be rich and plentiful. In that day your cattle will graze in broad meadows. 24The oxen and donkeys that work the soil will eat fodder and mash, spread out with fork and shovel. 25In the day of great slaughter, when the towers fall, streams of water will flow on every high mountain and every lofty hill. 26The moon will shine like the sun, and the sunlight will be seven times brighter, like the light of seven full days, when the LORD binds up the bruises of his people and heals the wounds he inflicted.

27See, the Name of the LORD comes from afar,
    with burning anger and dense clouds of
        smoke;
his lips are full of wrath,
    and his tongue is a consuming fire.
28His breath is like a rushing torrent,
    rising up to the neck.
He shakes the nations in the sieve of
        destruction;
    he places in the jaws of the peoples
    a bit that leads them astray.
29And you will sing
    as on the night you celebrate a holy festival;
your hearts will rejoice
    as when people go up with flutes
to the mountain of the LORD,
    to the Rock of Israel.
30The LORD will cause men to hear his majestic
        voice
    and will make them see his arm coming down
    with raging anger and consuming fire,
    with cloudburst, thunderstorm and hail.
31The voice of the LORD will shatter Assyria;
    with his scepter he will strike them down.

Living Bible

Israel, says: Only in returning to me and waiting for me will you be saved; in quietness and confidence is your strength; but you'll have none of this.

16"No," you say. "We will get our help from Egypt; they will give us swift horses for riding to battle." But the only swiftness you are going to see is the swiftness of your enemies chasing you! 17One of them will chase a thousand of you! Five of them will scatter you until not two of you are left together. You will be like lonely trees on the distant mountain tops. 18Yet the Lord still waits for you to come to him, so he can show you his love; he will conquer you to bless you, just as he said. For the Lord is faithful to his promises. Blessed are all those who wait for him to help them.

19O my people in Jerusalem, you shall weep no more, for he will surely be gracious to you at the sound of your cry. He will answer you. 20Though he give you the bread of adversity and water of affliction, yet he will be with you to teach you—with your own eyes you will see your Teacher. 21And if you leave God's paths and go astray, you will hear a Voice behind you say, "No, this is the way; walk here." 22And you will destroy all your silver idols and gold images and cast them out like filthy things you hate to touch. "Ugh!" you'll say to them. "Be gone!"

23Then God will bless you with rain at planting time and with wonderful harvests and with ample pastures for your cows. 24The oxen and young donkeys that till the ground will eat grain, its chaff blown away by the wind. 25In that day when God steps in to destroy your enemies, he will give you streams of water flowing down each mountain and every hill. 26The moon will be as bright as the sun, and the sunlight brighter than seven days! So it will be when the Lord begins to heal his people and to cure the wounds he gave them.

27See, the Lord comes from afar, aflame with wrath, surrounded by thick rising smoke. His lips are filled with fury; his words consume like fire. 28His wrath pours out like floods upon them all, to sweep them all away. He will sift out the proud nations and bridle them and lead them off to their doom.

29But the people of God will sing a song of solemn joy, like songs in the night when holy feasts are held; his people will have gladness of heart, as when a flutist leads a pilgrim band to Jerusalem to the Mountain of the Lord, the Rock of Israel. 30And the Lord shall cause his majestic voice to be heard and shall crush down his mighty arm upon his enemies with angry indignation and with devouring flames and tornados and terrible storms and huge hailstones. 31The voice of the Lord shall punish the Assyrians, who had been his rod of punishment. 32And when the Lord smites them, his peo-

New Revised Standard

15 For thus said the Lord GOD, the Holy One of
    Israel:
In returning and rest you shall be saved;
    in quietness and in trust shall be your
        strength.
But you refused 16and said,
"No! We will flee upon horses"—
    therefore you shall flee!
and, "We will ride upon swift steeds"—
    therefore your pursuers shall be swift!
17 A thousand shall flee at the threat of one,
    at the threat of five you shall flee,
until you are left
    like a flagstaff on the top of a mountain,
    like a signal on a hill.

God's Promise to Zion

18 Therefore the LORD waits to be gracious to
        you;
    therefore he will rise up to show mercy to
        you.
    For the LORD is a God of justice;
        blessed are all those who wait for him.

19 Truly, O people in Zion, inhabitants of Jerusalem, you shall weep no more. He will surely be gracious to you at the sound of your cry; when he hears it, he will answer you. 20Though the Lord may give you the bread of adversity and the water of affliction, yet your Teacher will not hide himself any more, but your eyes shall see your Teacher. 21And when you turn to the right or when you turn to the left, your ears shall hear a word behind you, saying, "This is the way; walk in it." 22Then you will defile your silver-covered idols and your gold-plated images. You will scatter them like filthy rags; you will say to them, "Away with you!"

23 He will give rain for the seed with which you sow the ground, and grain, the produce of the ground, which will be rich and plenteous. On that day your cattle will graze in broad pastures; 24and the oxen and donkeys that till the ground will eat silage, which has been winnowed with shovel and fork. 25On every lofty mountain and every high hill there will be brooks running with water—on a day of the great slaughter, when the towers fall. 26Moreover the light of the moon will be like the light of the sun, and the light of the sun will be sevenfold, like the light of seven days, on the day when the LORD binds up the injuries of his people, and heals the wounds inflicted by his blow.

Judgment on Assyria

27 See, the name of the LORD comes from far
        away,
    burning with his anger, and in thick rising
        smoke;ᵃ
    his lips are full of indignation,
        and his tongue is like a devouring fire;
28 his breath is like an overflowing stream
        that reaches up to the neck—
    to sift the nations with the sieve of
        destruction,
        and to place on the jaws of the peoples a
        bridle that leads them astray.

29 You shall have a song as in the night when a holy festival is kept; and gladness of heart, as when one sets out to the sound of the flute to go to the mountain of the LORD, to the Rock of Israel. 30And the LORD will cause his majestic voice to be heard and the descending blow of his arm to be seen, in furious anger and a flame of devouring fire, with a cloudburst and tempest and hailstones. 31The Assyrian will be terror-stricken at the voice of the LORD, when he strikes with his rod. 32And

ᵃ Meaning of Heb uncertain

King James

32And *in* every place where the grounded staff shall pass, which the LORD shall lay upon him, *it* shall be with tabrets and harps: and in battles of shaking will he fight with it.

33For Tophet *is* ordained of old; yea, for the king it is prepared; he hath made *it* deep *and* large: the pile thereof *is* fire and much wood; the breath of the LORD, like a stream of brimstone, doth kindle it.

31 WOE TO them that go down to Egypt for help; and stay on horses, and trust in chariots, because *they are* many; and in horsemen, because they are very strong; but they look not unto the Holy One of Israel, neither seek the LORD!

2Yet he also *is* wise, and will bring evil, and will not call back his words: but will arise against the house of the evildoers, and against the help of them that work iniquity.

3Now the Egyptians *are* men, and not God; and their horses flesh, and not spirit. When the LORD shall stretch out his hand, both he that helpeth shall fall, and he that is helped shall fall down, and they all shall fail together.

4For thus hath the LORD spoken unto me, Like as the lion and the young lion roaring on his prey, when a multitude of shepherds is called forth against him, *he* will not be afraid of their voice, nor abase himself for the noise of them: so shall the LORD of hosts come down to fight for mount Zion, and for the hill thereof.

5As birds flying, so will the LORD of hosts defend Jerusalem; defending also he will deliver *it; and* passing over he will preserve *it*.

6¶ Turn ye unto *him from* whom the children of Israel have deeply revolted.

7For in that day every man shall cast away his idols of silver, and his idols of gold, which your own hands have made unto you *for* a sin.

8¶ Then shall the Assyrian fall with the sword, not of a mighty man; and the sword, not of a mean man, shall devour him: but he shall flee from the sword, and his young men shall be discomfited.

9And he shall pass over to his strong hold for fear, and his princes shall be afraid of the ensign, saith the LORD, whose fire *is* in Zion, and his furnace in Jerusalem.

New International

32Every stroke the LORD lays on them
  with his punishing rod
will be to the music of tambourines and harps,
  as he fights them in battle with the blows of
    his arm.
33Topheth has long been prepared;
  it has been made ready for the king.
Its fire pit has been made deep and wide,
  with an abundance of fire and wood;
the breath of the LORD,
  like a stream of burning sulfur,
  sets it ablaze.

Woe to Those Who Rely on Egypt

31 WOE TO those who go down to Egypt for help,
  who rely on horses,
who trust in the multitude of their chariots
  and in the great strength of their horsemen,
but do not look to the Holy One of Israel,
  or seek help from the LORD.
2Yet he too is wise and can bring disaster;
  he does not take back his words.
He will rise up against the house of the wicked,
  against those who help evildoers.
3But the Egyptians are men and not God;
  their horses are flesh and not spirit.
When the LORD stretches out his hand,
  he who helps will stumble,
  he who is helped will fall;
  both will perish together.

4This is what the LORD says to me:

"As a lion growls,
  a great lion over his prey—
and though a whole band of shepherds
  is called together against him,
he is not frightened by their shouts
  or disturbed by their clamor—
so the LORD Almighty will come down
  to do battle on Mount Zion and on its
    heights.
5Like birds hovering overhead,
  the LORD Almighty will shield Jerusalem;
he will shield it and deliver it,
  he will 'pass over' it and will rescue it."

6Return to him you have so greatly revolted against, O Israelites. 7For in that day every one of you will reject the idols of silver and gold your sinful hands have made.

8"Assyria will fall by a sword that is not of man;
  a sword, not of mortals, will devour them.
They will flee before the sword
  and their young men will be put to forced
    labor.
9Their stronghold will fall because of terror;
  at sight of the battle standard their
    commanders will panic,"
declares the LORD,
  whose fire is in Zion,
  whose furnace is in Jerusalem.

Living Bible

ple will rejoice with music and song. 33The funeral pyre has long been ready, prepared for Molech, the Assyrian god; it is piled high with wood. The breath of the Lord, like fire from a volcano, will set it all on fire.

31 WOE TO those who run to Egypt for help, trusting their mighty cavalry and chariots instead of looking to the Holy One of Israel and consulting him. 2In his wisdom, he will send great evil on his people and will not change his mind. He will rise against them for the evil they have done, and crush their allies too. 3For these Egyptians are mere men, not God! Their horses are puny flesh, not mighty spirits! When the Lord clenches his fist against them, they will stumble and fall among those they are trying to help. All will fail together.

4, 5But the Lord has told me this: When a lion, even a young one, kills a sheep, he pays no attention to the shepherd's shouts and noise. He goes right on and eats. In such manner the Lord will come and fight upon Mount Zion. He will not be frightened away! He, the Lord Almighty, will hover over Jerusalem as birds hover round their nests, and he will defend the city and deliver it.

6Therefore, O my people, though you are such wicked rebels, come, return to God. 7I know the glorious day will come when every one of you will throw away his gold idols and silver images—which in your sinfulness you have made. 8And the Assyrians will be destroyed, but not by swords of men. The "sword of God" will smite them. They will panic and flee, and the strong young Assyrians will be taken away as slaves. 9Even their generals will quake with terror and flee when they see the battle flags of Israel, says the Lord. For the flame of God burns brightly in Jerusalem.

New Revised Standard

every stroke of the staff of punishment that the LORD lays upon him will be to the sound of timbrels and lyres; battling with brandished arm he will fight with him. 33For his burning placea has long been prepared; truly it is made ready for the king,b its pyre made deep and wide, with fire and wood in abundance; the breath of the LORD, like a stream of sulfur, kindles it.

Alliance with Egypt Is Futile

31 ALAS FOR those who go down to Egypt for help
and who rely on horses,
who trust in chariots because they are many
and in horsemen because they are very
strong,
but do not look to the Holy One of Israel
or consult the LORD!
2 Yet he too is wise and brings disaster;
he does not call back his words,
but will rise against the house of the
evildoers,
and against the helpers of those who work
iniquity.
3 The Egyptians are human, and not God;
their horses are flesh, and not spirit.
When the LORD stretches out his hand,
the helper will stumble, and the one helped
will fall,
and they will all perish together.

4 For thus the LORD said to me,
As a lion or a young lion growls over its prey,
and—when a band of shepherds is called
out against it—
is not terrified by their shouting
or daunted at their noise,
so the LORD of hosts will come down
to fight upon Mount Zion and upon its hill.
5 Like birds hovering overhead, so the LORD of
hosts
will protect Jerusalem;
he will protect and deliver it,
he will spare and rescue it.

6 Turn back to him whom youc have deeply betrayed, O people of Israel. 7For on that day all of you shall throw away your idols of silver and idols of gold, which your hands have sinfully made for you.
8 "Then the Assyrian shall fall by a sword, not
of mortals;
and a sword, not of humans, shall devour
him;
he shall flee from the sword,
and his young men shall be put to forced
labor.
9 His rock shall pass away in terror,
and his officers desert the standard in
panic,"
says the LORD, whose fire is in Zion,
and whose furnace is in Jerusalem.

a Or Topheth   b Or Molech   c Heb they

King James

32 BEHOLD, A king shall reign in righteousness, and princes shall rule in judgment.

2And a man shall be as an hiding place from the wind, and a covert from the tempest; as rivers of water in a dry place, as the shadow of a great rock in a weary land.

3And the eyes of them that see shall not be dim, and the ears of them that hear shall hearken.

4The heart also of the rash shall understand knowledge, and the tongue of the stammerers shall be ready to speak plainly.

5The vile person shall be no more called liberal, nor the churl said *to be* bountiful.

6For the vile person will speak villany, and his heart will work iniquity, to practise hypocrisy, and to utter error against the LORD, to make empty the soul of the hungry, and he will cause the drink of the thirsty to fail.

7The instruments also of the churl *are* evil: he deviseth wicked devices to destroy the poor with lying words, even when the needy speaketh right.

8But the liberal deviseth liberal things; and by liberal things shall he stand.

9¶ Rise up, ye women that are at ease; hear my voice, ye careless daughters; give ear unto my speech.

10Many days and years shall ye be troubled, ye careless women: for the vintage shall fail, the gathering shall not come.

11Tremble, ye women that are at ease; be troubled, ye careless ones: strip you, and make you bare, and gird *sackcloth* upon *your* loins.

12They shall lament for the teats, for the pleasant fields, for the fruitful vine.

13Upon the land of my people shall come up thorns *and* briers; Yea, upon all the houses of joy *in* the joyous city:

14Because the palaces shall be forsaken; the multitude of the city shall be left; the forts and towers shall be for dens for ever, a joy of wild asses, a pasture of flocks;

15Until the spirit be poured upon us from on high, and the wilderness be a fruitful field, and the fruitful field be counted for a forest.

16Then judgment shall dwell in the wilderness, and righteousness remain in the fruitful field.

17And the work of righteousness shall be peace; and the effect of righteousness quietness and assurance for ever.

18And my people shall dwell in a peaceable habitation, and in sure dwellings, and in quiet resting places;

New International

The Kingdom of Righteousness

32 SEE, A king will reign in righteousness and rulers will rule with justice.

2Each man will be like a shelter from the wind
  and a refuge from the storm,
like streams of water in the desert
  and the shadow of a great rock in a thirsty
    land.

3Then the eyes of those who see will no longer
    be closed,
  and the ears of those who hear will listen.
4The mind of the rash will know and understand,
  and the stammering tongue will be fluent and
    clear.
5No longer will the fool be called noble
  nor the scoundrel be highly respected.
6For the fool speaks folly,
  his mind is busy with evil:
He practices ungodliness
  and spreads error concerning the LORD;
the hungry he leaves empty
  and from the thirsty he withholds water.
7The scoundrel's methods are wicked,
  he makes up evil schemes
to destroy the poor with lies,
  even when the plea of the needy is just.
8But the noble man makes noble plans,
  and by noble deeds he stands.

The Women of Jerusalem

9You women who are so complacent,
  rise up and listen to me;
you daughters who feel secure,
  hear what I have to say!
10In little more than a year
  you who feel secure will tremble;
the grape harvest will fail,
  and the harvest of fruit will not come.
11Tremble, you complacent women;
  shudder, you daughters who feel secure!
Strip off your clothes,
  put sackcloth around your waists.
12Beat your breasts for the pleasant fields,
  for the fruitful vines
13and for the land of my people,
  a land overgrown with thorns and briers—
yes, mourn for all houses of merriment
  and for this city of revelry.
14The fortress will be abandoned,
  the noisy city deserted;
citadel and watchtower will become a wasteland
    forever,
  the delight of donkeys, a pasture for flocks,
15till the Spirit is poured upon us from on high,
  and the desert becomes a fertile field,
  and the fertile field seems like a forest.
16Justice will dwell in the desert
  and righteousness live in the fertile field.
17The fruit of righteousness will be peace;
  the effect of righteousness will be quietness
    and confidence forever.
18My people will live in peaceful dwelling places,
  in secure homes,
  in undisturbed places of rest.

Living Bible

32 LOOK, A righteous King is coming, with honest princes! ²He will shelter Israel from the storm and wind. He will refresh her as a river in the desert and as the cooling shadow of a mighty rock within a hot and weary land. ³Then at last the eyes of Israel will open wide to God; his people will listen to his voice. ⁴Even the hotheads among them will be full of sense and understanding, and those who stammer in uncertainty will speak out plainly.

⁵In those days the ungodly, the atheists, will not be heroes! Wealthy cheaters will not be spoken of as generous, outstanding men! ⁶Everyone will recognize an evil man when he sees him, and hypocrites will fool no one at all. Their lies about God and their cheating of the hungry will be plain for all to see. ⁷The smooth tricks of evil men will be exposed, as will all the lies they use to oppress the poor in the courts. ⁸But good men will be generous to others and will be blessed of God for all they do.

⁹Listen, you women who loll around in lazy ease; listen to me and I will tell you your reward: ¹⁰In a short time—in just a little more than a year—suddenly you'll care, O careless ones. For the crops of fruit will fail; the harvest will not take place. ¹¹Tremble, O women of ease; throw off your unconcern. Strip off your pretty clothes—wear sackcloth for your grief. ¹²Beat your breasts in sorrow for those bountiful farms of yours that will soon be gone, and for those fruitful vines of other years. ¹³For your lands will thrive with thorns and briars; your joyous homes and happy cities will be gone. ¹⁴Palaces and mansions will all be deserted, the crowded cities empty. Wild herds of donkeys and goats will graze upon the mountains where the watchtowers are, ¹⁵until at last the Spirit is poured down on us from heaven. Then once again enormous crops will come. ¹⁶Then justice will rule through all the land, ¹⁷and out of justice, peace. Quietness and confidence will reign forever more.

¹⁸My people will live in safety, quietly at home, ¹⁹but

New Revised Standard

Government with Justice Predicted

32 SEE, A king will reign in righteousness,
and princes will rule with justice.
2 Each will be like a hiding place from the wind,
a covert from the tempest,
like streams of water in a dry place,
like the shade of a great rock in a weary land.
3 Then the eyes of those who have sight will not be closed,
and the ears of those who have hearing will listen.
4 The minds of the rash will have good judgment,
and the tongues of stammerers will speak readily and distinctly.
5 A fool will no longer be called noble,
nor a villain said to be honorable.
6 For fools speak folly,
and their minds plot iniquity:
to practice ungodliness,
to utter error concerning the LORD,
to leave the craving of the hungry unsatisfied,
and to deprive the thirsty of drink.
7 The villainies of villains are evil;
they devise wicked devices
to ruin the poor with lying words,
even when the plea of the needy is right.
8 But those who are noble plan noble things,
and by noble things they stand.

Complacent Women Warned of Disaster

9 Rise up, you women who are at ease, hear my voice;
you complacent daughters, listen to my speech.
10 In little more than a year
you will shudder, you complacent ones;
for the vintage will fail,
the fruit harvest will not come.
11 Tremble, you women who are at ease,
shudder, you complacent ones;
strip, and make yourselves bare,
and put sackcloth on your loins.
12 Beat your breasts for the pleasant fields,
for the fruitful vine,
13 for the soil of my people
growing up in thorns and briers;
yes, for all the joyous houses
in the jubilant city.
14 For the palace will be forsaken,
the populous city deserted;
the hill and the watchtower
will become dens forever,
the joy of wild asses,
a pasture for flocks;
15 until a spirit from on high is poured out on us,
and the wilderness becomes a fruitful field,
and the fruitful field is deemed a forest.

The Peace of God's Reign

16 Then justice will dwell in the wilderness,
and righteousness abide in the fruitful field.
17 The effect of righteousness will be peace,
and the result of righteousness, quietness and trust forever.
18 My people will abide in a peaceful habitation,
in secure dwellings, and in quiet resting places.

King James

19When it shall hail, coming down on the forest; and the city shall be low in a low place.

20Blessed *are* ye that sow beside all waters, that send forth *thither* the feet of the ox and the ass.

33 WOE TO thee that spoilest, and thou *wast* not spoiled; and dealest treacherously, and they dealt not treacherously with thee! when thou shalt cease to spoil, thou shalt be spoiled; *and* when thou shalt make an end to deal treacherously, they shall deal treacherously with thee.

2O LORD, be gracious unto us; we have waited for thee: be thou their arm every morning, our salvation also in the time of trouble.

3At the noise of the tumult the people fled; at the lifting up of thyself the nations were scattered.

4And your spoil shall be gathered *like* the gathering of the caterpillar: as the running to and fro of locusts shall he run upon them.

5The LORD is exalted; for he dwelleth on high: he hath filled Zion with judgment and righteousness.

6And wisdom and knowledge shall be the stability of thy times, *and* strength of salvation: the fear of the LORD *is* his treasure.

7Behold, their valiant ones shall cry without: the ambassadors of peace shall weep bitterly.

8The highways lie waste, the wayfaring man ceaseth: he hath broken the covenant, he hath despised the cities, he regardeth no man.

9The earth mourneth *and* languisheth: Lebanon is ashamed *and* hewn down: Sharon is like a wilderness; and Bashan and Carmel shake off *their fruits.*

10Now will I rise, saith the LORD; now will I be exalted; now will I lift up myself.

11Ye shall conceive chaff, ye shall bring forth stubble: your breath, *as* fire, shall devour you.

12And the people shall be *as* the burnings of lime: *as* thorns cut up shall they be burned in the fire.

13¶ Hear, ye *that are* far off, what I have done; and, ye *that are* near, acknowledge my might.

14The sinners in Zion are afraid; fearfulness hath surprised the hypocrites. Who among us shall dwell with the devouring fire? who among us shall dwell with everlasting burnings?

New International

19Though hail flattens the forest
    and the city is leveled completely,
20how blessed you will be,
    sowing your seed by every stream,
    and letting your cattle and donkeys range
        free.

Distress and Help

33 WOE TO you, O destroyer,
    you who have not been destroyed!
Woe to you, O traitor,
    you who have not been betrayed!
When you stop destroying,
    you will be destroyed;
when you stop betraying,
    you will be betrayed.

2O LORD, be gracious to us;
    we long for you.
Be our strength every morning,
    our salvation in time of distress.
3At the thunder of your voice, the peoples flee;
    when you rise up, the nations scatter.
4Your plunder, O nations, is harvested as by
        young locusts;
    like a swarm of locusts men pounce on it.

5The LORD is exalted, for he dwells on high;
    he will fill Zion with justice and
        righteousness.
6He will be the sure foundation for your times,
    a rich store of salvation and wisdom and
        knowledge;
    the fear of the LORD is the key to this
        treasure.a

7Look, their brave men cry aloud in the streets;
    the envoys of peace weep bitterly.
8The highways are deserted,
    no travelers are on the roads.
 The treaty is broken,
    its witnessesb are despised,
    no one is respected.
9The land mournsc and wastes away,
    Lebanon is ashamed and withers;
 Sharon is like the Arabah,
    and Bashan and Carmel drop their leaves.

10"Now will I arise," says the LORD.
    "Now will I be exalted;
    now will I be lifted up.
11You conceive chaff,
    you give birth to straw;
    your breath is a fire that consumes you.
12The peoples will be burned as if to lime;
    like cut thornbushes they will be set ablaze."

13You who are far away, hear what I have done;
    you who are near, acknowledge my power!
14The sinners in Zion are terrified;
    trembling grips the godless:
 "Who of us can dwell with the consuming fire?
    Who of us can dwell with everlasting
        burning?"

---

a 6 Or *is a treasure from him*   b 8 Dead Sea Scrolls; Masoretic Text / *the cities*   c 9 Or *dries up*

Living Bible

the Assyrians[d] will be destroyed and their cities laid low. 20And God will greatly bless his people. Wherever they plant, bountiful crops will spring up, and their flocks and herds will graze in green pastures.

33 WOE TO you, Assyrians,[e] who have destroyed everything around you but have never felt destruction for yourselves. You expect others to respect their promises to you, while you betray them! Now you, too, will be betrayed and destroyed.

2But to us, O Lord, be merciful, for we have waited for you. Be our strength each day and our salvation in the time of trouble. 3The enemy runs at the sound of your voice. When you stand up, the nations flee. 4Just as locusts strip the fields and vines, so Jerusalem will strip the fallen army of Assyria![f]

5The Lord is very great, and lives in heaven. He will make Jerusalem the home of justice and goodness and righteousness. 6An abundance of salvation is stored up for Judah in a safe place, along with wisdom and knowledge and reverence for God.

7But now your ambassadors weep in bitter disappointment, for Assyria has refused their cry for peace. 8Your roads lie in ruins; travelers detour on back roads. The Assyrians have broken their peace pact[g] and care nothing for the promises they made in the presence of witnesses—they have no respect for anyone. 9All the land of Israel is in trouble; Lebanon has been destroyed; Sharon has become a wilderness; Bashan and Carmel are plundered.

10But the Lord says, I will stand up and show my power and might. 11You Assyrians will gain nothing by all your efforts. Your own breath will turn to fire and kill you. 12Your armies will be burned to lime, like thorns cut down and tossed in the fire.

13Listen to what I have done, O nations far away! And you that are near, acknowledge my might! 14The sinners among my people shake with fear. "Which one of us," they cry, "can live here in the presence of this all-consuming, Everlasting Fire?" 15I will tell you who

New Revised Standard

19 The forest will disappear completely,[h]
   and the city will be utterly laid low.
20 Happy will you be who sow beside every
     stream,
   who let the ox and the donkey range freely.

A Prophecy of Deliverance from Foes

33 AH, YOU destroyer,
     who yourself have not been destroyed;
   you treacherous one,
     with whom no one has dealt treacherously!
   When you have ceased to destroy,
     you will be destroyed;
   and when you have stopped dealing
       treacherously,
     you will be dealt with treacherously.

2 O LORD, be gracious to us; we wait for you.
   Be our arm every morning,
     our salvation in the time of trouble.
3 At the sound of tumult, peoples fled;
     before your majesty, nations scattered.
4 Spoil was gathered as the caterpillar gathers;
     as locusts leap, they leaped[i] upon it.
5 The LORD is exalted, he dwells on high;
     he filled Zion with justice and
       righteousness;
6 he will be the stability of your times,
   abundance of salvation, wisdom, and
       knowledge;
     the fear of the LORD is Zion's treasure.[j]

7 Listen! the valiant[i] cry in the streets;
     the envoys of peace weep bitterly.
8 The highways are deserted,
     travelers have quit the road.
   The treaty is broken,
     its oaths[k] are despised,
     its obligation[l] is disregarded.
9 The land mourns and languishes;
     Lebanon is confounded and withers away;
   Sharon is like a desert;
     and Bashan and Carmel shake off their
       leaves.

10 "Now I will arise," says the LORD,
     "now I will lift myself up;
     now I will be exalted.
11 You conceive chaff, you bring forth stubble;
     your breath is a fire that will consume you.
12 And the peoples will be as if burned to lime,
     like thorns cut down, that are burned in the
       fire."

13 Hear, you who are far away, what I have
       done;
     and you who are near, acknowledge my
       might.
14 The sinners in Zion are afraid;
     trembling has seized the godless:
   "Who among us can live with the devouring
       fire?
   Who among us can live with everlasting
       flames?"

---

d 32:19 But the Assyrians, implied.   e 33:1 Assyrians, implied.
f 33:4 fallen army of Assyria, see 2 Kings 19:35.   g 33:8 peace pact, see
2 Kings 18:14-17.

h Cn: Heb And it will hail when the forest comes down   i Meaning of Heb
uncertain   j Heb his treasure; meaning of Heb uncertain   k Q Ms: MT cities
l Or everyone

King James

15He that walketh righteously, and speaketh uprightly; he that despiseth the gain of oppressions, that shaketh
his hands from holding of bribes, that stoppeth his ears
from hearing of blood, and shutteth his eyes from seeing
evil;
16He shall dwell on high: his place of defence *shall
be* the munitions of rocks: bread shall be given him; his
waters *shall be* sure.
17Thine eyes shall see the king in his beauty: they
shall behold the land that is very far off.
18Thine heart shall meditate terror. Where *is* the
scribe? where *is* the receiver? where *is* he that counted
the towers?
19Thou shalt not see a fierce people, a people of a
deeper speech than thou canst perceive; of a stammering
tongue, *that thou canst* not understand.
20Look upon Zion, the city of our solemnities: thine
eyes shall see Jerusalem a quiet habitation, a tabernacle
that shall not be taken down; not one of the stakes thereof shall ever be removed, neither shall any of the cords
thereof be broken.
21But there the glorious LORD *will be* unto us a place
of broad rivers *and* streams; wherein shall go no galley
with oars, neither shall gallant ship pass thereby.
22For the LORD *is* our judge, the LORD *is* our lawgiver, the LORD *is* our king; he will save us.
23Thy tacklings are loosed; they could not well
strengthen their mast, they could not spread the sail: then
is the prey of a great spoil divided; the lame take the
prey.
24And the inhabitant shall not say, I am sick: the
people that dwell therein *shall be* forgiven *their* iniquity.

34 COME NEAR, ye nations, to hear; and heark-
en, ye people: let the earth hear, and all that is
therein; the world, and all things that come forth of it.
2For the indignation of the LORD *is* upon all nations,
and *his* fury upon all their armies: he hath utterly destroyed them, he hath delivered them to the slaughter.
3Their slain also shall be cast out, and their stink shall
come up out of their carcases, and the mountains shall
be melted with their blood.

New International

15He who walks righteously
    and speaks what is right,
who rejects gain from extortion
    and keeps his hand from accepting bribes,
who stops his ears against plots of murder
    and shuts his eyes against contemplating
        evil—
16this is the man who will dwell on the heights,
    whose refuge will be the mountain fortress.
His bread will be supplied,
    and water will not fail him.

17Your eyes will see the king in his beauty
    and view a land that stretches afar.
18In your thoughts you will ponder the former
        terror:
    "Where is that chief officer?
Where is the one who took the revenue?
Where is the officer in charge of the towers?"
19You will see those arrogant people no more,
    those people of an obscure speech,
    with their strange, incomprehensible tongue.

20Look upon Zion, the city of our festivals;
    your eyes will see Jerusalem,
    a peaceful abode, a tent that will not be
        moved;
    its stakes will never be pulled up,
    nor any of its ropes broken.
21There the LORD will be our Mighty One.
    It will be like a place of broad rivers and
        streams.
    No galley with oars will ride them,
    no mighty ship will sail them.
22For the LORD is our judge,
    the LORD is our lawgiver,
    the LORD is our king;
    it is he who will save us.

23Your rigging hangs loose:
    The mast is not held secure,
    the sail is not spread.
Then an abundance of spoils will be divided
    and even the lame will carry off plunder.
24No one living in Zion will say, "I am ill";
    and the sins of those who dwell there will be
        forgiven.

Judgment Against the Nations

34 COME NEAR, you nations, and listen;
    pay attention, you peoples!
Let the earth hear, and all that is in it,
    the world, and all that comes out of it!
2The LORD is angry with all nations;
    his wrath is upon all their armies.
He will totally destroy[a] them,
    he will give them over to slaughter.
3Their slain will be thrown out,
    their dead bodies will send up a stench;
    the mountains will be soaked with their
        blood.

---

[a] 2 The Hebrew term refers to the irrevocable giving over of things or persons
to the LORD, often by totally destroying them; also in verse 5.

Living Bible

can live here: All who are honest and fair, who reject making profit by fraud, who hold back their hands from taking bribes, who refuse to listen to those who plot murder, who shut their eyes to all enticement to do wrong. 16Such as these shall dwell on high. The rocks of the mountains will be their fortress of safety; food will be supplied to them and they will have all the water they need.

17Your eyes will see the King in his beauty, and the highlands of heaven far away. 18Your mind will think back to this time of terror when the Assyrian officers outside your walls are counting your towers and estimating how much they will get from your fallen city. 19But soon they will all be gone. These fierce, violent people, with a strange, jabbering language you can't understand, will disappear.

20Instead you will see Jerusalem at peace, a place where God is worshiped, a city quiet and unmoved. 21The glorious Lord will be to us as a wide river of protection, and no enemy can cross. 22For the Lord is our Judge, our Lawgiver and our King; he will care for us and save us. 23The enemies' sails hang loose on broken masts with useless tackle. Their treasure will be divided by the people of God; even the lame will win their share. 24The people of Israel will no longer say, "We are sick and helpless," for the Lord will forgive them their sins and bless them.

New Revised Standard

15 Those who walk righteously and speak uprightly,
    who despise the gain of oppression,
  who wave away a bribe instead of accepting it,
    who stop their ears from hearing of bloodshed
    and shut their eyes from looking on evil,
16 they will live on the heights;
    their refuge will be the fortresses of rocks;
    their food will be supplied, their water assured.

The Land of the Majestic King

17 Your eyes will see the king in his beauty;
    they will behold a land that stretches far away.
18 Your mind will muse on the terror:
    "Where is the one who counted?
    Where is the one who weighed the tribute?
    Where is the one who counted the towers?"
19 No longer will you see the insolent people,
    the people of an obscure speech that you cannot comprehend,
    stammering in a language that you cannot understand.
20 Look on Zion, the city of our appointed festivals!
    Your eyes will see Jerusalem,
    a quiet habitation, an immovable tent,
    whose stakes will never be pulled up,
    and none of whose ropes will be broken.
21 But there the LORD in majesty will be for us
    a place of broad rivers and streams,
    where no galley with oars can go,
    nor stately ship can pass.
22 For the LORD is our judge, the LORD is our ruler,
    the LORD is our king; he will save us.

23 Your rigging hangs loose;
    it cannot hold the mast firm in its place,
    or keep the sail spread out.

  Then prey and spoil in abundance will be divided;
    even the lame will fall to plundering.
24 And no inhabitant will say, "I am sick";
    the people who live there will be forgiven their iniquity.

Judgment on the Nations

34 COME HERE and listen, O nations of the earth; let the world and everything in it hear my words. 2For the Lord is enraged against the nations; his fury is against their armies. He will utterly destroy them and deliver them to slaughter. 3Their dead will be left unburied, and the stench of rotting bodies will fill the land, and the mountains will flow with their blood. 4At

34 DRAW NEAR, O nations, to hear;
    O peoples, give heed!
  Let the earth hear, and all that fills it;
    the world, and all that comes from it.
2 For the LORD is enraged against all the nations,
    and furious against all their hoards;
    he has doomed them, has given them over for slaughter.
3 Their slain shall be cast out,
    and the stench of their corpses shall rise;
    the mountains shall flow with their blood.

King James

⁴And all the host of heaven shall be dissolved, and the heavens shall be rolled together as a scroll: and all their host shall fall down, as the leaf falleth off from the vine, and as a falling *fig* from the fig tree.

⁵For my sword shall be bathed in heaven: behold, it shall come down upon Idumea, and upon the people of my curse, to judgment.

⁶The sword of the LORD is filled with blood, it is made fat with fatness, *and* with the blood of lambs and goats, with the fat of the kidneys of rams: for the LORD hath a sacrifice in Bozrah, and a great slaughter in the land of Idumea.

⁷And the unicorns shall come down with them, and the bullocks with the bulls; and their land shall be soaked with blood, and their dust made fat with fatness.

⁸For *it is* the day of the LORD's vengeance, *and* the year of recompences for the controversy of Zion.

⁹And the streams thereof shall be turned into pitch, and the dust thereof into brimstone, and the land thereof shall become burning pitch.

¹⁰It shall not be quenched night nor day; the smoke thereof shall go up for ever: from generation to generation it shall lie waste; none shall pass through it for ever and ever.

¹¹¶ But the cormorant and the bittern shall possess it; the owl also and the raven shall dwell in it: and he shall stretch out upon it the line of confusion, and the stones of emptiness.

¹²They shall call the nobles thereof to the kingdom, but none *shall be* there, and all her princes shall be nothing.

¹³And thorns shall come up in her palaces, nettles and brambles in the fortresses thereof: and it shall be an habitation of dragons, *and* a court for owls.

¹⁴The wild beasts of the desert shall also meet with the wild beasts of the island, and the satyr shall cry to his fellow; the screech owl also shall rest there, and find for herself a place of rest.

¹⁵There shall the great owl make her nest, and lay, and hatch, and gather under her shadow: there shall the vultures also be gathered, every one with her mate.

¹⁶¶ Seek ye out of the book of the LORD, and read: no one of these shall fail, none shall want her mate: for my mouth it hath commanded, and his spirit it hath gathered them.

¹⁷And he hath cast the lot for them, and his hand hath divided it unto them by line: they shall possess it for ever, from generation to generation shall they dwell therein.

New International

⁴All the stars of the heavens will be dissolved
and the sky rolled up like a scroll;
all the starry host will fall
like withered leaves from the vine,
like shriveled figs from the fig tree.

⁵My sword has drunk its fill in the heavens;
see, it descends in judgment on Edom,
the people I have totally destroyed.
⁶The sword of the LORD is bathed in blood,
it is covered with fat—
the blood of lambs and goats,
fat from the kidneys of rams.
For the LORD has a sacrifice in Bozrah
and a great slaughter in Edom.
⁷And the wild oxen will fall with them,
the bull calves and the great bulls.
Their land will be drenched with blood,
and the dust will be soaked with fat.

⁸For the LORD has a day of vengeance,
a year of retribution, to uphold Zion's cause.
⁹Edom's streams will be turned into pitch,
her dust into burning sulfur;
her land will become blazing pitch!
¹⁰It will not be quenched night and day;
its smoke will rise forever.
From generation to generation it will lie
desolate;
no one will ever pass through it again.
¹¹The desert owl[a] and screech owl[a] will possess
it;
the great owl[a] and the raven will nest there.
God will stretch out over Edom
the measuring line of chaos
and the plumb line of desolation.
¹²Her nobles will have nothing there to be called
a kingdom,
all her princes will vanish away.
¹³Thorns will overrun her citadels,
nettles and brambles her strongholds.
She will become a haunt for jackals,
a home for owls.
¹⁴Desert creatures will meet with hyenas,
and wild goats will bleat to each other;
there the night creatures will also repose
and find for themselves places of rest.
¹⁵The owl will nest there and lay eggs,
she will hatch them, and care for her young
under the shadow of her wings;
there also the falcons will gather,
each with its mate.

¹⁶Look in the scroll of the LORD and read:

None of these will be missing,
not one will lack her mate.
For it is his mouth that has given the order,
and his Spirit will gather them together.
¹⁷He allots their portions;
his hand distributes them by measure.
They will possess it forever
and dwell there from generation to generation.

---

^a *11* The precise identification of these birds is uncertain.

Living Bible

that time the heavens above will melt away and disappear just like a rolled-up scroll, and the stars will fall as leaves, as ripe fruit from the trees.

⁵And when my sword has finished its work in the heavens, then watch, for it will fall upon Edom, the people I have doomed. ⁶The sword of the Lord is sated with blood; it is gorged with flesh as though used for slaying lambs and goats for sacrifice. For the Lord will slay a great sacrifice in Edom and make a mighty slaughter there. ⁷The strongest will perish, young boys and veterans too. The land will be soaked with blood, and the soil made rich with fat. ⁸For it is the day of vengeance, the year of recompense for what Edom has done to Israel. ⁹The streams of Edom will be filled with burning pitch, and the ground will be covered with fire.

¹⁰This judgment on Edom will never end. Its smoke will rise up forever. The land will lie deserted from generation to generation; no one will live there anymore. ¹¹There the hawks and porcupines will live, and owls and ravens. For God will observe that land and find it worthy of destruction. He will test its nobles and find them worthy of death. ¹²It will be called "The Land of Nothing," and its princes soon will all be gone. ¹³Thorns will overrun the palaces, and nettles will grow in its forts, and it will become the haunt of jackals and a home for ostriches. ¹⁴The wild animals of the desert will mingle there with wolves and hyenas. Their howls will fill the night. There the night-monsters will scream at each other, and the demons will come there to rest. ¹⁵There the owl will make her nest and lay her eggs and hatch her young and nestle them beneath her wings, and the kites will come, each one with its mate.

¹⁶Search the Book of the Lord and see all that he will do; not one detail will he miss; not one kite will be there without a mate, for the Lord has said it, and his Spirit will make it all come true. ¹⁷He has surveyed and subdivided the land and deeded it to those doleful creatures; they shall possess it forever, from generation to generation.

New Revised Standard

4   All the host of heaven shall rot away,
      and the skies roll up like a scroll.
    All their host shall wither
      like a leaf withering on a vine,
      or fruit withering on a fig tree.

5   When my sword has drunk its fill in the
        heavens,
      lo, it will descend upon Edom,
      upon the people I have doomed to
        judgment.
6   The LORD has a sword; it is sated with blood,
      it is gorged with fat,
      with the blood of lambs and goats,
      with the fat of the kidneys of rams.
    For the LORD has a sacrifice in Bozrah,
      a great slaughter in the land of Edom.
7   Wild oxen shall fall with them,
      and young steers with the mighty bulls.
    Their land shall be soaked with blood,
      and their soil made rich with fat.

8   For the LORD has a day of vengeance,
      a year of vindication by Zion's cause.ᵇ
9   And the streams of Edomᶜ shall be turned
        into pitch,
      and her soil into sulfur;
      her land shall become burning pitch.
10 Night and day it shall not be quenched;
      its smoke shall go up forever.
    From generation to generation it shall lie
        waste;
      no one shall pass through it forever and
        ever.
11 But the hawkᵈ and the hedgehogᵈ shall
        possess it;
      the owlᵈ and the raven shall live in it.
    He shall stretch the line of confusion over it,
      and the plummet of chaos overᵉ its nobles.
12 They shall name it No Kingdom There,
      and all its princes shall be nothing.
13 Thorns shall grow over its strongholds,
      nettles and thistles in its fortresses.
    It shall be the haunt of jackals,
      an abode for ostriches.
14 Wildcats shall meet with hyenas,
      goat-demons shall call to each other;
    there too Lilith shall repose,
      and find a place to rest.
15 There shall the owl nest
      and lay and hatch and brood in its shadow;
    there too the buzzards shall gather,
      each one with its mate.
16 Seek and read from the book of the LORD:
      Not one of these shall be missing;
      none shall be without its mate.
    For the mouth of the LORD has commanded,
      and his spirit has gathered them.
17 He has cast the lot for them,
      his hand has portioned it out to them with
        the line;
    they shall possess it forever,
      from generation to generation they shall live
        in it.

ᵇ Or of recompense by Zion's defender   ᶜ Heb her streams   ᵈ Identification
uncertain   ᵉ Heb lacks over

King James

35 THE WILDERNESS and the solitary place shall be glad for them; and the desert shall rejoice, and blossom as the rose.

2It shall blossom abundantly, and rejoice even with joy and singing: the glory of Lebanon shall be given unto it, the excellency of Carmel and Sharon, they shall see the glory of the LORD, *and* the excellency of our God.

3¶ Strengthen ye the weak hands, and confirm the feeble knees.

4Say to them *that are* of a fearful heart, Be strong, fear not: behold, your God will come *with* vengeance, *even* God *with* a recompence; he will come and save you.

5Then the eyes of the blind shall be opened, and the ears of the deaf shall be unstopped.

6Then shall the lame *man* leap as an hart, and the tongue of the dumb sing: for in the wilderness shall waters break out, and streams in the desert.

7And the parched ground shall become a pool, and the thirsty land springs of water: in the habitation of dragons, where each lay, *shall be* grass with reeds and rushes.

8And an highway shall be there, and a way, and it shall be called The way of holiness; the unclean shall not pass over it; but it *shall be* for those: the wayfaring men, though fools, shall not err *therein*.

9No lion shall be there, nor *any* ravenous beast shall go up thereon, it shall not be found there; but the redeemed shall walk *there*:

10And the ransomed of the LORD shall return, and come to Zion with songs and everlasting joy upon their heads: they shall obtain joy and gladness, and sorrow and sighing shall flee away.

36 NOW IT came to pass in the fourteenth year of king Hezekiah, *that* Sennacherib king of Assyria came up against all the defenced cities of Judah, and took them.

2And the king of Assyria sent Rab-shakeh from Lachish to Jerusalem unto king Hezekiah with a great army. And he stood by the conduit of the upper pool in the highway of the fuller's field.

3Then came forth unto him Eliakim, Hilkiah's son, which was over the house, and Shebna the scribe, and Joah, Asaph's son, the recorder.

4¶ And Rab-shakeh said unto them, Say ye now to Hezekiah, Thus saith the great king, the king of Assyria, What confidence *is* this wherein thou trustest?

5I say, *sayest thou,* (but *they are but* vain words) I *have* counsel and strength for war: now on whom dost thou trust, that thou rebellest against me?

6Lo, thou trustest in the staff of this broken reed, on Egypt; whereon if a man lean, it will go into his hand, and pierce it: so *is* Pharaoh king of Egypt to all that trust in him.

New International

Joy of the Redeemed

35 THE DESERT and the parched land will be glad;
the wilderness will rejoice and blossom.
Like the crocus, 2it will burst into bloom;
it will rejoice greatly and shout for joy.
The glory of Lebanon will be given to it,
the splendor of Carmel and Sharon;
they will see the glory of the LORD,
the splendor of our God.

3Strengthen the feeble hands,
steady the knees that give way;
4say to those with fearful hearts,
"Be strong, do not fear;
your God will come,
he will come with vengeance;
with divine retribution
he will come to save you."

5Then will the eyes of the blind be opened
and the ears of the deaf unstopped.
6Then will the lame leap like a deer,
and the mute tongue shout for joy.
Water will gush forth in the wilderness
and streams in the desert.
7The burning sand will become a pool,
the thirsty ground bubbling springs.
In the haunts where jackals once lay,
grass and reeds and papyrus will grow.

8And a highway will be there;
it will be called the Way of Holiness.
The unclean will not journey on it;
it will be for those who walk in that Way;
wicked fools will not go about on it.[a]
9No lion will be there,
nor will any ferocious beast get up on it;
they will not be found there.
But only the redeemed will walk there,
10 and the ransomed of the LORD will return.
They will enter Zion with singing;
everlasting joy will crown their heads.
Gladness and joy will overtake them,
and sorrow and sighing will flee away.

Sennacherib Threatens Jerusalem

36 IN THE fourteenth year of King Hezekiah's reign, Sennacherib king of Assyria attacked all the fortified cities of Judah and captured them. 2Then the king of Assyria sent his field commander with a large army from Lachish to King Hezekiah at Jerusalem. When the commander stopped at the aqueduct of the Upper Pool, on the road to the Washerman's Field, 3Eliakim son of Hilkiah the palace administrator, Shebna the secretary, and Joah son of Asaph the recorder went out to him.

4The field commander said to them, "Tell Hezekiah,

" 'This is what the great king, the king of Assyria, says: On what are you basing this confidence of yours? 5You say you have strategy and military strength—but you speak only empty words. On whom are you depending, that you rebel against me? 6Look now, you are depending on Egypt, that splintered reed of a staff, which pierces a man's hand and wounds him if he leans on it! Such is Pharaoh king of Egypt to all who depend on him.

---

a 8 Or / *the simple will not stray from it*

Living Bible

New Revised Standard

The Return of the Redeemed to Zion

35 EVEN THE wilderness and desert will rejoice in those days; the desert will blossom with flowers. 2Yes, there will be an abundance of flowers and singing and joy! The deserts will become as green as the Lebanon mountains, as lovely as Mount Carmel's pastures and Sharon's meadows; for the Lord will display his glory there, the excellency of our God.

3With this news bring cheer to all discouraged ones. 4Encourage those who are afraid. Tell them, "Be strong, fear not, for your God is coming to destroy your enemies. He is coming to save you." 5And when he comes, he will open the eyes of the blind, and unstop the ears of the deaf. 6The lame man will leap up like a deer, and those who could not speak will shout and sing! Springs will burst forth in the wilderness, and streams in the desert. 7The parched ground will become a pool, with springs of water in the thirsty land. Where desert jackals lived, there will be reeds and rushes!

8And a main road will go through that once-deserted land; it will be named "The Holy Highway." No evil-hearted men may walk upon it. God will walk there with you; even the most stupid cannot miss the way. 9No lion will lurk along its course, nor will there be any other dangers; only the redeemed will travel there. 10These, the ransomed of the Lord, will go home along that road to Zion, singing the songs of everlasting joy. For them all sorrow and all sighing will be gone forever; only joy and gladness will be there.

35 THE WILDERNESS and the dry land shall be glad,
the desert shall rejoice and blossom;
like the crocus 2it shall blossom abundantly,
and rejoice with joy and singing.
The glory of Lebanon shall be given to it,
the majesty of Carmel and Sharon.
They shall see the glory of the LORD,
the majesty of our God.

3 Strengthen the weak hands,
and make firm the feeble knees.
4 Say to those who are of a fearful heart,
"Be strong, do not fear!
Here is your God.
He will come with vengeance,
with terrible recompense.
He will come and save you."

5 Then the eyes of the blind shall be opened,
and the ears of the deaf unstopped;
6 then the lame shall leap like a deer,
and the tongue of the speechless sing for joy.
For waters shall break forth in the wilderness,
and streams in the desert;
7 the burning sand shall become a pool,
and the thirsty ground springs of water;
the haunt of jackals shall become a swamp,b
the grass shall become reeds and rushes.

8 A highway shall be there,
and it shall be called the Holy Way;
the unclean shall not travel on it,c
but it shall be for God's people;d
no traveler, not even fools, shall go astray.
9 No lion shall be there,
nor shall any ravenous beast come up on it;
they shall not be found there,
but the redeemed shall walk there.
10 And the ransomed of the LORD shall return,
and come to Zion with singing;
everlasting joy shall be upon their heads;
they shall obtain joy and gladness,
and sorrow and sighing shall flee away.

Sennacherib Threatens Jerusalem

36 SO IN the fourteenth year of King Hezekiah's reign, Sennacherib, king of Assyria, came to fight against the walled cities of Judah and conquered them. 2Then he sent his personal representative with a great army from Lachish to confer with King Hezekiah in Jerusalem. He camped near the outlet of the upper pool, along the road going past the field where cloth is bleached.

3Then Eliakim, Hilkiah's son, who was the prime minister of Israel, and Shebna, the king's scribe, and Joah (Asaph's son), the royal secretary, formed a truce team and went out of the city to meet with him. 4The Assyrian ambassador told them to go and say to Hezekiah, "The mighty king of Assyria says you are a fool to think that the king of Egypt will help you. 5What are the Pharaoh's promises worth? Mere words won't substitute for strength, yet you rely on him for help, and have rebelled against me! 6Egypt is a dangerous ally. She is a sharpened stick that will pierce your hand if you lean on it. That is the experience of everyone who has ever looked to her for help. 7But perhaps you say, 'We are

36 IN THE fourteenth year of King Hezekiah, King Sennacherib of Assyria came up against all the fortified cities of Judah and captured them. 2The king of Assyria sent the Rabshakeh from Lachish to King Hezekiah at Jerusalem, with a great army. He stood by the conduit of the upper pool on the highway to the Fuller's Field. 3And there came out to him Eliakim son of Hilkiah, who was in charge of the palace, and Shebna the secretary, and Joah son of Asaph, the recorder.

4 The Rabshakeh said to them, "Say to Hezekiah: Thus says the great king, the king of Assyria: On what do you base this confidence of yours? 5Do you think that mere words are strategy and power for war? On whom do you now rely, that you have rebelled against me? 6See, you are relying on Egypt, that broken reed of a staff, which will pierce the hand of anyone who leans on it. Such is Pharaoh king of Egypt to all who rely on him. 7But if you say to me, 'We rely on the LORD our

b Cn: Heb *in the haunt of jackals is her resting place*   c Or *pass it by*   d Cn:
Heb *for them*

King James

7But if thou say to me, We trust in the LORD our God: *is it* not he, whose high places and whose altars Hezekiah hath taken away, and said to Judah and to Jerusalem, Ye shall worship before this altar?

8Now therefore give pledges, I pray thee, to my master the king of Assyria, and I will give thee two thousand horses, if thou be able on thy part to set riders upon them.

9How then wilt thou turn away the face of one captain of the least of my master's servants, and put thy trust on Egypt for chariots and for horsemen?

10And am I now come up without the LORD against this land to destroy it? the LORD said unto me, Go up against this land, and destroy it.

11¶ Then said Eliakim and Shebna and Joah unto Rab-shakeh, Speak, I pray thee, unto thy servants in the Syrian language; for we understand *it:* and speak not to us in the Jews' language, in the ears of the people that *are* on the wall.

12¶ But Rab-shakeh said, Hath my master sent me to thy master and to thee to speak these words? *hath he* not *sent me* to the men that sit upon the wall, that they may eat their own dung, and drink their own piss with you?

13Then Rab-shakeh stood, and cried with a loud voice in the Jews' language, and said, Hear ye the words of the great king, the king of Assyria.

14Thus saith the king, Let not Hezekiah deceive you: for he shall not be able to deliver you.

15Neither let Hezekiah make you trust in the LORD, saying, The LORD will surely deliver us: this city shall not be delivered into the hand of the king of Assyria.

16Hearken not to Hezekiah: for thus saith the king of Assyria, Make *an agreement* with me *by* a present, and come out to me: and eat ye every one of his vine, and every one of his fig tree, and drink ye every one the waters of his own cistern;

17Until I come and take you away to a land like your own land, a land of corn and wine, a land of bread and vineyards.

18*Beware* lest Hezekiah persuade you, saying, The LORD will deliver us. Hath any of the gods of the nations delivered his land out of the hand of the king of Assyria?

19Where *are* the gods of Hamath and Arphad? where *are* the gods of Sepharvaim? and have they delivered Samaria out of my hand?

20Who *are they* among all the gods of these lands, that have delivered their land out of my hand, that the LORD should deliver Jerusalem out of my hand?

21But they held their peace, and answered him not a word: for the king's commandment was, saying, Answer him not.

22¶ Then came Eliakim, the son of Hilkiah, that *was* over the household, and Shebna the scribe, and Joah, the son of Asaph, the recorder, to Hezekiah with *their* clothes rent, and told him the words of Rab-shakeh.

37 AND IT came to pass, when king Hezekiah heard *it,* that he rent his clothes, and covered himself with sackcloth, and went into the house of the LORD.

2And he sent Eliakim, who *was* over the household, and Shebna the scribe, and the elders of the priests covered with sackcloth, unto Isaiah the prophet the son of Amoz.

3And they said unto him, Thus saith Hezekiah, This day *is* a day of trouble, and of rebuke, and of blasphemy: for the children are come to the birth, and *there is* not strength to bring forth.

New International

7And if you say to me, "We are depending on the LORD our God"—isn't he the one whose high places and altars Hezekiah removed, saying to Judah and Jerusalem, "You must worship before this altar"?

8" 'Come now, make a bargain with my master, the king of Assyria: I will give you two thousand horses—if you can put riders on them! 9How then can you repulse one officer of the least of my master's officials, even though you are depending on Egypt for chariots and horsemen? 10Furthermore, have I come to attack and destroy this land without the LORD? The LORD himself told me to march against this country and destroy it.' "

11Then Eliakim, Shebna and Joah said to the field commander, "Please speak to your servants in Aramaic, since we understand it. Don't speak to us in Hebrew in the hearing of the people on the wall."

12But the commander replied, "Was it only to your master and you that my master sent me to say these things, and not to the men sitting on the wall—who, like you, will have to eat their own filth and drink their own urine?"

13Then the commander stood and called out in Hebrew, "Hear the words of the great king, the king of Assyria! 14This is what the king says: Do not let Hezekiah deceive you! He cannot deliver you! 15Do not let Hezekiah persuade you to trust in the LORD when he says, 'The LORD will surely deliver us; this city will not be given into the hand of the king of Assyria.'

16"Do not listen to Hezekiah. This is what the king of Assyria says: Make peace with me and come out to me. Then every one of you will eat from his own vine and fig tree and drink water from his own cistern, 17until I come and take you to a land like your own—a land of grain and new wine, a land of bread and vineyards.

18"Do not let Hezekiah mislead you when he says, 'The LORD will deliver us.' Has the god of any nation ever delivered his land from the hand of the king of Assyria? 19Where are the gods of Hamath and Arpad? Where are the gods of Sepharvaim? Have they rescued Samaria from my hand? 20Who of all the gods of these countries has been able to save his land from me? How then can the LORD deliver Jerusalem from my hand?"

21But the people remained silent and said nothing in reply, because the king had commanded, "Do not answer him."

22Then Eliakim son of Hilkiah the palace administrator, Shebna the secretary, and Joah son of Asaph the recorder went to Hezekiah, with their clothes torn, and told him what the field commander had said.

Jerusalem's Deliverance Foretold

37 WHEN KING Hezekiah heard this, he tore his clothes and put on sackcloth and went into the temple of the LORD. 2He sent Eliakim the palace administrator, Shebna the secretary, and the leading priests, all wearing sackcloth, to the prophet Isaiah son of Amoz. 3They told him, "This is what Hezekiah says: This day is a day of distress and rebuke and disgrace, as when children come to the point of birth and there is no strength to deliver them. 4It may be that the LORD your

Living Bible

trusting in the Lord our God!' Oh? Isn't he the one your king insulted, tearing down his temples and altars in the hills and making everyone in Judah worship only at the altars here in Jerusalem? 8. 9My master, the king of Assyria, wants to make a little bet with you!—that you don't have 2,000 men left in your entire army! If you do, he will give you 2,000 horses for them to ride on! With that tiny army, how can you think of proceeding against even the smallest and worst contingent of my master's troops? For you'll get no help from Egypt. 10What's more, do you think I have come here without the Lord's telling me to take this land? The Lord said to me, 'Go and destroy it!' "

11Then Eliakim and Shebna and Joah said to him, "Please talk to us in Aramaic[a] for we understand it quite well. Don't speak in Hebrew, for the people on the wall will hear."

12But he replied, "My master wants everyone in Jerusalem to hear this, not just you. He wants them to know that if you don't surrender, this city will be put under siege until everyone is so hungry and thirsty that he will eat his own dung and drink his own urine."

13Then he shouted in Hebrew to the Jews listening on the wall, "Hear the words of the great king, the king of Assyria:

14"Don't let Hezekiah fool you—nothing he can do will save you. 15Don't let him talk you into trusting in the Lord by telling you the Lord won't let you be conquered by the king of Assyria. 16Don't listen to Hezekiah, for here is the king of Assyria's offer to you: Give me a present as a token of surrender; open the gates and come out, and I will let you each have your own farm and garden and water, 17until I can arrange to take you to a country very similar to this one—a country where there are bountiful harvests of grain and grapes, a land of plenty. 18Don't let Hezekiah deprive you of all this by saying the Lord will deliver you from my armies. Have any other nation's gods ever gained victory over the armies of the king of Assyria? 19Don't you remember what I did to Hamath and Arpad? Did their gods save them? And what about Sepharvaim and Samaria? Where are their gods now? 20Of all the gods of these lands, which one has ever delivered their people from my power? Name just one! And do you think this God of yours can deliver Jerusalem from me? Don't be ridiculous!"

21But the people were silent and answered not a word, for Hezekiah had told them to say nothing in reply. 22Then Eliakim (son of Hilkiah), the prime minister, and Shebna, the royal scribe, and Joah (son of Asaph), the royal secretary, went back to Hezekiah with clothes ripped to shreds as a sign of their despair and told him all that had happened.

37 WHEN KING Hezekiah heard the results of the meeting, he tore his robes and wound himself in coarse cloth used for making sacks, as a sign of humility and mourning, and went over to the Temple to pray. 2Meanwhile he sent Eliakim his prime minister, and Shebna his royal scribe, and the older priests—all dressed in sackcloth—to Isaiah the prophet, son of Amoz. 3They brought him this message from Hezekiah:

"This is a day of trouble and frustration and blasphemy; it is a serious time, as when a woman is in heavy labor trying to give birth, and the child does not come.

New Revised Standard

God,' is it not he whose high places and altars Hezekiah has removed, saying to Judah and to Jerusalem, 'You shall worship before this altar'? 8Come now, make a wager with my master the king of Assyria: I will give you two thousand horses, if you are able on your part to set riders on them. 9How then can you repulse a single captain among the least of my master's servants, when you rely on Egypt for chariots and for horsemen? 10Moreover, is it without the LORD that I have come up against this land to destroy it? The LORD said to me, Go up against this land, and destroy it."

11 Then Eliakim, Shebna, and Joah said to the Rabshakeh, "Please speak to your servants in Aramaic, for we understand it; do not speak to us in the language of Judah within the hearing of the people who are on the wall." 12But the Rabshakeh said, "Has my master sent me to speak these words to your master and to you, and not to the people sitting on the wall, who are doomed with you to eat their own dung and drink their own urine?"

13 Then the Rabshakeh stood and called out in a loud voice in the language of Judah, "Hear the words of the great king, the king of Assyria! 14Thus says the king: 'Do not let Hezekiah deceive you, for he will not be able to deliver you. 15Do not let Hezekiah make you rely on the LORD by saying, The LORD will surely deliver us; this city will not be given into the hand of the king of Assyria.' 16Do not listen to Hezekiah; for thus says the king of Assyria: 'Make your peace with me and come out to me; then everyone of you will eat from your own vine and your own fig tree and drink water from your own cistern, 17until I come and take you away to a land like your own land, a land of grain and wine, a land of bread and vineyards. 18Do not let Hezekiah mislead you by saying, The LORD will save us. Has any of the gods of the nations saved their land out of the hand of the king of Assyria? 19Where are the gods of Hamath and Arpad? Where are the gods of Sepharvaim? Have they delivered Samaria out of my hand? 20Who among all the gods of these countries have saved their countries out of my hand, that the LORD should save Jerusalem out of my hand?' "

21 But they were silent and answered him not a word, for the king's command was, "Do not answer him." 22Then Eliakim son of Hilkiah, who was in charge of the palace, and Shebna the secretary, and Joah son of Asaph, the recorder, came to Hezekiah with their clothes torn, and told him the words of the Rabshakeh.

Hezekiah Consults Isaiah

37 WHEN KING Hezekiah heard it, he tore his clothes, covered himself with sackcloth, and went into the house of the LORD. 2And he sent Eliakim, who was in charge of the palace, and Shebna the secretary, and the senior priests, covered with sackcloth, to the prophet Isaiah son of Amoz. 3They said to him, "Thus says Hezekiah, This day is a day of distress, of rebuke, and of disgrace; children have come to the birth, and there is no strength to bring them forth. 4It may be

---

a 36:11 Please talk to us in Aramaic. Aramaic was the language used in international diplomacy at this time.

King James

4It may be the LORD thy God will hear the words of Rab-shakeh, whom the king of Assyria his master hath sent to reproach the living God, and will reprove the words which the LORD thy God hath heard: wherefore lift up *thy* prayer for the remnant that is left.

5So the servants of king Hezekiah came to Isaiah.

6¶ And Isaiah said unto them, Thus shall ye say unto your master, Thus saith the LORD, Be not afraid of the words that thou hast heard, wherewith the servants of the king of Assyria have blasphemed me.

7Behold, I will send a blast upon him, and he shall hear a rumour, and return to his own land; and I will cause him to fall by the sword in his own land.

8¶ So Rab-shakeh returned, and found the king of Assyria warring against Libnah: for he had heard that he was departed from Lachish.

9And he heard say concerning Tirhakah king of Ethiopia, He is come forth to make war with thee. And when he heard *it,* he sent messengers to Hezekiah, saying,

10Thus shall ye speak to Hezekiah king of Judah, saying, Let not thy God, in whom thou trustest, deceive thee, saying, Jerusalem shall not be given into the hand of the king of Assyria.

11Behold, thou hast heard what the kings of Assyria have done to all lands by destroying them utterly; and shalt thou be delivered?

12Have the gods of the nations delivered them which my fathers have destroyed, *as* Gozan, and Haran, and Rezeph, and the children of Eden which *were* in Telassar?

13Where *is* the king of Hamath, and the king of Arphad, and the king of the city of Sepharvaim, Hena, and Ivah?

14¶ And Hezekiah received the letter from the hand of the messengers, and read it: and Hezekiah went up unto the house of the LORD, and spread it before the LORD.

15And Hezekiah prayed unto the LORD, saying,

16O LORD of hosts, God of Israel, that dwellest *between* the cherubims, thou *art* the God, *even* thou alone, of all the kingdoms of the earth: thou hast made heaven and earth.

17Incline thine ear, O LORD, and hear; open thine eyes, O LORD, and see: and hear all the words of Sennacherib, which hath sent to reproach the living God.

18Of a truth, LORD, the kings of Assyria have laid waste all the nations, and their countries,

19And have cast their gods into the fire: for they *were* no gods, but the work of men's hands, wood and stone: therefore they have destroyed them.

20Now therefore, O LORD our God, save us from his hand, that all the kingdoms of the earth may know that thou *art* the LORD, *even* thou only.

21¶ Then Isaiah the son of Amoz sent unto Hezekiah, saying, Thus saith the LORD God of Israel, Whereas thou hast prayed to me against Sennacherib king of Assyria:

22This *is* the word which the LORD hath spoken concerning him; The virgin, the daughter of Zion, hath despised thee, *and* laughed thee to scorn; the daughter of Jerusalem hath shaken her head at thee.

23Whom hast thou reproached and blasphemed? and against whom hast thou exalted *thy* voice, and lifted up thine eyes on high? *even* against the Holy One of Israel.

New International

God will hear the words of the field commander, whom his master, the king of Assyria, has sent to ridicule the living God, and that he will rebuke him for the words the LORD your God has heard. Therefore pray for the remnant that still survives."

5When King Hezekiah's officials came to Isaiah, 6Isaiah said to them, "Tell your master, 'This is what the LORD says: Do not be afraid of what you have heard—those words with which the underlings of the king of Assyria have blasphemed me. 7Listen! I am going to put a spirit in him so that when he hears a certain report, he will return to his own country, and there I will have him cut down with the sword.' "

8When the field commander heard that the king of Assyria had left Lachish, he withdrew and found the king fighting against Libnah.

9Now Sennacherib received a report that Tirhakah, the Cushite[a] king of Egypt, was marching out to fight against him. When he heard it, he sent messengers to Hezekiah with this word: 10"Say to Hezekiah king of Judah: Do not let the god you depend on deceive you when he says, 'Jerusalem will not be handed over to the king of Assyria.' 11Surely you have heard what the kings of Assyria have done to all the countries, destroying them completely. And will you be delivered? 12Did the gods of the nations that were destroyed by my forefathers deliver them—the gods of Gozan, Haran, Rezeph and the people of Eden who were in Tel Assar? 13Where is the king of Hamath, the king of Arpad, the king of the city of Sepharvaim, or of Hena or Ivvah?"

Hezekiah's Prayer

14Hezekiah received the letter from the messengers and read it. Then he went up to the temple of the LORD and spread it out before the LORD. 15And Hezekiah prayed to the LORD: 16"O LORD Almighty, God of Israel, enthroned between the cherubim, you alone are God over all the kingdoms of the earth. You have made heaven and earth. 17Give ear, O LORD, and hear; open your eyes, O LORD, and see; listen to all the words Sennacherib has sent to insult the living God.

18"It is true, O LORD, that the Assyrian kings have laid waste all these peoples and their lands. 19They have thrown their gods into the fire and destroyed them, for they were not gods but only wood and stone, fashioned by human hands. 20Now, O LORD our God, deliver us from his hand, so that all kingdoms on earth may know that you alone, O LORD, are God.[b]"

Sennacherib's Fall

21Then Isaiah son of Amoz sent a message to Hezekiah: "This is what the LORD, the God of Israel, says: Because you have prayed to me concerning Sennacherib king of Assyria, 22this is the word the LORD has spoken against him:

"The Virgin Daughter of Zion
    despises and mocks you.
The Daughter of Jerusalem
    tosses her head as you flee.
23Who is it you have insulted and blasphemed?
    Against whom have you raised your voice
and lifted your eyes in pride?
    Against the Holy One of Israel!

a 9 That is, from the upper Nile region   b 20 Dead Sea Scrolls (see also 2 Kings 19:19); Masoretic Text *alone are the LORD*

Living Bible

4But perhaps the Lord your God heard the blasphemy of the king of Assyria's representative as he scoffed at the Living God. Surely God won't let him get away with this. Surely God will rebuke him for those words. Oh, Isaiah, pray for us who are left!"

5So they took the king's message to Isaiah.

6Then Isaiah replied, "Tell King Hezekiah that the Lord says, Don't be disturbed by this speech from the servant of the king of Assyria, and his blasphemy. 7For a report from Assyria will reach the king that he is needed at home at once, and he will return to his own land, where I will have him killed."

8, 9Now the Assyrian envoy left Jerusalem and went to consult his king, who had left Lachish and was besieging Libnah. But at this point the Assyrian king received word that Tirhakah, crown prince of Ethiopia, was leading an army against him [from the south^c]. Upon hearing this, he sent messengers back to Jerusalem to Hezekiah with this message:

10"Don't let this God you trust in fool you by promising that Jerusalem will not be captured by the king of Assyria! 11Just remember what has happened wherever the kings of Assyria have gone, for they have crushed everyone who has opposed them. Do you think you will be any different? 12Did their gods save the cities of Gozan, Haran, or Rezeph, or the people of Eden in Telassar? No, the Assyrian kings completely destroyed them! 13And don't forget what happened to the king of Hamath, to the king of Arpad, and to the kings of the cities of Sepharvaim, Hena, and Ivvah."

14As soon as King Hezekiah had read this letter, he went over to the Temple and spread it out before the Lord, 15and prayed, saying, 16, 17"O Lord, Almighty God of Israel enthroned between the Guardian Angels, *you alone* are God of all the kingdoms of the earth. You alone made heaven and earth. Listen as I plead; see me as I pray. Look at this letter from King Sennacherib, for he has mocked the Living God. 18It is true, O Lord, that the kings of Assyria have destroyed all those nations, just as the letter says, 19and thrown their gods into the fire; for they weren't gods at all, but merely idols, carved by men from wood and stone. Of course the Assyrians could destroy them. 20O Lord our God, save us so that all the kingdoms of the earth will know that you are God, and you alone."

21Then Isaiah, the son of Amoz, sent this message to King Hezekiah: "The Lord God of Israel says, This is my answer to your prayer against Sennacherib, Assyria's king.

22"The Lord says to him: My people—the helpless virgin daughter of Zion—laughs at you and scoffs and shakes her head at you in scorn. 23Who is it you scoffed against and mocked? Whom did you revile? At whom did you direct your violence and pride? It was against the Holy One of Israel! 24You have sent your messengers

New Revised Standard

that the LORD your God heard the words of the Rabshakeh, whom his master the king of Assyria has sent to mock the living God, and will rebuke the words that the LORD your God has heard; therefore lift up your prayer for the remnant that is left."

5 When the servants of King Hezekiah came to Isaiah, 6Isaiah said to them, "Say to your master, 'Thus says the LORD: Do not be afraid because of the words that you have heard, with which the servants of the king of Assyria have reviled me. 7I myself will put a spirit in him, so that he shall hear a rumor, and return to his own land; I will cause him to fall by the sword in his own land.' "

8 The Rabshakeh returned, and found the king of Assyria fighting against Libnah; for he had heard that the king had left Lachish. 9Now the king^d heard concerning King Tirhakah of Ethiopia,^e "He has set out to fight against you." When he heard it, he sent messengers to Hezekiah, saying, 10"Thus shall you speak to King Hezekiah of Judah: Do not let your God on whom you rely deceive you by promising that Jerusalem will not be given into the hand of the king of Assyria. 11See, you have heard what the kings of Assyria have done to all lands, destroying them utterly. Shall you be delivered? 12Have the gods of the nations delivered them, the nations that my predecessors destroyed, Gozan, Haran, Rezeph, and the people of Eden who were in Telassar? 13Where is the king of Hamath, the king of Arpad, the king of the city of Sepharvaim, the king of Hena, or the king of Ivvah?"

Hezekiah's Prayer

14 Hezekiah received the letter from the hand of the messengers and read it; then Hezekiah went up to the house of the LORD and spread it before the LORD. 15And Hezekiah prayed to the LORD, saying: 16"O LORD of hosts, God of Israel, who are enthroned above the cherubim, you are God, you alone, of all the kingdoms of the earth; you have made heaven and earth. 17Incline your ear, O LORD, and hear; open your eyes, O LORD, and see; hear all the words of Sennacherib, which he has sent to mock the living God. 18Truly, O LORD, the kings of Assyria have laid waste all the nations and their lands, 19and have hurled their gods into the fire—though they were no gods, but the work of human hands—wood and stone—and so they were destroyed. 20So now, O LORD our God, save us from his hand, so that all the kingdoms of the earth may know that you alone are the LORD."

21 Then Isaiah son of Amoz sent to Hezekiah, saying: "Thus says the LORD, the God of Israel: Because you have prayed to me concerning King Sennacherib of Assyria, 22this is the word that the LORD has spoken concerning him:

> She despises you, she scorns you—
>   virgin daughter Zion;
> she tosses her head—behind your back,
>   daughter Jerusalem.

> 23 Whom have you mocked and reviled?
>   Against whom have you raised your voice
> and haughtily lifted your eyes?
>   Against the Holy One of Israel!

---

^c 37:8, 9 *from the south*, implied.   ^d Heb *he*   ^e Or Nubia; Heb *Cush*

King James

24By thy servants hast thou reproached the Lord, and hast said, By the multitude of my chariots am I come up to the height of the mountains, to the sides of Lebanon; and I will cut down the tall cedars thereof, *and* the choice fir trees thereof: and I will enter into the height of his border, *and* the forest of his Carmel.

25I have digged, and drunk water; and with the sole of my feet have I dried up all the rivers of the besieged places.

26Hast thou not heard long ago, *how* I have done it; *and* of ancient times, that I have formed it? now have I brought it to pass, that thou shouldest be to lay waste defenced cities *into* ruinous heaps.

27Therefore their inhabitants *were* of small power, they were dismayed and confounded: they were *as* the grass of the field, and *as* the green herb, *as* the grass on the housetops, and *as corn* blasted before it be grown up.

28But I know thy abode, and thy going out, and thy coming in, and thy rage against me.

29Because thy rage against me, and thy tumult, is come up into mine ears, therefore will I put my hook in thy nose, and my bridle in thy lips, and I will turn thee back by the way by which thou camest.

30And this *shall be* a sign unto thee, Ye shall eat *this* year such as groweth of itself; and the second year that which springeth of the same: and in the third year sow ye, and reap, and plant vineyards, and eat the fruit thereof.

31And the remnant that is escaped of the house of Judah shall again take root downward, and bear fruit upward:

32For out of Jerusalem shall go forth a remnant, and they that escape out of mount Zion: the zeal of the LORD of hosts shall do this.

33Therefore thus saith the LORD concerning the king of Assyria, He shall not come into this city, nor shoot an arrow there, nor come before it with shields, nor cast a bank against it.

34By the way that he came, by the same shall he return, and shall not come into this city, saith the LORD.

35For I will defend this city to save it for mine own sake, and for my servant David's sake.

36Then the angel of the LORD went forth, and smote in the camp of the Assyrians a hundred and fourscore and five thousand: and when they arose early in the morning, behold, they *were* all dead corpses.

37¶ So Sennacherib king of Assyria departed, and went and returned, and dwelt at Nineveh.

New International

24By your messengers
    you have heaped insults on the Lord.
And you have said,
    'With my many chariots
I have ascended the heights of the mountains,
    the utmost heights of Lebanon.
I have cut down its tallest cedars,
    the choicest of its pines.
I have reached its remotest heights,
    the finest of its forests.
25I have dug wells in foreign landsa
    and drunk the water there.
With the soles of my feet
    I have dried up all the streams of Egypt.'

26"Have you not heard?
    Long ago I ordained it.
In days of old I planned it;
    now I have brought it to pass,
that you have turned fortified cities
    into piles of stone.
27Their people, drained of power,
    are dismayed and put to shame.
They are like plants in the field,
    like tender green shoots,
like grass sprouting on the roof,
    scorchedb before it grows up.

28"But I know where you stay
    and when you come and go
    and how you rage against me.
29Because you rage against me
    and because your insolence has reached my
        ears,
I will put my hook in your nose
    and my bit in your mouth,
and I will make you return
    by the way you came.

30"This will be the sign for you, O Hezekiah:

"This year you will eat what grows by itself,
    and the second year what springs from that.
But in the third year sow and reap,
    plant vineyards and eat their fruit.
31Once more a remnant of the house of Judah
    will take root below and bear fruit above.
32For out of Jerusalem will come a remnant,
    and out of Mount Zion a band of survivors.
The zeal of the LORD Almighty
    will accomplish this.

33"Therefore this is what the LORD says concerning the king of Assyria:

"He will not enter this city
    or shoot an arrow here.
He will not come before it with shield
    or build a siege ramp against it.
34By the way that he came he will return;
    he will not enter this city,"
                                    declares the LORD.
35"I will defend this city and save it,
    for my sake and for the sake of David my
        servant!"

36Then the angel of the LORD went out and put to death a hundred and eighty-five thousand men in the Assyrian camp. When the people got up the next morning—there were all the dead bodies! 37So Sennacherib king of Assyria broke camp and withdrew. He returned to Nineveh and stayed there.

---

a 25 Dead Sea Scrolls (see also 2 Kings 19:24); Masoretic Text does not have *in foreign lands.*   b 27 Some manuscripts of the Masoretic Text, Dead Sea Scrolls and some Septuagint manuscripts (see also 2 Kings 19:26); most manuscripts of the Masoretic Text *roof / and terraced fields*

Living Bible

to mock the Lord. You boast, 'I came with my mighty army against the nations of the west. I cut down the tallest cedars and choicest cypress trees. I conquered their highest mountains and destroyed their thickest forests.'

25"You boast of wells you've dug in many a conquered land, and Egypt with all its armies is no obstacle to you! 26But do you not yet know that it was I who decided all this long ago? That it was I who gave you all this power from ancient times? I have caused all this to happen as I planned—that you should crush walled cities into ruined heaps. 27That's why their people had so little power, and were such easy prey for you. They were as helpless as the grass, as tender plants you trample down beneath your feet, as grass upon the housetops, burnt yellow by the sun. 28But I know you well—your comings and goings and all you do—and the way you have raged against me. 29Because of your anger against the Lord—and I heard it all!—I have put a hook in your nose and a bit in your mouth and led you back to your own land by the same road you came."

30Then God said to Hezekiah, "Here is the proof that I am the one who is delivering this city from the king of Assyria: This yearᶜ he will abandon his siege. Although it is too late now to plant your crops, and you will have only volunteer grain this fall, still it will give you enough seed for a small harvest next year, and two years from nowᵈ you will be living in luxury again. 31And you who are left in Judah will take root again in your own soil and flourish and multiply. 32For a remnant shall go out from Jerusalem to repopulate the land; the power of the Lord Almighty will cause all this to come to pass.

33"As for the king of Assyria, his armies shall not enter Jerusalem, nor shoot their arrows there, nor march outside its gates, nor build up an earthen bank against its walls. 34He will return to his own country by the road he came on, and will not enter this city, says the Lord. 35For my own honor I will defend it, and in memory of my servant David."

36That night the Angel of the Lord went out to the camp of the Assyrians and killed 185,000 soldiers; when the living wakened the next morning, all these lay dead before them. 37Then Sennacherib, king of Assyria, returned to his own country, to Nineveh. 38And one day

New Revised Standard

24 By your servants you have mocked the Lord,
 and you have said, 'With my many chariots
I have gone up the heights of the mountains,
 to the far recesses of Lebanon;
I felled its tallest cedars,
 its choicest cypresses;
I came to its remotest height,
 its densest forest.
25 I dug wells
 and drank waters,
I dried up with the sole of my foot
 all the streams of Egypt.'

26 Have you not heard
 that I determined it long ago?
I planned from days of old
 what now I bring to pass,
that you should make fortified cities
 crash into heaps of ruins,
27 while their inhabitants, shorn of strength,
 are dismayed and confounded;
they have become like plants of the field
 and like tender grass,
like grass on the housetops,
 blightedᵉ before it is grown.

28 I know your rising upᶠ and your sitting down,
 your going out and coming in,
 and your raging against me.
29 Because you have raged against me
 and your arrogance has come to my ears,
I will put my hook in your nose
 and my bit in your mouth;
I will turn you back on the way
 by which you came.

30 "And this shall be the sign for you: This year eat what grows of itself, and in the second year what springs from that; then in the third year sow, reap, plant vineyards, and eat their fruit. 31 The surviving remnant of the house of Judah shall again take root downward, and bear fruit upward; 32 for from Jerusalem a remnant shall go out, and from Mount Zion a band of survivors. The zeal of the LORD of hosts will do this.

33 "Therefore thus says the LORD concerning the king of Assyria: He shall not come into this city, shoot an arrow there, come before it with a shield, or cast up a siege ramp against it. 34 By the way that he came, by the same he shall return; he shall not come into this city, says the LORD. 35 For I will defend this city to save it, for my own sake and for the sake of my servant David."

Sennacherib's Defeat and Death

36 Then the angel of the LORD set out and struck down one hundred eighty-five thousand in the camp of the Assyrians; when morning dawned, they were all dead bodies. 37 Then King Sennacherib of Assyria left, went home, and lived at Nineveh. 38 As he was worship-

---

ᶜ 37:30 *This year,* implied.   ᵈ 37:30 *two years from now you will be living in luxury again.* The third harvest from then would yield a bumper crop.   ᵉ With 2 Kings 19.26: Heb *field*   ᶠ Q Ms Gk: MT lacks *your rising up*

King James

38And it came to pass, as he was worshipping in the house of Nisroch his god, that Adrammelech and Share-zer his sons smote him with the sword; and they escaped into the land of Armenia: and Esar-haddon his son reigned in his stead.

38 IN THOSE days was Hezekiah sick unto death. And Isaiah the prophet the son of Amoz came unto him, and said unto him, Thus saith the LORD, Set thine house in order: for thou shalt die, and not live.

2Then Hezekiah turned his face toward the wall, and prayed unto the LORD,

3And said, Remember now, O LORD, I beseech thee, how I have walked before thee in truth and with a perfect heart, and have done *that which is* good in thy sight. And Hezekiah wept sore.

4¶ Then came the word of the LORD to Isaiah, saying,

5Go, and say to Hezekiah, Thus saith the LORD, the God of David thy father, I have heard thy prayer, I have seen thy tears: behold, I will add unto thy days fifteen years.

6And I will deliver thee and this city out of the hand of the king of Assyria: and I will defend this city.

7And this *shall be* a sign unto thee from the LORD, that the LORD will do this thing that he hath spoken;

8Behold, I will bring again the shadow of the degrees, which is gone down in the sun dial of Ahaz, ten degrees backward. So the sun returned ten degrees, by which degrees it was gone down.

9¶ The writing of Hezekiah king of Judah, when he had been sick, and was recovered of his sickness:

10I said in the cutting off of my days, I shall go to the gates of the grave; I am deprived of the residue of my years.

11I said, I shall not see the LORD, *even* the LORD, in the land of the living: I shall behold man no more with the inhabitants of the world.

12Mine age is departed, and is removed from me as a shepherd's tent: I have cut off like a weaver my life: he will cut me off with pining sickness: from day *even* to night wilt thou make an end of me.

13I reckoned till morning, *that,* as a lion, so will he break all my bones: from day *even* to night wilt thou make an end of me.

14Like a crane *or* a swallow, so did I chatter: I did mourn as a dove: mine eyes fail *with looking* upward: O LORD, I am oppressed; undertake for me.

15What shall I say? he hath both spoken unto me, and himself hath done *it:* I shall go softly all my years in the bitterness of my soul.

16O Lord, by these *things men* live, and in all these *things is* the life of my spirit: so wilt thou recover me, and make me to live.

17Behold, for peace I had great bitterness: but thou hast in love to my soul *delivered it* from the pit of corruption: for thou hast cast all my sins behind thy back.

New International

38One day, while he was worshiping in the temple of his god Nisroch, his sons Adrammelech and Sharezer cut him down with the sword, and they escaped to the land of Ararat. And Esarhaddon his son succeeded him as king.

Hezekiah's Illness

38 IN THOSE days Hezekiah became ill and was at the point of death. The prophet Isaiah son of Amoz went to him and said, "This is what the LORD says: Put your house in order, because you are going to die; you will not recover."

2Hezekiah turned his face to the wall and prayed to the LORD, 3"Remember, O LORD, how I have walked before you faithfully and with wholehearted devotion and have done what is good in your eyes." And Hezekiah wept bitterly.

4Then the word of the LORD came to Isaiah: 5"Go and tell Hezekiah, 'This is what the LORD, the God of your father David, says: I have heard your prayer and seen your tears; I will add fifteen years to your life. 6And I will deliver you and this city from the hand of the king of Assyria. I will defend this city.

7" 'This is the LORD's sign to you that the LORD will do what he has promised: 8I will make the shadow cast by the sun go back the ten steps it has gone down on the stairway of Ahaz.' " So the sunlight went back the ten steps it had gone down.

9A writing of Hezekiah king of Judah after his illness and recovery:

10I said, "In the prime of my life
    must I go through the gates of death[a]
    and be robbed of the rest of my years?"
11I said, "I will not again see the LORD,
    the LORD, in the land of the living;
no longer will I look on mankind,
    or be with those who now dwell in this
    world.[b]
12Like a shepherd's tent my house
    has been pulled down and taken from me.
Like a weaver I have rolled up my life,
    and he has cut me off from the loom;
    day and night you made an end of me.
13I waited patiently till dawn,
    but like a lion he broke all my bones;
    day and night you made an end of me.
14I cried like a swift or thrush,
    I moaned like a mourning dove.
My eyes grew weak as I looked to the heavens.
    I am troubled; O Lord, come to my aid!"

15But what can I say?
    He has spoken to me, and he himself has
    done this.
I will walk humbly all my years
    because of this anguish of my soul.
16Lord, by such things men live;
    and my spirit finds life in them too.
You restored me to health
    and let me live.
17Surely it was for my benefit
    that I suffered such anguish.
In your love you kept me
    from the pit of destruction;
you have put all my sins
    behind your back.

a *10* Hebrew *Sheol*   b *11* A few Hebrew manuscripts; most Hebrew manuscripts *in the place of cessation*

Living Bible

while he was worshiping in the temple of Nisroch his god, his sons Adrammelech and Sharezer killed him with their swords; then they escaped into the land of Ararat, and Esar-haddon his son became king.

38 IT WAS just before all this that Hezekiah became deathly sick and Isaiah the prophet (Amoz' son) went to visit him and gave him this message from the Lord:

"Set your affairs in order, for you are going to die; you will not recover from this illness."

2When Hezekiah heard this, he turned his face to the wall and prayed:

3"O Lord, don't you remember how true I've been to you and how I've always tried to obey you in everything you said?" Then he broke down with great sobs.

4So the Lord sent another message to Isaiah:

5"Go and tell Hezekiah that the Lord God of your forefather David hears you praying and sees your tears and will let you live fifteen more years. 6He will deliver you and this city from the king of Assyria. I will defend you, says the Lord, 7and here is my guarantee: 8I will send the sun backwards ten degrees as measured on Ahaz' sundial!"

So the sun retraced ten degrees that it had gone down!

9When King Hezekiah was well again, he wrote this poem about his experience:

10"My life is but half done and I must leave it all. I am robbed of my normal years, and now I must enter the gates of Sheol. 11Never again will I see the Lord in the land of the living. Never again will I see my friends in this world. 12My life is blown away like a shepherd's tent; it is cut short as when a weaver stops his working at the loom. In one short day my life hangs by a thread.

13"All night I moaned; it was like being torn apart by lions. 14Delirious, I chattered like a swallow and mourned like a dove; my eyes grew weary of looking up for help. 'O God,' I cried, 'I am in trouble—help me.' 15But what can I say? For he himself has sent this sickness. All my sleep has fled because of my soul's bitterness. 16O Lord, your discipline is good and leads to life and health. Oh, heal me and make me live!

17"Yes, now I see it all—it was good for me to undergo this bitterness, for you have lovingly delivered me from death; you have forgiven all my sins. 18For dead

New Revised Standard

ing in the house of his god Nisroch, his sons Adrammelech and Sharezer killed him with the sword, and they escaped into the land of Ararat. His son Esar-haddon succeeded him.

Hezekiah's Illness

38 IN THOSE days Hezekiah became sick and was at the point of death. The prophet Isaiah son of Amoz came to him, and said to him, "Thus says the LORD: Set your house in order, for you shall die; you shall not recover." 2Then Hezekiah turned his face to the wall, and prayed to the LORD: 3"Remember now, O LORD, I implore you, how I have walked before you in faithfulness with a whole heart, and have done what is good in your sight." And Hezekiah wept bitterly.

4 Then the word of the LORD came to Isaiah: 5"Go and say to Hezekiah, Thus says the LORD, the God of your ancestor David: I have heard your prayer, I have seen your tears; I will add fifteen years to your life. 6I will deliver you and this city out of the hand of the king of Assyria, and defend this city.

7 "This is the sign to you from the LORD, that the LORD will do this thing that he has promised: 8See, I will make the shadow cast by the declining sun on the dial of Ahaz turn back ten steps." So the sun turned back on the dial the ten steps by which it had declined.c

9 A writing of King Hezekiah of Judah, after he had been sick and had recovered from his sickness:

10 I said: In the noontide of my days
    I must depart;
I am consigned to the gates of Sheol
    for the rest of my years.

11 I said, I shall not see the LORD
    in the land of the living;
I shall look upon mortals no more
    among the inhabitants of the world.

12 My dwelling is plucked up and removed from
    me
    like a shepherd's tent;
like a weaver I have rolled up my life;
    he cuts me off from the loom;
from day to night you bring me to an end;c

13   I cry for helpd until morning;
like a lion he breaks all my bones;
    from day to night you bring me to an end.c

14 Like a swallow or a cranec I clamor,
    I moan like a dove.
My eyes are weary with looking upward.
    O Lord, I am oppressed; be my security!

15 But what can I say? For he has spoken to me,
    and he himself has done it.
All my sleep has flede
    because of the bitterness of my soul.

16 O Lord, by these things people live,
    and in all these is the life of my spirit.c
    Oh, restore me to health and make me live!

17 Surely it was for my welfare
    that I had great bitterness;
but you have held backf my life
    from the pit of destruction,
for you have cast all my sins
    behind your back.

c Meaning of Heb uncertain   d Cn: Meaning of Heb uncertain   e Cn
Compare Syr: Heb I will walk slowly all my years   f Cn Compare Gk Vg:
Heb loved

King James

18For the grave cannot praise thee, death can *not* celebrate thee: they that go down into the pit cannot hope for thy truth.

19The living, the living, he shall praise thee, as I *do* this day: the father to the children shall make known thy truth.

20The LORD *was ready* to save me: therefore we will sing my songs to the stringed instruments all the days of our life in the house of the LORD.

21For Isaiah had said, Let them take a lump of figs, and lay *it* for a plaster upon the boil, and he shall recover.

22Hezekiah also had said, What *is* the sign that I shall go up to the house of the LORD?

39 AT THAT time Merodach-baladan, the son of Baladan, king of Babylon, sent letters and a present to Hezekiah: for he had heard that he had been sick, and was recovered.

2And Hezekiah was glad of them, and showed them the house of his precious things, the silver, and the gold, and the spices, and the precious ointment, and all the house of his armour, and all that was found in his treasures: there was nothing in his house, nor in all his dominion, that Hezekiah showed them not.

3¶ Then came Isaiah the prophet unto king Hezekiah, and said unto him, What said these men? and from whence came they unto thee? And Hezekiah said, They are come from a far country unto me, *even* from Babylon.

4Then said he, What have they seen in thine house? And Hezekiah answered, All that *is* in mine house have they seen: there is nothing among my treasures that I have not shown them.

5Then said Isaiah to Hezekiah, Hear the word of the LORD of hosts:

6Behold, the days come, that all that *is* in thine house, and *that* which thy fathers have laid up in store until this day, shall be carried to Babylon: nothing shall be left, saith the LORD.

7And of thy sons that shall issue from thee, which thou shalt beget, shall they take away; and they shall be eunuchs in the palace of the king of Babylon.

8Then said Hezekiah to Isaiah, Good *is* the word of the LORD which thou hast spoken. He said moreover, For there shall be peace and truth in my days.

40 COMFORT YE, comfort ye my people, saith your God.

2Speak ye comfortably to Jerusalem, and cry unto her, that her warfare is accomplished, that her iniquity is pardoned: for she hath received of the LORD's hand double for all her sins.

New International

18For the gravea cannot praise you,
    death cannot sing your praise;
those who go down to the pit
    cannot hope for your faithfulness.
19The living, the living—they praise you,
    as I am doing today;
fathers tell their children
    about your faithfulness.

20The LORD will save me,
    and we will sing with stringed instruments
all the days of our lives
    in the temple of the LORD.

21Isaiah had said, "Prepare a poultice of figs and apply it to the boil, and he will recover."

22Hezekiah had asked, "What will be the sign that I will go up to the temple of the LORD?"

Envoys From Babylon

39 AT THAT time Merodach-Baladan son of Baladan king of Babylon sent Hezekiah letters and a gift, because he had heard of his illness and recovery.

2Hezekiah received the envoys gladly and showed them what was in his storehouses—the silver, the gold, the spices, the fine oil, his entire armory and everything found among his treasures. There was nothing in his palace or in all his kingdom that Hezekiah did not show them.

3Then Isaiah the prophet went to King Hezekiah and asked, "What did those men say, and where did they come from?"

"From a distant land," Hezekiah replied. "They came to me from Babylon."

4The prophet asked, "What did they see in your palace?"

"They saw everything in my palace," Hezekiah said. "There is nothing among my treasures that I did not show them."

5Then Isaiah said to Hezekiah, "Hear the word of the LORD Almighty: 6The time will surely come when everything in your palace, and all that your fathers have stored up until this day, will be carried off to Babylon. Nothing will be left, says the LORD. 7And some of your descendants, your own flesh and blood who will be born to you, will be taken away, and they will become eunuchs in the palace of the king of Babylon."

8"The word of the LORD you have spoken is good," Hezekiah replied. For he thought, "There will be peace and security in my lifetime."

Comfort for God's People

40 COMFORT, COMFORT my people,
    says your God.
2Speak tenderly to Jerusalem,
    and proclaim to her
that her hard service has been completed,
    that her sin has been paid for,
that she has received from the LORD's hand
    double for all her sins.

a 18 Hebrew *Sheol*

Living Bible

men cannot praise you.b They cannot be filled with hope
and joy. 19The living, only the living, can praise you as
I do today. One generation makes known your faithfulness to the next. 20Think of it! The Lord healed me!
Every day of my life from now on I will sing my songs
of praise in the Temple, accompanied by the orchestra."

21(For Isaiah had told Hezekiah's servants, "Make an
ointment of figs and spread it over the boil, and he will
get well again."

22And then Hezekiah had asked, "What sign will the
Lord give me to prove that he will heal me?")

39 SOON AFTERWARDS, the king of Babylon
(Merodach-baladan, the son of Baladan) sent
Hezekiah a present and his best wishes,c for he had
heard that Hezekiah had been very sick and now was
well again. 2Hezekiah appreciated this and took the envoys from Babylon on a tour of the palace, showing
them his treasure house full of silver, gold, spices and
perfumes. He took them into his jewel rooms, too, and
opened to them all his treasures—everything.

3Then Isaiah the prophet came to the king and said,
"What did they say? Where are they from?"

"From far away in Babylon," Hezekiah replied.

4"How much have they seen?" asked Isaiah.

And Hezekiah replied, "I showed them everything I
own, all my priceless treasures."

5Then Isaiah said to him, "Listen to this message
from the Lord Almighty:

6"The time is coming when everything you have—all
the treasures stored up by your fathers—will be carried
off to Babylon. Nothing will be left. 7And some of your
own sons will become slaves, yes, eunuchs, in the palace of the king of Babylon."

8"All right," Hezekiah replied. "Whatever the Lord
says is good. At least there will be peace during my
lifetime!"

40 COMFORT, YES, comfort my people, says
your God. 2Speak tenderly to Jerusalem and tell
her that her sad days are gone. Her sins are pardoned,
and I have punished her in full for all her sins.

New Revised Standard

18 For Sheol cannot thank you,
    death cannot praise you;
  those who go down to the Pit cannot hope
    for your faithfulness.

19 The living, the living, they thank you,
    as I do this day;
  fathers make known to children
    your faithfulness.

20 The LORD will save me,
    and we will sing to stringed instrumentsd
  all the days of our lives,
    at the house of the LORD.

21 Now Isaiah had said, "Let them take a lump of
figs, and apply it to the boil, so that he may recover."
22Hezekiah also had said, "What is the sign that I shall
go up to the house of the LORD?"

Envoys from Babylon Welcomed

39 AT THAT time King Merodach-baladan son of
Baladan of Babylon sent envoys with letters and
a present to Hezekiah, for he heard that he had been sick
and had recovered. 2Hezekiah welcomed them; he
showed them his treasure house, the silver, the gold, the
spices, the precious oil, his whole armory, all that was
found in his storehouses. There was nothing in his house
or in all his realm that Hezekiah did not show them.
3Then the prophet Isaiah came to King Hezekiah and
said to him, "What did these men say? From where did
they come to you?" Hezekiah answered, "They have
come to me from a far country, from Babylon." 4He
said, "What have they seen in your house?" Hezekiah
answered, "They have seen all that is in my house; there
is nothing in my storehouses that I did not show them."

5 Then Isaiah said to Hezekiah, "Hear the word of
the LORD of hosts: 6Days are coming when all that is in
your house, and that which your ancestors have stored
up until this day, shall be carried to Babylon; nothing
shall be left, says the LORD. 7Some of your own sons
who are born to you shall be taken away; they shall be
eunuchs in the palace of the king of Babylon." 8Then
Hezekiah said to Isaiah, "The word of the LORD that you
have spoken is good." For he thought, "There will be
peace and security in my days."

God's People Are Comforted

40 COMFORT, O comfort my people,
    says your God.
2 Speak tenderly to Jerusalem,
    and cry to her
  that she has served her term,
    that her penalty is paid,
  that she has received from the LORD's hand
    double for all her sins.

---

b *38:18 For dead men cannot praise you.* The meaning is unclear. Perhaps
Hezekiah was unaware of the blessedness of the future life for those who
trust in God (57:1, 2). Or perhaps his meaning is, "Dead bodies cannot praise
you." c *39:1 Merodach-baladan . . . sent Hezekiah a present and his best
wishes.* Merodach-baladan was at this time planning a revolt in the east against
Sennacherib, so he was especially interested in Hezekiah's activities in the
west.

d Heb *my stringed instruments*

King James

3¶ The voice of him that crieth in the wilderness, Prepare ye the way of the LORD, make straight in the desert a highway for our God.

4Every valley shall be exalted, and every mountain and hill shall be made low: and the crooked shall be made straight, and the rough places plain:

5And the glory of the LORD shall be revealed, and all flesh shall see it together: for the mouth of the LORD hath spoken it.

6The voice said, Cry. And he said, What shall I cry? All flesh is grass, and all the goodliness thereof is as the flower of the field:

7The grass withereth, the flower fadeth: because the spirit of the LORD bloweth upon it: surely the people is grass.

8The grass withereth, the flower fadeth: but the word of our God shall stand for ever.

9¶ O Zion, that bringest good tidings, get thee up into the high mountain; O Jerusalem, that bringest good tidings, lift up thy voice with strength; lift it up, be not afraid; say unto the cities of Judah, Behold your God!

10Behold, the Lord GOD will come with strong hand, and his arm shall rule for him: behold, his reward is with him, and his work before him.

11He shall feed his flock like a shepherd: he shall gather the lambs with his arm, and carry them in his bosom, and shall gently lead those that are with young.

12¶ Who hath measured the waters in the hollow of his hand, and meted out heaven with the span, and comprehended the dust of the earth in a measure, and weighed the mountains in scales, and the hills in a balance?

13Who hath directed the spirit of the LORD, or being his counsellor hath taught him?

14With whom took he counsel, and who instructed him, and taught him in the path of judgment, and taught him knowledge, and showed to him the way of understanding?

15Behold, the nations are as a drop of a bucket, and are counted as the small dust of the balance: behold, he taketh up the isles as a very little thing.

16And Lebanon is not sufficient to burn, nor the beasts thereof sufficient for a burnt offering.

17All nations before him are as nothing; and they are counted to him less than nothing, and vanity.

18¶ To whom then will ye liken God? or what likeness will ye compare unto him?

19The workman melteth a graven image, and the goldsmith spreadeth it over with gold, and casteth silver chains.

New International

3A voice of one calling:
"In the desert prepare
    the way for the LORD[a];
make straight in the wilderness
    a highway for our God.[b]
4Every valley shall be raised up,
    every mountain and hill made low;
the rough ground shall become level,
    the rugged places a plain.
5And the glory of the LORD will be revealed,
    and all mankind together will see it.
      For the mouth of the LORD has spoken."

6A voice says, "Cry out."
    And I said, "What shall I cry?"

"All men are like grass,
    and all their glory is like the flowers of the
    field.
7The grass withers and the flowers fall,
    because the breath of the LORD blows on
    them.
Surely the people are grass.
8The grass withers and the flowers fall,
    but the word of our God stands forever."

9You who bring good tidings to Zion,
    go up on a high mountain.
You who bring good tidings to Jerusalem,[c]
    lift up your voice with a shout,
lift it up, do not be afraid;
    say to the towns of Judah,
    "Here is your God!"
10See, the Sovereign LORD comes with power,
    and his arm rules for him.
See, his reward is with him,
    and his recompense accompanies him.
11He tends his flock like a shepherd:
    He gathers the lambs in his arms
and carries them close to his heart;
    he gently leads those that have young.

12Who has measured the waters in the hollow of
    his hand,
    or with the breadth of his hand marked off
    the heavens?
Who has held the dust of the earth in a basket,
    or weighed the mountains on the scales
    and the hills in a balance?
13Who has understood the mind[d] of the LORD,
    or instructed him as his counselor?
14Whom did the LORD consult to enlighten him,
    and who taught him the right way?
Who was it that taught him knowledge
    or showed him the path of understanding?

15Surely the nations are like a drop in a bucket;
    they are regarded as dust on the scales;
he weighs the islands as though they were
    fine dust.
16Lebanon is not sufficient for altar fires,
    nor its animals enough for burnt offerings.
17Before him all the nations are as nothing;
    they are regarded by him as worthless
    and less than nothing.

18To whom, then, will you compare God?
    What image will you compare him to?
19As for an idol, a craftsman casts it,
    and a goldsmith overlays it with gold
    and fashions silver chains for it.

---

a 3 Or A voice of one calling in the desert: | "Prepare the way for the LORD
b 3 Hebrew; Septuagint make straight the paths of our God   c 9 Or O Zion, bringer of good tidings, | go up on a high mountain. | O Jerusalem, bringer of good tidings   d 13 Or Spirit; or spirit

Living Bible

³Listen! I hear the voice of someone shouting, "Make a road for the Lord through the wilderness; make him a straight, smooth road through the desert. ⁴Fill the valleys; level the hills; straighten out the crooked paths and smooth off the rough spots in the road. ⁵The glory of the Lord will be seen by all mankind together." The Lord has spoken—it shall be.

⁶The voice says, "Shout!"

"What shall I shout?" I asked.

"Shout that man is like the grass that dies away, and all his beauty fades like dying flowers. ⁷The grass withers, the flower fades beneath the breath of God. And so it is with fragile man. ⁸The grass withers, the flowers fade, but the Word of our God shall stand forever."

⁹O Crier of Good News, shout to Jerusalem from the mountain tops! Shout louder—don't be afraid—tell the cities of Judah, "Your God is coming!" ¹⁰Yes, the Lord God is coming with mighty power; he will rule with awesome strength. See, his reward is with him, to each as he has done. ¹¹He will feed his flock like a shepherd; he will carry the lambs in his arms and gently lead the ewes with young.

¹²Who else has held the oceans in his hands and measured off the heavens with his ruler? Who else knows the weight of all the earth and weighs the mountains and the hills? ¹³Who can advise the Spirit of the Lord or be his teacher or give him counsel? ¹⁴Has he ever needed anyone's advice? Did he need instruction as to what is right and best? ¹⁵No, for all the peoples of the world are nothing in comparison with him—they are but a drop in the bucket, dust on the scales. He picks up the islands as though they had no weight at all. ¹⁶All of Lebanon's forests do not contain sufficient fuel to consume a sacrifice large enough to honor him, nor are all its animals enough to offer to our God. ¹⁷All the nations are as nothing to him; in his eyes they are less than nothing—mere emptiness and froth.

¹⁸How can we describe God? With what can we compare him? ¹⁹With an idol? An idol, made from a mold, overlaid with gold, and with silver chains around its neck? ²⁰The man too poor to buy expensive gods like

New Revised Standard

3 A voice cries out:
"In the wilderness prepare the way of the
   Lord,
   make straight in the desert a highway for
      our God.
4 Every valley shall be lifted up,
   and every mountain and hill be made low;
the uneven ground shall become level,
   and the rough places a plain.
5 Then the glory of the Lord shall be revealed,
   and all people shall see it together,
   for the mouth of the Lord has spoken."

6 A voice says, "Cry out!"
   And I said, "What shall I cry?"
All people are grass,
   their constancy is like the flower of the
      field.
7 The grass withers, the flower fades,
   when the breath of the Lord blows upon it;
   surely the people are grass.
8 The grass withers, the flower fades;
   but the word of our God will stand forever.
9 Get you up to a high mountain,
   O Zion, herald of good tidings;ᵉ
lift up your voice with strength,
   O Jerusalem, herald of good tidings,ᶠ
lift it up, do not fear;
   say to the cities of Judah,
   "Here is your God!"
10 See, the Lord God comes with might,
   and his arm rules for him;
his reward is with him,
   and his recompense before him.
11 He will feed his flock like a shepherd;
   he will gather the lambs in his arms,
and carry them in his bosom,
   and gently lead the mother sheep.

12 Who has measured the waters in the hollow of
      his hand
   and marked off the heavens with a span,
enclosed the dust of the earth in a measure,
   and weighed the mountains in scales
   and the hills in a balance?
13 Who has directed the spirit of the Lord,
   or as his counselor has instructed him?
14 Whom did he consult for his enlightenment,
   and who taught him the path of justice?
Who taught him knowledge,
   and showed him the way of understanding?
15 Even the nations are like a drop from a
      bucket,
   and are accounted as dust on the scales;
   see, he takes up the isles like fine dust.
16 Lebanon would not provide fuel enough,
   nor are its animals enough for a burnt
      offering.
17 All the nations are as nothing before him;
   they are accounted by him as less than
      nothing and emptiness.

18 To whom then will you liken God,
   or what likeness compare with him?
19 An idol? —A workman casts it,
   and a goldsmith overlays it with gold,
   and casts for it silver chains.

ᵉ Or *O herald of good tidings to Zion*   ᶠ Or *O herald of good tidings to Jerusalem*

King James

20He that *is* so impoverished that he hath no oblation chooseth a tree *that* will not rot; he seeketh unto him a cunning workman to prepare a graven image, *that* shall not be moved.

21Have ye not known? have ye not heard? hath it not been told you from the beginning? have ye not understood from the foundations of the earth?

22*It is* he that sitteth upon the circle of the earth, and the inhabitants thereof *are* as grasshoppers; that stretcheth out the heavens as a curtain, and spreadeth them out as a tent to dwell in:

23That bringeth the princes to nothing; he maketh the judges of the earth as vanity.

24Yea, they shall not be planted; yea, they shall not be sown: yea, their stock shall not take root in the earth: and he shall also blow upon them, and they shall wither, and the whirlwind shall take them away as stubble.

25To whom then will ye liken me, or shall I be equal? saith the Holy One.

26Lift up your eyes on high, and behold who hath created these *things,* that bringeth out their host by number: he calleth them all by names by the greatness of his might, for that *he is* strong in power; not one faileth.

27Why sayest thou, O Jacob, and speakest, O Israel, My way is hid from the LORD, and my judgment is passed over from my God?

28¶ Hast thou not known? hast thou not heard, *that* the everlasting God, the LORD, the Creator of the ends of the earth, fainteth not, neither is weary? *there is* no searching of his understanding.

29He giveth power to the faint; and to *them that have* no might he increaseth strength.

30Even the youths shall faint and be weary, and the young men shall utterly fall:

31But they that wait upon the LORD shall renew *their* strength; they shall mount up with wings as eagles; they shall run, and not be weary; *and* they shall walk, and not faint.

41 KEEP SILENCE before me, O islands; and let the people renew *their* strength: let them come near; then let them speak: let us come near together to judgment.

2Who raised up the righteous *man* from the east, called him to his foot, gave the nations before him, and made *him* rule over kings? he gave *them* as the dust to his sword, *and* as driven stubble to his bow.

3He pursued them, *and* passed safely; *even* by the way *that* he had not gone with his feet.

New International

20A man too poor to present such an offering
   selects wood that will not rot.
He looks for a skilled craftsman
   to set up an idol that will not topple.

21Do you not know?
   Have you not heard?
Has it not been told you from the beginning?
   Have you not understood since the earth was
      founded?

22He sits enthroned above the circle of the earth,
   and its people are like grasshoppers.
He stretches out the heavens like a canopy,
   and spreads them out like a tent to live in.

23He brings princes to naught
   and reduces the rulers of this world to
      nothing.

24No sooner are they planted,
   no sooner are they sown,
   no sooner do they take root in the ground,
than he blows on them and they wither,
   and a whirlwind sweeps them away like
      chaff.

25"To whom will you compare me?
   Or who is my equal?" says the Holy One.

26Lift your eyes and look to the heavens:
   Who created all these?
He who brings out the starry host one by one,
   and calls them each by name.
Because of his great power and mighty strength,
   not one of them is missing.

27Why do you say, O Jacob,
   and complain, O Israel,
"My way is hidden from the LORD;
   my cause is disregarded by my God"?

28Do you not know?
   Have you not heard?
The LORD is the everlasting God,
   the Creator of the ends of the earth.
He will not grow tired or weary,
   and his understanding no one can fathom.

29He gives strength to the weary
   and increases the power of the weak.

30Even youths grow tired and weary,
   and young men stumble and fall;

31but those who hope in the LORD
   will renew their strength.
They will soar on wings like eagles;
   they will run and not grow weary,
   they will walk and not be faint.

The Helper of Israel

41 "BE SILENT before me, you islands!
   Let the nations renew their strength!
Let them come forward and speak;
   let us meet together at the place of judgment.

2"Who has stirred up one from the east,
   calling him in righteousness to his service[a]?
He hands nations over to him
   and subdues kings before him.
He turns them to dust with his sword,
   to windblown chaff with his bow.

3He pursues them and moves on unscathed,
   by a path his feet have not traveled before.

---

[a] 2 Or *I whom victory meets at every step*

Living Bible

that will find a tree free from rot and hire a man to carve a face on it, and that's his god—a god that cannot even move!

21Are you so ignorant? Are you so deaf to the words of God—the words he gave before the world began? Have you never heard nor understood? 22It is God who sits above the circle of the earth. (The people below must seem to him like grasshoppers!) He is the one who stretches out the heavens like a curtain and makes his tent from them. 23He dooms the great men of the world and brings them all to naught. 24They hardly get started, barely take root, when he blows on them and their work withers and the wind carries them off like straw.

25"With whom will you compare me? Who is my equal?" asks the Holy One.

26Look up into the heavens! Who created all these stars? As a shepherdb leads his sheep, calling each by its pet name, and counts them to see that none are lost or strayed, so God does with stars and planets!

27O Jacob, O Israel, how can you say that the Lord doesn't see your troubles and isn't being fair? 28Don't you yet understand? Don't you know by now that the everlasting God, the Creator of the farthest parts of the earth, never grows faint or weary? No one can fathom the depths of his understanding. 29He gives power to the tired and worn out, and strength to the weak. 30Even the youths shall be exhausted, and the young men will all-give up. 31But they that wait upon the Lord shall renew their strength. They shall mount up with wings like eagles; they shall run and not be weary; they shall walk and not faint.

41 LISTEN IN silence before me, O lands beyond the sea. Bring your strongest arguments. Come now and speak. The court is ready for your case.

2Who has stirred up this one from the east,c whom victory meets at every step? Who, indeed, but the Lord? God has given him victory over many nations and permitted him to trample kings underfoot and to put entire armies to the sword. 3He chases them away and goes on safely, though the paths he treads are new. 4Who has

New Revised Standard

20 As a gift one chooses mulberry woodd
    —wood that will not rot—
  then seeks out a skilled artisan
    to set up an image that will not topple.

21 Have you not known? Have you not heard?
    Has it not been told you from the
      beginning?
  Have you not understood from the
    foundations of the earth?
22 It is he who sits above the circle of the earth,
    and its inhabitants are like grasshoppers;
  who stretches out the heavens like a curtain,
    and spreads them like a tent to live in;
23 who brings princes to naught,
    and makes the rulers of the earth as
      nothing.

24 Scarcely are they planted, scarcely sown,
    scarcely has their stem taken root in the
      earth,
  when he blows upon them, and they wither,
    and the tempest carries them off like
      stubble.

25 To whom then will you compare me,
    or who is my equal? says the Holy One.
26 Lift up your eyes on high and see:
    Who created these?
  He who brings out their host and numbers
      them,
    calling them all by name;
  because he is great in strength,
    mighty in power,
    not one is missing.

27 Why do you say, O Jacob,
    and speak, O Israel,
  "My way is hidden from the LORD,
    and my right is disregarded by my God"?
28 Have you not known? Have you not heard?
  The LORD is the everlasting God,
    the Creator of the ends of the earth.
  He does not faint or grow weary;
    his understanding is unsearchable.
29 He gives power to the faint,
    and strengthens the powerless.
30 Even youths will faint and be weary,
    and the young will fall exhausted;
31 but those who wait for the LORD shall renew
      their strength,
  they shall mount up with wings like eagles,
  they shall run and not be weary,
  they shall walk and not faint.

Israel Assured of God's Help

41 LISTEN TO me in silence, O coastlands;
    let the peoples renew their strength;
  let them approach, then let them speak;
    let us together draw near for judgment.

2 Who has roused a victor from the east,
    summoned him to his service?
  He delivers up nations to him,
    and tramples kings under foot;
  he makes them like dust with his sword,
    like driven stubble with his bow.
3 He pursues them and passes on safely,
    scarcely touching the path with his feet.

b 40:26 As a shepherd leads his sheep, implied.   c 41:2 this one from the east. Doubtless Cyrus the Great of Persia. See 44:28.

d Meaning of Heb uncertain

King James

⁴Who hath wrought and done *it,* calling the generations from the beginning? I the LORD, the first, and with the last; I *am* he.

⁵The isles saw *it,* and feared; the ends of the earth were afraid, drew near, and came.

⁶They helped every one his neighbour; and *every one* said to his brother, Be of good courage.

⁷So the carpenter encouraged the goldsmith, *and* he that smootheth *with* the hammer him that smote the anvil, saying, It *is* ready for the soldering: and he fastened it with nails, *that* it should not be moved.

⁸But thou, Israel, *art* my servant, Jacob whom I have chosen, the seed of Abraham my friend.

⁹*Thou* whom I have taken from the ends of the earth, and called thee from the chief men thereof, and said unto thee, Thou *art* my servant; I have chosen thee, and not cast thee away.

¹⁰¶ Fear thou not; for I *am* with thee: be not dismayed; for I *am* thy God: I will strengthen thee; yea, I will help thee; yea, I will uphold thee with the right hand of my righteousness.

¹¹Behold, all they that were incensed against thee shall be ashamed and confounded: they shall be as nothing; and they that strive with thee shall perish.

¹²Thou shalt seek them, and shalt not find them, *even* them that contended with thee: they that war against thee shall be as nothing, and as a thing of nought.

¹³For I the LORD thy God will hold thy right hand, saying unto thee, Fear not; I will help thee.

¹⁴Fear not, thou worm Jacob, *and* ye men of Israel; I will help thee, saith the LORD, and thy redeemer, the Holy One of Israel.

¹⁵Behold, I will make thee a new sharp threshing instrument having teeth: thou shalt thresh the mountains, and beat *them* small, and shalt make the hills as chaff.

¹⁶Thou shalt fan them, and the wind shall carry them away, and the whirlwind shall scatter them: and thou shalt rejoice in the LORD, *and* shalt glory in the Holy One of Israel.

¹⁷*When* the poor and needy seek water, and *there is* none, *and* their tongue faileth for thirst, I the LORD will hear them, *I* the God of Israel will not forsake them.

¹⁸I will open rivers in high places, and fountains in the midst of the valleys: I will make the wilderness a pool of water, and the dry land springs of water.

¹⁹I will plant in the wilderness the cedar, the shittah tree, and the myrtle, and the oil tree; I will set in the desert the fir tree, *and* the pine, and the box tree together:

New International

⁴Who has done this and carried it through,
    calling forth the generations from the
      beginning?
I, the LORD—with the first of them
    and with the last—I am he."

⁵The islands have seen it and fear;
    the ends of the earth tremble.
They approach and come forward;
⁶ each helps the other
    and says to his brother, "Be strong!"
⁷The craftsman encourages the goldsmith,
    and he who smooths with the hammer
    spurs on him who strikes the anvil.
He says of the welding, "It is good."
    He nails down the idol so it will not topple.

⁸"But you, O Israel, my servant,
    Jacob, whom I have chosen,
    you descendants of Abraham my friend,
⁹I took you from the ends of the earth,
    from its farthest corners I called you.
I said, 'You are my servant';
    I have chosen you and have not rejected you.
¹⁰So do not fear, for I am with you;
    do not be dismayed, for I am your God.
I will strengthen you and help you;
    I will uphold you with my righteous right
      hand.

¹¹"All who rage against you
    will surely be ashamed and disgraced;
those who oppose you
    will be as nothing and perish.
¹²Though you search for your enemies,
    you will not find them.
Those who wage war against you
    will be as nothing at all.
¹³For I am the LORD, your God,
    who takes hold of your right hand
and says to you, Do not fear;
    I will help you.
¹⁴Do not be afraid, O worm Jacob,
    O little Israel,
for I myself will help you," declares the LORD,
    your Redeemer, the Holy One of Israel.
¹⁵"See, I will make you into a threshing sledge,
    new and sharp, with many teeth.
You will thresh the mountains and crush them,
    and reduce the hills to chaff.
¹⁶You will winnow them, the wind will pick them
      up,
    and a gale will blow them away.
But you will rejoice in the LORD
    and glory in the Holy One of Israel.

¹⁷"The poor and needy search for water,
    but there is none;
    their tongues are parched with thirst.
But I the LORD will answer them;
    I, the God of Israel, will not forsake them.
¹⁸I will make rivers flow on barren heights,
    and springs within the valleys.
I will turn the desert into pools of water,
    and the parched ground into springs.
¹⁹I will put in the desert
    the cedar and the acacia, the myrtle and the
      olive.
I will set pines in the wasteland,
    the fir and the cypress together,

Living Bible

done such mighty deeds, directing the affairs of generations of mankind as they march by? It is I, the Lord, the
First and Last; I alone am he.

⁵The lands beyond the sea watch in fear and wait for
word of Cyrus'ᵃ new campaigns. Remote lands tremble
and mobilize for war. ⁶, ⁷The craftsmen encourage each
other as they rush to make new idols to protect them.
The carver hurries the goldsmith, and the molder helps
at the anvil. "Good," they say. "It's coming along fine.
Now we can solder on the arms." Carefully they join the
parts together, and then fasten the thing in place so it
won't fall over!

⁸But as for you, O Israel, you are mine, my chosen
ones; for you are Abraham's family, and he was my
friend. ⁹I have called you back from the ends of the earth
and said that you must serve but me alone, for I have
chosen you and will not throw you away. ¹⁰Fear not, for
I am with you. Do not be dismayed. I am your God. I
will strengthen you; I will help you; I will uphold you
with my victorious right hand.ᵇ

¹¹See, all your angry enemies lie confused and shattered. Anyone opposing you will die. ¹²You will look
for them in vain—they will all be gone. ¹³I am holding
you by your right hand—I, the Lord your God—and I
say to you, Don't be afraid; I am here to help you.
¹⁴Despised though you are, fear not, O Israel; for I will
help you. I am the Lord, your Redeemer; I am the Holy
One of Israel. ¹⁵You shall be a new and sharp-toothed
threshing instrument to tear all enemies apart, making
chaff of mountains. ¹⁶You shall toss them in the air; the
wind shall blow them all away; whirlwinds shall scatter
them. And the joy of the Lord shall fill you full; you
shall glory in the God of Israel.

¹⁷When the poor and needy seek water and there is
none and their tongues are parched from thirst, then I
will answer when they cry to me. I, Israel's God, will
not ever forsake them. ¹⁸I will open up rivers for them
on high plateaus! I will give them fountains of water in
the valleys! In the deserts will be pools of water, and
rivers fed by springs shall flow across the dry, parched
ground. ¹⁹I will plant trees—cedars, myrtle, olive trees,
the cypress, fir and pine—on barren land. ²⁰Everyone

New Revised Standard

4 Who has performed and done this,
  calling the generations from the beginning?
  I, the Lord, am first,
  and will be with the last.

5 The coastlands have seen and are afraid,
  the ends of the earth tremble;
  they have drawn near and come.

6 Each one helps the other,
  saying to one another, "Take courage!"

7 The artisan encourages the goldsmith,
  and the one who smooths with the hammer
    encourages the one who strikes the
    anvil,
saying of the soldering, "It is good";
  and they fasten it with nails so that it cannot
  be moved.

8 But you, Israel, my servant,
  Jacob, whom I have chosen,
  the offspring of Abraham, my friend;

9 you whom I took from the ends of the earth,
  and called from its farthest corners,
saying to you, "You are my servant,
  I have chosen you and not cast you off";

10 do not fear, for I am with you,
  do not be afraid, for I am your God;
I will strengthen you, I will help you,
  I will uphold you with my victorious right
  hand.

11 Yes, all who are incensed against you
  shall be ashamed and disgraced;
those who strive against you
  shall be as nothing and shall perish.

12 You shall seek those who contend with you,
  but you shall not find them;
those who war against you
  shall be as nothing at all.

13 For I, the Lord your God,
  hold your right hand;
it is I who say to you, "Do not fear,
  I will help you."

14 Do not fear, you worm Jacob,
  you insectᶜ Israel!
I will help you, says the Lord;
  your Redeemer is the Holy One of Israel.

15 Now, I will make of you a threshing sledge,
  sharp, new, and having teeth;
you shall thresh the mountains and crush
    them,
  and you shall make the hills like chaff.

16 You shall winnow them and the wind shall
    carry them away,
  and the tempest shall scatter them.
Then you shall rejoice in the Lord;
  in the Holy One of Israel you shall glory.

17 When the poor and needy seek water,
  and there is none,
  and their tongue is parched with thirst,
I the Lord will answer them,
  I the God of Israel will not forsake them.

18 I will open rivers on the bare heights,ᵈ
  and fountains in the midst of the valleys;
I will make the wilderness a pool of water,
  and the dry land springs of water.

19 I will put in the wilderness the cedar,
  the acacia, the myrtle, and the olive;
I will set in the desert the cypress,
  the plane and the pine together,

ᵃ 41:5 Cyrus', implied from 45:1.   ᵇ 41:10 with my victorious right hand,
or, "with the right hand of my righteousness."

ᶜ Syr: Heb men of   ᵈ Or trails

King James

20That they may see, and know, and consider, and understand together, that the hand of the LORD hath done this, and the Holy One of Israel hath created it.

21Produce your cause, saith the LORD; bring forth your strong *reasons*, saith the King of Jacob.

22Let them bring *them* forth, and show us what shall happen: let them show the former things, what they *be*, that we may consider them, and know the latter end of them; or declare us things for to come.

23Show the things that are to come hereafter, that we may know that ye *are* gods: yea, do good, or do evil, that we may be dismayed, and behold *it* together.

24Behold, ye *are* of nothing, and your work of nought: an abomination *is he that* chooseth you.

25I have raised up *one* from the north, and he shall come: from the rising of the sun shall he call upon my name: and he shall come upon princes as *upon* mortar, and as the potter treadeth clay.

26Who hath declared from the beginning, that we may know? and beforetime, that we may say, *He is* righteous? yea, *there is* none that showeth, yea, *there is* none that declareth, yea, *there is* none that heareth your words.

27The first *shall say* to Zion, Behold, behold them: and I will give to Jerusalem one that bringeth good tidings.

28For I beheld, and *there was* no man; even among them, and *there was* no counsellor, that, when I asked of them, could answer a word.

29Behold, they *are* all vanity; their works *are* nothing: their molten images *are* wind and confusion.

New International

20so that people may see and know,
    may consider and understand,
  that the hand of the LORD has done this,
    that the Holy One of Israel has created it.

21"Present your case," says the LORD.
  "Set forth your arguments," says Jacob's
    King.
22"Bring in ˏyour idolsˏ to tell us
    what is going to happen.
  Tell us what the former things were,
    so that we may consider them
    and know their final outcome.
  Or declare to us the things to come,
23   tell us what the future holds,
    so we may know that you are gods.
  Do something, whether good or bad,
    so that we will be dismayed and filled with
      fear.
24But you are less than nothing
    and your works are utterly worthless;
  he who chooses you is detestable.

25"I have stirred up one from the north, and he
      comes—
    one from the rising sun who calls on my
      name.
  He treads on rulers as if they were mortar,
    as if he were a potter treading the clay.
26Who told of this from the beginning, so we
      could know,
    or beforehand, so we could say, 'He was
      right'?
  No one told of this,
    no one foretold it,
    no one heard any words from you.
27I was the first to tell Zion, 'Look, here they
      are!'
  I gave to Jerusalem a messenger of good
      tidings.
28I look but there is no one—
    no one among them to give counsel,
    no one to give answer when I ask them.
29See, they are all false!
  Their deeds amount to nothing;
    their images are but wind and confusion.

The Servant of the LORD

42 BEHOLD MY servant, whom I uphold; mine elect, *in whom* my soul delighteth; I have put my spirit upon him: he shall bring forth judgment to the Gentiles.

2He shall not cry, nor lift up, nor cause his voice to be heard in the street.

3A bruised reed shall he not break, and the smoking flax shall he not quench: he shall bring forth judgment unto truth.

4He shall not fail nor be discouraged, till he have set judgment in the earth: and the isles shall wait for his law.

5¶ Thus saith God the LORD, he that created the heavens, and stretched them out; he that spread forth the earth, and that which cometh out of it; he that giveth breath unto the people upon it, and spirit to them that walk therein:

42 "HERE IS my servant, whom I uphold,
    my chosen one in whom I delight;
  I will put my Spirit on him
    and he will bring justice to the nations.
2He will not shout or cry out,
    or raise his voice in the streets.
3A bruised reed he will not break,
    and a smoldering wick he will not snuff out.
  In faithfulness he will bring forth justice;
4   he will not falter or be discouraged
  till he establishes justice on earth.
    In his law the islands will put their hope."

5This is what God the LORD says—
  he who created the heavens and stretched them
      out,
    who spread out the earth and all that comes
      out of it,
  who gives breath to its people,
    and life to those who walk on it:

Living Bible

will see this miracle and understand that it is God who did it, Israel's Holy One.

21Can your idols make such claims as these? Let them come and show what they can do! says God, the King of Israel. 22Let them try to tell us what occurred in years gone by, or what the future holds. 23Yes, that's it! If you are gods, tell what will happen in the days ahead! Or do some mighty miracle that makes us stare, amazed. 24But no! You are less than nothing, and can do nothing at all. Anyone who chooses you needs to have his head examined!

25But I have stirred up (Cyrus) from the north and east; he will come against the nations and call on my name, and I will give him victory over kings and princes. He will tread them as a potter tramples clay.

26Who but I have told you this would happen? Who else predicted this, making you admit that he was right? No one else! None other said one word! 27I was the first to tell Jerusalem, "Look! Look! Help is on the way!" 28Not one of your idols told you this. Not one gave any answer when I asked. 29See, they are all foolish, worthless things; your idols are all as empty as the wind.

42 SEE MY servant,a whom I uphold; my Chosen One, in whom I delight. I have put my Spirit upon him; he will reveal justice to the nations of the world. 2He will be gentle—he will not shout nor quarrel in the streets. 3He will not break the bruised reed, nor quench the dimly burning flame. He will encourage the fainthearted, those tempted to despair. He will see full justice given to all who have been wronged. 4He won't be satisfiedb until truth and righteousness prevail throughout the earth, nor until even distant lands beyond the seas have put their trust in him.

5The Lord God who created the heavens and stretched them out and created the earth and everything in it, and gives life and breath and spirit to everyone in all the world, he is the one who says [to his Servant, the Messiahc],

New Revised Standard

20 so that all may see and know,
      all may consider and understand,
    that the hand of the LORD has done this,
      the Holy One of Israel has created it.

The Futility of Idols

21 Set forth your case, says the LORD;
      bring your proofs, says the King of Jacob.
22 Let them bring them, and tell us
      what is to happen.
    Tell us the former things, what they are,
      so that we may consider them,
    and that we may know their outcome;
      or declare to us the things to come.
23 Tell us what is to come hereafter,
      that we may know that you are gods;
    do good, or do harm,
      that we may be afraid and terrified.
24 You, indeed, are nothing
      and your work is nothing at all;
      whoever chooses you is an abomination.

25 I stirred up one from the north, and he has
        come,
      from the rising of the sun he was
        summoned by name.d
    He shall tramplee on rulers as on mortar,
      as the potter treads clay.
26 Who declared it from the beginning, so that
        we might know,
      and beforehand, so that we might say, "He
        is right"?
    There was no one who declared it, none who
        proclaimed,
      none who heard your words.
27 I first have declared it to Zion,f
      and I give to Jerusalem a herald of good
        tidings.
28 But when I look there is no one;
      among these there is no counselor
    who, when I ask, gives an answer.
29 No, they are all a delusion;
      their works are nothing;
      their images are empty wind.

The Servant, a Light to the Nations

42 HERE IS my servant, whom I uphold,
      my chosen, in whom my soul delights;
    I have put my spirit upon him;
      he will bring forth justice to the nations.
2 He will not cry or lift up his voice,
      or make it heard in the street;
3 a bruised reed he will not break,
      and a dimly burning wick he will not
        quench;
    he will faithfully bring forth justice.
4 He will not grow faint or be crushed
      until he has established justice in the earth;
    and the coastlands wait for his teaching.

5 Thus says God, the LORD,
      who created the heavens and stretched them
        out,
    who spread out the earth and what comes
        from it,
    who gives breath to the people upon it
      and spirit to those who walk in it:

---

a 42:1 See my servant. Not Cyrus, as in chapter 41, but Christ.   b 42:4 He won't be satisfied, literally, "He will not burn dimly or be bruised until. . . ."   c 42:5 to his Servant, the Messiah, implied.

d Cn Compare Q Ms Gk: MT and he shall call on my name   e Cn: Heb come   f Cn: Heb First to Zion—Behold, behold them

King James

6I the LORD have called thee in righteousness, and will hold thine hand, and will keep thee, and give thee for a covenant of the people, for a light of the Gentiles;

7To open the blind eyes, to bring out the prisoners from the prison, *and* them that sit in darkness out of the prison house.

8I *am* the LORD: that *is* my name: and my glory will I not give to another, neither my praise to graven images.

9Behold, the former things are come to pass, and new things do I declare: before they spring forth I tell you of them.

10Sing unto the LORD a new song, *and* his praise from the end of the earth, ye that go down to the sea, and all that is therein; the isles, and the inhabitants thereof.

11Let the wilderness and the cities thereof lift up *their* voice, the villages *that* Kedar doth inhabit: let the inhabitants of the rock sing, let them shout from the top of the mountains.

12Let them give glory unto the LORD, and declare his praise in the islands.

13The LORD shall go forth as a mighty man, he shall stir up jealousy like a man of war: he shall cry, yea, roar; he shall prevail against his enemies.

14I have long time holden my peace; I have been still, *and* refrained myself: *now* will I cry like a travailing woman; I will destroy and devour at once.

15I will make waste mountains and hills, and dry up all their herbs; and I will make the rivers islands, and I will dry up the pools.

16And I will bring the blind by a way *that* they knew not; I will lead them in paths *that* they have not known: I will make darkness light before them, and crooked things straight. These things will I do unto them, and not forsake them.

17¶ They shall be turned back, they shall be greatly ashamed, that trust in graven images, that say to the molten images, Ye *are* our gods.

18Hear, ye deaf; and look, ye blind, that ye may see.

19Who *is* blind, but my servant? or deaf, as my messenger *that* I sent? who *is* blind as *he that is* perfect, and blind as the LORD's servant?

20Seeing many things, but thou observest not; opening the ears, but he heareth not.

21The LORD is well pleased for his righteousness' sake; he will magnify the law, and make *it* honourable.

New International

6"I, the LORD, have called you in righteousness;
  I will take hold of your hand.
I will keep you and will make you
  to be a covenant for the people
  and a light for the Gentiles,
7to open eyes that are blind,
  to free captives from prison
  and to release from the dungeon those who sit
    in darkness.

8"I am the LORD; that is my name!
  I will not give my glory to another
  or my praise to idols.
9See, the former things have taken place,
  and new things I declare;
before they spring into being
  I announce them to you."

Song of Praise to the LORD

10Sing to the LORD a new song,
  his praise from the ends of the earth,
you who go down to the sea, and all that is in
    it,
  you islands, and all who live in them.
11Let the desert and its towns raise their voices;
  let the settlements where Kedar lives rejoice.
Let the people of Sela sing for joy;
  let them shout from the mountaintops.
12Let them give glory to the LORD
  and proclaim his praise in the islands.
13The LORD will march out like a mighty man,
  like a warrior he will stir up his zeal;
with a shout he will raise the battle cry
  and will triumph over his enemies.

14"For a long time I have kept silent,
  I have been quiet and held myself back.
But now, like a woman in childbirth,
  I cry out, I gasp and pant.
15I will lay waste the mountains and hills
  and dry up all their vegetation;
I will turn rivers into islands
  and dry up the pools.
16I will lead the blind by ways they have not
    known,
  along unfamiliar paths I will guide them;
I will turn the darkness into light before them
  and make the rough places smooth.
These are the things I will do;
  I will not forsake them.
17But those who trust in idols,
  who say to images, 'You are our gods,'
  will be turned back in utter shame.

Israel Blind and Deaf

18"Hear, you deaf;
  look, you blind, and see!
19Who is blind but my servant,
  and deaf like the messenger I send?
Who is blind like the one committed to me,
  blind like the servant of the LORD?
20You have seen many things, but have paid no
    attention;
  your ears are open, but you hear nothing."
21It pleased the LORD
  for the sake of his righteousness
  to make his law great and glorious.

Living Bible

6"I the Lord have called you to demonstrate my righteousness. I will guard and support you, for I have given you to my people as the personal confirmation of my covenant with them.ᵃ You shall also be a light to guide the nations unto me. 7You will open the eyes of the blind, and release those who sit in prison darkness and despair. 8I am the Lord! That is my name, and I will not give my glory to anyone else; I will not share my praise with carved idols. 9Everything I prophesied came true, and now I will prophesy again. I will tell you the future before it happens."

10Sing a new song to the Lord; sing his praises, all you who live in earth's remotest corners! Sing, O sea! Sing, all you who live in distant lands beyond the sea! 11Join in the chorus, you desert cities—Kedar and Sela! And you, too, dwellers in the mountain tops. 12Let the western coastlands glorify the Lord and sing his mighty power.

13The Lord will be a mighty warrior, full of fury toward his foes. He will give a great shout and prevail. 14Long has he been silent; he has restrained himself. But now he will give full vent to his wrath; he will groan and cry like a woman delivering her child. 15He will level the mountains and hills and blight their greenery. He will dry up the rivers and pools. 16He will bring blind Israel along a path they have not seen before. He will make the darkness bright before them and smooth and straighten out the road ahead. He will not forsake them. 17But those who trust in idols and call them gods will be greatly disappointed; they will be turned away.

18Oh, how blind and deaf you are towards God! Why won't you listen? Why won't you see? 19Who in all the world is as blind as my own people,ᵇ who are designed to be my messengers of truth? Who is so blind as my "dedicated one," the "servant of the Lord"? 20You see and understand what is right but won't heed nor do it; you hear but you won't listen.

21The Lord has magnified his law and made it truly glorious. Through it he had planned to show the world that he is righteous. 22But what a sight his people are—

New Revised Standard

6 I am the LORD, I have called you in
      righteousness,
    I have taken you by the hand and kept you;
  I have given you as a covenant to the
      people,ᶜ
    a light to the nations,
7   to open the eyes that are blind,
  to bring out the prisoners from the dungeon,
    from the prison those who sit in darkness.
8 I am the LORD, that is my name;
    my glory I give to no other,
    nor my praise to idols.
9 See, the former things have come to pass,
    and new things I now declare;
  before they spring forth,
    I tell you of them.

A Hymn of Praise

10 Sing to the LORD a new song,
    his praise from the end of the earth!
  Let the sea roarᵈ and all that fills it,
    the coastlands and their inhabitants.
11 Let the desert and its towns lift up their voice,
    the villages that Kedar inhabits;
  let the inhabitants of Sela sing for joy,
    let them shout from the tops of the
      mountains.
12 Let them give glory to the LORD,
    and declare his praise in the coastlands.
13 The LORD goes forth like a soldier,
    like a warrior he stirs up his fury;
  he cries out, he shouts aloud,
    he shows himself mighty against his foes.

14 For a long time I have held my peace,
    I have kept still and restrained myself;
  now I will cry out like a woman in labor,
    I will gasp and pant.
15 I will lay waste mountains and hills,
    and dry up all their herbage;
  I will turn the rivers into islands,
    and dry up the pools.
16 I will lead the blind
    by a road they do not know,
  by paths they have not known
    I will guide them.
  I will turn the darkness before them into light,
    the rough places into level ground.
  These are the things I will do,
    and I will not forsake them.
17 They shall be turned back and utterly put to
      shame—
    those who trust in carved images,
  who say to cast images,
    "You are our gods."

18 Listen, you that are deaf;
    and you that are blind, look up and see!
19 Who is blind but my servant,
    or deaf like my messenger whom I send?
  Who is blind like my dedicated one,
    or blind like the servant of the LORD?
20 He sees many things, but doesᵉ not observe
      them;
    his ears are open, but he does not hear.

Israel's Disobedience

21 The LORD was pleased, for the sake of his
      righteousness,
    to magnify his teaching and make it
      glorious.

ᵃ *42:6 I have given you to my people as the personal confirmation of my covenant with them,* or, "You will be my convenant with all the people. . . ."
ᵇ *42:19 as my own people,* literally, "as my servant."

ᶜ Meaning of Heb uncertain   ᵈ Cn Compare Ps 96.11; 98.7: Heb *Those who go down to the sea*   ᵉ Heb *You see many things but do*

King James

22But this *is* a people robbed and spoiled; *they are* all of them snared in holes, and they are hid in prison houses: they are for a prey, and none delivereth; for a spoil, and none saith, Restore.

23Who among you will give ear to this? *who* will hearken and hear for the time to come?

24Who gave Jacob for a spoil, and Israel to the robbers? did not the Lord, he against whom we have sinned? for they would not walk in his ways, neither were they obedient unto his law.

25Therefore he hath poured upon him the fury of his anger, and the strength of battle: and it hath set him on fire round about, yet he knew not; and it burned him, yet he laid *it* not to heart.

43 BUT NOW thus saith the Lord that created thee, O Jacob, and he that formed thee, O Israel, Fear not: for I have redeemed thee, I have called *thee* by thy name; thou *art* mine.

2When thou passest through the waters, I *will be* with thee; and through the rivers, they shall not overflow thee: when thou walkest through the fire, thou shalt not be burned; neither shall the flame kindle upon thee.

3For I *am* the Lord thy God, the Holy One of Israel, thy Saviour: I gave Egypt *for* thy ransom, Ethiopia and Seba for thee.

4Since thou wast precious in my sight, thou hast been honourable, and I have loved thee: therefore will I give men for thee, and people for thy life.

5Fear not: for I *am* with thee: I will bring thy seed from the east, and gather thee from the west;

6I will say to the north, Give up; and to the south, Keep not back: bring my sons from far, and my daughters from the ends of the earth;

7*Even* every one that is called by my name: for I have created him for my glory, I have formed him; yea, I have made him.

8¶ Bring forth the blind people that have eyes, and the deaf that have ears.

9Let all the nations be gathered together, and let the people be assembled: who among them can declare this, and show us former things? let them bring forth their witnesses, that they may be justified: or let them hear, and say, *It is* truth.

New International

22But this is a people plundered and looted,
    all of them trapped in pits
    or hidden away in prisons.
They have become plunder,
    with no one to rescue them;
they have been made loot,
    with no one to say, "Send them back."

23Which of you will listen to this
    or pay close attention in time to come?
24Who handed Jacob over to become loot,
    and Israel to the plunderers?
Was it not the Lord,
    against whom we have sinned?
For they would not follow his ways;
    they did not obey his law.
25So he poured out on them his burning anger,
    the violence of war.
It enveloped them in flames, yet they did not
        understand;
    it consumed them, but they did not take it to
        heart.

Israel's Only Savior

43 BUT NOW, this is what the Lord says—
    he who created you, O Jacob,
    he who formed you, O Israel:
"Fear not, for I have redeemed you;
    I have summoned you by name; you are
        mine.
2When you pass through the waters,
    I will be with you;
and when you pass through the rivers,
    they will not sweep over you.
When you walk through the fire,
    you will not be burned;
    the flames will not set you ablaze.
3For I am the Lord, your God,
    the Holy One of Israel, your Savior;
I give Egypt for your ransom,
    Cush[a] and Seba in your stead.
4Since you are precious and honored in my sight,
    and because I love you,
I will give men in exchange for you,
    and people in exchange for your life.
5Do not be afraid, for I am with you;
    I will bring your children from the east
    and gather you from the west.
6I will say to the north, 'Give them up!'
    and to the south, 'Do not hold them back.'
Bring my sons from afar
    and my daughters from the ends of the
        earth—
7everyone who is called by my name,
    whom I created for my glory,
    whom I formed and made."

8Lead out those who have eyes but are blind,
    who have ears but are deaf.
9All the nations gather together
    and the peoples assemble.
Which of them foretold this
    and proclaimed to us the former things?
Let them bring in their witnesses to prove they
        were right,
    so that others may hear and say, "It is true."

---

[a] 3 That is, the upper Nile region

Living Bible

these who were to demonstrate to all the world the glory of his law;b for they are robbed, enslaved, imprisoned, trapped, fair game for all, with no one to protect them. 23Won't even one of you apply these lessons from the past and see the ruin that awaits you up ahead? 24Who let Israel be robbed and hurt? Did not the Lord? It is the Lord they sinned against, for they would not go where he sent them nor listen to his laws. 25That is why God poured out such fury and wrath on his people and destroyed them in battle. Yet, though set on fire and burned, they will not understand the reason why—that it is God, wanting them to repent.c

43 BUT NOW the Lord who created you, O Israel, says, Don't be afraid, for I have ransomed you; I have called you by name; you are mine. 2When you go through deep waters and great trouble, I will be with you. When you go through rivers of difficulty, you will not drown! When you walk through the fire of oppression, you will not be burned up—the flames will not consume you. 3For I am the Lord your God, your Savior, the Holy One of Israel. I gave Egypt and Ethiopia and Seba [to Cyrusd] in exchange for your freedom, as your ransom. 4Others died that you might live; I traded their lives for yours because you are precious to me and honored, and I love you.

5Don't be afraid, for I am with you. I will gather you from east and west, 6from north and south. I will bring my sons and daughters back to Israel from the farthest corners of the earth. 7All who claim me as their God will come, for I have made them for my glory; I created them. 8Bring them back to me—blind as they are and deaf when I call (although they see and hear!).

9Gather the nations together! Which of all their idols ever has foretold such things? Which can predict a single day ahead? Where are the witnesses of anything they said? If there are no witnesses, then they must confess that only God can prophesy.

New Revised Standard

22 But this is a people robbed and plundered,
    all of them are trapped in holes
    and hidden in prisons;
they have become a prey with no one to
    rescue,
    a spoil with no one to say, "Restore!"
23 Who among you will give heed to this,
    who will attend and listen for the time to
    come?
24 Who gave up Jacob to the spoiler,
    and Israel to the robbers?
Was it not the LORD, against whom we have
    sinned,
    in whose ways they would not walk,
    and whose law they would not obey?
25 So he poured upon him the heat of his anger
    and the fury of war;
it set him on fire all around, but he did not
    understand;
    it burned him, but he did not take it to
    heart.

Restoration and Protection Promised

43 BUT NOW thus says the LORD,
    he who created you, O Jacob,
    he who formed you, O Israel:
Do not fear, for I have redeemed you;
    I have called you by name, you are mine.
2 When you pass through the waters, I will be
    with you;
    and through the rivers, they shall not
    overwhelm you;
when you walk through fire you shall not be
    burned,
    and the flame shall not consume you.
3 For I am the LORD your God,
    the Holy One of Israel, your Savior.
I give Egypt as your ransom,
    Ethiopiae and Seba in exchange for you.
4 Because you are precious in my sight,
    and honored, and I love you,
I give people in return for you,
    nations in exchange for your life.
5 Do not fear, for I am with you;
    I will bring your offspring from the east,
    and from the west I will gather you;
6 I will say to the north, "Give them up,"
    and to the south, "Do not withhold;
bring my sons from far away
    and my daughters from the end of the
    earth—
7 everyone who is called by my name,
    whom I created for my glory,
    whom I formed and made."

8 Bring forth the people who are blind, yet have
    eyes,
    who are deaf, yet have ears!
9 Let all the nations gather together,
    and let the peoples assemble.
Who among them declared this,
    and foretold to us the former things?
Let them bring their witnesses to justify them,
    and let them hear and say, "It is true."

---

b 42:22 these who were to demonstrate to all the world the glory of his law, implied in previous verse.   c 42:25 wanting them to repent, implied. d 43:3 to Cyrus, implied.

e Or Nubia; Heb Cush

King James

¹⁰Ye *are* my witnesses, saith the LORD, and my servant whom I have chosen: that ye may know and believe me, and understand that I *am* he: before me there was no God formed, neither shall there be after me.

¹¹I, *even* I, *am* the LORD; and beside me *there is* no saviour.

¹²I have declared, and have saved, and I have shown, when *there was* no strange *god* among you: therefore ye *are* my witnesses, saith the LORD, that I *am* God.

¹³Yea, before the day *was* I *am* he; and *there is* none that can deliver out of my hand: I will work, and who shall let it?

¹⁴Thus saith the LORD, your redeemer, the Holy One of Israel; For your sake I have sent to Babylon, and have brought down all their nobles, and the Chaldeans, whose cry *is* in the ships.

¹⁵I *am* the LORD, your Holy One, the creator of Israel, your King.

¹⁶Thus saith the LORD, which maketh a way in the sea, and a path in the mighty waters;

¹⁷Which bringeth forth the chariot and horse, the army and the power; they shall lie down together, they shall not rise: they are extinct, they are quenched as tow.

¹⁸¶ Remember ye not the former things, neither consider the things of old.

¹⁹Behold, I will do a new thing; now it shall spring forth; shall ye not know it? I will even make a way in the wilderness, *and* rivers in the desert.

²⁰The beast of the field shall honour me, the dragons and the owls: because I give waters in the wilderness, *and* rivers in the desert, to give drink to my people, my chosen.

²¹This people have I formed for myself; they shall show forth my praise.

²²¶ But thou hast not called upon me, O Jacob; but thou hast been weary of me, O Israel.

²³Thou hast not brought me the small cattle of thy burnt offerings; neither hast thou honoured me with thy sacrifices. I have not caused thee to serve with an offering, nor wearied thee with incense.

²⁴Thou hast bought me no sweet cane with money, neither hast thou filled me with the fat of thy sacrifices: but thou hast made me to serve with thy sins, thou hast wearied me with thine iniquities.

²⁵I, *even* I, *am* he that blotteth out thy transgressions for mine own sake, and will not remember thy sins.

²⁶Put me in remembrance: let us plead together: declare thou, that thou mayest be justified.

²⁷Thy first father hath sinned, and thy teachers have transgressed against me.

New International

¹⁰"You are my witnesses," declares the LORD,
    "and my servant whom I have chosen,
so that you may know and believe me
    and understand that I am he.
Before me no god was formed,
    nor will there be one after me.
¹¹I, even I, am the LORD,
    and apart from me there is no savior.
¹²I have revealed and saved and proclaimed—
    I, and not some foreign god among you.
You are my witnesses," declares the LORD,
    "that I am God.
¹³ Yes, and from ancient days I am he.
No one can deliver out of my hand.
    When I act, who can reverse it?"

God's Mercy and Israel's Unfaithfulness

¹⁴This is what the LORD says—
    your Redeemer, the Holy One of Israel:
"For your sake I will send to Babylon
    and bring down as fugitives all the
        Babylonians,ᵃ
    in the ships in which they took pride.
¹⁵I am the LORD, your Holy One,
    Israel's Creator, your King."

¹⁶This is what the LORD says—
    he who made a way through the sea,
    a path through the mighty waters,
¹⁷who drew out the chariots and horses,
    the army and reinforcements together,
and they lay there, never to rise again,
    extinguished, snuffed out like a wick:
¹⁸"Forget the former things;
    do not dwell on the past.
¹⁹See, I am doing a new thing!
    Now it springs up; do you not perceive it?
I am making a way in the desert
    and streams in the wasteland.
²⁰The wild animals honor me,
    the jackals and the owls,
because I provide water in the desert
    and streams in the wasteland,
to give drink to my people, my chosen,
²¹ the people I formed for myself
    that they may proclaim my praise.

²²"Yet you have not called upon me, O Jacob,
    you have not wearied yourselves for me,
        O Israel.
²³You have not brought me sheep for burnt
        offerings,
    nor honored me with your sacrifices.
I have not burdened you with grain offerings
    nor wearied you with demands for incense.
²⁴You have not bought any fragrant calamus for
        me,
    or lavished on me the fat of your sacrifices.
But you have burdened me with your sins
    and wearied me with your offenses.

²⁵"I, even I, am he who blots out
    your transgressions, for my own sake,
    and remembers your sins no more.
²⁶Review the past for me,
    let us argue the matter together;
    state the case for your innocence.
²⁷Your first father sinned;
    your spokesmen rebelled against me.

ᵃ *14 Or Chaldeans*

Living Bible

10But I have witnesses, O Israel, says the Lord! You are my witnesses and my servants, chosen to know and to believe me and to understand that I alone am God. There is no other God; there never was and never will be. 11I am the Lord, and there is no other Savior. 12Whenever you have thrown away your idols, I have shown you my power. With one word I have saved you. You have seen me do it; you are my witnesses that it is true. 13From eternity to eternity I am God. No one can oppose what I do.

14The Lord, your Redeemer, the Holy One of Israel, says:

For your sakes I will send an invading army against Babylon that will walk in, almost unscathed. The boasts of the Babylonians will turn to cries of fear. 15I am the Lord, your Holy One, Israel's Creator and King. 16I am the Lord, who opened a way through the waters, making a path right through the sea. 17I called forth the mighty army of Egypt with all its chariots and horses, to lie beneath the waves, dead, their lives snuffed out like candlewicks.

18But forget all that—it is nothing compared to what I'm going to do! 19For I'm going to do a brand new thing. See, I have already begun! Don't you see it? I will make a road through the wilderness of the world for my people to go home, and create rivers for them in the desert! 20The wild animals in the fields will thank me, the jackals and ostriches too, for giving them water in the wilderness, yes, springs in the desert, so that my people, my chosen ones, can be refreshed. 21I have made Israel for myself, and these my people will some day honor me before the world.

22But O my people, you won't ask my help; you have grown tired of me! 23You have not brought me the lambs for burnt offerings; you have not honored me with sacrifices. Yet my requests for offerings and incense have been very few! I have not treated you as slaves. 24You have brought me no sweet-smelling incense nor pleased me with the sacrificial fat. No, you have presented me only with sins, and wearied me with all your faults.

25I, yes, I alone am he who blots away your sins for my own sake and will never think of them again. 26Oh, remind me of this promise of forgiveness, for we must talk about your sins. Plead your case for my forgiving you. 27From the very first your ancestors sinned against

New Revised Standard

10 You are my witnesses, says the LORD,
  and my servant whom I have chosen,
so that you may know and believe me
  and understand that I am he.
Before me no god was formed,
  nor shall there be any after me.
11 I, I am the LORD,
  and besides me there is no savior.
12 I declared and saved and proclaimed,
  when there was no strange god among you;
  and you are my witnesses, says the LORD.
13 I am God, and also henceforth I am He;
  there is no one who can deliver from my
    hand;
  I work and who can hinder it?

14 Thus says the LORD,
  your Redeemer, the Holy One of Israel:
For your sake I will send to Babylon
  and break down all the bars,
  and the shouting of the Chaldeans will be
    turned to lamentation.b
15 I am the LORD, your Holy One,
  the Creator of Israel, your King.
16 Thus says the LORD,
  who makes a way in the sea,
  a path in the mighty waters,
17 who brings out chariot and horse,
  army and warrior;
they lie down, they cannot rise,
  they are extinguished, quenched like a wick:
18 Do not remember the former things,
  or consider the things of old.
19 I am about to do a new thing;
  now it springs forth, do you not perceive it?
I will make a way in the wilderness
  and rivers in the desert.
20 The wild animals will honor me,
  the jackals and the ostriches;
for I give water in the wilderness,
  rivers in the desert,
to give drink to my chosen people,
21 the people whom I formed for myself
so that they might declare my praise.

22 Yet you did not call upon me, O Jacob;
  but you have been weary of me, O Israel!
23 You have not brought me your sheep for burnt
    offerings,
  or honored me with your sacrifices.
I have not burdened you with offerings,
  or wearied you with frankincense.
24 You have not bought me sweet cane with
    money,
  or satisfied me with the fat of your
    sacrifices.
But you have burdened me with your sins;
  you have wearied me with your iniquities.

25 I, I am He
  who blots out your transgressions for my
    own sake,
  and I will not remember your sins.
26 Accuse me, let us go to trial;
  set forth your case, so that you may be
    proved right.
27 Your first ancestor sinned,
  and your interpreters transgressed against
    me.

b Meaning of Heb uncertain

King James

²⁸Therefore I have profaned the princes of the sanctuary, and have given Jacob to the curse, and Israel to reproaches.

44 YET NOW hear, O Jacob my servant; and Israel, whom I have chosen:

²Thus saith the LORD that made thee, and formed thee from the womb, *which* will help thee; Fear not, O Jacob, my servant; and thou, Jesurun, whom I have chosen.

³For I will pour water upon him that is thirsty, and floods upon the dry ground: I will pour my spirit upon thy seed, and my blessing upon thine offspring:

⁴And they shall spring up *as* among the grass, as willows by the water courses.

⁵One shall say, I *am* the LORD's; and another shall call *himself* by the name of Jacob; and another shall subscribe *with* his hand unto the LORD, and surname *himself* by the name of Israel.

⁶Thus saith the LORD the King of Israel, and his redeemer the LORD of hosts; I *am* the first, and I *am* the last; and beside me *there is* no God.

⁷And who, as I, shall call, and shall declare it, and set it in order for me, since I appointed the ancient people? and the things that are coming, and shall come, let them show unto them.

⁸Fear ye not, neither be afraid: have not I told thee from that time, and have declared *it?* ye *are* even my witnesses. Is there a God beside me? yea, *there is* no God; I know not *any.*

⁹¶ They that make a graven image *are* all of them vanity; and their delectable things shall not profit; and they *are* their own witnesses; they see not, nor know; that they may be ashamed.

¹⁰Who hath formed a god, or molten a graven image *that* is profitable for nothing?

¹¹Behold, all his fellows shall be ashamed: and the workmen, they *are* of men: let them all be gathered together, let them stand up; *yet* they shall fear, *and* they shall be ashamed together.

¹²The smith with the tongs both worketh in the coals, and fashioneth it with hammers, and worketh it with the strength of his arms: yea, he is hungry, and his strength faileth: he drinketh no water, and is faint.

New International

²⁸So I will disgrace the dignitaries of your temple,
and I will consign Jacob to destructionᵃ
and Israel to scorn.

Israel the Chosen

44 "BUT NOW listen, O Jacob, my servant,
Israel, whom I have chosen.
²This is what the LORD says—
he who made you, who formed you in the womb,
and who will help you:
Do not be afraid, O Jacob, my servant,
Jeshurun, whom I have chosen.
³For I will pour water on the thirsty land,
and streams on the dry ground;
I will pour out my Spirit on your offspring,
and my blessing on your descendants.
⁴They will spring up like grass in a meadow,
like poplar trees by flowing streams.
⁵One will say, 'I belong to the LORD';
another will call himself by the name of Jacob;
still another will write on his hand, 'The LORD's,'
and will take the name Israel.

The LORD, Not Idols

⁶"This is what the LORD says—
Israel's King and Redeemer, the LORD Almighty:
I am the first and I am the last;
apart from me there is no God.
⁷Who then is like me? Let him proclaim it.
Let him declare and lay out before me
what has happened since I established my ancient people,
and what is yet to come—
yes, let him foretell what will come.
⁸Do not tremble, do not be afraid.
Did I not proclaim this and foretell it long ago?
You are my witnesses. Is there any God besides me?
No, there is no other Rock; I know not one."

⁹All who make idols are nothing,
and the things they treasure are worthless.
Those who would speak up for them are blind;
they are ignorant, to their own shame.
¹⁰Who shapes a god and casts an idol,
which can profit him nothing?
¹¹He and his kind will be put to shame;
craftsmen are nothing but men.
Let them all come together and take their stand;
they will be brought down to terror and infamy.

¹²The blacksmith takes a tool
and works with it in the coals;
he shapes an idol with hammers,
he forges it with the might of his arm.
He gets hungry and loses his strength;
he drinks no water and grows faint.

ᵃ *28* The Hebrew term refers to the irrevocable giving over of things or persons to the LORD, often by totally destroying them.

Living Bible

me—all your forebears transgressed my law. 28That is why I have deposed your priests and destroyed Israel, leaving her to shame.

44 LISTEN TO me, O my servant Israel, O my chosen ones:

2The Lord who made you, who will help you, says, O servant of mine, don't be afraid. O Jerusalem, my chosen ones, don't be afraid. 3For I will give you abundant water for your thirst and for your parched fields. And I will pour out my Spirit and my blessings on your children. 4They shall thrive like watered grass, like willows on a river bank. 5"I am the Lord's," they'll proudlyb say, or, "I am a Jew," and tattoo upon their hands the name of God or the honored name of Israel.

6The Lord, the King of Israel, says—yes, it is Israel's Redeemer, the Lord Almighty, who says it—I am the First and Last; there is no other God. 7Who else can tell you what is going to happen in the days ahead? Let them tell you if they can, and prove their power. Let them do as I have done since ancient times. 8Don't, don't be afraid. Haven't I proclaimed from ages past [that I would save youc]? You are my witnesses—is there any other God? No! None that I know about! There is no other Rock!

9What fools they are who manufacture idols for their gods. Their hopes remain unanswered. They themselves are witnesses that this is so, for their idols neither see nor know. No wonder those who worship them are so ashamed. 10Who but a fool would make his own god—an idol that can help him not one whit! 11All that worship these will stand before the Lord in shame, along with all these carpenters—mere men—who claim that they have made a god. Together they will stand in terror. 12The metalsmith stands at his forge to make an axe, pounding on it with all his might. He grows hungry and thirsty, weak and faint. 13Then the woodcarver takes the axe and

New Revised Standard

28 Therefore I profaned the princes of the
     sanctuary,
   I delivered Jacob to utter destruction,
     and Israel to reviling.

God's Blessing on Israel

44 BUT NOW hear, O Jacob my servant,
     Israel whom I have chosen!
2   Thus says the LORD who made you,
     who formed you in the womb and will help
       you:
   Do not fear, O Jacob my servant,
     Jeshurun whom I have chosen.
3   For I will pour water on the thirsty land,
     and streams on the dry ground;
   I will pour my spirit upon your descendants,
     and my blessing on your offspring.
4   They shall spring up like a green tamarisk,
     like willows by flowing streams.
5   This one will say, "I am the LORD's,"
     another will be called by the name of Jacob,
   yet another will write on the hand, "The
       LORD's,"
     and adopt the name of Israel.

6   Thus says the LORD, the King of Israel,
     and his Redeemer, the LORD of hosts:
   I am the first and I am the last;
     besides me there is no god.
7   Who is like me? Let them proclaim it,
     let them declare and set it forth before me.
   Who has announced from of old the things to
       come?d
     Let them tell use what is yet to be.
8   Do not fear, or be afraid;
     have I not told you from of old and
       declared it?
   You are my witnesses!
   Is there any god besides me?
     There is no other rock; I know not one.

The Absurdity of Idol Worship

9 All who make idols are nothing, and the things they delight in do not profit; their witnesses neither see nor know. And so they will be put to shame. 10Who would fashion a god or cast an image that can do no good? 11Look, all its devotees shall be put to shame; the artisans too are merely human. Let them all assemble, let them stand up; they shall be terrified, they shall all be put to shame.

12 The ironsmith fashions itf and works it over the coals, shaping it with hammers, and forging it with his strong arm; he becomes hungry and his strength fails, he drinks no water and is faint. 13The carpenter stretches

---

b 44:5 proudly, implied.   c 44:8 that I would save you, implied.

d Cn: Heb from my placing an eternal people and things to come   e Tg: Heb them   f Cn: Heb an ax

King James

13The carpenter stretcheth out *his* rule; he marketh it out with a line; he fitteth it with planes, and he marketh it out with the compass, and maketh it after the figure of a man, according to the beauty of a man; that it may remain in the house.

14He heweth him down cedars, and taketh the cypress and the oak, which he strengtheneth for himself among the trees of the forest: he planteth an ash, and the rain doth nourish *it*.

15Then shall it be for a man to burn: for he will take thereof, and warm himself; yea, he kindleth *it,* and baketh bread; yea, he maketh a god, and worshippeth *it;* he maketh it a graven image, and falleth down thereto.

16He burneth part thereof in the fire; with part thereof he eateth flesh; he roasteth roast, and is satisfied: yea, he warmeth *himself,* and saith, Aha, I am warm, I have seen the fire:

17And the residue thereof he maketh a god, *even* his graven image: he falleth down unto it, and worshippeth *it,* and prayeth unto it, and saith, Deliver me; for thou *art* my god.

18They have not known nor understood: for he hath shut their eyes, that they cannot see; *and* their hearts, that they cannot understand.

19And none considereth in his heart, neither *is there* knowledge nor understanding to say, I have burned part of it in the fire; yea, also I have baked bread upon the coals thereof; I have roasted flesh, and eaten *it:* and shall I make the residue thereof an abomination? shall I fall down to the stock of a tree?

20He feedeth on ashes: a deceived heart hath turned him aside, that he cannot deliver his soul, nor say, *Is there* not a lie in my right hand?

21¶ Remember these, O Jacob and Israel; for thou *art* my servant: I have formed thee; thou *art* my servant: O Israel, thou shalt not be forgotten of me.

22I have blotted out, as a thick cloud, thy transgressions, and, as a cloud, thy sins: return unto me; for I have redeemed thee.

23Sing, O ye heavens; for the LORD hath done *it:* shout, ye lower parts of the earth: break forth into singing, ye mountains, O forest, and every tree therein: for the LORD hath redeemed Jacob, and glorified himself in Israel.

24Thus saith the LORD, thy redeemer, and he that formed thee from the womb, I *am* the LORD that maketh all *things;* that stretcheth forth the heavens alone; that spreadeth abroad the earth by myself;

25That frustrateth the tokens of the liars, and maketh diviners mad; that turneth wise *men* backward, and maketh their knowledge foolish;

New International

13The carpenter measures with a line
  and makes an outline with a marker;
he roughs it out with chisels
  and marks it with compasses.
He shapes it in the form of man,
  of man in all his glory,
  that it may dwell in a shrine.
14He cut down cedars,
  or perhaps took a cypress or oak.
He let it grow among the trees of the forest,
  or planted a pine, and the rain made it grow.
15It is man's fuel for burning;
  some of it he takes and warms himself,
  he kindles a fire and bakes bread.
But he also fashions a god and worships it;
  he makes an idol and bows down to it.
16Half of the wood he burns in the fire;
  over it he prepares his meal,
  he roasts his meat and eats his fill.
He also warms himself and says,
  "Ah! I am warm; I see the fire."
17From the rest he makes a god, his idol;
  he bows down to it and worships.
He prays to it and says,
  "Save me; you are my god."
18They know nothing, they understand nothing;
  their eyes are plastered over so they cannot
    see,
  and their minds closed so they cannot
    understand.
19No one stops to think,
  no one has the knowledge or understanding to
    say,
"Half of it I used for fuel;
  I even baked bread over its coals,
  I roasted meat and I ate.
Shall I make a detestable thing from what is
    left?
  Shall I bow down to a block of wood?"
20He feeds on ashes, a deluded heart misleads
    him;
  he cannot save himself, or say,
  "Is not this thing in my right hand a lie?"

21"Remember these things, O Jacob,
  for you are my servant, O Israel.
I have made you, you are my servant;
  O Israel, I will not forget you.
22I have swept away your offenses like a cloud,
  your sins like the morning mist.
Return to me,
  for I have redeemed you."

23Sing for joy, O heavens, for the LORD has done
    this;
  shout aloud, O earth beneath.
Burst into song, you mountains,
  you forests and all your trees,
for the LORD has redeemed Jacob,
  he displays his glory in Israel.

Jerusalem to Be Inhabited

24"This is what the LORD says—
  your Redeemer, who formed you in the
    womb:

I am the LORD,
  who has made all things,
who alone stretched out the heavens,
  who spread out the earth by myself,

25who foils the signs of false prophets
  and makes fools of diviners,
who overthrows the learning of the wise
  and turns it into nonsense,

Living Bible

uses it to make an idol. He measures and marks out a block of wood and carves the figure of a man. Now he has a wonderful idol that can't so much as move from where it is placed. 14He cuts down cedars, he selects the cypress and the oak, he plants the ash in the forest to be nourished by the rain. 15And after his care, he uses part of the wood to make a fire to warm himself and bake his bread, and then—he really does—he takes the rest of it and makes himself a god—a god for men to worship! An idol to fall down before and praise! 16Part of the tree he burns to roast his meat and to keep him warm and fed and well content, 17and with what's left he makes his god: a carved idol! He falls down before it and worships it and prays to it. "Deliver me," he says. "You are my god!"

18Such stupidity and ignorance! God has shut their eyes so that they cannot see, and closed their minds from understanding. 19The man never stops to think or figure out, "Why, it's just a block of wood! I've burned it for heat and used it to bake my bread and roast my meat. How can the rest of it be a god? Should I fall down before a chunk of wood?" 20The poor, deluded fool feeds on ashes; he is trusting what can never give him any help at all. Yet he cannot bring himself to ask, "Is this thing, this idol that I'm holding in my hand, a lie?"

21Pay attention, Israel, for you are my servant; I made you, and I will not forget to help you. 22I've blotted out your sins; they are gone like morning mist at noon! Oh, return to me, for I have paid the price to set you free.

23Sing, O heavens, for the Lord has done this wondrous thing. Shout, O earth; break forth into song, O mountains and forests, yes, and every tree; for the Lord redeemed Jacob and is glorified in Israel! 24The Lord, your Redeemer who made you, says, All things were made by me; I alone stretched out the heavens. By myself I made the earth and everything in it.

25I am the one who shows what liars all false prophets are, by causing something else to happen than the things they say. I make wise men give opposite advice to what they should, and make them into fools. 26But what my

New Revised Standard

a line, marks it out with a stylus, fashions it with planes, and marks it with a compass; he makes it in human form, with human beauty, to be set up in a shrine. 14He cuts down cedars or chooses a holm tree or an oak and lets it grow strong among the trees of the forest. He plants a cedar and the rain nourishes it. 15Then it can be used as fuel. Part of it he takes and warms himself; he kindles a fire and bakes bread. Then he makes a god and worships it, makes it a carved image and bows down before it. 16Half of it he burns in the fire; over this half he roasts meat, eats it and is satisfied. He also warms himself and says, "Ah, I am warm, I can feel the fire!" 17The rest of it he makes into a god, his idol, bows down to it and worships it; he prays to it and says, "Save me, for you are my god!"

18 They do not know, nor do they comprehend; for their eyes are shut, so that they cannot see, and their minds as well, so that they cannot understand. 19No one considers, nor is there knowledge or discernment to say, "Half of it I burned in the fire; I also baked bread on its coals, I roasted meat and have eaten. Now shall I make the rest of it an abomination? Shall I fall down before a block of wood?" 20He feeds on ashes; a deluded mind has led him astray, and he cannot save himself or say, "Is not this thing in my right hand a fraud?"

Israel Is Not Forgotten

21 Remember these things, O Jacob,
and Israel, for you are my servant;
I formed you, you are my servant;
O Israel, you will not be forgotten by me.
22 I have swept away your transgressions like a
cloud,
and your sins like mist;
return to me, for I have redeemed you.

23 Sing, O heavens, for the LORD has done it;
shout, O depths of the earth;
break forth into singing, O mountains,
O forest, and every tree in it!
For the LORD has redeemed Jacob,
and will be glorified in Israel.

24 Thus says the LORD, your Redeemer,
who formed you in the womb:
I am the LORD, who made all things,
who alone stretched out the heavens,
who by myself spread out the earth;
25 who frustrates the omens of liars,
and makes fools of diviners;
who turns back the wise,
and makes their knowledge foolish;

King James

26That confirmeth the word of his servant, and performeth the counsel of his messengers; that saith to Jerusalem, Thou shalt be inhabited; and to the cities of Judah, Ye shall be built, and I will raise up the decayed places thereof:

27That saith to the deep, Be dry, and I will dry up thy rivers:

28That saith of Cyrus, *He is* my shepherd, and shall perform all my pleasure: even saying to Jerusalem, Thou shalt be built; and to the temple, Thy foundation shall be laid.

45 THUS SAITH the LORD to his anointed, to Cyrus, whose right hand I have holden, to subdue nations before him; and I will loose the loins of kings, to open before him the two leaved gates; and the gates shall not be shut;

2I will go before thee, and make the crooked places straight: I will break in pieces the gates of brass, and cut in sunder the bars of iron:

3And I will give thee the treasures of darkness, and hidden riches of secret places, that thou mayest know that I, the LORD, which call *thee* by thy name, *am* the God of Israel.

4For Jacob my servant's sake, and Israel mine elect, I have even called thee by thy name: I have surnamed thee, though thou hast not known me.

5¶ *I am* the LORD, and *there is* none else, *there is* no God beside me: I girded thee, though thou hast not known me:

6That they may know from the rising of the sun, and from the west, that *there is* none beside me. I *am* the LORD, and *there is* none else.

7I form the light, and create darkness: I make peace, and create evil: I the LORD do all these *things*.

8Drop down, ye heavens, from above, and let the skies pour down righteousness: let the earth open, and let them bring forth salvation, and let righteousness spring up together; I the LORD have created it.

9Woe unto him that striveth with his Maker! *Let* the potsherd *strive* with the potsherds of the earth. Shall the clay say to him that fashioneth it, What makest thou? or thy work, He hath no hands?

10Woe unto him that saith unto *his* father, What begettest thou? or to the woman, What hast thou brought forth?

New International

26who carries out the words of his servants
　and fulfills the predictions of his messengers,

who says of Jerusalem, 'It shall be inhabited,'
　of the towns of Judah, 'They shall be built,'
　and of their ruins, 'I will restore them,'
27who says to the watery deep, 'Be dry,
　and I will dry up your streams,'
28who says of Cyrus, 'He is my shepherd
　and will accomplish all that I please;
he will say of Jerusalem, "Let it be rebuilt,"
　and of the temple, "Let its foundations be
　　laid." '

45 "THIS IS what the LORD says to his
　anointed,
　to Cyrus, whose right hand I take hold of
to subdue nations before him
　and to strip kings of their armor,
to open doors before him
　so that gates will not be shut:
2I will go before you
　and will level the mountains[a];
I will break down gates of bronze
　and cut through bars of iron.
3I will give you the treasures of darkness,
　riches stored in secret places,
so that you may know that I am the LORD,
　the God of Israel, who summons you by
　　name.
4For the sake of Jacob my servant,
　of Israel my chosen,
I summon you by name
　and bestow on you a title of honor,
　though you do not acknowledge me.
5I am the LORD, and there is no other;
　apart from me there is no God.
I will strengthen you,
　though you have not acknowledged me,
6so that from the rising of the sun
　to the place of its setting
men may know there is none besides me.
　I am the LORD, and there is no other.
7I form the light and create darkness,
　I bring prosperity and create disaster;
　I, the LORD, do all these things.

8"You heavens above, rain down righteousness;
　let the clouds shower it down.
Let the earth open wide,
　let salvation spring up,
let righteousness grow with it;
　I, the LORD, have created it.

9"Woe to him who quarrels with his Maker,
　to him who is but a potsherd among the
　　potsherds on the ground.
Does the clay say to the potter,
　'What are you making?'
Does your work say,
　'He has no hands'?
10Woe to him who says to his father,
　'What have you begotten?'
or to his mother,
　'What have you brought to birth?'

---

[a] 2 Dead Sea Scrolls and Septuagint; the meaning of the word in the Masoretic Text is uncertain.

Living Bible

prophets say, I do; when they say Jerusalem will be delivered and the cities of Judah lived in once again—it shall be done! 27When I speak to the rivers and say, "Be dry!" they shall be dry. 28When I say of Cyrus,b "He is my shepherd," he will certainly do as I say; and Jerusalem will be rebuilt and the Temple restored, for I have spoken it.

45 THIS IS Jehovah's message to Cyrus, God's anointed, whom he has chosen to conquer many lands. God shall empower his right hand and he shall crush the strength of mighty kings. God shall open the gates of Babylon to him; the gates shall not be shut against him any more. 2I will go before you, Cyrus, and level the mountains and smash down the city gates of brass and iron bars. 3And I will give you treasures hidden in the darkness, secret riches; and you will know that I am doing this—I, the Lord, the God of Israel, the one who calls you by your name.

4And why have I named you for this work? For the sake of Jacob, my servant—Israel, my chosen. I called you by name when you didn't know me. 5I am Jehovah; there is no other God. I will strengthen you and send you out to victory even though you don't know me, 6and all the world from east to west will know there is no other God. I am Jehovah and there is no one else. I alone am God. 7I form the light and make the dark. I send good times and bad. I, Jehovah, am he who does these things. 8Open up, O heavens. Let salvation and righteousness sprout up together from the earth. I, Jehovah, created them.

9Woe to the man who fights with his Creator. Does the pot argue with its maker? Does the clay dispute with him who forms it, saying, "Stop, you're doing it wrong!" or the pot exclaim, "How clumsy can you be!"? 10Woe to the baby just being born who squalls to his father and mother, "Why have you produced me? Can't you do anything right at all?"

New Revised Standard

26 who confirms the word of his servant,
    and fulfills the prediction of his messengers;
who says of Jerusalem, "It shall be inhabited,"
    and of the cities of Judah, "They shall be
    rebuilt,
    and I will raise up their ruins";
27 who says to the deep, "Be dry—
    I will dry up your rivers";
28 who says of Cyrus, "He is my shepherd,
    and he shall carry out all my purpose";
and who says of Jerusalem, "It shall be
    rebuilt,"
    and of the temple, "Your foundation shall
    be laid."

Cyrus, God's Instrument

45 THUS SAYS the LORD to his anointed, to Cyrus,
    whose right hand I have grasped
to subdue nations before him
    and strip kings of their robes,
to open doors before him—
    and the gates shall not be closed:
2 I will go before you
    and level the mountains,c
I will break in pieces the doors of bronze
    and cut through the bars of iron,
3 I will give you the treasures of darkness
    and riches hidden in secret places,
so that you may know that it is I, the LORD,
    the God of Israel, who call you by your
    name.
4 For the sake of my servant Jacob,
    and Israel my chosen,
I call you by your name,
    I surname you, though you do not know
    me.
5 I am the LORD, and there is no other;
    besides me there is no god.
I arm you, though you do not know me,
6 so that they may know, from the rising of the
    sun
    and from the west, that there is no one
    besides me;
I am the LORD, and there is no other.
7 I form light and create darkness,
    I make weal and create woe;
    I the LORD do all these things.

8 Shower, O heavens, from above,
    and let the skies rain down righteousness;
let the earth open, that salvation may spring
    up,d
    and let it cause righteousness to sprout up
    also;
I the LORD have created it.

9 Woe to you who strive with your Maker,
    earthen vessels with the potter!e
Does the clay say to the one who fashions it,
    "What are you making"?
    or "Your work has no handles"?
10 Woe to anyone who says to a father, "What
    are you begetting?"
    or to a woman, "With what are you in
    labor?"

---

b 44:28 This was written many years before Cyrus began his meteoric rise to power.

c Q Ms Gk: MT *the swellings*   d Q Ms: MT *that they may bring forth salvation*
e Cn: Heb *with the potsherds*, or *with the potters*

King James

11Thus saith the LORD, the Holy One of Israel, and his Maker, Ask me of things to come concerning my sons, and concerning the work of my hands command ye me.

12I have made the earth, and created man upon it: I, *even* my hands, have stretched out the heavens, and all their host have I commanded.

13I have raised him up in righteousness, and I will direct all his ways: he shall build my city, and he shall let go my captives, not for price nor reward, saith the LORD of hosts.

14Thus saith the LORD, The labour of Egypt, and merchandise of Ethiopia and of the Sabeans, men of stature, shall come over unto thee, and they shall be thine: they shall come after thee; in chains they shall come over, and they shall fall down unto thee, they shall make supplication unto thee, *saying*, Surely God *is* in thee; and *there is* none else, *there is* no God.

15Verily thou *art* a God that hidest thyself, O God of Israel, the Saviour.

16They shall be ashamed, and also confounded, all of them: they shall go to confusion together *that are* makers of idols.

17*But* Israel shall be saved in the LORD with an everlasting salvation: ye shall not be ashamed nor confounded world without end.

18For thus saith the LORD that created the heavens; God himself that formed the earth and made it; he hath established it, he created it not in vain, he formed it to be inhabited: I *am* the LORD; and *there is* none else.

19I have not spoken in secret, in a dark place of the earth: I said not unto the seed of Jacob, Seek ye me in vain: I the LORD speak righteousness, I declare things that are right.

20¶ Assemble yourselves and come; draw near together, ye *that are* escaped of the nations: they have no knowledge that set up the wood of their graven image, and pray unto a god *that* cannot save.

21Tell ye, and bring *them* near; yea, let them take counsel together: who hath declared this from ancient time? *who* hath told it from that time? *have* not I the LORD? and *there is* no God else beside me; a just God and a Saviour; *there is* none beside me.

22Look unto me, and be ye saved, all the ends of the earth: for I *am* God, and *there is* none else.

New International

11"This is what the LORD says—
the Holy One of Israel, and its Maker:
Concerning things to come,
do you question me about my children,
or give me orders about the work of my
hands?
12It is I who made the earth
and created mankind upon it.
My own hands stretched out the heavens;
I marshaled their starry hosts.
13I will raise up Cyrus[a] in my righteousness:
I will make all his ways straight.
He will rebuild my city
and set my exiles free,
but not for a price or reward,
says the LORD Almighty."

14This is what the LORD says:

"The products of Egypt and the merchandise of
Cush,[b]
and those tall Sabeans—
they will come over to you
and will be yours;
they will trudge behind you,
coming over to you in chains.
They will bow down before you
and plead with you, saying,
'Surely God is with you, and there is no other;
there is no other god.' "

15Truly you are a God who hides himself,
O God and Savior of Israel.
16All the makers of idols will be put to shame
and disgraced;
they will go off into disgrace together.
17But Israel will be saved by the LORD
with an everlasting salvation;
you will never be put to shame or disgraced,
to ages everlasting.

18For this is what the LORD says—
he who created the heavens,
he is God;
he who fashioned and made the earth,
he founded it;
he did not create it to be empty,
but formed it to be inhabited—
he says:
"I am the LORD,
and there is no other.
19I have not spoken in secret,
from somewhere in a land of darkness;
I have not said to Jacob's descendants,
'Seek me in vain.'
I, the LORD, speak the truth;
I declare what is right.

20"Gather together and come;
assemble, you fugitives from the nations.
Ignorant are those who carry about idols of
wood,
who pray to gods that cannot save.
21Declare what is to be, present it—
let them take counsel together.
Who foretold this long ago,
who declared it from the distant past?
Was it not I, the LORD?
And there is no God apart from me,
a righteous God and a Savior;
there is none but me.

22"Turn to me and be saved,
all you ends of the earth;
for I am God, and there is no other.

---

a 13 Hebrew *him*　　b 14 That is, the upper Nile region

Living Bible

11Jehovah, the Holy One of Israel, Israel's Creator, says: What right have you to question what I do? Who are you to command me concerning the work of my hands? 12I have made the earth and created man upon it. With my hands I have stretched out the heavens and commanded all the vast myriads of stars. 13I have raised up Cyrus[c] to fulfill my righteous purpose, and I will direct all his paths. He shall restore my city and free my captive people—and not for a reward!

14Jehovah says: The Egyptians, Ethiopians and Sabeans shall be subject to you. They shall come to you with all their merchandise and it shall all be yours. They shall follow you as prisoners in chains, and fall down on their knees before you and say, "The only God there is, is your God!"

15Truly, O God of Israel, Savior, you work in strange, mysterious ways. 16All who worship idols shall be disappointed and ashamed. 17But Israel shall be saved by Jehovah with eternal salvation; they shall never be disappointed in their God through all eternity. 18For Jehovah created the heavens and earth and put everything in place, and he made the world to be lived in, not to be an empty chaos. I am Jehovah, he says, and there is no other! 19I publicly proclaim bold promises; I do not whisper obscurities in some dark corner so that no one can know what I mean. And I didn't tell Israel to ask me for what I didn't plan to give! No, for I, Jehovah, speak only truth and righteousness.

20Gather together and come, you nations that escape from Cyrus' hand. What fools they are who carry around the wooden idols and pray to gods that cannot save! 21Consult together, argue your case and state your proofs that idol-worship pays! Who but God has said that these things concerning Cyrus would come true? What idol ever told you they would happen? For there is no other God but me—a just God and a Savior—no, not one! 22Let all the world look to me for salvation! For I am God; there is no other. 23I have sworn by myself

New Revised Standard

11 Thus says the LORD,
   the Holy One of Israel, and its Maker:
Will you question me[d] about my children,
   or command me concerning the work of my
      hands?
12 I made the earth,
   and created humankind upon it;
it was my hands that stretched out the
      heavens,
   and I commanded all their host.
13 I have aroused Cyrus[e] in righteousness,
   and I will make all his paths straight;
he shall build my city
   and set my exiles free,
not for price or reward,
   says the LORD of hosts.

14 Thus says the LORD:
The wealth of Egypt and the merchandise of
      Ethiopia,[f]
   and the Sabeans, tall of stature,
shall come over to you and be yours,
   they shall follow you;
they shall come over in chains and bow
      down to you.
They will make supplication to you, saying,
   "God is with you alone, and there is no
      other;
   there is no god besides him."
15 Truly, you are a God who hides himself,
   O God of Israel, the Savior.
16 All of them are put to shame and confounded,
   the makers of idols go in confusion
      together.
17 But Israel is saved by the LORD
   with everlasting salvation;
you shall not be put to shame or confounded
   to all eternity.

18 For thus says the LORD,
who created the heavens
   (he is God!),
who formed the earth and made it
   (he established it;
he did not create it a chaos,
   he formed it to be inhabited!):
I am the LORD, and there is no other.
19 I did not speak in secret,
   in a land of darkness;
I did not say to the offspring of Jacob,
   "Seek me in chaos."
I the LORD speak the truth,
   I declare what is right.

Idols Cannot Save Babylon

20 Assemble yourselves and come together,
   draw near, you survivors of the nations!
They have no knowledge—
   those who carry about their wooden idols,
and keep on praying to a god
   that cannot save.
21 Declare and present your case;
   let them take counsel together!
Who told this long ago?
   Who declared it of old?
Was it not I, the LORD?
   There is no other god besides me,
a righteous God and a Savior;
   there is no one besides me.

22 Turn to me and be saved,
   all the ends of the earth!
For I am God, and there is no other.

---

c *45:13 I have raised up Cyrus,* literally, "I have raised up him. . . ." The reference probably is also to Christ in the more distant future, as well as to Cyrus.

d Cn: Heb *Ask me of things to come*   e Heb *him*   f Or *Nubia;* Heb *Cush*

King James

23I have sworn by myself, the word is gone out of my mouth *in* righteousness, and shall not return, That unto me every knee shall bow, every tongue shall swear.

24Surely, shall *one* say, in the LORD have I righteousness and strength: *even* to him shall *men* come; and all that are incensed against him shall be ashamed.

25In the LORD shall all the seed of Israel be justified, and shall glory.

46 BEL BOWETH down, Nebo stoopeth, their idols were upon the beasts, and upon the cattle: your carriages *were* heavy laden; *they are* a burden to the weary *beast.*

2They stoop, they bow down together; they could not deliver the burden, but themselves are gone into captivity.

3¶ Hearken unto me, O house of Jacob, and all the remnant of the house of Israel, which are borne *by me* from the belly, which are carried from the womb:

4And *even* to *your* old age I *am* he; and *even* to hoar hairs will I carry *you:* I have made, and I will bear; even I will carry, and will deliver *you.*

5¶ To whom will ye liken me, and make *me* equal, and compare me, that we may be like?

6They lavish gold out of the bag, and weigh silver in the balance, *and* hire a goldsmith; and he maketh it a god: they fall down, yea, they worship.

7They bear him upon the shoulder, they carry him, and set him in his place, and he standeth; from his place shall he not remove: yea, *one* shall cry unto him, yet can he not answer, nor save him out of his trouble.

8Remember this, and show yourselves men: bring *it* again to mind, O ye transgressors.

9Remember the former things of old: for I *am* God, and *there is* none else; *I am* God, and *there is* none like me,

10Declaring the end from the beginning, and from ancient times *the things* that are not *yet* done, saying, My counsel shall stand, and I will do all my pleasure:

11Calling a ravenous bird from the east, the man that executeth my counsel from a far country: yea, I have spoken *it,* I will also bring it to pass; I have purposed *it,* I will also do it.

12¶ Hearken unto me, ye stouthearted, that *are* far from righteousness:

13I bring near my righteousness; it shall not be far off, and my salvation shall not tarry: and I will place salvation in Zion for Israel my glory.

New International

23By myself I have sworn,
   my mouth has uttered in all integrity
   a word that will not be revoked:
Before me every knee will bow;
   by me every tongue will swear.
24They will say of me, 'In the LORD alone
   are righteousness and strength.' "
All who have raged against him
   will come to him and be put to shame.
25But in the LORD all the descendants of Israel
   will be found righteous and will exult.

Gods of Babylon

46 BEL BOWS down, Nebo stoops low;
   their idols are borne by beasts of burden.[a]
The images that are carried about are
      burdensome,
   a burden for the weary.
2They stoop and bow down together;
   unable to rescue the burden,
   they themselves go off into captivity.

3"Listen to me, O house of Jacob,
   all you who remain of the house of Israel,
you whom I have upheld since you were
      conceived,
   and have carried since your birth.
4Even to your old age and gray hairs
   I am he, I am he who will sustain you.
I have made you and I will carry you;
   I will sustain you and I will rescue you.

5"To whom will you compare me or count me
      equal?
   To whom will you liken me that we may be
      compared?
6Some pour out gold from their bags
   and weigh out silver on the scales;
they hire a goldsmith to make it into a god,
   and they bow down and worship it.
7They lift it to their shoulders and carry it;
   they set it up in its place, and there it stands.
   From that spot it cannot move.
Though one cries out to it, it does not answer;
   it cannot save him from his troubles.

8"Remember this, fix it in mind,
   take it to heart, you rebels.
9Remember the former things, those of long ago;
   I am God, and there is no other;
   I am God, and there is none like me.
10I make known the end from the beginning,
   from ancient times, what is still to come.
I say: My purpose will stand,
   and I will do all that I please.
11From the east I summon a bird of prey;
   from a far-off land, a man to fulfill my
      purpose.
What I have said, that will I bring about;
   what I have planned, that will I do.
12Listen to me, you stubborn-hearted,
   you who are far from righteousness.
13I am bringing my righteousness near,
   it is not far away;
   and my salvation will not be delayed.
I will grant salvation to Zion,
   my splendor to Israel.

a 1 Or are but beasts and cattle

Living Bible

and I will never go back on my word, for it is true—that every knee in all the world shall bow to me, and every tongue shall swear allegiance to my name. 24"In Jehovah is all my righteousness and strength," the people shall declare. And all who were angry with him shall come to him and be ashamed. 25In Jehovah all the generations of Israel shall be justified, triumphant.

46 THE IDOLS of Babylon, Bel and Nebo,b are being hauled away on ox carts! But look! The beasts are stumbling! The cart is turning over! The gods are falling out onto the ground! Is that the best that they can do? If they cannot even save themselves from such a fall, how can they save their worshipers from Cyrus? 3"Listen to me, all Israel who are left; I have created you and cared for you since you were born. 4I will be your God through all your lifetime, yes, even when your hair is white with age. I made you and I will care for you. I will carry you along and be your Savior.

5"With what in all of heaven and earth do I compare? Whom can you find who equals me? 6Will you compare me with an idol made lavishly with silver and with gold? They hire a goldsmith to take your wealth and make a god from it! Then they fall down and worship it! 7They carry it around on their shoulders, and when they set it down it stays there, for it cannot move! And when someone prays to it there is no answer, for it cannot get him out of his trouble.

8"Don't forget this, O guilty ones. 9And don't forget the many times I clearly told you what was going to happen in the future. For I am God—I only—and there is no other like me 10who can tell you what is going to happen. All I say will come to pass, for I do whatever I wish. 11I will call that swift bird of prey from the east—that man Cyrus from far away. And he will come and do my bidding. I have said I would do it and I will. 12Listen to me, you stubborn, evil men! 13For I am offering you my deliverance; not in the distant future, but right now! I am ready to save you, and I will restore Jerusalem, and Israel, who is my glory.

New Revised Standard

23 By myself I have sworn,
    from my mouth has gone forth in
      righteousness
    a word that shall not return:
  "To me every knee shall bow,
    every tongue shall swear."

24 Only in the LORD, it shall be said of me,
    are righteousness and strength;
  all who were incensed against him
    shall come to him and be ashamed.
25 In the LORD all the offspring of Israel
    shall triumph and glory.

46 BEL BOWS down, Nebo stoops,
    their idols are on beasts and cattle;
  these things you carry are loaded
    as burdens on weary animals.
2 They stoop, they bow down together;
    they cannot save the burden,
  but themselves go into captivity.

3 Listen to me, O house of Jacob,
    all the remnant of the house of Israel,
  who have been borne by me from your birth,
    carried from the womb;
4 even to your old age I am he,
    even when you turn gray I will carry you.
  I have made, and I will bear;
    I will carry and will save.

5 To whom will you liken me and make me
      equal,
    and compare me, as though we were alike?
6 Those who lavish gold from the purse,
    and weigh out silver in the scales—
  they hire a goldsmith, who makes it into a
      god;
    then they fall down and worship!
7 They lift it to their shoulders, they carry it,
    they set it in its place, and it stands there;
  it cannot move from its place.
  If one cries out to it, it does not answer
    or save anyone from trouble.

8 Remember this and consider,c
    recall it to mind, you transgressors,
9   remember the former things of old;
  for I am God, and there is no other;
    I am God, and there is no one like me,
10 declaring the end from the beginning
    and from ancient times things not yet done,
  saying, "My purpose shall stand,
    and I will fulfill my intention,"
11 calling a bird of prey from the east,
    the man for my purpose from a far country.
  I have spoken, and I will bring it to pass;
    I have planned, and I will do it.

12 Listen to me, you stubborn of heart,
    you who are far from deliverance:
13 I bring near my deliverance, it is not far off,
    and my salvation will not tarry;
  I will put salvation in Zion,
    for Israel my glory.

---

b 46:1 *Bel and Nebo.* Names of Marduk and Nabu, the two principal gods in the Babylonian pantheon.

c Meaning of Heb uncertain

King James

47 COME DOWN, and sit in the dust, O virgin daughter of Babylon, sit on the ground: *there is* no throne, O daughter of the Chaldeans: for thou shalt no more be called tender and delicate.

²Take the millstones, and grind meal: uncover thy locks, make bare the leg, uncover the thigh, pass over the rivers.

³Thy nakedness shall be uncovered, yea, thy shame shall be seen: I will take vengeance, and I will not meet *thee as* a man.

⁴*As for* our redeemer, the Lᴏʀᴅ of hosts *is* his name, the Holy One of Israel.

⁵Sit thou silent, and get thee into darkness, O daughter of the Chaldeans: for thou shalt no more be called, The lady of kingdoms.

⁶¶ I was wroth with my people, I have polluted mine inheritance, and given them into thine hand: thou didst show them no mercy; upon the ancient hast thou very heavily laid thy yoke.

⁷¶ And thou saidst, I shall be a lady for ever: *so that* thou didst not lay these *things* to thy heart, neither didst remember the latter end of it.

⁸Therefore hear now this, *thou that art* given to pleasures, that dwellest carelessly, that sayest in thine heart, I *am,* and none else beside me; I shall not sit *as* a widow, neither shall I know the loss of children:

⁹But these two *things* shall come to thee in a moment in one day, the loss of children, and widowhood: they shall come upon thee in their perfection for the multitude of thy sorceries, *and* for the great abundance of thine enchantments.

¹⁰¶ For thou hast trusted in thy wickedness: thou hast said, None seeth me. Thy wisdom and thy knowledge, it hath perverted thee; and thou hast said in thine heart, I *am,* and none else beside me.

¹¹¶ Therefore shall evil come upon thee; thou shalt not know from whence it riseth: and mischief shall fall upon thee; thou shalt not be able to put it off: and desolation shall come upon thee suddenly, *which* thou shalt not know.

¹²Stand now with thine enchantments, and with the multitude of thy sorceries, wherein thou hast laboured from thy youth; if so be thou shalt be able to profit, if so be thou mayest prevail.

New International

The Fall of Babylon

47 "GO DOWN, sit in the dust,
    Virgin Daughter of Babylon;
sit on the ground without a throne,
    Daughter of the Babylonians.ᵃ
No more will you be called
    tender or delicate.
²Take millstones and grind flour;
    take off your veil.
Lift up your skirts, bare your legs,
    and wade through the streams.
³Your nakedness will be exposed
    and your shame uncovered.
I will take vengeance;
    I will spare no one."

⁴Our Redeemer—the Lᴏʀᴅ Almighty is his
    name—
    is the Holy One of Israel.

⁵"Sit in silence, go into darkness,
    Daughter of the Babylonians;
no more will you be called
    queen of kingdoms.
⁶I was angry with my people
    and desecrated my inheritance;
I gave them into your hand,
    and you showed them no mercy.
Even on the aged
    you laid a very heavy yoke.
⁷You said, 'I will continue forever—
    the eternal queen!'
But you did not consider these things
    or reflect on what might happen.

⁸"Now then, listen, you wanton creature,
    lounging in your security
and saying to yourself,
    'I am, and there is none besides me.
I will never be a widow
    or suffer the loss of children.'
⁹Both of these will overtake you
    in a moment, on a single day:
    loss of children and widowhood.
They will come upon you in full measure,
    in spite of your many sorceries
    and all your potent spells.
¹⁰You have trusted in your wickedness
    and have said, 'No one sees me.'
Your wisdom and knowledge mislead you
    when you say to yourself,
    'I am, and there is none besides me.'
¹¹Disaster will come upon you,
    and you will not know how to conjure it
    away.
A calamity will fall upon you
    that you cannot ward off with a ransom;
a catastrophe you cannot foresee
    will suddenly come upon you.

¹²"Keep on, then, with your magic spells
    and with your many sorceries,
    which you have labored at since childhood.
Perhaps you will succeed,
    perhaps you will cause terror.

ᵃ *1* Or *Chaldeans*; also in verse 5

Living Bible

47 "O BABYLON, the unconquered, come sit in the dust; for your days of glory, pomp and honor are ended. O daughter of Chaldea, never again will you be the lovely princess, tender and delicate. ²Take heavy millstones and grind the corn; remove your veil;ᵇ strip off your robe; expose yourself to public view. ³You shall be in nakedness and shame. I will take vengeance upon you and will not repent."

⁴So speaks our Redeemer, who will save Israel from Babylon's mighty power; the Lord Almighty is his name, the Holy One of Israel.

⁵Sit in darkness and silence, O Babylon; never again will you be called "The Queen of Kingdoms." ⁶For I was angry with my people Israel and began to punish them a little by letting them fall into your hands, O Babylon. But you showed them no mercy. You have made even the old folks carry heavy burdens. ⁷You thought your reign would never end, Queen Kingdom of the world. You didn't care a whit about my people or think about the fate of those who do them harm.

⁸O pleasure-mad kingdom, living at ease, bragging as the greatest in the world—listen to the sentence of my court upon your sins. You say, "I alone am God! I'll never be a widow; I'll never lose my children." ⁹Well, those two things shall come upon you in one moment, in full measure in one day: widowhood and the loss of your children, despite all your witchcraft and magic.

¹⁰You felt secure in all your wickedness. "No one sees me," you said. Your "wisdom" and "knowledge" have caused you to turn away from me and claim that you yourself are Jehovah. ¹¹That is why disaster shall overtake you suddenly—so suddenly that you won't know where it comes from. And there will be no atonement then to cleanse away your sins.

¹²Call out the demon hordes you've worshiped all these years. Call on them to help you strike deep terror into many hearts again. ¹³You have advisors by the

New Revised Standard

The Humiliation of Babylon

47 COME DOWN and sit in the dust,
virgin daughter Babylon!
Sit on the ground without a throne,
daughter Chaldea!
For you shall no more be called
tender and delicate.
2 Take the millstones and grind meal,
remove your veil,
strip off your robe, uncover your legs,
pass through the rivers.
3 Your nakedness shall be uncovered,
and your shame shall be seen.
I will take vengeance,
and I will spare no one.
4 Our Redeemer—the LORD of hosts is his
name—
is the Holy One of Israel.

5 Sit in silence, and go into darkness,
daughter Chaldea!
For you shall no more be called
the mistress of kingdoms.
6 I was angry with my people,
I profaned my heritage;
I gave them into your hand,
you showed them no mercy;
on the aged you made your yoke
exceedingly heavy.
7 You said, "I shall be mistress forever,"
so that you did not lay these things to heart
or remember their end.

8 Now therefore hear this, you lover of
pleasures,
who sit securely,
who say in your heart,
"I am, and there is no one besides me;
I shall not sit as a widow
or know the loss of children"—
9 both these things shall come upon you
in a moment, in one day:
the loss of children and widowhood
shall come upon you in full measure,
in spite of your many sorceries
and the great power of your enchantments.

10 You felt secure in your wickedness;
you said, "No one sees me."
Your wisdom and your knowledge
led you astray,
and you said in your heart,
"I am, and there is no one besides me."
11 But evil shall come upon you,
which you cannot charm away;
disaster shall fall upon you,
which you will not be able to ward off;
and ruin shall come on you suddenly,
of which you know nothing.

12 Stand fast in your enchantments
and your many sorceries,
with which you have labored from your
youth;
perhaps you may be able to succeed,
perhaps you may inspire terror.

ᵇ *47:2 remove your veil.* In ancient Babylonia (and in many eastern lands today) only harlots were permitted to go without veils.

King James

13Thou art wearied in the multitude of thy counsels. Let now the astrologers, the stargazers, the monthly prognosticators, stand up, and save thee from *these things* that shall come upon thee.

14Behold, they shall be as stubble; the fire shall burn them; they shall not deliver themselves from the power of the flame: *there shall* not *be* a coal to warm at, *nor* fire to sit before it.

15Thus shall they be unto thee with whom thou hast laboured, *even* thy merchants, from thy youth: they shall wander every one to his quarter; none shall save thee.

48 HEAR YE this, O house of Jacob, which are called by the name of Israel, and are come forth out of the waters of Judah, which swear by the name of the LORD, and make mention of the God of Israel, *but* not in truth, nor in righteousness.

2For they call themselves of the holy city, and stay themselves upon the God of Israel; The LORD of hosts *is* his name.

3I have declared the former things from the beginning; and they went forth out of my mouth, and I showed them; I did *them* suddenly, and they came to pass.

4Because I knew that thou *art* obstinate, and thy neck *is* an iron sinew, and thy brow brass;

5I have even from the beginning declared *it* to thee; before it came to pass I showed *it* thee: lest thou shouldest say, Mine idol hath done them, and my graven image, and my molten image, hath commanded them.

6Thou hast heard, see all this; and will not ye declare *it?* I have shown thee new things from this time, even hidden things, and thou didst not know them.

7They are created now, and not from the beginning; even before the day when thou heardest them not; lest thou shouldest say, Behold, I knew them.

8Yea, thou heardest not; yea, thou knewest not; yea, from that time *that* thine ear was not opened: for I knew that thou wouldest deal very treacherously, and wast called a transgressor from the womb.

9¶ For my name's sake will I defer mine anger, and for my praise will I refrain for thee, that I cut thee not off.

New International

13All the counsel you have received has only
   worn you out!
Let your astrologers come forward,
those stargazers who make predictions month by
   month,
   let them save you from what is coming upon
     you.
14Surely they are like stubble;
   the fire will burn them up.
They cannot even save themselves
   from the power of the flame.
Here are no coals to warm anyone;
   here is no fire to sit by.
15That is all they can do for you—
   these you have labored with
   and trafficked with since childhood.
Each of them goes on in his error;
   there is not one that can save you.

Stubborn Israel

48 "LISTEN TO this, O house of Jacob,
   you who are called by the name of Israel
and come from the line of Judah,
you who take oaths in the name of the LORD
   and invoke the God of Israel—
   but not in truth or righteousness—
2you who call yourselves citizens of the holy city
   and rely on the God of Israel—
   the LORD Almighty is his name:
3I foretold the former things long ago,
   my mouth announced them and I made them
     known;
   then suddenly I acted, and they came to pass.
4For I knew how stubborn you were;
   the sinews of your neck were iron,
   your forehead was bronze.
5Therefore I told you these things long ago;
   before they happened I announced them to
     you
so that you could not say,
   'My idols did them;
   my wooden image and metal god ordained
     them.'
6You have heard these things; look at them all.
   Will you not admit them?

"From now on I will tell you of new things,
   of hidden things unknown to you.
7They are created now, and not long ago;
   you have not heard of them before today.
So you cannot say,
   'Yes, I knew of them.'
8You have neither heard nor understood;
   from of old your ear has not been open.
Well do I know how treacherous you are;
   you were called a rebel from birth.
9For my own name's sake I delay my wrath;
   for the sake of my praise I hold it back from
     you,
   so as not to cut you off.

Living Bible

ton—your astrologers and stargazers, who try to tell you what the future holds. 14But they are as useless as dried grass burning in the fire. They cannot even deliver themselves! You'll get no help from them at all. Theirs is no fire to sit beside to make you warm! 15And all your friends of childhood days shall slip away and disappear, unable to help.

48 HEAR ME, my people: you swear allegiance to the Lord without meaning a word of it, when you boast of living in the Holy City and brag about depending on the God of Israel. 3Time and again I told you what was going to happen in the future. My words were scarcely spoken when suddenly I did just what I said. 4I knew how hard and obstinate you are. Your necks are as unbending as iron; you are as hardheaded as brass. 5That is why I told you ahead of time what I was going to do, so that you could never say, "My idol did it; my carved image commanded it to happen!" 6You have heard my predictions and seen them fulfilled, but you refuse to agree it is so. Now I will tell you new things I haven't mentioned before, secrets you haven't heard.

7Then you can't say, "We knew that all the time!" 8Yes, I'll tell you things entirely new, for I know so well what traitors you are, rebels from earliest childhood, rotten through and through. 9Yet for my own sake and for the honor of my name I will hold back my anger and not wipe you out. 10I refined you in the furnace of

New Revised Standard

13 You are wearied with your many
      consultations;
   let those who studya the heavens
stand up and save you,
      those who gaze at the stars,
   and at each new moon predict
      whatb shall befall you.

14 See, they are like stubble,
      the fire consumes them;
   they cannot deliver themselves
      from the power of the flame.
   No coal for warming oneself is this,
      no fire to sit before!

15 Such to you are those with whom you have
      labored,
   who have trafficked with you from your
      youth;
   they all wander about in their own paths;
      there is no one to save you.

God the Creator and Redeemer

48 HEAR THIS, O house of Jacob,
      who are called by the name of Israel,
   and who came forth from the loinsc of
      Judah;
   who swear by the name of the LORD,
      and invoke the God of Israel,
      but not in truth or right.
2   For they call themselves after the holy city,
      and lean on the God of Israel;
      the LORD of hosts is his name.

3   The former things I declared long ago,
      they went out from my mouth and I made
         them known;
   then suddenly I did them and they came to
         pass.
4   Because I know that you are obstinate,
      and your neck is an iron sinew
      and your forehead brass,
5   I declared them to you from long ago,
      before they came to pass I announced them
         to you,
   so that you would not say, "My idol did them,
      my carved image and my cast image
         commanded them."

6   You have heard; now see all this;
      and will you not declare it?
   From this time forward I make you hear new
         things,
      hidden things that you have not known.
7   They are created now, not long ago;
      before today you have never heard of them,
   so that you could not say, "I already knew
         them."
8   You have never heard, you have never known,
      from of old your ear has not been opened.
   For I knew that you would deal very
         treacherously,
      and that from birth you were called a rebel.

9   For my name's sake I defer my anger,
      for the sake of my praise I restrain it for
         you,
   so that I may not cut you off.

a Meaning of Heb uncertain   b Gk Syr Compare Vg: Heb from what   c Cn:
Heb waters

King James

10Behold, I have refined thee, but not with silver; I have chosen thee in the furnace of affliction.

11For mine own sake, *even* for mine own sake, will I do *it:* for how should *my name* be polluted? and I will not give my glory unto another.

12¶ Hearken unto me, O Jacob and Israel, my called; I *am* he; I *am* the first, I also *am* the last.

13Mine hand also hath laid the foundation of the earth, and my right hand hath spanned the heavens: *when* I call unto them, they stand up together.

14All ye, assemble yourselves, and hear; which among them hath declared these *things?* The LORD hath loved him: he will do his pleasure on Babylon, and his arm *shall be on* the Chaldeans.

15I, *even* I, have spoken; yea, I have called him: I have brought him, and he shall make his way prosperous.

16¶ Come ye near unto me, hear ye this; I have not spoken in secret from the beginning; from the time that it was, there *am* I: and now the Lord GOD, and his spirit, hath sent me.

17Thus saith the LORD, thy Redeemer, the Holy One of Israel; I *am* the LORD thy God which teacheth thee to profit, which leadeth thee by the way *that* thou shouldest go.

18O that thou hadst hearkened to my commandments! then had thy peace been as a river, and thy righteousness as the waves of the sea:

19Thy seed also had been as the sand, and the offspring of thy bowels like the gravel thereof; his name should not have been cut off nor destroyed from before me.

20¶ Go ye forth of Babylon, flee ye from the Chaldeans, with a voice of singing declare ye, tell this, utter it *even* to the end of the earth; say ye, The LORD hath redeemed his servant Jacob.

21And they thirsted not *when* he led them through the deserts: he caused the waters to flow out of the rock for them: he clave the rock also, and the waters gushed out.

22*There is* no peace, saith the LORD, unto the wicked.

49 LISTEN, O isles, unto me; and hearken, ye people, from far; The LORD hath called me from the womb; from the bowels of my mother hath he made mention of my name.

New International

10See, I have refined you, though not as silver;
    I have tested you in the furnace of affliction.
11For my own sake, for my own sake, I do this.
    How can I let myself be defamed?
    I will not yield my glory to another.

Israel Freed

12"Listen to me, O Jacob,
    Israel, whom I have called:
I am he;
    I am the first and I am the last.
13My own hand laid the foundations of the earth,
    and my right hand spread out the heavens;
when I summon them,
    they all stand up together.

14"Come together, all of you, and listen:
    Which of ˌthe idolsˌ has foretold these things?
The LORD's chosen ally
    will carry out his purpose against Babylon;
    his arm will be against the Babylonians.a
15I, even I, have spoken;
    yes, I have called him.
I will bring him,
    and he will succeed in his mission.

16"Come near me and listen to this:

"From the first announcement I have not spoken in secret;
    at the time it happens, I am there."

And now the Sovereign LORD has sent me,
    with his Spirit.

17This is what the LORD says—
    your Redeemer, the Holy One of Israel:
"I am the LORD your God,
    who teaches you what is best for you,
    who directs you in the way you should go.
18If only you had paid attention to my commands,
    your peace would have been like a river,
    your righteousness like the waves of the sea.
19Your descendants would have been like the sand,
    your children like its numberless grains;
their name would never be cut off
    nor destroyed from before me."

20Leave Babylon,
    flee from the Babylonians!
Announce this with shouts of joy
    and proclaim it.
Send it out to the ends of the earth;
    say, "The LORD has redeemed his servant Jacob."
21They did not thirst when he led them through the deserts;
    he made water flow for them from the rock;
he split the rock
    and water gushed out.

22"There is no peace," says the LORD, "for the wicked."

The Servant of the LORD

49 LISTEN TO me, you islands;
    hear this, you distant nations:
Before I was born the LORD called me;
    from my birth he has made mention of my name.

---

a *14 Or Chaldeans;* also in verse 20

Living Bible

affliction, but found no silver there. You are worthless, with nothing good in you at all. 11Yet for my own sake—yes, *for my own sake*—I will save you from my anger and not destroy you lest the heathen say their gods have conquered me. I will not let them have my glory.

12Listen to me, my people, my chosen ones! I alone am God. I am the First; I am the Last. 13It was my hand that laid the foundations of the earth; the palm of my right hand spread out the heavens above; I spoke and they came into being.

14Come, all of you, and listen. Among all your idols, which one has ever told you this: "The Lord loves Cyrus. He will use him to put an end to the empire of Babylonia. He will utterly rout the armies of the Chaldeans"? 15But I am saying it. I have called Cyrus; I have sent him on this errand and I will prosper him.

16Come closer and listen. I have always told you plainly what would happen, so that you could clearly understand. And now the Lord God and his Spirit have sent me (with this message):

17The Lord, your Redeemer, the Holy One of Israel, says, I am the Lord your God, who punishes you for your own good and leads you along the paths that you should follow.

18Oh, that you had listened to my laws! Then you would have had peace flowing like a gentle river, and great waves of righteousness. 19Then you would have become as numerous as the sands along the seashores of the world, too many to count, and there would have been no need for your destruction.

20Yet even now, be free from your captivity! Leave Babylon, singing as you go; shout to the ends of the earth that the Lord has redeemed his servants, the Jews. 21They were not thirsty when he led them through the deserts; he divided the rock, and water gushed out for them to drink. 22But there is no peace, says the Lord, for the wicked.

49 LISTEN TO me, all of you in far-off lands: The Lord called me before my birth. From within the womb he called me by my name. 2God will make

New Revised Standard

10 See, I have refined you, but not like[b] silver;
  I have tested you in the furnace of
    adversity.
11 For my own sake, for my own sake, I do it,
  for why should my name[c] be profaned?
  My glory I will not give to another.

12 Listen to me, O Jacob,
  and Israel, whom I called:
I am He; I am the first,
  and I am the last.
13 My hand laid the foundation of the earth,
  and my right hand spread out the heavens;
when I summon them,
  they stand at attention.

14 Assemble, all of you, and hear!
  Who among them has declared these things?
The LORD loves him;
  he shall perform his purpose on Babylon,
  and his arm shall be against the Chaldeans.
15 I, even I, have spoken and called him,
  I have brought him, and he will prosper in
    his way.
16 Draw near to me, hear this!
  From the beginning I have not spoken in
    secret,
  from the time it came to be I have been
    there.
And now the Lord GOD has sent me and his
  spirit.

17 Thus says the LORD,
  your Redeemer, the Holy One of Israel:
I am the LORD your God,
  who teaches you for your own good,
  who leads you in the way you should go.
18 O that you had paid attention to my
    commandments!
Then your prosperity would have been like
    a river,
  and your success like the waves of the sea;
19 your offspring would have been like the sand,
  and your descendants like its grains;
their name would never be cut off
  or destroyed from before me.

20 Go out from Babylon, flee from Chaldea,
  declare this with a shout of joy, proclaim it,
send it forth to the end of the earth;
  say, "The LORD has redeemed his servant
    Jacob!"
21 They did not thirst when he led them through
    the deserts;
  he made water flow for them from the rock;
  he split open the rock and the water gushed
    out.

22 "There is no peace," says the LORD, "for the
  wicked."

The Servant's Mission

49 LISTEN TO me, O coastlands,
  pay attention, you peoples from far away!
The LORD called me before I was born,
  while I was in my mother's womb he
    named me.

King James

2And he hath made my mouth like a sharp sword; in the shadow of his hand hath he hid me, and made me a polished shaft; in his quiver hath he hid me;

3And said unto me, Thou *art* my servant, O Israel, in whom I will be glorified.

4Then I said, I have laboured in vain, I have spent my strength for nought, and in vain: *yet* surely my judgment *is* with the LORD, and my work with my God.

5¶ And now, saith the LORD that formed me from the womb *to be* his servant, to bring Jacob again to him, Though Israel be not gathered, yet shall I be glorious in the eyes of the LORD, and my God shall be my strength.

6And he said, It is a light thing that thou shouldest be my servant to raise up the tribes of Jacob, and to restore the preserved of Israel: I will also give thee for a light to the Gentiles, that thou mayest be my salvation unto the end of the earth.

7Thus saith the LORD, the Redeemer of Israel, *and* his Holy One, to him whom man despiseth, to him whom the nation abhorreth, to a servant of rulers, Kings shall see and arise, princes also shall worship, because of the LORD that is faithful, *and* the Holy One of Israel, and he shall choose thee.

8Thus saith the LORD, In an acceptable time have I heard thee, and in a day of salvation have I helped thee: and I will preserve thee, and give thee for a covenant of the people, to establish the earth, to cause to inherit the desolate heritages;

9That thou mayest say to the prisoners, Go forth; to them that *are* in darkness, Show yourselves. They shall feed in the ways, and their pastures *shall be* in all high places.

10They shall not hunger nor thirst; neither shall the heat nor sun smite them: for he that hath mercy on them shall lead them, even by the springs of water shall he guide them.

11And I will make all my mountains a way, and my highways shall be exalted.

12Behold, these shall come from far: and, lo, these from the north and from the west; and these from the land of Sinim.

13¶ Sing, O heavens; and be joyful, O earth; and break forth into singing, O mountains: for the LORD hath comforted his people, and will have mercy upon his afflicted.

New International

2He made my mouth like a sharpened sword,
   in the shadow of his hand he hid me;
he made me into a polished arrow
   and concealed me in his quiver.
3He said to me, "You are my servant,
   Israel, in whom I will display my splendor."
4But I said, "I have labored to no purpose;
   I have spent my strength in vain and for
      nothing.
Yet what is due me is in the LORD's hand,
   and my reward is with my God."

5And now the LORD says—
   he who formed me in the womb to be his
      servant
to bring Jacob back to him
   and gather Israel to himself,
for I am honored in the eyes of the LORD
   and my God has been my strength—
6he says:
"It is too small a thing for you to be my servant
   to restore the tribes of Jacob
   and bring back those of Israel I have kept.
I will also make you a light for the Gentiles,
   that you may bring my salvation to the ends
      of the earth."

7This is what the LORD says—
   the Redeemer and Holy One of Israel—
to him who was despised and abhorred by the
      nation,
   to the servant of rulers:
"Kings will see you and rise up,
   princes will see and bow down,
because of the LORD, who is faithful,
   the Holy One of Israel, who has chosen you."

Restoration of Israel

8This is what the LORD says:

"In the time of my favor I will answer you,
   and in the day of salvation I will help you;
I will keep you and will make you
   to be a covenant for the people,
to restore the land
   and to reassign its desolate inheritances,
9to say to the captives, 'Come out,'
   and to those in darkness, 'Be free!'

"They will feed beside the roads
   and find pasture on every barren hill.
10They will neither hunger nor thirst,
   nor will the desert heat or the sun beat upon
      them.
He who has compassion on them will guide
      them
   and lead them beside springs of water.
11I will turn all my mountains into roads,
   and my highways will be raised up.
12See, they will come from afar—
   some from the north, some from the west,
   some from the region of Aswan.ᵃ"

13Shout for joy, O heavens;
   rejoice, O earth;
   burst into song, O mountains!
For the LORD comforts his people
   and will have compassion on his afflicted
      ones.

ᵃ *12* Dead Sea Scrolls; Masoretic Text *Sinim*

Living Bible

my words of judgment sharp as swords. He has hidden me in the shadow of his hand; I am like a sharp arrow in his quiver.

³He said to me: "You are my Servant, a Prince of Powerᵇ with God, and you shall bring me glory."

⁴I replied, "But my work for them seems all in vain; I have spent my strength for them without response. Yet I leave it all with God for my reward."

⁵"And now," said the Lord—the Lord who formed me from my mother's womb to serve him who commissioned me to restore to him his people Israel, who has given me the strength to perform this task and honored me for doing it!— ⁶"you shall do more than restore Israel to me. I will make you a Light to the nations of the world to bring my salvation to them too."

⁷The Lord, the Redeemer and Holy One of Israel, says to the one who is despised, rejected by mankind, and kept beneath the heel of the world's rulers: "Kings shall stand at attention when you pass by; princes shall bow low because the Lord has chosen you; he, the faithful Lord, the Holy One of Israel, chooses you."

⁸, ⁹The Lord says, "Your request has come at a favorable time. I will keep you from harm and give you as a token and pledge to Israel, proof that I will reestablish the land of Israel and reassign it to its own people again. Through you I am saying to the prisoners of darkness, 'Come out! I am giving you your freedom!' They will be my sheep, grazing in green pastures and on the grassy hills. ¹⁰They shall neither hunger nor thirst; the searing sun and scorching desert winds will not reach them any more. For the Lord in his mercy will lead them beside the cool waters. ¹¹And I will make my mountains into level paths for them; the highways shall be raised above the valleys. ¹²See, my people shall return from far away, from north and west and south."

¹³Sing for joy, O heavens; shout, O earth. Break forth with song, O mountains, for the Lord has comforted his people, and will have compassion upon them in their sorrow.

New Revised Standard

2 He made my mouth like a sharp sword,
   in the shadow of his hand he hid me;
he made me a polished arrow,
   in his quiver he hid me away.
3 And he said to me, "You are my servant,
   Israel, in whom I will be glorified."
4 But I said, "I have labored in vain,
   I have spent my strength for nothing and
      vanity;
yet surely my cause is with the LORD,
   and my reward with my God."

5 And now the LORD says,
   who formed me in the womb to be his
      servant,
to bring Jacob back to him,
   and that Israel might be gathered to him,
for I am honored in the sight of the LORD,
   and my God has become my strength—
6 he says,
"It is too light a thing that you should be my
      servant
   to raise up the tribes of Jacob
   and to restore the survivors of Israel;
I will give you as a light to the nations,
   that my salvation may reach to the end of
      the earth."

7 Thus says the LORD,
   the Redeemer of Israel and his Holy One,
to one deeply despised, abhorred by the
      nations,
   the slave of rulers,
"Kings shall see and stand up,
   princes, and they shall prostrate themselves,
because of the LORD, who is faithful,
   the Holy One of Israel, who has chosen
      you."

Zion's Children to Be Brought Home

8 Thus says the LORD:
In a time of favor I have answered you,
   on a day of salvation I have helped you;
I have kept you and given you
   as a covenant to the people,ᶜ
to establish the land,
   to apportion the desolate heritages;
9 saying to the prisoners, "Come out,"
   to those who are in darkness, "Show
      yourselves."
They shall feed along the ways,
   on all the bare heightsᵈ shall be their
      pasture;
10 they shall not hunger or thirst,
   neither scorching wind nor sun shall strike
      them down,
for he who has pity on them will lead them,
   and by springs of water will guide them.
11 And I will turn all my mountains into a road,
   and my highways shall be raised up.
12 Lo, these shall come from far away,
   and lo, these from the north and from the
      west,
   and these from the land of Syene.ᵉ

13 Sing for joy, O heavens, and exult, O earth;
   break forth, O mountains, into singing!
For the LORD has comforted his people,
   and will have compassion on his suffering
      ones.

ᵇ 49:3 a Prince of Power. or, "Israel."   ᶜ Meaning of Heb uncertain   ᵈ Or the trails   ᵉ Q Ms: MT Sinim

King James

14But Zion said, The LORD hath forsaken me, and my Lord hath forgotten me.

15Can a woman forget her sucking child, that she should not have compassion on the son of her womb? yea, they may forget, yet will I not forget thee.

16Behold, I have graven thee upon the palms of *my* hands; thy walls *are* continually before me.

17Thy children shall make haste; thy destroyers and they that made thee waste shall go forth of thee.

18¶ Lift up thine eyes round about, and behold: all these gather themselves together, *and* come to thee. *As* I live, saith the LORD, thou shalt surely clothe thee with them all, as with an ornament, and bind them *on thee*, as a bride *doeth*.

19For thy waste and thy desolate places, and the land of thy destruction, shall even now be too narrow by reason of the inhabitants, and they that swallowed thee up shall be far away.

20The children which thou shalt have, after thou hast lost the other, shall say again in thine ears, The place *is* too strait for me: give place to me that I may dwell.

21Then shalt thou say in thine heart, Who hath begotten me these, seeing I have lost my children, and am desolate, a captive, and removing to and fro? and who hath brought up these? Behold, I was left alone; these, where *had* they *been*?

22Thus saith the Lord GOD, Behold, I will lift up mine hand to the Gentiles, and set up my standard to the people: and they shall bring thy sons in *their* arms, and thy daughters shall be carried upon *their* shoulders.

23And kings shall be thy nursing fathers, and their queens thy nursing mothers: they shall bow down to thee with *their* face toward the earth, and lick up the dust of thy feet; and thou shalt know that I *am* the LORD: for they shall not be ashamed that wait for me.

24¶ Shall the prey be taken from the mighty, or the lawful captive delivered?

25But thus saith the LORD, Even the captives of the mighty shall be taken away, and the prey of the terrible shall be delivered: for I will contend with him that contendeth with thee, and I will save thy children.

26And I will feed them that oppress thee with their own flesh; and they shall be drunken with their own blood, as with sweet wine: and all flesh shall know that I the LORD *am* thy Saviour and thy Redeemer, the mighty One of Jacob.

New International

14But Zion said, "The LORD has forsaken me,
  the Lord has forgotten me."

15"Can a mother forget the baby at her breast
  and have no compassion on the child she has
    borne?
Though she may forget,
  I will not forget you!
16See, I have engraved you on the palms of my
    hands;
  your walls are ever before me.
17Your sons hasten back,
  and those who laid you waste depart from
    you.
18Lift up your eyes and look around;
  all your sons gather and come to you.
As surely as I live," declares the LORD,
  "you will wear them all as ornaments;
  you will put them on, like a bride.

19"Though you were ruined and made desolate
  and your land laid waste,
now you will be too small for your people,
  and those who devoured you will be far
    away.
20The children born during your bereavement
  will yet say in your hearing,
'This place is too small for us;
  give us more space to live in.'
21Then you will say in your heart,
  'Who bore me these?
I was bereaved and barren;
  I was exiled and rejected.
Who brought these up?
  I was left all alone,
but these—where have they come from?' "

22This is what the Sovereign LORD says:

"See, I will beckon to the Gentiles,
  I will lift up my banner to the peoples;
they will bring your sons in their arms
  and carry your daughters on their shoulders.
23Kings will be your foster fathers,
  and their queens your nursing mothers.
They will bow down before you with their faces
    to the ground;
  they will lick the dust at your feet.
Then you will know that I am the LORD;
  those who hope in me will not be
    disappointed."

24Can plunder be taken from warriors,
  or captives rescued from the fierce[a]?

25But this is what the LORD says:

"Yes, captives will be taken from warriors,
  and plunder retrieved from the fierce;
I will contend with those who contend with
    you,
  and your children I will save.
26I will make your oppressors eat their own flesh;
  they will be drunk on their own blood, as
    with wine.
Then all mankind will know
  that I, the LORD, am your Savior,
  your Redeemer, the Mighty One of Jacob."

---

[a] 24 Dead Sea Scrolls, Vulgate and Syriac (see also Septuagint and verse 25); Masoretic Text *righteous*

Living Bible

14Yet they say, "My Lord deserted us; he has forgotten us."

15"Never! Can a mother forget her little child and not have love for her own son? Yet even if that should be, I will not forget you. 16See, I have tattooed your name upon my palm and ever before me is a picture of Jerusalem's walls in ruins. 17Soon your rebuilders shall come and chase away all those destroying you. 18Look and see, for the Lord has vowed that all your enemies shall come and be your slaves. They will be as jewels to display, as bridal ornaments.

19"Even the most desolate parts of your abandoned land shall soon be crowded with your people, and your enemies who enslaved you shall be far away. 20The generations born in exile shall return and say, 'We need more room! It's crowded here!' 21Then you will think to yourself, 'Who has given me all these? For most of my children were killed and the rest were carried away into exile, leaving me here alone. Who bore these? Who raised them for me?' "

22The Lord God says, "See, I will give a signal to the Gentiles and they shall carry your little sons back to you in their arms, and your daughters on their shoulders. 23Kings and queens shall serve you; they shall care for all your needs. They shall bow to the earth before you, and lick the dust from off your feet; then you shall know I am the Lord. Those who wait for me shall never be ashamed."

24Who can snatch the prey from the hands of a mighty man? Who can demand that a tyrant let his captives go? 25But the Lord says, "Even the captives of the most mighty and most terrible shall all be freed; for I will fight those who fight you, and I will save your children. 26I will feed your enemies with their own flesh and they shall be drunk with rivers of their own blood. All the world shall know that I, the Lord, am your Savior and Redeemer, the Mighty One of Israel."

New Revised Standard

14 But Zion said, "The LORD has forsaken me,
my Lord has forgotten me."
15 Can a woman forget her nursing child,
or show no compassion for the child of her
womb?
Even these may forget,
yet I will not forget you.
16 See, I have inscribed you on the palms of my
hands;
your walls are continually before me.
17 Your builders outdo your destroyers,b
and those who laid you waste go away from
you.
18 Lift up your eyes all around and see;
they all gather, they come to you.
As I live, says the LORD,
you shall put all of them on like an
ornament,
and like a bride you shall bind them on.

19 Surely your waste and your desolate places
and your devastated land—
surely now you will be too crowded for your
inhabitants,
and those who swallowed you up will be far
away.
20 The children born in the time of your
bereavement
will yet say in your hearing:
"The place is too crowded for me;
make room for me to settle."
21 Then you will say in your heart,
"Who has borne me these?
I was bereaved and barren,
exiled and put away—
so who has reared these?
I was left all alone—
where then have these come from?"

22 Thus says the Lord GOD:
I will soon lift up my hand to the nations,
and raise my signal to the peoples;
and they shall bring your sons in their bosom,
and your daughters shall be carried on their
shoulders.
23 Kings shall be your foster fathers,
and their queens your nursing mothers.
With their faces to the ground they shall bow
down to you,
and lick the dust of your feet.
Then you will know that I am the LORD;
those who wait for me shall not be put to
shame.

24 Can the prey be taken from the mighty,
or the captives of a tyrantc be rescued?
25 But thus says the LORD:
Even the captives of the mighty shall be
taken,
and the prey of the tyrant be rescued;
for I will contend with those who contend
with you,
and I will save your children.
26 I will make your oppressors eat their own
flesh,
and they shall be drunk with their own
blood as with wine.
Then all flesh shall know
that I am the LORD your Savior,
and your Redeemer, the Mighty One of
Jacob.

b Or Your children come swiftly; your destroyers   c Q Ms Syr Vg: MT of
a righteous person

King James

50 THUS SAITH the Lord, Where *is* the bill of your mother's divorcement, whom I have put away? or which of my creditors *is it* to whom I have sold you? Behold, for your iniquities have ye sold yourselves, and for your transgressions is your mother put away.

2Wherefore, when I came, *was there* no man? when I called, *was there* none to answer? Is my hand shortened at all, that it cannot redeem? or have I no power to deliver? behold, at my rebuke I dry up the sea, I make the rivers a wilderness: their fish stinketh, because *there is* no water, and dieth for thirst.

3I clothe the heavens with blackness, and I make sackcloth their covering.

4The Lord God hath given me the tongue of the learned, that I should know how to speak a word in season to *him that is* weary: he wakeneth morning by morning, he wakeneth mine ear to hear as the learned.

5¶ The Lord God hath opened mine ear, and I was not rebellious, neither turned away back.

6I gave my back to the smiters, and my cheeks to them that plucked off the hair: I hid not my face from shame and spitting.

7¶ For the Lord God will help me; therefore shall I not be confounded: therefore have I set my face like a flint, and I know that I shall not be ashamed.

8*He is* near that justifieth me; who will contend with me? let us stand together: who *is* mine adversary? let him come near to me.

9Behold, the Lord God will help me; who *is* he *that* shall condemn me? lo, they all shall wax old as a garment; the moth shall eat them up.

10¶ Who *is* among you that feareth the Lord, that obeyeth the voice of his servant, that walketh in darkness, and hath no light? let him trust in the name of the Lord, and stay upon his God.

11Behold, all ye that kindle a fire, that compass *your-selves* about with sparks: walk in the light of your fire, and in the sparks *that* ye have kindled. This shall ye have of mine hand; ye shall lie down in sorrow.

New International

Israel's Sin and the Servant's Obedience

50 THIS IS what the Lord says:
"Where is your mother's certificate of
    divorce
  with which I sent her away?
Or to which of my creditors
  did I sell you?
Because of your sins you were sold;
  because of your transgressions your mother
      was sent away.
2When I came, why was there no one?
  When I called, why was there no one to
      answer?
Was my arm too short to ransom you?
  Do I lack the strength to rescue you?
By a mere rebuke I dry up the sea,
  I turn rivers into a desert;
their fish rot for lack of water
  and die of thirst.
3I clothe the sky with darkness
  and make sackcloth its covering."

4The Sovereign Lord has given me an instructed
      tongue,
  to know the word that sustains the weary.
He wakens me morning by morning,
  wakens my ear to listen like one being taught.
5The Sovereign Lord has opened my ears,
  and I have not been rebellious;
  I have not drawn back.
6I offered my back to those who beat me,
  my cheeks to those who pulled out my beard;
I did not hide my face
  from mocking and spitting.
7Because the Sovereign Lord helps me,
  I will not be disgraced.
Therefore have I set my face like flint,
  and I know I will not be put to shame.
8He who vindicates me is near.
  Who then will bring charges against me?
  Let us face each other!
Who is my accuser?
  Let him confront me!
9It is the Sovereign Lord who helps me.
  Who is he that will condemn me?
They will all wear out like a garment;
  the moths will eat them up.

10Who among you fears the Lord
  and obeys the word of his servant?
Let him who walks in the dark,
  who has no light,
trust in the name of the Lord
  and rely on his God.
11But now, all you who light fires
  and provide yourselves with flaming torches,
go, walk in the light of your fires
  and of the torches you have set ablaze.
This is what you shall receive from my hand:
  You will lie down in torment.

Living Bible

50 THE LORD asks, Did I sell you to my creditors? Is that why you aren't here? Is your mother gone because I divorced her and sent her away? No, you went away as captives because of your sins. And your mother, too, was taken in payment for your sins. [2]Was I too weak to save you? Is that why the house is silent and empty when I come home? Have I no longer power to deliver? No, that is not the reason! For I can rebuke the sea and make it dry! I can turn the rivers into deserts, covered with dying fish. [3]I am the one who sends the darkness out across the skies.

[4]The Lord God has given me his words of wisdom so that I may know what I should say to all these weary ones. Morning by morning he wakens me and opens my understanding to his will. [5]The Lord God has spoken to me and I have listened; I do not rebel nor turn away. [6]I give my back to the whip, and my cheeks to those who pull out the beard. I do not hide from shame—they spit in my face.

[7]Because the Lord God helps me, I will not be dismayed; therefore, I have set my face like flint to do his will, and I know that I will triumph. [8]He who gives me justice is near. Who will dare to fight against me now? Where are my enemies? Let them appear! [9]See, the Lord God is for me! Who shall declare me guilty? All my enemies shall be destroyed like old clothes eaten up by moths!

[10]Who among you fears the Lord and obeys his Servant? If such men walk in darkness, without one ray of light, let them trust the Lord, let them rely upon their God. [11]But see here, you who live in your own light, and warm yourselves from your own fires and not from God's; you will live among sorrows.

New Revised Standard

50 THUS SAYS the LORD:
Where is your mother's bill of divorce
with which I put her away?
Or which of my creditors is it
to whom I have sold you?
No, because of your sins you were sold,
and for your transgressions your mother was
put away.
[2] Why was no one there when I came?
Why did no one answer when I called?
Is my hand shortened, that it cannot redeem?
Or have I no power to deliver?
By my rebuke I dry up the sea,
I make the rivers a desert;
their fish stink for lack of water,
and die of thirst.[a]
[3] I clothe the heavens with blackness,
and make sackcloth their covering.

The Servant's Humiliation and Vindication

[4] The Lord GOD has given me
the tongue of a teacher,[b]
that I may know how to sustain
the weary with a word.
Morning by morning he wakens—
wakens my ear
to listen as those who are taught.
[5] The Lord GOD has opened my ear,
and I was not rebellious,
I did not turn backward.
[6] I gave my back to those who struck me,
and my cheeks to those who pulled out the
beard;
I did not hide my face
from insult and spitting.

[7] The Lord GOD helps me;
therefore I have not been disgraced;
therefore I have set my face like flint,
and I know that I shall not be put to shame;
[8] he who vindicates me is near.
Who will contend with me?
Let us stand up together.
Who are my adversaries?
Let them confront me.
[9] It is the Lord GOD who helps me;
who will declare me guilty?
All of them will wear out like a garment;
the moth will eat them up.

[10] Who among you fears the LORD
and obeys the voice of his servant,
who walks in darkness
and has no light,
yet trusts in the name of the LORD
and relies upon his God?
[11] But all of you are kindlers of fire,
lighters of firebrands.[c]
Walk in the flame of your fire,
and among the brands that you have
kindled!
This is what you shall have from my hand:
you shall lie down in torment.

[a] Or *die on the thirsty ground*   [b] Cn: Heb *of those who are taught*   [c] Syr: Heb *you gird yourselves with firebrands*

King James

51 HEARKEN TO me, ye that follow after righteousness, ye that seek the LORD: look unto the rock *whence* ye are hewn, and to the hole of the pit *whence* ye are digged.

2Look unto Abraham your father, and unto Sarah *that* bare you: for I called him alone, and blessed him, and increased him.

3For the LORD shall comfort Zion: he will comfort all her waste places; and he will make her wilderness like Eden, and her desert like the garden of the LORD; joy and gladness shall be found therein, thanksgiving, and the voice of melody.

4¶ Hearken unto me, my people; and give ear unto me, O my nation: for a law shall proceed from me, and I will make my judgment to rest for a light of the people.

5My righteousness *is* near; my salvation is gone forth, and mine arms shall judge the people; the isles shall wait upon me, and on mine arm shall they trust.

6Lift up your eyes to the heavens, and look upon the earth beneath: for the heavens shall vanish away like smoke, and the earth shall wax old like a garment, and they that dwell therein shall die in like manner: but my salvation shall be for ever, and my righteousness shall not be abolished.

7¶ Hearken unto me, ye that know righteousness, the people in whose heart *is* my law; fear ye not the reproach of men, neither be ye afraid of their revilings.

8For the moth shall eat them up like a garment, and the worm shall eat them like wool: but my righteousness shall be for ever, and my salvation from generation to generation.

9¶ Awake, awake, put on strength, O arm of the LORD; awake, as in the ancient days, in the generations of old. *Art* thou not it that hath cut Rahab, *and* wounded the dragon?

10*Art* thou not it which hath dried the sea, the waters of the great deep; that hath made the depths of the sea a way for the ransomed to pass over?

11Therefore the redeemed of the LORD shall return, and come with singing unto Zion; and everlasting joy *shall be* upon their head: they shall obtain gladness and joy; *and* sorrow and mourning shall flee away.

12I, *even* I, *am* he that comforteth you: who *art* thou, that thou shouldest be afraid of a man *that* shall die, and of the son of man *which* shall be made *as* grass;

New International

Everlasting Salvation for Zion

51 "LISTEN TO me, you who pursue righteousness
  and who seek the LORD:
Look to the rock from which you were cut
  and to the quarry from which you were hewn;
2look to Abraham, your father,
  and to Sarah, who gave you birth.
When I called him he was but one,
  and I blessed him and made him many.
3The LORD will surely comfort Zion
  and will look with compassion on all her ruins;
he will make her deserts like Eden,
  her wastelands like the garden of the LORD.
Joy and gladness will be found in her,
  thanksgiving and the sound of singing.

4"Listen to me, my people;
  hear me, my nation:
The law will go out from me;
  my justice will become a light to the nations.
5My righteousness draws near speedily,
  my salvation is on the way,
  and my arm will bring justice to the nations.
The islands will look to me
  and wait in hope for my arm.
6Lift up your eyes to the heavens,
  look at the earth beneath;
the heavens will vanish like smoke,
  the earth will wear out like a garment
  and its inhabitants die like flies.
But my salvation will last forever,
  my righteousness will never fail.

7"Hear me, you who know what is right,
  you people who have my law in your hearts:
Do not fear the reproach of men
  or be terrified by their insults.
8For the moth will eat them up like a garment;
  the worm will devour them like wool.
But my righteousness will last forever,
  my salvation through all generations."

9Awake, awake! Clothe yourself with strength,
  O arm of the LORD;
awake, as in days gone by,
  as in generations of old.
Was it not you who cut Rahab to pieces,
  who pierced that monster through?
10Was it not you who dried up the sea,
  the waters of the great deep,
who made a road in the depths of the sea
  so that the redeemed might cross over?
11The ransomed of the LORD will return.
  They will enter Zion with singing;
  everlasting joy will crown their heads.
Gladness and joy will overtake them,
  and sorrow and sighing will flee away.

12"I, even I, am he who comforts you.
  Who are you that you fear mortal men,
  the sons of men, who are but grass,

Living Bible

51 LISTEN TO me, all who hope for deliverance, who seek the Lord! Consider the quarry from which you were mined, the rock from which you were cut! Yes, think about your ancestors Abraham and Sarah, from whom you came. You worry at being so small and few, but Abraham was only *one* when I called him. But when I blessed him, he became a great nation. ³And the Lord will bless Israel again, and make her deserts blossom; her barren wilderness will become as beautiful as the Garden of Eden. Joy and gladness will be found there, thanksgiving and lovely songs.

⁴Listen to me, my people; listen, O Israel, for I will see that right prevails. ⁵My mercy and justice are coming soon; your salvation is on the way. I will rule the nations; they shall wait for me and long for me to come. ⁶Look high in the skies and watch the earth beneath, for the skies shall disappear like smoke, the earth shall wear out like a garment, and the people of the earth shall die like flies. But my salvation lasts forever; my righteous rule will never die nor end.

⁷Listen to me, you who know the right from wrong and cherish my laws in your hearts: don't be afraid of people's scorn or their slanderous talk. ⁸For the moth shall destroy them like garments; the worm shall eat them like wool; but my justice and mercy shall last forever, and my salvation from generation to generation.

⁹Awake, O Lord! Rise up and robe yourself with strength. Rouse yourself as in the days of old when you slew Egypt, the dragon of the Nile.ᵃ ¹⁰Are you not the same today, the mighty God who dried up the sea, making a path right through it for your ransomed ones? ¹¹The time will come when God's redeemed will all come home again. They shall come with singing to Jerusalem, filled with joy and everlasting gladness; sorrow and mourning will all disappear.

¹²I, even I, am he who comforts you and gives you all this joy. So what right have you to fear mere mortal men, who wither like the grass and disappear? ¹³And yet

New Revised Standard

Blessings in Store for God's People

51 LISTEN TO me, you that pursue righteousness,
    you that seek the LORD.
Look to the rock from which you were hewn,
    and to the quarry from which you were dug.
2 Look to Abraham your father
    and to Sarah who bore you;
for he was but one when I called him,
    but I blessed him and made him many.
3 For the LORD will comfort Zion;
    he will comfort all her waste places,
and will make her wilderness like Eden,
    her desert like the garden of the LORD;
joy and gladness will be found in her,
    thanksgiving and the voice of song.

4 Listen to me, my people,
    and give heed to me, my nation;
for a teaching will go out from me,
    and my justice for a light to the peoples.
5 I will bring near my deliverance swiftly,
    my salvation has gone out
    and my arms will rule the peoples;
the coastlands wait for me,
    and for my arm they hope.
6 Lift up your eyes to the heavens,
    and look at the earth beneath;
for the heavens will vanish like smoke,
    the earth will wear out like a garment,
    and those who live on it will die like
        gnats;ᵇ
but my salvation will be forever,
    and my deliverance will never be ended.

7 Listen to me, you who know righteousness,
    you people who have my teaching in your
        hearts;
do not fear the reproach of others,
    and do not be dismayed when they revile
        you.
8 For the moth will eat them up like a garment,
    and the worm will eat them like wool;
but my deliverance will be forever,
    and my salvation to all generations.

9 Awake, awake, put on strength,
    O arm of the LORD!
Awake, as in days of old,
    the generations of long ago!
Was it not you who cut Rahab in pieces,
    who pierced the dragon?
10 Was it not you who dried up the sea,
    the waters of the great deep;
who made the depths of the sea a way
    for the redeemed to cross over?
11 So the ransomed of the LORD shall return,
    and come to Zion with singing;
everlasting joy shall be upon their heads;
    they shall obtain joy and gladness,
    and sorrow and sighing shall flee away.

12 I, I am he who comforts you;
    why then are you afraid of a mere mortal
        who must die,
    a human being who fades like grass?

ᵃ 51:9 Egypt, the dragon, literally, "Rahab, the dragon."   ᵇ Or *in like manner*

King James

13And forgettest the LORD thy maker, that hath stretched forth the heavens, and laid the foundations of the earth; and hast feared continually every day because of the fury of the oppressor, as if he were ready to destroy? and where *is* the fury of the oppressor?

14The captive exile hasteneth that he may be loosed, and that he should not die in the pit, nor that his bread should fail.

15But I *am* the LORD thy God, that divided the sea, whose waves roared: The LORD of hosts *is* his name.

16And I have put my words in thy mouth, and I have covered thee in the shadow of mine hand, that I may plant the heavens, and lay the foundations of the earth, and say unto Zion, Thou *art* my people.

17¶ Awake, awake, stand up, O Jerusalem, which hast drunk at the hand of the LORD the cup of his fury; thou hast drunken the dregs of the cup of trembling, *and* wrung *them* out.

18*There is* none to guide her among all the sons *whom* she hath brought forth; neither *is there any* that taketh her by the hand of all the sons *that* she hath brought up.

19These two *things* are come unto thee; who shall be sorry for thee? desolation, and destruction, and the famine, and the sword: by whom shall I comfort thee?

20Thy sons have fainted, they lie at the head of all the streets, as a wild bull in a net: they are full of the fury of the LORD, the rebuke of thy God.

21¶ Therefore hear now this, thou afflicted, and drunken, but not with wine:

22Thus saith thy Lord the LORD, and thy God *that* pleadeth the cause of his people, Behold, I have taken out of thine hand the cup of trembling, *even* the dregs of the cup of my fury; thou shalt no more drink it again:

23But I will put it into the hand of them that afflict thee; which have said to thy soul, Bow down, that we may go over: and thou hast laid thy body as the ground, and as the street, to them that went over.

New International

13that you forget the LORD your Maker,
    who stretched out the heavens
    and laid the foundations of the earth,
that you live in constant terror every day
    because of the wrath of the oppressor,
    who is bent on destruction?
For where is the wrath of the oppressor?
14   The cowering prisoners will soon be set free;
    they will not die in their dungeon,
    nor will they lack bread.
15For I am the LORD your God,
    who churns up the sea so that its waves
        roar—
    the LORD Almighty is his name.
16I have put my words in your mouth
    and covered you with the shadow of my
        hand—
I who set the heavens in place,
    who laid the foundations of the earth,
    and who say to Zion, 'You are my people.' "

The Cup of the LORD's Wrath

17Awake, awake!
    Rise up, O Jerusalem,
you who have drunk from the hand of the LORD
    the cup of his wrath,
you who have drained to its dregs
    the goblet that makes men stagger.
18Of all the sons she bore
    there was none to guide her;
of all the sons she reared
    there was none to take her by the hand.
19These double calamities have come upon you—
    who can comfort you?—
ruin and destruction, famine and sword—
    who can[a] console you?
20Your sons have fainted;
    they lie at the head of every street,
    like antelope caught in a net.
They are filled with the wrath of the LORD
    and the rebuke of your God.

21Therefore hear this, you afflicted one,
    made drunk, but not with wine.
22This is what your Sovereign LORD says,
    your God, who defends his people:
"See, I have taken out of your hand
    the cup that made you stagger;
from that cup, the goblet of my wrath,
    you will never drink again.
23I will put it into the hands of your tormentors,
    who said to you,
    'Fall prostrate that we may walk over you.'
And you made your back like the ground,
    like a street to be walked over."

52 AWAKE, AWAKE; put on thy strength, O Zion; put on thy beautiful garments, O Jerusalem, the holy city: for henceforth there shall no more come into thee the uncircumcised and the unclean.

2Shake thyself from the dust; arise, *and* sit down, O Jerusalem: loose thyself from the bands of thy neck, O captive daughter of Zion.

52 AWAKE, AWAKE, O Zion,
    clothe yourself with strength.
Put on your garments of splendor,
    O Jerusalem, the holy city.
The uncircumcised and defiled
    will not enter you again.
2Shake off your dust;
    rise up, sit enthroned, O Jerusalem.
Free yourself from the chains on your neck,
    O captive Daughter of Zion.

---

a *19* Dead Sea Scrolls, Septuagint, Vulgate and Syriac; Masoretic Text / *how can I*

Living Bible

you have no fear of God, your Maker—you have forgotten him, the one who spread the stars throughout the skies and made the earth. Will you be in constant dread of men's oppression, and fear their anger all day long? [14]Soon, soon you slaves shall be released; dungeon, starvation and death are not your fate. [15]For I am the Lord your God, the Lord Almighty, who dried a path for you right through the sea, between the roaring waves. [16]And I have put my words in your mouth and hidden you safe within my hand. I planted the stars in place and molded all the earth. I am the one who says to Israel, "You are mine."

[17]Wake up, wake up, Jerusalem! You have drunk enough from the cup of the fury of the Lord. You have drunk to the dregs the cup of terror and squeezed out the last drops. [18]Not one of her sons is left alive to help or tell her what to do. [19]These two things have been your lot: desolation and destruction. Yes, famine and the sword. And who is left to sympathize? Who is left to comfort you? [20]For your sons have fainted and lie in the streets, helpless as wild goats caught in a net. The Lord has poured out his fury and rebuke upon them. [21]But listen now to this, afflicted ones—full of troubles and in a stupor (but not from being drunk)— [22]this is what the Lord says, the Lord your God who cares for his people: "See, I take from your hands the terrible cup; you shall drink no more of my fury; it is gone at last. [23]But I will put that terrible cup into the hands of those who tormented you and trampled your souls to the dust and walked upon your backs."

52 WAKE UP, wake up, Jerusalem, and clothe yourselves with strength [from God[b]]. Put on your beautiful clothes, O Zion, Holy City; for sinners—those who turn from God—will no longer enter your gates. [2]Rise from the dust, Jerusalem; take off the slave bands from your neck, O captive daughter of Zion. [3]For

[b] 52:1 from God, implied.

New Revised Standard

[13] You have forgotten the LORD, your Maker,
     who stretched out the heavens
     and laid the foundations of the earth.
You fear continually all day long
     because of the fury of the oppressor,
who is bent on destruction.
     But where is the fury of the oppressor?
[14] The oppressed shall speedily be released;
     they shall not die and go down to the Pit,
     nor shall they lack bread.
[15] For I am the LORD your God,
     who stirs up the sea so that its waves
          roar—
     the LORD of hosts is his name.
[16] I have put my words in your mouth,
     and hidden you in the shadow of my hand,
stretching out[c] the heavens
     and laying the foundations of the earth,
     and saying to Zion, "You are my people."

[17] Rouse yourself, rouse yourself!
     Stand up, O Jerusalem,
you who have drunk at the hand of the LORD
     the cup of his wrath,
who have drunk to the dregs
     the bowl of staggering.
[18] There is no one to guide her
     among all the children she has borne;
there is no one to take her by the hand
     among all the children she has brought up.
[19] These two things have befallen you
     —who will grieve with you?—
devastation and destruction, famine and
          sword—
     who will comfort you?[d]
[20] Your children have fainted,
     they lie at the head of every street
     like an antelope in a net;
they are full of the wrath of the LORD,
     the rebuke of your God.

[21] Therefore hear this, you who are wounded,[e]
     who are drunk, but not with wine:
[22] Thus says your Sovereign, the LORD,
     your God who pleads the cause of his
          people:
See, I have taken from your hand the cup of
          staggering;
you shall drink no more
     from the bowl of my wrath.
[23] And I will put it into the hand of your
          tormentors,
     who have said to you,
     "Bow down, that we may walk on you";
and you have made your back like the ground
     and like the street for them to walk on.

Let Zion Rejoice

52 AWAKE, AWAKE,
     put on your strength, O Zion!
Put on your beautiful garments,
     O Jerusalem, the holy city;
for the uncircumcised and the unclean
     shall enter you no more.
[2] Shake yourself from the dust, rise up,
     O captive[f] Jerusalem;
loose the bonds from your neck,
     O captive daughter Zion!

[c] Syr: Heb planting   [d] Q Ms Gk Syr Vg: MT how may I comfort you?   [e] Or humbled   [f] Cn: Heb rise up, sit

King James

³For thus saith the LORD, Ye have sold yourselves for nought; and ye shall be redeemed without money.

⁴For thus saith the Lord GOD, My people went down aforetime into Egypt to sojourn there; and the Assyrian oppressed them without cause.

⁵Now therefore, what have I here, saith the LORD, that my people is taken away for nought? they that rule over them make them to howl, saith the LORD; and my name continually every day *is* blasphemed.

⁶Therefore my people shall know my name: therefore *they shall know* in that day that I *am* he that doth speak: behold, *it is* I.

⁷¶ How beautiful upon the mountains are the feet of him that bringeth good tidings, that publisheth peace; that bringeth good tidings of good, that publisheth salvation; that saith unto Zion, Thy God reigneth!

⁸Thy watchmen shall lift up the voice; with the voice together shall they sing: for they shall see eye to eye, when the LORD shall bring again Zion.

⁹¶ Break forth into joy, sing together, ye waste places of Jerusalem: for the LORD hath comforted his people, he hath redeemed Jerusalem.

¹⁰The LORD hath made bare his holy arm in the eyes of all the nations; and all the ends of the earth shall see the salvation of our God.

¹¹¶ Depart, depart ye, go ye out from thence; touch no unclean *thing;* go ye out of the midst of her; be ye clean, that bear the vessels of the LORD.

¹²For ye shall not go out with haste, nor go by flight: for the LORD will go before you; and the God of Israel *will be* your rearward.

¹³¶ Behold, my servant shall deal prudently, he shall be exalted and extolled, and be very high.

¹⁴As many were astonied at thee; his visage was so marred more than any man, and his form more than the sons of men:

¹⁵So shall he sprinkle many nations; the kings shall shut their mouths at him: for *that* which had not been told them shall they see; and *that* which they had not heard shall they consider.

New International

³For this is what the LORD says:

"You were sold for nothing,
  and without money you will be redeemed."

⁴For this is what the Sovereign LORD says:

"At first my people went down to Egypt to live;
  lately, Assyria has oppressed them.

⁵"And now what do I have here?" declares the LORD.

"For my people have been taken away for
    nothing,
  and those who rule them mock,^a"
               declares the LORD.
"And all day long
  my name is constantly blasphemed.
⁶Therefore my people will know my name;
  therefore in that day they will know
that it is I who foretold it.
  Yes, it is I."

⁷How beautiful on the mountains
  are the feet of those who bring good news,
who proclaim peace,
  who bring good tidings,
  who proclaim salvation,
who say to Zion,
  "Your God reigns!"
⁸Listen! Your watchmen lift up their voices;
  together they shout for joy.
When the LORD returns to Zion,
  they will see it with their own eyes.
⁹Burst into songs of joy together,
  you ruins of Jerusalem,
for the LORD has comforted his people,
  he has redeemed Jerusalem.
¹⁰The LORD will lay bare his holy arm
  in the sight of all the nations,
and all the ends of the earth will see
  the salvation of our God.

¹¹Depart, depart, go out from there!
  Touch no unclean thing!
Come out from it and be pure,
  you who carry the vessels of the LORD.
¹²But you will not leave in haste
  or go in flight;
for the LORD will go before you,
  the God of Israel will be your rear guard.

The Suffering and Glory of the Servant

¹³See, my servant will act wisely^b;
  he will be raised and lifted up and highly
    exalted.
¹⁴Just as there were many who were appalled at
    him^c—
  his appearance was so disfigured beyond that
    of any man
  and his form marred beyond human
    likeness—
¹⁵so will he sprinkle many nations,^d
  and kings will shut their mouths because of
    him.
For what they were not told, they will see,
  and what they have not heard, they will
    understand.

^a 5 Dead Sea Scrolls and Vulgate; Masoretic Text *wail*   ^b 13 Or *will prosper*   ^c 14 Hebrew *you*   ^d 15 Hebrew; Septuagint *so will many nations marvel at him*

Living Bible

the Lord says, When I sold you into exile I asked no fee from your oppressors; now I can take you back again and owe them not a cent! 4My people were tyrannized without cause by Egypt and Assyria, and I delivered them.

5And now, what is this? asks the Lord. Why are my people enslaved again, and oppressed without excuse? Those who rule them shout in exultation, and my name is constantly blasphemed, day by day. 6Therefore I will reveal my name to my people and they shall know the power in that name. Then at last they will recognize that it is I, yes, I, who speaks to them.

7How beautiful upon the mountains are the feet of those who bring the happy news of peace and salvation, the news that the God of Israel reigns. 8The watchmen shout and sing with joy, for right before their eyes they see the Lord God bring his people home again. 9Let the ruins of Jerusalem break into joyous song, for the Lord has comforted his people; he has redeemed Jerusalem. 10The Lord has bared his holy arm before the eyes of all the nations; the ends of the earth shall see the salvation of our God.

11Go now, leave your bonds and slavery. Put Babylon and all it represents far behind you—it is unclean to you. You are the holy people of the Lord; purify yourselves, all you who carry home the vessels of the Lord. 12You shall not leave in haste, running for your lives; for the Lord will go ahead of you, and he, the God of Israel, will protect you from behind.

13See, my Servante shall prosper; he shall be highly exalted. 14, 15Yet many shall be amazed when they see him—yes, even far-off foreign nations and their kings; they shall stand dumbfounded, speechless in his presence. For they shall see and understand what they had not been told before. They shall see my Servant beaten and bloodied, so disfigured one would scarcely know it was a person standing there. So shall he cleansef many nations.

New Revised Standard

3 For thus says the LORD: You were sold for nothing, and you shall be redeemed without money. 4For thus says the Lord GOD: Long ago, my people went down into Egypt to reside there as aliens; the Assyrian, too, has oppressed them without cause. 5Now therefore what am I doing here, says the LORD, seeing that my people are taken away without cause? Their rulers howl, says the LORD, and continually, all day long, my name is despised. 6Therefore my people shall know my name; therefore in that day they shall know that it is I who speak; here am I.

7 How beautiful upon the mountains
    are the feet of the messenger who
        announces peace,
    who brings good news,
        who announces salvation,
        who says to Zion, "Your God reigns."
8 Listen! Your sentinels lift up their voices,
        together they sing for joy;
    for in plain sight they see
        the return of the LORD to Zion.
9 Break forth together into singing,
        you ruins of Jerusalem;
    for the LORD has comforted his people,
        he has redeemed Jerusalem.
10 The LORD has bared his holy arm
        before the eyes of all the nations;
    and all the ends of the earth shall see
        the salvation of our God.

11 Depart, depart, go out from there!
        Touch no unclean thing;
    go out from the midst of it, purify yourselves,
        you who carry the vessels of the LORD.
12 For you shall not go out in haste,
        and you shall not go in flight;
    for the LORD will go before you,
        and the God of Israel will be your rear
        guard.

The Suffering Servant
13 See, my servant shall prosper;
        he shall be exalted and lifted up,
        and shall be very high.
14 Just as there were many who were astonished
        at himg
        —so marred was his appearance, beyond
            human semblance,
        and his form beyond that of mortals—
15 so he shall startleh many nations;
        kings shall shut their mouths because of
            him;
    for that which had not been told them they
        shall see,
    and that which they had not heard they shall
        contemplate.

e 52:13 my Servant. The Servant of the Lord, as the term is used here, is the Messiah, our Lord Jesus. This was the interpretation of this passage by Christ himself, and the writers of the New Testament, and orthodox Christianity ever since.   f 52:15 So shall he cleanse many nations, or, "So shall he startle many nations." The meaning of the Hebrew word is uncertain.

g Syr Tg: Heb you   h Meaning of Heb uncertain

King James

53 WHO HATH believed our report? and to whom is the arm of the LORD revealed?

2For he shall grow up before him as a tender plant, and as a root out of a dry ground: he hath no form nor comeliness; and when we shall see him, *there is* no beauty that we should desire him.

3He is despised and rejected of men; a man of sorrows, and acquainted with grief: and we hid as it were *our* faces from him; he was despised, and we esteemed him not.

4¶ Surely he hath borne our griefs, and carried our sorrows: yet we did esteem him stricken, smitten of God, and afflicted.

5But he *was* wounded for our transgressions, *he was* bruised for our iniquities: the chastisement of our peace *was* upon him; and with his stripes we are healed.

6All we like sheep have gone astray; we have turned every one to his own way; and the LORD hath laid on him the iniquity of us all.

7He was oppressed, and he was afflicted, yet he opened not his mouth: he is brought as a lamb to the slaughter, and as a sheep before her shearers is dumb, so he openeth not his mouth.

8He was taken from prison and from judgment: and who shall declare his generation? for he was cut off out of the land of the living: for the transgression of my people was he stricken.

9And he made his grave with the wicked, and with the rich in his death; because he had done no violence, neither *was any* deceit in his mouth.

10¶ Yet it pleased the LORD to bruise him; he hath put *him* to grief: when thou shalt make his soul an offering for sin, he shall see *his* seed, he shall prolong *his* days, and the pleasure of the LORD shall prosper in his hand.

11He shall see of the travail of his soul, *and* shall be satisfied: by his knowledge shall my righteous servant justify many; for he shall bear their iniquities.

12Therefore will I divide him *a portion* with the great, and he shall divide the spoil with the strong; because he hath poured out his soul unto death: and he was numbered with the transgressors; and he bare the sin of many, and made intercession for the transgressors.

New International

53 WHO HAS believed our message and to whom has the arm of the LORD been revealed?

2He grew up before him like a tender shoot, and like a root out of dry ground.
He had no beauty or majesty to attract us to him, nothing in his appearance that we should desire him.

3He was despised and rejected by men, a man of sorrows, and familiar with suffering.
Like one from whom men hide their faces he was despised, and we esteemed him not.

4Surely he took up our infirmities and carried our sorrows, yet we considered him stricken by God, smitten by him, and afflicted.

5But he was pierced for our transgressions, he was crushed for our iniquities; the punishment that brought us peace was upon him, and by his wounds we are healed.

6We all, like sheep, have gone astray, each of us has turned to his own way; and the LORD has laid on him the iniquity of us all.

7He was oppressed and afflicted, yet he did not open his mouth; he was led like a lamb to the slaughter, and as a sheep before her shearers is silent, so he did not open his mouth.

8By oppressiona and judgment he was taken away.
And who can speak of his descendants?
For he was cut off from the land of the living; for the transgression of my people he was stricken.b

9He was assigned a grave with the wicked, and with the rich in his death, though he had done no violence, nor was any deceit in his mouth.

10Yet it was the LORD's will to crush him and cause him to suffer, and though the LORD makesc his life a guilt offering, he will see his offspring and prolong his days, and the will of the LORD will prosper in his hand.

11After the suffering of his soul, he will see the light ˌof lifeˌd and be satisfiede; by his knowledgef my righteous servant will justify many, and he will bear their iniquities.

12Therefore I will give him a portion among the great,g and he will divide the spoils with the strong,h because he poured out his life unto death, and was numbered with the transgressors.
For he bore the sin of many, and made intercession for the transgressors.

ᵃ 8 Or *From arrest*   ᵇ 8 Or *away.* / *Yet who of his generation considered* / *that he was cut off from the land of the living* / *for the transgression of my people,* / *to whom the blow was due?*   ᶜ 10 Hebrew *though you make*   ᵈ 11 Dead Sea Scrolls (see also Septuagint); Masoretic Text does not have *the light ˌof life,.*   ᵉ 11 Or (with Masoretic Text) ¹¹*He will see the result of the suffering of his soul* / *and be satisfied*   ᶠ 11 Or *by knowledge of him*   ᵍ 12 Or *many*   ʰ 12 Or *numerous*

Living Bible

53 BUT, OH, how few believe it! Who will listen? To whom will God reveal his saving power? ²In God's eyesⁱ he was like a tender green shoot, sprouting from a root in dry and sterile ground. But in our eyes there was no attractiveness at all, nothing to make us want him. ³We despised him and rejected him—a man of sorrows, acquainted with bitterest grief. We turned our backs on him and looked the other way when he went by. He was despised and we didn't care.

⁴Yet it was *our* grief he bore, *our* sorrows that weighed him down. And we thought his troubles were a punishment from God, for his *own* sins! ⁵But he was wounded and bruised for *our* sins. He was beaten that we might have peace; he was lashed—and we were healed! ⁶*We*—every one of us—have strayed away like sheep! *We,* who left God's paths to follow our own. Yet God laid on *him* the guilt and sins of every one of us!

⁷He was oppressed and he was afflicted, yet he never said a word. He was brought as a lamb to the slaughter; and as a sheep before her shearers is dumb, so he stood silent before the ones condemning him. ⁸From prison and trial they led him away to his death. But who among the people of that day realized it was their sins that he was dying for—that he was suffering their punishment? ⁹He was buried like a criminal, but in a rich man's grave; but he had done no wrong, and had never spoken an evil word.

¹⁰But it was the Lord's good plan to bruise him and fill him with grief. However when his soul has been made an offering for sin, then he shall have a multitude of children, many heirs. He shall live againʲ and God's program shall prosper in his hands. ¹¹And when he sees all that is accomplished by the anguish of his soul, he shall be satisfied; and because of what he has experienced, my righteous Servant shall make many to be counted righteous before God, for he shall bear all their sins. ¹²Therefore I will give him the honors of one who is mighty and great, because he has poured out his soul unto death. He was counted as a sinner, and he bore the sins of many, and he pled with God for sinners.

New Revised Standard

53 WHO HAS believed what we have heard? And to whom has the arm of the LORD been revealed?
² For he grew up before him like a young plant, and like a root out of dry ground; he had no form or majesty that we should look at him, nothing in his appearance that we should desire him.
³ He was despised and rejected by others; a man of sufferingᵏ and acquainted with infirmity; and as one from whom others hide their facesˡ he was despised, and we held him of no account.

⁴ Surely he has borne our infirmities and carried our diseases; yet we accounted him stricken, struck down by God, and afflicted.
⁵ But he was wounded for our transgressions, crushed for our iniquities; upon him was the punishment that made us whole, and by his bruises we are healed.
⁶ All we like sheep have gone astray; we have all turned to our own way, and the LORD has laid on him the iniquity of us all.

⁷ He was oppressed, and he was afflicted, yet he did not open his mouth; like a lamb that is led to the slaughter, and like a sheep that before its shearers is silent, so he did not open his mouth.
⁸ By a perversion of justice he was taken away. Who could have imagined his future? For he was cut off from the land of the living, stricken for the transgression of my people.
⁹ They made his grave with the wicked and his tombᵐ with the rich,ⁿ although he had done no violence, and there was no deceit in his mouth.

¹⁰ Yet it was the will of the LORD to crush him with pain.º When you make his life an offering for sin,ᵖ he shall see his offspring, and shall prolong his days; through him the will of the LORD shall prosper.
¹¹ Out of his anguish he shall see light;q he shall find satisfaction through his knowledge. The righteous one,ʳ my servant, shall make many righteous, and he shall bear their iniquities.
¹² Therefore I will allot him a portion with the great, and he shall divide the spoil with the strong; because he poured out himself to death, and was numbered with the transgressors; yet he bore the sin of many, and made intercession for the transgressors.

ᵏ Or *a man of sorrows*   ˡ Or *as one who hides his face from us*   ᵐ Q Ms: MT *and in his death*   ⁿ Cn: Heb *with a rich person*   º Or *by disease*; meaning of Heb uncertain   ᵖ Meaning of Heb uncertain   q Q Mss: MT lacks *light*   ʳ Or *and he shall find satisfaction. Through his knowledge, the righteous one*

ⁱ 53:2 *In God's eyes,* literally, "before him."   ʲ 53:10 *He shall live again,* literally, "He shall prolong his days."

King James

54 SING, O barren, thou *that* didst not bear; break forth into singing, and cry aloud, thou *that* didst not travail with child: for more *are* the children of the desolate than the children of the married wife, saith the LORD.

2Enlarge the place of thy tent, and let them stretch forth the curtains of thine habitations: spare not, lengthen thy cords, and strengthen thy stakes;

3For thou shalt break forth on the right hand and on the left; and thy seed shall inherit the Gentiles and make the desolate cities to be inhabited.

4Fear not; for thou shalt not be ashamed: neither be thou confounded; for thou shalt not be put to shame: for thou shalt forget the shame of thy youth, and shalt not remember the reproach of thy widowhood any more.

5For thy Maker *is* thine husband; the LORD of hosts *is* his name; and thy Redeemer the Holy One of Israel; The God of the whole earth shall he be called.

6For the LORD hath called thee as a woman forsaken and grieved in spirit, and a wife of youth, when thou wast refused, saith thy God.

7For a small moment have I forsaken thee; but with great mercies will I gather thee.

8In a little wrath I hid my face from thee for a moment; but with everlasting kindness will I have mercy on thee, saith the LORD thy Redeemer.

9For this *is as* the waters of Noah unto me: for *as* I have sworn that the waters of Noah should no more go over the earth; so have I sworn that I would not be wroth with thee, nor rebuke thee.

10For the mountains shall depart, and the hills be removed; but my kindness shall not depart from thee, neither shall the covenant of my peace be removed, saith the LORD that hath mercy on thee.

11¶ O thou afflicted, tossed with tempest, *and* not comforted, behold, I will lay thy stones with fair colours, and lay thy foundations with sapphires.

12And I will make thy windows of agates, and thy gates of carbuncles, and all thy borders of pleasant stones.

13And all thy children *shall be* taught of the LORD; and great *shall be* the peace of thy children.

14In righteousness shalt thou be established: thou shalt be far from oppression; for thou shalt not fear: and from terror; for it shall not come near thee.

New International

The Future Glory of Zion

54 "SING, O barren woman,
you who never bore a child;
burst into song, shout for joy,
you who were never in labor;
because more are the children of the desolate
woman
than of her who has a husband,"
says the LORD.

2"Enlarge the place of your tent,
stretch your tent curtains wide,
do not hold back;
lengthen your cords,
strengthen your stakes.

3For you will spread out to the right and to the
left;
your descendants will dispossess nations
and settle in their desolate cities.

4"Do not be afraid; you will not suffer shame.
Do not fear disgrace; you will not be
humiliated.
You will forget the shame of your youth
and remember no more the reproach of your
widowhood.

5For your Maker is your husband—
the LORD Almighty is his name—
the Holy One of Israel is your Redeemer;
he is called the God of all the earth.

6The LORD will call you back
as if you were a wife deserted and distressed
in spirit—
a wife who married young,
only to be rejected," says your God.

7"For a brief moment I abandoned you,
but with deep compassion I will bring you
back.

8In a surge of anger
I hid my face from you for a moment,
but with everlasting kindness
I will have compassion on you,"
says the LORD your Redeemer.

9"To me this is like the days of Noah,
when I swore that the waters of Noah would
never again cover the earth.
So now I have sworn not to be angry with you,
never to rebuke you again.

10Though the mountains be shaken
and the hills be removed,
yet my unfailing love for you will not be shaken
nor my covenant of peace be removed,"
says the LORD, who has compassion on you.

11"O afflicted city, lashed by storms and not
comforted,
I will build you with stones of turquoise,a
your foundations with sapphires.b

12I will make your battlements of rubies,
your gates of sparkling jewels,
and all your walls of precious stones.

13All your sons will be taught by the LORD,
and great will be your children's peace.

14In righteousness you will be established:
Tyranny will be far from you;
you will have nothing to fear.
Terror will be far removed;
it will not come near you.

a 11 The meaning of the Hebrew for this word is uncertain.   b 11 Or lapis lazuli

Living Bible

54 SING, O childless woman! Break out into loud and joyful song, Jerusalem,[c] for she who was abandoned has more blessings[d] now than she whose husband stayed! [2]Enlarge your house; build on additions; spread out your home! [3]For you will soon be bursting at the seams! And your descendants will possess the cities left behind during the exile, and rule the nations that took their lands.

[4]Fear not; you will no longer live in shame. The shame of your youth and the sorrows of widowhood will be remembered no more, [5]for your Creator will be your "husband." The Lord Almighty is his name; he is your Redeemer, the Holy One of Israel, the God of all the earth. [6]For the Lord has called you back from your grief—a young wife abandoned by her husband. [7]For a brief moment I abandoned you. But with great compassion I will take you back. [8]In a moment of anger I turned my face a little while; but with everlasting love I will have pity on you, says the Lord, your Redeemer.

[9]Just as in the time of Noah I swore that I would never again permit the waters of a flood to cover the earth and destroy its life, so now I swear that I will never again pour out my anger on you. [10]For the mountains may depart and the hills disappear, but my kindness shall not leave you. My promise of peace for you will never be broken, says the Lord who has mercy upon you.

[11]O my afflicted people, tempest-tossed and troubled, I will rebuild you on a foundation of sapphires and make the walls of your houses from precious jewels. [12]I will make your towers of sparkling agate, and your gates and walls of shining gems. [13]And all your citizens shall be taught by me, and their prosperity shall be great. [14]You will live under a government that is just and fair. Your enemies will stay far away; you will live in peace. Terror shall not come near. [15]If any nation comes to fight

New Revised Standard

The Eternal Covenant of Peace

54 SING, O barren one who did not bear;
    burst into song and shout,
  you who have not been in labor!
For the children of the desolate woman will be more
    than the children of her that is married, says the Lord.
[2] Enlarge the site of your tent,
    and let the curtains of your habitations be stretched out;
do not hold back; lengthen your cords
    and strengthen your stakes.
[3] For you will spread out to the right and to the left,
    and your descendants will possess the nations
    and will settle the desolate towns.

[4] Do not fear, for you will not be ashamed;
    do not be discouraged, for you will not suffer disgrace;
for you will forget the shame of your youth,
    and the disgrace of your widowhood you will remember no more.
[5] For your Maker is your husband,
    the Lord of hosts is his name;
the Holy One of Israel is your Redeemer,
    the God of the whole earth he is called.
[6] For the Lord has called you
    like a wife forsaken and grieved in spirit,
like the wife of a man's youth when she is cast off,
    says your God.
[7] For a brief moment I abandoned you,
    but with great compassion I will gather you.
[8] In overflowing wrath for a moment
    I hid my face from you,
but with everlasting love I will have compassion on you,
    says the Lord, your Redeemer.

[9] This is like the days of Noah to me:
    Just as I swore that the waters of Noah would never again go over the earth,
so I have sworn that I will not be angry with you
    and will not rebuke you.
[10] For the mountains may depart
    and the hills be removed,
but my steadfast love shall not depart from you,
    and my covenant of peace shall not be removed,
    says the Lord, who has compassion on you.

[11] O afflicted one, storm-tossed, and not comforted,
    I am about to set your stones in antimony,
    and lay your foundations with sapphires.[e]
[12] I will make your pinnacles of rubies,
    your gates of jewels,
    and all your wall of precious stones.
[13] All your children shall be taught by the Lord,
    and great shall be the prosperity of your children.
[14] In righteousness you shall be established;
    you shall be far from oppression, for you shall not fear;
    and from terror, for it shall not come near you.

---

[c] *54:1* Jerusalem, implied.   [d] *54:1* blessings, literally, "children."   [e] Or *lapis lazuli*

King James

15Behold, they shall surely gather together, *but* not by me: whosoever shall gather together against thee shall fall for thy sake.

16Behold, I have created the smith that bloweth the coals in the fire, and that bringeth forth an instrument for his work; and I have created the waster to destroy.

17¶ No weapon that is formed against thee shall prosper; and every tongue *that* shall rise against thee in judgment thou shalt condemn. This *is* the heritage of the servants of the LORD, and their righteousness *is* of me, saith the LORD.

55 HO, EVERY one that thirsteth, come ye to the waters, and he that hath no money; come ye, buy, and eat; yea, come, buy wine and milk without money and without price.

2Wherefore do ye spend money for *that which is* not bread? and your labour for *that which* satisfieth not? hearken diligently unto me, and eat ye *that which is* good, and let your soul delight itself in fatness.

3Incline your ear, and come unto me: hear, and your soul shall live; and I will make an everlasting covenant with you, *even* the sure mercies of David.

4Behold, I have given him *for* a witness to the people, a leader and commander to the people.

5Behold, thou shalt call a nation *that* thou knowest not, and nations *that* knew not thee shall run unto thee because of the LORD thy God, and for the Holy One of Israel; for he hath glorified thee.

6¶ Seek ye the LORD while he may be found, call ye upon him while he is near:

7Let the wicked forsake his way, and the unrighteous man his thoughts: and let him return unto the LORD, and he will have mercy upon him; and to our God, for he will abundantly pardon.

8¶ For my thoughts *are* not your thoughts, neither *are* your ways my ways, saith the LORD.

9For *as* the heavens are higher than the earth, so are my ways higher than your ways, and my thoughts than your thoughts.

10For as the rain cometh down, and the snow from heaven, and returneth not thither, but watereth the earth, and maketh it bring forth and bud, that it may give seed to the sower, and bread to the eater:

11So shall my word be that goeth forth out of my mouth: it shall not return unto me void, but it shall accomplish that which I please, and it shall prosper in the thing whereto I sent it.

New International

15If anyone does attack you, it will not be my doing;
    whoever attacks you will surrender to you.

16"See, it is I who created the blacksmith
    who fans the coals into flame
    and forges a weapon fit for its work.
And it is I who have created the destroyer to work havoc;
17   no weapon forged against you will prevail,
    and you will refute every tongue that accuses you.
This is the heritage of the servants of the LORD,
    and this is their vindication from me,"
        declares the LORD.

Invitation to the Thirsty

55 "COME, ALL you who are thirsty,
    come to the waters;
and you who have no money,
    come, buy and eat!
Come, buy wine and milk
    without money and without cost.
2Why spend money on what is not bread,
    and your labor on what does not satisfy?
Listen, listen to me, and eat what is good,
    and your soul will delight in the richest of fare.
3Give ear and come to me;
    hear me, that your soul may live.
I will make an everlasting covenant with you,
    my faithful love promised to David.
4See, I have made him a witness to the peoples,
    a leader and commander of the peoples.
5Surely you will summon nations you know not,
    and nations that do not know you will hasten to you,
because of the LORD your God,
    the Holy One of Israel,
    for he has endowed you with splendor."

6Seek the LORD while he may be found;
    call on him while he is near.
7Let the wicked forsake his way
    and the evil man his thoughts.
Let him turn to the LORD, and he will have mercy on him,
    and to our God, for he will freely pardon.

8"For my thoughts are not your thoughts,
    neither are your ways my ways,"
        declares the LORD.
9"As the heavens are higher than the earth,
    so are my ways higher than your ways
    and my thoughts than your thoughts.
10As the rain and the snow
    come down from heaven,
and do not return to it
    without watering the earth
and making it bud and flourish,
    so that it yields seed for the sower and bread for the eater,
11so is my word that goes out from my mouth:
    It will not return to me empty,
but will accomplish what I desire
    and achieve the purpose for which I sent it.

Living Bible

you, it will not be sent by me to punish you. Therefore it will be routed, for I am on your side.a 16I have created the smith who blows the coals beneath the forge and makes the weapons of destruction. And I have created the armies that destroy. 17But in that coming day, no weapon turned against you shall succeed, and you will have justice against every courtroom lie. This is the heritage of the servants of the Lord. This is the blessing I have given you, says the Lord.

55 SAY THERE! Is anyone thirsty? Come and drink—even if you have no money! Come, take your choice of wine and milk—it's all free! 2Why spend your money on food that doesn't give you strength? Why pay for groceries that do you no good? Listen and I'll tell you where to get good food that fattens up the soul! 3Come to me with your ears wide open. Listen, for the life of your soul is at stake. I am ready to make an everlasting covenant with you, to give you all the unfailing mercies and love that I had for King David.b 4He proved my power by conquering foreign nations.c 5You also will command the nations and they will come running to obey, not because of your own power or virtue but because I, the Lord your God, have glorified you.

6Seek the Lord while you can find him. Call upon him now while he is near. 7Let men cast off their wicked deeds; let them banish from their minds the very thought of doing wrong! Let them turn to the Lord that he may have mercy upon them, and to our God, for he will abundantly pardon! 8This plan of mine is not what you would work out, neither are my thoughts the same as yours! 9For just as the heavens are higher than the earth, so are my ways higher than yours, and my thoughts than yours.

10As the rain and snow come down from heaven and stay upon the ground to water the earth, and cause the grain to grow and to produce seed for the farmer and bread for the hungry, 11so also is my Word. I send it out and it always produces fruit. It shall accomplish all I want it to, and prosper everywhere I send it. 12You will

New Revised Standard

15 If anyone stirs up strife,
       it is not from me;
    whoever stirs up strife with you
       shall fall because of you.
16 See it is I who have created the smith
       who blows the fire of coals,
       and produces a weapon fit for its purpose;
    I have also created the ravager to destroy.
17   No weapon that is fashioned against you
          shall prosper,
       and you shall confute every tongue that rises
          against you in judgment.
    This is the heritage of the servants of the
       LORD
       and their vindication from me, says the
       LORD.

An Invitation to Abundant Life

55 HO, EVERYONE who thirsts,
       come to the waters;
    and you that have no money,
       come, buy and eat!
    Come, buy wine and milk
       without money and without price.
2   Why do you spend your money for that which
          is not bread,
       and your labor for that which does not
          satisfy?
    Listen carefully to me, and eat what is good,
       and delight yourselves in rich food.
3   Incline your ear, and come to me;
       listen, so that you may live.
    I will make with you an everlasting covenant,
       my steadfast, sure love for David.
4   See, I made him a witness to the peoples,
       a leader and commander for the peoples.
5   See, you shall call nations that you do not
          know,
       and nations that do not know you shall run
          to you,
    because of the LORD your God, the Holy One
       of Israel,
       for he has glorified you.

6   Seek the LORD while he may be found,
       call upon him while he is near;
7   let the wicked forsake their way,
       and the unrighteous their thoughts;
    let them return to the LORD, that he may have
          mercy on them,
       and to our God, for he will abundantly
          pardon.
8   For my thoughts are not your thoughts,
       nor are your ways my ways, says the LORD.
9   For as the heavens are higher than the earth,
       so are my ways higher than your ways
       and my thoughts than your thoughts.

10 For as the rain and the snow come down from
          heaven,
       and do not return there until they have
          watered the earth,
    making it bring forth and sprout,
       giving seed to the sower and bread to the
          eater,
11 so shall my word be that goes out from my
          mouth;
       it shall not return to me empty,
    but it shall accomplish that which I purpose,
       and succeed in the thing for which I sent it.

King James

¹²For ye shall go out with joy, and be led forth with peace: the mountains and the hills shall break forth before you into singing, and all the trees of the field shall clap *their* hands.

¹³Instead of the thorn shall come up the fir tree, and instead of the brier shall come up the myrtle tree: and it shall be to the LORD for a name, for an everlasting sign *that* shall not be cut off.

56 THUS SAITH the LORD, Keep ye judgment, and do justice: for my salvation *is* near to come, and my righteousness to be revealed.

²Blessed *is* the man *that* doeth this, and the son of man *that* layeth hold on it; that keepeth the sabbath from polluting it, and keepeth his hand from doing any evil.

³¶ Neither let the son of the stranger, that hath joined himself to the LORD, speak, saying, The LORD hath utterly separated me from his people: neither let the eunuch say, Behold, I *am* a dry tree.

⁴For thus saith the LORD unto the eunuchs that keep my sabbaths, and choose *the things* that please me, and take hold of my covenant;

⁵Even unto them will I give in mine house and within my walls a place and a name better than of sons and of daughters: I will give them an everlasting name, that shall not be cut off.

⁶Also the sons of the stranger, that join themselves to the LORD, to serve him, and to love the name of the LORD, to be his servants, every one that keepeth the sabbath from polluting it, and taketh hold of my covenant;

⁷Even them will I bring to my holy mountain, and make them joyful in my house of prayer: their burnt offerings and their sacrifices *shall be* accepted upon mine altar; for mine house shall be called an house of prayer for all people.

⁸The Lord GOD which gathereth the outcasts of Israel saith, Yet will I gather *others* to him, beside those that are gathered unto him.

⁹¶ All ye beasts of the field, come to devour, *yea,* all ye beasts in the forest.

New International

¹²You will go out in joy
    and be led forth in peace;
the mountains and hills
    will burst into song before you,
and all the trees of the field
    will clap their hands.
¹³Instead of the thornbush will grow the pine tree,
    and instead of briers the myrtle will grow.
This will be for the LORD's renown,
    for an everlasting sign,
    which will not be destroyed."

Salvation for Others

56 THIS IS what the LORD says:

    "Maintain justice
    and do what is right,
for my salvation is close at hand
    and my righteousness will soon be revealed.
²Blessed is the man who does this,
    the man who holds it fast,
who keeps the Sabbath without desecrating it,
    and keeps his hand from doing any evil."

³Let no foreigner who has bound himself to the
    LORD say,
    "The LORD will surely exclude me from his
      people."
And let not any eunuch complain,
    "I am only a dry tree."

⁴For this is what the LORD says:

    "To the eunuchs who keep my Sabbaths,
    who choose what pleases me
    and hold fast to my covenant—
⁵to them I will give within my temple and its
      walls
    a memorial and a name
    better than sons and daughters;
I will give them an everlasting name
    that will not be cut off.
⁶And foreigners who bind themselves to the
    LORD
    to serve him,
to love the name of the LORD,
    and to worship him,
all who keep the Sabbath without desecrating it
    and who hold fast to my covenant—
⁷these I will bring to my holy mountain
    and give them joy in my house of prayer.
Their burnt offerings and sacrifices
    will be accepted on my altar;
for my house will be called
    a house of prayer for all nations."
⁸The Sovereign LORD declares—
    he who gathers the exiles of Israel:
"I will gather still others to them
    besides those already gathered."

God's Accusation Against the Wicked

⁹Come, all you beasts of the field,
    come and devour, all you beasts of the forest!

Living Bible

live in joy and peace. The mountains and hills, the trees of the field—all the world around you—will rejoice. 13Where once were thorns, fir trees will grow; where briars grew, the myrtle trees will sprout up. This miracle will make the Lord's name very great and be an everlasting sign [of God's power and lovea].

56 BE JUST and fair to all, the Lord God says. Do what's right and good, for I am coming soon to rescue you. 2Blessed is the man who refuses to work during my Sabbath days of rest, but honors them; and blessed is the man who checks himself from doing wrong.

3And my blessings are for Gentiles, too, when they accept the Lord; don't let them think that I will make them second-class citizens. And this is for the eunuchs too. They can be as much mine as anyone. 4For I say this to the eunuchs who keep my Sabbaths holy and choose the things that please me, and obey my laws: 5I will give them—in my house, within my walls—a name far greater than the honor they would receive from having sons and daughters. For the name that I will give them is an everlasting one; it will never disappear.

6As for the Gentiles, the outsiders who join the people of the Lord and serve him and love his name, and are his servants and don't desecrate the Sabbath, and have accepted his covenant and promises, 7I will bring them also to my holy mountain of Jerusalem, and make them full of joy within my House of Prayer.

I will accept their sacrifices and offerings, for my Temple shall be called "A House of Prayer for All People"! 8For the Lord God who brings back the outcasts of Israel says, I will bring others too besides my people Israel.

9Come, wild animals of the field; come, tear apart the sheep; come, wild animals of the forest, devour my people.b 10For the leaders of my people—the Lord's

New Revised Standard

12 For you shall go out in joy,
    and be led back in peace;
the mountains and the hills before you
    shall burst into song,
and all the trees of the field shall clap their
    hands.
13 Instead of the thorn shall come up the cypress;
    instead of the brier shall come up the
    myrtle;
and it shall be to the LORD for a memorial,
    for an everlasting sign that shall not be cut
    off.

The Covenant Extended to All Who Obey

56 THUS SAYS the LORD:
    Maintain justice, and do what is right,
for soon my salvation will come,
    and my deliverance be revealed.

2 Happy is the mortal who does this,
    the one who holds it fast,
who keeps the sabbath, not profaning it,
    and refrains from doing any evil.

3 Do not let the foreigner joined to the LORD
    say,
    "The LORD will surely separate me from his
    people";
and do not let the eunuch say,
    "I am just a dry tree."
4 For thus says the LORD:
To the eunuchs who keep my sabbaths,
    who choose the things that please me
    and hold fast my covenant,
5 I will give, in my house and within my walls,
    a monument and a name
    better than sons and daughters;
I will give them an everlasting name
    that shall not be cut off.

6 And the foreigners who join themselves to the
    LORD,
    to minister to him, to love the name of the
    LORD,
    and to be his servants,
all who keep the sabbath, and do not profane
    it,
    and hold fast my covenant—
7 these I will bring to my holy mountain,
    and make them joyful in my house of
    prayer;
their burnt offerings and their sacrifices
    will be accepted on my altar;
for my house shall be called a house of prayer
    for all peoples.
8 Thus says the Lord GOD,
    who gathers the outcasts of Israel,
I will gather others to them
    besides those already gathered.c

The Corruption of Israel's Rulers

9 All you wild animals,
    all you wild animals in the forest, come to
    devour!

---

a 55:13 of God's power and love, implied.   b 56:9 devour my people,
implied.   c Heb besides his gathered ones

King James

10His watchmen *are* blind: they are all ignorant, they *are* all dumb dogs, they cannot bark; sleeping, lying down, loving to slumber.

11Yea, *they are* greedy dogs *which* can never have enough, and they *are* shepherds *that* cannot understand: they all look to their own way, every one for his gain, from his quarter.

12Come ye, *say they*, I will fetch wine, and we will fill ourselves with strong drink; and tomorrow shall be as this day, *and* much more abundant.

57 THE RIGHTEOUS perisheth, and no man layeth *it* to heart: and merciful men *are* taken away, none considering that the righteous is taken away from the evil *to come*.

2He shall enter into peace: they shall rest in their beds, *each one* walking *in* his uprightness.

3¶ But draw near hither, ye sons of the sorceress, the seed of the adulterer and the whore.

4Against whom do ye sport yourselves? against whom make ye a wide mouth, *and* draw out the tongue? *are* ye not children of transgression, a seed of falsehood,

5Enflaming yourselves with idols under every green tree, slaying the children in the valleys under the clefts of the rocks?

6Among the smooth *stones* of the stream *is* thy portion; they, they *are* thy lot: even to them hast thou poured a drink offering, thou hast offered a meat offering. Should I receive comfort in these?

7Upon a lofty and high mountain hast thou set thy bed: even thither wentest thou up to offer sacrifice.

8Behind the doors also and the posts hast thou set up thy remembrance: for thou hast discovered *thyself to another* than me, and art gone up; thou hast enlarged thy bed, and made thee *a covenant* with them; thou lovedst their bed where thou sawest *it*.

9And thou wentest to the king with ointment, and didst increase thy perfumes, and didst send thy messengers far off, and didst debase *thyself even* unto hell.

10Thou art wearied in the greatness of thy way; *yet* saidst thou not, There is no hope: thou hast found the life of thine hand; therefore thou wast not grieved.

New International

10Israel's watchmen are blind,
    they all lack knowledge;
they are all mute dogs,
    they cannot bark;
they lie around and dream,
    they love to sleep.
11They are dogs with mighty appetites;
    they never have enough.
They are shepherds who lack understanding;
    they all turn to their own way,
    each seeks his own gain.
12"Come," each one cries, "let me get wine!
    Let us drink our fill of beer!
And tomorrow will be like today,
    or even far better."

57 THE RIGHTEOUS perish,
    and no one ponders it in his heart;
devout men are taken away,
    and no one understands
that the righteous are taken away
    to be spared from evil.
2Those who walk uprightly
    enter into peace;
    they find rest as they lie in death.

3"But you—come here, you sons of a sorceress,
    you offspring of adulterers and prostitutes!
4Whom are you mocking?
    At whom do you sneer
    and stick out your tongue?
Are you not a brood of rebels,
    the offspring of liars?
5You burn with lust among the oaks
    and under every spreading tree;
you sacrifice your children in the ravines
    and under the overhanging crags.
6The idols among the smooth stones of the
        ravines are your portion;
    they, they are your lot.
Yes, to them you have poured out drink
        offerings
    and offered grain offerings.
    In the light of these things, should I relent?
7You have made your bed on a high and lofty
        hill;
    there you went up to offer your sacrifices.
8Behind your doors and your doorposts
    you have put your pagan symbols.
Forsaking me, you uncovered your bed,
    you climbed into it and opened it wide;
you made a pact with those whose beds you
        love,
    and you looked on their nakedness.
9You went to Molech[a] with olive oil
    and increased your perfumes.
You sent your ambassadors[b] far away;
    you descended to the grave[c] itself!
10You were wearied by all your ways,
    but you would not say, 'It is hopeless.'
You found renewal of your strength,
    and so you did not faint.

Living Bible

watchmen, his shepherds—are all blind to every danger. They are featherbrained and give no warning when danger comes. They love to lie there, love to sleep, to dream. 11And they are as greedy as dogs, never satisfied; they are stupid shepherds who only look after their own interest, each trying to get as much as he can for himself from every possible source.

12"Come," they say. "We'll get some wine and have a party; let's all get drunk. This is really living; let it go on and on, and tomorrow will be even better!"

57 THE GOOD men perish; the godly die before their time and no one seems to care or wonder why. No one seems to realize that God is taking them away from evil days ahead. 2For the godly who die shall rest in peace.

3But you—come here, you witches' sons, you offspring of adulterers and harlots! 4Who is it you mock, making faces and sticking out your tongues? You children of sinners and liars! 5You worship your idols with great zeal beneath the shade of every tree, and slay your children as human sacrifices down in the valleys, under overhanging rocks. 6Your gods are the smooth stones in the valleys. You worship them and they, not I, are your inheritance. Does all this make me happy? 7, 8You have committed adultery on the tops of the mountains, for you worship idols there, deserting me. Behind closed doors you set your idols up and worship someone other than me. This is adultery, for you are giving these idols your love, instead of loving me. 9You have taken pleasant incense and perfume to Molech as your gift. You have traveled far, even to hell itself, to find new gods to love. 10You grew weary in your search, but you never gave up. You strengthened yourself and went on. 11Why were

New Revised Standard

10   Israel'sd sentinels are blind,
        they are all without knowledge;
     they are all silent dogs
        that cannot bark;
     dreaming, lying down,
        loving to slumber.
11   The dogs have a mighty appetite;
        they never have enough.
     The shepherds also have no understanding;
        they have all turned to their own way,
        to their own gain, one and all.
12   "Come," they say, "let use get wine;
        let us fill ourselves with strong drink.
     And tomorrow will be like today,
        great beyond measure."

Israel's Futile Idolatry

57   THE RIGHTEOUS perish,
        and no one takes it to heart;
     the devout are taken away,
        while no one understands.
     For the righteous are taken away from
        calamity,
2   and they enter into peace;
     those who walk uprightly
        will rest on their couches.
3   But as for you, come here,
        you children of a sorceress,
        you offspring of an adulterer and a whore.f
4   Whom are you mocking?
        Against whom do you open your mouth
           wide
        and stick out your tongue?
     Are you not children of transgression,
        the offspring of deceit—
5   you that burn with lust among the oaks,
        under every green tree;
     you that slaughter your children in the valleys,
        under the clefts of the rocks?
6   Among the smooth stones of the valley is your
           portion;
        they, they, are your lot;
     to them you have poured out a drink offering,
        you have brought a grain offering.
        Shall I be appeased for these things?
7   Upon a high and lofty mountain
        you have set your bed,
     and there you went up to offer sacrifice.
8   Behind the door and the doorpost
        you have set up your symbol;
     for, in deserting me,g you have uncovered
           your bed,
        you have gone up to it,
        you have made it wide;
     and you have made a bargain for yourself with
           them,
        you have loved their bed,
        you have gazed on their nakedness.h
9   You journeyed to Molechi with oil,
        and multiplied your perfumes;
     you sent your envoys far away,
        and sent down even to Sheol.
10   You grew weary from your many wanderings,
        but you did not say, "It is useless."
     You found your desire rekindled,
        and so you did not weaken.

---

d Heb *His*   e Q Ms Syr Vg Tg: MT *me*   f Heb *an adulterer and she plays*
the whore   g Meaning of Heb uncertain   h Or *their phallus*; Heb *the hand*
i Or *the king*

King James

11And of whom hast thou been afraid or feared, that thou hast lied, and hast not remembered me, nor laid *it* to thy heart? have not I held my peace even of old, and thou fearest me not?

12I will declare thy righteousness, and thy works; for they shall not profit thee.

13¶ When thou criest, let thy companies deliver thee; but the wind shall carry them all away; vanity shall take *them:* but he that putteth his trust in me shall possess the land, and shall inherit my holy mountain;

14And shall say, Cast ye up, cast ye up, prepare the way, take up the stumblingblock out of the way of my people.

15For thus saith the high and lofty One that inhabiteth eternity, whose name *is* Holy; I dwell in the high and holy *place,* with him also *that is* of a contrite and humble spirit, to revive the spirit of the humble, and to revive the heart of the contrite ones.

16For I will not contend for ever, neither will I be always wroth: for the spirit should fail before me, and the souls *which* I have made.

17For the iniquity of his covetousness was I wroth, and smote him: I hid me, and was wroth, and he went on frowardly in the way of his heart.

18I have seen his ways, and will heal him: I will lead him also, and restore comforts unto him and to his mourners.

19I create the fruit of the lips; Peace, peace to *him that is* far off, and to *him that is* near, saith the LORD; and I will heal him.

20But the wicked *are* like the troubled sea, when it cannot rest, whose waters cast up mire and dirt.

21*There is* no peace, saith my God, to the wicked.

58 CRY ALOUD, spare not, lift up thy voice like a trumpet, and show my people their transgression, and the house of Jacob their sins.

2Yet they seek me daily, and delight to know my ways, as a nation that did righteousness, and forsook not the ordinance of their God: they ask of me the ordinances of justice; they take delight in approaching to God.

New International

11"Whom have you so dreaded and feared
    that you have been false to me,
and have neither remembered me
    nor pondered this in your hearts?
Is it not because I have long been silent
    that you do not fear me?
12I will expose your righteousness and your
        works,
    and they will not benefit you.
13When you cry out for help,
    let your collection of idols save you!
The wind will carry all of them off,
    a mere breath will blow them away.
But the man who makes me his refuge
    will inherit the land
    and possess my holy mountain."

Comfort for the Contrite

14And it will be said:

"Build up, build up, prepare the road!
    Remove the obstacles out of the way of my
        people."
15For this is what the high and lofty One says—
    he who lives forever, whose name is holy:
"I live in a high and holy place,
    but also with him who is contrite and lowly
        in spirit,
to revive the spirit of the lowly
    and to revive the heart of the contrite.
16I will not accuse forever,
    nor will I always be angry,
for then the spirit of man would grow faint
        before me—
    the breath of man that I have created.
17I was enraged by his sinful greed;
    I punished him, and hid my face in anger,
    yet he kept on in his willful ways.
18I have seen his ways, but I will heal him;
    I will guide him and restore comfort to him,
19   creating praise on the lips of the mourners in
        Israel.
Peace, peace, to those far and near,"
    says the LORD. "And I will heal them."
20But the wicked are like the tossing sea,
    which cannot rest,
    whose waves cast up mire and mud.
21"There is no peace," says my God, "for the
        wicked."

True Fasting

58 "SHOUT IT aloud, do not hold back.
    Raise your voice like a trumpet.
Declare to my people their rebellion
    and to the house of Jacob their sins.
2For day after day they seek me out;
    they seem eager to know my ways,
as if they were a nation that does what is right
    and has not forsaken the commands of its
        God.
They ask me for just decisions
    and seem eager for God to come near them.

Living Bible

you more afraid of them than of me? How is it that you gave not even a second thought to me? Is it because I've been too gentle, that you have no fear of me? 12And then there is your "righteousness" and your "good works"—none of which will save you. 13Let's see if the whole collection of your idols can help you when you cry to them to save you! They are so weak that the wind can carry them off! A breath can puff them away. But he who trusts in me shall possess the land and inherit my Holy Mountain. 14I will say, Rebuild the road! Clear away the rocks and stones. Prepare a glorious highway for my people's return from captivity.

15The high and lofty one who inhabits eternity, the Holy One, says this: I live in that high and holy place where those with contrite, humble spirits dwell; and I refresh the humble and give new courage to those with repentant hearts. 16For I will not fight against you forever, nor always show my wrath; if I did, all mankind would perish—the very souls that I have made. 17I was angry and smote these greedy men. But they went right on sinning, doing everything their evil hearts desired. 18I have seen what they do, but I will heal them anyway! I will lead them and comfort them, helping them to mourn and to confess their sins. 19Peace, peace to them, both near and far, for I will heal them all. 20But those who still reject mea are like the restless sea, which is never still, but always churns up mire and dirt. 21There is no peace, says my God, for them!

58 SHOUT WITH the voice of a trumpet blast; tell my people of their sins! 2Yet they act so pious! They come to the Temple every day and are so delighted to hear the reading of my laws—just as though they would obey them—just as though they don't despise the commandments of their God! How anxious they are to worship correctly; oh, how they love the Temple services!

New Revised Standard

11 Whom did you dread and fear
    so that you lied,
  and did not remember me
    or give me a thought?
  Have I not kept silent and closed my eyes,b
    and so you do not fear me?
12 I will concede your righteousness and your
      works,
    but they will not help you.
13 When you cry out, let your collection of idols
      deliver you!
    The wind will carry them off,
    a breath will take them away.
  But whoever takes refuge in me shall possess
      the land
    and inherit my holy mountain.

A Promise of Help and Healing

14 It shall be said,
  "Build up, build up, prepare the way,
    remove every obstruction from my people's
      way."
15 For thus says the high and lofty one
    who inhabits eternity, whose name is Holy:
  I dwell in the high and holy place,
    and also with those who are contrite and
      humble in spirit,
  to revive the spirit of the humble,
    and to revive the heart of the contrite.
16 For I will not continually accuse,
    nor will I always be angry;
  for then the spirits would grow faint before
      me,
    even the souls that I have made.
17 Because of their wicked covetousness I
      was angry;
    I struck them, I hid and was angry;
  but they kept turning back to their own
      ways.
18 I have seen their ways, but I will heal them;
    I will lead them and repay them with
      comfort,
  creating for their mourners the fruit of the
      lips.c
19 Peace, peace, to the far and the near, says the
      LORD;
    and I will heal them.
20 But the wicked are like the tossing sea
    that cannot keep still;
    its waters toss up mire and mud.
21 There is no peace, says my God, for the
      wicked.

False and True Worship

58 SHOUT OUT, do not hold back!
    Lift up your voice like a trumpet!
  Announce to my people their rebellion,
    to the house of Jacob their sins.
2 Yet day after day they seek me
    and delight to know my ways,
  as if they were a nation that practiced
      righteousness
    and did not forsake the ordinance of their
      God;
  they ask of me righteous judgments,
    they delight to draw near to God.

---

a 57:20 But those who still reject me, literally, "the wicked."   b Gk Vg: Heb silent even for a long time   c Meaning of Heb uncertain

King James

3¶ Wherefore have we fasted, *say they,* and thou seest not? *wherefore* have we afflicted our soul, and thou takest no knowledge? Behold, in the day of your fast ye find pleasure, and exact all your labours.

4Behold, ye fast for strife and debate, and to smite with the fist of wickedness: ye shall not fast as *ye do this* day, to make your voice to be heard on high.

5Is it such a fast that I have chosen? a day for a man to afflict his soul? *is it* to bow down his head as a bulrush, and to spread sackcloth and ashes *under him?* wilt thou call this a fast, and an acceptable day to the LORD?

6*Is* not this the fast that I have chosen? to loose the bands of wickedness, to undo the heavy burdens, and to let the oppressed go free, and that ye break every yoke?

7*Is it* not to deal thy bread to the hungry, and that thou bring the poor that are cast out to thy house? when thou seest the naked, that thou cover him; and that thou hide not thyself from thine own flesh?

8¶ Then shall thy light break forth as the morning, and thine health shall spring forth speedily: and thy righteousness shall go before thee; the glory of the LORD shall be thy rearward.

9Then shalt thou call, and the LORD shall answer; thou shalt cry, and he shall say, Here I *am.* If thou take away from the midst of thee the yoke, the putting forth of the finger, and speaking vanity;

10And *if* thou draw out thy soul to the hungry, and satisfy the afflicted soul; then shall thy light rise in obscurity, and thy darkness *be* as the noonday:

11And the LORD shall guide thee continually, and satisfy thy soul in drought, and make fat thy bones: and thou shalt be like a watered garden, and like a spring of water, whose waters fail not.

12And *they that shall be* of thee shall build the old waste places: thou shalt raise up the foundations of many generations; and thou shalt be called, The repairer of the breach, The restorer of paths to dwell in.

13¶ If thou turn away thy foot from the sabbath, *from* doing thy pleasure on my holy day; and call the sabbath a delight, the holy of the LORD, honourable; and shalt honour him, not doing thine own ways, nor finding thine own pleasure, nor speaking *thine own* words:

14Then shalt thou delight thyself in the LORD; and I will cause thee to ride upon the high places of the earth, and feed thee with the heritage of Jacob thy father: for the mouth of the LORD hath spoken *it.*

New International

3'Why have we fasted,' they say,
  'and you have not seen it?
Why have we humbled ourselves,
  and you have not noticed?'

"Yet on the day of your fasting, you do as you
    please
  and exploit all your workers.
4Your fasting ends in quarreling and strife,
  and in striking each other with wicked fists.
You cannot fast as you do today
  and expect your voice to be heard on high.
5Is this the kind of fast I have chosen,
  only a day for a man to humble himself?
Is it only for bowing one's head like a reed
  and for lying on sackcloth and ashes?
Is that what you call a fast,
  a day acceptable to the LORD?

6"Is not this the kind of fasting I have chosen:
  to loose the chains of injustice
    and untie the cords of the yoke,
  to set the oppressed free
    and break every yoke?
7Is it not to share your food with the hungry
  and to provide the poor wanderer with
    shelter—
when you see the naked, to clothe him,
  and not to turn away from your own flesh and
    blood?
8Then your light will break forth like the dawn,
  and your healing will quickly appear;
then your righteousness[a] will go before you,
  and the glory of the LORD will be your rear
    guard.
9Then you will call, and the LORD will answer;
  you will cry for help, and he will say: Here
    am I.

"If you do away with the yoke of oppression,
  with the pointing finger and malicious talk,
10and if you spend yourselves in behalf of the
    hungry
  and satisfy the needs of the oppressed,
then your light will rise in the darkness,
  and your night will become like the noonday.
11The LORD will guide you always;
  he will satisfy your needs in a sun-scorched
    land
  and will strengthen your frame.
You will be like a well-watered garden,
  like a spring whose waters never fail.
12Your people will rebuild the ancient ruins
  and will raise up the age-old foundations;
you will be called Repairer of Broken Walls,
  Restorer of Streets with Dwellings.

13"If you keep your feet from breaking the
    Sabbath
  and from doing as you please on my holy
    day,
if you call the Sabbath a delight
  and the LORD's holy day honorable,
and if you honor it by not going your own way
  and not doing as you please or speaking idle
    words,
14then you will find your joy in the LORD,
  and I will cause you to ride on the heights of
    the land
  and to feast on the inheritance of your father
    Jacob."
The mouth of the LORD has spoken.

---

a 8 Or *your righteous One*

Living Bible

3"We have fasted before you," they say. "Why aren't you impressed? Why don't you see our sacrifices? Why don't you hear our prayers? We have done much penance, and you don't even notice it!" I'll tell you why! Because you are living in evil pleasure even while you are fasting, and you keep right on oppressing your workers. 4Look, what good is fasting when you keep on fighting and quarreling? This kind of fasting will never get you anywhere with me. 5Is this what I want—this doing of penance and bowing like reeds in the wind and putting on sackcloth and covering yourselves with ashes? Is this what you call fasting?

6No, the kind of fast I want is that you stop oppressing those who work for you and treat them fairly and give them what they earn. 7I want you to share your food with the hungry and bring right into your own homes those who are helpless, poor and destitute. Clothe those who are cold and don't hide from relatives who need your help.

8If you do these things, God will shed his own glorious light upon you. He will heal you; your godliness will lead you forward, and goodness will be a shield before you, and the glory of the Lord will protect you from behind. 9Then, when you call, the Lord will answer. "Yes, I am here," he will quickly reply. All you need to do is to stop oppressing the weak, and to stop making false accusations and spreading vicious rumors!

10Feed the hungry! Help those in trouble! Then your light will shine out from the darkness, and the darkness around you shall be as bright as day. 11And the Lord will guide you continually, and satisfy you with all good things, and keep you healthy too; and you will be like a well-watered garden, like an ever-flowing spring. 12Your sons will rebuild the long-deserted ruins of your cities, and you will be known as "The People Who Rebuild Their Walls and Cities."

13If you keep the Sabbath holy, not having your own fun and business on that day, but enjoying the Sabbath and speaking of it with delight as the Lord's holy day, and honoring the Lord in what you do, not following your own desires and pleasure, nor talking idly— 14then the Lord will be your delight, and I will see to it that you ride high, and get your full share of the blessings I promised to Jacob, your father. The Lord has spoken.

New Revised Standard

3 "Why do we fast, but you do not see?
   Why humble ourselves, but you do not
       notice?"
Look, you serve your own interest on your
       fast day,
   and oppress all your workers.
4 Look, you fast only to quarrel and to fight
   and to strike with a wicked fist.
Such fasting as you do today
   will not make your voice heard on high.
5 Is such the fast that I choose,
   a day to humble oneself?
Is it to bow down the head like a bulrush,
   and to lie in sackcloth and ashes?
Will you call this a fast,
   a day acceptable to the Lord?

6 Is not this the fast that I choose:
   to loose the bonds of injustice,
   to undo the thongs of the yoke,
to let the oppressed go free,
   and to break every yoke?
7 Is it not to share your bread with the hungry,
   and bring the homeless poor into your
       house;
when you see the naked, to cover them,
   and not to hide yourself from your own kin?
8 Then your light shall break forth like the
       dawn,
   and your healing shall spring up quickly;
your vindicator[b] shall go before you,
   the glory of the Lord shall be your rear
       guard.
9 Then you shall call, and the Lord will
       answer;
   you shall cry for help, and he will say,
       Here I am.

If you remove the yoke from among you,
   the pointing of the finger, the speaking of
       evil,
10 if you offer your food to the hungry
   and satisfy the needs of the afflicted,
then your light shall rise in the darkness
   and your gloom be like the noonday.
11 The Lord will guide you continually,
   and satisfy your needs in parched places,
   and make your bones strong;
and you shall be like a watered garden,
   like a spring of water,
   whose waters never fail.
12 Your ancient ruins shall be rebuilt;
   you shall raise up the foundations of many
       generations;
you shall be called the repairer of the breach,
   the restorer of streets to live in.

13 If you refrain from trampling the sabbath,
   from pursuing your own interests on my
       holy day;
if you call the sabbath a delight
   and the holy day of the Lord honorable;
if you honor it, not going your own ways,
   serving your own interests, or pursuing your
       own affairs;[c]
14 then you shall take delight in the Lord,
   and I will make you ride upon the heights
       of the earth;
I will feed you with the heritage of your
       ancestor Jacob,
   for the mouth of the Lord has spoken.

b Or vindication   c Heb or speaking words

King James

New International

Sin, Confession and Redemption

59 BEHOLD, THE Lord's hand is not shortened, that it cannot save; neither his ear heavy, that it cannot hear:

2But your iniquities have separated between you and your God, and your sins have hid *his* face from you, that he will not hear.

3For your hands are defiled with blood, and your fingers with iniquity; your lips have spoken lies, your tongue hath muttered perverseness.

4None calleth for justice, nor *any* pleadeth for truth: they trust in vanity, and speak lies; they conceive mischief, and bring forth iniquity.

5They hatch cockatrice' eggs, and weave the spider's web: he that eateth of their eggs dieth, and that which is crushed breaketh out into a viper.

6Their webs shall not become garments, neither shall they cover themselves with their works: their works *are* works of iniquity, and the act of violence *is* in their hands.

7Their feet run to evil, and they make haste to shed innocent blood: their thoughts *are* thoughts of iniquity; wasting and destruction *are* in their paths.

8The way of peace they know not; and *there is* no judgment in their goings: they have made them crooked paths: whosoever goeth therein shall not know peace.

9¶ Therefore is judgment far from us, neither doth justice overtake us: we wait for light, but behold obscurity; for brightness, *but* we walk in darkness.

10We grope for the wall like the blind, and we grope as if *we had* no eyes: we stumble at noonday as in the night; *we are* in desolate places as dead *men*.

11We roar all like bears, and mourn sore like doves: we look for judgment, but *there is* none; for salvation, *but* it is far off from us.

12For our transgressions are multiplied before thee, and our sins testify against us: for our transgressions *are* with us; and *as for* our iniquities, we know them;

13In transgressing and lying against the Lord, and departing away from our God, speaking oppression and revolt, conceiving and uttering from the heart words of falsehood.

14And judgment is turned away backward, and justice standeth afar off: for truth is fallen in the street, and equity cannot enter.

15Yea, truth faileth; and he *that* departeth from evil maketh himself a prey: and the Lord saw *it*, and it displeased him that *there was* no judgment.

16¶ And he saw that *there was* no man, and wondered that *there was* no intercessor: therefore his arm brought salvation unto him; and his righteousness, it sustained him.

59 SURELY THE arm of the Lord is not too
    short to save,
  nor his ear too dull to hear.
2But your iniquities have separated
    you from your God;
  your sins have hidden his face from you,
    so that he will not hear.
3For your hands are stained with blood,
    your fingers with guilt.
  Your lips have spoken lies,
    and your tongue mutters wicked things.
4No one calls for justice;
  no one pleads his case with integrity.
  They rely on empty arguments and speak lies;
    they conceive trouble and give birth to evil.
5They hatch the eggs of vipers
    and spin a spider's web.
  Whoever eats their eggs will die,
    and when one is broken, an adder is hatched.
6Their cobwebs are useless for clothing;
    they cannot cover themselves with what they
      make.
  Their deeds are evil deeds,
    and acts of violence are in their hands.
7Their feet rush into sin;
    they are swift to shed innocent blood.
  Their thoughts are evil thoughts;
    ruin and destruction mark their ways.
8The way of peace they do not know;
    there is no justice in their paths.
  They have turned them into crooked roads;
    no one who walks in them will know peace.

9So justice is far from us,
    and righteousness does not reach us.
  We look for light, but all is darkness;
    for brightness, but we walk in deep shadows.
10Like the blind we grope along the wall,
    feeling our way like men without eyes.
  At midday we stumble as if it were twilight;
    among the strong, we are like the dead.
11We all growl like bears;
    we moan mournfully like doves.
  We look for justice, but find none;
    for deliverance, but it is far away.

12For our offenses are many in your sight,
    and our sins testify against us.
  Our offenses are ever with us,
    and we acknowledge our iniquities:
13rebellion and treachery against the Lord,
    turning our backs on our God,
  fomenting oppression and revolt,
    uttering lies our hearts have conceived.
14So justice is driven back,
    and righteousness stands at a distance;
  truth has stumbled in the streets,
    honesty cannot enter.
15Truth is nowhere to be found,
    and whoever shuns evil becomes a prey.

  The Lord looked and was displeased
    that there was no justice.
16He saw that there was no one,
    he was appalled that there was no one to
      intervene;
  so his own arm worked salvation for him,
    and his own righteousness sustained him.

Living Bible

59 LISTEN NOW! The Lord isn't too weak to save you. And he isn't getting deaf! He can hear you when you call! ²But the trouble is that your sins have cut you off from God. Because of sin he has turned his face away from you and will not listen anymore. ³For your hands are those of murderers and your fingers are filthy with sin. You lie and grumble and oppose the good. ⁴No one cares about being fair and true. Your lawsuits are based on lies; you spend your time plotting evil deeds and doing them. ⁵You spend your time and energy in spinning evil plans which end up in deadly actions. ⁶You cheat and shortchange everyone. Everything you do is filled with sin; violence is your trademark. ⁷Your feet run to do evil and rush to murder; your thoughts are only of sinning, and wherever you go you leave behind a trail of misery and death. ⁸You don't know what true peace is, nor what it means to be just and good; you continually do wrong and those who follow you won't experience any peace, either.

⁹It is because of all this evil that you aren't finding God's blessings; that's why he doesn't punish those who injure you. No wonder you are in darkness when you expected light. No wonder you are walking in the gloom. ¹⁰No wonder you grope like blind men and stumble along in broad daylight, yes, even at brightest noon-time, as though it were the darkest night! No wonder you are like corpses when compared with vigorous young men! ¹¹You roar like hungry bears; you moan with mournful cries like doves. You look for God to keep you, but he doesn't. He has turned away. ¹²For your sins keep piling up before the righteous God, and testify against you.

Yes, we know what sinners we are. ¹³We know our disobedience; we have denied the Lord our God. We know what rebels we are and how unfair we are, for we carefully plan our lies. ¹⁴Our courts oppose the righteous man; fairness is unknown. Truth falls dead in the streets, and justice is outlawed.

¹⁵Yes, truth is gone, and anyone who tries a better life is soon attacked. The Lord saw all the evil and was displeased to find no steps taken against sin. ¹⁶He saw no one was helping you, and wondered that no one inter-vened. Therefore he himself stepped in to save you through his mighty power and justice. ¹⁷He put on righ-

New Revised Standard

Injustice and Oppression to Be Punished

59 SEE, THE LORD's hand is not too short to save,
    nor his ear too dull to hear.
2 Rather, your iniquities have been barriers
    between you and your God,
  and your sins have hidden his face from you
    so that he does not hear.
3 For your hands are defiled with blood,
    and your fingers with iniquity;
  your lips have spoken lies,
    your tongue mutters wickedness.
4 No one brings suit justly,
    no one goes to law honestly;
  they rely on empty pleas, they speak lies,
    conceiving mischief and begetting iniquity.
5 They hatch adders' eggs,
    and weave the spider's web;
  whoever eats their eggs dies,
    and the crushed egg hatches out a viper.
6 Their webs cannot serve as clothing;
    they cannot cover themselves with what
      they make.
  Their works are works of iniquity,
    and deeds of violence are in their hands.
7 Their feet run to evil,
    and they rush to shed innocent blood;
  their thoughts are thoughts of iniquity,
    desolation and destruction are in
      their highways.
8 The way of peace they do not know,
    and there is no justice in their paths.
  Their roads they have made crooked;
    no one who walks in them knows peace.

9 Therefore justice is far from us,
    and righteousness does not reach us;
  we wait for light, and lo! there is darkness;
    and for brightness, but we walk in gloom.
10 We grope like the blind along a wall,
    groping like those who have no eyes;
  we stumble at noon as in the twilight,
    among the vigorousᵃ as though we were
      dead.
11 We all growl like bears;
    like doves we moan mournfully.
  We wait for justice, but there is none;
    for salvation, but it is far from us.
12 For our transgressions before you are many,
    and our sins testify against us.
  Our transgressions indeed are with us,
    and we know our iniquities:
13 transgressing, and denying the LORD,
    and turning away from following our God,
  talking oppression and revolt,
    conceiving lying words and uttering them
      from the heart.
14 Justice is turned back,
    and righteousness stands at a distance;
  for truth stumbles in the public square,
    and uprightness cannot enter.
15 Truth is lacking,
    and whoever turns from evil is despoiled.

  The LORD saw it, and it displeased him
    that there was no justice.
16 He saw that there was no one,
    and was appalled that there was no one to
      intervene;
  so his own arm brought him victory,
    and his righteousness upheld him.

ᵃ Meaning of Heb uncertain

King James

17For he put on righteousness as a breastplate, and an helmet of salvation upon his head; and he put on the garments of vengeance *for* clothing, and was clad with zeal as a cloak.

18According to *their* deeds, accordingly he will repay, fury to his adversaries, recompence to his enemies; to the islands he will repay recompence.

19So shall they fear the name of the LORD from the west, and his glory from the rising of the sun. When the enemy shall come in like a flood, the spirit of the LORD shall lift up a standard against him.

20¶ And the Redeemer shall come to Zion, and unto them that turn from transgression in Jacob, saith the LORD.

21As for me, this *is* my covenant with them, saith the LORD; My spirit that *is* upon thee, and my words which I have put in thy mouth, shall not depart out of thy mouth, nor out of the mouth of thy seed, nor out of the mouth of thy seed's seed, saith the LORD, from henceforth and for ever.

60 ARISE, SHINE; for thy light is come, and the glory of the LORD is risen upon thee.

2For, behold, the darkness shall cover the earth, and gross darkness the people: but the LORD shall arise upon thee, and his glory shall be seen upon thee.

3And the Gentiles shall come to thy light, and kings to the brightness of thy rising.

4Lift up thine eyes round about, and see: all they gather themselves together, they come to thee: thy sons shall come from far, and thy daughters shall be nursed at *thy* side.

5Then thou shalt see, and flow together, and thine heart shall fear, and be enlarged; because the abundance of the sea shall be converted unto thee, the forces of the Gentiles shall come unto thee.

6The multitude of camels shall cover thee, the dromedaries of Midian and Ephah; all they from Sheba shall come: they shall bring gold and incense; and they shall show forth the praises of the LORD.

7All the flocks of Kedar shall be gathered together unto thee, the rams of Nebaioth shall minister unto thee: they shall come up with acceptance on mine altar, and I will glorify the house of my glory.

8Who *are* these *that* fly as a cloud, and as the doves to their windows?

9Surely the isles shall wait for me, and the ships of Tarshish first, to bring thy sons from far, their silver and their gold with them, unto the name of the LORD thy God, and to the Holy One of Israel, because he hath glorified thee.

New International

17He put on righteousness as his breastplate,
  and the helmet of salvation on his head;
he put on the garments of vengeance
  and wrapped himself in zeal as in a cloak.
18According to what they have done,
  so will he repay
wrath to his enemies
  and retribution to his foes;
he will repay the islands their due.
19From the west, men will fear the name of the
  LORD,
  and from the rising of the sun, they will
    revere his glory.
For he will come like a pent-up flood
  that the breath of the LORD drives along.[a]

20"The Redeemer will come to Zion,
  to those in Jacob who repent of their sins,"
              declares the LORD.

21"As for me, this is my covenant with them," says the LORD. "My Spirit, who is on you, and my words that I have put in your mouth will not depart from your mouth, or from the mouths of your children, or from the mouths of their descendants from this time on and forever," says the LORD.

The Glory of Zion

60 "ARISE, SHINE, for your light has come,
  and the glory of the LORD rises upon you.
2See, darkness covers the earth
  and thick darkness is over the peoples,
but the LORD rises upon you
  and his glory appears over you.
3Nations will come to your light,
  and kings to the brightness of your dawn.

4"Lift up your eyes and look about you:
  All assemble and come to you;
your sons come from afar,
  and your daughters are carried on the arm.
5Then you will look and be radiant,
  your heart will throb and swell with joy;
the wealth on the seas will be brought to you,
  to you the riches of the nations will come.
6Herds of camels will cover your land,
  young camels of Midian and Ephah.
And all from Sheba will come,
  bearing gold and incense
  and proclaiming the praise of the LORD.
7All Kedar's flocks will be gathered to you,
  the rams of Nebaioth will serve you;
they will be accepted as offerings on my altar,
  and I will adorn my glorious temple.

8"Who are these that fly along like clouds,
  like doves to their nests?
9Surely the islands look to me;
  in the lead are the ships of Tarshish,[b]
bringing your sons from afar,
  with their silver and gold,
to the honor of the LORD your God,
  the Holy One of Israel,
for he has endowed you with splendor.

Living Bible

teousness as armor, and the helmet of salvation on his head. He clothed himself with robes of vengeance and of godly fury. 18He will repay his enemies for their evil deeds—fury for his foes in distant lands. 19Then at last they will reverence and glorify the name of God from west to east. For he will come like a flood-tide driven by Jehovah's breath. 20He will come as a Redeemer to those in Zion who have turned away from sin.

21"As for me, this is my promise to them," says the Lord: "My Holy Spirit shall not leave them, and they shall want the good and hate the wrong—they and their children and their children's children forever."

60 ARISE, MY people! Let your light shine for all the nations to see! For the glory of the Lord is streaming from you. 2Darkness as black as night shall cover all the peoples of the earth, but the glory of the Lord will shine from you. 3All nations will come to your light; mighty kings will come to see the glory of the Lord upon you.

4Lift up your eyes and see! For your sons and daughters are coming home to you from distant lands. 5Your eyes will shine with joy, your hearts will thrill, for merchants from around the world will flow to you, bringing you the wealth of many lands. 6Vast droves of camels will converge upon you, dromedaries from Midian and Sheba and Ephah, too, bringing gold and incense to add to the praise of God. 7The flocks of Kedar shall be given you, and the rams of Nabaioth for my altars, and I will glorify my glorious Temple in that day.

8And who are these who fly like a cloud to Israel, like doves to their nests? 9I have reserved the ships of many lands, the very best,ᶜ to bring the sons of Israel home again from far away, bringing their wealth with them. For the Holy One of Israel, known around the world, has glorified you in the eyes of all.

New Revised Standard

17 He put on righteousness like a breastplate,
   and a helmet of salvation on his head;
   he put on garments of vengeance for clothing,
   and wrapped himself in fury as in a mantle.
18 According to their deeds, so will he repay;
   wrath to his adversaries, requital to his
      enemies;
   to the coastlands he will render requital.
19 So those in the west shall fear the name of the
      LORD,
   and those in the east, his glory;
   for he will come like a pent-up stream
   that the wind of the LORD drives on.

20 And he will come to Zion as Redeemer,
   to those in Jacob who turn from
      transgression, says the LORD.
21 And as for me, this is my covenant with them, says the LORD: my spirit that is upon you, and my words that I have put in your mouth, shall not depart out of your mouth, or out of the mouths of your children, or out of the mouths of your children's children, says the LORD, from now on and forever.

The Ingathering of the Dispersed

60 ARISE, SHINE; for your light has come,
   and the glory of the LORD has risen upon
      you.
2 For darkness shall cover the earth,
   and thick darkness the peoples;
   but the LORD will arise upon you,
   and his glory will appear over you.
3 Nations shall come to your light,
   and kings to the brightness of your dawn.

4 Lift up your eyes and look around;
   they all gather together, they come to you;
   your sons shall come from far away,
   and your daughters shall be carried on their
      nurses' arms.
5 Then you shall see and be radiant;
   your heart shall thrill and rejoice,ᵈ
   because the abundance of the sea shall be
      brought to you,
   the wealth of the nations shall come to you.
6 A multitude of camels shall cover you,
   the young camels of Midian and Ephah;
   all those from Sheba shall come.
   They shall bring gold and frankincense,
   and shall proclaim the praise of the LORD.
7 All the flocks of Kedar shall be gathered to
      you,
   the rams of Nebaioth shall minister to you;
   they shall be acceptable on my altar,
   and I will glorify my glorious house.

8 Who are these that fly like a cloud,
   and like doves to their windows?
9 For the coastlands shall wait for me,
   the ships of Tarshish first,
   to bring your children from far away,
   their silver and gold with them,
   for the name of the LORD your God,
   and for the Holy One of Israel,
   because he has glorified you.

ᶜ 60:9 the very best, literally, "the ships of Tarshish."   ᵈ Heb be enlarged

King James

10And the sons of strangers shall build up thy walls, and their kings shall minister unto thee: for in my wrath I smote thee, but in my favour have I had mercy on thee.

11Therefore thy gates shall be open continually; they shall not be shut day nor night; that *men* may bring unto thee the forces of the Gentiles, and *that* their kings *may be* brought.

12For the nation and kingdom that will not serve thee shall perish; yea, *those* nations shall be utterly wasted.

13The glory of Lebanon shall come unto thee, the fir tree, the pine tree, and the box together, to beautify the place of my sanctuary; and I will make the place of my feet glorious.

14The sons also of them that afflicted thee shall come bending unto thee; and all they that despised thee shall bow themselves down at the soles of thy feet; and they shall call thee, The city of the LORD, The Zion of the Holy One of Israel.

15Whereas thou hast been forsaken and hated, so that no man went through *thee*, I will make thee an eternal excellency, a joy of many generations.

16Thou shalt also suck the milk of the Gentiles, and shalt suck the breast of kings: and thou shalt know that I the LORD *am* thy Saviour and thy Redeemer, the mighty One of Jacob.

17For brass I will bring gold, and for iron I will bring silver, and for wood brass, and for stones iron: I will also make thy officers peace, and thine exactors righteousness.

18Violence shall no more be heard in thy land, wasting nor destruction within thy borders; but thou shalt call thy walls Salvation, and thy gates Praise.

19The sun shall be no more thy light by day; neither for brightness shall the moon give light unto thee: but the LORD shall be unto thee an everlasting light, and thy God thy glory.

20Thy sun shall no more go down; neither shall thy moon withdraw itself: for the LORD shall be thine everlasting light, and the days of thy mourning shall be ended.

21Thy people also *shall be* all righteous: they shall inherit the land for ever, the branch of my planting, the work of my hands, that I may be glorified.

22A little one shall become a thousand, and a small one a strong nation: I the LORD will hasten it in his time.

New International

10"Foreigners will rebuild your walls,
    and their kings will serve you.
Though in anger I struck you,
    in favor I will show you compassion.
11Your gates will always stand open,
    they will never be shut, day or night,
so that men may bring you the wealth of the
    nations—
    their kings led in triumphal procession.
12For the nation or kingdom that will not serve
    you will perish;
    it will be utterly ruined.

13"The glory of Lebanon will come to you,
    the pine, the fir and the cypress together,
to adorn the place of my sanctuary;
    and I will glorify the place of my feet.
14The sons of your oppressors will come bowing
    before you;
all who despise you will bow down at your
    feet
and will call you the City of the LORD,
    Zion of the Holy One of Israel.

15"Although you have been forsaken and hated,
    with no one traveling through,
I will make you the everlasting pride
    and the joy of all generations.
16You will drink the milk of nations
    and be nursed at royal breasts.
Then you will know that I, the LORD, am your
    Savior,
    your Redeemer, the Mighty One of Jacob.
17Instead of bronze I will bring you gold,
    and silver in place of iron.
Instead of wood I will bring you bronze,
    and iron in place of stones.
I will make peace your governor
    and righteousness your ruler.
18No longer will violence be heard in your land,
    nor ruin or destruction within your borders,
but you will call your walls Salvation
    and your gates Praise.
19The sun will no more be your light by day,
    nor will the brightness of the moon shine on
    you,
for the LORD will be your everlasting light,
    and your God will be your glory.
20Your sun will never set again,
    and your moon will wane no more;
the LORD will be your everlasting light,
    and your days of sorrow will end.
21Then will all your people be righteous
    and they will possess the land forever.
They are the shoot I have planted,
    the work of my hands,
    for the display of my splendor.
22The least of you will become a thousand,
    the smallest a mighty nation.
I am the LORD;
    in its time I will do this swiftly."

Living Bible

10Foreigners will come and build your cities. Presidents and kings will send you aid. For though I destroyed you in my anger, I will have mercy on you through my grace. 11Your gates will stay wide open around the clock to receive the wealth of many lands. The kings of the world will cater to you. 12For the nations refusing to be your alliesa will perish; they shall be destroyed. 13The glory of Lebanon will be yours—the forests of firs and pines, and box trees—to beautify my sanctuary. My Temple will be glorious.

14The sons of anti-Semites will come and bow before you! They will kiss your feet! They will call Jerusalem "The City of the Lord" and "The Glorious Mountain of the Holy One of Israel.

15Though once despised and hated and rebuffed by all, you will be beautiful forever, a joy for all the generations of the world, for I will make you so. 16Powerful kings and mighty nations shall provide you with the choicest of their goods to satisfy your every need, and you will know at last and really understand that I, the Lord, am your Savior and Redeemer, the Mighty One of Israel. 17I will exchange your brass for gold, your iron for silver, your wood for brass, your stones for iron. Peace and righteousness shall be your taskmasters! 18Violence will disappear out of your land—all war will end. Your walls will be "Salvation" and your gates "Praise."

19No longer will you need the sun or moon to give you light, for the Lord your God will be your everlasting light, and he will be your glory. 20Your sun shall never set; the moon shall not go down—for the Lord will be your everlasting light; your days of mourning all will end. 21All your people will be good. They will possess their land forever, for I will plant them there with my own hands; this will bring me glory. 22The smallest family shall multiply into a clan; the tiny group shall be a mighty nation. I, the Lord, will bring it all to pass when it is time.

New Revised Standard

10 Foreigners shall build up your walls,
   and their kings shall minister to you;
for in my wrath I struck you down,
   but in my favor I have had mercy on you.
11 Your gates shall always be open;
   day and night they shall not be shut,
so that nations shall bring you their wealth,
   with their kings led in procession.
12 For the nation and kingdom
   that will not serve you shall perish;
   those nations shall be utterly laid waste.
13 The glory of Lebanon shall come to you,
   the cypress, the plane, and the pine,
to beautify the place of my sanctuary;
   and I will glorify where my feet rest.
14 The descendants of those who oppressed you
   shall come bending low to you,
and all who despised you
   shall bow down at your feet;
they shall call you the City of the LORD,
   the Zion of the Holy One of Israel.
15 Whereas you have been forsaken and hated,
   with no one passing through,
I will make you majestic forever,
   a joy from age to age.
16 You shall suck the milk of nations,
   you shall suck the breasts of kings;
and you shall know that I, the LORD, am your
   Savior
   and your Redeemer, the Mighty One of
   Jacob.

17 Instead of bronze I will bring gold,
   instead of iron I will bring silver;
instead of wood, bronze,
   instead of stones, iron.
I will appoint Peace as your overseer
   and Righteousness as your taskmaster.
18 Violence shall no more be heard in your land,
   devastation or destruction within your
   borders;
you shall call your walls Salvation,
   and your gates Praise.

God the Glory of Zion

19 The sun shall no longer be
   your light by day,
nor for brightness shall the moon
   give light to you by night;b
but the LORD will be your everlasting light,
   and your God will be your glory.
20 Your sun shall no more go down,
   or your moon withdraw itself;
for the LORD will be your everlasting light,
   and your days of mourning shall be ended.
21 Your people shall all be righteous;
   they shall possess the land forever.
They are the shoot that I planted, the work of
   my hands,
   so that I might be glorified.
22 The least of them shall become a clan,
   and the smallest one a mighty nation;
I am the LORD;
   in its time I will accomplish it quickly.

---

a 60:12 For the nations refusing to be your allies, literally, "that will not serve you."

b Q Ms Gk Old Latin Tg: MT lacks by night

King James

New International

The Year of the Lord's Favor

61 THE SPIRIT of the Lord GOD *is* upon me; because the LORD hath anointed me to preach good tidings unto the meek; he hath sent me to bind up the brokenhearted, to proclaim liberty to the captives, and the opening of the prison to *them that are* bound;

2To proclaim the acceptable year of the LORD, and the day of vengeance of our God; to comfort all that mourn;

3To appoint unto them that mourn in Zion, to give unto them beauty for ashes, the oil of joy for mourning, the garment of praise for the spirit of heaviness; that they might be called trees of righteousness, the planting of the LORD, that he might be glorified.

4¶ And they shall build the old wastes, they shall raise up the former desolations, and they shall repair the waste cities, the desolations of many generations.

5And strangers shall stand and feed your flocks, and the sons of the alien *shall be* your plowmen and your vinedressers.

6But ye shall be named the Priests of the LORD: *men* shall call you the Ministers of our God: ye shall eat the riches of the Gentiles, and in their glory shall ye boast yourselves.

7¶ For your shame *ye shall have* double; and *for* confusion they shall rejoice in their portion: therefore in their land they shall possess the double: everlasting joy shall be unto them.

8For I the LORD love judgment, I hate robbery for burnt offering; and I will direct their work in truth, and I will make an everlasting covenant with them.

9And their seed shall be known among the Gentiles, and their offspring among the people: all that see them shall acknowledge them, that they *are* the seed *which* the LORD hath blessed.

10I will greatly rejoice in the LORD, my soul shall be joyful in my God; for he hath clothed me with the garments of salvation, he hath covered me with the robe of righteousness, as a bridegroom decketh *himself* with ornaments, and as a bride adorneth *herself* with her jewels.

11For as the earth bringeth forth her bud, and as the garden causeth the things that are sown in it to spring forth; so the Lord GOD will cause righteousness and praise to spring forth before all the nations.

61 THE SPIRIT of the Sovereign LORD is on
  me,
because the LORD has anointed me
  to preach good news to the poor.
He has sent me to bind up the brokenhearted,
  to proclaim freedom for the captives
  and release from darkness for the prisoners,[a]
2to proclaim the year of the LORD's favor
  and the day of vengeance of our God,
to comfort all who mourn,
3 and provide for those who grieve in Zion—
to bestow on them a crown of beauty
  instead of ashes,
the oil of gladness
  instead of mourning,
and a garment of praise
  instead of a spirit of despair.
They will be called oaks of righteousness,
  a planting of the LORD
  for the display of his splendor.

4They will rebuild the ancient ruins
  and restore the places long devastated;
they will renew the ruined cities
  that have been devastated for generations.
5Aliens will shepherd your flocks;
  foreigners will work your fields and
  vineyards.
6And you will be called priests of the LORD,
  you will be named ministers of our God.
You will feed on the wealth of nations,
  and in their riches you will boast.

7Instead of their shame
  my people will receive a double portion,
and instead of disgrace
  they will rejoice in their inheritance;
and so they will inherit a double portion in their
  land,
  and everlasting joy will be theirs.

8"For I, the LORD, love justice;
  I hate robbery and iniquity.
In my faithfulness I will reward them
  and make an everlasting covenant with them.
9Their descendants will be known among the
  nations
  and their offspring among the peoples.
All who see them will acknowledge
  that they are a people the LORD has blessed."

10I delight greatly in the LORD;
  my soul rejoices in my God.
For he has clothed me with garments of
  salvation
  and arrayed me in a robe of righteousness,
as a bridegroom adorns his head like a priest,
  and as a bride adorns herself with her jewels.
11For as the soil makes the sprout come up
  and a garden causes seeds to grow,
so the Sovereign LORD will make righteousness
  and praise
  spring up before all nations.

Zion's New Name

62 FOR ZION'S sake will I not hold my peace, and for Jerusalem's sake I will not rest, until the righteousness thereof go forth as brightness, and the salvation thereof as a lamp *that* burneth.

62 FOR ZION'S sake I will not keep silent,
  for Jerusalem's sake I will not remain quiet,
till her righteousness shines out like the dawn,
  her salvation like a blazing torch.

---

[a] *1* Hebrew; Septuagint *the blind*

Living Bible

61 THE SPIRIT of the Lord God is upon me, because the Lord has anointed me to bring good news to the suffering and afflicted. He has sent me to comfort the brokenhearted, to announce liberty to captives and to open the eyes of the blind. 2He has sent me to tell those who mourn that the time of God's favor to them has come, and the day of his wrath to their enemies. 3To all who mourn in Israel he will give:

Beauty for ashes;
Joy instead of mourning;
Praise instead of heaviness.

For God has planted them like strong and graceful oaks for his own glory.

4And they shall rebuild the ancient ruins, repairing cities long ago destroyed, reviving them though they have lain there many generations. 5Foreigners shall be your servants; they shall feed your flocks and plow your fields and tend your vineyards. 6You shall be called priests of the Lord, ministers of our God. You shall be fed with the treasures of the nations and shall glory in their riches. 7Instead of shame and dishonor, you shall have a double portion of prosperity and everlasting joy.

8For I, the Lord, love justice; I hate robbery and wrong. I will faithfully reward my people for their suffering and make an everlasting covenant with them. 9Their descendants shall be known and honored among the nations; all shall realize that they are a people God has blessed.

10Let me tell you how happy God has made me! For he has clothed me with garments of salvation and draped about me the robe of righteousness. I am like a bridegroom in his wedding suit or a bride with her jewels. 11The Lord will show the nations of the world his justice; all will praise him. His righteousness shall be like a budding tree, or like a garden in early spring, full of young plants springing up everywhere.

62 BECAUSE I love Zion, because my heart yearns for Jerusalem, I will not cease to pray for her or to cry out to God on her behalf until she shines forth in his righteousness and is glorious in his salvation.

New Revised Standard

The Good News of Deliverance

61 THE SPIRIT of the Lord GOD is upon me, because the LORD has anointed me;
he has sent me to bring good news to the oppressed,
to bind up the brokenhearted,
to proclaim liberty to the captives,
and release to the prisoners;
2 to proclaim the year of the LORD's favor,
and the day of vengeance of our God;
to comfort all who mourn;
3 to provide for those who mourn in Zion—
to give them a garland instead of ashes,
the oil of gladness instead of mourning,
the mantle of praise instead of a faint spirit.
They will be called oaks of righteousness,
the planting of the LORD, to display his glory.
4 They shall build up the ancient ruins,
they shall raise up the former devastations;
they shall repair the ruined cities,
the devastations of many generations.

5 Strangers shall stand and feed your flocks,
foreigners shall till your land and dress your vines;
6 but you shall be called priests of the LORD,
you shall be named ministers of our God;
you shall enjoy the wealth of the nations,
and in their riches you shall glory.
7 Because their[b] shame was double,
and dishonor was proclaimed as their lot,
therefore they shall possess a double portion;
everlasting joy shall be theirs.

8 For I the LORD love justice,
I hate robbery and wrongdoing;[c]
I will faithfully give them their recompense,
and I will make an everlasting covenant with them.
9 Their descendants shall be known among the nations,
and their offspring among the peoples;
all who see them shall acknowledge
that they are a people whom the LORD has blessed.
10 I will greatly rejoice in the LORD,
my whole being shall exult in my God;
for he has clothed me with the garments of salvation,
he has covered me with the robe of righteousness,
as a bridegroom decks himself with a garland,
and as a bride adorns herself with her jewels.
11 For as the earth brings forth its shoots,
and as a garden causes what is sown in it to spring up,
so the Lord GOD will cause righteousness and praise
to spring up before all the nations.

The Vindication and Salvation of Zion

62 FOR ZION'S sake I will not keep silent,
and for Jerusalem's sake I will not rest,
until her vindication shines out like the dawn,
and her salvation like a burning torch.

b Heb *your*   c Or *robbery with a burnt offering*

King James

2And the Gentiles shall see thy righteousness, and all kings thy glory: and thou shalt be called by a new name, which the mouth of the LORD shall name.

3Thou shalt also be a crown of glory in the hand of the LORD, and a royal diadem in the hand of thy God.

4Thou shalt no more be termed Forsaken; neither shall thy land any more be termed Desolate: but thou shalt be called Hephzibah, and thy land Beulah: for the LORD delighteth in thee, and thy land shall be married.

5¶ For *as* a young man marrieth a virgin, *so* shall thy sons marry thee: and *as* the bridegroom rejoiceth over the bride, *so* shall thy God rejoice over thee.

6I have set watchmen upon thy walls, O Jerusalem, *which* shall never hold their peace day nor night: ye that make mention of the LORD, keep not silence;

7And give him no rest, till he establish, and till he make Jerusalem a praise in the earth.

8The LORD hath sworn by his right hand, and by the arm of his strength, Surely I will no more give thy corn *to be* meat for thine enemies; and the sons of the stranger shall not drink thy wine, for the which thou hast laboured:

9But they that have gathered it shall eat it, and praise the LORD; and they that have brought it together shall drink it in the courts of my holiness.

10¶ Go through, go through the gates; prepare ye the way of the people; cast up, cast up the highway; gather out the stones; lift up a standard for the people.

11Behold, the LORD hath proclaimed unto the end of the world, Say ye to the daughter of Zion, Behold, thy salvation cometh; behold, his reward *is* with him, and his work before him.

12And they shall call them, The holy people, The redeemed of the LORD: and thou shalt be called, Sought out, A city not forsaken.

63 WHO *IS* this that cometh from Edom, with dyed garments from Bozrah? this *that is* glorious in his apparel, travelling in the greatness of his strength? I that speak in righteousness, mighty to save.

2Wherefore *art thou* red in thine apparel, and thy garments like him that treadeth in the winevat?

New International

2The nations will see your righteousness,
  and all kings your glory;
you will be called by a new name
  that the mouth of the LORD will bestow.
3You will be a crown of splendor in the LORD's hand,
  a royal diadem in the hand of your God.
4No longer will they call you Deserted,
  or name your land Desolate.
But you will be called Hephzibah,[a]
  and your land Beulah[b];
for the LORD will take delight in you,
  and your land will be married.
5As a young man marries a maiden,
  so will your sons[c] marry you;
as a bridegroom rejoices over his bride,
  so will your God rejoice over you.

6I have posted watchmen on your walls,
  O Jerusalem;
  they will never be silent day or night.
You who call on the LORD,
  give yourselves no rest,
7and give him no rest till he establishes Jerusalem
  and makes her the praise of the earth.

8The LORD has sworn by his right hand
  and by his mighty arm:
"Never again will I give your grain
  as food for your enemies,
and never again will foreigners drink the new wine
  for which you have toiled;
9but those who harvest it will eat it
  and praise the LORD,
and those who gather the grapes will drink it
  in the courts of my sanctuary."

10Pass through, pass through the gates!
  Prepare the way for the people.
Build up, build up the highway!
  Remove the stones.
Raise a banner for the nations.

11The LORD has made proclamation
  to the ends of the earth:
"Say to the Daughter of Zion,
  'See, your Savior comes!
See, his reward is with him,
  and his recompense accompanies him.' "
12They will be called the Holy People,
  the Redeemed of the LORD;
and you will be called Sought After,
  the City No Longer Deserted.

God's Day of Vengeance and Redemption

63 WHO IS this coming from Edom,
  from Bozrah, with his garments stained crimson?
Who is this, robed in splendor,
  striding forward in the greatness of his strength?

"It is I, speaking in righteousness,
  mighty to save."

2Why are your garments red,
  like those of one treading the winepress?

Living Bible

2The nations shall see your righteousness. Kings shall be blinded by your glory; and God will confer on you a new name. 3He will hold you aloft in his hands for all to see—a splendid crown for the King of kings. 4Never again shall you be called "The God-forsaken Land" or the "Land that God Forgot." Your new name will be "The Land of God's Delight" and "The Bride," for the Lord delights in you and will claim you as his own. 5Your children will care for you, O Jerusalem, with joy like that of a young man who marries a virgin; and God will rejoice over you as a bridegroom with his bride.

6,7O Jerusalem, I have set intercessorsd on your walls who shall cry to God all day and all night for the fulfillment of his promises. Take no rest, all you who pray, and give God no rest until he establishes Jerusalem and makes her respected and admired throughout the earth. 8The Lord has sworn to Jerusalem with all his integrity: "I will never again give you to your enemies; never again shall foreign soldiers come and take away your grain and wine. 9You raised it; you shall keep it, praising God. Within the Temple courts you yourselves shall drink the wine you pressed.

10"Go out! Go out! Prepare the roadway for my people to return! Build the roads, pull out the boulders, raise the flag of Israel."

11See, the Lord has sent his messengers to every land and said, "Tell my people, I, the Lord your God, am coming to save you and will bring you many gifts." 12And they shall be called "The Holy People" and "The Lord's Redeemed," and Jerusalem shall be called "The Land of Desire" and "The City God Has Blessed."

New Revised Standard

2 The nations shall see your vindication,
    and all the kings your glory;
  and you shall be called by a new name
    that the mouth of the LORD will give.
3 You shall be a crown of beauty in the hand of
    the LORD,
    and a royal diadem in the hand of your
    God.
4 You shall no more be termed Forsaken,e
    and your land shall no more be termed
    Desolate;f
  but you shall be called My Delight Is in Her,g
    and your land Married;h
  for the LORD delights in you,
    and your land shall be married.
5 For as a young man marries a young woman,
    so shall your builderi marry you,
  and as the bridegroom rejoices over the bride,
    so shall your God rejoice over you.
6 Upon your walls, O Jerusalem,
    I have posted sentinels;
  all day and all night
    they shall never be silent.
  You who remind the LORD,
    take no rest,
7 and give him no rest
    until he establishes Jerusalem
    and makes it renowned throughout the earth.
8 The LORD has sworn by his right hand
    and by his mighty arm:
  I will not again give your grain
    to be food for your enemies,
  and foreigners shall not drink the wine
    for which you have labored;
9 but those who garner it shall eat it
    and praise the LORD,
  and those who gather it shall drink it
    in my holy courts.

10 Go through, go through the gates,
    prepare the way for the people;
  build up, build up the highway,
    clear it of stones,
    lift up an ensign over the peoples.
11 The LORD has proclaimed
    to the end of the earth:
  Say to daughter Zion,
    "See, your salvation comes;
  his reward is with him,
    and his recompense before him."
12 They shall be called, "The Holy People,
    The Redeemed of the LORD";
  and you shall be called, "Sought Out,
    A City Not Forsaken."

Vengeance on Edom

63 "WHO IS this that comes from Edom,
    from Bozrah in garments stained crimson?
Who is this so splendidly robed,
    marching in his great might?"

"It is I, announcing vindication,
    mighty to save."

2 "Why are your robes red,
    and your garments like theirs who tread the
    wine press?"

63 WHO IS this who comes from Edom, from the city of Bozrah, with his magnificent garments of crimson? Who is this in royal robes, marching in the greatness of his strength?

"It is I, the Lord, announcing your salvation; I, the Lord, the one who is mighty to save!"

2"Why are your clothes so red, as from treading out the grapes?"

---

d 62:6, 7 intercessors, literally, "watchmen."

e Heb *Azubah*   f Heb *Shemamah*   g Heb *Hephzibah*   h Heb *Beulah*
i Cn: Heb *your sons*

King James

3I have trodden the winepress alone; and of the people *there was* none with me: for I will tread them in mine anger, and trample them in my fury; and their blood shall be sprinkled upon my garments, and I will stain all my raiment.

4For the day of vengeance *is* in mine heart, and the year of my redeemed is come.

5And I looked, and *there was* none to help; and I wondered that *there was* none to uphold: therefore mine own arm brought salvation unto me; and my fury, it upheld me.

6And I will tread down the people in mine anger, and make them drunk in my fury, and I will bring down their strength to the earth.

7¶ I will mention the lovingkindnesses of the LORD, *and* the praises of the LORD, according to all that the LORD hath bestowed on us, and the great goodness toward the house of Israel, which he hath bestowed on them according to his mercies, and according to the multitude of his lovingkindnesses.

8For he said, Surely they *are* my people, children *that* will not lie: so he was their Saviour.

9In all their affliction he was afflicted, and the angel of his presence saved them: in his love and in his pity he redeemed them; and he bare them, and carried them all the days of old.

10¶ But they rebelled, and vexed his holy spirit: therefore he was turned to be their enemy, *and* he fought against them.

11Then he remembered the days of old, Moses, *and* his people, *saying,* Where *is* he that brought them up out of the sea with the shepherd of his flock? where *is* he that put his holy spirit within him?

12That led *them* by the right hand of Moses with his glorious arm, dividing the water before them, to make himself an everlasting name?

13That led them through the deep, as an horse in the wilderness, *that* they should not stumble?

14As a beast goeth down into the valley, the spirit of the LORD caused him to rest: so didst thou lead thy people, to make thyself a glorious name.

15¶ Look down from heaven, and behold from the habitation of thy holiness and of thy glory: where *is* thy zeal and thy strength, the sounding of thy bowels and of thy mercies toward me? are they restrained?

New International

3"I have trodden the winepress alone;
    from the nations no one was with me.
I trampled them in my anger
    and trod them down in my wrath;
their blood spattered my garments,
    and I stained all my clothing.
4For the day of vengeance was in my heart,
    and the year of my redemption has come.
5I looked, but there was no one to help,
    I was appalled that no one gave support;
so my own arm worked salvation for me,
    and my own wrath sustained me.
6I trampled the nations in my anger;
    in my wrath I made them drunk
    and poured their blood on the ground."

Praise and Prayer

7I will tell of the kindnesses of the LORD,
    the deeds for which he is to be praised,
    according to all the LORD has done for us—
yes, the many good things he has done
    for the house of Israel,
    according to his compassion and many
       kindnesses.
8He said, "Surely they are my people,
    sons who will not be false to me";
    and so he became their Savior.
9In all their distress he too was distressed,
    and the angel of his presence saved them.
In his love and mercy he redeemed them;
    he lifted them up and carried them
    all the days of old.
10Yet they rebelled
    and grieved his Holy Spirit.
So he turned and became their enemy
    and he himself fought against them.

11Then his people recalled[a] the days of old,
    the days of Moses and his people—
where is he who brought them through the sea,
    with the shepherd of his flock?
Where is he who set
    his Holy Spirit among them,
12who sent his glorious arm of power
    to be at Moses' right hand,
who divided the waters before them,
    to gain for himself everlasting renown,
13who led them through the depths?
Like a horse in open country,
    they did not stumble;
14like cattle that go down to the plain,
    they were given rest by the Spirit of the
       LORD.
This is how you guided your people
    to make for yourself a glorious name.

15Look down from heaven and see
    from your lofty throne, holy and glorious.
Where are your zeal and your might?
    Your tenderness and compassion are withheld
       from us.

a 11 Or *But may he recall*

Living Bible

3"I have trodden the winepress alone. No one was there to help me. In my wrath I have trodden my enemies like grapes. In my fury I trampled my foes. It is their blood you see upon my clothes. 4For the time has come for me to avenge my people, to redeem them from the hands of their oppressors. 5I looked but no one came to help them; I was amazed and appalled. So I executed vengeance alone; unaided, I meted out judgment. 6I crushed the heathen nations in my anger and made them stagger and fall to the ground."

7I will tell of the lovingkindnesses of God. I will praise him for all he has done; I will rejoice in his great goodness to Israel, which he has granted in accordance with his mercy and love. 8He said, "They are my very own; surely they will not be false again." And he became their Savior. 9In all their affliction he was afflicted, and he personallyᵇ saved them. In his love and pity he redeemed them and lifted them up and carried them through all the years.

10But they rebelled against him and grieved his Holy Spirit. That is why he became their enemy and personally fought against them. 11Then they remembered those days of old when Moses, God's servant, led his people out of Egypt and they cried out, "Where is the one who brought Israel through the sea, with Moses as their shepherd? Where is the God who sent his Holy Spirit to be among his people? 12Where is he whose mighty power divided the sea before them when Moses lifted up his hand, and established his reputation forever? 13Who led them through the bottom of the sea? Like fine stallions racing through the desert, they never stumbled. 14Like cattle grazing in the valleys, so the Spirit of the Lord gave them rest. Thus he gave himself a magnificent reputation."

15O Lord, look down from heaven and see us from your holy, glorious home; where is the love for us you used to show—your power, your mercy and your compassion? Where are they now? 16Surely you are still our

New Revised Standard

3 "I have trodden the wine press alone,
    and from the peoples no one was with me;
I trod them in my anger
    and trampled them in my wrath;
their juice spattered on my garments,
    and stained all my robes.
4 For the day of vengeance was in my heart,
    and the year for my redeeming work had
       come.
5 I looked, but there was no helper;
    I stared, but there was no one to sustain me;
so my own arm brought me victory,
    and my wrath sustained me.
6 I trampled down peoples in my anger,
    I crushed them in my wrath,
    and I poured out their lifeblood on the
      earth."

God's Mercy Remembered

7 I will recount the gracious deeds of the LORD,
    the praiseworthy acts of the LORD,
because of all that the LORD has done for us,
    and the great favor to the house of Israel
that he has shown them according to his
      mercy,
    according to the abundance of his steadfast
      love.
8 For he said, "Surely they are my people,
    children who will not deal falsely";
and he became their savior
9   in all their distress.
It was no messengerᶜ or angel
    but his presence that saved them;ᵈ
in his love and in his pity he redeemed them;
    he lifted them up and carried them all the
      days of old.

10 But they rebelled
    and grieved his holy spirit;
therefore he became their enemy;
    he himself fought against them.
11 Then theyᵉ remembered the days of old,
    of Moses his servant.ᶠ
Where is the one who brought them up out of
      the sea
    with the shepherds of his flock?
Where is the one who put within them
    his holy spirit,
12 who caused his glorious arm
    to march at the right hand of Moses,
who divided the waters before them
    to make for himself an everlasting name,
13   who led them through the depths?
Like a horse in the desert,
    they did not stumble.
14 Like cattle that go down into the valley,
    the spirit of the LORD gave them rest.
Thus you led your people,
    to make for yourself a glorious name.

A Prayer of Penitence

15 Look down from heaven and see,
    from your holy and glorious habitation.
Where are your zeal and your might?
    The yearning of your heart and your
      compassion?
    They are withheld from me.

ᵇ 63:9 *he personally saved them,* or, "The Angel of his Presence saved them out of their affliction."

ᶜ Gk: Heb *anguish*   ᵈ Or *savior.* ⁹*In all their distress he was distressed; the angel of his presence saved them;* ᵉ Heb *he* ᶠ Cn: Heb *his people*

King James

16Doubtless thou *art* our father, though Abraham be ignorant of us, and Israel acknowledge us not: thou, O LORD, *art* our father, our redeemer; thy name *is* from everlasting.

17¶ O LORD, why hast thou made us to err from thy ways, *and* hardened our heart from thy fear? Return for thy servants' sake, the tribes of thine inheritance.

18The people of thy holiness have possessed *it* but a little while: our adversaries have trodden down thy sanctuary.

19We are *thine:* thou never barest rule over them; they were not called by thy name.

64 OH THAT thou wouldest rend the heavens, that thou wouldest come down, that the mountains might flow down at thy presence,

2As *when* the melting fire burneth, the fire causeth the waters to boil, to make thy name known to thine adversaries, *that* the nations may tremble at thy presence!

3When thou didst terrible things *which* we looked not for, thou camest down, the mountains flowed down at thy presence.

4For since the beginning of the world *men* have not heard, nor perceived by the ear, neither hath the eye seen, O God, beside thee, *what* he hath prepared for him that waiteth for him.

5Thou meetest him that rejoiceth and worketh righteousness, *those that* remember thee in thy ways: behold, thou art wroth; for we have sinned: in those is continuance, and we shall be saved.

6But we are all as an unclean *thing*, and all our righteousnesses *are* as filthy rags; and we all do fade as a leaf; and our iniquities, like the wind, have taken us away.

7And *there is* none that calleth upon thy name, that stirreth up himself to take hold of thee: for thou hast hid thy face from us, and hast consumed us, because of our iniquities.

8But now, O LORD, thou *art* our father; we *are* the clay, and thou our potter; and we all *are* the work of thy hand.

9¶ Be not wroth very sore, O LORD, neither remember iniquity for ever: behold, see, we beseech thee, we *are* all thy people.

10Thy holy cities are a wilderness, Zion is a wilderness, Jerusalem a desolation.

11Our holy and our beautiful house, where our fathers praised thee, is burned up with fire: and all our pleasant things are laid waste.

New International

16But you are our Father,
      though Abraham does not know us
      or Israel acknowledge us;
   you, O LORD, are our Father,
      our Redeemer from of old is your name.
17Why, O LORD, do you make us wander from
         your ways
      and harden our hearts so we do not revere
         you?
   Return for the sake of your servants,
      the tribes that are your inheritance.
18For a little while your people possessed your
         holy place,
      but now our enemies have trampled down
         your sanctuary.
19We are yours from of old;
      but you have not ruled over them,
      they have not been called by your name.[a]

64 OH, THAT you would rend the heavens and
         come down,
      that the mountains would tremble before you!
2As when fire sets twigs ablaze
      and causes water to boil,
   come down to make your name known to your
         enemies
      and cause the nations to quake before you!
3For when you did awesome things that we did
         not expect,
      you came down, and the mountains trembled
         before you.
4Since ancient times no one has heard,
      no ear has perceived,
   no eye has seen any God besides you,
      who acts on behalf of those who wait for
         him.
5You come to the help of those who gladly do
         right,
      who remember your ways.
   But when we continued to sin against them,
      you were angry.
   How then can we be saved?
6All of us have become like one who is unclean,
      and all our righteous acts are like filthy rags;
   we all shrivel up like a leaf,
      and like the wind our sins sweep us away.
7No one calls on your name
      or strives to lay hold of you;
   for you have hidden your face from us
      and made us waste away because of our sins.

8Yet, O LORD, you are our Father.
      We are the clay, you are the potter;
      we are all the work of your hand.
9Do not be angry beyond measure, O LORD;
      do not remember our sins forever.
   Oh, look upon us, we pray,
      for we are all your people.
10Your sacred cities have become a desert;
      even Zion is a desert, Jerusalem a desolation.
11Our holy and glorious temple, where our fathers
         praised you,
      has been burned with fire,
      and all that we treasured lies in ruins.

---

a *19 Or* We are like those you have never ruled, / like those never called *by your name*

Living Bible

Father! Even if Abraham and Jacob would disown us, still you would be our Father, our Redeemer from ages past. 17O Lord, why have you hardened our hearts and made us sin and turn against you? Return and help us, for we who belong to you need you so.b 18How briefly we possessed Jerusalem! And now our enemies have destroyed her. 19O God, why do you treat us as though we weren't your people, as though we were a heathen nation that never called you "Lord"?

64 OH, THAT you would burst forth from the skies and come down! How the mountains would quake in your presence! 2The consuming fire of your glory would burn down the forests and boil the oceans dry. The nations would tremble before you; then your enemies would learn the reason for your fame! 3So it was before when you came down, for you did awesome things beyond our highest expectations, and how the mountains quaked! 4For since the world began no one has seen or heard of such a God as ours, who works for those who wait for him! 5You welcome those who cheerfully do good, who follow godly ways.

But we are not godly; we are constant sinners and have been all our lives. Therefore your wrath is heavy on us. How can such as we be saved? 6We are all infected and impure with sin. When we put on our prized robes of righteousness we find they are but filthy rags.c Like autumn leaves we fade, wither and fall. And our sins, like the wind, sweep us away. 7Yet no one calls upon your name or pleads with you for mercy. Therefore you have turned away from us and turned us over to our sins.

8And yet, O Lord, you are our Father. We are the clay and you are the Potter. We are all formed by your hand. 9Oh, be not so angry with us, Lord, nor forever remember our sins. Oh, look and see that we are all your people.

10Your holy cities are destroyed; Jerusalem is a desolate wilderness. 11Our holy, beautiful Temple where our fathers praised you is burned down, and all the things

New Revised Standard

16 For you are our father,
    though Abraham does not know us
    and Israel does not acknowledge us;
  you, O Lord, are our father;
    our Redeemer from of old is your name.
17 Why, O Lord, do you make us stray from
        your ways
    and harden our heart, so that we do not fear
        you?
  Turn back for the sake of your servants,
    for the sake of the tribes that are your
        heritage.
18 Your holy people took possession for a little
        while;
    but now our adversaries have trampled
        down your sanctuary.
19 We have long been like those whom you do
        not rule,
    like those not called by your name.

64 O THAT you would tear open the heavens
      and come down,
    so that the mountains would quake at your
        presence—
2d as when fire kindles brushwood
    and the fire causes water to boil—
  to make your name known to your
        adversaries,
    so that the nations might tremble at your
        presence!
3 When you did awesome deeds that we did not
        expect,
    you came down, the mountains quaked at
        your presence.
4 From ages past no one has heard,
    no ear has perceived,
  no eye has seen any God besides you,
    who works for those who wait for him.
5 You meet those who gladly do right,
    those who remember you in your ways.
  But you were angry, and we sinned;
    because you hid yourself we transgressed.e
6 We have all become like one who is unclean,
    and all our righteous deeds are like a filthy
        cloth.
  We all fade like a leaf,
    and our iniquities, like the wind, take us
        away.
7 There is no one who calls on your name,
    or attempts to take hold of you;
  for you have hidden your face from us,
    and have deliveredf us into the hand of our
        iniquity.
8 Yet, O Lord, you are our Father;
    we are the clay, and you are our potter;
    we are all the work of your hand.
9 Do not be exceedingly angry, O Lord,
    and do not remember iniquity forever.
  Now consider, we are all your people.
10 Your holy cities have become a wilderness,
    Zion has become a wilderness,
    Jerusalem a desolation.
11 Our holy and beautiful house,
    where our ancestors praised you,
  has been burned by fire,
    and all our pleasant places have become
        ruins.

---

b 63:17 for we who belong to you need you so, literally, "for your servants' sake."   c 64:6 filthy rags, literally, "filthy as a menstruating woman's rags."

d Ch 64.1 in Heb   e Meaning of Heb uncertain   f Gk Syr Old Latin Tg: Heb melted

King James

12Wilt thou refrain thyself for these *things,* O LORD? wilt thou hold thy peace, and afflict us very sore?

65 I AM sought of *them that* asked not *for me;* I am found of *them that* sought me not: I said, Behold me, behold me, unto a nation *that* was not called by my name.

2I have spread out my hands all the day unto a rebellious people, which walketh in a way *that was* not good, after their own thoughts;

3A people that provoketh me to anger continually to my face; that sacrificeth in gardens, and burneth incense upon altars of brick;

4Which remain among the graves, and lodge in the monuments, which eat swine's flesh, and broth of abominable *things is in* their vessels;

5Which say, Stand by thyself, come not near to me; for I am holier than thou. These *are* a smoke in my nose, a fire that burneth all the day.

6Behold, *it is* written before me: I will not keep silence, but will recompense, even recompense into their bosom,

7Your iniquities, and the iniquities of your fathers together, saith the LORD, which have burned incense upon the mountains, and blasphemed me upon the hills: therefore will I measure their former work into their bosom.

8¶ Thus saith the LORD, As the new wine is found in the cluster, and *one* saith, Destroy it not; for a blessing *is* in it: so will I do for my servants' sakes, that I may not destroy them all.

9And I will bring forth a seed out of Jacob, and out of Judah an inheritor of my mountains: and mine elect shall inherit it, and my servants shall dwell there.

10And Sharon shall be a fold of flocks, and the valley of Achor a place for the herds to lie down in, for my people that have sought me.

11¶ But ye *are* they that forsake the LORD, that forget my holy mountain, that prepare a table for that troop, and that furnish the drink offering unto that number.

12Therefore will I number you to the sword, and ye shall all bow down to the slaughter: because when I called, ye did not answer; when I spake, ye did not hear; but did evil before mine eyes, and did choose *that* wherein I delighted not.

New International

12After all this, O LORD, will you hold yourself back?
  Will you keep silent and punish us beyond measure?

Judgment and Salvation

65 "I REVEALED myself to those who did not ask for me;
  I was found by those who did not seek me.
To a nation that did not call on my name,
  I said, 'Here am I, here am I.'
2All day long I have held out my hands
  to an obstinate people,
who walk in ways not good,
  pursuing their own imaginations—
3a people who continually provoke me
  to my very face,
offering sacrifices in gardens
  and burning incense on altars of brick;
4who sit among the graves
  and spend their nights keeping secret vigil;
who eat the flesh of pigs,
  and whose pots hold broth of unclean meat;
5who say, 'Keep away; don't come near me,
  for I am too sacred for you!'
Such people are smoke in my nostrils,
  a fire that keeps burning all day.

6"See, it stands written before me:
  I will not keep silent but will pay back in full;
  I will pay it back into their laps—
7both your sins and the sins of your fathers,"
  says the LORD.
"Because they burned sacrifices on the mountains
  and defied me on the hills,
I will measure into their laps
  the full payment for their former deeds."

8This is what the LORD says:

"As when juice is still found in a cluster of grapes
  and men say, 'Don't destroy it,
  there is yet some good in it,'
so will I do in behalf of my servants;
  I will not destroy them all.
9I will bring forth descendants from Jacob,
  and from Judah those who will possess my mountains;
my chosen people will inherit them,
  and there will my servants live.
10Sharon will become a pasture for flocks,
  and the Valley of Achor a resting place for herds,
  for my people who seek me.

11"But as for you who forsake the LORD
  and forget my holy mountain,
who spread a table for Fortune
  and fill bowls of mixed wine for Destiny,
12I will destine you for the sword,
  and you will all bend down for the slaughter;
for I called but you did not answer,
  I spoke but you did not listen.
You did evil in my sight
  and chose what displeases me."

Living Bible

of beauty are destroyed. 12After all of this, must you still refuse to help us, Lord? Will you stand silent and still punish us?

65 THE LORD says, Peoplea who never before inquired about me are now seeking me out. Nationsa who never before searched for me are finding me.

2But my own people—though I have been spreading out my arms to welcome them all day long—have rebelled; they follow their own evil paths and thoughts. 3All day long they insult me to my face by worshiping idols in many gardens and burning incense on the rooftops of their homes. 4At night they go out among the graves and caves to worship evil spirits, and they eat pork and other forbidden foods. 5Yet they say to one another, "Don't come too close, you'll defile me! For I am holier than you!" They stifle me. Day in and day out they infuriate me.

6See, here is my decree all written out before me: *I will not stand silent; I will repay. Yes, I will repay them*— 7not only for their own sins but for those of their fathers too, says the Lord, for they also burned incense on the mountains and insulted me upon the hills. I will pay them back in full.

8But I will not destroy them all, says the Lord; for just as good grapes are found among a cluster of bad ones (and someone will say, "Don't throw them all away— there are some good grapes there!") so I will not destroy all Israel, for I have true servants there. 9I will preserve a remnant of my people to possess the land of Israel; those I select will inherit it and serve me there. 10As for my people who have sought me, the plains of Sharon shall again be filled with flocks, and the valley of Achor shall be a place to pasture herds.

11But because the rest of you have forsaken the Lord and his Temple and worship gods of "Fate" and "Destiny," 12therefore I will "destine" you to the sword, and your "fate" shall be a dark one; for when I called, you didn't answer; when I spoke, you wouldn't listen. You deliberately sinned before my very eyes, choosing to do what you know I despise. 13Therefore the Lord God

New Revised Standard

12 After all this, will you restrain yourself,
         O LORD?
      Will you keep silent, and punish us so
         severely?

The Righteousness of God's Judgment

65 I WAS ready to be sought out by those who
         did not ask,
      to be found by those who did not seek me.
   I said, "Here I am, here I am,"
      to a nation that did not call on my name.
2 I held out my hands all day long
      to a rebellious people,
   who walk in a way that is not good,
      following their own devices;
3 a people who provoke me
      to my face continually,
   sacrificing in gardens
      and offering incense on bricks;
4 who sit inside tombs,
      and spend the night in secret places;
   who eat swine's flesh,
      with broth of abominable things in their
         vessels;
5 who say, "Keep to yourself,
      do not come near me, for I am too holy for
         you."
   These are a smoke in my nostrils,
      a fire that burns all day long.
6 See, it is written before me:
      I will not keep silent, but I will repay;
   I will indeed repay into their laps
7   theirb iniquities and theirb ancestors'
         iniquities together,
                                    says the LORD;
   because they offered incense on the mountains
      and reviled me on the hills,
   I will measure into their laps
      full payment for their actions.
8 Thus says the LORD:
   As the wine is found in the cluster,
      and they say, "Do not destroy it,
      for there is a blessing in it,"
   so I will do for my servants' sake,
      and not destroy them all.
9 I will bring forth descendantsc from Jacob,
      and from Judah inheritorsd of my
         mountains;
   my chosen shall inherit it,
      and my servants shall settle there.
10 Sharon shall become a pasture for flocks,
      and the Valley of Achor a place for herds to
         lie down,
   for my people who have sought me.
11 But you who forsake the LORD,
      who forget my holy mountain,
   who set a table for Fortune
      and fill cups of mixed wine for Destiny;
12 I will destine you to the sword,
      and all of you shall bow down to the
         slaughter;
   because, when I called, you did not answer,
      when I spoke, you did not listen,
   but you did what was evil in my sight,
      and chose what I did not delight in.

---

a 65:1 *People*, literally, "those." Some believe this verse as well as the next applies to Israelites rather than to the nations. But see Rom 10:20, 21.   b Gk Syr: Heb *your*   c Or *a descendant*   d Or *an inheritor*

King James

13Therefore thus saith the Lord GOD, Behold, my servants shall eat, but ye shall be hungry: behold, my servants shall drink, but ye shall be thirsty: behold, my servants shall rejoice, but ye shall be ashamed:

14Behold, my servants shall sing for joy of heart, but ye shall cry for sorrow of heart, and shall howl for vexation of spirit.

15And ye shall leave your name for a curse unto my chosen: for the Lord GOD shall slay thee, and call his servants by another name:

16That he who blesseth himself in the earth shall bless himself in the God of truth; and he that sweareth in the earth shall swear by the God of truth; because the former troubles are forgotten, and because they are hid from mine eyes.

17¶ For, behold, I create new heavens and a new earth: and the former shall not be remembered, nor come into mind.

18But be ye glad and rejoice for ever in that which I create: for, behold, I create Jerusalem a rejoicing, and her people a joy.

19And I will rejoice in Jerusalem, and joy in my people: and the voice of weeping shall be no more heard in her, nor the voice of crying.

20There shall be no more thence an infant of days, nor an old man that hath not filled his days; for the child shall die an hundred years old; but the sinner being an hundred years old shall be accursed.

21And they shall build houses, and inhabit them; and they shall plant vineyards, and eat the fruit of them.

22They shall not build, and another inhabit; they shall not plant, and another eat: for as the days of a tree are the days of my people, and mine elect shall long enjoy the work of their hands.

23They shall not labour in vain, nor bring forth for trouble; for they are the seed of the blessed of the LORD, and their offspring with them.

24And it shall come to pass, that before they call, I will answer; and while they are yet speaking, I will hear.

25The wolf and the lamb shall feed together, and the lion shall eat straw like the bullock: and dust shall be the serpent's meat. They shall not hurt nor destroy in all my holy mountain, saith the LORD.

New International

13Therefore this is what the Sovereign LORD says:

"My servants will eat,
    but you will go hungry;
my servants will drink,
    but you will go thirsty;
my servants will rejoice,
    but you will be put to shame.
14My servants will sing
    out of the joy of their hearts,
but you will cry out
    from anguish of heart
    and wail in brokenness of spirit.
15You will leave your name
    to my chosen ones as a curse;
the Sovereign LORD will put you to death,
    but to his servants he will give another name.
16Whoever invokes a blessing in the land
    will do so by the God of truth;
he who takes an oath in the land
    will swear by the God of truth.
For the past troubles will be forgotten
    and hidden from my eyes.

New Heavens and a New Earth

17"Behold, I will create
    new heavens and a new earth.
The former things will not be remembered,
    nor will they come to mind.
18But be glad and rejoice forever
    in what I will create,
for I will create Jerusalem to be a delight
    and its people a joy.
19I will rejoice over Jerusalem
    and take delight in my people;
the sound of weeping and of crying
    will be heard in it no more.

20"Never again will there be in it
    an infant who lives but a few days,
    or an old man who does not live out his
        years;
he who dies at a hundred
    will be thought a mere youth;
he who fails to reach a hundred
    will be considered accursed.
21They will build houses and dwell in them;
    they will plant vineyards and eat their fruit.
22No longer will they build houses and others live
        in them,
    or plant and others eat.
For as the days of a tree,
    so will be the days of my people;
my chosen ones will long enjoy
    the works of their hands.
23They will not toil in vain
    or bear children doomed to misfortune;
for they will be a people blessed by the LORD,
    they and their descendants with them.
24Before they call I will answer;
    while they are still speaking I will hear.
25The wolf and the lamb will feed together,
    and the lion will eat straw like the ox,
    but dust will be the serpent's food.
They will neither harm nor destroy
    on all my holy mountain,"
                                    says the LORD.

a 20 Or / the sinner who reaches

Living Bible

says, You shall starve, but my servants shall eat; you shall be thirsty while they drink; you shall be sad and ashamed, but they shall rejoice. [14]You shall cry in sorrow and vexation and despair, while they sing for joy. [15]Your name shall be a curse word among my people, for the Lord God will slay you and call his true servants by another name.[b]

[16]And yet, the days will come[c] when all who invoke a blessing or take an oath shall swear by the God of Truth; for I will put aside my anger and forget the evil that you did. [17]For see, I am creating new heavens and a new earth—so wonderful that no one will even think about the old ones anymore. [18]Be glad; rejoice forever in my creation. Look! I will recreate Jerusalem as a place of happiness, and her people shall be a joy! [19]And I will rejoice in Jerusalem, and in my people; and the voice of weeping and crying shall not be heard there any more.

[20]No longer will babies die when only a few days old; no longer will men be considered old at 100! Only sinners will die that young! [21, 22]In those days, when a man builds a house, he will keep on living in it—it will not be destroyed by invading armies as in the past. My people will plant vineyards and eat the fruit themselves—their enemies will not confiscate it. For my people will live as long as trees and will long enjoy their hard-won gains. [23]Their harvests will not be eaten by their enemies; their children will not be born to be cannon fodder. For they are the children of those the Lord has blessed; and their children, too, shall be blessed. [24]I will answer them before they even call to me. While they are still talking to me about their needs, I will go ahead and answer their prayers! [25]The wolf and lamb shall feed together, the lion shall eat straw as the ox does, and poisonous snakes shall strike[d] no more! In those days nothing and no one shall be hurt or destroyed in all my Holy Mountain, says the Lord.

New Revised Standard

13 Therefore thus says the Lord GOD:
  My servants shall eat,
    but you shall be hungry;
  my servants shall drink,
    but you shall be thirsty;
  my servants shall rejoice,
    but you shall be put to shame;
14 my servants shall sing for gladness of heart,
    but you shall cry out for pain of heart,
    and shall wail for anguish of spirit.
15 You shall leave your name to my chosen to
    use as a curse,
  and the Lord GOD will put you to death;
  but to his servants he will give a different
    name.
16 Then whoever invokes a blessing in the land
    shall bless by the God of faithfulness,
  and whoever takes an oath in the land
    shall swear by the God of faithfulness;
  because the former troubles are forgotten
    and are hidden from my sight.

The Glorious New Creation

17 For I am about to create new heavens
    and a new earth;
  the former things shall not be remembered
    or come to mind.
18 But be glad and rejoice forever
    in what I am creating;
  for I am about to create Jerusalem as a joy,
    and its people as a delight.
19 I will rejoice in Jerusalem,
    and delight in my people;
  no more shall the sound of weeping be heard
    in it,
    or the cry of distress.
20 No more shall there be in it
    an infant that lives but a few days,
  or an old person who does not live out a
    lifetime;
  for one who dies at a hundred years will be
    considered a youth,
  and one who falls short of a hundred will be
    considered accursed.
21 They shall build houses and inhabit them;
    they shall plant vineyards and eat their fruit.
22 They shall not build and another inhabit;
    they shall not plant and another eat;
  for like the days of a tree shall the days of my
    people be,
  and my chosen shall long enjoy the work of
    their hands.
23 They shall not labor in vain,
    or bear children for calamity;[e]
  for they shall be offspring blessed by the
    LORD—
    and their descendants as well.
24 Before they call I will answer,
    while they are yet speaking I will hear.
25 The wolf and the lamb shall feed together,
    the lion shall eat straw like the ox;
    but the serpent—its food shall be dust!
  They shall not hurt or destroy
    on all my holy mountain,
               says the LORD.

---

[b] *65:15 by another name*, i.e., "Christians"? See Acts 11:26.   [c] *65:16 the days will come*, implied.   [d] *65:25 snakes shall strike no more*, literally, "dust (i.e., not men!) shall be the serpent's food."

[e] Or *sudden terror*

King James

66 THUS SAITH the LORD, The heaven *is* my throne, and the earth *is* my footstool: where *is* the house that ye build unto me? and where *is* the place of my rest?

2For all those *things* hath mine hand made, and all those *things* have been, saith the LORD: but to this *man* will I look, *even* to *him that is* poor and of a contrite spirit, and trembleth at my word.

3He that killeth an ox *is as if* he slew a man; he that sacrificeth a lamb, *as if* he cut off a dog's neck; he that offereth an oblation, *as if he offered* swine's blood; he that burneth incense, *as if* he blessed an idol. Yea, they have chosen their own ways, and their soul delighteth in their abominations.

4I also will choose their delusions, and will bring their fears upon them; because when I called, none did answer; when I spake, they did not hear: but they did evil before mine eyes, and chose *that* in which I delighted not.

5¶ Hear the word of the LORD, ye that tremble at his word; Your brethren that hated you, that cast you out for my name's sake, said, Let the LORD be glorified: but he shall appear to your joy, and they shall be ashamed.

6A voice of noise from the city, a voice from the temple, a voice of the LORD that rendereth recompence to his enemies.

7Before she travailed, she brought forth; before her pain came, she was delivered of a man child.

8Who hath heard such a thing? who hath seen such things? Shall the earth be made to bring forth in one day? *or* shall a nation be born at once? for as soon as Zion travailed, she brought forth her children.

9Shall I bring to the birth, and not cause to bring forth? saith the LORD: shall I cause to bring forth, and shut *the womb?* saith thy God.

10Rejoice ye with Jerusalem, and be glad with her, all ye that love her: rejoice for joy with her, all ye that mourn for her:

11That ye may suck, and be satisfied with the breasts of her consolations; that ye may milk out, and be delighted with the abundance of her glory.

New International

Judgment and Hope

66 THIS IS what the LORD says:

"Heaven is my throne,
and the earth is my footstool.
Where is the house you will build for me?
Where will my resting place be?
2Has not my hand made all these things,
and so they came into being?"
declares the LORD.

"This is the one I esteem:
he who is humble and contrite in spirit,
and trembles at my word.
3But whoever sacrifices a bull
is like one who kills a man,
and whoever offers a lamb,
like one who breaks a dog's neck;
whoever makes a grain offering
is like one who presents pig's blood,
and whoever burns memorial incense,
like one who worships an idol.
They have chosen their own ways,
and their souls delight in their abominations;
4so I also will choose harsh treatment for them
and will bring upon them what they dread.
For when I called, no one answered,
when I spoke, no one listened.
They did evil in my sight
and chose what displeases me."

5Hear the word of the LORD,
you who tremble at his word:
"Your brothers who hate you,
and exclude you because of my name, have
said,
'Let the LORD be glorified,
that we may see your joy!'
Yet they will be put to shame.
6Hear that uproar from the city,
hear that noise from the temple!
It is the sound of the LORD
repaying his enemies all they deserve.

7"Before she goes into labor,
she gives birth;
before the pains come upon her,
she delivers a son.
8Who has ever heard of such a thing?
Who has ever seen such things?
Can a country be born in a day
or a nation be brought forth in a moment?
Yet no sooner is Zion in labor
than she gives birth to her children.
9Do I bring to the moment of birth
and not give delivery?" says the LORD.
"Do I close up the womb
when I bring to delivery?" says your God.
10"Rejoice with Jerusalem and be glad for her,
all you who love her;
rejoice greatly with her,
all you who mourn over her.
11For you will nurse and be satisfied
at her comforting breasts;
you will drink deeply
and delight in her overflowing abundance."

Living Bible

66 HEAVEN IS my throne and the earth is my footstool: What Temple can you build for me as good as that? ²My hand has made both earth and skies, and they are mine. Yet I will look with pity on the man who has a humble and a contrite heart, who trembles at my word.

³But those who choose their own ways, delighting in their sins, are cursed. God will not accept their offerings. When such men sacrifice an ox on the altar of God, it is no more acceptable to him than human sacrifice. If they sacrifice a lamb, or bring an offering of grain, it is as loathsome to God as putting a dog or the blood of a swine on his altar! When they burn incense to him, he counts it the same as though they blessed an idol. ⁴I will send great troubles upon them—all the things they feared, for when I called them, they refused to answer, and when I spoke to them, they would not hear. Instead, they did wrong before my eyes, and chose what they knew I despised.

⁵Hear the words of God, all you who fear him, and tremble at his words: Your brethren hate you and cast you out for being loyal to my name. "Glory to God," they scoff. "Be happy in the Lord!" But they shall be put to shame.

⁶What is all the commotion in the city? What is that terrible noise from the Temple? It is the voice of the Lord taking vengeance upon his enemies.

⁷, ⁸Who has heard or seen anything as strange as this? For in one day, suddenly, a nation, Israel, shall be born, even before the birth pains come. In a moment, just as Israel's anguish starts, the baby is born; the nation begins. ⁹Shall I bring to the point of birth and then not deliver? asks the Lord your God. No! Never!

¹⁰Rejoice with Jerusalem; be glad with her, all you who love her, you who mourned for her. ¹¹Delight in Jerusalem; drink deep of her glory even as an infant at a mother's generous breasts. ¹²Prosperity shall overflow

New Revised Standard

The Worship God Demands

66 THUS SAYS the Lord:
   Heaven is my throne
   and the earth is my footstool;
what is the house that you would build for
   me,
   and what is my resting place?
2 All these things my hand has made,
   and so all these things are mine,ᵃ
          says the Lord.
But this is the one to whom I will look,
   to the humble and contrite in spirit,
   who trembles at my word.

3 Whoever slaughters an ox is like one who
      kills a human being;
   whoever sacrifices a lamb, like one who
      breaks a dog's neck;
   whoever presents a grain offering, like one
      who offers swine's blood;ᵇ
   whoever makes a memorial offering of
      frankincense, like one who blesses an
      idol.
These have chosen their own ways,
   and in their abominations they take delight;
4 I also will choose to mockᶜ them,
   and bring upon them what they fear;
because, when I called, no one answered,
   when I spoke, they did not listen;
but they did what was evil in my sight,
   and chose what did not please me.

The Lord Vindicates Zion

5 Hear the word of the Lord,
   you who tremble at his word:
Your own people who hate you
   and reject you for my name's sake
have said, "Let the Lord be glorified,
   so that we may see your joy";
   but it is they who shall be put to shame.

6 Listen, an uproar from the city!
   A voice from the temple!
The voice of the Lord,
   dealing retribution to his enemies!

7 Before she was in labor
   she gave birth;
before her pain came upon her
   she delivered a son.
8 Who has heard of such a thing?
   Who has seen such things?
Shall a land be born in one day?
   Shall a nation be delivered in one moment?
Yet as soon as Zion was in labor
   she delivered her children.
9 Shall I open the womb and not deliver?
   says the Lord;
shall I, the one who delivers, shut the womb?
   says your God.

10 Rejoice with Jerusalem, and be glad for her,
   all you who love her;
rejoice with her in joy,
   all you who mourn over her—
11 that you may nurse and be satisfied
   from her consoling breast;
that you may drink deeply with delight
   from her glorious bosom.

ᵃ Gk Syr: Heb *these things came to be*   ᵇ Meaning of Heb uncertain   ᶜ Or *to punish*

King James

12For thus saith the LORD, Behold, I will extend peace to her like a river, and the glory of the Gentiles like a flowing stream: then shall ye suck, ye shall be borne upon *her* sides, and be dandled upon *her* knees.

13As one whom his mother comforteth, so will I comfort you; and ye shall be comforted in Jerusalem.

14And when ye see *this,* your heart shall rejoice, and your bones shall flourish like an herb: and the hand of the LORD shall be known toward his servants, and *his* indignation toward his enemies.

15For, behold, the LORD will come with fire, and with his chariots like a whirlwind, to render his anger with fury, and his rebuke with flames of fire.

16For by fire and by his sword will the LORD plead with all flesh: and the slain of the LORD shall be many.

17They that sanctify themselves, and purify themselves in the gardens behind one *tree* in the midst, eating swine's flesh, and the abomination, and the mouse, shall be consumed together, saith the LORD.

18For I *know* their works and their thoughts: it shall come, that I will gather all nations and tongues; and they shall come, and see my glory.

19And I will set a sign among them, and I will send those that escape of them unto the nations, *to* Tarshish, Pul, and Lud, that draw the bow, *to* Tubal, and Javan, *to* the isles afar off, that have not heard my fame, neither have seen my glory; and they shall declare my glory among the Gentiles.

20And they shall bring all your brethren *for* an offering unto the LORD out of all nations upon horses, and in chariots, and in litters, and upon mules, and upon swift beasts, to my holy mountain Jerusalem, saith the LORD, as the children of Israel bring an offering in a clean vessel into the house of the LORD.

21And I will also take of them for priests *and* for Levites, saith the LORD.

22For as the new heavens and the new earth, which I will make, shall remain before me, saith the LORD, so shall your seed and your name remain.

23And it shall come to pass, *that* from one new moon to another, and from one sabbath to another, shall all flesh come to worship before me, saith the LORD.

24And they shall go forth, and look upon the carcases of the men that have transgressed against me: for their worm shall not die, neither shall their fire be quenched; and they shall be an abhorring unto all flesh.

New International

12For this is what the LORD says:

"I will extend peace to her like a river,
  and the wealth of nations like a flooding
    stream;
you will nurse and be carried on her arm
  and dandled on her knees.
13As a mother comforts her child,
  so will I comfort you;
  and you will be comforted over Jerusalem."
14When you see this, your heart will rejoice
  and you will flourish like grass;
the hand of the LORD will be made known to
    his servants,
  but his fury will be shown to his foes.
15See, the LORD is coming with fire,
  and his chariots are like a whirlwind;
he will bring down his anger with fury,
  and his rebuke with flames of fire.
16For with fire and with his sword
  the LORD will execute judgment upon all
    men,
  and many will be those slain by the LORD.

17"Those who consecrate and purify themselves to go into the gardens, following the one in the midst of[a] those who eat the flesh of pigs and rats and other abominable things—they will meet their end together," declares the LORD.

18"And I, because of their actions and their imaginations, am about to come[b] and gather all nations and tongues, and they will come and see my glory.

19"I will set a sign among them, and I will send some of those who survive to the nations—to Tarshish, to the Libyans[c] and Lydians (famous as archers), to Tubal and Greece, and to the distant islands that have not heard of my fame or seen my glory. They will proclaim my glory among the nations. 20And they will bring all your brothers, from all the nations, to my holy mountain in Jerusalem as an offering to the LORD—on horses, in chariots and wagons, and on mules and camels," says the LORD. "They will bring them, as the Israelites bring their grain offerings, to the temple of the LORD in ceremonially clean vessels. 21And I will select some of them also to be priests and Levites," says the LORD.

22"As the new heavens and the new earth that I make will endure before me," declares the LORD, "so will your name and descendants endure. 23From one New Moon to another and from one Sabbath to another, all mankind will come and bow down before me," says the LORD. 24"And they will go out and look upon the dead bodies of those who rebelled against me; their worm will not die, nor will their fire be quenched, and they will be loathsome to all mankind."

---

a *17* Or *gardens behind one of your temples, and*   b *18* The meaning of the Hebrew for this clause is uncertain.   c *19* Some Septuagint manuscripts *Put* (Libyans); Hebrew *Pul*

Living Bible

Jerusalem like a river, says the Lord, for I will send it; the riches of the Gentiles will flow to her. Her children shall be nursed at her breasts, carried on her hips and dandled on her knees. 13I will comfort you there as a little one is comforted by its mother. 14When you see Jerusalem, your heart will rejoice; vigorous health will be yours. All the world will see the good hand of God upon his people, and his wrath upon his enemies.

15For see, the Lord will come with fire and with swift chariots of doom to pour out the fury of his anger and his hot rebuke with flames of fire. 16For the Lord will punish the world by fire and by his sword, and the slain of the Lord shall be many! 17Those who worship idols that are hidden behind a tree in the garden, feasting there on pork and mouse and all forbidden meat—they will come to an evil end, says Jehovah. 18I see full well what they are doing; I know what they are thinking, so I will gather together all nations and people against Jerusalem, where they shall see my glory. 19I will perform a mighty miracle against them, and I will send thosed who escape, as missionaries to the nations—to Tarshish, Put, Lud, Meshech, Rosh, Tubal, Javan, and the lands beyond the sea that have not heard my fame nor seen my glory. There they shall declare my glory to the Gentiles. 20And they shall bring back all your brethren from every nation as a gift to the Lord, transporting them gentlye on horses and in chariots, and in litters, and on mules and camels, to my holy mountain, to Jerusalem, says the Lord. It will be like offerings flowing into the Temple of the Lord at harvest time, carried in vessels consecrated to the Lord. 21And I will appoint some of those returning to be my priests and Levites, says the Lord. 22As surely as my new heavens and earth shall remain, so surely shall you always be my people, with a name that shall never disappear. 23All mankind shall come to worship me from week to week and month to month. 24And they shall go out and look at the dead bodies of those who have rebelled against me, for their worm shall never die; their fire shall not be quenched, and they shall be a disgusting sight to all mankind.

New Revised Standard

12 For thus says the LORD:
I will extend prosperity to her like a river,
and the wealth of the nations like an
overflowing stream;
and you shall nurse and be carried on her arm,
and dandled on her knees.
13 As a mother comforts her child,
so I will comfort you;
you shall be comforted in Jerusalem.

The Reign and Indignation of God

14 You shall see, and your heart shall rejoice;
your bodiesf shall flourish like the grass;
and it shall be known that the hand of the
LORD is with his servants,
and his indignation is against his enemies.
15 For the LORD will come in fire,
and his chariots like the whirlwind,
to pay back his anger in fury,
and his rebuke in flames of fire.
16 For by fire will the LORD execute judgment,
and by his sword, on all flesh;
and those slain by the LORD shall be many.

17 Those who sanctify and purify themselves to go into the gardens, following the one in the center, eating the flesh of pigs, vermin, and rodents, shall come to an end together, says the LORD.

18 For I knowg their works and their thoughts, and I amh coming to gather all nations and tongues; and they shall come and shall see my glory, 19and I will set a sign among them. From them I will send survivors to the nations, to Tarshish, Put,i and Lud—which draw the bow—to Tubal and Javan, to the coastlands far away that have not heard of my fame or seen my glory; and they shall declare my glory among the nations. 20They shall bring all your kindred from all the nations as an offering to the LORD, on horses, and in chariots, and in litters, and on mules, and on dromedaries, to my holy mountain Jerusalem, says the LORD, just as the Israelites bring a grain offering in a clean vessel to the house of the LORD. 21And I will also take some of them as priests and as Levites, says the LORD.

22 For as the new heavens and the new earth,
which I will make,
shall remain before me, says the LORD;
so shall your descendants and your name
remain.
23 From new moon to new moon,
and from sabbath to sabbath,
all flesh shall come to worship before me,
says the LORD.

24 And they shall go out and look at the dead bodies of the people who have rebelled against me; for their worm shall not die, their fire shall not be quenched, and they shall be an abhorrence to all flesh.

---

d *66:19 I will send those who escape.* It is not clear from the Hebrew whether "those who escape" means survivors of the armies of the nations, or survivors of the Jews in Israel. The context seems to favor the former. Put and Lud were in North Africa; Meshech, Rosh, and Tubal were in Asia Minor and Armenia. e *66:20 transporting them gently,* implied.

f Heb *bones*   g Gk Syr: Heb lacks *know*   h Gk Syr Vg Tg: Heb *it is*   i Gk: Heb *Pul*

THE BOOK OF THE PROPHET

Jeremiah

Jeremiah

1 THE WORDS of Jeremiah the son of Hilkiah, of the priests that *were* in Anathoth in the land of Benjamin:

²To whom the word of the LORD came in the days of Josiah the son of Amon king of Judah, in the thirteenth year of his reign.

³It came also in the days of Jehoiakim the son of Josiah king of Judah, unto the end of the eleventh year of Zedekiah the son of Josiah king of Judah, unto the carrying away of Jerusalem captive in the fifth month.

⁴Then the word of the LORD came unto me, saying,

⁵Before I formed thee in the belly I knew thee; and before thou camest forth out of the womb I sanctified thee, *and* I ordained thee a prophet unto the nations.

⁶Then said I, Ah, Lord GOD! behold, I cannot speak: for I *am* a child.

⁷¶ But the LORD said unto me, Say not, I *am* a child: for thou shalt go to all that I shall send thee, and whatsoever I command thee thou shalt speak.

⁸Be not afraid of their faces: for I *am* with thee to deliver thee, saith the LORD.

⁹Then the LORD put forth his hand, and touched my mouth. And the LORD said unto me, Behold, I have put my words in thy mouth.

¹⁰See, I have this day set thee over the nations and over the kingdoms, to root out, and to pull down, and to destroy, and to throw down, to build, and to plant.

¹¹¶ Moreover the word of the LORD came unto me, saying, Jeremiah, what seest thou? And I said, I see a rod of an almond tree.

¹²Then said the LORD unto me, Thou hast well seen: for I will hasten my word to perform it.

¹³And the word of the LORD came unto me the second time, saying, What seest thou? And I said, I see a seething pot; and the face thereof *is* toward the north.

¹⁴Then the LORD said unto me, Out of the north an evil shall break forth upon all the inhabitants of the land.

¹⁵For, lo, I will call all the families of the kingdoms of the north, saith the LORD; and they shall come, and they shall set every one his throne at the entering of the gates of Jerusalem, and against all the walls thereof round about, and against all the cities of Judah.

¹⁶And I will utter my judgments against them touching all their wickedness, who have forsaken me, and have burned incense unto other gods, and worshipped the works of their own hands.

¹⁷¶ Thou therefore gird up thy loins, and arise, and speak unto them all that I command thee: be not dismayed at their faces, lest I confound thee before them.

1 THE WORDS of Jeremiah son of Hilkiah, one of the priests at Anathoth in the territory of Benjamin. ²The word of the LORD came to him in the thirteenth year of the reign of Josiah son of Amon king of Judah, ³and through the reign of Jehoiakim son of Josiah king of Judah, down to the fifth month of the eleventh year of Zedekiah son of Josiah king of Judah, when the people of Jerusalem went into exile.

The Call of Jeremiah

⁴The word of the LORD came to me, saying,

⁵"Before I formed you in the womb I knewᵃ you,
  before you were born I set you apart;
  I appointed you as a prophet to the nations."

⁶"Ah, Sovereign LORD," I said, "I do not know how to speak; I am only a child."

⁷But the LORD said to me, "Do not say, 'I am only a child.' You must go to everyone I send you to and say whatever I command you. ⁸Do not be afraid of them, for I am with you and will rescue you," declares the LORD.

⁹Then the LORD reached out his hand and touched my mouth and said to me, "Now, I have put my words in your mouth. ¹⁰See, today I appoint you over nations and kingdoms to uproot and tear down, to destroy and overthrow, to build and to plant."

¹¹The word of the LORD came to me: "What do you see, Jeremiah?"

"I see the branch of an almond tree," I replied.

¹²The LORD said to me, "You have seen correctly, for I am watchingᵇ to see that my word is fulfilled."

¹³The word of the LORD came to me again: "What do you see?"

"I see a boiling pot, tilting away from the north," I answered.

¹⁴The LORD said to me, "From the north disaster will be poured out on all who live in the land. ¹⁵I am about to summon all the peoples of the northern kingdoms," declares the LORD.

  "Their kings will come and set up their thrones
    in the entrance of the gates of Jerusalem;
  they will come against all her surrounding walls
    and against all the towns of Judah.
¹⁶I will pronounce my judgments on my people
  because of their wickedness in forsaking me,
  in burning incense to other gods
  and in worshiping what their hands have
    made.

¹⁷"Get yourself ready! Stand up and say to them whatever I command you. Do not be terrified by them, or I will terrify you before them. ¹⁸Today I have made

---

ᵃ 5 Or *chose*   ᵇ 12 The Hebrew for *watching* sounds like the Hebrew for *almond tree.*

Living Bible	New Revised Standard

Jeremiah

Jeremiah

1 THESE ARE God's messages to Jeremiah the priest (the son of Hilkiah) who lived in the town of Anathoth in the land of Benjamin. The first of these messages came to him in the thirteenth year of the reign of Amon's son Josiah, king of Judah. ³Others came during the reign of Josiah's son Jehoiakim, king of Judah, and at various other times until July of the eleventh year of the reign of Josiah's son Zedekiah, king of Judah, when Jerusalem was captured and the people were taken away as slaves.

⁴The Lord said to me, ⁵"I knew you before you were formed within your mother's womb; before you were born I sanctified you and appointed you as my spokesman to the world."

⁶"O Lord God," I said, "I can't do that! I'm far too young! I'm only a youth!"

⁷"Don't say that," he replied, "for you will go wherever I send you and speak whatever I tell you to. ⁸And don't be afraid of the people, for I, the Lord, will be with you and see you through."

⁹Then he touched my mouth and said, "See, I have put my words in your mouth! ¹⁰Today your work begins, to warn the nations and the kingdoms of the world. In accord with my words spoken through your mouth I will tear down some and destroy them, and plant others and nurture them and make them strong and great."

¹¹Then the Lord said to me, "Look, Jeremiah! What do you see?"

And I replied, "I see a whip made from the branch of an almond tree."

¹²And the Lord replied, "That's right, and it means that I will surely carry out my threats of punishment."ᶜ

¹³Then the Lord asked me, "What do you see now?"

And I replied, "I see a pot of boiling water, tipping southward, spilling over Judah."ᵈ

¹⁴"Yes," he said, "for terror from the north will boil out upon all the people of this land. ¹⁵I am calling the armies of the kingdoms of the north to come to Jerusalem and set their thrones at the gates of the city and all along its walls, and in all the other cities of Judah. ¹⁶This is the way I will punish my people for deserting me and for worshiping other gods—yes, idols they themselves have made! ¹⁷Get up and dress and go out and tell them whatever I tell you to say. Don't be afraid of them, or else I will make a fool of you in front of them. ¹⁸For see,

1 THE WORDS of Jeremiah son of Hilkiah, of the priests who were in Anathoth in the land of Benjamin, ²to whom the word of the LORD came in the days of King Josiah son of Amon of Judah, in the thirteenth year of his reign. ³It came also in the days of King Jehoiakim son of Josiah of Judah, and until the end of the eleventh year of King Zedekiah son of Josiah of Judah, until the captivity of Jerusalem in the fifth month.

Jeremiah's Call and Commission

4 Now the word of the LORD came to me saying,
5   "Before I formed you in the womb I knew
        you,
    and before you were born I consecrated you;
    I appointed you a prophet to the nations."
⁶Then I said, "Ah, Lord GOD! Truly I do not know how to speak, for I am only a boy." ⁷But the LORD said to me,
    "Do not say, 'I am only a boy';
    for you shall go to all to whom I send you,
    and you shall speak whatever I command you,
8   Do not be afraid of them,
    for I am with you to deliver you,
                            says the LORD."
⁹Then the LORD put out his hand and touched my mouth; and the LORD said to me,
    "Now I have put my words in your mouth.
10 See, today I appoint you over nations and
        over kingdoms,
    to pluck up and to pull down,
    to destroy and to overthrow,
    to build and to plant."

11 The word of the LORD came to me, saying, "Jeremiah, what do you see?" And I said, "I see a branch of an almond tree."ᵉ ¹²Then the LORD said to me, "You have seen well, for I am watchingᶠ over my word to perform it." ¹³The word of the LORD came to me a second time, saying, "What do you see?" And I said, "I see a boiling pot, tilted away from the north."

14 Then the LORD said to me: Out of the north disaster shall break out on all the inhabitants of the land. ¹⁵For now I am calling all the tribes of the kingdoms of the north, says the LORD; and they shall come and all of them shall set their thrones at the entrance of the gates of Jerusalem, against all its surrounding walls and against all the cities of Judah. ¹⁶And I will utter my judgments against them, for all their wickedness in forsaking me; they have made offerings to other gods, and worshiped the works of their own hands. ¹⁷But you, gird up your loins; stand up and tell them everything that I command you. Do not break down before them, or I will break you before them. ¹⁸And I for my part have made

---

ᶜ *1:12 I will surely carry out my threats of punishment.* There is a word play here between *shaqedh* (almond) in vs 11 and *shoqedh* (watching) in vs 12: "For I am watching over my word to perform it."   ᵈ *1:13 spilling over Judah,* implied.

ᵉ Heb *shaqed*   ᶠ Heb *shoqed*

King James

18For, behold, I have made thee this day a defenced city, and an iron pillar, and brasen walls against the whole land, against the kings of Judah, against the princes thereof, against the priests thereof, and against the people of the land.

19And they shall fight against thee; but they shall not prevail against thee; for I *am* with thee, saith the LORD, to deliver thee.

2 MOREOVER THE word of the LORD came to me, saying,

2Go and cry in the ears of Jerusalem, saying, Thus saith the LORD; I remember thee, the kindness of thy youth, the love of thine espousals, when thou wentest after me in the wilderness, in a land *that was* not sown.

3Israel *was* holiness unto the LORD, *and* the firstfruits of his increase: all that devour him shall offend; evil shall come upon them, saith the LORD.

4Hear ye the word of the LORD, O house of Jacob, and all the families of the house of Israel:

5¶ Thus saith the LORD, What iniquity have your fathers found in me, that they are gone far from me, and have walked after vanity, and are become vain?

6Neither said they, Where *is* the LORD that brought us up out of the land of Egypt, that led us through the wilderness, through a land of deserts and of pits, through a land of drought, and of the shadow of death, through a land that no man passed through, and where no man dwelt?

7And I brought you into a plentiful country, to eat the fruit thereof and the goodness thereof; but when ye entered, ye defiled my land, and made mine heritage an abomination.

8The priests said not, Where *is* the LORD? and they that handle the law knew me not: the pastors also transgressed against me, and the prophets prophesied by Baal, and walked after *things* that do not profit.

9¶ Wherefore I will yet plead with you, saith the LORD, and with your children's children will I plead.

10For pass over the isles of Chittim, and see; and send unto Kedar, and consider diligently, and see if there be such a thing.

11Hath a nation changed *their* gods, which *are* yet no gods? but my people have changed their glory for *that which* doth not profit.

12Be astonished, O ye heavens, at this, and be horribly afraid, be ye very desolate, saith the LORD.

13For my people have committed two evils; they have forsaken me the fountain of living waters, *and* hewed them out cisterns, broken cisterns, that can hold no water.

New International

you a fortified city, an iron pillar and a bronze wall to stand against the whole land—against the kings of Judah, its officials, its priests and the people of the land. 19They will fight against you but will not overcome you, for I am with you and will rescue you," declares the LORD.

Israel Forsakes God

2 THE WORD of the LORD came to me: 2"Go and proclaim in the hearing of Jerusalem:

" 'I remember the devotion of your youth,
  how as a bride you loved me
and followed me through the desert,
  through a land not sown.
3Israel was holy to the LORD,
  the firstfruits of his harvest;
all who devoured her were held guilty,
  and disaster overtook them,' "
                          declares the LORD.

4Hear the word of the LORD, O house of Jacob,
  all you clans of the house of Israel.

5This is what the LORD says:

"What fault did your fathers find in me,
  that they strayed so far from me?
They followed worthless idols
  and became worthless themselves.
6They did not ask, 'Where is the LORD,
  who brought us up out of Egypt
and led us through the barren wilderness,
  through a land of deserts and rifts,
a land of drought and darkness,[a]
  a land where no one travels and no one
    lives?'
7I brought you into a fertile land
  to eat its fruit and rich produce.
But you came and defiled my land
  and made my inheritance detestable.
8The priests did not ask,
  'Where is the LORD?'
Those who deal with the law did not know me;
  the leaders rebelled against me.
The prophets prophesied by Baal,
  following worthless idols.

9"Therefore I bring charges against you again,"
                          declares the LORD.
  "And I will bring charges against your
    children's children.
10Cross over to the coasts of Kittim[b] and look,
  send to Kedar[c] and observe closely;
  see if there has ever been anything like this:
11Has a nation ever changed its gods?
  (Yet they are not gods at all.)
But my people have exchanged their[d] Glory
  for worthless idols.
12Be appalled at this, O heavens,
  and shudder with great horror,"
                          declares the LORD.
13"My people have committed two sins:
They have forsaken me,
  the spring of living water,
and have dug their own cisterns,
  broken cisterns that cannot hold water.

---

[a] *6* Or *and the shadow of death*   [b] *10* That is, Cyprus and western coastlands
[c] *10* The home of Bedouin tribes in the Syro-Arabian desert   [d] *11* Masoretic Text; an ancient Hebrew scribal tradition *my*

Living Bible

today I have made you impervious to their attacks. They cannot harm you. You are strong like a fortified city that cannot be captured, like an iron pillar and heavy gates of brass. All the kings of Judah and its officers and priests and people will not be able to prevail against you. 19They will try, but they will fail. For I am with you," says the Lord. "I will deliver you."

2 AGAIN THE Lord spoke to me and said: 2Go and shout this in Jerusalem's streets: The Lord says, I remember how eager you were to please me as a young bride long ago and how you loved me and followed me even through the barren deserts. 3In those days Israel was a holy people, the first of my children.e All who harmed them were counted deeply guilty, and great evil fell on anyone who touched them.

4,5O Israel, says the Lord, why did your fathers desert me? What sin did they find in me that turned them away and changed them into fools who worship idols? 6They ignore the fact that it was I, the Lord, who brought them safely out of Egypt and led them through the barren wilderness, a land of deserts and rocks, of drought and death, where no one lives or even travels. 7And I brought them into a fruitful land, to eat of its bounty and goodness, but they made it into a land of sin and corruption and turned my inheritance into an evil thing. 8Even their priests cared nothing for the Lord, and their judges ignored me; their rulers turned against me, and their prophets worshiped Baal and wasted their time on nonsense.

9But I will not give you up—I will plead for you to return to me, and will keep on pleading; yes, even with your children's children in the years to come!

10, 11Look around you and see if you can find another nation anywhere that has traded in its old gods for new ones—even though their gods are nothing. Send to the west to the island of Cyprus; send to the east to the deserts of Kedar. See if anyone there has ever heard so strange a thing as this. And yet my people have given up their glorious God for silly idols! 12The heavens are shocked at such a thing and shrink back in horror and dismay. 13For my people have done two evil things: They have forsaken me, the Fountain of Life-giving Water; and they have built for themselves broken cisterns that can't hold water!

New Revised Standard

you today a fortified city, an iron pillar, and a bronze wall, against the whole land—against the kings of Judah, its princes, its priests, and the people of the land. 19They will fight against you; but they shall not prevail against you, for I am with you, says the LORD, to deliver you.

God Pleads with Israel to Repent

2 THE WORD of the LORD came to me, saying: 2Go and proclaim in the hearing of Jerusalem, Thus says the LORD:

I remember the devotion of your youth,
  your love as a bride,
how you followed me in the wilderness,
  in a land not sown.
3 Israel was holy to the LORD,
  the first fruits of his harvest.
All who ate of it were held guilty;
  disaster came upon them,
                                says the LORD.

4 Hear the word of the LORD, O house of Jacob, and all the families of the house of Israel. 5Thus says the LORD:

What wrong did your ancestors find in me
  that they went far from me,
and went after worthless things, and became
  worthless themselves?
6 They did not say, "Where is the LORD
  who brought us up from the land of Egypt,
who led us in the wilderness,
  in a land of deserts and pits,
in a land of drought and deep darkness,
  in a land that no one passes through,
  where no one lives?"
7 I brought you into a plentiful land
  to eat its fruits and its good things.
But when you entered you defiled my land,
  and made my heritage an abomination.
8 The priests did not say, "Where is the LORD?"
  Those who handle the law did not know
  me;
the rulersf transgressed against me;
  the prophets prophesied by Baal,
  and went after things that do not profit.

9 Therefore once more I accuse you,
                                says the LORD,
  and I accuse your children's children.
10 Cross to the coasts of Cyprus and look,
  send to Kedar and examine with care;
  see if there has ever been such a thing.
11 Has a nation changed its gods,
  even though they are no gods?
But my people have changed their glory
  for something that does not profit.
12 Be appalled, O heavens, at this,
  be shocked, be utterly desolate,
                                says the LORD,
13 for my people have committed two evils:
  they have forsaken me,
  the fountain of living water,
  and dug out cisterns for themselves,
cracked cisterns
  that can hold no water.

---

e 2:3 the first of my children, literally, "the firstfruits of his harvest."   f Heb shepherds

King James

14¶ *Is* Israel a servant? *is* he a homeborn *slave?* why is he spoiled?

15The young lions roared upon him, *and* yelled, and they made his land waste: his cities are burned without inhabitant.

16Also the children of Noph and Tahapanes have broken the crown of thy head.

17Hast thou not procured this unto thyself, in that thou hast forsaken the LORD thy God, when he led thee by the way?

18And now what hast thou to do in the way of Egypt, to drink the waters of Sihor? or what hast thou to do in the way of Assyria, to drink the waters of the river?

19Thine own wickedness shall correct thee, and thy backslidings shall reprove thee: know therefore and see that *it is* an evil *thing* and bitter, that thou hast forsaken the LORD thy God, and that my fear *is* not in thee, saith the Lord GOD of hosts.

20¶ For of old time I have broken thy yoke, *and* burst thy bands; and thou saidst, I will not transgress; when upon every high hill and under every green tree thou wanderest, playing the harlot.

21Yet I had planted thee a noble vine, wholly a right seed: how then art thou turned into the degenerate plant of a strange vine unto me?

22For though thou wash thee with nitre, and take thee much soap, *yet* thine iniquity is marked before me, saith the Lord GOD.

23How canst thou say, I am not polluted, I have not gone after Baalim? see thy way in the valley, know what thou hast done: *thou art* a swift dromedary traversing her ways;

24A wild ass used to the wilderness, *that* snuffeth up the wind at her pleasure; in her occasion who can turn her away? all they that seek her will not weary themselves; in her month they shall find her.

25Withhold thy foot from being unshod, and thy throat from thirst: but thou saidst, There is no hope: no; for I have loved strangers, and after them will I go.

26As the thief is ashamed when he is found, so is the house of Israel ashamed; they, their kings, their princes, and their priests, and their prophets,

27Saying to a stock, Thou *art* my father; and to a stone, Thou hast brought me forth: for they have turned *their* back unto me, and not *their* face: but in the time of their trouble they will say, Arise, and save us.

28But where *are* thy gods that thou hast made thee? let them arise, if they can save thee in the time of thy trouble: for *according to* the number of thy cities are thy gods, O Judah.

New International

14Is Israel a servant, a slave by birth?
  Why then has he become plunder?
15Lions have roared;
  they have growled at him.
They have laid waste his land;
  his towns are burned and deserted.
16Also, the men of Memphis[a] and Tahpanhes
  have shaved the crown of your head.[b]
17Have you not brought this on yourselves
  by forsaking the LORD your God
  when he led you in the way?
18Now why go to Egypt
  to drink water from the Shihor[c]?
And why go to Assyria
  to drink water from the River[d]?
19Your wickedness will punish you;
  your backsliding will rebuke you.
Consider then and realize
  how evil and bitter it is for you
when you forsake the LORD your God
  and have no awe of me,"
    declares the Lord, the LORD Almighty.

20"Long ago you broke off your yoke
  and tore off your bonds;
  you said, 'I will not serve you!'
Indeed, on every high hill
  and under every spreading tree
  you lay down as a prostitute.
21I had planted you like a choice vine
  of sound and reliable stock.
How then did you turn against me
  into a corrupt, wild vine?
22Although you wash yourself with soda
  and use an abundance of soap,
  the stain of your guilt is still before me,"
    declares the Sovereign LORD.
23"How can you say, 'I am not defiled;
  I have not run after the Baals'?
See how you behaved in the valley;
  consider what you have done.
You are a swift she-camel
  running here and there,
24a wild donkey accustomed to the desert,
  sniffing the wind in her craving—
  in her heat who can restrain her?
Any males that pursue her need not tire
    themselves;
  at mating time they will find her.
25Do not run until your feet are bare
  and your throat is dry.
But you said, 'It's no use!
  I love foreign gods,
  and I must go after them.'

26"As a thief is disgraced when he is caught,
  so the house of Israel is disgraced—
they, their kings and their officials,
  their priests and their prophets.
27They say to wood, 'You are my father,'
  and to stone, 'You gave me birth.'
They have turned their backs to me
  and not their faces;
yet when they are in trouble, they say,
  'Come and save us!'
28Where then are the gods you made for
    yourselves?
  Let them come if they can save you
  when you are in trouble!
For you have as many gods
  as you have towns, O Judah.

a 16 Hebrew *Noph*   b 16 Or *have cracked your skull*   c 18 That is, a branch of the Nile   d 18 That is, the Euphrates

Living Bible

¹⁴Why has Israel become a nation of slaves? Why is she captured and led far away?

¹⁵I see great armies marching on Jerusalem with mighty shouts[e] to destroy her and leave her cities in ruins, burned and desolate. ¹⁶I see the armies of Egypt rising against her, marching from their cities of Memphis and Tahpanhes to utterly destroy Israel's glory and power. ¹⁷And you have brought this on yourselves by rebelling against the Lord your God when he wanted to lead you and show you the way!

¹⁸What have you gained by your alliances with Egypt and with Assyria? ¹⁹Your own wickedness will punish you. You will see what an evil, bitter thing it is to rebel against the Lord your God, fearlessly forsaking him, says the Lord Almighty. ²⁰Long ago you shook off my yoke and broke away from my ties. Defiant, you would not obey me. On every hill and under every tree you've bowed low before idols.

²¹How could this happen? How could this be? For when I planted you, I chose my seed so carefully—the very best. Why have you become this degenerate race of evil men? ²²No amount of soap or lye can make you clean. You are stained with guilt that cannot ever be washed away. I see it always before me, the Lord God says. ²³You say it isn't so, that you haven't worshiped idols? How can you say a thing like that? Go and look in any valley in the land! Face the awful sins that you have done, O restless female camel, seeking for a male! ²⁴You are a wild donkey, sniffing the wind at mating time. (Who can restrain her lust?) Any jack wanting you need not search, for you come running to him! ²⁵Why don't you turn from all this weary running after other gods? But you say, "Don't waste your breath. I've fallen in love with these strangers and I can't stop loving them now!"

^{26, 27}Like a thief, the only shame that Israel knows is getting caught. Kings, princes, priests and prophets—all are alike in this. They call a carved-up wooden post their father, and for their mother they have an idol chiseled out from stone. Yet in time of trouble they cry to me to save them! ²⁸Why don't you call on these gods you have made? When danger comes, let *them* go out and save you if they can! For you have as many gods as there are cities in Judah. ²⁹Don't come to me—you are all

New Revised Standard

¹⁴ Is Israel a slave? Is he a homeborn servant?
    Why then has he become plunder?
¹⁵ The lions have roared against him,
      they have roared loudly.
   They have made his land a waste;
      his cities are in ruins, without inhabitant.
¹⁶ Moreover, the people of Memphis and
      Tahpanhes
      have broken the crown of your head.
¹⁷ Have you not brought this upon yourself
      by forsaking the LORD your God,
   while he led you in the way?
¹⁸ What then do you gain by going to Egypt,
      to drink the waters of the Nile?
   Or what do you gain by going to Assyria,
      to drink the waters of the Euphrates?
¹⁹ Your wickedness will punish you,
      and your apostasies will convict you.
   Know and see that it is evil and bitter
      for you to forsake the LORD your God;
      the fear of me is not in you,
         says the Lord GOD of hosts.

²⁰ For long ago you broke your yoke
      and burst your bonds,
      and you said, "I will not serve!"
   On every high hill
      and under every green tree
      you sprawled and played the whore.
²¹ Yet I planted you as a choice vine,
      from the purest stock.
   How then did you turn degenerate
      and become a wild vine?
²² Though you wash yourself with lye
      and use much soap,
      the stain of your guilt is still before me,
         says the Lord GOD.
²³ How can you say, "I am not defiled,
      I have not gone after the Baals"?
   Look at your way in the valley;
      know what you have done—
   a restive young camel interlacing her tracks,
²⁴   a wild ass at home in the wilderness,
   in her heat sniffing the wind!
      Who can restrain her lust?
   None who seek her need weary themselves;
      in her month they will find her.
²⁵ Keep your feet from going unshod
      and your throat from thirst.
   But you said, "It is hopeless,
      for I have loved strangers,
      and after them I will go."

²⁶ As a thief is shamed when caught,
      so the house of Israel shall be shamed—
   they, their kings, their officials,
      their priests, and their prophets,
²⁷ who say to a tree, "You are my father,"
      and to a stone, "You gave me birth."
   For they have turned their backs to me,
      and not their faces.
   But in the time of their trouble they say,
      "Come and save us!"
²⁸ But where are your gods
      that you made for yourself?
   Let them come, if they can save you,
      in your time of trouble;
   for you have as many gods
      as you have towns, O Judah.

---

e *2:15 I see great armies marching on Jerusalem with mighty shouts,* literally, "The lions have roared against him."

King James

29Wherefore will ye plead with me? ye all have transgressed against me, saith the LORD.
30In vain have I smitten your children; they received no correction: your own sword hath devoured your prophets, like a destroying lion.
31¶ O generation, see ye the word of the LORD. Have I been a wilderness unto Israel? a land of darkness? wherefore say my people, We are lords; we will come no more unto thee?
32Can a maid forget her ornaments, *or* a bride her attire? yet my people have forgotten me days without number.
33Why trimmest thou thy way to seek love? therefore hast thou also taught the wicked ones thy ways.
34Also in thy skirts is found the blood of the souls of the poor innocents: I have not found it by secret search, but upon all these.
35Yet thou sayest, Because I am innocent, surely his anger shall turn from me. Behold, I will plead with thee, because thou sayest, I have not sinned.
36Why gaddest thou about so much to change thy way? thou also shalt be ashamed of Egypt, as thou wast ashamed of Assyria.
37Yea, thou shalt go forth from him, and thine hands upon thine head: for the LORD hath rejected thy confidences, and thou shalt not prosper in them.

3 THEY SAY, If a man put away his wife, and she go from him, and become another man's, shall he return unto her again? shall not that land be greatly polluted? but thou hast played the harlot with many lovers; yet return again to me, saith the LORD.
2Lift up thine eyes unto the high places, and see where thou hast not been lain with. In the ways hast thou sat for them, as the Arabian in the wilderness; and thou hast polluted the land with thy whoredoms and with thy wickedness.
3Therefore the showers have been withholden, and there hath been no latter rain; and thou hadst a whore's forehead, thou refusedst to be ashamed.
4Wilt thou not from this time cry unto me, My father, thou *art* the guide of my youth?
5Will he reserve *his anger* for ever? will he keep *it* to the end? Behold, thou hast spoken and done evil things as thou couldest.

New International

29"Why do you bring charges against me?
    You have all rebelled against me,"
                        declares the LORD.
30"In vain I punished your people;
    they did not respond to correction.
Your sword has devoured your prophets
    like a ravening lion.

31"You of this generation, consider the word of the LORD:

"Have I been a desert to Israel
    or a land of great darkness?
Why do my people say, 'We are free to roam;
    we will come to you no more'?
32Does a maiden forget her jewelry,
    a bride her wedding ornaments?
Yet my people have forgotten me,
    days without number.
33How skilled you are at pursuing love!
    Even the worst of women can learn from your
        ways.
34On your clothes men find
    the lifeblood of the innocent poor,
    though you did not catch them breaking in.
    Yet in spite of all this
35 you say, 'I am innocent;
    he is not angry with me.'
But I will pass judgment on you
    because you say, 'I have not sinned.'
36Why do you go about so much,
    changing your ways?
You will be disappointed by Egypt
    as you were by Assyria.
37You will also leave that place
    with your hands on your head,
for the LORD has rejected those you trust;
    you will not be helped by them.

3 "IF A man divorces his wife
and she leaves him and marries another man,
    should he return to her again?
    Would not the land be completely defiled?
But you have lived as a prostitute with many
        lovers—
    would you now return to me?"
                        declares the LORD.
2"Look up to the barren heights and see.
    Is there any place where you have not been
        ravished?
By the roadside you sat waiting for lovers,
    sat like a nomad[a] in the desert.
You have defiled the land
    with your prostitution and wickedness.
3Therefore the showers have been withheld,
    and no spring rains have fallen.
Yet you have the brazen look of a prostitute;
    you refuse to blush with shame.
4Have you not just called to me:
    'My Father, my friend from my youth,
5will you always be angry?
    Will your wrath continue forever?'
This is how you talk,
    but you do all the evil you can."

a 2 *Or an Arab*

Living Bible

rebels, says the Lord. ³⁰I have punished your children but it did them no good; they still will not obey. And you yourselves have killed my prophets as a lion kills its prey.

³¹O my people, listen to the words of God: Have I been unjust to Israel? Have I been to them a land of darkness and of evil? Why then do my people say, "At last we are free from God; we won't have anything to do with him again!" ³²How can you disown your God like that?ᵇ Can a girl forget her jewels? What bride will seek to hide her wedding dress? Yet for years on end my people have forgotten me—the most precious of their treasures.ᶜ

³³How you plot and scheme to win your lovers. The most experienced harlot could learn a lot from you! ³⁴Your clothing is stained with the blood of the innocent and the poor. Brazenly you murder without a cause. ³⁵And yet you say, "I haven't done a thing to anger God. I'm sure he isn't angry!"ᵈ I will punish you severely because you say, "I haven't sinned!"

³⁶First here, then there, you flit about, going from one ally to another for their help; but it's all no good— your new friends in Egypt will forsake you as Assyria did before. ³⁷You will be left in despair, and cover your face with your hands, for the Lord has rejected the ones that you trust. You will not succeed despite their aid.

3 THERE IS a lawᵉ that if a man divorces a woman who then remarries, he is not to take her back again, for she has become corrupted. But though you have left me and married many lovers, yet I have invited you to come to me again, the Lord says. ²Is there a single spot in all the land where you haven't been defiled by your worshiping these other gods?ᶠ You sit like a prostitute beside the road waiting for a client! You sit alone like a Bedouin in the desert. You have polluted the land with your vile prostitution. ³That is why even the springtime rains have failed. For you are a prostitute, and completely unashamed. ⁴, ⁵And yet you say to me, "O Father, you have always been my Friend; surely you won't be angry about such a little thing! Surely you will just forget it?" So you talk, and keep right on doing all the evil that you can.

New Revised Standard

29 Why do you complain against me?
    You have all rebelled against me,
                        says the LORD.
30 In vain I have struck down your children;
    they accepted no correction.
   Your own sword devoured your prophets
    like a ravening lion.
31 And you, O generation, behold the word of
    the LORD!ᵍ
   Have I been a wilderness to Israel,
    or a land of thick darkness?
   Why then do my people say, "We are free,
    we will come to you no more"?
32 Can a girl forget her ornaments,
    or a bride her attire?
   Yet my people have forgotten me,
    days without number.

33 How well you direct your course
    to seek lovers!
   So that even to wicked women
    you have taught your ways.
34 Also on your skirts is found
    the lifeblood of the innocent poor,
   though you did not catch them breaking in.
    Yet in spite of all these thingsᵍ
35 you say, "I am innocent;
    surely his anger has turned from me."
   Now I am bringing you to judgment
    for saying, "I have not sinned."
36 How lightly you gad about,
    changing your ways!
   You shall be put to shame by Egypt
    as you were put to shame by Assyria.
37 From there also you will come away
    with your hands on your head;
   for the LORD has rejected those in whom you
    trust,
   and you will not prosper through them.

Unfaithful Israel

3 IFʰ A man divorces his wife
   and she goes from him
   and becomes another man's wife,
    will he return to her?
   Would not such a land be greatly polluted?
   You have played the whore with many lovers;
    and would you return to me?
                        says the LORD.
2 Look up to the bare heights,ⁱ and see!
    Where have you not been lain with?
   By the waysides you have sat waiting for
    lovers,
    like a nomad in the wilderness.
   You have polluted the land
    with your whoring and wickedness.
3 Therefore the showers have been withheld,
    and the spring rain has not come;
   yet you have the forehead of a whore,
    you refuse to be ashamed.
4 Have you not just now called to me,
    "My Father, you are the friend of my
     youth—
5 will he be angry forever,
    will he be indignant to the end?"
   This is how you have spoken,
    but you have done all the evil that you
     could.

ᵇ 2:32 *How can you disown your God like that?* Implied. ᶜ 2:32 *The most precious of their treasures,* implied. ᵈ 2:35 *he isn't angry,* implied. ᵉ 3:1 *There is a law,* Deut 24:1-4. ᶠ 3:2 *your worshiping these other gods,* implied.

ᵍ Meaning of Heb uncertain   ʰ Q Ms Gk Syr: MT *Saying, If*   ⁱ Or *the trails*

King James

6¶ The LORD said also unto me in the days of Josiah the king, Hast thou seen *that* which backsliding Israel hath done? she is gone up upon every high mountain and under every green tree, and there hath played the harlot.

7And I said after she had done all these *things,* Turn thou unto me. But she returned not. And her treacherous sister Judah saw *it.*

8And I saw, when for all the causes whereby backsliding Israel committed adultery I had put her away, and given her a bill of divorce; yet her treacherous sister Judah feared not, but went and played the harlot also.

9And it came to pass through the lightness of her whoredom, that she defiled the land, and committed adultery with stones and with stocks.

10And yet for all this her treacherous sister Judah hath not turned unto me with her whole heart, but feignedly, saith the LORD.

11And the LORD said unto me, The backsliding Israel hath justified herself more than treacherous Judah.

12¶ Go and proclaim these words toward the north, and say, Return, thou backsliding Israel, saith the LORD; *and* I will not cause mine anger to fall upon you: for I *am* merciful, saith the LORD, *and* I will not keep *anger* for ever.

13Only acknowledge thine iniquity, that thou hast transgressed against the LORD thy God, and hast scattered thy ways to the strangers under every green tree, and ye have not obeyed my voice, saith the LORD.

14Turn, O backsliding children, saith the LORD; for I am married unto you: and I will take you one of a city, and two of a family, and I will bring you to Zion:

15And I will give you pastors according to mine heart, which shall feed you with knowledge and understanding.

16And it shall come to pass, when ye be multiplied and increased in the land, in those days, saith the LORD, they shall say no more, The ark of the covenant of the LORD: neither shall it come to mind: neither shall they remember it; neither shall they visit *it;* neither shall *that* be done any more.

17At that time they shall call Jerusalem the throne of the LORD; and all the nations shall be gathered unto it, to the name of the LORD, to Jerusalem: neither shall they walk any more after the imagination of their evil heart.

18In those days the house of Judah shall walk with the house of Israel, and they shall come together out of the land of the north to the land that I have given for an inheritance unto your fathers.

19But I said, How shall I put thee among the children, and give thee a pleasant land, a goodly heritage of the hosts of nations? and I said, Thou shalt call me, My father; and shalt not turn away from me.

20¶ Surely *as* a wife treacherously departeth from her husband, so have ye dealt treacherously with me, O house of Israel, saith the LORD.

21A voice was heard upon the high places, weeping *and* supplications of the children of Israel: for they have perverted their way, *and* they have forgotten the LORD their God.

New International

Unfaithful Israel

6During the reign of King Josiah, the LORD said to me, "Have you seen what faithless Israel has done? She has gone up on every high hill and under every spreading tree and has committed adultery there. 7I thought that after she had done all this she would return to me but she did not, and her unfaithful sister Judah saw it. 8I gave faithless Israel her certificate of divorce and sent her away because of all her adulteries. Yet I saw that her unfaithful sister Judah had no fear; she also went out and committed adultery. 9Because Israel's immorality mattered so little to her, she defiled the land and committed adultery with stone and wood. 10In spite of all this, her unfaithful sister Judah did not return to me with all her heart, but only in pretense," declares the LORD.

11The LORD said to me, "Faithless Israel is more righteous than unfaithful Judah. 12Go, proclaim this message toward the north:

"'Return, faithless Israel,' declares the LORD,
    'I will frown on you no longer,
for I am merciful,' declares the LORD,
    'I will not be angry forever.
13Only acknowledge your guilt—
    you have rebelled against the LORD your God,
you have scattered your favors to foreign gods
    under every spreading tree,
    and have not obeyed me,'"

declares the LORD.

14"Return, faithless people," declares the LORD, "for I am your husband. I will choose you—one from a town and two from a clan—and bring you to Zion. 15Then I will give you shepherds after my own heart, who will lead you with knowledge and understanding. 16In those days, when your numbers have increased greatly in the land," declares the LORD, "men will no longer say, 'The ark of the covenant of the LORD.' It will never enter their minds or be remembered; it will not be missed, nor will another one be made. 17At that time they will call Jerusalem The Throne of the LORD, and all nations will gather in Jerusalem to honor the name of the LORD. No longer will they follow the stubbornness of their evil hearts. 18In those days the house of Judah will join the house of Israel, and together they will come from a northern land to the land I gave your forefathers as an inheritance.

19"I myself said,

"'How gladly would I treat you like sons
    and give you a desirable land,
    the most beautiful inheritance of any nation.'
I thought you would call me 'Father'
    and not turn away from following me.
20But like a woman unfaithful to her husband,
    so you have been unfaithful to me, O house
        of Israel,"

declares the LORD.

21A cry is heard on the barren heights,
    the weeping and pleading of the people of
        Israel,
because they have perverted their ways
    and have forgotten the LORD their God.

Living Bible

6This message from the Lord came to me during the reign of King Josiah:

Have you seen what Israel does? Like a wanton wife who gives herself to other men at every chance, so Israel has worshiped other gods on every hill, beneath every shady tree. 7I thought that someday she would return to me and once again be mine; but she didn't come back. And her faithless sister Judah saw the continued rebellion of Israel. 8Yet she paid no attention, even though she saw that I divorced faithless Israel. But now Judah too has left me and given herself to prostitution, for she has gone to other gods to worship them. 9She treated it all so lightly—to her it was nothing at all that she should worship idols made of wood and stone. And so the land was greatly polluted and defiled. 10Then, afterwards, this faithless one "returned" to me, but her "sorrow" was only faked, the Lord God says. 11In fact, faithless Israel is less guilty than treacherous Judah!

12Therefore go and say to Israel, O Israel, my sinful people, come home to me again, for I am merciful; I will not be forever angry with you. 13Only acknowledge your guilt; admit that you rebelled against the Lord your God and committed adultery against him by worshiping idols under every tree; confess that you refused to follow me. 14O sinful children, come home, for I am your Master and I will bring you again to the land of Israel—one from here and two from there, wherever you are scattered. 15And I will give you leaders after my own heart, who will guide you with wisdom and understanding.

16Then, when your land is once more filled with people, says the Lord, you will no longer wish for "the good old days of long ago" when you possessed the Ark of God's covenant. Those days will not be missed or even thought about, and the Ark will not be reconstructed, 17for the Lord himself will be among you, and the whole city of Jerusalem will be known as the throne of the Lord, and all nations will come to him there and no longer stubbornly follow their evil desires. 18At that time the people of Judah and of Israel will return together from their exile in the north, to the land I gave their fathers as an inheritance forever. 19And I thought how wonderful it would be for you to be here among my children. I planned to give you part of this beautiful land, the finest in the world. I looked forward to your calling me "Father," and thought that you would never turn away from me again. 20But you have betrayed me; you have gone off and given yourself to a host of foreign gods; you have been like a faithless wife who leaves her husband.

21I hear voices high upon the windswept mountains, crying, crying. It is the sons of Israel who have turned their backs on God and wandered far away. 22O my

New Revised Standard

A Call to Repentance

6 The LORD said to me in the days of King Josiah: Have you seen what she did, that faithless one, Israel, how she went up on every high hill and under every green tree, and played the whore there? 7And I thought, "After she has done all this she will return to me"; but she did not return, and her false sister Judah saw it. 8Shea saw that for all the adulteries of that faithless one, Israel, I had sent her away with a decree of divorce; yet her false sister Judah did not fear, but she too went and played the whore. 9Because she took her whoredom so lightly, she polluted the land, committing adultery with stone and tree. 10Yet for all this her false sister Judah did not return to me with her whole heart, but only in pretense, says the LORD.

11 Then the LORD said to me: Faithless Israel has shown herself less guilty than false Judah. 12Go, and proclaim these words toward the north, and say:

Return, faithless Israel,

                                                    says the LORD.

I will not look on you in anger,
    for I am merciful,

                                                    says the LORD;

I will not be angry forever.
13 Only acknowledge your guilt,
        that you have rebelled against the LORD
            your God,
    and scattered your favors among strangers
            under every green tree,
    and have not obeyed my voice,

                                                    says the LORD.

14 Return, O faithless children,

                                                    says the LORD,

    for I am your master;
    I will take you, one from a city and two from
        a family,
    and I will bring you to Zion.

15 I will give you shepherds after my own heart, who will feed you with knowledge and understanding. 16And when you have multiplied and increased in the land, in those days, says the LORD, they shall no longer say, "The ark of the covenant of the LORD." It shall not come to mind, or be remembered, or missed; nor shall another one be made. 17At that time Jerusalem shall be called the throne of the LORD, and all nations shall gather to it, to the presence of the LORD in Jerusalem, and they shall no longer stubbornly follow their own evil will. 18In those days the house of Judah shall join the house of Israel, and together they shall come from the land of the north to the land that I gave your ancestors for a heritage.

19 I thought
        how I would set you among my children,
    and give you a pleasant land,
        the most beautiful heritage of all the
            nations.
    And I thought you would call me, My Father,
        and would not turn from following me.
20 Instead, as a faithless wife leaves her husband,
        so you have been faithless to me, O house
            of Israel,

                                                    says the LORD.

21 A voice on the bare heightsb is heard,
        the plaintive weeping of Israel's children,
    because they have perverted their way,
        they have forgotten the LORD their God:

---

a Q Ms Gk Mss Syr: MT *I*   b Or *the trails*

King James

22Return, ye backsliding children, *and* I will heal your backslidings. Behold, we come unto thee; for thou *art* the LORD our God.

23Truly in vain *is salvation hoped for* from the hills, *and from* the multitude of mountains: truly in the LORD our God *is* the salvation of Israel.

24For shame hath devoured the labour of our fathers from our youth; their flocks and their herds, their sons and their daughters.

25We lie down in our shame, and our confusion covereth us: for we have sinned against the LORD our God, we and our fathers, from our youth even unto this day, and have not obeyed the voice of the LORD our God.

4 IF THOU wilt return, O Israel, saith the LORD, return unto me: and if thou wilt put away thine abominations out of my sight, then shalt thou not remove.

2And thou shalt swear, The LORD liveth, in truth, in judgment, and in righteousness; and the nations shall bless themselves in him, and in him shall they glory.

3¶ For thus saith the LORD to the men of Judah and Jerusalem, Break up your fallow ground, and sow not among thorns.

4Circumcise yourselves to the LORD, and take away the foreskins of your heart, ye men of Judah and inhabitants of Jerusalem: lest my fury come forth like fire, and burn that none can quench *it,* because of the evil of your doings.

5Declare ye in Judah, and publish in Jerusalem; and say, Blow ye the trumpet in the land: cry, gather together, and say, Assemble yourselves, and let us go into the defenced cities.

6Set up the standard toward Zion: retire, stay not: for I will bring evil from the north, and a great destruction.

7The lion is come up from his thicket, and the destroyer of the Gentiles is on his way; he is gone forth from his place to make thy land desolate; *and* thy cities shall be laid waste, without an inhabitant.

8For this gird you with sackcloth, lament and howl: for the fierce anger of the LORD is not turned back from us.

9And it shall come to pass at that day, saith the LORD, *that* the heart of the king shall perish, and the heart of the princes; and the priests shall be astonished, and the prophets shall wonder.

New International

22"Return, faithless people;
    I will cure you of backsliding."

"Yes, we will come to you,
    for you are the LORD our God.
23Surely the idolatrous commotion on the hills
    and mountains is a deception;
surely in the LORD our God
    is the salvation of Israel.
24From our youth shameful gods have consumed
    the fruits of our fathers' labor—
their flocks and herds,
    their sons and daughters.
25Let us lie down in our shame,
    and let our disgrace cover us.
We have sinned against the LORD our God,
    both we and our fathers;
from our youth till this day
    we have not obeyed the LORD our God."

4 "IF YOU will return, O Israel,
    return to me,"
                    declares the LORD.
"If you put your detestable idols out of my sight
    and no longer go astray,
2and if in a truthful, just and righteous way
    you swear, 'As surely as the LORD lives,'
then the nations will be blessed by him
    and in him they will glory."

3This is what the LORD says to the men of Judah and to Jerusalem:

"Break up your unplowed ground
    and do not sow among thorns.
4Circumcise yourselves to the LORD,
    circumcise your hearts,
    you men of Judah and people of Jerusalem,
or my wrath will break out and burn like fire
    because of the evil you have done—
    burn with no one to quench it.

Disaster From the North

5"Announce in Judah and proclaim in Jerusalem
        and say:
    'Sound the trumpet throughout the land!'
Cry aloud and say:
    'Gather together!
Let us flee to the fortified cities!'
6Raise the signal to go to Zion!
    Flee for safety without delay!
For I am bringing disaster from the north,
    even terrible destruction."

7A lion has come out of his lair;
    a destroyer of nations has set out.
He has left his place
    to lay waste your land.
Your towns will lie in ruins
    without inhabitant.
8So put on sackcloth,
    lament and wail,
for the fierce anger of the LORD
    has not turned away from us.

9"In that day," declares the LORD,
    "the king and the officials will lose heart,
the priests will be horrified,
    and the prophets will be appalled."

Living Bible

rebellious children, come back to me again and I will heal you from your sins.

And they reply, Yes, we will come, for you are the Lord our God. 23We are weary of worshiping idols on the hills and of having orgies on the mountains. It is all a farce. Only in the Lord our God can Israel ever find her help and her salvation. 24From our childhood we have seen everything our fathers had—flocks and herds and sons and daughters—squandered on priests and idols. 25We lie in shame and in dishonor, for we and our fathers have sinned from childhood against the Lord our God; we have not obeyed him.

4 O ISRAEL, if you will truly return to me and absolutely discard your idols, 2and if you will swear by me alone, the living God, and begin to live good, honest, clean lives, then you will be a testimony to the nations of the world and they will come to me and glorify my name.

3The Lord is saying to the men of Judah and Jerusalem, Plow up the hardness of your hearts; otherwise the good seed will be wasted among the thorns. 4Cleanse your minds and hearts,a not just your bodies, or else my anger will burn you to a crisp because of all your sins. And no one will be able to put the fire out.

5Shout to Jerusalem and to all Judea, telling them to sound the alarm throughout the land. "Run for your lives! Flee to the fortified cities!" 6Send a signal from Jerusalem: "Flee now, don't delay!" For I the Lord am bringing vast destruction on you from the north.b 7A lion—a destroyer of nations—stalks from his lair; and he is headed for your land. Your cities will lie in ruin without inhabitant. 8Put on clothes of mourning and weep with broken hearts, for the fierce anger of the Lord has not stopped yet. 9In that day, says the Lord, the king and the princes will tremble in fear; and the priests and the prophets will be stricken with horror.

New Revised Standard

22 Return, O faithless children,
    I will heal your faithlessness.

    "Here we come to you;
      for you are the LORD our God.
23 Truly the hills arec a delusion,
      the orgies on the mountains.
    Truly in the LORD our God
      is the salvation of Israel.

24 "But from our youth the shameful thing has devoured all for which our ancestors had labored, their flocks and their herds, their sons and their daughters. 25Let us lie down in our shame, and let our dishonor cover us; for we have sinned against the LORD our God, we and our ancestors, from our youth even to this day; and we have not obeyed the voice of the LORD our God."

4 IF YOU return, O Israel,
                                    says the LORD,
      if you return to me,
    if you remove your abominations from my
        presence,
      and do not waver,
2   and if you swear, "As the LORD lives!"
      in truth, in justice, and in uprightness,
    then nations shall be blessedd by him,
      and by him they shall boast.

3   For thus says the LORD to the people of Judah and to the inhabitants of Jerusalem:
    Break up your fallow ground,
      and do not sow among thorns.
4   Circumcise yourselves to the LORD,
      remove the foreskin of your hearts,
    O people of Judah and inhabitants of
        Jerusalem,
    or else my wrath will go forth like fire,
      and burn with no one to quench it,
      because of the evil of your doings.

Invasion and Desolation of Judah Threatened

5   Declare in Judah, and proclaim in Jerusalem, and
say:
    Blow the trumpet through the land;
      shout aloude and say,
    "Gather together, and let us go
      into the fortified cities!"
6   Raise a standard toward Zion,
      flee for safety, do not delay;
    for I am bringing evil from the north,
      and a great destruction.
7   A lion has gone up from its thicket,
      a destroyer of nations has set out;
    he has gone out from his place
      to make your land a waste;
    your cities will be ruins
      without inhabitant.
8   Because of this put on sackcloth,
      lament and wail:
    "The fierce anger of the LORD
      has not turned away from us."

9On that day, says the LORD, courage shall fail the king and the officials; the priests shall be appalled and the prophets astounded. 10Then I said, "Ah, Lord GOD, how

---

a *4:4 Cleanse your minds and hearts*, literally, "Circumcise yourselves . . . remove the foreskin of your hearts."   b *4:6 from the north*, i.e., from Babylon. Nabopolasser and Nebuchadnezzar II soon attacked.

c Gk Syr Vg: Heb *Truly from the hills is*   d Or *shall bless themselves*   e Or *shout, take your weapons*: Heb *shout, fill* (your hand)

King James

10Then said I, Ah, Lord GOD! surely thou hast greatly deceived this people and Jerusalem, saying, Ye shall have peace; whereas the sword reacheth unto the soul.

11At that time shall it be said to this people and to Jerusalem, A dry wind of the high places in the wilderness toward the daughter of my people, not to fan, nor to cleanse,

12Even a full wind from those places shall come unto me: now also will I give sentence against them.

13Behold, he shall come up as clouds, and his chariots shall be as a whirlwind: his horses are swifter than eagles. Woe unto us! for we are spoiled.

14O Jerusalem, wash thine heart from wickedness, that thou mayest be saved. How long shall thy vain thoughts lodge within thee?

15For a voice declareth from Dan, and publisheth affliction from mount Ephraim.

16Make ye mention to the nations; behold, publish against Jerusalem, that watchers come from a far country, and give out their voice against the cities of Judah.

17As keepers of a field, are they against her round about; because she hath been rebellious against me, saith the LORD.

18Thy way and thy doings have procured these things unto thee; this is thy wickedness, because it is bitter, because it reacheth unto thine heart.

19¶ My bowels, my bowels! I am pained at my very heart; my heart maketh a noise in me; I cannot hold my peace, because thou hast heard, O my soul, the sound of the trumpet, the alarm of war.

20Destruction upon destruction is cried; for the whole land is spoiled: suddenly are my tents spoiled, and my curtains in a moment.

21How long shall I see the standard, and hear the sound of the trumpet?

22For my people is foolish, they have not known me; they are sottish children, and they have none understanding: they are wise to do evil, but to do good they have no knowledge.

23I beheld the earth, and, lo, it was without form, and void; and the heavens, and they had no light.

24I beheld the mountains, and, lo, they trembled, and all the hills moved lightly.

25I beheld, and, lo, there was no man, and all the birds of the heavens were fled.

26I beheld, and, lo, the fruitful place was a wilderness, and all the cities thereof were broken down at the presence of the LORD, and by his fierce anger.

27For thus hath the LORD said, The whole land shall be desolate; yet will I not make a full end.

28For this shall the earth mourn, and the heavens above be black: because I have spoken it, I have purposed it, and will not repent, neither will I turn back from it.

New International

10Then I said, "Ah, Sovereign LORD, how completely you have deceived this people and Jerusalem by saying, 'You will have peace,' when the sword is at our throats."

11At that time this people and Jerusalem will be told, "A scorching wind from the barren heights in the desert blows toward my people, but not to winnow or cleanse;
12a wind too strong for that comes from me.a Now I pronounce my judgments against them."

13Look! He advances like the clouds,
　　his chariots come like a whirlwind,
his horses are swifter than eagles.
　　Woe to us! We are ruined!
14O Jerusalem, wash the evil from your heart and
　　be saved.
　　How long will you harbor wicked thoughts?
15A voice is announcing from Dan,
　　proclaiming disaster from the hills of
　　　Ephraim.
16"Tell this to the nations,
　　proclaim it to Jerusalem:
'A besieging army is coming from a distant
　　land,
　　raising a war cry against the cities of Judah.
17They surround her like men guarding a field,
　　because she has rebelled against me,' "
　　　　　　　　　　　　declares the LORD.
18"Your own conduct and actions
　　have brought this upon you.
This is your punishment.
　　How bitter it is!
　　How it pierces to the heart!"

19Oh, my anguish, my anguish!
　　I writhe in pain.
Oh, the agony of my heart!
　　My heart pounds within me,
　　I cannot keep silent.
For I have heard the sound of the trumpet;
　　I have heard the battle cry.
20Disaster follows disaster;
　　the whole land lies in ruins.
In an instant my tents are destroyed,
　　my shelter in a moment.
21How long must I see the battle standard
　　and hear the sound of the trumpet?

22"My people are fools;
　　they do not know me.
They are senseless children;
　　they have no understanding.
They are skilled in doing evil;
　　they know not how to do good."

23I looked at the earth,
　　and it was formless and empty;
and at the heavens,
　　and their light was gone.
24I looked at the mountains,
　　and they were quaking;
all the hills were swaying.
25I looked, and there were no people;
　　every bird in the sky had flown away.
26I looked, and the fruitful land was a desert;
　　all its towns lay in ruins
　　before the LORD, before his fierce anger.

27This is what the LORD says:

"The whole land will be ruined,
　　though I will not destroy it completely.
28Therefore the earth will mourn
　　and the heavens above grow dark,
because I have spoken and will not relent,
　　I have decided and will not turn back."

a 12 Or comes at my command

Living Bible

10(Then I said, "But Lord, the people have been deceived by what you said, for you promised great blessings on Jerusalem. Yet the sword is even now poised to strike them dead!")

11, 12At that time he will send a burning wind from the desert upon them—not in little gusts but in a roaring blast—and he will pronounce their doom. 13The enemy shall roll down upon us like a storm wind; his chariots are like a whirlwind; his steeds are swifter than eagles. Woe, woe upon us, for we are doomed.

14O Jerusalem, cleanse your hearts while there is time. You can yet be saved by casting out your evil thoughts. 15From Dan and from Mount Ephraim your doom has been announced. 16Warn the other nations that the enemy is coming from a distant land and they shout against Jerusalem and the cities of Judah. 17They surround Jerusalem like shepherds moving in on some wild animal! For my people have rebelled against me, says the Lord. 18Your ways have brought this down upon you; it is a bitter dose of your own medicine, striking deep within your hearts.

19My heart, my heart—I writhe in pain; my heart pounds within me. I cannot be still because I have heard, O my soul, the blast of the enemies' trumpets and the enemies' battle cries. 20Wave upon wave of destruction rolls over the land, until it lies in utter ruin; suddenly, in a moment, every house is crushed. 21How long must this go on? How long must I see war and death surrounding me?

22"Until my people leave their foolishness, for they refuse to listen to me; they are dull, retarded children who have no understanding. They are smart enough at doing wrong, but for doing right they have no talent, none at all."

23I looked down upon their land and as far as I could see in all directions everything was ruins. And all the heavens were dark. 24I looked at the mountains and saw that they trembled and shook. 25I looked, and mankind was gone and the birds of the heavens had fled.

26The fertile valleys were wilderness and all the cities were broken down before the presence of the Lord, and crushed by his fierce anger. 27The Lord's decree of desolation covers all the land.

"Yet," he says, "there will be a little remnant of my people left. 28The earth shall mourn, the heavens shall be draped with black, because of my decree against my people, but I have made up my mind and I will not change it."

New Revised Standard

utterly you have deceived this people and Jerusalem, saying, 'It shall be well with you,' even while the sword is at the throat!"

11 At that time it will be said to this people and to Jerusalem: A hot wind comes from me out of the bare heights[b] in the desert toward my poor people, not to winnow or cleanse— 12 a wind too strong for that. Now it is I who speak in judgment against them.

13 Look! He comes up like clouds,
    his chariots like the whirlwind;
his horses are swifter than eagles—
    woe to us, for we are ruined!
14 O Jerusalem, wash your heart clean of
    wickedness
so that you may be saved.
How long shall your evil schemes
    lodge within you?
15 For a voice declares from Dan
    and proclaims disaster from Mount
      Ephraim.
16 Tell the nations, "Here they are!"
    Proclaim against Jerusalem,
"Besiegers come from a distant land;
    they shout against the cities of Judah.
17 They have closed in around her like watchers
    of a field,
    because she has rebelled against me,
                  says the LORD.
18 Your ways and your doings
    have brought this upon you.
This is your doom; how bitter it is!
    It has reached your very heart."

Sorrow for a Doomed Nation

19 My anguish, my anguish! I writhe in pain!
    Oh, the walls of my heart!
My heart is beating wildly;
    I cannot keep silent;
for I[c] hear the sound of the trumpet,
    the alarm of war.
20 Disaster overtakes disaster,
    the whole land is laid waste.
Suddenly my tents are destroyed,
    my curtains in a moment.
21 How long must I see the standard,
    and hear the sound of the trumpet?
22 "For my people are foolish,
    they do not know me;
they are stupid children,
    they have no understanding.
They are skilled in doing evil,
    but do not know how to do good."

23 I looked on the earth, and lo, it was waste and
      void;
    and to the heavens, and they had no light.
24 I looked on the mountains, and lo, they were
      quaking,
    and all the hills moved to and fro.
25 I looked, and lo, there was no one at all,
    and all the birds of the air had fled.
26 I looked, and lo, the fruitful land was a
      desert,
    and all its cities were laid in ruins
    before the LORD, before his fierce anger.
27 For thus says the LORD: The whole land shall be
a desolation; yet I will not make a full end.
28 Because of this the earth shall mourn,
    and the heavens above grow black;
for I have spoken, I have purposed;
    I have not relented nor will I turn back.

b Or the trails   c Another reading is for you, O my soul,

King James

29The whole city shall flee for the noise of the horsemen and bowmen; they shall go into thickets, and climb up upon the rocks: every city *shall be* forsaken, and not a man dwell therein.

30And *when* thou *art* spoiled, what wilt thou do? Though thou clothest thyself with crimson, though thou deckest thee with ornaments of gold, though thou rentest thy face with painting, in vain shalt thou make thyself fair; *thy* lovers will despise thee, they will seek thy life.

31For I have heard a voice as of a woman in travail, *and* the anguish as of her that bringeth forth her first child, the voice of the daughter of Zion, *that* bewaileth herself, *that* spreadeth her hands, *saying,* Woe *is* me now! for my soul is wearied because of murderers.

5 RUN YE to and fro through the streets of Jerusalem, and see now, and know, and seek in the broad places thereof, if ye can find a man, if there be *any* that executeth judgment, that seeketh the truth; and I will pardon it.

2And though they say, The LORD liveth; surely they swear falsely.

3O LORD, *are* not thine eyes upon the truth? thou hast stricken them, but they have not grieved; thou hast consumed them, *but* they have refused to receive correction: they have made their faces harder than a rock; they have refused to return.

4Therefore I said, Surely these *are* poor; they are foolish: for they know not the way of the LORD, *nor* the judgment of their God.

5I will get me unto the great men, and will speak unto them; for they have known the way of the LORD, *and* the judgment of their God: but these have altogether broken the yoke, *and* burst the bonds.

6Wherefore a lion out of the forest shall slay them, *and* a wolf of the evenings shall spoil them, a leopard shall watch over their cities: every one that goeth out thence shall be torn in pieces: because their transgressions are many, *and* their backslidings are increased.

7¶ How shall I pardon thee for this? thy children have forsaken me, and sworn by *them that are* no gods: when I had fed them to the full, they then committed adultery, and assembled themselves by troops in the harlots' houses.

8They were *as* fed horses in the morning: every one neighed after his neighbour's wife.

New International

29At the sound of horsemen and archers
  every town takes to flight.
Some go into the thickets;
  some climb up among the rocks.
All the towns are deserted;
  no one lives in them.

30What are you doing, O devastated one?
  Why dress yourself in scarlet
  and put on jewels of gold?
Why shade your eyes with paint?
  You adorn yourself in vain.
Your lovers despise you;
  they seek your life.

31I hear a cry as of a woman in labor,
  a groan as of one bearing her first child—
the cry of the Daughter of Zion gasping for
    breath,
  stretching out her hands and saying,
"Alas! I am fainting;
  my life is given over to murderers."

Not One Is Upright

5 "GO UP and down the streets of Jerusalem,
  look around and consider,
  search through her squares.
If you can find but one person
  who deals honestly and seeks the truth,
  I will forgive this city.
2Although they say, 'As surely as the LORD
    lives,'
  still they are swearing falsely."

3O LORD, do not your eyes look for truth?
  You struck them, but they felt no pain;
  you crushed them, but they refused
    correction.
They made their faces harder than stone
  and refused to repent.
4I thought, "These are only the poor;
  they are foolish,
for they do not know the way of the LORD,
  the requirements of their God.
5So I will go to the leaders
  and speak to them;
surely they know the way of the LORD,
  the requirements of their God."
But with one accord they too had broken off the
    yoke
  and torn off the bonds.
6Therefore a lion from the forest will attack
    them,
  a wolf from the desert will ravage them,
a leopard will lie in wait near their towns
  to tear to pieces any who venture out,
for their rebellion is great
  and their backslidings many.

7"Why should I forgive you?
  Your children have forsaken me
  and sworn by gods that are not gods.
I supplied all their needs,
  yet they committed adultery
  and thronged to the houses of prostitutes.
8They are well-fed, lusty stallions,
  each neighing for another man's wife.

Living Bible

29All the cities flee in terror at the noise of marching armies coming near. The people hide in the bushes and flee to the mountains. All the cities are abandoned—all have fled in terror. 30Why do you put on your most beautiful clothing and jewelry and brighten your eyes with mascara? It will do you no good! Your allies despise you and will kill you.

31I have heard great crying like that of a woman giving birth to her first child; it is the cry of my people gasping for breath, pleading for help, prostrate before their murderers.

5 RUN UP and down through every street in all Jerusalem; search high and low and see if you can find even one person who is fair and honest! Search every square, and if you find just one, I'll not destroy the city! 2Even under oath, they all lie. 3O Lord, you are looking for faithfulness. You have tried to get them to be honest, for you have punished them, but they won't change! You have destroyed them but they refuse to turn from their sins. They are determined, with faces hard as rock, not to repent.

4Then I said, "But what can we expect from the poor and ignorant? They don't know the ways of God. How can they obey him?"

5I will go now to their leaders, the men of importance, and speak to them, for they know the ways of the Lord and the judgment that follows sin. But they too had utterly rejected their God.

6So I will send upon them the wild fury of the "lion from the forest"; the "desert wolves" shall pounce upon them, and a "leopard" shall lurk around their cities so that all who go out shall be torn apart. For their sins are very many; their rebellion against me is great.

7How can I pardon you? For even your children have turned away, and worship gods that are not gods at all. I fed my people until they were fully satisfied, and their thanks was to commit adultery wholesale and to gang up at the city's brothels. 8They are well-fed, lusty stallions, each neighing for his neighbor's mate. 9Shall I not pun-

New Revised Standard

29 At the noise of horseman and archer
 every town takes to flight;
they enter thickets; they climb among rocks;
 all the towns are forsaken,
 and no one lives in them.
30 And you, O desolate one,
what do you mean that you dress in crimson,
 that you deck yourself with ornaments of
  gold,
 that you enlarge your eyes with paint?
In vain you beautify yourself.
 Your lovers despise you;
 they seek your life.
31 For I heard a cry as of a woman in labor,
 anguish as of one bringing forth her first
  child,
the cry of daughter Zion gasping for breath,
 stretching out her hands,
"Woe is me! I am fainting before killers!"

The Utter Corruption of God's People

5 RUN TO and fro through the streets of
 Jerusalem,
 look around and take note!
Search its squares and see
 if you can find one person
who acts justly
 and seeks truth—
so that I may pardon Jerusalem.a
2 Although they say, "As the LORD lives,"
 yet they swear falsely.
3 O LORD, do your eyes not look for truth?
You have struck them,
 but they felt no anguish;
you have consumed them,
 but they refused to take correction.
They have made their faces harder than rock;
 they have refused to turn back.

4 Then I said, "These are only the poor,
 they have no sense;
for they do not know the way of the LORD,
 the law of their God.
5 Let me go to the richb
 and speak to them;
surely they know the way of the LORD,
 the law of their God."
But they all alike had broken the yoke,
 they had burst the bonds.

6 Therefore a lion from the forest shall kill
  them,
 a wolf from the desert shall destroy them.
A leopard is watching against their cities;
 everyone who goes out of them shall be
  torn in pieces—
because their transgressions are many,
 their apostasies are great.

7 How can I pardon you?
 Your children have forsaken me,
 and have sworn by those who are no gods.
When I fed them to the full,
 they committed adultery
 and trooped to the houses of prostitutes.
8 They were well-fed lusty stallions,
 each neighing for his neighbor's wife.

a Heb it   b Or the great

King James

9Shall I not visit for these *things?* saith the LORD: and shall not my soul be avenged on such a nation as this?

10¶ Go ye up upon her walls, and destroy; but make not a full end: take away her battlements; for they *are* not the LORD's.

11For the house of Israel and the house of Judah have dealt very treacherously against me, saith the LORD.

12They have belied the LORD, and said, *It is* not he; neither shall evil come upon us; neither shall we see sword nor famine:

13And the prophets shall become wind, and the word *is* not in them: thus shall it be done unto them.

14Wherefore thus saith the LORD God of hosts, Because ye speak this word, behold, I will make my words in thy mouth fire, and this people wood, and it shall devour them.

15Lo, I will bring a nation upon you from far, O house of Israel, saith the LORD: it *is* a mighty nation, it *is* an ancient nation, a nation whose language thou knowest not, neither understandest what they say.

16Their quiver *is* as an open sepulchre, they *are* all mighty men.

17And they shall eat up thine harvest, and thy bread, *which* thy sons and thy daughters should eat: they shall eat up thy flocks and thine herds: they shall eat up thy vines and thy fig trees: they shall impoverish thy fenced cities, wherein thou trustedst, with the sword.

18Nevertheless in those days, saith the LORD, I will not make a full end with you.

19¶ And it shall come to pass, when ye shall say, Wherefore doeth the LORD our God all these *things* unto us? then shalt thou answer them, Like as ye have forsaken me, and served strange gods in your land, so shall ye serve strangers in a land *that is* not yours.

20Declare this in the house of Jacob, and publish it in Judah, saying,

21Hear now this, O foolish people, and without understanding; which have eyes, and see not; which have ears, and hear not:

22Fear ye not me? saith the LORD: will ye not tremble at my presence, which have placed the sand *for* the bound of the sea by a perpetual decree, that it cannot pass it: and though the waves thereof toss themselves, yet can they not prevail; though they roar, yet can they not pass over it?

New International

9Should I not punish them for this?"
    declares the LORD.
"Should I not avenge myself
    on such a nation as this?

10"Go through her vineyards and ravage them,
    but do not destroy them completely.
Strip off her branches,
    for these people do not belong to the LORD.
11The house of Israel and the house of Judah
    have been utterly unfaithful to me,"
                  declares the LORD.

12They have lied about the LORD;
    they said, "He will do nothing!
No harm will come to us;
    we will never see sword or famine.
13The prophets are but wind
    and the word is not in them;
    so let what they say be done to them."

14Therefore this is what the LORD God Almighty says:

"Because the people have spoken these words,
    I will make my words in your mouth a fire
    and these people the wood it consumes.
15O house of Israel," declares the LORD,
    "I am bringing a distant nation against you—
    an ancient and enduring nation,
    a people whose language you do not know,
    whose speech you do not understand.
16Their quivers are like an open grave;
    all of them are mighty warriors.
17They will devour your harvests and food,
    devour your sons and daughters;
they will devour your flocks and herds,
    devour your vines and fig trees.
With the sword they will destroy
    the fortified cities in which you trust.

18"Yet even in those days," declares the LORD, "I will not destroy you completely. 19And when the people ask, 'Why has the LORD our God done all this to us?' you will tell them, 'As you have forsaken me and served foreign gods in your own land, so now you will serve foreigners in a land not your own.'

20"Announce this to the house of Jacob
    and proclaim it in Judah:
21Hear this, you foolish and senseless people,
    who have eyes but do not see,
    who have ears but do not hear:
22Should you not fear me?" declares the LORD.
    "Should you not tremble in my presence?
I made the sand a boundary for the sea,
    an everlasting barrier it cannot cross.
The waves may roll, but they cannot prevail;
    they may roar, but they cannot cross it.

Living Bible

ish them for this? Shall I not send my vengeance on such a nation as this? 10Go down the rows of the vineyards and destroy them! But leave a scattered few to live. Strip the branches from each vine, for they are not the Lord's.

11For the people of Israel and Judah are full of treachery against me, says the Lord. 12They have lied and said, "He won't bother us! No evil will come upon us! There will be neither famine nor war! 13God's prophets," they say, "are windbags full of words with no divine authority. Their claims of doom will fall upon themselves, not us!"

14Therefore this is what the Lord God of Hosts says to his prophets: Because of talk like this I'll take your words and prophecies and turn them into raging fire and burn up these people like kindling wood. 15See, I will bring a distant nation against you, O Israel, says the Lord—a mighty nation, an ancienta nation whose language you don't understand. 16Their weapons are deadly; the men are all mighty. 17And they shall eat your harvest and your children's bread, and your flocks of sheep and herds of cattle, yes, and your grapes and figs; and they shall sack your walled cities that you think are safe.

18But I will not completely blot you out. So says the Lord.

19And when your people ask, "Why is it that the Lord is doing this to us?" then you shall say, "You rejected him and gave yourselves to other gods while in your land; now you must be slaves to foreigners in their lands."

20Make this announcement to Judah and to Israel:

21Listen, O foolish, senseless people—you with the eyes that do not see and the ears that do not listen—22have you no respect at all for me? the Lord God asks. How can it be that you don't even tremble in my presence? I set the shorelines of the world by perpetual decrees, so that the oceans, though they toss and roar, can never pass those bounds. Isn't such a God to be feared and worshiped?

New Revised Standard

9 Shall I not punish them for these things?
                                    says the LORD;
     and shall I not bring retribution
        on a nation such as this?

10 Go up through her vine-rows and destroy,
        but do not make a full end;
     strip away her branches,
        for they are not the LORD's.
11 For the house of Israel and the house of Judah
        have been utterly faithless to me,
                                    says the LORD.
12 They have spoken falsely of the LORD,
        and have said, "He will do nothing.
     No evil will come upon us,
        and we shall not see sword or famine."
13 The prophets are nothing but wind,
        for the word is not in them.
     Thus shall it be done to them!

14 Therefore thus says the LORD, the God of
        hosts:
     Because theyb have spoken this word,
     I am now making my words in your mouth a
        fire,
        and this people wood, and the fire shall
        devour them.
15 I am going to bring upon you
        a nation from far away, O house of Israel,
                                    says the LORD.
     It is an enduring nation,
        it is an ancient nation,
     a nation whose language you do not know,
        nor can you understand what they say.
16 Their quiver is like an open tomb;
        all of them are mighty warriors.
17 They shall eat up your harvest and your food;
        they shall eat up your sons and your
           daughters;
     they shall eat up your flocks and your herds;
        they shall eat up your vines and your fig
           trees;
     they shall destroy with the sword
        your fortified cities in which you trust.

18 But even in those days, says the LORD, I will not make a full end of you. 19And when your people say, "Why has the LORD our God done all these things to us?" you shall say to them, "As you have forsaken me and served foreign gods in your land, so you shall serve strangers in a land that is not yours."

20 Declare this in the house of Jacob,
        proclaim it in Judah:
21 Hear this, O foolish and senseless people,
        who have eyes, but do not see,
        who have ears, but do not hear.
22 Do you not fear me? says the LORD;
        Do you not tremble before me?
     I placed the sand as a boundary for the sea,
        a perpetual barrier that it cannot pass;
     though the waves toss, they cannot prevail,
        though they roar, they cannot pass over it.

---

a 5:15 *an ancient nation.* The kingdom of Babylonia, being revived in Jeremiah's time (around 626 B.C.) had a long and illustrious history. The old Babylonian Empire lasted from about 1900 B.C. to 1550 B.C. (the days of the Hebrew patriarchs), and earlier kingdoms had ruled on Babylonian soil as early as 3000 B.C.

b Heb *you*

King James

23But this people hath a revolting and a rebellious heart; they are revolted and gone.

24Neither say they in their heart, Let us now fear the LORD our God, that giveth rain, both the former and the latter, in his season: he reserveth unto us the appointed weeks of the harvest.

25¶ Your iniquities have turned away these *things,* and your sins have withholden good *things* from you.

26For among my people are found wicked *men:* they lay wait, as he that setteth snares; they set a trap, they catch men.

27As a cage is full of birds, so *are* their houses full of deceit: therefore they are become great, and waxen rich.

28They are waxen fat, they shine: yea, they overpass the deeds of the wicked: they judge not the cause, the cause of the fatherless, yet they prosper; and the right of the needy do they not judge.

29Shall I not visit for these *things?* saith the LORD: shall not my soul be avenged on such a nation as this?

30¶ A wonderful and horrible thing is committed in the land;

31The prophets prophesy falsely, and the priests bear rule by their means; and my people love *to have it* so: and what will ye do in the end thereof?

6 O YE children of Benjamin, gather yourselves to flee out of the midst of Jerusalem, and blow the trumpet in Tekoa, and set up a sign of fire in Beth-haccerem: for evil appeareth out of the north, and great destruction.

2I have likened the daughter of Zion to a comely and delicate *woman.*

3The shepherds with their flocks shall come unto her; they shall pitch *their* tents against her round about; they shall feed every one in his place.

4Prepare ye war against her; arise, and let us go up at noon. Woe unto us! for the day goeth away, for the shadows of the evening are stretched out.

5Arise, and let us go by night, and let us destroy her palaces.

6¶ For thus hath the LORD of hosts said, Hew ye down trees, and cast a mount against Jerusalem: this *is* the city to be visited; she *is* wholly oppression in the midst of her.

7As a fountain casteth out her waters, so she casteth out her wickedness: violence and spoil is heard in her; before me continually *is* grief and wounds.

8Be thou instructed, O Jerusalem, lest my soul depart from thee; lest I make thee desolate, a land not inhabited.

New International

23But these people have stubborn and rebellious hearts;
  they have turned aside and gone away.
24They do not say to themselves,
  'Let us fear the LORD our God,
who gives autumn and spring rains in season,
  who assures us of the regular weeks of
    harvest.'
25Your wrongdoings have kept these away;
  your sins have deprived you of good.

26"Among my people are wicked men
  who lie in wait like men who snare birds
  and like those who set traps to catch men.
27Like cages full of birds,
  their houses are full of deceit;
they have become rich and powerful
28 and have grown fat and sleek.
Their evil deeds have no limit;
  they do not plead the case of the fatherless to
    win it,
  they do not defend the rights of the poor.
29Should I not punish them for this?"
  declares the LORD.
"Should I not avenge myself
  on such a nation as this?

30"A horrible and shocking thing
  has happened in the land:
31The prophets prophesy lies,
  the priests rule by their own authority,
and my people love it this way.
  But what will you do in the end?

Jerusalem Under Siege

6 "FLEE FOR safety, people of Benjamin!
  Flee from Jerusalem!
Sound the trumpet in Tekoa!
  Raise the signal over Beth Hakkerem!
For disaster looms out of the north,
  even terrible destruction.
2I will destroy the Daughter of Zion,
  so beautiful and delicate.
3Shepherds with their flocks will come against
    her;
  they will pitch their tents around her,
  each tending his own portion."

4"Prepare for battle against her!
  Arise, let us attack at noon!
But, alas, the daylight is fading,
  and the shadows of evening grow long.
5So arise, let us attack at night
  and destroy her fortresses!"

6This is what the LORD Almighty says:

"Cut down the trees
  and build siege ramps against Jerusalem.
This city must be punished;
  it is filled with oppression.
7As a well pours out its water,
  so she pours out her wickedness.
Violence and destruction resound in her;
  her sickness and wounds are ever before me.
8Take warning, O Jerusalem,
  or I will turn away from you
and make your land desolate
  so no one can live in it."

Living Bible

23, 24But my people have rebellious hearts; they have turned against me and gone off into idolatry. Though I am the one who gives them rain each year in spring and fall and sends the harvest times, yet they have no respect or fear for me. 25And so I have taken away these wondrous blessings from them. This sin has robbed them of all of these good things.

26Among my people are wicked men who lurk for victims like a hunter hiding in a blind. They set their traps for men. 27Like a coop full of chickens their homes are full of evil plots. And the result? Now they are great and rich, 28and well fed and well groomed, and there is no limit to their wicked deeds. They refuse justice to orphans and the rights of the poor. 29Should I sit back and act as though nothing is going on? the Lord God asks. Shouldn't I punish a nation such as this?

30A horrible thing has happened in this land— 31the priests are ruled by false prophets, and my people like it so! But your doom is certain.

6 RUN, PEOPLE of Benjamin, run for your lives! Flee from Jerusalem! Sound the alarm in Tekoa; send up a smoke signal at Beth-haccherem; warn everyone that a powerful army is on the way from the north, coming to destroy this nation! 2Helpless as a girl, you are beautiful and delicate—and doomed. 3Evil shepherds shall surround you. They shall set up camp around the city, and divide your pastures for their flocks. 4See them prepare for battle. At noon it has begun. All afternoon it rages, until the evening shadows fall. 5"Come," they say. "Let us attack by night and destroy her palaces!"

6For the Lord Almighty has said to them, Cut down her trees for battering rams; smash down the walls of Jerusalem. This is the city to be punished, for she is vile through and through. 7She spouts evil like a fountain! Her streets echo with the sounds of violence; her sickness and wounds are ever before me.

8This is your last warning, O Jerusalem. If you don't listen, I will empty the land. 9Disaster on disaster shall

New Revised Standard

23 But this people has a stubborn and rebellious
          heart;
    they have turned aside and gone away.
24 They do not say in their hearts,
    "Let us fear the LORD our God,
    who gives the rain in its season,
    the autumn rain and the spring rain,
    and keeps for us
    the weeks appointed for the harvest."
25 Your iniquities have turned these away,
    and your sins have deprived you of good.
26 For scoundrels are found among my people;
    they take over the goods of others.
    Like fowlers they set a trap;a
    they catch human beings.
27 Like a cage full of birds,
    their houses are full of treachery;
    therefore they have become great and rich,
28   they have grown fat and sleek.
    They know no limits in deeds of wickedness;
    they do not judge with justice
    the cause of the orphan, to make it prosper,
    and they do not defend the rights of the
          needy.
29 Shall I not punish them for these things?
                                 says the LORD,
    and shall I not bring retribution
    on a nation such as this?

30 An appalling and horrible thing
    has happened in the land:
31 the prophets prophesy falsely,
    and the priests rule as the prophets direct;b
    my people love to have it so,
    but what will you do when the end comes?

The Imminence and Horror of the Invasion

6 FLEE FOR safety, O children of Benjamin,
    from the midst of Jerusalem!
    Blow the trumpet in Tekoa,
    and raise a signal on Beth-haccherem;
    for evil looms out of the north,
    and great destruction.
2 I have likened daughter Zion
    to the loveliest pasture.c
3 Shepherds with their flocks shall come against
          her.
    They shall pitch their tents around her;
    they shall pasture, all in their places.
4 "Prepare war against her;
    up, and let us attack at noon!"
    "Woe to us, for the day declines,
    the shadows of evening lengthen!"
5 "Up, and let us attack by night,
    and destroy her palaces!"
6 For thus says the LORD of hosts:
    Cut down her trees;
    cast up a siege ramp against Jerusalem.
    This is the city that must be punished;d
    there is nothing but oppression within her.
7 As a well keeps its water fresh,
    so she keeps fresh her wickedness;
    violence and destruction are heard within her;
    sickness and wounds are ever before me.
8 Take warning, O Jerusalem,
    or I shall turn from you in disgust,
    and make you a desolation,
    an uninhabited land.

---

a Meaning of Heb uncertain   b Or *rule by their own authority*   c Or *I will destroy daughter Zion, the loveliest pasture*   d Or *the city of license*

King James

9¶ Thus saith the Lord of hosts, They shall thoroughly glean the remnant of Israel as a vine: turn back thine hand as a grapegatherer into the baskets.

10To whom shall I speak, and give warning, that they may hear? behold, their ear *is* uncircumcised, and they cannot hearken: behold, the word of the Lord is unto them a reproach; they have no delight in it.

11Therefore I am full of the fury of the Lord; I am weary with holding in: I will pour it out upon the children abroad, and upon the assembly of young men together: for even the husband with the wife shall be taken, the aged with *him that is* full of days.

12And their houses shall be turned unto others, *with their* fields and wives together: for I will stretch out my hand upon the inhabitants of the land, saith the Lord.

13For from the least of them even unto the greatest of them every one *is* given to covetousness; and from the prophet even unto the priest every one dealeth falsely.

14They have healed also the hurt *of the daughter* of my people slightly, saying, Peace, peace; when *there is* no peace.

15Were they ashamed when they had committed abomination? nay, they were not at all ashamed, neither could they blush: therefore they shall fall among them that fall: at the time *that* I visit them they shall be cast down, saith the Lord.

16Thus saith the Lord, Stand ye in the ways, and see, and ask for the old paths, where *is* the good way, and walk therein, and ye shall find rest for your souls. But they said, We will not walk *therein*.

17Also I set watchmen over you, *saying*, Hearken to the sound of the trumpet. But they said, We will not hearken.

18¶ Therefore hear, ye nations, and know, O congregation, what *is* among them.

19Hear, O earth: behold, I will bring evil upon this people, *even* the fruit of their thoughts, because they have not hearkened unto my words, nor to my law, but rejected it.

20To what purpose cometh there to me incense from Sheba, and the sweet cane from a far country? your burnt offerings *are* not acceptable, nor your sacrifices sweet unto me.

21Therefore thus saith the Lord, Behold, I will lay stumblingblocks before this people, and the fathers and the sons together shall fall upon them; the neighbour and his friend shall perish.

New International

9This is what the Lord Almighty says:

"Let them glean the remnant of Israel
    as thoroughly as a vine;
pass your hand over the branches again,
    like one gathering grapes."

10To whom can I speak and give warning?
    Who will listen to me?
Their ears are closed[a]
    so they cannot hear.
The word of the Lord is offensive to them;
    they find no pleasure in it.
11But I am full of the wrath of the Lord,
    and I cannot hold it in.

"Pour it out on the children in the street
    and on the young men gathered together;
both husband and wife will be caught in it,
    and the old, those weighed down with years.
12Their houses will be turned over to others,
    together with their fields and their wives,
when I stretch out my hand
    against those who live in the land,"
               declares the Lord.
13"From the least to the greatest,
    all are greedy for gain;
prophets and priests alike,
    all practice deceit.
14They dress the wound of my people
    as though it were not serious.
'Peace, peace,' they say,
    when there is no peace.
15Are they ashamed of their loathsome conduct?
    No, they have no shame at all;
    they do not even know how to blush.
So they will fall among the fallen;
    they will be brought down when I punish
      them,"
               says the Lord.

16This is what the Lord says:

"Stand at the crossroads and look;
    ask for the ancient paths,
ask where the good way is, and walk in it,
    and you will find rest for your souls.
    But you said, 'We will not walk in it.'
17I appointed watchmen over you and said,
    'Listen to the sound of the trumpet!'
    But you said, 'We will not listen.'
18Therefore hear, O nations;
    observe, O witnesses,
    what will happen to them.
19Hear, O earth:
I am bringing disaster on this people,
    the fruit of their schemes,
because they have not listened to my words
    and have rejected my law.
20What do I care about incense from Sheba
    or sweet calamus from a distant land?
Your burnt offerings are not acceptable;
    your sacrifices do not please me."

21Therefore this is what the Lord says:

"I will put obstacles before this people.
    Fathers and sons alike will stumble over
      them;
neighbors and friends will perish."

a *10* Hebrew *uncircumcised*

Living Bible

befall you. Even the few who remain in Israel shall be gleaned again, the Lord Almighty has said; for as a grape-gatherer checks each vine to pick what he has missed, so the remnant of my people shall be destroyed again. 10But who will listen when I warn them? Their ears are closed and they refuse to hear. The word of God has angered them; they don't want it at all.

11For all this I am full of the wrath of God against them. I am weary of holding it in. I will pour it out over Jerusalem, even upon the children playing in the streets, upon the gatherings of young men, and on husbands and wives and grandparents. 12Their enemies shall live in their homes and take their fields and wives. For I will punish the people of this land, the Lord has said. 13They are swindlers and liars, from the least of them right to the top! Yes, even my prophets and priests! 14You can't heal a wound by saying it's not there! Yet the priests and prophets give assurances of peace when all is war. 15Were my people ashamed when they worshiped idols? No, not at all—they didn't even blush. Therefore they shall lie among the slain. They shall die beneath my anger.

16Yet the Lord pleads with you still: Ask where the good road is, the godly paths you used to walk in, in the days of long ago. Travel there, and you will find rest for your souls. But you reply, "No, that is not the road we want!" 17I set watchmen over you who warned you: "Listen for the sound of the trumpet! It will let you know when trouble comes." But you said, "No! We won't pay any attention!"

18, 19This, then, is my decree against my people: (Listen to it, distant lands; listen to it, O my people in Jerusalem; listen to it, all the earth!) I will bring evil upon this people; it will be the fruit of their own sin, because they will not listen to me. They reject my law. 20There is no use now in burning sweet incense from Sheba before me! Keep your expensive perfumes! I cannot accept your offerings; they have no sweet fragrance for me. 21I will make an obstacle course of the pathway of my people; fathers and sons shall be frustrated; neighbors and friends shall collapse together. 22The Lord God

New Revised Standard

9 Thus says the LORD of hosts:
Gleanb thoroughly as a vine
    the remnant of Israel;
like a grape-gatherer, pass your hand again
    over its branches.

10 To whom shall I speak and give warning,
    that they may hear?
See, their ears are closed,c
    they cannot listen.
The word of the LORD is to them an object of
        scorn;
    they take no pleasure in it.

11 But I am full of the wrath of the LORD;
    I am weary of holding it in.

Pour it out on the children in the street,
    and on the gatherings of young men as well;
both husband and wife shall be taken,
    the old folk and the very aged.

12 Their houses shall be turned over to others,
    their fields and wives together;
for I will stretch out my hand
    against the inhabitants of the land,
                    says the LORD.

13 For from the least to the greatest of them,
    everyone is greedy for unjust gain;
and from prophet to priest,
    everyone deals falsely.

14 They have treated the wound of my people
        carelessly,
    saying, "Peace, peace,"
    when there is no peace.

15 They acted shamefully, they committed
        abomination;
    yet they were not ashamed,
    they did not know how to blush.
Therefore they shall fall among those who fall;
    at the time that I punish them, they shall be
        overthrown,
                    says the LORD.

16 Thus says the LORD:
Stand at the crossroads, and look,
    and ask for the ancient paths,
where the good way lies; and walk in it,
    and find rest for your souls.
But they said, "We will not walk in it."

17 Also I raised up sentinels for you:
    "Give heed to the sound of the trumpet!"
But they said, "We will not give heed."

18 Therefore hear, O nations,
    and know, O congregation, what will
        happen to them.

19 Hear, O earth; I am going to bring disaster on
        this people,
    the fruit of their schemes,
because they have not given heed to my
        words;
    and as for my teaching, they have rejected
        it.

20 Of what use to me is frankincense that comes
        from Sheba,
    or sweet cane from a distant land?
Your burnt offerings are not acceptable,
    nor are your sacrifices pleasing to me.

21 Therefore thus says the LORD:
See, I am laying before this people
    stumbling blocks against which they shall
        stumble;
parents and children together,
    neighbor and friend shall perish.

b Cn: Heb *They shall glean*   c Heb *are uncircumcised*

King James

22Thus saith the LORD, Behold, a people cometh from the north country, and a great nation shall be raised from the sides of the earth.

23They shall lay hold on bow and spear; they *are* cruel, and have no mercy; their voice roareth like the sea; and they ride upon horses, set in array as men for war against thee, O daughter of Zion.

24We have heard the fame thereof: our hands wax feeble: anguish hath taken hold of us, *and* pain, as of a woman in travail.

25Go not forth into the field, nor walk by the way; for the sword of the enemy *and* fear *is* on every side.

26¶ O daughter of my people, gird *thee* with sackcloth, and wallow thyself in ashes: make thee mourning, *as for* an only son, most bitter lamentation: for the spoiler shall suddenly come upon us.

27I have set thee *for* a tower *and* a fortress among my people, that thou mayest know and try their way.

28They *are* all grievous revolters, walking with slanders: *they are* brass and iron; they *are* all corrupters.

29The bellows are burned, the lead is consumed of the fire; the founder melteth in vain: for the wicked are not plucked away.

30Reprobate silver shall *men* call them, because the LORD hath rejected them.

---

7 THE WORD that came to Jeremiah from the LORD, saying,

2Stand in the gate of the LORD's house, and proclaim there this word, and say, Hear the word of the LORD, all ye of Judah, that enter in at these gates to worship the LORD.

3Thus saith the LORD of hosts, the God of Israel, Amend your ways and your doings, and I will cause you to dwell in this place.

4Trust ye not in lying words, saying, The temple of the LORD, The temple of the LORD, The temple of the LORD, *are* these.

5For if ye thoroughly amend your ways and your doings; if ye thoroughly execute judgment between a man and his neighbour;

6*If* ye oppress not the stranger, the fatherless, and the widow, and shed not innocent blood in this place, neither walk after other gods to your hurt:

7Then will I cause you to dwell in this place, in the land that I gave to your fathers, for ever and ever.

8¶ Behold, ye trust in lying words, that cannot profit.

9Will ye steal, murder, and commit adultery, and swear falsely, and burn incense unto Baal, and walk after other gods whom ye know not;

10And come and stand before me in this house, which is called by my name, and say, We are delivered to do all these abominations?

New International

22This is what the LORD says:

"Look, an army is coming
  from the land of the north;
a great nation is being stirred up
  from the ends of the earth.
23They are armed with bow and spear;
  they are cruel and show no mercy.
They sound like the roaring sea
  as they ride on their horses;
they come like men in battle formation
  to attack you, O Daughter of Zion."

24We have heard reports about them,
  and our hands hang limp.
Anguish has gripped us,
  pain like that of a woman in labor.
25Do not go out to the fields
  or walk on the roads,
for the enemy has a sword,
  and there is terror on every side.
26O my people, put on sackcloth
  and roll in ashes;
mourn with bitter wailing
  as for an only son,
for suddenly the destroyer
  will come upon us.

27"I have made you a tester of metals
  and my people the ore,
that you may observe
  and test their ways.
28They are all hardened rebels,
  going about to slander.
They are bronze and iron;
  they all act corruptly.
29The bellows blow fiercely
  to burn away the lead with fire,
but the refining goes on in vain;
  the wicked are not purged out.
30They are called rejected silver,
  because the LORD has rejected them."

False Religion Worthless

7 THIS IS the word that came to Jeremiah from the LORD: 2"Stand at the gate of the LORD's house and there proclaim this message:

" 'Hear the word of the LORD, all you people of Judah who come through these gates to worship the LORD. 3This is what the LORD Almighty, the God of Israel, says: Reform your ways and your actions, and I will let you live in this place. 4Do not trust in deceptive words and say, "This is the temple of the LORD, the temple of the LORD, the temple of the LORD!" 5If you really change your ways and your actions and deal with each other justly, 6if you do not oppress the alien, the fatherless or the widow and do not shed innocent blood in this place, and if you do not follow other gods to your own harm, 7then I will let you live in this place, in the land I gave your forefathers for ever and ever. 8But look, you are trusting in deceptive words that are worthless.

9" 'Will you steal and murder, commit adultery and perjury,[a] burn incense to Baal and follow other gods you have not known, 10and then come and stand before me in this house, which bears my Name, and say, "We are safe"—safe to do all these detestable things? 11Has

---

a 9 Or *and swear by false gods*

Living Bible

says, See the armies marching from the north—a great nation is rising against you. 23They are a cruel, merciless people, fully armed, mounted for war. The noise of their army is like a roaring sea.

24We have heard the fame of their armies and we are weak with fright. Fright and pain have gripped us like that of women in travail. 25Don't go out to the fields! Don't travel the roads! For the enemy is everywhere, ready to kill; we are terrorized at every turn.

26O Jerusalem, pride of my people, put on mourning clothes and sit in ashes and weep bitterly as for an only son. For suddenly the destroying armies will be upon you.

27Jeremiah, I have made you an assayer of metals, that you may test this my people and determine their value. Listen to what they are saying and watch what they are doing. 28Are they not the worst of rebels, full of evil talk against the Lord? They are insolent as brass, hard and cruel as iron. 29The bellows blow fiercely; the refining fire grows hotter, but it can never cleanse them, for there is no pureness in them to bring out. Why continue the process longer? All is dross. No matter how hot the fire, they continue in their wicked ways. 30I must label them "Impure, Rejected Silver," and I have discarded them.

7 THEN THE Lord said to Jeremiah:
2Go over to the entrance of the Temple of the Lord and give this message to the people: O Judah, listen to this message from God. Listen to it, all of you who worship here. 3The Lord, the God of Israel says: Even yet, if you quit your evil ways I will let you stay in your own land. 4But don't be fooled by those who lie to you and say that since the Temple of the Lord is here, God will never let Jerusalem be destroyed. 5You may remain under these conditions only: If you stop your wicked thoughts and deeds, and are fair to others, 6and stop exploiting orphans, widows and foreigners. And stop your murdering. And stop worshiping idols as you do now to your hurt. 7Then, and only then, will I let you stay in this land that I gave to your fathers to keep forever.

8You think that because the Temple is here, you will never suffer? Don't fool yourselves! 9Do you really think that you can steal, murder, commit adultery, lie, and worship Baal and all of those new gods of yours, 10and then come here and stand before me in my Temple and chant, "We are saved!"—only to go right back to all these evil things again? 11Is my Temple but a den of

New Revised Standard

22 Thus says the LORD:
   See, a people is coming from the land of the
       north,
   a great nation is stirring from the farthest
       parts of the earth.
23 They grasp the bow and the javelin,
   they are cruel and have no mercy,
   their sound is like the roaring sea;
   they ride on horses,
   equipped like a warrior for battle,
   against you, O daughter Zion!

24 "We have heard news of them,
   our hands fall helpless;
   anguish has taken hold of us,
   pain as of a woman in labor.
25 Do not go out into the field,
   or walk on the road;
   for the enemy has a sword,
   terror is on every side."

26 O my poor people, put on sackcloth,
   and roll in ashes;
   make mourning as for an only child,
   most bitter lamentation:
   for suddenly the destroyer
   will come upon us.

27 I have made you a tester and a refinerb among
       my people
   so that you may know and test their ways.
28 They are all stubbornly rebellious,
   going about with slanders;
   they are bronze and iron,
   all of them act corruptly.
29 The bellows blow fiercely,
   the lead is consumed by the fire;
   in vain the refining goes on,
   for the wicked are not removed.
30 They are called "rejected silver,"
   for the LORD has rejected them.

Jeremiah Proclaims God's Judgment on the Nation

7 THE WORD that came to Jeremiah from the LORD: 2Stand in the gate of the LORD's house, and proclaim there this word, and say, Hear the word of the LORD, all you people of Judah, you that enter these gates to worship the LORD. 3Thus says the LORD of hosts, the God of Israel: Amend your ways and your doings, and let me dwell with youc in this place. 4Do not trust in these deceptive words: "This isd the temple of the LORD, the temple of the LORD, the temple of the LORD."

5 For if you truly amend your ways and your doings, if you truly act justly one with another, 6if you do not oppress the alien, the orphan, and the widow, or shed innocent blood in this place, and if you do not go after other gods to your own hurt, 7then I will dwell with you in this place, in the land that I gave of old to your ancestors forever and ever.

8 Here you are, trusting in deceptive words to no avail. 9Will you steal, murder, commit adultery, swear falsely, make offerings to Baal, and go after other gods that you have not known, 10and then come and stand before me in this house, which is called by my name, and say, "We are safe!"—only to go on doing all these abominations? 11Has this house, which is called by my

b Or a fortress   c Or and I will let you dwell   d Heb They are

King James

11Is this house, which is called by my name, become a den of robbers in your eyes? Behold, even I have seen *it*, saith the LORD.

12But go ye now unto my place which *was* in Shiloh, where I set my name at the first, and see what I did to it for the wickedness of my people Israel.

13And now, because ye have done all these works, saith the LORD, and I spake unto you, rising up early and speaking, but ye heard not; and I called you, but ye answered not;

14Therefore will I do unto *this* house, which is called by my name, wherein ye trust, and unto the place which I gave to you and to your fathers, as I have done to Shiloh.

15And I will cast you out of my sight, as I have cast out all your brethren, *even* the whole seed of Ephraim.

16Therefore pray not thou for this people, neither lift up cry nor prayer for them, neither make intercession to me: for I will not hear thee.

17¶ Seest thou not what they do in the cities of Judah and in the streets of Jerusalem?

18The children gather wood, and the fathers kindle the fire, and the women knead *their* dough, to make cakes to the queen of heaven, and to pour out drink offerings unto other gods, that they may provoke me to anger.

19Do they provoke me to anger? saith the LORD: *do they* not *provoke* themselves to the confusion of their own faces?

20Therefore thus saith the Lord GOD; Behold, mine anger and my fury shall be poured out upon this place, upon man, and upon beast, and upon the trees of the field, and upon the fruit of the ground; and it shall burn, and shall not be quenched.

21¶ Thus saith the LORD of hosts, the God of Israel; Put your burnt offerings unto your sacrifices, and eat flesh.

22For I spake not unto your fathers, nor commanded them in the day that I brought them out of the land of Egypt, concerning burnt offerings or sacrifices:

23But this thing commanded I them, saying, Obey my voice, and I will be your God, and ye shall be my people: and walk ye in all the ways that I have commanded you, that it may be well unto you.

24But they hearkened not, nor inclined their ear, but walked in the counsels *and* in the imagination of their evil heart, and went backward, and not forward.

25Since the day that your fathers came forth out of the land of Egypt unto this day I have even sent unto you all my servants the prophets, daily rising up early and sending *them:*

26Yet they hearkened not unto me, nor inclined their ear, but hardened their neck: they did worse than their fathers.

27Therefore thou shalt speak all these words unto them; but they will not hearken to thee: thou shalt also call unto them; but they will not answer thee.

28But thou shalt say unto them, This *is* a nation that obeyeth not the voice of the LORD their God, nor receiveth correction: truth is perished, and is cut off from their mouth.

29¶ Cut off thine hair, *O Jerusalem*, and cast *it* away, and take up a lamentation on high places; for the LORD hath rejected and forsaken the generation of his wrath.

30For the children of Judah have done evil in my sight, saith the LORD: they have set their abominations in the house which is called by my name, to pollute it.

31And they have built the high places of Tophet, which *is* in the valley of the son of Hinnom, to burn their sons and their daughters in the fire; which I commanded *them* not, neither came it into my heart.

32¶ Therefore, behold, the days come, saith the LORD, that it shall no more be called Tophet, nor the valley of the son of Hinnom, but the valley of slaughter: for they shall bury in Tophet, till there be no place.

New International

this house, which bears my Name, become a den of robbers to you? But I have been watching! declares the LORD.

12" 'Go now to the place in Shiloh where I first made a dwelling for my Name, and see what I did to it because of the wickedness of my people Israel. 13While you were doing all these things, declares the LORD, I spoke to you again and again, but you did not listen; I called you, but you did not answer. 14Therefore, what I did to Shiloh I will now do to the house that bears my Name, the temple you trust in, the place I gave to you and your fathers. 15I will thrust you from my presence, just as I did all your brothers, the people of Ephraim.'

16"So do not pray for this people nor offer any plea or petition for them; do not plead with me, for I will not listen to you. 17Do you not see what they are doing in the towns of Judah and in the streets of Jerusalem? 18The children gather wood, the fathers light the fire, and the women knead the dough and make cakes of bread for the Queen of Heaven. They pour out drink offerings to other gods to provoke me to anger. 19But am I the one they are provoking? declares the LORD. Are they not rather harming themselves, to their own shame?

20" 'Therefore this is what the Sovereign LORD says: My anger and my wrath will be poured out on this place, on man and beast, on the trees of the field and on the fruit of the ground, and it will burn and not be quenched.

21" 'This is what the LORD Almighty, the God of Israel, says: Go ahead, add your burnt offerings to your other sacrifices and eat the meat yourselves! 22For when I brought your forefathers out of Egypt and spoke to them, I did not just give them commands about burnt offerings and sacrifices, 23but I gave them this command: Obey me, and I will be your God and you will be my people. Walk in all the ways I command you, that it may go well with you. 24But they did not listen or pay attention; instead, they followed the stubborn inclinations of their evil hearts. They went backward and not forward. 25From the time your forefathers left Egypt until now, day after day, again and again I sent you my servants the prophets. 26But they did not listen to me or pay attention. They were stiff-necked and did more evil than their forefathers.'

27"When you tell them all this, they will not listen to you; when you call to them, they will not answer. 28Therefore say to them, 'This is the nation that has not obeyed the LORD its God or responded to correction. Truth has perished; it has vanished from their lips. 29Cut off your hair and throw it away; take up a lament on the barren heights, for the LORD has rejected and abandoned this generation that is under his wrath.

The Valley of Slaughter

30" 'The people of Judah have done evil in my eyes, declares the LORD. They have set up their detestable idols in the house that bears my Name and have defiled it. 31They have built the high places of Topheth in the Valley of Ben Hinnom to burn their sons and daughters in the fire—something I did not command, nor did it enter my mind. 32So beware, the days are coming, declares the LORD, when people will no longer call it Topheth or the Valley of Ben Hinnom, but the Valley of Slaughter, for they will bury the dead in Topheth until there is no more room. 33Then the carcasses of this peo-

Living Bible

robbers in your eyes? For I see all the evil going on in there.

12Go to Shiloh, the city I first honored with my name, and see what I did to her because of all the wickedness of my people Israel. 13, 14And now, says the Lord, I will do the same thing here because of all this evil you have done. Again and again I spoke to you about it, rising up early and calling, but you refused to hear or answer. Yes, I will destroy this Temple, as I did in Shiloh—this Temple called by my name, which you trust for help, and this place I gave to you and to your fathers. 15And I will send you into exile, just as I did your brothers, the people of Ephraim.

16Pray no more for these people, Jeremiah. Neither weep for them nor pray nor beg that I should help them, for I will not listen. 17Don't you see what they are doing throughout the cities of Judah and in the streets of Jerusalem? 18No wonder my anger is great! Watch how the children gather wood and the fathers build fires, and the women knead dough and make cakes to offer to "The Queen of Heaven"a and to their other idol-gods! 19Am I the one that they are hurting? asks the Lord. Most of all they hurt themselves, to their own shame. 20So the Lord God says, I will pour out my anger, yes, my fury on this place—people, animals, trees and plants will be consumed by the unquenchable fire of my anger.

21The Lord, the God of Israel says, Away with your offerings and sacrifices! 22It wasn't offerings and sacrifices I wanted from your fathers when I led them out of Egypt. That was not the point of my command. 23But what I told them was: *Obey* me and I will be your God and you shall be my people; only do as I say and all shall be well!

24But they wouldn't listen; they kept on doing whatever they wanted to, following their own stubborn, evil thoughts. They went backward instead of forward. 25Ever since the day your fathers left Egypt until now, I have kept on sending them my prophets, day after day. 26But they wouldn't listen to them or even try to hear. They are hard and stubborn and rebellious—worse even than their fathers were.

27Tell them everything that I will do to them, but don't expect them to listen. Cry out your warnings, but don't expect them to respond. 28Say to them: This is the nation that refuses to obey the Lord its God, and refuses to be taught. She continues to live a lie.

29O Jerusalem, shave your head in shame and weep alone upon the mountains; for the Lord has rejected and forsaken this people of his wrath. 30For the people of Judah have sinned before my very eyes, says the Lord. They have set up their idols right in my own Temple, polluting it. 31They have built the altar called Topheth in the Valley of Ben-Hinnom, and there they burn to death their little sons and daughters as sacrifices to their gods—a deed so horrible I've never even thought of it, let alone commanded it to be done. 32The time is coming, says the Lord, when that valley's name will be changed from "Topheth," or the "Valley of Ben-Hinnom," to the "Valley of Slaughter"; for there will be so many slain to bury that there won't be room enough for all the graves and they will dump the bodies in that valley.

New Revised Standard

name, become a den of robbers in your sight? You know, I too am watching, says the LORD. 12Go now to my place that was in Shiloh, where I made my name dwell at first, and see what I did to it for the wickedness of my people Israel. 13And now, because you have done all these things, says the LORD, and when I spoke to you persistently, you did not listen, and when I called you, you did not answer, 14therefore I will do to the house that is called by my name, in which you trust, and to the place that I gave to you and to your ancestors, just what I did to Shiloh. 15And I will cast you out of my sight, just as I cast out all your kinsfolk, all the offspring of Ephraim.

The People's Disobedience

16 As for you, do not pray for this people, do not raise a cry or prayer on their behalf, and do not intercede with me, for I will not hear you. 17Do you not see what they are doing in the towns of Judah and in the streets of Jerusalem? 18The children gather wood, the fathers kindle fire, and the women knead dough, to make cakes for the queen of heaven; and they pour out drink offerings to other gods, to provoke me to anger. 19Is it I whom they provoke? says the LORD. Is it not themselves, to their own hurt? 20Therefore thus says the Lord GOD: My anger and my wrath shall be poured out on this place, on human beings and animals, on the trees of the field and the fruit of the ground; it will burn and not be quenched.

21 Thus says the LORD of hosts, the God of Israel: Add your burnt offerings to your sacrifices, and eat the flesh. 22For in the day that I brought your ancestors out of the land of Egypt, I did not speak to them or command them concerning burnt offerings and sacrifices. 23But this command I gave them, "Obey my voice, and I will be your God, and you shall be my people; and walk only in the way that I command you, so that it may be well with you." 24Yet they did not obey or incline their ear, but, in the stubbornness of their evil will, they walked in their own counsels, and looked backward rather than forward. 25From the day that your ancestors came out of the land of Egypt until this day, I have persistently sent all my servants the prophets to them, day after day; 26yet they did not listen to me, or pay attention, but they stiffened their necks. They did worse than their ancestors did.

27 So you shall speak all these words to them, but they will not listen to you. You shall call to them, but they will not answer you. 28You shall say to them: This is the nation that did not obey the voice of the LORD their God, and did not accept discipline; truth has perished; it is cut off from their lips.

29 Cut off your hair and throw it away;
   raise a lamentation on the bare heights,b
for the LORD has rejected and forsaken
   the generation that provoked his wrath.

30 For the people of Judah have done evil in my sight, says the LORD; they have set their abominations in the house that is called by my name, defiling it. 31And they go on building the high placec of Topheth, which is in the valley of the son of Hinnom, to burn their sons and their daughters in the fire—which I did not command, nor did it come into my mind. 32Therefore, the days are surely coming, says the LORD, when it will no more be called Topheth, or the valley of the son of Hinnom, but the valley of Slaughter: for they will bury in Topheth until there is no more room. 33The corpses

---

a 7:18 *The Queen of Heaven.* A name by which Ishtar, the Mesopotamian goddess of love and war, was called. After the fall of Jerusalem the refugees who fled to Egypt continued to worship her (ch 44). A papyrus dating from the fifth century B.C. found at Hermopolis in Egypt mentions the "Queen of Heaven" among the gods honored by the Jewish community.

b Or *the trails*   c Gk Tg: Heb *high places*

King James

33And the carcases of this people shall be meat for the fowls of the heaven, and for the beasts of the earth; and none shall fray *them* away.

34Then will I cause to cease from the cities of Judah, and from the streets of Jerusalem, the voice of mirth, and the voice of gladness, the voice of the bridegroom, and the voice of the bride: for the land shall be desolate.

8 AT THAT time, saith the LORD, they shall bring out the bones of the kings of Judah, and the bones of his princes, and the bones of the priests, and the bones of the prophets, and the bones of the inhabitants of Jerusalem, out of their graves:

2And they shall spread them before the sun, and the moon, and all the host of heaven, whom they have loved, and whom they have served, and after whom they have walked, and whom they have sought, and whom they have worshipped: they shall not be gathered, nor be buried; they shall be for dung upon the face of the earth.

3And death shall be chosen rather than life by all the residue of them that remain of this evil family, which remain in all the places whither I have driven them, saith the LORD of hosts.

4¶ Moreover thou shalt say unto them, Thus saith the LORD; Shall they fall, and not arise? shall he turn away, and not return?

5Why *then* is this people of Jerusalem slidden back by a perpetual backsliding? they hold fast deceit, they refuse to return.

6I hearkened and heard, *but* they spake not aright: no man repented him of his wickedness, saying, What have I done? every one turned to his course, as the horse rusheth into the battle.

7Yea, the stork in the heaven knoweth her appointed times; and the turtle and the crane and the swallow observe the time of their coming; but my people know not the judgment of the LORD.

8How do ye say, We *are* wise, and the law of the LORD *is* with us? Lo, certainly in vain made he *it;* the pen of the scribes *is* in vain.

9The wise *men* are ashamed, they are dismayed and taken: lo, they have rejected the word of the LORD; and what wisdom *is* in them?

10Therefore will I give their wives unto others, *and* their fields to them that shall inherit *them:* for every one from the least even unto the greatest is given to covetousness, from the prophet even unto the priest every one dealeth falsely.

11For they have healed the hurt of the daughter of my people slightly, saying, Peace, peace; when *there is* no peace.

New International

ple will become food for the birds of the air and the beasts of the earth, and there will be no one to frighten them away. 34I will bring an end to the sounds of joy and gladness and to the voices of bride and bridegroom in the towns of Judah and the streets of Jerusalem, for the land will become desolate.

8 " 'AT THAT time, declares the LORD, the bones of the kings and officials of Judah, the bones of the priests and prophets, and the bones of the people of Jerusalem will be removed from their graves. 2They will be exposed to the sun and the moon and all the stars of the heavens, which they have loved and served and which they have followed and consulted and worshiped. They will not be gathered up or buried, but will be like refuse lying on the ground. 3Wherever I banish them, all the survivors of this evil nation will prefer death to life, declares the LORD Almighty.'

Sin and Punishment

4"Say to them, 'This is what the LORD says:

" 'When men fall down, do they not get up?
　When a man turns away, does he not return?
5Why then have these people turned away?
　Why does Jerusalem always turn away?
They cling to deceit;
　they refuse to return.
6I have listened attentively,
　but they do not say what is right.
No one repents of his wickedness,
　saying, "What have I done?"
Each pursues his own course
　like a horse charging into battle.
7Even the stork in the sky
　knows her appointed seasons,
and the dove, the swift and the thrush
　observe the time of their migration.
But my people do not know
　the requirements of the LORD.

8" 'How can you say, "We are wise,
　for we have the law of the LORD,"
when actually the lying pen of the scribes
　has handled it falsely?
9The wise will be put to shame;
　they will be dismayed and trapped.
Since they have rejected the word of the LORD,
　what kind of wisdom do they have?
10Therefore I will give their wives to other men
　and their fields to new owners.
From the least to the greatest,
　all are greedy for gain;
prophets and priests alike,
　all practice deceit.
11They dress the wound of my people
　as though it were not serious.
"Peace, peace," they say,
　when there is no peace.

Living Bible

33The bodies of my people shall be food for the birds and animals, and no one shall be left to scare them away. 34I will end the happy singing and laughter in the streets of Jerusalem and in the cities of Judah, and the joyous voices of the bridegrooms and brides. For the land shall lie in desolation.

8 THEN, SAYS the Lord, the enemy shall break open the graves of the kings of Judah and of the princes and priests and prophets and people, 2and dig out their bones and spread them out on the ground before the sun and moon and stars—the gods of my people!—whom they have loved and worshiped. Their bones shall not be gathered up again nor buried but shall be scattered like dung upon the ground. 3And those of this evil nation who are still left alive shall long to die, rather than live where I will scatter them, says the Lord Almighty.

4, 5Once again give them this message from the Lord: When a person falls, he jumps up again; when he is on the wrong road and discovers his mistake, he goes back to the fork where he made the wrong turn. But these people keep on along their evil path, even though I warn them. 6I listen to their conversation and what do I hear? Is anyone sorry for sin? Does anyone say, "What a terrible thing I have done?" No, all are rushing pell-mell down the path of sin as swiftly as a horse rushing to the battle! 7The stork knows the time of her migration, as does the turtledove, and the crane, and the swallow. They all return at God's appointed time each year; but not my people! They don't accept the laws of God.

8How can you say, "We understand his laws," when your teachers have twisted them up to mean a thing I never said? 9These wise teachers of yours will be shamed by exile for this sin, for they have rejected the word of the Lord. Are they then so wise? 10I will give their wives and their farms to others; for all of them, great and small, prophet and priest, have one purpose in mind—to get what isn't theirs. 11They give useless medicine for my people's grievous wounds, for they assure them all is well when that isn't so at all! 12Are they

New Revised Standard

of this people will be food for the birds of the air, and for the animals of the earth; and no one will frighten them away. 34 And I will bring to an end the sound of mirth and gladness, the voice of the bride and bridegroom in the cities of Judah and in the streets of Jerusalem; for the land shall become a waste.

8 AT THAT time, says the LORD, the bones of the kings of Judah, the bones of its officials, the bones of the priests, the bones of the prophets, and the bones of the inhabitants of Jerusalem shall be brought out of their tombs; 2 and they shall be spread before the sun and the moon and all the host of heaven, which they have loved and served, which they have followed, and which they have inquired of and worshiped; and they shall not be gathered or buried; they shall be like dung on the surface of the ground. 3 Death shall be preferred to life by all the remnant that remains of this evil family in all the places where I have driven them, says the LORD of hosts.

The Blind Perversity of the Whole Nation

4　You shall say to them, Thus says the LORD:
　　When people fall, do they not get up again?
　　　If they go astray, do they not turn back?
5　Why then has this peoplea turned away
　　　in perpetual backsliding?
　　They have held fast to deceit,
　　　they have refused to return.
6　I have given heed and listened,
　　　but they do not speak honestly;
　　no one repents of wickedness,
　　　saying, "What have I done!"
　　All of them turn to their own course,
　　　like a horse plunging headlong into battle.
7　Even the stork in the heavens
　　　knows its times;
　　and the turtledove, swallow, and craneb
　　　observe the time of their coming;
　　but my people do not know
　　　the ordinance of the LORD.

8　How can you say, "We are wise,
　　　and the law of the LORD is with us,"
　　when, in fact, the false pen of the scribes
　　　has made it into a lie?
9　The wise shall be put to shame,
　　　they shall be dismayed and taken;
　　since they have rejected the word of the
　　　LORD,
　　　what wisdom is in them?
10　Therefore I will give their wives to others
　　　and their fields to conquerors,
　　because from the least to the greatest
　　　everyone is greedy for unjust gain;
　　from prophet to priest
　　　everyone deals falsely.
11　They have treated the wound of my people
　　　carelessly,
　　　saying, "Peace, peace,"
　　　when there is no peace.

a One Ms Gk: MT *this people, Jerusalem*,   b Meaning of Heb uncertain

King James

12Were they ashamed when they had committed abomination? nay, they were not at all ashamed, neither could they blush: therefore shall they fall among them that fall: in the time of their visitation they shall be cast down, saith the LORD.

13¶ I will surely consume them, saith the LORD: *there shall be* no grapes on the vine, nor figs on the fig tree, and the leaf shall fade; and *the things that* I have given them shall pass away from them.

14Why do we sit still? assemble yourselves, and let us enter into the defenced cities, and let us be silent there: for the LORD our God hath put us to silence, and given us water of gall to drink, because we have sinned against the LORD.

15We looked for peace, but no good *came; and* for a time of health, and behold trouble!

16The snorting of his horses was heard from Dan: the whole land trembled at the sound of the neighing of his strong ones; for they are come, and have devoured the land, and all that is in it; the city, and those that dwell therein.

17For, behold, I will send serpents, cockatrices, among you, which *will* not *be* charmed, and they shall bite you, saith the LORD.

18¶ *When* I would comfort myself against sorrow, my heart *is* faint in me.

19Behold the voice of the cry of the daughter of my people because of them that dwell in a far country: *Is* not the LORD in Zion? *is* not her king in her? Why have they provoked me to anger with their graven images, *and* with strange vanities?

20The harvest is past, the summer is ended, and we are not saved.

21For the hurt of the daughter of my people am I hurt; I am black; astonishment hath taken hold on me.

22*Is there* no balm in Gilead; *is there* no physician there? why then is not the health of the daughter of my people recovered?

New International

12Are they ashamed of their loathsome conduct?
    No, they have no shame at all;
    they do not even know how to blush.
So they will fall among the fallen;
    they will be brought down when they are punished,
                        says the LORD.

13" 'I will take away their harvest,
                        declares the LORD.
    There will be no grapes on the vine.
There will be no figs on the tree,
    and their leaves will wither.
What I have given them
    will be taken from them.a' "

14"Why are we sitting here?
    Gather together!
Let us flee to the fortified cities
    and perish there!
For the LORD our God has doomed us to perish
    and given us poisoned water to drink,
    because we have sinned against him.
15We hoped for peace
    but no good has come,
for a time of healing
    but there was only terror.
16The snorting of the enemy's horses
    is heard from Dan;
at the neighing of their stallions
    the whole land trembles.
They have come to devour
    the land and everything in it,
    the city and all who live there."

17"See, I will send venomous snakes among you,
    vipers that cannot be charmed,
    and they will bite you,"
                        declares the LORD.

18O my Comforterb in sorrow,
    my heart is faint within me.
19Listen to the cry of my people
    from a land far away:
"Is the LORD not in Zion?
    Is her King no longer there?"

"Why have they provoked me to anger with
        their images,
    with their worthless foreign idols?"

20"The harvest is past,
    the summer has ended,
    and we are not saved."

21Since my people are crushed, I am crushed;
    I mourn, and horror grips me.
22Is there no balm in Gilead?
    Is there no physician there?
Why then is there no healing
    for the wound of my people?

9 OH THAT my head were waters, and mine eyes a fountain of tears, that I might weep day and night for the slain of the daughter of my people!

9 OH, THAT my head were a spring of water
    and my eyes a fountain of tears!
I would weep day and night
    for the slain of my people.

---

a *13* The meaning of the Hebrew for this sentence is uncertain.   b *18* The meaning of the Hebrew for this word is uncertain.

Living Bible

ashamed because they worship idols? No, not in the least; they don't even know how to blush! That is why I will see to it that they lie among the fallen. I will visit them with death. [13]Their figs and grapes will disappear, their fruit trees will die, and all the good things I prepared for them will soon be gone.

[14]Then the people will say, "Why should we wait here to die? Come, let us go to the walled cities and perish there. For the Lord our God has decreed our doom and given us a cup of poison to drink because of all our sins. [15]We expected peace, but no peace came; we looked for health but there was only terror."

[16]The noise of war resounds from the northern border.[c] The whole land trembles at the approach of the terrible army, for the enemy is coming, and is devouring the land and everything in it—the cities and people alike. [17]For I will send these enemy troops among you like poisonous snakes which you cannot charm. No matter what you do, they will bite you and you shall die.

[18]My grief is beyond healing; my heart is broken. [19]Listen to the weeping of my people all across the land. "Where is the Lord?" they ask. "Has God deserted us?"

"Oh, why have they angered me with their carved idols and strange evil rites?" the Lord replies.

[20]"The harvest is finished; the summer is over and we are not saved."

[21]I weep for the hurt of my people; I stand amazed, silent, dumb with grief. [22]Is there no medicine in Gilead? Is there no physician there? Why doesn't God do something? Why doesn't he help?

9 OH, THAT my eyes were a fountain of tears; I would weep forever; I would sob day and night for the slain of my people! [2]Oh, that I could go away and

New Revised Standard

[12] They acted shamefully, they committed abomination;
  yet they were not at all ashamed,
  they did not know how to blush.
Therefore they shall fall among those who fall;
  at the time when I punish them, they shall be overthrown,
               says the LORD.

[13] When I wanted to gather them, says the LORD,
  there are[d] no grapes on the vine,
  nor figs on the fig tree;
even the leaves are withered,
  and what I gave them has passed away from them.[e]

[14] Why do we sit still?
Gather together, let us go into the fortified cities
  and perish there;
for the LORD our God has doomed us to perish,
  and has given us poisoned water to drink,
  because we have sinned against the LORD.

[15] We look for peace, but find no good,
  for a time of healing, but there is terror instead.

[16] The snorting of their horses is heard from Dan;
  at the sound of the neighing of their stallions
  the whole land quakes.
They come and devour the land and all that fills it,
  the city and those who live in it.

[17] See, I am letting snakes loose among you,
  adders that cannot be charmed,
  and they shall bite you,
               says the LORD.

The Prophet Mourns for the People

[18] My joy is gone, grief is upon me,
  my heart is sick.
[19] Hark, the cry of my poor people
  from far and wide in the land:
"Is the LORD not in Zion?
  Is her King not in her?"
("Why have they provoked me to anger with their images,
  with their foreign idols?")
[20] "The harvest is past, the summer is ended,
  and we are not saved."
[21] For the hurt of my poor people I am hurt,
  I mourn, and dismay has taken hold of me.

[22] Is there no balm in Gilead?
  Is there no physician there?
Why then has the health of my poor people not been restored?

9 [f] O THAT my head were a spring of water,
  and my eyes a fountain of tears,
so that I might weep day and night
  for the slain of my poor people!

---

[c] 8:16 *The noise of war resounds from the northern border,* literally, "The snorting of their war horses can be heard all the way from Dan in the north."

[d] Or *I will make an end of them, says the LORD. There are* [e] Meaning of Heb uncertain [f] Ch 8.23 in Heb

King James

2Oh that I had in the wilderness a lodging place of wayfaring men; that I might leave my people, and go from them! for they *be* all adulterers, an assembly of treacherous men.

3And they bend their tongues *like* their bow *for* lies: but they are not valiant for the truth upon the earth; for they proceed from evil to evil, and they know not me, saith the LORD.

4Take ye heed every one of his neighbour, and trust ye not in any brother: for every brother will utterly supplant, and every neighbour will walk with slanders.

5And they will deceive every one his neighbour, and will not speak the truth: they have taught their tongue to speak lies, *and* weary themselves to commit iniquity.

6Thine habitation *is* in the midst of deceit; through deceit they refuse to know me, saith the LORD.

7Therefore thus saith the LORD of hosts, Behold, I will melt them, and try them; for how shall I do for the daughter of my people?

8Their tongue *is as* an arrow shot out; it speaketh deceit: *one* speaketh peaceably to his neighbour with his mouth, but in heart he layeth his wait.

9¶ Shall I not visit them for these *things?* saith the LORD: shall not my soul be avenged on such a nation as this?

10For the mountains will I take up a weeping and wailing, and for the habitations of the wilderness a lamentation, because they are burned up, so that none can pass through *them;* neither can *men* hear the voice of the cattle; both the fowl of the heavens and the beast are fled; they are gone.

11And I will make Jerusalem heaps, *and* a den of dragons; and I will make the cities of Judah desolate, without an inhabitant.

12¶ Who *is* the wise man, that may understand this? and *who is he* to whom the mouth of the LORD hath spoken, that he may declare it, for what the land perisheth *and* is burned up like a wilderness, that none passeth through?

13And the LORD saith, Because they have forsaken my law which I set before them, and have not obeyed my voice, neither walked therein;

14But have walked after the imagination of their own heart, and after Baalim, which their fathers taught them:

15Therefore thus saith the LORD of hosts, the God of Israel; Behold, I will feed them, *even* this people, with wormwood, and give them water of gall to drink.

16I will scatter them also among the heathen, whom neither they nor their fathers have known: and I will send a sword after them, till I have consumed them.

New International

2Oh, that I had in the desert
　　a lodging place for travelers,
so that I might leave my people
　　and go away from them;
for they are all adulterers,
　　a crowd of unfaithful people.
3"They make ready their tongue
　　like a bow, to shoot lies;
it is not by truth
　　that they triumpha in the land.
They go from one sin to another;
　　they do not acknowledge me,"
　　　　　　　　　　declares the LORD.
4"Beware of your friends;
　　do not trust your brothers.
For every brother is a deceiver,b
　　and every friend a slanderer.
5Friend deceives friend,
　　and no one speaks the truth.
They have taught their tongues to lie;
　　they weary themselves with sinning.
6Youc live in the midst of deception;
　　in their deceit they refuse to acknowledge
　　me,"
　　　　　　　　　　declares the LORD.

7Therefore this is what the LORD Almighty says:

"See, I will refine and test them,
　　for what else can I do
　　because of the sin of my people?
8Their tongue is a deadly arrow;
　　it speaks with deceit.
With his mouth each speaks cordially to his
　　neighbor,
but in his heart he sets a trap for him.
9Should I not punish them for this?"
　　declares the LORD.
"Should I not avenge myself
　　on such a nation as this?"

10I will weep and wail for the mountains
　　and take up a lament concerning the desert
　　pastures.
They are desolate and untraveled,
　　and the lowing of cattle is not heard.
The birds of the air have fled
　　and the animals are gone.

11"I will make Jerusalem a heap of ruins,
　　a haunt of jackals;
and I will lay waste the towns of Judah
　　so no one can live there."

12What man is wise enough to understand this? Who has been instructed by the LORD and can explain it? Why has the land been ruined and laid waste like a desert that no one can cross?

13The LORD said, "It is because they have forsaken my law, which I set before them; they have not obeyed me or followed my law. 14Instead, they have followed the stubbornness of their hearts; they have followed the Baals, as their fathers taught them." 15Therefore, this is what the LORD Almighty, the God of Israel, says: "See, I will make this people eat bitter food and drink poisoned water. 16I will scatter them among nations that neither they nor their fathers have known, and I will pursue them with the sword until I have destroyed them."

---

a 3 Or *lies; / they are not valiant for truth*　　b 4 Or *a deceiving Jacob*
c 6 That is, Jeremiah (the Hebrew is singular)

Living Bible

forget them and live in some wayside shack in the desert, for they are all adulterous, treacherous men.

³"They bend their tongues like bows to shoot their arrows of untruth. They care nothing for right and go from bad to worse; they care nothing for me," says the Lord.

⁴Beware of your neighbor! Beware of your brother! All take advantage of one another and spread their slanderous lies. ⁵With practiced tongues they fool and defraud each other; they wear themselves out with all their sinning.

⁶"They pile evil upon evil, lie upon lie, and utterly refuse to come to me," says the Lord.

⁷Therefore the Lord Almighty says this: "See, I will melt them in a crucible of affliction. I will refine them and test them like metal. What else can I do with them? ⁸For their tongues aim lies like poisoned spears. They speak cleverly to their neighbors while planning to kill them. ⁹Should not I punish them for such things as this?" asks the Lord. "Shall not my soul be avenged on such a nation as this?"

¹⁰Sobbing and weeping, I point to their mountains and pastures, for now they are desolate, without a living soul. Gone is the lowing of cattle, gone the birds and wild animals. All have fled.

¹¹"And I will turn Jerusalem into heaps of ruined houses where only jackals have their dens. The cities of Judah shall be ghost towns, with no one living in them."

¹²Who is wise enough to understand all this? Where is the Lord's messenger to explain it? Why is the land a wilderness so that no one dares even to travel through?

¹³"Because," the Lord replies, "my people have forsaken my commandments and not obeyed my laws. ¹⁴Instead they have done whatever they pleased and worshiped the idols of Baal, as their fathers told them to. ¹⁵Therefore this is what the Lord, the God of Israel, says: Look! I will feed them with bitterness and give them poison to drink. ¹⁶I will scatter them around the world, to be strangers in distant lands; and even there the sword of destruction shall chase them until I have utterly destroyed them.

New Revised Standard

²ᵈ O that I had in the desert
    a traveler's lodging place,
  that I might leave my people
    and go away from them!
  For they are all adulterers,
    a band of traitors.
³ They bend their tongues like bows;
    they have grown strong in the land for
        falsehood, and not for truth;
  for they proceed from evil to evil,
    and they do not know me, says the Lord.

⁴ Beware of your neighbors,
    and put no trust in any of your kin;ᵉ
  for all your kinᶠ are supplanters,
    and every neighbor goes around like a
        slanderer.
⁵ They all deceive their neighbors,
    and no one speaks the truth;
  they have taught their tongues to speak lies;
    they commit iniquity and are too weary to
        repent.ᵍ
⁶ Oppression upon oppression, deceitʰ upon
        deceit!
  They refuse to know me, says the Lord.

⁷ Therefore thus says the Lord of hosts:
  I will now refine and test them,
    for what else can I do with my sinful
        people?ⁱ
⁸ Their tongue is a deadly arrow;
    it speaks deceit through the mouth.
  They all speak friendly words to their
        neighbors,
    but inwardly are planning to lay an ambush.
⁹ Shall I not punish them for these things? says
        the Lord;
    and shall I not bring retribution
      on a nation such as this?

¹⁰ Take upʲ weeping and wailing for the
        mountains,
    and a lamentation for the pastures of the
        wilderness,
  because they are laid waste so that no one
        passes through,
    and the lowing of cattle is not heard;
  both the birds of the air and the animals
    have fled and are gone.
¹¹ I will make Jerusalem a heap of ruins,
    a lair of jackals;
  and I will make the towns of Judah a
        desolation,
    without inhabitant.

12 Who is wise enough to understand this? To whom has the mouth of the Lord spoken, so that they may declare it? Why is the land ruined and laid waste like a wilderness, so that no one passes through? 13 And the Lord says: Because they have forsaken my law that I set before them, and have not obeyed my voice, or walked in accordance with it, 14 but have stubbornly followed their own hearts and have gone after the Baals, as their ancestors taught them. 15 Therefore thus says the Lord of hosts, the God of Israel: I am feeding this people with wormwood, and giving them poisonous water to drink. 16 I will scatter them among nations that neither they nor their ancestors have known; and I will send the sword after them, until I have consumed them.

ᵈ Ch 9.1 in Heb   ᵉ Heb *in a brother*   ᶠ Heb *for every brother*   ᵍ Cn
Compare Gk: Heb *they weary themselves with iniquity.* ⁶*Your dwelling*   ʰ Cn:
Heb *Your dwelling in the midst of deceit*   ⁱ Or *my poor people*   ʲ Gk Syr:
Heb *I will take up*

King James

17¶ Thus saith the Lord of hosts, Consider ye, and call for the mourning women, that they may come; and send for cunning *women,* that they may come:

18And let them make haste, and take up a wailing for us, that our eyes may run down with tears, and our eyelids gush out with waters.

19For a voice of wailing is heard out of Zion, How are we spoiled! we are greatly confounded, because we have forsaken the land, because our dwellings have cast *us* out.

20Yet hear the word of the Lord, O ye women, and let your ear receive the word of his mouth, and teach your daughters wailing, and every one her neighbour lamentation.

21For death is come up into our windows, *and* is entered into our palaces, to cut off the children from without, *and* the young men from the streets.

22Speak, Thus saith the Lord, Even the carcases of men shall fall as dung upon the open field, and as the handful after the harvestman, and none shall gather *them.*

23¶ Thus saith the Lord, Let not the wise *man* glory in his wisdom, neither let the mighty *man* glory in his might, let not the rich *man* glory in his riches:

24But let him that glorieth glory in this, that he understandeth and knoweth me, that I *am* the Lord which exercise lovingkindness, judgment, and righteousness, in the earth: for in these *things* I delight, saith the Lord.

25¶ Behold, the days come, saith the Lord, that I will punish all *them which are* circumcised with the uncircumcised;

26Egypt, and Judah, and Edom, and the children of Ammon, and Moab, and all *that are* in the utmost corners, that dwell in the wilderness: for all *these* nations *are* uncircumcised, and all the house of Israel *are* uncircumcised in the heart.

10 HEAR YE the word which the Lord speaketh unto you, O house of Israel:

2Thus saith the Lord, Learn not the way of the heathen, and be not dismayed at the signs of heaven; for the heathen are dismayed at them.

3For the customs of the people *are* vain: for *one* cutteth a tree out of the forest, the work of the hands of the workman, with the axe.

4They deck it with silver and with gold; they fasten it with nails and with hammers, that it move not.

5They *are* upright as the palm tree, but speak not: they must needs be borne, because they cannot go. Be not afraid of them; for they cannot do evil, neither also *is it* in them to do good.

New International

17This is what the Lord Almighty says:

"Consider now! Call for the wailing women to
    come;
  send for the most skillful of them.
18Let them come quickly
    and wail over us
  till our eyes overflow with tears
    and water streams from our eyelids.
19The sound of wailing is heard from Zion:
  'How ruined we are!
    How great is our shame!
  We must leave our land
    because our houses are in ruins.' "

20Now, O women, hear the word of the Lord;
  open your ears to the words of his mouth.
  Teach your daughters how to wail;
    teach one another a lament.
21Death has climbed in through our windows
    and has entered our fortresses;
  it has cut off the children from the streets
    and the young men from the public squares.

22Say, "This is what the Lord declares:

" 'The dead bodies of men will lie
    like refuse on the open field,
  like cut grain behind the reaper,
    with no one to gather them.' "

23This is what the Lord says:

"Let not the wise man boast of his wisdom
    or the strong man boast of his strength
    or the rich man boast of his riches,
24but let him who boasts boast about this:
    that he understands and knows me,
  that I am the Lord, who exercises kindness,
    justice and righteousness on earth,
    for in these I delight,"
                      declares the Lord.

25"The days are coming," declares the Lord, "when I will punish all who are circumcised only in the flesh— 26Egypt, Judah, Edom, Ammon, Moab and all who live in the desert in distant places.[a] For all these nations are really uncircumcised, and even the whole house of Israel is uncircumcised in heart."

God and Idols

10 HEAR WHAT the Lord says to you, O house of Israel. 2This is what the Lord says:

"Do not learn the ways of the nations
    or be terrified by signs in the sky,
    though the nations are terrified by them.
3For the customs of the peoples are worthless;
    they cut a tree out of the forest,
    and a craftsman shapes it with his chisel.
4They adorn it with silver and gold;
    they fasten it with hammer and nails
    so it will not totter.
5Like a scarecrow in a melon patch,
    their idols cannot speak;
  they must be carried
    because they cannot walk.
  Do not fear them;
    they can do no harm
    nor can they do any good."

<hr>

a 26 Or *desert and who clip the hair by their foreheads*

Living Bible

17, 18"The Lord Almighty says: Send for the mourners! Quick! Begin your crying! Let the tears flow from your eyes. 19Hear Jerusalem weeping in despair. 'We are ruined! Disaster has befallen us! We must leave our land and homes!'" 20Listen to the words of God, O women who wail. Teach your daughters to wail and your neighbors too. 21For death has crept in through your windows into your homes. He has killed off the flower of your youth. Children no longer play in the streets; the young men gather no more in the squares.

22Tell them this, says the Lord: Bodies shall be scattered across the fields like manure, like sheaves after the mower, and no one will bury them.

23The Lord says: Let not the wise man bask in his wisdom, nor the mighty man in his might, nor the rich man in his riches. 24Let them boast in this alone: That they truly know me, and understand that I am the Lord of justice and of righteousness whose love is steadfast; and that I love to be this way.

25, 26A time is coming, says the Lord, when I will punish all those who are circumcised in body but not in spirit—the Egyptians, Edomites, Ammonites, Moabites, Arabs, and yes, even you people of Judah. For all these pagan nations also circumcise themselves. Unless you circumcise your hearts by loving me, your circumcision is only a heathen rite like theirs, and nothing more.

New Revised Standard

The People Mourn in Judgment

17 Thus says the LORD of hosts:
Consider, and call for the mourning women to come;
    send for the skilled women to come;
18 let them quickly raise a dirge over us,
    so that our eyes may run down with tears,
    and our eyelids flow with water.
19 For a sound of wailing is heard from Zion:
    "How we are ruined!
We are utterly shamed,
because we have left the land,
    because they have cast down our
        dwellings."

20 Hear, O women, the word of the LORD,
    and let your ears receive the word of his
        mouth;
teach to your daughters a dirge,
    and each to her neighbor a lament.
21 "Death has come up into our windows,
    it has entered our palaces,
to cut off the children from the streets
    and the young men from the squares."
22 Speak! Thus says the LORD:
"Human corpses shall fall
    like dung upon the open field,
like sheaves behind the reaper,
    and no one shall gather them."

23 Thus says the LORD: Do not let the wise boast in their wisdom, do not let the mighty boast in their might, do not let the wealthy boast in their wealth; 24but let those who boast boast in this, that they understand and know me, that I am the LORD; I act with steadfast love, justice, and righteousness in the earth, for in these things I delight, says the LORD.

25 The days are surely coming, says the LORD, when I will attend to all those who are circumcised only in the foreskin: 26Egypt, Judah, Edom, the Ammonites, Moab, and all those with shaven temples who live in the desert. For all these nations are uncircumcised, and all the house of Israel is uncircumcised in heart.

---

10 HEAR THE word of the Lord, O Israel:
2, 3Don't act like the people who make horoscopes and try to read their fate and future in the stars! Don't be frightened by predictions such as theirs, for it is all a pack of lies. Their ways are futile and foolish. They cut down a tree and carve an idol, 4and decorate it with gold and silver and fasten it securely in place with hammer and nails, so that it won't fall over, 5and there stands their god like a helpless scarecrow in a garden! It cannot speak, and it must be carried, for it cannot walk. Don't be afraid of such a god for it can neither harm nor help, nor do you any good.

Idolatry Has Brought Ruin on Israel

10 HEAR THE word that the LORD speaks to you,
O house of Israel. 2Thus says the LORD:
Do not learn the way of the nations,
    or be dismayed at the signs of the heavens;
    for the nations are dismayed at them.
3 For the customs of the peoples are false:
a tree from the forest is cut down,
    and worked with an ax by the hands of an
        artisan;
4 people deck it with silver and gold;
    they fasten it with hammer and nails
    so that it cannot move.
5 Their idolsb are like scarecrows in a cucumber
        field,
    and they cannot speak;
they have to be carried,
    for they cannot walk.
Do not be afraid of them,
    for they cannot do evil,
    nor is it in them to do good.

b Heb *They*

King James

6Forasmuch as *there is* none like unto thee, O LORD; thou *art* great, and thy name *is* great in might.

7Who would not fear thee, O King of nations? for to thee doth it appertain: forasmuch as among all the wise *men* of the nations, and in all their kingdoms, *there is* none like unto thee.

8But they are altogether brutish and foolish: the stock *is* a doctrine of vanities.

9Silver spread into plates is brought from Tarshish, and gold from Uphaz, the work of the workman, and of the hands of the founder: blue and purple *is* their clothing: they *are* all the work of cunning *men*.

10But the LORD *is* the true God, he *is* the living God, and an everlasting king: at his wrath the earth shall tremble, and the nations shall not be able to abide his indignation.

11Thus shall ye say unto them, The gods that have not made the heavens and the earth, *even* they shall perish from the earth, and from under these heavens.

12He hath made the earth by his power, he hath established the world by his wisdom, and hath stretched out the heavens by his discretion.

13When he uttereth his voice, *there is* a multitude of waters in the heavens, and he causeth the vapours to ascend from the ends of the earth; he maketh lightnings with rain, and bringeth forth the wind out of his treasures.

14Every man is brutish in *his* knowledge: every founder is confounded by the graven image: for his molten image *is* falsehood, and *there is* no breath in them.

15They *are* vanity, *and* the work of errors: in the time of their visitation they shall perish.

16The portion of Jacob *is* not like them: for he *is* the former of all *things;* and Israel *is* the rod of his inheritance: The LORD of hosts *is* his name.

17¶ Gather up thy wares out of the land, O inhabitant of the fortress.

18For thus saith the LORD, Behold, I will sling out the inhabitants of the land at this once, and will distress them, that they may find *it so.*

19¶ Woe is me for my hurt! my wound is grievous: but I said, Truly this *is* a grief, and I must bear it.

New International

6No one is like you, O LORD;
    you are great,
    and your name is mighty in power.
7Who should not revere you,
    O King of the nations?
    This is your due.
Among all the wise men of the nations
    and in all their kingdoms,
    there is no one like you.
8They are all senseless and foolish;
    they are taught by worthless wooden idols.
9Hammered silver is brought from Tarshish
    and gold from Uphaz.
What the craftsman and goldsmith have made
    is then dressed in blue and purple—
    all made by skilled workers.
10But the LORD is the true God;
    he is the living God, the eternal King.
When he is angry, the earth trembles;
    the nations cannot endure his wrath.

11"Tell them this: 'These gods, who did not make the heavens and the earth, will perish from the earth and from under the heavens.' "[a]

12But God made the earth by his power;
    he founded the world by his wisdom
    and stretched out the heavens by his
        understanding.
13When he thunders, the waters in the heavens
        roar;
    he makes clouds rise from the ends of the
        earth.
He sends lightning with the rain
    and brings out the wind from his storehouses.

14Everyone is senseless and without knowledge;
    every goldsmith is shamed by his idols.
His images are a fraud;
    they have no breath in them.
15They are worthless, the objects of mockery;
    when their judgment comes, they will perish.
16He who is the Portion of Jacob is not like these,
    for he is the Maker of all things,
including Israel, the tribe of his inheritance—
    the LORD Almighty is his name.

Coming Destruction

17Gather up your belongings to leave the land,
    you who live under siege.
18For this is what the LORD says:
    "At this time I will hurl out
    those who live in this land;
I will bring distress on them
    so that they may be captured."

19Woe to me because of my injury!
    My wound is incurable!
Yet I said to myself,
    "This is my sickness, and I must endure it."

---

a *11* The text of this verse is in Aramaic.

Living Bible

6O Lord, there is no other god like you. For you are great and your name is full of power. 7Who would not fear you, O King of nations? (And that title belongs to you alone!) Among all the wise men of the earth and in all the kingdoms of the world there isn't anyone like you.

8The wisest of men who worship idols are altogether stupid and foolish. 9They bring beaten sheets of silver from Tarshish and gold from Uphaz, and give them to skillful goldsmiths who make their idols; then they clothe these gods in royal purple robes that expert tailors make.

10But the Lord is the only true God, the living God, the everlasting King. The whole earth shall tremble at his anger; the world shall hide before his displeasure. 11Say this to those who worship other gods: Your so-called gods, who have not made the heavens and earth, shall vanish from the earth, 12but our God formed the earth by his power and wisdom, and by his intelligence he hung the stars in space and stretched out the heavens. 13It is his voice that echoes in the thunder of the storm clouds. He causes mist to rise upon the earth; he sends the lightning and brings the rain, and from his treasuries he brings the wind.

14But foolish men without knowledge of God bow before their idols. It is a shameful business that these men are in, for what they make are frauds, gods without life or power in them. 15All are worthless, silly; they will be crushed when their makers perish. 16But the God of Jacob is not like these foolish idols. He is the Creator of all, and Israel is his chosen nation. The Lord Almighty is his name.

17Pack your bags, he says. Get ready now to leave; the siege will soon begin. 18For suddenly I'll fling you from this land and pour great troubles down; at last you shall feel my wrath.

19*Desperate is my wound. My grief is great. My sickness is incurable, but I must bear it.* 20*My home is gone;*

New Revised Standard

6 There is none like you, O LORD;
   you are great, and your name is great in
      might.
7 Who would not fear you, O King of the
      nations?
   For that is your due;
   among all the wise ones of the nations
      and in all their kingdoms
      there is no one like you.
8 They are both stupid and foolish;
      the instruction given by idols
      is no better than wood!b
9 Beaten silver is brought from Tarshish,
      and gold from Uphaz.
   They are the work of the artisan and of the
      hands of the goldsmith;
      their clothing is blue and purple;
      they are all the product of skilled workers.
10 But the LORD is the true God;
      he is the living God and the everlasting
         King.
   At his wrath the earth quakes,
      and the nations cannot endure his
         indignation.

11 Thus shall you say to them: The gods who did not make the heavens and the earth shall perish from the earth and from under the heavens.c

12 It is he who made the earth by his power,
      who established the world by his wisdom,
      and by his understanding stretched out the
         heavens.
13 When he utters his voice, there is a tumult of
         waters in the heavens,
      and he makes the mist rise from the ends of
         the earth.
   He makes lightnings for the rain,
      and he brings out the wind from his
         storehouses.
14 Everyone is stupid and without knowledge;
      goldsmiths are all put to shame by their
         idols;
      for their images are false,
      and there is no breath in them.
15 They are worthless, a work of delusion;
      at the time of their punishment they shall
         perish.
16 Not like these is the LORD,d the portion of
         Jacob,
      for he is the one who formed all things,
      and Israel is the tribe of his inheritance;
      the LORD of hosts is his name.

The Coming Exile

17 Gather up your bundle from the ground,
      O you who live under siege!
18 For thus says the LORD:
   I am going to sling out the inhabitants of the
         land
      at this time,
   and I will bring distress on them,
      so that they shall feel it.

19 Woe is me because of my hurt!
      My wound is severe.
   But I said, "Truly this is my punishment,
      and I must bear it."

b Meaning of Heb uncertain   c This verse is in Aramaic   d Heb lacks *the* LORD

King James

20My tabernacle is spoiled, and all my cords are broken: my children are gone forth of me, and they *are* not: *there is* none to stretch forth my tent any more, and to set up my curtains.

21For the pastors are become brutish, and have not sought the LORD: therefore they shall not prosper, and all their flocks shall be scattered.

22Behold, the noise of the bruit is come, and a great commotion out of the north country, to make the cities of Judah desolate, *and* a den of dragons.

23¶ O LORD, I know that the way of man *is* not in himself: *it is* not in man that walketh to direct his steps.

24O LORD, correct me, but with judgment; not in thine anger, lest thou bring me to nothing.

25Pour out thy fury upon the heathen that know thee not, and upon the families that call not on thy name: for they have eaten up Jacob, and devoured him, and consumed him, and have made his habitation desolate.

11 THE WORD that came to Jeremiah from the LORD, saying,

2Hear ye the words of this covenant, and speak unto the men of Judah, and to the inhabitants of Jerusalem;

3And say thou unto them, Thus saith the LORD God of Israel; Cursed *be* the man that obeyeth not the words of this covenant,

4Which I commanded your fathers in the day *that* I brought them forth out of the land of Egypt, from the iron furnace, saying, Obey my voice, and do them, according to all which I command you: so shall ye be my people, and I will be your God:

5That I may perform the oath which I have sworn unto your fathers, to give them a land flowing with milk and honey, as *it is* this day. Then answered I, and said, So be it, O LORD.

6Then the LORD said unto me, Proclaim all these words in the cities of Judah, and in the streets of Jerusalem, saying, Hear ye the words of this covenant, and do them.

7For I earnestly protested unto your fathers in the day *that* I brought them up out of the land of Egypt, *even* unto this day, rising early and protesting, saying, Obey my voice.

8Yet they obeyed not, nor inclined their ear, but walked every one in the imagination of their evil heart: therefore I will bring upon them all the words of this covenant, which I commanded *them* to do; but they did *them* not.

9And the LORD said unto me, A conspiracy is found among the men of Judah, and among the inhabitants of Jerusalem.

10They are turned back to the iniquities of their forefathers, which refused to hear my words; and they went after other gods to serve them: the house of Israel and the house of Judah have broken my covenant which I made with their fathers.

New International

20My tent is destroyed;
    all its ropes are snapped.
My sons are gone from me and are no more;
    no one is left now to pitch my tent
    or to set up my shelter.
21The shepherds are senseless
    and do not inquire of the LORD;
so they do not prosper
    and all their flock is scattered.
22Listen! The report is coming—
    a great commotion from the land of the north!
It will make the towns of Judah desolate,
    a haunt of jackals.

Jeremiah's Prayer

23I know, O LORD, that a man's life is not his own;
    it is not for man to direct his steps.
24Correct me, LORD, but only with justice—
    not in your anger,
    lest you reduce me to nothing.
25Pour out your wrath on the nations
    that do not acknowledge you,
    on the peoples who do not call on your name.
For they have devoured Jacob;
    they have devoured him completely
    and destroyed his homeland.

The Covenant Is Broken

11 THIS IS the word that came to Jeremiah from the LORD: 2"Listen to the terms of this covenant and tell them to the people of Judah and to those who live in Jerusalem. 3Tell them that this is what the LORD, the God of Israel, says: 'Cursed is the man who does not obey the terms of this covenant— 4the terms I commanded your forefathers when I brought them out of Egypt, out of the iron-smelting furnace.' I said, 'Obey me and do everything I command you, and you will be my people, and I will be your God. 5Then I will fulfill the oath I swore to your forefathers, to give them a land flowing with milk and honey'—the land you possess today."

I answered, "Amen, LORD."

6The LORD said to me, "Proclaim all these words in the towns of Judah and in the streets of Jerusalem: 'Listen to the terms of this covenant and follow them. 7From the time I brought your forefathers up from Egypt until today, I warned them again and again, saying, "Obey me." 8But they did not listen or pay attention; instead, they followed the stubbornness of their evil hearts. So I brought on them all the curses of the covenant I had commanded them to follow but that they did not keep.' "

9Then the LORD said to me, "There is a conspiracy among the people of Judah and those who live in Jerusalem. 10They have returned to the sins of their forefathers, who refused to listen to my words. They have followed other gods to serve them. Both the house of Israel and the house of Judah have broken the covenant I made with their forefathers. 11Therefore this is what

Living Bible

my children have been taken away and I will never see them again. There is no one left to help me rebuild my home. 21The shepherds of my people have lost their senses; they no longer follow God nor ask his will. Therefore they perish and their flocks are scattered. 22Listen! Hear the terrible sound of great armies coming from the north. The cities of Judah shall become dens of jackals.

23O Lord, I know it is not within the power of man to map his life and plan his course— 24so you correct me, Lord; but please be gentle. Don't do it in your anger, for I would die. 25Pour out your fury on the nations who don't obey the Lord, for they have destroyed Israel and made a wasteland of this entire country.

11 THEN THE Lord spoke to Jeremiah once again and said:

Remind the men of Judah and all the people of Jerusalem that I made a contract with their fathers—and cursed is the man who does not heed it! 4For I told them at the time I brought them out of slavery in Egypt that if they would obey me and do whatever I commanded them, then they and all their children would be mine and I would be their God. 5And now, Israel, obey me, says the Lord, so that I can do for you the wonderful things I swore I would if you obeyed. I want to give you a land that "flows with milk and honey," as it is today. Then I replied, "So be it, Lord!"

6Then the Lord said: Broadcast this message in Jerusalem's streets—go from city to city throughout the land and say, Remember this agreement that your fathers made with God, and do all the things they promised him they would. 7For I solemnly said to your fathers when I brought them out of Egypt—and have kept on saying it over and over again until this day: Obey my every command! 8But your fathers didn't do it. They wouldn't even listen. Each followed his own stubborn will and his proud heart. Because they refused to obey, I did to them all the evils stated in the contract.

9Again the Lord spoke to me and said: I have discovered a conspiracy against me among the men of Judah and Jerusalem. 10They have returned to the sins of their fathers, refusing to listen to me and worshiping idols. The agreement I made with their fathers is broken and canceled. 11Therefore, the Lord says, I am going to

New Revised Standard

20 My tent is destroyed,
      and all my cords are broken;
   my children have gone from me,
      and they are no more;
   there is no one to spread my tent again,
      and to set up my curtains.
21 For the shepherds are stupid,
      and do not inquire of the LORD;
   therefore they have not prospered,
      and all their flock is scattered.

22 Hear, a noise! Listen, it is coming—
      a great commotion from the land of the
         north
   to make the cities of Judah a desolation,
      a lair of jackals.

23 I know, O LORD, that the way of human
         beings is not in their control,
      that mortals as they walk cannot direct their
         steps.
24 Correct me, O LORD, but in just measure;
      not in your anger, or you will bring me to
         nothing.

25 Pour out your wrath on the nations that do not
         know you,
      and on the peoples that do not call on your
         name;
   for they have devoured Jacob;
      they have devoured him and consumed him,
      and have laid waste his habitation.

Israel and Judah Have Broken the Covenant

11 THE WORD that came to Jeremiah from the LORD: 2Hear the words of this covenant, and speak to the people of Judah and the inhabitants of Jerusalem. 3You shall say to them, Thus says the LORD, the God of Israel: Cursed be anyone who does not heed the words of this covenant, 4which I commanded your ancestors when I brought them out of the land of Egypt, from the iron-smelter, saying, Listen to my voice, and do all that I command you. So shall you be my people, and I will be your God, 5that I may perform the oath that I swore to your ancestors, to give them a land flowing with milk and honey, as at this day. Then I answered, "So be it, LORD."

6 And the LORD said to me: Proclaim all these words in the cities of Judah, and in the streets of Jerusalem: Hear the words of this covenant and do them. 7For I solemnly warned your ancestors when I brought them up out of the land of Egypt, warning them persistently, even to this day, saying, Obey my voice. 8Yet they did not obey or incline their ear, but everyone walked in the stubbornness of an evil will. So I brought upon them all the words of this covenant, which I commanded them to do, but they did not.

9 And the LORD said to me: Conspiracy exists among the people of Judah and the inhabitants of Jerusalem. 10They have turned back to the iniquities of their ancestors of old, who refused to heed my words; they have gone after other gods to serve them; the house of Israel and the house of Judah have broken the covenant that I made with their ancestors. 11Therefore, thus says

King James

11¶ Therefore thus saith the LORD, Behold, I will bring evil upon them, which they shall not be able to escape; and though they shall cry unto me, I will not hearken unto them.

12Then shall the cities of Judah and inhabitants of Jerusalem go, and cry unto the gods unto whom they offer incense: but they shall not save them at all in the time of their trouble.

13For *according to* the number of thy cities were thy gods, O Judah; and *according to* the number of the streets of Jerusalem have ye set up altars to *that* shameful thing, *even* altars to burn incense unto Baal.

14Therefore pray not thou for this people, neither lift up a cry or prayer for them: for I will not hear *them* in the time that they cry unto me for their trouble.

15What hath my beloved to do in mine house, *seeing* she hath wrought lewdness with many, and the holy flesh is passed from thee? when thou doest evil, then thou rejoicest.

16The LORD called thy name, A green olive tree, fair, *and* of goodly fruit: with the noise of a great tumult he hath kindled fire upon it, and the branches of it are broken.

17For the LORD of hosts, that planted thee, hath pronounced evil against thee, for the evil of the house of Israel and of the house of Judah, which they have done against themselves to provoke me to anger in offering incense unto Baal.

18¶ And the LORD hath given me knowledge *of it,* and I know *it:* then thou showedst me their doings.

19But I *was* like a lamb *or* an ox *that* is brought to the slaughter; and I knew not that they had devised devices against me, *saying,* Let us destroy the tree with the fruit thereof, and let us cut him off from the land of the living, that his name may be no more remembered.

20But, O LORD of hosts, that judgest righteously, that triest the reins and the heart, let me see thy vengeance on them: for unto thee have I revealed my cause.

21Therefore thus saith the LORD of the men of Anathoth, that seek thy life, saying, Prophesy not in the name of the LORD, that thou die not by our hand:

22Therefore thus saith the LORD of hosts, Behold, I will punish them: the young men shall die by the sword; their sons and their daughters shall die by famine:

23And there shall be no remnant of them: for I will bring evil upon the men of Anathoth, *even* the year of their visitation.

12 RIGHTEOUS *ART* thou, O LORD, when I plead with thee: yet let me talk with thee of *thy* judgments: Wherefore doth the way of the wicked prosper? *wherefore* are all they happy that deal very treacherously?

2Thou hast planted them, yea, they have taken root: they grow, yea, they bring forth fruit: thou *art* near in their mouth, and far from their reins.

New International

the LORD says: 'I will bring on them a disaster they cannot escape. Although they cry out to me, I will not listen to them. 12The towns of Judah and the people of Jerusalem will go and cry out to the gods to whom they burn incense, but they will not help them at all when disaster strikes. 13You have as many gods as you have towns, O Judah; and the altars you have set up to burn incense to that shameful god Baal are as many as the streets of Jerusalem.'

14"Do not pray for this people nor offer any plea or petition for them, because I will not listen when they call to me in the time of their distress.

15"What is my beloved doing in my temple
    as she works out her evil schemes with
        many?
    Can consecrated meat avert ⌊your
        punishment⌋?
    When you engage in your wickedness,
        then you rejoice.a"

16The LORD called you a thriving olive tree
    with fruit beautiful in form.
But with the roar of a mighty storm
    he will set it on fire,
    and its branches will be broken.

17The LORD Almighty, who planted you, has decreed disaster for you, because the house of Israel and the house of Judah have done evil and provoked me to anger by burning incense to Baal.

Plot Against Jeremiah

18Because the LORD revealed their plot to me, I knew it, for at that time he showed me what they were doing. 19I had been like a gentle lamb led to the slaughter; I did not realize that they had plotted against me, saying,

    "Let us destroy the tree and its fruit;
        let us cut him off from the land of the living,
        that his name be remembered no more."

20But, O LORD Almighty, you who judge
        righteously
    and test the heart and mind,
    let me see your vengeance upon them,
        for to you I have committed my cause.

21"Therefore this is what the LORD says about the men of Anathoth who are seeking your life and saying, 'Do not prophesy in the name of the LORD or you will die by our hands'— 22therefore this is what the LORD Almighty says: 'I will punish them. Their young men will die by the sword, their sons and daughters by famine. 23Not even a remnant will be left to them, because I will bring disaster on the men of Anathoth in the year of their punishment.' "

Jeremiah's Complaint

12 YOU ARE always righteous, O LORD,
    when I bring a case before you.
Yet I would speak with you about your justice:
    Why does the way of the wicked prosper?
    Why do all the faithless live at ease?
2You have planted them, and they have taken
        root;
    they grow and bear fruit.
You are always on their lips
    but far from their hearts.

---

a 15 Or *Could consecrated meat avert your punishment? | Then you would rejoice*

Living Bible

bring calamity down upon them and they shall not escape. Though they cry for mercy, I will not listen to their pleas. 12Then they will pray to their idols and burn incense before them, but that cannot save them from their time of anguish and despair. 13O my people, you have as many gods as there are cities, and your altars of shame (your altars to burn incense to Baal) are along every street in Jerusalem.

14Therefore, Jeremiah, pray no longer for this people, neither weep nor plead for them; for I will not listen to them when they are finally desperate enough to beg me for help. 15What right do my beloved people have to come any more to my Temple? For you have been unfaithful and worshiped other gods. Can promises and sacrifices now avert your doom and give you life and joy again? 16The Lord used to call you his green olive tree, beautiful to see and full of good fruit; but now he has sent the fury of your enemies to burn you up and leave you broken and charred. 17It is because of the wickedness of Israel and Judah in offering incense to Baal that the Lord Almighty who planted the tree has ordered it destroyed.

18Then the Lord told me all about their plans and showed me their evil plots. 19I had been as unsuspecting as a lamb or ox on the way to slaughter. I didn't know that they were planning to kill me! "Let's destroy this man and all his messages," they said. "Let's kill him so that his name will be forever forgotten."

20O Lord Almighty, you are just. See the hearts and motives of these men. Repay them for all that they have planned! I look to you for justice.

21, 22And the Lord replied, The men of the city of Anathoth shall be punished for planning to kill you. They will tell you not to prophesy in God's name on pain of death. And so their young men shall die in battle; their boys and girls shall starve. 23Not one of these plotters of Anathoth shall survive, for I will bring a great disaster upon them. Their time has come.

12 O LORD, you always give me justice when I bring a case before you to decide. Now let me bring you this complaint: Why are the wicked so prosperous? Why are evil men so happy? 2You plant them. They take root and their business grows. Their profits multiply, and they are rich. They say, "Thank God!" But in their hearts they give no credit to you. 3But as for

New Revised Standard

the LORD, assuredly I am going to bring disaster upon them that they cannot escape; though they cry out to me, I will not listen to them. 12Then the cities of Judah and the inhabitants of Jerusalem will go and cry out to the gods to whom they make offerings, but they will never save them in the time of their trouble. 13For your gods have become as many as your towns, O Judah; and as many as the streets of Jerusalem are the altars you have set up to shame, altars to make offerings to Baal.

14 As for you, do not pray for this people, or lift up a cry or prayer on their behalf, for I will not listen when they call to me in the time of their trouble. 15What right has my beloved in my house, when she has done vile deeds? Can vowsb and sacrificial flesh avert your doom? Can you then exult? 16The LORD once called you, "A green olive tree, fair with goodly fruit"; but with the roar of a great tempest he will set fire to it, and its branches will be consumed. 17The LORD of hosts, who planted you, has pronounced evil against you, because of the evil that the house of Israel and the house of Judah have done, provoking me to anger by making offerings to Baal.

Jeremiah's Life Threatened

18 It was the LORD who made it known to me,
        and I knew;
      then you showed me their evil deeds.
19 But I was like a gentle lamb
        led to the slaughter.
    And I did not know it was against me
        that they devised schemes, saying,
    "Let us destroy the tree with its fruit,
        let us cut him off from the land of the
            living,
        so that his name will no longer be
            remembered!"
20 But you, O LORD of hosts, who judge
        righteously,
      who try the heart and the mind,
    let me see your retribution upon them,
        for to you I have committed my cause.

21 Therefore thus says the LORD concerning the people of Anathoth, who seek your life, and say, "You shall not prophesy in the name of the LORD, or you will die by our hand"— 22therefore thus says the LORD of hosts: I am going to punish them; the young men shall die by the sword; their sons and their daughters shall die by famine; 23and not even a remnant shall be left of them. For I will bring disaster upon the people of Anathoth, the year of their punishment.

Jeremiah Complains to God

12 YOU WILL be in the right, O LORD,
      when I lay charges against you;
    but let me put my case to you.
    Why does the way of the guilty prosper?
      Why do all who are treacherous thrive?
2   You plant them, and they take root;
      they grow and bring forth fruit;
    you are near in their mouths
      yet far from their hearts.

King James

3But thou, O LORD, knowest me: thou hast seen me, and tried mine heart toward thee: pull them out like sheep for the slaughter, and prepare them for the day of slaughter.

4How long shall the land mourn, and the herbs of every field wither, for the wickedness of them that dwell therein? the beasts are consumed, and the birds; because they said, He shall not see our last end.

5¶ If thou hast run with the footmen, and they have wearied thee, then how canst thou contend with horses? and *if* in the land of peace, *wherein* thou trustedst, *they wearied thee,* then how wilt thou do in the swelling of Jordan?

6For even thy brethren, and the house of thy father, even they have dealt treacherously with thee; yea, they have called a multitude after thee: believe them not, though they speak fair words unto thee.

7¶ I have forsaken mine house, I have left mine heritage; I have given the dearly beloved of my soul into the hand of her enemies.

8Mine heritage is unto me as a lion in the forest; it crieth out against me: therefore have I hated it.

9Mine heritage *is* unto me *as* a speckled bird, the birds round about *are* against her; come ye, assemble all the beasts of the field, come to devour.

10Many pastors have destroyed my vineyard, they have trodden my portion under foot, they have made my pleasant portion a desolate wilderness.

11They have made it desolate, *and being* desolate it mourneth unto me; the whole land is made desolate, because no man layeth *it* to heart.

12The spoilers are come upon all high places through the wilderness: for the sword of the LORD shall devour from the *one* end of the land even to the *other* end of the land: no flesh shall have peace.

13They have sown wheat, but shall reap thorns: they have put themselves to pain, *but* shall not profit: and they shall be ashamed of your revenues because of the fierce anger of the LORD.

14¶ Thus saith the LORD against all mine evil neighbours, that touch the inheritance which I have caused my people Israel to inherit; Behold, I will pluck them out of their land, and pluck out the house of Judah from among them.

15And it shall come to pass, after that I have plucked them out I will return, and have compassion on them, and will bring them again, every man to his heritage, and every man to his land.

16And it shall come to pass, if they will diligently learn the ways of my people, to swear by my name, The LORD liveth; as they taught my people to swear by Baal; then shall they be built in the midst of my people.

17But if they will not obey, I will utterly pluck up and destroy that nation, saith the LORD.

New International

3Yet you know me, O LORD;
  you see me and test my thoughts about you.
Drag them off like sheep to be butchered!
  Set them apart for the day of slaughter!
4How long will the land lie parched[a]
  and the grass in every field be withered?
Because those who live in it are wicked,
  the animals and birds have perished.
Moreover, the people are saying,
  "He will not see what happens to us."

God's Answer

5"If you have raced with men on foot
  and they have worn you out,
  how can you compete with horses?
If you stumble in safe country,[b]
  how will you manage in the thickets by[c] the
    Jordan?
6Your brothers, your own family—
  even they have betrayed you;
  they have raised a loud cry against you.
Do not trust them,
  though they speak well of you.

7"I will forsake my house,
  abandon my inheritance;
I will give the one I love
  into the hands of her enemies.
8My inheritance has become to me
  like a lion in the forest.
She roars at me;
  therefore I hate her.
9Has not my inheritance become to me
  like a speckled bird of prey
  that other birds of prey surround and attack?
Go and gather all the wild beasts;
  bring them to devour.
10Many shepherds will ruin my vineyard
  and trample down my field;
they will turn my pleasant field
  into a desolate wasteland.
11It will be made a wasteland,
  parched and desolate before me;
the whole land will be laid waste
  because there is no one who cares.
12Over all the barren heights in the desert
  destroyers will swarm,
for the sword of the LORD will devour
  from one end of the land to the other;
  no one will be safe.
13They will sow wheat but reap thorns;
  they will wear themselves out but gain
    nothing.
So bear the shame of your harvest
  because of the LORD's fierce anger."

14This is what the LORD says: "As for all my wicked neighbors who seize the inheritance I gave my people Israel, I will uproot them from their lands and I will uproot the house of Judah from among them. 15But after I uproot them, I will again have compassion and will bring each of them back to his own inheritance and his own country. 16And if they learn well the ways of my people and swear by my name, saying, 'As surely as the LORD lives'—even as they once taught my people to swear by Baal—then they will be established among my people. 17But if any nation does not listen, I will completely uproot and destroy it," declares the LORD.

a 4 Or *land mourn*   b 5 Or *If you put your trust in a land of safety*   c 5 Or *the flooding of*

Living Bible

me—Lord, you know my heart—you know how much it longs for you. (And I am poor,d O Lord!) Lord, drag them off like helpless sheep to the slaughter. Judge them, O God!

4How long must this land of yours put up with all their goings on? Even the grass of the field groans and weeps over their wicked deeds! The wild animals and birds have moved away, leaving the land deserted. Yet the people say, "God won't bring judgment on us. We're perfectly safe!"

5The Lord replied to me: If racing with mere men—these men of Anathothe—has wearied you, how will you race against horses, against the king, his court and all his evil priests?e If you stumble and fall on open ground, what will you do in Jordan's jungles? 6Even your own brothers, your own family, have turned against you. They have plotted to call for a mob to lynch you. Don't trust them, no matter how pleasantly they speak. Don't believe them.

7Then the Lord said: I have abandoned my people, my inheritance; I have surrendered my dearest ones to their enemies. 8My people have roared at me like a lion of the forest, so I have treated them as though I hated them. 9My people have fallen. I will bring upon them swarms of vultures and wild animals to pick the flesh from their corpses.

10Many foreign rulers have ravaged my vineyard, trampling down the vines, and turning all its beauty into barren wilderness. 11They have made it desolate; I hear its mournful cry. The whole land is desolate and no one cares. 12Destroying armies plunder the land; the sword of the Lord devours from one end of the nation to the other; nothing shall escape. 13My people have sown wheat but reaped thorns; they have worked hard but it does them no good. They shall harvest a crop of shame, for the fierce anger of the Lord is upon them.

14And now the Lord says this to the evil nations, the nations surrounding the land God gave his people Israel: See, I will force you from your land just as Judah will be forced from hers; 15but afterwards I will return and have compassion on all of you, and will bring you home to your own land again, each man to his inheritance. 16And if these heathen nations quickly learn my people's ways and claim me as their God instead of Baal (whom they taught my people to worship), then they shall be strong among my people. 17But any nation refusing to obey me will be expelled again and finished, says the Lord.

New Revised Standard

3 But you, O LORD, know me;
   You see me and test me—my heart is with
      you.
Pull them out like sheep for the slaughter,
   and set them apart for the day of slaughter.
4 How long will the land mourn,
   and the grass of every field wither?
For the wickedness of those who live in it
   the animals and the birds are swept away,
   and because people said, "He is blind to our
      ways."f

God Replies to Jeremiah

5 If you have raced with foot-runners and they
      have wearied you,
   how will you compete with horses?
And if in a safe land you fall down,
   how will you fare in the thickets of the
      Jordan?
6 For even your kinsfolk and your own family,
   even they have dealt treacherously with you;
   they are in full cry after you;
do not believe them,
   though they speak friendly words to you.

7 I have forsaken my house,
   I have abandoned my heritage;
I have given the beloved of my heart
   into the hands of her enemies.
8 My heritage has become to me
   like a lion in the forest;
she has lifted up her voice against me—
   therefore I hate her.
9 Is the hyena greedyg for my heritage at my
      command?
   Are the birds of prey all around her?
Go, assemble all the wild animals;
   bring them to devour her.
10 Many shepherds have destroyed my vineyard,
   they have trampled down my portion,
they have made my pleasant portion
   a desolate wilderness.
11 They have made it a desolation;
   desolate, it mourns to me.
The whole land is made desolate,
   but no one lays it to heart.
12 Upon all the bare heightsh in the desert
   spoilers have come;
for the sword of the LORD devours
   from one end of the land to the other;
   no one shall be safe.
13 They have sown wheat and have reaped
      thorns,
   they have tired themselves out but profit
      nothing.
They shall be ashamed of theiri harvests
   because of the fierce anger of the LORD.

14 Thus says the LORD concerning all my evil neighbors who touch the heritage that I have given my people Israel to inherit: I am about to pluck them up from their land, and I will pluck up the house of Judah from among them. 15 And after I have plucked them up, I will again have compassion on them, and I will bring them again to their heritage and to their land, everyone of them. 16 And then, if they will diligently learn the ways of my people, to swear by my name, "As the LORD lives," as they taught my people to swear by Baal, then they shall be built up in the midst of my people. 17 But if any nation will not listen, then I will completely uproot it and destroy it, says the LORD.

---

d 12:3 I am poor, implied.   e 12:5 these men of Anathoth . . . against the king, his court and all his evil priests, implied.

f Gk: Heb to our future   g Cn: Heb Is the hyena, the bird of prey   h Or the trails   i Heb your

King James

13 THUS SAITH the LORD unto me, Go and get thee a linen girdle, and put it upon thy loins, and put it not in water.

2So I got a girdle according to the word of the LORD, and put *it* on my loins.

3And the word of the LORD came unto me the second time, saying,

4Take the girdle that thou hast got, which *is* upon thy loins, and arise, go to Euphrates, and hide it there in a hole of the rock.

5So I went, and hid it by Euphrates, as the LORD commanded me.

6And it came to pass after many days, that the LORD said unto me, Arise, go to Euphrates, and take the girdle from thence, which I commanded thee to hide there.

7Then I went to Euphrates, and digged, and took the girdle from the place where I had hid it: and, behold, the girdle was marred, it was profitable for nothing.

8Then the word of the LORD came unto me, saying,

9Thus saith the LORD, After this manner will I mar the pride of Judah, and the great pride of Jerusalem.

10This evil people, which refuse to hear my words, which walk in the imagination of their heart, and walk after other gods, to serve them, and to worship them, shall even be as this girdle, which is good for nothing.

11For as the girdle cleaveth to the loins of a man, so have I caused to cleave unto me the whole house of Israel and the whole house of Judah, saith the LORD; that they might be unto me for a people, and for a name, and for a praise, and for a glory: but they would not hear.

12¶ Therefore thou shalt speak unto them this word; Thus saith the LORD God of Israel, Every bottle shall be filled with wine: and they shall say unto thee, Do we not certainly know that every bottle shall be filled with wine?

13Then shalt thou say unto them, Thus saith the LORD, Behold, I will fill all the inhabitants of this land, even the kings that sit upon David's throne, and the priests, and the prophets, and all the inhabitants of Jerusalem, with drunkenness.

14And I will dash them one against another, even the fathers and the sons together, saith the LORD: I will not pity, nor spare, nor have mercy, but destroy them.

15¶ Hear ye, and give ear; be not proud: for the LORD hath spoken.

16Give glory to the LORD your God, before he cause darkness, and before your feet stumble upon the dark mountains, and, while ye look for light, he turn it into the shadow of death, *and* make *it* gross darkness.

17But if ye will not hear it, my soul shall weep in secret places for *your* pride; and mine eye shall weep sore, and run down with tears, because the LORD's flock is carried away captive.

18Say unto the king and to the queen, Humble yourselves, sit down: for your principalities shall come down, *even* the crown of your glory.

19The cities of the south shall be shut up, and none shall open *them*: Judah shall be carried away captive all of it, it shall be wholly carried away captive.

New International

A Linen Belt

13 THIS IS what the LORD said to me: "Go and buy a linen belt and put it around your waist, but do not let it touch water." 2So I bought a belt, as the LORD directed, and put it around my waist.

3Then the word of the LORD came to me a second time: 4"Take the belt you bought and are wearing around your waist, and go now to Perath[a] and hide it there in a crevice in the rocks." 5So I went and hid it at Perath, as the LORD told me.

6Many days later the LORD said to me, "Go now to Perath and get the belt I told you to hide there." 7So I went to Perath and dug up the belt and took it from the place where I had hidden it, but now it was ruined and completely useless.

8Then the word of the LORD came to me: 9"This is what the LORD says: 'In the same way I will ruin the pride of Judah and the great pride of Jerusalem. 10These wicked people, who refuse to listen to my words, who follow the stubbornness of their hearts and go after other gods to serve and worship them, will be like this belt—completely useless! 11For as a belt is bound around a man's waist, so I bound the whole house of Israel and the whole house of Judah to me,' declares the LORD, 'to be my people for my renown and praise and honor. But they have not listened.'

Wineskins

12"Say to them: 'This is what the LORD, the God of Israel, says: Every wineskin should be filled with wine.' And if they say to you, 'Don't we know that every wineskin should be filled with wine?' 13then tell them, 'This is what the LORD says: I am going to fill with drunkenness all who live in this land, including the kings who sit on David's throne, the priests, the prophets and all those living in Jerusalem. 14I will smash them one against the other, fathers and sons alike, declares the LORD. I will allow no pity or mercy or compassion to keep me from destroying them.' "

Threat of Captivity

15Hear and pay attention,
  do not be arrogant,
  for the LORD has spoken.
16Give glory to the LORD your God
  before he brings the darkness,
before your feet stumble
  on the darkening hills.
You hope for light,
  but he will turn it to thick darkness
  and change it to deep gloom.
17But if you do not listen,
  I will weep in secret
  because of your pride;
my eyes will weep bitterly,
  overflowing with tears,
  because the LORD's flock will be taken
    captive.

18Say to the king and to the queen mother,
  "Come down from your thrones,
for your glorious crowns
  will fall from your heads."
19The cities in the Negev will be shut up,
  and there will be no one to open them.
All Judah will be carried into exile,
  carried completely away.

a 4 Or possibly *the Euphrates*; also in verses 5-7

Living Bible

13 THE LORD said to me, Go and buy a linen loincloth and wear it, but don't wash it—don't put it in water at all. ²So I bought the loincloth and put it on. ³Then the Lord's message came to me again. This time he said, ⁴Take the loincloth out to the Euphrates River and hide it in a hole in the rocks.

⁵So I did; I hid it as the Lord had told me to. ⁶Then, a long time afterwards, the Lord said: Go out to the river again and get the loincloth. ⁷And I did; I dug it out of the hole where I had hidden it. But now it was mildewed and falling apart. It was utterly useless!

8, ⁹Then the Lord said: This illustrates the way that I will rot the pride of Judah and Jerusalem. ¹⁰This evil nation refuses to listen to me, and follows its own evil desires and worships idols; therefore it shall become as this loincloth—good for nothing. ¹¹Even as a loincloth clings to a man's loins, so I made Judah and Israel to cling to me, says the Lord. They were my people, an honor to my name. But then they turned away.

¹²Tell them this: The Lord God of Israel says, All your wine jugs will be full of wine. And they will reply, Of course, you don't need to tell us how prosperous we will be!ᵇ ¹³Then tell them: That's not what I mean.ᶜ I mean that I will fill everyone living in this land with helpless bewilderment—from the king sitting on David's throne, and the priests and the prophets right on down to all the people. ¹⁴And I will smash fathers and sons against each other, says the Lord. I will not let pity nor mercy spare them from utter destruction.

¹⁵Oh, that you were not so proud and stubborn! Then you would listen to the Lord, for he has spoken. ¹⁶Give glory to the Lord your God before it is too late, before he causes deep, impenetrable darkness to fall upon you so that you stumble and fall upon the dark mountains; then, when you look for light, you will find only terrible darkness. ¹⁷Do you still refuse to listen? Then in loneliness my breaking heart shall mourn because of your pride. My eyes will overflow with tears because the Lord's flock shall be carried away as slaves.

¹⁸Say to the king and queen-mother,ᵈ Come down from your thrones and sit in the dust, for your glorious crowns are removed from your heads. They are no longer yours. ¹⁹The cities of the Negeb to the south of Jerusalem have closed their gates against the enemy. They must defend themselves, for Jerusalem cannot help;ᵉ and all Judah shall be taken away as slaves. ²⁰See

New Revised Standard

The Linen Loincloth

13 THUS SAID the LORD to me, "Go and buy yourself a linen loincloth, and put it on your loins, but do not dip it in water." ²So I bought a loincloth according to the word of the LORD, and put it on my loins. ³And the word of the LORD came to me a second time, saying, ⁴"Take the loincloth that you bought and are wearing, and go now to the Euphrates,ᶠ and hide it there in a cleft of the rock." ⁵So I went, and hid it by the Euphrates,ᵍ as the LORD commanded me. ⁶And after many days the LORD said to me, "Go now to the Euphrates,ᶠ and take from there the loincloth that I commanded you to hide there." ⁷Then I went to the Euphrates,ᶠ and dug, and I took the loincloth from the place where I had hidden it. But now the loincloth was ruined; it was good for nothing.

8 Then the word of the LORD came to me: ⁹Thus says the LORD: Just so I will ruin the pride of Judah and the great pride of Jerusalem. ¹⁰This evil people, who refuse to hear my words, who stubbornly follow their own will and have gone after other gods to serve them and worship them, shall be like this loincloth, which is good for nothing. ¹¹For as the loincloth clings to one's loins, so I made the whole house of Israel and the whole house of Judah cling to me, says the LORD, in order that they might be for me a people, a name, a praise, and a glory. But they would not listen.

Symbol of the Wine-Jars

12 You shall speak to them this word: Thus says the LORD, the God of Israel: Every wine-jar should be filled with wine. And they will say to you, "Do you think we do not know that every wine-jar should be filled with wine?" ¹³Then you shall say to them: Thus says the LORD: I am about to fill all the inhabitants of this land—the kings who sit on David's throne, the priests, the prophets, and all the inhabitants of Jerusalem—with drunkenness. ¹⁴And I will dash them one against another, parents and children together, says the LORD. I will not pity or spare or have compassion when I destroy them.

Exile Threatened

15 Hear and give ear; do not be haughty,
      for the LORD has spoken.
16 Give glory to the LORD your God
      before he brings darkness,
   and before your feet stumble
      on the mountains at twilight;
   while you look for light,
      he turns it into gloom
      and makes it deep darkness.
17 But if you will not listen,
      my soul will weep in secret for your pride;
   my eyes will weep bitterly and run down with
         tears,
   because the LORD's flock has been taken
         captive.

18 Say to the king and the queen mother;
      "Take a lowly seat,
   for your beautiful crown
      has come down from your head."ʰ
19 The towns of the Negeb are shut up
      with no one to open them;
   all Judah is taken into exile,
      wholly taken into exile.

ᵇ *13:12 Of course, you don't need to tell us how prosperous we will be,* literally, "that every bottle will be filled with wine."   ᶜ *13:13 That's not what I mean,* implied.   ᵈ *13:18 Say to the king and queen-mother,* i.e., to King Jehoiachin and his mother Nehashta.   ᵉ *13:19 for Jerusalem cannot help,* literally, "the cities are closed and none can open them." Perhaps the meaning is that they are permanently abandoned.

ᶠ Or *to Parah*; Heb *perath*   ᵍ Or *by Parah*; Heb *perath*   ʰ Gk Syr Vg: Meaning of Heb uncertain

King James

20Lift up your eyes, and behold them that come from the north: where *is* the flock *that* was given thee, thy beautiful flock?

21What wilt thou say when he shall punish thee? for thou hast taught them *to be* captains, *and* as chief over thee: shall not sorrows take thee, as a woman in travail?

22¶ And if thou say in thine heart, Wherefore come these things upon me? For the greatness of thine iniquity are thy skirts discovered, *and* thy heels made bare.

23Can the Ethiopian change his skin, or the leopard his spots? *then* may ye also do good, that are accustomed to do evil.

24Therefore will I scatter them as the stubble that passeth away by the wind of the wilderness.

25This *is* thy lot, the portion of thy measures from me, saith the LORD; because thou hast forgotten me, and trusted in falsehood.

26Therefore will I discover thy skirts upon thy face, that thy shame may appear.

27I have seen thine adulteries, and thy neighings, the lewdness of thy whoredom, *and* thine abominations on the hills in the fields. Woe unto thee, O Jerusalem! wilt thou not be made clean? when *shall it* once *be?*

14 THE WORD of the LORD that came to Jeremiah concerning the dearth.

2Judah mourneth, and the gates thereof languish; they are black unto the ground; and the cry of Jerusalem is gone up.

3And their nobles have sent their little ones to the waters: they came to the pits, *and* found no water; they returned with their vessels empty; they were ashamed and confounded, and covered their heads.

4Because the ground is chapt, for there was no rain in the earth, the plowmen were ashamed, they covered their heads.

5Yea, the hind also calved in the field, and forsook *it,* because there was no grass.

6And the wild asses did stand in the high places, they snuffed up the wind like dragons; their eyes did fail, because *there was* no grass.

7¶ O LORD, though our iniquities testify against us, do thou *it* for thy name's sake: for our backslidings are many; we have sinned against thee.

New International

20Lift up your eyes and see
   those who are coming from the north.
Where is the flock that was entrusted to you,
   the sheep of which you boasted?
21What will you say when the LORD sets over you
   those you cultivated as your special allies?
Will not pain grip you
   like that of a woman in labor?
22And if you ask yourself,
   "Why has this happened to me?"—
it is because of your many sins
   that your skirts have been torn off
   and your body mistreated.
23Can the Ethiopiana change his skin
   or the leopard its spots?
Neither can you do good
   who are accustomed to doing evil.

24"I will scatter you like chaff
   driven by the desert wind.
25This is your lot,
   the portion I have decreed for you,"
                         declares the LORD,
"because you have forgotten me
   and trusted in false gods.
26I will pull up your skirts over your face
   that your shame may be seen—
27your adulteries and lustful neighings,
   your shameless prostitution!
I have seen your detestable acts
   on the hills and in the fields.
Woe to you, O Jerusalem!
   How long will you be unclean?"

Drought, Famine, Sword

14 THIS IS the word of the LORD to Jeremiah concerning the drought:

2"Judah mourns,
   her cities languish;
they wail for the land,
   and a cry goes up from Jerusalem.
3The nobles send their servants for water;
   they go to the cisterns
   but find no water.
They return with their jars unfilled;
   dismayed and despairing,
   they cover their heads.
4The ground is cracked
   because there is no rain in the land;
the farmers are dismayed
   and cover their heads.
5Even the doe in the field
   deserts her newborn fawn
   because there is no grass.
6Wild donkeys stand on the barren heights
   and pant like jackals;
their eyesight fails
   for lack of pasture."

7Although our sins testify against us,
   O LORD, do something for the sake of your name.
For our backsliding is great;
   we have sinned against you.

a 23 Hebrew *Cushite* (probably a person from the upper Nile region)

Living Bible

the armies marching from the north! Where is your flock, Jerusalem,[b] your beautiful flock I gave you to take care of? 21How will you feel when I set your allies over you as your rulers? You will writhe in pain like a woman having a child. 22And if you ask yourself, Why is all this happening to me? It is because of the grossness of your sins; that is why you have been raped and destroyed by the invading army.

23Can the Ethiopian change the color of his skin? or a leopard take away his spots? Nor can you who are so used to doing evil now start being good. 24, 25Because you have put me out of your mind and put your trust in false gods, I will scatter you as chaff is scattered by the fierce winds off the desert. This then is your allotment, that which is due you, which I have measured out especially for you. 26I myself will expose you to utter shame. 27I am keenly aware of your apostasy, your faithlessness to me, and your abominable idol worship in the fields and on the hills. Woe upon you, O Jerusalem! How long before you will be pure?

14 THIS MESSAGE came to Jeremiah from the Lord, explaining why he was holding back the rain:

2Judah mourns; business has ground to a halt; all the people prostrate themselves to the earth and a great cry rises from Jerusalem. 3The nobles send servants for water from the wells, but the wells are dry. The servants return, baffled and desperate, and cover their heads in grief. 4The ground is parched and cracked for lack of rain; the farmers are afraid. 5The deer deserts her fawn because there is no grass. 6The wild donkeys stand upon the bare hills panting like thirsty jackals. They strain their eyes looking for grass to eat, but there is none to be found.

7O Lord, we have sinned against you grievously, yet help us for the sake of your own reputation! 8O Hope of

New Revised Standard

20 Lift up your eyes and see
    those who come from the north.
Where is the flock that was given you,
    your beautiful flock?
21 What will you say when they set as head over
        you
    those whom you have trained
    to be your allies?
Will not pangs take hold of you,
    like those of a woman in labor?
22 And if you say in your heart,
    "Why have these things come upon me?"
it is for the greatness of your iniquity
    that your skirts are lifted up,
    and you are violated.
23 Can Ethiopians[c] change their skin
    or leopards their spots?
Then also you can do good
    who are accustomed to do evil.
24 I will scatter you[d] like chaff
    driven by the wind from the desert.
25 This is your lot,
    the portion I have measured out to you,
        says the LORD,
because you have forgotten me
    and trusted in lies.
26 I myself will lift up your skirts over your
        face,
    and your shame will be seen.
27 I have seen your abominations,
    your adulteries and neighings, your
        shameless prostitutions
    on the hills of the countryside.
Woe to you, O Jerusalem!
    How long will it be
    before you are made clean?

The Great Drought

14 THE WORD of the LORD that came to Jeremiah concerning the drought:
2 Judah mourns
    and her gates languish;
they lie in gloom on the ground,
    and the cry of Jerusalem goes up.
3 Her nobles send their servants for water;
    they come to the cisterns,
they find no water,
    they return with their vessels empty.
They are ashamed and dismayed
    and cover their heads,
4 because the ground is cracked.
    Because there has been no rain on the land
the farmers are dismayed;
    they cover their heads.
5 Even the doe in the field forsakes her newborn
        fawn
    because there is no grass.
6 The wild asses stand on the bare heights,[e]
    they pant for air like jackals;
their eyes fail
    because there is no herbage.

7 Although our iniquities testify against us,
    act, O LORD, for your name's sake;
our apostasies indeed are many,
    and we have sinned against you.

---

b 13:20 Jerusalem, implied.   c Or Nubians; Heb Cushites   d Heb them   e Or the trails

King James

8O the hope of Israel, the saviour thereof in time of trouble, why shouldest thou be as a stranger in the land, and as a wayfaring man *that* turneth aside to tarry for a night?

9Why shouldest thou be as a man astonied, as a mighty man *that* cannot save? yet thou, O LORD, *art* in the midst of us, and we are called by thy name; leave us not.

10¶ Thus saith the LORD unto this people, Thus have they loved to wander, they have not refrained their feet, therefore the LORD doth not accept them; he will now remember their iniquity, and visit their sins.

11Then said the LORD unto me, Pray not for this people for *their* good.

12When they fast, I will not hear their cry; and when they offer burnt offering and an oblation, I will not accept them: but I will consume them by the sword, and by the famine, and by the pestilence.

13¶ Then said I, Ah, Lord GOD! behold, the prophets say unto them, Ye shall not see the sword, neither shall ye have famine; but I will give you assured peace in this place.

14Then the LORD said unto me, The prophets prophesy lies in my name: I sent them not, neither have I commanded them, neither spake unto them: they prophesy unto you a false vision and divination, and a thing of nought, and the deceit of their heart.

15Therefore thus saith the LORD concerning the prophets that prophesy in my name, and I sent them not, yet they say, Sword and famine shall not be in this land; By sword and famine shall those prophets be consumed.

16And the people to whom they prophesy shall be cast out in the streets of Jerusalem because of the famine and the sword; and they shall have none to bury them, them, their wives, nor their sons, nor their daughters: for I will pour their wickedness upon them.

17¶ Therefore thou shalt say this word unto them; Let mine eyes run down with tears night and day, and let them not cease: for the virgin daughter of my people is broken with a great breach, with a very grievous blow.

18If I go forth into the field, then behold the slain with the sword! and if I enter into the city, then behold them that are sick with famine! yea, both the prophet and the priest go about into a land that they know not.

19Hast thou utterly rejected Judah? hath thy soul loathed Zion? why hast thou smitten us, and *there is* no healing for us? we looked for peace, and *there is* no good; and for the time of healing, and behold trouble!

20We acknowledge, O LORD, our wickedness, *and* the iniquity of our fathers: for we have sinned against thee.

21Do not abhor *us*, for thy name's sake, do not disgrace the throne of thy glory: remember, break not thy covenant with us.

New International

8O Hope of Israel,
  its Savior in times of distress,
why are you like a stranger in the land,
  like a traveler who stays only a night?
9Why are you like a man taken by surprise,
  like a warrior powerless to save?
You are among us, O LORD,
  and we bear your name;
  do not forsake us!

10This is what the LORD says about this people:

"They greatly love to wander;
  they do not restrain their feet.
So the LORD does not accept them;
  he will now remember their wickedness
  and punish them for their sins."

11Then the LORD said to me, "Do not pray for the well-being of this people. 12Although they fast, I will not listen to their cry; though they offer burnt offerings and grain offerings, I will not accept them. Instead, I will destroy them with the sword, famine and plague."

13But I said, "Ah, Sovereign LORD, the prophets keep telling them, 'You will not see the sword or suffer famine. Indeed, I will give you lasting peace in this place.' "

14Then the LORD said to me, "The prophets are prophesying lies in my name. I have not sent them or appointed them or spoken to them. They are prophesying to you false visions, divinations, idolatries[a] and the delusions of their own minds. 15Therefore, this is what the LORD says about the prophets who are prophesying in my name: I did not send them, yet they are saying, 'No sword or famine will touch this land.' Those same prophets will perish by sword and famine. 16And the people they are prophesying to will be thrown out into the streets of Jerusalem because of the famine and sword. There will be no one to bury them or their wives, their sons or their daughters. I will pour out on them the calamity they deserve.

17"Speak this word to them:

" 'Let my eyes overflow with tears
  night and day without ceasing;
for my virgin daughter—my people—
  has suffered a grievous wound,
  a crushing blow.
18If I go into the country,
  I see those slain by the sword;
if I go into the city,
  I see the ravages of famine.
Both prophet and priest
  have gone to a land they know not.' "

19Have you rejected Judah completely?
  Do you despise Zion?
Why have you afflicted us
  so that we cannot be healed?
We hoped for peace
  but no good has come,
for a time of healing
  but there is only terror.
20O LORD, we acknowledge our wickedness
  and the guilt of our fathers;
  we have indeed sinned against you.
21For the sake of your name do not despise us;
  do not dishonor your glorious throne.
Remember your covenant with us
  and do not break it.

a *14* Or *visions, worthless divinations*

Living Bible

Israel, our Savior in times of trouble, why are you as a stranger to us, as one passing through the land who is merely stopping for the night? 9Are you also baffled? Are you helpless to save us? O Lord, you are right here among us, and we carry your name; we are known as your people. O Lord, don't desert us now!

10But the Lord replies: You have loved to wander far from me and have not tried to follow in my paths. Now I will no longer accept you as my people; now I will remember all the evil you have done, and punish your sins.

11The Lord told me again: Don't ask me any more to bless this people. Don't pray for them any more. 12When they fast, I will not pay any attention; when they present their offerings and sacrifices to me, I will not accept them. What I will give them in return is war and famine and disease.

13Then I said, O Lord God, their prophets are telling them that all is well—that no war or famine will come. They tell the people you will surely send them peace, that you will bless them.

14Then the Lord said: The prophets are telling lies in my name. I didn't send them or tell them to speak or give them any message. They prophesy of visions and revelations they have never seen nor heard; they speak foolishness concocted out of their own lying hearts. 15Therefore, the Lord says, I will punish these lying prophets who have spoken in my name though I did not send them, who say no war shall come nor famine. By war and famine they themselves shall die! 16And the people to whom they prophesy—their bodies shall be thrown out into the streets of Jerusalem, victims of famine and war; there shall be no one to bury them. Husbands, wives, sons and daughters—all will be gone. For I will pour out terrible punishment upon them for their sins.

17Therefore, tell them this: Night and day my eyes shall overflow with tears; I cannot stop my crying, for my people have been run through with a sword and lie mortally wounded on the ground. 18If I go out in the fields, there lie the bodies of those the sword has killed; and if I walk in the streets, there lie those dead from starvation and disease. And yet the prophets and priests alike have made it their business to travel through the whole country, reassuring everyone that all is well, speaking of things they know nothing about.

19"O Lord," the people will cry, "have you completely rejected Judah? Do you abhor Jerusalem? Even after punishment, will there be no peace? We thought, Now at last he will heal us and bind our wounds. But no peace has come and there is only trouble and terror everywhere. 20O Lord, we confess our wickedness, and that of our fathers too. 21Do not hate us, Lord, for the sake of your own name. Do not disgrace yourself and the throne of your glory by forsaking your promise to bless us! 22What heathen god can give us rain? Who but you

New Revised Standard

8 O hope of Israel,
    its savior in time of trouble,
why should you be like a stranger in the land,
    like a traveler turning aside for the night?
9 Why should you be like someone confused,
    like a mighty warrior who cannot give help?
Yet you, O LORD, are in the midst of us,
    and we are called by your name;
    do not forsake us!

10 Thus says the LORD concerning this people:
Truly they have loved to wander,
    they have not restrained their feet;
therefore the LORD does not accept them,
    now he will remember their iniquity
    and punish their sins.

11 The LORD said to me: Do not pray for the welfare of this people. 12Although they fast, I do not hear their cry, and although they offer burnt offering and grain offering, I do not accept them; but by the sword, by famine, and by pestilence I consume them.

Denunciation of Lying Prophets

13 Then I said: "Ah, Lord GOD! Here are the prophets saying to them, 'You shall not see the sword, nor shall you have famine, but I will give you true peace in this place.' " 14And the LORD said to me: The prophets are prophesying lies in my name; I did not send them, nor did I command them or speak to them. They are prophesying to you a lying vision, worthless divination, and the deceit of their own minds. 15Therefore thus says the LORD concerning the prophets who prophesy in my name though I did not send them, and who say, "Sword and famine shall not come on this land": By sword and famine those prophets shall be consumed. 16And the people to whom they prophesy shall be thrown out into the streets of Jerusalem, victims of famine and sword. There shall be no one to bury them—themselves, their wives, their sons, and their daughters. For I will pour out their wickedness upon them.

17 You shall say to them this word:
Let my eyes run down with tears night and
        day,
    and let them not cease,
for the virgin daughter—my people—is struck
        down with a crushing blow,
    with a very grievous wound.
18 If I go out into the field,
    look—those killed by the sword!
And if I enter the city,
    look—those sick with[b] famine!
For both prophet and priest ply their trade
        throughout the land,
    and have no knowledge.

The People Plead for Mercy

19 Have you completely rejected Judah?
    Does your heart loathe Zion?
Why have you struck us down
    so that there is no healing for us?
We look for peace, but find no good;
    for a time of healing, but there is terror
        instead.
20 We acknowledge our wickedness, O LORD,
    the iniquity of our ancestors,
    for we have sinned against you.
21 Do not spurn us, for your name's sake;
    do not dishonor your glorious throne;
    remember and do not break your covenant
        with us.

[b] Heb *look—the sicknesses of*

King James

22Are there *any* among the vanities of the Gentiles that can cause rain? or can the heavens give showers? *art* not thou he, O LORD our God? therefore we will wait upon thee: for thou hast made all these *things*.

15 THEN SAID the LORD unto me, Though Moses and Samuel stood before me, *yet* my mind *could* not *be* toward this people: cast *them* out of my sight, and let them go forth.

2And it shall come to pass, if they say unto thee, Whither shall we go forth? then thou shalt tell them, Thus saith the LORD; Such as *are* for death, to death; and such as *are* for the sword, to the sword; and such as *are* for the famine, to the famine; and such as *are* for the captivity, to the captivity.

3And I will appoint over them four kinds, saith the LORD: the sword to slay, and the dogs to tear, and the fowls of the heaven, and the beasts of the earth, to devour and destroy.

4And I will cause them to be removed into all kingdoms of the earth, because of Manasseh the son of Hezekiah king of Judah, for *that* which he did in Jerusalem.

5For who shall have pity upon thee, O Jerusalem? or who shall bemoan thee? or who shall go aside to ask how thou doest?

6Thou hast forsaken me, saith the LORD, thou art gone backward: therefore will I stretch out my hand against thee, and destroy thee; I am weary with repenting.

7And I will fan them with a fan in the gates of the land; I will bereave *them* of children, I will destroy my people, *since* they return not from their ways.

8Their widows are increased to me above the sand of the seas: I have brought upon them against the mother of the young men a spoiler at noonday: I have caused *him* to fall upon it suddenly, and terrors upon the city.

9She that hath borne seven languisheth: she hath given up the ghost; her sun is gone down while *it was* yet day: she hath been ashamed and confounded: and the residue of them will I deliver to the sword before their enemies, saith the LORD.

10¶ Woe is me, my mother, that thou hast borne me a man of strife and a man of contention to the whole earth! I have neither lent on usury, nor men have lent to me on usury; *yet* every one of them doth curse me.

11The LORD said, Verily it shall be well with thy remnant; verily I will cause the enemy to entreat thee *well* in the time of evil and in the time of affliction.

New International

22Do any of the worthless idols of the nations
    bring rain?
Do the skies themselves send down showers?
No, it is you, O LORD our God.
Therefore our hope is in you,
    for you are the one who does all this.

15 THEN THE LORD said to me: "Even if Moses and Samuel were to stand before me, my heart would not go out to this people. Send them away from my presence! Let them go! 2And if they ask you, 'Where shall we go?' tell them, 'This is what the LORD says:

" 'Those destined for death, to death;
    those for the sword, to the sword;
    those for starvation, to starvation;
    those for captivity, to captivity.'

3"I will send four kinds of destroyers against them," declares the LORD, "the sword to kill and the dogs to drag away and the birds of the air and the beasts of the earth to devour and destroy. 4I will make them abhorrent to all the kingdoms of the earth because of what Manasseh son of Hezekiah king of Judah did in Jerusalem.

5"Who will have pity on you, O Jerusalem?
    Who will mourn for you?
    Who will stop to ask how you are?
6You have rejected me," declares the LORD.
    "You keep on backsliding.
So I will lay hands on you and destroy you;
    I can no longer show compassion.
7I will winnow them with a winnowing fork
    at the city gates of the land.
I will bring bereavement and destruction on my
    people,
    for they have not changed their ways.
8I will make their widows more numerous
    than the sand of the sea.
At midday I will bring a destroyer
    against the mothers of their young men;
suddenly I will bring down on them
    anguish and terror.
9The mother of seven will grow faint
    and breathe her last.
Her sun will set while it is still day;
    she will be disgraced and humiliated.
I will put the survivors to the sword
    before their enemies,"
                            declares the LORD.

10Alas, my mother, that you gave me birth,
    a man with whom the whole land strives and
        contends!
I have neither lent nor borrowed,
    yet everyone curses me.

11The LORD said,

"Surely I will deliver you for a good purpose;
    surely I will make your enemies plead with
        you
    in times of disaster and times of distress.

Living Bible | New Revised Standard

alone, O Lord our God, can do such things as this? Therefore we will wait for you to help us."

22 Can any idols of the nations bring rain?
    Or can the heavens give showers?
Is it not you, O LORD our God?
    We set our hope on you,
    for it is you who do all this.

Punishment Is Inevitable

15 THEN THE Lord said to me, Even if Moses and Samuel stood before me pleading for these people, even then I wouldn't help them—away with them! Get them out of my sight! 2And if they say to you, But where can we go? tell them the Lord says: Those who are destined for death, to death; those who must die by the sword, to the sword; those doomed to starvation, to famine; and those for captivity, to captivity. 3I will appoint over them four kinds of destroyers, says the Lord—the sword to kill, the dogs to tear, and the vultures and wild animals to finish up what's left. 4Because of the wicked things Manasseh, son of Hezekiah, king of Judah, did in Jerusalem, I will punish you so severely that your fate will horrify the peoples of the world.

5Who will feel sorry for you, Jerusalem? Who will weep for you? Who will even bother to ask how you are? 6You have forsaken me and turned your backs upon me. Therefore I will clench my fists against you to destroy you. I am tired of always giving you another chance. 7I will sift you at the gates of your cities and take from you all that you hold dear, and I will destroy my own people because they refuse to turn back to me from all their evil ways. 8There shall be countless widows; at noon time I will bring death to the young men and sorrow to their mothers. I will cause anguish and terror to fall upon them suddenly. 9The mother of seven sickens and faints, for all her sons are dead. Her sun is gone down while it is yet day. She sits childless now, disgraced, for all her children have been killed.

10Then Jeremiah said, "What sadness is mine, my mother; oh, that I had died at birth. For I am hated everywhere I go. I am neither a creditor soon to foreclose nor a debtor refusing to pay—yet they all curse me. 11Well, let them curse! Lord, you know how I have pled with you on their behalf—how I have begged you to spare these enemies of mine."

15 THEN THE LORD said to me: Though Moses and Samuel stood before me, yet my heart would not turn toward this people. Send them out of my sight, and let them go! 2And when they say to you, "Where shall we go?" you shall say to them: Thus says the LORD:

> Those destined for pestilence, to pestilence,
>   and those destined for the sword, to the
>   sword;
> those destined for famine, to famine,
>   and those destined for captivity, to
>   captivity.

3And I will appoint over them four kinds of destroyers, says the LORD: the sword to kill, the dogs to drag away, and the birds of the air and the wild animals of the earth to devour and destroy. 4I will make them a horror to all the kingdoms of the earth because of what King Manasseh son of Hezekiah of Judah did in Jerusalem.

5   Who will have pity on you, O Jerusalem,
    or who will bemoan you?
Who will turn aside
    to ask about your welfare?
6 You have rejected me, says the LORD,
    you are going backward;
so I have stretched out my hand against you
    and destroyed you—
I am weary of relenting.
7 I have winnowed them with a winnowing fork
    in the gates of the land;
I have bereaved them, I have destroyed my
    people;
    they did not turn from their ways.
8 Their widows became more numerous
    than the sand of the seas;
I have brought against the mothers of youths
    a destroyer at noonday;
I have made anguish and terror
    fall upon her suddenly.
9 She who bore seven has languished;
    she has swooned away;
her sun went down while it was yet day;
    she has been shamed and disgraced.
And the rest of them I will give to the sword
    before their enemies,
            says the LORD.

Jeremiah Complains Again and Is Reassured

10 Woe is me, my mother, that you ever bore me, a man of strife and contention to the whole land! I have not lent, nor have I borrowed, yet all of them curse me. 11The LORD said: Surely I have intervened in your life[a] for good, surely I have imposed enemies on you in a

---

[a] Heb *intervened with you*

King James

12Shall iron break the northern iron and the steel?

13Thy substance and thy treasures will I give to the spoil without price, and *that* for all thy sins, even in all thy borders.

14And I will make *thee* to pass with thine enemies into a land *which* thou knowest not: for a fire is kindled in mine anger, *which* shall burn upon you.

15¶ O LORD, thou knowest: remember me, and visit me, and revenge me of my persecutors; take me not away in thy longsuffering: know that for thy sake I have suffered rebuke.

16Thy words were found, and I did eat them; and thy word was unto me the joy and rejoicing of mine heart: for I am called by thy name, O LORD God of hosts.

17I sat not in the assembly of the mockers, nor rejoiced; I sat alone because of thy hand: for thou hast filled me with indignation.

18Why is my pain perpetual, and my wound incurable, *which* refuseth to be healed? wilt thou be altogether unto me as a liar, *and as* waters *that* fail?

19¶ Therefore thus saith the LORD, If thou return, then will I bring thee again, *and* thou shalt stand before me: and if thou take forth the precious from the vile, thou shalt be as my mouth: let them return unto thee; but return not thou unto them.

20And I will make thee unto this people a fenced brasen wall: and they shall fight against thee, but they shall not prevail against thee: for I *am* with thee to save thee and to deliver thee, saith the LORD.

21And I will deliver thee out of the hand of the wicked, and I will redeem thee out of the hand of the terrible.

16 THE WORD of the LORD came also unto me, saying,

2Thou shalt not take thee a wife, neither shalt thou have sons or daughters in this place.

3For thus saith the LORD concerning the sons and concerning the daughters that are born in this place, and concerning their mothers that bare them, and concerning their fathers that begat them in this land;

4They shall die of grievous deaths; they shall not be lamented; neither shall they be buried; *but* they shall be as dung upon the face of the earth: and they shall be consumed by the sword, and by famine; and their carcases shall be meat for the fowls of heaven, and for the beasts of the earth.

5For thus saith the LORD, Enter not into the house of mourning, neither go to lament nor bemoan them: for I have taken away my peace from this people, saith the LORD, *even* lovingkindness and mercies.

6Both the great and the small shall die in this land: they shall not be buried, neither shall *men* lament for them, nor cut themselves, nor make themselves bald for them:

New International

12"Can a man break iron—
  iron from the north—or bronze?

13Your wealth and your treasures
  I will give as plunder, without charge,
because of all your sins
  throughout your country.

14I will enslave you to your enemies
  in[a] a land you do not know,
for my anger will kindle a fire
  that will burn against you."

15You understand, O LORD;
  remember me and care for me.
  Avenge me on my persecutors.
You are long-suffering—do not take me away;
  think of how I suffer reproach for your sake.

16When your words came, I ate them;
  they were my joy and my heart's delight,
for I bear your name,
  O LORD God Almighty.

17I never sat in the company of revelers,
  never made merry with them;
I sat alone because your hand was on me
  and you had filled me with indignation.

18Why is my pain unending
  and my wound grievous and incurable?
Will you be to me like a deceptive brook,
  like a spring that fails?

19Therefore this is what the LORD says:

"If you repent, I will restore you
  that you may serve me;
if you utter worthy, not worthless, words,
  you will be my spokesman.
Let this people turn to you,
  but you must not turn to them.

20I will make you a wall to this people,
  a fortified wall of bronze;
they will fight against you
  but will not overcome you,
for I am with you
  to rescue and save you,"
              declares the LORD.

21"I will save you from the hands of the wicked
  and redeem you from the grasp of the cruel."

Day of Disaster

16 THEN THE word of the LORD came to me: 2"You must not marry and have sons or daughters in this place." 3For this is what the LORD says about the sons and daughters born in this land and about the women who are their mothers and the men who are their fathers: 4"They will die of deadly diseases. They will not be mourned or buried but will be like refuse lying on the ground. They will perish by sword and famine, and their dead bodies will become food for the birds of the air and the beasts of the earth."

5For this is what the LORD says: "Do not enter a house where there is a funeral meal; do not go to mourn or show sympathy, because I have withdrawn my blessing, my love and my pity from this people," declares the LORD. 6"Both high and low will die in this land. They will not be buried or mourned, and no one will cut himself or shave his head for them. 7No one will offer

---

a *14* Some Hebrew manuscripts, Septuagint and Syriac (see also Jer. 17:4); most Hebrew manuscripts *I will cause your enemies to bring you / into*

Living Bible

12, 13Can a man break bars of northern iron or bronze? This people's stubborn will can't be broken either. So, because of all your sins against me, I will deliver your wealth and treasures as loot to the enemy. 14I will have your enemies take you as slaves to a land where you have never been before, for my anger burns like fire, and it shall consume you.

15Then Jeremiah replied, "Lord, you know it is for your sake that I am suffering. They are persecuting me because I have proclaimed your word to them. Don't let them kill me! Rescue me from their clutches, and give them what they deserve! 16Your words are what sustain me; they are food to my hungry soul. They bring joy to my sorrowing heart and delight me. How proud I am to bear your name, O Lord. 17, 18I have not joined the people in their merry feasts. I sit alone beneath the hand of God. I burst with indignation at their sins. Yet you have failed me in my time of need! You have let them keep right on with all their persecutions. Will they never stop hurting me? Your help is as uncertain as a seasonal mountain brook—sometimes a flood, sometimes as dry as a bone."

19The Lord replied: "Stop this foolishness and talk some sense! Only if you return to trusting me will I let you continue as my spokesman. You are to influence *them*, not let them influence *you!* 20They will fight against you like a besieging army against a high city wall. But they will not conquer you for I am with you to protect and deliver you, says the Lord. 21Yes, I will certainly deliver you from these wicked men and rescue you from their ruthless hands."

16 ON YET another occasion God spoke to me, and said:

2You must not marry and have children here. 3For the children born in this city, and their mothers and fathers, 4shall die from terrible diseases. No one shall mourn for them or bury them, but their bodies shall lie on the ground to rot and fertilize the soil. They shall die from war and famine, and their bodies shall be picked apart by vultures and wild animals. 5Do not mourn or weep for them, for I have removed my protection and my peace from them—taken away my lovingkindness and my mercies. 6Both great and small shall die in this land, unburied and unmourned, and their friends shall not cut themselves nor shave their heads as signs of sorrow (as is their heathen custom). 7No one shall comfort the

New Revised Standard

time of trouble and in a time of distress. b12Can iron and bronze break iron from the north?

13 Your wealth and your treasures I will give as plunder, without price, for all your sins, throughout all your territory. 14I will make you serve your enemies in a land that you do not know, for in my anger a fire is kindled that shall burn forever.

15 O Lord, you know;
  remember me and visit me,
  and bring down retribution for me on my
    persecutors.
In your forbearance do not take me away;
  know that on your account I suffer insult.
16 Your words were found, and I ate them,
  and your words became to me a joy
  and the delight of my heart;
for I am called by your name,
  O Lord, God of hosts.
17 I did not sit in the company of merrymakers,
  nor did I rejoice;
under the weight of your hand I sat alone,
  for you had filled me with indignation.
18 Why is my pain unceasing,
  my wound incurable,
  refusing to be healed?
Truly, you are to me like a deceitful brook,
  like waters that fail.

19 Therefore thus says the Lord:
If you turn back, I will take you back,
  and you shall stand before me.
If you utter what is precious, and not what is
    worthless,
  you shall serve as my mouth.
It is they who will turn to you,
  not you who will turn to them.
20 And I will make you to this people
  a fortified wall of bronze;
they will fight against you,
  but they shall not prevail over you,
for I am with you
  to save you and deliver you,
                          says the Lord.
21 I will deliver you out of the hand of the
    wicked,
  and redeem you from the grasp of the
    ruthless.

Jeremiah's Celibacy and Message

16 THE WORD of the Lord came to me: 2You shall not take a wife, nor shall you have sons or daughters in this place. 3For thus says the Lord concerning the sons and daughters who are born in this place, and concerning the mothers who bear them and the fathers who beget them in this land: 4They shall die of deadly diseases. They shall not be lamented, nor shall they be buried; they shall become like dung on the surface of the ground. They shall perish by the sword and by famine, and their dead bodies shall become food for the birds of the air and for the wild animals of the earth.

5 For thus says the Lord: Do not enter the house of mourning, or go to lament, or bemoan them; for I have taken away my peace from this people, says the Lord, my steadfast love and mercy. 6Both great and small shall die in this land; they shall not be buried, and no one shall lament for them; there shall be no gashing, no shaving of the head for them. 7No one shall break

b Meaning of Heb uncertain

King James

7Neither shall *men* tear *themselves* for them in mourning, to comfort them for the dead; neither shall *men* give them the cup of consolation to drink for their father or for their mother.

8Thou shalt not also go into the house of feasting, to sit with them to eat and to drink.

9For thus saith the LORD of hosts, the God of Israel; Behold, I will cause to cease out of this place in your eyes, and in your days, the voice of mirth, and the voice of gladness, the voice of the bridegroom, and the voice of the bride.

10¶ And it shall come to pass, when thou shalt show this people all these words, and they shall say unto thee, Wherefore hath the LORD pronounced all this great evil against us? or what *is* our iniquity? or what *is* our sin that we have committed against the LORD our God?

11Then shalt thou say unto them, Because your fathers have forsaken me, saith the LORD, and have walked after other gods, and have served them, and have worshipped them, and have forsaken me, and have not kept my law;

12And ye have done worse than your fathers; for, behold, ye walk every one after the imagination of his evil heart, that they may not hearken unto me:

13Therefore will I cast you out of this land into a land that ye know not, *neither* ye nor your fathers; and there shall ye serve other gods day and night; where I will not show you favour.

14¶ Therefore, behold, the days come, saith the LORD, that it shall no more be said, The LORD liveth, that brought up the children of Israel out of the land of Egypt;

15But, The LORD liveth, that brought up the children of Israel from the land of the north, and from all the lands whither he had driven them: and I will bring them again into their land that I gave unto their fathers.

16¶ Behold, I will send for many fishers, saith the LORD, and they shall fish them; and after will I send for many hunters, and they shall hunt them from every mountain, and from every hill, and out of the holes of the rocks.

17For mine eyes *are* upon all their ways: they are not hid from my face, neither is their iniquity hid from mine eyes.

18And first I will recompense their iniquity and their sin double; because they have defiled my land, they have filled mine inheritance with the carcases of their detestable and abominable things.

19O LORD, my strength, and my fortress, and my refuge in the day of affliction, the Gentiles shall come unto thee from the ends of the earth, and shall say, Surely our fathers have inherited lies, vanity, and *things* wherein *there is* no profit.

20Shall a man make gods unto himself, and they *are* no gods?

21Therefore, behold, I will this once cause them to know, I will cause them to know mine hand and my might; and they shall know that my name *is* The LORD.

17 THE SIN of Judah *is* written with a pen of iron, *and* with the point of a diamond: *it is* graven upon the table of their heart, and upon the horns of your altars;

New International

food to comfort those who mourn for the dead—not even for a father or a mother—nor will anyone give them a drink to console them.

8"And do not enter a house where there is feasting and sit down to eat and drink. 9For this is what the LORD Almighty, the God of Israel, says: Before your eyes and in your days I will bring an end to the sounds of joy and gladness and to the voices of bride and bridegroom in this place.

10"When you tell these people all this and they ask you, 'Why has the LORD decreed such a great disaster against us? What wrong have we done? What sin have we committed against the LORD our God?' 11then say to them, 'It is because your fathers forsook me,' declares the LORD, 'and followed other gods and served and worshiped them. They forsook me and did not keep my law. 12But you have behaved more wickedly than your fathers. See how each of you is following the stubbornness of his evil heart instead of obeying me. 13So I will throw you out of this land into a land neither you nor your fathers have known, and there you will serve other gods day and night, for I will show you no favor.'

14"However, the days are coming," declares the LORD, "when men will no longer say, 'As surely as the LORD lives, who brought the Israelites up out of Egypt,' 15but they will say, 'As surely as the LORD lives, who brought the Israelites up out of the land of the north and out of all the countries where he had banished them.' For I will restore them to the land I gave their forefathers.

16"But now I will send for many fishermen," declares the LORD, "and they will catch them. After that I will send for many hunters, and they will hunt them down on every mountain and hill and from the crevices of the rocks. 17My eyes are on all their ways; they are not hidden from me, nor is their sin concealed from my eyes. 18I will repay them double for their wickedness and their sin, because they have defiled my land with the lifeless forms of their vile images and have filled my inheritance with their detestable idols."

19O LORD, my strength and my fortress,
　my refuge in time of distress,
to you the nations will come
　from the ends of the earth and say,
"Our fathers possessed nothing but false gods,
　worthless idols that did them no good.
20Do men make their own gods?
　Yes, but they are not gods!"

21"Therefore I will teach them—
　this time I will teach them
　my power and might.
Then they will know
　that my name is the LORD.

17 "JUDAH'S SIN is engraved with an iron tool,
　inscribed with a flint point,
on the tablets of their hearts
　and on the horns of their altars.

Living Bible

mourners with a meal, or send them a cup of wine expressing grief for their parents' death.

8As a sign to them of these sad days ahead,a don't you join them any more in their feasts and parties—don't even eat a meal with them. 9For the Lord Almighty, the God of Israel, says: In your own lifetime, before your very eyes, I will end all laughter in this land—the happy songs, the marriage feasts, the songs of bridegrooms and of brides.

10And when you tell the people all these things and they ask, "Why has the Lord decreed such terrible things against us? What have we done to merit such treatment? What is our sin against the Lord our God?" 11tell them the Lord's reply is this: Because your fathers forsook me. They worshiped other gods and served them; they did not keep my laws, 12*and you have been worse than your fathers were!* You follow evil to your hearts' content and refuse to listen to me. 13Therefore I will throw you out of this land and chase you into a foreign land where neither you nor your fathers have been before, and there you can go ahead and worship your idols all you like—and I will grant you no favors!

14, 15But there will come a glorious day, says the Lord, when the whole topic of conversation will be that God is bringing his people home from a nation in the north, and from many other lands where he had scattered them. You will look back no longer to the time when I rescued you from your slavery in Egypt. That mighty miracle will scarcely be mentioned any more. Yes, I will bring you back again, says the Lord, to this same land I gave your fathers.

16Now I am sending for many fishermen to fish you from the deeps where you are hiding from my wrath. I am sending for hunters to chase you down like deer in the forests or mountain goats on inaccessible crags. Wherever you run to escape my judgment, I will find you and punish you. 17For I am closely watching you and I see every sin. You cannot hope to hide from me.

18And I will punish you doubly for all your sins because you have defiled my land with your detestable idols, and filled it up with all your evil deeds.

19O Lord, my Strength and Fortress, my Refuge in the day of trouble, nations from around the world will come to you saying, "Our fathers have been foolish, for they have worshiped worthless idols! 20Can men make God? The gods they made are not real gods at all." 21And when they come in that spirit, I will show themb my power and might and make them understand at last that I alone am God.

17 MY PEOPLE sin as though commanded to, as though their evil were laws chiseled with an iron pen or diamond point upon their stony hearts or on the corners of their altars. 2, 3Their youths do not forget

New Revised Standard

breadc for the mourner, to offer comfort for the dead; nor shall anyone give them the cup of consolation to drink for their fathers or their mothers. 8You shall not go into the house of feasting to sit with them, to eat and drink. 9For thus says the LORD of hosts, the God of Israel: I am going to banish from this place, in your days and before your eyes, the voice of mirth and the voice of gladness, the voice of the bridegroom and the voice of the bride.

10 And when you tell this people all these words, and they say to you, "Why has the LORD pronounced all this great evil against us? What is our iniquity? What is the sin that we have committed against the LORD our God?" 11then you shall say to them: It is because your ancestors have forsaken me, says the LORD, and have gone after other gods and have served and worshiped them, and have forsaken me and have not kept my law; 12and because you have behaved worse than your ancestors, for here you are, every one of you, following your stubborn evil will, refusing to listen to me. 13Therefore I will hurl you out of this land into a land that neither you nor your ancestors have known, and there you shall serve other gods day and night, for I will show you no favor.

God Will Restore Israel

14 Therefore, the days are surely coming, says the LORD, when it shall no longer be said, "As the LORD lives who brought the people of Israel up out of the land of Egypt," 15but "As the LORD lives who brought the people of Israel up out of the land of the north and out of all the lands where he had driven them." For I will bring them back to their own land that I gave to their ancestors.

16 I am now sending for many fishermen, says the LORD, and they shall catch them; and afterward I will send for many hunters, and they shall hunt them from every mountain and every hill, and out of the clefts of the rocks. 17For my eyes are on all their ways; they are not hidden from my presence, nor is their iniquity concealed from my sight. 18Andd I will doubly repay their iniquity and their sin, because they have polluted my land with the carcasses of their detestable idols, and have filled my inheritance with their abominations.

19 O LORD, my strength and my stronghold,
   my refuge in the day of trouble,
to you shall the nations come
   from the ends of the earth and say:
Our ancestors have inherited nothing but lies,
   worthless things in which there is no profit.
20 Can mortals make for themselves gods?
   Such are no gods!

21 "Therefore I am surely going to teach them, this time I am going to teach them my power and my might, and they shall know that my name is the LORD."

Judah's Sin and Punishment

17 THE SIN of Judah is written with an iron pen; with a diamond point it is engraved on the tablet of their hearts, and on the horns of their altars, 2while

---

a *16:8 As a sign to them of these sad days ahead,* implied.   b *16:21 I will show them,* literally, "Therefore, behold, I will cause them to know."   c Two Mss Gk: MT *break for them*   d Gk: Heb *And first*

King James

²Whilst their children remember their altars and their groves by the green trees upon the high hills.

³O my mountain in the field, I will give thy substance *and* all thy treasures to the spoil, *and* thy high places for sin, throughout all thy borders.

⁴And thou, even thyself, shalt discontinue from thine heritage that I gave thee; and I will cause thee to serve thine enemies in the land which thou knowest not: for ye have kindled a fire in mine anger, *which* shall burn for ever.

⁵¶ Thus saith the LORD; Cursed *be* the man that trusteth in man, and maketh flesh his arm, and whose heart departeth from the LORD.

⁶For he shall be like the heath in the desert, and shall not see when good cometh; but shall inhabit the parched places in the wilderness, *in* a salt land and not inhabited.

⁷Blessed *is* the man that trusteth in the LORD, and whose hope the LORD is.

⁸For he shall be as a tree planted by the waters, and *that* spreadeth out her roots by the river, and shall not see when heat cometh, but her leaf shall be green; and shall not be careful in the year of drought, neither shall cease from yielding fruit.

⁹¶ The heart *is* deceitful above all *things,* and desperately wicked: who can know it?

¹⁰I the LORD search the heart, *I* try the reins, even to give every man according to his ways, *and* according to the fruit of his doings.

¹¹*As* the partridge sitteth *on eggs,* and hatcheth *them* not; *so* he that getteth riches, and not by right, shall leave them in the midst of his days, and at his end shall be a fool.

¹²¶ A glorious high throne from the beginning *is* the place of our sanctuary.

¹³O LORD, the hope of Israel, all that forsake thee shall be ashamed, *and* they that depart from me shall be written in the earth, because they have forsaken the LORD, the fountain of living waters.

¹⁴Heal me, O LORD, and I shall be healed; save me, and I shall be saved: for thou *art* my praise.

¹⁵¶ Behold, they say unto me, Where *is* the word of the LORD? let it come now.

¹⁶As for me, I have not hastened from *being* a pastor to follow thee: neither have I desired the woeful day; thou knowest: that which came out of my lips was *right* before thee.

¹⁷Be not a terror unto me: thou *art* my hope in the day of evil.

New International

²Even their children remember
　　their altars and Asherah poles[a]
beside the spreading trees
　　and on the high hills.
³My mountain in the land
　　and your[b] wealth and all your treasures
I will give away as plunder,
　　together with your high places,
　　because of sin throughout your country.
⁴Through your own fault you will lose
　　the inheritance I gave you.
I will enslave you to your enemies
　　in a land you do not know,
for you have kindled my anger,
　　and it will burn forever."

⁵This is what the LORD says:

"Cursed is the one who trusts in man,
　　who depends on flesh for his strength
　　and whose heart turns away from the LORD.
⁶He will be like a bush in the wastelands;
　　he will not see prosperity when it comes.
He will dwell in the parched places of the
　　desert,
　　in a salt land where no one lives.

⁷"But blessed is the man who trusts in the LORD,
　　whose confidence is in him.
⁸He will be like a tree planted by the water
　　that sends out its roots by the stream.
It does not fear when heat comes;
　　its leaves are always green.
It has no worries in a year of drought
　　and never fails to bear fruit."

⁹The heart is deceitful above all things
　　and beyond cure.
　　Who can understand it?

¹⁰"I the LORD search the heart
　　and examine the mind,
to reward a man according to his conduct,
　　according to what his deeds deserve."

¹¹Like a partridge that hatches eggs it did not lay
　　is the man who gains riches by unjust means.
When his life is half gone, they will desert him,
　　and in the end he will prove to be a fool.

¹²A glorious throne, exalted from the beginning,
　　is the place of our sanctuary.
¹³O LORD, the hope of Israel,
　　all who forsake you will be put to shame.
Those who turn away from you will be written
　　in the dust
because they have forsaken the LORD,
　　the spring of living water.

¹⁴Heal me, O LORD, and I will be healed;
　　save me and I will be saved,
　　for you are the one I praise.
¹⁵They keep saying to me,
　　"Where is the word of the LORD?
　　Let it now be fulfilled!"
¹⁶I have not run away from being your shepherd;
　　you know I have not desired the day of
　　despair.
What passes my lips is open before you.
¹⁷Do not be a terror to me;
　　you are my refuge in the day of disaster.

ᵃ 2 That is, symbols of the goddess Asherah　ᵇ 2,3 Or *hills* / ³*and the mountains of the land.* / *Your*

Living Bible

to sin, worshiping idols beneath each tree, high in the mountains or in the open country down below. And so I will give all your treasures to your enemies as the price that you must pay for all your sins. 4And the wonderful heritage I reserved for you will slip out of your hand, and I will send you away as slaves to your enemies in distant lands. For you have kindled a fire of my anger that shall burn forever.

5The Lord says: Cursed is the man who puts his trust in mortal man and turns his heart away from God. 6He is like a stunted shrub in the desert, with no hope for the future; he lives on the salt-encrusted plains in the barren wilderness; good times pass him by forever.

7But blessed is the man who trusts in the Lord and has made the Lord his hope and confidence. 8He is like a tree planted along a riverbank, with its roots reaching deep into the water—a tree not bothered by the heat nor worried by long months of drought. Its leaves stay green and it goes right on producing all its luscious fruit.

9The heart is the most deceitful thing there is, and desperately wicked. No one can really know how bad it is! 10Only the Lord knows! He searches all hearts and examines deepest motives so he can give to each person his right reward, according to his deeds—how he has lived.

11Like a bird that fills her nest with young she has not hatched and which will soon desert her and fly away, so is the man who gets his wealth by unjust means. Sooner or later he will lose his riches and at the end of his life become a poor old fool.

12But our refuge is your throne, eternal, high and glorious. 13O Lord, the Hope of Israel, all who turn away from you shall be disgraced and shamed; they are registered for earth and not for glory, for they have forsaken the Lord, the Fountain of living waters. 14Lord, you alone can heal me, you alone can save, and my praises are for you alone.

15Men scoff at me and say, "What is this word of the Lord you keep talking about? If these threats of yours are really from God, why don't they come true?"

16Lord, I don't want the people crushed by terrible calamity. The plan is yours, not mine. It is *your* message I've given them, not my own. *I* don't want them doomed! 17Lord, don't desert me now! You alone are my hope. 18Bring confusion and trouble on all who per-

New Revised Standard

their children remember their altars and their sacred poles,c beside every green tree, and on the high hills, 3 on the mountains in the open country. Your wealth and all your treasures I will give for spoil as the price of your sind throughout all your territory. 4 By your own act you shall lose the heritage that I gave you, and I will make you serve your enemies in a land that you do not know, for in my anger a fire is kindlede that shall burn forever.

5 Thus says the LORD:
  Cursed are those who trust in mere mortals
    and make mere flesh their strength,
    whose hearts turn away from the LORD.
6 They shall be like a shrub in the desert,
    and shall not see when relief comes.
  They shall live in the parched places of the
      wilderness,
    in an uninhabited salt land.

7 Blessed are those who trust in the LORD,
    whose trust is the LORD.
8 They shall be like a tree planted by water,
    sending out its roots by the stream.
  It shall not fear when heat comes,
    and its leaves shall stay green;
  in the year of drought it is not anxious,
    and it does not cease to bear fruit.

9 The heart is devious above all else;
    it is perverse—
    who can understand it?
10 I the LORD test the mind
    and search the heart,
  to give to all according to their ways,
    according to the fruit of their doings.

11 Like the partridge hatching what it did not
      lay,
  so are all who amass wealth unjustly;
  in mid-life it will leave them,
    and at their end they will prove to be fools.

12 O glorious throne, exalted from the beginning,
    shrine of our sanctuary!
13 O hope of Israel! O LORD!
  All who forsake you shall be put to shame;
  those who turn away from youf shall be
      recorded in the underworld,g
  for they have forsaken the fountain of living
      water, the LORD.

Jeremiah Prays for Vindication

14 Heal me, O LORD, and I shall be healed;
    save me, and I shall be saved;
    for you are my praise.
15 See how they say to me,
    "Where is the word of the LORD?
    Let it come!"
16 But I have not run away from being a
      shepherdh in your service,
    nor have I desired the fatal day.
  You know what came from my lips;
    it was before your face.
17 Do not become a terror to me;
    you are my refuge in the day of disaster;

---

c Heb *Asherim*   d Cn: Heb *spoil your high places for sin*   e Two Mss Theodotion: *you kindled*   f Heb *me*   g Or *in the earth*   h Meaning of Heb uncertain

King James

18Let them be confounded that persecute me, but let not me be confounded: let them be dismayed, but let not me be dismayed: bring upon them the day of evil, and destroy them with double destruction.

19¶ Thus said the LORD unto me; Go and stand in the gate of the children of the people, whereby the kings of Judah come in, and by the which they go out, and in all the gates of Jerusalem;

20And say unto them, Hear ye the word of the LORD, ye kings of Judah, and all Judah, and all the inhabitants of Jerusalem, that enter in by these gates:

21Thus saith the LORD; Take heed to yourselves, and bear no burden on the sabbath day, nor bring it in by the gates of Jerusalem;

22Neither carry forth a burden out of your houses on the sabbath day, neither do ye any work, but hallow ye the sabbath day, as I commanded your fathers.

23But they obeyed not, neither inclined their ear, but made their neck stiff, that they might not hear, nor receive instruction.

24And it shall come to pass, if ye diligently hearken unto me, saith the LORD, to bring in no burden through the gates of this city on the sabbath day, but hallow the sabbath day, to do no work therein;

25Then shall there enter into the gates of this city kings and princes sitting upon the throne of David, riding in chariots and on horses, they, and their princes, the men of Judah, and the inhabitants of Jerusalem: and this city shall remain for ever.

26And they shall come from the cities of Judah, and from the places about Jerusalem, and from the land of Benjamin, and from the plain, and from the mountains, and from the south, bringing burnt offerings, and sacrifices, and meat offerings, and incense, and bringing sacrifices of praise, unto the house of the LORD.

27But if ye will not hearken unto me to hallow the sabbath day, and not to bear a burden, even entering in at the gates of Jerusalem on the sabbath day; then will I kindle a fire in the gates thereof, and it shall devour the palaces of Jerusalem, and it shall not be quenched.

18 THE WORD which came to Jeremiah from the LORD, saying,

2Arise, and go down to the potter's house, and there I will cause thee to hear my words.

3Then I went down to the potter's house, and, behold, he wrought a work on the wheels.

4And the vessel that he made of clay was marred in the hand of the potter: so he made it again another vessel, as seemed good to the potter to make it.

5Then the word of the LORD came to me, saying,

6O house of Israel, cannot I do with you as this potter? saith the LORD. Behold, as the clay is in the potter's hand, so are ye in mine hand, O house of Israel.

7At what instant I shall speak concerning a nation, and concerning a kingdom, to pluck up, and to pull down, and to destroy it;

8If that nation, against whom I have pronounced, turn from their evil, I will repent of the evil that I thought to do unto them.

9And at what instant I shall speak concerning a nation, and concerning a kingdom, to build and to plant it;

10If it do evil in my sight, that it obey not my voice, then I will repent of the good, wherewith I said I would benefit them.

11¶ Now therefore go to, speak to the men of Judah, and to the inhabitants of Jerusalem, saying, Thus saith the LORD; Behold, I frame evil against you, and devise a device against you: return ye now every one from his evil way, and make your ways and your doings good.

New International

18Let my persecutors be put to shame,
　　but keep me from shame;
let them be terrified,
　　but keep me from terror.
Bring on them the day of disaster;
　　destroy them with double destruction.

Keeping the Sabbath Holy

19This is what the LORD said to me: "Go and stand at the gate of the people, through which the kings of Judah go in and out; stand also at all the other gates of Jerusalem. 20Say to them, 'Hear the word of the LORD, O kings of Judah and all people of Judah and everyone living in Jerusalem who come through these gates. 21This is what the LORD says: Be careful not to carry a load on the Sabbath day or bring it through the gates of Jerusalem. 22Do not bring a load out of your houses or do any work on the Sabbath, but keep the Sabbath day holy, as I commanded your forefathers. 23Yet they did not listen or pay attention; they were stiff-necked and would not listen or respond to discipline. 24But if you are careful to obey me, declares the LORD, and bring no load through the gates of this city on the Sabbath, but keep the Sabbath day holy by not doing any work on it, 25then kings who sit on David's throne will come through the gates of this city with their officials. They and their officials will come riding in chariots and on horses, accompanied by the men of Judah and those living in Jerusalem, and this city will be inhabited forever. 26People will come from the towns of Judah and the villages around Jerusalem, from the territory of Benjamin and the western foothills, from the hill country and the Negev, bringing burnt offerings and sacrifices, grain offerings, incense and thank offerings to the house of the LORD. 27But if you do not obey me to keep the Sabbath day holy by not carrying any load as you come through the gates of Jerusalem on the Sabbath day, then I will kindle an unquenchable fire in the gates of Jerusalem that will consume her fortresses.'"

At the Potter's House

18 THIS IS the word that came to Jeremiah from the LORD: 2"Go down to the potter's house, and there I will give you my message." 3So I went down to the potter's house, and I saw him working at the wheel. 4But the pot he was shaping from the clay was marred in his hands; so the potter formed it into another pot, shaping it as seemed best to him.

5Then the word of the LORD came to me: 6"O house of Israel, can I not do with you as this potter does?" declares the LORD. "Like clay in the hand of the potter, so are you in my hand, O house of Israel. 7If at any time I announce that a nation or kingdom is to be uprooted, torn down and destroyed, 8and if that nation I warned repents of its evil, then I will relent and not inflict on it the disaster I had planned. 9And if at another time I announce that a nation or kingdom is to be built up and planted, 10and if it does evil in my sight and does not obey me, then I will reconsider the good I had intended to do for it.

11"Now therefore say to the people of Judah and those living in Jerusalem, 'This is what the LORD says: Look! I am preparing a disaster for you and devising a plan against you. So turn from your evil ways, each one of you, and reform your ways and your actions.' 12But they

Living Bible

secute me, but give me peace. Yes, bring double destruction upon them!

19Then the Lord said to me, Go and stand in the gates of Jerusalem, first at the gate where the king goes out, and then at each of the other gates, 20and say to all the people: Hear the word of the Lord, kings of Judah and all the people of this nation, and all you citizens of Jerusalem. 21, 22The Lord says: Take warning and live; do no unnecessarya work on the Sabbath day but make it a holy day. I gave this commandment to your fathers, 23but they didn't listen or obey. They stubbornly refused to pay attention and be taught.

24But if you obey me, says the Lord, and refuse to work on the Sabbath day and keep it separate, special and holy, 25then this nation shall continue forever. There shall always be descendants of David sitting on the throne here in Jerusalem; there shall always be kings and princes riding in pomp and splendor among the people, and this city shall remain forever. 26And from all around Jerusalem and from the cities of Judah and Benjamin, and from the Negeb and from the lowlands west of Judah, the people shall come with their burnt offerings and grain offerings and incense, bringing their sacrifices to praise the Lord in his Temple.

27But if you will not listen to me, if you refuse to keep the Sabbath holy, if on the Sabbath you bring in loads of merchandise through these gates of Jerusalem, just as on other days, then I will set fire to these gates. The fire shall spread to the palaces and utterly destroy them, and no one shall be able to put out the raging flames.

18 HERE IS another message to Jeremiah from the Lord:

2Go down to the shop where clay pots and jars are made and I will talk to you there. 3I did as he told me, and found the potter working at his wheel. 4But the jar that he was forming didn't turn out as he wished, so he kneaded it into a lump and started again.

5Then the Lord said:

6O Israel, can't I do to you as this potter has done to his clay? As the clay is in the potter's hand, so are you in my hand. 7Whenever I announce that a certain nation or kingdom is to be taken up and destroyed, 8then if that nation renounces its evil ways, I will not destroy it as I had planned. 9And if I announce that I will make a certain nation strong and great, 10but then that nation changes its mind and turns to evil and refuses to obey me, then I too will change my mind and not bless that nation as I had said I would.

11Therefore go and warn all Judah and Jerusalem, saying: Hear the word of the Lord. I am planning evil against you now instead of good; turn back from your evil paths and do what is right.

New Revised Standard

18 Let my persecutors be shamed,
    but do not let me be shamed;
  let them be dismayed,
    but do not let me be dismayed;
  bring on them the day of disaster;
    destroy them with double destruction!

Hallow the Sabbath Day

19 Thus said the LORD to me: Go and stand in the People's Gate, by which the kings of Judah enter and by which they go out, and in all the gates of Jerusalem, 20and say to them: Hear the word of the LORD, you kings of Judah, and all Judah, and all the inhabitants of Jerusalem, who enter by these gates. 21Thus says the LORD: For the sake of your lives, take care that you do not bear a burden on the sabbath day or bring it in by the gates of Jerusalem. 22And do not carry a burden out of your houses on the sabbath or do any work, but keep the sabbath day holy, as I commanded your ancestors. 23Yet they did not listen or incline their ear; they stiffened their necks and would not hear or receive instruction.

24 But if you listen to me, says the LORD, and bring in no burden by the gates of this city on the sabbath day, but keep the sabbath day holy and do no work on it, 25then there shall enter by the gates of this city kingsb who sit on the throne of David, riding in chariots and on horses, they and their officials, the people of Judah and the inhabitants of Jerusalem; and this city shall be inhabited forever. 26And people shall come from the towns of Judah and the places around Jerusalem, from the land of Benjamin, from the Shephelah, from the hill country, and from the Negeb, bringing burnt offerings and sacrifices, grain offerings and frankincense, and bringing thank offerings to the house of the LORD. 27But if you do not listen to me, to keep the sabbath day holy, and to carry in no burden through the gates of Jerusalem on the sabbath day, then I will kindle a fire in its gates; it shall devour the palaces of Jerusalem and shall not be quenched.

The Potter and the Clay

18 THE WORD that came to Jeremiah from the LORD: 2"Come, go down to the potter's house, and there I will let you hear my words." 3So I went down to the potter's house, and there he was working at his wheel. 4The vessel he was making of clay was spoiled in the potter's hand, and he reworked it into another vessel, as seemed good to him.

5 Then the word of the LORD came to me: 6Can I not do with you, O house of Israel, just as this potter has done? says the LORD. Just like the clay in the potter's hand, so are you in my hand, O house of Israel. 7At one moment I may declare concerning a nation or a kingdom, that I will pluck up and break down and destroy it, 8but if that nation, concerning which I have spoken, turns from its evil, I will change my mind about the disaster that I intended to bring on it. 9And at another moment I may declare concerning a nation or a kingdom that I will build and plant it, 10but if it does evil in my sight, not listening to my voice, then I will change my mind about the good that I had intended to do to it. 11Now, therefore, say to the people of Judah and the inhabitants of Jerusalem: Thus says the LORD: Look, I am a potter shaping evil against you and devising a plan against you. Turn now, all of you from your evil way, and amend your ways and your doings.

---

a 17:21, 22 unnecessary, implied.

b Cn: Heb kings and officials

King James

12And they said, There is no hope: but we will walk after our own devices, and we will every one do the imagination of his evil heart.

13Therefore thus saith the LORD; Ask ye now among the heathen, who hath heard such things: the virgin of Israel hath done a very horrible thing.

14Will *a man* leave the snow of Lebanon *which cometh* from the rock of the field? *or* shall the cold flowing waters that come from another place be forsaken?

15Because my people hath forgotten me, they have burned incense to vanity, and they have caused them to stumble in their ways *from* the ancient paths, to walk in paths, *in* a way not cast up;

16To make their land desolate, *and* a perpetual hissing; every one that passeth thereby shall be astonished, and wag his head.

17I will scatter them as with an east wind before the enemy; I will show them the back, and not the face, in the day of their calamity.

18¶ Then said they, Come, and let us devise devices against Jeremiah; for the law shall not perish from the priest, nor counsel from the wise, nor the word from the prophet. Come, and let us smite him with the tongue, and let us not give heed to any of his words.

19Give heed to me, O LORD, and hearken to the voice of them that contend with me.

20Shall evil be recompensed for good? for they have digged a pit for my soul. Remember that I stood before thee to speak good for them, *and* to turn away thy wrath from them.

21Therefore deliver up their children to the famine, and pour out their *blood* by the force of the sword; and let their wives be bereaved of their children, and *be* widows; and let their men be put to death; *let* their young men *be* slain by the sword in battle.

22Let a cry be heard from their houses, when thou shalt bring a troop suddenly upon them: for they have digged a pit to take me, and hid snares for my feet.

23Yet, LORD, thou knowest all their counsel against me to slay *me:* forgive not their iniquity, neither blot out their sin from thy sight, but let them be overthrown before thee; deal *thus* with them in the time of thine anger.

New International

will reply, 'It's no use. We will continue with our own plans; each of us will follow the stubbornness of his evil heart.' "

13Therefore this is what the LORD says:

"Inquire among the nations:
  Who has ever heard anything like this?
A most horrible thing has been done
  by Virgin Israel.
14Does the snow of Lebanon
  ever vanish from its rocky slopes?
Do its cool waters from distant sources
  ever cease to flow?[a]
15Yet my people have forgotten me;
  they burn incense to worthless idols,
which made them stumble in their ways
  and in the ancient paths.
They made them walk in bypaths
  and on roads not built up.
16Their land will be laid waste,
  an object of lasting scorn;
all who pass by will be appalled
  and will shake their heads.
17Like a wind from the east,
  I will scatter them before their enemies;
I will show them my back and not my face
  in the day of their disaster."

18They said, "Come, let's make plans against Jeremiah; for the teaching of the law by the priest will not be lost, nor will counsel from the wise, nor the word from the prophets. So come, let's attack him with our tongues and pay no attention to anything he says."

19Listen to me, O LORD;
  hear what my accusers are saying!
20Should good be repaid with evil?
  Yet they have dug a pit for me.
Remember that I stood before you
  and spoke in their behalf
  to turn your wrath away from them.
21So give their children over to famine;
  hand them over to the power of the sword.
Let their wives be made childless and widows;
  let their men be put to death,
  their young men slain by the sword in battle.
22Let a cry be heard from their houses
  when you suddenly bring invaders against
    them,
for they have dug a pit to capture me
  and have hidden snares for my feet.
23But you know, O LORD,
  all their plots to kill me.
Do not forgive their crimes
  or blot out their sins from your sight.
Let them be overthrown before you;
  deal with them in the time of your anger.

19 THUS SAITH the LORD, Go and get a potter's earthen bottle, and *take* of the ancients of the people, and of the ancients of the priests;

2And go forth unto the valley of the son of Hinnom, which *is* by the entry of the east gate, and proclaim there the words that I shall tell thee,

19 THIS IS what the LORD says: "Go and buy a clay jar from a potter. Take along some of the elders of the people and of the priests 2and go out to the Valley of Ben Hinnom, near the entrance of the Potsherd Gate. There proclaim the words I tell you, 3and say,

---

[a] *14 The meaning of the Hebrew for this sentence is uncertain.*

Living Bible

12But they replied, "Don't waste your breath. We have no intention whatever of doing what God says. We will continue to live as we want to, free from any restraint, full of stubbornness and wickedness!"

13Then the Lord said: Even among the heathen, no one has ever heard of such a thing! My people have done something too horrible to understand. 14The snow never melts high up in the Lebanon mountains. The cold, flowing streams from the crags of Mount Hermon never run dry. 15These can be counted on. But not my people! For they have deserted me and turned to foolish idols. They have turned away from the ancient highways of good, and walk the muddy paths of sin. 16Therefore their land shall become desolate, so that all who pass by will gasp and shake their heads in amazement at its utter desolation. 17I will scatter my people before their enemies as the east wind scatters dust; and in all their trouble I will turn my back on them and refuse to notice their distress.

18Then the people said, "Come, let's get rid of Jeremiah. We have our own priests and wise men and prophets—we don't need his advice. Let's silence him that he may speak no more against us, nor bother us again."

19O Lord, help me! See what they are planning to do to me! 20Should they repay evil for good? They have set a trap to kill me, yet I spoke well of them to you and tried to defend them from your anger. 21Now, Lord, let their children starve to death and let the sword pour out their blood! Let their wives be widows and be bereft of all their children! Let their men die in epidemics and their youths die in battle! 22Let screaming be heard from their homes as troops of soldiers come suddenly upon them, for they have dug a pit for me to fall in, and they have hidden traps along my path. 23Lord, you know all their murderous plots against me. Don't forgive them, don't blot out their sin, but let them perish before you; deal with them in your anger.

19 THE LORD said, Buy a clay jar and take it out into the valley of Ben-Hinnom by the east gate of the city. Take some of the elders of the people and some of the older priests with you, and speak to them whatever words I give you.

New Revised Standard

Israel's Stubborn Idolatry

12 But they say, "It is no use! We will follow our own plans, and each of us will act according to the stubbornness of our evil will."

13 Therefore thus says the LORD:
Ask among the nations:
Who has heard the like of this?
The virgin Israel has done
a most horrible thing.
14 Does the snow of Lebanon leave
the crags of Sirion?b
Do the mountainc waters run dry,d
the cold flowing streams?
15 But my people have forgotten me,
they burn offerings to a delusion;
they have stumblede in their ways,
in the ancient roads,
and have gone into bypaths,
not the highway,
16 making their land a horror,
a thing to be hissed at forever.
All who pass by it are horrified
and shake their heads.
17 Like the wind from the east,
I will scatter them before the enemy.
I will show them my back, not my face,
in the day of their calamity.

A Plot against Jeremiah

18 Then they said, "Come, let us make plots against Jeremiah—for instruction shall not perish from the priest, nor counsel from the wise, nor the word from the prophet. Come, let us bring charges against him,f and let us not heed any of his words."

19 Give heed to me, O LORD,
and listen to what my adversaries say!
20 Is evil a recompense for good?
Yet they have dug a pit for my life.
Remember how I stood before you
to speak good for them,
to turn away your wrath from them.
21 Therefore give their children over to famine;
hurl them out to the power of the sword,
let their wives become childless and widowed.
May their men meet death by pestilence,
their youths be slain by the sword in battle.
22 May a cry be heard from their houses,
when you bring the marauder suddenly upon
them!
For they have dug a pit to catch me,
and laid snares for my feet.
23 Yet you, O LORD, know
all their plotting to kill me.
Do not forgive their iniquity,
do not blot out their sin from your sight.
Let them be tripped up before you;
deal with them while you are angry.

The Broken Earthenware Jug

19 THUS SAID the LORD: Go and buy a potter's earthenware jug. Take with youg some of the elders of the people and some of the senior priests, 2and go out to the valley of the son of Hinnom at the entry of the Potsherd Gate, and proclaim there the words that I tell you. 3You shall say: Hear the word of the LORD,

---

b Cn: Heb of the field   c Cn: Heb foreign   d Cn: Heb Are . . . plucked up?
e Gk Syr Vg: Heb they made them stumble   f Heb strike him with the tongue
g Syr Tg Compare Gk: Heb lacks take with you

King James

3And say, Hear ye the word of the LORD, O kings of Judah, and inhabitants of Jerusalem; Thus saith the LORD of hosts, the God of Israel; Behold, I will bring evil upon this place, the which whosoever heareth, his ears shall tingle.

4Because they have forsaken me, and have estranged this place, and have burned incense in it unto other gods, whom neither they nor their fathers have known, nor the kings of Judah, and have filled this place with the blood of innocents;

5They have built also the high places of Baal, to burn their sons with fire for burnt offerings unto Baal, which I commanded not, nor spake it, neither came it into my mind:

6Therefore, behold, the days come, saith the LORD, that this place shall no more be called Tophet, nor The valley of the son of Hinnom, but The valley of slaughter.

7And I will make void the counsel of Judah and Jerusalem in this place; and I will cause them to fall by the sword before their enemies, and by the hands of them that seek their lives: and their carcases will I give to be meat for the fowls of the heaven, and for the beasts of the earth.

8And I will make this city desolate, and an hissing; every one that passeth thereby shall be astonished and hiss because of all the plagues thereof.

9And I will cause them to eat the flesh of their sons and the flesh of their daughters, and they shall eat every one the flesh of his friend in the siege and straitness, wherewith their enemies, and they that seek their lives, shall straiten them.

10Then shalt thou break the bottle in the sight of the men that go with thee,

11And shalt say unto them, Thus saith the LORD of hosts; Even so will I break this people and this city, as one breaketh a potter's vessel, that cannot be made whole again: and they shall bury them in Tophet, till there be no place to bury.

12Thus will I do unto this place, saith the LORD, and to the inhabitants thereof, and even make this city as Tophet:

13And the houses of Jerusalem, and the houses of the kings of Judah, shall be defiled as the place of Tophet, because of all the houses upon whose roofs they have burned incense unto all the host of heaven, and have poured out drink offerings unto other gods.

14Then came Jeremiah from Tophet, whither the LORD had sent him to prophesy; and he stood in the court of the LORD's house; and said to all the people,

15Thus saith the LORD of hosts, the God of Israel; Behold, I will bring upon this city and upon all her towns all the evil that I have pronounced against it, because they have hardened their necks, that they might not hear my words.

20 NOW PASHUR the son of Immer the priest, who was also chief governor in the house of the LORD, heard that Jeremiah prophesied these things.

2Then Pashur smote Jeremiah the prophet, and put him in the stocks that were in the high gate of Benjamin, which was by the house of the LORD.

3And it came to pass on the morrow, that Pashur brought forth Jeremiah out of the stocks. Then said Jeremiah unto him, The LORD hath not called thy name Pashur, but Magor-missabib.

New International

'Hear the word of the LORD, O kings of Judah and people of Jerusalem. This is what the LORD Almighty, the God of Israel, says: Listen! I am going to bring a disaster on this place that will make the ears of everyone who hears of it tingle. 4For they have forsaken me and made this a place of foreign gods; they have burned sacrifices in it to gods that neither they nor their fathers nor the kings of Judah ever knew, and they have filled this place with the blood of the innocent. 5They have built the high places of Baal to burn their sons in the fire as offerings to Baal—something I did not command or mention, nor did it enter my mind. 6So beware, the days are coming, declares the LORD, when people will no longer call this place Topheth or the Valley of Ben Hinnom, but the Valley of Slaughter.

7" 'In this place I will ruina the plans of Judah and Jerusalem. I will make them fall by the sword before their enemies, at the hands of those who seek their lives, and I will give their carcasses as food to the birds of the air and the beasts of the earth. 8I will devastate this city and make it an object of scorn; all who pass by will be appalled and will scoff because of all its wounds. 9I will make them eat the flesh of their sons and daughters, and they will eat one another's flesh during the stress of the siege imposed on them by the enemies who seek their lives.'

10"Then break the jar while those who go with you are watching, 11and say to them, 'This is what the LORD Almighty says: I will smash this nation and this city just as this potter's jar is smashed and cannot be repaired. They will bury the dead in Topheth until there is no more room. 12This is what I will do to this place and to those who live here, declares the LORD. I will make this city like Topheth. 13The houses in Jerusalem and those of the kings of Judah will be defiled like this place, Topheth—all the houses where they burned incense on the roofs to all the starry hosts and poured out drink offerings to other gods.' "

14Jeremiah then returned from Topheth, where the LORD had sent him to prophesy, and stood in the court of the LORD's temple and said to all the people, 15"This is what the LORD Almighty, the God of Israel, says: 'Listen! I am going to bring on this city and the villages around it every disaster I pronounced against them, because they were stiff-necked and would not listen to my words.' "

Jeremiah and Pashhur

20 WHEN THE priest Pashhur son of Immer, the chief officer in the temple of the LORD, heard Jeremiah prophesying these things, 2he had Jeremiah the prophet beaten and put in the stocks at the Upper Gate of Benjamin at the LORD's temple. 3The next day, when Pashhur released him from the stocks, Jeremiah said to him, "The LORD's name for you is not Pashhur, but Magor-Missabib.b 4For this is what the LORD says: 'I

---

a 7 The Hebrew for ruin sounds like the Hebrew for jar (see verses 1 and 10).   b 3 Magor-Missabib means terror on every side.

Living Bible

3Then the Lord spoke to them and said: Listen to the word of the Lord, kings of Judah and citizens of Jerusalem! The Lord Almighty, the God of Israel, says, I will bring terrible evil upon this place, so terrible that the ears of those who hear it will prickle. 4For Israel has forsaken me and turned this valley into a place of shame and wickedness. The people burn incense to idols—idols that neither this generation nor their forefathers nor the kings of Judah have worshiped before—and they have filled this place with the blood of innocent children. 5They have built high altars to Baal and there they burn their sons in sacrifice—a thing I never commanded them nor even thought of!

6The day is coming, says the Lord, when this valley shall no longer be called "Topheth" or "Ben-Hinnom Valley," but "The Valley of Slaughter." 7For I will upset the battle plans of Judah and Jerusalem and I will let invading armies kill you here and leave your dead bodies for vultures and wild animals to feed upon. 8And I will wipe Jerusalem off the earth, so that everyone going by will gasp with astonishment at all that I have done to her. 9I will see to it that your enemies lay siege to the city until all food is gone, and those trapped inside begin to eat their own children and friends.

10And now, Jeremiah, as these men watch, smash the jar you brought with you, 11and say to them, This is the message to you from the Lord Almighty: As this jar lies shattered, so I will shatter the people of Jerusalem; and as this jar cannot be mended, neither can they. The slaughter shall be so great that there won't be room enough for decent burial anywhere, and their bodies shall be heaped in this valley. 12And as it will be in this valley, so it will be in Jerusalem. For I will fill Jerusalem with dead bodies too. 13And I will defile all the homes in Jerusalem, including the palace of the kings of Judah—wherever incense has been burned upon the roofs to your stargods, and libations poured out to them.

14As Jeremiah returned from Topheth where he had delivered this message, he stopped in front of the Temple of the Lord and said to all the people, 15The Lord Almighty, the God of Israel, says: I will bring upon this city and her surrounding towns all the evil I have promised, because you have stubbornly refused to listen to the Lord.

New Revised Standard

O kings of Judah and inhabitants of Jerusalem. Thus says the LORD of hosts, the God of Israel: I am going to bring such disaster upon this place that the ears of everyone who hears of it will tingle. 4Because the people have forsaken me, and have profaned this place by making offerings in it to other gods whom neither they nor their ancestors nor the kings of Judah have known; and because they have filled this place with the blood of the innocent, 5and gone on building the high places of Baal to burn their children in the fire as burnt offerings to Baal, which I did not command or decree, nor did it enter my mind. 6Therefore the days are surely coming, says the LORD, when this place shall no more be called Topheth, or the valley of the son of Hinnom, but the valley of Slaughter. 7And in this place I will make void the plans of Judah and Jerusalem, and will make them fall by the sword before their enemies, and by the hand of those who seek their life. I will give their dead bodies for food to the birds of the air and to the wild animals of the earth. 8And I will make this city a horror, a thing to be hissed at; everyone who passes by it will be horrified and will hiss because of all its disasters. 9And I will make them eat the flesh of their sons and the flesh of their daughters, and all shall eat the flesh of their neighbors in the siege, and in the distress with which their enemies and those who seek their life afflict them.

10 Then you shall break the jug in the sight of those who go with you, 11and shall say to them: Thus says the LORD of hosts: So will I break this people and this city, as one breaks a potter's vessel, so that it can never be mended. In Topheth they shall bury until there is no more room to bury. 12Thus will I do to this place, says the LORD, and to its inhabitants, making this city like Topheth. 13And the houses of Jerusalem and the houses of the kings of Judah shall be defiled like the place of Topheth—all the houses upon whose roofs offerings have been made to the whole host of heaven, and libations have been poured out to other gods.

14 When Jeremiah came from Topheth, where the LORD had sent him to prophesy, he stood in the court of the LORD's house and said to all the people: 15Thus says the LORD of hosts, the God of Israel: I am now bringing upon this city and upon all its towns all the disaster that I have pronounced against it, because they have stiffened their necks, refusing to hear my words.

Jeremiah Persecuted by Pashhur

20 NOW WHEN Pashhur (son of Immer), the priest in charge of the Temple of the Lord, heard what Jeremiah was saying, 2he arrested Jeremiah and had him whipped and put in the stocks at Benjamin Gate near the Temple. 3He left him there all night.

The next day when Pashhur finally released him, Jeremiah said, "Pashhur, the Lord has changed your name. He says from now on to call you 'The Man Who Lives in Terror.' 4For the Lord will send terror on you and all

20 NOW THE priest Pashhur son of Immer, who was chief officer in the house of the LORD, heard Jeremiah prophesying these things. 2Then Pashhur struck the prophet Jeremiah, and put him in the stocks that were in the upper Benjamin Gate of the house of the LORD. 3The next morning when Pashhur released Jeremiah from the stocks, Jeremiah said to him, The LORD has named you not Pashhur but "Terror-all-around." 4For thus says the LORD: I am making you a

King James

4For thus saith the LORD, Behold, I will make thee a terror to thyself, and to all thy friends: and they shall fall by the sword of their enemies, and thine eyes shall behold *it:* and I will give all Judah into the hand of the king of Babylon, and he shall carry them captive into Babylon, and shall slay them with the sword.

5Moreover I will deliver all the strength of this city, and all the labours thereof, and all the precious things thereof, and all the treasures of the kings of Judah will I give into the hand of their enemies, which shall spoil them, and take them, and carry them to Babylon.

6And thou, Pashur, and all that dwell in thine house shall go into captivity: and thou shalt come to Babylon, and there thou shalt die, and shalt be buried there, thou, and all thy friends, to whom thou hast prophesied lies.

7¶ O LORD, thou hast deceived me, and I was deceived: thou art stronger than I, and hast prevailed: I am in derision daily, every one mocketh me.

8For since I spake, I cried out, I cried violence and spoil; because the word of the LORD was made a reproach unto me, and a derision, daily.

9Then I said, I will not make mention of him, nor speak any more in his name. But *his word* was in mine heart as a burning fire shut up in my bones, and I was weary with forbearing, and I could not *stay.*

10¶ For I heard the defaming of many, fear on every side. Report, *say they,* and we will report it. All my familiars watched for my halting, *saying,* Peradventure he will be enticed, and we shall prevail against him, and we shall take our revenge on him.

11But the LORD *is* with me as a mighty terrible one: therefore my persecutors shall stumble, and they shall not prevail: they shall be greatly ashamed; for they shall not prosper: *their* everlasting confusion shall never be forgotten.

12But, O LORD of hosts, that triest the righteous, *and* seest the reins and the heart, let me see thy vengeance on them: for unto thee have I opened my cause.

13Sing unto the LORD, praise ye the LORD: for he hath delivered the soul of the poor from the hand of evildoers.

14¶ Cursed *be* the day wherein I was born: let not the day wherein my mother bare me be blessed.

15Cursed *be* the man who brought tidings to my father, saying, A man child is born unto thee; making him very glad.

16And let that man be as the cities which the LORD overthrew, and repented not: and let him hear the cry in the morning, and the shouting at noontide;

17Because he slew me not from the womb; or that my mother might have been my grave, and her womb *to be* always great *with me.*

New International

will make you a terror to yourself and to all your friends; with your own eyes you will see them fall by the sword of their enemies. I will hand all Judah over to the king of Babylon, who will carry them away to Babylon or put them to the sword. 5I will hand over to their enemies all the wealth of this city—all its products, all its valuables and all the treasures of the kings of Judah. They will take it away as plunder and carry it off to Babylon. 6And you, Pashhur, and all who live in your house will go into exile to Babylon. There you will die and be buried, you and all your friends to whom you have prophesied lies.'"

Jeremiah's Complaint

7O LORD, you deceiveda me, and I was
        deceiveda;
    you overpowered me and prevailed.
I am ridiculed all day long;
    everyone mocks me.
8Whenever I speak, I cry out
    proclaiming violence and destruction.
So the word of the LORD has brought me
    insult and reproach all day long.
9But if I say, "I will not mention him
    or speak any more in his name,"
his word is in my heart like a fire,
    a fire shut up in my bones.
I am weary of holding it in;
    indeed, I cannot.
10I hear many whispering,
    "Terror on every side!
    Report him! Let's report him!"
All my friends
    are waiting for me to slip, saying,
"Perhaps he will be deceived;
    then we will prevail over him
    and take our revenge on him."

11But the LORD is with me like a mighty warrior;
    so my persecutors will stumble and not
        prevail.
They will fail and be thoroughly disgraced;
    their dishonor will never be forgotten.
12O LORD Almighty, you who examine the
        righteous
    and probe the heart and mind,
let me see your vengeance upon them,
    for to you I have committed my cause.

13Sing to the LORD!
    Give praise to the LORD!
He rescues the life of the needy
    from the hands of the wicked.

14Cursed be the day I was born!
    May the day my mother bore me not be
        blessed!
15Cursed be the man who brought my father the
        news,
    who made him very glad, saying,
    "A child is born to you—a son!"
16May that man be like the towns
    the LORD overthrew without pity.
May he hear wailing in the morning,
    a battle cry at noon.
17For he did not kill me in the womb,
    with my mother as my grave,
    her womb enlarged forever.

a 7 Or *persuaded*

Living Bible

your friends, and you will see them die by the swords of their enemies. I will hand over Judah to the king of Babylon, says the Lord, and he shall take away these people as slaves to Babylon and kill them. 5And I will let your enemies loot Jerusalem. All the famed treasures of the city, with the precious jewels and gold and silver of your kings, shall be carried off to Babylon. 6And as for you, Pashhur, you and all your family and household shall become slaves in Babylon and die there—you and those to whom you lied when you prophesied that everything would be all right."

7Then I said, O Lord, you deceived me when you promised me your help. I have to give them your messages because you are stronger than I am, but now I am the laughingstock of the city, mocked by all. 8You have never once let me speak a word of kindness to them; always it is disaster and horror and destruction. No wonder they scoff and mock and make my name a household joke. 9And I can't quit! For if I say I'll never again mention the Lord—never more speak in his name—then his word in my heart is like fire that burns in my bones, and I can't hold it in any longer. 10Yet on every side I hear their whispered threats, and am afraid. "We will report," they say. Even those who were my friends are watching me, waiting for a fatal slip. "He will trap himself," they say, "and then we will get our revenge on him."

11But the Lord stands beside me like a great warrior, and before him, the Mighty, Terrible One, they shall stumble. They cannot defeat me; they shall be shamed and thoroughly humiliated, and they shall have a stigma upon them forever. 12O Lord Almighty, who knows those who are righteous and examines the deepest thoughts of hearts and minds, let me see your vengeance on them. For I have committed my cause to you. 13Therefore I will sing out in thanks to the Lord! Praise him! For he has delivered me, poor and needy, from my oppressors.

14Yet, cursed be the day that I was born! 15Cursed be the man who brought my father the news that a son was born. 16Let that messenger be destroyed like the cities of old which God overthrew without mercy. Terrify him all day long with battle shouts, 17because he did not kill me at my birth! Oh, that I had died within my mother's

New Revised Standard

terror to yourself and to all your friends; and they shall fall by the sword of their enemies while you look on. And I will give all Judah into the hand of the king of Babylon; he shall carry them captive to Babylon, and shall kill them with the sword. 5I will give all the wealth of this city, all its gains, all its prized belongings, and all the treasures of the kings of Judah into the hand of their enemies, who shall plunder them, and seize them, and carry them to Babylon. 6And you, Pashhur, and all who live in your house, shall go into captivity, and to Babylon you shall go; there you shall die, and there you shall be buried, you and all your friends, to whom you have prophesied falsely.

Jeremiah Denounces His Persecutors

7 O LORD, you have enticed me,
   and I was enticed;
you have overpowered me,
   and you have prevailed.
I have become a laughingstock all day long;
   everyone mocks me.
8 For whenever I speak, I must cry out,
   I must shout, "Violence and destruction!"
For the word of the LORD has become for me
   a reproach and derision all day long.
9 If I say, "I will not mention him,
   or speak any more in his name,"
then within me there is something like a
     burning fire
   shut up in my bones;
I am weary with holding it in,
   and I cannot.
10 For I hear many whispering:
   "Terror is all around!
Denounce him! Let us denounce him!"
   All my close friends
   are watching for me to stumble.
"Perhaps he can be enticed,
   and we can prevail against him,
   and take our revenge on him."
11 But the LORD is with me like a dread warrior;
   therefore my persecutors will stumble,
   and they will not prevail.
They will be greatly shamed,
   for they will not succeed.
Their eternal dishonor
   will never be forgotten.
12 O LORD of hosts, you test the righteous,
   you see the heart and the mind;
let me see your retribution upon them,
   for to you I have committed my cause.

13 Sing to the LORD;
   praise the LORD!
For he has delivered the life of the needy
   from the hands of evildoers.

14 Cursed be the day
   on which I was born!
The day when my mother bore me,
   let it not be blessed!
15 Cursed be the man
   who brought the news to my father, saying,
"A child is born to you, a son,"
   making him very glad.
16 Let that man be like the cities
   that the LORD overthrew without pity;
let him hear a cry in the morning
   and an alarm at noon,
17 because he did not kill me in the womb;
   so my mother would have been my grave,
   and her womb forever great.

King James

18Wherefore came I forth out of the womb to see labour and sorrow, that my days should be consumed with shame?

21 THE WORD which came unto Jeremiah from the LORD, when king Zedekiah sent unto him Pashur the son of Melchiah, and Zephaniah the son of Maaseiah the priest, saying,

2Inquire, I pray thee, of the LORD for us; for Nebuchadrezzar king of Babylon maketh war against us; if so be that the LORD will deal with us according to all his wondrous works, that he may go up from us.

3¶ Then said Jeremiah unto them, Thus shall ye say to Zedekiah:

4Thus saith the LORD God of Israel; Behold, I will turn back the weapons of war that *are* in your hands, wherewith ye fight against the king of Babylon, and *against* the Chaldeans, which besiege you without the walls, and I will assemble them into the midst of this city.

5And I myself will fight against you with an outstretched hand and with a strong arm, even in anger, and in fury, and in great wrath.

6And I will smite the inhabitants of this city, both man and beast: they shall die of a great pestilence.

7And afterward, saith the LORD, I will deliver Zedekiah king of Judah, and his servants, and the people, and such as are left in this city from the pestilence, from the sword, and from the famine, into the hand of Nebuchadrezzar king of Babylon, and into the hand of their enemies, and into the hand of those that seek their life: and he shall smite them with the edge of the sword; he shall not spare them, neither have pity, nor have mercy.

8¶ And unto this people thou shalt say, Thus saith the LORD; Behold, I set before you the way of life, and the way of death.

9He that abideth in this city shall die by the sword, and by the famine, and by the pestilence: but he that goeth out, and falleth to the Chaldeans that besiege you, he shall live, and his life shall be unto him for a prey.

10For I have set my face against this city for evil, and not for good, saith the LORD: it shall be given into the hand of the king of Babylon, and he shall burn it with fire.

11¶ And touching the house of the king of Judah, *say*, Hear ye the word of the LORD;

12O house of David, thus saith the LORD; Execute judgment in the morning, and deliver *him that is* spoiled out of the hand of the oppressor, lest my fury go out like fire, and burn that none can quench *it*, because of the evil of your doings.

13Behold, I *am* against thee, O inhabitant of the valley, *and* rock of the plain, saith the LORD; which say, Who shall come down against us? or who shall enter into our habitations?

14But I will punish you according to the fruit of your doings, saith the LORD: and I will kindle a fire in the forest thereof, and it shall devour all things round about it.

New International

18Why did I ever come out of the womb
to see trouble and sorrow
and to end my days in shame?

God Rejects Zedekiah's Request

21 THE WORD came to Jeremiah from the LORD when King Zedekiah sent to him Pashhur son of Malkijah and the priest Zephaniah son of Maaseiah. They said: 2"Inquire now of the LORD for us because Nebuchadnezzar[a] king of Babylon is attacking us. Perhaps the LORD will perform wonders for us as in times past so that he will withdraw from us."

3But Jeremiah answered them, "Tell Zedekiah, 4'This is what the LORD, the God of Israel, says: I am about to turn against you the weapons of war that are in your hands, which you are using to fight the king of Babylon and the Babylonians[b] who are outside the wall besieging you. And I will gather them inside this city. 5I myself will fight against you with an outstretched hand and a mighty arm in anger and fury and great wrath. 6I will strike down those who live in this city—both men and animals—and they will die of a terrible plague. 7After that, declares the LORD, I will hand over Zedekiah king of Judah, his officials and the people in this city who survive the plague, sword and famine, to Nebuchadnezzar king of Babylon and to their enemies who seek their lives. He will put them to the sword; he will show them no mercy or pity or compassion.'

8"Furthermore, tell the people, 'This is what the LORD says: See, I am setting before you the way of life and the way of death. 9Whoever stays in this city will die by the sword, famine or plague. But whoever goes out and surrenders to the Babylonians who are besieging you will live; he will escape with his life. 10I have determined to do this city harm and not good, declares the LORD. It will be given into the hands of the king of Babylon, and he will destroy it with fire.'

11"Moreover, say to the royal house of Judah, 'Hear the word of the LORD; 12O house of David, this is what the LORD says:

" 'Administer justice every morning;
rescue from the hand of his oppressor
the one who has been robbed,
or my wrath will break out and burn like fire
because of the evil you have done—
burn with no one to quench it.
13I am against you, ˻Jerusalem˼,
you who live above this valley
on the rocky plateau,
             declares the LORD—
you who say, "Who can come against us?
Who can enter our refuge?"
14I will punish you as your deeds deserve,
             declares the LORD.
I will kindle a fire in your forests
that will consume everything around you.' "

---

 a 2 Hebrew *Nebuchadrezzar*, of which *Nebuchadnezzar* is a variant; here and often in Jeremiah and Ezekiel   b 4 Or *Chaldeans*; also in verse 9

Living Bible

womb, that it had been my grave! 18Why was I ever born? For my life has been but trouble and sorrow and shame.

21 THEN KING Zedekiah sent Pashhur (son of Malchiah) and Zephaniah the priest (son of Maaseiah) to Jeremiah, and begged, "Ask the Lord to help us, for Nebuchadnezzar, king of Babylon, has declared war on us! 2Perhaps the Lord will be gracious to us and do a mighty miracle as in olden times*c* and force Nebuchadnezzar to withdraw his forces."

3, 4Jeremiah replied, "Go back to King Zedekiah and tell him the Lord God of Israel says, I will make all your weapons useless against the king of Babylon and the Chaldeans besieging you. In fact, I will bring your enemies right into the heart of this city, 5and I myself will fight against you, for I am very angry. 6And I will send a terrible plague on this city, and both men and animals shall die. 7And finally I will deliver King Zedekiah himself and all the remnant left in the city into the hands of King Nebuchadnezzar of Babylon, to slaughter them without pity or mercy.

8"Tell these people, the Lord says: Take your choice of life or death! 9Stay here in Jerusalem and die—slaughtered by your enemies, killed by starvation and disease—or go out and surrender to the Chaldean army and live. 10For I have set my face against this city; I will be its enemy and not its friend, says the Lord. It shall be captured by the king of Babylon and he shall reduce it to ashes.

11"And to the king of Judah, the Lord says: 12I am ready to judge you because of all the evil you are doing. Quick! Give justice to these you judge! Begin doing what is right before my burning fury flashes out upon you like a fire no man can quench. 13I will fight against this city of Jerusalem, which boasts, 'We are safe; no one can touch us here!' 14And I myself will destroy you for your sinfulness, says the Lord. I will light a fire in the forests that will burn up everything in its path."

New Revised Standard

18 Why did I come forth from the womb
     to see toil and sorrow,
     and spend my days in shame?

Jerusalem Will Fall to Nebuchadrezzar

21 THIS IS the word that came to Jeremiah from the LORD, when King Zedekiah sent to him Pashhur son of Malchiah and the priest Zephaniah son of Maaseiah, saying, 2"Please inquire of the LORD on our behalf, for King Nebuchadrezzar of Babylon is making war against us; perhaps the LORD will perform a wonderful deed for us, as he has often done, and will make him withdraw from us."

3 Then Jeremiah said to them: 4Thus you shall say to Zedekiah: Thus says the LORD, the God of Israel: I am going to turn back the weapons of war that are in your hands and with which you are fighting against the king of Babylon and against the Chaldeans who are besieging you outside the walls; and I will bring them together into the center of this city. 5I myself will fight against you with outstretched hand and mighty arm, in anger, in fury, and in great wrath. 6And I will strike down the inhabitants of this city, both human beings and animals; they shall die of a great pestilence. 7Afterward, says the LORD, I will give King Zedekiah of Judah, and his servants, and the people in this city—those who survive the pestilence, sword, and famine—into the hands of King Nebuchadrezzar of Babylon, into the hands of their enemies, into the hands of those who seek their lives. He shall strike them down with the edge of the sword; he shall not pity them, or spare them, or have compassion.

8 And to this people you shall say: Thus says the LORD: See, I am setting before you the way of life and the way of death. 9Those who stay in this city shall die by the sword, by famine, and by pestilence; but those who go out and surrender to the Chaldeans who are besieging you shall live and shall have their lives as a prize of war. 10For I have set my face against this city for evil and not for good, says the LORD: it shall be given into the hands of the king of Babylon, and he shall burn it with fire.

Message to the House of David

11 To the house of the king of Judah say: Hear the word of the LORD, 12O house of David! Thus says the LORD:

> Execute justice in the morning,
>   and deliver from the hand of the oppressor
>   anyone who has been robbed,
> or else my wrath will go forth like fire,
>   and burn, with no one to quench it,
>   because of your evil doings.

13 See, I am against you, O inhabitant of the
          valley,
     O rock of the plain,
                         says the LORD;
     you who say, "Who can come down against
          us,
     or who can enter our places of refuge?"
14 I will punish you according to the fruit of
          your doings,
                         says the LORD;
     I will kindle a fire in its forest,
     and it shall devour all that is around it.

---

c 21:2 as in olden times. King Zedekiah doubtless had in mind God's deliverances of Jerusalem from Sennacherib, king of Assyria, in the days of Hezekiah (Isa 36-37). But Zedekiah's hopes were dashed. He was Judah's last ruler before the exile of 597 B.C.

King James

22 THUS SAITH the LORD; Go down to the house of the king of Judah, and speak there this word,

²And say, Hear the word of the LORD, O king of Judah, that sittest upon the throne of David, thou, and thy servants, and thy people that enter in by these gates.

³Thus saith the LORD; Execute ye judgment and righteousness, and deliver the spoiled out of the hand of the oppressor: and do no wrong, do no violence to the stranger, the fatherless, nor the widow, neither shed innocent blood in this place.

⁴For if ye do this thing indeed, then shall there enter in by the gates of this house kings sitting upon the throne of David, riding in chariots and on horses, he, and his servants, and his people.

⁵But if ye will not hear these words, I swear by myself, saith the LORD, that this house shall become a desolation.

⁶For thus saith the LORD unto the king's house of Judah; Thou *art* Gilead unto me, *and* the head of Lebanon: *yet* surely I will make thee a wilderness; *and* cities *which* are not inhabited.

⁷And I will prepare destroyers against thee, every one with his weapons: and they shall cut down thy choice cedars, and cast *them* into the fire.

⁸And many nations shall pass by this city, and they shall say every man to his neighbour, Wherefore hath the LORD done thus unto this great city?

⁹Then they shall answer, Because they have forsaken the covenant of the LORD their God, and worshipped other gods, and served them.

¹⁰¶ Weep ye not for the dead, neither bemoan him: *but* weep sore for him that goeth away: for he shall return no more, nor see his native country.

¹¹For thus saith the LORD touching Shallum the son of Josiah king of Judah, which reigned instead of Josiah his father, which went forth out of this place; He shall not return thither any more:

¹²But he shall die in the place whither they have led him captive, and shall see this land no more.

¹³¶ Woe unto him that buildeth his house by unrighteousness, and his chambers by wrong; *that* useth his neighbour's service without wages, and giveth him not for his work;

¹⁴That saith, I will build me a wide house and large chambers, and cutteth him out windows; and *it is* ceiled with cedar, and painted with vermilion.

¹⁵Shalt thou reign, because thou closest *thyself* in cedar? did not thy father eat and drink, and do judgment and justice, *and* then *it was* well with him?

¹⁶He judged the cause of the poor and needy; then *it was* well *with him: was* not this to know me? saith the LORD.

¹⁷But thine eyes and thine heart *are* not but for thy covetousness, and for to shed innocent blood, and for oppression, and for violence, to do *it*.

New International

Judgment Against Evil Kings

22 THIS IS what the LORD says: "Go down to the palace of the king of Judah and proclaim this message there: ²'Hear the word of the LORD, O king of Judah, you who sit on David's throne—you, your officials and your people who come through these gates. ³This is what the LORD says: Do what is just and right. Rescue from the hand of his oppressor the one who has been robbed. Do no wrong or violence to the alien, the fatherless or the widow, and do not shed innocent blood in this place. ⁴For if you are careful to carry out these commands, then kings who sit on David's throne will come through the gates of this palace, riding in chariots and on horses, accompanied by their officials and their people. ⁵But if you do not obey these commands, declares the LORD, I swear by myself that this palace will become a ruin.'"

⁶For this is what the LORD says about the palace of the king of Judah:

"Though you are like Gilead to me,
    like the summit of Lebanon,
I will surely make you like a desert,
    like towns not inhabited.
⁷I will send destroyers against you,
    each man with his weapons,
and they will cut up your fine cedar beams
    and throw them into the fire.

⁸"People from many nations will pass by this city and will ask one another, 'Why has the LORD done such a thing to this great city?' ⁹And the answer will be: 'Because they have forsaken the covenant of the LORD their God and have worshiped and served other gods.'"

¹⁰Do not weep for the dead ₍king₎ or mourn his loss;
    rather, weep bitterly for him who is exiled,
because he will never return
    nor see his native land again.

¹¹For this is what the LORD says about Shallum[a] son of Josiah, who succeeded his father as king of Judah but has gone from this place: "He will never return. ¹²He will die in the place where they have led him captive; he will not see this land again."

¹³"Woe to him who builds his palace by unrighteousness,
    his upper rooms by injustice,
making his countrymen work for nothing,
    not paying them for their labor.
¹⁴He says, 'I will build myself a great palace
    with spacious upper rooms.'
So he makes large windows in it,
    panels it with cedar
    and decorates it in red.

¹⁵"Does it make you a king
    to have more and more cedar?
Did not your father have food and drink?
    He did what was right and just,
    so all went well with him.
¹⁶He defended the cause of the poor and needy,
    and so all went well.
Is that not what it means to know me?"
    declares the LORD.
¹⁷"But your eyes and your heart
    are set only on dishonest gain,
on shedding innocent blood
    and on oppression and extortion."

---

a 11 Also called *Jehoahaz*

Living Bible

22 THEN THE Lord said to me: Go over and speak directly to the king of Judah and say, ²Listen to this message from God, O king of Judah, sitting on David's throne; and let your servants and your people listen too.

³The Lord says: Be fair-minded. Do what is right! Help those in need of justice! Quit your evil deeds! Protect the rights of aliens and immigrants, orphans and widows; stop murdering the innocent! ⁴If you put an end to all these terrible deeds you are doing, then I will deliver this nation and once more give kings to sit on David's throne, and there shall be prosperity for all.

⁵But if you refuse to pay attention to this warning, I swear by my own name, says the Lord, that this palace shall become a shambles. ⁶For this is the Lord's message concerning the palace: You are as beloved to me as fruitful Gilead and the green forests of Lebanon; but I will destroy you and leave you deserted and uninhabited. ⁷I will call for a wrecking crew to bring out its tools to dismantle you. They will tear out all of your fine cedar beams and throw them on the fire. ⁸Men from many nations will pass by the ruins of this city and say to one another, "Why did the Lord do it? Why did he destroy such a great city?" ⁹And the answer will be, "Because the people living here forgot the Lord their God and violated his agreement with them, for they worshiped idols."

¹⁰Don't weep for the dead! Instead weep for the captives led away! For they will never return to see their native land again. ¹¹For the Lord says this about Jehoahaz who succeeded his father[b] King Josiah, and was taken away as a captive: ¹²He shall die in a distant land[c] and never again see his own country.

¹³And woe to you, King Jehoiakim,[d] for you are building your great palace with forced labor. By not paying wages you are building injustice into its walls and oppression into its doorframes and ceilings. ¹⁴You say, "I will build a magnificent palace with huge rooms and many windows, paneled throughout with fragrant cedar and painted a lovely red." ¹⁵But a beautiful palace does not make a great king! Why did your father Josiah reign so long? Because he was just and fair in all his dealings. That is why God blessed him. ¹⁶He saw to it that justice and help were given the poor and the needy and all went well for him. This is how a man lives close to God. ¹⁷But you! You are full of selfish greed and all dishonesty! You murder the innocent, oppress the poor and reign with ruthlessness.

New Revised Standard

Exhortation to Repent

22 THUS SAYS the LORD: Go down to the house of the king of Judah, and speak there this word, ²and say: Hear the word of the LORD, O King of Judah sitting on the throne of David—you, and your servants, and your people who enter these gates. ³Thus says the LORD: Act with justice and righteousness, and deliver from the hand of the oppressor anyone who has been robbed. And do no wrong or violence to the alien, the orphan, and the widow, or shed innocent blood in this place. ⁴For if you will indeed obey this word, then through the gates of this house shall enter kings who sit on the throne of David, riding in chariots and on horses, they, and their servants, and their people. ⁵But if you will not heed these words, I swear by myself, says the LORD, that this house shall become a desolation. ⁶For thus says the LORD concerning the house of the king of Judah:

You are like Gilead to me,
   like the summit of Lebanon;
but I swear that I will make you a desert,
   an uninhabited city.[e]
7 I will prepare destroyers against you,
   all with their weapons;
they shall cut down your choicest cedars
   and cast them into the fire.

8 And many nations will pass by this city, and all of them will say one to another, "Why has the LORD dealt in this way with that great city?" ⁹And they will answer, "Because they abandoned the covenant of the LORD their God, and worshiped other gods and served them."

10 Do not weep for him who is dead,
   nor bemoan him;
weep rather for him who goes away,
   for he shall return no more
   to see his native land.

Message to the Sons of Josiah

11 For thus says the LORD concerning Shallum son of King Josiah of Judah, who succeeded his father Josiah, and who went away from this place: He shall return here no more, ¹²but in the place where they have carried him captive he shall die, and he shall never see this land again.

13 Woe to him who builds his house by
      unrighteousness,
   and his upper rooms by injustice;
who makes his neighbors work for nothing,
   and does not give them their wages;
14 who says, "I will build myself a spacious
      house
   with large upper rooms,"
and who cuts out windows for it,
   paneling it with cedar,
   and painting it with vermilion.
15 Are you a king
   because you compete in cedar?
Did not your father eat and drink
   and do justice and righteousness?
   Then it was well with him.
16 He judged the cause of the poor and needy;
   then it was well.
Is not this to know me?
   says the LORD.
17 But your eyes and heart
   are only on your dishonest gain,
for shedding innocent blood,
   and for practicing oppression and violence.

King James

18Therefore thus saith the LORD concerning Jehoia-kim the son of Josiah king of Judah; They shall not lament for him, *saying,* Ah my brother! or, Ah sister! they shall not lament for him, *saying,* Ah lord! or, Ah his glory!

19He shall be buried with the burial of an ass, drawn and cast forth beyond the gates of Jerusalem.

20¶ Go up to Lebanon, and cry; and lift up thy voice in Bashan, and cry from the passages: for all thy lovers are destroyed.

21I spake unto thee in thy prosperity; *but* thou saidst, I will not hear. This *hath been* thy manner from thy youth, that thou obeyedst not my voice.

22The wind shall eat up all thy pastors, and thy lovers shall go into captivity: surely then shalt thou be ashamed and confounded for all thy wickedness.

23O inhabitant of Lebanon, that makest thy nest in the cedars, how gracious shalt thou be when pangs come upon thee, the pain as of a woman in travail!

24*As* I live, saith the LORD, though Coniah the son of Jehoiakim king of Judah were the signet upon my right hand, yet would I pluck thee thence;

25And I will give thee into the hand of them that seek thy life, and into the hand *of them* whose face thou fearest, even into the hand of Nebuchadrezzar king of Babylon, and into the hand of the Chaldeans.

26And I will cast thee out, and thy mother that bare thee, into another country, where ye were not born; and there shall ye die.

27But to the land whereunto they desire to return, thither shall they not return.

28*Is* this man Coniah a despised broken idol? *is he* a vessel wherein *is* no pleasure? wherefore are they cast out, he and his seed, and are cast into a land which they know not?

29O earth, earth, earth, hear the word of the LORD.

30Thus saith the LORD, Write ye this man childless, a man *that* shall not prosper in his days: for no man of his seed shall prosper, sitting upon the throne of David, and ruling any more in Judah.

23 WOE BE unto the pastors that destroy and scatter the sheep of my pasture! saith the LORD.

2Therefore thus saith the LORD God of Israel against the pastors that feed my people; Ye have scattered my flock, and driven them away, and have not visited them: behold, I will visit upon you the evil of your doings, saith the LORD.

3And I will gather the remnant of my flock out of all countries whither I have driven them, and will bring them again to their folds; and they shall be fruitful and increase.

New International

18Therefore this is what the LORD says about Jehoiakim son of Josiah king of Judah:

"They will not mourn for him:
  'Alas, my brother! Alas, my sister!'
They will not mourn for him:
  'Alas, my master! Alas, his splendor!'
19He will have the burial of a donkey—
  dragged away and thrown
  outside the gates of Jerusalem."

20"Go up to Lebanon and cry out,
  let your voice be heard in Bashan,
cry out from Abarim,
  for all your allies are crushed.
21I warned you when you felt secure,
  but you said, 'I will not listen!'
This has been your way from your youth;
  you have not obeyed me.
22The wind will drive all your shepherds away,
  and your allies will go into exile.
Then you will be ashamed and disgraced
  because of all your wickedness.
23You who live in 'Lebanon,'a
  who are nestled in cedar buildings,
how you will groan when pangs come upon
  you,
  pain like that of a woman in labor!

24"As surely as I live," declares the LORD, "even if you, Jehoiachinb son of Jehoiakim king of Judah, were a signet ring on my right hand, I would still pull you off. 25I will hand you over to those who seek your life, those you fear—to Nebuchadnezzar king of Babylon and to the Babylonians.c 26I will hurl you and the mother who gave you birth into another country, where neither of you was born, and there you both will die. 27You will never come back to the land you long to return to."

28Is this man Jehoiachin a despised, broken pot,
  an object no one wants?
Why will he and his children be hurled out,
  cast into a land they do not know?
29O land, land, land,
  hear the word of the LORD!
30This is what the LORD says:
"Record this man as if childless,
  a man who will not prosper in his lifetime,
for none of his offspring will prosper,
  none will sit on the throne of David
  or rule anymore in Judah."

The Righteous Branch

23 "WOE TO the shepherds who are destroying and scattering the sheep of my pasture!" declares the LORD. 2Therefore this is what the LORD, the God of Israel, says to the shepherds who tend my people: "Because you have scattered my flock and driven them away and have not bestowed care on them, I will bestow punishment on you for the evil you have done," declares the LORD. 3"I myself will gather the remnant of my flock out of all the countries where I have driven them and will bring them back to their pasture, where they will be fruitful and increase in number. 4I will place shepherds

---

a 23 That is, the palace in Jerusalem (see 1 Kings 7:2)   b 24 Hebrew *Coniah,* a variant of *Jehoiachin;* also in verse 28   c 25 Or *Chaldeans*

Living Bible

18Therefore this is God's decree of punishment against King Jehoiakim, who succeeded his father Josiah on the throne: His family will not weep for him when he dies. His subjects will not even care that he is dead. 19He shall be buried like a dead donkey—dragged out of Jerusalem and thrown on the garbage dump beyond the gate! 20Weep, for your allies are gone. Search for them in Lebanon; shout for them at Bashan; seek them at the fording points of Jordan. See, they are all destroyed. Not one is left to help you! 21When you were prosperous I warned you, but you replied, "Don't bother me." Since childhood you have been that way—you just won't listen! 22And now all your allies have disappeared with a puff of wind; all your friends are taken off as slaves. Surely at last you will see your wickedness and be ashamed. 23It's very nice to live graciously in a beautiful palace among the cedars of Lebanon, but soon you will cry and groan in anguish—anguish as of a woman in labor.

24, 25And as for you, Coniah,d son of Jehoiakim king of Judah—even if you were the signet ring on my right hand, I would pull you off and give you to those who seek to kill you, of whom you are so desperately afraid—to Nebuchadnezzar, king of Babylon, and his mighty army. 26I will throw you and your mother out of this country, and you shall die in a foreign land. 27You will never again return to the land of your desire. 28This man Coniah is like a discarded, broken dish. He and his children will be exiled to distant lands.

29O earth, earth, earth! Hear the word of the Lord! 30The Lord says:

Record this man Coniah as childless, for none of his children shall ever sit upon the throne of David or rule in Judah.e His life will amount to nothing.

23 THE LORD declares:
I will send disaster upon the leaders of my people—the shepherds of my sheep—for they have destroyed and scattered the very ones they were to care for. 2Instead of leading my flock to safety, you have deserted them and driven them to destruction. And now I will pour out judgment upon you for the evil you have done to them. 3And I will gather together the remnant of my flock from wherever I have sent them, and bring them back into their own fold, and they shall be fruitful and increase. 4And I will appoint responsible shepherds to

---

d 22:24, 25 Coniah. Coniah is an abbreviation—perhaps a disparaging nickname for Jeconiah and Jehoiachin, his other names. His name means, "The Lord will establish my throne!" e 22:30 none of his children shall ever sit upon the throne of David or rule in Judah. This man Coniah's grandson, Zerubbabel, was briefly governor, but not king.

New Revised Standard

18 Therefore thus says the LORD concerning King Jehoiakim son of Josiah of Judah:
They shall not lament for him, saying,
"Alas, my brother!" or "Alas, sister!"
They shall not lament for him, saying,
"Alas, lord!" or "Alas, his majesty!"
19 With the burial of a donkey he shall be
buried—
dragged off and thrown out beyond the
gates of Jerusalem.

20 Go up to Lebanon, and cry out,
and lift up your voice in Bashan;
cry out from Abarim,
for all your lovers are crushed.
21 I spoke to you in your prosperity,
but you said, "I will not listen."
This has been your way from your youth,
for you have not obeyed my voice.
22 The wind shall shepherd all your shepherds,
and your lovers shall go into captivity;
then you will be ashamed and dismayed
because of all your wickedness.
23 O inhabitant of Lebanon,
nested among the cedars,
how you will groanf when pangs come upon
you,
pain as of a woman in labor!

Judgment on Coniah (Jehoiachin)

24 As I live, says the LORD, even if King Coniah son of Jehoiakim of Judah were the signet ring on my right hand, even from there I would tear you off 25and give you into the hands of those who seek your life, into the hands of those of whom you are afraid, even into the hands of King Nebuchadrezzar of Babylon and into the hands of the Chaldeans. 26I will hurl you and the mother who bore you into another country, where you were not born, and there you shall die. 27But they shall not return to the land to which they long to return.
28 Is this man Coniah a despised broken pot,
a vessel no one wants?
Why are he and his offspring hurled out
and cast away in a land that they do not
know?
29 O land, land, land,
hear the word of the LORD!
30 Thus says the LORD:
Record this man as childless,
a man who shall not succeed in his days;
for none of his offspring shall succeed
in sitting on the throne of David,
and ruling again in Judah.

Restoration after Exile

23 WOE TO the shepherds who destroy and scatter the sheep of my pasture! says the LORD. 2Therefore thus says the LORD, the God of Israel, concerning the shepherds who shepherd my people: It is you who have scattered my flock, and have driven them away, and you have not attended to them. So I will attend to you for your evil doings, says the LORD. 3Then I myself will gather the remnant of my flock out of all the lands where I have driven them, and I will bring them back to their fold, and they shall be fruitful and multiply. 4I will raise up shepherds over them who will

---

f Gk Vg Syr: Heb will be pitied

King James

4And I will set up shepherds over them which shall feed them: and they shall fear no more, nor be dismayed, neither shall they be lacking, saith the LORD.

5¶ Behold, the days come, saith the LORD, that I will raise unto David a righteous Branch, and a King shall reign and prosper, and shall execute judgment and justice in the earth.

6In his days Judah shall be saved, and Israel shall dwell safely: and this *is* his name whereby he shall be called, THE LORD OUR RIGHTEOUSNESS.

7Therefore, behold, the days come, saith the LORD, that they shall no more say, The LORD liveth, which brought up the children of Israel out of the land of Egypt;

8But, The LORD liveth, which brought up and which led the seed of the house of Israel out of the north country, and from all countries whither I had driven them; and they shall dwell in their own land.

9¶ Mine heart within me is broken because of the prophets; all my bones shake; I am like a drunken man, and like a man whom wine hath overcome, because of the LORD, and because of the words of his holiness.

10For the land is full of adulterers; for because of swearing the land mourneth; the pleasant places of the wilderness are dried up, and their course is evil, and their force *is* not right.

11For both prophet and priest are profane; yea, in my house have I found their wickedness, saith the LORD.

12Wherefore their way shall be unto them as slippery *ways* in the darkness: they shall be driven on, and fall therein: for I will bring evil upon them, *even* the year of their visitation, saith the LORD.

13And I have seen folly in the prophets of Samaria; they prophesied in Baal, and caused my people Israel to err.

14I have seen also in the prophets of Jerusalem an horrible thing: they commit adultery, and walk in lies: they strengthen also the hands of evildoers, that none doth return from his wickedness: they are all of them unto me as Sodom, and the inhabitants thereof as Gomorrah.

15Therefore thus saith the LORD of hosts concerning the prophets; Behold, I will feed them with wormwood, and make them drink the water of gall: for from the prophets of Jerusalem is profaneness gone forth into all the land.

16Thus saith the LORD of hosts, Hearken not unto the words of the prophets that prophesy unto you: they make you vain: they speak a vision of their own heart, *and* not out of the mouth of the LORD.

New International

over them who will tend them, and they will no longer be afraid or terrified, nor will any be missing," declares the LORD.

5"The days are coming," declares the LORD,
  "when I will raise up to David[a] a righteous
    Branch,
a King who will reign wisely
  and do what is just and right in the land.
6In his days Judah will be saved
  and Israel will live in safety.
This is the name by which he will be called:
  The LORD Our Righteousness.

7"So then, the days are coming," declares the LORD, "when people will no longer say, 'As surely as the LORD lives, who brought the Israelites up out of Egypt,' 8but they will say, 'As surely as the LORD lives, who brought the descendants of Israel up out of the land of the north and out of all the countries where he had banished them.' Then they will live in their own land."

Lying Prophets

9Concerning the prophets:

My heart is broken within me;
  all my bones tremble.
I am like a drunken man,
  like a man overcome by wine,
because of the LORD
  and his holy words.
10The land is full of adulterers;
  because of the curse[b] the land lies parched[c]
  and the pastures in the desert are withered.
The ‚prophets‚ follow an evil course
  and use their power unjustly.

11"Both prophet and priest are godless;
  even in my temple I find their wickedness,"
                  declares the LORD.
12"Therefore their path will become slippery;
  they will be banished to darkness
  and there they will fall.
I will bring disaster on them
  in the year they are punished,"
                  declares the LORD.

13"Among the prophets of Samaria
  I saw this repulsive thing:
They prophesied by Baal
  and led my people Israel astray.
14And among the prophets of Jerusalem
  I have seen something horrible:
They commit adultery and live a lie.
  They strengthen the hands of evildoers,
  so that no one turns from his wickedness.
They are all like Sodom to me;
  the people of Jerusalem are like Gomorrah."

15Therefore, this is what the LORD Almighty says concerning the prophets:

"I will make them eat bitter food
  and drink poisoned water,
because from the prophets of Jerusalem
  ungodliness has spread throughout the land."

16This is what the LORD Almighty says:

"Do not listen to what the prophets are
    prophesying to you;
  they fill you with false hopes.
They speak visions from their own minds,
  not from the mouth of the LORD.

a 5 Or *up from David's line*   b 10 Or *because of these things*   c 10 Or *land mourns*

Living Bible

care for them, and they shall not need to be afraid again; all of them shall be accounted for continually.

5, 6For the time is coming, says the Lord, when I will place a righteous Branch upon King David's throne. He shall be a King who shall rule with wisdom and justice and cause righteousness to prevail everywhere throughout the earth.d And this is his name: *The Lord Our Righteousness.* At that time Judah will be saved and Israel will live in peace.

7In that day people will no longer say when taking an oath, "As the Lord lives who rescued the people of Israel from the land of Egypt," 8but they will say, "As the Lord lives who brought the Jews back to their own land of Israel from the countries to which he had exiled them."

9My heart is broken for the false prophets, full of deceit. I awake with fear and stagger as a drunkard does from wine, because of the awful fate awaiting them,e for God has decreed holy words of judgment against them. 10For the land is full of adultery and the curse of God is on it. The land itself is mourning—the pastures are dried up—for the prophets do evil and their power is used wrongly. 11And the priests are like the prophets, all ungodly, wicked men. I have seen their despicable acts right here in my own Temple, says the Lord. 12Therefore their paths will be dark and slippery; they will be chased down dark and treacherous trails, and fall. For I will bring evil upon them and see to it, when their time has come, that they pay their penalty in full for all their sins.

13I knew the prophets of Samaria were unbelievably evil, for they prophesied by Baal and led my people Israel into sin; 14but the prophets of Jerusalem are even worse! The things they do are horrible; they commit adultery and love dishonesty. They encourage and compliment those who are doing evil, instead of turning them back from their sins. These prophets are as thoroughly depraved as the men of Sodom and Gomorrah were.

15Therefore the Lord Almighty says: I will feed them with bitterness and give them poison to drink. For it is because of them that wickedness fills this land. 16This is my warning to my people, says the Lord Almighty. Don't listen to these false prophets when they prophesy to you, filling you with futile hopes. They are making up everything they say. They do not speak for me!

New Revised Standard

shepherd them, and they shall not fear any longer, or be dismayed, nor shall any be missing, says the LORD.

The Righteous Branch of David

5 The days are surely coming, says the LORD, when I will raise up for David a righteous Branch, and he shall reign as king and deal wisely, and shall execute justice and righteousness in the land. 6In his days Judah shall be saved and Israel will live in safety. And this is the name by which he will be called: "The LORD is our righteousness."

7 Therefore, the days are surely coming, says the LORD, when it shall no longer be said, "As the LORD lives who brought the people of Israel up out of the land of Egypt," 8but "As the LORD lives who brought out and led the offspring of the house of Israel out of the land of the north and out of all the lands where hef had driven them." Then they shall live in their own land.

False Prophets of Hope Denounced

9 Concerning the prophets:
My heart is crushed within me,
    all my bones shake;
I have become like a drunkard,
    like one overcome by wine,
because of the LORD
    and because of his holy words.
10 For the land is full of adulterers;
    because of the curse the land mourns,
    and the pastures of the wilderness are dried up.
Their course has been evil,
    and their might is not right.
11 Both prophet and priest are ungodly;
    even in my house I have found their wickedness,
                                    says the LORD.
12 Therefore their way shall be to them
    like slippery paths in the darkness,
    into which they shall be driven and fall;
for I will bring disaster upon them
    in the year of their punishment,
                                    says the LORD.
13 In the prophets of Samaria
    I saw a disgusting thing:
they prophesied by Baal
    and led my people Israel astray.
14 But in the prophets of Jerusalem
    I have seen a more shocking thing:
they commit adultery and walk in lies;
    they strengthen the hands of evildoers,
    so that no one turns from wickedness;
all of them have become like Sodom to me,
    and its inhabitants like Gomorrah.
15 Therefore thus says the LORD of hosts
                                    concerning the prophets:
"I am going to make them eat wormwood,
    and give them poisoned water to drink;
for from the prophets of Jerusalem
    ungodliness has spread throughout the land."

16 Thus says the LORD of hosts: Do not listen to the words of the prophets who prophesy to you; they are deluding you. They speak visions of their own minds, not from the mouth of the LORD. 17They keep saying to

---

d 23:5, 6 *throughout the earth,* or, "throughout the land."   e 23:9 *because of the awful fate awaiting them,* implied.

f Gk: Heb *I*

King James

17They say still unto them that despise me, The LORD hath said, Ye shall have peace; and they say unto every one that walketh after the imagination of his own heart, No evil shall come upon you.

18For who hath stood in the counsel of the LORD, and hath perceived and heard his word? who hath marked his word, and heard *it*?

19Behold, a whirlwind of the LORD is gone forth in fury, even a grievous whirlwind: it shall fall grievously upon the head of the wicked.

20The anger of the LORD shall not return, until he have executed, and till he have performed the thoughts of his heart: in the latter days ye shall consider it perfectly.

21I have not sent these prophets, yet they ran: I have not spoken to them, yet they prophesied.

22But if they had stood in my counsel, and had caused my people to hear my words, then they should have turned them from their evil way, and from the evil of their doings.

23*Am* I a God at hand, saith the LORD, and not a God afar off ?

24Can any hide himself in secret places that I shall not see him? saith the LORD. Do not I fill heaven and earth? saith the LORD.

25I have heard what the prophets said, that prophesy lies in my name, saying, I have dreamed, I have dreamed.

26How long shall *this* be in the heart of the prophets that prophesy lies? yea, *they are* prophets of the deceit of their own heart;

27Which think to cause my people to forget my name by their dreams which they tell every man to his neighbour, as their fathers have forgotten my name for Baal.

28The prophet that hath a dream, let him tell a dream; and he that hath my word, let him speak my word faithfully. What *is* the chaff to the wheat? saith the LORD.

29*Is* not my word like as a fire? saith the LORD; and like a hammer *that* breaketh the rock in pieces?

30Therefore, behold, I *am* against the prophets, saith the LORD, that steal my words every one from his neighbour.

31Behold, I *am* against the prophets, saith the LORD, that use their tongues, and say, He saith.

32Behold, I *am* against them that prophesy false dreams, saith the LORD, and do tell them, and cause my people to err by their lies, and by their lightness; yet I sent them not, nor commanded them: therefore they shall not profit this people at all, saith the LORD.

33¶ And when this people, or the prophet, or a priest, shall ask thee, saying, What *is* the burden of the LORD? thou shalt then say unto them, What burden? I will even forsake you, saith the LORD.

34And *as for* the prophet, and the priest, and the people, that shall say, The burden of the LORD, I will even punish that man and his house.

35Thus shall ye say every one to his neighbour, and every one to his brother, What hath the LORD answered? and, What hath the LORD spoken?

New International

17They keep saying to those who despise me,
  'The LORD says: You will have peace.'
And to all who follow the stubbornness of their
      hearts
  they say, 'No harm will come to you.'
18But which of them has stood in the council of
      the LORD
  to see or to hear his word?
  Who has listened and heard his word?
19See, the storm of the LORD
  will burst out in wrath,
a whirlwind swirling down
  on the heads of the wicked.
20The anger of the LORD will not turn back
  until he fully accomplishes
  the purposes of his heart.
In days to come
  you will understand it clearly.
21I did not send these prophets,
  yet they have run with their message;
I did not speak to them,
  yet they have prophesied.
22But if they had stood in my council,
  they would have proclaimed my words to my
      people
and would have turned them from their evil
      ways
  and from their evil deeds.
23"Am I only a God nearby,"

                        declares the LORD,
  "and not a God far away?
24Can anyone hide in secret places
  so that I cannot see him?"

                        declares the LORD.
  "Do not I fill heaven and earth?"

                        declares the LORD.

25"I have heard what the prophets say who prophesy lies in my name. They say, 'I had a dream! I had a dream!' 26How long will this continue in the hearts of these lying prophets, who prophesy the delusions of their own minds? 27They think the dreams they tell one another will make my people forget my name, just as their fathers forgot my name through Baal worship. 28Let the prophet who has a dream tell his dream, but let the one who has my word speak it faithfully. For what has straw to do with grain?" declares the LORD. 29"Is not my word like fire," declares the LORD, "and like a hammer that breaks a rock in pieces?

30"Therefore," declares the LORD, "I am against the prophets who steal from one another words supposedly from me. 31Yes," declares the LORD, "I am against the prophets who wag their own tongues and yet declare, 'The LORD declares.' 32Indeed, I am against those who prophesy false dreams," declares the LORD. "They tell them and lead my people astray with their reckless lies, yet I did not send or appoint them. They do not benefit these people in the least," declares the LORD.

False Oracles and False Prophets

33"When these people, or a prophet or a priest, ask you, 'What is the oraclea of the LORD?' say to them, 'What oracle?b I will forsake you, declares the LORD.' 34If a prophet or a priest or anyone else claims, 'This is the oracle of the LORD,' I will punish that man and his household. 35This is what each of you keeps on saying to his friend or relative: 'What is the LORD's answer?' or 'What has the LORD spoken?' 36But you must not

---

a *33* Or *burden* (see Septuagint and Vulgate)   b *33* Hebrew; Septuagint and Vulgate *'You are the burden.* (The Hebrew for *oracle* and *burden* is the same.)

Living Bible

17They keep saying to these rebels who despise me. "Don't worry! All is well"; and to those who live the way they want to, "The Lord has said you shall have peace!"

18But can you name even one of these prophets who lives close enough to God to hear what he is saying? Has even one of them cared enough to listen? 19See, the Lord is sending a furious whirlwind to sweep away these wicked men. 20The terrible anger of the Lord will not abate until it has carried out the full penalty he decrees against them. Later, when Jerusalem has fallen,c you will see what I mean.

21I have not sent these prophets, yet they claim to speak for me; I gave them no message, yet they say their words are mine. 22If they were mine, they would try to turn my people from their evil ways. 23Am I a God who is only in one place and cannot see what they are doing? 24Can anyone hide from me? Am I not everywhere in all of heaven and earth?

25"Listen to the dream I had from God last night," they say. And then they proceed to lie in my name. 26How long will this continue? If they are "prophets," they are prophets of deceit, inventing everything they say. 27By telling these false dreams they are trying to get my people to forget me in the same way as their fathers did, who turned away to the idols of Baal. 28Let these false prophets tell their dreams and let my true messengers faithfully proclaim my every word. There is a difference between chaff and wheat! 29Does not my word burn like fire? asks the Lord. Is it not like a mighty hammer that smashed the rock to pieces? 30, 31So I stand against these "prophets" who get their messages from each other—these smooth-tongued prophets who say, "This message is from God!" 32Their made-up dreams are flagrant lies that lead my people into sin. I did not send them and they have no message at all for my people, says the Lord.

33When one of the people or one of their "prophets" or priests asks you, "Well, Jeremiah, what is the sad news from the Lord today?" you shall reply, "What sad news? You are the sad news, for the Lord has cast you away!" 34And as for the false prophets and priests and people who joke about "today's sad news from God," I will punish them and their families for saying this. 35You can ask each other, "What is God's message? What is he saying?" 36But stop using this term, "God's

New Revised Standard

those who despise the word of the LORD, "It shall be well with you"; and to all who stubbornly follow their own stubborn hearts, they say, "No calamity shall come upon you."

18 For who has stood in the council of the LORD
       so as to see and to hear his word?
     Who has given heed to his word so as to
         proclaim it?
19 Look, the storm of the LORD!
       Wrath has gone forth,
     a whirling tempest;
       it will burst upon the head of the wicked.
20 The anger of the LORD will not turn back
       until he has executed and accomplished
       the intents of his mind.
     In the latter days you will understand it
         clearly.

21 I did not send the prophets,
       yet they ran;
     I did not speak to them,
       yet they prophesied.
22 But if they had stood in my council,
       then they would have proclaimed my words
         to my people,
     and they would have turned them from their
         evil way,
     and from the evil of their doings.

23 Am I a God near by, says the LORD, and not a God far off? 24Who can hide in secret places so that I cannot see them? says the LORD. Do I not fill heaven and earth? says the LORD. 25I have heard what the prophets have said who prophesy lies in my name, saying, "I have dreamed, I have dreamed!" 26How long? Will the hearts of the prophets ever turn back—those who prophesy lies, and who prophesy the deceit of their own heart? 27They plan to make my people forget my name by their dreams that they tell one another, just as their ancestors forgot my name for Baal. 28Let the prophet who has a dream tell the dream, but let the one who has my word speak my word faithfully. What has straw in common with wheat? says the LORD. 29Is not my word like fire, says the LORD, and like a hammer that breaks a rock in pieces? 30See, therefore, I am against the prophets, says the LORD, who steal my words from one another. 31See, I am against the prophets, says the LORD, who use their own tongues and say, "Says the LORD." 32See, I am against those who prophesy lying dreams, says the LORD, and who tell them, and who lead my people astray by their lies and their recklessness, when I did not send them or appoint them; so they do not profit this people at all, says the LORD.

33 When this people, or a prophet, or a priest asks you, "What is the burden of the LORD?" you shall say to them, "You are the burden,d and I will cast you off, says the LORD." 34And as for the prophet, priest, or the people who say, "The burden of the LORD," I will punish them and their households. 35Thus shall you say to one another, among yourselves, "What has the LORD answered?" or "What has the LORD spoken?" 36But "the

---

c 23:20 *Later, when Jerusalem has fallen*, literally, "in the latter days."   d Gk Vg: Heb *What burden*

King James

36And the burden of the LORD shall ye mention no more: for every man's word shall be his burden; for ye have perverted the words of the living God, of the LORD of hosts our God.

37Thus shalt thou say to the prophet, What hath the LORD answered thee? and, What hath the LORD spoken?

38But since ye say, The burden of the LORD; therefore thus saith the LORD; Because ye say this word, The burden of the LORD, and I have sent unto you, saying, Ye shall not say, The burden of the LORD;

39Therefore, behold, I, even I, will utterly forget you, and I will forsake you, and the city that I gave you and your fathers, *and cast you* out of my presence:

40And I will bring an everlasting reproach upon you, and a perpetual shame, which shall not be forgotten.

24 THE LORD showed me, and, behold, two baskets of figs *were* set before the temple of the LORD, after that Nebuchadrezzar king of Babylon had carried away captive Jeconiah the son of Jehoiakim king of Judah, and the princes of Judah, with the carpenters and smiths, from Jerusalem, and had brought them to Babylon.

2One basket *had* very good figs, *even* like the figs *that are* first ripe: and the other basket *had* very naughty figs, which could not be eaten, they were so bad.

3Then said the LORD unto me, What seest thou, Jeremiah? And I said, Figs; the good figs, very good; and the evil, very evil, that cannot be eaten, they are so evil.

4¶ Again the word of the LORD came unto me, saying,

5Thus saith the LORD, the God of Israel; Like these good figs, so will I acknowledge them that are carried away captive of Judah, whom I have sent out of this place into the land of the Chaldeans for *their* good.

6For I will set mine eyes upon them for good, and I will bring them again to this land: and I will build them, and not pull *them* down; and I will plant them, and not pluck *them* up.

7And I will give them an heart to know me, that I *am* the LORD: and they shall be my people, and I will be their God: for they shall return unto me with their whole heart.

8¶ And as the evil figs, which cannot be eaten, they are so evil; surely thus saith the LORD, So will I give Zedekiah the king of Judah, and his princes, and the residue of Jerusalem, that remain in this land, and them that dwell in the land of Egypt:

9And I will deliver them to be removed into all the kingdoms of the earth for *their* hurt, *to be* a reproach and a proverb, a taunt and a curse, in all places whither I shall drive them.

10And I will send the sword, the famine, and the pestilence, among them, till they be consumed from off the land that I gave unto them and to their fathers.

25 THE WORD that came to Jeremiah concerning all the people of Judah in the fourth year of Jehoiakim the son of Josiah king of Judah, that *was* the first year of Nebuchadrezzar king of Babylon;

New International

mention 'the oracle of the LORD' again, because every man's own word becomes his oracle and so you distort the words of the living God, the LORD Almighty, our God. 37This is what you keep saying to a prophet: 'What is the LORD's answer to you?' or 'What has the LORD spoken?' 38Although you claim, 'This is the oracle of the LORD,' this is what the LORD says: You used the words, 'This is the oracle of the LORD,' even though I told you that you must not claim, 'This is the oracle of the LORD.' 39Therefore, I will surely forget you and cast you out of my presence along with the city I gave to you and your fathers. 40I will bring upon you everlasting disgrace— everlasting shame that will not be forgotten."

Two Baskets of Figs

24 AFTER JEHOIACHIN[a] son of Jehoiakim king of Judah and the officials, the craftsmen and the artisans of Judah were carried into exile from Jerusalem to Babylon by Nebuchadnezzar king of Babylon, the LORD showed me two baskets of figs placed in front of the temple of the LORD. 2One basket had very good figs, like those that ripen early; the other basket had very poor figs, so bad they could not be eaten.

3Then the LORD asked me, "What do you see, Jeremiah?"

"Figs," I answered. "The good ones are very good, but the poor ones are so bad they cannot be eaten."

4Then the word of the LORD came to me: 5"This is what the LORD, the God of Israel, says: 'Like these good figs, I regard as good the exiles from Judah, whom I sent away from this place to the land of the Babylonians.[b] 6My eyes will watch over them for their good, and I will bring them back to this land. I will build them up and not tear them down; I will plant them and not uproot them. 7I will give them a heart to know me, that I am the LORD. They will be my people, and I will be their God, for they will return to me with all their heart.

8"'But like the poor figs, which are so bad they cannot be eaten,' says the LORD, 'so will I deal with Zedekiah king of Judah, his officials and the survivors from Jerusalem, whether they remain in this land or live in Egypt. 9I will make them abhorrent and an offense to all the kingdoms of the earth, a reproach and a byword, an object of ridicule and cursing, wherever I banish them. 10I will send the sword, famine and plague against them until they are destroyed from the land I gave to them and their fathers.' "

Seventy Years of Captivity

25 THE WORD came to Jeremiah concerning all the people of Judah in the fourth year of Jehoiakim son of Josiah king of Judah, which was the first year of Nebuchadnezzar king of Babylon. 2So Jeremiah the

a *1* Hebrew *Jeconiah,* a variant of *Jehoiachin*   b *5* Or *Chaldeans*

Living Bible

sad news." For what is sad is you and your lying. You are twisting my words and inventing "messages from God" that I didn't speak. 37You may respectfully ask Jeremiah, "What is the Lord's message? What has he said to you?" 38, 39But if you ask him about "today's sad news from God," when I have warned you not to mock like that, then I, the Lord God, will unburden myself of the burdenc you are to me. I will cast you out of my presence, you and this city I gave to you and your fathers. 40And I will bring reproach upon you and your name shall be infamous through the ages.

24 AFTER NEBUCHADNEZZAR, king of Babylon, had captured and enslaved Jeconiah (son of Jehoiakim), king of Judah, and exiled him to Babylon along with the princes of Judah and the skilled tradesmen—the carpenters and blacksmiths—the Lord gave me this vision. 2I saw two baskets of figs placed in front of the Temple in Jerusalem. In one basket there were fresh, just-ripened figs, but in the other the figs were spoiled and moldy—too rotten to eat. 3Then the Lord said to me, "What do you see, Jeremiah?"

I replied, "Figs, some very good and some very bad."

4, 5Then the Lord said: "The good figs represent the exiles sent to Babylon. I have done it for their good. 6I will see that they are well treated and I will bring them back here again. I will help them and not hurt them; I will plant them and not pull them up. 7I will give them hearts that respond to me. They shall be my people and I will be their God, for they shall return to me with great joy.

8"But the rotten figs represent Zedekiah, king of Judah, his officials and all the others of Jerusalem left here in this land; those too who live in Egypt. I will treat them like spoiled figs, too bad to use. 9I will make them repulsive to every nation of the earth, and they shall be mocked and taunted and cursed wherever I compel them to go. 10And I will send massacre and famine and disease among them until they are destroyed from the land of Israel, which I gave to them and to their fathers."

25 THIS MESSAGE for all the people of Judah came from the Lord to Jeremiah during the fourth year of the reign of King Jehoiakim of Judah (son of Josiah). This was the year Nebuchadnezzar, king of Babylon, began his reign.

New Revised Standard

burden of the LORD" you shall mention no more, for the burden is everyone's own word, and so you pervert the words of the living God, the LORD of hosts, our God. 37Thus you shall ask the prophet, "What has the LORD answered you?" or "What has the LORD spoken?" 38But if you say, "the burden of the LORD," thus says the LORD: Because you have said these words, "the burden of the LORD," when I sent to you, saying, You shall not say, "the burden of the LORD," 39therefore, I will surely lift you upd and cast you away from my presence, you and the city that I gave to you and your ancestors. 40And I will bring upon you everlasting disgrace and perpetual shame, which shall not be forgotten.

The Good and the Bad Figs

24 THE LORD showed me two baskets of figs placed before the temple of the LORD. This was after King Nebuchadrezzar of Babylon had taken into exile from Jerusalem King Jeconiah son of Jehoiakim of Judah, together with the officials of Judah, the artisans, and the smiths, and had brought them to Babylon. 2One basket had very good figs, like first-ripe figs, but the other basket had very bad figs, so bad that they could not be eaten. 3And the LORD said to me, "What do you see, Jeremiah?" I said, "Figs, the good figs very good, and the bad figs very bad, so bad that they cannot be eaten."

4 Then the word of the LORD came to me: 5Thus says the LORD, the God of Israel: Like these good figs, so I will regard as good the exiles from Judah, whom I have sent away from this place to the land of the Chaldeans. 6I will set my eyes upon them for good, and I will bring them back to this land. I will build them up, and not tear them down; I will plant them, and not pluck them up. 7I will give them a heart to know that I am the LORD; and they shall be my people and I will be their God, for they shall return to me with their whole heart.

8 But thus says the LORD: Like the bad figs that are so bad they cannot be eaten, so will I treat King Zedekiah of Judah, his officials, the remnant of Jerusalem who remain in this land, and those who live in the land of Egypt. 9I will make them a horror, an evil thing, to all the kingdoms of the earth—a disgrace, a byword, a taunt, and a curse in all the places where I shall drive them. 10And I will send sword, famine, and pestilence upon them, until they are utterly destroyed from the land that I gave to them and their ancestors.

The Babylonian Captivity Foretold

25 THE WORD that came to Jeremiah concerning all the people of Judah, in the fourth year of King Jehoiakim son of Josiah of Judah (that was the first year of King Nebuchadrezzar of Babylon), 2which the

---

c 23:38, 39 will unburden myself of the burden, literally, either, "the burden of the Lord," or, "the message of the Lord." This is a Hebrew pun.

d Heb Mss Gk Vg: MT forget you

King James

2The which Jeremiah the prophet spake unto all the people of Judah, and to all the inhabitants of Jerusalem, saying,

3From the thirteenth year of Josiah the son of Amon king of Judah, even unto this day, that is the three and twentieth year, the word of the LORD hath come unto me, and I have spoken unto you, rising early and speaking; but ye have not hearkened.

4And the LORD hath sent unto you all his servants the prophets, rising early and sending them; but ye have not hearkened, nor inclined your ear to hear.

5They said, Turn ye again now every one from his evil way, and from the evil of your doings, and dwell in the land that the LORD hath given unto you and to your fathers for ever and ever:

6And go not after other gods to serve them, and to worship them, and provoke me not to anger with the works of your hands; and I will do you no hurt.

7Yet ye have not hearkened unto me, saith the LORD; that ye might provoke me to anger with the works of your hands to your own hurt.

8¶ Therefore thus saith the LORD of hosts; Because ye have not heard my words,

9Behold, I will send and take all the families of the north, saith the LORD, and Nebuchadrezzar the king of Babylon, my servant, and will bring them against this land, and against the inhabitants thereof, and against all these nations round about, and will utterly destroy them, and make them an astonishment, and an hissing, and perpetual desolations.

10Moreover I will take from them the voice of mirth, and the voice of gladness, the voice of the bridegroom, and the voice of the bride, the sound of the millstones, and the light of the candle.

11And this whole land shall be a desolation, and an astonishment; and these nations shall serve the king of Babylon seventy years.

12¶ And it shall come to pass, when seventy years are accomplished, that I will punish the king of Babylon, and that nation, saith the LORD, for their iniquity, and the land of the Chaldeans, and will make it perpetual desolations.

13And I will bring upon that land all my words which I have pronounced against it, even all that is written in this book, which Jeremiah hath prophesied against all the nations.

14For many nations and great kings shall serve themselves of them also: and I will recompense them according to their deeds, and according to the works of their own hands.

15¶ For thus saith the LORD God of Israel unto me; Take the wine cup of this fury at my hand, and cause all the nations, to whom I send thee, to drink it.

16And they shall drink, and be moved, and be mad, because of the sword that I will send among them.

17Then took I the cup at the LORD's hand, and made all the nations to drink, unto whom the LORD had sent me:

18To wit, Jerusalem, and the cities of Judah, and the kings thereof, and the princes thereof, to make them a desolation, an astonishment, an hissing, and a curse; as it is this day;

19Pharaoh king of Egypt, and his servants, and his princes, and all his people;

20And all the mingled people, and all the kings of the land of Uz, and all the kings of the land of the Philistines, and Ashkelon, and Azzah, and Ekron, and the remnant of Ashdod,

21Edom, and Moab, and the children of Ammon,

22And all the kings of Tyrus, and all the kings of Zidon, and the kings of the isles which are beyond the sea,

23Dedan, and Tema, and Buz, and all that are in the utmost corners,

New International

prophet said to all the people of Judah and to all those living in Jerusalem: 3For twenty-three years—from the thirteenth year of Josiah son of Amon king of Judah until this very day—the word of the LORD has come to me and I have spoken to you again and again, but you have not listened.

4And though the LORD has sent all his servants the prophets to you again and again, you have not listened or paid any attention. 5They said, "Turn now, each of you, from your evil ways and your evil practices, and you can stay in the land the LORD gave to you and your fathers for ever and ever. 6Do not follow other gods to serve and worship them; do not provoke me to anger with what your hands have made. Then I will not harm you."

7"But you did not listen to me," declares the LORD, "and you have provoked me with what your hands have made, and you have brought harm to yourselves."

8Therefore the LORD Almighty says this: "Because you have not listened to my words, 9I will summon all the peoples of the north and my servant Nebuchadnezzar king of Babylon," declares the LORD, "and I will bring them against this land and its inhabitants and against all the surrounding nations. I will completely destroy[a] them and make them an object of horror and scorn, and an everlasting ruin. 10I will banish from them the sounds of joy and gladness, the voices of bride and bridegroom, the sound of millstones and the light of the lamp. 11This whole country will become a desolate wasteland, and these nations will serve the king of Babylon seventy years.

12"But when the seventy years are fulfilled, I will punish the king of Babylon and his nation, the land of the Babylonians,[b] for their guilt," declares the LORD, "and will make it desolate forever. 13I will bring upon that land all the things I have spoken against it, all that are written in this book and prophesied by Jeremiah against all the nations. 14They themselves will be enslaved by many nations and great kings; I will repay them according to their deeds and the work of their hands."

The Cup of God's Wrath

15This is what the LORD, the God of Israel, said to me: "Take from my hand this cup filled with the wine of my wrath and make all the nations to whom I send you drink it. 16When they drink it, they will stagger and go mad because of the sword I will send among them."

17So I took the cup from the LORD's hand and made all the nations to whom he sent me drink it: 18Jerusalem and the towns of Judah, its kings and officials, to make them a ruin and an object of horror and scorn and cursing, as they are today; 19Pharaoh king of Egypt, his attendants, his officials and all his people, 20and all the foreign people there; all the kings of Uz; all the kings of the Philistines (those of Ashkelon, Gaza, Ekron, and the people left at Ashdod); 21Edom, Moab and Ammon; 22all the kings of Tyre and Sidon; the kings of the coastlands across the sea; 23Dedan, Tema, Buz and all who are in distant places[c]; 24all the kings of Arabia and all

---

a 9 The Hebrew term refers to the irrevocable giving over of things or persons to the LORD, often by totally destroying them.   b 12 Or Chaldeans   c 23 Or who clip the hair by their foreheads

Living Bible

2, 3For the past twenty-three years, Jeremiah said, from the thirteenth year of the reign of Josiah (son of Amon) king of Judah, until now, God has been sending me his messages. I have faithfully passed them on to you, but you haven't listened. 4Again and again down through the years, God has sent you his prophets, but you have refused to hear. 5Each time the message was this: Turn from the evil road you are traveling and from the evil things you are doing. Only then can you continue to live here in this land which the Lord gave to you and to your ancestors forever. 6*Don't anger me by worshiping idols; but if you are true to me, then I'll not harm you.* 7But you won't listen; you have gone ahead and made me furious with your idols. So you have brought upon yourselves all the evil that has come your way.

8, 9And now the Lord God says, Because you have not listened to me, I will gather together all the armies of the north under Nebuchadnezzar, king of Babylon (I have appointed him as my deputy), and I will bring them all against this land and its people and against the other nations near you, and I will utterly destroy you and make you a byword of contempt forever. 10I will take away your joy, your gladness and your wedding feasts; your businesses shall fail and all your homes shall lie in silent darkness. 11This entire land shall become a desolate wasteland; all the world will be shocked at the disaster that befalls you. Israel and her neighboring lands shall serve the king of Babylon for seventy years.

12Then, after these yearsd of slavery are ended, I will punish the king of Babylone and his people for their sins; I will make the land of Chaldea an everlasting waste. 13I will bring upon them all the terrors I have promised in this book—all the penalties announced by Jeremiah against the nations. 14For many nations and great kings shall enslave the Chaldeans, just as they enslaved my people; I will punish them in proportion to their treatment of my people.

15For the Lord God said to me: "Take from my hand this wine cup filled to the brim with my fury, and make all the nations to whom I send you drink from it. 16They shall drink from it and reel, crazed by the death blows I rain upon them."

17So I took the cup of fury from the Lord and made all the nations drink from it—every nation God had sent me to; 18I went to Jerusalem and to the cities of Judah, and their kings and princes drank of the cup so that from that day until this they have been desolate, hated and cursed, just as they are today. 19, 20I went to Egypt, and Pharaoh and his servants, the princes and the people— they too drank from that terrible cup, along with all the foreign population living in his land. So did all the kings of the land of Uz and the kings of the Philistine cities: Ashkelon, Gaza, Ekron, and what remains of Ashdod, 21and I visited the nations of Edom, Moab and Ammon; 22and all the kings of Tyre and Sidon, and the kings of the regions across the sea; 23Dedan and Tema and Buz, and the other heathen there; 24and all the kings of Arabia

New Revised Standard

prophet Jeremiah spoke to all the people of Judah and all the inhabitants of Jerusalem: 3For twenty-three years, from the thirteenth year of King Josiah son of Amon of Judah, to this day, the word of the LORD has come to me, and I have spoken persistently to you, but you have not listened. 4And though the LORD persistently sent you all his servants the prophets, you have neither listened nor inclined your ears to hear 5when they said, "Turn now, everyone of you, from your evil way and wicked doings, and you will remain upon the land that the LORD has given to you and your ancestors from of old and forever; 6do not go after other gods to serve and worship them, and do not provoke me to anger with the work of your hands. Then I will do you no harm." 7Yet you did not listen to me, says the LORD, and so you have provoked me to anger with the work of your hands to your own harm.

8 Therefore thus says the LORD of hosts: Because you have not obeyed my words, 9I am going to send for all the tribes of the north, says the LORD, even for King Nebuchadrezzar of Babylon, my servant, and I will bring them against this land and its inhabitants, and against all these nations around; I will utterly destroy them, and make them an object of horror and of hissing, and an everlasting disgrace.f 10And I will banish from them the sound of mirth and the sound of gladness, the voice of the bridegroom and the voice of the bride, the sound of the millstones and the light of the lamp. 11This whole land shall become a ruin and a waste, and these nations shall serve the king of Babylon seventy years. 12Then after seventy years are completed, I will punish the king of Babylon and that nation, the land of the Chaldeans, for their iniquity, says the LORD, making the land an everlasting waste. 13I will bring upon that land all the words that I have uttered against it, everything written in this book, which Jeremiah prophesied against all the nations. 14For many nations and great kings shall make slaves of them also; and I will repay them according to their deeds and the work of their hands.

The Cup of God's Wrath

15 For thus the LORD, the God of Israel, said to me: Take from my hand this cup of the wine of wrath, and make all the nations to whom I send you drink it. 16They shall drink and stagger and go out of their minds because of the sword that I am sending among them.

17 So I took the cup from the LORD's hand, and made all the nations to whom the LORD sent me drink it: 18Jerusalem and the towns of Judah, its kings and officials, to make them a desolation and a waste, an object of hissing and of cursing, as they are today; 19Pharaoh king of Egypt, his servants, his officials, and all his people; 20all the mixed people;g all the kings of the land of Uz; all the kings of the land of the Philistines—Ashkelon, Gaza, Ekron, and the remnant of Ashdod; 21Edom, Moab, and the Ammonites; 22all the kings of Tyre, all the kings of Sidon, and the kings of the coastland across the sea; 23Dedan, Tema, Buz, and all who have shaven temples; 24all the kings of

---

d *25:12 after these years,* literally, "the seventy years." e *25:12 I will punish the king of Babylon.* This event is further described in Daniel 5. The troops of Cyrus the Great entered Babylon in 539 B.C. and killed Belshazzar, the last Babylonian ruler.

f Gk Compare Syr: Heb *and everlasting desolations* g Meaning of Heb uncertain

King James

24And all the kings of Arabia, and all the kings of the mingled people that dwell in the desert,

25And all the kings of Zimri, and all the kings of Elam, and all the kings of the Medes,

26And all the kings of the north, far and near, one with another, and all the kingdoms of the world, which *are* upon the face of the earth: and the king of Sheshach shall drink after them.

27Therefore thou shalt say unto them, Thus saith the LORD of hosts, the God of Israel; Drink ye, and be drunken, and spew, and fall, and rise no more, because of the sword which I will send among you.

28And it shall be, if they refuse to take the cup at thine hand to drink, then shalt thou say unto them, Thus saith the LORD of hosts; Ye shall certainly drink.

29For, lo, I begin to bring evil on the city which is called by my name, and should ye be utterly unpunished? Ye shall not be unpunished: for I will call for a sword upon all the inhabitants of the earth, saith the LORD of hosts.

30Therefore prophesy thou against them all these words, and say unto them, The LORD shall roar from on high, and utter his voice from his holy habitation; he shall mightily roar upon his habitation; he shall give a shout, as they that tread *the grapes,* against all the inhabitants of the earth.

31A noise shall come *even* to the ends of the earth; for the LORD hath a controversy with the nations, he will plead with all flesh; he will give them *that are* wicked to the sword, saith the LORD.

32Thus saith the LORD of hosts, Behold, evil shall go forth from nation to nation, and a great whirlwind shall be raised up from the coasts of the earth.

33And the slain of the LORD shall be at that day from *one* end of the earth even unto the *other* end of the earth: they shall not be lamented, neither gathered, nor buried; they shall be dung upon the ground.

34¶ Howl, ye shepherds, and cry; and wallow yourselves *in the ashes,* ye principal of the flock: for the days of your slaughter and of your dispersions are accomplished; and ye shall fall like a pleasant vessel.

35And the shepherds shall have no way to flee, nor the principal of the flock to escape.

36A voice of the cry of the shepherds, and an howling of the principal of the flock, *shall be heard:* for the LORD hath spoiled their pasture.

37And the peaceable habitations are cut down because of the fierce anger of the LORD.

38He hath forsaken his covert, as the lion: for their land is desolate because of the fierceness of the oppressor, and because of his fierce anger.

New International

the kings of the foreign people who live in the desert; 25all the kings of Zimri, Elam and Media; 26and all the kings of the north, near and far, one after the other—all the kingdoms on the face of the earth. And after all of them, the king of Sheshach[a] will drink it too.

27"Then tell them, 'This is what the LORD Almighty, the God of Israel, says: Drink, get drunk and vomit, and fall to rise no more because of the sword I will send among you.' 28But if they refuse to take the cup from your hand and drink, tell them, 'This is what the LORD Almighty says: You must drink it! 29See, I am beginning to bring disaster on the city that bears my Name, and will you indeed go unpunished? You will not go unpunished, for I am calling down a sword upon all who live on the earth, declares the LORD Almighty.'

30"Now prophesy all these words against them and say to them:

" 'The LORD will roar from on high;
   he will thunder from his holy dwelling
   and roar mightily against his land.
He will shout like those who tread the grapes,
   shout against all who live on the earth.
31The tumult will resound to the ends of the
      earth,
   for the LORD will bring charges against the
      nations;
he will bring judgment on all mankind
   and put the wicked to the sword,' "
                              declares the LORD.

32This is what the LORD Almighty says:

"Look! Disaster is spreading
   from nation to nation;
a mighty storm is rising
   from the ends of the earth."

33At that time those slain by the LORD will be everywhere—from one end of the earth to the other. They will not be mourned or gathered up or buried, but will be like refuse lying on the ground.

34Weep and wail, you shepherds;
   roll in the dust, you leaders of the flock.
For your time to be slaughtered has come;
   you will fall and be shattered like fine
      pottery.
35The shepherds will have nowhere to flee,
   the leaders of the flock no place to escape.
36Hear the cry of the shepherds,
   the wailing of the leaders of the flock,
   for the LORD is destroying their pasture.
37The peaceful meadows will be laid waste
   because of the fierce anger of the LORD.
38Like a lion he will leave his lair,
   and their land will become desolate
because of the sword[b] of the oppressor
   and because of the LORD's fierce anger.

26 IN THE beginning of the reign of Jehoiakim the son of Josiah king of Judah came this word from the LORD, saying,

2Thus saith the LORD; Stand in the court of the LORD's house, and speak unto all the cities of Judah, which come to worship in the LORD's house, all the words that I command thee to speak unto them; diminish not a word:

Jeremiah Threatened With Death

26 EARLY IN the reign of Jehoiakim son of Josiah king of Judah, this word came from the LORD: 2"This is what the LORD says: Stand in the courtyard of the LORD's house and speak to all the people of the towns of Judah who come to worship in the house of the LORD. Tell them everything I command you; do not omit a word. 3Perhaps they will listen and each will turn from

---

a 26 *Sheshach* is a cryptogram for Babylon. b 38 Some Hebrew manuscripts and Septuagint (see also Jer. 46:16 and 50:16); most Hebrew manuscripts *anger*

Living Bible

and of the nomadic tribes of the desert; 25and all the kings of Zimri, Elam and Media; 26and all the kings of the northern countries, far and near, one after the other; and all the kingdoms of the world. And finally, the king of Babylon himself drank from this cup of God's wrath. 27Tell them, "The Lord of heaven's armies, the God of Israel, says, Drink from this cup of my wrath until you are drunk and vomit and fall and rise no more, for I am sending terrible wars upon you." 28And if they refuse to accept the cup, tell them, "The Lord of heaven's armies says you *must* drink it! You cannot escape! 29I have begun to punish my own people, so should you go free? No, you shall not evade punishment. I will call for war against all the peoples of the earth."

30Therefore prophesy against them. Tell them the Lord will shout against his own from his holy temple in heaven, and against all those living on the earth. He will shout as the harvesters do who tread the juice from the grapes. 31That cry of judgment will reach the farthest ends of the earth, for the Lord has a case against all the nations—all mankind. He will slaughter all the wicked. 32See, declares the Lord Almighty, the punishment shall go from nation to nation—a great whirlwind of wrath shall rise against the farthest corners of the earth. 33On that day those the Lord has slain shall fill the earth from one end to the other. No one shall mourn for them nor gather up the bodies to bury them; they shall fertilize the earth.

34Weep and moan, O evil shepherds; let the leaders of mankind beat their heads upon the stones, for their time has come to be slaughtered and scattered; they shall fall like fragile women. 35And you will find no place to hide, no way to escape.

36Listen to the frantic cries of the shepherds and to the leaders shouting in despair, for the Lord has spoiled their pastures. 37People now living undisturbed will be cut down by the fierceness of the anger of the Lord. 38He has left his lair like a lion seeking prey; their land has been laid waste by warring armies—because of the fierce anger of the Lord.

26 THIS MESSAGE came to Jeremiah from the Lord during the first year of the reign of Jehoiakim (son of Josiah), king of Judah:

2Stand out in front of the Temple of the Lord and make an announcement to all the people who have come there to worship from many parts of Judah. Give them the entire message; don't leave out one word of all I have for them to hear. 3For perhaps they will listen and turn

New Revised Standard

Arabia and all the kings of the mixed peoples[c] that live in the desert; 25 all the kings of Zimri, all the kings of Elam, and all the kings of Media; 26 all the kings of the north, far and near, one after another, and all the kingdoms of the world that are on the face of the earth. And after them the king of Sheshach[d] shall drink.

27 Then you shall say to them, Thus says the Lord of hosts, the God of Israel: Drink, get drunk and vomit, fall and rise no more, because of the sword that I am sending among you.

28 And if they refuse to accept the cup from your hand to drink, then you shall say to them: Thus says the Lord of hosts: You must drink! 29 See, I am beginning to bring disaster on the city that is called by my name, and how can you possibly avoid punishment? You shall not go unpunished, for I am summoning a sword against all the inhabitants of the earth, says the Lord of hosts.

30 You, therefore, shall prophesy against them all these words, and say to them:

The Lord will roar from on high,
    and from his holy habitation utter his voice;
he will roar mightily against his fold,
    and shout, like those who tread grapes,
    against all the inhabitants of the earth.
31 The clamor will resound to the ends of the earth,
    for the Lord has an indictment against the nations;
he is entering into judgment with all flesh,
    and the guilty he will put to the sword,
                               says the Lord.

32 Thus says the Lord of hosts:
    See, disaster is spreading
        from nation to nation,
    and a great tempest is stirring
        from the farthest parts of the earth!
33 Those slain by the Lord on that day shall extend from one end of the earth to the other. They shall not be lamented, or gathered, or buried; they shall become dung on the surface of the ground.
34 Wail, you shepherds, and cry out;
    roll in ashes, you lords of the flock,
    for the days of your slaughter have
        come—and your dispersions,[c]
    and you shall fall like a choice vessel.
35 Flight shall fail the shepherds,
    and there shall be no escape for the lords of the flock.
36 Hark! the cry of the shepherds,
    and the wail of the lords of the flock!
    For the Lord is despoiling their pasture,
37 and the peaceful folds are devastated,
        because of the fierce anger of the Lord.
38 Like a lion he has left his covert;
    for their land has become a waste
because of the cruel sword,
    and because of his fierce anger.

Jeremiah's Prophecies in the Temple

26 AT THE beginning of the reign of King Jehoiakim son of Josiah of Judah, this word came from the Lord: 2Thus says the Lord: Stand in the court of the Lord's house, and speak to all the cities of Judah that come to worship in the house of the Lord; speak to them all the words that I command you; do not hold back a word. 3It may be that they will listen, all of them, and

---

[c] Meaning of Heb uncertain   [d] *Sheshach* is a cryptogram for *Babel*, Babylon

King James

³If so be they will hearken, and turn every man from his evil way, that I may repent me of the evil, which I purpose to do unto them because of the evil of their doings.

⁴And thou shalt say unto them, Thus saith the LORD; If ye will not hearken to me, to walk in my law, which I have set before you,

⁵To hearken to the words of my servants the prophets, whom I sent unto you, both rising up early, and sending *them,* but ye have not hearkened;

⁶Then will I make this house like Shiloh, and will make this city a curse to all the nations of the earth.

⁷So the priests and the prophets and all the people heard Jeremiah speaking these words in the house of the LORD.

⁸¶ Now it came to pass, when Jeremiah had made an end of speaking all that the LORD had commanded *him* to speak unto all the people, that the priests and the prophets and all the people took him, saying, Thou shalt surely die.

⁹Why hast thou prophesied in the name of the LORD, saying, This house shall be like Shiloh, and this city shall be desolate without an inhabitant? And all the people were gathered against Jeremiah in the house of the LORD.

¹⁰¶ When the princes of Judah heard these things, then they came up from the king's house unto the house of the LORD, and sat down in the entry of the new gate of the LORD's *house.*

¹¹Then spake the priests and the prophets unto the princes and to all the people, saying, This man *is* worthy to die; for he hath prophesied against this city, as ye have heard with your ears.

¹²¶ Then spake Jeremiah unto all the princes and to all the people, saying, The LORD sent me to prophesy against this house and against this city all the words that ye have heard.

¹³Therefore now amend your ways and your doings, and obey the voice of the LORD your God; and the LORD will repent him of the evil that he hath pronounced against you.

¹⁴As for me, behold, I *am* in your hand: do with me as seemeth good and meet unto you.

¹⁵But know ye for certain, that if ye put me to death, ye shall surely bring innocent blood upon yourselves, and upon this city, and upon the inhabitants thereof: for of a truth the LORD hath sent me unto you to speak all these words in your ears.

¹⁶¶ Then said the princes and all the people unto the priests and to the prophets; This man *is* not worthy to die: for he hath spoken to us in the name of the LORD our God.

¹⁷Then rose up certain of the elders of the land, and spake to all the assembly of the people, saying,

¹⁸Micah the Morasthite prophesied in the days of Hezekiah king of Judah, and spake to all the people of Judah, saying, Thus saith the LORD of hosts; Zion shall be plowed *like* a field, and Jerusalem shall become heaps, and the mountain of the house as the high places of a forest.

¹⁹Did Hezekiah king of Judah and all Judah put him at all to death? did he not fear the LORD, and besought the LORD, and the LORD repented him of the evil which he had pronounced against them? Thus might we procure great evil against our souls.

²⁰And there was also a man that prophesied in the name of the LORD, Urijah the son of Shemaiah of Kirjath-jearim, who prophesied against this city and against this land according to all the words of Jeremiah:

²¹And when Jehoiakim the king, with all his mighty men, and all the princes, heard his words, the king sought to put him to death: but when Urijah heard it, he was afraid, and fled, and went into Egypt;

New International

his evil way. Then I will relent and not bring on them the disaster I was planning because of the evil they have done. ⁴Say to them, 'This is what the LORD says: If you do not listen to me and follow my law, which I have set before you, ⁵and if you do not listen to the words of my servants the prophets, whom I have sent to you again and again (though you have not listened), ⁶then I will make this house like Shiloh and this city an object of cursing among all the nations of the earth.' "

⁷The priests, the prophets and all the people heard Jeremiah speak these words in the house of the LORD. ⁸But as soon as Jeremiah finished telling all the people everything the LORD had commanded him to say, the priests, the prophets and all the people seized him and said, "You must die! ⁹Why do you prophesy in the LORD's name that this house will be like Shiloh and this city will be desolate and deserted?" And all the people crowded around Jeremiah in the house of the LORD.

¹⁰When the officials of Judah heard about these things, they went up from the royal palace to the house of the LORD and took their places at the entrance of the New Gate of the LORD's house. ¹¹Then the priests and the prophets said to the officials and all the people, "This man should be sentenced to death because he has prophesied against this city. You have heard it with your own ears!"

¹²Then Jeremiah said to all the officials and all the people: "The LORD sent me to prophesy against this house and this city all the things you have heard. ¹³Now reform your ways and your actions and obey the LORD your God. Then the LORD will relent and not bring the disaster he has pronounced against you. ¹⁴As for me, I am in your hands; do with me whatever you think is good and right. ¹⁵Be assured, however, that if you put me to death, you will bring the guilt of innocent blood on yourselves and on this city and on those who live in it, for in truth the LORD has sent me to you to speak all these words in your hearing."

¹⁶Then the officials and all the people said to the priests and the prophets, "This man should not be sentenced to death! He has spoken to us in the name of the LORD our God."

¹⁷Some of the elders of the land stepped forward and said to the entire assembly of people, ¹⁸"Micah of Moresheth prophesied in the days of Hezekiah king of Judah. He told all the people of Judah, 'This is what the LORD Almighty says:

" 'Zion will be plowed like a field,
    Jerusalem will become a heap of rubble,
    the temple hill a mound overgrown with
        thickets.'ᵃ

¹⁹"Did Hezekiah king of Judah or anyone else in Judah put him to death? Did not Hezekiah fear the LORD and seek his favor? And did not the LORD relent, so that he did not bring the disaster he pronounced against them? We are about to bring a terrible disaster on ourselves!"

²⁰(Now Uriah son of Shemaiah from Kiriath Jearim was another man who prophesied in the name of the LORD; he prophesied the same things against this city and this land as Jeremiah did. ²¹When King Jehoiakim and all his officers and officials heard his words, the king sought to put him to death. But Uriah heard of it and fled in fear to Egypt. ²²King Jehoiakim, however,

---

ᵃ *18* Micah 3:12

Living Bible

from their evil ways, and then I can withhold all the punishment I am ready to pour out upon them because of their evil deeds. 4Tell them the Lord says: If you will not listen to me and obey the laws I have given you, 5and if you will not listen to my servants, the prophets—for I sent them again and again to warn you, but you would not listen to them— 6then I will destroy this Temple as I destroyed the Tabernacle at Shiloh, and I will make Jerusalem a curse word in every nation of the earth.

7, 8When Jeremiah had finished his message, saying everything the Lord had told him to, the priests and false prophets and all the people in the Temple mobbed him, shouting, "Kill him! Kill him! 9What right do you have to say the Lord will destroy this Temple like the one at Shiloh?" they yelled. "What do you mean—Jerusalem destroyed and not one survivor?"

10When the high officials of Judah heard what was going on, they rushed over from the palace and sat down at the door of the Temple to hold court. 11Then the priests and the false prophets presented their accusations to the officials and the people. "This man should die!" they said. "You have heard with your own ears what a traitor he is, for he has prophesied against this city."

12Then Jeremiah spoke in his defense. "The Lord sent me," he said, "to prophesy against this Temple and this city. He gave me every word of all that I have spoken. 13But if you stop your sinning and begin obeying the Lord your God, he will cancel all the punishment he has announced against you. 14As for me, I am helpless and in your power—do with me as you think best. 15But there is one thing sure, if you kill me, you will be killing an innocent man and the responsibility will lie upon you and upon this city and upon every person living in it; for it is absolutely true that the Lord sent me to speak every word that you have heard from me."

16Then the officials and people said to the priests and false prophets, "This man does not deserve the death sentence, for he has spoken to us in the name of the Lord our God."

17Then some of the wise old men stood and spoke to all the people standing around and said:

18"The decision is right; for back in the days when Micah the Morasthite prophesied in the days of King Hezekiah of Judah, he told the people that God said: 'This hill shall be plowed like an open field and this city of Jerusalem razed into heaps of stone, and a forest shall grow at the top where the great Temple now stands!' 19But did King Hezekiah and the people kill him for saying this? No, they turned from their wickedness and worshiped the Lord and begged the Lord to have mercy upon them; and the Lord held back the terrible punishment he had pronounced against them. If we kill Jeremiah for giving us the messages of God, who knows what God will do to us!"

20Another true prophet of the Lord, Uriah (son of Shemaiah) from Kiriathjearim, was also denouncing the city and the nation at the same time as Jeremiah was. 21But when King Jehoiakim and the army officers and officials heard what he was saying, the king sent to kill him. Uriah heard about it and fled to Egypt. 22Then King

New Revised Standard

will turn from their evil way, that I may change my mind about the disaster that I intend to bring on them because of their evil doings. 4You shall say to them: Thus says the LORD: If you will not listen to me, to walk in my law that I have set before you, 5and to heed the words of my servants the prophets whom I send to you urgently—though you have not heeded— 6then I will make this house like Shiloh, and I will make this city a curse for all the nations of the earth.

7 The priests and the prophets and all the people heard Jeremiah speaking these words in the house of the LORD. 8And when Jeremiah had finished speaking all that the LORD had commanded him to speak to all the people, then the priests and the prophets and all the people laid hold of him, saying, "You shall die! 9Why have you prophesied in the name of the LORD, saying, 'This house shall be like Shiloh, and this city shall be desolate, without inhabitant'?" And all the people gathered around Jeremiah in the house of the LORD.

10 When the officials of Judah heard these things, they came up from the king's house to the house of the LORD and took their seat in the entry of the New Gate of the house of the LORD. 11Then the priests and the prophets said to the officials and to all the people, "This man deserves the sentence of death because he has prophesied against this city, as you have heard with your own ears."

12 Then Jeremiah spoke to all the officials and all the people, saying, "It is the LORD who sent me to prophesy against this house and this city all the words you have heard. 13Now therefore amend your ways and your doings, and obey the voice of the LORD your God, and the LORD will change his mind about the disaster that he has pronounced against you. 14But as for me, here I am in your hands. Do with me as seems good and right to you. 15Only know for certain that if you put me to death, you will be bringing innocent blood upon yourselves and upon this city and its inhabitants, for in truth the LORD sent me to you to speak all these words in your ears."

16 Then the officials and all the people said to the priests and the prophets, "This man does not deserve the sentence of death, for he has spoken to us in the name of the LORD our God." 17And some of the elders of the land arose and said to all the assembled people, 18"Micah of Moresheth, who prophesied during the days of King Hezekiah of Judah, said to all the people of Judah: 'Thus says the LORD of hosts,

Zion shall be plowed as a field;
  Jerusalem shall become a heap of ruins,
  and the mountain of the house a wooded
    height.'

19Did King Hezekiah of Judah and all Judah actually put him to death? Did he not fear the LORD and entreat the favor of the LORD, and did not the LORD change his mind about the disaster that he had pronounced against them? But we are about to bring great disaster on ourselves!"

20 There was another man prophesying in the name of the LORD, Uriah son of Shemaiah from Kiriathjearim. He prophesied against this city and against this land in words exactly like those of Jeremiah. 21And when King Jehoiakim, with all his warriors and all the officials, heard his words, the king sought to put him to death; but when Uriah heard of it, he was afraid and fled and escaped to Egypt. 22Then King Jehoiakim sent[b]

King James

22And Jehoiakim the king sent men into Egypt, *namely*, Elnathan the son of Achbor, and *certain* men with him into Egypt.

23And they fetched forth Urijah out of Egypt, and brought him unto Jehoiakim the king; who slew him with the sword, and cast his dead body into the graves of the common people.

24Nevertheless the hand of Ahikam the son of Shaphan was with Jeremiah, that they should not give him into the hand of the people to put him to death.

27 IN THE beginning of the reign of Jehoiakim the son of Josiah king of Judah came this word unto Jeremiah from the LORD, saying,

2Thus saith the LORD to me; Make thee bonds and yokes, and put them upon thy neck,

3And send them to the king of Edom, and to the king of Moab, and to the king of the Ammonites, and to the king of Tyrus, and to the king of Zidon, by the hand of the messengers which come to Jerusalem unto Zedekiah king of Judah;

4And command them to say unto their masters, Thus saith the LORD of hosts, the God of Israel; Thus shall ye say unto your masters;

5I have made the earth, the man and the beast that *are* upon the ground, by my great power and by my outstretched arm, and have given it unto whom it seemed meet unto me.

6And now have I given all these lands into the hand of Nebuchadnezzar the king of Babylon, my servant; and the beasts of the field have I given him also to serve him.

7And all nations shall serve him, and his son, and his son's son, until the very time of his land come: and then many nations and great kings shall serve themselves of him.

8And it shall come to pass, *that* the nation and kingdom which will not serve the same Nebuchadnezzar the king of Babylon, and that will not put their neck under the yoke of the king of Babylon, that nation will I punish, saith the LORD, with the sword, and with the famine, and with the pestilence, until I have consumed them by his hand.

9Therefore hearken not ye to your prophets, nor to your diviners, nor to your dreamers, nor to your enchanters, nor to your sorcerers, which speak unto you, saying, Ye shall not serve the king of Babylon:

10For they prophesy a lie unto you, to remove you far from your land; and that I should drive you out, and ye should perish.

11But the nations that bring their neck under the yoke of the king of Babylon, and serve him, those will I let remain still in their own land, saith the LORD; and they shall till it, and dwell therein.

12¶ I spake also to Zedekiah king of Judah according to all these words, saying, Bring your necks under the yoke of the king of Babylon, and serve him and his people, and live.

13Why will ye die, thou and thy people, by the sword, by the famine, and by the pestilence, as the LORD hath spoken against the nation that will not serve the king of Babylon?

14Therefore hearken not unto the words of the prophets that speak unto you, saying, Ye shall not serve the king of Babylon: for they prophesy a lie unto you.

15For I have not sent them, saith the LORD, yet they prophesy a lie in my name; that I might drive you out, and that ye might perish, ye, and the prophets that prophesy unto you.

New International

sent Elnathan son of Acbor to Egypt, along with some other men. 23They brought Uriah out of Egypt and took him to King Jehoiakim, who had him struck down with a sword and his body thrown into the burial place of the common people.)

24Furthermore, Ahikam son of Shaphan supported Jeremiah, and so he was not handed over to the people to be put to death.

Judah to Serve Nebuchadnezzar

27 EARLY IN the reign of Zedekiah[a] son of Josiah king of Judah, this word came to Jeremiah from the LORD: 2This is what the LORD said to me: "Make a yoke out of straps and crossbars and put it on your neck. 3Then send word to the kings of Edom, Moab, Ammon, Tyre and Sidon through the envoys who have come to Jerusalem to Zedekiah king of Judah. 4Give them a message for their masters and say, 'This is what the LORD Almighty, the God of Israel, says: "Tell this to your masters: 5With my great power and outstretched arm I made the earth and its people and the animals that are on it, and I give it to anyone I please. 6Now I will hand all your countries over to my servant Nebuchadnezzar king of Babylon; I will make even the wild animals subject to him. 7All nations will serve him and his son and his grandson until the time for his land comes; then many nations and great kings will subjugate him.

8" ' "If, however, any nation or kingdom will not serve Nebuchadnezzar king of Babylon or bow its neck under his yoke, I will punish that nation with the sword, famine and plague, declares the LORD, until I destroy it by his hand. 9So do not listen to your prophets, your diviners, your interpreters of dreams, your mediums or your sorcerers who tell you, 'You will not serve the king of Babylon.' 10They prophesy lies to you that will only serve to remove you far from your lands; I will banish you and you will perish. 11But if any nation will bow its neck under the yoke of the king of Babylon and serve him, I will let that nation remain in its own land to till it and to live there, declares the LORD." ' "

12I gave the same message to Zedekiah king of Judah. I said, "Bow your neck under the yoke of the king of Babylon; serve him and his people, and you will live. 13Why will you and your people die by the sword, famine and plague with which the LORD has threatened any nation that will not serve the king of Babylon? 14Do not listen to the words of the prophets who say to you, 'You will not serve the king of Babylon,' for they are prophesying lies to you. 15'I have not sent them,' declares the LORD. 'They are prophesying lies in my name. Therefore, I will banish you and you will perish, both you and the prophets who prophesy to you.' "

a 1 A few Hebrew manuscripts and Syriac (see also Jer. 27:3, 12 and 28:1); most Hebrew manuscripts *Jehoiakim* (Most Septuagint manuscripts do not have this verse.)

Living Bible

Jehoiakim sent Elnathan (son of Achbor) to Egypt along with several other men to capture Uriah. 23They took him prisoner and brought him back to King Jehoiakim, who butchered him with a sword and had him buried in an unmarked grave.

24But Ahikam (son of Shaphan), the royal secretary,b stood with Jeremiah and persuaded the court not to turn him over to the mob to kill him.

27 THIS MESSAGE came to Jeremiah from the Lord at the beginning of the reign of Jehoiakimc (son of Josiah), king of Judah:

2Make a yoke and fasten it on your neck with leather thongs as you would strap a yoke on a plow-ox. 3Then send messages to the kings of Edom, Moab, Ammon, Tyre and Sidon, through their ambassadors in Jerusalem, 4saying, Tell your masters that the Lord, the God of Israel, sends you this message:

5"By my great power I have made the earth and all mankind and every animal; and I give these things of mine to anyone I want to. 6So now I have given all your countries to King Nebuchadnezzar of Babylon, who is my deputy. And I have handed over to him all your cattle for his use. 7All the nations shall serve him and his son and his grandson until his time is up, and then many nations and great kings shall conquer Babylon and make him their slave. 8Submit to him and serve him—put your neck under Babylon's yoke! I will punish any nation refusing to be his slave; I will send war, famine and disease upon that nation until he has conquered it.

9"Do not listen to your false prophets, fortune-tellers, dreamers, mediums and magicians who say the king of Babylon will not enslave you. 10For they are all liars, and if you follow their advice and refuse to submit to the king of Babylon, I will drive you out of your land and send you far away to perish. 11But the people of any nation submitting to the king of Babylon will be permitted to stay in their own country and farm the land as usual."

12Jeremiah repeated all these prophecies to Zedekiah, king of Judah. "If you want to live, submit to the king of Babylon," he said. 13"Why do you insist on dying—you and your people? Why should you choose war and famine and disease, which the Lord has promised to every nation that will not submit to Babylon's king? 14Don't listen to the false prophets who keep telling you the king of Babylon will not conquer you, for they are liars. 15I have not sent them, says the Lord, and they are telling you lies in my name. If you insist on heeding them, I must drive you from this land to die—you and all these 'prophets' too."

New Revised Standard

Elnathan son of Achbor and men with him to Egypt, 23and they took Uriah from Egypt and brought him to King Jehoiakim, who struck him down with the sword and threw his dead body into the burial place of the common people.

24 But the hand of Ahikam son of Shaphan was with Jeremiah so that he was not given over into the hands of the people to be put to death.

The Sign of the Yoke

27 IN THE beginning of the reign of King Zedekiahd son of Josiah of Judah, this word came to Jeremiah from the LORD. 2Thus the LORD said to me: Make yourself a yoke of straps and bars, and put them on your neck. 3Send worde to the king of Edom, the king of Moab, the king of the Ammonites, the king of Tyre, and the king of Sidon by the hand of the envoys who have come to Jerusalem to King Zedekiah of Judah. 4Give them this charge for their masters: Thus says the LORD of hosts, the God of Israel: This is what you shall say to your masters: 5It is I who by my great power and my outstretched arm have made the earth, with the people and animals that are on the earth, and I give it to whomever I please. 6Now I have given all these lands into the hand of King Nebuchadnezzar of Babylon, my servant, and I have given him even the wild animals of the field to serve him. 7All the nations shall serve him and his son and his grandson, until the time of his own land comes; then many nations and great kings shall make him their slave.

8 But if any nation or kingdom will not serve this king, Nebuchadnezzar of Babylon, and put its neck under the yoke of the king of Babylon, then I will punish that nation with the sword, with famine, and with pestilence, says the LORD, until I have completed itsf destruction by his hand. 9You, therefore, must not listen to your prophets, your diviners, your dreamers,g your soothsayers, or your sorcerers, who are saying to you, 'You shall not serve the king of Babylon.' 10For they are prophesying a lie to you, with the result that you will be removed far from your land; I will drive you out, and you will perish. 11But any nation that will bring its neck under the yoke of the king of Babylon and serve him, I will leave on its own land, says the LORD, to till it and live there.

12 I spoke to King Zedekiah of Judah in the same way: Bring your necks under the yoke of the king of Babylon, and serve him and his people, and live. 13Why should you and your people die by the sword, by famine, and by pestilence, as the LORD has spoken concerning any nation that will not serve the king of Babylon? 14Do not listen to the words of the prophets who are telling you not to serve the king of Babylon, for they are prophesying a lie to you. 15I have not sent them, says the LORD, but they are prophesying falsely in my name, with the result that I will drive you out and you will perish, you and the prophets who are prophesying to you.

---

b 26:24 the royal secretary, implied. See 2 Kgs 22:12.   c 27:1 reign of Jehoiakim. Some versions read "Zedekiah."

d Another reading is Jehoiakim   e Cn: Heb send them   f Heb their   g Gk Syr Vg: Heb dreams

King James

16Also I spake to the priests and to all this people, saying, Thus saith the LORD; Hearken not to the words of your prophets that prophesy unto you, saying, Behold, the vessels of the LORD's house shall now shortly be brought again from Babylon: for they prophesy a lie unto you.

17Hearken not unto them; serve the king of Babylon, and live: wherefore should this city be laid waste?

18But if they be prophets, and if the word of the LORD be with them, let them now make intercession to the LORD of hosts, that the vessels which are left in the house of the LORD, and in the house of the king of Judah, and at Jerusalem, go not to Babylon.

19¶ For thus saith the LORD of hosts concerning the pillars, and concerning the sea, and concerning the bases, and concerning the residue of the vessels that remain in this city,

20Which Nebuchadnezzar king of Babylon took not, when he carried away captive Jeconiah the son of Jehoiakim king of Judah from Jerusalem to Babylon, and all the nobles of Judah and Jerusalem;

21Yea, thus saith the LORD of hosts, the God of Israel, concerning the vessels that remain in the house of the LORD, and in the house of the king of Judah and of Jerusalem;

22They shall be carried to Babylon, and there shall they be until the day that I visit them, saith the LORD; then will I bring them up, and restore them to this place.

28 AND IT came to pass the same year, in the beginning of the reign of Zedekiah king of Judah, in the fourth year, and in the fifth month, that Hananiah the son of Azur the prophet, which was of Gibeon, spake unto me in the house of the LORD, in the presence of the priests and of all the people, saying,

2Thus speaketh the LORD of hosts, the God of Israel, saying, I have broken the yoke of the king of Babylon.

3Within two full years will I bring again into this place all the vessels of the LORD's house, that Nebuchadnezzar king of Babylon took away from this place, and carried them to Babylon:

4And I will bring again to this place Jeconiah the son of Jehoiakim king of Judah, with all the captives of Judah, that went into Babylon, saith the LORD: for I will break the yoke of the king of Babylon.

5¶ Then the prophet Jeremiah said unto the prophet Hananiah in the presence of the priests, and in the presence of all the people that stood in the house of the LORD,

6Even the prophet Jeremiah said, Amen: the LORD do so: the LORD perform thy words which thou hast prophesied, to bring again the vessels of the LORD's house, and all that is carried away captive, from Babylon into this place.

7Nevertheless hear thou now this word that I speak in thine ears, and in the ears of all the people;

8The prophets that have been before me and before thee of old prophesied both against many countries, and against great kingdoms, of war, and of evil, and of pestilence.

9The prophet which prophesieth of peace, when the word of the prophet shall come to pass, then shall the prophet be known, that the LORD hath truly sent him.

10¶ Then Hananiah the prophet took the yoke from off the prophet Jeremiah's neck, and brake it.

11And Hananiah spake in the presence of all the people, saying, Thus saith the LORD; Even so will I break the yoke of Nebuchadnezzar king of Babylon from the neck of all nations within the space of two full years. And the prophet Jeremiah went his way.

New International

16Then I said to the priests and all these people, "This is what the LORD says: Do not listen to the prophets who say, 'Very soon now the articles from the LORD's house will be brought back from Babylon.' They are prophesying lies to you. 17Do not listen to them. Serve the king of Babylon, and you will live. Why should this city become a ruin? 18If they are prophets and have the word of the LORD, let them plead with the LORD Almighty that the furnishings remaining in the house of the LORD and in the palace of the king of Judah and in Jerusalem not be taken to Babylon. 19For this is what the LORD Almighty says about the pillars, the Sea, the movable stands and the other furnishings that are left in this city, 20which Nebuchadnezzar king of Babylon did not take away when he carried Jehoiachin[a] son of Jehoiakim king of Judah into exile from Jerusalem to Babylon, along with all the nobles of Judah and Jerusalem— 21yes, this is what the LORD Almighty, the God of Israel, says about the things that are left in the house of the LORD and in the palace of the king of Judah and in Jerusalem: 22'They will be taken to Babylon and there they will remain until the day I come for them,' declares the LORD. 'Then I will bring them back and restore them to this place.'"

The False Prophet Hananiah

28 IN THE fifth month of that same year, the fourth year, early in the reign of Zedekiah king of Judah, the prophet Hananiah son of Azzur, who was from Gibeon, said to me in the house of the LORD in the presence of the priests and all the people: 2"This is what the LORD Almighty, the God of Israel, says: 'I will break the yoke of the king of Babylon. 3Within two years I will bring back to this place all the articles of the LORD's house that Nebuchadnezzar king of Babylon removed from here and took to Babylon. 4I will also bring back to this place Jehoiachin[a] son of Jehoiakim king of Judah and all the other exiles from Judah who went to Babylon,' declares the LORD, 'for I will break the yoke of the king of Babylon.'"

5Then the prophet Jeremiah replied to the prophet Hananiah before the priests and all the people who were standing in the house of the LORD. 6He said, "Amen! May the LORD do so! May the LORD fulfill the words you have prophesied by bringing the articles of the LORD's house and all the exiles back to this place from Babylon. 7Nevertheless, listen to what I have to say in your hearing and in the hearing of all the people: 8From early times the prophets who preceded you and me have prophesied war, disaster and plague against many countries and great kingdoms. 9But the prophet who prophesies peace will be recognized as one truly sent by the LORD only if his prediction comes true."

10Then the prophet Hananiah took the yoke off the neck of the prophet Jeremiah and broke it, 11and he said before all the people, "This is what the LORD says: 'In the same way will I break the yoke of Nebuchadnezzar king of Babylon off the neck of all the nations within two years.'" At this, the prophet Jeremiah went on his way.

Living Bible

16I spoke again and again to the priests and all the people and told them: "The Lord says, Don't listen to your prophets who are telling you that soon the gold dishes taken from the Temple will be returned from Babylon. It is all a lie. 17Don't listen to them. Surrender to the king of Babylon and live, for otherwise this whole city will be destroyed. 18If they are really God's prophets, then let them pray to the Lord Almighty that the gold dishes still here in the Temple, left from before; and that those in the palace of the king of Judah and in the palaces in Jerusalem will not be carried away with you to Babylon!

19, 20, 21"For the Lord Almighty says, The pillars of bronze standing before the Temple, and the great bronze basin in the Temple court, and the metal stands and all the other ceremonial articles left here by Nebuchadnezzar, king of Babylon, when he exiled all the important people of Judah and Jerusalem to Babylon, along with Jeconiah (son of Jehoiakim), king of Judah, 22will all yet be carried away to Babylon and will stay there until I send for them. Then I will bring them all back to Jerusalem again."

28 ON A December day in that same year—the fourth year of the reign of Zedekiah, king of Judah—Hananiah (son of Azzur), a false prophet from Gibeon, addressed me publicly in the Temple while all the priests and people listened. He said:

2"The Lord of Hosts, the God of Israel, declares: I have removed the yoke of the king of Babylon from your necks. 3Within two years I will bring back all the Temple treasures that Nebuchadnezzar carried off to Babylon, 4and I will bring back King Jeconiah,b son of Jehoiakim, king of Judah, and all the other captives exiled to Babylon, says the Lord. I will surely remove the yoke put on your necks by the king of Babylon."

5Then Jeremiah said to Hananiah, in front of all the priests and people, 6"Amen! May your prophecies come true! I hope the Lord will do everything you say and bring back from Babylon the treasures of this Temple, with all our loved ones. 7But listen now to the solemn words I speak to you in the presence of all these people. 8The ancient prophets who preceded you and me spoke against many nations, always warning of *war, famine* and *plague*. 9So a prophet who foretells *peace* has the burden of proof on him to prove that God has really sent him. Only when his message comes true can it be known that he really is from God."

10Then Hananiah, the false prophet, took the yoke off Jeremiah's neck and broke it. 11And Hananiah said again to the crowd that had gathered, "The Lord has promised that within two years he will release all the nations now in slavery to King Nebuchadnezzar of Babylon." At that point Jeremiah walked out.

New Revised Standard

16 Then I spoke to the priests and to all this people, saying, Thus says the LORD: Do not listen to the words of your prophets who are prophesying to you, saying, "The vessels of the LORD's house will soon be brought back from Babylon," for they are prophesying a lie to you. 17Do not listen to them; serve the king of Babylon and live. Why should this city become a desolation? 18If indeed they are prophets, and if the word of the LORD is with them, then let them intercede with the LORD of hosts, that the vessels left in the house of the LORD, in the house of the king of Judah, and in Jerusalem may not go to Babylon. 19For thus says the LORD of hosts concerning the pillars, the sea, the stands, and the rest of the vessels that are left in this city, 20which King Nebuchadnezzar of Babylon did not take away when he took into exile from Jerusalem to Babylon King Jeconiah son of Jehoiakim of Judah, and all the nobles of Judah and Jerusalem— 21thus says the LORD of hosts, the God of Israel, concerning the vessels left in the house of the LORD, in the house of the king of Judah, and in Jerusalem: 22They shall be carried to Babylon, and there they shall stay, until the day when I give attention to them, says the LORD. Then I will bring them up and restore them to this place.

Hananiah Opposes Jeremiah and Dies

28 IN THAT same year, at the beginning of the reign of King Zedekiah of Judah, in the fifth month of the fourth year, the prophet Hananiah son of Azzur, from Gibeon, spoke to me in the house of the LORD, in the presence of the priests and all the people, saying, 2"Thus says the LORD of hosts, the God of Israel: I have broken the yoke of the king of Babylon. 3Within two years I will bring back to this place all the vessels of the LORD's house, which King Nebuchadnezzar of Babylon took away from this place and carried to Babylon. 4I will also bring back to this place King Jeconiah son of Jehoiakim of Judah, and all the exiles from Judah who went to Babylon, says the LORD, for I will break the yoke of the king of Babylon."

5 Then the prophet Jeremiah spoke to the prophet Hananiah in the presence of the priests and all the people who were standing in the house of the LORD; 6and the prophet Jeremiah said, "Amen! May the LORD do so; may the LORD fulfill the words that you have prophesied, and bring back to this place from Babylon the vessels of the house of the LORD, and all the exiles. 7But listen now to this word that I speak in your hearing and in the hearing of all the people. 8The prophets who preceded you and me from ancient times prophesied war, famine, and pestilence against many countries and great kingdoms. 9As for the prophet who prophesies peace, when the word of that prophet comes true, then it will be known that the LORD has truly sent the prophet."

10 Then the prophet Hananiah took the yoke from the neck of the prophet Jeremiah, and broke it. 11And Hananiah spoke in the presence of all the people, saying, "Thus says the LORD: This is how I will break the yoke of King Nebuchadnezzar of Babylon from the neck of all the nations within two years." At this, the prophet Jeremiah went his way.

b 28:4 *Jeconiah,* or "Jehoiachin," as he is also called.

King James

12¶ Then the word of the LORD came unto Jeremiah *the prophet,* after that Hananiah the prophet had broken the yoke from off the neck of the prophet Jeremiah, saying,

13Go and tell Hananiah, saying, Thus saith the LORD; Thou hast broken the yokes of wood; but thou shalt make for them yokes of iron.

14For thus saith the LORD of hosts, the God of Israel; I have put a yoke of iron upon the neck of all these nations, that they may serve Nebuchadnezzar king of Babylon; and they shall serve him: and I have given him the beasts of the field also.

15¶ Then said the prophet Jeremiah unto Hananiah the prophet, Hear now, Hananiah; The LORD hath not sent thee; but thou makest this people to trust in a lie.

16Therefore thus saith the LORD; Behold, I will cast thee from off the face of the earth: this year thou shalt die, because thou hast taught rebellion against the LORD.

17So Hananiah the prophet died the same year in the seventh month.

29　NOW THESE *are* the words of the letter that Jeremiah the prophet sent from Jerusalem unto the residue of the elders which were carried away captives, and to the priests, and to the prophets, and to all the people whom Nebuchadnezzar had carried away captive from Jerusalem to Babylon;

2(After that Jeconiah the king, and the queen, and the eunuchs, the princes of Judah and Jerusalem, and the carpenters, and the smiths, were departed from Jerusalem;)

3By the hand of Elasah the son of Shaphan, and Gemariah the son of Hilkiah, (whom Zedekiah king of Judah sent unto Babylon to Nebuchadnezzar king of Babylon) saying,

4Thus saith the LORD of hosts, the God of Israel, unto all that are carried away captives, whom I have caused to be carried away from Jerusalem unto Babylon;

5Build ye houses, and dwell *in them;* and plant gardens, and eat the fruit of them;

6Take ye wives, and beget sons and daughters; and take wives for your sons, and give your daughters to husbands, that they may bear sons and daughters; that ye may be increased there, and not diminished.

7And seek the peace of the city whither I have caused you to be carried away captives, and pray unto the LORD for it: for in the peace thereof shall ye have peace.

8¶ For thus saith the LORD of hosts, the God of Israel; Let not your prophets and your diviners, that *be* in the midst of you, deceive you, neither hearken to your dreams which ye cause to be dreamed.

9For they prophesy falsely unto you in my name: I have not sent them, saith the LORD.

10¶ For thus saith the LORD, That after seventy years be accomplished at Babylon I will visit you, and perform my good word toward you, in causing you to return to this place.

11For I know the thoughts that I think toward you, saith the LORD, thoughts of peace, and not of evil, to give you an expected end.

12Then shall ye call upon me, and ye shall go and pray unto me, and I will hearken unto you.

13And ye shall seek me, and find *me,* when ye shall search for me with all your heart.

14And I will be found of you, saith the LORD: and I will turn away your captivity, and I will gather you from all the nations, and from all the places whither I have driven you, saith the LORD; and I will bring you again into the place whence I caused you to be carried away captive.

New International

12Shortly after the prophet Hananiah had broken the yoke off the neck of the prophet Jeremiah, the word of the LORD came to Jeremiah: 13"Go and tell Hananiah, 'This is what the LORD says: You have broken a wooden yoke, but in its place you will get a yoke of iron. 14This is what the LORD Almighty, the God of Israel, says: I will put an iron yoke on the necks of all these nations to make them serve Nebuchadnezzar king of Babylon, and they will serve him. I will even give him control over the wild animals.' "

15Then the prophet Jeremiah said to Hananiah the prophet, "Listen, Hananiah! The LORD has not sent you, yet you have persuaded this nation to trust in lies. 16Therefore, this is what the LORD says: 'I am about to remove you from the face of the earth. This very year you are going to die, because you have preached rebellion against the LORD.' "

17In the seventh month of that same year, Hananiah the prophet died.

A Letter to the Exiles

29　THIS IS the text of the letter that the prophet Jeremiah sent from Jerusalem to the surviving elders among the exiles and to the priests, the prophets and all the other people Nebuchadnezzar had carried into exile from Jerusalem to Babylon. 2(This was after King Jehoiachin[a] and the queen mother, the court officials and the leaders of Judah and Jerusalem, the craftsmen and the artisans had gone into exile from Jerusalem.) 3He entrusted the letter to Elasah son of Shaphan and to Gemariah son of Hilkiah, whom Zedekiah king of Judah sent to King Nebuchadnezzar in Babylon. It said:

4This is what the LORD Almighty, the God of Israel, says to all those I carried into exile from Jerusalem to Babylon: 5"Build houses and settle down; plant gardens and eat what they produce. 6Marry and have sons and daughters; find wives for your sons and give your daughters in marriage, so that they too may have sons and daughters. Increase in number there; do not decrease. 7Also, seek the peace and prosperity of the city to which I have carried you into exile. Pray to the LORD for it, because if it prospers, you too will prosper." 8Yes, this is what the LORD Almighty, the God of Israel, says: "Do not let the prophets and diviners among you deceive you. Do not listen to the dreams you encourage them to have. 9They are prophesying lies to you in my name. I have not sent them," declares the LORD.

10This is what the LORD says: "When seventy years are completed for Babylon, I will come to you and fulfill my gracious promise to bring you back to this place. 11For I know the plans I have for you," declares the LORD, "plans to prosper you and not to harm you, plans to give you hope and a future. 12Then you will call upon me and come and pray to me, and I will listen to you. 13You will seek me and find me when you seek me with all your heart. 14I will be found by you," declares the LORD, "and will bring you back from captivity.[b] I will gather you from all the nations and places where I have banished you," declares the LORD, "and will bring you back to the place from which I carried you into exile."

---

[a] 2 Hebrew *Jeconiah,* a variant of *Jehoiachin*　　[b] 14 Or *will restore your fortunes*

Living Bible

12Soon afterwards, the Lord gave this message to Jeremiah:

13Go and tell Hananiah that the Lord says, You have broken a wooden yoke but these people have yokes of iron on their necks. 14The Lord, the God of Israel, says: I have put a yoke of iron on the necks of all these nations, forcing them into slavery to Nebuchadnezzar, king of Babylon. And nothing will change this decree, for I have even given him all your flocks and herds.

15Then Jeremiah said to Hananiah, the false prophet, "Listen, Hananiah, the Lord has not sent you, and the people are believing your lies. 16Therefore the Lord says you must die. This very year your life will end because you have rebelled against the Lord."

17And sure enough, two months later Hananiah died.

29 AFTER JECONIAH the king, and the queen-mother, and the court officials, and the tribal officers and craftsmen had been deported to Babylon by Nebuchadnezzar, Jeremiah wrote them a letter from Jerusalem, addressing it to the Jewish elders and priests and prophets, and to all the people. 3He sent the letter with Elasah (son of Shaphan) and Gemariah (son of Hilkiah) when they went to Babylon as King Zedekiah's ambassadors to Nebuchadnezzar. And this is what the letter said:

4The Lord Almighty, the God of Israel, sends this message to all the captives he has exiled to Babylon from Jerusalem:

5Build homes and plan to stay; plant vineyards, for you will be there many years. 6Marry and have children, and then find mates for them and have many grandchildren. Multiply! Don't dwindle away! 7And work for the peace and prosperity of Babylon. Pray for her, for if Babylon has peace, so will you.

8The Lord Almighty, the God of Israel, says: Don't let the false prophets and mediums who are there among you fool you. Don't listen to the dreams that they invent, 9for they prophesy lies in my name. I have not sent them, says the Lord. 10The truth is this: You will be in Babylon for seventy years. But then I will come and do for you all the good things I have promised, and bring you home again. 11For I know the plans I have for you, says the Lord. They are plans for good and not for evil, to give you a future and a hope. 12In those days when you pray, I will listen. 13You will find me when you seek me, if you look for me in earnest.

14Yes, says the Lord, I will be found by you, and I will end your slavery and restore your fortunes, and gather you out of the nations where I sent you and bring you back home again to your own land.

New Revised Standard

12 Sometime after the prophet Hananiah had broken the yoke from the neck of the prophet Jeremiah, the word of the LORD came to Jeremiah: 13Go, tell Hananiah, Thus says the LORD: You have broken wooden bars only to forge iron bars in place of them! 14For thus says the LORD of hosts, the God of Israel: I have put an iron yoke on the neck of all these nations so that they may serve King Nebuchadnezzar of Babylon, and they shall indeed serve him; I have even given him the wild animals. 15And the prophet Jeremiah said to the prophet Hananiah, "Listen, Hananiah, the LORD has not sent you, and you made this people trust in a lie. 16Therefore thus says the LORD: I am going to send you off the face of the earth. Within this year you will be dead, because you have spoken rebellion against the LORD."

17 In that same year, in the seventh month, the prophet Hananiah died.

Jeremiah's Letter to the Exiles in Babylon

29 THESE ARE the words of the letter that the prophet Jeremiah sent from Jerusalem to the remaining elders among the exiles, and to the priests, the prophets, and all the people, whom Nebuchadnezzar had taken into exile from Jerusalem to Babylon. 2This was after King Jeconiah, and the queen mother, the court officials, the leaders of Judah and Jerusalem, the artisans, and the smiths had departed from Jerusalem. 3The letter was sent by the hand of Elasah son of Shaphan and Gemariah son of Hilkiah, whom King Zedekiah of Judah sent to Babylon to King Nebuchadnezzar of Babylon. It said: 4Thus says the LORD of hosts, the God of Israel, to all the exiles whom I have sent into exile from Jerusalem to Babylon: 5Build houses and live in them; plant gardens and eat what they produce. 6Take wives and have sons and daughters; take wives for your sons, and give your daughters in marriage, that they may bear sons and daughters; multiply there, and do not decrease. 7But seek the welfare of the city where I have sent you into exile, and pray to the LORD on its behalf, for in its welfare you will find your welfare. 8For thus says the LORD of hosts, the God of Israel: Do not let the prophets and the diviners who are among you deceive you, and do not listen to the dreams that they dream,c 9for it is a lie that they are prophesying to you in my name; I did not send them, says the LORD.

10 For thus says the LORD: Only when Babylon's seventy years are completed will I visit you, and I will fulfill to you my promise and bring you back to this place. 11For surely I know the plans I have for you, says the LORD, plans for your welfare and not for harm, to give you a future with hope. 12Then when you call upon me and come and pray to me, I will hear you. 13When you search for me, you will find me; if you seek me with all your heart, 14I will let you find me, says the LORD, and I will restore your fortunes and gather you from all the nations and all the places where I have driven you, says the LORD, and I will bring you back to the place from which I sent you into exile.

c Cn: Heb *your dreams that you cause to dream*

King James

15¶ Because ye have said, The LORD hath raised us up prophets in Babylon;

16*Know* that thus saith the LORD of the king that sitteth upon the throne of David, and of all the people that dwelleth in this city, *and* of your brethren that are not gone forth with you into captivity;

17Thus saith the LORD of hosts; Behold, I will send upon them the sword, the famine, and the pestilence, and will make them like vile figs, that cannot be eaten, they are so evil.

18And I will persecute them with the sword, with the famine, and with the pestilence, and will deliver them to be removed to all the kingdoms of the earth, to be a curse, and an astonishment, and an hissing, and a reproach, among all the nations whither I have driven them:

19Because they have not hearkened to my words, saith the LORD, which I sent unto them by my servants the prophets, rising up early and sending *them;* but ye would not hear, saith the LORD.

20¶ Hear ye therefore the word of the LORD, all ye of the captivity, whom I have sent from Jerusalem to Babylon:

21Thus saith the LORD of hosts, the God of Israel, of Ahab the son of Kolaiah, and of Zedekiah the son of Maaseiah, which prophesy a lie unto you in my name; Behold, I will deliver them into the hand of Nebuchadrezzar king of Babylon; and he shall slay them before your eyes;

22And of them shall be taken up a curse by all the captivity of Judah which *are* in Babylon, saying, The LORD make thee like Zedekiah and like Ahab, whom the king of Babylon roasted in the fire;

23Because they have committed villainy in Israel, and have committed adultery with their neighbours' wives, and have spoken lying words in my name, which I have not commanded them; even I know, and *am* a witness, saith the LORD.

24¶ *Thus* shalt thou also speak to Shemaiah the Nehelamite, saying,

25Thus speaketh the LORD of hosts, the God of Israel, saying, Because thou hast sent letters in thy name unto all the people that *are* at Jerusalem, and to Zephaniah the son of Maaseiah the priest, and to all the priests, saying,

26The LORD hath made thee priest in the stead of Jehoiada the priest, that ye should be officers in the house of the LORD, for every man *that is* mad, and maketh himself a prophet, that thou shouldest put him in prison, and in the stocks.

27Now therefore why hast thou not reproved Jeremiah of Anathoth, which maketh himself a prophet to you?

28For therefore he sent unto us *in* Babylon, saying, This *captivity is* long: build ye houses, and dwell *in them;* and plant gardens, and eat the fruit of them.

29And Zephaniah the priest read this letter in the ears of Jeremiah the prophet.

30¶ Then came the word of the LORD unto Jeremiah, saying,

31Send to all them of the captivity, saying, Thus saith the LORD concerning Shemaiah the Nehelamite; Because that Shemaiah hath prophesied unto you, and I sent him not, and he caused you to trust in a lie:

32Therefore thus saith the LORD; Behold, I will punish Shemaiah the Nehelamite, and his seed: he shall not have a man to dwell among this people; neither shall he behold the good that I will do for my people, saith the LORD; because he hath taught rebellion against the LORD.

New International

15You may say, "The LORD has raised up prophets for us in Babylon," 16but this is what the LORD says about the king who sits on David's throne and all the people who remain in this city, your countrymen who did not go with you into exile— 17yes, this is what the LORD Almighty says: "I will send the sword, famine and plague against them and I will make them like poor figs that are so bad they cannot be eaten. 18I will pursue them with the sword, famine and plague and will make them abhorrent to all the kingdoms of the earth and an object of cursing and horror, of scorn and reproach, among all the nations where I drive them. 19For they have not listened to my words," declares the LORD, "words that I sent to them again and again by my servants the prophets. And you exiles have not listened either," declares the LORD.

20Therefore, hear the word of the LORD, all you exiles whom I have sent away from Jerusalem to Babylon. 21This is what the LORD Almighty, the God of Israel, says about Ahab son of Kolaiah and Zedekiah son of Maaseiah, who are prophesying lies to you in my name: "I will hand them over to Nebuchadnezzar king of Babylon, and he will put them to death before your very eyes. 22Because of them, all the exiles from Judah who are in Babylon will use this curse: 'The LORD treat you like Zedekiah and Ahab, whom the king of Babylon burned in the fire.' 23For they have done outrageous things in Israel; they have committed adultery with their neighbors' wives and in my name have spoken lies, which I did not tell them to do. I know it and am a witness to it," declares the LORD.

Message to Shemaiah

24Tell Shemaiah the Nehelamite, 25"This is what the LORD Almighty, the God of Israel, says: You sent letters in your own name to all the people in Jerusalem, to Zephaniah son of Maaseiah the priest, and to all the other priests. You said to Zephaniah, 26'The LORD has appointed you priest in place of Jehoiada to be in charge of the house of the LORD; you should put any madman who acts like a prophet into the stocks and neck-irons. 27So why have you not reprimanded Jeremiah from Anathoth, who poses as a prophet among you? 28He has sent this message to us in Babylon: It will be a long time. Therefore build houses and settle down; plant gardens and eat what they produce.'"

29Zephaniah the priest, however, read the letter to Jeremiah the prophet. 30Then the word of the LORD came to Jeremiah: 31"Send this message to all the exiles: 'This is what the LORD says about Shemaiah the Nehelamite: Because Shemaiah has prophesied to you, even though I did not send him, and has led you to believe a lie, 32this is what the LORD says: I will surely punish Shemaiah the Nehelamite and his descendants. He will have no one left among this people, nor will he see the good things I will do for my people, declares the LORD, because he has preached rebellion against me.'"

Living Bible

15But now, because you accept the false prophets among you and say the Lord has sent them, 16, 17I will send war, famine and plague upon the people left here in Jerusalem—on your relatives who were not exiled to Babylon, and on the king who sits on David's throne—and make them like rotting figs, too bad to eat. 18And I will scatter them around the world. And in every nation where I place them they will be cursed and hissed and mocked, 19for they refuse to listen to me though I spoke to them again and again through my prophets.

20Therefore listen to the word of God, all you Jewish captives over there in Babylon. 21The Lord Almighty, the God of Israel, says this about your false prophets, Ahab (son of Kolaiah) and Zedekiah (son of Ma-aseiah), who are declaring lies to you in my name: Look, I am turning them over to Nebuchadnezzar to execute publicly. 22Their fate shall become proverbial of all evil, so that whenever anyone wants to curse someone he will say, "The Lord make you like Zedekiah and Ahab whom the king of Babylon burned alive!" 23For these men have done a terrible thing among my people. They have committed adultery with their neighbors' wives and have lied in my name. I know, for I have seen everything they do, says the Lord. 24And say this to Shemaiah the dreamer:a

25The Lord, the God of Israel, says: You have written a letter to Zephaniah (son of Ma-aseiah) the priest, and sent copies to all the other priests and to everyone in Jerusalem. 26And in this letter you have said to Zephaniah, "The Lord has appointed you to replace Jehoiada as priest in Jerusalem. And it is your responsibility to arrest any madman who claims to be a prophet, and to put him in the stocks and collar. 27Why haven't you done something about this false prophet Jeremiah of Anathoth? 28For he has written to us here in Babylon saying that our captivity will be long, and that we should build permanent homes and plan to stay many years, that we should plant fruit trees, for we will be here to eat the fruit from them for a long time to come."

29Zephaniah took the letter over to Jeremiah and read it to him! 30Then the Lord gave this message to Jeremiah:

31Send an open letter to all the exiles in Babylon and tell them this: The Lord says that because Shemaiah the Nehelamite has "prophesied" to you when I didn't send him, and has fooled you into believing his lies, 32I will punish him and his family. None of his descendants shall see the good I have waiting for my people, for he has taught you to rebel against the Lord.

New Revised Standard

15 Because you have said, "The LORD has raised up prophets for us in Babylon,"— 16Thus says the LORD concerning the king who sits on the throne of David, and concerning all the people who live in this city, your kinsfolk who did not go out with you into exile: 17Thus says the LORD of hosts, I am going to let loose on them sword, famine, and pestilence, and I will make them like rotten figs that are so bad they cannot be eaten. 18I will pursue them with the sword, with famine, and with pestilence, and will make them a horror to all the kingdoms of the earth, to be an object of cursing, and horror, and hissing, and a derision among all the nations where I have driven them, 19because they did not heed my words, says the LORD, when I persistently sent to you my servants the prophets, but theyb would not listen, says the LORD. 20But now, all you exiles whom I sent away from Jerusalem to Babylon, hear the word of the LORD: 21Thus says the LORD of hosts, the God of Israel, concerning Ahab son of Kolaiah and Zedekiah son of Maaseiah, who are prophesying a lie to you in my name: I am going to deliver them into the hand of King Nebuchadrezzar of Babylon, and he shall kill them before your eyes. 22And on account of them this curse shall be used by all the exiles from Judah in Babylon: "The LORD make you like Zedekiah and Ahab, whom the king of Babylon roasted in the fire," 23because they have perpetrated outrage in Israel and have committed adultery with their neighbors' wives, and have spoken in my name lying words that I did not command them; I am the one who knows and bears witness, says the LORD.

The Letter of Shemaiah

24 To Shemaiah of Nehelam you shall say: 25Thus says the LORD of hosts, the God of Israel: In your own name you sent a letter to all the people who are in Jerusalem, and to the priest Zephaniah son of Maaseiah, and to all the priests, saying, 26The LORD himself has made you priest instead of the priest Jehoiada, so that there may be officers in the house of the LORD to control any madman who plays the prophet, to put him in the stocks and the collar. 27So now why have you not rebuked Jeremiah of Anathoth who plays the prophet for you? 28For he has actually sent to us in Babylon, saying, "It will be a long time; build houses and live in them, and plant gardens and eat what they produce."

29 The priest Zephaniah read this letter in the hearing of the prophet Jeremiah. 30Then the word of the LORD came to Jeremiah: 31Send to all the exiles, saying, Thus says the LORD concerning Shemaiah of Nehelam: Because Shemaiah has prophesied to you, though I did not send him, and has led you to trust in a lie, 32therefore thus says the LORD: I am going to punish Shemaiah of Nehelam and his descendants; he shall not have anyone living among this people to seec the good that I am going to do to my people, says the LORD, for he has spoken rebellion against the LORD.

---

a 29:24 *Shemaiah the dreamer,* literally, "the Nehelamite." Nehelem was Shemaiah's home town, the name of which means "Dreamer." This seems to be another of the frequent puns in the prophetic books.

b Syr: Heb *you*   c Gk: Heb *and he shall not see*

King James

30 THE WORD that came to Jeremiah from the LORD, saying,

2Thus speaketh the LORD God of Israel, saying, Write thee all the words that I have spoken unto thee in a book.

3For, lo, the days come, saith the LORD, that I will bring again the captivity of my people Israel and Judah, saith the LORD: and I will cause them to return to the land that I gave to their fathers, and they shall possess it.

4¶ And these *are* the words that the LORD spake concerning Israel and concerning Judah.

5For thus saith the LORD; We have heard a voice of trembling, of fear, and not of peace.

6Ask ye now, and see whether a man doth travail with child? wherefore do I see every man with his hands on his loins, as a woman in travail, and all faces are turned into paleness?

7Alas! for that day *is* great, so that none *is* like it: it *is* even the time of Jacob's trouble; but he shall be saved out of it.

8For it shall come to pass in that day, saith the LORD of hosts, *that* I will break his yoke from off thy neck, and will burst thy bonds, and strangers shall no more serve themselves of him:

9But they shall serve the LORD their God, and David their king, whom I will raise up unto them.

10¶ Therefore fear thou not, O my servant Jacob, saith the LORD; neither be dismayed, O Israel: for, lo, I will save thee from afar, and thy seed from the land of their captivity; and Jacob shall return, and shall be in rest, and be quiet, and none shall make *him* afraid.

11For I *am* with thee, saith the LORD, to save thee: though I make a full end of all nations whither I have scattered thee, yet will I not make a full end of thee: but I will correct thee in measure, and will not leave thee altogether unpunished.

12For thus saith the LORD, Thy bruise *is* incurable, *and* thy wound *is* grievous.

13*There is* none to plead thy cause, that thou mayest be bound up: thou hast no healing medicines.

14All thy lovers have forgotten thee; they seek thee not; for I have wounded thee with the wound of an enemy, with the chastisement of a cruel one, for the multitude of thine iniquity; *because* thy sins were increased.

15Why criest thou for thine affliction? thy sorrow *is* incurable for the multitude of thine iniquity: *because* thy sins were increased, I have done these things unto thee.

16Therefore all they that devour thee shall be devoured; and all thine adversaries, every one of them, shall go into captivity; and they that spoil thee shall be a spoil, and all that prey upon thee will I give for a prey.

New International

Restoration of Israel

30 THIS IS the word that came to Jeremiah from the LORD: 2"This is what the LORD, the God of Israel, says: 'Write in a book all the words I have spoken to you. 3The days are coming,' declares the LORD, 'when I will bring my people Israel and Judah back from captivity[a] and restore them to the land I gave their forefathers to possess,' says the LORD.''

4These are the words the LORD spoke concerning Israel and Judah: 5"This is what the LORD says:

" 'Cries of fear are heard—
terror, not peace.
6Ask and see:
Can a man bear children?
Then why do I see every strong man
with his hands on his stomach like a woman
in labor,
every face turned deathly pale?
7How awful that day will be!
None will be like it.
It will be a time of trouble for Jacob,
but he will be saved out of it.

8" 'In that day,' declares the LORD Almighty,
'I will break the yoke off their necks
and will tear off their bonds;
no longer will foreigners enslave them.
9Instead, they will serve the LORD their God
and David their king,
whom I will raise up for them.

10" 'So do not fear, O Jacob my servant;
do not be dismayed, O Israel,'
declares the LORD.
'I will surely save you out of a distant place,
your descendants from the land of their exile.
Jacob will again have peace and security,
and no one will make him afraid.
11I am with you and will save you,'
declares the LORD.
'Though I completely destroy all the nations
among which I scatter you,
I will not completely destroy you.
I will discipline you but only with justice;
I will not let you go entirely unpunished.'

12"This is what the LORD says:

" 'Your wound is incurable,
your injury beyond healing.
13There is no one to plead your cause,
no remedy for your sore,
no healing for you.
14All your allies have forgotten you;
they care nothing for you.
I have struck you as an enemy would
and punished you as would the cruel,
because your guilt is so great
and your sins so many.
15Why do you cry out over your wound,
your pain that has no cure?
Because of your great guilt and many sins
I have done these things to you.

16" 'But all who devour you will be devoured;
all your enemies will go into exile.
Those who plunder you will be plundered;
all who make spoil of you I will despoil.

ª 3 Or *will restore the fortunes of my people Israel and Judah*

Living Bible

30 THIS IS another of the Lord's messages to Jeremiah: 2The Lord God of Israel says, Write down for the record all that I have said to you. 3For the time is coming when I will restore the fortunes of my people, Israel and Judah, and I will bring them home to this land that I gave to their fathers; they shall possess it and live here again.

4And write this also concerning Israel and Judah:

5"Where shall we find peace?" they cry. "There is only fear and trembling. 6Do men give birth? Then why do they stand there, ashen-faced, hands pressed against their sides like women in labor?"

7Alas, in all history when has there ever been a time of terror such as in that coming day? It is a time of trouble for my people—for Jacob—such as they have never known before. Yet God will rescue them! 8For on that day, says the Lord Almighty, I will break the yoke from their necks and snap their chains, and foreigners shall no longer be their masters! 9For they shall serve the Lord their God, and David their King,b whom I will raise up for them, says the Lord.

10So don't be afraid, O Jacob my servant; don't be dismayed, O Israel; for I will bring you home again from distant lands, and your children from their exile. They shall have rest and quiet in their own land, and no one shall make them afraid. 11For I am with you and I will save you, says the Lord. Even if I utterly destroy the nations where I scatter you, I will not exterminate you; I will punish you, yes—you will not go unpunished.

12For your sin is an incurable bruise, a terrible wound. 13There is no one to help you or to bind up your wound and no medicine does any good. 14All your lovers have left you and don't care anything about you any more; for I have wounded you cruelly, as though I were your enemy; mercilessly, as though I were an implacable foe; for your sins are so many, your guilt is so great.

15Why do you protest your punishment? Your sin is so scandalous that your sorrow should never end! It is because your guilt is great that I have had to punish you so much.

16But in that coming day, all who are destroying you shall be destroyed, and all your enemies shall be slaves. Those who rob you shall be robbed; and those attacking you shall be attacked. 17I will give you back your health

New Revised Standard

Restoration Promised for Israel and Judah

30 THE WORD that came to Jeremiah from the Lord: 2Thus says the Lord, the God of Israel: Write in a book all the words that I have spoken to you. 3For the days are surely coming, says the Lord, when I will restore the fortunes of my people, Israel and Judah, says the Lord, and I will bring them back to the land that I gave to their ancestors and they shall take possession of it.

4 These are the words that the Lord spoke concerning Israel and Judah:

5 Thus says the Lord:
We have heard a cry of panic,
    of terror, and no peace.
6 Ask now, and see,
    can a man bear a child?
Why then do I see every man
    with his hands on his loins like a woman in labor?
    Why has every face turned pale?
7 Alas! that day is so great
    there is none like it;
it is a time of distress for Jacob;
    yet he shall be rescued from it.

8 On that day, says the Lord of hosts, I will break the yoke from off hisc neck, and I will burst hisc bonds, and strangers shall no more make a servant of him. 9But they shall serve the Lord their God and David their king, whom I will raise up for them.

10 But as for you, have no fear, my servant
        Jacob, says the Lord,
    and do not be dismayed, O Israel;
for I am going to save you from far away,
    and your offspring from the land of their
        captivity.
Jacob shall return and have quiet and ease,
    and no one shall make him afraid.
11 For I am with you, says the Lord, to save
        you;
I will make an end of all the nations
    among which I scattered you,
    but of you I will not make an end.
I will chastise you in just measure,
    and I will by no means leave you
        unpunished.

12 For thus says the Lord:
Your hurt is incurable,
    your wound is grievous.
13 There is no one to uphold your cause,
    no medicine for your wound,
    no healing for you.
14 All your lovers have forgotten you;
    they care nothing for you;
for I have dealt you the blow of an enemy,
    the punishment of a merciless foe,
because your guilt is great,
    because your sins are so numerous.
15 Why do you cry out over your hurt?
    Your pain is incurable.
Because your guilt is great,
    because your sins are so numerous,
    I have done these things to you.
16 Therefore all who devour you shall be
        devoured,
    and all your foes, everyone of them, shall
        go into captivity;
those who plunder you shall be plundered,
    and all who prey on you I will make a prey.

---

b 30:9 David their King. The Messiah, David's greater Son, whom God has raised up for them.

c Cn: Heb your

King James

17For I will restore health unto thee, and I will heal thee of thy wounds, saith the LORD; because they called thee an Outcast, *saying,* This *is* Zion, whom no man seeketh after.

18¶ Thus saith the LORD; Behold, I will bring again the captivity of Jacob's tents, and have mercy on his dwellingplaces; and the city shall be builded upon her own heap, and the palace shall remain after the manner thereof.

19And out of them shall proceed thanksgiving and the voice of them that make merry: and I will multiply them, and they shall not be few; I will also glorify them, and they shall not be small.

20Their children also shall be as aforetime, and their congregation shall be established before me, and I will punish all that oppress them.

21And their nobles shall be of themselves, and their governor shall proceed from the midst of them; and I will cause him to draw near, and he shall approach unto me: for who *is* this that engaged his heart to approach unto me? saith the LORD.

22And ye shall be my people, and I will be your God.

23Behold, the whirlwind of the LORD goeth forth with fury, a continuing whirlwind: it shall fall with pain upon the head of the wicked.

24The fierce anger of the LORD shall not return, until he have done *it,* and until he have performed the intents of his heart: in the latter days ye shall consider it.

31 AT THE same time, saith the LORD, will I be the God of all the families of Israel, and they shall be my people.

2Thus saith the LORD, The people *which were* left of the sword found grace in the wilderness; *even* Israel, when I went to cause him to rest.

3The LORD hath appeared of old unto me, *saying,* Yea, I have loved thee with an everlasting love: therefore with lovingkindness have I drawn thee.

4Again I will build thee, and thou shalt be built, O virgin of Israel: thou shalt again be adorned with thy tabrets, and shalt go forth in the dances of them that make merry.

5Thou shalt yet plant vines upon the mountains of Samaria: the planters shall plant, and shall eat *them* as common things.

6For there shall be a day, *that* the watchmen upon the mount Ephraim shall cry, Arise ye, and let us go up to Zion unto the LORD our God.

New International

17But I will restore you to health
  and heal your wounds,'
                declares the LORD,
'because you are called an outcast,
  Zion for whom no one cares.'

18"This is what the LORD says:

" 'I will restore the fortunes of Jacob's tents
  and have compassion on his dwellings;
the city will be rebuilt on her ruins,
  and the palace will stand in its proper place.
19From them will come songs of thanksgiving
  and the sound of rejoicing.
I will add to their numbers,
  and they will not be decreased;
I will bring them honor,
  and they will not be disdained.
20Their children will be as in days of old,
  and their community will be established
    before me;
I will punish all who oppress them.
21Their leader will be one of their own;
  their ruler will arise from among them.
I will bring him near and he will come close to
  me,
for who is he who will devote himself
  to be close to me?'
                declares the LORD.
22" 'So you will be my people,
  and I will be your God.' "

23See, the storm of the LORD
  will burst out in wrath,
a driving wind swirling down
  on the heads of the wicked.
24The fierce anger of the LORD will not turn back
  until he fully accomplishes
  the purposes of his heart.
In days to come
  you will understand this.

31 "AT THAT time," declares the LORD, "I will be the God of all the clans of Israel, and they will be my people."

2This is what the LORD says:

"The people who survive the sword
  will find favor in the desert;
I will come to give rest to Israel."

3The LORD appeared to us in the past,[a] saying:

"I have loved you with an everlasting love;
I have drawn you with loving-kindness.
4I will build you up again
  and you will be rebuilt, O Virgin Israel.
Again you will take up your tambourines
  and go out to dance with the joyful.
5Again you will plant vineyards
  on the hills of Samaria;
the farmers will plant them
  and enjoy their fruit.
6There will be a day when watchmen cry out
  on the hills of Ephraim,
'Come, let us go up to Zion,
  to the LORD our God.' "

Living Bible

again and heal your wounds. Now you are called "The Outcast" and "Jerusalem, the Place Nobody Wants."

18But, says the Lord, when I bring you home again from your captivity and restore your fortunes, Jerusalem will be rebuilt upon her ruins; the palace will be reconstructed as it was before. 19The cities will be filled with joy and great thanksgiving, and I will multiply my people and make of them a great and honored nation. 20Their children shall prosper as in David's reign; their nations shall be established before me, and I will punish anyone who hurts them. 21They will have their own ruler again.b He will not be a foreigner. And I will invite him to be a priest at my altars, and he shall approach me, for who would dare to come unless invited. 22And you shall be my people and I will be your God.

23Suddenly the devastating whirlwind of the Lord roars with fury; it shall burst upon the heads of the wicked. 24The Lord will not call off the fierceness of his wrath until it has finished all the terrible destruction he has planned. Later onc you will understand what I am telling you.

31 AT THAT time, says the Lord, all the families of Israel shall recognize me as the Lord; they shall act like my people. 2I will care for them as I did those who escaped from Egypt, to whom I showed my mercies in the wilderness, when Israel sought for rest. 3For long ago the Lord had said to Israel: I have loved you, O my people, with an everlasting love; with loving-kindness I have drawn you to me. 4I will rebuild your nation, O virgin of Israel. You will again be happy and dance merrily with the timbrels. 5Again you shall plant your vineyards upon the mountains of Samaria and eat from your own gardens there.

6The day shall come when watchmen on the hills of Ephraim will call out and say, "Arise, and let us go up to Zion to the Lord our God." 7For the Lord says, Sing

New Revised Standard

17 For I will restore health to you,
    and your wounds I will heal,
                            says the Lord,
    because they have called you an outcast:
    "It is Zion; no one cares for her!"

18 Thus says the Lord:
    I am going to restore the fortunes of the tents
        of Jacob,
    and have compassion on his dwellings;
    the city shall be rebuilt upon its mound,
    and the citadel set on its rightful site.
19 Out of them shall come thanksgiving,
    and the sound of merrymakers.
    I will make them many, and they shall not be
        few;
    I will make them honored, and they shall
        not be disdained.
20 Their children shall be as of old,
        their congregation shall be established
        before me;
    and I will punish all who oppress them.
21 Their prince shall be one of their own,
        their ruler shall come from their midst;
    I will bring him near, and he shall approach
        me,
    for who would otherwise dare to approach
        me?
                            says the Lord.
22 And you shall be my people,
    and I will be your God.

23 Look, the storm of the Lord!
    Wrath has gone forth,
    a whirlingd tempest;
    it will burst upon the head of the wicked.
24 The fierce anger of the Lord will not turn
        back
    until he has executed and accomplished
    the intents of his mind.
    In the latter days you will understand this.

The Joyful Return of the Exiles

31 AT THAT time, says the Lord, I will be the God of all the families of Israel, and they shall be my people.
2 Thus says the Lord:
    The people who survived the sword
        found grace in the wilderness;
    when Israel sought for rest,
3   the Lord appeared to hime from far away.f
    I have loved you with an everlasting love;
        therefore I have continued my faithfulness
            to you.
4 Again I will build you, and you shall be built,
        O virgin Israel!
    Again you shall takeg your tambourines,
        and go forth in the dance of the
            merrymakers.
5 Again you shall plant vineyards
        on the mountains of Samaria;
    the planters shall plant,
        and shall enjoy the fruit.
6 For there shall be a day when sentinels will
        call
    in the hill country of Ephraim:
    "Come, let us go up to Zion,
        to the Lord our God."

---

b 30:21 They will have their own ruler again. This verse probably refers to the restoration after the Babylonian captivity (the rulers of the Maccabean period were priests as well as kings) as well as to the final restoration under Christ.   c 30:24 Later on, literally, "in the latter days."

d One Ms: Meaning of MT uncertain   e Gk: Heb me   f Or to him long ago
g Or adorn yourself with

King James

7For thus saith the LORD; Sing with gladness for Jacob, and shout among the chief of the nations: publish ye, praise ye, and say, O LORD, save thy people, the remnant of Israel.

8Behold, I will bring them from the north country, and gather them from the coasts of the earth, *and* with them the blind and the lame, the woman with child and her that travaileth with child together: a great company shall return thither.

9They shall come with weeping, and with supplications will I lead them: I will cause them to walk by the rivers of waters in a straight way, wherein they shall not stumble: for I am a father to Israel, and Ephraim *is* my firstborn.

10¶ Hear the word of the LORD, O ye nations, and declare *it* in the isles afar off, and say, He that scattered Israel will gather him, and keep him, as a shepherd *doth* his flock.

11For the LORD hath redeemed Jacob, and ransomed him from the hand of *him that was* stronger than he.

12Therefore they shall come and sing in the height of Zion, and shall flow together to the goodness of the LORD, for wheat, and for wine, and for oil, and for the young of the flock and of the herd: and their soul shall be as a watered garden; and they shall not sorrow any more at all.

13Then shall the virgin rejoice in the dance, both young men and old together: for I will turn their mourning into joy, and will comfort them, and make them rejoice from their sorrow.

14And I will satiate the soul of the priests with fatness, and my people shall be satisfied with my goodness, saith the LORD.

15¶ Thus saith the LORD; A voice was heard in Ramah, lamentation, *and* bitter weeping; Rahel weeping for her children refused to be comforted for her children, because they *were* not.

16Thus saith the LORD; Refrain thy voice from weeping, and thine eyes from tears: for thy work shall be rewarded, saith the LORD; and they shall come again from the land of the enemy.

17And there is hope in thine end, saith the LORD, that thy children shall come again to their own border.

New International

7This is what the LORD says:

"Sing with joy for Jacob;
    shout for the foremost of the nations.
Make your praises heard, and say,
    'O LORD, save your people,
    the remnant of Israel.'
8See, I will bring them from the land of the
        north
    and gather them from the ends of the earth.
Among them will be the blind and the lame,
    expectant mothers and women in labor;
    a great throng will return.
9They will come with weeping;
    they will pray as I bring them back.
I will lead them beside streams of water
    on a level path where they will not stumble,
because I am Israel's father,
    and Ephraim is my firstborn son.

10"Hear the word of the LORD, O nations;
    proclaim it in distant coastlands:
'He who scattered Israel will gather them
    and will watch over his flock like a
        shepherd.'
11For the LORD will ransom Jacob
    and redeem them from the hand of those
        stronger than they.
12They will come and shout for joy on the heights
        of Zion;
    they will rejoice in the bounty of the LORD—
the grain, the new wine and the oil,
    the young of the flocks and herds.
They will be like a well-watered garden,
    and they will sorrow no more.
13Then maidens will dance and be glad,
    young men and old as well.
I will turn their mourning into gladness;
    I will give them comfort and joy instead of
        sorrow.
14I will satisfy the priests with abundance,
    and my people will be filled with my
        bounty,"
                            declares the LORD.

15This is what the LORD says:

"A voice is heard in Ramah,
    mourning and great weeping,
Rachel weeping for her children
    and refusing to be comforted,
    because her children are no more."

16This is what the LORD says:

"Restrain your voice from weeping
    and your eyes from tears,
for your work will be rewarded,"
                            declares the LORD.
"They will return from the land of the enemy.
17So there is hope for your future,"
                            declares the LORD.
"Your children will return to their own land.

Living Bible

with joy for all that I will do for Israel, the greatest of the nations! Shout out with praise and joy: "The Lord has saved his people, the remnant of Israel." [8]For I will bring them from the north and from earth's farthest ends, not forgetting their blind and lame, young mothers with their little ones, those ready to give birth. It will be a great company who comes. [9]Tears of joy shall stream down their faces, and I will lead them home with great care. They shall walk beside the quiet streams and not stumble. For I am a Father to Israel, and Ephraim is my oldest child.

[10]Listen to this message from the Lord, you nations of the world, and publish it abroad: The Lord who scattered his people will gather them back together again and watch over them as a shepherd does his flock. [11]He will save Israel from those who are too strong for them! [12]They shall come home and sing songs of joy upon the hills of Zion, and shall be radiant over the goodness of the Lord—the good crops, the wheat and the wine and the oil, and the healthy flocks and herds. Their life shall be like a watered garden, and all their sorrows shall be gone. [13]The young girls will dance for joy, and men folk—old and young—will take their part in all the fun; for I will turn their mourning into joy and I will comfort them and make them rejoice, for their captivity with all its sorrows will be behind them. [14]I will feast the priests with the abundance of offerings brought to them at the Temple; I will satisfy my people with my bounty, says the Lord.

[15]The Lord spoke to me again, saying: In Ramah there is bitter weeping—Rachel[a] weeping for her children and cannot be comforted, for they are gone. [16]But the Lord says: Don't cry any longer, for I have heard your prayers[b] and you will see them again; they will come back to you from the distant land of the enemy. [17]There is hope for your future, says the Lord, and your children will come again to their own land.

New Revised Standard

[7] For thus says the LORD:
Sing aloud with gladness for Jacob,
    and raise shouts for the chief of the nations;
proclaim, give praise, and say,
    "Save, O LORD, your people,
    the remnant of Israel."
[8] See, I am going to bring them from the land
        of the north,
    and gather them from the farthest parts of
        the earth,
among them the blind and the lame,
    those with child and those in labor,
        together;
    a great company, they shall return here.
[9] With weeping they shall come,
    and with consolations[c] I will lead them
        back,
I will let them walk by brooks of water,
    in a straight path in which they shall not
        stumble;
for I have become a father to Israel,
    and Ephraim is my firstborn.

[10] Hear the word of the LORD, O nations,
    and declare it in the coastlands far away;
say, "He who scattered Israel will gather him,
    and will keep him as a shepherd a flock."
[11] For the LORD has ransomed Jacob,
    and has redeemed him from hands too
        strong for him.
[12] They shall come and sing aloud on the height
        of Zion,
    and they shall be radiant over the goodness
        of the LORD,
over the grain, the wine, and the oil,
    and over the young of the flock and the
        herd;
their life shall become like a watered garden,
    and they shall never languish again.
[13] Then shall the young women rejoice in the
        dance,
    and the young men and the old shall be
        merry.
I will turn their mourning into joy,
    I will comfort them, and give them gladness
        for sorrow.
[14] I will give the priests their fill of fatness,
    and my people shall be satisfied with my
        bounty,
                            says the LORD.

[15] Thus says the LORD:
A voice is heard in Ramah,
    lamentation and bitter weeping.
Rachel is weeping for her children;
    she refuses to be comforted for her children,
        because they are no more.
[16] Thus says the LORD:
Keep your voice from weeping,
    and your eyes from tears;
for there is a reward for your work,
                            says the LORD:
    they shall come back from the land of the
        enemy;
[17] there is hope for your future,
                            says the LORD:
    your children shall come back to their own
        country.

---

a *31:15 Rachel*, symbolic mother of the Northern tribes, who were taken away by the Assyrians as slaves.   b *31:16 for I have heard your prayers*, literally, "for your work shall be rewarded."

c Gk Compare Vg Tg: Heb *supplications*

King James

18¶ I have surely heard Ephraim bemoaning himself *thus;* Thou hast chastised me, and I was chastised, as a bullock unaccustomed *to the yoke:* turn thou me, and I shall be turned; for thou *art* the LORD my God.

19Surely after that I was turned, I repented; and after that I was instructed, I smote upon *my* thigh: I was ashamed, yea, even confounded, because I did bear the reproach of my youth.

20*Is* Ephraim my dear son? *is he* a pleasant child? for since I spake against him, I do earnestly remember him still: therefore my bowels are troubled for him; I will surely have mercy upon him, saith the LORD.

21Set thee up waymarks, make thee high heaps: set thine heart toward the highway, *even* the way *which* thou wentest: turn again, O virgin of Israel, turn again to these thy cities.

22¶ How long wilt thou go about, O thou backsliding daughter? for the LORD hath created a new thing in the earth, A woman shall compass a man.

23Thus saith the LORD of hosts, the God of Israel; As yet they shall use this speech in the land of Judah and in the cities thereof, when I shall bring again their captivity; The LORD bless thee, O habitation of justice, *and* mountain of holiness.

24And there shall dwell in Judah itself, and in all the cities thereof together, husbandmen, and they *that* go forth with flocks.

25For I have satiated the weary soul, and I have replenished every sorrowful soul.

26Upon this I awaked, and beheld; and my sleep was sweet unto me.

27¶ Behold, the days come, saith the LORD, that I will sow the house of Israel and the house of Judah with the seed of man, and with the seed of beast.

28And it shall come to pass, *that* like as I have watched over them, to pluck up, and to break down, and to throw down, and to destroy, and to afflict; so will I watch over them, to build, and to plant, saith the LORD.

29In those days they shall say no more, The fathers have eaten a sour grape, and the children's teeth are set on edge.

30But every one shall die for his own iniquity: every man that eateth the sour grape, his teeth shall be set on edge.

31¶ Behold, the days come, saith the LORD, that I will make a new covenant with the house of Israel, and with the house of Judah:

32Not according to the covenant that I made with their fathers in the day *that* I took them by the hand to bring them out of the land of Egypt; which my covenant they brake, although I was an husband unto them, saith the LORD:

33But this *shall be* the covenant that I will make with the house of Israel; After those days, saith the LORD, I will put my law in their inward parts, and write it in their hearts; and will be their God, and they shall be my people.

New International

18"I have surely heard Ephraim's moaning:
    'You disciplined me like an unruly calf,
    and I have been disciplined.
Restore me, and I will return,
    because you are the LORD my God.
19After I strayed,
    I repented;
after I came to understand,
    I beat my breast.
I was ashamed and humiliated
    because I bore the disgrace of my youth.'
20Is not Ephraim my dear son,
    the child in whom I delight?
Though I often speak against him,
    I still remember him.
Therefore my heart yearns for him;
    I have great compassion for him,"
                    declares the LORD.

21"Set up road signs;
    put up guideposts.
Take note of the highway,
    the road that you take.
Return, O Virgin Israel,
    return to your towns.
22How long will you wander,
    O unfaithful daughter?
The LORD will create a new thing on earth—
    a woman will surround[a] a man."

23This is what the LORD Almighty, the God of Israel, says: "When I bring them back from captivity,[b] the people in the land of Judah and in its towns will once again use these words: 'The LORD bless you, O righteous dwelling, O sacred mountain.' 24People will live together in Judah and all its towns—farmers and those who move about with their flocks. 25I will refresh the weary and satisfy the faint."

26At this I awoke and looked around. My sleep had been pleasant to me.

27"The days are coming," declares the LORD, "when I will plant the house of Israel and the house of Judah with the offspring of men and of animals. 28Just as I watched over them to uproot and tear down, and to overthrow, destroy and bring disaster, so I will watch over them to build and to plant," declares the LORD. 29"In those days people will no longer say,

    'The fathers have eaten sour grapes,
    and the children's teeth are set on edge.'

30Instead, everyone will die for his own sin; whoever eats sour grapes—his own teeth will be set on edge.

31"The time is coming," declares the LORD,
    "when I will make a new covenant
with the house of Israel
    and with the house of Judah.
32It will not be like the covenant
    I made with their forefathers
when I took them by the hand
    to lead them out of Egypt,
because they broke my covenant,
    though I was a husband to[c] them,[d]"
                    declares the LORD.
33"This is the covenant I will make with the
        house of Israel
    after that time," declares the LORD.
"I will put my law in their minds
    and write it on their hearts.
I will be their God,
    and they will be my people.

---

a 22 Or *will go about seeking;* or *will protect*   b 23 Or *I restore their fortunes*   c 32 Hebrew; Septuagint and Syriac / *and I turned away from*   d 32 Or *was their master*

Living Bible

18I have heard Ephraim's groans: "You have punished me greatly; but I needed it all, as a calf must be trained for the yoke. Turn me again to you and restore me, for you alone are the Lord, my God. 19I turned away from God but I was sorry afterwards. I kicked myself for my stupidity. I was thoroughly ashamed of all I did in younger days."

20And the Lord replies: Ephraim is still my son, my darling child. I had to punish him, but I still love him. I long for him and surely will have mercy on him.

21As you travel into exile, set up road signs pointing back to Israel. Mark your pathway well. For you shall return again, O virgin Israel, to your cities here. 22How long will you vacillate, O wayward daughter? For the Lord will cause something new and different to happen—Israel will search for God.e

23The Lord, the God of Israel, says: When I bring them back again they shall say in Judah and her cities, "The Lord bless you, O center of righteousness, O holy hill!" 24And city dwellers and farmers and shepherds alike shall live together in peace and happiness. 25For I have given rest to the weary and joy to all the sorrowing.

26(Then Jeremiah wakened. "Such sleep is very sweet!" he said.)

27The Lord says: The time will come when I will greatly increase the population and multiply the number of cattle here in Israel. 28In the past I painstakingly destroyed the nation but now I will carefully build it up. 29The people shall no longer quote this proverb—"Children pay for their fathers' sins."f 30For everyone shall die for his own sins—the person eating sour grapes is the one whose teeth are set on edge.

31The day will come, says the Lord, when I will make a new contract with the people of Israel and Judah. 32It won't be like the one I made with their fathers when I took them by the hand to bring them out of the land of Egypt—a contract they broke, forcing me to reject them,g says the Lord. 33But this is the new contract I will make with them: I will inscribe my laws upon their hearts,h so that they shall want to honor me;i then they shall truly be my people and I will be their God. 34At

New Revised Standard

18 Indeed I heard Ephraim pleading:
    "You disciplined me, and I took the discipline;
        I was like a calf untrained.
    Bring me back, let me come back,
        for you are the LORD my God.
19 For after I had turned away I repented;
        and after I was discovered, I struck my thigh;
    I was ashamed, and I was dismayed
        because I bore the disgrace of my youth."
20 Is Ephraim my dear son?
        Is he the child I delight in?
    As often as I speak against him,
        I still remember him.
    Therefore I am deeply moved for him;
        I will surely have mercy on him,
                                            says the LORD.

21 Set up road markers for yourself,
        make yourself guideposts;
    consider well the highway,
        the road by which you went.
    Return, O virgin Israel,
        return to these your cities.
22 How long will you waver,
        O faithless daughter?
    For the LORD has created a new thing on the earth:
        a woman encompassesj a man.

23 Thus says the LORD of hosts, the God of Israel: Once more they shall use these words in the land of Judah and in its towns when I restore their fortunes:
    "The LORD bless you, O abode of righteousness,
        O holy hill!"
24 And Judah and all its towns shall live there together, and the farmers and those who wanderk with their flocks.
25 I will satisfy the weary,
        and all who are faint I will replenish.
26 Thereupon I awoke and looked, and my sleep was pleasant to me.

Individual Retribution

27 The days are surely coming, says the LORD, when I will sow the house of Israel and the house of Judah with the seed of humans and the seed of animals. 28 And just as I have watched over them to pluck up and break down, to overthrow, destroy, and bring evil, so I will watch over them to build and to plant, says the LORD. 29 In those days they shall no longer say:
    "The parents have eaten sour grapes,
        and the children's teeth are set on edge."
30 But all shall die for their own sins; the teeth of everyone who eats sour grapes shall be set on edge.

A New Covenant

31 The days are surely coming, says the LORD, when I will make a new covenant with the house of Israel and the house of Judah. 32 It will not be like the covenant that I made with their ancestors when I took them by the hand to bring them out of the land of Egypt—a covenant that they broke, though I was their husband,l says the LORD. 33 But this is the covenant that I will make with the house of Israel after those days, says the LORD: I will put my law within them, and I will write it on their hearts; and I will be their God, and they shall be my people. 34 No longer shall they teach one another,

---

e 31:22 Israel will search for God, literally, "a woman shall court a suitor," or, "a woman shall encompass a man."   f 31:29 Children pay for their fathers' sins, literally, "The fathers eat the sour grapes and the children's teeth are set on edge."   g 31:32 a contract they broke, forcing me to reject them. Some versions read, "a covenant they broke, even though I cared for them as a husband does his wife." See Heb 8:9b.   h 31:33 upon their hearts, i.e., rather than upon tablets of stone, as were the Ten Commandments. i 31:33 so that they shall want to honor me. In Jeremiah 17:1 their sin was inscribed on their hearts, so that they wanted above all to disobey. This change seems to describe an experience very much like, if not the same as, the new birth.

j Meaning of Heb uncertain   k Cn Compare Syr Vg Tg: Heb and they shall wander   l Or master

King James

34And they shall teach no more every man his neighbour, and every man his brother, saying, Know the LORD: for they shall all know me, from the least of them unto the greatest of them, saith the LORD: for I will forgive their iniquity, and I will remember their sin no more.

35¶ Thus saith the LORD, which giveth the sun for a light by day, *and* the ordinances of the moon and of the stars for a light by night, which divideth the sea when the waves thereof roar; The LORD of hosts *is* his name:

36If those ordinances depart from before me, saith the LORD, *then* the seed of Israel also shall cease from being a nation before me for ever.

37Thus saith the LORD; If heaven above can be measured, and the foundations of the earth searched out beneath, I will also cast off all the seed of Israel for all that they have done, saith the LORD.

38¶ Behold, the days come, saith the LORD, that the city shall be built to the LORD from the tower of Hananeel unto the gate of the corner.

39And the measuring line shall yet go forth over against it upon the hill Gareb, and shall compass about to Goath.

40And the whole valley of the dead bodies, and of the ashes, and all the fields unto the brook of Kidron, unto the corner of the horse gate toward the east, *shall be* holy unto the LORD; it shall not be plucked up, nor thrown down any more for ever.

New International

34No longer will a man teach his neighbor,
  or a man his brother, saying, 'Know the
    LORD,'
because they will all know me,
  from the least of them to the greatest,"
                    declares the LORD.
"For I will forgive their wickedness
  and will remember their sins no more."

35This is what the LORD says,

he who appoints the sun
  to shine by day,
who decrees the moon and stars
  to shine by night,
who stirs up the sea
  so that its waves roar—
the LORD Almighty is his name:
36"Only if these decrees vanish from my sight,"
  declares the LORD,
"will the descendants of Israel ever cease
  to be a nation before me."

37This is what the LORD says:

"Only if the heavens above can be measured
  and the foundations of the earth below be
    searched out
will I reject all the descendants of Israel
  because of all they have done,"
                    declares the LORD.

38"The days are coming," declares the LORD, "when this city will be rebuilt for me from the Tower of Hananel to the Corner Gate. 39The measuring line will stretch from there straight to the hill of Gareb and then turn to Goah. 40The whole valley where dead bodies and ashes are thrown, and all the terraces out to the Kidron Valley on the east as far as the corner of the Horse Gate, will be holy to the LORD. The city will never again be uprooted or demolished."

Jeremiah Buys a Field

32 THE WORD that came to Jeremiah from the LORD in the tenth year of Zedekiah king of Judah, which *was* the eighteenth year of Nebuchadrezzar. 2For then the king of Babylon's army besieged Jerusalem: and Jeremiah the prophet was shut up in the court of the prison, which *was* in the king of Judah's house.

3For Zedekiah king of Judah had shut him up, saying, Wherefore dost thou prophesy, and say, Thus saith the LORD, Behold, I will give this city into the hand of the king of Babylon, and he shall take it;

4And Zedekiah king of Judah shall not escape out of the hand of the Chaldeans, but shall surely be delivered into the hand of the king of Babylon, and shall speak with him mouth to mouth, and his eyes shall behold his eyes;

5And he shall lead Zedekiah to Babylon, and there shall he be until I visit him, saith the LORD: though ye fight with the Chaldeans, ye shall not prosper.

6¶ And Jeremiah said, The word of the LORD came unto me, saying,

7Behold, Hanameel the son of Shallum thine uncle shall come unto thee, saying, Buy thee my field that *is* in Anathoth: for the right of redemption *is* thine to buy *it*.

8So Hanameel mine uncle's son came to me in the court of the prison according to the word of the LORD, and said unto me, Buy my field, I pray thee, that *is* in Anathoth, which *is* in the country of Benjamin: for the right of inheritance *is* thine, and the redemption *is* thine; buy *it* for thyself. Then I knew that this *was* the word of the LORD.

32 THIS IS the word that came to Jeremiah from the LORD in the tenth year of Zedekiah king of Judah, which was the eighteenth year of Nebuchadnezzar. 2The army of the king of Babylon was then besieging Jerusalem, and Jeremiah the prophet was confined in the courtyard of the guard in the royal palace of Judah.

3Now Zedekiah king of Judah had imprisoned him there, saying, "Why do you prophesy as you do? You say, 'This is what the LORD says: I am about to hand this city over to the king of Babylon, and he will capture it. 4Zedekiah king of Judah will not escape out of the hands of the Babyloniansa but will certainly be handed over to the king of Babylon, and will speak with him face to face and see him with his own eyes. 5He will take Zedekiah to Babylon, where he will remain until I deal with him, declares the LORD. If you fight against the Babylonians, you will not succeed.' "

6Jeremiah said, "The word of the LORD came to me: 7Hanamel son of Shallum your uncle is going to come to you and say, 'Buy my field at Anathoth, because as nearest relative it is your right and duty to buy it.'

8"Then, just as the LORD had said, my cousin Hanamel came to me in the courtyard of the guard and said, 'Buy my field at Anathoth in the territory of Benjamin. Since it is your right to redeem it and possess it, buy it for yourself.'

"I knew that this was the word of the LORD; 9so I

---
a *4 Or Chaldeans;* also in verses 5, 24, 25, 28, 29 and 43

Living Bible

that time it will no longer be necessary to admonish one another to know the Lord. For everyone, both great and small, shall really know me then, says the Lord, and I will forgive and forget their sins.

35The Lord who gives us sunlight in the daytime and the moon and stars to light the night, and who stirs the sea to make the roaring waves—his name is Lord Almighty—says this:

36I am as likely to reject my people Israel as I am to do away with these laws of nature! 37Not until the heavens can be measured and the foundations of the earth explored, will I consider casting them away forever for their sins!

38, 39For the time is coming, says the Lord, when all Jerusalem shall be rebuilt for the Lord, from the Tower of Hananel at the northeast corner,b to the Corner Gate at the northwest; and from the Hill of Gareb at the southwest, across to Goah on the southeast. 40And the entire city including the graveyard and ash dump in the valley shall be holy to the Lord, and so shall all the fields out to the brook of Kidron, and from there to the Horse Gate on the east side of the city; it shall never again be captured or destroyed.

32 THE FOLLOWING message came to Jeremiah from the Lord in the tenth year of the reign of Zedekiah, king of Judah (which was the eighteenth year of Nebuchadnezzar's reign). 2At this time Jeremiah was imprisoned in the dungeon beneathc the palace, while the Babylonian army was besieging Jerusalem. 3King Zedekiah had put him there for continuing to prophesy that the city would be conquered by the king of Babylon, 4and that King Zedekiah would be caught and taken as a prisoner before the king of Babylon for trial and sentencing.

5"He shall take you to Babylon and imprison you there for many years until you die. Why fight the facts? You can't win! Surrender now!" Jeremiah had told him again and again.

6,7Then this message from the Lord came to Jeremiah: Your cousin Hanamel (son of Shallum) will soon arrive to ask you to buy the farm he owns in Anathoth, for by law you have a chance to buy before it is offered to anyone else. 8So Hanamel came, as the Lord had said he would, and visited me in the prison. "Buy my field in Anathoth, in the land of Benjamin," he said, "for the law gives you the first right to purchase it." Then I knew for sure that the message I had heard was really from the Lord.

New Revised Standard

or say to each other, "Know the LORD," for they shall all know me, from the least of them to the greatest, says the LORD; for I will forgive their iniquity, and remember their sin no more.

35 Thus says the LORD,
  who gives the sun for light by day
    and the fixed order of the moon and the
      stars for light by night;
  who stirs up the sea so that its waves roar—
    the LORD of hosts is his name:
36 If this fixed order were ever to cease
    from my presence, says the LORD,
  then also the offspring of Israel would cease
    to be a nation before me forever.

37 Thus says the LORD:
  If the heavens above can be measured,
    and the foundations of the earth below can
      be explored,
  then I will reject all the offspring of Israel
    because of all they have done,
              says the LORD.

Jerusalem to Be Enlarged

38 The days are surely coming, says the LORD, when the city shall be rebuilt for the LORD from the tower of Hananel to the Corner Gate. 39And the measuring line shall go out farther, straight to the hill Gareb, and shall then turn to Goah. 40The whole valley of the dead bodies and the ashes, and all the fields as far as the Wadi Kidron, to the corner of the Horse Gate toward the east, shall be sacred to the LORD. It shall never again be uprooted or overthrown.

Jeremiah Buys a Field During the Siege

32 THE WORD that came to Jeremiah from the LORD in the tenth year of King Zedekiah of Judah, which was the eighteenth year of Nebuchadrezzar. 2At that time the army of the king of Babylon was besieging Jerusalem, and the prophet Jeremiah was confined in the court of the guard that was in the palace of the king of Judah, 3where King Zedekiah of Judah had confined him. Zedekiah had said, "Why do you prophesy and say: Thus says the LORD: I am going to give this city into the hand of the king of Babylon, and he shall take it; 4King Zedekiah of Judah shall not escape out of the hands of the Chaldeans, but shall surely be given into the hands of the king of Babylon, and shall speak with him face to face and see him eye to eye; 5and he shall take Zedekiah to Babylon, and there he shall remain until I attend to him, says the LORD; though you fight against the Chaldeans, you shall not succeed?"

6 Jeremiah said, The word of the LORD came to me: 7Hanamel son of your uncle Shallum is going to come to you and say, "Buy my field that is at Anathoth, for the right of redemption by purchase is yours." 8Then my cousin Hanamel came to me in the court of the guard, in accordance with the word of the LORD, and said to me, "Buy my field that is at Anathoth in the land of Benjamin, for the right of possession and redemption is yours; buy it for yourself." Then I knew that this was the word of the LORD.

b 31:38, 39 northeast corner . . . northwest . . . southwest . . . southeast, implied.   c 32:2 in the dungeon beneath, literally, "in the court of the prison in the palace."

King James

9And I bought the field of Hanameel my uncle's son, that *was* in Anathoth, and weighed him the money, *even* seventeen shekels of silver.

10And I subscribed the evidence, and sealed *it*, and took witnesses, and weighed *him* the money in the balances.

11So I took the evidence of the purchase, *both* that which was sealed *according* to the law and custom, and that which was open:

12And I gave the evidence of the purchase unto Baruch the son of Neriah, the son of Maaseiah, in the sight of Hanameel mine uncle's *son*, and in the presence of the witnesses that subscribed the book of the purchase, before all the Jews that sat in the court of the prison.

13¶ And I charged Baruch before them, saying,

14Thus saith the LORD of hosts, the God of Israel; Take these evidences, this evidence of the purchase, both which is sealed, and this evidence which is open; and put them in an earthen vessel, that they may continue many days.

15For thus saith the LORD of hosts, the God of Israel; Houses and fields and vineyards shall be possessed again in this land.

16¶ Now when I had delivered the evidence of the purchase unto Baruch the son of Neriah, I prayed unto the LORD, saying,

17Ah Lord GOD! behold, thou hast made the heaven and the earth by thy great power and stretched out arm, *and* there is nothing too hard for thee:

18Thou showest lovingkindness unto thousands, and recompensest the iniquity of the fathers into the bosom of their children after them: the Great, the Mighty God, the LORD of hosts, *is* his name,

19Great in counsel, and mighty in work: for thine eyes *are* open upon all the ways of the sons of men: to give every one according to his ways, and according to the fruit of his doings:

20Which hast set signs and wonders in the land of Egypt, *even* unto this day, and in Israel, and among *other* men; and hast made thee a name, as at this day;

21And hast brought forth thy people Israel out of the land of Egypt with signs, and with wonders, and with a strong hand, and with a stretched out arm, and with great terror;

22And hast given them this land, which thou didst swear to their fathers to give them, a land flowing with milk and honey;

23And they came in, and possessed it; but they obeyed not thy voice, neither walked in thy law; they have done nothing of all that thou commandedst them to do: therefore thou hast caused all this evil to come upon them:

24Behold the mounts, they are come unto the city to take it; and the city is given into the hand of the Chaldeans, that fight against it, because of the sword, and of the famine, and of the pestilence: and what thou hast spoken is come to pass; and, behold, thou seest *it*.

25And thou hast said unto me, O Lord GOD, Buy thee the field for money, and take witnesses; for the city is given into the hand of the Chaldeans.

26¶ Then came the word of the LORD unto Jeremiah, saying,

27Behold, I *am* the LORD, the God of all flesh: is there any thing too hard for me?

28Therefore thus saith the LORD; Behold, I will give this city into the hand of the Chaldeans, and into the hand of Nebuchadrezzar king of Babylon, and he shall take it:

29And the Chaldeans, that fight against this city, shall come and set fire on this city, and burn it with the houses, upon whose roofs they have offered incense unto Baal, and poured out drink offerings unto other gods, to provoke me to anger.

New International

bought the field at Anathoth from my cousin Hanamel and weighed out for him seventeen shekelsa of silver. 10I signed and sealed the deed, had it witnessed, and weighed out the silver on the scales. 11I took the deed of purchase—the sealed copy containing the terms and conditions, as well as the unsealed copy— 12and I gave this deed to Baruch son of Neriah, the son of Mahseiah, in the presence of my cousin Hanamel and of the witnesses who had signed the deed and of all the Jews sitting in the courtyard of the guard.

13"In their presence I gave Baruch these instructions: 14'This is what the LORD Almighty, the God of Israel, says: Take these documents, both the sealed and unsealed copies of the deed of purchase, and put them in a clay jar so they will last a long time. 15For this is what the LORD Almighty, the God of Israel, says: Houses, fields and vineyards will again be bought in this land.'

16"After I had given the deed of purchase to Baruch son of Neriah, I prayed to the LORD:

17"Ah, Sovereign LORD, you have made the heavens and the earth by your great power and outstretched arm. Nothing is too hard for you. 18You show love to thousands but bring the punishment for the fathers' sins into the laps of their children after them. O great and powerful God, whose name is the LORD Almighty, 19great are your purposes and mighty are your deeds. Your eyes are open to all the ways of men; you reward everyone according to his conduct and as his deeds deserve. 20You performed miraculous signs and wonders in Egypt and have continued them to this day, both in Israel and among all mankind, and have gained the renown that is still yours. 21You brought your people Israel out of Egypt with signs and wonders, by a mighty hand and an outstretched arm and with great terror. 22You gave them this land you had sworn to give their forefathers, a land flowing with milk and honey. 23They came in and took possession of it, but they did not obey you or follow your law; they did not do what you commanded them to do. So you brought all this disaster upon them.

24"See how the siege ramps are built up to take the city. Because of the sword, famine and plague, the city will be handed over to the Babylonians who are attacking it. What you said has happened, as you now see. 25And though the city will be handed over to the Babylonians, you, O Sovereign LORD, say to me, 'Buy the field with silver and have the transaction witnessed.' "

26Then the word of the LORD came to Jeremiah: 27"I am the LORD, the God of all mankind. Is anything too hard for me? 28Therefore, this is what the LORD says: I am about to hand this city over to the Babylonians and to Nebuchadnezzar king of Babylon, who will capture it. 29The Babylonians who are attacking this city will come in and set it on fire; they will burn it down, along with the houses where the people provoked me to anger by burning incense on the roofs to Baal and by pouring out drink offerings to other gods.

a 9 That is, about 7 ounces (about 200 grams)

Living Bible

9So I bought the field, paying Hanamel seventeen pieces of silver. 10I signed and sealed the deed of purchase before witnesses, and weighed out the silver and paid him. 11Then I took the sealed deed containing the terms and conditions, and also the unsealed copy, 12and publicly, in the presence of my cousin Hanamel and the witnesses who had signed the deed, and as the prison guards watched, I handed the papers to Baruch (son of Neriah, who was the son of Mahseiah). 13And I said to him as they all listened:

14"The Lord, God of Israel, says: Take both this sealed deed and the copy and put them into a pottery jar to preserve them for a long time. 15For the Lord, God of Israel, says, In the future these papers will be valuable.b Someday people will again own property here in this country and will be buying and selling houses and vineyards and fields."

16Then after I had given the papers to Baruch I prayed:

17"O Lord God! You have made the heavens and earth by your great power; nothing is too hard for you! 18You are loving and kind to thousands, yet children suffer for their fathers' sins; you are the great and mighty God, the Lord Almighty. 19You have all wisdom and do great and mighty miracles; for your eyes are open to all the ways of men, and you reward everyone according to his life and deeds. 20You have done incredible things in the land of Egypt—things still remembered to this day. And you have continued to do great miracles in Israel and all around the world. You have made your name very great, as it is today.

21"You brought Israel out of Egypt with mighty miracles and great power and terror. 22You gave Israel this land that you promised their fathers long ago—a wonderful land that 'flows with milk and honey.' 23Our fathers came and conquered it and lived in it, but they refused to obey you or to follow your laws; they have hardly done one thing you told them to. That is why you have sent all this terrible evil upon them. 24See how the siege mounds have been built against the city walls, and the Babylonians shall conquer the city by sword, famine and disease. Everything has happened just as you said— as you determined it should! 25And yet you say to buy the field—paying good money for it before these witnesses—even though the city will belong to our enemies."

26Then this message came to Jeremiah:

27I am the Lord, the God of all mankind; is there anything too hard for me? 28Yes, I will give this city to the Babylonians and to Nebuchadnezzar, king of Babylon; he shall conquer it. 29And the Babylonians outside the walls shall come in and set fire to the city and burn down all these houses where the roofs have been used to offer incense to Baal, and to pour out libations to other gods, causing my fury to rise! 30For Israel and Judah

New Revised Standard

9 And I bought the field at Anathoth from my cousin Hanamel, and weighed out the money to him, seventeen shekels of silver. 10I signed the deed, sealed it, got witnesses, and weighed the money on scales. 11Then I took the sealed deed of purchase, containing the terms and conditions, and the open copy; 12and I gave the deed of purchase to Baruch son of Neriah son of Mahseiah, in the presence of my cousin Hanamel, in the presence of the witnesses who signed the deed of purchase, and in the presence of all the Judeans who were sitting in the court of the guard. 13In their presence I charged Baruch, saying, 14Thus says the LORD of hosts, the God of Israel: Take these deeds, both this sealed deed of purchase and this open deed, and put them in an earthenware jar, in order that they may last for a long time. 15For thus says the LORD of hosts, the God of Israel: Houses and fields and vineyards shall again be bought in this land.

Jeremiah Prays for Understanding

16 After I had given the deed of purchase to Baruch son of Neriah, I prayed to the LORD, saying: 17Ah Lord GOD! It is you who made the heavens and the earth by your great power and by your outstretched arm! Nothing is too hard for you. 18You show steadfast love to the thousandth generation,c but repay the guilt of parents into the laps of their children after them, O great and mighty God whose name is the LORD of hosts, 19great in counsel and mighty in deed; whose eyes are open to all the ways of mortals, rewarding all according to their ways and according to the fruit of their doings. 20You showed signs and wonders in the land of Egypt, and to this day in Israel and among all humankind, and have made yourself a name that continues to this very day. 21You brought your people Israel out of the land of Egypt with signs and wonders, with a strong hand and outstretched arm, and with great terror; 22and you gave them this land, which you swore to their ancestors to give them, a land flowing with milk and honey; 23and they entered and took possession of it. But they did not obey your voice or follow your law; of all you commanded them to do, they did nothing. Therefore you have made all these disasters come upon them. 24See, the siege ramps have been cast up against the city to take it, and the city, faced with sword, famine, and pestilence, has been given into the hands of the Chaldeans who are fighting against it. What you spoke has happened, as you yourself can see. 25Yet you, O Lord GOD, have said to me, "Buy the field for money and get witnesses"—though the city has been given into the hands of the Chaldeans.

God's Assurance of the People's Return

26 The word of the LORD came to Jeremiah: 27See, I am the LORD, the God of all flesh; is anything too hard for me? 28Therefore, thus says the LORD: I am going to give this city into the hands of the Chaldeans and into the hand of King Nebuchadrezzar of Babylon, and he shall take it. 29The Chaldeans who are fighting against this city shall come, set it on fire, and burn it, with the houses on whose roofs offerings have been made to Baal and libations have been poured out to other gods, to provoke me to anger. 30For the people of Israel and the

---

b 32:15 *In the future these papers will be valuable,* implied.

c *Or* to thousands

King James

30For the children of Israel and the children of Judah have only done evil before me from their youth: for the children of Israel have only provoked me to anger with the work of their hands, saith the LORD.

31For this city hath been to me *as* a provocation of mine anger and of my fury from the day that they built it even unto this day; that I should remove it from before my face,

32Because of all the evil of the children of Israel and of the children of Judah, which they have done to provoke me to anger, they, their kings, their princes, their priests, and their prophets, and the men of Judah, and the inhabitants of Jerusalem.

33And they have turned unto me the back, and not the face: though I taught them, rising up early and teaching *them,* yet they have not hearkened to receive instruction.

34But they set their abominations in the house, which is called by my name, to defile it.

35And they built the high places of Baal, which *are* in the valley of the son of Hinnom, to cause their sons and their daughters to pass through *the fire* unto Molech; which I commanded them not, neither came it into my mind, that they should do this abomination, to cause Judah to sin.

36¶ And now therefore thus saith the LORD, the God of Israel, concerning this city, whereof ye say, It shall be delivered into the hand of the king of Babylon by the sword, and by the famine, and by the pestilence;

37Behold, I will gather them out of all countries, whither I have driven them in mine anger, and in my fury, and in great wrath; and I will bring them again unto this place, and I will cause them to dwell safely:

38And they shall be my people, and I will be their God:

39And I will give them one heart, and one way, that they may fear me for ever, for the good of them, and of their children after them:

40And I will make an everlasting covenant with them, that I will not turn away from them, to do them good; but I will put my fear in their hearts, that they shall not depart from me.

41Yea, I will rejoice over them to do them good, and I will plant them in this land assuredly with my whole heart and with my whole soul.

42For thus saith the LORD; Like as I have brought all this great evil upon this people, so will I bring upon them all the good that I have promised them.

43And fields shall be bought in this land, whereof ye say, *It is* desolate without man or beast; it is given into the hand of the Chaldeans.

44Men shall buy fields for money, and subscribe evidences, and seal *them,* and take witnesses in the land of Benjamin, and in the places about Jerusalem, and in the cities of Judah, and in the cities of the mountains, and in the cities of the valley, and in the cities of the south: for I will cause their captivity to return, saith the LORD.

33 MOREOVER THE word of the LORD came unto Jeremiah the second time, while he was yet shut up in the court of the prison, saying,

2Thus saith the LORD the maker thereof, the LORD that formed it, to establish it; the LORD *is* his name;

3Call unto me, and I will answer thee, and show thee great and mighty things, which thou knowest not.

4For thus saith the LORD, the God of Israel, concerning the houses of this city, and concerning the houses of the kings of Judah, which are thrown down by the mounts, and by the sword;

New International

30"The people of Israel and Judah have done nothing but evil in my sight from their youth; indeed, the people of Israel have done nothing but provoke me with what their hands have made, declares the LORD. 31From the day it was built until now, this city has so aroused my anger and wrath that I must remove it from my sight. 32The people of Israel and Judah have provoked me by all the evil they have done—they, their kings and officials, their priests and prophets, the men of Judah and the people of Jerusalem. 33They turned their backs to me and not their faces; though I taught them again and again, they would not listen or respond to discipline. 34They set up their abominable idols in the house that bears my Name and defiled it. 35They built high places for Baal in the Valley of Ben Hinnom to sacrifice their sons and daughtersa to Molech, though I never commanded, nor did it enter my mind, that they should do such a detestable thing and so make Judah sin.

36"You are saying about this city, 'By the sword, famine and plague it will be handed over to the king of Babylon'; but this is what the LORD, the God of Israel, says: 37I will surely gather them from all the lands where I banish them in my furious anger and great wrath; I will bring them back to this place and let them live in safety. 38They will be my people, and I will be their God. 39I will give them singleness of heart and action, so that they will always fear me for their own good and the good of their children after them. 40I will make an everlasting covenant with them: I will never stop doing good to them, and I will inspire them to fear me, so that they will never turn away from me. 41I will rejoice in doing them good and will assuredly plant them in this land with all my heart and soul.

42"This is what the LORD says: As I have brought all this great calamity on this people, so I will give them all the prosperity I have promised them. 43Once more fields will be bought in this land of which you say, 'It is a desolate waste, without men or animals, for it has been handed over to the Babylonians.' 44Fields will be bought for silver, and deeds will be signed, sealed and witnessed in the territory of Benjamin, in the villages around Jerusalem, in the towns of Judah and in the towns of the hill country, of the western foothills and of the Negev, because I will restore their fortunes,b declares the LORD."

Promise of Restoration

33 WHILE JEREMIAH was still confined in the courtyard of the guard, the word of the LORD came to him a second time: 2"This is what the LORD says, he who made the earth, the LORD who formed it and established it—the LORD is his name: 3'Call to me and I will answer you and tell you great and unsearchable things you do not know.' 4For this is what the LORD, the God of Israel, says about the houses in this city and the royal palaces of Judah that have been torn down to be used against the siege ramps and the sword

---

a 35 Or *to make their sons and daughters pass through the fire* b 44 Or *will bring them back from captivity*

Living Bible

have done nothing but wrong since their earliest days; they have infuriated me with all their evil deeds. 31From the time this city was built until now it has done nothing but anger me; so I am determined to be rid of it.

32The sins of Israel and Judah—the sins of the people, of their kings, officers, priests and prophets—stir me up. 33They have turned their backs upon me and refused to return; day after day, year after year, I taught them right from wrong, but they would not listen or obey. 34They have even defiled my own Temple by worshiping their abominable idols there. 35And they have built high altars to Baal in the Valley of Hinnom. There they have burnt their children as sacrifices to Molech—something I never commanded, and cannot imagine suggesting. What an incredible evil, causing Judah to sin so greatly!

36Now therefore the Lord God of Israel says concerning this city that it will fall to the king of Babylon through warfare, famine and disease, 37but I will bring my people back again from all the countries where in my fury I will scatter them. I will bring them back to this very city, and make them live in peace and safety. 38And they shall be my people and I will be their God. 39And I will give them one heart and mind to worship me forever, for their own good and for the good of all their descendants.

40And I will make an everlasting covenant with them, promising never again to desert them, but only to do them good. I will put a desire into their hearts to worship me, and they shall never leave me. 41I will rejoice to do them good and will replant them in this land, with great joy. 42Just as I have sent all these terrors and evils upon them, so will I do all the good I have promised them.

43Fields will again be bought and sold in this land, now ravaged by the Babylonians, where men and animals alike have disappeared. 44Yes, fields shall once again be bought and sold—deeds signed and sealed and witnessed—in the country of Benjamin and here in Jerusalem, in the cities of Judah and in the hill country, in the Philistine plain and in the Negeb too, for some day I will restore prosperity to them.

33 WHILE JEREMIAH was still in jail, the Lord sent him this second message:

2The Lord, the Maker of heaven and earth—Jehovah is his name—says this:

3Ask me and I will tell you some remarkable secrets about what is going to happen here. 4For though you have torn down the houses of this city, and the king's palace too, for materials to strengthen the walls against the siege weapons of the enemy, 5yet the Babylonians

New Revised Standard

people of Judah have done nothing but evil in my sight from their youth; the people of Israel have done nothing but provoke me to anger by the work of their hands, says the LORD. 31This city has aroused my anger and wrath, from the day it was built until this day, so that I will remove it from my sight 32because of all the evil of the people of Israel and the people of Judah that they did to provoke me to anger—they, their kings and their officials, their priests and their prophets, the citizens of Judah and the inhabitants of Jerusalem. 33They have turned their backs to me, not their faces; though I have taught them persistently, they would not listen and accept correction. 34They set up their abominations in the house that bears my name, and defiled it. 35They built the high places of Baal in the valley of the son of Hinnom, to offer up their sons and daughters to Molech, though I did not command them, nor did it enter my mind that they should do this abomination, causing Judah to sin.

36 Now therefore thus says the LORD, the God of Israel, concerning this city of which you say, "It is being given into the hand of the king of Babylon by the sword, by famine, and by pestilence": 37See, I am going to gather them from all the lands to which I drove them in my anger and my wrath and in great indignation; I will bring them back to this place, and I will settle them in safety. 38They shall be my people, and I will be their God. 39I will give them one heart and one way, that they may fear me for all time, for their own good and the good of their children after them. 40I will make an everlasting covenant with them, never to draw back from doing good to them; and I will put the fear of me in their hearts, so that they may not turn from me. 41I will rejoice in doing good to them, and I will plant them in this land in faithfulness, with all my heart and all my soul.

42 For thus says the LORD: Just as I have brought all this great disaster upon this people, so I will bring upon them all the good fortune that I now promise them. 43Fields shall be bought in this land of which you are saying, It is a desolation, without human beings or animals; it has been given into the hands of the Chaldeans. 44Fields shall be bought for money, and deeds shall be signed and sealed and witnessed, in the land of Benjamin, in the places around Jerusalem, and in the cities of Judah, of the hill country, of the Shephelah, and of the Negeb; for I will restore their fortunes, says the LORD.

Healing after Punishment

33 THE WORD of the LORD came to Jeremiah a second time, while he was still confined in the court of the guard: 2Thus says the LORD who made the earth,c the LORD who formed it to establish it—the LORD is his name: 3Call to me and I will answer you, and will tell you great and hidden things that you have not known. 4For thus says the LORD, the God of Israel, concerning the houses of this city and the houses of the kings of Judah that were torn down to make a defense against the siege ramps and before the sword:d 5The

c Gk: Heb it   d Meaning of Heb uncertain

King James

5They come to fight with the Chaldeans, but *it is* to fill them with the dead bodies of men, whom I have slain in mine anger and in my fury, and for all whose wickedness I have hid my face from this city.

6Behold, I will bring it health and cure, and I will cure them, and will reveal unto them the abundance of peace and truth.

7And I will cause the captivity of Judah and the captivity of Israel to return, and will build them, as at the first.

8And I will cleanse them from all their iniquity, whereby they have sinned against me; and I will pardon all their iniquities, whereby they have sinned, and whereby they have transgressed against me.

9¶ And it shall be to me a name of joy, a praise and an honour before all the nations of the earth, which shall hear all the good that I do unto them: and they shall fear and tremble for all the goodness and for all the prosperity that I procure unto it.

10Thus saith the LORD; Again there shall be heard in this place, which ye say *shall be* desolate without man and without beast, *even* in the cities of Judah, and in the streets of Jerusalem, that are desolate, without man, and without inhabitant, and without beast,

11The voice of joy, and the voice of gladness, the voice of the bridegroom, and the voice of the bride, the voice of them that shall say, Praise the LORD of hosts: for the LORD *is* good; for his mercy *endureth* for ever: *and* of them that shall bring the sacrifice of praise into the house of the LORD. For I will cause to return the captivity of the land, as at the first, saith the LORD.

12Thus saith the LORD of hosts; Again in this place, which is desolate without man and without beast, and in all the cities thereof, shall be an habitation of shepherds causing *their* flocks to lie down.

13In the cities of the mountains, in the cities of the vale, and in the cities of the south, and in the land of Benjamin, and in the places about Jerusalem, and in the cities of Judah, shall the flocks pass again under the hands of him that telleth *them*, saith the LORD.

14Behold, the days come, saith the LORD, that I will perform that good thing which I have promised unto the house of Israel and to the house of Judah.

15¶ In those days, and at that time, will I cause the Branch of righteousness to grow up unto David; and he shall execute judgment and righteousness in the land.

16In those days shall Judah be saved, and Jerusalem shall dwell safely: and this *is the name* wherewith she shall be called, The LORD our righteousness.

17¶ For thus saith the LORD; David shall never want a man to sit upon the throne of the house of Israel;

18Neither shall the priests the Levites want a man before me to offer burnt offerings, and to kindle meat offerings, and to do sacrifice continually.

19¶ And the word of the LORD came unto Jeremiah, saying,

20Thus saith the LORD; if ye can break my covenant of the day, and my covenant of the night, and that there should not be day and night in their season;

21*Then* may also my covenant be broken with David my servant, that he should not have a son to reign upon his throne; and with the Levites the priests, my ministers.

22As the host of heaven cannot be numbered, neither the sand of the sea measured: so will I multiply the seed of David my servant, and the Levites that minister unto me.

23Moreover the word of the LORD came to Jeremiah, saying,

24Considerest thou not what this people have spoken, saying, The two families which the LORD hath chosen, he hath even cast them off? thus they have despised my people, that they should be no more a nation before them.

New International

5in the fight with the Babylonians[a]: 'They will be filled with the dead bodies of the men I will slay in my anger and wrath. I will hide my face from this city because of all its wickedness.

6" 'Nevertheless, I will bring health and healing to it; I will heal my people and will let them enjoy abundant peace and security. 7I will bring Judah and Israel back from captivity[b] and will rebuild them as they were before. 8I will cleanse them from all the sin they have committed against me and will forgive all their sins of rebellion against me. 9Then this city will bring me renown, joy, praise and honor before all nations on earth that hear of all the good things I do for it; and they will be in awe and will tremble at the abundant prosperity and peace I provide for it.'

10"This is what the LORD says: 'You say about this place, "It is a desolate waste, without men or animals." Yet in the towns of Judah and the streets of Jerusalem that are deserted, inhabited by neither men nor animals, there will be heard once more 11the sounds of joy and gladness, the voices of bride and bridegroom, and the voices of those who bring thank offerings to the house of the LORD, saying,

"Give thanks to the LORD Almighty,
    for the LORD is good;
    his love endures forever."

For I will restore the fortunes of the land as they were before,' says the LORD.

12"This is what the LORD Almighty says: 'In this place, desolate and without men or animals—in all its towns there will again be pastures for shepherds to rest their flocks. 13In the towns of the hill country, of the western foothills and of the Negev, in the territory of Benjamin, in the villages around Jerusalem and in the towns of Judah, flocks will again pass under the hand of the one who counts them,' says the LORD.

14" 'The days are coming,' declares the LORD, 'when I will fulfill the gracious promise I made to the house of Israel and to the house of Judah.

15" 'In those days and at that time
    I will make a righteous Branch sprout from
        David's line;
    he will do what is just and right in the land.
16In those days Judah will be saved
    and Jerusalem will live in safety.
This is the name by which it[c] will be called:
    The LORD Our Righteousness.'

17For this is what the LORD says: 'David will never fail to have a man to sit on the throne of the house of Israel, 18nor will the priests, who are Levites, ever fail to have a man to stand before me continually to offer burnt offerings, to burn grain offerings and to present sacrifices.' "

19The word of the LORD came to Jeremiah: 20"This is what the LORD says: 'If you can break my covenant with the day and my covenant with the night, so that day and night no longer come at their appointed time, 21then my covenant with David my servant—and my covenant with the Levites who are priests ministering before me—can be broken and David will no longer have a descendant to reign on his throne. 22I will make the descendants of David my servant and the Levites who minister before me as countless as the stars of the sky and as measureless as the sand on the seashore.' "

23The word of the LORD came to Jeremiah: 24"Have you not noticed that these people are saying, 'The LORD has rejected the two kingdoms[d] he chose'? So they despise my people and no longer regard them as a nation.

---

a 5 Or *Chaldeans*   b 7 Or *will restore the fortunes of Judah and Israel*
c 16 Or *he*   d 24 Or *families*

Living Bible

will enter, and the men of this city are already as good as dead, for I have determined to destroy them in my furious anger. I have abandoned them because of all their wickedness, and I will not pity them when they cry for help.

6Nevertheless the time will come when I will heal Jerusalem's damage and give her prosperity and peace. 7I will rebuild the cities of both Judah and Israel and restore their fortunes. 8And I will cleanse away all their sins against me, and pardon them. 9Then this city will be an honor to me, and it will give me joy and be a source of praise and glory to me before all the nations of the earth! The people of the world will see the good I do for my people and will tremble with awe!

10, 11The Lord declares that the happy voices of bridegrooms and of brides, and the joyous song of those bringing thanksgiving offerings to the Lord will be heard again in this doomed land. The people will sing: "Praise the Lord! For he is good and his mercy endures forever!" For I will make this land happier and more prosperous than it has ever been before. 12This land—though every man and animal and city is doomed—will once more see shepherds leading sheep and lambs. 13Once again their flocks will prosper in the mountain villages and in the cities east of the Philistine plain, in all the cities of the Negeb, in the land of Benjamin, in the vicinity of Jerusalem and in all the cities of Judah. 14Yes, the day will come, says the Lord, when I will do for Israel and Judah all the good I promised them.

15At that time I will bring to the throne the true Son of David,e and he shall rule justly. 16In that day the people of Judah and Jerusalem shall live in safety and their motto will be, "The Lord is our righteousness!" 17For the Lord declares that from then on, David shall forever have an heir sitting on the throne of Israel. 18And there shall always be Levites to offer burnt offerings and meal offerings and sacrifices to the Lord.

19Then this message came to Jeremiah from the Lord: 20, 21If you can break my covenant with the day and with the night so that day and night don't come on their usual schedule, only then will my covenant with David, my servant, be broken so that he shall not have a son to reign upon his throne; and my covenant with the Levite priests, my ministers, is non-cancelable. 22And as the stars cannot be counted nor the sand upon the seashores measured, so the descendants of David my servant and the line of the Levites who minister to me will be multiplied.

23The Lord spoke to Jeremiah again and said: 24Have you heard what people are saying?—that the Lord chose Judah and Israel and then abandoned them! They are sneering and saying that Israel isn't worthy to be counted as a nation. 25, 26But this is the Lord's reply:

New Revised Standard

Chaldeans are coming in to fightf and to fill them with the dead bodies of those whom I shall strike down in my anger and my wrath, for I have hidden my face from this city because of all their wickedness. 6I am going to bring it recovery and healing; I will heal them and reveal to them abundanceg of prosperity and security. 7I will restore the fortunes of Judah and the fortunes of Israel, and rebuild them as they were at first. 8I will cleanse them from all the guilt of their sin against me, and I will forgive all the guilt of their sin and rebellion against me. 9And this cityh shall be to me a name of joy, a praise and a glory before all the nations of the earth who shall hear of all the good that I do for them; they shall fear and tremble because of all the good and all the prosperity I provide for it.

10 Thus says the Lord: In this place of which you say, "It is a waste without human beings or animals," in the towns of Judah and the streets of Jerusalem that are desolate, without inhabitants, human or animal, there shall once more be heard 11the voice of mirth and the voice of gladness, the voice of the bridegroom and the voice of the bride, the voices of those who sing, as they bring thank offerings to the house of the Lord:

"Give thanks to the Lord of hosts,
 for the Lord is good,
 for his steadfast love endures forever!"

For I will restore the fortunes of the land as at first, says the Lord.

12 Thus says the Lord of hosts: In this place that is waste, without human beings or animals, and in all its towns there shall again be pasture for shepherds resting their flocks. 13In the towns of the hill country, of the Shephelah, and of the Negeb, in the land of Benjamin, the places around Jerusalem, and in the towns of Judah, flocks shall again pass under the hands of the one who counts them, says the Lord.

The Righteous Branch and the Covenant with David

14 The days are surely coming, says the Lord, when I will fulfill the promise I made to the house of Israel and the house of Judah. 15In those days and at that time I will cause a righteous Branch to spring up for David; and he shall execute justice and righteousness in the land. 16In those days Judah will be saved and Jerusalem will live in safety. And this is the name by which it will be called: "The Lord is our righteousness."

17 For thus says the Lord: David shall never lack a man to sit on the throne of the house of Israel, 18and the levitical priests shall never lack a man in my presence to offer burnt offerings, to make grain offerings, and to make sacrifices for all time.

19 The word of the Lord came to Jeremiah: 20Thus says the Lord: If any of you could break my covenant with the day and my covenant with the night, so that day and night would not come at their appointed time, 21only then could my covenant with my servant David be broken, so that he would not have a son to reign on his throne, and my covenant with my ministers the Levites. 22Just as the host of heaven cannot be numbered and the sands of the sea cannot be measured, so I will increase the offspring of my servant David, and the Levites who minister to me.

23 The word of the Lord came to Jeremiah: 24Have you not observed how these people say, "The two families that the Lord chose have been rejected by him," and how they hold my people in such contempt that they no longer regard them as a nation? 25Thus says the Lord:

---

e *33:15 the true Son of David,* or, "the true vine from the roots of David." Christ was the true vine, the only true expression of David, the man after God's own heart.

f Cn: Heb *They are coming in to fight against the Chaldeans*   g Meaning of Heb uncertain   h Heb *And it*

King James

25Thus saith the LORD; If my covenant *be* not with day and night, *and if* I have not appointed the ordinances of heaven and earth;

26Then will I cast away the seed of Jacob, and David my servant, *so* that I will not take *any* of his seed *to be* rulers over the seed of Abraham, Isaac, and Jacob: for I will cause their captivity to return, and have mercy on them.

34 THE WORD which came unto Jeremiah from the LORD, when Nebuchadnezzar king of Babylon, and all his army, and all the kingdoms of the earth of his dominion, and all the people, fought against Jerusalem, and against all the cities thereof, saying,

2Thus saith the LORD, the God of Israel; Go and speak to Zedekiah king of Judah, and tell him, Thus saith the LORD; Behold, I will give this city into the hand of the king of Babylon, and he shall burn it with fire:

3And thou shalt not escape out of his hand, but shalt surely be taken, and delivered into his hand; and thine eyes shall behold the eyes of the king of Babylon, and he shall speak with thee mouth to mouth, and thou shalt go to Babylon.

4Yet hear the word of the LORD, O Zedekiah king of Judah; Thus saith the LORD of thee, Thou shalt not die by the sword:

5*But* thou shalt die in peace: and with the burnings of thy fathers, the former kings which were before thee, so shall they burn *odours* for thee; and they will lament thee, *saying,* Ah lord! for I have pronounced the word, saith the LORD.

6Then Jeremiah the prophet spake all these words unto Zedekiah king of Judah in Jerusalem,

7When the king of Babylon's army fought against Jerusalem, and against all the cities of Judah that were left, against Lachish, and against Azekah: for these defenced cities remained of the cities of Judah.

8¶ *This is* the word that came unto Jeremiah from the LORD, after that the king Zedekiah had made a covenant with all the people which *were* at Jerusalem, to proclaim liberty unto them;

9That every man should let his manservant, and every man his maidservant, *being* an Hebrew or an Hebrewess, go free; that none should serve himself of them, *to wit,* of a Jew his brother.

10Now when all the princes, and all the people, which had entered into the covenant, heard that every one should let his manservant, and every one his maidservant, go free, that none should serve themselves of them any more, then they obeyed, and let *them* go.

11But afterward they turned, and caused the servants and the handmaids, whom they had let go free, to return, and brought them into subjection for servants and for handmaids.

12¶ Therefore the word of the LORD came to Jeremiah from the LORD, saying,

13Thus saith the LORD, the God of Israel; I made a covenant with your fathers in the day that I brought them forth out of the land of Egypt, out of the house of bondmen, saying,

14At the end of seven years let ye go every man his brother an Hebrew, which hath been sold unto thee; and when he hath served thee six years, thou shalt let him go free from thee: but your fathers hearkened not unto me, neither inclined their ear.

15And ye were now turned, and had done right in my sight, in proclaiming liberty every man to his neighbour; and ye had made a covenant before me in the house which is called by my name:

New International

25This is what the LORD says: 'If I have not established my covenant with day and night and the fixed laws of heaven and earth, 26then I will reject the descendants of Jacob and David my servant and will not choose one of his sons to rule over the descendants of Abraham, Isaac and Jacob. For I will restore their fortunes[a] and have compassion on them.' "

Warning to Zedekiah

34 WHILE NEBUCHADNEZZAR king of Babylon and all his army and all the kingdoms and peoples in the empire he ruled were fighting against Jerusalem and all its surrounding towns, this word came to Jeremiah from the LORD: 2"This is what the LORD, the God of Israel, says: Go to Zedekiah king of Judah and tell him, 'This is what the LORD says: I am about to hand this city over to the king of Babylon, and he will burn it down. 3You will not escape from his grasp but will surely be captured and handed over to him. You will see the king of Babylon with your own eyes, and he will speak with you face to face. And you will go to Babylon.

4" 'Yet hear the promise of the LORD, O Zedekiah king of Judah. This is what the LORD says concerning you: You will not die by the sword; 5you will die peacefully. As people made a funeral fire in honor of your fathers, the former kings who preceded you, so they will make a fire in your honor and lament, "Alas, O master!" I myself make this promise, declares the LORD.' "

6Then Jeremiah the prophet told all this to Zedekiah king of Judah, in Jerusalem, 7while the army of the king of Babylon was fighting against Jerusalem and the other cities of Judah that were still holding out—Lachish and Azekah. These were the only fortified cities left in Judah.

Freedom for Slaves

8The word came to Jeremiah from the LORD after King Zedekiah had made a covenant with all the people in Jerusalem to proclaim freedom for the slaves. 9Everyone was to free his Hebrew slaves, both male and female; no one was to hold a fellow Jew in bondage. 10So all the officials and people who entered into this covenant agreed that they would free their male and female slaves and no longer hold them in bondage. They agreed, and set them free. 11But afterward they changed their minds and took back the slaves they had freed and enslaved them again.

12Then the word of the LORD came to Jeremiah: 13"This is what the LORD, the God of Israel, says: I made a covenant with your forefathers when I brought them out of Egypt, out of the land of slavery. I said, 14'Every seventh year each of you must free any fellow Hebrew who has sold himself to you. After he has served you six years, you must let him go free.'[b] Your fathers, however, did not listen to me or pay attention to me. 15Recently you repented and did what is right in my sight: Each of you proclaimed freedom to his countrymen. You even made a covenant before me in the house that bears my Name. 16But now you have turned around and profaned

---

Living Bible

I would no more reject my people than I would change my laws of night and day, of earth and sky. I will never abandon the Jews, or David my servant, or change the plan that his Child will someday rule these descendants of Abraham, Isaac and Jacob. Instead I will restore their prosperity and have mercy on them.

34 THIS IS the message that came to Jeremiah from the Lord when Nebuchadnezzar, king of Babylon, and all his armies from all the kingdoms he ruled, came and fought against Jerusalem and the cities of Judah:

2Go tell Zedekiah, king of Judah, that the Lord says this: I will give this city to the king of Babylon and he shall burn it. 3You shall not escape; you shall be captured and taken before the king of Babylon and he shall pronounce sentence against you and you shall be exiled to Babylon. 4But listen to this, O Zedekiah, king of Judah: God says you won't be killed in war and carnage, 5but that you will die quietly among your people, and they will burn incense in your memory, just as they did for your fathers. They will weep for you and say, "Alas, our king is dead!" This I have decreed, says the Lord.

6So Jeremiah delivered the message to King Zedekiah. 7At this time the Babylonian army was besieging Jerusalem, Lachish and Azekah—the only walled cities of Judah still standing.

8This is the message that came to Jeremiah from the Lord after King Zedekiah of Judah had freed all the slaves in Jerusalem— 9(for King Zedekiah had ordered everyone to free his Hebrew slaves, both men and women. He had said that no Jew should be the master of another Jew for all were brothers. 10The princes and all the people had obeyed the king's command and freed their slaves, but the action was only temporary. 11They changed their minds and made their servants slaves again.c 12That is why the Lord gave the following message to Jerusalem.)

13The Lord, the God of Israel, says:

I made a covenant with your fathers long ago when I brought them from their slavery in Egypt. 14I told them that every Hebrew slave must be freed after serving six years. But this was not done. 15Recently you began doing what was right, as I commanded you, and freed your slaves. You had solemnly promised me in my Temple that you would do it. 16But now you refuse and have

New Revised Standard

Only if I had not established my covenant with day and night and the ordinances of heaven and earth, 26would I reject the offspring of Jacob and of my servant David and not choose any of his descendants as rulers over the offspring of Abraham, Isaac, and Jacob. For I will restore their fortunes, and will have mercy upon them.

Death in Captivity Predicted for Zedekiah

34 THE WORD that came to Jeremiah from the LORD, when King Nebuchadrezzar of Babylon and all his army and all the kingdoms of the earth and all the peoples under his dominion were fighting against Jerusalem and all its cities: 2"Thus says the LORD, the God of Israel: Go and speak to King Zedekiah of Judah and say to him: Thus says the LORD: I am going to give this city into the hand of the king of Babylon, and he shall burn it with fire. 3And you yourself shall not escape from his hand, but shall surely be captured and handed over to him; you shall see the king of Babylon eye to eye and speak with him face to face; and you shall go to Babylon. 4Yet hear the word of the LORD, O King Zedekiah of Judah! Thus says the LORD concerning you: You shall not die by the sword; 5you shall die in peace. And as spices were burnedd for your ancestors, the earlier kings who preceded you, so they shall burn spicese for you and lament for you, saying, "Alas, lord!" For I have spoken the word, says the LORD.

6 Then the prophet Jeremiah spoke all these words to Zedekiah king of Judah, in Jerusalem, 7when the army of the king of Babylon was fighting against Jerusalem and against all the cities of Judah that were left, Lachish and Azekah; for these were the only fortified cities of Judah that remained.

Treacherous Treatment of Slaves

8 The word that came to Jeremiah from the LORD, after King Zedekiah had made a covenant with all the people in Jerusalem to make a proclamation of liberty to them, 9that all should set free their Hebrew slaves, male and female, so that no one should hold another Judean in slavery. 10And they obeyed, all the officials and all the people who had entered into the covenant that all would set free their slaves, male or female, so that they would not be enslaved again; they obeyed and set them free. 11 But afterward they turned around and took back the male and female slaves they had set free, and brought them again into subjection as slaves. 12The word of the LORD came to Jeremiah from the LORD: 13Thus says the LORD, the God of Israel: I myself made a covenant with your ancestors when I brought them out of the land of Egypt, out of the house of slavery, saying, 14"Every seventh year each of you must set free any Hebrews who have been sold to you and have served you six years; you must set them free from your service." But your ancestors did not listen to me or incline their ears to me. 15You yourselves recently repented and did what was right in my sight by proclaiming liberty to one another, and you made a covenant before me in the house that is called by my name; 16but then you turned around

---

c 34:11 They changed their minds and made their servants slaves again. When the siege was temporarily lifted (37:6-11) they became bold and returned to their sins.

d Heb as there was burning   e Heb shall burn

King James

16But ye turned and polluted my name, and caused every man his servant, and every man his handmaid, whom ye had set at liberty at their pleasure, to return, and brought them into subjection, to be unto you for servants and for handmaids.

17Therefore thus saith the LORD; Ye have not hearkened unto me, in proclaiming liberty, every one to his brother, and every man to his neighbour: behold, I proclaim a liberty for you, saith the LORD, to the sword, to the pestilence, and to the famine; and I will make you to be removed into all the kingdoms of the earth.

18And I will give the men that have transgressed my covenant, which have not performed the words of the covenant which they had made before me, when they cut the calf in twain, and passed between the parts thereof,

19The princes of Judah, and the princes of Jerusalem, the eunuchs, and the priests, and all the people of the land, which passed between the parts of the calf;

20I will even give them into the hand of their enemies, and into the hand of them that seek their life: and their dead bodies shall be for meat unto the fowls of the heaven, and to the beasts of the earth.

21And Zedekiah king of Judah and his princes will I give into the hand of their enemies, and into the hand of them that seek their life, and into the hand of the king of Babylon's army, which are gone up from you.

22Behold, I will command, saith the LORD, and cause them to return to this city; and they shall fight against it, and take it, and burn it with fire: and I will make the cities of Judah a desolation without an inhabitant.

35 THE WORD which came unto Jeremiah from the LORD in the days of Jehoiakim the son of Josiah king of Judah, saying,

2Go unto the house of the Rechabites, and speak unto them, and bring them into the house of the LORD, into one of the chambers, and give them wine to drink.

3Then I took Jaazaniah the son of Jeremiah, the son of Habaziniah, and his brethren, and all his sons, and the whole house of the Rechabites;

4And I brought them into the house of the LORD, into the chamber of the sons of Hanan, the son of Igdaliah, a man of God, which was by the chamber of the princes, which was above the chamber of Maaseiah the son of Shallum, the keeper of the door:

5And I set before the sons of the house of the Rechabites pots full of wine, and cups, and I said unto them, Drink ye wine.

6But they said, We will drink no wine: for Jonadab the son of Rechab our father commanded us, saying, Ye shall drink no wine, neither ye, nor your sons for ever:

7Neither shall ye build house, nor sow seed, nor plant vineyard, nor have any: but all your days ye shall dwell in tents; that ye may live many days in the land where ye be strangers.

8Thus have we obeyed the voice of Jonadab the son of Rechab our father in all that he hath charged us, to drink no wine all our days, we, our wives, our sons, nor our daughters;

9Nor to build houses for us to dwell in: neither have we vineyard, nor field, nor seed:

10But we have dwelt in tents, and have obeyed, and done according to all that Jonadab our father commanded us.

11But it came to pass, when Nebuchadrezzar king of Babylon came up into the land, that we said, Come, and let us go to Jerusalem for fear of the army of the Chaldeans, and for fear of the army of the Syrians: so we dwell at Jerusalem.

12¶ Then came the word of the LORD unto Jeremiah, saying,

New International

my name; each of you has taken back the male and female slaves you had set free to go where they wished. You have forced them to become your slaves again.

17"Therefore, this is what the LORD says: You have not obeyed me; you have not proclaimed freedom for your fellow countrymen. So I now proclaim 'freedom' for you, declares the LORD—'freedom' to fall by the sword, plague and famine. I will make you abhorrent to all the kingdoms of the earth. 18The men who have violated my covenant and have not fulfilled the terms of the covenant they made before me, I will treat like the calf they cut in two and then walked between its pieces. 19The leaders of Judah and Jerusalem, the court officials, the priests and all the people of the land who walked between the pieces of the calf, 20I will hand over to their enemies who seek their lives. Their dead bodies will become food for the birds of the air and the beasts of the earth.

21"I will hand Zedekiah king of Judah and his officials over to their enemies who seek their lives, to the army of the king of Babylon, which has withdrawn from you. 22I am going to give the order, declares the LORD, and I will bring them back to this city. They will fight against it, take it and burn it down. And I will lay waste the towns of Judah so no one can live there."

The Recabites

35 THIS IS the word that came to Jeremiah from the LORD during the reign of Jehoiakim son of Josiah king of Judah: 2"Go to the Recabite family and invite them to come to one of the side rooms of the house of the LORD and give them wine to drink."

3So I went to get Jaazaniah son of Jeremiah, the son of Habazziniah, and his brothers and all his sons—the whole family of the Recabites. 4I brought them into the house of the LORD, into the room of the sons of Hanan son of Igdaliah the man of God. It was next to the room of the officials, which was over that of Maaseiah son of Shallum the doorkeeper. 5Then I set bowls full of wine and some cups before the men of the Recabite family and said to them, "Drink some wine."

6But they replied, "We do not drink wine, because our forefather Jonadab son of Recab gave us this command: 'Neither you nor your descendants must ever drink wine. 7Also you must never build houses, sow seed or plant vineyards; you must never have any of these things, but must always live in tents. Then you will live a long time in the land where you are nomads.' 8We have obeyed everything our forefather Jonadab son of Recab commanded us. Neither we nor our wives nor our sons and daughters have ever drunk wine 9or built houses to live in or had vineyards, fields or crops. 10We have lived in tents and have fully obeyed everything our forefather Jonadab commanded us. 11But when Nebuchadnezzar king of Babylon invaded this land, we said, 'Come, we must go to Jerusalem to escape the Babylonian[a] and Aramean armies.' So we have remained in Jerusalem."

12Then the word of the LORD came to Jeremiah, saying: 13"This is what the LORD Almighty, the God of

ᵃ 11 Or Chaldean

Living Bible

defiled my name by shrugging off your oath and have made them slaves again.

17Therefore, says the Lord, because you will not listen to me and release them, I will release you to the power of death by war and famine and disease. And I will scatter you over all the world as exiles. 18, 19Because you have refused the terms of our contract I will cut you apart just as you cut apart the calf when you walked between its halves to solemnize your vows. Yes, I will butcher you, whether you are princes, court officials, priests or people—for you have broken your oath. 20I will give you to your enemies and they shall kill you. I will feed your dead bodies to the vultures and wild animals. 21And I will surrender Zedekiah, king of Judah, and his officials to the army of the king of Babylon, though he has departed from the city for a little while. 22I will summon the Babylonian armies back again and they will fight against it and capture this city and burn it. And I will see to it that the cities of Judah are completely destroyed and left desolate without a living soul.

35 THIS IS the message the Lord gave Jeremiah when Jehoiakim (son of Josiah) was the king of Judah:b

2Go to the settlement where the families of the Rechabites live and invite them to the Temple. Take them into one of the inner rooms and offer them a drink of wine.

3So I went over to see Ja-azaniah (son of Jeremiah, who was the son of Habazziniah), and brought him and all his brothers and sons—representing all the Rechab families— 4to the Temple, into the room assigned for the use of the sons of Hanan the prophet (the son of Igdaliah). This room was located next to the one used by the palace official, directly above the room of Maaseiah (son of Shallum), who was the temple doorman. 5I set cups and jugs of wine before them and invited them to have a drink, 6but they refused.

"No," they said. "We don't drink, for Jonadab our father (son of Rechab) commanded that none of us should ever drink, neither we nor our children forever. 7He also told us not to build houses or plant crops or vineyards and not to own farms, but always to live in tents; and that if we obeyed we would live long, good lives in our own land. 8And we have obeyed him in all these things. We have never had a drink of wine since then, nor our wives or our sons or daughters either. 9We haven't built houses or owned farms or planted crops. 10We have lived in tents and have fully obeyed everything that Jonadab our father commanded us. 11But when Nebuchadnezzar, king of Babylon, arrived in this country, we were afraid and decided to move to Jerusalem. That's why we are here."

12Then the Lord gave this message to Jeremiah:

New Revised Standard

and profaned my name when each of you took back your male and female slaves, whom you had set free according to their desire, and you brought them again into subjection to be your slaves. 17Therefore, thus says the LORD: You have not obeyed me by granting a release to your neighbors and friends; I am going to grant a release to you, says the LORD—a release to the sword, to pestilence, and to famine. I will make you a horror to all the kingdoms of the earth. 18And those who transgressed my covenant and did not keep the terms of the covenant that they made before me, I will make likec the calf when they cut it in two and passed between its parts: 19the officials of Judah, the officials of Jerusalem, the eunuchs, the priests, and all the people of the land who passed between the parts of the calf 20shall be handed over to their enemies and to those who seek their lives. Their corpses shall become food for the birds of the air and the wild animals of the earth. 21And as for King Zedekiah of Judah and his officials, I will hand them over to their enemies and to those who seek their lives, to the army of the king of Babylon, which has withdrawn from you. 22I am going to command, says the LORD, and will bring them back to this city; and they will fight against it, and take it, and burn it with fire. The towns of Judah I will make a desolation without inhabitant.

The Rechabites Commended

35 THE WORD that came to Jeremiah from the LORD in the days of King Jehoiakim son of Josiah of Judah: 2Go to the house of the Rechabites, and speak with them, and bring them to the house of the LORD, into one of the chambers; then offer them wine to drink. 3So I took Jaazaniah son of Jeremiah son of Habazziniah, and his brothers, and all his sons, and the whole house of the Rechabites. 4I brought them to the house of the LORD into the chamber of the sons of Hanan son of Igdaliah, the man of God, which was near the chamber of the officials, above the chamber of Maaseiah son of Shallum, keeper of the threshold. 5Then I set before the Rechabites pitchers full of wine, and cups; and I said to them, "Have some wine." 6But they answered, "We will drink no wine, for our ancestor Jonadab son of Rechab commanded us, 'You shall never drink wine, neither you nor your children; 7nor shall you ever build a house, or sow seed; nor shall you plant a vineyard, or even own one; but you shall live in tents all your days, that you may live many days in the land where you reside.' 8We have obeyed the charge of our ancestor Jonadab son of Rechab in all that he commanded us, to drink no wine all our days, ourselves, our wives, our sons, or our daughters, 9and not to build houses to live in. We have no vineyard or field or seed; 10but we have lived in tents, and have obeyed and done all that our ancestor Jonadab commanded us. 11But when King Nebuchadrezzar of Babylon came up against the land, we said, 'Come, and let us go to Jerusalem for fear of the army of the Chaldeans and the army of the Arameans.' That is why we are living in Jerusalem."

12 Then the word of the LORD came to Jeremiah:

b 35:1 when Jehoiakim . . . was the king of Judah. This is apparently an early message of Jeremiah, and is not here in its chronological order with the other messages.

c Cn: Heb lacks like

King James

13Thus saith the LORD of hosts, the God of Israel; Go and tell the men of Judah and the inhabitants of Jerusalem, Will ye not receive instruction to hearken to my words? saith the LORD.

14The words of Jonadab the son of Rechab, that he commanded his sons not to drink wine, are performed; for unto this day they drink none, but obey their father's commandment: notwithstanding I have spoken unto you, rising early and speaking; but ye hearkened not unto me.

15I have sent also unto you all my servants the prophets, rising up early and sending them, saying, Return ye now every man from his evil way, and amend your doings, and go not after other gods to serve them, and ye shall dwell in the land which I have given to you and to your fathers: but ye have not inclined your ear, nor hearkened unto me.

16Because the sons of Jonadab the son of Rechab have performed the commandment of their father, which he commanded them; but this people hath not hearkened unto me:

17Therefore thus saith the LORD God of hosts, the God of Israel; Behold, I will bring upon Judah and upon all the inhabitants of Jerusalem all the evil that I have pronounced against them: because I have spoken unto them, but they have not heard; and I have called unto them, but they have not answered.

18¶ And Jeremiah said unto the house of the Rechabites, Thus saith the LORD of hosts, the God of Israel; Because ye have obeyed the commandment of Jonadab your father, and kept all his precepts, and done according unto all that he hath commanded you:

19Therefore thus saith the LORD of hosts, the God of Israel; Jonadab the son of Rechab shall not want a man to stand before me for ever.

36 AND IT came to pass in the fourth year of Jehoiakim the son of Josiah king of Judah, that this word came unto Jeremiah from the LORD, saying,

2Take thee a roll of a book, and write therein all the words that I have spoken unto thee against Israel, and against Judah, and against all the nations, from the day I spake unto thee, from the days of Josiah, even unto this day.

3It may be that the house of Judah will hear all the evil which I purpose to do unto them; that they may return every man from his evil way; that I may forgive their iniquity and their sin.

4Then Jeremiah called Baruch the son of Neriah: and Baruch wrote from the mouth of Jeremiah all the words of the LORD, which he had spoken unto him, upon a roll of a book.

5And Jeremiah commanded Baruch, saying, I am shut up; I cannot go into the house of the LORD:

6Therefore go thou, and read in the roll, which thou hast written from my mouth, the words of the LORD in the ears of the people in the LORD's house upon the fasting day: and also thou shalt read them in the ears of all Judah that come out of their cities.

7It may be they will present their supplication before the LORD, and will return every one from his evil way: for great is the anger and the fury that the LORD hath pronounced against this people.

8And Baruch the son of Neriah did according to all that Jeremiah the prophet commanded him, reading in the book the words of the LORD in the LORD's house.

9And it came to pass in the fifth year of Jehoiakim the son of Josiah king of Judah, in the ninth month, that they proclaimed a fast before the LORD to all the people in Jerusalem, and to all the people that came from the cities of Judah unto Jerusalem.

New International

Israel, says: Go and tell the men of Judah and the people of Jerusalem, 'Will you not learn a lesson and obey my words?' declares the LORD. 14'Jonadab son of Recab ordered his sons not to drink wine and this command has been kept. To this day they do not drink wine, because they obey their forefather's command. But I have spoken to you again and again, yet you have not obeyed me. 15Again and again I sent all my servants the prophets to you. They said, "Each of you must turn from your wicked ways and reform your actions; do not follow other gods to serve them. Then you will live in the land I have given to you and your fathers." But you have not paid attention or listened to me. 16The descendants of Jonadab son of Recab have carried out the command their forefather gave them, but these people have not obeyed me.'

17"Therefore, this is what the LORD God Almighty, the God of Israel, says: 'Listen! I am going to bring on Judah and on everyone living in Jerusalem every disaster I pronounced against them. I spoke to them, but they did not listen; I called to them, but they did not answer.' "

18Then Jeremiah said to the family of the Recabites, "This is what the LORD Almighty, the God of Israel, says: 'You have obeyed the command of your forefather Jonadab and have followed all his instructions and have done everything he ordered.' 19Therefore, this is what the LORD Almighty, the God of Israel, says: 'Jonadab son of Recab will never fail to have a man to serve me.' "

Jehoiakim Burns Jeremiah's Scroll

36 IN THE fourth year of Jehoiakim son of Josiah king of Judah, this word came to Jeremiah from the LORD: 2"Take a scroll and write on it all the words I have spoken to you concerning Israel, Judah and all the other nations from the time I began speaking to you in the reign of Josiah till now. 3Perhaps when the people of Judah hear about every disaster I plan to inflict on them, each of them will turn from his wicked way; then I will forgive their wickedness and their sin."

4So Jeremiah called Baruch son of Neriah, and while Jeremiah dictated all the words the LORD had spoken to him, Baruch wrote them on the scroll. 5Then Jeremiah told Baruch, "I am restricted; I cannot go to the LORD's temple. 6So you go to the house of the LORD on a day of fasting and read to the people from the scroll the words of the LORD that you wrote as I dictated. Read them to all the people of Judah who come in from their towns. 7Perhaps they will bring their petition before the LORD, and each will turn from his wicked ways, for the anger and wrath pronounced against this people by the LORD are great."

8Baruch son of Neriah did everything Jeremiah the prophet told him to do; at the LORD's temple he read the words of the LORD from the scroll. 9In the ninth month of the fifth year of Jehoiakim son of Josiah king of Judah, a time of fasting before the LORD was proclaimed for all the people in Jerusalem and those who had come from the towns of Judah. 10From the room of Gemariah

Living Bible

13The Lord, the God of Israel, says: Go and say to Judah and Jerusalem, Won't you learn a lesson from the families of Rechab? 14They don't drink, because their father told them not to. But I have spoken to you again and again and you won't listen or obey. 15I have sent you prophet after prophet to tell you to turn back from your wicked ways and to stop worshiping other gods and that if you obeyed, then I would let you live in peace here in the land I gave to you and your fathers. But you wouldn't listen or obey. 16The families of Rechab have obeyed their father completely, but you have refused to listen to me. 17Therefore the Lord Almighty, the God of Israel, says: Because you refuse to listen or answer when I call, I will send upon Judah and Jerusalem all the evil I have ever threatened.

18, 19Then Jeremiah turned to the Rechabites and said: "The Lord, the God of Israel, says that because you have obeyed your father in every respect, he shall always have descendants who will worship me."

36 IN THE fourth year of the reign of King Jehoiakim[a] of Judah (son of Josiah) the Lord gave this message to Jeremiah:

2"Get a scroll and write down all my messages against Israel, Judah and the other nations. Begin with the first message back in the days of Josiah, and write down every one of them. 3Perhaps when the people of Judah see in writing all the terrible things I will do to them, they will repent. And then I can forgive them."

4So Jeremiah sent for Baruch (son of Neriah), and as Jeremiah dictated, Baruch wrote down all the prophecies.

5When all was finished, Jeremiah said to Baruch, "Since I am a prisoner here, 6you read the scroll in the Temple on the next Day of Fasting, for on that day people will be there from all over Judah. 7Perhaps even yet they will turn from their evil ways and ask the Lord to forgive them before it is too late, even though these curses of God have been pronounced upon them."

8Baruch did as Jeremiah told him to, and read all these messages to the people at the Temple. 9This occurred on the Day of Fasting held in December of the fifth year of the reign of King Jehoiakim (son of Josiah). People came from all over Judah to attend the services at the Temple that day. 10Baruch went to the office of

New Revised Standard

13 Thus says the LORD of hosts, the God of Israel: Go and say to the people of Judah and the inhabitants of Jerusalem, Can you not learn a lesson and obey my words? says the LORD. 14 The command has been carried out that Jonadab son of Rechab gave to his descendants to drink no wine; and they drink none to this day, for they have obeyed their ancestor's command. But I myself have spoken to you persistently, and you have not obeyed me. 15 I have sent to you all my servants the prophets, sending them persistently, saying, 'Turn now everyone of you from your evil way, and amend your doings, and do not go after other gods to serve them, and then you shall live in the land that I gave to you and your ancestors.' But you did not incline your ear or obey me. 16 The descendants of Jonadab son of Rechab have carried out the command that their ancestor gave them, but this people has not obeyed me. 17 Therefore, thus says the LORD, the God of hosts, the God of Israel: I am going to bring on Judah and on all the inhabitants of Jerusalem every disaster that I have pronounced against them; because I have spoken to them and they have not listened, I have called to them and they have not answered.

18 But to the house of the Rechabites Jeremiah said: Thus says the LORD of hosts, the God of Israel: Because you have obeyed the command of your ancestor Jonadab, and kept all his precepts, and done all that he commanded you, 19therefore thus says the LORD of hosts, the God of Israel: Jonadab son of Rechab shall not lack a descendant to stand before me for all time.

The Scroll Read in the Temple

36 IN THE fourth year of King Jehoiakim son of Josiah of Judah, this word came to Jeremiah from the LORD: 2Take a scroll and write on it all the words that I have spoken to you against Israel and Judah and all the nations, from the day I spoke to you, from the days of Josiah until today. 3 It may be that when the house of Judah hears of all the disasters that I intend to do to them, all of them may turn from their evil ways, so that I may forgive their iniquity and their sin.

4 Then Jeremiah called Baruch son of Neriah, and Baruch wrote on a scroll at Jeremiah's dictation all the words of the LORD that he had spoken to him. 5 And Jeremiah ordered Baruch, saying, "I am prevented from entering the house of the LORD; 6 so you go yourself, and on a fast day in the hearing of the people in the LORD's house you shall read the words of the LORD from the scroll that you have written at my dictation. You shall read them also in the hearing of all the people of Judah who come up from their towns. 7 It may be that their plea will come before the LORD, and that all of them will turn from their evil ways, for great is the anger and wrath that the LORD has pronounced against this people." 8 And Baruch son of Neriah did all that the prophet Jeremiah ordered him about reading from the scroll the words of the LORD in the LORD's house.

9 In the fifth year of King Jehoiakim son of Josiah of Judah, in the ninth month, all the people in Jerusalem and all the people who came from the towns of Judah to Jerusalem proclaimed a fast before the LORD. 10 Then,

---

[a] 36:1 In the fourth year of . . . King Jehoiakim. Probably in the summer of 605 B.C., shortly after Nebuchadnezzar's victory over the Egyptian army at Carchemish.

King James

10Then read Baruch in the book the words of Jeremiah in the house of the LORD, in the chamber of Gemariah the son of Shaphan the scribe, in the higher court, at the entry of the new gate of the LORD's house, in the ears of all the people.

11¶ When Michaiah the son of Gemariah, the son of Shaphan, had heard out of the book all the words of the LORD,

12Then he went down into the king's house, into the scribe's chamber: and, lo, all the princes sat there, even Elishama the scribe, and Delaiah the son of Shemaiah, and Elnathan the son of Achbor, and Gemariah the son of Shaphan, and Zedekiah the son of Hananiah, and all the princes.

13Then Michaiah declared unto them all the words that he had heard, when Baruch read the book in the ears of the people.

14Therefore all the princes sent Jehudi the son of Nethaniah, the son of Shelemiah, the son of Cushi, unto Baruch, saying, Take in thine hand the roll wherein thou hast read in the ears of the people, and come. So Baruch the son of Neriah took the roll in his hand, and came unto them.

15And they said unto him, Sit down now, and read it in our ears. So Baruch read it in their ears.

16Now it came to pass, when they had heard all the words, they were afraid both one and other, and said unto Baruch, We will surely tell the king of all these words.

17And they asked Baruch, saying, Tell us now, How didst thou write all these words at his mouth?

18Then Baruch answered them, He pronounced all these words unto me with his mouth, and I wrote them with ink in the book.

19Then said the princes unto Baruch, Go, hide thee, thou and Jeremiah; and let no man know where ye be.

20¶ And they went in to the king into the court, but they laid up the roll in the chamber of Elishama the scribe, and told all the words in the ears of the king.

21So the king sent Jehudi to fetch the roll: and he took it out of Elishama the scribe's chamber. And Jehudi read it in the ears of the king, and in the ears of all the princes which stood beside the king.

22Now the king sat in the winterhouse in the ninth month: and there was a fire on the hearth burning before him.

23And it came to pass, that when Jehudi had read three or four leaves, he cut it with the penknife, and cast it into the fire that was on the hearth, until all the roll was consumed in the fire that was on the hearth.

24Yet they were not afraid, nor rent their garments, neither the king, nor any of his servants that heard all these words.

25Nevertheless Elnathan and Delaiah and Gemariah had made intercession to the king that he would not burn the roll: but he would not hear them.

26But the king commanded Jerahmeel the son of Hammelech, and Seraiah the son of Azriel, and Shelemiah the son of Abdeel, to take Baruch the scribe and Jeremiah the prophet: but the LORD hid them.

27¶ Then the word of the LORD came to Jeremiah, after that the king had burned the roll, and the words which Baruch wrote at the mouth of Jeremiah, saying,

28Take thee again another roll, and write in it all the former words that were in the first roll, which Jehoiakim the king of Judah hath burned.

29And thou shalt say to Jehoiakim king of Judah, Thus saith the LORD; Thou hast burned this roll, saying, Why hast thou written therein, saying, The king of Babylon shall certainly come and destroy this land, and shall cause to cease from thence man and beast?

30Therefore thus saith the LORD of Jehoiakim king of Judah; He shall have none to sit upon the throne of David: and his dead body shall be cast out in the day to the heat, and in the night to the frost.

New International

son of Shaphan the secretary, which was in the upper courtyard at the entrance of the New Gate of the temple, Baruch read to all the people at the LORD's temple the words of Jeremiah from the scroll.

11When Micaiah son of Gemariah, the son of Shaphan, heard all the words of the LORD from the scroll, 12he went down to the secretary's room in the royal palace, where all the officials were sitting: Elishama the secretary, Delaiah son of Shemaiah, Elnathan son of Acbor, Gemariah son of Shaphan, Zedekiah son of Hananiah, and all the other officials. 13After Micaiah told them everything he had heard Baruch read to the people from the scroll, 14all the officials sent Jehudi son of Nethaniah, the son of Shelemiah, the son of Cushi, to say to Baruch, "Bring the scroll from which you have read to the people and come." So Baruch son of Neriah went to them with the scroll in his hand. 15They said to him, "Sit down, please, and read it to us."

So Baruch read it to them. 16When they heard all these words, they looked at each other in fear and said to Baruch, "We must report all these words to the king." 17Then they asked Baruch, "Tell us, how did you come to write all this? Did Jeremiah dictate it?"

18"Yes," Baruch replied, "he dictated all these words to me, and I wrote them in ink on the scroll."

19Then the officials said to Baruch, "You and Jeremiah, go and hide. Don't let anyone know where you are."

20After they put the scroll in the room of Elishama the secretary, they went to the king in the courtyard and reported everything to him. 21The king sent Jehudi to get the scroll, and Jehudi brought it from the room of Elishama the secretary and read it to the king and all the officials standing beside him. 22It was the ninth month and the king was sitting in the winter apartment, with a fire burning in the firepot in front of him. 23Whenever Jehudi had read three or four columns of the scroll, the king cut them off with a scribe's knife and threw them into the firepot, until the entire scroll was burned in the fire. 24The king and all his attendants who heard all these words showed no fear, nor did they tear their clothes. 25Even though Elnathan, Delaiah and Gemariah urged the king not to burn the scroll, he would not listen to them. 26Instead, the king commanded Jerahmeel, a son of the king, Seraiah son of Azriel and Shelemiah son of Abdeel to arrest Baruch the scribe and Jeremiah the prophet. But the LORD had hidden them.

27After the king burned the scroll containing the words that Baruch had written at Jeremiah's dictation, the word of the LORD came to Jeremiah: 28"Take another scroll and write on it all the words that were on the first scroll, which Jehoiakim king of Judah burned up. 29Also tell Jehoiakim king of Judah, 'This is what the LORD says: You burned that scroll and said, "Why did you write on it that the king of Babylon would certainly come and destroy this land and cut off both men and animals from it?" 30Therefore, this is what the LORD says about Jehoiakim king of Judah: He will have no one to sit on the throne of David; his body will be thrown out and exposed to the heat by day and the frost by night. 31I will

Living Bible

Gemariah the Scribe (son of Shaphan) to read the scroll. (This room was just off the upper assembly hall of the Temple, near the door of the New Gate.)

11When Micaiah (son of Gemariah, son of Shaphan) heard the messages from God, 12he went down to the palace to the conference room where the administrative officials were meeting. Elishama (the scribe) was there, as well as Delaiah (son of Shamaiah), Elnathan (son of Achbor), Gemariah (son of Shaphan), Zedekiah (son of Hananiah), and all the others with similar responsibilities. 13When Micaiah told them about the messages Baruch was reading to the people, 14, 15the officials sent Jehudi (son of Nethaniah, son of Shelemiah, son of Cushi) to ask Baruch to come and read the messages to them too, and Baruch did.

16By the time he finished they were badly frightened. "We must tell the king," they said. 17"But first, tell us how you got these messages. Did Jeremiah himself dictate them to you?" 18So Baruch explained that Jeremiah had dictated them to him word by word, and he had written them down in ink upon the scroll. 19"You and Jeremiah both hide," the officials said to Baruch. "Don't tell a soul where you are!" 20Then the officials hid the scroll in the room of Elishama the scribe and went to tell the king.

21The king sent Jehudi to get the scroll. Jehudi brought it from Elishama the scribe and read it to the king as all his officials stood by. 22The king was in a winterized part of the palace at the time, sitting in front of a fireplace,a for it was December, and cold. 23And whenever Jehudi finished reading three or four columns, the king would take his knife, and slit off the section and throw it into the fire, until the whole scroll was destroyed. 24, 25And no one protested except Elnathan, Delaiah and Gemariah. They pled with the king not to burn the scroll, but he wouldn't listen to them. Not another of the king's officials showed any signs of fear or anger at what he had done.

26Then the king commanded Jerahmeel (a member of the royal familyb) and Seraiah (son of Azri-el) and Shelemiah (son of Abdeel) to arrest Baruch and Jeremiah. But the Lord hid them!

27After the king had burned the scroll, the Lord said to Jeremiah:

28Get another scroll and write everything again just as you did before, 29and say this to the king: "The Lord says, You burned the scroll because it said the king of Babylon would destroy this country and everything in it. 30And now the Lord adds this concerning you, Jehoiakim, king of Judah: He shall have no one to sit upon the thronec of David. His dead body shall be thrown out to the hot sun and frosty nights, 31and I will punish him and

New Revised Standard

in the hearing of all the people, Baruch read the words of Jeremiah from the scroll, in the house of the LORD, in the chamber of Gemariah son of Shaphan the secretary, which was in the upper court, at the entry of the New Gate of the LORD's house.

The Scroll Read in the Palace

11 When Micaiah son of Gemariah son of Shaphan heard all the words of the LORD from the scroll, 12he went down to the king's house, into the secretary's chamber; and all the officials were sitting there: Elishama the secretary, Delaiah son of Shemaiah, Elnathan son of Achbor, Gemariah son of Shaphan, Zedekiah son of Hananiah, and all the officials. 13And Micaiah told them all the words that he had heard, when Baruch read the scroll in the hearing of the people. 14Then all the officials sent Jehudi son of Nethaniah son of Shelemiah son of Cushi to say to Baruch, "Bring the scroll that you read in the hearing of the people, and come." So Baruch son of Neriah took the scroll in his hand and came to them. 15And they said to him, "Sit down and read it to us." So Baruch read it to them. 16When they heard all the words, they turned to one another in alarm, and said to Baruch, "We certainly must report all these words to the king." 17Then they questioned Baruch, "Tell us now, how did you write all these words? Was it at his dictation?" 18Baruch answered them, "He dictated all these words to me, and I wrote them with ink on the scroll." 19Then the officials said to Baruch, "Go and hide, you and Jeremiah, and let no one know where you are."

Jehoiakim Burns the Scroll

20 Leaving the scroll in the chamber of Elishama the secretary, they went to the court of the king; and they reported all the words to the king. 21Then the king sent Jehudi to get the scroll, and he took it from the chamber of Elishama the secretary; and Jehudi read it to the king and all the officials who stood beside the king. 22Now the king was sitting in his winter apartment (it was the ninth month), and there was a fire burning in the brazier before him. 23As Jehudi read three or four columns, the kingd would cut them off with a penknife and throw them into the fire in the brazier, until the entire scroll was consumed in the fire that was in the brazier. 24Yet neither the king, nor any of his servants who heard all these words, was alarmed, nor did they tear their garments. 25Even when Elnathan and Delaiah and Gemariah urged the king not to burn the scroll, he would not listen to them. 26And the king commanded Jerahmeel the king's son and Seraiah son of Azriel and Shelemiah son of Abdeel to arrest the secretary Baruch and the prophet Jeremiah. But the LORD hid them.

Jeremiah Dictates Another

27 Now, after the king had burned the scroll with the words that Baruch wrote at Jeremiah's dictation, the word of the LORD came to Jeremiah: 28Take another scroll and write on it all the former words that were in the first scroll, which King Jehoiakim of Judah has burned. 29And concerning King Jehoiakim of Judah you shall say: Thus says the LORD, You have dared to burn this scroll, saying, Why have you written in it that the king of Babylon will certainly come and destroy this land, and will cut off from it human beings and animals? 30Therefore thus says the LORD concerning King Jehoiakim of Judah: He shall have no one to sit upon the throne of David, and his dead body shall be cast out to the heat by day and the frost by night. 31And I will punish him

---

a 36:22 *sitting in front of a fireplace,* more literally, "a large brazier in which a fire was burning." b 36:26 *a member of the royal family,* i.e., "a son of the king." c 36:30 *He shall have no one to sit upon the throne.* A three-month inter-regnum by his son Jehoiachin (also called Coniah and Jeconiah) evidently did not qualify as "sitting on the throne" under the meaning of permanence in the Hebrew expression used here.

d Heb *he*

King James

31And I will punish him and his seed and his servants for their iniquity; and I will bring upon them, and upon the inhabitants of Jerusalem, and upon the men of Judah, all the evil that I have pronounced against them; but they hearkened not.

32¶ Then took Jeremiah another roll, and gave it to Baruch the scribe, the son of Neriah; who wrote therein from the mouth of Jeremiah all the words of the book which Jehoiakim king of Judah had burned in the fire: and there were added besides unto them many like words.

37 AND KING Zedekiah the son of Josiah reigned instead of Coniah the son of Jehoiakim, whom Nebuchadrezzar king of Babylon made king in the land of Judah.

2But neither he, nor his servants, nor the people of the land, did hearken unto the words of the LORD, which he spake by the prophet Jeremiah.

3And Zedekiah the king sent Jehucal the son of Shelemiah and Zephaniah the son of Maaseiah the priest to the prophet Jeremiah, saying, Pray now unto the LORD our God for us.

4Now Jeremiah came in and went out among the people: for they had not put him into prison.

5Then Pharaoh's army was come forth out of Egypt: and when the Chaldeans that besieged Jerusalem heard tidings of them, they departed from Jerusalem.

6¶ Then came the word of the LORD unto the prophet Jeremiah, saying,

7Thus saith the LORD, the God of Israel; Thus shall ye say to the king of Judah, that sent you unto me to inquire of me; Behold, Pharaoh's army, which is come forth to help you, shall return to Egypt into their own land.

8And the Chaldeans shall come again, and fight against this city, and take it, and burn it with fire.

9Thus saith the LORD; Deceive not yourselves, saying, The Chaldeans shall surely depart from us: for they shall not depart.

10For though ye had smitten the whole army of the Chaldeans that fight against you, and there remained but wounded men among them, yet should they rise up every man in his tent, and burn this city with fire.

11¶ And it came to pass, that when the army of the Chaldeans was broken up from Jerusalem for fear of Pharaoh's army,

12Then Jeremiah went forth out of Jerusalem to go into the land of Benjamin, to separate himself thence in the midst of the people.

13And when he was in the gate of Benjamin, a captain of the ward was there, whose name was Irijah, the son of Shelemiah, the son of Hananiah; and he took Jeremiah the prophet, saying, Thou fallest away to the Chaldeans.

14Then said Jeremiah, It is false; I fall not away to the Chaldeans. But he hearkened not to him: so Irijah took Jeremiah, and brought him to the princes.

15Wherefore the princes were wroth with Jeremiah, and smote him, and put him in prison in the house of Jonathan the scribe: for they had made that the prison.

16¶ When Jeremiah was entered into the dungeon, and into the cabins, and Jeremiah had remained there many days;

17Then Zedekiah the king sent, and took him out: and the king asked him secretly in his house, and said, Is there any word from the LORD? And Jeremiah said, There is: for, said he, thou shalt be delivered into the hand of the king of Babylon.

New International

punish him and his children and his attendants for their wickedness; I will bring on them and those living in Jerusalem and the people of Judah every disaster I pronounced against them, because they have not listened.' "

32So Jeremiah took another scroll and gave it to scribe Baruch son of Neriah, and as Jeremiah dictated, Baruch wrote on it all the words of the scroll that Jehoiakim king of Judah had burned in the fire. And many similar words were added to them.

Jeremiah in Prison

37 ZEDEKIAH SON of Josiah was made king of Judah by Nebuchadnezzar king of Babylon; he reigned in place of Jehoiachina son of Jehoiakim. 2Neither he nor his attendants nor the people of the land paid any attention to the words the LORD had spoken through Jeremiah the prophet.

3King Zedekiah, however, sent Jehucal son of Shelemiah with the priest Zephaniah son of Maaseiah to Jeremiah the prophet with this message: "Please pray to the LORD our God for us."

4Now Jeremiah was free to come and go among the people, for he had not yet been put in prison. 5Pharaoh's army had marched out of Egypt, and when the Babyloniansb who were besieging Jerusalem heard the report about them, they withdrew from Jerusalem.

6Then the word of the LORD came to Jeremiah the prophet: 7"This is what the LORD, the God of Israel, says: Tell the king of Judah, who sent you to inquire of me, 'Pharaoh's army, which has marched out to support you, will go back to its own land, to Egypt. 8Then the Babylonians will return and attack this city; they will capture it and burn it down.'

9"This is what the LORD says: Do not deceive yourselves, thinking, 'The Babylonians will surely leave us.' They will not! 10Even if you were to defeat the entire Babylonianc army that is attacking you and only wounded men were left in their tents, they would come out and burn this city down."

11After the Babylonian army had withdrawn from Jerusalem because of Pharaoh's army, 12Jeremiah started to leave the city to go to the territory of Benjamin to get his share of the property among the people there. 13But when he reached the Benjamin Gate, the captain of the guard, whose name was Irijah son of Shelemiah, the son of Hananiah, arrested him and said, "You are deserting to the Babylonians!"

14"That's not true!" Jeremiah said. "I am not deserting to the Babylonians." But Irijah would not listen to him; instead, he arrested Jeremiah and brought him to the officials. 15They were angry with Jeremiah and had him beaten and imprisoned in the house of Jonathan the secretary, which they had made into a prison.

16Jeremiah was put into a vaulted cell in a dungeon, where he remained a long time. 17Then King Zedekiah sent for him and had him brought to the palace, where he asked him privately, "Is there any word from the LORD?"

"Yes," Jeremiah replied, "you will be handed over to the king of Babylon."

a 1 Hebrew Coniah, a variant of Jehoiachin   b 5 Or Chaldeans; also in verses 8, 9, 13 and 14   c 10 Or Chaldean; also in verse 11

Living Bible

his family and his officials because of their sins. I will pour out upon them all the evil I promised—upon them and upon all the people of Judah and Jerusalem, for they wouldn't listen to my warnings."

32Then Jeremiah took another scroll and dictated again to Baruch all he had written before, only this time the Lord added a lot more!

37 NEBUCHADNEZZAR, KING of Babylon, did not appoint Coniah (King Jehoiakim's son) to be the new king of Judah.d Instead he chose Zedekiah (son of Josiah). 2But neither King Zedekiah nor his officials nor the people who were left in the land listened to what the Lord said through Jeremiah. 3Nevertheless, King Zedekiah sent Jehucal (son of Shelemiah) and Zephaniah the priest (son of Ma-aseiah) to ask Jeremiah to pray for them. 4(Jeremiah had not been imprisoned yet, so he could go and come as he pleased.)

5When the army of Pharaoh Hophra of Egypt appeared at the southern border of Judah to relieve the besieged city of Jerusalem, the Babylonian army withdrew from Jerusalem to fight the Egyptians.

6Then the Lord sent this message to Jeremiah: 7"The Lord, the God of Israel, says: Tell the king of Judah, who sent you to ask me what is going to happen, that Pharaoh's army, though it came here to help you, is about to return in flight to Egypt! The Babylonians shall defeat them and send them scurrying home. 8These Babylonians shall capture this city and burn it to the ground. 9Don't fool yourselves that the Babylonians are gone for good. They aren't! 10Even if you destroyed the entire Babylonian army until there was only a handful of survivors and they lay wounded in their tents, yet they would stagger out and defeat you and put this city to the torch!"

11When the Babylonian army set out from Jerusalem to engage Pharaoh's army in battle, 12Jeremiah started to leave the city to go to the land of Benjamin, to see the property he had bought.e 13But as he was walking through the Benjamin Gate, a sentry arrested him as a traitor, claiming he was defecting to the Babylonians. The guard making the arrest was Irijah (son of Shelemiah, grandson of Hananiah).

14"That's not true," Jeremiah said. "I have no intention whatever of doing any such thing!"

But Irijah wouldn't listen; he took Jeremiah before the city officials. 15, 16They were incensed with Jeremiah and had him flogged and put into the dungeon under the house of Jonathan the scribe, which had been converted into a prison. Jeremiah was kept there for several days, 17but eventually King Zedekiah sent for him to come to the palace secretly. The king asked him if there was any recent message from the Lord. "Yes," said Jeremiah, "there is! You shall be defeated by the king of Babylon!"

New Revised Standard

and his offspring and his servants for their iniquity; I will bring on them, and on the inhabitants of Jerusalem, and on the people of Judah, all the disasters with which I have threatened them—but they would not listen.

32 Then Jeremiah took another scroll and gave it to the secretary Baruch son of Neriah, who wrote on it at Jeremiah's dictation all the words of the scroll that King Jehoiakim of Judah had burned in the fire; and many similar words were added to them.

Zedekiah's Vain Hope

37 ZEDEKIAH SON of Josiah, whom King Nebuchadrezzar of Babylon made king in the land of Judah, succeeded Coniah son of Jehoiakim. 2But neither he nor his servants nor the people of the land listened to the words of the LORD that he spoke through the prophet Jeremiah.

3 King Zedekiah sent Jehucal son of Shelemiah and the priest Zephaniah son of Maaseiah to the prophet Jeremiah saying, "Please pray for us to the LORD our God." 4Now Jeremiah was still going in and out among the people, for he had not yet been put in prison. 5Meanwhile, the army of Pharaoh had come out of Egypt; and when the Chaldeans who were besieging Jerusalem heard news of them, they withdrew from Jerusalem.

6 Then the word of the LORD came to the prophet Jeremiah: 7Thus says the LORD, God of Israel: This is what the two of you shall say to the king of Judah, who sent you to me to inquire of me, Pharaoh's army, which set out to help you, is going to return to its own land, to Egypt. 8And the Chaldeans shall return and fight against this city; they shall take it and burn it with fire. 9Thus says the LORD: Do not deceive yourselves, saying, "The Chaldeans will surely go away from us," for they will not go away. 10Even if you defeated the whole army of Chaldeans who are fighting against you, and there remained of them only wounded men in their tents, they would rise up and burn this city with fire.

Jeremiah Is Imprisoned

11 Now when the Chaldean army had withdrawn from Jerusalem at the approach of Pharaoh's army, 12Jeremiah set out from Jerusalem to go to the land of Benjamin to receive his share of propertyf among the people there. 13When he reached the Benjamin Gate, a sentinel there named Irijah son of Shelemiah son of Hananiah arrested the prophet Jeremiah saying, "You are deserting to the Chaldeans." 14And Jeremiah said, "That is a lie; I am not deserting to the Chaldeans." But Irijah would not listen to him, and arrested Jeremiah and brought him to the officials. 15The officials were enraged at Jeremiah, and they beat him and imprisoned him in the house of the secretary Jonathan, for it had been made a prison. 16Thus Jeremiah was put in the cistern house, in the cells, and remained there many days.

17 Then King Zedekiah sent for him, and received him. The king questioned him secretly in his house, and said, "Is there any word from the LORD?" Jeremiah said, "There is!" Then he said, "You shall be handed over to the king of Babylon." 18Jeremiah also said to King Zed-

---

d 37:1 to be the new king of Judah. The people of Jerusalem who had assassinated King Jehoiakim appointed his son Coniah as ruler before Nebuchadnezzar captured the city. The Babylonians took Coniah to Babylon as a political hostage. e 37:12 he had bought, see chapter 32:6-15.

f Meaning of Heb uncertain

King James

18Moreover Jeremiah said unto king Zedekiah, What have I offended against thee, or against thy servants, or against this people, that ye have put me in prison?

19Where *are* now your prophets which prophesied unto you, saying, The king of Babylon shall not come against you, nor against this land?

20Therefore hear now, I pray thee, O my lord the king: let my supplication, I pray thee, be accepted before thee; that thou cause me not to return to the house of Jonathan the scribe, lest I die there.

21Then Zedekiah the king commanded that they should commit Jeremiah into the court of the prison, and that they should give him daily a piece of bread out of the bakers' street, until all the bread in the city were spent. Thus Jeremiah remained in the court of the prison.

38 THEN SHEPHATIAH the son of Mattan, and Gedaliah the son of Pashur, and Jucal the son of Shelemiah, and Pashur the son of Malchiah, heard the words that Jeremiah had spoken unto all the people, saying,

2Thus saith the LORD, He that remaineth in this city shall die by the sword, by the famine, and by the pestilence: but he that goeth forth to the Chaldeans shall live; for he shall have his life for a prey, and shall live.

3Thus saith the LORD, This city shall surely be given into the hand of the king of Babylon's army, which shall take it.

4Therefore the princes said unto the king, We beseech thee, let this man be put to death: for thus he weakeneth the hands of the men of war that remain in this city, and the hands of all the people, in speaking such words unto them: for this man seeketh not the welfare of this people, but the hurt.

5Then Zedekiah the king said, Behold, he *is* in your hand: for the king *is* not *he that* can do *any* thing against you.

6Then took they Jeremiah, and cast him into the dungeon of Malchiah the son of Hammelech, that *was* in the court of the prison: and they let down Jeremiah with cords. And in the dungeon *there was* no water, but mire: so Jeremiah sunk in the mire.

7¶ Now when Ebed-melech the Ethiopian, one of the eunuchs which was in the king's house, heard that they had put Jeremiah in the dungeon; the king then sitting in the gate of Benjamin;

8Ebed-melech went forth out of the king's house, and spake to the king, saying,

9My lord the king, these men have done evil in all that they have done to Jeremiah the prophet, whom they have cast into the dungeon; and he is like to die for hunger in the place where he is: for *there is* no more bread in the city.

10Then the king commanded Ebed-melech the Ethiopian, saying, Take from hence thirty men with thee, and take up Jeremiah the prophet out of the dungeon, before he die.

11So Ebed-melech took the men with him, and went into the house of the king under the treasury, and took thence old cast clouts and old rotten rags, and let them down by cords into the dungeon to Jeremiah.

12And Ebed-melech the Ethiopian said unto Jeremiah, Put now *these* old cast clouts and rotten rags under thine armholes under the cords. And Jeremiah did so.

13So they drew up Jeremiah with cords, and took him up out of the dungeon: and Jeremiah remained in the court of the prison.

New International

18Then Jeremiah said to King Zedekiah, "What crime have I committed against you or your officials or this people, that you have put me in prison? 19Where are your prophets who prophesied to you, 'The king of Babylon will not attack you or this land'? 20But now, my lord the king, please listen. Let me bring my petition before you: Do not send me back to the house of Jonathan the secretary, or I will die there."

21King Zedekiah then gave orders for Jeremiah to be placed in the courtyard of the guard and given bread from the street of the bakers each day until all the bread in the city was gone. So Jeremiah remained in the courtyard of the guard.

Jeremiah Thrown Into a Cistern

38 SHEPHATIAH SON of Mattan, Gedaliah son of Pashhur, Jehucala son of Shelemiah, and Pashhur son of Malkijah heard what Jeremiah was telling all the people when he said, 2"This is what the LORD says: 'Whoever stays in this city will die by the sword, famine or plague, but whoever goes over to the Babyloniansb will live. He will escape with his life; he will live.' 3And this is what the LORD says: 'This city will certainly be handed over to the army of the king of Babylon, who will capture it.' "

4Then the officials said to the king, "This man should be put to death. He is discouraging the soldiers who are left in this city, as well as all the people, by the things he is saying to them. This man is not seeking the good of these people but their ruin."

5"He is in your hands," King Zedekiah answered. "The king can do nothing to oppose you."

6So they took Jeremiah and put him into the cistern of Malkijah, the king's son, which was in the courtyard of the guard. They lowered Jeremiah by ropes into the cistern; it had no water in it, only mud, and Jeremiah sank down into the mud.

7But Ebed-Melech, a Cushite,c an officiald in the royal palace, heard that they had put Jeremiah into the cistern. While the king was sitting in the Benjamin Gate, 8Ebed-Melech went out of the palace and said to him, 9"My lord the king, these men have acted wickedly in all they have done to Jeremiah the prophet. They have thrown him into a cistern, where he will starve to death when there is no longer any bread in the city."

10Then the king commanded Ebed-Melech the Cushite, "Take thirty men from here with you and lift Jeremiah the prophet out of the cistern before he dies."

11So Ebed-Melech took the men with him and went to a room under the treasury in the palace. He took some old rags and worn-out clothes from there and let them down with ropes to Jeremiah in the cistern. 12Ebed-Melech the Cushite said to Jeremiah, "Put these old rags and worn-out clothes under your arms to pad the ropes." Jeremiah did so, 13and they pulled him up with the ropes and lifted him out of the cistern. And Jeremiah remained in the courtyard of the guard.

---

a 1 Hebrew *Jucal*, a variant of *Jehucal*   b 2 Or *Chaldeans*; also in verses 18, 19 and 23   c 7 Probably from the upper Nile region   d 7 Or *a eunuch*

Living Bible

18Then Jeremiah broached the subject of his imprisonment. "What have I ever done to deserve this?" he asked the king. "What crime have I committed? Tell me what I have done against you or your officials or the people? 19Where are those prophets now who told you that the king of Babylon would not come? 20Listen, O my lord the king: I beg you, don't send me back to that dungeon, for I'll die there."

21Then King Zedekiah commanded that Jeremiah not be returned to the dungeon, but be placed in the palace prison instead, and that he be given a small loaf of fresh bread every day as long as there was any left in the city. So Jeremiah was kept in the palace prison.e

38 BUT WHEN Shephatiah (son of Mattan) and Gedaliah (son of Pashhur) and Jucal (son of Shelemiah) and Pashhur (son of Malchiah) heard what Jeremiah had been telling the people— 2that everyone remaining in Jerusalem would die by sword, starvation or disease, but anyone surrendering to the Babylonians would live, 3and that the city of Jerusalem would surely be captured by the king of Babylon— 4they went to the king and said: "Sir, this fellow must die. That kind of talk will undermine the morale of the few soldiers we have left, and of all the people too. This man is a traitor."

5So King Zedekiah agreed. "All right," he said. "Do as you like—I can't stop you."

6They took Jeremiah from his cell and lowered him by ropes into an empty cistern in the prison yard. (It belonged to Malchiah, a member of the royal family.) There was no water in it, but there was a thick layer of mire at the bottom, and Jeremiah sank down into it.

7When Ebed-melech the Ethiopian, an important palace official, heard that Jeremiah was in the cistern, 8he rushed out to the Gate of Benjamin where the king was holding court.

9"My lord the king," he said, "these men have done a very evil thing in putting Jeremiah into the cistern. He will die of hunger, for almost all the bread in the city is gone."

10Then the king commanded Ebed-melech to take thirty men with him and pull Jeremiah out before he died. 11So Ebed-melech took thirty men and went to a palace depot for discarded supplies where used clothing was kept. There he found some old rags and discarded garments which he took to the cistern and lowered to Jeremiah on a rope. 12Ebed-melech called down to Jeremiah, "Use these rags under your armpits to protect you from the ropes." Then, when Jeremiah was ready, 13they pulled him out and returned him to the palace prison, where he remained.

New Revised Standard

ekiah, "What wrong have I done to you or your servants or this people, that you have put me in prison? 19Where are your prophets who prophesied to you, saying, 'The king of Babylon will not come against you and against this land'? 20Now please hear me, my lord king: be good enough to listen to my plea, and do not send me back to the house of the secretary Jonathan to die there." 21So King Zedekiah gave orders, and they committed Jeremiah to the court of the guard; and a loaf of bread was given him daily from the bakers' street, until all the bread of the city was gone. So Jeremiah remained in the court of the guard.

Jeremiah in the Cistern

38 NOW SHEPHATIAH son of Mattan, Gedaliah son of Pashhur, Jucal son of Shelemiah, and Pashhur son of Malchiah heard the words that Jeremiah was saying to all the people, 2Thus says the LORD, Those who stay in this city shall die by the sword, by famine, and by pestilence; but those who go out to the Chaldeans shall live; they shall have their lives as a prize of war, and live. 3Thus says the LORD, This city shall surely be handed over to the army of the king of Babylon and be taken. 4Then the officials said to the king, "This man ought to be put to death, because he is discouraging the soldiers who are left in this city, and all the people, by speaking such words to them. For this man is not seeking the welfare of this people, but their harm." 5King Zedekiah said, "Here he is; he is in your hands; for the king is powerless against you." 6So they took Jeremiah and threw him into the cistern of Malchiah, the king's son, which was in the court of the guard, letting Jeremiah down by ropes. Now there was no water in the cistern, but only mud, and Jeremiah sank in the mud.

Jeremiah Is Rescued by Ebed-melech

7 Ebed-melech the Ethiopian,f a eunuch in the king's house, heard that they had put Jeremiah into the cistern. The king happened to be sitting at the Benjamin Gate, 8So Ebed-melech left the king's house and spoke to the king, 9"My lord king, these men have acted wickedly in all they did to the prophet Jeremiah by throwing him into the cistern to die there of hunger, for there is no bread left in the city." 10Then the king commanded Ebed-melech the Ethiopian,f "Take three men with you from here, and pull the prophet Jeremiah up from the cistern before he dies." 11So Ebed-melech took the men with him and went to the house of the king, to a wardrobe ofg the storehouse, and took from there old rags and worn-out clothes, which he let down to Jeremiah in the cistern by ropes. 12Then Ebed-melech the Ethiopianf said to Jeremiah, "Just put the rags and clothes between your armpits and the ropes." Jeremiah did so. 13Then they drew Jeremiah up by the ropes and pulled him out of the cistern. And Jeremiah remained in the court of the guard.

---

e 37:21 in the palace prison, literally, "the court of the guard."

f Or Nubian; Heb Cushite   g Cn: Heb to under

King James

14¶ Then Zedekiah the king sent, and took Jeremiah the prophet unto him into the third entry that *is* in the house of the LORD: and the king said unto Jeremiah, I will ask thee a thing; hide nothing from me.

15Then Jeremiah said unto Zedekiah, If I declare *it* unto thee, wilt thou not surely put me to death? and if I give thee counsel, wilt thou not hearken unto me?

16So Zedekiah the king sware secretly unto Jeremiah, saying, *As* the LORD liveth, that made us this soul, I will not put thee to death, neither will I give thee into the hand of these men that seek thy life.

17Then said Jeremiah unto Zedekiah, Thus saith the LORD, the God of hosts, the God of Israel; If thou wilt assuredly go forth unto the king of Babylon's princes, then thy soul shall live, and this city shall not be burned with fire; and thou shalt live, and thine house:

18But if thou wilt not go forth to the king of Babylon's princes, then shall this city be given into the hand of the Chaldeans, and they shall burn it with fire, and thou shalt not escape out of their hand.

19And Zedekiah the king said unto Jeremiah, I am afraid of the Jews that are fallen to the Chaldeans, lest they deliver me into their hand, and they mock me.

20But Jeremiah said, They shall not deliver *thee.* Obey, I beseech thee, the voice of the LORD, which I speak unto thee: so it shall be well unto thee, and thy soul shall live.

21But if thou refuse to go forth, this *is* the word that the LORD hath shown me:

22And, behold, all the women that are left in the king of Judah's house *shall be* brought forth to the king of Babylon's princes, and those *women* shall say, Thy friends have set thee on, and have prevailed against thee: thy feet are sunk in the mire, *and* they are turned away back.

23So they shall bring out all thy wives and thy children to the Chaldeans: and thou shalt not escape out of their hand, but shalt be taken by the hand of the king of Babylon: and thou shalt cause this city to be burned with fire.

24¶ Then said Zedekiah unto Jeremiah, Let no man know of these words, and thou shalt not die.

25But if the princes hear that I have talked with thee, and they come unto thee, and say unto thee, Declare unto us now what thou hast said unto the king, hide it not from us, and we will not put thee to death; also what the king said unto thee:

26Then thou shalt say unto them, I presented my supplication before the king, that he would not cause me to return to Jonathan's house, to die there.

27Then came all the princes unto Jeremiah, and asked him: and he told them according to all these words that the king had commanded. So they left off speaking with him; for the matter was not perceived.

28So Jeremiah abode in the court of the prison until the day that Jerusalem was taken: and he was *there* when Jerusalem was taken.

39 IN THE ninth year of Zedekiah king of Judah, in the tenth month, came Nebuchadrezzar king of Babylon and all his army against Jerusalem, and they besieged it.

2*And* in the eleventh year of Zedekiah, in the fourth month, the ninth *day* of the month, the city was broken up.

New International

Zedekiah Questions Jeremiah Again

14Then King Zedekiah sent for Jeremiah the prophet and had him brought to the third entrance to the temple of the LORD. "I am going to ask you something," the king said to Jeremiah. "Do not hide anything from me."

15Jeremiah said to Zedekiah, "If I give you an answer, will you not kill me? Even if I did give you counsel, you would not listen to me."

16But King Zedekiah swore this oath secretly to Jeremiah: "As surely as the LORD lives, who has given us breath, I will neither kill you nor hand you over to those who are seeking your life."

17Then Jeremiah said to Zedekiah, "This is what the LORD God Almighty, the God of Israel, says: 'If you surrender to the officers of the king of Babylon, your life will be spared and this city will not be burned down; you and your family will live. 18But if you will not surrender to the officers of the king of Babylon, this city will be handed over to the Babylonians and they will burn it down; you yourself will not escape from their hands.' "

19King Zedekiah said to Jeremiah, "I am afraid of the Jews who have gone over to the Babylonians, for the Babylonians may hand me over to them and they will mistreat me."

20"They will not hand you over," Jeremiah replied. "Obey the LORD by doing what I tell you. Then it will go well with you, and your life will be spared. 21But if you refuse to surrender, this is what the LORD has revealed to me: 22All the women left in the palace of the king of Judah will be brought out to the officials of the king of Babylon. Those women will say to you:

> " 'They misled you and overcame you—
>   those trusted friends of yours.
> Your feet are sunk in the mud;
>   your friends have deserted you.'

23"All your wives and children will be brought out to the Babylonians. You yourself will not escape from their hands but will be captured by the king of Babylon; and this city will[a] be burned down."

24Then Zedekiah said to Jeremiah, "Do not let anyone know about this conversation, or you may die. 25If the officials hear that I talked with you, and they come to you and say, 'Tell us what you said to the king and what the king said to you; do not hide it from us or we will kill you,' 26then tell them, 'I was pleading with the king not to send me back to Jonathan's house to die there.' "

27All the officials did come to Jeremiah and question him, and he told them everything the king had ordered him to say. So they said no more to him, for no one had heard his conversation with the king.

28And Jeremiah remained in the courtyard of the guard until the day Jerusalem was captured.

The Fall of Jerusalem

39 THIS IS how Jerusalem was taken: 1In the ninth year of Zedekiah king of Judah, in the tenth month, Nebuchadnezzar king of Babylon marched against Jerusalem with his whole army and laid siege to it. 2And on the ninth day of the fourth month of Zedekiah's eleventh year, the city wall was broken through.

---

a 23 Or *and you will cause this city to*

Living Bible

14One day King Zedekiah sent for Jeremiah to meet him at the side entrance of the Temple.

"I want to ask you something," the king said, "and don't try to hide the truth."

15Jeremiah said, "If I tell you the truth, you will kill me. And you won't listen to me anyway."

16So King Zedekiah swore before Almighty God his Creator that he would not kill Jeremiah or give him to the men who were after his life.

17Then Jeremiah said to Zedekiah, "The Almighty Lord, the God of Israel, says: If you will surrender to Babylon, you and your family shall live and the city will not be burned. 18If you refuse to surrender, this city shall be set afire by the Babylonian army and you will not escape."

19"But I am afraid to surrender," the king said, "for the Babylonians will hand me over to the Jews who have defected to them, and who knows what they will do to me?"

20Jeremiah replied, "You won't get into their hands if only you will obey the Lord; your life will be spared and all will go well for you. 21, 22But if you refuse to surrender, the Lord has said that all the women left in your palace will be brought out and given to the officers of the Babylonian army; and these women will taunt you with bitterness. 'Fine friends you have,' they'll say, 'those Egyptians. They have betrayed you and left you to your fate!' 23All your wives and children will be led out to the Babylonians, and you will not escape. You will be seized by the king of Babylon, and this city will be burned."

24Then Zedekiah said to Jeremiah, "On pain of death, don't tell anyone you told me this! 25And if my officials hear that I talked with you and they threaten you with death unless you tell them what we discussed, 26just say that you begged me not to send you back to the dungeon in Jonathan's house, for you would die there."

27And sure enough, it wasn't long before all the city officials came to Jeremiah and asked him why the king had called for him. So he said what the king had told him to, and they left without finding out the truth, for the conversation had not been overheard by anyone. 28And Jeremiah remained confined to the prison yard until the day Jerusalem was captured.

New Revised Standard

Zedekiah Consults Jeremiah Again

14   King Zedekiah sent for the prophet Jeremiah and received him at the third entrance of the temple of the LORD. The king said to Jeremiah, "I have something to ask you; do not hide anything from me." 15Jeremiah said to Zedekiah, "If I tell you, you will put me to death, will you not? And if I give you advice, you will not listen to me." 16So King Zedekiah swore an oath in secret to Jeremiah, "As the LORD lives, who gave us our lives, I will not put you to death or hand you over to these men who seek your life."

17   Then Jeremiah said to Zedekiah, "Thus says the LORD, the God of hosts, the God of Israel, If you will only surrender to the officials of the king of Babylon, then your life shall be spared, and this city shall not be burned with fire, and you and your house shall live. 18But if you do not surrender to the officials of the king of Babylon, then this city shall be handed over to the Chaldeans, and they shall burn it with fire, and you yourself shall not escape from their hand." 19King Zedekiah said to Jeremiah, "I am afraid of the Judeans who have deserted to the Chaldeans, for I might be handed over to them and they would abuse me." 20Jeremiah said, "That will not happen. Just obey the voice of the LORD in what I say to you, and it shall go well with you, and your life shall be spared. 21But if you are determined not to surrender, this is what the LORD has shown me— 22a vision of all the women remaining in the house of the king of Judah being led out to the officials of the king of Babylon and saying,

'Your trusted friends have seduced you
    and have overcome you;
Now that your feet are stuck in the mud,
    they desert you.'

23All your wives and your children shall be led out to the Chaldeans, and you yourself shall not escape from their hand, but shall be seized by the king of Babylon; and this city shall be burned with fire."

24   Then Zedekiah said to Jeremiah, "Do not let anyone else know of this conversation, or you will die. 25If the officials should hear that I have spoken with you, and they should come and say to you, 'Just tell us what you said to the king; do not conceal it from us, or we will put you to death. What did the king say to you?' 26then you shall say to them, 'I was presenting my plea to the king not to send me back to the house of Jonathan to die there.' " 27All the officials did come to Jeremiah and questioned him; and he answered them in the very words the king had commanded. So they stopped questioning him, for the conversation had not been overheard. 28And Jeremiah remained in the court of the guard until the day that Jerusalem was taken.

39 IT WAS in January of the ninth year of the reign of King Zedekiah of Judah, that King Nebuchadnezzar and all his army came against Jerusalem again and besieged it. 2Two years later, in the month of July, they breached the wall, and the city fell, 3and all

The Fall of Jerusalem

39 IN THE ninth year of King Zedekiah of Judah, in the tenth month, King Nebuchadrezzar of Babylon and all his army came against Jerusalem and besieged it; 2in the eleventh year of Zedekiah, in the fourth month, on the ninth day of the month, a breach was made in the city. 3When Jerusalem was taken,b all

b This clause has been transposed from 38.28

King James

3And all the princes of the king of Babylon came in, and sat in the middle gate, *even* Nergal-sharezer, Samgar-nebo, Sarsechim, Rabsaris, Nergal-sharezer, Rabmag, with all the residue of the princes of the king of Babylon.

4¶ And it came to pass, *that* when Zedekiah the king of Judah saw them, and all the men of war, then they fled, and went forth out of the city by night, by the way of the king's garden, by the gate betwixt the two walls: and he went out the way of the plain.

5But the Chaldeans' army pursued after them, and overtook Zedekiah in the plains of Jericho: and when they had taken him, they brought him up to Nebuchadnezzar king of Babylon to Riblah in the land of Hamath, where he gave judgment upon him.

6Then the king of Babylon slew the sons of Zedekiah in Riblah before his eyes: also the king of Babylon slew all the nobles of Judah.

7Moreover he put out Zedekiah's eyes, and bound him with chains, to carry him to Babylon.

8¶ And the Chaldeans burned the king's house, and the houses of the people, with fire, and brake down the walls of Jerusalem.

9Then Nebuzar-adan the captain of the guard carried away captive into Babylon the remnant of the people that remained in the city, and those that fell away, that fell to him, with the rest of the people that remained.

10But Nebuzar-adan the captain of the guard left of the poor of the people, which had nothing, in the land of Judah, and gave them vineyards and fields at the same time.

11¶ Now Nebuchadrezzar king of Babylon gave charge concerning Jeremiah to Nebuzar-adan the captain of the guard, saying,

12Take him, and look well to him, and do him no harm; but do unto him even as he shall say unto thee.

13So Nebuzar-adan the captain of the guard sent, and Nebushasban, Rabsaris, and Nergal-sharezer, Rab-mag, and all the king of Babylon's princes;

14Even they sent, and took Jeremiah out of the court of the prison, and committed him unto Gedaliah the son of Ahikam the son of Shaphan, that he should carry him home: so he dwelt among the people.

15¶ Now the word of the LORD came unto Jeremiah, while he was shut up in the court of the prison, saying,

16Go and speak to Ebed-melech the Ethiopian, saying, Thus saith the LORD of hosts, the God of Israel; Behold, I will bring my words upon this city for evil, and not for good; and they shall be *accomplished* in that day before thee.

17But I will deliver thee in that day, saith the LORD: and thou shalt not be given into the hand of the men of whom thou *art* afraid.

18For I will surely deliver thee, and thou shalt not fall by the sword, but thy life shall be for a prey unto thee: because thou hast put thy trust in me, saith the LORD.

40 THE WORD that came to Jeremiah from the LORD, after that Nebuzar-adan the captain of the guard had let him go from Ramah, when he had taken him being bound in chains among all that were carried away captive of Jerusalem and Judah, which were carried away captive unto Babylon.

New International

3Then all the officials of the king of Babylon came and took seats in the Middle Gate: Nergal-Sharezer of Samgar, Nebo-Sarsekim[a] a chief officer, Nergal-Sharezer a high official and all the other officials of the king of Babylon. 4When Zedekiah king of Judah and all the soldiers saw them, they fled; they left the city at night by way of the king's garden, through the gate between the two walls, and headed toward the Arabah.[b]

5But the Babylonian[c] army pursued them and overtook Zedekiah in the plains of Jericho. They captured him and took him to Nebuchadnezzar king of Babylon at Riblah in the land of Hamath, where he pronounced sentence on him. 6There at Riblah the king of Babylon slaughtered the sons of Zedekiah before his eyes and also killed all the nobles of Judah. 7Then he put out Zedekiah's eyes and bound him with bronze shackles to take him to Babylon.

8The Babylonians[d] set fire to the royal palace and the houses of the people and broke down the walls of Jerusalem. 9Nebuzaradan commander of the imperial guard carried into exile to Babylon the people who remained in the city, along with those who had gone over to him, and the rest of the people. 10But Nebuzaradan the commander of the guard left behind in the land of Judah some of the poor people, who owned nothing; and at that time he gave them vineyards and fields.

11Now Nebuchadnezzar king of Babylon had given these orders about Jeremiah through Nebuzaradan commander of the imperial guard: 12"Take him and look after him; don't harm him but do for him whatever he asks." 13So Nebuzaradan the commander of the guard, Nebushazban a chief officer, Nergal-Sharezer a high official and all the other officers of the king of Babylon 14sent and had Jeremiah taken out of the courtyard of the guard. They turned him over to Gedaliah son of Ahikam, the son of Shaphan, to take him back to his home. So he remained among his own people.

15While Jeremiah had been confined in the courtyard of the guard, the word of the LORD came to him: 16"Go and tell Ebed-Melech the Cushite, 'This is what the LORD Almighty, the God of Israel, says: I am about to fulfill my words against this city through disaster, not prosperity. At that time they will be fulfilled before your eyes. 17But I will rescue you on that day, declares the LORD; you will not be handed over to those you fear. 18I will save you; you will not fall by the sword but will escape with your life, because you trust in me, declares the LORD.' "

Jeremiah Freed

40 THE WORD came to Jeremiah from the LORD after Nebuzaradan commander of the imperial guard had released him at Ramah. He had found Jeremiah bound in chains among all the captives from Jerusalem and Judah who were being carried into exile to Babylon. 2When the commander of the guard found Jer-

---

a 3 Or *Nergal-Sharezer, Samgar-Nebo, Sarsekim*   b 4 Or *the Jordan Valley*
c 5 Or *Chaldean*   d 8 Or *Chaldeans*

Living Bible

the officers of the Babylonian army came in and sat in triumph at the middle gate. Nergal-sharezer was there, and Samgar-nebo and Sarsechim and Nergal-sharezer the king's chief assistant, and many others.

⁴When King Zedekiah and his soldiers realized that the city was lost, they fled during the night, going out through the gate between the two walls back of the palace garden and across the fields toward the Jordan valley. ⁵But the Babylonians chased the king and caught him on the plains of Jericho and brought him to Nebuchadnezzar, king of Babylon who was at Riblah, in the land of Hamath, where he pronounced judgment upon him. ⁶The king of Babylon made Zedekiah watch as they killed his children and all the nobles of Judah. ⁷Then he gouged out Zedekiah's eyes and bound him in chains to send him away to Babylon as a slave.

⁸Meanwhile the army burned Jerusalem, including the palace, and tore down the walls of the city. ⁹Then Nebuzaradan, the captain of the guard, and his men sent the remnant of the population and all those who had defected to him to Babylon. ¹⁰But throughout the land of Judah he left a few people, the very poor, and gave them fields and vineyards.

¹¹, ¹²Meanwhile King Nebuchadnezzar had told Nebuzaradan to find Jeremiah. "See that he isn't hurt," he said. "Look after him well and give him anything he wants." ¹³So Nebuzaradan, the captain of the guard, and Nebushazban, the chief of the eunuchs, and Nergal-sharezer, the king's advisor, and all the officials took steps to do as the king had commanded. ¹⁴They sent soldiers to bring Jeremiah out of the prison, and put him into the care of Gedaliah (son of Ahikam, son of Shaphan), to take him back to his home. And Jeremiah lived there among his people who were left in the land.

¹⁵The Lord gave the following message to Jeremiah before the Babylonians arrived, while he was still in prison:

¹⁶"Send this word to Ebed-melech the Ethiopian: The Lord, the God of Israel, says: I will do to this city everything I threatened; I will destroy it before your eyes, ¹⁷but I will deliver you. You shall not be killed by those you fear so much. ¹⁸As a reward for trusting me, I will preserve your life and keep you safe."

40 NEBUZARADAN, CAPTAIN of the guard, took Jeremiah to Ramah along with all the exiled people of Jerusalem and Judah who were being sent to Babylon, but then released him.

New Revised Standard

the officials of the king of Babylon came and sat in the middle gate: Nergal-sharezer, Samgar-nebo, Sarsechim the Rabsaris, Nergal-sharezer the Rabmag, with all the rest of the officials of the king of Babylon. ⁴When King Zedekiah of Judah and all the soldiers saw them, they fled, going out of the city at night by way of the king's garden through the gate between the two walls; and they went toward the Arabah. ⁵But the army of the Chaldeans pursued them, and overtook Zedekiah in the plains of Jericho; and when they had taken him, they brought him up to King Nebuchadrezzar of Babylon, at Riblah, in the land of Hamath; and he passed sentence on him. ⁶The king of Babylon slaughtered the sons of Zedekiah at Riblah before his eyes; also the king of Babylon slaughtered all the nobles of Judah. ⁷He put out the eyes of Zedekiah, and bound him in fetters to take him to Babylon. ⁸The Chaldeans burned the king's house and the houses of the people, and broke down the walls of Jerusalem. ⁹Then Nebuzaradan the captain of the guard exiled to Babylon the rest of the people who were left in the city, those who had deserted to him, and the people who remained. ¹⁰Nebuzaradan the captain of the guard left in the land of Judah some of the poor people who owned nothing, and gave them vineyards and fields at the same time.

Jeremiah, Set Free, Remembers Ebed-melech

11 King Nebuchadrezzar of Babylon gave command concerning Jeremiah through Nebuzaradan, the captain of the guard, saying, ¹²"Take him, look after him well and do him no harm, but deal with him as he may ask you." ¹³So Nebuzaradan the captain of the guard, Nebushazban the Rabsaris, Nergal-sharezer the Rabmag, and all the chief officers of the king of Babylon sent ¹⁴and took Jeremiah from the court of the guard. They entrusted him to Gedaliah son of Ahikam son of Shaphan to be brought home. So he stayed with his own people.

15 The word of the LORD came to Jeremiah while he was confined in the court of the guard: ¹⁶Go and say to Ebed-melech the Ethiopian:ᶜ Thus says the LORD of hosts, the God of Israel: I am going to fulfill my words against this city for evil and not for good, and they shall be accomplished in your presence on that day. ¹⁷But I will save you on that day, says the LORD, and you shall not be handed over to those whom you dread. ¹⁸For I will surely save you, and you shall not fall by the sword; but you shall have your life as a prize of war, because you have trusted in me, says the LORD.

Jeremiah with Gedaliah the Governor

40 THE WORD that came to Jeremiah from the LORD after Nebuzaradan the captain of the guard had let him go from Ramah, when he took him bound in fetters along with all the captives of Jerusalem and Judah who were being exiled to Babylon. ²The cap-

ᶜ Or *Nubian*; Heb *Cushite*

King James

2And the captain of the guard took Jeremiah, and said unto him, The LORD thy God hath pronounced this evil upon this place.

3Now the LORD hath brought *it*, and done according as he hath said: because ye have sinned against the LORD, and have not obeyed his voice, therefore this thing is come upon you.

4And now, behold, I loose thee this day from the chains which *were* upon thine hand. If it seem good unto thee to come with me into Babylon, come; and I will look well unto thee: but if it seem ill unto thee to come with me into Babylon, forbear: behold, all the land *is* before thee: whither it seemeth good and convenient for thee to go, thither go.

5Now while he was not yet gone back, *he said,* Go back also to Gedaliah the son of Ahikam the son of Shaphan, whom the king of Babylon hath made governor over the cities of Judah, and dwell with him among the people: or go wheresoever it seemeth convenient unto thee to go. So the captain of the guard gave him victuals and a reward, and let him go.

6Then went Jeremiah unto Gedaliah the son of Ahikam to Mizpah; and dwelt with him among the people that were left in the land.

7¶ Now when all the captains of the forces which *were* in the fields, *even* they and their men, heard that the king of Babylon had made Gedaliah the son of Ahikam governor in the land, and had committed unto him men, and women, and children, and of the poor of the land, of them that were not carried away captive to Babylon;

8Then they came to Gedaliah to Mizpah, even Ishmael the son of Nethaniah, and Johanan and Jonathan the sons of Kareah, and Seraiah the son of Tanhumeth, and the sons of Ephai the Netophathite, and Jezaniah the son of a Maachathite, they and their men.

9And Gedaliah the son of Ahikam the son of Shaphan sware unto them and to their men, saying, Fear not to serve the Chaldeans: dwell in the land, and serve the king of Babylon, and it shall be well with you.

10As for me, behold, I will dwell at Mizpah to serve the Chaldeans, which will come unto us: but ye, gather ye wine, and summer fruits, and oil, and put them in your vessels, and dwell in your cities that ye have taken.

11Likewise when all the Jews that *were* in Moab, and among the Ammonites, and in Edom, and that *were* in all the countries, heard that the king of Babylon had left a remnant of Judah, and that he had set over them Gedaliah the son of Ahikam the son of Shaphan;

12Even all the Jews returned out of all places whither they were driven, and came to the land of Judah, to Gedaliah, unto Mizpah, and gathered wine and summer fruits very much.

13¶ Moreover Johanan the son of Kareah, and all the captains of the forces that *were* in the fields, came to Gedaliah to Mizpah,

14And said unto him, Dost thou certainly know that Baalis the king of the Ammonites hath sent Ishmael the son of Nethaniah to slay thee? But Gedaliah the son of Ahikam believed them not.

15Then Johanan the son of Kareah spake to Gedaliah in Mizpah secretly, saying, Let me go, I pray thee, and I will slay Ishmael the son of Nethaniah, and no man shall know *it:* wherefore should he slay thee, that all the Jews which are gathered unto thee should be scattered, and the remnant in Judah perish?

16But Gedaliah the son of Ahikam said unto Johanan the son of Kareah, Thou shalt not do this thing: for thou speakest falsely of Ishmael.

New International

emiah, he said to him, "The LORD your God decreed this disaster for this place. 3And now the LORD has brought it about; he has done just as he said he would. All this happened because you people sinned against the LORD and did not obey him. 4But today I am freeing you from the chains on your wrists. Come with me to Babylon, if you like, and I will look after you; but if you do not want to, then don't come. Look, the whole country lies before you; go wherever you please." 5However, before Jeremiah turned to go,[a] Nebuzaradan added, "Go back to Gedaliah son of Ahikam, the son of Shaphan, whom the king of Babylon has appointed over the towns of Judah, and live with him among the people, or go anywhere else you please."

Then the commander gave him provisions and a present and let him go. 6So Jeremiah went to Gedaliah son of Ahikam at Mizpah and stayed with him among the people who were left behind in the land.

Gedaliah Assassinated

7When all the army officers and their men who were still in the open country heard that the king of Babylon had appointed Gedaliah son of Ahikam as governor over the land and had put him in charge of the men, women and children who were the poorest in the land and who had not been carried into exile to Babylon, 8they came to Gedaliah at Mizpah—Ishmael son of Nethaniah, Johanan and Jonathan the sons of Kareah, Seraiah son of Tanhumeth, the sons of Ephai the Netophathite, and Jaazaniah[b] the son of the Maacathite, and their men. 9Gedaliah son of Ahikam, the son of Shaphan, took an oath to reassure them and their men. "Do not be afraid to serve the Babylonians,[c]" he said. "Settle down in the land and serve the king of Babylon, and it will go well with you. 10I myself will stay at Mizpah to represent you before the Babylonians who come to us, but you are to harvest the wine, summer fruit and oil, and put them in your storage jars, and live in the towns you have taken over."

11When all the Jews in Moab, Ammon, Edom and all the other countries heard that the king of Babylon had left a remnant in Judah and had appointed Gedaliah son of Ahikam, the son of Shaphan, as governor over them, 12they all came back to the land of Judah, to Gedaliah at Mizpah, from all the countries where they had been scattered. And they harvested an abundance of wine and summer fruit.

13Johanan son of Kareah and all the army officers still in the open country came to Gedaliah at Mizpah 14and said to him, "Don't you know that Baalis king of the Ammonites has sent Ishmael son of Nethaniah to take your life?" But Gedaliah son of Ahikam did not believe them.

15Then Johanan son of Kareah said privately to Gedaliah in Mizpah, "Let me go and kill Ishmael son of Nethaniah, and no one will know it. Why should he take your life and cause all the Jews who are gathered around you to be scattered and the remnant of Judah to perish?"

16But Gedaliah son of Ahikam said to Johanan son of Kareah, "Don't do such a thing! What you are saying about Ishmael is not true."

Living Bible

2, 3The captain called for Jeremiah and said, "The Lord your God has brought this disaster on this land, just as he said he would. For these people have sinned against the Lord. That is why it happened. 4Now I am going to take off your chains and let you go. If you want to come with me to Babylon, fine; I will see that you are well cared for. But if you don't want to come, don't. The world is before you—go where you like. 5If you decide to stay, then return to Gedaliah, who has been appointed as governor of Judah by the king of Babylon, and stay with the remnant he rules. But it's up to you; go where you like."

Then Nebuzaradan gave Jeremiah some food and money and let him go. 6So Jeremiah returned to Gedaliah and lived in Judah with the people left in the land.

7Now when the leaders of the Jewish guerrilla bands in the countryside heard that the king of Babylon had appointed Gedaliah as governor over the poor of the land who were left behind, and had not exiled everyone to Babylon, 8they came to see Gedaliah at Mizpah, where his headquarters were. These are the names of the leaders who came: Ishmael (son of Nethaniah), Johanan and Jonathan (sons of Kareah), Seraiah (son of Tanhumeth), the sons of Ephai (the Netophathite), Jezaniah (son of a Ma-acathite), and their men. 9And Gedaliah assured them that it would be safe to surrender to the Babylonians.

"Stay here and serve the king of Babylon," he said, "and all will go well for you. 10As for me, I will stay at Mizpah and intercede for you with the Babylonians who will come here to oversee my administration. Settle in any city you wish and live off the land. Harvest the grapes and summer fruits and olives and store them away."

11When the Jews in Moab and among the Ammonites and in Edom and the other nearby countries heard that a few people were still left in Judah, and that the king of Babylon had not taken them all away, and that Gedaliah was the governor, 12they all began to return to Judah from the many places to which they had fled. They stopped at Mizpah to discuss their plans with Gedaliah and then went out to the deserted farms and gathered a great harvest of wine grapes and other crops.

13, 14But soon afterwards Johanan (son of Kareah) and the other guerrilla leaders came to Mizpah to warn Gedaliah that Baalis, king of the Ammonites, had sent Ishmael (son of Nethaniah) to assassinate him. But Gedaliah wouldn't believe them. 15Then Johanan had a private conference with Gedaliah. Johanan volunteered to kill Ishmael secretly.

"Why should we let him come and murder you?" Johanan asked. "What will happen then to the Jews who have returned? Why should this remnant be scattered and lost?"

16But Gedaliah said, "I forbid you to do any such thing, for you are lying about Ishmael."

New Revised Standard

tain of the guard took Jeremiah and said to him, "The LORD your God threatened this place with this disaster; 3and now the LORD has brought it about, and has done as he said, because all of you sinned against the LORD and did not obey his voice. Therefore this thing has come upon you. 4Now look, I have just released you today from the fetters on your hands. If you wish to come with me to Babylon, come, and I will take good care of you; but if you do not wish to come with me to Babylon, you need not come. See, the whole land is before you; go wherever you think it good and right to go. 5If you remain,d then return to Gedaliah son of Ahikam son of Shaphan, whom the king of Babylon appointed governor of the towns of Judah, and stay with him among the people; or go wherever you think it right to go." So the captain of the guard gave him an allowance of food and a present, and let him go. 6Then Jeremiah went to Gedaliah son of Ahikam at Mizpah, and stayed with him among the people who were left in the land.

7 When all the leaders of the forces in the open country and their troops heard that the king of Babylon had appointed Gedaliah son of Ahikam governor in the land, and had committed to him men, women, and children, those of the poorest of the land who had not been taken into exile to Babylon, 8they went to Gedaliah at Mizpah—Ishmael son of Nethaniah, Johanan son of Kareah, Seraiah son of Tanhumeth, the sons of Ephai the Netophathite, Jezaniah son of the Maacathite, they and their troops. 9Gedaliah son of Ahikam son of Shaphan swore to them and their troops, saying, "Do not be afraid to serve the Chaldeans. Stay in the land and serve the king of Babylon, and it shall go well with you. 10As for me, I am staying at Mizpah to represent you before the Chaldeans who come to us; but as for you, gather wine and summer fruits and oil, and store them in your vessels, and live in the towns that you have taken over." 11Likewise, when all the Judeans who were in Moab and among the Ammonites and in Edom and in other lands heard that the king of Babylon had left a remnant in Judah and had appointed Gedaliah son of Ahikam son of Shaphan as governor over them, 12then all the Judeans returned from all the places to which they had been scattered and came to the land of Judah, to Gedaliah at Mizpah; and they gathered wine and summer fruits in great abundance.

13 Now Johanan son of Kareah and all the leaders of the forces in the open country came to Gedaliah at Mizpah 14and said to him, "Are you at all aware that Baalis king of the Ammonites has sent Ishmael son of Nethaniah to take your life?" But Gedaliah son of Ahikam would not believe them. 15Then Johanan son of Kareah spoke secretly to Gedaliah at Mizpah, "Please let me go and kill Ishmael son of Nethaniah, and no one else will know. Why should he take your life, so that all the Judeans who are gathered around you would be scattered, and the remnant of Judah would perish?" 16But Gedaliah son of Ahikam said to Johanan son of Kareah, "Do not do such a thing, for you are telling a lie about Ishmael."

d Syr: Meaning of Heb uncertain

King James

41 NOW IT came to pass in the seventh month, *that* Ishmael the son of Nethaniah the son of Elishama, of the seed royal, and the princes of the king, even ten men with him, came unto Gedaliah the son of Ahikam to Mizpah; and there they did eat bread together in Mizpah.

2Then arose Ishmael the son of Nethaniah, and the ten men that were with him, and smote Gedaliah the son of Ahikam the son of Shaphan with the sword, and slew him, whom the king of Babylon had made governor over the land.

3Ishmael also slew all the Jews that were with him, *even* with Gedaliah, at Mizpah, and the Chaldeans that were found there, *and* the men of war.

4And it came to pass the second day after he had slain Gedaliah, and no man knew *it*,

5That there came certain from Shechem, from Shiloh, and from Samaria, *even* fourscore men, having their beards shaven, and their clothes rent, and having cut themselves, with offerings and incense in their hand, to bring *them* to the house of the LORD.

6And Ishmael the son of Nethaniah went forth from Mizpah to meet them, weeping all along as he went: and it came to pass, as he met them, he said unto them, Come to Gedaliah the son of Ahikam.

7And it was *so*, when they came into the midst of the city, that Ishmael the son of Nethaniah slew them, *and cast them* into the midst of the pit, he, and the men that *were* with him.

8But ten men were found among them that said unto Ishmael, Slay us not: for we have treasures in the field, of wheat, and of barley, and of oil, and of honey. So he forbare, and slew them not among their brethren.

9Now the pit wherein Ishmael had cast all the dead bodies of the men, whom he had slain because of Gedaliah, *was* it which Asa the king had made for fear of Baasha king of Israel: *and* Ishmael the son of Nethaniah filled it with *them that were* slain.

10Then Ishmael carried away captive all the residue of the people that *were* in Mizpah, *even* the king's daughters, and all the people that remained in Mizpah, whom Nebuzar-adan the captain of the guard had committed to Gedaliah the son of Ahikam: and Ishmael the son of Nethaniah carried them away captive, and departed to go over to the Ammonites.

11¶ But when Johanan the son of Kareah, and all the captains of the forces that *were* with him, heard of all the evil that Ishmael the son of Nethaniah had done,

12Then they took all the men, and went to fight with Ishmael the son of Nethaniah, and found him by the great waters that *are* in Gibeon.

13Now it came to pass, *that* when all the people which *were* with Ishmael saw Johanan the son of Kareah, and all the captains of the forces that *were* with him, then they were glad.

14So all the people that Ishmael had carried away captive from Mizpah cast about and returned, and went unto Johanan the son of Kareah.

15But Ishmael the son of Nethaniah escaped from Johanan with eight men, and went to the Ammonites.

16Then took Johanan the son of Kareah, and all the captains of the forces that *were* with him, all the remnant of the people whom he had recovered from Ishmael the son of Nethaniah, from Mizpah, after *that* he had slain Gedaliah the son of Ahikam, *even* mighty men of war, and the women, and the children, and the eunuchs, whom he had brought again from Gibeon:

17And they departed, and dwelt in the habitation of Chimham, which is by Bethlehem, to go to enter into Egypt,

New International

41 IN THE seventh month Ishmael son of Nethaniah, the son of Elishama, who was of royal blood and had been one of the king's officers, came with ten men to Gedaliah son of Ahikam at Mizpah. While they were eating together there, 2Ishmael son of Nethaniah and the ten men who were with him got up and struck down Gedaliah son of Ahikam, the son of Shaphan, with the sword, killing the one whom the king of Babylon had appointed as governor over the land. 3Ishmael also killed all the Jews who were with Gedaliah at Mizpah, as well as the Babyloniana soldiers who were there.

4The day after Gedaliah's assassination, before anyone knew about it, 5eighty men who had shaved off their beards, torn their clothes and cut themselves came from Shechem, Shiloh and Samaria, bringing grain offerings and incense with them to the house of the LORD. 6Ishmael son of Nethaniah went out from Mizpah to meet them, weeping as he went. When he met them, he said, "Come to Gedaliah son of Ahikam." 7When they went into the city, Ishmael son of Nethaniah and the men who were with him slaughtered them and threw them into a cistern. 8But ten of them said to Ishmael, "Don't kill us! We have wheat and barley, oil and honey, hidden in a field." So he let them alone and did not kill them with the others. 9Now the cistern where he threw all the bodies of the men he had killed along with Gedaliah was the one King Asa had made as part of his defense against Baasha king of Israel. Ishmael son of Nethaniah filled it with the dead.

10Ishmael made captives of all the rest of the people who were in Mizpah—the king's daughters along with all the others who were left there, over whom Nebuzaradan commander of the imperial guard had appointed Gedaliah son of Ahikam. Ishmael son of Nethaniah took them captive and set out to cross over to the Ammonites.

11When Johanan son of Kareah and all the army officers who were with him heard about all the crimes Ishmael son of Nethaniah had committed, 12they took all their men and went to fight Ishmael son of Nethaniah. They caught up with him near the great pool in Gibeon. 13When all the people Ishmael had with him saw Johanan son of Kareah and the army officers who were with him, they were glad. 14All the people Ishmael had taken captive at Mizpah turned and went over to Johanan son of Kareah. 15But Ishmael son of Nethaniah and eight of his men escaped from Johanan and fled to the Ammonites.

Flight to Egypt

16Then Johanan son of Kareah and all the army officers who were with him led away all the survivors from Mizpah whom he had recovered from Ishmael son of Nethaniah after he had assassinated Gedaliah son of Ahikam: the soldiers, women, children and court officials he had brought from Gibeon. 17And they went on, stopping at Geruth Kimham near Bethlehem on their

Living Bible

41 BUT IN October, Ishmael (son of Nethaniah, son of Elishama), who was a member of the royal family and one of the king's top officials, arrived in Mizpah with Gedaliah. Gedaliah invited them to dinner. ²While they were eating, Ishmael and the ten men in league with him suddenly jumped up, pulled out their swords and killed Gedaliah. ³Then they went out and slaughtered all the Jewish officials and Babylonian soldiers who were in Mizpah with Gedaliah.

⁴The next day, before the outside world knew what had happened, ⁵eighty men approached Mizpah from Shechem, Shiloh and Samaria, to worship at the Temple of the Lord. They had shaved off their beards, torn their clothes and cut themselves, and were bringing offerings and incense. ⁶Ishmael went out from the city to meet them, crying as he went. When he faced them he said, "Oh, come and see what has happened to Gedaliah!"

⁷Then, when they were all inside the city, Ishmael and his men killed all but ten of them and threw their bodies into a cistern. ⁸The ten had talked Ishmael into letting them go by promising to bring him their treasures of wheat, barley, oil and honey they had hidden away. ⁹The cistern where Ishmael dumped the bodies of the men he murdered was the large one constructed by King Asa when he fortified Mizpah to protect himself against Baasha, king of Israel.ᵇ

¹⁰Ishmael made captives of the king's daughters and of the people who had been left under Gedaliah's care in Mizpah by Nebuzaradan, captain of the guard. Soon after he took them with him when he headed toward the country of the Ammonites.

¹¹But when Johanan (son of Kareah) and the rest of the guerrilla leaders heard what Ishmael had done, ¹²they took all their men and set out to stop him. They caught up with him at the pool near Gibeon. ¹³, ¹⁴The people with Ishmael shouted for joy when they saw Johanan and his men, and ran to meet them.

¹⁵Meanwhile Ishmael escaped with eight of his men into the land of the Ammonites.

¹⁶, ¹⁷Then Johanan and his men went to the village of Geruth Chimham, near Bethlehem, taking with them all those they had rescued—soldiers, women, children and eunuchs, to prepare to leave for Egypt. ¹⁸For they were

New Revised Standard

Insurrection against Gedaliah

41 IN THE seventh month, Ishmael son of Nethaniah son of Elishama, of the royal family, one of the chief officers of the king, came with ten men to Gedaliah son of Ahikam, at Mizpah. As they ate bread together there at Mizpah, ²Ishmael son of Nethaniah and the ten men with him got up and struck down Gedaliah son of Ahikam son of Shaphan with the sword and killed him, because the king of Babylon had appointed him governor in the land. ³Ishmael also killed all the Judeans who were with Gedaliah at Mizpah, and the Chaldean soldiers who happened to be there.

4 On the day after the murder of Gedaliah, before anyone knew of it, ⁵eighty men arrived from Shechem and Shiloh and Samaria, with their beards shaved and their clothes torn, and their bodies gashed, bringing grain offerings and incense to present at the temple of the LORD. ⁶And Ishmael son of Nethaniah came out from Mizpah to meet them, weeping as he came. As he met them, he said to them, "Come to Gedaliah son of Ahikam." ⁷When they reached the middle of the city, Ishmael son of Nethaniah and the men with him slaughtered them, and threw themᶜ into a cistern. ⁸But there were ten men among them who said to Ishmael, "Do not kill us, for we have stores of wheat, barley, oil, and honey hidden in the fields." So he refrained, and did not kill them along with their companions.

9 Now the cistern into which Ishmael had thrown all the bodies of the men whom he had struck down was the large cisternᵈ that King Asa had made for defense against King Baasha of Israel; Ishmael son of Nethaniah filled that cistern with those whom he had killed. ¹⁰Then Ishmael took captive all the rest of the people who were in Mizpah, the king's daughters and all the people who were left at Mizpah, whom Nebuzaradan, the captain of the guard, had committed to Gedaliah son of Ahikam. Ishmael son of Nethaniah took them captive and set out to cross over to the Ammonites.

11 But when Johanan son of Kareah and all the leaders of the forces with him heard of all the crimes that Ishmael son of Nethaniah had done, ¹²they took all their men and went to fight against Ishmael son of Nethaniah. They came upon him at the great pool that is in Gibeon. ¹³And when all the people who were with Ishmael saw Johanan son of Kareah and all the leaders of the forces with him, they were glad. ¹⁴So all the people whom Ishmael had carried away captive from Mizpah turned around and came back, and went to Johanan son of Kareah. ¹⁵But Ishmael son of Nethaniah escaped from Johanan with eight men, and went to the Ammonites. ¹⁶Then Johanan son of Kareah and all the leaders of the forces with him took all the rest of the people whom Ishmael son of Nethaniah had carried away captiveᵉ from Mizpah after he had slain Gedaliah son of Ahikam—soldiers, women, children, and eunuchs, whom Johanan brought back from Gibeon.ᶠ ¹⁷And they set out, and stopped at Geruth Chimham near Bethle-

---

ᵇ *41:9 he fortified Mizpah to protect himself against Baasha, king of Israel.* See 1 Kgs 15:22. Fifty-three cisterns have been uncovered by excavators at the site of ancient Mizpah.

ᶜ Syr: Heb lacks *and threw them*; compare verse 9   ᵈ Gk: Heb *whom he had killed by the hand of Gedaliah*   ᵉ Cn: Heb *whom he recovered from Ishmael son of Nethaniah*   ᶠ Meaning of Heb uncertain

King James

18Because of the Chaldeans: for they were afraid of them, because Ishmael the son of Nethaniah had slain Gedaliah the son of Ahikam, whom the king of Babylon made governor in the land.

42 THEN ALL the captains of the forces, and Johanan the son of Kareah, and Jezaniah the son of Hoshaiah, and all the people from the least even unto the greatest, came near,

2And said unto Jeremiah the prophet, Let, we beseech thee, our supplication be accepted before thee, and pray for us unto the LORD thy God, *even* for all this remnant; (for we are left *but* a few of many, as thine eyes do behold us:)

3That the LORD thy God may show us the way wherein we may walk, and the thing that we may do.

4Then Jeremiah the prophet said unto them, I have heard *you;* behold, I will pray unto the LORD your God according to your words; and it shall come to pass, *that* whatsoever thing the LORD shall answer you, I will declare *it* unto you; I will keep nothing back from you.

5Then they said to Jeremiah, The LORD be a true and faithful witness between us, if we do not even according to all things for the which the LORD thy God shall send thee to us.

6Whether *it be* good, or whether *it be* evil, we will obey the voice of the LORD our God, to whom we send thee; that it may be well with us, when we obey the voice of the LORD our God.

7¶ And it came to pass after ten days, that the word of the LORD came unto Jeremiah.

8Then called he Johanan the son of Kareah, and all the captains of the forces which *were* with him, and all the people from the least even to the greatest,

9And said unto them, Thus saith the LORD, the God of Israel, unto whom ye sent me to present your supplication before him;

10If ye will still abide in this land, then will I build you, and not pull *you* down, and I will plant you, and not pluck *you* up: for I repent me of the evil that I have done unto you.

11Be not afraid of the king of Babylon, of whom ye are afraid; be not afraid of him, saith the LORD: for I *am* with you to save you, and to deliver you from his hand.

12And I will show mercies unto you, that he may have mercy upon you, and cause you to return to your own land.

13¶ But if ye say, We will not dwell in this land, neither obey the voice of the LORD your God,

14Saying, No; but we will go into the land of Egypt, where we shall see no war, nor hear the sound of the trumpet, nor have hunger of bread; and there will we dwell:

15And now therefore hear the word of the LORD, ye remnant of Judah; Thus saith the LORD of hosts, the God of Israel; If ye wholly set your faces to enter into Egypt, and go to sojourn there;

16Then it shall come to pass, *that* the sword, which ye feared, shall overtake you there in the land of Egypt, and the famine, whereof ye were afraid, shall follow close after you there in Egypt; and there ye shall die.

New International

way to Egypt 18to escape the Babylonians.a They were afraid of them because Ishmael son of Nethaniah had killed Gedaliah son of Ahikam, whom the king of Babylon had appointed as governor over the land.

42 THEN ALL the army officers, including Johanan son of Kareah and Jezaniahb son of Hoshaiah, and all the people from the least to the greatest approached 2Jeremiah the prophet and said to him, "Please hear our petition and pray to the LORD your God for this entire remnant. For as you now see, though we were once many, now only a few are left. 3Pray that the LORD your God will tell us where we should go and what we should do."

4"I have heard you," replied Jeremiah the prophet. "I will certainly pray to the LORD your God as you have requested; I will tell you everything the LORD says and will keep nothing back from you."

5Then they said to Jeremiah, "May the LORD be a true and faithful witness against us if we do not act in accordance with everything the LORD your God sends you to tell us. 6Whether it is favorable or unfavorable, we will obey the LORD our God, to whom we are sending you, so that it will go well with us, for we will obey the LORD our God."

7Ten days later the word of the LORD came to Jeremiah. 8So he called together Johanan son of Kareah and all the army officers who were with him and all the people from the least to the greatest. 9He said to them, "This is what the LORD, the God of Israel, to whom you sent me to present your petition, says: 10'If you stay in this land, I will build you up and not tear you down; I will plant you and not uproot you, for I am grieved over the disaster I have inflicted on you. 11Do not be afraid of the king of Babylon, whom you now fear. Do not be afraid of him, declares the LORD, for I am with you and will save you and deliver you from his hands. 12I will show you compassion so that he will have compassion on you and restore you to your land.'

13"However, if you say, 'We will not stay in this land,' and so disobey the LORD your God, 14and if you say, 'No, we will go and live in Egypt, where we will not see war or hear the trumpet or be hungry for bread,' 15then hear the word of the LORD, O remnant of Judah. This is what the LORD Almighty, the God of Israel, says: 'If you are determined to go to Egypt and you do go to settle there, 16then the sword you fear will overtake you there, and the famine you dread will follow you into Egypt, and there you will die. 17Indeed, all who are

---

a *18* Or *Chaldeans* b *1* Hebrew; Septuagint (see also 43:2) *Azariah*

Living Bible

afraid of what the Babylonians would do when the news reached them that Ishmael had killed Gedaliah the governor, for he had been chosen and appointed by the Babylonian emperor.

42 THEN JOHANAN and the army captains and all the people, great and small, came to Jeremiah 2and said, "Please pray for us to the Lord your God, for as you know so well, we are only a tiny remnant of what we were before. 3Beg the Lord your God to show us what to do and where to go."

4"All right," Jeremiah replied. "I will ask him and I will tell you what he says. I will hide nothing from you."

5Then they said to Jeremiah, "May the curse of God be on us if we refuse to obey whatever he says we should do! 6Whether we like it or not, we will obey the Lord our God, to whom we send you with our plea. For if we obey him, everything will turn out well for us."

7Ten days later the Lord gave his reply to Jeremiah. 8So he called for Johanan and the captains of his forces, and for all the people, great and small, 9and said to them: "You sent me to the Lord, the God of Israel, with your request, and this is his reply:

10"Stay here in this land. If you do, I will bless you and no one will harm you. For I am sorry for all the punishment I have had to give to you. 11Don't fear the king of Babylon any more, for I am with you to save you and to deliver you from his hand. 12And I will be merciful to you by making him kind so that he will not kill you or make slaves of you but will let you stay here in your land.

13, 14"But if you refuse to obey the Lord and say, 'We will not stay here,'—and insist on going to Egypt where you think you will be free from war and hunger and alarms, 15then this is what the Lord replies, O remnant of Judah: The Lord Almighty, the God of Israel, says: If you insist on going to Egypt, 16the war and famine you fear will follow close behind you and you will perish there. 17That is the fate awaiting every one of you who

New Revised Standard

hem, intending to go to Egypt 18because of the Chaldeans; for they were afraid of them, because Ishmael son of Nethaniah had killed Gedaliah son of Ahikam, whom the king of Babylon had made governor over the land.

Jeremiah Advises Survivors Not to Migrate

42 THEN ALL the commanders of the forces, and Johanan son of Kareah and Azariahc son of Hoshaiah, and all the people from the least to the greatest, approached 2the prophet Jeremiah and said, "Be good enough to listen to our plea, and pray to the LORD your God for us—for all this remnant. For there are only a few of us left out of many, as your eyes can see. 3Let the LORD your God show us where we should go and what we should do." 4The prophet Jeremiah said to them, "Very well: I am going to pray to the LORD your God as you request, and whatever the LORD answers you I will tell you; I will keep nothing back from you." 5They in their turn said to Jeremiah, "May the LORD be a true and faithful witness against us if we do not act according to everything that the LORD your God sends us through you. 6Whether it is good or bad, we will obey the voice of the LORD our God to whom we are sending you, in order that it may go well with us when we obey the voice of the LORD our God."

7 At the end of ten days the word of the LORD came to Jeremiah. 8Then he summoned Johanan son of Kareah and all the commanders of the forces who were with him, and all the people from the least to the greatest, 9and said to them, "Thus says the LORD, the God of Israel, to whom you sent me to present your plea before him: 10If you will only remain in this land, then I will build you up and not pull you down; I will plant you, and not pluck you up; for I am sorry for the disaster that I have brought upon you. 11Do not be afraid of the king of Babylon, as you have been; do not be afraid of him, says the LORD, for I am with you, to save you and to rescue you from his hand. 12I will grant you mercy, and he will have mercy on you and restore you to your native soil. 13But if you continue to say, 'We will not stay in this land,' thus disobeying the voice of the LORD your God 14and saying, 'No, we will go to the land of Egypt, where we shall not see war, or hear the sound of the trumpet, or be hungry for bread, and there we will stay,' 15then hear the word of the LORD, O remnant of Judah. Thus says the LORD of hosts, the God of Israel: If you are determined to enter Egypt and go to settle there, 16then the sword that you fear shall overtake you there, in the land of Egypt; and the famine that you dread shall follow close after you into Egypt; and there you shall die. 17All the people who have determined to go to

c Gk: Heb *Jezaniah*

King James

17So shall it be with all the men that set their faces to go into Egypt to sojourn there; they shall die by the sword, by the famine, and by the pestilence: and none of them shall remain or escape from the evil that I will bring upon them.

18For thus saith the LORD of hosts, the God of Israel; As mine anger and my fury hath been poured forth upon the inhabitants of Jerusalem; so shall my fury be poured forth upon you, when ye shall enter into Egypt: and ye shall be an execration, and an astonishment, and a curse, and a reproach; and ye shall see this place no more.

19¶ The LORD hath said concerning you, O ye remnant of Judah; Go ye not into Egypt: know certainly that I have admonished you this day.

20For ye dissembled in your hearts, when ye sent me unto the LORD your God, saying, Pray for us unto the LORD our God; and according unto all that the LORD our God shall say, so declare unto us, and we will do *it*.

21And *now* I have this day declared *it* to you; but ye have not obeyed the voice of the LORD your God, nor any *thing* for the which he hath sent me unto you.

22Now therefore know certainly that ye shall die by the sword, by the famine, and by the pestilence, in the place whither ye desire to go *and* to sojourn.

43 AND IT came to pass, *that* when Jeremiah had made an end of speaking unto all the people all the words of the LORD their God, for which the LORD their God had sent him to them, *even* all these words,

2Then spake Azariah the son of Hoshaiah, and Johanan the son of Kareah, and all the proud men, saying unto Jeremiah, Thou speakest falsely: the LORD our God hath not sent thee to say, Go not into Egypt to sojourn there:

3But Baruch the son of Neriah setteth thee on against us, for to deliver us into the hand of the Chaldeans, that they might put us to death, and carry us away captives into Babylon.

4So Johanan the son of Kareah, and all the captains of the forces, and all the people, obeyed not the voice of the LORD, to dwell in the land of Judah.

5But Johanan the son of Kareah, and all the captains of the forces, took all the remnant of Judah, that were returned from all nations, whither they had been driven, to dwell in the land of Judah;

6*Even* men, and women, and children, and the king's daughters, and every person that Nebuzar-adan the captain of the guard had left with Gedaliah the son of Ahikam the son of Shaphan, and Jeremiah the prophet, and Baruch the son of Neriah.

7So they came into the land of Egypt: for they obeyed not the voice of the LORD: thus came they *even* to Tahpanhes.

8¶ Then came the word of the LORD unto Jeremiah in Tahpanhes, saying,

9Take great stones in thine hand, and hide them in the clay in the brickkiln, which *is* at the entry of Pharaoh's house in Tahpanhes, in the sight of the men of Judah;

10And say unto them, Thus saith the LORD of hosts, the God of Israel; Behold, I will send and take Nebuchadrezzar the king of Babylon, my servant, and will set his throne upon these stones that I have hid; and he shall spread his royal pavilion over them.

11And when he cometh, he shall smite the land of Egypt, *and deliver* such *as are* for death to death; and such *as are* for captivity to captivity; and such *as are* for the sword to the sword.

New International

determined to go to Egypt to settle there will die by the sword, famine and plague; not one of them will survive or escape the disaster I will bring on them.' 18This is what the LORD Almighty, the God of Israel, says: 'As my anger and wrath have been poured out on those who lived in Jerusalem, so will my wrath be poured out on you when you go to Egypt. You will be an object of cursing and horror, of condemnation and reproach; you will never see this place again.'

19"O remnant of Judah, the LORD has told you, 'Do not go to Egypt.' Be sure of this: I warn you today 20that you made a fatal mistake[a] when you sent me to the LORD your God and said, 'Pray to the LORD our God for us; tell us everything he says and we will do it.' 21I have told you today, but you still have not obeyed the LORD your God in all he sent me to tell you. 22So now, be sure of this: You will die by the sword, famine and plague in the place where you want to go to settle."

43 WHEN JEREMIAH finished telling the people all the words of the LORD their God—everything the LORD had sent him to tell them— 2Azariah son of Hoshaiah and Johanan son of Kareah and all the arrogant men said to Jeremiah, "You are lying! The LORD our God has not sent you to say, 'You must not go to Egypt to settle there.' 3But Baruch son of Neriah is inciting you against us to hand us over to the Babylonians,[b] so they may kill us or carry us into exile to Babylon."

4So Johanan son of Kareah and all the army officers and all the people disobeyed the LORD's command to stay in the land of Judah. 5Instead, Johanan son of Kareah and all the army officers led away all the remnant of Judah who had come back to live in the land of Judah from all the nations where they had been scattered. 6They also led away all the men, women and children and the king's daughters whom Nebuzaradan commander of the imperial guard had left with Gedaliah son of Ahikam, the son of Shaphan, and Jeremiah the prophet and Baruch son of Neriah. 7So they entered Egypt in disobedience to the LORD and went as far as Tahpanhes.

8In Tahpanhes the word of the LORD came to Jeremiah: 9"While the Jews are watching, take some large stones with you and bury them in clay in the brick pavement at the entrance to Pharaoh's palace in Tahpanhes. 10Then say to them, 'This is what the LORD Almighty, the God of Israel, says: I will send for my servant Nebuchadnezzar king of Babylon, and I will set his throne over these stones I have buried here; he will spread his royal canopy above them. 11He will come and attack Egypt, bringing death to those destined for death, captivity to those destined for captivity, and the sword to those destined for the sword. 12He[c] will set fire to the

Living Bible

insists on going to live in Egypt. Yes, you will die from sword, famine and disease. None of you will escape from the evil I will bring upon you there.

18"For the Lord, the God of Israel, says: Just as my anger and fury were poured out upon the people of Jerusalem, so it will be poured out on you when you enter Egypt. You will be received with disgust and with hatred—you will be cursed and reviled. And you will never again see your own land. 19For the Lord has said: O remnant of Judah, do not go to Egypt!"

Jeremiah concluded: "Never forget the warning I have given you today. 20If you go, it will be at the cost of your lives. For you were deceitful when you sent me to pray for you and said, 'Just tell us what God says and we will do it!' 21And today I have told you exactly what he said, but you will not obey any more now than you did the other times. 22Therefore know for a certainty that you will die by sword, famine and disease in Egypt, where you insist on going."

43 WHEN JEREMIAH had finished giving this message from God to all the people, 2, 3Azariah (son of Hoshaiah) and Johanan (son of Kareah) and all the other proud men, said to Jeremiah, "You lie! The Lord our God hasn't told you to tell us not to go to Egypt! Baruch (son of Neriah) has plotted against us and told you to say this so that we will stay here and be killed by the Babylonians or carried off to Babylon as slaves."

4So Johanan and all the guerrilla leaders and all the people refused to obey the Lord and stay in Judah. 5All of them, including all those who had returned from the nearby countries where they had fled, now started off for Egypt with Johanan and the other captains in command. 6In the crowd were men, women and children, the king's daughters and all those whom Nebuzaradan, the captain of the guard, had left with Gedaliah. They even forced Jeremiah and Baruch to go with them too. 7And so they arrived in Egypt at the city of Tahpanhes, for they would not obey the Lord.

8Then at Tahpanhes, the Lord spoke to Jeremiah again and said:

9"Call together the men of Judah and, as they watch you, bury large rocks between the pavement stones at the entrance of Pharaoh's palace here in Tahpanhes, 10and tell the men of Judah this: The Lord Almighty, the God of Israel, says: I will surely bring Nebuchadnezzar, king of Babylon, here to Egypt, for he is my servant. I will set his throne upon these stones that I have hidden. He shall spread his royal canopy over them. 11And when he comes he shall destroy the land of Egypt, killing all those I want killed, and capturing those I want captured, and many shall die of plague. 12He will set fire to the

New Revised Standard

Egypt to settle there shall die by the sword, by famine, and by pestilence; they shall have no remnant or survivor from the disaster that I am bringing upon them.

18 "For thus says the LORD of hosts, the God of Israel: Just as my anger and my wrath were poured out on the inhabitants of Jerusalem, so my wrath will be poured out on you when you go to Egypt. You shall become an object of execration and horror, of cursing and ridicule. You shall see this place no more. 19The LORD has said to you, O remnant of Judah, Do not go to Egypt. Be well aware that I have warned you today 20that you have made a fatal mistake. For you yourselves sent me to the LORD your God, saying, 'Pray for us to the LORD our God, and whatever the LORD our God says, tell us and we will do it.' 21So I have told you today, but you have not obeyed the voice of the LORD your God in anything that he sent me to tell you. 22Be well aware, then, that you shall die by the sword, by famine, and by pestilence in the place where you desire to go and settle."

Taken to Egypt, Jeremiah Warns of Judgment

43 WHEN JEREMIAH finished speaking to all the people all these words of the LORD their God, with which the LORD their God had sent him to them, 2Azariah son of Hoshaiah and Johanan son of Kareah and all the other insolent men said to Jeremiah, "You are telling a lie. The LORD our God did not send you to say, 'Do not go to Egypt to settle there'; 3but Baruch son of Neriah is inciting you against us, to hand us over to the Chaldeans, in order that they may kill us or take us into exile in Babylon." 4So Johanan son of Kareah and all the commanders of the forces and all the people did not obey the voice of the LORD, to stay in the land of Judah. 5But Johanan son of Kareah and all the commanders of the forces took all the remnant of Judah who had returned to settle in the land of Judah from all the nations to which they had been driven— 6the men, the women, the children, the princesses, and everyone whom Nebuzaradan the captain of the guard had left with Gedaliah son of Ahikam son of Shaphan; also the prophet Jeremiah and Baruch son of Neriah. 7And they came into the land of Egypt, for they did not obey the voice of the LORD. And they arrived at Tahpanhes.

8 Then the word of the LORD came to Jeremiah in Tahpanhes: 9Take some large stones in your hands, and bury them in the clay pavementd that is at the entrance to Pharaoh's palace in Tahpanhes. Let the Judeans see you do it, 10and say to them, Thus says the LORD of hosts, the God of Israel: I am going to send and take my servant King Nebuchadrezzar of Babylon, and hee will set his throne above these stones that I have buried, and he will spread his royal canopy over them. 11He shall come and ravage the land of Egypt, giving

> those who are destined for pestilence, to
>   pestilence,
> and those who are destined for captivity, to
>   captivity,
> and those who are destined for the sword,
>   to the sword.

King James

12And I will kindle a fire in the houses of the gods of Egypt; and he shall burn them, and carry them away captives: and he shall array himself with the land of Egypt, as a shepherd putteth on his garment; and he shall go forth from thence in peace.

13He shall break also the images of Beth-shemesh, that *is* in the land of Egypt; and the houses of the gods of the Egyptians shall he burn with fire.

44 THE WORD that came to Jeremiah concerning all the Jews which dwell in the land of Egypt, which dwell at Migdol, and at Tahpanhes, and at Noph, and in the country of Pathros, saying,

2Thus saith the LORD of hosts, the God of Israel; Ye have seen all the evil that I have brought upon Jerusalem, and upon all the cities of Judah; and, behold, this day they *are* a desolation, and no man dwelleth therein,

3Because of their wickedness which they have committed to provoke me to anger, in that they went to burn incense, *and* to serve other gods, whom they knew not, *neither* they, ye, nor your fathers.

4Howbeit I sent unto you all my servants the prophets, rising early and sending *them*, saying, Oh, do not this abominable thing that I hate.

5But they hearkened not, nor inclined their ear to turn from their wickedness, to burn no incense unto other gods.

6Wherefore my fury and mine anger was poured forth, and was kindled in the cities of Judah and in the streets of Jerusalem; and they are wasted *and* desolate, as at this day.

7Therefore now thus saith the LORD, the God of hosts, the God of Israel; Wherefore commit ye *this* great evil against your souls, to cut off from you man and woman, child and suckling, out of Judah, to leave you none to remain;

8In that ye provoke me unto wrath with the works of your hands, burning incense unto other gods in the land of Egypt, whither ye be gone to dwell, that ye might cut yourselves off, and that ye might be a curse and a reproach among all the nations of the earth?

9Have ye forgotten the wickedness of your fathers, and the wickedness of the kings of Judah, and the wickedness of their wives, and your own wickedness, and the wickedness of your wives, which they have committed in the land of Judah, and in the streets of Jerusalem?

10They are not humbled *even* unto this day, neither have they feared, nor walked in my law, nor in my statutes, that I set before you and before your fathers.

11¶ Therefore thus saith the LORD of hosts, the God of Israel; Behold, I will set my face against you for evil, and to cut off all Judah.

12And I will take the remnant of Judah, that have set their faces to go into the land of Egypt to sojourn there, and they shall all be consumed, *and* fall in the land of Egypt; they shall *even* be consumed by the sword *and* by the famine: they shall die, from the least even unto the greatest, by the sword and by the famine: and they shall be an execration, *and* an astonishment, and a curse, and a reproach.

13For I will punish them that dwell in the land of Egypt, as I have punished Jerusalem, by the sword, by the famine, and by the pestilence:

14So that none of the remnant of Judah, which are gone into the land of Egypt to sojourn there, shall escape or remain, that they should return into the land of Judah, to the which they have a desire to return to dwell there: for none shall return but such as shall escape.

New International

temples of the gods of Egypt; he will burn their temples and take their gods captive. As a shepherd wraps his garment around him, so will he wrap Egypt around himself and depart from there unscathed. 13There in the temple of the suna in Egypt he will demolish the sacred pillars and will burn down the temples of the gods of Egypt.' "

Disaster Because of Idolatry

44 THIS WORD came to Jeremiah concerning all the Jews living in Lower Egypt—in Migdol, Tahpanhes and Memphisb—and in Upper Egypt: 2"This is what the LORD Almighty, the God of Israel, says: You saw the great disaster I brought on Jerusalem and on all the towns of Judah. Today they lie deserted and in ruins 3because of the evil they have done. They provoked me to anger by burning incense and by worshiping other gods that neither they nor you nor your fathers ever knew. 4Again and again I sent my servants the prophets, who said, 'Do not do this detestable thing that I hate!' 5But they did not listen or pay attention; they did not turn from their wickedness or stop burning incense to other gods. 6Therefore, my fierce anger was poured out; it raged against the towns of Judah and the streets of Jerusalem and made them the desolate ruins they are today.

7"Now this is what the LORD God Almighty, the God of Israel, says: Why bring such great disaster on yourselves by cutting off from Judah the men and women, the children and infants, and so leave yourselves without a remnant? 8Why provoke me to anger with what your hands have made, burning incense to other gods in Egypt, where you have come to live? You will destroy yourselves and make yourselves an object of cursing and reproach among all the nations on earth. 9Have you forgotten the wickedness committed by your fathers and by the kings and queens of Judah and the wickedness committed by you and your wives in the land of Judah and the streets of Jerusalem? 10To this day they have not humbled themselves or shown reverence, nor have they followed my law and the decrees I set before you and your fathers.

11"Therefore, this is what the LORD Almighty, the God of Israel, says: I am determined to bring disaster on you and to destroy all Judah. 12I will take away the remnant of Judah who were determined to go to Egypt to settle there. They will all perish in Egypt; they will fall by the sword or die from famine. From the least to the greatest, they will die by sword or famine. They will become an object of cursing and horror, of condemnation and reproach. 13I will punish those who live in Egypt with the sword, famine and plague, as I punished Jerusalem. 14None of the remnant of Judah who have gone to live in Egypt will escape or survive to return to the land of Judah, to which they long to return and live; none will return except a few fugitives."

a 13 Or in Heliopolis   b 1 Hebrew Noph   c 1 Hebrew in Pathros

Living Bible

temples of the gods of Egypt and burn the idols and carry off the people as his captives. And he shall plunder the land of Egypt as a shepherd picks fleas from his cloak! And he himself shall leave unharmed. 13And he shall break down the obelisks standing in the city of Heliopolis, and burn down the temples of the gods of Egypt."

44 THIS IS the message God gave to Jeremiah concerning all the Jews who were living in the north of Egypt in the cities of Migdol, Tahpanhes and Memphis, and throughout southern Egypt as well: 2, 3The Lord Almighty, the God of Israel, says: You saw what I did to Jerusalem and to all the cities of Judah. Because of all their wickedness they lie in heaps and ashes, without a living soul. For my anger rose high against them for worshiping other gods—"gods" that neither they nor you nor any of your fathers have ever known.

4I sent my servants, the prophets, to protest over and over again and to plead with them not to do this horrible thing I hate, 5but they wouldn't listen and wouldn't turn back from their wicked ways; they have kept right on with their sacrifices to these "gods." 6And so my fury and anger boiled over and fell as fire upon the cities of Judah and into the streets of Jerusalem, and there is desolation until this day.

7And now the Lord, the Lord Almighty, the God of Israel, asks you: Why are you destroying yourselves? For not one of you shall live—not a man, woman or child among you who has come here from Judah, not even the babies in arms. 8For you are rousing my anger with the idols you have made and worshiped here in Egypt, burning incense to them, and causing me to destroy you completely and to make you a curse and a stench in the nostrils of all the nations of the earth. 9Have you forgotten the sins of your fathers, and the sins of the kings and queens of Judah, and your own sins, and the sins of your wives in Judah and Jerusalem? 10And even until this very hour there has been no apology; no one has wanted to return to me, or follow the laws I gave you and your fathers before you.

11Therefore the Lord, the God of Israel, says: There is fury in my face and I will destroy every one of you! 12I will take this remnant of Judah that insisted on coming here to Egypt and I will consume them. They shall fall here in Egypt, killed by famine and sword; all shall die, from the least important to the greatest. They shall be despised and loathed, cursed and hated. 13I will punish them in Egypt just as I punished them in Jerusalem, by sword, famine and disease. 14Not one of them shall escape from my wrath except those who repent of their coming and escape from the others by returning again to their own land.

New Revised Standard

12He^d shall kindle a fire in the temples of the gods of Egypt; and he shall burn them and carry them away captive; and he shall pick clean the land of Egypt, as a shepherd picks his cloak clean of vermin; and he shall depart from there safely. 13He shall break the obelisks of Heliopolis, which is in the land of Egypt; and the temples of the gods of Egypt he shall burn with fire.

Denunciation of Persistent Idolatry

44 THE WORD that came to Jeremiah for all the Judeans living in the land of Egypt, at Migdol, at Tahpanhes, at Memphis, and in the land of Pathros, 2Thus says the LORD of hosts, the God of Israel: You yourselves have seen all the disaster that I have brought on Jerusalem and on all the towns of Judah. Look at them; today they are a desolation, without an inhabitant in them, 3because of the wickedness that they committed, provoking me to anger, in that they went to make offerings and serve other gods that they had not known, neither they, nor you, nor your ancestors. 4Yet I persistently sent to you all my servants the prophets, saying, "I beg you not to do this abominable thing that I hate!" 5But they did not listen or incline their ear, to turn from their wickedness and make no offerings to other gods. 6So my wrath and my anger were poured out and kindled in the towns of Judah and in the streets of Jerusalem; and they became a waste and a desolation, as they still are today. 7And now thus says the LORD God of hosts, the God of Israel: Why are you doing such great harm to yourselves, to cut off man and woman, child and infant, from the midst of Judah, leaving yourselves without a remnant? 8Why do you provoke me to anger with the works of your hands, making offerings to other gods in the land of Egypt where you have come to settle? Will you be cut off and become an object of cursing and ridicule among all the nations of the earth? 9Have you forgotten the crimes of your ancestors, of the kings of Judah, of their wives, your own crimes and those of your wives, which they committed in the land of Judah and in the streets of Jerusalem? 10They have shown no contrition or fear to this day, nor have they walked in my law and my statutes that I set before you and before your ancestors.

11 Therefore thus says the LORD of hosts, the God of Israel: I am determined to bring disaster on you, to bring all Judah to an end. 12I will take the remnant of Judah who are determined to come to the land of Egypt to settle, and they shall perish, everyone; in the land of Egypt they shall fall; by the sword and by famine they shall perish; from the least to the greatest, they shall die by the sword and by famine; and they shall become an object of execration and horror, of cursing and ridicule. 13I will punish those who live in the land of Egypt, as I have punished Jerusalem, with the sword, with famine, and with pestilence, 14so that none of the remnant of Judah who have come to settle in the land of Egypt shall escape or survive or return to the land of Judah. Although they long to go back to live there, they shall not go back, except some fugitives.

---

^d Gk Syr Vg: Heb *I*   ^e Heb *his*

King James

15¶ Then all the men which knew that their wives had burned incense unto other gods, and all the women that stood by, a great multitude, even all the people that dwelt in the land of Egypt, in Pathros, answered Jeremiah, saying,

16*As for* the word that thou hast spoken unto us in the name of the LORD, we will not hearken unto thee.

17But we will certainly do whatsoever thing goeth forth out of our own mouth, to burn incense unto the queen of heaven, and to pour out drink offerings unto her, as we have done, we, and our fathers, our kings, and our princes, in the cities of Judah, and in the streets of Jerusalem: for *then* had we plenty of victuals, and were well, and saw no evil.

18But since we left off to burn incense to the queen of heaven, and to pour out drink offerings unto her, we have wanted all *things*, and have been consumed by the sword and by the famine.

19And when we burned incense to the queen of heaven, and poured out drink offerings unto her, did we make her cakes to worship her, and pour out drink offerings unto her, without our men?

20¶ Then Jeremiah said unto all the people, to the men, and to the women, and to all the people which had given him *that* answer, saying,

21The incense that ye burned in the cities of Judah, and in the streets of Jerusalem, ye, and your fathers, your kings, and your princes, and the people of the land, did not the LORD remember them, and came it *not* into his mind?

22So that the LORD could no longer bear, because of the evil of your doings, *and* because of the abominations which ye have committed; therefore is your land a desolation, and an astonishment, and a curse, without an inhabitant, as at this day.

23Because ye have burned incense, and because ye have sinned against the LORD, and have not obeyed the voice of the LORD, nor walked in his law, nor in his statutes, nor in his testimonies; therefore this evil is happened unto you, as at this day.

24Moreover Jeremiah said unto all the people, and to all the women, Hear the word of the LORD, all Judah that *are* in the land of Egypt:

25Thus saith the LORD of hosts, the God of Israel, saying; Ye and your wives have both spoken with your mouths, and fulfilled with your hand, saying, We will surely perform our vows that we have vowed, to burn incense to the queen of heaven, and to pour out drink offerings unto her: ye will surely accomplish your vows, and surely perform your vows.

26Therefore hear ye the word of the LORD, all Judah that dwell in the land of Egypt; Behold, I have sworn by my great name, saith the LORD, that my name shall no more be named in the mouth of any man of Judah in all the land of Egypt, saying, The Lord GOD liveth.

27Behold, I will watch over them for evil, and not for good: and all the men of Judah that *are* in the land of Egypt shall be consumed by the sword and by the famine, until there be an end of them.

28Yet a small number that escape the sword shall return out of the land of Egypt into the land of Judah, and all the remnant of Judah, that are gone into the land of Egypt to sojourn there, shall know whose words shall stand, mine, or theirs.

29¶ And this *shall be* a sign unto you, saith the LORD, that I will punish you in this place, that ye may know that my words shall surely stand against you for evil:

30Thus saith the LORD; Behold, I will give Pharaoh-hophra king of Egypt into the hand of his enemies, and into the hand of them that seek his life; as I gave Zedekiah king of Judah into the hand of Nebuchadrezzar king of Babylon, his enemy, and that sought his life.

New International

15Then all the men who knew that their wives were burning incense to other gods, along with all the women who were present—a large assembly—and all the people living in Lower and Upper Egypt,[a] said to Jeremiah, 16"We will not listen to the message you have spoken to us in the name of the LORD! 17We will certainly do everything we said we would: We will burn incense to the Queen of Heaven and will pour out drink offerings to her just as we and our fathers, our kings and our officials did in the towns of Judah and in the streets of Jerusalem. At that time we had plenty of food and were well off and suffered no harm. 18But ever since we stopped burning incense to the Queen of Heaven and pouring out drink offerings to her, we have had nothing and have been perishing by sword and famine."

19The women added, "When we burned incense to the Queen of Heaven and poured out drink offerings to her, did not our husbands know that we were making cakes like her image and pouring out drink offerings to her?"

20Then Jeremiah said to all the people, both men and women, who were answering him, 21"Did not the LORD remember and think about the incense burned in the towns of Judah and the streets of Jerusalem by you and your fathers, your kings and your officials and the people of the land? 22When the LORD could no longer endure your wicked actions and the detestable things you did, your land became an object of cursing and a desolate waste without inhabitants, as it is today. 23Because you have burned incense and have sinned against the LORD and have not obeyed him or followed his law or his decrees or his stipulations, this disaster has come upon you, as you now see."

24Then Jeremiah said to all the people, including the women, "Hear the word of the LORD, all you people of Judah in Egypt. 25This is what the LORD Almighty, the God of Israel, says: You and your wives have shown by your actions what you promised when you said, 'We will certainly carry out the vows we made to burn incense and pour out drink offerings to the Queen of Heaven.'

"Go ahead then, do what you promised! Keep your vows! 26But hear the word of the LORD, all Jews living in Egypt: 'I swear by my great name,' says the LORD, 'that no one from Judah living anywhere in Egypt will ever again invoke my name or swear, "As surely as the Sovereign LORD lives." 27For I am watching over them for harm, not for good; the Jews in Egypt will perish by sword and famine until they are all destroyed. 28Those who escape the sword and return to the land of Judah from Egypt will be very few. Then the whole remnant of Judah who came to live in Egypt will know whose word will stand—mine or theirs.

29" 'This will be the sign to you that I will punish you in this place,' declares the LORD, 'so that you will know that my threats of harm against you will surely stand.' 30This is what the LORD says: 'I am going to hand Pharaoh Hophra king of Egypt over to his enemies who seek his life, just as I handed Zedekiah king of Judah over to Nebuchadnezzar king of Babylon, the enemy who was seeking his life.' "

---

a 15 Hebrew *in Egypt and Pathros*

Living Bible

15Then all the women present and all the men who knew that their wives had burned incense to idols (it was a great crowd of all the Jews in southern Egypt) answered Jeremiah:

16"We will not listen to your false 'Messages from God'! 17We will do whatever we want to. We will burn incense to the 'Queen of Heaven'b and sacrifice to her just as much as we like—just as we and our fathers before us, and our kings and princes have always done in the cities of Judah and in the streets of Jerusalem; for in those days we had plenty to eat and we were well off and happy! 18But ever since we quit burning incense to the 'Queen of Heaven' and stopped worshiping her we have been in great trouble and have been destroyed by sword and famine."

19"And," the women added, "do you suppose that we were worshiping the 'Queen of Heaven' and pouring out our libations to her and making cakes for her with her image on them, without our husbands knowing it and helping us? Of course not!"

20Then Jeremiah said to all of them, men and women alike, who had given him that answer:

21"Do you think the Lord didn't know that you and your fathers and your kings and princes and all the people were burning incense to idols in the cities of Judah and in the streets of Jerusalem? 22It was because he could no longer bear all the evil things you were doing that he made your land desolate, an incredible ruin, cursed, without an inhabitant, as it is today. 23The very reason all these terrible things have befallen you is because you have burned incense and sinned against the Lord and refused to obey him."

24Then Jeremiah said to them all, including the women: "Listen to the word of the Lord, all you citizens of Judah who are here in Egypt! 25The Lord, the God of Israel, says: Both you and your wives have said that you will never give up your devotion and sacrifices to the 'Queen of Heaven,' and you have proved it by your actions. Then go ahead and carry out your promises and vows to her! 26But listen to the word of the Lord, all you Jews who are living in the land of Egypt: I have sworn by my great name, says the Lord, that it will do you no good to seek my help and blessing any more, saying, 'O Lord our God, help us!' 27For I will watch over you, but *not* for good! I will see to it that evil befalls you, and you shall be destroyed by war and famine until all of you are dead.

28"Only those who return to Judah (it will be but a tiny remnant) shall escape my wrath, but all who refuse to go back—who insist on living in Egypt—shall find out who tells the truth, I or they! 29And this is the proof I give you that all I have threatened will happen to you, and that I will punish you here: 30I will turn Pharaoh Hophra,c king of Egypt, over to thosed who seek his life, just as I turned Zedekiah, king of Judah, over to Nebuchadnezzar, king of Babylon."

New Revised Standard

15 Then all the men who were aware that their wives had been making offerings to other gods, and all the women who stood by, a great assembly, all the people who lived in Pathros in the land of Egypt, answered Jeremiah: 16"As for the word that you have spoken to us in the name of the LORD, we are not going to listen to you. 17Instead, we will do everything that we have vowed, make offerings to the queen of heaven and pour out libations to her, just as we and our ancestors, our kings and our officials, used to do in the towns of Judah and in the streets of Jerusalem. We used to have plenty of food, and prospered, and saw no misfortune. 18But from the time we stopped making offerings to the queen of heaven and pouring out libations to her, we have lacked everything and have perished by the sword and by famine." 19And the women said,e "Indeed we will go on making offerings to the queen of heaven and pouring out libations to her; do you think that we made cakes for her, marked with her image, and poured out libations to her without our husbands' being involved?"

20 Then Jeremiah said to all the people, men and women, all the people who were giving him this answer: 21"As for the offerings that you made in the towns of Judah and in the streets of Jerusalem, you and your ancestors, your kings and your officials, and the people of the land, did not the LORD remember them? Did it not come into his mind? 22The LORD could no longer bear the sight of your evil doings, the abominations that you committed; therefore your land became a desolation and a waste and a curse, without inhabitant, as it is to this day. 23It is because you burned offerings, and because you sinned against the LORD and did not obey the voice of the LORD or walk in his law and in his statutes and in his decrees, that this disaster has befallen you, as is still evident today."

24 Jeremiah said to all the people and all the women, "Hear the word of the LORD, all you Judeans who are in the land of Egypt, 25Thus says the LORD of hosts, the God of Israel: You and your wives have accomplished in deeds what you declared in words, saying, 'We are determined to perform the vows that we have made, to make offerings to the queen of heaven and to pour out libations to her.' By all means, keep your vows and make your libations! 26Therefore hear the word of the LORD, all you Judeans who live in the land of Egypt: Lo, I swear by my great name, says the LORD, that my name shall no longer be pronounced on the lips of any of the people of Judah in all the land of Egypt, saying, 'As the Lord GOD lives.' 27I am going to watch over them for harm and not for good; all the people of Judah who are in the land of Egypt shall perish by the sword and by famine, until not one is left. 28And those who escape the sword shall return from the land of Egypt to the land of Judah, few in number; and all the remnant of Judah, who have come to the land of Egypt to settle, shall know whose words will stand, mine or theirs! 29This shall be the sign to you, says the LORD, that I am going to punish you in this place, in order that you may know that my words against you will surely be carried out: 30Thus says the LORD, I am going to give Pharaoh Hophra, king of Egypt, into the hands of his enemies, those who seek his life, just as I gave King Zedekiah of Judah into the hand of King Nebuchadrezzar of Babylon, his enemy who sought his life."

---

b 44:17 *Queen of Heaven.* See note to 7:18.   c 44:30 *Pharaoh Hophra.* Hophra, or Apries, ruled Egypt from 588 to 568 B.C.   d 44:30 *over to those.* Pharaoh Hophra was killed by Amasis, one of his generals who had revolted and who was then crowned in his place.

e Compare Syr: Heb lacks *And the women said*

King James

45 THE WORD that Jeremiah the prophet spake unto Baruch the son of Neriah, when he had written these words in a book at the mouth of Jeremiah, in the fourth year of Jehoiakim the son of Josiah king of Judah, saying,

2Thus saith the LORD, the God of Israel, unto thee, O Baruch;

3Thou didst say, Woe is me now! for the LORD hath added grief to my sorrow; I fainted in my sighing, and I find no rest.

4¶ Thus shalt thou say unto him, The LORD saith thus; Behold, *that* which I have built will I break down, and that which I have planted I will pluck up, even this whole land.

5And seekest thou great things for thyself ? seek *them* not: for, behold, I will bring evil upon all flesh, saith the LORD: but thy life will I give unto thee for a prey in all places whither thou goest.

46 THE WORD of the LORD which came to Jeremiah the prophet against the Gentiles;

2Against Egypt, against the army of Pharaoh-necho king of Egypt, which was by the river Euphrates in Carchemish, which Nebuchadrezzar king of Babylon smote in the fourth year of Jehoiakim the son of Josiah king of Judah.

3Order ye the buckler and shield, and draw near to battle.

4Harness the horses; and get up, ye horsemen, and stand forth with *your* helmets; furbish the spears, *and* put on the brigandines.

5Wherefore have I seen them dismayed *and* turned away back? and their mighty ones are beaten down, and are fled apace, and look not back: *for* fear *was* round about, saith the LORD.

6Let not the swift flee away, nor the mighty man escape; they shall stumble, and fall toward the north by the river Euphrates.

7Who *is* this *that* cometh up as a flood, whose waters are moved as the rivers?

8Egypt riseth up like a flood, and *his* waters are moved like the rivers; and he saith, I will go up, *and* will cover the earth; I will destroy the city and the inhabitants thereof.

9Come up, ye horses; and rage, ye chariots; and let the mighty men come forth; the Ethiopians and the Libyans, that handle the shield; and the Lydians, that handle *and* bend the bow.

New International

A Message to Baruch

45 THIS IS what Jeremiah the prophet told Baruch son of Neriah in the fourth year of Jehoiakim son of Josiah king of Judah, after Baruch had written on a scroll the words Jeremiah was then dictating: 2"This is what the LORD, the God of Israel, says to you, Baruch: 3You said, 'Woe to me! The LORD has added sorrow to my pain; I am worn out with groaning and find no rest.' "

4The LORD said, "Say this to him: 'This is what the LORD says: I will overthrow what I have built and uproot what I have planted, throughout the land. 5Should you then seek great things for yourself? Seek them not. For I will bring disaster on all people, declares the LORD, but wherever you go I will let you escape with your life.' "

A Message About Egypt

46 THIS IS the word of the LORD that came to Jeremiah the prophet concerning the nations:

2Concerning Egypt:

This is the message against the army of Pharaoh Neco king of Egypt, which was defeated at Carchemish on the Euphrates River by Nebuchadnezzar king of Babylon in the fourth year of Jehoiakim son of Josiah king of Judah:

3"Prepare your shields, both large and small,
and march out for battle!
4Harness the horses,
mount the steeds!
Take your positions
with helmets on!
Polish your spears,
put on your armor!
5What do I see?
They are terrified,
they are retreating,
their warriors are defeated.
They flee in haste
without looking back,
and there is terror on every side,"
declares the LORD.
6"The swift cannot flee
nor the strong escape.
In the north by the River Euphrates
they stumble and fall.

7"Who is this that rises like the Nile,
like rivers of surging waters?
8Egypt rises like the Nile,
like rivers of surging waters.
She says, 'I will rise and cover the earth;
I will destroy cities and their people.'
9Charge, O horses!
Drive furiously, O charioteers!
March on, O warriors—
men of Cush[a] and Put who carry shields,
men of Lydia who draw the bow.

---

a 9 That is, the upper Nile region

Living Bible

New Revised Standard

A Word of Comfort to Baruch

45 THIS IS the message[b] Jeremiah gave to Baruch in the fourth year of the reign of King Jehoiakim (son of Josiah), after Baruch had written down all God's messages as Jeremiah was dictating them to him:

2O Baruch, the Lord God of Israel says this to you: 3You have said, Woe is me! Don't I have troubles enough already? And now the Lord has added more! I am weary of my own sighing and I find no rest. 4But tell Baruch this, The Lord says: I will destroy this nation that I built; I will wipe out what I established. 5Are you seeking great things for yourself? Don't do it! For though I will bring great evil upon all these people, I will protect you wherever you go, as your reward.

46 HERE ARE the messages given to Jeremiah concerning foreign nations.

The Egyptians

2This message was given against Egypt at the occasion of the battle of Carchemish when Pharaoh Necho, king of Egypt, and his army were defeated beside the Euphrates River by Nebuchadnezzar, king of Babylon, in the fourth year of the reign of Jehoiakim (son of Josiah), king of Judah:

3Buckle on your armor, you Egyptians and advance to battle! 4Harness the horses and prepare to mount them—don your helmets, sharpen your spears, put on your armor. 5But look! The Egyptian army flees in terror; the mightiest of its soldiers run without a backward glance. Yes, terror shall surround them on every side, says the Lord. 6The swift will not escape, nor the mightiest of warriors. In the north, by the river Euphrates, they have stumbled and fallen.

7What is this mighty army, rising like the Nile at flood time, overflowing all the land? 8It is the Egyptian army, boasting that it will cover the earth like a flood, destroying every foe. 9Then come, O horses and chariots and mighty soldiers of Egypt! Come, all of you from Cush and Put and Lud who handle the shield and bend the bow! 10For this is the day of the Lord, the Lord

45 THE WORD that the prophet Jeremiah spoke to Baruch son of Neriah, when he wrote these words in a scroll at the dictation of Jeremiah, in the fourth year of King Jehoiakim son of Josiah of Judah: 2Thus says the LORD, the God of Israel, to you, O Baruch: 3You said, "Woe is me! The LORD has added sorrow to my pain; I am weary with my groaning, and I find no rest." 4Thus you shall say to him, "Thus says the LORD: I am going to break down what I have built, and pluck up what I have planted—that is, the whole land. 5And you, do you seek great things for yourself? Do not seek them; for I am going to bring disaster upon all flesh, says the LORD; but I will give you your life as a prize of war in every place to which you may go."

Judgment on Egypt

46 THE WORD of the LORD that came to the prophet Jeremiah concerning the nations.

2 Concerning Egypt, about the army of Pharaoh Neco, king of Egypt, which was by the river Euphrates at Carchemish and which King Nebuchadrezzar of Babylon defeated in the fourth year of King Jehoiakim son of Josiah of Judah:

3 Prepare buckler and shield,
   and advance for battle!
4 Harness the horses;
   mount the steeds!
Take your stations with your helmets,
   whet your lances,
   put on your coats of mail!
5 Why do I see them terrified?
   They have fallen back;
their warriors are beaten down,
   and have fled in haste.
They do not look back—
   terror is all around!
                              says the LORD.

6 The swift cannot flee away,
   nor can the warrior escape;
in the north by the river Euphrates
   they have stumbled and fallen.

7 Who is this, rising like the Nile,
   like rivers whose waters surge?
8 Egypt rises like the Nile,
   like rivers whose waters surge.
It said, Let me rise, let me cover the earth,
   let me destroy cities and their inhabitants.
9 Advance, O horses,
   and dash madly, O chariots!
Let the warriors go forth:
   Ethiopia[c] and Put who carry the shield,
   the Ludim, who draw[d] the bow.

---

b *45:1 This is the message.* This message, in point of time, follows chapter 36.   c Or *Nubia*; Heb *Cush*   d Cn: Heb *who grasp, who draw*

King James

¹⁰For this *is* the day of the Lord GOD of hosts, a day of vengeance, that he may avenge him of his adversaries: and the sword shall devour, and it shall be satiate and made drunk with their blood: for the Lord GOD of hosts hath a sacrifice in the north country by the river Euphrates.

¹¹Go up into Gilead, and take balm, O virgin, the daughter of Egypt: in vain shalt thou use many medicines; *for* thou shalt not be cured.

¹²The nations have heard of thy shame, and thy cry hath filled the land: for the mighty man hath stumbled against the mighty, *and* they are fallen both together.

¹³¶ The word that the LORD spake to Jeremiah the prophet, how Nebuchadrezzar king of Babylon should come *and* smite the land of Egypt.

¹⁴Declare ye in Egypt, and publish in Migdol, and publish in Noph and in Tahpanhes: say ye, Stand fast, and prepare thee; for the sword shall devour round about thee.

¹⁵Why are thy valiant *men* swept away? they stood not, because the LORD did drive them.

¹⁶He made many to fall, yea, one fell upon another: and they said, Arise, and let us go again to our own people, and to the land of our nativity, from the oppressing sword.

¹⁷They did cry there, Pharaoh king of Egypt *is but* a noise; he hath passed the time appointed.

¹⁸*As* I live, saith the King, whose name *is* the LORD of hosts, Surely as Tabor *is* among the mountains, and as Carmel by the sea, *so* shall he come.

¹⁹O thou daughter dwelling in Egypt, furnish thyself to go into captivity: for Noph shall be waste and desolate without an inhabitant.

²⁰Egypt *is like* a very fair heifer, *but* destruction cometh; it cometh out of the north.

²¹Also her hired men *are* in the midst of her like fatted bullocks; for they also are turned back, *and* are fled away together: they did not stand, because the day of their calamity was come upon them, *and* the time of their visitation.

²²The voice thereof shall go like a serpent; for they shall march with an army, and come against her with axes, as hewers of wood.

²³They shall cut down her forest, saith the LORD, though it cannot be searched; because they are more than the grasshoppers, and *are* innumerable.

²⁴The daughter of Egypt shall be confounded; she shall be delivered into the hand of the people of the north.

New International

¹⁰But that day belongs to the Lord, the LORD Almighty—
  a day of vengeance, for vengeance on his foes.
The sword will devour till it is satisfied,
  till it has quenched its thirst with blood.
For the Lord, the LORD Almighty, will offer sacrifice
  in the land of the north by the River Euphrates.

¹¹"Go up to Gilead and get balm,
  O Virgin Daughter of Egypt.
But you multiply remedies in vain;
  there is no healing for you.
¹²The nations will hear of your shame;
  your cries will fill the earth.
One warrior will stumble over another;
  both will fall down together."

¹³This is the message the LORD spoke to Jeremiah the prophet about the coming of Nebuchadnezzar king of Babylon to attack Egypt:

¹⁴"Announce this in Egypt, and proclaim it in Migdol;
  proclaim it also in Memphisᵃ and Tahpanhes:
'Take your positions and get ready,
  for the sword devours those around you.'
¹⁵Why will your warriors be laid low?
  They cannot stand, for the LORD will push them down.
¹⁶They will stumble repeatedly;
  they will fall over each other.
They will say, 'Get up, let us go back
  to our own people and our native lands,
  away from the sword of the oppressor.'
¹⁷There they will exclaim,
  'Pharaoh king of Egypt is only a loud noise;
  he has missed his opportunity.'

¹⁸"As surely as I live," declares the King,
  whose name is the LORD Almighty,
"one will come who is like Tabor among the mountains,
  like Carmel by the sea.
¹⁹Pack your belongings for exile,
  you who live in Egypt,
for Memphis will be laid waste
  and lie in ruins without inhabitant.

²⁰"Egypt is a beautiful heifer,
  but a gadfly is coming
  against her from the north.
²¹The mercenaries in her ranks
  are like fattened calves.
They too will turn and flee together,
  they will not stand their ground,
for the day of disaster is coming upon them,
  the time for them to be punished.
²²Egypt will hiss like a fleeing serpent
  as the enemy advances in force;
they will come against her with axes,
  like men who cut down trees.
²³They will chop down her forest,"
            declares the LORD,
  "dense though it be.
They are more numerous than locusts,
  they cannot be counted.
²⁴The Daughter of Egypt will be put to shame,
  handed over to the people of the north."

ᵃ *14* Hebrew *Noph*; also in verse 19

Living Bible

Almighty, a day of vengeance upon his enemies. The sword shall devour until it is sated, yes, drunk with your blood, for the Lord, the Lord Almighty will receive a sacrifice today in the north country beside the river Euphrates! 11Go up to Gilead for medicine, O virgin daughter of Egypt! Yet there is no cure for your wounds. Though you have used many medicines, there is no healing for you. 12The nations have heard of your shame. The earth is filled with your cry of despair and defeat; your mightiest soldiers will stumble across each other and fall together.

13Then God gave Jeremiah this message concerning the coming of Nebuchadnezzar, king of Babylon, to attack Egypt:

14Shout it out in Egypt; publish it in the cities of Migdol, Memphis and Tahpanhes! Mobilize for battle, for the sword of destruction shall devour all around you. 15Why has Apis, your bull god, fled in terror? Because the Lord knocked him down before your enemies. 16Vast multitudes fall in heaps. (Then the remnant of the Jews will say, "Come, let us return again to Judah where we were born and get away from all this slaughter here!")

17Rename Pharaoh Hophra and call him "The Man with No Power But with Plenty of Noise!"

18As I live, says the King, the Lord of Hosts, one is coming against Egypt who is as tall as Mount Tabor or Mount Carmel by the sea! 19Pack up; get ready to leave for exile, you citizens of Egypt, for the city of Memphis shall be utterly destroyed, and left without a soul alive. 20, 21Egypt is sleek as a heifer, but a gadfly sends her running—a gadfly from the north! Even her famed mercenaries have become like frightened calves. They turn and run, for it is the day of great calamity for Egypt, a time of great punishment. 22, 23Silent as a serpent gliding away, Egypt flees; the invading army marches in. The numberless soldiers cut down your people like woodsmen who clear a forest of its trees. 24Egypt is as helpless as a girl before these men from the north.

New Revised Standard

10 That day is the day of the Lord GOD of hosts,
    a day of retribution,
      to gain vindication from his foes.
The sword shall devour and be sated,
    and drink its fill of their blood.
For the Lord GOD of hosts holds a sacrifice
    in the land of the north by the river
      Euphrates.
11 Go up to Gilead, and take balm,
    O virgin daughter Egypt!
In vain you have used many medicines;
    there is no healing for you.
12 The nations have heard of your shame,
    and the earth is full of your cry;
for warrior has stumbled against warrior;
    both have fallen together.

Babylonia Will Strike Egypt

13 The word that the LORD spoke to the prophet Jeremiah about the coming of King Nebuchadrezzar of Babylon to attack the land of Egypt:

14 Declare in Egypt, and proclaim in Migdol;
    proclaim in Memphis and Tahpanhes;
Say, "Take your stations and be ready,
    for the sword shall devour those around
      you."
15 Why has Apis fled?[b]
    Why did your bull not stand?
    —because the LORD thrust him down.
16 Your multitude[c] stumbled and fell,
    and one said to another,[d]
"Come, let us go back to our own people
    and to the land of our birth,
    because of the destroying sword."
17 Give Pharaoh, king of Egypt, the name
    "Braggart who missed his chance."

18 As I live, says the King,
    whose name is the LORD of hosts,
one is coming
    like Tabor among the mountains,
    and like Carmel by the sea.
19 Pack your bags for exile,
    sheltered daughter Egypt!
For Memphis shall become a waste,
    a ruin, without inhabitant.

20 A beautiful heifer is Egypt—
    a gadfly from the north lights upon her.
21 Even her mercenaries in her midst
    are like fatted calves;
they too have turned and fled together,
    they did not stand;
for the day of their calamity has come upon
      them,
    the time of their punishment.

22 She makes a sound like a snake gliding away;
    for her enemies march in force,
and come against her with axes,
    like those who fell trees.
23 They shall cut down her forest,
              says the LORD,
    though it is impenetrable,
because they are more numerous
    than locusts;
    they are without number.
24 Daughter Egypt shall be put to shame;
    she shall be handed over to a people from
      the north.

---

b Gk: Heb *Why was it swept away*   c Gk: Meaning of Heb uncertain   d Gk: Heb *and fell one to another and they said*

King James

25The LORD of hosts, the God of Israel, saith; Behold, I will punish the multitude of No, and Pharaoh, and Egypt, with their gods, and their kings: even Pharaoh, and *all* them that trust in him:

26And I will deliver them into the hand of those that seek their lives, and into the hand of Nebuchadrezzar king of Babylon, and into the hand of his servants: and afterward it shall be inhabited, as in the days of old, saith the LORD.

27¶ But fear not thou, O my servant Jacob, and be not dismayed, O Israel: for, behold, I will save thee from afar off, and thy seed from the land of their captivity; and Jacob shall return, and be in rest and at ease, and none shall make *him* afraid.

28Fear thou not, O Jacob my servant, saith the LORD: for I *am* with thee; for I will make a full end of all the nations whither I have driven thee: but I will not make a full end of thee, but correct thee in measure; yet will I not leave thee wholly unpunished.

47 THE WORD of the LORD that came to Jeremiah the prophet against the Philistines, before that Pharaoh smote Gaza.

2Thus saith the LORD; Behold, waters rise up out of the north, and shall be an overflowing flood, and shall overflow the land, and all that is therein; the city, and them that dwell therein: then the men shall cry, and all the inhabitants of the land shall howl.

3At the noise of the stamping of the hoofs of his strong *horses,* at the rushing of his chariots, *and at* the rumbling of his wheels, the fathers shall not look back to *their* children for feebleness of hands;

4Because of the day that cometh to spoil all the Philistines, *and* to cut off from Tyrus and Zidon every helper that remaineth: for the LORD will spoil the Philistines, the remnant of the country of Caphtor.

5Baldness is come upon Gaza; Ashkelon is cut off *with* the remnant of their valley: how long wilt thou cut thyself?

6O thou sword of the LORD, how long *will it be* ere thou be quiet? put up thyself into thy scabbard, rest, and be still.

7How can it be quiet, seeing the LORD hath given it a charge against Ashkelon, and against the sea shore? there hath he appointed it.

New International

25The LORD Almighty, the God of Israel, says: "I am about to bring punishment on Amon god of Thebes,[a] on Pharaoh, on Egypt and her gods and her kings, and on those who rely on Pharaoh. 26I will hand them over to those who seek their lives, to Nebuchadnezzar king of Babylon and his officers. Later, however, Egypt will be inhabited as in times past," declares the LORD.

27"Do not fear, O Jacob my servant;
    do not be dismayed, O Israel.
I will surely save you out of a distant place,
    your descendants from the land of their exile.
Jacob will again have peace and security,
    and no one will make him afraid.
28Do not fear, O Jacob my servant,
    for I am with you," declares the LORD.
"Though I completely destroy all the nations
    among which I scatter you,
    I will not completely destroy you.
I will discipline you but only with justice;
    I will not let you go entirely unpunished."

A Message About the Philistines

47 THIS IS the word of the LORD that came to Jeremiah the prophet concerning the Philistines before Pharaoh attacked Gaza:

2This is what the LORD says:

"See how the waters are rising in the north;
    they will become an overflowing torrent.
They will overflow the land and everything in it,
    the towns and those who live in them.
The people will cry out;
    all who dwell in the land will wail
3at the sound of the hoofs of galloping steeds,
    at the noise of enemy chariots
    and the rumble of their wheels.
Fathers will not turn to help their children;
    their hands will hang limp.
4For the day has come
    to destroy all the Philistines
and to cut off all survivors
    who could help Tyre and Sidon.
The LORD is about to destroy the Philistines,
    the remnant from the coasts of Caphtor.[b]
5Gaza will shave her head in mourning;
    Ashkelon will be silenced.
O remnant on the plain,
    how long will you cut yourselves?

6" 'Ah, sword of the LORD,' ⌊you cry,⌋
    'how long till you rest?
Return to your scabbard;
    cease and be still.'
7But how can it rest
    when the LORD has commanded it,
when he has ordered it
    to attack Ashkelon and the coast?' "

Living Bible

25The Lord, the God of Israel, says: I will punish Amon, god of Thebes, and all the other gods of Egypt. I will punish Pharaoh too, and all who trust in him. 26I will deliver them into the hands of those who want them killed—into the hands of Nebuchadnezzar, king of Babylon, and his army. But afterwards the land shall recover from the ravages of war.

27But don't you be afraid, O my people who return to your own land, don't be dismayed; for I will save you from far away and bring your children from a distant land. Yes, Israel shall return and be at rest and nothing shall make her afraid. 28Fear not, O Jacob, my servant, says the Lord, for I am with you. I will destroy all the nations to which I have exiled you, but I will not destroy you. I will punish you, but only enough to correct you.

The Philistines

47 THIS IS God's message to Jeremiah concerning the Philistines of Gaza, before the city was captured[c] by the Egyptian army.

2The Lord says: A flood is coming from the north to overflow the land of the Philistines; it will destroy their cities and everything in them. Strong men will scream in terror and all the land will weep. 3Hear the clattering hoofs and rumbling wheels as the chariots go rushing by; fathers flee without a backward glance at their helpless children, 4for the time has come when all the Philistines and their allies from Tyre and Sidon will be destroyed. For the Lord is destroying the Philistines, those colonists from Caphtor. 5The cities of Gaza and Ashkelon will be razed to the ground and lie in ruins. O descendants of the Anakim, how you will lament and mourn!

6O sword of the Lord, when will you be at rest again? Go back into your scabbard; rest and be still! 7But how can it be still when the Lord has sent it on an errand? For the city of Ashkelon and those living along the sea must be destroyed.

New Revised Standard

25 The LORD of hosts, the God of Israel, said: See, I am bringing punishment upon Amon of Thebes, and Pharaoh, and Egypt and her gods and her kings, upon Pharaoh and those who trust in him. 26I will hand them over to those who seek their life, to King Nebuchadrezzar of Babylon and his officers. Afterward Egypt shall be inhabited as in the days of old, says the LORD.

God Will Save Israel

27 But as for you, have no fear, my servant
    Jacob,
  and do not be dismayed, O Israel;
for I am going to save you from far away,
  and your offspring from the land of their
    captivity.
Jacob shall return and have quiet and ease,
  and no one shall make him afraid.
28 As for you, have no fear, my servant Jacob,
                              says the LORD,
  for I am with you.
I will make an end of all the nations
  among which I have banished you,
  but I will not make an end of you!
I will chastise you in just measure,
  and I will by no means leave you
    unpunished.

Judgment on the Philistines

47 THE WORD of the LORD that came to the prophet Jeremiah concerning the Philistines, before Pharaoh attacked Gaza:
2 Thus says the LORD:
  See, waters are rising out of the north
    and shall become an overflowing torrent;
  they shall overflow the land and all that fills
    it,
    the city and those who live in it.
  People shall cry out,
    and all the inhabitants of the land shall
      wail.
3 At the noise of the stamping of the hoofs of
      his stallions,
    at the clatter of his chariots, at the rumbling
      of their wheels,
  parents do not turn back for children,
    so feeble are their hands,
4 because of the day that is coming
    to destroy all the Philistines,
  to cut off from Tyre and Sidon
    every helper that remains.
  For the LORD is destroying the Philistines,
    the remnant of the coastland of Caphtor.
5 Baldness has come upon Gaza,
    Ashkelon is silenced.
  O remnant of their power![d]
    How long will you gash yourselves?
6 Ah, sword of the LORD!
    How long until you are quiet?
  Put yourself into your scabbard,
    rest and be still!
7 How can it[e] be quiet,
    when the LORD has given it an order?
  Against Ashkelon and against the seashore—
    there he has appointed it.

---

c 47:1 before the city was captured. In 609 B.C., the year King Josiah died.   d Gk: Heb their valley   e Gk Vg: Heb you

King James

48 AGAINST MOAB thus saith the LORD of hosts, the God of Israel; Woe unto Nebo! for it is spoiled: Kiriathaim is confounded *and* taken: Misgab is confounded and dismayed.

2*There shall be* no more praise of Moab: in Heshbon they have devised evil against it; come, and let us cut it off from *being* a nation. Also thou shalt be cut down, O Madmen; the sword shall pursue thee.

3A voice of crying *shall be* from Horonaim, spoiling and great destruction.

4Moab is destroyed; her little ones have caused a cry to be heard.

5For in the going up of Luhith continual weeping shall go up; for in the going down of Horonaim the enemies have heard a cry of destruction.

6Flee, save your lives, and be like the heath in the wilderness.

7¶ For because thou hast trusted in thy works and in thy treasures, thou shalt also be taken: and Chemosh shall go forth into captivity *with* his priests and his princes together.

8And the spoiler shall come upon every city, and no city shall escape: the valley also shall perish, and the plain shall be destroyed, as the LORD hath spoken.

9Give wings unto Moab, that it may flee and get away: for the cities thereof shall be desolate, without any to dwell therein.

10Cursed *be* he that doeth the work of the LORD deceitfully, and cursed *be* he that keepeth back his sword from blood.

11¶ Moab hath been at ease from his youth, and he hath settled on his lees, and hath not been emptied from vessel to vessel, neither hath he gone into captivity: therefore his taste remained in him, and his scent is not changed.

12Therefore, behold, the days come, saith the LORD, that I will send unto him wanderers, that shall cause him to wander, and shall empty his vessels, and break their bottles.

13And Moab shall be ashamed of Chemosh, as the house of Israel was ashamed of Beth-el their confidence.

14¶ How say ye, We *are* mighty and strong men for the war?

15Moab is spoiled, and gone up *out of* her cities, and his chosen young men are gone down to the slaughter, saith the King, whose name *is* the LORD of hosts.

16The calamity of Moab *is* near to come, and his affliction hasteth fast.

New International

A Message About Moab

48 CONCERNING MOAB:

This is what the LORD Almighty, the God of Israel, says:

"Woe to Nebo, for it will be ruined.
    Kiriathaim will be disgraced and captured;
    the strongholda will be disgraced and
      shattered.
2Moab will be praised no more;
    in Heshbonb men will plot her downfall:
    'Come, let us put an end to that nation.'
You too, O Madmen,c will be silenced;
    the sword will pursue you.
3Listen to the cries from Horonaim,
    cries of great havoc and destruction.
4Moab will be broken;
    her little ones will cry out.d
5They go up the way to Luhith,
    weeping bitterly as they go;
on the road down to Horonaim
    anguished cries over the destruction are heard.
6Flee! Run for your lives;
    become like a bushe in the desert.
7Since you trust in your deeds and riches,
    you too will be taken captive,
and Chemosh will go into exile,
    together with his priests and officials.
8The destroyer will come against every town,
    and not a town will escape.
The valley will be ruined
    and the plateau destroyed,
    because the LORD has spoken.
9Put salt on Moab,
    for she will be laid wastef;
her towns will become desolate,
    with no one to live in them.

10"A curse on him who is lax in doing the LORD's work!
    A curse on him who keeps his sword from
      bloodshed!

11"Moab has been at rest from youth,
    like wine left on its dregs,
not poured from one jar to another—
    she has not gone into exile.
So she tastes as she did,
    and her aroma is unchanged.
12But days are coming,"
    declares the LORD,
"when I will send men who pour from jars,
    and they will pour her out;
they will empty her jars
    and smash her jugs.
13Then Moab will be ashamed of Chemosh,
    as the house of Israel was ashamed
    when they trusted in Bethel.

14"How can you say, 'We are warriors,
    men valiant in battle'?
15Moab will be destroyed and her towns invaded;
    her finest young men will go down in the
      slaughter,"
    declares the King, whose name is the LORD
      Almighty.
16"The fall of Moab is at hand;
    her calamity will come quickly.

a 1 Or / Misgab   b 2 The Hebrew for *Heshbon* sounds like the Hebrew for *plot.*   c 2 The name of the Moabite town Madmen sounds like the Hebrew for *be silenced.*   d 4 Hebrew; Septuagint / *proclaim it to Zoar*   e 6 Or like *Aroer*   f 9 Or *Give wings to Moab, / for she will fly away*

Living Bible

The Moabites

48 THIS IS the message of the Lord of Hosts, the God of Israel, against Moab:

Woe to the city of Nebo, for it shall lie in ruins. The city of Kiriathaim and its forts are overwhelmed and captured. 2, 3, 4No one will ever brag about Moab any more, for there is a plot against her life. In Heshbon, plans have been completed to destroy her. "Come," they say, "we will cut her off from being a nation." In Madmen all is silent. And then the roar of battle will surge against Horonaim, for all Moab is being destroyed. Her crying will be heard as far away as Zoar. 5Her refugees will climb the hills of Luhith, weeping bitterly, while cries of terror rise from the city below. 6Flee for your lives; hide in the wilderness! 7For you trusted in your wealth and skill; therefore you shall perish. Your god Chemosh, with his priests and princes, shall be taken away to distant lands!

8All the villages and cities, whether they be on the plateaus or in the valleys, shall be destroyed, for the Lord has said it. 9Oh, for wings for Moab that she could fly away, for her cities shall be left without a living soul. 10Cursed be those withholding their swords from your blood, refusing to do the work that God has given them!

11From her earliest history Moab has lived there undisturbed from all invasions. She is like wine that has not been poured from flask to flask, and is fragrant and smooth. But now she shall have the pouring out of exile! 12The time is coming soon, the Lord has said, when he will send troublemakers to spill her out from jar to jar and then shatter the jars! 13Then at last Moab shall be ashamed of her idol Chemosh, as Israel was of her calf-idol at Bethel.

14Do you remember that boast of yours: "We are heroes, mighty men of war"? 15But now Moab is to be destroyed; her destroyer is on the way; her choicest youth are doomed to slaughter, says the King, the Lord Almighty. 16Calamity is coming fast to Moab.

New Revised Standard

Judgment on Moab

48 CONCERNING MOAB.

Thus says the LORD of hosts, the God of Israel:
  Alas for Nebo, it is laid waste!
    Kiriathaim is put to shame, it is taken;
  the fortress is put to shame and broken down;
2   the renown of Moab is no more.
In Heshbon they planned evil against her:
  "Come, let us cut her off from being a
    nation!"
You also, O Madmen, shall be brought to
    silence;g
  the sword shall pursue you.

3 Hark! a cry from Horonaim,
    "Desolation and great destruction!"
4 "Moab is destroyed!"
    her little ones cry out.
5 For at the ascent of Luhith
    they goh up weeping bitterly;
  for at the descent of Horonaim
    they have heard the distressing cry of
      anguish.
6 Flee! Save yourselves!
    Be like a wild assi in the desert!

7 Surely, because you trusted in your
      strongholdsj and your treasures,
  you also shall be taken;
  Chemosh shall go out into exile,
    with his priests and his attendants.
8 The destroyer shall come upon every town,
    and no town shall escape;
  the valley shall perish,
    and the plain shall be destroyed,
    as the LORD has spoken.

9 Set aside salt for Moab,
    for she will surely fall;
  her towns shall become a desolation,
    with no inhabitant in them.

10 Accursed is the one who is slack in doing the work of the LORD; and accursed is the one who keeps back the sword from bloodshed.

11 Moab has been at ease from his youth,
    settled like winek on its dregs;
  he has not been emptied from vessel to vessel,
    nor has he gone into exile;
  therefore his flavor has remained
    and his aroma is unspoiled.
12 Therefore, the time is surely coming, says the LORD, when I shall send to him decanters to decant him, and empty his vessels, and break hisl jars in pieces. 13Then Moab shall be ashamed of Chemosh, as the house of Israel was ashamed of Bethel, their confidence.

14 How can you say, "We are heroes
    and mighty warriors"?
15 The destroyer of Moab and his towns has
      come up,
  and the choicest of his young men have
      gone down to slaughter,
  says the King, whose name is the LORD of
    hosts.
16 The calamity of Moab is near at hand
    and his doom approaches swiftly.

---

g The place-name *Madmen* sounds like the Hebrew verb *to be silent* h Cn: Heb *he goes* i Gk Aquila: Heb *like Aroer* j Gk: Heb *works* k Heb lacks *like wine* l Gk Aquila: Heb *their*

King James

17All ye that are about him, bemoan him; and all ye that know his name, say, How is the strong staff broken, *and* the beautiful rod!

18Thou daughter that dost inhabit Dibon, come down from *thy* glory, and sit in thirst; for the spoiler of Moab shall come upon thee, *and* he shall destroy thy strong holds.

19O inhabitant of Aroer, stand by the way, and espy; ask him that fleeth, and her that escapeth, *and* say, What is done?

20Moab is confounded; for it is broken down: howl and cry; tell ye it in Arnon, that Moab is spoiled,

21And judgment is come upon the plain country; upon Holon, and upon Jahazah, and upon Mephaath,

22And upon Dibon, and upon Nebo, and upon Beth-diblathaim,

23And upon Kiriathaim, and upon Beth-gamul, and upon Beth-meon,

24And upon Kerioth, and upon Bozrah, and upon all the cities of the land of Moab, far or near.

25The horn of Moab is cut off, and his arm is broken, saith the LORD.

26¶ Make ye him drunken: for he magnified *himself* against the LORD: Moab also shall wallow in his vomit, and he also shall be in derision.

27For was not Israel a derision unto thee? was he found among thieves? for since thou spakest of him, thou skippedst for joy.

28O ye that dwell in Moab, leave the cities, and dwell in the rock, and be like the dove *that* maketh her nest in the sides of the hole's mouth.

29We have heard the pride of Moab, (he is exceeding proud) his loftiness, and his arrogancy, and his pride, and the haughtiness of his heart.

30I know his wrath, saith the LORD; but *it shall* not *be* so; his lies shall not so effect *it.*

31Therefore will I howl for Moab, and I will cry out for all Moab; *mine heart* shall mourn for the men of Kir-heres.

32O vine of Sibmah, I will weep for thee with the weeping of Jazer: thy plants are gone over the sea, they reach *even* to the sea of Jazer: the spoiler is fallen upon thy summer fruits and upon thy vintage.

33And joy and gladness is taken from the plentiful field, and from the land of Moab; and I have caused wine to fail from the winepresses: none shall tread with shouting; *their* shouting *shall be* no shouting.

34From the cry of Heshbon *even* unto Elealeh, *and even* unto Jahaz, have they uttered their voice, from Zoar *even* unto Horonaim, *as* an heifer of three years old: for the waters also of Nimrim shall be desolate.

New International

17Mourn for her, all who live around her,
　all who know her fame;
say, 'How broken is the mighty scepter,
　how broken the glorious staff!'

18"Come down from your glory
　and sit on the parched ground,
　O inhabitants of the Daughter of Dibon,
for he who destroys Moab
　will come up against you
　and ruin your fortified cities.
19Stand by the road and watch,
　you who live in Aroer.
Ask the man fleeing and the woman escaping,
　ask them, 'What has happened?'
20Moab is disgraced, for she is shattered.
　Wail and cry out!
Announce by the Arnon
　that Moab is destroyed.
21Judgment has come to the plateau—
　to Holon, Jahzah and Mephaath,
22　to Dibon, Nebo and Beth Diblathaim,
23　to Kiriathaim, Beth Gamul and Beth Meon,
24　to Kerioth and Bozrah—
　to all the towns of Moab, far and near.
25Moab's horn[a] is cut off;
　her arm is broken,"

　　　　　　　　　　　declares the LORD.

26"Make her drunk,
　for she has defied the LORD.
Let Moab wallow in her vomit;
　let her be an object of ridicule.
27Was not Israel the object of your ridicule?
　Was she caught among thieves,
that you shake your head in scorn
　whenever you speak of her?
28Abandon your towns and dwell among the
　　rocks,
　you who live in Moab.
Be like a dove that makes its nest
　at the mouth of a cave.

29"We have heard of Moab's pride—
　her overweening pride and conceit,
her pride and arrogance
　and the haughtiness of her heart.
30I know her insolence but it is futile,"

　　　　　　　　　　　declares the LORD,
　"and her boasts accomplish nothing.
31Therefore I wail over Moab,
　for all Moab I cry out,
　I moan for the men of Kir Hareseth.
32I weep for you, as Jazer weeps,
　O vines of Sibmah.
Your branches spread as far as the sea;
　they reached as far as the sea of Jazer.
The destroyer has fallen
　on your ripened fruit and grapes.
33Joy and gladness are gone
　from the orchards and fields of Moab.
I have stopped the flow of wine from the
　　presses;
　no one treads them with shouts of joy.
Although there are shouts,
　they are not shouts of joy.

34"The sound of their cry rises
　from Heshbon to Elealeh and Jahaz,
from Zoar as far as Horonaim and Eglath
　　Shelishiyah,
　for even the waters of Nimrim are dried up.

---

a 25 *Horn* here symbolizes strength.

Living Bible

17O friends of Moab, weep for her and cry! See how the strong, the beautiful is shattered! 18Come down from your glory and sit in the dust, O people of Dibon, for those destroying Moab shall shatter Dibon too, and tear down all her towers. 19Those in Aroer stand anxiously beside the road to watch, and shout to those who flee from Moab, "What has happened there?"

20And they reply, "Moab lies in ruins; weep and wail. Tell it by the banks of the Arnon, that Moab is destroyed."

21All the cities of the tableland lie in ruins too, for God's judgment has been poured out upon them all—on Holon and Jahzah and Mepha-ath, 22and Dibon and Nebo and Beth-diblathaim, 23and Kiria-thaim and Beth-gamul and Beth-meon, 24and Keri-oth and Bozrah—and all the cities of the land of Moab, far and near.

25The strength of Moab is ended—her horns are cut off; her arms are broken. 26Let her stagger and fall like a drunkard, for she has rebelled against the Lord. Moab shall wallow in her vomit, scorned by all. 27For you scorned Israel and robbed her, and were happy at her fall.

28O people of Moab, flee from your cities and live in the caves like doves that nest in the clefts of the rocks. 29We have all heard of the pride of Moab, for it is very great. We know your loftiness, your arrogance and your haughty heart. 30I know her insolence, the Lord has said, but her boasts are false—her helplessness is great. 31Yes, I wail for Moab, my heart is broken for the men of Kir-heres.

32O men of Sibmah, rich in vineyards, I weep for you even more than for Jazer. For the destroyer has cut off your spreading tendrils and harvested your grapes and summer fruits. He has plucked you bare! 33Joy and gladness are gone from fruitful Moab. The presses yield no wine; no one treads the grapes with shouts of joy. There is shouting, yes, but not the shouting of joy. 34Instead the awful cries of terror and pain rise from all over the land—from Heshbon clear across to Elealeh and to Ja-haz; from Zoar to Horonaim and to Eglath-she-lishiyah. The pastures of Nimrim are deserted now.

New Revised Standard

17 Mourn over him, all you his neighbors,
    and all who know his name;
    say, "How the mighty scepter is broken,
    the glorious staff!"

18 Come down from glory,
    and sit on the parched ground,
    enthroned daughter Dibon!
    For the destroyer of Moab has come up
        against you;
    he has destroyed your strongholds.
19 Stand by the road and watch,
    you inhabitant of Aroer!
    Ask the man fleeing and the woman escaping;
    say, "What has happened?"
20 Moab is put to shame, for it is broken down;
    wail and cry!
    Tell it by the Arnon,
    that Moab is laid waste.

21 Judgment has come upon the tableland, upon Holon, and Jahzah, and Mephaath, 22and Dibon, and Nebo, and Beth-diblathaim, 23and Kiriathaim, and Beth-gamul, and Beth-meon, 24and Kerioth, and Bozrah, and all the towns of the land of Moab, far and near. 25The horn of Moab is cut off, and his arm is broken, says the LORD.

26 Make him drunk, because he magnified himself against the LORD; let Moab wallow in his vomit; let him too shall become a laughingstock. 27Israel was a laughingstock for you, though he was not caught among thieves; but whenever you spoke of him you shook your head!

28 Leave the towns, and live on the rock,
    O inhabitants of Moab!
    Be like the dove that nests
    on the sides of the mouth of a gorge.
29 We have heard of the pride of Moab—
    he is very proud—
    of his loftiness, his pride, and his arrogance,
    and the haughtiness of his heart.
30 I myself know his insolence, says the LORD;
    his boasts are false,
    his deeds are false.
31 Therefore I wail for Moab;
    I cry out for all Moab;
    for the people of Kir-heres I mourn.
32 More than for Jazer I weep for you,
    O vine of Sibmah!
    Your branches crossed over the sea,
    reached as far as Jazer;b
    upon your summer fruits and your vintage
    the destroyer has fallen.
33 Gladness and joy have been taken away
    from the fruitful land of Moab;
    I have stopped the wine from the wine
        presses;
    no one treads them with shouts of joy;
    the shouting is not the shout of joy.

34 Heshbon and Elealeh cry out;c as far as Jahaz they utter their voice, from Zoar to Horonaim and Eglath-shelishiyah. For even the waters of Nimrim have become desolate. 35And I will bring to an end in Moab,

b Two Mss and Isa 16.8: MT the sea of Jazer   c Cn: Heb From the cry of Heshbon to Elealeh

King James

35Moreover I will cause to cease in Moab, saith the LORD, him that offereth in the high places, and him that burneth incense to his gods.

36Therefore mine heart shall sound for Moab like pipes, and mine heart shall sound like pipes for the men of Kir-heres: because the riches *that* he hath gotten are perished.

37For every head *shall be* bald, and every beard clipped: upon all the hands *shall be* cuttings, and upon the loins sackcloth.

38*There shall be* lamentation generally upon all the housetops of Moab, and in the streets thereof: for I have broken Moab like a vessel wherein *is* no pleasure, saith the LORD.

39They shall howl, *saying,* How is it broken down! how hath Moab turned the back with shame! so shall Moab be a derision and a dismaying to all them about him.

40For thus saith the LORD; Behold, he shall fly as an eagle. and shall spread his wings over Moab.

41Kerioth is taken, and the strong holds are surprised, and the mighty men's hearts in Moab at that day shall be as the heart of a woman in her pangs.

42And Moab shall be destroyed from *being* a people, because he hath magnified *himself* against the LORD.

43Fear, and the pit, and the snare, *shall be* upon thee, O inhabitant of Moab, saith the LORD.

44He that fleeth from the fear shall fall into the pit; and he that getteth up out of the pit shall be taken in the snare: for I will bring upon it, *even* upon Moab, the year of their visitation, saith the LORD.

45They that fled stood under the shadow of Heshbon because of the force: but a fire shall come forth out of Heshbon, and a flame from the midst of Sihon, and shall devour the corner of Moab, and the crown of the head of the tumultuous ones.

46Woe be unto thee, O Moab! the people of Chemosh perisheth: for thy sons are taken captives, and thy daughters captives.

47¶ Yet will I bring again the captivity of Moab in the latter days, saith the LORD. Thus far *is* the judgment of Moab.

New International

35In Moab I will put an end
   to those who make offerings on the high
      places
   and burn incense to their gods,"
                              declares the LORD.
36"So my heart laments for Moab like a flute;
   it laments like a flute for the men of Kir
      Hareseth.
   The wealth they acquired is gone.
37Every head is shaved
   and every beard cut off;
   every hand is slashed
   and every waist is covered with sackcloth.
38On all the roofs in Moab
   and in the public squares
   there is nothing but mourning,
   for I have broken Moab
      like a jar that no one wants,"
                              declares the LORD.
39"How shattered she is! How they wail!
   How Moab turns her back in shame!
   Moab has become an object of ridicule,
      an object of horror to all those around her."

40This is what the LORD says:

   "Look! An eagle is swooping down,
      spreading its wings over Moab.
41Kerioth[a] will be captured
      and the strongholds taken.
   In that day the hearts of Moab's warriors
      will be like the heart of a woman in labor.
42Moab will be destroyed as a nation
      because she defied the LORD.
43Terror and pit and snare await you,
      O people of Moab,"
                              declares the LORD.
44"Whoever flees from the terror
      will fall into a pit,
   whoever climbs out of the pit
      will be caught in a snare;
   for I will bring upon Moab
      the year of her punishment,"
                              declares the LORD.

45"In the shadow of Heshbon
      the fugitives stand helpless,
   for a fire has gone out from Heshbon,
      a blaze from the midst of Sihon;
   it burns the foreheads of Moab,
      the skulls of the noisy boasters.
46Woe to you, O Moab!
      The people of Chemosh are destroyed;
   your sons are taken into exile
      and your daughters into captivity.

47"Yet I will restore the fortunes of Moab
      in days to come,"
                              declares the LORD.

Here ends the judgment on Moab.

A Message About Ammon

49 CONCERNING THE Ammonites, thus saith the LORD; Hath Israel no sons? hath he no heir? why *then* doth their king inherit Gad, and his people dwell in his cities?

49 CONCERNING THE Ammonites:

   This is what the LORD says:

   "Has Israel no sons?
      Has she no heirs?
   Why then has Molech[b] taken possession of
         Gad?
   Why do his people live in its towns?

---

[a] *41 Or The cities*   [b] *1 Or their king;* Hebrew *malcam;* also in verse 3

Living Bible

35For the Lord says: I have put a stop to Moab's worshiping false gods and burning incense to idols. 36Sad sings my heart for Moab and Kir-heres, for all their wealth has disappeared. 37They shave their heads and beards in anguish, and slash their hands and put on clothes of sackcloth. 38Crying and sorrow will be in every Moabite home and on the streets; for I have smashed and shattered Moab like an old, unwanted bottle. 39How it is broken! Hear the wails! See the shame of Moab! For she is a sign of horror and of scoffing to her neighbors now.

40A vulture circles ominously above the land of Moab, says the Lord. 41Her cities are fallen; her strongholds are seized. The hearts of her mightiest warriors fail with fear like women in the pains of giving birth. 42Moab shall no longer be a nation, for she has boasted against the Lord. 43Fear and traps and treachery shall be your lot, O Moab, says the Lord. 44He who flees shall fall in a trap and he who escapes from the trap shall run into a snare. I will see to it that you do not get away, for the time of your judgment has come. 45They flee to Heshbon, unable to go farther. But a fire comes from Heshbon—Sihon's ancestral home—and devours the land from end to end with all its rebellious people.

46Woe to you, O Moab; the people of the god Chemosh are destroyed, and your sons and daughters are taken away as slaves. 47But in the latter days, says the Lord, I will reestablish Moab.

(Here the prophecy concerning Moab ends.)

New Revised Standard

says the LORD, those who offer sacrifice at a high place and make offerings to their gods. 36Therefore my heart moans for Moab like a flute, and my heart moans like a flute for the people of Kir-heres; for the riches they gained have perished.

37 For every head is shaved and every beard cut off; on all the hands there are gashes, and on the loins sackcloth. 38On all the housetops of Moab and in the squares there is nothing but lamentation; for I have broken Moab like a vessel that no one wants, says the LORD. 39How it is broken! How they wail! How Moab has turned his back in shame! So Moab has become a derision and a horror to all his neighbors.

40 For thus says the LORD:
Look, he shall swoop down like an eagle,
    and spread his wings against Moab;
41 the townse shall be taken
    and the strongholds seized.
The hearts of the warriors of Moab, on that day,
    shall be like the heart of a woman in labor.
42 Moab shall be destroyed as a people,
    because he magnified himself against the LORD.
43 Terror, pit, and trap
    are before you, O inhabitants of Moab!
            says the LORD.
44 Everyone who flees from the terror
    shall fall into the pit,
and everyone who climbs out of the pit
    shall be caught in the trap.
For I will bring these thingsd upon Moab
    in the year of their punishment,
            says the LORD.

45 In the shadow of Heshbon
    fugitives stop exhausted;
for a fire has gone out from Heshbon,
    a flame from the house of Sihon;
it has destroyed the forehead of Moab,
    the scalp of the people of tumult.e
46 Woe to you, O Moab!
    The people of Chemosh have perished,
for your sons have been taken captive,
    and your daughters into captivity.
47 Yet I will restore the fortunes of Moab
    in the latter days, says the LORD.
Thus far is the judgment on Moab.

The Ammonites

49 WHAT IS this you are doing? Why are you living in the cities of the Jews? Aren't there Jews enough to fill them up? Didn't they inherit them from me? Why then have you, who worship Milcom, taken over Gad and all its cities? 2I will punish you for

Judgment on the Ammonites

49 CONCERNING THE Ammonites.

Thus says the LORD:
    Has Israel no sons?
    Has he no heir?
Why then has Milcom dispossessed Gad,
    and his people settled in its towns?

c Or Kerioth   d Gk Syr: Heb bring upon it   e Or of Shaon

King James

2Therefore, behold, the days come, saith the LORD, that I will cause an alarm of war to be heard in Rabbah of the Ammonites; and it shall be a desolate heap, and her daughters shall be burned with fire: then shall Israel be heir unto them that were his heirs, saith the LORD.

3Howl, O Heshbon, for Ai is spoiled: cry, ye daughters of Rabbah, gird you with sackcloth; lament, and run to and fro by the hedges; for their king shall go into captivity, *and* his priests and his princes together.

4Wherefore gloriest thou in the valleys, thy flowing valley, O backsliding daughter? that trusted in her treasures, *saying,* Who shall come unto me?

5Behold, I will bring a fear upon thee, saith the Lord GOD of hosts, from all those that be about thee; and ye shall be driven out every man right forth; and none shall gather up him that wandereth.

6And afterward I will bring again the captivity of the children of Ammon, saith the LORD.

7¶ Concerning Edom, thus saith the LORD of hosts; *Is* wisdom no more in Teman? is counsel perished from the prudent? is their wisdom vanished?

8Flee ye, turn back, dwell deep, O inhabitants of Dedan; for I will bring the calamity of Esau upon him, the time *that* I will visit him.

9If grapegatherers come to thee, would they not leave *some* gleaning grapes? if thieves by night, they will destroy till they have enough.

10But I have made Esau bare, I have uncovered his secret places, and he shall not be able to hide himself: his seed is spoiled, and his brethren, and his neighbours, and he *is* not.

11Leave thy fatherless children, I will preserve *them* alive; and let thy widows trust in me.

12For thus saith the LORD; Behold, they whose judgment *was* not to drink of the cup have assuredly drunken; and *art* thou he *that* shall altogether go unpunished? thou shalt not go unpunished, but thou shalt surely drink *of it.*

13For I have sworn by myself, saith the LORD, that Bozrah shall become a desolation, a reproach, a waste, and a curse; and all the cities thereof shall be perpetual wastes.

14I have heard a rumour from the LORD, and an ambassador is sent unto the heathen, *saying,* Gather ye together, and come against her, and rise up to the battle.

15For, lo, I will make thee small among the heathen, *and* despised among men.

New International

2But the days are coming,"
　　declares the LORD,
"when I will sound the battle cry
　　against Rabbah of the Ammonites;
it will become a mound of ruins,
　　and its surrounding villages will be set on
　　　fire.
Then Israel will drive out
　　those who drove her out,"
　　　　　　　　　　　　says the LORD.

3"Wail, O Heshbon, for Ai is destroyed!
　　Cry out, O inhabitants of Rabbah!
Put on sackcloth and mourn;
　　rush here and there inside the walls,
for Molech will go into exile,
　　together with his priests and officials.

4Why do you boast of your valleys,
　　boast of your valleys so fruitful?
O unfaithful daughter,
　　you trust in your riches and say,
　　'Who will attack me?'

5I will bring terror on you
　　from all those around you,"
　　　　declares the Lord, the LORD Almighty.
"Every one of you will be driven away,
　　and no one will gather the fugitives.

6"Yet afterward, I will restore the fortunes of the
　　Ammonites,"
　　　　　　　　　　declares the LORD.

A Message About Edom

7Concerning Edom:

This is what the LORD Almighty says:

"Is there no longer wisdom in Teman?
　　Has counsel perished from the prudent?
　　Has their wisdom decayed?
8Turn and flee, hide in deep caves,
　　you who live in Dedan,
for I will bring disaster on Esau
　　at the time I punish him.
9If grape pickers came to you,
　　would they not leave a few grapes?
If thieves came during the night,
　　would they not steal only as much as they
　　　wanted?
10But I will strip Esau bare;
　　I will uncover his hiding places,
　　so that he cannot conceal himself.
His children, relatives and neighbors will perish,
　　and he will be no more.
11Leave your orphans; I will protect their lives.
　　Your widows too can trust in me."

12This is what the LORD says: "If those who do not deserve to drink the cup must drink it, why should you go unpunished? You will not go unpunished, but must drink it. 13I swear by myself," declares the LORD, "that Bozrah will become a ruin and an object of horror, of reproach and of cursing; and all its towns will be in ruins forever."

14I have heard a message from the LORD:
　　An envoy was sent to the nations to say,
"Assemble yourselves to attack it!
　　Rise up for battle!"

15"Now I will make you small among the nations,
　　despised among men.

Living Bible

this, the Lord declares, by destroying your city of Rabbah. It shall become a desolate heap, and the neighboring towns shall be burned. Then Israel shall come and take back her land from you again. She shall dispossess those who dispossessed her, says the Lord. ³Cry out, O Heshbon, for Ai is destroyed! Weep, daughter of Rabbah! Put on garments of mourning; weep and wail, hiding in the hedges, for your god Milcom shall be exiled along with his princes and priests. ⁴You are proud of your fertile valleys, but they will soon be ruined. O wicked daughter, you trusted in your wealth and thought no one could ever harm you. ⁵But see, I will bring terror upon you, says the Lord, the Lord Almighty. For all your neighbors shall drive you from your land and none shall help your exiles as they flee. ⁶But afterward I will restore the fortunes of the Ammonites, says the Lord.

The Edomites

⁷The Lord says: Where are all your wise men of days gone by? Is there not one left in all of Teman? ⁸Flee to the remotest parts of the desert, O people of Dedan;ª for when I punish Edom, I will punish you! ⁹, ¹⁰Those who gather grapes leave a few for the poor, and even thieves don't take everything, but I will strip bare the land of Esau, and there will be no place to hide. Her children, her brothers, her neighbors—all will be destroyed—and she herself will perish too. ¹¹(But I will preserve your fatherless children who remain, and let your widows depend upon me.)

¹²The Lord says to Edom: If the innocent must suffer, how much more must you! You shall not go unpunished! You must drink this cup of judgment! ¹³For I have sworn by my own name, says the Lord, that Bozrah shall become heaps of ruins, cursed and mocked; and her cities shall be eternal wastes.

¹⁴I have heard this message from the Lord:

He has sent a messenger to call the nations to form a coalition against Edom and destroy her. ¹⁵I will make her weak among the nations and despised by all, says the Lord. ¹⁶You have been fooled by your fame and your

New Revised Standard

2 Therefore, the time is surely coming,
  says the LORD,
when I will sound the battle alarm
  against Rabbah of the Ammonites;
it shall become a desolate mound,
  and its villages shall be burned with fire;
then Israel shall dispossess those who
  dispossessed him,
  says the LORD.

3 Wail, O Heshbon, for Ai is laid waste!
  Cry out, O daughtersᵇ of Rabbah!
Put on sackcloth,
  lament, and slash yourselves with whips!ᶜ
For Milcom shall go into exile,
  with his priests and his attendants.
4 Why do you boast in your strength?
  Your strength is ebbing,
O faithless daughter.
  You trusted in your treasures, saying,
  "Who will attack me?"
5 I am going to bring terror upon you,
  says the Lord GOD of hosts,
  from all your neighbors,
and you will be scattered, each headlong,
  with no one to gather the fugitives.

6 But afterward I will restore the fortunes of the Ammonites, says the LORD.

Judgment on Edom

7 Concerning Edom.

Thus says the LORD of hosts:
  Is there no longer wisdom in Teman?
  Has counsel perished from the prudent?
  Has their wisdom vanished?
8 Flee, turn back, get down low,
  inhabitants of Dedan!
For I will bring the calamity of Esau upon
  him,
  the time when I punish him.
9 If grape-gatherers came to you,
  would they not leave gleanings?
If thieves came by night,
  even they would pillage only what they
    wanted.
10 But as for me, I have stripped Esau bare,
  I have uncovered his hiding places,
  and he is not able to conceal himself.
His offspring are destroyed, his kinsfolk
  and his neighbors; and he is no more.
11 Leave your orphans, I will keep them alive;
  and let your widows trust in me.

12 For thus says the LORD: If those who do not deserve to drink the cup still have to drink it, shall you be the one to go unpunished? You shall not go unpunished; you must drink it. ¹³For by myself I have sworn, says the LORD, that Bozrah shall become an object of horror and ridicule, a waste, and an object of cursing; and all her towns shall be perpetual wastes.

14 I have heard tidings from the LORD,
  and a messenger has been sent among the
    nations:
"Gather yourselves together and come against
  her,
  and rise up for battle!"
15 For I will make you least among the nations,
  despised by humankind.

ª 49:8 *Dedan* was in Northern Arabia and was a flourishing caravan city at the time of Jeremiah and Ezekiel.

ᵇ Or *villages* ᶜ Cn: Meaning of Heb uncertain

King James

16Thy terribleness hath deceived thee, *and* the pride of thine heart, O thou that dwellest in the clefts of the rock, that holdest the height of the hill: though thou shouldest make thy nest as high as the eagle, I will bring thee down from thence, saith the LORD.

17Also Edom shall be a desolation: every one that goeth by it shall be astonished, and shall hiss at all the plagues thereof.

18As in the overthrow of Sodom and Gomorrah and the neighbour *cities* thereof, saith the LORD, no man shall abide there, neither shall a son of man dwell in it.

19Behold, he shall come up like a lion from the swelling of Jordan against the habitation of the strong: but I will suddenly make him run away from her: and who *is* a chosen *man, that* I may appoint over her? for who *is* like me? and who will appoint me the time? and who *is* that shepherd that will stand before me?

20Therefore hear the counsel of the LORD, that he hath taken against Edom; and his purposes, that he hath purposed against the inhabitants of Teman: Surely the least of the flock shall draw them out: surely he shall make their habitations desolate with them.

21The earth is moved at the noise of their fall, at the cry the noise thereof was heard in the Red sea.

22Behold, he shall come up and fly as the eagle, and spread his wings over Bozrah: and at that day shall the heart of the mighty men of Edom be as the heart of a woman in her pangs.

23¶ Concerning Damascus. Hamath is confounded, and Arpad: for they have heard evil tidings: they are fainthearted; *there is* sorrow on the sea; it cannot be quiet.

24Damascus is waxed feeble, *and* turneth herself to flee, and fear hath seized on *her:* anguish and sorrows have taken her, as a woman in travail.

25How is the city of praise not left, the city of my joy!

26Therefore her young men shall fall in her streets, and all the men of war shall be cut off in that day, saith the LORD of hosts.

27And I will kindle a fire in the wall of Damascus, and it shall consume the palaces of Ben-hadad.

28¶ Concerning Kedar, and concerning the kingdoms of Hazor, which Nebuchadrezzar king of Babylon shall smite, thus saith the LORD; Arise ye, go up to Kedar, and spoil the men of the east.

29Their tents and their flocks shall they take away: they shall take to themselves their curtains, and all their vessels, and their camels; and they shall cry unto them, Fear *is* on every side.

New International

16The terror you inspire
  and the pride of your heart have deceived
    you,
you who live in the clefts of the rocks,
  who occupy the heights of the hill.
Though you build your nest as high as the
    eagle's,
  from there I will bring you down,"
                              declares the LORD.
17"Edom will become an object of horror;
  all who pass by will be appalled and will
    scoff
  because of all its wounds.
18As Sodom and Gomorrah were overthrown,
  along with their neighboring towns,"
                              says the LORD,
"so no one will live there;
  no man will dwell in it.

19"Like a lion coming up from Jordan's thickets
    to a rich pastureland,
I will chase Edom from its land in an instant.
  Who is the chosen one I will appoint for this?
Who is like me and who can challenge me?
  And what shepherd can stand against me?"
20Therefore, hear what the LORD has planned
    against Edom,
  what he has purposed against those who live
    in Teman:
The young of the flock will be dragged away;
  he will completely destroy their pasture
    because of them.
21At the sound of their fall the earth will tremble;
  their cry will resound to the Red Sea.[a]
22Look! An eagle will soar and swoop down,
  spreading its wings over Bozrah.
In that day the hearts of Edom's warriors
  will be like the heart of a woman in labor.

A Message About Damascus

23Concerning Damascus:

"Hamath and Arpad are dismayed,
  for they have heard bad news.
They are disheartened,
  troubled like[b] the restless sea.
24Damascus has become feeble,
  she has turned to flee
  and panic has gripped her;
anguish and pain have seized her,
  pain like that of a woman in labor.
25Why has the city of renown not been
    abandoned,
  the town in which I delight?
26Surely, her young men will fall in the streets;
  all her soldiers will be silenced in that day,"
                        declares the LORD Almighty.
27"I will set fire to the walls of Damascus;
  it will consume the fortresses of Ben-Hadad."

A Message About Kedar and Hazor

28Concerning Kedar and the kingdoms of Hazor, which Nebuchadnezzar king of Babylon attacked:

This is what the LORD says:

"Arise, and attack Kedar
  and destroy the people of the East.
29Their tents and their flocks will be taken;
  their shelters will be carried off
  with all their goods and camels.
Men will shout to them,
  'Terror on every side!'

---

a 21 Hebrew *Yam Suph*; that is, Sea of Reeds   b 23 Hebrew *on* or *by*

Living Bible

pride, living there in the mountains of Petra, in the clefts of the rocks. But though you live among the peaks with the eagles, I will bring you down, says the Lord.

17The fate of Edom will be horrible; all who go by will be appalled, and gasp at the sight. 18Your cities will become as silent as Sodom and Gomorrah and their neighboring towns, says the Lord. No one will live there anymore. 19I will send against them one who will come like a lion from the wilds of Jordan stalking the sheep in the fold. Suddenly Edom shall be destroyed, and I will appoint over the Edomites the person of my choice. For who is like me and who can call me to account? 20What shepherd can defy me? Take note: The Lord will certainly do this to Edom and also the people of Teman—even little children will be dragged away as slaves! It will be a shocking thing to see.

21The earth shakes with the noise of Edom's fall; the cry of the people is heard as far away as the Red Sea. 22The one who will come will fly as swift as a vulture and will spread his wings against Bozrah. Then the courage of the mightiest warriors will disappear like that of women in labor.

Damascus

23The cities of Hamath and Arpad are stricken with fear, for they have heard the news of their doom. Their hearts are troubled like a wild sea in a raging storm. 24Damascus has become feeble and all her people turn to flee. Fear, anguish and sorrow have gripped her as they do women in labor. 25O famous city, city of joy, how you are forsaken now! 26Your young men lie dead in the streets; your entire army shall be destroyed in one day, says the Lord Almighty. 27And I will start a fire at the edge of Damascus that shall burn up the palaces of Benhadad.

Kedar and Hazor

28This prophecy is about Kedar[c] and the kingdoms of Hazor, which are going to be destroyed by Nebuchadnezzar, king of Babylon, for the Lord will send him to destroy them. 29Their flocks and their tents will be captured, says the Lord, with all their household goods. Their camels will be taken away, and all around will be the shouts of panic, "We are surrounded and doomed!"

New Revised Standard

16 The terror you inspire
 and the pride of your heart have deceived
 you,
 you who live in the clefts of the rock,[d]
 who hold the height of the hill.
 Although you make your nest as high as the
 eagle's,
 from there I will bring you down,
 says the LORD.

17 Edom shall become an object of horror; everyone who passes by it will be horrified and will hiss because of all its disasters. 18As when Sodom and Gomorrah and their neighbors were overthrown, says the LORD, no one shall live there, nor shall anyone settle in it. 19Like a lion coming up from the thickets of the Jordan against a perennial pasture, I will suddenly chase Edom[e] away from it; and I will appoint over it whomever I choose.[f] For who is like me? Who can summon me? Who is the shepherd who can stand before me? 20Therefore hear the plan that the LORD has made against Edom and the purposes that he has formed against the inhabitants of Teman: Surely the little ones of the flock shall be dragged away; surely their fold shall be appalled at their fate. 21At the sound of their fall the earth shall tremble; the sound of their cry shall be heard at the Red Sea.[g] 22Look, he shall mount up and swoop down like an eagle, and spread his wings against Bozrah, and the heart of the warriors of Edom in that day shall be like the heart of a woman in labor.

Judgment on Damascus

23 Concerning Damascus.

 Hamath and Arpad are confounded,
 for they have heard bad news;
 they melt in fear, they are troubled like the
 sea[h]
 that cannot be quiet.
24 Damascus has become feeble, she turned to
 flee,
 and panic seized her;
 anguish and sorrows have taken hold of her,
 as of a woman in labor.
25 How the famous city is forsaken,[i]
 the joyful town![j]
26 Therefore her young men shall fall in her
 squares,
 and all her soldiers shall be destroyed in
 that day,
 says the LORD of hosts.
27 And I will kindle a fire at the wall of
 Damascus,
 and it shall devour the strongholds of
 Ben-hadad.

Judgment on Kedar and Hazor

28 Concerning Kedar and the kingdoms of Hazor that King Nebuchadrezzar of Babylon defeated.

 Thus says the LORD:
 Rise up, advance against Kedar!
 Destroy the people of the east!
29 Take their tents and their flocks,
 their curtains and all their goods;
 carry off their camels for yourselves,
 and a cry shall go up: "Terror is all
 around!"

---

c 49:28 Kedar, an Arab tribe living in the desert east of Palestine. Hazor, not the Hazor mentioned in Joshua and Judges—a great city north of the Sea of Galilee; but rather, a group of Arab tribes.

d Or of Sela   e Heb him   f Or and I will single out the choicest of his rams: Meaning of Heb uncertain   g Or Sea of Reeds   h Cn: Heb there is trouble in the sea   i Vg: Heb is not forsaken   j Syr Vg Tg: Heb the town of my joy

King James

30¶ Flee, get you far off, dwell deep, O ye inhabitants of Hazor, saith the LORD; for Nebuchadrezzar king of Babylon hath taken counsel against you, and hath conceived a purpose against you.

31Arise, get you up unto the wealthy nation, that dwelleth without care, saith the LORD, which have neither gates nor bars, *which* dwell alone.

32And their camels shall be a booty, and the multitude of their cattle a spoil: and I will scatter into all winds them *that are* in the utmost corners; and I will bring their calamity from all sides thereof, saith the LORD.

33And Hazor shall be a dwelling for dragons, *and* a desolation for ever: there shall no man abide there, nor *any* son of man dwell in it.

34¶ The word of the LORD that came to Jeremiah the prophet against Elam in the beginning of the reign of Zedekiah king of Judah, saying,

35Thus saith the LORD of hosts; Behold, I will break the bow of Elam, the chief of their might.

36And upon Elam will I bring the four winds from the four quarters of heaven, and will scatter them toward all those winds; and there shall be no nation whither the outcasts of Elam shall not come.

37For I will cause Elam to be dismayed before their enemies, and before them that seek their life: and I will bring evil upon them, *even* my fierce anger, saith the LORD; and I will send the sword after them, till I have consumed them:

38And I will set my throne in Elam, and will destroy from thence the king and the princes, saith the LORD.

39¶ But it shall come to pass in the latter days, *that* I will bring again the captivity of Elam, saith the LORD.

50 THE WORD that the LORD spake against Babylon *and* against the land of the Chaldeans by Jeremiah the prophet.

2Declare ye among the nations, and publish, and set up a standard; publish, *and* conceal not: say, Babylon is taken, Bel is confounded, Merodach is broken in pieces; her idols are confounded, her images are broken in pieces.

3For out of the north there cometh up a nation against her, which shall make her land desolate, and none shall dwell therein: they shall remove, they shall depart, both man and beast.

New International

30"Flee quickly away!
    Stay in deep caves, you who live in Hazor,"
        declares the LORD.
"Nebuchadnezzar king of Babylon has plotted
        against you;
    he has devised a plan against you.
31"Arise and attack a nation at ease,
    which lives in confidence,"
        declares the LORD,
"a nation that has neither gates nor bars;
    its people live alone.
32Their camels will become plunder,
    and their large herds will be booty.
I will scatter to the winds those who are in
        distant places[a]
    and will bring disaster on them from every
        side,"
        declares the LORD.
33"Hazor will become a haunt of jackals,
    a desolate place forever.
No one will live there;
    no man will dwell in it."

A Message About Elam

34This is the word of the LORD that came to Jeremiah the prophet concerning Elam, early in the reign of Zedekiah king of Judah:

35This is what the LORD Almighty says:

"See, I will break the bow of Elam,
    the mainstay of their might.
36I will bring against Elam the four winds
    from the four quarters of the heavens;
I will scatter them to the four winds,
    and there will not be a nation
    where Elam's exiles do not go.
37I will shatter Elam before their foes,
    before those who seek their lives;
I will bring disaster upon them,
    even my fierce anger,"
        declares the LORD.
"I will pursue them with the sword
    until I have made an end of them.
38I will set my throne in Elam
    and destroy her king and officials,"
        declares the LORD.
39"Yet I will restore the fortunes of Elam
    in days to come,"
        declares the LORD.

A Message About Babylon

50 THIS IS the word the LORD spoke through Jeremiah the prophet concerning Babylon and the land of the Babylonians[b]:

2"Announce and proclaim among the nations,
    lift up a banner and proclaim it;
    keep nothing back, but say,
'Babylon will be captured;
    Bel will be put to shame,
    Marduk filled with terror.
Her images will be put to shame
    and her idols filled with terror.'
3A nation from the north will attack her
    and lay waste her land.
No one will live in it;
    both men and animals will flee away.

---

[a] 32 Or *who clip the hair by their foreheads*   [b] 1 Or *Chaldeans*; also in verses 8, 25, 35 and 45

Living Bible

30Flee for your lives, says the Lord. Go deep into the deserts, O people of Hazor, for Nebuchadnezzar, king of Babylon, has plotted against you and is preparing to destroy you.

31"Go," said the Lord to King Nebuchadnezzar. "Attack those wealthy Bedouin tribes living alone in the desert without a care in the world, boasting that they are self-sufficient—that they need neither walls nor gates. **32**Their camels and cattle shall all be yours, and I will scatter these heathenᶜ to the winds. From all directions I will bring calamity upon them."

33Hazor shall be a home for wild animals of the desert. No one shall ever live there again. It shall be desolate forever.

Elam

34God's message against Elam came to Jeremiah in the beginning of the reign of Zedekiah, king of Judah:

35The Lord says: I will destroy the army of Elam, **36**and I will scatter the people of Elam to the four winds; they shall be exiled to countries throughout the world. **37**My fierce anger will bring great evil upon Elam, says the Lord, and I will cause her enemies to wipe her out. **38**And I will set my throne in Elam, says the Lord. I will destroy her king and princes. **39**But in the latter days I will bring the people back, says the Lord.

Babylon

50 THIS IS the message from the Lord against Babylon and the Chaldeans, spoken by Jeremiah the prophet:

2Tell all the world that Babylon will be destroyed; her god Marduk will be utterly disgraced! **3**For a nation shall come down upon her from the north with such destruction that no one shall live in her again; all shall be gone—both men and animals shall flee.

New Revised Standard

30 Flee, wander far away, hide in deep places,
　　O inhabitants of Hazor!
　　　　　　　　　　says the LORD.
For King Nebuchadrezzar of Babylon
　　has made a plan against you
　　and formed a purpose against you.

31 Rise up, advance against a nation at ease,
　　that lives secure,
　　　　　　　　　　says the LORD,
　　that has no gates or bars,
　　that lives alone.

32 Their camels shall become booty,
　　their herds of cattle a spoil.
I will scatter to every wind
　　those who have shaven temples,
and I will bring calamity
　　against them from every side,
　　　　　　　　　　says the LORD.

33 Hazor shall become a lair of jackals,
　　an everlasting waste;
no one shall live there,
　　nor shall anyone settle in it.

Judgment on Elam

34 The word of the LORD that came to the prophet Jeremiah concerning Elam, at the beginning of the reign of King Zedekiah of Judah.

35 Thus says the LORD of hosts: I am going to break the bow of Elam, the mainstay of their might; 36 and I will bring upon Elam the four winds from the four quarters of heaven; and I will scatter them to all these winds, and there shall be no nation to which the exiles from Elam shall not come. 37 I will terrify Elam before their enemies, and before those who seek their life; I will bring disaster upon them, my fierce anger, says the LORD. I will send the sword after them, until I have consumed them; 38 and I will set my throne in Elam, and destroy their king and officials, says the LORD.

39 But in the latter days I will restore the fortunes of Elam, says the LORD.

Judgment on Babylon

50 THE WORD that the LORD spoke concerning Babylon, concerning the land of the Chaldeans, by the prophet Jeremiah:

2 Declare among the nations and proclaim,
　　set up a banner and proclaim,
　　do not conceal it, say:
Babylon is taken,
　　Bel is put to shame,
　　Merodach is dismayed.
Her images are put to shame,
　　her idols are dismayed.

3 For out of the north a nation has come up against her; it shall make her land a desolation, and no one shall live in it; both human beings and animals shall flee away.

ᶜ 49:32 *these heathen*, literally, "those who cut the corners of their hair."

King James

4¶ In those days, and in that time, saith the LORD, the children of Israel shall come, they and the children of Judah together, going and weeping: they shall go, and seek the LORD their God.

5They shall ask the way to Zion with their faces thitherward, *saying*, Come, and let us join ourselves to the LORD in a perpetual covenant *that* shall not be forgotten.

6My people hath been lost sheep: their shepherds have caused them to go astray, they have turned them away *on* the mountains: they have gone from mountain to hill, they have forgotten their restingplace.

7All that found them have devoured them: and their adversaries said, We offend not, because they have sinned against the LORD, the habitation of justice, even the LORD, the hope of their fathers.

8Remove out of the midst of Babylon, and go forth out of the land of the Chaldeans, and be as the he goats before the flocks.

9¶ For, lo, I will raise and cause to come up against Babylon an assembly of great nations from the north country: and they shall set themselves in array against her; from thence she shall be taken: their arrows *shall be* as of a mighty expert man; none shall return in vain.

10And Chaldea shall be a spoil: all that spoil her shall be satisfied, saith the LORD.

11Because ye were glad, because ye rejoiced, O ye destroyers of mine heritage, because ye are grown fat as the heifer at grass, and bellow as bulls;

12Your mother shall be sore confounded; she that bare you shall be ashamed: behold, the hindermost of the nations *shall be* a wilderness, a dry land, and a desert.

13Because of the wrath of the LORD it shall not be inhabited, but it shall be wholly desolate: every one that goeth by Babylon shall be astonished, and hiss at all her plagues.

14Put yourselves in array against Babylon round about: all ye that bend the bow, shoot at her, spare no arrows: for she hath sinned against the LORD.

15Shout against her round about: she hath given her hand: her foundations are fallen, her walls are thrown down: for it *is* the vengeance of the LORD: take vengeance upon her; as she hath done, do unto her.

16Cut off the sower from Babylon, and him that handleth the sickle in the time of harvest: for fear of the oppressing sword they shall turn every one to his people, and they shall flee every one to his own land.

17¶ Israel *is* a scattered sheep; the lions have driven *him* away: first the king of Assyria hath devoured him; and last this Nebuchadrezzar king of Babylon hath broken his bones.

New International

4"In those days, at that time,"
　　declares the LORD,
"the people of Israel and the people of Judah together
　　will go in tears to seek the LORD their God.
5They will ask the way to Zion
　　and turn their faces toward it.
They will come and bind themselves to the LORD
　　in an everlasting covenant
　　that will not be forgotten.

6"My people have been lost sheep;
　　their shepherds have led them astray
　　and caused them to roam on the mountains.
They wandered over mountain and hill
　　and forgot their own resting place.
7Whoever found them devoured them;
　　their enemies said, 'We are not guilty,
for they sinned against the LORD, their true pasture,
　　the LORD, the hope of their fathers.'

8"Flee out of Babylon;
　　leave the land of the Babylonians,
　　and be like the goats that lead the flock.
9For I will stir up and bring against Babylon
　　an alliance of great nations from the land of the north.
They will take up their positions against her,
　　and from the north she will be captured.
Their arrows will be like skilled warriors
　　who do not return empty-handed.
10So Babylonia[a] will be plundered;
　　all who plunder her will have their fill,"
　　　　　　　　　　　declares the LORD.

11"Because you rejoice and are glad,
　　you who pillage my inheritance,
because you frolic like a heifer threshing grain
　　and neigh like stallions,
12your mother will be greatly ashamed;
　　she who gave you birth will be disgraced.
She will be the least of the nations—
　　a wilderness, a dry land, a desert.
13Because of the LORD's anger she will not be inhabited
　　but will be completely desolate.
All who pass Babylon will be horrified and scoff
　　because of all her wounds.

14"Take up your positions around Babylon,
　　all you who draw the bow.
Shoot at her! Spare no arrows,
　　for she has sinned against the LORD.
15Shout against her on every side!
　　She surrenders, her towers fall,
　　her walls are torn down.
Since this is the vengeance of the LORD,
　　take vengeance on her;
　　do to her as she has done to others.
16Cut off from Babylon the sower,
　　and the reaper with his sickle at harvest.
Because of the sword of the oppressor
　　let everyone return to his own people,
　　let everyone flee to his own land.

17"Israel is a scattered flock
　　that lions have chased away.
The first to devour him
　　was the king of Assyria;
the last to crush his bones
　　was Nebuchadnezzar king of Babylon."

Living Bible

4Then the people of Israel and Judah shall join together, weeping and seeking the Lord their God. 5They shall ask the way to Zion and start back home again. "Come," they will say, "let us be united to the Lord with an eternal pledge that will never be broken again."

6My people have been lost sheep. Their shepherds led them astray and then turned them loose in the mountains. They lost their way and didn't remember how to get back to the fold. 7All who found them devoured them and said, "We are permitted to attack them freely, for they have sinned against the Lord, the God of justice, the hope of their fathers."

8But now, flee from Babylon, the land of the Chaldeans; lead my people home again, 9for see, I am raising up an army of great nations from the north and I will bring them against Babylon to attack her, and she shall be destroyed. The enemies' arrows go straight to the mark; they do not miss! 10And Babylon shall be sacked until everyone is sated with loot, says the Lord.

11Though you were glad, O Chaldeans, plunderers of my people, and are fat as cows that feed in lush pastures, and neigh like stallions, 12yet your mother shall be overwhelmed with shame, for you shall become the least of the nations—a wilderness, a dry and desert land. 13Because of the anger of the Lord, Babylon shall become deserted wasteland, and all who pass by shall be appalled and shall mock at her for all her wounds.

14Yes, prepare to fight with Babylon, all you nations round about; let the archers shoot at her; spare no arrows, for she has sinned against the Lord. 15Shout against her from every side. Look! She surrenders! Her walls have fallen. The Lord has taken vengeance. Do to her as she has done! 16Let the farm hands all depart. Let them rush back to their own lands as the enemies advance.

17The Israelites are like sheep the lions chase. First the king of Assyria ate them up; then Nebuchadnezzar, the king of Babylon, crunched their bones. 18Therefore

New Revised Standard

4 In those days and in that time, says the LORD, the people of Israel shall come, they and the people of Judah together; they shall come weeping as they seek the LORD their God. 5They shall ask the way to Zion, with faces turned toward it, and they shall come and joinb themselves to the LORD by an everlasting covenant that will never be forgotten.

6 My people have been lost sheep; their shepherds have led them astray, turning them away on the mountains; from mountain to hill they have gone, they have forgotten their fold. 7All who found them have devoured them, and their enemies have said, "We are not guilty, because they have sinned against the LORD, the true pasture, the LORD, the hope of their ancestors."

8 Flee from Babylon, and go out of the land of the Chaldeans, and be like male goats leading the flock. 9For I am going to stir up and bring against Babylon a company of great nations from the land of the north; and they shall array themselves against her; from there she shall be taken. Their arrows are like the arrows of a skilled warrior who does not return empty-handed. 10Chaldea shall be plundered; all who plunder her shall be sated, says the LORD.

11 Though you rejoice, though you exult,
      O plunderers of my heritage,
    though you frisk about like a heifer on the
        grass,
      and neigh like stallions,
12 your mother shall be utterly shamed,
      and she who bore you shall be disgraced.
    Lo, she shall be the last of the nations,
      a wilderness, dry land, and a desert.
13 Because of the wrath of the LORD she shall
        not be inhabited,
      but shall be an utter desolation;
    everyone who passes by Babylon shall be
        appalled
      and hiss because of all her wounds.
14 Take up your positions around Babylon,
      all you that bend the bow;
    shoot at her, spare no arrows,
      for she has sinned against the LORD.
15 Raise a shout against her from all sides,
      "She has surrendered;
    her bulwarks have fallen,
      her walls are thrown down."
    For this is the vengeance of the LORD:
      take vengeance on her,
      do to her as she has done.
16 Cut off from Babylon the sower,
      and the wielder of the sickle in time of
        harvest;
    because of the destroying sword
      all of them shall return to their own people,
      and all of them shall flee to their own land.

17 Israel is a hunted sheep driven away by lions. First the king of Assyria devoured it, and now at the end King Nebuchadrezzar of Babylon has gnawed its bones.

King James

¹⁸Therefore thus saith the LORD of hosts, the God of Israel; Behold, I will punish the king of Babylon and his land, as I have punished the king of Assyria.

¹⁹And I will bring Israel again to his habitation, and he shall feed on Carmel and Bashan, and his soul shall be satisfied upon mount Ephraim and Gilead.

²⁰In those days, and in that time, saith the LORD, the iniquity of Israel shall be sought for, and *there shall be* none; and the sins of Judah, and they shall not be found: for I will pardon them whom I reserve.

²¹¶ Go up against the land of Merathaim, *even* against it, and against the inhabitants of Pekod: waste and utterly destroy after them, saith the LORD, and do according to all that I have commanded thee.

²²A sound of battle *is* in the land, and of great destruction.

²³How is the hammer of the whole earth cut asunder and broken! how is Babylon become a desolation among the nations!

²⁴I have laid a snare for thee, and thou art also taken, O Babylon, and thou wast not aware: thou art found, and also caught, because thou hast striven against the LORD.

²⁵The LORD hath opened his armoury, and hath brought forth the weapons of his indignation: for this *is* the work of the Lord GOD of hosts in the land of the Chaldeans.

²⁶Come against her from the utmost border, open her storehouses: cast her up as heaps, and destroy her utterly: let nothing of her be left.

²⁷Slay all her bullocks; let them go down to the slaughter: woe unto them! for their day is come, the time of their visitation.

²⁸The voice of them that flee and escape out of the land of Babylon, to declare in Zion the vengeance of the LORD our God, the vengeance of his temple.

²⁹Call together the archers against Babylon: all ye that bend the bow, camp against it round about; let none thereof escape: recompense her according to her work; according to all that she hath done, do unto her: for she hath been proud against the LORD, against the Holy One of Israel.

³⁰Therefore shall her young men fall in the streets, and all her men of war shall be cut off in that day, saith the LORD.

³¹Behold, I *am* against thee, *O thou* most proud, saith the Lord GOD of hosts: for thy day is come, the time *that* I will visit thee.

³²And the most proud shall stumble and fall, and none shall raise him up: and I will kindle a fire in his cities, and it shall devour all round about him.

New International

¹⁸Therefore this is what the LORD Almighty, the God of Israel, says:

"I will punish the king of Babylon and his land
as I punished the king of Assyria.
¹⁹But I will bring Israel back to his own pasture
and he will graze on Carmel and Bashan;
his appetite will be satisfied
on the hills of Ephraim and Gilead.
²⁰In those days, at that time,"
declares the LORD,
"search will be made for Israel's guilt,
but there will be none,
and for the sins of Judah,
but none will be found,
for I will forgive the remnant I spare.

²¹"Attack the land of Merathaim
and those who live in Pekod.
Pursue, kill and completely destroy^a them,"
declares the LORD.
"Do everything I have commanded you.
²²The noise of battle is in the land,
the noise of great destruction!
²³How broken and shattered
is the hammer of the whole earth!
How desolate is Babylon
among the nations!
²⁴I set a trap for you, O Babylon,
and you were caught before you knew it;
you were found and captured
because you opposed the LORD.
²⁵The LORD has opened his arsenal
and brought out the weapons of his wrath,
for the Sovereign LORD Almighty has work to do
in the land of the Babylonians.
²⁶Come against her from afar.
Break open her granaries;
pile her up like heaps of grain.
Completely destroy her
and leave her no remnant.
²⁷Kill all her young bulls;
let them go down to the slaughter!
Woe to them! For their day has come,
the time for them to be punished.
²⁸Listen to the fugitives and refugees from
Babylon
declaring in Zion
how the LORD our God has taken vengeance,
vengeance for his temple.

²⁹"Summon archers against Babylon,
all those who draw the bow.
Encamp all around her;
let no one escape.
Repay her for her deeds;
do to her as she has done.
For she has defied the LORD,
the Holy One of Israel.
³⁰Therefore, her young men will fall in the
streets;
all her soldiers will be silenced in that day,"
declares the LORD.
³¹"See, I am against you, O arrogant one,"
declares the Lord, the LORD Almighty,
"for your day has come,
the time for you to be punished.
³²The arrogant one will stumble and fall
and no one will help her up;
I will kindle a fire in her towns
that will consume all who are around her."

^a *21* The Hebrew term refers to the irrevocable giving over of things or persons to the LORD, often by totally destroying them; also in verse 26.

Living Bible

the Lord, the God of Israel, says: Now I will punish the king of Babylon and his land as I punished the king of Assyria. ¹⁹And I will bring Israel home again to her own land, to feed in the fields of Carmel and Bashan and to be happy once more on Mount Ephraim and Mount Gilead. ²⁰In those days, says the Lord, no sin shall be found in Israel or in Judah, for I will pardon the remnant I preserve.

²¹Go up, O my warriors, against the land of Merathaim[b] and against the people of Pekod.[c] Yes, march against Babylon, the land of rebels, a land that I will judge! Annihilate them, as I have commanded you. ²²Let there be the shout of battle in the land, a shout of great destruction. ²³Babylon, the mightiest hammer in all the earth, lies broken and shattered. Babylon is desolate among the nations! ²⁴O Babylon, I have set a trap for you and you are caught, for you have fought against the Lord.

²⁵The Lord has opened his armory and brought out weapons to explode his wrath upon his enemies. The terror that befalls Babylon will be the work of the Lord God. ²⁶Yes, come against her from distant lands; break open her granaries; knock down her walls and houses into heaps of ruins and utterly destroy her; let nothing be left. ²⁷Not even her cattle—woe to them, too! Kill them all! For the time has come for Babylon to be devastated.

²⁸But my people will flee; they will escape back to their own country to tell how the Lord their God has broken forth in fury upon those who destroyed his Temple.

²⁹Send out a call for archers to come to Babylon; surround the city so that none can escape. Do to her as she has done to others, for she has haughtily defied the Lord, the Holy One of Israel. ³⁰Her young men will fall in the streets and die; her warriors will all be killed. ³¹For see, I am against you, O people so proud; and now your day of reckoning has come. ³²Land of pride, you will stumble and fall and no one will raise you up, for the Lord will light a fire in the cities of Babylon that will burn everything around them.

New Revised Standard

¹⁸Therefore, thus says the Lord of hosts, the God of Israel: I am going to punish the king of Babylon and his land, as I punished the king of Assyria. ¹⁹I will restore Israel to its pasture, and it shall feed on Carmel and in Bashan, and on the hills of Ephraim and in Gilead its hunger shall be satisfied. ²⁰In those days and at that time, says the Lord, the iniquity of Israel shall be sought, and there shall be none; and the sins of Judah, and none shall be found; for I will pardon the remnant that I have spared.

21 Go up to the land of Merathaim;[d]
    go up against her,
and attack the inhabitants of Pekod[e]
    and utterly destroy the last of them,[f]
               says the Lord;
    do all that I have commanded you.
22 The noise of battle is in the land,
    and great destruction!
23 How the hammer of the whole earth
    is cut down and broken!
How Babylon has become
    a horror among the nations!
24 You set a snare for yourself and you were
    caught, O Babylon,
    but you did not know it;
you were discovered and seized,
    because you challenged the Lord.
25 The Lord has opened his armory,
    and brought out the weapons of his wrath,
for the Lord God of hosts has a task to do
    in the land of the Chaldeans.
26 Come against her from every quarter;
    open her granaries;
pile her up like heaps of grain, and destroy
    her utterly;
    let nothing be left of her.
27 Kill all her bulls,
    let them go down to the slaughter.
Alas for them, their day has come,
    the time of their punishment!

28 Listen! Fugitives and refugees from the land of Babylon are coming to declare in Zion the vengeance of the Lord our God, vengeance for his temple.

29 Summon archers against Babylon, all who bend the bow. Encamp all around her; let no one escape. Repay her according to her deeds; just as she has done, do to her—for she has arrogantly defied the Lord, the Holy One of Israel. ³⁰Therefore her young men shall fall in her squares, and all her soldiers shall be destroyed on that day, says the Lord.

31 I am against you, O arrogant one,
    says the Lord God of hosts;
for your day has come,
    the time when I will punish you.
32 The arrogant one shall stumble and fall,
    with no one to raise him up,
and I will kindle a fire in his cities,
    and it will devour everything around him.

---

b 50:21 *Merathaim*, meaning *double rebellion*, refers to southern Babylonia.
c 50:21 *Pekod*, meaning *punishment*, refers to a people in eastern Babylonia.

d Or *of Double Rebellion*   e Or *of Punishment*   f Tg: Heb *destroy after them*

King James

33¶ Thus saith the LORD of hosts; The children of Israel and the children of Judah *were* oppressed together: and all that took them captives held them fast; they refused to let them go.

34Their Redeemer *is* strong; the LORD of hosts *is* his name: he shall thoroughly plead their cause, that he may give rest to the land, and disquiet the inhabitants of Babylon.

35¶ A sword *is* upon the Chaldeans, saith the LORD, and upon the inhabitants of Babylon, and upon her princes, and upon her wise *men.*

36A sword *is* upon the liars; and they shall dote: a sword *is* upon her mighty men; and they shall be dismayed.

37A sword *is* upon their horses, and upon their chariots, and upon all the mingled people that *are* in the midst of her; and they shall become as women: a sword *is* upon her treasures; and they shall be robbed.

38A drought *is* upon her waters; and they shall be dried up: for it *is* the land of graven images, and they are mad upon *their* idols.

39Therefore the wild beasts of the desert with the wild beasts of the islands shall dwell *there,* and the owls shall dwell therein: and it shall be no more inhabited for ever; neither shall it be dwelt in from generation to generation.

40As God overthrew Sodom and Gomorrah and the neighbour *cities* thereof, saith the LORD; *so* shall no man abide there, neither shall any son of man dwell therein.

41Behold, a people shall come from the north, and a great nation, and many kings shall be raised up from the coasts of the earth.

42They shall hold the bow and the lance: they *are* cruel, and will not show mercy: their voice shall roar like the sea, and they shall ride upon horses, *every one* put in array, like a man to the battle, against thee, O daughter of Babylon.

43The king of Babylon hath heard the report of them, and his hands waxed feeble: anguish took hold of him, *and* pangs as of a woman in travail.

44Behold, he shall come up like a lion from the swelling of Jordan unto the habitation of the strong: but I will make them suddenly run away from her: and who *is* a chosen *man, that* I may appoint over her? for who *is* like me? and who will appoint me the time? and who *is* that shepherd that will stand before me?

45Therefore hear ye the counsel of the LORD, that he hath taken against Babylon; and his purposes, that he hath purposed against the land of the Chaldeans: Surely the least of the flock shall draw them out: surely he shall make *their* habitation desolate with them.

46At the noise of the taking of Babylon the earth is moved, and the cry is heard among the nations.

New International

33This is what the LORD Almighty says:

"The people of Israel are oppressed,
 and the people of Judah as well.
All their captors hold them fast,
 refusing to let them go.
34Yet their Redeemer is strong;
 the LORD Almighty is his name.
He will vigorously defend their cause
 so that he may bring rest to their land,
 but unrest to those who live in Babylon.

35"A sword against the Babylonians!"
 declares the LORD—
"against those who live in Babylon
 and against her officials and wise men!
36A sword against her false prophets!
 They will become fools.
A sword against her warriors!
 They will be filled with terror.
37A sword against her horses and chariots
 and all the foreigners in her ranks!
 They will become women.
A sword against her treasures!
 They will be plundered.
38A drought on[a] her waters!
 They will dry up.
For it is a land of idols,
 idols that will go mad with terror.

39"So desert creatures and hyenas will live there,
 and there the owl will dwell.
It will never again be inhabited
 or lived in from generation to generation.
40As God overthrew Sodom and Gomorrah
 along with their neighboring towns,"
 declares the LORD,
"so no one will live there;
 no man will dwell in it.

41"Look! An army is coming from the north;
 a great nation and many kings
 are being stirred up from the ends of the
 earth.
42They are armed with bows and spears;
 they are cruel and without mercy.
They sound like the roaring sea
 as they ride on their horses;
they come like men in battle formation
 to attack you, O Daughter of Babylon.
43The king of Babylon has heard reports about
 them,
 and his hands hang limp.
Anguish has gripped him,
 pain like that of a woman in labor.
44Like a lion coming up from Jordan's thickets
 to a rich pastureland,
I will chase Babylon from its land in an instant.
 Who is the chosen one I will appoint for this?
Who is like me and who can challenge me?
 And what shepherd can stand against me?"
45Therefore, hear what the LORD has planned
 against Babylon,
 what he has purposed against the land of the
 Babylonians:
The young of the flock will be dragged away;
 he will completely destroy their pasture
 because of them.
46At the sound of Babylon's capture the earth will
 tremble;
 its cry will resound among the nations.

---

a 38 Or *A sword against*

Living Bible

33The Lord says: The people of Israel and Judah have been wronged. Their captors hold them and refuse to let them go. 34But their Redeemer is strong. His name is the Lord Almighty. He will plead for them and see that they are freed to live again in quietness in Israel.

As for the people of Babylon—there is no rest for them! 35The sword of destruction shall smite the Chaldeans, says the Lord. It shall smite the people of Babylon—her princes and wise men too. 36All her wise counselors shall become fools! Panic shall seize her mightiest warriors! 37War shall devour her horses and chariots, and her allies from other lands shall become as weak as women. Her treasures shall all be robbed; 38even her water supply will fail. And why? Because the whole land is full of images, and the people are madly in love with their idols.

39Therefore this city of Babylon shall become inhabited by ostriches and jackals; it shall be a home for the wild animals of the desert. Never again shall it be lived in by human beings; it shall lie desolate forever. 40The Lord declares that he will destroy Babylon just as he destroyed Sodom and Gomorrah and their neighboring towns. No one has lived in them since, and no one will live again in Babylon.

41See them coming! A great army from the north! It is accompanied by many kings called by God from many lands. 42They are fully armed for slaughter; they are cruel and show no mercy; their battle cry roars like the surf against the shoreline. O Babylon, they ride against you fully ready for the battle.

43When the king of Babylon received the dispatch, his hands fell helpless at his sides; pangs of terror gripped him like the pangs of a woman in labor.

44*I will send against them an invader who will come upon them suddenly, like a lion from the jungles of Jordan that leaps upon the grazing sheep. I will put her defenders to flight and appoint over them whomsoever I please. For who is like me? What ruler can oppose my will? Who can call me to account?* 45*Listen to the plan of the Lord against Babylon, the land of the Chaldeans. For even little children shall be dragged away as slaves; oh, the horror; oh, the terror.* 46The whole earth shall shake at Babylon's fall, and her cry of despair shall be heard around the world.

New Revised Standard

33 Thus says the Lord of hosts: The people of Israel are oppressed, and so too are the people of Judah; all their captors have held them fast and refuse to let them go. 34 Their Redeemer is strong; the Lord of hosts is his name. He will surely plead their cause, that he may give rest to the earth, but unrest to the inhabitants of Babylon.

35 A sword against the Chaldeans, says the
    Lord,
    and against the inhabitants of Babylon,
    and against her officials and her sages!
36 A sword against the diviners,
    so that they may become fools!
A sword against her warriors,
    so that they may be destroyed!
37 A sword against her[b] horses and against her[b]
    chariots,
    and against all the foreign troops in her
    midst,
    so that they may become women!
A sword against all her treasures,
    that they may be plundered!
38 A drought[c] against her waters,
    that they may be dried up!
For it is a land of images,
    and they go mad over idols.

39 Therefore wild animals shall live with hyenas in Babylon,[d] and ostriches shall inhabit her; she shall never again be peopled, or inhabited for all generations. 40As when God overthrew Sodom and Gomorrah and their neighbors, says the Lord, so no one shall live there, nor shall anyone settle in her.

41 Look, a people is coming from the north;
    a mighty nation and many kings
    are stirring from the farthest parts of the
    earth.
42 They wield bow and spear,
    they are cruel and have no mercy.
The sound of them is like the roaring sea;
    they ride upon horses,
set in array as a warrior for battle,
    against you, O daughter Babylon!

43 The king of Babylon heard news of them,
    and his hands fell helpless;
anguish seized him,
    pain like that of a woman in labor.

44 Like a lion coming up from the thickets of the Jordan against a perennial pasture, I will suddenly chase them away from her; and I will appoint over her whomever I choose.[e] For who is like me? Who can summon me? Who is the shepherd who can stand before me? 45Therefore hear the plan that the Lord has made against Babylon, and the purposes that he has formed against the land of the Chaldeans: Surely the little ones of the flock shall be dragged away; surely their[f] fold shall be appalled at their fate. 46At the sound of the capture of Babylon the earth shall tremble, and her cry shall be heard among the nations.

b Cn: Heb *his*   c Another reading is *A sword*   d Heb lacks *in Babylon*   e Or *and I will single out the choicest of her rams*: Meaning of Heb uncertain   f Syr Gk Tg Compare 49.20: Heb lacks *their*

King James

51 THUS SAITH the LORD; Behold, I will raise up against Babylon, and against them that dwell in the midst of them that rise up against me, a destroying wind;

2And will send unto Babylon fanners, that shall fan her, and shall empty her land: for in the day of trouble they shall be against her round about.

3Against *him that* bendeth let the archer bend his bow, and against *him that* lifteth himself up in his brigandine: and spare ye not her young men; destroy ye utterly all her host.

4Thus the slain shall fall in the land of the Chaldeans, and *they that are* thrust through in her streets.

5For Israel *hath* not *been* forsaken, nor Judah of his God, of the LORD of hosts; though their land was filled with sin against the Holy One of Israel.

6Flee out of the midst of Babylon, and deliver every man his soul: be not cut off in her iniquity; for this *is* the time of the LORD's vengeance; he will render unto her a recompence.

7Babylon *hath been* a golden cup in the LORD's hand, that made all the earth drunken: the nations have drunken of her wine; therefore the nations are mad.

8Babylon is suddenly fallen and destroyed: howl for her; take balm for her pain, if so be she may be healed.

9We would have healed Babylon, but she is not healed: forsake her, and let us go every one into his own country: for her judgment reacheth unto heaven, and is lifted up *even* to the skies.

10The LORD hath brought forth our righteousness: come, and let us declare in Zion the work of the LORD our God.

11Make bright the arrows; gather the shields: the LORD hath raised up the spirit of the kings of the Medes: for his device *is* against Babylon, to destroy it; because it *is* the vengeance of the LORD, the vengeance of his temple.

12Set up the standard upon the walls of Babylon, make the watch strong, set up the watchmen, prepare the ambushes: for the LORD hath both devised and done that which he spake against the inhabitants of Babylon.

13O thou that dwellest upon many waters, abundant in treasures, thine end is come, *and* the measure of thy covetousness.

14The LORD of hosts hath sworn by himself, *saying,* Surely I will fill thee with men, as with caterpillars; and they shall lift up a shout against thee.

New International

51 THIS IS what the LORD says:

"See, I will stir up the spirit of a destroyer
against Babylon and the people of Leb
Kamai.[a]
2I will send foreigners to Babylon
to winnow her and to devastate her land;
they will oppose her on every side
in the day of her disaster.
3Let not the archer string his bow,
nor let him put on his armor.
Do not spare her young men;
completely destroy[b] her army.
4They will fall down slain in Babylon,[c]
fatally wounded in her streets.
5For Israel and Judah have not been forsaken
by their God, the LORD Almighty,
though their land[d] is full of guilt
before the Holy One of Israel.

6"Flee from Babylon!
Run for your lives!
Do not be destroyed because of her sins.
It is time for the LORD's vengeance;
he will pay her what she deserves.
7Babylon was a gold cup in the LORD's hand;
she made the whole earth drunk.
The nations drank her wine;
therefore they have now gone mad.
8Babylon will suddenly fall and be broken.
Wail over her!
Get balm for her pain;
perhaps she can be healed.

9" 'We would have healed Babylon,
but she cannot be healed;
let us leave her and each go to his own land,
for her judgment reaches to the skies,
it rises as high as the clouds.'

10" 'The LORD has vindicated us;
come, let us tell in Zion
what the LORD our God has done.'

11"Sharpen the arrows,
take up the shields!
The LORD has stirred up the kings of the
Medes,
because his purpose is to destroy Babylon.
The LORD will take vengeance,
vengeance for his temple.
12Lift up a banner against the walls of Babylon!
Reinforce the guard,
station the watchmen,
prepare an ambush!
The LORD will carry out his purpose,
his decree against the people of Babylon.
13You who live by many waters
and are rich in treasures,
your end has come,
the time for you to be cut off.
14The LORD Almighty has sworn by himself:
I will surely fill you with men, as with a
swarm of locusts,
and they will shout in triumph over you.

---

a *1 Leb Kamai* is a cryptogram for Chaldea, that is, Babylonia.   b *3* The Hebrew term refers to the irrevocable giving over of things or persons to the LORD, often by totally destroying them.   c *4* Or *Chaldea*   d *5* Or *l and the land of the Babylonians*

Living Bible

51 THE LORD says: I will stir up a destroyer against Babylon, against that whole land of the Chaldeans, and destroy it. ²Winnowers shall come and winnow her and blow her away; they shall come from every side to rise against her in her day of trouble. ³The arrows of the enemy shall strike down the bowmen of Babylon and pierce her warriors in their coats of mail. No one shall be spared; both young and old alike shall be destroyed. ⁴They shall fall down slain in the land of the Chaldeans, slashed to death in her streets. ⁵For the Lord Almighty has not forsaken Israel and Judah. He is still their God, but the land of the Chaldeans^c is filled with sin against the Holy One of Israel.

⁶Flee from Babylon! Save yourselves! Don't get trapped! If you stay, you will be destroyed when God takes his vengeance on all of Babylon's sins. ⁷Babylon has been as a gold cup in the Lord's hands, a cup from which he made the whole earth drink and go mad. ⁸But now, suddenly Babylon too has fallen. Weep for her; give her medicine; perhaps she can yet be healed. ⁹We would help her if we could, but nothing can save her now. Let her go. Abandon her and return to your own land, for God is judging her from heaven. ¹⁰The Lord has vindicated us. Come, let us declare in Jerusalem all the Lord our God has done.

¹¹Sharpen the arrows! Lift up the shields! For the Lord has stirred up the spirit of the kings of the Medes to march on Babylon and destroy her. This is his vengeance on those who wronged his people and desecrated his Temple. ¹²Prepare your defenses, Babylon! Set many watchmen on your walls; send out an ambush, for the Lord will do all he has said he would concerning Babylon. ¹³O wealthy port, great center of commerce, your end has come; the thread of your life is cut. ¹⁴The Lord Almighty has taken this vow, and sworn to it in his own name: Your cities shall be filled with enemies, like fields filled with locusts in a plague, and they shall lift to the skies their mighty shouts of victory.

New Revised Standard

51 THUS SAYS the LORD:
I am going to stir up a destructive wind^f
    against Babylon
    and against the inhabitants of Leb-qamai;^g
2 and I will send winnowers to Babylon,
    and they shall winnow her.
They shall empty her land
    when they come against her from every side
    on the day of trouble.
3 Let not the archer bend his bow,
    and let him not array himself in his coat of
        mail.
Do not spare her young men;
    utterly destroy her entire army.
4 They shall fall down slain in the land of the
        Chaldeans,
    and wounded in her streets.
5 Israel and Judah have not been forsaken
    by their God, the LORD of hosts,
though their land is full of guilt
    before the Holy One of Israel.

6 Flee from the midst of Babylon,
    save your lives, each of you!
Do not perish because of her guilt,
    for this is the time of the LORD's
        vengeance;
    he is repaying her what is due.
7 Babylon was a golden cup in the LORD's
        hand,
    making all the earth drunken;
the nations drank of her wine,
    and so the nations went mad.
8 Suddenly Babylon has fallen and is shattered;
    wail for her!
Bring balm for her wound;
    perhaps she may be healed.
9 We tried to heal Babylon,
    but she could not be healed.
Forsake her, and let each of us go
    to our own country;
for her judgment has reached up to heaven
    and has been lifted up even to the skies.
10 The LORD has brought forth our vindication;
    come, let us declare in Zion
    the work of the LORD our God.

11 Sharpen the arrows!
    Fill the quivers!
The LORD has stirred up the spirit of the kings of the Medes, because his purpose concerning Babylon is to destroy it, for that is the vengeance of the LORD, vengeance for his temple.
12 Raise a standard against the walls of Babylon;
    make the watch strong;
post sentinels;
    prepare the ambushes;
    for the LORD has both planned and done
        what he spoke concerning the inhabitants of
            Babylon.
13 You who live by mighty waters,
    rich in treasures,
your end has come,
    the thread of your life is cut.
14 The LORD of hosts has sworn by himself:
Surely I will fill you with troops like a swarm
        of locusts,
    and they shall raise a shout of victory over
        you.

---

^e 51:5 *the land of the Chaldeans,* implied.

^f Or *stir up the spirit of a destroyer*   ^g *Leb-qamai* is a cryptogram for *Kasdim,* Chaldea

King James

15He hath made the earth by his power, he hath established the world by his wisdom, and hath stretched out the heaven by his understanding.

16When he uttereth *his* voice, *there is* a multitude of waters in the heavens; and he causeth the vapours to ascend from the ends of the earth: he maketh lightnings with rain, and bringeth forth the wind out of his treasures.

17Every man is brutish by *his* knowledge; every founder is confounded by the graven image: for his molten image *is* falsehood, and *there is* no breath in them.

18They *are* vanity, the work of errors: in the time of their visitation they shall perish.

19The portion of Jacob *is* not like them; for he *is* the former of all things: and *Israel is* the rod of his inheritance: the LORD of hosts *is* his name.

20Thou *art* my battle axe *and* weapons of war: for with thee will I break in pieces the nations, and with thee will I destroy kingdoms;

21And with thee will I break in pieces the horse and his rider; and with thee will I break in pieces the chariot and his rider;

22With thee also will I break in pieces man and woman; and with thee will I break in pieces old and young; and with thee will I break in pieces the young man and the maid;

23I will also break in pieces with thee the shepherd and his flock; and with thee will I break in pieces the husbandman and his yoke of oxen; and with thee will I break in pieces captains and rulers.

24And I will render unto Babylon and to all the inhabitants of Chaldea all their evil that they have done in Zion in your sight, saith the LORD.

25Behold, I *am* against thee, O destroying mountain, saith the LORD, which destroyest all the earth: and I will stretch out mine hand upon thee, and roll thee down from the rocks, and will make thee a burnt mountain.

26And they shall not take of thee a stone for a corner, nor a stone for foundations; but thou shalt be desolate for ever, saith the LORD.

27Set ye up a standard in the land, blow the trumpet among the nations, prepare the nations against her, call together against her the kingdoms of Ararat, Minni, and Ashchenaz; appoint a captain against her; cause the horses to come up as the rough caterpillars.

28Prepare against her the nations with the kings of the Medes, the captains thereof, and all the rulers thereof, and all the land of his dominion.

29And the land shall tremble and sorrow: for every purpose of the LORD shall be performed against Babylon, to make the land of Babylon a desolation without an inhabitant.

New International

15"He made the earth by his power;
　　he founded the world by his wisdom
　　and stretched out the heavens by his
　　　understanding.
16When he thunders, the waters in the heavens
　　　roar;
　　he makes clouds rise from the ends of the
　　　earth.
He sends lightning with the rain
　　and brings out the wind from his storehouses.

17"Every man is senseless and without knowledge;
　　every goldsmith is shamed by his idols.
His images are a fraud;
　　they have no breath in them.
18They are worthless, the objects of mockery;
　　when their judgment comes, they will perish.
19He who is the Portion of Jacob is not like these,
　　for he is the Maker of all things,
including the tribe of his inheritance—
　　the LORD Almighty is his name.

20"You are my war club,
　　my weapon for battle—
with you I shatter nations,
　　with you I destroy kingdoms,
21with you I shatter horse and rider,
　　with you I shatter chariot and driver,
22with you I shatter man and woman,
　　with you I shatter old man and youth,
　　with you I shatter young man and maiden,
23with you I shatter shepherd and flock,
　　with you I shatter farmer and oxen,
　　with you I shatter governors and officials.

24"Before your eyes I will repay Babylon and all who live in Babylonia[a] for all the wrong they have done in Zion," declares the LORD.

25"I am against you, O destroying mountain,
　　you who destroy the whole earth,"
　　　　　　　　　　　　declares the LORD.
"I will stretch out my hand against you,
　　roll you off the cliffs,
　　and make you a burned-out mountain.
26No rock will be taken from you for a
　　　cornerstone,
　　nor any stone for a foundation,
　　for you will be desolate forever,"
　　　　　　　　　　　　declares the LORD.

27"Lift up a banner in the land!
　　Blow the trumpet among the nations!
Prepare the nations for battle against her;
　　summon against her these kingdoms:
　　Ararat, Minni and Ashkenaz.
Appoint a commander against her;
　　send up horses like a swarm of locusts.
28Prepare the nations for battle against her—
　　the kings of the Medes,
their governors and all their officials,
　　and all the countries they rule.
29The land trembles and writhes,
　　for the LORD's purposes against Babylon
　　　stand—
to lay waste the land of Babylon
　　so that no one will live there.

Living Bible

15God made the earth by his power and wisdom. He stretched out the heavens by his understanding. 16When he speaks there is thunder in the heavens and he causes the vapors to rise around the world; he brings the lightning with the rain and the winds from his treasuries. 17Compared to him, all men are stupid beasts. They have no wisdom—none at all! The silversmith is dulled by the images he makes, for in making them he lies; for he calls them gods, when there is not a breath of life in them at all! 18Idols are nothing! They are lies! And the time is coming when God will come and see, and shall destroy them all. 19But the God of Israel is no idol! For he made everything there is, and Israel is his nation; the Lord Almighty is his name.

20Cyrusb is God's battleaxe and sword. I will use you, says the Lord, to break nations in pieces and to destroy many kingdoms. 21With you I will crush armies, destroying the horse and his rider, the chariot and the charioteer— 22yes, and the civilians too, both old and young, young men and maidens, 23shepherds and flocks, farmers and oxen, captains and rulers; 24before your eyes I will repay Babylon and all the Chaldeans for all the evil they have done to my people, says the Lord.

25For see, I am against you, O mighty mountain, Babylon, destroyer of the earth! I will lift my hand against you and roll you down from your heights and leave you, a burnt-out mountain. 26You shall be desolate forever;c even your stones shall never be used for building again. You shall be completely wiped out.

27Signal many nations to mobilize for war on Babylon. Sound the battle cry; bring out the armies of Ararat, Minni, and Ashkenaz. Appoint a leader; bring a multitude of horses! 28Bring against her the armies of the kings of the Medes and their generals, and the armies of all the countries they rule.

29Babylon trembles and writhes in pain, for all that the Lord has planned against her stands unchanged. Babylon will be left desolate without a living soul. 30Her

New Revised Standard

15 It is he who made the earth by his power,
  who established the world by his wisdom,
and by his understanding stretched out the
  heavens.
16 When he utters his voice there is a tumult of
  waters in the heavens,
  and he makes the mist rise from the ends of
  the earth.
He makes lightnings for the rain,
  and he brings out the wind from his
  storehouses.
17 Everyone is stupid and without knowledge;
  goldsmiths are all put to shame by their
  idols;
for their images are false,
  and there is no breath in them.
18 They are worthless, a work of delusion;
  at the time of their punishment they shall
  perish.
19 Not like these is the LORD,d the portion of
  Jacob,
  for he is the one who formed all things,
and Israel is the tribe of his inheritance;
  the LORD of hosts is his name.

Israel the Creator's Instrument

20 You are my war club, my weapon of battle:
  with you I smash nations;
  with you I destroy kingdoms;
21 with you I smash the horse and its rider;
  with you I smash the chariot and the
  charioteer;
22 with you I smash man and woman;
  with you I smash the old man and the boy;
  with you I smash the young man and the girl;
23 with you I smash shepherds and their flocks;
  with you I smash farmers and their teams;
  with you I smash governors and deputies.

The Doom of Babylon

24 I will repay Babylon and all the inhabitants of Chaldea before your very eyes for all the wrong that they have done in Zion, says the LORD.

25 I am against you, O destroying mountain,
                    says the LORD,
  that destroys the whole earth;
I will stretch out my hand against you,
  and roll you down from the crags,
  and make you a burned-out mountain.
26 No stone shall be taken from you for a corner
  and no stone for a foundation,
but you shall be a perpetual waste,
  says the LORD.

27 Raise a standard in the land,
  blow the trumpet among the nations;
prepare the nations for war against her,
  summon against her the kingdoms,
  Ararat, Minni, and Ashkenaz;
appoint a marshal against her,
  bring up horses like bristling locusts.
28 Prepare the nations for war against her,
  the kings of the Medes, with their governors
  and deputies,
  and every land under their dominion.
29 The land trembles and writhes,
  for the LORD's purposes against Babylon
  stand,
to make the land of Babylon a desolation,
  without inhabitant.

b 51:20 Cyrus, literally, "You are . . ." Cyrus was used of God to conquer Babylon. See also Isa 44:28; 45:1.   c 51:26 You shall be desolate forever. This complete destruction of the city of Babylon was accomplished by later Persian kings. Jeremiah here sees the long-range picture of the city's history, and does not confine himself to Cyrus.

d Heb lacks the LORD

King James

30The mighty men of Babylon have forborne to fight, they have remained in *their* holds: their might hath failed; they became as women: they have burned her dwellingplaces; her bars are broken.

31One post shall run to meet another, and one messenger to meet another, to show the king of Babylon that his city is taken at *one* end,

32And that the passages are stopped, and the reeds they have burned with fire, and the men of war are affrighted.

33For thus saith the LORD of hosts, the God of Israel; The daughter of Babylon *is* like a threshingfloor, *it is* time to thresh her: yet a little while, and the time of her harvest shall come.

34Nebuchadrezzar the king of Babylon hath devoured me, he hath crushed me, he hath made me an empty vessel, he hath swallowed me up like a dragon, he hath filled his belly with my delicates, he hath cast me out.

35The violence done to me and to my flesh *be* upon Babylon, shall the inhabitant of Zion say; and my blood upon the inhabitants of Chaldea, shall Jerusalem say.

36Therefore thus saith the LORD; Behold, I will plead thy cause, and take vengeance for thee; and I will dry up her sea, and make her springs dry.

37And Babylon shall become heaps, a dwellingplace for dragons, an astonishment, and an hissing, without an inhabitant.

38They shall roar together like lions: they shall yell as lions' whelps.

39In their heat I will make their feasts, and I will make them drunken, that they may rejoice, and sleep a perpetual sleep, and not wake, saith the LORD.

40I will bring them down like lambs to the slaughter, like rams with he goats.

41How is Sheshach taken! and how is the praise of the whole earth surprised! how is Babylon become an astonishment among the nations!

42The sea is come up upon Babylon: she is covered with the multitude of the waves thereof.

43Her cities are a desolation, a dry land, and a wilderness, a land wherein no man dwelleth, neither doth *any* son of man pass thereby.

44And I will punish Bel in Babylon, and I will bring forth out of his mouth that which he hath swallowed up: and the nations shall not flow together any more unto him: yea, the wall of Babylon shall fall.

New International

30Babylon's warriors have stopped fighting;
 they remain in their strongholds.
Their strength is exhausted;
 they have become like women.
Her dwellings are set on fire;
 the bars of her gates are broken.
31One courier follows another
 and messenger follows messenger
to announce to the king of Babylon
 that his entire city is captured,
32the river crossings seized,
 the marshes set on fire,
 and the soldiers terrified."

33This is what the LORD Almighty, the God of Israel, says:

"The Daughter of Babylon is like a threshing floor
 at the time it is trampled;
 the time to harvest her will soon come."

34"Nebuchadnezzar king of Babylon has devoured us,
 he has thrown us into confusion,
 he has made us an empty jar.
Like a serpent he has swallowed us
 and filled his stomach with our delicacies,
 and then has spewed us out.
35May the violence done to our flesh[a] be upon Babylon,"
 say the inhabitants of Zion.
"May our blood be on those who live in Babylonia,"
 says Jerusalem.

36Therefore, this is what the LORD says:

"See, I will defend your cause
 and avenge you;
I will dry up her sea
 and make her springs dry.
37Babylon will be a heap of ruins,
 a haunt of jackals,
an object of horror and scorn,
 a place where no one lives.
38Her people all roar like young lions,
 they growl like lion cubs.
39But while they are aroused,
 I will set out a feast for them
 and make them drunk,
so that they shout with laughter—
 then sleep forever and not awake,"
                 declares the LORD.
40"I will bring them down
 like lambs to the slaughter,
 like rams and goats.

41"How Sheshach[b] will be captured,
 the boast of the whole earth seized!
What a horror Babylon will be
 among the nations!
42The sea will rise over Babylon;
 its roaring waves will cover her.
43Her towns will be desolate,
 a dry and desert land,
a land where no one lives,
 through which no man travels.
44I will punish Bel in Babylon
 and make him spew out what he has swallowed.
The nations will no longer stream to him.
And the wall of Babylon will fall.

---

a 35 Or *done to us and to our children*   b 41 *Sheshach* is a cryptogram for Babylon.

Living Bible

mightiest soldiers no longer fight; they stay in their barracks. Their courage is gone; they have become as women. The invaders have burned the houses and broken down the city gates. 31Messengers from every side come running to the king to tell him all is lost! 32All the escape routes are blocked; the fortifications are burning and the army is in panic.

33For the Lord, the God of Israel, says: Babylon is like the wheat upon a threshing floor; in just a little while the flailing will begin.

34, 35The Jews in Babylon say, "Nebuchadnezzar, king of Babylon, has eaten and crushed us and emptied out our strength; he has swallowed us like a great monster and filled his belly with our riches and cast us out of our own country. May Babylon be repaid for all she did to us! May she be paid in full for all our blood she spilled!"

36And the Lord replies: I will be your lawyer; I will plead your case; I will avenge you. I will dry up her river, her water supply, 37and Babylon shall become a heap of ruins, haunted by jackals, a land horrible to see, incredible, without a living soul. 38In their drunken feasts, the men of Babylon roar like lions. 39And while they lie inflamed with all their wine, I will prepare a different kind of feast for them, and make them drink until they fall unconscious to the floor, to sleep forever, never to waken again, says the Lord. 40I will bring them like lambs to the slaughter, like rams and goats.

41How Babylon is fallen—great Babylon, lauded by all the earth! The world can scarcely believe its eyes at Babylon's fall! 42The sea has risen upon Babylon; she is covered by its waves. 43Her cities lie in ruins—she is a dry wilderness where no one lives nor even travelers pass by. 44And I will punish Bel, the god of Babylon, and pull from his mouth what he has taken. The nations shall no longer come and worship him; the wall of Babylon has fallen.

New Revised Standard

30 The warriors of Babylon have given up
      fighting,
   they remain in their strongholds;
their strength has failed,
   they have become women;
her buildings are set on fire,
   her bars are broken.
31 One runner runs to meet another,
   and one messenger to meet another,
to tell the king of Babylon
   that his city is taken from end to end:
32 the fords have been seized,
   the marshes have been burned with fire,
   and the soldiers are in panic.
33 For thus says the LORD of hosts, the God of
      Israel:
Daughter Babylon is like a threshing floor
   at the time when it is trodden;
yet a little while
   and the time of her harvest will come.

34 "King Nebuchadrezzar of Babylon has
      devoured me,
   he has crushed me;
he has made me an empty vessel,
   he has swallowed me like a monster;
he has filled his belly with my delicacies,
   he has spewed me out.
35 May my torn flesh be avenged on Babylon,"
   the inhabitants of Zion shall say.
"May my blood be avenged on the inhabitants
   of Chaldea,"
   Jerusalem shall say.
36 Therefore thus says the LORD:
I am going to defend your cause
   and take vengeance for you.
I will dry up her sea
   and make her fountain dry;
37 and Babylon shall become a heap of ruins,
   a den of jackals,
an object of horror and of hissing,
   without inhabitant.

38 Like lions they shall roar together;
   they shall growl like lions' whelps.
39 When they are inflamed, I will set out their
      drink
   and make them drunk, until they become
      merry
and then sleep a perpetual sleep
   and never wake, says the LORD.
40 I will bring them down like lambs to the
      slaughter,
   like rams and goats.

41 How Sheshach[c] is taken,
   the pride of the whole earth seized!
How Babylon has become
   an object of horror among the nations!
42 The sea has risen over Babylon;
   she has been covered by its tumultuous
      waves.
43 Her cities have become an object of horror,
   a land of drought and a desert,
a land in which no one lives,
   and through which no mortal passes.
44 I will punish Bel in Babylon,
   and make him disgorge what he has
      swallowed.
The nations shall no longer stream to him;
   the wall of Babylon has fallen.

c Sheshach is a cryptogram for Babel, Babylon

King James

45My people, go ye out of the midst of her, and deliver ye every man his soul from the fierce anger of the LORD.

46And lest your heart faint, and ye fear for the rumour that shall be heard in the land; a rumour shall both come *one* year, and after that in *another* year *shall come* a rumour, and violence in the land, ruler against ruler.

47Therefore, behold, the days come, that I will do judgment upon the graven images of Babylon: and her whole land shall be confounded, and all her slain shall fall in the midst of her.

48Then the heaven and the earth, and all that *is* therein, shall sing for Babylon: for the spoilers shall come unto her from the north, saith the LORD.

49As Babylon *hath caused* the slain of Israel to fall, so at Babylon shall fall the slain of all the earth.

50Ye that have escaped the sword, go away, stand not still: remember the LORD afar off, and let Jerusalem come into your mind.

51We are confounded, because we have heard reproach: shame hath covered our faces: for strangers are come into the sanctuaries of the LORD's house.

52Wherefore, behold, the days come, saith the LORD, that I will do judgment upon her graven images: and through all her land the wounded shall groan.

53Though Babylon should mount up to heaven, and though she should fortify the height of her strength, *yet* from me shall spoilers come unto her, saith the LORD.

54A sound of a cry *cometh* from Babylon, and great destruction from the land of the Chaldeans:

55Because the LORD hath spoiled Babylon, and destroyed out of her the great voice; when her waves do roar like great waters, a noise of their voice is uttered:

56Because the spoiler is come upon her, *even* upon Babylon, and her mighty men are taken, every one of their bows is broken: for the LORD God of recompences shall surely requite.

57And I will make drunk her princes, and her wise *men*, her captains, and her rulers, and her mighty men: and they shall sleep a perpetual sleep, and not wake, saith the King, whose name *is* the LORD of hosts.

New International

45"Come out of her, my people!
  Run for your lives!
  Run from the fierce anger of the LORD.
46Do not lose heart or be afraid
  when rumors are heard in the land;
one rumor comes this year, another the next,
  rumors of violence in the land
  and of ruler against ruler.
47For the time will surely come
  when I will punish the idols of Babylon;
her whole land will be disgraced
  and her slain will all lie fallen within her.
48Then heaven and earth and all that is in them
  will shout for joy over Babylon,
for out of the north
  destroyers will attack her,"
                    declares the LORD.

49"Babylon must fall because of Israel's slain,
  just as the slain in all the earth
  have fallen because of Babylon.
50You who have escaped the sword,
  leave and do not linger!
Remember the LORD in a distant land,
  and think on Jerusalem."

51"We are disgraced,
  for we have been insulted
  and shame covers our faces,
because foreigners have entered
  the holy places of the LORD's house."

52"But days are coming," declares the LORD,
  "when I will punish her idols,
and throughout her land
  the wounded will groan.
53Even if Babylon reaches the sky
  and fortifies her lofty stronghold,
  I will send destroyers against her,"
                    declares the LORD.

54"The sound of a cry comes from Babylon,
  the sound of great destruction
  from the land of the Babylonians.ᵃ
55The LORD will destroy Babylon;
  he will silence her noisy din.
Waves of enemies will rage like great waters;
  the roar of their voices will resound.
56A destroyer will come against Babylon;
  her warriors will be captured,
  and their bows will be broken.
For the LORD is a God of retribution;
  he will repay in full.
57I will make her officials and wise men drunk,
  her governors, officers and warriors as well;
they will sleep forever and not awake,"
  declares the King, whose name is the LORD
  Almighty.

Living Bible

45O my people, flee from Babylon; save yourselves from the fierce anger of the Lord. 46But don't panic when you hear the first rumor of approaching forces. For rumors will keep coming year by year. Then there will be a time of civil war as the governors of Babylon fight against each other. 47For the time is surely coming when I will punish this great city and all her idols; her dead shall lie in the streets. 48Heaven and earth shall rejoice, for out of the north shall come destroying armies against Babylon, says the Lord. 49Just as Babylon killed the people of Israel, so must she be killed. 50Go, you who escaped the sword! Don't stand and watch—flee while you can! Remember the Lord and return to Jerusalem far away!

51*"We are ashamed because the Temple of the Lord has been defiled by foreigners from Babylon."*

52Yes, says the Lord. But the time is coming for the destruction of the idols of Babylon. All through the land will be heard the groans of the wounded. 53Though Babylon be as powerful as heaven, though she increase her strength immeasurably, she shall die, says the Lord.

54Listen! Hear the cry of great destruction out of Babylon, the land the Chaldeans rule! 55For the Lord is destroying Babylon; her mighty voice is stilled as the waves roar in upon her. 56Destroying armies come and slay her mighty men; all her weapons break in her hands, for the Lord God gives just punishment and is giving Babylon all her due. 57I will make drunk her princes, wise men, rulers, captains, warriors. They shall sleep and not wake up again! So says the King, the Lord Almighty. 58For the wide walls of Babylon shall be lev-

New Revised Standard

45 Come out of her, my people!
    Save your lives, each of you,
      from the fierce anger of the LORD!
46 Do not be fainthearted or fearful
    at the rumors heard in the land—
  one year one rumor comes,
    the next year another,
rumors of violence in the land
    and of ruler against ruler.

47 Assuredly, the days are coming
    when I will punish the images of Babylon;
    her whole land shall be put to shame,
      and all her slain shall fall in her midst.
48 Then the heavens and the earth,
    and all that is in them,
shall shout for joy over Babylon;
    for the destroyers shall come against them
      out of the north,
           says the LORD.
49 Babylon must fall for the slain of Israel,
    as the slain of all the earth have fallen
      because of Babylon.

50 You survivors of the sword,
    go, do not linger!
Remember the LORD in a distant land,
    and let Jerusalem come into your mind:
51 We are put to shame, for we have heard
      insults;
    dishonor has covered our face,
for aliens have come
    into the holy places of the LORD's house.

52 Therefore the time is surely coming, says the
    LORD,
    when I will punish her idols,
and through all her land
    the wounded shall groan.
53 Though Babylon should mount up to heaven,
    and though she should fortify her strong
      height,
from me destroyers would come upon her,
    says the LORD.

54 Listen!—a cry from Babylon!
    A great crashing from the land of the
      Chaldeans!
55 For the LORD is laying Babylon waste,
    and stilling her loud clamor.
Their waves roar like mighty waters,
    the sound of their clamor resounds;
56 for a destroyer has come against her,
    against Babylon;
her warriors are taken,
    their bows are broken;
for the LORD is a God of recompense,
    he will repay in full.
57 I will make her officials and her sages drunk,
    also her governors, her deputies, and her
      warriors;
they shall sleep a perpetual sleep and never
      wake,
    says the King, whose name is the LORD of
      hosts.

King James

58Thus saith the LORD of hosts; The broad walls of Babylon shall be utterly broken, and her high gates shall be burned with fire; and the people shall labour in vain, and the folk in the fire, and they shall be weary.

59¶ The word which Jeremiah the prophet commanded Seraiah the son of Neriah, the son of Maaseiah, when he went with Zedekiah the king of Judah into Babylon in the fourth year of his reign. And *this* Seraiah *was* a quiet prince.

60So Jeremiah wrote in a book all the evil that should come upon Babylon, *even* all these words that are written against Babylon.

61And Jeremiah said to Seraiah, When thou comest to Babylon, and shalt see, and shalt read all these words;

62Then shalt thou say, O LORD, thou hast spoken against this place, to cut it off, that none shall remain in it, neither man nor beast, but that it shall be desolate for ever.

63And it shall be, when thou hast made an end of reading this book, *that* thou shalt bind a stone to it, and cast it into the midst of Euphrates:

64And thou shalt say, Thus shall Babylon sink, and shall not rise from the evil that I will bring upon her: and they shall be weary. Thus far *are* the words of Jeremiah.

New International

58This is what the LORD Almighty says:

"Babylon's thick wall will be leveled
    and her high gates set on fire;
the peoples exhaust themselves for nothing,
    the nations' labor is only fuel for the flames."

59This is the message Jeremiah gave to the staff officer Seraiah son of Neriah, the son of Mahseiah, when he went to Babylon with Zedekiah king of Judah in the fourth year of his reign. 60Jeremiah had written on a scroll about all the disasters that would come upon Babylon—all that had been recorded concerning Babylon. 61He said to Seraiah, "When you get to Babylon, see that you read all these words aloud. 62Then say, 'O LORD, you have said you will destroy this place, so that neither man nor animal will live in it; it will be desolate forever.' 63When you finish reading this scroll, tie a stone to it and throw it into the Euphrates. 64Then say, 'So will Babylon sink to rise no more because of the disaster I will bring upon her. And her people will fall.' "

The words of Jeremiah end here.

---

52 ZEDEKIAH *WAS* one and twenty years old when he began to reign, and he reigned eleven years in Jerusalem. And his mother's name *was* Hamutal the daughter of Jeremiah of Libnah.

2And he did *that which was* evil in the eyes of the LORD, according to all that Jehoiakim had done.

3For through the anger of the LORD it came to pass in Jerusalem and Judah, till he had cast them out from his presence, that Zedekiah rebelled against the king of Babylon.

4¶ And it came to pass in the ninth year of his reign, in the tenth month, in the tenth *day* of the month, *that* Nebuchadrezzar king of Babylon came, he and all his army, against Jerusalem, and pitched against it, and built forts against it round about.

5So the city was besieged unto the eleventh year of king Zedekiah.

6And in the fourth month, in the ninth *day* of the month, the famine was sore in the city, so that there was no bread for the people of the land.

7Then the city was broken up, and all the men of war fled, and went forth out of the city by night by the way of the gate between the two walls, which *was* by the king's garden; (now the Chaldeans *were* by the city round about:) and they went by the way of the plain.

8¶ But the army of the Chaldeans pursued after the king, and overtook Zedekiah in the plains of Jericho; and all his army was scattered from him.

9Then they took the king, and carried him up unto the king of Babylon to Riblah in the land of Hamath; where he gave judgment upon him.

10And the king of Babylon slew the sons of Zedekiah before his eyes: he slew also all the princes of Judah in Riblah.

11Then he put out the eyes of Zedekiah; and the king of Babylon bound him in chains, and carried him to Babylon, and put him in prison till the day of his death.

12¶ Now in the fifth month, in the tenth *day* of the month, which *was* the nineteenth year of Nebuchadrezzar king of Babylon, came Nebuzar-adan, captain of the guard, *which* served the king of Babylon, into Jerusalem,

The Fall of Jerusalem

52 ZEDEKIAH WAS twenty-one years old when he became king, and he reigned in Jerusalem eleven years. His mother's name was Hamutal daughter of Jeremiah; she was from Libnah. 2He did evil in the eyes of the LORD, just as Jehoiakim had done. 3It was because of the LORD's anger that all this happened to Jerusalem and Judah, and in the end he thrust them from his presence.

Now Zedekiah rebelled against the king of Babylon.

4So in the ninth year of Zedekiah's reign, on the tenth day of the tenth month, Nebuchadnezzar king of Babylon marched against Jerusalem with his whole army. They camped outside the city and built siege works all around it. 5The city was kept under siege until the eleventh year of King Zedekiah.

6By the ninth day of the fourth month the famine in the city had become so severe that there was no food for the people to eat. 7Then the city wall was broken through, and the whole army fled. They left the city at night through the gate between the two walls near the king's garden, though the Babylonians[a] were surrounding the city. They fled toward the Arabah,[b] 8but the Babylonian[c] army pursued King Zedekiah and overtook him in the plains of Jericho. All his soldiers were separated from him and scattered, 9and he was captured.

He was taken to the king of Babylon at Riblah in the land of Hamath, where he pronounced sentence on him. 10There at Riblah the king of Babylon slaughtered the sons of Zedekiah before his eyes; he also killed all the officials of Judah. 11Then he put out Zedekiah's eyes, bound him with bronze shackles and took him to Babylon, where he put him in prison till the day of his death.

12On the tenth day of the fifth month, in the nineteenth year of Nebuchadnezzar king of Babylon, Nebuzaradan commander of the imperial guard, who served the king of Babylon, came to Jerusalem. 13He set fire to

---

a 7 Or *Chaldeans*; also in verse 17   b 7 Or *the Jordan Valley*   c 8 Or *Chaldean*; also in verse 14

Living Bible

eled to the ground and her high gates shall be burned; the builders from many lands have worked in vain— their work shall be destroyed by fire!

59During the fourth year of Zedekiah's reign, this message came to Jeremiah to give to Seraiah (son of Neriah, son of Mahseiah), concerning Seraiah's captured and exile to Babylon along with Zedekiah, king of Judah. (Seraiah was quartermaster of Zedekiah's army.) 60Jeremiah wrote on a scroll all the terrible things God had scheduled against Babylon—all the words written above— 61, 62and gave the scroll to Seraiah and said to him, "When you get to Babylon, read what I have written and say, 'Lord, you have said that you will destroy Babylon so that not a living creature will remain, and it will be abandoned forever.' 63Then, when you have finished reading the scroll, tie a rock to it and throw it into the Euphrates River, 64and say, 'So shall Babylon sink, never more to rise, because of the evil I am bringing upon her.' "

(This ends Jeremiah's messages.)

(Events told about in chapter 39.)

52 ZEDEKIAH WAS twenty-one years old when he became king, and he reigned eleven years in Jerusalem. His mother's name was Hamutal (daughter of Jeremiah of Libnah). 2But he was a wicked king, just as Jehoiakim had been. 3Things became so bad at last that the Lord, in his anger, saw to it that Zedekiah rebelled against the king of Babylon until he and the people of Israel were ejected from the Lord's presence in Jerusalem and Judah, and were taken away as captives to Babylon.

4In the ninth year of Zedekiah's reign, on the tenth day of the tenth month, Nebuchadnezzar, king of Babylon, came with all his army against Jerusalem and built forts around it, 5and laid siege to the city for two years. 6Then finally, on the ninth day of the fourth month, when the famine in the city was very serious, with the last of the food entirely gone, 7the people in the city tore a hole in the city wall and all the soldiers fled from the city during the night, going out by the gate between the two walls near the king's gardens (for the city was surrounded by the Chaldeans), and made a dash for it across the fields, toward Arabah.

8But the Chaldean soldiers chased them and caught King Zedekiah in some fields near Jericho—for all his army was scattered from him. 9They brought him to the king of Babylon who was staying in the city of Riblah in the kingdom of Hamath, and there judgment was passed upon him. 10He made Zedekiah watch while his sons and all the princes of Judah were killed before his eyes, 11and then his eyes were gouged out and he was taken in chains to Babylon and put in prison for the rest of his life.

12On the tenth day of the fifth month during the nineteenth yearc of the reign of Nebuchadnezzar, king of Babylon, Nebuzaradan, captain of the guard, arrived in Jerusalem, 13and burned the Temple and the palace and

New Revised Standard

58 Thus says the LORD of hosts:
The broad wall of Babylon
    shall be leveled to the ground,
and her high gates
    shall be burned with fire.
The peoples exhaust themselves for nothing,
    and the nations weary themselves only for
    fire.f

Jeremiah's Command to Seraiah

59 The word that the prophet Jeremiah commanded Seraiah son of Neriah son of Mahseiah, when he went with King Zedekiah of Judah to Babylon, in the fourth year of his reign. Seraiah was the quartermaster. 60Jeremiah wrote in ag scroll all the disasters that would come on Babylon, all these words that are written concerning Babylon. 61And Jeremiah said to Seraiah: "When you come to Babylon, see that you read all these words, 62and say, 'O LORD, you yourself threatened to destroy this place so that neither human beings nor animals shall live in it, and it shall be desolate forever.' 63When you finish reading this scroll, tie a stone to it, and throw it into the middle of the Euphrates, 64and say, 'Thus shall Babylon sink, to rise no more, because of the disasters that I am bringing on her.' "h

Thus far are the words of Jeremiah.

The Destruction of Jerusalem Reviewed

52 ZEDEKIAH WAS twenty-one years old when he began to reign; he reigned eleven years in Jerusalem. His mother's name was Hamutal daughter of Jeremiah of Libnah. 2He did what was evil in the sight of the LORD, just as Jehoiakim had done. 3Indeed, Jerusalem and Judah so angered the LORD that he expelled them from his presence.

Zedekiah rebelled against the king of Babylon. 4And in the ninth year of his reign, in the tenth month, on the tenth day of the month, King Nebuchadrezzar of Babylon came with all his army against Jerusalem, and they laid siege to it; they built siegeworks against it all around. 5So the city was besieged until the eleventh year of King Zedekiah. 6On the ninth day of the fourth month the famine became so severe in the city that there was no food for the people of the land. 7Then a breach was made in the city wall;i and all the soldiers fled and went out from the city by night by the way of the gate between the two walls, by the king's garden, though the Chaldeans were all around the city. They went in the direction of the Arabah. 8But the army of the Chaldeans pursued the king, and overtook Zedekiah in the plains of Jericho; and all his army was scattered, deserting him. 9Then they captured the king, and brought him up to the king of Babylon at Riblah in the land of Hamath, and he passed sentence on him. 10The king of Babylon killed the sons of Zedekiah before his eyes, and also killed all the officers of Judah at Riblah. 11He put out the eyes of Zedekiah, and bound him in fetters, and the king of Babylon took him to Babylon, and put him in prison until the day of his death.

12 In the fifth month, on the tenth day of the month—which was the nineteenth year of King Nebuchadrezzar, king of Babylon—Nebuzaradan the captain of the bodyguard who served the king of Babylon, entered Jerusalem. 13He burned the house of the LORD, the

---

d 51:59 concerning Seraiah's capture. This event occurred six years after this prophecy.   c 52:12 the nineteenth year, late in July, 587 B.C.

f Gk Syr Compare Hab 2.13: Heb and the nations for fire, and they are weary   g Or one   h Gk: Heb on her. And they shall weary themselves   i Heb lacks wall

King James

13And burned the house of the LORD, and the king's house; and all the houses of Jerusalem, and all the houses of the great *men,* burned he with fire:

14And all the army of the Chaldeans, that *were* with the captain of the guard, brake down all the walls of Jerusalem round about.

15Then Nebuzar-adan the captain of the guard carried away captive *certain* of the poor of the people, and the residue of the people that remained in the city, and those that fell away, that fell to the king of Babylon, and the rest of the multitude.

16But Nebuzar-adan the captain of the guard left *certain* of the poor of the land for vinedressers and for husbandmen.

17Also the pillars of brass that *were* in the house of the LORD, and the bases, and the brasen sea that *was* in the house of the LORD, the Chaldeans brake, and carried all the brass of them to Babylon.

18The caldrons also, and the shovels, and the snuffers, and the bowls, and the spoons, and all the vessels of brass wherewith they ministered, took they away.

19And the basins, and the firepans, and the bowls, and the caldrons, and the candlesticks, and the spoons, and the cups; *that* which *was* of gold *in* gold, and *that* which *was* of silver *in* silver, took the captain of the guard away.

20The two pillars, one sea, and twelve brasen bulls that *were* under the bases, which king Solomon had made in the house of the LORD: the brass of all these vessels was without weight.

21And *concerning* the pillars, the height of one pillar *was* eighteen cubits; and a fillet of twelve cubits did compass it; and the thickness thereof *was* four fingers: *it was* hollow.

22And a chapiter of brass *was* upon it; and the height of one chapiter *was* five cubits, with network and pomegranates upon the chapiters round about, all *of* brass. The second pillar also and the pomegranates *were* like unto these.

23And there were ninety and six pomegranates on a side; *and* all the pomegranates upon the network *were* an hundred round about.

24¶ And the captain of the guard took Seraiah the chief priest, and Zephaniah the second priest, and the three keepers of the door:

25He took also out of the city an eunuch, which had the charge of the men of war; and seven men of them that were near the king's person, which were found in the city; and the principal scribe of the host, who mustered the people of the land; and threescore men of the people of the land, that were found in the midst of the city.

26So Nebuzar-adan the captain of the guard took them, and brought them to the king of Babylon to Riblah.

27And the king of Babylon smote them, and put them to death in Riblah in the land of Hamath. Thus Judah was carried away captive out of his own land.

28This *is* the people whom Nebuchadrezzar carried away captive: in the seventh year three thousand Jews and three and twenty:

29In the eighteenth year of Nebuchadrezzar he carried away captive from Jerusalem eight hundred thirty and two persons:

30In the three and twentieth year of Nebuchadrezzar Nebuzar-adan the captain of the guard carried away captive of the Jews seven hundred forty and five persons: all the persons *were* four thousand and six hundred.

31¶ And it came to pass in the seven and thirtieth year of the captivity of Jehoiachin king of Judah, in the twelfth month, in the five and twentieth *day* of the month, *that* Evil-merodach king of Babylon in the *first* year of his reign lifted up the head of Jehoiachin king of Judah, and brought him forth out of prison,

New International

the temple of the LORD, the royal palace and all the houses of Jerusalem. Every important building he burned down. 14The whole Babylonian army under the commander of the imperial guard broke down all the walls around Jerusalem. 15Nebuzaradan the commander of the guard carried into exile some of the poorest people and those who remained in the city, along with the rest of the craftsmena and those who had gone over to the king of Babylon. 16But Nebuzaradan left behind the rest of the poorest people of the land to work the vineyards and fields.

17The Babylonians broke up the bronze pillars, the movable stands and the bronze Sea that were at the temple of the LORD and they carried all the bronze to Babylon. 18They also took away the pots, shovels, wick trimmers, sprinkling bowls, dishes and all the bronze articles used in the temple service. 19The commander of the imperial guard took away the basins, censers, sprinkling bowls, pots, lampstands, dishes and bowls used for drink offerings—all that were made of pure gold or silver.

20The bronze from the two pillars, the Sea and the twelve bronze bulls under it, and the movable stands, which King Solomon had made for the temple of the LORD, was more than could be weighed. 21Each of the pillars was eighteen cubits high and twelve cubits in circumferenceb; each was four fingers thick, and hollow. 22The bronze capital on top of the one pillar was five cubitsc high and was decorated with a network and pomegranates of bronze all around. The other pillar, with its pomegranates, was similar. 23There were ninety-six pomegranates on the sides; the total number of pomegranates above the surrounding network was a hundred.

24The commander of the guard took as prisoners Seraiah the chief priest, Zephaniah the priest next in rank and the three doorkeepers. 25Of those still in the city, he took the officer in charge of the fighting men, and seven royal advisers. He also took the secretary who was chief officer in charge of conscripting the people of the land and sixty of his men who were found in the city. 26Nebuzaradan the commander took them all and brought them to the king of Babylon at Riblah. 27There at Riblah, in the land of Hamath, the king had them executed.

So Judah went into captivity, away from her land. 28This is the number of the people Nebuchadnezzar carried into exile:

in the seventh year, 3,023 Jews;
29in Nebuchadnezzar's eighteenth year,
    832 people from Jerusalem;
30in his twenty-third year,
    745 Jews taken into exile by Nebuzaradan the commander of the imperial guard.
There were 4,600 people in all.

Jehoiachin Released

31In the thirty-seventh year of the exile of Jehoiachin king of Judah, in the year Evil-Merodachd became king of Babylon, he released Jehoiachin king of Judah and freed him from prison on the twenty-fifth day of the twelfth month. 32He spoke kindly to him and gave him

---

a *15* Or *populace*   b *21* That is, about 27 feet (about 8.1 meters) high and 18 feet (about 5.4 meters) in circumference   c *22* That is, about 7 1/2 feet (about 2.3 meters)   d *31* Also called *Amel-Marduk*

Living Bible

all the larger homes, 14and set the Chaldean army to work tearing down the walls of the city. 15Then he took to Babylon, as captives, some of the poorest of the people—along with those who survived the city's destruction, and those who had deserted Zedekiah and had come over to the Babylonian army, and the tradesmen who were left. 16But he left some of the poorest people to care for the crops as vinedressers and plowmen.

17The Babylonians dismantled the two large bronze pillars that stood at the entrance of the Temple, and the bronze laver and bronze bulls on which it stood, and carted them off to Babylon. 18And he took along all the bronze pots and kettles, and ash shovels used at the altar, and the snuffers, spoons, bowls, and all the other items used in the Temple. 19He also took the firepans and the solid gold and silver candlesticks and cups and bowls.

20The weight of the two enormous pillars and the laver and twelve bulls was tremendous. They had no way of estimating it. (They had been made in the days of King Solomon.) 21For the pillars were each twenty-seven feet high and eighteen feet in circumference, hollow, with three-inch walls. 22The top 7½ feet of each column had bronze carvings, a network of bronze pomegranates. 23There were ninety-six pomegranates on the sides, and on the network round about there were a hundred more.

24, 25The captain of the guard took along with him, as his prisoners, Seraiah the chief priest, and Zephaniah his assistant, the three chief Temple guards, one of the commanding officers of the army, seven of the king's special counselors discovered in the city, and the secretary of the general-in-chief of the Jewish army (who was in charge of recruitment) and sixty other men of importance found hiding. 26He took them to the king of Babylon at Riblah, 27where the king killed them all.

So it was that Judah's exile was accomplished.

28The number of captives taken to Babylon in the seventh year of Nebuchadnezzar's reign was 3,023. 29Then, eleven years later, he took 832 more; 30five years after that he sent Nebuzaradan, his captain of the guard, and took 745—a total of 4,600 captives in all.

31On February 25, of the 37th year of the imprisonment in Babylon of Jehoiachin, king of Judah, Evil-merodach, who became king of Babylon that year, was kind to King Jehoiachin and brought him out of prison,

New Revised Standard

king's house, and all the houses of Jerusalem; every great house he burned down. 14All the army of the Chaldeans, who were with the captain of the guard, broke down all the walls around Jerusalem. 15Nebuzaradan the captain of the guard carried into exile some of the poorest of the people and the rest of the people who were left in the city and the deserters who had defected to the king of Babylon, together with the rest of the artisans. 16But Nebuzaradan the captain of the guard left some of the poorest people of the land to be vinedressers and tillers of the soil.

17 The pillars of bronze that were in the house of the LORD, and the stands and the bronze sea that were in the house of the LORD, the Chaldeans broke in pieces, and carried all the bronze to Babylon. 18They took away the pots, the shovels, the snuffers, the basins, the ladles, and all the vessels of bronze used in the temple service. 19The captain of the guard took away the small bowls also, the firepans, the basins, the pots, the lampstands, the ladles, and the bowls for libation, both those of gold and those of silver. 20As for the two pillars, the one sea, the twelve bronze bulls that were under the sea, and the stands,e which King Solomon had made for the house of the LORD, the bronze of all these vessels was beyond weighing. 21As for the pillars, the height of the one pillar was eighteen cubits, its circumference was twelve cubits; it was hollow and its thickness was four fingers. 22Upon it was a capital of bronze; the height of the one capital was five cubits; latticework and pomegranates, all of bronze, encircled the top of the capital. And the second pillar had the same, with pomegranates. 23There were ninety-six pomegranates on the sides; all the pomegranates encircling the latticework numbered one hundred.

24 The captain of the guard took the chief priest Seraiah, the second priest Zephaniah, and the three guardians of the threshold; 25and from the city he took an officer who had been in command of the soldiers, and seven men of the king's council who were found in the city; the secretary of the commander of the army who mustered the people of the land; and sixty men of the people of the land who were found inside the city. 26Then Nebuzaradan the captain of the guard took them, and brought them to the king of Babylon at Riblah. 27And the king of Babylon struck them down, and put them to death at Riblah in the land of Hamath. So Judah went into exile out of its land.

28 This is the number of the people whom Nebuchadrezzar took into exile: in the seventh year, three thousand twenty-three Judeans; 29in the eighteenth year of Nebuchadrezzar he took into exile from Jerusalem eight hundred thirty-two persons; 30in the twenty-third year of Nebuchadrezzar, Nebuzaradan the captain of the guard took into exile of the Judeans seven hundred forty-five persons; all the persons were four thousand six hundred.

Jehoiachin Favored in Captivity

31 In the thirty-seventh year of the exile of King Jehoiachin of Judah, in the twelfth month, on the twenty-fifth day of the month, King Evil-merodach of Babylon, in the year he began to reign, showed favor to King Jehoiachin of Judah and brought him out of prison;

---

e Cn: Heb *that were under the stands*

King James

32And spake kindly unto him, and set his throne above the throne of the kings that *were* with him in Babylon,

33And changed his prison garments: and he did continually eat bread before him all the days of his life.

34And *for* his diet, there was a continual diet given him of the king of Babylon, every day a portion until the day of his death, all the days of his life.

New International

a seat of honor higher than those of the other kings who were with him in Babylon. 33So Jehoiachin put aside his prison clothes and for the rest of his life ate regularly at the king's table. 34Day by day the king of Babylon gave Jehoiachin a regular allowance as long as he lived, till the day of his death.

Living Bible

32and spoke pleasantly to him and gave him preference over all the other kings in Babylon, 33and gave him new clothes and fed him from the king's kitchen as long as he lived. 34And he was given a regular allowance to cover his daily needs until the day of his death.

New Revised Standard

32 he spoke kindly to him, and gave him a seat above the seats of the other kings who were with him in Babylon. 33 So Jehoiachin put aside his prison clothes, and every day of his life he dined regularly at the king's table. 34 For his allowance, a regular daily allowance was given him by the king of Babylon, as long as he lived, up to the day of his death.

THE

Lamentations　Lamentations

OF JEREMIAH

King James

1 HOW DOTH the city sit solitary, *that was* full of people! *how* is she become as a widow! she *that was* great among the nations, *and* princess among the provinces, *how* is she become tributary!

²She weepeth sore in the night, and her tears *are* on her cheeks: among all her lovers she hath none to comfort *her:* all her friends have dealt treacherously with her, they are become her enemies.

³Judah is gone into captivity because of affliction, and because of great servitude: she dwelleth among the heathen, she findeth no rest: all her persecutors overtook her between the straits.

⁴The ways of Zion do mourn, because none come to the solemn feasts: all her gates are desolate: her priests sigh, her virgins are afflicted, and she *is* in bitterness.

⁵Her adversaries are the chief, her enemies prosper; for the LORD hath afflicted her for the multitude of her transgressions: her children are gone into captivity before the enemy.

⁶And from the daughter of Zion all her beauty is departed: her princes are become like harts *that* find no pasture, and they are gone without strength before the pursuer.

⁷Jerusalem remembered in the days of her affliction and of her miseries all her pleasant things that she had in the days of old, when her people fell into the hand of the enemy, and none did help her: the adversaries saw her, *and* did mock at her sabbaths.

New International

1 ᵃ HOW DESERTED lies the city,
　once so full of people!
How like a widow is she,
　who once was great among the nations!
She who was queen among the provinces
　has now become a slave.

²Bitterly she weeps at night,
　tears are upon her cheeks.
Among all her lovers
　there is none to comfort her.
All her friends have betrayed her;
　they have become her enemies.

³After affliction and harsh labor,
　Judah has gone into exile.
She dwells among the nations;
　she finds no resting place.
All who pursue her have overtaken her
　in the midst of her distress.

⁴The roads to Zion mourn,
　for no one comes to her appointed feasts.
All her gateways are desolate,
　her priests groan,
her maidens grieve,
　and she is in bitter anguish.

⁵Her foes have become her masters;
　her enemies are at ease.
The LORD has brought her grief
　because of her many sins.
Her children have gone into exile,
　captive before the foe.

⁶All the splendor has departed
　from the Daughter of Zion.
Her princes are like deer
　that find no pasture;
in weakness they have fled
　before the pursuer.

⁷In the days of her affliction and wandering
　Jerusalem remembers all the treasures
　that were hers in days of old.
When her people fell into enemy hands,
　there was no one to help her.
Her enemies looked at her
　and laughed at her destruction.

ᵃ This chapter is an acrostic poem, the verses of which begin with the successive letters of the Hebrew alphabet.

Living Bible

Lamentations

1 JERUSALEM'S STREETS, once thronged with people, are silent now. Like a widow broken with grief, she sits alone in her mourning. She, once queen of nations, is now a slave.

²She sobs through the night; tears run down her cheeks. Among all her lovers,[b] there is none to help her. All her friends are now her enemies.

³Why is Judah led away, a slave? Because of all the wrong she did to others, making them her slaves. Now she sits in exile far away. There is no rest, for those she persecuted have turned and conquered her.

⁴The roads to Zion mourn, no longer filled with joyous throngs who come to celebrate the Temple feasts; the city gates are silent, her priests groan, her virgins have been dragged away. Bitterly she weeps.

⁵Her enemies prosper, for the Lord has punished Jerusalem for all her many sins; her young children are captured and taken far away as slaves.

⁶All her beauty and her majesty are gone; her princes are like starving deer that search for pasture—helpless game too weak to keep on running from their foes.

⁷And now in the midst of all Jerusalem's sadness she remembers happy bygone days. She thinks of all the precious joys she had before her mocking enemy struck her down—and there was no one to give her aid.

New Revised Standard

Lamentations

The Deserted City

1 HOW LONELY sits the city
  that once was full of people!
How like a widow she has become,
  she that was great among the nations!
She that was a princess among the provinces
  has become a vassal.

2 She weeps bitterly in the night,
  with tears on her cheeks;
among all her lovers
  she has no one to comfort her;
all her friends have dealt treacherously with
  her,
  they have become her enemies.

3 Judah has gone into exile with suffering
  and hard servitude;
she lives now among the nations,
  and finds no resting place;
her pursuers have all overtaken her
  in the midst of her distress.

4 The roads to Zion mourn,
  for no one comes to the festivals;
all her gates are desolate,
  her priests groan;
her young girls grieve,[c]
  and her lot is bitter.

5 Her foes have become the masters,
  her enemies prosper,
because the LORD has made her suffer
  for the multitude of her transgressions;
her children have gone away,
  captives before the foe.

6 From daughter Zion has departed
  all her majesty.
Her princes have become like stags
  that find no pasture;
they fled without strength
  before the pursuer.

7 Jerusalem remembers,
  in the days of her affliction and wandering,
all the precious things
  that were hers in days of old.
When her people fell into the hand of the foe,
  and there was no one to help her,
the foe looked on mocking
  over her downfall.

King James

8Jerusalem hath grievously sinned; therefore she is removed: all that honoured her despise her, because they have seen her nakedness: yea, she sigheth, and turneth backward.

9Her filthiness *is* in her skirts; she remembereth not her last end; therefore she came down wonderfully: she had no comforter. O LORD, behold my affliction: for the enemy hath magnified *himself*.

10The adversary hath spread out his hand upon all her pleasant things: for she hath seen *that* the heathen entered into her sanctuary, whom thou didst command *that* they should not enter into thy congregation.

11All her people sigh, they seek bread; they have given their pleasant things for meat to relieve the soul: see, O LORD, and consider; for I am become vile.

12¶ *Is it* nothing to you, all ye that pass by? behold, and see if there be any sorrow like unto my sorrow, which is done unto me, wherewith the LORD hath afflicted *me* in the day of his fierce anger.

13From above hath he sent fire into my bones, and it prevaileth against them: he hath spread a net for my feet, he hath turned me back: he hath made me desolate *and* faint all the day.

14The yoke of my transgressions is bound by his hand: they are wreathed, *and* come up upon my neck: he hath made my strength to fall, the Lord hath delivered me into *their* hands, *from whom* I am not able to rise up.

15The Lord hath trodden under foot all my mighty *men* in the midst of me: he hath called an assembly against me to crush my young men: the Lord hath trodden the virgin, the daughter of Judah, *as* in a winepress.

16For these *things* I weep; mine eye, mine eye runneth down with water, because the comforter that should relieve my soul is far from me: my children are desolate, because the enemy prevailed.

17Zion spreadeth forth her hands, *and there is* none to comfort her: the LORD hath commanded concerning Jacob, *that* his adversaries *should be* round about him: Jerusalem is as a menstruous woman among them.

New International

8Jerusalem has sinned greatly
    and so has become unclean.
All who honored her despise her,
    for they have seen her nakedness;
she herself groans
    and turns away.

9Her filthiness clung to her skirts;
    she did not consider her future.
Her fall was astounding;
    there was none to comfort her.
"Look, O LORD, on my affliction,
    for the enemy has triumphed."

10The enemy laid hands
    on all her treasures;
she saw pagan nations
    enter her sanctuary—
those you had forbidden
    to enter your assembly.

11All her people groan
    as they search for bread;
they barter their treasures for food
    to keep themselves alive.
"Look, O LORD, and consider,
    for I am despised."

12"Is it nothing to you, all you who pass by?
    Look around and see.
Is any suffering like my suffering
    that was inflicted on me,
that the LORD brought on me
    in the day of his fierce anger?

13"From on high he sent fire,
    sent it down into my bones.
He spread a net for my feet
    and turned me back.
He made me desolate,
    faint all the day long.

14"My sins have been bound into a yoke[a];
    by his hands they were woven together.
They have come upon my neck
    and the Lord has sapped my strength.
He has handed me over
    to those I cannot withstand.

15"The Lord has rejected
    all the warriors in my midst;
he has summoned an army against me
    to[b] crush my young men.
In his winepress the Lord has trampled
    the Virgin Daughter of Judah.

16"This is why I weep
    and my eyes overflow with tears.
No one is near to comfort me,
    no one to restore my spirit.
My children are destitute
    because the enemy has prevailed."

17Zion stretches out her hands,
    but there is no one to comfort her.
The LORD has decreed for Jacob
    that his neighbors become his foes;
Jerusalem has become
    an unclean thing among them.

a *14* Most Hebrew manuscripts; Septuagint *He kept watch over my sins*
b *15* Or *has set a time for me / when he will*

Living Bible

8For Jerusalem sinned so horribly; therefore she is tossed away like dirty rags. All who honored her despise her now, for they have seen her stripped naked and humiliated. She groans and hides her face.

9She indulged herself in immorality, and refused to face the fact that punishment was sure to come. Now she lies in the gutter with no one left to lift her out. "O Lord," she cries, "see my plight. The enemy has triumphed."

10Her enemies have plundered her completely, taking everything precious she owns. She has seen foreign nations violate her sacred Temple—foreigners you had forbidden even to enter.

11Her people groan and cry for bread; they have sold all they have for food to give a little strength. "Look, O Lord," she prays, "and see how I'm despised."

12Is it nothing to you, all you who pass by? Look and see if there is any sorrow like my sorrow, because of all the Lord has done to me in the day of his fierce wrath.

13He has sent fire from heaven that burns within my bones; he has placed a pitfall in my path and turned me back. He has left me sick and desolate the whole day through.

14He wove my sins into ropes to hitch me to a yoke of slavery. He sapped my strength and gave me to my enemies; I am helpless in their hands.

15The Lord has trampled all my mighty men. A great army has come at his command to crush the noblest youth. The Lord has trampled his beloved city as grapes in a winepress.

16For all these things I weep; tears flow down my cheeks. My Comforter is far away—he who alone could help me. My children have no future; we are a conquered land.

17Jerusalem pleads for help but no one comforts her. For the Lord has spoken: "Let her neighbors be her foes! Let her be thrown out like filthy rags!"

New Revised Standard

8 Jerusalem sinned grievously,
    so she has become a mockery;
all who honored her despise her,
    for they have seen her nakedness;
she herself groans,
    and turns her face away.

9 Her uncleanness was in her skirts;
    she took no thought of her future;
her downfall was appalling,
    with none to comfort her.
"O Lord, look at my affliction,
    for the enemy has triumphed!"

10 Enemies have stretched out their hands
    over all her precious things;
she has even seen the nations
    invade her sanctuary,
those whom you forbade
    to enter your congregation.

11 All her people groan
    as they search for bread;
they trade their treasures for food
    to revive their strength.
Look, O Lord, and see
    how worthless I have become.

12 Is it nothing to you,c all you who pass by?
    Look and see
if there is any sorrow like my sorrow,
    which was brought upon me,
which the Lord inflicted
    on the day of his fierce anger.

13 From on high he sent fire;
    it went deep into my bones;
he spread a net for my feet;
    he turned me back;
he has left me stunned,
    faint all day long.

14 My transgressions were bounde into a yoke;
    by his hand they were fastened together;
they weigh on my neck,
    sapping my strength;
the Lord handed me over
    to those whom I cannot withstand.

15 The Lord has rejected
    all my warriors in the midst of me;
he proclaimed a time against me
    to crush my young men;
the Lord has trodden as in a wine press
    the virgin daughter Judah.

16 For these things I weep;
    my eyes flow with tears;
for a comforter is far from me,
    one to revive my courage;
my children are desolate,
    for the enemy has prevailed.

17 Zion stretches out her hands,
    but there is no one to comfort her;
the Lord has commanded against Jacob
    that his neighbors should become his foes;
Jerusalem has become
    a filthy thing among them.

c Meaning of Heb uncertain

King James

18¶ The Lord is righteous; for I have rebelled against his commandment: hear, I pray you, all people, and behold my sorrow: my virgins and my young men are gone into captivity.

19I called for my lovers, *but* they deceived me: my priests and mine elders gave up the ghost in the city, while they sought their meat to relieve their souls.

20Behold, O Lord; for I *am* in distress: my bowels are troubled; mine heart is turned within me; for I have grievously rebelled: abroad the sword bereaveth, at home *there is* as death.

21They have heard that I sigh: *there is* none to comfort me: all mine enemies have heard of my trouble; they are glad that thou hast done *it:* thou wilt bring the day *that* thou hast called, and they shall be like unto me.

22Let all their wickedness come before thee; and do unto them, as thou hast done unto me for all my transgressions: for my sighs *are* many, and my heart *is* faint.

2 HOW HATH the Lord covered the daughter of Zion with a cloud in his anger, *and* cast down from heaven unto the earth the beauty of Israel, and remembered not his footstool in the day of his anger!

2The Lord hath swallowed up all the habitations of Jacob, and hath not pitied: he hath thrown down in his wrath the strong holds of the daughter of Judah; he hath brought *them* down to the ground: he hath polluted the kingdom and the princes thereof.

3He hath cut off in *his* fierce anger all the horn of Israel: he hath drawn back his right hand from before the enemy, and he burned against Jacob like a flaming fire, *which* devoureth round about.

4He hath bent his bow like an enemy: he stood with his right hand as an adversary, and slew all *that were* pleasant to the eye in the tabernacle of the daughter of Zion: he poured out his fury like fire.

New International

18"The Lord is righteous,
    yet I rebelled against his command.
Listen, all you peoples;
    look upon my suffering.
My young men and maidens
    have gone into exile.

19"I called to my allies
    but they betrayed me.
My priests and my elders
    perished in the city
while they searched for food
    to keep themselves alive.

20"See, O Lord, how distressed I am!
    I am in torment within,
and in my heart I am disturbed,
    for I have been most rebellious.
Outside, the sword bereaves;
    inside, there is only death.

21"People have heard my groaning,
    but there is no one to comfort me.
All my enemies have heard of my distress;
    they rejoice at what you have done.
May you bring the day you have announced
    so they may become like me.

22"Let all their wickedness come before you;
    deal with them
as you have dealt with me
    because of all my sins.
My groans are many
    and my heart is faint."

2[a] HOW THE Lord has covered the Daughter of Zion
    with the cloud of his anger[b]!
He has hurled down the splendor of Israel
    from heaven to earth;
he has not remembered his footstool
    in the day of his anger.

2Without pity the Lord has swallowed up
    all the dwellings of Jacob;
in his wrath he has torn down
    the strongholds of the Daughter of Judah.
He has brought her kingdom and its princes
    down to the ground in dishonor.

3In fierce anger he has cut off
    every horn[c] of Israel.
He has withdrawn his right hand
    at the approach of the enemy.
He has burned in Jacob like a flaming fire
    that consumes everything around it.

4Like an enemy he has strung his bow;
    his right hand is ready.
Like a foe he has slain
    all who were pleasing to the eye;
he has poured out his wrath like fire
    on the tent of the Daughter of Zion.

---

[a] This chapter is an acrostic poem, the verses of which begin with the successive letters of the Hebrew alphabet.   [b] *1* Or *How the Lord in his anger / has treated the Daughter of Zion with contempt*   [c] *3* Or / *all the strength*; or *every king; horn* here symbolizes strength.

Living Bible

18And the Lord is right, for we rebelled. And yet, O people everywhere, behold and see my anguish and despair, for my sons and daughters are taken far away as slaves to distant lands.

19I begged my alliesd for their help. False hope—they could not help at all. Nor could my priests and elders—they were starving in the streets while searching through the garbage dumps for bread.

20See, O Lord, my anguish; my heart is broken and my soul despairs, for I have terribly rebelled. In the streets the sword awaits me; at home, disease and death.

21Hear my groans! And there is no one anywhere to help. All my enemies have heard my troubles and they are glad to see what you have done. And yet, O Lord, the time will surely come—for you have promised it—when you will do to them as you have done to me.

22Look also on their sins, O Lord, and punish them as you have punished me, for my sighs are many and my heart is faint.

2 A CLOUD of anger from the Lord has overcast Jerusalem; the fairest city of Israel lies in the dust of the earth, cast from the heights of heaven at his command. In his day of awesome fury he has shown no mercy even to his Temple.e

2The Lord without mercy has destroyed every home in Israel. In his wrath he has broken every fortress, every wall. He has brought the kingdom to dust, with all its rulers.

3All the strength of Israel vanishes beneath his wrath. He has withdrawn his protection as the enemy attacks. God burns across the land of Israel like a raging fire.

4He bends his bow against his people as though he were an enemy. His strength is used against them to kill their finest youth. His fury is poured out like fire upon them.

New Revised Standard

18 The LORD is in the right,
    for I have rebelled against his word;
but hear, all you peoples,
    and behold my suffering;
my young women and young men
    have gone into captivity.

19 I called to my lovers
    but they deceived me;
my priests and elders
    perished in the city
while seeking food
    to revive their strength.

20 See, O LORD, how distressed I am;
    my stomach churns,
my heart is wrung within me,
    because I have been very rebellious.
In the street the sword bereaves;
    in the house it is like death.

21 They heard how I was groaning,
    with no one to comfort me.
All my enemies heard of my trouble;
    they are glad that you have done it.
Bring on the day you have announced,
    and let them be as I am.

22 Let all their evil doing come before you;
    and deal with them
as you have dealt with me
    because of all my transgressions;
for my groans are many
    and my heart is faint.

God's Warnings Fulfilled

2 HOW THE Lord in his anger
    has humiliatedf daughter Zion!
He has thrown down from heaven to earth
    the splendor of Israel;
he has not remembered his footstool
    in the day of his anger.

2 The Lord has destroyed without mercy
    all the dwellings of Jacob;
in his wrath he has broken down
    the strongholds of daughter Judah;
he has brought down to the ground in
        dishonor
    the kingdom and its rulers.

3 He has cut down in fierce anger
    all the might of Israel;
he has withdrawn his right hand from them
    in the face of the enemy;
he has burned like a flaming fire in Jacob,
    consuming all around.

4 He has bent his bow like an enemy,
    with his right hand set like a foe;
he has killed all in whom we took pride
    in the tent of daughter Zion;
he has poured out his fury like fire.

---

d 1:19 allies, literally, "lovers," which probably refers to Egypt.
e 2:1 Temple, literally, "footstool."

f Meaning of Heb uncertain

King James

5The Lord was as an enemy: he hath swallowed up Israel, he hath swallowed up all her palaces: he hath destroyed his strong holds, and hath increased in the daughter of Judah mourning and lamentation.

6And he hath violently taken away his tabernacle, as *if it were of* a garden: he hath destroyed his places of the assembly: the LORD hath caused the solemn feasts and sabbaths to be forgotten in Zion, and hath despised in the indignation of his anger the king and the priest.

7The Lord hath cast off his altar, he hath abhorred his sanctuary, he hath given up into the hand of the enemy the walls of her palaces; they have made a noise in the house of the LORD, as in the day of a solemn feast.

8The LORD hath purposed to destroy the wall of the daughter of Zion: he hath stretched out a line, he hath not withdrawn his hand from destroying: therefore he made the rampart and the wall to lament; they languished together.

9Her gates are sunk into the ground; he hath destroyed and broken her bars: her king and her princes *are* among the Gentiles: the law *is* no *more;* her prophets also find no vision from the LORD.

10The elders of the daughter of Zion sit upon the ground, *and* keep silence: they have cast up dust upon their heads; they have girded themselves with sackcloth: the virgins of Jerusalem hang down their heads to the ground.

11Mine eyes do fail with tears, my bowels are troubled, my liver is poured upon the earth, for the destruction of the daughter of my people; because the children and the sucklings swoon in the streets of the city.

12They say to their mothers, Where *is* corn and wine? when they swooned as the wounded in the streets of the city, when their soul was poured out into their mothers' bosom.

13What thing shall I take to witness for thee? what thing shall I liken to thee, O daughter of Jerusalem? what shall I equal to thee, that I may comfort thee, O virgin daughter of Zion? for thy breach *is* great like the sea: who can heal thee?

14Thy prophets have seen vain and foolish things for thee: and they have not discovered thine iniquity, to turn away thy captivity; but have seen for thee false burdens and causes of banishment.

New International

5The Lord is like an enemy;
  he has swallowed up Israel.
He has swallowed up all her palaces
  and destroyed her strongholds.
He has multiplied mourning and lamentation
  for the Daughter of Judah.

6He has laid waste his dwelling like a garden;
  he has destroyed his place of meeting.
The LORD has made Zion forget
  her appointed feasts and her Sabbaths;
in his fierce anger he has spurned
  both king and priest.

7The Lord has rejected his altar
  and abandoned his sanctuary.
He has handed over to the enemy
  the walls of her palaces;
they have raised a shout in the house of the
    LORD
  as on the day of an appointed feast.

8The LORD determined to tear down
  the wall around the Daughter of Zion.
He stretched out a measuring line
  and did not withhold his hand from
    destroying.
He made ramparts and walls lament;
  together they wasted away.

9Her gates have sunk into the ground;
  their bars he has broken and destroyed.
Her king and her princes are exiled among the
    nations,
  the law is no more,
and her prophets no longer find
  visions from the LORD.

10The elders of the Daughter of Zion
  sit on the ground in silence;
they have sprinkled dust on their heads
  and put on sackcloth.
The young women of Jerusalem
  have bowed their heads to the ground.

11My eyes fail from weeping,
  I am in torment within,
my heart is poured out on the ground
  because my people are destroyed,
because children and infants faint
  in the streets of the city.

12They say to their mothers,
  "Where is bread and wine?"
as they faint like wounded men
  in the streets of the city,
as their lives ebb away
  in their mothers' arms.

13What can I say for you?
  With what can I compare you,
  O Daughter of Jerusalem?
To what can I liken you,
  that I may comfort you,
  O Virgin Daughter of Zion?
Your wound is as deep as the sea.
  Who can heal you?

14The visions of your prophets
  were false and worthless;
they did not expose your sin
  to ward off your captivity.
The oracles they gave you
  were false and misleading.

Living Bible

⁵Yes, the Lord has vanquished Israel like an enemy. He has destroyed her forts and palaces. Sorrows and tears are his portion for Jerusalem.

⁶He has violently broken down his Temple as though it were a booth of leaves and branches in a garden! No longer can the people celebrate their holy feasts and Sabbaths. Kings and priests together fall before his wrath.

⁷The Lord has rejected his own altar, for he despises the false "worship" of his people; he has given their palaces to their enemies, who carouse in the Temple as Israel used to do on days of holy feasts!

⁸The Lord determined to destroy Jerusalem. He laid out an unalterable line of destruction. Therefore the ramparts and walls fell down before him.

⁹Jerusalem's gates are useless. All their locks and bars are broken, for he has crushed them. Her kings and princes are enslaved in far-off lands, without a temple, without a divine law to govern them, or prophetic vision to guide them.

¹⁰The elders of Jerusalem sit upon the ground in silence, clothed in sackcloth; they throw dust upon their heads in sorrow and despair. The virgins of Jerusalem hang their heads in shame.

¹¹I have cried until the tears no longer come; my heart is broken, my spirit poured out, as I see what has happened to my people; little children and tiny babies are fainting and dying in the streets.

¹²"Mama, Mama, we want food," they cry, and then collapse upon their mothers' shrunken breasts. Their lives ebb away like those wounded in battle.

¹³In all the world has there ever been such sorrow? O Jerusalem, what can I compare your anguish to? How can I comfort you? For your wound is deep as the sea. Who can heal you?

¹⁴Your "prophets" have said so many foolish things, false to the core. They have not tried to hold you back from slavery by pointing out your sins. They lied and said that all was well.

New Revised Standard

5 The Lord has become like an enemy;
   he has destroyed Israel;
He has destroyed all its palaces,
   laid in ruins its strongholds,
and multiplied in daughter Judah
   mourning and lamentation.

6 He has broken down his booth like a garden,
   he has destroyed his tabernacle;
the Lord has abolished in Zion
   festival and sabbath,
and in his fierce indignation has spurned
   king and priest.

7 The Lord has scorned his altar,
   disowned his sanctuary;
he has delivered into the hand of the enemy
   the walls of her palaces;
a clamor was raised in the house of the Lord
   as on a day of festival.

8 The Lord determined to lay in ruins
   the wall of daughter Zion;
he stretched the line;
   he did not withhold his hand from
      destroying;
he caused rampart and wall to lament;
   they languish together.

9 Her gates have sunk into the ground;
   he has ruined and broken her bars;
her king and princes are among the nations;
   guidance is no more,
and her prophets obtain
   no vision from the Lord.

10 The elders of daughter Zion
   sit on the ground in silence;
they have thrown dust on their heads
   and put on sackcloth;
the young girls of Jerusalem
   have bowed their heads to the ground.

11 My eyes are spent with weeping;
   my stomach churns;
my bile is poured out on the ground
   because of the destruction of my people,
because infants and babes faint
   in the streets of the city.

12 They cry to their mothers,
   "Where is bread and wine?"
as they faint like the wounded
   in the streets of the city,
as their life is poured out
   on their mothers' bosom.

13 What can I say for you, to what compare you,
   O daughter Jerusalem?
To what can I liken you, that I may comfort
      you,
   O virgin daughter Zion?
For vast as the sea is your ruin;
   who can heal you?

14 Your prophets have seen for you
   false and deceptive visions;
they have not exposed your iniquity
   to restore your fortunes,
but have seen oracles for you
   that are false and misleading.

King James

15All that pass by clap *their* hands at thee; they hiss and wag their head at the daughter of Jerusalem, *saying, Is* this the city that *men* call The perfection of beauty, The joy of the whole earth?

16All thine enemies have opened their mouth against thee: they hiss and gnash the teeth: they say, We have swallowed *her* up: certainly this *is* the day that we looked for; we have found, we have seen *it.*

17The LORD hath done *that* which he had devised; he hath fulfilled his word that he had commanded in the days of old: he hath thrown down, and hath not pitied: and he hath caused *thine* enemy to rejoice over thee, he hath set up the horn of thine adversaries.

18Their heart cried unto the Lord, O wall of the daughter of Zion, let tears run down like a river day and night: give thyself no rest: let not the apple of thine eye cease.

19Arise, cry out in the night: in the beginning of the watches pour out thine heart like water before the face of the Lord: lift up thy hands toward him for the life of thy young children, that faint for hunger in the top of every street.

20¶ Behold, O LORD, and consider to whom thou hast done this. Shall the women eat their fruit, *and* children of a span long? shall the priest and the prophet be slain in the sanctuary of the Lord?

21The young and the old lie on the ground in the streets: my virgins and my young men are fallen by the sword; thou hast slain *them* in the day of thine anger; thou hast killed, *and* not pitied.

22Thou hast called as in a solemn day my terrors round about, so that in the day of the LORD's anger none escaped nor remained: those that I have swaddled and brought up hath mine enemy consumed.

New International

15All who pass your way
  clap their hands at you;
they scoff and shake their heads
  at the Daughter of Jerusalem:
"Is this the city that was called
  the perfection of beauty,
  the joy of the whole earth?"

16All your enemies open their mouths
  wide against you;
they scoff and gnash their teeth
  and say, "We have swallowed her up.
This is the day we have waited for;
  we have lived to see it."

17The LORD has done what he planned;
  he has fulfilled his word,
  which he decreed long ago.
He has overthrown you without pity,
  he has let the enemy gloat over you,
  he has exalted the horn[a] of your foes.

18The hearts of the people
  cry out to the Lord.
O wall of the Daughter of Zion,
  let your tears flow like a river
  day and night;
give yourself no relief,
  your eyes no rest.

19Arise, cry out in the night,
  as the watches of the night begin;
pour out your heart like water
  in the presence of the Lord.
Lift up your hands to him
  for the lives of your children,
who faint from hunger
  at the head of every street.

20"Look, O LORD, and consider:
  Whom have you ever treated like this?
Should women eat their offspring,
  the children they have cared for?
Should priest and prophet be killed
  in the sanctuary of the Lord?

21"Young and old lie together
  in the dust of the streets;
my young men and maidens
  have fallen by the sword.
You have slain them in the day of your anger;
  you have slaughtered them without pity.

22"As you summon to a feast day,
  so you summoned against me terrors on every
    side.
In the day of the LORD's anger
  no one escaped or survived;
those I cared for and reared,
  my enemy has destroyed."

3 I AM the man *that* hath seen affliction by the rod of his wrath.

2He hath led me, and brought *me into* darkness, but not *into* light.

3Surely against me is he turned; he turneth his hand *against me* all the day.

3[b] I AM the man who has seen affliction
  by the rod of his wrath.
2He has driven me away and made me walk
  in darkness rather than light;
3indeed, he has turned his hand against me
  again and again, all day long.

---

a 17 *Horn* here symbolizes strength.   b This chapter is an acrostic poem; the verses of each stanza begin with the successive letters of the Hebrew alphabet, and the verses within each stanza begin with the same letter.

Living Bible

15All who pass by scoff and shake their heads and say, "Is this the city called 'Most Beautiful in All the World,' and 'Joy of All the Earth'?"

16All your enemies deride you. They hiss and grind their teeth and say, "We have destroyed her at last! Long have we waited for this hour and it is finally here! With our own eyes we've seen her fall."

17But it is the Lord who did it, just as he had warned. He has fulfilled the promises of doom he made so long ago. He has destroyed Jerusalem without mercy and caused her enemies to rejoice over her and boast of their power.

18Then the people wept before the Lord. O walls of Jerusalem, let tears fall down upon you like a river; give yourselves no rest from weeping day or night.

19Rise in the night and cry to your God. Pour out your hearts like water to the Lord; lift up your hands to him; plead for your children as they faint with hunger in the streets.

20*O Lord, think! These are your own people to whom you are doing this.* Shall mothers eat their little children, those they bounced upon their knees? Shall priests and prophets die within the Temple of the Lord?

21See them lying in the streets—old and young, boys and girls, killed by the enemies' swords. You have killed them, Lord, in your anger; you have killed them without mercy.

22You have deliberately called for this destruction; in the day of your anger none escaped or remained. All my little children lie dead upon the streets before the enemy.

3 I AM the man who has seen the afflictions that come from the rod of God's wrath. 2He has brought me into deepest darkness, shutting out all light. 3He has turned against me. Day and night his hand is

New Revised Standard

15 All who pass along the way
      clap their hands at you;
they hiss and wag their heads
      at daughter Jerusalem;
"Is this the city that was called
      the perfection of beauty,
      the joy of all the earth?"

16 All your enemies
      open their mouths against you;
they hiss, they gnash their teeth,
      they cry: "We have devoured her!
Ah, this is the day we longed for;
      at last we have seen it!"

17 The LORD has done what he purposed,
      he has carried out his threat;
as he ordained long ago,
      he has demolished without pity;
he has made the enemy rejoice over you,
      and exalted the might of your foes.

18 Cry aloud[c] to the Lord!
      O wall of daughter Zion!
Let tears stream down like a torrent
      day and night!
Give yourself no rest,
      your eyes no respite!

19 Arise, cry out in the night,
      at the beginning of the watches!
Pour out your heart like water
      before the presence of the Lord!
Lift your hands to him
      for the lives of your children,
who faint for hunger
      at the head of every street.

20 Look, O LORD, and consider!
      To whom have you done this?
Should women eat their offspring,
      the children they have borne?
Should priest and prophet be killed
      in the sanctuary of the Lord?

21 The young and the old are lying
      on the ground in the streets;
my young women and my young men
      have fallen by the sword;
in the day of your anger you have killed them,
      slaughtering without mercy.

22 You invited my enemies from all around
      as if for a day of festival;
and on the day of the anger of the LORD
      no one escaped or survived;
those whom I bore and reared
      my enemy has destroyed.

God's Steadfast Love Endures

3 I AM one who has seen affliction
      under the rod of God's[d] wrath;
2 he has driven and brought me
      into darkness without any light;
3 against me alone he turns his hand,
      again and again, all day long.

---

c Cn: Heb *Their heart cried*   d Heb *his*

King James

4My flesh and my skin hath he made old; he hath broken my bones.

5He hath builded against me, and compassed *me* with gall and travail.

6He hath set me in dark places, as *they that be* dead of old.

7He hath hedged me about, that I cannot get out: he hath made my chain heavy.

8Also when I cry and shout, he shutteth out my prayer.

9He hath inclosed my ways with hewn stone, he hath made my paths crooked.

10He *was* unto me *as* a bear lying in wait, *and as a* lion in secret places.

11He hath turned aside my ways, and pulled me in pieces: he hath made me desolate.

12He hath bent his bow, and set me as a mark for the arrow.

13He hath caused the arrows of his quiver to enter into my reins.

14I was a derision to all my people; *and* their song all the day.

15He hath filled me with bitterness, he hath made me drunken with wormwood.

16He hath also broken my teeth with gravel stones, he hath covered me with ashes.

17And thou hast removed my soul far off from peace: I forgat prosperity.

18And I said, My strength and my hope is perished from the LORD:

19Remembering mine affliction and my misery, the wormwood and the gall.

20My soul hath *them* still in remembrance, and is humbled in me.

21This I recall to my mind, therefore have I hope.

22¶ *It is of* the LORD's mercies that we are not consumed, because his compassions fail not.

23*They are* new every morning: great *is* thy faithfulness.

24The LORD *is* my portion, saith my soul; therefore will I hope in him.

25The LORD *is* good unto them that wait for him, to the soul *that* seeketh him.

26*It is* good that *a man* should both hope and quietly wait for the salvation of the LORD.

27*It is* good for a man that he bear the yoke in his youth.

28He sitteth alone and keepeth silence, because he hath borne *it* upon him.

29He putteth his mouth in the dust; if so be there may be hope.

30He giveth *his* cheek to him that smiteth him: he is filled full with reproach.

31For the Lord will not cast off for ever:

New International

4He has made my skin and my flesh grow old
  and has broken my bones.
5He has besieged me and surrounded me
  with bitterness and hardship.
6He has made me dwell in darkness
  like those long dead.

7He has walled me in so I cannot escape;
  he has weighed me down with chains.
8Even when I call out or cry for help,
  he shuts out my prayer.
9He has barred my way with blocks of stone;
  he has made my paths crooked.

10Like a bear lying in wait,
  like a lion in hiding,
11he dragged me from the path and mangled me
  and left me without help.
12He drew his bow
  and made me the target for his arrows.

13He pierced my heart
  with arrows from his quiver.
14I became the laughingstock of all my people;
  they mock me in song all day long.
15He has filled me with bitter herbs
  and sated me with gall.

16He has broken my teeth with gravel;
  he has trampled me in the dust.
17I have been deprived of peace;
  I have forgotten what prosperity is.
18So I say, "My splendor is gone
  and all that I had hoped from the LORD."

19I remember my affliction and my wandering,
  the bitterness and the gall.
20I well remember them,
  and my soul is downcast within me.
21Yet this I call to mind
  and therefore I have hope:

22Because of the LORD's great love we are not
  consumed,
  for his compassions never fail.
23They are new every morning;
  great is your faithfulness.
24I say to myself, "The LORD is my portion;
  therefore I will wait for him."

25The LORD is good to those whose hope is in
  him,
  to the one who seeks him;
26it is good to wait quietly
  for the salvation of the LORD.
27It is good for a man to bear the yoke
  while he is young.

28Let him sit alone in silence,
  for the LORD has laid it on him.
29Let him bury his face in the dust—
  there may yet be hope.
30Let him offer his cheek to one who would strike
  him,
  and let him be filled with disgrace.

31For men are not cast off
  by the Lord forever.

Living Bible

heavy on me. 4He has made me old and has broken my bones.

5He has built forts against me and surrounded me with anguish and distress. 6He buried me in dark places, like those long dead. 7He has walled me in; I cannot escape; he has fastened me with heavy chains. 8And though I cry and shout, he will not hear my prayers! 9He has shut me into a place of high, smooth walls;a he has filled my path with detours.

10He lurks like a bear, like a lion, waiting to attack me. 11He has dragged me into the underbrush and torn me with his claws, and left me bleeding and desolate. 12He has bent his bow and aimed it squarely at me, 13and sent his arrows deep within my heart.

14My own people laugh at me; all day long they sing their ribald songs.

15He has filled me with bitterness, and given me a cup of deepest sorrows to drink. 16He has made me eat gravel and broken my teeth; he has rolled me in ashes and dirt. 17O Lord, all peace and all prosperity have long since gone, for you have taken them away. I have forgotten what enjoyment is. 18All hope is gone; my strength has turned to water, for the Lord has left me. 19Oh, remember the bitterness and suffering you have dealt to me! 20For I can never forget these awful years; always my soul will live in utter shame.

21Yet there is one ray of hope: 22his compassion never ends. It is only the Lord's mercies that have kept us from complete destruction. 23Great is his faithfulness; his lovingkindness begins afresh each day. 24My soul claims the Lord as my inheritance; therefore I will hope in him. 25The Lord is wonderfully good to those who wait for him, to those who seek for him. 26It is good both to hope and wait quietly for the salvation of the Lord.

27It is good for a young man to be under discipline, 28for it causes him to sit apart in silence beneath the Lord's demands, 29to lie face downward in the dust; then at last there is hope for him. 30Let him turn the other cheek to those who strike him, and accept their awful insults, 31for the Lord will not abandon him forever.

New Revised Standard

4 He has made my flesh and my skin waste
      away,
   and broken my bones;
5 he has besieged and enveloped me
   with bitterness and tribulation;
6 he has made me sit in darkness
   like the dead of long ago.

7 He has walled me about so that I cannot
      escape;
   he has put heavy chains on me;
8 though I call and cry for help,
   he shuts out my prayer;
9 he has blocked my ways with hewn stones,
   he has made my paths crooked.

10 He is a bear lying in wait for me,
   a lion in hiding;
11 he led me off my way and tore me to pieces;
   he has made me desolate;
12 he bent his bow and set me
   as a mark for his arrow.

13 He shot into my vitals
   the arrows of his quiver;
14 I have become the laughingstock of all my
      people,
   the object of their taunt-songs all day long.
15 He has filled me with bitterness,
   he has sated me with wormwood.

16 He has made my teeth grind on gravel,
   and made me cower in ashes;
17 my soul is bereft of peace;
   I have forgotten what happiness is;
18 so I say, "Gone is my glory,
   and all that I had hoped for from the
      LORD."

19 The thought of my affliction and my
      homelessness
   is wormwood and gall!
20 My soul continually thinks of it
   and is bowed down within me.
21 But this I call to mind,
   and therefore I have hope:

22 The steadfast love of the LORD never ceases,b
   his mercies never come to an end;
23 they are new every morning;
   great is your faithfulness.
24 "The LORD is my portion," says my soul,
   "therefore I will hope in him."

25 The LORD is good to those who wait for him,
   to the soul that seeks him.
26 It is good that one should wait quietly
   for the salvation of the LORD.
27 It is good for one to bear
   the yoke in youth,
28 to sit alone in silence
   when the Lord has imposed it,
29 to put one's mouth to the dust
   (there may yet be hope),
30 to give one's cheek to the smiter,
   and be filled with insults.

31 For the Lord will not
   reject forever.

a 3:9 He has shut me into a place of high, smooth walls, literally, "He has walled up my ways with hewn stone."

b Syr Tg: Heb LORD, we are not cut off

King James

32But though he cause grief, yet will he have compassion according to the multitude of his mercies.

33For he doth not afflict willingly nor grieve the children of men.

34To crush under his feet all the prisoners of the earth,

35To turn aside the right of a man before the face of the most High,

36To subvert a man in his cause, the Lord approveth not.

37¶ Who *is* he *that* saith, and it cometh to pass, *when* the Lord commandeth *it* not?

38Out of the mouth of the most High proceedeth not evil and good?

39Wherefore doth a living man complain, a man for the punishment of his sins?

40Let us search and try our ways, and turn again to the Lord.

41Let us lift up our heart with *our* hands unto God in the heavens.

42We have transgressed and have rebelled: thou hast not pardoned.

43Thou hast covered with anger, and persecuted us: thou hast slain, thou hast not pitied.

44Thou hast covered thyself with a cloud, that *our* prayer should not pass through.

45Thou hast made us *as* the offscouring and refuse in the midst of the people.

46All our enemies have opened their mouths against us.

47Fear and a snare is come upon us, desolation and destruction.

48Mine eye runneth down with rivers of water for the destruction of the daughter of my people.

49Mine eye trickleth down, and ceaseth not, without any intermission,

50Till the Lord look down, and behold from heaven.

51Mine eye affecteth mine heart because of all the daughters of my city.

52Mine enemies chased me sore, like a bird, without cause.

53They have cut off my life in the dungeon, and cast a stone upon me.

54Waters flowed over mine head; *then* I said, I am cut off.

55¶ I called upon thy name, O Lord, out of the low dungeon.

56Thou hast heard my voice: hide not thine ear at my breathing, at my cry.

57Thou drewest near in the day *that* I called upon thee: thou saidst, Fear not.

58O Lord, thou hast pleaded the causes of my soul; thou hast redeemed my life.

59O Lord, thou hast seen my wrong: judge thou my cause.

60Thou hast seen all their vengeance *and* all their imaginations against me.

61Thou hast heard their reproach, O Lord, *and* all their imaginations against me;

New International

32Though he brings grief, he will show
    compassion,
  so great is his unfailing love.
33For he does not willingly bring affliction
  or grief to the children of men.

34To crush underfoot
  all prisoners in the land,
35to deny a man his rights
  before the Most High,
36to deprive a man of justice—
  would not the Lord see such things?

37Who can speak and have it happen
  if the Lord has not decreed it?
38Is it not from the mouth of the Most High
  that both calamities and good things come?
39Why should any living man complain
  when punished for his sins?

40Let us examine our ways and test them,
  and let us return to the Lord.
41Let us lift up our hearts and our hands
  to God in heaven, and say:
42"We have sinned and rebelled
  and you have not forgiven.

43"You have covered yourself with anger and
    pursued us;
  you have slain without pity.
44You have covered yourself with a cloud
  so that no prayer can get through.
45You have made us scum and refuse
  among the nations.

46"All our enemies have opened their mouths
  wide against us.
47We have suffered terror and pitfalls,
  ruin and destruction."
48Streams of tears flow from my eyes
  because my people are destroyed.

49My eyes will flow unceasingly,
  without relief,
50until the Lord looks down
  from heaven and sees.
51What I see brings grief to my soul
  because of all the women of my city.

52Those who were my enemies without cause
  hunted me like a bird.
53They tried to end my life in a pit
  and threw stones at me;
54the waters closed over my head,
  and I thought I was about to be cut off.

55I called on your name, O Lord,
  from the depths of the pit.
56You heard my plea: "Do not close your ears
  to my cry for relief."
57You came near when I called you,
  and you said, "Do not fear."

58O Lord, you took up my case;
  you redeemed my life.
59You have seen, O Lord, the wrong done to me.
  Uphold my cause!
60You have seen the depth of their vengeance,
  all their plots against me.

61O Lord, you have heard their insults,
  all their plots against me—

Living Bible

32Although God gives him grief, yet he will show compassion too, according to the greatness of his loving-kindness. 33For he does not enjoy afflicting men and causing sorrow.

34, 35, 36But you have trampled and crushed beneath your feet the lowly of the world, and deprived men of their God-given rights, and refused them justice. No wonder the Lord has had to deal with you! 37For who can act against you without the Lord's permission? 38It is the Lord who helps one and harms another.

39Why then should we, mere humans as we are, murmur and complain when punished for our sins? 40Let us examine ourselves instead, and repent and turn again to the Lord. 41Let us lift our hearts and hands to him in heaven, 42for we have sinned; we have rebelled against the Lord, and he has not forgotten it.

43You have engulfed us by your anger, Lord, and slain us without mercy. 44You have veiled yourself as with a cloud so that our prayers do not reach through. 45You have made us as refuse and garbage among the nations. 46All our enemies have spoken out against us. 47We are filled with fear, for we are trapped and desolate, destroyed.

48, 49My eyes flow day and night with never-ending streams of tears because of the destruction of my people. 50Oh, that the Lord might look down from heaven and respond to my cry! 51My heart is breaking over what is happening to the young girls of Jerusalem.

52My enemies, whom I have never harmed, chased me as though I were a bird. 53They threw me in a well and capped it with a rock. 54The water flowed above my head. I thought, This is the end! 55But I called upon your name, O Lord, from deep within the well, 56and you heard me! You listened to my pleading; you heard my weeping! 57Yes, you came at my despairing cry and told me not to fear.

58O Lord, you are my lawyer! Plead my case! For you have redeemed my life. 59You have seen the wrong they did to me; be my Judge, to prove me right. 60You have seen the plots my foes have laid against me. 61You have heard the vile names they have called me, 62and all

New Revised Standard

32 Although he causes grief, he will have
       compassion
    according to the abundance of his steadfast
       love;
33 for he does not willingly afflict
    or grieve anyone.

34 When all the prisoners of the land
    are crushed under foot,
35 when human rights are perverted
    in the presence of the Most High,
36 when one's case is subverted
    —does the Lord not see it?

37 Who can command and have it done,
    if the Lord has not ordained it?
38 Is it not from the mouth of the Most High
    that good and bad come?
39 Why should any who draw breath complain
    about the punishment of their sins?

40 Let us test and examine our ways,
    and return to the LORD.
41 Let us lift up our hearts as well as our hands
    to God in heaven.
42 We have transgressed and rebelled,
    and you have not forgiven.

43 You have wrapped yourself with anger and
       pursued us,
    killing without pity;
44 you have wrapped yourself with a cloud
    so that no prayer can pass through.
45 You have made us filth and rubbish
    among the peoples.

46 All our enemies
    have opened their mouths against us;
47 panic and pitfall have come upon us,
    devastation and destruction.
48 My eyes flow with rivers of tears
    because of the destruction of my people.

49 My eyes will flow without ceasing,
    without respite,
50 until the LORD from heaven
    looks down and sees.
51 My eyes cause me grief
    at the fate of all the young women in my
       city.

52 Those who were my enemies without cause
    have hunted me like a bird;
53 they flung me alive into a pit
    and hurled stones on me;
54 water closed over my head;
    I said, "I am lost."

55 I called on your name, O LORD,
    from the depths of the pit;
56 you heard my plea, "Do not close your ear
    to my cry for help, but give me relief!"
57 You came near when I called on you;
    you said, "Do not fear!"

58 You have taken up my cause, O Lord,
    you have redeemed my life.
59 You have seen the wrong done to me,
       O LORD;
    judge my cause.
60 You have seen all their malice,
    all their plots against me.

61 You have heard their taunts, O LORD,
    all their plots against me.

King James

62The lips of those that rose up against me, and their device against me all the day.

63Behold their sitting down, and their rising up; I *am* their music.

64¶ Render unto them a recompence, O LORD, according to the work of their hands.

65Give them sorrow of heart, thy curse unto them.

66Persecute and destroy them in anger from under the heavens of the LORD.

4 HOW IS the gold become dim! *how* is the most fine gold changed! the stones of the sanctuary are poured out in the top of every street.

2The precious sons of Zion, comparable to fine gold, how are they esteemed as earthen pitchers, the work of the hands of the potter!

3Even the sea monsters draw out the breast, they give suck to their young ones: the daughter of my people *is become* cruel, like the ostriches in the wilderness.

4The tongue of the sucking child cleaveth to the roof of his mouth for thirst: the young children ask bread, *and* no man breaketh *it* unto them.

5They that did feed delicately are desolate in the streets: they that were brought up in scarlet embrace dunghills.

6For the punishment of the iniquity of the daughter of my people is greater than the punishment of the sin of Sodom, that was overthrown as in a moment, and no hands stayed on her.

7Her Nazarites were purer than snow, they were whiter than milk, they were more ruddy in body than rubies, their polishing *was* of sapphire:

8Their visage is blacker than a coal; they are not known in the streets: their skin cleaveth to their bones; it is withered, it is become like a stick.

9*They that be* slain with the sword are better than *they that be* slain with hunger: for these pine away, stricken through for *want of* the fruits of the field.

10The hands of the pitiful women have sodden their own children: they were their meat in the destruction of the daughter of my people.

11The LORD hath accomplished his fury; he hath poured out his fierce anger, and hath kindled a fire in Zion, and it hath devoured the foundations thereof.

New International

62what my enemies whisper and mutter
  against me all day long.
63Look at them! Sitting or standing,
  they mock me in their songs.

64Pay them back what they deserve, O LORD,
  for what their hands have done.
65Put a veil over their hearts,
  and may your curse be on them!
66Pursue them in anger and destroy them
  from under the heavens of the LORD.

4[a] HOW THE gold has lost its luster,
  the fine gold become dull!
The sacred gems are scattered
  at the head of every street.

2How the precious sons of Zion,
  once worth their weight in gold,
are now considered as pots of clay,
  the work of a potter's hands!

3Even jackals offer their breasts
  to nurse their young,
but my people have become heartless
  like ostriches in the desert.

4Because of thirst the infant's tongue
  sticks to the roof of its mouth;
the children beg for bread,
  but no one gives it to them.

5Those who once ate delicacies
  are destitute in the streets.
Those nurtured in purple
  now lie on ash heaps.

6The punishment of my people
  is greater than that of Sodom,
which was overthrown in a moment
  without a hand turned to help her.

7Their princes were brighter than snow
  and whiter than milk,
their bodies more ruddy than rubies,
  their appearance like sapphires.[b]

8But now they are blacker than soot;
  they are not recognized in the streets.
Their skin has shriveled on their bones;
  it has become as dry as a stick.

9Those killed by the sword are better off
  than those who die of famine;
racked with hunger, they waste away
  for lack of food from the field.

10With their own hands compassionate women
  have cooked their own children,
who became their food
  when my people were destroyed.

11The LORD has given full vent to his wrath;
  he has poured out his fierce anger.
He kindled a fire in Zion
  that consumed her foundations.

---

[a] This chapter is an acrostic poem, the verses of which begin with the successive letters of the Hebrew alphabet.   [b] *7* Or *lapis lazuli*

Living Bible

they say about me and their whispered plans. 63See how they laugh and sing with glee, preparing my doom.

64O Lord, repay them well for all the evil they have done. 65Harden their hearts and curse them, Lord. 66Go after them in fierce pursuit and wipe them off the earth, beneath the heavens of the Lord.

4 HOW THE finest gold has lost its luster! For the inlaidᶜ Temple walls are scattered in the streets! 2The cream of our youth—the finest of the gold—are treated as earthenware pots. 3, 4Even the jackals feed their young, but not my people, Israel. They are like cruel desert ostriches, heedless of their babies' cries. The children's tongues stick to the roofs of their mouths for thirst, for there is not a drop of water left. Babies cry for bread but no one can give them any. 5Those who used to eat fastidiously are begging in the streets for anything at all. Those brought up in palaces now scratch in garbage pits for food. 6For the sin of my people is greater than that of Sodom, where utter disaster struck in a moment without the hand of man.

7Our princes were lean and tanned,ᵈ the finest specimens of men; 8but now their faces are as black as soot. No one can recognize them. Their skin sticks to their bones; it is dry and hard and withered. 9Those killed by the sword are far better off than those who die of slow starvation. 10Tenderhearted women have cooked and eaten their own children; thus they survived the siege. 11But now at last the anger of the Lord is satisfied; his fiercest anger has been poured out. He started a fire in Jerusalem that burned it down to its foundations.

New Revised Standard

62 The whispers and murmurs of my assailants
      are against me all day long.
63 Whether they sit or rise—see,
      I am the object of their taunt-songs.

64 Pay them back for their deeds, O LORD,
      according to the work of their hands!
65 Give them anguish of heart;
      your curse be on them!
66 Pursue them in anger and destroy them
      from under the LORD's heavens.

The Punishment of Zion

4 HOW THE gold has grown dim,
   how the pure gold is changed!
   The sacred stones lie scattered
      at the head of every street.

2 The precious children of Zion,
      worth their weight in fine gold—
   how they are reckoned as earthen pots,
      the work of a potter's hands!

3 Even the jackals offer the breast
      and nurse their young,
   but my people has become cruel,
      like the ostriches in the wilderness.

4 The tongue of the infant sticks
      to the roof of its mouth for thirst;
   the children beg for food,
      but no one gives them anything.

5 Those who feasted on delicacies
      perish in the streets;
   those who were brought up in purple
      cling to ash heaps.

6 For the chastisementᵉ of my people has been
         greater
      than the punishmentᶠ of Sodom,
   which was overthrown in a moment,
      though no hand was laid on it.ᵍ

7 Her princes were purer than snow,
      whiter than milk;
   their bodies were more ruddy than coral,
      their hairᵍ like sapphire.ʰ

8 Now their visage is blacker than soot;
      they are not recognized in the streets.
   Their skin has shriveled on their bones;
      it has become as dry as wood.

9 Happier were those pierced by the sword
      than those pierced by hunger,
   whose life drains away, deprived
      of the produce of the field.

10 The hands of compassionate women
      have boiled their own children;
   they became their food
      in the destruction of my people.

11 The LORD gave full vent to his wrath;
      he poured out his hot anger,
   and kindled a fire in Zion
      that consumed its foundations.

ᶜ *4:1 inlaid.* Implied.   ᵈ *4:7 Our princes were lean and tanned,* literally, "were purer than snow, whiter than milk, more ruddy than rubies, polished like sapphires."

ᵉ Or *iniquity*   ᶠ Or *sin*   ᵍ Meaning of Heb uncertain   ʰ Or *lapis lazuli*

King James

12The kings of the earth, and all the inhabitants of the world, would not have believed that the adversary and the enemy should have entered into the gates of Jerusalem.

13¶ For the sins of her prophets, *and* the iniquities of her priests, that have shed the blood of the just in the midst of her,

14They have wandered *as* blind *men* in the streets, they have polluted themselves with blood, so that men could not touch their garments.

15They cried unto them, Depart ye; *It is* unclean; depart, depart, touch not: when they fled away and wandered, they said among the heathen, They shall no more sojourn *there*.

16The anger of the LORD hath divided them; he will no more regard them: they respected not the persons of the priests, they favoured not the elders.

17As for us, our eyes as yet failed for our vain help: in our watching we have watched for a nation *that* could not save *us*.

18They hunt our steps, that we cannot go in our streets: our end is near, our days are fulfilled; for our end is come.

19Our persecutors are swifter than the eagles of the heaven: they pursued us upon the mountains, they laid wait for us in the wilderness.

20The breath of our nostrils, the anointed of the LORD, was taken in their pits, of whom we said, Under his shadow we shall live among the heathen.

21¶ Rejoice and be glad, O daughter of Edom, that dwellest in the land of Uz; the cup also shall pass through unto thee: thou shalt be drunken, and shalt make thyself naked.

22¶ The punishment of thine iniquity is accomplished, O daughter of Zion; he will no more carry thee away into captivity: he will visit thine iniquity, O daughter of Edom; he will discover thy sins.

New International

12The kings of the earth did not believe,
    nor did any of the world's people,
that enemies and foes could enter
    the gates of Jerusalem.

13But it happened because of the sins of her
        prophets
    and the iniquities of her priests,
who shed within her
    the blood of the righteous.

14Now they grope through the streets
    like men who are blind.
They are so defiled with blood
    that no one dares to touch their garments.

15"Go away! You are unclean!" men cry to them.
    "Away! Away! Don't touch us!"
When they flee and wander about,
    people among the nations say,
    "They can stay here no longer."

16The LORD himself has scattered them;
    he no longer watches over them.
The priests are shown no honor,
    the elders no favor.

17Moreover, our eyes failed,
    looking in vain for help;
from our towers we watched
    for a nation that could not save us.

18Men stalked us at every step,
    so we could not walk in our streets.
Our end was near, our days were numbered,
    for our end had come.

19Our pursuers were swifter
    than eagles in the sky;
they chased us over the mountains
    and lay in wait for us in the desert.

20The LORD's anointed, our very life breath,
    was caught in their traps.
We thought that under his shadow
    we would live among the nations.

21Rejoice and be glad, O Daughter of Edom,
    you who live in the land of Uz.
But to you also the cup will be passed;
    you will be drunk and stripped naked.

22O Daughter of Zion, your punishment will end;
    he will not prolong your exile.
But, O Daughter of Edom, he will punish your
        sin
    and expose your wickedness.

5 REMEMBER, O LORD, what is come upon us: consider, and behold our reproach.

2Our inheritance is turned to strangers, our houses to aliens.

3We are orphans and fatherless, our mothers *are* as widows.

4We have drunken our water for money; our wood is sold unto us.

5 REMEMBER, O LORD, what has happened to
        us;
    look, and see our disgrace.

2Our inheritance has been turned over to aliens,
    our homes to foreigners.

3We have become orphans and fatherless,
    our mothers like widows.

4We must buy the water we drink;
    our wood can be had only at a price.

Living Bible

12Not a king in all the earth—no one in all the world—would have believed an enemy could enter through Jerusalem's gates! 13Yet God permitted it because of the sins of her prophets and priests, who defiled the city by shedding innocent blood. 14Now these same men are blindly staggering through the streets, covered with blood, defiling everything they touch.

15"Get away!" the people shout at them. "You are defiled!" They flee to distant lands and wander there among the foreigners; but none will let them stay. 16The Lord himself has dealt with them; he no longer helps them, for they persecuted the priests and elders who stayed true to God.

17We look for our alliesa to come and save us, but we look in vain. The nation we expected most to help us makes no move at all.

18We can't go into the streets without danger to our lives. Our end is near—our days are numbered. We are doomed. 19Our enemies are swifter than the eagles; if we flee to the mountains they find us. If we hide in the wilderness, they are waiting for us there. 20Our king—the life of our life, the Lord's anointed—was captured in their snares. Yes, even our mighty king, about whom we had boasted that under his protection we could hold our own against any nation on earth!

21Do you rejoice, O people of Edom, in the land of Uz? But you too will feel the awful anger of the Lord. 22Israel's exile for her sins will end at last, but Edom's never.

New Revised Standard

12 The kings of the earth did not believe,
    nor did any of the inhabitants of the world,
that foe or enemy could enter
    the gates of Jerusalem.

13 It was for the sins of her prophets
    and the iniquities of her priests,
who shed the blood of the righteous
    in the midst of her.

14 Blindly they wandered through the streets,
    so defiled with blood
that no one was able
    to touch their garments.

15 "Away! Unclean!" people shouted at them;
    "Away! Away! Do not touch!"
So they became fugitives and wanderers;
    it was said among the nations,
    "They shall stay here no longer."

16 The LORD himself has scattered them,
    he will regard them no more;
no honor was shown to the priests,
    no favor to the elders.

17 Our eyes failed, ever watching
    vainly for help;
we were watching eagerly
    for a nation that could not save.

18 They dogged our steps
    so that we could not walk in our streets;
our end drew near; our days were numbered;
    for our end had come.

19 Our pursuers were swifter
    than the eagles in the heavens;
they chased us on the mountains,
    they lay in wait for us in the wilderness.

20 The LORD's anointed, the breath of our life,
    was taken in their pits—
the one of whom we said, "Under his shadow
    we shall live among the nations."

21 Rejoice and be glad, O daughter Edom,
    you that live in the land of Uz;
but to you also the cup shall pass;
    you shall become drunk and strip yourself
    bare.

22 The punishment of your iniquity, O daughter
    Zion, is accomplished,
he will keep you in exile no longer;
but your iniquity, O daughter Edom, he will
    punish,
he will uncover your sins.

A Plea for Mercy

5 O LORD, remember all that has befallen us; see what sorrows we must bear! 2Our homes, our nation, now are filled with foreigners. 3We are orphans—our fathers dead, our mothers widowed. 4We must even pay for water to drink; our fuel is sold to us at the highest of prices. 5We bow our necks beneath the victors' feet;

5 REMEMBER, O LORD, what has befallen us;
    look, and see our disgrace!
2 Our inheritance has been turned over to
        strangers,
    our homes to aliens.
3 We have become orphans, fatherless;
    our mothers are like widows.
4 We must pay for the water we drink;
    the wood we get must be bought.

---

a *4:17 allies,* probably the reference is to Egypt.

King James

⁵Our necks *are* under persecution: we labour, *and* have no rest.

⁶We have given the hand *to* the Egyptians, *and to* the Assyrians, to be satisfied with bread.

⁷Our fathers have sinned, *and are* not; and we have borne their iniquities.

⁸Servants have ruled over us: *there is* none that doth deliver *us* out of their hand.

⁹We gat our bread with *the peril of* our lives because of the sword of the wilderness.

¹⁰Our skin was black like an oven because of the terrible famine.

¹¹They ravished the women in Zion, *and* the maids in the cities of Judah.

¹²Princes are hanged up by their hand: the faces of elders were not honoured.

¹³They took the young men to grind, and the children fell under the wood.

¹⁴The elders have ceased from the gate, the young men from their music.

¹⁵The joy of our heart is ceased; our dance is turned into mourning.

¹⁶The crown is fallen *from* our head: woe unto us, that we have sinned!

¹⁷For this our heart is faint; for these *things* our eyes are dim.

¹⁸Because of the mountain of Zion, which is desolate, the foxes walk upon it.

¹⁹Thou, O LORD, remainest for ever; thy throne from generation to generation.

²⁰Wherefore dost thou forget us for ever, *and* forsake us so long time?

²¹Turn thou us unto thee, O LORD, and we shall be turned; renew our days as of old.

²²But thou hast utterly rejected us; thou art very wroth against us.

New International

⁵Those who pursue us are at our heels;
    we are weary and find no rest.
⁶We submitted to Egypt and Assyria
    to get enough bread.
⁷Our fathers sinned and are no more,
    and we bear their punishment.
⁸Slaves rule over us,
    and there is none to free us from their hands.
⁹We get our bread at the risk of our lives
    because of the sword in the desert.
¹⁰Our skin is hot as an oven,
    feverish from hunger.
¹¹Women have been ravished in Zion,
    and virgins in the towns of Judah.
¹²Princes have been hung up by their hands;
    elders are shown no respect.
¹³Young men toil at the millstones;
    boys stagger under loads of wood.
¹⁴The elders are gone from the city gate;
    the young men have stopped their music.
¹⁵Joy is gone from our hearts;
    our dancing has turned to mourning.
¹⁶The crown has fallen from our head.
    Woe to us, for we have sinned!
¹⁷Because of this our hearts are faint,
    because of these things our eyes grow dim
¹⁸for Mount Zion, which lies desolate,
    with jackals prowling over it.

¹⁹You, O LORD, reign forever;
    your throne endures from generation to
        generation.
²⁰Why do you always forget us?
    Why do you forsake us so long?
²¹Restore us to yourself, O LORD, that we may
        return;
    renew our days as of old
²²unless you have utterly rejected us
    and are angry with us beyond measure.

Living Bible

unending work is now our lot. 6We beg for bread from Egypt, and Assyria too.

7Our fathers sinned but died before the hand of judgment fell. We have borne the blow that they deserved!

8Our former servants have become our masters; there is no one left to save us. 9We went into the wilderness to hunt for food, risking death from enemies. 10Our skin was black from famine. 11They rape the women of Jerusalem and the girls in Judah's cities. 12Our princes are hanged by their thumbs. Even aged men are treated with contempt. 13They take away the young men to grind their grain and the little children stagger beneath their heavy loads.

14The old men sit no longer in the city gates; the young no longer dance and sing. 15The joy of our hearts has ended; our dance has turned to death.a 16Our glory is gone. The crown is fallen from our head. Woe upon us for our sins. 17Our hearts are faint and weary; our eyes grow dim. 18Jerusalem and the Temple of the Lord are desolate, deserted by all but wild animals lurking in the ruins.

19O Lord, forever you remain the same! Your throne continues from generation to generation. 20Why do you forget us forever? Why do you forsake us for so long? 21Turn us around and bring us back to you again! That is our only hope! Give us back the joys we used to have! 22*Or have you utterly rejected us? Are you angry with us still?*

New Revised Standard

5 With a yokeb on our necks we are hard driven;
   we are weary, we are given no rest.
6 We have made a pact withc Egypt and Assyria,
   to get enough bread.
7 Our ancestors sinned; they are no more,
   and we bear their iniquities.
8 Slaves rule over us;
   there is no one to deliver us from their hand.
9 We get our bread at the peril of our lives,
   because of the sword in the wilderness.
10 Our skin is black as an oven
   from the scorching heat of famine.
11 Women are raped in Zion,
   virgins in the towns of Judah.
12 Princes are hung up by their hands;
   no respect is shown to the elders.
13 Young men are compelled to grind,
   and boys stagger under loads of wood.
14 The old men have left the city gate,
   the young men their music.
15 The joy of our hearts has ceased;
   our dancing has been turned to mourning.
16 The crown has fallen from our head;
   woe to us, for we have sinned!
17 Because of this our hearts are sick,
   because of these things our eyes have grown dim:
18 because of Mount Zion, which lies desolate;
   jackals prowl over it.

19 But you, O LORD, reign forever;
   your throne endures to all generations.
20 Why have you forgotten us completely?
   Why have you forsaken us these many days?
21 Restore us to yourself, O LORD, that we may be restored;
   renew our days as of old—
22 unless you have utterly rejected us,
   and are angry with us beyond measure.

---

a *5:15 to death*, literally, "to mourning."

b Symmachus: Heb lacks *With a yoke*   c Heb *have given the hand to*

King James	New International

THE BOOK OF THE PROPHET

Ezekiel

Ezekiel

King James

1 NOW IT came to pass in the thirtieth year, in the fourth *month*, in the fifth *day* of the month, as I *was* among the captives by the river of Chebar, *that* the heavens were opened, and I saw visions of God.

2In the fifth *day* of the month, which *was* the fifth year of king Jehoiachin's captivity,

3The word of the LORD came expressly unto Ezekiel the priest, the son of Buzi, in the land of the Chaldeans by the river Chebar; and the hand of the LORD was there upon him.

4¶ And I looked, and, behold, a whirlwind came out of the north, a great cloud, and a fire infolding itself, and a brightness *was* about it, and out of the midst thereof as the colour of amber, out of the midst of the fire.

5Also out of the midst thereof *came* the likeness of four living creatures. And this *was* their appearance; they had the likeness of a man.

6And every one had four faces, and every one had four wings.

7And their feet *were* straight feet; and the sole of their feet *was* like the sole of a calf's foot: and they sparkled like the colour of burnished brass.

8And *they had* the hands of a man under their wings on their four sides; and they four had their faces and their wings.

9Their wings *were* joined one to another; they turned not when they went; they went every one straight forward.

10As for the likeness of their faces, they four had the face of a man, and the face of a lion, on the right side: and they four had the face of an ox on the left side; they four also had the face of an eagle.

11Thus *were* their faces: and their wings *were* stretched upward; two *wings* of every one *were* joined one to another, and two covered their bodies.

12And they went every one straight forward: whither the spirit was to go, they went; *and* they turned not when they went.

13As for the likeness of the living creatures, their appearance *was* like burning coals of fire, *and* like the appearance of lamps: it went up and down among the living creatures; and the fire was bright, and out of the fire went forth lightning.

14And the living creatures ran and returned as the appearance of a flash of lightning.

15¶ Now as I beheld the living creatures, behold one wheel upon the earth by the living creatures, with his four faces.

16The appearance of the wheels and their work *was* like unto the colour of a beryl: and they four had one likeness: and their appearance and their work *was* as it were a wheel in the middle of a wheel.

17When they went, they went upon their four sides: *and* they turned not when they went.

18As for their rings, they were so high that they were dreadful; and their rings *were* full of eyes round about them four.

New International

The Living Creatures and the Glory of the LORD

1 IN THE[a] thirtieth year, in the fourth month on the fifth day, while I was among the exiles by the Kebar River, the heavens were opened and I saw visions of God.

2On the fifth of the month—it was the fifth year of the exile of King Jehoiachin— 3the word of the LORD came to Ezekiel the priest, the son of Buzi,[b] by the Kebar River in the land of the Babylonians.[c] There the hand of the LORD was upon him.

4I looked, and I saw a windstorm coming out of the north—an immense cloud with flashing lightning and surrounded by brilliant light. The center of the fire looked like glowing metal, 5and in the fire was what looked like four living creatures. In appearance their form was that of a man, 6but each of them had four faces and four wings. 7Their legs were straight; their feet were like those of a calf and gleamed like burnished bronze. 8Under their wings on their four sides they had the hands of a man. All four of them had faces and wings, 9and their wings touched one another. Each one went straight ahead; they did not turn as they moved.

10Their faces looked like this: Each of the four had the face of a man, and on the right side each had the face of a lion, and on the left the face of an ox; each also had the face of an eagle. 11Such were their faces. Their wings were spread out upward; each had two wings, one touching the wing of another creature on either side, and two wings covering its body. 12Each one went straight ahead. Wherever the spirit would go, they would go, without turning as they went. 13The appearance of the living creatures was like burning coals of fire or like torches. Fire moved back and forth among the creatures; it was bright, and lightning flashed out of it. 14The creatures sped back and forth like flashes of lightning.

15As I looked at the living creatures, I saw a wheel on the ground beside each creature with its four faces. 16This was the appearance and structure of the wheels: They sparkled like chrysolite, and all four looked alike. Each appeared to be made like a wheel intersecting a wheel. 17As they moved, they would go in any one of the four directions the creatures faced; the wheels did not turn about[d] as the creatures went. 18Their rims were high and awesome, and all four rims were full of eyes all around.

---

a *1* Or *my;*   b *3* Or *Ezekiel son of Buzi the priest*   c *3* Or *Chaldeans*   d *17* Or *aside*

Ezekiel

Ezekiel

1 EZEKIEL WAS a priest (the son of Buzi) who lived with the Jewish exiles beside the Chebar Canal in Babylon.

One day late in June, when I was thirty years old,[e] the heavens were suddenly opened to me and I saw visions from God. [4]I saw, in this vision, a great storm coming toward me from the north, driving before it a huge cloud glowing with fire, with a mass of fire inside that flashed continually; and in the fire there was something that shone like polished brass.

[5]Then from the center of the cloud, four strange forms appeared that looked like men, [6]except that each had four faces and two pairs of wings! [7]Their legs were like those of men, but their feet were cloven like calves' feet, and shone like burnished brass. [8]And beneath each of their wings I could see human hands.

[9]The four living beings were joined wing to wing, and they flew straight forward without turning. [10]Each had the face of a man [in front[f]], with a lion's face on the right side [of his head[g]], and the face of an ox on the left side, and the face of an eagle at the back! [11]Each had two pairs of wings spreading out from the middle of his back. One pair stretched out to attach to the wings of the living beings on each side, and the other pair covered his body. [12]Wherever their spirit[h] went they went, going straight forward without turning.

[13]Going up and down among them were other forms that glowed like bright coals of fire or brilliant torches, and it was from these the lightning flashed. [14]The living beings darted to and fro, swift as lightning.

[15]As I stared at all of this, I saw four wheels on the ground beneath them, one wheel belonging to each. [16]The wheels looked as if they were made of polished amber and each wheel was constructed with a second wheel crosswise inside.[i] [17]They could go in any of the four directions without having to face around. [18]The four wheels had rims and spokes, and the rims were filled with eyes around their edges.

The Vision of the Chariot

1 IN THE thirtieth year, in the fourth month, on the fifth day of the month, as I was among the exiles by the river Chebar, the heavens were opened, and I saw visions of God. [2]On the fifth day of the month (it was the fifth year of the exile of King Jehoiachin), [3]the word of the LORD came to the priest Ezekiel son of Buzi, in the land of the Chaldeans by the river Chebar; and the hand of the LORD was on him there.

4 As I looked, a stormy wind came out of the north: a great cloud with brightness around it and fire flashing forth continually, and in the middle of the fire, something like gleaming amber. [5]In the middle of it was something like four living creatures. This was their appearance: they were of human form. [6]Each had four faces, and each of them had four wings. [7]Their legs were straight, and the soles of their feet were like the sole of a calf's foot; and they sparkled like burnished bronze. [8]Under their wings on their four sides they had human hands. And the four had their faces and their wings thus: [9]their wings touched one another; each of them moved straight ahead, without turning as they moved. [10]As for the appearance of their faces: the four had the face of a human being, the face of a lion on the right side, the face of an ox on the left side, and the face of an eagle; [11]such were their faces. Their wings were spread out above; each creature had two wings, each of which touched the wing of another, while two covered their bodies. [12]Each moved straight ahead; wherever the spirit would go, they went, without turning as they went. [13]In the middle of[j] the living creatures there was something that looked like burning coals of fire, like torches moving to and fro among the living creatures; the fire was bright, and lightning issued from the fire. [14]The living creatures darted to and fro, like a flash of lightning.

15 As I looked at the living creatures, I saw a wheel on the earth beside the living creatures, one for each of the four of them.[k] [16]As for the appearance of the wheels and their construction: their appearance was like the gleaming of beryl; and the four had the same form, their construction being something like a wheel within a wheel. [17]When they moved, they moved in any of the four directions without veering as they moved. [18]Their rims were tall and awesome, for the rims of all four were full of eyes all around. [19]When the living creatures

e 1:1-3 when I was thirty years old, literally, "in the thirtieth year."
f 1:10 in front, implied.   g 1:10 of his head, implied.   h 1:12 Wherever their spirit, literally, "the spirit."   i 1:16 a second wheel crosswise inside, literally, "a wheel within a wheel," perhaps as in a gyroscope.

j Gk OL: Heb And the appearance of   k Heb of their faces

King James

19And when the living creatures went, the wheels went by them: and when the living creatures were lifted up from the earth, the wheels were lifted up.

20Whithersoever the spirit was to go, they went, thither was their spirit to go; and the wheels were lifted up over against them: for the spirit of the living creature was in the wheels.

21When those went, these went; and when those stood, these stood; and when those were lifted up from the earth, the wheels were lifted up over against them: for the spirit of the living creature was in the wheels.

22And the likeness of the firmament upon the heads of the living creature was as the colour of the terrible crystal, stretched forth over their heads above.

23And under the firmament were their wings straight, the one toward the other: every one had two, which covered on this side, and every one had two, which covered on that side, their bodies.

24And when they went, I heard the noise of their wings, like the noise of great waters, as the voice of the Almighty, the voice of speech, as the noise of an host: when they stood, they let down their wings.

25And there was a voice from the firmament that was over their heads, when they stood, and had let down their wings.

26¶ And above the firmament that was over their heads was the likeness of a throne, as the appearance of a sapphire stone: and upon the likeness of the throne was the likeness as the appearance of a man above upon it.

27And I saw as the colour of amber, as the appearance of fire round about within it, from the appearance of his loins even upward, and from the appearance of his loins even downward, I saw as it were the appearance of fire, and it had brightness round about.

28As the appearance of the bow that is in the cloud in the day of rain, so was the appearance of the brightness round about. This was the appearance of the likeness of the glory of the LORD. And when I saw it, I fell upon my face, and I heard a voice of one that spake.

2 AND HE said unto me, Son of man, stand upon thy feet, and I will speak unto thee.

2And the spirit entered into me when he spake unto me, and set me upon my feet, that I heard him that spake unto me.

3And he said unto me, Son of man, I send thee to the children of Israel, to a rebellious nation that hath rebelled against me: they and their fathers have transgressed against me, even unto this very day.

4For they are impudent children and stiffhearted. I do send thee unto them; and thou shalt say unto them, Thus saith the Lord GOD.

5And they, whether they will hear, or whether they will forbear, (for they are a rebellious house,) yet shall know that there hath been a prophet among them.

6¶ And thou, son of man, be not afraid of them, neither be afraid of their words, though briers and thorns be with thee, and thou dost dwell among scorpions: be not afraid of their words, nor be dismayed at their looks, though they be a rebellious house.

7And thou shalt speak my words unto them, whether they will hear, or whether they will forbear: for they are most rebellious.

8But thou, son of man, hear what I say unto thee; Be not thou rebellious like that rebellious house: open thy mouth, and eat that I give thee.

9¶ And when I looked, behold, an hand was sent unto me; and, lo, a roll of a book was therein;

10And he spread it before me; and it was written within and without: and there was written therein lamentations, and mourning, and woe.

New International

19When the living creatures moved, the wheels beside them moved; and when the living creatures rose from the ground, the wheels also rose. 20Wherever the spirit would go, they would go, and the wheels would rise along with them, because the spirit of the living creatures was in the wheels. 21When the creatures moved, they also moved; when the creatures stood still, they also stood still; and when the creatures rose from the ground, the wheels rose along with them, because the spirit of the living creatures was in the wheels.

22Spread out above the heads of the living creatures was what looked like an expanse, sparkling like ice, and awesome. 23Under the expanse their wings were stretched out one toward the other, and each had two wings covering its body. 24When the creatures moved, I heard the sound of their wings, like the roar of rushing waters, like the voice of the Almighty,[a] like the tumult of an army. When they stood still, they lowered their wings.

25Then there came a voice from above the expanse over their heads as they stood with lowered wings. 26Above the expanse over their heads was what looked like a throne of sapphire,[b] and high above on the throne was a figure like that of a man. 27I saw that from what appeared to be his waist up he looked like glowing metal, as if full of fire, and that from there down he looked like fire; and brilliant light surrounded him. 28Like the appearance of a rainbow in the clouds on a rainy day, so was the radiance around him.

This was the appearance of the likeness of the glory of the LORD. When I saw it, I fell facedown, and I heard the voice of one speaking.

Ezekiel's Call

2 HE SAID to me, "Son of man, stand up on your feet and I will speak to you." 2As he spoke, the Spirit came into me and raised me to my feet, and I heard him speaking to me.

3He said: "Son of man, I am sending you to the Israelites, to a rebellious nation that has rebelled against me; they and their fathers have been in revolt against me to this very day. 4The people to whom I am sending you are obstinate and stubborn. Say to them, 'This is what the Sovereign LORD says.' 5And whether they listen or fail to listen—for they are a rebellious house—they will know that a prophet has been among them. 6And you, son of man, do not be afraid of them or their words. Do not be afraid, though briers and thorns are all around you and you live among scorpions. Do not be afraid of what they say or terrified by them, though they are a rebellious house. 7You must speak my words to them, whether they listen or fail to listen, for they are rebellious. 8But you, son of man, listen to what I say to you. Do not rebel like that rebellious house; open your mouth and eat what I give you."

9Then I looked, and I saw a hand stretched out to me. In it was a scroll, 10which he unrolled before me. On both sides of it were written words of lament and mourning and woe.

<hr>

a 24 Hebrew Shaddai   b 26 Or lapis lazuli

Living Bible

19, 20, 21When the four living beings flew forward, the wheels moved forward with them. When they flew upwards, the wheels went up too. When the living beings stopped, the wheels stopped. For the spirit of the four living beings was in the wheels; so wherever their spirit went, the wheels and the living beings went there too.

22The sky spreading out above them looked as though it were made of crystal; it was inexpressibly beautiful.

23The wings of each stretched straight out to touch the others' wings, and each had two wings covering his body. 24And as they flew, their wings roared like waves against the shore, or like the voice of God, or like the shouting of a mighty army. When they stopped they let down their wings. 25And every time they stopped, there came a voice from the crystal sky above them.c

26For high in the sky above them was what looked like a throne made of beautiful blue sapphire stones, and upon it sat someone who appeared to be a Man.

27, 28From his waist up, he seemed to be all glowing bronze, dazzling like fire; and from his waist down he seemed to be entirely flame, and there was a glowing halo like a rainbow all around him. That was the way the glory of the Lord appeared to me. And when I saw it, I fell face downward on the ground, and heard the voice of someone speaking to me:

2 AND HE said to me: "Stand up, son of dust,d and I will talk to you."

2And the Spirit entered into me as he spoke, and set me on my feet.

3"Son of dust," he said, "I am sending you to the nation of Israel, to a nation rebelling against me. They and their fathers have kept on sinning against me until this very hour. 4For they are a hardhearted, stiff-necked people. But I am sending you to give them my messages—the messages of the Lord God. 5And whether they listen or not (for remember, they are rebels), they will at least know they have had a prophet among them.

6"Son of dust, don't be afraid of them; don't be frightened even though their threats are sharp and barbed and sting like scorpions. Don't be dismayed by their dark scowls. For remember, they are rebels! 7You must give them my messages whether they listen or not (but they won't,e for they are utter rebels). 8Listen, son of dust, to what I say to you. Don't you be a rebel too! Open your mouth and eat what I give you."

9, 10Then I looked and saw a hand holding out to me a scroll, with writing on both sides. He unrolled it, and I saw that it was full of warnings and sorrows and pronouncements of doom.

New Revised Standard

moved, the wheels moved beside them; and when the living creatures rose from the earth, the wheels rose. 20Wherever the spirit would go, they went, and the wheels rose along with them; for the spirit of the living creatures was in the wheels. 21When they moved, the others moved; when they stopped, the others stopped; and when they rose from the earth, the wheels rose along with them; for the spirit of the living creatures was in the wheels.

22 Over the heads of the living creatures there was something like a dome, shining like crystal,f spread out above their heads. 23Under the dome their wings were stretched out straight, one toward another; and each of the creatures had two wings covering its body. 24When they moved, I heard the sound of their wings like the sound of mighty waters, like the thunder of the Almighty,g a sound of tumult like the sound of an army; when they stopped, they let down their wings. 25And there came a voice from above the dome over their heads; when they stopped, they let down their wings.

26 And above the dome over their heads there was something like a throne, in appearance like sapphire;h and seated above the likeness of a throne was something that seemed like a human form. 27Upward from what appeared like the loins I saw something like gleaming amber, something that looked like fire enclosed all around; and downward from what looked like the loins I saw something that looked like fire, and there was a splendor all around. 28Like the bow in a cloud on a rainy day, such was the appearance of the splendor all around. This was the appearance of the likeness of the glory of the LORD.

When I saw it, I fell on my face, and I heard the voice of someone speaking.

The Vision of the Scroll

2 HE SAID to me: O mortal,i stand up on your feet, and I will speak with you. 2And when he spoke to me, a spirit entered into me and set me on my feet; and I heard him speaking to me. 3He said to me, Mortal, I am sending you to the people of Israel, to a nationj of rebels who have rebelled against me; they and their ancestors have transgressed against me to this very day. 4The descendants are impudent and stubborn. I am sending you to them, and you shall say to them, "Thus says the Lord GOD." 5Whether they hear or refuse to hear (for they are a rebellious house), they shall know that there has been a prophet among them. 6And you, O mortal, do not be afraid of them, and do not be afraid of their words, though briers and thorns surround you and you live among scorpions; do not be afraid of their words, and do not be dismayed at their looks, for they are a rebellious house. 7You shall speak my words to them, whether they hear or refuse to hear; for they are a rebellious house.

8 But you, mortal, hear what I say to you; do not be rebellious like that rebellious house; open your mouth and eat what I give you. 9I looked, and a hand was stretched out to me, and a written scroll was in it. 10He spread it before me; it had writing on the front and on the back, and written on it were words of lamentation and mourning and woe.

---

c 1:25 from the crystal sky above them, literally, "from above the firmament, over their heads." d 2:1 son of dust, or "son of man.". . . and so also eighty-seven times throughout the book of Ezekiel. The connotation is "mortal man." In Daniel 7:13, the corresponding Aramaic expression is used for the Messiah as representative of the human race of which he is the head. e 2:7 but they won't, implied.

f Gk: Heb like the awesome crystal   g Traditional rendering of Heb Shaddai   h Or lapis lazuli   i Or son of man; Heb ben adam (and so throughout the book when Ezekiel is addressed)   j Syr: Heb to nations

King James

3 MOREOVER HE said unto me, Son of man, eat that thou findest; eat this roll, and go speak unto the house of Israel.

2So I opened my mouth, and he caused me to eat that roll.

3And he said unto me, Son of man, cause thy belly to eat, and fill thy bowels with this roll that I give thee. Then did I eat *it;* and it was in my mouth as honey for sweetness.

4¶ And he said unto me, Son of man, go, get thee unto the house of Israel, and speak with my words unto them.

5For thou *art* not sent to a people of a strange speech and of an hard language, *but* to the house of Israel;

6Not to many people of a strange speech and of an hard language, whose words thou canst not understand. Surely, had I sent thee to them, they would have hearkened unto thee.

7But the house of Israel will not hearken unto thee; for they will not hearken unto me: for all the house of Israel *are* impudent and hardhearted.

8Behold, I have made thy face strong against their faces, and thy forehead strong against their foreheads.

9As an adamant harder than flint have I made thy forehead: fear them not, neither be dismayed at their looks, though they *be* a rebellious house.

10Moreover he said unto me, Son of man, all my words that I shall speak unto thee receive in thine heart, and hear with thine ears.

11And go, get thee to them of the captivity, unto the children of thy people, and speak unto them, and tell them, Thus saith the Lord GOD; whether they will hear, or whether they will forbear.

12Then the spirit took me up, and I heard behind me a voice of a great rushing, *saying,* Blessed *be* the glory of the LORD from his place.

13I *heard* also the noise of the wings of the living creatures that touched one another, and the noise of the wheels over against them, and a noise of a great rushing.

14So the spirit lifted me up, and took me away, and I went in bitterness, in the heat of my spirit; but the hand of the LORD was strong upon me.

15¶ Then I came to them of the captivity at Tel-abib, that dwelt by the river of Chebar, and I sat where they sat, and remained there astonished among them seven days.

16And it came to pass at the end of seven days, that the word of the LORD came unto me, saying,

17Son of man, I have made thee a watchman unto the house of Israel: therefore hear the word at my mouth, and give them warning from me.

18When I say unto the wicked, Thou shalt surely die; and thou givest him not warning, nor speakest to warn the wicked from his wicked way, to save his life; the same wicked *man* shall die in his iniquity; but his blood will I require at thine hand.

19Yet if thou warn the wicked, and he turn not from his wickedness, nor from his wicked way, he shall die in his iniquity; but thou hast delivered thy soul.

20Again, When a righteous *man* doth turn from his righteousness, and commit iniquity, and I lay a stumblingblock before him, he shall die: because thou hast not given him warning, he shall die in his sin, and his righteousness which he hath done shall not be remembered; but his blood will I require at thine hand.

21Nevertheless if thou warn the righteous *man,* that the righteous sin not, and he doth not sin, he shall surely live, because he is warned; also thou hast delivered thy soul.

22¶ And the hand of the LORD was there upon me; and he said unto me, Arise, go forth into the plain, and I will there talk with thee.

23Then I arose, and went forth into the plain: and, behold, the glory of the LORD stood there, as the glory which I saw by the river of Chebar: and I fell on my face.

New International

3 AND HE said to me, "Son of man, eat what is before you, eat this scroll; then go and speak to the house of Israel." 2So I opened my mouth, and he gave me the scroll to eat.

3Then he said to me, "Son of man, eat this scroll I am giving you and fill your stomach with it." So I ate it, and it tasted as sweet as honey in my mouth.

4He then said to me: "Son of man, go now to the house of Israel and speak my words to them. 5You are not being sent to a people of obscure speech and difficult language, but to the house of Israel— 6not to many peoples of obscure speech and difficult language, whose words you cannot understand. Surely if I had sent you to them, they would have listened to you. 7But the house of Israel is not willing to listen to you because they are not willing to listen to me, for the whole house of Israel is hardened and obstinate. 8But I will make you as unyielding and hardened as they are. 9I will make your forehead like the hardest stone, harder than flint. Do not be afraid of them or terrified by them, though they are a rebellious house."

10And he said to me, "Son of man, listen carefully and take to heart all the words I speak to you. 11Go now to your countrymen in exile and speak to them. Say to them, 'This is what the Sovereign LORD says,' whether they listen or fail to listen."

12Then the Spirit lifted me up, and I heard behind me a loud rumbling sound—May the glory of the LORD be praised in his dwelling place!— 13the sound of the wings of the living creatures brushing against each other and the sound of the wheels beside them, a loud rumbling sound. 14The Spirit then lifted me up and took me away, and I went in bitterness and in the anger of my spirit, with the strong hand of the LORD upon me. 15I came to the exiles who lived at Tel Abib near the Kebar River. And there, where they were living, I sat among them for seven days—overwhelmed.

Warning to Israel

16At the end of seven days the word of the LORD came to me: 17"Son of man, I have made you a watchman for the house of Israel; so hear the word I speak and give them warning from me. 18When I say to a wicked man, 'You will surely die,' and you do not warn him or speak out to dissuade him from his evil ways in order to save his life, that wicked man will die for[a] his sin, and I will hold you accountable for his blood. 19But if you do warn the wicked man and he does not turn from his wickedness or from his evil ways, he will die for his sin; but you will have saved yourself.

20"Again, when a righteous man turns from his righteousness and does evil, and I put a stumbling block before him, he will die. Since you did not warn him, he will die for his sin. The righteous things he did will not be remembered, and I will hold you accountable for his blood. 21But if you do warn the righteous man not to sin and he does not sin, he will surely live because he took warning, and you will have saved yourself."

22The hand of the LORD was upon me there, and he said to me, "Get up and go out to the plain, and there I will speak to you." 23So I got up and went out to the plain. And the glory of the LORD was standing there, like the glory I had seen by the Kebar River, and I fell facedown.

---

a *18 Or* in; *also in verses 19 and 20*

Living Bible

3 AND HE said to me: "Son of dust, eat what I am giving you—eat this scroll! Then go and give its message to the people of Israel."

2So I took the scroll.

3"Eat it all," he said. And when I ate it, it tasted sweet as honey.

4Then he said: "Son of dust, I am sending you to the people of Israel with my messages. 5I am not sending you to some far-off foreign land where you can't understand the language— 6no, not to tribes with strange, difficult tongues. (If I did, they would listen!) 7I am sending you to the people of Israel, and they won't listen to you any more than they listen to me! For the whole lot of them are hard, impudent and stubborn. 8But see, I have made you hard and stubborn too—as tough as they are. 9I have made your forehead as hard as rock. So don't be afraid of them, or fear their sullen, angry looks, even though they are such rebels."

10Then he added: "Son of dust, let all my words sink deep into your own heart first; listen to them carefully for yourself. 11Then, afterward, go to your people in exile, and whether or not they will listen, tell them: This is what the Lord God says!"

12Then the Spirit lifted me up and the glory of the Lord began to move away, accompanied by the sound of a great earthquake.b 13It was the noise of the wings of the living beings as they touched against each other, and the sound of their wheels beside them.

14, 15The Spirit lifted me up and took me away to Tel Abib, another colony of Jewish exiles beside the Chebar River. I went in bitterness and anger,c but the hand of the Lord was strong upon me. And I sat among them, overwhelmed, for seven days.

16At the end of the seven days, the Lord said to me:

17"Son of dust, I have appointed you as a watchman for Israel; whenever I send my people a warning, pass it on to them at once. 18If you refuse to warn the wicked when I want you to tell them, you are under the penalty of death, therefore repent and save your life—they will die in their sins, but I will punish you. I will demand your blood for theirs. 19But if you warn them and they keep on sinning, and refuse to repent, they will die in their sins, but you are blameless—you have done all you could. 20And if a good man becomes bad, and you refuse to warn him of the consequences, and the Lord destroys him, his previous good deeds won't help him—he shall die in his sin. But I will hold you responsible for his death, and punish you. 21But if you warn him and he repents, he shall live and you have saved your own life too."

22I was helpless in the hand of God, and when he said to me, "Go out into the valley and I will talk to you there"— 23I arose and went, and oh, I saw the glory of the Lord there, just as in my first vision! And I fell to the ground on my face.

New Revised Standard

3 HE SAID to me, O mortal, eat what is offered to you; eat this scroll, and go, speak to the house of Israel. 2So I opened my mouth, and he gave me the scroll to eat. 3He said to me, Mortal, eat this scroll that I give you and fill your stomach with it. Then I ate it; and in my mouth it was as sweet as honey.

4 He said to me: Mortal, go to the house of Israel and speak my very words to them. 5For you are not sent to a people of obscure speech and difficult language, but to the house of Israel— 6not to many peoples of obscure speech and difficult language, whose words you cannot understand. Surely, if I sent you to them, they would listen to you. 7But the house of Israel will not listen to you, for they are not willing to listen to me; because all the house of Israel have a hard forehead and a stubborn heart. 8See, I have made your face hard against their faces, and your forehead hard against their foreheads. 9Like the hardest stone, harder than flint, I have made your forehead; do not fear them or be dismayed at their looks, for they are a rebellious house. 10He said to me: Mortal, all my words that I shall speak to you receive in your heart and hear with your ears; 11then go to the exiles, to your people, and speak to them. Say to them, "Thus says the Lord GOD"; whether they hear or refuse to hear.

Ezekiel at the River Chebar

12 Then the spirit lifted me up, and as the glory of the LORD rosed from its place, I heard behind me the sound of loud rumbling; 13it was the sound of the wings of the living creatures brushing against one another, and the sound of the wheels beside them, that sounded like a loud rumbling. 14The spirit lifted me up and bore me away; I went in bitterness in the heat of my spirit, the hand of the LORD being strong upon me. 15I came to the exiles at Tel-abib, who lived by the river Chebar.e And I sat there among them, stunned, for seven days.

16 At the end of seven days, the word of the LORD came to me: 17Mortal, I have made you a sentinel for the house of Israel; whenever you hear a word from my mouth, you shall give them warning from me. 18If I say to the wicked, "You shall surely die," and you give them no warning, or speak to warn the wicked from their wicked way, in order to save their life, those wicked persons shall die for their iniquity; but their blood I will require at your hand. 19But if you warn the wicked, and they do not turn from their wickedness, or from their wicked way, they shall die for their iniquity; but you will have saved your life. 20Again, if the righteous turn from their righteousness and commit iniquity, and I lay a stumbling block before them, they shall die; because you have not warned them, they shall die for their sin, and their righteous deeds that they have done shall not be remembered; but their blood I will require at your hand. 21If, however, you warn the righteous not to sin, and they do not sin, they shall surely live, because they took warning; and you will have saved your life.

Ezekiel Isolated and Silenced

22 Then the hand of the LORD was upon me there; and he said to me, Rise up, go out into the valley, and there I will speak with you. 23So I rose up and went out into the valley; and the glory of the LORD stood there, like the glory that I had seen by the river Chebar; and I fell on my face. 24The spirit entered into me, and set

---

b 3:12 *accompanied by the sound of a great earthquake*, literally, "I heard behind me the sound of a great earthquake." c *3:14, 15 I went in bitterness and anger*, literally, "I went in the heat of my spirit"—not necessarily anger, but indicated here by this reaction.

d Cn: Heb *and blessed be the glory of the* LORD   e Two Mss Syr: Heb *Chebar, and to where they lived*. Another reading is *Chebar, and I sat where they sat*

King James

24Then the spirit entered into me, and set me upon my feet, and spake with me, and said unto me, Go, shut thyself within thine house.

25But thou, O son of man, behold, they shall put bands upon thee, and shall bind thee with them, and thou shalt not go out among them:

26And I will make my tongue cleave to the roof of thy mouth, that thou shalt be dumb, and shalt not be to them a reprover: for they *are* a rebellious house.

27But when I speak with thee, I will open thy mouth, and thou shalt say unto them, Thus saith the Lord GOD; He that heareth, let him hear; and he that forbeareth, let him forbear: for they *are* a rebellious house.

4 THOU ALSO, son of man, take thee a tile, and lay it before thee, and portray upon it the city, *even* Jerusalem:

2And lay siege against it, and build a fort against it, and cast a mount against it; set the camp also against it, and set *battering* rams against it round about.

3Moreover take thou unto thee an iron pan, and set it *for* a wall of iron between thee and the city: and set thy face against it, and it shall be besieged, and thou shalt lay siege against it. This *shall be* a sign to the house of Israel.

4Lie thou also upon thy left side, and lay the iniquity of the house of Israel upon it: *according* to the number of the days that thou shalt lie upon it thou shalt bear their iniquity.

5For I have laid upon thee the years of their iniquity, according to the number of the days, three hundred and ninety days: so shalt thou bear the iniquity of the house of Israel.

6And when thou hast accomplished them, lie again on thy right side, and thou shalt bear the iniquity of the house of Judah forty days: I have appointed thee each day for a year.

7Therefore thou shalt set thy face toward the siege of Jerusalem, and thine arm *shall be* uncovered, and thou shalt prophesy against it.

8And, behold, I will lay bands upon thee, and thou shalt not turn thee from one side to another, till thou hast ended the days of thy siege.

9¶ Take thou also unto thee wheat, and barley, and beans, and lentils, and millet, and fitches, and put them in one vessel, and make thee bread thereof, *according* to the number of the days that thou shalt lie upon thy side, three hundred and ninety days shalt thou eat thereof.

10And thy meat which thou shalt eat *shall be* by weight, twenty shekels a day: from time to time shalt thou eat it.

11Thou shalt drink also water by measure, the sixth part of an hin: from time to time shalt thou drink.

12And thou shalt eat it *as* barley cakes, and thou shalt bake it with dung that cometh out of man, in their sight.

13And the LORD said, Even thus shall the children of Israel eat their defiled bread among the Gentiles, whither I will drive them.

14Then said I, Ah Lord GOD! behold, my soul hath not been polluted: for from my youth up even till now have I not eaten of that which dieth of itself, or is torn in pieces; neither came there abominable flesh into my mouth.

15Then he said unto me, Lo, I have given thee cow's dung for man's dung, and thou shalt prepare thy bread therewith.

16Moreover he said unto me, Son of man, behold, I will break the staff of bread in Jerusalem: and they shall eat bread by weight, and with care; and they shall drink water by measure, and with astonishment:

New International

24Then the Spirit came into me and raised me to my feet. He spoke to me and said: "Go, shut yourself inside your house. 25And you, son of man, they will tie with ropes; you will be bound so that you cannot go out among the people. 26I will make your tongue stick to the roof of your mouth so that you will be silent and unable to rebuke them, though they are a rebellious house. 27But when I speak to you, I will open your mouth and you shall say to them, 'This is what the Sovereign LORD says.' Whoever will listen let him listen, and whoever will refuse let him refuse; for they are a rebellious house.

Siege of Jerusalem Symbolized

4 "NOW, SON of man, take a clay tablet, put it in front of you and draw the city of Jerusalem on it. 2Then lay siege to it: Erect siege works against it, build a ramp up to it, set up camps against it and put battering rams around it. 3Then take an iron pan, place it as an iron wall between you and the city and turn your face toward it. It will be under siege, and you shall besiege it. This will be a sign to the house of Israel.

4"Then lie on your left side and put the sin of the house of Israel upon yourself.[a] You are to bear their sin for the number of days you lie on your side. 5I have assigned you the same number of days as the years of their sin. So for 390 days you will bear the sin of the house of Israel.

6"After you have finished this, lie down again, this time on your right side, and bear the sin of the house of Judah. I have assigned you 40 days, a day for each year. 7Turn your face toward the siege of Jerusalem and with bared arm prophesy against her. 8I will tie you up with ropes so that you cannot turn from one side to the other until you have finished the days of your siege.

9"Take wheat and barley, beans and lentils, millet and spelt; put them in a storage jar and use them to make bread for yourself. You are to eat it during the 390 days you lie on your side. 10Weigh out twenty shekels[b] of food to eat each day and eat it at set times. 11Also measure out a sixth of a hin[c] of water and drink it at set times. 12Eat the food as you would a barley cake; bake it in the sight of the people, using human excrement for fuel." 13The LORD said, "In this way the people of Israel will eat defiled food among the nations where I will drive them."

14Then I said, "Not so, Sovereign LORD! I have never defiled myself. From my youth until now I have never eaten anything found dead or torn by wild animals. No unclean meat has ever entered my mouth."

15"Very well," he said, "I will let you bake your bread over cow manure instead of human excrement."

16He then said to me: "Son of man, I will cut off the supply of food in Jerusalem. The people will eat rationed food in anxiety and drink rationed water in despair, 17for

---

a *4* Or *your side*   b *10* That is, about 8 ounces (about 0.2 kilogram)
c *11* That is, about 2/3 quart (about 0.6 liter)

Living Bible

24Then the Spirit entered into me and set me on my feet. He talked to me and said: "Go, imprison yourself in your house, 25and I will paralyze youᵈ so you can't leave; 26and I will make your tongue stick to the roof of your mouth so that you can't reprove them; for they are rebels. 27But whenever I give you a message, then I will loosen your tongue and let you speak, and you shall say to them: The Lord God says, Let anyone listen who wants to, and let anyone refuse who wants to, for they are rebels.

4 "AND NOW, son of dust, take a large brick and lay it before you and draw a map of the city of Jerusalem on it. Draw a picture of siege mounds being built against the city, and enemy camps around it, and battering rams surrounding the walls. 3And put an iron plate between you and the city, like a wall of iron. Demonstrate how an enemy army will capture Jerusalem!

"There is special meaning in each detail of what I have told you to do. For it is a warning to the people of Israel.

4, 5"Now lie on your left side for 390 days,ᵉ to show that Israel will be punished for 390 years by captivity and doom. Each day you lie there represents a year of punishment ahead for Israel. 6Afterwards, turn over and lie on your right side for forty days, to signify the years of Judah's punishment. Each day will represent one year.

7"Meanwhile continue your demonstration of the siege of Jerusalem; lie there with your arm bared [to signify great strength and power in the attack against herᶠ]. This will prophesy her doom. 8And I will paralyze youᵍ so that you can't turn over from one side to the other until you have completed all the days of your siege.

9"During the first 390 days eat bread made of flour mixed from wheat, barley, beans, lentils, and spelt. Mix the various kinds of flour together in a jar. 10You are to ration this out to yourself at the rate of eight ounces at a time, one meal a day. 11And use one quart of water a day; don't use more than that. 12Each day take flour from the barrel and prepare it as you would barley cakes. While all the people are watching, bake it over a fire, using dried human dung as fuel, and eat it. 13For the Lord declares, Israel shall eat defiled bread in the Gentile lands to which I exile them!"

14Then I said, "O Lord God, must I be defiled by using dung? For I have never been defiled before in all my life. From the time I was a child until now I have never eaten any animal that died of sickness or that I found injured or dead; and I have never eaten any of the kinds of animals our law forbids."ʰ

15Then the Lord said, "All right, you may use cow dung instead of human dung."

16Then he told me, "Son of dust, bread will be tightly rationed in Jerusalem. It will be weighed out with great care and eaten fearfully. And the water will be portioned out in driblets, and the people will drink it with dismay.

New Revised Standard

me on my feet; and he spoke with me and said to me: Go, shut yourself inside your house. 25As for you, mortal, cords shall be placed on you, and you shall be bound with them, so that you cannot go out among the people; 26and I will make your tongue cling to the roof of your mouth, so that you shall be speechless and unable to reprove them; for they are a rebellious house. 27But when I speak with you, I will open your mouth, and you shall say to them, "Thus says the Lord GOD"; let those who will hear, hear; and let those who refuse to hear, refuse; for they are a rebellious house.

The Siege of Jerusalem Portrayed

4 AND YOU, O mortal, take a brick and set it before you. On it portray a city, Jerusalem; 2and put siegeworks against it, and build a siege wall against it, and cast up a ramp against it; set camps also against it, and plant battering rams against it all around. 3Then take an iron plate and place it as an iron wall between you and the city; set your face toward it, and let it be in a state of siege, and press the siege against it. This is a sign for the house of Israel.

4 Then lie on your left side, and place the punishment of the house of Israel upon it; you shall bear their punishment for the number of the days that you lie there. 5For I assign to you a number of days, three hundred ninety days, equal to the number of the years of their punishment; and so you shall bear the punishment of the house of Israel. 6When you have completed these, you shall lie down a second time, but on your right side, and bear the punishment of the house of Judah; forty days I assign you, one day for each year. 7You shall set your face toward the siege of Jerusalem, and with your arm bared you shall prophesy against it. 8See, I am putting cords on you so that you cannot turn from one side to the other until you have completed the days of your siege.

9 And you, take wheat and barley, beans and lentils, millet and spelt; put them into one vessel, and make bread for yourself. During the number of days that you lie on your side, three hundred ninety days, you shall eat it. 10The food that you eat shall be twenty shekels a day by weight; at fixed times you shall eat it. 11And you shall drink water by measure, one-sixth of a hin; at fixed times you shall drink. 12You shall eat it as a barley-cake, baking it in their sight on human dung. 13The LORD said, "Thus shall the people of Israel eat their bread, unclean, among the nations to which I will drive them." 14Then I said, "Ah Lord GOD! I have never defiled myself; from my youth up until now I have never eaten what died of itself or was torn by animals, nor has carrion flesh come into my mouth." 15Then he said to me, "See, I will let you have cow's dung instead of human dung, on which you may prepare your bread."

16 Then he said to me, Mortal, I am going to break the staff of bread in Jerusalem; they shall eat bread by weight and with fearfulness; and they shall drink water by measure and in dismay. 17Lacking bread and water,

---

ᵈ 3:25 will paralyze you, literally, "lay bands upon you."   ᵉ 4:4, 5 for 390 days. Some versions read, "190 days."   ᶠ 4:7 to signify great strength and power in the attack against her, implied.   ᵍ 4:8 I will paralyze you, literally, "I will lay bands upon you."   ʰ 4:14 the kinds of animals our law forbids. See Leviticus 11 for the dietary laws Ezekiel refers to here.

King James

17That they may want bread and water, and be astonied one with another, and consume away for their iniquity.

5 AND THOU, son of man, take thee a sharp knife, take thee a barber's razor, and cause it to pass upon thine head and upon thy beard: then take thee balances to weigh, and divide the *hair*.

2Thou shalt burn with fire a third part in the midst of the city, when the days of the siege are fulfilled: and thou shalt take a third part, *and* smite about it with a knife: and a third part thou shalt scatter in the wind; and I will draw out a sword after them.

3Thou shalt also take thereof a few in number, and bind them in thy skirts.

4Then take of them again, and cast them into the midst of the fire, and burn them in the fire; *for* thereof shall a fire come forth into all the house of Israel.

5¶ Thus saith the Lord GOD; This *is* Jerusalem: I have set it in the midst of the nations and countries *that are* round about her.

6And she hath changed my judgments into wickedness more than the nations, and my statutes more than the countries that *are* round about her: for they have refused my judgments and my statutes, they have not walked in them.

7Therefore thus saith the Lord GOD; Because ye multiplied more than the nations that *are* round about you, *and* have not walked in my statutes, neither have kept my judgments, neither have done according to the judgments of the nations that *are* round about you;

8Therefore thus saith the Lord GOD; Behold, I, even I, *am* against thee, and will execute judgments in the midst of thee in the sight of the nations.

9And I will do in thee that which I have not done, and whereunto I will not do any more the like, because of all thine abominations.

10Therefore the fathers shall eat the sons in the midst of thee, and the sons shall eat their fathers; and I will execute judgments in thee, and the whole remnant of thee will I scatter into all the winds.

11Wherefore, *as* I live, saith the Lord GOD; Surely, because thou hast defiled my sanctuary with all thy detestable things, and with all thine abominations, therefore will I also diminish *thee;* neither shall mine eye spare, neither will I have any pity.

12¶ A third part of thee shall die with the pestilence, and with famine shall they be consumed in the midst of thee: and a third part shall fall by the sword round about thee; and I will scatter a third part into all the winds, and I will draw out a sword after them.

13Thus shall mine anger be accomplished, and I will cause my fury to rest upon them, and I will be comforted: and they shall know that I the LORD have spoken *it* in my zeal, when I have accomplished my fury in them.

14Moreover I will make thee waste, and a reproach among the nations that *are* round about thee, in the sight of all that pass by.

15So it shall be a reproach and a taunt, an instruction and an astonishment unto the nations that *are* round about thee, when I shall execute judgments in thee in anger and in fury and in furious rebukes. I the LORD have spoken *it*.

16When I shall send upon them the evil arrows of famine, which shall be for *their* destruction, *and* which I will send to destroy you: and I will increase the famine upon you, and will break your staff of bread:

17So will I send upon you famine and evil beasts, and they shall bereave thee; and pestilence and blood shall pass through thee; and I will bring the sword upon thee. I the LORD have spoken *it*.

New International

food and water will be scarce. They will be appalled at the sight of each other and will waste away because of[a] their sin.

5 "NOW, SON of man, take a sharp sword and use it as a barber's razor to shave your head and your beard. Then take a set of scales and divide up the hair. 2When the days of your siege come to an end, burn a third of the hair with fire inside the city. Take a third and strike it with the sword all around the city. And scatter a third to the wind. For I will pursue them with drawn sword. 3But take a few strands of hair and tuck them away in the folds of your garment. 4Again, take a few of these and throw them into the fire and burn them up. A fire will spread from there to the whole house of Israel.

5"This is what the Sovereign LORD says: This is Jerusalem, which I have set in the center of the nations, with countries all around her. 6Yet in her wickedness she has rebelled against my laws and decrees more than the nations and countries around her. She has rejected my laws and has not followed my decrees.

7"Therefore this is what the Sovereign LORD says: You have been more unruly than the nations around you and have not followed my decrees or kept my laws. You have not even[b] conformed to the standards of the nations around you.

8"Therefore this is what the Sovereign LORD says: I myself am against you, Jerusalem, and I will inflict punishment on you in the sight of the nations. 9Because of all your detestable idols, I will do to you what I have never done before and will never do again. 10Therefore in your midst fathers will eat their children, and children will eat their fathers. I will inflict punishment on you and will scatter all your survivors to the winds. 11Therefore as surely as I live, declares the Sovereign LORD, because you have defiled my sanctuary with all your vile images and detestable practices, I myself will withdraw my favor; I will not look on you with pity or spare you. 12A third of your people will die of the plague or perish by famine inside you; a third will fall by the sword outside your walls; and a third I will scatter to the winds and pursue with drawn sword.

13"Then my anger will cease and my wrath against them will subside, and I will be avenged. And when I have spent my wrath upon them, they will know that I the LORD have spoken in my zeal.

14"I will make you a ruin and a reproach among the nations around you, in the sight of all who pass by. 15You will be a reproach and a taunt, a warning and an object of horror to the nations around you when I inflict punishment on you in anger and in wrath and with stinging rebuke. I the LORD have spoken. 16When I shoot at you with my deadly and destructive arrows of famine, I will shoot to destroy you. I will bring more and more famine upon you and cut off your supply of food. 17I will send famine and wild beasts against you, and they will leave you childless. Plague and bloodshed will sweep through you, and I will bring the sword against you. I the LORD have spoken."

Living Bible

17I will cause the people to lack both bread and water, and to look at one another in frantic terror, and to waste away beneath their punishment.

5 "SON OF dust, take a sharp sword and use it as a barber's razor to shave your head and beard; use balances to weigh the hair into three equal parts. 2Place a third of it at the center of your map of Jerusalem. After your siege, burn it there. Scatter another third across your map and slash at it with a knife. Scatter the last third to the wind, for I will chase my people with the sword. 3Keep just a bit of the hair and tie it up in your robe; 4then take a few hairs out and throw them into the fire, for a fire shall come from this remnant and destroy all Israel."

5,6,7The Lord God says, "This illustrates what will happen to Jerusalem, for she has turned away from my laws and has been even more wicked than the nations surrounding her." 8Therefore the Lord God says, I, even I, am against you and will punish you publicly while all the nations watch. 9Because of the terrible sins you have committed, I will punish you more terribly than I have ever done before or ever will again. 10Fathers will eat their own sons, and sons will eat their fathers; and those who survive will be scattered into all the world.

11"For I promise you: Because you have defiled my Temple with idols and evil sacrifices, therefore I will not spare you nor pity you at all. 12One-third of you will die from famine and disease; one-third will be slaughtered by the enemy; and one-third I will scatter to the winds, sending the sword of the enemy chasing after you. 13Then at last my anger will be appeased. And all Israel will know that what I threaten, I do.

14"So I will make a public example of you before all the surrounding nations and before everyone traveling past the ruins of your land. 15You will become a laughingstock to the world and an awesome example to everyone, for all to see what happens when the Lord turns against an entire nation in furious rebuke. I, the Lord, have spoken it!

16"I will shower you with deadly arrows of famine to destroy you. The famine will become more and more serious until every bit of bread is gone. 17And not only famine will come, but wild animals will attack you and kill you and your families; disease and war will stalk your land, and the sword of the enemy will slay you; I, the Lord, have spoken it!"

New Revised Standard

they will look at one another in dismay, and waste away under their punishment.

A Sword against Jerusalem

5 AND YOU, O mortal, take a sharp sword; use it as a barber's razor and run it over your head and your beard; then take balances for weighing, and divide the hair. 2One third of the hair you shall burn in the fire inside the city, when the days of the siege are completed; one third you shall take and strike with the sword all around the city;c and one third you shall scatter to the wind, and I will unsheathe the sword after them. 3Then you shall take from these a small number, and bind them in the skirts of your robe. 4From these, again, you shall take some, throw them into the fire and burn them up; from there a fire will come out against all the house of Israel.

5 Thus says the Lord GOD: This is Jerusalem; I have set her in the center of the nations, with countries all around her. 6But she has rebelled against my ordinances and my statutes, becoming more wicked than the nations and the countries all around her, rejecting my ordinances and not following my statutes. 7Therefore thus says the Lord GOD: Because you are more turbulent than the nations that are all around you, and have not followed my statutes or kept my ordinances, but have acted according to the ordinances of the nations that are all around you; 8therefore thus says the Lord GOD: I, I myself, am coming against you; I will execute judgments among you in the sight of the nations. 9And because of all your abominations, I will do to you what I have never yet done, and the like of which I will never do again. 10Surely, parents shall eat their children in your midst, and children shall eat their parents; I will execute judgments on you, and any of you who survive I will scatter to every wind. 11Therefore, as I live, says the Lord GOD, surely, because you have defiled my sanctuary with all your detestable things and with all your abominations—therefore I will cut you down;d my eye will not spare, and I will have no pity. 12One third of you shall die of pestilence or be consumed by famine among you; one third shall fall by the sword around you; and one third I will scatter to every wind and will unsheathe the sword after them.

13 My anger shall spend itself, and I will vent my fury on them and satisfy myself; and they shall know that I, the LORD, have spoken in my jealousy, when I spend my fury on them. 14Moreover I will make you a desolation and an object of mocking among the nations around you, in the sight of all that pass by. 15You shall bee a mockery and a taunt, a warning and a horror, to the nations around you, when I execute judgments on you in anger and fury, and with furious punishments—I, the LORD, have spoken— 16when I loose against youf my deadly arrows of famine, arrows for destruction, which I will let loose to destroy you, and when I bring more and more famine upon you, and break your staff of bread. 17I will send famine and wild animals against you, and they shall rob you of your children; pestilence and bloodshed shall pass through you; and I will bring the sword upon you. I, the LORD, have spoken.

c Heb it   d Another reading is *I will withdraw*   e Gk Syr Vg Tg: Heb *It shall be*   f Heb *them*

King James

6 AND THE word of the LORD came unto me, saying,

2Son of man, set thy face toward the mountains of Israel, and prophesy against them,

3And say, Ye mountains of Israel, hear the word of the Lord GOD; Thus saith the Lord GOD to the mountains, and to the hills, to the rivers, and to the valleys; Behold, I, *even* I, will bring a sword upon you, and I will destroy your high places.

4And your altars shall be desolate, and your images shall be broken: and I will cast down your slain *men* before your idols.

5And I will lay the dead carcases of the children of Israel before their idols; and I will scatter your bones round about your altars.

6In all your dwellingplaces the cities shall be laid waste, and the high places shall be desolate; that your altars may be laid waste and made desolate, and your idols may be broken and cease, and your images may be cut down, and your works may be abolished.

7And the slain shall fall in the midst of you, and ye shall know that I *am* the LORD.

8¶ Yet will I leave a remnant, that ye may have *some* that shall escape the sword among the nations, when ye shall be scattered through the countries.

9And they that escape of you shall remember me among the nations whither they shall be carried captives, because I am broken with their whorish heart, which hath departed from me, and with their eyes, which go a-whoring after their idols: and they shall loathe themselves for the evils which they have committed in all their abominations.

10And they shall know that I *am* the LORD, *and that* I have not said in vain that I would do this evil unto them.

11¶ Thus saith the Lord GOD; Smite with thine hand, and stamp with thy foot, and say, Alas for all the evil abominations of the house of Israel! for they shall fall by the sword, by the famine, and by the pestilence.

12He that is far off shall die of the pestilence; and he that is near shall fall by the sword; and he that remaineth and is besieged shall die by the famine: thus will I accomplish my fury upon them.

13Then shall ye know that I *am* the LORD, when their slain *men* shall be among their idols round about their altars, upon every high hill, in all the tops of the mountains, and under every green tree, and under every thick oak, the place where they did offer sweet savour to all their idols.

14So will I stretch out my hand upon them, and make the land desolate, yea, more desolate than the wilderness toward Diblath, in all their habitations: and they shall know that I *am* the LORD.

7 MOREOVER THE word of the LORD came unto me, saying,

2Also, thou son of man, thus saith the Lord GOD unto the land of Israel; An end, the end is come upon the four corners of the land.

3Now *is* the end *come* upon thee, and I will send mine anger upon thee, and will judge thee according to thy ways, and will recompense upon thee all thine abominations.

4And mine eye shall not spare thee, neither will I have pity: but I will recompense thy ways upon thee, and thine abominations shall be in the midst of thee: and ye shall know that I *am* the LORD.

New International

A Prophecy Against the Mountains of Israel

6 THE WORD of the LORD came to me: 2"Son of man, set your face against the mountains of Israel; prophesy against them 3and say: 'O mountains of Israel, hear the word of the Sovereign LORD. This is what the Sovereign LORD says to the mountains and hills, to the ravines and valleys: I am about to bring a sword against you, and I will destroy your high places. 4Your altars will be demolished and your incense altars will be smashed; and I will slay your people in front of your idols. 5I will lay the dead bodies of the Israelites in front of their idols, and I will scatter your bones around your altars. 6Wherever you live, the towns will be laid waste and the high places demolished, so that your altars will be laid waste and devastated, your idols smashed and ruined, your incense altars broken down, and what you have made wiped out. 7Your people will fall slain among you, and you will know that I am the LORD.

8" 'But I will spare some, for some of you will escape the sword when you are scattered among the lands and nations. 9Then in the nations where they have been carried captive, those who escape will remember me—how I have been grieved by their adulterous hearts, which have turned away from me, and by their eyes, which have lusted after their idols. They will loathe themselves for the evil they have done and for all their detestable practices. 10And they will know that I am the LORD; I did not threaten in vain to bring this calamity on them.

11" 'This is what the Sovereign LORD says: Strike your hands together and stamp your feet and cry out "Alas!" because of all the wicked and detestable practices of the house of Israel, for they will fall by the sword, famine and plague. 12He that is far away will die of the plague, and he that is near will fall by the sword, and he that survives and is spared will die of famine. So will I spend my wrath upon them. 13And they will know that I am the LORD, when their people lie slain among their idols around their altars, on every high hill and on all the mountaintops, under every spreading tree and every leafy oak—places where they offered fragrant incense to all their idols. 14And I will stretch out my hand against them and make the land a desolate waste from the desert to Diblah[a]—wherever they live. Then they will know that I am the LORD.' "

The End Has Come

7 THE WORD of the LORD came to me: 2"Son of man, this is what the Sovereign LORD says to the land of Israel: The end! The end has come upon the four corners of the land. 3The end is now upon you and I will unleash my anger against you. I will judge you according to your conduct and repay you for all your detestable practices. 4I will not look on you with pity or spare you; I will surely repay you for your conduct and the detestable practices among you. Then you will know that I am the LORD.

---

[a] *14* Most Hebrew manuscripts; a few Hebrew manuscripts *Riblah*

Living Bible

6 AGAIN A message came from the Lord: 2"Son of dust, look over toward the mountains of Israel and prophesy against them. 3Say to them, O mountains of Israel, hear the message of the Lord God against you and against the rivers and valleys. I, even I the Lord, will bring war upon you to destroy your idols. 4–7All your cities will be smashed and burned, and the idol altars abandoned. Your gods will be shattered; the bones of their worshipers will lie scattered among the altars. Then at last you will know I am the Lord.

8"But I will let a few of my people escape—to be scattered among the nations of the world. 9Then when they are exiled among the nations, they will remember me, for I will take away their adulterous hearts—their love of idols—and I will blind their lecherous eyes that long for other gods. Then at last they will loathe themselves for all this wickedness. 10They will realize that I alone am God, and that I wasn't fooling when I told them that all this would happen to them.

11"The Lord God says: Raise your hands in horror and shake your headb with deep remorse and say, Alas for all the evil we have done! For you are going to perish from war and famine and disease. 12Disease will strike down those in exile; war will destroy those in the land of Israel; and any who remain will die by famine and siege. So at last I will expend my fury on you. 13When your slain lie scattered among your idols and altars on every hill and mountain and under every green tree and great oak where they offered incense to their gods—you will realize that I alone am God. 14I will crush you and make your cities desolate from the wilderness in the south to Riblah in the north. Then you will know I am the Lord."

7 THIS FURTHER message came to me from God: 2"Tell Israel, Wherever you look—east, west, north or south—your land is finished. 3No hope remains, for I will loose my anger on you for your worshiping of idols. 4I will turn my eyes away and show no pity; I will repay you in full, and you shall know I am the Lord."

New Revised Standard

Judgment on Idolatrous Israel

6 THE WORD of the LORD came to me: 2O mortal, set your face toward the mountains of Israel, and prophesy against them, 3and say, You mountains of Israel, hear the word of the Lord GOD! Thus says the Lord GOD to the mountains and the hills, to the ravines and the valleys: I, I myself will bring a sword upon you, and I will destroy your high places. 4Your altars shall become desolate, and your incense stands shall be broken; and I will throw down your slain in front of your idols. 5I will lay the corpses of the people of Israel in front of their idols; and I will scatter your bones around your altars. 6Wherever you live, your towns shall be waste and your high places ruined, so that your altars will be waste and ruined,c your idols broken and destroyed, your incense stands cut down, and your works wiped out. 7The slain shall fall in your midst; then you shall know that I am the LORD.

8 But I will spare some. Some of you shall escape the sword among the nations and be scattered through the countries. 9Those of you who escape shall remember me among the nations where they are carried captive, how I was crushed by their wanton heart that turned away from me, and their wanton eyes that turned after their idols. Then they will be loathsome in their own sight for the evils that they have committed, for all their abominations. 10And they shall know that I am the LORD; I did not threaten in vain to bring this disaster upon them.

11 Thus says the Lord GOD: Clap your hands and stamp your foot, and say, Alas for all the vile abominations of the house of Israel! For they shall fall by the sword, by famine, and by pestilence. 12Those far off shall die of pestilence; those nearby shall fall by the sword; and any who are left and are spared shall die of famine. Thus I will spend my fury upon them. 13And you shall know that I am the LORD, when their slain lie among their idols around their altars, on every high hill, on all the mountain tops, under every green tree, and under every leafy oak, wherever they offered pleasing odor to all their idols. 14I will stretch out my hand against them, and make the land desolate and waste, throughout all their settlements, from the wilderness to Riblah.d Then they shall know that I am the LORD.

Impending Disaster

7 THE WORD of the LORD came to me: 2You, O mortal, thus says the Lord GOD to the land of Israel:

An end! The end has come
    upon the four corners of the land.
3 Now the end is upon you,
    I will loose my anger upon you;
I will judge you according to your ways,
    I will punish you for all your abominations.
4 My eye will not spare you, I will have no
    pity.
I will punish you for your ways,
    while your abominations are among you.
Then you shall know that I am the LORD.

---

b 6:11 *Raise your hands in horror and shake your head,* literally, "Clap your hands and stamp your feet."

c Syr Vg Tg: Heb *and be made guilty*   d Another reading is *Diblah*

King James

5Thus saith the Lord GOD; An evil, an only evil, behold, is come.

6An end is come, the end is come: it watcheth for thee; behold, it is come.

7The morning is come unto thee, O thou that dwellest in the land: the time is come, the day of trouble *is* near, and not the sounding again of the mountains.

8Now will I shortly pour out my fury upon thee, and accomplish mine anger upon thee: and I will judge thee according to thy ways, and will recompense thee for all thine abominations.

9And mine eye shall not spare, neither will I have pity: I will recompense thee according to thy ways and thine abominations *that* are in the midst of thee; and ye shall know that I *am* the LORD that smiteth.

10Behold the day, behold, it is come: the morning is gone forth; the rod hath blossomed, pride hath budded.

11Violence is risen up into a rod of wickedness: none of them *shall remain*, nor of their multitude, nor of any of theirs: neither *shall there be* wailing for them.

12The time is come, the day draweth near: let not the buyer rejoice, nor the seller mourn: for wrath *is* upon all the multitude thereof.

13For the seller shall not return to that which is sold, although they were yet alive: for the vision *is* touching the whole multitude thereof, *which* shall not return; neither shall any strengthen himself in the iniquity of his life.

14They have blown the trumpet, even to make all ready; but none goeth to the battle: for my wrath *is* upon all the multitude thereof.

15The sword *is* without, and the pestilence and the famine within: he that *is* in the field shall die with the sword; and he that *is* in the city, famine and pestilence shall devour him.

16¶ But they that escape of them shall escape, and shall be on the mountains like doves of the valleys, all of them mourning, every one for his iniquity.

17All hands shall be feeble, and all knees shall be weak *as* water.

18They shall also gird *themselves* with sackcloth, and horror shall cover them; and shame *shall be* upon all faces, and baldness upon all their heads.

19They shall cast their silver in the streets, and their gold shall be removed: their silver and their gold shall not be able to deliver them in the day of the wrath of the LORD: they shall not satisfy their souls, neither fill their bowels: because it is the stumblingblock of their iniquity.

20¶ As for the beauty of his ornament, he set it in majesty: but they made the images of their abominations *and* of their detestable things therein: therefore have I set it far from them.

21And I will give it into the hands of the strangers for a prey, and to the wicked of the earth for a spoil; and they shall pollute it.

22My face will I turn also from them, and they shall pollute my secret *place:* for the robbers shall enter into it, and defile it.

23¶ Make a chain: for the land is full of bloody crimes, and the city is full of violence.

New International

5"This is what the Sovereign LORD says: Disaster! An unheard-of[a] disaster is coming. 6The end has come! The end has come! It has roused itself against you. It has come! 7Doom has come upon you—you who dwell in the land. The time has come, the day is near; there is panic, not joy, upon the mountains. 8I am about to pour out my wrath on you and spend my anger against you; I will judge you according to your conduct and repay you for all your detestable practices. 9I will not look on you with pity or spare you; I will repay you in accordance with your conduct and the detestable practices among you. Then you will know that it is I the LORD who strikes the blow.

10"The day is here! It has come! Doom has burst forth, the rod has budded, arrogance has blossomed! 11Violence has grown into[b] a rod to punish wickedness; none of the people will be left, none of that crowd—no wealth, nothing of value. 12The time has come, the day has arrived. Let not the buyer rejoice nor the seller grieve, for wrath is upon the whole crowd. 13The seller will not recover the land he has sold as long as both of them live, for the vision concerning the whole crowd will not be reversed. Because of their sins, not one of them will preserve his life. 14Though they blow the trumpet and get everything ready, no one will go into battle, for my wrath is upon the whole crowd.

15"Outside is the sword, inside are plague and famine; those in the country will die by the sword, and those in the city will be devoured by famine and plague. 16All who survive and escape will be in the mountains, moaning like doves of the valleys, each because of his sins. 17Every hand will go limp, and every knee will become as weak as water. 18They will put on sackcloth and be clothed with terror. Their faces will be covered with shame and their heads will be shaved. 19They will throw their silver into the streets, and their gold will be an unclean thing. Their silver and gold will not be able to save them in the day of the LORD's wrath. They will not satisfy their hunger or fill their stomachs with it, for it has made them stumble into sin. 20They were proud of their beautiful jewelry and used it to make their detestable idols and vile images. Therefore I will turn these into an unclean thing for them. 21I will hand it all over as plunder to foreigners and as loot to the wicked of the earth, and they will defile it. 22I will turn my face away from them, and they will desecrate my treasured place; robbers will enter it and desecrate it.

23"Prepare chains, because the land is full of bloodshed and the city is full of violence. 24I will bring the

---

a 5 Most Hebrew manuscripts; some Hebrew manuscripts and Syriac *Disaster after*   b 11 Or *The violent one has become*

Living Bible

5, 6The Lord God says: "With one blow after another I will finish you. The end has come; your final doom is waiting. 7O Israel, the day of your damnation dawns; the time has come; the day of trouble nears. It is a day of shouts of anguish, not shouts of joy! 8, 9Soon I will pour out my fury and let it finish its work of punishing you for all your evil deeds. I will not spare nor pity you, and you will know that I, the Lord, am doing it. 10, 11The day of judgment has come; the morning dawns, for your wickedness and pride have run their course and reached their climax—none of these rich and wicked men of pride shall live. All your boasting will die away, and no one will be left to bewail your fate.

12"Yes, the time has come; the day draws near. There will be nothing to buy or sell, for the wrath of God is on the land. 13And even if a merchant lives, his business will be gone, for God has spoken against all the people of Israel; all will be destroyed. Not one of those whose lives are filled with sin will recover.

14"The trumpets shout to Israel's army, 'Mobilize!' but no one listens, for my wrath is on them all. 15If you go outside the walls, there stands the enemy to kill you. If you stay inside, famine and disease will devour you. 16Any who escape will be lonely as mourning doves hiding on the mountains, each weeping for his sins. 17All hands shall be feeble, and all knees as weak as water. 18You shall clothe yourselves with sackcloth, and horror and shame shall cover you; you shall shave your heads in sorrow and remorse.

19"Throw away your money! Toss it out like worthless rubbish, for it will have no value in that day of wrath. It will neither satisfy nor feed you, for your love of money is the reason for your sin. 20I gave you gold to use in decorating the Temple, and you used it instead to make idols! Therefore I will take it all away from you. 21I will give it to foreigners and to wicked men as booty. They shall defile my Temple. 22I will not look when they defile it, nor will I stop them. Like robbers, they will loot the treasures and leave the Temple in ruins.

23"Prepare chains for my people, for the land is full of bloody crimes. Jerusalem is filled with violence, so I will enslave her people. 24I will crush your pride by

New Revised Standard

5 Thus says the Lord GOD:
   Disaster after disaster! See, it comes.
6   An end has come, the end has come.
   It has awakened against you; see, it comes!
7 Your doomc has come to you,
   O inhabitant of the land.
   The time has come, the day is near—
   of tumult, not of reveling on the mountains.
8 Soon now I will pour out my wrath upon you;
   I will spend my anger against you.
   I will judge you according to your ways,
   and punish you for all your abominations.
9 My eye will not spare; I will have no pity.
   I will punish you according to your ways,
   while your abominations are among you.
Then you shall know that it is I the LORD who strike.
10 See, the day! See, it comes!
   Your doomc has gone out.
   The rod has blossomed, pride has budded.
11   Violence has grown into a rod
        of wickedness.
   None of them shall remain,
      not their abundance, not their wealth;
      no pre-eminence among them.c
12 The time has come, the day draws near;
      let not the buyer rejoice, nor the seller
        mourn,
      for wrath is upon all their multitude.
13For the sellers shall not return to what has been sold as long as they remain alive. For the vision concerns all their multitude; it shall not be revoked. Because of their iniquity, they cannot maintain their lives.c
14 They have blown the horn and made
        everything ready;
      but no one goes to battle,
      for my wrath is upon all their multitude.
15 The sword is outside, pestilence and famine
        are inside;
      those in the field die by the sword;
      those in the city—famine and pestilence
        devour them.
16 If any survivors escape,
      they shall be found on the mountains
      like doves of the valleys,
   all of them moaning over their iniquity.
17 All hands shall grow feeble,
      all knees turn to water.
18 They shall put on sackcloth,
      horror shall cover them.
   Shame shall be on all faces,
      baldness on all their heads.
19 They shall fling their silver into the streets,
      their gold shall be treated as unclean.
Their silver and gold cannot save them on the day of the wrath of the LORD. They shall not satisfy their hunger or fill their stomachs with it. For it was the stumbling block of their iniquity. 20From theird beautiful ornament, in which they took pride, they made their abominable images, their detestable things; therefore I will make of it an unclean thing to them.
21 I will hand it over to strangers as booty,
      to the wicked of the earth as plunder;
      they shall profane it.
22 I will avert my face from them,
      so that they may profane my treasurede
        place;
   the violent shall enter it,
      they shall profane it.
23 Make a chain!c
   For the land is full of bloody crimes;
      the city is full of violence.

c Meaning of Heb uncertain   d Syr Symmachus: Heb its   e Or secret

King James

24Wherefore I will bring the worst of the heathen, and they shall possess their houses: I will also make the pomp of the strong to cease; and their holy places shall be defiled.

25Destruction cometh; and they shall seek peace, and *there shall be* none.

26Mischief shall come upon mischief, and rumour shall be upon rumour; then shall they seek a vision of the prophet; but the law shall perish from the priest, and counsel from the ancients.

27The king shall mourn, and the prince shall be clothed with desolation, and the hands of the people of the land shall be troubled: I will do unto them after their way, and according to their deserts will I judge them; and they shall know that I *am* the LORD.

8 AND IT came to pass in the sixth year, in the sixth *month,* in the fifth *day* of the month, *as* I sat in mine house, and the elders of Judah sat before me, that the hand of the Lord GOD fell there upon me.

2Then I beheld, and lo a likeness as the appearance of fire: from the appearance of his loins even downward, fire; and from his loins even upward, as the appearance of brightness, as the colour of amber.

3And he put forth the form of an hand, and took me by a lock of mine head; and the spirit lifted me up between the earth and the heaven, and brought me in the visions of God to Jerusalem, to the door of the inner gate that looketh toward the north; where *was* the seat of the image of jealousy, which provoketh to jealousy.

4And, behold, the glory of the God of Israel *was* there, according to the vision that I saw in the plain.

5¶ Then said he unto me, Son of man, lift up thine eyes now the way toward the north. So I lifted up mine eyes the way toward the north, and behold northward at the gate of the altar this image of jealousy in the entry.

6He said furthermore unto me, Son of man, seest thou what they do? *even* the great abominations that the house of Israel committeth here, that I should go far off from my sanctuary? but turn thee yet again, *and* thou shalt see greater abominations.

7¶ And he brought me to the door of the court; and when I looked, behold a hole in the wall.

8Then said he unto me, Son of man, dig now in the wall: and when I had digged in the wall, behold a door.

9And he said unto me, Go in, and behold the wicked abominations that they do here.

10So I went in and saw; and behold every form of creeping things, and abominable beasts, and all the idols of the house of Israel, portrayed upon the wall round about.

11And there stood before them seventy men of the ancients of the house of Israel, and in the midst of them stood Jaazaniah the son of Shaphan, with every man his censer in his hand; and a thick cloud of incense went up.

12Then said he unto me, Son of man, hast thou seen what the ancients of the house of Israel do in the dark, every man in the chambers of his imagery? for they say, The LORD seeth us not; the LORD hath forsaken the earth.

13¶ He said also unto me, Turn thee yet again, *and* thou shalt see greater abominations that they do.

14Then he brought me to the door of the gate of the LORD's house which *was* toward the north; and, behold, there sat women weeping for Tammuz.

New International

most wicked of the nations to take possession of their houses; I will put an end to the pride of the mighty, and their sanctuaries will be desecrated. 25When terror comes, they will seek peace, but there will be none. 26Calamity upon calamity will come, and rumor upon rumor. They will try to get a vision from the prophet; the teaching of the law by the priest will be lost, as will the counsel of the elders. 27The king will mourn, the prince will be clothed with despair, and the hands of the people of the land will tremble. I will deal with them according to their conduct, and by their own standards I will judge them. Then they will know that I am the LORD."

Idolatry in the Temple

8 IN THE sixth year, in the sixth month on the fifth day, while I was sitting in my house and the elders of Judah were sitting before me, the hand of the Sovereign LORD came upon me there. 2I looked, and I saw a figure like that of a man.[a] From what appeared to be his waist down he was like fire, and from there up his appearance was as bright as glowing metal. 3He stretched out what looked like a hand and took me by the hair of my head. The Spirit lifted me up between earth and heaven and in visions of God he took me to Jerusalem, to the entrance to the north gate of the inner court, where the idol that provokes to jealousy stood. 4And there before me was the glory of the God of Israel, as in the vision I had seen in the plain.

5Then he said to me, "Son of man, look toward the north." So I looked, and in the entrance north of the gate of the altar I saw this idol of jealousy.

6And he said to me, "Son of man, do you see what they are doing—the utterly detestable things the house of Israel is doing here, things that will drive me far from my sanctuary? But you will see things that are even more detestable."

7Then he brought me to the entrance to the court. I looked, and I saw a hole in the wall. 8He said to me, "Son of man, now dig into the wall." So I dug into the wall and saw a doorway there.

9And he said to me, "Go in and see the wicked and detestable things they are doing here." 10So I went in and looked, and I saw portrayed all over the walls all kinds of crawling things and detestable animals and all the idols of the house of Israel. 11In front of them stood seventy elders of the house of Israel, and Jaazaniah son of Shaphan was standing among them. Each had a censer in his hand, and a fragrant cloud of incense was rising.

12He said to me, "Son of man, have you seen what the elders of the house of Israel are doing in the darkness, each at the shrine of his own idol? They say, 'The LORD does not see us; the LORD has forsaken the land.' " 13Again, he said, "You will see them doing things that are even more detestable."

14Then he brought me to the entrance to the north gate of the house of the LORD, and I saw women sitting there, mourning for Tammuz. 15He said to me, "Do you see

---

[a] 2 Or *saw a fiery figure*

Living Bible

bringing to Jerusalem the worst of the nations to occupy your homes, break down your fortifications you are so proud of, and defile your Temple. 25For the time has come for the cutting off of Israel. You will sue for peace, but you won't get it. 26, 27Calamity upon calamity will befall you; woe upon woe, disaster upon disaster! You will long for a prophet to guide you, but the priests and elders and the kings and princes will stand helpless, weeping in despair. The people will tremble with fear, for I will do to them the evil they have done, and give them all their just deserts. They shall learn that I am the Lord."

8 THEN, LATE in August of the sixth year of King Jehoiachin's captivity,b as I was talking with the elders of Judah in my home, the power of the Lord God fell upon me. 2I saw what appeared to be a Man; from his waist down, he was made of fire; from his waist up, he was all amber-colored brightness. 3He put out what seemed to be a hand and took me by the hair. And the Spirit lifted me up into the sky and seemed to transport me to Jerusalem, to the entrance of the north gate, where the large idol was that had made the Lord so angry. 4Suddenly the glory of the God of Israel was there, just as I had seen it before in the valley.

5He said to me, "Son of dust, look toward the north." So I looked and, sure enough, north of the altar gate, in the entrance, stood the idol.

6And he said: "Son of dust, do you see what they are doing? Do you see what great sins the people of Israel are doing here, to push me from my Temple? But come, and I will show you greater sins than these!"

7Then he brought me to the door of the Temple court, where I could see an opening in the wall.

8"Now dig into the wall," he said. I did, and uncovered a door to a hidden room.

9"Go in," he said, "and see the wickedness going on in there!"

10So I went in. The walls were covered with pictures of all kinds of snakes, lizards and hideous creatures, besides all the various idols worshiped by the people of Israel. 11Seventy elders of Israel were standing there along with Ja-azaniah (son of Shaphan) worshiping the pictures. Each of them held a censer of burning incense, so there was a thick cloud of smoke above their heads.

12Then the Lord said to me: "Son of dust, have you seen what the elders of Israel are doing in their minds? For they say, 'The Lord doesn't see us; he has gone away!'" 13Then he added, "Come, and I will show you greater sins than these!"

14He brought me to the north gate of the Temple, and there sat women weeping for Tammuz,c their god.

New Revised Standard

24 I will bring the worst of the nations
        to take possession of their houses.
    I will put an end to the arrogance of the
        strong,
        and their holy places shall be profaned.
25 When anguish comes, they will seek peace,
        but there shall be none.
26 Disaster comes upon disaster,
        rumor follows rumor;
    they shall keep seeking a vision from the
        prophet;
    instruction shall perish from the priest,
        and counsel from the elders.
27 The king shall mourn,
        the prince shall be wrapped in despair,
        and the hands of the people of the land shall
            tremble.
    According to their way I will deal with them;
        according to their own judgments I will
            judge them.
And they shall know that I am the Lord.

Abominations in the Temple

8 IN THE sixth year, in the sixth month, on the fifth day of the month, as I sat in my house, with the elders of Judah sitting before me, the hand of the Lord God fell upon me there. 2I looked, and there was a figure that looked like a human being;d below what appeared to be its loins it was fire, and above the loins it was like the appearance of brightness, like gleaming amber. 3It stretched out the form of a hand, and took me by a lock of my head; and the spirit lifted me up between earth and heaven, and brought me in visions of God to Jerusalem, to the entrance of the gateway of the inner court that faces north, to the seat of the image of jealousy, which provokes to jealousy. 4And the glory of the God of Israel was there, like the vision that I had seen in the valley.

5 Then Gode said to me, "O mortal, lift up your eyes now in the direction of the north." So I lifted up my eyes toward the north, and there, north of the altar gate, in the entrance, was this image of jealousy. 6He said to me, "Mortal, do you see what they are doing, the great abominations that the house of Israel are committing here, to drive me far from my sanctuary? Yet you will see still greater abominations."

7 And he brought me to the entrance of the court; I looked, and there was a hole in the wall. 8Then he said to me, "Mortal, dig through the wall"; and when I dug through the wall, there was an entrance. 9He said to me, "Go in, and see the vile abominations that they are committing here." 10So I went in and looked; there, portrayed on the wall all around, were all kinds of creeping things, and loathsome animals, and all the idols of the house of Israel. 11Before them stood seventy of the elders of the house of Israel, with Jaazaniah son of Shaphan standing among them. Each had his censer in his hand, and the fragrant cloud of incense was ascending. 12Then he said to me, "Mortal, have you seen what the elders of the house of Israel are doing in the dark, each in his room of images? For they say, 'The Lord does not see us, the Lord has forsaken the land.'" 13He said also to me, "You will see still greater abominations that they are committing."

14 Then he brought me to the entrance of the north gate of the house of the Lord; women were sitting there weeping for Tammuz. 15Then he said to me, "Have you

b 8:1 the sixth year of King Jehoiachin's captivity, implied. c 8:14 there sat women weeping for Tammuz. The women wept for Tammuz, the god of fertility, because, according to Mesopotamian myths, he had been killed, and fertility had vanished with him.

d Gk: Heb like fire   e Heb he

King James

15¶ Then said he unto me, Hast thou seen *this*, O son of man? turn thee yet again, *and* thou shalt see greater abominations than these.

16And he brought me into the inner court of the LORD's house, and, behold, at the door of the temple of the LORD, between the porch and the altar, *were* about five and twenty men, with their backs toward the temple of the LORD, and their faces toward the east; and they worshipped the sun toward the east.

17¶ Then he said unto me, Hast thou seen *this*, O son of man? Is it a light thing to the house of Judah that they commit the abominations which they commit here? for they have filled the land with violence, and have returned to provoke me to anger: and, lo, they put the branch to their nose.

18Therefore will I also deal in fury: mine eye shall not spare, neither will I have pity: and though they cry in mine ears with a loud voice, *yet* will I not hear them.

9 HE CRIED also in mine ears with a loud voice, saying, Cause them that have charge over the city to draw near, even every man *with* his destroying weapon in his hand.

2And, behold, six men came from the way of the higher gate, which lieth toward the north, and every man a slaughter weapon in his hand; and one man among them *was* clothed with linen, with a writer's inkhorn by his side: and they went in, and stood beside the brasen altar.

3And the glory of the God of Israel was gone up from the cherub, whereupon he was, to the threshold of the house. And he called to the man clothed with linen, which *had* the writer's inkhorn by his side;

4And the LORD said unto him, Go through the midst of the city, through the midst of Jerusalem, and set a mark upon the foreheads of the men that sigh and that cry for all the abominations that be done in the midst thereof.

5¶ And to the others he said in mine hearing, Go ye after him through the city, and smite: let not your eye spare, neither have ye pity:

6Slay utterly old *and* young, both maids, and little children, and women: but come not near any man upon whom *is* the mark; and begin at my sanctuary. Then they began at the ancient men which *were* before the house.

7And he said unto them, Defile the house, and fill the courts with the slain: go ye forth. And they went forth, and slew in the city.

8¶ And it came to pass, while they were slaying them, and I was left, that I fell upon my face, and cried, and said, Ah Lord GOD! wilt thou destroy all the residue of Israel in thy pouring out of thy fury upon Jerusalem?

9Then said he unto me, The iniquity of the house of Israel and Judah *is* exceeding great, and the land is full of blood, and the city full of perverseness: for they say, The LORD hath forsaken the earth, and the LORD seeth not.

10And as for me also, mine eye shall not spare, neither will I have pity, *but* I will recompense their way upon their head.

11And, behold, the man clothed with linen, which *had* the inkhorn by his side, reported the matter, saying, I have done as thou hast commanded me.

New International

this, son of man? You will see things that are even more detestable than this."

16He then brought me into the inner court of the house of the LORD, and there at the entrance to the temple, between the portico and the altar, were about twenty-five men. With their backs toward the temple of the LORD and their faces toward the east, they were bowing down to the sun in the east.

17He said to me, "Have you seen this, son of man? Is it a trivial matter for the house of Judah to do the detestable things they are doing here? Must they also fill the land with violence and continually provoke me to anger? Look at them putting the branch to their nose! 18Therefore I will deal with them in anger; I will not look on them with pity or spare them. Although they shout in my ears, I will not listen to them."

Idolaters Killed

9 THEN I heard him call out in a loud voice, "Bring the guards of the city here, each with a weapon in his hand." 2And I saw six men coming from the direction of the upper gate, which faces north, each with a deadly weapon in his hand. With them was a man clothed in linen who had a writing kit at his side. They came in and stood beside the bronze altar.

3Now the glory of the God of Israel went up from above the cherubim, where it had been, and moved to the threshold of the temple. Then the LORD called to the man clothed in linen who had the writing kit at his side 4and said to him, "Go throughout the city of Jerusalem and put a mark on the foreheads of those who grieve and lament over all the detestable things that are done in it."

5As I listened, he said to the others, "Follow him through the city and kill, without showing pity or compassion. 6Slaughter old men, young men and maidens, women and children, but do not touch anyone who has the mark. Begin at my sanctuary." So they began with the elders who were in front of the temple.

7Then he said to them, "Defile the temple and fill the courts with the slain. Go!" So they went out and began killing throughout the city. 8While they were killing and I was left alone, I fell facedown, crying out, "Ah, Sovereign LORD! Are you going to destroy the entire remnant of Israel in this outpouring of your wrath on Jerusalem?"

9He answered me, "The sin of the house of Israel and Judah is exceedingly great; the land is full of bloodshed and the city is full of injustice. They say, 'The LORD has forsaken the land; the LORD does not see.' 10So I will not look on them with pity or spare them, but I will bring down on their own heads what they have done."

11Then the man in linen with the writing kit at his side brought back word, saying, "I have done as you commanded."

Living Bible

15"Have you seen this?" he asked. "But I will show you greater evils than these!"

16Then he brought me into the inner court of the Temple and there at the door, between the porch and the bronze altar, were about twenty-five men standing with their backs to the Temple of the Lord, facing east, worshiping the sun!

17"Have you seen this?" he asked. "Is it nothing to the people of Judah that they commit these terrible sins, leading the whole nation into idolatry, thumbing their noses at me and arousing my fury against them? 18Therefore I will deal with them in fury. I will neither pity nor spare. And though they scream for mercy, I will not listen."

9 THEN HE thundered, "Call those to whom I have given the city! Tell them to bring their weapons with them!"

2Six men appeared at his call, coming from the upper north gate, each one with his sword. One of them wore linen clothing and carried a writer's case strapped to his side. They all went into the Temple and stood beside the bronze altar. 3And the glory of the God of Israel rose from between the Guardian Angels where it had rested and stood above the entrance[a] to the Temple.

And the Lord called to the man with the writer's case, 4and said to him, "Walk through the streets of Jerusalem and put a mark on the foreheads of the men who weep and sigh because of all the sins they see around them." 5Then I heard the Lord tell the other men: "Follow him through the city and kill everyone whose forehead isn't marked. Spare not nor pity them— 6kill them all— old and young, girls, women and little children; but don't touch anyone with the mark. And begin right here at the Temple." And so they began by killing the seventy elders.

7And he said, "Defile the Temple! Fill its courts with the bodies of those you kill! Go!" And they went out through the city and did as they were told.

8While they were fulfilling their orders, I was alone. I fell to the ground on my face and cried out: "O Lord God! Will your fury against Jerusalem wipe out everyone left in Israel?"

9But he said to me, "The sins of the people of Israel and Judah are very great and all the land is full of murder and injustice, for they say, 'The Lord doesn't see it! He has gone away!' 10And so I will not spare them nor have any pity on them, and I will fully repay them for all that they have done."

11Just then the man in linen clothing, carrying the writer's case, reported back and said, "I have finished the work you gave me to do."

New Revised Standard

seen this, O mortal? You will see still greater abominations than these."

16 And he brought me into the inner court of the house of the LORD; there, at the entrance of the temple of the LORD, between the porch and the altar, were about twenty-five men, with their backs to the temple of the LORD, and their faces toward the east, prostrating themselves to the sun toward the east. 17Then he said to me, "Have you seen this, O mortal? Is it not bad enough that the house of Judah commits the abominations done here? Must they fill the land with violence, and provoke my anger still further? See, they are putting the branch to their nose! 18Therefore I will act in wrath; my eye will not spare, nor will I have pity; and though they cry in my hearing with a loud voice, I will not listen to them."

The Slaughter of the Idolaters

9 THEN HE cried in my hearing with a loud voice, saying, "Draw near, you executioners of the city, each with his destroying weapon in his hand." 2And six men came from the direction of the upper gate, which faces north, each with his weapon for slaughter in his hand; among them was a man clothed in linen, with a writing case at his side. They went in and stood beside the bronze altar.

3 Now the glory of the God of Israel had gone up from the cherub on which it rested to the threshold of the house. The LORD called to the man clothed in linen, who had the writing case at his side; 4and said to him, "Go through the city, through Jerusalem, and put a mark on the foreheads of those who sigh and groan over all the abominations that are committed in it." 5To the others he said in my hearing, "Pass through the city after him, and kill; your eye shall not spare, and you shall show no pity. 6Cut down old men, young men and young women, little children and women, but touch no one who has the mark. And begin at my sanctuary." So they began with the elders who were in front of the house. 7Then he said to them, "Defile the house, and fill the courts with the slain. Go!" So they went out and killed in the city. 8While they were killing, and I was left alone, I fell prostrate on my face and cried out, "Ah Lord GOD! will you destroy all who remain of Israel as you pour out your wrath upon Jerusalem?" 9He said to me, "The guilt of the house of Israel and Judah is exceedingly great; the land is full of bloodshed and the city full of perversity; for they say, 'The LORD has forsaken the land, and the LORD does not see.' 10As for me, my eye will not spare, nor will I have pity, but I will bring down their deeds upon their heads."

11 Then the man clothed in linen, with the writing case at his side, brought back word, saying, "I have done as you commanded me."

---

a 9:3 *above the entrance,* literally, "above the threshold of . . ."

King James

10 THEN I looked, and, behold, in the firmament that was above the head of the cherubims there appeared over them as it were a sapphire stone, as the appearance of the likeness of a throne.

2And he spake unto the man clothed with linen, and said, Go in between the wheels, *even* under the cherub, and fill thine hand with coals of fire from between the cherubims, and scatter *them* over the city. And he went in in my sight.

3Now the cherubims stood on the right side of the house, when the man went in; and the cloud filled the inner court.

4Then the glory of the LORD went up from the cherub, *and stood* over the threshold of the house; and the house was filled with the cloud, and the court was full of the brightness of the LORD's glory.

5And the sound of the cherubims' wings was heard *even* to the outer court, as the voice of the Almighty God when he speaketh.

6And it came to pass, *that* when he had commanded the man clothed with linen, saying, Take fire from between the wheels, from between the cherubims; then he went in, and stood beside the wheels.

7And *one* cherub stretched forth his hand from between the cherubims unto the fire that *was* between the cherubims, and took *thereof,* and put *it* into the hands of *him that was* clothed with linen: who took *it,* and went out.

8¶ And there appeared in the cherubims the form of a man's hand under their wings.

9And when I looked, behold the four wheels by the cherubims, one wheel by one cherub, and another wheel by another cherub: and the appearance of the wheels *was* as the colour of a beryl stone.

10And *as for* their appearances, they four had one likeness, as if a wheel had been in the midst of a wheel.

11When they went, they went upon their four sides; they turned not as they went, but to the place whither the head looked they followed it; they turned not as they went.

12And their whole body, and their backs, and their hands, and their wings, and the wheels, *were* full of eyes round about, *even* the wheels that they four had.

13As for the wheels, it was cried unto them in my hearing, O wheel.

14And every one had four faces: the first face *was* the face of a cherub, and the second face *was* the face of a man, and the third the face of a lion, and the fourth the face of an eagle.

15And the cherubims were lifted up. This *is* the living creature that I saw by the river of Chebar.

16And when the cherubims went, the wheels went by them: and when the cherubims lifted up their wings to mount up from the earth, the same wheels also turned not from beside them.

17When they stood, *these* stood; and when they were lifted up, *these* lifted up themselves *also:* for the spirit of the living creature *was* in them.

18Then the glory of the LORD departed from off the threshold of the house, and stood over the cherubims.

19And the cherubims lifted up their wings, and mounted up from the earth in my sight: when they went out, the wheels also *were* beside them, and *every one* stood at the door of the east gate of the LORD's house; and the glory of the God of Israel *was* over them above.

20This *is* the living creature that I saw under the God of Israel by the river of Chebar; and I knew that they *were* the cherubims.

21Every one had four faces apiece, and every one four wings; and the likeness of the hands of a man *was* under their wings.

New International

The Glory Departs From the Temple

10 I LOOKED, and I saw the likeness of a throne of sapphire[a] above the expanse that was over the heads of the cherubim. 2The LORD said to the man clothed in linen, "Go in among the wheels beneath the cherubim. Fill your hands with burning coals from among the cherubim and scatter them over the city." And as I watched, he went in.

3Now the cherubim were standing on the south side of the temple when the man went in, and a cloud filled the inner court. 4Then the glory of the LORD rose from above the cherubim and moved to the threshold of the temple. The cloud filled the temple, and the court was full of the radiance of the glory of the LORD. 5The sound of the wings of the cherubim could be heard as far away as the outer court, like the voice of God Almighty[b] when he speaks.

6When the LORD commanded the man in linen, "Take fire from among the wheels, from among the cherubim," the man went in and stood beside a wheel. 7Then one of the cherubim reached out his hand to the fire that was among them. He took up some of it and put it into the hands of the man in linen, who took it and went out. 8(Under the wings of the cherubim could be seen what looked like the hands of a man.)

9I looked, and I saw beside the cherubim four wheels, one beside each of the cherubim; the wheels sparkled like chrysolite. 10As for their appearance, the four of them looked alike; each was like a wheel intersecting a wheel. 11As they moved, they would go in any one of the four directions the cherubim faced; the wheels did not turn about[c] as the cherubim went. The cherubim went in whatever direction the head faced, without turning as they went. 12Their entire bodies, including their backs, their hands and their wings, were completely full of eyes, as were their four wheels. 13I heard the wheels being called "the whirling wheels." 14Each of the cherubim had four faces: One face was that of a cherub, the second the face of a man, the third the face of a lion, and the fourth the face of an eagle.

15Then the cherubim rose upward. These were the living creatures I had seen by the Kebar River. 16When the cherubim moved, the wheels beside them moved; and when the cherubim spread their wings to rise from the ground, the wheels did not leave their side. 17When the cherubim stood still, they also stood still; and when the cherubim rose, they rose with them, because the spirit of the living creatures was in them.

18Then the glory of the LORD departed from over the threshold of the temple and stopped above the cherubim. 19While I watched, the cherubim spread their wings and rose from the ground, and as they went, the wheels went with them. They stopped at the entrance to the east gate of the LORD's house, and the glory of the God of Israel was above them.

20These were the living creatures I had seen beneath the God of Israel by the Kebar River, and I realized that they were cherubim. 21Each had four faces and four wings, and under their wings was what looked like the hands of a man. 22Their faces had the same appearance

Living Bible

10 SUDDENLY A throne of beautiful blue sapphired appeared in the sky above the heads of the Guardian Angels.e

2Then the Lord spoke to the man in linen clothing and said: "Go in between the whirling wheels beneath the Guardian Angels, and take a handful of glowing coals and scatter them over the city."

He did so while I watched. 3The Guardian Angels were standing at the south end of the Temple when the man went in. And the cloud of glory filled the inner court. 4Then the glory of the Lord rose from above the Guardian Angels and went over to the door of the Temple. The Temple was filled with the cloud of glory, and the court of the Temple was filled with the brightness of the glory of the Lord. 5And the sound of the wings of the Guardian Angels was as the voice of Almighty God when he speaks and could be heard clear out in the outer court.

6When the Lord told the man in linen clothing to go between the Guardian Angels and take some burning coals from between the wheels, the man went in and stood beside one of the wheels, 7, 8and one of the Guardian Angels reached out his hand (for each of the mighty angels had, beneath his wings, what looked like human hands) and took some live coals from the flames between the Angels and put them into the hands of the man in linen clothes, who took them and went out.

9-13Each of the four Guardian Angels had a wheel beside him—"The Whirl-Wheels," as I heard them called, for each one had a second wheel crosswise within—sparkling like chrysolite, giving off a greenish-yellow glow. Because of the construction of these wheels,f the Angels could go straight forward in each of four directions; they did not turn when they changed direction but could go in any of the four ways their faces looked. Each of the four wheels was covered with eyes, including the rims and spokes. 14Each of the four Guardian Angels had four faces—the first was that of an ox;g the second, a man's; the third, a lion's; and the fourth, an eagle's.

15, 16These were the same beings I had seen beside the Chebar Canal, and when they rose into the air the wheels rose with them, and stayed beside them as they flew. 17When the Guardian Angels stood still, so did the wheels, for the spirit of the Guardian Angels was in the wheels.h

18Then the glory of the Lord moved from the door of the Temple and stood above the Guardian Angels. 19And as I watched, the Guardian Angels flew with their wheels beside them to the east gate of the Temple. And the glory of the God of Israel was above them.

20These were the living beings I had seen beneath the God of Israel beside the Chebar Canal. I knew they were the same, 21for each had four faces and four wings, with what looked like human hands under their wings.

New Revised Standard

God's Glory Leaves Jerusalem

10 THEN I looked, and above the dome that was over the heads of the cherubim there appeared above them something like a sapphire,i in form resembling a throne. 2He said to the man clothed in linen, "Go within the wheelwork underneath the cherubim; fill your hands with burning coals from among the cherubim, and scatter them over the city." He went in as I looked on. 3Now the cherubim were standing on the south side of the house when the man went in; and a cloud filled the inner court. 4Then the glory of the LORD rose up from the cherub to the threshold of the house; the house was filled with the cloud, and the court was full of the brightness of the glory of the LORD. 5The sound of the wings of the cherubim was heard as far as the outer court, like the voice of God Almightyj when he speaks.

6 When he commanded the man clothed in linen, "Take fire from within the wheelwork, from among the cherubim," he went in and stood beside a wheel. 7And a cherub stretched out his hand from among the cherubim to the fire that was among the cherubim, took some of it and put it into the hands of the man clothed in linen, who took it and went out. 8The cherubim appeared to have the form of a human hand under their wings.

9 I looked, and there were four wheels beside the cherubim, one beside each cherub; and the appearance of the wheels was like gleaming beryl. 10And as for their appearance, the four looked alike, something like a wheel within a wheel. 11When they moved, they moved in any of the four directions without veering as they moved; but in whatever direction the front wheel faced, the others followed without veering as they moved. 12Their entire body, their rims, their spokes, their wings, and the wheels—the wheels of the four of them—were full of eyes all around. 13As for the wheels, they were called in my hearing "the wheelwork." 14Each one had four faces: the first face was that of the cherub, the second face was that of a human being, the third that of a lion, and the fourth that of an eagle.

15 The cherubim rose up. These were the living creatures that I saw by the river Chebar. 16When the cherubim moved, the wheels moved beside them; and when the cherubim lifted up their wings to rise up from the earth, the wheels at their side did not veer. 17When they stopped, the others stopped, and when they rose up, the others rose up with them; for the spirit of the living creatures was in them.

18 Then the glory of the LORD went out from the threshold of the house and stopped above the cherubim. 19The cherubim lifted up their wings and rose up from the earth in my sight as they went out with the wheels beside them. They stopped at the entrance of the east gate of the house of the LORD; and the glory of the God of Israel was above them.

20 These were the living creatures that I saw underneath the God of Israel by the river Chebar; and I knew that they were cherubim. 21Each had four faces, each four wings, and underneath their wings something like human hands. 22As for what their faces were like, they

---

d 10:1 blue sapphire, literally, "lapis lazuli." e 10:1 Guardian Angels, literally, "cherubim." f 10:9-13 Because of the construction of these wheels, implied. g 10:14 ox, literally, "cherub's face." See 1:10. h 10:17 for the spirit of the Guardian Angels was in the wheels. That is, the wheel was a living part of the bodies of the cherubim. Hence it could not be separated from the cherubim.

i Or lapis lazuli j Traditional rendering of Heb El Shaddai

King James

22And the likeness of their faces *was* the same faces which I saw by the river of Chebar, their appearances and themselves: they went every one straight forward.

11 MOREOVER THE spirit lifted me up, and brought me unto the east gate of the LORD's house, which looketh eastward: and behold at the door of the gate five and twenty men; among whom I saw Jaazaniah the son of Azur, and Pelatiah the son of Benaiah, princes of the people.

2Then said he unto me, Son of man, these *are* the men that devise mischief, and give wicked counsel in this city:

3Which say, *It is* not near; let us build houses: this *city is* the caldron, and we *be* the flesh.

4¶ Therefore prophesy against them, prophesy, O son of man.

5And the spirit of the LORD fell upon me, and said unto me, Speak; Thus saith the LORD; Thus have ye said, O house of Israel: for I know the things that come into your mind, *every one of* them.

6Ye have multiplied your slain in this city, and ye have filled the streets thereof with the slain.

7Therefore thus saith the Lord GOD; Your slain whom ye have laid in the midst of it, they *are* the flesh, and this *city is* the caldron: but I will bring you forth out of the midst of it.

8Ye have feared the sword; and I will bring a sword upon you, saith the Lord GOD.

9And I will bring you out of the midst thereof, and deliver you into the hands of strangers, and will execute judgments among you.

10Ye shall fall by the sword; I will judge you in the border of Israel; and ye shall know that I *am* the LORD.

11This *city* shall not be your caldron, neither shall ye be the flesh in the midst thereof; *but* I will judge you in the border of Israel:

12And ye shall know that I *am* the LORD: for ye have not walked in my statutes, neither executed my judgments, but have done after the manners of the heathen that *are* round about you.

13¶ And it came to pass, when I prophesied, that Pelatiah the son of Benaiah died. Then fell I down upon my face, and cried with a loud voice, and said, Ah Lord GOD! wilt thou make a full end of the remnant of Israel?

14Again the word of the LORD came unto me, saying,

15Son of man, thy brethren, *even* thy brethren, the men of thy kindred, and all the house of Israel wholly, *are* they unto whom the inhabitants of Jerusalem have said, Get you far from the LORD: unto us is this land given in possession.

16Therefore say, Thus saith the Lord GOD; Although I have cast them far off among the heathen, and although I have scattered them among the countries, yet will I be to them as a little sanctuary in the countries where they shall come.

17Therefore say, Thus saith the Lord GOD; I will even gather you from the people, and assemble you out of the countries where ye have been scattered, and I will give you the land of Israel.

18And they shall come thither, and they shall take away all the detestable things thereof and all the abominations thereof from thence.

19And I will give them one heart, and I will put a new spirit within you; and I will take the stony heart out of their flesh, and will give them an heart of flesh:

20That they may walk in my statutes, and keep mine ordinances, and do them: and they shall be my people, and I will be their God.

New International

as those I had seen by the Kebar River. Each one went straight ahead.

Judgment on Israel's Leaders

11 THEN THE Spirit lifted me up and brought me to the gate of the house of the LORD that faces east. There at the entrance to the gate were twenty-five men, and I saw among them Jaazaniah son of Azzur and Pelatiah son of Benaiah, leaders of the people. 2The LORD said to me, "Son of man, these are the men who are plotting evil and giving wicked advice in this city. 3They say, 'Will it not soon be time to build houses?a This city is a cooking pot, and we are the meat.' 4Therefore prophesy against them; prophesy, son of man."

5Then the Spirit of the LORD came upon me, and he told me to say: "This is what the LORD says: That is what you are saying, O house of Israel, but I know what is going through your mind. 6You have killed many people in this city and filled its streets with the dead.

7"Therefore this is what the Sovereign LORD says: The bodies you have thrown there are the meat and this city is the pot, but I will drive you out of it. 8You fear the sword, and the sword is what I will bring against you, declares the Sovereign LORD. 9I will drive you out of the city and hand you over to foreigners and inflict punishment on you. 10You will fall by the sword, and I will execute judgment on you at the borders of Israel. Then you will know that I am the LORD. 11This city will not be a pot for you, nor will you be the meat in it; I will execute judgment on you at the borders of Israel. 12And you will know that I am the LORD, for you have not followed my decrees or kept my laws but have conformed to the standards of the nations around you."

13Now as I was prophesying, Pelatiah son of Benaiah died. Then I fell facedown and cried out in a loud voice, "Ah, Sovereign LORD! Will you completely destroy the remnant of Israel?"

14The word of the LORD came to me: 15"Son of man, your brothers—your brothers who are your blood relativesb and the whole house of Israel—are those of whom the people of Jerusalem have said, 'They arec far away from the LORD; this land was given to us as our possession.'

Promised Return of Israel

16"Therefore say: 'This is what the Sovereign LORD says: Although I sent them far away among the nations and scattered them among the countries, yet for a little while I have been a sanctuary for them in the countries where they have gone.'

17"Therefore say: 'This is what the Sovereign LORD says: I will gather you from the nations and bring you back from the countries where you have been scattered, and I will give you back the land of Israel again.'

18"They will return to it and remove all its vile images and detestable idols. 19I will give them an undivided heart and put a new spirit in them; I will remove from them their heart of stone and give them a heart of flesh. 20Then they will follow my decrees and be careful to keep my laws. They will be my people, and I will be their God. 21But as for those whose hearts are devoted

---

a 3 *Or* This is not the time to build houses.   b 15 *Or* are in exile with you (see Septuagint and Syriac)   c 15 *Or* those to whom the people of Jerusalem have said, 'Stay

Living Bible

22Their faces too were identical to the faces of those I had seen at the Canal, and they traveled straight ahead, just as the others did.

11 THEN THE Spirit lifted me and brought me over to the east gate of the Temple, where I saw twenty-five of the most prominent men of the city, including two officers, Ja-azaniah (son of Azzur) and Pelatiah (son of Benaiah).

Then the Spirit said to me, "Son of dust, these are the men who are responsible for all of the wicked counsel being given out in this city. 3For they say to the people, 'It is time to rebuild Jerusalem, for our city is an iron shield and will protect us from all harm.'d 4Therefore, son of dust, prophesy against them loudly and clearly."

5Then the Spirit of the Lord came upon me and told me to say: "The Lord says to the people of Israel: Is that what you are saying? Yes, I know it is, for I know everything you think—every thought that comes into your minds. 6You have murdered endlessly and filled your streets with the dead.

7"Therefore the Lord God says: You think this city is an iron shield? No, it isn't! It will not protect you. Your slain will lie within it, but you will be dragged out and slaughtered.e 8I will expose you to the war you have so greatly feared, says the Lord God, 9and I will take you from Jerusalem and hand you over to foreigners who will carry out my judgments against you. 10You will be slaughtered all the way to the borders of Israel, and you will know I am the Lord. 11No, this city will not be an iron shield for you, and you safe within. I will chase you even to the borders of Israel, 12and you will know I am the Lord—you who have not obeyed me, but rather have copied the nations all around you."

13While I was still speaking and telling them this, Pelatiah (son of Benaiah) suddenly died. Then I fell to the ground on my face and cried out: "O Lord God, are you going to kill everyone in all Israel?"

14Again a message came from the Lord:

15"Son of dust, the remnant left in Jerusalem are saying about your brother exiles: 'It is because they were so wicked that the Lord has deported them. Now the Lord has given us their land!'

16"But tell the exiles that the Lord God says: Although I have scattered you in the countries of the world, yet I will be a sanctuary to you for the time that you are there, 17and I will gather you back from the nations where you are scattered and give you the land of Israel again. 18And when you return you will remove every trace of all this idol worship. 19I will give you one heart and a new spirit; I will take from you your hearts of stone and give you tender hearts of love for God, 20so that you can obey my laws and be my people, and I will be your God. 21But as for those now in Jerusalem,f who long

New Revised Standard

were the same faces whose appearance I had seen by the river Chebar. Each one moved straight ahead.

Judgment on Wicked Counselors

11 THE SPIRIT lifted me up and brought me to the east gate of the house of the LORD, which faces east. There, at the entrance of the gateway, were twenty-five men; among them I saw Jaazaniah son of Azzur, and Pelatiah son of Benaiah, officials of the people. 2He said to me, "Mortal, these are the men who devise iniquity and who give wicked counsel in this city; 3they say, 'The time is not near to build houses; this city is the pot, and we are the meat.' 4Therefore prophesy against them; prophesy, O mortal."

5 Then the spirit of the LORD fell upon me, and he said to me, "Say, Thus says the LORD: This is what you think, O house of Israel; I know the things that come into your mind. 6You have killed many in this city, and have filled its streets with the slain. 7Therefore thus says the Lord GOD: The slain whom you have placed within it are the meat, and this city is the pot; but you shall be taken out of it. 8You have feared the sword; and I will bring the sword upon you, says the Lord GOD. 9I will take you out of it and give you over to the hands of foreigners, and execute judgments upon you. 10You shall fall by the sword; I will judge you at the border of Israel. And you shall know that I am the LORD. 11This city shall not be your pot, and you shall not be the meat inside it; I will judge you at the border of Israel. 12Then you shall know that I am the LORD, whose statutes you have not followed, and whose ordinances you have not kept, but you have acted according to the ordinances of the nations that are around you."

13 Now, while I was prophesying, Pelatiah son of Benaiah died. Then I fell down on my face, cried with a loud voice, and said, "Ah Lord GOD! will you make a full end of the remnant of Israel?"

God Will Restore Israel

14 Then the word of the LORD came to me: 15Mortal, your kinsfolk, your own kin, your fellow exiles,g the whole house of Israel, all of them, are those of whom the inhabitants of Jerusalem have said, "They have gone far from the LORD; to us this land is given for a possession." 16Therefore say: Thus says the Lord GOD: Though I removed them far away among the nations, and though I scattered them among the countries, yet I have been a sanctuary to them for a little whileh in the countries where they have gone. 17Therefore say: Thus says the Lord GOD: I will gather you from the peoples, and assemble you out of the countries where you have been scattered, and I will give you the land of Israel. 18When they come there, they will remove from it all its detestable things and all its abominations. 19I will give them onei heart, and put a new spirit within them; I will remove the heart of stone from their flesh and give them a heart of flesh, 20so that they may follow my statutes and keep my ordinances and obey them. Then they shall be my people, and I will be their God. 21But

---

d 11:3 for our city is an iron shield and will protect us from all harm, literally, "this city the caldron and we the flesh." e 11:7 but you will be dragged out and slaughtered, literally, "Your slain . . . are the flesh and this is the caldron; but you will be brought out from it." f 11:21 as for those now in Jerusalem, implied.

g Gk Syr: Heb people of your kindred h Or to some extent i Another reading is a new

King James

21But *as for them* whose heart walketh after the heart of their detestable things and their abominations, I will recompense their way upon their own heads, saith the Lord GOD.

22¶ Then did the cherubims lift up their wings, and the wheels beside them; and the glory of the God of Israel *was* over them above.

23And the glory of the LORD went up from the midst of the city, and stood upon the mountain which *is* on the east side of the city.

24¶ Afterwards the spirit took me up, and brought me in a vision by the spirit of God into Chaldea, to them of the captivity. So the vision that I had seen went up from me.

25Then I spake unto them of the captivity all the things that the LORD had shown me.

12 THE WORD of the LORD also came unto me, saying,

2Son of man, thou dwellest in the midst of a rebellious house, which have eyes to see, and see not; they have ears to hear, and hear not: for they *are* a rebellious house.

3Therefore, thou son of man, prepare thee stuff for removing, and remove by day in their sight; and thou shalt remove from thy place to another place in their sight: it may be they will consider, though they *be* a rebellious house.

4Then shalt thou bring forth thy stuff by day in their sight, as stuff for removing: and thou shalt go forth at even in their sight, as they that go forth into captivity.

5Dig thou through the wall in their sight, and carry out thereby.

6In their sight shalt thou bear *it* upon *thy* shoulders, *and* carry *it* forth in the twilight: thou shalt cover thy face, that thou see not the ground: for I have set thee *for* a sign unto the house of Israel.

7And I did so as I was commanded: I brought forth my stuff by day, as stuff for captivity, and in the even I digged through the wall with mine hand; I brought *it* forth in the twilight, *and* I bare *it* upon *my* shoulder in their sight.

8¶ And in the morning came the word of the LORD unto me, saying,

9Son of man, hath not the house of Israel, the rebellious house, said unto thee, What doest thou?

10Say thou unto them, Thus saith the Lord GOD; This burden *concerneth* the prince in Jerusalem, and all the house of Israel that *are* among them.

11Say, I *am* your sign: like as I have done, so shall it be done unto them: they shall remove *and* go into captivity.

12And the prince that *is* among them shall bear upon *his* shoulder in the twilight, and shall go forth: they shall dig through the wall to carry out thereby: he shall cover his face, that he see not the ground with *his* eyes.

13My net also will I spread upon him, and he shall be taken in my snare: and I will bring him to Babylon *to* the land of the Chaldeans; yet shall he not see it, though he shall die there.

14And I will scatter toward every wind all that *are* about him to help him, and all his bands; and I will draw out the sword after them.

15And they shall know that I *am* the LORD, when I shall scatter them among the nations, and disperse them in the countries.

16But I will leave a few men of them from the sword, from the famine, and from the pestilence; that they may declare all their abominations among the heathen whither they come; and they shall know that I *am* the LORD.

17¶ Moreover the word of the LORD came to me, saying,

New International

to their vile images and detestable idols, I will bring down on their own heads what they have done, declares the Sovereign LORD."

22Then the cherubim, with the wheels beside them, spread their wings, and the glory of the God of Israel was above them. 23The glory of the LORD went up from within the city and stopped above the mountain east of it. 24The Spirit lifted me up and brought me to the exiles in Babyloniaa in the vision given by the Spirit of God.

Then the vision I had seen went up from me, 25and I told the exiles everything the LORD had shown me.

The Exile Symbolized

12 THE WORD of the LORD came to me: 2"Son of man, you are living among a rebellious people. They have eyes to see but do not see and ears to hear but do not hear, for they are a rebellious people.

3"Therefore, son of man, pack your belongings for exile and in the daytime, as they watch, set out and go from where you are to another place. Perhaps they will understand, though they are a rebellious house. 4During the daytime, while they watch, bring out your belongings packed for exile. Then in the evening, while they are watching, go out like those who go into exile. 5While they watch, dig through the wall and take your belongings out through it. 6Put them on your shoulder as they are watching and carry them out at dusk. Cover your face so that you cannot see the land, for I have made you a sign to the house of Israel."

7So I did as I was commanded. During the day I brought out my things packed for exile. Then in the evening I dug through the wall with my hands. I took my belongings out at dusk, carrying them on my shoulders while they watched.

8In the morning the word of the LORD came to me: 9"Son of man, did not that rebellious house of Israel ask you, 'What are you doing?'

10"Say to them, 'This is what the Sovereign LORD says: This oracle concerns the prince in Jerusalem and the whole house of Israel who are there.' 11Say to them, 'I am a sign to you.'

"As I have done, so it will be done to them. They will go into exile as captives.

12"The prince among them will put his things on his shoulder at dusk and leave, and a hole will be dug in the wall for him to go through. He will cover his face so that he cannot see the land. 13I will spread my net for him, and he will be caught in my snare; I will bring him to Babylonia, the land of the Chaldeans, but he will not see it, and there he will die. 14I will scatter to the winds all those around him—his staff and all his troops—and I will pursue them with drawn sword.

15"They will know that I am the LORD, when I disperse them among the nations and scatter them through the countries. 16But I will spare a few of them from the sword, famine and plague, so that in the nations where they go they may acknowledge all their detestable practices. Then they will know that I am the LORD."

17The word of the LORD came to me: 18"Son of man,

Living Bible

for idols, I will repay them fully for their sins," the Lord God says.

22Then the Guardian Angels lifted their wings and rose into the air with their wheels beside them, and the glory of the God of Israel stood above them. 23Then the glory of the Lord rose from over the city and stood above the mountain on the east side.

24Afterwards the Spirit of God carried me back again to Babylon, to the Jews in exile there. And so ended the vision of my visit to Jerusalem. 25And I told the exiles everything the Lord had shown me.

12 AGAIN A message came to me from the Lord: 2"Son of dust," he said, "you live among rebels who could know the truth if they wanted to, but they don't want to; they could hear me if they would listen, but they won't, 3for they are rebels. So now put on a demonstration, to show them what being exiled will be like. Pack whatever you can carry on your back and leave your home—go somewhere else. Go in the daylight so they can see, for perhaps even yet they will consider what this means, even though they are such rebels. 4Bring your baggage outside your house during the daylight so they can watch. Then leave the house at night, just as captives do when they begin their long march to distant lands. 5Dig a tunnel through the city wall while they are observing and carry your possessions out through the hole. 6As they watch, lift your pack to your shoulders and walk away into the night; muffle your face and don't gaze around. All this is a sign to the people of Israel of the evil that will come upon Jerusalem."

7So I did as I was told. I brought my pack outside in the daylight—all I could take into exile—and in the evening I dug through the wall with my hands. I went out into the darkness with my pack on my shoulder while the people looked on. 8The next morning this message came to me from the Lord:

9"Son of dust, these rebels, the people of Israel, have asked what all this means. 10Tell them the Lord God says it is a message to King Zedekiahᵇ in Jerusalem and to all the people of Israel. 11Explain that what you did was a demonstration of what is going to happen to them, for they shall be driven out of their homes and sent away into exile.

12"Even King Zedekiah shall go out at night through a hole in the wall, taking only what he can carry with him, with muffled face, for he won't be able to see.ᶜ 13I will capture him in my net and bring him to Babylon, the land of the Chaldeans; but he shall not see it, and he shall die there. 14I will scatter his servants and guards to the four winds and send the sword after them. 15And when I scatter them among the nations, then they shall know I am the Lord. 16But I will spare a few of them from death by war and famine and disease. I will save them to confess to the nations how wicked they have been, and they shall know I am the Lord."

17Then this message came to me from the Lord:

New Revised Standard

as for those whose heart goes after their detestable things and their abominations,ᵈ I will bring their deeds upon their own heads, says the Lord GOD.

22 Then the cherubim lifted up their wings, with the wheels beside them; and the glory of the God of Israel was above them. 23 And the glory of the LORD ascended from the middle of the city, and stopped on the mountain east of the city. 24The spirit lifted me up and brought me in a vision by the spirit of God into Chaldea, to the exiles. Then the vision that I had seen left me. 25And I told the exiles all the things that the LORD had shown me.

Judah's Captivity Portrayed

12 THE WORD of the LORD came to me: 2Mortal, you are living in the midst of a rebellious house, who have eyes to see but do not see, who have ears to hear but do not hear; 3for they are a rebellious house. Therefore, mortal, prepare for yourself an exile's baggage, and go into exile by day in their sight; you shall go like an exile from your place to another place in their sight. Perhaps they will understand, though they are a rebellious house. 4You shall bring out your baggage by day in their sight, as baggage for exile; and you shall go out yourself at evening in their sight, as those do who go into exile. 5Dig through the wall in their sight, and carry the baggage through it. 6In their sight you shall lift the baggage on your shoulder, and carry it out in the dark; you shall cover your face, so that you may not see the land; for I have made you a sign for the house of Israel.

7 I did just as I was commanded. I brought out my baggage by day, as baggage for exile, and in the evening I dug through the wall with my own hands; I brought it out in the dark, carrying it on my shoulder in their sight.

8 In the morning the word of the LORD came to me: 9Mortal, has not the house of Israel, the rebellious house, said to you, "What are you doing?" 10Say to them, "Thus says the Lord GOD: This oracle concerns the prince in Jerusalem and all the house of Israel in it." 11Say, "I am a sign for you: as I have done, so shall it be done to them; they shall go into exile, into captivity." 12And the prince who is among them shall lift his baggage on his shoulder in the dark, and shall go out; heᵉ shall dig through the wall and carry it through; he shall cover his face, so that he may not see the land with his eyes. 13I will spread my net over him, and he shall be caught in my snare; and I will bring him to Babylon, the land of the Chaldeans, yet he shall not see it; and he shall die there. 14I will scatter to every wind all who are around him, his helpers and all his troops; and I will unsheathe the sword behind them. 15And they shall know that I am the LORD, when I disperse them among the nations and scatter them through the countries. 16But I will let a few of them escape from the sword, from famine and pestilence, so that they may tell of all their abominations among the nations where they go; then they shall know that I am the LORD.

Judgment Not Postponed

17 The word of the LORD came to me: 18Mortal, eat

ᵇ *12:10 King Zedekiah,* literally, "to the prince in Jerusalem." ᶜ *12:12 for he won't be able to see,* literally, "that he may not see the land with his eyes." Apparently a reference to the fact that his eyes were put out before he was taken to Babylon, Jer 52:11. Also in vs 13.

ᵈ Cn: Heb *And to the heart of their detestable things and their abominations their heart goes* ᵉ Gk Syr: Heb *they*

King James

18Son of man, eat thy bread with quaking, and drink thy water with trembling and with carefulness;

19And say unto the people of the land, Thus saith the Lord GOD of the inhabitants of Jerusalem, and of the land of Israel; They shall eat their bread with carefulness, and drink their water with astonishment, that her land may be desolate from all that is therein, because of the violence of all them that dwell therein.

20And the cities that are inhabited shall be laid waste, and the land shall be desolate; and ye shall know that I am the LORD.

21¶ And the word of the LORD came unto me, saying,

22Son of man, what is that proverb that ye have in the land of Israel, saying, The days are prolonged, and every vision faileth?

23Tell them therefore, Thus saith the Lord GOD; I will make this proverb to cease, and they shall no more use it as a proverb in Israel; but say unto them, The days are at hand, and the effect of every vision.

24For there shall be no more any vain vision nor flattering divination within the house of Israel.

25For I am the LORD: I will speak, and the word that I shall speak shall come to pass; it shall be no more prolonged: for in your days, O rebellious house, will I say the word, and will perform it, saith the Lord GOD.

26¶ Again the word of the LORD came to me, saying,

27Son of man, behold, they of the house of Israel say, The vision that he seeth is for many days to come, and he prophesieth of the times that are far off.

28Therefore say unto them, Thus saith the Lord GOD; There shall none of my words be prolonged any more, but the word which I have spoken shall be done, saith the Lord GOD.

13 AND THE word of the LORD came unto me, saying,

2Son of man, prophesy against the prophets of Israel that prophesy, and say thou unto them that prophesy out of their own hearts, Hear ye the word of the LORD;

3Thus saith the Lord GOD; Woe unto the foolish prophets, that follow their own spirit, and have seen nothing!

4O Israel, thy prophets are like the foxes in the deserts.

5Ye have not gone up into the gaps, neither made up the hedge for the house of Israel to stand in the battle in the day of the LORD.

6They have seen vanity and lying divination, saying, The LORD saith: and the LORD hath not sent them: and they have made others to hope that they would confirm the word.

7Have ye not seen a vain vision, and have ye not spoken a lying divination, whereas ye say, The LORD saith it; albeit I have not spoken?

8Therefore thus saith the Lord GOD; Because ye have spoken vanity, and seen lies, therefore, behold, I am against you, saith the Lord GOD.

9And mine hand shall be upon the prophets that see vanity, and that divine lies: they shall not be in the assembly of my people, neither shall they be written in the writing of the house of Israel, neither shall they enter into the land of Israel; and ye shall know that I am the Lord GOD.

10¶ Because, even because they have seduced my people, saying, Peace; and there was no peace; and one built up a wall, and, lo, others daubed it with untempered mortar:

11Say unto them which daub it with untempered mortar, that it shall fall: there shall be an overflowing shower; and ye, O great hailstones, shall fall; and a stormy wind shall rend it.

New International

tremble as you eat your food, and shudder in fear as you drink your water. 19Say to the people of the land: 'This is what the Sovereign LORD says about those living in Jerusalem and in the land of Israel: They will eat their food in anxiety and drink their water in despair, for their land will be stripped of everything in it because of the violence of all who live there. 20The inhabited towns will be laid waste and the land will be desolate. Then you will know that I am the LORD.' "

21The word of the LORD came to me: 22"Son of man, what is this proverb you have in the land of Israel: 'The days go by and every vision comes to nothing'? 23Say to them, 'This is what the Sovereign LORD says: I am going to put an end to this proverb, and they will no longer quote it in Israel.' Say to them, 'The days are near when every vision will be fulfilled. 24For there will be no more false visions or flattering divinations among the people of Israel. 25But I the LORD will speak what I will, and it shall be fulfilled without delay. For in your days, you rebellious house, I will fulfill whatever I say, declares the Sovereign LORD.' "

26The word of the LORD came to me: 27"Son of man, the house of Israel is saying, 'The vision he sees is for many years from now, and he prophesies about the distant future.'

28"Therefore say to them, 'This is what the Sovereign LORD says: None of my words will be delayed any longer; whatever I say will be fulfilled, declares the Sovereign LORD.' "

False Prophets Condemned

13 THE WORD of the LORD came to me: 2"Son of man, prophesy against the prophets of Israel who are now prophesying. Say to those who prophesy out of their own imagination: 'Hear the word of the LORD! 3This is what the Sovereign LORD says: Woe to the foolisha prophets who follow their own spirit and have seen nothing! 4Your prophets, O Israel, are like jackals among ruins. 5You have not gone up to the breaks in the wall to repair it for the house of Israel so that it will stand firm in the battle on the day of the LORD. 6Their visions are false and their divinations a lie. They say, "The LORD declares," when the LORD has not sent them; yet they expect their words to be fulfilled. 7Have you not seen false visions and uttered lying divinations when you say, "The LORD declares," though I have not spoken?

8" 'Therefore this is what the Sovereign LORD says: Because of your false words and lying visions, I am against you, declares the Sovereign LORD. 9My hand will be against the prophets who see false visions and utter lying divinations. They will not belong to the council of my people or be listed in the records of the house of Israel, nor will they enter the land of Israel. Then you will know that I am the Sovereign LORD.

10" 'Because they lead my people astray, saying, "Peace," when there is no peace, and because, when a flimsy wall is built, they cover it with whitewash, 11therefore tell those who cover it with whitewash that it is going to fall. Rain will come in torrents, and I will send hailstones hurtling down, and violent winds will burst forth. 12When the wall collapses, will people not

a 3 Or wicked

Living Bible

18"Son of dust, tremble as you eat your meals; ration out your water as though it were your last, 19and say to the people, the Lord God says that the people of Israel and Jerusalem shall ration their food with utmost care and sip their tiny portions of water in utter despair because of all their sins. 20Your cities shall be destroyed and your farmlands deserted, and you shall know I am the Lord."

21Again a message came to me from the Lord:

22"Son of dust, what is that proverb they quote in Israel—'The days as they pass make liars out of every prophet.' 23The Lord God says, I will put an end to this proverb and they will soon stop saying it. Give them this one instead: 'The time has come for all these prophecies to be fulfilled.'

24"Then you will see what becomes of all the false predictions of safety and security for Jerusalem. 25For I am the Lord! What I threaten always happens. There will be no more delays, O rebels of Israel! I will do it in your own lifetime!" says the Lord God.

26Then this message came:

27"Son of dust, the people of Israel say, 'His visions won't come true for a long, long time.' 28Therefore say to them: 'The Lord God says, All delay has ended! I will do it now!'"

13 THEN THIS message came to me: 2, 3"Son of dust, prophesy against the false prophets of Israel who are inventing their own visions and claiming to have messages from me when I have never told them anything at all. Woe upon them!

4"O Israel, these 'prophets' of yours are as useless as foxes for rebuilding your walls! 5O evil prophets, what have you ever done to strengthen the walls of Israel against her enemies—by strengthening Israel in the Lord? 6Instead you have lied when you said, 'My message is from God!' God did not send you. And yet you expect him to fulfill your prophecies. 7Can you deny that you have claimed to see 'visions' you never saw, and that you have said, 'This message is from God,' when I never spoke to you at all?

8"Therefore the Lord God says: I will destroy you for these 'visions' and lies. 9My hand shall be against you, and you shall be cut off from among the leaders of Israel; I will blot out your names and you will never see your own country again. And you shall know I am the Lord. 10For these evil men deceive my people by saying, 'God will send peace,' when that is not my plan at all! My people build a flimsy wall and these prophets praise them for it—and cover it with whitewash!

11"Tell these evil builders that their wall will fall. A heavy rainstorm will undermine it; great hailstones and mighty winds will knock it down. 12And when the wall

New Revised Standard

your bread with quaking, and drink your water with trembling and with fearfulness; 19 and say to the people of the land, Thus says the Lord GOD concerning the inhabitants of Jerusalem in the land of Israel: They shall eat their bread with fearfulness, and drink their water in dismay, because their land shall be stripped of all it contains, on account of the violence of all those who live in it. 20 The inhabited cities shall be laid waste, and the land shall become a desolation; and you shall know that I am the LORD.

21 The word of the LORD came to me: 22Mortal, what is this proverb of yours about the land of Israel, which says, "The days are prolonged, and every vision comes to nothing"? 23Tell them therefore, "Thus says the Lord GOD: I will put an end to this proverb, and they shall use it no more as a proverb in Israel." But say to them, The days are near, and the fulfillment of every vision. 24 For there shall no longer be any false vision or flattering divination within the house of Israel. 25 But I the LORD will speak the word that I speak, and it will be fulfilled. It will no longer be delayed; but in your days, O rebellious house, I will speak the word and fulfill it, says the Lord GOD.

26 The word of the LORD came to me: 27Mortal, the house of Israel is saying, "The vision that he sees is for many years ahead; he prophesies for distant times." 28Therefore say to them, Thus says the Lord GOD: None of my words will be delayed any longer, but the word that I speak will be fulfilled, says the Lord GOD.

False Prophets Condemned

13 THE WORD of the LORD came to me: 2Mortal, prophesy against the prophets of Israel who are prophesying; say to those who prophesy out of their own imagination: "Hear the word of the LORD!" 3Thus says the Lord GOD, Alas for the senseless prophets who follow their own spirit, and have seen nothing! 4 Your prophets have been like jackals among ruins, O Israel. 5 You have not gone up into the breaches, or repaired a wall for the house of Israel, so that it might stand in battle on the day of the LORD. 6They have envisioned falsehood and lying divination; they say, "Says the LORD," when the LORD has not sent them, and yet they wait for the fulfillment of their word! 7Have you not seen a false vision or uttered a lying divination, when you have said, "Says the LORD," even though I did not speak?

8 Therefore thus says the Lord GOD: Because you have uttered falsehood and envisioned lies, I am against you, says the Lord GOD. 9My hand will be against the prophets who see false visions and utter lying divinations; they shall not be in the council of my people, nor be enrolled in the register of the house of Israel, nor shall they enter the land of Israel; and you shall know that I am the Lord GOD. 10Because, in truth, because they have misled my people, saying, "Peace," when there is no peace; and because, when the people build a wall, these prophetsb smear whitewash on it. 11Say to those who smear whitewash on it that it shall fall. There will be a deluge of rain,c great hailstones will fall, and a stormy wind will break out. 12When the wall falls, will

---

b Heb *they*   c Heb *rain and you*

King James

12Lo, when the wall is fallen, shall it not be said unto you, Where *is* the daubing wherewith ye have daubed *it?*

13Therefore thus saith the Lord GOD; I will even rend *it* with a stormy wind in my fury; and there shall be an overflowing shower in mine anger, and great hailstones in *my* fury to consume *it.*

14So will I break down the wall that ye have daubed with untempered *mortar,* and bring it down to the ground, so that the foundation thereof shall be discovered, and it shall fall, and ye shall be consumed in the midst thereof: and ye shall know that I *am* the LORD.

15Thus will I accomplish my wrath upon the wall, and upon them that have daubed it with untempered *mortar,* and will say unto you, The wall *is* no *more,* neither they that daubed it;

16*To wit,* the prophets of Israel which prophesy concerning Jerusalem, and which see visions of peace for her, and *there is* no peace, saith the Lord GOD.

17¶ Likewise, thou son of man, set thy face against the daughters of thy people, which prophesy out of their own heart; and prophesy thou against them,

18And say, Thus saith the Lord GOD; Woe to the *women* that sew pillows to all armholes, and make kerchiefs upon the head of every stature to hunt souls! Will ye hunt the souls of my people, and will ye save the souls alive *that come* unto you?

19And will ye pollute me among my people for handfuls of barley and for pieces of bread, to slay the souls that should not die, and to save the souls alive that should not live, by your lying to my people that hear *your* lies?

20Wherefore thus saith the Lord GOD; Behold, I *am* against your pillows, wherewith ye there hunt the souls to make *them* fly, and I will tear them from your arms, and will let the souls go, *even* the souls that ye hunt to make *them* fly.

21Your kerchiefs also will I tear, and deliver my people out of your hand, and they shall be no more in your hand to be hunted; and ye shall know that I *am* the LORD.

22Because with lies ye have made the heart of the righteous sad, whom I have not made sad; and strengthened the hands of the wicked, that he should not return from his wicked way, by promising him life:

23Therefore ye shall see no more vanity, nor divine divinations: for I will deliver my people out of your hand: and ye shall know that I *am* the LORD.

14 THEN CAME certain of the elders of Israel unto me, and sat before me.

2And the word of the LORD came unto me, saying,

3Son of man, these men have set up their idols in their heart, and put the stumblingblock of their iniquity before their face: should I be inquired of at all by them?

4Therefore speak unto them, and say unto them, Thus saith the Lord GOD; Every man of the house of Israel that setteth up his idols in his heart, and putteth the stumblingblock of his iniquity before his face, and cometh to the prophet; I the LORD will answer him that cometh according to the multitude of his idols;

5That I may take the house of Israel in their own heart, because they are all estranged from me through their idols.

New International

ask you, "Where is the whitewash you covered it with?"

13" 'Therefore this is what the Sovereign LORD says: In my wrath I will unleash a violent wind, and in my anger hailstones and torrents of rain will fall with destructive fury. 14I will tear down the wall you have covered with whitewash and will level it to the ground so that its foundation will be laid bare. When ita falls, you will be destroyed in it; and you will know that I am the LORD. 15So I will spend my wrath against the wall and against those who covered it with whitewash. I will say to you, "The wall is gone and so are those who whitewashed it, 16those prophets of Israel who prophesied to Jerusalem and saw visions of peace for her when there was no peace, declares the Sovereign LORD." '

17"Now, son of man, set your face against the daughters of your people who prophesy out of their own imagination. Prophesy against them 18and say, 'This is what the Sovereign LORD says: Woe to the women who sew magic charms on all their wrists and make veils of various lengths for their heads in order to ensnare people. Will you ensnare the lives of my people but preserve your own? 19You have profaned me among my people for a few handfuls of barley and scraps of bread. By lying to my people, who listen to lies, you have killed those who should not have died and have spared those who should not live.

20" 'Therefore this is what the Sovereign LORD says: I am against your magic charms with which you ensnare people like birds and I will tear them from your arms; I will set free the people that you ensnare like birds. 21I will tear off your veils and save my people from your hands, and they will no longer fall prey to your power. Then you will know that I am the LORD. 22Because you disheartened the righteous with your lies, when I had brought them no grief, and because you encouraged the wicked not to turn from their evil ways and so save their lives, 23therefore you will no longer see false visions or practice divination. I will save my people from your hands. And then you will know that I am the LORD.' "

Idolaters Condemned

14 SOME OF the elders of Israel came to me and sat down in front of me. 2Then the word of the LORD came to me: 3"Son of man, these men have set up idols in their hearts and put wicked stumbling blocks before their faces. Should I let them inquire of me at all? 4Therefore speak to them and tell them, 'This is what the Sovereign LORD says: When any Israelite sets up idols in his heart and puts a wicked stumbling block before his face and then goes to a prophet, I the LORD will answer him myself in keeping with his great idolatry. 5I will do this to recapture the hearts of the people of Israel, who have all deserted me for their idols.'

---

a 14 Or *the city*

Living Bible

falls, the people will cry out, 'Why didn't you tell us that it wasn't good enough? Why did you whitewash it and cover up its faults?' 13Yes, it will surely fall. The Lord God says: I will sweep it away with a storm of indignation and with a great flood of anger and with hailstones of wrath. 14I will break down your whitewashed wall, and it will fall on you and crush you, and you shall know I am the Lord. 15Then at last my wrath against the wall will be completed; and concerning those who praised it, I will say: The wall and its builders both are gone. 16For they were lying prophets, claiming Jerusalem will have peace when there is no peace, says the Lord God.

17"Son of dust, speak out against the women prophets too who pretend the Lord has given them his messages. 18Tell them the Lord God says: Woe to these women who are damning the souls of my people, of both young and old alike, by tying magic charms on their wrists and furnishing them with magic veils and selling them indulgences. They refuse to even offer help unless they get a profit from it.b 19For the sake of a few paltry handfuls of barley or a piece of bread will you turn away my people from me? You have led those to death who should not die! And you have promised life to those who should not live, by lying to my people—and how they love it!

20"And so the Lord says: I will crush you because you hunt my people's souls with all your magic charms. I will tear off the charms and set my people free like birds from cages. 21I will tear off the magic veils and save my people from you; they will no longer be your victims, and you shall know I am the Lord. 22Your lies have discouraged the righteous, when I didn't want it so. And you have encouraged the wicked by promising life, though they continue in their sins. 23But you will lie no more; no longer will you talk of seeing 'visions' that you never saw, nor practice your magic, for I will deliver my people out of your hands by destroying you, and you shall know I am the Lord."

14 THEN SOME of the elders of Israel visited me, to ask me for a message from the Lord, 2and this is the message that came to me to give to them: 3"Son of dust, these men worship idols in their hearts—should I let them ask me anything? 4Tell them, the Lord God says: I the Lord will personally deal with anyone in Israel who worships idols and then comes to ask my help. 5For I will punish the minds and hearts of those who turn from me to idols.

New Revised Standard

it not be said to you, "Where is the whitewash you smeared on it?" 13Therefore thus says the Lord GOD: In my wrath I will make a stormy wind break out, and in my anger there shall be a deluge of rain, and hailstones in wrath to destroy it. 14I will break down the wall that you have smeared with whitewash, and bring it to the ground, so that its foundation will be laid bare; when it falls, you shall perish within it; and you shall know that I am the LORD. 15Thus I will spend my wrath upon the wall, and upon those who have smeared it with whitewash; and I will say to you, The wall is no more, nor those who smeared it— 16the prophets of Israel who prophesied concerning Jerusalem and saw visions of peace for it, when there was no peace, says the Lord GOD.

17 As for you, mortal, set your face against the daughters of your people, who prophesy out of their own imagination; prophesy against them 18and say, Thus says the Lord GOD: Woe to the women who sew bands on all wrists, and make veils for the heads of persons of every height, in the hunt for human lives! Will you hunt down lives among my people, and maintain your own lives? 19You have profaned me among my people for handfuls of barley and for pieces of bread, putting to death persons who should not die and keeping alive persons who should not live, by your lies to my people, who listen to lies.

20 Therefore thus says the Lord GOD: I am against your bands with which you hunt lives;c I will tear them from your arms, and let the lives go free, the lives that you hunt down like birds. 21I will tear off your veils, and save my people from your hands; they shall no longer be prey in your hands; and you shall know that I am the LORD. 22Because you have disheartened the righteous falsely, although I have not disheartened them, and you have encouraged the wicked not to turn from their wicked way and save their lives; 23therefore you shall no longer see false visions or practice divination; I will save my people from your hand. Then you will know that I am the LORD.

God's Judgments Justified

14 CERTAIN ELDERS of Israel came to me and sat down before me. 2And the word of the LORD came to me: 3Mortal, these men have taken their idols into their hearts, and placed their iniquity as a stumbling block before them; shall I let myself be consulted by them? 4Therefore speak to them, and say to them, Thus says the Lord GOD: Any of those of the house of Israel who take their idols into their hearts and place their iniquity as a stumbling block before them, and yet come to the prophet—I the LORD will answer those who come with the multitude of their idols, 5in order that I may take hold of the hearts of the house of Israel, all of whom are estranged from me through their idols.

---

b 13:18 unless they get a profit from it, literally, "Will you hunt the souls of my people and save your own souls alive?"

c Gk Syr: Heb lives for birds

King James

6¶ Therefore say unto the house of Israel, Thus saith the Lord GOD; Repent, and turn *yourselves* from your idols; and turn away your faces from all your abominations.

7For every one of the house of Israel, or of the stranger that sojourneth in Israel, which separateth himself from me, and setteth up his idols in his heart, and putteth the stumblingblock of his iniquity before his face, and cometh to a prophet to inquire of him concerning me; I the LORD will answer him by myself:

8And I will set my face against that man, and will make him a sign and a proverb, and I will cut him off from the midst of my people; and ye shall know that I *am* the LORD.

9And if the prophet be deceived when he hath spoken a thing, I the LORD have deceived that prophet, and I will stretch out my hand upon him, and will destroy him from the midst of my people Israel.

10And they shall bear the punishment of their iniquity: the punishment of the prophet shall be even as the punishment of him that seeketh *unto him;*

11That the house of Israel may go no more astray from me, neither be polluted any more with all their transgressions; but that they may be my people, and I may be their God, saith the Lord GOD.

12¶ The word of the LORD came again to me, saying,

13Son of man, when the land sinneth against me by trespassing grievously, then will I stretch out mine hand upon it, and will break the staff of the bread thereof, and will send famine upon it, and will cut off man and beast from it:

14Though these three men, Noah, Daniel, and Job, were in it, they should deliver *but* their own souls by their righteousness, saith the Lord GOD.

15¶ If I cause noisome beasts to pass through the land, and they spoil it, so that it be desolate, that no man may pass through because of the beasts:

16*Though* these three men *were* in it, *as* I live, saith the Lord GOD, they shall deliver neither sons nor daughters; they only shall be delivered, but the land shall be desolate.

17¶ Or *if* I bring a sword upon that land, and say, Sword, go through the land; so that I cut off man and beast from it:

18Though these three men *were* in it, *as* I live, saith the Lord GOD, they shall deliver neither sons nor daughters, but they only shall be delivered themselves.

19¶ Or *if* I send a pestilence into that land, and pour out my fury upon it in blood, to cut off from it man and beast:

20Though Noah, Daniel, and Job, *were* in it, *as* I live, saith the Lord GOD, they shall deliver neither son nor daughter; they shall *but* deliver their own souls by their righteousness.

21For thus saith the Lord GOD; How much more when I send my four sore judgments upon Jerusalem, the sword, and the famine, and the noisome beast, and the pestilence, to cut off from it man and beast?

22¶ Yet, behold, therein shall be left a remnant that shall be brought forth, *both* sons and daughters: behold, they shall come forth unto you, and ye shall see their way and their doings: and ye shall be comforted concerning the evil that I have brought upon Jerusalem, *even* concerning all that I have brought upon it.

23And they shall comfort you, when ye see their ways and their doings: and ye shall know that I have not done without cause all that I have done in it, saith the Lord GOD.

New International

6"Therefore say to the house of Israel, 'This is what the Sovereign LORD says: Repent! Turn from your idols and renounce all your detestable practices!

7" 'When any Israelite or any alien living in Israel separates himself from me and sets up idols in his heart and puts a wicked stumbling block before his face and then goes to a prophet to inquire of me, I the LORD will answer him myself. 8I will set my face against that man and make him an example and a byword. I will cut him off from my people. Then you will know that I am the LORD.

9" 'And if the prophet is enticed to utter a prophecy, I the LORD have enticed that prophet, and I will stretch out my hand against him and destroy him from among my people Israel. 10They will bear their guilt—the prophet will be as guilty as the one who consults him. 11Then the people of Israel will no longer stray from me, nor will they defile themselves anymore with all their sins. They will be my people, and I will be their God, declares the Sovereign LORD.' "

Judgment Inescapable

12The word of the LORD came to me: 13"Son of man, if a country sins against me by being unfaithful and I stretch out my hand against it to cut off its food supply and send famine upon it and kill its men and their animals, 14even if these three men—Noah, Daniel[a] and Job—were in it, they could save only themselves by their righteousness, declares the Sovereign LORD.

15"Or if I send wild beasts through that country and they leave it childless and it becomes desolate so that no one can pass through it because of the beasts, 16as surely as I live, declares the Sovereign LORD, even if these three men were in it, they could not save their own sons or daughters. They alone would be saved, but the land would be desolate.

17"Or if I bring a sword against that country and say, 'Let the sword pass throughout the land,' and I kill its men and their animals, 18as surely as I live, declares the Sovereign LORD, even if these three men were in it, they could not save their own sons or daughters. They alone would be saved.

19"Or if I send a plague into that land and pour out my wrath upon it through bloodshed, killing its men and their animals, 20as surely as I live, declares the Sovereign LORD, even if Noah, Daniel and Job were in it, they could save neither son nor daughter. They would save only themselves by their righteousness.

21"For this is what the Sovereign LORD says: How much worse will it be when I send against Jerusalem my four dreadful judgments—sword and famine and wild beasts and plague—to kill its men and their animals! 22Yet there will be some survivors—sons and daughters who will be brought out of it. They will come to you, and when you see their conduct and their actions, you will be consoled regarding the disaster I have brought upon Jerusalem—every disaster I have brought upon it. 23You will be consoled when you see their conduct and their actions, for you will know that I have done nothing in it without cause, declares the Sovereign LORD."

---

a *14* Or *Danel*; the Hebrew spelling may suggest a person other than the prophet Daniel; also in verse 20.

Living Bible

6, 7"Therefore warn them that the Lord God says: Repent and destroy your idols, and stop worshiping them in your hearts. I the Lord will personally punish everyone, whether people of Israel or the foreigners living among you, who rejects me for idols, and then comes to a prophet to ask for my help and advice. 8I will turn upon him and make a terrible example of him, destroying him; and you shall know I am the Lord. 9And if one of the false prophets gives him a message anyway, it is a lie. His prophecy will not come true, and I will stand against that 'prophet' and destroy him from among my people Israel. 10False prophets and hypocrites—evil people who say they want my words—all will be punished for their sins, 11so that the people of Israel will learn not to desert me and not to be polluted any longer with sin, but to be my people and I their God. So says the Lord."

12Then this message of the Lord came to me: 13"Son of dust, when the people of this land sin against me, then I will crush them with my fist and break off their food supply and send famine to destroy both man and beast. 14If Noah, Daniel and Job were here today, they alone would be saved by their righteousness, and I would destroy the remainder of Israel, says the Lord God.

15"When I send an invasion of dangerous wild animals into the land to devastate the land, 16even if these three men were here, the Lord God swears that it would do no good—it would not save the people from their doom. Those three only would be saved, but the land would be devastated.

17"Or when I bring war against that land and tell the armies of the enemy to come and destroy everything, 18even if these three men were in the land, the Lord God declares that they alone would be saved.

19"And when I pour out my fury by sending an epidemic of disease into the land, and the plague kills man and beast alike, 20though Noah, Daniel and Job were living there, the Lord God says that only they would be saved, because of their righteousness.

21"And the Lord says: Four great punishments await Jerusalem to destroy all life: war, famine, ferocious beasts, plague. 22If there are survivors and they come here to join you as exiles in Babylon, you will see with your own eyes how wicked they are, and you will know it was right for me to destroy Jerusalem. 23You will agree, when you meet them, that it is not without cause that all these things are being done to Israel."

New Revised Standard

6 Therefore say to the house of Israel, Thus says the Lord GOD: Repent and turn away from your idols; and turn away your faces from all your abominations. 7For any of those of the house of Israel, or of the aliens who reside in Israel, who separate themselves from me, taking their idols into their hearts and placing their iniquity as a stumbling block before them, and yet come to a prophet to inquire of me by him, I the LORD will answer them myself. 8I will set my face against them; I will make them a sign and a byword and cut them off from the midst of my people; and you shall know that I am the LORD.

9 If a prophet is deceived and speaks a word, I, the LORD, have deceived that prophet, and I will stretch out my hand against him, and will destroy him from the midst of my people Israel. 10And they shall bear their punishment—the punishment of the inquirer and the punishment of the prophet shall be the same— 11so that the house of Israel may no longer go astray from me, nor defile themselves any more with all their transgressions. Then they shall be my people, and I will be their God, says the LORD.

12 The word of the LORD came to me: 13Mortal, when a land sins against me by acting faithlessly, and I stretch out my hand against it, and break its staff of bread and send famine upon it, and cut off from it human beings and animals, 14even if Noah, Daniel,b and Job, these three, were in it, they would save only their own lives by their righteousness, says the Lord GOD. 15If I send wild animals through the land to ravage it, so that it is made desolate, and no one may pass through because of the animals; 16even if these three men were in it, as I live, says the Lord GOD, they would save neither sons nor daughters; they alone would be saved, but the land would be desolate. 17Or if I bring a sword upon that land and say, 'Let a sword pass through the land,' and I cut off human beings and animals from it; 18though these three men were in it, as I live, says the Lord GOD, they would save neither sons nor daughters, but they alone would be saved. 19Or if I send a pestilence into that land, and pour out my wrath upon it with blood, to cut off humans and animals from it; 20even if Noah, Daniel,b and Job were in it, as I live, says the Lord GOD, they would save neither son nor daughter; they would save only their own lives by their righteousness.

21 For thus says the Lord GOD: How much more when I send upon Jerusalem my four deadly acts of judgment, sword, famine, wild animals, and pestilence, to cut off humans and animals from it! 22Yet, survivors shall be left in it, sons and daughters who will be brought out; they will come out to you. When you see their ways and their deeds, you will be consoled for the evil that I have brought upon Jerusalem, for all that I have brought upon it. 23They shall console you, when you see their ways and their deeds; and you shall know that it was not without cause that I did all that I have done in it, says the Lord GOD.

b Or, as otherwise read, *Danel*

King James

15 AND THE word of the LORD came unto me, saying,

2Son of man, What is the vine tree more than any tree, *or than* a branch which is among the trees of the forest?

3Shall wood be taken thereof to do any work? or will *men* take a pin of it to hang any vessel thereon?

4Behold, it is cast into the fire for fuel; the fire devoureth both the ends of it, and the midst of it is burned. Is it meet for *any* work?

5Behold, when it was whole, it was meet for no work: how much less shall it be meet yet for *any* work, when the fire hath devoured it, and it is burned?

6¶ Therefore thus saith the Lord GOD; As the vine tree among the trees of the forest, which I have given to the fire for fuel, so will I give the inhabitants of Jerusalem.

7And I will set my face against them; they shall go out from *one* fire, and *another* fire shall devour them; and ye shall know that I *am* the LORD, when I set my face against them.

8And I will make the land desolate, because they have committed a trespass, saith the Lord GOD.

16 AGAIN THE word of the LORD came unto me, saying,

2Son of man, cause Jerusalem to know her abominations,

3And say, Thus saith the Lord GOD unto Jerusalem; Thy birth and thy nativity *is* of the land of Canaan; thy father *was* an Amorite, and thy mother an Hittite.

4And *as for* thy nativity, in the day thou wast born thy navel was not cut, neither wast thou washed in water to supple *thee;* thou wast not salted at all, nor swaddled at all.

5None eye pitied thee, to do any of these unto thee, to have compassion upon thee; but thou wast cast out in the open field, to the loathing of thy person, in the day that thou wast born.

6¶ And when I passed by thee, and saw thee polluted in thine own blood, I said unto thee *when thou wast* in thy blood, Live; yea, I said unto thee *when thou wast* in thy blood, Live.

7I have caused thee to multiply as the bud of the field, and thou hast increased and waxen great, and thou art come to excellent ornaments: *thy* breasts are fashioned, and thine hair is grown, whereas thou *wast* naked and bare.

8Now when I passed by thee, and looked upon thee, behold, thy time *was* the time of love; and I spread my skirt over thee, and covered thy nakedness: yea, I sware unto thee, and entered into a covenant with thee, saith the Lord GOD, and thou becamest mine.

9Then washed I thee with water; yea, I thoroughly washed away thy blood from thee, and I anointed thee with oil.

10I clothed thee also with broidered work, and shod thee with badgers' skin, and I girded thee about with fine linen, and I covered thee with silk.

11I decked thee also with ornaments, and I put bracelets upon thy hands, and a chain on thy neck.

12And I put a jewel on thy forehead, and earrings in thine ears, and a beautiful crown upon thine head.

New International

15 THE WORD of the LORD came to me: 2"Son of man, how is the wood of a vine better than that of a branch on any of the trees in the forest? 3Is wood ever taken from it to make anything useful? Do they make pegs from it to hang things on? 4And after it is thrown on the fire as fuel and the fire burns both ends and chars the middle, is it then useful for anything? 5If it was not useful for anything when it was whole, how much less can it be made into something useful when the fire has burned it and it is charred?

6"Therefore this is what the Sovereign LORD says: As I have given the wood of the vine among the trees of the forest as fuel for the fire, so will I treat the people living in Jerusalem. 7I will set my face against them. Although they have come out of the fire, the fire will yet consume them. And when I set my face against them, you will know that I am the LORD. 8I will make the land desolate because they have been unfaithful, declares the Sovereign LORD."

An Allegory of Unfaithful Jerusalem

16 THE WORD of the LORD came to me: 2"Son of man, confront Jerusalem with her detestable practices 3and say, 'This is what the Sovereign LORD says to Jerusalem: Your ancestry and birth were in the land of the Canaanites; your father was an Amorite and your mother a Hittite. 4On the day you were born your cord was not cut, nor were you washed with water to make you clean, nor were you rubbed with salt or wrapped in cloths. 5No one looked on you with pity or had compassion enough to do any of these things for you. Rather, you were thrown out into the open field, for on the day you were born you were despised.

6"'Then I passed by and saw you kicking about in your blood, and as you lay there in your blood I said to you, "Live!"[a] 7I made you grow like a plant of the field. You grew up and developed and became the most beautiful of jewels.[b] Your breasts were formed and your hair grew, you who were naked and bare.

8"'Later I passed by, and when I looked at you and saw that you were old enough for love, I spread the corner of my garment over you and covered your nakedness. I gave you my solemn oath and entered into a covenant with you, declares the Sovereign LORD, and you became mine.

9"'I bathed[c] you with water and washed the blood from you and put ointments on you. 10I clothed you with an embroidered dress and put leather sandals on you. I dressed you in fine linen and covered you with costly garments. 11I adorned you with jewelry: I put bracelets on your arms and a necklace around your neck, 12and I put a ring on your nose, earrings on your ears and a beautiful crown on your head. 13So you were adorned

---

[a] 6 A few Hebrew manuscripts, Septuagint and Syriac; most Hebrew manuscripts *"Live!" And as you lay there in your blood I said to you, "Live!"*   [b] 7 Or *became mature*   [c] 9 Or *I had bathed*

Living Bible

15

THEN THIS message came to me from the Lord:

2"Son of dust, what good are vines from the forest? Are they as useful as trees? Are they even as valuable as a single branch? 3No, for vines can't be used even for making pegs to hang up pots and pans! 4All they are good for is fuel—and even so, they burn but poorly! 5, 6So they are useless both before and after being put in the fire!

"This is what I mean, the Lord God says: The people of Jerusalem are like the vines of the forest—useless before being burned and certainly useless afterwards! 7And I will set myself against them to see to it that if they escape from one fire, they will fall into another; and then you shall know I am the Lord. 8And I will make the land desolate because they worship idols," says the Lord God.

16

THEN AGAIN a message came to me from the Lord.

2"Son of dust," he said, "speak to Jerusalem about her loathsome sins. 3Tell her, the Lord God says: You are no better than the people of Canaan—your father must have been an Amorite and your mother a Hittite!d 4When you were born, no one cared for you. When I first saw you, your umbilical cord was uncut, and you had been neither washed nor rubbed with salt nor clothed. 5No one had the slightest interest in you; no one pitied you or cared for you. On that day when you were born, you were dumped out into a field and left to die, unwanted.

6, 7"But I came by and saw you there, covered with your own blood, and I said, 'Live! Thrive like a plant in the field!' And you did! You grew up and became tall, slender and supple, a jewel among jewels. And when you reached the age of maidenhood your breasts were full-formed and your pubic hair had grown; yet you were naked.

8"Later, when I passed by and saw you again, you were old enough for marriage; and I wrapped my cloak around you to legally declare my marriage vow. I signed a covenant with you, and you became mine. 9, 10Then, when the marriage had taken place, I gave you beautiful clothes of linens and silk, embroidered, and sandals made of dolphin hide. 11I gave you lovely ornaments, bracelets and beautiful necklaces, 12a ring for your nose and two more for your ears, and a lovely tiara for your head. 13And so you were made beautiful with gold and

New Revised Standard

The Useless Vine

15

THE WORD of the LORD came to me: 2 O mortal, how does the wood of the vine surpass all other wood—
　the vine branch that is among the trees of
　the forest?
3 Is wood taken from it to make anything?
　Does one take a peg from it on which to
　hang any object?
4 It is put in the fire for fuel;
　when the fire has consumed both ends of it
　and the middle of it is charred,
　is it useful for anything?
5 When it was whole it was used for nothing;
　how much less—when the fire has
　consumed it,
　and it is charred—
　can it ever be used for anything!

6 Therefore thus says the Lord GOD: Like the wood of the vine among the trees of the forest, which I have given to the fire for fuel, so I will give up the inhabitants of Jerusalem. 7I will set my face against them; although they escape from the fire, the fire shall still consume them; and you shall know that I am the LORD, when I set my face against them. 8And I will make the land desolate, because they have acted faithlessly, says the Lord GOD.

God's Faithless Bride

16

THE WORD of the LORD came to me: 2Mortal, make known to Jerusalem her abominations, 3and say, Thus says the Lord GOD to Jerusalem: Your origin and your birth were in the land of the Canaanites; your father was an Amorite, and your mother a Hittite. 4As for your birth, on the day you were born your navel cord was not cut, nor were you washed with water to cleanse you, nor rubbed with salt, nor wrapped in cloths. 5No eye pitied you, to do any of these things for you out of compassion for you; but you were thrown out in the open field, for you were abhorred on the day you were born.

6 I passed by you, and saw you flailing about in your blood. As you lay in your blood, I said to you, "Live! 7and grow upe like a plant of the field." You grew up and became tall and arrived at full womanhood;f your breasts were formed, and your hair had grown; yet you were naked and bare.

8 I passed by you again and looked on you; you were at the age for love. I spread the edge of my cloak over you, and covered your nakedness: I pledged myself to you and entered into a covenant with you, says the Lord GOD, and you became mine. 9Then I bathed you with water and washed off the blood from you, and anointed you with oil. 10I clothed you with embroidered cloth and with sandals of fine leather; I bound you in fine linen and covered you with rich fabric.g 11I adorned you with ornaments: I put bracelets on your arms, a chain on your neck, 12a ring on your nose, earrings in your ears, and a beautiful crown upon your head. 13You were adorned

---

d 16:3 your mother a Hittite! The Amorites and Hittites were nations who turned their backs to all knowledge of God.

e Gk Syr: Heb Live! I made you a myriad　f Cn: Heb ornament of ornaments
g Meaning of Heb uncertain

King James

13Thus wast thou decked with gold and silver; and thy raiment *was of* fine linen, and silk, and broidered work; thou didst eat fine flour, and honey, and oil: and thou wast exceeding beautiful, and thou didst prosper into a kingdom.

14And thy renown went forth among the heathen for thy beauty: for it *was* perfect through my comeliness, which I had put upon thee, saith the Lord GOD.

15¶ But thou didst trust in thine own beauty, and playedst the harlot because of thy renown, and pouredst out thy fornications on every one that passed by; his it was.

16And of thy garments thou didst take, and deckedst thy high places with divers colours, and playedst the harlot thereupon: *the like things* shall not come, neither shall it be *so*.

17Thou hast also taken thy fair jewels of my gold and of my silver, which I had given thee, and madest to thyself images of men, and didst commit whoredom with them,

18And tookest thy broidered garments, and coveredst them: and thou hast set mine oil and mine incense before them.

19My meat also which I gave thee, fine flour, and oil, and honey, *wherewith* I fed thee, thou hast even set it before them for a sweet savour: and *thus* it was, saith the Lord GOD.

20Moreover thou hast taken thy sons and thy daughters, whom thou hast borne unto me, and these hast thou sacrificed unto them to be devoured. *Is this* of thy whoredoms a small matter,

21That thou hast slain my children, and delivered them to cause them to pass through *the fire* for them?

22And in all thine abominations and thy whoredoms thou hast not remembered the days of thy youth, when thou wast naked and bare, *and* wast polluted in thy blood.

23And it came to pass after all thy wickedness, (woe, woe unto thee! saith the Lord GOD;)

24*That* thou hast also built unto thee an eminent place, and hast made thee an high place in every street.

25Thou hast built thy high place at every head of the way, and hast made thy beauty to be abhorred, and hast opened thy feet to every one that passed by, and multiplied thy whoredoms.

26Thou hast also committed fornication with the Egyptians thy neighbours, great of flesh; and hast increased thy whoredoms, to provoke me to anger.

27Behold, therefore I have stretched out my hand over thee, and have diminished thine ordinary *food*, and delivered thee unto the will of them that hate thee, the daughters of the Philistines, which are ashamed of thy lewd way.

28Thou hast played the whore also with the Assyrians, because thou wast unsatiable; yea, thou hast played the harlot with them, and yet couldest not be satisfied.

29Thou hast moreover multiplied thy fornication in the land of Canaan unto Chaldea; and yet thou wast not satisfied herewith.

30How weak is thine heart, saith the Lord GOD, seeing thou doest all these *things*, the work of an imperious whorish woman;

31In that thou buildest thine eminent place in the head of every way, and makest thine high place in every street; and hast not been as an harlot, in that thou scornest hire;

32*But as* a wife that committeth adultery, *which* taketh strangers instead of her husband!

33They give gifts to all whores: but thou givest thy gifts to all thy lovers, and hirest them, that they may come unto thee on every side for thy whoredom.

34And the contrary is in thee from *other* women in thy whoredoms, whereas none followeth thee to commit whoredoms: and in that thou givest a reward, and no reward is given unto thee, therefore thou art contrary.

New International

with gold and silver; your clothes were of fine linen and costly fabric and embroidered cloth. Your food was fine flour, honey and olive oil. You became very beautiful and rose to be a queen. 14And your fame spread among the nations on account of your beauty, because the splendor I had given you made your beauty perfect, declares the Sovereign LORD.

15" 'But you trusted in your beauty and used your fame to become a prostitute. You lavished your favors on anyone who passed by and your beauty became his.a 16You took some of your garments to make gaudy high places, where you carried on your prostitution. Such things should not happen, nor should they ever occur. 17You also took the fine jewelry I gave you, the jewelry made of my gold and silver, and you made for yourself male idols and engaged in prostitution with them. 18And you took your embroidered clothes to put on them, and you offered my oil and incense before them. 19Also the food I provided for you—the fine flour, olive oil and honey I gave you to eat—you offered as fragrant incense before them. That is what happened, declares the Sovereign LORD.

20" 'And you took your sons and daughters whom you bore to me and sacrificed them as food to the idols. Was your prostitution not enough? 21You slaughtered my children and sacrificed themb to the idols. 22In all your detestable practices and your prostitution you did not remember the days of your youth, when you were naked and bare, kicking about in your blood.

23" 'Woe! Woe to you, declares the Sovereign LORD. In addition to all your other wickedness, 24you built a mound for yourself and made a lofty shrine in every public square. 25At the head of every street you built your lofty shrines and degraded your beauty, offering your body with increasing promiscuity to anyone who passed by. 26You engaged in prostitution with the Egyptians, your lustful neighbors, and provoked me to anger with your increasing promiscuity. 27So I stretched out my hand against you and reduced your territory; I gave you over to the greed of your enemies, the daughters of the Philistines, who were shocked by your lewd conduct. 28You engaged in prostitution with the Assyrians too, because you were insatiable; and even after that, you still were not satisfied. 29Then you increased your promiscuity to include Babylonia,c a land of merchants, but even with this you were not satisfied.

30" 'How weak-willed you are, declares the Sovereign LORD, when you do all these things, acting like a brazen prostitute! 31When you built your mounds at the head of every street and made your lofty shrines in every public square, you were unlike a prostitute, because you scorned payment.

32" 'You adulterous wife! You prefer strangers to your own husband! 33Every prostitute receives a fee, but you give gifts to all your lovers, bribing them to come to you from everywhere for your illicit favors. 34So in your prostitution you are the opposite of others; no one runs after you for your favors. You are the very opposite, for you give payment and none is given to you.

a *15 Most Hebrew manuscripts; one Hebrew manuscript (see some Septuagint manuscripts) by. Such a thing should not happen* b *21 Or and made them pass through the fire* c *29 Or Chaldea*

Living Bible

silver, and your clothes were silk and linen and beautifully embroidered. You ate the finest foods and became more beautiful than ever. You looked like a queen, and so you were! 14Your reputation was great among the nations for your beauty; it was perfect because of all the gifts I gave you, says the Lord God.

15"But you thought you could get along without me—you trusted in your beauty instead; and you gave yourself as a prostitute to every man who came along. Your beauty was his for the asking. 16You used the lovely things I gave you for making idol shrines and to decorate your bed of prostitution. Unbelievable! There has never been anything like it before! 17You took the very jewels and gold and silver ornaments I gave to you and made statues of men and worshiped them, which is adultery against me. 18You used the beautifully embroidered clothes I gave you—to cover your idols! And used my oil and incense to worship *them!* 19You set before them—imagine it—the fine flour and oil and honey I gave you; you used it as a lovely sacrifice to *them!* 20And you took my sons and daughters you had borne to me, and sacrificed them to your gods; and they are gone. Wasn't it enough that you should be a prostitute? 21Must you also slay my children by sacrificing them to idols?

22"And in all these years of adultery and sin you have not thought of those days long ago when you were naked and covered with blood.

23"And then, in addition to all your other wickedness—woe, woe upon you, says the Lord God— 24you built a spacious brothel for your lovers, and idol altars on every street, 25and there you offered your beauty to every man who came by, in an endless stream of prostitution. 26And you added lustful Egypt to your prostitutions by your alliance with her. My anger is great.

27"Therefore I have crushed you with my fist; I have reduced your boundaries and delivered you into the hands of those who hate you—the Philistines—and even they are ashamed of you.

28"You have committed adultery with the Assyrians too [by making them your allies and worshiping their gods[d]]; it seems that you can never find enough new gods. After your adultery there, you still weren't satisfied, 29so you worshiped the gods of that great merchant land of Babylon—and you still weren't satisfied. 30What a filthy heart you have, says the Lord God, to do such things as these; you are a brazen prostitute, 31building your idol altars, your brothels, on every street. You have been worse than a prostitute, so eager for sin that you have not even charged for your love! 32Yes, you are an adulterous wife who lives with other men instead of her own husband. 33, 34Prostitutes charge for their services—men pay with many gifts. But not you, you give *them* gifts, bribing them to come to you! So you are different from other prostitutes. But you had to pay them, for no one wanted you.

New Revised Standard

with gold and silver, while your clothing was of fine linen, rich fabric,[e] and embroidered cloth. You had choice flour and honey and oil for food. You grew exceedingly beautiful, fit to be a queen. 14Your fame spread among the nations on account of your beauty, for it was perfect because of my splendor that I had bestowed on you, says the Lord GOD.

15 But you trusted in your beauty, and played the whore because of your fame, and lavished your whorings on any passer-by.[f] 16You took some of your garments, and made for yourself colorful shrines, and on them played the whore; nothing like this has ever been or ever shall be.[e] 17You also took your beautiful jewels of my gold and my silver that I had given you, and made for yourself male images, and with them played the whore; 18and you took your embroidered garments to cover them, and set my oil and my incense before them. 19Also my bread that I gave you—I fed you with choice flour and oil and honey—you set it before them as a pleasing odor; and so it was, says the Lord GOD. 20You took your sons and your daughters, whom you had borne to me, and these you sacrificed to them to be devoured. As if your whorings were not enough! 21You slaughtered my children and delivered them up as an offering to them. 22And in all your abominations and your whorings you did not remember the days of your youth, when you were naked and bare, flailing about in your blood.

23 After all your wickedness (woe, woe to you! says the Lord GOD), 24you built yourself a platform and made yourself a lofty place in every square; 25at the head of every street you built your lofty place and prostituted your beauty, offering yourself to every passer-by, and multiplying your whoring. 26You played the whore with the Egyptians, your lustful neighbors, multiplying your whoring, to provoke me to anger. 27Therefore I stretched out my hand against you, reduced your rations, and gave you up to the will of your enemies, the daughters of the Philistines, who were ashamed of your lewd behavior. 28You played the whore with the Assyrians, because you were insatiable; you played the whore with them, and still you were not satisfied. 29You multiplied your whoring with Chaldea, the land of merchants; and even with this you were not satisfied.

30 How sick is your heart, says the Lord GOD, that you did all these things, the deeds of a brazen whore; 31building your platform at the head of every street, and making your lofty place in every square! Yet you were not like a whore, because you scorned payment. 32Adulterous wife, who receives strangers instead of her husband! 33Gifts are given to all whores; but you gave your gifts to all your lovers, bribing them to come to you from all around for your whorings. 34So you were different from other women in your whorings: no one solicited you to play the whore; and you gave payment, while no payment was given to you; you were different.

---

d 16:28 *by making them your allies and worshiping their gods*, implied.   e Meaning of Heb uncertain   f Heb adds *let it be his*

King James

35¶ Wherefore, O harlot, hear the word of the LORD:
36Thus saith the Lord GOD; Because thy filthiness
was poured out, and thy nakedness discovered through
thy whoredoms with thy lovers, and with all the idols of
thy abominations, and by the blood of thy children,
which thou didst give unto them;

37Behold, therefore I will gather all thy lovers, with
whom thou hast taken pleasure, and all *them* that thou
hast loved, with all *them* that thou hast hated; I will even
gather them round about against thee, and will discover
thy nakedness unto them, that they may see all thy nakedness.

38And I will judge thee, as women that break wedlock
and shed blood are judged; and I will give thee blood in
fury and jealousy.

39And I will also give thee into their hand, and they
shall throw down thine eminent place, and shall break
down thy high places: they shall strip thee also of thy
clothes, and shall take thy fair jewels, and leave thee
naked and bare.

40They shall also bring up a company against thee,
and they shall stone thee with stones, and thrust thee
through with their swords.

41And they shall burn thine houses with fire, and
execute judgments upon thee in the sight of many wom-
en: and I will cause thee to cease from playing the harlot,
and thou also shalt give no hire any more.

42So will I make my fury toward thee to rest, and my
jealousy shall depart from thee, and I will be quiet, and
will be no more angry.

43Because thou hast not remembered the days of thy
youth, but hast fretted me in all these *things;* behold,
therefore I also will recompense thy way upon *thine*
head, saith the Lord GOD: and thou shalt not commit this
lewdness above all thine abominations.

44¶ Behold, every one that useth proverbs shall use
this proverb against thee, saying, As *is* the mother, *so
is* her daughter.

45Thou *art* thy mother's daughter, that loatheth her
husband and her children; and thou *art* the sister of thy
sisters, which loathed their husbands and their children:
your mother *was* an Hittite, and your father an Amorite.

46And thine elder sister *is* Samaria, she and her
daughters that dwell at thy left hand: and thy younger
sister, that dwelleth at thy right hand, *is* Sodom and her
daughters.

47Yet hast thou not walked after their ways, nor done
after their abominations: but, as *if that were* a very little
thing, thou wast corrupted more than they in all thy
ways.

48*As* I live, saith the Lord GOD, Sodom thy sister hath
not done, she nor her daughters, as thou hast done, thou
and thy daughters.

49Behold, this was the iniquity of thy sister Sodom,
pride, fulness of bread, and abundance of idleness was
in her and in her daughters, neither did she strengthen
the hand of the poor and needy.

50And they were haughty, and committed abomination before me: therefore I took them away as I saw
good.

51Neither hath Samaria committed half of thy sins;
but thou hast multiplied thine abominations more than
they, and hast justified thy sisters in all thine abominations which thou hast done.

52Thou also, which hast judged thy sisters, bear thine
own shame for thy sins that thou hast committed more
abominable than they: they are more righteous than
thou: yea, be thou confounded also, and bear thy shame,
in that thou hast justified thy sisters.

53When I shall bring again their captivity, the captivity of Sodom and her daughters, and the captivity of
Samaria and her daughters, then *will I bring again* the
captivity of thy captives in the midst of them:

New International

35" 'Therefore, you prostitute, hear the word of the
LORD! 36This is what the Sovereign LORD says: Because
you poured out your wealth[a] and exposed your nakedness in your promiscuity with your lovers, and because
of all your detestable idols, and because you gave them
your children's blood, 37therefore I am going to gather
all your lovers, with whom you found pleasure, those
you loved as well as those you hated. I will gather them
against you from all around and will strip you in front
of them, and they will see all your nakedness. 38I will
sentence you to the punishment of women who commit
adultery and who shed blood; I will bring upon you the
blood vengeance of my wrath and jealous anger. 39Then
I will hand you over to your lovers, and they will tear
down your mounds and destroy your lofty shrines. They
will strip you of your clothes and take your fine jewelry
and leave you naked and bare. 40They will bring a mob
against you, who will stone you and hack you to pieces
with their swords. 41They will burn down your houses
and inflict punishment on you in the sight of many wom-
en. I will put a stop to your prostitution, and you will
no longer pay your lovers. 42Then my wrath against you
will subside and my jealous anger will turn away from
you; I will be calm and no longer angry.

43" 'Because you did not remember the days of your
youth but enraged me with all these things, I will surely
bring down on your head what you have done, declares
the Sovereign LORD. Did you not add lewdness to all
your other detestable practices?

44" 'Everyone who quotes proverbs will quote this
proverb about you: "Like mother, like daughter." 45You
are a true daughter of your mother, who despised her
husband and her children; and you are a true sister of
your sisters, who despised their husbands and their children. Your mother was a Hittite and your father an Amorite. 46Your older sister was Samaria, who lived to the
north of you with her daughters; and your younger sister,
who lived to the south of you with her daughters, was
Sodom. 47You not only walked in their ways and copied
their detestable practices, but in all your ways you soon
became more depraved than they. 48As surely as I live,
declares the Sovereign LORD, your sister Sodom and her
daughters never did what you and your daughters have
done.

49" 'Now this was the sin of your sister Sodom: She
and her daughters were arrogant, overfed and unconcerned; they did not help the poor and needy. 50They
were haughty and did detestable things before me.
Therefore I did away with them as you have seen. 51Sa-
maria did not commit half the sins you did. You have
done more detestable things than they, and have made
your sisters seem righteous by all these things you have
done. 52Bear your disgrace, for you have furnished some
justification for your sisters. Because your sins were
more vile than theirs, they appear more righteous than
you. So then, be ashamed and bear your disgrace, for
you have made your sisters appear righteous.

53" 'However, I will restore the fortunes of Sodom
and her daughters and of Samaria and her daughters, and
your fortunes along with them, 54so that you may bear

Living Bible

35"O prostitute, hear the word of the Lord:

36"The Lord God says: Because I see your filthy sins, your adultery with your lovers—your worshiping of idols—and the slaying of your children as sacrifices to your gods, 37this is what I am going to do: I will gather together all your allies—these lovers of yours you have sinned with, both those you loved and those you hated—and I will make you naked before them, that they may see you. 38I will punish you as a murderess is punished and as a woman breaking wedlock living with other men. 39I will give you to your lovers—these many nations—to destroy, and they will knock down your brothels and idol altars, and strip you and take your beautiful jewels and leave you naked and ashamed. 40, 41They will burn your homes, punishing you before the eyes of many women. And I will see to it that you stop your adulteries with other gods and end your payments to your allies for their love.

42"Then at last my fury against you will die away; my jealousy against you will end, and I will be quiet and not be angry with you anymore. 43But first, because you have not remembered your youth, but have angered me by all these evil things you do, I will fully repay you for all of your sins, says the Lord. For you are thankless in addition to all your other faults.

44" 'Like mother, like daughter'—that is what everyone will say of you. 45For your mother loathed her husband and her children, and you do too. And you are exactly like your sisters, for they despised their husbands and their children. Truly, your mother must have been a Hittite and your father an Amorite.

46"Your older sister is Samaria, living with her daughters north of you; your younger sister is Sodom and her daughters, in the south. 47You have not merely sinned as they do—no, that was nothing to you; in a very short time you far surpassed them.

48"As I live, the Lord God says, Sodom and her daughters have never been as wicked as you and your daughters. 49Your sister Sodom's sins were pride and laziness and too much food, while the poor and needy suffered outside her door. 50She insolently worshiped many idols as I watched. Therefore I crushed her.

51"Even Samaria has not committed half your sins. You have worshiped idols far more than your sisters have; they seem almost righteous in comparison with you! 52Don't be surprised then by the lighter punishment they get. For your sins are so awful that in comparison with you, your sisters seem innocent! 53(But someday I will restore the fortunes of Sodom and Samaria again, and those of Judah too.) 54Your terrible punishment will

New Revised Standard

35 Therefore, O whore, hear the word of the LORD: 36Thus says the Lord GOD, Because your lust was poured out and your nakedness uncovered in your whoring with your lovers, and because of all your abominable idols, and because of the blood of your children that you gave to them, 37therefore, I will gather all your lovers, with whom you took pleasure, all those you loved and all those you hated; I will gather them against you from all around, and will uncover your nakedness to them, so that they may see all your nakedness. 38I will judge you as women who commit adultery and shed blood are judged, and bring blood upon you in wrath and jealousy. 39I will deliver you into their hands, and they shall throw down your platform and break down your lofty places; they shall strip you of your clothes and take your beautiful objects and leave you naked and bare. 40They shall bring up a mob against you, and they shall stone you and cut you to pieces with their swords. 41They shall burn your houses and execute judgments on you in the sight of many women; I will stop you from playing the whore, and you shall also make no more payments. 42So I will satisfy my fury on you, and my jealousy shall turn away from you; I will be calm, and will be angry no longer. 43Because you have not remembered the days of your youth, but have enraged me with all these things; therefore, I have returned your deeds upon your head, says the Lord GOD.

Have you not committed lewdness beyond all your abominations? 44See, everyone who uses proverbs will use this proverb about you, "Like mother, like daughter." 45You are the daughter of your mother, who loathed her husband and her children; and you are the sister of your sisters, who loathed their husbands and their children. Your mother was a Hittite and your father an Amorite. 46Your elder sister is Samaria, who lived with her daughters to the north of you; and your younger sister, who lived to the south of you, is Sodom with her daughters. 47You not only followed their ways, and acted according to their abominations; within a very little time you were more corrupt than they in all your ways. 48As I live, says the Lord GOD, your sister Sodom and her daughters have not done as you and your daughters have done. 49This was the guilt of your sister Sodom: she and her daughters had pride, excess of food, and prosperous ease, but did not aid the poor and needy. 50They were haughty, and did abominable things before me; therefore I removed them when I saw it. 51Samaria has not committed half your sins; you have committed more abominations than they, and have made your sisters appear righteous by all the abominations that you have committed. 52Bear your disgrace, you also, for you have brought about for your sisters a more favorable judgment; because of your sins in which you acted more abominably than they, they are more in the right than you. So be ashamed, you also, and bear your disgrace, for you have made your sisters appear righteous.

53 I will restore their fortunes, the fortunes of Sodom and her daughters and the fortunes of Samaria and her daughters, and I will restore your own fortunes along with theirs, 54in order that you may bear your disgrace

King James

⁵⁴That thou mayest bear thine own shame, and mayest be confounded in all that thou hast done, in that thou art a comfort unto them.

⁵⁵When thy sisters, Sodom and her daughters, shall return to their former estate, and Samaria and her daughters shall return to their former estate, then thou and thy daughters shall return to your former estate.

⁵⁶For thy sister Sodom was not mentioned by thy mouth in the day of thy pride,

⁵⁷Before thy wickedness was discovered, as at the time of *thy* reproach of the daughters of Syria, and all *that are* round about her, the daughters of the Philistines, which despise thee round about.

⁵⁸Thou hast borne thy lewdness and thine abominations, saith the LORD.

⁵⁹For thus saith the Lord GOD; I will even deal with thee as thou hast done, which hast despised the oath in breaking the covenant.

⁶⁰¶ Nevertheless I will remember my covenant with thee in the days of thy youth, and I will establish unto thee an everlasting covenant.

⁶¹Then thou shalt remember thy ways, and be ashamed, when thou shalt receive thy sisters, thine elder and thy younger: and I will give them unto thee for daughters, but not by thy covenant.

⁶²And I will establish my covenant with thee; and thou shalt know that I *am* the LORD:

⁶³That thou mayest remember, and be confounded, and never open thy mouth any more because of thy shame, when I am pacified toward thee for all that thou hast done, saith the Lord GOD.

17 AND THE word of the LORD came unto me, saying,

²Son of man, put forth a riddle, and speak a parable unto the house of Israel;

³And say, Thus saith the Lord GOD; A great eagle with great wings, longwinged, full of feathers, which had divers colours, came unto Lebanon, and took the highest branch of the cedar:

⁴He cropped off the top of his young twigs, and carried it into a land of traffic; he set it in a city of merchants.

⁵He took also of the seed of the land, and planted it in a fruitful field; he placed *it* by great waters, *and* set it *as* a willow tree.

⁶And it grew, and became a spreading vine of low stature, whose branches turned toward him, and the roots thereof were under him: so it became a vine, and brought forth branches, and shot forth sprigs.

⁷There was also another great eagle with great wings and many feathers: and, behold, this vine did bend her roots toward him, and shot forth her branches toward him, that he might water it by the furrows of her plantation.

⁸It was planted in a good soil by great waters, that it might bring forth branches, and that it might bear fruit, that it might be a goodly vine.

New International

your disgrace and be ashamed of all you have done in giving them comfort. ⁵⁵And your sisters, Sodom with her daughters and Samaria with her daughters, will return to what they were before; and you and your daughters will return to what you were before. ⁵⁶You would not even mention your sister Sodom in the day of your pride, ⁵⁷before your wickedness was uncovered. Even so, you are now scorned by the daughters of Edom[a] and all her neighbors and the daughters of the Philistines— all those around you who despise you. ⁵⁸You will bear the consequences of your lewdness and your detestable practices, declares the LORD.

⁵⁹"'This is what the Sovereign LORD says: I will deal with you as you deserve, because you have despised my oath by breaking the covenant. ⁶⁰Yet I will remember the covenant I made with you in the days of your youth, and I will establish an everlasting covenant with you. ⁶¹Then you will remember your ways and be ashamed when you receive your sisters, both those who are older than you and those who are younger. I will give them to you as daughters, but not on the basis of my covenant with you. ⁶²So I will establish my covenant with you, and you will know that I am the LORD. ⁶³Then, when I make atonement for you for all you have done, you will remember and be ashamed and never again open your mouth because of your humiliation, declares the Sovereign LORD.'"

Two Eagles and a Vine

17 THE WORD of the LORD came to me: ²"Son of man, set forth an allegory and tell the house of Israel a parable. ³Say to them, 'This is what the Sovereign LORD says: A great eagle with powerful wings, long feathers and full plumage of varied colors came to Lebanon. Taking hold of the top of a cedar, ⁴he broke off its topmost shoot and carried it away to a land of merchants, where he planted it in a city of traders.

⁵"'He took some of the seed of your land and put it in fertile soil. He planted it like a willow by abundant water, ⁶and it sprouted and became a low, spreading vine. Its branches turned toward him, but its roots remained under it. So it became a vine and produced branches and put out leafy boughs.

⁷"'But there was another great eagle with powerful wings and full plumage. The vine now sent out its roots toward him from the plot where it was planted and stretched out its branches to him for water. ⁸It had been planted in good soil by abundant water so that it would produce branches, bear fruit and become a splendid vine.'

a 57 Many Hebrew manuscripts and Syriac; most Hebrew manuscripts, Septuagint and Vulgate *Aram*

Living Bible

be a consolation to them, for it will be greater than theirs.

55"Yes, your sisters, Sodom and Samaria, and all their people will be restored again, and Judah too will prosper in that day. 56In your proud days you held Sodom in unspeakable contempt. 57But now your greater wickedness has been exposed to all the world, and you are the one who is scorned—by Edom and all her neighbors and by all the Philistines. 58This is part of your punishment for all your sins, says the Lord.

59, 60"For the Lord God says: I will repay you for your broken promises. You lightly broke your solemn vows to me, yet I will keep the pledge I made to you when you were young. I will establish an everlasting covenant with you forever, 61and you will remember with shame all the evil you have done; and you will be overcome by my favor when I take your sisters, Samaria and Sodom, and make them your daughters, for you to rule over. You will know you don't deserve this gracious act, for you did not keep my covenant. 62I will reaffirm my covenant with you, and you will know I am the Lord. 63Despite all you have done, I will be kind to you again; you will cover your mouth in silence and in shame when I forgive you all that you have done, says the Lord God."

17 THEN THIS message came to me from the Lord:

2"Son of dust, give this riddle to the people of Israel: 3, 4"A great eagle with broad wings full of many-colored feathers came to Lebanon and plucked off the shoot at the top of the tallest cedar tree and carried it into a city filled with merchants. 5There he planted itᵇ in fertile ground beside a broad river, where it would grow as quickly as a willow tree. 6It took root and grew and became a low but spreading vine that turned toward the eagle and produced strong branches and luxuriant leaves. 7But when another great, broad-winged, full-feathered eagle came along, this tree sent its roots and branches out toward him instead, even though it was already in good soil with plenty of water to become a splendid vine, producing leaves and fruit.

New Revised Standard

and be ashamed of all that you have done, becoming a consolation to them. 55As for your sisters, Sodom and her daughters shall return to their former state, Samaria and her daughters shall return to their former state, and you and your daughters shall return to your former state. 56Was not your sister Sodom a byword in your mouth in the day of your pride, 57before your wickedness was uncovered? Now you are a mockery to the daughters of Aramᶜ and all her neighbors, and to the daughters of the Philistines, those all around who despise you. 58You must bear the penalty of your lewdness and your abominations, says the LORD.

An Everlasting Covenant

59 Yes, thus says the Lord GOD: I will deal with you as you have done, you who have despised the oath, breaking the covenant; 60yet I will remember my covenant with you in the days of your youth, and I will establish with you an everlasting covenant. 61Then you will remember your ways, and be ashamed when Iᵈ take your sisters, both your elder and your younger, and give them to you as daughters, but not on account of myᵉ covenant with you. 62I will establish my covenant with you, and you shall know that I am the LORD, 63in order that you may remember and be confounded, and never open your mouth again because of your shame, when I forgive you all that you have done, says the Lord GOD.

The Two Eagles and the Vine

17 THE WORD of the LORD came to me: 2O mortal, propound a riddle, and speak an allegory to the house of Israel. 3Say: Thus says the Lord GOD:

A great eagle, with great wings and long
    pinions,
  rich in plumage of many colors,
    came to the Lebanon.
He took the top of the cedar,
4   broke off its topmost shoot;
He carried it to a land of trade,
    set it in a city of merchants.
5 Then he took a seed from the land,
    placed it in fertile soil;
A plantᶠ by abundant waters,
    he set it like a willow twig.
6 It sprouted and became a vine
    spreading out, but low;
Its branches turned toward him,
    its roots remained where it stood.
So it became a vine;
    it brought forth branches,
    put forth foliage.

7 There was another great eagle,
    with great wings and much plumage.
And see! This vine stretched out
    its roots toward him;
It shot out its branches toward him,
    so that he might water it.
From the bed where it was planted
8   it was transplanted
to good soil by abundant waters,
    so that it might produce branches
    and bear fruit
    and become a noble vine.

ᵇ 17:5 planted it, literally, "planted the seed of the land."

ᶜ Another reading is Edom   ᵈ Syr: Heb you   ᵉ Heb lacks my   ᶠ Meaning of Heb uncertain

King James

9Say thou, Thus saith the Lord GOD; Shall it prosper? shall he not pull up the roots thereof, and cut off the fruit thereof, that it wither? it shall wither in all the leaves of her spring, even without great power or many people to pluck it up by the roots thereof.

10Yea, behold, *being* planted, shall it prosper? shall it not utterly wither, when the east wind toucheth it? it shall wither in the furrows where it grew.

11¶ Moreover the word of the LORD came unto me, saying,

12Say now to the rebellious house, Know ye not what these *things mean?* tell *them,* Behold, the king of Babylon is come to Jerusalem, and hath taken the king thereof, and the princes thereof, and led them with him to Babylon;

13And hath taken of the king's seed, and made a covenant with him, and hath taken an oath of him: he hath also taken the mighty of the land:

14That the kingdom might be base, that it might not lift itself up, *but* that by keeping of his covenant it might stand.

15But he rebelled against him in sending his ambassadors into Egypt, that they might give him horses and much people. Shall he prosper? shall he escape that doeth such *things?* or shall he break the covenant, and be delivered?

16As I live, saith the Lord GOD, surely in the place *where* the king *dwelleth* that made him king, whose oath he despised, and whose covenant he brake, *even* with him in the midst of Babylon he shall die.

17Neither shall Pharaoh with *his* mighty army and great company make for him in the war, by casting up mounts, and building forts, to cut off many persons:

18Seeing he despised the oath by breaking the covenant, when, lo, he had given his hand, and hath done all these *things,* he shall not escape.

19Therefore thus saith the Lord GOD; *As* I live, surely mine oath that he hath despised, and my covenant that he hath broken, even it will I recompense upon his own head.

20And I will spread my net upon him, and he shall be taken in my snare, and I will bring him to Babylon, and will plead with him there for his trespass that he hath trespassed against me.

21And all his fugitives with all his bands shall fall by the sword, and they that remain shall be scattered toward all winds: and ye shall know that I the LORD have spoken *it.*

22¶ Thus saith the Lord GOD; I will also take of the highest branch of the high cedar, and will set *it;* I will crop off from the top of his young twigs a tender one, and will plant *it* upon an high mountain and eminent:

23In the mountain of the height of Israel will I plant it: and it shall bring forth boughs, and bear fruit, and be a goodly cedar: and under it shall dwell all fowl of every wing; in the shadow of the branches thereof shall they dwell.

24And all the trees of the field shall know that I the LORD have brought down the high tree, have exalted the low tree, have dried up the green tree, and have made the dry tree to flourish: I the LORD have spoken and have done *it.*

New International

9"Say to them, 'This is what the Sovereign LORD says: Will it thrive? Will it not be uprooted and stripped of its fruit so that it withers? All its new growth will wither. It will not take a strong arm or many people to pull it up by the roots. 10Even if it is transplanted, will it thrive? Will it not wither completely when the east wind strikes it—wither away in the plot where it grew?' "

11Then the word of the LORD came to me: 12"Say to this rebellious house, 'Do you not know what these things mean?' Say to them: 'The king of Babylon went to Jerusalem and carried off her king and her nobles, bringing them back with him to Babylon. 13Then he took a member of the royal family and made a treaty with him, putting him under oath. He also carried away the leading men of the land, 14so that the kingdom would be brought low, unable to rise again, surviving only by keeping his treaty. 15But the king rebelled against him by sending his envoys to Egypt to get horses and a large army. Will he succeed? Will he who does such things escape? Will he break the treaty and yet escape?

16"'As surely as I live, declares the Sovereign LORD, he shall die in Babylon, in the land of the king who put him on the throne, whose oath he despised and whose treaty he broke. 17Pharaoh with his mighty army and great horde will be of no help to him in war, when ramps are built and siege works erected to destroy many lives. 18He despised the oath by breaking the covenant. Because he had given his hand in pledge and yet did all these things, he shall not escape.

19"'Therefore this is what the Sovereign LORD says: As surely as I live, I will bring down on his head my oath that he despised and my covenant that he broke. 20I will spread my net for him, and he will be caught in my snare. I will bring him to Babylon and execute judgment upon him there because he was unfaithful to me. 21All his fleeing troops will fall by the sword, and the survivors will be scattered to the winds. Then you will know that I the LORD have spoken.

22"'This is what the Sovereign LORD says: I myself will take a shoot from the very top of a cedar and plant it; I will break off a tender sprig from its topmost shoots and plant it on a high and lofty mountain. 23On the mountain heights of Israel I will plant it; it will produce branches and bear fruit and become a splendid cedar. Birds of every kind will nest in it; they will find shelter in the shade of its branches. 24All the trees of the field will know that I the LORD bring down the tall tree and make the low tree grow tall. I dry up the green tree and make the dry tree flourish.

" 'I the LORD have spoken, and I will do it.' "

<table>
<tr><th>Living Bible</th><th>New Revised Standard</th></tr>
</table>

Living Bible

9"The Lord God asks: Shall I let this tree grow and prosper? No! I will pull it out, roots and all! I will cut off its branches and let its leaves wither and die. It will pull out easily enough—it won't take a big crew or a lot of equipment to do that. 10Though the vine began so well, will it thrive? No, it will wither away completely when the east wind touches it, dying in the same choice soil where it had grown so well."

11Then this message came to me from the Lord:

12, 13"Ask these rebels of Israel: Don't you understand what this riddle of the eagles means? I will tell you. Nebuchadnezzar, king of Babylon [the first of the two eaglesa], came to Jerusalem and took away her king and princes [her topmost buds and shoots] and brought them to Babylon. Nebuchadnezzar made a covenant with a member of the royal family [Zedekiah], and made him take an oath of loyalty. He took a seedling and planted it in fertile ground beside a broad river and he exiled the top men of Israel's government, 14so that Israel would not be strong again and revolt. But by keeping her promises, Israel could be respected and maintain her identity.

15"Nevertheless, Zedekiah rebelled against Babylon, sending ambassadors to Egypt to seek for a great army and many horses to fight against Nebuchadnezzar. But will Israel prosper after breaking all her promises like that? Will she succeed? 16No! For as I live, says the Lord, the king of Israel shall die. (Nebuchadnezzar will pull out the tree, roots and all!) Zedekiah shall die in Babylon, where the king lives who gave him his power, and whose covenant he despised and broke. 17Pharaoh and all his mighty army shall fail to help Israel when the king of Babylon lays siege to Jerusalem again and slaughters many lives. 18For the king of Israel broke his promise after swearing to obey; therefore he shall not escape.

19"The Lord God says: As I live, surely I will punish him for despising the solemn oath he made in my name. 20I will throw my net over him and he shall be captured in my snare, and I will bring him to Babylon and deal with him there for this treason against me. 21And all the best soldiers of Israel will be killed by the sword, and those remaining in the city will be scattered to the four winds. Then you will know that I, the Lord, have spoken these words.

22, 23"The Lord God says: I will take a tender sprout from the top of a tall cedar, and I will plant it on the top of Israel's highest mountain. It shall become a noble cedar, bringing forth branches and bearing seed. Animals of every sort will gather under it; its branches will shelter every kind of bird. 24And everyone shall know that it is I, the Lord, who cuts down the high trees and exalts the low, that I make the green tree wither and the dead tree grow. I, the Lord, have said that I would do it, and I will."

New Revised Standard

9Say: Thus says the Lord GOD:
Will it prosper?
Will he not pull up its roots,
    cause its fruit to rotb and wither,
    its fresh sprouting leaves to fade?
No strong arm or mighty army will be needed
    to pull it from its roots.
10 When it is transplanted, will it thrive?
When the east wind strikes it,
    will it not utterly wither,
    wither on the bed where it grew?

11 Then the word of the LORD came to me: 12Say now to the rebellious house: Do you not know what these things mean? Tell them: The king of Babylon came to Jerusalem, took its king and its officials, and brought them back with him to Babylon. 13He took one of the royal offspring and made a covenant with him, putting him under oath (he had taken away the chief men of the land), 14so that the kingdom might be humble and not lift itself up, and that by keeping his covenant it might stand. 15But he rebelled against him by sending ambassadors to Egypt, in order that they might give him horses and a large army. Will he succeed? Can one escape who does such things? Can he break the covenant and yet escape? 16As I live, says the Lord GOD, surely in the place where the king resides who made him king, whose oath he despised, and whose covenant with him he broke—in Babylon he shall die. 17Pharaoh with his mighty army and great company will not help him in war, when ramps are cast up and siege walls built to cut off many lives. 18Because he despised the oath and broke the covenant, because he gave his hand and yet did all these things, he shall not escape. 19Therefore thus says the Lord GOD: As I live, I will surely return upon his head my oath that he despised, and my covenant that he broke. 20I will spread my net over him, and he shall be caught in my snare; I will bring him to Babylon and enter into judgment with him there for the treason he has committed against me. 21All the pickc of his troops shall fall by the sword, and the survivors shall be scattered to every wind; and you shall know that I, the LORD, have spoken.

Israel Exalted at Last

22 Thus says the Lord GOD:
I myself will take a sprig
    from the lofty top of a cedar;
    I will set it out.
I will break off a tender one
    from the topmost of its young twigs;
I myself will plant it
    on a high and lofty mountain.
23 On the mountain height of Israel
    I will plant it,
in order that it may produce boughs and bear
        fruit,
    and become a noble cedar.
Under it every kind of bird will live;
    in the shade of its branches will nest
    winged creatures of every kind.
24 All the trees of the field shall know
    that I am the LORD.
I bring low the high tree,
    I make high the low tree;
I dry up the green tree
    and make the dry tree flourish.
I the LORD have spoken;
    I will accomplish it.

---

a 17:12, 13 the first of the two eagles . . . her topmost buds and shoots . . . Zedekiah, implied. So also in vs 16.

b Meaning of Heb uncertain   c Another reading is fugitives

King James

18 THE WORD of the LORD came unto me again, saying,

2What mean ye, that ye use this proverb concerning the land of Israel, saying, The fathers have eaten sour grapes, and the children's teeth are set on edge?

3*As* I live, saith the Lord GOD, ye shall not have *occasion* any more to use this proverb in Israel.

4Behold, all souls are mine; as the soul of the father, so also the soul of the son is mine: the soul that sinneth, it shall die.

5¶ But if a man be just, and do that which is lawful and right,

6*And* hath not eaten upon the mountains, neither hath lifted up his eyes to the idols of the house of Israel, neither hath defiled his neighbour's wife, neither hath come near to a menstruous woman,

7And hath not oppressed any, *but* hath restored to the debtor his pledge, hath spoiled none by violence, hath given his bread to the hungry, and hath covered the naked with a garment;

8He *that* hath not given forth upon usury, neither hath taken any increase, *that* hath withdrawn his hand from iniquity, hath executed true judgment between man and man,

9Hath walked in my statutes, and hath kept my judgments, to deal truly; he *is* just, he shall surely live, saith the Lord GOD.

10¶ If he beget a son *that is* a robber, a shedder of blood, and *that* doeth the like to *any* one of these *things*,

11And that doeth not any of those *duties*, but even hath eaten upon the mountains, and defiled his neighbour's wife,

12Hath oppressed the poor and needy, hath spoiled by violence, hath not restored the pledge, and hath lifted up his eyes to the idols, hath committed abomination,

13Hath given forth upon usury, and hath taken increase: shall he then live? he shall not live: he hath done all these abominations; he shall surely die; his blood shall be upon him.

14¶ Now, lo, *if* he beget a son, that seeth all his father's sins which he hath done, and considereth, and doeth not such like,

15*That* hath not eaten upon the mountains, neither hath lifted up his eyes to the idols of the house of Israel, hath not defiled his neighbour's wife,

16Neither hath oppressed any, hath not withholden the pledge, neither hath spoiled by violence, *but* hath given his bread to the hungry, and hath covered the naked with a garment,

17*That* hath taken off his hand from the poor, *that* hath not received usury nor increase, hath executed my judgments, hath walked in my statutes; he shall not die for the iniquity of his father, he shall surely live.

18*As for* his father, because he cruelly oppressed, spoiled his brother by violence, and did *that* which *is* not good among his people, lo, even he shall die in his iniquity.

19¶ Yet say ye, Why? doth not the son bear the iniquity of the father? When the son hath done that which is lawful and right, *and* hath kept all my statutes, and hath done them, he shall surely live.

New International

The Soul Who Sins Will Die

18 THE WORD of the LORD came to me: 2"What do you people mean by quoting this proverb about the land of Israel:

"'The fathers eat sour grapes,
and the children's teeth are set on edge'?

3"As surely as I live, declares the Sovereign LORD, you will no longer quote this proverb in Israel. 4For every living soul belongs to me, the father as well as the son—both alike belong to me. The soul who sins is the one who will die.

5"Suppose there is a righteous man
who does what is just and right.
6He does not eat at the mountain shrines
or look to the idols of the house of Israel.
He does not defile his neighbor's wife
or lie with a woman during her period.
7He does not oppress anyone,
but returns what he took in pledge for a loan.
He does not commit robbery
but gives his food to the hungry
and provides clothing for the naked.
8He does not lend at usury
or take excessive interest.a
He withholds his hand from doing wrong
and judges fairly between man and man.
9He follows my decrees
and faithfully keeps my laws.
That man is righteous;
he will surely live,
　　　　　declares the Sovereign LORD.

10"Suppose he has a violent son, who sheds blood or does any of these other thingsb 11(though the father has done none of them):

"He eats at the mountain shrines.
He defiles his neighbor's wife.
12He oppresses the poor and needy.
He commits robbery.
He does not return what he took in pledge.
He looks to the idols.
He does detestable things.
13He lends at usury and takes excessive interest.

Will such a man live? He will not! Because he has done all these detestable things, he will surely be put to death and his blood will be on his own head.

14"But suppose this son has a son who sees all the sins his father commits, and though he sees them, he does not do such things:

15"He does not eat at the mountain shrines
or look to the idols of the house of Israel.
He does not defile his neighbor's wife.
16He does not oppress anyone
or require a pledge for a loan.
He does not commit robbery
but gives his food to the hungry
and provides clothing for the naked.
17He withholds his hand from sinc
and takes no usury or excessive interest.
He keeps my laws and follows my decrees.

He will not die for his father's sin; he will surely live. 18But his father will die for his own sin, because he practiced extortion, robbed his brother and did what was wrong among his people.

19"Yet you ask, 'Why does the son not share the guilt of his father?' Since the son has done what is just and right and has been careful to keep all my decrees, he will surely live. 20The soul who sins is the one who will die.

---

a *8* Or *take interest*; similarly in verses 13 and 17　　b *10* Or *things to a brother*
c *17* Septuagint (see also verse 8); Hebrew *from the poor*

Living Bible

18 THEN THE Lord's message came to me again. 2"Why do people use this proverb about the land of Israel: The children are punished for their fathers' sins?d 3As I live, says the Lord God, you will not use this proverb any more in Israel, 4for all souls are mine to judge—fathers and sons alike—and my rule is this: It is for a man's own sins that he will die.

5"But if a man is just and does what is lawful and right, 6and has not gone out to the mountains to feast before the idols of Israel and worship them, and does not commit adultery, nor lie with any woman during the time of her menstruation, 7and is a merciful creditor, not holding on to the items given to him in pledge by poor debtors, and is no robber, but gives food to the hungry and clothes to those in need, 8and grants loans without interest,e and stays away from sin, and is honest and fair when judging others, 9and obeys my laws—that man is just, says the Lord, and he shall surely live.

10"But if that man has a son who is a robber or murderer and who fulfills none of his responsibilities, 11who refuses to obey the laws of God, but worships idols on the mountains and commits adultery, 12and oppresses the poor and helpless, and robs his debtors by refusing to let them redeem what they have given him in pledge, and loves idols and worships them, 13and loans out his money at interestf—shall that man live? No! He shall surely die, and it is his own fault.

14"But if this sinful man has, in turn, a son who sees all his father's wickedness, so that he fears God and decides against that kind of life, 15and doesn't go up on the mountains to feast before the idols and worship them, and does not commit adultery, 16and is fair to those who borrow from him and doesn't rob them, but feeds the hungry and clothes the needy, 17and helps the poor and does not loan money at interest, and obeys my laws—he shall not die because of his father's sins; he shall surely live. 18But his father shall die for his own sins because he is cruel and robs and does wrong.

19" 'What?' you ask. 'Doesn't the son pay for his father's sins?' No! For if the son does what is right and keeps my laws, he shall surely live. 20The one who sins

New Revised Standard

Individual Retribution

18 THE WORD of the Lord came to me: 2What do you mean by repeating this proverb concerning the land of Israel, "The parents have eaten sour grapes, and the children's teeth are set on edge"? 3As I live, says the Lord God, this proverb shall no more be used by you in Israel. 4Know that all lives are mine; the life of the parent as well as the life of the child is mine: it is only the person who sins that shall die.

5 If a man is righteous and does what is lawful and right— 6if he does not eat upon the mountains or lift up his eyes to the idols of the house of Israel, does not defile his neighbor's wife or approach a woman during her menstrual period, 7does not oppress anyone, but restores to the debtor his pledge, commits no robbery, gives his bread to the hungry and covers the naked with a garment, 8does not take advance or accrued interest, withholds his hand from iniquity, executes true justice between contending parties, 9follows my statutes, and is careful to observe my ordinances, acting faithfully— such a one is righteous; he shall surely live, says the Lord God.

10 If he has a son who is violent, a shedder of blood, 11who does any of these things (though his fatherg does none of them), who eats upon the mountains, defiles his neighbor's wife, 12oppresses the poor and needy, commits robbery, does not restore the pledge, lifts up his eyes to the idols, commits abomination, 13takes advance or accrued interest; shall he then live? He shall not. He has done all these abominable things; he shall surely die; his blood shall be upon himself.

14 But if this man has a son who sees all the sins that his father has done, considers, and does not do likewise, 15who does not eat upon the mountains or lift up his eyes to the idols of the house of Israel, does not defile his neighbor's wife, 16does not wrong anyone, exacts no pledge, commits no robbery, but gives his bread to the hungry and covers the naked with a garment, 17withholds his hand from iniquity,h takes no advance or accrued interest, observes my ordinances, and follows my statutes; he shall not die for his father's iniquity; he shall surely live. 18As for his father, because he practiced extortion, robbed his brother, and did what is not good among his people, he dies for his iniquity.

19 Yet you say, "Why should not the son suffer for the iniquity of the father?" When the son has done what is lawful and right, and has been careful to observe all my statutes, he shall surely live. 20The person who sins

---

d *18:2 The children are punished for their fathers' sins?* Literally, "The fathers have eaten sour grapes and the children's teeth are set on edge." e *18:8 without interest,* or, "without any usury." f *18:13 at interest,* or, "at usurious interest."

g Heb *he*   h Gk: Heb *the poor*

King James

20The soul that sinneth, it shall die. The son shall not bear the iniquity of the father, neither shall the father bear the iniquity of the son: the righteousness of the righteous shall be upon him, and the wickedness of the wicked shall be upon him.

21But if the wicked will turn from all his sins that he hath committed, and keep all my statutes, and do that which is lawful and right, he shall surely live, he shall not die.

22All his transgressions that he hath committed, they shall not be mentioned unto him: in his righteousness that he hath done he shall live.

23Have I any pleasure at all that the wicked should die? saith the Lord GOD: *and* not that he should return from his ways, and live?

24¶ But when the righteous turneth away from his righteousness, and committeth iniquity, *and* doeth according to all the abominations that the wicked *man* doeth, shall he live? All his righteousness that he hath done shall not be mentioned: in his trespass that he hath trespassed, and in his sin that he hath sinned, in them shall he die.

25¶ Yet ye say, The way of the Lord is not equal. Hear now, O house of Israel; Is not my way equal? are not your ways unequal?

26When a righteous *man* turneth away from his righteousness, and committeth iniquity, and dieth in them; for his iniquity that he hath done shall he die.

27Again, when the wicked *man* turneth away from his wickedness that he hath committed, and doeth that which is lawful and right, he shall save his soul alive.

28Because he considereth, and turneth away from all his transgressions that he hath committed, he shall surely live, he shall not die.

29Yet saith the house of Israel, The way of the Lord is not equal. O house of Israel, are not my ways equal? are not your ways unequal?

30Therefore I will judge you, O house of Israel, every one according to his ways, saith the Lord GOD. Repent, and turn *yourselves* from all your transgressions; so iniquity shall not be your ruin.

31¶ Cast away from you all your transgressions, whereby ye have transgressed; and make you a new heart and a new spirit: for why will ye die, O house of Israel?

32For I have no pleasure in the death of him that dieth, saith the Lord GOD: wherefore turn *yourselves,* and live ye.

New International

The son will not share the guilt of the father, nor will the father share the guilt of the son. The righteousness of the righteous man will be credited to him, and the wickedness of the wicked will be charged against him.

21"But if a wicked man turns away from all the sins he has committed and keeps all my decrees and does what is just and right, he will surely live; he will not die. 22None of the offenses he has committed will be remembered against him. Because of the righteous things he has done, he will live. 23Do I take any pleasure in the death of the wicked? declares the Sovereign LORD. Rather, am I not pleased when they turn from their ways and live?

24"But if a righteous man turns from his righteousness and commits sin and does the same detestable things the wicked man does, will he live? None of the righteous things he has done will be remembered. Because of the unfaithfulness he is guilty of and because of the sins he has committed, he will die.

25"Yet you say, 'The way of the Lord is not just.' Hear, O house of Israel: Is my way unjust? Is it not your ways that are unjust? 26If a righteous man turns from his righteousness and commits sin, he will die for it; because of the sin he has committed he will die. 27But if a wicked man turns away from the wickedness he has committed and does what is just and right, he will save his life. 28Because he considers all the offenses he has committed and turns away from them, he will surely live; he will not die. 29Yet the house of Israel says, 'The way of the Lord is not just.' Are my ways unjust, O house of Israel? Is it not your ways that are unjust?

30"Therefore, O house of Israel, I will judge you, each one according to his ways, declares the Sovereign LORD. Repent! Turn away from all your offenses; then sin will not be your downfall. 31Rid yourselves of all the offenses you have committed, and get a new heart and a new spirit. Why will you die, O house of Israel? 32For I take no pleasure in the death of anyone, declares the Sovereign LORD. Repent and live!

---

19 MOREOVER TAKE thou up a lamentation for the princes of Israel,

2And say, What *is* thy mother? A lioness: she lay down among lions, she nourished her whelps among young lions.

3And she brought up one of her whelps: it became a young lion, and it learned to catch the prey; it devoured men.

4The nations also heard of him; he was taken in their pit, and they brought him with chains unto the land of Egypt.

5Now when she saw that she had waited, *and* her hope was lost, then she took another of her whelps, *and* made him a young lion.

A Lament for Israel's Princes

19 "TAKE UP a lament concerning the princes of Israel 2and say:

" 'What a lioness was your mother
    among the lions!
She lay down among the young lions
    and reared her cubs.
3She brought up one of her cubs,
    and he became a strong lion.
He learned to tear the prey
    and he devoured men.
4The nations heard about him,
    and he was trapped in their pit.
They led him with hooks
    to the land of Egypt.

5" 'When she saw her hope unfulfilled,
    her expectation gone,
she took another of her cubs
    and made him a strong lion.

Living Bible

is the one who dies. The son shall not be punished for his father's sins, nor the father for his son's. The righteous person will be rewarded for his own goodness and the wicked person for his wickedness. 21But if a wicked person turns away from all his sins and begins to obey my laws and do what is just and right, he shall surely live and not die. 22All his past sins will be forgotten, and he shall live because of his goodness.

23"Do you think I like to see the wicked die? asks the Lord. Of course not! I only want him to turn from his wicked ways and live. 24However, if a righteous person turns to sinning and acts like any other sinner, should he be allowed to live? No, of course not. All his previous goodness will be forgotten and he shall die for his sins.

25"Yet you say: The Lord isn't being fair! Listen to me, O people of Israel. Am I the one who is unfair, or is it you? 26When a good man turns away from being good and begins sinning and dies in his sins, he dies for the evil he has done. 27And if a wicked person turns away from his wickedness and obeys the law, and does right, he shall save his soul, 28for he has thought it over and decided to turn from his sins and live a good life. He shall surely live—he shall not die.

29"And yet the people of Israel keep saying: 'The Lord is unfair!' O people of Israel, it is you who are unfair, not I. 30I will judge each of you, O Israel, and punish or reward each according to your own actions. Oh, turn from your sins while there is yet time. 31Put them behind you and receive a new heart and a new spirit. For why will you die, O Israel? 32I do not enjoy seeing you die, the Lord God says. Turn, turn and live!

19 "SING THIS death dirge for the leaders of Israel: 2What a woman your mother was—like a lioness! Her children were like lion's cubs! 3One of her cubs [King Jehoahaz[a]] grew into a strong young lion, and learned to catch prey and became a man-eater. 4Then the nations called out their hunters and trapped him in a pit and brought him in chains to Egypt.

5"When Israel, the mother lion, saw that all her hopes for him were gone, she took another of her cubs [King Jehoiachin] and taught him to be 'king of the beasts.'

New Revised Standard

shall die. A child shall not suffer for the iniquity of a parent, nor a parent suffer for the iniquity of a child; the righteousness of the righteous shall be his own, and the wickedness of the wicked shall be his own.

21 But if the wicked turn away from all their sins that they have committed, and keep all my statutes and do what is lawful and right, they shall surely live; they shall not die. 22None of the transgressions that they have committed shall be remembered against them; for the righteousness that they have done they shall live. 23Have I any pleasure in the death of the wicked, says the Lord God, and not rather that they should turn from their ways and live? 24But when the righteous turn away from their righteousness and commit iniquity and do the same abominable things that the wicked do, shall they live? None of the righteous deeds that they have done shall be remembered; for the treachery of which they are guilty and the sin they have committed, they shall die.

25 Yet you say, "The way of the Lord is unfair." Hear now, O house of Israel: Is my way unfair? Is it not your ways that are unfair? 26When the righteous turn away from their righteousness and commit iniquity, they shall die for it; for the iniquity that they have committed they shall die. 27Again, when the wicked turn away from the wickedness they have committed and do what is lawful and right, they shall save their life. 28Because they considered and turned away from all the transgressions that they had committed, they shall surely live; they shall not die. 29Yet the house of Israel says, "The way of the Lord is unfair." O house of Israel, are my ways unfair? Is it not your ways that are unfair?

30 Therefore I will judge you, O house of Israel, all of you according to your ways, says the Lord God. Repent and turn from all your transgressions; otherwise iniquity will be your ruin.[b] 31Cast away from you all the transgressions that you have committed against me, and get yourselves a new heart and a new spirit! Why will you die, O house of Israel? 32For I have no pleasure in the death of anyone, says the Lord God. Turn, then, and live.

Israel Degraded

19 AS FOR you, raise up a lamentation for the princes of Israel, 2and say:
What a lioness was your mother
    among lions!
She lay down among young lions,
    rearing her cubs.
3 She raised up one of her cubs;
    he became a young lion,
and he learned to catch prey;
    he devoured humans.
4 The nations sounded an alarm against him;
    he was caught in their pit;
and they brought him with hooks
    to the land of Egypt.
5 When they saw that she was thwarted,
    that her hope was lost,
she took another of her cubs
    and made him a young lion.

---

a 19:3 *King Jehoahaz,* implied.

b *Or so that they shall not be a stumbling block of iniquity to you*

King James

6And he went up and down among the lions, he became a young lion, and learned to catch the prey, *and* devoured men.

7And he knew their desolate palaces, and he laid waste their cities; and the land was desolate, and the fulness thereof, by the noise of his roaring.

8Then the nations set against him on every side from the provinces, and spread their net over him: he was taken in their pit.

9And they put him in ward in chains, and brought him to the king of Babylon: they brought him into holds, that his voice should no more be heard upon the mountains of Israel.

10¶ Thy mother *is* like a vine in thy blood, planted by the waters: she was fruitful and full of branches by reason of many waters.

11And she had strong rods for the sceptres of them that bare rule, and her stature was exalted among the thick branches, and she appeared in her height with the multitude of her branches.

12But she was plucked up in fury, she was cast down to the ground, and the east wind dried up her fruit: her strong rods were broken and withered; the fire consumed them.

13And now she *is* planted in the wilderness, in a dry and thirsty ground.

14And fire is gone out of a rod of her branches, *which* hath devoured her fruit, so that she hath no strong rod *to be* a sceptre to rule. This *is* a lamentation, and shall be for a lamentation.

20 AND IT came to pass in the seventh year, in the fifth *month,* the tenth *day* of the month, *that* certain of the elders of Israel came to inquire of the LORD, and sat before me.

2Then came the word of the LORD unto me, saying,

3Son of man, speak unto the elders of Israel, and say unto them, Thus saith the Lord GOD; Are ye come to inquire of me? *As* I live, saith the Lord GOD, I will not be inquired of by you.

4Wilt thou judge them, son of man, wilt thou judge *them?* cause them to know the abominations of their fathers:

5¶ And say unto them, Thus saith the Lord GOD; In the day when I chose Israel, and lifted up mine hand unto the seed of the house of Jacob, and made myself known unto them in the land of Egypt, when I lifted up mine hand unto them, saying, I *am* the LORD your God;

6In the day *that* I lifted up mine hand unto them, to bring them forth of the land of Egypt into a land that I had espied for them, flowing with milk and honey, which *is* the glory of all lands:

7Then said I unto them, Cast ye away every man the abominations of his eyes, and defile not yourselves with the idols of Egypt: I *am* the LORD your God.

New International

6He prowled among the lions,
    for he was now a strong lion.
He learned to tear the prey
    and he devoured men.
7He broke downa their strongholds
    and devastated their towns.
The land and all who were in it
    were terrified by his roaring.
8Then the nations came against him,
    those from regions round about.
They spread their net for him,
    and he was trapped in their pit.
9With hooks they pulled him into a cage
    and brought him to the king of Babylon.
They put him in prison,
    so his roar was heard no longer
    on the mountains of Israel.

10" 'Your mother was like a vine in your
        vineyardb
    planted by the water;
it was fruitful and full of branches
    because of abundant water.
11Its branches were strong,
    fit for a ruler's scepter.
It towered high
    above the thick foliage,
conspicuous for its height
    and for its many branches.
12But it was uprooted in fury
    and thrown to the ground.
The east wind made it shrivel,
    it was stripped of its fruit;
its strong branches withered
    and fire consumed them.
13Now it is planted in the desert,
    in a dry and thirsty soil.
14Fire spread from one of its mainc branches
    and consumed its fruit.
No strong branch is left on it
    fit for a ruler's scepter.'

This is a lament and is to be used as a lament."

Rebellious Israel

20 IN THE seventh year, in the fifth month on the tenth day, some of the elders of Israel came to inquire of the LORD, and they sat down in front of me.

2Then the word of the LORD came to me: 3"Son of man, speak to the elders of Israel and say to them, 'This is what the Sovereign LORD says: Have you come to inquire of me? As surely as I live, I will not let you inquire of me, declares the Sovereign LORD.'

4"Will you judge them? Will you judge them, son of man? Then confront them with the detestable practices of their fathers 5and say to them: 'This is what the Sovereign LORD says: On the day I chose Israel, I swore with uplifted hand to the descendants of the house of Jacob and revealed myself to them in Egypt. With uplifted hand I said to them, "I am the LORD your God." 6On that day I swore to them that I would bring them out of Egypt into a land I had searched out for them, a land flowing with milk and honey, the most beautiful of all lands. 7And I said to them, "Each of you, get rid of the vile images you have set your eyes on, and do not defile yourselves with the idols of Egypt. I am the LORD your God."

---

a 7 Targum (see Septuagint); Hebrew *He knew*   b 10 Two Hebrew manuscripts; most Hebrew manuscripts *your blood*   c 14 Or *from under its*

Living Bible

6He became a leader among the lions and learned to catch prey, and he too became a man-eater. 7He demolished the palaces of the surrounding nations and ruined their cities; their farms were desolated, their crops destroyed; everyone in the land shook with terror when they heard him roar. 8Then the armies of the nations surrounded him, coming from every side, and trapped him in a pit and captured him. 9They prodded him into a cage and brought him before the king of Babylon. He was held in captivity so that his voice could never again be heard upon the mountains of Israel.

10"Your mother was like a vine beside an irrigation ditch, with lush, green foliage because of all the water. 11Its strongest branch became a ruler's scepter and it was very great, towering above the others and noticed from far away. 12But the vine was uprooted in fury and thrown down to the ground. Its branches were broken and withered by a strong wind from the east; the fruit was destroyed by fire. 13Now the vine is planted in the wilderness where the ground is hard and dry. 14It is decaying from within;d no strong branch remains. The fulfillment of this sad prophecy has already begun, and there is more ahead."

20 LATE IN July, six years after King Jeconiah was captured,e some of the elders of Israel came to ask instructions from the Lord, and sat before me awaiting his reply.

2Then the Lord gave me this message:

3"Son of dust, say to the elders of Israel: The Lord God says: How dare you come to ask my help? I swear that I will tell you nothing. 4Judge them, son of dust; condemn them; tell them of all the sins of this nation from the times of their fathers until now. 5, 6Tell them the Lord God says: When I chose Israel and revealed myself to her in Egypt, I swore to her and her descendants that I would bring them out of Egypt to a land I had discovered and explored for them—a good land, flowing as it were with milk and honey, the best of all lands anywhere.

7"Then I said to them: Get rid of every idol; do not defile yourselves with the Egyptian gods, for I am the Lord your God. 8But they rebelled against me and would

New Revised Standard

6 He prowled among the lions;
    he became a young lion,
and he learned to catch prey;
    he devoured people.
7 And he ravaged their strongholds,f
    and laid waste their towns;
the land was appalled, and all in it,
    at the sound of his roaring.
8 The nations set upon him
    from the provinces all around;
they spread their net over him;
    he was caught in their pit.
9 With hooks they put him in a cage,
    and brought him to the king of Babylon;
    they brought him into custody,
so that his voice should be heard no more
    on the mountains of Israel.

10 Your mother was like a vine in a vineyard
    transplanted by the water,
fruitful and full of branches
    from abundant water.
11 Its strongest stem became
    a ruler's scepter;h
it towered aloft
    among the thick boughs;
it stood out in its height
    with its mass of branches.
12 But it was plucked up in fury,
    cast down to the ground;
the east wind dried it up;
    its fruit was stripped off,
its strong stem was withered;
    the fire consumed it.
13 Now it is transplanted into the wilderness,
    into a dry and thirsty land.
14 And fire has gone out from its stem,
    has consumed its branches and fruit,
so that there remains in it no strong stem,
    no scepter for ruling.

This is a lamentation, and it is used as a lamentation.

Israel's Continuing Rebellion

20 IN THE seventh year, in the fifth month, on the tenth day of the month, certain elders of Israel came to consult the LORD, and sat down before me. 2And the word of the LORD came to me: 3Mortal, speak to the elders of Israel, and say to them: Thus says the Lord GOD: Why are you coming? To consult me? As I live, says the Lord GOD, I will not be consulted by you. 4Will you judge them, mortal, will you judge them? Then let them know the abominations of their ancestors, 5and say to them: Thus says the Lord GOD: On the day when I chose Israel, I swore to the offspring of the house of Jacob—making myself known to them in the land of Egypt—I swore to them, saying, I am the LORD your God. 6On that day I swore to them that I would bring them out of the land of Egypt into a land that I had searched out for them, a land flowing with milk and honey, the most glorious of all lands. 7And I said to them, Cast away the detestable things your eyes feast on, every one of you, and do not defile yourselves with the idols of Egypt; I am the LORD your God. 8But they

---

d 19:14 It is decaying from within, literally, "A fire is gone out of its branches and devoured its fruit." e 20:1 six years after King Jeconiah was captured, literally, "in the seventh year of Jeconiah's captivity."

f Heb his widows g Cn: Heb in your blood h Heb Its strongest stems became rulers' scepters

King James

8But they rebelled against me, and would not hearken unto me: they did not every man cast away the abominations of their eyes, neither did they forsake the idols of Egypt: then I said, I will pour out my fury upon them, to accomplish my anger against them in the midst of the land of Egypt.

9But I wrought for my name's sake, that it should not be polluted before the heathen, among whom they *were,* in whose sight I made myself known unto them, in bringing them forth out of the land of Egypt.

10¶ Wherefore I caused them to go forth out of the land of Egypt, and brought them into the wilderness.

11And I gave them my statutes, and showed them my judgments, which *if* a man do, he shall even live in them.

12Moreover also I gave them my sabbaths, to be a sign between me and them, that they might know that I *am* the LORD that sanctify them.

13But the house of Israel rebelled against me in the wilderness: they walked not in my statutes, and they despised my judgments, which *if* a man do, he shall even live in them; and my sabbaths they greatly polluted: then I said, I would pour out my fury upon them in the wilderness, to consume them.

14But I wrought for my name's sake, that it should not be polluted before the heathen, in whose sight I brought them out.

15Yet also I lifted up my hand unto them in the wilderness, that I would not bring them into the land which I had given *them,* flowing with milk and honey, which *is* the glory of all lands;

16Because they despised my judgments, and walked not in my statutes, but polluted my sabbaths: for their heart went after their idols.

17Nevertheless mine eye spared them from destroying them, neither did I make an end of them in the wilderness.

18But I said unto their children in the wilderness, Walk ye not in the statutes of your fathers, neither observe their judgments, nor defile yourselves with their idols:

19I *am* the LORD your God; walk in my statutes, and keep my judgments, and do them;

20And hallow my sabbaths; and they shall be a sign between me and you, that ye may know that I *am* the LORD your God.

21Notwithstanding the children rebelled against me: they walked not in my statutes, neither kept my judgments to do them, which *if* a man do, he shall even live in them; they polluted my sabbaths: then I said, I would pour out my fury upon them, to accomplish my anger against them in the wilderness.

22Nevertheless I withdrew mine hand, and wrought for my name's sake, that it should not be polluted in the sight of the heathen, in whose sight I brought them forth.

23I lifted up mine hand unto them also in the wilderness, that I would scatter them among the heathen, and disperse them through the countries;

24Because they had not executed my judgments, but had despised my statutes, and had polluted my sabbaths, and their eyes were after their fathers' idols.

25Wherefore I gave them also statutes *that were* not good, and judgments whereby they should not live;

26And I polluted them in their own gifts, in that they caused to pass through *the fire* all that openeth the womb, that I might make them desolate, to the end that they might know that I *am* the LORD.

New International

8" 'But they rebelled against me and would not listen to me; they did not get rid of the vile images they had set their eyes on, nor did they forsake the idols of Egypt. So I said I would pour out my wrath on them and spend my anger against them in Egypt. 9But for the sake of my name I did what would keep it from being profaned in the eyes of the nations they lived among and in whose sight I had revealed myself to the Israelites by bringing them out of Egypt. 10Therefore I led them out of Egypt and brought them into the desert. 11I gave them my decrees and made known to them my laws, for the man who obeys them will live by them. 12Also I gave them my Sabbaths as a sign between us, so they would know that I the LORD made them holy.

13" 'Yet the people of Israel rebelled against me in the desert. They did not follow my decrees but rejected my laws—although the man who obeys them will live by them—and they utterly desecrated my Sabbaths. So I said I would pour out my wrath on them and destroy them in the desert. 14But for the sake of my name I did what would keep it from being profaned in the eyes of the nations in whose sight I had brought them out. 15Also with uplifted hand I swore to them in the desert that I would not bring them into the land I had given them—a land flowing with milk and honey, most beautiful of all lands— 16because they rejected my laws and did not follow my decrees and desecrated my Sabbaths. For their hearts were devoted to their idols. 17Yet I looked on them with pity and did not destroy them or put an end to them in the desert. 18I said to their children in the desert, "Do not follow the statutes of your fathers or keep their laws or defile yourselves with their idols. 19I am the LORD your God; follow my decrees and be careful to keep my laws. 20Keep my Sabbaths holy, that they may be a sign between us. Then you will know that I am the LORD your God."

21" 'But the children rebelled against me: They did not follow my decrees, they were not careful to keep my laws—although the man who obeys them will live by them—and they desecrated my Sabbaths. So I said I would pour out my wrath on them and spend my anger against them in the desert. 22But I withheld my hand, and for the sake of my name I did what would keep it from being profaned in the eyes of the nations in whose sight I had brought them out. 23Also with uplifted hand I swore to them in the desert that I would disperse them among the nations and scatter them through the countries, 24because they had not obeyed my laws but had rejected my decrees and desecrated my Sabbaths, and their eyes lusted after their fathers' idols. 25I also gave them over to statutes that were not good and laws they could not live by; 26I let them become defiled through their gifts—the sacrifice of every firstborna—that I might fill them with horror so they would know that I am the LORD.'

---

a 26 Or *—making every firstborn pass through the fire*

Living Bible

not listen. They didn't get rid of their idols, nor forsake the gods of Egypt. Then I thought, I will pour out my fury upon them and fulfill my anger against them while they are still in Egypt.

9, 10"But I didn't do it, for I acted to protect the honor of my name, lest the Egyptians laugh at Israel's God who couldn't keep them back from harm. So I brought my people out of Egypt right before the Egyptians' eyes, and led them into the wilderness. 11There I gave them my laws so they could live by keeping them. If anyone keeps them, he shall live. 12And I gave them the Sabbath—a day of rest every seventh day—as a symbol between them and me, to remind them that it is I, the Lord, who sanctifies them, that they are truly my people.

13"But Israel rebelled against me. There in the wilderness they refused my laws. They would not obey my rules even though obeying them means life. And they misused my Sabbaths. Then I thought, I will pour out my fury upon them and utterly consume them in the desert.

14"But again I refrained in order to protect the honor of my name, lest the nations who saw me bring them out of Egypt would say that it was because I couldn't care for them that I destroyed them. 15But I swore to them in the wilderness that I would not bring them into the land I had given them, a land full of milk and honey, the choicest spot on earth, 16because they laughed at my laws, ignored my wishes, and violated my Sabbaths—their hearts were with their idols! 17Nevertheless, I spared them. I didn't finish them off in the wilderness.

18"Then I spoke to their children and said: Don't follow your fathers' footsteps. Don't defile yourselves with their idols, 19for I am the Lord your God. Follow my laws; keep my ordinances; 20hallow my Sabbaths; for they are a symbol of the contract between us to help you remember that I am the Lord your God.

21"But their children too rebelled against me. They refused my laws—the laws that, if a person keeps them, he shall live. And they defiled my Sabbaths. So then I said: Now at last I will pour out my fury upon you in the wilderness.

22"Nevertheless, again I withdrew my judgment against them to protect my name among the nations who had seen my power in bringing them out of Egypt. 23, 24But I took a solemn oath against them while they were in the wilderness that I would scatter them, dispersing them to the ends of the earth because they did not obey my laws but scorned them and violated my Sabbaths and longed for their fathers' idols. 25I let them adopt[b] customs and laws which were worthless. Through the keeping of them they could not attain life.[c] 26In the hope that they would draw back in horror, and know that I alone am God, I let them pollute themselves with the very gifts I gave them. They burnt their firstborn children as offerings to their gods!

New Revised Standard

rebelled against me and would not listen to me; not one of them cast away the detestable things their eyes feasted on, nor did they forsake the idols of Egypt.

Then I thought I would pour out my wrath upon them and spend my anger against them in the midst of the land of Egypt. 9But I acted for the sake of my name, that it should not be profaned in the sight of the nations among whom they lived, in whose sight I made myself known to them in bringing them out of the land of Egypt. 10So I led them out of the land of Egypt and brought them into the wilderness. 11I gave them my statutes and showed them my ordinances, by whose observance everyone shall live. 12Moreover I gave them my sabbaths, as a sign between me and them, so that they might know that I the LORD sanctify them. 13But the house of Israel rebelled against me in the wilderness; they did not observe my statutes but rejected my ordinances, by whose observance everyone shall live; and my sabbaths they greatly profaned.

Then I thought I would pour out my wrath upon them in the wilderness, to make an end of them. 14But I acted for the sake of my name, so that it should not be profaned in the sight of the nations, in whose sight I had brought them out. 15Moreover I swore to them in the wilderness that I would not bring them into the land that I had given them, a land flowing with milk and honey, the most glorious of all lands, 16because they rejected my ordinances and did not observe my statutes, and profaned my sabbaths; for their heart went after their idols. 17Nevertheless my eye spared them, and I did not destroy them or make an end of them in the wilderness.

18 I said to their children in the wilderness, Do not follow the statutes of your parents, nor observe their ordinances, nor defile yourselves with their idols. 19I the LORD am your God; follow my statutes, and be careful to observe my ordinances, 20and hallow my sabbaths that they may be a sign between me and you, so that you may know that I the LORD am your God. 21But the children rebelled against me; they did not follow my statutes, and were not careful to observe my ordinances, by whose observance everyone shall live; they profaned my sabbaths.

Then I thought I would pour out my wrath upon them and spend my anger against them in the wilderness. 22But I withheld my hand, and acted for the sake of my name, so that it should not be profaned in the sight of the nations, in whose sight I had brought them out. 23Moreover I swore to them in the wilderness that I would scatter them among the nations and disperse them through the countries, 24because they had not executed my ordinances, but had rejected my statutes and profaned my sabbaths, and their eyes were set on their ancestors' idols. 25Moreover I gave them statutes that were not good and ordinances by which they could not live. 26I defiled them through their very gifts, in their offering up all their firstborn, in order that I might horrify them, so that they might know that I am the LORD.

b 20:25 let them adopt, literally, "gave them."   c 20:25 Through the keeping of them they could not attain life, literally, "ordinances by which they could not have life." Doubtless, the reference is to the pagan customs of vss 18 and 26. In contrast, see vs 11.

King James

27¶ Therefore, son of man, speak unto the house of Israel, and say unto them, Thus saith the Lord GOD; Yet in this your fathers have blasphemed me, in that they have committed a trespass against me.

28For when I had brought them into the land, *for* the which I lifted up mine hand to give it to them, then they saw every high hill, and all the thick trees, and they offered there their sacrifices, and there they presented the provocation of their offering: there also they made their sweet savour, and poured out there their drink offerings.

29Then I said unto them, What *is* the high place whereunto ye go? And the name thereof is called Bamah unto this day.

30Wherefore say unto the house of Israel, Thus saith the Lord GOD; Are ye polluted after the manner of your fathers? and commit ye whoredom after their abominations?

31For when ye offer your gifts, when ye make your sons to pass through the fire, ye pollute yourselves with all your idols, even unto this day: and shall I be inquired of by you, O house of Israel? *As* I live, saith the Lord GOD, I will not be inquired of by you.

32And that which cometh into your mind shall not be at all, that ye say, We will be as the heathen, as the families of the countries, to serve wood and stone.

33¶ *As* I live, saith the Lord GOD, surely with a mighty hand, and with a stretched out arm, and with fury poured out, will I rule over you:

34And I will bring you out from the people, and will gather you out of the countries wherein ye are scattered, with a mighty hand, and with a stretched out arm, and with fury poured out.

35And I will bring you into the wilderness of the people, and there will I plead with you face to face.

36Like as I pleaded with your fathers in the wilderness of the land of Egypt, so will I plead with you, saith the Lord GOD.

37And I will cause you to pass under the rod, and I will bring you into the bond of the covenant:

38And I will purge out from among you the rebels, and them that transgress against me: I will bring them forth out of the country where they sojourn, and they shall not enter into the land of Israel: and ye shall know that I *am* the LORD.

39As for you, O house of Israel, thus saith the Lord GOD; Go ye, serve ye every one his idols, and hereafter *also*, if ye will not hearken unto me: but pollute ye my holy name no more with your gifts, and with your idols.

40For in mine holy mountain, in the mountain of the height of Israel, saith the Lord GOD, there shall all the house of Israel, all of them in the land, serve me: there will I accept them, and there will I require your offerings, and the firstfruits of your oblations, with all your holy things.

41I will accept you with your sweet savour, when I bring you out from the people, and gather you out of the countries wherein ye have been scattered; and I will be sanctified in you before the heathen.

42And ye shall know that I *am* the LORD, when I shall bring you into the land of Israel, into the country *for* the which I lifted up mine hand to give it to your fathers.

43And there shall ye remember your ways, and all your doings, wherein ye have been defiled; and ye shall loathe yourselves in your own sight for all your evils that ye have committed.

44And ye shall know that I *am* the LORD, when I have wrought with you for my name's sake, not according to your wicked ways, nor according to your corrupt doings, O ye house of Israel, saith the Lord GOD.

45¶ Moreover the word of the LORD came unto me, saying,

46Son of man, set thy face toward the south, and drop *thy word* toward the south, and prophesy against the forest of the south field;

New International

27"Therefore, son of man, speak to the people of Israel and say to them, 'This is what the Sovereign LORD says: In this also your fathers blasphemed me by forsaking me: 28When I brought them into the land I had sworn to give them and they saw any high hill or any leafy tree, there they offered their sacrifices, made offerings that provoked me to anger, presented their fragrant incense and poured out their drink offerings. 29Then I said to them: What is this high place you go to?' " (It is called Bamah[a] to this day.)

Judgment and Restoration

30"Therefore say to the house of Israel: 'This is what the Sovereign LORD says: Will you defile yourselves the way your fathers did and lust after their vile images? 31When you offer your gifts—the sacrifice of your sons in[b] the fire—you continue to defile yourselves with all your idols to this day. Am I to let you inquire of me, O house of Israel? As surely as I live, declares the Sovereign LORD, I will not let you inquire of me.

32"'You say, "We want to be like the nations, like the peoples of the world, who serve wood and stone." But what you have in mind will never happen. 33As surely as I live, declares the Sovereign LORD, I will rule over you with a mighty hand and an outstretched arm and with outpoured wrath. 34I will bring you from the nations and gather you from the countries where you have been scattered—with a mighty hand and an outstretched arm and with outpoured wrath. 35I will bring you into the desert of the nations and there, face to face, I will execute judgment upon you. 36As I judged your fathers in the desert of the land of Egypt, so I will judge you, declares the Sovereign LORD. 37I will take note of you as you pass under my rod, and I will bring you into the bond of the covenant. 38I will purge you of those who revolt and rebel against me. Although I will bring them out of the land where they are living, yet they will not enter the land of Israel. Then you will know that I am the LORD.

39"'As for you, O house of Israel, this is what the Sovereign LORD says: Go and serve your idols, every one of you! But afterward you will surely listen to me and no longer profane my holy name with your gifts and idols. 40For on my holy mountain, the high mountain of Israel, declares the Sovereign LORD, there in the land the entire house of Israel will serve me, and there I will accept them. There I will require your offerings and your choice gifts,[c] along with all your holy sacrifices. 41I will accept you as fragrant incense when I bring you out from the nations and gather you from the countries where you have been scattered, and I will show myself holy among you in the sight of the nations. 42Then you will know that I am the LORD, when I bring you into the land of Israel, the land I had sworn with uplifted hand to give to your fathers. 43There you will remember your conduct and all the actions by which you have defiled yourselves, and you will loathe yourselves for all the evil you have done. 44You will know that I am the LORD, when I deal with you for my name's sake and not according to your evil ways and your corrupt practices, O house of Israel, declares the Sovereign LORD.' "

Prophecy Against the South

45The word of the LORD came to me: 46"Son of man, set your face toward the south; preach against the south and prophesy against the forest of the southland. 47Say

---

a *29 Bamah* means *high place.*   b *31* Or —*making your sons pass through*
c *40* Or *and the gifts of your firstfruits*

Living Bible

27, 28"Son of dust, tell them that the Lord God says: Your fathers continued to blaspheme and betray me when I brought them into the land I promised them, for they offered sacrifices and incense on every high hill and under every tree! They roused my fury as they offered up their sacrifices to those 'gods.' They brought their perfumes and incense and poured out their drink offerings to them! 29I said to them: 'What is this place of sacrificed where you go?' And so it is still called 'The Place of Sacrifice'—that is how it got its name.

30"The Lord God wants to know whether you are going to pollute yourselves just as your fathers did, and keep on worshiping idols? 31For when you offer gifts to them and give your little sons to be burned to ashes as you do even today, shall I listen to you or help you, Israel? As I live, the Lord God says, I will not give you any message, though you have come to me to ask.

32"What you have in mind will not be done—to be like the nations all around you, serving gods of wood and stone. 33I will rule you with an iron fist and in great anger and with power. 34With might and fury I will bring you out from the lands where you are scattered, 35, 36and will bring you into my desert judgment hall.e I will judge you there, and get rid of the rebels, just as I did in the wilderness after I brought you out of Egypt. 37I will count you carefully and let only a small quota return. 38And the others—the rebels and all those who sin against me—I will purge from among you. They shall not enter Israel, but I will bring them out of the countries where they are in exile. And when that happens, you will know I am the Lord.

39"O Israel, the Lord God says: If you insist on worshiping your idols, go right ahead, but then don't bring your gifts to me as well! Such desecration of my holy name must stop!

40"For at Jerusalem in my holy mountain, says the Lord, all Israel shall worship me. There I will accept you, and require you to bring me your offerings and the finest of your gifts. 41You will be to me as an offering of perfumed incense when I bring you back from exile, and the nations will see the great change in your hearts. 42Then, when I have brought you home to the land I promised your fathers, you will know I am the Lord. 43Then you will look back at all your sins and loathe yourselves because of the evil you have done. 44And when I have honored my name by blessing you despite your wickedness, then, O Israel, you will know I am the Lord."

45Then this message came to me from the Lord: 46"Son of dust, look toward Jerusalem and speak out against it and the forest lands of the Negeb. 47Prophesy

New Revised Standard

27 Therefore, mortal, speak to the house of Israel and say to them, Thus says the Lord GOD: In this again your ancestors blasphemed me, by dealing treacherously with me. 28For when I had brought them into the land that I swore to give them, then wherever they saw any high hill or any leafy tree, there they offered their sacrifices and presented the provocation of their offering; there they sent up their pleasing odors, and there they poured out their drink offerings. 29(I said to them, What is the high place to which you go? So it is called Bamahf to this day.) 30Therefore say to the house of Israel, Thus says the Lord GOD: Will you defile yourselves after the manner of your ancestors and go astray after their detestable things? 31When you offer your gifts and make your children pass through the fire, you defile yourselves with all your idols to this day. And shall I be consulted by you, O house of Israel? As I live, says the Lord GOD, I will not be consulted by you.

32 What is in your mind shall never happen—the thought, "Let us be like the nations, like the tribes of the countries, and worship wood and stone."

God Will Restore Israel

33 As I live, says the Lord GOD, surely with a mighty hand and an outstretched arm, and with wrath poured out, I will be king over you. 34I will bring you out from the peoples and gather you out of the countries where you are scattered, with a mighty hand and an outstretched arm, and with wrath poured out; 35and I will bring you into the wilderness of the peoples, and there I will enter into judgment with you face to face. 36As I entered into judgment with your ancestors in the wilderness of the land of Egypt, so I will enter into judgment with you, says the Lord GOD. 37I will make you pass under the staff, and will bring you within the bond of the covenant. 38I will purge out the rebels among you, and those who transgress against me; I will bring them out of the land where they reside as aliens, but they shall not enter the land of Israel. Then you shall know that I am the LORD.

39 As for you, O house of Israel, thus says the Lord GOD: Go serve your idols, everyone of you now and hereafter, if you will not listen to me; but my holy name you shall no more profane with your gifts and your idols.

40 For on my holy mountain, the mountain height of Israel, says the Lord GOD, there all the house of Israel, all of them, shall serve me in the land; there I will accept them, and there I will require your contributions and the choicest of your gifts, with all your sacred things. 41As a pleasing odor I will accept you, when I bring you out from the peoples, and gather you out of the countries where you have been scattered; and I will manifest my holiness among you in the sight of the nations. 42You shall know that I am the LORD, when I bring you into the land of Israel, the country that I swore to give to your ancestors. 43There you shall remember your ways and all the deeds by which you have polluted yourselves; and you shall loathe yourselves for all the evils that you have committed. 44And you shall know that I am the LORD, when I deal with you for my name's sake, not according to your evil ways, or corrupt deeds, O house of Israel, says the Lord GOD.

A Prophecy against the Negeb

45g The word of the LORD came to me: 46Mortal, set your face toward the south, preach against the south, and prophesy against the forest land in the Negeb; 47say to

---

d 20:29 place of sacrifice, literally, "bamah"—a hilltop area where sacrifices were made to the gods.   e 20:35, 36 desert judgment hall, literally, "the wilderness of the people," meaning the Syro-Arabian deserts, peopled by nomadic tribes. This desert would be traversed in returning to Israel from Babylon.

f That is High Place   g Ch 21.1 in Heb

King James

47And say to the forest of the south, Hear the word of the LORD; Thus saith the Lord GOD; Behold, I will kindle a fire in thee, and it shall devour every green tree in thee, and every dry tree: the flaming flame shall not be quenched, and all faces from the south to the north shall be burned therein.

48And all flesh shall see that I the LORD have kindled it: it shall not be quenched.

49Then said I, Ah Lord GOD! they say of me, Doth he not speak parables?

21 AND THE word of the LORD came unto me, saying,

2Son of man, set thy face toward Jerusalem, and drop *thy word* toward the holy places, and prophesy against the land of Israel,

3And say to the land of Israel, Thus saith the LORD; Behold, I *am* against thee, and will draw forth my sword out of his sheath, and will cut off from thee the righteous and the wicked.

4Seeing then that I will cut off from thee the righteous and the wicked, therefore shall my sword go forth out of his sheath against all flesh from the south to the north:

5That all flesh may know that I the LORD have drawn forth my sword out of his sheath: it shall not return any more.

6Sigh therefore, thou son of man, with the breaking of *thy* loins; and with bitterness sigh before their eyes.

7And it shall be, when they say unto thee, Wherefore sighest thou? that thou shalt answer, For the tidings; because it cometh: and every heart shall melt, and all hands shall be feeble, and every spirit shall faint, and all knees shall be weak *as* water: behold, it cometh, and shall be brought to pass, saith the Lord GOD.

8¶ Again the word of the LORD came unto me, saying,

9Son of man, prophesy, and say, Thus saith the LORD; Say, A sword, a sword is sharpened, and also furbished:

10It is sharpened to make a sore slaughter; it is furbished that it may glitter: should we then make mirth? it contemneth the rod of my son, *as* every tree.

11And he hath given it to be furbished, that it may be handled: this sword is sharpened, and it is furbished, to give it into the hand of the slayer.

12Cry and howl, son of man: for it shall be upon my people, it *shall be* upon all the princes of Israel: terrors by reason of the sword shall be upon my people: smite therefore upon *thy* thigh.

13Because *it is* a trial, and what if *the sword* contemn even the rod? it shall be no *more*, saith the Lord GOD.

14Thou therefore, son of man, prophesy, and smite *thine* hands together, and let the sword be doubled the third time, the sword of the slain: it *is* the sword of the great *men that are* slain, which entereth into their privy chambers.

15I have set the point of the sword against all their gates, that *their* heart may faint, and *their* ruins be multiplied: ah! *it is* made bright, *it is* wrapped up for the slaughter.

16Go thee one way or other, *either* on the right hand, *or* on the left, whithersoever thy face *is* set.

New International

to the southern forest: 'Hear the word of the LORD. This is what the Sovereign LORD says: I am about to set fire to you, and it will consume all your trees, both green and dry. The blazing flame will not be quenched, and every face from south to north will be scorched by it. 48Everyone will see that I the LORD have kindled it; it will not be quenched.' "

49Then I said, "Ah, Sovereign LORD! They are saying of me, 'Isn't he just telling parables?' "

Babylon, God's Sword of Judgment

21 THE WORD of the LORD came to me: 2"Son of man, set your face against Jerusalem and preach against the sanctuary. Prophesy against the land of Israel 3and say to her: 'This is what the LORD says: I am against you. I will draw my sword from its scabbard and cut off from you both the righteous and the wicked. 4Because I am going to cut off the righteous and the wicked, my sword will be unsheathed against everyone from south to north. 5Then all people will know that I the LORD have drawn my sword from its scabbard; it will not return again.'

6"Therefore groan, son of man! Groan before them with broken heart and bitter grief. 7And when they ask you, 'Why are you groaning?' you shall say, 'Because of the news that is coming. Every heart will melt and every hand go limp; every spirit will become faint and every knee become as weak as water.' It is coming! It will surely take place, declares the Sovereign LORD."

8The word of the LORD came to me: 9"Son of man, prophesy and say, 'This is what the Lord says:

" 'A sword, a sword,
　　sharpened and polished—
10sharpened for the slaughter,
　　polished to flash like lightning!

" 'Shall we rejoice in the scepter of my son ˌJudahˌ? The sword despises every such stick.

11" 'The sword is appointed to be polished,
　　to be grasped with the hand;
it is sharpened and polished,
　　made ready for the hand of the slayer.
12Cry out and wail, son of man,
　　for it is against my people;
it is against all the princes of Israel.
They are thrown to the sword
　　along with my people.
Therefore beat your breast.

13" 'Testing will surely come. And what if the scepter ˌof Judahˌ, which the sword despises, does not continue? declares the Sovereign LORD.'

14"So then, son of man, prophesy
　　and strike your hands together.
Let the sword strike twice,
　　even three times.
It is a sword for slaughter—
　　a sword for great slaughter,
　　closing in on them from every side.
15So that hearts may melt
　　and the fallen be many,
I have stationed the sword for slaughterª
　　at all their gates.
Oh! It is made to flash like lightning,
　　it is grasped for slaughter.
16O sword, slash to the right,
　　then to the left,
　　wherever your blade is turned.

ª 15 Septuagint; the meaning of the Hebrew for this word is uncertain.

Living Bible

to it and say: Hear the word of the Lord. I will set you on fire, O forest, and every tree will die, green and dry alike. The terrible flames will not be quenched and they will scorch the world. ⁴⁸And all the world will see that I, the Lord, have set the fire. It shall not be put out."

⁴⁹Then I said, "O Lord God, they say of me, 'He only talks in riddles!' "

21 THEN THIS message came to me from the Lord:

²"Son of dust, face toward Jerusalem and prophesy against Israel and against my Temple!ᵇ ³For the Lord says: I am against you, Israel. I will unsheath my sword and destroy your people, good and bad alike— ⁴I will not spare even the righteous. I will make a clean sweep throughout the land from the Negeb to your northern borders. ⁵All the world shall know that it is I, the Lord. His sword is in his hand, and it will not return to its sheath again until its work is finished.

⁶"Sigh and groan before the people, son of dust, in your bitter anguish; sigh with grief and broken heart. ⁷When they ask you why, tell them: Because of the fearsome news that God has given me. When it comes true, the boldest heart will melt with fear; all strength will disappear. Every spirit will faint; strong knees will tremble and become as weak as water. And the Lord God says: Your doom is on the way; my judgments will be fulfilled!"

⁸Then again this message came to me from God:

⁹, ¹⁰, ¹¹"Son of dust, tell them this: A sword is being sharpened and polished for terrible slaughter. Now will you laugh? For those far stronger than you have perished beneath its power. It is ready now to hand to the executioner. ¹²Son of dust, with sobbing, beat upon your thigh, for that sword shall slay my people and all their leaders. All alike shall die. ¹³It will put them all to the test—and what chance do they have? The Lord God asks.

¹⁴"Prophesy to them in this way: Clap your hands vigorously, then take a sword and brandish it twice, thrice, to symbolize the great massacre they face! ¹⁵Let their hearts melt with terror, for a sword glitters at every gate; it flashes like lightning; it is razor-edged for slaughter. ¹⁶O sword, slash to the right and slash to the left, wherever you will, wherever you want. ¹⁷And you

New Revised Standard

the forest of the Negeb, Hear the word of the LORD: Thus says the Lord GOD, I will kindle a fire in you, and it shall devour every green tree in you and every dry tree; the blazing flame shall not be quenched, and all faces from south to north shall be scorched by it. ⁴⁸All flesh shall see that I the LORD have kindled it; it shall not be quenched. ⁴⁹Then I said, "Ah Lord GOD! they are saying of me, 'Is he not a maker of allegories?' "

The Drawn Sword of God

21ᶜ THE WORD of the LORD came to me: ²Mortal, set your face toward Jerusalem and preach against the sanctuaries; prophesy against the land of Israel ³and say to the land of Israel, Thus says the LORD: I am coming against you, and will draw my sword out of its sheath, and will cut off from you both righteous and wicked. ⁴Because I will cut off from you both righteous and wicked, therefore my sword shall go out of its sheath against all flesh from south to north; ⁵and all flesh shall know that I the LORD have drawn my sword out of its sheath; it shall not be sheathed again. ⁶Moan therefore, mortal; moan with breaking heart and bitter grief before their eyes. ⁷And when they say to you, "Why do you moan?" you shall say, "Because of the news that has come. Every heart will melt and all hands will be feeble, every spirit will faint and all knees will turn to water. See, it comes and it will be fulfilled," says the Lord GOD.

⁸ And the word of the LORD came to me: ⁹Mortal, prophesy and say: Thus says the Lord; Say:

A sword, a sword is sharpened,
    it is also polished;
¹⁰ It is sharpened for slaughter,
    honed to flash like lightning!
How can we make merry?
    You have despised the rod,
    and all discipline.ᵈ
¹¹ The swordᵉ is given to be polished,
    to be grasped in the hand;
It is sharpened, the sword is polished,
    to be placed in the slayer's hand.
¹² Cry and wail, O mortal,
    for it is against my people;
it is against all Israel's princes;
    they are thrown to the sword,
    together with my people.
Ah! Strike the thigh!
¹³For consider: What! If you despise the rod, will it not happen?ᵈ says the Lord GOD.
¹⁴ And you, mortal, prophesy;
    Strike hand to hand.
Let the sword fall twice, thrice;
    it is a sword for killing.
A sword for great slaughter—
    it surrounds them;
¹⁵ therefore hearts melt
    and many stumble.
At all their gates I have set
    the pointᵈ of the sword.
Ah! It is made for flashing,
    it is polishedᶠ for slaughter.
¹⁶ Attack to the right!
    Engage to the left!
    Wherever your edge is directed.

ᵇ *21:2 against my Temple,* literally, "against the sanctuaries."

ᶜ Ch 21.6 in Heb   ᵈ Meaning of Heb uncertain   ᵉ Heb *It*   ᶠ Tg: Heb *wrapped up*

King James

17I will also smite mine hands together, and I will cause my fury to rest: I the LORD have said *it*.

18¶ The word of the LORD came unto me again, saying,

19Also, thou son of man, appoint thee two ways, that the sword of the king of Babylon may come: both twain shall come forth out of one land: and choose thou a place, choose *it* at the head of the way to the city.

20Appoint a way, that the sword may come to Rabbath of the Ammonites, and to Judah in Jerusalem the defenced.

21For the king of Babylon stood at the parting of the way, at the head of the two ways, to use divination: he made *his* arrows bright, he consulted with images, he looked in the liver.

22At his right hand was the divination for Jerusalem, to appoint captains, to open the mouth in the slaughter, to lift up the voice with shouting, to appoint *battering* rams against the gates, to cast a mount, *and* to build a fort.

23And it shall be unto them as a false divination in their sight, to them that have sworn oaths: but he will call to remembrance the iniquity, that they may be taken.

24Therefore thus saith the Lord GOD; Because ye have made your iniquity to be remembered, in that your transgressions are discovered, so that in all your doings your sins do appear; because, *I say*, that ye are come to remembrance, ye shall be taken with the hand.

25¶ And thou, profane wicked prince of Israel, whose day is come, when iniquity *shall have* an end,

26Thus saith the Lord GOD; Remove the diadem, and take off the crown: this *shall* not *be* the same: exalt *him that is* low, and abase *him that is* high.

27I will overturn, overturn, overturn, it: and it shall be no *more*, until he come whose right it is; and I will give it *him*.

28¶ And thou, son of man, prophesy and say, Thus saith the Lord GOD concerning the Ammonites, and concerning their reproach; even say thou, The sword, the sword *is* drawn: for the slaughter *it is* furbished, to consume because of the glittering:

29Whiles they see vanity unto thee, whiles they divine a lie unto thee, to bring thee upon the necks of *them that are* slain, of the wicked, whose day is come, when their iniquity *shall have* an end.

30Shall I cause *it* to return into his sheath? I will judge thee in the place where thou wast created, in the land of thy nativity.

31And I will pour out mine indignation upon thee, I will blow against thee in the fire of my wrath, and deliver thee into the hand of brutish men, *and* skilful to destroy.

32Thou shalt be for fuel to the fire; thy blood shall be in the midst of the land; thou shalt be no *more* remembered: for I the LORD have spoken *it*.

22 MOREOVER THE word of the LORD came unto me, saying,

2Now, thou son of man, wilt thou judge, wilt thou judge the bloody city? yea, thou shalt show her all her abominations.

New International

17I too will strike my hands together,
   and my wrath will subside.
I the LORD have spoken."

18The word of the LORD came to me: 19"Son of man, mark out two roads for the sword of the king of Babylon to take, both starting from the same country. Make a signpost where the road branches off to the city. 20Mark out one road for the sword to come against Rabbah of the Ammonites and another against Judah and fortified Jerusalem. 21For the king of Babylon will stop at the fork in the road, at the junction of the two roads, to seek an omen: He will cast lots with arrows, he will consult his idols, he will examine the liver. 22Into his right hand will come the lot for Jerusalem, where he is to set up battering rams, to give the command to slaughter, to sound the battle cry, to set battering rams against the gates, to build a ramp and to erect siege works. 23It will seem like a false omen to those who have sworn allegiance to him, but he will remind them of their guilt and take them captive.

24"Therefore this is what the Sovereign LORD says: 'Because you people have brought to mind your guilt by your open rebellion, revealing your sins in all that you do—because you have done this, you will be taken captive.

25" 'O profane and wicked prince of Israel, whose day has come, whose time of punishment has reached its climax, 26this is what the Sovereign LORD says: Take off the turban, remove the crown. It will not be as it was: The lowly will be exalted and the exalted will be brought low. 27A ruin! A ruin! I will make it a ruin! It will not be restored until he comes to whom it rightfully belongs; to him I will give it.'

28"And you, son of man, prophesy and say, 'This is what the Sovereign LORD says about the Ammonites and their insults:

" 'A sword, a sword,
   drawn for the slaughter,
polished to consume
   and to flash like lightning!
29Despite false visions concerning you
   and lying divinations about you,
it will be laid on the necks
   of the wicked who are to be slain,
whose day has come,
   whose time of punishment has reached its
      climax.
30Return the sword to its scabbard.
   In the place where you were created,
in the land of your ancestry,
   I will judge you.
31I will pour out my wrath upon you
   and breathe out my fiery anger against you;
I will hand you over to brutal men,
   men skilled in destruction.
32You will be fuel for the fire,
   your blood will be shed in your land,
you will be remembered no more;
   for I the LORD have spoken.' "

Jerusalem's Sins

22 THE WORD of the LORD came to me: 2"Son of man, will you judge her? Will you judge this city of bloodshed? Then confront her with all her detestable practices 3and say: 'This is what the Sovereign

Living Bible

have prophesied with clapping hands that I, the Lord, will smite Jerusalem and satisfy my fury."

18Then this message came to me. The Lord said:

19, 20"Son of dust, make a map and on it trace two routes for the king of Babylon to follow—one to Jerusalem and the other to Rabbah in Trans-Jordan.a And put a signpost at the fork in the road from Babylon. 21For the king of Babylon stands at a fork, uncertain whether to attack Jerusalem or Rabbah. He will call his magicians to use divination; they will cast lots by shaking arrows from the quiver; they will sacrifice to idols and inspect the liverb of their sacrifice. 22They will decide to turn toward Jerusalem! With battering rams they will go against the gates, shouting for the kill; they will build siege towers and make a hill against the walls to reach the top. 23Jerusalem won't understand this treachery; how could the diviners make this terrible mistake? For Babylon is Judah's ally and has sworn to defend Jerusalem! But (the king of Babylon) will think only of the times the people rebelled. He will attack and defeat them.

24"The Lord God says: Again and again your guilt cries out against you, for your sins are open and unashamed. Wherever you go, whatever you do, all is filled with sin. And now the time of punishment has come.

25"O King Zedekiah,c evil prince of Israel, your final day of reckoning is here. 26Take off your jeweled crown, the Lord God says. The old order changes. Now the poor are exalted, and the rich brought very low. 27I will overturn, overturn, overturn the kingdom, so that even the new order that emerges will not succeed until the Man appears who has a right to it. And I will give it all to him.

28"Son of dust, prophesy to the Ammonites too, for they mocked my people in their woe. Tell them this:

"Against you also my glittering sword is drawn from its sheath; it is sharpened and polished and flashed like lightning. 29Your magicians and false prophets have told you lies of safety and success—that your gods will save you from the king of Babylon. Thus they have caused your death along with all the other wicked, for when the day of final reckoning has come you will be wounded unto death. 30Shall I return my sword to its sheath before I deal with you? No, I will destroy you in your own country where you were born. 31I will pour out my fury upon you and blow upon the fire of my wrath until it becomes a roaring conflagration, and I will deliver you into the hands of cruel men skilled in destruction. 32You are the fuel for the fire; your blood will be spilled in your own country and you will be utterly wiped out, your memory lost in history. For I, the Lord, have spoken it."

22 NOW ANOTHER message came from the Lord. He said:

2"Son of dust, indict Jerusalem as the City of Murder. Publicly denounce her terrible deeds. 3City of Murder,

---

a 21:19, 20 Rabbah in Trans-Jordan, literally, "Rabbah of the Ammonites."
b 21:21 inspect the liver. A very common type of divination by which ancients thought they could obtain information from the gods.   c 21:25 O King Zedekiah, implied.

New Revised Standard

17 I too will strike hand to hand,
    I will satisfy my fury;
    I the LORD have spoken.

18 The word of the LORD came to me: 19Mortal, mark out two roads for the sword of the king of Babylon to come; both of them shall issue from the same land. And make a signpost, make it for a fork in the road leading to a city; 20mark out the road for the sword to come to Rabbah of the Ammonites or to Judah and tod Jerusalem the fortified. 21For the king of Babylon stands at the parting of the way, at the fork in the two roads, to use divination; he shakes the arrows, he consults the teraphim,e he inspects the liver. 22Into his right hand comes the lot for Jerusalem, to set battering rams, to call out for slaughter, for raising the battle cry, to set battering rams against the gates, to cast up ramps, to build siege towers. 23But to them it will seem like a false divination; they have sworn solemn oaths; but he brings their guilt to remembrance, bringing about their capture.

24 Therefore thus says the Lord GOD: Because you have brought your guilt to remembrance, in that your transgressions are uncovered, so that in all your deeds your sins appear—because you have come to remembrance, you shall be taken in hand.f

25 As for you, vile, wicked prince of Israel,
    you whose day has come,
    the time of final punishment,
26 thus says the Lord GOD:
Remove the turban, take off the crown;
    things shall not remain as they are.
Exalt that which is low,
    abase that which is high.
27 A ruin, a ruin, a ruin—
    I will make it!
(Such has never occurred.)
Until he comes whose right it is;
    to him I will give it.

28 As for you, mortal, prophesy, and say, Thus says the Lord GOD concerning the Ammonites, and concerning their reproach; say:
A sword, a sword! Drawn for slaughter
    Polished to consume,g to flash like
        lightning.
29 Offering false visions for you,
    divining lies for you,
they place you over the necks
    of the vile, wicked ones—
those whose day has come,
    the time of final punishment.
30 Return it to its sheath!
In the place where you were created,
    in the land of your origin,
    I will judge you.
31 I will pour out my indignation upon you,
    with the fire of my wrath
    I will blow upon you.
I will deliver you into brutish hands,
    those skillful to destroy.
32 You shall be fuel for the fire,
    your blood shall enter the earth;
You shall be remembered no more,
    for I the LORD have spoken.

The Bloody City

22 THE WORD of the LORD came to me: 2You, mortal, will you judge, will you judge the bloody city? Then declare to it all its abominable deeds.

---

d Gk Syr: Heb Judah in   e Or the household gods   f Or be taken captive
g Cn: Heb to contain

King James

3Then say thou, Thus saith the Lord GOD, The city sheddeth blood in the midst of it, that her time may come, and maketh idols against herself to defile herself.

4Thou art become guilty in thy blood that thou hast shed; and hast defiled thyself in thine idols which thou hast made; and thou hast caused thy days to draw near, and art come *even* unto thy years: therefore have I made thee a reproach unto the heathen, and a mocking to all countries.

5*Those that be* near, and *those that be* far from thee, shall mock thee, *which art* infamous *and* much vexed.

6Behold, the princes of Israel, every one were in thee to their power to shed blood.

7In thee have they set light by father and mother: in the midst of thee have they dealt by oppression with the stranger: in thee have they vexed the fatherless and the widow.

8Thou hast despised mine holy things, and hast profaned my sabbaths.

9In thee are men that carry tales to shed blood: and in thee they eat upon the mountains: in the midst of thee they commit lewdness.

10In thee have they discovered their fathers' nakedness: in thee have they humbled her that was set apart for pollution.

11And one hath committed abomination with his neighbour's wife; and another hath lewdly defiled his daughter-in-law; and another in thee hath humbled his sister, his father's daughter.

12In thee have they taken gifts to shed blood; thou hast taken usury and increase, and thou hast greedily gained of thy neighbours by extortion, and hast forgotten me, saith the Lord GOD.

13¶ Behold, therefore I have smitten mine hand at thy dishonest gain which thou hast made, and at thy blood which hath been in the midst of thee.

14Can thine heart endure, or can thine hands be strong, in the days that I shall deal with thee? I the LORD have spoken *it,* and will do *it.*

15And I will scatter thee among the heathen, and disperse thee in the countries, and will consume thy filthiness out of thee.

16And thou shalt take thine inheritance in thyself in the sight of the heathen, and thou shalt know that I *am* the LORD.

17And the word of the LORD came unto me, saying,

18Son of man, the house of Israel is to me become dross: all they *are* brass, and tin, and iron, and lead, in the midst of the furnace; they are *even* the dross of silver.

19Therefore thus saith the Lord GOD; Because ye are all become dross, behold, therefore I will gather you into the midst of Jerusalem.

20*As* they gather silver, and brass, and iron, and lead, and tin, into the midst of the furnace, to blow the fire upon it, to melt *it;* so will I gather *you* in mine anger and in my fury, and I will leave *you there,* and melt you.

21Yea, I will gather you, and blow upon you in the fire of my wrath, and ye shall be melted in the midst thereof.

22As silver is melted in the midst of the furnace, so shall ye be melted in the midst thereof; and ye shall know that I the LORD have poured out my fury upon you.

23¶ And the word of the LORD came unto me, saying,

24Son of man, say unto her, Thou *art* the land that is not cleansed, nor rained upon in the day of indignation.

25*There is* a conspiracy of her prophets in the midst thereof, like a roaring lion ravening the prey; they have devoured souls; they have taken the treasure and precious things; they have made her many widows in the midst thereof.

New International

LORD says: O city that brings on herself doom by shedding blood in her midst and defiles herself by making idols, 4you have become guilty because of the blood you have shed and have become defiled by the idols you have made. You have brought your days to a close, and the end of your years has come. Therefore I will make you an object of scorn to the nations and a laughingstock to all the countries. 5Those who are near and those who are far away will mock you, O infamous city, full of turmoil.

6" 'See how each of the princes of Israel who are in you uses his power to shed blood. 7In you they have treated father and mother with contempt; in you they have oppressed the alien and mistreated the fatherless and the widow. 8You have despised my holy things and desecrated my Sabbaths. 9In you are slanderous men bent on shedding blood; in you are those who eat at the mountain shrines and commit lewd acts. 10In you are those who dishonor their fathers' bed; in you are those who violate women during their period, when they are ceremonially unclean. 11In you one man commits a detestable offense with his neighbor's wife, another shamefully defiles his daughter-in-law, and another violates his sister, his own father's daughter. 12In you men accept bribes to shed blood; you take usury and excessive interest[a] and make unjust gain from your neighbors by extortion. And you have forgotten me, declares the Sovereign LORD.

13" 'I will surely strike my hands together at the unjust gain you have made and at the blood you have shed in your midst. 14Will your courage endure or your hands be strong in the day I deal with you? I the LORD have spoken, and I will do it. 15I will disperse you among the nations and scatter you through the countries; and I will put an end to your uncleanness. 16When you have been defiled[b] in the eyes of the nations, you will know that I am the LORD.' "

17Then the word of the LORD came to me: 18"Son of man, the house of Israel has become dross to me; all of them are the copper, tin, iron and lead left inside a furnace. They are but the dross of silver. 19Therefore this is what the Sovereign LORD says: 'Because you have all become dross, I will gather you into Jerusalem. 20As men gather silver, copper, iron, lead and tin into a furnace to melt it with a fiery blast, so will I gather you in my anger and my wrath and put you inside the city and melt you. 21I will gather you and I will blow on you with my fiery wrath, and you will be melted inside her. 22As silver is melted in a furnace, so you will be melted inside her, and you will know that I the LORD have poured out my wrath upon you.' "

23Again the word of the LORD came to me: 24"Son of man, say to the land, 'You are a land that has had no rain or showers[c] in the day of wrath.' 25There is a conspiracy of her princes[d] within her like a roaring lion tearing its prey; they devour people, take treasures and precious things and make many widows within her.

---

[a] 12 Or *usury and interest* [b] 16 Or *When I have allotted you your inheritance* [c] 24 Septuagint; Hebrew *has not been cleansed or rained on* [d] 25 Septuagint; Hebrew *prophets*

Living Bible

doomed and damned—City of Idols, filthy and foul—⁴you are guilty both of murder and idolatry. Now comes your day of doom. You have reached the limit of your years. I will make you a laughingstock and a reproach to all the nations of the world. ⁵Near and far they will mock you, a city of infamous rebels.

⁶"Every leader in Israel who lives within your walls is bent on murder. ⁷Fathers and mothers are contemptuously ignored; immigrants and visitors are forced to pay you for your 'protection'; orphans and widows are wronged and oppressed. ⁸The things of God are all despised; my Sabbaths are ignored. ⁹Prisoners are falsely accused and sent to their death. Every mountain top is filled with idols; lewdness is everywhere. ¹⁰There are men who commit adultery with their fathers' wives and lie with menstruous women.ᶜ ¹¹Adultery with a neighbor's wife, a daughter-in-law, a half sister—this is common. ¹²Hired murderers, loan racketeers and extortioners are everywhere. You never even think of me and my commands, the Lord God says.

¹³"But now I snap my fingers and call a halt to your dishonest gain and bloodshed. ¹⁴How strong and courageous will you be then, in my day of reckoning? For I, the Lord, have spoken, and I will do all that I have said. ¹⁵I will scatter you throughout the world and burn out the wickedness within you. ¹⁶You will be dishonored among the nations, and you shall know I am the Lord."

¹⁷Then the Lord said this:

¹⁸, ¹⁹, ²⁰"Son of dust, the people of Israel are the worthless slag left when silver is smelted. They are the dross, compounded from the brass, the tin, the iron and the lead. Therefore the Lord God says: Because you are worthless dross, I will bring you to my crucible in Jerusalem, to smelt you with the heat of my wrath. ²¹I will blow the fire of my wrath upon you, ²²and you will melt like silver in fierce heat, and you will know that I, the Lord, have poured my wrath upon you."

²³Again the message of the Lord came to me, saying: ²⁴"Son of dust, say to the people of Israel: In the day of my indignation you shall be like an uncleared wilderness, or a desert without rain. ²⁵Your 'prophets' have plotted against you like lions stalking prey. They devour many lives; they seize treasures and extort wealth; they multiply the widows in the land. ²⁶Your priests have

New Revised Standard

³You shall say, Thus says the Lord GOD: A city! Shedding blood within itself; its time has come; making its idols, defiling itself. ⁴You have become guilty by the blood that you have shed, and defiled by the idols that you have made; you have brought your day near, the appointed time of your years has come. Therefore I have made you a disgrace before the nations, and a mockery to all the countries. ⁵Those who are near and those who are far from you will mock you, you infamous one, full of tumult.

6 The princes of Israel in you, everyone according to his power, have been bent on shedding blood. ⁷Father and mother are treated with contempt in you; the alien residing within you suffers extortion; the orphan and the widow are wronged in you. ⁸You have despised my holy things, and profaned my sabbaths. ⁹In you are those who slander to shed blood, those in you who eat upon the mountains, who commit lewdness in your midst. ¹⁰In you they uncover their fathers' nakedness; in you they violate women in their menstrual periods. ¹¹One commits abomination with his neighbor's wife; another lewdly defiles his daughter-in-law; another in you defiles his sister, his father's daughter. ¹²In you, they take bribes to shed blood; you take both advance interest and accrued interest, and make gain of your neighbors by extortion; and you have forgotten me, says the Lord GOD.

13 See, I strike my hands together at the dishonest gain you have made, and at the blood that has been shed within you. ¹⁴Can your courage endure, or can your hands remain strong in the days when I shall deal with you? I the LORD have spoken, and I will do it. ¹⁵I will scatter you among the nations and disperse you through the countries, and I will purge your filthiness out of you. ¹⁶And Iᶠ shall be profaned through you in the sight of the nations; and you shall know that I am the LORD.

17 The word of the LORD came to me: ¹⁸Mortal, the house of Israel has become dross to me; all of them, silver,ᵍ bronze, tin, iron, and lead. In the smelter they have become dross. ¹⁹Therefore thus says the Lord GOD: Because you have all become dross, I will gather you into the midst of Jerusalem. ²⁰As one gathers silver, bronze, iron, lead, and tin into a smelter, to blow the fire upon them in order to melt them; so I will gather you in my anger and in my wrath, and I will put you in and melt you. ²¹I will gather you and blow upon you with the fire of my wrath, and you shall be melted within it. ²²As silver is melted in a smelter, so you shall be melted in it; and you shall know that I the LORD have poured out my wrath upon you.

23 The word of the LORD came to me: ²⁴Mortal, say to it: You are a land that is not cleansed, not rained upon in the day of indignation. ²⁵Its princesʰ within it are like a roaring lion tearing the prey; they have devoured human lives; they have taken treasure and precious things; they have made many widows within it. ²⁶Its priests

---

King James

26Her priests have violated my law, and have profaned mine holy things: they have put no difference between the holy and profane, neither have they shown *difference* between the unclean and the clean, and have hid their eyes from my sabbaths, and I am profaned among them.

27Her princes in the midst thereof *are* like wolves ravening the prey, to shed blood, *and* to destroy souls, to get dishonest gain.

28And her prophets have daubed them with untempered *mortar,* seeing vanity, and divining lies unto them, saying, Thus saith the Lord GOD, when the LORD hath not spoken.

29The people of the land have used oppression, and exercised robbery, and have vexed the poor and needy: yea, they have oppressed the stranger wrongfully.

30And I sought for a man among them, that should make up the hedge, and stand in the gap before me for the land, that I should not destroy it: but I found none.

31Therefore have I poured out mine indignation upon them; I have consumed them with the fire of my wrath: their own way have I recompensed upon their heads, saith the Lord GOD.

23 THE WORD of the LORD came again unto me, saying,

2Son of man, there were two women, the daughters of one mother:

3And they committed whoredoms in Egypt; they committed whoredoms in their youth: there were their breasts pressed, and there they bruised the teats of their virginity.

4And the names of them *were* Aholah the elder, and Aholibah her sister: and they were mine, and they bare sons and daughters. Thus *were* their names; Samaria *is* Aholah, and Jerusalem Aholibah.

5And Aholah played the harlot when she was mine; and she doted on her lovers, on the Assyrians *her* neighbours,

6*Which were* clothed with blue, captains and rulers, all of them desirable young men, horsemen riding upon horses.

7Thus she committed her whoredoms with them, with all them *that were* the chosen men of Assyria, and with all on whom she doted: with all their idols she defiled herself.

8Neither left she her whoredoms *brought* from Egypt: for in her youth they lay with her, and they bruised the breasts of her virginity, and poured their whoredom upon her.

9Wherefore I have delivered her into the hand of her lovers, into the hand of the Assyrians, upon whom she doted.

10These discovered her nakedness: they took her sons and her daughters, and slew her with the sword: and she became famous among women; for they had executed judgment upon her.

11And when her sister Aholibah saw *this,* she was more corrupt in her inordinate love than she, and in her whoredoms more than her sister in *her* whoredoms.

12She doted upon the Assyrians *her* neighbours, captains and rulers clothed most gorgeously, horsemen riding upon horses, all of them desirable young men.

13Then I saw that she was defiled, *that* they *took* both one way,

New International

26Her priests do violence to my law and profane my holy things; they do not distinguish between the holy and the common; they teach that there is no difference between the unclean and the clean; and they shut their eyes to the keeping of my Sabbaths, so that I am profaned among them. 27Her officials within her are like wolves tearing their prey; they shed blood and kill people to make unjust gain. 28Her prophets whitewash these deeds for them by false visions and lying divinations. They say, 'This is what the Sovereign LORD says'—when the LORD has not spoken. 29The people of the land practice extortion and commit robbery; they oppress the poor and needy and mistreat the alien, denying them justice.

30"I looked for a man among them who would build up the wall and stand before me in the gap on behalf of the land so I would not have to destroy it, but I found none. 31So I will pour out my wrath on them and consume them with my fiery anger, bringing down on their own heads all they have done, declares the Sovereign LORD."

Two Adulterous Sisters

23 THE WORD of the LORD came to me: 2"Son of man, there were two women, daughters of the same mother. 3They became prostitutes in Egypt, engaging in prostitution from their youth. In that land their breasts were fondled and their virgin bosoms caressed. 4The older was named Oholah, and her sister was Oholibah. They were mine and gave birth to sons and daughters. Oholah is Samaria, and Oholibah is Jerusalem.

5"Oholah engaged in prostitution while she was still mine; and she lusted after her lovers, the Assyrians—warriors 6clothed in blue, governors and commanders, all of them handsome young men, and mounted horsemen. 7She gave herself as a prostitute to all the elite of the Assyrians and defiled herself with all the idols of everyone she lusted after. 8She did not give up the prostitution she began in Egypt, when during her youth men slept with her, caressed her virgin bosom and poured out their lust upon her.

9"Therefore I handed her over to her lovers, the Assyrians, for whom she lusted. 10They stripped her naked, took away her sons and daughters and killed her with the sword. She became a byword among women, and punishment was inflicted on her.

11"Her sister Oholibah saw this, yet in her lust and prostitution she was more depraved than her sister. 12She too lusted after the Assyrians—governors and commanders, warriors in full dress, mounted horsemen, all handsome young men. 13I saw that she too defiled herself; both of them went the same way.

Living Bible

violated my laws and defiled my Temple and my holiness. To them the things of God are no more important than any daily task. They have not taught my people the difference between right and wrong, and they disregard my Sabbaths, so my holy name is greatly defiled among them. 27Your leaders are like wolves, who tear apart their victims, and they destroy lives for profit. 28Your 'prophets' describe false visions and speak false messages they claim are from God, when he hasn't spoken one word to them at all. Thus they repair the walls with whitewash! 29Even the common people oppress and rob the poor and needy and cruelly extort from aliens.

30"I looked in vain for anyone who would build again the wall of righteousness that guards the land, who could stand in the gap and defend you from my just attacks, but I found not one. 31And so the Lord God says: I will pour out my anger upon you; I will consume you with the fire of my wrath. I have heaped upon you the full penalty for all your sins."

23 THE LORD'S message came to me again, saying:
2, 3"Son of dust, there were two sisters who as young girls became prostitutes in Egypt.
4, 5"The older girl was named Oholah; her sister was Oholibah. (I am speaking of Samaria and Jerusalem!) I married them, and they bore me sons and daughters. But then Oholah turned to other gods instead of me, and gave her love to the Assyrians, her neighbors, 6for they were all attractive young men, captains and commanders, in handsome blue, dashing about on their horses. 7And so she sinned with them—the choicest men of Assyria—worshiping their idols, defiling herself. 8For when she left Egypt, she did not leave her spirit of prostitution behind, but was still as lewd as in her youth, when the Egyptians poured out their lusts upon her and robbed her of her virginity.

9"And so I delivered her into the evil clutches of the Assyrians whose gods she loved so much. 10They stripped her and killed her and took away her children as their slaves. Her name was known to every woman in the land as a sinner who had received what she deserved.

11"But when Oholibah (Jerusalem) saw what had happened to her sister she went right ahead in the same way, and sinned even more than her sister. 12She fawned over her Assyrian neighbors,a those handsome young men on fine steeds, those army officers in handsome uniforms—all of them desirable. 13I saw the way she was going, following right along behind her older sister.

New Revised Standard

have done violence to my teaching and have profaned my holy things; they have made no distinction between the holy and the common, neither have they taught the difference between the unclean and the clean, and they have disregarded my sabbaths, so that I am profaned among them. 27 Its officials within it are like wolves tearing the prey, shedding blood, destroying lives to get dishonest gain. 28 Its prophets have smeared whitewash on their behalf, seeing false visions and divining lies for them, saying, "Thus says the Lord GOD," when the LORD has not spoken. 29 The people of the land have practiced extortion and committed robbery; they have oppressed the poor and needy, and have extorted from the alien without redress. 30 And I sought for anyone among them who would repair the wall and stand in the breach before me on behalf of the land, so that I would not destroy it; but I found no one. 31 Therefore I have poured out my indignation upon them; I have consumed them with the fire of my wrath; I have returned their conduct upon their heads, says the Lord GOD.

Oholah and Oholibah

23 THE WORD of the LORD came to me: 2Mortal, there were two women, the daughters of one mother; 3they played the whore in Egypt; they played the whore in their youth; their breasts were caressed there, and their virgin bosoms were fondled. 4Oholah was the name of the elder and Oholibah the name of her sister. They became mine, and they bore sons and daughters. As for their names, Oholah is Samaria, and Oholibah is Jerusalem.

5 Oholah played the whore while she was mine; she lusted after her lovers the Assyrians, warriorsb 6clothed in blue, governors and commanders, all of them handsome young men, mounted horsemen. 7She bestowed her favors upon them, the choicest men of Assyria all of them; and she defiled herself with all the idols of everyone for whom she lusted. 8She did not give up her whorings that she had practiced since Egypt; for in her youth men had lain with her and fondled her virgin bosom and poured out their lust upon her. 9Therefore I delivered her into the hands of her lovers, into the hands of the Assyrians, for whom she lusted. 10These uncovered her nakedness; they seized her sons and her daughters; and they killed her with the sword. Judgment was executed upon her, and she became a byword among women.

11 Her sister Oholibah saw this, yet she was more corrupt than she in her lusting and in her whorings, which were worse than those of her sister. 12She lusted after the Assyrians, governors and commanders, warriorsb clothed in full armor, mounted horsemen, all of them handsome young men. 13And I saw that she was defiled; they both took the same way. 14But she carried

---

a 23:12 She fawned over her Assyrian neighbors, i.e., when Ahaz paid "protection money" to Tiglath-pileser II (2 Kgs 16:7, 8).

b Meaning of Heb uncertain

King James

14And *that* she increased her whoredoms: for when she saw men portrayed upon the wall, the images of the Chaldeans portrayed with vermilion,

15Girded with girdles upon their loins, exceeding in dyed attire upon their heads, all of them princes to look to, after the manner of the Babylonians of Chaldea, the land of their nativity:

16And as soon as she saw them with her eyes, she doted upon them, and sent messengers unto them into Chaldea.

17And the Babylonians came to her into the bed of love, and they defiled her with their whoredom, and she was polluted with them, and her mind was alienated from them.

18So she discovered her whoredoms, and discovered her nakedness: then my mind was alienated from her, like as my mind was alienated from her sister.

19Yet she multiplied her whoredoms, in calling to remembrance the days of her youth, wherein she had played the harlot in the land of Egypt.

20For she doted upon their paramours, whose flesh *is as* the flesh of asses, and whose issue *is like* the issue of horses.

21Thus thou calledst to remembrance the lewdness of thy youth, in bruising thy teats by the Egyptians for the paps of thy youth.

22¶ Therefore, O Aholibah, thus saith the Lord GOD; Behold, I will raise up thy lovers against thee, from whom thy mind is alienated, and I will bring them against thee on every side;

23The Babylonians, and all the Chaldeans, Pekod, and Shoa, and Koa, *and* all the Assyrians with them: all of them desirable young men, captains and rulers, great lords and renowned, all of them riding upon horses.

24And they shall come against thee with chariots, wagons, and wheels, and with an assembly of people, *which* shall set against thee buckler and shield and helmet round about: and I will set judgment before them, and they shall judge thee according to their judgments.

25And I will set my jealousy against thee, and they shall deal furiously with thee: they shall take away thy nose and thine ears; and thy remnant shall fall by the sword: they shall take thy sons and thy daughters; and thy residue shall be devoured by the fire.

26They shall also strip thee out of thy clothes, and take away thy fair jewels.

27Thus will I make thy lewdness to cease from thee, and thy whoredom *brought* from the land of Egypt: so that thou shalt not lift up thine eyes unto them, nor remember Egypt any more.

28For thus saith the Lord GOD; Behold, I will deliver thee into the hand *of them* whom thou hatest, into the hand *of them* from whom thy mind is alienated:

29And they shall deal with thee hatefully, and shall take away all thy labour, and shall leave thee naked and bare: and the nakedness of thy whoredoms shall be discovered, both thy lewdness and thy whoredoms.

30I will do these *things* unto thee, because thou hast gone awhoring after the heathen, *and* because thou art polluted with their idols.

31Thou hast walked in the way of thy sister; therefore will I give her cup into thine hand.

32Thus saith the Lord GOD; Thou shalt drink of thy sister's cup deep and large: thou shalt be laughed to scorn and had in derision; it containeth much.

33Thou shalt be filled with drunkenness and sorrow, with the cup of astonishment and desolation, with the cup of thy sister Samaria.

34Thou shalt even drink it and suck *it* out, and thou shalt break the sherds thereof, and pluck off thine own breasts: for I have spoken *it,* saith the Lord GOD.

35Therefore thus saith the Lord GOD; Because thou hast forgotten me, and cast me behind thy back, therefore bear thou also thy lewdness and thy whoredoms.

New International

14"But she carried her prostitution still further. She saw men portrayed on a wall, figures of Chaldeans[a] portrayed in red, 15with belts around their waists and flowing turbans on their heads; all of them looked like Babylonian chariot officers, natives of Chaldea.[b] 16As soon as she saw them, she lusted after them and sent messengers to them in Chaldea. 17Then the Babylonians came to her, to the bed of love, and in their lust they defiled her. After she had been defiled by them, she turned away from them in disgust. 18When she carried on her prostitution openly and exposed her nakedness, I turned away from her in disgust, just as I had turned away from her sister. 19Yet she became more and more promiscuous as she recalled the days of her youth, when she was a prostitute in Egypt. 20There she lusted after her lovers, whose genitals were like those of donkeys and whose emission was like that of horses. 21So you longed for the lewdness of your youth, when in Egypt your bosom was caressed and your young breasts fondled.[c]

22"Therefore, Oholibah, this is what the Sovereign LORD says: I will stir up your lovers against you, those you turned away from in disgust, and I will bring them against you from every side— 23the Babylonians and all the Chaldeans, the men of Pekod and Shoa and Koa, and all the Assyrians with them, handsome young men, all of them governors and commanders, chariot officers and men of high rank, all mounted on horses. 24They will come against you with weapons,[d] chariots and wagons and with a throng of people; they will take up positions against you on every side with large and small shields and with helmets. I will turn you over to them for punishment, and they will punish you according to their standards. 25I will direct my jealous anger against you, and they will deal with you in fury. They will cut off your noses and your ears, and those of you who are left will fall by the sword. They will take away your sons and daughters, and those of you who are left will be consumed by fire. 26They will also strip you of your clothes and take your fine jewelry. 27So I will put a stop to the lewdness and prostitution you began in Egypt. You will not look on these things with longing or remember Egypt anymore.

28"For this is what the Sovereign LORD says: I am about to hand you over to those you hate, to those you turned away from in disgust. 29They will deal with you in hatred and take away everything you have worked for. They will leave you naked and bare, and the shame of your prostitution will be exposed. Your lewdness and promiscuity 30have brought this upon you, because you lusted after the nations and defiled yourself with their idols. 31You have gone the way of your sister; so I will put her cup into your hand.

32"This is what the Sovereign LORD says:

"You will drink your sister's cup,
    a cup large and deep;
it will bring scorn and derision,
    for it holds so much.
33You will be filled with drunkenness and sorrow,
    the cup of ruin and desolation,
    the cup of your sister Samaria.
34You will drink it and drain it dry;
    you will dash it to pieces
    and tear your breasts.

I have spoken, declares the Sovereign LORD.

35"Therefore this is what the Sovereign LORD says: Since you have forgotten me and thrust me behind your back, you must bear the consequences of your lewdness and prostitution."

---

a 14 Or *Babylonians* b 15 Or *Babylonia*; also in verse 16 c 21 Syriac (see also verse 3); Hebrew *caressed because of your young breasts* d 24 The meaning of the Hebrew for this word is uncertain.

Living Bible

14, 15"She was in fact more debased than Samaria, for she fell in love with pictures she saw painted on a wall! They were pictures of Babylonian military officers, outfitted in striking red uniforms, with handsome belts, and flowing turbans on their heads. 16When she saw these paintings she longed to give herself to the men pictured, so she sent messengers to Chaldeae to invite them to come to her. 17And they came and committed adultery with her, defiling her in the bed of love, but afterward she hated them and broke off all relations with them.f

18"And I despised her just as I despised her sister, because she flaunted herself before them and gave herself to their lust. 19, 20But that didn't bother her. She turned to even greater prostitution, sinning with the lustful men she remembered from her youth when she was a prostitute in Egypt.g 21And thus you celebrated those former days when as a young girl you gave your virginity to those from Egypt.

22"And now the Lord God says that he will raise against you, O Oholibah (Jerusalem), those very nations from which you turned away, disgusted. 23For the Babylonians will come, and all the Chaldeans from Pekod and Shoa and Koa; and all the Assyrians with them—handsome young men of high rank, riding their steeds. 24They will come against you from the north with chariots and wagons and a great army fully prepared for attack. They will surround you on every side with armored men and I will let them at you, to do with you as they wish. 25And I will send my jealousy against you and deal furiously with you, and cut off your nose and ears; your survivors will be killed; your children will be taken away as slaves, and everything left will be burned. 26They will strip you of your beautiful clothes and jewels.

27"And so I will put a stop to your lewdness and prostitution brought from the land of Egypt; you will no more long for Egypt and her gods. 28For the Lord God says: I will surely deliver you over to your enemies, to those you loathe. 29They will deal with you in hatred, and rob you of all you own, leaving you naked and bare. And the shame of your prostitution shall be exposed to all the world.

30"You brought all this upon yourself by worshiping the gods of other nations, defiling yourself with all their idols. 31You have followed in your sister's footsteps, so I will punish you with the same terrors that destroyed her. 32Yes, the terrors that fell upon her will fall upon you—and the cup from which she drank was full and large. And all the world will mock you for your woe. 33You will reel like a drunkard beneath the awful blows of sorrow and distress, just as your sister Samaria did. 34In deep anguish you will drain that cup of terror to the very bottom and will lick the inside to get every drop. For I have spoken, says the Lord. 35Because you have forgotten me and turned your backs upon me, therefore you must bear the consequence of all your sin.

New Revised Standard

her whorings further; she saw male figures carved on the wall, images of the Chaldeans portrayed in vermilion, 15with belts around their waists, with flowing turbans on their heads, all of them looking like officers—a picture of Babylonians whose native land was Chaldea. 16When she saw them she lusted after them, and sent messengers to them in Chaldea. 17And the Babylonians came to her into the bed of love, and they defiled her with their lust; and after she defiled herself with them, she turned from them in disgust. 18When she carried on her whorings so openly and flaunted her nakedness, I turned in disgust from her, as I had turned from her sister. 19Yet she increased her whorings, remembering the days of her youth, when she played the whore in the land of Egypt 20and lusted after her paramours there, whose members were like those of donkeys, and whose emission was like that of stallions. 21Thus you longed for the lewdness of your youth, when the Egyptiansh fondled your bosom and caressedi your young breasts.

22 Therefore, O Oholibah, thus says the Lord GOD: I will rouse against you your lovers from whom you turned in disgust, and I will bring them against you from every side: 23the Babylonians and all the Chaldeans, Pekod and Shoa and Koa, and all the Assyrians with them, handsome young men, governors and commanders all of them, officers and warriors,j all of them riding on horses. 24They shall come against you from the northk with chariots and wagons and a host of peoples; they shall set themselves against you on every side with buckler, shield, and helmet, and I will commit the judgment to them, and they shall judge you according to their ordinances. 25I will direct my indignation against you, in order that they may deal with you in fury. They shall cut off your nose and your ears, and your survivors shall fall by the sword. They shall seize your sons and your daughters, and your survivors shall be devoured by fire. 26They shall also strip you of your clothes and take away your fine jewels. 27So I will put an end to your lewdness and your whoring brought from the land of Egypt; you shall not long for them, or remember Egypt any more. 28For thus says the Lord GOD: I will deliver you into the hands of those whom you hate, into the hands of those from whom you turned in disgust; 29and they shall deal with you in hatred, and take away all the fruit of your labor, and leave you naked and bare, and the nakedness of your whorings shall be exposed. Your lewdness and your whorings 30have brought this upon you, because you played the whore with the nations, and polluted yourself with their idols. 31You have gone the way of your sister; therefore I will give her cup into your hand. 32Thus says the Lord GOD:

You shall drink your sister's cup,
    deep and wide;
you shall be scorned and derided,
    it holds so much.
33 You shall be filled with drunkenness and
    sorrow.
A cup of horror and desolation
    is the cup of your sister Samaria;
34 you shall drink it and drain it out,
    and gnaw its sherds,
    and tear out your breasts;
for I have spoken, says the Lord GOD. 35Therefore thus says the Lord GOD: Because you have forgotten me and cast me behind your back, therefore bear the consequences of your lewdness and whorings.

---

e 23:16 so she sent messengers to Chaldea. This occurred when Hezekiah entertained the embassy from Babylon (Isa 38-39), also during the reign of Manasseh. f 23:17 and broke off all relations with them. The anti-Babylonian party in Judah looked to Egypt for help during the reigns of the last two Judean kings, Jehoiakim and Zedekiah. g 23:19, 20 when she was a prostitute in Egypt, i.e., during the reign of Josiah.

h Two Mss: MT from Egypt   i Cn: Heb for the sake of   j Compare verses 6 and 12: Heb officers and called ones   k Gk: Meaning of Heb uncertain

King James

36¶ The LORD said moreover unto me; Son of man, wilt thou judge Aholah and Aholibah? yea, declare unto them their abominations;

37That they have committed adultery, and blood *is* in their hands, and with their idols have they committed adultery, and have also caused their sons, whom they bare unto me, to pass for them through *the fire*, to devour *them*.

38Moreover this they have done unto me: they have defiled my sanctuary in the same day, and have profaned my sabbaths.

39For when they had slain their children to their idols, then they came the same day into my sanctuary to profane it; and, lo, thus have they done in the midst of mine house.

40And furthermore, that ye have sent for men to come from far, unto whom a messenger *was* sent; and, lo, they came: for whom thou didst wash thyself, paintedst thy eyes, and deckedst thyself with ornaments,

41And satest upon a stately bed, and a table prepared before it, whereupon thou hast set mine incense and mine oil.

42And a voice of a multitude being at ease *was* with her: and with the men of the common sort *were* brought Sabeans from the wilderness, which put bracelets upon their hands, and beautiful crowns upon their heads.

43Then said I unto *her that was* old in adulteries, Will they now commit whoredoms with her, and she *with them?*

44Yet they went in unto her, as they go in unto a woman that playeth the harlot: so went they in unto Aholah and unto Aholibah, the lewd women.

45¶ And the righteous men, they shall judge them after the manner of adulteresses, and after the manner of women that shed blood; because they *are* adulteresses, and blood *is* in their hands.

46For thus saith the Lord GOD; I will bring up a company upon them, and will give them to be removed and spoiled.

47And the company shall stone them with stones, and dispatch them with their swords; they shall slay their sons and their daughters, and burn up their houses with fire.

48Thus will I cause lewdness to cease out of the land, that all women may be taught not to do after your lewdness.

49And they shall recompense your lewdness upon you, and ye shall bear the sins of your idols: and ye shall know that I *am* the Lord GOD.

24 AGAIN IN the ninth year, in the tenth month, in the tenth *day* of the month, the word of the LORD come unto me, saying,

2Son of man, write thee the name of the day, *even* of this same day: the king of Babylon set himself against Jerusalem this same day.

3And utter a parable unto the rebellious house, and say unto them, Thus saith the Lord GOD; Set on a pot, set *it* on, and also pour water into it:

4Gather the pieces thereof into it, *even* every good piece, the thigh, and the shoulder; fill *it* with the choice bones.

5Take the choice of the flock, and burn also the bones under it, *and* make it boil well, and let them seethe the bones of it therein.

New International

36The LORD said to me: "Son of man, will you judge Oholah and Oholibah? Then confront them with their detestable practices, 37for they have committed adultery and blood is on their hands. They committed adultery with their idols; they even sacrificed their children, whom they bore to me,[a] as food for them. 38They have also done this to me: At that same time they defiled my sanctuary and desecrated my Sabbaths. 39On the very day they sacrificed their children to their idols, they entered my sanctuary and desecrated it. That is what they did in my house.

40"They even sent messengers for men who came from far away, and when they arrived you bathed yourself for them, painted your eyes and put on your jewelry. 41You sat on an elegant couch, with a table spread before it on which you had placed the incense and oil that belonged to me.

42"The noise of a carefree crowd was around her; Sabeans[b] were brought from the desert along with men from the rabble, and they put bracelets on the arms of the woman and her sister and beautiful crowns on their heads. 43Then I said about the one worn out by adultery, 'Now let them use her as a prostitute, for that is all she is.' 44And they slept with her. As men sleep with a prostitute, so they slept with those lewd women, Oholah and Oholibah. 45But righteous men will sentence them to the punishment of women who commit adultery and shed blood, because they are adulterous and blood is on their hands.

46"This is what the Sovereign LORD says: Bring a mob against them and give them over to terror and plunder. 47The mob will stone them and cut them down with their swords; they will kill their sons and daughters and burn down their houses.

48"So I will put an end to lewdness in the land, that all women may take warning and not imitate you. 49You will suffer the penalty for your lewdness and bear the consequences of your sins of idolatry. Then you will know that I am the Sovereign LORD."

The Cooking Pot

24 IN THE ninth year, in the tenth month on the tenth day, the word of the LORD came to me: 2"Son of man, record this date, this very date, because the king of Babylon has laid siege to Jerusalem this very day. 3Tell this rebellious house a parable and say to them: 'This is what the Sovereign LORD says:

" 'Put on the cooking pot; put it on
    and pour water into it.
4Put into it the pieces of meat,
    all the choice pieces—the leg and the
      shoulder.
Fill it with the best of these bones;
5 take the pick of the flock.
Pile wood beneath it for the bones;
    bring it to a boil
    and cook the bones in it.

---

a 37 Or *even made the children they bore to me pass through the fire*
b 42 Or *drunkards*

Living Bible

New Revised Standard

<table>
<tr><td>

36"Son of dust, you must accuse Jerusalem and Samaria of all their awful deeds. 37For they have committed both adultery and murder; they have worshiped idols and murdered my children whom they bore to me, burning them as sacrifices on their altars. 38On the same day they defiled my Temple and ignored my Sabbaths, 39for when they had murdered their children in front of their idols, then even that same day they actually came into my Temple to worship! That is how much regard they have for me!

40"You even sent away to distant lands for priests to come with other gods for you to serve, and they have come and been welcomed! You bathed yourself, painted your eyelids, and put on your finest jewels for them. 41You sat together on a beautifully embroidered bed and put my incense and my oil upon a table spread before you. 42From your apartment came the sound of many men carousing—lewd men and drunkards from the wilderness, who put bracelets on your wrists and beautiful crowns upon your head. 43Will they commit adultery with these who have become old harlot hags? 44Yet that is what they did. They went in to them—to Samaria and Jerusalem, these shameless harlots—with all the zest of lustful men who visit prostitutes. 45But just persons everywhere will judge them for what they really are—adulteresses and murderers. They will mete out to them the sentences the law demands.

46"The Lord God says: Bring an army against them and hand them out to be crushed and despised. 47For their enemies will stone them and kill them with swords; they will butcher their sons and daughters and burn their homes. 48Thus will I make lewdness and idolatry to cease from the land. My judgment will be a lesson against idolatry for all to see. 49For you will be fully repaid for all your harlotry, your worshiping of idols. You will suffer the full penalty, and you will know that I alone am God."

</td><td>

36 The LORD said to me: Mortal, will you judge Oholah and Oholibah? Then declare to them their abominable deeds. 37For they have committed adultery, and blood is on their hands; with their idols they have committed adultery; and they have even offered up to them for food the children whom they had borne to me. 38Moreover this they have done to me: they have defiled my sanctuary on the same day and profaned my sabbaths. 39For when they had slaughtered their children for their idols, on the same day they came into my sanctuary to profane it. This is what they did in my house.

40 They even sent for men to come from far away, to whom a messenger was sent, and they came. For them you bathed yourself, painted your eyes, and decked yourself with ornaments; 41you sat on a stately couch, with a table spread before it on which you had placed my incense and my oil. 42The sound of a raucous multitude was around her, with many of the rabble brought in drunken from the wilderness; and they put bracelets on the armsᶜ of the women, and beautiful crowns upon their heads.

43 Then I said, Ah, she is worn out with adulteries, but they carry on their sexual acts with her. 44For they have gone in to her, as one goes in to a whore. Thus they went in to Oholah and to Oholibah, wanton women. 45But righteous judges shall declare them guilty of adultery and of bloodshed; because they are adulteresses and blood is on their hands.

46 For thus says the Lord GOD: Bring up an assembly against them, and make them an object of terror and of plunder. 47The assembly shall stone them and with their swords they shall cut them down; they shall kill their sons and their daughters, and burn up their houses. 48Thus will I put an end to lewdness in the land, so that all women may take warning and not commit lewdness as you have done. 49They shall repay you for your lewdness, and you shall bear the penalty for your sinful idolatry; and you shall know that I am the Lord GOD.

</td></tr>
</table>

<table>
<tr><td>

24 ONE DAY late in December of the ninth year (of King Jehoiachin's captivity), another message came to me from the Lord.

2"Son of dust," he said, "write down this date, for today the king of Babylon has attacked Jerusalem. 3And now give this parable to these rebels, Israel; tell them the Lord God says: Put a pot of water on the fire to boil. 4Fill it with choicest mutton, the rump and shoulder and all the most tender cuts. 5Use only the best sheep from the flock, and heap fuel on the fire beneath the pot. Boil the meat well, until the flesh falls off the bones.

</td><td>

The Boiling Pot

24 IN THE ninth year, in the tenth month, on the tenth day of the month, the word of the LORD came to me: 2Mortal, write down the name of this day, this very day. The king of Babylon has laid siege to Jerusalem this very day. 3And utter an allegory to the rebellious house and say to them, Thus says the Lord GOD:

Set on the pot, set it on,
   pour in water also;
4 put in it the pieces,
   all the good pieces, the thigh and the
      shoulder;
   fill it with choice bones.
5 Take the choicest one of the flock,
   pile the logsᵈ under it;
boil its pieces,ᵉ
   seetheᶠ also its bones in it.

</td></tr>
</table>

ᶜ Heb *hands*   ᵈ Compare verse 10: Heb *the bones*   ᵉ Two Mss: Heb *its boilings*   ᶠ Cn: Heb *its bones seethe*

King James

6¶ Wherefore thus saith the Lord GOD; Woe to the bloody city, to the pot whose scum *is* therein, and whose scum is not gone out of it! bring it out piece by piece; let no lot fall upon it.

7For her blood is in the midst of her; she set it upon the top of a rock; she poured it not upon the ground, to cover it with dust;

8That it might cause fury to come up to take vengeance; I have set her blood upon the top of a rock, that it should not be covered.

9Therefore thus saith the Lord GOD; Woe to the bloody city! I will even make the pile for fire great.

10Heap on wood, kindle the fire, consume the flesh, and spice it well, and let the bones be burned.

11Then set it empty upon the coals thereof, that the brass of it may be hot, and may burn, and *that* the filthiness of it may be molten in it, *that* the scum of it may be consumed.

12She hath wearied *herself* with lies, and her great scum went not forth out of her: her scum *shall be* in the fire.

13In thy filthiness *is* lewdness: because I have purged thee, and thou wast not purged, thou shalt not be purged from thy filthiness any more, till I have caused my fury to rest upon thee.

14I the LORD have spoken *it:* it shall come to pass, and I will do *it;* I will not go back, neither will I spare, neither will I repent; according to thy ways, and according to thy doings, shall they judge thee, saith the Lord GOD.

15¶ Also the word of the LORD came unto me, saying,

16Son of man, behold, I take away from thee the desire of thine eyes with a stroke: yet neither shalt thou mourn nor weep, neither shall thy tears run down.

17Forbear to cry, make no mourning for the dead, bind the tire of thine head upon thee, and put on thy shoes upon thy feet, and cover not *thy* lips, and eat not the bread of men.

18So I spake unto the people in the morning: and at even my wife died; and I did in the morning as I was commanded.

19¶ And the people said unto me, Wilt thou not tell us what these *things are* to us, that thou doest *so?*

20Then I answered them, The word of the LORD came unto me, saying,

21Speak unto the house of Israel, Thus saith the Lord GOD; Behold, I will profane my sanctuary, the excellency of your strength, the desire of your eyes, and that which your soul pitieth; and your sons and your daughters whom ye have left shall fall by the sword.

22And ye shall do as I have done: ye shall not cover *your* lips, nor eat the bread of men.

23And your tires *shall be* upon your heads, and your shoes upon your feet: ye shall not mourn nor weep; but ye shall pine away for your iniquities, and mourn one toward another.

24Thus Ezekiel is unto you a sign: according to all that he hath done shall ye do: and when this cometh, ye shall know that I *am* the Lord GOD.

25Also, thou son of man, *shall it* not *be* in the day when I take from them their strength, the joy of their glory, the desire of their eyes, and that whereupon they set their minds, their sons and their daughters,

26*That* he that escapeth in that day shall come unto thee, to cause *thee* to hear *it* with *thine* ears?

New International

6 'For this is what the Sovereign LORD says:

" 'Woe to the city of bloodshed,
　to the pot now encrusted,
　whose deposit will not go away!
Empty it piece by piece
　without casting lots for them.

7" 'For the blood she shed is in her midst:
　She poured it on the bare rock;
　she did not pour it on the ground,
　where the dust would cover it.
8To stir up wrath and take revenge
　I put her blood on the bare rock,
　so that it would not be covered.

9 'Therefore this is what the Sovereign LORD says:

" 'Woe to the city of bloodshed!
　I, too, will pile the wood high.
10So heap on the wood
　and kindle the fire.
Cook the meat well,
　mixing in the spices;
　and let the bones be charred.
11Then set the empty pot on the coals
　till it becomes hot and its copper glows
　so its impurities may be melted
　and its deposit burned away.
12It has frustrated all efforts;
　its heavy deposit has not been removed,
　not even by fire.

13 'Now your impurity is lewdness. Because I tried to cleanse you but you would not be cleansed from your impurity, you will not be clean again until my wrath against you has subsided.

14 'I the LORD have spoken. The time has come for me to act. I will not hold back; I will not have pity, nor will I relent. You will be judged according to your conduct and your actions, declares the Sovereign LORD.' "

Ezekiel's Wife Dies

15The word of the LORD came to me: 16"Son of man, with one blow I am about to take away from you the delight of your eyes. Yet do not lament or weep or shed any tears. 17Groan quietly; do not mourn for the dead. Keep your turban fastened and your sandals on your feet; do not cover the lower part of your face or eat the customary food of mourners." "

18So I spoke to the people in the morning, and in the evening my wife died. The next morning I did as I had been commanded.

19Then the people asked me, "Won't you tell us what these things have to do with us?"

20So I said to them, "The word of the LORD came to me: 21Say to the house of Israel, 'This is what the Sovereign LORD says: I am about to desecrate my sanctuary—the stronghold in which you take pride, the delight of your eyes, the object of your affection. The sons and daughters you left behind will fall by the sword. 22And you will do as I have done. You will not cover the lower part of your face or eat the customary food of mourners. 23You will keep your turbans on your heads and your sandals on your feet. You will not mourn or weep but will waste away because of[a] your sins and groan among yourselves. 24Ezekiel will be a sign to you; you will do just as he has done. When this happens, you will know that I am the Sovereign LORD.'

25"And you, son of man, on the day I take away their stronghold, their joy and glory, the delight of their eyes, their heart's desire, and their sons and daughters as well— 26on that day a fugitive will come to tell you the news. 27At that time your mouth will be opened; you will

Living Bible

6"For the Lord God says: Woe to Jerusalem, City of Murderers; you are a pot that is pitted with rust and with wickedness. So take out the meat chunk by chunk in whatever order it comes—for none is better than any other.b 7For her wickedness is evident to all—she boldly murders, leaving blood upon the rocks in open view for all to see; she does not even try to cover it. 8And I have left it there, uncovered, to shout to me against her and arouse my wrath and vengeance.

9"Woe to Jerusalem, City of Murderers. I will pile on the fuel beneath her. 10Heap on the wood; let the fire roar and the pot boil. Cook the meat well and then empty the pot and burn the bones. 11Now set it empty on the coals to scorch away the rust and corruption. 12But all for naught—it all remains despite the hottest fire. 13It is the rust and corruption of your filthy lewdness, of worshiping your idols. And now, because I wanted to cleanse you and you refused, remain filthy until my fury has accomplished all its terrors upon you! 14I, the Lord, have spoken it; it shall come to pass and I will do it."

15Again a message came to me from the Lord, saying: 16"Son of dust, I am going to take away your lovely wife. Suddenly, she will die. Yet you must show no sorrow. Do not weep; let there be no tears. 17You may sigh, but only quietly. Let there be no wailing at her grave; don't bare your head nor feet, and don't accept the food brought to you by consoling friends."

18I proclaimed this to the people in the morning, and in the evening my wife died. The next morning I did all the Lord had told me to.

19Then the people said: "What does all this mean? What are you trying to tell us?"

20, 21And I answered, "The Lord told me to say to the people of Israel: I will destroy my lovely, beautiful Temple, the strength of your nation. And your sons and daughters in Judea will be slaughtered by the sword. 22And you will do as I have done; you may not mourn in public or console yourself by eating the food brought to you by sympathetic friends. 23Your head and feet shall not be bared; you shall not mourn or weep. But you will sorrow to one another for your sins, and mourn privately for all the evil you have done. 24Ezekiel is an example to you, the Lord God says. You will do as he has done. And when that time comes, then you will know I am the Lord."

25"Son of dust, on the day I finish taking from them in Jerusalem the joy of their hearts and their glory and joys—their wives and their sons and their daughters— 26on that day a refugee from Jerusalem will start on a journey to come to you in Babylon to tell you what has happened. 27And on the day of his arrival, your voice

New Revised Standard

6 Therefore thus says the Lord GOD:
   Woe to the bloody city,
      the pot whose rust is in it,
      whose rust has not gone out of it!
   Empty it piece by piece,
      making no choice at all.c
7 For the blood she shed is inside it;
      she placed it on a bare rock;
   she did not pour it out on the ground,
      to cover it with earth.
8 To rouse my wrath, to take vengeance,
   I have placed the blood she shed
      on a bare rock,
      so that it may not be covered.
9 Therefore thus says the Lord GOD:
   Woe to the bloody city!
      I will even make the pile great.
10 Heap up the logs, kindle the fire;
      boil the meat well, mix in the spices,
      let the bones be burned.
11 Stand it empty upon the coals,
      so that it may become hot, its copper glow,
      its filth melt in it, its rust be consumed.
12 In vain I have wearied myself;d
      its thick rust does not depart.
   To the fire with its rust!e
13 Yet, when I cleansed you in your filthy
         lewdness,
      you did not become clean from your filth;
      you shall not again be cleansed
      until I have satisfied my fury upon you.
14 I the LORD have spoken; the time is coming, I will act. I will not refrain, I will not spare, I will not relent. According to your ways and your doings I will judge you, says the Lord GOD.

Ezekiel's Bereavement

15 The word of the LORD came to me: 16Mortal, with one blow I am about to take away from you the delight of your eyes; yet you shall not mourn or weep, nor shall your tears run down. 17Sigh, but not aloud; make no mourning for the dead. Bind on your turban, and put your sandals on your feet; do not cover your upper lip or eat the bread of mourners.f 18So I spoke to the people in the morning, and at evening my wife died. And on the next morning I did as I was commanded.

19 Then the people said to me, "Will you not tell us what these things mean for us, that you are acting this way?" 20Then I said to them: The word of the LORD came to me: 21Say to the house of Israel, Thus says the Lord GOD: I will profane my sanctuary, the pride of your power, the delight of your eyes, and your heart's desire; and your sons and your daughters whom you left behind shall fall by the sword. 22And you shall do as I have done; you shall not cover your upper lip or eat the bread of mourners.f 23Your turbans shall be on your heads and your sandals on your feet; you shall not mourn or weep, but you shall pine away in your iniquities and groan to one another. 24Thus Ezekiel shall be a sign to you; you shall do just as he has done. When this comes, then you shall know that I am the Lord GOD.

25 And you, mortal, on the day when I take from them their stronghold, their joy and glory, the delight of their eyes and their heart's affection, and alsog their sons and their daughters, 26on that day, one who has escaped will come to you to report to you the news. 27On

---

b 24:6 *for none is better than any other*, literally, "no lot has fallen upon it."

c Heb *piece, no lot has fallen on it*   d Cn: Meaning of Heb uncertain   e Meaning of Heb uncertain   f Vg Tg: Heb *of men*   g Heb lacks *and also*

King James

27In that day shall thy mouth be opened to him which is escaped, and thou shalt speak, and be no more dumb: and thou shalt be a sign unto them; and they shall know that I *am* the LORD.

25 THE WORD of the LORD came again unto me, saying,

2Son of man, set thy face against the Ammonites, and prophesy against them;

3And say unto the Ammonites, Hear the word of the Lord GOD; Thus saith the Lord GOD; Because thou saidst, Aha, against my sanctuary, when it was profaned; and against the land of Israel, when it was desolate; and against the house of Judah, when they went into captivity;

4Behold, therefore I will deliver thee to the men of the east for a possession, and they shall set their palaces in thee, and make their dwellings in thee: they shall eat thy fruit, and they shall drink thy milk.

5And I will make Rabbah a stable for camels, and the Ammonites a couching place for flocks: and ye shall know that I *am* the LORD.

6For thus saith the Lord GOD; Because thou hast clapped *thine* hands, and stamped with the feet, and rejoiced in heart with all thy despite against the land of Israel;

7Behold, therefore I will stretch out mine hand upon thee, and will deliver thee for a spoil to the heathen; and I will cut thee off from the people, and I will cause thee to perish out of the countries: I will destroy thee; and thou shalt know that I *am* the LORD.

8¶ Thus saith the Lord GOD; Because that Moab and Seir do say, Behold, the house of Judah *is* like unto all the heathen;

9Therefore, behold, I will open the side of Moab from the cities, from his cities *which are* on his frontiers, the glory of the country, Beth-jeshimoth, Baal-meon, and Kiriathaim,

10Unto the men of the east with the Ammonites, and will give them in possession, that the Ammonites may not be remembered among the nations.

11And I will execute judgments upon Moab; and they shall know that I *am* the LORD.

12¶ Thus saith the Lord GOD; Because that Edom hath dealt against the house of Judah by taking vengeance, and hath greatly offended, and revenged himself upon them;

13Therefore thus saith the Lord GOD; I will also stretch out mine hand upon Edom, and will cut off man and beast from it; and I will make it desolate from Teman; and they of Dedan shall fall by the sword.

14And I will lay my vengeance upon Edom by the hand of my people Israel: and they shall do in Edom according to mine anger and according to my fury; and they shall know my vengeance, saith the Lord GOD.

15¶ Thus saith the Lord GOD; Because the Philistines have dealt by revenge, and have taken vengeance with a despiteful heart, to destroy *it* for the old hatred;

16Therefore thus saith the Lord GOD; Behold, I will stretch out mine hand upon the Philistines, and I will cut off the Cherethims, and destroy the remnant of the sea coast.

17And I will execute great vengeance upon them with furious rebukes; and they shall know that I *am* the LORD, when I shall lay my vengeance upon them.

New International

speak with him and will no longer be silent. So you will be a sign to them, and they will know that I am the LORD."

A Prophecy Against Ammon

25 THE WORD of the LORD came to me: 2"Son of man, set your face against the Ammonites and prophesy against them. 3Say to them, 'Hear the word of the Sovereign LORD. This is what the Sovereign LORD says: Because you said "Aha!" over my sanctuary when it was desecrated and over the land of Israel when it was laid waste and over the people of Judah when they went into exile, 4therefore I am going to give you to the people of the East as a possession. They will set up their camps and pitch their tents among you; they will eat your fruit and drink your milk. 5I will turn Rabbah into a pasture for camels and Ammon into a resting place for sheep. Then you will know that I am the LORD. 6For this is what the Sovereign LORD says: Because you have clapped your hands and stamped your feet, rejoicing with all the malice of your heart against the land of Israel, 7therefore I will stretch out my hand against you and give you as plunder to the nations. I will cut you off from the nations and exterminate you from the countries. I will destroy you, and you will know that I am the LORD.' "

A Prophecy Against Moab

8"This is what the Sovereign LORD says: 'Because Moab and Seir said, "Look, the house of Judah has become like all the other nations," 9therefore I will expose the flank of Moab, beginning at its frontier towns—Beth Jeshimoth, Baal Meon and Kiriathaim—the glory of that land. 10I will give Moab along with the Ammonites to the people of the East as a possession, so that the Ammonites will not be remembered among the nations; 11and I will inflict punishment on Moab. Then they will know that I am the LORD.' "

A Prophecy Against Edom

12"This is what the Sovereign LORD says: 'Because Edom took revenge on the house of Judah and became very guilty by doing so, 13therefore this is what the Sovereign LORD says: I will stretch out my hand against Edom and kill its men and their animals. I will lay it waste, and from Teman to Dedan they will fall by the sword. 14I will take vengeance on Edom by the hand of my people Israel, and they will deal with Edom in accordance with my anger and my wrath; they will know my vengeance, declares the Sovereign LORD.' "

A Prophecy Against Philistia

15"This is what the Sovereign LORD says: 'Because the Philistines acted in vengeance and took revenge with malice in their hearts, and with ancient hostility sought to destroy Judah, 16therefore this is what the Sovereign LORD says: I am about to stretch out my hand against the Philistines, and I will cut off the Kerethites and destroy those remaining along the coast. 17I will carry out great vengeance on them and punish them in my wrath. Then they will know that I am the LORD, when I take vengeance on them.' "

Living Bible

will suddenly return to you so that you can talk with him; and you will be a symbol for these people and they shall know I am the Lord."

25 THEN THE Lord's message came to me again. He said:

2"Son of dust, look toward the land of Ammon and prophesy against its people. 3Tell them: Listen to what the Lord God says. Because you scoffed when my Temple was destroyed, and mocked Israel in her anguish, and laughed at Judah when she was marched away captive, 4therefore I will let the Bedouins from the desert to the east of you overrun your land. They will set up their encampments among you. They will harvest all your fruit and steal your dairy cattle. 5And I will turn the city of Rabbah into a pasture for camels and all the country of the Ammonites into a waste land where flocks of sheep can graze. Then you will know I am the Lord.

6"For the Lord God says: Because you clapped and stamped and cheered with glee at the destruction of my people, 7therefore I will lay my hand heavily upon you, delivering you to many nations for devastation. I will cut you off from being a nation any more. I will destroy you; then you shall know I am the Lord.

8"And the Lord God says: Because the Moabites have said that Judah is no better off than any other nation, 9, 10therefore I will open up the eastern flank of Moab, wiping out her frontier cities, the glory of the nation— Beth-jeshimoth, Baal-meon and Kiriathaim. And Bedouin tribes from the desert to the east will pour in upon her, just as they will upon Ammon. And Moab will no longer be counted among the nations. 11Thus I will bring down my judgment upon the Moabites, and they shall know I am the Lord.

12"And the Lord God says: Because the people of Edom have sinned so greatly by avenging themselves upon the people of Judah, 13I will smash Edom with my fist and wipe out her people, her cattle and her flocks. The sword will destroy everything from Teman to Dedan. 14By the hand of my people, Israel, this shall be done. They will carry out my furious vengeance.

15"And the Lord God says: Because the Philistines have acted against Judah out of revenge and long-standing hatred, 16I will shake my fist over the land of the Philistines, and I will wipe out the Cherithites and utterly destroy those along the sea coast. 17I will execute terrible vengeance upon them to rebuke them for what they have done. And when all this happens, then they shall know I am the Lord."

New Revised Standard

that day your mouth shall be opened to the one who has escaped, and you shall speak and no longer be silent. So you shall be a sign to them; and they shall know that I am the LORD.

Proclamation against Ammon

25 THE WORD of the LORD came to me: 2Mortal, set your face toward the Ammonites and prophesy against them. 3Say to the Ammonites, Hear the word of the Lord GOD: Thus says the Lord GOD, Because you said, "Aha!" over my sanctuary when it was profaned, and over the land of Israel when it was made desolate, and over the house of Judah when it went into exile; 4therefore I am handing you over to the people of the east for a possession. They shall set their encampments among you and pitch their tents in your midst; they shall eat your fruit, and they shall drink your milk. 5I will make Rabbah a pasture for camels and Ammon a fold for flocks. Then you shall know that I am the LORD. 6For thus says the Lord GOD: Because you have clapped your hands and stamped your feet and rejoiced with all the malice within you against the land of Israel, 7therefore I have stretched out my hand against you, and will hand you over as plunder to the nations. I will cut you off from the peoples and will make you perish out of the countries; I will destroy you. Then you shall know that I am the LORD.

Proclamation against Moab

8 Thus says the Lord GOD: Because Moaba said, The house of Judah is like all the other nations, 9therefore I will lay open the flank of Moab from the townsb on its frontier, the glory of the country, Beth-jeshimoth, Baal-meon, and Kiriathaim. 10I will give it along with Ammon to the people of the east as a possession. Thus Ammon shall be remembered no more among the nations, 11and I will execute judgments upon Moab. Then they shall know that I am the LORD.

Proclamation against Edom

12 Thus says the Lord GOD: Because Edom acted revengefully against the house of Judah and has grievously offended in taking vengeance upon them, 13therefore thus says the Lord GOD, I will stretch out my hand against Edom, and cut off from it humans and animals, and I will make it desolate; from Teman even to Dedan they shall fall by the sword. 14I will lay my vengeance upon Edom by the hand of my people Israel; and they shall act in Edom according to my anger and according to my wrath; and they shall know my vengeance, says the Lord GOD.

Proclamation against Philistia

15 Thus says the Lord GOD: Because with unending hostilities the Philistines acted in vengeance, and with malice of heart took revenge in destruction; 16therefore thus says the Lord GOD, I will stretch out my hand against the Philistines, cut off the Cherethites, and destroy the rest of the seacoast. 17I will execute great vengeance on them with wrathful punishments. Then they shall know that I am the LORD, when I lay my vengeance on them.

---

a Gk Old Latin: Heb *Moab and Seir*   b Heb *towns from its towns*

King James

26 AND IT came to pass in the eleventh year, in the first *day* of the month, *that* the word of the LORD came unto me, saying,

2Son of man, because that Tyrus hath said against Jerusalem, Aha, she is broken *that was* the gates of the people: she is turned unto me: I shall be replenished, *now* she is laid waste:

3Therefore thus saith the Lord GOD; Behold, I *am* against thee, O Tyrus, and will cause many nations to come up against thee, as the sea causeth his waves to come up.

4And they shall destroy the walls of Tyrus, and break down her towers: I will also scrape her dust from her, and make her like the top of a rock.

5It shall be *a place for* the spreading of nets in the midst of the sea: for I have spoken *it*, saith the Lord GOD: and it shall become a spoil to the nations.

6And her daughters which *are* in the field shall be slain by the sword; and they shall know that I *am* the LORD.

7¶ For thus saith the Lord GOD; Behold, I will bring upon Tyrus Nebuchadrezzar king of Babylon, a king of kings, from the north, with horses, and with chariots, and with horsemen, and companies, and much people.

8He shall slay with the sword thy daughters in the field: and he shall make a fort against thee, and cast a mount against thee, and lift up the buckler against thee.

9And he shall set engines of war against thy walls, and with his axes he shall break down thy towers.

10By reason of the abundance of his horses their dust shall cover thee: thy walls shall shake at the noise of the horsemen, and of the wheels, and of the chariots, when he shall enter into thy gates, as men enter into a city wherein is made a breach.

11With the hoofs of his horses shall he tread down all thy streets: he shall slay thy people by the sword, and thy strong garrisons shall go down to the ground.

12And they shall make a spoil of thy riches, and make a prey of thy merchandise: and they shall break down thy walls, and destroy thy pleasant houses: and they shall lay thy stones and thy timber and thy dust in the midst of the water.

13And I will cause the noise of thy songs to cease; and the sound of thy harps shall be no more heard.

14And I will make thee like the top of a rock: thou shalt be *a place* to spread nets upon; thou shalt be built no more: for I the LORD have spoken *it*, saith the Lord GOD.

15¶ Thus saith the Lord GOD to Tyrus; Shall not the isles shake at the sound of thy fall, when the wounded cry, when the slaughter is made in the midst of thee?

16Then all the princes of the sea shall come down from their thrones, and lay away their robes, and put off their broidered garments: they shall clothe themselves with trembling; they shall sit upon the ground, and shall tremble at *every* moment, and be astonished at thee.

New International

A Prophecy Against Tyre

26 IN THE eleventh year, on the first day of the month, the word of the LORD came to me: 2"Son of man, because Tyre has said of Jerusalem, 'Aha! The gate to the nations is broken, and its doors have swung open to me; now that she lies in ruins I will prosper,' 3therefore this is what the Sovereign LORD says: I am against you, O Tyre, and I will bring many nations against you, like the sea casting up its waves. 4They will destroy the walls of Tyre and pull down her towers; I will scrape away her rubble and make her a bare rock. 5Out in the sea she will become a place to spread fishnets, for I have spoken, declares the Sovereign LORD. She will become plunder for the nations, 6and her settlements on the mainland will be ravaged by the sword. Then they will know that I am the LORD.

7"For this is what the Sovereign LORD says: From the north I am going to bring against Tyre Nebuchadnezzar[a] king of Babylon, king of kings, with horses and chariots, with horsemen and a great army. 8He will ravage your settlements on the mainland with the sword; he will set up siege works against you, build a ramp up to your walls and raise his shields against you. 9He will direct the blows of his battering rams against your walls and demolish your towers with his weapons. 10His horses will be so many that they will cover you with dust. Your walls will tremble at the noise of the war horses, wagons and chariots when he enters your gates as men enter a city whose walls have been broken through. 11The hoofs of his horses will trample all your streets; he will kill your people with the sword, and your strong pillars will fall to the ground. 12They will plunder your wealth and loot your merchandise; they will break down your walls and demolish your fine houses and throw your stones, timber and rubble into the sea. 13I will put an end to your noisy songs, and the music of your harps will be heard no more. 14I will make you a bare rock, and you will become a place to spread fishnets. You will never be rebuilt, for I the LORD have spoken, declares the Sovereign LORD.

15"This is what the Sovereign LORD says to Tyre: Will not the coastlands tremble at the sound of your fall, when the wounded groan and the slaughter takes place in you? 16Then all the princes of the coast will step down from their thrones and lay aside their robes and take off their embroidered garments. Clothed with terror, they will sit on the ground, trembling every moment, ap-

---

a 7 Hebrew *Nebuchadrezzar*, of which *Nebuchadnezzar* is a variant; here and often in Ezekiel and Jeremiah

Living Bible

26 ANOTHER MESSAGE came to me from the Lord on the first day of the month, in the eleventh year (after King Jehoiachin was taken away to captivity).

2"Son of dust, Tyre has rejoiced over the fall of Jerusalem, saying, 'Ha! She who controlled the lucrative north-south trade routes along the coast and along the course of the Jordan River[b] has been broken, and I have fallen heir! Because she has been laid waste, I shall become wealthy!'

3"Therefore the Lord God says: I stand against you, Tyre, and I will bring nations against you like ocean waves. 4They will destroy the walls of Tyre and tear down her towers. I will scrape away her soil and make her a bare rock! 5Her island shall become uninhabited, a place for fishermen to spread their nets, for I have spoken it, says the Lord God. Tyre shall become the prey of many nations, 6and her mainland city shall perish by the sword. Then they shall know I am the Lord.

7"For the Lord God says: I will bring Nebuchadnezzar, king of Babylon—the king of kings from the north—against Tyre with a great army and cavalry and chariots. 8First he will destroy your suburbs; then he will attack your mainland city by building a siege wall and raising a roof of shields against it. 9He will set up battering rams against your walls and with sledge hammers demolish your forts. 10The hoofs of his cavalry will choke the city with dust, and your walls will shake as the horses gallop through your broken gates, pulling chariots behind them. 11Horsemen will occupy every street in the city; they will butcher your people, and your famous, huge pillars will topple.

12"They will plunder all your riches and merchandise and break down your walls. They will destroy your lovely homes and dump your stones and timber and even your dust into the sea. 13I will stop the music of your songs. No more will there be the sound of harps among you. 14I will make your island a bare rock,[c] a place for fishermen to spread their nets. You will never be rebuilt, for I, the Lord, have spoken it. So says the Lord. 15The whole country will shake with your fall; the wounded will scream as the slaughter goes on.

16"Then all the seaport rulers shall come down from their thrones and lay aside their robes and beautiful garments and sit on the ground shaking with fear at what they have seen. 17And they shall wail for you, singing

New Revised Standard

Proclamation against Tyre

26 IN THE eleventh year, on the first day of the month, the word of the LORD came to me: 2Mortal, because Tyre said concerning Jerusalem,
"Aha, broken is the gateway of the peoples;
  it has swung open to me;
I shall be replenished,
  now that it is wasted."
3Therefore, thus says the Lord GOD:
See, I am against you, O Tyre!
  I will hurl many nations against you,
  as the sea hurls its waves.
4 They shall destroy the walls of Tyre
    and break down its towers.
  I will scrape its soil from it
    and make it a bare rock.
5 It shall become, in the midst of the sea,
    a place for spreading nets.
I have spoken, says the Lord GOD.
  It shall become plunder for the nations,
6   and its daughter-towns in the country
    shall be killed by the sword.
Then they shall know that I am the LORD.

7 For thus says the Lord GOD: I will bring against Tyre from the north King Nebuchadrezzar of Babylon, king of kings, together with horses, chariots, cavalry, and a great and powerful army.
8 Your daughter-towns in the country
    he shall put to the sword.
  He shall set up a siege wall against you,
    cast up a ramp against you,
    and raise a roof of shields against you.
9 He shall direct the shock of his battering rams
    against your walls
    and break down your towers with his axes.
10 His horses shall be so many
    that their dust shall cover you.
  At the noise of cavalry, wheels, and chariots
    your very walls shall shake,
  when he enters your gates
    like those entering a breached city.
11 With the hoofs of his horses
    he shall trample all your streets.
  He shall put your people to the sword,
    and your strong pillars shall fall to the
      ground.
12 They will plunder your riches
    and loot your merchandise;
  they shall break down your walls
    and destroy your fine houses.
  Your stones and timber and soil
    they shall cast into the water.
13 I will silence the music of your songs;
    the sound of your lyres shall be heard no
      more.
14 I will make you a bare rock;
    you shall be a place for spreading nets.
  You shall never again be rebuilt,
    for I the LORD have spoken,
    says the Lord GOD.

15 Thus says the Lord GOD to Tyre: Shall not the coastlands shake at the sound of your fall, when the wounded groan, when slaughter goes on within you? 16Then all the princes of the sea shall step down from their thrones; they shall remove their robes and strip off their embroidered garments. They shall clothe themselves with trembling, and shall sit on the ground; they shall tremble every moment, and be appalled at you.

---

b *26:2 the course of the Jordan River,* literally, "the gate of the peoples."
c *26:14 I will make your island a bare rock.* Certain aspects of vss 12 and 14 exceed the actual damage done to Tyre by Nebuchadnezzar, and foreshadow what happened to the island settlement later as a result of the conquest by Alexander the Great.

King James

17And they shall take up a lamentation for thee, and say to thee, How art thou destroyed, *that wast* inhabited of seafaring men, the renowned city, which wast strong in the sea, she and her inhabitants, which cause their terror *to be* on all that haunt it!

18Now shall the isles tremble in the day of thy fall; yea, the isles that *are* in the sea shall be troubled at thy departure.

19For thus saith the Lord GOD; When I shall make thee a desolate city, like the cities that are not inhabited; when I shall bring up the deep upon thee, and great waters shall cover thee;

20When I shall bring thee down with them that descend into the pit, with the people of old time, and shall set thee in the low parts of the earth, in places desolate of old, with them that go down to the pit, that thou be not inhabited; and I shall set glory in the land of the living;

21I will make thee a terror, and thou *shalt be* no *more:* though thou be sought for, yet shalt thou never be found again, saith the Lord GOD.

27 THE WORD of the LORD came again unto me, saying,

2Now, thou son of man, take up a lamentation for Tyrus;

3And say unto Tyrus, O thou that art situate at the entry of the sea, *which art* a merchant of the people for many isles, Thus saith the Lord GOD; O Tyrus, thou hast said, I *am* of perfect beauty.

4Thy borders *are* in the midst of the seas, thy builders have perfected thy beauty.

5They have made all thy *ship* boards of fir trees of Senir: they have taken cedars from Lebanon to make masts for thee.

6Of the oaks of Bashan have they made thine oars; the company of the Ashurites have made thy benches *of* ivory, *brought* out of the isles of Chittim.

7Fine linen with broidered work from Egypt was that which thou spreadest forth to be thy sail; blue and purple from the isles of Elishah was that which covered thee.

8The inhabitants of Zidon and Arvad were thy mariners: thy wise *men,* O Tyrus, *that* were in thee, were thy pilots.

9The ancients of Gebal and the wise *men* thereof were in thee thy calkers: all the ships of the sea with their mariners were in thee to occupy thy merchandise.

10They of Persia and of Lud and of Phut were in thine army, thy men of war: they hanged the shield and helmet in thee; they set forth thy comeliness.

11The men of Arvad with thine army *were* upon thy walls round about, and the Gammadims were in thy towers: they hanged their shields upon thy walls round about; they have made thy beauty perfect.

New International

palled at you. 17Then they will take up a lament concerning you and say to you:

" 'How you are destroyed, O city of renown,
    peopled by men of the sea!
You were a power on the seas,
    you and your citizens;
you put your terror
    on all who lived there.
18Now the coastlands tremble
    on the day of your fall;
the islands in the sea
    are terrified at your collapse.'

19"This is what the Sovereign LORD says: When I make you a desolate city, like cities no longer inhabited, and when I bring the ocean depths over you and its vast waters cover you, 20then I will bring you down with those who go down to the pit, to the people of long ago. I will make you dwell in the earth below, as in ancient ruins, with those who go down to the pit, and you will not return or take your placea in the land of the living. 21I will bring you to a horrible end and you will be no more. You will be sought, but you will never again be found, declares the Sovereign LORD."

A Lament for Tyre

27 THE WORD of the LORD came to me: 2"Son of man, take up a lament concerning Tyre. 3Say to Tyre, situated at the gateway to the sea, merchant of peoples on many coasts, 'This is what the Sovereign LORD says:

" 'You say, O Tyre,
    "I am perfect in beauty."
4Your domain was on the high seas;
    your builders brought your beauty to
        perfection.
5They made all your timbers
    of pine trees from Senirb;
they took a cedar from Lebanon
    to make a mast for you.
6Of oaks from Bashan
    they made your oars;
of cypress woodc from the coasts of Cyprusd
    they made your deck, inlaid with ivory.
7Fine embroidered linen from Egypt was your
        sail
    and served as your banner;
your awnings were of blue and purple
    from the coasts of Elishah.
8Men of Sidon and Arvad were your oarsmen;
    your skilled men, O Tyre, were aboard as
        your seamen.
9Veteran craftsmen of Gebale were on board
    as shipwrights to caulk your seams.
All the ships of the sea and their sailors
    came alongside to trade for your wares.

10" 'Men of Persia, Lydia and Put
    served as soldiers in your army.
They hung their shields and helmets on your
        walls,
    bringing you splendor.
11Men of Arvad and Helech
    manned your walls on every side;
men of Gammad
    were in your towers.
They hung their shields around your walls;
    they brought your beauty to perfection.

---

a 20 Septuagint; Hebrew *return, and I will give glory*   b 5 That is, Hermon
c 6 Targum; the Masoretic Text has a different division of the consonants.
d 6 Hebrew *Kittim*   e 9 That is, Byblos

Living Bible

this dirge: 'O mighty island city, with your naval power that terrorized the mainland, how you have vanished from the seas! 18How the islands tremble at your fall! They watch dismayed.'

19"For the Lord God says: I will destroy Tyre to the ground. You will sink beneath the terrible waves of enemy attack. Great seas shall swallow you. 20I will send you to the pit of hell to lie there with those of long ago. Your city will lie in ruins, dead, like the bodies of those in the underworld who entered long ago the nether world of the dead. Never again will you be inhabited or be given beauty here in the land of those who live. 21I will bring you to a dreadful end; no search will be enough to find you, says the Lord."

27 THEN THIS message came to me from the Lord. He said:

2"Son of dust, sing this sad dirge for Tyre:

3"O mighty seaport city, merchant center of the world, the Lord God speaks. You say, 'I am the most beautiful city in all the world.' 4You have extended your boundaries out into the sea; your architects have made you glorious. 5You are like a ship built of finest fir from Senir. They took a cedar from Lebanon to make a mast for you. 6They made your oars from oaks of Bashan. The walls of your cabin are of cypress from the southern coast of Cyprus. 7Your sails are made of Egypt's finest linens; you stand beneath awnings bright with purple and scarlet dyes from eastern Cyprus.

8"Your sailors come from Sidon and Arvad; your helmsmen are skilled men from Zemer. 9Wise old craftsmen from Gebal do the calking. Ships come from every land with all their goods to barter for your trade.

10"Your army includes men from far-off Paras, Lud and Put.f They serve you—it is a feather in your cap to have their shields hang upon your walls; it is the ultimate of honor. 11Men from Arvad and from Helechg are the sentinels upon your walls; your towers are manned by men from Gamad. Their shields hang row on row upon the walls, perfecting your glory.

New Revised Standard

17And they shall raise a lamentation over you, and say to you:

How you have vanishedh from the seas,
    O city renowned,
once mighty on the sea,
    you and your inhabitants,i
who imposed youri terror
    on all the mainland!k
18 Now the coastlands tremble
    on the day of your fall;
the coastlands by the sea
    are dismayed at your passing.

19 For thus says the Lord God: When I make you a city laid waste, like cities that are not inhabited, when I bring up the deep over you, and the great waters cover you, 20then I will thrust you down with those who descend into the Pit, to the people of long ago, and I will make you live in the world below, among primeval ruins, with those who go down to the Pit, so that you will not be inhabited or have a placel in the land of the living. 21I will bring you to a dreadful end, and you shall be no more; though sought for, you will never be found again, says the Lord God.

Lamentation over Tyre

27 THE WORD of the Lord came to me: 2Now you, mortal, raise a lamentation over Tyre, 3and say to Tyre, which sits at the entrance to the sea, merchant of the peoples on many coastlands, Thus says the Lord God:

O Tyre, you have said,
    "I am perfect in beauty."
4 Your borders are in the heart of the seas;
    your builders made perfect your beauty.
5 They made all your planks
    of fir trees from Senir;
they took a cedar from Lebanon
    to make a mast for you.
6 From oaks of Bashan
    they made your oars;
they made your deck of pinesm
    from the coasts of Cyprus,
    inlaid with ivory.
7 Of fine embroidered linen from Egypt
    was your sail,
    serving as your ensign;
blue and purple from the coasts of Elishah
    was your awning.
8 The inhabitants of Sidon and Arvad
    were your rowers;
skilled men of Zemern were within you,
    they were your pilots.
9 The elders of Gebal and its artisans were
        within you,
    caulking your seams;
all the ships of the sea with their mariners
        were within you,
    to barter for your wares.
10 Paraso and Lud and Put
    were in your army,
    your mighty warriors;
they hung shield and helmet in you;
    they gave you splendor.
11 Men of Arvad and Helechp
    were on your walls all around;
    men of Gamad were at your towers.
They hung their quivers all around your walls;
    they made perfect your beauty.

---

f 27:10 Paras, Lud and Put. These were three cities of ancient North Africa.
g 27:11 Helech, a region in ancient Cilicia known from Assyrian records as Hilakku.

h Gk OL Aquila: Heb *have vanished, O inhabited one,* i Heb *it and its inhabitants* j Heb *their* k Cn: Heb *its inhabitants* l Gk: Heb *I will give beauty* m Or *boxwood* n Cn Compare Gen 10.18: Heb *your skilled men, O Tyre* o Or *Persia* p Or *and your army*

King James

12Tarshish *was* thy merchant by reason of the multitude of all *kind of* riches; with silver, iron, tin, and lead, they traded in thy fairs.

13Javan, Tubal, and Meshech, they *were* thy merchants: they traded the persons of men and vessels of brass in thy market.

14They of the house of Togarmah traded in thy fairs with horses and horsemen and mules.

15The men of Dedan *were* thy merchants; many isles *were* the merchandise of thine hand: they brought thee *for* a present horns of ivory and ebony.

16Syria *was* thy merchant by reason of the multitude of the wares of thy making: they occupied in thy fairs with emeralds, purple, and broidered work, and fine linen, and coral, and agate.

17Judah, and the land of Israel, they *were* thy merchants: they traded in thy market wheat of Minnith, and Pannag, and honey, and oil, and balm.

18Damascus *was* thy merchant in the multitude of the wares of thy making, for the multitude of all riches; in the wine of Helbon, and white wool.

19Dan also and Javan going to and fro occupied in thy fairs: bright iron, cassia, and calamus, were in thy market.

20Dedan *was* thy merchant in precious clothes for chariots.

21Arabia, and all the princes of Kedar, they occupied with thee in lambs, and rams, and goats: in these *were* *they* thy merchants.

22The merchants of Sheba and Raamah, they *were* thy merchants: they occupied in thy fairs with chief of all spices, and with all precious stones, and gold.

23Haran, and Canneh, and Eden, the merchants of Sheba, Asshur, *and* Chilmad, *were* thy merchants.

24These *were* thy merchants in all sorts *of things*, in blue clothes, and broidered work, and in chests of rich apparel, bound with cords, and made of cedar, among thy merchandise.

25The ships of Tarshish did sing of thee in thy market: and thou wast replenished, and made very glorious in the midst of the seas.

26¶ Thy rowers have brought thee into great waters: the east wind hath broken thee in the midst of the seas.

27Thy riches, and thy fairs, thy merchandise, thy mariners, and thy pilots, thy calkers, and the occupiers of thy merchandise, and all thy men of war, that *are* in thee, and in all thy company which *is* in the midst of thee, shall fall into the midst of the seas in the day of thy ruin.

28The suburbs shall shake at the sound of the cry of thy pilots.

29And all that handle the oar, the mariners, *and* all the pilots of the sea, shall come down from their ships, they shall stand upon the land;

30And shall cause their voice to be heard against thee, and shall cry bitterly, and shall cast up dust upon their heads, they shall wallow themselves in the ashes:

31And they shall make themselves utterly bald for thee, and gird them with sackcloth, and they shall weep for thee with bitterness of heart *and* bitter wailing.

32And in their wailing they shall take up a lamentation for thee, and lament over thee, *saying*, What *city is* like Tyrus, like the destroyed in the midst of the sea?

New International

12" 'Tarshish did business with you because of your great wealth of goods; they exchanged silver, iron, tin and lead for your merchandise.

13" 'Greece, Tubal and Meshech traded with you; they exchanged slaves and articles of bronze for your wares.

14" 'Men of Beth Togarmah exchanged work horses, war horses and mules for your merchandise.

15" 'The men of Rhodes[a] traded with you, and many coastlands were your customers; they paid you with ivory tusks and ebony.

16" 'Aram[b] did business with you because of your many products; they exchanged turquoise, purple fabric, embroidered work, fine linen, coral and rubies for your merchandise.

17" 'Judah and Israel traded with you; they exchanged wheat from Minnith and confections,[c] honey, oil and balm for your wares.

18" 'Damascus, because of your many products and great wealth of goods, did business with you in wine from Helbon and wool from Zahar.

19" 'Danites and Greeks from Uzal bought your merchandise; they exchanged wrought iron, cassia and calamus for your wares.

20" 'Dedan traded in saddle blankets with you.

21" 'Arabia and all the princes of Kedar were your customers; they did business with you in lambs, rams and goats.

22" 'The merchants of Sheba and Raamah traded with you; for your merchandise they exchanged the finest of all kinds of spices and precious stones, and gold.

23" 'Haran, Canneh and Eden and merchants of Sheba, Asshur and Kilmad traded with you. 24In your marketplace they traded with you beautiful garments, blue fabric, embroidered work and multicolored rugs with cords twisted and tightly knotted.

25" 'The ships of Tarshish serve
as carriers for your wares.
You are filled with heavy cargo
in the heart of the sea.
26Your oarsmen take you
out to the high seas.
But the east wind will break you to pieces
in the heart of the sea.
27Your wealth, merchandise and wares,
your mariners, seamen and shipwrights,
your merchants and all your soldiers,
and everyone else on board
will sink into the heart of the sea
on the day of your shipwreck.
28The shorelands will quake
when your seamen cry out.
29All who handle the oars
will abandon their ships;
the mariners and all the seamen
will stand on the shore.
30They will raise their voice
and cry bitterly over you;
they will sprinkle dust on their heads
and roll in ashes.
31They will shave their heads because of you
and will put on sackcloth.
They will weep over you with anguish of soul
and with bitter mourning.
32As they wail and mourn over you,
they will take up a lament concerning you:
"Who was ever silenced like Tyre,
surrounded by the sea?"

---

a 15 Septuagint; Hebrew *Dedan*   b 16 Most Hebrew manuscripts; some Hebrew manuscripts and Syriac *Edom*   c 17 The meaning of the Hebrew for this word is uncertain.

Living Bible

12"From Tarshish come all kinds of riches to your markets—silver, iron, tin and lead. 13Merchants from Javan, Tubal and Meshechd bring slaves and bronze dishes, 14while from Togarmah come chariot horses, steeds and mules.

15"Merchants come to you from Rhodes, and many coastlands are your captive markets, giving payment in ebony and ivory. 16Edom sends her traders to buy your many wares. They bring emeralds, purple dyes, embroidery, fine linen, and jewelry of coral and agate. 17Judah and the cities in what was once the kingdom of Israel send merchants with wheat from Minnith and Pannag,e and with honey, oil and balm. 18Damascus comes. She brings wines from Helbon, and white Syrian wool to trade for all the rich variety of goods you make. 19Vedan and Javan bring Arabian yarn,f wrought iron, cassia and calamus, 20while Dedan brings expensive saddlecloths for riding.

21"The Arabians, and Kedar's wealthy merchant princes bring you lambs and rams and goats. 22The merchants of Sheba and Raamah come with all kinds of spices, jewels and gold. 23Haran and Canneh, Eden, Asshur and Chilmad all send their wares. 24They bring choice fabrics to trade—blue cloth, embroidery and many-colored carpets bound with cords and made secure. 25The ships of Tarshish are your ocean caravans; your island warehouse is filled to the brim!

26"But now your statesmen bring your ship of state into a hurricane! Your mighty vessel flounders in the heavy eastern gale,g and you are wrecked in the heart of the seas! 27Everything is lost. Your riches and wares, your sailors and pilots, your shipwrights and merchants and soldiers and all the people sink into the sea on the day of your vast ruin.

28"The surrounding cities quake at the sound as your pilots scream with fright. 29All your sailors out at sea come to land and watch upon the mainland shore, 30weeping bitterly and casting dust upon their heads and wallowing in ashes. 31They shave their heads in grief and put on sackcloth and weep for you with bitterness of heart and deep mourning.

32"And this is the song of their sorrow: 'Where in all the world was there ever such a wondrous city as Tyre, destroyed in the midst of the sea? 33Your merchandise

New Revised Standard

12 Tarshish did business with you out of the abundance of your great wealth; silver, iron, tin, and lead they exchanged for your wares. 13Javan, Tubal, and Meshech traded with you; they exchanged human beings and vessels of bronze for your merchandise. 14Beth-togarmah exchanged for your wares horses, war horses, and mules. 15The Rhodiansh traded with you; many coastlands were your own special markets; they brought you in payment ivory tusks and ebony. 16Edomi did business with you because of your abundant goods; they exchanged for your wares turquoise, purple, embroidered work, fine linen, coral, and rubies. 17Judah and the land of Israel traded with you; they exchanged for your merchandise wheat from Minnith, millet,j honey, oil, and balm. 18Damascus traded with you for your abundant goods—because of your great wealth of every kind—wine of Helbon, and white wool. 19Vedan and Javan from Uzalj entered into trade for your wares; wrought iron, cassia, and sweet cane were bartered for your merchandise. 20Dedan traded with you in saddlecloths for riding. 21Arabia and all the princes of Kedar were your favored dealers in lambs, rams, and goats; in these they did business with you. 22The merchants of Sheba and Raamah traded with you; they exchanged for your wares the best of all kinds of spices, and all precious stones, and gold. 23Haran, Canneh, Eden, the merchants of Sheba, Asshur, and Chilmad traded with you. 24These traded with you in choice garments, in clothes of blue and embroidered work, and in carpets of colored material, bound with cords and made secure; in these they traded with you.k 25The ships of Tarshish traveled for you in your trade.

So you were filled and heavily laden
   in the heart of the seas.
26 Your rowers have brought you
   into the high seas.
The east wind has wrecked you
   in the heart of the seas.
27 Your riches, your wares, your merchandise,
   your mariners and your pilots,
your caulkers, your dealers in merchandise,
   and all your warriors within you,
with all the company
   that is with you,
sink into the heart of the seas
   on the day of your ruin.
28 At the sound of the cry of your pilots
   the countryside shakes,
29 and down from their ships
   come all that handle the oar.
The mariners and all the pilots of the sea
   stand on the shore
30 and wail aloud over you,
   and cry bitterly.
They throw dust on their heads
   and wallow in ashes;
31 they make themselves bald for you,
   and put on sackcloth,
and they weep over you in bitterness of soul,
   with bitter mourning.
32 In their wailing they raise a lamentation for
   you,
   and lament over you:
"Who was ever destroyedl like Tyre
   in the midst of the sea?

---

d 27:13, 14 Javan, Tubal and Meshech . . . from Togarmah. Regions of Asia Minor, now in Turkey.   e 27:17 with wheat from Minnith and Pannag, or, "with wheat, minnith and pannag." If these were commodities, their identification is uncertain.   f 27:19 Vedan and Javan bring Arabian yarn, or, probably better, "They exchanged wine from Uzal for your wares." The text here is uncertain.   g 27:26 Your mighty vessel flounders in the heavy eastern gale, i.e., Nebuchadnezzar of Babylonia.

h Gk: Heb The Dedanites   i Another reading is Aram   j Meaning of Heb uncertain   k Cn: Heb in your market   l Tg Vg: Heb like silence

King James

33When thy wares went forth out of the seas, thou filledst many people; thou didst enrich the kings of the earth with the multitude of thy riches and of thy merchandise.

34In the time *when* thou shalt be broken by the seas in the depths of the waters thy merchandise and all thy company in the midst of thee shall fall.

35All the inhabitants of the isles shall be astonished at thee, and their kings shall be sore afraid, they shall be troubled in *their* countenance.

36The merchants among the people shall hiss at thee; thou shalt be a terror, and never *shalt be* any more.

28 THE WORD of the LORD came again unto me, saying,

2Son of man, say unto the prince of Tyrus, Thus saith the Lord GOD; Because thine heart *is* lifted up, and thou hast said, I *am* a God, I sit *in* the seat of God, in the midst of the seas; yet thou *art* a man, and not God, though thou set thine heart as the heart of God:

3Behold, thou *art* wiser than Daniel; there is no secret that they can hide from thee:

4With thy wisdom and with thine understanding thou hast gotten thee riches, and hast gotten gold and silver into thy treasures:

5By thy great wisdom *and* by thy traffic hast thou increased thy riches, and thine heart is lifted up because of thy riches:

6Therefore thus saith the Lord GOD; Because thou hast set thine heart as the heart of God;

7Behold, therefore I will bring strangers upon thee, the terrible of the nations: and they shall draw their swords against the beauty of thy wisdom, and they shall defile thy brightness.

8They shall bring thee down to the pit, and thou shalt die the deaths of *them that are* slain in the midst of the seas.

9Wilt thou yet say before him that slayeth thee, I *am* God? but thou *shalt be* a man, and no God, in the hand of him that slayeth thee.

10Thou shalt die the deaths of the uncircumcised by the hand of strangers: for I have spoken *it*, saith the Lord GOD.

11¶ Moreover the word of the LORD came unto me, saying,

12Son of man, take up a lamentation upon the king of Tyrus, and say unto him, Thus saith the Lord GOD; Thou sealest up the sum, full of wisdom, and perfect in beauty.

New International

33When your merchandise went out on the seas,
    you satisfied many nations;
with your great wealth and your wares
    you enriched the kings of the earth.
34Now you are shattered by the sea
    in the depths of the waters;
your wares and all your company
    have gone down with you.
35All who live in the coastlands
    are appalled at you;
their kings shudder with horror
    and their faces are distorted with fear.
36The merchants among the nations hiss at you;
    you have come to a horrible end
    and will be no more.' "

A Prophecy Against the King of Tyre

28 THE WORD of the LORD came to me: 2"Son of man, say to the ruler of Tyre, 'This is what the Sovereign LORD says:

" 'In the pride of your heart
    you say, "I am a god;
I sit on the throne of a god
    in the heart of the seas."
But you are a man and not a god,
    though you think you are as wise as a god.
3Are you wiser than Daniela?
    Is no secret hidden from you?
4By your wisdom and understanding
    you have gained wealth for yourself
and amassed gold and silver
    in your treasuries.
5By your great skill in trading
    you have increased your wealth,
and because of your wealth
    your heart has grown proud.

6" 'Therefore this is what the Sovereign LORD says:

" 'Because you think you are wise,
    as wise as a god,
7I am going to bring foreigners against you,
    the most ruthless of nations;
they will draw their swords against your beauty
    and wisdom
    and pierce your shining splendor.
8They will bring you down to the pit,
    and you will die a violent death
    in the heart of the seas.
9Will you then say, "I am a god,"
    in the presence of those who kill you?
You will be but a man, not a god,
    in the hands of those who slay you.
10You will die the death of the uncircumcised
    at the hands of foreigners.

I have spoken, declares the Sovereign LORD.' "

11The word of the LORD came to me: 12"Son of man, take up a lament concerning the king of Tyre and say to him: 'This is what the Sovereign LORD says:

" 'You were the model of perfection,
    full of wisdom and perfect in beauty.

---

a 3 Or *Danel*; the Hebrew spelling may suggest a person other than the prophet Daniel.

Living Bible

satisfied the desires of many nations. Kings at the ends of the earth rejoiced in the riches you sent them. 34Now you lie broken beneath the sea; all your merchandise and all your crew have perished with you. 35All who live along the coastlands watch, incredulous. Their kings are horribly afraid and look on with twisted faces. 36The merchants of the nations shake their heads, for your fate is dreadful; you have forever perished.' "

28 HERE IS another message given to me from the Lord:

2, 3"Son of dust, say to the prince of Tyre: The Lord God says: You are so proud you think you are God, sitting on the throne of a god on your island home in the midst of the seas. But you are only a man, and not a god, though you boast yourself to be like God. You are wiser than Daniel, for no secret is hidden from you. 4You have used your wisdom and understanding to get great wealth—gold and silver and many treasures. 5Yes, your wisdom has made you very rich and very proud.

6"Therefore the Lord God says: Because you claim that you are as wise as God, 7an enemy army, the terror of the nations, shall suddenly draw their swords against your marvelous wisdom and defile your splendor! 8They will bring you to the pit of hell and you shall die as those pierced with many wounds, there on your island in the heart of the seas. 9Then will you boast as a god? At least to these invaders you will be no god, but merely man! 10You will die like an outcast at the hands of foreigners. For I have spoken it, the Lord God says."

11Then this further message came to me from the Lord:

12"Son of dust, weep for the king of Tyre.b Tell him, the Lord God says: You were the perfection of wisdom and beauty. 13You were in Eden, the garden of God;

New Revised Standard

33 When your wares came from the seas,
    you satisfied many peoples;
with your abundant wealth and merchandise
    you enriched the kings of the earth.
34 Now you are wrecked by the seas,
    in the depths of the waters;
your merchandise and all your crew
    have sunk with you.
35 All the inhabitants of the coastlands
    are appalled at you;
and their kings are horribly afraid,
    their faces are convulsed.
36 The merchants among the peoples hiss at you;
    you have come to a dreadful end
    and shall be no more forever."

Proclamation against the King of Tyre

28 THE WORD of the LORD came to me: 2Mortal, say to the prince of Tyre, Thus says the Lord GOD:

Because your heart is proud
    and you have said, "I am a god;
I sit in the seat of the gods,
    in the heart of the seas,"
yet you are but a mortal, and no god,
    though you compare your mind
    with the mind of a god.
3 You are indeed wiser than Daniel;c
    no secret is hidden from you;
4 by your wisdom and your understanding
    you have amassed wealth for yourself,
and have gathered gold and silver
    into your treasuries.
5 By your great wisdom in trade
    you have increased your wealth,
    and your heart has become proud in your
        wealth.
6 Therefore thus says the Lord GOD:
Because you compare your mind
    with the mind of a god,
7 therefore, I will bring strangers against you,
    the most terrible of the nations;
they shall draw their swords against the beauty
        of your wisdom
    and defile your splendor.
8 They shall thrust you down to the Pit,
    and you shall die a violent death
    in the heart of the seas.
9 Will you still say, "I am a god,"
    in the presence of those who kill you,
though you are but a mortal, and no god,
    in the hands of those who wound you?
10 You shall die the death of the uncircumcised
    by the hand of foreigners;
    for I have spoken, says the Lord GOD.

Lamentation over the King of Tyre

11 Moreover the word of the LORD came to me: 12Mortal, raise a lamentation over the king of Tyre, and say to him, Thus says the Lord GOD:
You were the signet of perfection,d
    full of wisdom and perfect in beauty.

---

b 28:12 *weep for the king of Tyre.* In this passage (vss 11-19) some descriptive phrases apply to a human king of Tyre, and some seem to apply to Satan. Great care therefore must be taken to apply these verses with discernment.   c Or, as otherwise read, *Danel*   d Meaning of Heb uncertain

King James

13Thou hast been in Eden the garden of God; every precious stone *was* thy covering, the sardius, topaz, and the diamond, the beryl, the onyx, and the jasper, the sapphire, the emerald, and the carbuncle, and gold: the workmanship of thy tabrets and of thy pipes was prepared in thee in the day that thou wast created.

14Thou *art* the anointed cherub that covereth; and I have set thee *so:* thou wast upon the holy mountain of God; thou hast walked up and down in the midst of the stones of fire.

15Thou *wast* perfect in thy ways from the day that thou wast created, till iniquity was found in thee.

16By the multitude of thy merchandise they have filled the midst of thee with violence, and thou hast sinned: therefore I will cast thee as profane out of the mountain of God: and I will destroy thee, O covering cherub, from the midst of the stones of fire.

17Thine heart was lifted up because of thy beauty, thou hast corrupted thy wisdom by reason of thy brightness: I will cast thee to the ground, I will lay thee before kings, that they may behold thee.

18Thou hast defiled thy sanctuaries by the multitude of thine iniquities, by the iniquity of thy traffic; therefore will I bring forth a fire from the midst of thee, it shall devour thee, and I will bring thee to ashes upon the earth in the sight of all them that behold thee.

19All they that know thee among the people shall be astonished at thee: thou shalt be a terror, and never *shalt* thou *be* any more.

20¶ Again the word of the LORD came unto me, saying,

21Son of man, set thy face against Zidon, and prophesy against it,

22And say, Thus saith the Lord GOD; Behold, I *am* against thee, O Zidon; and I will be glorified in the midst of thee: and they shall know that I *am* the LORD, when I shall have executed judgments in her, and shall be sanctified in her.

23For I will send into her pestilence, and blood into her streets; and the wounded shall be judged in the midst of her by the sword upon her on every side; and they shall know that I *am* the LORD.

24¶ And there shall be no more a pricking brier unto the house of Israel, nor *any* grieving thorn of all *that are* round about them, that despised them; and they shall know that I *am* the Lord GOD.

25Thus saith the Lord GOD; When I shall have gathered the house of Israel from the people among whom they are scattered, and shall be sanctified in them in the sight of the heathen, then shall they dwell in their land that I have given to my servant Jacob.

26And they shall dwell safely therein, and shall build houses, and plant vineyards; yea, they shall dwell with confidence, when I have executed judgments upon all those that despise them round about them; and they shall know that I *am* the LORD their God.

New International

13You were in Eden,
    the garden of God;
every precious stone adorned you:
    ruby, topaz and emerald,
    chrysolite, onyx and jasper,
    sapphire,[a] turquoise and beryl.[b]
Your settings and mountings[c] were made of
        gold;
    on the day you were created they were
        prepared.
14You were anointed as a guardian cherub,
    for so I ordained you.
You were on the holy mount of God;
    you walked among the fiery stones.
15You were blameless in your ways
    from the day you were created
    till wickedness was found in you.
16Through your widespread trade
    you were filled with violence,
    and you sinned.
So I drove you in disgrace from the mount of
        God,
    and I expelled you, O guardian cherub,
    from among the fiery stones.
17Your heart became proud
    on account of your beauty,
and you corrupted your wisdom
    because of your splendor.
So I threw you to the earth;
    I made a spectacle of you before kings.
18By your many sins and dishonest trade
    you have desecrated your sanctuaries.
So I made a fire come out from you,
    and it consumed you,
and I reduced you to ashes on the ground
    in the sight of all who were watching.
19All the nations who knew you
    are appalled at you;
you have come to a horrible end
    and will be no more.' "

A Prophecy Against Sidon

20The word of the LORD came to me: 21"Son of man, set your face against Sidon; prophesy against her 22and say: 'This is what the Sovereign LORD says:

" 'I am against you, O Sidon,
    and I will gain glory within you.
They will know that I am the LORD,
    when I inflict punishment on her
    and show myself holy within her.
23I will send a plague upon her
    and make blood flow in her streets.
The slain will fall within her,
    with the sword against her on every side.
Then they will know that I am the LORD.

24" 'No longer will the people of Israel have malicious neighbors who are painful briers and sharp thorns. Then they will know that I am the Sovereign LORD.

25" 'This is what the Sovereign LORD says: When I gather the people of Israel from the nations where they have been scattered, I will show myself holy among them in the sight of the nations. Then they will live in their own land, which I gave to my servant Jacob. 26They will live there in safety and will build houses and plant vineyards; they will live in safety when I inflict punishment on all their neighbors who maligned them. Then they will know that I am the LORD their God.' "

---

a *13* Or *lapis lazuli*   b *13* The precise identification of some of these precious stones is uncertain.   c *13* The meaning of the Hebrew for this phrase is uncertain.

Living Bible

your clothing was bejeweled with every precious stone—ruby, topaz, diamond, chrysolite, onyx, jasper, sapphire, carbuncle, and emerald—all in beautiful settings of finest gold. They were given to you on the day you were created. 14I appointed you to be the anointed Guardian Angel. You had access to the holy mountain of God. You walked among the stones of fire.d

15"You were perfect in all you did from the day you were created until that time when wrong was found in you. 16Your great wealth filled you with internal turmoil and you sinned. Therefore, I cast you out of the mountain of God like a common sinner. I destroyed you, O Guardian Angel, from the midst of the stones of fire.e 17Your heart was filled with pride because of all your beauty; you corrupted your wisdom for the sake of your splendor. Therefore I have cast you down to the ground and exposed you helpless before the curious gaze of kings. 18You defiled your holiness with lust for gain;f therefore I brought forth fire from your own actionsg and let it burn you to ashes upon the earth in the sight of all those watching you. 19All who know you are appalled at your fate; you are an example of horror; you are destroyed forever."

20Then another message came to me from the Lord: 21"Son of dust, look toward the city of Sidon and prophesy against it. Say to it: 22"The Lord God says: I am your enemy, O Sidon, and I will reveal my power over you. When I destroy you and show forth my holiness upon you then all who see shall know I am the Lord. 23I will send an epidemic of disease and an army to destroy; the wounded shall be slain in your streets by troops on every side. Then you will know I am the Lord. 24No longer shall you and Israel's other neighbor nations prick and tear at Israel like thorns and briars, though they formerly despised her and treated her with great contempt.

25"The people of Israel will once more live in their own land, the land I gave their father Jacob. For I will gather them back again from distant lands where I have scattered them and I will show the nations of the world my holiness among my people. 26They will live safely in Israel, and build their homes and plant their vineyards. When I punish all the bordering nations that treated them with such contempt, then they shall know I am the Lord their God."

New Revised Standard

13 You were in Eden, the garden of God;
        every precious stone was your covering,
    carnelian, chrysolite, and moonstone,
        beryl, onyx, and jasper,
    sapphire,h turquoise, and emerald;
        and worked in gold were your settings
        and your engravings.i
    On the day that you were created
        they were prepared.
14 With an anointed cherub as guardian I placed you;i
        you were on the holy mountain of God;
        you walked among the stones of fire.
15 You were blameless in your ways
        from the day that you were created,
        until iniquity was found in you.
16 In the abundance of your trade
        you were filled with violence, and you sinned;
    so I cast you as a profane thing from the
        mountain of God,
        and the guardian cherub drove you out
        from among the stones of fire.
17 Your heart was proud because of your beauty;
        you corrupted your wisdom for the sake of
        your splendor.
    I cast you to the ground;
        I exposed you before kings,
        to feast their eyes on you.
18 By the multitude of your iniquities,
        in the unrighteousness of your trade,
        you profaned your sanctuaries.
    So I brought out fire from within you;
        it consumed you,
    and I turned you to ashes on the earth
        in the sight of all who saw you.
19 All who know you among the peoples
        are appalled at you;
    you have come to a dreadful end
        and shall be no more forever.

Proclamation against Sidon

20 The word of the LORD came to me: 21Mortal, set your face toward Sidon, and prophesy against it, 22and say, Thus says the Lord GOD:
    I am against you, O Sidon,
        and I will gain glory in your midst.
    They shall know that I am the LORD
        when I execute judgments in it,
        and manifest my holiness in it;
23 for I will send pestilence into it,
        and bloodshed into its streets;
    and the dead shall fall in its midst,
        by the sword that is against it on every side.
    And they shall know that I am the LORD.

24 The house of Israel shall no longer find a pricking brier or a piercing thorn among all their neighbors who have treated them with contempt. And they shall know that I am the Lord GOD.

Future Blessing for Israel

25 Thus says the Lord GOD: When I gather the house of Israel from the peoples among whom they are scattered, and manifest my holiness in them in the sight of the nations, then they shall settle on their own soil that I gave to my servant Jacob. 26They shall live in safety in it, and shall build houses and plant vineyards. They shall live in safety, when I execute judgments upon all their neighbors who have treated them with contempt. And they shall know that I am the LORD their God.

---

d 28:14 You walked among the stones of fire. Probably a symbol of the angels.
e 28:16 O Guardian Angel, from the midst of the stones of fire, or, "and the guardian cherub drove you out from the midst of the stones of fire."
f 28:18 with lust for gain, literally, "in the unrighteousness of your trade."
g 28:18 I brought forth fire from your own actions, literally, "I brought fire from the midst of you."

h Or lapis lazuli   i Meaning of Heb uncertain

King James

29 IN THE tenth year, in the tenth *month*, in the twelfth *day* of the month, the word of the LORD came unto me, saying,

2Son of man, set thy face against Pharaoh king of Egypt, and prophesy against him, and against all Egypt:

3Speak, and say, Thus saith the Lord GOD; Behold, I *am* against thee, Pharaoh king of Egypt, the great dragon that lieth in the midst of his rivers, which hath said, My river *is* mine own, and I have made *it* for myself.

4But I will put hooks in thy jaws, and I will cause the fish of thy rivers to stick unto thy scales, and I will bring thee up out of the midst of thy rivers, and all the fish of thy rivers shall stick unto thy scales.

5And I will leave thee *thrown* into the wilderness, thee and all the fish of thy rivers: thou shalt fall upon the open fields; thou shalt not be brought together, nor gathered: I have given thee for meat to the beasts of the field and to the fowls of the heaven.

6And all the inhabitants of Egypt shall know that I *am* the LORD, because they have been a staff of reed to the house of Israel.

7When they took hold of thee by thy hand, thou didst break, and rend all their shoulder: and when they leaned upon thee, thou brakest, and madest all their loins to be at a stand.

8¶ Therefore thus saith the Lord GOD; Behold, I will bring a sword upon thee, and cut off man and beast out of thee.

9And the land of Egypt shall be desolate and waste; and they shall know that I *am* the LORD: because he hath said, The river *is* mine, and I have made *it*.

10Behold, therefore I *am* against thee, and against thy rivers, and I will make the land of Egypt utterly waste *and* desolate, from the tower of Syene even unto the border of Ethiopia.

11No foot of man shall pass through it, nor foot of beast shall pass through it, neither shall it be inhabited forty years.

12And I will make the land of Egypt desolate in the midst of the countries *that are* desolate, and her cities among the cities *that are* laid waste shall be desolate forty years: and I will scatter the Egyptians among the nations, and will disperse them through the countries.

13¶ Yet thus saith the Lord GOD; At the end of forty years will I gather the Egyptians from the people whither they were scattered:

14And I will bring again the captivity of Egypt, and will cause them to return *into* the land of Pathros, into the land of their habitation; and they shall be there a base kingdom.

15It shall be the basest of the kingdoms; neither shall it exalt itself any more above the nations: for I will diminish them, that they shall no more rule over the nations.

16And it shall be no more the confidence of the house of Israel, which bringeth *their* iniquity to remembrance, when they shall look after them: but they shall know that I *am* the Lord GOD.

17¶ And it came to pass in the seven and twentieth year, in the first *month*, in the first *day* of the month, the word of the LORD came unto me, saying,

18Son of man, Nebuchadrezzar king of Babylon caused his army to serve a great service against Tyrus: every head *was* made bald, and every shoulder *was* peeled: yet had he no wages, nor his army, for Tyrus, for the service that he had served against it:

New International

A Prophecy Against Egypt

29 IN THE tenth year, in the tenth month on the twelfth day, the word of the LORD came to me: 2"Son of man, set your face against Pharaoh king of Egypt and prophesy against him and against all Egypt. 3Speak to him and say: 'This is what the Sovereign LORD says:

" 'I am against you, Pharaoh king of Egypt,
　you great monster lying among your streams.
You say, "The Nile is mine;
　I made it for myself."
4But I will put hooks in your jaws
　and make the fish of your streams stick to
　　your scales.
I will pull you out from among your streams,
　with all the fish sticking to your scales.
5I will leave you in the desert,
　you and all the fish of your streams.
You will fall on the open field
　and not be gathered or picked up.
I will give you as food
　to the beasts of the earth and the birds of the
　　air.

6Then all who live in Egypt will know that I am the LORD.

" 'You have been a staff of reed for the house of Israel. 7When they grasped you with their hands, you splintered and you tore open their shoulders; when they leaned on you, you broke and their backs were wrenched.[a]

8" 'Therefore this is what the Sovereign LORD says: I will bring a sword against you and kill your men and their animals. 9Egypt will become a desolate wasteland. Then they will know that I am the LORD.

" 'Because you said, "The Nile is mine; I made it," 10therefore I am against you and against your streams, and I will make the land of Egypt a ruin and a desolate waste from Migdol to Aswan, as far as the border of Cush.[b] 11No foot of man or animal will pass through it; no one will live there for forty years. 12I will make the land of Egypt desolate among devastated lands, and her cities will lie desolate forty years among ruined cities. And I will disperse the Egyptians among the nations and scatter them through the countries.

13" 'Yet this is what the Sovereign LORD says: At the end of forty years I will gather the Egyptians from the nations where they were scattered. 14I will bring them back from captivity and return them to Upper Egypt,[c] the land of their ancestry. There they will be a lowly kingdom. 15It will be the lowliest of kingdoms and will never again exalt itself above the other nations. I will make it so weak that it will never again rule over the nations. 16Egypt will no longer be a source of confidence for the people of Israel but will be a reminder of their sin in turning to her for help. Then they will know that I am the Sovereign LORD.' "

17In the twenty-seventh year, in the first month on the first day, the word of the LORD came to me: 18"Son of man, Nebuchadnezzar king of Babylon drove his army in a hard campaign against Tyre; every head was rubbed bare and every shoulder made raw. Yet he and his army got no reward from the campaign he led against Tyre.

Living Bible

29 LATE IN December of the tenth year (of the imprisonment of King Jehoiachin), this message came to me from the Lord:

2"Son of dust, face toward Egypt and prophesy against Pharaoh her king and all her people. 3Tell them that the Lord God says: I am your enemy, Pharaoh, king of Egypt—mighty dragon lying in the middle of your rivers. For you have said, 'The Nile is mine; I have made it for myself!' 4I will put hooks into your jaws and drag you out onto the land with fish sticking to your scales. 5And I will leave you and all the fish stranded in the desert to die, and you won't be buried, for I have given you as food to the wild animals and birds.

6"Because of the way your might collapsed when Israel called on you for aid [instead of trusting me], all of you shall know I am the Lord. 7Israel leaned on you but, like a cracked staff, you snapped beneath her hand and wrenched her shoulder out of joint and made her stagger with the pain. 8Therefore the Lord God says: I will bring an army against you, O Egypt, and destroy both men and herds. 9The land of Egypt shall become a desolate wasteland, and the Egyptians will know that I, the Lord, have done it.

10"Because you said: 'The Nile is mine! I made it!' therefore I am against you and your river and I will utterly destroy the land of Egypt, from Migdol to Syene, as far south as the border of Ethiopia. 11For forty years not a soul will pass that way, neither men nor animals. It will be completely uninhabited. 12I will make Egypt desolate, surrounded by desolate nations, and her cities will lie as wastelands for forty years. I will exile the Egyptians to other lands.

13"But the Lord God says that at the end of the forty years he will bring the Egyptians home again from the nations to which they will be banished. 14And I will restore the fortunes of Egypt and bring her people back to the land of Pathros in southern Egypt where they were born, but she will be an unimportant, minor kingdom. 15She will be the lowliest of all the nations; never again will she raise herself above the other nations; never again will Egypt be great enough for that.

16"Israel will no longer expect any help from Egypt. Whenever she thinks of asking for it, then she will remember her sin in seeking it before. Then Israel will know that I alone am God."

17In the twenty-seventh year of King Jehoiachin's captivity,d around the middle of March, this message came to me from the Lord:

18"Son of dust, the army of King Nebuchadnezzar of Babylon fought hard against Tyre. The soldiers' heads were bald (from carrying heavy basketfuls of earth); their shoulders were raw and blistered (from burdens of stones for the siege). And Nebuchadnezzar received no compensation and could not pay the army for all this work.e 19Therefore, the Lord God says, I will give the

New Revised Standard

Proclamation against Egypt

29 IN THE tenth year, in the tenth month, on the twelfth day of the month, the word of the LORD came to me: 2Mortal, set your face against Pharaoh king of Egypt, and prophesy against him and against all Egypt; 3speak, and say, Thus says the Lord GOD:

I am against you,
    Pharaoh king of Egypt,
the great dragon sprawling
    in the midst of its channels,
saying, "My Nile is my own;
    I made it for myself."
4 I will put hooks in your jaws,
    and make the fish of your channels stick to
        your scales.
I will draw you up from your channels,
    with all the fish of your channels
        sticking to your scales.
5 I will fling you into the wilderness,
    you and all the fish of your channels;
you shall fall in the open field,
    and not be gathered and buried.
To the animals of the earth and to the birds of
        the air
    I have given you as food.
6 Then all the inhabitants of Egypt shall know
        that I am the LORD
because youf were a staff of reed
    to the house of Israel;
7 when they grasped you with the hand, you
        broke,
    and tore all their shoulders;
and when they leaned on you, you broke,
    and made all their legs unsteady.g

8 Therefore, thus says the Lord GOD: I will bring a sword upon you, and will cut off from you human being and animal; 9and the land of Egypt shall be a desolation and a waste. Then they shall know that I am the LORD.

Because youh said, "The Nile is mine, and I made it," 10therefore, I am against you, and against your channels, and I will make the land of Egypt an utter waste and desolation, from Migdol to Syene, as far as the border of Ethiopia.i 11No human foot shall pass through it, and no animal foot shall pass through it; it shall be uninhabited forty years. 12I will make the land of Egypt a desolation among desolated countries; and her cities shall be a desolation forty years among cities that are laid waste. I will scatter the Egyptians among the nations, and disperse them among the countries.

13 Further, thus says the Lord GOD: At the end of forty years I will gather the Egyptians from the peoples among whom they were scattered; 14and I will restore the fortunes of Egypt, and bring them back to the land of Pathros, the land of their origin; and there they shall be a lowly kingdom. 15It shall be the most lowly of the kingdoms, and never again exalt itself above the nations; and I will make them so small that they will never again rule over the nations. 16The Egyptiansj shall never again be the reliance of the house of Israel; they will recall their iniquity, when they turned to them for aid. Then they shall know that I am the Lord GOD.

Babylonia Will Plunder Egypt

17 In the twenty-seventh year, in the first month, on the first day of the month, the word of the LORD came to me: 18Mortal, King Nebuchadrezzar of Babylon made his army labor hard against Tyre; every head was made bald and every shoulder was rubbed bare; yet neither he nor his army got anything from Tyre to pay for the labor that he had expended against it. 19Therefore thus says

---

d 29:17 *King Jehoiachin's captivity,* implied.   e 29:18 *and could not pay the army for all this work.* Tyre capitulated to Nebuchadnezzar at the end of a thirteen-year siege (587-574 B.C.) There was little left to pay the "salary" of Nebuchadnezzar, so the Lord was giving Egypt to him to make up for what he was "shortchanged" at Tyre.

f Gk Syr Vg: Heb *they*   g Syr: Heb *stand*   h Gk Syr Vg: Heb *he*   i Or Nubia; Heb *Cush*   j Heb *It*

King James

¹⁹Therefore thus saith the Lord GOD; Behold, I will give the land of Egypt unto Nebuchadrezzar king of Babylon; and he shall take her multitude, and take her spoil, and take her prey; and it shall be the wages for his army.

²⁰I have given him the land of Egypt *for* his labour wherewith he served against it, because they wrought for me, saith the Lord GOD.

²¹¶ In that day will I cause the horn of the house of Israel to bud forth, and I will give thee the opening of the mouth in the midst of them; and they shall know that I *am* the LORD.

30 THE WORD of the LORD came again unto me, saying,

²Son of man, prophesy and say, Thus saith the Lord GOD; Howl ye, Woe worth the day!

³For the day *is* near, even the day of the LORD *is* near, a cloudy day; it shall be the time of the heathen.

⁴And the sword shall come upon Egypt, and great pain shall be in Ethiopia, when the slain shall fall in Egypt, and they shall take away her multitude, and her foundations shall be broken down.

⁵Ethiopia, and Libya, and Lydia, and all the mingled people, and Chub, and the men of the land that is in league, shall fall with them by the sword.

⁶Thus saith the LORD; They also that uphold Egypt shall fall; and the pride of her power shall come down: from the tower of Syene shall they fall in it by the sword, saith the Lord GOD.

⁷And they shall be desolate in the midst of the countries *that are* desolate, and her cities shall be in the midst of the cities *that are* wasted.

⁸And they shall know that I *am* the LORD, when I have set a fire in Egypt, and *when* all her helpers shall be destroyed.

⁹In that day shall messengers go forth from me in ships to make the careless Ethiopians afraid, and great pain shall come upon them, as in the day of Egypt: for, lo, it cometh.

¹⁰Thus saith the Lord GOD; I will also make the multitude of Egypt to cease by the hand of Nebuchadrezzar king of Babylon.

¹¹He and his people with him, the terrible of the nations, shall be brought to destroy the land: and they shall draw their swords against Egypt, and fill the land with the slain.

¹²And I will make the rivers dry, and sell the land into the hand of the wicked: and I will make the land waste, and all that is therein, by the hand of strangers: I the LORD have spoken *it*.

New International

¹⁹Therefore this is what the Sovereign LORD says: I am going to give Egypt to Nebuchadnezzar king of Babylon, and he will carry off its wealth. He will loot and plunder the land as pay for his army. ²⁰I have given him Egypt as a reward for his efforts because he and his army did it for me, declares the Sovereign LORD.

²¹"On that day I will make a horn[a] grow for the house of Israel, and I will open your mouth among them. Then they will know that I am the LORD."

A Lament for Egypt

30 THE WORD of the LORD came to me: ²"Son of man, prophesy and say: 'This is what the Sovereign LORD says:

" 'Wail and say,
  "Alas for that day!"
³For the day is near,
  the day of the LORD is near—
a day of clouds,
  a time of doom for the nations.
⁴A sword will come against Egypt,
  and anguish will come upon Cush.[b]
When the slain fall in Egypt,
  her wealth will be carried away
  and her foundations torn down.

⁵Cush and Put, Lydia and all Arabia, Libya[c] and the people of the covenant land will fall by the sword along with Egypt.

⁶" 'This is what the LORD says:

" 'The allies of Egypt will fall
  and her proud strength will fail.
From Migdol to Aswan
  they will fall by the sword within her,
            declares the Sovereign LORD.
⁷" 'They will be desolate
  among desolate lands,
and their cities will lie
  among ruined cities.
⁸Then they will know that I am the LORD,
  when I set fire to Egypt
  and all her helpers are crushed.

⁹" 'On that day messengers will go out from me in ships to frighten Cush out of her complacency. Anguish will take hold of them on the day of Egypt's doom, for it is sure to come.

¹⁰" 'This is what the Sovereign LORD says:

" 'I will put an end to the hordes of Egypt
  by the hand of Nebuchadnezzar king of
    Babylon.
¹¹He and his army—the most ruthless of
    nations—
  will be brought in to destroy the land.
They will draw their swords against Egypt
  and fill the land with the slain.
¹²I will dry up the streams of the Nile
  and sell the land to evil men;
by the hand of foreigners
  I will lay waste the land and everything in it.

I the LORD have spoken.

---

^a *21 Horn* here symbolizes strength.   ^b *4* That is, the upper Nile region; also in verses 5 and 9   ^c *5* Hebrew *Cub*

Living Bible

land of Egypt to Nebuchadnezzar, king of Babylon, and he will carry off her wealth, plundering everything she has, for his army. [20]Yes, I have given him the land of Egypt for his salary, because he was working for me during those thirteen years at Tyre, says the Lord. [21]And the day will come when I will cause the ancient glory of Israel to revive, and then at last her words will be respected, and Egypt shall know I am the Lord."

30 ANOTHER MESSAGE from the Lord! [2, 3]"Son of dust, prophesy and say: The Lord God says, Weep, for the terrible day is almost here; the day of the Lord; a day of clouds and gloom; a day of despair for the nations! [4]A sword shall fall on Egypt; the slain shall cover the ground. Her wealth is taken away, her foundations destroyed. The land of Cush has been ravished. [5]For Cush and Put and Lud, Arabia and Libya and all the countries leagued with them shall perish in that war.

[6]"For the Lord says: All Egypt's allies shall fall, and the pride of her power shall end. From Migdol to Syene they shall perish by the sword. [7]She shall be desolate, surrounded by desolate nations, and her cities shall be in ruins, surrounded by other ruined cities. [8]And they will know I am the Lord when I have set Egypt on fire and destroyed her allies. [9]At that time I will send swift messengers to bring panic to the Ethiopians; great terror shall befall them at that time of Egypt's doom. This will all come true.

[10]"For the Lord God says: Nebuchadnezzar, king of Babylon, will destroy the multitudes of Egypt. [11]He and his armies—the terror of the nations—are sent to demolish the land. They shall war against Egypt and cover the ground with the slain. [12]I will dry up the Nile and sell the whole land to wicked men. I will destroy Egypt and everything in it, using foreigners to do it. I, the Lord, have spoken it.

New Revised Standard

the Lord GOD: I will give the land of Egypt to King Nebuchadrezzar of Babylon; and he shall carry off its wealth and despoil it and plunder it; and it shall be the wages for his army. [20]I have given him the land of Egypt as his payment for which he labored, because they worked for me, says the Lord GOD.

21 On that day I will cause a horn to sprout up for the house of Israel, and I will open your lips among them. Then they shall know that I am the LORD.

Lamentation for Egypt

30 THE WORD of the LORD came to me: [2]Mortal, prophesy, and say, Thus says the Lord GOD:
Wail, "Alas for the day!"
3   For a day is near,
    the day of the LORD is near;
  it will be a day of clouds,
    a time of doom[d] for the nations.
4   A sword shall come upon Egypt,
    and anguish shall be in Ethiopia,[e]
  when the slain fall in Egypt,
    and its wealth is carried away,
    and its foundations are torn down.
5 Ethiopia,[e] and Put, and Lud, and all Arabia, and Libya,[f] and the people of the allied lands[g] shall fall with them by the sword.

6   Thus says the LORD:
  Those who support Egypt shall fall,
    and its proud might shall come down;
  from Migdol to Syene
    they shall fall within it by the sword,
  says the Lord GOD.
7   They shall be desolated among other desolated
    countries,
  and their cities shall lie among cities laid
    waste.
8   Then they shall know that I am the LORD,
    when I have set fire to Egypt,
    and all who help it are broken.

9 On that day, messengers shall go out from me in ships to terrify the unsuspecting Ethiopians;[h] and anguish shall come upon them on the day of Egypt's doom;[i] for it is coming!

10 Thus says the Lord GOD:
  I will put an end to the hordes of Egypt,
    by the hand of King Nebuchadrezzar of
    Babylon.
11 He and his people with him, the most terrible
    of the nations,
  shall be brought in to destroy the land;
  and they shall draw their swords against
    Egypt,
    and fill the land with the slain.
12 I will dry up the channels,
    and will sell the land into the hand of
    evildoers;
  I will bring desolation upon the land and
    everything in it
    by the hand of foreigners;
  I the LORD have spoken.

---

[d] Heb lacks *of doom*   [e] Or *Nubia*; Heb *Cush*   [f] Compare Gk Syr Vg: Heb *Cub*   [g] Meaning of Heb uncertain   [h] Or *Nubians*; Heb *Cush*   [i] Heb *the day of Egypt*

King James

13Thus saith the Lord GOD; I will also destroy the idols, and I will cause *their* images to cease out of Noph; and there shall be no more a prince of the land of Egypt: and I will put a fear in the land of Egypt.

14And I will make Pathros desolate, and will set fire in Zoan, and will execute judgments in No.

15And I will pour my fury upon Sin, the strength of Egypt; and I will cut off the multitude of No.

16And I will set fire in Egypt: Sin shall have great pain, and No shall be rent asunder, and Noph *shall have* distresses daily.

17The young men of Aven and of Pi-beseth shall fall by the sword: and these *cities* shall go into captivity.

18At Tehaphnehes also the day shall be darkened, when I shall break there the yokes of Egypt: and the pomp of her strength shall cease in her: as for her, a cloud shall cover her, and her daughters shall go into captivity.

19Thus will I execute judgments in Egypt: and they shall know that I *am* the LORD.

20¶ And it came to pass in the eleventh year, in the first *month*, in the seventh *day* of the month, *that* the word of the LORD came unto me, saying,

21Son of man, I have broken the arm of Pharaoh king of Egypt; and, lo, it shall not be bound up to be healed, to put a roller to bind it, to make it strong to hold the sword.

22Therefore thus saith the Lord GOD; Behold, I *am* against Pharaoh king of Egypt, and will break his arms, the strong, and that which was broken; and I will cause the sword to fall out of his hand.

23And I will scatter the Egyptians among the nations, and will disperse them through the countries.

24And I will strengthen the arms of the king of Babylon, and put my sword in his hand: but I will break Pharaoh's arms, and he shall groan before him with the groanings of a deadly wounded *man*.

25But I will strengthen the arms of the king of Babylon, and the arms of Pharaoh shall fall down; and they shall know that I *am* the LORD, when I shall put my sword into the hand of the king of Babylon, and he shall stretch it out upon the land of Egypt.

26And I will scatter the Egyptians among the nations, and disperse them among the countries; and they shall know that I *am* the LORD.

New International

13" 'This is what the Sovereign LORD says:

" 'I will destroy the idols
    and put an end to the images in Memphis.a
No longer will there be a prince in Egypt,
    and I will spread fear throughout the land.
14I will lay waste Upper Egypt,b
    set fire to Zoan
    and inflict punishment on Thebes.c
15I will pour out my wrath on Pelusium,d
    the stronghold of Egypt,
    and cut off the hordes of Thebes.
16I will set fire to Egypt;
    Pelusium will writhe in agony.
Thebes will be taken by storm;
    Memphis will be in constant distress.
17The young men of Heliopolise and Bubastisf
    will fall by the sword,
    and the cities themselves will go into
        captivity.
18Dark will be the day at Tahpanhes
    when I break the yoke of Egypt;
    there her proud strength will come to an end.
She will be covered with clouds,
    and her villages will go into captivity.
19So I will inflict punishment on Egypt,
    and they will know that I am the LORD.' "

20In the eleventh year, in the first month on the seventh day, the word of the LORD came to me: 21"Son of man, I have broken the arm of Pharaoh king of Egypt. It has not been bound up for healing or put in a splint so as to become strong enough to hold a sword. 22Therefore this is what the Sovereign LORD says: I am against Pharaoh king of Egypt. I will break both his arms, the good arm as well as the broken one, and make the sword fall from his hand. 23I will disperse the Egyptians among the nations and scatter them through the countries. 24I will strengthen the arms of the king of Babylon and put my sword in his hand, but I will break the arms of Pharaoh, and he will groan before him like a mortally wounded man. 25I will strengthen the arms of the king of Babylon, but the arms of Pharaoh will fall limp. Then they will know that I am the LORD, when I put my sword into the hand of the king of Babylon and he brandishes it against Egypt. 26I will disperse the Egyptians among the nations and scatter them through the countries. Then they will know that I am the LORD."

A Cedar in Lebanon

31 AND IT came to pass in the eleventh year, in the third *month,* in the first *day* of the month, *that* the word of the LORD came unto me, saying,

31 IN THE eleventh year, in the third month on the first day, the word of the LORD came to me:

---

a 13 Hebrew *Noph*; also in verse 16   b 14 Hebrew *waste Pathros*
c 14 Hebrew *No*; also in verses 15 and 16   d 15 Hebrew *Sin*; also in verse
16   e 17 Hebrew *Awen* (or *On*)   f 17 Hebrew *Pi Beseth*

Living Bible

13"And I will smash the idols of Egypt and the images at Memphis, and there will be no king in Egypt; anarchy shall reign!

14"The cities of Pathros [along the upper Nileg], and Zoan and Thebes shall lie in ruins by my hand. 15And I will pour out my fury upon Pelusium, the strongest fortress of Egypt, and I will stamp out the people of Thebes. 16Yes, I will set fire to Egypt, Pelusium will be racked with pain, Thebes will be torn apart, Memphis will be in daily terror. 17The young men of Heliopolis and Bubastis shall die by the sword and the women will be taken away as slaves. 18When I come to break the power of Egypt it will be a dark day for Tehaphnehes too; a dark cloud will cover her, and her daughters will be taken away as captives. 19And so I will greatly punish Egypt and they shall know I am the Lord."

20A year later,h around the middle of March of the eleventh year of King Jehoiachin's captivity, this message came to me:

21"Son of dust, I have broken the arm of Pharaoh,i king of Egypt, and it has not been set nor put into a cast to make it strong enough to hold a sword again. 22For, the Lord God says, I am against Pharaoh, king of Egypt, and I will break both his arms—the strong one and the one that was broken before, and I will make his sword clatter to the ground. 23And I will banish the Egyptians to many lands. 24And I will strengthen the arms of the king of Babylon and place my sword in his hand. But I will break the arms of Pharaoh, king of Egypt, and he shall groan before the king of Babylon as one who has been wounded unto death. 25I will strengthen the hands of the king of Babylon, while the arms of Pharaoh fall useless to his sides. Yes, when I place my sword into the hand of the king of Babylon, and he swings it over the land of Egypt, Egypt shall know I am the Lord. 26I will scatter the Egyptians among the nations; then they shall know I am the Lord."

31 IN MID-MAY of the eleventh year of King Jehoiachin's captivity,j this message came to me from the Lord:

New Revised Standard

13 Thus says the Lord GOD:
  I will destroy the idols
    and put an end to the images in Memphis;
  there shall no longer be a prince in the land of
      Egypt;
    so I will put fear in the land of Egypt.
14 I will make Pathros a desolation,
    and will set fire to Zoan,
    and will execute acts of judgment on
      Thebes.
15 I will pour my wrath upon Pelusium,
    the stronghold of Egypt,
    and cut off the hordes of Thebes.
16 I will set fire to Egypt;
    Pelusium shall be in great agony;
  Thebes shall be breached,
    and Memphis face adversaries by day.
17 The young men of On and of Pi-beseth shall
      fall by the sword;
    and the cities themselvesk shall go into
      captivity.
18 At Tehaphnehes the day shall be dark,
    when I break there the dominion of Egypt,
  and its proud might shall come to an end;
    the cityl shall be covered by a cloud,
    and its daughter-towns shall go into
      captivity.
19 Thus I will execute acts of judgment on
      Egypt.
    Then they shall know that I am the LORD.

Proclamation against Pharaoh

20 In the eleventh year, in the first month, on the seventh day of the month, the word of the LORD came to me: 21Mortal, I have broken the arm of Pharaoh king of Egypt; it has not been bound up for healing or wrapped with a bandage, so that it may become strong to wield the sword. 22Therefore thus says the Lord GOD: I am against Pharaoh king of Egypt, and will break his arms, both the strong arm and the one that was broken; and I will make the sword fall from his hand. 23I will scatter the Egyptians among the nations, and disperse them throughout the lands. 24I will strengthen the arms of the king of Babylon, and put my sword in his hand; but I will break the arms of Pharaoh, and he will groan before him with the groans of one mortally wounded. 25I will strengthen the arms of the king of Babylon, but the arms of Pharaoh shall fall. And they shall know that I am the LORD, when I put my sword into the hand of the king of Babylon. He shall stretch it out against the land of Egypt, 26and I will scatter the Egyptians among the nations and disperse them throughout the countries. Then they shall know that I am the LORD.

The Lofty Cedar

31 IN THE eleventh year, in the third month, on the first day of the month, the word of the LORD

---

g 30:14 *along the upper Nile,* implied.   h 30:20 *A year later,* 587 B.C., the year Jerusalem fell to Nebuchadnezzar and was destroyed. *the eleventh year of King Jehoiachin's captivity,* literally, the eleventh year of our exile. i 30:21 *I have broken the arm of Pharaoh.* When Pharoah Hophra sent an army to relieve Jerusalem in 588 B.C., Nebuchadnezzar withdrew from the siege just long enough to defeat the Egyptian force. This is what Ezekiel means by the first "broken arm." j 31:1 *the eleventh year of King Jehoiachin's captivity,* implied. It was the year 587 B.C., the year Jerusalem fell.

k Heb *and they*   l Heb *she*

King James

²Son of man, speak unto Pharaoh king of Egypt, and to his multitude; Whom art thou like in thy greatness?

³¶ Behold, the Assyrian was a cedar in Lebanon with fair branches, and with a shadowing shroud, and of an high stature; and his top was among the thick boughs.

⁴The waters made him great, the deep set him up on high with her rivers running round about his plants, and sent out her little rivers unto all the trees of the field.

⁵Therefore his height was exalted above all the trees of the field, and his boughs were multiplied, and his branches became long because of the multitude of waters, when he shot forth.

⁶All the fowls of heaven made their nests in his boughs, and under his branches did all the beasts of the field bring forth their young, and under his shadow dwelt all great nations.

⁷Thus was he fair in his greatness, in the length of his branches: for his root was by great waters.

⁸The cedars in the garden of God could not hide him: the fir trees were not like his boughs, and the chestnut trees were not like his branches; nor any tree in the garden of God was like unto him in his beauty.

⁹I have made him fair by the multitude of his branches: so that all the trees of Eden, that were in the garden of God, envied him.

¹⁰¶ Therefore thus saith the Lord GOD; Because thou hast lifted up thyself in height, and he hath shot up his top among the thick boughs, and his heart is lifted up in his height;

¹¹I have therefore delivered him into the hand of the mighty one of the heathen; he shall surely deal with him: I have driven him out for his wickedness.

¹²And strangers, the terrible of the nations, have cut him off, and have left him: upon the mountains and in all the valleys his branches are fallen, and his boughs are broken by all the rivers of the land; and all the people of the earth are gone down from his shadow, and have left him.

¹³Upon his ruin shall all the fowls of the heaven remain, and all the beasts of the field shall be upon his branches:

¹⁴To the end that none of all the trees by the waters exalt themselves for their height, neither shoot up their top among the thick boughs, neither their trees stand up in their height, all that drink water: for they are all delivered unto death, to the nether parts of the earth, in the midst of the children of men, with them that go down to the pit.

¹⁵Thus saith the Lord GOD; In the day when he went down to the grave I caused a mourning: I covered the deep for him, and I restrained the floods thereof, and the great waters were stayed: and I caused Lebanon to mourn for him, and all the trees of the field fainted for him.

¹⁶I made the nations to shake at the sound of his fall, when I cast him down to hell with them that descend into the pit: and all the trees of Eden, the choice and best of Lebanon, all that drink water, shall be comforted in the nether parts of the earth.

New International

²"Son of man, say to Pharaoh king of Egypt and to his hordes:

" 'Who can be compared with you in majesty?
³Consider Assyria, once a cedar in Lebanon,
　　with beautiful branches overshadowing the
　　　　forest;
it towered on high,
　　its top above the thick foliage.
⁴The waters nourished it,
　　deep springs made it grow tall;
their streams flowed
　　all around its base
and sent their channels
　　to all the trees of the field.
⁵So it towered higher
　　than all the trees of the field;
its boughs increased
　　and its branches grew long,
　　spreading because of abundant waters.
⁶All the birds of the air
　　nested in its boughs,
all the beasts of the field
　　gave birth under its branches;
all the great nations
　　lived in its shade.
⁷It was majestic in beauty,
　　with its spreading boughs,
for its roots went down
　　to abundant waters.
⁸The cedars in the garden of God
　　could not rival it,
nor could the pine trees
　　equal its boughs,
nor could the plane trees
　　compare with its branches—
no tree in the garden of God
　　could match its beauty.
⁹I made it beautiful
　　with abundant branches,
the envy of all the trees of Eden
　　in the garden of God.

¹⁰" 'Therefore this is what the Sovereign LORD says: Because it towered on high, lifting its top above the thick foliage, and because it was proud of its height, ¹¹I handed it over to the ruler of the nations, for him to deal with according to its wickedness. I cast it aside, ¹²and the most ruthless of foreign nations cut it down and left it. Its boughs fell on the mountains and in all the valleys; its branches lay broken in all the ravines of the land. All the nations of the earth came out from under its shade and left it. ¹³All the birds of the air settled on the fallen tree, and all the beasts of the field were among its branches. ¹⁴Therefore no other trees by the waters are ever to tower proudly on high, lifting their tops above the thick foliage. No other trees so well-watered are ever to reach such a height; they are all destined for death, for the earth below, among mortal men, with those who go down to the pit.

¹⁵" 'This is what the Sovereign LORD says: On the day it was brought down to the graveᵃ I covered the deep springs with mourning for it; I held back its streams, and its abundant waters were restrained. Because of it I clothed Lebanon with gloom, and all the trees of the field withered away. ¹⁶I made the nations tremble at the sound of its fall when I brought it down to the grave with those who go down to the pit. Then all the trees of Eden, the choicest and best of Lebanon, all the trees that were well-watered, were consoled in the earth below. ¹⁷Those

---

ᵃ 15 Hebrew Sheol; also in verses 16 and 17

Living Bible

2, 3"Son of dust, tell Pharaoh, king of Egypt, and all his people: You are as Assyria was—a great and mighty nation—like a cedar of Lebanon, full of thick branches and forest shade, with its head high up among the clouds. 4Its roots went deep into the moist earth. It grew luxuriantly and gave streamlets of water to all the trees around. 5It towered above all the other trees. It prospered and grew long thick branches because of all the water at its roots. 6The birds nested in its branches, and in its shade the flocks and herds gave birth to young. All the great nations of the world lived beneath its shadow. 7It was strong and beautiful, for its roots went deep to water. 8This tree was taller than any other in the garden of God; no cypress had branches equal to it; none had boughs to compare; none equaled it in beauty. 9Because of the magnificence that I gave it, it was the envy of all the other trees of Eden.

10"But Egyptb has become proud and arrogant, the Lord God says. Therefore because she has set herself so high above the others, reaching to the clouds, 11I will deliver her into the hands of a mighty nation, to destroy her as her wickedness deserves. I, myself, will cut her down. 12A foreign army (from Babylon)—the terror of the nations—will invade her land and cut her down and leave her fallen on the ground. Her branches will be scattered across the mountains and valleys and rivers of the land. All those who live beneath her shade will go away and leave her lying there. 13The birds will pluck off her twigs and the wild animals will lie among her branches; 14let no other nation exult with pride for its own prosperity, though it be higher than the clouds, for all are doomed and they will land in hell, along with all the proud men of the world.

15"The Lord God says: When she fell I made the oceans mourn for her and restrained their tides.c I clothed Lebanon in black and caused the trees of Lebanon to weep. 16I made the nations shake with fear at the sound of her fall, for I threw her down to hell with all the others like her. And all the other proud trees of Eden, the choicest and the best of Lebanon, the ones whose roots went deep into the water, are comforted to find her there with them in hell. 17Her allies too are all destroyed

New Revised Standard

came to me: 2Mortal, say to Pharaoh king of Egypt and to his hordes:

Whom are you like in your greatness?
3   Consider Assyria, a cedar of Lebanon,
with fair branches and forest shade,
    and of great height,
    its top among the clouds.d
4 The waters nourished it,
    the deep made it grow tall,
making its rivers flowe
    around the place it was planted,
sending forth its streams
    to all the trees of the field.
5 So it towered high
    above all the trees of the field;
its boughs grew large
    and its branches long,
    from abundant water in its shoots.
6 All the birds of the air
    made their nests in its boughs;
under its branches all the animals of the field
    gave birth to their young;
and in its shade
    all great nations lived.
7 It was beautiful in its greatness,
    in the length of its branches;
for its roots went down
    to abundant water.
8 The cedars in the garden of God could not
    rival it,
    nor the fir trees equal its boughs;
the plane trees were as nothing
    compared with its branches;
no tree in the garden of God
    was like it in beauty.
9 I made it beautiful
    with its mass of branches,
    the envy of all the trees of Eden
    that were in the garden of God.

10 Therefore thus says the Lord GOD: Because itf towered high and set its top among the clouds,d and its heart was proud of its height, 11I gave it into the hand of the prince of the nations; he has dealt with it as its wickedness deserves. I have cast it out. 12Foreigners from the most terrible of the nations have cut it down and left it. On the mountains and in all the valleys its branches have fallen, and its boughs lie broken in all the watercourses of the land; and all the peoples of the earth went away from its shade and left it.

13 On its fallen trunk settle
    all the birds of the air,
    and among its boughs lodge
    all the wild animals.
14All this is in order that no trees by the waters may grow to lofty height or set their tops among the clouds,d and that no trees that drink water may reach up to them in height.

For all of them are handed over to death,
    to the world below;
along with all mortals,
    with those who go down to the Pit.

15 Thus says the Lord GOD: On the day it went down to Sheol I closed the deep over it and covered it; I restrained its rivers, and its mighty waters were checked. I clothed Lebanon in gloom for it, and all the trees of the field fainted because of it. 16I made the nations quake at the sound of its fall, when I cast it down to Sheol with those who go down to the Pit; and all the trees of Eden, the choice and best of Lebanon, all that were well watered, were consoled in the world below.

b 31:10 But Egypt, implied.   c 31:15 restrained their tides, literally, "the great waters were held back."

d Gk: Heb thick boughs   e Gk: Heb rivers going   f Syr Vg: Heb you

King James

17They also went down into hell with him unto *them that be* slain with the sword; and *they that were* his arm, *that* dwelt under his shadow in the midst of the heathen.

18¶ To whom art thou thus like in glory and in greatness among the trees of Eden? yet shalt thou be brought down with the trees of Eden unto the nether parts of the earth: thou shalt lie in the midst of the uncircumcised with *them that be* slain by the sword. This *is* Pharaoh and all his multitude, saith the Lord GOD.

32 AND IT came to pass in the twelfth year, in the twelfth month, in the first *day* of the month, *that* the word of the LORD came unto me, saying,

2Son of man, take up a lamentation for Pharaoh king of Egypt, and say unto him, Thou art like a young lion of the nations, and thou *art* as a whale in the seas: and thou camest forth with thy rivers, and troubledst the waters with thy feet, and fouledst their rivers.

3Thus saith the Lord GOD; I will therefore spread out my net over thee with a company of many people; and they shall bring thee up in my net.

4Then will I leave thee upon the land, I will cast thee forth upon the open field, and will cause all the fowls of the heaven to remain upon thee, and I will fill the beasts of the whole earth with thee.

5And I will lay thy flesh upon the mountains, and fill the valleys with thy height.

6I will also water with thy blood the land wherein thou swimmest, *even* to the mountains; and the rivers shall be full of thee.

7And when I shall put thee out, I will cover the heaven, and make the stars thereof dark; I will cover the sun with a cloud, and the moon shall not give her light.

8All the bright lights of heaven will I make dark over thee, and set darkness upon thy land, saith the Lord GOD.

9I will also vex the hearts of many people, when I shall bring thy destruction among the nations, into the countries which thou hast not known.

10Yea, I will make many people amazed at thee, and their kings shall be horribly afraid for thee, when I shall brandish my sword before them; and they shall tremble at *every* moment, every man for his own life, in the day of thy fall.

11¶ For thus saith the Lord GOD; The sword of the king of Babylon shall come upon thee.

12By the swords of the mighty will I cause thy multitude to fall, the terrible of the nations, all of them: and they shall spoil the pomp of Egypt, and all the multitude thereof shall be destroyed.

13I will destroy also all the beasts thereof from beside the great waters; neither shall the foot of man trouble them any more, nor the hoofs of beasts trouble them.

New International

who lived in its shade, its allies among the nations, had also gone down to the grave with it, joining those killed by the sword.

18" 'Which of the trees of Eden can be compared with you in splendor and majesty? Yet you, too, will be brought down with the trees of Eden to the earth below; you will lie among the uncircumcised, with those killed by the sword.

" 'This is Pharaoh and all his hordes, declares the Sovereign LORD.' "

A Lament for Pharaoh

32 IN THE twelfth year, in the twelfth month on the first day, the word of the LORD came to me: 2"Son of man, take up a lament concerning Pharaoh king of Egypt and say to him:

" 'You are like a lion among the nations;
    you are like a monster in the seas
thrashing about in your streams,
    churning the water with your feet
    and muddying the streams.

3" 'This is what the Sovereign LORD says:

" 'With a great throng of people
    I will cast my net over you,
    and they will haul you up in my net.
4I will throw you on the land
    and hurl you on the open field.
I will let all the birds of the air settle on you
    and all the beasts of the earth gorge
        themselves on you.
5I will spread your flesh on the mountains
    and fill the valleys with your remains.
6I will drench the land with your flowing blood
    all the way to the mountains,
    and the ravines will be filled with your flesh.
7When I snuff you out, I will cover the heavens
    and darken their stars;
I will cover the sun with a cloud,
    and the moon will not give its light.
8All the shining lights in the heavens
    I will darken over you;
    I will bring darkness over your land,
                    declares the Sovereign LORD.
9I will trouble the hearts of many peoples
    when I bring about your destruction among
        the nations,
    among[a] lands you have not known.
10I will cause many peoples to be appalled at you,
    and their kings will shudder with horror
        because of you
    when I brandish my sword before them.
On the day of your downfall
    each of them will tremble
    every moment for his life.

11" 'For this is what the Sovereign LORD says:

" 'The sword of the king of Babylon
    will come against you.
12I will cause your hordes to fall
    by the swords of mighty men—
    the most ruthless of all nations.
They will shatter the pride of Egypt,
    and all her hordes will be overthrown.
13I will destroy all her cattle
    from beside abundant waters
no longer to be stirred by the foot of man
    or muddied by the hoofs of cattle.

---

a 9 Hebrew; Septuagint *bring you into captivity among the nations, / to*

Living Bible

and perish with her. They went down with her to the
nether world—those nations that had lived beneath her
shade.

18"O Egypt, you are great and glorious among the
trees of Eden—the nations of the world. And you will
be brought down to the pit of hell with all these other
nations. You will be among the nations you despise,
killed by the sword. This is the fate of Pharaoh and all
his teeming masses, says the Lord."

32 IN MID-FEBRUARY of the twelfth year of
King Jehoiachin's captivity, this message came
to me from the Lord:

2"Son of dust, mourn for Pharaoh, king of Egypt, and
say to him: You think of yourself as a strong young lion
among the nations, but you are merely a crocodile[b]
along the banks of the Nile, making bubbles and muddying the stream.

3"The Lord God says: I will send a great army to catch
you with my net. I will haul you out, 4and leave you
stranded on the land to die. And all the birds of the
heavens will light upon you and the wild animals of the
whole earth will devour you until they are glutted and
full. 5And I will cover the hills with your flesh and fill
the valleys with your bones. 6And I will drench the earth
with your gushing blood, filling the ravines to the tops
of the mountains. 7I will blot you out, and I will veil the
heavens and darken the stars. I will cover the sun with
a cloud, and the moon shall not give you her light. 8Yes,
darkness will be everywhere across your land—even the
bright stars will be dark above you.

9"And when I destroy you,[c] grief will be in many
hearts among the distant nations you have never seen.
10Yes, terror shall strike in many lands, and their kings
shall be terribly afraid because of all I do to you. They
shall shudder with terror when I brandish my sword
before them. They shall greatly tremble for their lives
on the day of your fall.

11"For the Lord God says: The sword of the king of
Babylon shall come upon you. 12I will destroy you with
Babylon's mighty army—the terror of the nations. It
will smash the pride of Egypt and all her people; all will
perish. 13I will destroy all your flocks and herds that
graze beside the streams, and neither man nor animal
will disturb those waters any more. 14Therefore the wa-

New Revised Standard

17They also went down to Sheol with it, to those killed
by the sword, along with its allies,[d] those who lived in
its shade among the nations.

18 Which among the trees of Eden was like you in
glory and in greatness? Now you shall be brought down
with the trees of Eden to the world below; you shall lie
among the uncircumcised, with those who are killed by
the sword. This is Pharaoh and all his horde, says the
Lord GOD.

Lamentation over Pharaoh and Egypt

32 IN THE twelfth year, in the twelfth month, on
the first day of the month, the word of the LORD
came to me: 2Mortal, raise a lamentation over Pharaoh
king of Egypt, and say to him:
    You consider yourself a lion among the
        nations,
    but you are like a dragon in the seas;
    you thrash about in your streams,
        trouble the water with your feet,
        and foul your[e] streams.
3 Thus says the Lord GOD:
    In an assembly of many peoples
    I will throw my net over you;
        and I[f] will haul you up in my dragnet.
4 I will throw you on the ground,
        on the open field I will fling you,
    and will cause all the birds of the air to settle
        on you,
        and I will let the wild animals of the whole
            earth gorge themselves with you.
5 I will strew your flesh on the mountains,
        and fill the valleys with your carcass.[g]
6 I will drench the land with your flowing blood
        up to the mountains,
        and the watercourses will be filled with you.
7 When I blot you out, I will cover the heavens,
        and make their stars dark;
    I will cover the sun with a cloud,
        and the moon shall not give its light.
8 All the shining lights of the heavens
        I will darken above you,
        and put darkness on your land,
                            says the Lord GOD.
9 I will trouble the hearts of many peoples,
        as I carry you captive[h] among the nations,
        into countries you have not known.
10 I will make many peoples appalled at you;
        their kings shall shudder because of you.
    When I brandish my sword before them,
        they shall tremble every moment
    for their lives, each one of them,
        on the day of your downfall.
11 For thus says the Lord GOD:
    The sword of the king of Babylon shall come
        against you.
12 I will cause your hordes to fall
        by the swords of mighty ones,
        all of them most terrible among the nations.
    They shall bring to ruin the pride of Egypt,
        and all its hordes shall perish.
13 I will destroy all its livestock
        from beside abundant waters;
    and no human foot shall trouble them any
                            more,
        nor shall the hoofs of cattle trouble them.

---

b 32:2 crocodile, or, "sea serpent."   c 32:9 when I destroy you, or, "when
I carry you captive among the nations."

d Heb its arms   e Heb their   f Gk Vg: Heb they   g Symmachus Syr Vg:
Heb your height   h Gk: Heb bring your destruction

King James

14Then will I make their waters deep, and cause their rivers to run like oil, saith the Lord GOD.

15When I shall make the land of Egypt desolate, and the country shall be destitute of that whereof it was full, when I shall smite all them that dwell therein, then shall they know that I *am* the LORD.

16This *is* the lamentation wherewith they shall lament her: the daughters of the nations shall lament her: they shall lament for her, *even* for Egypt, and for all her multitude, saith the Lord GOD.

17¶ It came to pass also in the twelfth year, in the fifteenth *day* of the month, *that* the word of the LORD came unto me, saying,

18Son of man, wail for the multitude of Egypt, and cast them down, *even* her, and the daughters of the famous nations, unto the nether parts of the earth, with them that go down into the pit.

19Whom dost thou pass in beauty? go down, and be thou laid with the uncircumcised.

20They shall fall in the midst of *them that are* slain by the sword: she is delivered to the sword: draw her and all her multitudes.

21The strong among the mighty shall speak to him out of the midst of hell with them that help him: they are gone down, they lie uncircumcised, slain by the sword.

22Asshur *is* there and all her company: his graves *are* about him: all of them slain, fallen by the sword:

23Whose graves are set in the sides of the pit, and her company is round about her grave: all of them slain, fallen by the sword, which caused terror in the land of the living.

24There *is* Elam and all her multitude round about her grave, all of them slain, fallen by the sword, which are gone down uncircumcised into the nether parts of the earth, which caused their terror in the land of the living; yet have they borne their shame with them that go down to the pit.

25They have set her a bed in the midst of the slain with all her multitude: her graves *are* round about him: all of them uncircumcised, slain by the sword: though their terror was caused in the land of the living, yet have they borne their shame with them that go down to the pit: he is put in the midst of *them that be* slain.

26There *is* Meshech, Tubal, and all her multitude: her graves *are* round about him: all of them uncircumcised, slain by the sword, though they caused their terror in the land of the living.

27And they shall not lie with the mighty *that are* fallen of the uncircumcised, which are gone down to hell with their weapons of war: and they have laid their swords under their heads, but their iniquities shall be upon their bones, though *they were* the terror of the mighty in the land of the living.

28Yea, thou shalt be broken in the midst of the uncircumcised, and shalt lie with *them that are* slain with the sword.

29There *is* Edom, her kings, and all her princes, which with their might are laid by *them that were* slain by the sword: they shall lie with the uncircumcised, and with them that go down to the pit.

30There *be* the princes of the north, all of them, and all the Zidonians, which are gone down with the slain; with their terror they are ashamed of their might; and they lie uncircumcised with *them that be* slain by the sword, and bear their shame with them that go down to the pit.

New International

14Then I will let her waters settle
and make her streams flow like oil,
　　　　　declares the Sovereign LORD.
15When I make Egypt desolate
and strip the land of everything in it,
when I strike down all who live there,
then they will know that I am the LORD.'

16"This is the lament they will chant for her. The daughters of the nations will chant it; for Egypt and all her hordes they will chant it, declares the Sovereign LORD."

17In the twelfth year, on the fifteenth day of the month, the word of the LORD came to me: 18"Son of man, wail for the hordes of Egypt and consign to the earth below both her and the daughters of mighty nations, with those who go down to the pit. 19Say to them, 'Are you more favored than others? Go down and be laid among the uncircumcised.' 20They will fall among those killed by the sword. The sword is drawn; let her be dragged off with all her hordes. 21From within the gravea the mighty leaders will say of Egypt and her allies, 'They have come down and they lie with the uncircumcised, with those killed by the sword.'

22"Assyria is there with her whole army; she is surrounded by the graves of all her slain, all who have fallen by the sword. 23Their graves are in the depths of the pit and her army lies around her grave. All who had spread terror in the land of the living are slain, fallen by the sword.

24"Elam is there, with all her hordes around her grave. All of them are slain, fallen by the sword. All who had spread terror in the land of the living went down uncircumcised to the earth below. They bear their shame with those who go down to the pit. 25A bed is made for her among the slain, with all her hordes around her grave. All of them are uncircumcised, killed by the sword. Because their terror had spread in the land of the living, they bear their shame with those who go down to the pit; they are laid among the slain.

26"Meshech and Tubal are there, with all their hordes around their graves. All of them are uncircumcised, killed by the sword because they spread their terror in the land of the living. 27Do they not lie with the other uncircumcised warriors who have fallen, who went down to the grave with their weapons of war, whose swords were placed under their heads? The punishment for their sins rested on their bones, though the terror of these warriors had stalked through the land of the living.

28"You too, O Pharaoh, will be broken and will lie among the uncircumcised, with those killed by the sword.

29"Edom is there, her kings and all her princes; despite their power, they are laid with those killed by the sword. They lie with the uncircumcised, with those who go down to the pit.

30"All the princes of the north and all the Sidonians are there; they went down with the slain in disgrace despite the terror caused by their power. They lie uncircumcised with those killed by the sword and bear their shame with those who go down to the pit.

---

a 21 Hebrew *Sheol*; also in verse 27

Living Bible

ters of Egypt will be as clear and flow as smoothly as olive oil, the Lord God says. 15And when I destroy Egypt and wipe out everything she has, then she shall know that I, the Lord, have done it. 16Yes, cry for the sorrows of Egypt. Let all the nations weep for her and for her people, says the Lord."

17Two weeks later,b another message came to me from the Lord. He said:

18"Son of dust, weep for the people of Egypt and for the other mighty nations. Send them down to the nether world among the denizens of death. 19What nation is as beautiful as you, O Egypt? Yet your doom is the pit; you will be laid beside the people you despise. 20The Egyptians will die with the multitudes slain by the sword, for the sword is drawn against the land of Egypt. She will be drawn down to judgment. 21The mighty warriors in the nether world will welcome her as she arrives with all her friends, to lie there beside the nations she despised, all victims of the sword.

22"The princes of Assyria lie there surrounded by the graves of all her people, those the sword has slain. 23Their graves are in the depths of hell, surrounded by their allies. All these mighty men who once struck terror into the hearts of everyone are now dead at the hands of their foes.

24"Great kings of Elam lie there with their people. They scourged the nations while they lived, and now they lie undone in hell; their fate is the same as that of ordinary men. 25They have a resting place among the slain, surrounded by the graves of all their people. Yes, they terrorized the nations while they lived, but now they lie in shame in the pit, slain by the sword.

26"The princes of Meshech and Tubal are there, surrounded by the graves of all their armies—all of them idolaters—who once struck terror to the hearts of all; now they lie dead. 27They are buried in a common grave, and not as the fallen lords who are buried in great honor with their weapons beside them, with their shields covering them and their swords beneath their heads.c They were a terror to all while they lived. 28Now you will lie crushed and broken among the idolaters, among those who are slain by the sword.

29"Edom is there with her kings and her princes; mighty as they were, they too lie among the others whom the sword has slain, with the idolaters who have gone down to the pit. 30All the princes of the north are there, and the Sidonians, all slain. Once a terror, now they lie in shame; they lie in ignominy with all the other slain who go down to the pit.

New Revised Standard

14 Then I will make their waters clear,
      and cause their streams to run like oil, says
          the Lord GOD.
15 When I make the land of Egypt desolate
      and when the land is stripped of all that fills
          it,
    when I strike down all who live in it,
      then they shall know that I am the LORD.
16 This is a lamentation; it shall be chanted.
      The women of the nations shall chant it.
    Over Egypt and all its hordes they shall chant
        it,
      says the Lord GOD.

Dirge over Egypt

17 In the twelfth year, in the first month,d on the fifteenth day of the month, the word of the LORD came to me:

18 Mortal, wail over the hordes of Egypt,
      and send them down,
    with Egypte and the daughters of majestic
        nations,
    to the world below,
      with those who go down to the Pit.
19 "Whom do you surpass in beauty?
      Go down! Be laid to rest with the
          uncircumcised!"

20They shall fall among those who are killed by the sword. Egyptf has been handed over to the sword; carry away both it and its hordes. 21The mighty chiefs shall speak of them, with their helpers, out of the midst of Sheol: "They have come down, they lie still, the uncircumcised, killed by the sword."

22 Assyria is there, and all its company, their graves all around it, all of them killed, fallen by the sword. 23Their graves are set in the uttermost parts of the Pit. Its company is all around its grave, all of them killed, fallen by the sword, who spread terror in the land of the living.

24 Elam is there, and all its hordes around its grave; all of them killed, fallen by the sword, who went down uncircumcised into the world below, who spread terror in the land of the living. They bear their shame with those who go down to the Pit. 25They have made Elame a bed among the slain with all its hordes, their graves all around it, all of them uncircumcised, killed by the sword; for terror of them was spread in the land of the living, and they bear their shame with those who go down to the Pit; they are placed among the slain.

26 Meshech and Tubal are there, and all their multitude, their graves all around them, all of them uncircumcised, killed by the sword; for they spread terror in the land of the living. 27And they do not lie with the fallen warriors of long agog who went down to Sheol with their weapons of war, whose swords were laid under their heads, and whose shieldsh are upon their bones; for the terror of the warriors was in the land of the living. 28So you shall be broken and lie among the uncircumcised, with those who are killed by the sword.

29 Edom is there, its kings and all its princes, who for all their might are laid with those who are killed by the sword; they lie with the uncircumcised, with those who go down to the Pit.

30 The princes of the north are there, all of them, and all the Sidonians, who have gone down in shame with the slain, for all the terror that they caused by their might; they lie uncircumcised with those who are killed by the sword, and bear their shame with those who go down to the Pit.

---

b *32:17 Two weeks later*, literally, "In the twelfth year, on the fifteenth day of the month."   c *32:27 and their swords beneath their heads*, literally, "their iniquity (iniquities) upon their bones."

d Gk: Heb lacks *in the first month*   e Heb *it*   f Heb *It*   g Gk Old Latin: Heb *of the uncircumcised*   h Cn: Heb *iniquities*

King James

31Pharaoh shall see them, and shall be comforted over all his multitude, *even* Pharaoh and all his army slain by the sword, saith the Lord GOD.

32For I have caused my terror in the land of the living: and he shall be laid in the midst of the uncircumcised with *them that are* slain with the sword, *even* Pharaoh and all his multitude, saith the Lord GOD.

33 AGAIN THE word of the LORD came unto me, saying,

2Son of man, speak to the children of thy people, and say unto them, When I bring the sword upon a land, if the people of the land take a man of their coasts, and set him for their watchman:

3If when he seeth the sword come upon the land, he blow the trumpet, and warn the people;

4Then whosoever heareth the sound of the trumpet, and taketh not warning; if the sword come, and take him away, his blood shall be upon his own head.

5He heard the sound of the trumpet, and took not warning; his blood shall be upon him. But he that taketh warning shall deliver his soul.

6But if the watchman see the sword come, and blow not the trumpet, and the people be not warned; if the sword come, and take *any* person from among them, he is taken away in his iniquity; but his blood will I require at the watchman's hand.

7¶ So thou, O son of man, I have set thee a watchman unto the house of Israel; therefore thou shalt hear the word at my mouth, and warn them from me.

8When I say unto the wicked, O wicked *man,* thou shalt surely die; if thou dost not speak to warn the wicked from his way, that wicked *man* shall die in his iniquity; but his blood will I require at thine hand.

9Nevertheless, if thou warn the wicked of his way to turn from it; if he do not turn from his way, he shall die in his iniquity; but thou hast delivered thy soul.

10Therefore, O thou son of man, speak unto the house of Israel; Thus ye speak, saying, If our transgressions and our sins *be* upon us, and we pine away in them, how should we then live?

11Say unto them, As I live, saith the Lord GOD, I have no pleasure in the death of the wicked; but that the wicked turn from his way and live: turn ye, turn ye from your evil ways; for why will ye die, O house of Israel?

12Therefore, thou son of man, say unto the children of thy people, The righteousness of the righteous shall not deliver him in the day of his transgression: as for the wickedness of the wicked, he shall not fall thereby in the day that he turneth from his wickedness; neither shall the righteous be able to live for his *righteousness* in the day that he sinneth.

13When I shall say to the righteous, *that* he shall surely live; if he trust to his own righteousness, and commit iniquity, all his righteousnesses shall not be remembered; but for his iniquity that he hath committed, he shall die for it.

14Again, when I say unto the wicked, Thou shalt surely die; if he turn from his sin, and do that which is lawful and right;

15If the wicked restore the pledge, give again that he had robbed, walk in the statutes of life, without committing iniquity; he shall surely live, he shall not die.

16None of his sins that he hath committed shall be mentioned unto him: he hath done that which is lawful and right; he shall surely live.

17¶ Yet the children of thy people say, The way of the Lord is not equal: but as for them, their way is not equal.

18When the righteous turneth from his righteousness, and committeth iniquity, he shall even die thereby.

19But if the wicked turn from his wickedness, and do that which is lawful and right, he shall live thereby.

New International

31"Pharaoh—he and all his army—will see them and he will be consoled for all his hordes that were killed by the sword, declares the Sovereign LORD. 32Although I had him spread terror in the land of the living, Pharaoh and all his hordes will be laid among the uncircumcised, with those killed by the sword, declares the Sovereign LORD."

Ezekiel a Watchman

33 THE WORD of the LORD came to me: 2"Son of man, speak to your countrymen and say to them: 'When I bring the sword against a land, and the people of the land choose one of their men and make him their watchman, 3and he sees the sword coming against the land and blows the trumpet to warn the people, 4then if anyone hears the trumpet but does not take warning and the sword comes and takes his life, his blood will be on his own head. 5Since he heard the sound of the trumpet but did not take warning, his blood will be on his own head. If he had taken warning, he would have saved himself. 6But if the watchman sees the sword coming and does not blow the trumpet to warn the people and the sword comes and takes the life of one of them, that man will be taken away because of his sin, but I will hold the watchman accountable for his blood.'

7"Son of man, I have made you a watchman for the house of Israel; so hear the word I speak and give them warning from me. 8When I say to the wicked, 'O wicked man, you will surely die,' and you do not speak out to dissuade him from his ways, that wicked man will die fora his sin, and I will hold you accountable for his blood. 9But if you do warn the wicked man to turn from his ways and he does not do so, he will die for his sin, but you will have saved yourself.

10"Son of man, say to the house of Israel, 'This is what you are saying: "Our offenses and sins weigh us down, and we are wasting away because ofb them. How then can we live?"' 11Say to them, 'As surely as I live, declares the Sovereign LORD, I take no pleasure in the death of the wicked, but rather that they turn from their ways and live. Turn! Turn from your evil ways! Why will you die, O house of Israel?'

12"Therefore, son of man, say to your countrymen, 'The righteousness of the righteous man will not save him when he disobeys, and the wickedness of the wicked man will not cause him to fall when he turns from it. The righteous man, if he sins, will not be allowed to live because of his former righteousness.' 13If I tell the righteous man that he will surely live, but then he trusts in his righteousness and does evil, none of the righteous things he has done will be remembered; he will die for the evil he has done. 14And if I say to the wicked man, 'You will surely die,' but he then turns away from his sin and does what is just and right— 15if he gives back what he took in pledge for a loan, returns what he has stolen, follows the decrees that give life, and does no evil, he will surely live; he will not die. 16None of the sins he has committed will be remembered against him. He has done what is just and right; he will surely live.

17"Yet your countrymen say, 'The way of the Lord is not just.' But it is their way that is not just. 18If a righteous man turns from his righteousness and does evil, he will die for it. 19And if a wicked man turns away from his wickedness and does what is just and right, he will live by doing so. 20Yet, O house of Israel, you say,

---

a 8 Or *in*; also in verse 9   b 10 Or *away in*

Living Bible

31"When Pharaoh arrives, he will be comforted to find that he is not alone in having all his army slain, says the Lord God. 32For I have caused my terror to fall upon all the living. And Pharaoh and his army shall lie among the idolaters who are slain by the sword."

33 ONCE AGAIN a message came to me from the Lord. He said:

2"Son of dust, tell your people: When I bring an army against a country, and the people of that land choose a watchman, 3and when he sees the army coming, and blows the alarm to warn them, 4then anyone who hears the alarm and refuses to heed it—well, if he dies the fault is his own. 5For he heard the warning and wouldn't listen; the fault is his. If he had heeded the warning, he would have saved his life. 6But if the watchman sees the enemy coming and doesn't sound the alarm and warn the people, he is responsible for their deaths. They will die in their sins, but I will charge the watchman with their deaths.

7"So with you, son of dust. I have appointed you as a watchman for the people of Israel; therefore listen to what I say and warn them for me. 8When I say to the wicked, 'O wicked man, you will die!' and you don't tell him what I say, so that he does not repent—that wicked person will die in his sins, but I will hold you responsible for his death. 9But if you warn him to repent and he doesn't, he will die in his sin, and you will not be responsible.

10"O people of Israel, you are saying: 'Our sins are heavy upon us; we pine away with guilt. How can we live?' 11Tell them: As I live, says the Lord God, I have no pleasure in the death of the wicked; *I desire that the wicked turn from his evil ways and live*. Turn, turn from your wickedness, for why will you die, O Israel? 12For the good works of a righteous man will not save him if he turns to sin; and the sins of an evil man will not destroy him if he repents and turns from his sins.

13"I have said the good man will live. But if he sins, expecting his past goodness to save him, then none of his good deeds will be remembered. I will destroy him for his sins. 14And when I tell the wicked he will die and then he turns from his sins and does what is fair and right— 15if he gives back the borrower's pledge and returns what he has stolen and walks along the paths of right, not doing evil—he shall surely live. He shall not die. 16None of his past sins shall be brought up against him, for he has turned to the good and shall surely live.

17"And yet your people are saying the Lord isn't fair. The trouble is *they* aren't fair. 18For again I say, when the good man turns to evil, he shall die. 19But if the wicked turns from his wickedness and does what's fair and just, he shall live. 20Yet you are saying the Lord

New Revised Standard

31 When Pharaoh sees them, he will be consoled for all his hordes—Pharaoh and all his army, killed by the sword, says the Lord GOD. 32For hec spread terror in the land of the living; therefore he shall be laid to rest among the uncircumcised, with those who are slain by the sword—Pharaoh and all his multitude, says the Lord GOD.

Ezekiel Israel's Sentry

33 THE WORD of the LORD came to me: 2O Mortal, speak to your people and say to them, If I bring the sword upon a land, and the people of the land take one of their number as their sentinel; 3and if the sentinel sees the sword coming upon the land and blows the trumpet and warns the people; 4then if any who hear the sound of the trumpet do not take warning, and the sword comes and takes them away, their blood shall be upon their own heads. 5They heard the sound of the trumpet and did not take warning; their blood shall be upon themselves. But if they had taken warning, they would have saved their lives. 6But if the sentinel sees the sword coming and does not blow the trumpet, so that the people are not warned, and the sword comes and takes any of them, they are taken away in their iniquity, but their blood I will require at the sentinel's hand.

7 So you, mortal, I have made a sentinel for the house of Israel; whenever you hear a word from my mouth, you shall give them warning from me. 8If I say to the wicked, "O wicked ones, you shall surely die," and you do not speak to warn the wicked to turn from their ways, the wicked shall die in their iniquity, but their blood I will require at your hand. 9But if you warn the wicked to turn from their ways, and they do not turn from their ways, the wicked shall die in their iniquity, but you will have saved your life.

God's Justice and Mercy

10 Now you, mortal, say to the house of Israel, Thus you have said: "Our transgressions and our sins weigh upon us, and we waste away because of them; how then can we live?" 11Say to them, As I live, says the Lord GOD, I have no pleasure in the death of the wicked, but that the wicked turn from their ways and live; turn back, turn back from your evil ways; for why will you die, O house of Israel? 12And you, mortal, say to your people, The righteousness of the righteous shall not save them when they transgress; and as for the wickedness of the wicked, it shall not make them stumble when they turn from their wickedness; and the righteous shall not be able to live by their righteousnessd when they sin. 13Though I say to the righteous that they shall surely live, yet if they trust in their righteousness and commit iniquity, none of their righteous deeds shall be remembered; but in the iniquity that they have committed they shall die. 14Again, though I say to the wicked, "You shall surely die," yet if they turn from their sin and do what is lawful and right— 15if the wicked restore the pledge, give back what they have taken by robbery, and walk in the statutes of life, committing no iniquity—they shall surely live, they shall not die. 16None of the sins that they have committed shall be remembered against them; they have done what is lawful and right, they shall surely live.

17 Yet your people say, "The way of the Lord is not just," when it is their own way that is not just. 18When the righteous turn from their righteousness, and commit iniquity, they shall die for it.e 19And when the wicked turn from their wickedness, and do what is lawful and right, they shall live by it.e 20Yet you say, "The way

King James

20¶ Yet ye say, The way of the Lord is not equal. O ye house of Israel, I will judge you every one after his ways.

21And it came to pass in the twelfth year of our captivity, in the tenth *month*, in the fifth *day* of the month, *that* one that had escaped out of Jerusalem came unto me, saying, The city is smitten.

22Now the hand of the LORD was upon me in the evening, afore he that was escaped came; and had opened my mouth, until he came to me in the morning; and my mouth was opened, and I was no more dumb.

23Then the word of the LORD came unto me, saying, 24Son of man, they that inhabit those wastes of the land of Israel speak, saying, Abraham was one, and he inherited the land: but we *are* many; the land is given us for inheritance.

25Wherefore say unto them, Thus saith the Lord GOD; Ye eat with the blood, and lift up your eyes toward your idols, and shed blood: and shall ye possess the land? 26Ye stand upon your sword, ye work abomination, and ye defile every one his neighbour's wife: and shall ye possess the land?

27Say thou thus unto them, Thus saith the Lord GOD; As I live, surely they that *are* in the wastes shall fall by the sword, and him that *is* in the open field will I give to the beasts to be devoured, and they that *be* in the forts and in the caves shall die of the pestilence.

28For I will lay the land most desolate, and the pomp of her strength shall cease; and the mountains of Israel shall be desolate, that none shall pass through.

29Then shall they know that I *am* the LORD, when I have laid the land most desolate because of all their abominations which they have committed.

30¶ Also, thou son of man, the children of thy people still are talking against thee by the walls and in the doors of the houses, and speak one to another, every one to his brother, saying, Come, I pray you, and hear what is the word that cometh forth from the LORD.

31And they come unto thee as the people cometh, and they sit before thee *as* my people, and they hear thy words, but they will not do them: for with their mouth they show much love, *but* their heart goeth after their covetousness.

32And, lo, thou *art* unto them as a very lovely song of one that hath a pleasant voice, and can play well on an instrument: for they hear thy words, but they do them not.

33And when this cometh to pass, (lo, it will come,) then shall they know that a prophet hath been among them.

34 AND THE word of the LORD came unto me, saying,

2Son of man, prophesy against the shepherds of Israel, prophesy, and say unto them, Thus saith the Lord GOD unto the shepherds; Woe *be* to the shepherds of Israel that do feed themselves! should not the shepherds feed the flocks?

3Ye eat the fat, and ye clothe you with the wool, ye kill them that are fed: *but* ye feed not the flock.

4The diseased have ye not strengthened, neither have ye healed that which was sick, neither have ye bound up *that which was* broken, neither have ye brought again that which was driven away, neither have ye sought that which was lost; but with force and with cruelty have ye ruled them.

5And they were scattered, because *there is* no shepherd: and they became meat to all the beasts of the field, when they were scattered.

New International

'The way of the Lord is not just.' But I will judge each of you according to his own ways."

Jerusalem's Fall Explained

21In the twelfth year of our exile, in the tenth month on the fifth day, a man who had escaped from Jerusalem came to me and said, "The city has fallen!" 22Now the evening before the man arrived, the hand of the LORD was upon me, and he opened my mouth before the man came to me in the morning. So my mouth was opened and I was no longer silent.

23Then the word of the LORD came to me: 24"Son of man, the people living in those ruins in the land of Israel are saying, 'Abraham was only one man, yet he possessed the land. But we are many; surely the land has been given to us as our possession.' 25Therefore say to them, 'This is what the Sovereign LORD says: Since you eat meat with the blood still in it and look to your idols and shed blood, should you then possess the land? 26You rely on your sword, you do detestable things, and each of you defiles his neighbor's wife. Should you then possess the land?'

27"Say this to them: 'This is what the Sovereign LORD says: As surely as I live, those who are left in the ruins will fall by the sword, those out in the country I will give to the wild animals to be devoured, and those in strongholds and caves will die of a plague. 28I will make the land a desolate waste, and her proud strength will come to an end, and the mountains of Israel will become desolate so that no one will cross them. 29Then they will know that I am the LORD, when I have made the land a desolate waste because of all the detestable things they have done.'

30"As for you, son of man, your countrymen are talking together about you by the walls and at the doors of the houses, saying to each other, 'Come and hear the message that has come from the LORD.' 31My people come to you, as they usually do, and sit before you to listen to your words, but they do not put them into practice. With their mouths they express devotion, but their hearts are greedy for unjust gain. 32Indeed, to them you are nothing more than one who sings love songs with a beautiful voice and plays an instrument well, for they hear your words but do not put them into practice.

33"When all this comes true—and it surely will—then they will know that a prophet has been among them."

Shepherds and Sheep

34 THE WORD of the LORD came to me: 2"Son of man, prophesy against the shepherds of Israel; prophesy and say to them: 'This is what the Sovereign LORD says: Woe to the shepherds of Israel who only take care of themselves! Should not shepherds take care of the flock? 3You eat the curds, clothe yourselves with the wool and slaughter the choice animals, but you do not take care of the flock. 4You have not strengthened the weak or healed the sick or bound up the injured. You have not brought back the strays or searched for the lost. You have ruled them harshly and brutally. 5So they were scattered because there was no shepherd, and when they were scattered they became food for all the wild animals. 6My sheep wandered over all the mountains and

Living Bible

isn't fair. But I will judge each of you in accordance with his deeds."

21In the eleventh yeara of our exile, late in December, one of those who escaped from Jerusalem arrived to tell me, "The city has fallen!" 22Now the hand of the Lord had been upon me the previous evening, and he had healed me so that I could speak again by the time the man arrived.

23Then this message came to me:

24"Son of dust, the scattered remnants of Judah living among the ruined cities keep saying, 'Abraham was only one man and yet he got possession of the whole country! We are many, so we should certainly be able to get it back!' 25But the Lord God says: You are powerless, for you do evil! You eat meat with the blood; you worship idols, and murder. Do you suppose I'll let you have the land? 26Murderers! Idolators! Adulterers! Should you possess the land?

27"Tell them: The Lord God says: As I live, surely those living in the ruins shall die by the sword. Those living in the open fields shall be eaten by wild animals, and those in the forts and caves shall die of disease. 28I will desolate the land and her pride, and her power shall come to an end. And the mountain villages of Israel shall be so ruined that no one will even travel through them. 29When I have ruined the land because of their sins, then they shall know I am the Lord.

30"Son of dust, your people are whispering behind your back. They talk about you in their houses and whisper about you at the doors, saying, 'Come on, let's have some fun! Let's go hear him tell us what the Lord is saying!'b 31So they come as though they are sincere and sit before you listening. But they have no intention of doing what I tell them to; they talk very sweetly about loving the Lord, but with their hearts they are loving their money. 32You are very entertaining to them, like someone who sings lovely songs with a beautiful voice or plays well on an instrument. They hear what you say but don't pay any attention to it! 33But when all these terrible things happen to them—as they will—then they will know a prophet has been among them."

34 THEN THIS message came to me from the Lord:

2"Son of dust, prophesy against the shepherds, the leaders of Israel, and say to them: The Lord God says to you: Woe to the shepherds who feed themselves instead of their flocks. Shouldn't shepherds feed the sheep? 3You eat the best food and wear the finest clothes, but you let your flocks starve. 4You haven't taken care of the weak nor tended the sick nor bound up the broken bones nor gone looking for those who have wandered away and are lost. Instead you have ruled them with force and cruelty. 5So they were scattered, without a shepherd. They have become a prey to every animal that comes along. 6My sheep wandered through

New Revised Standard

of the Lord is not just." O house of Israel, I will judge all of you according to your ways!

The Fall of Jerusalem

21 In the twelfth year of our exile, in the tenth month, on the fifth day of the month, someone who had escaped from Jerusalem came to me and said, "The city has fallen." 22Now the hand of the LORD had been upon me the evening before the fugitive came; but he had opened my mouth by the time the fugitive came to me in the morning; so my mouth was opened, and I was no longer unable to speak.

The Survivors in Judah

23 The word of the LORD came to me: 24Mortal, the inhabitants of these waste places in the land of Israel keep saying, "Abraham was only one man, yet he got possession of the land; but we are many; the land is surely given us to possess." 25Therefore say to them, Thus says the Lord GOD: You eat flesh with the blood, and lift up your eyes to your idols, and shed blood; shall you then possess the land? 26You depend on your swords, you commit abominations, and each of you defiles his neighbor's wife; shall you then possess the land? 27Say this to them, Thus says the Lord GOD: As I live, surely those who are in the waste places shall fall by the sword; and those who are in the open field I will give to the wild animals to be devoured; and those who are in strongholds and in caves shall die by pestilence. 28I will make the land a desolation and a waste, and its proud might shall come to an end; and the mountains of Israel shall be so desolate that no one will pass through. 29Then they shall know that I am the LORD, when I have made the land a desolation and a waste because of all their abominations that they have committed.

30 As for you, mortal, your people who talk together about you by the walls, and at the doors of the houses, say to one another, each to a neighbor, "Come and hear what the word is that comes from the LORD." 31They come to you as people come, and they sit before you as my people, and they hear your words, but they will not obey them. For flattery is on their lips, but their heart is set on their gain. 32To them you are like a singer of love songs,c one who has a beautiful voice and plays well on an instrument; they hear what you say, but they will not do it. 33When this comes—and come it will!— then they shall know that a prophet has been among them.

Israel's False Shepherds

34 THE WORD of the LORD came to me: 2Mortal, prophesy against the shepherds of Israel: prophesy, and say to them—to the shepherds: Thus says the Lord GOD: Ah, you shepherds of Israel who have been feeding yourselves! Should not shepherds feed the sheep? 3You eat the fat, you clothe yourselves with the wool, you slaughter the fatlings; but you do not feed the sheep. 4You have not strengthened the weak, you have not healed the sick, you have not bound up the injured, you have not brought back the strayed, you have not sought the lost, but with force and harshness you have ruled them. 5So they were scattered, because there was no shepherd; and scattered, they became food for all the wild animals. 6My sheep were scattered, they wandered

---

a 33:21 *In the eleventh year.* Some manuscripts read, "In the twelfth year."
b 33:30 *Come on, let's have some fun! Let's go hear him tell us what the Lord is saying!* Literally, "Come and let us hear what the word is that comes from the Lord!"

c Cn: Heb *like a love song*

King James

6My sheep wandered through all the mountains, and upon every high hill: yea, my flock was scattered upon all the face of the earth, and none did search or seek *after them*.

7¶ Therefore, ye shepherds, hear the word of the LORD;

8*As* I live, saith the Lord GOD, surely because my flock became a prey, and my flock became meat to every beast of the field, because *there was* no shepherd, neither did my shepherds search for my flock, but the shepherds fed themselves, and fed not my flock;

9Therefore, O ye shepherds, hear the word of the LORD;

10Thus saith the Lord GOD; Behold, I *am* against the shepherds; and I will require my flock at their hand, and cause them to cease from feeding the flock; neither shall the shepherds feed themselves any more; for I will deliver my flock from their mouth, that they may not be meat for them.

11¶ For thus saith the Lord GOD; Behold, I, *even* I, will both search my sheep, and seek them out.

12As a shepherd seeketh out his flock in the day that he is among his sheep *that are* scattered; so will I seek out my sheep, and will deliver them out of all places where they have been scattered in the cloudy and dark day.

13And I will bring them out from the people, and gather them from the countries, and will bring them to their own land, and feed them upon the mountains of Israel by the rivers, and in all the inhabited places of the country.

14I will feed them in a good pasture, and upon the high mountains of Israel shall their fold be: there shall they lie in a good fold, and *in* a fat pasture shall they feed upon the mountains of Israel.

15I will feed my flock, and I will cause them to lie down, saith the Lord GOD.

16I will seek that which was lost, and bring again that which was driven away, and will bind up *that which was* broken, and will strengthen that which was sick: but I will destroy the fat and the strong; I will feed them with judgment.

17And *as for* you, O my flock, thus saith the Lord GOD; Behold, I judge between cattle and cattle, between the rams and the he goats.

18*Seemeth it* a small thing unto you to have eaten up the good pasture, but ye must tread down with your feet the residue of your pastures? and to have drunk of the deep waters, but ye must foul the residue with your feet?

19And *as for* my flock, they eat that which ye have trodden with your feet; and they drink that which ye have fouled with your feet.

20¶ Therefore thus saith the Lord GOD unto them; Behold, I, *even* I, will judge between the fat cattle and between the lean cattle.

21Because ye have thrust with side and with shoulder, and pushed all the diseased with your horns, till ye have scattered them abroad;

22Therefore will I save my flock, and they shall no more be a prey; and I will judge between cattle and cattle.

23And I will set up one shepherd over them, and he shall feed them, *even* my servant David; he shall feed them, and he shall be their shepherd.

24And I the LORD will be their God, and my servant David a prince among them; I the LORD have spoken *it*.

25And I will make with them a covenant of peace, and will cause the evil beasts to cease out of the land: and they shall dwell safely in the wilderness, and sleep in the woods.

26And I will make them and the places round about my hill a blessing; and I will cause the shower to come down in his season; there shall be showers of blessing.

New International

on every high hill. They were scattered over the whole earth, and no one searched or looked for them.

7" 'Therefore, you shepherds, hear the word of the LORD: 8As surely as I live, declares the Sovereign LORD, because my flock lacks a shepherd and so has been plundered and has become food for all the wild animals, and because my shepherds did not search for my flock but cared for themselves rather than for my flock, 9therefore, O shepherds, hear the word of the LORD: 10This is what the Sovereign LORD says: I am against the shepherds and will hold them accountable for my flock. I will remove them from tending the flock so that the shepherds can no longer feed themselves. I will rescue my flock from their mouths, and it will no longer be food for them.

11" 'For this is what the Sovereign LORD says: I myself will search for my sheep and look after them. 12As a shepherd looks after his scattered flock when he is with them, so will I look after my sheep. I will rescue them from all the places where they were scattered on a day of clouds and darkness. 13I will bring them out from the nations and gather them from the countries, and I will bring them into their own land. I will pasture them on the mountains of Israel, in the ravines and in all the settlements in the land. 14I will tend them in a good pasture, and the mountain heights of Israel will be their grazing land. There they will lie down in good grazing land, and there they will feed in a rich pasture on the mountains of Israel. 15I myself will tend my sheep and have them lie down, declares the Sovereign LORD. 16I will search for the lost and bring back the strays. I will bind up the injured and strengthen the weak, but the sleek and the strong I will destroy. I will shepherd the flock with justice.

17" 'As for you, my flock, this is what the Sovereign LORD says: I will judge between one sheep and another, and between rams and goats. 18Is it not enough for you to feed on the good pasture? Must you also trample the rest of your pasture with your feet? Is it not enough for you to drink clear water? Must you also muddy the rest with your feet? 19Must my flock feed on what you have trampled and drink what you have muddied with your feet?

20" 'Therefore this is what the Sovereign LORD says to them: See, I myself will judge between the fat sheep and the lean sheep. 21Because you shove with flank and shoulder, butting all the weak sheep with your horns until you have driven them away, 22I will save my flock, and they will no longer be plundered. I will judge between one sheep and another. 23I will place over them one shepherd, my servant David, and he will tend them; he will tend them and be their shepherd. 24I the LORD will be their God, and my servant David will be prince among them. I the LORD have spoken.

25" 'I will make a covenant of peace with them and rid the land of wild beasts so that they may live in the desert and sleep in the forests in safety. 26I will bless them and the places surrounding my hill.[a] I will send down showers in season; there will be showers of blessing. 27The trees of the field will yield their fruit and the

---

a 26 Or *I will make them and the places surrounding my hill a blessing*

Living Bible

the mountains and hills and over the face of the earth, and there was no one to search for them or care about them.

7"Therefore, O shepherds, hear the word of the Lord: 8"As I live, says the Lord God, you abandoned my flock, leaving them to be attacked and destroyed, and you were no real shepherds at all, for you didn't search for them. You fed yourselves and let them starve; 9, 10therefore I am against the shepherds, and I will hold them responsible for what has happened to my flock. I will take away their right to feed the flock—and take away their right to eat. I will save my flock from being taken for their food.

11"For the Lord God says: I will search and find my sheep. 12I will be like a shepherd looking for his flock. I will find my sheep and rescue them from all the places they were scattered in that dark and cloudy day. 13And I will bring them back from among the people and nations where they were, back home to their own land of Israel, and I will feed them upon the mountains of Israel and by the rivers where the land is fertile and good. 14Yes, I will give them good pasture on the high hills of Israel. There they will lie down in peace and feed in luscious mountain pastures. 15, 16I myself will be the Shepherd of my sheep, and cause them to lie down in peace, the Lord God says. I will seek my lost ones, those who strayed away, and bring them safely home again. I will put splints and bandages upon their broken limbs and heal the sick. And I will destroy the powerful, fat shepherds; I will feed them, yes—feed them punishment!

17"And as for you, O my flock—my people—the Lord God says, I will judge you and separate good from bad, sheep from goats.

18"Is it a small thing to you, O evil shepherds, that you not only keep the best of the pastures for yourselves, but trample down the rest? That you take the best water for yourselves, and muddy the rest with your feet? 19All that's left for my flock is what you've trampled down; all they have to drink is water that you've fouled.

20"Therefore the Lord God says: I will surely judge between these fat shepherds and their scrawny sheep. 21For these shepherds push and butt and crowd my sick and hungry flock until they're scattered far away. 22So I myself will save my flock; no more will they be picked on and destroyed. And I will notice which is plump and which is thin, and why!

23"And I will set one Shepherd over all my people, even my Servant, David. He shall feed them and be a Shepherd to them.

24"And I, the Lord, will be their God, and my Servant David shall be a Prince among my people. I, the Lord, have spoken it.

25"I will make a peace pact with them, and drive away the dangerous animals from the land so that my people can safely camp in the wildest places and sleep safely in the woods. 26I will make my people and their homes around my hill a blessing. And there shall be showers, showers of blessing, for I will not shut off the rains but send them in their seasons. 27Their fruit trees and fields

New Revised Standard

over all the mountains and on every high hill; my sheep were scattered over all the face of the earth, with no one to search or seek for them.

7 Therefore, you shepherds, hear the word of the LORD: 8 As I live, says the Lord GOD, because my sheep have become a prey, and my sheep have become food for all the wild animals, since there was no shepherd; and because my shepherds have not searched for my sheep, but the shepherds have fed themselves, and have not fed my sheep; 9 therefore, you shepherds, hear the word of the LORD: 10 Thus says the Lord GOD, I am against the shepherds; and I will demand my sheep at their hand, and put a stop to their feeding the sheep; no longer shall the shepherds feed themselves. I will rescue my sheep from their mouths, so that they may not be food for them.

God, the True Shepherd

11 For thus says the Lord GOD: I myself will search for my sheep, and will seek them out. 12 As shepherds seek out their flocks when they are among their scattered sheep, so I will seek out my sheep. I will rescue them from all the places to which they have been scattered on a day of clouds and thick darkness. 13 I will bring them out from the peoples and gather them from the countries, and will bring them into their own land; and I will feed them on the mountains of Israel, by the watercourses, and in all the inhabited parts of the land. 14 I will feed them with good pasture, and the mountain heights of Israel shall be their pasture; there they shall lie down in good grazing land, and they shall feed on rich pasture on the mountains of Israel. 15 I myself will be the shepherd of my sheep, and I will make them lie down, says the Lord GOD. 16 I will seek the lost, and I will bring back the strayed, and I will bind up the injured, and I will strengthen the weak, but the fat and the strong I will destroy. I will feed them with justice.

17 As for you, my flock, thus says the Lord GOD: I shall judge between sheep and sheep, between rams and goats: 18 Is it not enough for you to feed on the good pasture, but you must tread down with your feet the rest of your pasture? When you drink of clear water, must you foul the rest with your feet? 19 And must my sheep eat what you have trodden with your feet, and drink what you have fouled with your feet?

20 Therefore, thus says the Lord GOD to them: I myself will judge between the fat sheep and the lean sheep. 21 Because you pushed with flank and shoulder, and butted at all the weak animals with your horns until you scattered them far and wide, 22 I will save my flock, and they shall no longer be ravaged; and I will judge between sheep and sheep.

23 I will set up over them one shepherd, my servant David, and he shall feed them: he shall feed them and be their shepherd. 24 And I, the LORD, will be their God, and my servant David shall be prince among them; I, the LORD, have spoken.

25 I will make with them a covenant of peace and banish wild animals from the land, so that they may live in the wild and sleep in the woods securely. 26 I will make them and the region around my hill a blessing; and I will send down the showers in their season; they shall be showers of blessing. 27 The trees of the field shall

King James

27And the tree of the field shall yield her fruit, and the earth shall yield her increase, and they shall be safe in their land, and shall know that I *am* the LORD, when I have broken the bands of their yoke, and delivered them out of the hand of those that served themselves of them.

28And they shall no more be a prey to the heathen, neither shall the beast of the land devour them; but they shall dwell safely, and none shall make *them* afraid.

29And I will raise up for them a plant of renown, and they shall be no more consumed with hunger in the land, neither bear the shame of the heathen any more.

30Thus shall they know that I the LORD their God *am* with them, and *that* they, *even* the house of Israel, *are* my people, saith the Lord GOD.

31And ye my flock, the flock of my pasture, *are* men, *and* I *am* your God, saith the Lord GOD.

35 MOREOVER THE word of the LORD came unto me, saying,

2Son of man, set thy face against mount Seir, and prophesy against it,

3And say unto it, Thus saith the Lord GOD; Behold, O mount Seir, I *am* against thee, and I will stretch out mine hand against thee, and I will make thee most desolate.

4I will lay thy cities waste, and thou shalt be desolate, and thou shalt know that I *am* the LORD.

5Because thou hast had a perpetual hatred, and hast shed *the blood of* the children of Israel by the force of the sword in the time of their calamity, in the time *that their* iniquity *had* an end:

6Therefore, *as* I live, saith the Lord GOD, I will prepare thee unto blood, and blood shall pursue thee: since thou hast not hated blood, even blood shall pursue thee.

7Thus will I make mount Seir most desolate, and cut off from it him that passeth out and him that returneth.

8And I will fill his mountains with his slain *men:* in thy hills, and in thy valleys, and in all thy rivers, shall they fall that are slain with the sword.

9I will make thee perpetual desolations, and thy cities shall not return: and ye shall know that I *am* the LORD.

10Because thou hast said, These two nations and these two countries shall be mine, and we will possess it; whereas the LORD was there:

11Therefore, *as* I live, saith the Lord GOD, I will even do according to thine anger, and according to thine envy which thou hast used out of thy hatred against them; and I will make myself known among them, when I have judged thee.

12And thou shalt know that I *am* the LORD, *and that* I have heard all thy blasphemies which thou hast spoken against the mountains of Israel, saying, They are laid desolate, they are given us to consume.

13Thus with your mouth ye have boasted against me, and have multiplied your words against me: I have heard *them*.

14Thus saith the Lord GOD; When the whole earth rejoiceth, I will make thee desolate.

15As thou didst rejoice at the inheritance of the house of Israel, because it was desolate, so will I do unto thee: thou shalt be desolate, O mount Seir, and all Idumea, *even* all of it: and they shall know that I *am* the LORD.

New International

ground will yield its crops; the people will be secure in their land. They will know that I am the LORD, when I break the bars of their yoke and rescue them from the hands of those who enslaved them. 28They will no longer be plundered by the nations, nor will wild animals devour them. They will live in safety, and no one will make them afraid. 29I will provide for them a land renowned for its crops, and they will no longer be victims of famine in the land or bear the scorn of the nations. 30Then they will know that I, the LORD their God, am with them and that they, the house of Israel, are my people, declares the Sovereign LORD. 31You my sheep, the sheep of my pasture, are people, and I am your God, declares the Sovereign LORD.' "

A Prophecy Against Edom

35 THE WORD of the LORD came to me: 2"Son of man, set your face against Mount Seir; prophesy against it 3and say: 'This is what the Sovereign LORD says: I am against you, Mount Seir, and I will stretch out my hand against you and make you a desolate waste. 4I will turn your towns into ruins and you will be desolate. Then you will know that I am the LORD.

5" 'Because you harbored an ancient hostility and delivered the Israelites over to the sword at the time of their calamity, the time their punishment reached its climax, 6therefore as surely as I live, declares the Sovereign LORD, I will give you over to bloodshed and it will pursue you. Since you did not hate bloodshed, bloodshed will pursue you. 7I will make Mount Seir a desolate waste and cut off from it all who come and go. 8I will fill your mountains with the slain; those killed by the sword will fall on your hills and in your valleys and in all your ravines. 9I will make you desolate forever; your towns will not be inhabited. Then you will know that I am the LORD.

10" 'Because you have said, "These two nations and countries will be ours and we will take possession of them," even though I the LORD was there, 11therefore as surely as I live, declares the Sovereign LORD, I will treat you in accordance with the anger and jealousy you showed in your hatred of them and I will make myself known among them when I judge you. 12Then you will know that I the LORD have heard all the contemptible things you have said against the mountains of Israel. You said, "They have been laid waste and have been given over to us to devour." 13You boasted against me and spoke against me without restraint, and I heard it. 14This is what the Sovereign LORD says: While the whole earth rejoices, I will make you desolate. 15Because you rejoiced when the inheritance of the house of Israel became desolate, that is how I will treat you. You will be desolate, O Mount Seir, you and all of Edom. Then they will know that I am the LORD.' "

Living Bible

will yield bumper crops, and everyone will live in safety. When I have broken off their chains of slavery and
delivered them from those who profiteered at their expense, they shall know I am the Lord. 28No more will
other nations conquer them nor wild animals attack.
They shall live in safety and no one shall make them
afraid.

29"And I will raise up a notable Vine [the Messiaha],
in Israel so that my people will never again go hungry
nor be shamed by heathen conquest. 30In this way they
will know that I, the Lord their God, am with them, and
that they, the people of Israel, are my people, says the
Lord God. 31You are my flock, the sheep of my pasture.
You are my men and I am your God, so says the Lord."

35 AGAIN A message came from the Lord. He
said:

2"Son of dust, face toward Mount Seir and prophesy
against the people saying:

3"The Lord God says: I am against you and I will
smash you with my fist and utterly destroy you. 4, 5Be-
cause you hate my people Israel, I will demolish your
cities and make you desolate, and then you shall know
I am the Lord. You butchered my people when they were
helpless, when I had punished them for all their sins. 6As
I live, the Lord God says, since you enjoy blood so
much, I will give you a blood bath—your turn has
come! 7I will utterly wipe out the people of Mount Seir,
killing off all those who try to escape and all those who
return. 8I will fill your mountains with the dead—your
hills, your valleys and your rivers will be filled with
those the sword has killed. 9Never again will you revive.
You will be abandoned forever; your cities will never be
rebuilt. Then you shall know I am the Lord.

10"For you said, 'Both Israel and Judah shall be mine.
We will take possession of them. What do we care that
God is there!' 11Therefore as I live, the Lord God says,
I will pay back your angry deeds with mine—I will
punish you for all your acts of envy and of hate. And
I will honor my name in Israel by what I do to you.
12And you shall know that I have heard each evil word
you spoke against the Lord, saying, 'His people are
helpless; they are food for us to eat!' 13Saying that, you
boasted great words against the Lord. And I have heard
them all!

14"The whole world will rejoice when I make you
desolate. 15You rejoiced at Israel's fearful fate. Now I
will rejoice at yours! You will be wiped out, O people
of Mount Seir and all who live in Edom! And then you
will know I am the Lord!

New Revised Standard

yield their fruit, and the earth shall yield its increase.
They shall be secure on their soil; and they shall know
that I am the Lord, when I break the bars of their yoke,
and save them from the hands of those who enslaved
them. 28They shall no more be plunder for the nations,
nor shall the animals of the land devour them; they shall
live in safety, and no one shall make them afraid. 29I
will provide for them a splendid vegetation so that they
shall no more be consumed with hunger in the land, and
no longer suffer the insults of the nations. 30They shall
know that I, the Lord their God, am with them, and that
they, the house of Israel, are my people, says the Lord
God. 31You are my sheep, the sheep of my pastureb and
I am your God, says the Lord God.

Judgment on Mount Seir

35 THE WORD of the Lord came to me: 2Mortal,
set your face against Mount Seir, and prophesy
against it, 3and say to it, Thus says the Lord God:
    I am against you, Mount Seir;
        I stretch out my hand against you
        to make you a desolation and a waste.
4   I lay your towns in ruins;
        you shall become a desolation,
        and you shall know that I am the Lord.
5Because you cherished an ancient enmity, and gave
over the people of Israel to the power of the sword at the
time of their calamity, at the time of their final punishment; 6therefore, as I live, says the Lord God, I will
prepare you for blood, and blood shall pursue you; since
you did not hate bloodshed, bloodshed shall pursue you.
7I will make Mount Seir a waste and a desolation; and
I will cut off from it all who come and go. 8I will fill
its mountains with the slain; on your hills and in your
valleys and in all your watercourses those killed with the
sword shall fall. 9I will make you a perpetual desolation,
and your cities shall never be inhabited. Then you shall
know that I am the Lord.

10 Because you said, "These two nations and these
two countries shall be mine, and we will take possession
of them,"—although the Lord was there— 11therefore,
as I live, says the Lord God, I will deal with you according to the anger and envy that you showed because of
your hatred against them; and I will make myself known
among you,c when I judge you. 12You shall know that
I, the Lord, have heard all the abusive speech that you
uttered against the mountains of Israel, saying, "They
are laid desolate, they are given us to devour." 13And
you magnified yourselves against me with your mouth,
and multiplied your words against me; I heard it. 14Thus
says the Lord God: As the whole earth rejoices, I will
make you desolate. 15As you rejoiced over the inheritance of the house of Israel, because it was desolate, so
I will deal with you; you shall be desolate, Mount Seir,
and all Edom, all of it. Then they shall know that I am
the Lord.

---

a 34:29 And I will raise up a notable Vine (the Messiah), literally, "a plant
of renown"; so perhaps the meaning is, "I will give them bumper crops."
Either translation is permissible, but the word for "plant" is in the singular.

b Gk OL: Heb pasture, you are people   c Gk: Heb them

King James

36 ALSO, THOU son of man, prophesy unto the mountains of Israel, and say, Ye mountains of Israel, hear the word of the LORD:

2Thus saith the Lord GOD; Because the enemy hath said against you, Aha, even the ancient high places are ours in possession:

3Therefore prophesy and say, Thus saith the Lord GOD; Because they have made *you* desolate, and swallowed you up on every side, that ye might be a possession unto the residue of the heathen, and ye are taken up in the lips of talkers, and *are* an infamy of the people:

4Therefore, ye mountains of Israel, hear the word of the Lord GOD; Thus saith the Lord GOD to the mountains, and to the hills, to the rivers, and to the valleys, to the desolate wastes, and to the cities that are forsaken, which became a prey and derision to the residue of the heathen that *are* round about;

5Therefore thus saith the Lord GOD; Surely in the fire of my jealousy have I spoken against the residue of the heathen, and against all Idumea, which have appointed my land into their possession with the joy of all *their* heart, with despiteful minds, to cast it out for a prey.

6Prophesy therefore concerning the land of Israel, and say unto the mountains, and to the hills, to the rivers, and to the valleys, Thus saith the Lord GOD; Behold, I have spoken in my jealousy and in my fury, because ye have borne the shame of the heathen:

7Therefore thus saith the Lord GOD; I have lifted up mine hand, Surely the heathen that *are* about you, they shall bear their shame.

8¶ But ye, O mountains of Israel, ye shall shoot forth your branches, and yield your fruit to my people of Israel; for they are at hand to come.

9For, behold, I *am* for you, and I will turn unto you, and ye shall be tilled and sown:

10And I will multiply men upon you, all the house of Israel, *even* all of it: and the cities shall be inhabited, and the wastes shall be builded:

11And I will multiply upon you man and beast; and they shall increase and bring fruit: and I will settle you after your old estates, and will do better *unto you* than at your beginnings: and ye shall know that I *am* the LORD.

12Yea, I will cause men to walk upon you, *even* my people Israel; and they shall possess thee, and thou shalt be their inheritance, and thou shalt no more henceforth bereave them *of men.*

13Thus saith the Lord GOD; Because they say unto you, Thou *land* devourest up men, and hast bereaved thy nations;

14Therefore thou shalt devour men no more, neither bereave thy nations any more, saith the Lord GOD.

15Neither will I cause *men* to hear in thee the shame of the heathen any more, neither shalt thou bear the reproach of the people any more, neither shalt thou cause thy nations to fall any more, saith the Lord GOD.

16¶ Moreover the word of the LORD came unto me, saying,

17Son of man, when the house of Israel dwelt in their own land, they defiled it by their own way and by their doings: their way was before me as the uncleanness of a removed woman.

18Wherefore I poured my fury upon them for the blood that they had shed upon the land, and for their idols *wherewith* they had polluted it:

19And I scattered them among the heathen, and they were dispersed through the countries: according to their way and according to their doings I judged them.

20And when they entered unto the heathen, whither they went, they profaned my holy name, when they said to them, These *are* the people of the LORD, and are gone forth out of his land.

New International

A Prophecy to the Mountains of Israel

36 "SON OF man, prophesy to the mountains of Israel and say, 'O mountains of Israel, hear the word of the LORD. 2This is what the Sovereign LORD says: The enemy said of you, "Aha! The ancient heights have become our possession." ' 3Therefore prophesy and say, 'This is what the Sovereign LORD says: Because they ravaged and hounded you from every side so that you became the possession of the rest of the nations and the object of people's malicious talk and slander, 4therefore, O mountains of Israel, hear the word of the Sovereign LORD: This is what the Sovereign LORD says to the mountains and hills, to the ravines and valleys, to the desolate ruins and the deserted towns that have been plundered and ridiculed by the rest of the nations around you— 5this is what the Sovereign LORD says: In my burning zeal I have spoken against the rest of the nations, and against all Edom, for with glee and with malice in their hearts they made my land their own possession so that they might plunder its pastureland.' 6Therefore prophesy concerning the land of Israel and say to the mountains and hills, to the ravines and valleys: 'This is what the Sovereign LORD says: I speak in my jealous wrath because you have suffered the scorn of the nations. 7Therefore this is what the Sovereign LORD says: I swear with uplifted hand that the nations around you will also suffer scorn.

8" 'But you, O mountains of Israel, will produce branches and fruit for my people Israel, for they will soon come home. 9I am concerned for you and will look on you with favor; you will be plowed and sown, 10and I will multiply the number of people upon you, even the whole house of Israel. The towns will be inhabited and the ruins rebuilt. 11I will increase the number of men and animals upon you, and they will be fruitful and become numerous. I will settle people on you as in the past and will make you prosper more than before. Then you will know that I am the LORD. 12I will cause people, my people Israel, to walk upon you. They will possess you, and you will be their inheritance; you will never again deprive them of their children.

13" 'This is what the Sovereign LORD says: Because people say to you, "You devour men and deprive your nation of its children," 14therefore you will no longer devour men or make your nation childless, declares the Sovereign LORD. 15No longer will I make you hear the taunts of the nations, and no longer will you suffer the scorn of the peoples or cause your nation to fall, declares the Sovereign LORD.' "

16Again the word of the LORD came to me: 17"Son of man, when the people of Israel were living in their own land, they defiled it by their conduct and their actions. Their conduct was like a woman's monthly uncleanness in my sight. 18So I poured out my wrath on them because they had shed blood in the land and because they had defiled it with their idols. 19I dispersed them among the nations, and they were scattered through the countries; I judged them according to their conduct and their actions. 20And wherever they went among the nations they profaned my holy name, for it was said of them, 'These are the LORD's people, and yet they had to leave his land.' 21I had concern for my holy name, which the

Living Bible

36 "SON OF dust, prophesy to Israel's mountains. Tell them: Listen to this message from the Lord. 2"Your enemies have sneered at you and claimed your ancient heights as theirs, 3and destroyed you on every side and sent you away as slaves to many lands. You are mocked and slandered. 4Therefore, O mountains of Israel, hear the word of the Lord God. He says to the hills and mountains, dales and valleys, and to the ruined farms and the long-deserted cities, destroyed and mocked by heathen nations all around: 5My anger is afire against these nations, especially Edom, for grabbing my land with relish, in utter contempt for me, to take it for themselves.

6"Therefore prophesy and say to the hills and mountains, dales and valleys of Israel: The Lord God says, I am full of fury because you suffered shame before the surrounding nations. 7Therefore I have sworn with hand held high, that those nations are going to have their turn of being covered with shame, 8but for Israel, good times will return. There will be heavy crops of fruit to prepare for my people's return—and they will be coming home again soon! 9See, I am for you, and I will come and help you as you prepare the ground and sow your crops. 10I will greatly increase your population throughout all Israel, and the ruined cities will be rebuilt and filled with people. 11Not only the people, but your flocks and herds will also greatly multiply. O mountains of Israel, again you will be filled with homes. I will do even more for you than I did before. Then you shall know I am the Lord. 12My people will walk upon you once again, and you will belong to them again; and you will no longer be a place for burning their children on idol altars.

13"The Lord God says: Now the other nations taunt you, saying, 'Israel is a land that devours her people!' 14But they will not say this any more. Your birth rate will rise and your infant mortality rate will drop off sharply, says the Lord. 15No longer will those heathen nations sneer, for you will no longer be a nation of sinners, the Lord God says."

16Then this further word came to me from the Lord: 17"Son of dust, when the people of Israel were living in their own country, they defiled it by their evil deeds; to me their worship was as foul as filthy rags.a 18They polluted the land with murder and with the worshiping of idols, so I poured out my fury upon them. 19And I exiled them to many lands; that is how I punished them for the evil way they lived. 20But when they were scattered out among the nations, then they were a blight upon my holy name because the nations said, 'These are the people of God and he couldn't protect them from

New Revised Standard

Blessing on Israel

36 AND YOU, mortal, prophesy to the mountains of Israel, and say: O mountains of Israel, hear the word of the LORD. 2Thus says the Lord GOD: Because the enemy said of you, "Aha!" and, "The ancient heights have become our possession," 3therefore prophesy, and say: Thus says the Lord GOD: Because they made you desolate indeed, and crushed you from all sides, so that you became the possession of the rest of the nations, and you became an object of gossip and slander among the people; 4therefore, O mountains of Israel, hear the word of the Lord GOD: Thus says the Lord GOD to the mountains and the hills, the watercourses and the valleys, the desolate wastes and the deserted towns, which have become a source of plunder and an object of derision to the rest of the nations all around; 5therefore thus says the Lord GOD: I am speaking in my hot jealousy against the rest of the nations, and against all Edom, who, with wholehearted joy and utter contempt, took my land as their possession, because of its pasture, to plunder it. 6Therefore prophesy concerning the land of Israel, and say to the mountains and hills, to the watercourses and valleys, Thus says the Lord GOD: I am speaking in my jealous wrath, because you have suffered the insults of the nations; 7therefore thus says the Lord GOD: I swear that the nations that are all around you shall themselves suffer insults.

8 But you, O mountains of Israel, shall shoot out your branches, and yield your fruit to my people Israel; for they shall soon come home. 9See now, I am for you; I will turn to you, and you shall be tilled and sown; 10and I will multiply your population, the whole house of Israel, all of it; the towns shall be inhabited and the waste places rebuilt; 11and I will multiply human beings and animals upon you. They shall increase and be fruitful; and I will cause you to be inhabited as in your former times, and will do more good to you than ever before. Then you shall know that I am the LORD. 12I will lead people upon you—my people Israel—and they shall possess you, and you shall be their inheritance. No longer shall you bereave them of children.

13 Thus says the Lord GOD: Because they say to you, "You devour people, and you bereave your nation of children," 14therefore you shall no longer devour people and no longer bereave your nation of children, says the Lord GOD; 15and no longer will I let you hear the insults of the nations, no longer shall you bear the disgrace of the peoples; and no longer shall you cause your nation to stumble, says the Lord GOD.

The Renewal of Israel

16 The word of the LORD came to me: 17Mortal, when the house of Israel lived on their own soil, they defiled it with their ways and their deeds; their conduct in my sight was like the uncleanness of a woman in her menstrual period. 18So I poured out my wrath upon them for the blood that they had shed upon the land, and for the idols with which they had defiled it. 19I scattered them among the nations, and they were dispersed through the countries; in accordance with their conduct and their deeds I judged them. 20But when they came to the nations, wherever they came, they profaned my holy name, in that it was said of them, "These are the people of the LORD, and yet they had to go out of his land." 21But I had concern for my holy name, which the

---

a 36:17 *as filthy rags*, literally, "as a menstruous cloth."

King James

21¶ But I had pity for mine holy name, which the house of Israel had profaned among the heathen, whither they went.

22Therefore say unto the house of Israel, Thus saith the Lord GOD; I do not *this* for your sakes, O house of Israel, but for mine holy name's sake, which ye have profaned among the heathen, whither ye went.

23And I will sanctify my great name, which was profaned among the heathen, which ye have profaned in the midst of them; and the heathen shall know that I *am* the LORD, saith the Lord GOD, when I shall be sanctified in you before their eyes.

24For I will take you from among the heathen, and gather you out of all countries, and will bring you into your own land.

25¶ Then will I sprinkle clean water upon you, and ye shall be clean: from all your filthiness, and from all your idols, will I cleanse you.

26A new heart also will I give you, and a new spirit will I put within you: and I will take away the stony heart out of your flesh, and I will give you an heart of flesh.

27And I will put my spirit within you, and cause you to walk in my statutes, and ye shall keep my judgments, and do *them.*

28And ye shall dwell in the land that I gave to your fathers; and ye shall be my people, and I will be your God.

29I will also save you from all your uncleannesses: and I will call for the corn, and will increase it, and lay no famine upon you.

30And I will multiply the fruit of the tree, and the increase of the field, that ye shall receive no more reproach of famine among the heathen.

31Then shall ye remember your own evil ways, and your doings that *were* not good, and shall loathe yourselves in your own sight for your iniquities and for your abominations.

32Not for your sakes do I *this,* saith the Lord GOD, be it known unto you: be ashamed and confounded for your own ways, O house of Israel.

33Thus saith the Lord GOD; In the day that I shall have cleansed you from all your iniquities I will also cause *you* to dwell in the cities, and the wastes shall be builded.

34And the desolate land shall be tilled, whereas it lay desolate in the sight of all that passed by.

35And they shall say, This land that was desolate is become like the garden of Eden; and the waste and desolate and ruined cities *are become* fenced, *and* are inhabited.

36Then the heathen that are left round about you shall know that I the LORD build the ruined *places, and* plant that that was desolate: I the LORD have spoken *it,* and I will do *it.*

37Thus saith the Lord GOD; I will yet *for* this be inquired of by the house of Israel, to do *it* for them; I will increase them with men like a flock.

38As the holy flock, as the flock of Jerusalem in her solemn feasts; so shall the waste cities be filled with flocks of men: and they shall know that I *am* the LORD.

37 THE HAND of the LORD was upon me, and carried me out in the spirit of the LORD, and set me down in the midst of the valley which *was* full of bones,

2And caused me to pass by them round about: and, behold, *there were* very many in the open valley; and, lo, *they were* very dry.

3And he said unto me, Son of man, can these bones live? And I answered, O Lord GOD, thou knowest.

New International

house of Israel profaned among the nations where they had gone.

22"Therefore say to the house of Israel, 'This is what the Sovereign LORD says: It is not for your sake, O house of Israel, that I am going to do these things, but for the sake of my holy name, which you have profaned among the nations where you have gone. 23I will show the holiness of my great name, which has been profaned among the nations, the name you have profaned among them. Then the nations will know that I am the LORD, declares the Sovereign LORD, when I show myself holy through you before their eyes.

24" 'For I will take you out of the nations; I will gather you from all the countries and bring you back into your own land. 25I will sprinkle clean water on you, and you will be clean; I will cleanse you from all your impurities and from all your idols. 26I will give you a new heart and put a new spirit in you; I will remove from you your heart of stone and give you a heart of flesh. 27And I will put my Spirit in you and move you to follow my decrees and be careful to keep my laws. 28You will live in the land I gave your forefathers; you will be my people, and I will be your God. 29I will save you from all your uncleanness. I will call for the grain and make it plentiful and will not bring famine upon you. 30I will increase the fruit of the trees and the crops of the field, so that you will no longer suffer disgrace among the nations because of famine. 31Then you will remember your evil ways and wicked deeds, and you will loathe yourselves for your sins and detestable practices. 32I want you to know that I am not doing this for your sake, declares the Sovereign LORD. Be ashamed and disgraced for your conduct, O house of Israel!

33" 'This is what the Sovereign LORD says: On the day I cleanse you from all your sins, I will resettle your towns, and the ruins will be rebuilt. 34The desolate land will be cultivated instead of lying desolate in the sight of all who pass through it. 35They will say, "This land that was laid waste has become like the garden of Eden; the cities that were lying in ruins, desolate and destroyed, are now fortified and inhabited." 36Then the nations around you that remain will know that I the LORD have rebuilt what was destroyed and have replanted what was desolate. I the LORD have spoken, and I will do it.'

37"This is what the Sovereign LORD says: Once again I will yield to the plea of the house of Israel and do this for them: I will make their people as numerous as sheep, 38as numerous as the flocks for offerings at Jerusalem during her appointed feasts. So will the ruined cities be filled with flocks of people. Then they will know that I am the LORD."

The Valley of Dry Bones

37 THE HAND of the LORD was upon me, and he brought me out by the Spirit of the LORD and set me in the middle of a valley; it was full of bones. 2He led me back and forth among them, and I saw a great many bones on the floor of the valley, bones that were very dry. 3He asked me, "Son of man, can these bones live?"

I said, "O Sovereign LORD, you alone know."

Living Bible

harm!' 21I am concerned about my reputation that was ruined by my people throughout the world.

22"Therefore say to the people of Israel: The Lord God says, I am bringing you back again, but not because you deserve it; I am doing it to protect my holy name which you tarnished among the nations. 23I will honor my great name that you defiled, and the people of the world shall know I am the Lord. I will be honored before their eyes by delivering you from exile among them.a 24For I will bring you back home again to the land of Israel.

25"Then it will be as though I had sprinkled clean water on you, for you will be clean—your filthiness will be washed away, your idol worship gone. 26And I will give you a new heart—I will give you new and right desires—and put a new spirit within you. I will take out your stony hearts of sin and give you new hearts of love.b 27And I will put my Spirit within you so that you will obey my laws and do whatever I command.

28"And you shall live in Israel, the land which I gave your fathers long ago. And you shall be my people and I will be your God. 29I will cleanse away your sins. I will abolish crop failures and famine. 30I will give you huge harvests from your fruit trees and fields, and never again will the surrounding nations be able to scoff at your land for its famines. 31Then you will remember your past sins and loathe yourselves for all the evils you did. 32But always remember this: It is not for your own sakes that I will do this, but for mine. O my people Israel, be utterly ashamed of all that you have done!

33"The Lord God says: When I cleanse you from your sins, I will bring you home again to Israel, and rebuild the ruins. 34Acreage will be cultivated again that through the years of exile lay empty as a barren wilderness; all who passed by were shocked to see the extent of ruin in your land. 35But when I bring you back they will say, 'This God-forsaken land has become like Eden's garden! The ruined cities are rebuilt and walled and filled with people!' 36Then the nations all around—all those still left—will know that I, the Lord, rebuilt the ruins and planted lush crops in the wilderness. For I, the Lord, have promised it, and I will do it.

37, 38"The Lord God says: I am ready to hear Israel's prayers for these blessings, and to grant them their requests. Let them but ask and I will multiply them like the flocks that fill Jerusalem's streets at time of sacrifice. The ruined cities will be crowded once more, and everyone will know I am the Lord."

37 THE POWER of the Lord was upon me and I was carried away by the Spirit of the Lord to a valley full of old, dry bones that were scattered everywhere across the ground. He led me around among them, 3and then he said to me:

"Son of dust, can these bones become people again?"

I replied, "Lord, you alone know the answer to that."

New Revised Standard

house of Israel had profaned among the nations to which they came.

22   Therefore say to the house of Israel, Thus says the Lord GOD: It is not for your sake, O house of Israel, that I am about to act, but for the sake of my holy name, which you have profaned among the nations to which you came. 23I will sanctify my great name, which has been profaned among the nations, and which you have profaned among them; and the nations shall know that I am the LORD, says the Lord GOD, when through you I display my holiness before their eyes. 24I will take you from the nations, and gather you from all the countries, and bring you into your own land. 25I will sprinkle clean water upon you, and you shall be clean from all your uncleannesses, and from all your idols I will cleanse you. 26A new heart I will give you, and a new spirit I will put within you; and I will remove from your body the heart of stone and give you a heart of flesh. 27I will put my spirit within you, and make you follow my statutes and be careful to observe my ordinances. 28Then you shall live in the land that I gave to your ancestors; and you shall be my people, and I will be your God. 29I will save you from all your uncleannesses, and I will summon the grain and make it abundant and lay no famine upon you. 30I will make the fruit of the tree and the produce of the field abundant, so that you may never again suffer the disgrace of famine among the nations. 31Then you shall remember your evil ways, and your dealings that were not good; and you shall loathe yourselves for your iniquities and your abominable deeds. 32It is not for your sake that I will act, says the Lord GOD; let that be known to you. Be ashamed and dismayed for your ways, O house of Israel.

33   Thus says the Lord GOD: On the day that I cleanse you from all your iniquities, I will cause the towns to be inhabited, and the waste places shall be rebuilt. 34The land that was desolate shall be tilled, instead of being the desolation that it was in the sight of all who passed by. 35And they will say, "This land that was desolate has become like the garden of Eden; and the waste and desolate and ruined towns are now inhabited and fortified." 36Then the nations that are left all around you shall know that I, the LORD, have rebuilt the ruined places, and replanted that which was desolate; I, the LORD, have spoken, and I will do it.

37   Thus says the Lord GOD: I will also let the house of Israel ask me to do this for them: to increase their population like a flock. 38Like the flock for sacrifices,c like the flock at Jerusalem during her appointed festivals, so shall the ruined towns be filled with flocks of people. Then they shall know that I am the LORD.

The Valley of Dry Bones

37 THE HAND of the LORD came upon me, and he brought me out by the spirit of the LORD and set me down in the middle of a valley; it was full of bones. 2He led me all around them; there were very many lying in the valley, and they were very dry. 3He said to me, "Mortal, can these bones live?" I answered, "O Lord GOD, you know." 4Then he said to me,

---

a 36:23 by delivering you from exile among them, implied.   b 36:26 hearts of love, literally, "hearts of flesh," in contrast to "hearts of stone."

c Heb flock of holy things

King James

4Again he said unto me, Prophesy upon these bones, and say unto them, O ye dry bones, hear the word of the LORD.

5Thus saith the Lord GOD unto these bones; Behold, I will cause breath to enter into you, and ye shall live:

6And I will lay sinews upon you, and will bring up flesh upon you, and cover you with skin, and put breath in you, and ye shall live; and ye shall know that I *am* the LORD.

7So I prophesied as I was commanded: and as I prophesied, there was a noise, and behold a shaking, and the bones came together, bone to his bone.

8And when I beheld, lo, the sinews and the flesh came up upon them, and the skin covered them above: but *there was* no breath in them.

9Then said he unto me, Prophesy unto the wind, prophesy, son of man, and say to the wind, Thus saith the Lord GOD; Come from the four winds, O breath, and breathe upon these slain, that they may live.

10So I prophesied as he commanded me, and the breath came into them, and they lived, and stood up upon their feet, an exceeding great army.

11¶ Then he said unto me, Son of man, these bones are the whole house of Israel: behold, they say, Our bones are dried, and our hope is lost: we are cut off for our parts.

12Therefore prophesy and say unto them, Thus saith the Lord GOD; Behold, O my people, I will open your graves, and cause you to come up out of your graves, and bring you into the land of Israel.

13And ye shall know that I *am* the LORD, when I have opened your graves, O my people, and brought you up out of your graves,

14And shall put my spirit in you, and ye shall live, and I shall place you in your own land: then shall ye know that I the LORD have spoken *it,* and performed *it,* saith the LORD.

15¶ The word of the LORD came again unto me, saying,

16Moreover, thou son of man, take thee one stick, and write upon it, For Judah, and for the children of Israel his companions: then take another stick, and write upon it, For Joseph, the stick of Ephraim, and *for* all the house of Israel his companions:

17And join them one to another into one stick; and they shall become one in thine hand.

18¶ And when the children of thy people shall speak unto thee, saying, Wilt thou not show us what thou *meanest* by these?

19Say unto them, Thus saith the Lord GOD; Behold, I will take the stick of Joseph, which *is* in the hand of Ephraim, and the tribes of Israel his fellows, and will put them with him, *even* with the stick of Judah, and make them one stick, and they shall be one in mine hand.

20¶ And the sticks whereon thou writest shall be in thine hand before their eyes.

21And say unto them, Thus saith the Lord GOD; Behold, I will take the children of Israel from among the heathen, whither they be gone, and will gather them on every side, and bring them into their own land:

22And I will make them one nation in the land upon the mountains of Israel; and one king shall be king to them all: and they shall be no more two nations, neither shall they be divided into two kingdoms any more at all:

23Neither shall they defile themselves any more with their idols, nor with their detestable things, nor with any of their transgressions: but I will save them out of all their dwellingplaces, wherein they have sinned, and will cleanse them: so shall they be my people, and I will be their God.

24And David my servant *shall be* king over them; and they all shall have one shepherd: they shall also walk in my judgments, and observe my statutes, and do them.

New International

4Then he said to me, "Prophesy to these bones and say to them, 'Dry bones, hear the word of the LORD! 5This is what the Sovereign LORD says to these bones: I will make breatha enter you, and you will come to life. 6I will attach tendons to you and make flesh come upon you and cover you with skin; I will put breath in you, and you will come to life. Then you will know that I am the LORD.' "

7So I prophesied as I was commanded. And as I was prophesying, there was a noise, a rattling sound, and the bones came together, bone to bone. 8I looked, and tendons and flesh appeared on them and skin covered them, but there was no breath in them.

9Then he said to me, "Prophesy to the breath; prophesy, son of man, and say to it, 'This is what the Sovereign LORD says: Come from the four winds, O breath, and breathe into these slain, that they may live.' " 10So I prophesied as he commanded me, and breath entered them; they came to life and stood up on their feet—a vast army.

11Then he said to me: "Son of man, these bones are the whole house of Israel. They say, 'Our bones are dried up and our hope is gone; we are cut off.' 12Therefore prophesy and say to them: 'This is what the Sovereign LORD says: O my people, I am going to open your graves and bring you up from them; I will bring you back to the land of Israel. 13Then you, my people, will know that I am the LORD, when I open your graves and bring you up from them. 14I will put my Spirit in you and you will live, and I will settle you in your own land. Then you will know that I the LORD have spoken, and I have done it, declares the LORD.' "

One Nation Under One King

15The word of the LORD came to me: 16"Son of man, take a stick of wood and write on it, 'Belonging to Judah and the Israelites associated with him.' Then take another stick of wood, and write on it, 'Ephraim's stick, belonging to Joseph and all the house of Israel associated with him.' 17Join them together into one stick so that they will become one in your hand.

18"When your countrymen ask you, 'Won't you tell us what you mean by this?' 19say to them, 'This is what the Sovereign LORD says: I am going to take the stick of Joseph—which is in Ephraim's hand—and of the Israelite tribes associated with him, and join it to Judah's stick, making them a single stick of wood, and they will become one in my hand.' 20Hold before their eyes the sticks you have written on 21and say to them, 'This is what the Sovereign LORD says: I will take the Israelites out of the nations where they have gone. I will gather them from all around and bring them back into their own land. 22I will make them one nation in the land, on the mountains of Israel. There will be one king over all of them and they will never again be two nations or be divided into two kingdoms. 23They will no longer defile themselves with their idols and vile images or with any of their offenses, for I will save them from all their sinful backsliding,b and I will cleanse them. They will be my people, and I will be their God.

24" 'My servant David will be king over them, and they will all have one shepherd. They will follow my laws and be careful to keep my decrees. 25They will live

---

a *5* The Hebrew for this word can also mean *wind* or *spirit* (see verses 6-14).
b *23* Many Hebrew manuscripts (see also Septuagint); most Hebrew manuscripts *all their dwelling places where they sinned*

Living Bible

4Then he told me to speak to the bones and say: "O dry bones, listen to the words of God, 5for the Lord God says, See! I am going to make you live and breathe again! 6I will replace the flesh and muscles on you and cover you with skin. I will put breath into you, and you shall live and know I am the Lord."

7So I spoke these words from God, just as he told me to; and suddenly there was a rattling noise from all across the valley, and the bones of each body came together and attached to each other as they used to be. 8Then, as I watched, the muscles and flesh formed over the bones, and skin covered them, but the bodies had no breath. 9Then he told me to call to the wind and say: "The Lord God says: Come from the four winds, O Spirit, and breathe upon these slain bodies, that they may live again." 10So I spoke to the winds as he commanded me and the bodies began breathing; they lived, and stood up—a very great army.

11Then he told me what the vision meant: "These bones," he said, "represent all the people of Israel. They say: 'We have become a heap of dried-out bones—all hope is gone.' 12But tell them, the Lord God says: My people, I will open your graves of exile and cause you to rise again and return to the land of Israel. 13And, then at last, O my people, you will know I am the Lord. 14I will put my Spirit into you, and you shall live and return home again to your own land. Then you will know that I, the Lord, have done just what I promised you."

15Again a message from the Lord came to me, saying: 16"Take a stick and carve on it these words: 'This stick represents Judah and her allied tribes.' Then take another stick and carve these words on it: 'This stick represents all the other tribes of Israel.' 17Now hold them together in your hand as one stick. 18, 19, 20Tell these people (holding the sticks so they can see what you are doing), the Lord God says: I will take the tribes of Israel and join them to Judah and make them one stick in my hand.

21"For the Lord God says: I am gathering the people of Israel from among the nations, and bringing them home from around the world to their own land, 22to unify them into one nation. One king shall be king of them all; no longer shall they be divided into two nations. 23They shall stop polluting themselves with idols and their other sins, for I will save them from all this foulness. Then they shall truly be my people and I their God.

24"And David, my Servant—the Messiah—shall be their King, their only Shepherd; and they shall obey my laws and all my wishes. 25They shall live in the land of

New Revised Standard

"Prophesy to these bones, and say to them: O dry bones, hear the word of the LORD. 5Thus says the Lord GOD to these bones: I will cause breathc to enter you, and you shall live. 6I will lay sinews on you, and will cause flesh to come upon you, and cover you with skin, and put breathc in you, and you shall live; and you shall know that I am the LORD."

7 So I prophesied as I had been commanded; and as I prophesied, suddenly there was a noise, a rattling, and the bones came together, bone to its bone. 8I looked, and there were sinews on them, and flesh had come upon them, and skin had covered them; but there was no breath in them. 9Then he said to me, "Prophesy to the breath, prophesy, mortal, and say to the breath:d Thus says the Lord GOD: Come from the four winds, O breath,d and breathe upon these slain, that they may live." 10I prophesied as he commanded me, and the breath came into them, and they lived, and stood on their feet, a vast multitude.

11 Then he said to me, "Mortal, these bones are the whole house of Israel. They say, 'Our bones are dried up, and our hope is lost; we are cut off completely.' 12Therefore prophesy, and say to them, Thus says the Lord GOD: I am going to open your graves, and bring you up from your graves, O my people; and I will bring you back to the land of Israel. 13 And you shall know that I am the LORD, when I open your graves, and bring you up from your graves, O my people. 14I will put my spirit within you, and you shall live, and I will place you on your own soil; then you shall know that I, the LORD, have spoken and will act," says the LORD.

The Two Sticks

15 The word of the LORD came to me: 16Mortal, take a stick and write on it, "For Judah, and the Israelites associated with it"; then take another stick and write on it, "For Joseph (the stick of Ephraim) and all the house of Israel associated with it"; 17and join them together into one stick, so that they may become one in your hand. 18And when your people say to you, "Will you not show us what you mean by these?" 19say to them, Thus says the Lord GOD: I am about to take the stick of Joseph (which is in the hand of Ephraim) and the tribes of Israel associated with it; and I will put the stick of Judah upon it,e and make them one stick, in order that they may be one in my hand. 20When the sticks on which you write are in your hand before their eyes, 21then say to them, Thus says the Lord GOD: I will take the people of Israel from the nations among which they have gone, and will gather them from every quarter, and bring them to their own land. 22I will make them one nation in the land, on the mountains of Israel; and one king shall be king over them all. Never again shall they be two nations, and never again shall they be divided into two kingdoms. 23They shall never again defile themselves with their idols and their detestable things, or with any of their transgressions. I will save them from all the apostasies into which they have fallen,f and will cleanse them. Then they shall be my people, and I will be their GOD.

24 My servant David shall be king over them; and they shall all have one shepherd. They shall follow my ordinances and be careful to observe my statutes.

King James

25And they shall dwell in the land that I have given unto Jacob my servant, wherein your fathers have dwelt; and they shall dwell therein, *even* they, and their children, and their children's children for ever: and my servant David *shall be* their prince for ever.

26Moreover I will make a covenant of peace with them; it shall be an everlasting covenant with them: and I will place them, and multiply them, and will set my sanctuary in the midst of them for evermore.

27My tabernacle also shall be with them: yea, I will be their God, and they shall be my people.

28And the heathen shall know that I the LORD do sanctify Israel, when my sanctuary shall be in the midst of them for evermore.

38 AND THE word of the LORD came unto me, saying,

2Son of man, set thy face against Gog, the land of Magog, the chief prince of Meshech and Tubal, and prophesy against him,

3And say, Thus saith the Lord GOD; Behold, I *am* against thee, O Gog, the chief prince of Meshech and Tubal:

4And I will turn thee back, and put hooks into thy jaws, and I will bring thee forth, and all thine army, horses and horsemen, all of them clothed with all sorts *of armour, even* a great company *with* bucklers and shields, all of them handling swords:

5Persia, Ethiopia, and Libya with them; all of them with shield and helmet:

6Gomer, and all his bands; the house of Togarmah of the north quarters, and all his bands: *and* many people with thee.

7Be thou prepared, and prepare for thyself, thou, and all thy company that are assembled unto thee, and be thou a guard unto them.

8¶ After many days thou shalt be visited: in the latter years thou shalt come into the land *that is* brought back from the sword, *and is* gathered out of many people, against the mountains of Israel, which have been always waste: but it is brought forth out of the nations, and they shall dwell safely all of them.

9Thou shalt ascend and come like a storm, thou shalt be like a cloud to cover the land, thou, and all thy bands, and many people with thee.

10Thus saith the Lord GOD; It shall also come to pass, *that* at the same time shall things come into thy mind, and thou shalt think an evil thought:

11And thou shalt say, I will go up to the land of unwalled villages; I will go to them that are at rest, that dwell safely, all of them dwelling without walls, and having neither bars nor gates,

12To take a spoil, and to take a prey; to turn thine hand upon the desolate places *that are now* inhabited, and upon the people *that are* gathered out of the nations, which have gotten cattle and goods, that dwell in the midst of the land.

13Sheba, and Dedan, and the merchants of Tarshish, with all the young lions thereof, shall say unto thee, Art thou come to take a spoil? hast thou gathered thy company to take a prey? to carry away silver and gold, to take away cattle and goods, to take a great spoil?

14¶ Therefore, son of man, prophesy and say unto Gog, Thus saith the Lord GOD; In that day when my people of Israel dwelleth safely, shalt thou not know *it*?

New International

in the land I gave to my servant Jacob, the land where your fathers lived. They and their children and their children's children will live there forever, and David my servant will be their prince forever. 26I will make a covenant of peace with them; it will be an everlasting covenant. I will establish them and increase their numbers, and I will put my sanctuary among them forever. 27My dwelling place will be with them; I will be their God, and they will be my people. 28Then the nations will know that I the LORD make Israel holy, when my sanctuary is among them forever.' "

A Prophecy Against Gog

38 THE WORD of the LORD came to me: 2"Son of man, set your face against Gog, of the land of Magog, the chief prince of[a] Meshech and Tubal; prophesy against him 3and say: 'This is what the Sovereign LORD says: I am against you, O Gog, chief prince of[b] Meshech and Tubal. 4I will turn you around, put hooks in your jaws and bring you out with your whole army—your horses, your horsemen fully armed, and a great horde with large and small shields, all of them brandishing their swords. 5Persia, Cush[c] and Put will be with them, all with shields and helmets, 6also Gomer with all its troops, and Beth Togarmah from the far north with all its troops—the many nations with you.

7" 'Get ready; be prepared, you and all the hordes gathered about you, and take command of them. 8After many days you will be called to arms. In future years you will invade a land that has recovered from war, whose people were gathered from many nations to the mountains of Israel, which had long been desolate. They had been brought out from the nations, and now all of them live in safety. 9You and all your troops and the many nations with you will go up, advancing like a storm; you will be like a cloud covering the land.

10" 'This is what the Sovereign LORD says: On that day thoughts will come into your mind and you will devise an evil scheme. 11You will say, "I will invade a land of unwalled villages; I will attack a peaceful and unsuspecting people—all of them living without walls and without gates and bars. 12I will plunder and loot and turn my hand against the resettled ruins and the people gathered from the nations, rich in livestock and goods, living at the center of the land." 13Sheba and Dedan and the merchants of Tarshish and all her villages[d] will say to you, "Have you come to plunder? Have you gathered your hordes to loot, to carry off silver and gold, to take away livestock and goods and to seize much plunder?" '

14"Therefore, son of man, prophesy and say to Gog: 'This is what the Sovereign LORD says: In that day, when my people Israel are living in safety, will you not take notice of it? 15You will come from your place in the far

Living Bible

Israel where their fathers lived, the land I gave my servant Jacob. They and their children after them shall live there, and their grandchildren, for all generations. And my Servant David, their Messiah, shall be their Prince forever. 26And I will make a covenant of peace with them, an everlasting pact. I will bless them and multiply them and put my Temple among them forever. 27And I will make my home among them. Yes, I will be their God and they shall be my people. 28And when my Temple remains among them forever, then the nations will know that I, the Lord, have chosen Israel as my very own."

38 HERE IS another message to me from the Lord: 2, 3"Son of dust, face northwarde toward the land of Magog, and prophesy against Gogf king of Meshech and Tubal. Tell him that the Lord God says: I am against you, Gog. 4I will put hooks into your jaws and pull you to your doom. I will mobilize your troops and armored cavalry, and make you a mighty host, all fully armed. 5Peras, Cush and Put shall join you too with all their weaponry, 6and so shall Gomer and all his hordes and the armies of Togarmah from the distant north, as well as many others. 7Be prepared! Stay mobilized. You are their leader, Gog!

8"A long time from now you will be called to action. In distant years you will swoop down onto the land of Israel, that will be lying in peace after the return of its people from many lands. 9You and all your allies—a vast and awesome army—will roll down upon them like a storm and cover the land like a cloud. 10For at that time an evil thought will have come to your mind. 11You will have said, 'Israel is an unprotected land of unwalled villages! I will march against her and destroy these people living in such confidence! 12I will go to those once-desolate cities that are now filled with people again—those who have returned from all the nations—and I will capture vast amounts of loot and many slaves. For the people are rich with cattle now, and the whole earth revolves around them!'

13"But Sheba and Dedang and the merchant princes of Tarshish with whom she tradesh will ask, 'Who are you to rob them of silver and gold and drive away their cattle and seize their goods and make them poor?'

14"The Lord God says to Gog: When my people are living in peace in their land, then you will rouse yourself. 15, 16You will come from all over the north with

---

e 38:2, 3 face northward, implied.   f 38:2, 3 against Gog. The names of Gog's confederates (Meshech, Tubal, Gomer, Beth-togarmah) can be identified as Muschki, Tabal, Gimaraya, Tegerama, peoples who lived in the mountainous area southeast of the Black Sea and southwest of the Caspian, currently in central Turkey. It therefore seems that Gog was, or is to be, the leader of one of these nations. But from the context Gog seems to be a symbol rather than a historical figure like Nebuchadnezzar. In any event he represents the aggregate military might of the forces opposed to God, especially in a mighty battle of the end times. See also Rev 20:7-9.   g 38:13 Sheba and Dedan, great trading centers in Arabia.   h 38:13 the merchant princes of Tarshish with whom she trades, implied.

New Revised Standard

25They shall live in the land that I gave to my servant Jacob, in which your ancestors lived; they and their children and their children's children shall live there forever; and my servant David shall be their prince forever. 26I will make a covenant of peace with them; it shall be an everlasting covenant with them; and I will blessi them and multiply them, and will set my sanctuary among them forevermore. 27My dwelling place shall be with them; and I will be their God, and they shall be my people. 28Then the nations shall know that I the LORD sanctify Israel, when my sanctuary is among them forevermore.

Invasion by Gog

38 THE WORD of the LORD came to me: 2Mortal, set your face toward Gog, of the land of Magog, the chief prince of Meshech and Tubal. Prophesy against him 3and say: Thus says the Lord GOD: I am against you, O Gog, chief prince of Meshech and Tubal; 4I will turn you around and put hooks into your jaws, and I will lead you out with all your army, horses and horsemen, all of them clothed in full armor, a great company, all of them with shield and buckler, wielding swords. 5Persia, Ethiopia,j and Put are with them, all of them with buckler and helmet; 6Gomer and all its troops; Beth-togarmah from the remotest parts of the north with all its troops—many peoples are with you.

7 Be ready and keep ready, you and all the companies that are assembled around you, and hold yourselves in reserve for them. 8After many days you shall be mustered; in the latter years you shall go against a land restored from war, a land where people were gathered from many nations on the mountains of Israel, which had long lain waste; its people were brought out from the nations and now are living in safety, all of them. 9You shall advance, coming on like a storm; you shall be like a cloud covering the land, you and all your troops, and many peoples with you.

10 Thus says the Lord GOD: On that day thoughts will come into your mind, and you will devise an evil scheme. 11You will say, "I will go up against the land of unwalled villages; I will fall upon the quiet people who live in safety, all of them living without walls, and having no bars or gates"; 12to seize spoil and carry off plunder; to assail the waste places that are now inhabited, and the people who were gathered from the nations, who are acquiring cattle and goods, who live at the centerk of the earth. 13Sheba and Dedan and the merchants of Tarshish and all its young warriorsl will say to you, "Have you come to seize spoil? Have you assembled your horde to carry off plunder, to carry away silver and gold, to take away cattle and goods, to seize a great amount of booty?"

14 Therefore, mortal, prophesy, and say to Gog: Thus says the Lord GOD: On that day when my people Israel are living securely, you will rouse yourselfm 15and

---

i Tg: Heb give   j Or Nubia; Heb Cush   k Heb navel   l Heb young lions   m Gk: Heb will you not know?

King James

15And thou shalt come from thy place out of the north parts, thou, and many people with thee, all of them riding upon horses, a great company, and a mighty army:

16And thou shalt come up against my people of Israel, as a cloud to cover the land; it shall be in the latter days, and I will bring thee against my land, that the heathen may know me, when I shall be sanctified in thee, O Gog, before their eyes.

17Thus saith the Lord GOD; Art thou he of whom I have spoken in old time by my servants the prophets of Israel, which prophesied in those days many years that I would bring thee against them?

18And it shall come to pass at the same time when Gog shall come against the land of Israel, saith the Lord GOD, that my fury shall come up in my face.

19For in my jealousy and in the fire of my wrath have I spoken, Surely in that day there shall be a great shaking in the land of Israel;

20So that the fishes of the sea, and the fowls of the heaven, and the beasts of the field, and all creeping things that creep upon the earth, and all the men that are upon the face of the earth, shall shake at my presence, and the mountains shall be thrown down, and the steep places shall fall, and every wall shall fall to the ground.

21And I will call for a sword against him throughout all my mountains, saith the Lord GOD: every man's sword shall be against his brother.

22And I will plead against him with pestilence and with blood; and I will rain upon him, and upon his bands, and upon the many people that are with him, an overflowing rain, and great hailstones, fire, and brimstone.

23Thus will I magnify myself, and sanctify myself; and I will be known in the eyes of many nations, and they shall know that I am the LORD.

39 THEREFORE, THOU son of man, prophesy against Gog, and say, Thus saith the Lord GOD; Behold, I am against thee, O Gog, the chief prince of Meshech and Tubal:

2And I will turn thee back, and leave but the sixth part of thee, and will cause thee to come up from the north parts, and will bring thee upon the mountains of Israel:

3And I will smite thy bow out of thy left hand, and will cause thine arrows to fall out of thy right hand.

4Thou shalt fall upon the mountains of Israel, thou, and all thy bands, and the people that is with thee: I will give thee unto the ravenous birds of every sort, and to the beasts of the field to be devoured.

5Thou shalt fall upon the open field: for I have spoken it, saith the Lord GOD.

6And I will send a fire on Magog, and among them that dwell carelessly in the isles: and they shall know that I am the LORD.

7So will I make my holy name known in the midst of my people Israel; and I will not let them pollute my holy name any more: and the heathen shall know that I am the LORD, the Holy One in Israel.

8¶ Behold, it is come, and it is done, saith the Lord GOD; this is the day whereof I have spoken.

9And they that dwell in the cities of Israel shall go forth, and shall set on fire and burn the weapons, both the shields and the bucklers, the bows and the arrows, and the handstaves, and the spears, and they shall burn them with fire seven years:

10So that they shall take no wood out of the field, neither cut down any out of the forests; for they shall burn the weapons with fire: and they shall spoil those that spoiled them, and rob those that robbed them, saith the Lord GOD.

New International

north, you and many nations with you, all of them riding on horses, a great horde, a mighty army. 16You will advance against my people Israel like a cloud that covers the land. In days to come, O Gog, I will bring you against my land, so that the nations may know me when I show myself holy through you before their eyes.

17" 'This is what the Sovereign LORD says: Are you not the one I spoke of in former days by my servants the prophets of Israel? At that time they prophesied for years that I would bring you against them. 18This is what will happen in that day: When Gog attacks the land of Israel, my hot anger will be aroused, declares the Sovereign LORD. 19In my zeal and fiery wrath I declare that at that time there shall be a great earthquake in the land of Israel. 20The fish of the sea, the birds of the air, the beasts of the field, every creature that moves along the ground, and all the people on the face of the earth will tremble at my presence. The mountains will be overturned, the cliffs will crumble and every wall will fall to the ground. 21I will summon a sword against Gog on all my mountains, declares the Sovereign LORD. Every man's sword will be against his brother. 22I will execute judgment upon him with plague and bloodshed; I will pour down torrents of rain, hailstones and burning sulfur on him and on his troops and on the many nations with him. 23And so I will show my greatness and my holiness, and I will make myself known in the sight of many nations. Then they will know that I am the LORD.'

39 "SON OF man, prophesy against Gog and say: 'This is what the Sovereign LORD says: I am against you, O Gog, chief prince of[a] Meshech and Tubal. 2I will turn you around and drag you along. I will bring you from the far north and send you against the mountains of Israel. 3Then I will strike your bow from your left hand and make your arrows drop from your right hand. 4On the mountains of Israel you will fall, you and all your troops and the nations with you. I will give you as food to all kinds of carrion birds and to the wild animals. 5You will fall in the open field, for I have spoken, declares the Sovereign LORD. 6I will send fire on Magog and on those who live in safety in the coastlands, and they will know that I am the LORD.

7" 'I will make known my holy name among my people Israel. I will no longer let my holy name be profaned, and the nations will know that I the LORD am the Holy One in Israel. 8It is coming! It will surely take place, declares the Sovereign LORD. This is the day I have spoken of.

9" 'Then those who live in the towns of Israel will go out and use the weapons for fuel and burn them up—the small and large shields, the bows and arrows, the war clubs and spears. For seven years they will use them for fuel. 10They will not need to gather wood from the fields or cut it from the forests, because they will use the weapons for fuel. And they will plunder those who plundered them and loot those who looted them, declares the Sovereign LORD.

---

a 1 Or Gog, prince of Rosh,

Living Bible

your vast host of cavalry and cover the land like a cloud. This will happen in the distant future—in the latter years of history.b I will bring you against my land, and my holiness will be vindicated in your terrible destruction before their eyes, so that all the nations will know that I am God.

17"The Lord God says: You are the one I spoke of long ago through the prophets of Israel, saying that after many years had passed, I would bring you against my people. 18But when you come to destroy the land of Israel, my fury will rise! 19For in my jealousy and blazing wrath, I promise a mighty shaking in the land of Israel on that day. 20All living things shall quake in terror at my presence; mountains shall be thrown down; cliffs shall tumble; walls shall crumble to the earth. 21I will summon every kind of terror against you, says the Lord God, and you will fight against yourselves in mortal combat! 22I will fight you with sword, disease, torrential floods, great hailstones, fire and brimstone! 23Thus will I show my greatness and bring honor upon my name, and all the nations of the world will hear what I have done, and know that I am God!

39 "SON OF dust, prophesy this also against Gog. Tell him:

I stand against you, Gog, leader of Meshech and Tubal. 2I will turn you and drive you toward the mountains of Israel, bringing you from the distant north. And I will destroy 85 percentc of your army in the mountains. 3I will knock your weapons from your hands and leave you helpless. 4You and all your vast armies will die upon the mountains. I will give you to the vultures and wild animals to devour you. 5You will never reach the cities—you will fall upon the open fields; for I have spoken, the Lord God says. 6And I will rain down fire on Magog and on all your allies who live safely on the coasts, and they shall know I am the Lord.

7"Thus I will make known my holy name among my people Israel; I will not let it be mocked at anymore. And the nations too shall know I am the Lord, the Holy One of Israel. 8That day of judgment will come; everything will happen just as I have declared it.

9"The people of the cities of Israel will go out and pick up your shields and bucklers, bows and arrows, javelins and spears, to use for fuel—enough to last them seven years. 10For seven years they will need nothing else for their fires. They won't cut wood from the fields or forests, for these weapons will give them all they need. They will use the possessions of those who abused them.

New Revised Standard

come from your place out of the remotest parts of the north, you and many peoples with you, all of them riding on horses, a great horde, a mighty army; 16you will come up against my people Israel, like a cloud covering the earth. In the latter days I will bring you against my land, so that the nations may know me, when through you, O Gog, I display my holiness before their eyes.

Judgment on Gog

17 Thus says the Lord GOD: Are you he of whom I spoke in former days by my servants the prophets of Israel, who in those days prophesied for years that I would bring you against them? 18On that day, when Gog comes against the land of Israel, says the Lord GOD, my wrath shall be aroused. 19For in my jealousy and in my blazing wrath I declare: On that day there shall be a great shaking in the land of Israel; 20the fish of the sea, and the birds of the air, and the animals of the field, and all creeping things that creep on the ground, and all human beings that are on the face of the earth, shall quake at my presence, and the mountains shall be thrown down, and the cliffs shall fall, and every wall shall tumble to the ground. 21I will summon the sword against Gogd ine all my mountains, says the Lord GOD; the swords of all will be against their comrades. 22With pestilence and bloodshed I will enter into judgment with him; and I will pour down torrential rains and hailstones, fire and sulfur, upon him and his troops and the many peoples that are with him. 23So I will display my greatness and my holiness and make myself known in the eyes of many nations. Then they shall know that I am the LORD.

Gog's Armies Destroyed

39 AND YOU, mortal, prophesy against Gog, and say: Thus says the Lord GOD: I am against you, O Gog, chief prince of Meshech and Tubal! 2I will turn you around and drive you forward, and bring you up from the remotest parts of the north, and lead you against the mountains of Israel. 3I will strike your bow from your left hand, and will make your arrows drop out of your right hand. 4You shall fall upon the mountains of Israel, you and all your troops and the peoples that are with you; I will give you to birds of prey of every kind and to the wild animals to be devoured. 5You shall fall in the open field; for I have spoken, says the Lord GOD. 6I will send fire on Magog and on those who live securely in the coastlands; and they shall know that I am the LORD.

7 My holy name I will make known among my people Israel; and I will not let my holy name be profaned any more; and the nations shall know that I am the LORD, the Holy One in Israel. 8It has come! It has happened, says the Lord GOD. This is the day of which I have spoken.

9 Then those who live in the towns of Israel will go out and make fires of the weapons and burn them— bucklers and shields, bows and arrows, handpikes and spears—and they will make fires of them for seven years. 10They will not need to take wood out of the field or cut down any trees in the forests, for they will make their fires of the weapons; they will despoil those who despoiled them, and plunder those who plundered them, says the Lord GOD.

---

b 38:15, 16 in the latter years of history, implied. Literally, "in the latter days," an expression which does not, in Hebrew usage, necessarily mean "the end times."   c 39:2 I will destroy 85 percent, literally, "leave one-sixth of you."

d Heb him   e Heb to or for

King James

11¶ And it shall come to pass in that day, *that* I will give unto Gog a place there of graves in Israel, the valley of the passengers on the east of the sea: and it shall stop the *noses* of the passengers: and there shall they bury Gog and all his multitude: and they shall call *it* The valley of Hamon-gog.

12And seven months shall the house of Israel be burying of them, that they may cleanse the land.

13Yea, all the people of the land shall bury *them;* and it shall be to them a renown the day that I shall be glorified, saith the Lord GOD.

14And they shall sever out men of continual employment, passing through the land to bury with the passengers those that remain upon the face of the earth, to cleanse it: after the end of seven months shall they search.

15And the passengers *that* pass through the land, when *any* seeth a man's bone, then shall he set up a sign by it, till the buriers have buried it in the valley of Hamon-gog.

16And also the name of the city *shall be* Hamonah. Thus shall they cleanse the land.

17¶ And, thou son of man, thus saith the Lord GOD; Speak unto every feathered fowl, and to every beast of the field, Assemble yourselves, and come; gather yourselves on every side to my sacrifice that I do sacrifice for you, *even* a great sacrifice upon the mountains of Israel, that ye may eat flesh, and drink blood.

18Ye shall eat the flesh of the mighty, and drink the blood of the princes of the earth, of rams, of lambs, and of goats, of bullocks, all of them fatlings of Bashan.

19And ye shall eat fat till ye be full, and drink blood till ye be drunken, of my sacrifice which I have sacrificed for you.

20Thus ye shall be filled at my table with horses and chariots, with mighty men, and with all men of war, saith the Lord GOD.

21And I will set my glory among the heathen, and all the heathen shall see my judgment that I have executed, and my hand that I have laid upon them.

22So the house of Israel shall know that I *am* the LORD their God from that day and forward.

23¶ And the heathen shall know that the house of Israel went into captivity for their iniquity: because they trespassed against me, therefore hid I my face from them, and gave them into the hand of their enemies: so fell they all by the sword.

24According to their uncleanness and according to their transgressions have I done unto them, and hid my face from them.

25Therefore thus saith the Lord GOD; Now will I bring again the captivity of Jacob, and have mercy upon the whole house of Israel, and will be jealous for my holy name;

26After that they have borne their shame, and all their trespasses whereby they have trespassed against me, when they dwelt safely in their land, and none made *them* afraid.

27When I have brought them again from the people, and gathered them out of their enemies' lands, and am sanctified in them in the sight of many nations;

28Then shall they know that I *am* the LORD their God, which caused them to be led into captivity among the heathen: but I have gathered them unto their own land, and have left none of them any more there.

29Neither will I hide my face any more from them: for I have poured out my spirit upon the house of Israel, saith the Lord GOD.

New International

11 'On that day I will give Gog a burial place in Israel, in the valley of those who travel east toward[a] the Sea.[b] It will block the way of travelers, because Gog and all his hordes will be buried there. So it will be called the Valley of Hamon Gog.[c]

12 'For seven months the house of Israel will be burying them in order to cleanse the land. 13All the people of the land will bury them, and the day I am glorified will be a memorable day for them, declares the Sovereign LORD.

14 'Men will be regularly employed to cleanse the land. Some will go throughout the land and, in addition to them, others will bury those that remain on the ground. At the end of the seven months they will begin their search. 15As they go through the land and one of them sees a human bone, he will set up a marker beside it until the gravediggers have buried it in the Valley of Hamon Gog. 16(Also a town called Hamonah[d] will be there.) And so they will cleanse the land.'

17"Son of man, this is what the Sovereign LORD says: Call out to every kind of bird and all the wild animals: 'Assemble and come together from all around to the sacrifice I am preparing for you, the great sacrifice on the mountains of Israel. There you will eat flesh and drink blood. 18You will eat the flesh of mighty men and drink the blood of the princes of the earth as if they were rams and lambs, goats and bulls—all of them fattened animals from Bashan. 19At the sacrifice I am preparing for you, you will eat fat till you are glutted and drink blood till you are drunk. 20At my table you will eat your fill of horses and riders, mighty men and soldiers of every kind,' declares the Sovereign LORD.

21"I will display my glory among the nations, and all the nations will see the punishment I inflict and the hand I lay upon them. 22From that day forward the house of Israel will know that I am the LORD their God. 23And the nations will know that the people of Israel went into exile for their sin, because they were unfaithful to me. So I hid my face from them and handed them over to their enemies, and they all fell by the sword. 24I dealt with them according to their uncleanness and their offenses, and I hid my face from them.

25"Therefore this is what the Sovereign LORD says: I will now bring Jacob back from captivity[e] and will have compassion on all the people of Israel, and I will be zealous for my holy name. 26They will forget their shame and all the unfaithfulness they showed toward me when they lived in safety in their land with no one to make them afraid. 27When I have brought them back from the nations and have gathered them from the countries of their enemies, I will show myself holy through them in the sight of many nations. 28Then they will know that I am the LORD their God, for though I sent them into exile among the nations, I will gather them to their own land, not leaving any behind. 29I will no longer hide my face from them, for I will pour out my Spirit on the house of Israel, declares the Sovereign LORD."

---

a *11* Or *of*   b *11* That is, the Dead Sea   c *11 Hamon Gog* means *hordes of Gog.*   d *16 Hamonah* means *horde.*   e *25* Or *now restore the fortunes of Jacob*

Living Bible

11"And I will make a vast graveyard for Gog and his armies in the Valley of the Travelers, east of the Dead Sea. It will block the path of the travelers. There Gog and all his armies will be buried. And they will change the name of the place to 'The Valley of Gog's Army.' 12It will take seven months for the people of Israel to bury the bodies. 13Everyone in Israel will help, for it will be a glorious victory for Israel on that day when I demonstrate my glory, says the Lord. 14At the end of the seven months, they will appoint men to search the land systematically for any skeletons left and bury them, so that the land will be cleansed. 15, 16Whenever anyone sees some bones, he will put up a marker beside them so that the buriers will see them and take them to the Valley of Gog's Army to bury them. A city named 'Multitude' is there! And so the land will finally be cleansed.

17"And now, son of dust, call all the birds and animals and say to them: Gather together for a mighty sacrificial feast. Come from far and near to the mountains of Israel. Come, eat the flesh and drink the blood! 18Eat the flesh of mighty men and drink the blood of princes— they are the rams, the lambs, the goats and the fat young bulls of Bashan for my feast! 19Gorge yourselves with flesh until you are glutted, drink blood until you are drunk; this is the sacrificial feast I have prepared for you. 20Feast at my banquet table—feast on horses, riders and valiant warriors, says the Lord God. 21Thus I will demonstrate my glory among the nations; all shall see the punishment of Gog and know that I have done it.

22"And from that time onward, the people of Israel will know I am the Lord their God. 23And the nations will know why Israel was sent away to exile—it was punishment for sin, for they acted in treachery against their God. Therefore I turned my face away from them and let their enemies destroy them. 24I turned my face away and punished them in proportion to the vileness of their sins.

25"But now, the Lord God says, I will end the captivity of my people and have mercy upon them and restore their fortunes, for I am concerned about my reputation! 26Their time of treachery and shame will all be in the past; they will be home again, in peace and safety in their own land, with no one bothering them or making them afraid. 27I will bring them home from the lands of their enemies—and my glory shall be evident to all the nations when I do it. Through them I will vindicate my holiness before the nations. 28Then my people will know I am the Lord their God—responsible for sending them away to exile, and responsible for bringing them home. I will leave none of them remaining among the nations. 29And I will never hide my face from them again, for I will pour out my Spirit upon them, says the Lord God."

New Revised Standard

The Burial of Gog

11 On that day I will give to Gog a place for burial in Israel, the Valley of the Travelers[f] east of the sea; it shall block the path of the travelers, for there Gog and all his horde will be buried; it shall be called the Valley of Hamon-gog.[g] 12 Seven months the house of Israel shall spend burying them, in order to cleanse the land. 13 All the people of the land shall bury them; and it will bring them honor on the day that I show my glory, says the Lord GOD. 14 They will set apart men to pass through the land regularly and bury any invaders[h] who remain on the face of the land, so as to cleanse it; for seven months they shall make their search. 15 As the searchers[h] pass through the land, anyone who sees a human bone shall set up a sign by it, until the buriers have buried it in the Valley of Hamon-gog.[g] 16 (A city Hamonah[i] is there also.) Thus they shall cleanse the land.

17 As for you, mortal, thus says the Lord GOD: Speak to the birds of every kind and to all the wild animals: Assemble and come, gather from all around to the sacrificial feast that I am preparing for you, a great sacrificial feast on the mountains of Israel, and you shall eat flesh and drink blood. 18 You shall eat the flesh of the mighty, and drink the blood of the princes of the earth—of rams, of lambs, and of goats, of bulls, all of them fatlings of Bashan. 19 You shall eat fat until you are filled, and drink blood until you are drunk, at the sacrificial feast that I am preparing for you. 20 And you shall be filled at my table with horses and charioteers,[j] with warriors and all kinds of soldiers, says the Lord GOD.

Israel Restored to the Land

21 I will display my glory among the nations; and all the nations shall see my judgment that I have executed, and my hand that I have laid on them. 22 The house of Israel shall know that I am the LORD their God, from that day forward. 23 And the nations shall know that the house of Israel went into captivity for their iniquity, because they dealt treacherously with me. So I hid my face from them and gave them into the hand of their adversaries, and they all fell by the sword. 24 I dealt with them according to their uncleanness and their transgressions, and hid my face from them.

25 Therefore thus says the Lord GOD: Now I will restore the fortunes of Jacob, and have mercy on the whole house of Israel; and I will be jealous for my holy name. 26 They shall forget[k] their shame, and all the treachery they have practiced against me, when they live securely in their land with no one to make them afraid, 27 when I have brought them back from the peoples and gathered them from their enemies' lands, and through them have displayed my holiness in the sight of many nations. 28 Then they shall know that I am the LORD their God because I sent them into exile among the nations, and then gathered them into their own land. I will leave none of them behind; 29 and I will never again hide my face from them, when I pour out my spirit upon the house of Israel, says the Lord GOD.

f Or of the Abarim   g That is, the Horde of Gog   h Heb travelers   i That is The Horde   j Heb chariots   k Another reading is They shall bear

King James

40 IN THE five and twentieth year of our captivity, in the beginning of the year, in the tenth *day* of the month, in the fourteenth year after that the city was smitten, in the selfsame day the hand of the LORD was upon me, and brought me thither.

2In the visions of God brought he me into the land of Israel, and set me upon a very high mountain, by which *was* as the frame of a city on the south.

3And he brought me thither, and, behold, *there was* a man, whose appearance *was* like the appearance of brass, with a line of flax in his hand, and a measuring reed; and he stood in the gate.

4And the man said unto me, Son of man, behold with thine eyes, and hear with thine ears, and set thine heart upon all that I shall show thee; for to the intent that I might show *them* unto thee *art* thou brought hither: declare all that thou seest to the house of Israel.

5And behold a wall on the outside of the house round about, and in the man's hand a measuring reed of six cubits *long* by the cubit and an handbreadth: so he measured the breadth of the building, one reed; and the height, one reed.

6¶ Then came he unto the gate which looketh toward the east, and went up the stairs thereof, and measured the threshold of the gate, *which was* one reed broad; and the other threshold *of the gate, which was* one reed broad.

7And *every* little chamber *was* one reed long, and one reed broad; and between the little chambers *were* five cubits; and the threshold of the gate by the porch of the gate within *was* one reed.

8He measured also the porch of the gate within, one reed.

9Then measured he the porch of the gate, eight cubits; and the posts thereof, two cubits; and the porch of the gate *was* inward.

10And the little chambers of the gate eastward *were* three on this side, and three on that side; they three *were* of one measure: and the posts had one measure on this side and on that side.

11And he measured the breadth of the entry of the gate, ten cubits; *and* the length of the gate, thirteen cubits.

12The space also before the little chambers *was* one cubit *on this side*, and the space *was* one cubit on that side: and the little chambers *were* six cubits on this side, and six cubits on that side.

13He measured then the gate from the roof of *one* little chamber to the roof of another: the breadth *was* five and twenty cubits, door against door.

14He made also posts of threescore cubits, even unto the post of the court round about the gate.

15And from the face of the gate of the entrance unto the face of the porch of the inner gate *were* fifty cubits.

16And *there were* narrow windows to the little chambers, and to their posts within the gate round about, and likewise to the arches: and windows *were* round about inward: and upon *each* post *were* palm trees.

17Then brought he me into the outward court, and, lo, *there were* chambers, and a pavement made for the court round about: thirty chambers *were* upon the pavement.

18And the pavement by the side of the gates over against the length of the gates *was* the lower pavement.

19Then he measured the breadth from the forefront of the lower gate unto the forefront of the inner court without, an hundred cubits eastward and northward.

New International

The New Temple Area

40 IN THE twenty-fifth year of our exile, at the beginning of the year, on the tenth of the month, in the fourteenth year after the fall of the city—on that very day the hand of the LORD was upon me and he took me there. 2In visions of God he took me to the land of Israel and set me on a very high mountain, on whose south side were some buildings that looked like a city. 3He took me there, and I saw a man whose appearance was like bronze; he was standing in the gateway with a linen cord and a measuring rod in his hand. 4The man said to me, "Son of man, look with your eyes and hear with your ears and pay attention to everything I am going to show you, for that is why you have been brought here. Tell the house of Israel everything you see."

The East Gate to the Outer Court

5I saw a wall completely surrounding the temple area. The length of the measuring rod in the man's hand was six long cubits, each of which was a cubit[a] and a handbreadth.[b] He measured the wall; it was one measuring rod thick and one rod high.

6Then he went to the gate facing east. He climbed its steps and measured the threshold of the gate; it was one rod deep.[c] 7The alcoves for the guards were one rod long and one rod wide, and the projecting walls between the alcoves were five cubits thick. And the threshold of the gate next to the portico facing the temple was one rod deep.

8Then he measured the portico of the gateway; 9it[d] was eight cubits deep and its jambs were two cubits thick. The portico of the gateway faced the temple.

10Inside the east gate were three alcoves on each side; the three had the same measurements, and the faces of the projecting walls on each side had the same measurements. 11Then he measured the width of the entrance to the gateway; it was ten cubits and its length was thirteen cubits. 12In front of each alcove was a wall one cubit high, and the alcoves were six cubits square. 13Then he measured the gateway from the top of the rear wall of one alcove to the top of the opposite one; the distance was twenty-five cubits from one parapet opening to the opposite one. 14He measured along the faces of the projecting walls all around the inside of the gateway—sixty cubits. The measurement was up to the portico[e] facing the courtyard.[f] 15The distance from the entrance of the gateway to the far end of its portico was fifty cubits. 16The alcoves and the projecting walls inside the gateway were surmounted by narrow parapet openings all around, as was the portico; the openings all around faced inward. The faces of the projecting walls were decorated with palm trees.

The Outer Court

17Then he brought me into the outer court. There I saw some rooms and a pavement that had been constructed all around the court; there were thirty rooms along the pavement. 18It abutted the sides of the gateways and was as wide as they were long; this was the lower pavement. 19Then he measured the distance from the inside of the lower gateway to the outside of the inner court; it was a hundred cubits on the east side as well as on the north.

---

a 5 The common cubit was about 1 1/2 feet (about 0.5 meter).   b 5 That is, about 3 inches (about 8 centimeters)   c 6 Septuagint; Hebrew *deep, the first threshold, one rod deep*   d 8,9 Many Hebrew manuscripts, Septuagint, Vulgate and Syriac; most Hebrew manuscripts *gateway facing the temple; it was one rod deep.* 9*Then he measured the portico of the gateway; it* e 14 Septuagint; Hebrew *projecting wall*   f 14 The meaning of the Hebrew for this verse is uncertain.

Living Bible

40 EARLY IN April of the twenty-fifth year of our exile—the fourteenth year after Jerusalem was captured—the hand of the Lord was upon me, ²and in a vision he took me to the land of Israel and set me down on a high mountain where I saw what appeared to be a city opposite me. ³Going nearer, I saw a man whose face shone like bronze, standing beside the Temple gate,g holding in his hand a measuring tape and a measuring stick.

⁴He said to me: "Son of dust, watch and listen and take to heart everything I show you, for you have been brought here so I can show you many things; and then you are to return to the people of Israel to tell them all you have seen." ⁵The man began to measure the wall around the outside of the Temple area with his measuring stick, which was 10½ feet long. He told me, "This wall is 10½ feet high and 10½ feet wide." ⁶Then he took me over to the passageway that goes through the eastern wall. We climbed the seven steps into the entrance and he measured the entry hall of the passage; it was 10½ feet wide.

⁷⁻¹²Walking on through the passageway I saw that there were three guardrooms on each side; each of these rooms was 10½ feet square, with a distance of 8¾ feet along the wall between them. In front of these rooms was a low barrier eighteen inches high and eighteen inches wide.h Beyond the guardrooms was a 10½-foot doorway opening into a 14-foot hall with 3½-foot columns. Beyond this hall, at the inner end of the passageway was a vestibule 22¾ feet wide and 17½ feet long.

¹³Then he measured the entire outside width of the passageway, measuring across the roof from the outside doors of the guardrooms; this distance was 43¾ feet. ¹⁴Then he estimated the pillars on each side of the porch to be about 100 feet high. ¹⁵The full length of the entrance passage was 87½ feet from one end to the other. ¹⁶There were windows that narrowed inward through the walls along both sides of the passageway and along the guardroom walls. The windows were also in the exit and in the entrance halls. The pillars were decorated with palm tree decorations.

¹⁷And so we passed through the passageway to the court inside. A stone pavement ran around the inside of the walls, and thirty rooms were built against the walls, opening onto this pavement. ¹⁸This was called "the lower pavement." It extended out from the walls into the court the same distance as the passageway did.

¹⁹Then he measured across to the wall on the other side of this court (which was called "the outer court" of the Templei) and found that the distance was 175 feet.

New Revised Standard

The Vision of the New Temple

40 IN THE twenty-fifth year of our exile, at the beginning of the year, on the tenth day of the month, in the fourteenth year after the city was struck down, on that very day, the hand of the LORD was upon me, and he brought me there. ²He brought me, in visions of God, to the land of Israel, and set me down upon a very high mountain, on which was a structure like a city to the south. ³When he brought me there, a man was there, whose appearance shone like bronze, with a linen cord and a measuring reed in his hand; and he was standing in the gateway. ⁴The man said to me, "Mortal, look closely and listen attentively, and set your mind upon all that I shall show you, for you were brought here in order that I might show it to you; declare all that you see to the house of Israel."

5 Now there was a wall all around the outside of the temple area. The length of the measuring reed in the man's hand was six long cubits, each being a cubit and a handbreadth in length; so he measured the thickness of the wall, one reed; and the height, one reed. ⁶Then he went into the gateway facing east, going up its steps, and measured the threshold of the gate, one reed deep.j There were ⁷recesses, and each recess was one reed wide and one reed deep; and the space between the recesses, five cubits; and the threshold of the gate by the vestibule of the gate at the inner end was one reed deep. ⁸Then he measured the inner vestibule of the gateway, one cubit. ⁹Then he measured the vestibule of the gateway, eight cubits; and its pilasters, two cubits; and the vestibule of the gate was at the inner end. ¹⁰There were three recesses on either side of the east gate; the three were of the same size; and the pilasters on either side were of the same size. ¹¹Then he measured the width of the opening of the gateway, ten cubits; and the width of the gateway, thirteen cubits. ¹²There was a barrier before the recesses, one cubit on either side; and the recesses were six cubits on either side. ¹³Then he measured the gate from the backk of the one recess to the backk of the other, a width of twenty-five cubits, from wall to wall.¹ ¹⁴He measuredm also the vestibule, twenty cubits; and the gate next to the pilaster on every side of the court.n ¹⁵From the front of the gate at the entrance to the end of the inner vestibule of the gate was fifty cubits. ¹⁶The recesses and their pilasters had windows, with shuttersn on the inside of the gateway all around, and the vestibules also had windows on the inside all around; and on the pilasters were palm trees.

17 Then he brought me into the outer court; there were chambers there, and a pavement, all around the court; thirty chambers fronted on the pavement. ¹⁸The pavement ran along the side of the gates, corresponding to the length of the gates; this was the lower pavement. ¹⁹Then he measured the distance from the inner front ofo the lower gate to the outer front of the inner court, one hundred cubits.p

---

g 40:3 *standing beside the Temple gate*, implied.   h 40:7-12 *eighteen inches wide*, or, an eighteen-inch pillar in front of (or between) the guardrooms, projecting out into the hallway.   i 40:19 *which was called "the outer court" of the Temple*, implied.

j Heb *deep, and one threshold, one reed deep*   k Gk: Heb *roof*   l Heb *opening facing opening*   m Heb *made*   n Meaning of Heb uncertain   o Compare Gk: Heb *from before*   p Heb adds *the east and the north*

King James

20¶ And the gate of the outward court that looked toward the north, he measured the length thereof, and the breadth thereof.

21And the little chambers thereof *were* three on this side and three on that side; and the posts thereof and the arches thereof were after the measure of the first gate: the length thereof *was* fifty cubits, and the breadth five and twenty cubits.

22And their windows, and their arches, and their palm trees, *were* after the measure of the gate that looketh toward the east; and they went up unto it by seven steps; and the arches thereof *were* before them.

23And the gate of the inner court *was* over against the gate toward the north, and toward the east; and he measured from gate to gate an hundred cubits.

24¶ After that he brought me toward the south, and behold a gate toward the south: and he measured the posts thereof and the arches thereof according to these measures.

25And *there were* windows in it and in the arches thereof round about, like those windows: the length *was* fifty cubits, and the breadth five and twenty cubits.

26And *there were* seven steps to go up to it, and the arches thereof *were* before them: and it had palm trees, one on this side, and another on that side, upon the posts thereof.

27And *there was* a gate in the inner court toward the south: and he measured from gate to gate toward the south an hundred cubits.

28And he brought me to the inner court by the south gate: and he measured the south gate according to these measures;

29And the little chambers thereof, and the posts thereof, and the arches thereof, according to these measures: and *there were* windows in it and in the arches thereof round about: *it was* fifty cubits long, and five and twenty cubits broad.

30And the arches round about *were* five and twenty cubits long, and five cubits broad.

31And the arches thereof *were* toward the utter court; and palm trees *were* upon the posts thereof: and the going up to it *had* eight steps.

32¶ And he brought me into the inner court toward the east: and he measured the gate according to these measures.

33And the little chambers thereof, and the posts thereof, and the arches thereof, *were* according to these measures: and *there were* windows therein and in the arches thereof round about: *it was* fifty cubits long, and five and twenty cubits broad.

34And the arches thereof *were* toward the outward court; and palm trees *were* upon the posts thereof, on this side, and on that side: and the going up to it *had* eight steps.

35¶ And he brought me to the north gate, and measured *it* according to these measures;

36The little chambers thereof, the posts thereof, and the arches thereof, and the windows to it round about: the length *was* fifty cubits, and the breadth five and twenty cubits.

37And the posts thereof *were* toward the utter court; and palm trees *were* upon the posts thereof, on this side, and on that side: and the going up to it *had* eight steps.

38And the chambers and the entries thereof *were* by the posts of the gates, where they washed the burnt offering.

39¶ And in the porch of the gate *were* two tables on this side, and two tables on that side, to slay thereon the burnt offering and the sin offering and the trespass offering.

40And at the side without, as one goeth up to the entry of the north gate, *were* two tables; and on the other side, which *was* at the porch of the gate, *were* two tables.

New International

The North Gate

20Then he measured the length and width of the gate facing north, leading into the outer court. 21Its alcoves—three on each side—its projecting walls and its portico had the same measurements as those of the first gateway. It was fifty cubits long and twenty-five cubits wide. 22Its openings, its portico and its palm tree decorations had the same measurements as those of the gate facing east. Seven steps led up to it, with its portico opposite them. 23There was a gate to the inner court facing the north gate, just as there was on the east. He measured from one gate to the opposite one; it was a hundred cubits.

The South Gate

24Then he led me to the south side and I saw a gate facing south. He measured its jambs and its portico, and they had the same measurements as the others. 25The gateway and its portico had narrow openings all around, like the openings of the others. It was fifty cubits long and twenty-five cubits wide. 26Seven steps led up to it, with its portico opposite them; it had palm tree decorations on the faces of the projecting walls on each side. 27The inner court also had a gate facing south, and he measured from this gate to the outer gate on the south side; it was a hundred cubits.

Gates to the Inner Court

28Then he brought me into the inner court through the south gate, and he measured the south gate; it had the same measurements as the others. 29Its alcoves, its projecting walls and its portico had the same measurements as the others. The gateway and its portico had openings all around. It was fifty cubits long and twenty-five cubits wide. 30(The porticoes of the gateways around the inner court were twenty-five cubits wide and five cubits deep.) 31Its portico faced the outer court; palm trees decorated its jambs, and eight steps led up to it.

32Then he brought me to the inner court on the east side, and he measured the gateway; it had the same measurements as the others. 33Its alcoves, its projecting walls and its portico had the same measurements as the others. The gateway and its portico had openings all around. It was fifty cubits long and twenty-five cubits wide. 34Its portico faced the outer court; palm trees decorated the jambs on either side, and eight steps led up to it.

35Then he brought me to the north gate and measured it. It had the same measurements as the others, 36as did its alcoves, its projecting walls and its portico, and it had openings all around. It was fifty cubits long and twenty-five cubits wide. 37Its portico[a] faced the outer court; palm trees decorated the jambs on either side, and eight steps led up to it.

The Rooms for Preparing Sacrifices

38A room with a doorway was by the portico in each of the inner gateways, where the burnt offerings were washed. 39In the portico of the gateway were two tables on each side, on which the burnt offerings, sin offerings and guilt offerings were slaughtered. 40By the outside wall of the portico of the gateway, near the steps at the entrance to the north gateway were two tables, and on the other side of the steps were two tables. 41So there

---

a 37 Septuagint (see also verses 31 and 34); Hebrew *jambs*

Living Bible

20As I followed, he left the eastern passageway and went over to the passage through the northern wall and measured it. 21Here too there were three guardrooms on each side, and all the measurements were the same as for the east passageway—87½ feet long and 43¾ feet from side to side across the top of the guardrooms. 22There were windows, an entry hall and the palm tree decorations just the same as on the east side. And there were seven steps leading up to the doorway to the entry hall inside.

23Here at the north entry, just as at the east, if one walked through the passageway into the court, and straight across it, he came to an inner wall and a passageway through it to an inner court. The distance between the two passageways was 175 feet. 24Then he took me around to the south gate and measured the various sections of its passageway and found they were just the same as in the others. 25It had windows along the walls as the others did, and an entry hall. And like the others, it was 87½ feet long and 43¾ feet wide. 26It too had a stairway of seven steps leading up to it, and there were palm tree decorations along the walls. 27And here again, if one walked through the passageway into the court and straight across it, he came to the inner wall and a passageway through it to the inner court. And the distance between the passageways was 175 feet.

28Then he took me over to the inner wall and its south passageway. He measured this passageway and found that it had the same measurements as the passageways of the outer wall.b 29,30c Its guardrooms, pillars and entrance and exit hall were identical to all the others, and so were the windows along its walls and entry. And, like the others, it was 87½ feet long by 43¾ feet wide. 31The only difference was that it had eight steps leading up to it instead of seven. It had palm tree decorations on the pillars, just as the others.

32Then he took me along the court to the eastern entrance of the inner wall, and measured it. It too had the same measurements as the others. 33Its guardrooms, pillars and entrance hall were the same size as those of the other passageways, and there were windows along the walls and in the entry hall; and it was 87½ feet long by 43¾ feet wide. 34Its entry hall faced the outer court and there were palm tree decorations on its columns, but there were eight steps instead of seven going up to the entrance.

35Then he took me around to the north gate of the inner wall, and the measurements there were just like the others: 36The guardrooms, pillars and entry hall of this passageway were the same as the others, with a length of 87½ feet and a width of 43¾ feet. 37Its entry hall faced toward the outer court, and it had palm tree decorations on the walls of each side of the passageway, and there were eight steps leading up to the entrance.

38But a door led from its entry hall into a side room where the flesh of the sacrifices was washed before being taken to the altar; 39on each side of the entry hall of the passageway there were two tables where the animals for sacrifice were slaughtered for the burnt offerings, sin offerings and guilt offerings to be presented in the Temple. 40Outside the entry hall, on each side of the stairs going up to the north entrance, there were two more tables. 41So, in all, there were eight tables, four inside

New Revised Standard

20   Then he measured the gate of the outer court that faced north—its depth and width. 21Its recesses, three on either side, and its pilasters and its vestibule were of the same size as those of the first gate; its depth was fifty cubits, and its width twenty-five cubits. 22Its windows, its vestibule, and its palm trees were of the same size as those of the gate that faced toward the east. Seven steps led up to it; and its vestibule was on the inside.d 23Opposite the gate on the north, as on the east, was a gate to the inner court; he measured from gate to gate, one hundred cubits.

24   Then he led me toward the south, and there was a gate on the south; and he measured its pilasters and its vestibule; they had the same dimensions as the others. 25There were windows all around in it and in its vestibule, like the windows of the others; its depth was fifty cubits, and its width twenty-five cubits. 26There were seven steps leading up to it; its vestibule was on the inside.d It had palm trees on its pilasters, one on either side. 27There was a gate on the south of the inner court; and he measured from gate to gate toward the south, one hundred cubits.

28   Then he brought me to the inner court by the south gate, and he measured the south gate; it was of the same dimensions as the others. 29Its recesses, its pilasters, and its vestibule were of the same size as the others; and there were windows all around in it and in its vestibule; its depth was fifty cubits, and its width twenty-five cubits. 30There were vestibules all around, twenty-five cubits deep and five cubits wide. 31Its vestibule faced the outer court, and palm trees were on its pilasters, and its stairway had eight steps.

32   Then he brought me to the inner court on the east side, and he measured the gate; it was of the same size as the others. 33Its recesses, its pilasters, and its vestibule were of the same dimensions as the others; and there were windows all around in it and in its vestibule; its depth was fifty cubits, and its width twenty-five cubits. 34Its vestibule faced the outer court, and it had palm trees on its pilasters, on either side; and its stairway had eight steps.

35   Then he brought me to the north gate, and he measured it; it had the same dimensions as the others. 36Its recesses, its pilasters, and its vestibule were of the same size as the others;e and it had windows all around. Its depth was fifty cubits, and its width twenty-five cubits. 37Its vestibulef faced the outer court, and it had palm trees on its pilasters, on either side; and its stairway had eight steps.

38   There was a chamber with its door in the vestibule of the gate,g where the burnt offering was to be washed. 39And in the vestibule of the gate were two tables on either side, on which the burnt offering and the sin offering and the guilt offering were to be slaughtered. 40On the outside of the vestibuleh at the entrance of the north gate were two tables; and on the other side of the vestibule of the gate were two tables. 41Four

---

b 40:28 Some manuscripts add to this verse: "And the arches around it were 37½ feet by 8¾ feet broad."   c 40:30 Verse 30, omitted in the Septuagint and several other of the ancient manuscripts, reads, "There were vestibules round about, and they were 37½ feet long and 8¾ feet broad."

d Gk: Heb before them   e One Ms: Compare verses 29 and 33: MT lacks were of the same size as the others   f Gk Vg Compare verses 26, 31, 34: Heb pilasters   g Cn: Heb at the pilasters of the gates   h Cn: Heb to him who goes up

King James

41Four tables *were* on this side, and four tables on that side, by the side of the gate; eight tables, whereupon they slew *their sacrifices.*

42And the four tables *were* of hewn stone for the burnt offering, of a cubit and an half long, and a cubit and an half broad, and one cubit high: whereupon also they laid the instruments wherewith they slew the burnt offering and the sacrifice.

43And within *were* hooks, an hand broad, fastened round about: and upon the tables *was* the flesh of offering.

44¶ And without the inner gate *were* the chambers of the singers in the inner court, which *was* at the side of the north gate; and their prospect *was* toward the south: one at the side of the east gate *having* the prospect toward the north.

45And he said unto me, This chamber, whose prospect *is* toward the south, *is* for the priests, the keepers of the charge of the house.

46And the chamber whose prospect *is* toward the north *is* for the priests, the keepers of the charge of the altar: these *are* the sons of Zadok among the sons of Levi, which come near to the LORD to minister unto him.

47So he measured the court, an hundred cubits long, and an hundred cubits broad, foursquare; and the altar *that was* before the house.

48¶ And he brought me to the porch of the house, and measured *each* post of the porch, five cubits on this side, and five cubits on that side: and the breadth of the gate *was* three cubits on this side, and three cubits on that side.

49The length of the porch *was* twenty cubits, and the breadth eleven cubits; and *he brought me* by the steps whereby they went up to it: and *there were* pillars by the posts, one on this side, and another on that side.

41 AFTERWARD HE brought me to the temple, and measured the posts, six cubits broad on the one side, and six cubits broad on the other side, *which was* the breadth of the tabernacle.

2And the breadth of the door *was* ten cubits; and the sides of the door *were* five cubits on the one side, and five cubits on the other side: and he measured the length thereof, forty cubits: and the breadth, twenty cubits.

3Then went he inward, and measured the post of the door, two cubits; and the door, six cubits; and the breadth of the door, seven cubits.

4So he measured the length thereof, twenty cubits; and the breadth, twenty cubits, before the temple: and he said unto me, This *is* the most holy *place.*

5After he measured the wall of the house, six cubits; and the breadth of *every* side chamber, four cubits, round about the house on every side.

6And the side chambers *were* three, one over another, and thirty in order; and they entered into the wall which *was* of the house for the side chambers round about, that they might have hold, but they had not hold in the wall of the house.

7And *there was* an enlarging, and a winding about still upward to the side chambers: for the winding about of the house went still upward round about the house: therefore the breadth of the house *was still* upward, and so increased *from* the lowest *chamber* to the highest by the midst.

New International

were four tables on one side of the gateway and four on the other—eight tables in all—on which the sacrifices were slaughtered. 42There were also four tables of dressed stone for the burnt offerings, each a cubit and a half long, a cubit and a half wide and a cubit high. On them were placed the utensils for slaughtering the burnt offerings and the other sacrifices. 43And double-pronged hooks, each a handbreadth long, were attached to the wall all around. The tables were for the flesh of the offerings.

Rooms for the Priests

44Outside the inner gate, within the inner court, were two rooms, onea at the side of the north gate and facing south, and another at the side of the southb gate and facing north. 45He said to me, "The room facing south is for the priests who have charge of the temple, 46and the room facing north is for the priests who have charge of the altar. These are the sons of Zadok, who are the only Levites who may draw near to the LORD to minister before him."

47Then he measured the court: It was square—a hundred cubits long and a hundred cubits wide. And the altar was in front of the temple.

The Temple

48He brought me to the portico of the temple and measured the jambs of the portico; they were five cubits wide on either side. The width of the entrance was fourteen cubits and its projecting walls werec three cubits wide on either side. 49The portico was twenty cubits wide, and twelved cubits from front to back. It was reached by a flight of stairs,e and there were pillars on each side of the jambs.

41 THEN THE man brought me to the outer sanctuary and measured the jambs; the width of the jambs was six cubitsf on each side.g 2The entrance was ten cubits wide, and the projecting walls on each side of it were five cubits wide. He also measured the outer sanctuary; it was forty cubits long and twenty cubits wide.

3Then he went into the inner sanctuary and measured the jambs of the entrance; each was two cubits wide. The entrance was six cubits wide, and the projecting walls on each side of it were seven cubits wide. 4And he measured the length of the inner sanctuary; it was twenty cubits, and its width was twenty cubits across the end of the outer sanctuary. He said to me, "This is the Most Holy Place."

5Then he measured the wall of the temple; it was six cubits thick, and each side room around the temple was four cubits wide. 6The side rooms were on three levels, one above another, thirty on each level. There were ledges all around the wall of the temple to serve as supports for the side rooms, so that the supports were not inserted into the wall of the temple. 7The side rooms all around the temple were wider at each successive level. The structure surrounding the temple was built in ascending stages, so that the rooms widened as one went upward. A stairway went up from the lowest floor to the top floor through the middle floor.

---

a 44 Septuagint; Hebrew *were rooms for singers, which were*
b 44 Septuagint; Hebrew *east*　　c 48 Septuagint; Hebrew *entrance was*
d 49 Septuagint; Hebrew *eleven*　　e 49 Hebrew; Septuagint *Ten steps led up to it*　　f 1 The common cubit was about 1 1/2 feet (about 0.5 meter).
g 1 One Hebrew manuscript and Septuagint; most Hebrew manuscripts *side, the width of the tent*

Living Bible

and four outside, where the sacrifices were cut up and prepared. 42There were also four stone tables where the butchering knives and other implements were laid. These tables were about 2⅝ feet square and 1¾ feet high. 43There were hooks, three or four inches long, fastened along the walls of the entry hall, and on the tables the flesh of the offering was to be laid.

44In the inner court, there were two one-room buildings, one beside the northern entrance, facing south, and one beside the southern entrance, facing north.

45And he said to me: "The building beside the inner northern gate is for the priests who supervise the maintenance. 46The building beside the inner southern entrance is for the priests in charge of the altar—the descendants of Zadok—for they alone of all the Levites may come near to the Lord to minister to him."

47Then he measured the inner court [in front of the Templeʰ] and found it to be 175 feet square, and there was an altar in the court, standing in front of the Temple. 48, 49Then he brought me to the entrance hall of the Temple. Ten steps led up to it from the inner court. Its walls extended up on either side to form two pillars, each of them 8¾ feet thick. The entrance was 24½ feet wide with 5¼-foot walls. Thus the entry hall was 35 feet wide and 19¼ feet long.

41 AFTERWARD HE brought me into the nave, the large main room of the Temple, and measured the pillars that formed its doorway. They were 10½ feet square. 2The entrance hall was 17½ feet wide and 8¾ feet deep. The nave itself was seventy feet long by thirty-five feet.

3Then he went into the inner room at the end of the nave and measured the columns at the entrance and found them to be 3½ feet thick; its doorway was 10½ feet wide, with a hallway 12¼ feet deep behind it. 4The inner room was thirty-five feet square. "This," he told me, "is the Most Holy Place."

5Then he measured the wall of the Temple and found that it was 10½ feet thick, with a row of rooms along the outside. Each room was seven feet wide. 6These rooms were in three tiers, one above the other, with thirty rooms in each tier. The whole structure was supported by girders and not attached to the Temple wall for support. 7Each tier was wider than the one below it, corresponding to the narrowing of the Temple wall as it rose higher. A stairway at the side of the Temple led up from floor to floor.

New Revised Standard

tables were on the inside, and four tables on the outside of the side of the gate, eight tables, on which the sacrifices were to be slaughtered. 42There were also four tables of hewn stone for the burnt offering, a cubit and a half long, and one cubit and a half wide, and one cubit high, on which the instruments were to be laid with which the burnt offerings and the sacrifices were slaughtered. 43There were pegs, one handbreadth long, fastened all around the inside. And on the tables the flesh of the offering was to be laid.

44 On the outside of the inner gateway there were chambers for the singers in the inner court, oneⁱ at the side of the north gate facing south, the other at the side of the east gate facing north. 45He said to me, "This chamber that faces south is for the priests who have charge of the temple, 46and the chamber that faces north is for the priests who have charge of the altar; these are the descendants of Zadok, who alone among the descendants of Levi may come near to the Lᴏʀᴅ to minister to him." 47He measured the court, one hundred cubits deep, and one hundred cubits wide, a square; and the altar was in front of the temple.

The Temple

48 Then he brought me to the vestibule of the temple and measured the pilasters of the vestibule, five cubits on either side; and the width of the gate was fourteen cubits; and the sidewalls of the gate were three cubitsʲ on either side. 49The depth of the vestibule was twenty cubits, and the width twelveᵏ cubits; ten steps led upˡ to it; and there were pillars beside the pilasters on either side.

41 THEN HE brought me to the nave, and measured the pilasters; on each side six cubits was the width of the pilasters.ᵐ 2The width of the entrance was ten cubits; and the sidewalls of the entrance were five cubits on either side. He measured the length of the nave, forty cubits, and its width, twenty cubits. 3Then he went into the inner room and measured the pilasters of the entrance, two cubits; and the width of the entrance, six cubits; and the sidewallsⁿ of the entrance, seven cubits. 4He measured the depth of the room, twenty cubits, and its width, twenty cubits, beyond the nave. And he said to me, This is the most holy place.

5 Then he measured the wall of the temple, six cubits thick; and the width of the side chambers, four cubits, all around the temple. 6The side chambers were in three stories, one over another, thirty in each story. There were offsetsᵒ all around the wall of the temple to serve as supports for the side chambers, so that they should not be supported by the wall of the temple. 7The passagewayᵖ of the side chambers widened from story to story; for the structure was supplied with a stairway all around the temple. For this reason the structure became wider from story to story. One ascended from the bottom story to the uppermost story by way of the middle one. 8I saw also that the temple had a raised platform

---

ʰ 40:47 *in front of the Temple,* implied.

ⁱ Heb lacks *one*   ʲ Gk: Heb *and the width of the gate was three cubits*   ᵏ Gk: Heb *eleven*   ˡ Gk: Heb *and by steps that went up*   ᵐ Compare Gk: Heb *tent*   ⁿ Gk: Heb *width*   ᵒ Gk Compare 1 Kings 6.6: Heb *they entered*   ᵖ Cn: Heb *it was surrounded*

King James

8I saw also the height of the house round about: the foundations of the side chambers *were* a full reed of six great cubits.

9The thickness of the wall, which *was* for the side chamber without, *was* five cubits: and *that* which *was* left *was* the place of the side chambers that *were* within.

10And between the chambers *was* the wideness of twenty cubits round about the house on every side.

11And the doors of the side chambers *were* toward *the place that was* left, one door toward the north, and another door toward the south: and the breadth of the place that was left *was* five cubits round about.

12Now the building that *was* before the separate place at the end toward the west *was* seventy cubits broad; and the wall of the building *was* five cubits thick round about, and the length thereof ninety cubits.

13So he measured the house, an hundred cubits long; and the separate place, and the building, with the walls thereof, an hundred cubits long;

14Also the breadth of the face of the house, and of the separate place toward the east, an hundred cubits.

15And he measured the length of the building over against the separate place which *was* behind it, and the galleries thereof on the one side and on the other side, an hundred cubits, with the inner temple, and the porches of the court;

16The door posts, and the narrow windows, and the galleries round about on their three stories, over against the door, ceiled with wood round about, and from the ground up to the windows, and the windows *were* covered;

17To that above the door, even unto the inner house, and without, and by all the wall round about within and without, by measure.

18And *it was* made with cherubims and palm trees, so that a palm tree *was* between a cherub and a cherub; and *every* cherub had two faces;

19So that the face of a man *was* toward the palm tree on the one side, and the face of a young lion toward the palm tree on the other side: *it was* made through all the house round about.

20From the ground unto above the door *were* cherubims and palm trees made, and *on* the wall of the temple.

21The posts of the temple *were* squared, *and* the face of the sanctuary; the appearance *of the one* as the appearance *of the other.*

22The altar of wood *was* three cubits high, and the length thereof two cubits; and the corners thereof, and the length thereof, and the walls thereof, *were* of wood: and he said unto me, This *is* the table that *is* before the LORD.

23And the temple and the sanctuary had two doors.

24And the doors had two leaves *apiece,* two turning leaves; two *leaves* for the one door, and two leaves for the other *door.*

25And *there were* made on them, on the doors of the temple, cherubims and palm trees, like as *were* made upon the walls; and *there were* thick planks upon the face of the porch without.

26And *there were* narrow windows and palm trees on the one side and on the other side, on the sides of the porch, and *upon* the side chambers of the house, and thick planks.

New International

8I saw that the temple had a raised base all around it, forming the foundation of the side rooms. It was the length of the rod, six long cubits. 9The outer wall of the side rooms was five cubits thick. The open area between the side rooms of the temple 10and the ╻priests'╻ rooms was twenty cubits wide all around the temple. 11There were entrances to the side rooms from the open area, one on the north and another on the south; and the base adjoining the open area was five cubits wide all around.

12The building facing the temple courtyard on the west side was seventy cubits wide. The wall of the building was five cubits thick all around, and its length was ninety cubits.

13Then he measured the temple; it was a hundred cubits long, and the temple courtyard and the building with its walls were also a hundred cubits long. 14The width of the temple courtyard on the east, including the front of the temple, was a hundred cubits.

15Then he measured the length of the building facing the courtyard at the rear of the temple, including its galleries on each side; it was a hundred cubits.

The outer sanctuary, the inner sanctuary and the portico facing the court, 16as well as the thresholds and the narrow windows and galleries around the three of them—everything beyond and including the threshold was covered with wood. The floor, the wall up to the windows, and the windows were covered. 17In the space above the outside of the entrance to the inner sanctuary and on the walls at regular intervals all around the inner and outer sanctuary 18were carved cherubim and palm trees. Palm trees alternated with cherubim. Each cherub had two faces: 19the face of a man toward the palm tree on one side and the face of a lion toward the palm tree on the other. They were carved all around the whole temple. 20From the floor to the area above the entrance, cherubim and palm trees were carved on the wall of the outer sanctuary.

21The outer sanctuary had a rectangular doorframe, and the one at the front of the Most Holy Place was similar. 22There was a wooden altar three cubits high and two cubits square[a]; its corners, its base[b] and its sides were of wood. The man said to me, "This is the table that is before the LORD." 23Both the outer sanctuary and the Most Holy Place had double doors. 24Each door had two leaves—two hinged leaves for each door. 25And on the doors of the outer sanctuary were carved cherubim and palm trees like those carved on the walls, and there was a wooden overhang on the front of the portico. 26On the sidewalls of the portico were narrow windows with palm trees carved on each side. The side rooms of the temple also had overhangs.

Living Bible

8I noticed that the Temple was built on a terrace and that the bottom row of rooms extended out 10½ feet onto the terrace. 9The outer wall of these rooms was 8¾ feet thick, leaving a free space of 8¾ feet out to the edge of the terrace, the same on both sides.

10Thirty-five feet away from the terrace, on both sides of the Temple, was another row of rooms down in the inner court. 11Two doors opened from the tiers of rooms to the terrace yard, which was 8¾ feet wide; one door faced north and the other south.

12A large building stood on the west, facing the Temple yard, measuring 122½ feet wide by 157½ feet long. Its walls were 8¾ feet thick. 13Then he measured the Temple and its immediately surrounding yards. The area was 175 feet square. 14The inner court at the east of the Temple was also 175 feet wide, 15, 16and so was the building west of the Temple, including its two walls.

The nave of the Temple and the Holy of Holies and the entry hall were paneled, and all three had recessed windows. The inner walls of the Temple were paneled with wood above and below the windows. 17, 18The space above the door leading into the Holy of Holies was also paneled. The walls were decorated with carvings of Guardian Angels, each with two faces, and of palm trees alternating with the Guardian Angels. 19, 20One face—that of a man—looked toward the palm tree on one side, and the other face—that of a young lion—looked toward the palm tree on the other side. And so it was, all around the inner wall of the Temple.

21There were square doorposts at the doors of the nave, and in front of the Holy of Holies was what appeared to be an altar, but it was made of wood. 22This altar was 3½ feet square, and 5¼ feet high; its corners, base and sides were all of wood. "This," he told me, "is the Table of the Lord."c

23Both the nave and the Holy of Holies had double doors, 24each with two swinging sections. 25The doors leading into the nave were decorated with cherubim and palm trees, just as on the walls. And there was a wooden canopy over the entry hall. 26There were recessed windows and carved palm trees on both sides of the entry hall, the hallways beside the Temple, and on the canopy over the entrance.

New Revised Standard

all around; the foundations of the side chambers measured a full reed of six long cubits. 9The thickness of the outer wall of the side chambers was five cubits; and the free space between the side chambers of the temple 10and the chambers of the court was a width of twenty cubits all around the temple on every side. 11The side chambers opened onto the area left free, one door toward the north, and another door toward the south; and the width of the part that was left free was five cubits all around.

12 The building that was facing the temple yard on the west side was seventy cubits wide; and the wall of the building was five cubits thick all around, and its depth ninety cubits.

13 Then he measured the temple, one hundred cubits deep; and the yard and the building with its walls, one hundred cubits deep; 14also the width of the east front of the temple and the yard, one hundred cubits.

15 Then he measured the depth of the building facing the yard at the west, together with its galleriesd on either side, one hundred cubits.

The nave of the temple and the inner room and the outere vestibule 16were paneled,f and, all around, all three had windows with recessedg frames. Facing the threshold the temple was paneled with wood all around, from the floor up to the windows (now the windows were covered), 17to the space above the door, even to the inner room, and on the outside. And on all the walls all around in the inner room and the nave there was a pattern.h 18It was formed of cherubim and palm trees, a palm tree between cherub and cherub. Each cherub had two faces: 19a human face turned toward the palm tree on the one side, and the face of a young lion turned toward the palm tree on the other side. They were carved on the whole temple all around; 20from the floor to the area above the door, cherubim and palm trees were carved on the wall.i

21 The doorposts of the nave were square. In front of the holy place was something resembling 22an altar of wood, three cubits high, two cubits long, and two cubits wide;j its corners, its base,k and its walls were of wood. He said to me, "This is the table that stands before the Lord." 23The nave and the holy place had each a double door. 24The doors had two leaves apiece, two swinging leaves for each door. 25On the doors of the nave were carved cherubim and palm trees, such as were carved on the walls; and there was a canopy of wood in front of the vestibule outside. 26And there were recessed windows and palm trees on either side, on the sidewalls of the vestibule.l

---

c 41:22 the Table of the Lord, literally, "the table which is before the Lord."

d Cn: Meaning of Heb uncertain   e Gk: Heb of the court   f Gk: Heb the thresholds   g Cn Compare Gk 1 Kings 6.4: Meaning of Heb uncertain   h Heb measures   i Cn Compare verse 25: Heb and the wall   j Gk: Heb lacks two cubits wide   k Gk: Heb length   l Cn: Heb vestibule. And the side chambers of the temple and the canopies

King James

42 THEN HE brought me forth into the utter court, the way toward the north: and he brought me into the chamber that *was* over against the separate place, and which *was* before the building toward the north.

2Before the length of an hundred cubits *was* the north door, and the breadth *was* fifty cubits.

3Over against the twenty *cubits* which *were* for the inner court, and over against the pavement which *was* for the utter court, *was* gallery against gallery in three *stories*.

4And before the chambers *was* a walk of ten cubits breadth inward, a way of one cubit; and their doors toward the north.

5Now the upper chambers *were* shorter: for the galleries were higher than these, than the lower, and than the middlemost of the building.

6For they *were* in three *stories*, but had not pillars as the pillars of the courts: therefore *the building* was straitened more than the lowest and the middlemost from the ground.

7And the wall that *was* without over against the chambers, toward the utter court on the forepart of the chambers, the length thereof *was* fifty cubits.

8For the length of the chambers that *were* in the utter court *was* fifty cubits: and, lo, before the temple *were* an hundred cubits.

9And from under these chambers *was* the entry on the east side, as one goeth into them from the utter court.

10The chambers *were* in the thickness of the wall of the court toward the east, over against the separate place, and over against the building.

11And the way before them *was* like the appearance of the chambers which *were* toward the north, as long as they, *and* as broad as they: and all their goings out *were* both according to their fashions, and according to their doors.

12And according to the doors of the chambers that *were* toward the south *was* a door in the head of the way, *even* the way directly before the wall toward the east, as one entereth into them.

13¶ Then said he unto me, The north chambers *and* the south chambers, which *are* before the separate place, they *be* holy chambers, where the priests that approach unto the LORD shall eat the most holy things: there shall they lay the most holy things, and the meat offering, and the sin offering, and the trespass offering; for the place *is* holy.

14When the priests enter therein, then shall they not go out of the holy *place* into the utter court, but there they shall lay their garments wherein they minister; for they *are* holy; and shall put on other garments, and shall approach to *those things* which *are* for the people.

15Now when he had made an end of measuring the inner house, he brought me forth toward the gate whose prospect *is* toward the east, and measured it round about.

16He measured the east side with the measuring reed, five hundred reeds, with the measuring reed round about.

17He measured the north side, five hundred reeds, with the measuring reed round about.

18He measured the south side, five hundred reeds, with the measuring reed.

19¶ He turned about to the west side, *and* measured five hundred reeds with the measuring reed.

20He measured it by the four sides: it had a wall round about, five hundred *reeds* long, and five hundred broad, to make a separation between the sanctuary and the profane place.

New International

Rooms for the Priests

42 THEN THE man led me northward into the outer court and brought me to the rooms opposite the temple courtyard and opposite the outer wall on the north side. 2The building whose door faced north was a hundred cubitsa long and fifty cubits wide. 3Both in the section twenty cubits from the inner court and in the section opposite the pavement of the outer court, gallery faced gallery at the three levels. 4In front of the rooms was an inner passageway ten cubits wide and a hundred cubitsb long. Their doors were on the north. 5Now the upper rooms were narrower, for the galleries took more space from them than from the rooms on the lower and middle floors of the building. 6The rooms on the third floor had no pillars, as the courts had; so they were smaller in floor space than those on the lower and middle floors. 7There was an outer wall parallel to the rooms and the outer court; it extended in front of the rooms for fifty cubits. 8While the row of rooms on the side next to the outer court was fifty cubits long, the row on the side nearest the sanctuary was a hundred cubits long. 9The lower rooms had an entrance on the east side as one enters them from the outer court,

10On the south sidec along the length of the wall of the outer court, adjoining the temple courtyard and opposite the outer wall, were rooms 11with a passageway in front of them. These were like the rooms on the north; they had the same length and width, with similar exits and dimensions. Similar to the doorways on the north 12were the doorways of the rooms on the south. There was a doorway at the beginning of the passageway that was parallel to the corresponding wall extending eastward, by which one enters the rooms.

13Then he said to me, "The north and south rooms facing the temple courtyard are the priests' rooms, where the priests who approach the LORD will eat the most holy offerings. There they will put the most holy offerings—the grain offerings, the sin offerings and the guilt offerings—for the place is holy. 14Once the priests enter the holy precincts, they are not to go into the outer court until they leave behind the garments in which they minister, for these are holy. They are to put on other clothes before they go near the places that are for the people."

15When he had finished measuring what was inside the temple area, he led me out by the east gate and measured the area all around: 16He measured the east side with the measuring rod; it was five hundred cubits.d 17He measured the north side; it was five hundred cubitse by the measuring rod. 18He measured the south side; it was five hundred cubits by the measuring rod. 19Then he turned to the west side and measured; it was five hundred cubits by the measuring rod. 20So he measured the area on all four sides. It had a wall around it, five hundred cubits long and five hundred cubits wide, to separate the holy from the common.

---

a 2 The common cubit was about 1 1/2 feet (about 0.5 meter). b 4 Septuagint and Syriac; Hebrew *and one cubit* c 10 Septuagint; Hebrew *Eastward* d 16 See Septuagint of verse 17; Hebrew *rods*; also in verses 18 and 19. e 17 Septuagint; Hebrew *rods*

Living Bible

42 THEN HE led me out of the Temple, back into the inner court to the rooms north of the Temple yard, and to another building. 2This group of structures was 175 feet long by 87½ feet wide. 3The rows of rooms behind this building were the inner wall of the court. The rooms were in three tiers, overlooking the outer court on one side, and having a 35-foot strip of inner court on the other. 4A 17½-foot walk ran between the building and the tiers of rooms, extending the entire length, with the doors of the building facing north. 5The upper two tiers of rooms were not as wide as the lower one, because the upper tiers had wider walkways beside them. 6And since the building was not built with girders as those in the outer court were, the upper stories were set back from the ground floor.

7, 8The north tiers, next to the outer court, were 87½ feet long—only half as long as the inner wing that faced the Temple court, which was 175 feet long. But a wall extended from the end of the shorter wing, parallel to the longer wing. 9, 10And there was an entrance from the outer court to these rooms from the east. On the opposite side of the Temple a similar building composed of two units of tiers was on the south side of the inner court, between the Temple and the outer court, arranged the same as the other. 11There was a walk between the two wings of the building, the same as in the other building across the court—the same length and width and the same exits and doors—they were identical units. 12And there was a door from the outer courtf at the east.

13Then he told me: "These north and south tiers of rooms facing the Temple yard are holy; there the priests who offer up the sacrifices to the Lord shall eat of the most holy offerings and store them—the cereal offerings, sin offerings, and guilt offerings, for these rooms are holy. 14When the priests leave the Holy Place—the nave of the Temple—they must change their clothes before going out to the outer court. The special robes in which they have been ministering must first be removed, for these robes are holy. They must put on other clothes before entering the parts of the building open to the public."

15When he had finished making these measurements, he led me out through the east passageway to measure the entire Temple area. 16–20He found that it was in the form of a square, 875 feet long on each side, with a wall all around it to separate the restricted area from the public places.g

New Revised Standard

The Holy Chambers and the Outer Wall

42 THEN HE led me out into the outer court, toward the north, and he brought me to the chambers that were opposite the temple yard and opposite the building on the north. 2The length of the building that was on the north sideh wasi one hundred cubits, and the width fifty cubits. 3Across the twenty cubits that belonged to the inner court, and facing the pavement that belonged to the outer court, the chambers rosej galleryk by galleryk in three stories. 4In front of the chambers was a passage on the inner side, ten cubits wide and one hundred cubits deep,l and itsm entrances were on the north. 5Now the upper chambers were narrower, for the galleriesk took more away from them than from the lower and middle chambers in the building. 6For they were in three stories, and they had no pillars like the pillars of the outern court; for this reason the upper chambers were set back from the ground more than the lower and the middle ones. 7There was a wall outside parallel to the chambers, toward the outer court, opposite the chambers, fifty cubits long. 8For the chambers on the outer court were fifty cubits long, while those opposite the temple were one hundred cubits long. 9At the foot of these chambers ran a passage that one entered from the east in order to enter them from the outer court. 10The width of the passageo is fixed by the wall of the court.

On the southp also, opposite the vacant area and opposite the building, there were chambers 11with a passage in front of them; they were similar to the chambers on the north, of the same length and width, with the same exitsq and arrangements and doors. 12So the entrances of the chambers to the south were entered through the entrance at the head of the corresponding passage, from the east, along the matching wall.k

13 Then he said to me, "The north chambers and the south chambers opposite the vacant area are the holy chambers, where the priests who approach the LORD shall eat the most holy offerings; there they shall deposit the most holy offerings—the grain offering, the sin offering, and the guilt offering, for the place is holy. 14When the priests enter the holy place, they shall not go out of it into the outer court without laying there the vestments in which they minister, for these are holy; they shall put on other garments before they go near to the area open to the people."

15 When he had finished measuring the interior of the temple area, he led me out by the gate that faces east, and measured the temple area all around. 16He measured the east side with the measuring reed, five hundred cubits by the measuring reed. 17Then he turned and measuredr the north side, five hundred cubits by the measuring reed. 18Then he turned and measuredr the south side, five hundred cubits by the measuring reed. 19Then he turned to the west side and measured, five hundred cubits by the measuring reed. 20He measured it on the four sides. It had a wall around it, five hundred cubits long and five hundred cubits wide, to make a separation between the holy and the common.

---

f 42:12 *from the outer court,* implied.   g 42:16-20 *to separate the restricted area from the public places,* literally, "between the holy and the common."

h Gk: Heb *door*   i Gk: Heb *before the length*   j Heb lacks *the chambers rose*   k Meaning of Heb uncertain   l Gk Syr: Heb *a way of one cubit*   m Heb *their*   n Gk: Heb backs *outer*   o Heb lacks *of the passage*   p Gk: Heb *east*   q Heb *and all their exits*   r Gk: Heb *measuring reed all around. He measured*

King James

43 AFTERWARD HE brought me to the gate, *even* the gate that looketh toward the east:

2And, behold, the glory of the God of Israel came from the way of the east: and his voice *was* like a noise of many waters: and the earth shined with his glory.

3And *it was* according to the appearance of the vision which I saw, *even* according to the vision that I saw when I came to destroy the city: and the visions *were* like the vision that I saw by the river Chebar; and I fell upon my face.

4And the glory of the LORD came into the house by the way of the gate whose prospect *is* toward the east.

5So the spirit took me up, and brought me into the inner court; and, behold, the glory of the LORD filled the house.

6And I heard *him* speaking unto me out of the house; and the man stood by me.

7¶ And he said unto me, Son of man, the place of my throne, and the place of the soles of my feet, where I will dwell in the midst of the children of Israel for ever, and my holy name, shall the house of Israel no more defile, *neither* they, nor their kings, by their whoredom, nor by the carcases of their kings in their high places.

8In their setting of their threshold by my thresholds, and their post by my posts, and the wall between me and them, they have even defiled my holy name by their abominations that they have committed: wherefore I have consumed them in mine anger.

9Now let them put away their whoredom, and the carcases of their kings, far from me, and I will dwell in the midst of them for ever.

10¶ Thou son of man, show the house to the house of Israel, that they may be ashamed of their iniquities: and let them measure the pattern.

11And if they be ashamed of all that they have done, show them the form of the house, and the fashion thereof, and the goings out thereof, and the comings in thereof, and all the forms thereof, and all the ordinances thereof, and all the forms thereof, and all the laws thereof: and write *it* in their sight, that they may keep the whole form thereof, and all the ordinances thereof, and do them.

12This *is* the law of the house; Upon the top of the mountain the whole limit thereof round about *shall be* most holy. Behold, this *is* the law of the house.

13¶ And these *are* the measures of the altar after the cubits: The cubit *is* a cubit and an handbreadth; even the bottom *shall be* a cubit, and the breadth a cubit, and the border thereof by the edge thereof round about *shall be* a span: and this *shall be* the higher place of the altar.

14And from the bottom *upon* the ground *even* to the lower settle *shall be* two cubits, and the breadth one cubit; and from the lesser settle *even* to the greater settle *shall be* four cubits, and the breadth *one* cubit.

15So the altar *shall be* four cubits; and from the altar and upward *shall be* four horns.

16And the altar *shall be* twelve *cubits* long, twelve broad, square in the four squares thereof.

17And the settle *shall be* fourteen *cubits* long and fourteen broad in the four squares thereof; and the border about it *shall be* half a cubit; and the bottom thereof *shall be* a cubit about; and his stairs shall look toward the east.

18¶ And he said unto me, Son of man, thus saith the Lord GOD; These *are* the ordinances of the altar in the day when they shall make it, to offer burnt offerings thereon, and to sprinkle blood thereon.

19And thou shalt give to the priests the Levites that be of the seed of Zadok, which approach unto me, to minister unto me, saith the Lord GOD, a young bullock for a sin offering.

New International

The Glory Returns to the Temple

43 THEN THE man brought me to the gate facing east, 2and I saw the glory of the God of Israel coming from the east. His voice was like the roar of rushing waters, and the land was radiant with his glory. 3The vision I saw was like the vision I had seen when hea came to destroy the city and like the visions I had seen by the Kebar River, and I fell facedown. 4The glory of the LORD entered the temple through the gate facing east. 5Then the Spirit lifted me up and brought me into the inner court, and the glory of the LORD filled the temple.

6While the man was standing beside me, I heard someone speaking to me from inside the temple. 7He said: "Son of man, this is the place of my throne and the place for the soles of my feet. This is where I will live among the Israelites forever. The house of Israel will never again defile my holy name—neither they nor their kings—by their prostitutionb and the lifeless idolsc of their kings at their high places. 8When they placed their threshold next to my threshold and their doorposts beside my doorposts, with only a wall between me and them, they defiled my holy name by their detestable practices. So I destroyed them in my anger. 9Now let them put away from me their prostitution and the lifeless idols of their kings, and I will live among them forever.

10"Son of man, describe the temple to the people of Israel, that they may be ashamed of their sins. Let them consider the plan, 11and if they are ashamed of all they have done, make known to them the design of the temple—its arrangement, its exits and entrances—its whole design and all its regulationsd and laws. Write these down before them so that they may be faithful to its design and follow all its regulations.

12"This is the law of the temple: All the surrounding area on top of the mountain will be most holy. Such is the law of the temple.

The Altar

13"These are the measurements of the altar in long cubits, that cubit being a cubite and a handbreadthf: Its gutter is a cubit deep and a cubit wide, with a rim of one spang around the edge. And this is the height of the altar: 14From the gutter on the ground up to the lower ledge it is two cubits high and a cubit wide, and from the smaller ledge up to the larger ledge it is four cubits high and a cubit wide. 15The altar hearth is four cubits high, and four horns project upward from the hearth. 16The altar hearth is square, twelve cubits long and twelve cubits wide. 17The upper ledge also is square, fourteen cubits long and fourteen cubits wide, with a rim of half a cubit and a gutter of a cubit all around. The steps of the altar face east."

18Then he said to me, "Son of man, this is what the Sovereign LORD says: These will be the regulations for sacrificing burnt offerings and sprinkling blood upon the altar when it is built: 19You are to give a young bull as a sin offering to the priests, who are Levites, of the family of Zadok, who come near to minister before me, declares the Sovereign LORD. 20You are to take some of

---

a 3 Some Hebrew manuscripts and Vulgate; most Hebrew manuscripts *I*   b 7 Or *their spiritual adultery*; also in verse 9   c 7 Or *the corpses*; also in verse 9   d 11 Some Hebrew manuscripts and Septuagint; most Hebrew manuscripts *regulations and its whole design*   e 13 The common cubit was about 1 1/2 feet (about 0.5 meter).   f 13 That is, about 3 inches (about 8 centimeters)   g 13 That is, about 9 inches (about 22 centimeters)

Living Bible

43 AFTERWARD HE brought me out again to the passageway through the outer wall leading to the east. 2And suddenly the glory of the God of Israel appeared from the east. The sound of his coming was like the roar of rushing waters and the whole landscape lighted up with his glory. 3It was just as I had seen it in the other visions, first by the Chebar Canal, and then later at Jerusalemh when he came to destroy the city. And I fell down before him with my face in the dust. 4And the glory of the Lord came into the Temple through the eastern passageway.

5Then the Spirit took me up and brought me into the inner court; and the glory of the Lord filled the Temple. 6And I heard the Lord speaking to me from within the Temple (the man who had been measuring was still standing beside me).

7And the Lord said to me:

"Son of dust, this is the place of my throne, and my footstool, where I shall remain, living among the people of Israel forever. They and their kings will not defile my holy name any longer through the adulterous worship of other gods or by worshiping the totem poles erected by their kings. 8They built their idol temples beside mine, with only a wall between, and worshiped their idols. Because they sullied my holy name by such wickedness, I consumed them in my anger. 9Now let them put away their idols and the totem polesi erected by their kings, and I will live among them forever.

10"Son of dust, describe the Temple I have shown you to the people of Israel. Tell them its appearance and its plan so they will be ashamed of all their sins. 11And if they are truly ashamed of what they have done, then explain to them the details of its construction—its doors and entrances—and everything about it. Write out all the directions and the rules for them to keep. 12And this is the basic law of the Temple: *Holiness!* The entire top of the hill where the Temple is built is *holy.* Yes, this is the primary law concerning it.

13"And these are the measurements of the altar: The base is twenty-one inches high, with a nine-inch rim around its edge, and it extends twenty-one inches beyond the altar on all sides. 14The first stage of the altar is a stone platform 3½ feet high. This platform is twenty-one inches narrower than the base block on all sides. Rising from this is a narrower platform, twenty-one inches narrower on all sides, and seven feet high. 15From it a still narrower platform rises seven feet, and this is the top of the altar, with four horns projecting twenty-one inches up from the corners. 16This top platform of the altar is twenty-one feet square. 17The platform beneath it is 24½ feet square with a 10½-inch curb around the edges. The entire platform extends out from the top twenty-one inches on all sides. On the east side are steps to climb the altar."

18And he said to me:

"Son of dust, the Lord God says: These are the measurements of the altar to be made in the future, when it is erected for the burning of offerings and the sprinkling of blood upon it. 19At that time the Zadok family of the Levite tribe, who are my ministers, are to be given a bullock for a sin offering. 20You shall take some of its

New Revised Standard

The Divine Glory Returns to the Temple

43 THEN HE brought me to the gate, the gate facing east. 2And there, the glory of the God of Israel was coming from the east; the sound was like the sound of mighty waters; and the earth shone with his glory. 3Thej vision I saw was like the vision that I had seen when he came to destroy the city, andk like the vision that I had seen by the river Chebar; and I fell upon my face. 4As the glory of the LORD entered the temple by the gate facing east, the spirit lifted me up, and brought me into the inner court; and the glory of the LORD filled the temple.

6 While the man was standing beside me, I heard someone speaking to me out of the temple. 7He said to me: Mortal, this is the place of my throne and the place for the soles of my feet, where I will reside among the people of Israel forever. The house of Israel shall no more defile my holy name, neither they nor their kings, by their whoring, and by the corpses of their kings at their death.l 8When they placed their threshold by my threshold and their doorposts beside my doorposts, with only a wall between me and them, they were defiling my holy name by their abominations that they committed; therefore I have consumed them in my anger. 9Now let them put away their idolatry and the corpses of their kings far from me, and I will reside among them forever.

10 As for you, mortal, describe the temple to the house of Israel, and let them measure the pattern; and let them be ashamed of their iniquities. 11When they are ashamed of all that they have done, make known to them the plan of the temple, its arrangement, its exits and its entrances, and its whole form—all its ordinances and its entire plan and all its laws; and write it down in their sight, so that they may observe and follow the entire plan and all its ordinances. 12This is the law of the temple: the whole territory on the top of the mountain all around shall be most holy. This is the law of the temple.

The Altar

13 These are the dimensions of the altar by cubits (the cubit being one cubit and a handbreadth): its base shall be one cubit high,m and one cubit wide, with a rim of one span around its edge. This shall be the height of the altar: 14From the base on the ground to the lower ledge, two cubits, with a width of one cubit; and from the smaller ledge to the larger ledge, four cubits, with a width of one cubit; 15and the altar hearth, four cubits; and from the altar hearth projecting upward, four horns. 16The altar hearth shall be square, twelve cubits long by twelve wide. 17The ledge also shall be square, fourteen cubits long by fourteen wide, with a rim around it half a cubit wide, and its surrounding base, one cubit. Its steps shall face east.

18 Then he said to me: Mortal, thus says the Lord GOD: These are the ordinances for the altar: On the day when it is erected for offering burnt offerings upon it and for dashing blood against it, 19you shall give to the levitical priests of the family of Zadok, who draw near to me to minister to me, says the Lord GOD, a bull for a sin offering. 20And you shall take some of its blood,

---

h 43:3 *at Jerusalem,* implied.   i 43:9 *totem poles,* literally, "stellae."

j Gk: Heb *Like the vision*   k Syr: Heb *and the visions*   l Or *on their high places*   m Gk: Heb lacks *high*

King James

20And thou shalt take of the blood thereof, and put *it* on the four horns of it, and on the four corners of the settle, and upon the border round about: thus shalt thou cleanse and purge it.

21Thou shalt take the bullock also of the sin offering, and he shall burn it in the appointed place of the house, without the sanctuary.

22And on the second day thou shalt offer a kid of the goats without blemish for a sin offering; and they shall cleanse the altar, as they did cleanse *it* with the bullock.

23When thou hast made an end of cleansing *it,* thou shalt offer a young bullock without blemish, and a ram out of the flock without blemish.

24And thou shalt offer them before the LORD, and the priests shall cast salt upon them, and they shall offer them up *for* a burnt offering unto the LORD.

25Seven days shalt thou prepare every day a goat *for* a sin offering: they shall also prepare a young bullock, and a ram out of the flock, without blemish.

26Seven days shall they purge the altar and purify it; and they shall consecrate themselves.

27And when these days are expired, it shall be, *that* upon the eighth day, and *so* forward, the priests shall make your burnt offerings upon the altar, and your peace offerings; and I will accept you, saith the Lord GOD.

44 THEN HE brought me back the way of the gate of the outward sanctuary which looketh toward the east; and it *was* shut.

2Then said the LORD unto me; This gate shall be shut, it shall not be opened, and no man shall enter in by it; because the LORD, the God of Israel, hath entered in by it, therefore it shall be shut.

3*It is* for the prince; the prince, he shall sit in it to eat bread before the LORD; he shall enter by the way of the porch of *that* gate, and shall go out by the way of the same.

4¶ Then brought he me the way of the north gate before the house: and I looked, and, behold, the glory of the LORD filled the house of the LORD: and I fell upon my face.

5And the LORD said unto me, Son of man, mark well, and behold with thine eyes, and hear with thine ears all that I say unto thee concerning all the ordinances of the house of the LORD, and all the laws thereof; and mark well the entering in of the house, with every going forth of the sanctuary.

6And thou shalt say to the rebellious, *even* to the house of Israel, Thus saith the Lord GOD; O ye house of Israel, let it suffice you of all your abominations.

7In that ye have brought *into my sanctuary* strangers, uncircumcised in heart, and uncircumcised in flesh, to be in my sanctuary, to pollute it, *even* my house, when ye offer my bread, the fat and the blood, and they have broken my covenant because of all your abominations.

8And ye have not kept the charge of mine holy things: but ye have set keepers of my charge in my sanctuary for yourselves.

9¶ Thus saith the Lord GOD; No stranger, uncircumcised in heart, nor uncircumcised in flesh, shall enter into my sanctuary, of any stranger that *is* among the children of Israel.

10And the Levites that are gone away far from me, when Israel went astray, which went astray away from me after their idols; they shall even bear their iniquity.

11Yet they shall be ministers in my sanctuary, *having* charge at the gates of the house, and ministering to the house: they shall slay the burnt offering and the sacrifice for the people, and they shall stand before them to minister unto them.

New International

its blood and put it on the four horns of the altar and on the four corners of the upper ledge and all around the rim, and so purify the altar and make atonement for it. 21You are to take the bull for the sin offering and burn it in the designated part of the temple area outside the sanctuary.

22"On the second day you are to offer a male goat without defect for a sin offering, and the altar is to be purified as it was purified with the bull. 23When you have finished purifying it, you are to offer a young bull and a ram from the flock, both without defect. 24You are to offer them before the LORD, and the priests are to sprinkle salt on them and sacrifice them as a burnt offering to the LORD.

25"For seven days you are to provide a male goat daily for a sin offering; you are also to provide a young bull and a ram from the flock, both without defect. 26For seven days they are to make atonement for the altar and cleanse it; thus they will dedicate it. 27At the end of these days, from the eighth day on, the priests are to present your burnt offerings and fellowship offeringsa on the altar. Then I will accept you, declares the Sovereign LORD."

The Prince, the Levites, the Priests

44 THEN THE man brought me back to the outer gate of the sanctuary, the one facing east, and it was shut. 2The LORD said to me, "This gate is to remain shut. It must not be opened; no one may enter through it. It is to remain shut because the LORD, the God of Israel, has entered through it. 3The prince himself is the only one who may sit inside the gateway to eat in the presence of the LORD. He is to enter by way of the portico of the gateway and go out the same way."

4Then the man brought me by way of the north gate to the front of the temple. I looked and saw the glory of the LORD filling the temple of the LORD, and I fell facedown.

5The LORD said to me, "Son of man, look carefully, listen closely and give attention to everything I tell you concerning all the regulations regarding the temple of the LORD. Give attention to the entrance of the temple and all the exits of the sanctuary. 6Say to the rebellious house of Israel, 'This is what the Sovereign LORD says: Enough of your detestable practices, O house of Israel! 7In addition to all your other detestable practices, you brought foreigners uncircumcised in heart and flesh into my sanctuary, desecrating my temple while you offered me food, fat and blood, and you broke my covenant. 8Instead of carrying out your duty in regard to my holy things, you put others in charge of my sanctuary. 9This is what the Sovereign LORD says: No foreigner uncircumcised in heart and flesh is to enter my sanctuary, not even the foreigners who live among the Israelites.

10"'The Levites who went far from me when Israel went astray and who wandered from me after their idols must bear the consequences of their sin. 11They may serve in my sanctuary, having charge of the gates of the temple and serving in it; they may slaughter the burnt offerings and sacrifices for the people and stand before the people and serve them. 12But because they served

---

a 27 Traditionally *peace offerings*

Living Bible

blood and smear it on the four horns of the altar and on the four corners of the top platform and in the curb around it. This will cleanse and make atonement for the altar. 21Then take the bullock for the sin offering and burn it at the appointed place outside the Temple area.

22"The second day, sacrifice a young male goat without any defects—without sickness, deformities, cuts or scars—for a sin offering. Thus the altar shall be cleansed, as it was by the bullock. 23When you have finished this cleansing ceremony, offer another perfect bullock and a perfect ram from the flock. 24Present them before the Lord, and the priests shall sprinkle salt upon them as a burnt offering.

25"Every day for seven days a male goat, a bullock and a ram from the flock shall be sacrificed as a sin offering. None are to have any defects or unhealthiness of any kind. 26Do this each day for seven days to cleanse and make atonement for the altar, thus consecrating it. 27On the eighth day, and on each day afterward, the priests will sacrifice on the altar the burnt offerings and thank offerings of the people, and I will accept you, says the Lord God."

44 THEN THE Lord brought me back to the outer wall's eastern passageway, but it was closed. 2And he said to me:

"This gate shall remain closed; it shall never be opened. No man shall pass through it; for the Lord, the God of Israel, entered here and so it shall remain shut. 3Only the prince—because he is the prince—may sit inside the passageway to feast there before the Lord. But he shall go and come only through the entry hall of the passage."

4Then he brought me through the north passageway to the front of the Temple. I looked and saw that the glory of the Lord filled the Temple of the Lord, and I fell to the ground with my face in the dust.

5And the Lord said to me:

"Son of dust, notice carefully; use your eyes and ears. Listen to all I tell you about the laws and rules of the Temple of the Lord. Note carefully who may be admitted to the Temple, and who is to be excluded from it. 6And say to these rebels, the people of Israel, The Lord God says: O Israel, you have sinned greatly, 7by letting the uncircumcised into my sanctuary—those who have no heart for God—when you offer me my food, the fat and the blood. Thus you have broken my covenant in addition to all your other sins. 8You have not kept the laws I gave you concerning these holy affairs, for you have hired foreigners to take charge of my sanctuary.

9"The Lord God says: No foreigner of all the many among you shall enter my sanctuary if he has not been circumcised and does not love the Lord. 10And the men of the tribe of Levi who abandoned me when Israel strayed away from God to idols must be punished for their unfaithfulness. 11They may be Temple guards and gatemen; they may slay the animals brought for burnt offerings and be present to help the people. 12But be-

New Revised Standard

and put it on the four horns of the altar, and on the four corners of the ledge, and upon the rim all around; thus you shall purify it and make atonement for it. 21You shall also take the bull of the sin offering, and it shall be burnt in the appointed place belonging to the temple, outside the sacred area.

22 On the second day you shall offer a male goat without blemish for a sin offering; and the altar shall be purified, as it was purified with the bull. 23When you have finished purifying it, you shall offer a bull without blemish and a ram from the flock without blemish. 24You shall present them before the LORD, and the priests shall throw salt on them and offer them up as a burnt offering to the LORD. 25For seven days you shall provide daily a goat for a sin offering; also a bull and a ram from the flock, without blemish, shall be provided. 26Seven days shall they make atonement for the altar and cleanse it, and so consecrate it. 27When these days are over, then from the eighth day onward the priests shall offer upon the altar your burnt offerings and your offerings of well-being; and I will accept you, says the Lord GOD.

The Closed Gate

44 THEN HE brought me back to the outer gate of the sanctuary, which faces east; and it was shut. 2The LORD said to me: This gate shall remain shut; it shall not be opened, and no one shall enter by it; for the LORD, the God of Israel, has entered by it; therefore it shall remain shut. 3Only the prince, because he is a prince, may sit in it to eat food before the LORD; he shall enter by way of the vestibule of the gate, and shall go out by the same way.

Admission to the Temple

4 Then he brought me by way of the north gate to the front of the temple; and I looked, and lo! the glory of the LORD filled the temple of the LORD; and I fell upon my face. 5The LORD said to me: Mortal, mark well, look closely, and listen attentively to all that I shall tell you concerning all the ordinances of the temple of the LORD and all its laws; and mark well those who may be admitted tob the temple and all those who are to be excluded from the sanctuary. 6Say to the rebellious house,c to the house of Israel, Thus says the Lord GOD: O house of Israel, let there be an end to all your abominations 7in admitting foreigners, uncircumcised in heart and flesh, to be in my sanctuary, profaning my temple when you offer to me my food, the fat and the blood. Youd have broken my covenant with all your abominations. 8And you have not kept charge of my sacred offerings; but you have appointed foreignerse to act for you in keeping my charge in my sanctuary.

9 Thus says the Lord GOD: No foreigner, uncircumcised in heart and flesh, of all the foreigners who are among the people of Israel, shall enter my sanctuary. 10But the Levites who went far from me, going astray from me after their idols when Israel went astray, shall bear their punishment. 11They shall be ministers in my sanctuary, having oversight at the gates of the temple, and serving in the temple; they shall slaughter the burnt offering and the sacrifice for the people, and they shall attend on them and serve them. 12Because they minis-

b Cn: Heb the entrance of   c Gk: Heb lacks house   d Gk Syr Vg: Heb They
e Heb lacks foreigners

King James

12Because they ministered unto them before their idols, and caused the house of Israel to fall into iniquity; therefore have I lifted up mine hand against them, saith the Lord GOD, and they shall bear their iniquity.

13And they shall not come near unto me, to do the office of a priest unto me, nor to come near to any of my holy things, in the most holy *place:* but they shall bear their shame, and their abominations which they have committed.

14But I will make them keepers of the charge of the house, for all the service thereof, and for all that shall be done therein.

15¶ But the priests the Levites, the sons of Zadok, that kept the charge of my sanctuary when the children of Israel went astray from me, they shall come near to me to minister unto me, and they shall stand before me to offer unto me the fat and the blood, saith the Lord GOD:

16They shall enter into my sanctuary, and they shall come near to my table, to minister unto me, and they shall keep my charge.

17¶ And it shall come to pass, *that* when they enter in at the gates of the inner court, they shall be clothed with linen garments; and no wool shall come upon them, whiles they minister in the gates of the inner court, and within.

18They shall have linen bonnets upon their heads, and shall have linen breeches upon their loins; they shall not gird *themselves* with any thing that causeth sweat.

19And when they go forth into the utter court, *even* into the utter court to the people, they shall put off their garments wherein they ministered, and lay them in the holy chambers, and they shall put on other garments; and they shall not sanctify the people with their garments.

20Neither shall they shave their heads, nor suffer their locks to grow long; they shall only poll their heads.

21Neither shall any priest drink wine, when they enter into the inner court.

22Neither shall they take for their wives a widow, nor her that is put away: but they shall take maidens of the seed of the house of Israel, or a widow that had a priest before.

23And they shall teach my people the *difference* between the holy and profane, and cause them to discern between the unclean and the clean.

24And in controversy they shall stand in judgment; *and* they shall judge it according to my judgments: and they shall keep my laws and my statutes in all mine assemblies; and they shall hallow my sabbaths.

25And they shall come at no dead person to defile themselves: but for father, or for mother, or for son, or for daughter, for brother, or for sister that hath had no husband, they may defile themselves.

26And after he is cleansed, they shall reckon unto him seven days.

27And in the day that he goeth into the sanctuary, unto the inner court, to minister in the sanctuary, he shall offer his sin offering, saith the Lord GOD.

28And it shall be unto them for an inheritance: I *am* their inheritance: and ye shall give them no possession in Israel: I *am* their possession.

29They shall eat the meat offering, and the sin offering, and the trespass offering; and every dedicated thing in Israel shall be theirs.

30And the first of all the firstfruits of all *things,* and every oblation of all, of every *sort* of your oblations, shall be the priest's: ye shall also give unto the priest the first of your dough, that he may cause the blessing to rest in thine house.

31The priests shall not eat of any thing that is dead of itself, or torn, whether it be fowl or beast.

New International

them in the presence of their idols and made the house of Israel fall into sin, therefore I have sworn with uplifted hand that they must bear the consequences of their sin, declares the Sovereign LORD. 13They are not to come near to serve me as priests or come near any of my holy things or my most holy offerings; they must bear the shame of their detestable practices. 14Yet I will put them in charge of the duties of the temple and all the work that is to be done in it.

15" 'But the priests, who are Levites and descendants of Zadok and who faithfully carried out the duties of my sanctuary when the Israelites went astray from me, are to come near to minister before me; they are to stand before me to offer sacrifices of fat and blood, declares the Sovereign LORD. 16They alone are to enter my sanctuary; they alone are to come near my table to minister before me and perform my service.

17" 'When they enter the gates of the inner court, they are to wear linen clothes; they must not wear any woolen garment while ministering at the gates of the inner court or inside the temple. 18They are to wear linen turbans on their heads and linen undergarments around their waists. They must not wear anything that makes them perspire. 19When they go out into the outer court where the people are, they are to take off the clothes they have been ministering in and are to leave them in the sacred rooms, and put on other clothes, so that they do not consecrate the people by means of their garments.

20" 'They must not shave their heads or let their hair grow long, but they are to keep the hair of their heads trimmed. 21No priest is to drink wine when he enters the inner court. 22They must not marry widows or divorced women; they may marry only virgins of Israelite descent or widows of priests. 23They are to teach my people the difference between the holy and the common and show them how to distinguish between the unclean and the clean.

24" 'In any dispute, the priests are to serve as judges and decide it according to my ordinances. They are to keep my laws and my decrees for all my appointed feasts, and they are to keep my Sabbaths holy.

25" 'A priest must not defile himself by going near a dead person; however, if the dead person was his father or mother, son or daughter, brother or unmarried sister, then he may defile himself. 26After he is cleansed, he must wait seven days. 27On the day he goes into the inner court of the sanctuary to minister in the sanctuary, he is to offer a sin offering for himself, declares the Sovereign LORD.

28" 'I am to be the only inheritance the priests have. You are to give them no possession in Israel; I will be their possession. 29They will eat the grain offerings, the sin offerings and the guilt offerings; and everything in Israel devoted[a] to the LORD will belong to them. 30The best of all the firstfruits and of all your special gifts will belong to the priests. You are to give them the first portion of your ground meal so that a blessing may rest on your household. 31The priests must not eat anything, bird or animal, found dead or torn by wild animals.

a 29 The Hebrew term refers to the irrevocable giving over of things or persons to the LORD.

Living Bible

cause they encouraged the people to worship other gods, causing Israel to fall into deep sin, I have raised my hand and taken oath, says the Lord God, that they must be punished. 13They shall not come near me to minister as priests; they may not touch any of my holy things, for they must bear their shame for all the sins they have committed. 14They are the Temple caretakers, to do maintenance work and to assist the people in a general way.

15"However, the sons of Zadok, of the tribe of Levi, continued as my priests in the Temple when Israel abandoned me for idols. These men shall be my ministers; they shall stand before me to offer the fat and blood of the sacrifices, says the Lord God. 16They shall enter my sanctuary and come to my Table to minister to me; they shall fulfill my requirements.

17"They must wear only linen clothing when they enter the passageway to the inner court, for they must wear no wool while on duty in the inner court or in the Temple. 18They must wear linen turbans and linen trousers; they must not wear anything that would cause them to perspire. 19When they return to the outer court, they must take off the clothes they wear while ministering to me, leaving them in the sacred chambers, and put on other clothes lest they harm the people by touching them with this clothing.

20"They must not let their hair grow too long, nor shave it off. Regular, moderate haircuts are all they are allowed. 21No priest may drink wine before coming to the inner court. 22He may marry only a Jewish maiden, or the widow of a priest; he may not marry a divorced woman.

23"He shall teach my people the difference between what is holy and what is secular, what is right and what is wrong.b

24"They will serve as judges to resolve any disagreements among my people. Their decisions must be based upon my laws. And the priests themselves shall obey my rules and regulations at all the sacred festivals, and they shall see to it that the Sabbath is kept a sacred day.

25"A priest must not defile himself by being in the presence of a dead person, unless it is his father, mother, child, brother or unmarried sister. In such cases it is all right. 26But afterward he must wait seven days before he is cleansed and able to perform his Temple duties again. 27The first day he returns to work and enters the inner court and the sanctuary, he must offer a sin offering for himself, the Lord God says.

28"As to property, they shall not own any, for I am their heritage! That is enough!c

29"Their food shall be the gifts and sacrifices brought to the Temple by the people—the cereal offerings, the sin offerings and the guilt offerings. Whatever anyone gives to the Lord shall be the priests'. 30The first of the first-ripe fruits and all the gifts for the Lord shall go to the priests. The first samples of each harvest of grain shall be donated to the priests too, so that the Lord will bless your homes. 31Priests may never eat meat from any bird or animal that dies a natural death or that dies after being attacked by other animals.

New Revised Standard

tered to them before their idols and made the house of Israel stumble into iniquity, therefore I have sworn concerning them, says the Lord GOD, that they shall bear their punishment. 13They shall not come near to me, to serve me as priest, nor come near any of my sacred offerings, the things that are most sacred; but they shall bear their shame, and the consequences of the abominations that they have committed. 14Yet I will appoint them to keep charge of the temple, to do all its chores, all that is to be done in it.

The Levitical Priests

15 But the levitical priests, the descendants of Zadok, who kept the charge of my sanctuary when the people of Israel went astray from me, shall come near to me to minister to me; and they shall attend me to offer me the fat and the blood, says the Lord GOD. 16It is they who shall enter my sanctuary, it is they who shall approach my table, to minister to me, and they shall keep my charge. 17When they enter the gates of the inner court, they shall wear linen vestments; they shall have nothing of wool on them, while they minister at the gates of the inner court, and within. 18They shall have linen turbans on their heads, and linen undergarments on their loins; they shall not bind themselves with anything that causes sweat. 19When they go out into the outer court to the people, they shall remove the vestments in which they have been ministering, and lay them in the holy chambers; and they shall put on other garments, so that they may not communicate holiness to the people with their vestments. 20They shall not shave their heads or let their locks grow long; they shall only trim the hair of their heads. 21No priest shall drink wine when he enters the inner court. 22They shall not marry a widow, or a divorced woman, but only a virgin of the stock of the house of Israel, or a widow who is the widow of a priest. 23They shall teach my people the difference between the holy and the common, and show them how to distinguish between the unclean and the clean. 24In a controversy they shall act as judges, and they shall decide it according to my judgments. They shall keep my laws and my statutes regarding all my appointed festivals, and they shall keep my sabbaths holy. 25They shall not defile themselves by going near to a dead person: for father or mother, however, and for son or daughter, and for brother or unmarried sister they may defile themselves. 26After he has become clean, they shall count seven days for him. 27On the day that he goes into the holy place, into the inner court, to minister in the holy place, he shall offer his sin offering, says the Lord GOD.

28 This shall be their inheritance: I am their inheritance; and you shall give them no holding in Israel; I am their holding. 29They shall eat the grain offering, the sin offering, and the guilt offering; and every devoted thing in Israel shall be theirs. 30The first of all the first fruits of all kinds, and every offering of all kinds from all your offerings, shall belong to the priests; you shall also give to the priests the first of your dough, in order that a blessing may rest on your house. 31The priests shall not eat of anything, whether bird or animal, that died of itself or was torn by animals.

---

b 44:23 between what is holy and what is secular, what is right and what is wrong, literally, "between what is ritually clean and ritually unclean."
c 44:28 That is enough! Implied.

King James

New International

45 MOREOVER, WHEN ye shall divide by lot the land for inheritance, ye shall offer an oblation unto the LORD, an holy portion of the land: the length *shall be* the length of five and twenty thousand *reeds,* and the breadth *shall be* ten thousand. This *shall be* holy in all the borders thereof round about.

2Of this there shall be for the sanctuary five hundred *in length,* with five hundred *in breadth,* square round about; and fifty cubits round about for the suburbs thereof.

3And of this measure shalt thou measure the length of five and twenty thousand, and the breadth of ten thousand: and in it shall be the sanctuary *and* the most holy *place.*

4The holy *portion* of the land shall be for the priests the ministers of the sanctuary, which shall come near to minister unto the LORD: and it shall be a place for their houses, and an holy place for the sanctuary.

5And the five and twenty thousand of length, and the ten thousand of breadth, shall also the Levites, the ministers of the house, have for themselves, for a possession for twenty chambers.

6¶ And ye shall appoint the possession of the city five thousand broad, and five and twenty thousand long, over against the oblation of the holy *portion:* it shall be for the whole house of Israel.

7¶ And *a portion shall be* for the prince on the one side and on the other side of the oblation of the holy *portion,* and of the possession of the city, before the oblation of the holy *portion,* and before the possession of the city, from the west side westward, and from the east side eastward: and the length *shall be* over against one of the portions, from the west border unto the east border.

8In the land shall be his possession in Israel: and my princes shall no more oppress my people; and *the rest of* the land shall they give to the house of Israel according to their tribes.

9¶ Thus saith the Lord GOD; Let it suffice you, O princes of Israel: remove violence and spoil, and execute judgment and justice, take away your exactions from my people, saith the Lord GOD.

10Ye shall have just balances, and a just ephah, and a just bath.

11The ephah and the bath shall be of one measure, that the bath may contain the tenth part of an homer, and the ephah the tenth part of an homer: the measure thereof shall be after the homer.

12And the shekel *shall be* twenty gerahs: twenty shekels, five and twenty shekels, fifteen shekels, shall be your maneh.

13This *is* the oblation that ye shall offer; the sixth part of an ephah of an homer of wheat, and ye shall give the sixth part of an ephah of an homer of barley:

14Concerning the ordinance of oil, the bath of oil, *ye shall offer* the tenth part of a bath out of the cor, *which is* an homer of ten baths; for ten baths *are* an homer:

15And one lamb out of the flock, out of two hundred, out of the fat pastures of Israel; for a meat offering, and for a burnt offering, and for peace offerings, to make reconciliation for them, saith the Lord GOD.

16All the people of the land shall give this oblation for the prince in Israel.

17And it shall be the prince's part *to give* burnt offerings, and meat offerings, and drink offerings, in the feasts, and in the new moons, and in the sabbaths, in all solemnities of the house of Israel: he shall prepare the sin offering, and the meat offering, and the burnt offering, and the peace offerings, to make reconciliation for the house of Israel.

18Thus saith the Lord GOD; In the first *month,* in the first *day* of the month, thou shalt take a young bullock without blemish, and cleanse the sanctuary:

Division of the Land

45 " 'WHEN YOU allot the land as an inheritance, you are to present to the LORD a portion of the land as a sacred district, 25,000 cubits long and 20,000[a] cubits wide; the entire area will be holy. 2Of this, a section 500 cubits square is to be for the sanctuary, with 50 cubits around it for open land. 3In the sacred district, measure off a section 25,000 cubits[b] long and 10,000 cubits[c] wide. In it will be the sanctuary, the Most Holy Place. 4It will be the sacred portion of the land for the priests, who minister in the sanctuary and who draw near to minister before the LORD. It will be a place for their houses as well as a holy place for the sanctuary. 5An area 25,000 cubits long and 10,000 cubits wide will belong to the Levites, who serve in the temple, as their possession for towns to live in.[d]

6" 'You are to give the city as its property an area 5,000 cubits wide and 25,000 cubits long, adjoining the sacred portion; it will belong to the whole house of Israel.

7" 'The prince will have the land bordering each side of the area formed by the sacred district and the property of the city. It will extend westward from the west side and eastward from the east side, running lengthwise from the western to the eastern border parallel to one of the tribal portions. 8This land will be his possession in Israel. And my princes will no longer oppress my people but will allow the house of Israel to possess the land according to their tribes.

9" 'This is what the Sovereign LORD says: You have gone far enough, O princes of Israel! Give up your violence and oppression and do what is just and right. Stop dispossessing my people, declares the Sovereign LORD. 10You are to use accurate scales, an accurate ephah[e] and an accurate bath.[f] 11The ephah and the bath are to be the same size, the bath containing a tenth of a homer[g] and the ephah a tenth of a homer; the homer is to be the standard measure for both. 12The shekel[h] is to consist of twenty gerahs. Twenty shekels plus twenty-five shekels plus fifteen shekels equal one mina.[i]

Offerings and Holy Days

13" 'This is the special gift you are to offer: a sixth of an ephah from each homer of wheat and a sixth of an ephah from each homer of barley. 14The prescribed portion of oil, measured by the bath, is a tenth of a bath from each cor (which consists of ten baths or one homer, for ten baths are equivalent to a homer). 15Also one sheep is to be taken from every flock of two hundred from the well-watered pastures of Israel. These will be used for the grain offerings, burnt offerings and fellowship offerings[j] to make atonement for the people, declares the Sovereign LORD. 16All the people of the land will participate in this special gift for the use of the prince in Israel. 17It will be the duty of the prince to provide the burnt offerings, grain offerings and drink offerings at the festivals, the New Moons and the Sabbaths—at all the appointed feasts of the house of Israel. He will provide the sin offerings, grain offerings, burnt offerings and fellowship offerings to make atonement for the house of Israel.

18" 'This is what the Sovereign LORD says: In the first month on the first day you are to take a young bull without defect and purify the sanctuary. 19The priest is

a *1* Septuagint (see also verses 3 and 5 and 48:9); Hebrew *10,000*   b *3* That is, about 7 miles (about 12 kilometers)   c *3* That is, about 3 miles (about 5 kilometers)   d *5* Septuagint; Hebrew *temple; they will have as their possession 20 rooms*   e *10* An ephah was a dry measure.   f *10* A bath was a liquid measure.   g *11* A homer was a dry measure.   h *12* A shekel weighed about 2/5 ounce (about 11.5 grams).   i *12* That is, 60 shekels; the common mina was 50 shekels.   j *15* Traditionally *peace offerings*; also in verse 17

Living Bible

45 "WHEN YOU divide the land among the tribes of Israel, you shall first give a section of it to the Lord as his holy portion. This piece shall be 8 1/3 miles long and 6 2/3 miles wide. It shall all be holy ground.

2"A section of this land, 875 feet square, shall be designated for the Temple. An additional 87½-foot strip all around is to be left empty. 3The Temple shall be built within the area which is 8 1/3 miles long and 3 1/3 miles wide. 4All this section shall be holy land; it will be used by the priests, who minister in the sanctuary, for their homes and for my Temple.

5"The strip next to it, 8 1/3 miles long and 3 1/3 miles wide, shall be the residence area for the Levites who work at the Temple. 6Adjacent to the holy lands will be a section 8 1/3 miles by 1 2/3 miles for a city open to everyone in Israel.

7"Two special sections of land shall be set apart for the prince—one on each side of the holy lands and city; it is contiguous with them in length, and its eastern and western boundaries are the same as those of the tribal sections. 8This shall be his allotment. My princes shall no longer oppress and rob my people, but shall assign all the remainder of the land to the people, giving a portion to each tribe. 9For the Sovereign Lord says to the rulers: Quit robbing and cheating my people out of their land, and expelling them from their homes. Always be fair and honest.

10"You must use honest scales, honest bushels, honest gallons. 11A homer [about five bushels] shall be your standard unit of measurement for both liquid and dry measure. Smaller units shall be the ephah [about one half bushel] for dry measure, and the bath [about seventeen quarts] for liquid. 12The unit of weight shall be the silver shekel [about half an ounce]; it must always be exchanged for twenty gerahs, no less; five shekels shall be valued at five shekels, no less; and ten shekels at ten shekels! Fifty shekels[k] shall always equal one mina.

13"This is the tax you must give to the prince: a bushel of wheat or barley for every sixty you reap; 14and one percent of your olive oil; 15from each 200 sheep in all your flocks in Israel, give him one sheep. These are the meal offerings, burnt offerings and thank offerings to make atonement for those who bring them, says the Lord God. 16All the people of Israel shall bring their offerings to the prince.

17"The prince shall be required to furnish the people with sacrifices for public worship—sin offerings, burnt offerings, meal offerings, drink offerings and thank offerings—to make reconciliation for the people of Israel. This shall be done at the time of the religious feasts, the new moon ceremonies, the Sabbaths and all other similar occasions.

18"The Lord God says: On each New Year's Day[l] sacrifice a young bull with no blemishes, to purify the Temple. 19The priest shall take some of the blood of this

[k] *45:12 fifty shekels*, or, sixty shekels, the manuscripts are unclear.
[l] *45:18 On each New Year's Day*, literally, "on the first day of the first month. The first month of the Hebrew year corresponded approximately to March 15-April 15 of our calendar.

New Revised Standard

The Holy District

45 WHEN YOU allot the land as an inheritance, you shall set aside for the LORD a portion of the land as a holy district, twenty-five thousand cubits long and twenty[m] thousand cubits wide; it shall be holy throughout its entire extent. 2Of this, a square plot of five hundred by five hundred cubits shall be for the sanctuary, with fifty cubits for an open space around it. 3In the holy district you shall measure off a section twenty-five thousand cubits long and ten thousand wide, in which shall be the sanctuary, the most holy place. 4It shall be a holy portion of the land; it shall be for the priests, who minister in the sanctuary and approach the LORD to minister to him; and it shall be both a place for their houses and a holy place for the sanctuary. 5Another section, twenty-five thousand cubits long and ten thousand cubits wide, shall be for the Levites who minister at the temple, as their holding for cities to live in.[n]

6 Alongside the portion set apart as the holy district you shall assign as a holding for the city an area five thousand cubits wide, and twenty-five thousand cubits long; it shall belong to the whole house of Israel.

7 And to the prince shall belong the land on both sides of the holy district and the holding of the city, alongside the holy district and the holding of the city, on the west and on the east, corresponding in length to one of the tribal portions, and extending from the western to the eastern boundary 8of the land. It is to be his property in Israel. And my princes shall no longer oppress my people; but they shall let the house of Israel have the land according to their tribes.

9 Thus says the Lord GOD: Enough, O princes of Israel! Put away violence and oppression, and do what is just and right. Cease your evictions of my people, says the Lord GOD.

Weights and Measures

10 You shall have honest balances, an honest ephah, and an honest bath.[o] 11The ephah and the bath shall be of the same measure, the bath containing one-tenth of a homer, and the ephah one-tenth of a homer; the homer shall be the standard measure. 12The shekel shall be twenty gerahs. Twenty shekels, twenty-five shekels, and fifteen shekels shall make a mina for you.

Offerings

13 This is the offering that you shall make: one-sixth of an ephah from each homer of wheat, and one-sixth of an ephah from each homer of barley, 14and as the fixed portion of oil,[p] one-tenth of a bath from each cor (the cor,[q] like the homer, contains ten baths); 15and one sheep from every flock of two hundred, from the pastures of Israel. This is the offering for grain offerings, burnt offerings, and offerings of well-being, to make atonement for them, says the Lord GOD. 16All the people of the land shall join with the prince in Israel in making this offering. 17But this shall be the obligation of the prince regarding the burnt offerings, grain offerings, and drink offerings, at the festivals, the new moons, and the sabbaths, all the appointed festivals of the house of Israel: he shall provide the sin offerings, grain offerings, the burnt offerings, and the offerings of well-being, to make atonement for the house of Israel.

Festivals

18 Thus says the Lord GOD: In the first month, on the first day of the month, you shall take a young bull without blemish, and purify the sanctuary. 19The priest

[m] Gk: Heb *ten* [n] Gk: Heb *as their holding, twenty chambers* [o] A Heb measure of volume [p] Cn: Heb *oil, the bath the oil* [q] Vg: Heb *homer*

King James

19And the priest shall take of the blood of the sin offering, and put it upon the posts of the house, and upon the four corners of the settle of the altar, and upon the posts of the gate of the inner court.

20And so thou shalt do the seventh day of the month for every one that erreth, and for him that is simple: so shall ye reconcile the house.

21In the first month, in the fourteenth day of the month, ye shall have the passover, a feast of seven days; unleavened bread shall be eaten.

22And upon that day shall the prince prepare for himself and for all the people of the land a bullock for a sin offering.

23And seven days of the feast he shall prepare a burnt offering to the LORD, seven bullocks and seven rams without blemish daily the seven days; and a kid of the goats daily for a sin offering.

24And he shall prepare a meat offering of an ephah for a bullock, and an ephah for a ram, and an hin of oil for an ephah.

25In the seventh month, in the fifteenth day of the month, shall he do the like in the feast of the seven days, according to the sin offering, according to the burnt offering, and according to the meat offering, and according to the oil.

46 THUS SAITH the Lord GOD; The gate of the inner court that looketh toward the east shall be shut the six working days; but on the sabbath it shall be opened, and in the day of the new moon it shall be opened.

2And the prince shall enter by the way of the porch of that gate without, and shall stand by the post of the gate, and the priests shall prepare his burnt offering and his peace offerings, and he shall worship at the threshold of the gate: then he shall go forth; but the gate shall not be shut until the evening.

3Likewise the people of the land shall worship at the door of this gate before the LORD in the sabbaths and in the new moons.

4And the burnt offering that the prince shall offer unto the LORD in the sabbath day shall be six lambs without blemish, and a ram without blemish.

5And the meat offering shall be an ephah for a ram, and the meat offering for the lambs as he shall be able to give, and an hin of oil to an ephah.

6And in the day of the new moon it shall be a young bullock without blemish, and six lambs, and a ram: they shall be without blemish.

7And he shall prepare a meat offering, an ephah for a bullock, and an ephah for a ram, and for the lambs according as his hand shall attain unto, and an hin of oil to an ephah.

8And when the prince shall enter, he shall go in by the way of the porch of that gate, and he shall go forth by the way thereof.

9¶ But when the people of the land shall come before the LORD in the solemn feasts, he that entereth in by the way of the north gate to worship shall go out by the way of the south gate; and he that entereth by the way of the south gate shall go forth by the way of the north gate: he shall not return by the way of the gate whereby he came in, but shall go forth over against it.

10And the prince in the midst of them, when they go in, shall go in; and when they go forth, shall go forth.

11And in the feasts and in the solemnities the meat offering shall be an ephah to a bullock, and an ephah to a ram, and to the lambs as he is able to give, and an hin of oil to an ephah.

New International

to take some of the blood of the sin offering and put it on the doorposts of the temple, on the four corners of the upper ledge of the altar and on the gateposts of the inner court. 20You are to do the same on the seventh day of the month for anyone who sins unintentionally or through ignorance; so you are to make atonement for the temple.

21 'In the first month on the fourteenth day you are to observe the Passover, a feast lasting seven days, during which you shall eat bread made without yeast. 22On that day the prince is to provide a bull as a sin offering for himself and for all the people of the land. 23Every day during the seven days of the Feast he is to provide seven bulls and seven rams without defect as a burnt offering to the LORD, and a male goat for a sin offering. 24He is to provide as a grain offering an ephah for each bull and an ephah for each ram, along with a hina of oil for each ephah.

25 'During the seven days of the Feast, which begins in the seventh month on the fifteenth day, he is to make the same provision for sin offerings, burnt offerings, grain offerings and oil.

46 " 'THIS IS what the Sovereign LORD says: The gate of the inner court facing east is to be shut on the six working days, but on the Sabbath day and on the day of the New Moon it is to be opened. 2The prince is to enter from the outside through the portico of the gateway and stand by the gatepost. The priests are to sacrifice his burnt offering and his fellowship offerings.b He is to worship at the threshold of the gateway and then go out, but the gate will not be shut until evening. 3On the Sabbaths and New Moons the people of the land are to worship in the presence of the LORD at the entrance to that gateway. 4The burnt offering the prince brings to the LORD on the Sabbath day is to be six male lambs and a ram, all without defect. 5The grain offering given with the ram is to be an ephah,c and the grain offering with the lambs is to be as much as he pleases, along with a hina of oil for each ephah. 6On the day of the New Moon he is to offer a young bull, six lambs and a ram, all without defect. 7He is to provide as a grain offering one ephah with the bull, one ephah with the ram, and with the lambs as much as he wants to give, along with a hin of oil with each ephah. 8When the prince enters, he is to go in through the portico of the gateway, and he is to come out the same way.

9 'When the people of the land come before the LORD at the appointed feasts, whoever enters by the north gate to worship is to go out the south gate; and whoever enters by the south gate is to go out the north gate. No one is to return through the gate by which he entered, but each is to go out the opposite gate. 10The prince is to be among them, going in when they go in and going out when they go out.

11 'At the festivals and the appointed feasts, the grain offering is to be an ephah with a bull, an ephah with a ram, and with the lambs as much as one pleases, along with a hin of oil for each ephah. 12When the prince

a 24,5 That is, probably about 4 quarts (about 4 liters)   b 2 Traditionally peace offerings; also in verse 12   c 5 That is, probably about 3/5 bushel (about 22 liters)

Living Bible

sin offering and put it on the door posts of the Temple and upon the four corners of the base of the altar and upon the walls at the entry of the inner court. 20Do this also on the seventh day of that month for anyone who has sinned through error or ignorance, and so the Temple will be cleansed.

21"On the fourteenth day of the same month, you shall celebrate the Passover. It will be a seven-day feast. Only bread without yeast shall be eaten during those days. 22On the day of Passover the prince shall provide a young bull for a sin offering for himself and all the people of Israel. 23On each of the seven days of the feast he shall prepare a burnt offering to the Lord. This daily offering will consist of seven young bulls and seven rams without blemish. A male goat shall also be given each day for a sin offering. 24And the prince shall provide one half bushel of grain with each bullock and ram for a meal offering, and three quarts of olive oil.

25"Early in October, during each of the seven days of the annual festival of shelters, he shall provide these same sacrifices for the sin offering, burnt offering, meal offering and oil offering.

46 "THE LORD God says, the inner wall's eastern entrance shall be closed during the six work days but open on the Sabbath and on the days of the new moon celebrations. 2The prince shall enter the outside entry hall of the passageway and proceed to the inner wall at the other end while the priest offers his burnt offering and peace offering. He shall worship inside the passageway and then return back to the entrance, which shall not be closed until evening. 3The people shall worship the Lord in front of this passageway on the Sabbaths and on the days of the new moon celebrations.

4"The burnt offering which the prince sacrifices to the Lord on the Sabbath days shall be six lambs and a ram, all unblemished. 5He shall present a meal offering of one half bushel of flour to go with the ram, and whatever amount he is willing for, to go with each lamb. And he shall bring three quarts of olive oil for each half bushel of flour. 6At the new moon celebration, he shall bring one young bull, in perfect condition; six lambs and one ram, all without any blemish. 7With the young bull, he must bring one half busheld of flour for a meal offering. With the ram, he must bring one half busheld of flour. With the lamb, he is to bring whatever he is willing to give. With each half bushel of grain he is to bring three quarts of olive oil.

8"The prince shall go in at the entry hall of the passageway and out the same way; 9but when the people come in through the north passageway to sacrifice during the religious feasts, they must go out through the south passageway. Those coming in from the south must go out by the north. They must never go out the same way they come in, but must always use the opposite passageway. 10The prince shall enter and leave with the common people on these occasions.

11"To summarize: At the special feasts and sacred festivals the meal offering shall be one half bushel with the young bull; one half bushel with the ram; as much as the prince is willing to give with each lamb; and three quarts of oil with each half bushel of grain. 12Whenever

New Revised Standard

shall take some of the blood of the sin offering and put it on the doorposts of the temple, the four corners of the ledge of the altar, and the posts of the gate of the inner court. 20 You shall do the same on the seventh day of the month for anyone who has sinned through error or ignorance; so you shall make atonement for the temple.

21 In the first month, on the fourteenth day of the month, you shall celebrate the festival of the passover, and for seven days unleavened bread shall be eaten. 22On that day the prince shall provide for himself and all the people of the land a young bull for a sin offering. 23And during the seven days of the festival he shall provide as a burnt offering to the LORD seven young bulls and seven rams without blemish, on each of the seven days; and a male goat daily for a sin offering. 24He shall provide as a grain offering an ephah for each bull, an ephah for each ram, and a hin of oil to each ephah. 25In the seventh month, on the fifteenth day of the month and for the seven days of the festival, he shall make the same provision for sin offerings, burnt offerings, and grain offerings, and for the oil.

Miscellaneous Regulations

46 THUS SAYS the Lord GOD: The gate of the inner court that faces east shall remain closed on the six working days; but on the sabbath day it shall be opened and on the day of the new moon it shall be opened. 2The prince shall enter by the vestibule of the gate from outside, and shall take his stand by the post of the gate. The priests shall offer his burnt offering and his offerings of well-being, and he shall bow down at the threshold of the gate. Then he shall go out, but the gate shall not be closed until evening. 3The people of the land shall bow down at the entrance of that gate before the LORD on the sabbaths and on the new moons. 4The burnt offering that the prince offers to the LORD on the sabbath day shall be six lambs without blemish and a ram without blemish; 5and the grain offering with the ram shall be an ephah, and the grain offering with the lambs shall be as much as he wishes to give, together with a hin of oil to each ephah. 6On the day of the new moon he shall offer a young bull without blemish, and six lambs and a ram, which shall be without blemish; 7as a grain offering he shall provide an ephah with the bull and an ephah with the ram, and with the lambs as much as he wishes, together with a hin of oil to each ephah. 8When the prince enters, he shall come in by the vestibule of the gate, and he shall go out by the same way.

9 When the people of the land come before the LORD at the appointed festivals, whoever enters by the north gate to worship shall go out by the south gate; and whoever enters by the south gate shall go out by the north gate: they shall not return by way of the gate by which they entered, but shall go out straight ahead. 10When they come in, the prince shall come in with them; and when they go out, he shall go out.

11 At the festivals and the appointed seasons the grain offering with a young bull shall be an ephah, and with a ram an ephah, and with the lambs as much as one wishes to give, together with a hin of oil to an ephah.

---

d 46:7 bushel, literally, "one ephah."

King James

12Now when the prince shall prepare a voluntary burnt offering or peace offerings voluntarily unto the LORD, *one* shall then open him the gate that looketh toward the east, and he shall prepare his burnt offering and his peace offerings, as he did on the sabbath day: then he shall go forth; and after his going forth *one* shall shut the gate.

13Thus shalt daily prepare a burnt offering unto the LORD *of* a lamb of the first year without blemish: thou shalt prepare it every morning.

14And thou shalt prepare a meat offering for it every morning, the sixth part of an ephah, and the third part of an hin of oil, to temper with the fine flour; a meat offering continually by a perpetual ordinance unto the LORD.

15Thus shall they prepare the lamb, and the meat offering, and the oil, every morning *for* a continual burnt offering.

16¶ Thus saith the Lord GOD; If the prince give a gift unto any of his sons, the inheritance thereof shall be his sons'; it *shall be* their possession by inheritance.

17But if he give a gift of his inheritance to one of his servants, then it shall be his to the year of liberty; after it shall return to the prince: but his inheritance shall be his sons' for them.

18Moreover the prince shall not take of the people's inheritance by oppression, to thrust them out of their possession; *but* he shall give his sons inheritance out of his own possession: that my people be not scattered every man from his possession.

19¶ After he brought me through the entry, which *was* at the side of the gate, into the holy chambers of the priests, which looked toward the north: and, behold, there *was* a place on the two sides westward.

20Then said he unto me, This *is* the place where the priests shall boil the trespass offering and the sin offering, where they shall bake the meat offering; that they bear *them* not out into the utter court, to sanctify the people.

21Then he brought me forth into the utter court, and caused me to pass by the four corners of the court; and, behold, in every corner of the court *there was* a court.

22In the four corners of the court *there were* courts joined of forty *cubits* long and thirty broad: these four corners *were* of one measure.

23And *there was* a row *of building* round about in them, round about them four, and *it was* made with boiling places under the rows round about.

24Then said he unto me, These *are* the places of them that boil, where the ministers of the house shall boil the sacrifice of the people.

47 AFTERWARD HE brought me again unto the door of the house; and, behold, waters issued out from under the threshold of the house eastward: for the forefront of the house *stood toward* the east, and the waters came down from under from the right side of the house, at the south *side* of the altar.

2Then brought he me out of the way of the gate northward, and led me about the way without unto the utter gate by the way that looketh eastward; and, behold, there ran out waters on the right side.

3And when the man that had the line in his hand went forth eastward, he measured a thousand cubits, and he brought me through the waters; the waters *were* to the ankles.

4Again he measured a thousand, and brought me through the waters; the waters *were* to the knees. Again he measured a thousand, and brought me through; the waters *were* to the loins.

New International

provides a freewill offering to the LORD—whether a burnt offering or fellowship offerings—the gate facing east is to be opened for him. He shall offer his burnt offering or his fellowship offerings as he does on the Sabbath day. Then he shall go out, and after he has gone out, the gate will be shut.

13" 'Every day you are to provide a year-old lamb without defect for a burnt offering to the LORD; morning by morning you shall provide it. 14You are also to provide with it morning by morning a grain offering, consisting of a sixth of an ephah with a third of a hin of oil to moisten the flour. The presenting of this grain offering to the LORD is a lasting ordinance. 15So the lamb and the grain offering and the oil shall be provided morning by morning for a regular burnt offering.

16" 'This is what the Sovereign LORD says: If the prince makes a gift from his inheritance to one of his sons, it will also belong to his descendants; it is to be their property by inheritance. 17If, however, he makes a gift from his inheritance to one of his servants, the servant may keep it until the year of freedom; then it will revert to the prince. His inheritance belongs to his sons only; it is theirs. 18The prince must not take any of the inheritance of the people, driving them off their property. He is to give his sons their inheritance out of his own property, so that none of my people will be separated from his property.' "

19Then the man brought me through the entrance at the side of the gate to the sacred rooms facing north, which belonged to the priests, and showed me a place at the western end. 20He said to me, "This is the place where the priests will cook the guilt offering and the sin offering and bake the grain offering, to avoid bringing them into the outer court and consecrating the people."

21He then brought me to the outer court and led me around to its four corners, and I saw in each corner another court. 22In the four corners of the outer court were encloseda courts, forty cubits long and thirty cubits wide; each of the courts in the four corners was the same size. 23Around the inside of each of the four courts was a ledge of stone, with places for fire built all around under the ledge. 24He said to me, "These are the kitchens where those who minister at the temple will cook the sacrifices of the people."

The River From the Temple

47 THE MAN brought me back to the entrance of the temple, and I saw water coming out from under the threshold of the temple toward the east (for the temple faced east). The water was coming down from under the south side of the temple, south of the altar. 2He then brought me out through the north gate and led me around the outside to the outer gate facing east, and the water was flowing from the south side.

3As the man went eastward with a measuring line in his hand, he measured off a thousand cubitsb and then led me through water that was ankle-deep. 4He measured off another thousand cubits and led me through water that was knee-deep. He measured off another thousand and led me through water that was up to the waist. 5He measured off another thousand, but now it

---

a 22 The meaning of the Hebrew for this word is uncertain.　　b 3 That is, about 1,500 feet (about 450 meters)

Living Bible

the prince offers an extra burnt offering or peace offering to be sacrificed to the Lord, the inner eastern gate shall be opened up for him to enter and he shall offer his sacrifices just as on the Sabbaths. Then he shall turn around and go out, and the passage shall be shut behind him.

13"Each morning a yearling lamb must be sacrificed as a burnt offering to the Lord. 14, 15And there must be a meal offering each morning—five pounds of flour with one quart of oil with which to mix it. This is a permanent ordinance—the lamb, the grain offering and the olive oil shall be provided every morning for the daily sacrifice.

16"The Sovereign Lord says: If the prince gives a gift of land to one of his sons, it will belong to him forever. 17But if he gives a gift of land to one of his servants, the servant may keep it only until the Year of Release (every seventh year) when he is set free; then the land returns to the prince. Only gifts to his sons are permanent. 18And the prince may never take anyone's property by force. If he gives property to his sons, it must be from his own land, for I don't want my people losing their property and having to move away."

19, 20After that, using the door through the wall at the side of the main passageway, he led me through the entrance to the block of sacred chambers that faced north. There, at the extreme west end of these rooms, I saw a place where, my guide told me, the priests boil the meat of the trespass offering and sin offering and bake the flour of the flour offerings into bread. They do it here to avoid the necessity of carrying the sacrifices through the outer court, in case they harm the people.

21, 22Then he brought me out to the outer court again and led me to each of the four corners of the court. I saw that in each corner there was a room 70 feet long by 52½ feet wide, enclosed by walls. 23Around the inside of these walls there ran a line of brick boiling vats, with ovens underneath. 24He said these rooms were where the Temple assistants—the Levites—boil the sacrifices the people offer.

47 THEN HE brought me back to the door of the Temple. I saw a stream flowing eastward from beneath the Temple and passing to the right of the altar, that is, on its south side. 2Then he brought me outside the wall through the north passagewayᶜ and around to the eastern entrance, where I saw the stream flowing along on the south side [of the eastern passagewayᵈ]. 3Measuring as he went, he took me 1,500 feet east along the stream and told me to go across. At that point the water was up to my ankles. 4He measured off another 1,500 feet and told me to cross again. This time the water was up to my knees. 5Fifteen hundred feet after

New Revised Standard

12When the prince provides a freewill offering, either a burnt offering or offerings of well-being as a freewill offering to the Lord, the gate facing east shall be opened for him; and he shall offer his burnt offering or his offerings of well-being as he does on the sabbath day. Then he shall go out, and after he has gone out the gate shall be closed.

13 He shall provide a lamb, a yearling, without blemish, for a burnt offering to the Lord daily; morning by morning he shall provide it. 14And he shall provide a grain offering with it morning by morning regularly, one-sixth of an ephah, and one-third of a hin of oil to moisten the choice flour, as a grain offering to the Lord; this is the ordinance for all time. 15Thus the lamb and the grain offering and the oil shall be provided, morning by morning, as a regular burnt offering.

16 Thus says the Lord God: If the prince makes a gift to any of his sons out of his inheritance,ᵉ it shall belong to his sons, it is their holding by inheritance. 17But if he makes a gift out of his inheritance to one of his servants, it shall be his to the year of liberty; then it shall revert to the prince; only his sons may keep a gift from his inheritance. 18The prince shall not take any of the inheritance of the people, thrusting them out of their holding; he shall give his sons their inheritance out of his own holding, so that none of my people shall be dispossessed of their holding.

19 Then he brought me through the entrance, which was at the side of the gate, to the north row of the holy chambers for the priests; and there I saw a place at the extreme western end of them. 20He said to me, "This is the place where the priests shall boil the guilt offering and the sin offering, and where they shall bake the grain offering, in order not to bring them out into the outer court and so communicate holiness to the people."

21 Then he brought me out to the outer court, and led me past the four corners of the court; and in each corner of the court there was a court— 22in the four corners of the court were smallᶠ courts, forty cubits long and thirty wide; the four were of the same size. 23On the inside, around each of the four courtsᵍ was a row of masonry, with hearths made at the bottom of the rows all around. 24Then he said to me, "These are the kitchens where those who serve at the temple shall boil the sacrifices of the people."

Water Flowing from the Temple

47 THEN HE brought me back to the entrance of the temple; there, water was flowing from below the threshold of the temple toward the east (for the temple faced east); and the water was flowing down from below the south end of the threshold of the temple, south of the altar. 2Then he brought me out by way of the north gate, and led me around on the outside to the outer gate that faces toward the east;ʰ and the water was coming out on the south side.

3 Going on eastward with a cord in his hand, the man measured one thousand cubits, and then led me through the water; and it was ankle-deep. 4Again he measured one thousand, and led me through the water; and it was knee-deep. Again he measured one thousand, and led me through the water; and it was up to the waist.

c 47:2 *through the north passageway.* The eastern passageway was closed.
d 47:2 *of the eastern passageway,* implied.

e Gk: Heb *it is his inheritance*   f Gk Syr Vg: Meaning of Heb uncertain
g Heb *the four of them*   h Meaning of Heb uncertain

King James

5Afterward he measured a thousand; *and it was* a river that I could not pass over: for the waters were risen, waters to swim in, a river that could not be passed over.

6¶ And he said unto me, Son of man, hast thou seen *this?* Then he brought me, and caused me to return to the brink of the river.

7Now when I had returned, behold, at the bank of the river *were* very many trees on the one side and on the other.

8Then said he unto me, These waters issue out toward the east country, and go down into the desert, and go into the sea: *which being* brought forth into the sea, the waters shall be healed.

9And it shall come to pass, *that* every thing that liveth, which moveth, whithersoever the rivers shall come, shall live: and there shall be a very great multitude of fish, because these waters shall come thither: for they shall be healed; and every thing shall live whither the river cometh.

10And it shall come to pass, *that* the fishers shall stand upon it from En-gedi even unto En-eglaim; they shall be a *place* to spread forth nets; their fish shall be according to their kinds, as the fish of the great sea, exceeding many.

11But the miry places thereof and the marshes thereof shall not be healed; they shall be given to salt.

12And by the river upon the bank thereof, on this side and on that side, shall grow all trees for meat, whose leaf shall not fade, neither shall the fruit thereof be consumed: it shall bring forth new fruit according to his months, because their waters they issued out of the sanctuary: and the fruit thereof shall be for meat, and the leaf thereof for medicine.

13¶ Thus saith the Lord GOD; This *shall be* the border, whereby ye shall inherit the land according to the twelve tribes of Israel: Joseph *shall have two* portions.

14And ye shall inherit it, one as well as another: *concerning* the which I lifted up mine hand to give it unto your fathers: and this land shall fall unto you for inheritance.

15And this *shall be* the border of the land toward the north side, from the great sea, the way of Hethlon, as men go to Zedad;

16Hamath, Berothah, Sibraim, which *is* between the border of Damascus and the border of Hamath; Hazar-hatticon, which *is* by the coast of Hauran.

17And the border from the sea shall be Hazar-enan, the border of Damascus, and the north northward, and the border of Hamath. And *this is* the north side.

18And the east side ye shall measure from Hauran, and from Damascus, and from Gilead, and from the land of Israel *by* Jordan, from the border unto the east sea. And *this is* the east side.

19And the south side southward, from Tamar *even* to the waters of strife *in* Kadesh, the river to the great sea. And *this is* the south side southward.

20The west side also *shall be* the great sea from the border, till a man come over against Hamath. This *is* the west side.

21So shall ye divide this land unto you according to the tribes of Israel.

22¶ And it shall come to pass, *that* ye shall divide it by lot for an inheritance unto you, and to the strangers that sojourn among you, which shall beget children among you: and they shall be unto you as born in the country among the children of Israel; they shall have inheritance with you among the tribes of Israel.

23And it shall come to pass, *that* in what tribe the stranger sojourneth, there shall ye give *him* his inheritance, saith the Lord GOD.

New International

was a river that I could not cross, because the water had risen and was deep enough to swim in—a river that no one could cross. 6He asked me, "Son of man, do you see this?"

Then he led me back to the bank of the river. 7When I arrived there, I saw a great number of trees on each side of the river. 8He said to me, "This water flows toward the eastern region and goes down into the Arabah,a where it enters the Sea.b When it empties into the Sea,b the water there becomes fresh. 9Swarms of living creatures will live wherever the river flows. There will be large numbers of fish, because this water flows there and makes the salt water fresh; so where the river flows everything will live. 10Fishermen will stand along the shore; from En Gedi to En Eglaim there will be places for spreading nets. The fish will be of many kinds—like the fish of the Great Sea.c 11But the swamps and marshes will not become fresh; they will be left for salt. 12Fruit trees of all kinds will grow on both banks of the river. Their leaves will not wither, nor will their fruit fail. Every month they will bear, because the water from the sanctuary flows to them. Their fruit will serve for food and their leaves for healing."

The Boundaries of the Land

13This is what the Sovereign LORD says: "These are the boundaries by which you are to divide the land for an inheritance among the twelve tribes of Israel, with two portions for Joseph. 14You are to divide it equally among them. Because I swore with uplifted hand to give it to your forefathers, this land will become your inheritance.

15"This is to be the boundary of the land:

"On the north side it will run from the Great Sea by the Hethlon road past Lebod Hamath to Zedad, 16Berothahe and Sibraim (which lies on the border between Damascus and Hamath), as far as Hazer Hatticon, which is on the border of Hauran. 17The boundary will extend from the sea to Hazar Enan,f along the northern border of Damascus, with the border of Hamath to the north. This will be the north boundary.

18"On the east side the boundary will run between Hauran and Damascus, along the Jordan between Gilead and the land of Israel, to the eastern sea and as far as Tamar.g This will be the east boundary.

19"On the south side it will run from Tamar as far as the waters of Meribah Kadesh, then along the Wadi of Egypt to the Great Sea. This will be the south boundary.

20"On the west side, the Great Sea will be the boundary to a point opposite Leboh Hamath. This will be the west boundary.

21"You are to distribute this land among yourselves according to the tribes of Israel. 22You are to allot it as an inheritance for yourselves and for the aliens who have settled among you and who have children. You are to consider them as native-born Israelites; along with you they are to be allotted an inheritance among the tribes of Israel. 23In whatever tribe the alien settles, there you are to give him his inheritance," declares the Sovereign LORD.

---

a 8 Or *the Jordan Valley*   b 8 That is, the Dead Sea   c 10 That is, the Mediterranean; also in verses 15, 19 and 20   d 15 Or *past the entrance to*   e 15,16 See Septuagint and Ezekiel 48:1; Hebrew *road to go into Zedad,* 16Hamath, Berothah   f 17 Hebrew Enon, a variant of Enan   g 18 Septuagint and Syriac; Hebrew Israel. You will measure to the eastern sea   h 20 Or *opposite the entrance to*

Living Bible

that it was up to my waist. Another 1,500 feet and it had become a river so deep I wouldn't be able to get across unless I were to swim. It was too deep to cross on foot.

6He told me to keep in mind what I had seen, then led me back along the bank. 7And now, to my surprise,i many trees were growing on both sides of the river!

8He told me: "This river flows east through the desert and the Jordan Valley to the Dead Sea, where it will heal the salty waters and make them fresh and pure. 9Everything touching the water of this river shall live. Fish will abound in the Dead Sea, for its waters will be healed. Wherever this water flows, everything will live. 10Fishermen will stand along the shores of the Dead Sea, fishing all the way from En-gedi to En-eglaim. The shores will be filled with nets drying in the sun. Fish of every kind will fill the Dead Sea just as they do the Mediterranean! 11But the marshes and swamps will not be healed; they will still be salty. 12All kinds of fruit trees will grow along the river banks. The leaves will never turn brown and fall, and there will always be fruit. There will be a new crop every month—without fail! For they are watered by the river flowing from the Temple. The fruit will be for food and the leaves for medicine.

13"The Lord God says: Here are the instructions for dividing the land to the twelve tribes of Israel: The tribe of Joseph (Ephraim and Manassehj) shall be given two sections. 14Otherwise, each tribe will have an equal share. I promised with hand raised in oath of truth to give the land to your fathers, and you shall inherit it now.

15"The northern boundary will run from the Mediterranean toward Hethlon, then on through Labwehk to Zedad; 16then to Berothah and Sibraim, which are on the border between Damascus and Hamath, and finally to Hazer-hatticon, on the border of Hauran. 17So the northern border will be from the Mediterranean to Hazarenon, on the border with Hamath to the north and Damascus to the south.

18"The eastern border will run south from Hazar-enon to Mount Hauran, where it will bend westward to the Jordan at the southern tip of the Sea of Galilee, and down along the Jordan River separating Israel from Gilead, past the Dead Sea to Tamar.

19"The southern border will go west from Tamar to the springs at Meribath-kadesh and then follow the course of the Brook of Egypt (Wadi el-Arish) to the Mediterranean.

20"On the west side, the Mediterranean itself will be your boundary, from the southern boundary to the point where the northern boundary begins.

21"Divide the land within these boundaries among the tribes of Israel. 22Distribute the land as an inheritance for yourselves and for the foreigners who live among you with their families. All children born in the land—whether or not their parents are foreigners—are to be considered citizens and have the same rights your own children have. 23All these immigrants are to be given land according to the tribe where they now live.

New Revised Standard

5Again he measured one thousand, and it was a river that I could not cross, for the water had risen; it was deep enough to swim in, a river that could not be crossed. 6He said to me, "Mortal, have you seen this?"

Then he led me back along the bank of the river. 7As I came back, I saw on the bank of the river a great many trees on the one side and on the other. 8He said to me, "This water flows toward the eastern region and goes down into the Arabah; and when it enters the sea, the sea of stagnant waters, the water will become fresh. 9Wherever the river goes,l every living creature that swarms will live, and there will be very many fish, once these waters reach there. It will become fresh; and everything will live where the river goes. 10People will stand fishing beside the seam from En-gedi to En-eglaim; it will be a place for the spreading of nets; its fish will be of a great many kinds, like the fish of the Great Sea. 11But its swamps and marshes will not become fresh; they are to be left for salt. 12On the banks, on both sides of the river, there will grow all kinds of trees for food. Their leaves will not wither nor their fruit fail, but they will bear fresh fruit every month, because the water for them flows from the sanctuary. Their fruit will be for food, and their leaves for healing."

The New Boundaries of the Land

13 Thus says the Lord God: These are the boundaries by which you shall divide the land for inheritance among the twelve tribes of Israel. Joseph shall have two portions. 14You shall divide it equally; I swore to give it to your ancestors, and this land shall fall to you as your inheritance.

15 This shall be the boundary of the land: On the north side, from the Great Sea by way of Hethlon to Lebo-hamath, and on to Zedad,n 16Berothah, Sibraim (which lies between the border of Damascus and the border of Hamath), as far as Hazer-hatticon, which is on the border of Hauran. 17So the boundary shall run from the sea to Hazar-enon, which is north of the border of Damascus, with the border of Hamath to the north.o This shall be the north side.

18 On the east side, between Hauran and Damascus; along the Jordan between Gilead and the land of Israel; to the eastern sea and as far as Tamar.p This shall be the east side.

19 On the south side, it shall run from Tamar as far as the waters of Meribath-kadesh, from there along the Wadi of Egyptq to the Great Sea. This shall be the south side.

20 On the west side, the Great Sea shall be the boundary to a point opposite Lebo-hamath. This shall be the west side.

21 So you shall divide this land among you according to the tribes of Israel. 22You shall allot it as an inheritance for yourselves and for the aliens who reside among you and have begotten children among you. They shall be to you as citizens of Israel; with you they shall be allotted an inheritance among the tribes of Israel. 23In whatever tribe aliens reside, there you shall assign them their inheritance, says the Lord God.

---

i 47:7 to my surprise, implied.   j 47:13 Ephraim and Manasseh, implied.
k 47:15 Labweh. The present village on this site is so named. It was originally called Lebo-Hamath.

l Gk Syr Vg Tg: Heb the two rivers go   m Heb it   n Gk: Heb Lebo-zedad, 16Hamath   o Meaning of Heb uncertain   p Compare Syr: Heb you shall measure   q Heb lacks of Egypt

King James

48 NOW THESE *are* the names of the tribes. From the north end to the coast of the way of Hethlon, as one goeth to Hamath, Hazar-enan, the border of Damascus northward, to the coast of Hamath; for these are his sides east *and* west; a *portion for* Dan.

2And by the border of Dan, from the east side unto the west side, a *portion for* Asher.

3And by the border of Asher, from the east side even unto the west side, a *portion for* Naphtali.

4And by the border of Naphtali, from the east side unto the west side, a *portion for* Manasseh.

5And by the border of Manasseh, from the east side unto the west side, a *portion for* Ephraim.

6And by the border of Ephraim, from the east side even unto the west side, a *portion for* Reuben.

7And by the border of Reuben, from the east side unto the west side, a *portion for* Judah.

8¶ And by the border of Judah, from the east side unto the west side, shall be the offering which ye shall offer of five and twenty thousand *reeds in* breadth, and *in* length as one of the *other* parts, from the east side unto the west side: and the sanctuary shall be in the midst of it.

9The oblation that ye shall offer unto the LORD *shall be* of five and twenty thousand in length, and of ten thousand in breadth.

10And for them, *even* for the priests, shall be *this* holy oblation; toward the north five and twenty thousand in *length,* and toward the west ten thousand in breadth, and toward the east ten thousand in breadth, and toward the south five and twenty thousand in length: and the sanctuary of the LORD shall be in the midst thereof.

11*It shall be* for the priests that are *sanctified of the* sons of Zadok; which have kept my charge, which went not astray when the children of Israel went astray, as the Levites went astray.

12And *this* oblation of the land that is offered shall be unto them a thing most holy by the border of the Levites.

13And over against the border of the priests the Levites *shall have* five and twenty thousand in length, and ten thousand in breadth: all the length *shall be* five and twenty thousand, and the breadth ten thousand.

14And they shall not sell of it, neither exchange, nor alienate the firstfruits of the land: for *it is* holy unto the LORD.

15¶ And the five thousand, that are left in the breadth over against the five and twenty thousand, shall be a profane *place* for the city, for dwelling, and for suburbs: and the city shall be in the midst thereof.

16And these *shall be* the measures thereof; the north side four thousand and five hundred, and the south side four thousand and five hundred, and on the east side four thousand and five hundred, and the west side four thousand and five hundred.

17And the suburbs of the city shall be toward the north two hundred and fifty, and toward the south two hundred and fifty, and toward the east two hundred and fifty, and toward the west two hundred and fifty.

18And the residue in length over against the oblation of the holy *portion shall be* ten thousand eastward, and ten thousand westward: and it shall be over against the oblation of the holy *portion;* and the increase thereof shall be for food unto them that serve the city.

19And they that serve the city shall serve it out of all the tribes of Israel.

20All the oblation *shall be* five and twenty thousand by five and twenty thousand: ye shall offer the holy oblation foursquare, with the possession of the city.

New International

The Division of the Land

48 "THESE ARE the tribes, listed by name: At the northern frontier, Dan will have one portion; it will follow the Hethlon road to Leboa Hamath; Hazar Enan and the northern border of Damascus next to Hamath will be part of its border from the east side to the west side.

2"Asher will have one portion; it will border the territory of Dan from east to west.

3"Naphtali will have one portion; it will border the territory of Asher from east to west.

4"Manasseh will have one portion; it will border the territory of Naphtali from east to west.

5"Ephraim will have one portion; it will border the territory of Manasseh from east to west.

6"Reuben will have one portion; it will border the territory of Ephraim from east to west.

7"Judah will have one portion; it will border the territory of Reuben from east to west.

8"Bordering the territory of Judah from east to west will be the portion you are to present as a special gift. It will be 25,000 cubitsb wide, and its length from east to west will equal one of the tribal portions; the sanctuary will be in the center of it.

9"The special portion you are to offer to the LORD will be 25,000 cubits long and 10,000 cubitsc wide. 10This will be the sacred portion for the priests. It will be 25,000 cubits long on the north side, 10,000 cubits wide on the west side, 10,000 cubits wide on the east side and 25,000 cubits long on the south side. In the center of it will be the sanctuary of the LORD. 11This will be for the consecrated priests, the Zadokites, who were faithful in serving me and did not go astray as the Levites did when the Israelites went astray. 12It will be a special gift to them from the sacred portion of the land, a most holy portion, bordering the territory of the Levites.

13"Alongside the territory of the priests, the Levites will have an allotment 25,000 cubits long and 10,000 cubits wide. Its total length will be 25,000 cubits and its width 10,000 cubits. 14They must not sell or exchange any of it. This is the best of the land and must not pass into other hands, because it is holy to the LORD.

15"The remaining area, 5,000 cubits wide and 25,000 cubits long, will be for the common use of the city, for houses and for pastureland. The city will be in the center of it 16and will have these measurements: the north side 4,500 cubits, the south side 4,500 cubits, the east side 4,500 cubits, and the west side 4,500 cubits. 17The pastureland for the city will be 250 cubits on the north, 250 cubits on the south, 250 cubits on the east, and 250 cubits on the west. 18What remains of the area, bordering on the sacred portion and running the length of it, will be 10,000 cubits on the east side and 10,000 cubits on the west side. Its produce will supply food for the workers of the city. 19The workers from the city who farm it will come from all the tribes of Israel. 20The entire portion will be a square, 25,000 cubits on each side. As a special gift you will set aside the sacred portion, along with the property of the city.

---

a *1* Or *to the entrance to* b *8* That is, about 7 miles (about 12 kilometers)
c *9* That is, about 3 miles (about 5 kilometers)

Living Bible

48 "HERE IS the list of the tribes and the territory each is to get. For Dan: From the northwest boundary at the Mediterranean, across to Hethlon, then to Labweh, and then on to Hazar-enon on the border between Damascus to the south and Hamath to the north. Those are the eastern and western limits of the land. 2Asher's territory lies south of Dan's and has the same east and west boundaries. 3Naphtali's land lies south of Asher's, with the same boundary lines on the east and the west. 4Then comes Manasseh, south of Naphtali, with the same eastern and western boundary lines. 5, 6, 7Next, to the south, is Ephraim, and then Reuben and then Judah, all with the same boundaries on the east and the west.

8"South of Judah is the land set aside for the Temple. It has the same eastern and western boundaries as the tribal units, with the Temple in the center. 9This Temple area will be 8 1/3 miles long and 6 2/3 miles wide.

10"A strip of land measuring 8 1/3 miles long by 3 1/3 miles wide, north to south, surrounds the Temple. 11It is for the priests, that is, the sons of Zadok who obeyed me and didn't go into sin when the people of Israel and the rest of their tribe of Levi did. 12It is their special portion when the land is distributed, the most sacred land of all. Next to it lies the area where the other Levites will live. 13It will be of the same size and shape as the first. Together they measure 8 1/3 miles by 6 2/3 miles. 14None of this special land shall ever be sold or traded or used by others, for it belongs to the Lord; it is holy.

15"The strip of land 8 1/3 miles long by 1 2/3 miles wide, south of the Temple section, is for public use— homes, pasture and parks, with a city in the center. 16The city itself is to be 1½ miles square. 17Open land for pastures shall surround the city for approximately a tenth of a mile.d 18Outside the city, stretching east and west for three miles alongside the holy grounds, is garden area belonging to the city, for public use. 19It is open to anyone working in the city, no matter where he comes from in Israel.

20"The entire area—including sacred lands and city lands—is 8 1/3 miles square.

New Revised Standard

The Tribal Portions

48 THESE ARE the names of the tribes: Beginning at the northern border, on the Hethlon road,e from Lebo-hamath, as far as Hazar-enon (which is on the border of Damascus, with Hamath to the north), andf extending from the east side to the west,g Dan, one portion. 2Adjoining the territory of Dan, from the east side to the west, Asher, one portion. 3Adjoining the territory of Asher, from the east side to the west, Naphtali, one portion. 4Adjoining the territory of Naphtali, from the east side to the west, Manasseh, one portion. 5Adjoining the territory of Manasseh, from the east side to the west, Ephraim, one portion. 6Adjoining the territory of Ephraim, from the east side to the west, Reuben, one portion. 7Adjoining the territory of Reuben, from the east side to the west, Judah, one portion.

8 Adjoining the territory of Judah, from the east side to the west, shall be the portion that you shall set apart, twenty-five thousand cubits in width, and in length equal to one of the tribal portions, from the east side to the west, with the sanctuary in the middle of it. 9The portion that you shall set apart for the LORD shall be twenty-five thousand cubits in length, and twentyh thousand in width. 10These shall be the allotments of the holy portion: the priests shall have an allotment measuring twenty-five thousand cubits on the northern side, ten thousand cubits in width on the western side, ten thousand in width on the eastern side, and twenty-five thousand in length on the southern side, with the sanctuary of the LORD in the middle of it. 11This shall be for the consecrated priests, the descendantsi of Zadok, who kept my charge, who did not go astray when the people of Israel went astray, as the Levites did. 12It shall belong to them as a special portion from the holy portion of the land, a most holy place, adjoining the territory of the Levites. 13Alongside the territory of the priests, the Levites shall have an allotment twenty-five thousand cubits in length and ten thousand in width. The whole length shall be twenty-five thousand cubits and the width twentyj thousand. 14They shall not sell or exchange any of it; they shall not transfer this choice portion of the land, for it is holy to the LORD.

15 The remainder, five thousand cubits in width and twenty-five thousand in length, shall be for ordinary use for the city, for dwellings and for open country. In the middle of it shall be the city; 16and these shall be its dimensions: the north side four thousand five hundred cubits, the south side four thousand five hundred, the east side four thousand five hundred, and the west side four thousand and five hundred. 17The city shall have open land: on the north two hundred fifty cubits, on the south two hundred fifty, on the east two hundred fifty, on the west two hundred fifty. 18The remainder of the length alongside the holy portion shall be ten thousand cubits to the east, and ten thousand to the west, and it shall be alongside the holy portion. Its produce shall be food for the workers of the city. 19The workers of the city, from all the tribes of Israel, shall cultivate it. 20The whole portion that you shall set apart shall be twenty-five thousand cubits square, that is, the holy portion together with the property of the city.

---

d 48:17 *for approximately a tenth of a mile,* literally, "437½ feet" in every direction.

e Compare 47.15: Heb *by the side of the way*   f Cn: Heb *and they shall be his*   g Gk Compare verses 2-8: Heb *the east side the west*   h Compare 45.1: Heb *ten*   i One Ms Gk: Heb *of the descendants*   j Gk: Heb *ten*

King James

21¶ And the residue *shall be* for the prince, on the one side and on the other of the holy oblation, and of the possession of the city, over against the five and twenty thousand of the oblation toward the east border, and westward over against the five and twenty thousand toward the west border, over against the portions for the prince: and it shall be the holy oblation; and the sanctuary of the house *shall be* in the midst thereof.

22Moreover from the possession of the Levites, and from the possession of the city, *being* in the midst *of that* which is the prince's, between the border of Judah and the border of Benjamin, shall be for the prince.

23As for the rest of the tribes, from the east side unto the west side, Benjamin *shall have* a *portion*.

24And by the border of Benjamin, from the east side unto the west side, Simeon *shall have* a *portion*.

25And by the border of Simeon, from the east side unto the west side, Issachar a *portion*.

26And by the border of Issachar, from the east side unto the west side, Zebulun a *portion*.

27And by the border of Zebulun, from the east side unto the west side, Gad a *portion*.

28And by the border of Gad, at the south side southward, the border shall be even from Tamar *unto* the waters of strife *in* Kadesh, *and* to the river toward the great sea.

29This *is* the land which ye shall divide by lot unto the tribes of Israel for inheritance, and these *are* their portions, saith the Lord God.

30¶ And these *are* the goings out of the city on the north side, four thousand and five hundred measures.

31And the gates of the city *shall be* after the names of the tribes of Israel: three gates northward; one gate of Reuben, one gate of Judah, one gate of Levi.

32And at the east side four thousand and five hundred: and three gates; and one gate of Joseph, one gate of Benjamin, one gate of Dan.

33And at the south side four thousand and five hundred measures: and three gates; one gate of Simeon, one gate of Issachar, one gate of Zebulun.

34At the west side four thousand and five hundred, *with* their three gates; one gate of Gad, one gate of Asher, one gate of Naphtali.

35*It was* round about eighteen thousand *measures:* and the name of the city from *that* day *shall be,* The Lord *is* there.

New International

21"What remains on both sides of the area formed by the sacred portion and the city property will belong to the prince. It will extend eastward from the 25,000 cubits of the sacred portion to the eastern border, and westward from the 25,000 cubits to the western border. Both these areas running the length of the tribal portions will belong to the prince, and the sacred portion with the temple sanctuary will be in the center of them. 22So the property of the Levites and the property of the city will lie in the center of the area that belongs to the prince. The area belonging to the prince will lie between the border of Judah and the border of Benjamin.

23"As for the rest of the tribes: Benjamin will have one portion; it will extend from the east side to the west side.

24"Simeon will have one portion; it will border the territory of Benjamin from east to west.

25"Issachar will have one portion; it will border the territory of Simeon from east to west.

26"Zebulun will have one portion; it will border the territory of Issachar from east to west.

27"Gad will have one portion; it will border the territory of Zebulun from east to west.

28"The southern boundary of Gad will run south from Tamar to the waters of Meribah Kadesh, then along the Wadi of Egypt, to the Great Sea.[a]

29"This is the land you are to allot as an inheritance to the tribes of Israel, and these will be their portions," declares the Sovereign Lord.

The Gates of the City

30"These will be the exits of the city: Beginning on the north side, which is 4,500 cubits long, 31the gates of the city will be named after the tribes of Israel. The three gates on the north side will be the gate of Reuben, the gate of Judah and the gate of Levi.

32"On the east side, which is 4,500 cubits long, will be three gates: the gate of Joseph, the gate of Benjamin and the gate of Dan.

33"On the south side, which measures 4,500 cubits, will be three gates: the gate of Simeon, the gate of Issachar and the gate of Zebulun.

34"On the west side, which is 4,500 cubits long, will be three gates: the gate of Gad, the gate of Asher and the gate of Naphtali.

35"The distance all around will be 18,000 cubits.

"And the name of the city from that time on will be:

THE LORD IS THERE."

---

a 28 That is, the Mediterranean

Living Bible

21, 22"The land on both sides of this area, extending clear out to the eastern and western boundaries of Israel, shall belong to the prince. This land, lying between the sections alloted to Judah and Benjamin, is 8 1/3 miles square on each side of the sacred and city lands.

23"The sections given to the remaining tribes are as follows: Benjamin's section extends across the entire country of Israel, from its eastern border clear across to the western border. 24South of Benjamin's area lies that of Simeon, also extending out to these same eastern and western borders. 25Next is Issachar, with the same boundaries. 26Then comes Zebulun, also extending all the way across. 27, 28Then Gad, with the same borders on east and west, while its south border runs from Tamar to the Spring at Meribath-kadesh, and then follows the Brook of Egypt (Wadi el-Arish) to the Mediterranean. 29These are the allotments to be made to each tribe, says the Lord God.

30, 31"Each city gate will be named in honor of one of the tribes of Israel. On the north side, with its 1½-mile wall, there will be three gates, one named for Reuben, one for Judah and one for Levi. 32On the east side, with its 1½-mile wall, the gates will be named for Joseph, Benjamin and Dan. 33The south wall, also the same length, will have the gates of Simeon, Issachar and Zebulun; 34on the 1½ miles of the west side, they will be named for Gad, Asher and Naphtali.

35"The entire circumference of the city is six miles. And the name of the city will be 'The City of God.' "b

New Revised Standard

21   What remains on both sides of the holy portion and of the property of the city shall belong to the prince. Extending from the twenty-five thousand cubits of the holy portion to the east border, and westward from the twenty-five thousand cubits to the west border, parallel to the tribal portions, it shall belong to the prince. The holy portion with the sanctuary of the temple in the middle of it, 22 and the property of the Levites and of the city, shall be in the middle of that which belongs to the prince. The portion of the prince shall lie between the territory of Judah and the territory of Benjamin.

23   As for the rest of the tribes: from the east side to the west, Benjamin, one portion. 24 Adjoining the territory of Benjamin, from the east side to the west, Simeon, one portion. 25 Adjoining the territory of Simeon, from the east side to the west, Issachar, one portion. 26 Adjoining the territory of Issachar, from the east side to the west, Zebulun, one portion. 27 Adjoining the territory of Zebulun, from the east side to the west, Gad, one portion. 28 And adjoining the territory of Gad to the south, the boundary shall run from Tamar to the waters of Meribath-kadesh, from there along the Wadi of Egyptᶜ to the Great Sea. 29 This is the land that you shall allot as an inheritance among the tribes of Israel, and these are their portions, says the Lord GOD.

30   These shall be the exits of the city: On the north side, which is to be four thousand five hundred cubits by measure, 31 three gates, the gate of Reuben, the gate of Judah, and the gate of Levi, the gates of the city being named after the tribes of Israel. 32 On the east side, which is to be four thousand five hundred cubits, three gates, the gate of Joseph, the gate of Benjamin, and the gate of Dan. 33 On the south side, which is to be four thousand five hundred cubits by measure, three gates, the gate of Simeon, the gate of Issachar, and the gate of Zebulun. 34 On the west side, which is to be four thousand five hundred cubits, three gates,ᵈ the gate of Gad, the gate of Asher, and the gate of Naphtali. 35 The circumference of the city shall be eighteen thousand cubits. And the name of the city from that time on shall be, The LORD is There.

ᵇ *48:35 The City of God*, literally, "Jehovah-Shammah," "The Lord is there."   ᶜ Heb lacks *of Egypt*   ᵈ One Ms Gk Syr: MT *their gates three*

THE BOOK OF

Daniel

Daniel

Daniel's Training in Babylon

1 IN THE third year of the reign of Jehoiakim king of Judah came Nebuchadnezzar king of Babylon unto Jerusalem, and besieged it.

2And the Lord gave Jehoiakim king of Judah into his hand, with part of the vessels of the house of God: which he carried into the land of Shinar to the house of his god; and he brought the vessels into the treasure house of his god.

3¶ And the king spake unto Ashpenaz the master of his eunuchs, that he should bring *certain* of the children of Israel, and of the king's seed, and of the princes;

4Children in whom *was* no blemish, but well-favoured, and skilful in all wisdom, and cunning in knowledge, and understanding science, and such as *had* ability in them to stand in the king's palace, and whom they might teach the learning and the tongue of the Chaldeans.

5And the king appointed them a daily provision of the king's meat, and of the wine which he drank: so nourishing them three years, that at the end thereof they might stand before the king.

6Now among these were of the children of Judah, Daniel, Hananiah, Mishael, and Azariah:

7Unto whom the prince of the eunuchs gave names: for he gave unto Daniel *the name* of Belteshazzar; and to Hananiah, of Shadrach; and to Mishael, of Meshach; and to Azariah, of Abed-nego.

8¶ But Daniel purposed in his heart that he would not defile himself with the portion of the king's meat, nor with the wine which he drank: therefore he requested of the prince of the eunuchs that he might not defile himself.

9Now God had brought Daniel into favour and tender love with the prince of the eunuchs.

10And the prince of the eunuchs said unto Daniel, I fear my lord the king, who hath appointed your meat and your drink: for why should he see your faces worse liking than the children which *are* of your sort? then shall ye make *me* endanger my head to the king.

11Then said Daniel to Melzar, whom the prince of the eunuchs had set over Daniel, Hananiah, Mishael, and Azariah,

12Prove thy servants, I beseech thee, ten days; and let them give us pulse to eat, and water to drink.

13Then let our countenances be looked upon before thee, and the countenance of the children that eat of the portion of the king's meat: and as thou seest, deal with thy servants.

14So he consented to them in this matter, and proved them ten days.

1 IN THE third year of the reign of Jehoiakim king of Judah, Nebuchadnezzar king of Babylon came to Jerusalem and besieged it. 2And the Lord delivered Jehoiakim king of Judah into his hand, along with some of the articles from the temple of God. These he carried off to the temple of his god in Babylonia[a] and put in the treasure house of his god.

3Then the king ordered Ashpenaz, chief of his court officials, to bring in some of the Israelites from the royal family and the nobility— 4young men without any physical defect, handsome, showing aptitude for every kind of learning, well informed, quick to understand, and qualified to serve in the king's palace. He was to teach them the language and literature of the Babylonians.[b] 5The king assigned them a daily amount of food and wine from the king's table. They were to be trained for three years, and after that they were to enter the king's service.

6Among these were some from Judah: Daniel, Hananiah, Mishael and Azariah. 7The chief official gave them new names: to Daniel, the name Belteshazzar; to Hananiah, Shadrach; to Mishael, Meshach; and to Azariah, Abednego.

8But Daniel resolved not to defile himself with the royal food and wine, and he asked the chief official for permission not to defile himself this way. 9Now God had caused the official to show favor and sympathy to Daniel, 10but the official told Daniel, "I am afraid of my lord the king, who has assigned your[c] food and drink. Why should he see you looking worse than the other young men your age? The king would then have my head because of you."

11Daniel then said to the guard whom the chief official had appointed over Daniel, Hananiah, Mishael and Azariah, 12"Please test your servants for ten days: Give us nothing but vegetables to eat and water to drink. 13Then compare our appearance with that of the young men who eat the royal food, and treat your servants in accordance with what you see." 14So he agreed to this and tested them for ten days.

---

a 2 Hebrew *Shinar*   b 4 Or *Chaldeans*   c 10 The Hebrew for *your* and *you* in this verse is plural.

Daniel   # Daniel

Four Young Israelites at the Babylonian Court

1 THREE YEARS after King Jehoiakim began to rule in Judah, Babylon's King Nebuchadnezzar attacked Jerusalem with his armies, and the Lord gave him victory over Jehoiakim. When he returned to Babylon, he took along some of the sacred cups from the Temple of God, and placed them in the treasury of his god in the land of Shinar.

3, 4Then he ordered Ashpenaz, who was in charge of his palace personnel,d to select some of the Jewish youths brought back as captives—young men of the royal family and nobility of Judah—and to teach them the Chaldean language and literature.e "Pick strong, healthy, good-looking lads," he said; "those who have read widely in many fields, are well informed, alert and sensible, and have enough poise to look good around the palace."

5The king assigned them the best of food and wine from his own kitchen during their three-year training period, planning to make them his counselors when they graduated.

6Daniel, Hananiah, Misha-el, and Azariah were four of the young men chosen, all from the tribe of Judah. 7However, their superintendent gave them Babylonian names, as follows:

Daniel was called Belteshazzar;
Hananiah was called Shadrach;
Misha-el was called Meshach;
Azariah was called Abednego.

8But Daniel made up his mind not to eat the food and wine given to them by the king.f He asked the superintendent for permission to eat other things instead.g 9Now as it happened, God had given the superintendent a special appreciation for Daniel, and sympathy for his predicament. 10But he was alarmed by Daniel's suggestion.

"I'm afraid you will become pale and thin compared with the other youths your age," he said, "and then the king will behead me for neglecting my responsibilities."

11Daniel talked it over with the steward who was appointed by the superintendent to look after Daniel, Hananiah, Misha-el, and Azariah, 12and suggested a ten-day diet of only vegetables and water; 13then, at the end of this trial period the steward could see how they looked in comparison with the other fellows who ate the king's rich food, and decide whether or not to let them continue their diet.

14The steward finally agreed to the test. 15Well, at the

1 IN THE third year of the reign of King Jehoiakim of Judah, King Nebuchadnezzar of Babylon came to Jerusalem and besieged it. 2The Lord let King Jehoiakim of Judah fall into his power, as well as some of the vessels of the house of God. These he brought to the land of Shinar,h and placed the vessels in the treasury of his gods.

3 Then the king commanded his palace master Ashpenaz to bring some of the Israelites of the royal family and of the nobility, 4young men without physical defect and handsome, versed in every branch of wisdom, endowed with knowledge and insight, and competent to serve in the king's palace; they were to be taught the literature and language of the Chaldeans. 5The king assigned them a daily portion of the royal rations of food and wine. They were to be educated for three years, so that at the end of that time they could be stationed in the king's court. 6Among them were Daniel, Hananiah, Mishael, and Azariah, from the tribe of Judah. 7The palace master gave them other names: Daniel he called Belteshazzar, Hananiah he called Shadrach, Mishael he called Meshach, and Azariah he called Abednego.

8 But Daniel resolved that he would not defile himself with the royal rations of food and wine; so he asked the palace master to allow him not to defile himself. 9Now God allowed Daniel to receive favor and compassion from the palace master. 10The palace master said to Daniel, "I am afraid of my lord the king; he has appointed your food and your drink. If he should see you in poorer condition than the other young men of your own age, you would endanger my head with the king." 11Then Daniel asked the guard whom the palace master had appointed over Daniel, Hananiah, Mishael, and Azariah: 12"Please test your servants for ten days. Let us be given vegetables to eat and water to drink. 13You can then compare our appearance with the appearance of the young men who eat the royal rations, and deal with your servants according to what you observe." 14So he agreed to this proposal and tested them for ten days. 15At the

---

d 1:3, 4 who was in charge of his palace personnel, literally, "his chief eunuch." See 2 Kgs 20:17, 18. e 1:3, 4 to teach them the Chaldean language and literature. The language was Aramaic; the literature would have included mathematics, astronomy, and history—plus a strong dose of alchemy and magic! f 1:8 not to eat the food and wine given to them by the king, literally, "determined . . . that he would not defile himself." The defilement was probably in eating pork or other foods outlawed in Lev 11 and Deut 14:3-21. g 1:8 He asked the superintendent for permission to eat other things instead, literally, "He asked . . . to allow him not to defile himself."

h Gk Theodotion: Heb adds to the house of his own gods

King James

15And at the end of ten days their countenances appeared fairer and fatter in flesh than all the children which did eat the portion of the king's meat.

16Thus Melzar took away the portion of their meat, and the wine that they should drink; and gave them pulse.

17¶ As for these four children, God gave them knowledge and skill in all learning and wisdom: and Daniel had understanding in all visions and dreams.

18Now at the end of the days that the king had said he should bring them in, then the prince of the eunuchs brought them in before Nebuchadnezzar.

19And the king communed with them; and among them all was found none like Daniel, Hananiah, Mishael, and Azariah: therefore stood they before the king.

20And in all matters of wisdom *and* understanding, that the king inquired of them, he found them ten times better than all the magicians *and* astrologers that *were* in all his realm.

21And Daniel continued *even* unto the first year of king Cyrus.

2 AND IN the second year of the reign of Nebuchadnezzar, Nebuchadnezzar dreamed dreams, wherewith his spirit was troubled, and his sleep brake from him.

2Then the king commanded to call the magicians, and the astrologers, and the sorcerers, and the Chaldeans, for to show the king his dreams. So they came and stood before the king.

3And the king said unto them, I have dreamed a dream, and my spirit was troubled to know the dream.

4Then spake the Chaldeans to the king in Syriac, O king, live for ever: tell thy servants the dream, and we will show the interpretation.

5The king answered and said to the Chaldeans, The thing is gone from me: if ye will not make known unto me the dream, with the interpretation thereof, ye shall be cut in pieces, and your houses shall be made a dunghill.

6But if ye show the dream, and the interpretation thereof, ye shall receive of me gifts and rewards and great honour: therefore show me the dream, and the interpretation thereof.

7They answered again and said, Let the king tell his servants the dream, and we will show the interpretation of it.

8The king answered and said, I know of certainty that ye would gain the time, because ye see the thing is gone from me.

9But if ye will not make known unto me the dream, *there is but* one decree for you: for ye have prepared lying and corrupt words to speak before me, till the time be changed: therefore tell me the dream, and I shall know that ye can show me the interpretation thereof.

10¶ The Chaldeans answered before the king, and said, There is not a man upon the earth that can show the king's matter: therefore *there is* no king, lord, nor ruler, *that* asked such things at any magician, or astrologer, or Chaldean.

11And *it is* a rare thing that the king requireth, and there is none other that can show it before the king, except the gods, whose dwelling is not with flesh.

12For this cause the king was angry and very furious, and commanded to destroy all the wise *men* of Babylon.

13And the decree went forth that the wise *men* should be slain; and they sought Daniel and his fellows to be slain.

14¶ Then Daniel answered with counsel and wisdom to Arioch the captain of the king's guard, which was gone forth to slay the wise *men* of Babylon:

New International

15At the end of the ten days they looked healthier and better nourished than any of the young men who ate the royal food. 16So the guard took away their choice food and the wine they were to drink and gave them vegetables instead.

17To these four young men God gave knowledge and understanding of all kinds of literature and learning. And Daniel could understand visions and dreams of all kinds.

18At the end of the time set by the king to bring them in, the chief official presented them to Nebuchadnezzar. 19The king talked with them, and he found none equal to Daniel, Hananiah, Mishael and Azariah; so they entered the king's service. 20In every matter of wisdom and understanding about which the king questioned them, he found them ten times better than all the magicians and enchanters in his whole kingdom.

21And Daniel remained there until the first year of King Cyrus.

Nebuchadnezzar's Dream

2 IN THE second year of his reign, Nebuchadnezzar had dreams; his mind was troubled and he could not sleep. 2So the king summoned the magicians, enchanters, sorcerers and astrologersa to tell him what he had dreamed. When they came in and stood before the king, 3he said to them, "I have had a dream that troubles me and I want to know what it means.b"

4Then the astrologers answered the king in Aramaic,c "O king, live forever! Tell your servants the dream, and we will interpret it."

5The king replied to the astrologers, "This is what I have firmly decided: If you do not tell me what my dream was and interpret it, I will have you cut into pieces and your houses turned into piles of rubble. 6But if you tell me the dream and explain it, you will receive from me gifts and rewards and great honor. So tell me the dream and interpret it for me."

7Once more they replied, "Let the king tell his servants the dream, and we will interpret it."

8Then the king answered, "I am certain that you are trying to gain time, because you realize that this is what I have firmly decided: 9If you do not tell me the dream, there is just one penalty for you. You have conspired to tell me misleading and wicked things, hoping the situation will change. So then, tell me the dream, and I will know that you can interpret it for me."

10The astrologers answered the king, "There is not a man on earth who can do what the king asks! No king, however great and mighty, has ever asked such a thing of any magician or enchanter or astrologer. 11What the king asks is too difficult. No one can reveal it to the king except the gods, and they do not live among men."

12This made the king so angry and furious that he ordered the execution of all the wise men of Babylon. 13So the decree was issued to put the wise men to death, and men were sent to look for Daniel and his friends to put them to death.

14When Arioch, the commander of the king's guard, had gone out to put to death the wise men of Babylon, Daniel spoke to him with wisdom and tact. 15He asked

---

a 2 Or *Chaldeans*; also in verses 4, 5 and 10   b 3 Or *was*   c 4 The text from here through chapter 7 is in Aramaic.

Living Bible

end of the ten days, Daniel and his three friends looked healthier and better nourished than the youths who had been eating the food supplied by the king! 16So after that the steward fed them only vegetables and water, without the rich foods and wines!

17God gave these four youths great ability to learn and they soon mastered all the literature and science of the time, and God gave to Daniel special ability in understanding the meanings of dreams and visions.

18, 19When the three-year training period was completed, the superintendent brought all the young men to the king for oral exams, as he had been ordered to do. King Nebuchadnezzar had long talks with each of them, and none of them impressed him as much as Daniel, Hananiah, Misha-el, and Azariah. So they were put on his regular staff of advisors. 20And in all matters requiring information and balanced judgment, the king found these young men's advice ten times better than that of all the skilled magicians and wise astrologers in his realm.

21Daniel held this appointment as the king's counselor until the first year of the reign of King Cyrus.

2 ONE NIGHT in the second year of his reign, Nebuchadnezzar had a terrifying nightmare, and awoke trembling with fear. And to make matters worse, he couldn't remember his dream! He immediately called in all his magicians, incantationists, sorcerers, and astrologers, and demanded that they tell him what his dream had been.

"I've had a terrible nightmare," he said as they stood before him, "and I can't remember what it was. Tell me, for I fear some tragedy awaits me."

4Then the astrologers (speaking in Aramaic) said to the king, "Sir, tell us the dream and then we can tell you what it means."

5But the king replied, "I tell you, the dream is gone—I can't remember it. And if you won't tell me what it was and what it means, I'll have you torn limb from limb and your houses made into heaps of rubble! 6But I will give you many wonderful gifts and honors if you tell me what the dream was and what it means. So, begin!"

7They said again, "How can we tell you what the dream means unless you tell us what it was?"

8, 9The king retorted, "I can see your trick! You're trying to stall for time until the calamity befalls me that the dream foretells. But if you don't tell me the dream, you certainly can't expect me to believe your interpretation!"

10The astrologers replied to the king, "There isn't a man alive who can tell others what they have dreamed! And there isn't a king in all the world who would ask such a thing! 11This is an impossible thing the king requires. No one except the gods can tell you your dream, and they are not here to help."

12Upon hearing this, the king was furious, and sent out orders to execute all the wise men of Babylon. 13And Daniel and his companions were rounded up with the others to be killed.

14But when Ari-och, the chief executioner, came to kill them, Daniel handled the situation with great wis-

New Revised Standard

end of ten days it was observed that they appeared better and fatter than all the young men who had been eating the royal rations. 16So the guard continued to withdraw their royal rations and the wine they were to drink, and gave them vegetables. 17To these four young men God gave knowledge and skill in every aspect of literature and wisdom; Daniel also had insight into all visions and dreams.

18 At the end of the time that the king had set for them to be brought in, the palace master brought them into the presence of Nebuchadnezzar, 19and the king spoke with them. And among them all, no one was found to compare with Daniel, Hananiah, Mishael, and Azariah; therefore they were stationed in the king's court. 20In every matter of wisdom and understanding concerning which the king inquired of them, he found them ten times better than all the magicians and enchanters in his whole kingdom. 21And Daniel continued there until the first year of King Cyrus.

Nebuchadnezzar's Dream

2 IN THE second year of Nebuchadnezzar's reign, Nebuchadnezzar dreamed such dreams that his spirit was troubled and his sleep left him. 2So the king commanded that the magicians, the enchanters, the sorcerers, and the Chaldeans be summoned to tell the king his dreams. When they came in and stood before the king, 3he said to them, "I have had such a dream that my spirit is troubled by the desire to understand it." 4The Chaldeans said to the king (in Aramaic),d "O king, live forever! Tell your servants the dream, and we will reveal the interpretation." 5The king answered the Chaldeans, "This is a public decree: if you do not tell me both the dream and its interpretation, you shall be torn limb from limb, and your houses shall be laid in ruins. 6But if you do tell me the dream and its interpretation, you shall receive from me gifts and rewards and great honor. Therefore tell me the dream and its interpretation." 7They answered a second time, "Let the king first tell his servants the dream, then we can give its interpretation." 8The king answered, "I know with certainty that you are trying to gain time, because you see I have firmly decreed: 9if you do not tell me the dream, there is but one verdict for you. You have agreed to speak lying and misleading words to me until things take a turn. Therefore, tell me the dream, and I shall know that you can give me its interpretation." 10The Chaldeans answered the king, "There is no one on earth who can reveal what the king demands! In fact no king, however great and powerful, has ever asked such a thing of any magician or enchanter or Chaldean. 11The thing that the king is asking is too difficult, and no one can reveal it to the king except the gods, whose dwelling is not with mortals."

12 Because of this the king flew into a violent rage and commanded that all the wise men of Babylon be destroyed. 13The decree was issued, and the wise men were about to be executed; and they looked for Daniel and his companions, to execute them. 14Then Daniel responded with prudence and discretion to Arioch, the king's chief executioner, who had gone out to execute the wise men of Babylon; 15he asked Arioch, the royal

---

d The text from this point to the end of chapter 7 is in Aramaic

King James

15He answered and said to Arioch the king's captain, Why *is* the decree *so* hasty from the king? Then Arioch made the thing known to Daniel.

16Then Daniel went in, and desired of the king that he would give him time, and that he would show the king the interpretation.

17Then Daniel went to his house, and made the thing known to Hananiah, Mishael, and Azariah, his companions:

18That they would desire mercies of the God of heaven concerning this secret; that Daniel and his fellows should not perish with the rest of the wise *men* of Babylon.

19¶ Then was the secret revealed unto Daniel in a night vision. Then Daniel blessed the God of heaven.

20Daniel answered and said, Blessed be the name of God for ever and ever: for wisdom and might are his:

21And he changeth the times and the seasons: he removeth kings, and setteth up kings: he giveth wisdom unto the wise, and knowledge to them that know understanding:

22He revealeth the deep and secret things: he knoweth what *is* in the darkness, and the light dwelleth with him.

23I thank thee, and praise thee, O thou God of my fathers, who hast given me wisdom and might, and hast made known unto me now what we desired of thee: for thou hast *now* made known unto us the king's matter.

24¶ Therefore Daniel went in unto Arioch, whom the king had ordained to destroy the wise *men* of Babylon: he went and said thus unto him; Destroy not the wise *men* of Babylon: bring me in before the king, and I will show unto the king the interpretation.

25Then Arioch brought in Daniel before the king in haste, and said thus unto him, I have found a man of the captives of Judah, that will make known unto the king the interpretation.

26The king answered and said to Daniel, whose name *was* Belteshazzar, Art thou able to make known unto me the dream which I have seen, and the interpretation thereof?

27Daniel answered in the presence of the king, and said, The secret which the king hath demanded cannot the wise *men*, the astrologers, the magicians, the soothsayers, show unto the king;

28But there is a God in heaven that revealeth secrets, and maketh known to the king Nebuchadnezzar what shall be in the latter days. Thy dream, and the visions of thy head upon thy bed, are these;

29As for thee, O king, thy thoughts came *into thy mind* upon thy bed, what should come to pass hereafter: and he that revealeth secrets maketh known to thee what shall come to pass.

30But as for me, this secret is not revealed to me for *any* wisdom that I have more than any living, but for *their* sakes that shall make known the interpretation to the king, and that thou mightest know the thoughts of thy heart.

31¶ Thou, O king, sawest, and behold a great image. This great image, whose brightness *was* excellent, stood before thee; and the form thereof *was* terrible.

32This image's head *was* of fine gold, his breast and his arms of silver, his belly and his thighs of brass,

33His legs of iron, his feet part of iron and part of clay.

34Thou sawest till that a stone was cut out without hands, which smote the image upon his feet *that were* of iron and clay, and brake them to pieces.

35Then was the iron, the clay, the brass, the silver, and the gold, broken to pieces together, and became like the chaff of the summer threshingfloors; and the wind carried them away, that no place was found for them: and the stone that smote the image became a great mountain, and filled the whole earth.

36¶ This *is* the dream; and we will tell the interpretation thereof before the king.

New International

the king's officer, "Why did the king issue such a harsh decree?" Arioch then explained the matter to Daniel. 16At this, Daniel went in to the king and asked for time, so that he might interpret the dream for him.

17Then Daniel returned to his house and explained the matter to his friends Hananiah, Mishael and Azariah. 18He urged them to plead for mercy from the God of heaven concerning this mystery, so that he and his friends might not be executed with the rest of the wise men of Babylon. 19During the night the mystery was revealed to Daniel in a vision. Then Daniel praised the God of heaven 20and said:

"Praise be to the name of God for ever and
ever;
wisdom and power are his.
21He changes times and seasons;
he sets up kings and deposes them.
He gives wisdom to the wise
and knowledge to the discerning.
22He reveals deep and hidden things;
he knows what lies in darkness,
and light dwells with him.
23I thank and praise you, O God of my fathers:
You have given me wisdom and power,
you have made known to me what we asked of
you,
you have made known to us the dream of the
king."

Daniel Interprets the Dream

24Then Daniel went to Arioch, whom the king had appointed to execute the wise men of Babylon, and said to him, "Do not execute the wise men of Babylon. Take me to the king, and I will interpret his dream for him."

25Arioch took Daniel to the king at once and said, "I have found a man among the exiles from Judah who can tell the king what his dream means."

26The king asked Daniel (also called Belteshazzar), "Are you able to tell me what I saw in my dream and interpret it?"

27Daniel replied, "No wise man, enchanter, magician or diviner can explain to the king the mystery he has asked about, 28but there is a God in heaven who reveals mysteries. He has shown King Nebuchadnezzar what will happen in days to come. Your dream and the visions that passed through your mind as you lay on your bed are these:

29"As you were lying there, O king, your mind turned to things to come, and the revealer of mysteries showed you what is going to happen. 30As for me, this mystery has been revealed to me, not because I have greater wisdom than other living men, but so that you, O king, may know the interpretation and that you may understand what went through your mind.

31"You looked, O king, and there before you stood a large statue—an enormous, dazzling statue, awesome in appearance. 32The head of the statue was made of pure gold, its chest and arms of silver, its belly and thighs of bronze, 33its legs of iron, its feet partly of iron and partly of baked clay. 34While you were watching, a rock was cut out, but not by human hands. It struck the statue on its feet of iron and clay and smashed them. 35Then the iron, the clay, the bronze, the silver and the gold were broken to pieces at the same time and became like chaff on a threshing floor in the summer. The wind swept them away without leaving a trace. But the rock that struck the statue became a huge mountain and filled the whole earth.

36"This was the dream, and now we will interpret it to the king. 37You, O king, are the king of kings. The

Living Bible

dom by asking, 15"Why is the king so angry? What is the matter?"

Then Ari-och told him all that had happened.

16So Daniel went in to see the king. "Give me a little time," he said, "and I will tell you the dream and what it means."

17Then he went home and told Hananiah, Misha-el, and Azariah, his companions. 18They asked the God of heaven to show them his mercy by telling them the secret, so they would not die with the others. 19And that night in a vision God told Daniel what the king had dreamed.

Then Daniel praised the God of heaven, 20saying, "Blessed be the name of God forever and ever, for he alone has all wisdom and all power. 21World events are under his control. He removes kings and sets others on their thrones. He gives wise men their wisdom, and scholars their intelligence. 22He reveals profound mysteries beyond man's understanding. He knows all hidden things, for he is light, and darkness is no obstacle to him. 23I thank and praise you, O God of my fathers, for you have given me wisdom and glowing health, and now, even this vision of the king's dream, and the understanding of what it means."

24Then Daniel went in to see Ari-och, who had been ordered to execute the wise men of Babylon, and said, "Don't kill them. Take me to the king and I will tell him what he wants to know."

25Then Ari-och hurried Daniel in to the king and said, "I've found one of the Jewish captives who will tell you your dream!"

26The king said to Daniel, "Is this true? Can you tell me what my dream was and what it means?"

27Daniel replied, "No wise man, astrologer, magician, or wizard can tell the king such things, 28but there is a God in heaven who reveals secrets, and he has told you in your dream what will happen in the future. This was your dream:

29"You dreamed of coming events. He who reveals secrets was speaking to you. 30(But remember, it's not because I am wiser than any living person that I know this secret of your dream, for God showed it to me for your benefit.)

31"O king, you saw a huge and powerful statue of a man, shining brilliantly, frightening and terrible. 32The head of the statue was made of purest gold, its chest and arms were of silver, its belly and thighs of brass, 33its legs of iron, its feet part iron and part clay. 34But as you watched, a Rock was cut from the mountainsidea by supernatural means. It came hurtling toward the statue and crushed the feet of iron and clay, smashing them to bits. 35Then the whole statue collapsed into a heap of iron, clay, brass, silver, and gold; its pieces were crushed as small as chaff, and the wind blew them all away. But the Rock that knocked the statue down became a great mountain that covered the whole earth.

36"That was the dream; now for its meaning:

---
a 2:34 a Rock was cut from the mountainside, implied.

New Revised Standard

official, "Why is the decree of the king so urgent?" Arioch then explained the matter to Daniel. 16So Daniel went in and requested that the king give him time and he would tell the king the interpretation.

God Reveals Nebuchadnezzar's Dream

17 Then Daniel went to his home and informed his companions, Hananiah, Mishael, and Azariah, 18and told them to seek mercy from the God of heaven concerning this mystery, so that Daniel and his companions with the rest of the wise men of Babylon might not perish. 19Then the mystery was revealed to Daniel in a vision of the night, and Daniel blessed the God of heaven.

20 Daniel said:

"Blessed be the name of God from age to age,
    for wisdom and power are his.
21 He changes times and seasons,
    deposes kings and sets up kings;
he gives wisdom to the wise
    and knowledge to those who have
        understanding.
22 He reveals deep and hidden things;
    he knows what is in the darkness,
    and light dwells with him.
23 To you, O God of my ancestors,
    I give thanks and praise,
for you have given me wisdom and power,
    and have now revealed to me what we
        asked of you,
    for you have revealed to us what the king
        ordered."

Daniel Interprets the Dream

24 Therefore Daniel went to Arioch, whom the king had appointed to destroy the wise men of Babylon, and said to him, "Do not destroy the wise men of Babylon; bring me in before the king, and I will give the king the interpretation."

25 Then Arioch quickly brought Daniel before the king and said to him: "I have found among the exiles from Judah a man who can tell the king the interpretation." 26The king said to Daniel, whose name was Belteshazzar, "Are you able to tell me the dream that I have seen and its interpretation?" 27Daniel answered the king, "No wise men, enchanters, magicians, or diviners can show to the king the mystery that the king is asking, 28but there is a God in heaven who reveals mysteries, and he has disclosed to King Nebuchadnezzar what will happen at the end of days. Your dream and the visions of your head as you lay in bed were these: 29To you, O king, as you lay in bed, came thoughts of what would be hereafter, and the revealer of mysteries disclosed to you what is to be. 30But as for me, this mystery has not been revealed to me because of any wisdom that I have more than any other living being, but in order that the interpretation may be known to the king and that you may understand the thoughts of your mind.

31 "You were looking, O king, and lo! there was a great statue. This statue was huge, its brilliance extraordinary; it was standing before you, and its appearance was frightening. 32The head of that statue was of fine gold, its chest and arms of silver, its middle and thighs of bronze, 33its legs of iron, its feet partly of iron and partly of clay. 34As you looked on, a stone was cut out, not by human hands, and it struck the statue on its feet of iron and clay and broke them in pieces. 35Then the iron, the clay, the bronze, the silver, and the gold, were all broken in pieces and became like the chaff of the summer threshing floors; and the wind carried them away, so that not a trace of them could be found. But the stone that struck the statue became a great mountain and filled the whole earth.

36 "This was the dream; now we will tell the king its interpretation. 37You, O king, the king of kings—to

King James

37Thou, O king, *art* a king of kings: for the God of heaven hath given thee a kingdom, power, and strength, and glory.

38And wheresoever the children of men dwell, the beasts of the field and the fowls of the heaven hath he given into thine hand, and hath made thee ruler over them all. Thou *art* this head of gold.

39And after thee shall arise another kingdom inferior to thee, and another third kingdom of brass, which shall bear rule over all the earth.

40And the fourth kingdom shall be strong as iron: forasmuch as iron breaketh in pieces and subdueth all *things;* and as iron that breaketh all these, shall it break in pieces and bruise.

41And whereas thou sawest the feet and toes, part of potters' clay, and part of iron, the kingdom shall be divided; but there shall be in it of the strength of the iron, forasmuch as thou sawest the iron mixed with miry clay.

42And *as* the toes of the feet *were* part of iron, and part of clay, *so* the kingdom shall be partly strong, and partly broken.

43And whereas thou sawest iron mixed with miry clay, they shall mingle themselves with the seed of men: but they shall not cleave one to another, even as iron is not mixed with clay.

44And in the days of these kings shall the God of heaven set up a kingdom, which shall never be destroyed: and the kingdom shall not be left to other people, *but* it shall break in pieces and consume all these kingdoms, and it shall stand for ever.

45Forasmuch as thou sawest that the stone was cut out of the mountain without hands, and that it brake in pieces the iron, the brass, the clay, the silver, and the gold; the great God hath made known to the king what shall come to pass hereafter: and the dream *is* certain, and the interpretation thereof sure.

46¶ Then the king Nebuchadnezzar fell upon his face, and worshipped Daniel, and commanded that they should offer an oblation and sweet odours unto him.

47The king answered unto Daniel, and said, Of a truth *it is,* that your God *is* a God of gods, and a Lord of kings, and a revealer of secrets, seeing thou couldest reveal this secret.

48Then the king made Daniel a great man, and gave him many great gifts, and made him ruler over the whole province of Babylon, and chief of the governors over all the wise *men* of Babylon.

49Then Daniel requested of the king, and he set Shadrach, Meshach, and Abed-nego, over the affairs of the province of Babylon: but Daniel *sat* in the gate of the king.

3 NEBUCHADNEZZAR THE king made an image of gold, whose height *was* threescore cubits, *and* the breadth thereof six cubits: he set it up in the plain of Dura, in the province of Babylon.

2Then Nebuchadnezzar the king sent to gather together the princes, the governors, and the captains, the judges, the treasurers, the counsellors, the sheriffs, and all the rulers of the provinces, to come to the dedication of the image which Nebuchadnezzar the king had set up.

3Then the princes, the governors, and captains, the judges, the treasurers, the counsellors, the sheriffs, and all the rulers of the provinces, were gathered together unto the dedication of the image that Nebuchadnezzar the king had set up; and they stood before the image that Nebuchadnezzar had set up.

4Then an herald cried aloud, To you it is commanded, O people, nations, and languages,

New International

God of heaven has given you dominion and power and might and glory; 38in your hands he has placed mankind and the beasts of the field and the birds of the air. Wherever they live, he has made you ruler over them all. You are that head of gold.

39"After you, another kingdom will rise, inferior to yours. Next, a third kingdom, one of bronze, will rule over the whole earth. 40Finally, there will be a fourth kingdom, strong as iron—for iron breaks and smashes everything—and as iron breaks things to pieces, so it will crush and break all the others. 41Just as you saw that the feet and toes were partly of baked clay and partly of iron, so this will be a divided kingdom; yet it will have some of the strength of iron in it, even as you saw iron mixed with clay. 42As the toes were partly iron and partly clay, so this kingdom will be partly strong and partly brittle. 43And just as you saw the iron mixed with baked clay, so the people will be a mixture and will not remain united, any more than iron mixes with clay.

44"In the time of those kings, the God of heaven will set up a kingdom that will never be destroyed, nor will it be left to another people. It will crush all those kingdoms and bring them to an end, but it will itself endure forever. 45This is the meaning of the vision of the rock cut out of a mountain, but not by human hands—a rock that broke the iron, the bronze, the clay, the silver and the gold to pieces.

"The great God has shown the king what will take place in the future. The dream is true and the interpretation is trustworthy."

46Then King Nebuchadnezzar fell prostrate before Daniel and paid him honor and ordered that an offering and incense be presented to him. 47The king said to Daniel, "Surely your God is the God of gods and the Lord of kings and a revealer of mysteries, for you were able to reveal this mystery."

48Then the king placed Daniel in a high position and lavished many gifts on him. He made him ruler over the entire province of Babylon and placed him in charge of all its wise men. 49Moreover, at Daniel's request the king appointed Shadrach, Meshach and Abednego administrators over the province of Babylon, while Daniel himself remained at the royal court.

The Image of Gold and the Fiery Furnace

3 KING NEBUCHADNEZZAR made an image of gold, ninety feet high and nine feeta wide, and set it up on the plain of Dura in the province of Babylon. 2He then summoned the satraps, prefects, governors, advisers, treasurers, judges, magistrates and all the other provincial officials to come to the dedication of the image he had set up. 3So the satraps, prefects, governors, advisers, treasurers, judges, magistrates and all the other provincial officials assembled for the dedication of the image that King Nebuchadnezzar had set up, and they stood before it.

4Then the herald loudly proclaimed, "This is what you are commanded to do, O peoples, nations and men of every language: 5As soon as you hear the sound of the

---

a *1* Aramaic *sixty cubits high and six cubits wide* (about 27 meters high and 2.7 meters wide)

Living Bible

37"Your Majesty, you are a king over many kings, for the God of heaven has given you your kingdom, power, strength and glory. 38You rule the farthest provinces, and even animals and birds are under your control, as God decreed. You are that head of gold.

39"But after your kingdom has come to an end, another world powerᵇ will arise to take your place. This empire will be inferior to yours. And after that kingdom has fallen, yet a third great powerᶜ—represented by the bronze belly of the statue—will rise to rule the world. 40Following it, the fourth kingdomᵈ will be strong as iron—smashing, bruising, and conquering. 41, 42The feet and toes you saw—part iron and part clay—show that later on, this kingdom will be divided. Some parts of it will be as strong as iron, and some as weak as clay. 43This mixture of iron with clay also shows that these kingdoms will try to strengthen themselves by forming alliances with each other through intermarriage of their rulers; but this will not succeed, for iron and clay don't mix.

44"During the reigns of those kings, the God of heaven will set up a kingdom that will never be destroyed; no one will ever conquer it. It will shatter all these kingdoms into nothingness, but it shall stand forever, indestructible. 45That is the meaning of the Rock cut from the mountain without human hands—the Rock that crushed to powder all the iron and brass, the clay, the silver, and the gold.

"Thus the great God has shown what will happen in the future, and this interpretation of your dream is as sure and certain as my description of it."

46Then Nebuchadnezzar fell to the ground before Daniel and worshiped him, and commanded his people to offer sacrifices and burn sweet incense before him.

47"Truly, O Daniel," the king said, "your God is the God of gods, Ruler of kings, the Revealer of mysteries, because he has told you this secret."

48Then the king made Daniel very great; he gave him many valuable gifts, and appointed him to be ruler over the whole province of Babylon, as well as chief over all his wise men.

49Then, at Daniel's request, the king appointed Shadrach, Meshach, and Abednego as Daniel's assistants, to be in charge of all the affairs of the province of Babylon; Daniel served as chief magistrate in the king's court.

3 KING NEBUCHADNEZZAR made a gold statue ninety feet high and nine feet wide and set it up on the Plain of Dura, in the province of Babylon; 2then he sent messages to all the princes, governors, captains, judges, treasurers, counselors, sheriffs, and rulers of all the provinces of his empire, to come to the dedication of his statue. 3When they had all arrived and were standing before the monument, 4a herald shouted out, "O people of all nations and languages, this is the king's command:

New Revised Standard

whom the God of heaven has given the kingdom, the power, the might, and the glory, 38into whose hand he has given human beings, wherever they live, the wild animals of the field, and the birds of the air, and whom he has established as ruler over them all—you are the head of gold. 39After you shall arise another kingdom inferior to yours, and yet a third kingdom of bronze, which shall rule over the whole earth. 40And there shall be a fourth kingdom, strong as iron; just as iron crushes and smashes everything,ᵉ it shall crush and shatter all these. 41As you saw the feet and toes partly of potter's clay and partly of iron, it shall be a divided kingdom; but some of the strength of iron shall be in it, as you saw the iron mixed with the clay. 42As the toes of the feet were part iron and part clay, so the kingdom shall be partly strong and partly brittle. 43As you saw the iron mixed with clay, so will they mix with one another in marriage,ᶠ but they will not hold together, just as iron does not mix with clay. 44And in the days of those kings the God of heaven will set up a kingdom that shall never be destroyed, nor shall this kingdom be left to another people. It shall crush all these kingdoms and bring them to an end, and it shall stand forever; 45just as you saw that a stone was cut from the mountain not by hands, and that it crushed the iron, the bronze, the clay, the silver, and the gold. The great God has informed the king what shall be hereafter. The dream is certain, and its interpretation trustworthy."

Daniel and His Friends Promoted

46 Then King Nebuchadnezzar fell on his face, worshiped Daniel, and commanded that a grain offering and incense be offered to him. 47The king said to Daniel, "Truly, your God is God of gods and Lord of kings and a revealer of mysteries, for you have been able to reveal this mystery!" 48Then the king promoted Daniel, gave him many great gifts, and made him ruler over the whole province of Babylon and chief prefect over all the wise men of Babylon. 49Daniel made a request of the king, and he appointed Shadrach, Meshach, and Abednego over the affairs of the province of Babylon. But Daniel remained at the king's court.

The Golden Image

3 KING NEBUCHADNEZZAR made a golden statue whose height was sixty cubits and whose width was six cubits; he set it up on the plain of Dura in the province of Babylon. 2Then King Nebuchadnezzar sent for the satraps, the prefects, and the governors, the counselors, the treasurers, the justices, the magistrates, and all the officials of the provinces to assemble and come to the dedication of the statue that King Nebuchadnezzar had set up. 3So the satraps, the prefects, and the governors, the counselors, the treasurers, the justices, the magistrates, and all the officials of the provinces, assembled for the dedication of the statue that King Nebuchadnezzar had set up. When they were standing before the statue that Nebuchadnezzar had set up, 4the herald proclaimed aloud, "You are commanded, O peoples, nations, and languages, 5that when you hear

---

ᵇ 2:39 another world power. The Medo-Persian Empire, whose first great ruler was Cyrus.   ᶜ 2:39 yet a third great power. The Greek Empire founded by Alexander the Great.   ᵈ 2:40 the fourth kingdom. Apparently the Roman Empire.

ᵉ Gk Theodotion Syr Vg: Aram adds and like iron that crushes   ᶠ Aram by human seed

King James

5*That* at what time ye hear the sound of the cornet, flute, harp, sackbut, psaltery, dulcimer, and all kinds of music, ye fall down and worship the golden image that Nebuchadnezzar the king hath set up:

6And whoso falleth not down and worshippeth shall the same hour be cast into the midst of a burning fiery furnace.

7Therefore at that time, when all the people heard the sound of the cornet, flute, harp, sackbut, psaltery, and all kinds of music, all the people, the nations, and the languages, fell down *and* worshipped the golden image that Nebuchadnezzar the king had set up.

8¶ Wherefore at that time certain Chaldeans came near, and accused the Jews.

9They spake and said to the king Nebuchadnezzar, O king, live for ever.

10Thou, O king, hast made a decree, that every man that shall hear the sound of the cornet, flute, harp, sackbut, psaltery, and dulcimer, and all kinds of music, shall fall down and worship the golden image:

11And whoso falleth not down and worshippeth, *that* he should be cast into the midst of a burning fiery furnace.

12There are certain Jews whom thou hast set over the affairs of the province of Babylon, Shadrach, Meshach, and Abed-nego; these men, O king, have not regarded thee: they serve not thy gods, nor worship the golden image which thou hast set up.

13¶ Then Nebuchadnezzar in *his* rage and fury commanded to bring Shadrach, Meshach, and Abed-nego. Then they brought these men before the king.

14Nebuchadnezzar spake and said unto them, *Is it* true, O Shadrach, Meshach, and Abed-nego, do not ye serve my gods, nor worship the golden image which I have set up?

15Now if ye be ready that at what time ye hear the sound of the cornet, flute, harp, sackbut, psaltery, and dulcimer, and all kinds of music, ye fall down and worship the image which I have made; *well:* but if ye worship not, ye shall be cast the same hour into the midst of a burning fiery furnace; and who *is* that God that shall deliver you out of my hands?

16Shadrach, Meshach, and Abed-nego, answered and said to the king, O Nebuchadnezzar, we *are* not careful to answer thee in this matter.

17If it be *so,* our God whom we serve is able to deliver us from the burning fiery furnace, and he will deliver *us* out of thine hand, O king.

18But if not, be it known unto thee, O king, that we will not serve thy gods, nor worship the golden image which thou hast set up.

19¶ Then was Nebuchadnezzar full of fury, and the form of his visage was changed against Shadrach, Meshach, and Abed-nego: *therefore* he spake, and commanded that they should heat the furnace one seven times more than it was wont to be heated.

20And he commanded the most mighty men that *were* in his army to bind Shadrach, Meshach, and Abed-nego, *and* to cast *them* into the burning fiery furnace.

21Then these men were bound in their coats, their hosen, and their hats, and their *other* garments, and were cast into the midst of the burning fiery furnace.

22Therefore because the king's commandment was urgent, and the furnace exceeding hot, the flame of the fire slew those men that took up Shadrach, Meshach, and Abed-nego.

23And these three men, Shadrach, Meshach, and Abed-nego, fell down bound into the midst of the burning fiery furnace.

24Then Nebuchadnezzar the king was astonied, and rose up in haste, *and* spake, and said unto his counsellors, Did not we cast three men bound into the midst of the fire? They answered and said unto the king, True, O king.

New International

horn, flute, zither, lyre, harp, pipes and all kinds of music, you must fall down and worship the image of gold that King Nebuchadnezzar has set up. 6Whoever does not fall down and worship will immediately be thrown into a blazing furnace."

7Therefore, as soon as they heard the sound of the horn, flute, zither, lyre, harp and all kinds of music, all the peoples, nations and men of every language fell down and worshiped the image of gold that King Nebuchadnezzar had set up.

8At this time some astrologersa came forward and denounced the Jews. 9They said to King Nebuchadnezzar, "O king, live forever! 10You have issued a decree, O king, that everyone who hears the sound of the horn, flute, zither, lyre, harp, pipes and all kinds of music must fall down and worship the image of gold, 11and that whoever does not fall down and worship will be thrown into a blazing furnace. 12But there are some Jews whom you have set over the affairs of the province of Babylon—Shadrach, Meshach and Abednego—who pay no attention to you, O king. They neither serve your gods nor worship the image of gold you have set up."

13Furious with rage, Nebuchadnezzar summoned Shadrach, Meshach and Abednego. So these men were brought before the king, 14and Nebuchadnezzar said to them, "Is it true, Shadrach, Meshach and Abednego, that you do not serve my gods or worship the image of gold I have set up? 15Now when you hear the sound of the horn, flute, zither, lyre, harp, pipes and all kinds of music, if you are ready to fall down and worship the image I made, very good. But if you do not worship it, you will be thrown immediately into a blazing furnace. Then what god will be able to rescue you from my hand?"

16Shadrach, Meshach and Abednego replied to the king, "O Nebuchadnezzar, we do not need to defend ourselves before you in this matter. 17If we are thrown into the blazing furnace, the God we serve is able to save us from it, and he will rescue us from your hand, O king. 18But even if he does not, we want you to know, O king, that we will not serve your gods or worship the image of gold you have set up."

19Then Nebuchadnezzar was furious with Shadrach, Meshach and Abednego, and his attitude toward them changed. He ordered the furnace heated seven times hotter than usual 20and commanded some of the strongest soldiers in his army to tie up Shadrach, Meshach and Abednego and throw them into the blazing furnace. 21So these men, wearing their robes, trousers, turbans and other clothes, were bound and thrown into the blazing furnace. 22The king's command was so urgent and the furnace so hot that the flames of the fire killed the soldiers who took up Shadrach, Meshach and Abednego, 23and these three men, firmly tied, fell into the blazing furnace.

24Then King Nebuchadnezzar leaped to his feet in amazement and asked his advisers, "Weren't there three men that we tied up and threw into the fire?"

They replied, "Certainly, O king."

a 8 Or *Chaldeans*

Living Bible

5"When the band[b] strikes up, you are to fall flat on the ground to worship King Nebuchadnezzar's gold statue; 6anyone who refuses to obey will immediately be thrown into a flaming furnace."

7So when the band began to play, everyone—whatever his nation, language, or religion[c]—fell to the ground and worshiped the statue.

8But some officials went to the king and accused some of the Jews of refusing to worship!

9"Your Majesty," they said to him, 10"you made a law that everyone must fall down and worship the gold statue when the band begins to play, 11and that anyone who refuses will be thrown into a flaming furnace. 12But there are some Jews out there—Shadrach, Meshach, and Abednego, whom you have put in charge of Babylonian affairs—who have defied you, refusing to serve your gods or to worship the gold statue you set up."

13Then Nebuchadnezzar, in a terrible rage, ordered Shadrach, Meshach, and Abednego to be brought in before him.

14"Is it true, O Shadrach, Meshach, and Abednego," he demanded, "that you are refusing to serve my gods or to worship the gold statue I set up? 15I'll give you one more chance. When the music plays, if you fall down and worship the statue, all will be well. But if you refuse, you will be thrown into a flaming furnace within the hour. And what god can deliver you out of my hands then?"

16Shadrach, Meshach, and Abednego replied, "O Nebuchadnezzar, we are not worried about what will happen to us. 17If we are thrown into the flaming furnace, our God is able to deliver us; and he will deliver us out of your hand, Your Majesty. 18But if he doesn't, please understand, sir, that even then we will never under any circumstance serve your gods or worship the gold statue you have erected." 19Then Nebuchadnezzar was filled with fury and his face became dark with anger at Shadrach, Meshach, and Abednego. He commanded that the furnace be heated up seven times hotter than usual, 20and called for some of the strongest men of his army to bind Shadrach, Meshach, and Abednego, and throw them into the fire.

21So they bound them tight with ropes and threw them into the furnace, fully clothed. 22And because the king, in his anger, had demanded such a hot fire in the furnace, the flames leaped out and killed the soldiers as they threw them in! 23So Shadrach, Meshach, and Abednego fell down bound into the roaring flames.

24But suddenly, as he was watching, Nebuchadnezzar jumped up in amazement and exclaimed to his advisors, "Didn't we throw three men into the furnace?"

"Yes," they said, "we did indeed, Your Majesty."

New Revised Standard

the sound of the horn, pipe, lyre, trigon, harp, drum, and entire musical ensemble, you are to fall down and worship the golden statue that King Nebuchadnezzar has set up. 6Whoever does not fall down and worship shall immediately be thrown into a furnace of blazing fire." 7Therefore, as soon as all the peoples heard the sound of the horn, pipe, lyre, trigon, harp, drum, and entire musical ensemble, all the peoples, nations, and languages fell down and worshiped the golden statue that King Nebuchadnezzar had set up.

8 Accordingly, at this time certain Chaldeans came forward and denounced the Jews. 9They said to King Nebuchadnezzar, "O king, live forever! 10You, O king, have made a decree, that everyone who hears the sound of the horn, pipe, lyre, trigon, harp, drum, and entire musical ensemble, shall fall down and worship the golden statue, 11and whoever does not fall down and worship shall be thrown into a furnace of blazing fire. 12There are certain Jews whom you have appointed over the affairs of the province of Babylon: Shadrach, Meshach, and Abednego. These pay no heed to you, O King. They do not serve your gods and they do not worship the golden statue that you have set up."

13 Then Nebuchadnezzar in furious rage commanded that Shadrach, Meshach, and Abednego be brought in; so they brought those men before the king. 14Nebuchadnezzar said to them, "Is it true, O Shadrach, Meshach, and Abednego, that you do not serve my gods and you do not worship the golden statue that I have set up? 15Now if you are ready when you hear the sound of the horn, pipe, lyre, trigon, harp, drum, and entire musical ensemble, to fall down and worship the statue that I have made, well and good.[d] But if you do not worship, you shall immediately be thrown into a furnace of blazing fire, and who is the god that will deliver you out of my hands?"

16 Shadrach, Meshach, and Abednego answered the king, "O Nebuchadnezzar, we have no need to present a defense to you in this matter. 17If our God whom we serve is able to deliver us from the furnace of blazing fire and out of your hand, O king, let him deliver us.[e] 18But if not, be it known to you, O king, that we will not serve your gods and we will not worship the golden statue that you have set up."

The Fiery Furnace

19 Then Nebuchadnezzar was so filled with rage against Shadrach, Meshach, and Abednego that his face was distorted. He ordered the furnace heated up seven times more than was customary, 20and ordered some of the strongest guards in his army to bind Shadrach, Meshach, and Abednego and to throw them into the furnace of blazing fire. 21So the men were bound, still wearing their tunics,[f] their trousers,[f] their hats, and their other garments, and they were thrown into the furnace of blazing fire. 22Because the king's command was urgent and the furnace was so overheated, the raging flames killed the men who lifted Shadrach, Meshach, and Abednego. 23But the three men, Shadrach, Meshach, and Abednego, fell down, bound, into the furnace of blazing fire.

24 Then King Nebuchadnezzar was astonished and rose up quickly. He said to his counselors, "Was it not three men that we threw bound into the fire?" They answered the king, "True, O king." 25He replied, "But

---

b 3:5 When the band, literally, "the cornet, flute, harp, sackbut, psaltry, dulcimer, and every other sort of instrument." So also in vss 7 and 10.
c 3:7 whatever his nation, language, or religion, implied.

d Aram lacks well and good   e Or If our God whom we serve is able to deliver us, he will deliver us from the furnace of blazing fire and out of your hand, O king.   f Meaning of Aram word uncertain

King James

25He answered and said, Lo, I see four men loose, walking in the midst of the fire, and they have no hurt; and the form of the fourth is like the Son of God.

26¶ Then Nebuchadnezzar came near to the mouth of the burning fiery furnace, *and* spake, and said, Shadrach, Meshach, and Abed-nego, ye servants of the most high God, come forth, and come *hither*. Then Shadrach, Meshach, and Abed-nego, came forth of the midst of the fire.

27And the princes, governors, and captains, and the king's counsellors, being gathered together, saw these men, upon whose bodies the fire had no power, nor was an hair of their head singed, neither were their coats changed, nor the smell of fire had passed on them.

28*Then* Nebuchadnezzar spake, and said, Blessed *be* the God of Shadrach, Meshach, and Abed-nego, who hath sent his angel, and delivered his servants that trusted in him, and have changed the king's word, and yielded their bodies, that they might not serve nor worship any god, except their own God.

29Therefore I make a decree, That every people, nation, and language, which speak any thing amiss against the God of Shadrach, Meshach, and Abed-nego, shall be cut in pieces, and their houses shall be made a dunghill: because there is no other God that can deliver after this sort.

30Then the king promoted Shadrach, Meshach, and Abed-nego, in the province of Babylon.

4 NEBUCHADNEZZAR THE king, unto all people, nations, and languages, that dwell in all the earth; Peace be multiplied unto you.

2I thought it good to show the signs and wonders that the high God hath wrought toward me.

3How great *are* his signs! and how mighty *are* his wonders! his kingdom *is* an everlasting kingdom, and his dominion *is* from generation to generation.

4¶ I Nebuchadnezzar was at rest in mine house, and flourishing in my palace:

5I saw a dream which made me afraid, and the thoughts upon my bed and the visions of my head troubled me.

6Therefore made I a decree to bring in all the wise *men* of Babylon before me, that they might make known unto me the interpretation of the dream.

7Then came in the magicians, the astrologers, the Chaldeans, and the soothsayers: and I told the dream before them; but they did not make known unto me the interpretation thereof.

8¶ But at the last Daniel came in before me, whose name *was* Belteshazzar, according to the name of my god, and in whom *is* the spirit of the holy gods: and before him I told the dream, *saying,*

9O Belteshazzar, master of the magicians, because I know that the spirit of the holy gods *is* in thee, and no secret troubleth thee, tell me the visions of my dream that I have seen, and the interpretation thereof.

New International

25He said, "Look! I see four men walking around in the fire, unbound and unharmed, and the fourth looks like a son of the gods."

26Nebuchadnezzar then approached the opening of the blazing furnace and shouted, "Shadrach, Meshach and Abednego, servants of the Most High God, come out! Come here!"

So Shadrach, Meshach and Abednego came out of the fire, 27and the satraps, prefects, governors and royal advisers crowded around them. They saw that the fire had not harmed their bodies, nor was a hair of their heads singed; their robes were not scorched, and there was no smell of fire on them.

28Then Nebuchadnezzar said, "Praise be to the God of Shadrach, Meshach and Abednego, who has sent his angel and rescued his servants! They trusted in him and defied the king's command and were willing to give up their lives rather than serve or worship any god except their own God. 29Therefore I decree that the people of any nation or language who say anything against the God of Shadrach, Meshach and Abednego be cut into pieces and their houses be turned into piles of rubble, for no other god can save in this way."

30Then the king promoted Shadrach, Meshach and Abednego in the province of Babylon.

Nebuchadnezzar's Dream of a Tree

4 KING NEBUCHADNEZZAR,

To the peoples, nations and men of every language, who live in all the world:

May you prosper greatly!

2It is my pleasure to tell you about the miraculous signs and wonders that the Most High God has performed for me.

3How great are his signs,
    how mighty his wonders!
His kingdom is an eternal kingdom;
    his dominion endures from generation to
        generation.

4I, Nebuchadnezzar, was at home in my palace, contented and prosperous. 5I had a dream that made me afraid. As I was lying in my bed, the images and visions that passed through my mind terrified me. 6So I commanded that all the wise men of Babylon be brought before me to interpret the dream for me. 7When the magicians, enchanters, astrologersa and diviners came, I told them the dream, but they could not interpret it for me. 8Finally, Daniel came into my presence and I told him the dream. (He is called Belteshazzar, after the name of my god, and the spirit of the holy gods is in him.)

9I said, "Belteshazzar, chief of the magicians, I know that the spirit of the holy gods is in you, and no mystery is too difficult for you. Here is my dream; interpret it for me. 10These are the visions

---

a 7 Or *Chaldeans*

Living Bible

25"Well, look!" Nebuchadnezzar shouted. "I see *four* men, unbound, walking around in the fire, and they aren't even hurt by the flames! And the fourth looks like a god!"b

26Then Nebuchadnezzar came as close as he could to the open door of the flaming furnace and yelled: "Shadrach, Meshach, and Abednego, servants of the Most High God! Come out! Come here!" So they stepped out of the fire.

27Then the princes, governors, captains, and counselors crowded around them and saw that the fire hadn't touched them—not a hair of their heads was singed; their coats were unscorched, and they didn't even smell of smoke!

28Then Nebuchadnezzar said, "Blessed be the God of Shadrach, Meshach, and Abednego, for he sent his angel to deliver his trusting servants when they defied the king's commandment, and were willing to die rather than serve or worship any god except their own. 29Therefore, I make this decree, that any person of any nation, language, or religionc who speaks a word against the God of Shadrach, Meshach, and Abednego shall be torn limb from limb and his house knocked into a heap of rubble. For no other God can do what this one does."

30Then the king gave promotions to Shadrach, Meshach, and Abednego, so that they prospered greatly there in the province of Babylon.

4 THIS IS the proclamation of Nebuchadnezzar the king, which he sent to people of every language in every nation of the world:

Greetings:

2I want you all to know about the strange thing that the Most High God did to me. 3It was incredible—a mighty miracle! And now I know for sure that his kingdom is everlasting; he reigns forever and ever.

4I, Nebuchadnezzar, was living in peace and prosperity, 5when one night I had a dream that greatly frightened me. 6I called in all the wise men of Babylon to tell me the meaning of my dream, 7but when they came—the magicians, astrologers, fortunetellers, and wizards—and I told them the dream, they couldn't interpret it. 8At last Daniel came in—the man I named Belteshazzar after my god—the man in whom is the spirit of the holy gods, and I told him the dream.

9"O Belteshazzar, master magician," I said, "I know that the spirit of the holy gods is in you and no mystery is too great for you to solve. Tell me what my dream means:

New Revised Standard

I see four men unbound, walking in the middle of the fire, and they are not hurt; and the fourth has the appearance of a god."d 26Nebuchadnezzar then approached the door of the furnace of blazing fire and said, "Shadrach, Meshach, and Abednego, servants of the Most High God, come out! Come here!" So Shadrach, Meshach, and Abednego came out from the fire. 27And the satraps, the prefects, the governors, and the king's counselors gathered together and saw that the fire had not had any power over the bodies of those men; the hair of their heads was not singed, their tunicse were not harmed, and not even the smell of fire came from them. 28Nebuchadnezzar said, "Blessed be the God of Shadrach, Meshach, and Abednego, who has sent his angel and delivered his servants who trusted in him. They disobeyed the king's command and yielded up their bodies rather than serve and worship any god except their own God. 29Therefore I make a decree: Any people, nation, or language that utters blasphemy against the God of Shadrach, Meshach, and Abednego shall be torn limb from limb, and their houses laid in ruins; for there is no other god who is able to deliver in this way." 30Then the king promoted Shadrach, Meshach, and Abednego in the province of Babylon.

Nebuchadnezzar's Second Dream

4f KING NEBUCHADNEZZAR to all peoples, nations, and languages that live throughout the earth: May you have abundant prosperity! 2The signs and wonders that the Most High God has worked for me I am pleased to recount.

3   How great are his signs,
         how mighty his wonders!
     His kingdom is an everlasting kingdom,
         and his sovereignty is from generation to
             generation.

4g I, Nebuchadnezzar, was living at ease in my home and prospering in my palace. 5I saw a dream that frightened me; my fantasies in bed and the visions of my head terrified me. 6So I made a decree that all the wise men of Babylon should be brought before me, in order that they might tell me the interpretation of the dream. 7Then the magicians, the enchanters, the Chaldeans, and the diviners came in, and I told them the dream, but they could not tell me its interpretation. 8At last Daniel came in before me—he who was named Belteshazzar after the name of my god, and who is endowed with a spirit of the holy godsh—and I told him the dream: 9"O Belteshazzar, chief of the magicians, I know that you are endowed with a spirit of the holy godsh and that no mystery is too difficult for you. Heari the dream that I saw; tell me its interpretation.

---

b *3:25* Literally, "looks like a son of the gods."   c *3:29 of any nation, language, or religion,* implied.

d Aram *a son of the gods*   e Meaning of Aram word uncertain   f Ch 3.31 in Aram   g Ch 4.1 in Aram   h Or *a holy, divine spirit*   i Theodotion: Aram *The visions of*

King James

10Thus *were* the visions of mine head in my bed; I saw, and behold a tree in the midst of the earth, and the height thereof *was* great.

11The tree grew, and was strong, and the height thereof reached unto heaven, and the sight thereof to the end of all the earth:

12The leaves thereof *were* fair, and the fruit thereof much, and in it *was* meat for all: the beasts of the field had shadow under it, and the fowls of the heaven dwelt in the boughs thereof, and all flesh was fed of it.

13I saw in the visions of my head upon my bed, and, behold, a watcher and an holy one came down from heaven;

14He cried aloud, and said thus, Hew down the tree, and cut off his branches, shake off his leaves, and scatter his fruit: let the beasts get away from under it, and the fowls from his branches:

15Nevertheless leave the stump of his roots in the earth, even with a band of iron and brass, in the tender grass of the field; and let it be wet with the dew of heaven, and *let* his portion *be* with the beasts in the grass of the earth:

16Let his heart be changed from man's, and let a beast's heart be given unto him; and let seven times pass over him.

17This matter *is* by the decree of the watchers, and the demand by the word of the holy ones: to the intent that the living may know that the most High ruleth in the kingdom of men, and giveth it to whomsoever he will, and setteth up over it the basest of men.

18This dream I king Nebuchadnezzar have seen. Now thou, O Belteshazzar, declare the interpretation thereof, forasmuch as all the wise *men* of my kingdom are not able to make known unto me the interpretation: but thou *art* able; for the spirit of the holy gods *is* in thee.

19¶ Then Daniel, whose name *was* Belteshazzar, was astonied for one hour, and his thoughts troubled him. The king spake, and said, Belteshazzar, let not the dream, or the interpretation thereof, trouble thee. Belteshazzar answered and said, My lord, the dream *be* to them that hate thee, and the interpretation thereof to thine enemies.

20The tree that thou sawest, which grew, and was strong, whose height reached unto the heaven, and the sight thereof to all the earth;

21Whose leaves *were* fair, and the fruit thereof much, and in it *was* meat for all; under which the beasts of the field dwelt, and upon whose branches the fowls of the heaven had their habitation:

22It *is* thou, O king, that art grown and become strong: for thy greatness is grown, and reacheth unto heaven, and thy dominion to the end of the earth.

New International

I saw while lying in my bed: I looked, and there before me stood a tree in the middle of the land. Its height was enormous. 11The tree grew large and strong and its top touched the sky; it was visible to the ends of the earth. 12Its leaves were beautiful, its fruit abundant, and on it was food for all. Under it the beasts of the field found shelter, and the birds of the air lived in its branches; from it every creature was fed.

13"In the visions I saw while lying in my bed, I looked, and there before me was a messenger,[a] a holy one, coming down from heaven. 14He called in a loud voice: 'Cut down the tree and trim off its branches; strip off its leaves and scatter its fruit. Let the animals flee from under it and the birds from its branches. 15But let the stump and its roots, bound with iron and bronze, remain in the ground, in the grass of the field.

" 'Let him be drenched with the dew of heaven, and let him live with the animals among the plants of the earth. 16Let his mind be changed from that of a man and let him be given the mind of an animal, till seven times[b] pass by for him.

17" 'The decision is announced by messengers, the holy ones declare the verdict, so that the living may know that the Most High is sovereign over the kingdoms of men and gives them to anyone he wishes and sets over them the lowliest of men.'

18"This is the dream that I, King Nebuchadnezzar, had. Now, Belteshazzar, tell me what it means, for none of the wise men in my kingdom can interpret it for me. But you can, because the spirit of the holy gods is in you."

Daniel Interprets the Dream

19Then Daniel (also called Belteshazzar) was greatly perplexed for a time, and his thoughts terrified him. So the king said, "Belteshazzar, do not let the dream or its meaning alarm you."

Belteshazzar answered, "My lord, if only the dream applied to your enemies and its meaning to your adversaries! 20The tree you saw, which grew large and strong, with its top touching the sky, visible to the whole earth, 21with beautiful leaves and abundant fruit, providing food for all, giving shelter to the beasts of the field, and having nesting places in its branches for the birds of the air— 22you, O king, are that tree! You have become great and strong; your greatness has grown until it reaches the sky, and your dominion extends to distant parts of the earth.

---

[a] *13* Or *watchman;* also in verses 17 and 23   [b] *16* Or *years;* also in verses 23, 25 and 32

Living Bible

10, 11"I saw a very tall tree out in a field, growing higher and higher into the sky until it could be seen by everyone in all the world. 12Its leaves were fresh and green, and its branches were weighted down with fruit, enough for everyone to eat. Wild animals rested beneath its shade and birds sheltered in its branches, and all the world was fed from it. 13Then as I lay there dreaming, I saw one of God's angels[c] coming down from heaven.

14"He shouted, 'Cut down the tree; lop off its branches; shake off its leaves, and scatter its fruit. Get the animals out from under it and the birds from its branches, 15but leave its stump and roots in the ground, banded with a chain of iron and brass, surrounded by the tender grass. Let the dews of heaven drench him and let him eat grass with the wild animals! 16For seven years let him have the mind of an animal instead of a man. 17For this has been decreed by the Watchers, demanded by the Holy Ones. The purpose of this decree is that all the world may understand that the Most High dominates the kingdoms of the world, and gives them to anyone he wants to, even the lowliest of men!'

18"O Belteshazzar, that was my dream; now tell me what it means. For no one else can help me; all the wisest men of my kingdom have failed me. But you can tell me, for the spirit of the holy gods is in you."

19Then Daniel[d] sat there stunned and silent for an hour, aghast at the meaning of the dream. Finally the king said to him: "Belteshazzar, don't be afraid to tell me what it means."

Daniel replied: "Oh, that the events foreshadowed in this dream would happen to your enemies, my lord, and not to you! 20For the tree you saw growing so tall, reaching high into the heavens for all the world to see, 21with its fresh green leaves, loaded with fruit for all to eat, the wild animals living in its shade, with its branches full of birds— 22that tree, Your Majesty, is you. For you have grown strong and great; your greatness reaches up to heaven, and your rule to the ends of the earth.

New Revised Standard

10e Upon my bed this is what I saw;
　　there was a tree at the center of the earth,
　　and its height was great.
11　The tree grew great and strong,
　　its top reached to heaven,
　　and it was visible to the ends of the whole
　　　earth.
12　Its foliage was beautiful,
　　its fruit abundant,
　　and it provided food for all.
　　The animals of the field found shade under it,
　　the birds of the air nested in its branches,
　　and from it all living beings were fed.

13I continued looking, in the visions of my head as I lay in bed, and there was a holy watcher, coming down from heaven. 14He cried aloud and said:
'Cut down the tree and chop off its branches,
　strip off its foliage and scatter its fruit.
Let the animals flee from beneath it
　and the birds from its branches.
15　But leave its stump and roots in the ground,
　　with a band of iron and bronze,
　　in the tender grass of the field.
Let him be bathed with the dew of heaven,
　and let his lot be with the animals of the
　　field
　in the grass of the earth.
16　Let his mind be changed from that of a
　　　human,
　　and let the mind of an animal be given to
　　　him.
　　And let seven times pass over him.
17　The sentence is rendered by decree of the
　　　watchers,
　　the decision is given by order of the holy
　　　ones,
　　in order that all who live may know
　　that the Most High is sovereign over the
　　　kingdom of mortals;
　　he gives it to whom he will
　　and sets over it the lowliest of human
　　　beings.'

18This is the dream that I, King Nebuchadnezzar, saw. Now you, Belteshazzar, declare the interpretation, since all the wise men of my kingdom are unable to tell me the interpretation. You are able, however, for you are endowed with a spirit of the holy gods."[f]

Daniel Interprets the Second Dream

19　Then Daniel, who was called Belteshazzar, was severely distressed for a while. His thoughts terrified him. The king said, "Belteshazzar, do not let the dream or the interpretation terrify you." Belteshazzar answered, "My lord, may the dream be for those who hate you, and its interpretation for your enemies! 20The tree that you saw, which grew great and strong, so that its top reached to heaven and was visible to the end of the whole earth, 21whose foliage was beautiful and its fruit abundant, and which provided food for all, under which animals of the field lived, and in whose branches the birds of the air had nests— 22it is you, O king! You have grown great and strong. Your greatness has increased and reaches to heaven, and your sovereignty to the ends of the earth. 23And whereas the king saw a holy

---

c 4:13 one of God's angels, literally, "a watcher, a holy one."　d 4:19 Then Daniel, literally, "Daniel, whose name was Belteshazzar."

e Theodotion Syr Compare Gk: Aram adds The visions of my head　f Or a holy, divine spirit

King James

23And whereas the king saw a watcher and an holy one coming down from heaven, and saying, Hew the tree down, and destroy it; yet leave the stump of the roots thereof in the earth, even with a band of iron and brass, in the tender grass of the field; and let it be wet with the dew of heaven, and *let* his portion *be* with the beasts of the field, till seven times pass over him;

24This *is* the interpretation, O king, and this *is* the decree of the most High, which is come upon my lord the king:

25That they shall drive thee from men, and thy dwelling shall be with the beasts of the field, and they shall make thee to eat grass as oxen, and they shall wet thee with the dew of heaven, and seven times shall pass over thee, till thou know that the most High ruleth in the kingdom of men, and giveth it to whomsoever he will.

26And whereas they commanded to leave the stump of the tree roots; thy kingdom shall be sure unto thee, after that thou shalt have known that the heavens do rule.

27Wherefore, O king, let my counsel be acceptable unto thee, and break off thy sins by righteousness, and thine iniquities by showing mercy to the poor; if it may be a lengthening of thy tranquillity.

28¶ All this came upon the king Nebuchadnezzar.

29At the end of twelve months he walked in the palace of the kingdom of Babylon.

30The king spake, and said, Is not this great Babylon, that I have built for the house of the kingdom by the might of my power, and for the honour of my majesty?

31While the word *was* in the king's mouth, there fell a voice from heaven, *saying*, O king Nebuchadnezzar, to thee it is spoken; The kingdom is departed from thee.

32And they shall drive thee from men, and thy dwelling *shall be* with the beasts of the field: they shall make thee to eat grass as oxen, and seven times shall pass over thee, until thou know that the most High ruleth in the kingdom of men, and giveth it to whomsoever he will.

33The same hour was the thing fulfilled upon Nebuchadnezzar: and he was driven from men, and did eat grass as oxen, and his body was wet with the dew of heaven, till his hairs were grown like eagles' *feathers*, and his nails like birds' *claws*.

34And at the end of the days I Nebuchadnezzar lifted up mine eyes unto heaven, and mine understanding returned unto me, and I blessed the most High, and I praised and honoured him that liveth for ever, whose dominion *is* an everlasting dominion, and his kingdom *is* from generation to generation:

35And all the inhabitants of the earth *are* reputed as nothing: and he doeth according to his will in the army of heaven, and *among* the inhabitants of the earth: and none can stay his hand, or say unto him, What doest thou?

36At the same time my reason returned unto me; and for the glory of my kingdom, mine honour and brightness returned unto me; and my counsellors and my lords sought unto me; and I was established in my kingdom, and excellent majesty was added unto me.

37Now I Nebuchadnezzar praise and extol and honour the King of heaven, all whose works *are* truth, and his ways judgment: and those that walk in pride he is able to abase.

New International

23"You, O king, saw a messenger, a holy one, coming down from heaven and saying, 'Cut down the tree and destroy it, but leave the stump, bound with iron and bronze, in the grass of the field, while its roots remain in the ground. Let him be drenched with the dew of heaven; let him live like the wild animals, until seven times pass by for him.'

24"This is the interpretation, O king, and this is the decree the Most High has issued against my lord the king: 25You will be driven away from people and will live with the wild animals; you will eat grass like cattle and be drenched with the dew of heaven. Seven times will pass by for you until you acknowledge that the Most High is sovereign over the kingdoms of men and gives them to anyone he wishes. 26The command to leave the stump of the tree with its roots means that your kingdom will be restored to you when you acknowledge that Heaven rules. 27Therefore, O king, be pleased to accept my advice: Renounce your sins by doing what is right, and your wickedness by being kind to the oppressed. It may be that then your prosperity will continue."

The Dream Is Fulfilled

28All this happened to King Nebuchadnezzar. 29Twelve months later, as the king was walking on the roof of the royal palace of Babylon, 30he said, "Is not this the great Babylon I have built as the royal residence, by my mighty power and for the glory of my majesty?"

31The words were still on his lips when a voice came from heaven, "This is what is decreed for you, King Nebuchadnezzar: Your royal authority has been taken from you. 32You will be driven away from people and will live with the wild animals; you will eat grass like cattle. Seven times will pass by for you until you acknowledge that the Most High is sovereign over the kingdoms of men and gives them to anyone he wishes."

33Immediately what had been said about Nebuchadnezzar was fulfilled. He was driven away from people and ate grass like cattle. His body was drenched with the dew of heaven until his hair grew like the feathers of an eagle and his nails like the claws of a bird.

34At the end of that time, I, Nebuchadnezzar, raised my eyes toward heaven, and my sanity was restored. Then I praised the Most High; I honored and glorified him who lives forever.

His dominion is an eternal dominion;
  his kingdom endures from generation to
    generation.
35All the peoples of the earth
  are regarded as nothing.
He does as he pleases
  with the powers of heaven
  and the peoples of the earth.
No one can hold back his hand
  or say to him: "What have you done?"

36At the same time that my sanity was restored, my honor and splendor were returned to me for the glory of my kingdom. My advisers and nobles sought me out, and I was restored to my throne and became even greater than before. 37Now I, Nebuchadnezzar, praise and exalt and glorify the King of heaven, because everything he does is right and all his ways are just. And those who walk in pride he is able to humble.

Living Bible

23"Then you saw God's angel[a] coming down from heaven and saying, 'Cut down the tree and destroy it, but leave the stump and the roots in the earth surrounded by tender grass, banded with a chain of iron and brass. Let him be wet with the dew of heaven. For seven years let him eat grass with the animals of the field.'

24"Your Majesty, the Most High God has decreed—and it will surely happen— 25that your people will chase you from your palace, and you will live in the fields like an animal, eating grass like a cow, your back wet with dew from heaven. For seven years this will be your life, until you learn that the Most High God dominates the kingdoms of men, and gives power to anyone he chooses. 26But the stump and the roots were left in the ground! This means that you will get your kingdom back again, when you have learned that heaven rules.

27"O King Nebuchadnezzar, listen to me—stop sinning; do what you know is right; be merciful to the poor. Perhaps even yet God will spare you."

28But all these things happened to Nebuchadnezzar. 29Twelve months after this dream, he was strolling on the roof of the royal palace in Babylon, 30and saying, "I, by my own mighty power, have built this beautiful city as my royal residence, and as the capital of my empire."

31While he was still speaking these words, a voice called down from heaven, "O King Nebuchadnezzar, this message is for you: You are no longer ruler of this kingdom. 32You will be forced out of the palace to live with the animals in the fields, and to eat grass like the cows for seven years until you finally realize that God parcels out the kingdoms of men and gives them to anyone he chooses."

33That very same hour this prophecy was fulfilled. Nebuchadnezzar was chased from his palace and ate grass like the cows, and his body was wet with dew; his hair grew as long as eagles' feathers, and his nails were like birds' claws.

34"At the end of seven years[b] I, Nebuchadnezzar, looked up to heaven, and my sanity returned, and I praised and worshiped the Most High God and honored him who lives forever, whose rule is everlasting, his kingdom evermore. 35All the people of the earth are nothing when compared to him; he does whatever he thinks best among the angels of heaven, as well as here on earth. No one can stop him or challenge him, saying, 'What do you mean by doing these things?' 36When my mind returned to me, so did my honor and glory and kingdom. My counselors and officers came back to me and I was reestablished as head of my kingdom, with even greater honor than before.

37"Now, I, Nebuchadnezzar, praise and glorify and honor the King of Heaven, the Judge of all, whose every act is right and good; for he is able to take those who walk proudly and push them into the dust!"

New Revised Standard

watcher coming down from heaven and saying, 'Cut down the tree and destroy it, but leave its stump and roots in the ground, with a band of iron and bronze, in the grass of the field; and let him be bathed with the dew of heaven, and let his lot be with the animals of the field, until seven times pass over him'— 24this is the interpretation, O king, and it is a decree of the Most High that has come upon my lord the king: 25You shall be driven away from human society, and your dwelling shall be with the wild animals. You shall be made to eat grass like oxen, you shall be bathed with the dew of heaven, and seven times shall pass over you, until you have learned that the Most High has sovereignty over the kingdom of mortals, and gives it to whom he will. 26As it was commanded to leave the stump and roots of the tree, your kingdom shall be re-established for you from the time that you learn that Heaven is sovereign. 27Therefore, O king, may my counsel be acceptable to you: atone for[c] your sins with righteousness, and your iniquities with mercy to the oppressed, so that your prosperity may be prolonged."

Nebuchadnezzar's Humiliation

28 All this came upon King Nebuchadnezzar. 29At the end of twelve months he was walking on the roof of the royal palace of Babylon, 30and the king said, "Is this not magnificent Babylon, which I have built as a royal capital by my mighty power and for my glorious majesty?" 31While the words were still in the king's mouth, a voice came from heaven: "O King Nebuchadnezzar, to you it is declared: The kingdom has departed from you! 32You shall be driven away from human society, and your dwelling shall be with the animals of the field. You shall be made to eat grass like oxen, and seven times shall pass over you, until you have learned that the Most High has sovereignty over the kingdom of mortals and gives it to whom he will." 33Immediately the sentence was fulfilled against Nebuchadnezzar. He was driven away from human society, ate grass like oxen, and his body was bathed with the dew of heaven, until his hair grew as long as eagles' feathers and his nails became like birds' claws.

Nebuchadnezzar Praises God

34 When that period was over, I, Nebuchadnezzar, lifted my eyes to heaven, and my reason returned to me.
I blessed the Most High,
    and praised and honored the one who lives forever.
For his sovereignty is an everlasting sovereignty,
    and his kingdom endures from generation to generation.
35 All the inhabitants of the earth are accounted as nothing,
    and he does what he wills with the host of heaven
    and the inhabitants of the earth.
There is no one who can stay his hand
    or say to him, "What are you doing?"
36At that time my reason returned to me; and my majesty and splendor were restored to me for the glory of my kingdom. My counselors and my lords sought me out, I was re-established over my kingdom, and still more greatness was added to me. 37Now I, Nebuchadnezzar, praise and extol and honor the King of heaven,
    for all his works are truth,
    and his ways are justice;
and he is able to bring low
    those who walk in pride.

---

[a] 4:23 God's angel, literally, "a holy watcher." [b] 4:34 At the end of seven years, literally, "At the end of the days."

[c] Aram break off

King James

5 BELSHAZZAR THE king made a great feast to a
   thousand of his lords, and drank wine before the
thousand.

2Belshazzar, whiles he tasted the wine, commanded
to bring the golden and silver vessels which his father
Nebuchadnezzar had taken out of the temple which *was*
in Jerusalem; that the king, and his princes, his wives,
and his concubines, might drink therein.

3Then they brought the golden vessels that were taken
out of the temple of the house of God which *was* at
Jerusalem; and the king, and his princes, his wives, and
his concubines, drank in them.

4They drank wine, and praised the gods of gold, and
of silver, of brass, of iron, of wood, and of stone.

5¶ In the same hour came forth fingers of a man's
hand, and wrote over against the candlestick upon the
plaster of the wall of the king's palace: and the king saw
the part of the hand that wrote.

6Then the king's countenance was changed, and his
thoughts troubled him, so that the joints of his loins
were loosed, and his knees smote one against another.

7The king cried aloud to bring in the astrologers, the
Chaldeans, and the soothsayers. *And* the king spake, and
said to the wise *men* of Babylon, Whosoever shall read
this writing, and show me the interpretation thereof,
shall be clothed with scarlet, and *have* a chain of gold
about his neck, and shall be the third ruler in the kingdom.

8Then came in all the king's wise *men:* but they could
not read the writing, nor make known to the king the
interpretation thereof.

9Then was king Belshazzar greatly troubled, and his
countenance was changed in him, and his lords were
astonied.

10¶ *Now* the queen, by reason of the words of the king
and his lords, came into the banquet house: *and* the
queen spake and said, O king, live for ever: let not thy
thoughts trouble thee, nor let thy countenance be
changed:

11There is a man in thy kingdom, in whom *is* the spirit
of the holy gods; and in the days of thy father light and
understanding and wisdom, like the wisdom of the gods,
was found in him; whom the king Nebuchadnezzar thy
father, the king, *I say,* thy father, made master of the
magicians, astrologers, Chaldeans, *and* soothsayers;

12Forasmuch as an excellent spirit, and knowledge,
and understanding, interpreting of dreams, and showing
of hard sentences, and dissolving of doubts, were found
in the same Daniel, whom the king named Belteshazzar:
now let Daniel be called, and he will show the interpretation.

13Then was Daniel brought in before the king. *And*
the king spake and said unto Daniel, *Art* thou that Daniel, which *art* of the children of the captivity of Judah,
whom the king my father brought out of Jewry?

14I have even heard of thee, that the spirit of the gods
is in thee, and *that* light and understanding and excellent
wisdom is found in thee.

15And now the wise *men,* the astrologers, have been
brought in before me, that they should read this writing,
and make known unto me the interpretation thereof: but
they could not show the interpretation of the thing:

16And I have heard of thee, that thou canst make
interpretations, and dissolve doubts: now if thou canst
read the writing, and make known to me the interpretation thereof, thou shalt be clothed with scarlet, and *have*
a chain of gold about thy neck, and shalt be the third
ruler in the kingdom.

17¶ Then Daniel answered and said before the king,
Let thy gifts be to thyself, and give thy rewards to another; yet I will read the writing unto the king, and make
known to him the interpretation.

New International

The Writing on the Wall

5 KING BELSHAZZAR gave a great banquet for a
   thousand of his nobles and drank wine with them.
2While Belshazzar was drinking his wine, he gave orders to bring in the gold and silver goblets that Nebuchadnezzar his fathera had taken from the temple in
Jerusalem, so that the king and his nobles, his wives and
his concubines might drink from them. 3So they brought
in the gold goblets that had been taken from the temple
of God in Jerusalem, and the king and his nobles, his
wives and his concubines drank from them. 4As they
drank the wine, they praised the gods of gold and silver,
of bronze, iron, wood and stone.

5Suddenly the fingers of a human hand appeared and
wrote on the plaster of the wall, near the lampstand in
the royal palace. The king watched the hand as it wrote.
6His face turned pale and he was so frightened that his
knees knocked together and his legs gave way.

7The king called out for the enchanters, astrologersb
and diviners to be brought and said to these wise men
of Babylon, "Whoever reads this writing and tells me
what it means will be clothed in purple and have a gold
chain placed around his neck, and he will be made the
third highest ruler in the kingdom."

8Then all the king's wise men came in, but they could
not read the writing or tell the king what it meant. 9So
King Belshazzar became even more terrified and his
face grew more pale. His nobles were baffled.

10The queen,c hearing the voices of the king and his
nobles, came into the banquet hall. "O king, live forever!" she said. "Don't be alarmed! Don't look so pale!
11There is a man in your kingdom who has the spirit of
the holy gods in him. In the time of your father he was
found to have insight and intelligence and wisdom like
that of the gods. King Nebuchadnezzar your father—
your father the king, I say—appointed him chief of the
magicians, enchanters, astrologers and diviners. 12This
man Daniel, whom the king called Belteshazzar, was
found to have a keen mind and knowledge and understanding, and also the ability to interpret dreams, explain riddles and solve difficult problems. Call for Daniel, and he will tell you what the writing means."

13So Daniel was brought before the king, and the king
said to him, "Are you Daniel, one of the exiles my father
the king brought from Judah? 14I have heard that the
spirit of the gods is in you and that you have insight,
intelligence and outstanding wisdom. 15The wise men
and enchanters were brought before me to read this writing and tell me what it means, but they could not explain
it. 16Now I have heard that you are able to give interpretations and to solve difficult problems. If you can read
this writing and tell me what it means, you will be
clothed in purple and have a gold chain placed around
your neck, and you will be made the third highest ruler
in the kingdom."

17Then Daniel answered the king, "You may keep
your gifts for yourself and give your rewards to someone
else. Nevertheless, I will read the writing for the king
and tell him what it means.

a 2 Or *ancestor*; or *predecessor*; also in verses 11, 13 and 18   b 7 Or
Chaldeans; also in verse 11   c 10 Or *queen mother*

Living Bible

5 BELSHAZZAR THE king invited a thousand of his officers to a great feast where the wine flowed freely. 2, 3, 4While Belshazzar was drinking he was reminded of the gold and silver cups taken long before from the Temple in Jerusalem during Nebuchadnezzar's reign, and brought to Babylon. Belshazzar ordered that these sacred cups be brought in to the feast, and when they arrived he and his princes, wives, and concubines drank toasts from them to their idols made of gold and silver, brass and iron, wood and stone.

5Suddenly, as they were drinking from these cups, they saw the fingers of a man's hand writing on the plaster of the wall opposite the lampstand. The king himself saw the fingers as they wrote. 6His face blanched with fear, and such terror gripped him that his knees knocked together and his legs gave way beneath him.

7"Bring the magicians and astrologers!" he screamed. "Bring the Chaldeans! Whoever reads that writing on the wall, and tells me what it means, will be dressed in purple robes of royal honor with a gold chain around his neck, and become the third ruler in the kingdom!"d

8But when they came, none of them could understand the writing or tell him what it meant.

9The king grew more and more hysterical; his face reflected the terror he felt, and his officers too were shaken. 10But when the queen-mother heard what was happening, she rushed to the banquet hall and said to Belshazzar, "Calm yourself, Your Majesty, don't be so pale and frightened over this. 11For there is a man in your kingdom who has within him the spirit of the holy gods. In the days of your father this man was found to be as full of wisdom and understanding as though he were himself a god. And in the reign of King Nebuchadnezzar,e he was made chief of all the magicians, astrologers, Chaldeans and soothsayers of Babylon. 12Call for this man, Daniel—or Belteshazzar, as the king called him—for his mind is filled with divine knowledge and understanding. He can interpret dreams, explain riddles, and solve knotty problems. He will tell you what the writing means."

13So Daniel was rushed in to see the king. The king asked him, "Are you the Daniel brought from Israel as a captive by King Nebuchadnezzar? 14I have heard that you have the spirit of the gods within you and that you are filled with enlightenment and wisdom. 15My wise men and astrologers have tried to read that writing on the wall, and tell me what it means, but they can't. 16I am told you can solve all kinds of mysteries. If you can tell me the meaning of those words, I will clothe you in purple robes, with a gold chain around your neck, and make you the third ruler in the kingdom."

17Daniel answered, "Keep your gifts, or give them to someone else, but I will tell you what the writing means.

New Revised Standard

Belshazzar's Feast

5 KING BELSHAZZAR made a great festival for a thousand of his lords, and he was drinking wine in the presence of the thousand.

2 Under the influence of the wine, Belshazzar commanded that they bring in the vessels of gold and silver that his father Nebuchadnezzar had taken out of the temple in Jerusalem, so that the king and his lords, his wives, and his concubines might drink from them. 3So they brought in the vessels of gold and silverf that had been taken out of the temple, the house of God in Jerusalem, and the king and his lords, his wives, and his concubines drank from them. 4They drank the wine and praised the gods of gold and silver, bronze, iron, wood, and stone.

The Writing on the Wall

5 Immediately the fingers of a human hand appeared and began writing on the plaster of the wall of the royal palace, next to the lampstand. The king was watching the hand as it wrote. 6Then the king's face turned pale, and his thoughts terrified him. His limbs gave way, and his knees knocked together. 7The king cried aloud to bring in the enchanters, the Chaldeans, and the diviners; and the king said to the wise men of Babylon, "Whoever can read this writing and tell me its interpretation shall be clothed in purple, have a chain of gold around his neck, and rank third in the kingdom." 8Then all the king's wise men came in, but they could not read the writing or tell the king the interpretation. 9Then King Belshazzar became greatly terrified and his face turned pale, and his lords were perplexed.

10 The queen, when she heard the discussion of the king and his lords, came into the banqueting hall. The queen said, "O king, live forever! Do not let your thoughts terrify you or your face grow pale. 11There is a man in your kingdom who is endowed with a spirit of the holy gods.g In the days of your father he was found to have enlightenment, understanding, and wisdom like the wisdom of the gods. Your father, King Nebuchadnezzar, made him chief of the magicians, enchanters, Chaldeans, and diviners,h 12because an excellent spirit, knowledge, and understanding to interpret dreams, explain riddles, and solve problems were found in this Daniel, whom the king named Belteshazzar. Now let Daniel be called, and he will give the interpretation."

The Writing on the Wall Interpreted

13 Then Daniel was brought in before the king. The king said to Daniel, "So you are Daniel, one of the exiles of Judah, whom my father the king brought from Judah? 14I have heard of you that a spirit of the godsi is in you, and that enlightenment, understanding, and excellent wisdom are found in you. 15Now the wise men, the enchanters, have been brought in before me to read this writing and tell me its interpretation, but they were not able to give the interpretation of the matter. 16But I have heard that you can give interpretations and solve problems. Now if you are able to read the writing and tell me its interpretation, you shall be clothed in purple, have a chain of gold around your neck, and rank third in the kingdom."

17 Then Daniel answered in the presence of the king, "Let your gifts be for yourself, or give your rewards to someone else! Nevertheless I will read the writing to the king and let him know the interpretation.

King James

18O thou king, the most high God gave Nebuchadnezzar thy father a kingdom, and majesty, and glory, and honour:

19And for the majesty that he gave him, all people, nations, and languages, trembled and feared before him: whom he would he slew; and whom he would he kept alive; and whom he would he set up; and whom he would he put down.

20But when his heart was lifted up, and his mind hardened in pride, he was deposed from his kingly throne, and they took his glory from him:

21And he was driven from the sons of men; and his heart was made like the beasts, and his dwelling *was* with the wild asses: they fed him with grass like oxen, and his body was wet with the dew of heaven; till he knew that the most high God ruled in the kingdom of men, and *that* he appointeth over it whomsoever he will.

22And thou his son, O Belshazzar, hast not humbled thine heart, though thou knewest all this;

23But hast lifted up thyself against the Lord of heaven; and they have brought the vessels of his house before thee, and thou, and thy lords, thy wives, and thy concubines, have drunk wine in them; and thou hast praised the gods of silver, and gold, of brass, iron, wood, and stone, which see not, nor hear, nor know: and the God in whose hand thy breath *is,* and whose *are* all thy ways, hast thou not glorified:

24Then was the part of the hand sent from him; and this writing was written.

25¶ And this *is* the writing that was written, MENE, MENE, TEKEL, UPHARSIN.

26This *is* the interpretation of the thing: MENE; God hath numbered thy kingdom, and finished it.

27TEKEL; Thou art weighed in the balances, and art found wanting.

28PERES; Thy kingdom is divided, and given to the Medes and Persians.

29Then commanded Belshazzar, and they clothed Daniel with scarlet, and *put* a chain of gold about his neck, and made a proclamation concerning him, that he should be the third ruler in the kingdom.

30¶ In that night was Belshazzar the king of the Chaldeans slain.

31And Darius the Median took the kingdom, *being* about threescore and two years old.

6 IT PLEASED Darius to set over the kingdom an hundred and twenty princes, which should be over the whole kingdom;

2And over these three presidents; of whom Daniel *was* first: that the princes might give accounts unto them, and the king should have no damage.

3Then this Daniel was preferred above the presidents and princes, because an excellent spirit *was* in him; and the king thought to set him over the whole realm.

4¶ Then the presidents and princes sought to find occasion against Daniel concerning the kingdom; but they could find none occasion nor fault; forasmuch as he *was* faithful, neither was there any error or fault found in him.

5Then said these men, We shall not find any occasion against this Daniel, except we find *it* against him concerning the law of his God.

6Then these presidents and princes assembled together to the king, and said thus unto him, King Darius, live for ever.

New International

18"O king, the Most High God gave your father Nebuchadnezzar sovereignty and greatness and glory and splendor. 19Because of the high position he gave him, all the peoples and nations and men of every language dreaded and feared him. Those the king wanted to put to death, he put to death; those he wanted to spare, he spared; those he wanted to promote, he promoted; and those he wanted to humble, he humbled. 20But when his heart became arrogant and hardened with pride, he was deposed from his royal throne and stripped of his glory. 21He was driven away from people and given the mind of an animal; he lived with the wild donkeys and ate grass like cattle; and his body was drenched with the dew of heaven, until he acknowledged that the Most High God is sovereign over the kingdoms of men and sets over them anyone he wishes.

22"But you his son,[a] O Belshazzar, have not humbled yourself, though you knew all this. 23Instead, you have set yourself up against the Lord of heaven. You had the goblets from his temple brought to you, and you and your nobles, your wives and your concubines drank wine from them. You praised the gods of silver and gold, of bronze, iron, wood and stone, which cannot see or hear or understand. But you did not honor the God who holds in his hand your life and all your ways. 24Therefore he sent the hand that wrote the inscription.

25"This is the inscription that was written:

MENE, MENE, TEKEL, PARSIN[b]

26"This is what these words mean:

Mene[c]: God has numbered the days of your reign and brought it to an end.
27*Tekel*[d]: You have been weighed on the scales and found wanting.
28*Peres*[e]: Your kingdom is divided and given to the Medes and Persians."

29Then at Belshazzar's command, Daniel was clothed in purple, a gold chain was placed around his neck, and he was proclaimed the third highest ruler in the kingdom.

30That very night Belshazzar, king of the Babylonians,[f] was slain, 31and Darius the Mede took over the kingdom, at the age of sixty-two.

Daniel in the Den of Lions

6 IT PLEASED Darius to appoint 120 satraps to rule throughout the kingdom, 2with three administrators over them, one of whom was Daniel. The satraps were made accountable to them so that the king might not suffer loss. 3Now Daniel so distinguished himself among the administrators and the satraps by his exceptional qualities that the king planned to set him over the whole kingdom. 4At this, the administrators and the satraps tried to find grounds for charges against Daniel in his conduct of government affairs, but they were unable to do so. They could find no corruption in him, because he was trustworthy and neither corrupt nor negligent. 5Finally these men said, "We will never find any basis for charges against this man Daniel unless it has something to do with the law of his God."

6So the administrators and the satraps went as a group to the king and said: "O King Darius, live forever! 7The

---

a 22 Or *descendant*; or *successor*   b 25 Aramaic UPARSIN (that is, *AND PARSIN*)   c 26 *Mene* can mean *numbered* or *mina* (a unit of money). d 27 *Tekel* can mean *weighed* or *shekel*.   e 28 *Peres* (the singular of *Parsin*) can mean *divided* or *Persia* or *a half mina* or *a half shekel*.   f 30 Or *Chaldeans*

Living Bible

18Your Majesty, the Most High God gave Nebuchadnezzar, who long ago preceded you, a kingdom and majesty and glory and honor. 19He gave him such majesty that all the nations of the world trembled before him in fear. He killed any who offended him, and spared any he liked. At his whim they rose or fell. 20But when his heart and mind were hardened in pride, God removed him from his royal throne and took away his glory, 21and he was chased out of his palace into the fields. His thoughts and feelings became those of an animal, and he lived among the wild donkeys; he ate grass like the cows and his body was wet with the dew of heaven, until at last he knew that the Most High overrules the kingdoms of men, and that he appoints anyone he desires to reign over them.

22"And you, his successor, O Belshazzar—you knew all this, yet you have not been humble. 23For you have defied the Lord of Heaven, and brought here these cups from his Temple; and you and your officers and wives and concubines have been drinking wine from them while praising gods of silver, gold, brass, iron, wood, and stone—gods that neither see nor hear, nor know anything at all. But you have not praised the God who gives you the breath of life and controls your destiny! 24, 25And so God sent those fingers to write this message: 'Mene,' 'Mene,' 'Tekel,' 'Parsin.'

26"This is what it means:

"Mene means 'numbered'—God has numbered the days of your reign, and they are ended.

27"Tekel means 'weighed'—you have been weighed in God's balances and have failed the test.

28"Parsin means 'divided'—your kingdom will be divided and given to the Medes and Persians."

29Then at Belshazzar's command, Daniel was robed in purple, and a gold chain was hung around his neck, and he was proclaimed third ruler in the kingdom.

30That very night Belshazzar, the Chaldean king, was killed, 31and Darius the Medeg entered the city and began reigning at the age of sixty-two.

6 DARIUS DIVIDED the kingdom into 120 provinces, each under a governor. 2The governors were accountable to three presidents (Daniel was one of them) so the king could administer the kingdom efficiently.

3Daniel soon proved himself more capable than all the other presidents and governors, for he had great ability, and the king began to think of placing him over the entire empire as his administrative officer.

4This made the other presidents and governors very jealous, and they began searching for some fault in the way Daniel was handling his affairs so that they could complain to the king about him. But they couldn't find anything to criticize! He was faithful and honest, and made no mistakes. 5So they concluded, "Our only chance is his religion!"

6They decided to go to the king and say, "King Darius, live forever! 7We presidents, governors, counselors

New Revised Standard

18O king, the Most High God gave your father Nebuchadnezzar kingship, greatness, glory, and majesty. 19And because of the greatness that he gave him, all peoples, nations, and languages trembled and feared before him. He killed those he wanted to kill, kept alive those he wanted to keep alive, honored those he wanted to honor, and degraded those he wanted to degrade. 20But when his heart was lifted up and his spirit was hardened so that he acted proudly, he was deposed from his kingly throne, and his glory was stripped from him. 21He was driven from human society, and his mind was made like that of an animal. His dwelling was with the wild asses, he was fed grass like oxen, and his body was bathed with the dew of heaven, until he learned that the Most High God has sovereignty over the kingdom of mortals, and sets over it whomever he will. 22And you, Belshazzar his son, have not humbled your heart, even though you knew all this! 23You have exalted yourself against the Lord of heaven! The vessels of his temple have been brought in before you, and you and your lords, your wives and your concubines have been drinking wine from them. You have praised the gods of silver and gold, of bronze, iron, wood, and stone, which do not see or hear or know; but the God in whose power is your very breath, and to whom belong all your ways, you have not honored.

24 "So from his presence the hand was sent and this writing was inscribed. 25And this is the writing that was inscribed: MENE, MENE, TEKEL, and PARSIN. 26This is the interpretation of the matter: MENE, God has numbered the days ofh your kingdom and brought it to an end; 27TEKEL, you have been weighed on the scales and found wanting; 28PERES,i your kingdom is divided and given to the Medes and Persians."

29 Then Belshazzar gave the command, and Daniel was clothed in purple, a chain of gold was put around his neck, and a proclamation was made concerning him that he should rank third in the kingdom.

30 That very night Belshazzar, the Chaldean king, was killed. 31j And Darius the Mede received the kingdom, being about sixty-two years old.

The Plot against Daniel

6 IT PLEASED Darius to set over the kingdom one hundred twenty satraps, stationed throughout the whole kingdom, 2and over them three presidents, including Daniel; to these the satraps gave account, so that the king might suffer no loss. 3Soon Daniel distinguished himself above all the other presidents and satraps because an excellent spirit was in him, and the king planned to appoint him over the whole kingdom. 4So the presidents and the satraps tried to find grounds for complaint against Daniel in connection with the kingdom. But they could find no grounds for complaint or any corruption, because he was faithful, and no negligence or corruption could be found in him. 5The men said, "We shall not find any ground for complaint against this Daniel unless we find it in connection with the law of his God."

6 So the presidents and satraps conspired and came to the king and said to him, "O King Darius, live forever! 7All the presidents of the kingdom, the prefects and

---

g 5:31 Darius the Mede. Darius the Mede is not to be confused with Darius the Persian mentioned in Ezra, Haggai, and Zechariah, nor with the one in Neh 12:22.

h Aram lacks the days of i The singular of Parsin j Ch 6.1 in Aram

King James

7All the presidents of the kingdom, the governors, and the princes, the counsellors, and the captains, have consulted together to establish a royal statute, and to make a firm decree, that whosoever shall ask a petition of any God or man for thirty days, save of thee, O king, he shall be cast into the den of lions.

8Now, O king, establish the decree, and sign the writing, that it be not changed, according to the law of the Medes and Persians, which altereth not.

9Wherefore king Darius signed the writing and the decree.

10¶ Now when Daniel knew that the writing was signed, he went into his house; and his windows being open in his chamber toward Jerusalem, he kneeled upon his knees three times a day, and prayed, and gave thanks before his God, as he did aforetime.

11Then these men assembled, and found Daniel praying and making supplication before his God.

12Then they came near, and spake before the king concerning the king's decree; Hast thou not signed a decree, that every man that shall ask *a petition* of any God or man within thirty days, save of thee, O king, shall be cast into the den of lions? The king answered and said, The thing *is* true, according to the law of the Medes and Persians, which altereth not.

13Then answered they and said before the king, That Daniel, which *is* of the children of the captivity of Judah, regardeth not thee, O king, nor the decree that thou hast signed, but maketh his petition three times a day.

14Then the king, when he heard *these* words, was sore displeased with himself, and set *his* heart on Daniel to deliver him: and he laboured till the going down of the sun to deliver him.

15Then these men assembled unto the king, and said unto the king, Know, O king, that the law of the Medes and Persians *is,* That no decree nor statute which the king establisheth may be changed.

16Then the king commanded, and they brought Daniel, and cast *him* into the den of lions. *Now* the king spake and said unto Daniel, Thy God whom thou servest continually, he will deliver thee.

17And a stone was brought, and laid upon the mouth of the den; and the king sealed it with his own signet, and with the signet of his lords; that the purpose might not be changed concerning Daniel.

18¶ Then the king went to his palace, and passed the night fasting: neither were instruments of music brought before him: and his sleep went from him.

19Then the king arose very early in the morning, and went in haste unto the den of lions.

20And when he came to the den, he cried with a lamentable voice unto Daniel: *and* the king spake and said to Daniel, O Daniel, servant of the living God, is thy God, whom thou servest continually, able to deliver thee from the lions?

21Then said Daniel unto the king, O king, live for ever.

22My God hath sent his angel, and hath shut the lions' mouths, that they have not hurt me: forasmuch as before him innocency was found in me; and also before thee, O king, have I done no hurt.

23Then was the king exceeding glad for him, and commanded that they should take Daniel up out of the den. So Daniel was taken up out of the den, and no manner of hurt was found upon him, because he believed in his God.

24¶ And the king commanded, and they brought those men which had accused Daniel, and they cast *them* into the den of lions, them, their children, and their wives; and the lions had the mastery of them, and brake all their bones in pieces or ever they came at the bottom of the den.

New International

royal administrators, prefects, satraps, advisers and governors have all agreed that the king should issue an edict and enforce the decree that anyone who prays to any god or man during the next thirty days, except to you, O king, shall be thrown into the lions' den. 8Now, O king, issue the decree and put it in writing so that it cannot be altered—in accordance with the laws of the Medes and Persians, which cannot be repealed." 9So King Darius put the decree in writing.

10Now when Daniel learned that the decree had been published, he went home to his upstairs room where the windows opened toward Jerusalem. Three times a day he got down on his knees and prayed, giving thanks to his God, just as he had done before. 11Then these men went as a group and found Daniel praying and asking God for help. 12So they went to the king and spoke to him about his royal decree: "Did you not publish a decree that during the next thirty days anyone who prays to any god or man except to you, O king, would be thrown into the lions' den?"

The king answered, "The decree stands—in accordance with the laws of the Medes and Persians, which cannot be repealed."

13Then they said to the king, "Daniel, who is one of the exiles from Judah, pays no attention to you, O king, or to the decree you put in writing. He still prays three times a day." 14When the king heard this, he was greatly distressed; he was determined to rescue Daniel and made every effort until sundown to save him.

15Then the men went as a group to the king and said to him, "Remember, O king, that according to the law of the Medes and Persians no decree or edict that the king issues can be changed."

16So the king gave the order, and they brought Daniel and threw him into the lions' den. The king said to Daniel, "May your God, whom you serve continually, rescue you!"

17A stone was brought and placed over the mouth of the den, and the king sealed it with his own signet ring and with the rings of his nobles, so that Daniel's situation might not be changed. 18Then the king returned to his palace and spent the night without eating and without any entertainment being brought to him. And he could not sleep.

19At the first light of dawn, the king got up and hurried to the lions' den. 20When he came near the den, he called to Daniel in an anguished voice, "Daniel, servant of the living God, has your God, whom you serve continually, been able to rescue you from the lions?"

21Daniel answered, "O king, live forever! 22My God sent his angel, and he shut the mouths of the lions. They have not hurt me, because I was found innocent in his sight. Nor have I ever done any wrong before you, O king."

23The king was overjoyed and gave orders to lift Daniel out of the den. And when Daniel was lifted from the den, no wound was found on him, because he had trusted in his God.

24At the king's command, the men who had falsely accused Daniel were brought in and thrown into the lions' den, along with their wives and children. And before they reached the floor of the den, the lions overpowered them and crushed all their bones.

Living Bible

and deputies have unanimously decided that you should make a law, irrevocable under any circumstance, that for the next thirty days anyone who asks a favor of God or man—except from you, Your Majesty—shall be thrown to the lions. 8Your Majesty, we request your signature on this law; sign it so that it cannot be canceled or changed; it will be a 'law of the Medes and Persians' that cannot be revoked."

9So King Darius signed the law.

10But though Daniel knew about it, he went home and knelt down as usual in his upstairs bedroom, with its windows open toward Jerusalem, and prayed three times a day, just as he always had, giving thanks to his God.

11Then the men thronged to Daniel's house and found him praying there, asking favors of his God. 12They rushed back to the king and reminded him about his law. "Haven't you signed a decree," they demanded, "that permits no petitions to any God or man—except you—for thirty days? And anyone disobeying will be thrown to the lions?"

"Yes," the king replied, "it is 'a law of the Medes and Persians,' that cannot be altered or revoked."

13Then they told the king, "That fellow Daniel, one of the Jewish captives, is paying no attention to you or your law. He is asking favors of his God three times a day."

14Hearing this, the king was very angry with himself for signing the law, and determined to save Daniel. He spent the rest of the day trying to think of some way to get Daniel out of this predicament.

15In the evening the men came again to the king and said, "Your Majesty, there is nothing you can do. You signed the law and it cannot be changed."

16So at last the king gave the order for Daniel's arrest, and he was taken to the den of lions. The king said to him, "May your God, whom you worship continually, deliver you." And then they threw him in. 17A stone was brought and placed over the mouth of the den; and the king sealed it with his own signet ring, and that of his government, so that no one could rescue Daniel from the lions.

18Then the king returned to his palace and went to bed without dinner. He refused his usual entertainment and didn't sleep all night. 19Very early the next morning he hurried out to the lions' den, 20and called out in anguish, "O Daniel, servant of the Living God, was your God, whom you worship continually, able to deliver you from the lions?"

21Then he heard a voice! "Your Majesty, live forever!" It was Daniel! 22"My God has sent his angel," he said, "to shut the lions' mouths so that they can't touch me; for I am innocent before God, nor, sir, have I wronged you."

23The king was beside himself with joy and ordered Daniel lifted from the den. And not a scratch was found on him, because he believed in his God.

24Then the king issued a command to bring the men who had accused Daniel, and throw them into the den along with their children and wives, and the lions leaped upon them and tore them apart before they even hit the bottom of the den.

New Revised Standard

the satraps, the counselors and the governors are agreed that the king should establish an ordinance and enforce an interdict, that whoever prays to anyone, divine or human, for thirty days, except to you, O king, shall be thrown into a den of lions. 8Now, O king, establish the interdict and sign the document, so that it cannot be changed, according to the law of the Medes and the Persians, which cannot be revoked." 9Therefore King Darius signed the document and interdict.

Daniel in the Lions' Den

10 Although Daniel knew that the document had been signed, he continued to go to his house, which had windows in its upper room open toward Jerusalem, and to get down on his knees three times a day to pray to his God and praise him, just as he had done previously. 11The conspirators came and found Daniel praying and seeking mercy before his God. 12Then they approached the king and said concerning the interdict, "O king! Did you not sign an interdict, that anyone who prays to anyone, divine or human, within thirty days except to you, O king, shall be thrown into a den of lions?" The king answered, "The thing stands fast, according to the law of the Medes and Persians, which cannot be revoked." 13Then they responded to the king, "Daniel, one of the exiles from Judah, pays no attention to you, O king, or to the interdict you have signed, but he is saying his prayers three times a day."

14 When the king heard the charge, he was very much distressed. He was determined to save Daniel, and until the sun went down he made every effort to rescue him. 15Then the conspirators came to the king and said to him, "Know, O king, that it is a law of the Medes and Persians that no interdict or ordinance that the king establishes can be changed."

16 Then the king gave the command, and Daniel was brought and thrown into the den of lions. The king said to Daniel, "May your God, whom you faithfully serve, deliver you!" 17A stone was brought and laid on the mouth of the den, and the king sealed it with his own signet and with the signet of his lords, so that nothing might be changed concerning Daniel. 18Then the king went to his palace and spent the night fasting; no food was brought to him, and sleep fled from him.

Daniel Saved from the Lions

19 Then, at break of day, the king got up and hurried to the den of lions. 20When he came near the den where Daniel was, he cried out anxiously to Daniel, "O Daniel, servant of the living God, has your God whom you faithfully serve been able to deliver you from the lions?" 21Daniel then said to the king, "O king, live forever! 22My God sent his angel and shut the lions' mouths so that they would not hurt me, because I was found blameless before him; and also before you, O king, I have done no wrong." 23Then the king was exceedingly glad and commanded that Daniel be taken up out of the den. So Daniel was taken up out of the den, and no kind of harm was found on him, because he had trusted in his God. 24The king gave a command, and those who had accused Daniel were brought and thrown into the den of lions—they, their children, and their wives. Before they reached the bottom of the den the lions overpowered them and broke all their bones in pieces.

King James

25¶ Then king Darius wrote unto all people, nations, and languages, that dwell in all the earth; Peace be multiplied unto you.

26I make a decree, That in every dominion of my kingdom men tremble and fear before the God of Daniel: for he *is* the living God, and stedfast for ever, and his kingdom *that* which shall not be destroyed, and his dominion *shall be even* unto the end.

27He delivereth and rescueth, and he worketh signs and wonders in heaven and in earth, who hath delivered Daniel from the power of the lions.

28So this Daniel prospered in the reign of Darius, and in the reign of Cyrus the Persian.

7 IN THE first year of Belshazzar king of Babylon Daniel had a dream and visions of his head upon his bed: then he wrote the dream, *and* told the sum of the matters.

2Daniel spake and said, I saw in my vision by night, and, behold, the four winds of the heaven strove upon the great sea.

3And four great beasts came up from the sea, diverse one from another.

4The first *was* like a lion, and had eagle's wings: I beheld till the wings thereof were plucked, and it was lifted up from the earth, and made stand upon the feet as a man, and a man's heart was given to it.

5And behold another beast, a second, like to a bear, and it raised up itself on one side, and *it had* three ribs in the mouth of it between the teeth of it: and they said thus unto it, Arise, devour much flesh.

6After this I beheld, and lo another, like a leopard, which had upon the back of it four wings of a fowl; the beast had also four heads; and dominion was given to it.

7After this I saw in the night visions, and behold a fourth beast, dreadful and terrible, and strong exceedingly; and it had great iron teeth: it devoured and brake in pieces, and stamped the residue with the feet of it: and it *was* diverse from all the beasts that *were* before it; and it had ten horns.

8I considered the horns, and, behold, there came up among them another little horn, before whom there were three of the first horns plucked up by the roots: and, behold, in this horn *were* eyes like the eyes of man, and a mouth speaking great things.

9¶ I beheld till the thrones were cast down, and the Ancient of days did sit, whose garment *was* white as snow, and the hair of his head like the pure wool: his throne *was like* the fiery flame, *and* his wheels *as* burning fire.

10A fiery stream issued and came forth from before him: thousand thousands ministered unto him, and ten thousand times ten thousand stood before him: the judgment was set, and the books were opened.

New International

25Then King Darius wrote to all the peoples, nations and men of every language throughout the land:

"May you prosper greatly!

26"I issue a decree that in every part of my kingdom people must fear and reverence the God of Daniel.

"For he is the living God
    and he endures forever;
his kingdom will not be destroyed,
    his dominion will never end.
27He rescues and he saves;
    he performs signs and wonders
    in the heavens and on the earth.
He has rescued Daniel
    from the power of the lions."

28So Daniel prospered during the reign of Darius and the reign of Cyrus[a] the Persian.

Daniel's Dream of Four Beasts

7 IN THE first year of Belshazzar king of Babylon, Daniel had a dream, and visions passed through his mind as he was lying on his bed. He wrote down the substance of his dream.

2Daniel said: "In my vision at night I looked, and there before me were the four winds of heaven churning up the great sea. 3Four great beasts, each different from the others, came up out of the sea.

4"The first was like a lion, and it had the wings of an eagle. I watched until its wings were torn off and it was lifted from the ground so that it stood on two feet like a man, and the heart of a man was given to it.

5"And there before me was a second beast, which looked like a bear. It was raised up on one of its sides, and it had three ribs in its mouth between its teeth. It was told, 'Get up and eat your fill of flesh!'

6"After that, I looked, and there before me was another beast, one that looked like a leopard. And on its back it had four wings like those of a bird. This beast had four heads, and it was given authority to rule.

7"After that, in my vision at night I looked, and there before me was a fourth beast—terrifying and frightening and very powerful. It had large iron teeth; it crushed and devoured its victims and trampled underfoot whatever was left. It was different from all the former beasts, and it had ten horns.

8"While I was thinking about the horns, there before me was another horn, a little one, which came up among them; and three of the first horns were uprooted before it. This horn had eyes like the eyes of a man and a mouth that spoke boastfully.

9"As I looked,

"thrones were set in place,
    and the Ancient of Days took his seat.
His clothing was as white as snow;
    the hair of his head was white like wool.
His throne was flaming with fire,
    and its wheels were all ablaze.
10A river of fire was flowing,
    coming out from before him.
Thousands upon thousands attended him;
    ten thousand times ten thousand stood before
    him.
The court was seated,
    and the books were opened.

a 28 Or Darius, that is, the reign of Cyrus

Living Bible

25, 26Afterward King Darius wrote this message addressed to everyone in his empire:

"Greetings! I decree that everyone shall tremble and fear before the God of Daniel in every part of my kingdom. For his God is the living, unchanging God whose kingdom shall never be destroyed and whose power shall never end. 27He delivers his people, preserving them from harm; he does great miracles in heaven and earth; it is he who delivered Daniel from the power of the lions."

28So Daniel prospered in the reign of Darius, and in the reign of Cyrus the Persian.

7 ONE NIGHT during the first year of Belshazzar's reign over the Babylonian empire, Daniel had a dream and he wrote it down. This is his description of what he saw:

2In my dream I saw a great storm on a mighty ocean, with strong winds blowing from every direction. 3Then four huge animals came up out of the water, each different from the other. 4The first was like a lion, but it had eagle's wings! And as I watched, its wings were pulled off so that it could no longer fly, and it was left standing on the ground, on two feet, like a man; and a man's mind was given to it. 5The second animal looked like a bear with its paw raised, ready to strike. It held three ribs between its teeth, and I heard a voice saying to it, "Get up! Devour many people!" 6The third of these strange animals looked like a leopard, but on its back it had wings like those of birds, and it had four heads! And great power was given to it over all mankind.

7Then, as I watched in my dream, a fourth animal rose up out of the ocean, too dreadful to describe and incredibly strong. It devoured some of its victims by tearing them apart with its huge iron teeth, and others it crushed beneath its feet. It was far more brutal and vicious than any of the other animals, and it had ten horns.

8As I was looking at the horns, suddenly another small horn appeared among them, and three of the first ones were yanked out, roots and all, to give it room; this little horn had a man's eyes and a bragging mouth.

9I watched as thrones were put in place and the Ancient of Days—the Almighty God—sat down to judge. His clothing was as white as snow, his hair like whitest wool. He sat upon a fiery throne brought in on flaming wheels, and 10a river of fire flowed from before him. Millions of angels ministered to him and hundreds of millions of people stood before him, waiting to be judged. Then the court began its session and The Books were opened.

New Revised Standard

25 Then King Darius wrote to all peoples and nations of every language throughout the whole world: "May you have abundant prosperity! 26I make a decree, that in all my royal dominion people should tremble and fear before the God of Daniel:

For he is the living God,
    enduring forever.
His kingdom shall never be destroyed,
    and his dominion has no end.
27 He delivers and rescues,
    he works signs and wonders in heaven and
        on earth;
for he has saved Daniel
    from the power of the lions."

28So this Daniel prospered during the reign of Darius and the reign of Cyrus the Persian.

Visions of the Four Beasts

7 IN THE first year of King Belshazzar of Babylon, Daniel had a dream and visions of his head as he lay in bed. Then he wrote down the dream:b 2I,c Daniel, saw in my vision by night the four winds of heaven stirring up the great sea, 3and four great beasts came up out of the sea, different from one another. 4The first was like a lion and had eagles' wings. Then, as I watched, its wings were plucked off, and it was lifted up from the ground and made to stand on two feet like a human being; and a human mind was given to it. 5Another beast appeared, a second one, that looked like a bear. It was raised up on one side, had three tusksd in its mouth among its teeth, and was told, "Arise, devour many bodies!" 6After this, as I watched, another appeared, like a leopard. The beast had four wings of a bird on its back and four heads; and dominion was given to it. 7After this I saw in the visions by night a fourth beast, terrifying and dreadful and exceedingly strong. It had great iron teeth and was devouring, breaking in pieces, and stamping what was left with its feet. It was different from all the beasts that preceded it, and it had ten horns. 8I was considering the horns, when another horn appeared, a little one coming up among them; to make room for it, three of the earlier horns were plucked up by the roots. There were eyes like human eyes in this horn, and a mouth speaking arrogantly.

Judgment before the Ancient One

9 As I watched,
    thrones were set in place,
    and an Ancient Onee took his throne,
his clothing was white as snow,
    and the hair of his head like pure wool;
his throne was fiery flames,
    and its wheels were burning fire.
10 A stream of fire issued
    and flowed out from his presence.
A thousand thousands served him,
    and ten thousand times ten thousand stood
        attending him.
The court sat in judgment,
    and the books were opened.

---

b Q Ms Theodotion: MT adds *the beginning of the words; he said*
c Theodotion: Aram *Daniel answered and said, "I*   d Or *ribs*   e Aram *an Ancient of Days*

King James

11I beheld then because of the voice of the great words which the horn spake: I beheld *even* till the beast was slain, and his body destroyed, and given to the burning flame.

12As concerning the rest of the beasts, they had their dominion taken away: yet their lives were prolonged for a season and time.

13I saw in the night visions, and, behold, *one* like the Son of man came with the clouds of heaven, and came to the Ancient of days, and they brought him near before him.

14And there was given him dominion, and glory, and a kingdom, that all people, nations, and languages, should serve him: his dominion *is* an everlasting dominion, which shall not pass away, and his kingdom *that* which shall not be destroyed.

15¶ I Daniel was grieved in my spirit in the midst of *my* body, and the visions of my head troubled me.

16I came near unto one of them that stood by, and asked him the truth of all this. So he told me, and made me know the interpretation of the things.

17These great beasts, which are four, *are* four kings, *which* shall arise out of the earth.

18But the saints of the most High shall take the kingdom, and possess the kingdom for ever, even for ever and ever.

19Then I would know the truth of the fourth beast, which was diverse from all the others, exceeding dreadful, whose teeth *were of* iron, and his nails *of* brass; *which* devoured, brake in pieces, and stamped the residue with his feet;

20And of the ten horns that *were* in his head, and *of* the other which came up, and before whom three fell; even *of* that horn that had eyes, and a mouth that spake very great things, whose look *was* more stout than his fellows.

21I beheld, and the same horn made war with the saints, and prevailed against them;

22Until the Ancient of days came, and judgment was given to the saints of the most High; and the time came that the saints possessed the kingdom.

23Thus he said, The fourth beast shall be the fourth kingdom upon earth, which shall be diverse from all kingdoms, and shall devour the whole earth, and shall tread it down, and break it in pieces.

24And the ten horns out of this kingdom *are* ten kings *that* shall arise: and another shall rise after them; and he shall be diverse from the first, and he shall subdue three kings.

25And he shall speak *great* words against the most High, and shall wear out the saints of the most High, and think to change times and laws: and they shall be given into his hand until a time and times and the dividing of time.

26But the judgment shall sit, and they shall take away his dominion, to consume and to destroy *it* unto the end.

New International

11"Then I continued to watch because of the boastful words the horn was speaking. I kept looking until the beast was slain and its body destroyed and thrown into the blazing fire. 12(The other beasts had been stripped of their authority, but were allowed to live for a period of time.)

13"In my vision at night I looked, and there before me was one like a son of man, coming with the clouds of heaven. He approached the Ancient of Days and was led into his presence. 14He was given authority, glory and sovereign power; all peoples, nations and men of every language worshiped him. His dominion is an everlasting dominion that will not pass away, and his kingdom is one that will never be destroyed.

The Interpretation of the Dream

15"I, Daniel, was troubled in spirit, and the visions that passed through my mind disturbed me. 16I approached one of those standing there and asked him the true meaning of all this.

"So he told me and gave me the interpretation of these things: 17'The four great beasts are four kingdoms that will rise from the earth. 18But the saints of the Most High will receive the kingdom and will possess it forever— yes, for ever and ever.'

19"Then I wanted to know the true meaning of the fourth beast, which was different from all the others and most terrifying, with its iron teeth and bronze claws— the beast that crushed and devoured its victims and trampled underfoot whatever was left. 20I also wanted to know about the ten horns on its head and about the other horn that came up, before which three of them fell—the horn that looked more imposing than the others and that had eyes and a mouth that spoke boastfully. 21As I watched, this horn was waging war against the saints and defeating them, 22until the Ancient of Days came and pronounced judgment in favor of the saints of the Most High, and the time came when they possessed the kingdom.

23"He gave me this explanation: 'The fourth beast is a fourth kingdom that will appear on earth. It will be different from all the other kingdoms and will devour the whole earth, trampling it down and crushing it. 24The ten horns are ten kings who will come from this kingdom. After them another king will arise, different from the earlier ones; he will subdue three kings. 25He will speak against the Most High and oppress his saints and try to change the set times and the laws. The saints will be handed over to him for a time, times and half a time.[a]

26"'But the court will sit, and his power will be taken away and completely destroyed forever. 27Then the sov-

Living Bible

11As I watched, the brutal fourth animal was killed and its body handed over to be burned because of its arrogance against Almighty God, and the boasting of its little horn. 12As for the other three animals, their kingdoms were taken from them, but they were allowed to live a short time longer.b

13Next I saw the arrival of a Man—or so he seemed to be—brought there on clouds from heaven; he approached the Ancient of Days and was presented to him. 14He was given the ruling power and glory over all the nations of the world, so that all people of every language must obey him. His power is eternal—it will never end; his government shall never fall.

15I was confused and disturbed by all I had seen [Daniel wrote in his report], 16so I approached one of those standing beside the throne and asked him the meaning of all these things, and he explained them to me.

17"These four huge animals," he said, "represent four kings who will someday rule the earth. 18But in the end the people of the Most High God shall rule the governments of the world forever and forever."

19Then I asked about the fourth animal, the one so brutal and shocking, with its iron teeth and brass claws that tore men apart and that stamped others to death with its feet. 20I asked, too, about the ten horns and the little horn that came up afterward and destroyed three of the others—the horn with the eyes, and the loud, bragging mouth, the one which was stronger than the others. 21For I had seen this horn warring against God's people and winning, 22until the Ancient of Days came and opened his court and vindicated his people, giving them worldwide powers of government.

23"This fourth animal," he told me, "is the fourth world powerc that will rule the earth. It will be more brutal than any of the others; it will devour the whole world, destroying everything before it. 24His ten horns are ten kings that will rise out of his empire; then another kingd will arise, more brutal than the other ten, and will destroy three of them. 25He will defy the Most High God, and wear down the saints with persecution, and try to change all laws, morals, and customs.e God's people will be helpless in his hands for three and a half years.

26"But then the Ancient of Days will comef and open his court of justice and take all power from this vicious king, to consume and destroy it until the end. 27Then

New Revised Standard

11 I watched then because of the noise of the arrogant words that the horn was speaking. And as I watched, the beast was put to death, and its body destroyed and given over to be burned with fire. 12 As for the rest of the beasts, their dominion was taken away, but their lives were prolonged for a season and a time. 13 As I watched in the night visions,

I saw one like a human beingg
coming with the clouds of heaven.
And he came to the Ancient Oneh
and was presented before him.
14 To him was given dominion
and glory and kingship,
that all peoples, nations, and languages
should serve him.
His dominion is an everlasting dominion
that shall not pass away,
and his kingship is one
that shall never be destroyed.

Daniel's Visions Interpreted

15 As for me, Daniel, my spirit was troubled within me,i and the visions of my head terrified me. 16 I approached one of the attendants to ask him the truth concerning all this. So he said that he would disclose to me the interpretation of the matter: 17"As for these four great beasts, four kings shall arise out of the earth. 18 But the holy ones of the Most High shall receive the kingdom and possess the kingdom forever—forever and ever."

19 Then I desired to know the truth concerning the fourth beast, which was different from all the rest, exceedingly terrifying, with its teeth of iron and claws of bronze, and which devoured and broke in pieces, and stamped what was left with its feet; 20 and concerning the ten horns that were on its head, and concerning the other horn, which came up and to make room for which three of them fell out—the horn that had eyes and a mouth that spoke arrogantly, and that seemed greater than the others. 21 As I looked, this horn made war with the holy ones and was prevailing over them, 22until the Ancient Oneh came; then judgment was given for the holy ones of the Most High, and the time arrived when the holy ones gained possession of the kingdom.

23 This is what he said: "As for the fourth beast,
there shall be a fourth kingdom on earth
that shall be different from all the other
kingdoms;
it shall devour the whole earth,
and trample it down, and break it to pieces.
24 As for the ten horns,
out of this kingdom ten kings shall arise,
and another shall arise after them.
This one shall be different from the former
ones,
and shall put down three kings.
25 He shall speak words against the Most High,
shall wear out the holy ones of the Most
High,
and shall attempt to change the sacred
seasons and the law;
and they shall be given into his power
for a time, two times,j and half a time.
26 Then the court shall sit in judgment,
and his dominion shall be taken away,
to be consumed and totally destroyed.

---

b 7:12 *a short time longer,* literally, "for a season and a time."   c 7:23 *the fourth world power.* Usually believed to be a revived Roman Empire. See 2:40.   d 7:24 *then another king,* probably the future Antichrist of 2 Thess 2:3, 4.   e 7:25 *change all laws, morals, and customs,* literally, "change the times and the law." Perhaps the meaning is, "change right to wrong and wrong to right."   f 7:26 *the Ancient of Days will come,* implied in vs 22.

g Aram *one like a son of man*   h Aram *the Ancient of Days*   i Aram *troubled in its sheath*   j Aram *a time, times*

King James

27And the kingdom and dominion, and the greatness of the kingdom under the whole heaven, shall be given to the people of the saints of the most High, whose kingdom *is* an everlasting kingdom, and all dominions shall serve and obey him.

28Hitherto *is* the end of the matter. As for me Daniel, my cogitations much troubled me, and my countenance changed in me: but I kept the matter in my heart.

8 IN THE third year of the reign of king Belshazzar a vision appeared unto me, *even unto* me Daniel, after that which appeared unto me at the first.

2And I saw in a vision; and it came to pass, when I saw, that I *was* at Shushan *in* the palace, which *is* in the province of Elam; and I saw in a vision, and I was by the river of Ulai.

3Then I lifted up mine eyes, and saw, and, behold, there stood before the river a ram which had *two* horns: and the *two* horns *were* high; but one *was* higher than the other, and the higher came up last.

4I saw the ram pushing westward, and northward, and southward; so that no beasts might stand before him, neither *was there any* that could deliver out of his hand; but he did according to his will, and became great.

5And as I was considering, behold, an he goat came from the west on the face of the whole earth, and touched not the ground: and the goat *had* a notable horn between his eyes.

6And he came to the ram that had *two* horns, which I had seen standing before the river, and ran unto him in the fury of his power.

7And I saw him come close unto the ram, and he was moved with choler against him, and smote the ram, and brake his two horns: and there was no power in the ram to stand before him, but he cast him down to the ground, and stamped upon him: and there was none that could deliver the ram out of his hand.

8Therefore the he goat waxed very great: and when he was strong, the great horn was broken; and for it came up four notable ones toward the four winds of heaven.

9And out of one of them came forth a little horn, which waxed exceeding great, toward the south, and toward the east, and toward the pleasant *land*.

10And it waxed great, *even* to the host of heaven; and it cast down *some* of the host and of the stars to the ground, and stamped upon them.

11Yea, he magnified *himself* even to the prince of the host, and by him the daily *sacrifice* was taken away, and the place of his sanctuary was cast down.

12And an host was given *him* against the daily *sacrifice* by reason of transgression, and it cast down the truth to the ground; and it practised, and prospered.

13¶ Then I heard one saint speaking, and another saint said unto that certain *saint* which spake, How long *shall be* the vision *concerning* the daily *sacrifice,* and the transgression of desolation, to give both the sanctuary and the host to be trodden under foot?

14And he said unto me, Unto two thousand and three hundred days; then shall the sanctuary be cleansed.

15¶ And it came to pass, when I, *even* I Daniel, had seen the vision, and sought for the meaning, then, behold, there stood before me as the appearance of a man.

16And I heard a man's voice between *the banks of* Ulai, which called, and said, Gabriel, make this *man* to understand the vision.

New International

ereignty, power and greatness of the kingdoms under the whole heaven will be handed over to the saints, the people of the Most High. His kingdom will be an everlasting kingdom, and all rulers will worship and obey him.

28"This is the end of the matter. I, Daniel, was deeply troubled by my thoughts, and my face turned pale, but I kept the matter to myself."

Daniel's Vision of a Ram and a Goat

8 IN THE third year of King Belshazzar's reign, I, Daniel, had a vision, after the one that had already appeared to me. 2In my vision I saw myself in the citadel of Susa in the province of Elam; in the vision I was beside the Ulai Canal. 3I looked up, and there before me was a ram with two horns, standing beside the canal, and the horns were long. One of the horns was longer than the other but grew up later. 4I watched the ram as he charged toward the west and the north and the south. No animal could stand against him, and none could rescue from his power. He did as he pleased and became great.

5As I was thinking about this, suddenly a goat with a prominent horn between his eyes came from the west, crossing the whole earth without touching the ground. 6He came toward the two-horned ram I had seen standing beside the canal and charged at him in great rage. 7I saw him attack the ram furiously, striking the ram and shattering his two horns. The ram was powerless to stand against him; the goat knocked him to the ground and trampled on him, and none could rescue the ram from his power. 8The goat became very great, but at the height of his power his large horn was broken off, and in its place four prominent horns grew up toward the four winds of heaven.

9Out of one of them came another horn, which started small but grew in power to the south and to the east and toward the Beautiful Land. 10It grew until it reached the host of the heavens, and it threw some of the starry host down to the earth and trampled on them. 11It set itself up to be as great as the Prince of the host; it took away the daily sacrifice from him, and the place of his sanctuary was brought low. 12Because of rebellion, the host ,of the saints,a and the daily sacrifice were given over to it. It prospered in everything it did, and truth was thrown to the ground.

13Then I heard a holy one speaking, and another holy one said to him, "How long will it take for the vision to be fulfilled—the vision concerning the daily sacrifice, the rebellion that causes desolation, and the surrender of the sanctuary and of the host that will be trampled underfoot?"

14He said to me, "It will take 2,300 evenings and mornings; then the sanctuary will be reconsecrated."

The Interpretation of the Vision

15While I, Daniel, was watching the vision and trying to understand it, there before me stood one who looked like a man. 16And I heard a man's voice from the Ulai calling, "Gabriel, tell this man the meaning of the vision."

---

a 12 Or *rebellion, the armies*

Living Bible

every nation under heaven, and all their power, shall be given to the people of God;[b] they shall rule all things forever, and all rulers shall serve and obey them."

28That was the end of the dream. When I awoke, I was greatly disturbed, and my face was pale with fright, but I told no one what I had seen.

8 IN THE third year of the reign of King Belshazzar, I had another dream similar to the first.

2This time I was at Susa,[c] the capital in the province of Elam, standing beside the Ulai River. 3As I was looking around, I saw a ram with two long horns standing on the river bank; and as I watched, one of these horns began to grow, so that it was longer than the other. 4The ram butted everything out of its way and no one could stand against it or help its victims. It did as it pleased and became very great.

5While I was wondering what this could mean, suddenly a buck goat appeared from the west, so swiftly that it didn't even touch the ground. This goat, which had one very large horn between its eyes, 6rushed furiously at the two-horned ram. 7And the closer he came, the angrier he was. He charged into the ram and broke off both his horns. Now the ram was helpless and the buck goat knocked him down and trampled him, for there was no one to rescue him.

8The victor became both proud and powerful, but suddenly, at the height of his power, his horn was broken, and in its place grew four good-sized horns[d] pointing in four directions. 9One of these, growing slowly at first, soon became very strong and attacked the south and east, and warred against the land of Israel.[e] 10He fought against the people of God[f] and defeated some of their leaders.[f] 11He even challenged the Commander[g] of the army of heaven by canceling the daily sacrifices offered to him, and by defiling his Temple. 12But the army of heaven was restrained from destroying him for this transgression. As a result, truth and righteousness perished, and evil triumphed and prospered.[h]

13Then I heard two of the holy angels talking to each other. One of them said, "How long will it be until the daily sacrifice is restored again? How long until the destruction of the Temple is avenged and God's people triumph?"

14The other replied, "Twenty-three hundred days[i] must first go by."

15As I was trying to understand the meaning of this vision, suddenly a man was standing in front of me—or at least he looked like a man— 16and I heard a man's voice calling from across the river, "Gabriel, tell Daniel the meaning of his dream."

---

b 7:27 *the people of God*, literally, "the people of the saints of the Most High."
c 8:2 *Susa*. Susa was one of several capitals of the empire at this time.
d 8:8 *in its place grew four good-sized horns*. The four principal successors of Alexander the Great were Ptolemy I of Egypt, Seleucus of Babylonia, Antigonus of Syria and Asia Minor, and Antipater of Macedonia and Greece.
e 8:9 *the land of Israel*, literally, "the glorious land." Israel was attacked by Antiochus IV Epiphanes, with a further fulfillment of this prophecy indicated for the future; see vss 17, 19, 23.   f 8:10 *the people of God and . . . some of their leaders*, literally, "host of heaven" and the "starry host." See 8:24.
g 8:11 *the Commander*. Compare Josh 5:13-15.   h 8:12 *and evil triumphed and prospered*, or, "and great indignities were perpetrated against the Temple ceremonies, so truth and righteousness perished." The Hebrew text is obscure.
i 8:14 *Twenty-three hundred days*, literally, "Twenty-three hundred mornings and evenings."

New Revised Standard

27 The kingship and dominion
and the greatness of the kingdoms under the whole heaven
shall be given to the people of the holy ones of the Most High;
their kingdom shall be an everlasting kingdom,
and all dominions shall serve and obey them."

28 Here the account ends. As for me, Daniel, my thoughts greatly terrified me, and my face turned pale; but I kept the matter in my mind.

Vision of a Ram and a Goat

8 IN THE third year of the reign of King Belshazzar a vision appeared to me, Daniel, after the one that had appeared to me at first. 2 In the vision I was looking and saw myself in Susa the capital, in the province of Elam,[j] and I was by the river Ulai.[k] 3 I looked up and saw a ram standing beside the river.[l] It had two horns. Both horns were long, but one was longer than the other, and the longer one came up second. 4 I saw the ram charging westward and northward and southward. All beasts were powerless to withstand it, and no one could rescue from its power; it did as it pleased and became strong.

5 As I was watching, a male goat appeared from the west, coming across the face of the whole earth without touching the ground. The goat had a horn[m] between its eyes. 6 It came toward the ram with the two horns that I had seen standing beside the river,[l] and it ran at it with savage force. 7 I saw it approaching the ram. It was enraged against it and struck the ram, breaking its two horns. The ram did not have power to withstand it; it threw the ram down to the ground and trampled upon it, and there was no one who could rescue the ram from its power. 8 Then the male goat grew exceedingly great; but at the height of its power, the great horn was broken, and in its place there came up four prominent horns toward the four winds of heaven.

9 Out of one of them came another[n] horn, a little one, which grew exceedingly great toward the south, toward the east, and toward the beautiful land. 10 It grew as high as the host of heaven. It threw down to the earth some of the host and some of the stars, and trampled on them. 11 Even against the prince of the host it acted arrogantly; it took the regular burnt offering away from him and overthrew the place of his sanctuary. 12 Because of wickedness, the host was given over to it together with the regular burnt offering;[o] it cast truth to the ground, and kept prospering in what it did. 13 Then I heard a holy one speaking, and another holy one said to the one that spoke, "For how long is this vision concerning the regular burnt offering, the transgression that makes desolate, and the giving over of the sanctuary and host to be trampled?"[o] 14 And he answered him,[p] "For two thousand three hundred evenings and mornings; then the sanctuary shall be restored to its rightful state."

Gabriel Interprets the Vision

15 When I, Daniel, had seen the vision, I tried to understand it. Then someone appeared standing before me, having the appearance of a man, 16and I heard a human voice by the Ulai, calling, "Gabriel, help this man understand the vision." 17So he came near where

---

j Gk Theodotion: MT Q Ms repeat *in the vision I was looking*   k Or *the Ulai Gate*   l Or *gate*   m Theodotion: Gk *one horn*; Heb *a horn of vision*   n Cn Compare 7.8: Heb *one*   o Meaning of Heb uncertain   p Gk Theodotion Syr Vg: Heb *me*

King James

17So he came near where I stood: and when he came, I was afraid, and fell upon my face: but he said unto me, Understand, O son of man: for at the time of the end *shall be* the vision.

18Now as he was speaking with me, I was in a deep sleep on my face toward the ground: but he touched me, and set me upright.

19And he said, Behold, I will make thee know what shall be in the last end of the indignation: for at the time appointed the end *shall be*.

20The ram which thou sawest having *two* horns *are* the kings of Media and Persia.

21And the rough goat *is* the king of Grecia: and the great horn that *is* between his eyes *is* the first king.

22Now that being broken, whereas four stood up for it, four kingdoms shall stand up out of the nation, but not in his power.

23And in the latter time of their kingdom, when the transgressors are come to the full, a king of fierce countenance, and understanding dark sentences, shall stand up.

24And his power shall be mighty, but not by his own power: and he shall destroy wonderfully, and shall prosper, and practise, and shall destroy the mighty and the holy people.

25And through his policy also he shall cause craft to prosper in his hand; and he shall magnify *himself* in his heart, and by peace shall destroy many: he shall also stand up against the Prince of princes; but he shall be broken without hand.

26And the vision of the evening and the morning which was told *is* true: wherefore shut thou up the vision; for it *shall be* for many days.

27And I Daniel fainted, and was sick *certain* days; afterward I rose up, and did the king's business; and I was astonished at the vision, but none understood *it*.

9 IN THE first year of Darius the son of Ahasuerus, of the seed of the Medes, which was made king over the realm of the Chaldeans;

2In the first year of his reign I Daniel understood by books the number of the years, whereof the word of the LORD came to Jeremiah the prophet, that he would accomplish seventy years in the desolations of Jerusalem.

3¶ And I set my face unto the Lord God, to seek by prayer and supplications, with fasting, and sackcloth, and ashes:

4And I prayed unto the LORD my God, and made my confession, and said, O Lord, the great and dreadful God, keeping the covenant and mercy to them that love him, and to them that keep his commandments;

5We have sinned, and have committed iniquity, and have done wickedly, and have rebelled, even by departing from thy precepts and from thy judgments:

6Neither have we hearkened unto thy servants the prophets, which spake in thy name to our kings, our princes, and our fathers, and to all the people of the land.

New International

17As he came near the place where I was standing, I was terrified and fell prostrate. "Son of man," he said to me, "understand that the vision concerns the time of the end."

18While he was speaking to me, I was in a deep sleep, with my face to the ground. Then he touched me and raised me to my feet.

19He said: "I am going to tell you what will happen later in the time of wrath, because the vision concerns the appointed time of the end.a 20The two-horned ram that you saw represents the kings of Media and Persia. 21The shaggy goat is the king of Greece, and the large horn between his eyes is the first king. 22The four horns that replaced the one that was broken off represent four kingdoms that will emerge from his nation but will not have the same power.

23"In the latter part of their reign, when rebels have become completely wicked, a stern-faced king, a master of intrigue, will arise. 24He will become very strong, but not by his own power. He will cause astounding devastation and will succeed in whatever he does. He will destroy the mighty men and the holy people. 25He will cause deceit to prosper, and he will consider himself superior. When they feel secure, he will destroy many and take his stand against the Prince of princes. Yet he will be destroyed, but not by human power.

26"The vision of the evenings and mornings that has been given you is true, but seal up the vision, for it concerns the distant future."

27I, Daniel, was exhausted and lay ill for several days. Then I got up and went about the king's business. I was appalled by the vision; it was beyond understanding.

Daniel's Prayer

9 IN THE first year of Darius son of Xerxesb (a Mede by descent), who was made ruler over the Babylonianc kingdom— 2in the first year of his reign, I, Daniel, understood from the Scriptures, according to the word of the LORD given to Jeremiah the prophet, that the desolation of Jerusalem would last seventy years. 3So I turned to the Lord God and pleaded with him in prayer and petition, in fasting, and in sackcloth and ashes.

4I prayed to the LORD my God and confessed:

"O Lord, the great and awesome God, who keeps his covenant of love with all who love him and obey his commands, 5we have sinned and done wrong. We have been wicked and have rebelled; we have turned away from your commands and laws. 6We have not listened to your servants the prophets, who spoke in your name to our kings, our princes and our fathers, and to all the people of the land.

a 19 Or because the end will be at the appointed time   b 1 Hebrew Ahasuerus
c 1 Or Chaldean

Living Bible

17So Gabriel started toward me. But as he approached, I was too frightened to stand, and fell down with my face to the ground. "Son of man," he said, "you must understand that the events you have seen in your vision will not take place until the end times come."

18Then I fainted, lying face downward on the ground. But he roused me with a touch, and helped me to my feet. 19"I am here," he said, "to tell you what is going to happen in the last days of the coming time of terror—for what you have seen pertains to that final event in history.

20"The two horns of the ram you saw are the kings of Media and Persia; 21the shaggy-haired goat is the nation of Greece, and its long horn represents the first great king of that country. 22When you saw the horn break off, and four smaller horns replace it, this meant that the Grecian Empire will break into four sections with four kings, none of them as great as the first.

23"Toward the end of their kingdoms, when they have become morally rotten, an angry king shall rise to power with great shrewdness and intelligence.d 24His power shall be mighty, but it will be satanic strength and not his own.e Prospering wherever he turns, he will destroy all who oppose him, though their armies be mighty, and he will devastate God's people.

25"He will be a master of deception, defeating many by catching them off guard as they bask in false security. Without warning he will destroy them. So great will he fancy himself to be that he will even take on the Prince of Princes in battle; but in so doing he will seal his own doom, for he shall be broken by the hand of God, though no human means could overpower him.

26"And then in your vision you heard about the twenty-three hundred days to pass before the rights of worship are restored. This number is literal, and means just that.f But none of these things will happen for a long time, so don't tell anyone about them yet."

27Then I grew faint and was sick for several days. Afterward I was up and around again and performed my duties for the king, but I was greatly distressed by the dream and did not understand it.

9 IT WAS now the first year of the reign of King Darius, the son of Ahasuerus. (Darius was a Mede but became king of the Chaldeans.) 2In that first year of his reign, I, Daniel, learned from the book of Jeremiah the prophet, that Jerusalem must lie desolate for seventy years.g 3So I earnestly pleaded with the Lord God [to end our captivity and send us back to our own landh].

As I prayed, I fasted, and wore rough sackcloth, and sprinkled myself with ashes, 4and confessed my sins and those of my people.

"O Lord," I prayed, "you are a great and awesome God; you always fulfill your promises of mercy to those who love you and who keep your laws. 5But we have sinned so much; we have rebelled against you and scorned your commands. 6We have refused to listen to your servants the prophets, whom you sent again and again down through the years, with your messages to our kings and princes and to all the people.

---

d 8:23 with great shrewdness and intelligence, literally, "one who understands riddles"; an alternate rendering might read, "skilled in intrigues." Probably a reference to Antiochus Epiphanes and further future fulfillment by the Antichrist at the end of human history. e 8:24 but it will be satanic strength and not his own, implied. Literally, "but not with his power." f 8:26 This number is literal, and means just that, literally, "The vision of the evenings and the mornings which has been told is true." Vs 14 is the basis for the meaning expressed in the paraphrase. g 9:2 Jerusalem must lie desolate for seventy years. Jeremiah 25:11, 12; 29:10. This interval had now almost expired. h 9:3 to end our captivity and send us back to our own land, implied.

New Revised Standard

I stood; and when he came, I became frightened and fell prostrate. But he said to me, "Understand, O mortal,i that the vision is for the time of the end."

18 As he was speaking to me, I fell into a trance, face to the ground; then he touched me and set me on my feet. 19He said, "Listen, and I will tell you what will take place later in the period of wrath; for it refers to the appointed time of the end. 20As for the ram that you saw with the two horns, these are the kings of Media and Persia. 21The male goati is the king of Greece, and the great horn between its eyes is the first king. 22As for the horn that was broken, in place of which four others arose, four kingdoms shall arise from hisk nation, but not with his power.

23 At the end of their rule,
     when the transgressions have reached their
          full measure,
   a king of bold countenance shall arise,
          skilled in intrigue.
24 He shall grow strong in power,l
          shall cause fearful destruction,
          and shall succeed in what he does.
   He shall destroy the powerful
          and the people of the holy ones.
25 By his cunning
   he shall make deceit prosper under his hand,
          and in his own mind he shall be great.
   Without warning he shall destroy many
          and shall even rise up against the Prince of
               princes.
   But he shall be broken, and not by human
               hands.

26The vision of the evenings and the mornings that has been told is true. As for you, seal up the vision, for it refers to many days from now."

27 So I, Daniel, was overcome and lay sick for some days; then I arose and went about the king's business. But I was dismayed by the vision and did not understand it.

Daniel's Prayer for the People

9 IN THE first year of Darius son of Ahasuerus, by birth a Mede, who became king over the realm of the Chaldeans— 2in the first year of his reign, I, Daniel, perceived in the books the number of years that, according to the word of the LORD to the prophet Jeremiah, must be fulfilled for the devastation of Jerusalem, namely, seventy years.

3 Then I turned to the Lord God, to seek an answer by prayer and supplication with fasting and sackcloth and ashes. 4I prayed to the LORD my God and made confession, saying,

"Ah, Lord, great and awesome God, keeping covenant and steadfast love with those who love you and keep your commandments, 5we have sinned and done wrong, acted wickedly and rebelled, turning aside from your commandments and ordinances. 6We have not listened to your servants the prophets, who spoke in your name to our kings, our princes, and our ancestors, and to all the people of the land.

---

i Heb son of man j Or shaggy male goat k Gk Theodotion Vg: Heb the l Theodotion and one Gk Ms: Heb repeats (from 8.22) but not with his power

King James

7O Lord, righteousness *belongeth* unto thee, but unto us confusion of faces, as at this day; to the men of Judah, and to the inhabitants of Jerusalem, and unto all Israel, *that are* near, and *that are* far off, through all the countries whither thou hast driven them, because of their trespass that they have trespassed against thee.

8O Lord, to us *belongeth* confusion of face, to our kings, to our princes, and to our fathers, because we have sinned against thee.

9To the Lord our God *belong* mercies and forgivenesses, though we have rebelled against him;

10Neither have we obeyed the voice of the LORD our God, to walk in his laws, which he set before us by his servants the prophets.

11Yea, all Israel have transgressed thy law, even by departing, that they might not obey thy voice; therefore the curse is poured upon us, and the oath that *is* written in the law of Moses the servant of God, because we have sinned against him.

12And he hath confirmed his words, which he spake against us, and against our judges that judged us, by bringing upon us a great evil: for under the whole heaven hath not been done as hath been done upon Jerusalem.

13As *it is* written in the law of Moses, all this evil is come upon us: yet made we not our prayer before the LORD our God, that we might turn from our iniquities, and understand thy truth.

14Therefore hath the LORD watched upon the evil, and brought it upon us: for the LORD our God *is* righteous in all his works which he doeth: for we obeyed not his voice.

15And now, O Lord our God, that hast brought thy people forth out of the land of Egypt with a mighty hand, and hast gotten thee renown, as at this day; we have sinned, we have done wickedly.

16¶ O Lord, according to all thy righteousness, I beseech thee, let thine anger and thy fury be turned away from thy city Jerusalem, thy holy mountain: because for our sins, and for the iniquities of our fathers, Jerusalem and thy people *are become* a reproach to all *that are* about us.

17Now therefore, O our God, hear the prayer of thy servant, and his supplications, and cause thy face to shine upon thy sanctuary that is desolate, for the Lord's sake.

18O my God, incline thine ear, and hear; open thine eyes, and behold our desolations, and the city which is called by thy name: for we do not present our supplications before thee for our righteousnesses, but for thy great mercies.

19O Lord, hear; O Lord, forgive; O Lord, hearken and do; defer not, for thine own sake, O my God: for thy city and thy people are called by thy name.

20¶ And whiles I *was* speaking, and praying, and confessing my sin and the sin of my people Israel, and presenting my supplication before the LORD my God for the holy mountain of my God;

21Yea, whiles I *was* speaking in prayer, even the man Gabriel, whom I had seen in the vision at the beginning, being caused to fly swiftly, touched me about the time of the evening oblation.

22And he informed *me,* and talked with me, and said, O Daniel, I am now come forth to give thee skill and understanding.

23At the beginning of thy supplications the commandment came forth, and I am come to show *thee;* for thou *art* greatly beloved: therefore understand the matter, and consider the vision.

24Seventy weeks are determined upon thy people and upon thy holy city, to finish the transgression, and to make an end of sins, and to make reconciliation for iniquity, and to bring in everlasting righteousness, and to seal up the vision and prophecy, and to anoint the most Holy.

New International

7"Lord, you are righteous, but this day we are covered with shame—the men of Judah and people of Jerusalem and all Israel, both near and far, in all the countries where you have scattered us because of our unfaithfulness to you. 8O LORD, we and our kings, our princes and our fathers are covered with shame because we have sinned against you. 9The Lord our God is merciful and forgiving, even though we have rebelled against him; 10we have not obeyed the LORD our God or kept the laws he gave us through his servants the prophets. 11All Israel has transgressed your law and turned away, refusing to obey you.

"Therefore the curses and sworn judgments written in the Law of Moses, the servant of God, have been poured out on us, because we have sinned against you. 12You have fulfilled the words spoken against us and against our rulers by bringing upon us great disaster. Under the whole heaven nothing has ever been done like what has been done to Jerusalem. 13Just as it is written in the Law of Moses, all this disaster has come upon us, yet we have not sought the favor of the LORD our God by turning from our sins and giving attention to your truth. 14The LORD did not hesitate to bring the disaster upon us, for the LORD our God is righteous in everything he does; yet we have not obeyed him.

15"Now, O Lord our God, who brought your people out of Egypt with a mighty hand and who made for yourself a name that endures to this day, we have sinned, we have done wrong. 16O Lord, in keeping with all your righteous acts, turn away your anger and your wrath from Jerusalem, your city, your holy hill. Our sins and the iniquities of our fathers have made Jerusalem and your people an object of scorn to all those around us.

17"Now, our God, hear the prayers and petitions of your servant. For your sake, O Lord, look with favor on your desolate sanctuary. 18Give ear, O God, and hear; open your eyes and see the desolation of the city that bears your Name. We do not make requests of you because we are righteous, but because of your great mercy. 19O Lord, listen! O Lord, forgive! O Lord, hear and act! For your sake, O my God, do not delay, because your city and your people bear your Name."

The Seventy "Sevens"

20While I was speaking and praying, confessing my sin and the sin of my people Israel and making my request to the LORD my God for his holy hill— 21while I was still in prayer, Gabriel, the man I had seen in the earlier vision, came to me in swift flight about the time of the evening sacrifice. 22He instructed me and said to me, "Daniel, I have now come to give you insight and understanding. 23As soon as you began to pray, an answer was given, which I have come to tell you, for you are highly esteemed. Therefore, consider the message and understand the vision:

24"Seventy 'sevens'[a] are decreed for your people and your holy city to finish[b] transgression, to put an end to sin, to atone for wickedness, to bring in everlasting righteousness, to seal up vision and prophecy and to anoint the most holy.[c]

---

[a] 24 Or 'weeks'; also in verses 25 and 26   [b] 24 Or restrain   [c] 24 Or Most Holy Place; or most holy One

Living Bible

7"O Lord, you are righteous; but as for us, we are always shamefaced with sin, just as you see us now; yes, all of us—the men of Judah, the people of Jerusalem, and all Israel, scattered near and far wherever you have driven us because of our disloyalty to you. 8O Lord, we and our kings and princes and fathers are weighted down with shame because of all our sins.

9"But the Lord our God is merciful, and pardons even those who have rebelled against him.

10"O Lord our God, we have disobeyed you; we have flouted all the laws you gave us through your servants, the prophets. 11All Israel has disobeyed; we have turned away from you and haven't listened to your voice. And so the awesome curse of God has crushed us—the curse written in the law of Moses your servant. 12And you have done exactly as you warned us you would do, for never in all history has there been a disaster like what happened at Jerusalem to us and our rulers. 13Every curse against us written in the law of Moses has come true; all the evils he predicted—all have come. But even so we still refuse to satisfy the Lord our God by turning from our sins and doing right.

14"And so the Lord deliberately crushed us with the calamity he prepared; he is fair in everything he does, but we would not obey. 15O Lord our God, you brought lasting honor to your name by removing your people from Egypt in a great display of power. Lord, do it again! Though we have sinned so much and are full of wickedness, 16yet because of all your faithful mercies, Lord, please turn away your furious anger from Jerusalem, your own city, your holy mountain. For the heathen mock at you because your city lies in ruins for our sins.

17"O our God, hear your servant's prayer! Listen as I plead! Let your face shine again with peace and joy upon your desolate sanctuary—for your own glory, Lord.

18"O my God, bend down your ear and listen to my plea. Open your eyes and see our wretchedness, how your city lies in ruins—for everyone knows that it is yours. We don't ask because we merit help, but because you are so merciful despite our grievous sins.

19"O Lord, hear; O Lord, forgive. O Lord, listen to me and act! Don't delay—for your own sake, O my God, because your people and your city bear your name."

20Even while I was praying and confessing my sin and the sins of my people, and desperately pleading with the Lord my God for Jerusalem, his holy mountain, 21Gabriel, whom I had seen in the earlier vision, flew swiftly to me at the time of the evening sacrifice, 22and said to me, "Daniel, I am here to help you understand God's plans. 23The moment you began praying, a command was given. I am here to tell you what it was, for God loves you very much. Listen, and try to understand the meaning of the vision that you saw!

24"The Lord has commanded 490 years[d] of further punishment upon Jerusalem and your people. Then at last they will learn to stay away from sin, and their guilt will be cleansed; then the kingdom of everlasting righteousness will begin, and the Most Holy Place (in the Temple) will be rededicated, as the prophets have declared. 25Now listen! It will be forty-nine years plus 434

New Revised Standard

7 "Righteousness is on your side, O Lord, but open shame, as at this day, falls on us, the people of Judah, the inhabitants of Jerusalem, and all Israel, those who are near and those who are far away, in all the lands to which you have driven them, because of the treachery that they have committed against you. 8Open shame, O Lord, falls on us, our kings, our officials, and our ancestors, because we have sinned against you. 9To the Lord our God belong mercy and forgiveness, for we have rebelled against him, 10and have not obeyed the voice of the Lord our God by following his laws, which he set before us by his servants the prophets.

11 "All Israel has transgressed your law and turned aside, refusing to obey your voice. So the curse and the oath written in the law of Moses, the servant of God, have been poured out upon us, because we have sinned against you. 12He has confirmed his words, which he spoke against us and against our rulers, by bringing upon us a calamity so great that what has been done against Jerusalem has never before been done under the whole heaven. 13Just as it is written in the law of Moses, all this calamity has come upon us. We did not entreat the favor of the Lord our God, turning from our iniquities and reflecting on his[e] fidelity. 14So the Lord kept watch over this calamity until he brought it upon us. Indeed, the Lord our God is right in all that he has done; for we have disobeyed his voice.

15 "And now, O Lord our God, who brought your people out of the land of Egypt with a mighty hand and made your name renowned even to this day—we have sinned, we have done wickedly. 16O Lord, in view of all your righteous acts, let your anger and wrath, we pray, turn away from your city Jerusalem, your holy mountain; because of our sins and the iniquities of our ancestors, Jerusalem and your people have become a disgrace among all our neighbors. 17Now therefore, O our God, listen to the prayer of your servant and to his supplication, and for your own sake, Lord,[f] let your face shine upon your desolated sanctuary. 18Incline your ear, O my God, and hear. Open your eyes and look at our desolation and the city that bears your name. We do not present our supplication before you on the ground of our righteousness, but on the ground of your great mercies. 19O Lord, hear; O Lord, forgive; O Lord, listen and act and do not delay! For your own sake, O my God, because your city and your people bear your name!"

The Seventy Weeks

20 While I was speaking, and was praying and confessing my sin and the sin of my people Israel, and presenting my supplication before the Lord my God on behalf of the holy mountain of my God— 21while I was speaking in prayer, the man Gabriel, whom I had seen before in a vision, came to me in swift flight at the time of the evening sacrifice. 22He came[g] and said to me, "Daniel, I have now come out to give you wisdom and understanding. 23At the beginning of your supplications a word went out, and I have come to declare it, for you are greatly beloved. So consider the word and understand the vision:

24 "Seventy weeks are decreed for your people and your holy city: to finish the transgression, to put an end to sin, and to atone for iniquity, to bring in everlasting righteousness, to seal both vision and prophet, and to anoint a most holy place.[h] 25Know therefore and under-

---

[d] 9:24 490 years, literally, "seventy weeks" or "seventy sevens" (of years). These were not in uninterrupted sequence. See vss 25-27.

[e] Heb *your*   [f] Theodotion Vg Compare Syr: Heb *for the Lord's sake*   [g] Gk Syr: Heb *He made to understand*   [h] Or *thing* or *one*

King James

25Know therefore and understand, *that* from the going forth of the commandment to restore and to build Jerusalem unto the Messiah the Prince *shall be* seven weeks, and threescore and two weeks: the street shall be built again, and the wall, even in troublous times.

26And after threescore and two weeks shall Messiah be cut off, but not for himself: and the people of the prince that shall come shall destroy the city and the sanctuary; and the end thereof *shall be* with a flood, and unto the end of the war desolations are determined.

27And he shall confirm the covenant with many for one week: and in the midst of the week he shall cause the sacrifice and the oblation to cease, and for the overspreading of abominations he shall make *it* desolate, even until the consummation, and that determined shall be poured upon the desolate.

10 IN THE third year of Cyrus king of Persia a thing was revealed unto Daniel, whose name was called Belteshazzar; and the thing *was* true, but the time appointed *was* long: and he understood the thing, and had understanding of the vision.

2In those days I Daniel was mourning three full weeks.

3I ate no pleasant bread, neither came flesh nor wine in my mouth, neither did I anoint myself at all, till three whole weeks were fulfilled.

4And in the four and twentieth day of the first month, as I was by the side of the great river, which *is* Hiddekel;

5Then I lifted up mine eyes, and looked, and behold a certain man clothed in linen, whose loins *were* girded with fine gold of Uphaz:

6His body also *was* like the beryl, and his face as the appearance of lightning, and his eyes as lamps of fire, and his arms and his feet like in colour to polished brass, and the voice of his words like the voice of a multitude.

7And I Daniel alone saw the vision: for the men that were with me saw not the vision; but a great quaking fell upon them, so that they fled to hide themselves.

8Therefore I was left alone, and saw this great vision, and there remained no strength in me: for my comeliness was turned in me into corruption, and I retained no strength.

9Yet heard I the voice of his words: and when I heard the voice of his words, then was I in a deep sleep on my face, and my face toward the ground.

10¶ And, behold, an hand touched me, which set me upon my knees and *upon* the palms of my hands.

11And he said unto me, O Daniel, a man greatly beloved, understand the words that I speak unto thee, and stand upright: for unto thee am I now sent. And when he had spoken this word unto me, I stood trembling.

12Then said he unto me, Fear not, Daniel: for from the first day that thou didst set thine heart to understand, and to chasten thyself before thy God, thy words were heard, and I am come for thy words.

13But the prince of the kingdom of Persia withstood me one and twenty days: but, lo, Michael, one of the chief princes, came to help me; and I remained there with the kings of Persia.

14Now I am come to make thee understand what shall befall thy people in the latter days: for yet the vision *is* for *many* days.

15And when he had spoken such words unto me, I set my face toward the ground, and I became dumb.

16And, behold, *one* like the similitude of the sons of men touched my lips: then I opened my mouth, and spake, and said unto him that stood before me, O my lord, by the vision my sorrows are turned upon me, and I have retained no strength.

New International

25"Know and understand this: From the issuing of the decree[a] to restore and rebuild Jerusalem until the Anointed One,[b] the ruler, comes, there will be seven 'sevens,' and sixty-two 'sevens.' It will be rebuilt with streets and a trench, but in times of trouble. 26After the sixty-two 'sevens,' the Anointed One will be cut off and will have nothing.[c] The people of the ruler who will come will destroy the city and the sanctuary. The end will come like a flood: War will continue until the end, and desolations have been decreed. 27He will confirm a covenant with many for one 'seven.'[d] In the middle of the 'seven'[d] he will put an end to sacrifice and offering. And on a wing of the temple, he will set up an abomination that causes desolation, until the end that is decreed is poured out on him.[e]"[f]

Daniel's Vision of a Man

10 IN THE third year of Cyrus king of Persia, a revelation was given to Daniel (who was called Belteshazzar). Its message was true and it concerned a great war.[g] The understanding of the message came to him in a vision.

2At that time I, Daniel, mourned for three weeks. 3I ate no choice food; no meat or wine touched my lips; and I used no lotions at all until the three weeks were over.

4On the twenty-fourth day of the first month, as I was standing on the bank of the great river, the Tigris, 5I looked up and there before me was a man dressed in linen, with a belt of the finest gold around his waist. 6His body was like chrysolite, his face like lightning, his eyes like flaming torches, his arms and legs like the gleam of burnished bronze, and his voice like the sound of a multitude.

7I, Daniel, was the only one who saw the vision; the men with me did not see it, but such terror overwhelmed them that they fled and hid themselves. 8So I was left alone, gazing at this great vision; I had no strength left, my face turned deathly pale and I was helpless. 9Then I heard him speaking, and as I listened to him, I fell into a deep sleep, my face to the ground.

10A hand touched me and set me trembling on my hands and knees. 11He said, "Daniel, you who are highly esteemed, consider carefully the words I am about to speak to you, and stand up, for I have now been sent to you." And when he said this to me, I stood up trembling.

12Then he continued, "Do not be afraid, Daniel. Since the first day that you set your mind to gain understanding and to humble yourself before your God, your words were heard, and I have come in response to them. 13But the prince of the Persian kingdom resisted me twenty-one days. Then Michael, one of the chief princes, came to help me, because I was detained there with the king of Persia. 14Now I have come to explain to you what will happen to your people in the future, for the vision concerns a time yet to come."

15While he was saying this to me, I bowed with my face toward the ground and was speechless. 16Then one who looked like a man[h] touched my lips, and I opened my mouth and began to speak. I said to the one standing before me, "I am overcome with anguish because of the vision, my lord, and I am helpless. 17How can I, your

a 25 Or *word*   b 25 Or *an anointed one*; also in verse 26   c 26 Or *off and will have no one*; or *off, but not for himself*   d 27 Or '*week*'   e 27 Or *it*   f 27 Or *And one who causes desolation will come upon the pinnacle of the abominable temple,, until the end that is decreed is poured out on the desolated city,*   g 1 Or *true and burdensome*   h 16 Most manuscripts of the Masoretic Text; one manuscript of the Masoretic Text, Dead Sea Scrolls and Septuagint *Then something that looked like a man's hand*

Living Bible

years[i] from the time the command is given to rebuild Jerusalem, until the Anointed One comes! Jerusalem's streets and walls will be rebuilt despite the perilous times.

26"After this period of 434 years, the Anointed One will be killed, his kingdom still unrealized . . . and a king will arise whose armies will destroy the city and the Temple. They will be overwhelmed as with a flood, and war and its miseries are decreed from that time to the very end. 27This king will make a seven-year treaty with the people, but after half that time, he will break his pledge and stop the Jews from all their sacrifices and their offerings; then, as a climax to all his terrible deeds, the Enemy shall utterly defile the sanctuary of God. But in God's time and plan, his judgment will be poured out upon this Evil One."

10 IN THE third year of the reign of Cyrus, king of Persia, Daniel (also called Belteshazzar) had another vision. It concerned events certain to happen in the future: times of great tribulation—wars and sorrows, and this time he understood what the vision meant.

2When this vision came to me (Daniel said later) I had been in mourning for three full weeks. 3All that time I tasted neither wine nor meat, and of course I went without desserts. I neither washed nor shaved nor combed my hair.

4Then one day early in April, as I was standing beside the great Tigris River, 5, 6I looked up and suddenly there before me stood a person robed in linen garments, with a belt of purest gold around his waist, and glowing, lustrous skin! From his face came blinding flashes like lightning, and his eyes were pools of fire; his arms and feet shone like polished brass, and his voice was like the roaring of a vast multitude of people.

7I, Daniel, alone saw this great vision; the men with me saw nothing, but they were suddenly filled with unreasoning terror and ran to hide, 8and I was left alone. When I saw this frightening vision my strength left me, and I grew pale and weak with fright.

9Then he spoke to me, and I fell to the ground face downward in a deep faint. 10But a hand touched me and lifted me, still trembling, to my hands and knees. 11And I heard his voice—"O Daniel, greatly beloved of God," he said, "stand up and listen carefully to what I have to say to you, for God has sent me to you." So I stood up, still trembling with fear.

12Then he said, "Don't be frightened, Daniel, for your request has been heard in heaven and was answered the very first day you began to fast before the Lord and pray for understanding; that very day I was sent here to meet you. 13But for twenty-one days the mighty Evil Spirit[j] who overrules the kingdom of Persia blocked my way. Then Michael, one of the top officers of the heavenly army, came to help me, so that I was able to break through these spirit rulers of Persia. 14Now I am here to tell you what will happen to your people, the Jews, at the end times—for the fulfillment of this prophecy is many years away."

15All this time I was looking down, unable to speak a word. 16Then someone—he looked like a man—touched my lips and I could talk again, and I said to the messenger from heaven, "Sir, I am terrified by your appearance and have no strength. 17How can such a

New Revised Standard

stand: from the time that the word went out to restore and rebuild Jerusalem until the time of an anointed prince, there shall be seven weeks; and for sixty-two weeks it shall be built again with streets and moat, but in a troubled time. 26After the sixty-two weeks, an anointed one shall be cut off and shall have nothing, and the troops of the prince who is to come shall destroy the city and the sanctuary. Its[k] end shall come with a flood, and to the end there shall be war. Desolations are decreed. 27He shall make a strong covenant with many for one week, and for half of the week he shall make sacrifice and offering cease; and in their place[l] shall be an abomination that desolates, until the decreed end is poured out upon the desolator."

Conflict of Nations and Heavenly Powers

10 IN THE third year of King Cyrus of Persia a word was revealed to Daniel, who was named Belteshazzar. The word was true, and it concerned a great conflict. He understood the word, having received understanding in the vision.

2 At that time I, Daniel, had been mourning for three weeks. 3I had eaten no rich food, no meat or wine had entered my mouth, and I had not anointed myself at all, for the full three weeks. 4On the twenty-fourth day of the first month, as I was standing on the bank of the great river (that is, the Tigris), 5I looked up and saw a man clothed in linen, with a belt of gold from Uphaz around his waist. 6His body was like beryl, his face like lightning, his eyes like flaming torches, his arms and legs like the gleam of burnished bronze, and the sound of his words like the roar of a multitude. 7I, Daniel, alone saw the vision; the people who were with me did not see the vision, though a great trembling fell upon them, and they fled and hid themselves. 8So I was left alone to see this great vision. My strength left me, and my complexion grew deathly pale, and I retained no strength. 9Then I heard the sound of his words; and when I heard the sound of his words, I fell into a trance, face to the ground.

10 But then a hand touched me and roused me to my hands and knees. 11He said to me, "Daniel, greatly beloved, pay attention to the words that I am going to speak to you. Stand on your feet, for I have now been sent to you." So while he was speaking this word to me, I stood up trembling. 12He said to me, "Do not fear, Daniel, for from the first day that you set your mind to gain understanding and to humble yourself before your God, your words have been heard, and I have come because of your words. 13But the prince of the kingdom of Persia opposed me twenty-one days. So Michael, one of the chief princes, came to help me, and I left him there with the prince of the kingdom of Persia,[m] 14and have come to help you understand what is to happen to your people at the end of days. For there is a further vision for those days."

15 While he was speaking these words to me, I turned my face toward the ground and was speechless. 16Then one in human form touched my lips, and I opened my mouth to speak, and said to the one who stood before me, "My lord, because of the vision such pains have come upon me that I retain no strength.

i 9:25 *It will be forty-nine years plus 434 years.* This totals 483 years, instead of the 490 years mentioned in vs 24, leaving seven years unaccounted for at the time of Messiah's death. For their future fulfillment, see vs 27 and the Revelation. Or, consider the destruction of Jerusalem in A.D. 70 by Titus and the subsequent slaughter of 1,000,000 Jews during the following three and a half years as at least a partial fulfillment of this prophecy.   j 10:13 *the . . . Evil Spirit,* literally, "the prince of Persia."

k Or *His*   l Cn: Meaning of Heb uncertain   m Gk Theodotion: Heb *I was left there with the kings of Persia*

King James

¹⁷For how can the servant of this my lord talk with this my lord? for as for me, straightway there remained no strength in me, neither is there breath left in me.

¹⁸Then there came again and touched me *one* like the appearance of a man, and he strengthened me,

¹⁹And said, O man greatly beloved, fear not: peace *be* unto thee, be strong, yea, be strong. And when he had spoken unto me, I was strengthened, and said, Let my lord speak; for thou hast strengthened me.

²⁰Then said he, Knowest thou wherefore I come unto thee? and now will I return to fight with the prince of Persia: and when I am gone forth, lo, the prince of Grecia shall come.

²¹But I will show thee that which is noted in the scripture of truth: and *there is* none that holdeth with me in these things, but Michael your prince.

11 ALSO I in the first year of Darius the Mede, *even* I, stood to confirm and to strengthen him.

²And now will I show thee the truth. Behold, there shall stand up yet three kings in Persia; and the fourth shall be far richer than *they* all: and by his strength through his riches he shall stir up all against the realm of Grecia.

³And a mighty king shall stand up, that shall rule with great dominion, and do according to his will.

⁴And when he shall stand up, his kingdom shall be broken, and shall be divided toward the four winds of heaven; and not to his posterity, nor according to his dominion which he ruled: for his kingdom shall be plucked up, even for others beside those.

⁵¶ And the king of the south shall be strong, and *one* of his princes; and he shall be strong above him, and have dominion; his dominion *shall be* a great dominion.

⁶And in the end of years they shall join themselves together; for the king's daughter of the south shall come to the king of the north to make an agreement: but she shall not retain the power of the arm; neither shall he stand, nor his arm: but she shall be given up, and they that brought her, and he that begat her, and he that strengthened her in *these* times.

⁷But out of a branch of her roots shall *one* stand up in his estate, which shall come with an army, and shall enter into the fortress of the king of the north, and shall deal against them, and shall prevail:

⁸And shall also carry captives into Egypt their gods, with their princes, *and* with their precious vessels of silver and of gold; and he shall continue *more* years than the king of the north.

⁹So the king of the south shall come into *his* kingdom, and shall return into his own land.

¹⁰But his sons shall be stirred up, and shall assemble a multitude of great forces: and *one* shall certainly come, and overflow, and pass through: then shall he return, and be stirred up, *even* to his fortress.

¹¹And the king of the south shall be moved with choler, and shall come forth and fight with him, *even* with the king of the north: and he shall set forth a great multitude; but the multitude shall be given into his hand.

¹²*And* when he hath taken away the multitude, his heart shall be lifted up; and he shall cast down *many* ten thousands: but he shall not be strengthened *by it*.

¹³For the king of the north shall return, and shall set forth a multitude greater than the former, and shall certainly come after certain years with a great army and with much riches.

New International

servant, talk with you, my lord? My strength is gone and I can hardly breathe."

¹⁸Again the one who looked like a man touched me and gave me strength. ¹⁹"Do not be afraid, O man highly esteemed," he said. "Peace! Be strong now; be strong."

When he spoke to me, I was strengthened and said, "Speak, my lord, since you have given me strength."

²⁰So he said, "Do you know why I have come to you? Soon I will return to fight against the prince of Persia, and when I go, the prince of Greece will come; ²¹but first I will tell you what is written in the Book of Truth. (No one supports me against them except Michael, your prince.

11 AND IN the first year of Darius the Mede, I took my stand to support and protect him.)

The Kings of the South and the North

²"Now then, I tell you the truth: Three more kings will appear in Persia, and then a fourth, who will be far richer than all the others. When he has gained power by his wealth, he will stir up everyone against the kingdom of Greece. ³Then a mighty king will appear, who will rule with great power and do as he pleases. ⁴After he has appeared, his empire will be broken up and parceled out toward the four winds of heaven. It will not go to his descendants, nor will it have the power he exercised, because his empire will be uprooted and given to others.

⁵"The king of the South will become strong, but one of his commanders will become even stronger than he and will rule his own kingdom with great power. ⁶After some years, they will become allies. The daughter of the king of the South will go to the king of the North to make an alliance, but she will not retain her power, and he and his power*ᵃ* will not last. In those days she will be handed over, together with her royal escort and her father*ᵇ* and the one who supported her.

⁷"One from her family line will arise to take her place. He will attack the forces of the king of the North and enter his fortress; he will fight against them and be victorious. ⁸He will also seize their gods, their metal images and their valuable articles of silver and gold and carry them off to Egypt. For some years he will leave the king of the North alone. ⁹Then the king of the North will invade the realm of the king of the South but will retreat to his own country. ¹⁰His sons will prepare for war and assemble a great army, which will sweep on like an irresistible flood and carry the battle as far as his fortress.

¹¹"Then the king of the South will march out in a rage and fight against the king of the North, who will raise a large army, but it will be defeated. ¹²When the army is carried off, the king of the South will be filled with pride and will slaughter many thousands, yet he will not remain triumphant. ¹³For the king of the North will muster another army, larger than the first; and after several years, he will advance with a huge army fully equipped.

ᵃ 6 Or *offspring*   ᵇ 6 Or *child* (see Vulgate and Syriac)

Living Bible

person as I even talk to you? For my strength is gone and I can hardly breathe."

18Then the one who seemed to be a man touched me again, and I felt my strength returning. 19"God loves you very much," he said; "don't be afraid! Calm yourself; be strong—yes, strong!"

Suddenly, as he spoke these words, I felt stronger and said to him, "Now you can go ahead and speak, sir, for you have strengthened me."

20, 21He replied, "Do you know why I have come? I am here to tell you what is written in the 'Book of the Future.' Then, when I leave, I will go again to fight my way back, past the prince of Persia; and after him, the prince of Greece. Only Michael, the angel who guards your people Israel,c will be there to help me.

11 "I WAS the one sent to strengthen and help Darius the Mede in the first year of his reign. 2But now I will show you what the future holds. Three more Persian kings will reign, to be succeeded by a fourth,d far richer than the others. Using his wealth for political advantage, he will plan total war against Greece.

3"Then a mighty king will rise in Greece, a king who will rule a vast kingdom and accomplish everything he sets out to do.e 4But at the zenith of his power, his kingdom will break apart and be divided into four weaker nations, not even ruled by his sons. For his empire will be torn apart and given to others. 5One of them, the king of Egypt,f will increase in power, but this king's own officials will rebel against him and take away his kingdom and make it still more powerful.

6"Several years later an alliance will be formed between the king of Syriag and the king of Egypt. The daughter of the king of Egypt will be given in marriage to the king of Syria as a gesture of peace,h but she will lose her influence over him and not only will her hopes be blighted, but those of her father, the king of Egypt, and of her ambassador and child. 7But when her brotheri takes over as king of Egypt, he will raise an army against the king of Syria, and march against him and defeat him. 8When he returns again to Egypt he will carry back their idols with him, along with priceless gold and silver dishes and for many years afterward he will leave the Syrian king alone.

9"Meanwhile the king of Syria will invade Egypt briefly, but will soon return again to his own land. 10, 11However, the sons of this Syrian king will assemble a mighty army that will overflow across Israel into Egypt, to a fortress there. Then the king of Egypt,k in great anger, will rally against the vast forces of Syria and defeat them. 12Filled with pride after this great victory, he will have many thousands of his enemies killed, but his success will be short-lived.

13"A few years later the Syrian kingl will return with a fully-equipped army far greater than the one he lost,

New Revised Standard

17How can my lord's servant talk with my lord? For I am shaking,m no strength remains in me, and no breath is left in me."

18 Again one in human form touched me and strengthened me. 19He said, "Do not fear, greatly beloved, you are safe. Be strong and courageous!" When he spoke to me, I was strengthened and said, "Let my lord speak, for you have strengthened me." 20Then he said, "Do you know why I have come to you? Now I must return to fight against the prince of Persia, and when I am through with him, the prince of Greece will come. 21But I am to tell you what is inscribed in the book of truth. There is no one with me who contends against these princes except Michael, your prince.

11 AS FOR me, in the first year of Darius the Mede, I stood up to support and strengthen him.

2 "Now I will announce the truth to you. Three more kings shall arise in Persia. The fourth shall be far richer than all of them, and when he has become strong through his riches, he shall stir up all against the kingdom of Greece. 3Then a warrior king shall arise, who shall rule with great dominion and take action as he pleases. 4And while still rising in power, his kingdom shall be broken and divided toward the four winds of heaven, but not to his posterity, nor according to the dominion with which he ruled; for his kingdom shall be uprooted and go to others besides these.

5 "Then the king of the south shall grow strong, but one of his officers shall grow stronger than he and shall rule a realm greater than his own realm. 6After some years they shall make an alliance, and the daughter of the king of the south shall come to the king of the north to ratify the agreement. But she shall not retain her power, and his offspring shall not endure. She shall be given up, she and her attendants and her child and the one who supported her.

"In those times 7a branch from her roots shall rise up in his place. He shall come against the army and enter the fortress of the king of the north, and he shall take action against them and prevail. 8Even their gods, with their idols and with their precious vessels of silver and gold, he shall carry off to Egypt as spoils of war. For some years he shall refrain from attacking the king of the north; 9then the latter shall invade the realm of the king of the south, but will return to his own land.

10 "His sons shall wage war and assemble a multitude of great forces, which shall advance like a flood and pass through, and again shall carry the war as far as his fortress. 11Moved with rage, the king of the south shall go out and do battle against the king of the north, who shall muster a great multitude, which shall, however, be defeated by his enemy. 12When the multitude has been carried off, his heart shall be exalted, and he shall overthrow tens of thousands, but he shall not prevail. 13For the king of the north shall again raise a multitude, larger than the former, and after some yearsn he shall advance with a great army and abundant supplies.

c 10:20, 21 your people Israel, literally, "your prince."   d 11:2 by a fourth. Perhaps Xerxes (486-465 B.C.) who launched an all-out effort against Greece.   e 11:3 and accomplish everything he sets out to do. Doubtless Alexander the Great.   f 11:5 the king of Egypt, literally, "the southern king"—Ptolemy II.   g 11:6 the king of Syria, literally, "the king of the north," and so also throughout this passage. These prophecies seem to have been fulfilled many years later in the Seleucid wars between Egypt and Syria.   h 11:6 as a gesture of peace. In 252 B.C. Ptolemy II of Egypt gave his daughter Berenice in marriage to Antiochus II of Syria to conclude a treaty of peace between their two lands.   i 11:7 when her brother, literally, "from a branch." Berenice, murdered in Antioch by Antiochus II's former wife Laodice, was the sister of Ptolemy III, who now ascended the Egyptian throne and declared war against the Seleucids to avenge his sister's murder.   j 11:9 the king of Syria, Seleucus II.   k 11:10, 11 the king of Egypt, Ptolemy IV.   l 11:13 the Syrian king. Possibly Antiochus III the Great, who was later defeated by the Romans at Magnesia. Compare vs. 18.

m Gk: Heb from now   n Heb and at the end of the times years

King James

14And in those times there shall many stand up against the king of the south: also the robbers of thy people shall exalt themselves to establish the vision; but they shall fall.

15So the king of the north shall come, and cast up a mount, and take the most fenced cities: and the arms of the south shall not withstand, neither his chosen people, neither *shall there be any* strength to withstand.

16But he that cometh against him shall do according to his own will, and none shall stand before him: and he shall stand in the glorious land, which by his hand shall be consumed.

17He shall also set his face to enter with the strength of his whole kingdom, and upright ones with him; thus shall he do: and he shall give him the daughter of women, corrupting her: but she shall not stand *on his side,* neither be for him.

18After this shall he turn his face unto the isles, and shall take many: but a prince for his own behalf shall cause the reproach offered by him to cease; without his own reproach he shall cause *it* to turn upon him.

19Then he shall turn his face toward the fort of his own land: but he shall stumble and fall, and not be found.

20Then shall stand up in his estate a raiser of taxes *in* the glory of the kingdom: but within few days he shall be destroyed, neither in anger, nor in battle.

21And in his estate shall stand up a vile person, to whom they shall not give the honour of the kingdom: but he shall come in peaceably, and obtain the kingdom by flatteries.

22And with the arms of a flood shall they be overflown from before him, and shall be broken; yea, also the prince of the covenant.

23And after the league *made* with him he shall work deceitfully: for he shall come up, and shall become strong with a small people.

24He shall enter peaceably even upon the fattest places of the province; and he shall do *that* which his fathers have not done, nor his fathers' fathers; he shall scatter among them the prey, and spoil, and riches: *yea,* and he shall forecast his devices against the strong holds, even for a time.

25And he shall stir up his power and his courage against the king of the south with a great army; and the king of the south shall be stirred up to battle with a very great and mighty army; but he shall not stand: for they shall forecast devices against him.

26Yea, they that feed of the portion of his meat shall destroy him, and his army shall overflow: and many shall fall down slain.

27And both these kings' hearts *shall be* to do mischief, and they shall speak lies at one table; but it shall not prosper: for yet the end *shall be* at the time appointed.

28Then shall he return into his land with great riches; and his heart *shall be* against the holy covenant; and he shall do *exploits,* and return to his own land.

29At the time appointed he shall return, and come toward the south; but it shall not be as the former, or as the latter.

30¶ For the ships of Chittim shall come against him: therefore he shall be grieved, and return, and have indignation against the holy covenant: so shall he do; he shall even return, and have intelligence with them that forsake the holy covenant.

31And arms shall stand on his part, and they shall pollute the sanctuary of strength, and shall take away the daily *sacrifice,* and they shall place the abomination that maketh desolate.

32And such as do wickedly against the covenant shall he corrupt by flatteries: but the people that do know their God shall be strong, and do *exploits.*

New International

14"In those times many will rise against the king of the South. The violent men among your own people will rebel in fulfillment of the vision, but without success. 15Then the king of the North will come and build up siege ramps and will capture a fortified city. The forces of the South will be powerless to resist; even their best troops will not have the strength to stand. 16The invader will do as he pleases; no one will be able to stand against him. He will establish himself in the Beautiful Land and will have the power to destroy it. 17He will determine to come with the might of his entire kingdom and will make an alliance with the king of the South. And he will give him a daughter in marriage in order to overthrow the kingdom, but his plansa will not succeed or help him. 18Then he will turn his attention to the coastlands and will take many of them, but a commander will put an end to his insolence and will turn his insolence back upon him. 19After this, he will turn back toward the fortresses of his own country but will stumble and fall, to be seen no more.

20"His successor will send out a tax collector to maintain the royal splendor. In a few years, however, he will be destroyed, yet not in anger or in battle.

21"He will be succeeded by a contemptible person who has not been given the honor of royalty. He will invade the kingdom when its people feel secure, and he will seize it through intrigue. 22Then an overwhelming army will be swept away before him; both it and a prince of the covenant will be destroyed. 23After coming to an agreement with him, he will act deceitfully, and with only a few people he will rise to power. 24When the richest provinces feel secure, he will invade them and will achieve what neither his fathers nor his forefathers did. He will distribute plunder, loot and wealth among his followers. He will plot the overthrow of fortresses—but only for a time.

25"With a large army he will stir up his strength and courage against the king of the South. The king of the South will wage war with a large and very powerful army, but he will not be able to stand because of the plots devised against him. 26Those who eat from the king's provisions will try to destroy him; his army will be swept away, and many will fall in battle. 27The two kings, with their hearts bent on evil, will sit at the same table and lie to each other, but to no avail, because an end will still come at the appointed time. 28The king of the North will return to his own country with great wealth, but his heart will be set against the holy covenant. He will take action against it and then return to his own country.

29"At the appointed time he will invade the South again, but this time the outcome will be different from what it was before. 30Ships of the western coastlandsb will oppose him, and he will lose heart. Then he will turn back and vent his fury against the holy covenant. He will return and show favor to those who forsake the holy covenant.

31"His armed forces will rise up to desecrate the temple fortress and will abolish the daily sacrifice. Then they will set up the abomination that causes desolation. 32With flattery he will corrupt those who have violated the covenant, but the people who know their God will firmly resist him.

---

a 17 Or *but she*　　b 30 Hebrew *of Kittim*

Living Bible

14and other nations will join him in a crusade against Egypt. Insurgents among your own people, the Jews, will join them, thus fulfilling prophecy,c but they will not succeed. 15Then the Syrian king and his allies will come and lay siege to a fortified city of Egypt and capture it, and the proud armies of Egypt will go down to defeat.

16"The Syrian king will march onward unopposed; none will be able to stop him. And he will also enter 'The Glorious Land' of Israel, and pillage it. 17This will be his plot for conquering all Egypt: he too will form an alliance with the Egyptian king, giving him a daughter in marriage, so that she can work for him from within. But the plan will fail.

18"After this he will turn his attention to the coastal cities and conquer many. But a general will stop him and cause him to retreat in shame. 19He will turn homeward again, but will have trouble on the way, and disappear.

20"His successord will be remembered as the king who sent a tax collector into Israel, but after a very brief reign, he will die mysteriously, neither in battle nor in riot.

21"Next to come to power will be an evil man not directly in line for royal succession.e But during a crisis he will take over the kingdom by flattery and intrigue. 22Then all opposition will be swept away before him, including a leader of the priests.f 23His promises will be worthless. From the first his method will be deceit; with a mere handful of followers, he will become strong. 24He will enter the richest areas of the land without warning and do something never done before: he will take the property and wealth of the rich and scatter it out among the people. With great success he will besiege and capture powerful strongholds throughout his dominions, but this will last for only a short while. 25Then he will stir up his courage and raise a great army against Egypt; and Egypt, too, will raise a mighty army, but to no avail, for plots against him will succeed.

26"Those of his own household will bring his downfall; his army will desert, and many be killed.

27"Both these kingsg will be plotting against each other at the conference table, attempting to deceive each other. But it will make no difference, for neither can succeed until God's appointed time has come.

28"The Syrian king will then return home with great riches, first marching through Israel and destroying it. 29Then, at the predestined time, he will once again turn his armies southward, as he had threatened, but now it will be a very different story from those first two occasions. 30, 31For Roman warshipsh will scare him off, and he will withdraw and return home. Angered by having to retreat, the Syrian king will again pillage Jerusalem and pollute the sanctuary,i putting a stop to the daily sacrifices, and worshiping idols inside the Temple.j He will leave godless Jews in power when he leaves—men who have abandoned their fathers' faith. 32He will flatter those who hate the things of God,k and win them over to his side. But the people who know their Godl shall be strong and do great things.

---

c 11:14 thus fulfilling prophecy, literally, "in order to fulfill the vision." d 11:20 His successor. Seleucus IV, successor to Antiochus III, sent Heliodorus to rob and desecrate the Temple in Jerusalem. e 11:21 Next to come to power will be an evil man not directly in line for royal succession. This may refer to Antiochus IV Epiphanes who, when his brother Seleucus was assassinated, ingratiated himself with the Romans and took over. f 11:22 including a leader of the priests. Probably Jason, treacherously removed by the Hellenist Menelaus. g 11:27 Both these kings. Probably Antiochus IV and Ptolemy IV. h 11:30, 31 For Roman warships, or, "from Cyprus." i 11:30, 31 pollute the sanctuary. By offering swine on the altar. This event was fulfilled in 168-167 B.C. j 11:30, 31 worshiping idols inside the Temple, literally, "they shall set up the abomination that astonished." k 11:32 He will flatter those who hate the things of God. Menelaus, the High Priest, who conspired with Antiochus against the Jews who were loyal to God's laws. l 11:32 But the people who know their God. Perhaps the valiant Maccabees and their sympathizers. But a further fulfillment may lie in the future.

New Revised Standard

14 "In those times many shall rise against the king of the south. The lawless among your own people shall lift themselves up in order to fulfill the vision, but they shall fail. 15Then the king of the north shall come and throw up siegeworks, and take a well-fortified city. And the forces of the south shall not stand, not even his picked troops, for there shall be no strength to resist. 16But he who comes against him shall take the actions he pleases, and no one shall withstand him. He shall take a position in the beautiful land, and all of it shall be in his power. 17He shall set his mind to come with the strength of his whole kingdom, and he shall bring terms of peacem and perform them. In order to destroy the kingdom,n he shall give him a woman in marriage; but it shall not succeed or be to his advantage. 18Afterward he shall turn to the coastlands, and shall capture many. But a commander shall put an end to his insolence; indeed,o he shall turn his insolence back upon him. 19Then he shall turn back toward the fortresses of his own land, but he shall stumble and fall, and shall not be found.

20 "Then shall arise in his place one who shall send an official for the glory of the kingdom; but within a few days he shall be broken, though not in anger or in battle. 21In his place shall arise a contemptible person on whom royal majesty had not been conferred; he shall come in without warning and obtain the kingdom through intrigue. 22Armies shall be utterly swept away and broken before him, and the prince of the covenant as well. 23And after an alliance is made with him, he shall act deceitfully and become strong with a small party. 24Without warning he shall come into the richest partsp of the province and do what none of his predecessors had ever done, lavishing plunder, spoil, and wealth on them. He shall devise plans against strongholds, but only for a time. 25He shall stir up his power and determination against the king of the south with a great army, and the king of the south shall wage war with a much greater and stronger army. But he shall not succeed, for plots shall be devised against him 26by those who eat of the royal rations. They shall break him, his army shall be swept away, and many shall fall slain. 27The two kings, their minds bent on evil, shall sit at one table and exchange lies. But it shall not succeed, for there remains an end at the time appointed. 28He shall return to his land with great wealth, but his heart shall be set against the holy covenant. He shall work his will, and return to his own land.

29 "At the time appointed he shall return and come into the south, but this time it shall not be as it was before. 30For ships of Kittim shall come against him, and he shall lose heart and withdraw. He shall be enraged and take action against the holy covenant. He shall turn back and pay heed to those who forsake the holy covenant. 31Forces sent by him shall occupy and profane the temple and fortress. They shall abolish the regular burnt offering and set up the abomination that makes desolate. 32He shall seduce with intrigue those who violate the covenant; but the people who are loyal to their God shall stand firm and take action. 33The wise among

---

m Gk: Heb kingdom, and upright ones with him   n Heb it   o Meaning of Heb uncertain   p Or among the richest men

King James

33And they that understand among the people shall instruct many: yet they shall fall by the sword, and by flame, by captivity, and by spoil, *many* days.

34Now when they shall fall, they shall be helped with a little help: but many shall cleave to them with flatteries.

35And *some* of them of understanding shall fall, to try them, and to purge, and to make *them* white, *even* to the time of the end: because *it is* yet for a time appointed.

36And the king shall do according to his will; and he shall exalt himself, and magnify himself above every god, and shall speak marvellous things against the God of gods, and shall prosper till the indignation be accomplished: for that that is determined shall be done.

37Neither shall he regard the God of his fathers, nor the desire of women, nor regard any god: for he shall magnify himself above all.

38But in his estate shall he honour the God of forces: and a god whom his fathers knew not shall he honour with gold, and silver, and with precious stones, and pleasant things.

39Thus shall he do in the most strong holds with a strange god, whom he shall acknowledge *and* increase with glory: and he shall cause them to rule over many, and shall divide the land for gain.

40And at the time of the end shall the king of the south push at him: and the king of the north shall come against him like a whirlwind, with chariots, and with horsemen, and with many ships; and he shall enter into the countries, and shall overflow and pass over.

41He shall enter also into the glorious land, and many *countries* shall be overthrown: but these shall escape out of his hand, *even* Edom, and Moab, and the chief of the children of Ammon.

42He shall stretch forth his hand also upon the countries: and the land of Egypt shall not escape.

43But he shall have power over the treasures of gold and of silver, and over all the precious things of Egypt: and the Libyans and the Ethiopians *shall be* at his steps.

44But tidings out of the east and out of the north shall trouble him: therefore he shall go forth with great fury to destroy, and utterly to make away many.

45And he shall plant the tabernacles of his palace between the seas in the glorious holy mountain; yet he shall come to his end, and none shall help him.

12 AND AT that time shall Michael stand up, the great prince which standeth for the children of thy people: and there shall be a time of trouble, such as never was since there was a nation *even* to that same time: and at that time thy people shall be delivered, every one that shall be found written in the book.

2And many of them that sleep in the dust of the earth shall awake, some to everlasting life, and some to shame *and* everlasting contempt.

3And they that be wise shall shine as the brightness of the firmament; and they that turn many to righteousness as the stars for ever and ever.

4But thou, O Daniel, shut up the words, and seal the book, *even* to the time of the end: many shall run to and fro, and knowledge shall be increased.

New International

33"Those who are wise will instruct many, though for a time they will fall by the sword or be burned or captured or plundered. 34When they fall, they will receive a little help, and many who are not sincere will join them. 35Some of the wise will stumble, so that they may be refined, purified and made spotless until the time of the end, for it will still come at the appointed time.

The King Who Exalts Himself

36"The king will do as he pleases. He will exalt and magnify himself above every god and will say unheard-of things against the God of gods. He will be successful until the time of wrath is completed, for what has been determined must take place. 37He will show no regard for the gods of his fathers or for the one desired by women, nor will he regard any god, but will exalt himself above them all. 38Instead of them, he will honor a god of fortresses; a god unknown to his fathers he will honor with gold and silver, with precious stones and costly gifts. 39He will attack the mightiest fortresses with the help of a foreign god and will greatly honor those who acknowledge him. He will make them rulers over many people and will distribute the land at a price.[a]

40"At the time of the end the king of the South will engage him in battle, and the king of the North will storm out against him with chariots and cavalry and a great fleet of ships. He will invade many countries and sweep through them like a flood. 41He will also invade the Beautiful Land. Many countries will fall, but Edom, Moab and the leaders of Ammon will be delivered from his hand. 42He will extend his power over many countries; Egypt will not escape. 43He will gain control of the treasures of gold and silver and all the riches of Egypt, with the Libyans and Nubians in submission. 44But reports from the east and the north will alarm him, and he will set out in a great rage to destroy and annihilate many. 45He will pitch his royal tents between the seas at[b] the beautiful holy mountain. Yet he will come to his end, and no one will help him.

The End Times

12 "AT THAT time Michael, the great prince who protects your people, will arise. There will be a time of distress such as has not happened from the beginning of nations until then. But at that time your people—everyone whose name is found written in the book—will be delivered. 2Multitudes who sleep in the dust of the earth will awake: some to everlasting life, others to shame and everlasting contempt. 3Those who are wise[c] will shine like the brightness of the heavens, and those who lead many to righteousness, like the stars for ever and ever. 4But you, Daniel, close up and seal the words of the scroll until the time of the end. Many will go here and there to increase knowledge."

Living Bible

33"Those with spiritual understanding will have a wide ministry of teaching in those days. But they will be in constant danger, many of them dying by fire and sword, or being jailed and robbed. 34Eventually these pressures will subside, and some ungodly men will come, pretending to offer a helping hand, only to take advantage of them.

35"And some who are most gifted in the things of God will stumble in those days and fall, but this will only refine and cleanse them and make them pure until the final end of all their trials, at God's appointed time.

36"The king will do exactly as he pleases, claiming to be greater than every god there is, even blaspheming the God of gods, and prospering—until his time is up. For God's plans are unshakable. 37He will have no regard for the gods of his fathers, nor for the god beloved of women,d nor any other god, for he will boast that he is greater than them all. 38Instead of these he will worship the Fortress gode—a god his fathers never knew—and lavish on him costly gifts! 39Claiming his help he will have great success against the strongest fortresses. He will honor those who submit to him, appointing them to positions of authority and dividing the land to them as their reward.

40"Then at the time of the end,f the king of the south will attack him again, and the northern king will react with the strength and fury of a whirlwind; his vast army and navy will rush out to bury him with their might. 41He will invade various lands on the way, including Israel, the Pleasant Land, and overthrow the governments of many nations. Moab, Edom, and most of Ammon will escape, 42but Egypt and many other lands will be occupied. 43He will capture all the treasures of Egypt, and the Libyans and Ethiopians shall be his servants.

44"But then news from the east and north will alarm him and he will return in great anger to destroy as he goes. 45He will halt between Jerusalem and the sea, and there pitch his royal tents, but while he is there his time will suddenly run out and there will be no one to help him.

New Revised Standard

the people shall give understanding to many; for some days, however, they shall fall by sword and flame, and suffer captivity and plunder. 34When they fall victim, they shall receive a little help, and many shall join them insincerely. 35Some of the wise shall fall, so that they may be refined, purified, and cleansed,h until the time of the end, for there is still an interval until the time appointed.

36 "The king shall act as he pleases. He shall exalt himself and consider himself greater than any god, and shall speak horrendous things against the God of gods. He shall prosper until the period of wrath is completed, for what is determined shall be done. 37He shall pay no respect to the gods of his ancestors, or to the one beloved by women; he shall pay no respect to any other god, for he shall consider himself greater than all. 38He shall honor the god of fortresses instead of these; a god whom his ancestors did not know he shall honor with gold and silver, with precious stones and costly gifts. 39He shall deal with the strongest fortresses by the help of a foreign god. Those who acknowledge him he shall make more wealthy, and shall appoint them as rulers over many, and shall distribute the land for a price.

The Time of the End

40 "At the time of the end the king of the south shall attack him. But the king of the north shall rush upon him like a whirlwind, with chariots and horsemen, and with many ships. He shall advance against countries and pass through like a flood. 41He shall come into the beautiful land, and tens of thousands shall fall victim, but Edom and Moab and the main part of the Ammonites shall escape from his power. 42He shall stretch out his hand against the countries, and the land of Egypt shall not escape. 43He shall become ruler of the treasures of gold and of silver, and all the riches of Egypt; and the Libyans and the Ethiopiansi shall follow in his train. 44But reports from the east and the north shall alarm him, and he shall go out with great fury to bring ruin and complete destruction to many. 45He shall pitch his palatial tents between the sea and the beautiful holy mountain. Yet he shall come to his end, with no one to help him.

12 "AT THAT time Michael, the mighty angelic prince who stands guard over your nation, will stand up [and fight for you in heaven against satanic forcesg], and there will be a time of anguish for the Jews greater than any previous suffering in Jewish history. And yet every one of your people whose names are written in the Book will endure it.

2"And many of those whose bodies lie dead and buried will rise up, some to everlasting life and some to shame and everlasting contempt.

3"And those who are wise—the people of God—shall shine as brightly as the sun's brilliance, and those who turn many to righteousness will glitter like stars forever.

4"But Daniel, keep this prophecy a secret; seal it up so that it will not be understood until the end times, when travel and education shall be vastly increased!"

The Resurrection of the Dead

12 "AT THAT time Michael, the great prince, the protector of your people, shall arise. There shall be a time of anguish, such as has never occurred since nations first came into existence. But at that time your people shall be delivered, everyone who is found written in the book. 2Many of those who sleep in the dust of the earthj shall awake, some to everlasting life, and some to shame and everlasting contempt. 3Those who are wise shall shine like the brightness of the sky,k and those who lead many to righteousness, like the stars forever and ever. 4But you, Daniel, keep the words secret and the book sealed until the time of the end. Many shall be running back and forth, and evill shall increase."

---

d 11:37 the god beloved of women was probably Tammuz-Adonis, whose worship was popular among women (cf. Ezek 8:14).   e 11:38 the Fortress god, literally, "the god of Fortresses."   f 11:40 at the time of the end. The prophecy takes a turn here. Antiochus IV fades from view and the Antichrist of the last days becomes the center of attention from this point on.   g 12:1 and fight for you in heaven against satanic forces, implied.

h Heb made them white   i Or Nubians; Heb Cushites   j Or the land of dust   k Or dome   l Cn Compare Gk: Heb knowledge

King James

5¶ Then I Daniel looked, and, behold, there stood other two, the one on this side of the bank of the river, and the other on that side of the bank of the river.

6And *one* said to the man clothed in linen, which *was* upon the waters of the river, How long *shall it be to* the end of these wonders?

7And I heard the man clothed in linen, which *was* upon the waters of the river, when he held up his right hand and his left hand unto heaven, and sware by him that liveth for ever that *it shall be* for a time, times, and an half; and when he shall have accomplished to scatter the power of the holy people, all these *things* shall be finished.

8And I heard, but I understood not: then said I, O my Lord, what *shall be* the end of these *things?*

9And he said, Go thy way, Daniel: for the words *are* closed up and sealed till the time of the end.

10Many shall be purified, and made white, and tried; but the wicked shall do wickedly: and none of the wicked shall understand; but the wise shall understand.

11And from the time *that* the daily *sacrifice* shall be taken away, and the abomination that maketh desolate set up, *there shall be* a thousand two hundred and ninety days.

12Blessed *is* he that waiteth, and cometh to the thousand three hundred and five and thirty days.

13But go thou thy way till the end *be:* for thou shalt rest, and stand in thy lot at the end of the days.

New International

5Then I, Daniel, looked, and there before me stood two others, one on this bank of the river and one on the opposite bank. 6One of them said to the man clothed in linen, who was above the waters of the river, "How long will it be before these astonishing things are fulfilled?"

7The man clothed in linen, who was above the waters of the river, lifted his right hand and his left hand toward heaven, and I heard him swear by him who lives forever, saying, "It will be for a time, times and half a time.[a] When the power of the holy people has been finally broken, all these things will be completed."

8I heard, but I did not understand. So I asked, "My lord, what will the outcome of all this be?"

9He replied, "Go your way, Daniel, because the words are closed up and sealed until the time of the end. 10Many will be purified, made spotless and refined, but the wicked will continue to be wicked. None of the wicked will understand, but those who are wise will understand.

11"From the time that the daily sacrifice is abolished and the abomination that causes desolation is set up, there will be 1,290 days. 12Blessed is the one who waits for and reaches the end of the 1,335 days.

13"As for you, go your way till the end. You will rest, and then at the end of the days you will rise to receive your allotted inheritance."

Living Bible

5Then I, Daniel, looked and saw two menb on each bank of a river. 6And one of them asked the man in linen robes who was standing now above the river, "How long will it be until all these terrors end?"

7He replied, with both hands lifted to heaven, taking oath by him who lives forever and ever, that they will not end until three and a half yearsc after the power of God's people has been crushed.

8I heard what he said but I didn't understand what he meant, so I said, "Sir, how will all this finally end?"

9But he said, "Go now, Daniel, for what I have said is not to be understood until the time of the end. 10Many shall be purified by great trials and persecutions. But the wicked shall continue in their wickedness, and none of them will understand. Only those who are willing to learn will know what it means.

11"From the time the daily sacrifice is taken away and the Horrible Thing is set up to be worshiped, there will be 1,290 days.d 12And blessed are those who wait and remain until the 1335th day!

13"But go on now to the end of your life and your rest; for you will rise again and have your full share of those last days."e

New Revised Standard

5 Then I, Daniel, looked, and two others appeared, one standing on this bank of the stream and one on the other. 6One of them said to the man clothed in linen, who was upstream, "How long shall it be until the end of these wonders?" 7The man clothed in linen, who was upstream, raised his right hand and his left hand toward heaven. And I heard him swear by the one who lives forever that it would be for a time, two times, and half a time,f and that when the shattering of the power of the holy people comes to an end, all these things would be accomplished. 8I heard but could not understand; so I said, "My lord, what shall be the outcome of these things?" 9He said, "Go your way, Daniel, for the words are to remain secret and sealed until the time of the end. 10Many shall be purified, cleansed, and refined, but the wicked shall continue to act wickedly. None of the wicked shall understand, but those who are wise shall understand. 11From the time that the regular burnt offering is taken away and the abomination that desolates is set up, there shall be one thousand two hundred ninety days. 12Happy are those who persevere and attain the thousand three hundred thirty-five days. 13But you, go your way,g and rest; you shall rise for your reward at the end of the days."

Hosea

Hosea

1 THE WORD of the LORD that came unto Hosea, the son of Beeri, in the days of Uzziah, Jotham, Ahaz, *and* Hezekiah, kings of Judah, and in the days of Jeroboam the son of Joash, king of Israel.

2The beginning of the word of the LORD by Hosea. And the LORD said to Hosea, Go, take unto thee a wife of whoredoms and children of whoredoms: for the land hath committed great whoredom, *departing* from the LORD.

3So he went and took Gomer the daughter of Diblaim; which conceived, and bare him a son.

4And the LORD said unto him, Call his name Jezreel; for yet a little *while,* and I will avenge the blood of Jezreel upon the house of Jehu, and will cause to cease the kingdom of the house of Israel.

5And it shall come to pass at that day, that I will break the bow of Israel in the valley of Jezreel.

6¶ And she conceived again, and bare a daughter. And *God* said unto him, Call her name Lo-ruhamah: for I will no more have mercy upon the house of Israel; but I will utterly take them away.

7But I will have mercy upon the house of Judah, and will save them by the LORD their God, and will not save them by bow, nor by sword, nor by battle, by horses, nor by horsemen.

8¶ Now when she had weaned Lo-ruhamah, she conceived, and bare a son.

9Then said *God,* Call his name Lo-ammi: for ye *are* not my people, and I will not be your *God.*

10¶ Yet the number of the children of Israel shall be as the sand of the sea, which cannot be measured nor numbered; and it shall come to pass, *that* in the place where it was said unto them, Ye *are* not my people, *there* it shall be said unto them, *Ye are* the sons of the living God.

11Then shall the children of Judah and the children of Israel be gathered together, and appoint themselves one head, and they shall come up out of the land: for great *shall be* the day of Jezreel.

1 THE WORD of the LORD that came to Hosea son of Beeri during the reigns of Uzziah, Jotham, Ahaz and Hezekiah, kings of Judah, and during the reign of Jeroboam son of Jehoasha king of Israel:

Hosea's Wife and Children

2When the LORD began to speak through Hosea, the LORD said to him, "Go, take to yourself an adulterous wife and children of unfaithfulness, because the land is guilty of the vilest adultery in departing from the LORD." 3So he married Gomer daughter of Diblaim, and she conceived and bore him a son.

4Then the LORD said to Hosea, "Call him Jezreel, because I will soon punish the house of Jehu for the massacre at Jezreel, and I will put an end to the kingdom of Israel. 5In that day I will break Israel's bow in the Valley of Jezreel."

6Gomer conceived again and gave birth to a daughter. Then the LORD said to Hosea, "Call her Lo-Ruhamah,b for I will no longer show love to the house of Israel, that I should at all forgive them. 7Yet I will show love to the house of Judah; and I will save them—not by bow, sword or battle, or by horses and horsemen, but by the LORD their God."

8After she had weaned Lo-Ruhamah, Gomer had another son. 9Then the LORD said, "Call him Lo-Ammi,c for you are not my people, and I am not your God.

10"Yet the Israelites will be like the sand on the seashore, which cannot be measured or counted. In the place where it was said to them, 'You are not my people,' they will be called 'sons of the living God.' 11The people of Judah and the people of Israel will be reunited, and they will appoint one leader and will come up out of the land, for great will be the day of Jezreel.

a *1* Hebrew *Joash,* a variant of *Jehoash* b *6 Lo-Ruhamah* means *not loved.*
c *9 Lo-Ammi* means *not my people.*

Living Bible

Hosea

1 THESE ARE the messages from the Lord to Hosea, son of Beeri, during the reigns of these four kings of Judah:
Uzziah, Jotham, Ahaz, and Hezekiah; and one of the kings of Israel, Jeroboam, son of Joash.
²Here is the first message:
The Lord said to Hosea, "Go and marry a girl who is a prostitute, so that some of her children will be born to you from other men. This will illustrate the way my people have been untrue to me, committing open adultery against me by worshiping other gods."
³So Hosea married Gomer, daughter of Diblaim, and she conceived and bore him a son.
4, 5 And the Lord said, "Name the child Jezreel, for in the Valley of Jezreel I am about to punish King Jehu's dynasty to avenge the murders he committed;d in fact, I will put an end to Israel as an independent kingdom, breaking the power of the nation in the Valley of Jezreel."e
⁶Soon Gomer had another child—this one a daughter. And God said to Hosea, "Name her Lo-ruhamah (meaning 'No more mercy') for I will have no more mercy upon Israel, to forgive her again. ⁷But I *will* have mercy on the tribe of Judah. I will personally free her from her enemies without any help from her armies or her weapons."f
⁸After Gomer had weaned Lo-ruhamah, she again conceived and this time gave birth to a son. ⁹And God said, "Call him Lo-ammi (meaning 'Not mine'), for Israel is not mine and I am not her God.
¹⁰"Yet the time will come when Israel shall prosper and become a great nation; in that day her people will be too numerous to count—like sand along a seashore! Then, instead of saying to them, 'You are not my people,' I will tell them, 'You are my sons, children of the Living God.' ¹¹Then the people of Judah and Israel will unite and have one leader; they will return from exile together; what a day that will be—the day when God will sow his people in the fertile soil of their own land again."g

New Revised Standard

Hosea

1 THE WORD of the LORD that came to Hosea son of Beeri, in the days of Kings Uzziah, Jotham, Ahaz, and Hezekiah of Judah, and in the days of King Jeroboam son of Joash of Israel.

The Family of Hosea

2 When the LORD first spoke through Hosea, the LORD said to Hosea, "Go, take for yourself a wife of whoredom and have children of whoredom, for the land commits great whoredom by forsaking the LORD." ³So he went and took Gomer daughter of Diblaim, and she conceived and bore him a son.
4 And the LORD said to him, "Name him Jezreel;h for in a little while I will punish the house of Jehu for the blood of Jezreel, and I will put an end to the kingdom of the house of Israel. ⁵On that day I will break the bow of Israel in the valley of Jezreel."
6 She conceived again and bore a daughter. Then the LORD said to him, "Name her Lo-ruhamah,i for I will no longer have pity on the house of Israel or forgive them. ⁷But I will have pity on the house of Judah, and I will save them by the LORD their God; I will not save them by bow, or by sword, or by war, or by horses, or by horsemen."
8 When she had weaned Lo-ruhamah, she conceived and bore a son. ⁹Then the LORD said, "Name him Lo-ammi,j for you are not my people and I am not your God."k

The Restoration of Israel

10l Yet the number of the people of Israel shall be like the sand of the sea, which can be neither measured nor numbered; and in the place where it was said to them, "You are not my people," it shall be said to them, "Children of the living God." ¹¹ The people of Judah and the people of Israel shall be gathered together, and they shall appoint for themselves one head; and they shall take possession ofm the land, for great shall be the day of Jezreel.

---

d 1:4, 5 *avenge the murders he committed.* He went far beyond God's command to execute the family of Ahab. See 1 Kgs 21:21 and 2 Kgs 10:11. e 1:4, 5 *breaking the power of the nation in the Valley of Jezreel,* a prediction of the Assyrian conquest of Israel twenty-five years later. f 1:7 *I will personally free her* [Judah] *from her enemies without any help from her armies or her weapons.* Shortly after defeating Israel, the Assyrian Emperor Sennacherib invaded Judah and besieged Jerusalem. He was driven off by special intervention of God's angel (Isa 36-37). g 1:11 *the day when God will sow his people in the fertile soil of their own land again,* literally, "the day of Jezreel ('God sows')"; see 2:23.

h That is *God sows* i That is *Not pitied* j That is *Not my people* k Heb *I am not yours* l Ch 2.1 in Heb m Heb *rise up from*

King James

2 SAY YE unto your brethren, Ammi; and to your sisters, Ruhamah.

2Plead with your mother, plead: for she *is* not my wife, neither *am* I her husband: let her therefore put away her whoredoms out of her sight, and her adulteries from between her breasts;

3Lest I strip her naked, and set her as in the day that she was born, and make her as a wilderness, and set her like a dry land, and slay her with thirst.

4And I will not have mercy upon her children; for they *be* the children of whoredoms.

5For their mother hath played the harlot: she that conceived them hath done shamefully: for she said, I will go after my lovers, that give *me* my bread and my water, my wool and my flax, mine oil and my drink.

6¶ Therefore, behold, I will hedge up thy way with thorns, and make a wall, that she shall not find her paths.

7And she shall follow after her lovers, but she shall not overtake them; and she shall seek them, but shall not find *them:* then shall she say, I will go and return to my first husband; for then *was it* better with me than now.

8For she did not know that I gave her corn, and wine, and oil, and multiplied her silver and gold, *which they* prepared for Baal.

9Therefore will I return, and take away my corn in the time thereof, and my wine in the season thereof, and will recover my wool and my flax *given* to cover her nakedness.

10And now will I discover her lewdness in the sight of her lovers, and none shall deliver her out of mine hand.

11I will also cause all her mirth to cease, her feast days, her new moons, and her sabbaths, and all her solemn feasts.

12And I will destroy her vines and her fig trees, whereof she hath said, These *are* my rewards that my lovers have given me: and I will make them a forest, and the beasts of the field shall eat them.

13And I will visit upon her the days of Baalim, wherein she burned incense to them, and she decked herself with her earrings and her jewels, and she went after her lovers, and forgat me, saith the LORD.

14¶ Therefore, behold, I will allure her, and bring her into the wilderness, and speak comfortably unto her.

New International

2 "SAY OF your brothers, 'My people,' and of your sisters, 'My loved one.'

Israel Punished and Restored

2"Rebuke your mother, rebuke her,
    for she is not my wife,
    and I am not her husband.
Let her remove the adulterous look from her
        face
    and the unfaithfulness from between her
        breasts.
3Otherwise I will strip her naked
    and make her as bare as on the day she was
        born;
I will make her like a desert,
    turn her into a parched land,
    and slay her with thirst.
4I will not show my love to her children,
    because they are the children of adultery.
5Their mother has been unfaithful
    and has conceived them in disgrace.
She said, 'I will go after my lovers,
    who give me my food and my water,
    my wool and my linen, my oil and my
        drink.'
6Therefore I will block her path with
        thornbushes;
    I will wall her in so that she cannot find her
        way.
7She will chase after her lovers but not catch
        them;
    she will look for them but not find them.
Then she will say,
    'I will go back to my husband as at first,
    for then I was better off than now.'
8She has not acknowledged that I was the one
    who gave her the grain, the new wine and
        oil,
who lavished on her the silver and gold—
    which they used for Baal.

9"Therefore I will take away my grain when it
        ripens,
    and my new wine when it is ready.
I will take back my wool and my linen,
    intended to cover her nakedness.
10So now I will expose her lewdness
    before the eyes of her lovers;
    no one will take her out of my hands.
11I will stop all her celebrations:
    her yearly festivals, her New Moons,
    her Sabbath days—all her appointed feasts.
12I will ruin her vines and her fig trees,
    which she said were her pay from her lovers;
I will make them a thicket,
    and wild animals will devour them.
13I will punish her for the days
    she burned incense to the Baals;
she decked herself with rings and jewelry,
    and went after her lovers,
    but me she forgot,"

                                    declares the LORD.

14"Therefore I am now going to allure her;
    I will lead her into the desert
    and speak tenderly to her.

Living Bible

2 O JEZREEL,[a] rename your brother and sister. Call your brother Ammi (which means "Now you are mine"); name your sister Ruhamah ("Pitied"), for now God will have mercy upon her!

2Plead with your mother, for she has become another man's wife—I am no longer her husband. Beg her to stop her harlotry, to quit giving herself to others. 3If she doesn't, I will strip her as naked as the day she was born, and cause her to waste away and die of thirst as in a land riddled with famine and drought. 4And I will not give special favors to her children as I would to my own, for they are not my children; they belong to other men.

5For their mother has committed adultery. She did a shameful thing when she said, "I'll run after other men and sell myself to them for food and drinks and clothes."

6But I will fence her in with briars and thornbushes; I'll block the road before her to make her lose her way, so that 7when she runs after her lovers she will not catch up with them. She will search for them but not find them. Then she will think, "I might as well return to my husband, for I was better off with him than I am now."

8She doesn't realize that all she has, has come from me. It was I who gave her all the gold and silver she used in worshiping Baal, her god!

9But now I will take back the wine and ripened corn I constantly supplied, and the clothes I gave her to cover her nakedness—I will no longer give her rich harvests of grain in its season, or wine at the time of the grape harvest. 10Now I will expose her nakedness in public for all her lovers to see, and no one will be able to rescue her from my hand.

11I will put an end to all her joys, her parties, holidays, and feasts. 12I will destroy her vineyards and her orchards—gifts she claims her lovers gave her—and let them grow into a jungle; wild animals will eat their fruit.

13For all the incense she burned to Baal her idol and for the times when she put on her earrings and jewels and went out looking for her lovers, and deserted me: for all these things I will punish her, says the Lord.

14But I will court her again, and bring her into the wilderness, and speak to her tenderly there. 15There I

New Revised Standard

2[b] SAY TO your brother,[c] Ammi,[d] and to your sister,[e] Ruhamah.[f]

Israel's Infidelity, Punishment, and Redemption

2   Plead with your mother, plead—
        for she is not my wife,
        and I am not her husband—
     that she put away her whoring from her face,
        and her adultery from between her breasts,
3   or I will strip her naked
        and expose her as in the day she was born,
     and make her like a wilderness,
        and turn her into a parched land,
        and kill her with thirst.
4   Upon her children also I will have no pity,
        because they are children of whoredom.
5   For their mother has played the whore;
        she who conceived them has acted
            shamefully.
     For she said, "I will go after my lovers;
        they give me my bread and my water,
        my wool and my flax, my oil and my
            drink."
6   Therefore I will hedge up her[g] way with
            thorns;
        and I will build a wall against her,
        so that she cannot find her paths.
7   She shall pursue her lovers,
        but not overtake them;
     and she shall seek them,
        but shall not find them.
     Then she shall say, "I will go
        and return to my first husband,
        for it was better with me then than now."
8   She did not know
        that it was I who gave her
        the grain, the wine, and the oil,
     and who lavished upon her silver
        and gold that they used for Baal.
9   Therefore I will take back
        my grain in its time,
        and my wine in its season;
     and I will take away my wool and my flax,
        which were to cover her nakedness.
10 Now I will uncover her shame
        in the sight of her lovers,
        and no one shall rescue her out of my hand.
11 I will put an end to all her mirth,
        her festivals, her new moons, her sabbaths,
        and all her appointed festivals.
12 I will lay waste her vines and her fig trees,
        of which she said,
     "These are my pay,
        which my lovers have given me."
     I will make them a forest,
        and the wild animals shall devour them.
13 I will punish her for the festival days of the
            Baals,
        when she offered incense to them
     and decked herself with her ring and jewelry,
        and went after her lovers,
        and forgot me, says the LORD.

14 Therefore, I will now allure her,
        and bring her into the wilderness,
        and speak tenderly to her.

a *2:1 Jezreel* is implied in the preceding chapter and verse.

b Ch 2.3 in Heb   c Gk: Heb *brothers*   d That is *My People*   e Gk Vg: Heb *sisters*   f That is *Pitied*   g Gk Syr: Heb *your*

King James

15And I will give her her vineyards from thence, and the valley of Achor for a door of hope: and she shall sing there, as in the days of her youth, and as in the day when she came up out of the land of Egypt.

16And it shall be at that day, saith the LORD, *that* thou shalt call me Ishi; and shalt call me no more Baali.

17For I will take away the names of Baalim out of her mouth, and they shall no more be remembered by their name.

18And in that day will I make a covenant for them with the beasts of the field, and with the fowls of heaven, and *with* the creeping things of the ground: and I will break the bow and the sword and the battle out of the earth, and will make them to lie down safely.

19And I will betroth thee unto me for ever; yea, I will betroth thee unto me in righteousness, and in judgment, and in lovingkindness, and in mercies.

20I will even betroth thee unto me in faithfulness: and thou shalt know the LORD.

21And it shall come to pass in that day, I will hear, saith the LORD, I will hear the heavens, and they shall hear the earth;

22And the earth shall hear the corn, and the wine, and the oil; and they shall hear Jezreel.

23And I will sow her unto me in the earth; and I will have mercy upon her that had not obtained mercy; and I will say to *them which were* not my people, Thou *art* my people; and they shall say, *Thou art* my God.

3 THEN SAID the LORD unto me, Go yet, love a woman beloved of *her* friend, yet an adulteress, according to the love of the LORD toward the children of Israel, who look to other gods, and love flagons of wine.

2So I bought her to me for fifteen *pieces* of silver, and *for* an homer of barley, and an half homer of barley:

3And I said unto her, Thou shalt abide for me many days; thou shalt not play the harlot, and thou shalt not be for *another* man: so *will* I also *be* for thee.

4For the children of Israel shall abide many days without a king, and without a prince, and without a sacrifice, and without an image, and without an ephod, and *without* teraphim:

5Afterward shall the children of Israel return, and seek the LORD their God, and David their king; and shall fear the LORD and his goodness in the latter days.

4 HEAR THE word of the LORD, ye children of Israel: for the LORD hath a controversy with the inhabitants of the land, because *there is* no truth, nor mercy, nor knowledge of God in the land.

New International

15There I will give her back her vineyards,
    and will make the Valley of Achora a door of
        hope.
There she will singb as in the days of her
        youth,
    as in the day she came up out of Egypt.

16"In that day," declares the LORD,
    "you will call me 'my husband';
    you will no longer call me 'my master.c'
17I will remove the names of the Baals from her
        lips;
    no longer will their names be invoked.
18In that day I will make a covenant for them
    with the beasts of the field and the birds of
        the air
    and the creatures that move along the ground.
Bow and sword and battle
    I will abolish from the land,
    so that all may lie down in safety.
19I will betroth you to me forever;
    I will betroth you ind righteousness and
        justice,
    ine love and compassion.
20I will betroth you in faithfulness,
    and you will acknowledge the LORD.

21"In that day I will respond,"
    declares the LORD—
"I will respond to the skies,
    and they will respond to the earth;
22and the earth will respond to the grain,
    the new wine and oil,
    and they will respond to Jezreel.f
23I will plant her for myself in the land;
    I will show my love to the one I called 'Not
        my loved one.g'
    I will say to those called 'Not my people,h'
        'You are my people';
    and they will say, 'You are my God.'"

Hosea's Reconciliation With His Wife

3 THE LORD said to me, "Go, show your love to your wife again, though she is loved by another and is an adulteress. Love her as the LORD loves the Israelites, though they turn to other gods and love the sacred raisin cakes."

2So I bought her for fifteen shekelsi of silver and about a homer and a lethekj of barley. 3Then I told her, "You are to live withk me many days; you must not be a prostitute or be intimate with any man, and I will live withk you."

4For the Israelites will live many days without king or prince, without sacrifice or sacred stones, without ephod or idol. 5Afterward the Israelites will return and seek the LORD their God and David their king. They will come trembling to the LORD and to his blessings in the last days.

The Charge Against Israel

4 HEAR THE word of the LORD, you Israelites, because the LORD has a charge to bring
        against you who live in the land:
"There is no faithfulness, no love,
    no acknowledgment of God in the land.

---

a *15* Achor means *trouble.* b *15* Or *respond* c *16* Hebrew *baal* d *19* Or *with*; also in verse 20 e *19* Or *with* f *22* Jezreel means *God plants.* g *23* Hebrew *Lo-Ruhamah* h *23* Hebrew *Lo-Ammi* i *2* That is, about 6 ounces (about 170 grams) j *2* That is, probably about 10 bushels (about 330 liters) k *3* Or *wait for*

Living Bible

will give back her vineyards to her, and transform her Valley of Troubles into a Door of Hope. She will respond to me there, singing with joy as in days long ago in her youth, after I had freed her from captivity in Egypt.

16In that coming day, says the Lord, she will call me "My Husband" instead of "My Master."l 17O Israel, I will cause you to forget your idols, and their names will not be spoken anymore.

18At that time I will make a treaty between you and the wild animals, birds, and snakes, not to fear each other any more; and I will destroy all weapons, and all wars will end.

Then you will lie down in peace and safety, unafraid; 19and I will bind you to me forever with chains of righteousness and justice and love and mercy. 20I will betroth you to me in faithfulness and love, and you will really know me then as you never have before.

21, 22In that day, says the Lord, I will answer the pleading of the sky for clouds, to pour down water on the earth in answer to its cry for rain. Then the earth can answer the parched cry of the grain, the grapes, and the olive trees for moisture and for dew—and the whole grand chorus shall sing together that "God sows!"m He has given all!

23At that time I will sow a crop of Israelites and raise them for myself! I will pity those who are "not pitied,"n and I will say to those who are "not my people," "Now you are my people"; and they will reply, "You are our God!"

3 THEN THE Lord said to me, "Go, and get your wife again and bring her back to you and love her, even though she loves adultery. For the Lord still loves Israel though she has turned to other gods and offered them choice gifts."

2So I bought her [back from her slaveryo] for a couple of dollars and eight bushels of barley, 3and I said to her, "You must live alone for many days; do not go out with other men nor be a prostitute, and I will wait for you."

4This illustrates the fact that Israel will be a long time without a king or prince, and without an altar, temple, priests, or even idols!

5Afterward they will return to the Lord their God, and to the Messiah, their King,p and they shall come trembling, submissive to the Lord and to his blessings, in the end times.

4 HEAR THE word of the Lord, O people of Israel. The Lord has filed a lawsuit against you listing the following charges: There is no faithfulness, no kindness, no knowledge of God in your land. 2You swear and lie

---

l 2:16 "My Husband" instead of "My Master," literally, "my Baal," meaning "my Lord," but this was a tainted word because applied to idols, so it will no longer be used in reference to the true God.   m 2:21, 22 "God sows," literally, "Jezreel."   n 2:23 "not pitied," see 1:6, 9, 10.   o 3:2 back from her slavery, implied.   p 3:5 to the Messiah, their King, literally, "to David, their king." Christ was "the Greater David."

New Revised Standard

15 From there I will give her her vineyards,
     and make the Valley of Achor a door of
        hope.
   There she shall respond as in the days of her
        youth,
     as at the time when she came out of the
        land of Egypt.
16On that day, says the Lord, you will call me, "My husband," and no longer will you call me, "My Baal."q 17For I will remove the names of the Baals from her mouth, and they shall be mentioned by name no more. 18I will make for your a covenant on that day with the wild animals, the birds of the air, and the creeping things of the ground; and I will abolishs the bow, the sword, and war from the land; and I will make you lie down in safety. 19And I will take you for my wife forever; I will take you for my wife in righteousness and in justice, in steadfast love, and in mercy. 20I will take you for my wife in faithfulness; and you shall know the Lord.

21 On that day I will answer, says the Lord,
     I will answer the heavens
        and they shall answer the earth;
22 and the earth shall answer the grain, the wine,
        and the oil,
     and they shall answer Jezreel;t
23   and I will sow himu for myself in the land.
   And I will have pity on Lo-ruhamah,v
     and I will say to Lo-ammi,w "You are my
        people";
     and he shall say, "You are my God."

Further Assurances of God's Redeeming Love

3 THE LORD said to me again, "Go, love a woman who has a lover and is an adulteress, just as the Lord loves the people of Israel, though they turn to other gods and love raisin cakes." 2So I bought her for fifteen shekels of silver and a homer of barley and a measure of wine.x 3And I said to her, "You must remain as mine for many days; you shall not play the whore, you shall not have intercourse with a man, nor I with you." 4For the Israelites shall remain many days without king or prince, without sacrifice or pillar, without ephod or teraphim. 5Afterward the Israelites shall return and seek the Lord their God, and David their king; they shall come in awe to the Lord and to his goodness in the latter days.

God Accuses Israel

4 HEAR THE word of the Lord, O people of
     Israel;
   for the Lord has an indictment against the
        inhabitants of the land.
   There is no faithfulness or loyalty,
     and no knowledge of God in the land.

---

q That is, "My master"   r Heb them   s Heb break   t That is God sows   u Cn: Heb her   v That is Not pitied   w That is Not my people   x Gk: Heb a homer of barley and a lethech of barley

King James

2By swearing, and lying, and killing, and stealing, and committing adultery, they break out, and blood toucheth blood.

3Therefore shall the land mourn, and every one that dwelleth therein shall languish, with the beasts of the field, and with the fowls of heaven; yea, the fishes of the sea also shall be taken away.

4Yet let no man strive, nor reprove another: for thy people *are* as they that strive with the priest.

5Therefore shalt thou fall in the day, and the prophet also shall fall with thee in the night, and I will destroy thy mother.

6¶ My people are destroyed for lack of knowledge: because thou hast rejected knowledge, I will also reject thee, that thou shalt be no priest to me: seeing thou hast forgotten the law of thy God, I will also forget thy children.

7As they were increased, so they sinned against me: *therefore* will I change their glory into shame.

8They eat up the sin of my people, and they set their heart on their iniquity.

9And there shall be, like people, like priest: and I will punish them for their ways, and reward them their doings.

10For they shall eat, and not have enough: they shall commit whoredom, and shall not increase: because they have left off to take heed to the LORD.

11Whoredom and wine and new wine take away the heart.

12¶ My people ask counsel at their stocks, and their staff declareth unto them: for the spirit of whoredoms hath caused *them* to err, and they have gone a-whoring from under their God.

13They sacrifice upon the tops of the mountains, and burn incense upon the hills, under oaks and poplars and elms, because the shadow thereof *is* good: therefore your daughters shall commit whoredom, and your spouses shall commit adultery.

14I will not punish your daughters when they commit whoredom, nor your spouses when they commit adultery: for themselves are separated with whores, and they sacrifice with harlots: therefore the people *that* doth not understand shall fall.

15¶ Though thou, Israel, play the harlot, *yet* let not Judah offend; and come not ye unto Gilgal, neither go ye up to Beth-aven, nor swear, The LORD liveth.

16For Israel slideth back as a backsliding heifer: now the LORD will feed them as a lamb in a large place.

New International

2There is only cursing,[a] lying and murder,
  stealing and adultery;
 they break all bounds,
  and bloodshed follows bloodshed.
3Because of this the land mourns,[b]
  and all who live in it waste away;
 the beasts of the field and the birds of the air
  and the fish of the sea are dying.

4"But let no man bring a charge,
  let no man accuse another,
 for your people are like those
  who bring charges against a priest.
5You stumble day and night,
  and the prophets stumble with you.
 So I will destroy your mother—
6 my people are destroyed from lack of
   knowledge.

"Because you have rejected knowledge,
  I also reject you as my priests;
 because you have ignored the law of your God,
  I also will ignore your children.
7The more the priests increased,
  the more they sinned against me;
 they exchanged[c] their[d] Glory for something
   disgraceful.
8They feed on the sins of my people
  and relish their wickedness.
9And it will be: Like people, like priests.
  I will punish both of them for their ways
  and repay them for their deeds.

10"They will eat but not have enough;
  they will engage in prostitution but not
   increase,
 because they have deserted the LORD
  to give themselves 11to prostitution,
 to old wine and new,
  which take away the understanding 12of my
   people.
 They consult a wooden idol
  and are answered by a stick of wood.
 A spirit of prostitution leads them astray;
  they are unfaithful to their God.
13They sacrifice on the mountaintops
  and burn offerings on the hills,
 under oak, poplar and terebinth,
  where the shade is pleasant.
 Therefore your daughters turn to prostitution
  and your daughters-in-law to adultery.

14"I will not punish your daughters
  when they turn to prostitution,
 nor your daughters-in-law
  when they commit adultery,
 because the men themselves consort with harlots
  and sacrifice with shrine prostitutes—
 a people without understanding will come to
   ruin!

15"Though you commit adultery, O Israel,
  let not Judah become guilty.

"Do not go to Gilgal;
  do not go up to Beth Aven.[e]
 And do not swear, 'As surely as the LORD
   lives!'
16The Israelites are stubborn,
  like a stubborn heifer.
 How then can the LORD pasture them
  like lambs in a meadow?

---

a 2 That is, to pronounce a curse upon   b 3 Or *dries up*   c 7 Syriac and an ancient Hebrew scribal tradition; Masoretic Text *I will exchange*   d 7 Masoretic Text; an ancient Hebrew scribal tradition *my*   e 15 *Beth Aven* means *house of wickedness* (a name for Bethel, which means *house of God*).

Living Bible

and kill and steal and commit adultery. There is violence everywhere, with one murder after another.

³That is why your land is not producing; it is filled with sadness, and all living things grow sick and die; the animals, the birds, and even the fish begin to disappear.

⁴Don't point your finger at someone else, and try to pass the blame to him! Look, priest, I am pointing my finger at *you*. ⁵As a sentence for your crimes, you priests will stumble in broad daylight as well as in the night, and so will your false "prophets" too; and I will destroy your mother, Israel. ⁶My people are destroyed because they don't know me, and it is all your fault, you priests, for you yourselves refuse to know me; therefore I refuse to recognize you as my priests. Since you have forgotten my laws, I will "forget" to bless your children. ⁷The more my people multiplied, the more they sinned against me. They exchanged the glory of God for the disgrace of idols.

⁸The priests rejoice in the sins of the people; they lap it up and lick their lips for more! ⁹And thus it is: "Like priests, like people"—because the priests are wicked, the people are too. Therefore, I will punish both priests and people for all their wicked deeds. ¹⁰They will eat and still be hungry. Though they do a big business as prostitutes, they shall have no children, for they have deserted me and turned to other gods.

¹¹Wine, women, and song have robbed my people of their brains. ¹²For they are asking a piece of wood to tell them what to do. "Divine Truth" comes to them through tea leaves!ᶠ Longing after idols has made them foolish. For they have played the harlot, serving other gods, deserting me. ¹³They sacrifice to idols on the tops of mountains; they go up into the hills to burn incense in the pleasant shade of oaks and poplars and sumac trees. There your daughters turn to prostitution and your brides commit adultery. ¹⁴But why should I punish them? For you men are doing the same thing, sinning with harlots and temple prostitutes. Fools! Your doom is sealed, for you refuse to understand.

¹⁵But though Israel is a prostitute, may Judah stay far from such a life. O Judah, do not join with those who insincerely worship me at Gilgal and at Bethel. Their worship is mere pretense. ¹⁶Don't be like Israel, stubborn as a heifer, resisting the Lord's attempts to lead her

New Revised Standard

² Swearing, lying, and murder,
    and stealing and adultery break out;
    bloodshed follows bloodshed.
³ Therefore the land mourns,
    and all who live in it languish;
together with the wild animals
    and the birds of the air,
    even the fish of the sea are perishing.

⁴ Yet let no one contend,
    and let none accuse,
    for with you is my contention, O priest.ᵍ
⁵ You shall stumble by day;
    the prophet also shall stumble with you by
        night,
    and I will destroy your mother.
⁶ My people are destroyed for lack of
        knowledge;
    because you have rejected knowledge,
    I reject you from being a priest to me.
And since you have forgotten the law of your
        God,
    I also will forget your children.

⁷ The more they increased,
    the more they sinned against me;
    they changedʰ their glory into shame.
⁸ They feed on the sin of my people;
    they are greedy for their iniquity.
⁹ And it shall be like people, like priest;
    I will punish them for their ways,
    and repay them for their deeds.
¹⁰ They shall eat, but not be satisfied;
    they shall play the whore, but not multiply;
because they have forsaken the LORD
    to devote themselves to ¹¹whoredom.

The Idolatry of Israel

    Wine and new wine
    take away the understanding.
¹² My people consult a piece of wood,
    and their divining rod gives them oracles.
For a spirit of whoredom has led them astray,
    and they have played the whore, forsaking
        their God.
¹³ They sacrifice on the tops of the mountains,
    and make offerings upon the hills,
under oak, poplar, and terebinth,
    because their shade is good.

    Therefore your daughters play the whore,
    and your daughters-in-law commit adultery.
¹⁴ I will not punish your daughters when they
        play the whore,
    nor your daughters-in-law when they
        commit adultery;
for the men themselves go aside with whores,
    and sacrifice with temple prostitutes;
thus a people without understanding comes to
        ruin.

¹⁵ Though you play the whore, O Israel,
    do not let Judah become guilty.
Do not enter into Gilgal,
    or go up to Beth-aven,
    and do not swear, "As the LORD lives."
¹⁶ Like a stubborn heifer,
    Israel is stubborn;
can the LORD now feed them
    like a lamb in a broad pasture?

ᶠ *4:12 "Divine Truth" comes to them through tea leaves*, literally, "their staff." There is no modern parallel to this ancient practice used by sorcerers, whose predictions were based on how their staffs landed on the ground when thrown or allowed to fall.

ᵍ Cn: Meaning of Heb uncertain   ʰ Ancient Heb tradition: MT *I will change*

King James

17Ephraim *is* joined to idols: let him alone.

18Their drink is sour: they have committed whoredom continually: her rulers *with* shame do love, Give ye.

19The wind hath bound her up in her wings, and they shall be ashamed because of their sacrifices.

5 HEAR YE this, O priests; and hearken, ye house of Israel; and give ye ear, O house of the king; for judgment *is* toward you, because ye have been a snare on Mizpah, and a net spread upon Tabor.

2And the revolters are profound to make slaughter, though I *have been* a rebuker of them all.

3I know Ephraim, and Israel is not hid from me: for now, O Ephraim, thou committest whoredom, *and* Israel is defiled.

4 They will not frame their doings to turn unto their God: for the spirit of whoredoms *is* in the midst of them, and they have not known the LORD.

5And the pride of Israel doth testify to his face: therefore shall Israel and Ephraim fall in their iniquity; Judah also shall fall with them.

6They shall go with their flocks and with their herds to seek the LORD; but they shall not find *him;* he hath withdrawn himself from them.

7They have dealt treacherously against the LORD: for they have begotten strange children: now shall a month devour them with their portions.

8Blow ye the cornet in Gibeah, *and* the trumpet in Ramah: cry aloud *at* Beth-aven, after thee, O Benjamin.

9Ephraim shall be desolate in the day of rebuke: among the tribes of Israel have I made known that which shall surely be.

10The princes of Judah were like them that remove the bound: *therefore* I will pour out my wrath upon them like water.

11Ephraim *is* oppressed *and* broken in judgment, because he willingly walked after the commandment.

12Therefore *will* I *be* unto Ephraim as a moth, and to the house of Judah as rottenness.

13When Ephraim saw his sickness, and Judah *saw* his wound, then went Ephraim to the Assyrian, and sent to king Jareb: yet could he not heal you, nor cure you of your wound.

14For I *will be* unto Ephraim as a lion, and as a young lion to the house of Judah: I, *even* I, will tear and go away; I will take away, and none shall rescue *him*.

New International

17Ephraim is joined to idols;
    leave him alone!
18Even when their drinks are gone,
    they continue their prostitution;
    their rulers dearly love shameful ways.
19A whirlwind will sweep them away,
    and their sacrifices will bring them shame.

Judgment Against Israel

5 "HEAR THIS, you priests!
    Pay attention, you Israelites!
    Listen, O royal house!
    This judgment is against you:
    You have been a snare at Mizpah,
        a net spread out on Tabor.
2The rebels are deep in slaughter.
    I will discipline all of them.
3I know all about Ephraim;
    Israel is not hidden from me.
    Ephraim, you have now turned to prostitution;
        Israel is corrupt.

4"Their deeds do not permit them
    to return to their God.
A spirit of prostitution is in their heart;
    they do not acknowledge the LORD.
5Israel's arrogance testifies against them;
    the Israelites, even Ephraim, stumble in their
        sin;
    Judah also stumbles with them.
6When they go with their flocks and herds
    to seek the LORD,
they will not find him;
    he has withdrawn himself from them.
7They are unfaithful to the LORD;
    they give birth to illegitimate children.
Now their New Moon festivals
    will devour them and their fields.

8"Sound the trumpet in Gibeah,
    the horn in Ramah.
Raise the battle cry in Beth Aven[a];
    lead on, O Benjamin.
9Ephraim will be laid waste
    on the day of reckoning.
Among the tribes of Israel
    I proclaim what is certain.
10Judah's leaders are like those
    who move boundary stones.
I will pour out my wrath on them
    like a flood of water.
11Ephraim is oppressed,
    trampled in judgment,
    intent on pursuing idols.[b]
12I am like a moth to Ephraim,
    like rot to the people of Judah.

13"When Ephraim saw his sickness,
    and Judah his sores,
then Ephraim turned to Assyria,
    and sent to the great king for help.
But he is not able to cure you,
    not able to heal your sores.
14For I will be like a lion to Ephraim,
    like a great lion to Judah.
I will tear them to pieces and go away;
    I will carry them off, with no one to rescue
        them.

a 8 Beth Aven means house of wickedness (a name for Bethel, which means house of God).   b 11 The meaning of the Hebrew for this word is uncertain.

Living Bible

in green pastures. 17Stay away from her, for she is wedded to idolatry.

18The men of Israel finish up their drinking bouts, and off they go to find some whores. Their love for shame is greater than for honor.c

19Therefore, a mighty wind shall sweep them away;d they shall die in shame, because they sacrifice to idols.

5 LISTEN TO this, you priests and all of Israel's leaders; listen, all you men of the royal family: You are doomed! For you have deluded the people with idols at Mizpah and Tabor, 2and dug a deep pit to trap them at Acacia. But never forget—I will settle up with all of you for what you've done.

3I have seen your evil deeds: Israel, you have left me as a prostitute leaves her husband; you are utterly defiled. 4Your deeds won't let you come to God again, for the spirit of adultery is deep within you, and you cannot know the Lord.

5The very arrogance of Israel testifies against her in my court. She will stumble under her load of guilt, and Judah, too, shall fall. 6Then at last, they will come with their flocks and herds to sacrifice to God, but it will be too late—they will not find him. He has withdrawn from them and they are left alone.

7For they have betrayed the honor of the Lord, bearing children that aren't his. Suddenly they and all their wealth will disappear. 8Sound the alarm! Warn with trumpet blasts in Gibeah and Ramah, and on over to Beth-aven; tremble, land of Benjamin! 9Hear this announcement, Israel: When your day of punishment comes, you will become a heap of rubble.

10The leaders of Judah have become the lowest sort of thieves.e Therefore, I will pour my anger down upon them like a waterfall, 11and Ephraim will be crushed and broken by my sentence because she is determined to follow idols. 12I will destroy her as a moth does wool; I will sap away the strength of Judah like dry rot.

13When Ephraim and Judah see how sick they are, Ephraim will turn to Assyria, to the great king there, but he can neither help nor cure.

14I will tear Ephraim and Judah as a lion rips apart its prey; I will carry them off and chase all rescuers away.

New Revised Standard

17   Ephraim is joined to idols—
        let him alone.
18   When their drinking is ended, they indulge in
           sexual orgies;
        they love lewdness more than their glory.f
19   A wind has wrapped themg in its wings,
        and they shall be ashamed because of their
           altars.h

Impending Judgment on Israel and Judah

5 HEAR THIS, O priests!
        Give heed, O house of Israel!
     Listen, O house of the king!
        For the judgment pertains to you;
     for you have been a snare at Mizpah,
        and a net spread upon Tabor,
2   and a pit dug deep in Shittim;i
        but I will punish all of them.

3   I know Ephraim,
        and Israel is not hidden from me;
     for now, O Ephraim, you have played the
           whore;
        Israel is defiled.
4   Their deeds do not permit them
        to return to their God.
     For the spirit of whoredom is within them,
        and they do not know the Lord.

5   Israel's pride testifies against him;
        Ephraimj stumbles in his guilt;
        Judah also stumbles with them.
6   With their flocks and herds they shall go
        to seek the Lord,
     but they will not find him;
        he has withdrawn from them.
7   They have dealt faithlessly with the Lord;
        for they have borne illegitimate children.
     Now the new moon shall devour them along
           with their fields.

8   Blow the horn in Gibeah,
        the trumpet in Ramah.
     Sound the alarm at Beth-aven;
        look behind you, Benjamin!
9   Ephraim shall become a desolation
        in the day of punishment;
     among the tribes of Israel
        I declare what is sure.
10   The princes of Judah have become
        like those who remove the landmark;
     on them I will pour out
        my wrath like water.
11   Ephraim is oppressed, crushed in judgment,
        because he was determined to go after
           vanity.k
12   Therefore I am like maggots to Ephraim,
        and like rottenness to the house of Judah.
13   When Ephraim saw his sickness,
        and Judah his wound,
     then Ephraim went to Assyria,
        and sent to the great king.l
     But he is not able to cure you
        or heal your wound.
14   For I will be like a lion to Ephraim,
        and like a young lion to the house of Judah.
     I myself will tear and go away;
        I will carry off, and no one shall rescue.

---

c 4:18 Their love for shame is greater than for honor. The Hebrew text is uncertain. The translation follows the Greek version.   d 4:19 a mighty wind shall sweep them away. The Assyrian invasion came about twenty years later and the nation disappeared.   e 5:10 the lowest sort of thieves, literally, "as those who move a boundary marker." See Deut 19:14; 27:17.

f Cn Compare Gk: Meaning of Heb uncertain   g Heb her   h Gk Syr: Heb sacrifices   i Cn: Meaning of Heb uncertain   j Heb Israel and Ephraim   k Gk: Meaning of Heb uncertain   l Cn: Heb to a king who will contend

King James

15¶ I will go *and* return to my place, till they acknowledge their offence, and seek my face: in their affliction they will seek me early.

6 COME, AND let us return unto the LORD: for he hath torn, and he will heal us; he hath smitten, and he will bind us up.

2After two days will he revive us: in the third day he will raise us up, and we shall live in his sight.

3Then shall we know, *if* we follow on to know the LORD: his going forth is prepared as the morning; and he shall come unto us as the rain, as the latter *and* former rain unto the earth.

4¶ O Ephraim, what shall I do unto thee? O Judah, what shall I do unto thee? for your goodness *is* as a morning cloud, and as the early dew it goeth away.

5Therefore have I hewed *them* by the prophets; I have slain them by the words of my mouth: and thy judgments *are as* the light *that* goeth forth.

6For I desired mercy, and not sacrifice; and the knowledge of God more than burnt offerings.

7But they like men have transgressed the covenant: there have they dealt treacherously against me.

8Gilead *is* a city of them that work iniquity, *and is* polluted with blood.

9And as troops of robbers wait for a man, *so* the company of priests murder in the way by consent: for they commit lewdness.

10I have seen an horrible thing in the house of Israel: there *is* the whoredom of Ephraim, Israel is defiled.

11Also, O Judah, he hath set an harvest for thee, when I returned the captivity of my people.

7 WHEN I would have healed Israel, then the iniquity of Ephraim was discovered, and the wickedness of Samaria: for they commit falsehood; and the thief cometh in, *and* the troop of robbers spoileth without.

2And they consider not in their hearts *that* I remember all their wickedness: now their own doings have beset them about; they are before my face.

3They make the king glad with their wickedness, and the princes with their lies.

New International

15Then I will go back to my place
  until they admit their guilt.
And they will seek my face;
  in their misery they will earnestly seek me."

Israel Unrepentant

6 "COME, LET us return to the LORD.
He has torn us to pieces
  but he will heal us;
he has injured us
  but he will bind up our wounds.
2After two days he will revive us;
  on the third day he will restore us,
  that we may live in his presence.
3Let us acknowledge the LORD;
  let us press on to acknowledge him.
As surely as the sun rises,
  he will appear;
he will come to us like the winter rains,
  like the spring rains that water the earth."

4"What can I do with you, Ephraim?
  What can I do with you, Judah?
Your love is like the morning mist,
  like the early dew that disappears.
5Therefore I cut you in pieces with my prophets,
  I killed you with the words of my mouth;
  my judgments flashed like lightning upon
    you.
6For I desire mercy, not sacrifice,
  and acknowledgment of God rather than burnt
    offerings.
7Like Adam,a they have broken the covenant—
  they were unfaithful to me there.
8Gilead is a city of wicked men,
  stained with footprints of blood.
9As marauders lie in ambush for a man,
  so do bands of priests;
they murder on the road to Shechem,
  committing shameful crimes.
10I have seen a horrible thing
  in the house of Israel.
There Ephraim is given to prostitution
  and Israel is defiled.

11"Also for you, Judah,
  a harvest is appointed.

"Whenever I would restore the fortunes of my
    people,

7 WHENEVER I would heal Israel,
  the sins of Ephraim are exposed
  and the crimes of Samaria revealed.
They practice deceit,
  thieves break into houses,
  bandits rob in the streets;
2but they do not realize
  that I remember all their evil deeds.
Their sins engulf them;
  they are always before me.

3"They delight the king with their wickedness,
  the princes with their lies.

---

a 7 Or *As at Adam;* or *Like men*

Living Bible

15I will abandon them and return to my home until they admit their guilt and look to me for help again, for as soon as trouble comes, they will search for me and say:

6 "COME, LET us return to the Lord; it is he who has torn us—he will heal us. He has wounded—he will bind us up. 2In just a couple of days,b or three at the most, he will set us on our feet again, to live in his kindness! 3Oh, that we might know the Lord! Let us press on to know him, and he will respond to us as surely as the coming of dawn or the rain of early spring."

4O Ephraim and Judah, what shall I do with you? For your love vanishes like morning clouds, and disappears like dew. 5I sent my prophets to warn you of your doom; I have slain you with the words of my mouth, threatening you with death. Suddenly, without warning, my judgment will strike you as surely as day follows night.

6I don't want your sacrifices—I want your love; I don't want your offerings—I want you to know me. 7But like Adam, you broke my covenant; you refused my love. 8Gilead is a city of sinners, tracked with footprints of blood. 9Her citizens are gangs of robbers, lying in ambush for their victims; packs of priests murder along the road to Shechem and practice every kind of sin. 10Yes, I have seen a horrible thing in Israel—Ephraim chasing other gods, Israel utterly defiled.

11O Judah, for you also there is a plentiful harvest of punishment waiting—and I wanted so much to bless you!

7 I WANTED to forgive Israel, but her sins were far too great—no one can even live in Samaria without being a liar, thief, and bandit!

2Her people never seem to recognize that I am watching them. Their sinful deeds give them away on every side; I see them all. 3The king is glad about their wickedness; the princes laugh about their lies. 4They are all

New Revised Standard

15 I will return again to my place
   until they acknowledge their guilt and seek
      my face.
   In their distress they will beg my favor:

A Call to Repentance

6 "COME, LET us return to the Lord;
   for it is he who has torn, and he will heal
      us;
   he has struck down, and he will bind us up.
2 After two days he will revive us;
   on the third day he will raise us up,
      that we may live before him.
3 Let us know, let us press on to know the
      Lord;
   his appearing is as sure as the dawn;
he will come to us like the showers,
   like the spring rains that water the earth."

Impenitence of Israel and Judah

4 What shall I do with you, O Ephraim?
   What shall I do with you, O Judah?
Your love is like a morning cloud,
   like the dew that goes away early.
5 Therefore I have hewn them by the prophets,
   I have killed them by the words of my
      mouth,
   and myc judgment goes forth as the light.
6 For I desire steadfast love and not sacrifice,
   the knowledge of God rather than burnt
      offerings.

7 But atd Adam they transgressed the covenant;
   there they dealt faithlessly with me.
8 Gilead is a city of evildoers,
   tracked with blood.
9 As robbers lie in waite for someone,
   so the priests are banded together;f
they murder on the road to Shechem,
   they commit a monstrous crime.
10 In the house of Israel I have seen a horrible
      thing;
   Ephraim's whoredom is there, Israel is
      defiled.

11 For you also, O Judah, a harvest is appointed.

   When I would restore the fortunes of my
      people,

7 WHEN I would heal Israel,
   the corruption of Ephraim is revealed,
   and the wicked deeds of Samaria;
for they deal falsely,
   the thief breaks in,
   and the bandits raid outside.
2 But they do not consider
   that I remember all their wickedness.
Now their deeds surround them,
   they are before my face.
3 By their wickedness they make the king glad,
   and the officials by their treachery.

b 6:2 In just a couple of days, literally, "In two days."

c Gk Syr: Heb your   d Cn: Heb like   e Cn: Meaning of Heb uncertain
f Syr: Heb are a company

King James

⁴They *are* all adulterers, as an oven heated by the baker, *who* ceaseth from raising after he hath kneaded the dough, until it be leavened.

⁵In the day of our king the princes have made *him* sick with bottles of wine; he stretched out his hand with scorners.

⁶For they have made ready their heart like an oven, whiles they lie in wait: their baker sleepeth all the night; in the morning it burneth as a flaming fire.

⁷They are all hot as an oven, and have devoured their judges; all their kings are fallen: *there is* none among them that calleth unto me.

⁸Ephraim, he hath mixed himself among the people; Ephraim is a cake not turned.

⁹Strangers have devoured his strength, and he knoweth *it* not: yea, gray hairs are here and there upon him, yet he knoweth not.

¹⁰And the pride of Israel testifieth to his face: and they do not return to the Lord their God, nor seek him for all this.

¹¹¶ Ephraim also is like a silly dove without heart: they call to Egypt, they go to Assyria.

¹²When they shall go, I will spread my net upon them; I will bring them down as the fowls of the heaven; I will chastise them, as their congregation hath heard.

¹³Woe unto them! for they have fled from me: destruction unto them! because they have transgressed against me: though I have redeemed them, yet they have spoken lies against me.

¹⁴And they have not cried unto me with their heart, when they howled upon their beds: they assemble themselves for corn and wine, *and* they rebel against me.

¹⁵Though I have bound *and* strengthened their arms, yet do they imagine mischief against me.

¹⁶They return, *but* not to the most High: they are like a deceitful bow: their princes shall fall by the sword for the rage of their tongue: this *shall be* their derision in the land of Egypt.

8 SET THE trumpet to thy mouth. *He shall come* as an eagle against the house of the Lord, because they have transgressed my covenant, and trespassed against my law.

²Israel shall cry unto me, My God, we know thee.

³Israel hath cast off *the thing that is* good: the enemy shall pursue him.

New International

⁴They are all adulterers,
  burning like an oven
whose fire the baker need not stir
  from the kneading of the dough till it rises.
⁵On the day of the festival of our king
  the princes become inflamed with wine,
  and he joins hands with the mockers.
⁶Their hearts are like an oven;
  they approach him with intrigue.
Their passion smolders all night;
  in the morning it blazes like a flaming fire.
⁷All of them are hot as an oven;
  they devour their rulers.
All their kings fall,
  and none of them calls on me.

⁸"Ephraim mixes with the nations;
  Ephraim is a flat cake not turned over.
⁹Foreigners sap his strength,
  but he does not realize it.
His hair is sprinkled with gray,
  but he does not notice.
¹⁰Israel's arrogance testifies against him,
  but despite all this
he does not return to the Lord his God
  or search for him.

¹¹"Ephraim is like a dove,
  easily deceived and senseless—
now calling to Egypt,
  now turning to Assyria.
¹²When they go, I will throw my net over them;
  I will pull them down like birds of the air.
When I hear them flocking together,
  I will catch them.
¹³Woe to them,
  because they have strayed from me!
Destruction to them,
  because they have rebelled against me!
I long to redeem them
  but they speak lies against me.
¹⁴They do not cry out to me from their hearts
  but wail upon their beds.
They gather togetherᵃ for grain and new wine
  but turn away from me.
¹⁵I trained them and strengthened them,
  but they plot evil against me.
¹⁶They do not turn to the Most High;
  they are like a faulty bow.
Their leaders will fall by the sword
  because of their insolent words.
For this they will be ridiculed
  in the land of Egypt.

Israel to Reap the Whirlwind

8 "PUT THE trumpet to your lips!
An eagle is over the house of the Lord
because the people have broken my covenant
  and rebelledagainst my law.
²Israel cries out to me,
  'O our God, we acknowledge you!'
³But Israel has rejected what is good;
  an enemy will pursue him.

ᵃ *14* Most Hebrew manuscripts; some Hebrew manuscripts and Septuagint
They slash themselves

Living Bible

adulterers; as a baker's oven is constantly aflame—except after he kneads the dough and waits for it to rise again—so are these people constantly aflame with lust.

5On the king's birthday, the princes get him drunk; he makes a fool of himself and drinks with those who mock him. 6Their hearts blaze like a furnace with intrigue. Their plot smolders through the night, and in the morning it flames forth like raging fire.

7They kill their kings one after another,b and none cries out to me for help.

8My people mingle with the heathen, picking up their evil ways; thus they become as good-for-nothing as a half-baked cake!

9Worshiping foreign gods has sapped their strength, but they don't know it. Ephraim's hair is turning gray, and he doesn't even realize how weak and old he is. 10His pride in other gods has openly condemned him; yet he doesn't return to his God, nor even try to find him.

11Ephraim is a silly, witless dove, calling to Egypt, flying to Assyria. 12But as she flies, I throw my net over her and bring her down like a bird from the sky; I will punish her for all her evil ways.

13Woe to my people for deserting me; let them perish, for they have sinned against me. I wanted to redeem them but their hard hearts would not accept the truth. 14They lie there sleepless with anxiety, but won't ask my help. Instead, they worship heathen gods, asking them for crops and for prosperity.

15I have helped them, and made them strong, yet now they turn against me.

16They look everywhere except to heaven, to the Most High God. They are like a crooked bow that always misses targets; their leaders will perish by the sword of the enemy for their insolence to me. And all Egypt will laugh at them.

8 SOUND THE alarm! They are coming! Like a vulture, the enemy descends upon the people of God because they have broken my treaty and revolted against my laws.

2Now Israel pleads with me and says, "Help us, for you are our God!" 3But it is too late! Israel has thrown away her chance with contempt, and now her enemies will chase her. 4She has appointed kings and princes, but

New Revised Standard

4 They are all adulterers;
    they are like a heated oven,
  whose baker does not need to stir the fire,
    from the kneading of the dough until it is
      leavened.
5 On the day of our king the officials
    became sick with the heat of wine;
  he stretched out his hand with mockers.
6 For they are kindledc like an oven, their heart
      burns within them;
  all night their anger smolders;
    in the morning it blazes like a flaming fire.
7 All of them are hot as an oven,
    and they devour their rulers.
  All their kings have fallen;
    none of them calls upon me.

8 Ephraim mixes himself with the peoples;
    Ephraim is a cake not turned.
9 Foreigners devour his strength,
    but he does not know it;
  gray hairs are sprinkled upon him,
    but he does not know it.
10 Israel's pride testifies againstd him;
    yet they do not return to the LORD their
      God,
  or seek him, for all this.

Futile Reliance on the Nations

11 Ephraim has become like a dove,
    silly and without sense;
  they call upon Egypt, they go to Assyria.
12 As they go, I will cast my net over them;
    I will bring them down like birds of the air;
  I will discipline them according to the report
      made to their assembly.e
13 Woe to them, for they have strayed from me!
    Destruction to them, for they have rebelled
      against me!
  I would redeem them,
    but they speak lies against me.

14 They do not cry to me from the heart,
    but they wail upon their beds;
  they gash themselves for grain and wine;
    they rebel against me.
15 It was I who trained and strengthened their
      arms,
    yet they plot evil against me.
16 They turn to that which does not profit;f
    they have become like a defective bow;
  their officials shall fall by the sword
    because of the rage of their tongue.
  So much for their babbling in the land of
      Egypt.

Israel's Apostasy

8 SET THE trumpet to your lips!
    One like a vulturee is over the house of the
      LORD,
  because they have broken my covenant,
    and transgressed my law.
2 Israel cries to me,
    "My God, we—Israel—know you!"
3 Israel has spurned the good;
    the enemy shall pursue him.

---

b 7:7 They kill their kings one after another. Three Israelite kings were assassinated during Hosea's lifetime—Zechariah, Shallum, and Pekahiah.

c Gk Syr: Heb brought near   d Or humbles   e Meaning of Heb uncertain
f Cn: Meaning of Heb uncertain

King James

New International

4They have set up kings, but not by me: they have made princes, and I knew *it* not: of their silver and their gold have they made them idols, that they may be cut off.

5¶ Thy calf, O Samaria, hath cast *thee* off; mine anger is kindled against them: how long *will it be* ere they attain to innocency?

6For from Israel *was* it also: the workman made it; therefore it *is* not God: but the calf of Samaria shall be broken in pieces.

7For they have sown the wind, and they shall reap the whirlwind: it hath no stalk: the bud shall yield no meal: if so be it yield, the strangers shall swallow it up.

8Israel is swallowed up: now shall they be among the Gentiles as a vessel wherein *is* no pleasure.

9For they are gone up to Assyria, a wild ass alone by himself: Ephraim hath hired lovers.

10Yea, though they have hired among the nations, now will I gather them, and they shall sorrow a little for the burden of the king of princes.

11Because Ephraim hath made many altars to sin, altars shall be unto him to sin.

12I have written to him the great things of my law, *but* they were counted as a strange thing.

13They sacrifice flesh *for* the sacrifices of mine offerings, and eat *it; but* the LORD accepteth them not; now will he remember their iniquity, and visit their sins: they shall return to Egypt.

14For Israel hath forgotten his Maker, and buildeth temples; and Judah hath multiplied fenced cities: but I will send a fire upon his cities, and it shall devour the palaces thereof.

4They set up kings without my consent;
    they choose princes without my approval.
With their silver and gold
    they make idols for themselves
    to their own destruction.
5Throw out your calf-idol, O Samaria!
    My anger burns against them.
How long will they be incapable of purity?
6   They are from Israel!
This calf—a craftsman has made it;
    it is not God.
It will be broken in pieces,
    that calf of Samaria.

7"They sow the wind
    and reap the whirlwind.
The stalk has no head;
    it will produce no flour.
Were it to yield grain,
    foreigners would swallow it up.
8Israel is swallowed up;
    now she is among the nations
    like a worthless thing.
9For they have gone up to Assyria
    like a wild donkey wandering alone.
    Ephraim has sold herself to lovers.
10Although they have sold themselves among the
        nations,
    I will now gather them together.
They will begin to waste away
    under the oppression of the mighty king.

11"Though Ephraim built many altars for sin
        offerings,
    these have become altars for sinning.
12I wrote for them the many things of my law,
    but they regarded them as something alien.
13They offer sacrifices given to me
    and they eat the meat,
    but the LORD is not pleased with them.
Now he will remember their wickedness
    and punish their sins:
    They will return to Egypt.
14Israel has forgotten his Maker
    and built palaces;
    Judah has fortified many towns.
But I will send fire upon their cities
    that will consume their fortresses."

Punishment for Israel

9 REJOICE NOT, O Israel, for joy, as *other* people: for thou hast gone a-whoring from thy God, thou hast loved a reward upon every cornfloor.

2The floor and the winepress shall not feed them, and the new wine shall fail in her.

3They shall not dwell in the LORD's land; but Ephraim shall return to Egypt, and they shall eat unclean *things* in Assyria.

9 DO NOT rejoice, O Israel;
    do not be jubilant like the other nations.
For you have been unfaithful to your God;
    you love the wages of a prostitute
    at every threshing floor.
2Threshing floors and winepresses will not feed
        the people;
    the new wine will fail them.
3They will not remain in the LORD's land;
    Ephraim will return to Egypt
    and eat uncleana food in Assyria.

---

a 3 That is, ceremonially unclean

Living Bible

not with my consent. They have cut themselves off from my help by worshiping the idols that they made from their silver and gold.

5O Samaria, I reject this calf—this idol you have made. My fury burns against you. How long will it be before one honest man is found among you? 6When will you admit this calf you worship was made by human hands! It is not God! Therefore, it must be smashed to bits.

7They have sown the wind and they will reap the whirlwind. Their cornstalks stand there barren, withered, sickly, with no grain; if it has any, foreigners will eat it.

8Israel is destroyed; she lies among the nations as a broken pot. 9She is a lonely, wandering wild ass. The only friends she has are those she hires; Assyria is one of them.

10But though she hires "friends" from many lands, I will send her off to exile. Then for a while at least she will be free of the burden of her wonderful king! 11Ephraim has built many altars, but they are not to worship me! They are altars of sin! 12Even if I gave her ten thousand laws, she'd say they weren't for her—that they applied to someone far away. 13Her people love the ritual of their sacrifice, but to me it is meaningless! I will call for an accounting of their sins and punish them; they shall return to Egypt.

14Israel has built great palaces; Judah has constructed great defenses for her cities, but they have forgotten their Maker. Therefore, I will send down fire upon those palaces and burn those fortresses.

9 O ISRAEL, rejoice no more as others do, for you have deserted your God and sacrificed to other gods on every threshing floor.

2Therefore your harvests will be small; your grapes will blight upon the vine.

3You may no longer stay here in this land of God; you will be carried off to Egypt and Assyria, and live there on scraps of food. 4There, far from home, you are not

New Revised Standard

4 They made kings, but not through me;
    they set up princes, but without my
        knowledge.
With their silver and gold they made idols
    for their own destruction.
5 Your calf is rejected, O Samaria.
    My anger burns against them.
How long will they be incapable of
        innocence?
6   For it is from Israel,
an artisan made it;
    it is not God.
The calf of Samaria
    shall be broken to pieces.b

7 For they sow the wind,
    and they shall reap the whirlwind.
The standing grain has no heads,
    it shall yield no meal;
if it were to yield,
    foreigners would devour it.
8 Israel is swallowed up;
    now they are among the nations
    as a useless vessel.
9 For they have gone up to Assyria,
    a wild ass wandering alone;
Ephraim has bargained for lovers.
10 Though they bargain with the nations,
    I will now gather them up.
They shall soon writhe
    under the burden of kings and princes.

11 When Ephraim multiplied altars to expiate sin,
    they became to him altars for sinning.
12 Though I write for him the multitude of my
        instructions,
    they are regarded as a strange thing.
13 Though they offer choice sacrifices,c
    though they eat flesh,
    the LORD does not accept them.
Now he will remember their iniquity,
    and punish their sins;
    they shall return to Egypt.
14 Israel has forgotten his Maker,
    and built palaces;
and Judah has multiplied fortified cities;
    but I will send a fire upon his cities,
    and it shall devour his strongholds.

Punishment for Israel's Sin

9 DO NOT rejoice, O Israel!
Do not exultd as other nations do;
for you have played the whore, departing from
    your God.
    You have loved a prostitute's pay
    on all threshing floors.
2 Threshing floor and wine vat shall not feed
    them,
    and the new wine shall fail them.
3 They shall not remain in the land of the LORD;
    but Ephraim shall return to Egypt,
    and in Assyria they shall eat unclean food.

b Or shall go up in flames   c Cn: Meaning of Heb uncertain   d Gk: Heb
To exultation

King James

⁴They shall not offer wine *offerings* to the LORD, neither shall they be pleasing unto him: their sacrifices *shall be* unto them as the bread of mourners; all that eat thereof shall be polluted: for their bread for their soul shall not come into the house of the LORD.

⁵What will ye do in the solemn day, and in the day of the feast of the LORD?

⁶For, lo, they are gone because of destruction: Egypt shall gather them up, Memphis shall bury them: the pleasant *places* for their silver, nettles shall possess them: thorns *shall be* in their tabernacles.

⁷The days of visitation are come, the days of recompence are come; Israel shall know *it:* the prophet *is* a fool, the spiritual man *is* mad, for the multitude of thine iniquity, and the great hatred.

⁸The watchman of Ephraim *was* with my God: *but* the prophet *is* a snare of a fowler in all his ways, *and* hatred in the house of his God.

⁹They have deeply corrupted *themselves,* as in the days of Gibeah: *therefore* he will remember their iniquity, he will visit their sins.

¹⁰I found Israel like grapes in the wilderness; I saw your fathers as the firstripe in the fig tree at her first time: *but* they went to Baal-peor, and separated themselves unto *that* shame; and *their* abominations were according as they loved.

¹¹*As for* Ephraim, their glory shall fly away like a bird, from the birth, and from the womb, and from the conception.

¹²Though they bring up their children, yet will I bereave them, *that there shall* not *be* a man *left:* yea, woe also to them when I depart from them!

¹³Ephraim, as I saw Tyrus, *is* planted in a pleasant place: but Ephraim shall bring forth his children to the murderer.

¹⁴Give them, O LORD: what wilt thou give? give them a miscarrying womb and dry breasts.

¹⁵All their wickedness *is* in Gilgal: for there I hated them: for the wickedness of their doings I will drive them out of mine house, I will love them no more: all their princes *are* revolters.

¹⁶Ephraim is smitten, their root is dried up, they shall bear no fruit: yea, though they bring forth, yet will I slay *even* the beloved *fruit* of their womb.

New International

⁴They will not pour out wine offerings to the
      LORD,
   nor will their sacrifices please him.
Such sacrifices will be to them like the bread of
      mourners;
   all who eat them will be unclean.
This food will be for themselves;
   it will not come into the temple of the LORD.

⁵What will you do on the day of your appointed
      feasts,
   on the festival days of the LORD?
⁶Even if they escape from destruction,
   Egypt will gather them,
   and Memphis will bury them.
Their treasures of silver will be taken over by
      briers,
   and thorns will overrun their tents.
⁷The days of punishment are coming,
   the days of reckoning are at hand.
   Let Israel know this.
Because your sins are so many
   and your hostility so great,
the prophet is considered a fool,
   the inspired man a maniac.
⁸The prophet, along with my God,
   is the watchman over Ephraim,[a]
yet snares await him on all his paths,
   and hostility in the house of his God.
⁹They have sunk deep into corruption,
   as in the days of Gibeah.
God will remember their wickedness
   and punish them for their sins.

¹⁰"When I found Israel,
   it was like finding grapes in the desert;
when I saw your fathers,
   it was like seeing the early fruit on the fig
      tree.
But when they came to Baal Peor,
   they consecrated themselves to that shameful
      idol
   and became as vile as the thing they loved.
¹¹Ephraim's glory will fly away like a bird—
   no birth, no pregnancy, no conception.
¹²Even if they rear children,
   I will bereave them of every one.
Woe to them
   when I turn away from them!
¹³I have seen Ephraim, like Tyre,
   planted in a pleasant place.
But Ephraim will bring out
   their children to the slayer."

¹⁴Give them, O LORD—
   what will you give them?
Give them wombs that miscarry
   and breasts that are dry.

¹⁵"Because of all their wickedness in Gilgal,
   I hated them there.
Because of their sinful deeds,
   I will drive them out of my house.
I will no longer love them;
   all their leaders are rebellious.
¹⁶Ephraim is blighted,
   their root is withered,
   they yield no fruit.
Even if they bear children,
   I will slay their cherished offspring."

---

a 8 Or *The prophet is the watchman over Ephraim, / the people of my God*

Living Bible

allowed to pour out wine for sacrifice to God. For no sacrifice that is offered there can please him; it is polluted, just as food of mourners is; all who eat such sacrifices are defiled. They may eat this food to feed themselves, but may not offer it to God. 5What then will you do on holy days, on days of feasting to the Lord, 6when you are carried off to Assyria as slaves? Who will inherit your possessions left behind? Egypt will! She will gather your dead; Memphis will bury them. And thorns and thistles will grow up among the ruins.

7The time of Israel's punishment has come; the day of recompense is almost here and soon Israel will know it all too well. "The prophets are crazy"; "The inspired men are mad." Yes, so they mock, for the nation is weighted with sin, and shows only hatred for those who love God.

8I appointed the prophets to guard my people, but the people have blocked them at every turn and publicly declared their hatred, even in the Temple of the Lord. 9The things my people do are as depraved as what they did in Gibeahᵇ long ago. The Lord does not forget. He will surely punish them.

10O Israel, how well I remember those first delightful days when I led you through the wilderness! How refreshing was your love! How satisfying, like the early figs of summer in their first season! But then you deserted me for Baal-peor,ᶜ to give yourselves to other gods, and soon you were as foul as they. 11The glory of Israel flies away like a bird, for your children will die at birth, or perish in the womb, or never even be conceived. 12And if your children grow, I will take them from you; all are doomed. Yes, it will be a sad day when I turn away and leave you alone.

13In my vision I have seen the sons of Israel doomed. The fathers are forced to lead their sons to slaughter. 14O Lord, what shall I ask for your people? I will ask for wombs that don't give birth, for breasts that cannot nourish.

15All their wickedness began at Gilgal;ᵈ there I began to hate them. I will drive them from myland because of their idolatry. I will love them no more, for all their leaders are rebels. 16Ephraim is doomed. The roots of Israel are dried up; she shall bear no more fruit. And if she gives birth, I will slay even her beloved child.

New Revised Standard

4 They shall not pour drink offerings of wine to
    the LORD,
  and their sacrifices shall not please him.
Such sacrifices shall be like mourners' bread;
  all who eat of it shall be defiled;
for their bread shall be for their hunger only;
  it shall not come to the house of the LORD.

5 What will you do on the day of appointed
    festival,
  and on the day of the festival of the LORD?
6 For even if they escape destruction,
  Egypt shall gather them,
  Memphis shall bury them.
Nettles shall possess their precious things of
    silver;ᵉ
  thorns shall be in their tents.

7 The days of punishment have come,
  the days of recompense have come;
  Israel cries,ᶠ
"The prophet is a fool,
  the man of the spirit is mad!"
Because of your great iniquity,
  your hostility is great.
8 The prophet is a sentinel for my God over
    Ephraim,
  yet a fowler's snare is on all his ways,
  and hostility in the house of his God.
9 They have deeply corrupted themselves
  as in the days of Gibeah;
he will remember their iniquity,
  he will punish their sins.

10 Like grapes in the wilderness,
  I found Israel.
Like the first fruit on the fig tree,
  in its first season,
  I saw your ancestors.
But they came to Baal-peor,
  and consecrated themselves to a thing of
    shame,
  and became detestable like the thing they
    loved.
11 Ephraim's glory shall fly away like a bird—
  no birth, no pregnancy, no conception!
12 Even if they bring up children,
  I will bereave them until no one is left.
Woe to them indeed
  when I depart from them!
13 Once I saw Ephraim as a young palm planted
  in a lovely meadow,ᵉ
but now Ephraim must lead out his children
  for slaughter.
14 Give them, O LORD—
  what will you give?
Give them a miscarrying womb
  and dry breasts.

15 Every evil of theirs began at Gilgal;
  there I came to hate them.
Because of the wickedness of their deeds
  I will drive them out of my house.
I will love them no more;
  all their officials are rebels.

16 Ephraim is stricken,
  their root is dried up,
  they shall bear no fruit.
Even though they give birth,
  I will kill the cherished offspring of their
    womb.

ᵇ 9:9 what they did in Gibeah. See Judg 19:14ff.   ᶜ 9:10 But then you deserted me for Baal-peor, the god of Peor, a city of Moab (Num 23). ᵈ 9:15 Gilgal, the town where Baal-worship flourished (Hosea 4:15; 12:11), and where the monarchy, hated of God, was instituted (1 Sam 11:15).

ᵉ Meaning of Heb uncertain   ᶠ Cn Compare Gk: Heb shall know

King James

17My God will cast them away, because they did not hearken unto him: and they shall be wanderers among the nations.

10 ISRAEL *IS* an empty vine, he bringeth forth fruit unto himself: according to the multitude of his fruit he hath increased the altars; according to the goodness of his land they have made goodly images.

2Their heart is divided; now shall they be found faulty: he shall break down their altars, he shall spoil their images.

3For now they shall say, We have no king, because we feared not the LORD; what then should a king do to us?

4They have spoken words, swearing falsely in making a covenant: thus judgment springeth up as hemlock in the furrows of the field.

5The inhabitants of Samaria shall fear because of the calves of Beth-aven: for the people thereof shall mourn over it, and the priests thereof *that* rejoiced on it, for the glory thereof, because it is departed from it.

6It shall be also carried unto Assyria *for* a present to king Jareb: Ephraim shall receive shame, and Israel shall be ashamed of his own counsel.

7*As for* Samaria, her king is cut off as the foam upon the water.

8The high places also of Aven, the sin of Israel, shall be destroyed: the thorn and the thistle shall come up on their altars; and they shall say to the mountains, Cover us; and to the hills, Fall on us.

9O Israel, thou hast sinned from the days of Gibeah: there they stood: the battle in Gibeah against the children of iniquity did not overtake them.

10*It is* in my desire that I should chastise them; and the people shall be gathered against them, when they shall bind themselves in their two furrows.

11And Ephraim *is as* an heifer *that is* taught, *and* loveth to tread out *the corn;* but I passed over upon her fair neck: I will make Ephraim to ride; Judah shall plow, *and* Jacob shall break his clods.

12Sow to yourselves in righteousness, reap in mercy; break up your fallow ground: for *it is* time to seek the LORD, till he come and rain righteousness upon you.

New International

17My God will reject them
because they have not obeyed him;
they will be wanderers among the nations.

10 ISRAEL WAS a spreading vine;
he brought forth fruit for himself.
As his fruit increased,
he built more altars;
as his land prospered,
he adorned his sacred stones.
2Their heart is deceitful,
and now they must bear their guilt.
The LORD will demolish their altars
and destroy their sacred stones.
3Then they will say, "We have no king
because we did not revere the LORD.
But even if we had a king,
what could he do for us?"
4They make many promises,
take false oaths
and make agreements;
therefore lawsuits spring up
like poisonous weeds in a plowed field.
5The people who live in Samaria fear
for the calf-idol of Beth Aven.[a]
Its people will mourn over it,
and so will its idolatrous priests,
those who had rejoiced over its splendor,
because it is taken from them into exile.
6It will be carried to Assyria
as tribute for the great king.
Ephraim will be disgraced;
Israel will be ashamed of its wooden idols.[b]
7Samaria and its king will float away
like a twig on the surface of the waters.
8The high places of wickedness[c] will be
destroyed—
it is the sin of Israel.
Thorns and thistles will grow up
and cover their altars.
Then they will say to the mountains, "Cover
us!"
and to the hills, "Fall on us!"

9"Since the days of Gibeah, you have sinned,
O Israel,
and there you have remained.[d]
Did not war overtake
the evildoers in Gibeah?
10When I please, I will punish them;
nations will be gathered against them
to put them in bonds for their double sin.
11Ephraim is a trained heifer
that loves to thresh;
so I will put a yoke
on her fair neck.
I will drive Ephraim,
Judah must plow,
and Jacob must break up the ground.
12Sow for yourselves righteousness,
reap the fruit of unfailing love,
and break up your unplowed ground;
for it is time to seek the LORD,
until he comes
and showers righteousness on you.

a 5 *Beth Aven* means *house of wickedness* (a name for Bethel, which means *house of God*).   b 6 Or *its counsel*   c 8 Hebrew *aven*, a reference to Beth Aven (a derogatory name for Bethel)   d 9 Or *there a stand was taken*

Living Bible

17My God will destroy the people of Israel because they will not listen or obey. They will be wandering Jews, homeless among the nations.

10 HOW PROSPEROUS Israel is—a luxuriant vine all filled with fruit! But the more wealth I give her, the more she pours it on the altars of her heathen gods; the richer the harvests I give her, the more beautiful the statues and idols she erects. 2The hearts of her people are false toward God. They are guilty and must be punished. God will break down their heathen altars and smash their idols. 3Then they will say, "We deserted the Lord and he took away our king. But what's the difference? We don't need one anyway!"

4They make promises they don't intend to keep. Therefore punishment will spring up among them like poisonous weeds in the furrows of the field. 5The people of Samaria tremble lest their calf-god idols at Beth-aven should be hurt; the priests and people, too, mourn over the departed honor of their shattered gods. 6This idol—this calf-god thing—will be carted with them when they go as slaves to Assyria, a present to the great king there. Ephraim will be laughed at for trusting in this idol; Israel will be put to shame. 7As for Samaria, her king shall disappear like a chip of wood upon an ocean wave. 8And the idol altars of Aven at Bethel where Israel sinned will crumble. Thorns and thistles will grow up to surround them. And the people will cry to the mountains and hills to fall upon them and crush them.

9O Israel, ever since that awful night in Gibeah,e there has been only sin, sin, sin! You have made no progress whatever. Was it not right that the men of Gibeah were wiped out? 10I will come against you for your disobedience; I will gather the armies of the nations against you to punish you for your heaped-up sins.

11Ephraim is accustomed to treading out the grain—an easy job she loves. I have never put her under a heavy yoke before; I have spared her tender neck. But now I will harness her to the plow and harrow. Her days of ease are gone.

12Plant the good seeds of righteousness and you will reap a crop of my love; plow the hard ground of your hearts, for now is the time to seek the Lord, that he may come and shower salvation upon you.

New Revised Standard

17 Because they have not listened to him,
    my God will reject them;
    they shall become wanderers among the
        nations.

Israel's Sin and Captivity

10 ISRAEL IS a luxuriant vine
    that yields its fruit.
The more his fruit increased
    the more altars he built;
as his country improved,
    he improved his pillars.
2 Their heart is false;
    now they must bear their guilt.
The Lordf will break down their altars,
    and destroy their pillars.

3 For now they will say:
    "We have no king,
for we do not fear the Lord,
    and a king—what could he do for us?"
4 They utter mere words;
    with empty oaths they make covenants;
so litigation springs up like poisonous weeds
    in the furrows of the field.
5 The inhabitants of Samaria tremble
    for the calfg of Beth-aven.
Its people shall mourn for it,
    and its idolatrous priests shall wailh over it,
    over its glory that has departed from it.
6 The thing itself shall be carried to Assyria
    as tribute to the great king.i
Ephraim shall be put to shame,
    and Israel shall be ashamed of his idol.j

7 Samaria's king shall perish
    like a chip on the face of the waters.
8 The high places of Aven, the sin of Israel,
    shall be destroyed.
Thorn and thistle shall grow up
    on their altars.
They shall say to the mountains, Cover us,
    and to the hills, Fall on us.

9 Since the days of Gibeah you have sinned,
    O Israel;
    there they have continued.
    Shall not war overtake them in Gibeah?
10 I will comek against the wayward people to
        punish them;
    and nations shall be gathered against them
    when they are punishedl for their double
        iniquity.

11 Ephraim was a trained heifer
    that loved to thresh,
    and I spared her fair neck;
but I will make Ephraim break the ground;
    Judah must plow;
    Jacob must harrow for himself.
12 Sow for yourselves righteousness;
    reap steadfast love;
    break up your fallow ground;
for it is time to seek the Lord,
    that he may come and rain righteousness
        upon you.

---

e 10:9 that awful night in Gibeah, for which see Judg 19, 20.

f Heb he   g Gk Syr: Heb calves   h Cn: Heb exult   i Cn: Heb to a king who will contend   j Cn: Heb counsel   k Cn Compare Gk: Heb In my desire
l Gk: Heb bound

King James

13Ye have plowed wickedness, ye have reaped iniquity; ye have eaten the fruit of lies: because thou didst trust in thy way, in the multitude of thy mighty men.

14Therefore shall a tumult arise among thy people, and all thy fortresses shall be spoiled, as Shalman spoiled Beth-arbel in the day of battle: the mother was dashed in pieces upon *her* children.

15So shall Beth-el do unto you because of your great wickedness: in a morning shall the king of Israel utterly be cut off.

11 WHEN ISRAEL *was* a child, then I loved him, and called my son out of Egypt.

2*As* they called them, so they went from them: they sacrificed unto Baalim, and burned incense to graven images.

3I taught Ephraim also to go, taking them by their arms; but they knew not that I healed them.

4I drew them with cords of a man, with bands of love: and I was to them as they that take off the yoke on their jaws, and I laid meat unto them.

5¶ He shall not return into the land of Egypt, but the Assyrian shall be his king, because they refused to return.

6And the sword shall abide on his cities, and shall consume his branches, and devour *them*, because of their own counsels.

7And my people are bent to backsliding from me: though they called them to the most High, none at all would exalt *him*.

8How shall I give thee up, Ephraim? *how* shall I deliver thee, Israel? how shall I make thee as Admah? *how* shall I set thee as Zeboim? mine heart is turned within me, my repentings are kindled together.

9I will not execute the fierceness of mine anger, I will not return to destroy Ephraim: for I *am* God, and not man; the Holy One in the midst of thee: and I will not enter into the city.

10They shall walk after the LORD: he shall roar like a lion: when he shall roar, then the children shall tremble from the west.

11They shall tremble as a bird out of Egypt, and as a dove out of the land of Assyria: and I will place them in their houses, saith the LORD.

New International

13But you have planted wickedness,
you have reaped evil,
you have eaten the fruit of deception.
Because you have depended on your own strength
and on your many warriors,
14the roar of battle will rise against your people,
so that all your fortresses will be devastated—
as Shalman devastated Beth Arbel on the day of battle,
when mothers were dashed to the ground with their children.
15Thus will it happen to you, O Bethel,
because your wickedness is great.
When that day dawns,
the king of Israel will be completely destroyed.

God's Love for Israel

11 "WHEN ISRAEL was a child, I loved him,
and out of Egypt I called my son.
2But the more Ia called Israel,
the further they went from me.b
They sacrificed to the Baals
and they burned incense to images.
3It was I who taught Ephraim to walk,
taking them by the arms;
but they did not realize
it was I who healed them.
4I led them with cords of human kindness,
with ties of love;
I lifted the yoke from their neck
and bent down to feed them.

5"Will they not return to Egypt
and will not Assyria rule over them
because they refuse to repent?
6Swords will flash in their cities,
will destroy the bars of their gates
and put an end to their plans.
7My people are determined to turn from me.
Even if they call to the Most High,
he will by no means exalt them.

8"How can I give you up, Ephraim?
How can I hand you over, Israel?
How can I treat you like Admah?
How can I make you like Zeboiim?
My heart is changed within me;
all my compassion is aroused.
9I will not carry out my fierce anger,
nor will I turn and devastate Ephraim.
For I am God, and not man—
the Holy One among you.
I will not come in wrath.c
10They will follow the LORD;
he will roar like a lion.
When he roars,
his children will come trembling from the west.
11They will come trembling
like birds from Egypt,
like doves from Assyria.
I will settle them in their homes,"
declares the LORD.

a 2 Some Septuagint manuscripts; Hebrew *they* b 2 Septuagint; Hebrew *them* c 9 Or *come against any city*

Living Bible

13But you have cultivated wickedness and raised a thriving crop of sins. You have earned the full reward of trusting in a lie—believing that military might and great armies can make a nation safe! 14Therefore the terrors of war shall rise among your people, and all your forts will fall, just as at Beth-arbel, which Shalmand destroyed; even mothers and children were dashed to death there. 15That will be your fate, too, you people of Israel, because of your great wickedness. In one morning the king of Israel shall be destroyed.

11 WHEN ISRAEL was a child I loved him as a son and brought him out of Egypt. 2But the more I called to him, the more he rebelled, sacrificing to Baal and burning incense to idols. 3I trained him from infancy, I taught him to walk, I held him in my arms. But he doesn't know or even care that it was I who raised him.

4As a man would lead his favorite ox,e so I led Israel with my ropes of love. I loosened his muzzle so he could eat. I myself have stooped and fed him. 5But my people shall return to Egypt and Assyria because they won't return to me.

6War will swirl through their cities; their enemies will crash through their gates and trap them in their own fortresses. 7For my people are determined to desert me. And so I have sentenced them to slavery, and no one shall set them free.

8Oh, how can I give you up, my Ephraim? How can I let you go? How can I forsake you like Admah and Zeboiim?f My heart cries out within me; how I long to help you! 9No, I will not punish you as much as my fierce anger tells me to. This is the last time I will destroy Ephraim. For I am God and not man; I am the Holy One living among you, and I did not come to destroy.

10For the people shall walk after the Lord. I shall roar as a lion [at their enemies] and my people shall return trembling from the west. 11Like a flock of birds, they will come from Egypt—like doves flying from Assyria. And I will bring them home again; it is a promise from the Lord.

New Revised Standard

13 You have plowed wickedness,
    you have reaped injustice,
    you have eaten the fruit of lies.
Because you have trusted in your power
    and in the multitude of your warriors,
14 therefore the tumult of war shall rise against
        your people,
    and all your fortresses shall be destroyed,
    as Shalman destroyed Beth-arbel on the day of
        battle
    when mothers were dashed in pieces with
        their children.
15 Thus it shall be done to you, O Bethel,
    because of your great wickedness.
At dawn the king of Israel
    shall be utterly cut off.

God's Compassion Despite Israel's Ingratitude

11 WHEN ISRAEL was a child, I loved him,
    and out of Egypt I called my son.
2 The more Ig called them,
    the more they went from me;h
they kept sacrificing to the Baals,
    and offering incense to idols.

3 Yet it was I who taught Ephraim to walk,
    I took them up in myi arms;
    but they did not know that I healed them.
4 I led them with cords of human kindness,
    with bands of love.
I was to them like those
    who lift infants to their cheeks.j
    I bent down to them and fed them.

5 They shall return to the land of Egypt,
    and Assyria shall be their king,
    because they have refused to return to me.
6 The sword rages in their cities,
    it consumes their oracle-priests,
    and devours because of their schemes.
7 My people are bent on turning away from me.
    To the Most High they call,
    but he does not raise them up at all.k

8 How can I give you up, Ephraim?
    How can I hand you over, O Israel?
How can I make you like Admah?
    How can I treat you like Zeboiim?
My heart recoils within me;
    my compassion grows warm and tender.
9 I will not execute my fierce anger;
    I will not again destroy Ephraim;
for I am God and no mortal,
    the Holy One in your midst,
    and I will not come in wrath.k

10 They shall go after the LORD,
    who roars like a lion;
when he roars,
    his children shall come trembling from the
        west.
11 They shall come trembling like birds from
        Egypt,
    and like doves from the land of Assyria;
    and I will return them to their homes, says
    the LORD.

---

d 10:14 Shalman: probably Salaman, king of Moab, who invaded Gilead around 740 B.C. e 11:4 As a man would lead his favorite ox, implied. f 11:8 Admah and Zeboiim, cities of the plain that perished with Sodom and Gomorrah (Deut 29:23).

g Gk: Heb they h Gk: Heb them i Gk Syr Vg: Heb his j Or who ease the yoke on their jaws k Meaning of Heb uncertain

King James

12Ephraim compasseth me about with lies, and the house of Israel with deceit: but Judah yet ruleth with God, and is faithful with the saints.

12 EPHRAIM FEEDETH on wind, and followeth after the east wind: he daily increaseth lies and desolation; and they do make a covenant with the Assyrians, and oil is carried into Egypt.

2The LORD hath also a controversy with Judah, and will punish Jacob according to his ways; according to his doings will he recompense him.

3¶ He took his brother by the heel in the womb, and by his strength he had power with God:

4Yea, he had power over the angel, and prevailed: he wept, and made supplication unto him: he found him *in* Beth-el, and there he spake with us;

5Even the LORD God of hosts; the LORD *is* his memorial.

6Therefore turn thou to thy God: keep mercy and judgment, and wait on thy God continually.

7¶ *He is* a merchant, the balances of deceit *are* in his hand: he loveth to oppress.

8And Ephraim said, Yet I am become rich, I have found me out substance: *in* all my labours they shall find none iniquity in me that *were* sin.

9And I *that am* the LORD thy God from the land of Egypt will yet make thee to dwell in tabernacles, as in the days of the solemn feast.

10I have also spoken by the prophets, and I have multiplied visions, and used similitudes, by the ministry of the prophets.

11*Is there* iniquity *in* Gilead? surely they are vanity: they sacrifice bullocks in Gilgal; yea, their altars *are* as heaps in the furrows of the fields.

12And Jacob fled into the country of Syria, and Israel served for a wife, and for a wife he kept *sheep*.

13And by a prophet the LORD brought Israel out of Egypt, and by a prophet was he preserved.

14Ephraim provoked *him* to anger most bitterly: therefore shall he leave his blood upon him, and his reproach shall his Lord return unto him.

13 WHEN EPHRAIM spake trembling, he exalted himself in Israel; but when he offended in Baal, he died.

New International

Israel's Sin

12Ephraim has surrounded me with lies,
    the house of Israel with deceit.
And Judah is unruly against God,
    even against the faithful Holy One.

12 EPHRAIM FEEDS on the wind;
    he pursues the east wind all day
    and multiplies lies and violence.
He makes a treaty with Assyria
    and sends olive oil to Egypt.
2The LORD has a charge to bring against Judah;
    he will punish Jacoba according to his ways
    and repay him according to his deeds.
3In the womb he grasped his brother's heel;
    as a man he struggled with God.
4He struggled with the angel and overcame him;
    he wept and begged for his favor.
He found him at Bethel
    and talked with him there—
5the LORD God Almighty,
    the LORD is his name of renown!
6But you must return to your God;
    maintain love and justice,
    and wait for your God always.

7The merchant uses dishonest scales;
    he loves to defraud.
8Ephraim boasts,
    "I am very rich; I have become wealthy.
With all my wealth they will not find in me
    any iniquity or sin."

9"I am the LORD your God,
    who brought you out ofb Egypt;
I will make you live in tents again,
    as in the days of your appointed feasts.
10I spoke to the prophets,
    gave them many visions
    and told parables through them."

11Is Gilead wicked?
    Its people are worthless!
Do they sacrifice bulls in Gilgal?
    Their altars will be like piles of stones
    on a plowed field.
12Jacob fled to the country of Aramc;
    Israel served to get a wife,
    and to pay for her he tended sheep.
13The LORD used a prophet to bring Israel up
        from Egypt,
    by a prophet he cared for him.
14But Ephraim has bitterly provoked him to anger;
    his Lord will leave upon him the guilt of his
        bloodshed
    and will repay him for his contempt.

The LORD's Anger Against Israel

13 WHEN EPHRAIM spoke, men trembled;
    he was exalted in Israel.
But he became guilty of Baal worship and
        died.

---

a 2 *Jacob* means *he grasps the heel* (figuratively, *he deceives*).   b 9 Or *God / ever since you were in*   c 12 That is, Northwest Mesopotamia

Living Bible

12Israel surrounds me with lies and deceit, but Judah still trusts in God and is faithful to the Holy One.

12 ISRAEL IS chasing the wind, yes, shepherding a whirlwind—a dangerous game!d For she has given gifts to Egypt and Assyria to get their help, and in return she gets their worthless promises.

2But the Lord is bringing a lawsuit against Judah. Jacob will be justly punished for his ways. 3When he was born, he struggled with his brother; when he became a man, he even fought with God. 4Yes, he wrestled with the Angel and prevailed. He wept and pleaded for a blessing from him. He met God there at Bethel face to face. God spoke to him— 5the Lord, the God of heaven's armies—Jehovah is his name.

6Oh, come back to God. Live by the principles of love and justice, and always be expecting much from him, your God.

7But no, my people are like crafty merchants selling from dishonest scales—they love to cheat. 8Ephraim boasts, "I am so rich! I have gotten it all by myself!" But riches can't make up for sin.

9I am the same Lord, the same God, who delivered you from slavery in Egypt, and I am the one who will consign you to living in tents again, as you do each year at the Tabernacle Feast. 10I sent my prophets to warn you with many a vision and many a parable and dream. 11But the sins of Gilgal flourish just the same. Row on row of altars—like furrows in a field—are used for sacrifices to your idols. And Gilead, too, is full of foolse who worship idols. 12Jacob fled to Syria and earned a wife by tending sheep. 13Then the Lord led his people out of Egypt by a prophet, who guided and protected them. 14But Ephraim has bitterly provoked the Lord. The Lord will sentence him to death as payment for his sins.

13 IT USED to be when Israel spoke, the nations shook with fear, for he was a mighty prince; but he worshiped Baal and sealed his doom.

New Revised Standard

12f Ephraim has surrounded me with lies,
    and the house of Israel with deceit;
but Judah still walksg with God,
    and is faithful to the Holy One.

12 EPHRAIM HERDS the wind,
    and pursues the east wind all day long;
they multiply falsehood and violence;
    they make a treaty with Assyria,
    and oil is carried to Egypt.

The Long History of Rebellion

2 The LORD has an indictment against Judah,
    and will punish Jacob according to his
      ways,
    and repay him according to his deeds.
3 In the womb he tried to supplant his brother,
    and in his manhood he strove with God.
4 He strove with the angel and prevailed,
    he wept and sought his favor;
he met him at Bethel,
    and there he spoke with him.h
5 The LORD the God of hosts,
    the LORD is his name!
6 But as for you, return to your God,
    hold fast to love and justice,
    and wait continually for your God.

7 A trader, in whose hands are false balances,
    he loves to oppress.
8 Ephraim has said, "Ah, I am rich,
    I have gained wealth for myself;
in all of my gain
    no offense has been found in me
    that would be sin."i
9 I am the LORD your God
    from the land of Egypt;
I will make you live in tents again,
    as in the days of the appointed festival.

10 I spoke to the prophets;
     it was I who multiplied visions,
     and through the prophets I will bring
         destruction.
11 In Gileadj there is iniquity,
     they shall surely come to nothing.
In Gilgal they sacrifice bulls,
     so their altars shall be like stone heaps
     on the furrows of the field.
12 Jacob fled to the land of Aram,
     there Israel served for a wife,
     and for a wife he guarded sheep.k
13 By a prophet the LORD brought Israel up from
         Egypt,
     and by a prophet he was guarded.
14 Ephraim has given bitter offense,
     so his Lord will bring his crimes down on
         him
     and pay him back for his insults.

Relentless Judgment on Israel

13 WHEN EPHRAIM spoke, there was
    trembling;
he was exalted in Israel;
    but he incurred guilt through Baal and died.

---

d 12:1 a dangerous game, implied.   e 12:11 fools, or, "vanity."

f Ch 12.1 in Heb   g Heb roams or rules   h Gk Syr: Heb us   i Meaning of Heb uncertain   j Compare Syr: Heb Gilead   k Heb lacks sheep

King James

2And now they sin more and more, and have made them molten images of their silver, *and* idols according to their own understanding, all of it the work of the craftsmen: they say of them, Let the men that sacrifice kiss the calves.

3Therefore they shall be as the morning cloud, and as the early dew that passeth away, as the chaff *that* is driven with the whirlwind out of the floor, and as the smoke out of the chimney.

4Yet I *am* the LORD thy God from the land of Egypt, and thou shalt know no god but me: for *there is* no saviour beside me.

5¶ I did know thee in the wilderness, in the land of great drought.

6According to their pasture, so were they filled; they were filled, and their heart was exalted; therefore have they forgotten me.

7Therefore I will be unto them as a lion: as a leopard by the way will I observe *them:*

8I will meet them as a bear *that is* bereaved *of her whelps,* and will rend the caul of their heart, and there will I devour them like a lion: the wild beast shall tear them.

9¶ O Israel, thou hast destroyed thyself; but in me *is* thine help.

10I will be thy king: where *is any other* that may save thee in all thy cities? and thy judges of whom thou saidst, Give me a king and princes?

11I gave thee a king in mine anger, and took *him* away in my wrath.

12The iniquity of Ephraim *is* bound up; his sin *is* hid.

13The sorrows of a travailing woman shall come upon him: he *is* an unwise son; for he should not stay long in *the place of* the breaking forth of children.

14I will ransom them from the power of the grave; I will redeem them from death: O death, I will be thy plagues; O grave, I will be thy destruction: repentance shall be hid from mine eyes.

15¶ Though he be fruitful among *his* brethren, an east wind shall come, the wind of the LORD shall come up from the wilderness, and his spring shall become dry, and his fountain shall be dried up: he shall spoil the treasure of all pleasant vessels.

16Samaria shall become desolate; for she hath rebelled against her God: they shall fall by the sword: their infants shall be dashed in pieces, and their women with child shall be ripped up.

New International

2Now they sin more and more;
  they make idols for themselves from their
    silver,
cleverly fashioned images,
  all of them the work of craftsmen.
It is said of these people,
  "They offer human sacrifice
  and kiss[a] the calf-idols."

3Therefore they will be like the morning mist,
  like the early dew that disappears,
  like chaff swirling from a threshing floor,
  like smoke escaping through a window.

4"But I am the LORD your God,
  ¡who brought you¡ out of[b] Egypt.
You shall acknowledge no God but me,
  no Savior except me.

5I cared for you in the desert,
  in the land of burning heat.

6When I fed them, they were satisfied;
  when they were satisfied, they became proud;
  then they forgot me.

7So I will come upon them like a lion,
  like a leopard I will lurk by the path.

8Like a bear robbed of her cubs,
  I will attack them and rip them open.
Like a lion I will devour them;
  a wild animal will tear them apart.

9"You are destroyed, O Israel,
  because you are against me, against your
    helper.

10Where is your king, that he may save you?
  Where are your rulers in all your towns,
of whom you said,
  'Give me a king and princes'?

11So in my anger I gave you a king,
  and in my wrath I took him away.

12The guilt of Ephraim is stored up,
  his sins are kept on record.

13Pains as of a woman in childbirth come to him,
  but he is a child without wisdom;
when the time arrives,
  he does not come to the opening of the
    womb.

14"I will ransom them from the power of the
    grave;
  I will redeem them from death.
Where, O death, are your plagues?
  Where, O grave,[c] is your destruction?

"I will have no compassion,
15 even though he thrives among his brothers.
An east wind from the LORD will come,
  blowing in from the desert;
his spring will fail
  and his well dry up.
His storehouse will be plundered
  of all its treasures.

16The people of Samaria must bear their guilt,
  because they have rebelled against their God.
They will fall by the sword;
  their little ones will be dashed to the ground,
  their pregnant women ripped open."

a 2 Or *"Men who sacrifice / kiss*   b 4 Or *God / ever since you were in*
c 14 Hebrew *Sheol*

Living Bible

2And now the people disobey more and more. They melt their silver to mold into idols, formed with skill by the hands of men. "Sacrifice to these!" they say—men kissing calves! 3They shall disappear like morning mist, like dew that quickly dries away, like chaff blown by the wind, like a cloud of smoke.

4I alone am God, your Lord, and have been ever since I brought you out from Egypt. You have no God but me, for there is no other Savior. 5I took care of you in the wilderness, in that dry and thirsty land. 6But when you had eaten and were satisfied, then you became proud and forgot me. 7So I will come upon you like a lion, or a leopard lurking along the road. 8I will rip you to pieces like a bear whose cubs have been taken away, and like a lion I will devour you.

9O Israel, if I destroy you, who can save you? 10Where is your king? Why don't you call on him for help? Where are all the leaders of the land? You asked for them, now let them save you! 11I gave you kings in my anger, and I took them awayd in my wrath. 12Ephraim's sins are harvested and stored away for punishment. 13New birth is offered him, but he is like a child resisting in the womb—how stubborn! how foolish! 14Shall I ransom him from hell? Shall I redeem him from Death? O Death, bring forth your terrors for his tasting! O Grave, demonstrate your plagues! For I will not relent!

15He was called the most fruitful of all his brothers, but the east wind—a wind of the Lord from the desert—will blow hard upon him and dry up his land. All his flowing springs and green oases will dry away, and he will die of thirst. 16Samaria must bear her guilt, for she rebelled against her God. Her people will be killed by the invading army, her babies dashed to death against the ground, her pregnant women ripped open with a sword.

New Revised Standard

2 And now they keep on sinning
    and make a cast image for themselves,
idols of silver made according to their
        understanding,
    all of them the work of artisans.
"Sacrifice to these," they say.e
    People are kissing calves!
3 Therefore they shall be like the morning mist
    or like the dew that goes away early,
like chaff that swirls from the threshing floor
    or like smoke from a window.

4 Yet I have been the LORD your God
    ever since the land of Egypt;
you know no God but me,
    and besides me there is no savior.
5 It was I who fedf you in the wilderness,
    in the land of drought.
6 When I fedg them, they were satisfied;
    they were satisfied, and their heart was
        proud;
    therefore they forgot me.
7 So I will become like a lion to them,
    like a leopard I will lurk beside the way.
8 I will fall upon them like a bear robbed of her
        cubs,
    and will tear open the covering
        of their heart;
there I will devour them like a lion,
    as a wild animal would mangle them.

9 I will destroy you, O Israel;
    who can help you?h
10 Where now isi your king, that he may save
        you?
    Where in all your cities are your rulers,
of whom you said,
    "Give me a king and rulers"?
11 I gave you a king in my anger,
    and I took him away in my wrath.

12 Ephraim's iniquity is bound up;
    his sin is kept in store.
13 The pangs of childbirth come for him,
    but he is an unwise son;
for at the proper time he does not present
        himself
    at the mouth of the womb.

14 Shall I ransom them from the power of Sheol?
    Shall I redeem them from Death?
O Death, where arej your plagues?
    O Sheol, where isj your destruction?
    Compassion is hidden from my eyes.

15 Although he may flourish among rushes,k
    the east wind shall come, a blast from the
        LORD,
    rising from the wilderness;
and his fountain shall dry up,
    his spring shall be parched.
It shall strip his treasury
    of every precious thing.
16l Samaria shall bear her guilt,
    because she has rebelled against her God;
they shall fall by the sword,
    their little ones shall be dashed in pieces,
    and their pregnant women ripped open.

---

d 13:11 I gave you kings in my anger, and I took them away. Probably an allusion to the kings of Israel assassinated during her last tempestuous years: Zechariah, Shallum, Pekahiah.

e Cn Compare Gk: Heb To these they say sacrifices of people   f Gk Syr: Heb knew   g Cn: Heb according to their pasture   h Gk Syr: Heb for in me is your help   i Gk Syr Vg: Heb I will be   j Gk Syr: Heb I will be   k Or among brothers   l Ch 14.1 in Heb

King James

14 O ISRAEL, return unto the LORD thy God; for thou hast fallen by thine iniquity.

²Take with you words, and turn to the LORD: say unto him, Take away all iniquity, and receive *us* graciously: so will we render the calves of our lips.

³Asshur shall not save us; we will not ride upon horses: neither will we say any more to the work of our hands, *Ye are* our gods: for in thee the fatherless findeth mercy.

⁴¶ I will heal their backsliding, I will love them freely: for mine anger is turned away from him.

⁵I will be as the dew unto Israel: he shall grow as the lily, and cast forth his roots as Lebanon.

⁶His branches shall spread, and his beauty shall be as the olive tree, and his smell as Lebanon.

⁷They that dwell under his shadow shall return; they shall revive *as* the corn, and grow as the vine: the scent thereof *shall be* as the wine of Lebanon.

⁸Ephraim *shall say,* What have I to do any more with idols? I have heard *him,* and observed him: I *am* like a green fir tree. From me is thy fruit found.

⁹Who *is* wise, and he shall understand these *things?* prudent, and he shall know them? for the ways of the LORD *are* right, and the just shall walk in them: but the transgressors shall fall therein.

New International

Repentance to Bring Blessing

14 RETURN, O Israel, to the LORD your God. Your sins have been your downfall!
²Take words with you
    and return to the LORD.
Say to him:
    "Forgive all our sins
and receive us graciously,
    that we may offer the fruit of our lips.ᵃ
³Assyria cannot save us;
    we will not mount war-horses.
We will never again say 'Our gods'
    to what our own hands have made,
    for in you the fatherless find compassion."

⁴"I will heal their waywardness
    and love them freely,
    for my anger has turned away from them.
⁵I will be like the dew to Israel;
    he will blossom like a lily.
Like a cedar of Lebanon
    he will send down his roots;
⁶   his young shoots will grow.
His splendor will be like an olive tree,
    his fragrance like a cedar of Lebanon.
⁷Men will dwell again in his shade.
    He will flourish like the grain.
He will blossom like a vine,
    and his fame will be like the wine from
        Lebanon.
⁸O Ephraim, what more have Iᵇ to do with
        idols?
    I will answer him and care for him.
I am like a green pine tree;
    your fruitfulness comes from me."

⁹Who is wise? He will realize these things.
    Who is discerning? He will understand them.
The ways of the LORD are right;
    the righteous walk in them,
    but the rebellious stumble in them.

Living Bible

14 O ISRAEL, return to the Lord, your God, for you have been crushed by your sins. 2Bring your petition. Come to the Lord and say, "O Lord, take away our sins; be gracious to us and receive us, and we will offer you the sacrifice of praise. 3Assyria cannot save us, nor can our strength in battle; never again will we call the idols we have made 'our gods'; for in you alone, O Lord, the fatherless find mercy."

4Then I will cure you of idolatry and faithlessness, and my love will know no bounds, for my anger will be forever gone! 5I will refresh Israel like the dew from heaven; she will blossom as the lily and root deeply in the soil like cedars in Lebanon. 6Her branches will spread out, as beautiful as olive trees, fragrant as the forests of Lebanon. 7Her people will return from exile far away and rest beneath my shadow. They will be a watered garden and blossom like grapes and be as fragrant as the wines of Lebanon.

8O Ephraim! Stay away from idols! I am living and strong! I look after you and care for you. I am like an evergreen tree, yielding my fruit to you throughout the year. My mercies never fail.

9Whoever is wise, let him understand these things. Whoever is intelligent, let him listen. For the paths of the Lord are true and right, and good men walk along them. But sinners trying it will fail.

New Revised Standard

A Plea for Repentance

14 RETURN, O Israel, to the LORD your God,
for you have stumbled because of your
iniquity.
2 Take words with you
and return to the LORD;
say to him,
"Take away all guilt;
accept that which is good,
and we will offer
the fruitc of our lips.
3 Assyria shall not save us;
we will not ride upon horses;
we will say no more, 'Our God,'
to the work of our hands.
In you the orphan finds mercy."

Assurance of Forgiveness

4 I will heal their disloyalty;
I will love them freely,
for my anger has turned from them.
5 I will be like the dew to Israel;
he shall blossom like the lily,
he shall strike root like the forests of
Lebanon.d
6 His shoots shall spread out;
his beauty shall be like the olive tree,
and his fragrance like that of Lebanon.
7 They shall again live beneath mye shadow,
they shall flourish as a garden;f
they shall blossom like the vine,
their fragrance shall be like the wine of
Lebanon.

8 O Ephraim, what have Ig to do with idols?
It is I who answer and look after you.h
I am like an evergreen cypress;
your faithfulnessi comes from me.
9 Those who are wise understand these things;
those who are discerning know them.
For the ways of the LORD are right,
and the upright walk in them,
but transgressors stumble in them.

---

c Gk Syr: Heb *bulls*   d Cn: Heb *like Lebanon*   e Heb *his*   f Cn: Heb *they shall grow grain*   g Or *What more has Ephraim*   h Heb *him*   i Heb *your fruit*

King James

Joel

1 THE WORD of the LORD that came to Joel the son of Pethuel.

2Hear this, ye old men, and give ear, all ye inhabitants of the land. Hath this been in your days, or even in the days of your fathers?

3Tell ye your children of it, and *let* your children *tell* their children, and their children another generation.

4That which the palmerworm hath left hath the locust eaten; and that which the locust hath left hath the cankerworm eaten; and that which the cankerworm hath left hath the caterpillar eaten.

5Awake, ye drunkards, and weep; and howl, all ye drinkers of wine, because of the new wine; for it is cut off from your mouth.

6For a nation is come up upon my land, strong, and without number, whose teeth *are* the teeth of a lion, and he hath the cheek teeth of a great lion.

7He hath laid my vine waste, and barked my fig tree: he hath made it clean bare, and cast *it* away; the branches thereof are made white.

8¶ Lament like a virgin girded with sackcloth for the husband of her youth.

9The meat offering and the drink offering is cut off from the house of the LORD; the priests, the LORD's ministers, mourn.

10The field is wasted, the land mourneth; for the corn is wasted: the new wine is dried up, the oil languisheth.

11Be ye ashamed, O ye husbandmen; howl, O ye vinedressers, for the wheat and for the barley; because the harvest of the field is perished.

12The vine is dried up, and the fig tree languisheth; the pomegranate tree, the palm tree also, and the apple tree, *even* all the trees of the field, are withered: because joy is withered away from the sons of men.

New International

Joel

1 THE WORD of the LORD that came to Joel son of Pethuel.

An Invasion of Locusts

2Hear this, you elders;
   listen, all who live in the land.
Has anything like this ever happened in your
      days
   or in the days of your forefathers?
3Tell it to your children,
   and let your children tell it to their children,
   and their children to the next generation.
4What the locust swarm has left
   the great locusts have eaten;
what the great locusts have left
   the young locusts have eaten;
what the young locusts have left
   other locustsa have eaten.

5Wake up, you drunkards, and weep!
   Wail, all you drinkers of wine;
wail because of the new wine,
   for it has been snatched from your lips.
6A nation has invaded my land,
   powerful and without number;
it has the teeth of a lion,
   the fangs of a lioness.
7It has laid waste my vines
   and ruined my fig trees.
It has stripped off their bark
   and thrown it away,
   leaving their branches white.

8Mourn like a virginb in sackcloth
   grieving for the husbandc of her youth.
9Grain offerings and drink offerings
   are cut off from the house of the LORD.
The priests are in mourning,
   those who minister before the LORD.
10The fields are ruined,
   the ground is dried upd;
the grain is destroyed,
   the new wine is dried up,
   the oil fails.
11Despair, you farmers,
   wail, you vine growers;
grieve for the wheat and the barley,
   because the harvest of the field is destroyed.
12The vine is dried up
   and the fig tree is withered;
the pomegranate, the palm and the apple tree—
   all the trees of the field—are dried up.
Surely the joy of mankind
   is withered away.

---

a 4 The precise meaning of the four Hebrew words used here for locusts is uncertain. b 8 Or *young woman* c 8 Or *betrothed* d 10 Or *ground mourns*

Joel

THE WORD of the LORD that came to Joel son of Pethuel:

THIS MESSAGE came from the Lord to Joel, son of Pethuel:

2Listen, you aged men of Israel! Everyone, listen! In all your lifetime, yes, in all your history, have you ever heard of such a thing as I am going to tell you? 3In years to come, tell your children about it; pass the awful story down from generation to generation. 4After the cutter-locusts finish eating your crops, the swarmer-locusts will take what's left! After them will come the hopper-locusts! And then the stripper-locusts, too!

5Wake up and weep, you drunkards, for all the grapes are ruined and all your wine is gone! 6A vast army of locusts[e] covers the land. It is a terrible army too numerous to count, with teeth as sharp as those of lions! 7They have ruined my vines and stripped the bark from the fig trees, leaving trunks and branches white and bare.

8Weep with sorrow, as a virgin weeps whose fiancé is dead. 9Gone are the offerings of grain and wine to bring to the Temple of the Lord; the priests are starving. Hear the crying of these ministers of God. 10The fields are bare of crops. Sorrow and sadness are everywhere. The grain, the grapes, the olive oil are gone.

11Well may you farmers stand so shocked and stricken; well may you vinedressers weep. Weep for the wheat and the barley too, for they are gone. 12The grapevines are dead; the fig trees are dying; the pomegranates wither; the apples shrivel on the trees; all joy has withered with them.

Joel

THE WORD of the LORD that came to Joel son of Pethuel:

Lament over the Ruin of the Country

2 Hear this, O elders,
   give ear, all inhabitants of the land!
 Has such a thing happened in your days,
   or in the days of your ancestors?
3 Tell your children of it,
   and let your children tell their children,
   and their children another generation.

4 What the cutting locust left,
   the swarming locust has eaten.
 What the swarming locust left,
   the hopping locust has eaten,
 and what the hopping locust left,
   the destroying locust has eaten.

5 Wake up, you drunkards, and weep;
   and wail, all you wine-drinkers,
 over the sweet wine,
   for it is cut off from your mouth.
6 For a nation has invaded my land,
   powerful and innumerable;
 its teeth are lions' teeth,
   and it has the fangs of a lioness.
7 It has laid waste my vines,
   and splintered my fig trees;
 it has stripped off their bark and thrown it
   down;
   their branches have turned white.

8 Lament like a virgin dressed in sackcloth
   for the husband of her youth.
9 The grain offering and the drink offering are
     cut off
   from the house of the LORD.
 The priests mourn,
   the ministers of the LORD.
10 The fields are devastated,
   the ground mourns;
 for the grain is destroyed,
   the wine dries up,
   the oil fails.

11 Be dismayed, you farmers,
   wail, you vinedressers,
 over the wheat and the barley;
   for the crops of the field are ruined.
12 The vine withers,
   the fig tree droops.
 Pomegranate, palm, and apple—
   all the trees of the field are dried up;
 surely, joy withers away
   among the people.

---

e *1:6 a vast army of locusts*, literally, "a nation."

King James

13Gird yourselves, and lament, ye priests: howl, ye ministers of the altar: come, lie all night in sackcloth, ye ministers of my God: for the meat offering and the drink offering is witholden from the house of your God.

14¶ Sanctify ye a fast, call a solemn assembly, gather the elders *and* all the inhabitants of the land *into* the house of the LORD your God, and cry unto the LORD.

15Alas for the day! for the day of the LORD *is* at hand, and as a destruction from the Almighty shall it come.

16Is not the meat cut off before our eyes, *yea,* joy and gladness from the house of our God?

17The seed is rotten under their clods, the garners are laid desolate, the barns are broken down; for the corn is withered.

18How do the beasts groan! the herds of cattle are perplexed, because they have no pasture; yea, the flocks of sheep are made desolate.

19O LORD, to thee will I cry: for the fire hath devoured the pastures of the wilderness, and the flame hath burned all the trees of the field.

20The beasts of the field cry also unto thee: for the rivers of waters are dried up, and the fire hath devoured the pastures of the wilderness.

2 BLOW YE the trumpet in Zion, and sound an alarm in my holy mountain: let all the inhabitants of the land tremble: for the day of the LORD cometh, for *it is* nigh at hand;

2A day of darkness and of gloominess, a day of clouds and of thick darkness, as the morning spread upon the mountains: a great people and a strong; there hath not been ever the like, neither shall be any more after it, *even* to the years of many generations.

3A fire devoureth before them; and behind them a flame burneth: the land *is* as the garden of Eden before them, and behind them a desolate wilderness; yea, and nothing shall escape them.

4The appearance of them *is* as the appearance of horses; and as horsemen, so shall they run.

New International

A Call to Repentance

13Put on sackcloth, O priests, and mourn;
  wail, you who minister before the altar.
Come, spend the night in sackcloth,
  you who minister before my God;
for the grain offerings and drink offerings
  are withheld from the house of your God.
14Declare a holy fast;
  call a sacred assembly.
Summon the elders
  and all who live in the land
to the house of the LORD your God,
  and cry out to the LORD.

15Alas for that day!
  For the day of the LORD is near;
  it will come like destruction from the
    Almighty.a

16Has not the food been cut off
  before our very eyes—
joy and gladness
  from the house of our God?
17The seeds are shriveled
  beneath the clods.b
The storehouses are in ruins,
  the granaries have been broken down,
  for the grain has dried up.
18How the cattle moan!
  The herds mill about
because they have no pasture;
  even the flocks of sheep are suffering.

19To you, O LORD, I call,
  for fire has devoured the open pastures
  and flames have burned up all the trees of the
    field.
20Even the wild animals pant for you;
  the streams of water have dried up
  and fire has devoured the open pastures.

An Army of Locusts

2 BLOW THE trumpet in Zion;
  sound the alarm on my holy hill.
Let all who live in the land tremble,
  for the day of the LORD is coming.
It is close at hand—
2 a day of darkness and gloom,
    a day of clouds and blackness.
Like dawn spreading across the mountains
  a large and mighty army comes,
such as never was of old
  nor ever will be in ages to come.

3Before them fire devours,
  behind them a flame blazes.
Before them the land is like the garden of Eden,
  behind them, a desert waste—
  nothing escapes them.
4They have the appearance of horses;
  they gallop along like cavalry.

---

a *15* Hebrew *Shaddai*   b *17* The meaning of the Hebrew for this word is uncertain.

Living Bible

13O priests, robe yourselves in sackcloth. O ministers of my God, lie all night before the altar, weeping. For there are no more offerings of grain and wine for you. 14Announce a fast; call a solemn meeting. Gather the elders and all the people into the Temple of the Lord your God, and weep before him there.

15Alas, this terrible day of punishmentᶜ is on the way. Destruction from the Almighty is almost here! 16Our food will disappear before our eyes; all joy and gladness will be ended in the Temple of our God. 17The seed rots in the ground; the barns and granaries are empty; the grain has dried up in the fields. 18The cattle groan with hunger; the herds stand perplexed for there is no pasture for them; the sheep bleat in misery.

19Lord, help us! For the heat has withered the pastures and burned up all the trees. 20Even the wild animals cry to you for help, for there is no water for them. The creeks are dry and the pastures are scorched.

New Revised Standard

A Call to Repentance and Prayer

13 Put on sackcloth and lament, you priests;
    wail, you ministers of the altar.
Come, pass the night in sackcloth,
    you ministers of my God!
Grain offering and drink offering
    are withheld from the house of your God.

14 Sanctify a fast,
    call a solemn assembly.
Gather the elders
    and all the inhabitants of the land
to the house of the LORD your God,
    and cry out to the LORD.

15 Alas for the day!
For the day of the LORD is near,
    and as destruction from the Almightyᵈ it
        comes.

16 Is not the food cut off
    before our eyes,
joy and gladness
    from the house of our God?

17 The seed shrivels under the clods,ᵉ
    the storehouses are desolate;
the granaries are ruined
    because the grain has failed.

18 How the animals groan!
    The herds of cattle wander about
because there is no pasture for them;
    even the flocks of sheep are dazed.ᶠ

19 To you, O LORD, I cry.
For fire has devoured
    the pastures of the wilderness,
and flames have burned
    all the trees of the field.

20 Even the wild animals cry to you
    because the watercourses are dried up,
and fire has devoured
    the pastures of the wilderness.

2 SOUND THE alarm in Jerusalem! Let the blast of the warning trumpet be heard upon my holy mountain! Let everyone tremble in fear, for the day of the Lord's judgment approaches.

2It is a day of darkness and gloom, of black clouds and thick darkness. What a mighty army! It covers the mountains like night! How great, how powerful these "people" are! The likes of them have not been seen before, and never will again throughout the generations of the world! 3Fire goes before them and follows them on every side! Ahead of them the land lies fair as Eden's Garden in all its beauty, but they destroy it to the ground; not one thing escapes. 4They look like tiny horses, and they run as fast. 5Look at them leaping along the tops

2 BLOW THE trumpet in Zion;
    sound the alarm on my holy mountain!
Let all the inhabitants of the land tremble,
    for the day of the LORD is coming, it is
        near—
2 a day of darkness and gloom,
    a day of clouds and thick darkness!
Like blackness spread upon the mountains
    a great and powerful army comes;
their like has never been from of old,
    nor will be again after them
        in ages to come.

3 Fire devours in front of them,
    and behind them a flame burns.
Before them the land is like the garden of
        Eden,
    but after them a desolate wilderness,
        and nothing escapes them.

4 They have the appearance of horses,
    and like war-horses they charge.

ᶜ *1:15 this terrible day of punishment,* or, "the Day of the Lord."

ᵈ Traditional rendering of Heb *Shaddai*   ᵉ Meaning of Heb uncertain
ᶠ Compare Gk Syr Vg: Meaning of Heb uncertain

King James

5Like the noise of chariots on the tops of mountains shall they leap, like the noise of a flame of fire that devoureth the stubble, as a strong people set in battle array.

6Before their face the people shall be much pained: all faces shall gather blackness.

7They shall run like mighty men; they shall climb the wall like men of war; and they shall march every one on his ways, and they shall not break their ranks:

8Neither shall one thrust another; they shall walk every one in his path: and *when* they fall upon the sword, they shall not be wounded.

9They shall run to and fro in the city; they shall run upon the wall, they shall climb up upon the houses; they shall enter in at the windows like a thief.

10The earth shall quake before them; the heavens shall tremble: the sun and the moon shall be dark, and the stars shall withdraw their shining:

11And the LORD shall utter his voice before his army: for his camp *is* very great: for *he is* strong that executeth his word: for the day of the LORD *is* great and very terrible; and who can abide it?

12¶ Therefore also now, saith the LORD, turn ye *even* to me with all your heart, and with fasting, and with weeping, and with mourning:

13And rend your heart, and not your garments, and turn unto the LORD your God: for he *is* gracious and merciful, slow to anger, and of great kindness, and repenteth him of the evil.

14Who knoweth *if* he will return and repent, and leave a blessing behind him; *even* a meat offering and a drink offering unto the LORD your God?

15¶ Blow the trumpet in Zion, sanctify a fast, call a solemn assembly:

16Gather the people, sanctify the congregation, assemble the elders, gather the children, and those that suck the breasts: let the bridegroom go forth of his chamber, and the bride out of her closet.

17Let the priests, the ministers of the LORD, weep between the porch and the altar, and let them say, Spare thy people, O LORD, and give not thine heritage to reproach, that the heathen should rule over them: wherefore should they say among the people, Where *is* their God?

New International

5With a noise like that of chariots
    they leap over the mountaintops,
like a crackling fire consuming stubble,
    like a mighty army drawn up for battle.
6At the sight of them, nations are in anguish;
    every face turns pale.
7They charge like warriors;
    they scale walls like soldiers.
They all march in line,
    not swerving from their course.
8They do not jostle each other;
    each marches straight ahead.
They plunge through defenses
    without breaking ranks.
9They rush upon the city;
    they run along the wall.
They climb into the houses;
    like thieves they enter through the windows.

10Before them the earth shakes,
    the sky trembles,
the sun and moon are darkened,
    and the stars no longer shine.
11The LORD thunders
    at the head of his army;
his forces are beyond number,
    and mighty are those who obey his command.
The day of the LORD is great;
    it is dreadful.
Who can endure it?

Rend Your Heart

12"Even now," declares the LORD,
    "return to me with all your heart,
    with fasting and weeping and mourning."

13Rend your heart
    and not your garments.
Return to the LORD your God,
    for he is gracious and compassionate,
slow to anger and abounding in love,
    and he relents from sending calamity.
14Who knows? He may turn and have pity
    and leave behind a blessing—
grain offerings and drink offerings
    for the LORD your God.

15Blow the trumpet in Zion,
    declare a holy fast,
    call a sacred assembly.
16Gather the people,
    consecrate the assembly;
bring together the elders,
    gather the children,
    those nursing at the breast.
Let the bridegroom leave his room
    and the bride her chamber.
17Let the priests, who minister before the LORD,
    weep between the temple porch and the altar.
Let them say, "Spare your people, O LORD.
    Do not make your inheritance an object of
        scorn,
    a byword among the nations.
Why should they say among the peoples,
    'Where is their God?' "

Living Bible

of the mountain! Listen to the noise they make, like the rumbling of chariots, or the roar of fire sweeping across a field, and like a mighty army moving into battle.

6Fear grips the waiting people; their faces grow pale with fright. 7These "soldiers" charge like infantry; they scale the walls like picked and trained commandos. Straight forward they march, never breaking ranks. 8They never crowd each other. Each is right in place. No weapon can stop them. 9They swarm upon the city; they run upon the walls; they climb up into the houses, coming like thieves through the windows. 10The earth quakes before them and the heavens tremble. The sun and moon are obscured and the stars are hid.

11The Lord leads them with a shout. This is his mighty army and they follow his orders. The day of the judgment of the Lord is an awesome, terrible thing. Who can endure it?

12That is why the Lord says, "Turn to me now, while there is time. Give me all your hearts. Come with fasting, weeping, mourning. 13Let your remorse tear at your hearts and not your garments." Return to the Lord your God, for he is gracious and merciful. He is not easily angered; he is full of kindness, and anxious not to punish you.

14Who knows? Perhaps even yet he will decide to let you alone and give you a blessing instead of his terrible curse. Perhaps he will give you so much that you can offer your grain and wine to the Lord as before!

15Sound the trumpet in Zion! Call a fast and gather all the people together for a solemn meeting. 16Bring everyone—the elders, the children, and even the babies. Call the bridegroom from his quarters and the bride from her privacy.

17The priests, the ministers of God, will stand between the people and the altar, weeping; and they will pray, "Spare your people, O our God; don't let the heathen rule them, for they belong to you. Don't let them be disgraced by the taunts of the heathen who say, 'Where is this God of theirs? How weak and helpless he must be!'"

New Revised Standard

5 As with the rumbling of chariots,
  they leap on the tops of the mountains,
like the crackling of a flame of fire
  devouring the stubble,
like a powerful army
  drawn up for battle.

6 Before them peoples are in anguish,
  all faces grow pale.[a]
7 Like warriors they charge,
  like soldiers they scale the wall.
Each keeps to its own course,
  they do not swerve from[b] their paths.
8 They do not jostle one another,
  each keeps to its own track;
they burst through the weapons
  and are not halted.
9 They leap upon the city,
  they run upon the walls;
they climb up into the houses,
  they enter through the windows like a thief.

10 The earth quakes before them,
  the heavens tremble.
The sun and the moon are darkened,
  and the stars withdraw their shining.
11 The LORD utters his voice
  at the head of his army;
how vast is his host!
  Numberless are those who obey his
    command.
Truly the day of the LORD is great;
  terrible indeed—who can endure it?

12 Yet even now, says the LORD,
  return to me with all your heart,
with fasting, with weeping, and with
    mourning;
13 rend your hearts and not your clothing.
Return to the LORD, your God,
  for he is gracious and merciful,
slow to anger, and abounding in steadfast
    love,
  and relents from punishing.
14 Who knows whether he will not turn and
    relent,
  and leave a blessing behind him,
a grain offering and a drink offering
  for the LORD, your God?

15 Blow the trumpet in Zion;
  sanctify a fast;
call a solemn assembly;
16   gather the people.
Sanctify the congregation;
  assemble the aged;
gather the children,
  even infants at the breast.
Let the bridegroom leave his room,
  and the bride her canopy.

17 Between the vestibule and the altar
  let the priests, the ministers of the LORD,
    weep.
Let them say, "Spare your people, O LORD,
  and do not make your heritage a mockery,
  a byword among the nations.
Why should it be said among the peoples,
  'Where is their God?'"

---

a Meaning of Heb uncertain   b Gk Syr Vg: Heb *they do not take a pledge along*

King James

18¶ Then will the LORD be jealous for his land, and pity his people.

19Yea, the LORD will answer and say unto his people, Behold, I will send you corn, and wine, and oil, and ye shall be satisfied therewith: and I will no more make you a reproach among the heathen:

20But I will remove far off from you the northern *army,* and will drive him into a land barren and desolate, with his face toward the east sea, and his hinder part toward the utmost sea, and his stink shall come up, and his ill savour shall come up, because he hath done great things.

21¶ Fear not, O land; be glad and rejoice: for the LORD will do great things.

22Be not afraid, ye beasts of the field: for the pastures of the wilderness do spring, for the tree beareth her fruit, the fig tree and the vine do yield their strength.

23Be glad then, ye children of Zion, and rejoice in the LORD your God: for he hath given you the former rain moderately, and he will cause to come down for you the rain, the former rain, and the latter rain in the first *month.*

24And the floors shall be full of wheat, and the vats shall overflow with wine and oil.

25And I will restore to you the years that the locust hath eaten, the cankerworm, and the caterpillar, and the palmerworm, my great army which I sent among you.

26And ye shall eat in plenty, and be satisfied, and praise the name of the LORD your God, that hath dealt wondrously with you: and my people shall never be ashamed.

27And ye shall know that I *am* in the midst of Israel, and *that* I *am* the LORD your God, and none else: and my people shall never be ashamed.

28¶ And it shall come to pass afterward, *that* I will pour out my spirit upon all flesh; and your sons and your daughters shall prophesy, your old men shall dream dreams, your young men shall see visions:

29And also upon the servants and upon the handmaids in those days will I pour out my spirit.

30And I will show wonders in the heavens and in the earth, blood, and fire, and pillars of smoke.

31The sun shall be turned into darkness, and the moon into blood, before the great and the terrible day of the LORD come.

New International

The LORD's Answer

18Then the LORD will be jealous for his land
    and take pity on his people.

19The LORD will reply[a] to them:

"I am sending you grain, new wine and oil,
    enough to satisfy you fully;
never again will I make you
    an object of scorn to the nations.

20"I will drive the northern army far from you,
    pushing it into a parched and barren land,
with its front columns going into the eastern
    sea[b]
and those in the rear into the western sea.[c]
And its stench will go up;
    its smell will rise."

Surely he has done great things.[d]
21   Be not afraid, O land;
    be glad and rejoice.
Surely the LORD has done great things.
22   Be not afraid, O wild animals,
    for the open pastures are becoming green.
The trees are bearing their fruit;
    the fig tree and the vine yield their riches.
23Be glad, O people of Zion,
    rejoice in the LORD your God,
for he has given you
    the autumn rains in righteousness.[e]
He sends you abundant showers,
    both autumn and spring rains, as before.
24The threshing floors will be filled with grain;
    the vats will overflow with new wine and oil.

25"I will repay you for the years the locusts have
    eaten—
the great locust and the young locust,
    the other locusts and the locust swarm[f]—
my great army that I sent among you.
26You will have plenty to eat, until you are full,
    and you will praise the name of the LORD
        your God,
who has worked wonders for you;
    never again will my people be shamed.
27Then you will know that I am in Israel,
    that I am the LORD your God,
    and that there is no other;
never again will my people be shamed.

The Day of the LORD

28"And afterward,
    I will pour out my Spirit on all people.
Your sons and daughters will prophesy,
    your old men will dream dreams,
    your young men will see visions.
29Even on my servants, both men and women,
    I will pour out my Spirit in those days.
30I will show wonders in the heavens
    and on the earth,
    blood and fire and billows of smoke.
31The sun will be turned to darkness
    and the moon to blood
    before the coming of the great and dreadful
        day of the LORD.

---

[a] *18,19* Or *LORD was jealous . . . / and took pity . . . / 19The LORD replied*
[b] *20* That is, the Dead Sea   [c] *20* That is, the Mediterranean   [d] *20* Or *rise.*
/ Surely it has done great things."   [e] *23* Or */ the teacher for righteousness;*
[f] *25* The precise meaning of the four Hebrew words used here for locusts is uncertain.

Living Bible

18Then the Lord will pity his people and be indignant for the honor of his land! 19He will reply, "See, I am sending you much corn and wine and oil, to fully satisfy your need. No longer will I make you a laughingstock among the nations. 20I will remove these armies from the north and send them far away; I will turn them back into the parched wastelands where they will die; half shall be driven into the Dead Sea and the rest into the Mediterranean, and then their rotting stench will rise upon the land. The Lord has done a mighty miracle for you."

21Fear not, my people; be glad now and rejoice, for he has done amazing things for you.

22"Let the flocks and herds forget their hunger; the pastures will turn green again. The trees will bear their fruit; the fig trees and grape vines will flourish once more.

23"Rejoice, O people of Jerusalem, rejoice in the Lord your God! For the rains he sends are tokens of forgiveness. Once more the autumn rains will come, as well as those of spring. 24The threshing floors will pile high again with wheat, and the presses overflow with olive oil and wine. 25And I will give you back the crops the locusts ate!—my great destroying army that I sent against you. 26Once again you will have all the food you want.

"Praise the Lord, who does these miracles for you. Never again will my people experience disaster such as this. 27And you will know that I am here among my people Israel, and that I alone am the Lord, your God. And my people shall never again be dealt a blow like this.

28"After I have poured out my rains again, I will pour out my Spirit upon all of you! Your sons and daughters will prophesy; your old men will dream dreams, and your young men see visions. 29And I will pour out my Spirit even on your slaves, men and women alike, 30and put strange symbols in the earth and sky—blood and fire and pillars of smoke.

31"The sun will be turned into darkness and the moon to blood before the great and terrible Day of the Lord shall come.

New Revised Standard

God's Response and Promise

18 Then the LORD became jealous for his land,
      and had pity on his people.
19 In response to his people the LORD said:
    I am sending you
      grain, wine, and oil,
      and you will be satisfied;
    and I will no more make you
      a mockery among the nations.

20 I will remove the northern army far from you,
      and drive it into a parched and desolate
         land,
    its front into the eastern sea,
      and its rear into the western sea;
    its stench and foul smell will rise up.
      Surely he has done great things!

21 Do not fear, O soil;
      be glad and rejoice,
      for the LORD has done great things!
22 Do not fear, you animals of the field,
      for the pastures of the wilderness are green;
    the tree bears its fruit,
      the fig tree and vine give their full yield.

23 O children of Zion, be glad
      and rejoice in the LORD your God;
    for he has given the early rain[g] for your
         vindication,
    he has poured down for you abundant rain,
      the early and the later rain, as before.
24 The threshing floors shall be full of grain,
      the vats shall overflow with wine and oil.

25 I will repay you for the years
      that the swarming locust has eaten,
    the hopper, the destroyer, and the cutter,
      my great army, which I sent against you.

26 You shall eat in plenty and be satisfied,
      and praise the name of the LORD your God,
      who has dealt wondrously with you.
    And my people shall never again
         be put to shame.
27 You shall know that I am in the midst of
         Israel,
      and that I, the LORD, am your God and
         there is no other.
    And my people shall never again
      be put to shame.

God's Spirit Poured Out

28[h] Then afterward
      I will pour out my spirit on all flesh;
      your sons and your daughters shall prophesy,
      your old men shall dream reams,
      and your young men shall see visions.
29 Even on the male and female slaves,
      in those days, I will pour out my spirit.

30 I will show portents in the heavens and on the earth, blood and fire and columns of smoke. 31The sun shall be turned to darkness, and the moon to blood, before the great and terrible day of the LORD comes.

g Meaning of Heb uncertain   h Ch 3.1 in Heb

King James

³²And it shall come to pass, *that* whosoever shall call on the name of the LORD shall be delivered: for in mount Zion and in Jerusalem shall be deliverance, as the LORD hath said, and in the remnant whom the LORD shall call.

3 FOR, BEHOLD, in those days, and in that time, when I shall bring again the captivity of Judah and Jerusalem,

²I will also gather all nations, and will bring them down into the valley of Jehoshaphat, and will plead with them there for my people and *for* my heritage Israel, whom they have scattered among the nations, and parted my land.

³And they have cast lots for my people; and have given a boy for an harlot, and sold a girl for wine, that they might drink.

⁴Yea, and what have ye to do with me, O Tyre, and Zidon, and all the coasts of Palestine? will ye render me a recompense? and if ye recompense me, swiftly *and* speedily will I return your recompense upon your own head;

⁵Because ye have taken my silver and my gold, and have carried into your temples my goodly pleasant things:

⁶The children also of Judah and the children of Jerusalem have ye sold unto the Grecians, that ye might remove them far from their border.

⁷Behold, I will raise them out of the place whither ye have sold them, and will return your recompense upon your own head:

⁸And I will sell your sons and your daughters into the hand of the children of Judah, and they shall sell them to the Sabeans, to a people far off: for the LORD hath spoken *it*.

⁹¶ Proclaim ye this among the Gentiles; Prepare war, wake up the mighty men, let all the men of war draw near; let them come up:

¹⁰Beat your plowshares into swords, and your pruning hooks into spears: let the weak say, I *am* strong.

¹¹Assemble yourselves, and come, all ye heathen, and gather yourselves together round about: thither cause thy mighty ones to come down, O LORD.

¹²Let the heathen be wakened, and come up to the valley of Jehoshaphat: for there will I sit to judge all the heathen round about.

¹³Put ye in the sickle, for the harvest is ripe: come, get you down; for the press is full, the vats overflow; for their wickedness *is* great.

¹⁴Multitudes, multitudes in the valley of decision: for the day of the LORD *is* near in the valley of decision.

¹⁵The sun and the moon shall be darkened, and the stars shall withdraw their shining.

New International

³²And everyone who calls
　on the name of the LORD will be saved;
for on Mount Zion and in Jerusalem
　there will be deliverance,
　as the LORD has said,
among the survivors
　whom the LORD calls.

The Nations Judged

3 "IN THOSE days and at that time,
　when I restore the fortunes of Judah and
　　Jerusalem,
²I will gather all nations
　and bring them down to the Valley of
　　Jehoshaphat.ᵃ
There I will enter into judgment against them
　concerning my inheritance, my people Israel,
for they scattered my people among the nations
　and divided up my land.
³They cast lots for my people
　and traded boys for prostitutes;
they sold girls for wine
　that they might drink.

⁴"Now what have you against me, O Tyre and Sidon and all you regions of Philistia? Are you repaying me for something I have done? If you are paying me back, I will swiftly and speedily return on your own heads what you have done. ⁵For you took my silver and my gold and carried off my finest treasures to your temples. ⁶You sold the people of Judah and Jerusalem to the Greeks, that you might send them far from their homeland.

⁷"See, I am going to rouse them out of the places to which you sold them, and I will return on your own heads what you have done. ⁸I will sell your sons and daughters to the people of Judah, and they will sell them to the Sabeans, a nation far away." The LORD has spoken.

⁹Proclaim this among the nations:
　Prepare for war!
Rouse the warriors!
　Let all the fighting men draw near and attack.
¹⁰Beat your plowshares into swords
　and your pruning hooks into spears.
Let the weakling say,
　"I am strong!"
¹¹Come quickly, all you nations from every side,
　and assemble there.

Bring down your warriors, O LORD!

¹²"Let the nations be roused;
　let them advance into the Valley of
　　Jehoshaphat,
for there I will sit
　to judge all the nations on every side.
¹³Swing the sickle,
　for the harvest is ripe.
Come, trample the grapes,
　for the winepress is full
　and the vats overflow—
so great is their wickedness!"

¹⁴Multitudes, multitudes
　in the valley of decision!
For the day of the LORD is near
　in the valley of decision.
¹⁵The sun and moon will be darkened,
　and the stars no longer shine.

ᵃ *2 Jehoshaphat* means *the* LORD *judges*; also in verse 12.

Living Bible

32"Everyone who calls upon the name of the Lord will be saved; even in Jerusalem some will escape, just as the Lord has promised, for he has chosen some to survive.

3 "AT THAT time, when I restore the prosperity of Judah and Jerusalem," says the Lord, 2"I will gather the armies of the world into the 'Valley Where Jehovah Judges'b and punish them there for harming my people, for scattering my inheritance among the nations and dividing up my land.

3"They divided up my people as their slaves; they traded a young lad for a prostitute, and a little girl for wine enough to get drunk. 4Tyre and Sidon, don't you try to interfere! Are you trying to take revenge on me, you cities of Philistia? Beware, for I will strike back swiftly, and return the harm to your own heads.

5"You have taken my silver and gold and all my precious treasures and carried them off to your heathen temples. 6You have sold the people of Judah and Jerusalem to the Greeks, who took them far from their own land. 7But I will bring them back again from all these places you have sold them to, and I will pay you back for all that you have done. 8I will sell your sons and daughters to the people of Judah and they will sell them to the Sabeans far away. This is a promise from the Lord."

9Announce this far and wide: Get ready for war! Conscript your best soldiers; collect all your armies. 10Melt your plowshares into swords and beat your pruning hooks into spears. Let the weak be strong. 11Gather together and come, all nations everywhere.

And now, O Lord, bring down your warriors! 12Collect the nations; bring them to the Valley of Jehoshaphat, for there I will sit to pronounce judgment on them all. 13Now let the sickle do its work; the harvest is ripe and waiting. Tread the winepress, for it is full to overflowing with the wickedness of these men.

14Multitudes, multitudes waiting in the valley for the verdict of their doom! For the Day of the Lord is near, in the Valley of Judgment.

15The sun and moon will be darkened and the stars withdraw their light. 16The Lord shouts from his Temple

New Revised Standard

32Then everyone who calls on the name of the LORD shall be saved; for in Mount Zion and in Jerusalem there shall be those who escape, as the LORD has said, and among the survivors shall be those whom the LORD calls.

3c FOR THEN, in those days and at that time, when I restore the fortunes of Judah and Jerusalem, 2I will gather all the nations and bring them down to the valley of Jehoshaphat, and I will enter into judgment with them there, on account of my people and my heritage Israel, because they have scattered them among the nations. They have divided my land, 3and cast lots for my people, and traded boys for prostitutes, and sold girls for wine, and drunk it down.

4 What are you to me, O Tyre and Sidon, and all the regions of Philistia? Are you paying me back for something? If you are paying me back, I will turn your deeds back upon your own heads swiftly and speedily. 5For you have taken my silver and my gold, and have carried my rich treasures into your temples.d 6You have sold the people of Judah and Jerusalem to the Greeks, removing them far from their own border. 7But now I will rouse them to leave the places to which you have sold them, and I will turn your deeds back upon your own heads. 8I will sell your sons and your daughters into the hand of the people of Judah, and they will sell them to the Sabeans, to a nation far away; for the LORD has spoken.

Judgment in the Valley of Jehoshaphat

9 Proclaim this among the nations:
   Prepare war,e
      stir up the warriors.
   Let all the soldiers draw near,
      let them come up.
10 Beat your plowshares into swords,
      and your pruning hooks into spears;
      let the weakling say, "I am a warrior."

11 Come quickly,f
      all you nations all around,
      gather yourselves there.
   Bring down your warriors, O LORD.
12 Let the nations rouse themselves,
      and come up to the valley of Jehoshaphat;
   for there I will sit to judge
      all the neighboring nations.

13 Put in the sickle,
      for the harvest is ripe.
   Go in, tread,
      for the wine press is full.
   The vats overflow,
      for their wickedness is great.

14 Multitudes, multitudes,
      in the valley of decision!
   For the day of the LORD is near
      in the valley of decision.
15 The sun and the moon are darkened,
      and the stars withdraw their shining.

b 3:2 Valley Where Jehovah Judges, or, "Valley of Jehoshaphat."

c Ch 4.1 in Heb   d Or palaces   e Heb sanctify war   f Meaning of Heb uncertain

King James

16The LORD also shall roar out of Zion, and utter his voice from Jerusalem; and the heavens and the earth shall shake: but the LORD *will be* the hope of his people, and the strength of the children of Israel.

17So shall ye know that I *am* the LORD your God dwelling in Zion, my holy mountain: then shall Jerusalem be holy, and there shall no strangers pass through her any more.

18¶ And it shall come to pass in that day, *that* the mountains shall drop down new wine, and the hills shall flow with milk, and all the rivers of Judah shall flow with waters, and a fountain shall come forth of the house of the LORD, and shall water the valley of Shittim.

19Egypt shall be a desolation, and Edom shall be a desolate wilderness, for the violence *against* the children of Judah, because they have shed innocent blood in their land.

20But Judah shall dwell for ever, and Jerusalem from generation to generation.

21For I will cleanse their blood *that* I have not cleansed: for the LORD dwelleth in Zion.

New International

16The LORD will roar from Zion
  and thunder from Jerusalem;
  the earth and the sky will tremble.
But the LORD will be a refuge for his people,
  a stronghold for the people of Israel.

Blessings for God's People

17"Then you will know that I, the LORD your
    God,
  dwell in Zion, my holy hill.
Jerusalem will be holy;
  never again will foreigners invade her.

18"In that day the mountains will drip new wine,
  and the hills will flow with milk;
  all the ravines of Judah will run with water.
A fountain will flow out of the LORD's house
  and will water the valley of acacias.a

19But Egypt will be desolate,
  Edom a desert waste,
because of violence done to the people of
    Judah,
  in whose land they shed innocent blood.

20Judah will be inhabited forever
  and Jerusalem through all generations.

21Their bloodguilt, which I have not pardoned,
  I will pardon."

  The LORD dwells in Zion!

---

a *18 Or Valley of Shittim*

Living Bible

in Jerusalem and the earth and sky begin to shake. But to his people Israel, the Lord will be very gentle. He is their Refuge and Strength. 17"Then you shall know at last that I am the Lord your God in Zion, my holy mountain. Jerusalem shall be mine forever; the time will come when no foreign armies will pass through her any more.

18"Sweet wine will drip from the mountains, and the hills shall flow with milk. Water will fill the dry stream beds of Judah, and a fountain will burst forth from the Temple of the Lord to water Acacia Valley. 19Egypt will be destroyed, and Edom too, because of their violence against the Jews, for they killed innocent people in those nations.

20"But Israel will prosper forever, and Jerusalem will thrive as generations pass. 21For I will avenge the blood of my people; I will not clear their oppressors of guilt. For my home is in Jerusalem with my people."

New Revised Standard

16 The LORD roars from Zion,
and utters his voice from Jerusalem,
and the heavens and the earth shake.
But the LORD is a refuge for his people,
a stronghold for the people of Israel.

The Glorious Future of Judah

17 So you shall know that I, the LORD your God,
dwell in Zion, my holy mountain.
And Jerusalem shall be holy,
and strangers shall never again pass through
it.

18 In that day
the mountains shall drip sweet wine,
the hills shall flow with milk,
and all the stream beds of Judah
shall flow with water;
a fountain shall come forth from the house of
the LORD
and water the Wadi Shittim.

19 Egypt shall become a desolation
and Edom a desolate wilderness,
because of the violence done to the people of
Judah,
in whose land they have shed innocent
blood.
20 But Judah shall be inhabited forever,
and Jerusalem to all generations.
21 I will avenge their blood, and I will not clear
the guilty,b
for the LORD dwells in Zion.

---

b Gk Syr: Heb *I will hold innocent their blood that I have not held innocent*

Amos

Amos

1 THE WORDS of Amos, who was among the herdmen of Tekoa, which he saw concerning Israel in
the days of Uzziah king of Judah, and in the days of
Jeroboam the son of Joash king of Israel, two years
before the earthquake.

2And he said, the LORD will roar from Zion, and utter
his voice from Jerusalem; and the habitations of the
shepherds shall mourn, and the top of Carmel shall
wither.

3Thus saith the LORD; For three transgressions of Damascus, and for four, I will not turn away *the punishment* thereof; because they have threshed Gilead with
threshing instruments of iron:

4But I will send a fire into the house of Hazael, which
shall devour the palaces of Ben-hadad.

5I will break also the bar of Damascus, and cut off
the inhabitant from the plain of Aven, and him that
holdeth the sceptre from the house of Eden: and the
people of Syria shall go into captivity unto Kir, saith the
LORD.

6¶ Thus saith the LORD; For three transgressions of
Gaza, and for four, I will not turn away *the punishment*
thereof; because they carried away captive the whole
captivity, to deliver *them* up to Edom:

7But I will send a fire on the wall of Gaza, which shall
devour the palaces thereof:

8And I will cut off the inhabitant from Ashdod, and
him that holdeth the sceptre from Ashkelon, and I will
turn mine hand against Ekron: and the remnant of the
Philistines shall perish, saith the Lord GOD.

1 THE WORDS of Amos, one of the shepherds of
Tekoa—what he saw concerning Israel two years
before the earthquake, when Uzziah was king of Judah
and Jeroboam son of Jehoasha was king of Israel.

2He said:

"The LORD roars from Zion
    and thunders from Jerusalem;
the pastures of the shepherds dry up,b
    and the top of Carmel withers."

Judgment on Israel's Neighbors

3This is what the LORD says:

"For three sins of Damascus,
    even for four, I will not turn back ⌞my wrath⌟.
Because she threshed Gilead
    with sledges having iron teeth,
4I will send fire upon the house of Hazael
    that will consume the fortresses of
        Ben-Hadad.
5I will break down the gate of Damascus;
    I will destroy the king who is inc the Valley
        of Avend
and the one who holds the scepter in Beth
    Eden.
The people of Aram will go into exile to
    Kir,"
                            says the LORD.

6This is what the LORD says:

"For three sins of Gaza,
    even for four, I will not turn back ⌞my wrath⌟.
Because she took captive whole communities
    and sold them to Edom,
7I will send fire upon the walls of Gaza
    that will consume her fortresses.
8I will destroy the kinge of Ashdod
    and the one who holds the scepter in
        Ashkelon.
I will turn my hand against Ekron,
    till the last of the Philistines is dead,"
                    says the Sovereign LORD.

---

a *1* Hebrew *Joash,* a variant of *Jehoash*   b *2* Or *shepherds mourn*   c *5* Or
the inhabitants of   d *5* Aven means *wickedness.*   e *8* Or *inhabitants*

Living Bible

Amos

1 AMOS WAS a herdsman living in the village of Tekoa. [All day long he sat on the hillsides watching the sheep, keeping them from straying.]f

²One day, in a vision, God told him some of the things that were going to happen to his nation, Israel. This vision came to him at the time Uzziah was king of Judah, and while Jeroboam (son of Joash) was king of Israel—two years before the earthquake.

This is his report of what he saw and heard: The Lord roared—like a ferocious lion from his lair—from his Temple on Mount Zion. And suddenly the lush pastures of Mount Carmel withered and dried, and all the shepherds mourned.

³The Lord says, "The people of Damascus have sinned again and again, and I will not forget it. I will not leave her unpunished any more. For they have threshed my people in Gilead as grain is threshed with iron rods. ⁴So I will set fire to King Hazael's palace, destroying the strong fortress of Ben-hadad. ⁵I will snap the bars that locked the gates of Damascus, and kill her people as far away as the plain of Aven, and the people of Syria shall return to Kirᵍ as slaves." The Lord has spoken.

⁶The Lord says, "Gaza has sinned again and again, and I will not forget it. I will not leave her unpunished any more. For she sent my people into exile, selling them as slaves in Edom. ⁷So I will set fire to the walls of Gaza, and all her forts shall be destroyed. ⁸I will kill the people of Ashdod, and destroy Ekron and the king of Ashkelon; all Philistines left will perish." The Lord has spoken.

New Revised Standard

Amos

1 THE WORDS of Amos, who was among the shepherds of Tekoa, which he saw concerning Israel in the days of King Uzziah of Judah and in the days of King Jeroboam son of Joash of Israel, two yearsh before the earthquake.

Judgment on Israel's Neighbors

²And he said:

The LORD roars from Zion,
    and utters his voice from Jerusalem;
the pastures of the shepherds wither,
    and the top of Carmel dries up.

³ Thus says the LORD:
For three transgressions of Damascus,
    and for four, I will not revoke the
        punishment;i
because they have threshed Gilead
    with threshing sledges of iron.
⁴ So I will send a fire on the house of Hazael,
    and it shall devour the strongholds of
        Ben-hadad.
⁵ I will break the gate bars of Damascus,
    and cut off the inhabitants from the Valley
        of Aven,
and the one who holds the scepter from
        Beth-eden;
    and the people of Aram shall go into exile
        to Kir,
                        says the LORD.

⁶ Thus says the LORD:
For three transgressions of Gaza,
    and for four, I will not revoke the
        punishment;i
because they carried into exile entire
        communities,
    to hand them over to Edom.
⁷ So I will send a fire on the wall of Gaza,
    fire that shall devour its strongholds.
⁸ I will cut off the inhabitants from Ashdod,
    and the one who holds the scepter from
        Ashkelon;
I will turn my hand against Ekron,
    and the remnant of the Philistines shall
        perish,
                        says the Lord GOD.

---

f *1:1 All day long he sat . . . keeping them from straying,* implied. g *1:5 the people of Syria shall return to Kir.* Decreeing that the Syrians should go back to Kir as slaves was like saying to the Israelites that they must go back to Egypt as slaves, for the Syrians had made their exodus from Kir and now were free. (See 9:7.)

h Or *during two years* i Heb *cause it to return*

King James

9¶ Thus saith the LORD; For three transgressions of Tyrus, and for four, I will not turn away *the punishment* thereof; because they delivered up the whole captivity to Edom, and remembered not the brotherly covenant:

10But I will send a fire on the wall of Tyrus, which shall devour the palaces thereof.

11¶ Thus saith the LORD; For three transgressions of Edom, and for four, I will not turn away *the punishment* thereof; because he did pursue his brother with the sword, and did cast off all pity, and his anger did tear perpetually, and he kept his wrath for ever:

12But I will send a fire upon Teman, which shall devour the palaces of Bozrah.

13¶ Thus saith the LORD; For three transgressions of the children of Ammon, and for four, I will not turn away *the punishment* thereof; because they have ripped up the women with child of Gilead, that they might enlarge their border:

14But I will kindle a fire in the wall of Rabbah, and it shall devour the palaces thereof, with shouting in the day of battle, with a tempest in the day of the whirlwind:

15And their king shall go into captivity, he and his princes together, saith the LORD.

2 THUS SAITH the LORD; For three transgressions of Moab, and for four, I will not turn away *the punishment* thereof; because he burned the bones of the king of Edom into lime:

2But I will send a fire upon Moab, and it shall devour the palaces of Kirioth: and Moab shall die with tumult, with shouting, *and* with the sound of the trumpet:

3And I will cut off the judge from the midst thereof, and will slay all the princes thereof with him, saith the LORD.

4¶ Thus saith the LORD; For three transgressions of Judah, and for four, I will not turn away *the punishment* thereof; because they have despised the law of the LORD, and have not kept his commandments, and their lies caused them to err, after the which their fathers have walked:

5But I will send a fire upon Judah, and it shall devour the palaces of Jerusalem.

New International

9This is what the LORD says:

"For three sins of Tyre,
　even for four, I will not turn back ⌐my wrath⌐.
Because she sold whole communities of captives
　to Edom,
　disregarding a treaty of brotherhood,
10I will send fire upon the walls of Tyre
　that will consume her fortresses."

11This is what the LORD says:

"For three sins of Edom,
　even for four, I will not turn back ⌐my wrath⌐.
Because he pursued his brother with a sword,
　stifling all compassion,[a]
because his anger raged continually
　and his fury flamed unchecked,
12I will send fire upon Teman
　that will consume the fortresses of Bozrah."

13This is what the LORD says:

"For three sins of Ammon,
　even for four, I will not turn back ⌐my wrath⌐.
Because he ripped open the pregnant women of
　Gilead
in order to extend his borders,
14I will set fire to the walls of Rabbah
　that will consume her fortresses
amid war cries on the day of battle,
　amid violent winds on a stormy day.
15Her king[b] will go into exile,
　he and his officials together,"
　　　　　　　　　　　　　　says the LORD.

2 THIS IS what the LORD says:

"For three sins of Moab,
　even for four, I will not turn back ⌐my wrath⌐.
Because he burned, as if to lime,
　the bones of Edom's king,
2I will send fire upon Moab
　that will consume the fortresses of Kerioth.[c]
Moab will go down in great tumult
　amid war cries and the blast of the trumpet.
3I will destroy her ruler
　and kill all her officials with him,"
　　　　　　　　　　　　　　says the LORD.

4This is what the LORD says:

"For three sins of Judah,
　even for four, I will not turn back ⌐my wrath⌐.
Because they have rejected the law of the LORD
　and have not kept his decrees,
because they have been led astray by false
　gods,[d]
　the gods[e] their ancestors followed,
5I will send fire upon Judah
　that will consume the fortresses of
　Jerusalem."

a 11 Or *sword* / *and destroyed his allies*　b 15 Or / *Molech*; Hebrew *malcam*
c 2 Or *of her cities*　d 4 Or *by lies*　e 4 Or *lies*

Living Bible

9The Lord says, "The people of Tyre have sinned again and again and I will not forget it. I will not leave them unpunished any more. For they broke their treaty with their brother, Israel; they attacked and conquered him, and led him into slavery to Edom. 10So I will set fire to the walls of Tyre, and it will burn down all his forts and palaces."

11The Lord says, "Edom has sinned again and again, and I will not forget it. I will not leave him unpunished any more. For he chased his brother, Israel, with the sword; he was pitiless in unrelenting anger. 12So I will set fire to Teman, and it will burn down all the forts of Bozrah."f

13The Lord says, "The people of Ammon have sinned again and again, and I will not forget it. I will not leave them unpunished any more. For in their wars in Gilead to enlarge their borders, they committed cruel crimes, ripping open pregnant women with their swords.

14"So I will set fire to the walls of Rabbah, and it will burn down their forts and palaces; there will be wild shouts of battle like a whirlwind in a mighty storm. 15And their king and his princes will go into exile together." The Lord has spoken.

2 THE LORD says, "The people of Moab have sinned again and again, and I will not forget it. I will not leave them unpunished any more. For they desecrated the tombs of the kings of Edom, with no respect for the dead. 2Now in return I will send fire upon Moab, and it will destroy all the palaces in Kerioth. Moab shall go down in tumult as the warriors shout and trumpets blare. 3And I will destroy their king and slay all the leaders under him." The Lord has spoken.

4The Lord says, "The people of Judah have sinned again and again, and I will not forget it. I will not leave them unpunished any more. For they have rejected the laws of God, refusing to obey him. They have hardened their hearts and sinned as their fathers did. 5So I will destroy Judah with fire, and burn down all Jerusalem's palaces and forts."

New Revised Standard

9 Thus says the LORD:
   For three transgressions of Tyre,
      and for four, I will not revoke the
         punishment;g
   because they delivered entire communities
         over to Edom,
      and did not remember the covenant of
         kinship.
10 So I will send a fire on the wall of Tyre,
      fire that shall devour its strongholds.

11 Thus says the LORD:
   For three transgressions of Edom,
      and for four, I will not revoke the
         punishment;g
   because he pursued his brother with the sword
      and cast off all pity;
   he maintained his anger perpetually,h
      and kept his wrathi forever.
12 So I will send a fire on Teman,
      and it shall devour the strongholds of
         Bozrah.

13 Thus says the LORD:
   For three transgressions of the Ammonites,
      and for four, I will not revoke the
         punishment;g
   because they have ripped open pregnant
         women in Gilead
      in order to enlarge their territory.
14 So I will kindle a fire against the wall of
         Rabbah,
      fire that shall devour its strongholds,
   with shouting on the day of battle,
      with a storm on the day of the whirlwind;
15 then their king shall go into exile,
      he and his officials together,
                              says the LORD.

2 THUS SAYS the LORD:
   For three transgressions of Moab,
      and for four, I will not revoke the
         punishment;g
   because he burned to lime
      the bones of the king of Edom.
2 So I will send a fire on Moab,
      and it shall devour the strongholds of
         Kerioth,
   and Moab shall die amid uproar,
      amid shouting and the sound of the trumpet;
3 I will cut off the ruler from its midst,
      and will kill all its officials with him,
                              says the LORD.

Judgment on Judah

4 Thus says the LORD:
   For three transgressions of Judah,
      and for four, I will not revoke the
         punishment;g
   because they have rejected the law of the
         LORD,
      and have not kept his statutes,
   but they have been led astray by the same lies
      after which their ancestors walked.
5 So I will send a fire on Judah,
      and it shall devour the strongholds of
         Jerusalem.

---

f 1:12 Teman and Bozrah. Teman was in the north of Edom, and Bozrah in the south. The entire country was to be devastated.

g Heb cause it to return   h Syr Vg: Heb and his anger tore perpetually   i Gk Syr Vg: Heb and his wrath kept

King James

6¶ Thus saith the LORD; For three transgressions of Israel, and for four, I will not turn away *the punishment* thereof; because they sold the righteous for silver, and the poor for a pair of shoes;

7That pant after the dust of the earth on the head of the poor, and turn aside the way of the meek: and a man and his father will go in unto the *same* maid, to profane my holy name:

8And they lay *themselves* down upon clothes laid to pledge by every altar, and they drink the wine of the condemned *in* the house of their god.

9¶ Yet destroyed I the Amorite before them, whose height *was* like the height of the cedars, and he *was* strong as the oaks; yet I destroyed his fruit from above, and his roots from beneath.

10Also I brought you up from the land of Egypt, and led you forty years through the wilderness, to possess the land of the Amorite.

11And I raised up of your sons for prophets, and of your young men for Nazarites. *Is it* not even thus, O ye children of Israel? saith the LORD.

12But ye gave the Nazarites wine to drink; and commanded the prophets, saying, Prophesy not.

13Behold, I am pressed under you, as a cart is pressed *that is* full of sheaves.

14Therefore the flight shall perish from the swift, and the strong shall not strengthen his force, neither shall the mighty deliver himself:

15Neither shall he stand that handleth the bow; and *he that is* swift of foot shall not deliver *himself:* neither shall he that rideth the horse deliver himself.

16And *he that is* courageous among the mighty shall flee away naked in that day, saith the LORD.

3 HEAR THIS word that the LORD hath spoken against you, O children of Israel, against the whole family which I brought up from the land of Egypt, saying,

2You only have I known of all the families of the earth: therefore I will punish you for all your iniquities.

3Can two walk together, except they be agreed?

4Will a lion roar in the forest, when he hath no prey? will a young lion cry out of his den, if he have taken nothing?

New International

Judgment on Israel

6This is what the LORD says:

"For three sins of Israel,
    even for four, I will not turn back ˌmy wrathˌ.
They sell the righteous for silver,
    and the needy for a pair of sandals.
7They trample on the heads of the poor
    as upon the dust of the ground
    and deny justice to the oppressed.
Father and son use the same girl
    and so profane my holy name.
8They lie down beside every altar
    on garments taken in pledge.
In the house of their god
    they drink wine taken as fines.

9"I destroyed the Amorite before them,
    though he was tall as the cedars
    and strong as the oaks.
I destroyed his fruit above
    and his roots below.
10"I brought you up out of Egypt,
    and I led you forty years in the desert
    to give you the land of the Amorites.
11I also raised up prophets from among your sons
    and Nazirites from among your young men.
Is this not true, people of Israel?"
                    declares the LORD.
12"But you made the Nazirites drink wine
    and commanded the prophets not to prophesy.

13"Now then, I will crush you
    as a cart crushes when loaded with grain.
14The swift will not escape,
    the strong will not muster their strength,
    and the warrior will not save his life.
15The archer will not stand his ground,
    the fleet-footed soldier will not get away,
    and the horseman will not save his life.
16Even the bravest warriors
    will flee naked on that day,"
                    declares the LORD.

Witnesses Summoned Against Israel

3 HEAR THIS word the LORD has spoken against you, O people of Israel—against the whole family I brought up out of Egypt:

2"You only have I chosen
    of all the families of the earth;
therefore I will punish you
    for all your sins."

3Do two walk together
    unless they have agreed to do so?
4Does a lion roar in the thicket
    when he has no prey?
Does he growl in his den
    when he has caught nothing?

Living Bible

6The Lord says, "The people of Israel have sinned again and again, and I will not forget it. I will not leave them unpunished any more. For they have perverted justice by accepting bribes, and sold into slavery the poor who can't repay their debts; they trade them for a pair of shoes. 7They trample the poor in the dust and kick aside the meek.

"And a man and his father defile the same temple-girl, corrupting my holy name. 8At their religious feasts they lounge in clothing stolen from their debtors, and in my own Temple they offer sacrifices of wine they purchased with stolen money.

9"Yet think of all I did for them! I cleared the land of the Amorites before them—the Amorites, as tall as cedar trees, and strong as oaks! But I lopped off their fruit and cut their roots. 10And I brought you out from Egypt and led you through the desert forty years, to possess the land of the Amorites. 11And I chose your sons to be Nazirites[a] and prophets—can you deny this, Israel?" asks the Lord. 12"But you caused the Nazirites to sin by urging them to drink your wine, and you silenced my prophets, telling them, 'Shut up!'

13"Therefore I will make you groan as a wagon groans that is loaded with sheaves. 14Your swiftest warriors will stumble in flight. The strong will all be weak, and the great ones can no longer save themselves. 15The archer's aim will fail, the swiftest runners won't be fast enough to flee, and even the best of horsemen can't outrun the danger then. 16The most courageous of your mighty men will drop their weapons and run for their lives that day." The Lord God has spoken.

3 LISTEN! THIS is your doom! It is spoken by the Lord against both Israel and Judah—against the entire family I brought from Egypt:

2"Of all the peoples of the earth, I have chosen you alone. That is why I must punish you the more for all your sins. 3For how can we walk together with your sins between us?

4"Would I be roaring as a lion unless I had a reason? The fact is, I am getting ready to destroy you. Even a young lion, when it growls, shows it is ready for its food. 5A trap doesn't snap shut unless it is stepped on;

New Revised Standard

Judgment on Israel

6 Thus says the LORD:
   For three transgressions of Israel,
      and for four, I will not revoke the
         punishment;[b]
   because they sell the righteous for silver,
      and the needy for a pair of sandals—
7 they who trample the head of the poor into the
         dust of the earth,
      and push the afflicted out of the way;
   father and son go in to the same girl,
      so that my holy name is profaned;
8 they lay themselves down beside every altar
      on garments taken in pledge;
   and in the house of their God they drink
      wine bought with fines they imposed.

9 Yet I destroyed the Amorite before them,
      whose height was like the height of cedars,
      and who was as strong as oaks;
   I destroyed his fruit above,
      and his roots beneath.
10 Also I brought you up out of the land of
         Egypt,
      and led you forty years in the wilderness,
      to possess the land of the Amorite.
11 And I raised up some of your children to be
         prophets
      and some of your youths to be nazirites.[c]
   Is it not indeed so, O people of Israel?
                                        says the LORD.

12 But you made the nazirites[c] drink wine,
      and commanded the prophets,
      saying, "You shall not prophesy."

13 So, I will press you down in your place,
      just as a cart presses down
         when it is full of sheaves.[d]
14 Flight shall perish from the swift,
      and the strong shall not retain their strength,
      nor shall the mighty save their lives;
15 those who handle the bow shall not stand,
      and those who are swift of foot shall not
         save themselves,
      nor shall those who ride horses save their
         lives;
16 and those who are stout of heart among the
         mighty
      shall flee away naked in that day,
                                        says the LORD.

Israel's Guilt and Punishment

3 HEAR THIS word that the LORD has spoken against you, O people of Israel, against the whole family that I brought up out of the land of Egypt:
2 You only have I known
      of all the families of the earth;
   therefore I will punish you
      for all your iniquities.

3 Do two walk together
      unless they have made an appointment?
4 Does a lion roar in the forest,
      when it has no prey?
   Does a young lion cry out from its den,
      if it has caught nothing?

---

a 2:11 to be Nazirites, see Num 6.

b Heb *cause it to return*   c That is, *those separated* or *those consecrated*
d Meaning of Heb uncertain

King James

5Can a bird fall in a snare upon the earth, where no gin *is* for him? shall *one* take up a snare from the earth, and have taken nothing at all?

6Shall a trumpet be blown in the city, and the people not be afraid? shall there be evil in a city, and the LORD hath not done *it?*

7Surely the Lord GOD will do nothing, but he revealeth his secret unto his servants the prophets.

8The lion hath roared, who will not fear? the Lord GOD hath spoken, who can but prophesy?

9¶ Publish in the palaces at Ashdod, and in the palaces in the land of Egypt, and say, Assemble yourselves upon the mountains of Samaria, and behold the great tumults in the midst thereof, and the oppressed in the midst thereof.

10For they know not to do right, saith the LORD, who store up violence and robbery in their palaces.

11Therefore thus saith the Lord GOD; An adversary *there shall be* even round about the land; and he shall bring down thy strength from thee, and thy palaces shall be spoiled.

12Thus saith the LORD; As the shepherd taketh out of the mouth of the lion two legs, or a piece of an ear; so shall the children of Israel be taken out that dwell in Samaria in the corner of a bed, and in Damascus *in* a couch.

13Hear ye, and testify in the house of Jacob, saith the Lord GOD, the God of hosts,

14That in the day that I shall visit the transgressions of Israel upon him I will also visit the altars of Beth-el: and the horns of the altar shall be cut off, and fall to ground.

15And I will smite the winter house with the summer house; and the houses of ivory shall perish, and the great houses shall have an end, saith the LORD.

4 HEAR THIS word, ye kine of Bashan, that *are* in the mountain of Samaria, which oppress the poor, which crush the needy, which say to their masters, Bring, and let us drink.

2The Lord GOD hath sworn by his holiness, that, lo, the days shall come upon you, that he will take you away with hooks, and your posterity with fishhooks.

3And ye shall go out at the breaches, every *cow at that which is* before her; and ye shall cast *them* into the palace, saith the LORD.

New International

5Does a bird fall into a trap on the ground
  where no snare has been set?
Does a trap spring up from the earth
  when there is nothing to catch?
6When a trumpet sounds in a city,
  do not the people tremble?
When disaster comes to a city,
  has not the LORD caused it?

7Surely the Sovereign LORD does nothing
  without revealing his plan
  to his servants the prophets.

8The lion has roared—
  who will not fear?
The Sovereign LORD has spoken—
  who can but prophesy?

9Proclaim to the fortresses of Ashdod
  and to the fortresses of Egypt:
"Assemble yourselves on the mountains of
    Samaria;
  see the great unrest within her
  and the oppression among her people."

10"They do not know how to do right," declares
    the LORD,
  "who hoard plunder and loot in their
    fortresses."

11Therefore this is what the Sovereign LORD says:

"An enemy will overrun the land;
  he will pull down your strongholds
  and plunder your fortresses."

12This is what the LORD says:

"As a shepherd saves from the lion's mouth
  only two leg bones or a piece of an ear,
so will the Israelites be saved,
  those who sit in Samaria
on the edge of their beds
  and in Damascus on their couches.a"

13"Hear this and testify against the house of Jacob," declares the Lord, the LORD God Almighty.

14"On the day I punish Israel for her sins,
  I will destroy the altars of Bethel;
the horns of the altar will be cut off
  and fall to the ground.
15I will tear down the winter house
  along with the summer house;
the houses adorned with ivory will be destroyed
  and the mansions will be demolished,"
                    declares the LORD.

Israel Has Not Returned to God

4 HEAR THIS word, you cows of Bashan on
    Mount Samaria,
  you women who oppress the poor and crush
    the needy
  and say to your husbands, "Bring us some
    drinks!"
2The Sovereign LORD has sworn by his holiness:
  "The time will surely come
when you will be taken away with hooks,
  the last of you with fishhooks.
3You will each go straight out
  through breaks in the wall,
  and you will be cast out toward Harmon,b"
                    declares the LORD.

a *12* The meaning of the Hebrew for this line is uncertain.   b *3* Masoretic Text; with a different word division of the Hebrew (see Septuagint) *out, O mountain of oppression*

Living Bible

your punishment is well deserved. 6The alarm has sounded—listen and fear! For I, the Lord, am sending disaster into your land.

7"But always, first of all, I warn you through my prophets. This I now have done."

8The Lion has roared—tremble in fear. The Lord God has sounded your doom—I dare not refuse to proclaim it.

9Call together the Assyrian and Egyptian leaders, saying, "Take your seats now on the mountains of Samaria to witness the scandalous spectacle of all Israel's crimes. 10My people have forgotten what it means to do right," says the Lord. "Their beautiful homes are full of the loot from their thefts and banditry. 11Therefore," the Lord God says, "an enemy is coming! He is surrounding them and will shatter their forts and plunder those beautiful homes."

12The Lord says, "A shepherd tried to rescue his sheep from a lion, but it was too late; he snatched from the lion's mouth two legs and a piece of ear. So it will be when the Israelites in Samaria are finally rescued—all they will have left is half a chair and a tattered pillow.

13"Listen to this announcement, and publish it throughout all Israel," says the Lord, the Lord Almighty: 14"On the same day that I punish Israel for her sins, I will also destroy the idol altars at Bethel. The horns of the altar will be cut off and fall to the ground.

15"And I will destroy the beautiful homes of the wealthy—their winter mansions and their summer houses, too—and demolish their ivory palaces."

4 LISTEN TO me, you "fat cows" of Bashan living in Samaria—you women who encourage your husbands to rob the poor and crush the needy—you who never have enough to drink! 2The Lord God has sworn by his holiness that the time will come when he will put hooks in your noses and lead you away like the cattle you are; they will drag the last of you away with fishhooks! 3You will be hauled from your beautiful homes and tossed out through the nearest breach in the wall. The Lord has said it.

New Revised Standard

5 Does a bird fall into a snare on the earth,
   when there is no trap for it?
Does a snare spring up from the ground,
   when it has taken nothing?
6 Is a trumpet blown in a city,
   and the people are not afraid?
Does disaster befall a city,
   unless the LORD has done it?
7 Surely the Lord GOD does nothing,
   without revealing his secret
   to his servants the prophets.
8 The lion has roared;
   who will not fear?
The Lord GOD has spoken;
   who can but prophesy?

9 Proclaim to the strongholds in Ashdod,
   and to the strongholds in the land of Egypt,
and say, "Assemble yourselves on Mount[c]
      Samaria,
   and see what great tumults are within it,
   and what oppressions are in its midst."
10 They do not know how to do right, says the
      LORD,
   those who store up violence and robbery in
      their strongholds.
11 Therefore thus says the Lord GOD:
An adversary shall surround the land,
   and strip you of your defense;
   and your strongholds shall be plundered.

12 Thus says the LORD: As the shepherd rescues from the mouth of the lion two legs, or a piece of an ear, so shall the people of Israel who live in Samaria be rescued, with the corner of a couch and part[d] of a bed.

13 Hear, and testify against the house of Jacob,
   says the Lord GOD, the God of hosts:
14 On the day I punish Israel for its
      transgressions,
   I will punish the altars of Bethel,
and the horns of the altar shall be cut off
   and fall to the ground.
15 I will tear down the winter house as well as
      the summer house;
   and the houses of ivory shall perish,
and the great houses[e] shall come to an end,
                              says the LORD.

4 HEAR THIS word, you cows of Bashan
   who are on Mount Samaria,
who oppress the poor, who crush the needy,
   who say to their husbands, "Bring
      something to drink!"
2 The Lord GOD has sworn by his holiness:
   The time is surely coming upon you,
when they shall take you away with hooks,
   even the last of you with fishhooks.
3 Through breaches in the wall you shall leave,
   each one straight ahead;
   and you shall be flung out into Harmon,[d]
                              says the LORD.

c Gk Syr: Heb the mountains of   d Meaning of Heb uncertain   e Or many houses

King James

4¶ Come to Beth-el, and transgress; at Gilgal multiply transgression; and bring your sacrifices every morning, *and* your tithes after three years:

5And offer a sacrifice of thanksgiving with leaven, and proclaim *and* publish the free offerings: for this liketh you, O ye children of Israel, saith the Lord God.

6¶ And I also have given you cleanness of teeth in all your cities, and want of bread in all your places: yet have ye not returned unto me, saith the Lord.

7And also I have withholden the rain from you, when *there were* yet three months to the harvest: and I caused it to rain upon one city, and caused it not to rain upon another city: one piece was rained upon, and the piece whereupon it rained not withered.

8So two *or* three cities wandered unto one city, to drink water; but they were not satisfied: yet have ye not returned unto me, saith the Lord.

9I have smitten you with blasting and mildew: when your gardens and your vineyards and your fig trees and your olive trees increased, the palmerworm devoured *them*: yet have ye not returned unto me, saith the Lord.

10I have sent among you the pestilence after the manner of Egypt: your young men have I slain with the sword, and have taken away your horses; and I have made the stink of your camps to come up unto your nostrils: yet have ye not returned unto me, saith the Lord.

11I have overthrown *some* of you, as God overthrew Sodom and Gomorrah, and ye were as a firebrand plucked out of the burning: yet have ye not returned unto me, saith the Lord.

12Therefore thus will I do unto thee, O Israel: *and* because I will do this unto thee, prepare to meet thy God, O Israel.

13For, lo, he that formeth the mountains, and createth the wind, and declareth unto man what *is* his thought, that maketh the morning darkness, and treadeth upon the high places of the earth, The Lord, The God of hosts, *is* his name.

New International

4"Go to Bethel and sin;
  go to Gilgal and sin yet more.
Bring your sacrifices every morning,
  your tithes every three years.a
5Burn leavened bread as a thank offering
  and brag about your freewill offerings—
boast about them, you Israelites,
  for this is what you love to do,"
        declares the Sovereign Lord.

6"I gave you empty stomachsb in every city
  and lack of bread in every town,
  yet you have not returned to me,"
        declares the Lord.

7"I also withheld rain from you
  when the harvest was still three months away.
I sent rain on one town,
  but withheld it from another.
One field had rain;
  another had none and dried up.
8People staggered from town to town for water
  but did not get enough to drink,
  yet you have not returned to me,"
        declares the Lord.

9"Many times I struck your gardens and
    vineyards,
  I struck them with blight and mildew.
Locusts devoured your fig and olive trees,
  yet you have not returned to me,"
        declares the Lord.

10"I sent plagues among you
  as I did to Egypt.
I killed your young men with the sword,
  along with your captured horses.
I filled your nostrils with the stench of your
    camps,
  yet you have not returned to me,"
        declares the Lord.

11"I overthrew some of you
  as Ic overthrew Sodom and Gomorrah.
You were like a burning stick snatched from the
    fire,
  yet you have not returned to me,"
        declares the Lord.

12"Therefore this is what I will do to you, Israel,
  and because I will do this to you,
  prepare to meet your God, O Israel."

13He who forms the mountains,
  creates the wind,
  and reveals his thoughts to man,
he who turns dawn to darkness,
  and treads the high places of the earth—
  the Lord God Almighty is his name.

a 4 Or *tithes on the third day*   b 6 Hebrew *you cleanness of teeth*
c 11 Hebrew *God*

Living Bible

⁴Go ahead and sacrifice to idols at Bethel and Gilgal. Keep disobeying—your sins are mounting up. Sacrifice each morning and bring your tithes twice a week! ⁵Go through all your proper forms and give extra offerings. How you pride yourselves and crow about it everywhere!

⁶"I sent you hunger," says the Lord, "but it did no good; you still would not return to me. ⁷I ruined your crops by holding back the rain three months before the harvest. I sent rain on one city, but not another. While rain fell on one field, another was dry and withered. ⁸People from two or three cities would make their weary journey for a drink of water to a city that had rain, but there wasn't ever enough. Yet you wouldn't return to me," says the Lord.

⁹"I sent blight and mildew on your farms and your vineyards; the locusts ate your figs and olive trees. And still you wouldn't return to me," says the Lord. ¹⁰"I sent you plagues like those of Egypt long ago. I killed your lads in war and drove away your horses. The stench of death was terrible to smell. And yet you refused to come. ¹¹I destroyed some of your cities, as I did Sodom and Gomorrah; those left are like half-burned firebrands snatched away from fire. And still you won't return to me," says the Lord.

¹²"Therefore I will bring upon you all these further evils I have spoken of. Prepare to meet your God in judgment, Israel. ¹³For you are dealing with the one who formed the mountains and made the winds, and knows your every thought; he turns the morning to darkness and crushes down the mountains underneath his feet: Jehovah, the Lord, the Lord Almighty, is his name."

New Revised Standard

4 Come to Bethel—and transgress;
    to Gilgal—and multiply transgression;
  bring your sacrifices every morning,
    your tithes every three days;
5 bring a thank offering of leavened bread,
    and proclaim freewill offerings, publish
    them;
  for so you love to do, O people of Israel!
                says the Lord GOD.

Israel Rejects Correction

6 I gave you cleanness of teeth in all your
    cities,
  and lack of bread in all your places,
  yet you did not return to me,
                says the LORD.

7 And I also withheld the rain from you
    when there were still three months to the
    harvest;
  I would send rain on one city,
    and send no rain on another city;
  one field would be rained upon,
    and the field on which it did not rain
    withered;
8 so two or three towns wandered to one town
    to drink water, and were not satisfied;
  yet you did not return to me,
                says the LORD.

9 I struck you with blight and mildew;
  I laid waste[d] your gardens and your
    vineyards;
  the locust devoured your fig trees and your
    olive trees;
  yet you did not return to me,
                says the LORD.

10 I sent among you a pestilence after the manner
    of Egypt;
  I killed your young men with the sword;
  I carried away your horses;[e]
  and I made the stench of your camp go up
    into your nostrils;
  yet you did not return to me,
                says the LORD.

11 I overthrew some of you,
    as when God overthrew Sodom and
    Gomorrah,
  and you were like a brand snatched from
    the fire;
  yet you did not return to me,
                says the LORD.

12 Therefore thus I will do to you, O Israel;
  because I will do this to you,
  prepare to meet your God, O Israel!

13 For lo, the one who forms the mountains,
    creates the wind,
  reveals his thoughts to mortals,
  makes the morning darkness,
  and treads on the heights of the earth—
  the LORD, the God of hosts, is his name!

---

d Cn: Heb *the multitude of*   e Heb *with the captivity of your horses*

King James

5 HEAR YE this word which I take up against you, *even* a lamentation, O house of Israel.

²The virgin of Israel is fallen; she shall no more rise: she is forsaken upon her land; *there is* none to raise her up.

³For thus saith the Lord God; The city that went out *by* a thousand shall leave an hundred, and that which went forth *by* an hundred shall leave ten, to the house of Israel.

⁴¶ For thus saith the Lord unto the house of Israel, Seek ye me, and ye shall live:

⁵But seek not Beth-el, nor enter into Gilgal, and pass not to Beer-sheba: for Gilgal shall surely go into captivity, and Beth-el shall come to nought.

⁶Seek the Lord, and ye shall live; lest he break out like fire in the house of Joseph, and devour *it,* and *there* be none to quench *it* in Beth-el.

⁷Ye who turn judgment to wormwood, and leave off righteousness in the earth,

⁸*Seek him* that maketh the seven stars and Orion, and turneth the shadow of death into the morning, and maketh the day dark with night: that calleth for the waters of the sea, and poureth them out upon the face of the earth: The Lord *is* his name:

⁹That strengtheneth the spoiled against the strong, so that the spoiled shall come against the fortress.

¹⁰They hate him that rebuketh in the gate, and they abhor him that speaketh uprightly.

¹¹Forasmuch therefore as your treading *is* upon the poor, and ye take from him burdens of wheat: ye have built houses of hewn stone, but ye shall not dwell in them; ye have planted pleasant vineyards, but ye shall not drink wine of them.

¹²For I know your manifold transgressions and your mighty sins: they afflict the just, they take a bribe, and they turn aside the poor in the gate *from their right.*

¹³Therefore the prudent shall keep silence in that time; for it *is* an evil time.

¹⁴Seek good, and not evil, that ye may live: and so the Lord, the God of hosts, shall be with you, as ye have spoken.

¹⁵Hate the evil, and love the good, and establish judgment in the gate: it may be that the Lord God of hosts will be gracious unto the remnant of Joseph.

New International

A Lament and Call to Repentance

5 HEAR THIS word, O house of Israel, this lament I take up concerning you:

²"Fallen is Virgin Israel,
    never to rise again,
deserted in her own land,
    with no one to lift her up."

³This is what the Sovereign Lord says:

"The city that marches out a thousand strong for Israel
    will have only a hundred left;
the town that marches out a hundred strong
    will have only ten left."

⁴This is what the Lord says to the house of Israel:

"Seek me and live;
⁵ do not seek Bethel,
do not go to Gilgal,
    do not journey to Beersheba.
For Gilgal will surely go into exile,
    and Bethel will be reduced to nothing.ᵃ"
⁶Seek the Lord and live,
    or he will sweep through the house of Joseph
        like a fire;
it will devour,
    and Bethel will have no one to quench it.

⁷You who turn justice into bitterness
    and cast righteousness to the ground
⁸(he who made the Pleiades and Orion,
    who turns blackness into dawn
    and darkens day into night,
who calls for the waters of the sea
    and pours them out over the face of the
        land—
    the Lord is his name—
⁹he flashes destruction on the stronghold
    and brings the fortified city to ruin),
¹⁰you hate the one who reproves in court
    and despise him who tells the truth.

¹¹You trample on the poor
    and force him to give you grain.
Therefore, though you have built stone
        mansions,
    you will not live in them;
though you have planted lush vineyards,
    you will not drink their wine.
¹²For I know how many are your offenses
    and how great your sins.

You oppress the righteous and take bribes
    and you deprive the poor of justice in the
        courts.
¹³Therefore the prudent man keeps quiet in such
        times,
    for the times are evil.

¹⁴Seek good, not evil,
    that you may live.
Then the Lord God Almighty will be with you,
    just as you say he is.
¹⁵Hate evil, love good;
    maintain justice in the courts.
Perhaps the Lord God Almighty will have
        mercy
    on the remnant of Joseph.

ᵃ 5 Or *grief;* or *wickedness;* Hebrew *aven,* a reference to Beth Aven (a derogatory name for Bethel)

Living Bible

5 SADLY I sing this song of grief for you, O Israel: 2"Beautiful Israel lies broken and crushed upon the ground and cannot rise. No one will help her. She is left alone to die." 3For the Lord God says, "The city that sends a thousand men to battle, a hundred will return. The city that sends a hundred, only ten will come back alive."

4The Lord says to the people of Israel, "Seek me—and live. 5Don't seek the idols of Bethel, Gilgal, or Beer-sheba; for the people of Gilgal will be carried off to exile, and those of Bethel shall surely come to grief."

6Seek the Lord and live, or else he will sweep like fire through Israel and consume her, and none of the idols in Bethel can put it out.

7O evil men, you make "justice" a bitter pill for the poor and oppressed. "Righteousness" and "fair play" are meaningless fictions to you!

8Seek him who created the Seven Stars and the constellation Orion, who turns darkness into morning, and day into night, who calls forth the water from the ocean and pours it out as rain upon the land. The Lord, Jehovah, is his name. 9With blinding speed and violence he brings destruction on the strong, breaking all defenses.

10How you hate honest judges! How you despise people who tell the truth! 11You trample the poor and steal their smallest crumb by all your taxes, fines, and usury; therefore you will never live in the beautiful stone houses you are building, nor drink the wine from the lush vineyards you are planting.

12For many and great are your sins. I know them all so well. You are the enemies of everything good; you take bribes; you refuse justice to the poor. 13Therefore those who are wise will not try to interfere with the Lord in the dread day of your punishment.

14Be good, flee evil—and live! Then the Lord, the Lord Almighty, will truly be your Helper, as you have claimed he is. 15Hate evil and love the good; remodel your courts into true halls of justice. Perhaps even yet the Lord God of Hosts will have mercy on his people who remain.

New Revised Standard

A Lament for Israel's Sin

5 HEAR THIS word that I take up over you in lamentation, O house of Israel:

2 Fallen, no more to rise,
  is maiden Israel;
forsaken on her land,
  with no one to raise her up.

3 For thus says the Lord GOD:
The city that marched out a thousand
  shall have a hundred left,
and that which marched out a hundred
  shall have ten left.b

4 For thus says the LORD to the house of Israel:
Seek me and live;
5   but do not seek Bethel,
and do not enter into Gilgal
  or cross over to Beer-sheba;
for Gilgal shall surely go into exile,
  and Bethel shall come to nothing.

6 Seek the LORD and live,
  or he will break out against the house of
    Joseph like fire,
  and it will devour Bethel, with no one to
    quench it.
7 Ah, you that turn justice to wormwood,
  and bring righteousness to the ground!

8 The one who made the Pleiades and Orion,
  and turns deep darkness into the morning,
  and darkens the day into night,
who calls for the waters of the sea,
  and pours them out on the surface of the
    earth,
the LORD is his name,
9 who makes destruction flash out against the
    strong,
  so that destruction comes upon the fortress.

10 They hate the one who reproves in the gate,
  and they abhor the one who speaks the
    truth.
11 Therefore because you trample on the poor
  and take from them levies of grain,
you have built houses of hewn stone,
  but you shall not live in them;
you have planted pleasant vineyards,
  but you shall not drink their wine.
12 For I know how many are your transgressions,
  and how great are your sins—
you who afflict the righteous, who take a
    bribe,
  and push aside the needy in the gate.
13 Therefore the prudent will keep silent in such
    a time;
  for it is an evil time.

14 Seek good and not evil,
  that you may live;
and so the LORD, the God of hosts, will be
    with you,
  just as you have said.
15 Hate evil and love good,
  and establish justice in the gate;
it may be that the LORD, the God of hosts,
  will be gracious to the remnant of Joseph.

b Heb adds *to the house of Israel*

King James

16Therefore the LORD, the God of hosts, the Lord, saith thus; Wailing *shall be* in all streets; and they shall say in all the highways, Alas! alas! and they shall call the husbandman to mourning, and such as are skilful of lamentation to Wailing.

17And in all vineyards *shall be* wailing: for I will pass through thee, saith the LORD.

18Woe unto you that desire the day of the LORD! to what end *is* it for you? the day of the LORD *is* darkness, and not light.

19As if a man did flee from a lion, and a bear met him; or went into the house, and leaned his hand on the wall, and a serpent bit him.

20*Shall* not the day of the LORD *be* darkness, and not light? even very dark, and no brightness in it?

21¶ I hate, I despise your feast days, and I will not smell in your solemn assemblies.

22Though ye offer me burnt offerings and your meat offerings, I will not accept *them:* neither will I regard the peace offerings of your fat beasts.

23Take thou away from me the noise of thy songs; for I will not hear the melody of thy viols.

24But let judgment run down as waters, and righteousness as a mighty stream.

25Have ye offered unto me sacrifices and offerings in the wilderness forty years, O house of Israel?

26But ye have borne the tabernacle of your Moloch and Chiun your images, the star of your god, which ye made to yourselves.

27Therefore will I cause you to go into captivity beyond Damascus, saith the LORD, whose name *is* The God of hosts.

6 WOE TO them *that are* at ease in Zion, and trust in the mountain of Samaria, *which are* named chief of the nations, to whom the house of Israel came!

2Pass ye unto Calneh, and see; and from thence go ye to Hamath the great: then go down to Gath of the Philistines: *be they* better than these kingdoms? or their border greater than your border?

3Ye that put far away the evil day, and cause the seat of violence to come near;

4That lie upon beds of ivory, and stretch themselves upon their couches, and eat the lambs out of the flock, and the calves out of the midst of the stall;

5That chant to the sound of the viol, *and* invent to themselves instruments of music, like David;

New International

16Therefore this is what the Lord, the LORD God Almighty, says:

"There will be wailing in all the streets
and cries of anguish in every public square.
The farmers will be summoned to weep
and the mourners to wail.
17There will be wailing in all the vineyards,
for I will pass through your midst,"
says the LORD.

The Day of the LORD

18Woe to you who long
for the day of the LORD!
Why do you long for the day of the LORD?
That day will be darkness, not light.
19It will be as though a man fled from a lion
only to meet a bear,
as though he entered his house
and rested his hand on the wall
only to have a snake bite him.
20Will not the day of the LORD be darkness, not
light—
pitch-dark, without a ray of brightness?

21"I hate, I despise your religious feasts;
I cannot stand your assemblies.
22Even though you bring me burnt offerings and
grain offerings,
I will not accept them.
Though you bring choice fellowship offerings,a
I will have no regard for them.
23Away with the noise of your songs!
I will not listen to the music of your harps.
24But let justice roll on like a river,
righteousness like a never-failing stream!

25"Did you bring me sacrifices and offerings
forty years in the desert, O house of Israel?
26You have lifted up the shrine of your king,
the pedestal of your idols,
the star of your godb—
which you made for yourselves.
27Therefore I will send you into exile beyond
Damascus,"
says the LORD, whose name is God Almighty.

Woe to the Complacent

6 WOE TO you who are complacent in Zion,
and to you who feel secure on Mount
Samaria,
you notable men of the foremost nation,
to whom the people of Israel come!
2Go to Calneh and look at it;
go from there to great Hamath,
and then go down to Gath in Philistia.
Are they better off than your two kingdoms?
Is their land larger than yours?
3You put off the evil day
and bring near a reign of terror.
4You lie on beds inlaid with ivory
and lounge on your couches.
You dine on choice lambs
and fattened calves.
5You strum away on your harps like David
and improvise on musical instruments.

---

a 22 Traditionally *peace offerings*   b 26 Or *lifted up Sakkuth your king* / *and
Kaiwan your idols,* / *your star-gods;* Septuagint *lifted up the shrine of Molech
* / *and the star of your god Rephan,* / *their idols*

Living Bible

16Therefore the Lord God says this: "There will be crying in all the streets and every road. Call for the farmers to weep with you, too; call for professional mourners to wail and lament. 17There will be sorrow and crying in every vineyard, for I will pass through and destroy. 18You say, 'If only the Day of the Lord were here, for then God would deliver us from all our foes.' But you have no idea what you ask. For that day will *not* be light and prosperity, but darkness and doom! How terrible the darkness will be for you; not a ray of joy or hope will shine. 19In that day you will be as a man who is chased by a lion—and met by a bear, or a man in a dark room who leans against a wall—and puts his hand on a snake. 20Yes, that will be a dark and hopeless day for you.

21"I hate your show and pretense—your hypocrisy of 'honoring' me with your religious feasts and solemn assemblies. 22I will not accept your burnt offerings and thank offerings. I will not look at your offerings of peace. 23Away with your hymns of praise—they are mere noise to my ears. I will not listen to your music, no matter how lovely it is.

24"I want to see a mighty flood of justice—a torrent of doing good.

25, 26, 27"You sacrificed to me for forty years while you were in the desert, Israel—but always your real interest has been in your heathen gods—in Sakkuth your king, and in Kaiwan, your god of the stars, and in all the images of them you made. So I will send them into captivity with you far to the east of Damascus," says the Lord, the Lord Almighty.

New Revised Standard

16 Therefore thus says the LORD, the God of
        hosts, the Lord:
    In all the squares there shall be wailing;
        and in all the streets they shall say, "Alas!
        alas!"
    They shall call the farmers to mourning,
        and those skilled in lamentation, to wailing;
17 in all the vineyards there shall be wailing,
        for I will pass through the midst of you,
                                        says the LORD.

The Day of the LORD a Dark Day

18 Alas for you who desire the day of the LORD!
        Why do you want the day of the LORD?
    It is darkness, not light;
19   as if someone fled from a lion,
        and was met by a bear;
    or went into the house and rested a hand
            against the wall,
        and was bitten by a snake.
20 Is not the day of the LORD darkness, not light,
        and gloom with no brightness in it?

21 I hate, I despise your festivals,
        and I take no delight in your solemn
            assemblies.
22 Even though you offer me your burnt offerings
            and grain offerings,
        I will not accept them;
    and the offerings of well-being of your fatted
            animals
        I will not look upon.
23 Take away from me the noise of your songs;
        I will not listen to the melody of your
            harps.
24 But let justice roll down like waters,
        and righteousness like an ever-flowing
            stream.

25 Did you bring to me sacrifices and offerings the forty years in the wilderness, O house of Israel? 26You shall take up Sakkuth your king, and Kaiwan your star-god, your images,c which you made for yourselves; 27therefore I will take you into exile beyond Damascus, says the LORD, whose name is the God of hosts.

Complacent Self-Indulgence Will Be Punished

6 WOE TO those lounging in luxury at Jerusalem and Samaria, so famous and popular among the people of Israel. 2Go over to Calneh and see what happened there; then go to great Hamath and down to Gath in the Philistines' land. Once they were better and greater than you, but look at them now. 3You push away all thought of punishment awaiting you, but by your deeds you bring the Day of Judgment near.

4You lie on ivory beds surrounded with luxury, eating the meat of the tenderest lambs and the choicest calves. 5You sing idle songs to the sound of the harp, and fancy yourselves to be as great musicians as King David was.

6 ALAS FOR those who are at ease in Zion,
        and for those who feel secure on Mount
            Samaria,
    the notables of the first of the nations,
        to whom the house of Israel resorts!
2 Cross over to Calneh, and see;
        from there go to Hamath the great;
        then go down to Gath of the Philistines.
    Are you betterd than these kingdoms?
        Or is youre territory greater than theirf
            territory,
3 O you that put far away the evil day,
        and bring near a reign of violence?

4 Alas for those who lie on beds of ivory,
        and lounge on their couches,
    and eat lambs from the flock,
        and calves from the stall;
5 who sing idle songs to the sound of the harp,
        and like David improvise on instruments of
            music;

c Heb *your images, your star-god*   d Or *Are they better*   e Heb *their*
f Heb *your*

King James

6That drink wine in bowls, and anoint themselves with the chief ointments: but they are not grieved for the affliction of Joseph.

7¶ Therefore now shall they go captive with the first that go captive, and the banquet of them that stretched themselves shall be removed.

8The Lord GOD hath sworn by himself, saith the LORD the God of hosts, I abhor the excellency of Jacob, and hate his palaces: therefore will I deliver up the city with all that is therein.

9And it shall come to pass, if there remain ten men in one house, that they shall die.

10And a man's uncle shall take him up, and he that burneth him, to bring out the bones out of the house, and shall say unto him that is by the sides of the house, Is there yet any with thee? and he shall say, No. Then shall he say, Hold thy tongue: for we may not make mention of the name of the LORD.

11For, behold, the LORD commandeth, and he will smite the great house with breaches, and the little house with clefts.

12¶ Shall horses run upon the rock? will one plow there with oxen? for ye have turned judgment into gall, and the fruit of righteousness into hemlock:

13Ye which rejoice in a thing of nought, which say, Have we not taken to us horns by our own strength?

14But, behold, I will raise up against you a nation, O house of Israel, saith the LORD the God of hosts; and they shall afflict you from the entering in of Hemath unto the river of the wilderness.

7 THUS HATH the Lord GOD shown unto me; and, behold, he formed grasshoppers in the beginning of the shooting up of the latter growth; and, lo, it was the latter growth after the king's mowings.

2And it came to pass, that when they had made an end of eating the grass of the land, then I said, O Lord GOD, forgive, I beseech thee: by whom shall Jacob arise? for he is small.

3The LORD repented for this: It shall not be, saith the LORD.

4¶ Thus hath the Lord GOD shown unto me: and, behold, the Lord GOD called to contend by fire, and it devoured the great deep, and did eat up a part.

5Then said I, O Lord GOD, cease, I beseech thee: by whom shall Jacob arise? for he is small.

6The LORD repented for this: This also shall not be, saith the Lord GOD.

7¶ Thus he showed me: and, behold, the Lord stood upon a wall made by a plumbline, with a plumbline in his hand.

New International

6You drink wine by the bowlful
   and use the finest lotions,
   but you do not grieve over the ruin of Joseph.
7Therefore you will be among the first to go into
      exile;
   your feasting and lounging will end.

The LORD Abhors the Pride of Israel

8The Sovereign LORD has sworn by himself—the
LORD God Almighty declares:

"I abhor the pride of Jacob
      and detest his fortresses;
   I will deliver up the city
      and everything in it."

9If ten men are left in one house, they too will die.
10And if a relative who is to burn the bodies comes to
carry them out of the house and asks anyone still hiding
there, "Is anyone with you?" and he says, "No," then he
will say, "Hush! We must not mention the name of the
LORD."

11For the LORD has given the command,
   and he will smash the great house into pieces
      and the small house into bits.

12Do horses run on the rocky crags?
   Does one plow there with oxen?
But you have turned justice into poison
   and the fruit of righteousness into bitterness—
13you who rejoice in the conquest of Lo Debar[a]
   and say, "Did we not take Karnaim[b] by our
      own strength?"

14For the LORD God Almighty declares,
   "I will stir up a nation against you, O house
      of Israel,
   that will oppress you all the way
      from Lebo[c] Hamath to the valley of the
         Arabah."

Locusts, Fire and a Plumb Line

7 THIS IS what the Sovereign LORD showed me: He
was preparing swarms of locusts after the king's
share had been harvested and just as the second crop was
coming up. 2When they had stripped the land clean, I
cried out, "Sovereign LORD, forgive! How can Jacob
survive? He is so small!"

3So the LORD relented.

"This will not happen," the LORD said.

4This is what the Sovereign LORD showed me: The
Sovereign LORD was calling for judgment by fire; it
dried up the great deep and devoured the land. 5Then I
cried out, "Sovereign LORD, I beg you, stop! How can
Jacob survive? He is so small!"

6So the LORD relented.

"This will not happen either," the Sovereign LORD
said.

7This is what he showed me: The Lord was standing
by a wall that had been built true to plumb, with a plumb

a 13 Lo Debar means nothing.   b 13 Karnaim means horns; horn here
symbolizes strength.   c 14 Or from the entrance to

Living Bible

6You drink wine by the bucketful and perfume yourselves with sweet ointments, caring nothing at all that your brothers need your help. 7Therefore you will be the first to be taken as slaves; suddenly your revelry will end.

8Jehovah the Almighty Lord has sworn by his own name, "I despise the pride and false glory of Israel, and hate their beautiful homes. I will turn over this city and everything in it to her enemies."

9If there are as few as ten of them left, and even one house, they too will perish. 10A man's uncle will be the only one left to bury him, and when he goes in to carry his body from the house, he will ask the only one still alive inside, "Are any others left?" And the answer will be, "No," and he will add, "Shhh . . . don't mention the name of the Lord—he might hear you."

11For the Lord commanded this: That homes both great and small should be smashed to pieces. 12Can horses run on rocks? Can oxen plow the sea? Stupid even to ask, but no more stupid than what you do when you make a mockery of justice, and corrupt and sour all that should be good and right. 13And just as stupid is your rejoicing in how great you are, when you are less than nothing! And priding yourselves on your own tiny power!

14"O Israel, I will bring against you a nation that will bitterly oppress you from your northern boundary to your southern tip, all the way from Hamath to the brook of Arabah," says the Lord, the Lord Almighty.

7 THIS IS what the Lord God showed me in a vision: He was preparing a vast swarm of locusts to destroy all the main crop that sprang up after the first mowing, which went as taxes to the king. 2They ate everything in sight. Then I said, "O Lord God, please forgive your people! Don't send them this plague! If you turn against Israel, what hope is there? For Israel is so small!" 3So the Lord relented, and did not fulfill the vision. "I won't do it," he told me.

4Then the Lord God showed me a great fire he had prepared to punish them; it had burned up the waters and was devouring the entire land.

5Then I said, "O Lord God, please don't do it. If you turn against them, what hope is there? For Israel is so small!"

6Then the Lord turned from this plan too, and said, "I won't do that either."

7Then he showed me this: The Lord was standing beside a wall built with a plumbline, checking it with a

New Revised Standard

6 who drink wine from bowls,
  and anoint themselves with the finest oils,
  but are not grieved over the ruin of Joseph!
7 Therefore they shall now be the first to go
  into exile,
  and the revelry of the loungers shall pass
  away.

8 The Lord GOD has sworn by himself
  (says the LORD, the God of hosts):
  I abhor the pride of Jacob
  and hate his strongholds;
  and I will deliver up the city and all that is
  in it.

9 If ten people remain in one house, they shall die. 10And if a relative, one who burns the dead,d shall take up the body to bring it out of the house, and shall say to someone in the innermost parts of the house, "Is anyone else with you?" the answer will come, "No." Then the relativee shall say, "Hush! We must not mention the name of the LORD."

11 See, the LORD commands,
  and the great house shall be shattered to
  bits,
  and the little house to pieces.
12 Do horses run on rocks?
  Does one plow the sea with oxen?f
  But you have turned justice into poison
  and the fruit of righteousness into
  wormwood—
13 you who rejoice in Lo-debar,g
  who say, "Have we not by our own strength
  taken Karnaimh for ourselves?"
14 Indeed, I am raising up against you a nation,
  O house of Israel, says the LORD, the God
  of hosts,
  and they shall oppress you from Lebo-hamath
  to the Wadi Arabah.

Locusts, Fire, and a Plumb Line

7 THIS IS what the Lord GOD showed me: he was forming locusts at the time the latter growth began to sprout (it was the latter growth after the king's mowings). 2When they had finished eating the grass of the land, I said,
  "O Lord GOD, forgive, I beg you!
  How can Jacob stand?
  He is so small!"
3 The LORD relented concerning this;
  "It shall not be," said the LORD.

4 This is what the Lord GOD showed me: the Lord GOD was calling for a shower of fire,i and it devoured the great deep and was eating up the land. 5Then I said,
  "O Lord GOD, cease, I beg you!
  How can Jacob stand?
  He is so small!"
6 The LORD relented concerning this;
  "This also shall not be," said the Lord GOD.

7 This is what he showed me: the Lord was standing beside a wall built with a plumb line, with a plumb line in his hand. 8And the LORD said to me, "Amos, what

---

d Or who makes a burning for him e Heb he f Or Does one plow them with oxen g Or in a thing of nothingness h Or horns i Or for a judgment by fire

King James

8And the LORD said unto me, Amos, what seest thou? And I said, A plumbline. Then said the Lord, Behold, I will set a plumbline in the midst of my people Israel: I will not again pass by them any more:

9And the high places of Isaac shall be desolate, and the sanctuaries of Israel shall be laid waste; and I will rise against the house of Jeroboam with the sword.

10¶ Then Amaziah the priest of Beth-el sent to Jeroboam king of Israel, saying, Amos hath conspired against thee in the midst of the house of Israel: the land is not able to bear all his words.

11For thus Amos saith, Jeroboam shall die by the sword, and Israel shall surely be led away captive out of their own land.

12Also Amaziah said unto Amos, O thou seer, go, flee thee away into the land of Judah, and there eat bread, and prophesy there:

13But prophesy not again any more at Beth-el: for it *is* the king's chapel, and it *is* the king's court.

14¶ Then answered Amos, and said to Amaziah, I *was* no prophet, neither *was* I a prophet's son; but I *was* an herdman, and a gatherer of sycamore fruit:

15And the LORD took me as I followed the flock, and the LORD said unto me, Go, prophesy unto my people Israel.

16¶ Now therefore hear thou the word of the LORD: Thou sayest, Prophesy not against Israel, and drop not *thy word* against the house of Isaac.

17Therefore thus saith the LORD; Thy wife shall be an harlot in the city, and thy sons and thy daughters shall fall by the sword, and thy land shall be divided by line; and thou shalt die in a polluted land: and Israel shall surely go into captivity forth of his land.

8 THUS HATH the Lord GOD shown unto me: and behold a basket of summer fruit.

2And he said, Amos, what seest thou? And I said, A basket of summer fruit. Then said the LORD unto me, The end is come upon my people of Israel; I will not again pass by them any more.

3And the songs of the temple shall be howlings in that day, saith the Lord GOD: *there shall be* many dead bodies in every place; they shall cast *them* forth with silence.

4¶ Hear this, O ye that swallow up the needy, even to make the poor of the land to fail,

5Saying, When will the new moon be gone, that we may sell corn? and the sabbath, that we may set forth wheat, making the ephah small, and the shekel great, and falsifying the balances by deceit?

New International

line in his hand. 8And the LORD asked me, "What do you see, Amos?"

"A plumb line," I replied.

Then the Lord said, "Look, I am setting a plumb line among my people Israel; I will spare them no longer.

9"The high places of Isaac will be destroyed
   and the sanctuaries of Israel will be ruined;
   with my sword I will rise against the house of
      Jeroboam."

Amos and Amaziah

10Then Amaziah the priest of Bethel sent a message to Jeroboam king of Israel: "Amos is raising a conspiracy against you in the very heart of Israel. The land cannot bear all his words. 11For this is what Amos is saying:

   " 'Jeroboam will die by the sword,
      and Israel will surely go into exile,
      away from their native land.' "

12Then Amaziah said to Amos, "Get out, you seer! Go back to the land of Judah. Earn your bread there and do your prophesying there. 13Don't prophesy anymore at Bethel, because this is the king's sanctuary and the temple of the kingdom."

14Amos answered Amaziah, "I was neither a prophet nor a prophet's son, but I was a shepherd, and I also took care of sycamore-fig trees. 15But the LORD took me from tending the flock and said to me, 'Go, prophesy to my people Israel.' 16Now then, hear the word of the LORD. You say,

   " 'Do not prophesy against Israel,
      and stop preaching against the house of
         Isaac.'

17"Therefore this is what the LORD says:

   " 'Your wife will become a prostitute in the
         city,
      and your sons and daughters will fall by the
         sword.
   Your land will be measured and divided up,
      and you yourself will die in a pagana
         country.
   And Israel will certainly go into exile,
      away from their native land.' "

A Basket of Ripe Fruit

8 THIS IS what the Sovereign LORD showed me: a basket of ripe fruit. 2"What do you see, Amos?" he asked.

"A basket of ripe fruit," I answered.

Then the LORD said to me, "The time is ripe for my people Israel; I will spare them no longer.

3"In that day," declares the Sovereign LORD, "the songs in the temple will turn to wailing.b Many, many bodies—flung everywhere! Silence!"

4Hear this, you who trample the needy
   and do away with the poor of the land,

5saying,

   "When will the New Moon be over
      that we may sell grain,
   and the Sabbath be ended
      that we may market wheat?"—
   skimping the measure,
      boosting the price
      and cheating with dishonest scales,

---

a 17 Hebrew *an unclean*   b 3 Or *"the temple singers will wail"*

Living Bible

plumbline to see if it was straight. 8And the Lord said to me, "Amos, what do you see?"

I answered, "A plumbline."

And he replied, "I will test my people with a plumbline. I will no longer turn away from punishing. 9The idol altars and temples of Israel will be destroyed, and I will destroy the dynasty of King Jeroboam by the sword."

10But when Amaziah, the priest of Bethel, heard what Amos was saying, he rushed a message to Jeroboam, the king: "Amos is a traitor to our nation and is plotting your death. This is intolerable. It will lead to rebellion all across the land. 11He says you will be killed, and Israel will be sent far away into exile and slavery."

12Then Amaziah sent orders to Amos, "Get out of here, you prophet, you! Flee to the land of Judah and do your prophesying there! 13Don't bother us here with your visions, not here in the capital, where the king's chapel is!"

14But Amos replied, "I am not really one of the prophets. I do not come from a family of prophets. I am just a herdsman and fruit picker. 15But the Lord took me from caring for the flocks and told me, 'Go and prophesy to my people Israel.'

16"Now therefore listen to this message to you from the Lord. You say, 'Don't prophesy against Israel.' 17The Lord's reply is this: 'Because of your interference, your wife will become a prostitute in this city, and your sons and daughters will be killed and your land divided up. You yourself will die in a heathen land, and the people of Israel will certainly become slaves in exile, far from their land.' "

8 THEN THE Lord God showed me, in a vision, a basket full of ripe fruit.

2"What do you see, Amos?" he asked.

I replied, "A basket full of ripe fruit."

Then the Lord said, "This fruit represents my people Israel—ripe for punishment. I will not defer their punishment again. 3The riotous sound of singing in the Temple will turn to weeping then. Dead bodies will be scattered everywhere. They will be carried out of the city in silence." The Lord has spoken.

4Listen, you merchants who rob the poor, trampling on the needy; 5you who long for the Sabbath to end and the religious holidays to be over, so you can get out and start cheating again—using your weighted scales and under-sized measures; 6you who make slaves of the

New Revised Standard

do you see?" And I said, "A plumb line." Then the Lord said,

> "See, I am setting a plumb line
> in the midst of my people Israel;
> I will never again pass them by;
> 9 the high places of Isaac shall be made
> desolate,
> and the sanctuaries of Israel shall be laid
> waste,
> and I will rise against the house of
> Jeroboam with the sword."

Amaziah Complains to the King

10 Then Amaziah, the priest of Bethel, sent to King Jeroboam of Israel, saying, "Amos has conspired against you in the very center of the house of Israel; the land is not able to bear all his words. 11For thus Amos has said,

> 'Jeroboam shall die by the sword,
> and Israel must go into exile
> away from his land.' "

12And Amaziah said to Amos, "O seer, go, flee away to the land of Judah, earn your bread there, and prophesy there; 13but never again prophesy at Bethel, for it is the king's sanctuary, and it is a temple of the kingdom."

14 Then Amos answered Amaziah, "I amc no prophet, nor a prophet's son; but I amc a herdsman, and a dresser of sycamore trees, 15and the LORD took me from following the flock, and the LORD said to me, 'Go, prophesy to my people Israel.'

16 "Now therefore hear the word of the LORD.
> You say, 'Do not prophesy against Israel,
> and do not preach against the house of
> Isaac.'
17 Therefore thus says the LORD:
> 'Your wife shall become a prostitute in the
> city,
> and your sons and your daughters shall fall
> by the sword,
> and your land shall be parceled out by line;
> you yourself shall die in an unclean land,
> and Israel shall surely go into exile away
> from its land.' "

The Basket of Fruit

8 THIS IS what the Lord GOD showed me—a basket of summer fruit.d 2He said, "Amos, what do you see?" And I said, "A basket of summer fruit."d Then the LORD said to me,

> "The ende has come upon my people Israel;
> I will never again pass them by.
> 3 The songs of the templef shall become
> wailings in that day,"
>   says the Lord GOD;
> "the dead bodies shall be many,
> cast out in every place. Be silent!"

> 4 Hear this, you that trample on the needy,
> and bring to ruin the poor of the land,
> 5 saying, "When will the new moon be over
> so that we may sell grain;
> and the sabbath,
> so that we may offer wheat for sale?
> We will make the ephah small and the shekel
> great,
> and practice deceit with false balances,

---

c Or was   d Heb qayits   e Heb qets   f Or palace

King James

6That we may buy the poor for silver, and the needy for a pair of shoes; *yea,* and sell the refuse of the wheat? 7The LORD hath sworn by the excellency of Jacob, Surely I will never forget any of their works.

8Shall not the land tremble for this, and every one mourn that dwelleth therein? and it shall rise up wholly as a flood; and it shall be cast out and drowned, as *by* the flood of Egypt.

9And it shall come to pass in that day, saith the Lord GOD, that I will cause the sun to go down at noon, and I will darken the earth in the clear day:

10And I will turn your feasts into mourning, and all your songs into lamentation; and I will bring up sackcloth upon all loins, and baldness upon every head; and I will make it as the mourning of an only *son,* and the end thereof as a bitter day.

11¶ Behold, the days come, saith the Lord GOD, that I will send a famine in the land, not a famine of bread, nor a thirst for water, but of hearing the words of the LORD:

12And they shall wander from sea to sea, and from the north even to the east, they shall run to and fro to seek the word of the LORD, and shall not find *it.*

13In that day shall the fair virgins and young men faint for thirst.

14They that swear by the sin of Samaria, and say, Thy god, O Dan, liveth; and, The manner of Beer-sheba liveth; even they shall fall, and never rise up again.

New International

6buying the poor with silver
and the needy for a pair of sandals,
selling even the sweepings with the wheat.

7The LORD has sworn by the Pride of Jacob: "I will never forget anything they have done.

8"Will not the land tremble for this,
and all who live in it mourn?
The whole land will rise like the Nile;
it will be stirred up and then sink
like the river of Egypt.

9"In that day," declares the Sovereign LORD,

"I will make the sun go down at noon
and darken the earth in broad daylight.
10I will turn your religious feasts into mourning
and all your singing into weeping.
I will make all of you wear sackcloth
and shave your heads.
I will make that time like mourning for an only
son
and the end of it like a bitter day.

11"The days are coming," declares the Sovereign LORD,
"when I will send a famine through the
land—
not a famine of food or a thirst for water,
but a famine of hearing the words of the
LORD.
12Men will stagger from sea to sea
and wander from north to east,
searching for the word of the LORD,
but they will not find it.

13"In that day

"the lovely young women and strong young
men
will faint because of thirst.
14They who swear by the shamea of Samaria,
or say, 'As surely as your god lives, O Dan,'
or, 'As surely as the godb of Beersheba
lives'—
they will fall,
never to rise again."

Israel to Be Destroyed

9 I SAW the Lord standing upon the altar: and he said, Smite the lintel of the door, that the posts may shake: and cut them in the head, all of them; and I will slay the last of them with the sword: he that fleeth of them shall not flee away, and he that escapeth of them shall not be delivered.

2Though they dig into hell, thence shall mine hand take them; though they climb up to heaven, thence will I bring them down:

3And though they hide themselves in the top of Carmel, I will search and take them out thence; and though they be hid from my sight in the bottom of the sea, thence will I command the serpent, and he shall bite them:

9 I SAW the Lord standing by the altar, and he said:

"Strike the tops of the pillars
so that the thresholds shake.
Bring them down on the heads of all the people;
those who are left I will kill with the sword.
Not one will get away,
none will escape.
2Though they dig down to the depths of the
grave,c
from there my hand will take them.
Though they climb up to the heavens,
from there I will bring them down.
3Though they hide themselves on the top of
Carmel,
there I will hunt them down and seize them.
Though they hide from me at the bottom of the
sea,
there I will command the serpent to bite
them.

---

a *14 Or by Ashima; or by the idol* b *14 Or power* c *2 Hebrew to Sheol*

Living Bible

poor, buying them for their debt of a piece of silver or a pair of shoes, or selling them your moldy wheat— 7the Lord, the Pride of Israel, has sworn: "I won't forget your deeds! 8The land will tremble as it awaits its doom, and everyone will mourn. It will rise up like the river Nile at floodtime, toss about, and sink again. 9At that time I will make the sun go down at noon and darken the earth in the daytime.

10"And I will turn your parties into times of mourning, and your songs of joy will be turned to cries of despair. You will wear funeral clothes and shave your heads as signs of sorrow, as if your only son had died; bitter, bitter will be that day. 11The time is surely coming," says the Lord God, "when I will send a famine on the land—not a famine of bread or water, but of hearing the words of the Lord. 12Men will wander everywhere from sea to sea, seeking the Word of the Lord, searching, running here and going there, but will not find it.

13"Beautiful girls and fine young men alike will grow faint and weary, thirsting for the Word of God. 14And those who worship the idols of Samaria, Dan, and Beersheba shall fall and never rise again."

9 I SAW the Lord standing beside the altar, saying, "Smash the tops of the pillars and shake the Temple until the pillars crumble and the roof crashes down upon the people below. Though they run, they will not escape; they all will be killed.

2"Though they dig down to Sheol, I will reach down and pull them up; though they climb into the heavens, I will bring them down. 3Though they hide among the rocks at the top of Carmel, I will search them out and capture them. Though they hide at the bottom of the ocean, I will send the sea-serpent after them to bite and destroy them. 4Though they volunteer for exile, I will

New Revised Standard

6 buying the poor for silver
   and the needy for a pair of sandals,
   and selling the sweepings of the wheat."

7 The LORD has sworn by the pride of Jacob:
   Surely I will never forget any of their deeds.
8 Shall not the land tremble on this account,
   and everyone mourn who lives in it,
and all of it rise like the Nile,
   and be tossed about and sink again, like the
      Nile of Egypt?

9 On that day, says the Lord GOD,
   I will make the sun go down at noon,
   and darken the earth in broad daylight.
10 I will turn your feasts into mourning,
   and all your songs into lamentation;
I will bring sackcloth on all loins,
   and baldness on every head;
I will make it like the mourning for an only
      son,
   and the end of it like a bitter day.

11 The time is surely coming, says the Lord
      GOD,
   when I will send a famine on the land;
not a famine of bread, or a thirst for water,
   but of hearing the words of the LORD.
12 They shall wander from sea to sea,
   and from north to east;
they shall run to and fro, seeking the word of
      the LORD,
   but they shall not find it.

13 In that day the beautiful young women and the
      young men
   shall faint for thirst.
14 Those who swear by Ashimah of Samaria,
   and say, "As your god lives, O Dan,"
and, "As the way of Beer-sheba lives"—
   they shall fall, and never rise again.

The Destruction of Israel

9 I SAW the LORD standing beside[d] the altar, and he said:
   Strike the capitals until the thresholds shake,
      and shatter them on the heads of all the
         people;[e]
and those who are left I will kill with the
      sword;
   not one of them shall flee away,
   not one of them shall escape.

2 Though they dig into Sheol,
   from there shall my hand take them;
though they climb up to heaven,
   from there I will bring them down.
3 Though they hide themselves on the top of
      Carmel,
   from there I will search out and take them;
and though they hide from my sight at the
      bottom of the sea,
   there I will command the sea-serpent, and it
      shall bite them.

d Or on   e Heb all of them

King James

4And though they go into captivity before their enemies, thence will I command the sword, and it shall slay them: and I will set mine eyes upon them for evil, and not for good.

5And the Lord GOD of hosts *is* he that toucheth the land, and it shall melt, and all that dwell therein shall mourn: and it shall rise up wholly like a flood; and shall be drowned, as *by* the flood of Egypt.

6*It is* he that buildeth his stories in the heaven, and hath founded his troop in the earth; he that calleth for the waters of the sea, and poureth them out upon the face of the earth: The LORD *is* his name.

7*Are* ye not as children of the Ethiopians unto me, O children of Israel? saith the LORD. Have not I brought up Israel out of the land of Egypt? and the Philistines from Caphtor, and the Syrians from Kir?

8Behold, the eyes of the Lord GOD *are* upon the sinful kingdom, and I will destroy it from off the face of the earth; saving that I will not utterly destroy the house of Jacob, saith the LORD.

9For, lo, I will command, and I will sift the house of Israel among all nations, like as *corn* is sifted in a sieve, yet shall not the least grain fall upon the earth.

10All the sinners of my people shall die by the sword, which say, The evil shall not overtake nor prevent us.

11¶ In that day will I raise up the tabernacle of David that is fallen, and close up the breaches thereof; and I will raise up his ruins, and I will build it as in the days of old:

12That they may possess the remnant of Edom, and of all the heathen, which are called by my name, saith the LORD that doeth this.

13Behold, the days come, saith the LORD, that the plowman shall overtake the reaper, and the treader of grapes him that soweth seed; and the mountains shall drop sweet wine, and all the hills shall melt.

New International

4Though they are driven into exile by their
   enemies,
  there I will command the sword to slay them.
I will fix my eyes upon them
  for evil and not for good."

5The Lord, the LORD Almighty,
  he who touches the earth and it melts,
  and all who live in it mourn—
the whole land rises like the Nile,
  then sinks like the river of Egypt—
6he who builds his lofty palace[a] in the heavens
  and sets its foundation[b] on the earth,
who calls for the waters of the sea
  and pours them out over the face of the
   land—
  the LORD is his name.

7"Are not you Israelites
  the same to me as the Cushites[c]?"
                     declares the LORD.
"Did I not bring Israel up from Egypt,
  the Philistines from Caphtor[d]
  and the Arameans from Kir?

8"Surely the eyes of the Sovereign LORD
  are on the sinful kingdom.
I will destroy it
  from the face of the earth—
yet I will not totally destroy
  the house of Jacob,"
                     declares the LORD.
9"For I will give the command,
  and I will shake the house of Israel
  among all the nations
as grain is shaken in a sieve,
  and not a pebble will reach the ground.
10All the sinners among my people
  will die by the sword,
all those who say,
  'Disaster will not overtake or meet us.'

Israel's Restoration

11"In that day I will restore
  David's fallen tent.
I will repair its broken places,
  restore its ruins,
  and build it as it used to be,
12so that they may possess the remnant of Edom
  and all the nations that bear my name,[e]"
                   declares the LORD,
              who will do these things.

13"The days are coming," declares the LORD,

"when the reaper will be overtaken by the
   plowman
  and the planter by the one treading grapes.
New wine will drip from the mountains
  and flow from all the hills.

---

a 6 The meaning of the Hebrew for this phrase is uncertain.   b 6 The meaning of the Hebrew for this word is uncertain.   c 7 That is, people from the upper Nile region   d 7 That is, Crete   e 12 Hebrew; Septuagint *so that the remnant of men / and all the nations that bear my name may seek the Lord,*

Living Bible

command the sword to kill them there. I will see to it that they receive evil and not good."

5The Lord Almighty touches the land and it melts, and all its people mourn. It rises like the river Nile in Egypt, and then sinks again. 6The upper stories of his home are in the heavens, the first floor on the earth. He calls for the vapor to rise from the ocean and pours it down as rain upon the ground. Jehovah, the Lord, is his name.

7"O people of Israel, are you any more to me than the Ethiopians are? Have not I, who brought you out of Egypt, done as much for other people, too? I brought the Philistines from Caphtor and the Syrians out of Kir.

8"The eyes of the Lord God are watching Israel, that sinful nation, and I will root her up and scatter her across the world. *Yet I have promised that this rooting out will not be permanent.* 9For I have commanded that Israel be sifted by the other nations as grain is sifted in a sieve, yet not one true kernel will be lost. 10But all these sinners who say, 'God will not touch us,' will die by the sword.

11"Then, at that time I will rebuild the City of David, which is now lying in ruins, and return it to its former glory, 12and Israel will possess what is left of Edom, and of all the nations that belong to me." For so the Lord, who plans it all, has said.

13"The time will come when there will be such abundance of crops, that the harvest time will scarcely end before the farmer starts again to sow another crop, and the terraces of grapes upon the hills of Israel will drip sweet wine! 14I will restore the fortunes of my people

New Revised Standard

4 And though they go into captivity in front of
        their enemies,
    there I will command the sword, and it shall
        kill them;
and I will fix my eyes on them
    for harm and not for good.

5 The Lord, GOD of hosts,
    he who touches the earth and it melts,
        and all who live in it mourn,
    and all of it rises like the Nile,
        and sinks again, like the Nile of Egypt;
6 who builds his upper chambers in the heavens,
        and founds his vault upon the earth;
    who calls for the waters of the sea,
        and pours them out upon the surface of the
            earth—
    the LORD is his name.

7 Are you not like the Ethiopiansf to me,
        O people of Israel? says the LORD.
    Did I not bring Israel up from the land of
        Egypt,
        and the Philistines from Caphtor and the
            Arameans from Kir?
8 The eyes of the Lord GOD are upon the sinful
        kingdom,
    and I will destroy it from the face of the
        earth
    —except that I will not utterly destroy the
        house of Jacob,
                                says the LORD.

9 For lo, I will command,
        and shake the house of Israel among all the
            nations
    as one shakes with a sieve,
        but no pebble shall fall to the ground.
10 All the sinners of my people shall die by the
        sword,
    who say, "Evil shall not overtake or meet
        us."

The Restoration of David's Kingdom

11 On that day I will raise up
        the booth of David that is fallen,
    and repair itsg breaches,
        and raise up itsh ruins,
        and rebuild it as in the days of old;
12 in order that they may possess the remnant of
        Edom
        and all the nations who are called by my
            name,
    says the LORD who does this.

13 The time is surely coming, says the LORD,
        when the one who plows shall overtake the
            one who reaps,
        and the treader of grapes the one who sows
            the seed;
    the mountains shall drip sweet wine,
        and all the hills shall flow with it.

f Or *Nubians*; Heb *Cushites*   g Gk: Heb *their*   h Gk: Heb *his*

King James

14And I will bring again the captivity of my people of Israel, and they shall build the waste cities, and inhabit *them;* and they shall plant vineyards, and drink the wine thereof; they shall also make gardens, and eat the fruit of them.

15And I will plant them upon their land, and they shall no more be pulled up out of their land which I have given them, saith the LORD thy God.

New International

14I will bring back my exileda people Israel;
  they will rebuild the ruined cities and live in
     them.
They will plant vineyards and drink their wine;
  they will make gardens and eat their fruit.
15I will plant Israel in their own land,
  never again to be uprooted
  from the land I have given them,"

          says the LORD your God.

Living Bible

Israel, and they shall rebuild their ruined cities, and live in them again, and they shall plant vineyards and gardens and eat their crops and drink their wine. 15I will firmly plant them there upon the land that I have given them; they shall not be pulled up again," says the Lord your God.

New Revised Standard

14 I will restore the fortunes of my people Israel,
      and they shall rebuild the ruined cities and
        inhabit them;
    they shall plant vineyards and drink their
        wine,
      and they shall make gardens and eat their
        fruit.
15 I will plant them upon their land,
      and they shall never again be plucked up
      out of the land that I have given them,
                              says the LORD your God.

Obadiah   # Obadiah

¹THE VISION of Obadiah. Thus saith the Lord GOD concerning Edom; We have heard a rumour from the LORD, and an ambassador is sent among the heathen, Arise ye, and let us rise up against her in battle.

²Behold, I have made thee small among the heathen: thou art greatly despised.

³¶ The pride of thine heart hath deceived thee, thou that dwellest in the clefts of the rock, whose habitation *is* high; that saith in his heart, Who shall bring me down to the ground?

⁴Though thou exalt *thyself* as the eagle, and though thou set thy nest among the stars, thence will I bring thee down, saith the LORD.

⁵If thieves came to thee, if robbers by night, (how art thou cut off!) would they not have stolen till they had enough? if the grapegatherers came to thee, would they not leave *some* grapes?

⁶How are *the things* of Esau searched out! *how* are his hidden things sought up!

⁷All the men of thy confederacy have brought thee *even* to the border: the men that were at peace with thee have deceived thee, *and* prevailed against thee; *they that eat* thy bread have laid a wound under thee: *there is* none understanding in him.

⁸Shall I not in that day, saith the LORD, even destroy the wise *men* out of Edom, and understanding out of the mount of Esau?

⁹And thy mighty *men*, O Teman, shall be dismayed, to the end that every one of the mount of Esau may be cut off by slaughter.

¹⁰¶ For *thy* violence against thy brother Jacob shame shall cover thee, and thou shalt be cut off for ever.

¹¹In the day that thou stoodest on the other side, in the day that the strangers carried away captive his forces, and foreigners entered into his gates, and cast lots upon Jerusalem, even thou *wast* as one of them.

¹THE VISION of Obadiah.

This is what the Sovereign LORD says about Edom—

> We have heard a message from the LORD:
> An envoy was sent to the nations to say,
> "Rise, and let us go against her for battle"—

²"See, I will make you small among the nations;
you will be utterly despised.
³The pride of your heart has deceived you,
you who live in the clefts of the rocksª
and make your home on the heights,
you who say to yourself,
'Who can bring me down to the ground?'
⁴Though you soar like the eagle
and make your nest among the stars,
from there I will bring you down,"
                    declares the LORD.
⁵"If thieves came to you,
if robbers in the night—
Oh, what a disaster awaits you—
would they not steal only as much as they
wanted?
If grape pickers came to you,
would they not leave a few grapes?
⁶But how Esau will be ransacked,
his hidden treasures pillaged!
⁷All your allies will force you to the border;
your friends will deceive and overpower you;
those who eat your bread will set a trap for
you,ᵇ
but you will not detect it.

⁸"In that day," declares the LORD,
"will I not destroy the wise men of Edom,
men of understanding in the mountains of
Esau?
⁹Your warriors, O Teman, will be terrified,
and everyone in Esau's mountains
will be cut down in the slaughter.
¹⁰Because of the violence against your brother
Jacob,
you will be covered with shame;
you will be destroyed forever.
¹¹On the day you stood aloof
while strangers carried off his wealth
and foreigners entered his gates
and cast lots for Jerusalem,
you were like one of them.

ª *3* Or *of Sela*   ᵇ *7* The meaning of the Hebrew for this clause is uncertain.

Obadiah

Obadiah

Living Bible column

¹*IN A vision the Lord God showed Obadiah the future of the land of Edom.*ᶜ

"A report has come from the Lord," he said, "that God has sent an ambassador to the nations with this message: 'Attention! You are to send your armies against Edom and destroy her!'"

²I will cut you down to size among the nations, Edom, making you small and despised.

³You are proud because you live in those high, inaccessible cliffs. "Who can ever reach us way up here!" you boast. Don't fool yourselves! ⁴Though you soar as high as eagles, and build your nest among the stars, I will bring you plummeting down, says the Lord.

⁵Far better it would be for you if thieves had come at night to plunder you—for they would not take everything! Or if your vineyards were robbed of all their fruit—for at least the gleanings would be left! ⁶Every nook and cranny will be searched and robbed, and every treasure found and taken.

⁷All your allies will turn against you and help to push you out of your land. They will promise peace while plotting your destruction. Your trusted friends will set traps for you and all your counterstrategy will fail. ⁸In that day not one wise man will be left in all of Edom! says the Lord. For I will fill the wise men of Edom with stupidity. ⁹The mightiest soldiers of Teman will be confused, and helpless to prevent the slaughter.

¹⁰And why? Because of what you did to your brother Israel. Now your sins will be exposed for all to see; ashamed and defenseless, you will be cut off forever. ¹¹For you deserted Israel in his time of need. You stood aloof, refusing to lift a finger to help him when invaders carried off his wealth and divided Jerusalem among them by lot; you were as one of his enemies.

New Revised Standard column

Proud Edom Will Be Brought Low

1 THE VISION of Obadiah.

Thus says the Lord GOD concerning Edom:
We have heard a report from the LORD,
    and a messenger has been sent among the
        nations:
"Rise up! Let us rise against it for battle!"
2 I will surely make you least among the
        nations;
    you shall be utterly despised.
3 Your proud heart has deceived you,
    you that live in the clefts of the rock,ᵈ
    whose dwelling is in the heights.
You say in your heart,
    "Who will bring me down to the ground?"
4 Though you soar aloft like the eagle,
    though your nest is set among the stars,
    from there I will bring you down,
                    says the LORD.

Pillage and Slaughter Will Repay Edom's Cruelty

5 If thieves came to you,
    if plunderers by night
    —how you have been destroyed!—
    would they not steal only what they wanted?
If grape-gatherers came to you,
    would they not leave gleanings?
6 How Esau has been pillaged,
    his treasures searched out!
7 All your allies have deceived you,
    they have driven you to the border;
your confederates have prevailed against you;
    those who ateᵉ your bread have set a trap
            for you—
    there is no understanding of it.
8 On that day, says the LORD,
    I will destroy the wise out of Edom,
    and understanding out of Mount Esau.
9 Your warriors shall be shattered, O Teman,
    so that everyone from Mount Esau will be
        cut off.

Edom Mistreated His Brother

10 For the slaughter and violence done to your
            brother Jacob,
    shame shall cover you,
    and you shall be cut off forever.
11 On the day that you stood aside,
    on the day that strangers carried off his
            wealth,
    and foreigners entered his gates
    and cast lots for Jerusalem,
    you too were like one of them.

ᶜ *1:1 Edom.* A nation southeast of Israel including Petra, the city hewn from rocks; her southern boundary was on the Gulf of Aqaba.

ᵈ Or *clefts of Sela*   ᵉ Cn: Heb lacks *those who ate*

King James

¹²But thou shouldest not have looked on the day of
thy brother in the day that he became a stranger; neither
shouldest thou have rejoiced over the children of Judah
in the day of their destruction; neither shouldest thou
have spoken proudly in the day of distress.

¹³Thou shouldest not have entered into the gate of my
people in the day of their calamity; yea, thou shouldest
not have looked on their affliction in the day of their
calamity, nor have laid *hands* on their substance in the
day of their calamity;

¹⁴Neither shouldest thou have stood in the crossway,
to cut off those of his that did escape; neither shouldest
thou have delivered up those of his that did remain in the
day of distress.

¹⁵For the day of the LORD *is* near upon all the heathen:
as thou hast done, it shall be done unto thee: thy reward
shall return upon thine own head.

¹⁶For as ye have drunk upon my holy mountain, *so*
shall all the heathen drink continually, yea, they shall
drink, and they shall swallow down, and they shall be
as though they had not been.

¹⁷¶ But upon mount Zion shall be deliverance, and
there shall be holiness; and the house of Jacob shall
possess their possessions.

¹⁸And the house of Jacob shall be a fire, and the house
of Joseph a flame, and the house of Esau for stubble, and
they shall kindle in them, and devour them; and there
shall not be *any* remaining of the house of Esau; for the
LORD hath spoken *it*.

¹⁹And *they of* the south shall possess the mount of
Esau; and *they of* the plain the Philistines: and they shall
possess the fields of Ephraim, and the fields of Samaria:
and Benjamin *shall possess* Gilead.

²⁰And the captivity of this host of the children of
Israel *shall possess* that of the Canaanites, *even* unto
Zarephath; and the captivity of Jerusalem, which *is* in
Sepharad, shall possess the cities of the south.

²¹And saviours shall come up on mount Zion to judge
the mount of Esau; and the kingdom shall be the LORD's.

New International

¹²You should not look down on your brother
    in the day of his misfortune,
nor rejoice over the people of Judah
    in the day of their destruction,
nor boast so much
    in the day of their trouble.
¹³You should not march through the gates of my
        people
    in the day of their disaster,
nor look down on them in their calamity
    in the day of their disaster,
nor seize their wealth
    in the day of their disaster.
¹⁴You should not wait at the crossroads
    to cut down their fugitives,
nor hand over their survivors
    in the day of their trouble.

¹⁵"The day of the LORD is near
    for all nations.
As you have done, it will be done to you;
    your deeds will return upon your own head.
¹⁶Just as you drank on my holy hill,
    so all the nations will drink continually;
they will drink and drink
    and be as if they had never been.
¹⁷But on Mount Zion will be deliverance;
    it will be holy,
and the house of Jacob
    will possess its inheritance.
¹⁸The house of Jacob will be a fire
    and the house of Joseph a flame;
the house of Esau will be stubble,
    and they will set it on fire and consume it.
There will be no survivors
    from the house of Esau."
                        The LORD has spoken.

¹⁹People from the Negev will occupy
    the mountains of Esau,
and people from the foothills will possess
    the land of the Philistines.
They will occupy the fields of Ephraim and
        Samaria,
    and Benjamin will possess Gilead.
²⁰This company of Israelite exiles who are in
        Canaan
    will possess the land as far as Zarephath;
the exiles from Jerusalem who are in Sepharad
    will possess the towns of the Negev.
²¹Deliverers will go up on^a Mount Zion
    to govern the mountains of Esau.
    And the kingdom will be the LORD's.

---

^a 21 Or *from*

Living Bible

12You should not have done it. You should not have gloated when they took him far away to foreign lands; you should not have rejoiced in the day of his misfortune; you should not have mocked in his time of need. 13You yourselves went into the land of Israel in the day of his calamity and looted him. You made yourselves rich at his expense. 14You stood at the crossroads and killed those trying to escape; you captured the survivors and returned them to their enemies in that terrible time of his distress.

15The Lord's vengeance will soon fall upon all Gentile nations. As you have done to Israel, so will it be done to you. Your acts will boomerang upon your heads. 16You drank my cup of punishment upon my holy mountain, and the nations round about will drink it, too; yes, drink and stagger back and disappear from history, no longer nations any more.

17But Jerusalem will become a refuge, a way of escape. Israel will reoccupy the land. 18Israel will be a fire that sets the dry fields of Edom aflame. There will be no survivors, for the Lord has spoken.

19Then my people who live in the Negeb shall occupy the hill country of Edom; those living in Judean lowlands shall possess the Philistine plains, and repossess the fields of Ephraim and Samaria. And the people of Benjamin shall possess Gilead.

20The Israeli exiles shall return and occupy the Phoenician coastal strip as far north as Zarephath. Those exiled in Asia Minor shall return to their homeland and conquer the Negeb's outlying villages. 21For deliverers will come to Jerusalem and rule all Edom. And the Lord shall be King!

New Revised Standard

12 But you should not have gloated[b] over[c] your brother
  on the day of his misfortune;
you should not have rejoiced over the people
    of Judah
  on the day of their ruin;
you should not have boasted
  on the day of distress.
13 You should not have entered the gate of my
    people
  on the day of their calamity;
you should not have joined in the gloating
    over Judah's[d] disaster
  on the day of his calamity;
you should not have looted his goods
  on the day of his calamity.
14 You should not have stood at the crossings
  to cut off his fugitives;
you should not have handed over his survivors
  on the day of distress.

15 For the day of the LORD is near against all the
    nations.
  As you have done, it shall be done to you;
  your deeds shall return on your own head.
16 For as you have drunk on my holy mountain,
  all the nations around you shall drink;
they shall drink and gulp down,[e]
  and shall be as though they had never been.

Israel's Final Triumph

17 But on Mount Zion there shall be those that
    escape,
  and it shall be holy;
and the house of Jacob shall take possession
    of those who dispossessed them.
18 The house of Jacob shall be a fire,
    the house of Joseph a flame,
  and the house of Esau stubble;
they shall burn them and consume them,
  and there shall be no survivor of the house
    of Esau;
                for the LORD has spoken.
19 Those of the Negeb shall possess Mount Esau,
    and those of the Shephelah the land of the
      Philistines;
they shall possess the land of Ephraim and the
      land of Samaria,
  and Benjamin shall possess Gilead.
20 The exiles of the Israelites who are in Halah[f]
    shall possess[g] Phoenicia as far
      as Zarephath;
and the exiles of Jerusalem who are in
      Sepharad
  shall possess the towns of the Negeb.
21 Those who have been saved[h] shall go up to
      Mount Zion
    to rule Mount Esau;
  and the kingdom shall be the LORD's.

---

b Heb *But do not gloat* (and similarly through verse 14)   c Heb *on the day of*   d Heb *his*   e Meaning of Heb uncertain   f Cn: Heb *in this army*   g Cn: Meaning of Heb uncertain   h Or *Saviors*

Jonah　　　　Jonah

1 NOW THE word of the LORD came unto Jonah the son of Amittai, saying,

²Arise, go to Nineveh, that great city, and cry against it; for their wickedness is come up before me.

³But Jonah rose up to flee unto Tarshish from the presence of the LORD, and went down to Joppa; and he found a ship going to Tarshish: so he paid the fare thereof, and went down into it, to go with them unto Tarshish from the presence of the LORD.

⁴¶ But the LORD sent out a great wind into the sea, and there was a mighty tempest in the sea, so that the ship was like to be broken.

⁵Then the mariners were afraid, and cried every man unto his god, and cast forth the wares that *were* in the ship into the sea, to lighten *it* of them. But Jonah was gone down into the sides of the ship; and he lay, and was fast asleep.

⁶So the shipmaster came to him, and said unto him, What meanest thou, O sleeper? arise, call upon thy God, if so be that God will think upon us, that we perish not.

⁷And they said every one to his fellow, Come, and let us cast lots, that we may know for whose cause this evil *is* upon us. So they cast lots, and the lot fell upon Jonah.

⁸Then said they unto him, Tell us, we pray thee, for whose cause this evil *is* upon us; What *is* thine occupation? and whence comest thou? what *is* thy country? and of what people *art* thou?

⁹And he said unto them, I *am* an Hebrew; and I fear the LORD, the God of heaven, which hath made the sea and the dry *land*.

¹⁰Then were the men exceedingly afraid, and said unto him, Why hast thou done this? For the men knew that he fled from the presence of the LORD, because he had told them.

¹¹¶ Then said they unto him, What shall we do unto thee, that the sea may be calm unto us? for the sea wrought, and was tempestuous.

¹²And he said unto them, Take me up, and cast me forth into the sea; so shall the sea be calm unto you: for I know that for my sake this great tempest *is* upon you.

¹³Nevertheless the men rowed hard to bring *it* to the land; but they could not: for the sea wrought, and was tempestuous against them.

¹⁴Wherefore they cried unto the LORD, and said, We beseech thee, O LORD, we beseech thee, let us not perish for this man's life, and lay not upon us innocent blood: for thou, O LORD, hast done as it pleased thee.

¹⁵So they took up Jonah, and cast him forth into the sea: and the sea ceased from her raging.

¹⁶Then the men feared the LORD exceedingly, and offered a sacrifice unto the LORD, and made vows.

¹⁷¶ Now the LORD had prepared a great fish to swallow up Jonah. And Jonah was in the belly of the fish three days and three nights.

Jonah Flees From the LORD

1 THE WORD of the LORD came to Jonah son of Amittai: ²"Go to the great city of Nineveh and preach against it, because its wickedness has come up before me."

³But Jonah ran away from the LORD and headed for Tarshish. He went down to Joppa, where he found a ship bound for that port. After paying the fare, he went aboard and sailed for Tarshish to flee from the LORD.

⁴Then the LORD sent a great wind on the sea, and such a violent storm arose that the ship threatened to break up. ⁵All the sailors were afraid and each cried out to his own god. And they threw the cargo into the sea to lighten the ship.

But Jonah had gone below deck, where he lay down and fell into a deep sleep. ⁶The captain went to him and said, "How can you sleep? Get up and call on your god! Maybe he will take notice of us, and we will not perish."

⁷Then the sailors said to each other, "Come, let us cast lots to find out who is responsible for this calamity." They cast lots and the lot fell on Jonah.

⁸So they asked him, "Tell us, who is responsible for making all this trouble for us? What do you do? Where do you come from? What is your country? From what people are you?"

⁹He answered, "I am a Hebrew and I worship the LORD, the God of heaven, who made the sea and the land."

¹⁰This terrified them and they asked, "What have you done?" (They knew he was running away from the LORD, because he had already told them so.)

¹¹The sea was getting rougher and rougher. So they asked him, "What should we do to you to make the sea calm down for us?"

¹²"Pick me up and throw me into the sea," he replied, "and it will become calm. I know that it is my fault that this great storm has come upon you."

¹³Instead, the men did their best to row back to land. But they could not, for the sea grew even wilder than before. ¹⁴Then they cried to the LORD, "O LORD, please do not let us die for taking this man's life. Do not hold us accountable for killing an innocent man, for you, O LORD, have done as you pleased." ¹⁵Then they took Jonah and threw him overboard, and the raging sea grew calm. ¹⁶At this the men greatly feared the LORD, and they offered a sacrifice to the LORD and made vows to him.

¹⁷But the LORD provided a great fish to swallow Jonah, and Jonah was inside the fish three days and three nights.

Living Bible	*New Revised Standard*

Jonah

Jonah

Jonah Tries to Run Away from God

1 THE LORD sent this message to Jonah, the son of Amittai:

2"Go to the great city of Nineveh, and give them this announcement from the Lord: 'I am going to destroy you, for your wickedness rises before me; it smells to highest heaven.'"

3But Jonah was afraid to go and ran away from the Lord. He went down to the seacoast, to the port of Joppa, where he found a ship leaving for Tarshish. He bought a ticket, went on board, and climbed down into the dark hold of the ship to hide there from the Lord.

4But as the ship was sailing along, suddenly the Lord flung a terrific wind over the sea, causing a great storm that threatened to send them to the bottom. 5Fearing for their lives, the desperate sailors shouted to their gods for help and threw the cargo overboard to lighten the ship. And all this time Jonah was sound asleep down in the hold.

6So the captain went down after him. "What do you mean," he roared, "sleeping at a time like this? Get up and cry to your god, and see if he will have mercy on us and save us!"

7Then the crew decided to draw straws to see which of them had offended the gods and caused this terrible storm; and Jonah drew the short one.

8"What have you done," they asked, "to bring this awful storm upon us? Who are you? What is your work? What country are you from? What is your nationality?"

9, 10And he said, "I am a Jew;a I worship Jehovah, the God of heaven, who made the earth and sea." Then he told them he was running away from the Lord.

The men were terribly frightened when they heard this. "Oh, why did you do it?" they shouted. 11"What should we do to you to stop the storm?" For it was getting worse and worse.

12"Throw me out into the sea," he said, "and it will become calm again. For I know this terrible storm has come because of me."

13They tried harder to row the boat ashore, but couldn't make it. The storm was too fierce to fight against. 14Then they shouted out a prayer to Jehovah, Jonah's God. "O Jehovah," they pleaded, "don't make us die for this man's sin, and don't hold us responsible for his death, for it is not our fault—you have sent this storm upon him for your own good reasons."

15Then they picked up Jonah and threw him overboard into the raging sea—and the storm stopped!

16The men stood there in awe before Jehovah, and sacrificed to him and vowed to serve him.

17Now the Lord had arranged for a great fish to swallow Jonah. And Jonah was inside the fish three days and three nights.

1 NOW THE word of the LORD came to Jonah son of Amittai, saying, 2"Go at once to Nineveh, that great city, and cry out against it; for their wickedness has come up before me." 3But Jonah set out to flee to Tarshish from the presence of the LORD. He went down to Joppa and found a ship going to Tarshish; so he paid his fare and went on board, to go with them to Tarshish, away from the presence of the LORD.

4 But the LORD hurled a great wind upon the sea, and such a mighty storm came upon the sea that the ship threatened to break up. 5Then the mariners were afraid, and each cried to his god. They threw the cargo that was in the ship into the sea, to lighten it for them. Jonah, meanwhile, had gone down into the hold of the ship and had lain down, and was fast asleep. 6The captain came and said to him, "What are you doing sound asleep? Get up, call on your god! Perhaps the god will spare us a thought so that we do not perish."

7 The sailorsb said to one another, "Come, let us cast lots, so that we may know on whose account this calamity has come upon us." So they cast lots, and the lot fell on Jonah. 8Then they said to him, "Tell us why this calamity has come upon us. What is your occupation? Where do you come from? What is your country? And of what people are you?" 9"I am a Hebrew," he replied. "I worship the LORD, the God of heaven, who made the sea and the dry land." 10Then the men were even more afraid, and said to him, "What is this that you have done!" For the men knew that he was fleeing from the presence of the LORD, because he had told them so.

11 Then they said to him, "What shall we do to you, that the sea may quiet down for us?" For the sea was growing more and more tempestuous. 12He said to them, "Pick me up and throw me into the sea; then the sea will quiet down for you; for I know it is because of me that this great storm has come upon you." 13Nevertheless the men rowed hard to bring the ship back to land, but they could not, for the sea grew more and more stormy against them. 14Then they cried out to the LORD, "Please, O LORD, we pray, do not let us perish on account of this man's life. Do not make us guilty of innocent blood; for you, O LORD, have done as it pleased you." 15So they picked Jonah up and threw him into the sea; and the sea ceased from its raging. 16Then the men feared the LORD even more, and they offered a sacrifice to the LORD and made vows.

17c But the LORD provided a large fish to swallow up Jonah; and Jonah was in the belly of the fish three days and three nights.

---

a 1:9 I am a Jew, literally, "a Hebrew."   b Heb They   c Ch 2.1 in Heb

King James

2 THEN JONAH prayed unto the LORD his God out of the fish's belly,

²And said, I cried by reason of mine affliction unto the LORD, and he heard me; out of the belly of hell cried I, *and* thou heardest my voice.

³For thou hadst cast me into the deep, in the midst of the seas; and the floods compassed me about: all thy billows and thy waves passed over me.

⁴Then I said, I am cast out of thy sight; yet I will look again toward thy holy temple.

⁵The waters compassed me about, *even* to the soul: the depth closed me round about, the weeds were wrapped about my head.

⁶I went down to the bottoms of the mountains; the earth with her bars *was* about me for ever: yet hast thou brought up my life from corruption, O LORD my God.

⁷When my soul fainted within me I remembered the LORD: and my prayer came in unto thee, into thine holy temple.

⁸They that observe lying vanities forsake their own mercy.

⁹But I will sacrifice unto thee with the voice of thanksgiving; I will pay *that* that I have vowed. Salvation *is* of the LORD.

¹⁰¶ And the LORD spake unto the fish, and it vomited out Jonah upon the dry *land*.

3 AND THE word of the LORD came unto Jonah the second time, saying,

²Arise, go unto Nineveh, that great city, and preach unto it the preaching that I bid thee.

³So Jonah arose, and went unto Nineveh, according to the word of the LORD. Now Nineveh was an exceeding great city of three days' journey.

⁴And Jonah began to enter into the city a day's journey, and he cried, and said, Yet forty days, and Nineveh shall be overthrown.

⁵¶ So the people of Nineveh believed God, and proclaimed a fast, and put on sackcloth, from the greatest of them even to the least of them.

⁶For word came unto the king of Nineveh, and he arose from his throne, and he laid his robe from him, and covered *him* with sackcloth, and sat in ashes.

⁷And he caused *it* to be proclaimed and published through Nineveh by the decree of the king and his nobles, saying, Let neither man nor beast, herd nor flock, taste any thing: let them not feed, nor drink water:

⁸But let man and beast be covered with sackcloth, and cry mightily unto God: yea, let them turn every one from his evil way, and from the violence that *is* in their hands.

⁹Who can tell *if* God will turn and repent, and turn away from his fierce anger, that we perish not?

New International

Jonah's Prayer

2 FROM INSIDE the fish Jonah prayed to the LORD his God. ²He said:

"In my distress I called to the LORD,
   and he answered me.
From the depths of the grave[a] I called for help,
   and you listened to my cry.
³You hurled me into the deep,
   into the very heart of the seas,
   and the currents swirled about me;
all your waves and breakers
   swept over me.
⁴I said, 'I have been banished
   from your sight;
yet I will look again
   toward your holy temple.'
⁵The engulfing waters threatened me,[b]
   the deep surrounded me;
   seaweed was wrapped around my head.
⁶To the roots of the mountains I sank down;
   the earth beneath barred me in forever.
But you brought my life up from the pit,
   O LORD my God.

⁷"When my life was ebbing away,
   I remembered you, LORD,
and my prayer rose to you,
   to your holy temple.

⁸"Those who cling to worthless idols
   forfeit the grace that could be theirs.
⁹But I, with a song of thanksgiving,
   will sacrifice to you.
What I have vowed I will make good.
   Salvation comes from the LORD."

¹⁰And the LORD commanded the fish, and it vomited Jonah onto dry land.

Jonah Goes to Nineveh

3 THEN THE word of the LORD came to Jonah a second time: ²"Go to the great city of Nineveh and proclaim to it the message I give you."

³Jonah obeyed the word of the LORD and went to Nineveh. Now Nineveh was a very important city—a visit required three days. ⁴On the first day, Jonah started into the city. He proclaimed: "Forty more days and Nineveh will be overturned." ⁵The Ninevites believed God. They declared a fast, and all of them, from the greatest to the least, put on sackcloth.

⁶When the news reached the king of Nineveh, he rose from his throne, took off his royal robes, covered himself with sackcloth and sat down in the dust. ⁷Then he issued a proclamation in Nineveh:

"By the decree of the king and his nobles:

Do not let any man or beast, herd or flock, taste anything; do not let them eat or drink. ⁸But let man and beast be covered with sackcloth. Let everyone call urgently on God. Let them give up their evil ways and their violence. ⁹Who knows? God may yet relent and with compassion turn from his fierce anger so that we will not perish."

ª 2 Hebrew *Sheol*   ᵇ 5 Or *waters were at my throat*

Living Bible

2 THEN JONAH prayed to the Lord his God from inside the fish:

2"In my great trouble I cried to the Lord and he answered me; from the depths of death I called, and Lord, you heard me! 3You threw me into the ocean depths; I sank down into the floods of waters and was covered by your wild and stormy waves. 4Then I said, 'O Lord, you have rejected me and cast me away. How shall I ever again see your holy Temple?'

5"I sank beneath the waves, and death was very near. The waters closed above me; the seaweed wrapped itself around my head. 6I went down to the bottoms of the mountains that rise from off the ocean floor. I was locked out of life and imprisoned in the land of death. But, O Lord my God, you have snatched me from the yawning jaws of death!

7"When I had lost all hope, I turned my thoughts once more to the Lord. And my earnest prayer went to you in your holy Temple. 8(Those who worship false gods have turned their backs on all the mercies waiting for them from the Lord!)

9"I will never worship anyone but you! For how can I thank you enough for all you have done? I will surely fulfill my promises. For my deliverance comes from the Lord alone."

10And the Lord ordered the fish to spit up Jonah on the beach, and it did.

3 THEN THE Lord spoke to Jonah again: "Go to that great city, Nineveh," he said, "and warn them of their doom, as I told you to before!"

3So Jonah obeyed, and went to Nineveh. Now Nineveh was a very large city, with many villages around it—so large that it would take three days to walk through it.c

4, 5But the very first day when Jonah entered the city and began to preach, the people repented. Jonah shouted to the crowds that gathered around him, "Forty days from now Nineveh will be destroyed!" And they believed him and declared a fast; from the king on down, everyone put on sackcloth—the rough, coarse garments worn at times of mourning.d

6For when the king of Nineveh heard what Jonah was saying, he stepped down from his throne and laid aside his royal robes and put on sackcloth and sat in ashes. 7And the king and his nobles sent this message throughout the city: "Let no one, not even the animals, eat anything at all, nor even drink any water. 8Everyone must wear sackcloth and cry mightily to God, and let everyone turn from his evil ways, from his violence and robbing. 9Who can tell? Perhaps even yet God will decide to let us live, and will hold back his fierce anger from destroying us."

New Revised Standard

A Psalm of Thanksgiving

2 THEN JONAH prayed to the LORD his God from the belly of the fish, 2saying,
"I called to the LORD out of my distress,
    and he answered me;
out of the belly of Sheol I cried,
    and you heard my voice.
3 You cast me into the deep,
    into the heart of the seas,
    and the flood surrounded me;
all your waves and your billows
    passed over me.
4 Then I said, 'I am driven away
    from your sight;
howe shall I look again
    upon your holy temple?'
5 The waters closed in over me;
    the deep surrounded me;
weeds were wrapped around my head
6   at the roots of the mountains.
I went down to the land
    whose bars closed upon me forever;
yet you brought up my life from the Pit,
    O LORD my God.
7 As my life was ebbing away,
    I remembered the LORD;
and my prayer came to you,
    into your holy temple.
8 Those who worship vain idols
    forsake their true loyalty.
9 But I with the voice of thanksgiving
    will sacrifice to you;
what I have vowed I will pay.
    Deliverance belongs to the LORD!"

10Then the LORD spoke to the fish, and it spewed Jonah out upon the dry land.

Conversion of Nineveh

3 THE WORD of the LORD came to Jonah a second time, saying, 2"Get up, go to Nineveh, that great city, and proclaim to it the message that I tell you." 3So Jonah set out and went to Nineveh, according to the word of the LORD. Now Nineveh was an exceedingly large city, a three days' walk across. 4Jonah began to go into the city, going a day's walk. And he cried out, "Forty days more, and Nineveh shall be overthrown!" 5And the people of Nineveh believed God; they proclaimed a fast, and everyone, great and small, put on sackcloth.

6 When the news reached the king of Nineveh, he rose from his throne, removed his robe, covered himself with sackcloth, and sat in ashes. 7Then he had a proclamation made in Nineveh: "By the decree of the king and his nobles: No human being or animal, no herd or flock, shall taste anything. They shall not feed, nor shall they drink water. 8Human beings and animals shall be covered with sackcloth, and they shall cry mightily to God. All shall turn from their evil ways and from the violence that is in their hands. 9Who knows? God may relent and change his mind; he may turn from his fierce anger, so that we do not perish."

---

c *3:3 so large that it would take three days to walk through it.* The Hebrew text makes no distinction between the city proper—the walls of which were only about eight miles in circumference, accommodating a population of about 175,000 persons—and the administrative district of Nineveh which was about thirty to sixty miles across.   d *3:4, 5 the rough, coarse garments worn at times of mourning,* implied.

e Theodotion: Heb *surely*

King James

10¶ And God saw their works, that they turned from their evil way; and God repented of the evil, that he had said that he would do unto them; and he did *it* not.

4 BUT IT displeased Jonah exceedingly, and he was very angry.

2And he prayed unto the LORD, and said, I pray thee, O LORD, *was* not this my saying, when I was yet in my country? Therefore I fled before unto Tarshish: for I knew that thou *art* a gracious God, and merciful, slow to anger, and of great kindness, and repentest thee of the evil.

3Therefore now, O LORD, take, I beseech thee, my life from me; for *it is* better for me to die than to live.

4¶ Then said the LORD, Doest thou well to be angry?

5So Jonah went out of the city, and sat on the east side of the city, and there made him a booth, and sat under it in the shadow, till he might see what would become of the city.

6And the LORD God prepared a gourd, and made *it* to come up over Jonah, that it might be a shadow over his head, to deliver him from his grief. So Jonah was exceeding glad of the gourd.

7But God prepared a worm when the morning rose the next day, and it smote the gourd that it withered.

8And it came to pass, when the sun did arise, that God prepared a vehement east wind; and the sun beat upon the head of Jonah, that he fainted, and wished in himself to die, and said, *It is* better for me to die than to live.

9And God said to Jonah, Doest thou well to be angry for the gourd? And he said, I do well to be angry, *even* unto death.

10Then said the LORD, Thou hast had pity on the gourd, for the which thou hast not laboured, neither madest it grow; which came up in a night, and perished in a night:

11And should not I spare Nineveh, that great city, wherein are more than sixscore thousand persons that cannot discern between their right hand and their left hand; and *also* much cattle?

New International

10When God saw what they did and how they turned from their evil ways, he had compassion and did not bring upon them the destruction he had threatened.

Jonah's Anger at the LORD's Compassion

4 BUT JONAH was greatly displeased and became angry. 2He prayed to the LORD, "O LORD, is this not what I said when I was still at home? That is why I was so quick to flee to Tarshish. I knew that you are a gracious and compassionate God, slow to anger and abounding in love, a God who relents from sending calamity. 3Now, O LORD, take away my life, for it is better for me to die than to live."

4But the LORD replied, "Have you any right to be angry?"

5Jonah went out and sat down at a place east of the city. There he made himself a shelter, sat in its shade and waited to see what would happen to the city. 6Then the LORD God provided a vine and made it grow up over Jonah to give shade for his head to ease his discomfort, and Jonah was very happy about the vine. 7But at dawn the next day God provided a worm, which chewed the vine so that it withered. 8When the sun rose, God provided a scorching east wind, and the sun blazed on Jonah's head so that he grew faint. He wanted to die, and said, "It would be better for me to die than to live."

9But God said to Jonah, "Do you have a right to be angry about the vine?"

"I do," he said. "I am angry enough to die."

10But the LORD said, "You have been concerned about this vine, though you did not tend it or make it grow. It sprang up overnight and died overnight. 11But Nineveh has more than a hundred and twenty thousand people who cannot tell their right hand from their left, and many cattle as well. Should I not be concerned about that great city?"

Living Bible

10And when God saw that they had put a stop to their evil ways, he abandoned his plan to destroy them, and didn't carry it through.

4 THIS CHANGE of plans made Jonah very angry. 2He complained to the Lord about it: "This is exactly what I thought you'd do, Lord, when I was there in my own country and you first told me to come here. That's why I ran away to Tarshish. For I knew you were a gracious God, merciful, slow to get angry, and full of kindness; I knew how easily you could cancel your plans for destroying these people.

3"Please kill me, Lord; I'd rather be dead than alive [when nothing that I told them happensa]."

4Then the Lord said, "Is it right to be *angry* about *this?"*

5So Jonah went out and sat sulkingb on the east side of the city, and he made a leafy shelter to shade him as he waited there to see if anything would happen to the city. 6And when the leaves of the shelter withered in the heat, the Lord arranged for a vine to grow up quickly and spread its broad leaves over Jonah's head to shade him. This made him comfortable and very grateful.

7But God also prepared a worm! The next morning the worm ate through the stem of the plant, so that it withered away and died.

8Then, when the sun was hot, God ordered a scorching east wind to blow on Jonah, and the sun beat down upon his head until he grew faint and wished to die. For he said, "Death is better than this!"

9And God said to Jonah, "Is it right for you to be angry because the plant died?"

"Yes," Jonah said, "it is; it is right for me to be angry enough to die!"

10Then the Lord said, "You feel sorry for yourself when your shelter is destroyed, though you did no work to put it there, and it is, at best, short-lived. 11And why shouldn't I feel sorry for a great city like Nineveh with its 120,000 people in utter spiritual darkness,c and all its cattle?"

New Revised Standard

10 When God saw what they did, how they turned from their evil ways, God changed his mind about the calamity that he had said he would bring upon them; and he did not do it.

Jonah's Anger

4 BUT THIS was very displeasing to Jonah, and he became angry. 2He prayed to the Lord and said, "O Lord! Is not this what I said while I was still in my own country? That is why I fled to Tarshish at the beginning; for I knew that you are a gracious God and merciful, slow to anger, and abounding in steadfast love, and ready to relent from punishing. 3And now, O Lord, please take my life from me, for it is better for me to die than to live." 4And the Lord said, "Is it right for you to be angry?" 5Then Jonah went out of the city and sat down east of the city, and made a booth for himself there. He sat under it in the shade, waiting to see what would become of the city.

6 The Lord God appointed a bush,d and made it come up over Jonah, to give shade over his head, to save him from his discomfort; so Jonah was very happy about the bush. 7But when dawn came up the next day, God appointed a worm that attacked the bush, so that it withered. 8When the sun rose, God prepared a sultry east wind, and the sun beat down on the head of Jonah so that he was faint and asked that he might die. He said, "It is better for me to die than to live."

Jonah Is Reproved

9 But God said to Jonah, "Is it right for you to be angry about the bush?" And he said, "Yes, angry enough to die." 10Then the Lord said, "You are concerned about the bush, for which you did not labor and which you did not grow; it came into being in a night and perished in a night. 11And should I not be concerned about Nineveh, that great city, in which there are more than a hundred and twenty thousand persons who do not know their right hand from their left, and also many animals?"

---

a 4:3 *when nothing that I told them happens,* implied.   b 4:5 *sat sulking,* implied.   c 4:11 *with its 120,000 people in utter spiritual darkness,* or "with its 120,000 children who don't know their right hands from their left."

d Heb *qiqayon,* possibly *the castor bean plant*

Micah   Micah

1 THE WORD of the LORD that came to Micah the Morasthite in the days of Jotham, Ahaz, *and* Hezekiah, kings of Judah, which he saw concerning Samaria and Jerusalem.

²Hear, all ye people; hearken, O earth, and all that therein is: and let the Lord GOD be witness against you, the Lord from his holy temple.

³For, behold, the LORD cometh forth out of his place, and will come down, and tread upon the high places of the earth.

⁴And the mountains shall be molten under him, and the valleys shall be cleft, as wax before the fire, *and* as the waters *that are* poured down a steep place.

⁵For the transgression of Jacob *is* all this, and for the sins of the house of Israel. What *is* the transgression of Jacob? *is it* not Samaria? and what *are* the high places of Judah? *are they* not Jerusalem?

⁶Therefore I will make Samaria as an heap of the field, *and* as plantings of a vineyard: and I will pour down the stones thereof into the valley, and I will discover the foundations thereof.

⁷And all the graven images thereof shall be beaten to pieces, and all the hires thereof shall be burned with the fire, and all the idols thereof will I lay desolate: for she gathered *it* of the hire of an harlot, and they shall return to the hire of an harlot.

⁸Therefore I will wail and howl, I will go stripped and naked: I will make a wailing like the dragons, and mourning as the owls.

⁹For her wound *is* incurable; for it is come unto Judah; he is come unto the gate of my people, *even* to Jerusalem.

¹⁰¶ Declare ye *it* not at Gath, weep ye not at all: in the house of Aphrah roll thyself in the dust.

---

1 THE WORD of the LORD that came to Micah of Moresheth during the reigns of Jotham, Ahaz and Hezekiah, kings of Judah—the vision he saw concerning Samaria and Jerusalem.

²Hear, O peoples, all of you,
 listen, O earth and all who are in it,
that the Sovereign LORD may witness against
  you,
 the Lord from his holy temple.

Judgment Against Samaria and Jerusalem

³Look! The LORD is coming from his dwelling
  place;
 he comes down and treads the high places of
  the earth.
⁴The mountains melt beneath him
 and the valleys split apart,
like wax before the fire,
 like water rushing down a slope.
⁵All this is because of Jacob's transgression,
 because of the sins of the house of Israel.
What is Jacob's transgression?
 Is it not Samaria?
What is Judah's high place?
 Is it not Jerusalem?

⁶"Therefore I will make Samaria a heap of
  rubble,
 a place for planting vineyards.
I will pour her stones into the valley
 and lay bare her foundations.
⁷All her idols will be broken to pieces;
 all her temple gifts will be burned with fire;
 I will destroy all her images.
Since she gathered her gifts from the wages of
  prostitutes,
 as the wages of prostitutes they will again be
  used."

Weeping and Mourning

⁸Because of this I will weep and wail;
 I will go about barefoot and naked.
I will howl like a jackal
 and moan like an owl.
⁹For her wound is incurable;
 it has come to Judah.
Itª has reached the very gate of my people,
 even to Jerusalem itself.
¹⁰Tell it not in Gathᵇ;
 weep not at all.ᶜ
In Beth Ophrahᵈ
 roll in the dust.

ª *9 Or He* ᵇ *10 Gath* sounds like the Hebrew for *tell.* ᶜ *10* Hebrew; Septuagint may suggest *not in Acco.* The Hebrew for *in Acco* sounds like the Hebrew for *weep.* ᵈ *10 Beth Ophrah* means *house of dust.*

Micah   # Micah

1 THESE ARE messages from the Lord to Micah, who lived in the town of Moresheth during the reigns of King Jotham, King Ahaz, and King Hezekiah, all kings of Judah. The messages were addressed to both Samaria and Judah, and came to Micah in the form of visions.
²Attention! Let all the peoples of the world listen. For the Lord in his holy Temple has made accusations against you!
³Look! He is coming! He leaves his throne in heaven and comes to earth, walking on the mountaintops. ⁴They melt beneath his feet, and flow into the valleys like wax in fire, like water pouring down a hill.
⁵And why is this happening? Because of the sins of Israel and Judah. What sins? The idolatry and oppression centering in the capital cities, Samaria and Jerusalem!
⁶Therefore the entire city of Samaria will crumble into a heap of rubble, and become an open field, her streets plowed up for planting grapes! The Lord will tear down her wall and her forts, exposing their foundations, and pour their stones into the valleys below. ⁷All her carved images will be smashed to pieces; her ornate idol temples, built with the gifts of worshipers, will all be burned.ᵉ
⁸I will wail and lament, howling as a jackal, mournful as an ostrich crying across the desert sands at night. I will walk naked and barefoot in sorrow and shame; ⁹for my people's wound is far too deep to heal. The Lord stands ready at Jerusalem's gates to punish her. ¹⁰Woe to the city of Gath. Weep, men of Bakah. In Beth-le-aphrah roll in the dust in your anguish and shame.

1 THE WORD of the LORD that came to Micah of Moresheth in the days of Kings Jotham, Ahaz, and Hezekiah of Judah, which he saw concerning Samaria and Jerusalem.

Judgment Pronounced against Samaria

2 Hear, you peoples, all of you;
       listen, O earth, and all that is in it;
       and let the Lord GOD be a witness against
           you,
       the Lord from his holy temple.
3 For lo, the LORD is coming out of his place,
       and will come down and tread upon the
           high places of the earth.
4 Then the mountains will melt under him
       and the valleys will burst open,
   like wax near the fire,
       like waters poured down a steep place.
5 All this is for the transgression of Jacob
       and for the sins of the house of Israel.
   What is the transgression of Jacob?
       Is it not Samaria?
   And what is the high placeᶠ of Judah?
       Is it not Jerusalem?
6 Therefore I will make Samaria a heap in the
           open country,
       a place for planting vineyards.
   I will pour down her stones into the valley,
       and uncover her foundations.
7 All her images shall be beaten to pieces,
       all her wages shall be burned with fire,
       and all her idols I will lay waste;
   for as the wages of a prostitute she gathered
           them,
       and as the wages of a prostitute they shall
           again be used.

The Doom of the Cities of Judah

8 For this I will lament and wail;
       I will go barefoot and naked;
   I will make lamentation like the jackals,
       and mourning like the ostriches.
9 For her woundᵍ is incurable.
       It has come to Judah;
   it has reached to the gate of my people,
       to Jerusalem.

10 Tell it not in Gath,
        weep not at all;
    in Beth-leaphrah
        roll yourselves in the dust.

ᵉ *1:7 will all be burned,* literally, "they shall return to the hire of an harlot."   ᶠ Heb *what are the high places*   ᵍ Gk Syr Vg: Heb *wounds*

King James

11Pass ye away, thou inhabitant of Saphir, having thy shame naked: the inhabitant of Zaanan came not forth in the mourning of Beth-ezel; he shall receive of you his standing.

12For the inhabitant of Maroth waited carefully for good: but evil came down from the LORD unto the gate of Jerusalem.

13O thou inhabitant of Lachish, bind the chariot to the swift beast: she *is* the beginning of the sin to the daughter of Zion: for the transgressions of Israel were found in thee.

14Therefore shalt thou give presents to Moresheth-gath: the houses of Achzib *shall be* a lie to the kings of Israel.

15Yet will I bring an heir unto thee, O inhabitant of Mareshah: he shall come unto Adullam the glory of Israel.

16Make thee bald, and poll thee for thy delicate children; enlarge thy baldness as the eagle; for they are gone into captivity from thee.

2 WOE TO them that devise iniquity, and work evil upon their beds! when the morning is light, they practice it, because it is in the power of their hand.

2And they covet fields, and take *them* by violence; and houses, and take *them* away: so they oppress a man and his house, even a man and his heritage.

3Therefore thus saith the LORD; Behold, against this family do I devise an evil, from which ye shall not remove your necks; neither shall ye go haughtily: for this time *is* evil.

4¶ In that day shall *one* take up a parable against you, and lament with a doleful lamentation, *and* say, We be utterly spoiled: he hath changed the portion of my people: how hath he removed *it* from me! turning away he hath divided our fields.

5Therefore thou shalt have none that shall cast a cord by lot in the congregation of the LORD.

6 Prophesy ye not, *say they to them that* prophesy: they shall not prophesy to them, *that* they shall not take shame.

7¶ O *thou that art* named the house of Jacob, is the spirit of the LORD straitened? *are* these his doings? do not my words do good to him that walketh uprightly?

New International

11Pass on in nakedness and shame,
    you who live in Shaphir.[a]
Those who live in Zaanan[b]
    will not come out.
Beth Ezel is in mourning;
    its protection is taken from you.
12Those who live in Maroth[c] writhe in pain,
    waiting for relief,
because disaster has come from the LORD,
    even to the gate of Jerusalem.
13You who live in Lachish,[d]
    harness the team to the chariot.
You were the beginning of sin
    to the Daughter of Zion,
for the transgressions of Israel
    were found in you.
14Therefore you will give parting gifts
    to Moresheth Gath.
The town of Aczib[e] will prove deceptive
    to the kings of Israel.
15I will bring a conqueror against you
    who live in Mareshah.[f]
He who is the glory of Israel
    will come to Adullam.
16Shave your heads in mourning
    for the children in whom you delight;
make yourselves as bald as the vulture,
    for they will go from you into exile.

Man's Plans and God's

2 WOE TO those who plan iniquity,
    to those who plot evil on their beds!
At morning's light they carry it out
    because it is in their power to do it.
2They covet fields and seize them,
    and houses, and take them.
They defraud a man of his home,
    a fellowman of his inheritance.

3Therefore, the LORD says:

"I am planning disaster against this people,
    from which you cannot save yourselves.
You will no longer walk proudly,
    for it will be a time of calamity.
4In that day men will ridicule you;
    they will taunt you with this mournful song:
'We are utterly ruined;
    my people's possession is divided up.
He takes it from me!
    He assigns our fields to traitors.' "

5Therefore you will have no one in the assembly
        of the LORD
    to divide the land by lot.

False Prophets

6"Do not prophesy," their prophets say.
    "Do not prophesy about these things;
    disgrace will not overtake us."
7Should it be said, O house of Jacob:
    "Is the Spirit of the LORD angry?
    Does he do such things?"

"Do not my words do good
    to him whose ways are upright?

a *11 Shaphir* means *pleasant.*   b *11 Zaanan* sounds like the Hebrew for *come out.*   c *12 Maroth* sounds like the Hebrew for *bitter.*   d *13 Lachish* sounds like the Hebrew for *team.*   e *14 Aczib* means *deception.*   f *15 Mareshah* sounds like the Hebrew for *conqueror.*

Living Bible

11There go the people of Shaphir,g led away as slaves—stripped, naked and ashamed. The people of Zaanang dare not show themselves outside their walls. The foundations of Beth-ezelg are swept away—the very ground on which it stood. 12The people of Maroth vainly hope for better days, but only bitterness awaits them as the Lord stands poised against Jerusalem.

13Quick! Use your swiftest chariots and flee, O people of Lachish, for you were the first of the cities of Judah to follow Israel in her sin of idol worship. Then all the cities of the south began to follow your example.

14Write off Moreshethh of Gath; there is no hope of saving her. The town of Achzib has deceived the kings of Israel, for she promised help she cannot give. 15You people of Mareshah will be a prize to your enemies. They will penetrate to Adullam, the "Pride of Israel."

16Weep, weep for your little ones. For they are snatched away and you will never see them again. They have gone as slaves to distant lands. Shave your heads in sorrow.

2 WOE TO you who lie awake at night, plotting wickedness; you rise at dawn to carry out your schemes; because you can, you do. 2You want a certain piece of land, or someone else's house (though it is all he has); you take it by fraud and threats and violence.

3But the Lord God says, I will reward your evil with evil; nothing can stop me; never again will you be proud and haughty after I am through with you. 4Then your enemies will taunt you and mock your dirge of despair: "We are finished, ruined. God has confiscated our land and sent us far away, and given what is ours to others." 5Others will set your boundaries then. "The People of the Lord" will live where they are sent.

6"Don't say such things," the people say. "Don't harp on things like that. It's disgraceful, that sort of talk. Such evils surely will not come our way."

7Is that the right reply for you to make, O House of Jacob? Do you think the Spirit of the Lord likes to talk to you so roughly? No! His threats are for your good, to get you on the path again.

New Revised Standard

11 Pass on your way,
   inhabitants of Shaphir,
   in nakedness and shame;
the inhabitants of Zaanan
   do not come forth;
Beth-ezel is wailing
   and shall remove its support from you.
12 For the inhabitants of Maroth
   wait anxiously for good,
yet disaster has come down from the LORD
   to the gate of Jerusalem.
13 Harness the steeds to the chariots,
   inhabitants of Lachish;
it was the beginning of sin
   to daughter Zion,
for in you were found
   the transgressions of Israel.
14 Therefore you shall give parting gifts
   to Moresheth-gath;
the houses of Achzib shall be a deception
   to the kings of Israel.
15 I will again bring a conqueror upon you,
   inhabitants of Mareshah;
the glory of Israel
   shall come to Adullam.
16 Make yourselves bald and cut off your hair
   for your pampered children;
make yourselves as bald as the eagle,
   for they have gone from you into exile.

Social Evils Denounced

2 ALAS FOR those who devise wickedness
   and evil deedsi on their beds!
When the morning dawns, they perform it,
   because it is in their power.
2 They covet fields, and seize them;
   houses, and take them away;
they oppress householder and house,
   people and their inheritance.
3 Therefore thus says the LORD:
Now, I am devising against this family an evil
   from which you cannot remove your necks;
and you shall not walk haughtily,
   for it will be an evil time.
4 On that day they shall take up a taunt song
      against you,
   and wail with bitter lamentation,
and say, "We are utterly ruined;
   the LORDj alters the inheritance of my
      people;
how he removes it from me!
   Among our captorsk he parcels out our
      fields."
5 Therefore you will have no one to cast the
      line by lot
   in the assembly of the LORD.

6 "Do not preach"—thus they preach—
   "one should not preach of such things;
   disgrace will not overtake us."
7 Should this be said, O house of Jacob?
   Is the LORD's patience exhausted?
   Are these his doings?
Do not my words do good
   to one who walks uprightly?

---

g *1:11 There go the people of Shaphir.* In the Hebrew there is frequent word play in vss 10-14. Micah bitterly declaims each town, demonstrating by the use of puns their failures. *Shaphir* sounds like the Hebrew word for "beauty," here contrasted with their shame; *Zaanan* sounds like the verb meaning "to go forth," here contrasted with the fear of its inhabitants to venture outside; *Beth-ezel* sounds like a word for "foundation," which had been taken away from them. h *1:14 Moresheth,* Micah's home town (1:1).

i Cn: Heb *work evil*   j Heb *he*   k Cn: Heb *the rebellious*

King James

8Even of late my people is risen up as an enemy: ye pull off the robe with the garment from them that pass by securely as men averse from war.

9The women of my people have ye cast out from their pleasant houses; from their children have ye taken away my glory for ever.

10Arise ye, and depart; for this *is* not *your* rest: because it is polluted, it shall destroy *you*, even with a sore destruction.

11If a man walking in the spirit and falsehood do lie, *saying,* I will prophesy unto thee of wine and of strong drink; he shall even be the prophet of this people.

12¶ I will surely assemble, O Jacob, all of thee; I will surely gather the remnant of Israel; I will put them together as the sheep of Bozrah, as the flock in the midst of their fold: they shall make great noise by reason of *the multitude of* men.

13The breaker is come up before them: they have broken up, and have passed through the gate, and are gone out by it: and their king shall pass before them, and the LORD on the head of them.

3 AND I said, Hear, I pray you, O heads of Jacob, and ye princes of the house of Israel; *Is it* not for you to know judgment?

2Who hate the good, and love the evil; who pluck off their skin from off them, and their flesh from off their bones;

3Who also eat the flesh of my people, and flay their skin from off them; and they break their bones, and chop them in pieces, as for the pot, and as flesh within the caldron.

4Then shall they cry unto the LORD, but he will not hear them: he will even hide his face from them at that time, as they have behaved themselves ill in their doings.

5¶ Thus saith the LORD concerning the prophets that make my people err, that bite with their teeth, and cry, Peace; and he that putteth not into their mouths, they even prepare war against him.

6Therefore night *shall be* unto you, that ye shall not have a vision; and it shall be dark unto you, that ye shall not divine; and the sun shall go down over the prophets, and the day shall be dark over them.

7Then shall the seers be ashamed, and the diviners confounded: yea, they shall all cover their lips; for *there is* no answer of God.

New International

8Lately my people have risen up
  like an enemy.
You strip off the rich robe
  from those who pass by without a care,
  like men returning from battle.
9You drive the women of my people
  from their pleasant homes.
You take away my blessing
  from their children forever.
10Get up, go away!
  For this is not your resting place,
  because it is defiled,
  it is ruined, beyond all remedy.
11If a liar and deceiver comes and says,
  'I will prophesy for you plenty of wine and
    beer,'
  he would be just the prophet for this people!

Deliverance Promised

12"I will surely gather all of you, O Jacob;
  I will surely bring together the remnant of
    Israel.
I will bring them together like sheep in a pen,
  like a flock in its pasture;
  the place will throng with people.
13One who breaks open the way will go up before
    them;
  they will break through the gate and go out.
Their king will pass through before them,
  the LORD at their head."

Leaders and Prophets Rebuked

3 THEN I said,

"Listen, you leaders of Jacob,
  you rulers of the house of Israel.
Should you not know justice,
2   you who hate good and love evil;
who tear the skin from my people
  and the flesh from their bones;
3who eat my people's flesh,
  strip off their skin
  and break their bones in pieces;
who chop them up like meat for the pan,
  like flesh for the pot?"

4Then they will cry out to the LORD,
  but he will not answer them.
At that time he will hide his face from them
  because of the evil they have done.

5This is what the LORD says:

"As for the prophets
  who lead my people astray,
if one feeds them,
  they proclaim 'peace';
if he does not,
  they prepare to wage war against him.
6Therefore night will come over you, without
    visions,
  and darkness, without divination.
The sun will set for the prophets,
  and the day will go dark for them.
7The seers will be ashamed
  and the diviners disgraced.
They will all cover their faces
  because there is no answer from God."

Living Bible

8Yet to this very hour my people rise against me. For you steal the shirts right off the backs of those who trusted you, who walk in peace.

9You have driven out the widows from their homes, and stripped their children of every God-given right. 10Up! Begone! This is no more your land and home, for you have filled it with sin and it will vomit you out. 11"I'll preach to you the joys of wine and drink"— that is the kind of drunken, lying prophet that you like! 12The time will come, O Israel, when I will gather you—all that are left—and bring you together again like sheep in a fold, like a flock in a pasture—a noisy, happy crowd. 13The Messiaha will lead you out of exile and bring you through the gates of your cities of captivity, back to your own land. Your King will go before you— the Lord leads on.

3 LISTEN, YOU leaders of Israel—you are supposed to know right from wrong, 2yet you are the very ones who hate good and love evil; you skin my people and strip them to the bone.

3You devour them, flog them, break their bones, and chop them up like meat for the cooking pot— 4and then you plead with the Lord for his help in times of trouble! Do you really expect him to listen? He will look the other way! 5You false prophets! You who lead his people astray! You who cry "Peace" to those who give you food, and threaten those who will not pay!

This is God's message to you: 6The night will close about you and cut off all your visions; darkness will cover you, with never a word from God. The sun will go down upon you, and your day will end. 7Then at last you will cover your faces in shame, and admit that your messages were not from God.

New Revised Standard

8 But you rise up against my peopleb as an
        enemy;
     you strip the robe from the peaceful,c
   from those who pass by trustingly
     with no thought of war.
9 The women of my people you drive out
        from their pleasant houses;
   from their young children you take away
        my glory forever.
10 Arise and go;
        for this is no place to rest,
   because of uncleanness that destroys
        with a grievous destruction.d
11 If someone were to go about uttering empty
        falsehoods,
     saying, "I will preach to you of wine and
        strong drink,"
     such a one would be the preacher for this
        people!

A Promise for the Remnant of Israel

12 I will surely gather all of you, O Jacob,
        I will gather the survivors of Israel;
   I will set them together
        like sheep in a fold,
   like a flock in its pasture;
        it will resound with people.
13 The one who breaks out will go up before
        them;
     they will break through and pass the gate,
        going out by it.
   Their king will pass on before them,
        the LORD at their head.

Wicked Rulers and Prophets

3 AND I said:
   Listen, you heads of Jacob
        and rulers of the house of Israel!
   Should you not know justice?—
2   you who hate the good and love the evil,
   who tear the skin off my people,e
        and the flesh off their bones;
3 who eat the flesh of my people,
        flay their skin off them,
   break their bones in pieces,
        and chop them up like meatf in a kettle,
        like flesh in a caldron.

4 Then they will cry to the LORD,
        but he will not answer them;
   he will hide his face from them at that time,
        because they have acted wickedly.

5 Thus says the LORD concerning the prophets
        who lead my people astray,
   who cry "Peace"
        when they have something to eat,
   but declare war against those
        who put nothing into their mouths.
6 Therefore it shall be night to you, without
        vision,
        and darkness to you, without revelation.
   The sun shall go down upon the prophets,
        and the day shall be black over them;
7 the seers shall be disgraced,
        and the diviners put to shame;
   they shall all cover their lips,
        for there is no answer from God.

---

a 2:13 The Messiah, literally, "He who opens the breach."

b Cn: Heb But yesterday my people rose   c Cn: Heb from before a garment
d Meaning of Heb uncertain   e Heb from them   f Gk: Heb as

King James

8¶ But truly I am full of power by the spirit of the LORD, and of judgment, and of might, to declare unto Jacob his transgression, and to Israel his sin.

9Hear this, I pray you, ye heads of the house of Jacob, and princes of the house of Israel, that abhor judgment, and pervert all equity.

10They build up Zion with blood, and Jerusalem with iniquity.

11The heads thereof judge for reward, and the priests thereof teach for hire, and the prophets thereof divine for money: yet will they lean upon the LORD, and say, *Is* not the LORD among us? none evil can come upon us.

12Therefore shall Zion for your sake be plowed *as* a field, and Jerusalem shall become heaps, and the mountain of the house as the high places of the forest.

4 BUT IN the last days it shall come to pass, *that* the mountain of the house of the LORD shall be established in the top of the mountains, and it shall be exalted above the hills; and people shall flow unto it.

2And many nations shall come, and say, Come, and let us go up to the mountain of the LORD, and to the house of the God of Jacob; and he will teach us of his ways, and we will walk in his paths: for the law shall go forth of Zion, and the word of the LORD from Jerusalem.

3¶ And he shall judge among many people, and rebuke strong nations afar off; and they shall beat their swords into plowshares, and their spears into pruninghooks: nation shall not lift up a sword against nation, neither shall they learn war any more.

4But they shall sit every man under his vine and under his fig tree; and none shall make *them* afraid: for the mouth of the LORD of hosts hath spoken *it*.

5For all people will walk every one in the name of his god, and we will walk in the name of the LORD our God for ever and ever.

6In that day, saith the LORD, will I assemble her that halteth, and I will gather her that is driven out, and her that I have afflicted;

7And I will make her that halted a remnant, and her that was cast far off a strong nation: and the LORD shall reign over them in mount Zion from henceforth, even for ever.

New International

8But as for me, I am filled with power,
   with the Spirit of the LORD,
   and with justice and might,
to declare to Jacob his transgression,
   to Israel his sin.

9Hear this, you leaders of the house of Jacob,
   you rulers of the house of Israel,
who despise justice
   and distort all that is right;
10who build Zion with bloodshed,
   and Jerusalem with wickedness.
11Her leaders judge for a bribe,
   her priests teach for a price,
   and her prophets tell fortunes for money.
Yet they lean upon the LORD and say,
   "Is not the LORD among us?
   No disaster will come upon us."
12Therefore because of you,
   Zion will be plowed like a field,
Jerusalem will become a heap of rubble,
   the temple hill a mound overgrown with
      thickets.

The Mountain of the LORD

4 IN THE last days

the mountain of the LORD's temple will be
      established
   as chief among the mountains;
it will be raised above the hills,
   and peoples will stream to it.

2Many nations will come and say,

"Come, let us go up to the mountain of the
      LORD,
   to the house of the God of Jacob.
He will teach us his ways,
   so that we may walk in his paths."
The law will go out from Zion,
   the word of the LORD from Jerusalem.
3He will judge between many peoples
   and will settle disputes for strong nations far
      and wide.
They will beat their swords into plowshares
   and their spears into pruning hooks.
Nation will not take up sword against nation,
   nor will they train for war anymore.
4Every man will sit under his own vine
   and under his own fig tree,
and no one will make them afraid,
   for the LORD Almighty has spoken.
5All the nations may walk
   in the name of their gods;
we will walk in the name of the LORD
   our God for ever and ever.

The LORD's Plan

6"In that day," declares the LORD,

"I will gather the lame;
   I will assemble the exiles
   and those I have brought to grief.
7I will make the lame a remnant,
   those driven away a strong nation.
The LORD will rule over them in Mount Zion
   from that day and forever.

Living Bible

8But as for me, I am filled with power, with the Spirit of the Lord, fearlessly announcing God's punishment on Israel for her sins.

9Listen to me, you leaders of Israel who hate justice and love unfairness, 10and fill Jerusalem with murder and sin of every kind— 11you leaders who take bribes; you priests and prophets who won't preach and prophesy until you're paid. (And yet you fawn upon the Lord and say, "All is well—the Lord is here among us. No harm can come to us.") 12It is because of you that Jerusalem will be plowed like a field, and become a heap of rubble; the mountaintop where the Temple stands will be overgrown with brush.

4 BUT IN the last days Mount Zion will be the most renowned of all the mountains of the world, praised by all nations; people from all over the world will make pilgrimages there.

2"Come," they will say to one another, "let us visit the mountain of the Lord, and see the Temple of the God of Israel; he will tell us what to do, and we will do it." For in those days the whole world will be ruled by the Lord from Jerusalem! He will issue his laws and announce his decrees from there.

3He will arbitrate among the nations, and dictate to strong nations far away. They will beat their swords into plowshares and their spears into pruning-hooks; nations shall no longer fight each other, for all war will end. There will be universal peace, and all the military academies and training camps will be closed down.

4Everyone will live quietly in his own home in peace and prosperity, for there will be nothing to fear. The Lord himself has promised this. 5(Therefore we will follow the Lord our God forever and ever, even though all the nations around us worship idols!)

6In that coming day, the Lord says that he will bring back his punished people—sick and lame and dispossessed— 7and make them strong again in their own land, a mighty nation, and the Lord himself shall be their King from Mount Zion forever. 8O Jerusalem—the

New Revised Standard

8 But as for me, I am filled with power,
    with the spirit of the LORD,
    and with justice and might,
to declare to Jacob his transgression
    and to Israel his sin.

9 Hear this, you rulers of the house of Jacob
    and chiefs of the house of Israel,
who abhor justice
    and pervert all equity,
10 who build Zion with blood
    and Jerusalem with wrong!
11 Its rulers give judgment for a bribe,
    its priests teach for a price,
    its prophets give oracles for money;
yet they lean upon the LORD and say,
    "Surely the LORD is with us!
    No harm shall come upon us."
12 Therefore because of you
    Zion shall be plowed as a field;
Jerusalem shall become a heap of ruins,
    and the mountain of the house a wooded
        height.

Peace and Security through Obedience

4 IN DAYS to come
    the mountain of the LORD's house
shall be established as the highest of the
        mountains,
    and shall be raised up above the hills.
Peoples shall stream to it,
2   and many nations shall come and say:
"Come, let us go up to the mountain of the
        LORD,
    to the house of the God of Jacob;
that he may teach us his ways
    and that we may walk in his paths."
For out of Zion shall go forth instruction,
    and the word of the LORD from Jerusalem.
3 He shall judge between many peoples,
    and shall arbitrate between strong nations
        far away;
they shall beat their swords into plowshares,
    and their spears into pruning hooks;
nation shall not lift up sword against nation,
    neither shall they learn war any more;
4 but they shall all sit under their own vines and
        under their own fig trees,
    and no one shall make them afraid;
for the mouth of the LORD of hosts has
        spoken.

5 For all the peoples walk,
    each in the name of its god,
but we will walk in the name of the LORD our
        God
    forever and ever.

Restoration Promised after Exile

6 In that day, says the LORD,
    I will assemble the lame
and gather those who have been driven away,
    and those whom I have afflicted.
7 The lame I will make the remnant,
    and those who were cast off, a strong
        nation;
and the LORD will reign over them in Mount
        Zion
    now and forevermore.

King James

8¶ And thou, O tower of the flock, the strong hold of the daughter of Zion, unto thee shall it come, even the first dominion; the kingdom shall come to the daughter of Jerusalem.

9Now why dost thou cry out aloud? *is there* no king in thee? is thy counsellor perished? for pangs have taken thee as a woman in travail.

10Be in pain, and labour to bring forth, O daughter of Zion, like a woman in travail: for now shalt thou go forth out of the city, and thou shalt dwell in the field, and thou shalt go *even* to Babylon; there shalt thou be delivered; there the LORD shall redeem thee from the hand of thine enemies.

11¶ Now also many nations are gathered against thee, that say, Let her be defiled, and let our eye look upon Zion.

12But they know not the thoughts of the LORD, neither understand they his counsel: for he shall gather them as the sheaves into the floor.

13Arise and thresh, O daughter of Zion: for I will make thine horn iron, and I will make thy hoofs brass: and thou shalt beat in pieces many people: and I will consecrate their gain unto the LORD, and their substance unto the Lord of the whole earth.

5 NOW GATHER thyself in troops, O daughter of troops: he hath laid siege against us: they shall smite the judge of Israel with a rod upon the cheek.

2But thou, Bethlehem Ephratah, *though* thou be little among the thousands of Judah, *yet* out of thee shall he come forth unto me *that is* to be ruler in Israel; whose goings forth *have been* from of old, from everlasting.

3Therefore will he give them up, until the time *that* she which travaileth hath brought forth: then the remnant of his brethren shall return unto the children of Israel.

4¶ And he shall stand and feed in the strength of the LORD, in the majesty of the name of the LORD his God; and they shall abide: for now shall he be great unto the ends of the earth.

5And this *man* shall be the peace, when the Assyrian shall come into our land: and when he shall tread in our palaces, then shall we raise against him seven shepherds, and eight principal men.

New International

8As for you, O watchtower of the flock,
    O strongholda of the Daughter of Zion,
the former dominion will be restored to you;
    kingship will come to the Daughter of
        Jerusalem."

9Why do you now cry aloud—
    have you no king?
Has your counselor perished,
    that pain seizes you like that of a woman in
        labor?
10Writhe in agony, O Daughter of Zion,
    like a woman in labor,
for now you must leave the city
    to camp in the open field.
You will go to Babylon;
    there you will be rescued.
There the LORD will redeem you
    out of the hand of your enemies.

11But now many nations
    are gathered against you.
They say, "Let her be defiled,
    let our eyes gloat over Zion!"
12But they do not know
    the thoughts of the LORD;
they do not understand his plan,
    he who gathers them like sheaves to the
        threshing floor.

13"Rise and thresh, O Daughter of Zion,
    for I will give you horns of iron;
I will give you hoofs of bronze
    and you will break to pieces many nations."

You will devote their ill-gotten gains to the
        LORD,
    their wealth to the Lord of all the earth.

A Promised Ruler From Bethlehem

5 MARSHAL YOUR troops, O city of troops,b
    for a siege is laid against us.
They will strike Israel's ruler
    on the cheek with a rod.

2"But you, Bethlehem Ephrathah,
    though you are small among the clansc of
        Judah,
out of you will come for me
    one who will be ruler over Israel,
whose originsd are from of old,
    from ancient times.e"

3Therefore Israel will be abandoned
    until the time when she who is in labor gives
        birth
and the rest of his brothers return
    to join the Israelites.

4He will stand and shepherd his flock
    in the strength of the LORD,
    in the majesty of the name of the LORD his
        God.
And they will live securely, for then his
        greatness
    will reach to the ends of the earth.
5 And he will be their peace.

Deliverance and Destruction

When the Assyrian invades our land
    and marches through our fortresses,
we will raise against him seven shepherds,
    even eight leaders of men.

a 8 Or *hill*   b 1 Or *Strengthen your walls, O walled city*   c 2 Or *rulers*
d 2 Hebrew *goings out*   e 2 Or *from days of eternity*

Living Bible

Watchtower of God's people—your royal might and power will come back to you again, just as before.

⁹But for now, now you scream in terror. Where is your king to lead you? He is dead! Where are your wise men? All are gone! Pain has gripped you like a woman in labor. ¹⁰Writhe and groan in your terrible pain, O people of Zion, for you must leave this city and live in the fields; you will be sent far away into exile in Babylon. But there I will rescue you and free you from the grip of your enemies.

¹¹True, many nations have gathered together against you, calling for your blood, eager to destroy you. ¹²But they do not know my thoughts nor understand my plan, for the time will come when the Lord will gather together the enemies of his people like sheaves upon the threshing floor, ¹³helpless before Israel.

Rise, thresh, O daughter of Zion; I will give you horns of iron and hoofs of brass and you will trample to pieces many people, and you will give their wealth as offerings to the Lord, the Lord of all the earth.

5 MOBILIZE! THE enemy lays siege to Jerusalem! With a rod they shall strike the Judge of Israel on the face.

²O Bethlehem Ephrathah, you are but a small Judean village, yet you will be the birthplace of my King who is alive from everlasting ages past! ³God will abandon his people to their enemies until she who is to give birth has her son; then at last his fellow countrymen—the exile remnants of Israel—will rejoin their brethren in their own land.

⁴And he shall stand and feed his flock in the strength of the Lord, in the majesty of the name of the Lord his God, and his people shall remain there undisturbed, for he will be greatly honored all around the world. ⁵He will be our Peace. And when the Assyrian[f] invades our land and marches across our hills, he will appoint seven shepherds to watch over us, eight princes to lead us. ⁶They

New Revised Standard

8 And you, O tower of the flock,
　　hill of daughter Zion,
to you it shall come,
　　the former dominion shall come,
　　the sovereignty of daughter Jerusalem.

9 Now why do you cry aloud?
　　Is there no king in you?
Has your counselor perished,
　　that pangs have seized you like a woman in
　　　labor?
10 Writhe and groan,[g] O daughter Zion,
　　like a woman in labor;
for now you shall go forth from the city
　　and camp in the open country;
　　you shall go to Babylon.
There you shall be rescued,
　　there the LORD will redeem you
　　from the hands of your enemies.

11 Now many nations
　　are assembled against you,
saying, "Let her be profaned,
　　and let our eyes gaze upon Zion."
12 But they do not know
　　the thoughts of the LORD;
they do not understand his plan,
　　that he has gathered them as sheaves to the
　　　threshing floor.
13 Arise and thresh,
　　O daughter Zion,
for I will make your horn iron
　　and your hoofs bronze;
you shall beat in pieces many peoples,
　　and shall[h] devote their gain to the LORD,
　　their wealth to the Lord of the whole earth.

5[i] NOW YOU are walled around with a wall;[j]
　　siege is laid against us;
with a rod they strike the ruler of Israel
　　upon the cheek.

The Ruler from Bethlehem

2[k] But you, O Bethlehem of Ephrathah,
　　who are one of the little clans of Judah,
from you shall come forth for me
　　one who is to rule in Israel,
whose origin is from of old,
　　from ancient days.
3 Therefore he shall give them up until the time
　　when she who is in labor has brought forth;
then the rest of his kindred shall return
　　to the people of Israel.
4 And he shall stand and feed his flock in the
　　　strength of the LORD,
　　in the majesty of the name of the LORD his
　　　God.
And they shall live secure, for now he shall
　　　be great
　　to the ends of the earth;
5 and he shall be the one of peace.

　　If the Assyrians come into our land
　　　and tread upon our soil,[l]
we will raise against them seven shepherds
　　and eight installed as rulers.

---

g Meaning of Heb uncertain　h Gk Syr Tg: Heb *and I will*　i Ch 4.14 in Heb　j Cn Compare Gk: Meaning of Heb uncertain　k Ch 5.1 in Heb　l Gk: Heb *in our palaces*

f 5:5 The area of ancient Assyria is now known as Iraq.

King James

6And they shall waste the land of Assyria with the sword, and the land of Nimrod in the entrances thereof: thus shall he deliver *us* from the Assyrian, when he cometh into our land, and when he treadeth within our borders.

7And the remnant of Jacob shall be in the midst of many people as a dew from the LORD, as the showers upon the grass, that tarrieth not for man, nor waiteth for the sons of men.

8¶ And the remnant of Jacob shall be among the Gentiles in the midst of many people as a lion among the beasts of the forest, as a young lion among the flocks of sheep: who, if he go through, both treadeth down, and teareth in pieces, and none can deliver.

9Thine hand shall be lifted up upon thine adversaries, and all thine enemies shall be cut off.

10And it shall come to pass in that day, saith the LORD, that I will cut off thy horses out of the midst of thee, and I will destroy thy chariots:

11And I will cut off the cities of thy land, and throw down all thy strong holds:

12And I will cut off witchcrafts out of thine hand; and thou shalt have no *more* soothsayers:

13Thy graven images also will I cut off, and thy standing images out of the midst of thee; and thou shalt no more worship the work of thine hands.

14And I will pluck up thy groves out of the midst of thee: so will I destroy thy cities.

15And I will execute vengeance in anger and fury upon the heathen, such as they have not heard.

6 HEAR YE now what the LORD saith; Arise, contend thou before the mountains, and let the hills hear thy voice.

2Hear ye, O mountains, the LORD's controversy, and ye strong foundations of the earth: for the LORD hath a controversy with his people, and he will plead with Israel.

3O my people, what have I done unto thee? and wherein have I wearied thee? testify against me.

4For I brought thee up out of the land of Egypt, and redeemed thee out of the house of servants; and I sent before thee Moses, Aaron, and Miriam.

5O my people, remember now what Balak king of Moab consulted, and what Balaam the son of Beor answered him from Shittim unto Gilgal; that ye may know the righteousness of the LORD.

New International

6They will rule[a] the land of Assyria with the sword,
　　the land of Nimrod with drawn sword.[b]
He will deliver us from the Assyrian
　when he invades our land
　and marches into our borders.

7The remnant of Jacob will be
　in the midst of many peoples
like dew from the LORD,
　like showers on the grass,
which do not wait for man
　or linger for mankind.
8The remnant of Jacob will be among the
　　nations,
　in the midst of many peoples,
like a lion among the beasts of the forest,
　like a young lion among flocks of sheep,
which mauls and mangles as it goes,
　and no one can rescue.
9Your hand will be lifted up in triumph over
　　your enemies,
　and all your foes will be destroyed.

10"In that day," declares the LORD,

"I will destroy your horses from among you
　and demolish your chariots.
11I will destroy the cities of your land
　and tear down all your strongholds.
12I will destroy your witchcraft
　and you will no longer cast spells.
13I will destroy your carved images
　and your sacred stones from among you;
you will no longer bow down
　to the work of your hands.
14I will uproot from among you your Asherah
　　poles[c]
　and demolish your cities.
15I will take vengeance in anger and wrath
　upon the nations that have not obeyed me."

The LORD's Case Against Israel

6 LISTEN TO what the LORD says:

"Stand up, plead your case before the
　　mountains;
　let the hills hear what you have to say.
2Hear, O mountains, the LORD's accusation;
　listen, you everlasting foundations of the
　　earth.
For the LORD has a case against his people;
　he is lodging a charge against Israel.

3"My people, what have I done to you?
　How have I burdened you? Answer me.
4I brought you up out of Egypt
　and redeemed you from the land of slavery.
I sent Moses to lead you,
　also Aaron and Miriam.
5My people, remember
　what Balak king of Moab counseled
　and what Balaam son of Beor answered.
Remember ˌyour journeyˌ from Shittim to
　　Gilgal,
　that you may know the righteous acts of the
　　LORD."

---

a 6 Or *crush*　　b 6 Or *Nimrod in its gates*　　c 14 That is, symbols of the goddess Asherah

Living Bible

will rule Assyria with drawn swords and enter the gates of the land of Nimrod. He will deliver us from the Assyrians when they invade our land.

7Then the nation of Israel will refresh the world like a gentle dew or the welcome showers of rain, 8and Israel will be as strong as a lion. The nations will be like helpless sheep before her! 9She will stand up to her foes; all her enemies will be wiped out.

10At that same time, says the Lord, I will destroy all the weapons you depend on, 11and tear down your walls and demolish the defenses of your cities. 12I will put an end to all witchcraft—there will be no more fortune-tellers to consult— 13and destroy all your idols. Never again will you worship what you have made, 14and I will abolish the heathen shrines from among you, and destroy the cities where your idol temples stand.

15And I will pour out my vengeance upon the nations who refuse to obey me.

6 LISTEN TO what the Lord is saying to his people: Stand up and state your case against me. Let the mountains and hills be called to witness your complaint.

2And now, O mountains, listen to the Lord's complaint! For he has a case against his people Israel! He will prosecute them to the full. 3O my people, what have I done that makes you turn away from me? Tell me why your patience is exhausted! Answer me! 4For I brought you out of Egypt, and cut your chains of slavery. I gave you Moses, Aaron, and Miriam to help you.

5Don't you remember, O my people, how Balak, king of Moab, tried to destroy you through the curse of Balaam, son of Beor, but I made him bless you instead? That is the kindness I showed you again and again. Have you no memory at all of what happened at Acacia and Gilgal, and how I blessed you there?

New Revised Standard

6 They shall rule the land of Assyria with the
    sword,
    and the land of Nimrod with the drawn
      sword;d
theye shall rescue us from the Assyrians
    if they come into our land
    or tread within our border.

The Future Role of the Remnant

7 Then the remnant of Jacob,
    surrounded by many peoples,
shall be like dew from the LORD,
    like showers on the grass,
which do not depend upon people
    or wait for any mortal.
8 And among the nations the remnant of Jacob,
    surrounded by many peoples,
shall be like a lion among the animals of the
      forest,
    like a young lion among the flocks of
      sheep,
which, when it goes through, treads down
    and tears in pieces, with no one to deliver.
9 Your hand shall be lifted up over your
      adversaries,
    and all your enemies shall be cut off.

10 In that day, says the LORD,
    I will cut off your horses from among you
    and will destroy your chariots;
11 and I will cut off the cities of your land
    and throw down all your strongholds;
12 and I will cut off sorceries from your hand,
    and you shall have no more soothsayers;
13 and I will cut off your images
    and your pillars from among you,
and you shall bow down no more
    to the work of your hands;
14 and I will uproot your sacred polesf from
      among you
    and destroy your towns.
15 And in anger and wrath I will execute
      vengeance
    on the nations that did not obey.

God Challenges Israel

6 HEAR WHAT the LORD says:
Rise, plead your case before the mountains,
    and let the hills hear your voice.
2 Hear, you mountains, the controversy of the
      LORD,
    and you enduring foundations of the earth;
for the LORD has a controversy with his
      people,
    and he will contend with Israel.

3 "O my people, what have I done to you?
    In what have I wearied you? Answer me!
4 For I brought you up from the land of Egypt,
    and redeemed you from the house of
      slavery;
    and I sent before you Moses,
    Aaron, and Miriam.
5 O my people, remember now what King Balak
    of Moab devised,
    what Balaam son of Beor answered him,
and what happened from Shittim to Gilgal,
    that you may know the saving acts of the
      LORD."

d Cn: Heb in its entrances   e Heb he   f Heb Asherim

King James

6¶ Wherewith shall I come before the LORD, *and* bow myself before the high God? shall I come before him with burnt offerings, with calves of a year old?

7Will the LORD be pleased with thousands of rams, *or* with ten thousands of rivers of oil? shall I give my firstborn *for* my transgression, the fruit of my body *for* the sin of my soul?

8He hath shown thee, O man, what *is* good; and what doth the LORD require of thee, but to do justly, and to love mercy, and to walk humbly with thy God?

9The LORD's voice crieth unto the city, and *the man of* wisdom shall see thy name: hear ye the rod, and who hath appointed it.

10¶ Are there yet the treasures of wickedness in the house of the wicked, and the scant measure *that is* abominable?

11Shall I count *them* pure with the wicked balances, and with the bag of deceitful weights?

12For the rich men thereof are full of violence, and the inhabitants thereof have spoken lies, and their tongue *is* deceitful in their mouth.

13Therefore also will I make *thee* sick in smiting thee, in making *thee* desolate because of thy sins.

14Thou shalt eat, but not be satisfied; and thy casting down *shall be* in the midst of thee; and thou shalt take hold, but shalt not deliver; and *that* which thou deliverest will I give up to the sword.

15Thou shalt sow, but thou shalt not reap; thou shalt tread the olives, but thou shalt not anoint thee with oil; and sweet wine, but shalt not drink wine.

16¶ For the statutes of Omri are kept, and all the works of the house of Ahab, and ye walk in their counsels; that I should make thee a desolation, and the inhabitants thereof an hissing: therefore ye shall bear the reproach of my people.

7 WOE IS me! for I am as when they have gathered the summer fruits, as the grapegleanings of the vintage: *there is* no cluster to eat: my soul desired the firstripe fruit.

2The good *man* is perished out of the earth: and *there is* none upright among men: they all lie in wait for blood; they hunt every man his brother with a net.

3¶ That they may do evil with both hands earnestly, the prince asketh, and the judge *asketh* for a reward; and the great *man*, he uttereth his mischievous desire: so they wrap it up.

4The best of them *is* as a brier: the most upright *is* sharper than a thorn hedge: the day of thy watchmen *and* thy visitation cometh; now shall be their perplexity.

New International

6With what shall I come before the LORD
    and bow down before the exalted God?
Shall I come before him with burnt offerings,
    with calves a year old?
7Will the LORD be pleased with thousands of
        rams,
    with ten thousand rivers of oil?
Shall I offer my firstborn for my transgression,
    the fruit of my body for the sin of my soul?
8He has showed you, O man, what is good.
    And what does the LORD require of you?
To act justly and to love mercy
    and to walk humbly with your God.

Israel's Guilt and Punishment

9Listen! The LORD is calling to the city—
    and to fear your name is wisdom—
    "Heed the rod and the One who appointed
        it.a
10Am I still to forget, O wicked house,
    your ill-gotten treasures
    and the short ephah,b which is accursed?
11Shall I acquit a man with dishonest scales,
    with a bag of false weights?
12Her rich men are violent;
    her people are liars
    and their tongues speak deceitfully.
13Therefore, I have begun to destroy you,
    to ruin you because of your sins.
14You will eat but not be satisfied;
    your stomach will still be empty.c
You will store up but save nothing,
    because what you save I will give to the
        sword.
15You will plant but not harvest;
    you will press olives but not use the oil on
        yourselves,
    you will crush grapes but not drink the wine.
16You have observed the statutes of Omri
    and all the practices of Ahab's house,
    and you have followed their traditions.
Therefore I will give you over to ruin
    and your people to derision;
    you will bear the scorn of the nations.d"

Israel's Misery

7 WHAT MISERY is mine!
    I am like one who gathers summer fruit
        at the gleaning of the vineyard;
there is no cluster of grapes to eat,
    none of the early figs that I crave.
2The godly have been swept from the land;
    not one upright man remains.
All men lie in wait to shed blood;
    each hunts his brother with a net.
3Both hands are skilled in doing evil;
    the ruler demands gifts,
the judge accepts bribes,
    the powerful dictate what they desire—
    they all conspire together.
4The best of them is like a brier,
    the most upright worse than a thorn hedge.
The day of your watchmen has come,
    the day God visits you.
    Now is the time of their confusion.

---

a *9* The meaning of the Hebrew for this line is uncertain.   b *10* An ephah was a dry measure.   c *14* The meaning of the Hebrew for this word is uncertain.   d *16* Septuagint; Hebrew *scorn due my people*

Living Bible

  6"How can we make up to you for what we've done?" you ask. "Shall we bow before the Lord with offerings of yearling calves?"

  Oh, no! 7For if you offered him thousands of rams and ten thousands of rivers of olive oil—would that please him? Would he be satisfied? If you sacrificed your oldest child, would that make him glad? Then would he forgive your sins? Of course not!

  8No, he has told you what he wants, and this is all it is: *to be fair and just and merciful, and to walk humbly with your God.* 9The Lord's voice calls out to all Jerusalem—listen to the Lord if you are wise! The armies of destruction are coming; the Lord is sending them.

  10For your sins are very great—is there to be no end of getting rich by cheating? The homes of the wicked are full of ungodly treasures and lying scales. 11Shall I say "Good!" to all your merchants with their bags of false, deceitful weights? How could God be just while saying that? 12Your rich men are wealthy through extortion and violence; your citizens are so used to lying that their tongues can't tell the truth!

  13Therefore I will wound you! I will make your hearts miserable for all your sins. 14You will eat but never have enough; hunger pangs and emptiness will still remain. And though you try and try to save your money, it will come to nothing at the end, and what little you succeed in storing up I'll give to those who conquer you!e 15You will plant crops but not harvest them; you will press out the oil from the olives, and not get enough to anoint yourself! You will trample the grapes, but get no juice to make your wine.

  16The only commands you keep are those of Omri; the only example you follow is that of Ahab! Therefore I will make an awesome example of you—I will destroy you. I will make you the laughingstock of the world; all who see you will snicker and sneer!

7 WOE IS me! It is as hard to find an honest man as grapes and figs when harvest days are over. Not a cluster to eat, not a single early fig, however much I long for it! The good men have disappeared from the earth; not one fairminded man is left. They are all murderers, turning against even their own brothers.

  3They go at their evil deeds with both hands, and how skilled they are in using them! The governor and judge alike demand bribes. The rich man pays them off and tells them whom to ruin. Justice is twisted between them. 4Even the best of them are prickly as briars; the straightest is more crooked than a hedge of thorns. But your judgment day is coming swiftly now; your time of punishment is almost here; confusion, destruction, and terror will be yours.

New Revised Standard

What God Requires

6 "With what shall I come before the Lord,
   and bow myself before God on high?
Shall I come before him with burnt offerings,
   with calves a year old?
7 Will the Lord be pleased with thousands of
   rams,
  with ten thousands of rivers of oil?
Shall I give my firstborn for my transgression,
   the fruit of my body for the sin of my
    soul?"
8 He has told you, O mortal, what is good;
   and what does the Lord require of you
but to do justice, and to love kindness,
   and to walk humbly with your God?

Cheating and Violence to Be Punished

9 The voice of the Lord cries to the city
   (it is sound wisdom to fear your name):
Hear, O tribe and assembly of the city!f
10   Can I forgetg the treasures of wickedness in
    the house of the wicked,
  and the scant measure that is accursed?
11 Can I tolerate wicked scales
   and a bag of dishonest weights?
12 Yourh wealthy are full of violence;
   youri inhabitants speak lies,
   with tongues of deceit in their mouths.
13 Therefore I have begunj to strike you down,
   making you desolate because of your sins.
14 You shall eat, but not be satisfied,
   and there shall be a gnawing hunger within
    you;
you shall put away, but not save,
   and what you save, I will hand over to the
    sword.
15 You shall sow, but not reap;
   you shall tread olives, but not anoint
    yourselves with oil;
   you shall tread grapes, but not drink wine.
16 For you have kept the statutes of Omrik
   and all the works of the house of Ahab,
   and you have followed their counsels.
Therefore I will make you a desolation, and
    yourl inhabitants an object of hissing;
so you shall bear the scorn of my people.

The Total Corruption of the People

7 WOE IS me! For I have become like one who,
  after the summer fruit has been gathered,
after the vintage has been gleaned,
finds no cluster to eat;
  there is no first-ripe fig for which I hunger.
2 The faithful have disappeared from the land,
  and there is no one left who is upright;
they all lie in wait for blood,
  and they hunt each other with nets.
3 Their hands are skilled to do evil;
  the official and the judge ask for a bribe,
and the powerful dictate what they desire;
  thus they pervert justice.m
4 The best of them is like a brier,
  the most upright of them a thorn hedge.
The day of theirn sentinels, of theirn
    punishment, has come;
  now their confusion is at hand.

---

e *6:14* See Haggai 1:6.

f Cn Compare Gk: Heb *tribe, and who has appointed it yet?*   g Cn: Meaning of Heb uncertain   h Heb *Whose*   i Heb *whose*   j Gk Syr Vg: Heb *have made sick*   k Gk Syr Vg Tg: Heb *the statutes of Omri are kept*   l Heb *its*   m Cn: Heb *they weave it*   n Heb *your*

King James

5¶ Trust ye not in a friend, put ye not confidence in a guide: keep the doors of thy mouth from her that lieth in thy bosom.

6For the son dishonoureth the father, the daughter riseth up against her mother, the daughter-in-law against her mother-in-law; a man's enemies *are* the men of his own house.

7Therefore I will look unto the LORD; I will wait for the God of my salvation: my God will hear me.

8¶ Rejoice not against me, O mine enemy: when I fall, I shall arise; when I sit in darkness, the LORD *shall be* a light unto me.

9I will bear the indignation of the LORD, because I have sinned against him, until he plead my cause, and execute judgment for me: he will bring me forth to the light, *and* I shall behold his righteousness.

10Then *she that is* mine enemy shall see *it*, and shame shall cover her which said unto me, Where is the LORD thy God? mine eyes shall behold her: now shall she be trodden down as the mire of the streets.

11*In* the day that thy walls are to be built, *in* that day shall the decree be far removed.

12*In* that day *also* he shall come even to thee from Assyria, and *from* the fortified cities, and from the fortress even to the river, and from sea to sea, and *from* mountain to mountain.

13Notwithstanding the land shall be desolate because of them that dwell therein, for the fruit of their doings.

14¶ Feed thy people with thy rod, the flock of thine heritage, which dwell solitarily *in* the wood, in the midst of Carmel: let them feed *in* Bashan and Gilead, as in the days of old.

15According to the days of thy coming out of the land of Egypt will I show unto him marvellous *things*.

16¶ The nations shall see and be confounded at all their might: they shall lay *their* hand upon *their* mouth, their ears shall be deaf.

17They shall lick the dust like a serpent, they shall move out of their holes like worms of the earth: they shall be afraid of the LORD our God, and shall fear because of thee.

18Who *is* a God like unto thee, that pardoneth iniquity, and passeth by the transgression of the remnant of his heritage? he retaineth not his anger for ever, because he delighteth *in* mercy.

New International

5Do not trust a neighbor;
   put no confidence in a friend.
Even with her who lies in your embrace
   be careful of your words.
6For a son dishonors his father,
   a daughter rises up against her mother,
a daughter-in-law against her mother-in-law—
   a man's enemies are the members of his own
      household.

7But as for me, I watch in hope for the LORD,
   I wait for God my Savior;
   my God will hear me.

Israel Will Rise

8Do not gloat over me, my enemy!
   Though I have fallen, I will rise.
Though I sit in darkness,
   the LORD will be my light.
9Because I have sinned against him,
   I will bear the LORD's wrath,
until he pleads my case
   and establishes my right.
He will bring me out into the light;
   I will see his righteousness.
10Then my enemy will see it
   and will be covered with shame,
she who said to me,
   "Where is the LORD your God?"
My eyes will see her downfall;
   even now she will be trampled underfoot
   like mire in the streets.

11The day for building your walls will come,
   the day for extending your boundaries.
12In that day people will come to you
   from Assyria and the cities of Egypt,
even from Egypt to the Euphrates
   and from sea to sea
   and from mountain to mountain.
13The earth will become desolate because of its
      inhabitants,
   as the result of their deeds.

Prayer and Praise

14Shepherd your people with your staff,
   the flock of your inheritance,
which lives by itself in a forest,
   in fertile pasturelands.a
Let them feed in Bashan and Gilead
   as in days long ago.

15"As in the days when you came out of Egypt,
   I will show them my wonders."

16Nations will see and be ashamed,
   deprived of all their power.
They will lay their hands on their mouths
   and their ears will become deaf.
17They will lick dust like a snake,
   like creatures that crawl on the ground.
They will come trembling out of their dens;
   they will turn in fear to the LORD our God
   and will be afraid of you.
18Who is a God like you,
   who pardons sin and forgives the
      transgression
   of the remnant of his inheritance?
You do not stay angry forever
   but delight to show mercy.

Living Bible

5Don't trust anyone, not your best friend—not even your wife! 6For the son despises his father; the daughter defies her mother; the bride curses her mother-in-law. Yes, a man's enemies will be found in his own home.

7As for me, I look to the Lord for his help; I wait for God to save me; he will hear me. 8Do not rejoice against me, O my enemy, for though I fall, I will rise again! When I sit in darkness, the Lord himself will be my Light. 9I will be patient while the Lord punishes me, for I have sinned against him; then he will defend me from my enemies, and punish them for all the evil they have done to me. God will bring me out of my darkness into the light, and I will see his goodness. 10Then my enemy will see that God is for me, and be ashamed for taunting me, "Where is that God of yours?" Now with my own eyes I see them trampled down like mud in the street.

11Your cities, people of God, will be rebuilt, much larger and more prosperous than before. 12Citizens of many lands will come and honor you—from Assyria to Egypt, and from Egypt to the Euphrates, from sea to sea and from distant hills and mountains.

13But first comes terrible destruction to Israelb for the great wickedness of her people. 14O Lord, come and rule your people; lead your flock; make them live in peace and prosperity; let them enjoy the fertile pastures of Bashan and Gilead as they did long ago.

15"Yes," replies the Lord, "I will do mighty miracles for you, like those when I brought you out of slavery in Egypt. 16All the world will stand amazed at what I will do for you, and be embarrassed at their puny might. They will stand in silent awe, deaf to all around them." 17They will see what snakes they are, lowly as worms crawling from their holes. They will come trembling out from their fortresses to meet the Lord our God. They will fear him; they will stand in awe.

18Where is another God like you, who pardons the sins of the survivors among his people? You cannot stay angry with your people, for you love to be merciful.

●

New Revised Standard

5 Put no trust in a friend,
    have no confidence in a loved one;
  guard the doors of your mouth
    from her who lies in your embrace;
6 for the son treats the father with contempt,
    the daughter rises up against her mother,
  the daughter-in-law against her mother-in-law;
    your enemies are members of your own
        household.
7 But as for me, I will look to the LORD,
    I will wait for the God of my salvation;
    my God will hear me.

Penitence and Trust in God

8 Do not rejoice over me, O my enemy;
    when I fall, I shall rise;
  when I sit in darkness,
    the LORD will be a light to me.
9 I must bear the indignation of the LORD,
    because I have sinned against him,
  until he takes my side
    and executes judgment for me.
  He will bring me out to the light;
    I shall see his vindication.
10 Then my enemy will see,
    and shame will cover her who said to me,
  "Where is the LORD your God?"
  My eyes will see her downfall;c
    now she will be trodden down
    like the mire of the streets.

A Prophecy of Restoration

11 A day for the building of your walls!
    In that day the boundary shall be far
        extended.
12 In that day they will come to you
    from Assyria tod Egypt,
  and from Egypt to the River,
    from sea to sea and from mountain to
        mountain.
13 But the earth will be desolate
    because of its inhabitants,
    for the fruit of their doings.

14 Shepherd your people with your staff,
    the flock that belongs to you,
  which lives alone in a forest
    in the midst of a garden land;
  let them feed in Bashan and Gilead
    as in the days of old.
15 As in the days when you came out of the land
        of Egypt,
    show use marvelous things.
16 The nations shall see and be ashamed
    of all their might;
  they shall lay their hands on their mouths;
    their ears shall be deaf;
17 they shall lick dust like a snake,
    like the crawling things of the earth;
  they shall come trembling out of their
        fortresses;
  they shall turn in dread to the LORD our
        God,
    and they shall stand in fear of you.

God's Compassion and Steadfast Love

18 Who is a God like you, pardoning iniquity
    and passing over the transgression
  of the remnant of yourf possession?
  He does not retain his anger forever,
    because he delights in showing clemency.

King James

19He will turn again, he will have compassion upon us; he will subdue our iniquities; and thou wilt cast all their sins into the depths of the sea.

20Thou wilt perform the truth to Jacob, *and* the mercy to Abraham, which thou hast sworn unto our fathers from the days of old.

New International

19You will again have compassion on us;
   you will tread our sins underfoot
   and hurl all our iniquities into the depths of
     the sea.
20You will be true to Jacob,
   and show mercy to Abraham,
   as you pledged on oath to our fathers
   in days long ago.

Living Bible

19Once again you will have compassion on us. You will tread our sins beneath your feet; you will throw them into the depths of the ocean! 20You will bless us as you promised Jacob long ago. You will set your love upon us, as you promised our father Abraham!

New Revised Standard

19 He will again have compassion upon us;
        he will tread our iniquities under foot.
    You will cast all oura sins
        into the depths of the sea.
20 You will show faithfulness to Jacob
        and unswerving loyalty to Abraham,
    as you have sworn to our ancestors
        from the days of old.

Nahum

Nahum

1 THE BURDEN of Nineveh. The book of the vision of Nahum the Elkoshite.

²God *is* jealous, and the LORD revengeth; the LORD revengeth, and *is* furious; the LORD will take vengeance on his adversaries, and he reserveth *wrath* for his enemies.

³The LORD *is* slow to anger, and great in power, and will not at all acquit *the wicked:* the LORD *hath* his way in the whirlwind and in the storm, and the clouds *are* the dust of his feet.

⁴He rebuketh the sea, and maketh it dry, and drieth up all the rivers: Bashan languisheth, and Carmel, and the flower of Lebanon languisheth.

⁵The mountains quake at him, and the hills melt, and the earth is burned at his presence, yea, the world, and all that dwell therein.

⁶Who can stand before his indignation? and who can abide in the fierceness of his anger? his fury is poured out like fire, and the rocks are thrown down by him.

⁷The LORD *is* good, a strong hold in the day of trouble; and he knoweth them that trust in him.

⁸But with an overrunning flood he will make an utter end of the place thereof, and darkness shall pursue his enemies.

⁹What do ye imagine against the LORD? he will make an utter end: affliction shall not rise up the second time.

¹⁰For while *they be* folden together *as* thorns, and while they are drunken *as* drunkards, they shall be devoured as stubble fully dry.

¹¹There is *one* come out of thee, that imagineth evil against the LORD, a wicked counsellor.

¹²Thus saith the LORD; Though *they be* quiet, and likewise many, yet thus shall they be cut down, when he shall pass through. Though I have afflicted thee, I will afflict thee no more.

¹³For now will I break his yoke from off thee, and will burst thy bonds in sunder.

1 AN ORACLE concerning Nineveh. The book of the vision of Nahum the Elkoshite.

The LORD's Anger Against Nineveh

²The LORD is a jealous and avenging God;
　the LORD takes vengeance and is filled with
　　wrath.
The LORD takes vengeance on his foes
　and maintains his wrath against his enemies.
³The LORD is slow to anger and great in power;
　the LORD will not leave the guilty
　　unpunished.
His way is in the whirlwind and the storm,
　and clouds are the dust of his feet.
⁴He rebukes the sea and dries it up;
　he makes all the rivers run dry.
Bashan and Carmel wither
　and the blossoms of Lebanon fade.
⁵The mountains quake before him
　and the hills melt away.
The earth trembles at his presence,
　the world and all who live in it.
⁶Who can withstand his indignation?
　Who can endure his fierce anger?
His wrath is poured out like fire;
　the rocks are shattered before him.

⁷The LORD is good,
　a refuge in times of trouble.
He cares for those who trust in him,
⁸ but with an overwhelming flood
he will make an end of ˌNineveh,ˌ;
　he will pursue his foes into darkness.

⁹Whatever they plot against the LORD
　heᵃ will bring to an end;
　trouble will not come a second time.
¹⁰They will be entangled among thorns
　and drunk from their wine;
　they will be consumed like dry stubble.ᵇ
¹¹From you, ˌO Nineveh,ˌ has one come forth
　who plots evil against the LORD
　and counsels wickedness.

¹²This is what the LORD says:

"Although they have allies and are numerous,
　they will be cut off and pass away.
Although I have afflicted you, ˌO Judah,ˌ
　I will afflict you no more.
¹³Now I will break their yoke from your neck
　and tear your shackles away."

ᵃ 9 Or *What do you foes plot against the LORD? / He*　ᵇ 10 The meaning of the Hebrew for this verse is uncertain.

Living Bible

Nahum

1 THIS IS the vision God gave to Nahum, who lived in Elkosh, concerning the impending doom of Nineveh:[c]

2God is jealous over those he loves; that is why he takes vengeance on those who hurt them. He furiously destroys their enemies. 3He is slow in getting angry, but when aroused, his power is incredible, and he does not easily forgive. He shows his power in the terrors of the cyclone and the raging storms; clouds are billowing dust beneath his feet! 4At his command the oceans and rivers become dry sand; the lush pastures of Bashan and Carmel fade away; the green forests of Lebanon wilt. 5In his presence mountains quake and hills melt; the earth crumbles and its people are destroyed.

6Who can stand before an angry God? His fury is like fire; the mountains tumble down before his anger.

7The Lord is good. When trouble comes, he is the place to go! And he knows everyone who trusts in him! 8But he sweeps away his enemies with an overwhelming flood; he pursues them all night long.

9What are you thinking of, Nineveh, to defy the Lord? He will stop you with one blow; he won't need to strike again. 10He tosses his enemies into the fire like a tangled mass of thorns. They burst into flames like straw. 11Who is this king[d] of yours who dares to plot against the Lord? 12But the Lord is not afraid of him! "Though he build his army millions strong," the Lord declares, "it will vanish.

"O my people, I have punished you enough! 13Now I will break your chains and release you from the yoke of slavery to this Assyrian king." 14And to the king he

New Revised Standard

Nahum

1 AN ORACLE concerning Nineveh. The book of the vision of Nahum of Elkosh.

The Consuming Wrath of God

2 A jealous and avenging God is the LORD,
   the LORD is avenging and wrathful;
the LORD takes vengeance on his adversaries
   and rages against his enemies.
3 The LORD is slow to anger but great in power,
   and the LORD will by no means clear the
   guilty.

His way is in whirlwind and storm,
   and the clouds are the dust of his feet.
4 He rebukes the sea and makes it dry,
   and he dries up all the rivers;
Bashan and Carmel wither,
   and the bloom of Lebanon fades.
5 The mountains quake before him,
   and the hills melt;
the earth heaves before him,
   the world and all who live in it.

6 Who can stand before his indignation?
   Who can endure the heat of his anger?
His wrath is poured out like fire,
   and by him the rocks are broken in pieces.
7 The LORD is good,
   a stronghold in a day of trouble;
he protects those who take refuge in him,
8   even in a rushing flood.
He will make a full end of his adversaries,[e]
   and will pursue his enemies into darkness.
9 Why do you plot against the LORD?
   He will make an end;
no adversary will rise up twice.
10 Like thorns they are entangled,
   like drunkards they are drunk;
   they are consumed like dry straw.
11 From you one has gone out
   who plots evil against the LORD,
   who counsels wickedness.

Good News for Judah

12 Thus says the LORD,
   "Though they are at full strength and many,[f]
they will be cut off and pass away.
Though I have afflicted you,
   I will afflict you no more.
13 And now I will break off his yoke from you
   and snap the bonds that bind you."

---

c *1:1* Nineveh was the capital of Assyria.   d *1:11* *Who is this king,* implied in vss 11, 13, and 3:18.

e Gk: Heb *of her place*   f Meaning of Heb uncertain

King James

14And the LORD hath given a commandment concerning thee, *that* no more of thy name be sown: out of the house of thy gods will I cut off the graven image and the molten image: I will make thy grave; for thou art vile.

15Behold upon the mountains the feet of him that bringeth good tidings, that publisheth peace! O Judah, keep thy solemn feasts, perform thy vows: for the wicked shall no more pass through thee; he is utterly cut off.

2 HE THAT dasheth in pieces is come up before thy face: keep the munition, watch the way, make *thy* loins strong, fortify *thy* power mightily.

2For the LORD hath turned away the excellency of Jacob, as the excellency of Israel: for the emptiers have emptied them out, and marred their vine branches.

3The shield of his mighty men is made red, the valiant men *are* in scarlet: the chariots *shall be* with flaming torches in the day of his preparation, and the fir trees shall be terribly shaken.

4The chariots shall rage in the streets, they shall justle one against another in the broad ways: they shall seem like torches, they shall run like the lightnings.

5He shall recount his worthies: they shall stumble in their walk; they shall make haste to the wall thereof, and the defence shall be prepared.

6The gates of the rivers shall be opened, and the palace shall be dissolved.

7And Huzzab shall be led away captive, she shall be brought up, and her maids shall lead *her* as with the voice of doves, tabering upon their breasts.

8But Nineveh *is* of old like a pool of water: yet they shall flee away. Stand, stand, *shall they cry;* but none shall look back.

9Take ye the spoil of silver, take the spoil of gold: for *there is* none end of the store *and* glory out of all the pleasant furniture.

10She is empty, and void, and waste: and the heart melteth, and the knees smite together, and much pain *is* in all loins, and the faces of them all gather blackness.

11Where *is* the dwelling of the lions, and the feeding-place of the young lions, where the lion, *even* the old lion, walked, *and* the lion's whelp, and none made *them* afraid?

New International

14The LORD has given a command concerning
    you, ˌNinevehˌ:
  "You will have no descendants to bear your
    name.
I will destroy the carved images and cast idols
  that are in the temple of your gods.
I will prepare your grave,
  for you are vile."

15Look, there on the mountains,
  the feet of one who brings good news,
    who proclaims peace!
Celebrate your festivals, O Judah,
  and fulfill your vows.
No more will the wicked invade you;
  they will be completely destroyed.

Nineveh to Fall

2 AN ATTACKER advances against you,
    ˌNinevehˌ.
  Guard the fortress,
  watch the road,
  brace yourselves,
  marshal all your strength!

2The LORD will restore the splendor of Jacob
  like the splendor of Israel,
though destroyers have laid them waste
  and have ruined their vines.

3The shields of his soldiers are red;
  the warriors are clad in scarlet.
The metal on the chariots flashes
  on the day they are made ready;
  the spears of pine are brandished.a
4The chariots storm through the streets,
  rushing back and forth through the squares.
They look like flaming torches;
  they dart about like lightning.

5He summons his picked troops,
  yet they stumble on their way.
They dash to the city wall;
  the protective shield is put in place.
6The river gates are thrown open
  and the palace collapses.
7It is decreedb that ˌthe cityˌ
  be exiled and carried away.
Its slave girls moan like doves
  and beat upon their breasts.
8Nineveh is like a pool,
  and its water is draining away.
"Stop! Stop!" they cry,
  but no one turns back.
9Plunder the silver!
  Plunder the gold!
The supply is endless,
  the wealth from all its treasures!
10She is pillaged, plundered, stripped!
  Hearts melt, knees give way,
  bodies tremble, every face grows pale.

11Where now is the lions' den,
  the place where they fed their young,
where the lion and lioness went,
  and the cubs, with nothing to fear?

---

a *3* Hebrew; Septuagint and Syriac / *the horsemen rush to and fro*   b *7* The meaning of the Hebrew for this word is uncertain.

Living Bible

says, "I have ordered an end to your dynasty; your sons will never sit upon your throne. And I will destroy your gods and temples, and I will bury you! For how you stink with sin!"

15See, the messengers come running down the mountains with glad news: "The invaders have been wiped out and we are safe!" O Judah, proclaim a day of thanksgiving, and worship only the Lord, as you have vowed. For this enemy from Nineveh will never come again. He is cut off forever; he will never be seen again.

2 NINEVEH, YOU are finished!c You are already surrounded by enemy armies! Sound the alarm! Man the ramparts! Muster your defenses, full force, and keep a sharp watch for the enemy attack to begin! 2For the land of the people of God lies empty and broken after your attacks but the Lord will restore their honor and power again!

3Shields flash red in the sunlight! The attack begins! See their scarlet uniforms! See their glittering chariots moving forward side by side, pulled by prancing steeds! 4Your own chariots race recklessly along the streets and through the squares, darting like lightning, gleaming like torches. 5The king shouts for his officers; they stumble in their haste, rushing to the walls to set up their defenses. 6But too late! The river gates are open! The enemy has entered! The palace is in panic!

7The queen of Nineveh is brought out naked to the streets, and led away, a slave, with all her maidens weeping after her; listen to them mourn like doves, and beat their breasts! 8Nineveh is like a leaking water tank! Her soldiers slip away, deserting her; she cannot hold them back. "Stop, stop," she shouts, but they keep on running.

9Loot the silver! Loot the gold! There seems to be no end of treasures. Her vast, uncounted wealth is stripped away. 10Soon the city is an empty shambles; hearts melt in horror; knees quake; her people stand aghast, pale-faced and trembling.

11Where now is that great Nineveh, lion of the nations, full of fight and boldness, where even the old and feeble, as well as the young and tender, lived unafraid?

New Revised Standard

14 The LORD has commanded concerning you:
  "Your name shall be perpetuated no longer;
from the house of your gods I will cut off
  the carved image and the cast image.
I will make your grave, for you
  are worthless."

15d Look! On the mountains the feet of one
  who brings good tidings,
  who proclaims peace!
Celebrate your festivals, O Judah,
  fulfill your vows,
for never again shall the wicked invade you;
  they are utterly cut off.

The Destruction of the Wicked City

2 A SHATTERERe has come up against you.
  Guard the ramparts;
  watch the road;
gird your loins;
  collect all your strength.

2 (For the LORD is restoring the majesty of
    Jacob,
  as well as the majesty of Israel,
though ravagers have ravaged them
  and ruined their branches.)

3 The shields of his warriors are red;
  his soldiers are clothed in crimson.
The metal on the chariots flashes
  on the day when he musters them;
  the chargersf prance.
4 The chariots race madly through the streets,
  they rush to and fro through the squares;
their appearance is like torches,
  they dart like lightning.
5 He calls his officers;
  they stumble as they come forward;
they hasten to the wall,
  and the manteletg is set up.
6 The river gates are opened,
  the palace trembles.
7 It is decreedg that the cityh be exiled,
  its slave women led away,
moaning like doves
  and beating their breasts.
8 Nineveh is like a pool
  whose watersi run away.
"Halt! Halt!"—
  but no one turns back.
9 "Plunder the silver,
  plunder the gold!
There is no end of treasure!
  An abundance of every precious thing!"

10 Devastation, desolation, and destruction!
  Hearts faint and knees tremble,
all loins quake,
  all faces grow pale!
11 What became of the lions' den,
  the cavej of the young lions,
where the lion goes,
  and the lion's cubs, with no one to disturb
    them?

---

c 2:1 Nineveh, you are finished! This chapter predicts the events of the year 612 B.C. when the combined armies of the Babylonians and Medes sacked the impregnable Nineveh.

d Ch 2.1 in Heb   e Cn: Heb scatterer   f Cn Compare Gk Syr: Heb cypresses
g Meaning of Heb uncertain   h Heb it   i Cn Compare Gk: Heb a pool, from
the days that she has become, and they   j Cn: Heb pasture

King James

12The lion did tear in pieces enough for his whelps, and strangled for his lionesses, and filled his holes with prey, and his dens with ravin.

13Behold, I *am* against thee, saith the LORD of hosts, and I will burn her chariots in the smoke, and the sword shall devour thy young lions: and I will cut off thy prey from the earth, and the voice of thy messengers shall no more be heard.

3 WOE TO the bloody city! it *is* all full of lies *and* robbery; the prey departeth not;

2The noise of a whip, and the noise of the rattling of the wheels, and of the prancing horses, and of the jumping chariots.

3The horseman lifteth up both the bright sword and the glittering spear: and *there is* a multitude of slain, and a great number of carcases; and *there is* none end of *their* corpses; they stumble upon their corpses:

4Because of the multitude of the whoredoms of the wellfavoured harlot, the mistress of witchcrafts, that selleth nations through her whoredoms, and families through her witchcrafts.

5Behold, I *am* against thee, saith the LORD of hosts; and I will discover thy skirts upon thy face, and I will show the nations thy nakedness, and the kingdoms thy shame.

6And I will cast abominable filth upon thee, and make thee vile, and will set thee as a gazingstock.

7And it shall come to pass, *that* all they that look upon thee shall flee from thee, and say, Nineveh is laid waste: who will bemoan her? whence shall I seek comforters for thee?

8Art thou better than populous No, that was situate among the rivers, *that had* the waters round about it, whose rampart *was* the sea, *and* her wall *was* from the sea?

9Ethiopia and Egypt *were* her strength, and *it was* infinite; Put and Lubim were thy helpers.

10Yet *was* she carried away, she went into captivity: her young children also were dashed in pieces at the top of all the streets: and they cast lots for her honourable men, and all her great men were bound in chains.

11Thou also shalt be drunken: thou shalt be hid, thou also shalt seek strength because of the enemy.

12All thy strong holds *shall be like* fig trees with the firstripe figs: if they be shaken, they shall even fall into the mouth of the eater.

New International

12The lion killed enough for his cubs
    and strangled the prey for his mate,
filling his lairs with the kill
    and his dens with the prey.

13"I am against you,"
    declares the LORD Almighty.
"I will burn up your chariots in smoke,
    and the sword will devour your young lions.
    I will leave you no prey on the earth.
The voices of your messengers
    will no longer be heard."

Woe to Nineveh

3 WOE TO the city of blood,
    full of lies,
full of plunder,
    never without victims!
2The crack of whips,
    the clatter of wheels,
galloping horses
    and jolting chariots!
3Charging cavalry,
    flashing swords
    and glittering spears!
Many casualties,
    piles of dead,
bodies without number,
    people stumbling over the corpses—
4all because of the wanton lust of a harlot,
    alluring, the mistress of sorceries,
who enslaved nations by her prostitution
    and peoples by her witchcraft.

5"I am against you," declares the LORD
        Almighty.
    "I will lift your skirts over your face.
I will show the nations your nakedness
    and the kingdoms your shame.
6I will pelt you with filth,
    I will treat you with contempt
    and make you a spectacle.
7All who see you will flee from you and say,
    'Nineveh is in ruins—who will mourn for
        her?'
    Where can I find anyone to comfort you?"

8Are you better than Thebes,[a]
    situated on the Nile,
    with water around her?
The river was her defense,
    the waters her wall.
9Cush[b] and Egypt were her boundless strength;
    Put and Libya were among her allies.
10Yet she was taken captive
    and went into exile.
Her infants were dashed to pieces
    at the head of every street.
Lots were cast for her nobles,
    and all her great men were put in chains.
11You too will become drunk;
    you will go into hiding
    and seek refuge from the enemy.

12All your fortresses are like fig trees
    with their first ripe fruit;
when they are shaken,
    the figs fall into the mouth of the eater.

a 8 Hebrew *No Amon*   b 9 That is, the upper Nile region

Living Bible

12O Nineveh, once mighty lion! You crushed your enemies to feed your children and your wives, and filled your city and your homes with captured goods and slaves.

13But now the Lord Almighty has turned against you. He destroys your weapons. Your chariots stand there, silent and unused. Your finest youth lie dead. Never again will you bring back slaves from conquered nations; never again will you rule the earth.

3 WOE TO Nineveh, City of Blood, full of lies, crammed with plunder. 2Listen! Hear the crack of the whips as the chariots rush forward against her, wheels rumbling, horses' hoofs pounding, and chariots clattering as they bump wildly through the streets! 3See the flashing swords and glittering spears in the upraised arms of the cavalry! The dead are lying in the streets— bodies, heaps of bodies, everywhere. Men stumble over them, scramble to their feet, and fall again.

4All this because Nineveh sold herself to the enemies of God. The beautiful and faithless city, mistress of deadly charms, enticed the nations with her beauty, then taught them all to worship her false gods,c bewitching people everywhere.

5"No wonder I stand against you," says the Lord Almighty; "and now all the earth will see your nakedness and shame. 6I will cover you with filth and show the world how really vile you are." 7All who see you will shrink back in horror: "Nineveh lies in utter ruin." Yet no one anywhere regrets your fate!

8Are you any better than Thebes,d straddling the Nile, protected on all sides by the river? 9Ethiopia and the whole land of Egypt were her mighty allies, and she could call on them for infinite assistance, as well as Put and Libya. 10Yet Thebes fell and her people were led off as slaves; her babies were dashed to death against the stones of the streets. Soldiers drew straws to see who would get her officers as servants. All her leaders were bound in chains.

11Nineveh, too, will stagger like a drunkard and hide herself in fear. 12All your forts will fall. They will be devoured like first-ripe figs that fall into the mouths of those who shake the trees. 13Your troops will be weak

New Revised Standard

12 The lion has torn enough for his whelps
   and strangled prey for his lionesses;
   he has filled his caves with prey
   and his dens with torn flesh.

13 See, I am against you, says the LORD of hosts, and I will burn your chariots in smoke, and the sword shall devour your young lions; I will cut off your prey from the earth, and the voice of your messengers shall be heard no more.

Ruin Imminent and Inevitable

3 AH! CITY of bloodshed,
   utterly deceitful, full of booty—
      no end to the plunder!
2 The crack of whip and rumble of wheel,
      galloping horse and bounding chariot!
3 Horsemen charging,
      flashing sword and glittering spear,
   piles of dead,
      heaps of corpses,
   dead bodies without end—
      they stumble over the bodies!
4 Because of the countless debaucheries of
         the prostitute,
      gracefully alluring, mistress of sorcery,
   who enslavesf nations through her
         debaucheries,
      and peoples through her sorcery,
5 I am against you,
      says the LORD of hosts,
   and will lift up your skirts over your face;
   and I will let nations look on your nakedness
      and kingdoms on your shame.
6 I will throw filth at you
      and treat you with contempt,
      and make you a spectacle.
7 Then all who see you will shrink from you
         and say,
   "Nineveh is devastated; who will bemoan
         her?"
      Where shall I seek comforters for you?

8 Are you better than Thebesg
      that sat by the Nile,
   with water around her,
      her rampart a sea,
      water her wall?
9 Ethiopiah was her strength,
      Egypt too, and that without limit;
      Put and the Libyans were heri helpers.

10 Yet she became an exile,
      she went into captivity;
   even her infants were dashed in pieces
      at the head of every street;
   lots were cast for her nobles,
      all her dignitaries were bound in fetters.
11 You also will be drunken,
      you will go into hiding;j
   you will seek
      a refuge from the enemy.
12 All your fortresses are like fig trees
         with first-ripe figs—
   if shaken they fall
      into the mouth of the eater.

---

c 3:4 taught them all to worship her false gods, literally, "who betrays nations with her harlotries."   d 3:8 Are you any better than Thebes . . . Thebes was conquered by the Assyrians fifty-one years before this prophecy.

e Heb her   f Heb sells   g Heb No-amon   h Or Nubia; Heb Cush   i Gk: Heb your   j Meaning of Heb uncertain

King James

13Behold, thy people in the midst of thee *are* women: the gates of thy land shall be set wide open unto thine enemies: the fire shall devour thy bars.

14Draw thee waters for the siege, fortify thy strong holds: go into clay, and tread the mortar, make strong the brickkiln.

15There shall the fire devour thee; the sword shall cut thee off, it shall eat thee up like the cankerworm: make thyself many as the cankerworm, make thyself many as the locusts.

16Thou hast multiplied thy merchants above the stars of heaven: the cankerworm spoileth, and flieth away.

17Thy crowned *are* as the locusts, and thy captains as the great grasshoppers, which camp in the hedges in the cold day, *but* when the sun ariseth they flee away, and their place is not known where they *are*.

18Thy shepherds slumber, O king of Assyria: thy nobles shall dwell *in the dust:* thy people is scattered upon the mountains, and no man gathereth *them*.

19*There is* no healing of thy bruise; thy wound is grievous: all that hear the bruit of thee shall clap the hands over thee: for upon whom hath not thy wickedness passed continually?

New International

13Look at your troops—
they are all women!
The gates of your land
are wide open to your enemies;
fire has consumed their bars.

14Draw water for the siege,
strengthen your defenses!
Work the clay,
tread the mortar,
repair the brickwork!

15There the fire will devour you;
the sword will cut you down
and, like grasshoppers, consume you.
Multiply like grasshoppers,
multiply like locusts!

16You have increased the number of your
merchants
till they are more than the stars of the sky,
but like locusts they strip the land
and then fly away.

17Your guards are like locusts,
your officials like swarms of locusts
that settle in the walls on a cold day—
but when the sun appears they fly away,
and no one knows where.

18O king of Assyria, your shepherdsa slumber;
your nobles lie down to rest.
Your people are scattered on the mountains
with no one to gather them.

19Nothing can heal your wound;
your injury is fatal.
Everyone who hears the news about you
claps his hands at your fall,
for who has not felt
your endless cruelty?

a 18 Or *rulers*

Living Bible

and helpless as women. The gates of your land will be opened wide to the enemy and set on fire and burned. 14Get ready for the siege! Store up water! Strengthen the forts! Prepare many bricks for repairing your walls! Go into the pits to trample the clay, and pack it in the molds!

15But in the middle of your preparations, the fire will devour you; the sword will cut you down; the enemy will consume you like young locusts that eat up everything before them. There is no escape, though you multiply like grasshoppers. 16Merchants, numerous as stars, filled your city with vast wealth, but your enemies swarm like locusts and carry it away. 17Your princes and officials crowd together like grasshoppers in the hedges in the cold, but all of them will flee away and disappear, like locusts when the sun comes up and warms the earth.

18O Assyrian king, your princes lie dead in the dust; your people are scattered across the mountains; there is no shepherd now to gather them. 19There is no healing for your wound—it is far too deep to cure. All who hear your fate will clap their hands for joy, for where can one be found who has not suffered from your cruelty?

New Revised Standard

13 Look at your troops:
   they are women in your midst.
The gates of your land
   are wide open to your foes;
   fire has devoured the bars of your gates.

14 Draw water for the siege,
   strengthen your forts;
trample the clay,
   tread the mortar,
   take hold of the brick mold!
15 There the fire will devour you,
   the sword will cut you off.
   It will devour you like the locust.

Multiply yourselves like the locust,
   multiply like the grasshopper!
16 You increased your merchants
   more than the stars of the heavens.
   The locust sheds its skin and flies away.
17 Your guards are like grasshoppers,
   your scribes like swarmsb of locusts
settling on the fences
   on a cold day—
when the sun rises, they fly away;
   no one knows where they have gone.

18 Your shepherds are asleep,
   O king of Assyria;
   your nobles slumber.
Your people are scattered on the mountains
   with no one to gather them.
19 There is no assuaging your hurt,
   your wound is mortal.
All who hear the news about you
   clap their hands over you.
For who has ever escaped
   your endless cruelty?

b Meaning of Heb uncertain

Habakkuk

Habakkuk

King James

1 THE BURDEN which Habakkuk the prophet did see.

2O LORD, how long shall I cry, and thou wilt not hear! *even* cry out unto thee *of* violence, and thou wilt not save!

3Why dost thou show me iniquity, and cause *me* to behold grievance? for spoiling and violence *are* before me: and there are *that* raise up strife and contention.

4Therefore the law is slacked, and judgment doth never go forth: for the wicked doth compass about the righteous; therefore wrong judgment proceedeth.

5¶ Behold ye among the heathen, and regard, and wonder marvellously: for *I* will work a work in your days, *which* ye will not believe, though it be told *you*.

6For, lo, I raise up the Chaldeans, *that* bitter and hasty nation, which shall march through the breadth of the land, to possess the dwellingplaces *that are* not theirs.

7They *are* terrible and dreadful: their judgment and their dignity shall proceed of themselves.

8Their horses also are swifter than the leopards, and are more fierce than the evening wolves: and their horsemen shall spread themselves, and their horsemen shall come from far; they shall fly as the eagle *that* hasteth to eat.

9They shall come all for violence: their faces shall sup up *as* the east wind, and they shall gather the captivity as the sand.

10And they shall scoff at the kings, and the princes shall be a scorn unto them: they shall deride every strong hold; for they shall heap dust, and take it.

11Then shall *his* mind change, and he shall pass over, and offend, *imputing* this his power unto his god.

12¶ *Art* thou not from everlasting, O LORD my God, mine Holy One? we shall not die. O LORD, thou hast ordained them for judgment; and, O mighty God, thou hast established them for correction.

New International

1 THE ORACLE that Habakkuk the prophet received.

Habakkuk's Complaint

2How long, O LORD, must I call for help,
  but you do not listen?
Or cry out to you, "Violence!"
  but you do not save?
3Why do you make me look at injustice?
  Why do you tolerate wrong?
Destruction and violence are before me;
  there is strife, and conflict abounds.
4Therefore the law is paralyzed,
  and justice never prevails.
The wicked hem in the righteous,
  so that justice is perverted.

The LORD's Answer

5"Look at the nations and watch—
  and be utterly amazed.
For I am going to do something in your days
  that you would not believe,
  even if you were told.
6I am raising up the Babylonians,[a]
  that ruthless and impetuous people,
who sweep across the whole earth
  to seize dwelling places not their own.
7They are a feared and dreaded people;
  they are a law to themselves
  and promote their own honor.
8Their horses are swifter than leopards,
  fiercer than wolves at dusk.
Their cavalry gallops headlong;
  their horsemen come from afar.
They fly like a vulture swooping to devour;
9 they all come bent on violence.
Their hordes[b] advance like a desert wind
  and gather prisoners like sand.
10They deride kings
  and scoff at rulers.
They laugh at all fortified cities;
  they build earthen ramps and capture them.
11Then they sweep past like the wind and go on—
  guilty men, whose own strength is their god."

Habakkuk's Second Complaint

12O LORD, are you not from everlasting?
  My God, my Holy One, we will not die.
O LORD, you have appointed them to execute judgment;
  O Rock, you have ordained them to punish.

---

[a] 6 Or *Chaldeans*   [b] 9 The meaning of the Hebrew for this word is uncertain.

Habakkuk

1 THIS IS the message that came to the prophet Habakkuk in a vision from God:

2O Lord, how long must I call for help before you will listen? I shout to you in vain; there is no answer. "Help! Murder!" I cry, but no one comes to save. 3Must I forever see this sin and sadness all around me?

Wherever I look there is oppression and bribery and men who love to argue and to fight. 4The law is not enforced and there is no justice given in the courts, for the wicked far outnumber the righteous, and bribes and trickery prevail.

5The Lord replied: "Look, and be amazed! You will be astounded at what I am about to do! For I am going to do something in your own lifetime that you will have to see to believe. 6I am raising a new force on the world scene, the Chaldeans,c a cruel and violent nation who will march across the world and conquer it. 7They are notorious for their cruelty. They do as they like, and no one can interfere. 8Their horses are swifter than leopards. They are a fierce people, more fierce than wolves at dusk. Their cavalry move proudly forward from a distant land; like eagles they come swooping down to pounce upon their prey. 9All opposition melts away before the terror of their presence. They collect captives like sand.

10"They scoff at kings and princes, and scorn their forts. They simply heap up dirt against their walls and capture them! 11dThey sweep past like wind and are gone, but their guilt is deep, for they claim their power is from their gods."

12O Lord my God, my Holy One, you who are eternal—is your plan in all of this to wipe us out? Surely not! O God our Rock, you have decreed the rise of these Chaldeans to chasten and correct us for our awful sins.

Habakkuk

1 THE ORACLE that the prophet Habakkuk saw.

The Prophet's Complaint

2 O LORD, how long shall I cry for help,
   and you will not listen?
   Or cry to you "Violence!"
   and you will not save?
3 Why do you make me see wrongdoing
   and look at trouble?
   Destruction and violence are before me;
   strife and contention arise.
4 So the law becomes slack
   and justice never prevails.
   The wicked surround the righteous—
   therefore judgment comes forth perverted.

5 Look at the nations, and see!
   Be astonished! Be astounded!
   For a work is being done in your days
   that you would not believe if you were told.
6 For I am rousing the Chaldeans,
   that fierce and impetuous nation,
   who march through the breadth of the earth
   to seize dwellings not their own.
7 Dread and fearsome are they;
   their justice and dignity proceed from
       themselves.
8 Their horses are swifter than leopards,
   more menacing than wolves at dusk;
   their horses charge.
   Their horsemen come from far away;
   they fly like an eagle swift to devour.
9 They all come for violence,
   with faces pressing forward;
   they gather captives like sand.
10 At kings they scoff,
   and of rulers they make sport.
   They laugh at every fortress,
   and heap up earth to take it.
11 Then they sweep by like the wind;
   they transgress and become guilty;
   their own might is their god!

12 Are you not from of old,
   O LORD my God, my Holy One?
   Youf shall not die.
   O LORD, you have marked them for judgment;
   and you, O Rock, have established them for
       punishment.

---

c *1:6 The Chaldeans:* a tribe of Semites living between Babylon and the Persian Gulf, who began to assert themselves against the Assyrians around 630 B.C., and twenty-five years later had mastered most of the Near East.   d *1:11* The Hebrew text of this verse is very uncertain.

e Meaning of Heb uncertain   f Ancient Heb tradition: MT *We*

King James

13Thou art of purer eyes than to behold evil, and canst not look on iniquity: wherefore lookest thou upon them that deal treacherously, *and* holdest thy tongue when the wicked devoureth *the man that is* more righteous than he?

14And makest men as the fishes of the sea, as the creeping things, *that have* no ruler over them?

15They take up all of them with the angle, they catch them in their net, and gather them in their drag: therefore they rejoice and are glad.

16Therefore they sacrifice unto their net, and burn incense unto their drag; because by them their portion *is* fat, and their meat plenteous.

17Shall they therefore empty their net, and not spare continually to slay the nations?

2 I WILL stand upon my watch, and set me upon the tower, and will watch to see what he will say unto me, and what I shall answer when I am reproved.

2And the LORD answered me, and said, Write the vision, and make *it* plain upon tables, that he may run that readeth it.

3For the vision *is* yet for an appointed time, but at the end it shall speak, and not lie: though it tarry, wait for it; because it will surely come, it will not tarry.

4Behold, his soul *which* is lifted up is not upright in him: but the just shall live by his faith.

5¶ Yea also, because he transgresseth by wine, *he is* a proud man, neither keepeth at home, who enlargeth his desire as hell, and *is* as death, and cannot be satisfied, but gathereth unto him all nations, and heapeth unto him all people:

6Shall not all these take up a parable against him, and a taunting proverb against him, and say, Woe to him that increaseth *that which is* not his! how long? and to him that ladeth himself with thick clay!

7Shall they not rise up suddenly that shall bite thee, and awake that shall vex thee, and thou shalt be for booties unto them?

8Because thou hast spoiled many nations, all the remnant of the people shall spoil thee; because of men's blood, and *for* the violence of the land, of the city, and of all that dwell therein.

9¶ Woe to him that coveteth an evil covetousness to his house, that he may set his nest on high, that he may be delivered from the power of evil!

New International

13Your eyes are too pure to look on evil;
 you cannot tolerate wrong.
Why then do you tolerate the treacherous?
 Why are you silent while the wicked
 swallow up those more righteous than
 themselves?
14You have made men like fish in the sea,
 like sea creatures that have no ruler.
15The wicked foe pulls all of them up with hooks,
 he catches them in his net,
he gathers them up in his dragnet;
 and so he rejoices and is glad.
16Therefore he sacrifices to his net
 and burns incense to his dragnet,
for by his net he lives in luxury
 and enjoys the choicest food.
17Is he to keep on emptying his net,
 destroying nations without mercy?

2 I WILL stand at my watch
 and station myself on the ramparts;
 I will look to see what he will say to me,
 and what answer I am to give to this
 complaint.[a]

The LORD's Answer

2Then the LORD replied:

"Write down the revelation
 and make it plain on tablets
 so that a herald[b] may run with it.
3For the revelation awaits an appointed time;
 it speaks of the end
 and will not prove false.
Though it linger, wait for it;
 it[c] will certainly come and will not delay.

4"See, he is puffed up;
 his desires are not upright—
 but the righteous will live by his faith[d]—
5indeed, wine betrays him;
 he is arrogant and never at rest.
Because he is as greedy as the grave[e]
 and like death is never satisfied,
he gathers to himself all the nations
 and takes captive all the peoples.

6"Will not all of them taunt him with ridicule and scorn, saying,

" 'Woe to him who piles up stolen goods
 and makes himself wealthy by extortion!
 How long must this go on?'
7Will not your debtors[f] suddenly arise?
 Will they not wake up and make you
 tremble?
 Then you will become their victim.
8Because you have plundered many nations,
 the peoples who are left will plunder you.
For you have shed man's blood;
 you have destroyed lands and cities and
 everyone in them.

9"Woe to him who builds his realm by unjust
 gain
 to set his nest on high,
 to escape the clutches of ruin!

[a] 1 Or *and what to answer when I am rebuked*　[b] 2 Or *so that whoever reads it*　[c] 3 Or *Though he linger, wait for him; I he*　[d] 4 Or *faithfulness*　[e] 5 Hebrew *Sheol*　[f] 7 Or *creditors*

Living Bible

13We are wicked, but they far more! Will you, who cannot allow sin in any form, stand idly by while they swallow us up? Should you be silent while the wicked destroy those who are better than they?

14Are we but fish, to be caught and killed? Are we but creeping things that have no leader to defend them from their foes? 15Must we be strung up on their hooks and dragged out in their nets, while they rejoice? 16Then they will worship their nets and burn incense before them! "These are the gods who make us rich," they'll say.

17Will you let them get away with this forever? Will they succeed forever in their heartless wars?

2 I WILL climb my watchtower now, and wait to see what answer God will give to my complaint.

2And the Lord said to me, "Write my answer on a billboard,g large and clear, so that anyone can read it at a glance and rush to tell the others. 3But these things I plan won't happen right away. Slowly, steadily, surely, the time approaches when the vision will be fulfilled. If it seems slow,h do not despair, for these things will surely come to pass. Just be patient! They will not be overdue a single day!

4"Note this: Wicked men trust themselves alone [as these Chaldeans doi], and fail; but the righteous man trusts in me, and lives!j 5What's more, these arrogant Chaldeans are betrayed by all their wine, for it is treacherous. In their greed they have collected many nations, but like death and hell, they are never satisfied. 6The time is coming when all their captives will taunt them, saying: 'You robbers! At last justice has caught up with you! Now you will get your just deserts for your oppression and extortion!'

7"Suddenly your debtors will rise up in anger and turn on you and take all you have, while you stand trembling and helpless. 8You have ruined many nations; now they will ruin you. You murderers! You have filled the countryside with lawlessness and all the cities too.

9"Woe to you for getting rich by evil means, attempting to live beyond the reach of danger. 10By the murders

New Revised Standard

13 Your eyes are too pure to behold evil,
    and you cannot look on wrongdoing;
why do you look on the treacherous,
    and are silent when the wicked swallow
    those more righteous than they?

14 You have made people like the fish of the sea,
    like crawling things that have no ruler.

15 The enemyk brings all of them up with a
    hook;
he drags them out with his net,
he gathers them in his seine;
    so he rejoices and exults.

16 Therefore he sacrifices to his net
    and makes offerings to his seine;
for by them his portion is lavish,
    and his food is rich.

17 Is he then to keep on emptying his net,
    and destroying nations without mercy?

God's Reply to the Prophet's Complaint

2 I WILL stand at my watchpost,
    and station myself on the rampart;
I will keep watch to see what he will say to
    me,
    and what hel will answer concerning my
    complaint.

2 Then the LORD answered me and said:
Write the vision;
    make it plain on tablets,
    so that a runner may read it.

3 For there is still a vision for the appointed
    time;
    it speaks of the end, and does not lie.
If it seems to tarry, wait for it;
    it will surely come, it will not delay.

4 Look at the proud!
    Their spirit is not right in them,
    but the righteous live by their faith.m

5 Moreover, wealthn is treacherous;
    the arrogant do not endure.
They open their throats wide as Sheol;
    like Death they never have enough.
They gather all nations for themselves,
    and collect all peoples as their own.

The Woes of the Wicked

6 Shall not everyone taunt such people and, with mocking riddles, say about them,
    "Alas for you who heap up what is not your
        own!"
    How long will you load yourselves with
        goods taken in pledge?

7 Will not your own creditors suddenly rise,
    and those who make you tremble wake up?
    Then you will be booty for them.

8 Because you have plundered many nations,
    all that survive of the peoples shall plunder
        you—
because of human bloodshed, and violence to
        the earth,
    to cities and all who live in them.

9 "Alas for you who get evil gain for your
        houses,
    setting your nest on high
    to be safe from the reach of harm!"

---

g 2:2 *on a billboard*, literally, "on the tablets." h 2:3 *if it seems slow*, or, "if he seems slow." i 2:4 *as these Chaldeans do*, implied. j 2:4 *the righteous trusts in me, and lives*, or, "the righteous shall live by his faith."

k Heb *He* l Syr: Heb *I* m Or *faithfulness* n Other Heb Mss read *wine*

King James

10Thou hast consulted shame to thy house by cutting off many people, and hast sinned *against* thy soul.

11For the stone shall cry out of the wall, and the beam out of the timber shall answer it.

12¶ Woe to him that buildeth a town with blood, and stablisheth a city by iniquity!

13Behold, *is it* not of the LORD of hosts that the people shall labour in the very fire, and the people shall weary themselves for very vanity?

14For the earth shall be filled with the knowledge of the glory of the LORD, as the waters cover the sea.

15¶ Woe unto him that giveth his neighbour drink, that puttest thy bottle to *him*, and makest *him* drunken also, that thou mayest look on their nakedness!

16Thou art filled with shame for glory: drink thou also, and let thy foreskin be uncovered: the cup of the LORD's right hand shall be turned unto thee, and shameful spewing *shall be* on thy glory.

17For the violence of Lebanon shall cover thee, and the spoil of beasts, *which* made them afraid, because of men's blood, and for the violence of the land, of the city, and of all that dwell therein.

18¶ What profiteth the graven image that the maker thereof hath graven it; the molten image, and a teacher of lies, that the maker of his work trusteth therein, to make dumb idols?

19Woe unto him that saith to the wood, Awake; to the dumb stone, Arise, it shall teach! Behold, it *is* laid over with gold and silver, and *there is* no breath at all in the midst of it.

20But the LORD *is* in his holy temple: let all the earth keep silence before him.

3 A PRAYER of Habakkuk the prophet upon Shigionoth.

2O LORD, I have heard thy speech, *and* was afraid: O LORD, revive thy work in the midst of the years, in the midst of the years make known; in wrath remember mercy.

3God came from Teman, and the Holy One from mount Paran. Selah. His glory covered the heavens, and the earth was full of his praise.

4And *his* brightness was as the light; he had horns *coming* out of his hand: and there *was* the hiding of his power.

New International

10You have plotted the ruin of many peoples, shaming your own house and forfeiting your life.

11The stones of the wall will cry out, and the beams of the woodwork will echo it.

12"Woe to him who builds a city with bloodshed and establishes a town by crime!

13Has not the LORD Almighty determined that the people's labor is only fuel for the fire, that the nations exhaust themselves for nothing?

14For the earth will be filled with the knowledge of the glory of the LORD, as the waters cover the sea.

15"Woe to him who gives drink to his neighbors, pouring it from the wineskin till they are drunk, so that he can gaze on their naked bodies.

16You will be filled with shame instead of glory. Now it is your turn! Drink and be exposed[a]! The cup from the LORD's right hand is coming around to you, and disgrace will cover your glory.

17The violence you have done to Lebanon will overwhelm you, and your destruction of animals will terrify you. For you have shed man's blood; you have destroyed lands and cities and everyone in them.

18"Of what value is an idol, since a man has carved it? Or an image that teaches lies? For he who makes it trusts in his own creation; he makes idols that cannot speak.

19Woe to him who says to wood, 'Come to life!' Or to lifeless stone, 'Wake up!' Can it give guidance? It is covered with gold and silver; there is no breath in it.

20But the LORD is in his holy temple; let all the earth be silent before him."

Habakkuk's Prayer

3 A PRAYER of Habakkuk the prophet. On *shigionoth*.[b]

2LORD, I have heard of your fame; I stand in awe of your deeds, O LORD. Renew them in our day, in our time make them known; in wrath remember mercy.

3God came from Teman, the Holy One from Mount Paran.   Selah[c] His glory covered the heavens and his praise filled the earth.

4His splendor was like the sunrise; rays flashed from his hand, where his power was hidden.

---

[a] *16* Masoretic Text; Dead Sea Scrolls, Aquila, Vulgate and Syriac (see also Septuagint) *and stagger*   [b] *1* Probably a literary or musical term   [c] *3* A word of uncertain meaning; possibly a musical term; also in verses 9 and 13

Living Bible

you commit, you have shamed your name and forfeited your lives. [11]The very stones in the walls of your homes cry out against you, and the beams in the ceilings echo what they say.

[12]"Woe to you who build cities with money gained from murdering and robbery! [13]Has not the Lord decreed that godless nations' gains will turn to ashes in their hands? They work so hard, but all in vain!

[14]("The time will come when all the earth is filled, as the waters fill the sea, with an awareness of the glory of the Lord.)

[15]"Woe to you for making your neighboring lands reel and stagger like drunkards beneath your blows, and then gloating over their nakedness and shame. [16]Soon your own glory will be replaced by shame. Drink down God's judgment on yourselves. Stagger and fall! [17]You cut down the forests of Lebanon—now you will be cut down! You terrified the wild animals you caught in your traps—now terror will strike you because of all your murdering and violence in cities everywhere.

[18]"What profit was there in worshiping all your man-made idols? What a foolish lie that they could help! What fools you were to trust what you yourselves had made. [19]Woe to those who command their lifeless wooden idols to arise and save them, who call out to the speechless stone to tell them what to do. Can images speak for God? They are overlaid with gold and silver, but there is no breath at all inside!

[20]"But the Lord is in his holy Temple; let all the earth be silent before him."

3 THIS IS the prayer of triumph[d] that Habakkuk sang before the Lord:

[2]O Lord, now I have heard your report, and I worship you in awe for the fearful things you are going to do. In this time of our deep need, begin again to help us, as you did in years gone by. Show us your power to save us. In your wrath, remember mercy.

[3]I see God moving across the deserts from Mount Sinai.[e] His brilliant splendor fills the earth and sky; his glory fills the heavens, and the earth is full of his praise! What a wonderful God he is! [4]From his hands flash rays of brilliant light. He rejoices in his awesome power.[f]

New Revised Standard

[10] You have devised shame for your house
      by cutting off many peoples;
      you have forfeited your life.
[11] The very stones will cry out from the wall,
      and the plaster[g] will respond from the
         woodwork.

[12] "Alas for you who build a town by bloodshed,
      and found a city on iniquity!"
[13] Is it not from the LORD of hosts
      that peoples labor only to feed the flames,
      and nations weary themselves for nothing?
[14] But the earth will be filled
      with the knowledge of the glory of the
         LORD,
      as the waters cover the sea.

[15] "Alas for you who make your neighbors drink,
      pouring out your wrath[h] until they are
         drunk,
      in order to gaze on their nakedness!"
[16] You will be sated with contempt instead of
         glory.
      Drink, you yourself, and stagger![i]
      The cup in the LORD's right hand
      will come around to you,
      and shame will come upon your glory!
[17] For the violence done to Lebanon will
         overwhelm you;
      the destruction of the animals will terrify
         you—[j]
      because of human bloodshed and violence to
         the earth,
      to cities and all who live in them.

[18] What use is an idol
      once its maker has shaped it—
      a cast image, a teacher of lies?
      For its maker trusts in what has been made,
      though the product is only an idol that
         cannot speak!
[19] Alas for you who say to the wood, "Wake
         up!"
      to silent stone, "Rouse yourself!"
      Can it teach?
      See, it is gold and silver plated,
      and there is no breath in it at all.

[20] But the LORD is in his holy temple;
      let all the earth keep silence before him!

3 A PRAYER of the prophet Habakkuk according to Shigionoth.

The Prophet's Prayer

[2] O LORD, I have heard of your renown,
     and I stand in awe, O LORD, of your work.
     In our own time revive it;
        in our own time make it known;
        in wrath may you remember mercy.
[3] God came from Teman,
        the Holy One from Mount Paran.   Selah
     His glory covered the heavens,
        and the earth was full of his praise.
[4] The brightness was like the sun;
     rays came forth from his hand,
        where his power lay hidden.

---

[d] *3:1 This is the prayer of triumph*, literally, "according to Shigionoth"—though by some to mean a mournful dirge.   [e] *3:3 from Mount Sinai*, literally, "from Teman . . . from Mount Paran."   [f] *3:4 He rejoices in his awesome power.* Or, "He veils his power."

[g] Or *beam*   [h] Or *poison*   [i] Q Ms Gk: MT *be uncircumcised*   [j] Gk Syr: Meaning of Heb uncertain

King James

5Before him went the pestilence, and burning coals went forth at his feet.

6He stood, and measured the earth: he beheld, and drove asunder the nations; and the everlasting mountains were scattered, the perpetual hills did bow: his ways *are* everlasting.

7I saw the tents of Cushan in affliction: *and* the curtains of the land of Midian did tremble.

8Was the LORD displeased against the rivers? *was* thine anger against the rivers? *was* thy wrath against the sea, that thou didst ride upon thine horses *and* thy chariots of salvation?

9Thy bow was made quite naked, *according* to the oaths of the tribes, *even thy* word. Selah. Thou didst cleave the earth with rivers.

10The mountains saw thee, *and* they trembled: the overflowing of the water passed by: the deep uttered his voice, *and* lifted up his hands on high.

11The sun *and* moon stood still in their habitation: at the light of thine arrows they went, *and* at the shining of thy glittering spear.

12Thou didst march through the land in indignation, thou didst thresh the heathen in anger.

13Thou wentest forth for the salvation of thy people, *even* for salvation with thine anointed; thou woundedst the head out of the house of the wicked, by discovering the foundation unto the neck. Selah.

14Thou didst strike through with his staves the head of his villages: they came out as a whirlwind to scatter me: their rejoicing *was* as to devour the poor secretly.

15Thou didst walk through the sea with thine horses, *through* the heap of great waters.

16When I heard, my belly trembled; my lips quivered at the voice: rottenness entered into my bones, and I trembled in myself, that I might rest in the day of trouble: when he cometh up unto the people, he will invade them with his troops.

17¶ Although the fig tree shall not blossom, neither *shall* fruit *be* in the vines; the labour of the olive shall fail, and the fields shall yield no meat; the flock shall be cut off from the fold, and *there shall be* no herd in the stalls:

18Yet I will rejoice in the LORD, I will joy in the God of my salvation.

19The LORD God *is* my strength, and he will make my feet like hinds' *feet,* and he will make me to walk upon mine high places. To the chief singer on my stringed instruments.

New International

5Plague went before him;
    pestilence followed his steps.
6He stood, and shook the earth;
    he looked, and made the nations tremble.
The ancient mountains crumbled
    and the age-old hills collapsed.
    His ways are eternal.
7I saw the tents of Cushan in distress,
    the dwellings of Midian in anguish.

8Were you angry with the rivers, O LORD?
    Was your wrath against the streams?
Did you rage against the sea
    when you rode with your horses
    and your victorious chariots?
9You uncovered your bow,
    you called for many arrows.   *Selah*
You split the earth with rivers;
10   the mountains saw you and writhed.
Torrents of water swept by;
    the deep roared
    and lifted its waves on high.

11Sun and moon stood still in the heavens
    at the glint of your flying arrows,
    at the lightning of your flashing spear.
12In wrath you strode through the earth
    and in anger you threshed the nations.
13You came out to deliver your people,
    to save your anointed one.
You crushed the leader of the land of
        wickedness,
    you stripped him from head to foot.   *Selah*
14With his own spear you pierced his head
    when his warriors stormed out to scatter us,
    gloating as though about to devour
    the wretched who were in hiding.
15You trampled the sea with your horses,
    churning the great waters.

16I heard and my heart pounded,
    my lips quivered at the sound;
decay crept into my bones,
    and my legs trembled.
Yet I will wait patiently for the day of calamity
    to come on the nation invading us.
17Though the fig tree does not bud
    and there are no grapes on the vines,
though the olive crop fails
    and the fields produce no food,
though there are no sheep in the pen
    and no cattle in the stalls,
18yet I will rejoice in the LORD,
    I will be joyful in God my Savior.

19The Sovereign LORD is my strength;
    he makes my feet like the feet of a deer,
    he enables me to go on the heights.

For the director of music. On my stringed
    instruments.

Living Bible

5Pestilence marches before him; plague follows close behind. 6He stops; he stands still for a moment, gazing at the earth. Then he shakes the nations, scattering the everlasting mountains and leveling the hills. His power is just the same as always! 7I see the people of Cushan and of Midian in mortal fear.

8,9aWas it in anger, Lord, you smote the rivers and parted the sea? Were you displeased with them? No, you were sending your chariots of salvation! All saw your power! Then springs burst forth upon the earth at your command! 10The mountains watched and trembled. Onward swept the raging water. The mighty deep cried out, announcing its surrender to the Lord.b 11The lofty sun and moon began to fade, obscured by brilliance from your arrows and the flashing of your glittering spear.

12You marched across the land in awesome anger, and trampled down the nations in your wrath. 13You went out to save your chosen people. You crushed the head of the wicked and laid bare his bones from head to toe. 14You destroyed with their own weapons those who came out like a whirlwind, thinking Israel would be an easy prey.

15Your horsemen marched across the sea; the mighty waters piled high. 16I tremble when I hear all this; my lips quiver with fear. My legs give way beneath me and I shake in terror. I will quietly wait for the day of trouble to come upon the people who invade us.

17Even though the fig trees are all destroyed, and there is neither blossom left nor fruit, and though the olive crops all fail, and the fields lie barren; even if the flocks die in the fields and the cattle barns are empty, 18yet I will rejoice in the Lord; I will be happy in the God of my salvation. 19The Lord God is my Strength, and he will give me the speed of a deer and bring me safely over the mountains.

(A note to the choir director: When singing this ode, the choir is to be accompanied by stringed instruments.)

New Revised Standard

5 Before him went pestilence,
     and plague followed close behind.
6 He stopped and shook the earth;
     he looked and made the nations tremble.
   The eternal mountains were shattered;
     along his ancient pathways
     the everlasting hills sank low.
7 I saw the tents of Cushan under affliction;
     the tent-curtains of the land of Midian
     trembled.
8 Was your wrath against the rivers,c O Lord?
     Or your anger against the rivers,c
     or your rage against the sea,d
   when you drove your horses,
     your chariots to victory?
9 You brandished your naked bow,
     satede were the arrows at your command.f
                                             Selah
   You split the earth with rivers.
10 The mountains saw you, and writhed;
      a torrent of water swept by;
    the deep gave forth its voice.
    The sung raised high its hands;
11 the moonh stood still in its exalted place,
      at the light of your arrows speeding by,
      at the gleam of your flashing spear.
12 In fury you trod the earth,
      in anger you trampled nations.
13 You came forth to save your people,
      to save your anointed.
    You crushed the head of the wicked house,
      laying it bare from foundation to roof.f
                                             Selah
14 You pierced with his own arrows the headi of
        his warriors,j
      who came like a whirlwind to scatter us,k
      gloating as if ready to devour the poor who
        were in hiding.
15 You trampled the sea with your horses,
      churning the mighty waters.

16 I hear, and I tremble within;
      my lips quiver at the sound.
    Rottenness enters into my bones,
      and my steps tremblel beneath me.
    I wait quietly for the day of calamity
      to come upon the people who attack us.

Trust and Joy in the Midst of Trouble

17 Though the fig tree does not blossom,
      and no fruit is on the vines;
    though the produce of the olive fails
      and the fields yield no food;
    though the flock is cut off from the fold
      and there is no herd in the stalls,
18 yet I will rejoice in the Lord;
      I will exult in the God of my salvation.
19 God, the Lord, is my strength;
      he makes my feet like the feet of a deer,
      and makes me tread upon the heights.m

    To the leader: with stringedn
      instruments.

---

a 3:8, 9 Literally, "Was the Lord displeased against the rivers? Were you angry with them? Was your wrath against their sin that you rode upon your horses? Your chariots were salvation. Your bow was pulled from its sheath and you put arrows to the string. You ribboned the earth with rivers."
b 3:10 announcing its surrender to the Lord, literally, "and lifts high its hands."

c Or against River   d Or against Sea   e Cn: Heb oaths   f Meaning of Heb uncertain   g Heb It   h Heb sun, moon   i Or leader   j Vg Compare Gk Syr: Meaning of Heb uncertain   k Heb me   l Cn Compare Gk: Meaning of Heb uncertain   m Heb my heights   n Heb my stringed

Zephaniah

Zephaniah

1 THE WORD of the LORD which came unto Zephaniah the son of Cushi, the son of Gedaliah, the son of Amariah, the son of Hizkiah, in the days of Josiah the son of Amon, king of Judah.

2I will utterly consume all *things* from off the land, saith the LORD.

3I will consume man and beast; I will consume the fowls of the heaven, and the fishes of the sea, and the stumblingblocks with the wicked; and I will cut off man from off the land, saith the LORD.

4I will also stretch out mine hand upon Judah, and upon all the inhabitants of Jerusalem; and I will cut off the remnant of Baal from this place, *and* the name of the Chemarims with the priests;

5And them that worship the host of heaven upon the housetops; and them that worship *and* that swear by the LORD, and that swear by Malcham;

6And them that are turned back from the LORD; and *those* that have not sought the LORD, nor inquired for him.

7Hold thy peace at the presence of the Lord GOD: for the day of the LORD *is* at hand: for the LORD hath prepared a sacrifice, he hath bid his guests.

8And it shall come to pass in the day of the LORD's sacrifice, that I will punish the princes, and the king's children, and all such as are clothed with strange apparel.

9In the same day also will I punish all those that leap on the threshold, which fill their masters' houses with violence and deceit.

10And it shall come to pass in that day, saith the LORD, *that there shall be* the noise of a cry from the fish gate, and an howling from the second, and a great crashing from the hills.

11Howl, ye inhabitants of Maktesh, for all the merchant people are cut down; all they that bear silver are cut off.

1 THE WORD of the LORD that came to Zephaniah son of Cushi, the son of Gedaliah, the son of Amariah, the son of Hezekiah, during the reign of Josiah son of Amon king of Judah:

Warning of Coming Destruction

2"I will sweep away everything
　from the face of the earth,"
　　　　　　　　declares the LORD.
3"I will sweep away both men and animals;
　I will sweep away the birds of the air
　and the fish of the sea.
The wicked will have only heaps of rubble[a]
　when I cut off man from the face of the
　　earth,"
　　　　　　　　declares the LORD.

Against Judah

4"I will stretch out my hand against Judah
　and against all who live in Jerusalem.
I will cut off from this place every remnant of
　　Baal,
　the names of the pagan and the idolatrous
　　priests—
5those who bow down on the roofs
　to worship the starry host,
　those who bow down and swear by the LORD
　and who also swear by Molech,[b]
6those who turn back from following the LORD
　and neither seek the LORD nor inquire of him.
7Be silent before the Sovereign LORD,
　for the day of the LORD is near.
The LORD has prepared a sacrifice;
　he has consecrated those he has invited.
8On the day of the LORD's sacrifice
　I will punish the princes
　and the king's sons
　and all those clad
　in foreign clothes.
9On that day I will punish
　all who avoid stepping on the threshold,[c]
　who fill the temple of their gods
　with violence and deceit.

10"On that day," declares the LORD,
　"a cry will go up from the Fish Gate,
　wailing from the New Quarter,
　and a loud crash from the hills.
11Wail, you who live in the market district[d];
　all your merchants will be wiped out,
　all who trade with[e] silver will be ruined.

---

a 3 The meaning of the Hebrew for this line is uncertain.　*b 5* Hebrew *Malcam,* that is, Milcom　*c 9* See 1 Samuel 5:5.　*d 11* Or *the Mortar*　*e 11* Or *in*

Zephaniah

1 SUBJECT: A message from the Lord.
To: Zephaniah (son of Cushi, grandson of Gedaliah, great-grandson of Amariah, and great-great-grandson of Hezekiah). *When:* During the reign of Josiah (son of Amon) king of Judah.f

2"I will sweep away everything in all your land," says the Lord. "I will destroy it to the ground. 3I will sweep away both men and animals alike. Mankind and all the idols that he worships—all will vanish. Even the birds of the air and the fish in the sea will perish. 4I will crush Judah and Jerusalem with my fist, and destroy every remnant of those who worship Baal; I will put an end to their idolatrous priests, so that even the memory of them will disappear. 5They go up on their roofs and bow to the sun, moon and stars. They 'follow the Lord,' but worship Molech, too! I will destroy them. 6And I will destroy those who formerly worshiped the Lord, but now no longer do, and those who never loved him and never wanted to."

7Stand in silence in the presence of the Lord. For the awesome Day of his Judgment has come; he has prepared a great slaughter of his people and has chosen their executioners.g 8"On that Day of Judgment I will punish the leaders and princes of Judah, and all others wearing heathen clothing.h 9Yes, I will punish those who follow heathen customs and who rob and kill to fill their masters' homes with evil gain of violence and fraud. 10A cry of alarm will begin at the farthest gate of Jerusalem, coming closer and closer until the noise of the advancing army reaches the very top of the hill where the city is built.

11"Wail in sorrow, you people of Jerusalem. All your greedy businessmen, all your loan sharks—all will die.

Zephaniah

1 THE WORD of the LORD that came to Zephaniah son of Cushi son of Gedaliah son of Amariah son of Hezekiah, in the days of King Josiah son of Amon of Judah.

The Coming Judgment on Judah

2 I will utterly sweep away everything
    from the face of the earth, says the LORD.
3 I will sweep away humans and animals;
    I will sweep away the birds of the air
    and the fish of the sea.
  I will make the wicked stumble.i
    I will cut off humanity
    from the face of the earth, says the LORD.
4 I will stretch out my hand against Judah,
    and against all the inhabitants of Jerusalem;
  and I will cut off from this place every
        remnant of Baal
    and the name of the idolatrous priests;j
5 those who bow down on the roofs
    to the host of the heavens;
  those who bow down and swear to the LORD,
    but also swear by Milcom;k
6 those who have turned back from following
        the LORD,
    who have not sought the LORD or inquired
        of him.

7 Be silent before the Lord GOD!
    For the day of the LORD is at hand;
  the LORD has prepared a sacrifice,
    he has consecrated his guests.
8 And on the day of the LORD's sacrifice
    I will punish the officials and the king's sons
    and all who dress themselves in foreign
        attire.
9 On that day I will punish
    all who leap over the threshold,
  who fill their master's house
    with violence and fraud.
10 On that day, says the LORD,
    a cry will be heard from the Fish Gate,
  a wail from the Second Quarter,
    a loud crash from the hills.
11 The inhabitants of the Mortar wail,
    for all the traders have perished;
  all who weigh out silver are cut off.

---

f *1:1* The Great Revival under King Josiah followed about ten years after this prophecy, and then, a dozen years later, the deportation and exile. The prophet Jeremiah was active during this same period.   g *1:7 Has chosen their executioners,* literally is: "He has prepared a sacrifice and sanctified his guests."   h *1:8 wearing heathen clothing,* i.e., showing their desire for foreign gods and foreign ways, and their contempt for the Lord.

i Cn: Heb *sea, and those who cause the wicked to stumble*   j Compare Gk: Heb *the idolatrous priests with the priests*   k Gk Mss Syr Vg: Heb *Malcam* (or, *their king*)

King James

12And it shall come to pass at that time, *that* I will search Jerusalem with candles, and punish the men that are settled on their lees: that say in their heart, The LORD will not do good, neither will he do evil.

13Therefore their goods shall become a booty, and their houses a desolation: they shall also build houses, but not inhabit *them;* and they shall plant vineyards, but not drink the wine thereof.

14The great day of the LORD *is* near, *it is* near, and hasteth greatly, *even* the voice of the day of the LORD: the mighty man shall cry there bitterly.

15That day *is* a day of wrath, a day of trouble and distress, a day of wasteness and desolation, a day of darkness and gloominess, a day of clouds and thick darkness,

16A day of the trumpet and alarm against the fenced cities, and against the high towers.

17And I will bring distress upon men, that they shall walk like blind men, because they have sinned against the LORD: and their blood shall be poured out as dust, and their flesh as the dung.

18Neither their silver nor their gold shall be able to deliver them in the day of the LORD's wrath; but the whole land shall be devoured by the fire of his jealousy: for he shall make even a speedy riddance of all them that dwell in the land.

2 GATHER YOURSELVES together, yea, gather together, O nation not desired;

2Before the decree bring forth, *before* the day pass as the chaff, before the fierce anger of the LORD come upon you, before the day of the LORD's anger come upon you.

3Seek ye the LORD, all ye meek of the earth, which have wrought his judgment; seek righteousness, seek meekness: it may be ye shall be hid in the day of the LORD's anger.

4¶ For Gaza shall be forsaken, and Ashkelon a desolation: they shall drive out Ashdod at the noon day, and Ekron shall be rooted up.

5Woe unto the inhabitants of the sea coast, the nation of the Cherethites! the word of the LORD *is* against you; O Canaan, the land of the Philistines, I will even destroy thee, that there shall be no inhabitant.

New International

12At that time I will search Jerusalem with lamps
    and punish those who are complacent,
    who are like wine left on its dregs,
who think, 'The LORD will do nothing,
    either good or bad.'
13Their wealth will be plundered,
    their houses demolished.
They will build houses
    but not live in them;
they will plant vineyards
    but not drink the wine.

The Great Day of the LORD

14"The great day of the LORD is near—
    near and coming quickly.
Listen! The cry on the day of the LORD will be
    bitter,
    the shouting of the warrior there.
15That day will be a day of wrath,
    a day of distress and anguish,
a day of trouble and ruin,
    a day of darkness and gloom,
    a day of clouds and blackness,
16a day of trumpet and battle cry
    against the fortified cities
    and against the corner towers.
17I will bring distress on the people
    and they will walk like blind men,
    because they have sinned against the LORD.
Their blood will be poured out like dust
    and their entrails like filth.
18Neither their silver nor their gold
    will be able to save them
    on the day of the LORD's wrath.
In the fire of his jealousy
    the whole world will be consumed,
for he will make a sudden end
    of all who live in the earth."

2 GATHER TOGETHER, gather together,
    O shameful nation,
2before the appointed time arrives
    and that day sweeps on like chaff,
    before the fierce anger of the LORD comes upon
        you,
    before the day of the LORD's wrath comes
        upon you.
3Seek the LORD, all you humble of the land,
    you who do what he commands.
Seek righteousness, seek humility;
    perhaps you will be sheltered
    on the day of the LORD's anger.

Against Philistia

4Gaza will be abandoned
    and Ashkelon left in ruins.
At midday Ashdod will be emptied
    and Ekron uprooted.
5Woe to you who live by the sea,
    O Kerethite people;
the word of the LORD is against you,
    O Canaan, land of the Philistines.

"I will destroy you,
    and none will be left."

Living Bible

12"I will search with lanterns in Jerusalem's darkest corners to find and punish those who sit contented in their sins, indifferent to God, thinking he will let them alone. 13They are the very ones whose property will be plundered by the enemy, whose homes will be ransacked; they will never have a chance to live in the new homes they have built. They will never drink wine from the vineyards they have planted."

14"That terrible day is near. Swiftly it comes—a day when strong men will weep bitterly. 15It is a day of the wrath of God poured out; it is a day of terrible distress and anguish, a day of ruin and desolation, of darkness, gloom, clouds, blackness, 16trumpet calls and battle cries; down go the walled cities and strongest battlements!

17"I will make you as helpless as a blind man searching for a path, because you have sinned against the Lord; therefore your blood will be poured out into the dust and your bodies will lie there rotting on the ground.

18Your silver and gold will be of no use to you in that day of the Lord's wrath. You cannot ransom yourselves with it.a For the whole land will be devoured by the fire of his jealousy. He will make a speedy riddance of all the people of Judah.

2 GATHER TOGETHER and pray, you shameless nation, 2while there still is time—before judgment begins, and your opportunity is blown away like chaff; before the fierce anger of the Lord falls and the terrible day of his wrath begins. 3Beg him to save you, all who are humble—all who have tried to obey.

Walk humbly and do what is right; perhaps even yet the Lord will protect you from his wrath in that day of doom.

4Gaza, Ashkelon, Ashdod, Ekron—these Philistine cities, too, will be rooted out and left in desolation. 5And woe to you Philistinesb living on the coast and in the land of Canaan, for the judgment is against you, too. The Lord will destroy you until not one of you is left.

New Revised Standard

12 At that time I will search Jerusalem with lamps,
    and I will punish the people
who rest complacentlyc on their dregs,
    those who say in their hearts,
"The LORD will not do good,
    nor will he do harm."
13 Their wealth shall be plundered,
    and their houses laid waste.
Though they build houses,
    they shall not inhabit them;
though they plant vineyards,
    they shall not drink wine from them.

The Great Day of the LORD

14 The great day of the LORD is near,
    near and hastening fast;
the sound of the day of the LORD is bitter,
    the warrior cries aloud there.
15 That day will be a day of wrath,
    a day of distress and anguish,
a day of ruin and devastation,
    a day of darkness and gloom,
a day of clouds and thick darkness,
16   a day of trumpet blast and battle cry
against the fortified cities
    and against the lofty battlements.

17 I will bring such distress upon people
    that they shall walk like the blind;
    because they have sinned against the LORD,
their blood shall be poured out like dust,
    and their flesh like dung.
18 Neither their silver nor their gold
    will be able to save them
    on the day of the LORD's wrath;
in the fire of his passion
    the whole earth shall be consumed;
for a full, a terrible end
    he will make of all the inhabitants of the
        earth.

Judgment on Israel's Enemies

2 GATHER TOGETHER, gather,
    O shameless nation,
2 before you are driven away
    like the drifting chaff,d
before there comes upon you
    the fierce anger of the LORD,
before there comes upon you
    the day of the LORD's wrath.
3 Seek the LORD, all you humble of the land,
    who do his commands;
seek righteousness, seek humility;
    perhaps you may be hidden
    on the day of the LORD's wrath.
4 For Gaza shall be deserted,
    and Ashkelon shall become a desolation;
Ashdod's people shall be driven out at noon,
    and Ekron shall be uprooted.

5 Ah, inhabitants of the seacoast,
    you nation of the Cherethites!
The word of the LORD is against you,
    O Canaan, land of the Philistines;
    and I will destroy you until no inhabitant is
        left.

---

a 1:18 you cannot ransom yourselves with it, implied.   b 2:5 Philistines, literally, "Cherethites [or Cretans]." With the Philistines they were part of a great wave of immigrants to the southern coast of Palestine around 1200 B.C.

c Heb who thicken   d Cn Compare Gk Syr: Heb before a decree is born; like chaff a day has passed away

King James

6And the sea coast shall be dwellings *and* cottages for shepherds, and folds for flocks.

7And the coast shall be for the remnant of the house of Judah; they shall feed thereupon: in the houses of Ashkelon shall they lie down in the evening: for the LORD their God shall visit them, and turn away their captivity.

8¶ I have heard the reproach of Moab, and the revilings of the children of Ammon, whereby they have reproached my people, and magnified *themselves* against their border.

9Therefore *as* I live, saith the LORD of hosts, the God of Israel, Surely Moab shall be as Sodom, and the children of Ammon as Gomorrah, *even* the breeding of nettles, and saltpits, and a perpetual desolation: the residue of my people shall spoil them, and the remnant of my people shall possess them.

10This shall they have for their pride, because they have reproached and magnified *themselves* against the people of the LORD of hosts.

11The LORD *will be* terrible unto them: for he will famish all the gods of the earth; and *men* shall worship him, every one from his place, *even* all the isles of the heathen.

12¶ Ye Ethiopians also, ye *shall be* slain by my sword.

13And he will stretch out his hand against the north, and destroy Assyria; and will make Nineveh a desolation, *and* dry like a wilderness.

14And flocks shall lie down in the midst of her, all the beasts of the nations: both the cormorant and the bittern shall lodge in the upper lintels of it; *their* voice shall sing in the windows; desolation *shall be* in the thresholds: for he shall uncover the cedar work.

15This *is* the rejoicing city that dwelt carelessly, that said in her heart, I *am*, and *there is* none beside me: how is she become a desolation, a place for beasts to lie down in! every one that passeth by her shall hiss, *and* wag his hand.

3 WOE TO her that is filthy and polluted, to the oppressing city!

New International

6The land by the sea, where the Kerethites[a]
    dwell,
will be a place for shepherds and sheep pens.
7It will belong to the remnant of the house of
    Judah;
    there they will find pasture.
In the evening they will lie down
    in the houses of Ashkelon.
The LORD their God will care for them;
    he will restore their fortunes.[b]

Against Moab and Ammon

8"I have heard the insults of Moab
    and the taunts of the Ammonites,
who insulted my people
    and made threats against their land.
9Therefore, as surely as I live,"
    declares the LORD Almighty, the God of
    Israel,
"surely Moab will become like Sodom,
    the Ammonites like Gomorrah—
a place of weeds and salt pits,
    a wasteland forever.
The remnant of my people will plunder them;
    the survivors of my nation will inherit their
    land."

10This is what they will get in return for their
    pride,
    for insulting and mocking the people of the
    LORD Almighty.
11The LORD will be awesome to them
    when he destroys all the gods of the land.
The nations on every shore will worship him,
    every one in its own land.

Against Cush

12"You too, O Cushites,[c]
    will be slain by my sword."

Against Assyria

13He will stretch out his hand against the north
    and destroy Assyria,
leaving Nineveh utterly desolate
    and dry as the desert.
14Flocks and herds will lie down there,
    creatures of every kind.
The desert owl and the screech owl
    will roost on her columns.
Their calls will echo through the windows,
    rubble will be in the doorways,
    the beams of cedar will be exposed.
15This is the carefree city
    that lived in safety.
She said to herself,
    "I am, and there is none besides me."
What a ruin she has become,
    a lair for wild beasts!
All who pass by her scoff
    and shake their fists.

The Future of Jerusalem

3 WOE TO the city of oppressors,
    rebellious and defiled!

---

[a] 6 The meaning of the Hebrew for this word is uncertain.   [b] 7 Or *will bring back their captives*   [c] 12 That is, people from the upper Nile region

Living Bible

6The coastland will become a pasture, a place of shepherd camps and folds for sheep.

7There the little remnant of the tribe of Judah will be pastured. They will lie down to rest in the abandoned houses in Ashkelon. For the Lord God will visit his people in kindness and restore their prosperity again.

8"I have heard the taunts of the people of Moab and Ammon, mocking my people and invading their land. 9Therefore as I live," says the Lord Almighty, God of Israel, "Moab and Ammon will be destroyed like Sodom and Gomorrah, and become a place of stinging nettles and salt pits and eternal desolation; those of my people who are left will plunder and possess them." 10They will receive the wages of their pride, for they have scoffed at the people of the Lord Almighty. 11The Lord will do terrible things to them. He will starve out all those gods of foreign powers, and everyone shall worship him, each in his own land throughout the world.

12You Ethiopians, too, will be slain by his sword, 13and so will the lands of the north; he will destroy Assyria and make its great capital Nineveh a desolate wasteland like a wilderness. 14That once proud city will become a pastureland for sheep. All sorts of wild animals will have their homes in her. Hedgehogs will burrow there; the vultures and the owls will live among the ruins of her palaces, hooting from the gaping windows; the ravens will croak from her doors. All her cedar paneling will lie open to the wind and weather.

15This is the fate of that vast, prosperous city that lived in such security, that said to herself, "In all the world there is no city as great as I." But now—see how she has become a place of utter ruins, a place for animals to live! Everyone passing that way will mock, or shake his head in disbelief.d

New Revised Standard

6 And you, O seacoast, shall be pastures,
  meadows for shepherds
  and folds for flocks.
7 The seacoast shall become the possession
  of the remnant of the house of Judah,
  on which they shall pasture,
and in the houses of Ashkelon
  they shall lie down at evening.
For the LORD their God will be mindful of
  them
  and restore their fortunes.

8 I have heard the taunts of Moab
  and the revilings of the Ammonites,
how they have taunted my people
  and made boasts against their territory.
9 Therefore, as I live, says the LORD of hosts,
  the God of Israel,
Moab shall become like Sodom
  and the Ammonites like Gomorrah,
a land possessed by nettles and salt pits,
  and a waste forever.
The remnant of my people shall plunder them,
  and the survivors of my nation shall possess
    them.
10 This shall be their lot in return for their pride,
  because they scoffed and boasted
  against the people of the LORD of hosts.
11 The LORD will be terrible against them;
  he will shrivel all the gods of the earth,
and to him shall bow down,
  each in its place,
  all the coasts and islands of the nations.

12 You also, O Ethiopians,e
  shall be killed by my sword.

13 And he will stretch out his hand against the
    north,
  and destroy Assyria;
and he will make Nineveh a desolation,
  a dry waste like the desert.
14 Herds shall lie down in it,
  every wild animal;f
the desert owlg and the screech owlg
  shall lodge on its capitals;
the owlh shall hoot at the window,
  the raveni croak on the threshold;
  for its cedar work will be laid bare.
15 Is this the exultant city
  that lived secure,
that said to itself,
  "I am, and there is no one else"?
What a desolation it has become,
  a lair for wild animals!
Everyone who passes by it
  hisses and shakes the fist.

The Wickedness of Jerusalem

3 WOE TO filthy, sinful Jerusalem, city of violence and crime. 2In her pride she won't listen even to

3 AH, SOILED, defiled,
  oppressing city!

---

d *2:15 will mock, or shake his head in disbelief.* "Nothing seemed more improbable than that the capital of so vast an empire, a city of sixty miles around with walls 100 feet high and so thick that three chariots could go abreast on them, and with 1500 towers, should be so totally destroyed that its site is with difficulty discovered."—Jamieson, Fausset and Brown Commentary

e Or *Nubians*; Heb *Cushites*   f Tg Compare Gk: Heb *nation*   g Meaning of Heb uncertain   h Cn: Heb *a voice*   i Gk Vg: Heb *desolation*

King James

2She obeyed not the voice; she received not correction; she trusted not in the LORD; she drew not near to her God.

3Her princes within her *are* roaring lions; her judges *are* evening wolves; they gnaw not the bones till the morrow.

4Her prophets *are* light *and* treacherous persons: her priests have polluted the sanctuary, they have done violence to the law.

5The just LORD *is* in the midst thereof; he will not do iniquity: every morning doth he bring his judgment to light, he faileth not; but the unjust knoweth no shame.

6I have cut off the nations: their towers are desolate; I made their streets waste, that none passeth by: their cities are destroyed, so that there is no man, that there is none inhabitant.

7I said, Surely thou wilt fear me, thou wilt receive instruction; so their dwelling should not be cut off, howsoever I punished them: but they rose early, *and* corrupted all their doings.

8¶ Therefore wait ye upon me, saith the LORD, until the day that I rise up to the prey: for my determination *is* to gather the nations, that I may assemble the kingdoms, to pour upon them mine indignation, *even* all my fierce anger: for all the earth shall be devoured with the fire of my jealousy.

9For then will I turn to the people a pure language, that they may all call upon the name of the LORD, to serve him with one consent.

10From beyond the rivers of Ethiopia my suppliants, *even* the daughter of my dispersed, shall bring mine offering.

11In that day shalt thou not be ashamed for all thy doings, wherein thou hast transgressed against me: for then I will take away out of the midst of thee them that rejoice in thy pride, and thou shalt no more be haughty because of my holy mountain.

12I will also leave in the midst of thee an afflicted and poor people, and they shall trust in the name of the LORD.

13The remnant of Israel shall not do iniquity, nor speak lies; neither shall a deceitful tongue be found in their mouth: for they shall feed and lie down, and none shall make *them* afraid.

New International

2She obeys no one,
　　she accepts no correction.
She does not trust in the LORD,
　　she does not draw near to her God.
3Her officials are roaring lions,
　　her rulers are evening wolves,
　　who leave nothing for the morning.
4Her prophets are arrogant;
　　they are treacherous men.
Her priests profane the sanctuary
　　and do violence to the law.
5The LORD within her is righteous;
　　he does no wrong.
Morning by morning he dispenses his justice,
　　and every new day he does not fail,
　　yet the unrighteous know no shame.

6"I have cut off nations;
　　their strongholds are demolished.
I have left their streets deserted,
　　with no one passing through.
Their cities are destroyed;
　　no one will be left—no one at all.
7I said to the city,
　　'Surely you will fear me
　　and accept correction!'
Then her dwelling would not be cut off,
　　nor all my punishments come upon her.
But they were still eager
　　to act corruptly in all they did.
8Therefore wait for me," declares the LORD,
　　"for the day I will stand up to testify.[a]
I have decided to assemble the nations,
　　to gather the kingdoms
and to pour out my wrath on them—
　　all my fierce anger.
The whole world will be consumed
　　by the fire of my jealous anger.

9"Then will I purify the lips of the peoples,
　　that all of them may call on the name of the
　　　LORD
　　and serve him shoulder to shoulder.
10From beyond the rivers of Cush[b]
　　my worshipers, my scattered people,
　　will bring me offerings.
11On that day you will not be put to shame
　　for all the wrongs you have done to me,
because I will remove from this city
　　those who rejoice in their pride.
Never again will you be haughty
　　on my holy hill.
12But I will leave within you
　　the meek and humble,
　　who trust in the name of the LORD.
13The remnant of Israel will do no wrong;
　　they will speak no lies,
　　nor will deceit be found in their mouths.
They will eat and lie down
　　and no one will make them afraid."

---

[a] 8 Septuagint and Syriac; Hebrew *will rise up to plunder*   [b] 10 That is, the upper Nile region

Living Bible

the voice of God. No one can tell her anything; she refuses all correction. She does not trust the Lord, nor seek for God.

3Her leaders are like roaring lions hunting for their victims—out for everything that they can get. Her judges are like ravenous wolves at evening time, who by dawn have left no trace of their prey.

4Her "prophets" are liars seeking their own gain; her priests defile the Temple by their disobedience to God's laws.

5But the Lord is there within the city, and he does no wrong. Day by day his justice is more evident, but no one heeds—the wicked know no shame.

6"I have cut off many nations, laying them waste to their farthest borders; I have left their streets in silent ruin and their cities deserted without a single survivor to remember what happened. 7I thought, 'Surely they will listen to me now—surely they will heed my warnings, so that I'll not need to strike again.' But no; however much I punish them, they continue all their evil ways from dawn to dusk and dusk to dawn. 8But the Lord says, "Be patient; the time is coming soon when I will stand up and accuse these evil nations. For it is my decision to gather together the kingdoms of the earth, and pour out my fiercest anger and wrath upon them. All the earth shall be devoured with the fire of my jealousy.

9"At that time I will change the speech of my returning people to pure Hebrewc so that all can worship the Lord together. 10My scattered people who live in the Sudan,d beyond the rivers of Ethiopia, will come with their offerings, asking me to be their God again. 11And then you will no longer need to be ashamed of yourselves, for you will no longer be rebels against me. I will remove all your proud and arrogant people from among you; there will be no pride or haughtiness on my holy mountain. 12Those who are left will be the poor and the humble, and they will trust in the name of the Lord. 13They will not be sinners, full of lies and deceit. They will live quietly, in peace, and lie down in safety, and no one will make them afraid."

New Revised Standard

2   It has listened to no voice;
        it has accepted no correction.
    It has not trusted in the LORD;
        it has not drawn near to its God.

3   The officials within it
        are roaring lions;
    its judges are evening wolves
        that leave nothing until the morning.
4   Its prophets are reckless,
        faithless persons;
    its priests have profaned what is sacred,
        they have done violence to the law.
5   The LORD within it is righteous;
        he does no wrong.
    Every morning he renders his judgment,
        each dawn without fail;
        but the unjust knows no shame.

6   I have cut off nations;
        their battlements are in ruins;
    I have laid waste their streets
        so that no one walks in them;
    their cities have been made desolate,
        without people, without inhabitants.
7   I said, "Surely the citye will fear me,
        it will accept correction;
    it will not lose sightf
        of all that I have brought upon it."
    But they were the more eager
        to make all their deeds corrupt.

Punishment and Conversion of the Nations

8   Therefore wait for me, says the LORD,
        for the day when I arise as a witness.
    For my decision is to gather nations,
        to assemble kingdoms,
    to pour out upon them my indignation,
        all the heat of my anger;
    for in the fire of my passion
        all the earth shall be consumed.

9   At that time I will change the speech of the
            peoples
        to a pure speech,
    that all of them may call on the name of the
            LORD
        and serve him with one accord.
10 From beyond the rivers of Ethiopiag
        my suppliants, my scattered ones,
        shall bring my offering.

11 On that day you shall not be put to shame
        because of all the deeds by which you have
            rebelled against me;
    for then I will remove from your midst
        your proudly exultant ones,
    and you shall no longer be haughty
        in my holy mountain.
12 For I will leave in the midst of you
        a people humble and lowly.
    They shall seek refuge in the name of the
            LORD—
13   the remnant of Israel;
    they shall do no wrong
        and utter no lies,
    nor shall a deceitful tongue
        be found in their mouths.
    Then they will pasture and lie down,
        and no one shall make them afraid.

---

c 3:9 *I will change the speech . . . to pure Hebrew*, literally "I will change the speech of the peoples to a pure speech. . . ." See Isa 19:18.   d *3:10 in the Sudan*, implied.

e Heb *it*   f Gk Syr: Heb *its dwelling will not be cut off*   g Or *Nubia*; Heb *Cush*

King James

14¶ Sing, O daughter of Zion; shout, O Israel; be glad and rejoice with all the heart, O daughter of Jerusalem.

15The LORD hath taken away thy judgments, he hath cast out thine enemy: the king of Israel, *even* the LORD, *is* in the midst of thee: thou shalt not see evil any more.

16In that day it shall be said to Jerusalem, Fear thou not: *and to* Zion, Let not thine hands be slack.

17The LORD thy God in the midst of thee *is* mighty; he will save, he will rejoice over thee with joy; he will rest in his love, he will joy over thee with singing.

18I will gather *them that are* sorrowful for the solemn assembly, *who* are of thee, *to whom* the reproach of it *was* a burden.

19Behold, at that time I will undo all that afflict thee: and I will save her that halteth, and gather her that was driven out; and I will get them praise and fame in every land where they have been put to shame.

20At that time will I bring you *again*, even in the time that I gather you: for I will make you a name and a praise among all people of the earth, when I turn back your captivity before your eyes, saith the LORD.

New International

14Sing, O Daughter of Zion;
    shout aloud, O Israel!
Be glad and rejoice with all your heart,
    O Daughter of Jerusalem!
15The LORD has taken away your punishment,
    he has turned back your enemy.
The LORD, the King of Israel, is with you;
    never again will you fear any harm.
16On that day they will say to Jerusalem,
    "Do not fear, O Zion;
    do not let your hands hang limp.
17The LORD your God is with you,
    he is mighty to save.
He will take great delight in you,
    he will quiet you with his love,
    he will rejoice over you with singing."

18"The sorrows for the appointed feasts
    I will remove from you;
    they are a burden and a reproach to you.a
19At that time I will deal
    with all who oppressed you;
I will rescue the lame
    and gather those who have been scattered.
I will give them praise and honor
    in every land where they were put to shame.
20At that time I will gather you;
    at that time I will bring you home.
I will give you honor and praise
    among all the peoples of the earth
when I restore your fortunesb
    before your very eyes,"
                                    says the LORD.

---

a 18 Or *"I will gather you who mourn for the appointed feasts; / your reproach is a burden to you*   b 20 Or *I bring back your captives*

Living Bible

14Sing, O daughter of Zion; shout, O Israel; be glad and rejoice with all your heart, O daughter of Jerusalem. 15For the Lord will remove his hand of judgment, and disperse the armies of your enemy. And the Lord himself, the King of Israel, will live among you! At last your troubles will be over—you need fear no more.

16On that day the announcement to Jerusalem will be, "Cheer up, don't be afraid. 17, 18For the Lord your God has arrived to live among you. He is a mighty Savior. He will give you victory. He will rejoice over you in great gladness; he will love you and not accuse you." Is that a joyous choir I hear? No, it is the Lord himself exulting over you in happy song:

"I have gathered your wounded and taken away your reproach. 19And I will deal severely with all who have oppressed you. I will save the weak and helpless ones, and bring together those who were chased away. I will give glory to my former exiles, mocked and shamed.

20"At that time, I will gather you together and bring you home again, and give you a good name, a name of distinction among all the peoples of the earth, and they will praise you when I restore your fortunes before your very eyes," says the Lord.

New Revised Standard

A Song of Joy

14 Sing aloud, O daughter Zion;
   shout, O Israel!
   Rejoice and exult with all your heart,
   O daughter Jerusalem!
15 The Lord has taken away the judgments
   against you,
   he has turned away your enemies.
   The king of Israel, the Lord, is in your midst;
   you shall fear disaster no more.
16 On that day it shall be said to Jerusalem:
   Do not fear, O Zion;
   do not let your hands grow weak.
17 The Lord, your God, is in your midst,
   a warrior who gives victory;
   he will rejoice over you with gladness,
   he will renew youc in his love;
   he will exult over you with loud singing
18 as on a day of festival.d
   I will remove disaster from you,e
   so that you will not bear reproach for it.
19 I will deal with all your oppressors
   at that time.
   And I will save the lame
   and gather the outcast,
   and I will change their shame into praise
   and renown in all the earth.
20 At that time I will bring you home,
   at the time when I gather you;
   for I will make you renowned and praised
   among all the peoples of the earth,
   when I restore your fortunes
   before your eyes, says the Lord.

---

c Gk Syr: Heb *he will be silent*   d Gk Syr: Meaning of Heb uncertain   e Cn:
Heb *I will remove from you; they were*

King James

Haggai

1 IN THE second year of Darius the king, in the sixth month, in the first day of the month, came the word of the LORD by Haggai the prophet unto Zerubbabel the son of Shealtiel, governor of Judah, and to Joshua the son of Josedech, the high priest, saying,

²Thus speaketh the LORD of hosts, saying, This people say, The time is not come, the time that the LORD's house should be built.

³Then came the word of the LORD by Haggai the prophet, saying,

⁴Is it time for you, O ye, to dwell in your ceiled houses, and this house lie waste?

⁵Now therefore thus saith the LORD of hosts; Consider your ways.

⁶Ye have sown much, and bring in little; ye eat, but ye have not enough; ye drink, but ye are not filled with drink; ye clothe you, but there is none warm; and he that earneth wages earneth wages to put it into a bag with holes.

⁷¶ Thus saith the LORD of hosts; Consider your ways.

⁸Go up to the mountain, and bring wood, and build the house; and I will take pleasure in it, and I will be glorified, saith the LORD.

⁹Ye looked for much, and, lo, it came to little; and when ye brought it home, I did blow upon it. Why? saith the LORD of hosts. Because of mine house that is waste, and ye run every man unto his own house.

¹⁰Therefore the heaven over you is stayed from dew, and the earth is stayed from her fruit.

¹¹And I called for a drought upon the land, and upon the mountains, and upon the corn, and upon the new wine, and upon the oil, and upon that which the ground bringeth forth, and upon men, and upon cattle, and upon all the labour of the hands.

¹²¶ Then Zerubbabel the son of Shealtiel, and Joshua the son of Josedech, the high priest, with all the remnant of the people, obeyed the voice of the LORD their God, and the words of Haggai the prophet, as the LORD their God had sent him, and the people did fear before the LORD.

¹³Then spake Haggai the LORD's messenger in the LORD's message unto the people, saying, I am with you, saith the LORD.

¹⁴And the LORD stirred up the spirit of Zerubbabel the son of Shealtiel, governor of Judah, and the spirit of Joshua the son of Josedech, the high priest, and the spirit of all the remnant of the people; and they came and did work in the house of the LORD of hosts, their God,

¹⁵In the four and twentieth day of the sixth month, in the second year of Darius the king.

New International

Haggai

A Call to Build the House of the LORD

1 IN THE second year of King Darius, on the first day of the sixth month, the word of the LORD came through the prophet Haggai to Zerubbabel son of Shealtiel, governor of Judah, and to Joshuaᵃ son of Jehozadak, the high priest:

²This is what the LORD Almighty says: "These people say, 'The time has not yet come for the LORD's house to be built.' "

³Then the word of the LORD came through the prophet Haggai: ⁴"Is it a time for you yourselves to be living in your paneled houses, while this house remains a ruin?"

⁵Now this is what the LORD Almighty says: "Give careful thought to your ways. ⁶You have planted much, but have harvested little. You eat, but never have enough. You drink, but never have your fill. You put on clothes, but are not warm. You earn wages, only to put them in a purse with holes in it."

⁷This is what the LORD Almighty says: "Give careful thought to your ways. ⁸Go up into the mountains and bring down timber and build the house, so that I may take pleasure in it and be honored," says the LORD. ⁹"You expected much, but see, it turned out to be little. What you brought home, I blew away. Why?" declares the LORD Almighty. "Because of my house, which remains a ruin, while each of you is busy with his own house. ¹⁰Therefore, because of you the heavens have withheld their dew and the earth its crops. ¹¹I called for a drought on the fields and the mountains, on the grain, the new wine, the oil and whatever the ground produces, on men and cattle, and on the labor of your hands."

¹²Then Zerubbabel son of Shealtiel, Joshua son of Jehozadak, the high priest, and the whole remnant of the people obeyed the voice of the LORD their God and the message of the prophet Haggai, because the LORD their God had sent him. And the people feared the LORD.

¹³Then Haggai, the LORD's messenger, gave this message of the LORD to the people: "I am with you," declares the LORD. ¹⁴So the LORD stirred up the spirit of Zerubbabel son of Shealtiel, governor of Judah, and the spirit of Joshua son of Jehozadak, the high priest, and the spirit of the whole remnant of the people. They came and began to work on the house of the LORD Almighty, their God, ¹⁵on the twenty-fourth day of the sixth month in the second year of King Darius.

ᵃ 1 A variant of Jeshua; here and elsewhere in Haggai

Living Bible

New Revised Standard

Haggai

Haggai

1 SUBJECT: A message from the Lord.
To: Haggai the prophet, who delivered it to Zerubbabel (son of Shealtiel), governor of Judah; and to Joshua (son of Josedech), the High Priest—for it was addressed to them.[b]
When: In late August of the second year of the reign of King Darius I.

2"Why is everyone saying it is not the right time for rebuilding my Temple?" asks the Lord.

3,4His reply to them is this: "Is it then the right time for you to live in luxurious homes, when the Temple lies in ruins? 5Look at the result: 6You plant much but harvest little. You have scarcely enough to eat or drink, and not enough clothes to keep you warm. Your income disappears, as though you were putting it into pockets filled with holes!

7"Think it over," says the Lord Almighty. "Consider how you have acted, and what has happened as a result! 8Then go up into the mountains and bring down timber, and rebuild my Temple, and I will be pleased with it and appear there in my glory," says the Lord.

9"You hope for much but get so little. And when you bring it home, I blow it away—it doesn't last at all. Why? Because my Temple lies in ruins and you don't care. Your only concern is your own fine homes. 10That is why I am holding back the rains from heaven and giving you such scant crops. 11In fact, I have called for a drought upon the land, yes, and in the highlands, too; a drought to wither the grain and grapes and olives and all your other crops, a drought to starve both you and all your cattle, and ruin everything you have worked so hard to get."

12Then Zerubbabel (son of Shealtiel), the governor of Judah, and Joshua (son of Josedech), the High Priest, and the few people remaining in the land obeyed Haggai's message from the Lord their God; they began to worship him in earnest.

13Then the Lord told them (again sending the message through Haggai, his messenger), "I am with you; I will bless you." 14, 15And the Lord gave them a desire to rebuild his Temple; so they all gathered in early September of the second year of King Darius' reign, and volunteered their help.

The Command to Rebuild the Temple

1 IN THE second year of King Darius, in the sixth month, on the first day of the month, the word of the LORD came by the prophet Haggai to Zerubbabel son of Shealtiel, governor of Judah, and to Joshua son of Jehozadak, the high priest: 2Thus says the LORD of hosts: These people say the time has not yet come to rebuild the LORD's house. 3Then the word of the LORD came by the prophet Haggai, saying: 4Is it a time for you yourselves to live in your paneled houses, while this house lies in ruins? 5Now therefore thus says the LORD of hosts: Consider how you have fared. 6You have sown much, and harvested little; you eat, but you never have enough; you drink, but you never have your fill; you clothe yourselves, but no one is warm; and you that earn wages earn wages to put them into a bag with holes.

7 Thus says the LORD of hosts: Consider how you have fared. 8Go up to the hills and bring wood and build the house, so that I may take pleasure in it and be honored, says the LORD. 9You have looked for much, and, lo, it came to little; and when you brought it home, I blew it away. Why? says the LORD of hosts. Because my house lies in ruins, while all of you hurry off to your own houses. 10Therefore the heavens above you have withheld the dew, and the earth has withheld its produce. 11And I have called for a drought on the land and the hills, on the grain, the new wine, the oil, on what the soil produces, on human beings and animals, and on all their labors.

12 Then Zerubbabel son of Shealtiel, and Joshua son of Jehozadak, the high priest, with all the remnant of the people, obeyed the voice of the LORD their God, and the words of the prophet Haggai, as the LORD their God had sent him; and the people feared the LORD. 13Then Haggai, the messenger of the LORD, spoke to the people with the LORD's message, saying, I am with you, says the LORD. 14And the LORD stirred up the spirit of Zerubbabel son of Shealtiel, governor of Judah, and the spirit of Joshua son of Jehozadak, the high priest, and the spirit of all the remnant of the people; and they came and worked on the house of the LORD of hosts, their God, 15on the twenty-fourth day of the month, in the sixth month.

---

b 1:1 *for it was addressed to them,* that is, to the exiles who had returned from Babylon to rebuild Jerusalem.

King James

2 IN THE seventh *month,* in the one and twentieth *day* of the month, came the word of the LORD by the prophet Haggai, saying,

2Speak now to Zerubbabel the son of Shealtiel, governor of Judah, and to Joshua the son of Josedech, the high priest, and to the residue of the people, saying,

3Who *is* left among you that saw this house in her first glory? and how do ye see it now? *is it* not in your eyes in comparison of it as nothing?

4Yet now be strong, O Zerubbabel, saith the LORD; and be strong, O Joshua, son of Josedech, the high priest; and be strong, all ye people of the land, saith the LORD, and work: for I *am* with you, saith the LORD of hosts:

5*According to* the word that I covenanted with you when ye came out of Egypt, so my spirit remaineth among you: fear ye not.

6For thus saith the LORD of hosts; Yet once, it *is* a little while, and I will shake the heavens, and the earth, and the sea, and the dry *land;*

7And I will shake all nations, and the desire of all nations shall come: and I will fill this house with glory, saith the LORD of hosts.

8The silver *is* mine, and the gold *is* mine, saith the LORD of hosts.

9The glory of this latter house shall be greater than of the former, saith the LORD of hosts: and in this place will I give peace, saith the LORD of hosts.

10¶ In the four and twentieth *day* of the ninth *month,* in the second year of Darius, came the word of the LORD by Haggai the prophet, saying,

11Thus saith the LORD of hosts; Ask now the priests *concerning* the law, saying,

12If one bear holy flesh in the skirt of his garment, and with his skirt do touch bread, or pottage, or wine, or oil, or any meat, shall it be holy? And the priests answered and said, No.

13Then said Haggai, If *one that is* unclean by a dead body touch any of these, shall it be unclean? And the priests answered and said, It shall be unclean.

14Then answered Haggai, and said, So *is* this people, and so *is* this nation before me, saith the LORD; and so *is* every work of their hands; and that which they offer there *is* unclean.

15And now, I pray you, consider from this day and upward, from before a stone was laid upon a stone in the temple of the LORD:

16Since those *days* were, when *one* came to an heap of twenty *measures,* there were *but* ten: when *one* came to the pressvat for to draw out fifty *vessels* out of the press, there were *but* twenty.

17I smote you with blasting and with mildew and with hail in all the labours of your hands; yet ye *turned* not to me, saith the LORD.

18Consider now from this day and upward, from the four and twentieth day of the ninth *month, even* from the day that the foundation of the LORD's temple was laid, consider *it.*

19Is the seed yet in the barn? yea, as yet the vine, and the fig tree, and the pomegranate, and the olive tree, hath not brought forth: from this day will I bless *you.*

20¶ And again the word of the LORD came unto Haggai in the four and twentieth *day* of the month, saying,

21Speak to Zerubbabel, governor of Judah, saying, I will shake the heavens and the earth;

22And I will overthrow the throne of kingdoms, and I will destroy the strength of the kingdoms of the heathen; and I will overthrow the chariots, and those that ride in them; and the horses and their riders shall come down, every one by the sword of his brother.

New International

The Promised Glory of the New House

2 ON THE twenty-first day of the seventh month, the word of the LORD came through the prophet Haggai: 2"Speak to Zerubbabel son of Shealtiel, governor of Judah, to Joshua son of Jehozadak, the high priest, and to the remnant of the people. Ask them, 3'Who of you is left who saw this house in its former glory? How does it look to you now? Does it not seem to you like nothing? 4But now be strong, O Zerubbabel,' declares the LORD. 'Be strong, O Joshua son of Jehozadak, the high priest. Be strong, all you people of the land,' declares the LORD, 'and work. For I am with you,' declares the LORD Almighty. 5'This is what I covenanted with you when you came out of Egypt. And my Spirit remains among you. Do not fear.'

6"This is what the LORD Almighty says: 'In a little while I will once more shake the heavens and the earth, the sea and the dry land. 7I will shake all nations, and the desired of all nations will come, and I will fill this house with glory,' says the LORD Almighty. 8'The silver is mine and the gold is mine,' declares the LORD Almighty. 9'The glory of this present house will be greater than the glory of the former house,' says the LORD Almighty. 'And in this place I will grant peace,' declares the LORD Almighty."

Blessings for a Defiled People

10On the twenty-fourth day of the ninth month, in the second year of Darius, the word of the LORD came to the prophet Haggai: 11"This is what the LORD Almighty says: 'Ask the priests what the law says: 12If a person carries consecrated meat in the fold of his garment, and that fold touches some bread or stew, some wine, oil or other food, does it become consecrated?' "

The priests answered, "No."

13Then Haggai said, "If a person defiled by contact with a dead body touches one of these things, does it become defiled?"

"Yes," the priests replied, "it becomes defiled."

14Then Haggai said, " 'So it is with this people and this nation in my sight,' declares the LORD. 'Whatever they do and whatever they offer there is defiled.

15" 'Now give careful thought to this from this day ona—consider how things were before one stone was laid on another in the LORD's temple. 16When anyone came to a heap of twenty measures, there were only ten. When anyone went to a wine vat to draw fifty measures, there were only twenty. 17I struck all the work of your hands with blight, mildew and hail, yet you did not turn to me,' declares the LORD. 18'From this day on, from this twenty-fourth day of the ninth month, give careful thought to the day when the foundation of the LORD's temple was laid. Give careful thought: 19Is there yet any seed left in the barn? Until now, the vine and the fig tree, the pomegranate and the olive tree have not borne fruit.

" 'From this day on I will bless you.' "

Zerubbabel the Lord's Signet Ring

20The word of the LORD came to Haggai a second time on the twenty-fourth day of the month: 21"Tell Zerubbabel governor of Judah that I will shake the heavens and the earth. 22I will overturn royal thrones and shatter the power of the foreign kingdoms. I will overthrow chariots and their drivers; horses and their riders will fall, each by the sword of his brother.

---

a 15 Or *to the days past*

Living Bible

2 IN EARLY October of the same year, the Lord sent them this message through Haggai:

2Ask this question of the governor and High Priest and everyone left in the land:

3"Who among you can remember the Temple as it was before? How glorious it was! In comparison, it is nothing now, is it? 4But take courage, O Zerubbabel and Joshua and all the people; take courage and work, for 'I am with you,' says the Lord Almighty. 5'For I promised when you left Egypt that my Spirit would remain among you; so don't be afraid.'

6"For the Lord Almighty says, 'In just a little while I will begin to shake the heavens and earth—and the oceans, too, and the dry land— 7I will shake all nations, and the Desire of All Nationsb shall come to this Temple, and I will fill this place with my glory,' says the Lord Almighty. 8, 9'The future splendor of this Temple will be greater than the splendor of the first one! For I have plenty of silver and gold to do it! And here I will give peace,'c says the Lord."

10In early December, in the second year of the reign of King Darius, this message came from the Lord through Haggai the prophet:

11Ask the priests this question about the law: 12"If one of you is carrying a holy sacrifice in his robes, and happens to brush against some bread or wine or meat, will it too become holy?"

"No," the priests replied. "Holiness does not pass to other things that way."

13Then Haggai asked, "But if someone touches a dead person, and so becomes ceremonially impure, and then brushes against something, does it become contaminated?"

And the priests answered, "Yes."

14Haggai then made his meaning clear. "You people," he said (speaking for the Lord), "were contaminating your sacrifices by living with selfish attitudes and evil hearts—and not only your sacrifices, but everything else that you did as a 'service' to me. 15And so everything you did went wrong. But all is different now, because you have begun to build the Temple. 16, 17Before, when you expected a twenty-bushel crop, there were only ten. When you came to draw fifty gallons from the olive press, there were only twenty. I rewarded all your labor with rust and mildew and hail. Yet, even so, you refused to return to me," says the Lord.

18, 19"But now note this: From today, this 24th day of the month,d as the foundation of the Lord's Temple is finished, and from this day onward, I will bless you. Notice, I am giving you this promise now before you have even begun to rebuild the Temple structure, and before you have harvested your grain, and before the grapes and figs and pomegranates and olives have produced their next crops: *From this day I will bless you.*"

20Another message came to Haggai from the Lord that same day:

21Tell Zerubbabel, the governor of Judah, "I am about to shake the heavens and the earth, 22and to overthrow thrones and destroy the strength of the kingdoms of the nations. I will overthrow their armed might, and brothers and companions will kill each other. 23But

New Revised Standard

The Future Glory of the Temple

2 IN THE second year of King Darius, 1in the seventh month, on the twenty-first day of the month, the word of the LORD came by the prophet Haggai, saying: 2Speak now to Zerubbabel son of Shealtiel, governor of Judah, and to Joshua son of Jehozadak, the high priest, and to the remnant of the people, and say, 3Who is left among you that saw this house in its former glory? How does it look to you now? Is it not in your sight as nothing? 4Yet now take courage, O Zerubbabel, says the LORD; take courage, O Joshua, son of Jehozadak, the high priest; take courage, all you people of the land, says the LORD; work, for I am with you, says the LORD of hosts, 5according to the promise that I made you when you came out of Egypt. My spirit abides among you; do not fear. 6For thus says the LORD of hosts: Once again, in a little while, I will shake the heavens and the earth and the sea and the dry land; 7and I will shake all the nations, so that the treasure of all nations shall come, and I will fill this house with splendor, says the LORD of hosts. 8The silver is mine, and the gold is mine, says the LORD of hosts. 9The latter splendor of this house shall be greater than the former, says the LORD of hosts; and in this place I will give prosperity, says the LORD of hosts.

A Rebuke and a Promise

10 On the twenty-fourth day of the ninth month, in the second year of Darius, the word of the LORD came by the prophet Haggai, saying: 11Thus says the LORD of hosts: Ask the priests for a ruling: 12If one carries consecrated meat in the fold of one's garment, and with the fold touches bread, or stew, or wine, or oil, or any kind of food, does it become holy? The priests answered, "No." 13Then Haggai said, "If one who is unclean by contact with a dead body touches any of these, does it become unclean?" The priests answered, "Yes, it becomes unclean." 14Haggai then said, So is it with this people, and with this nation before me, says the LORD; and so with every work of their hands; and what they offer there is unclean. 15But now, consider what will come to pass from this day on. Before a stone was placed upon a stone in the LORD's temple, 16how did you fare?e When one came to a heap of twenty measures, there were but ten; when one came to the winevat to draw fifty measures, there were but twenty. 17I struck you and all the products of your toil with blight and mildew and hail; yet you did not return to me, says the LORD. 18Consider from this day on, from the twenty-fourth day of the ninth month. Since the day that the foundation of the LORD's temple was laid, consider: 19Is there any seed left in the barn? Do the vine, the fig tree, the pomegranate, and the olive tree still yield nothing? From this day on I will bless you.

God's Promise to Zerubbabel

20 The word of the LORD came a second time to Haggai on the twenty-fourth day of the month: 21Speak to Zerubbabel, governor of Judah, saying, I am about to shake the heavens and the earth, 22and to overthrow the throne of kingdoms; I am about to destroy the strength of the kingdoms of the nations, and overthrow the chariots and their riders; and the horses and their riders shall fall, every one by the sword of a comrade. 23On that

---

b 2:7 *the Desire of All Nations*, i.e., Christ the Messiah. Literally, "The Treasures" or "that which is choice." But many commentators prefer this rendering: "The treasures of the nations will pour into this Temple, and I will fill it with splendor."   c 2:9 *I will give peace*, i.e., peace with God through Christ who, 500 years later, came often to this Temple. d 2:18, 19 *24th day of the month*, i.e., of Kislev, which is early in December, according to our calendar.

e Gk: Heb *since they were*

King James

23In that day, saith the LORD of hosts, will I take thee, O Zerubbabel, my servant, the son of Shealtiel, saith the LORD, and will make thee as a signet: for I have chosen thee, saith the LORD of hosts.

New International

23" 'On that day,' declares the LORD Almighty, 'I will take you, my servant Zerubbabel son of Shealtiel,' declares the LORD, 'and I will make you like my signet ring, for I have chosen you,' declares the LORD Almighty."

Living Bible

when that happens, I will take you, O Zerubbabel my servant, and honor you like a signet ring upon my finger; for I have specially chosen you," says the Lord Almighty.

New Revised Standard

day, says the LORD of hosts, I will take you, O Zerubbabel my servant, son of Shealtiel, says the LORD, and make you like a signet ring; for I have chosen you, says the LORD of hosts.

King James

New International

Zechariah

Zechariah

A Call to Return to the Lord

1 IN THE eighth month, in the second year of Darius, came the word of the Lord unto Zechariah, the son of Berechiah, the son of Iddo the prophet, saying,

2The Lord hath been sore displeased with your fathers.

3Therefore say thou unto them, Thus saith the Lord of hosts; Turn ye unto me, saith the Lord of hosts, and I will turn unto you, saith the Lord of hosts.

4Be ye not as your fathers, unto whom the former prophets have cried, saying, Thus saith the Lord of hosts; Turn ye now from your evil ways, and *from* your evil doings: but they did not hear, nor hearken unto me, saith the Lord.

5Your fathers, where *are* they? and the prophets, do they live for ever?

6But my words and my statutes, which I commanded my servants the prophets, did they not take hold of your fathers? and they returned and said, Like as the Lord of hosts thought to do unto us, according to our ways, and according to our doings, so hath he dealt with us.

7¶ Upon the four and twentieth day of the eleventh month, which *is* the month Sebat, in the second year of Darius, came the word of the Lord unto Zechariah, the son of Berechiah, the son of Iddo the prophet, saying,

8I saw by night, and behold a man riding upon a red horse, and he stood among the myrtle trees that *were* in the bottom; and behind him *were there* red horses, speckled, and white.

9Then said I, O my lord, what *are* these? And the angel that talked with me said unto me, I will shew thee what these *be*.

10And the man that stood among the myrtle trees answered and said, These *are they* whom the Lord hath sent to walk to and fro through the earth.

11And they answered the angel of the Lord that stood among the myrtle trees, and said, We have walked to and fro through the earth, and, behold, all the earth sitteth still, and is at rest.

12¶ Then the angel of the Lord answered and said, O Lord of hosts, how long wilt thou not have mercy on Jerusalem and on the cities of Judah, against which thou hast had indignation these threescore and ten years?

13And the Lord answered the angel that talked with me *with* good words *and* comfortable words.

14So the angel that communed with me said unto me, Cry thou, saying, Thus saith the Lord of hosts; I am jealous for Jerusalem and for Zion with a great jealousy.

15And I am very sore displeased with the heathen *that are* at ease: for I was but a little displeased, and they helped forward the affliction.

16Therefore thus saith the Lord; I am returned to Jerusalem with mercies: my house shall be built in it, saith the Lord of hosts, and a line shall be stretched forth upon Jerusalem.

17Cry yet, saying, Thus saith the Lord of hosts; My cities through prosperity shall yet be spread abroad; and the Lord shall yet comfort Zion, and shall yet choose Jerusalem.

A Call to Return to the Lord

1 IN THE eighth month of the second year of Darius, the word of the Lord came to the prophet Zechariah son of Berekiah, the son of Iddo:

2"The Lord was very angry with your forefathers. 3Therefore tell the people: This is what the Lord Almighty says: 'Return to me,' declares the Lord Almighty, 'and I will return to you,' says the Lord Almighty. 4Do not be like your forefathers, to whom the earlier prophets proclaimed: This is what the Lord Almighty says: 'Turn from your evil ways and your evil practices.' But they would not listen or pay attention to me, declares the Lord. 5Where are your forefathers now? And the prophets, do they live forever? 6But did not my words and my decrees, which I commanded my servants the prophets, overtake your forefathers?

"Then they repented and said, 'The Lord Almighty has done to us what our ways and practices deserve, just as he determined to do.' "

The Man Among the Myrtle Trees

7On the twenty-fourth day of the eleventh month, the month of Shebat, in the second year of Darius, the word of the Lord came to the prophet Zechariah son of Berekiah, the son of Iddo.

8During the night I had a vision—and there before me was a man riding a red horse! He was standing among the myrtle trees in a ravine. Behind him were red, brown and white horses.

9I asked, "What are these, my lord?"

The angel who was talking with me answered, "I will show you what they are."

10Then the man standing among the myrtle trees explained, "They are the ones the Lord has sent to go throughout the earth."

11And they reported to the angel of the Lord, who was standing among the myrtle trees, "We have gone throughout the earth and found the whole world at rest and in peace."

12Then the angel of the Lord said, "Lord Almighty, how long will you withhold mercy from Jerusalem and from the towns of Judah, which you have been angry with these seventy years?" 13So the Lord spoke kind and comforting words to the angel who talked with me.

14Then the angel who was speaking to me said, "Proclaim this word: This is what the Lord Almighty says: 'I am very jealous for Jerusalem and Zion, 15but I am very angry with the nations that feel secure. I was only a little angry, but they added to the calamity.'

16"Therefore, this is what the Lord says: 'I will return to Jerusalem with mercy, and there my house will be rebuilt. And the measuring line will be stretched out over Jerusalem,' declares the Lord Almighty.

17"Proclaim further: This is what the Lord Almighty says: 'My towns will again overflow with prosperity, and the Lord will again comfort Zion and choose Jerusalem.' "

Living Bible	New Revised Standard

Zechariah

Zechariah

Zechariah

1 SUBJECT: MESSAGES from the Lord. These messages from the Lord were given to Zechariah (son of Berechiah, and grandson of Iddo the prophet) in early November of the second year of the reign of King Darius.

2The Lord Almighty was very angry with your fathers. 3But he will turn again and favor you if only you return to him. 4Don't be like your fathers were! The earlier prophets pled in vain with them to turn from all their evil ways.

"Come, return to me," the Lord God said. But no, they wouldn't listen; they paid no attention at all.

5, 6Your fathers and their prophets are now long dead, but remember the lesson they learned, that *God's Word endures!* It caught up with them and punished them. Then at last they repented.

"We have gotten what we deserved from God," they said, "He has done just what he warned us he would."

7The following February, still in the second year of the reign of King Darius, another message from the Lord came to Zechariah (son of Berechiah and grandson of Iddo the prophet), in a vision in the night: 8I saw a Man sitting on a red horse that was standing among the myrtle trees beside a river. Behind him were other horses, red and bay and white, each with its rider.ª

9An angel stood beside me, and I asked him, "Sir, what are all those horses for?"

"I'll tell you," he replied.

10Then the rider on the red horse—he was the Angel of the Lord—answered me, "The Lord has sent them to patrol the earth for him."

11Then the other riders reported to the Angel of the Lord, "We have patrolled the whole earth, and everywhere there is prosperity and peace."

12Upon hearing this, the Angel of the Lord prayed this prayer: "O Lord Almighty, for seventy years your anger has raged against Jerusalem and the cities of Judah. How long will it be until you again show mercy to them?"

13And the Lord answered the angel who stood beside me, speaking words of comfort and assurance.

14Then the angel said, "Shout out this message from the Lord Almighty: Don't you think I care about what has happened to Judah and Jerusalem? I am as jealous as a husband for his captive wife. 15I am very angry with the heathen nations sitting around at ease, for I was only a little displeased with my people, but the nations afflicted them far beyond my intentions. 16Therefore the Lord declares: I have returned to Jerusalem filled with mercy; my Temple will be rebuilt, says the Lord Almighty, and so will all Jerusalem. 17Say it again: The Lord Almighty declares that the cities of Israel will again overflow with prosperity, and the Lord will again comfort Jerusalem and bless her and live in her."

Israel Urged to Repent

1 IN THE eighth month, in the second year of Darius, the word of the LORD came to the prophet Zechariah son of Berechiah son of Iddo, saying: 2The LORD was very angry with your ancestors. 3Therefore say to them, Thus says the LORD of hosts: Return to me, says the LORD of hosts, and I will return to you, says the LORD of hosts. 4Do not be like your ancestors, to whom the former prophets proclaimed, "Thus says the LORD of hosts, Return from your evil ways and from your evil deeds." But they did not hear or heed me, says the LORD. 5Your ancestors, where are they? And the prophets, do they live forever? 6But my words and my statutes, which I commanded my servants the prophets, did they not overtake your ancestors? So they repented and said, "The LORD of hosts has dealt with us according to our ways and deeds, just as he planned to do."

First Vision: The Horsemen

7 On the twenty-fourth day of the eleventh month, the month of Shebat, in the second year of Darius, the word of the LORD came to the prophet Zechariah son of Berechiah son of Iddo; and Zechariahᵇ said, 8In the night I saw a man riding on a red horse! He was standing among the myrtle trees in the glen; and behind him were red, sorrel, and white horses. 9Then I said, "What are these, my lord?" The angel who talked with me said to me, "I will show you what they are." 10So the man who was standing among the myrtle trees answered, "They are those whom the LORD has sent to patrol the earth." 11Then they spoke to the angel of the LORD who was standing among the myrtle trees, "We have patrolled the earth, and lo, the whole earth remains at peace." 12Then the angel of the LORD said, "O LORD of hosts, how long will you withhold mercy from Jerusalem and the cities of Judah, with which you have been angry these seventy years?" 13Then the LORD replied with gracious and comforting words to the angel who talked with me. 14So the angel who talked with me said to me, Proclaim this message: Thus says the LORD of hosts; I am very jealous for Jerusalem and for Zion. 15And I am extremely angry with the nations that are at ease; for while I was only a little angry, they made the disaster worse. 16Therefore, thus says the LORD, I have returned to Jerusalem with compassion; my house shall be built in it, says the LORD of hosts, and the measuring line shall be stretched out over Jerusalem. 17Proclaim further: Thus says the LORD of hosts: My cities shall again overflow with prosperity; the LORD will again comfort Zion and again choose Jerusalem.

ª *1:8 each with its rider*, implied.

ᵇ Heb *and he*

King James

18¶ Then lifted I up mine eyes, and saw, and behold four horns.

19And I said unto the angel that talked with me, What *be* these? And he answered me, These *are* the horns which have scattered Judah, Israel, and Jerusalem.

20And the LORD showed me four carpenters.

21Then said I, What come these to do? And he spake, saying, These *are* the horns which have scattered Judah, so that no man did lift up his head: but these are come to fray them, to cast out the horns of the Gentiles, which lifted up *their* horn over the land of Judah to scatter it.

2 I LIFTED up mine eyes again, and looked, and behold a man with a measuring line in his hand.

2Then said I, Whither goest thou? And he said unto me, To measure Jerusalem, to see what *is* the breadth thereof, and what *is* the length thereof.

3And, behold, the angel that talked with me went forth, and another angel went out to meet him,

4And said unto him, Run, speak to this young man, saying, Jerusalem shall be inhabited *as* towns without walls for the multitude of men and cattle therein:

5For I, saith the LORD, will be unto her a wall of fire round about, and will be the glory in the midst of her.

6¶ Ho, ho, *come forth*, and flee from the land of the north, saith the LORD: for I have spread you abroad as the four winds of the heaven, saith the LORD.

7Deliver thyself, O Zion, that dwellest *with* the daughter of Babylon.

8For thus saith the LORD of hosts; After the glory hath he sent me unto the nations which spoiled you: for he that toucheth you toucheth the apple of his eye.

9For, behold, I will shake mine hand upon them, and they shall be a spoil to their servants: and ye shall know that the LORD of hosts hath sent me.

10¶ Sing and rejoice, O daughter of Zion: for, lo, I come, and I will dwell in the midst of thee, saith the LORD.

11And many nations shall be joined to the LORD in that day, and shall be my people: and I will dwell in the midst of thee, and thou shalt know that the LORD of hosts hath sent me unto thee.

12And the LORD shall inherit Judah his portion in the holy land, and shall choose Jerusalem again.

13Be silent, O all flesh, before the LORD: for he is raised up out of his holy habitation.

3 AND HE showed me Joshua the high priest standing before the angel of the LORD, and Satan standing at his right hand to resist him.

2And the LORD said unto Satan, The LORD rebuke thee, O Satan; even the LORD that hath chosen Jerusalem rebuke thee: *is* not this a brand plucked out of the fire?

3Now Joshua was clothed with filthy garments, and stood before the angel.

4And he answered and spake unto those that stood before him, saying, Take away the filthy garments from him. And unto him he said, Behold, I have caused thine iniquity to pass from thee, and I will clothe thee with change of raiment.

New International

Four Horns and Four Craftsmen

18Then I looked up—and there before me were four horns! 19I asked the angel who was speaking to me, "What are these?"

He answered me, "These are the horns that scattered Judah, Israel and Jerusalem."

20Then the LORD showed me four craftsmen. 21I asked, "What are these coming to do?"

He answered, "These are the horns that scattered Judah so that no one could raise his head, but the craftsmen have come to terrify them and throw down these horns of the nations who lifted up their horns against the land of Judah to scatter its people."

A Man With a Measuring Line

2 THEN I looked up—and there before me was a man with a measuring line in his hand! 2I asked, "Where are you going?"

He answered me, "To measure Jerusalem, to find out how wide and how long it is."

3Then the angel who was speaking to me left, and another angel came to meet him 4and said to him: "Run, tell that young man, 'Jerusalem will be a city without walls because of the great number of men and livestock in it. 5And I myself will be a wall of fire around it,' declares the LORD, 'and I will be its glory within.'

6"Come! Come! Flee from the land of the north," declares the LORD, "for I have scattered you to the four winds of heaven," declares the LORD.

7"Come, O Zion! Escape, you who live in the Daughter of Babylon!" 8For this is what the LORD Almighty says: "After he has honored me and has sent me against the nations that have plundered you—for whoever touches you touches the apple of his eye— 9I will surely raise my hand against them so that their slaves will plunder them.[a] Then you will know that the LORD Almighty has sent me.

10"Shout and be glad, O Daughter of Zion. For I am coming, and I will live among you," declares the LORD. 11"Many nations will be joined with the LORD in that day and will become my people. I will live among you and you will know that the LORD Almighty has sent me to you. 12The LORD will inherit Judah as his portion in the holy land and will again choose Jerusalem. 13Be still before the LORD, all mankind, because he has roused himself from his holy dwelling."

Clean Garments for the High Priest

3 THEN HE showed me Joshua[b] the high priest standing before the angel of the LORD, and Satan[c] standing at his right side to accuse him. 2The LORD said to Satan, "The LORD rebuke you, Satan! The LORD, who has chosen Jerusalem, rebuke you! Is not this man a burning stick snatched from the fire?"

3Now Joshua was dressed in filthy clothes as he stood before the angel. 4The angel said to those who were standing before him, "Take off his filthy clothes."

Then he said to Joshua, "See, I have taken away your sin, and I will put rich garments on you."

---

a 8,9 Or *says after . . . eye:* 9"I *. . . plunder them."*   b 1 A variant of *Jeshua;* here and elsewhere in Zechariah   c 1 *Satan* means *accuser.*

Living Bible

18Then I looked and saw four animal horns!

19"What are these?" I asked the angel.

He replied, "They represent the four world powers that have scattered Judah, Israel, and Jerusalem."

20Then the Lord showed me four blacksmiths.

21"What have these men come to do?" I asked.

The angel replied, "They have come to take hold of the four horns that scattered Judah so terribly, and to pound them on the anvil and throw them away."

2 WHEN I looked around me again, I saw a man carrying a yardstick in his hand.

2"Where are you going?" I asked.

"To measure Jerusalem," he said. "I want to see whether it is big enough for all the people!"

3Then the angel who was talking to me went over to meet another angel coming toward him.

4"Go tell this young man," said the other angel, "that Jerusalem will some day be so full of people that she won't have room enough for all! Many will live outside the city walls, with all their many cattle—and yet they will be safe. 5For the Lord himself will be a wall of fire protecting them and all Jerusalem; he will be the glory of the city.

6, 7" 'Come, flee from the land of the north, from Babylon,' says the Lord to all his exiles there; 'I scattered you to the winds but I will bring you back again. Escape, escape to Zion now!' says the Lord.

8"The Lord of Glory has sent med against the nations that oppressed you, for he who harms you sticks his finger in Jehovah's eye!

9" 'I will smash them with my fist and their slaves will be their rulers! Then you will know it was the Lord Almighty who sent me. 10Sing, Jerusalem, and rejoice! For I have come to live among you,' says the Lord. 11, 12'At that time many nations will be converted to the Lord, and they too shall be my people; I will live among them all. Then you will know it was the Lord Almighty who sent me to you. And Judah shall be the Lord's inheritance in the Holy Land, for God shall once more choose to bless Jerusalem.'

13"Be silent, all mankind, before the Lord, for he has come to earth from heaven, from his holy home."

3 THEN THE Angel showed me (in my vision) Joshua the High Priest standing before the Angel of the Lord; and Satan was there too, at the Angel's right hand, accusing Joshua of many things.

2And the Lord said to Satan, "I reject your accusations, Satan;e yes, I, the Lord, for I have decided to be merciful to Jerusalem—I rebuke you. I have decreed mercy to Joshua and his nation; they are like a burning stick pulled out of the fire."

3Joshua's clothing was filthy as he stood before the Angel of the Lord.

4Then the Angel said to the others standing there, "Remove his filthy clothing." And turning to Joshua he said, "See, I have taken away your sins, and now I am giving you these fine new clothes."

New Revised Standard

Second Vision: The Horns and the Smiths

18f And I looked up and saw four horns. 19I asked the angel who talked with me, "What are these?" And he answered me, "These are the horns that have scattered Judah, Israel, and Jerusalem." 20Then the Lord showed me four blacksmiths. 21And I asked, "What are they coming to do?" He answered, "These are the horns that scattered Judah, so that no head could be raised; but these have come to terrify them, to strike down the horns of the nations that lifted up their horns against the land of Judah to scatter its people."g

Third Vision: The Man with a Measuring Line

2h I LOOKED up and saw a man with a measuring line in his hand. 2Then I asked, "Where are you going?" He answered me, "To measure Jerusalem, to see what is its width and what is its length." 3Then the angel who talked with me came forward, and another angel came forward to meet him, 4and said to him, "Run, say to that young man: Jerusalem shall be inhabited like villages without walls, because of the multitude of people and animals in it. 5For I will be a wall of fire all around it, says the Lord, and I will be the glory within it."

Interlude: An Appeal to the Exiles

6 Up, up! Flee from the land of the north, says the Lord; for I have spread you abroad like the four winds of heaven, says the Lord. 7Up! Escape to Zion, you that live with daughter Babylon. 8For thus said the Lord of hosts (after his gloryi sent me) regarding the nations that plundered you: Truly, one who touches you touches the apple of my eye.j 9See now, I am going to raisek my hand against them, and they shall become plunder for their own slaves. Then you will know that the Lord of hosts has sent me. 10Sing and rejoice, O daughter Zion! For lo, I will come and dwell in your midst, says the Lord. 11Many nations shall join themselves to the Lord on that day, and shall be my people; and I will dwell in your midst. And you shall know that the Lord of hosts has sent me to you. 12The Lord will inherit Judah as his portion in the holy land, and will again choose Jerusalem.

13 Be silent, all people, before the Lord; for he has roused himself from his holy dwelling.

Fourth Vision: Joshua and Satan

3 THEN HE showed me the high priest Joshua standing before the angel of the Lord, and Satanl standing at his right hand to accuse him. 2And the Lord said to Satan,l "The Lord rebuke you, O Satan!l The Lord who has chosen Jerusalem rebuke you! Is not this man a brand plucked from the fire?" 3Now Joshua was dressed with filthy clothes as he stood before the angel. 4The angel said to those who were standing before him, "Take off his filthy clothes." And to him he said, "See, I have taken your guilt away from you, and I will clothe you with festal apparel." 5And I said, "Let them put a

---

d 2:8 This passage evidently refers to the Messiah, here seen as one of the Godhead.   e 3:2 I reject your accusations, Satan, literally, "The Lord rebuke you, O Satan; even the Lord, who has chosen Jerusalem, rebuke you. Is not this a brand plucked out of the fire?"

f Ch 2.1 in Heb   g Heb it   h Ch 2.5 in Heb   i Cn: Heb after glory he   j Heb his eye   k Or wave   l Or the Accuser; Heb the Adversary

King James

5And I said, Let them set a fair mitre upon his head. So they set a fair mitre upon his head, and clothed him with garments. And the angel of the LORD stood by.

6And the angel of the LORD protested unto Joshua, saying,

7Thus saith the LORD of hosts; If thou wilt walk in my ways, and if thou wilt keep my charge, then thou shalt also judge my house, and shalt also keep my courts, and I will give thee places to walk among these that stand by.

8Hear now, O Joshua the high priest, thou, and thy fellows that sit before thee: for they *are* men wondered at: for, behold, I will bring forth my servant the BRANCH.

9For behold the stone that I have laid before Joshua; upon one stone *shall be* seven eyes: behold, I will engrave the graving thereof, saith the LORD of hosts, and I will remove the iniquity of that land in one day.

10In that day, saith the LORD of hosts, shall ye call every man his neighbour under the vine and under the fig tree.

4 AND THE angel that talked with me came again, and waked me, as a man that is wakened out of his sleep,

2And said unto me, What seest thou? And I said, I have looked, and behold a candlestick all *of* gold, with a bowl upon the top of it, and his seven lamps thereon, and seven pipes to the seven lamps, which *are* upon the top thereof:

3And two olive trees by it, one upon the right *side* of the bowl, and the other upon the left *side* thereof.

4So I answered and spake to the angel that talked with me, saying, What *are* these, my lord?

5Then the angel that talked with me answered and said unto me, Knowest thou not what these be? And I said, No, my lord.

6Then he answered and spake unto me, saying, This *is* the word of the LORD unto Zerubbabel, saying, Not by might, nor by power, but by my spirit, saith the LORD of hosts.

7Who *art* thou, O great mountain? before Zerubbabel *thou shalt become* a plain: and he shall bring forth the headstone *thereof with* shoutings, *crying,* Grace, grace unto it.

8Moreover the word of the LORD came unto me, saying,

9The hands of Zerubbabel have laid the foundation of this house; his hands shall also finish it; and thou shalt know that the LORD of hosts hath sent me unto you.

10For who hath despised the day of small things? for they shall rejoice, and shall see the plummet in the hand of Zerubbabel *with* those seven; they *are* the eyes of the LORD, which run to and fro through the whole earth.

11¶ Then answered I, and said unto him, What *are* these two olive trees upon the right *side* of the candlestick and upon the left *side* thereof ?

12And I answered again, and said unto him, What *be these* two olive branches which through the two golden pipes empty the golden *oil* out of themselves?

13And he answered me and said, Knowest thou not what these *be?* And I said, No, my lord.

14Then said he, These *are* the two anointed ones, that stand by the Lord of the whole earth.

New International

5Then I said, "Put a clean turban on his head." So they put a clean turban on his head and clothed him, while the angel of the LORD stood by.

6The angel of the LORD gave this charge to Joshua: 7"This is what the LORD Almighty says: 'If you will walk in my ways and keep my requirements, then you will govern my house and have charge of my courts, and I will give you a place among these standing here.

8" 'Listen, O high priest Joshua and your associates seated before you, who are men symbolic of things to come: I am going to bring my servant, the Branch. 9See, the stone I have set in front of Joshua! There are seven eyesa on that one stone, and I will engrave an inscription on it,' says the LORD Almighty, 'and I will remove the sin of this land in a single day.

10" 'In that day each of you will invite his neighbor to sit under his vine and fig tree,' declares the LORD Almighty."

The Gold Lampstand and the Two Olive Trees

4 THEN THE angel who talked with me returned and wakened me, as a man is wakened from his sleep. 2He asked me, "What do you see?"

I answered, "I see a solid gold lampstand with a bowl at the top and seven lights on it, with seven channels to the lights. 3Also there are two olive trees by it, one on the right of the bowl and the other on its left."

4I asked the angel who talked with me, "What are these, my lord?"

5He answered, "Do you not know what these are?"

"No, my lord," I replied.

6So he said to me, "This is the word of the LORD to Zerubbabel: 'Not by might nor by power, but by my Spirit,' says the LORD Almighty.

7"Whatb are you, O mighty mountain? Before Zerubbabel you will become level ground. Then he will bring out the capstone to shouts of 'God bless it! God bless it!' "

8Then the word of the LORD came to me: 9"The hands of Zerubbabel have laid the foundation of this temple; his hands will also complete it. Then you will know that the LORD Almighty has sent me to you.

10"Who despises the day of small things? Men will rejoice when they see the plumb line in the hand of Zerubbabel.

"(These seven are the eyes of the LORD, which range throughout the earth.)"

11Then I asked the angel, "What are these two olive trees on the right and the left of the lampstand?"

12Again I asked him, "What are these two olive branches beside the two gold pipes that pour out golden oil?"

13He replied, "Do you not know what these are?"

"No, my lord," I said.

14So he said, "These are the two who are anointed toc serve the Lord of all the earth."

---

a 9 Or facets   b 7 Or Who   c 14 Or two who bring oil and

Living Bible

5, 6 Then I said, "Please, could he also have a clean turban on his head?" So they gave him one.

Then the Angel of the Lord spoke very solemnly to Joshua and said, 7"The Lord Almighty declares: 'If you will follow the paths I set for you and do all I tell you to, then I will put you in charge of my Temple, to keep it holy; and I will let you walk in and out of my presence with these angels. 8Listen to me, O Joshua the High Priest, and all you other priests, you are illustrations of the good things to come. Don't you see?—Joshua represents my servant the Branchd whom I will send. 9He will be the Foundation Stone of the Temple that Joshua is standing beside, and I will engrave this inscription on it seven times:e *I will remove the sins of this land in a single day.* 10And after that,' the Lord Almighty declares, 'you will all live in peace and prosperity and each of you will own a home of your own where you can invite your neighbors.' "

4   THEN THE angel who had been talking with me woke me, as though I had been asleep.
2"What do you see now?" he asked.

I answered, "I see a gold lampstand holding seven lamps, and at the top there is a reservoir for the olive oil that feeds the lamps, flowing into them through seven tubes. 3And I see two olive trees carved upon the lampstand, one on each side of the reservoir. 4What is it, sir?" I asked. "What does this mean?"

5"Don't you really know?" the angel asked.

"No, sir," I said, "I don't."

6Then he said, "This is God's message to Zerubbabel:f 'Not by might, nor by power, but by my Spirit, says the Lord Almighty—you will succeed because of my Spirit, though you are few and weak.' 7Therefore no mountain, however high, can stand before Zerubbabel! For it will flatten out before him! And Zerubbabel will finish building this Templeg with mighty shouts of thanksgiving for God's mercy, declaring that all was done by grace alone."h

8Another message that I received from the Lord said: 9"Zerubbabel laid the foundation of this Temple, and he will complete it. (Then you will know these messages are from God, the Lord Almighty.) 10Do not despise this small beginning, for the eyes of the Lord rejoice to see the work begin, to see the plumbline in the hand of Zerubbabel. For these seven lamps represent the eyes of the Lord that see everywhere around the world."

11Then I asked him about the two olive trees on each side of the lampstand, 12and about the two olive branches that emptied oil into gold bowls through two gold tubes.

13"Don't you know?" he asked.

"No, sir," I said.

14Then he told me, "They represent the two anointed ones who assist the Lord of all the earth."

New Revised Standard

clean turban on his head." So they put a clean turban on his head and clothed him with the apparel; and the angel of the LORD was standing by.

6 Then the angel of the LORD assured Joshua, saying 7"Thus says the LORD of hosts: If you will walk in my ways and keep my requirements, then you shall rule my house and have charge of my courts, and I will give you the right of access among those who are standing here. 8Now listen, Joshua, high priest, you and your colleagues who sit before you! For they are an omen of things to come: I am going to bring my servant the Branch. 9For on the stone that I have set before Joshua, on a single stone with seven facets, I will engrave its inscription, says the LORD of hosts, and I will remove the guilt of this land in a single day. 10On that day, says the LORD of hosts, you shall invite each other to come under your vine and fig tree."

Fifth Vision: The Lampstand and Olive Trees

4   THE ANGEL who talked with me came again, and wakened me, as one is wakened from sleep. 2He said to me, "What do you see?" And I said, "I see a lampstand all of gold, with a bowl on the top of it; there are seven lamps on it, with seven lips on each of the lamps that are on the top of it. 3And by it there are two olive trees, one on the right of the bowl and the other on its left." 4I said to the angel who talked with me, "What are these, my lord?" 5Then the angel who talked with me answered me, "Do you not know what these are?" I said, "No, my lord." 6He said to me, "This is the word of the LORD to Zerubbabel: Not by might, nor by power, but by my spirit, says the LORD of hosts. 7What are you, O great mountain? Before Zerubbabel you shall become a plain; and he shall bring out the top stone amid shouts of 'Grace, grace to it!' "

8 Moreover the word of the LORD came to me, saying, 9"The hands of Zerubbabel have laid the foundation of this house; his hands shall also complete it. Then you will know that the LORD of hosts has sent me to you. 10For whoever has despised the day of small things shall rejoice, and shall see the plummet in the hand of Zerubbabel.

"These seven are the eyes of the LORD, which range through the whole earth." 11Then I said to him, "What are these two olive trees on the right and the left of the lampstand?" 12And a second time I said to him, "What are these two branches of the olive trees, which pour out the oili through the two golden pipes?" 13He said to me, "Do you not know what these are?" I said, "No, my lord." 14Then he said, "These are the two anointed ones who stand by the Lord of the whole earth."

---

d 3:8 *the Branch,* i.e., the Messiah, Christ.   e 3:9 *I will engrave this inscription on it seven times,* literally, "See the stone with seven facets I have set before Joshua, and I will engrave its inscription."   f 4:6 *to Zerubbabel:* Governor of Judah, who was given the responsibility for rebuilding the Temple. See Hag 1:1; 2:23, etc.   g 4:7 *will finish building this Temple,* literally, "He will bring forth the capstone."   h 4:7 *all was done by grace alone,* or, "with mighty shouts, 'How beautiful it is!' " or, "The Lord bless it!"

i Cn: Heb *gold*

King James

New International

The Flying Scroll

5 THEN I turned, and lifted up mine eyes, and looked, and behold a flying roll.

2And he said unto me, What seest thou? And I answered, I see a flying roll; the length thereof *is* twenty cubits, and the breadth thereof ten cubits.

3Then said he unto me, This *is* the curse that goeth forth over the face of the whole earth: for every one that stealeth shall be cut off *as* on this side according to it; and every one that sweareth shall be cut off *as* on that side according to it.

4I will bring it forth, saith the LORD of hosts, and it shall enter into the house of the thief, and into the house of him that sweareth falsely by my name: and it shall remain in the midst of his house, and shall consume it with the timber thereof and the stones thereof.

5¶ Then the angel that talked with me went forth, and said unto me, Lift up now thine eyes, and see what *is* this that goeth forth.

6And I said, What *is* it? And he said, This *is* an ephah that goeth forth. He said moreover, This *is* their resemblance through all the earth.

7And, behold, there was lifted up a talent of lead: and this *is* a woman that sitteth in the midst of the ephah.

8And he said, This *is* wickedness. And he cast it into the midst of the ephah; and he cast the weight of lead upon the mouth thereof.

9Then lifted I up mine eyes, and looked, and, behold, there came out two women, and the wind *was* in their wings; for they had wings like the wings of a stork: and they lifted up the ephah between the earth and the heaven.

10Then said I to the angel that talked with me, Whither do these bear the ephah?

11And he said unto me, To build it an house in the land of Shinar: and it shall be established, and set there upon her own base.

6 AND I turned, and lifted up mine eyes, and looked, and, behold, there came four chariots out from between two mountains; and the mountains *were* mountains of brass.

2In the first chariot *were* red horses; and in the second chariot black horses;

3And in the third chariot white horses; and in the fourth chariot grisled and bay horses.

4Then I answered and said unto the angel that talked with me, What *are* these, my lord?

5And the angel answered and said unto me, These *are* the four spirits of the heavens, which go forth from standing before the Lord of all the earth.

6The black horses which *are* therein go forth into the north country; and the white go forth after them; and the grisled go forth toward the south country.

7And the bay went forth, and sought to go that they might walk to and fro through the earth: and he said, Get you hence, walk to and fro through the earth. So they walked to and fro through the earth.

8Then cried he upon me, and spake unto me, saying, Behold, these that go toward the north country have quieted my spirit in the north country.

9¶ And the word of the LORD came unto me, saying,

The Flying Scroll

5 I LOOKED again—and there before me was a flying scroll!

2He asked me, "What do you see?"

I answered, "I see a flying scroll, thirty feet long and fifteen feet wide."[a]

3And he said to me, "This is the curse that is going out over the whole land; for according to what it says on one side, every thief will be banished, and according to what it says on the other, everyone who swears falsely will be banished. 4The LORD Almighty declares, 'I will send it out, and it will enter the house of the thief and the house of him who swears falsely by my name. It will remain in his house and destroy it, both its timbers and its stones.' "

The Woman in a Basket

5Then the angel who was speaking to me came forward and said to me, "Look up and see what this is that is appearing."

6I asked, "What is it?"

He replied, "It is a measuring basket.[b]" And he added, "This is the iniquity[c] of the people throughout the land."

7Then the cover of lead was raised, and there in the basket sat a woman! 8He said, "This is wickedness," and he pushed her back into the basket and pushed the lead cover down over its mouth.

9Then I looked up—and there before me were two women, with the wind in their wings! They had wings like those of a stork, and they lifted up the basket between heaven and earth.

10"Where are they taking the basket?" I asked the angel who was speaking to me.

11He replied, "To the country of Babylonia[d] to build a house for it. When it is ready, the basket will be set there in its place."

Four Chariots

6 I LOOKED up again—and there before me were four chariots coming out from between two mountains—mountains of bronze! 2The first chariot had red horses, the second black, 3the third white, and the fourth dappled—all of them powerful. 4I asked the angel who was speaking to me, "What are these, my lord?"

5The angel answered me, "These are the four spirits[e] of heaven, going out from standing in the presence of the Lord of the whole world. 6The one with the black horses is going toward the north country, the one with the white horses toward the west,[f] and the one with the dappled horses toward the south."

7When the powerful horses went out, they were straining to go throughout the earth. And he said, "Go throughout the earth!" So they went throughout the earth.

8Then he called to me, "Look, those going toward the north country have given my Spirit[g] rest in the land of the north."

A Crown for Joshua

9The word of the LORD came to me: 10"Take silver

a 2 Hebrew *twenty cubits long and ten cubits wide* (about 9 meters long and 4.5 meters wide) b 6 Hebrew *an ephah*; also in verses 7-11 c 6 Or *appearance* d 11 Hebrew *Shinar* e 5 Or *winds* f 6 Or *horses after them* g 8 Or *spirit*

Living Bible

5 I LOOKED up again and saw a scroll flying through the air.

2"What do you see?" he asked.

"A flying scroll!" I replied. "It appears to be about thirty feet long and fifteen feet wide!"

3"This scroll," he told me, "represents the words of God's curse going out over the entire land. It says that all who steal and lie have been judged and sentenced to death."

4"I am sending this curse into the home of every thief and everyone who swears falsely by my name," says the Lord Almighty. "And my curse shall remain upon his home and completely destroy it."

5Then the angel left me for awhile, but he returned and said, "Look up! Something is traveling through the sky!"

6"What is it?" I asked.

He replied, "It is a bushel basket filled with the sin prevailing everywhere throughout the land."

7Suddenly the heavy lead cover on the basket was lifted off, and I could see a woman sitting inside the basket!

8He said, "She represents wickedness," and he pushed her back into the basket and clamped down the heavy lid again.

9Then I saw two women flying toward us, with wings like those of a stork. And they took the bushel basket and flew off with it, high in the sky.

10"Where are they taking her?" I asked the angel.

11He replied, "To Babylonh where they will build a temple for the basket, to worship it!"

6 THEN I looked up again and saw four chariots coming from between what looked like two mountains made of brass. 2The first chariot was pulled by red horses, the second by black ones, 3the third by white horses and the fourth by dappled-greys.

4"And what are these, sir?" I asked the angel.

5He replied, "These are the four heavenly spirits who stand before the Lord of all the earth; they are going out to do his work. 6The chariot pulled by the black horses will go north, and the one pulled by white horses will follow it there,i while the dappled-greys will go south."

7The redj horses were impatient to be off, to patrol back and forth across the earth, so the Lord said, "Go. Begin your patrol." So they left at once.

8Then the Lord summoned me and said, "Those who went north have executed my judgmentk and quieted my anger there."

9In another message the Lord said:

New Revised Standard

Sixth Vision: The Flying Scroll

5 AGAIN I looked up and saw a flying scroll. 2And he said to me, "What do you see?" I answered, "I see a flying scroll; its length is twenty cubits, and its width ten cubits." 3Then he said to me, "This is the curse that goes out over the face of the whole land; for everyone who steals shall be cut off according to the writing on one side, and everyone who swears falselyl shall be cut off according to the writing on the other side. 4I have sent it out, says the LORD of hosts, and it shall enter the house of the thief, and the house of anyone who swears falsely by my name; and it shall abide in that house and consume it, both timber and stones."

Seventh Vision: The Woman in a Basket

5 Then the angel who talked with me came forward and said to me, "Look up and see what this is that is coming out." 6I said, "What is it?" He said, "This is a basketm coming out." And he said, "This is their iniquityn in all the land." 7Then a leaden cover was lifted, and there was a woman sitting in the basket!m 8And he said, "This is Wickedness." So he thrust her back into the basket,m and pressed the leaden weight down on its mouth. 9Then I looked up and saw two women coming forward. The wind was in their wings; they had wings like the wings of a stork, and they lifted up the basketm between earth and sky. 10Then I said to the angel who talked with me, "Where are they taking the basket?"m 11He said to me, "To the land of Shinar, to build a house for it; and when this is prepared, they will set the basketm down there on its base."

Eighth Vision: Four Chariots

6 AND AGAIN I looked up and saw four chariots coming out from between two mountains—mountains of bronze. 2The first chariot had red horses, the second chariot black horses, 3the third chariot white horses, and the fourth chariot dappled grayo horses. 4Then I said to the angel who talked with me, "What are these, my lord?" 5The angel answered me, "These are the four windsp of heaven going out, after presenting themselves before the LORD of all the earth. 6The chariot with the black horses goes toward the north country, the white ones go toward the west country,q and the dappled ones go toward the south country." 7When the steeds came out, they were impatient to get off and patrol the earth. And he said, "Go, patrol the earth." So they patrolled the earth. 8Then he cried out to me, "Lo, those who go toward the north country have set my spirit at rest in the north country."

The Coronation of the Branch

9 The word of the LORD came to me: 10Collect silver

---

h 5:11 *To Babylon* (the land of Shinar). Babylon had, by the time of Zechariah, become a symbol, the center of world idolatry and wickedness. i 6:6 *will follow it there,* or, "will go west." j 6:7 *red,* implied. k 6:8 *Those who went north have executed my judgment,* implied.

l The word *falsely* added from verse 4 m Heb *ephah* n Gk Compare Syr: Heb *their eye* o Compare Gk: Meaning of Heb uncertain p Or *spirits* q Cn: Heb *go after them*

King James

10Take of *them of* the captivity, *even* of Heldai, of Tobijah, and of Jedaiah, which are come from Babylon, and come thou the same day, and go into the house of Josiah the son of Zephaniah;

11Then take silver and gold, and make crowns, and set *them* upon the head of Joshua the son of Josedech, the high priest;

12And speak unto him, saying, Thus speaketh the LORD of hosts, saying, Behold the man whose name *is* The BRANCH; and he shall grow up out of his place, and he shall build the temple of the LORD:

13Even he shall build the temple of the LORD; and he shall bear the glory, and shall sit and rule upon his throne; and he shall be a priest upon his throne: and the counsel of peace shall be between them both.

14And the crowns shall be to Helem, and to Tobijah, and to Jedaiah, and to Hen the son of Zephaniah, for a memorial in the temple of the LORD.

15And they *that are* far off shall come and build in the temple of the LORD, and ye shall know that the LORD of hosts hath sent me unto you. And *this* shall come to pass, if ye will diligently obey the voice of the LORD your God.

7 AND IT came to pass in the fourth year of king Darius, *that* the word of the LORD came unto Zechariah in the fourth *day* of the ninth month, *even* in Chisleu;

2When they had sent unto the house of God Sherezer and Regem-melech, and their men, to pray before the LORD,

3*And* to speak unto the priests which *were* in the house of the LORD of hosts, and to the prophets, saying, Should I weep in the fifth month, separating myself, as I have done these so many years?

4¶ Then came the word of the LORD of hosts unto me, saying,

5Speak unto all the people of the land, and to the priests, saying, When ye fasted and mourned in the fifth and seventh *month*, even those seventy years, did ye at all fast unto me, *even* to me?

6And when ye did eat, and when ye did drink, did not ye eat *for yourselves*, and drink *for yourselves?*

7*Should* ye not *hear* the words which the LORD hath cried by the former prophets, when Jerusalem was inhabited and in prosperity, and the cities thereof round about her, when *men* inhabited the south and the plain?

8¶ And the word of the LORD came unto Zechariah, saying,

9Thus speaketh the LORD of hosts, saying, Execute true judgment, and show mercy and compassions every man to his brother:

10And oppress not the widow, nor the fatherless, the stranger, nor the poor; and let none of you imagine evil against his brother in your heart.

11But they refused to hearken, and pulled away the shoulder, and stopped their ears, that they should not hear.

12Yea, they made their hearts *as* an adamant stone, lest they should hear the law, and the words which the LORD of hosts hath sent in his spirit by the former prophets: therefore came a great wrath from the LORD of hosts.

13Therefore it is come to pass, *that* as he cried, and they would not hear; so they cried, and I would not hear, saith the LORD of hosts:

14But I scattered them with a whirlwind among all the nations whom they knew not. Thus the land was desolate after them, that no man passed through nor returned: for they laid the pleasant land desolate.

New International

and gold, from the exiles Heldai, Tobijah and Jedaiah, who have arrived from Babylon. Go the same day to the house of Josiah son of Zephaniah. 11Take the silver and gold and make a crown, and set it on the head of the high priest, Joshua son of Jehozadak. 12Tell him this is what the LORD Almighty says: 'Here is the man whose name is the Branch, and he will branch out from his place and build the temple of the LORD. 13It is he who will build the temple of the LORD, and he will be clothed with majesty and will sit and rule on his throne. And he will be a priest on his throne. And there will be harmony between the two.' 14The crown will be given to Heldai,[a] Tobijah, Jedaiah and Hen[b] son of Zephaniah as a memorial in the temple of the LORD. 15Those who are far away will come and help to build the temple of the LORD, and you will know that the LORD Almighty has sent me to you. This will happen if you diligently obey the LORD your God."

Justice and Mercy, Not Fasting

7 IN THE fourth year of King Darius, the word of the LORD came to Zechariah on the fourth day of the ninth month, the month of Kislev. 2The people of Bethel had sent Sharezer and Regem-Melech, together with their men, to entreat the LORD 3by asking the priests of the house of the LORD Almighty and the prophets, "Should I mourn and fast in the fifth month, as I have done for so many years?"

4Then the word of the LORD Almighty came to me: 5"Ask all the people of the land and the priests, 'When you fasted and mourned in the fifth and seventh months for the past seventy years, was it really for me that you fasted? 6And when you were eating and drinking, were you not just feasting for yourselves? 7Are these not the words the LORD proclaimed through the earlier prophets when Jerusalem and its surrounding towns were at rest and prosperous, and the Negev and the western foothills were settled?' "

8And the word of the LORD came again to Zechariah: 9"This is what the LORD Almighty says: 'Administer true justice; show mercy and compassion to one another. 10Do not oppress the widow or the fatherless, the alien or the poor. In your hearts do not think evil of each other.'

11"But they refused to pay attention; stubbornly they turned their backs and stopped up their ears. 12They made their hearts as hard as flint and would not listen to the law or to the words that the LORD Almighty had sent by his Spirit through the earlier prophets. So the LORD Almighty was very angry.

13" 'When I called, they did not listen; so when they called, I would not listen,' says the LORD Almighty. 14'I scattered them with a whirlwind among all the nations, where they were strangers. The land was left so desolate behind them that no one could come or go. This is how they made the pleasant land desolate.' "

---

a *14* Syriac; Hebrew *Helem*　　b *14* Or *and the gracious one, the*

Living Bible

10, 11"Heldai, Tobijah, and Jedaiah will bring gifts of silver and gold from the Jews exiled in Babylon. The same day they arrive, meet them at the home of Josiah (son of Zephaniah), where they will stay. Accept their gifts and make from them a crown from the silver and gold. Then put the crown on the head of Joshua (son of Josedech) the High Priest. 12Tell him that the Lord Almighty says, 'You represent the Man who will come, whose name is "The Branch"—he will grow up from himselfc—and will build the Temple of the Lord. 13To him belongs the royal title. He will rule both as King and as Priest, with perfect harmony between the two!'

14"Then put the crown in the Temple of the Lord, to honor those who gave it—Heldai, Tobijah, Jedaiah, and also Josiah. 15These three who have come from so far away represent many others who will some day come from distant lands to rebuild the Temple of the Lord. And when this happens you will know my messages have been from God, the Lord Almighty. But none of this will happen unless you carefully obey the commandments of the Lord your God."

7 ANOTHER MESSAGE came to me from the Lord in late November of the fourth year of the reign of King Darius.

2The Jews of the city of Bethel had sent a group of men headed by Sharezer, the chief administrative officer of the king, and Regem-melech, to the Lord's Temple at Jerusalem, to seek his blessing, 3and to speak with the priests and prophets about whether they must continue their traditional custom of fasting and mourning during the month of August each year, as they had been doing so long.

4This was the Lord's reply:

5"When you return to Bethel, say to all your people and your priests, 'During those seventy years of exile when you fasted and mourned in August and October, were you really in earnest about leaving your sins behind, and coming back to me? No, not at all! 6And even now in your holy feasts to God, you don't think of me, but only of the food and fellowship and fun. 7Long years ago, when Jerusalem was prosperous and her southern suburbs out along the plain were filled with people, the prophets warned them that this attitude would surely lead to ruin, as it has.' "

8, 9Then this message from the Lord came to Zechariah. "Tell them to be honest and fair—and not to take bribes—and to be merciful and kind to everyone. 10Tell them to stop oppressing widows and orphans, foreigners and poor people, and to stop plotting evil against each other. 11Your fathers would not listen to this message. They turned stubbornly away and put their fingers in their ears to keep from hearing me. 12They hardened their hearts like flint, afraid to hear the words that God, the Lord Almighty, commanded them—the laws he had revealed to them by his Spirit through the early prophets. That is why such great wrath came down on them from God. 13I called but they refused to listen, so when they cried to me, I turned away. 14I scattered them as with a whirlwind among the far-off nations. Their land became desolate; no one even traveled through it; the Pleasant Land lay bare and blighted."

New Revised Standard

and goldd from the exiles—from Heldai, Tobijah, and Jedaiah—who have arrived from Babylon; and go the same day to the house of Josiah son of Zephaniah. 11Take the silver and gold and make a crown,e and set it on the head of the high priest Joshua son of Jehozadak; 12say to him: Thus says the LORD of hosts: Here is a man whose name is Branch: for he shall branch out in his place, and he shall build the temple of the LORD. 13It is he that shall build the temple of the LORD; he shall bear royal honor, and shall sit and rule on his throne. There shall be a priest by his throne, with peaceful understanding between the two of them. 14And the crownf shall be in the care of Heldai,g Tobijah, Jedaiah, and Josiahh son of Zephaniah, as a memorial in the temple of the LORD.

15 Those who are far off shall come and help to build the temple of the LORD; and you shall know that the LORD of hosts has sent me to you. This will happen if you diligently obey the voice of the LORD your God.

Hypocritical Fasting Condemned

7 IN THE fourth year of King Darius, the word of the LORD came to Zechariah on the fourth day of the ninth month, which is Chislev. 2Now the people of Bethel had sent Sharezer and Regem-melech and their men, to entreat the favor of the LORD, 3and to ask the priests of the house of the LORD of hosts and the prophets, "Should I mourn and practice abstinence in the fifth month, as I have done for so many years?" 4Then the word of the LORD of hosts came to me: 5Say to all the people of the land and the priests: When you fasted and lamented in the fifth month and in the seventh, for these seventy years, was it for me that you fasted? 6And when you eat and when you drink, do you not eat and drink only for yourselves? 7Were not these the words that the LORD proclaimed by the former prophets, when Jerusalem was inhabited and in prosperity, along with the towns around it, and when the Negeb and the Shephelah were inhabited?

Punishment for Rejecting God's Demands

8 The word of the LORD came to Zechariah, saying: 9Thus says the LORD of hosts: Render true judgments, show kindness and mercy to one another; 10do not oppress the widow, the orphan, the alien, or the poor; and do not devise evil in your hearts against one another. 11But they refused to listen, and turned a stubborn shoulder, and stopped their ears in order not to hear. 12They made their hearts adamant in order not to hear the law and the words that the LORD of hosts had sent by his spirit through the former prophets. Therefore great wrath came from the LORD of hosts. 13Just as, when Ii called, they would not hear, so, when they called, I would not hear, says the LORD of hosts, 14and I scattered them with a whirlwind among all the nations that they had not known. Thus the land they left was desolate, so that no one went to and fro, and a pleasant land was made desolate.

---

c 6:12 he will grow up from himself, literally, "he will grow up in his place."

d Cn Compare verse 11: Heb lacks silver and gold   e Gk Mss Syr Tg: Heb crowns   f Gk Syr: Heb crowns   g Syr Compare verse 10: Heb Helem   h Syr Compare verse 10: Heb Hen   i Heb he

King James

8 AGAIN THE word of the LORD of hosts came *to me,* saying,

2Thus saith the LORD of hosts; I was jealous for Zion with great jealousy, and I was jealous for her with great fury.

3Thus saith the LORD; I am returned unto Zion, and will dwell in the midst of Jerusalem: and Jerusalem shall be called a city of truth; and the mountain of the LORD of hosts the holy mountain.

4Thus saith the LORD of hosts; There shall yet old men and old women dwell in the streets of Jerusalem, and every man with his staff in his hand for very age.

5And the streets of the city shall be full of boys and girls playing in the streets thereof.

6Thus saith the LORD of hosts; If it be marvellous in the eyes of the remnant of this people in these days, should it also be marvellous in mine eyes? saith the LORD of hosts.

7Thus saith the LORD of hosts; Behold, I will save my people from the east country, and from the west country;

8And I will bring them, and they shall dwell in the midst of Jerusalem: and they shall be my people, and I will be their God, in truth and in righteousness.

9¶ Thus saith the LORD of hosts; Let your hands be strong, ye that hear in these days these words by the mouth of the prophets, which *were* in the day *that* the foundation of the house of the LORD of hosts was laid, that the temple might be built.

10For before these days there was no hire for man, nor any hire for beast; neither *was there any* peace to him that went out or came in because of the affliction: for I set all men every one against his neighbour.

11But now I *will* not *be* unto the residue of this people as in the former days, saith the LORD of hosts.

12For the seed *shall be* prosperous; the vine shall give her fruit, and the ground shall give her increase, and the heavens shall give their dew; and I will cause the remnant of this people to possess all these *things.*

13And it shall come to pass, *that* as ye were a curse among the heathen, O house of Judah, and house of Israel; so will I save you, and ye shall be a blessing: fear not, *but* let your hands be strong.

14For thus saith the LORD of hosts; As I thought to punish you, when your fathers provoked me to wrath, saith the LORD of hosts, and I repented not:

15So again have I thought in these days to do well unto Jerusalem and to the house of Judah: fear ye not.

16¶ These *are* the things that ye shall do; Speak ye every man the truth to his neighbour; execute the judgment of truth and peace in your gates:

17And let none of you imagine evil in your hearts against his neighbour; and love no false oath: for all these *are things* that I hate, saith the LORD.

18¶ And the word of the LORD of hosts came unto me, saying,

19Thus saith the LORD of hosts; The fast of the fourth *month,* and the fast of the fifth, and the fast of the seventh, and the fast of the tenth, shall be to the house of Judah joy and gladness, and cheerful feasts; therefore love the truth and peace.

20Thus saith the LORD of hosts; *It shall* yet *come to pass,* that there shall come people, and the inhabitants of many cities:

21And the inhabitants of one *city* shall go to another, saying, Let us go speedily to pray before the LORD, and to seek the LORD of hosts: I will go also.

22Yea, many people and strong nations shall come to seek the LORD of hosts in Jerusalem, and to pray before the LORD.

New International

The LORD Promises to Bless Jerusalem

8 AGAIN THE word of the LORD Almighty came to me. 2This is what the LORD Almighty says: "I am very jealous for Zion; I am burning with jealousy for her."

3This is what the LORD says: "I will return to Zion and dwell in Jerusalem. Then Jerusalem will be called the City of Truth, and the mountain of the LORD Almighty will be called the Holy Mountain."

4This is what the LORD Almighty says: "Once again men and women of ripe old age will sit in the streets of Jerusalem, each with cane in hand because of his age. 5The city streets will be filled with boys and girls playing there."

6This is what the LORD Almighty says: "It may seem marvelous to the remnant of this people at that time, but will it seem marvelous to me?" declares the LORD Almighty.

7This is what the LORD Almighty says: "I will save my people from the countries of the east and the west. 8I will bring them back to live in Jerusalem; they will be my people, and I will be faithful and righteous to them as their God."

9This is what the LORD Almighty says: "You who now hear these words spoken by the prophets who were there when the foundation was laid for the house of the LORD Almighty, let your hands be strong so that the temple may be built. 10Before that time there were no wages for man or beast. No one could go about his business safely because of his enemy, for I had turned every man against his neighbor. 11But now I will not deal with the remnant of this people as I did in the past," declares the LORD Almighty.

12"The seed will grow well, the vine will yield its fruit, the ground will produce its crops, and the heavens will drop their dew. I will give all these things as an inheritance to the remnant of this people. 13As you have been an object of cursing among the nations, O Judah and Israel, so will I save you, and you will be a blessing. Do not be afraid, but let your hands be strong."

14This is what the LORD Almighty says: "Just as I had determined to bring disaster upon you and showed no pity when your fathers angered me," says the LORD Almighty, 15"so now I have determined to do good again to Jerusalem and Judah. Do not be afraid. 16These are the things you are to do: Speak the truth to each other, and render true and sound judgment in your courts; 17do not plot evil against your neighbor, and do not love to swear falsely. I hate all this," declares the LORD.

18Again the word of the LORD Almighty came to me. 19This is what the LORD Almighty says: "The fasts of the fourth, fifth, seventh and tenth months will become joyful and glad occasions and happy festivals for Judah. Therefore love truth and peace."

20This is what the LORD Almighty says: "Many peoples and the inhabitants of many cities will yet come, 21and the inhabitants of one city will go to another and say, 'Let us go at once to entreat the LORD and seek the LORD Almighty. I myself am going.' 22And many peoples and powerful nations will come to Jerusalem to seek the LORD Almighty and to entreat him."

Living Bible

8 AGAIN THE Lord's message came to me: 2"The Lord Almighty says, I am greatly concerned—yes, furiously angry—because of all that Jerusalem's enemies have done to her. 3Now I am going to return to my land and I, myself, will live within Jerusalem, and Jerusalem shall be called 'The Faithful City,' and 'The Holy Mountain,' and 'The Mountain of the Lord Almighty.' "

4The Lord Almighty declares that Jerusalem will have peace and prosperity so long that there will once again be aged men and women hobbling through her streets on canes, 5and the streets will be filled with boys and girls at play.

6The Lord says, "This seems unbelievable to you—a remnant, small, discouraged as you are—but it is no great thing for me. 7You can be sure that I will rescue my people from east and west, wherever they are scattered. 8I will bring them home again to live safely in Jerusalem, and they will be my people, and I will be their God, just and true and yet forgiving them their sins!"a

9The Lord Almighty says, "Get on with the job and finish it! You have been listening long enough! For since you began laying the foundation of the Temple, the prophets have been telling you about the blessings that await you when it's finished. 10Before the work began there were no jobs, no wages, no security; if you left the city, there was no assurance you would ever return, for crime was rampant.

11"But it is all so different now!" says the Lord Almighty. 12"For I am sowing peace and prosperity among you. Your crops will prosper; the grapevines will be weighted down with fruit; the ground will be fertile, with plenty of rain; all these blessings will be given to the people left in the land. 13'May you be as poor as Judah,' the heathen used to say to those they cursed! But no longer! For now 'Judah' is a word of blessing, not a curse. 'May you be as prosperous and happy as Judah is,' they'll say. So don't be afraid or discouraged! Get on with rebuilding the Temple! 14, 15If you do, I will certainly bless you. And don't think that I might change my mind. I did what I said I would when your fathers angered me and I promised to punish them, and I won't change this decision of mine to bless you. 16Here is your part: Tell the truth. Be fair. Live at peace with everyone. 17Don't plot harm to others; don't swear that something is true when it isn't! How I hate all that sort of thing!" says the Lord.

18Here is another message that came to me from the Lord Almighty: 19"The traditional fasts and times of mourning you have kept in July, August, October, and Januaryb are ended. They will be changed to joyous festivals if you love truth and peace! 20, 21People from around the world will come on pilgrimages and pour into Jerusalem from many foreign cities to attend these celebrations. People will write their friends in other cities and say, 'Let's go to Jerusalem to ask the Lord to bless us, and be merciful to us. I'm going! Please come with me. Let's go now!' 22Yes, many people, even strong nations, will come to the Lord Almighty in Jerusalem to ask for his blessing and help. 23In those days ten men from ten different

New Revised Standard

God's Promises to Zion

8 THE WORD of the LORD of hosts came to me, saying: 2Thus says the LORD of hosts: I am jealous for Zion with great jealousy, and I am jealous for her with great wrath. 3Thus says the LORD: I will return to Zion, and will dwell in the midst of Jerusalem; Jerusalem shall be called the faithful city, and the mountain of the LORD of hosts shall be called the holy mountain. 4Thus says the LORD of hosts: Old men and old women shall again sit in the streets of Jerusalem, each with staff in hand because of their great age. 5And the streets of the city shall be full of boys and girls playing in its streets. 6Thus says the LORD of hosts: Even though it seems impossible to the remnant of this people in these days, should it also seem impossible to me, says the LORD of hosts? 7Thus says the LORD of hosts: I will save my people from the east country and from the west country; 8and I will bring them to live in Jerusalem. They shall be my people and I will be their God, in faithfulness and in righteousness.

9 Thus says the LORD of hosts: Let your hands be strong—you that have recently been hearing these words from the mouths of the prophets who were present when the foundation was laid for the rebuilding of the temple, the house of the LORD of hosts. 10For before those days there were no wages for people or for animals, nor was there any safety from the foe for those who went out or came in, and I set them all against one other. 11But now I will not deal with the remnant of this people as in the former days, says the LORD of hosts. 12For there shall be a sowing of peace; the vine shall yield its fruit, the ground shall give its produce, and the skies shall give their dew; and I will cause the remnant of this people to possess all these things. 13Just as you have been a cursing among the nations, O house of Judah and house of Israel, so I will save you and you shall be a blessing. Do not be afraid, but let your hands be strong.

14 For thus says the LORD of hosts: Just as I purposed to bring disaster upon you, when your ancestors provoked me to wrath, and I did not relent, says the LORD of hosts, 15so again I have purposed in these days to do good to Jerusalem and to the house of Judah; do not be afraid. 16These are the things that you shall do: Speak the truth to one another, render in your gates judgments that are true and make for peace, 17do not devise evil in your hearts against one another, and love no false oath; for all these are things that I hate, says the LORD.

Joyful Fasting

18 The word of the LORD of hosts came to me, saying: 19Thus says the LORD of hosts: The fast of the fourth month, and the fast of the fifth, and the fast of the seventh, and the fast of the tenth, shall be seasons of joy and gladness, and cheerful festivals for the house of Judah: therefore love truth and peace.

Many Peoples Drawn to Jerusalem

20 Thus says the LORD of hosts: Peoples shall yet come, the inhabitants of many cities; 21the inhabitants of one city shall go to another, saying, "Come, let us go to entreat the favor of the LORD, and to seek the LORD of hosts; I myself am going." 22Many peoples and strong nations shall come to seek the LORD of hosts in Jerusalem, and to entreat the favor of the LORD. 23Thus says

---

a 8:8 *forgiving them their sins,* literally, "I will be their God in truth and in righteousness." b 8:19 *July, August, October, and January,* literally, "fourth, fifth, seventh, and tenth months," of the Hebrew calendar.

King James

23Thus saith the LORD of hosts; In those days *it shall come to pass*, that ten men shall take hold out of all languages of the nations, even shall take hold of the skirt of him that is a Jew, saying, We will go with you: for we have heard *that* God *is* with you.

9 THE BURDEN of the word of the LORD in the land of Hadrach, and Damascus *shall be* the rest thereof: when the eyes of man, as of all the tribes of Israel, *shall be* toward the LORD.

2And Hamath also shall border thereby; Tyrus, and Zidon, though it be very wise.

3And Tyrus did build herself a strong hold, and heaped up silver as the dust, and fine gold as the mire of the streets.

4Behold, the Lord will cast her out, and he will smite her power in the sea; and she shall be devoured with fire.

5Ashkelon shall see *it*, and fear; Gaza also *shall see it*, and be very sorrowful, and Ekron; for her expectation shall be ashamed; and the king shall perish from Gaza, and Ashkelon shall not be inhabited.

6And a bastard shall dwell in Ashdod, and I will cut off the pride of the Philistines.

7And I will take away his blood out of his mouth, and his abominations from between his teeth: but he that remaineth, even he, *shall be* for our God, and he shall be as a governor in Judah, and Ekron as a Jebusite.

8And I will encamp about mine house because of the army, because of him that passeth by, and because of him that returneth: and no oppressor shall pass through them any more: for now have I seen with mine eyes.

9¶ Rejoice greatly, O daughter of Zion; shout, O daughter of Jerusalem: behold, thy King cometh unto thee: he *is* just, and having salvation; lowly, and riding upon an ass, and upon a colt the foal of an ass.

10And I will cut off the chariot from Ephraim, and the horse from Jerusalem, and the battle bow shall be cut off: and he shall speak peace unto the heathen: and his dominion *shall be* from sea *even* to sea, and from the river *even* to the ends of the earth.

11As for thee also, by the blood of thy covenant I have sent forth thy prisoners out of the pit wherein *is* no water.

12¶ Turn you to the strong hold, ye prisoners of hope: even today do I declare *that* I will render double unto thee;

New International

23This is what the LORD Almighty says: "In those days ten men from all languages and nations will take firm hold of one Jew by the hem of his robe and say, 'Let us go with you, because we have heard that God is with you.' "

Judgment on Israel's Enemies
An Oracle

9 THE WORD of the LORD is against the land of Hadrach
   and will rest upon Damascus—
for the eyes of men and all the tribes of Israel
   are on the LORD—a
2and upon Hamath too, which borders on it,
   and upon Tyre and Sidon, though they are
      very skillful.
3Tyre has built herself a stronghold;
   she has heaped up silver like dust,
   and gold like the dirt of the streets.
4But the Lord will take away her possessions
   and destroy her power on the sea,
   and she will be consumed by fire.
5Ashkelon will see it and fear;
   Gaza will writhe in agony,
   and Ekron too, for her hope will wither.
Gaza will lose her king
   and Ashkelon will be deserted.
6Foreigners will occupy Ashdod,
   and I will cut off the pride of the Philistines.
7I will take the blood from their mouths,
   the forbidden food from between their teeth.
Those who are left will belong to our God
   and become leaders in Judah,
   and Ekron will be like the Jebusites.
8But I will defend my house
   against marauding forces.
Never again will an oppressor overrun my
      people,
   for now I am keeping watch.

The Coming of Zion's King

9Rejoice greatly, O Daughter of Zion!
   Shout, Daughter of Jerusalem!
See, your kingb comes to you,
   righteous and having salvation,
   gentle and riding on a donkey,
   on a colt, the foal of a donkey.
10I will take away the chariots from Ephraim
   and the war-horses from Jerusalem,
   and the battle bow will be broken.
He will proclaim peace to the nations.
   His rule will extend from sea to sea
   and from the Riverc to the ends of the
      earth.d
11As for you, because of the blood of my
      covenant with you,
   I will free your prisoners from the waterless
      pit.
12Return to your fortress, O prisoners of hope;
   even now I announce that I will restore twice
      as much to you.

Living Bible

nations will clutch at the coat sleeves of one Jew and say, 'Please be my friend, for I know that God is with you.' "

9 THIS IS the message concerning God's curse on the lands of Hadrach and Damascus, for the Lord is closely watching all mankind,e as well as Israel.
2"Doomed is Hamath, near Damascus, and Tyre, and Zidon, too, shrewd though they be. 3Though Tyre has armed herself to the hilt, and become so rich that silver is like dirt to her, and fine gold like dust in the street, 4yet the Lord will dispossess her, and hurl her fortifications into the sea; and she shall be set on fire and burned to the ground.
5"Ashkelon will see it happen and be filled with fear; Gaza will huddle in desperation and Ekron will shake with terror, for their hopes that Tyre would stop the enemies' advance will all be dashed. Gaza will be conquered, her king killed, and Ashkelon will be completely destroyed.
6"Foreigners will take over the city of Ashdod, the rich city of the Philistines. 7I will yank her idolatry out of her mouth, and pull from her teeth her sacrifices that she eats with blood. Everyone left will worship God and be adopted into Israel as a new clan: the Philistines of Ekron will intermarry with the Jews, just as the Jebusites did so long ago. 8And I will surround my Temple like a guard to keep invading armies from entering Israel. I am closely watching their movements and I will keep them away; no foreign oppressors will again overrun my people's land.
9"Rejoice greatly, O my people! Shout with joy! For look—your King is coming! He is the Righteous One, the Victor! Yet he is lowly, riding on a donkey's colt! 10I will disarm all peoples of the earth, including my people in Israel, and he shall bring peace among the nations. His realm shall stretch from sea to sea, from the river to the ends of the earth.f
11"I have delivered you from death in a waterless pit because of the covenant I made with you, sealed with blood. 12Come to the place of safety, all you prisoners, for there is yet hope! I promise right now, I will repay you two mercies for each of your woes! 13Judah, you are

New Revised Standard

the LORD of hosts: In those days ten men from nations of every language shall take hold of a Jew, grasping his garment and saying, "Let us go with you, for we have heard that God is with you."

Judgment on Israel's Enemies

9   An Oracle.

The word of the LORD is against the land of Hadrach
    and will rest upon Damascus.
For to the LORD belongs the capitalg of Aram,h
    as do all the tribes of Israel;
2 Hamath also, which borders on it,
    Tyre and Sidon, though they are very wise.
3 Tyre has built itself a rampart,
    and heaped up silver like dust,
    and gold like the dirt of the streets.
4 But now, the Lord will strip it of its possessions
    and hurl its wealth into the sea,
    and it shall be devoured by fire.

5 Ashkelon shall see it and be afraid;
    Gaza too, and shall writhe in anguish;
    Ekron also, because its hopes are withered.
The king shall perish from Gaza;
    Ashkelon shall be uninhabited;
6 a mongrel people shall settle in Ashdod,
    and I will make an end of the pride of Philistia.
7 I will take away its blood from its mouth,
    and its abominations from between its teeth;
it too shall be a remnant for our God;
    it shall be like a clan in Judah,
    and Ekron shall be like the Jebusites.
8 Then I will encamp at my house as a guard,
    so that no one shall march to and fro;
no oppressor shall again overrun them,
    for now I have seen with my own eyes.

The Coming Ruler of God's People

9 Rejoice greatly, O daughter Zion!
    Shout aloud, O daughter Jerusalem!
Lo, your king comes to you;
    triumphant and victorious is he,
humble and riding on a donkey,
    on a colt, the foal of a donkey.
10 Hei will cut off the chariot from Ephraim
    and the war horse from Jerusalem;
and the battle bow shall be cut off,
    and he shall command peace to the nations;
his dominion shall be from sea to sea,
    and from the River to the ends of the earth.

11 As for you also, because of the blood of my covenant with you,
    I will set your prisoners free from the waterless pit.
12 Return to your stronghold, O prisoners of hope;
    today I declare that I will restore to you double.

---

e 9:1 for the Lord is closely watching all mankind, or, "for the cities of Syria belong to the Lord, as much as do the tribes of Israel." f 9:10 from the river to the ends of the earth, or, "to the ends of the land" of Palestine. Either interpretation is possible from the Hebrew text, but many other passages indicate Christ's universal rule.

g Heb eye   h Cn: Heb of Adam (or of humankind)   i Gk: Heb I

King James

13When I have bent Judah for me, filled the bow with Ephraim, and raised up thy sons, O Zion, against thy sons, O Greece, and made thee as the sword of a mighty man.

14And the LORD shall be seen over them, and his arrow shall go forth as the lightning: and the Lord GOD shall blow the trumpet, and shall go with whirlwinds of the south.

15The LORD of hosts shall defend them; and they shall devour, and subdue with sling stones; and they shall drink, *and* make a noise as through wine; and they shall be filled like bowls, *and* as the corners of the altar.

16And the LORD their God shall save them in that day as the flock of his people: for *they shall be as* the stones of a crown, lifted up as an ensign upon his land.

17For how great *is* his goodness, and how great *is* his beauty! corn shall make the young men cheerful, and new wine the maids.

10 ASK YE of the LORD rain in the time of the latter rain; *so* the LORD shall make bright clouds, and give them showers of rain, to every one grass in the field.

2For the idols have spoken vanity, and the diviners have seen a lie, and have told false dreams; they comfort in vain: therefore they went their way as a flock, they were troubled, because *there was* no shepherd.

3Mine anger was kindled against the shepherds, and I punished the goats: for the LORD of hosts hath visited his flock the house of Judah, and hath made them as his goodly horse in the battle.

4Out of him came forth the corner, out of him the nail, out of him the battle bow, out of him every oppressor together.

5¶ And they shall be as mighty *men,* which tread down *their enemies* in the mire of the streets in the battle: and they shall fight, because the LORD *is* with them, and the riders on horses shall be confounded.

6And I will strengthen the house of Judah, and I will save the house of Joseph, and I will bring them again to place them; for I have mercy upon them: and they shall be as though I had not cast them off: for I *am* the LORD their God, and will hear them.

7And *they of* Ephraim shall be like a mighty *man,* and their heart shall rejoice as through wine: yea, their children shall see *it,* and be glad; their heart shall rejoice in the LORD.

New International

13I will bend Judah as I bend my bow
    and fill it with Ephraim.
I will rouse your sons, O Zion,
    against your sons, O Greece,
    and make you like a warrior's sword.

The LORD Will Appear

14Then the LORD will appear over them;
    his arrow will flash like lightning.
The Sovereign LORD will sound the trumpet;
    he will march in the storms of the south,
15   and the LORD Almighty will shield them.
They will destroy
    and overcome with slingstones.
They will drink and roar as with wine;
    they will be full like a bowl
    used for sprinklinga the corners of the altar.
16The LORD their God will save them on that day
    as the flock of his people.
They will sparkle in his land
    like jewels in a crown.
17How attractive and beautiful they will be!
    Grain will make the young men thrive,
    and new wine the young women.

The LORD Will Care for Judah

10 ASK THE LORD for rain in the springtime;
    it is the LORD who makes the storm clouds.
He gives showers of rain to men,
    and plants of the field to everyone.
2The idols speak deceit,
    diviners see visions that lie;
they tell dreams that are false,
    they give comfort in vain.
Therefore the people wander like sheep
    oppressed for lack of a shepherd.

3"My anger burns against the shepherds,
    and I will punish the leaders;
for the LORD Almighty will care
    for his flock, the house of Judah,
    and make them like a proud horse in battle.
4From Judah will come the cornerstone,
    from him the tent peg,
    from him the battle bow,
    from him every ruler.
5Together theyb will be like mighty men
    trampling the muddy streets in battle.
Because the LORD is with them,
    they will fight and overthrow the horsemen.

6"I will strengthen the house of Judah
    and save the house of Joseph.
I will restore them
    because I have compassion on them.
They will be as though
    I had not rejected them,
for I am the LORD their God
    and I will answer them.
7The Ephraimites will become like mighty men,
    and their hearts will be glad as with wine.
Their children will see it and be joyful;
    their hearts will rejoice in the LORD.

Living Bible

my bow! Ephraim, you are my arrow! Both of you will be my sword, like the sword of a mighty soldier brandished against the sons of Greece."

14The Lord shall lead his people as they fight! His arrows shall fly like lightning; the Lord God shall sound the trumpet call and go out against his enemies like a whirlwind off the desert from the south. 15He will defend his people and they will subdue their enemies, treading them beneath their feet. They will taste victory and shout with triumph. They will slaughter their foes, leaving horrible carnage everywhere. 16, 17The Lord their God will save his people in that day, as a Shepherd caring for his sheep. They shall shine in his land as glittering jewels in a crown. How wonderful and beautiful all shall be! The abundance of grain and grapes will make the young men and girls flourish; they will be radiant with health and happiness.

10 ASK THE Lord for rain in the springtime, and he will answer with lightning and showers. Every field will become a lush pasture. 2How foolish to ask the idols for anything like that! Fortune-tellers' predictions are all a bunch of silly lies; what comfort is there in promises that don't come true? Judah and Israel have been led astray and wander like lost sheep; everyone attacks them, for they have no shepherd to protect them.

3"My anger burns against your 'shepherds'—your leaders—and I will punish them—these goats. For the Lord Almighty has arrived to help his flock of Judah. I will make them strong and glorious like a proud steed in battle. 4From them will come the Cornerstone, the Peg on which all hope hangs, the Bow that wins the battle, the Ruler over all the earth.c 5They will be mighty warriors for God, grinding their enemies' faces into the dust beneath their feet. The Lord is with them as they fight; their enemy is doomed.

6"I will strengthen Judah, yes, and Israel too; I will re-establish them because I love them. It will be as though I had never cast them all away, for I, the Lord their God, will hear their cries. 7They shall be like mighty warriors. They shall be happy as with wine. Their children, too, shall see the mercies of the Lord and be glad. Their hearts shall rejoice in the Lord. 8When I

New Revised Standard

13 For I have bent Judah as my bow;
   I have made Ephraim its arrow.
I will arouse your sons, O Zion,
   against your sons, O Greece,
   and wield you like a warrior's sword.

14 Then the LORD will appear over them,
   and his arrow go forth like lightning;
the Lord GOD will sound the trumpet
   and march forth in the whirlwinds of the
      south.
15 The LORD of hosts will protect them,
   and they shall devour and tread down the
      slingers;d
they shall drink their bloode like wine,
   and be full like a bowl,
   drenched like the corners of the altar.

16 On that day the LORD their God will save
      them
   for they are the flock of his people;
for like the jewels of a crown
   they shall shine on his land.
17 For what goodness and beauty are his!
   Grain shall make the young men flourish,
   and new wine the young women.

Restoration of Judah and Israel

10 ASK RAIN from the LORD
   in the season of the spring rain,
from the LORD who makes the storm clouds,
   who gives showers of rain to you,f
   the vegetation in the field to everyone.
2 For the teraphimg utter nonsense,
   and the diviners see lies;
the dreamers tell false dreams,
   and give empty consolation.
Therefore the people wander like sheep;
   they suffer for lack of a shepherd.

3 My anger is hot against the shepherds,
   and I will punish the leaders;h
for the LORD of hosts cares for his flock, the
      house of Judah,
   and will make them like his proud war
      horse.
4 Out of them shall come the cornerstone,
   out of them the tent peg,
out of them the battle bow,
   out of them every commander.
5 Together they shall be like warriors in battle,
   trampling the foe in the mud of the streets;
they shall fight, for the LORD is with them,
   and they shall put to shame the riders on
      horses.

6 I will strengthen the house of Judah,
   and I will save the house of Joseph.
I will bring them back because I have
      compassion on them,
   and they shall be as though I had not
      rejected them;
   for I am the LORD their God and I will
      answer them.
7 Then the people of Ephraim shall become like
      warriors,
   and their hearts shall be glad as with wine.
Their children shall see it and rejoice,
   their hearts shall exult in the LORD.

---

c *10:4 the Ruler over all the earth,* i.e., the Messiah.

d Cn: Heb *the slingstones* e Gk: Heb *shall drink* f Heb *them* g Or *household gods* h Or *male goats*

King James

8I will hiss for them, and gather them; for I have redeemed them: and they shall increase as they have increased.

9And I will sow them among the people: and they shall remember me in far countries; and they shall live with their children, and turn again.

10I will bring them again also out of the land of Egypt, and gather them out of Assyria; and I will bring them into the land of Gilead and Lebanon; and *place* shall not be found for them.

11And he shall pass through the sea with affliction, and shall smite the waves in the sea, and all the deeps of the river shall dry up: and the pride of Assyria shall be brought down, and the sceptre of Egypt shall depart away.

12And I will strengthen them in the LORD; and they shall walk up and down in his name, saith the LORD.

11 OPEN THY doors, O Lebanon, that the fire may devour thy cedars.

2Howl, fir tree; for the cedar is fallen; because the mighty are spoiled: howl, O ye oaks of Bashan; for the forest of the vintage is come down.

3¶ *There is* a voice of the howling of the shepherds; for their glory is spoiled: a voice of the roaring of young lions; for the pride of Jordan is spoiled.

4Thus saith the LORD my God; Feed the flock of the slaughter;

5Whose possessors slay them, and hold themselves not guilty: and they that sell them say, Blessed *be* the LORD; for I am rich: and their own shepherds pity them not.

6For I will no more pity the inhabitants of the land, saith the LORD: but, lo, I will deliver the men every one into his neighbour's hand, and into the hand of his king: and they shall smite the land, and out of their hand I will not deliver *them*.

7And I will feed the flock of slaughter, *even* you, O poor of the flock. And I took unto me two staves; the one I called Beauty, and the other I called Bands; and I fed the flock.

8Three shepherds also I cut off in one month; and my soul loathed them, and their soul also abhorred me.

9Then said I, I will not feed you: that that dieth, let it die; and that that is to be cut off, let it be cut off; and let the rest eat every one the flesh of another.

10¶ And I took my staff, *even* Beauty, and cut it asunder, that I might break my covenant which I had made with all the people.

11And it was broken in that day: and so the poor of the flock that waited upon me knew that it *was* the word of the LORD.

12And I said unto them, If ye think good, give *me* my price; and if not, forbear. So they weighed for my price thirty *pieces* of silver.

New International

8I will signal for them
  and gather them in.
Surely I will redeem them;
  they will be as numerous as before.
9Though I scatter them among the peoples,
  yet in distant lands they will remember me.
They and their children will survive,
  and they will return.
10I will bring them back from Egypt
  and gather them from Assyria.
I will bring them to Gilead and Lebanon,
  and there will not be room enough for them.
11They will pass through the sea of trouble;
  the surging sea will be subdued
  and all the depths of the Nile will dry up.
Assyria's pride will be brought down
  and Egypt's scepter will pass away.
12I will strengthen them in the LORD
  and in his name they will walk,"

declares the LORD.

11 OPEN YOUR doors, O Lebanon,
  so that fire may devour your cedars!
2Wail, O pine tree, for the cedar has fallen;
  the stately trees are ruined!
Wail, oaks of Bashan;
  the dense forest has been cut down!
3Listen to the wail of the shepherds;
  their rich pastures are destroyed!
Listen to the roar of the lions;
  the lush thicket of the Jordan is ruined!

Two Shepherds

4This is what the LORD my God says: "Pasture the flock marked for slaughter. 5Their buyers slaughter them and go unpunished. Those who sell them say, 'Praise the LORD, I am rich!' Their own shepherds do not spare them. 6For I will no longer have pity on the people of the land," declares the LORD. "I will hand everyone over to his neighbor and his king. They will oppress the land, and I will not rescue them from their hands."

7So I pastured the flock marked for slaughter, particularly the oppressed of the flock. Then I took two staffs and called one Favor and the other Union, and I pastured the flock. 8In one month I got rid of the three shepherds.

The flock detested me, and I grew weary of them 9and said, "I will not be your shepherd. Let the dying die, and the perishing perish. Let those who are left eat one another's flesh."

10Then I took my staff called Favor and broke it, revoking the covenant I had made with all the nations. 11It was revoked on that day, and so the afflicted of the flock who were watching me knew it was the word of the LORD.

12I told them, "If you think it best, give me my pay; but if not, keep it." So they paid me thirty pieces of silver.

Living Bible

whistle to them, they'll come running, for I have bought them back again. From the few that are left, their population will grow again to former size. 9Though I have scattered them like seeds among the nations, still they will remember me and return again to God; with all their children, they will come home again to Israel. 10I will bring them back from Egypt and Assyria, and resettle them in Israel—in Gilead and Lebanon; there will scarcely be room for all of them! 11They shall pass safely through the sea of distress,a for the waves will be held back. The Nile will become dry—the rule of Assyria and Egypt over my people will end."

12The Lord says, "I will make my people strong with power from me! They will go wherever they wish, and wherever they go, they will be under my personal care."

11 OPEN YOUR doors, O Lebanon, to judgment.b You will be destroyed as though by fire raging through your forests. 2Weep, O cypress trees, for all the ruined cedars; the tallest and most beautiful of them are fallen. Cry in fear, you oaks of Bashan, as you watch the thickest forests felled. 3Listen to the wailing of Israel's leaders—all these evil shepherds—for their wealth is gone. Hear the young lions roaring—the princes are weeping, for their glorious Jordan valley lies in ruins.

4Then said the Lord my God to me, "Go and take a job as shepherd of a flock being fattened for the butcher. 5This will illustrate the way my people have been bought and slain by wicked leaders, who go unpunished. 'Thank God, now I am rich!' say those who have betrayed them—their own shepherds have sold them without mercy. 6And I won't spare them either," says the Lord, "for I will let them fall into the clutches of their own wicked leaders, and they will slay them. They shall turn the land into a wilderness and I will not protect it from them."

7So I took two shepherd's staffs, naming one "Grace" and the other "Union," and I fed the flock as I had been told to do. 8And I got rid of their three evil shepherds in a single month. But I became impatient with these sheep—this nation—and they hated me too.

9So I told them, "I won't be your shepherd any longer. If you die, you die; if you are killed, I don't care. Go ahead and destroy yourselves!"

10And I took my staff called "Grace" and snapped it in two, showing that I had broken my contract to lead and protect them. 11That was the end of the agreement. Then those who bought and sold sheep, who were watching, realized that God was telling them something through what I did.

12And I said to their leaders, "If you like, give me my pay, whatever I am worth; but only if you want to."

So they counted out thirty little silver coinsc as my wages.

New Revised Standard

8 I will signal for them and gather them in,
    for I have redeemed them,
    and they shall be as numerous as they were
        before.
9 Though I scattered them among the nations,
    yet in far countries they shall remember me,
    and they shall rear their children and return.
10 I will bring them home from the land of
        Egypt,
    and gather them from Assyria;
I will bring them to the land of Gilead and to
        Lebanon,
    until there is no room for them.
11 Theyd shall pass through the sea of distress,
    and the waves of the sea shall be struck
        down,
    and all the depths of the Nile dried up.
The pride of Assyria shall be laid low,
    and the scepter of Egypt shall depart.
12 I will make them strong in the LORD,
    and they shall walk in his name,
                            says the LORD.

11 OPEN YOUR doors, O Lebanon,
    so that fire may devour your cedars!
2 Wail, O cypress, for the cedar has fallen,
    for the glorious trees are ruined!
Wail, oaks of Bashan,
    for the thick forest has been felled!
3 Listen, the wail of the shepherds,
    for their glory is despoiled!
Listen, the roar of the lions,
    for the thickets of the Jordan are destroyed!

Two Kinds of Shepherds

4 Thus said the LORD my God: Be a shepherd of the flock doomed to slaughter. 5Those who buy them kill them and go unpunished; and those who sell them say, "Blessed be the LORD, for I have become rich"; and their own shepherds have no pity on them. 6For I will no longer have pity on the inhabitants of the earth, says the LORD. I will cause them, every one, to fall each into the hand of a neighbor, and each into the hand of the king; and they shall devastate the earth, and I will deliver no one from their hand.

7 So, on behalf of the sheep merchants, I became the shepherd of the flock doomed to slaughter. I took two staffs; one I named Favor, the other I named Unity, and I tended the sheep. 8In one month I disposed of the three shepherds, for I had become impatient with them, and they also detested me. 9So I said, "I will not be your shepherd. What is to die, let it die; what is to be destroyed, let it be destroyed; and let those that are left devour the flesh of one another!" 10I took my staff Favor and broke it, annulling the covenant that I had made with all the peoples. 11So it was annulled on that day, and the sheep merchants, who were watching me, knew that it was the word of the LORD. 12I then said to them, "If it seems right to you, give me my wages; but if not, keep them." So they weighed out as my wages thirty shekels of silver. 13Then the LORD said to me, "Throw it into

---

a *10:11 the sea of distress,* or, "the Sea of Egypt," referring to the Red Sea which the people of Israel were miraculously brought through when God delivered them out of slavery the first time. b *11:1 to judgment,* implied. c *11:12 thirty little silver coins,* the price of a slave. See Ex 21:32 and Mt 27:3-9.

d Gk: Heb *He*

King James

13And the LORD said unto me, Cast it unto the potter: a goodly price that I was prised at of them. And I took the thirty *pieces* of silver, and cast them to the potter in the house of the LORD.

14Then I cut asunder mine other staff, *even* Bands, that I might break the brotherhood between Judah and Israel.

15¶ And the LORD said unto me, Take unto thee yet the instruments of a foolish shepherd.

16For, lo, I will raise up a shepherd in the land, *which* shall not visit those that be cut off, neither shall seek the young one, nor heal that that is broken, nor feed that that standeth still: but he shall eat the flesh of the fat, and tear their claws in pieces.

17Woe to the idol shepherd that leaveth the flock! the sword *shall be* upon his arm, and upon his right eye: his arm shall be clean dried up, and his right eye shall be utterly darkened.

12 THE BURDEN of the word of the LORD for Israel, saith the LORD, which stretcheth forth the heavens, and layeth the foundation of the earth, and formeth the spirit of man within him.

2Behold, I will make Jerusalem a cup of trembling unto all the people round about, when they shall be in the siege both against Judah *and* against Jerusalem.

3¶ And in that day will I make Jerusalem a burdensome stone for all people: all that burden themselves with it shall be cut in pieces, though all the people of the earth be gathered together against it.

4In that day, saith the LORD, I will smite every horse with astonishment, and his rider with madness: and I will open mine eyes upon the house of Judah, and will smite every horse of the people with blindness.

5And the governors of Judah shall say in their heart, The inhabitants of Jerusalem *shall be* my strength in the LORD of hosts their God.

6¶ In that day will I make the governors of Judah like an hearth of fire among the wood, and like a torch of fire in a sheaf; and they shall devour all the people round about, on the right hand and on the left: and Jerusalem shall be inhabited again in her own place, *even* in Jerusalem.

7The LORD also shall save the tents of Judah first, that the glory of the house of David and the glory of the inhabitants of Jerusalem do not magnify *themselves* against Judah.

8In that day shall the LORD defend the inhabitants of Jerusalem; and he that is feeble among them at that day shall be as David; and the house of David *shall be* as God, as the angel of the LORD before them.

9¶ And it shall come to pass in that day, *that* I will seek to destroy all the nations that come against Jerusalem.

10And I will pour upon the house of David, and upon the inhabitants of Jerusalem, the spirit of grace and of supplications: and they shall look upon me whom they have pierced, and they shall mourn for him, as one mourneth for *his* only *son*, and shall be in bitterness for *him*, as one that is in bitterness for *his* firstborn.

11In that day shall there be a great mourning in Jerusalem, as the mourning of Hadadrimmon in the valley of Megiddon.

New International

13And the LORD said to me, "Throw it to the potter"—the handsome price at which they priced me! So I took the thirty pieces of silver and threw them into the house of the LORD to the potter.

14Then I broke my second staff called Union, breaking the brotherhood between Judah and Israel.

15Then the LORD said to me, "Take again the equipment of a foolish shepherd. 16For I am going to raise up a shepherd over the land who will not care for the lost, or seek the young, or heal the injured, or feed the healthy, but will eat the meat of the choice sheep, tearing off their hoofs.

17"Woe to the worthless shepherd,
    who deserts the flock!
May the sword strike his arm and his right eye!
    May his arm be completely withered,
    his right eye totally blinded!"

Jerusalem's Enemies to Be Destroyed
An Oracle

12 THIS IS the word of the LORD concerning Israel. The LORD, who stretches out the heavens, who lays the foundation of the earth, and who forms the spirit of man within him, declares: 2"I am going to make Jerusalem a cup that sends all the surrounding peoples reeling. Judah will be besieged as well as Jerusalem. 3On that day, when all the nations of the earth are gathered against her, I will make Jerusalem an immovable rock for all the nations. All who try to move it will injure themselves. 4On that day I will strike every horse with panic and its rider with madness," declares the LORD. "I will keep a watchful eye over the house of Judah, but I will blind all the horses of the nations. 5Then the leaders of Judah will say in their hearts, 'The people of Jerusalem are strong, because the LORD Almighty is their God.'

6"On that day I will make the leaders of Judah like a firepot in a woodpile, like a flaming torch among sheaves. They will consume right and left all the surrounding peoples, but Jerusalem will remain intact in her place.

7"The LORD will save the dwellings of Judah first, so that the honor of the house of David and of Jerusalem's inhabitants may not be greater than that of Judah. 8On that day the LORD will shield those who live in Jerusalem, so that the feeblest among them will be like David, and the house of David will be like God, like the Angel of the LORD going before them. 9On that day I will set out to destroy all the nations that attack Jerusalem.

Mourning for the One They Pierced

10"And I will pour out on the house of David and the inhabitants of Jerusalem a spirita of grace and supplication. They will look onb me, the one they have pierced, and they will mourn for him as one mourns for an only child, and grieve bitterly for him as one grieves for a firstborn son. 11On that day the weeping in Jerusalem will be great, like the weeping of Hadad Rimmon in the plain of Megiddo. 12The land will mourn, each clan by

Living Bible

13And the Lord told me, "Use it to buy a fieldc from the pottery makers—this magnificent sum they value you at!"

So I took the thirty coins and threw them into the Temple for the pottery makers. 14Then I broke my other staff, "Union," to show that the bond of unity between Judah and Israel was broken.

15Then the Lord told me to go again and get a job as a shepherd; this time I was to act the part of a worthless, wicked shepherd.

16And he said to me, "This illustrates how I will give this nation a shepherd who will not care for the dying ones, nor look after the young, nor heal the broken bones, nor feed the healthy ones, nor carry the lame that cannot walk; instead, he will eat the fat ones, even tearing off their feet. 17Woe to this worthless shepherd who doesn't care for the flock. God's sword will cut his arm and pierce through his right eye; his arm will become useless and his right eye blinded."

12 THIS IS the fate of Israel, as pronounced by the Lord, who stretched out the heavens and laid the foundation of the earth, and formed the spirit of man within him:

2"I will make Jerusalem and Judah like a cup of poison to all the nearby nations that send their armies to surround Jerusalem. 3Jerusalem will be a heavy stone burdening the world. And though all the nations of the earth unite in an attempt to move her, they will all be crushed.

4"In that day," says the Lord, "I will bewilder the armies drawn up against her, and make fools of them, for I will watch over the people of Judah, but blind all her enemies.

5"And the clans of Judah shall say to themselves, 'The people of Jerusalem have found strength in the Lord Almighty, their God.'

6"In that day I will make the clans of Judah like a little fire that sets the forest aflame—like a burning match among the sheaves; they will burn up all the neighboring nations right and left, while Jerusalem stands unmoved. 7The Lord will give victory to the rest of Judah first, before Jerusalem, so that the people of Jerusalem and the royal line of David won't be filled with pride at their success.

8"The Lord will defend the people of Jerusalem; the weakest among them will be as mighty as King David! And the royal line will be as God, like the Angel of the Lord who goes before them! 9For my plan is to destroy all the nations that come against Jerusalem.

10"Then I will pour out the spirit of grace and prayer on all the people of Jerusalem, and they will look on him they pierced, and mourn for him as for an only son, and grieve bitterly for him as for an oldest child who died. 11The sorrow and mourning in Jerusalem at that time will be even greater than the grievous mourning for the godly King Josiah,d who was killed in the valley of Megiddo.

New Revised Standard

the treasury"e—this lordly price at which I was valued by them. So I took the thirty shekels of silver and threw them into the treasurye in the house of the LORD. 14Then I broke my second staff Unity, annulling the family ties between Judah and Israel.

15 Then the LORD said to me: Take once more the implements of a worthless shepherd. 16For I am now raising up in the land a shepherd who does not care for the perishing, or seek the wandering,f or heal the maimed, or nourish the healthy,g but devours the flesh of the fat ones, tearing off even their hoofs.

17   Oh, my worthless shepherd,
        who deserts the flock!
    May the sword strike his arm
        and his right eye!
    Let his arm be completely withered,
        his right eye utterly blinded!

Jerusalem's Victory

12   An Oracle.

The word of the LORD concerning Israel: Thus says the LORD, who stretched out the heavens and founded the earth and formed the human spirit within: 2See, I am about to make Jerusalem a cup of reeling for all the surrounding peoples; it will be against Judah also in the siege against Jerusalem. 3On that day I will make Jerusalem a heavy stone for all the peoples; all who lift it shall grievously hurt themselves. And all the nations of the earth shall come together against it. 4On that day, says the LORD, I will strike every horse with panic, and its rider with madness. But on the house of Judah I will keep a watchful eye, when I strike every horse of the peoples with blindness. 5Then the clans of Judah shall say to themselves, "The inhabitants of Jerusalem have strength through the LORD of hosts, their God."

6 On that day I will make the clans of Judah like a blazing pot on a pile of wood, like a flaming torch among sheaves; and they shall devour to the right and to the left all the surrounding peoples, while Jerusalem shall again be inhabited in its place, in Jerusalem.

7 And the LORD will give victory to the tents of Judah first, that the glory of the house of David and the glory of the inhabitants of Jerusalem may not be exalted over that of Judah. 8On that day the LORD will shield the inhabitants of Jerusalem so that the feeblest among them on that day shall be like David, and the house of David shall be like God, like the angel of the LORD, at their head. 9And on that day I will seek to destroy all the nations that come against Jerusalem.

Mourning for the Pierced One

10 And I will pour out a spirit of compassion and supplication on the house of David and the inhabitants of Jerusalem, so that, when they look on the oneh whom they have pierced, they shall mourn for him, as one mourns for an only child, and weep bitterly over him, as one weeps over a firstborn. 11On that day the mourning in Jerusalem will be as great as the mourning for Hadad-rimmon in the plain of Megiddo. 12The land

---

c 11:13 Use it to buy a field, literally, "Throw it to the pottery-makers."
d 12:11 King Josiah. Implied in 2 Chron 35:24, 25. Literally, "Like the mourning of Hadad-rimmon in the valley of Megiddo."

e Syr: Heb it to the potter   f Syr Compare Gk Vg: Heb the youth   g Meaning of Heb uncertain   h Heb on me

King James

12And the land shall mourn, every family apart; the family of the house of David apart, and their wives apart; the family of the house of Nathan apart, and their wives apart;

13The family of the house of Levi apart, and their wives apart; the family of Shimei apart, and their wives apart;

14All the families that remain, every family apart, and their wives apart.

13 IN THAT day there shall be a fountain opened to the house of David and to the inhabitants of Jerusalem for sin and for uncleanness.

2¶ And it shall come to pass in that day, saith the LORD of hosts, *that* I will cut off the names of the idols out of the land, and they shall no more be remembered: and also I will cause the prophets and the unclean spirit to pass out of the land.

3And it shall come to pass, *that* when any shall yet prophesy, then his father and his mother that begat him shall say unto him, Thou shalt not live; for thou speakest lies in the name of the LORD: and his father and his mother that begat him shall thrust him through when he prophesieth.

4And it shall come to pass in that day, *that* the prophets shall be ashamed every one of his vision, when he hath prophesied; neither shall they wear a rough garment to deceive:

5But he shall say, I *am* no prophet, I *am* an husbandman; for man taught me to keep cattle from my youth.

6And *one* shall say unto him, What *are* these wounds in thine hands? Then he shall answer, *Those* with which I was wounded *in* the house of my friends.

7¶ Awake, O sword, against my shepherd, and against the man *that is* my fellow, saith the LORD of hosts: smite the shepherd, and the sheep shall be scattered: and I will turn mine hand upon the little ones.

8And it shall come to pass, *that* in all the land, saith the LORD, two parts therein shall be cut off *and* die; but the third shall be left therein.

9And I will bring the third part through the fire, and will refine them as silver is refined, and will try them as gold is tried: they shall call on my name, and I will hear them: I will say, It *is* my people: and they shall say, The LORD *is* my God.

14 BEHOLD, THE day of the LORD cometh, and thy spoil shall be divided in the midst of thee.

2For I will gather all nations against Jerusalem to battle; and the city shall be taken, and the houses rifled, and the women ravished; and half of the city shall go forth into captivity, and the residue of the people shall not be cut off from the city.

3Then shall the LORD go forth, and fight against those nations, as when he fought in the day of battle.

New International

itself, with their wives by themselves: the clan of the house of David and their wives, the clan of the house of Nathan and their wives, 13the clan of the house of Levi and their wives, the clan of Shimei and their wives, 14and all the rest of the clans and their wives.

Cleansing From Sin

13 "ON THAT day a fountain will be opened to the house of David and the inhabitants of Jerusalem, to cleanse them from sin and impurity.

2"On that day, I will banish the names of the idols from the land, and they will be remembered no more," declares the LORD Almighty. "I will remove both the prophets and the spirit of impurity from the land. 3And if anyone still prophesies, his father and mother, to whom he was born, will say to him, 'You must die, because you have told lies in the LORD's name.' When he prophesies, his own parents will stab him.

4"On that day every prophet will be ashamed of his prophetic vision. He will not put on a prophet's garment of hair in order to deceive. 5He will say, 'I am not a prophet. I am a farmer; the land has been my livelihood since my youth.a' 6If someone asks him, 'What are these wounds on your bodyb?' he will answer, 'The wounds I was given at the house of my friends.'

The Shepherd Struck, the Sheep Scattered

7"Awake, O sword, against my shepherd,
  against the man who is close to me!"
  declares the LORD Almighty.
"Strike the shepherd,
  and the sheep will be scattered,
  and I will turn my hand against the little
  ones.
8In the whole land," declares the LORD,
  "two-thirds will be struck down and perish;
  yet one-third will be left in it.
9This third I will bring into the fire;
  I will refine them like silver
  and test them like gold.
They will call on my name
  and I will answer them;
I will say, 'They are my people,'
  and they will say, 'The LORD is our God.'"

The LORD Comes and Reigns

14 A DAY of the LORD is coming when your plunder will be divided among you.

2I will gather all the nations to Jerusalem to fight against it; the city will be captured, the houses ransacked, and the women raped. Half of the city will go into exile, but the rest of the people will not be taken from the city.

3Then the LORD will go out and fight against those nations, as he fights in the day of battle. 4On that day

a 5 Or farmer; a man sold me in my youth   b 6 Or wounds between your hands

Living Bible

12, 13, 14"All of Israel will weep in profound sorrow. The whole nation will be bowed down with universal grief—king, prophet, priest, and people. Each family will go into private mourning, husbands and wives apart, to face their sorrow alone.

13 "AT THAT time a Fountain will be opened to the people of Israel and Jerusalem, a Fountain to cleanse them from all their sins and defilement."

2And the Lord Almighty declares, "In that day I will get rid of every vestige of idol worship throughout the land, so that even the names of the idols will be forgotten. All false prophets and fortune-tellers will be wiped out, 3and if anyone begins false prophecy again, his own father and mother will slay him! 'You must die,' they will tell him, 'for you are prophesying lies in the name of the Lord.'

4"No one will be boasting then of his prophetic gift! No one will wear prophet's clothes to try to fool the people then.

5" 'No,' he will say. 'I am not a prophet; I am a farmer. The soil has been my livelihood from my earliest youth.'

6"And if someone asks, 'Then what are these scars on your chest and your back?'c he will say, 'I got into a brawl at the home of a friend!'d

7"Awake, O sword, against my Shepherd, the man who is my associate and equal," says the Lord Almighty. "Strike down the Shepherd and the sheep will scatter, but I will come back and comfort and care for the lambs. 8Two-thirds of all the nation of Israel will be cut off and die,e but a third will be left in the land. 9I will bring the third that remain through the fire and make them pure, as gold and silver are refined and purified by fire. They will call upon my name and I will hear them; I will say, 'These are my people,' and they will say, 'The Lord is our God.' "

14 WATCH, FOR the day of the Lord is coming soon! On that day the Lord will gather together the nations to fight Jerusalem; the city will be taken, the houses rifled, the loot divided, the women raped; half the population will be taken away as slaves, and half will be left in what remains of the city.

3Then the Lord will go out fully armed for war, to fight against those nations. 4That day his feet will stand

New Revised Standard

shall mourn, each family by itself; the family of the house of David by itself, and their wives by themselves; the family of the house of Nathan by itself, and their wives by themselves; 13the family of the house of Levi by itself, and their wives by themselves; the family of the Shimeites by itself, and their wives by themselves; 14and all the families that are left, each by itself, and their wives by themselves.

13 ON THAT day a fountain shall be opened for the house of David and the inhabitants of Jerusalem, to cleanse them from sin and impurity.

Idolatry Cut Off

2 On that day, says the LORD of hosts, I will cut off the names of the idols from the land, so that they shall be remembered no more; and also I will remove from the land the prophets and the unclean spirit. 3And if any prophets appear again, their fathers and mothers who bore them will say to them, "You shall not live, for you speak lies in the name of the LORD"; and their fathers and their mothers who bore them shall pierce them through when they prophesy. 4On that day the prophets will be ashamed, every one, of their visions when they prophesy; they will not put on a hairy mantle in order to deceive, 5but each of them will say, "I am no prophet, I am a tiller of the soil; for the land has been my possessionf since my youth." 6And if anyone asks them, "What are these wounds on your chest?"g the answer will be "The wounds I received in the house of my friends."

The Shepherd Struck, the Flock Scattered

7   "Awake, O sword, against my shepherd,
        against the man who is my associate,"
                    says the LORD of hosts.
    Strike the shepherd, that the sheep may be
        scattered;
        I will turn my hand against the little ones.
8   In the whole land, says the LORD,
        two-thirds shall be cut off and perish,
        and one-third shall be left alive.
9   And I will put this third into the fire,
        refine them as one refines silver,
        and test them as gold is tested.
    They will call on my name,
        and I will answer them.
    I will say, "They are my people";
        and they will say, "The LORD is our God."

Future Warfare and Final Victory

14 SEE, A day is coming for the LORD, when the plunder taken from you will be divided in your midst. 2For I will gather all the nations against Jerusalem to battle, and the city shall be taken and the houses looted and the women raped; half the city shall go into exile, but the rest of the people shall not be cut off from the city. 3Then the LORD will go forth and fight against those nations as when he fights on a day of battle. 4On

---

c 13:6 these scars on your chest and your back. Evidently self-inflicted cuts, as practiced by false prophets. See 1 Kgs 18:28.   d 13:6 at the home of a friend, literally, "[These are] wounds I received in the house of my friends." Some think this refers to Christ; others believe this refers to a false prophet who is lying about the reasons for his scars.   e 13:8 Two-thirds of all the nation of Israel will be cut off and die. Something of this sort has already happened twice: two million Jews perished in the Roman wars, and six million under Hitler. Is a yet future disaster predicted here?

f Cn: Heb for humankind has caused me to possess   g Heb wounds between your hands

King James

4¶ And his feet shall stand in that day upon the mount of Olives, which *is* before Jerusalem on the east, and the mount of Olives shall cleave in the midst thereof toward the east and toward the west, *and there shall be* a very great valley; and half of the mountain shall remove toward the north, and half of it toward the south.

5And ye shall flee *to* the valley of the mountains; for the valley of the mountains shall reach unto Azal: yea, ye shall flee, like as ye fled from before the earthquake in the days of Uzziah king of Judah: and the LORD my God shall come, *and* all the saints with thee.

6And it shall come to pass in that day, *that* the light shall not be clear, *nor* dark:

7But it shall be one day which shall be known to the LORD, not day, nor night: but it shall come to pass, *that* at evening time it shall be light.

8And it shall be in that day, *that* living waters shall go out from Jerusalem; half of them toward the former sea, and half of them toward the hinder sea: in summer and in winter shall it be.

9And the LORD shall be king over all the earth: in that day shall there be one LORD, and his name one.

10All the land shall be turned as a plain from Geba to Rimmon south of Jerusalem: and it shall be lifted up, and inhabited in her place, from Benjamin's gate unto the place of the first gate, unto the corner gate, and *from* the tower of Hananeel unto the king's winepresses.

11And *men* shall dwell in it, and there shall be no more utter destruction; but Jerusalem shall be safely inhabited.

12¶ And this shall be the plague wherewith the LORD will smite all the people that have fought against Jerusalem; Their flesh shall consume away while they stand upon their feet, and their eyes shall consume away in their holes, and their tongue shall consume away in their mouth.

13And it shall come to pass in that day, *that* a great tumult from the LORD shall be among them; and they shall lay hold every one on the hand of his neighbour, and his hand shall rise up against the hand of his neighbour.

14And Judah also shall fight at Jerusalem; and the wealth of all the heathen round about shall be gathered together, gold, and silver, and apparel, in great abundance.

15And so shall be the plague of the horse, of the mule, of the camel, and of the ass, and of all the beasts that shall be in these tents, as this plague.

16¶ And it shall come to pass, *that* every one that is left of all the nations which came against Jerusalem shall even go up from year to year to worship the King, the LORD of hosts, and to keep the feast of tabernacles.

17And it shall be, *that* whoso will not come up of *all* the families of the earth unto Jerusalem to worship the King, the LORD of hosts, even upon them shall be no rain.

18And if the family of Egypt go not up, and come not, that *have* no *rain;* there shall be the plague, wherewith the LORD will smite the heathen that come not up to keep the feast of tabernacles.

19This shall be the punishment of Egypt, and the punishment of all nations that come not up to keep the feast of tabernacles.

20¶ In that day shall there be upon the bells of the horses, HOLINESS UNTO THE LORD; and the pots in the LORD's house shall be like the bowls before the altar.

21Yea, every pot in Jerusalem and in Judah shall be holiness unto the LORD of hosts: and all they that sacrifice shall come and take of them, and seethe therein: and in that day there shall be no more the Canaanite in the house of the LORD of hosts.

New International

his feet will stand on the Mount of Olives, east of Jerusalem, and the Mount of Olives will be split in two from east to west, forming a great valley, with half of the mountain moving north and half moving south. 5You will flee by my mountain valley, for it will extend to Azel. You will flee as you fled from the earthquakeª in the days of Uzziah king of Judah. Then the LORD my God will come, and all the holy ones with him.

6On that day there will be no light, no cold or frost. 7It will be a unique day, without daytime or nighttime— a day known to the LORD. When evening comes, there will be light.

8On that day living water will flow out from Jerusalem, half to the eastern seaᵇ and half to the western sea,ᶜ in summer and in winter.

9The LORD will be king over the whole earth. On that day there will be one LORD, and his name the only name.

10The whole land, from Geba to Rimmon, south of Jerusalem, will become like the Arabah. But Jerusalem will be raised up and remain in its place, from the Benjamin Gate to the site of the First Gate, to the Corner Gate, and from the Tower of Hananel to the royal winepresses. 11It will be inhabited; never again will it be destroyed. Jerusalem will be secure.

12This is the plague with which the LORD will strike all the nations that fought against Jerusalem: Their flesh will rot while they are still standing on their feet, their eyes will rot in their sockets, and their tongues will rot in their mouths. 13On that day men will be stricken by the LORD with great panic. Each man will seize the hand of another, and they will attack each other. 14Judah too will fight at Jerusalem. The wealth of all the surrounding nations will be collected—great quantities of gold and silver and clothing. 15A similar plague will strike the horses and mules, the camels and donkeys, and all the animals in those camps.

16Then the survivors from all the nations that have attacked Jerusalem will go up year after year to worship the King, the LORD Almighty, and to celebrate the Feast of Tabernacles. 17If any of the peoples of the earth do not go up to Jerusalem to worship the King, the LORD Almighty, they will have no rain. 18If the Egyptian people do not go up and take part, they will have no rain. The LORDᵈ will bring on them the plague he inflicts on the nations that do not go up to celebrate the Feast of Tabernacles. 19This will be the punishment of Egypt and the punishment of all the nations that do not go up to celebrate the Feast of Tabernacles.

20On that day HOLY TO THE LORD will be inscribed on the bells of the horses, and the cooking pots in the LORD's house will be like the sacred bowls in front of the altar. 21Every pot in Jerusalem and Judah will be holy to the LORD Almighty, and all who come to sacrifice will take some of the pots and cook in them. And on that day there will no longer be a Canaaniteᵉ in the house of the LORD Almighty.

ª 5 Or *⁵My mountain valley will be blocked and will extend to Azel. It will be blocked as it was blocked because of the earthquake*   ᵇ 8 That is, the Dead Sea   ᶜ 8 That is, the Mediterranean   ᵈ 18 Or *part, then the LORD*   ᵉ 21 Or *merchant*

Living Bible

upon the Mount of Olives, to the east of Jerusalem, and the Mount of Olives will split apart, making a very wide valley running from east to west, for half the mountain will move toward the north and half toward the south. ⁵You will escape through that valley, for it will reach across to the city gate.ᶠ Yes, you will escape as your people did long centuries ago from the earthquake in the days of Uzziah, king of Judah, and the Lord my God shall come, and all his saints and angelsᵍ with him.

⁶The sun and moon and stars will no longer shine,ʰ ⁷yet there will be continuous day! Only the Lord knows how! There will be no normal day and night—at evening time it will still be light. ⁸Life-giving waters will flow out from Jerusalem, half toward the Dead Sea and half toward the Mediterranean, flowing continuously both in winter and in summer.

⁹And the Lord shall be King over all the earth. In that day there shall be one Lord—his name alone will be worshiped. ¹⁰All the land from Geba (the northern border of Judah) to Rimmon (the southern border) will become one vast plain, but Jerusalem will be on an elevated site, covering the area all the way from the Gate of Benjamin over to the site of the old gate, then to the Corner Gate, and from the Tower of Hananel to the king's wine presses. ¹¹And Jerusalem shall be inhabited, safe at last, never again to be cursed and destroyed.

¹²And the Lord will send a plague on all the people who fought Jerusalem. They will become like walking corpses, their flesh rotting away; their eyes will shrivel in their sockets, and their tongues will decay in their mouths.

¹³They will be seized with terror, panic-stricken from the Lord, and will fight against each other in hand-to-hand combat. ¹⁴All Judah will be fighting at Jerusalem.ⁱ The wealth of all the neighboring nations will be confiscated—great quantities of gold and silver and fine clothing. ¹⁵(This same plague will strike the horses, mules, camels, donkeys, and all the other animals in the enemy camp.)

¹⁶In the end, those who survive the plague will go up to Jerusalem each year to worship the King, the Lord Almighty, to celebrate a timeʲ of thanksgiving. ¹⁷And any nation anywhere in all the world that refuses to come to Jerusalem to worship the King, the Lord Almighty, will have no rain. ¹⁸But if Egypt refuses to come, God will punish her with some other plague. ¹⁹And so Egypt and the other nations will all be punished if they refuse to come.

²⁰In that day the bells on the horses will have written on them, "These Are Holy Property";ᵏ and the trash cans in the Temple of the Lord will be as sacred as the bowls beside the altar. ²¹In fact, every container in Jerusalem and Judah shall be sacred to the Lord Almighty; all who come to worship may use any of them free of charge to boil their sacrifices in; there will be no more grasping traders in the Temple of the Lord Almighty!

New Revised Standard

that day his feet shall stand on the Mount of Olives, which lies before Jerusalem on the east; and the Mount of Olives shall be split in two from east to west by a very wide valley; so that one half of the Mount shall withdraw northward, and the other half southward. ⁵ And you shall flee by the valley of the Lord's mountain,ˡ for the valley between the mountains shall reach to Azal;ᵐ and you shall flee as you fled from the earthquake in the days of King Uzziah of Judah. Then the Lord my God will come, and all the holy ones with him.

6 On that day there shall not beⁿ either cold or frost.º ⁷ And there shall be continuous day (it is known to the Lord), not day and not night, for at evening time there shall be light.

8 On that day living waters shall flow out from Jerusalem, half of them to the eastern sea and half of them to the western sea; it shall continue in summer as in winter.

9 And the Lord will become king over all the earth; on that day the Lord will be one and his name one.

10 The whole land shall be turned into a plain from Geba to Rimmon south of Jerusalem. But Jerusalem shall remain aloft on its site from the Gate of Benjamin to the place of the former gate, to the Corner Gate, and from the Tower of Hananel to the king's wine presses. ¹¹ And it shall be inhabited, for never again shall it be doomed to destruction; Jerusalem shall abide in security.

12 This shall be the plague with which the Lord will strike all the peoples that wage war against Jerusalem: their flesh shall rot while they are still on their feet; their eyes shall rot in their sockets, and their tongues shall rot in their mouths. ¹³ On that day a great panic from the Lord shall fall on them, so that each will seize the hand of a neighbor, and the hand of the one will be raised against the hand of the other; ¹⁴ even Judah will fight at Jerusalem. And the wealth of all the surrounding nations shall be collected—gold, silver, and garments in great abundance. ¹⁵ And a plague like this plague shall fall on the horses, the mules, the camels, the donkeys, and whatever animals may be in those camps.

16 Then all who survive of the nations that have come against Jerusalem shall go up year after year to worship the King, the Lord of hosts, and to keep the festival of booths.ᵖ ¹⁷ If any of the families of the earth do not go up to Jerusalem to worship the King, the Lord of hosts, there will be no rain upon them. ¹⁸ And if the family of Egypt do not go up and present themselves, then on them shallᑫ come the plague that the Lord inflicts on the nations that do not go up to keep the festival of booths.ᵖ ¹⁹ Such shall be the punishment of Egypt and the punishment of all the nations that do not go up to keep the festival of booths.ᵖ

20 On that day there shall be inscribed on the bells of the horses, "Holy to the Lord." And the cooking pots in the house of the Lord shall be as holy asʳ the bowls in front of the altar; ²¹ and every cooking pot in Jerusalem and Judah shall be sacred to the Lord of hosts, so that all who sacrifice may come and use them to boil the flesh of the sacrifice. And there shall no longer be tradersˢ in the house of the Lord of hosts on that day.

ᶠ 14:5 for it will reach across to the city gate, literally, "for the valley of my mountain shall touch Azel"—apparently a hamlet on the eastern outskirts of Jerusalem.   ᵍ 14:5 all his saints and angels, literally, "his holy ones."   ʰ 14:6 The sun and moon and stars will no longer shine. The Hebrew is uncertain.   ⁱ 14:14 at Jerusalem, or, "against Jerusalem."   ʲ 14:16 to celebrate a time, literally, "the Feast of Tabernacles," or "Booths."   ᵏ 14:20 These Are Holy Property, literally, "Holy to the Lord."

ˡ Heb my mountains   ᵐ Meaning of Heb uncertain   ⁿ Cn: Heb there shall not be light   º Compare Gk Syr Vg Tg: Meaning of Heb uncertain   ᵖ Or tabernacles; Heb succoth   ᑫ Gk Syr: Heb shall not   ʳ Heb shall be like   ˢ Or Canaanites

Malachi

Malachi

1 THE BURDEN of the word of the LORD to Israel by Malachi.

2I have loved you, saith the LORD. Yet ye say, Wherein hast thou loved us? *Was* not Esau Jacob's brother? saith the LORD: yet I loved Jacob,

3And I hated Esau, and laid his mountains and his heritage waste for the dragons of the wilderness.

4Whereas Edom saith, We are impoverished, but we will return and build the desolate places; thus saith the LORD of hosts, They shall build, but I will throw down; and they shall call them, The border of wickedness, and, The people against whom the LORD hath indignation for ever.

5And your eyes shall see, and ye shall say, The LORD will be magnified from the border of Israel.

6¶ A son honoureth *his* father, and a servant his master: if then I *be* a father, where *is* mine honour? and if I *be* a master, where *is* my fear? saith the LORD of hosts unto you, O priests, that despise my name. And ye say, Wherein have we despised thy name?

7Ye offer polluted bread upon mine altar; and ye say, Wherein have we polluted thee? In that ye say, The table of the LORD *is* contemptible.

8And if ye offer the blind for sacrifice, *is it* not evil? and if ye offer the lame and sick, *is it* not evil? offer it now unto thy governor; will he be pleased with thee, or accept thy person? saith the LORD of hosts.

9And now, I pray you, beseech God that he will be gracious unto us: this hath been by your means: will he regard your persons? saith the LORD of hosts.

10Who *is there* even among you that would shut the doors *for nought?* neither do ye kindle *fire* on mine altar for nought. I have no pleasure in you, saith the LORD of hosts, neither will I accept an offering at your hand.

11For from the rising of the sun even unto the going down of the same my name *shall be* great among the Gentiles; and in every place incense *shall be* offered unto my name, and a pure offering: for my name *shall be* great among the heathen, saith the LORD of hosts.

12¶ But ye have profaned it, in that ye say, The table of the LORD *is* polluted; and the fruit thereof, *even* his meat, *is* contemptible.

13Ye said also, Behold, what a weariness *is it!* and ye have snuffed at it, saith the LORD of hosts; and ye brought *that which was* torn, and the lame, and the sick; thus ye brought an offering: should I accept this of your hand? saith the LORD.

1 AN ORACLE: The word of the LORD to Israel through Malachi.[a]

Jacob Loved, Esau Hated

2"I have loved you," says the LORD.

"But you ask, 'How have you loved us?'

"Was not Esau Jacob's brother?" the LORD says. "Yet I have loved Jacob, 3but Esau I have hated, and I have turned his mountains into a wasteland and left his inheritance to the desert jackals."

4Edom may say, "Though we have been crushed, we will rebuild the ruins."

But this is what the LORD Almighty says: "They may build, but I will demolish. They will be called the Wicked Land, a people always under the wrath of the LORD. 5You will see it with your own eyes and say, 'Great is the LORD—even beyond the borders of Israel!'

Blemished Sacrifices

6"A son honors his father, and a servant his master. If I am a father, where is the honor due me? If I am a master, where is the respect due me?" says the LORD Almighty. "It is you, O priests, who show contempt for my name.

"But you ask, 'How have we shown contempt for your name?'

7"You place defiled food on my altar.

"But you ask, 'How have we defiled you?'

"By saying that the LORD's table is contemptible. 8When you bring blind animals for sacrifice, is that not wrong? When you sacrifice crippled or diseased animals, is that not wrong? Try offering them to your governor! Would he be pleased with you? Would he accept you?" says the LORD Almighty.

9"Now implore God to be gracious to us. With such offerings from your hands, will he accept you?"—says the LORD Almighty.

10"Oh, that one of you would shut the temple doors, so that you would not light useless fires on my altar! I am not pleased with you," says the LORD Almighty, "and I will accept no offering from your hands. 11My name will be great among the nations, from the rising to the setting of the sun. In every place incense and pure offerings will be brought to my name, because my name will be great among the nations," says the LORD Almighty.

12"But you profane it by saying of the Lord's table, 'It is defiled,' and of its food, 'It is contemptible.' 13And you say, 'What a burden!' and you sniff at it contemptuously," says the LORD Almighty.

"When you bring injured, crippled or diseased animals and offer them as sacrifices, should I accept them from your hands?" says the LORD. 14"Cursed is the cheat

---

a *1 Malachi* means *my messenger*.

Malachi

Malachi

1 HERE IS the Lord's message to Israel, given through the prophet Malachi:

2, 3"I have loved you very deeply," says the Lord. But you retort, "Really? When was this?" And the Lord replies, "I showed my love for you by loving your father, Jacob. I didn't need to. I even rejected his very own brother, Esau, and destroyed Esau's mountains and inheritance, to give it to the jackals of the desert. 4And if his descendants should say, 'We will rebuild the ruins,' then the Lord Almighty will say, 'Try to if you like, but I will destroy it again,' for their country is named 'The Land of Wickedness' and their people are called 'Those Whom God Does Not Forgive.' "

5O Israel, lift your eyes to see what God is doing all around the world; then you will say, "Truly, the Lord's great power goes far beyond our borders!"

6"A son honors his father, a servant honors his master. I am your Father and Master, yet you don't honor me, O priests, but you despise my name."

"Who? Us?" you say. "When did we ever despise your name?"

7"When you offer polluted sacrifices on my altar."

"Polluted sacrifices? When have we ever done a thing like that?"

"Every time you say, 'Don't bother bringing anything very valuable to offer to God!' 8You tell the people, 'Lame animals are all right to offer on the altar of the Lord—yes, even the sick and the blind ones.' And you claim this isn't evil? Try it on your governor sometime—give him gifts like that—and see how pleased he is!

9" 'God have mercy on us,' you recite; 'God be gracious to us!' But when you bring that kind of gift, why should he show you any favor at all?

10"Oh, to find one priest among you who would shut the doors and refuse this kind of sacrifice. I have no pleasure in you," says the Lord Almighty, "and I will not accept your offerings.

11"But my name will be honored by the Gentiles from morning till night. All around the world they will offer sweet incense and pure offerings in honor of my name. For my name shall be great among the nations," says the Lord Almighty. 12"But you dishonor it, saying that my altar is not important, and encouraging people to bring cheap, sick animals to offer to me on it.

13"You say, 'Oh, it's too difficult to serve the Lord and do what he asks.' And you turn up your noses at the rules he has given you to obey. Think of it! Stolen animals, lame and sick—as offerings to God! Should I accept such offerings as these?" asks the Lord.

1 AN ORACLE. The word of the LORD to Israel by Malachi.b

Israel Preferred to Edom

2 I have loved you, says the LORD. But you say, "How have you loved us?" Is not Esau Jacob's brother? says the LORD. Yet I have loved Jacob 3but I have hated Esau; I have made his hill country a desolation and his heritage a desert for jackals. 4If Edom says, "We are shattered but we will rebuild the ruins," the LORD of hosts says: They may build, but I will tear down, until they are called the wicked country, the people with whom the LORD is angry forever. 5Your own eyes shall see this, and you shall say, "Great is the LORD beyond the borders of Israel!"

Corruption of the Priesthood

6 A son honors his father, and servants their master. If then I am a father, where is the honor due me? And if I am a master, where is the respect due me? says the LORD of hosts to you, O priests, who despise my name. You say, "How have we despised your name?" 7By offering polluted food on my altar. And you say, "How have we polluted it?"c By thinking that the LORD's table may be despised. 8When you offer blind animals in sacrifice, is that not wrong? And when you offer those that are lame or sick, is that not wrong? Try presenting that to your governor; will he be pleased with you or show you favor? says the LORD of hosts. 9And now implore the favor of God, that he may be gracious to us. The fault is yours. Will he show favor to any of you? says the LORD of hosts. 10Oh, that someone among you would shut the templed doors, so that you would not kindle fire on my altar in vain! I have no pleasure in you, says the LORD of hosts, and I will not accept an offering from your hands. 11For from the rising of the sun to its setting my name is great among the nations, and in every place incense is offered to my name, and a pure offering; for my name is great among the nations, says the LORD of hosts. 12But you profane it when you say that the Lord's table is polluted, and the food for ite may be despised. 13"What a weariness this is," you say, and you sniff at me,f says the LORD of hosts. You bring what has been taken by violence or is lame or sick, and this you bring as your offering! Shall I accept that from your hand? says the LORD. 14Cursed be the cheat who has a

b Or by my messenger   c Gk: Heb you   d Heb lacks temple   e Compare Syr Tg: Heb its fruit, its food   f Another reading is at it

King James

[14]But cursed *be* the deceiver, which hath in his flock a male, and voweth, and sacrificeth unto the Lord a corrupt thing: for I *am* a great King, saith the LORD of hosts, and my name *is* dreadful among the heathen.

2 AND NOW, O ye priests, this commandment *is* for you.

[2]If ye will not hear, and if ye will not lay *it* to heart, to give glory unto my name, saith the LORD of hosts, I will even send a curse upon you, and I will curse your blessings: yea, I have cursed them already, because ye do not lay *it* to heart.

[3]Behold, I will corrupt your seed, and spread dung upon your faces, *even* the dung of your solemn feasts; and *one* shall take you away with it.

[4]And ye shall know that I have sent this commandment unto you, that my covenant might be with Levi, saith the LORD of hosts.

[5]My covenant was with him of life and peace; and I gave them to him *for* the fear wherewith he feared me, and was afraid before my name.

[6]The law of truth was in his mouth, and iniquity was not found in his lips: he walked with me in peace and equity, and did turn many away from iniquity.

[7]For the priest's lips should keep knowledge, and they should seek the law at his mouth: for he *is* the messenger of the LORD of hosts.

[8]But ye are departed out of the way; ye have caused many to stumble at the law; ye have corrupted the covenant of Levi, saith the LORD of hosts.

[9]Therefore have I also made you contemptible and base before all the people, according as ye have not kept my ways, but have been partial in the law.

[10]Have we not all one father? hath not one God created us? why do we deal treacherously every man against his brother, by profaning the covenant of our fathers?

[11]¶ Judah hath dealt treacherously, and an abomination is committed in Israel and in Jerusalem; for Judah hath profaned the holiness of the LORD which he loved, and hath married the daughter of a strange god.

[12]The LORD will cut off the man that doeth this, the master and the scholar, out of the tabernacles of Jacob, and him that offereth an offering unto the LORD of hosts.

[13]And this have ye done again, covering the altar of the LORD with tears, with weeping, and with crying out, insomuch that he regardeth not the offering any more, or receiveth *it* with good will at your hand.

[14]¶ Yet ye say, Wherefore? Because the LORD hath been witness between thee and the wife of thy youth, against whom thou hast dealt treacherously: yet *is* she thy companion, and the wife of thy covenant.

[15]And did not he make one? Yet had he the residue of the spirit. And wherefore one? That he might seek a godly seed. Therefore take heed to your spirit, and let none deal treacherously against the wife of his youth.

[16]For the LORD, the God of Israel, saith that he hateth putting away: for *one* covereth violence with his garment, saith the LORD of hosts: therefore take heed to your spirit, that ye deal not treacherously.

New International

who has an acceptable male in his flock and vows to give it, but then sacrifices a blemished animal to the Lord. For I am a great king," says the LORD Almighty, "and my name is to be feared among the nations.

Admonition for the Priests

2 "AND NOW this admonition is for you, O priests. [2]If you do not listen, and if you do not set your heart to honor my name," says the LORD Almighty, "I will send a curse upon you, and I will curse your blessings. Yes, I have already cursed them, because you have not set your heart to honor me.

[3]"Because of you I will rebuke[a] your descendants[b]; I will spread on your faces the offal from your festival sacrifices, and you will be carried off with it. [4]And you will know that I have sent you this admonition so that my covenant with Levi may continue," says the LORD Almighty. [5]"My covenant was with him, a covenant of life and peace, and I gave them to him; this called for reverence and he revered me and stood in awe of my name. [6]True instruction was in his mouth and nothing false was found on his lips. He walked with me in peace and uprightness, and turned many from sin.

[7]"For the lips of a priest ought to preserve knowledge, and from his mouth men should seek instruction— because he is the messenger of the LORD Almighty. [8]But you have turned from the way and by your teaching have caused many to stumble; you have violated the covenant with Levi," says the LORD Almighty. [9]"So I have caused you to be despised and humiliated before all the people, because you have not followed my ways but have shown partiality in matters of the law."

Judah Unfaithful

[10]Have we not all one Father[c]? Did not one God create us? Why do we profane the covenant of our fathers by breaking faith with one another?

[11]Judah has broken faith. A detestable thing has been committed in Israel and in Jerusalem: Judah has desecrated the sanctuary the LORD loves, by marrying the daughter of a foreign god. [12]As for the man who does this, whoever he may be, may the LORD cut him off from the tents of Jacob[d]—even though he brings offerings to the LORD Almighty.

[13]Another thing you do: You flood the LORD's altar with tears. You weep and wail because he no longer pays attention to your offerings or accepts them with pleasure from your hands. [14]You ask, "Why?" It is because the LORD is acting as the witness between you and the wife of your youth, because you have broken faith with her, though she is your partner, the wife of your marriage covenant.

[15]Has not the LORD made them one? In flesh and spirit they are his. And why one? Because he was seeking godly offspring.[e] So guard yourself in your spirit, and do not break faith with the wife of your youth.

[16]"I hate divorce," says the LORD God of Israel, "and I hate a man's covering himself[f] with violence as well as with his garment," says the LORD Almighty.

So guard yourself in your spirit, and do not break faith.

ᵃ *3 Or cut off (see Septuagint)* ᵇ *3 Or will blight your grain* ᶜ *10 Or father* ᵈ *12 Or ¹²May the LORD cut off from the tents of Jacob anyone who gives testimony in behalf of the man who does this* ᵉ *15 Or ¹⁵But the one who is our father, did not do this, not as long as life remained in him. And what was he seeking? An offspring from God* ᶠ *16 Or his wife*

Living Bible

14"Cursed is that man who promises a fine ram from his flock, and substitutes a sick one to sacrifice to God. For I am a Great King," says the Lord Almighty, "and my name is to be mightily revered among the Gentiles."

2 LISTEN, YOU priests, to this warning from the Lord Almighty:
"If you don't change your ways and give glory to my name, then I will send terrible punishment upon you, and instead of giving you blessings as I would like to, I will turn on you with curses. Indeed, I have cursed you already because you haven't taken seriously the things that are most important to me.

3"Take note that I will rebuke your children and I will spread on your faces the manure of these animals you offer me, and throw you out like dung. 4Then at last you will know it was I who sent you this warning to return to the laws I gave your father Levi," says the Lord Almighty. 5"The purpose of these laws was to give him life and peace, to be a means of showing his respect and awe for me, by keeping them. 6He passed on to the people all the truth he got from me. He did not lie or cheat; he walked with me, living a good and righteous life, and turned many from their lives of sin.

7"Priests' lips should flow with the knowledge of God so the people will learn God's laws. The priests are the messengers of the Lord Almighty, and men should come to them for guidance. 8But not to you! For you have left God's paths. Your 'guidance' has caused many to stumble in sin. You have distorted the covenant of Levi, and made it into a grotesque parody," says the Lord Almighty. 9"Therefore I have made you contemptible in the eyes of all the people; for you have not obeyed me, but you let your favorites break the law without rebuke."

10We are children of the same father, Abraham, all created by the same God. And yet we are faithless to each other, violating the covenant of our fathers! 11In Judah, in Israel, and in Jerusalem, there is treachery, for the men of Judah have defiled God's holy and beloved Temple by marrying heathen women who worship idols. 12May the Lord cut off from his covenant every last man, whether priest or layman, who has done this thing!

13Yet you cover the altar with your tears because the Lord doesn't pay attention to your offerings anymore, and you receive no blessing from him. 14"Why has God abandoned us?" you cry. I'll tell you why; it is because the Lord has seen your treachery in divorcing your wives who have been faithful to you through the years, the companions you promised to care for and keep. 15You were united to your wife by the Lord. In God's wise plan, when you married, the two of you became one person in his sight. And what does he want? Godly children from your union. Therefore guard your passions! Keep faith with the wife of your youth.

16For the Lord, the God of Israel, says he hates divorce and cruel men. Therefore control your passions—let there be no divorcing of your wives.

New Revised Standard

male in the flock and vows to give it, and yet sacrifices to the Lord what is blemished; for I am a great King, says the LORD of hosts, and my name is reverenced among the nations.

2 AND NOW, O priests, this command is for you. 2If you will not listen, if you will not lay it to heart to give glory to my name, says the LORD of hosts, then I will send the curse on you and I will curse your blessings; indeed I have already cursed them,g because you do not lay it to heart. 3I will rebuke your offspring, and spread dung on your faces, the dung of your offerings, and I will put you out of my presence.h

4 Know, then, that I have sent this command to you, that my covenant with Levi may hold, says the LORD of hosts. 5My covenant with him was a covenant of life and well-being, which I gave him; this called for reverence, and he revered me and stood in awe of my name. 6True instruction was in his mouth, and no wrong was found on his lips. He walked with me in integrity and uprightness, and he turned many from iniquity. 7For the lips of a priest should guard knowledge, and people should seek instruction from his mouth, for he is the messenger of the LORD of hosts. 8But you have turned aside from the way; you have caused many to stumble by your instruction; you have corrupted the covenant of Levi, says the LORD of hosts, 9and so I make you despised and abased before all the people, inasmuch as you have not kept my ways but have shown partiality in your instruction.

The Covenant Profaned by Judah

10 Have we not all one father? Has not one God created us? Why then are we faithless to one another, profaning the covenant of our ancestors? 11Judah has been faithless, and abomination has been committed in Israel and in Jerusalem; for Judah has profaned the sanctuary of the LORD, which he loves, and has married the daughter of a foreign god. 12May the LORD cut off from the tents of Jacob anyone who does this—any to witnessi or answer, or to bring an offering to the LORD of hosts.

13 And this you do as well: You cover the LORD's altar with tears, with weeping and groaning because he no longer regards the offering or accepts it with favor at your hand. 14You ask, "Why does he not?" Because the LORD was a witness between you and the wife of your youth, to whom you have been faithless, though she is your companion and your wife by covenant. 15Did not one God make her?j Both flesh and spirit are his.k And what does the one Godl desire? Godly offspring. So look to yourselves, and do not let anyone be faithless to the wife of his youth. 16For I hatem divorce, says the LORD, the God of Israel, and covering one's garment with violence, says the LORD of hosts. So take heed to yourselves and do not be faithless.

---

g Heb it　h Cn Compare Gk Syr: Heb and he shall bear you to it　i Cn Compare Gk: Heb arouse　j Or Has he not made one?　k Cn: Heb and a remnant of spirit was his　l Heb he　m Cn: Heb he hates

King James

17¶ Ye have wearied the LORD with your words. Yet ye say, Wherein have we wearied *him?* When ye say, Every one that doeth evil *is* good in the sight of the LORD, and he delighteth in them; or, Where *is* the God of judgment?

3 BEHOLD, I will send my messenger, and he shall prepare the way before me: and the Lord, whom ye seek, shall suddenly come to his temple, even the messenger of the covenant, whom ye delight in: behold, he shall come, saith the LORD of hosts.

2But who may abide the day of his coming? and who shall stand when he appeareth? for he *is* like a refiner's fire, and like fullers' soap:

3And he shall sit *as* a refiner and purifier of silver: and he shall purify the sons of Levi, and purge them as gold and silver, that they may offer unto the LORD an offering in righteousness.

4Then shall the offering of Judah and Jerusalem be pleasant unto the LORD, as in the days of old, and as in former years.

5And I will come near to you to judgment; and I will be a swift witness against the sorcerers, and against the adulterers, and against false swearers, and against those that oppress the hireling in *his* wages, the widow, and the fatherless, and that turn aside the stranger *from his right,* and fear not me, saith the LORD of hosts.

6For I *am* the LORD, I change not; therefore ye sons of Jacob are not consumed.

7¶ Even from the days of your fathers ye are gone away from mine ordinances, and have not kept *them.* Return unto me, and I will return unto you, saith the LORD of hosts. But ye said, Wherein shall we return?

8¶ Will a man rob God? Yet ye have robbed me. But ye say, Wherein have we robbed thee? In tithes and offerings.

9Ye *are* cursed with a curse: for ye have robbed me, *even* this whole nation.

10Bring ye all the tithes into the storehouse, that there may be meat in mine house, and prove me now herewith, saith the LORD of hosts, if I will not open you the windows of heaven, and pour you out a blessing, that *there shall* not *be room* enough *to receive it.*

11And I will rebuke the devourer for your sakes, and he shall not destroy the fruits of your ground; neither shall your vine cast her fruit before the time in the field, saith the LORD of hosts.

12And all nations shall call you blessed: for ye shall be a delightsome land, saith the LORD of hosts.

13¶ Your words have been stout against me, saith the LORD. Yet ye say, What have we spoken *so much* against thee?

14Ye have said, It *is* vain to serve God: and what profit *is it* that we have kept his ordinance, and that we have walked mournfully before the LORD of hosts?

15And now we call the proud happy; yea, they that work wickedness are set up; yea, *they that* tempt God are even delivered.

16¶ Then they that feared the LORD spake often one to another: and the LORD hearkened, and heard *it,* and a book of remembrance was written before him for them that feared the LORD, and that thought upon his name.

17And they shall be mine, saith the LORD of hosts, in that day when I make up my jewels; and I will spare them, as a man spareth his own son that serveth him.

New International

The Day of Judgment

17You have wearied the LORD with your words.
"How have we wearied him?" you ask.
By saying, "All who do evil are good in the eyes of the LORD, and he is pleased with them" or "Where is the God of justice?"

3 "SEE, I will send my messenger, who will prepare the way before me. Then suddenly the Lord you are seeking will come to his temple; the messenger of the covenant, whom you desire, will come," says the LORD Almighty.

2But who can endure the day of his coming? Who can stand when he appears? For he will be like a refiner's fire or a launderer's soap. 3He will sit as a refiner and purifier of silver; he will purify the Levites and refine them like gold and silver. Then the LORD will have men who will bring offerings in righteousness, 4and the offerings of Judah and Jerusalem will be acceptable to the LORD, as in days gone by, as in former years.

5"So I will come near to you for judgment. I will be quick to testify against sorcerers, adulterers and perjurers, against those who defraud laborers of their wages, who oppress the widows and the fatherless, and deprive aliens of justice, but do not fear me," says the LORD Almighty.

Robbing God

6"I the LORD do not change. So you, O descendants of Jacob, are not destroyed. 7Ever since the time of your forefathers you have turned away from my decrees and have not kept them. Return to me, and I will return to you," says the LORD Almighty.
"But you ask, 'How are we to return?'
8"Will a man rob God? Yet you rob me.
"But you ask, 'How do we rob you?'
"In tithes and offerings. 9You are under a curse—the whole nation of you—because you are robbing me. 10Bring the whole tithe into the storehouse, that there may be food in my house. Test me in this," says the LORD Almighty, "and see if I will not throw open the floodgates of heaven and pour out so much blessing that you will not have room enough for it. 11I will prevent pests from devouring your crops, and the vines in your fields will not cast their fruit," says the LORD Almighty. 12"Then all the nations will call you blessed, for yours will be a delightful land," says the LORD Almighty.

13"You have said harsh things against me," says the LORD.
"Yet you ask, 'What have we said against you?'
14"You have said, 'It is futile to serve God. What did we gain by carrying out his requirements and going about like mourners before the LORD Almighty? 15But now we call the arrogant blessed. Certainly the evildoers prosper, and even those who challenge God escape.' "

16Then those who feared the LORD talked with each other, and the LORD listened and heard. A scroll of remembrance was written in his presence concerning those who feared the LORD and honored his name.

17"They will be mine," says the LORD Almighty, "in the day when I make up my treasured possession.a I will spare them, just as in compassion a man spares his son who serves him. 18And you will again see the distinction

---

a 17 Or *Almighty, "my treasured possession, in the day when I act*

Living Bible

17You have wearied the Lord with your words. "Wearied him?" you ask in fake surprise. "How have we wearied him?"

By saying that evil is good, that it pleases the Lord! Or by saying that God won't punish us—he doesn't care.

3 "LISTEN: I will send my messenger before me to prepare the way. And then the oneᵇ you are look-ing for will come suddenly to his Temple—the Messen-ger of God's promises, to bring you great joy. Yes, he is surely coming," says the Lord Almighty. 2"But who can live when he appears? Who can endure his coming? For he is like a blazing fire refining precious metal and he can bleach the dirtiest garments! 3Like a refiner of silver he will sit and closely watch as the dross is burned away. He will purify the Levites, the ministers of God, refining them like gold or silver, so that they will do their work for God with pure hearts. 4Then once more the Lord will enjoy the offerings brought to him by the people of Judah and Jerusalem, as he did before. 5At that time my punishments will be quick and certain; I will move swiftly against wicked men who trick the inno-cent, against adulterers, and liars, against all those who cheat their hired hands, or oppress widows and orphans, or defraud strangers, and do not fear me," says the Lord Almighty.

6"For I am the Lord—I do not change. That is why you are not already utterly destroyed [for my mercy endures foreverᶜ].

7"Though you have scorned my laws from earliest time, yet you may still return to me," says the Lord Almighty. "Come and I will forgive you.

"But you say, 'We have never even gone away!'

8"Will a man rob God? Surely not! And yet you have robbed me.

" 'What do you mean? When did we ever rob you?'

"You have robbed me of the tithes and offerings due to me. 9And so the awesome curse of God is cursing you, for your whole nation has been robbing me. 10Bring all the tithes into the storehouse so that there will be food enough in my Temple; if you do, I will open up the windows of heaven for you and pour out a blessing so great you won't have room enough to take it in!

"Try it! Let me prove it to you! 11Your crops will be large, for I will guard them from insects and plagues. Your grapes won't shrivel away before they ripen," says the Lord Almighty. 12"And all nations will call you blessed, for you will be a land sparkling with happiness. These are the promises of the Lord Almighty.

13"Your attitude toward me has been proud and arro-gant," says the Lord.

"But you say, 'What do you mean? What have we said that we shouldn't?'

14, 15"Listen; you have said, 'It is foolish to worship God and obey him. What good does it do to obey his laws, and to sorrow and mourn for our sins? From now on, as far as we're concerned, "Blessed are the arro-gant." For those who do evil shall prosper, and those who dare God to punish them shall get off scot-free.' "

16Then those who feared and loved the Lord spoke often of him to each other. And he had a Book of Re-membrance drawn up in which he recorded the names of those who feared him and loved to think about him.

17"They shall be mine," says the Lord Almighty, "in that day when I make up my jewels. And I will spare them as a man spares an obedient and dutiful son. 18Then

New Revised Standard

17 You have wearied the LORD with your words. Yet you say, "How have we wearied him?" By saying, "All who do evil are good in the sight of the LORD, and he delights in them." Or by asking, "Where is the God of justice?"

The Coming Messenger

3 SEE, I am sending my messenger to prepare the way before me, and the Lord whom you seek will suddenly come to his temple. The messenger of the cov-enant in whom you delight—indeed, he is coming, says the LORD of hosts. 2But who can endure the day of his coming, and who can stand when he appears?

For he is like a refiner's fire and like fullers' soap; 3he will sit as a refiner and purifier of silver, and he will purify the descendants of Levi and refine them like gold and silver, until they present offerings to the LORD in righteousness.ᵈ 4Then the offering of Judah and Jerusa-lem will be pleasing to the LORD as in the days of old and as in former years.

5 Then I will draw near to you for judgment; I will be swift to bear witness against the sorcerers, against the adulterers, against those who swear falsely, against those who oppress the hired workers in their wages, the widow and the orphan, against those who thrust aside the alien, and do not fear me, says the LORD of hosts.

6 For I the LORD do not change; therefore you, O children of Jacob, have not perished. 7Ever since the days of your ancestors you have turned aside from my statutes and have not kept them. Return to me, and I will return to you, says the LORD of hosts. But you say, "How shall we return?"

Do Not Rob God

8 Will anyone rob God? Yet you are robbing me! But you say, "How are we robbing you?" In your tithes and offerings! 9You are cursed with a curse, for you are robbing me—the whole nation of you! 10Bring the full tithe into the storehouse, so that there may be food in my house, and thus put me to the test, says the LORD of hosts; see if I will not open the windows of heaven for you and pour down for you an overflowing blessing. 11I will rebuke the locustᵉ for you, so that it will not destroy the produce of your soil; and your vine in the field shall not be barren, says the LORD of hosts. 12Then all nations will count you happy, for you will be a land of delight, says the LORD of hosts.

13 You have spoken harsh words against me, says the LORD. Yet you say, "How have we spoken against you?" 14You have said, "It is vain to serve God. What do we profit by keeping his command or by going about as mourners before the LORD of hosts? 15Now we count the arrogant happy; evildoers not only prosper, but when they put God to the test they escape."

The Reward of the Faithful

16 Then those who revered the LORD spoke with one another. The LORD took note and listened, and a book of remembrance was written before him of those who revered the LORD and thought on his name. 17They shall be mine, says the LORD of hosts, my special possession on the day when I act, and I will spare them as parents spare their children who serve them. 18Then once more

ᵇ 3:1 the one, literally, "the Lord."   ᶜ 3:6 for my mercy endures forever, implied.   ᵈ Or right offerings to the LORD   ᵉ Heb devourer

King James

18Then shall ye return, and discern between the righteous and the wicked, between him that serveth God and him that serveth him not.

4 FOR, BEHOLD, the day cometh, that shall burn as an oven; and all the proud, yea, and all that do wickedly, shall be stubble: and the day that cometh shall burn them up, saith the LORD of hosts, that it shall leave them neither root nor branch.

2¶ But unto you that fear my name shall the Sun of righteousness arise with healing in his wings; and ye shall go forth, and grow up as calves of the stall.

3And ye shall tread down the wicked; for they shall be ashes under the soles of your feet in the day that I shall do *this*, saith the LORD of hosts.

4¶ Remember ye the law of Moses my servant, which I commanded unto him in Horeb for all Israel, *with* the statutes and judgments.

5¶ Behold, I will send you Elijah the prophet before the coming of the great and dreadful day of the LORD:

6And he shall turn the heart of the fathers to the children, and the heart of the children to their fathers, lest I come and smite the earth with a curse.

New International

between the righteous and the wicked, between those who serve God and those who do not.

The Day of the LORD

4 "SURELY THE day is coming; it will burn like a furnace. All the arrogant and every evildoer will be stubble, and that day that is coming will set them on fire," says the LORD Almighty. "Not a root or a branch will be left to them. 2But for you who revere my name, the sun of righteousness will rise with healing in its wings. And you will go out and leap like calves released from the stall. 3Then you will trample down the wicked; they will be ashes under the soles of your feet on the day when I do these things," says the LORD Almighty.

4"Remember the law of my servant Moses, the decrees and laws I gave him at Horeb for all Israel.

5"See, I will send you the prophet Elijah before that great and dreadful day of the LORD comes. 6He will turn the hearts of the fathers to their children, and the hearts of the children to their fathers; or else I will come and strike the land with a curse."

Living Bible

you will see the difference between God's treatment of good men and bad, between those who serve him and those who don't.

4 "WATCH NOW," the Lord Almighty declares, "the day of judgment is coming, burning like a furnace. The proud and wicked will be burned up like straw; like a tree, they will be consumed—roots and all.

2"But for you who fear my name, the Sun of Righteousness will rise with healing in his wings. And you will go free, leaping with joy like calves let out to pasture. 3Then you will tread upon the wicked as ashes underfoot," says the Lord Almighty. 4"Remember to obey the laws I gave all Israel through Moses my servant on Mount Horeb.

5"See, I will send you another prophet like Elijaha before the coming of the great and dreadful judgment day of God. 6His preaching will bring fathers and children together again, to be of one mind and heart, for they will know that if they do not repent, I will come and utterly destroy their land."

New Revised Standard

you shall see the difference between the righteous and the wicked, between one who serves God and one who does not serve him.

The Great Day of the LORD

4b SEE, THE day is coming, burning like an oven, when all the arrogant and all evildoers will be stubble; the day that comes shall burn them up, says the LORD of hosts, so that it will leave them neither root nor branch. 2But for you who revere my name the sun of righteousness shall rise, with healing in its wings. You shall go out leaping like calves from the stall. 3And you shall tread down the wicked, for they will be ashes under the soles of your feet, on the day when I act, says the LORD of hosts.

4 Remember the teaching of my servant Moses, the statutes and ordinances that I commanded him at Horeb for all Israel.

5 Lo, I will send you the prophet Elijah before the great and terrible day of the LORD comes. 6He will turn the hearts of parents to their children and the hearts of children to their parents, so that I will not come and strike the land with a curse.c

---

a 4:5 *another prophet like Elijah*, literally, "like the prophet Elijah." Compare
Mt. 17:10-12 and Lk 1:17.   b Ch 4.1-6 are Ch 3.19-24 in Heb   c Or *a ban of utter destruction*

The New Testament

King James   *New International*

THE GOSPEL ACCORDING TO

St. Matthew   Matthew

The Genealogy of Jesus

1 THE BOOK of the generation of Jesus Christ, the son of David, the son of Abraham.

2Abraham begat Isaac; and Isaac begat Jacob; and Jacob begat Judas and his brethren;

3And Judas begat Phares and Zara of Thamar; and Phares begat Esrom; and Esrom begat Aram;

4And Aram begat Aminadab; and Aminadab begat Naasson; and Naasson begat Salmon;

5And Salmon begat Booz of Rachab; and Booz begat Obed of Ruth; and Obed begat Jesse;

6And Jesse begat David the king; and David the king begat Solomon of her *that had been the wife* of Urias;

7And Solomon begat Roboam; and Roboam begat Abia; and Abia begat Asa;

8And Asa begat Josaphat; and Josaphat begat Joram; and Joram begat Ozias;

9And Ozias begat Joatham; and Joatham begat Achaz; and Achaz begat Ezekias;

10And Ezekias begat Manasses; and Manasses begat Amon; and Amon begat Josias;

11And Josias begat Jechonias and his brethren, about the time they were carried away to Babylon:

12And after they were brought to Babylon, Jechonias begat Salathiel; and Salathiel begat Zorobabel;

13And Zorobabel begat Abiud; and Abiud begat Eliakim; and Eliakim begat Azor;

14And Azor begat Sadoc; and Sadoc begat Achim; and Achim begat Eliud;

15And Eliud begat Eleazar; and Eleazar begat Matthan; and Matthan begat Jacob;

16And Jacob begat Joseph the husband of Mary, of whom was born Jesus, who is called Christ.

17So all the generations from Abraham to David *are* fourteen generations; and from David until the carrying away into Babylon *are* fourteen generations; and from the carrying away into Babylon unto Christ *are* fourteen generations.

1 A RECORD of the genealogy of Jesus Christ the son of David, the son of Abraham:

2Abraham was the father of Isaac,
Isaac the father of Jacob,
Jacob the father of Judah and his brothers,
3Judah the father of Perez and Zerah, whose mother was Tamar,
Perez the father of Hezron,
Hezron the father of Ram,
4Ram the father of Amminadab,
Amminadab the father of Nahshon,
Nahshon the father of Salmon,
5Salmon the father of Boaz, whose mother was Rahab,
Boaz the father of Obed, whose mother was Ruth,
Obed the father of Jesse,
6and Jesse the father of King David.

David was the father of Solomon, whose mother had been Uriah's wife,
7Solomon the father of Rehoboam,
Rehoboam the father of Abijah,
Abijah the father of Asa,
8Asa the father of Jehoshaphat,
Jehoshaphat the father of Jehoram,
Jehoram the father of Uzziah,
9Uzziah the father of Jotham,
Jotham the father of Ahaz,
Ahaz the father of Hezekiah,
10Hezekiah the father of Manasseh,
Manasseh the father of Amon,
Amon the father of Josiah,
11and Josiah the father of Jeconiah[a] and his brothers at the time of the exile to Babylon.

12After the exile to Babylon:
Jeconiah was the father of Shealtiel,
Shealtiel the father of Zerubbabel,
13Zerubbabel the father of Abiud,
Abiud the father of Eliakim,
Eliakim the father of Azor,
14Azor the father of Zadok,
Zadok the father of Akim,
Akim the father of Eliud,
15Eliud the father of Eleazar,
Eleazar the father of Matthan,
Matthan the father of Jacob,
16and Jacob the father of Joseph, the husband of Mary, of whom was born Jesus, who is called Christ.

17Thus there were fourteen generations in all from Abraham to David, fourteen from David to the exile to Babylon, and fourteen from the exile to the Christ.[b]

---

a *11* That is, Jehoiachin; also in verse 12   b *17* Or *Messiah.* "The Christ" (Greek) and "the Messiah" (Hebrew) both mean "the Anointed One."

Living Bible

New Revised Standard

Matthew

Matthew

The Genealogy of Jesus the Messiah

1 THESE ARE the ancestors of Jesus Christ, a descendant of King David and of Abraham:

²Abraham was the father of Isaac; Isaac was the father of Jacob; Jacob was the father of Judah and his brothers.

³Judah was the father of Perez and Zerah (Tamar was their mother); Perez was the father of Hezron; Hezron was the father of Aram;

⁴Aram was the father of Amminadab; Amminadab was the father of Nahshon; Nahshon was the father of Salmon;

⁵Salmon was the father of Boaz (Rahab was his mother); Boaz was the father of Obed (Ruth was his mother); Obed was the father of Jesse;

⁶Jesse was the father of King David. David was the father of Solomon (his mother was the widow of Uriah);

⁷Solomon was the father of Rehoboam; Rehoboam was the father of Abijah; Abijah was the father of Asa;

⁸Asa was the father of Jehoshaphat; Jehoshaphat was the father of Joram; Joram was the father of Uzziah;

⁹Uzziah was the father of Jotham; Jotham was the father of Ahaz; Ahaz was the father of Hezekiah;

¹⁰Hezekiah was the father of Manasseh; Manasseh was the father of Amos; Amos was the father of Josiah;

¹¹Josiah was the father of Jechoniah and his brothers (born at the time of the exile to Babylon).

¹²After the exile: Jechoniah was the father of Shealtiel; Shealtiel was the father of Zerubbabel;

¹³Zerubbabel was the father of Abiud; Abiud was the father of Eliakim; Eliakim was the father of Azor;

¹⁴Azor was the father of Zadok; Zadok was the father of Achim; Achim was the father of Eliud;

¹⁵Eliud was the father of Eleazar; Eleazar was the father of Matthan; Matthan was the father of Jacob;

¹⁶Jacob was the father of Joseph (who was the husband of Mary, the mother of Jesus Christ the Messiah).

¹⁷These are fourteenᶜ of the generations from Abraham to King David; and fourteen from King David's time to the exile; and fourteen from the exile to Christ.

1 AN ACCOUNT of the genealogyᵈ of Jesus the Messiah,ᵉ the son of David, the son of Abraham.

2 Abraham was the father of Isaac, and Isaac the father of Jacob, and Jacob the father of Judah and his brothers, ³and Judah the father of Perez and Zerah by Tamar, and Perez the father of Hezron, and Hezron the father of Aram, ⁴and Aram the father of Aminadab, and Aminadab the father of Nahshon, and Nahshon the father of Salmon, ⁵and Salmon the father of Boaz by Rahab, and Boaz the father of Obed by Ruth, and Obed the father of Jesse, ⁶and Jesse the father of King David.

And David was the father of Solomon by the wife of Uriah, ⁷and Solomon the father of Rehoboam, and Rehoboam the father of Abijah, and Abijah the father of Asaph,ᶠ ⁸and Asaphᶠ the father of Jehoshaphat, and Jehoshaphat the father of Joram, and Joram the father of Uzziah, ⁹and Uzziah the father of Jotham, and Jotham the father of Ahaz, and Ahaz the father of Hezekiah, ¹⁰and Hezekiah the father of Manasseh, and Manasseh the father of Amos,ᵍ and Amosᵍ the father of Josiah, ¹¹and Josiah the father of Jechoniah and his brothers, at the time of the deportation to Babylon.

12 And after the deportation to Babylon: Jechoniah was the father of Salathiel, and Salathiel the father of Zerubbabel, ¹³and Zerubbabel the father of Abiud, and Abiud the father of Eliakim, and Eliakim the father of Azor, ¹⁴and Azor the father of Zadok, and Zadok the father of Achim, and Achim the father of Eliud, ¹⁵and Eliud the father of Eleazar, and Eleazar the father of Matthan, and Matthan the father of Jacob, ¹⁶and Jacob the father of Joseph the husband of Mary, of whom Jesus was born, who is called the Messiah.ʰ

17 So all the generations from Abraham to David are fourteen generations; and from David to the deportation to Babylon, fourteen generations; and from the deportation to Babylon to the Messiah,ʰ fourteen generations.

ᶜ *1:17 These are fourteen,* literally, "So all the generations from Abraham unto David are fourteen."

ᵈ Or *birth*   ᵉ Or *Jesus Christ*   ᶠ Other ancient authorities read *Asa*   ᵍ Other ancient authorities read *Amon*   ʰ Or *the Christ*

King James

18¶ Now the birth of Jesus Christ was on this wise: When as his mother Mary was espoused to Joseph, before they came together, she was found with child of the Holy Ghost.

19Then Joseph her husband, being a just *man*, and not willing to make her a public example, was minded to put her away privily.

20But while he thought on these things, behold, the angel of the Lord appeared unto him in a dream, saying, Joseph, thou son of David, fear not to take unto thee Mary thy wife: for that which is conceived in her is of the Holy Ghost.

21And she shall bring forth a son, and thou shalt call his name JESUS: for he shall save his people from their sins.

22Now all this was done, that it might be fulfilled which was spoken of the Lord by the prophet, saying,

23Behold, a virgin shall be with child, and shall bring forth a son, and they shall call his name Emmanuel, which being interpreted is, God with us.

24Then Joseph being raised from sleep did as the angel of the Lord had bidden him, and took unto him his wife:

25And knew her not till she had brought forth her firstborn son: and he called his name JESUS.

2 NOW WHEN Jesus was born in Bethlehem of Judaea in the days of Herod the king, behold, there came wise men from the east to Jerusalem,

2Saying, Where is he that is born King of the Jews? for we have seen his star in the east, and are come to worship him.

3When Herod the king had heard *these things*, he was troubled, and all Jerusalem with him.

4And when he had gathered all the chief priests and scribes of the people together, he demanded of them where Christ should be born.

5And they said unto him, In Bethlehem of Judaea: for thus it is written by the prophet,

6And thou Bethlehem, *in* the land of Juda, art not the least among the princes of Juda: for out of thee shall come a Governor, that shall rule my people Israel.

7Then Herod, when he had privily called the wise men, inquired of them diligently what time the star appeared.

8And he sent them to Bethlehem, and said, Go and search diligently for the young child; and when ye have found *him*, bring me word again, that I may come and worship him also.

9When they had heard the king, they departed; and, lo, the star, which they saw in the east, went before them, till it came and stood over where the young child was.

10When they saw the star, they rejoiced with exceeding great joy.

11¶ And when they were come into the house, they saw the young child with Mary his mother, and fell down, and worshipped him: and when they had opened their treasures, they presented unto him gifts; gold, and frankincense, and myrrh.

12And being warned of God in a dream that they should not return to Herod, they departed into their own country another way.

13And when they were departed, behold, the angel of the Lord appeareth to Joseph in a dream, saying, Arise, and take the young child and his mother, and flee into Egypt, and be thou there until I bring thee word: for Herod will seek the young child to destroy him.

14When he arose, he took the young child and his mother by night, and departed into Egypt:

New International

The Birth of Jesus Christ

18This is how the birth of Jesus Christ came about: His mother Mary was pledged to be married to Joseph, but before they came together, she was found to be with child through the Holy Spirit. 19Because Joseph her husband was a righteous man and did not want to expose her to public disgrace, he had in mind to divorce her quietly.

20But after he had considered this, an angel of the Lord appeared to him in a dream and said, "Joseph son of David, do not be afraid to take Mary home as your wife, because what is conceived in her is from the Holy Spirit. 21She will give birth to a son, and you are to give him the name Jesus,a because he will save his people from their sins."

22All this took place to fulfill what the Lord had said through the prophet: 23"The virgin will be with child and will give birth to a son, and they will call him Immanuel"b—which means, "God with us."

24When Joseph woke up, he did what the angel of the Lord had commanded him and took Mary home as his wife. 25But he had no union with her until she gave birth to a son. And he gave him the name Jesus.

The Visit of the Magi

2 AFTER JESUS was born in Bethlehem in Judea, during the time of King Herod, Magic from the east came to Jerusalem 2and asked, "Where is the one who has been born king of the Jews? We saw his star in the eastd and have come to worship him."

3When King Herod heard this he was disturbed, and all Jerusalem with him. 4When he had called together all the people's chief priests and teachers of the law, he asked them where the Christe was to be born. 5"In Bethlehem in Judea," they replied, "for this is what the prophet has written:

6" 'But you, Bethlehem, in the land of Judah,
   are by no means least among the rulers of
      Judah;
   for out of you will come a ruler
      who will be the shepherd of my people
         Israel.'f"

7Then Herod called the Magi secretly and found out from them the exact time the star had appeared. 8He sent them to Bethlehem and said, "Go and make a careful search for the child. As soon as you find him, report to me, so that I too may go and worship him."

9After they had heard the king, they went on their way, and the star they had seen in the eastg went ahead of them until it stopped over the place where the child was. 10When they saw the star, they were overjoyed. 11On coming to the house, they saw the child with his mother Mary, and they bowed down and worshiped him. Then they opened their treasures and presented him with gifts of gold and of incense and of myrrh. 12And having been warned in a dream not to go back to Herod, they returned to their country by another route.

The Escape to Egypt

13When they had gone, an angel of the Lord appeared to Joseph in a dream. "Get up," he said, "take the child and his mother and escape to Egypt. Stay there until I tell you, for Herod is going to search for the child to kill him."

14So he got up, took the child and his mother during the night and left for Egypt, 15where he stayed until the

---

a *21 Jesus* is the Greek form of *Joshua*, which means *the LORD saves.*
b *23* Isaiah 7:14   c *1* Traditionally *Wise Men*   d *2* Or *star when it rose*
e *4* Or *Messiah*   f *6* Micah 5:2   g *9* Or *seen when it rose*

Living Bible

18These are the facts concerning the birth of Jesus Christ: His mother, Mary, was engaged to be married to Joseph. But while she was still a virgin she became pregnant by the Holy Spirit. 19Then Joseph, her fiancé,h being a man of stern principle,i decided to break the engagement but to do it quietly, as he didn't want to publicly disgrace her.

20As he lay awakej considering this, he fell into a dream, and saw an angel standing beside him. "Joseph, son of David," the angel said, "don't hesitate to take Mary as your wife! For the child within her has been conceived by the Holy Spirit. 21And she will have a Son, and you shall name him Jesus (meaning 'Savior'), for he will save his people from their sins. 22This will fulfill God's message through his prophets—

23'Listen! The virgin shall conceive a child! She shall give birth to a Son, and he shall be called "Emmanuel" (meaning "God is with us").' "

24When Joseph awoke, he did as the angel commanded, and brought Mary home to be his wife, 25but she remained a virgin until her Son was born; and Joseph named him "Jesus."

2 JESUS WAS born in the town of Bethlehem, in Judea, during the reign of King Herod.

At about that time some astrologers from eastern lands arrived in Jerusalem, asking, 2"Where is the new-born King of the Jews? for we have seen his star in far-off eastern lands, and have come to worship him."

3King Herod was deeply disturbed by their question, and all Jerusalem was filled with rumors.k 4He called a meeting of the Jewish religious leaders.

"Did the prophets tell us where the Messiah would be born?" he asked.

5"Yes, in Bethlehem," they said, "for this is what the prophet Micahl wrote:

6'O little town of Bethlehem, you are not just an unimportant Judean village, for a Governor shall rise from you to rule my people Israel.' "

7Then Herod sent a private message to the astrologers, asking them to come to see him; at this meeting he found out from them the exact time when they first saw the star. Then he told them, 8"Go to Bethlehem and search for the child. And when you find him, come back and tell me so that I can go and worship him too!"

9After this interview the astrologers started out again. And look! The star appeared to them again, standing over Bethlehem.m 10Their joy knew no bounds!

11Entering the house where the baby and Mary his mother were, they threw themselves down before him, worshiping. Then they opened their presents and gave him gold, frankincense and myrrh. 12But when they returned to their own land, they didn't go through Jerusalem to report to Herod, for God had warned them in a dream to go home another way.

13After they were gone, an angel of the Lord appeared to Joseph in a dream. "Get up and flee to Egypt with the baby and his mother," the angel said, "and stay there until I tell you to return, for King Herod is going to try to kill the child." 14That samen night he left for Egypt with Mary and the baby, 15and stayed there until King

New Revised Standard

The Birth of Jesus the Messiah

18 Now the birth of Jesus the Messiaho took place in this way. When his mother Mary had been engaged to Joseph, but before they lived together, she was found to be with child from the Holy Spirit. 19Her husband Joseph, being a righteous man and unwilling to expose her to public disgrace, planned to dismiss her quietly. 20But just when he had resolved to do this, an angel of the Lord appeared to him in a dream and said, "Joseph, son of David, do not be afraid to take Mary as your wife, for the child conceived in her is from the Holy Spirit. 21She will bear a son, and you are to name him Jesus, for he will save his people from their sins." 22All this took place to fulfill what had been spoken by the Lord through the prophet:

23   "Look, the virgin shall conceive and bear a
        son,
    and they shall name him Emmanuel,"

which means, "God is with us." 24When Joseph awoke from sleep, he did as the angel of the Lord commanded him; he took her as his wife, 25but had no marital relations with her until she had borne a son;p and he named him Jesus.

The Visit of the Wise Men

2 IN THE time of King Herod, after Jesus was born in Bethlehem of Judea, wise menq from the East came to Jerusalem, 2asking, "Where is the child who has been born king of the Jews? For we observed his star at its rising,r and have come to pay him homage." 3When King Herod heard this, he was frightened, and all Jerusalem with him; 4and calling together all the chief priests and scribes of the people, he inquired of them where the Messiahs was to be born. 5They told him, "In Bethlehem of Judea; for so it has been written by the prophet:

6   'And you, Bethlehem, in the land of Judah,
        are by no means least among the rulers of
        Judah;
    for from you shall come a ruler
        who is to shepherdt my people Israel.' "

7 Then Herod secretly called for the wise menq and learned from them the exact time when the star had appeared. 8Then he sent them to Bethlehem, saying, "Go and search diligently for the child; and when you have found him, bring me word so that I may also go and pay him homage." 9When they had heard the king, they set out; and there, ahead of them, went the star that they had seen at its rising,r until it stopped over the place where the child was. 10When they saw that the star had stopped,u they were overwhelmed with joy. 11On entering the house, they saw the child with Mary his mother; and they knelt down and paid him homage. Then, opening their treasure chests, they offered him gifts of gold, frankincense, and myrrh. 12And having been warned in a dream not to return to Herod, they left for their own country by another road.

The Escape to Egypt

13 Now after they had left, an angel of the Lord appeared to Joseph in a dream and said, "Get up, take the child and his mother, and flee to Egypt, and remain there until I tell you; for Herod is about to search for the child, to destroy him." 14Then Josephv got up, took the child and his mother by night, and went to Egypt, 15and

---

h 1:19 her fiancé, literally, "her husband." i 1:19 a man of stern principle, literally, "a just man." j 1:20 As he lay awake, implied in remainder of verse. k 2:3 and all Jerusalem was filled with rumors, literally, "and all Jerusalem with him." l 2:5 Micah, implied. Micah 5:2. m 2:9 standing over Bethlehem, literally, "went before them until it came and stood over where the baby lay." n 2:14 same, implied.

o Or Jesus Christ p Other ancient authorities read her firstborn son q Or astrologers; Gk magi r Or in the East s Or the Christ t Or rule u Gk saw the star v Gk he

King James

15And was there until the death of Herod: that it might be fulfilled which was spoken of the Lord by the prophet, saying, Out of Egypt have I called my son.

16¶ Then Herod, when he saw that he was mocked of the wise men, was exceeding wroth, and sent forth, and slew all the children that were in Bethlehem, and in all the coasts thereof, from two years old and under, according to the time which he had diligently inquired of the wise men.

17Then was fulfilled that which was spoken by Jeremy the prophet, saying,

18In Rama was there a voice heard, lamentation, and weeping, and great mourning, Rachel weeping *for* her children, and would not be comforted, because they are not.

19¶ But when Herod was dead, behold, an angel of the Lord appeareth in a dream to Joseph in Egypt,

20Saying, Arise, and take the young child and his mother, and go into the land of Israel: for they are dead which sought the young child's life.

21And he arose, and took the young child and his mother, and came into the land of Israel.

22But when he heard that Archelaus did reign in Judaea in the room of his father Herod, he was afraid to go thither: notwithstanding, being warned of God in a dream, he turned aside into the parts of Galilee:

23And he came and dwelt in a city called Nazareth: that it might be fulfilled which was spoken by the prophets, He shall be called a Nazarene.

3 IN THOSE days came John the Baptist, preaching in the wilderness of Judaea,

2And saying, Repent ye: for the kingdom of heaven is at hand.

3For this is he that was spoken of by the prophet Esaias, saying, The voice of one crying in the wilderness, Prepare ye the way of the Lord, make his paths straight.

4And the same John had his raiment of camel's hair, and a leathern girdle about his loins; and his meat was locusts and wild honey.

5Then went out to him Jerusalem, and all Judaea, and all the region round about Jordan,

6And were baptized of him in Jordan, confessing their sins.

7¶ But when he saw many of the Pharisees and Sadducees come to his baptism, he said unto them, O generation of vipers, who hath warned you to flee from the wrath to come?

8Bring forth therefore fruits meet for repentance:

9And think not to say within yourselves, We have Abraham to *our* father: for I say unto you, that God is able of these stones to raise up children unto Abraham.

10And now also the axe is laid unto the root of the trees: therefore every tree which bringeth not forth good fruit is hewn down, and cast into the fire.

New International

death of Herod. And so was fulfilled what the Lord had said through the prophet: "Out of Egypt I called my son."a

16When Herod realized that he had been outwitted by the Magi, he was furious, and he gave orders to kill all the boys in Bethlehem and its vicinity who were two years old and under, in accordance with the time he had learned from the Magi. 17Then what was said through the prophet Jeremiah was fulfilled:

18"A voice is heard in Ramah,
    weeping and great mourning,
Rachel weeping for her children
    and refusing to be comforted,
because they are no more."b

The Return to Nazareth

19After Herod died, an angel of the Lord appeared in a dream to Joseph in Egypt 20and said, "Get up, take the child and his mother and go to the land of Israel, for those who were trying to take the child's life are dead."

21So he got up, took the child and his mother and went to the land of Israel. 22But when he heard that Archelaus was reigning in Judea in place of his father Herod, he was afraid to go there. Having been warned in a dream, he withdrew to the district of Galilee, 23and he went and lived in a town called Nazareth. So was fulfilled what was said through the prophets: "He will be called a Nazarene."

John the Baptist Prepares the Way

3 IN THOSE days John the Baptist came, preaching in the Desert of Judea 2and saying, "Repent, for the kingdom of heaven is near." 3This is he who was spoken of through the prophet Isaiah:

"A voice of one calling in the desert,
'Prepare the way for the Lord,
    make straight paths for him.' "c

4John's clothes were made of camel's hair, and he had a leather belt around his waist. His food was locusts and wild honey. 5People went out to him from Jerusalem and all Judea and the whole region of the Jordan. 6Confessing their sins, they were baptized by him in the Jordan River.

7But when he saw many of the Pharisees and Sadducees coming to where he was baptizing, he said to them: "You brood of vipers! Who warned you to flee from the coming wrath? 8Produce fruit in keeping with repentance. 9And do not think you can say to yourselves, 'We have Abraham as our father.' I tell you that out of these stones God can raise up children for Abraham. 10The ax is already at the root of the trees, and every tree that does not produce good fruit will be cut down and thrown into the fire.

Living Bible

Herod's death. This fulfilled the prophet's prediction, "I have called my Son from Egypt."[d]

16Herod was furious when he learned that the astrologers had disobeyed him. Sending soldiers to Bethlehem, he ordered them to kill every baby boy two years old and under, both in the town and on the nearby farms, for the astrologers had told him the star first appeared to them two years before. 17This brutal action of Herod's fulfilled the prophecy of Jeremiah:

18"Screams of anguish come from Ramah,[e]
Weeping unrestrained;
Rachel weeping for her children,
Uncomforted—
For they are dead."

19When Herod died, an angel of the Lord appeared in a dream to Joseph in Egypt, and told him, 20"Get up and take the baby and his mother back to Israel, for those who were trying to kill the child are dead."

21So he returned immediately to Israel with Jesus and his mother. 22But on the way he was frightened to learn that the new king was Herod's son, Archelaus. Then, in another dream, he was warned not to go to Judea, so they went to Galilee instead, 23and lived in Nazareth. This fulfilled the prediction of the prophets concerning the Messiah,

"He shall be called a Nazarene."

3 WHILE THEY were living in Nazareth,[f] John the Baptist began preaching out in the Judean wilderness. His constant theme was, 2"Turn from your sins . . . turn to God . . . for the Kingdom of Heaven is coming soon."[g] 3Isaiah the prophet had told about John's ministry centuries before! He had written,

"I hear[h] a shout from the wilderness, 'Prepare a road for the Lord—straighten out the path where he will walk.' "

4John's clothing was woven from camel's hair and he wore a leather belt; his food was locusts and wild honey. 5People from Jerusalem and from all over the Jordan Valley, and, in fact, from every section of Judea went out to the wilderness to hear him preach, 6and when they confessed their sins, he baptized them in the Jordan River.

7But when he saw many Pharisees[i] and Sadducees[j] coming to be baptized, he denounced them.

"You sons of snakes!" he warned. "Who said that you could escape the coming wrath of God? 8Before being baptized, prove that you have turned from sin by doing worthy deeds. 9Don't try to get by as you are, thinking, 'We are safe for we are Jews—descendants of Abraham.' That proves nothing. God can change these stones here into Jews![k]

10"And even now the axe of God's judgment is poised to chop down every unproductive tree. They will be chopped and burned.

New Revised Standard

remained there until the death of Herod. This was to fulfill what had been spoken by the Lord through the prophet, "Out of Egypt I have called my son."

The Massacre of the Infants

16 When Herod saw that he had been tricked by the wise men,[l] he was infuriated, and he sent and killed all the children in and around Bethlehem who were two years old or under, according to the time that he had learned from the wise men.[l] 17Then was fulfilled what had been spoken through the prophet Jeremiah:

18 "A voice was heard in Ramah,
    wailing and loud lamentation,
Rachel weeping for her children;
    she refused to be consoled, because they are
    no more."

The Return from Egypt

19 When Herod died, an angel of the Lord suddenly appeared in a dream to Joseph in Egypt and said, 20"Get up, take the child and his mother, and go to the land of Israel, for those who were seeking the child's life are dead." 21Then Joseph[m] got up, took the child and his mother, and went to the land of Israel. 22But when he heard that Archelaus was ruling over Judea in place of his father Herod, he was afraid to go there. And after being warned in a dream, he went away to the district of Galilee. 23There he made his home in a town called Nazareth, so that what had been spoken through the prophets might be fulfilled, "He will be called a Nazorean."

The Proclamation of John the Baptist

3 IN THOSE days John the Baptist appeared in the wilderness of Judea, proclaiming, 2"Repent, for the kingdom of heaven has come near."[n] 3This is the one of whom the prophet Isaiah spoke when he said,

"The voice of one crying out in
    the wilderness:
'Prepare the way of the Lord,
    make his paths straight.' "

4Now John wore clothing of camel's hair with a leather belt around his waist, and his food was locusts and wild honey. 5Then the people of Jerusalem and all Judea were going out to him, and all the region along the Jordan, 6and they were baptized by him in the river Jordan, confessing their sins.

7 But when he saw many Pharisees and Sadducees coming for baptism, he said to them, "You brood of vipers! Who warned you to flee from the wrath to come? 8Bear fruit worthy of repentance. 9Do not presume to say to yourselves, 'We have Abraham as our ancestor'; for I tell you, God is able from these stones to raise up children to Abraham. 10Even now the ax is lying at the root of the trees; every tree therefore that does not bear good fruit is cut down and thrown into the fire.

---

[d] 2:15 Hosea 11:1.   [e] 2:18 Ramah, or, "the region of Ramah."
[f] 3:1 While they were living in Nazareth, literally, "in those days."   [g] 3:2 is coming soon, or, "has arrived." Literally, "is at hand."   [h] 3:3 I hear, implied. Isa 40:3.   [i] 3:7 Pharisees, Jewish religious leaders who strictly followed the letter of the law but often violated its intent.   [j] 3:7 Sadducees, Jewish political leaders.   [k] 3:9 God can change these stones here into Jews, literally, "God is able of these stones to raise up children unto Abraham."

[l] Or astrologers; Gk magi   [m] Gk he   [n] Or is at hand

King James

11I indeed baptize you with water unto repentance: but he that cometh after me is mightier than I, whose shoes I am not worthy to bear: he shall baptize you with the Holy Ghost, and *with* fire:

12Whose fan *is* in his hand, and he will thoroughly purge his floor, and gather his wheat into the garner; but he will burn up the chaff with unquenchable fire.

13¶ Then cometh Jesus from Galilee to Jordan unto John, to be baptized of him.

14But John forbad him, saying, I have need to be baptized of thee, and comest thou to me?

15And Jesus answering said unto him, Suffer *it to be so* now: for thus it becometh us to fulfil all righteousness. Then he suffered him.

16And Jesus, when he was baptized, went up straightway out of the water: and, lo, the heavens were opened unto him, and he saw the Spirit of God descending like a dove, and lighting upon him:

17And lo a voice from heaven, saying, This is my beloved Son, in whom I am well pleased.

4 THEN WAS Jesus led up of the Spirit into the wilderness to be tempted of the devil.

2And when he had fasted forty days and forty nights, he was afterward an hungered.

3And when the tempter came to him, he said, If thou be the Son of God, command that these stones be made bread.

4But he answered and said, It is written, Man shall not live by bread alone, but by every word that proceedeth out of the mouth of God.

5Then the devil taketh him up into the holy city, and setteth him on a pinnacle of the temple,

6And saith unto him, If thou be the Son of God, cast thyself down: for it is written, He shall give his angels charge concerning thee: and in *their* hands they shall bear thee up, lest at any time thou dash thy foot against a stone.

7Jesus said unto him, It is written again, Thou shalt not tempt the Lord thy God.

8Again, the devil taketh him up into an exceeding high mountain, and showeth him all the kingdoms of the world, and the glory of them;

9And saith unto him, All these things will I give thee, if thou wilt fall down and worship me.

10Then saith Jesus unto him, Get thee hence, Satan: for it is written, Thou shalt worship the Lord thy God, and him only shalt thou serve.

11Then the devil leaveth him, and, behold, angels came and ministered unto him.

12¶ Now when Jesus had heard that John was cast into prison, he departed into Galilee;

13And leaving Nazareth, he came and dwelt in Capernaum, which is upon the sea coast, in the borders of Zabulon and Nephthalim:

14That it might be fulfilled which was spoken by Esaias the prophet, saying,

15The land of Zabulon, and the land of Nephthalim, *by* the way of the sea, beyond Jordan, Galilee of the Gentiles;

16The people which sat in darkness saw great light; and to them which sat in the region and shadow of death light is sprung up.

17¶ From that time Jesus began to preach, and to say, Repent: for the kingdom of heaven is at hand.

New International

11"I baptize you with[a] water for repentance. But after me will come one who is more powerful than I, whose sandals I am not fit to carry. He will baptize you with the Holy Spirit and with fire. 12His winnowing fork is in his hand, and he will clear his threshing floor, gathering his wheat into the barn and burning up the chaff with unquenchable fire."

The Baptism of Jesus

13Then Jesus came from Galilee to the Jordan to be baptized by John. 14But John tried to deter him, saying, "I need to be baptized by you, and do you come to me?"

15Jesus replied, "Let it be so now; it is proper for us to do this to fulfill all righteousness." Then John consented.

16As soon as Jesus was baptized, he went up out of the water. At that moment heaven was opened, and he saw the Spirit of God descending like a dove and lighting on him. 17And a voice from heaven said, "This is my Son, whom I love; with him I am well pleased."

The Temptation of Jesus

4 THEN JESUS was led by the Spirit into the desert to be tempted by the devil. 2After fasting forty days and forty nights, he was hungry. 3The tempter came to him and said, "If you are the Son of God, tell these stones to become bread."

4Jesus answered, "It is written: 'Man does not live on bread alone, but on every word that comes from the mouth of God.'[b]"

5Then the devil took him to the holy city and had him stand on the highest point of the temple. 6"If you are the Son of God," he said, "throw yourself down. For it is written:

" 'He will command his angels concerning you,
    and they will lift you up in their hands,
so that you will not strike your foot against a
    stone.'[c]"

7Jesus answered him, "It is also written: 'Do not put the Lord your God to the test.'[d]"

8Again, the devil took him to a very high mountain and showed him all the kingdoms of the world and their splendor. 9"All this I will give you," he said, "if you will bow down and worship me."

10Jesus said to him, "Away from me, Satan! For it is written: 'Worship the Lord your God, and serve him only.'[e]"

11Then the devil left him, and angels came and attended him.

Jesus Begins to Preach

12When Jesus heard that John had been put in prison, he returned to Galilee. 13Leaving Nazareth, he went and lived in Capernaum, which was by the lake in the area of Zebulun and Naphtali— 14to fulfill what was said through the prophet Isaiah:

15"Land of Zebulun and land of Naphtali,
    the way to the sea, along the Jordan,
    Galilee of the Gentiles—
16the people living in darkness
    have seen a great light;
on those living in the land of the shadow of
    death
    a light has dawned."[f]

17From that time on Jesus began to preach, "Repent, for the kingdom of heaven is near."

[a] *11* Or *in* [b] *4* Deut. 8:3 [c] *6* Psalm 91:11,12 [d] *7* Deut. 6:16
[e] *10* Deut. 6:13 [f] *16* Isaiah 9:1,2

Living Bible

11"With water⁸ I baptize those who repent of their sins; but someone else is coming, far greater than I am, so great that I am not worthy to carry his shoes! He shall baptize you with the Holy Spirit⁸ and with fire. 12He will separate the chaff from the grain, burning the chaff with never-ending fire, and storing away the grain."

13Then Jesus went from Galilee to the Jordan River to be baptized there by John. 14John didn't want to do it.

"This isn't proper," he said. "I am the one who needs to be baptized by you."

15But Jesus said, "Please do it, for I must do all that is right."ʰ So then John baptized him.

16After his baptism, as soon as Jesus came up out of the water, the heavens were opened to him and he saw the Spirit of God coming down in the form of a dove. 17And a voice from heaven said, "This is my beloved Son, and I am wonderfully pleased with him."

4 THEN JESUS was led out into the wilderness by the Holy Spirit, to be tempted there by Satan. 2For forty days and forty nights he ate nothing and became very hungry. 3Then Satan tempted him to get food by changing stones into loaves of bread.

"It will prove you are the Son of God," he said.

4But Jesus told him, "No! For the Scriptures tell us that bread won't feed men's souls: obedience to every word of God is what we need."

5Then Satan took him to Jerusalem to the roof of the Temple. 6"Jump off," he said, "and prove you are the Son of God; for the Scriptures declare, 'God will send his angels to keep you from harm,' . . . they will prevent you from smashing on the rocks below."

7Jesus retorted, "It also says not to put the Lord your God to a foolish test!"

8Next Satan took him to the peak of a very high mountain and showed him the nations of the world and all their glory. 9"I'll give it all to you," he said, "if you will only kneel and worship me."

10"Get out of here, Satan," Jesus told him. "The Scriptures say, 'Worship only the Lord God. Obey only him.'"

11Then Satan went away, and angels came and cared for Jesus.

12, 13When Jesus heard that John had been arrested, he left Judea and returned homeⁱ to Nazareth in Galilee; but soon he moved to Capernaum, beside the Lake of Galilee, close to Zebulun and Naphtali. 14This fulfilled Isaiah's prophecy:

15, 16"The land of Zebulun and the land of Naphtali, beside the Lake, and the countryside beyond the Jordan River, and Upper Galilee where so many foreigners live—there the people who sat in darkness have seen a great Light; they sat in the land of death, and the Light broke through upon them."ʲ

17From then on, Jesus began to preach, "Turn from sin, and turn to God, for the Kingdom of Heaven is near."ᵏ

New Revised Standard

11 "I baptize you withˡ water for repentance, but one who is more powerful than I is coming after me; I am not worthy to carry his sandals. He will baptize you withˡ the Holy Spirit and fire. 12His winnowing fork is in his hand, and he will clear his threshing floor and will gather his wheat into the granary; but the chaff he will burn with unquenchable fire."

The Baptism of Jesus

13 Then Jesus came from Galilee to John at the Jordan, to be baptized by him. 14John would have prevented him, saying, "I need to be baptized by you, and do you come to me?" 15But Jesus answered him, "Let it be so now; for it is proper for us in this way to fulfill all righteousness." Then he consented. 16And when Jesus had been baptized, just as he came up from the water, suddenly the heavens were opened to him and he saw the Spirit of God descending like a dove and alighting on him. 17And a voice from heaven said, "This is my Son, the Beloved,ᵐ with whom I am well pleased."

The Temptation of Jesus

4 THEN JESUS was led up by the Spirit into the wilderness to be tempted by the devil. 2He fasted forty days and forty nights, and afterwards he was famished. 3The tempter came and said to him, "If you are the Son of God, command these stones to become loaves of bread." 4But he answered, "It is written,

'One does not live by bread alone,
    but by every word that comes from the
        mouth of God.'"

5 Then the devil took him to the holy city and placed him on the pinnacle of the temple, 6saying to him, "If you are the Son of God, throw yourself down; for it is written,

'He will command his angels concerning you,'
    and 'On their hands they will bear you up,
so that you will not dash your foot against a
        stone.'"

7Jesus said to him, "Again it is written, 'Do not put the Lord your God to the test.'"

8 Again, the devil took him to a very high mountain and showed him all the kingdoms of the world and their splendor; 9and he said to him, "All these I will give you, if you will fall down and worship me." 10Jesus said to him, "Away with you, Satan! for it is written,

'Worship the Lord your God,
    and serve only him.'"

11Then the devil left him, and suddenly angels came and waited on him.

Jesus Begins His Ministry in Galilee

12 Now when Jesusⁿ heard that John had been arrested, he withdrew to Galilee. 13He left Nazareth and made his home in Capernaum by the sea, in the territory of Zebulun and Naphtali, 14so that what had been spoken through the prophet Isaiah might be fulfilled:

15 "Land of Zebulun, land of Naphtali,
    on the road by the sea, across the Jordan,
        Galilee of the Gentiles—
16 the people who sat in darkness
    have seen a great light,
    and for those who sat in the region and
        shadow of death
    light has dawned."

17From that time Jesus began to proclaim, "Repent, for the kingdom of heaven has come near."ᵒ

ᵍ 3:11 With water . . . with the Holy Spirit, or, "in water," and "in the Holy Spirit and in fire." ʰ 3:15 do all that is right, literally, "fulfill all righteousness." ⁱ 4:12, 13 returned home, implied. ʲ 4:15, 16 broke through upon them, Isa 9:1, 2. ᵏ 4:17 is near, or, "is at hand," or, "has arrived."

ˡ Or in   ᵐ Or my beloved Son   ⁿ Gk he   ᵒ Or is at hand

King James

18¶ And Jesus, walking by the sea of Galilee, saw two brethren, Simon called Peter, and Andrew his brother, casting a net into the sea: for they were fishers.

19And he saith unto them, Follow me, and I will make you fishers of men.

20And they straightway left *their* nets, and followed him.

21And going on from thence, he saw other two brethren, James *the son* of Zebedee, and John his brother, in a ship with Zebedee their father, mending their nets; and he called them.

22And they immediately left the ship and their father, and followed him.

23¶ And Jesus went about all Galilee, teaching in their synagogues, and preaching the gospel of the kingdom, and healing all manner of sickness and all manner of disease among the people.

24And his fame went throughout all Syria: and they brought unto him all sick people that were taken with divers diseases and torments, and those which were possessed with devils, and those which were lunatic, and those that had the palsy; and he healed them.

25And there followed him great multitudes of people from Galilee, and *from* Decapolis, and *from* Jerusalem, and *from* Judaea, and *from* beyond Jordan.

5 AND SEEING the multitudes, he went up into a mountain: and when he was set, his disciples came unto him:

2And he opened his mouth, and taught them, saying,

3Blessed *are* the poor in spirit: for theirs is the kingdom of heaven.

4Blessed *are* they that mourn: for they shall be comforted.

5Blessed *are* the meek: for they shall inherit the earth.

6Blessed *are* they which do hunger and thirst after righteousness: for they shall be filled.

7Blessed *are* the merciful: for they shall obtain mercy.

8Blessed *are* the pure in heart: for they shall see God.

9Blessed *are* the peacemakers: for they shall be called the children of God.

10Blessed *are* they which are persecuted for righteousness' sake: for theirs is the kingdom of heaven.

11Blessed are ye, when *men* shall revile you, and persecute *you,* and shall say all manner of evil against you falsely, for my sake.

12Rejoice, and be exceeding glad: for great *is* your reward in heaven: for so persecuted they the prophets which were before you.

13¶ Ye are the salt of the earth: but if the salt have lost his savour, wherewith shall it be salted? it is thenceforth good for nothing, but to be cast out, and to be trodden under foot of men.

14Ye are the light of the world. A city that is set on an hill cannot be hid.

15Neither do men light a candle, and put it under a bushel, but on a candlestick; and it giveth light unto all that are in the house.

16Let your light so shine before men, that they may see your good works, and glorify your Father which is in heaven.

New International

The Calling of the First Disciples

18As Jesus was walking beside the Sea of Galilee, he saw two brothers, Simon called Peter and his brother Andrew. They were casting a net into the lake, for they were fishermen. 19"Come, follow me," Jesus said, "and I will make you fishers of men." 20At once they left their nets and followed him.

21Going on from there, he saw two other brothers, James son of Zebedee and his brother John. They were in a boat with their father Zebedee, preparing their nets. Jesus called them, 22and immediately they left the boat and their father and followed him.

Jesus Heals the Sick

23Jesus went throughout Galilee, teaching in their synagogues, preaching the good news of the kingdom, and healing every disease and sickness among the people. 24News about him spread all over Syria, and people brought to him all who were ill with various diseases, those suffering severe pain, the demon-possessed, those having seizures, and the paralyzed, and he healed them. 25Large crowds from Galilee, the Decapolis,a Jerusalem, Judea and the region across the Jordan followed him.

The Beatitudes

5 NOW WHEN he saw the crowds, he went up on a mountainside and sat down. His disciples came to him, 2and he began to teach them, saying:

3"Blessed are the poor in spirit,
  for theirs is the kingdom of heaven.
4Blessed are those who mourn,
  for they will be comforted.
5Blessed are the meek,
  for they will inherit the earth.
6Blessed are those who hunger and thirst for
    righteousness,
  for they will be filled.
7Blessed are the merciful,
  for they will be shown mercy.
8Blessed are the pure in heart,
  for they will see God.
9Blessed are the peacemakers,
  for they will be called sons of God.
10Blessed are those who are persecuted because of
    righteousness,
  for theirs is the kingdom of heaven.

11"Blessed are you when people insult you, persecute you and falsely say all kinds of evil against you because of me. 12Rejoice and be glad, because great is your reward in heaven, for in the same way they persecuted the prophets who were before you.

Salt and Light

13"You are the salt of the earth. But if the salt loses its saltiness, how can it be made salty again? It is no longer good for anything, except to be thrown out and trampled by men.

14"You are the light of the world. A city on a hill cannot be hidden. 15Neither do people light a lamp and put it under a bowl. Instead they put it on its stand, and it gives light to everyone in the house. 16In the same way, let your light shine before men, that they may see your good deeds and praise your Father in heaven.

---

a 25 That is, the Ten Cities

Living Bible

18One day as he was walking along the beach beside the Lake of Galilee, he saw two brothers—Simon, also called Peter, and Andrew—out in a boatb fishing with a net, for they were commercial fishermen.

19Jesus called out, "Come along with me and I will show you how to fish for the souls of men!" 20And they left their nets at once and went with him.

21A little farther up the beach he saw two other brothers, James and John, sitting in a boat with their father Zebedee, mending their nets; and he called to them to come too. 22At once they stopped their work and, leaving their father behind, went with him.

23Jesus traveled all through Galilee teaching in the Jewish synagogues, everywhere preaching the Good News about the Kingdom of Heaven. And he healed every kind of sickness and disease. 24The report of his miracles spread far beyond the borders of Galilee so that sick folk were soon coming to be healed from as far away as Syria. And whatever their illness and pain, or if they were possessed by demons, or were insane, or paralyzed—he healed them all. 25Enormous crowds followed him wherever he went—people from Galilee, and the Ten Cities, and Jerusalem, and from all over Judea, and even from across the Jordan River.

5 ONE DAY as the crowds were gathering, he went up the hillside with his disciples and sat down and taught them there.

3"Humble men are very fortunate!" he told them, "for the Kingdom of Heaven is given to them. 4Those who mourn are fortunate! for they shall be comforted. 5The meek and lowly are fortunate! for the whole wide world belongs to them.

6"Happy are those who long to be just and good, for they shall be completely satisfied. 7Happy are the kind and merciful, for they shall be shown mercy. 8Happy are those whose hearts are pure, for they shall see God. 9Happy are those who strive for peace—they shall be called the sons of God. 10Happy are those who are persecuted because they are good, for the Kingdom of Heaven is theirs.

11"When you are reviled and persecuted and lied about because you are my followers—wonderful! 12Be happy about it! Be very glad! for a tremendous reward awaits you up in heaven. And remember, the ancient prophets were persecuted too.

13"You are the world's seasoning, to make it tolerable. If you lose your flavor, what will happen to the world? And you yourselves will be thrown out and trampled underfoot as worthless. 14You are the world's light—a city on a hill, glowing in the night for all to see. 15, 16Don't hide your light! Let it shine for all; let your good deeds glow for all to see, so that they will praise your heavenly Father.

New Revised Standard

Jesus Calls the First Disciples

18 As he walked by the Sea of Galilee, he saw two brothers, Simon, who is called Peter, and Andrew his brother, casting a net into the sea—for they were fishermen. 19And he said to them, "Follow me, and I will make you fish for people." 20Immediately they left their nets and followed him. 21As he went from there, he saw two other brothers, James son of Zebedee and his brother John, in the boat with their father Zebedee, mending their nets, and he called them. 22Immediately they left the boat and their father, and followed him.

Jesus Ministers to Crowds of People

23 Jesusc went throughout Galilee, teaching in their synagogues and proclaiming the good newsd of the kingdom and curing every disease and every sickness among the people. 24So his fame spread throughout all Syria, and they brought to him all the sick, those who were afflicted with various diseases and pains, demoniacs, epileptics, and paralytics, and he cured them. 25And great crowds followed him from Galilee, the Decapolis, Jerusalem, Judea, and from beyond the Jordan.

The Beatitudes

5 WHEN JESUSe saw the crowds, he went up the mountain; and after he sat down, his disciples came to him. 2Then he began to speak, and taught them, saying:

3 "Blessed are the poor in spirit, for theirs is the kingdom of heaven.

4 "Blessed are those who mourn, for they will be comforted.

5 "Blessed are the meek, for they will inherit the earth.

6 "Blessed are those who hunger and thirst for righteousness, for they will be filled.

7 "Blessed are the merciful, for they will receive mercy.

8 "Blessed are the pure in heart, for they will see God.

9 "Blessed are the peacemakers, for they will be called children of God.

10 "Blessed are those who are persecuted for righteousness' sake, for theirs is the kingdom of heaven.

11 "Blessed are you when people revile you and persecute you and utter all kinds of evil against you falselyf on my account. 12Rejoice and be glad, for your reward is great in heaven, for in the same way they persecuted the prophets who were before you.

Salt and Light

13 "You are the salt of the earth; but if salt has lost its taste, how can its saltiness be restored? It is no longer good for anything, but is thrown out and trampled under foot.

14 "You are the light of the world. A city built on a hill cannot be hid. 15No one after lighting a lamp puts it under the bushel basket, but on the lampstand, and it gives light to all in the house. 16In the same way, let your light shine before others, so that they may see your good works and give glory to your Father in heaven.

---

b 4:18 out in a boat, implied.

c Gk He   d Gk gospel   e Gk he   f Other ancient authorities lack falsely

King James

17¶ Think not that I am come to destroy the law, or the prophets: I am not come to destroy, but to fulfil.

18For verily I say unto you, Till heaven and earth pass, one jot or one tittle shall in no wise pass from the law, till all be fulfilled.

19Whosoever therefore shall break one of these least commandments, and shall teach men so, he shall be called the least in the kingdom of heaven: but whosoever shall do and teach *them,* the same shall be called great in the kingdom of heaven.

20For I say unto you, That except your righteousness shall exceed *the righteousness* of the scribes and Pharisees, ye shall in no case enter into the kingdom of heaven.

21¶ Ye have heard that it was said by them of old time, Thou shalt not kill; and whosoever shall kill shall be in danger of the judgment:

22But I say unto you, That whosoever is angry with his brother without a cause shall be in danger of the judgment: and whosoever shall say to his brother, Raca, shall be in danger of the council: but whosoever shall say, Thou fool, shall be in danger of hell fire.

23Therefore if thou bring thy gift to the altar, and there rememberest that thy brother hath aught against thee;

24Leave there thy gift before the altar, and go thy way; first be reconciled to thy brother, and then come and offer thy gift.

25Agree with thine adversary quickly, whiles thou art in the way with him; lest at any time the adversary deliver thee to the judge, and the judge deliver thee to the officer, and thou be cast into prison.

26Verily I say unto thee, Thou shalt by no means come out thence, till thou hast paid the uttermost farthing.

27¶ Ye have heard that it was said by them of old time, Thou shalt not commit adultery:

28But I say unto you, That whosoever looketh on a woman to lust after her hath committed adultery with her already in his heart.

29And if thy right eye offend thee, pluck it out, and cast *it* from thee: for it is profitable for thee that one of thy members should perish, and not *that* thy whole body should be cast into hell.

30And if thy right hand offend thee, cut it off, and cast *it* from thee: for it is profitable for thee that one of thy members should perish, and not *that* thy whole body should be cast into hell.

31It hath been said, Whosoever shall put away his wife, let him give her a writing of divorcement:

32But I say unto you, That whosoever shall put away his wife, saving for the cause of fornication, causeth her to commit adultery: and whosoever shall marry her that is divorced committeth adultery.

33¶ Again, ye have heard that it hath been said by them of old time, Thou shalt not forswear thyself, but shalt perform unto the Lord thine oaths:

34But I say unto you, Swear not at all; neither by heaven; for it is God's throne:

35Nor by the earth; for it is his footstool: neither by Jerusalem; for it is the city of the great King.

36Neither shalt thou swear by thy head, because thou canst not make one hair white or black.

37But let your communication be, Yea, yea; Nay, nay: for whatsoever is more than these cometh of evil.

38¶ Ye have heard that it hath been said, An eye for an eye, and a tooth for a tooth:

New International

The Fulfillment of the Law

17"Do not think that I have come to abolish the Law or the Prophets; I have not come to abolish them but to fulfill them. 18I tell you the truth, until heaven and earth disappear, not the smallest letter, not the least stroke of a pen, will by any means disappear from the Law until everything is accomplished. 19Anyone who breaks one of the least of these commandments and teaches others to do the same will be called least in the kingdom of heaven, but whoever practices and teaches these commands will be called great in the kingdom of heaven. 20For I tell you that unless your righteousness surpasses that of the Pharisees and the teachers of the law, you will certainly not enter the kingdom of heaven.

Murder

21"You have heard that it was said to the people long ago, 'Do not murder,a and anyone who murders will be subject to judgment.' 22But I tell you that anyone who is angry with his brotherb will be subject to judgment. Again, anyone who says to his brother, 'Raca,c' is answerable to the Sanhedrin. But anyone who says, 'You fool!' will be in danger of the fire of hell.

23"Therefore, if you are offering your gift at the altar and there remember that your brother has something against you, 24leave your gift there in front of the altar. First go and be reconciled to your brother; then come and offer your gift.

25"Settle matters quickly with your adversary who is taking you to court. Do it while you are still with him on the way, or he may hand you over to the judge, and the judge may hand you over to the officer, and you may be thrown into prison. 26I tell you the truth, you will not get out until you have paid the last penny.d

Adultery

27"You have heard that it was said, 'Do not commit adultery.'e 28But I tell you that anyone who looks at a woman lustfully has already committed adultery with her in his heart. 29If your right eye causes you to sin, gouge it out and throw it away. It is better for you to lose one part of your body than for your whole body to be thrown into hell. 30And if your right hand causes you to sin, cut it off and throw it away. It is better for you to lose one part of your body than for your whole body to go into hell.

Divorce

31"It has been said, 'Anyone who divorces his wife must give her a certificate of divorce.'f 32But I tell you that anyone who divorces his wife, except for marital unfaithfulness, causes her to become an adulteress, and anyone who marries the divorced woman commits adultery.

Oaths

33"Again, you have heard that it was said to the people long ago, 'Do not break your oath, but keep the oaths you have made to the Lord.' 34But I tell you, Do not swear at all: either by heaven, for it is God's throne; 35or by the earth, for it is his footstool; or by Jerusalem, for it is the city of the Great King. 36And do not swear by your head, for you cannot make even one hair white or black. 37Simply let your 'Yes' be 'Yes,' and your 'No,' 'No'; anything beyond this comes from the evil one.

An Eye for an Eye

38"You have heard that it was said, 'Eye for eye, and tooth for tooth.'g 39But I tell you, Do not resist an evil

---

a *21* Exodus 20:13   b *22* Some manuscripts *brother without cause*
c *22* An Aramaic term of contempt   d *26* Greek *kodrantes*   e *27* Exodus
20:14   f *31* Deut. 24:1   g *38* Exodus 21:24; Lev. 24:20; Deut. 19:21

Living Bible

17"Don't misunderstand why I have come—it isn't to cancel the laws of Moses and the warnings of the prophets. No, I came to fulfill them, and to make them all come true. 18With all the earnestness I have I say: Every law in the Book will continue until its purpose is achieved.h 19And so if anyone breaks the least commandment, and teaches others to, he shall be the least in the Kingdom of Heaven. But those who teach God's laws *and obey them* shall be great in the Kingdom of Heaven.

20"But I warn you—unless your goodnessi is greater than that of the Pharisees and other Jewish leaders, you can't get into the Kingdom of Heaven at all!

21"Under the laws of Moses the rule was, 'If you murder, you must die.' 22But I have added to that rule,j and tell you that if you are only *angry,* even in your own home,k you are in danger of judgment! If you call your friend an idiot, you are in danger of being brought before the court. And if you curse him, you are in danger of the fires of hell.l

23"So if you are standing before the altar in the Temple, offering a sacrifice to God, and suddenly remember that a friend has something against you, 24leave your sacrifice there beside the altar and go and apologize and be reconciled to him, and then come and offer your sacrifice to God. 25Come to terms quickly with your enemy before it is too late and he drags you into court and you are thrown into a debtor's cell, 26for you will stay there until you have paid the last penny.

27"The laws of Moses said, 'You shall not commit adultery.' 28But I say: Anyone who even looks at a woman with lust in his eye has already committed adultery with her in his heart. 29So if your eye—even if it is your best eye!m—causes you to lust, gouge it out and throw it away. Better for part of you to be destroyed than for all of you to be cast into hell. 30And if your hand—even your right hand—causes you to sin, cut it off and throw it away. Better that than find yourself in hell.

31"The law of Moses says, 'If anyone wants to be rid of his wife, he can divorce her merely by giving her a letter of dismissal.' 32But I say that a man who divorces his wife, except for fornication, causes her to commit adultery if she marries again. And he who marries her commits adultery.

33"Again, the law of Moses says, 'You shall not break your vows to God, but must fulfill them all.' 34But I say: Don't make any vows! And even to say, 'By heavens!' is a sacred vow to God, for the heavens are God's throne. 35And if you say 'By the earth!' it is a sacred vow, for the earth is his footstool. And don't swear 'By Jerusalem!' for Jerusalem is the capital of the great King. 36Don't even swear 'By my head!' for you can't turn one hair white or black. 37Say just a simple 'Yes, I will' or 'No, I won't.' Your word is enough. To strengthen your promise with a vow shows that something is wrong.

38"The law of Moses says, 'If a man gouges out another's eye, he must pay with his own eye. If a tooth gets knocked out, knock out the toothn of the one who did it.' 39But I say: Don't resist violence! If you are slapped

New Revised Standard

The Law and the Prophets

17 "Do not think that I have come to abolish the law or the prophets; I have come not to abolish but to fulfill. 18For truly I tell you, until heaven and earth pass away, not one letter,o not one stroke of a letter, will pass from the law until all is accomplished. 19Therefore, whoever breaksp one of the least of these commandments, and teaches others to do the same, will be called least in the kingdom of heaven; but whoever does them and teaches them will be called great in the kingdom of heaven. 20For I tell you, unless your righteousness exceeds that of the scribes and Pharisees, you will never enter the kingdom of heaven.

Concerning Anger

21 "You have heard that it was said to those of ancient times, 'You shall not murder'; and 'whoever murders shall be liable to judgment.' 22But I say to you that if you are angry with a brother or sister,q you will be liable to judgment; and if you insultr a brother or sister,s you will be liable to the council; and if you say, 'You fool,' you will be liable to the hellt of fire. 23So when you are offering your gift at the altar, if you remember that your brother or sisteru has something against you, 24leave your gift there before the altar and go; first be reconciled to your brother or sister,u and then come and offer your gift. 25Come to terms quickly with your accuser while you are on the way to courtv with him, or your accuser may hand you over to the judge, and the judge to the guard, and you will be thrown into prison. 26Truly I tell you, you will never get out until you have paid the last penny.

Concerning Adultery

27 "You have heard that it was said, 'You shall not commit adultery.' 28But I say to you that everyone who looks at a woman with lust has already committed adultery with her in his heart. 29If your right eye causes you to sin, tear it out and throw it away; it is better for you to lose one of your members than for your whole body to be thrown into hell.t 30And if your right hand causes you to sin, cut it off and throw it away; it is better for you to lose one of your members than for your whole body to go into hell.t

Concerning Divorce

31 "It was also said, 'Whoever divorces his wife, let him give her a certificate of divorce.' 32But I say to you that anyone who divorces his wife, except on the ground of unchastity, causes her to commit adultery; and whoever marries a divorced woman commits adultery.

Concerning Oaths

33 "Again, you have heard that it was said to those of ancient times, 'You shall not swear falsely, but carry out the vows you have made to the Lord.' 34But I say to you, Do not swear at all, either by heaven, for it is the throne of God, 35or by the earth, for it is his footstool, or by Jerusalem, for it is the city of the great King. 36And do not swear by your head, for you cannot make one hair white or black. 37Let your word be 'Yes, Yes' or 'No, No'; anything more than this comes from the evil one.w

Concerning Retaliation

38 "You have heard that it was said, 'An eye for an eye and a tooth for a tooth.' 39But I say to you, Do not

---

h *5:18 until its purpose is achieved,* literally, "until all things be accomplished."　　i *5:20 goodness,* literally, "righteousness."　j *5:21, 22 But I have added to that rule,* literally, "But I say."　k *5:21, 22 even in your own home,* literally, "with your brother."　l *5:21, 22 the fires of hell,* literally, "the hell of fire."　m *5:29 your best eye,* literally, "your right eye."　n *5:38 pay with his own eye . . . knock out the tooth,* literally, "an eye for an eye and a tooth for a tooth."

o Gk *one iota*　p Or *annuls*　q Gk *a brother*; other ancient authorities add *without cause*　r Gk *say Raca to* (an obscure term of abuse)　s Gk *a brother*　t Gk *Gehenna*　u Gk *your brother*　v Gk lacks *to court*　w Or *evil*

King James

39But I say unto you, That ye resist not evil: but whosoever shall smite thee on thy right cheek, turn to him the other also.

40And if any man will sue thee at the law, and take away thy coat, let him have *thy* cloak also.

41And whosoever shall compel thee to go a mile, go with him twain.

42Give to him that asketh thee, and from him that would borrow of thee turn not thou away.

43¶ Ye have heard that it hath been said, Thou shalt love thy neighbour, and hate thine enemy.

44But I say unto you, Love your enemies, bless them that curse you, do good to them that hate you, and pray for them which despitefully use you, and persecute you;

45That ye may be the children of your Father which is in heaven: for he maketh his sun to rise on the evil and on the good, and sendeth rain on the just and on the unjust.

46For if ye love them which love you, what reward have ye? do not even the publicans the same?

47And if ye salute your brethren only, what do ye more *than others?* do not even the publicans so?

48Be ye therefore perfect, even as your Father which is in heaven is perfect.

6 TAKE HEED that ye do not your alms before men, to be seen of them: otherwise ye have no reward of your Father which is in heaven.

2Therefore when thou doest *thine* alms, do not sound a trumpet before thee, as the hypocrites do in the synagogues and in the streets, that they may have glory of men. Verily I say unto you, They have their reward.

3But when thou doest alms, let not thy left hand know what thy right hand doeth:

4That thine alms may be in secret: and thy Father which seeth in secret himself shall reward thee openly.

5¶ And when thou prayest, thou shalt not be as the hypocrites *are:* for they love to pray standing in the synagogues and in the corners of the streets, that they may be seen of men. Verily I say unto you, They have their reward.

6But thou, when thou prayest, enter into thy closet, and when thou hast shut thy door, pray to thy Father which is in secret; and thy Father which seeth in secret shall reward thee openly.

7But when ye pray, use not vain repetitions, as the heathen *do:* for they think that they shall be heard for their much speaking.

8Be not ye therefore like unto them: for your Father knoweth what things ye have need of, before ye ask him.

9After this manner therefore pray ye: Our Father which art in heaven, Hallowed be thy name.

10Thy kingdom come. Thy will be done in earth, as *it is* in heaven.

11Give us this day our daily bread.

12And forgive us our debts, as we forgive our debtors.

13And lead us not into temptation, but deliver us from evil: For thine is the kingdom, and the power, and the glory, for ever. Amen.

14For if ye forgive men their trespasses, your heavenly Father will also forgive you:

15But if ye forgive not men their trespasses, neither will your Father forgive your trespasses.

New International

person. If someone strikes you on the right cheek, turn to him the other also. 40And if someone wants to sue you and take your tunic, let him have your cloak as well. 41If someone forces you to go one mile, go with him two miles. 42Give to the one who asks you, and do not turn away from the one who wants to borrow from you.

Love for Enemies

43"You have heard that it was said, 'Love your neighbora and hate your enemy.' 44But I tell you: Love your enemiesb and pray for those who persecute you, 45that you may be sons of your Father in heaven. He causes his sun to rise on the evil and the good, and sends rain on the righteous and the unrighteous. 46If you love those who love you, what reward will you get? Are not even the tax collectors doing that? 47And if you greet only your brothers, what are you doing more than others? Do not even pagans do that? 48Be perfect, therefore, as your heavenly Father is perfect.

Giving to the Needy

6 "BE CAREFUL not to do your 'acts of righteousness' before men, to be seen by them. If you do, you will have no reward from your Father in heaven.

2"So when you give to the needy, do not announce it with trumpets, as the hypocrites do in the synagogues and on the streets, to be honored by men. I tell you the truth, they have received their reward in full. 3But when you give to the needy, do not let your left hand know what your right hand is doing, 4so that your giving may be in secret. Then your Father, who sees what is done in secret, will reward you.

Prayer

5"And when you pray, do not be like the hypocrites, for they love to pray standing in the synagogues and on the street corners to be seen by men. I tell you the truth, they have received their reward in full. 6But when you pray, go into your room, close the door and pray to your Father, who is unseen. Then your Father, who sees what is done in secret, will reward you. 7And when you pray, do not keep on babbling like pagans, for they think they will be heard because of their many words. 8Do not be like them, for your Father knows what you need before you ask him.

9"This, then, is how you should pray:

" 'Our Father in heaven,
   hallowed be your name,
10your kingdom come,
   your will be done
     on earth as it is in heaven.
11Give us today our daily bread.
12Forgive us our debts,
   as we also have forgiven our debtors.
13And lead us not into temptation,
   but deliver us from the evil one.c '

14For if you forgive men when they sin against you, your heavenly Father will also forgive you. 15But if you do not forgive men their sins, your Father will not forgive your sins.

---

a 43 Lev. 19:18   b 44 Some late manuscripts *enemies, bless those who curse you, do good to those who hate you*   c 13 Or *from evil;* some late manuscripts *one, / for yours is the kingdom and the power and the glory forever. Amen.*

Living Bible

on one cheek, turn the other too. 40If you are ordered to court, and your shirt is taken from you, give your coat too. 41If the military demand that you carry their gear for a mile, carry it two. 42Give to those who ask, and don't turn away from those who want to borrow.

43"There is a saying, 'Love your *friends* and hate your enemies.' 44But I say: Love your *enemies!* Pray for those who *persecute* you! 45In that way you will be acting as true sons of your Father in heaven. For he gives his sunlight to both the evil and the good, and sends rain on the just and on the unjust too. 46If you love only those who love you, what good is that? Even scoundrels do that much. 47If you are friendly only to your friends, how are you different from anyone else? Even the heathen do that. 48But you are to be perfect, even as your Father in heaven is perfect.

6 "TAKE CARE! Don't do your good deeds publicly, to be admired, for then you will lose the reward from your Father in heaven. 2When you give a gift to a beggar, don't shout about it as the hypocrites do—blowing trumpets in the synagogues and streets to call attention to their acts of charity! I tell you in all earnestness, they have received all the reward they will ever get. 3But when you do a kindness to someone, do it secretly—don't tell your left hand what your right hand is doing. 4And your Father who knows all secrets will reward you.

5"And now about prayer. When you pray, don't be like the hypocrites who pretend piety by praying publicly on street corners and in the synagogues where everyone can see them. Truly, that is all the reward they will ever get. 6But when you pray, go away by yourself, all alone, and shut the door behind you and pray to your Father secretly, and your Father, who knows your secrets, will reward you.

7, 8"Don't recite the same prayer over and over as the heathen do, who think prayers are answered only by repeating them again and again. Remember, your Father knows exactly what you need even before you ask him! 9"Pray along these lines: 'Our Father in heaven, we honor your holy name. 10We ask that your kingdom will come now. May your will be done here on earth, just as it is in heaven. 11Give us our food again today, as usual, 12and forgive us our sins, just as we have forgiven those who have sinned against us. 13Don't bring us into temptation, but deliver us from the Evil One.d Amen.' 14, 15Your heavenly Father will forgive you if you forgive those who sin against you; but if *you* refuse to forgive *them, he* will not forgive *you.*

New Revised Standard

resist an evildoer. But if anyone strikes you on the right cheek, turn the other also; 40and if anyone wants to sue you and take your coat, give your cloak as well; 41and if anyone forces you to go one mile, go also the second mile. 42Give to everyone who begs from you, and do not refuse anyone who wants to borrow from you.

Love for Enemies

43 "You have heard that it was said, 'You shall love your neighbor and hate your enemy.' 44But I say to you, Love your enemies and pray for those who persecute you, 45so that you may be children of your Father in heaven; for he makes his sun rise on the evil and on the good, and sends rain on the righteous and on the unrighteous. 46For if you love those who love you, what reward do you have? Do not even the tax collectors do the same? 47And if you greet only your brothers and sisters,e what more are you doing than others? Do not even the Gentiles do the same? 48Be perfect, therefore, as your heavenly Father is perfect.

Concerning Almsgiving

6 "BEWARE OF practicing your piety before others in order to be seen by them; for then you have no reward from your Father in heaven.

2 "So whenever you give alms, do not sound a trumpet before you, as the hypocrites do in the synagogues and in the streets, so that they may be praised by others. Truly I tell you, they have received their reward. 3But when you give alms, do not let your left hand know what your right hand is doing, 4so that your alms may be done in secret; and your Father who sees in secret will reward you.f

Concerning Prayer

5 "And whenever you pray, do not be like the hypocrites; for they love to stand and pray in the synagogues and at the street corners, so that they may be seen by others. Truly I tell you, they have received their reward. 6But whenever you pray, go into your room and shut the door and pray to your Father who is in secret; and your Father who sees in secret will reward you.f

7 "When you are praying, do not heap up empty phrases as the Gentiles do; for they think that they will be heard because of their many words. 8Do not be like them, for your Father knows what you need before you ask him.

9 "Pray then in this way:
Our Father in heaven,
  hallowed be your name.
10 Your kingdom come.
  Your will be done,
    on earth as it is in heaven.
11 Give us this day our daily bread.g
12 And forgive us our debts,
    as we also have forgiven our debtors.
13 And do not bring us to the time of trial,h
    but rescue us from the evil one.i

14For if you forgive others their trespasses, your heavenly Father will also forgive you; 15but if you do not forgive others, neither will your Father forgive your trespasses.

---

e Gk *your brothers*   f Other ancient authorities add *openly*   g Or *our bread for tomorrow*   h Or *us into temptation*   i Or *from evil.* Other ancient authorities add, in some form, *For the kingdom and the power and the glory are yours forever. Amen.*

King James

16¶ Moreover when ye fast, be not, as the hypocrites, of a sad countenance: for they disfigure their faces, that they may appear unto men to fast. Verily I say unto you, They have their reward.

17But thou, when thou fastest, anoint thine head, and wash thy face;

18That thou appear not unto men to fast, but unto thy Father which is in secret: and thy Father, which seeth in secret, shall reward thee openly.

19¶ Lay not up for yourselves treasures upon earth, where moth and rust doth corrupt, and where thieves break through and steal:

20But lay up for yourselves treasures in heaven, where neither moth nor rust doth corrupt, and where thieves do not break through nor steal:

21For where your treasure is, there will your heart be also.

22The light of the body is the eye: if therefore thine eye be single, thy whole body shall be full of light.

23But if thine eye be evil, thy whole body shall be full of darkness. If therefore the light that is in thee be darkness, how great is that darkness!

24¶ No man can serve two masters: for either he will hate the one, and love the other; or else he will hold to the one, and despise the other. Ye cannot serve God and mammon.

25Therefore I say unto you, Take no thought for your life, what ye shall eat, or what ye shall drink; nor yet for your body, what ye shall put on. Is not the life more than meat, and the body than raiment?

26Behold the fowls of the air: for they sow not, neither do they reap, nor gather into barns; yet your heavenly Father feedeth them. Are ye not much better than they?

27Which of you by taking thought can add one cubit unto his stature?

28And why take ye thought for raiment? Consider the lilies of the field, how they grow; they toil not, neither do they spin:

29And yet I say unto you, That even Solomon in all his glory was not arrayed like one of these.

30Wherefore, if God so clothe the grass of the field, which today is, and tomorrow is cast into the oven, *shall he* not much more *clothe* you, O ye of little faith?

31Therefore take no thought, saying, What shall we eat? or, What shall we drink? or, Wherewithal shall we be clothed?

32(For after all these things do the Gentiles seek:) for your heavenly Father knoweth that ye have need of all these things.

33But seek ye first the kingdom of God, and his righteousness; and all these things shall be added unto you.

34Take therefore no thought for the morrow: for the morrow shall take thought for the things of itself. Sufficient unto the day *is* the evil thereof.

7 JUDGE NOT, that ye be not judged.
2For with what judgment ye judge, ye shall be judged: and with what measure ye mete, it shall be measured to you again.

3And why beholdest thou the mote that is in thy brother's eye, but considerest not the beam that is in thine own eye?

4Or how wilt thou say to thy brother, Let me pull out the mote out of thine eye; and, behold, a beam *is* in thine own eye?

5Thou hypocrite, first cast out the beam out of thine own eye; and then shalt thou see clearly to cast out the mote out of thy brother's eye.

New International

Fasting

16"When you fast, do not look somber as the hypocrites do, for they disfigure their faces to show men they are fasting. I tell you the truth, they have received their reward in full. 17But when you fast, put oil on your head and wash your face, 18so that it will not be obvious to men that you are fasting, but only to your Father, who is unseen; and your Father, who sees what is done in secret, will reward you.

Treasures in Heaven

19"Do not store up for yourselves treasures on earth, where moth and rust destroy, and where thieves break in and steal. 20But store up for yourselves treasures in heaven, where moth and rust do not destroy, and where thieves do not break in and steal. 21For where your treasure is, there your heart will be also.

22"The eye is the lamp of the body. If your eyes are good, your whole body will be full of light. 23But if your eyes are bad, your whole body will be full of darkness. If then the light within you is darkness, how great is that darkness!

24"No one can serve two masters. Either he will hate the one and love the other, or he will be devoted to the one and despise the other. You cannot serve both God and Money.

Do Not Worry

25"Therefore I tell you, do not worry about your life, what you will eat or drink; or about your body, what you will wear. Is not life more important than food, and the body more important than clothes? 26Look at the birds of the air; they do not sow or reap or store away in barns, and yet your heavenly Father feeds them. Are you not much more valuable than they? 27Who of you by worrying can add a single hour to his life[a]?

28"And why do you worry about clothes? See how the lilies of the field grow. They do not labor or spin. 29Yet I tell you that not even Solomon in all his splendor was dressed like one of these. 30If that is how God clothes the grass of the field, which is here today and tomorrow is thrown into the fire, will he not much more clothe you, O you of little faith? 31So do not worry, saying, 'What shall we eat?' or 'What shall we drink?' or 'What shall we wear?' 32For the pagans run after all these things, and your heavenly Father knows that you need them. 33But seek first his kingdom and his righteousness, and all these things will be given to you as well. 34Therefore do not worry about tomorrow, for tomorrow will worry about itself. Each day has enough trouble of its own.

Judging Others

7 "DO NOT judge, or you too will be judged. 2For in the same way you judge others, you will be judged, and with the measure you use, it will be measured to you.

3"Why do you look at the speck of sawdust in your brother's eye and pay no attention to the plank in your own eye? 4How can you say to your brother, 'Let me take the speck out of your eye,' when all the time there is a plank in your own eye? 5You hypocrite, first take the plank out of your own eye, and then you will see clearly to remove the speck from your brother's eye.

---

a 27 Or *single cubit to his height*

Living Bible

16"And now about fasting. When you fast, declining your food for a spiritual purpose, don't do it publicly, as the hypocrites do, who try to look wan and disheveled so people will feel sorry for them. Truly, that is the only reward they will ever get. 17But when you fast, put on festive clothing, 18so that no one will suspect you are hungry, except your Father who knows every secret. And he will reward you.

19"Don't store up treasures here on earth where they can erode away or may be stolen. 20Store them in heaven where they will never lose their value, and are safe from thieves. 21If your profits are in heaven your heart will be there too.

22"If your eye is pure, there will be sunshine in your soul. 23But if your eye is clouded with evil thoughts and desires, you are in deep spiritual darkness. And oh, how deep that darkness can be!

24"You cannot serve two masters: God and money. For you will hate one and love the other, or else the other way around.

25"So my counsel is: Don't worry about *things*—food, drink, and clothes. For you already have life and a body—and they are far more important than what to eat and wear. 26Look at the birds! They don't worry about what to eat—they don't need to sow or reap or store up food—for your heavenly Father feeds them. And you are far more valuable to him than they are. 27Will all your worries add a single moment to your life?

28"And why worry about your clothes? Look at the field lilies! They don't worry about theirs. 29Yet King Solomon in all his glory was not clothed as beautifully as they. 30And if God cares so wonderfully for flowers that are here today and gone tomorrow, won't he more surely care for you, O men of little faith?

31, 32"So don't worry at all about having enough food and clothing. Why be like the heathen? For they take pride in all these things and are deeply concerned about them. But your heavenly Father already knows perfectly well that you need them, 33and he will give them to you if you give him first place in your life and live as he wants you to.

34"So don't be anxious about tomorrow. God will take care of your tomorrow too. Live one day at a time.b

7   "DON'T CRITICIZE, and then you won't be criti-
     cized. 2For others will treat you as you treat them.
3And why worry about a speck in the eye of a brother when you have a board in your own? 4Should you say, 'Friend, let me help you get that speck out of your eye,' when you can't even see because of the board in your own? 5Hypocrite! First get rid of the board. Then you can see to help your brother.

New Revised Standard

Concerning Fasting

16 "And whenever you fast, do not look dismal, like the hypocrites, for they disfigure their faces so as to show others that they are fasting. Truly I tell you, they have received their reward. 17But when you fast, put oil on your head and wash your face, 18so that your fasting may be seen not by others but by your Father who is in secret; and your Father who sees in secret will reward you.c

Concerning Treasures

19 "Do not store up for yourselves treasures on earth, where moth and rustd consume and where thieves break in and steal; 20but store up for yourselves treasures in heaven, where neither moth nor rustd consumes and where thieves do not break in and steal. 21For where your treasure is, there your heart will be also.

The Sound Eye

22 "The eye is the lamp of the body. So, if your eye is healthy, your whole body will be full of light; 23but if your eye is unhealthy, your whole body will be full of darkness. If then the light in you is darkness, how great is the darkness!

Serving Two Masters

24 "No one can serve two masters; for a slave will either hate the one and love the other, or be devoted to the one and despise the other. You cannot serve God and wealth.e

Do Not Worry

25 "Therefore I tell you, do not worry about your life, what you will eat or what you will drink,f or about your body, what you will wear. Is not life more than food, and the body more than clothing? 26Look at the birds of the air; they neither sow nor reap nor gather into barns, and yet your heavenly Father feeds them. Are you not of more value than they? 27And can any of you by worrying add a single hour to your span of life?g 28And why do you worry about clothing? Consider the lilies of the field, how they grow; they neither toil nor spin, 29yet I tell you, even Solomon in all his glory was not clothed like one of these. 30But if God so clothes the grass of the field, which is alive today and tomorrow is thrown into the oven, will he not much more clothe you—you of little faith? 31Therefore do not worry, saying, 'What will we eat?' or 'What will we drink?' or 'What will we wear?' 32For it is the Gentiles who strive for all these things; and indeed your heavenly Father knows that you need all these things. 33But strive first for the kingdom of Godh and hisi righteousness, and all these things will be given to you as well.

34 "So do not worry about tomorrow, for tomorrow will bring worries of its own. Today's trouble is enough for today.

Judging Others

7   "DO NOT judge, so that you may not be judged.
     2For with the judgment you make you will be judged, and the measure you give will be the measure you get. 3Why do you see the speck in your neighbor'sj eye, but do not notice the log in your own eye? 4Or how can you say to your neighbor,k 'Let me take the speck out of your eye,' while the log is in your own eye? 5You hypocrite, first take the log out of your own eye, and then you will see clearly to take the speck out of your neighbor'sj eye.

c Other ancient authorities add *openly*   d Gk *eating*   e Gk *mammon*
f Other ancient authorities lack *or what you will drink*   g Or *add one cubit to your height*   h Other ancient authorities lack *of God*   i Or *its*   j Gk *brother's*   k Gk *brother*

b 6:34 *Live one day at a time*, literally, "Sufficient unto the day is the evil thereof."

King James

6¶ Give not that which is holy unto the dogs, neither cast ye your pearls before swine, lest they trample them under their feet, and turn again and rend you.

7¶ Ask, and it shall be given you; seek, and ye shall find; knock, and it shall be opened unto you:

8For every one that asketh receiveth; and he that seeketh findeth; and to him that knocketh it shall be opened.

9Or what man is there of you, whom if his son ask bread, will he give him a stone?

10Or if he ask a fish, will he give him a serpent?

11If ye then, being evil, know how to give good gifts unto your children, how much more shall your Father which is in heaven give good things to them that ask him?

12Therefore all things whatsoever ye would that men should do to you, do ye even so to them: for this is the law and the prophets.

13¶ Enter ye in at the strait gate: for wide is the gate, and broad is the way, that leadeth to destruction, and many there be which go in thereat:

14Because strait is the gate, and narrow is the way, which leadeth unto life, and few there be that find it.

15¶ Beware of false prophets, which come to you in sheep's clothing, but inwardly they are ravening wolves.

16Ye shall know them by their fruits. Do men gather grapes of thorns, or figs of thistles?

17Even so every good tree bringeth forth good fruit; but a corrupt tree bringeth forth evil fruit.

18A good tree cannot bring forth evil fruit, neither can a corrupt tree bring forth good fruit.

19Every tree that bringeth not forth good fruit is hewn down, and cast into the fire.

20Wherefore by their fruits ye shall know them.

21¶ Not every one that saith unto me, Lord, Lord, shall enter into the kingdom of heaven; but he that doeth the will of my Father which is in heaven.

22Many will say to me in that day, Lord, Lord, have we not prophesied in thy name? and in thy name have cast out devils? and in thy name done many wonderful works?

23And then will I profess unto them, I never knew you: depart from me, ye that work iniquity.

24¶ Therefore whosoever heareth these sayings of mine, and doeth them, I will liken him unto a wise man, which built his house upon a rock:

25And the rain descended, and the floods came, and the winds blew, and beat upon that house; and it fell not: for it was founded upon a rock.

26And every one that heareth these sayings of mine, and doeth them not, shall be likened unto a foolish man, which built his house upon the sand:

27And the rain descended, and the floods came, and the winds blew, and beat upon that house; and it fell: and great was the fall of it.

28And it came to pass, when Jesus had ended these sayings, the people were astonished at his doctrine:

29For he taught them as one having authority, and not as the scribes.

New International

6"Do not give dogs what is sacred; do not throw your pearls to pigs. If you do, they may trample them under their feet, and then turn and tear you to pieces.

Ask, Seek, Knock

7"Ask and it will be given to you; seek and you will find; knock and the door will be opened to you. 8For everyone who asks receives; he who seeks finds; and to him who knocks, the door will be opened.

9"Which of you, if his son asks for bread, will give him a stone? 10Or if he asks for a fish, will give him a snake? 11If you, then, though you are evil, know how to give good gifts to your children, how much more will your Father in heaven give good gifts to those who ask him! 12So in everything, do to others what you would have them do to you, for this sums up the Law and the Prophets.

The Narrow and Wide Gates

13"Enter through the narrow gate. For wide is the gate and broad is the road that leads to destruction, and many enter through it. 14But small is the gate and narrow the road that leads to life, and only a few find it.

A Tree and Its Fruit

15"Watch out for false prophets. They come to you in sheep's clothing, but inwardly they are ferocious wolves. 16By their fruit you will recognize them. Do people pick grapes from thornbushes, or figs from thistles? 17Likewise every good tree bears good fruit, but a bad tree bears bad fruit. 18A good tree cannot bear bad fruit, and a bad tree cannot bear good fruit. 19Every tree that does not bear good fruit is cut down and thrown into the fire. 20Thus, by their fruit you will recognize them.

21"Not everyone who says to me, 'Lord, Lord,' will enter the kingdom of heaven, but only he who does the will of my Father who is in heaven. 22Many will say to me on that day, 'Lord, Lord, did we not prophesy in your name, and in your name drive out demons and perform many miracles?' 23Then I will tell them plainly, 'I never knew you. Away from me, you evildoers!'

The Wise and Foolish Builders

24"Therefore everyone who hears these words of mine and puts them into practice is like a wise man who built his house on the rock. 25The rain came down, the streams rose, and the winds blew and beat against that house; yet it did not fall, because it had its foundation on the rock. 26But everyone who hears these words of mine and does not put them into practice is like a foolish man who built his house on sand. 27The rain came down, the streams rose, and the winds blew and beat against that house, and it fell with a great crash."

28When Jesus had finished saying these things, the crowds were amazed at his teaching, 29because he taught as one who had authority, and not as their teachers of the law.

Living Bible

6"Don't give holy things to depraved men. Don't give pearls to swine! They will trample the pearls and turn and attack you.

7"Ask, and you will be given what you ask for. Seek, and you will find. Knock, and the door will be opened. 8For everyone who asks, receives. Anyone who seeks, finds. If only you will knock, the door will open. 9If a child asks his father for a loaf of bread, will he be given a stone instead? 10If he asks for fish, will he be given a poisonous snake? Of course not! 11And if you hardhearted, sinful men know how to give good gifts to your children, won't your Father in heaven even more certainly give good gifts to those who ask him for them?

12"Do for others what you want them to do for you. This is the teaching of the laws of Moses in a nutshell.a

13"Heaven can be entered only through the narrow gate! The highway to hellb is broad, and its gate is wide enough for all the multitudes who choose its easy way. 14But the Gateway to Life is small, and the road is narrow, and only a few ever find it.

15"Beware of false teachers who come disguised as harmless sheep, but are wolves and will tear you apart. 16You can detect them by the way they act, just as you can identify a tree by its fruit. You need never confuse grapevines with thorn bushes or figs with thistles. 17Different kinds of fruit trees can quickly be identified by examining their fruit. 18A variety that produces delicious fruit never produces an inedible kind. And a tree producing an inedible kind can't produce what is good. 19So the trees having the inedible fruit are chopped down and thrown on the fire. 20Yes, the way to identify a tree or a personc is by the kind of fruit produced.

21"Not all who sound religious are really godly people. They may refer to me as 'Lord,' but still won't get to heaven. For the decisive question is whether they obey my Father in heaven. 22At the Judgmentd many will tell me, 'Lord, Lord, we told others about you and used your name to cast out demons and to do many other great miracles.' 23But I will reply, 'You have never been mine.e Go away, for your deeds are evil.'

24"All who listen to my instructions and follow them are wise, like a man who builds his house on solid rock. 25Though the rain comes in torrents, and the floods rise and the storm winds beat against his house, it won't collapse, for it is built on rock.

26"But those who hear my instructions and ignore them are foolish, like a man who builds his house on sand. 27For when the rains and floods come, and storm winds beat against his house, it will fall with a mighty crash." 28The crowds were amazed at Jesus' sermons, 29for he taught as one who had great authority, and not as their Jewish leaders.f

a 7:12 This is the teaching of the laws of Moses in a nutshell, literally, "This is the law and the prophets." b 7:13 The highway to hell, literally, "The way that leads to destruction." c 7:20 or a person, implied. d 7:22 At the Judgment, literally, "in that day." e 7:23 You have never been mine, literally, "I never knew you." f 7:29 not as their Jewish leaders, literally, "not as the scribes." These leaders only quoted others, and did not presume to present any fresh revelation.

New Revised Standard

Profaning the Holy

6 "Do not give what is holy to dogs; and do not throw your pearls before swine, or they will trample them under foot and turn and maul you.

Ask, Search, Knock

7 "Ask, and it will be given you; search, and you will find; knock, and the door will be opened for you. 8For everyone who asks receives, and everyone who searches finds, and for everyone who knocks, the door will be opened. 9Is there anyone among you who, if your child asks for bread, will give a stone? 10Or if the child asks for a fish, will give a snake? 11If you then, who are evil, know how to give good gifts to your children, how much more will your Father in heaven give good things to those who ask him!

The Golden Rule

12 "In everything do to others as you would have them do to you; for this is the law and the prophets.

The Narrow Gate

13 "Enter through the narrow gate; for the gate is wide and the road is easyg that leads to destruction, and there are many who take it. 14For the gate is narrow and the road is hard that leads to life, and there are few who find it.

A Tree and Its Fruit

15 "Beware of false prophets, who come to you in sheep's clothing but inwardly are ravenous wolves. 16You will know them by their fruits. Are grapes gathered from thorns, or figs from thistles? 17In the same way, every good tree bears good fruit, but the bad tree bears bad fruit. 18A good tree cannot bear bad fruit, nor can a bad tree bear good fruit. 19Every tree that does not bear good fruit is cut down and thrown into the fire. 20Thus you will know them by their fruits.

Concerning Self-Deception

21 "Not everyone who says to me, 'Lord, Lord,' will enter the kingdom of heaven, but only the one who does the will of my Father in heaven. 22On that day many will say to me, 'Lord, Lord, did we not prophesy in your name, and cast out demons in your name, and do many deeds of power in your name?' 23Then I will declare to them, 'I never knew you; go away from me, you evildoers.'

Hearers and Doers

24 "Everyone then who hears these words of mine and acts on them will be like a wise man who built his house on rock. 25The rain fell, the floods came, and the winds blew and beat on that house, but it did not fall, because it had been founded on rock. 26And everyone who hears these words of mine and does not act on them will be like a foolish man who built his house on sand. 27The rain fell, and the floods came, and the winds blew and beat against that house, and it fell—and great was its fall!"

28 Now when Jesus had finished saying these things, the crowds were astounded at his teaching, 29for he taught them as one having authority, and not as their scribes.

g Other ancient authorities read for the road is wide and easy

King James

8 WHEN HE was come down from the mountain, great multitudes followed him.

2And, behold, there came a leper and worshipped him, saying, Lord, if thou wilt, thou canst make me clean.

3And Jesus put forth *his* hand, and touched him, saying, I will; be thou clean. And immediately his leprosy was cleansed.

4And Jesus saith unto him, See thou tell no man; but go thy way, show thyself to the priest, and offer the gift that Moses commanded, for a testimony unto them.

5¶ And when Jesus was entered into Capernaum, there came unto him a centurion, beseeching him,

6And saying, Lord, my servant lieth at home sick of the palsy, grievously tormented.

7And Jesus saith unto him, I will come and heal him.

8The centurion answered and said, Lord, I am not worthy that thou shouldest come under my roof: but speak the word only, and my servant shall be healed.

9For I am a man under authority, having soldiers under me: and I say to this *man,* Go, and he goeth; and to another, Come, and he cometh; and to my servant, Do this, and he doeth *it.*

10When Jesus heard *it,* he marvelled, and said to them that followed, Verily I say unto you, I have not found so great faith, no, not in Israel.

11And I say unto you, That many shall come from the east and west, and shall sit down with Abraham, and Isaac, and Jacob, in the kingdom of heaven.

12But the children of the kingdom shall be cast out into outer darkness: there shall be weeping and gnashing of teeth.

13And Jesus said unto the centurion, Go thy way; and as thou hast believed, *so* be it done unto thee. And his servant was healed in the selfsame hour.

14¶ And when Jesus was come into Peter's house, he saw his wife's mother laid, and sick of a fever.

15And he touched her hand, and the fever left her: and she arose, and ministered unto them.

16¶ When the even was come, they brought unto him many that were possessed with devils: and he cast out the spirits with *his* word, and healed all that were sick:

17That it might be fulfilled which was spoken by Esaias the prophet, saying, Himself took our infirmities, and bare *our* sicknesses.

18¶ Now when Jesus saw great multitudes about him, he gave commandment to depart unto the other side.

19And a certain scribe came, and said unto him, Master, I will follow thee whithersoever thou goest.

20And Jesus saith unto him, The foxes have holes, and the birds of the air *have* nests; but the Son of man hath not where to lay *his* head.

21And another of his disciples said unto him, Lord, suffer me first to go and bury my father.

22But Jesus said unto him, Follow me; and let the dead bury their dead.

23¶ And when he was entered into a ship, his disciples followed him.

24And, behold, there arose a great tempest in the sea, insomuch that the ship was covered with the waves: but he was asleep.

25And his disciples came to *him,* and awoke him, saying, Lord, save us: we perish.

New International

The Man With Leprosy

8 WHEN HE came down from the mountainside, large crowds followed him. 2A man with leprosy[a] came and knelt before him and said, "Lord, if you are willing, you can make me clean."

3Jesus reached out his hand and touched the man. "I am willing," he said. "Be clean!" Immediately he was cured[b] of his leprosy. 4Then Jesus said to him, "See that you don't tell anyone. But go, show yourself to the priest and offer the gift Moses commanded, as a testimony to them."

The Faith of the Centurion

5When Jesus had entered Capernaum, a centurion came to him, asking for help. 6"Lord," he said, "my servant lies at home paralyzed and in terrible suffering."

7Jesus said to him, "I will go and heal him."

8The centurion replied, "Lord, I do not deserve to have you come under my roof. But just say the word, and my servant will be healed. 9For I myself am a man under authority, with soldiers under me. I tell this one, 'Go,' and he goes; and that one, 'Come,' and he comes. I say to my servant, 'Do this,' and he does it."

10When Jesus heard this, he was astonished and said to those following him, "I tell you the truth, I have not found anyone in Israel with such great faith. 11I say to you that many will come from the east and the west, and will take their places at the feast with Abraham, Isaac and Jacob in the kingdom of heaven. 12But the subjects of the kingdom will be thrown outside, into the darkness, where there will be weeping and gnashing of teeth."

13Then Jesus said to the centurion, "Go! It will be done just as you believed it would." And his servant was healed at that very hour.

Jesus Heals Many

14When Jesus came into Peter's house, he saw Peter's mother-in-law lying in bed with a fever. 15He touched her hand and the fever left her, and she got up and began to wait on him.

16When evening came, many who were demon-possessed were brought to him, and he drove out the spirits with a word and healed all the sick. 17This was to fulfill what was spoken through the prophet Isaiah:

"He took up our infirmities
and carried our diseases."[c]

The Cost of Following Jesus

18When Jesus saw the crowd around him, he gave orders to cross to the other side of the lake. 19Then a teacher of the law came to him and said, "Teacher, I will follow you wherever you go."

20Jesus replied, "Foxes have holes and birds of the air have nests, but the Son of Man has no place to lay his head."

21Another disciple said to him, "Lord, first let me go and bury my father."

22But Jesus told him, "Follow me, and let the dead bury their own dead."

Jesus Calms the Storm

23Then he got into the boat and his disciples followed him. 24Without warning, a furious storm came up on the lake, so that the waves swept over the boat. But Jesus was sleeping. 25The disciples went and woke him, saying, "Lord, save us! We're going to drown!"

---

a 2 The Greek word was used for various diseases affecting the skin—not necessarily leprosy.   b 3 Greek *made clean*   c 17 Isaiah 53:4

Living Bible

8 LARGE CROWDS followed Jesus as he came down the hillside.

2Look! A leper is approaching. He kneels before him, worshiping. "Sir," the leper pleads, "if you want to, you can heal me."

3Jesus touches the man. "I want to," he says. "Be healed." And instantly the leprosy disappears.

4Then Jesus says to him, "Don't stop to talkᵈ to anyone; go right over to the priest to be examined; and take with you the offering required by Moses' law for lepers who are healed—a public testimony of your cure."

5, 6When Jesus arrived in Capernaum, a Roman army captain came and pled with him to come to his home and heal his servant boy who was in bed paralyzed and racked with pain.

7"Yes," Jesus said, "I will come and heal him."

8, 9Then the officer said, "Sir, I am not worthy to have you in my home; [and it isn't necessary for you to comeᵉ]. If you will only stand here and say, 'Be healed,' my servant will get well! I know, because I am under the authority of my superior officers and I have authority over my soldiers, and I say to one, 'Go,' and he goes, and to another, 'Come,' and he comes, and to my slave boy, 'Do this or that,' and he does it. And I know you have authority to tell his sickness to go—and it will go!"

10Jesus stood there amazed! Turning to the crowd he said, "I haven't seen faith like this in all the land of Israel! 11And I tell you this, that many Gentiles [like this Roman officerᶠ], shall come from all over the world and sit down in the Kingdom of Heaven with Abraham, Isaac, and Jacob. 12And many an Israelite—those for whom the Kingdom was prepared—shall be cast into outer darkness, into the place of weeping and torment."

13Then Jesus said to the Roman officer, "Go on home. What you have believed has happened!" And the boy was healed that same hour!

14When Jesus arrived at Peter's house, Peter's mother-in-law was in bed with a high fever. 15But when Jesus touched her hand, the fever left her; and she got up and prepared a meal for them!ᵍ

16That evening several demon-possessed people were brought to Jesus; and when he spoke a single word, all the demons fled; and all the sick were healed. 17This fulfilled the prophecy of Isaiah, "He took our sicknesses and bore our diseases."ʰ

18When Jesus noticed how large the crowd was growing, he instructed his disciples to get ready to cross to the other side of the lake.

19Just thenⁱ one of the Jewish religious teachersʲ said to him, "Teacher, I will follow you no matter where you go!"

20But Jesus said, "Foxes have dens and birds have nests, but I, the Messiah,ᵏ have no home of my own—no place to lay my head."

21Another of his disciples said, "Sir, when my father is dead, then I will follow you."ˡ

22But Jesus told him, "Follow me now!ᵐ Let those who are spiritually deadⁿ care for their own dead."

23Then he got into a boat and started across the lake with his disciples. 24Suddenly a terrible storm came up, with waves higher than the boat. But Jesus was asleep.

25The disciples went to him and wakened him, shouting, "Lord, save us! We're sinking!"

New Revised Standard

Jesus Cleanses a Leper

8 WHEN JESUSᵒ had come down from the mountain, great crowds followed him; 2and there was a leperᵖ who came to him and knelt before him, saying, "Lord, if you choose, you can make me clean." 3He stretched out his hand and touched him, saying, "I do choose. Be made clean!" Immediately his leprosyᵖ was cleansed. 4Then Jesus said to him, "See that you say nothing to anyone; but go, show yourself to the priest, and offer the gift that Moses commanded, as a testimony to them."

Jesus Heals a Centurion's Servant

5 When he entered Capernaum, a centurion came to him, appealing to him 6and saying, "Lord, my servant is lying at home paralyzed, in terrible distress." 7And he said to him, "I will come and cure him." 8The centurion answered, "Lord, I am not worthy to have you come under my roof; but only speak the word, and my servant will be healed. 9For I also am a man under authority, with soldiers under me; and I say to one, 'Go,' and he goes, and to another, 'Come,' and he comes, and to my slave, 'Do this,' and the slave does it." 10When Jesus heard him, he was amazed and said to those who followed him, "Truly I tell you, in no oneᵍ in Israel have I found such faith. 11I tell you, many will come from east and west and will eat with Abraham and Isaac and Jacob in the kingdom of heaven, 12while the heirs of the kingdom will be thrown into the outer darkness, where there will be weeping and gnashing of teeth." 13And to the centurion Jesus said, "Go; let it be done for you according to your faith." And the servant was healed in that hour.

Jesus Heals Many at Peter's House

14 When Jesus entered Peter's house, he saw his mother-in-law lying in bed with a fever; 15he touched her hand, and the fever left her, and she got up and began to serve him. 16That evening they brought to him many who were possessed with demons; and he cast out the spirits with a word, and cured all who were sick. 17This was to fulfill what had been spoken through the prophet Isaiah, "He took our infirmities and bore our diseases."

Would-Be Followers of Jesus

18 Now when Jesus saw great crowds around him, he gave orders to go over to the other side. 19A scribe then approached and said, "Teacher, I will follow you wherever you go." 20And Jesus said to him, "Foxes have holes, and birds of the air have nests; but the Son of Man has nowhere to lay his head." 21Another of his disciples said to him, "Lord, first let me go and bury my father." 22But Jesus said to him, "Follow me, and let the dead bury their own dead."

Jesus Stills the Storm

23 And when he got into the boat, his disciples followed him. 24A windstorm arose on the sea, so great that the boat was being swamped by the waves; but he was asleep. 25And they went and woke him up, saying, "Lord, save us! We are perishing!" 26And he said to

---

ᵈ 8:4 talk, literally, "See you tell no man." ᵉ 8:8, 9 and it isn't necessary for you to come, implied. ᶠ 8:11 like this Roman officer, implied. ᵍ 8:15 prepared a meal for them, literally, "ministered unto them." ʰ 8:17 bore our diseases, Isa 53:4. ⁱ 8:19 Just then, implied. ʲ 8:19 one of the Jewish religious teachers, literally, "a scribe." ᵏ 8:20 Messiah, literally, "Son of Man." ˡ 8:21 then I will follow you, or, "let me first go and bury my father." ᵐ 8:22 now, implied. ⁿ 8:22 spiritually dead, implied.

ᵒ Gk he ᵖ The terms leper and leprosy can refer to several diseases ᵍ Other ancient authorities read Truly I tell you, not even

King James

26And he saith unto them, Why are ye fearful, O ye of little faith? Then he arose, and rebuked the winds and the sea; and there was a great calm.

27But the men marvelled, saying, What manner of man is this, that even the winds and the sea obey him!

28¶ And when he was come to the other side into the country of the Gergesenes, there met him two possessed with devils, coming out of the tombs, exceeding fierce, so that no man might pass by that way.

29And, behold, they cried out, saying, What have we to do with thee, Jesus, thou Son of God? art thou come hither to torment us before the time?

30And there was a good way off from them an herd of many swine feeding.

31So the devils besought him, saying, If thou cast us out, suffer us to go away into the herd of swine.

32And he said unto them, Go. And when they were come out, they went into the herd of swine: and, behold, the whole herd of swine ran violently down a steep place into the sea, and perished in the waters.

33And they that kept them fled, and went their ways into the city, and told every thing, and what was befallen to the possessed of the devils.

34And, behold, the whole city came out to meet Jesus: and when they saw him, they besought *him* that he would depart out of their coasts.

9 AND HE entered into a ship, and passed over, and came into his own city.

2And, behold, they brought to him a man sick of the palsy, lying on a bed: and Jesus seeing their faith said unto the sick of the palsy; Son, be of good cheer; thy sins be forgiven thee.

3And, behold, certain of the scribes said within themselves, This *man* blasphemeth.

4And Jesus knowing their thoughts said, Wherefore think ye evil in your hearts?

5For whether is easier, to say, *Thy* sins be forgiven thee; or to say, Arise, and walk?

6But that ye may know that the Son of man hath power on earth to forgive sins, (then saith he to the sick of the palsy,) Arise, take up thy bed, and go unto thine house.

7And he arose, and departed to his house.

8But when the multitudes saw *it*, they marvelled, and glorified God, which had given such power unto men.

9¶ And as Jesus passed forth from thence, he saw a man, named Matthew, sitting at the receipt of custom: and he saith unto him, Follow me. And he arose, and followed him.

10¶ And it came to pass, as Jesus sat at meat in the house, behold, many publicans and sinners came and sat down with him and his disciples.

11And when the Pharisees saw *it*, they said unto his disciples, Why eateth your Master with publicans and sinners?

12But when Jesus heard *that*, he said unto them, They that be whole need not a physician, but they that are sick.

13But go ye and learn what *that* meaneth, I will have mercy, and not sacrifice: for I am not come to call the righteous, but sinners to repentance.

14¶ Then came to him the disciples of John, saying, Why do we and the Pharisees fast oft, but thy disciples fast not?

New International

26He replied, "You of little faith, why are you so afraid?" Then he got up and rebuked the winds and the waves, and it was completely calm.

27The men were amazed and asked, "What kind of man is this? Even the winds and the waves obey him!"

The Healing of Two Demon-possessed Men

28When he arrived at the other side in the region of the Gadarenes,a two demon-possessed men coming from the tombs met him. They were so violent that no one could pass that way. 29"What do you want with us, Son of God?" they shouted. "Have you come here to torture us before the appointed time?"

30Some distance from them a large herd of pigs was feeding. 31The demons begged Jesus, "If you drive us out, send us into the herd of pigs."

32He said to them, "Go!" So they came out and went into the pigs, and the whole herd rushed down the steep bank into the lake and died in the water. 33Those tending the pigs ran off, went into the town and reported all this, including what had happened to the demon-possessed men. 34Then the whole town went out to meet Jesus. And when they saw him, they pleaded with him to leave their region.

Jesus Heals a Paralytic

9 JESUS STEPPED into a boat, crossed over and came to his own town. 2Some men brought to him a paralytic, lying on a mat. When Jesus saw their faith, he said to the paralytic, "Take heart, son; your sins are forgiven."

3At this, some of the teachers of the law said to themselves, "This fellow is blaspheming!"

4Knowing their thoughts, Jesus said, "Why do you entertain evil thoughts in your hearts? 5Which is easier: to say, 'Your sins are forgiven,' or to say, 'Get up and walk'? 6But so that you may know that the Son of Man has authority on earth to forgive sins. . . ." Then he said to the paralytic, "Get up, take your mat and go home." 7And the man got up and went home. 8When the crowd saw this, they were filled with awe; and they praised God, who had given such authority to men.

The Calling of Matthew

9As Jesus went on from there, he saw a man named Matthew sitting at the tax collector's booth. "Follow me," he told him, and Matthew got up and followed him.

10While Jesus was having dinner at Matthew's house, many tax collectors and "sinners" came and ate with him and his disciples. 11When the Pharisees saw this, they asked his disciples, "Why does your teacher eat with tax collectors and 'sinners'?"

12On hearing this, Jesus said, "It is not the healthy who need a doctor, but the sick. 13But go and learn what this means: 'I desire mercy, not sacrifice.'b For I have not come to call the righteous, but sinners."

Jesus Questioned About Fasting

14Then John's disciples came and asked him, "How is it that we and the Pharisees fast, but your disciples do not fast?"

---

a 28 Some manuscripts *Gergesenes*; others *Gerasenes*   b 13 Hosea 6:6

Living Bible

26But Jesus answered, "O you men of little faith! Why are you so frightened?" Then he stood up and rebuked the wind and waves, and the storm subsided and all was calm. 27The disciples just sat there, awed! "Who is this," they asked themselves, "that even the winds and the sea obey him?"

28When they arrived on the other side of the lake, in the country of the Gadarenes, two men with demons in them met him. They lived in a cemetery and were so dangerous that no one could go through that area.

29They began screaming at him, "What do you want with us, O Son of God? You have no right to torment us yet."c

30A herd of pigs was feeding in the distance, 31so the demons begged, "If you cast us out, send us into that herd of pigs."

32"All right," Jesus told them. "Begone."

And they came out of the men and entered the pigs, and the whole herd rushed over a cliff and drowned in the water below. 33The herdsmen fled to the nearest city with the story of what had happened, 34and the entire population came rushing out to see Jesus, and begged him to go away and leave them alone.

9 SO JESUS climbed into a boat and went across the lake to Capernaum, his home town.d

2Soon some men brought him a paralyzed boy on a mat. When Jesus saw their faith, he said to the sick boy, "Cheer up, son! For I have forgiven your sins!"

3"Blasphemy! This man is saying he is God!" exclaimed some of the religious leaders to themselves. 4Jesus knew what they were thinking and asked them, "Why are you thinking such evil thoughts? 5, 6I, the Messiah,e have the authority on earth to forgive sins. But talk is cheap—anybody could say that. So I'll prove it to you by healing this man." Then, turning to the paralyzed man, he commanded, "Pick up your stretcher and go on home, for you are healed."

7And the boy jumped up and left!

8A chill of fear swept through the crowd as they saw this happen right before their eyes. How they praised God for giving such authority to a man!

9As Jesus was going on down the road, he saw a tax collector, Matthew,f sitting at a tax collection booth. "Come and be my disciple," Jesus said to him, and Matthew jumped up and went along with him.

10Later, as Jesus and his disciples were eating dinner [at Matthew's house], there were many notorious swindlers there as guests!

11The Pharisees were indignant. "Why does your teacher associate with men like that?"

12"Because people who are well don't need a doctor! It's the sick people who do!" was Jesus' reply. 13Then he added, "Now go away and learn the meaning of this verse of Scripture,

'It isn't your sacrifices and your gifts I want—I want you to be merciful.'h

For I have come to urge sinners, not the self-righteous, back to God."

14One day the disciples of John the Baptist came to Jesus and asked him, "Why don't your disciples fast as we do and as the Pharisees do?"

New Revised Standard

them, "Why are you afraid, you of little faith?" Then he got up and rebuked the winds and the sea; and there was a dead calm. 27They were amazed, saying, "What sort of man is this, that even the winds and the sea obey him?"

Jesus Heals the Gadarene Demoniacs

28 When he came to the other side, to the country of the Gadarenes,i two demoniacs coming out of the tombs met him. They were so fierce that no one could pass that way. 29Suddenly they shouted, "What have you to do with us, Son of God? Have you come here to torment us before the time?" 30Now a large herd of swine was feeding at some distance from them. 31The demons begged him, "If you cast us out, send us into the herd of swine." 32And he said to them, "Go!" So they came out and entered the swine; and suddenly, the whole herd rushed down the steep bank into the sea and perished in the water. 33The swineherds ran off, and on going into the town, they told the whole story about what had happened to the demoniacs. 34Then the whole town came out to meet Jesus; and when they saw him, they begged him to leave their neighborhood.

9 AND AFTER getting into a boat he crossed the sea and came to his own town.

Jesus Heals a Paralytic

2 And just then some people were carrying a paralyzed man lying on a bed. When Jesus saw their faith, he said to the paralytic, "Take heart, son; your sins are forgiven." 3Then some of the scribes said to themselves, "This man is blaspheming." 4But Jesus, perceiving their thoughts, said, "Why do you think evil in your hearts? 5For which is easier, to say, 'Your sins are forgiven,' or to say, 'Stand up and walk'? 6But so that you may know that the Son of Man has authority on earth to forgive sins"—he then said to the paralytic—"Stand up, take your bed and go to your home." 7And he stood up and went to his home. 8When the crowds saw it, they were filled with awe, and they glorified God, who had given such authority to human beings.

The Call of Matthew

9 As Jesus was walking along, he saw a man called Matthew sitting at the tax booth; and he said to him, "Follow me." And he got up and followed him.

10 And as he sat at dinnerj in the house, many tax collectors and sinners came and were sittingk with him and his disciples. 11When the Pharisees saw this, they said to his disciples, "Why does your teacher eat with tax collectors and sinners?" 12But when he heard this, he said, "Those who are well have no need of a physician, but those who are sick. 13Go and learn what this means, 'I desire mercy, not sacrifice.' For I have come to call not the righteous but sinners."

The Question about Fasting

14 Then the disciples of John came to him, saying, "Why do we and the Pharisees fast often,l but your disciples do not fast?" 15And Jesus said to them, "The

---

c 8:29 You have no right to torment us yet, literally, "Have you come here to torment us before the time?" d 9:1 his home town, literally, "his own city." e 9:5, 6 the Messiah, literally, "the Son of Man." f 9:9 Matthew. The Matthew who wrote this book. g 9:10 at Matthew's house, implied. h 9:13 to be merciful, see Hosea 6:6.

i Other ancient authorities read Gergesenes; others, Gerasenes   j Gk reclined   k Gk were reclining   l Other ancient authorities lack often

King James

15And Jesus said unto them, Can the children of the bridechamber mourn, as long as the bridegroom is with them? but the days will come, when the bridegroom shall be taken from them, and then shall they fast.

16No man putteth a piece of new cloth unto an old garment, for that which is put in to fill it up taketh from the garment, and the rent is made worse.

17Neither do men put new wine into old bottles: else the bottles break, and the wine runneth out, and the bottles perish: but they put new wine into new bottles, and both are preserved.

18¶ While he spake these things unto them, behold, there came a certain ruler, and worshipped him, saying, My daughter is even now dead: but come and lay thy hand upon her, and she shall live.

19And Jesus arose, and followed him, and *so did* his disciples.

20¶ And, behold, a woman, which was diseased with an issue of blood twelve years, came behind *him*, and touched the hem of his garment:

21For she said within herself, If I may but touch his garment, I shall be whole.

22But Jesus turned him about, and when he saw her, he said, Daughter, be of good comfort; thy faith hath made thee whole. And the woman was made whole from that hour.

23And when Jesus came into the ruler's house, and saw the minstrels and the people making a noise,

24He said unto them, Give place: for the maid is not dead, but sleepeth. And they laughed him to scorn.

25But when the people were put forth, he went in, and took her by the hand, and the maid arose.

26And the fame hereof went abroad into all that land.

27¶ And when Jesus departed thence, two blind men followed him, crying, and saying, *Thou* Son of David, have mercy on us.

28And when he was come into the house, the blind men came to him: and Jesus saith unto them, Believe ye that I am able to do this? They said unto him, Yea, Lord.

29Then touched he their eyes, saying, According to your faith be it unto you.

30And their eyes were opened; and Jesus straitly charged them, saying, See *that* no man know *it*.

31But they, when they were departed, spread abroad his fame in all that country.

32¶ As they went out, behold, they brought to him a dumb man possessed with a devil.

33And when the devil was cast out, the dumb spake: and the multitudes marvelled, saying, It was never so seen in Israel.

34But the Pharisees said, He casteth out devils through the prince of the devils.

35And Jesus went about all the cities and villages, teaching in their synagogues, and preaching the gospel of the kingdom, and healing every sickness and every disease among the people.

36¶ But when he saw the multitudes, he was moved with compassion on them, because they fainted, and were scattered abroad, as sheep having no shepherd.

37Then saith he unto his disciples, The harvest truly *is* plenteous, but the labourers *are* few;

38Pray ye therefore the Lord of the harvest, that he will send forth labourers into his harvest.

10 AND WHEN he had called unto *him* his twelve disciples, he gave them power *against* unclean spirits, to cast them out, and to heal all manner of sickness and all manner of disease.

New International

15Jesus answered, "How can the guests of the bridegroom mourn while he is with them? The time will come when the bridegroom will be taken from them; then they will fast.

16"No one sews a patch of unshrunk cloth on an old garment, for the patch will pull away from the garment, making the tear worse. 17Neither do men pour new wine into old wineskins. If they do, the skins will burst, the wine will run out and the wineskins will be ruined. No, they pour new wine into new wineskins, and both are preserved."

A Dead Girl and a Sick Woman

18While he was saying this, a ruler came and knelt before him and said, "My daughter has just died. But come and put your hand on her, and she will live." 19Jesus got up and went with him, and so did his disciples.

20Just then a woman who had been subject to bleeding for twelve years came up behind him and touched the edge of his cloak. 21She said to herself, "If I only touch his cloak, I will be healed."

22Jesus turned and saw her. "Take heart, daughter," he said, "your faith has healed you." And the woman was healed from that moment.

23When Jesus entered the ruler's house and saw the flute players and the noisy crowd, 24he said, "Go away. The girl is not dead but asleep." But they laughed at him. 25After the crowd had been put outside, he went in and took the girl by the hand, and she got up. 26News of this spread through all that region.

Jesus Heals the Blind and Mute

27As Jesus went on from there, two blind men followed him, calling out, "Have mercy on us, Son of David!"

28When he had gone indoors, the blind men came to him, and he asked them, "Do you believe that I am able to do this?"

"Yes, Lord," they replied.

29Then he touched their eyes and said, "According to your faith will it be done to you"; 30and their sight was restored. Jesus warned them sternly, "See that no one knows about this." 31But they went out and spread the news about him all over that region.

32While they were going out, a man who was demon-possessed and could not talk was brought to Jesus. 33And when the demon was driven out, the man who had been mute spoke. The crowd was amazed and said, "Nothing like this has ever been seen in Israel."

34But the Pharisees said, "It is by the prince of demons that he drives out demons."

The Workers Are Few

35Jesus went through all the towns and villages, teaching in their synagogues, preaching the good news of the kingdom and healing every disease and sickness. 36When he saw the crowds, he had compassion on them, because they were harassed and helpless, like sheep without a shepherd. 37Then he said to his disciples, "The harvest is plentiful but the workers are few. 38Ask the Lord of the harvest, therefore, to send out workers into his harvest field."

Jesus Sends Out the Twelve

10 HE CALLED his twelve disciples to him and gave them authority to drive out evil[a] spirits and to heal every disease and sickness.

---

a *1* Greek *unclean*

Living Bible

15"Should the bridegroom's friends mourn and go without food while he is with them?" Jesus asked. "But the time is coming when I[b] will be taken from them. Time enough then for them to refuse to eat.

16"And who would patch an old garment with unshrunk cloth? For the patch would tear away and make the hole worse. 17And who would use old wineskins[c] to store new wine? For the old skins would burst with the pressure, and the wine would be spilled and skins ruined. Only new wineskins are used to store new wine. That way both are preserved."

18As he was saying this, the rabbi of the local synagogue came and worshiped him. "My little daughter has just died," he said, "but you can bring her back to life again if you will only come and touch her."

19As Jesus and the disciples were going to the rabbi's home, 20a woman who had been sick for twelve years with internal bleeding came up behind him and touched a tassel of his robe, 21for she thought, "If I only touch him, I will be healed."

22Jesus turned around and spoke to her. "Daughter," he said, "all is well! Your faith has healed you." And the woman was well from that moment.

23When Jesus arrived at the rabbi's home and saw the noisy crowds and heard the funeral music, 24he said, "Get them out, for the little girl isn't dead; she is only sleeping!" Then how they all scoffed and sneered at him!

25When the crowd was finally outside, Jesus went in where the little girl was lying and took her by the hand, and she jumped up and was all right again! 26The report of this wonderful miracle swept the entire countryside.

27As Jesus was leaving her home, two blind men followed along behind, shouting, "O Son of King David, have mercy on us."

28They went right into the house where he was staying, and Jesus asked them, "Do you believe I can make you see?"

"Yes, Lord," they told him, "we do."

29Then he touched their eyes and said, "Because of your faith it will happen."

30And suddenly they could see! Jesus sternly warned them not to tell anyone about it, 31but instead they spread his fame all over the town.[d]

32Leaving that place, Jesus met a man who couldn't speak because a demon was inside him. 33So Jesus cast out the demon, and instantly the man could talk. How the crowds marveled! "Never in all our lives have we seen anything like this," they exclaimed.

34But the Pharisees said, "The reason he can cast out demons is that he is demon-possessed himself—possessed by Satan, the demon king!"

35Jesus traveled around through all the cities and villages of that area, teaching in the Jewish synagogues and announcing the Good News about the Kingdom. And wherever he went he healed people of every sort of illness. 36And what pity he felt for the crowds that came, because their problems were so great and they didn't know what to do or where to go for help. They were like sheep without a shepherd.

37"The harvest is so great, and the workers are so few," he told his disciples. 38"So pray to the one in charge of the harvesting, and ask him to recruit more workers for his harvest fields."

10 JESUS CALLED his twelve disciples to him, and gave them authority to cast out evil spirits and to heal every kind of sickness and disease.

b 9:15 *I*, literally, "the Bridegroom." c 9:17 *old wineskins*. These were leather bags for storing wine. d 9:31 *all over the town*, literally, "in all that land."

New Revised Standard

wedding guests cannot mourn as long as the bridegroom is with them, can they? The days will come when the bridegroom is taken away from them, and then they will fast. 16No one sews a piece of unshrunk cloth on an old cloak, for the patch pulls away from the cloak, and a worse tear is made. 17Neither is new wine put into old wineskins; otherwise, the skins burst, and the wine is spilled, and the skins are destroyed; but new wine is put into fresh wineskins, and so both are preserved."

A Girl Restored to Life and a Woman Healed

18 While he was saying these things to them, suddenly a leader of the synagogue[e] came in and knelt before him, saying, "My daughter has just died; but come and lay your hand on her, and she will live." 19And Jesus got up and followed him, with his disciples. 20Then suddenly a woman who had been suffering from hemorrhages for twelve years came up behind him and touched the fringe of his cloak, 21for she said to herself, "If I only touch his cloak, I will be made well." 22Jesus turned, and seeing her he said, "Take heart, daughter; your faith has made you well." And instantly the woman was made well. 23When Jesus came to the leader's house and saw the flute players and the crowd making a commotion, 24he said, "Go away; for the girl is not dead but sleeping." And they laughed at him. 25But when the crowd had been put outside, he went in and took her by the hand, and the girl got up. 26And the report of this spread throughout that district.

Jesus Heals Two Blind Men

27 As Jesus went on from there, two blind men followed him, crying loudly, "Have mercy on us, Son of David!" 28When he entered the house, the blind men came to him; and Jesus said to them, "Do you believe that I am able to do this?" They said to him, "Yes, Lord." 29Then he touched their eyes and said, "According to your faith let it be done to you." 30And their eyes were opened. Then Jesus sternly ordered them, "See that no one knows of this." 31But they went away and spread the news about him throughout that district.

Jesus Heals One Who Was Mute

32 After they had gone away, a demoniac who was mute was brought to him. 33And when the demon had been cast out, the one who had been mute spoke; and the crowds were amazed and said, "Never has anything like this been seen in Israel." 34But the Pharisees said, "By the ruler of the demons he casts out the demons."[f]

The Harvest Is Great, the Laborers Few

35 Then Jesus went about all the cities and villages, teaching in their synagogues, and proclaiming the good news of the kingdom, and curing every disease and every sickness. 36When he saw the crowds, he had compassion for them, because they were harassed and helpless, like sheep without a shepherd. 37Then he said to his disciples, "The harvest is plentiful, but the laborers are few; 38therefore ask the Lord of the harvest to send out laborers into his harvest."

The Twelve Apostles

10 THEN JESUS[g] summoned his twelve disciples and gave them authority over unclean spirits, to cast them out, and to cure every disease and every sickness. 2These are the names of the twelve apostles: first,

e Gk lacks *of the synagogue* f Other ancient authorities lack this verse g Gk *he*

King James

2Now the names of the twelve apostles are these; The first, Simon, who is called Peter, and Andrew his brother; James *the son* of Zebedee, and John his brother;

3Philip, and Bartholomew; Thomas, and Matthew the publican; James *the son* of Alphaeus, and Lebbaeus, whose surname was Thaddaeus;

4Simon the Canaanite, and Judas Iscariot, who also betrayed him.

5These twelve Jesus sent forth, and commanded them, saying, Go not into the way of the Gentiles, and into *any* city of the Samaritans enter ye not:

6But go rather to the lost sheep of the house of Israel.

7And as ye go, preach, saying, The kingdom of heaven is at hand.

8Heal the sick, cleanse the lepers, raise the dead, cast out devils: freely ye have received, freely give.

9Provide neither gold, nor silver, nor brass in your purses,

10Nor scrip for *your* journey, neither two coats, neither shoes, nor yet staves: for the workman is worthy of his meat.

11And into whatsoever city or town ye shall enter, inquire who in it is worthy; and there abide till ye go thence.

12And when ye come into an house, salute it.

13And if the house be worthy, let your peace come upon it: but if it be not worthy, let your peace return to you.

14And whosoever shall not receive you, nor hear your words, when ye depart out of that house or city, shake off the dust of your feet.

15Verily I say unto you, It shall be more tolerable for the land of Sodom and Gomorrha in the day of judgment, than for that city.

16¶ Behold, I send you forth as sheep in the midst of wolves: be ye therefore wise as serpents, and harmless as doves.

17But beware of men: for they will deliver you up to the councils, and they will scourge you in their synagogues;

18And ye shall be brought before governors and kings for my sake, for a testimony against them and the Gentiles.

19But when they deliver you up, take no thought how or what ye shall speak: for it shall be given you in that same hour what ye shall speak.

20For it is not ye that speak, but the Spirit of your Father which speaketh in you.

21And the brother shall deliver up the brother to death, and the father the child: and the children shall rise up against *their* parents, and cause them to be put to death.

22And ye shall be hated of all *men* for my name's sake: but he that endureth to the end shall be saved.

23But when they persecute you in this city, flee ye into another: for verily I say unto you, Ye shall not have gone over the cities of Israel, till the Son of man be come.

24The disciple is not above *his* master, nor the servant above his lord.

25It is enough for the disciple that he be as his master, and the servant as his lord. If they have called the master of the house Beelzebub, how much more *shall they call* them of his household?

26Fear them not therefore: for there is nothing covered, that shall not be revealed; and hid, that shall not be known.

27What I tell you in darkness, *that* speak ye in light: and what ye hear in the ear, *that* preach ye upon the housetops.

28And fear not them which kill the body, but are not able to kill the soul: but rather fear him which is able to destroy both soul and body in hell.

29Are not two sparrows sold for a farthing? and one of them shall not fall on the ground without your Father.

New International

2These are the names of the twelve apostles: first, Simon (who is called Peter) and his brother Andrew; James son of Zebedee, and his brother John; 3Philip and Bartholomew; Thomas and Matthew the tax collector; James son of Alphaeus, and Thaddaeus; 4Simon the Zealot and Judas Iscariot, who betrayed him.

5These twelve Jesus sent out with the following instructions: "Do not go among the Gentiles or enter any town of the Samaritans. 6Go rather to the lost sheep of Israel. 7As you go, preach this message: 'The kingdom of heaven is near.' 8Heal the sick, raise the dead, cleanse those who have leprosy,a drive out demons. Freely you have received, freely give. 9Do not take along any gold or silver or copper in your belts; 10take no bag for the journey, or extra tunic, or sandals or a staff; for the worker is worth his keep.

11"Whatever town or village you enter, search for some worthy person there and stay at his house until you leave. 12As you enter the home, give it your greeting. 13If the home is deserving, let your peace rest on it; if it is not, let your peace return to you. 14If anyone will not welcome you or listen to your words, shake the dust off your feet when you leave that home or town. 15I tell you the truth, it will be more bearable for Sodom and Gomorrah on the day of judgment than for that town. 16I am sending you out like sheep among wolves. Therefore be as shrewd as snakes and as innocent as doves.

17"Be on your guard against men; they will hand you over to the local councils and flog you in their synagogues. 18On my account you will be brought before governors and kings as witnesses to them and to the Gentiles. 19But when they arrest you, do not worry about what to say or how to say it. At that time you will be given what to say, 20for it will not be you speaking, but the Spirit of your Father speaking through you.

21"Brother will betray brother to death, and a father his child; children will rebel against their parents and have them put to death. 22All men will hate you because of me, but he who stands firm to the end will be saved. 23When you are persecuted in one place, flee to another. I tell you the truth, you will not finish going through the cities of Israel before the Son of Man comes.

24"A student is not above his teacher, nor a servant above his master. 25It is enough for the student to be like his teacher, and the servant like his master. If the head of the house has been called Beelzebub,b how much more the members of his household!

26"So do not be afraid of them. There is nothing concealed that will not be disclosed, or hidden that will not be made known. 27What I tell you in the dark, speak in the daylight; what is whispered in your ear, proclaim from the roofs. 28Do not be afraid of those who kill the body but cannot kill the soul. Rather, be afraid of the One who can destroy both soul and body in hell. 29Are not two sparrows sold for a pennyc? Yet not one of them will fall to the ground apart from the will of your Father.

---

a 8 The Greek word was used for various diseases affecting the skin—not necessarily leprosy.   b 25 Greek *Beezeboul* or *Beelzeboul*   c 29 Greek *an assarion*

Living Bible

2, 3, 4Here are the names of his twelve disciples:
Simon (also called Peter),
Andrew (Peter's brother),
James (Zebedee's son),
John (James' brother),
Philip,
Bartholomew,
Thomas,
Matthew (the tax collector),
James (Alphaeus' son),
Thaddaeus,
Simon (a member of "The Zealots," a subversive
   political party),
Judas Iscariot (the one who betrayed him).

5Jesus sent them out with these instructions: "Don't
go to the Gentiles or the Samaritans, 6but only to the
people of Israel—God's lost sheep. 7Go and announce
to them that the Kingdom of Heaven is near.d 8Heal the
sick, raise the dead, cure the lepers, and cast out demons. Give as freely as you have received!

9"Don't take any money with you; 10don't even carry
a duffle bag with extra clothes and shoes, or even a
walking stick; for those you help should feed and care
for you. 11Whenever you enter a city or village, search
for a godly man and stay in his home until you leave for
the next town. 12When you ask permission to stay, be
friendly, 13and if it turns out to be a godly home, give
it your blessing; if not, keep the blessing. 14Any city or
home that doesn't welcome you—shake off the dust of
that place from your feet as you leave. 15Truly, the wicked cities of Sodom and Gomorrah will be better off at
Judgment Day than they.

16"I am sending you out as sheep among wolves. Be
as wary as serpents and harmless as doves. 17But beware! For you will be arrested and tried, and whipped
in the synagogues. 18Yes, and you must stand trial before governors and kings for my sake. This will give you
the opportunity to tell them about me, yes, to witness to
the world.

19"When you are arrested, don't worry about what to
say at your trial, for you will be given the right words
at the right time. 20For it won't be you doing the talking—it will be the Spirit of your heavenly Father speaking through you!

21"Brother shall betray brother to death, and fathers
shall betray their own children. And children shall rise
against their parents and cause their deaths. 22Everyone
shall hate you because you belong to me. But all of you
who endure to the end shall be saved.

23"When you are persecuted in one city, flee to the
next! Ie will return before you have reached them all!

24"A student is not greater than his teacher. A servant
is not above his master. 25The student shares his teacher's fate. The servant shares his master's! And since I,
the master of the household, have been called 'Satan,'f
how much more will you! 26But don't be afraid of those
who threaten you. For the time is coming when the truth
will be revealed: their secret plots will become public
information.

27"What I tell you now in the gloom, shout abroad
when daybreak comes. What I whisper in your ears,
proclaim from the housetops!

28"Don't be afraid of those who can kill only your
bodies—but can't touch your souls! Fear only God who
can destroy both soul and body in hell. 29Not one sparrow (What do they cost? Two for a penny?) can fall to
the ground without your Father knowing it. 30And the

New Revised Standard

Simon, also known as Peter, and his brother Andrew;
James son of Zebedee, and his brother John; 3Philip and
Bartholomew; Thomas and Matthew the tax collector;
James son of Alphaeus, and Thaddaeus;g 4Simon the
Cananaean, and Judas Iscariot, the one who betrayed
him.

The Mission of the Twelve

5 These twelve Jesus sent out with the following
instructions: "Go nowhere among the Gentiles, and enter no town of the Samaritans, 6but go rather to the lost
sheep of the house of Israel. 7As you go, proclaim the
good news, 'The kingdom of heaven has come near.'h
8Cure the sick, raise the dead, cleanse the lepers,i cast
out demons. You received without payment; give without payment. 9Take no gold, or silver, or copper in your
belts, 10no bag for your journey, or two tunics, or sandals, or a staff; for laborers deserve their food. 11What-
ever town or village you enter, find out who in it is
worthy, and stay there until you leave. 12As you enter
the house, greet it. 13If the house is worthy, let your
peace come upon it; but if it is not worthy, let your peace
return to you. 14If anyone will not welcome you or listen
to your words, shake off the dust from your feet as you
leave that house or town. 15Truly I tell you, it will be
more tolerable for the land of Sodom and Gomorrah on
the day of judgment than for that town.

Coming Persecutions

16 "See, I am sending you out like sheep into the
midst of wolves; so be wise as serpents and innocent as
doves. 17Beware of them, for they will hand you over
to councils and flog you in their synagogues; 18and you
will be dragged before governors and kings because of
me, as a testimony to them and the Gentiles. 19When
they hand you over, do not worry about how you are to
speak or what you are to say; for what you are to say will
be given to you at that time; 20for it is not you who
speak, but the Spirit of your Father speaking through
you. 21Brother will betray brother to death, and a father
his child, and children will rise against parents and have
them put to death; 22and you will be hated by all because
of my name. But the one who endures to the end will
be saved. 23When they persecute you in one town, flee
to the next; for truly I tell you, you will not have gone
through all the towns of Israel before the Son of Man
comes.

24 "A disciple is not above the teacher, nor a slave
above the master; 25it is enough for the disciple to be like
the teacher, and the slave like the master. If they have
called the master of the house Beelzebul, how much
more will they malign those of his household!

Whom to Fear

26 "So have no fear of them; for nothing is covered
up that will not be uncovered, and nothing secret that
will not become known. 27What I say to you in the dark,
tell in the light; and what you hear whispered, proclaim
from the housetops. 28Do not fear those who kill the
body but cannot kill the soul; rather fear him who can
destroy both soul and body in hell.j 29Are not two sparrows sold for a penny? Yet not one of them will fall to
the ground apart from your Father. 30And even the hairs

---

d 10:7 is near, or, "at hand," or, "has arrived."   e 10:23 I, literally, "the
Son of Man."   f 10:25 have been called Satan. See 9:34 where they called
him this.

g Other ancient authorities read Lebbaeus, or Lebbaeus called Thaddaeus
h Or is at hand   i The terms leper and leprosy can refer to several diseases
j Gk Gehenna

King James

30But the very hairs of your head are all numbered. 31Fear ye not therefore, ye are of more value than many sparrows.

32Whosoever therefore shall confess me before men, him will I confess also before my Father which is in heaven.

33But whosoever shall deny me before men, him will I also deny before my Father which is in heaven.

34Think not that I am come to send peace on earth: I came not to send peace, but a sword.

35For I am come to set a man at variance against his father, and the daughter against her mother, and the daughter-in-law against her mother-in-law.

36And a man's foes *shall be* they of his own household.

37He that loveth father or mother more than me is not worthy of me: and he that loveth son or daughter more than me is not worthy of me.

38And he that taketh not his cross, and followeth after me, is not worthy of me.

39He that findeth his life shall lose it: and he that loseth his life for my sake shall find it.

40¶ He that receiveth you receiveth me, and he that receiveth me receiveth him that sent me.

41He that receiveth a prophet in the name of a prophet shall receive a prophet's reward; and he that receiveth a righteous man in the name of a righteous man shall receive a righteous man's reward.

42And whosoever shall give to drink unto one of these little ones a cup of cold *water* only in the name of a disciple, verily I say unto you, he shall in no wise lose his reward.

11 AND IT came to pass, when Jesus had made an end of commanding his twelve disciples, he departed thence to teach and to preach in their cities.

2Now when John had heard in the prison the works of Christ, he sent two of his disciples,

3And said unto him, Art thou he that should come, or do we look for another?

4Jesus answered and said unto them, Go and show John again those things which ye do hear and see:

5The blind receive their sight, and the lame walk, the lepers are cleansed, and the deaf hear, the dead are raised up, and the poor have the gospel preached to them.

6And blessed is *he*, whosoever shall not be offended in me.

7¶ And as they departed, Jesus began to say unto the multitudes concerning John, What went ye out into the wilderness to see? A reed shaken with the wind?

8But what went ye out for to see? A man clothed in soft raiment? behold, they that wear soft *clothing* are in kings' houses.

9But what went ye out for to see? A prophet? yea, I say unto you, and more than a prophet.

10For this is *he*, of whom it is written, Behold, I send my messenger before thy face, which shall prepare thy way before thee.

11Verily I say unto you, Among them that are born of women there hath not risen a greater than John the Baptist: notwithstanding he that is least in the kingdom of heaven is greater than he.

New International

30And even the very hairs of your head are all numbered. 31So don't be afraid; you are worth more than many sparrows.

32"Whoever acknowledges me before men, I will also acknowledge him before my Father in heaven. 33But whoever disowns me before men, I will disown him before my Father in heaven.

34"Do not suppose that I have come to bring peace to the earth. I did not come to bring peace, but a sword. 35For I have come to turn

" 'a man against his father,
    a daughter against her mother,
    a daughter-in-law against her mother-in-law—
36   a man's enemies will be the members of his
        own household.'a

37"Anyone who loves his father or mother more than me is not worthy of me; anyone who loves his son or daughter more than me is not worthy of me; 38and anyone who does not take his cross and follow me is not worthy of me. 39Whoever finds his life will lose it, and whoever loses his life for my sake will find it.

40"He who receives you receives me, and he who receives me receives the one who sent me. 41Anyone who receives a prophet because he is a prophet will receive a prophet's reward, and anyone who receives a righteous man because he is a righteous man will receive a righteous man's reward. 42And if anyone gives even a cup of cold water to one of these little ones because he is my disciple, I tell you the truth, he will certainly not lose his reward."

Jesus and John the Baptist

11 AFTER JESUS had finished instructing his twelve disciples, he went on from there to teach and preach in the towns of Galilee.b

2When John heard in prison what Christ was doing, he sent his disciples 3to ask him, "Are you the one who was to come, or should we expect someone else?"

4Jesus replied, "Go back and report to John what you hear and see: 5The blind receive sight, the lame walk, those who have leprosyc are cured, the deaf hear, the dead are raised, and the good news is preached to the poor. 6Blessed is the man who does not fall away on account of me."

7As John's disciples were leaving, Jesus began to speak to the crowd about John: "What did you go out into the desert to see? A reed swayed by the wind? 8If not, what did you go out to see? A man dressed in fine clothes? No, those who wear fine clothes are in kings' palaces. 9Then what did you go out to see? A prophet? Yes, I tell you, and more than a prophet. 10This is the one about whom it is written:

" 'I will send my messenger ahead of you,
    who will prepare your way before you.'d

11I tell you the truth: Among those born of women there has not risen anyone greater than John the Baptist; yet he who is least in the kingdom of heaven is greater than he. 12From the days of John the Baptist until now, the

a *36* Micah 7:6   b *1* Greek *in their towns*   c *5* The Greek word was used for various diseases affecting the skin—not necessarily leprosy.   d *10* Mal. 3:1

Living Bible

very hairs of your head are all numbered. ³¹So don't worry! You are more valuable to him than many sparrows.

³²"If anyone publicly acknowledges me as his friend, I will openly acknowledge him as my friend before my Father in heaven. ³³But if anyone publicly denies me, I will openly deny him before my Father in heaven.

³⁴"Don't imagine that I came to bring peace to the earth! No, rather, a sword. ³⁵I have come to set a man against his father, and a daughter against her mother, and a daughter-in-law against her mother-in-law— ³⁶a man's worst enemies will be right in his own home! ³⁷If you love your father and mother more than you love me, you are not worthy of being mine; or if you love your son or daughter more than me, you are not worthy of being mine. ³⁸If you refuse to take up your cross and follow me, you are not worthy of being mine.

³⁹"If you cling to your life, you will lose it; but if you give it up for me, you will save it.

⁴⁰"Those who welcome you are welcoming me. And when they welcome me they are welcoming God who sent me. ⁴¹If you welcome a prophet because he is a man of God, you will be given the same reward a prophet gets. And if you welcome good and godly men because of their godliness, you will be given a reward like theirs.

⁴²"And if, as my representatives, you give even a cup of cold water to a little child, you will surely be rewarded."

11 WHEN JESUS had finished giving these instructions to his twelve disciples, he went off preaching in the cities where they were scheduled to go.^e

²John the Baptist, who was now in prison, heard about all the miracles the Messiah was doing, so he sent his disciples to ask Jesus, ³"Are you really the one we are waiting for, or shall we keep on looking?"

⁴Jesus told them, "Go back to John and tell him about the miracles you've seen me do— ⁵the blind people I've healed, and the lame people now walking without help, and the cured lepers, and the deaf who hear, and the dead raised to life; and tell him about my preaching the Good News to the poor. ⁶Then give him this message, 'Blessed are those who don't doubt me.' "

⁷When John's disciples had gone, Jesus began talking about him to the crowds. "When you went out into the barren wilderness to see John, what did you expect him to be like? Grass blowing in the wind? ⁸Or were you expecting to see a man dressed as a prince in a palace? ⁹Or a prophet of God? Yes, and he is more than just a prophet. ¹⁰For John is the man mentioned in the Scriptures—a messenger to precede me, to announce my coming, and prepare people to receive me.^f

¹¹"Truly, of all men ever born, none shines more brightly than John the Baptist. And yet, even the lesser lights in the Kingdom of Heaven will be greater than he is! ¹²And from the time John the Baptist began preaching

New Revised Standard

of your head are all counted. ³¹So do not be afraid; you are of more value than many sparrows.

³²"Everyone therefore who acknowledges me before others, I also will acknowledge before my Father in heaven; ³³but whoever denies me before others, I also will deny before my Father in heaven.

Not Peace, but a Sword

34 "Do not think that I have come to bring peace to the earth; I have not come to bring peace, but a sword.
35 For I have come to set a man against his
         father,
      and a daughter against her mother,
      and a daughter-in-law against her
         mother-in-law;
36   and one's foes will be members of one's own
         household.

³⁷Whoever loves father or mother more than me is not worthy of me; and whoever loves son or daughter more than me is not worthy of me; ³⁸and whoever does not take up the cross and follow me is not worthy of me. ³⁹Those who find their life will lose it, and those who lose their life for my sake will find it.

Rewards

40 "Whoever welcomes you welcomes me, and whoever welcomes me welcomes the one who sent me. ⁴¹Whoever welcomes a prophet in the name of a prophet will receive a prophet's reward; and whoever welcomes a righteous person in the name of a righteous person will receive the reward of the righteous; ⁴²and whoever gives even a cup of cold water to one of these little ones in the name of a disciple—truly I tell you, none of these will lose their reward."

11 NOW WHEN Jesus had finished instructing his twelve disciples, he went on from there to teach and proclaim his message in their cities.

Messengers from John the Baptist

2 When John heard in prison what the Messiah^g was doing, he sent word by his^h disciples ³and said to him, "Are you the one who is to come, or are we to wait for another?" ⁴Jesus answered them, "Go and tell John what you hear and see: ⁵the blind receive their sight, the lame walk, the lepersⁱ are cleansed, the deaf hear, the dead are raised, and the poor have good news brought to them. ⁶And blessed is anyone who takes no offense at me."

Jesus Praises John the Baptist

7 As they went away, Jesus began to speak to the crowds about John: "What did you go out into the wilderness to look at? A reed shaken by the wind? ⁸What then did you go out to see? Someone^j dressed in soft robes? Look, those who wear soft robes are in royal palaces. ⁹What then did you go out to see? A prophet?^k Yes, I tell you, and more than a prophet. ¹⁰This is the one about whom it is written,

   'See, I am sending my messenger ahead of
         you,
      who will prepare your way before you.'

¹¹Truly I tell you, among those born of women no one has arisen greater than John the Baptist; yet the least in the kingdom of heaven is greater than he. ¹²From the

---

^e *11:1 where they were scheduled to go,* literally, "to teach and preach in their cities." Lk 10:1 remarks, "The Lord now chose seventy other disciples and sent them on ahead in pairs to all the towns and villages he planned to visit later." ^f *11:10 prepare people to receive me,* literally, "prepare your way before you."

^g Or *the Christ* ^h Other ancient authorities read *two of his* ⁱ The terms *leper* and *leprosy* can refer to several diseases ^j Or *Why then did you go out? To see someone* ^k Other ancient authorities read *Why then did you go out? To see a prophet?*

King James

12And from the days of John the Baptist until now the kingdom of heaven suffereth violence, and the violent take it by force.

13For all the prophets and the law prophesied until John.

14And if ye will receive *it,* this is Elias, which was for to come.

15He that hath ears to hear, let him hear.

16¶ But whereunto shall I liken this generation? It is like unto children sitting in the markets, and calling unto their fellows,

17And saying, We have piped unto you, and ye have not danced; we have mourned unto you, and ye have not lamented.

18For John came neither eating nor drinking, and they say, He hath a devil.

19The Son of man came eating and drinking, and they say, Behold a man gluttonous, and a winebibber, a friend of publicans and sinners. But wisdom is justified of her children.

20¶ Then began he to upbraid the cities wherein most of his mighty works were done, because they repented not:

21Woe unto thee, Chorazin! woe unto thee, Bethsaida! for if the mighty works, which were done in you, had been done in Tyre and Sidon, they would have repented long ago in sackcloth and ashes.

22But I say unto you, It shall be more tolerable for Tyre and Sidon at the day of judgment, than for you.

23And thou, Capernaum, which art exalted unto heaven, shalt be brought down to hell: for if the mighty works, which have been done in thee, had been done in Sodom, it would have remained until this day.

24But I say unto you, That it shall be more tolerable for the land of Sodom in the day of judgment, than for thee.

25¶ At that time Jesus answered and said, I thank thee, O Father, Lord of heaven and earth, because thou hast hid these things from the wise and prudent, and hast revealed them unto babes.

26Even so, Father: for so it seemed good in thy sight.

27All things are delivered unto me of my Father: and no man knoweth the Son, but the Father; neither knoweth any man the Father, save the Son, and *he* to whomsoever the Son will reveal *him.*

28¶ Come unto me, all *ye* that labour and are heavy laden, and I will give you rest.

29Take my yoke upon you, and learn of me; for I am meek and lowly in heart: and ye shall find rest unto your souls.

30For my yoke *is* easy, and my burden is light.

12 AT THAT time Jesus went on the sabbath day through the corn; and his disciples were an hungered, and began to pluck the ears of corn, and to eat.

2But when the Pharisees saw *it,* they said unto him, Behold, thy disciples do that which is not lawful to do upon the sabbath day.

3But he said unto them, Have ye not read what David did, when he was an hungered, and they that were with him;

New International

kingdom of heaven has been forcefully advancing, and forceful men lay hold of it. 13For all the Prophets and the Law prophesied until John. 14And if you are willing to accept it, he is the Elijah who was to come. 15He who has ears, let him hear.

16"To what can I compare this generation? They are like children sitting in the marketplaces and calling out to others:

17" 'We played the flute for you,
    and you did not dance;
 we sang a dirge,
    and you did not mourn.'

18For John came neither eating nor drinking, and they say, 'He has a demon.' 19The Son of Man came eating and drinking, and they say, 'Here is a glutton and a drunkard, a friend of tax collectors and "sinners." ' But wisdom is proved right by her actions."

Woe on Unrepentant Cities

20Then Jesus began to denounce the cities in which most of his miracles had been performed, because they did not repent. 21"Woe to you, Korazin! Woe to you, Bethsaida! If the miracles that were performed in you had been performed in Tyre and Sidon, they would have repented long ago in sackcloth and ashes. 22But I tell you, it will be more bearable for Tyre and Sidon on the day of judgment than for you. 23And you, Capernaum, will you be lifted up to the skies? No, you will go down to the depths.a If the miracles that were performed in you had been performed in Sodom, it would have remained to this day. 24But I tell you that it will be more bearable for Sodom on the day of judgment than for you."

Rest for the Weary

25At that time Jesus said, "I praise you, Father, Lord of heaven and earth, because you have hidden these things from the wise and learned, and revealed them to little children. 26Yes, Father, for this was your good pleasure.

27"All things have been committed to me by my Father. No one knows the Son except the Father, and no one knows the Father except the Son and those to whom the Son chooses to reveal him.

28"Come to me, all you who are weary and burdened, and I will give you rest. 29Take my yoke upon you and learn from me, for I am gentle and humble in heart, and you will find rest for your souls. 30For my yoke is easy and my burden is light."

Lord of the Sabbath

12 AT THAT time Jesus went through the grainfields on the Sabbath. His disciples were hungry and began to pick some heads of grain and eat them. 2When the Pharisees saw this, they said to him, "Look! Your disciples are doing what is unlawful on the Sabbath."

3He answered, "Haven't you read what David did when he and his companions were hungry? 4He entered

---

Living Bible

and baptizing until now, ardent multitudes have been crowding toward the Kingdom of Heaven,b 13for all the laws and prophets looked forward [to the Messiahc]. Then John appeared, 14and if you are willing to understand what I mean, he is Elijah, the one the prophets said would come [at the time the Kingdom beginsd]. 15If ever you were willing to listen, listen now!

16"What shall I say about this nation? These people are like children playing, who say to their little friends, 17'We played wedding and you weren't happy, so we played funeral but you weren't sad.' 18For John the Baptist doesn't even drink wine and often goes without food, and you say, 'He's crazy.'e 19And I, the Messiah,f feast and drink, and you complain that I am 'a glutton and a drinking man, and hang around with the worst sort of sinners!' But brilliant men like you can justify your every inconsistency!"g

20Then he began to pour out his denunciations against the cities where he had done most of his miracles, because they hadn't turned to God.

21"Woe to you, Chorazin, and woe to you, Bethsaida! For if the miracles I did in your streets had been done in wicked Tyre and Sidonh their people would have repented long ago in shame and humility. 22Truly, Tyre and Sidon will be better off on the Judgment Day than you! 23And Capernaum, though highly honored,i shall go down to hell! For if the marvelous miracles I did in you had been done in Sodom,i it would still be here today. 24Truly, Sodom will be better off at the Judgment Day than you."

25And Jesus prayed this prayer: "O Father, Lord of heaven and earth, thank you for hiding the truth from those who think themselves so wise, and for revealing it to little children. 26Yes, Father, for it pleased you to do it this way! . . .

27"Everything has been entrusted to me by my Father. Only the Father knows the Son, and the Father is known only by the Son and by those to whom the Son reveals him. 28Come to me and I will give you rest—all of you who work so hard beneath a heavy yoke. 29, 30Wear my yoke—for it fits perfectly—and let me teach you; for I am gentle and humble, and you shall find rest for your souls; for I give you only light burdens."

12 ABOUT THAT time, Jesus was walking one day through some grainfields with his disciples. It was on the Sabbath, the Jewish day of worship, and his disciples were hungry; so they began breaking off heads of wheat and eating the grain.

2But some Pharisees saw them do it and protested, "Your disciples are breaking the law. They are harvesting on the Sabbath."

3But Jesus said to them, "Haven't you ever read what King David did when he and his friends were hungry?

New Revised Standard

days of John the Baptist until now the kingdom of heaven has suffered violence,j and the violent take it by force. 13For all the prophets and the law prophesied until John came; 14and if you are willing to accept it, he is Elijah who is to come. 15Let anyone with earsk listen!

16 "But to what will I compare this generation? It is like children sitting in the marketplaces and calling to one another,

17 'We played the flute for you, and you did not dance;
we wailed, and you did not mourn.'

18For John came neither eating nor drinking, and they say, 'He has a demon'; 19the Son of Man came eating and drinking, and they say, 'Look, a glutton and a drunkard, a friend of tax collectors and sinners!' Yet wisdom is vindicated by her deeds."l

Woes to Unrepentant Cities

20 Then he began to reproach the cities in which most of his deeds of power had been done, because they did not repent. 21"Woe to you, Chorazin! Woe to you, Bethsaida! For if the deeds of power done in you had been done in Tyre and Sidon, they would have repented long ago in sackcloth and ashes. 22But I tell you, on the day of judgment it will be more tolerable for Tyre and Sidon than for you. 23And you, Capernaum,
will you be exalted to heaven?
No, you will be brought down to Hades.
For if the deeds of power done in you had been done in Sodom, it would have remained until this day. 24But I tell you that on the day of judgment it will be more tolerable for the land of Sodom than for you."

Jesus Thanks His Father

25 At that time Jesus said, "I thankm you, Father, Lord of heaven and earth, because you have hidden these things from the wise and the intelligent and have revealed them to infants; 26yes, Father, for such was your gracious will.n 27All things have been handed over to me by my Father; and no one knows the Son except the Father, and no one knows the Father except the Son and anyone to whom the Son chooses to reveal him.

28 "Come to me, all you that are weary and are carrying heavy burdens, and I will give you rest. 29Take my yoke upon you, and learn from me; for I am gentle and humble in heart, and you will find rest for your souls. 30For my yoke is easy, and my burden is light."

Plucking Grain on the Sabbath

12 AT THAT time Jesus went through the grainfields on the sabbath; his disciples were hungry, and they began to pluck heads of grain and to eat. 2When the Pharisees saw it, they said to him, "Look, your disciples are doing what is not lawful to do on the sabbath." 3He said to them, "Have you not read what David did when he and his companions were hungry? 4He entered

---

b 11:12 ardent multitudes have been crowding toward the Kingdom of Heaven, literally, "the Kingdom of Heaven suffers violence and men of violence take it by force." c 11:13 to the Messiah, implied. d 11:14 at the time the Kingdom begins, implied. e 11:18 He's crazy, literally, "He has a demon." f 11:19 the Messiah, literally, "the Son of Man." g 11:19 you can justify your every inconsistency, literally, "wisdom is justified by her children." h 11:21 Tyre and Sidon, cities destroyed by God for their wickedness. Also Sodom in vs 23. i 11:23 highly honored, i.e., highly honored by Christ's being there.

j Or has been coming violently k Other ancient authorities add to hear l Other ancient authorities read children m Or praise n Or for so it was well-pleasing in your sight

King James

4How he entered into the house of God, and did eat the showbread, which was not lawful for him to eat, neither for them which were with him, but only for the priests?

5Or have ye not read in the law, how that on the sabbath days the priests in the temple profane the sabbath, and are blameless?

6But I say unto you, That in this place is *one* greater than the temple.

7But if ye had known what *this* meaneth, I will have mercy, and not sacrifice, ye would not have condemned the guiltless.

8For the Son of man is Lord even of the sabbath day.

9And when he was departed thence, he went into their synagogue:

10¶ And, behold, there was a man which had *his* hand withered. And they asked him, saying, Is it lawful to heal on the sabbath days? that they might accuse him.

11And he said unto them, What man shall there be among you, that shall have one sheep, and if it fall into a pit on the sabbath day, will he not lay hold on it, and lift *it* out?

12How much then is a man better than a sheep? Wherefore it is lawful to do well on the sabbath days.

13Then saith he to the man, Stretch forth thine hand. And he stretched *it* forth; and it was restored whole, like as the other.

14¶ Then the Pharisees went out, and held a council against him, how they might destroy him.

15But when Jesus knew *it,* he withdrew himself from thence: and great multitudes followed him, and he healed them all;

16And charged them that they should not make him known:

17That it might be fulfilled which was spoken by Esaias the prophet, saying,

18Behold my servant, whom I have chosen; my beloved, in whom my soul is well pleased: I will put my spirit upon him, and he shall show judgment to the Gentiles.

19He shall not strive, nor cry; neither shall any man hear his voice in the streets.

20A bruised reed shall he not break, and smoking flax shall he not quench, till he send forth judgment unto victory.

21And in his name shall the Gentiles trust.

22¶ Then was brought unto him one possessed with a devil, blind, and dumb: and he healed him, insomuch that the blind and dumb both spake and saw.

23And all the people were amazed, and said, Is not this the son of David?

24But when the Pharisees heard *it,* they said, This *fellow* doth not cast out devils, but by Beelzebub the prince of the devils.

25And Jesus knew their thoughts, and said unto them, Every kingdom divided against itself is brought to desolation; and every city or house divided against itself shall not stand:

26And if Satan cast out Satan, he is divided against himself; how shall then his kingdom stand?

27And if I by Beelzebub cast out devils, by whom do your children cast *them* out? therefore they shall be your judges.

28But if I cast out devils by the Spirit of God, then the kingdom of God is come unto you.

29Or else how can one enter into a strong man's house, and spoil his goods, except he first bind the strong man? and then he will spoil his house.

30He that is not with me is against me; and he that gathereth not with me scattereth abroad.

New International

the house of God, and he and his companions ate the consecrated bread—which was not lawful for them to do, but only for the priests. 5Or haven't you read in the Law that on the Sabbath the priests in the temple desecrate the day and yet are innocent? 6I tell you that one[a] greater than the temple is here. 7If you had known what these words mean, 'I desire mercy, not sacrifice,'[b] you would not have condemned the innocent. 8For the Son of Man is Lord of the Sabbath."

9Going on from that place, he went into their synagogue, 10and a man with a shriveled hand was there. Looking for a reason to accuse Jesus, they asked him, "Is it lawful to heal on the Sabbath?"

11He said to them, "If any of you has a sheep and it falls into a pit on the Sabbath, will you not take hold of it and lift it out? 12How much more valuable is a man than a sheep! Therefore it is lawful to do good on the Sabbath."

13Then he said to the man, "Stretch out your hand." So he stretched it out and it was completely restored, just as sound as the other. 14But the Pharisees went out and plotted how they might kill Jesus.

God's Chosen Servant

15Aware of this, Jesus withdrew from that place. Many followed him, and he healed all their sick, 16warning them not to tell who he was. 17This was to fulfill what was spoken through the prophet Isaiah:

18"Here is my servant whom I have chosen,
    the one I love, in whom I delight;
I will put my Spirit on him,
    and he will proclaim justice to the nations.
19He will not quarrel or cry out;
    no one will hear his voice in the streets.
20A bruised reed he will not break,
    and a smoldering wick he will not snuff out,
    till he leads justice to victory.
21 In his name the nations will put their hope."[c]

Jesus and Beelzebub

22Then they brought him a demon-possessed man who was blind and mute, and Jesus healed him, so that he could both talk and see. 23All the people were astonished and said, "Could this be the Son of David?"

24But when the Pharisees heard this, they said, "It is only by Beelzebub,[d] the prince of demons, that this fellow drives out demons."

25Jesus knew their thoughts and said to them, "Every kingdom divided against itself will be ruined, and every city or household divided against itself will not stand. 26If Satan drives out Satan, he is divided against himself. How then can his kingdom stand? 27And if I drive out demons by Beelzebub, by whom do your people drive them out? So then, they will be your judges. 28But if I drive out demons by the Spirit of God, then the kingdom of God has come upon you.

29"Or again, how can anyone enter a strong man's house and carry off his possessions unless he first ties up the strong man? Then he can rob his house. 30"He who is not with me is against me, and he who does not gather with me scatters. 31And so I tell you,

Living Bible

4He went into the Temple and they ate the special bread permitted to the priests alone. That was breaking the law too. 5And haven't you ever read in the law of Moses how the priests on duty in the Temple may work on the Sabbath? 6And truly, one is here who is greater than the Temple! 7But if you had known the meaning of this Scripture verse, 'I want you to be merciful more than I want your offerings,' you would not have condemned those who aren't guilty! 8For I, the Messiah,e am master even of the Sabbath."

9Then he went over to the synagogue, 10and noticed there a man with a deformed hand. The Phariseesf asked Jesus, "Is it legal to work by healing on the Sabbath day?" (They were, of course, hoping he would say "Yes," so they could arrestg him!) 11This was his answer: "If you had just one sheep, and it fell into a well on the Sabbath, would you work to rescue it that day? Of course you would.h 12And how much more valuable is a person than a sheep! Yes, it is right to do good on the Sabbath." 13Then he said to the man, "Stretch out your arm." And as he did, his hand became normal, just like the other one!

14Then the Pharisees called a meeting to plot Jesus' arrest and death.

15But he knew what they were planning, and left the synagogue, with many following him. He healed all the sick among them, 16but he cautioned them against spreading the news about his miracles. 17This fulfilled the prophecy of Isaiah concerning him:

18"Look at my Servant.
See my Chosen One.
He is my Beloved, in whom my soul delights.
I will put my Spirit upon him,
And he will judge the nations.
19He does not fight nor shout;
He does not raise his voice!
20He does not crush the weak,
Or quench the smallest hope;
He will end all conflict with his final victory,
21And his name shall be the hope
Of all the world."i

22Then a demon-possessed man—he was both blind and unable to talk—was brought to Jesus, and Jesus healed him so that he could both speak and see. 23The crowd was amazed. "Maybe Jesus is the Messiah!"j they exclaimed.

24But when the Pharisees heard about the miracle they said, "He can cast out demons because he is Satan,k king of devils."

25Jesus knew their thoughts and replied, "A divided kingdom ends in ruin. A city or home divided against itself cannot stand. 26And if Satan is casting out Satan, he is fighting himself, and destroying his own kingdom. 27And if, as you claim, I am casting out demons by invoking the powers of Satan, then what power do your own people use when they cast them out? Let them answer your accusation! 28But if I am casting out demons by the Spirit of God, then the Kingdom of God has arrived among you. 29One cannot rob Satan's kingdom without first binding Satan.l Only then can his demons be cast out!m 30Anyone who isn't helping me is harming me.

New Revised Standard

the house of God and ate the bread of the Presence, which it was not lawful for him or his companions to eat, but only for the priests. 5Or have you not read in the law that on the sabbath the priests in the temple break the sabbath and yet are guiltless? 6I tell you, something greater than the temple is here. 7But if you had known what this means, 'I desire mercy and not sacrifice,' you would not have condemned the guiltless. 8For the Son of Man is lord of the sabbath."

The Man with a Withered Hand

9 He left that place and entered their synagogue; 10a man was there with a withered hand, and they asked him, "Is it lawful to cure on the sabbath?" so that they might accuse him. 11He said to them, "Suppose one of you has only one sheep and it falls into a pit on the sabbath; will you not lay hold of it and lift it out? 12How much more valuable is a human being than a sheep! So it is lawful to do good on the sabbath." 13Then he said to the man, "Stretch out your hand." He stretched it out, and it was restored, as sound as the other. 14But the Pharisees went out and conspired against him, how to destroy him.

God's Chosen Servant

15 When Jesus became aware of this, he departed. Many crowdsn followed him, and he cured all of them, 16and he ordered them not to make him known. 17This was to fulfill what had been spoken through the prophet Isaiah:

18 "Here is my servant, whom I have chosen,
   my beloved, with whom my soul is well
      pleased.
   I will put my Spirit upon him,
      and he will proclaim justice to the Gentiles.
19 He will not wrangle or cry aloud,
      nor will anyone hear his voice in the streets.
20 He will not break a bruised reed
      or quench a smoldering wick
   until he brings justice to victory.
21   And in his name the Gentiles will hope."

Jesus and Beelzebul

22 Then they brought to him a demoniac who was blind and mute; and he cured him, so that the one who had been mute could speak and see. 23All the crowds were amazed and said, "Can this be the Son of David?" 24But when the Pharisees heard it, they said, "It is only by Beelzebul, the ruler of the demons, that this fellow casts out the demons." 25He knew what they were thinking and said to them, "Every kingdom divided against itself is laid waste, and no city or house divided against itself will stand. 26If Satan casts out Satan, he is divided against himself; how then will his kingdom stand? 27If I cast out demons by Beelzebul, by whom do your own exorcistso cast them out? Therefore they will be your judges. 28But if it is by the Spirit of God that I cast out demons, then the kingdom of God has come to you. 29Or how can one enter a strong man's house and plunder his property, without first tying up the strong man? Then indeed the house can be plundered. 30Whoever is not with me is against me, and whoever does not gather with me scatters. 31Therefore I tell you, people will be for-

---

e 12:8 the Messiah, literally, "the Son of Man." f 12:10 The Pharisees, implied. g 12:10 arrest, literally, "accuse." h 12:11 Of course you would, implied. i 12:21 Of all the world, see Isa 42:1-4. j 12:23 the Messiah, literally, "the Son of David." k 12:24 Satan, literally, "Beelzebub." l 12:29 without first binding Satan, literally, "the strong." m 12:29 Only then can his demons be cast out, literally, "Then will he spoil his house."

n Other ancient authorities lack crowds   o Gk sons

King James

31¶ Wherefore I say unto you, All manner of sin and blasphemy shall be forgiven unto men: but the blasphemy *against* the *Holy* Ghost shall not be forgiven unto men.

32And whosoever speaketh a word against the Son of man, it shall be forgiven him: but whosoever speaketh against the Holy Ghost, it shall not be forgiven him, neither in this world, neither in the *world* to come.

33Either make the tree good, and his fruit good; or else make the tree corrupt, and his fruit corrupt: for the tree is known by *his* fruit.

34O generation of vipers, how can ye, being evil, speak good things? for out of the abundance of the heart the mouth speaketh.

35A good man out of the good treasure of the heart bringeth forth good things: and an evil man out of the evil treasure bringeth forth evil things.

36But I say unto you, That every idle word that men shall speak, they shall give account thereof in the day of judgment.

37For by thy words thou shalt be justified, and by thy words thou shalt be condemned.

38¶ Then certain of the scribes and of the Pharisees answered, saying, Master, we would see a sign from thee.

39But he answered and said unto them, An evil and adulterous generation seeketh after a sign; and there shall no sign be given to it, but the sign of the prophet Jonas:

40For as Jonas was three days and three nights in the whale's belly; so shall the Son of man be three days and three nights in the heart of the earth.

41The men of Nineveh shall rise in judgment with this generation, and shall condemn it: because they repented at the preaching of Jonas; and, behold, a greater than Jonas *is* here.

42The queen of the south shall rise up in the judgment with this generation, and shall condemn it: for she came from the uttermost parts of the earth to hear the wisdom of Solomon; and, behold, a greater than Solomon *is* here.

43When the unclean spirit is gone out of a man, he walketh through dry places, seeking rest, and findeth none.

44Then he saith, I will return into my house from whence I came out; and when he is come, he findeth *it* empty, swept, and garnished.

45Then goeth he, and taketh with himself seven other spirits more wicked than himself, and they enter in and dwell there: and the last *state* of that man is worse than the first. Even so shall it be also unto this wicked generation.

46¶ While he yet talked to the people, behold, *his* mother and his brethren stood without, desiring to speak with him.

47Then one said unto him, Behold, thy mother and thy brethren stand without, desiring to speak with thee.

48But he answered and said unto him that told him, Who is my mother? and who are my brethren?

49And he stretched forth his hand toward his disciples, and said, Behold my mother and my brethren!

50For whosoever shall do the will of my Father which is in heaven, the same is my brother, and sister, and mother.

New International

every sin and blasphemy will be forgiven men, but the blasphemy against the Spirit will not be forgiven. 32Anyone who speaks a word against the Son of Man will be forgiven, but anyone who speaks against the Holy Spirit will not be forgiven, either in this age or in the age to come.

33"Make a tree good and its fruit will be good, or make a tree bad and its fruit will be bad, for a tree is recognized by its fruit. 34You brood of vipers, how can you who are evil say anything good? For out of the overflow of the heart the mouth speaks. 35The good man brings good things out of the good stored up in him, and the evil man brings evil things out of the evil stored up in him. 36But I tell you that men will have to give account on the day of judgment for every careless word they have spoken. 37For by your words you will be acquitted, and by your words you will be condemned."

The Sign of Jonah

38Then some of the Pharisees and teachers of the law said to him, "Teacher, we want to see a miraculous sign from you."

39He answered, "A wicked and adulterous generation asks for a miraculous sign! But none will be given it except the sign of the prophet Jonah. 40For as Jonah was three days and three nights in the belly of a huge fish, so the Son of Man will be three days and three nights in the heart of the earth. 41The men of Nineveh will stand up at the judgment with this generation and condemn it; for they repented at the preaching of Jonah, and now one[a] greater than Jonah is here. 42The Queen of the South will rise at the judgment with this generation and condemn it; for she came from the ends of the earth to listen to Solomon's wisdom, and now one greater than Solomon is here.

43"When an evil[b] spirit comes out of a man, it goes through arid places seeking rest and does not find it. 44Then it says, 'I will return to the house I left.' When it arrives, it finds the house unoccupied, swept clean and put in order. 45Then it goes and takes with it seven other spirits more wicked than itself, and they go in and live there. And the final condition of that man is worse than the first. That is how it will be with this wicked generation."

Jesus' Mother and Brothers

46While Jesus was still talking to the crowd, his mother and brothers stood outside, wanting to speak to him. 47Someone told him, "Your mother and brothers are standing outside, wanting to speak to you."[c]

48He replied to him, "Who is my mother, and who are my brothers?" 49Pointing to his disciples, he said, "Here are my mother and my brothers. 50For whoever does the will of my Father in heaven is my brother and sister and mother."

The Parable of the Sower

13 THE SAME day went Jesus out of the house, and sat by the sea side.

13 THAT SAME day Jesus went out of the house and sat by the lake. 2Such large crowds gath-

---

a 41 Or *something*; also in verse 42   b 43 Greek *unclean*   c 47 Some manuscripts do not have verse 47.

Living Bible

31, 32"Even blasphemy against me[d] or any other sin can be forgiven—all except one: speaking against the Holy Spirit shall never be forgiven, either in this world or in the world to come.

33"A tree is identified by its fruit. A tree from a select variety produces good fruit; poor varieties don't. 34You brood of snakes! How could evil men like you speak what is good and right? For a man's heart determines his speech. 35A good man's speech reveals the rich treasures within him. An evil-hearted man is filled with venom, and his speech reveals it. 36And I tell you this, that you must give account on Judgment Day for every idle word you speak. 37Your words now reflect your fate then: either you will be justified by them or you will be condemned."

38One day some of the Jewish leaders, including some Pharisees, came to Jesus asking him to show them a miracle.

39, 40But Jesus replied, "Only an evil, faithless nation would ask for further proof; and none will be given except what happened to Jonah the prophet! For as Jonah was in the great fish for three days and three nights, so I, the Messiah,[e] shall be in the heart of the earth three days and three nights. 41The men of Nineveh shall arise against this nation at the judgment and condemn you. For when Jonah preached to them, they repented and turned to God from all their evil ways. And now a greater than Jonah is here—and you refuse to believe him.[f] 42The Queen of Sheba shall rise against this nation in the judgment, and condemn it; for she came from a distant land to hear the wisdom of Solomon; and now a greater than Solomon is here—and you refuse to believe him.

43, 44, 45"This evil nation is like a man possessed by a demon. For if the demon leaves, it goes into the desert[g] for a while, seeking rest but finding none. Then it says, 'I will return to the man I came from.' So it returns and finds the man's heart clean but empty! Then the demon finds seven other spirits more evil than itself, and all enter the man and live in him. And so he is worse off than before."

46, 47As Jesus was speaking in a crowded house[h] his mother and brothers were outside, wanting to talk with him. When someone told him they were there, 48he remarked, "Who is my mother? Who are my brothers?" 49He pointed to his disciples. "Look!" he said, "these are my mother and brothers." 50Then he added, "Anyone who obeys my Father in heaven is my brother, sister and mother!"

New Revised Standard

given for every sin and blasphemy, but blasphemy against the Spirit will not be forgiven. 32Whoever speaks a word against the Son of Man will be forgiven, but whoever speaks against the Holy Spirit will not be forgiven, either in this age or in the age to come.

A Tree and Its Fruit

33 "Either make the tree good, and its fruit good; or make the tree bad, and its fruit bad; for the tree is known by its fruit. 34You brood of vipers! How can you speak good things, when you are evil? For out of the abundance of the heart the mouth speaks. 35The good person brings good things out of a good treasure, and the evil person brings evil things out of an evil treasure. 36I tell you, on the day of judgment you will have to give an account for every careless word you utter; 37for by your words you will be justified, and by your words you will be condemned."

The Sign of Jonah

38 Then some of the scribes and Pharisees said to him, "Teacher, we wish to see a sign from you." 39But he answered them, "An evil and adulterous generation asks for a sign, but no sign will be given to it except the sign of the prophet Jonah. 40For just as Jonah was three days and three nights in the belly of the sea monster, so for three days and three nights the Son of Man will be in the heart of the earth. 41The people of Nineveh will rise up at the judgment with this generation and condemn it, because they repented at the proclamation of Jonah, and see, something greater than Jonah is here! 42The queen of the South will rise up at the judgment with this generation and condemn it, because she came from the ends of the earth to listen to the wisdom of Solomon, and see, something greater than Solomon is here!

The Return of the Unclean Spirit

43 "When the unclean spirit has gone out of a person, it wanders through waterless regions looking for a resting place, but it finds none. 44Then it says, 'I will return to my house from which I came.' When it comes, it finds it empty, swept, and put in order. 45Then it goes and brings along seven other spirits more evil than itself, and they enter and live there; and the last state of that person is worse than the first. So will it be also with this evil generation."

The True Kindred of Jesus

46 While he was still speaking to the crowds, his mother and his brothers were standing outside, wanting to speak to him. 47Someone told him, "Look, your mother and your brothers are standing outside, wanting to speak to you."[i] 48But to the one who had told him this, Jesus[j] replied, "Who is my mother, and who are my brothers?" 49And pointing to his disciples, he said, "Here are my mother and my brothers! 50For whoever does the will of my Father in heaven is my brother and sister and mother."

The Parable of the Sower

13 LATER THAT same day, Jesus left the house and went down to the shore, 2, 3where an im-

13 THAT SAME day Jesus went out of the house and sat beside the sea. 2Such great crowds gath-

---

d *12:31, 32 me,* literally, "the Son of Man."   e *12:39, 40 the Messiah,* literally, "the Son of Man."   f *12:41 you refuse to believe him,* implied. Also in vs 42.   g *12:43-45 goes into the deserts,* literally, "passes through waterless places."   h *12:46, 47 in a crowded house,* implied in Mk 3:32.

i Other ancient authorities lack verse 47   j Gk *he*

King James

2And great multitudes were gathered together unto him, so that he went into a ship, and sat; and the whole multitude stood on the shore.

3And he spake many things unto them in parables, saying, Behold, a sower went forth to sow;

4And when he sowed, some *seeds* fell by the way side, and the fowls came and devoured them up:

5Some fell upon stony places, where they had not much earth: and forthwith they sprung up, because they had no deepness of earth:

6And when the sun was up, they were scorched; and because they had no root, they withered away.

7And some fell among thorns; and the thorns sprung up, and choked them:

8But other fell into good ground, and brought forth fruit, some an hundredfold, some sixtyfold, some thirtyfold.

9Who hath ears to hear, let him hear.

10And the disciples came, and said unto him, Why speakest thou unto them in parables?

11He answered and said unto them, Because it is given unto you to know the mysteries of the kingdom of heaven, but to them it is not given.

12For whosoever hath, to him shall be given, and he shall have more abundance: but whosoever hath not, from him shall be taken away even that he hath.

13Therefore speak I to them in parables: because they seeing see not; and hearing they hear not, neither do they understand.

14And in them is fulfilled the prophecy of Esaias, which saith, By hearing ye shall hear, and shall not understand; and seeing ye shall see, and shall not perceive:

15For this people's heart is waxed gross, and *their* ears are dull of hearing, and their eyes they have closed; lest at any time they should see with *their* eyes, and hear with *their* ears, and should understand with *their* heart, and should be converted, and I should heal them.

16But blessed *are* your eyes, for they see: and your ears, for they hear.

17For verily I say unto you, That many prophets and righteous *men* have desired to see *those things* which ye see, and have not seen *them;* and to hear *those things* which ye hear, and have not heard *them.*

18¶ Hear ye therefore the parable of the sower.

19When any one heareth the word of the kingdom, and understandeth *it* not, then cometh the wicked *one,* and catcheth away that which was sown in his heart. This is he which received seed by the way side.

20But he that received the seed into stony places, the same is he that heareth the word, and anon with joy receiveth it;

21Yet hath he not root in himself, but dureth for a while: for when tribulation or persecution ariseth because of the word, by and by he is offended.

22He also that received seed among the thorns is he that heareth the word; and the care of this world, and the deceitfulness of riches, choke the word, and he becometh unfruitful.

23But he that received seed into the good ground is he that heareth the word, and understandeth *it;* which also beareth fruit, and bringeth forth, some an hundredfold, some sixty, some thirty.

24¶ Another parable put he forth unto them, saying, The kingdom of heaven is likened unto a man which sowed good seed in his field:

25But while men slept, his enemy came and sowed tares among the wheat, and went his way.

26But when the blade was sprung up, and brought forth fruit, then appeared the tares also.

27So the servants of the householder came and said unto him, Sir, didst not thou sow good seed in thy field? from whence then hath it tares?

New International

ered around him that he got into a boat and sat in it, while all the people stood on the shore. 3Then he told them many things in parables, saying: "A farmer went out to sow his seed. 4As he was scattering the seed, some fell along the path, and the birds came and ate it up. 5Some fell on rocky places, where it did not have much soil. It sprang up quickly, because the soil was shallow. 6But when the sun came up, the plants were scorched, and they withered because they had no root. 7Other seed fell among thorns, which grew up and choked the plants. 8Still other seed fell on good soil, where it produced a crop—a hundred, sixty or thirty times what was sown. 9He who has ears, let him hear."

10The disciples came to him and asked, "Why do you speak to the people in parables?"

11He replied, "The knowledge of the secrets of the kingdom of heaven has been given to you, but not to them. 12Whoever has will be given more, and he will have an abundance. Whoever does not have, even what he has will be taken from him. 13This is why I speak to them in parables:

"Though seeing, they do not see;
    though hearing, they do not hear or
        understand.

14In them is fulfilled the prophecy of Isaiah:

" 'You will be ever hearing but never
        understanding;
    you will be ever seeing but never perceiving.
15For this people's heart has become calloused;
    they hardly hear with their ears,
    and they have closed their eyes.
Otherwise they might see with their eyes,
    hear with their ears,
    understand with their hearts
    and turn, and I would heal them.'[a]

16But blessed are your eyes because they see, and your ears because they hear. 17For I tell you the truth, many prophets and righteous men longed to see what you see but did not see it, and to hear what you hear but did not hear it.

18"Listen then to what the parable of the sower means: 19When anyone hears the message about the kingdom and does not understand it, the evil one comes and snatches away what was sown in his heart. This is the seed sown along the path. 20The one who received the seed that fell on rocky places is the man who hears the word and at once receives it with joy. 21But since he has no root, he lasts only a short time. When trouble or persecution comes because of the word, he quickly falls away. 22The one who received the seed that fell among the thorns is the man who hears the word, but the worries of this life and the deceitfulness of wealth choke it, making it unfruitful. 23But the one who received the seed that fell on good soil is the man who hears the word and understands it. He produces a crop, yielding a hundred, sixty or thirty times what was sown."

The Parable of the Weeds

24Jesus told them another parable: "The kingdom of heaven is like a man who sowed good seed in his field. 25But while everyone was sleeping, his enemy came and sowed weeds among the wheat, and went away. 26When the wheat sprouted and formed heads, then the weeds also appeared.

27"The owner's servants came to him and said, 'Sir, didn't you sow good seed in your field? Where then did the weeds come from?'

a *15* Isaiah 6:9,10

Living Bible

mense crowd soon gathered. He got into a boat and taught from it while the people listened on the beach. He used many illustrations such as this one in his sermon:

"A farmer was sowing grain in his fields. 4As he scattered the seed across the ground, some fell beside a path, and the birds came and ate it. 5And some fell on rocky soil where there was little depth of earth; the plants sprang up quickly enough in the shallow soil, 6but the hot sun soon scorched them and they withered and died, for they had so little root. 7Other seeds fell among thorns, and the thorns choked out the tender blades. 8But some fell on good soil, and produced a crop that was thirty, sixty, and even a hundred times as much as he had planted. 9If you have ears, listen!"

10His disciples came and asked him, "Why do you always use these hard-to-understand illustrations?"b

11Then he explained to them that only they were permitted to understand about the Kingdom of Heaven, and others were not.

12, 13"For to him who has will more be given," he told them, "and he will have great plenty; but from him who has not, even the little he has will be taken away. That is why I use these illustrations, so people will hear and see but not understand.c

14"This fulfills the prophecy of Isaiah:
'They hear, but don't understand; they look, but don't see! 15For their hearts are fat and heavy, and their ears are dull, and they have closed their eyes in sleep, 16so they won't see and hear and understand and turn to God again, and let me heal them.'
But blessed are your eyes, for they see; and your ears, for they hear. 17Many a prophet and godly man has longed to see what you have seen, and hear what you have heard, but couldn't.

18"Now here is the explanation of the story I told about the farmer planting grain: 19The hard path where some of the seeds fell represents the heart of a person who hears the Good News about the Kingdom and doesn't understand it; then Satand comes and snatches away the seeds from his heart. 20The shallow, rocky soil represents the heart of a man who hears the message and receives it with real joy, 21but he doesn't have much depth in his life, and the seeds don't root very deeply, and after a while when trouble comes, or persecution begins because of his beliefs, his enthusiasm fades, and he drops out. 22The ground covered with thistles represents a man who hears the message, but the cares of this life and his longing for money choke out God's Word, and he does less and less for God. 23The good ground represents the heart of a man who listens to the message and understands it and goes out and brings thirty, sixty, or even a hundred others into the Kingdom."e

24Here is another illustration Jesus used: "The Kingdom of Heaven is like a farmer sowing good seed in his field; 25but one night as he slept, his enemy came and sowed thistles among the wheat. 26When the crop began to grow, the thistles grew too.

27"The farmer's men came and told him, 'Sir, the field where you planted that choice seed is full of thistles!'

b 13:10 Why do you always use these hard-to-understand illustrations? is implied.   c 13:13 so people will hear and see but not understand. Those who were receptive to spiritual truth understood the illustrations. To others they were only stories without meaning.   d 13:19 Satan, literally, "the evil." e 13:23 even a hundred others into the Kingdom, literally, "produces a crop many times greater than the amount planted—thirty, sixty, or even a hundred times as much."

New Revised Standard

ered around him that he got into a boat and sat there, while the whole crowd stood on the beach. 3And he told them many things in parables, saying: "Listen! A sower went out to sow. 4And as he sowed, some seeds fell on the path, and the birds came and ate them up. 5Other seeds fell on rocky ground, where they did not have much soil, and they sprang up quickly, since they had no depth of soil. 6But when the sun rose, they were scorched; and since they had no root, they withered away. 7Other seeds fell among thorns, and the thorns grew up and choked them. 8Other seeds fell on good soil and brought forth grain, some a hundredfold, some sixty, some thirty. 9Let anyone with earsf listen!"

The Purpose of the Parables

10 Then the disciples came and asked him, "Why do you speak to them in parables?" 11He answered, "To you it has been given to know the secretsg of the kingdom of heaven, but to them it has not been given. 12For to those who have, more will be given, and they will have an abundance; but from those who have nothing, even what they have will be taken away. 13The reason I speak to them in parables is that 'seeing they do not perceive, and hearing they do not listen, nor do they understand.' 14With them indeed is fulfilled the prophecy of Isaiah that says:
'You will indeed listen, but never understand,
     and you will indeed look, but never perceive.
15 For this people's heart has grown dull,
     and their ears are hard of hearing,
     and they have shut their eyes;
     so that they might not look with their eyes,
     and listen with their ears,
     and understand with their heart and turn—
     and I would heal them.'
16But blessed are your eyes, for they see, and your ears, for they hear. 17Truly I tell you, many prophets and righteous people longed to see what you see, but did not see it, and to hear what you hear, but did not hear it.

The Parable of the Sower Explained

18 "Hear then the parable of the sower. 19When anyone hears the word of the kingdom and does not understand it, the evil one comes and snatches away what is sown in the heart; this is what was sown on the path. 20As for what was sown on rocky ground, this is the one who hears the word and immediately receives it with joy; 21yet such a person has no root, but endures only for a while, and when trouble or persecution arises on account of the word, that person immediately falls away.h 22As for what was sown among thorns, this is the one who hears the word, but the cares of the world and the lure of wealth choke the word, and it yields nothing. 23But as for what was sown on good soil, this is the one who hears the word and understands it, who indeed bears fruit and yields, in one case a hundredfold, in another sixty, and in another thirty."

The Parable of Weeds among the Wheat

24 He put before them another parable: "The kingdom of heaven may be compared to someone who sowed good seed in his field; 25but while everybody was asleep, an enemy came and sowed weeds among the wheat, and then went away. 26So when the plants came up and bore grain, then the weeds appeared as well. 27And the slaves of the householder came and said to him, 'Master, did you not sow good seed in your field? Where, then, did these weeds come from?' 28He an-

f Other ancient authorities add to hear   g Or mysteries   h Gk stumbles

King James

28He said unto them, An enemy hath done this. The servants said unto him, Wilt thou then that we go and gather them up?

29But he said, Nay; lest while ye gather up the tares, ye root up also the wheat with them.

30Let both grow together until the harvest: and in the time of harvest I will say to the reapers, Gather ye together first the tares, and bind them in bundles to burn them: but gather the wheat into my barn.

31¶ Another parable put he forth unto them, saying, The kingdom of heaven is like to a grain of mustard seed, which a man took, and sowed in his field:

32Which indeed is the least of all seeds: but when it is grown, it is the greatest among herbs, and becometh a tree, so that the birds of the air come and lodge in the branches thereof.

33¶ Another parable spake he unto them; The kingdom of heaven is like unto leaven, which a woman took, and hid in three measures of meal, till the whole was leavened.

34All these things spake Jesus unto the multitude in parables; and without a parable spake he not unto them:

35That it might be fulfilled which was spoken by the prophet, saying, I will open my mouth in parables; I will utter things which have been kept secret from the foundation of the world.

36Then Jesus sent the multitude away, and went into the house: and his disciples came unto him, saying, Declare unto us the parable of the tares of the field.

37He answered and said unto them, He that soweth the good seed is the Son of man;

38The field is the world; the good seed are the children of the kingdom; but the tares are the children of the wicked one;

39The enemy that sowed them is the devil; the harvest is the end of the world; and the reapers are the angels.

40As therefore the tares are gathered and burned in the fire; so shall it be in the end of this world.

41The Son of man shall send forth his angels, and they shall gather out of his kingdom all things that offend, and them which do iniquity;

42And shall cast them into a furnace of fire: there shall be wailing and gnashing of teeth.

43Then shall the righteous shine forth as the sun in the kingdom of their Father. Who hath ears to hear, let him hear.

44¶ Again, the kingdom of heaven is like unto treasure hid in a field; the which when a man hath found, he hideth, and for joy thereof goeth and selleth all that he hath, and buyeth that field.

45¶ Again, the kingdom of heaven is like unto a merchant man, seeking goodly pearls:

46Who, when he had found one pearl of great price, went and sold all that he had, and bought it.

47¶ Again, the kingdom of heaven is like unto a net, that was cast into the sea, and gathered of every kind:

48Which, when it was full, they drew to shore, and sat down, and gathered the good into vessels, but cast the bad away.

49So shall it be at the end of the world: the angels shall come forth, and sever the wicked from among the just,

50And shall cast them into the furnace of fire: there shall be wailing and gnashing of teeth.

51Jesus saith unto them, Have ye understood all these things? They say unto him, Yea, Lord.

New International

28" 'An enemy did this,' he replied.

"The servants asked him, 'Do you want us to go and pull them up?'

29" 'No,' he answered, 'because while you are pulling the weeds, you may root up the wheat with them. 30Let both grow together until the harvest. At that time I will tell the harvesters: First collect the weeds and tie them in bundles to be burned; then gather the wheat and bring it into my barn.' "

The Parables of the Mustard Seed and the Yeast

31He told them another parable: "The kingdom of heaven is like a mustard seed, which a man took and planted in his field. 32Though it is the smallest of all your seeds, yet when it grows, it is the largest of garden plants and becomes a tree, so that the birds of the air come and perch in its branches."

33He told them still another parable: "The kingdom of heaven is like yeast that a woman took and mixed into a large amount[a] of flour until it worked all through the dough."

34Jesus spoke all these things to the crowd in parables; he did not say anything to them without using a parable. 35So was fulfilled what was spoken through the prophet:

"I will open my mouth in parables,
    I will utter things hidden since the creation of
        the world."[b]

The Parable of the Weeds Explained

36Then he left the crowd and went into the house. His disciples came to him and said, "Explain to us the parable of the weeds in the field."

37He answered, "The one who sowed the good seed is the Son of Man. 38The field is the world, and the good seed stands for the sons of the kingdom. The weeds are the sons of the evil one, 39and the enemy who sows them is the devil. The harvest is the end of the age, and the harvesters are angels.

40"As the weeds are pulled up and burned in the fire, so it will be at the end of the age. 41The Son of Man will send out his angels, and they will weed out of his kingdom everything that causes sin and all who do evil. 42They will throw them into the fiery furnace, where there will be weeping and gnashing of teeth. 43Then the righteous will shine like the sun in the kingdom of their Father. He who has ears, let him hear.

The Parables of the Hidden Treasure and the Pearl

44"The kingdom of heaven is like treasure hidden in a field. When a man found it, he hid it again, and then in his joy went and sold all he had and bought that field.

45"Again, the kingdom of heaven is like a merchant looking for fine pearls. 46When he found one of great value, he went away and sold everything he had and bought it.

The Parable of the Net

47"Once again, the kingdom of heaven is like a net that was let down into the lake and caught all kinds of fish. 48When it was full, the fishermen pulled it up on the shore. Then they sat down and collected the good fish in baskets, but threw the bad away. 49This is how it will be at the end of the age. The angels will come and separate the wicked from the righteous 50and throw them into the fiery furnace, where there will be weeping and gnashing of teeth.

51"Have you understood all these things?" Jesus asked.

"Yes," they replied.

---

a 33 Greek three satas (probably about 1/2 bushel or 22 liters)   b 35 Psalm 78:2

Living Bible

28" 'An enemy has done it,' he exclaimed.

" 'Shall we pull out the thistles?' they asked.

29" 'No,' he replied. 'You'll hurt the wheat if you do. 30Let both grow together until the harvest, and I will tell the reapers to sort out the thistles and burn them, and put the wheat in the barn.' "

31, 32Here is another of his illustrations: "The Kingdom of Heaven is like a tiny mustard seed planted in a field. It is the smallest of all seeds, but becomes the largest of plants, and grows into a tree where birds can come and find shelter."

33He also used this example:

"The Kingdom of Heaven can be compared to a woman making bread. She takes a measure of flour and mixes in the yeast until it permeates every part of the dough."

34, 35Jesus constantly used these illustrations when speaking to the crowds. In fact, because the prophets said that he would use so many, he never spoke to them without at least one illustration. For it had been prophesied, "I will talk in parables; I will explain mysteries hidden since the beginning of time."c

36Then, leaving the crowds outside, he went into the house. His disciples asked him to explain to them the illustration of the thistles and the wheat.

37"All right," he said, "Id am the farmer who sows the choice seed. 38The field is the world, and the seed represents the people of the Kingdom; the thistles are the people belonging to Satan. 39The enemy who sowed the thistles among the wheat is the devil; the harvest is the end of the world, and the reapers are the angels.

40"Just as in this story the thistles are separated and burned, so shall it be at the end of the world: 41Id will send my angels and they will separate out of the Kingdom every temptation and all who are evil, 42and throw them into the furnace and burn them. There shall be weeping and gnashing of teeth. 43Then the godly shall shine as the sun in their Father's Kingdom. Let those with ears, listen!

44"The Kingdom of Heaven is like a treasure a man discovered in a field. In his excitement, he sold everything he owned to get enough money to buy the field— and get the treasure, too!

45"Again, the Kingdom of Heaven is like a pearl merchant on the lookout for choice pearls. 46He discovered a real bargain—a pearl of great value—and sold everything he owned to purchase it!

47, 48"Again, the Kingdom of Heaven can be illustrated by a fisherman—he casts a net into the water and gathers in fish of every kind, valuable and worthless. When the net is full, he drags it up onto the beach and sits down and sorts out the edible ones into crates and throws the others away. 49That is the way it will be at the end of the world—the angels will come and separate the wicked people from the godly, 50casting the wicked into the fire; there shall be weeping and gnashing of teeth. 51Do you understand?"

"Yes," they said, "we do."

New Revised Standard

swered, 'An enemy has done this.' The slaves said to him, 'Then do you want us to go and gather them?' 29But he replied, 'No; for in gathering the weeds you would uproot the wheat along with them. 30Let both of them grow together until the harvest; and at harvest time I will tell the reapers, Collect the weeds first and bind them in bundles to be burned, but gather the wheat into my barn.' "

The Parable of the Mustard Seed

31 He put before them another parable: "The kingdom of heaven is like a mustard seed that someone took and sowed in his field; 32it is the smallest of all the seeds, but when it has grown it is the greatest of shrubs and becomes a tree, so that the birds of the air come and make nests in its branches."

The Parable of the Yeast

33 He told them another parable: "The kingdom of heaven is like yeast that a woman took and mixed in withe three measures of flour until all of it was leavened."

The Use of Parables

34 Jesus told the crowds all these things in parables; without a parable he told them nothing. 35This was to fulfill what had been spoken through the prophet:f

"I will open my mouth to speak in parables;
I will proclaim what has been hidden from
   the foundation of the world."g

Jesus Explains the Parable of the Weeds

36 Then he left the crowds and went into the house. And his disciples approached him, saying, "Explain to us the parable of the weeds of the field." 37He answered, "The one who sows the good seed is the Son of Man; 38the field is the world, and the good seed are the children of the kingdom; the weeds are the children of the evil one, 39and the enemy who sowed them is the devil; the harvest is the end of the age, and the reapers are angels. 40Just as the weeds are collected and burned up with fire, so will it be at the end of the age. 41The Son of Man will send his angels, and they will collect out of his kingdom all causes of sin and all evildoers, 42and they will throw them into the furnace of fire, where there will be weeping and gnashing of teeth. 43Then the righteous will shine like the sun in the kingdom of their Father. Let anyone with earsh listen!

Three Parables

44 "The kingdom of heaven is like treasure hidden in a field, which someone found and hid; then in his joy he goes and sells all that he has and buys that field.

45 "Again, the kingdom of heaven is like a merchant in search of fine pearls; 46on finding one pearl of great value, he went and sold all that he had and bought it.

47 "Again, the kingdom of heaven is like a net that was thrown into the sea and caught fish of every kind; 48when it was full, they drew it ashore, sat down, and put the good into baskets but threw out the bad. 49So it will be at the end of the age. The angels will come out and separate the evil from the righteous 50and throw them into the furnace of fire, where there will be weeping and gnashing of teeth.

Treasures New and Old

51 "Have you understood all this?" They answered, "Yes." 52And he said to them, "Therefore every scribe

---

c 13:35 beginning of time, see Psalm 78:2.   d 13:37,13:41 I, literally, "the Son of Man."

e Gk hid in   f Other ancient authorities read the prophet Isaiah   g Other ancient authorities lack of the world   h Other ancient authorities add to hear

King James

⁵²Then said he unto them, Therefore every scribe *which is* instructed unto the kingdom of heaven is like unto a man *that is* an householder, which bringeth forth out of his treasure *things* new and old.

⁵³¶ And it came to pass, *that* when Jesus had finished these parables, he departed thence.

⁵⁴And when he was come into his own country, he taught them in their synagogue, insomuch that they were astonished, and said, Whence hath this *man* this wisdom, and *these* mighty works?

⁵⁵Is not this the carpenter's son? is not his mother called Mary? and his brethren, James, and Joses, and Simon, and Judas?

⁵⁶And his sisters, are they not all with us? Whence then hath this *man* all these things?

⁵⁷And they were offended in him. But Jesus said unto them, A prophet is not without honour, save in his own country, and in his own house.

⁵⁸And he did not many mighty works there because of their unbelief.

14 AT THAT time Herod the tetrarch heard of the fame of Jesus,

²And said unto his servants, This is John the Baptist; he is risen from the dead; and therefore mighty works do show forth themselves in him.

³¶ For Herod had laid hold on John, and bound him, and put *him* in prison for Herodias' sake, his brother Philip's wife.

⁴For John said unto him, It is not lawful for thee to have her.

⁵And when he would have put him to death, he feared the multitude, because they counted him as a prophet.

⁶But when Herod's birthday was kept, the daughter of Herodias danced before them, and pleased Herod.

⁷Whereupon he promised with an oath to give her whatsoever she would ask.

⁸And she, being before instructed of her mother, said, Give me here John Baptist's head in a charger.

⁹And the king was sorry: nevertheless for the oath's sake, and them which sat with him at meat, he commanded *it* to be given *her.*

¹⁰And he sent, and beheaded John in the prison.

¹¹And his head was brought in a charger, and given to the damsel: and she brought *it* to her mother.

¹²And his disciples came, and took up the body, and buried it, and went and told Jesus.

¹³¶ When Jesus heard *of it,* he departed thence by ship into a desert place apart: and when the people had heard *thereof,* they followed him on foot out of the cities.

¹⁴And Jesus went forth, and saw a great multitude, and was moved with compassion toward them, and he healed their sick.

¹⁵¶ And when it was evening, his disciples came to him, saying, This is a desert place, and the time is now past; send the multitude away, that they may go into the villages, and buy themselves victuals.

¹⁶But Jesus said unto them, They need not depart; give ye them to eat.

¹⁷And they say unto him, We have here but five loaves, and two fishes.

¹⁸He said, Bring them hither to me.

¹⁹And he commanded the multitude to sit down on the grass, and took the five loaves, and the two fishes, and looking up to heaven, he blessed, and brake, and gave the loaves to *his* disciples, and the disciples to the multitude.

New International

⁵²He said to them, "Therefore every teacher of the law who has been instructed about the kingdom of heaven is like the owner of a house who brings out of his storeroom new treasures as well as old."

A Prophet Without Honor

⁵³When Jesus had finished these parables, he moved on from there. ⁵⁴Coming to his hometown, he began teaching the people in their synagogue, and they were amazed. "Where did this man get this wisdom and these miraculous powers?" they asked. ⁵⁵"Isn't this the carpenter's son? Isn't his mother's name Mary, and aren't his brothers James, Joseph, Simon and Judas? ⁵⁶Aren't all his sisters with us? Where then did this man get all these things?" ⁵⁷And they took offense at him.

But Jesus said to them, "Only in his hometown and in his own house is a prophet without honor."

⁵⁸And he did not do many miracles there because of their lack of faith.

John the Baptist Beheaded

14 AT THAT time Herod the tetrarch heard the reports about Jesus, ²and he said to his attendants, "This is John the Baptist; he has risen from the dead! That is why miraculous powers are at work in him."

³Now Herod had arrested John and bound him and put him in prison because of Herodias, his brother Philip's wife, ⁴for John had been saying to him: "It is not lawful for you to have her." ⁵Herod wanted to kill John, but he was afraid of the people, because they considered him a prophet.

⁶On Herod's birthday the daughter of Herodias danced for them and pleased Herod so much ⁷that he promised with an oath to give her whatever she asked. ⁸Prompted by her mother, she said, "Give me here on a platter the head of John the Baptist." ⁹The king was distressed, but because of his oaths and his dinner guests, he ordered that her request be granted ¹⁰and had John beheaded in the prison. ¹¹His head was brought in on a platter and given to the girl, who carried it to her mother. ¹²John's disciples came and took his body and buried it. Then they went and told Jesus.

Jesus Feeds the Five Thousand

¹³When Jesus heard what had happened, he withdrew by boat privately to a solitary place. Hearing of this, the crowds followed him on foot from the towns. ¹⁴When Jesus landed and saw a large crowd, he had compassion on them and healed their sick.

¹⁵As evening approached, the disciples came to him and said, "This is a remote place, and it's already getting late. Send the crowds away, so they can go to the villages and buy themselves some food."

¹⁶Jesus replied, "They do not need to go away. You give them something to eat."

¹⁷"We have here only five loaves of bread and two fish," they answered.

¹⁸"Bring them here to me," he said. ¹⁹And he directed the people to sit down on the grass. Taking the five loaves and the two fish and looking up to heaven, he gave thanks and broke the loaves. Then he gave them to the disciples, and the disciples gave them to the people. ²⁰They all ate and were satisfied, and the disciples

Living Bible

52Then he added, "Those experts in Jewish law who are now my disciples have double treasures—from the Old Testament as well as from the New!"a

53, 54When Jesus had finished giving these illustrations, he returned to his home town, Nazareth in Galilee,b and taught there in the synagogue and astonished everyone with his wisdom and his miracles.

55"How is this possible?" the people exclaimed. "He's just a carpenter's son, and we know Mary his mother and his brothers—James, Joseph, Simon, and Judas. 56And his sisters—they all live here. How can he be so great?" 57And they became angry with him!

Then Jesus told them, "A prophet is honored everywhere except in his own country, and among his own people!" 58And so he did only a few great miracles there, because of their unbelief.

14 WHEN KING Herodc heard about Jesus, 2he said to his men, "This must be John the Baptist, come back to life again. That is why he can do these miracles." 3For Herod had arrested John and chained him in prison at the demand ofd his wife Herodias, his brother Philip's ex-wife, 4because John had told him it was wrong for him to marry her. 5He would have killed John but was afraid of a riot, for all the people believed John was a prophet.

6But at a birthday party for Herod, Herodias' daughter performed a dance that greatly pleased him, 7so he vowed to give her anything she wanted. 8Consequently, at her mother's urging, the girl asked for John the Baptist's head on a tray.

9The king was grieved, but because of his oath, and because he didn't want to back down in front of his guests, he issued the necessary orders.

10So John was beheaded in the prison, 11and his head was brought on a tray and given to the girl, who took it to her mother.

12Then John's disciples came for his body and buried it, and came to tell Jesus what had happened.

13As soon as Jesus heard the news, he went off by himself in a boat to a remote area to be alone. But the crowds saw where he was headed, and followed by land from many villages.

14So when Jesus came out of the wilderness, a vast crowd was waiting for him and he pitied them and healed their sick.

15That evening the disciples came to him and said, "It is already past time for supper, and there is nothing to eat here in the desert; send the crowds away so they can go to the villages and buy some food."

16But Jesus replied, "That isn't necessary—you feed them!"

17"What!" they exclaimed. "We have exactly five small loaves of bread and two fish!"

18"Bring them here," he said.

19Then he told the people to sit down on the grass; and he took the five loaves and two fish, looked up into the sky and asked God's blessing on the meal, then broke the loaves apart and gave them to the disciples to place before the people. 20And everyone ate until full! And

New Revised Standard

who has been trained for the kingdom of heaven is like the master of a household who brings out of his treasure what is new and what is old." 53When Jesus had finished these parables, he left that place.

The Rejection of Jesus at Nazareth

54 He came to his hometown and began to teach the peoplee in their synagogue, so that they were astounded and said, "Where did this man get this wisdom and these deeds of power? 55Is not this the carpenter's son? Is not his mother called Mary? And are not his brothers James and Joseph and Simon and Judas? 56And are not all his sisters with us? Where then did this man get all this?" 57And they took offense at him. But Jesus said to them, "Prophets are not without honor except in their own country and in their own house." 58And he did not do many deeds of power there, because of their unbelief.

The Death of John the Baptist

14 AT THAT time Herod the rulerf heard reports about Jesus; 2and he said to his servants, "This is John the Baptist; he has been raised from the dead, and for this reason these powers are at work in him." 3For Herod had arrested John, bound him, and put him in prison on account of Herodias, his brother Philip's wife,g 4because John had been telling him, "It is not lawful for you to have her." 5Though Herodh wanted to put him to death, he feared the crowd, because they regarded him as a prophet. 6But when Herod's birthday came, the daughter of Herodias danced before the company, and she pleased Herod 7so much that he promised on oath to grant her whatever she might ask. 8Prompted by her mother, she said, "Give me the head of John the Baptist here on a platter." 9The king was grieved, yet out of regard for his oaths and for the guests, he commanded it to be given; 10he sent and had John beheaded in the prison. 11The head was brought on a platter and given to the girl, who brought it to her mother. 12His disciples came and took the body and buried it; then they went and told Jesus.

Feeding the Five Thousand

13 Now when Jesus heard this, he withdrew from there in a boat to a deserted place by himself. But when the crowds heard it, they followed him on foot from the towns. 14When he went ashore, he saw a great crowd; and he had compassion for them and cured their sick. 15When it was evening, the disciples came to him and said, "This is a deserted place, and the hour is now late; send the crowds away so that they may go into the villages and buy food for themselves." 16Jesus said to them, "They need not go away; you give them something to eat." 17They replied, "We have nothing here but five loaves and two fish." 18And he said, "Bring them here to me." 19Then he ordered the crowds to sit down on the grass. Taking the five loaves and the two fish, he looked up to heaven, and blessed and broke the loaves, and gave them to the disciples, and the disciples gave them to the crowds. 20And all ate and were filled; and

---

a 13:52 *from the Old Testament as well as from the New,* literally, "brings back out of his treasure things both new and old." The paraphrase is of course highly anachronistic! b 13:53, 54 *Nazareth in Galilee,* implied. c 14:1 *King Herod,* literally, "the Tetrarch"—he was one of four "kings" over this area, his sovereignty being Galilee and Peraea. d 14:3 *at the demand of,* literally, "on account of."

e Gk *them* f Gk *tetrarch* g Other ancient authorities read *his brother's wife* h Gk *he*

King James

20And they did all eat, and were filled: and they took up of the fragments that remained twelve baskets full.

21And they that had eaten were about five thousand men, beside women and children.

22¶ And straightway Jesus constrained his disciples to get into a ship, and to go before him unto the other side, while he sent the multitudes away.

23And when he had sent the multitudes away, he went up into a mountain apart to pray: and when the evening was come, he was there alone.

24But the ship was now in the midst of the sea, tossed with waves: for the wind was contrary.

25And in the fourth watch of the night Jesus went unto them, walking on the sea.

26And when the disciples saw him walking on the sea, they were troubled, saying, It is a spirit; and they cried out for fear.

27But straightway Jesus spake unto them, saying, Be of good cheer; it is I; be not afraid.

28And Peter answered him and said, Lord, if it be thou, bid me come unto thee on the water.

29And he said, Come. And when Peter was come down out of the ship, he walked on the water, to go to Jesus.

30But when he saw the wind boisterous, he was afraid; and beginning to sink, he cried, saying, Lord, save me.

31And immediately Jesus stretched forth *his* hand, and caught him, and said unto him, O thou of little faith, wherefore didst thou doubt?

32And when they were come into the ship, the wind ceased.

33Then they that were in the ship came and worshipped him, saying, Of a truth thou art the Son of God.

34¶ And when they were gone over, they came into the land of Gennesaret.

35And when the men of that place had knowledge of him, they sent out into all that country round about, and brought unto him all that were diseased;

36And besought him that they might only touch the hem of his garment: and as many as touched were made perfectly whole.

15 THEN CAME to Jesus scribes and Pharisees, which were of Jerusalem, saying,

2Why do thy disciples transgress the tradition of the elders? for they wash not their hands when they eat bread.

3But he answered and said unto them, Why do ye also transgress the commandment of God by your tradition?

4For God commanded, saying, Honour thy father and mother: and, He that curseth father or mother, let him die the death.

5But ye say, Whosoever shall say to *his* father or *his* mother, *It is* a gift, by whatsoever thou mightest be profited by me;

6And honour not his father or his mother, *he shall be free.* Thus have ye made the commandment of God of none effect by your tradition.

7*Ye* hypocrites, well did Esaias prophesy of you, saying,

8This people draweth nigh unto me with their mouth, and honoureth me with *their* lips; but their heart is far from me.

9But in vain they do worship me, teaching *for* doctrines the commandments of men.

10¶ And he called the multitude, and said unto them, Hear, and understand:

11Not that which goeth into the mouth defileth a man; but that which cometh out of the mouth, this defileth a man.

New International

picked up twelve basketfuls of broken pieces that were left over. 21The number of those who ate was about five thousand men, besides women and children.

Jesus Walks on the Water

22Immediately Jesus made the disciples get into the boat and go on ahead of him to the other side, while he dismissed the crowd. 23After he had dismissed them, he went up on a mountainside by himself to pray. When evening came, he was there alone, 24but the boat was already a considerable distancea from land, buffeted by the waves because the wind was against it.

25During the fourth watch of the night Jesus went out to them, walking on the lake. 26When the disciples saw him walking on the lake, they were terrified. "It's a ghost," they said, and cried out in fear.

27But Jesus immediately said to them: "Take courage! It is I. Don't be afraid."

28"Lord, if it's you," Peter replied, "tell me to come to you on the water."

29"Come," he said.

Then Peter got down out of the boat, walked on the water and came toward Jesus. 30But when he saw the wind, he was afraid and, beginning to sink, cried out, "Lord, save me!"

31Immediately Jesus reached out his hand and caught him. "You of little faith," he said, "why did you doubt?"

32And when they climbed into the boat, the wind died down. 33Then those who were in the boat worshiped him, saying, "Truly you are the Son of God."

34When they had crossed over, they landed at Gennesaret. 35And when the men of that place recognized Jesus, they sent word to all the surrounding country. People brought all their sick to him 36and begged him to let the sick just touch the edge of his cloak, and all who touched him were healed.

Clean and Unclean

15 THEN SOME Pharisees and teachers of the law came to Jesus from Jerusalem and asked, 2"Why do your disciples break the tradition of the elders? They don't wash their hands before they eat!"

3Jesus replied, "And why do you break the command of God for the sake of your tradition? 4For God said, 'Honor your father and mother'b and 'Anyone who curses his father or mother must be put to death.'c 5But you say that if a man says to his father or mother, 'Whatever help you might otherwise have received from me is a gift devoted to God,' 6he is not to 'honor his fatherd' with it. Thus you nullify the word of God for the sake of your tradition. 7You hypocrites! Isaiah was right when he prophesied about you:

8" 'These people honor me with their lips,
but their hearts are far from me.
9They worship me in vain;
their teachings are but rules taught by
men.'e"

10Jesus called the crowd to him and said, "Listen and understand. 11What goes into a man's mouth does not make him 'unclean,' but what comes out of his mouth, that is what makes him 'unclean.' "

a 24 Greek *many stadia*   b 4 Exodus 20:12; Deut. 5:16   c 4 Exodus 21:17;
Lev. 20:9   d 6 Some manuscripts *father or his mother*   e 9 Isaiah 29:13

Living Bible

when the scraps were picked up afterwards, there were twelve basketfuls left over! 21(About 5,000 men were in the crowd that day, besides all the women and children.)

22Immediately after this, Jesus told his disciples to get into their boat and cross to the other side of the lake while he stayed to get the people started home.

23, 24Then afterwards he went up into the hills to pray. Night fell, and out on the lake the disciples were in trouble. For the wind had risen and they were fighting heavy seas.

25About four o'clock in the morning Jesus came to them, walking on the water! 26They screamed in terror, for they thought he was a ghost.

27But Jesus immediately spoke to them, reassuring them. "Don't be afraid!" he said.

28Then Peter called to him: "Sir, if it is really you, tell me to come over to you, walking on the water."

29"All right," the Lord said, "come along!"

So Peter went over the side of the boat and walked on the water toward Jesus. 30But when he looked around at the high waves, he was terrified and began to sink. "Save me, Lord!" he shouted.

31Instantly Jesus reached out his hand and rescued him. "O man of little faith," Jesus said. "Why did you doubt me?" 32And when they had climbed back into the boat, the wind stopped.

33The others sat there, awestruck. "You really are the Son of God!" they exclaimed.

34They landed at Gennesaret. 35The news of their arrival spread quickly throughout the city, and soon people were rushing around, telling everyone to bring in their sick to be healed. 36The sick begged him to let them touch even the tassel of his robe, and all who did were healed.

15 SOME PHARISEES and other Jewish leaders now arrived from Jerusalem to interview Jesus. 2"Why do your disciples disobey the ancient Jewish traditions?" they demanded. "For they ignore our ritual of ceremonial handwashing before they eat." 3He replied, "And why do your traditions violate the direct commandments of God? 4For instance, God's law is 'Honor your father and mother; anyone who reviles his parents must die.' 5, 6But you say, 'Even if your parents are in need, you may give their support money to the churchf instead.' And so, by your man-made rule, you nullify the direct command of God to honor and care for your parents. 7You hypocrites! Well did Isaiah prophesy of you, 8"These people say they honor me, but their hearts are far away. 9Their worship is worthless, for they teach their man-made laws instead of those from God.' "g

10Then Jesus called to the crowds and said, "Listen to what I say and try to understand: 11You aren't made unholy by eating non-kosher food! It is what you *say* and *think* that makes you unclean."h

New Revised Standard

they took up what was left over of the broken pieces, twelve baskets full. 21And those who ate were about five thousand men, besides women and children.

Jesus Walks on the Water

22 Immediately he made the disciples get into the boat and go on ahead to the other side, while he dismissed the crowds. 23And after he had dismissed the crowds, he went up the mountain by himself to pray. When evening came, he was there alone, 24but by this time the boat, battered by the waves, was far from the land,i for the wind was against them. 25And early in the morning he came walking toward them on the sea. 26But when the disciples saw him walking on the sea, they were terrified, saying, "It is a ghost!" And they cried out in fear. 27But immediately Jesus spoke to them and said, "Take heart, it is I; do not be afraid."

28 Peter answered him, "Lord, if it is you, command me to come to you on the water." 29He said, "Come." So Peter got out of the boat, started walking on the water, and came toward Jesus. 30But when he noticed the strong wind,j he became frightened, and beginning to sink, he cried out, "Lord, save me!" 31Jesus immediately reached out his hand and caught him, saying to him, "You of little faith, why did you doubt?" 32When they got into the boat, the wind ceased. 33And those in the boat worshiped him, saying, "Truly you are the Son of God."

Jesus Heals the Sick in Gennesaret

34 When they had crossed over, they came to land at Gennesaret. 35After the people of that place recognized him, they sent word throughout the region and brought all who were sick to him, 36and begged him that they might touch even the fringe of his cloak; and all who touched it were healed.

The Tradition of the Elders

15 THEN PHARISEES and scribes came to Jesus from Jerusalem and said, 2"Why do your disciples break the tradition of the elders? For they do not wash their hands before they eat." 3He answered them, "And why do you break the commandment of God for the sake of your tradition? 4For God said,k 'Honor your father and your mother,' and, 'Whoever speaks evil of father or mother must surely die.' 5But you say that whoever tells father or mother, 'Whatever support you might have had from me is given to God,'l then that person need not honor the father.m 6So, for the sake of your tradition, you make void the wordn of God. 7You hypocrites! Isaiah prophesied rightly about you when he said:

8 'This people honors me with their lips,
      but their hearts are far from me;
9 in vain do they worship me,
      teaching human precepts as doctrines.' "

Things That Defile

10 Then he called the crowd to him and said to them, "Listen and understand: 11it is not what goes into the mouth that defiles a person, but it is what comes out of the mouth that defiles." 12Then the disciples ap-

f *15:5, 6 to the church,* literally, "to God." g *15:9 those from God,* see Isa 29:13. h *15:11 It is what you say and think that makes you unclean,* implied. Literally, "what comes out of a man defiles a man."

i Other ancient authorities read *was out on the sea* j Other ancient authorities read *the wind* k Other ancient authorities read *commanded, saying* l Or *is an offering* m Other ancient authorities add *or the mother* n Other ancient authorities read *law;* others, *commandment*

King James

¹²Then came his disciples, and said unto him, Knowest thou that the Pharisees were offended, after they heard this saying?

¹³But he answered and said, Every plant, which my heavenly Father hath not planted, shall be rooted up.

¹⁴Let them alone: they be blind leaders of the blind. And if the blind lead the blind, both shall fall into the ditch.

¹⁵Then answered Peter and said unto him, Declare unto us this parable.

¹⁶And Jesus said, Are ye also yet without understanding?

¹⁷Do not ye yet understand, that whatsoever entereth in at the mouth goeth into the belly, and is cast out into the draught?

¹⁸But those things which proceed out of the mouth come forth from the heart; and they defile the man.

¹⁹For out of the heart proceed evil thoughts, murders, adulteries, fornications, thefts, false witness, blasphemies:

²⁰These are the things which defile a man: but to eat with unwashen hands defileth not a man.

²¹¶ Then Jesus went thence, and departed into the coasts of Tyre and Sidon.

²²And, behold, a woman of Canaan came out of the same coasts, and cried unto him, saying, Have mercy on me, O Lord, thou Son of David; my daughter is grievously vexed with a devil.

²³But he answered her not a word. And his disciples came and besought him, saying, Send her away; for she crieth after us.

²⁴But he answered and said, I am not sent but unto the lost sheep of the house of Israel.

²⁵Then came she and worshipped him, saying, Lord, help me.

²⁶But he answered and said, It is not meet to take the children's bread, and to cast it to dogs.

²⁷And she said, Truth, Lord: yet the dogs eat of the crumbs which fall from their masters' table.

²⁸Then Jesus answered and said unto her, O woman, great is thy faith: be it unto thee even as thou wilt. And her daughter was made whole from that very hour.

²⁹And Jesus departed from thence, and came nigh unto the sea of Galilee; and went up into a mountain, and sat down there.

³⁰And great multitudes came unto him, having with them those that were lame, blind, dumb, maimed, and many others, and cast them down at Jesus' feet; and he healed them:

³¹Insomuch that the multitude wondered, when they saw the dumb to speak, the maimed to be whole, the lame to walk, and the blind to see: and they glorified the God of Israel.

³²¶ Then Jesus called his disciples unto him, and said, I have compassion on the multitude, because they continue with me now three days, and have nothing to eat: and I will not send them away fasting, lest they faint in the way.

³³And his disciples say unto him, Whence should we have so much bread in the wilderness, as to fill so great a multitude?

³⁴And Jesus saith unto them, How many loaves have ye? And they said, Seven, and a few little fishes.

³⁵And he commanded the multitude to sit down on the ground.

³⁶And he took the seven loaves and the fishes, and gave thanks, and brake them, and gave to his disciples, and the disciples to the multitude.

³⁷And they did all eat, and were filled: and they took up of the broken meat that was left seven baskets full.

³⁸And they that did eat were four thousand men, beside women and children.

³⁹And he sent away the multitude, and took ship, and came into the coasts of Magdala.

New International

¹²Then the disciples came to him and asked, "Do you know that the Pharisees were offended when they heard this?"

¹³He replied, "Every plant that my heavenly Father has not planted will be pulled up by the roots. ¹⁴Leave them; they are blind guides.ᵃ If a blind man leads a blind man, both will fall into a pit."

¹⁵Peter said, "Explain the parable to us."

¹⁶"Are you still so dull?" Jesus asked them. ¹⁷"Don't you see that whatever enters the mouth goes into the stomach and then out of the body? ¹⁸But the things that come out of the mouth come from the heart, and these make a man 'unclean.' ¹⁹For out of the heart come evil thoughts, murder, adultery, sexual immorality, theft, false testimony, slander. ²⁰These are what make a man 'unclean'; but eating with unwashed hands does not make him 'unclean.'"

The Faith of the Canaanite Woman

²¹Leaving that place, Jesus withdrew to the region of Tyre and Sidon. ²²A Canaanite woman from that vicinity came to him, crying out, "Lord, Son of David, have mercy on me! My daughter is suffering terribly from demon-possession."

²³Jesus did not answer a word. So his disciples came to him and urged him, "Send her away, for she keeps crying out after us."

²⁴He answered, "I was sent only to the lost sheep of Israel."

²⁵The woman came and knelt before him. "Lord, help me!" she said.

²⁶He replied, "It is not right to take the children's bread and toss it to their dogs."

²⁷"Yes, Lord," she said, "but even the dogs eat the crumbs that fall from their masters' table."

²⁸Then Jesus answered, "Woman, you have great faith! Your request is granted." And her daughter was healed from that very hour.

Jesus Feeds the Four Thousand

²⁹Jesus left there and went along the Sea of Galilee. Then he went up on a mountainside and sat down. ³⁰Great crowds came to him, bringing the lame, the blind, the crippled, the mute and many others, and laid them at his feet; and he healed them. ³¹The people were amazed when they saw the mute speaking, the crippled made well, the lame walking and the blind seeing. And they praised the God of Israel.

³²Jesus called his disciples to him and said, "I have compassion for these people; they have already been with me three days and have nothing to eat. I do not want to send them away hungry, or they may collapse on the way."

³³His disciples answered, "Where could we get enough bread in this remote place to feed such a crowd?"

³⁴"How many loaves do you have?" Jesus asked.

"Seven," they replied, "and a few small fish."

³⁵He told the crowd to sit down on the ground. ³⁶Then he took the seven loaves and the fish, and when he had given thanks, he broke them and gave them to the disciples, and they in turn to the people. ³⁷They all ate and were satisfied. Afterward the disciples picked up seven basketfuls of broken pieces that were left over. ³⁸The number of those who ate was four thousand, besides women and children. ³⁹After Jesus had sent the crowd away, he got into the boat and went to the vicinity of Magadan.

ᵃ 14 Some manuscripts guides of the blind

Living Bible

12Then the disciples came and told him, "You offended the Pharisees by that remark."

13, 14Jesus replied, "Every plant not planted by my Father shall be rooted up, so ignore them. They are blind guides leading the blind, and both will fall into a ditch."

15Then Peter asked Jesus to explain what he meant when he said that people are not defiled by non-kosher food.

16"Don't you understand?" Jesus asked him. 17"Don't you see that anything you eat passes through the digestive tract and out again? 18But evil words come from an evil heart, and defile the man who says them. 19For from the heart come evil thoughts, murder, adultery, fornication, theft, lying and slander. 20These are what defile; but there is no spiritual defilement from eating without first going through the ritual of ceremonial handwashing!"

21Jesus then left that part of the country and walked the fifty milesᵇ to Tyre and Sidon.

22A woman from Canaan who was living there came to him, pleading, "Have mercy on me, O Lord, King David's Son! For my daughter has a demon within her, and it torments her constantly."

23But Jesus gave her no reply—not even a word. Then his disciples urged him to send her away. "Tell her to get going," they said, "for she is bothering us with all her begging."

24Then he said to the woman, "I was sent to help the Jews—the lost sheep of Israel—not the Gentiles."

25But she came and worshiped him and pled again, "Sir, help me!"

26"It doesn't seem right to take bread from the children and throw it to the dogs," he said.

27"Yes, it is!" she replied, "for even the puppies beneath the table are permitted to eat the crumbs that fall."

28"Woman," Jesus told her, "your faith is large, and your request is granted." And her daughter was healed right then.

29Jesus now returned to the Sea of Galilee, and climbed a hill and sat there. 30And a vast crowd brought him their lame, blind, maimed, and those who couldn't speak, and many others, and laid them before Jesus, and he healed them all. 31What a spectacle it was! Those who hadn't been able to say a word before were talking excitedly, and those with missing arms and legs had new ones; the crippled were walking and jumping around, and those who had been blind were gazing about them! The crowds just marveled, and praised the God of Israel.

32Then Jesus called his disciples to him and said, "I pity these people—they've been here with me for three days now, and have nothing left to eat; I don't want to send them away hungry or they will faint along the road."

33The disciples replied, "And where would we get enough here in the desert for all this mob to eat?"

34Jesus asked them, "How much food do you have?" And they replied, "Seven loaves of bread and a few small fish!"

35Then Jesus told all of the people to sit down on the ground, 36and he took the seven loaves and the fish, and gave thanks to God for them, and divided them into pieces, and gave them to the disciples who presented them to the crowd. 37, 38And everyone ate until full— 4,000 men besides the women and children! And afterwards, when the scraps were picked up, there were seven basketfuls left over!

39Then Jesus sent the people home and got into the boat and crossed to Magadan.

New Revised Standard

proached and said to him, "Do you know that the Pharisees took offense when they heard what you said?" 13He answered, "Every plant that my heavenly Father has not planted will be uprooted. 14Let them alone; they are blind guides of the blind.ᶜ And if one blind person guides another, both will fall into a pit." 15But Peter said to him, "Explain this parable to us." 16Then he said, "Are you also still without understanding? 17Do you not see that whatever goes into the mouth enters the stomach, and goes out into the sewer? 18But what comes out of the mouth proceeds from the heart, and this is what defiles. 19For out of the heart come evil intentions, murder, adultery, fornication, theft, false witness, slander. 20These are what defile a person, but to eat with unwashed hands does not defile."

The Canaanite Woman's Faith

21 Jesus left that place and went away to the district of Tyre and Sidon. 22Just then a Canaanite woman from that region came out and started shouting, "Have mercy on me, Lord, Son of David; my daughter is tormented by a demon." 23But he did not answer her at all. And his disciples came and urged him, saying, "Send her away, for she keeps shouting after us." 24He answered, "I was sent only to the lost sheep of the house of Israel." 25But she came and knelt before him, saying, "Lord, help me." 26He answered, "It is not fair to take the children's food and throw it to the dogs." 27She said, "Yes, Lord, yet even the dogs eat the crumbs that fall from their masters' table." 28Then Jesus answered her, "Woman, great is your faith! Let it be done for you as you wish." And her daughter was healed instantly.

Jesus Cures Many People

29 After Jesus had left that place, he passed along the Sea of Galilee, and he went up the mountain, where he sat down. 30Great crowds came to him, bringing with them the lame, the maimed, the blind, the mute, and many others. They put them at his feet, and he cured them, 31so that the crowd was amazed when they saw the mute speaking, the maimed whole, the lame walking, and the blind seeing. And they praised the God of Israel.

Feeding the Four Thousand

32 Then Jesus called his disciples to him and said, "I have compassion for the crowd, because they have been with me now for three days and have nothing to eat; and I do not want to send them away hungry, for they might faint on the way." 33The disciples said to him, "Where are we to get enough bread in the desert to feed so great a crowd?" 34Jesus asked them, "How many loaves have you?" They said, "Seven, and a few small fish." 35Then ordering the crowd to sit down on the ground, 36he took the seven loaves and the fish; and after giving thanks he broke them and gave them to the disciples, and the disciples gave them to the crowds. 37And all of them ate and were filled; and they took up the broken pieces left over, seven baskets full. 38Those who had eaten were four thousand men, besides women and children. 39After sending away the crowds, he got into the boat and went to the region of Magadan.ᵈ

ᵇ 15:21 walked the fifty miles, implied. Literally, "withdrew into the parts of Tyre and Sidon."

ᶜ Other ancient authorities lack of the blind   ᵈ Other ancient authorities read Magdala or Magdalan

King James

16 THE PHARISEES also with the Sadducees came, and tempting desired him that he would show them a sign from heaven.

2He answered and said unto them, When it is evening, ye say, *It will be* fair weather: for the sky is red.

3And in the morning, *It will be* foul weather today: for the sky is red and lowering. O *ye* hypocrites, ye can discern the face of the sky; but can ye not *discern* the signs of the times?

4A wicked and adulterous generation seeketh after a sign; and there shall no sign be given unto it, but the sign of the prophet Jonas. And he left them, and departed.

5And when his disciples were come to the other side, they had forgotten to take bread.

6¶ Then Jesus said unto them, Take heed and beware of the leaven of the Pharisees and of the Sadducees.

7And they reasoned among themselves, saying, *It is* because we have taken no bread.

8*Which* when Jesus perceived, he said unto them, O ye of little faith, why reason ye among yourselves, because ye have brought no bread?

9Do ye not yet understand, neither remember the five loaves of the five thousand, and how many baskets ye took up?

10Neither the seven loaves of the four thousand, and how many baskets ye took up?

11How is it that ye do not understand that I spake *it* not to you concerning bread, that ye should beware of the leaven of the Pharisees and of the Sadducees?

12Then understood they how that he bade *them* not beware of the leaven of bread, but of the doctrine of the Pharisees and of the Sadducees.

13¶ When Jesus came into the coasts of Caesarea Philippi, he asked his disciples, saying, Whom do men say that I the Son of man am?

14And they said, Some *say that thou art* John the Baptist: some, Elias; and others, Jeremias, or one of the prophets.

15He saith unto them, But whom say ye that I am?

16And Simon Peter answered and said, Thou art the Christ, the Son of the living God.

17And Jesus answered and said unto him, Blessed art thou, Simon Bar-jona: for flesh and blood hath not revealed *it* unto thee, but my Father which is in heaven.

18And I say also unto thee, That thou art Peter, and upon this rock I will build my church; and the gates of hell shall not prevail against it.

19And I will give unto thee the keys of the kingdom of heaven: and whatsoever thou shalt bind on earth shall be bound in heaven: and whatsoever thou shalt loose on earth shall be loosed in heaven.

20Then charged he his disciples that they should tell no man that he was Jesus the Christ.

21¶ From that time forth began Jesus to show unto his disciples, how that he must go unto Jerusalem, and suffer many things of the elders and chief priests and scribes, and be killed, and be raised again the third day.

22Then Peter took him, and began to rebuke him, saying, Be it far from thee, Lord: this shall not be unto thee.

23But he turned, and said unto Peter, Get thee behind me, Satan: thou art an offence unto me: for thou savourest not the things that be of God, but those that be of men.

24¶ Then said Jesus unto his disciples, If any *man* will come after me, let him deny himself, and take up his cross, and follow me.

New International

The Demand for a Sign

16 THE PHARISEES and Sadducees came to Jesus and tested him by asking him to show them a sign from heaven.

2He replied,a "When evening comes, you say, 'It will be fair weather, for the sky is red,' 3and in the morning, 'Today it will be stormy, for the sky is red and overcast.' You know how to interpret the appearance of the sky, but you cannot interpret the signs of the times.

4A wicked and adulterous generation looks for a miraculous sign, but none will be given it except the sign of Jonah." Jesus then left them and went away.

The Yeast of the Pharisees and Sadducees

5When they went across the lake, the disciples forgot to take bread. 6"Be careful," Jesus said to them. "Be on your guard against the yeast of the Pharisees and Sadducees."

7They discussed this among themselves and said, "It is because we didn't bring any bread."

8Aware of their discussion, Jesus asked, "You of little faith, why are you talking among yourselves about having no bread? 9Do you still not understand? Don't you remember the five loaves for the five thousand, and how many basketfuls you gathered? 10Or the seven loaves for the four thousand, and how many basketfuls you gathered? 11How is it you don't understand that I was not talking to you about bread? But be on your guard against the yeast of the Pharisees and Sadducees." 12Then they understood that he was not telling them to guard against the yeast used in bread, but against the teaching of the Pharisees and Sadducees.

Peter's Confession of Christ

13When Jesus came to the region of Caesarea Philippi, he asked his disciples, "Who do people say the Son of Man is?"

14They replied, "Some say John the Baptist; others say Elijah; and still others, Jeremiah or one of the prophets."

15"But what about you?" he asked. "Who do you say I am?"

16Simon Peter answered, "You are the Christ,b the Son of the living God."

17Jesus replied, "Blessed are you, Simon son of Jonah, for this was not revealed to you by man, but by my Father in heaven. 18And I tell you that you are Peter,c and on this rock I will build my church, and the gates of Hadesd will not overcome it.e 19I will give you the keys of the kingdom of heaven; whatever you bind on earth will bef bound in heaven, and whatever you loose on earth will bef loosed in heaven." 20Then he warned his disciples not to tell anyone that he was the Christ.

Jesus Predicts His Death

21From that time on Jesus began to explain to his disciples that he must go to Jerusalem and suffer many things at the hands of the elders, chief priests and teachers of the law, and that he must be killed and on the third day be raised to life.

22Peter took him aside and began to rebuke him. "Never, Lord!" he said. "This shall never happen to you!"

23Jesus turned and said to Peter, "Get behind me, Satan! You are a stumbling block to me; you do not have in mind the things of God, but the things of men."

24Then Jesus said to his disciples, "If anyone would come after me, he must deny himself and take up his cross and follow me. 25For whoever wants to save his

---

a 2 Some early manuscripts do not have the rest of verse 2 and all of verse 3.　b 16 Or *Messiah*; also in verse 20　c 18 *Peter* means rock.　d 18 Or hell　e 18 Or *not prove stronger than it*　f 19 Or *have been*

Living Bible

16 ONE DAY the Pharisees and Sadducees[g] came to test Jesus' claim of being the Messiah by asking him to show them some great demonstrations in the skies.

2, 3He replied, "You are good at reading the weather signs of the skies—red sky tonight means fair weather tomorrow; red sky in the morning means foul weather all day—but you can't read the obvious signs of the times! 4This evil, unbelieving nation is asking for some strange sign in the heavens, but no further proof will be given except the miracle that happened to Jonah." Then Jesus walked out on them.

5Arriving across the lake, the disciples discovered they had forgotten to bring any food.

6"Watch out!" Jesus warned them; "beware of the yeast of the Pharisees and Sadducees."

7They thought he was saying this because they had forgotten to bring bread.

8Jesus knew what they were thinking and told them, "O men of little faith! Why are you so worried about having no food? 9Won't you ever understand? Don't you remember at all the 5,000 I fed with five loaves, and the basketfuls left over? 10Don't you remember the 4,000 I fed, and all that was left? 11How could you even think I was talking about food? But again I say, 'Beware of the yeast of the Pharisees and Sadducees.' "

12Then at last they understood that by "yeast" he meant the *wrong teaching* of the Pharisees and Sadducees.

13When Jesus came to Caesarea Philippi, he asked his disciples, "Who are the people saying I[h] am?"

14"Well," they replied, "some say John the Baptist; some, Elijah; some, Jeremiah or one of the other prophets."

15Then he asked them, "Who do *you* think I am?"

16Simon Peter answered, "The Christ, the Messiah, the Son of the living God."

17"God has blessed you, Simon, son of Jonah," Jesus said, "for my Father in heaven has personally revealed this to you—this is not from any human source. 18You are Peter, a stone; and upon this rock I will build my church; and all the powers of hell shall not prevail against it. 19And I will give you the keys of the Kingdom of Heaven; whatever doors you lock on earth shall be locked in heaven; and whatever doors you open on earth shall be open in heaven!"

20Then he warned the disciples against telling others that he was the Messiah.

21From then on Jesus began to speak plainly to his disciples about going to Jerusalem, and what would happen to him there—that he would suffer at the hands of the Jewish leaders,[i] that he would be killed, and that three days later he would be raised to life again.

22But Peter took him aside to remonstrate with him. "Heaven forbid, sir," he said. "This is not going to happen to you!"

23Jesus turned on Peter and said, "Get away from me, you Satan! You are a dangerous trap to me. You are thinking merely from a human point of view, and not from God's."

24Then Jesus said to the disciples, "If anyone wants to be a follower of mine, let him deny himself and take up his cross and follow me. 25For anyone who keeps his

New Revised Standard

The Demand for a Sign

16 THE PHARISEES and Sadducees came, and to test Jesus[j] they asked him to show them a sign from heaven. 2He answered them, "When it is evening, you say, 'It will be fair weather, for the sky is red.' 3And in the morning, 'It will be stormy today, for the sky is red and threatening.' You know how to interpret the appearance of the sky, but you cannot interpret the signs of the times.[k] 4An evil and adulterous generation asks for a sign, but no sign will be given to it except the sign of Jonah." Then he left them and went away.

The Yeast of the Pharisees and Sadducees

5 When the disciples reached the other side, they had forgotten to bring any bread. 6Jesus said to them, "Watch out, and beware of the yeast of the Pharisees and Sadducees." 7They said to one another, "It is because we have brought no bread." 8And becoming aware of it, Jesus said, "You of little faith, why are you talking about having no bread? 9Do you still not perceive? Do you not remember the five loaves for the five thousand, and how many baskets you gathered? 10Or the seven loaves for the four thousand, and how many baskets you gathered? 11How could you fail to perceive that I was not speaking about bread? Beware of the yeast of the Pharisees and Sadducees!" 12Then they understood that he had not told them to beware of the yeast of bread, but of the teaching of the Pharisees and Sadducees.

Peter's Declaration about Jesus

13 Now when Jesus came into the district of Caesarea Philippi, he asked his disciples, "Who do people say that the Son of Man is?" 14And they said, "Some say John the Baptist, but others Elijah, and still others Jeremiah or one of the prophets." 15He said to them, "But who do you say that I am?" 16Simon Peter answered, "You are the Messiah,[l] the Son of the living God." 17And Jesus answered him, "Blessed are you, Simon son of Jonah! For flesh and blood has not revealed this to you, but my Father in heaven. 18And I tell you, you are Peter,[m] and on this rock[n] I will build my church, and the gates of Hades will not prevail against it. 19I will give you the keys of the kingdom of heaven, and whatever you bind on earth will be bound in heaven, and whatever you loose on earth will be loosed in heaven." 20Then he sternly ordered the disciples not to tell anyone that he was[o] the Messiah.[l]

Jesus Foretells His Death and Resurrection

21 From that time on, Jesus began to show his disciples that he must go to Jerusalem and undergo great suffering at the hands of the elders and chief priests and scribes, and be killed, and on the third day be raised. 22And Peter took him aside and began to rebuke him, saying, "God forbid it, Lord! This must never happen to you." 23But he turned and said to Peter, "Get behind me, Satan! You are a stumbling block to me; for you are setting your mind not on divine things but on human things."

The Cross and Self-Denial

24 Then Jesus told his disciples, "If any want to become my followers, let them deny themselves and take up their cross and follow me. 25For those who want

---

[g] *16:1 Pharisees and Sadducees.* Jewish politico-religious leaders of two different parties. [h] *16:13 I,* literally, "the Son of Man." [i] *16:21 the Jewish leaders,* literally, "of the elders, and chief priests, and scribes."

[j] Gk *him* [k] Other ancient authorities lack *2When it is . . . of the times* [l] Or *the Christ* [m] Gk *Petros* [n] Gk *petra* [o] Other ancient authorities add *Jesus*

King James

25For whosoever will save his life shall lose it: and whosoever will lose his life for my sake shall find it.

26For what is a man profited, if he shall gain the whole world, and lose his own soul? or what shall a man give in exchange for his soul?

27For the Son of man shall come in the glory of his Father with his angels; and then he shall reward every man according to his works.

28Verily I say unto you, There be some standing here, which shall not taste of death, till they see the Son of man coming in his kingdom.

17 AND AFTER six days Jesus taketh Peter, James, and John his brother, and bringeth them up into an high mountain apart,

2And was transfigured before them: and his face did shine as the sun, and his raiment was white as the light.

3And, behold, there appeared unto them Moses and Elias talking with him.

4Then answered Peter, and said unto Jesus, Lord, it is good for us to be here: if thou wilt, let us make here three tabernacles; one for thee, and one for Moses, and one for Elias.

5While he yet spake, behold, a bright cloud overshadowed them: and behold a voice out of the cloud, which said, This is my beloved Son, in whom I am well pleased; hear ye him.

6And when the disciples heard it, they fell on their face, and were sore afraid.

7And Jesus came and touched them, and said, Arise, and be not afraid.

8And when they had lifted up their eyes, they saw no man, save Jesus only.

9And as they came down from the mountain, Jesus charged them, saying, Tell the vision to no man, until the Son of man be risen again from the dead.

10And his disciples asked him, saying, Why then say the scribes that Elias must first come?

11And Jesus answered and said unto them, Elias truly shall first come, and restore all things.

12But I say unto you, That Elias is come already, and they knew him not, but have done unto him whatsoever they listed. Likewise shall also the Son of man suffer of them.

13Then the disciples understood that he spake unto them of John the Baptist.

14¶ And when they were come to the multitude, there came to him a *certain* man, kneeling down to him, and saying,

15Lord, have mercy on my son: for he is lunatic, and sore vexed: for ofttimes he falleth into the fire, and oft into the water.

16And I brought him to thy disciples, and they could not cure him.

17Then Jesus answered and said, O faithless and perverse generation, how long shall I be with you? how long shall I suffer you? bring him hither to me.

18And Jesus rebuked the devil; and he departed out of him: and the child was cured from that very hour.

19Then came the disciples to Jesus apart, and said, Why could not we cast him out?

20And Jesus said unto them, Because of your unbelief: for verily I say unto you, If ye have faith as a grain of mustard seed, ye shall say unto this mountain, Remove hence to yonder place; and it shall remove; and nothing shall be impossible unto you.

21Howbeit this kind goeth not out but by prayer and fasting.

New International

lifea will lose it, but whoever loses his life for me will find it. 26What good will it be for a man if he gains the whole world, yet forfeits his soul? Or what can a man give in exchange for his soul? 27For the Son of Man is going to come in his Father's glory with his angels, and then he will reward each person according to what he has done. 28I tell you the truth, some who are standing here will not taste death before they see the Son of Man coming in his kingdom."

The Transfiguration

17 AFTER SIX days Jesus took with him Peter, James and John the brother of James, and led them up a high mountain by themselves. 2There he was transfigured before them. His face shone like the sun, and his clothes became as white as the light. 3Just then there appeared before them Moses and Elijah, talking with Jesus.

4Peter said to Jesus, "Lord, it is good for us to be here. If you wish, I will put up three shelters—one for you, one for Moses and one for Elijah."

5While he was still speaking, a bright cloud enveloped them, and a voice from the cloud said, "This is my Son, whom I love; with him I am well pleased. Listen to him!"

6When the disciples heard this, they fell facedown to the ground, terrified. 7But Jesus came and touched them. "Get up," he said. "Don't be afraid." 8When they looked up, they saw no one except Jesus.

9As they were coming down the mountain, Jesus instructed them, "Don't tell anyone what you have seen, until the Son of Man has been raised from the dead." 10The disciples asked him, "Why then do the teachers of the law say that Elijah must come first?"

11Jesus replied, "To be sure, Elijah comes and will restore all things. 12But I tell you, Elijah has already come, and they did not recognize him, but have done to him everything they wished. In the same way the Son of Man is going to suffer at their hands." 13Then the disciples understood that he was talking to them about John the Baptist.

The Healing of a Boy With a Demon

14When they came to the crowd, a man approached Jesus and knelt before him. 15"Lord, have mercy on my son," he said. "He has seizures and is suffering greatly. He often falls into the fire or into the water. 16I brought him to your disciples, but they could not heal him."

17"O unbelieving and perverse generation," Jesus replied, "how long shall I stay with you? How long shall I put up with you? Bring the boy here to me." 18Jesus rebuked the demon, and it came out of the boy, and he was healed from that moment.

19Then the disciples came to Jesus in private and asked, "Why couldn't we drive it out?"

20He replied, "Because you have so little faith. I tell you the truth, if you have faith as small as a mustard seed, you can say to this mountain, 'Move from here to there' and it will move. Nothing will be impossible for you.b"

---

a *25* The Greek word means either *life* or *soul*; also in verse 26.   b *20* Some manuscripts *you.* *21But this kind does not go out except by prayer and fasting.*

Living Bible

life for himself shall lose it; and anyone who loses his life for me shall find it again. 26What profit is there if you gain the whole world—and lose eternal life? What can be compared with the value of eternal life? 27For I, the Son of Mankind, shall come with my angels in the glory of my Father and judge each person according to his deeds. 28And some of you standing right here now will certainly live to see me coming in my Kingdom."

17 SIX DAYS later Jesus took Peter, James, and his brother John to the top of a high and lonely hill, 2and as they watched, his appearance changed so that his face shone like the sun and his clothing became dazzling white.

3Suddenly Moses and Elijah appeared and were talking with him. 4Peter blurted out, "Sir, it's wonderful that we can be here! If you want me to, I'll make three shelters,c one for you and one for Moses and one for Elijah."

5But even as he said it, a bright cloud came over them, and a voice from the cloud said, "This is my beloved Son, and I am wonderfully pleased with him. Obey him."d

6At this the disciples fell face downward to the ground, terribly frightened. 7Jesus came over and touched them. "Get up," he said, "don't be afraid."

8And when they looked, only Jesus was with them.

9As they were going down the mountain, Jesus commanded them not to tell anyone what they had seen until after he had risen from the dead.

10His disciples asked, "Why do the Jewish leaders insist Elijah must return before the Messiah comes?"e

11Jesus replied, "They are right. Elijah must come and set everything in order. 12And, in fact, he has already come, but he wasn't recognized, and was badly mistreated by many. And I, the Messiah,f shall also suffer at their hands."

13Then the disciples realized he was speaking of John the Baptist.

14When they arrived at the bottom of the hill, a huge crowd was waiting for them. A man came and knelt before Jesus and said, 15"Sir, have mercy on my son, for he is mentally deranged, and in great trouble, for he often falls into the fire or into the water; 16so I brought him to your disciples, but they couldn't cure him."

17Jesus replied, "Oh, you stubborn, faithless people! How long shall I bear with you? Bring him here to me."

18Then Jesus rebuked the demon in the boy and it left him, and from that moment the boy was well.

19Afterwards the disciples asked Jesus privately, "Why couldn't we cast that demon out?"

20"Because of your little faith," Jesus told them. "For if you had faith even as small as a tiny mustard seed you could say to this mountain, 'Move!' and it would go far away. Nothing would be impossible. 21But this kind of demon won't leave unless you have prayed and gone without food."g

New Revised Standard

to save their life will lose it, and those who lose their life for my sake will find it. 26For what will it profit them if they gain the whole world but forfeit their life? Or what will they give in return for their life?

27 "For the Son of Man is to come with his angels in the glory of his Father, and then he will repay everyone for what has been done. 28Truly I tell you, there are some standing here who will not taste death before they see the Son of Man coming in his kingdom."

The Transfiguration

17 SIX DAYS later, Jesus took with him Peter and James and his brother John and led them up a high mountain, by themselves. 2And he was transfigured before them, and his face shone like the sun, and his clothes became dazzling white. 3Suddenly there appeared to them Moses and Elijah, talking with him. 4Then Peter said to Jesus, "Lord, it is good for us to be here; if you wish, Ih will make three dwellingsi here, one for you, one for Moses, and one for Elijah." 5While he was still speaking, suddenly a bright cloud overshadowed them, and from the cloud a voice said, "This is my Son, the Beloved;j with him I am well pleased; listen to him!" 6When the disciples heard this, they fell to the ground and were overcome by fear. 7But Jesus came and touched them, saying, "Get up and do not be afraid." 8And when they looked up, they saw no one except Jesus himself alone.

9 As they were coming down the mountain, Jesus ordered them, "Tell no one about the vision until after the Son of Man has been raised from the dead." 10And the disciples asked him, "Why, then, do the scribes say that Elijah must come first?" 11He replied, "Elijah is indeed coming and will restore all things; 12but I tell you that Elijah has already come, and they did not recognize him, but they did to him whatever they pleased. So also the Son of Man is about to suffer at their hands." 13Then the disciples understood that he was speaking to them about John the Baptist.

Jesus Cures a Boy with a Demon

14 When they came to the crowd, a man came to him, knelt before him, 15and said, "Lord, have mercy on my son, for he is an epileptic and he suffers terribly; he often falls into the fire and often into the water. 16And I brought him to your disciples, but they could not cure him." 17Jesus answered, "You faithless and perverse generation, how much longer must I be with you? How much longer must I put up with you? Bring him here to me." 18And Jesus rebuked the demon,k and itl came out of him, and the boy was cured instantly. 19Then the disciples came to Jesus privately and said, "Why could we not cast it out?" 20He said to them, "Because of your little faith. For truly I tell you, if you have faith the size of am mustard seed, you will say to this mountain, 'Move from here to there,' and it will move; and nothing will be impossible for you."n

---

c 17:4 three shelters, literally, "three tabernacles" or "tents." What was in Peter's mind is not explained.   d 17:5 Obey him, literally, "hear him."   e 17:10 Elijah must return before the Messiah comes, implied. Literally, "that Elijah must come first."   f 17:12 the Messiah, literally, "the Son of Man."   g 17:21 This verse is omitted in many of the ancient manuscripts.

h Other ancient authorities read we   i Or tents   j Or my beloved Son   k Gk it or him   l Gk the demon   m Gk faith as a grain of   n Other ancient authorities add verse 21, But this kind does not come out except by prayer and fasting

King James

New International

22¶ And while they abode in Galilee, Jesus said unto them, The Son of man shall be betrayed into the hands of men:

23And they shall kill him, and the third day he shall be raised again. And they were exceeding sorry.

24¶ And when they were come to Capernaum, they that received tribute *money* came to Peter, and said, Doth not your master pay tribute?

25He saith, Yes. And when he was come into the house, Jesus prevented him, saying, What thinkest thou, Simon? of whom do the kings of the earth take custom or tribute? of their own children, or of strangers?

26Peter saith unto him, Of strangers. Jesus saith unto him, Then are the children free.

27Notwithstanding, lest we should offend them, go thou to the sea, and cast an hook, and take up the fish that first cometh up; and when thou hast opened his mouth, thou shalt find a piece of money: that take, and give unto them for me and thee.

18 AT THE same time came the disciples unto Jesus, saying, Who is the greatest in the kingdom of heaven?

2And Jesus called a little child unto him, and set him in the midst of them,

3And said, Verily I say unto you, Except ye be converted, and become as little children, ye shall not enter into the kingdom of heaven.

4Whosoever therefore shall humble himself as this little child, the same is greatest in the kingdom of heaven.

5And whoso shall receive one such little child in my name receiveth me.

6But whoso shall offend one of these little ones which believe in me, it were better for him that a millstone were hanged about his neck, and *that* he were drowned in the depth of the sea.

7¶ Woe unto the world because of offences! for it must needs be that offences come; but woe to that man by whom the offence cometh!

8Wherefore if thy hand or thy foot offend thee, cut them off, and cast *them* from thee: it is better for thee to enter into life halt or maimed, rather than having two hands or two feet to be cast into everlasting fire.

9And if thine eye offend thee, pluck it out, and cast *it* from thee: it is better for thee to enter into life with one eye, rather than having two eyes to be cast into hell fire.

10Take heed that ye despise not one of these little ones; for I say unto you, That in heaven their angels do always behold the face of my Father which is in heaven.

11For the Son of man is come to save that which was lost.

12How think ye? if a man have an hundred sheep, and one of them be gone astray, doth he not leave the ninety and nine, and goeth into the mountains, and seeketh that which is gone astray?

13And if so be that he find it, verily I say unto you, he rejoiceth more of that *sheep,* than of the ninety and nine which went not astray.

14Even so it is not the will of your Father which is in heaven, that one of these little ones should perish.

15¶ Moreover if thy brother shall trespass against thee, go and tell him his fault between thee and him alone: if he shall hear thee, thou hast gained thy brother.

16But if he will not hear *thee, then* take with thee one or two more, that in the mouth of two or three witnesses every word may be established.

22When they came together in Galilee, he said to them, "The Son of Man is going to be betrayed into the hands of men. 23They will kill him, and on the third day he will be raised to life." And the disciples were filled with grief.

The Temple Tax

24After Jesus and his disciples arrived in Capernaum, the collectors of the two-drachma tax came to Peter and asked, "Doesn't your teacher pay the temple taxa?"

25"Yes, he does," he replied.

When Peter came into the house, Jesus was the first to speak. "What do you think, Simon?" he asked. "From whom do the kings of the earth collect duty and taxes— from their own sons or from others?"

26"From others," Peter answered.

"Then the sons are exempt," Jesus said to him. 27"But so that we may not offend them, go to the lake and throw out your line. Take the first fish you catch; open its mouth and you will find a four-drachma coin. Take it and give it to them for my tax and yours."

The Greatest in the Kingdom of Heaven

18 AT THAT time the disciples came to Jesus and asked, "Who is the greatest in the kingdom of heaven?"

2He called a little child and had him stand among them. 3And he said: "I tell you the truth, unless you change and become like little children, you will never enter the kingdom of heaven. 4Therefore, whoever humbles himself like this child is the greatest in the kingdom of heaven.

5"And whoever welcomes a little child like this in my name welcomes me. 6But if anyone causes one of these little ones who believe in me to sin, it would be better for him to have a large millstone hung around his neck and to be drowned in the depths of the sea.

7"Woe to the world because of the things that cause people to sin! Such things must come, but woe to the man through whom they come! 8If your hand or your foot causes you to sin, cut it off and throw it away. It is better for you to enter life maimed or crippled than to have two hands or two feet and be thrown into eternal fire. 9And if your eye causes you to sin, gouge it out and throw it away. It is better for you to enter life with one eye than to have two eyes and be thrown into the fire of hell.

The Parable of the Lost Sheep

10"See that you do not look down on one of these little ones. For I tell you that their angels in heaven always see the face of my Father in heaven.b

12"What do you think? If a man owns a hundred sheep, and one of them wanders away, will he not leave the ninety-nine on the hills and go to look for the one that wandered off? 13And if he finds it, I tell you the truth, he is happier about that one sheep than about the ninety-nine that did not wander off. 14In the same way your Father in heaven is not willing that any of these little ones should be lost.

A Brother Who Sins Against You

15"If your brother sins against you,c go and show him his fault, just between the two of you. If he listens to you, you have won your brother over. 16But if he will not listen, take one or two others along, so that 'every matter may be established by the testimony of two or three witnesses.'d 17If he refuses to listen to them, tell

---

a 24 Greek *the two drachmas*   b 10 Some manuscripts *heaven.* [11]*The Son of Man came to save what was lost.*   c 15 Some manuscripts do not have *against you.*   d 16 Deut. 19:15

Living Bible

22, 23One day while they were still in Galilee, Jesus told them, "I am going to be betrayed into the power of those who will kill me, and on the third day afterwards I will be brought back to life again." And the disciples' hearts were filled with sorrow and dread.

24On their arrival in Capernaum, the Temple tax collectors came to Peter and asked him, "Doesn't your master pay taxes?"

25"Of course he does," Peter replied.

Then he went into the house to talk to Jesus about it, but before he had a chance to speak, Jesus asked him, "What do you think, Peter? Do kings levy assessments against their own people, or against conquered foreigners?"

26, 27"Against the foreigners," Peter replied.

"Well, then," Jesus said, "the citizens are free! However, we don't want to offend them, so go down to the shore and throw in a line, and open the mouth of the first fish you catch. You will find a coin to cover the taxes for both of us; take it and pay them."

18 ABOUT THAT time the disciples came to Jesus to ask which of them would be greatest in the Kingdom of Heaven!

2Jesus called a small child over to him and set the little fellow down among them, 3and said, "Unless you turn to God from your sins and become as little children, you will never get into the Kingdom of Heaven. 4Therefore anyone who humbles himself as this little child, is the greatest in the Kingdom of Heaven. 5And any of you who welcomes a little child like this because you are mine, is welcoming me and caring for me. 6But if any of you causes one of these little ones who trusts in me to lose his faith,e it would be better for you to have a rock tied to your neck and be thrown into the sea.

7"Woe upon the world for all its evils.f Temptation to do wrong is inevitable, but woe to the man who does the tempting. 8So if your hand or foot causes you to sin, cut it off and throw it away. Better to enter heaven crippled than to be in hell with both of your hands and feet. 9And if your eye causes you to sin, gouge it out and throw it away. Better to enter heaven with one eye than to be in hell with two.

10"Beware that you don't look down upon a single one of these little children. For I tell you that in heaven their angels have constant accessg to my Father. 11And I, the Messiah,h came to save the lost.h

12"If a man has a hundred sheep, and one wanders away and is lost, what will he do? Won't he leave the ninety-nine others and go out into the hills to search for the lost one? 13And if he finds it, he will rejoice over it more than over the ninety-nine others safe at home! 14Just so, it is not my Father's will that even one of these little ones should perish.

15"If a brother sins against you, go to him privately and confront him with his fault. If he listens and confesses it, you have won back a brother. 16But if not, then take one or two others with you and go back to him again, proving everything you say by these witnesses.

New Revised Standard

Jesus Again Foretells His Death and Resurrection

22 As they were gatheringi in Galilee, Jesus said to them, "The Son of Man is going to be betrayed into human hands, 23and they will kill him, and on the third day he will be raised." And they were greatly distressed.

Jesus and the Temple Tax

24 When they reached Capernaum, the collectors of the temple taxi came to Peter and said, "Does your teacher not pay the temple tax?"j 25He said, "Yes, he does." And when he came home, Jesus spoke of it first, asking, "What do you think, Simon? From whom do kings of the earth take toll or tribute? From their children or from others?" 26When Peterk said, "From others," Jesus said to him, "Then the children are free. 27However, so that we do not give offense to them, go to the sea and cast a hook; take the first fish that comes up; and when you open its mouth, you will find a coin;l take that and give it to them for you and me."

True Greatness

18 AT THAT time the disciples came to Jesus and asked, "Who is the greatest in the kingdom of heaven?" 2He called a child, whom he put among them, 3and said, "Truly I tell you, unless you change and become like children, you will never enter the kingdom of heaven. 4Whoever becomes humble like this child is the greatest in the kingdom of heaven. 5Whoever welcomes one such child in my name welcomes me.

Temptations to Sin

6 "If any of you put a stumbling block before one of these little ones who believe in me, it would be better for you if a great millstone were fastened around your neck and you were drowned in the depth of the sea. 7Woe to the world because of stumbling blocks! Occasions for stumbling are bound to come, but woe to the one by whom the stumbling block comes!

8 "If your hand or your foot causes you to stumble, cut it off and throw it away; it is better for you to enter life maimed or lame than to have two hands or two feet and to be thrown into the eternal fire. 9And if your eye causes you to stumble, tear it out and throw it away; it is better for you to enter life with one eye than to have two eyes and to be thrown into the hellm of fire.

The Parable of the Lost Sheep

10 "Take care that you do not despise one of these little ones; for, I tell you, in heaven their angels continually see the face of my Father in heaven.n 12What do you think? If a shepherd has a hundred sheep, and one of them has gone astray, does he not leave the ninety-nine on the mountains and go in search of the one that went astray? 13And if he finds it, truly I tell you, he rejoices over it more than over the ninety-nine that never went astray. 14So it is not the will of youro Father in heaven that one of these little ones should be lost.

Reproving Another Who Sins

15 "If another member of the churchp sins against you,q go and point out the fault when the two of you are alone. If the member listens to you, you have regained that one.r 16But if you are not listened to, take one or two others along with you, so that every word may be confirmed by the evidence of two or three witnesses.

---

e *18:6 to lose his faith,* literally, "cause to stumble." f *18:7 for all its evils,* literally, "because of occasions of stumbling." g *18:10 have constant access,* or, "do always behold . . ." h *18:11 the Messiah,* literally, "the Son of Man." This verse is left out of many manuscripts, some ancient.

i Other ancient authorities read *living* j Gk *didrachma* k Gk *he* l Gk *stater*; the stater was worth two didrachmas m Gk *Gehenna* n Other ancient authorities add verse 11, *For the Son of Man came to save the lost* o Other ancient authorities read *my* p Gk *If your brother* q Other ancient authorities lack *against you* r Gk *the brother*

King James

17And if he shall neglect to hear them, tell *it* unto the church: but if he neglect to hear the church, let him be unto thee as an heathen man and a publican.

18Verily I say unto you, Whatsoever ye shall bind on earth shall be bound in heaven: and whatsoever ye shall loose on earth shall be loosed in heaven.

19Again I say unto you, That if two of you shall agree on earth as touching any thing that they shall ask, it shall be done for them of my Father which is in heaven.

20For where two or three are gathered together in my name, there am I in the midst of them.

21¶ Then came Peter to him, and said, Lord, how oft shall my brother sin against me, and I forgive him? till seven times?

22Jesus saith unto him, I say not unto thee, Until seven times: but, Until seventy times seven.

23¶ Therefore is the kingdom of heaven likened unto a certain king, which would take account of his servants.

24And when he had begun to reckon, one was brought unto him, which owed him ten thousand talents.

25But forasmuch as he had not to pay, his lord commanded him to be sold, and his wife, and children, and all that he had, and payment to be made.

26The servant therefore fell down, and worshipped him, saying, Lord, have patience with me, and I will pay thee all.

27Then the lord of that servant was moved with compassion, and loosed him, and forgave him the debt.

28But the same servant went out, and found one of his fellowservants, which owed him an hundred pence: and he laid hands on him, and took *him* by the throat, saying, Pay me that thou owest.

29And his fellowservant fell down at his feet, and besought him, saying, Have patience with me, and I will pay thee all.

30And he would not: but went and cast him into prison, till he should pay the debt.

31So when his fellowservants saw what was done, they were very sorry, and came and told unto their lord all that was done.

32Then his lord, after that he had called him, said unto him, O thou wicked servant, I forgave thee all that debt, because thou desiredst me:

33Shouldest not thou also have had compassion on thy fellowservant, even as I had pity on thee?

34And his lord was wroth, and delivered him to the tormentors, till he should pay all that was due unto him.

35So likewise shall my heavenly Father do also unto you, if ye from your hearts forgive not every one his brother their trespasses.

19 AND IT came to pass, *that* when Jesus had finished these sayings, he departed from Galilee, and came into the coasts of Judaea beyond Jordan;

2And great multitudes followed him; and he healed them there.

3¶ The Pharisees also came unto him, tempting him, and saying unto him, Is it lawful for a man to put away his wife for every cause?

4And he answered and said unto them, Have ye not read, that he which made *them* at the beginning made them male and female,

5And said, For this cause shall a man leave father and mother, and shall cleave to his wife: and they twain shall be one flesh?

6Wherefore they are no more twain, but one flesh. What therefore God hath joined together, let not man put asunder.

7They say unto him, Why did Moses then command to give a writing of divorcement, and to put her away?

New International

it to the church; and if he refuses to listen even to the church, treat him as you would a pagan or a tax collector.

18"I tell you the truth, whatever you bind on earth will bea bound in heaven, and whatever you loose on earth will bea loosed in heaven.

19"Again, I tell you that if two of you on earth agree about anything you ask for, it will be done for you by my Father in heaven. 20For where two or three come together in my name, there am I with them."

The Parable of the Unmerciful Servant

21Then Peter came to Jesus and asked, "Lord, how many times shall I forgive my brother when he sins against me? Up to seven times?"

22Jesus answered, "I tell you, not seven times, but seventy-seven times.b

23"Therefore, the kingdom of heaven is like a king who wanted to settle accounts with his servants. 24As he began the settlement, a man who owed him ten thousand talentsc was brought to him. 25Since he was not able to pay, the master ordered that he and his wife and his children and all that he had be sold to repay the debt.

26"The servant fell on his knees before him. 'Be patient with me,' he begged, 'and I will pay back everything.' 27The servant's master took pity on him, canceled the debt and let him go.

28"But when that servant went out, he found one of his fellow servants who owed him a hundred denarii.d He grabbed him and began to choke him. 'Pay back what you owe me!' he demanded.

29"His fellow servant fell to his knees and begged him, 'Be patient with me, and I will pay you back.'

30"But he refused. Instead, he went off and had the man thrown into prison until he could pay the debt. 31When the other servants saw what had happened, they were greatly distressed and went and told their master everything that had happened.

32"Then the master called the servant in. 'You wicked servant,' he said, 'I canceled all that debt of yours because you begged me to. 33Shouldn't you have had mercy on your fellow servant just as I had on you?' 34In anger his master turned him over to the jailers to be tortured, until he should pay back all he owed.

35"This is how my heavenly Father will treat each of you unless you forgive your brother from your heart."

Divorce

19 WHEN JESUS had finished saying these things, he left Galilee and went into the region of Judea to the other side of the Jordan. 2Large crowds followed him, and he healed them there.

3Some Pharisees came to him to test him. They asked, "Is it lawful for a man to divorce his wife for any and every reason?"

4"Haven't you read," he replied, "that at the beginning the Creator 'made them male and female,'e 5and said, 'For this reason a man will leave his father and mother and be united to his wife, and the two will become one flesh'f? 6So they are no longer two, but one. Therefore what God has joined together, let man not separate."

7"Why then," they asked, "did Moses command that a man give his wife a certificate of divorce and send her away?"

---

a 18 Or *have been*   b 22 Or *seventy times seven*   c 24 That is, millions of dollars   d 28 That is, a few dollars   e 4 Gen. 1:27   f 5 Gen. 2:24

Living Bible

17If he still refuses to listen, then take your case to the church, and if the church's verdict favors you, but he won't accept it, then the church should excommunicate him.g 18And I tell you this—whatever you bind on earth is bound in heaven, and whatever you free on earth will be freed in heaven.

19"I also tell you this—if two of you agree down here on earth concerning anything you ask for, my Father in heaven will do it for you. 20For where two or three gather together because they are mine, I will be right there among them."

21Then Peter came to him and asked, "Sir, how often should I forgive a brother who sins against me? Seven times?"

22"No!" Jesus replied, "seventy times seven!

23"The Kingdom of Heaven can be compared to a king who decided to bring his accounts up to date. 24In the process, one of his debtors was brought in who owed him $10,000,000!h 25He couldn't pay, so the king ordered him sold for the debt, also his wife and children and everything he had.

26"But the man fell down before the king, his face in the dust, and said, 'Oh, sir, be patient with me and I will pay it all.'

27"Then the king was filled with pity for him and released him and forgave his debt.

28"But when the man left the king, he went to a man who owed him $2,000i and grabbed him by the throat and demanded instant payment.

29"The man fell down before him and begged him to give him a little time. 'Be patient and I will pay it,' he pled.

30"But his creditor wouldn't wait. He had the man arrested and jailed until the debt would be paid in full.

31"Then the man's friends went to the king and told him what had happened. 32And the king called before him the man he had forgiven and said, 'You evil-hearted wretch! Here I forgave you all that tremendous debt, just because you asked me to— 33shouldn't you have mercy on others, just as I had mercy on you?'

34"Then the angry king sent the man to the torture chamber until he had paid every last penny due. 35So shall my heavenly Father do to you if you refuse to truly forgive your brothers."

19 AFTER JESUS had finished this address, he left Galilee and circled back to Judea from across the Jordan River. 2Vast crowds followed him, and he healed their sick. 3Some Pharisees came to interview him, and tried to trap him into saying something that would ruin him.

"Do you permit divorce?" they asked.

4"Don't you read the Scriptures?" he replied. "In them it is written that at the beginning God created man and woman, 5, 6and that a man should leave his father and mother, and be forever united to his wife. The two shall become one—no longer two, but one! And no man may divorce what God has joined together."

7"Then, why," they asked, "did Moses say a man may divorce his wife by merely writing her a letter of dismissal?"

New Revised Standard

17If the member refuses to listen to them, tell it to the church; and if the offender refuses to listen even to the church, let such a one be to you as a Gentile and a tax collector. 18Truly I tell you, whatever you bind on earth will be bound in heaven, and whatever you loose on earth will be loosed in heaven. 19Again, truly I tell you, if two of you agree on earth about anything you ask, it will be done for you by my Father in heaven. 20For where two or three are gathered in my name, I am there among them."

Forgiveness

21 Then Peter came and said to him, "Lord, if another member of the churchj sins against me, how often should I forgive? As many as seven times?" 22Jesus said to him, "Not seven times, but, I tell you, seventy-sevenk times.

The Parable of the Unforgiving Servant

23 "For this reason the kingdom of heaven may be compared to a king who wished to settle accounts with his slaves. 24When he began the reckoning, one who owed him ten thousand talentsl was brought to him; 25and, as he could not pay, his lord ordered him to be sold, together with his wife and children and all his possessions, and payment to be made. 26So the slave fell on his knees before him, saying, 'Have patience with me, and I will pay you everything.' 27And out of pity for him, the lord of that slave released him and forgave him the debt. 28But that same slave, as he went out, came upon one of his fellow slaves who owed him a hundred denarii;m and seizing him by the throat, he said, 'Pay what you owe.' 29Then his fellow slave fell down and pleaded with him, 'Have patience with me, and I will pay you.' 30But he refused; then he went and threw him into prison until he would pay the debt. 31When his fellow slaves saw what had happened, they were greatly distressed, and they went and reported to their lord all that had taken place. 32Then his lord summoned him and said to him, 'You wicked slave! I forgave you all that debt because you pleaded with me. 33Should you not have had mercy on your fellow slave, as I had mercy on you?' 34And in anger his lord handed him over to be tortured until he would pay his entire debt. 35So my heavenly Father will also do to every one of you, if you do not forgive your brother or sistern from your heart."

Teaching about Divorce

19 WHEN JESUS had finished saying these things, he left Galilee and went to the region of Judea beyond the Jordan. 2Large crowds followed him, and he cured them there.

3 Some Pharisees came to him, and to test him they asked, "Is it lawful for a man to divorce his wife for any cause?" 4He answered, "Have you not read that the one who made them at the beginning 'made them male and female,' 5and said, 'For this reason a man shall leave his father and mother and be joined to his wife, and the two shall become one flesh'? 6So they are no longer two, but one flesh. Therefore what God has joined together, let no one separate." 7They said to him, "Why then did Moses command us to give a certificate of dismissal and to divorce her?" 8He said to them, "It was

---

g 18:17 should excommunicate him, literally, "let him be to you as the Gentile and the publican." h 18:24 $10,000,000, literally, "10,000 talents." Approximately £3,000,000. i 18:28 $2,000, approximately £700.

j Gk if my brother k Or seventy times seven l A talent was worth more than fifteen years' wages of a laborer m The denarius was the usual day's wage for a laborer n Gk brother

King James

8He saith unto them, Moses because of the hardness of your hearts suffered you to put away your wives: but from the beginning it was not so.

9And I say unto you, Whosoever shall put away his wife, except *it be* for fornication, and shall marry another, committeth adultery: and whoso marrieth her which is put away doth commit adultery.

10¶ His disciples say unto him, If the case of the man be so with *his* wife, it is not good to marry.

11But he said unto them, All *men* cannot receive this saying, save *they* to whom it is given.

12For there are some eunuchs, which were so born from *their* mother's womb: and there are some eunuchs, which were made eunuchs of men: and there be eunuchs, which have made themselves eunuchs for the kingdom of heaven's sake. He that is able to receive *it,* let him receive *it.*

13¶ Then were there brought unto him little children, that he should put *his* hands on them, and pray: and the disciples rebuked them.

14But Jesus said, Suffer little children, and forbid them not, to come unto me: for of such is the kingdom of heaven.

15And he laid *his* hands on them, and departed thence.

16¶ And, behold, one came and said unto him, Good Master, what good thing shall I do, that I may have eternal life?

17And he said unto him, Why callest thou me good? *there is* none good but one, *that is,* God: but if thou wilt enter into life, keep the commandments.

18He saith unto him, Which? Jesus said, Thou shalt do no murder, Thou shalt not commit adultery, Thou shalt not steal, Thou shalt not bear false witness,

19Honour thy father and *thy* mother: and, Thou shalt love thy neighbour as thyself.

20The young man saith unto him, All these things have I kept from my youth up: what lack I yet?

21Jesus said unto him, If thou wilt be perfect, go *and* sell that thou hast, and give to the poor, and thou shalt have treasure in heaven: and come *and* follow me.

22But when the young man heard that saying, he went away sorrowful: for he had great possessions.

23¶ Then said Jesus unto his disciples, Verily I say unto you, That a rich man shall hardly enter into the kingdom of heaven.

24And again I say unto you, It is easier for a camel to go through the eye of a needle, than for a rich man to enter into the kingdom of God.

25When his disciples heard *it,* they were exceedingly amazed, saying, Who then can be saved?

26But Jesus beheld *them,* and said unto them, With men this is impossible; but with God all things are possible.

27¶ Then answered Peter and said unto him, Behold, we have forsaken all, and followed thee; what shall we have therefore?

28And Jesus said unto them, Verily I say unto you, That ye which have followed me, in the regeneration when the Son of man shall sit in the throne of his glory, ye also shall sit upon twelve thrones, judging the twelve tribes of Israel.

29And every one that hath forsaken houses, or brethren, or sisters, or father, or mother, or wife, or children, or lands, for my name's sake, shall receive an hundredfold, and shall inherit everlasting life.

30But many *that are* first shall be last; and the last *shall be* first.

New International

8Jesus replied, "Moses permitted you to divorce your wives because your hearts were hard. But it was not this way from the beginning. 9I tell you that anyone who divorces his wife, except for marital unfaithfulness, and marries another woman commits adultery."

10The disciples said to him, "If this is the situation between a husband and wife, it is better not to marry."

11Jesus replied, "Not everyone can accept this word, but only those to whom it has been given. 12For some are eunuchs because they were born that way; others were made that way by men; and others have renounced marriageª because of the kingdom of heaven. The one who can accept this should accept it."

The Little Children and Jesus

13Then little children were brought to Jesus for him to place his hands on them and pray for them. But the disciples rebuked those who brought them.

14Jesus said, "Let the little children come to me, and do not hinder them, for the kingdom of heaven belongs to such as these." 15When he had placed his hands on them, he went on from there.

The Rich Young Man

16Now a man came up to Jesus and asked, "Teacher, what good thing must I do to get eternal life?"

17"Why do you ask me about what is good?" Jesus replied. "There is only One who is good. If you want to enter life, obey the commandments."

18"Which ones?" the man inquired.

Jesus replied, " 'Do not murder, do not commit adultery, do not steal, do not give false testimony, 19honor your father and mother,'b and 'love your neighbor as yourself.'c"

20"All these I have kept," the young man said. "What do I still lack?"

21Jesus answered, "If you want to be perfect, go, sell your possessions and give to the poor, and you will have treasure in heaven. Then come, follow me."

22When the young man heard this, he went away sad, because he had great wealth.

23Then Jesus said to his disciples, "I tell you the truth, it is hard for a rich man to enter the kingdom of heaven. 24Again I tell you, it is easier for a camel to go through the eye of a needle than for a rich man to enter the kingdom of God."

25When the disciples heard this, they were greatly astonished and asked, "Who then can be saved?"

26Jesus looked at them and said, "With man this is impossible, but with God all things are possible."

27Peter answered him, "We have left everything to follow you! What then will there be for us?"

28Jesus said to them, "I tell you the truth, at the renewal of all things, when the Son of Man sits on his glorious throne, you who have followed me will also sit on twelve thrones, judging the twelve tribes of Israel. 29And everyone who has left houses or brothers or sisters or father or motherd or children or fields for my sake will receive a hundred times as much and will inherit eternal life. 30But many who are first will be last, and many who are last will be first.

ª *12* Or *have made themselves eunuchs*   b *19* Exodus 20:12-16; Deut. 5:16-20   c *19* Lev. 19:18   d *29* Some manuscripts *mother or wife*

Living Bible

8Jesus replied, "Moses did that in recognition of your hard and evil hearts, but it was not what God had originally intended. 9And I tell you this, that anyone who divorces his wife, except for fornication, and marries another, commits adultery."e

10Jesus' disciples then said to him, "If that is how it is, it is better not to marry!"

11"Not everyone can accept this statement," Jesus said. "Only those whom God helps. 12Some are born without the ability to marry,f and some are disabled by men, and some refuse to marry for the sake of the Kingdom of Heaven. Let anyone who can, accept my statement."

13Little children were brought for Jesus to lay his hands on them and pray. But the disciples scolded those who brought them. "Don't bother him," they said.

14But Jesus said, "Let the little children come to me, and don't prevent them. For of such is the Kingdom of Heaven." 15And he put his hands on their heads and blessed them before he left.

16Someone came to Jesus with this question: "Good master, what must I do to have eternal life?"

17"When you call me good you are calling me God," Jesus replied, "for God alone is truly good.g But to answer your question, you can get to heaven if you keep the commandments."

18"Which ones?" the man asked.

And Jesus replied, "Don't kill, don't commit adultery, don't steal, don't lie, 19honor your father and mother, and love your neighbor as yourself!"

20"I've always obeyed every one of them," the youth replied. "What else must I do?"

21Jesus told him, "If you want to be perfect, go and sell everything you have and give the money to the poor, and you will have treasure in heaven; and come, follow me." 22But when the young man heard this, he went away sadly, for he was very rich.

23Then Jesus said to his disciples, "It is almost impossible for a rich man to get into the Kingdom of Heaven. 24I say it again—it is easier for a camel to go through the eye of a needle than for a rich man to enter the Kingdom of God!"

25This remark confounded the disciples. "Then who in the world can be saved?" they asked.

26Jesus looked at them intently and said, "Humanly speaking, no one. But with God, everything is possible."

27Then Peter said to him, "We left everything to follow you. What will we get out of it?"

28And Jesus replied, "When I, the Messiah,h shall sit upon my glorious throne in the Kingdom,i you my disciples shall certainly sit on twelve thrones judging the twelve tribes of Israel. 29And anyone who gives up his home, brothers, sisters, father, mother, wife,j children, or property, to follow me, shall receive a hundred times as much in return, and shall have eternal life. 30But many who are first now will be last then; and some who are last now will be first then."

New Revised Standard

because you were so hard-hearted that Moses allowed you to divorce your wives, but from the beginning it was not so. 9And I say to you, whoever divorces his wife, except for unchastity, and marries another commits adultery."k

10 His disciples said to him, "If such is the case of a man with his wife, it is better not to marry." 11But he said to them, "Not everyone can accept this teaching, but only those to whom it is given. 12For there are eunuchs who have been so from birth, and there are eunuchs who have been made eunuchs by others, and there are eunuchs who have made themselves eunuchs for the sake of the kingdom of heaven. Let anyone accept this who can."

Jesus Blesses Little Children

13 Then little children were being brought to him in order that he might lay his hands on them and pray. The disciples spoke sternly to those who brought them; 14but Jesus said, "Let the little children come to me, and do not stop them; for it is to such as these that the kingdom of heaven belongs." 15And he laid his hands on them and went on his way.

The Rich Young Man

16 Then someone came to him and said, "Teacher, what good deed must I do to have eternal life?" 17And he said to him, "Why do you ask me about what is good? There is only one who is good. If you wish to enter into life, keep the commandments." 18He said to him, "Which ones?" And Jesus said, "You shall not murder; You shall not commit adultery; You shall not steal; You shall not bear false witness; 19Honor your father and mother; also, You shall love your neighbor as yourself." 20The young man said to him, "I have kept all these;l what do I still lack?" 21Jesus said to him, "If you wish to be perfect, go, sell your possessions, and give the moneym to the poor, and you will have treasure in heaven; then come, follow me." 22When the young man heard this word, he went away grieving, for he had many possessions.

23 Then Jesus said to his disciples, "Truly I tell you, it will be hard for a rich person to enter the kingdom of heaven. 24Again I tell you, it is easier for a camel to go through the eye of a needle than for someone who is rich to enter the kingdom of God." 25When the disciples heard this, they were greatly astounded and said, "Then who can be saved?" 26But Jesus looked at them and said, "For mortals it is impossible, but for God all things are possible."

27 Then Peter said in reply, "Look, we have left everything and followed you. What then will we have?" 28Jesus said to them, "Truly I tell you, at the renewal of all things, when the Son of Man is seated on the throne of his glory, you who have followed me will also sit on twelve thrones, judging the twelve tribes of Israel. 29And everyone who has left houses or brothers or sisters or father or mother or children or fields, for my name's sake, will receive a hundredfold,n and will inherit eternal life. 30But many who are first will be last, and the last will be first.

---

e 19:9 "And the man who marries a divorced woman commits adultery." This sentence is added in some ancient manuscripts.   f 19:12 Some are born without the ability to marry, literally, "born eunuchs," or, "born emasculated."   g 19:17 for God alone is truly good, implied from Lk 18:19.   h 19:28 the Messiah, literally, "the Son of Man."   i 19:28 in the Kingdom, literally, "in the regeneration."   j 19:29 wife, omitted here in many manuscripts but included in Lk 18:29.

k Other ancient authorities read except on the ground of unchastity, causes her to commit adultery; others add at the end of the verse and he who marries a divorced woman commits adultery   l Other ancient authorities add from my youth   m Gk lacks the money   n Other ancient authorities read manifold

King James

20 FOR THE kingdom of heaven is like unto a man *that is* an householder, which went out early in the morning to hire labourers into his vineyard.

2And when he had agreed with the labourers for a penny a day, he sent them into his vineyard.

3And he went out about the third hour, and saw others standing idle in the marketplace,

4And said unto them; Go ye also into the vineyard, and whatsoever is right I will give you. And they went their way.

5Again he went out about the sixth and ninth hour, and did likewise.

6And about the eleventh hour he went out, and found others standing idle, and saith unto them, Why stand ye here all the day idle?

7They say unto him, Because no man hath hired us. He saith unto them, Go ye also into the vineyard; and whatsoever is right, *that* shall ye receive.

8So when even was come, the lord of the vineyard saith unto his steward, Call the labourers, and give them *their* hire, beginning from the last unto the first.

9And when they came that *were hired* about the eleventh hour, they received every man a penny.

10But when the first came, they supposed that they should have received more; and they likewise received every man a penny.

11And when they had received *it*, they murmured against the goodman of the house,

12Saying, These last have wrought *but* one hour, and thou hast made them equal unto us, which have borne the burden and heat of the day.

13But he answered one of them, and said, Friend, I do thee no wrong: didst not thou agree with me for a penny?

14Take *that* thine *is*, and go thy way: I will give unto this last, even as unto thee.

15Is it not lawful for me to do what I will with mine own? Is thine eye evil, because I am good?

16So the last shall be first, and the first last: for many be called, but few chosen.

17¶ And Jesus going up to Jerusalem took the twelve disciples apart in the way, and said unto them,

18Behold, we go up to Jerusalem; and the Son of man shall be betrayed unto the chief priests and unto the scribes, and they shall condemn him to death,

19And shall deliver him to the Gentiles to mock, and to scourge, and to crucify *him:* and the third day he shall rise again.

20¶ Then came to him the mother of Zebedee's children with her sons, worshipping *him*, and desiring a certain thing of him.

21And he said unto her, What wilt thou? She saith unto him, Grant that these my two sons may sit, the one on thy right hand, and the other on the left, in thy kingdom.

22But Jesus answered and said, Ye know not what ye ask. Are ye able to drink of the cup that I shall drink of, and to be baptized with the baptism that I am baptized with? They say unto him, We are able.

23And he saith unto them, Ye shall drink indeed of my cup, and be baptized with the baptism that I am baptized with: but to sit on my right hand, and on my left, is not mine to give, but *it shall be given to them* for whom it is prepared of my Father.

24And when the ten heard *it*, they were moved with indignation against the two brethren.

25But Jesus called them *unto him*, and said, Ye know that the princes of the Gentiles exercise dominion over them, and they that are great exercise authority upon them.

26But it shall not be so among you: but whosoever will be great among you, let him be your minister;

New International

The Parable of the Workers in the Vineyard

20 "FOR THE kingdom of heaven is like a landowner who went out early in the morning to hire men to work in his vineyard. 2He agreed to pay them a denarius for the day and sent them into his vineyard.

3"About the third hour he went out and saw others standing in the marketplace doing nothing. 4He told them, 'You also go and work in my vineyard, and I will pay you whatever is right.' 5So they went.

"He went out again about the sixth hour and the ninth hour and did the same thing. 6About the eleventh hour he went out and found still others standing around. He asked them, 'Why have you been standing here all day long doing nothing?'

7" 'Because no one has hired us,' they answered.

"He said to them, 'You also go and work in my vineyard.'

8"When evening came, the owner of the vineyard said to his foreman, 'Call the workers and pay them their wages, beginning with the last ones hired and going on to the first.'

9"The workers who were hired about the eleventh hour came and each received a denarius. 10So when those came who were hired first, they expected to receive more. But each one of them also received a denarius. 11When they received it, they began to grumble against the landowner. 12'These men who were hired last worked only one hour,' they said, 'and you have made them equal to us who have borne the burden of the work and the heat of the day.'

13"But he answered one of them, 'Friend, I am not being unfair to you. Didn't you agree to work for a denarius? 14Take your pay and go. I want to give the man who was hired last the same as I gave you. 15Don't I have the right to do what I want with my own money? Or are you envious because I am generous?'

16"So the last will be first, and the first will be last."

Jesus Again Predicts His Death

17Now as Jesus was going up to Jerusalem, he took the twelve disciples aside and said to them, 18"We are going up to Jerusalem, and the Son of Man will be betrayed to the chief priests and the teachers of the law. They will condemn him to death 19and will turn him over to the Gentiles to be mocked and flogged and crucified. On the third day he will be raised to life!"

A Mother's Request

20Then the mother of Zebedee's sons came to Jesus with her sons and, kneeling down, asked a favor of him.

21"What is it you want?" he asked.

She said, "Grant that one of these two sons of mine may sit at your right and the other at your left in your kingdom."

22"You don't know what you are asking," Jesus said to them. "Can you drink the cup I am going to drink?"

"We can," they answered.

23Jesus said to them, "You will indeed drink from my cup, but to sit at my right or left is not for me to grant. These places belong to those for whom they have been prepared by my Father."

24When the ten heard about this, they were indignant with the two brothers. 25Jesus called them together and said, "You know that the rulers of the Gentiles lord it over them, and their high officials exercise authority over them. 26Not so with you. Instead, whoever wants to become great among you must be your servant, 27and

Living Bible

20 HERE IS another illustration of the Kingdom of Heaven. "The owner of an estate went out early one morning to hire workers for his harvest field. ²He agreed to pay them $20 a day[a] and sent them out to work.

³"A couple of hours later he was passing a hiring hall and saw some men standing around waiting for jobs, ⁴so he sent them also into his fields, telling them he would pay them whatever was right at the end of the day. ⁵At noon and again around three o'clock in the afternoon he did the same thing.

⁶"At five o'clock that evening he was in town again and saw some more men standing around and asked them, 'Why haven't you been working today?'

⁷" 'Because no one hired us,' they replied.

" 'Then go on out and join the others in my fields,' he told them.

⁸"That evening he told the paymaster to call the men in and pay them, beginning with the last men first. ⁹When the men hired at five o'clock were paid, each received $20. ¹⁰So when the men hired earlier came to get theirs, they assumed they would receive much more. But they, too, were paid $20.

¹¹, ¹²"They protested, 'Those fellows worked only one hour, and yet you've paid them just as much as those of us who worked all day in the scorching heat.'

¹³" 'Friend,' he answered one of them, 'I did you no wrong! Didn't you agree to work all day for $20? ¹⁴Take it and go. It is my desire to pay all the same; ¹⁵is it against the law to give away my money if I want to? Should you be angry because I am kind?' ¹⁶And so it is that the last shall be first, and the first, last."

¹⁷As Jesus was on the way to Jerusalem, he took the twelve disciples aside, ¹⁸and talked to them about what would happen to him when they arrived.

"I[b] will be betrayed to the chief priests and other Jewish leaders, and they will condemn me to die. ¹⁹And they will hand me over to the Roman government, and I will be mocked and crucified, and the third day I will rise to life again."

²⁰Then the mother of James and John, the sons of Zebedee, brought them to Jesus and respectfully asked a favor.

²¹"What is your request?" he asked. She replied, "In your Kingdom, will you let my two sons sit on two thrones[c] next to yours?"

²²But Jesus told her, "You don't know what you are asking!" Then he turned to James and John and asked them, "Are you able to drink from the terrible cup I am about to drink from?"

"Yes," they replied, "we are able!"

²³"You shall indeed drink from it," he told them. "But I have no right to say who will sit on the thrones next to mine. Those places are reserved for the persons my Father selects."

²⁴The other ten disciples were indignant when they heard what James and John had asked for.

²⁵But Jesus called them together and said, "Among the heathen, kings are tyrants and each minor official lords it over those beneath him. ²⁶But among you it is quite different. Anyone wanting to be a leader among you must be your servant. ²⁷And if you want to be right

New Revised Standard

The Laborers in the Vineyard

20 "FOR THE kingdom of heaven is like a landowner who went out early in the morning to hire laborers for his vineyard. ²After agreeing with the laborers for the usual daily wage,[d] he sent them into his vineyard. ³When he went out about nine o'clock, he saw others standing idle in the marketplace; ⁴and he said to them, 'You also go into the vineyard, and I will pay you whatever is right.' So they went. ⁵When he went out again about noon and about three o'clock, he did the same. ⁶And about five o'clock he went out and found others standing around; and he said to them, 'Why are you standing here idle all day?' ⁷They said to him, 'Because no one has hired us.' He said to them, 'You also go into the vineyard.' ⁸When evening came, the owner of the vineyard said to his manager, 'Call the laborers and give them their pay, beginning with the last and then going to the first.' ⁹When those hired about five o'clock came, each of them received the usual daily wage.[d] ¹⁰Now when the first came, they thought they would receive more; but each of them also received the usual daily wage.[d] ¹¹And when they received it, they grumbled against the landowner, ¹²saying, 'These last worked only one hour, and you have made them equal to us who have borne the burden of the day and the scorching heat.' ¹³But he replied to one of them, 'Friend, I am doing you no wrong; did you not agree with me for the usual daily wage?[d] ¹⁴Take what belongs to you and go; I choose to give to this last the same as I give to you. ¹⁵Am I not allowed to do what I choose with what belongs to me? Or are you envious because I am generous?'[e] ¹⁶So the last will be first, and the first will be last."[f]

A Third Time Jesus Foretells His Death and Resurrection

17 While Jesus was going up to Jerusalem, he took the twelve disciples aside by themselves, and said to them on the way, ¹⁸"See, we are going up to Jerusalem, and the Son of Man will be handed over to the chief priests and scribes, and they will condemn him to death; ¹⁹then they will hand him over to the Gentiles to be mocked and flogged and crucified; and on the third day he will be raised."

The Request of the Mother of James and John

20 Then the mother of the sons of Zebedee came to him with her sons, and kneeling before him, she asked a favor of him. ²¹And he said to her, "What do you want?" She said to him, "Declare that these two sons of mine will sit, one at your right hand and one at your left, in your kingdom." ²²But Jesus answered, "You do not know what you are asking. Are you able to drink the cup that I am about to drink?"[g] They said to him, "We are able." ²³He said to them, "You will indeed drink my cup, but to sit at my right hand and at my left, this is not mine to grant, but it is for those for whom it has been prepared by my Father."

24 When the ten heard it, they were angry with the two brothers. ²⁵But Jesus called them to him and said, "You know that the rulers of the Gentiles lord it over them, and their great ones are tyrants over them. ²⁶It will not be so among you; but whoever wishes to be great among you must be your servant, ²⁷and whoever wishes

---

a *20:2 $20 a day*, literally, "a denarius," the payment for a day's labor; equivalent to $20 in modern times, or £7.   b *20:18 I*, literally, "the Son of Man."   c *20:21 sit on two thrones*, implied. Also in vs 23.

d Gk *a denarius*   e Gk *is your eye evil because I am good?*   f Other ancient authorities add *for many are called but few are chosen*   g Other ancient authorities add *or to be baptized with the baptism that I am baptized with?*

King James

27And whosoever will be chief among you, let him be your servant:

28Even as the Son of man came not to be ministered unto, but to minister, and to give his life a ransom for many.

29And as they departed from Jericho, a great multitude followed him.

30¶ And, behold, two blind men sitting by the way side, when they heard that Jesus passed by, cried out, saying, Have mercy on us, O Lord, *thou* Son of David.

31And the multitude rebuked them, because they should hold their peace: but they cried the more, saying, Have mercy on us, O Lord, *thou* Son of David.

32And Jesus stood still, and called them, and said, What will ye that I shall do unto you?

33They say unto him, Lord, that our eyes may be opened.

34So Jesus had compassion *on them*, and touched their eyes: and immediately their eyes received sight, and they followed him.

21 AND WHEN they drew nigh unto Jerusalem, and were come to Bethphage, unto the mount of Olives, then sent Jesus two disciples,

2Saying unto them, Go into the village over against you, and straightway ye shall find an ass tied, and a colt with her: loose *them*, and bring *them* unto me.

3And if any *man* say aught unto you, ye shall say, The Lord hath need of them; and straightway he will send them.

4All this was done, that it might be fulfilled which was spoken by the prophet, saying,

5Tell ye the daughter of Zion, Behold, thy King cometh unto thee, meek, and sitting upon an ass, and a colt the foal of an ass.

6And the disciples went, and did as Jesus commanded them,

7And brought the ass, and the colt, and put on them their clothes, and they set *him* thereon.

8And a very great multitude spread their garments in the way; others cut down branches from the trees, and strawed *them* in the way.

9And the multitudes that went before, and that followed, cried, saying, Hosanna to the son of David: Blessed *is* he that cometh in the name of the Lord; Hosanna in the highest.

10And when he was come into Jerusalem, all the city was moved, saying, Who is this?

11And the multitude said, This is Jesus the prophet of Nazareth of Galilee.

12¶ And Jesus went into the temple of God, and cast out all them that sold and bought in the temple, and overthrew the tables of the moneychangers, and the seats of them that sold doves,

13And said unto them, It is written, My house shall be called the house of prayer; but ye have made it a den of thieves.

14And the blind and the lame came to him in the temple; and he healed them.

15And when the chief priests and scribes saw the wonderful things that he did, and the children crying in the temple, and saying, Hosanna to the son of David; they were sore displeased,

New International

whoever wants to be first must be your slave— 28just as the Son of Man did not come to be served, but to serve, and to give his life as a ransom for many."

Two Blind Men Receive Sight

29As Jesus and his disciples were leaving Jericho, a large crowd followed him. 30Two blind men were sitting by the roadside, and when they heard that Jesus was going by, they shouted, "Lord, Son of David, have mercy on us!"

31The crowd rebuked them and told them to be quiet, but they shouted all the louder, "Lord, Son of David, have mercy on us!"

32Jesus stopped and called them. "What do you want me to do for you?" he asked.

33"Lord," they answered, "we want our sight."

34Jesus had compassion on them and touched their eyes. Immediately they received their sight and followed him.

The Triumphal Entry

21 AS THEY approached Jerusalem and came to Bethphage on the Mount of Olives, Jesus sent two disciples, 2saying to them, "Go to the village ahead of you, and at once you will find a donkey tied there, with her colt by her. Untie them and bring them to me. 3If anyone says anything to you, tell him that the Lord needs them, and he will send them right away."

4This took place to fulfill what was spoken through the prophet:

5"Say to the Daughter of Zion,
'See, your king comes to you,
gentle and riding on a donkey,
on a colt, the foal of a donkey.' "a

6The disciples went and did as Jesus had instructed them. 7They brought the donkey and the colt, placed their cloaks on them, and Jesus sat on them. 8A very large crowd spread their cloaks on the road, while others cut branches from the trees and spread them on the road. 9The crowds that went ahead of him and those that followed shouted,

"Hosannab to the Son of David!"

"Blessed is he who comes in the name of the Lord!"c

"Hosannab in the highest!"

10When Jesus entered Jerusalem, the whole city was stirred and asked, "Who is this?"

11The crowds answered, "This is Jesus, the prophet from Nazareth in Galilee."

Jesus at the Temple

12Jesus entered the temple area and drove out all who were buying and selling there. He overturned the tables of the money changers and the benches of those selling doves. 13"It is written," he said to them, " 'My house will be called a house of prayer,'d but you are making it a 'den of robbers.'e"

14The blind and the lame came to him at the temple, and he healed them. 15But when the chief priests and the teachers of the law saw the wonderful things he did and the children shouting in the temple area, "Hosanna to the Son of David," they were indignant.

---

a 5 Zech. 9:9   b 9 A Hebrew expression meaning "Save!" which became an exclamation of praise; also in verse 15   c 9 Psalm 118:26   d 13 Isaiah 56:7   e 13 Jer. 7:11

Living Bible

at the top, you must serve like a slave. 28Your attitudef must be like my own, for I, the Messiah,g did not come to be served, but to serve, and to give my life as a ransom for many."

29As Jesus and the disciples left the city of Jericho, a vast crowd surged along behind.

30Two blind men were sitting beside the road and when they heard that Jesus was coming that way, they began shouting, "Sir, King David's Son, have mercy on us!"

31The crowd told them to be quiet, but they only yelled the louder.

32, 33When Jesus came to the place where they were he stopped in the road and called, "What do you want me to do for you?"

"Sir," they said, "we want to see!"

34Jesus was moved with pity for them and touched their eyes. And instantly they could see, and followed him.

21 AS JESUS and the disciples approached Jerusalem, and were near the town of Bethphage on the Mount of Olives, Jesus sent two of them into the village ahead.

2"Just as you enter," he said, "you will see a donkey tied there, with its colt beside it. Untie them and bring them here. 3If anyone asks you what you are doing, just say, 'The Master needs them,' and there will be no trouble."

4This was done to fulfill the ancient prophecy, 5"Tell Jerusalem her King is coming to her, riding humbly on a donkey's colt!"

6The two disciples did as Jesus said, 7and brought the animals to him and threw their garments over the colth for him to ride on. 8And some in the crowd threw down their coats along the road ahead of him, and others cut branches from the trees and spread them out before him.

9Then the crowds surged on ahead and pressed along behind, shouting, "God bless King David's Son!" . . . "God's Man is here!"i . . . Bless him, Lord!" . . . "Praise God in highest heaven!"

10The entire city of Jerusalem was stirred as he entered. "Who is this?" they asked.

11And the crowds replied, "It's Jesus, the prophet from Nazareth up in Galilee."

12Jesus went into the Temple, drove out the merchants, and knocked over the moneychangers' tables and the stalls of those selling doves.

13"The Scriptures say my Temple is a place of prayer," he declared, "but you have turned it into a den of thieves."

14And now the blind and crippled came to him and he healed them there in the Temple. 15But when the chief priests and other Jewish leaders saw these wonderful miracles, and heard even the little children in the Temple shouting, "God bless the Son of David," they were disturbed and indignant and asked him, "Do you hear what these children are saying?"

New Revised Standard

to be first among you must be your slave; 28just as the Son of Man came not to be served but to serve, and to give his life a ransom for many."

Jesus Heals Two Blind Men

29 As they were leaving Jericho, a large crowd followed him. 30There were two blind men sitting by the roadside. When they heard that Jesus was passing by, they shouted, "Lord,j have mercy on us, Son of David!" 31The crowd sternly ordered them to be quiet; but they shouted even more loudly, "Have mercy on us, Lord, Son of David!" 32Jesus stood still and called them, saying, "What do you want me to do for you?" 33They said to him, "Lord, let our eyes be opened." 34Moved with compassion, Jesus touched their eyes. Immediately they regained their sight and followed him.

Jesus' Triumphal Entry into Jerusalem

21 WHEN THEY had come near Jerusalem and had reached Bethphage, at the Mount of Olives, Jesus sent two disciples, 2saying to them, "Go into the village ahead of you, and immediately you will find a donkey tied, and a colt with her; untie them and bring them to me. 3If anyone says anything to you, just say this, 'The Lord needs them.' And he will send them immediately.k" 4This took place to fulfill what had been spoken through the prophet, saying,

5 "Tell the daughter of Zion,
Look, your king is coming to you,
humble, and mounted on a donkey,
and on a colt, the foal of a donkey."

6The disciples went and did as Jesus had directed them; 7they brought the donkey and the colt, and put their cloaks on them, and he sat on them. 8A very large crowdl spread their cloaks on the road, and others cut branches from the trees and spread them on the road. 9The crowds that went ahead of him and that followed were shouting,

"Hosanna to the Son of David!
Blessed is the one who comes in the name
of the Lord!
Hosanna in the highest heaven!"

10When he entered Jerusalem, the whole city was in turmoil, asking, "Who is this?" 11The crowds were saying, "This is the prophet Jesus from Nazareth in Galilee."

Jesus Cleanses the Temple

12 Then Jesus entered the templem and drove out all who were selling and buying in the temple, and he overturned the tables of the money changers and the seats of those who sold doves. 13He said to them, "It is written,

'My house shall be called a house of prayer';
but you are making it a den of robbers."

14 The blind and the lame came to him in the temple, and he cured them. 15But when the chief priests and the scribes saw the amazing things that he did, and heardn the children crying out in the temple, "Hosanna to the Son of David," they became angry 16and said to

---

f 20:28 Your attitude, implied.   g 20:28 the Messiah, literally, "the Son of Man."   h 21:7 threw their garments over the colt, implied.   i 21:9 God's Man is here, literally, "Blessed is he who comes in the name of the Lord."

j Other ancient authorities lack Lord   k Or 'The Lord needs them and will send them back immediately.'   l Or Most of the crowd   m Other ancient authorities add of God   n Gk lacks heard

King James

16And said unto him, Hearest thou what these say? And Jesus saith unto them, Yea; have ye never read, Out of the mouth of babes and sucklings thou hast perfected praise?

17¶ And he left them, and went out of the city into Bethany; and he lodged there.

18Now in the morning as he returned into the city, he hungered.

19And when he saw a fig tree in the way, he came to it, and found nothing thereon, but leaves only, and said unto it, Let no fruit grow on thee henceforward for ever. And presently the fig tree withered away.

20And when the disciples saw it, they marvelled, saying, How soon is the fig tree withered away!

21Jesus answered and said unto them, Verily I say unto you, If ye have faith, and doubt not, ye shall not only do this which is done to the fig tree, but also if ye shall say unto this mountain, Be thou removed, and be thou cast into the sea; it shall be done.

22And all things, whatsoever ye shall ask in prayer, believing, ye shall receive.

23¶ And when he was come into the temple, the chief priests and the elders of the people came unto him as he was teaching, and said, By what authority doest thou these things? and who gave thee this authority?

24And Jesus answered and said unto them, I also will ask you one thing, which if ye tell me, I in like wise will tell you by what authority I do these things.

25The baptism of John, whence was it? from heaven, or of men? And they reasoned with themselves, saying, If we shall say, From heaven; he will say unto us, Why did ye not then believe him?

26But if we shall say, Of men; we fear the people; for all hold John as a prophet.

27And they answered Jesus, and said, We cannot tell. And he said unto them, Neither tell I you by what authority I do these things.

28¶ But what think ye? A certain man had two sons; and he came to the first, and said, Son, go work today in my vineyard.

29He answered and said, I will not: but afterward he repented, and went.

30And he came to the second, and said likewise. And he answered and said, I go, sir: and went not.

31Whether of them twain did the will of his father? They say unto him, The first. Jesus saith unto them, Verily I say unto you, That the publicans and the harlots go into the kingdom of God before you.

32For John came unto you in the way of righteousness, and ye believed him not: but the publicans and the harlots believed him: and ye, when ye had seen it, repented not afterward, that ye might believe him.

33¶ Hear another parable: There was a certain householder, which planted a vineyard, and hedged it round about, and digged a winepress in it, and built a tower, and let it out to husbandmen, and went into a far country:

34And when the time of the fruit drew near, he sent his servants to the husbandmen, that they might receive the fruits of it.

35And the husbandmen took his servants, and beat one, and killed another, and stoned another.

36Again, he sent other servants more than the first: and they did unto them likewise.

37But last of all he sent unto them his son, saying, They will reverence my son.

New International

16"Do you hear what these children are saying?" they asked him.

"Yes," replied Jesus, "have you never read,

" 'From the lips of children and infants
    you have ordained praise'a?"

17And he left them and went out of the city to Bethany, where he spent the night.

The Fig Tree Withers

18Early in the morning, as he was on his way back to the city, he was hungry. 19Seeing a fig tree by the road, he went up to it but found nothing on it except leaves. Then he said to it, "May you never bear fruit again!" Immediately the tree withered.

20When the disciples saw this, they were amazed. "How did the fig tree wither so quickly?" they asked.

21Jesus replied, "I tell you the truth, if you have faith and do not doubt, not only can you do what was done to the fig tree, but also you can say to this mountain, 'Go, throw yourself into the sea,' and it will be done. 22If you believe, you will receive whatever you ask for in prayer."

The Authority of Jesus Questioned

23Jesus entered the temple courts, and, while he was teaching, the chief priests and the elders of the people came to him. "By what authority are you doing these things?" they asked. "And who gave you this authority?"

24Jesus replied, "I will also ask you one question. If you answer me, I will tell you by what authority I am doing these things. 25John's baptism—where did it come from? Was it from heaven, or from men?"

They discussed it among themselves and said, "If we say, 'From heaven,' he will ask, 'Then why didn't you believe him?' 26But if we say, 'From men'—we are afraid of the people, for they all hold that John was a prophet."

27So they answered Jesus, "We don't know."

Then he said, "Neither will I tell you by what authority I am doing these things.

The Parable of the Two Sons

28"What do you think? There was a man who had two sons. He went to the first and said, 'Son, go and work today in the vineyard.'

29" 'I will not,' he answered, but later he changed his mind and went.

30"Then the father went to the other son and said the same thing. He answered, 'I will, sir,' but he did not go.

31"Which of the two did what his father wanted?"

"The first," they answered.

Jesus said to them, "I tell you the truth, the tax collectors and the prostitutes are entering the kingdom of God ahead of you. 32For John came to you to show you the way of righteousness, and you did not believe him, but the tax collectors and the prostitutes did. And even after you saw this, you did not repent and believe him.

The Parable of the Tenants

33"Listen to another parable: There was a landowner who planted a vineyard. He put a wall around it, dug a winepress in it and built a watchtower. Then he rented the vineyard to some farmers and went away on a journey. 34When the harvest time approached, he sent his servants to the tenants to collect his fruit.

35"The tenants seized his servants; they beat one, killed another, and stoned a third. 36Then he sent other servants to them, more than the first time, and the tenants treated them the same way. 37Last of all, he sent his son to them. 'They will respect my son,' he said.

a 16 Psalm 8:2

Living Bible

16"Yes," Jesus replied. "Didn't you ever read the Scriptures? For they say, 'Even little babies shall praise him!'"

17Then he returned to Bethany, where he stayed overnight.

18In the morning, as he was returning to Jerusalem, he was hungry, 19and noticed a fig tree beside the road. He went over to see if there were any figs, but there were only leaves. Then he said to it, "Never bear fruit again!" And soonᵇ the fig tree withered up.

20The disciples were utterly amazed and asked, "How did the fig tree wither so quickly?"

21Then Jesus told them, "Truly, if you have faith, and don't doubt, you can do things like this and much more. You can even say to this Mount of Olives, 'Move over into the ocean,' and it will. 22You can get anything—anything you ask for in prayer—if you believe."

23When he had returned to the Temple and was teaching, the chief priests and other Jewish leaders came up to him and demanded to know by whose authority he had thrown out the merchants the day before.ᶜ

24"I'll tell you if you answer one question first," Jesus replied. 25"Was John the Baptist sent from God, or not?"

They talked it over among themselves. "If we say, 'From God,'" they said, "then he will ask why we didn't believe what John said. 26And if we deny that God sent him, we'll be mobbed, for the crowd all think he was a prophet." 27So they finally replied, "We don't know!"

And Jesus said, "Then I won't answer your question either.

28"But what do you think about this? A man with two sons told the older boy, 'Son, go out and work on the farm today.' 29'I won't,' he answered, but later he changed his mind and went. 30Then the father told the youngest, 'You go!' and he said, 'Yes, sir, I will.' But he didn't. 31Which of the two was obeying his father?"

They replied, "The first, of course."

Then Jesus explained his meaning: "Surely evil men and prostitutes will get into the Kingdom before you do. 32For John the Baptist told you to repent and turn to God, and you wouldn't, while very evil men and prostitutes did. And even when you saw this happening, you refused to repent, and so you couldn't believe.

33"Now listen to this story: A certain landowner planted a vineyard with a hedge around it, and built a platform for the watchman, then leased the vineyard to some farmers on a sharecrop basis, and went away to live in another country.

34"At the time of the grape harvest he sent his agents to the farmers to collect his share. 35But the farmers attacked his men, beat one, killed one and stoned another.

36"Then he sent a larger group of his men to collect for him, but the results were the same. 37Finally the owner sent his son, thinking they would surely respect him.

New Revised Standard

him, "Do you hear what these are saying?" Jesus said to them, "Yes; have you never read,

'Out of the mouths of infants and nursing babies
you have prepared praise for yourself'?"

17He left them, went out of the city to Bethany, and spent the night there.

Jesus Curses the Fig Tree

18 In the morning, when he returned to the city, he was hungry. 19And seeing a fig tree by the side of the road, he went to it and found nothing at all on it but leaves. Then he said to it, "May no fruit ever come from you again!" And the fig tree withered at once. 20When the disciples saw it, they were amazed, saying, "How did the fig tree wither at once?" 21Jesus answered them, "Truly I tell you, if you have faith and do not doubt, not only will you do what has been done to the fig tree, but even if you say to this mountain, 'Be lifted up and thrown into the sea,' it will be done. 22Whatever you ask for in prayer with faith, you will receive."

The Authority of Jesus Questioned

23 When he entered the temple, the chief priests and the elders of the people came to him as he was teaching, and said, "By what authority are you doing these things, and who gave you this authority?" 24Jesus said to them, "I will also ask you one question; if you tell me the answer, then I will also tell you by what authority I do these things. 25Did the baptism of John come from heaven, or was it of human origin?" And they argued with one another, "If we say, 'From heaven,' he will say to us, 'Why then did you not believe him?' 26But if we say, 'Of human origin,' we are afraid of the crowd; for all regard John as a prophet." 27So they answered Jesus, "We do not know." And he said to them, "Neither will I tell you by what authority I am doing these things.

The Parable of the Two Sons

28 "What do you think? A man had two sons; he went to the first and said, 'Son, go and work in the vineyard today.' 29He answered, 'I will not'; but later he changed his mind and went. 30The fatherᵈ went to the second and said the same; and he answered, 'I go, sir'; but he did not go. 31Which of the two did the will of his father?" They said, "The first." Jesus said to them, "Truly I tell you, the tax collectors and the prostitutes are going into the kingdom of God ahead of you. 32For John came to you in the way of righteousness and you did not believe him, but the tax collectors and the prostitutes believed him; and even after you saw it, you did not change your minds and believe him.

The Parable of the Wicked Tenants

33 "Listen to another parable. There was a landowner who planted a vineyard, put a fence around it, dug a wine press in it, and built a watchtower. Then he leased it to tenants and went to another country. 34When the harvest time had come, he sent his slaves to the tenants to collect his produce. 35But the tenants seized his slaves and beat one, killed another, and stoned another. 36Again he sent other slaves, more than the first; and they treated them in the same way. 37Finally he sent his son to them, saying, 'They will respect my son.' 38But

---

ᵇ 21:19 soon, or "immediately." ᶜ 21:23 by whose authority he had thrown out the merchants the day before, literally, "By what authority do you do these things?"

ᵈ Gk He

King James

38But when the husbandmen saw the son, they said among themselves, This is the heir; come, let us kill him, and let us seize on his inheritance.

39And they caught him, and cast *him* out of the vineyard, and slew *him*.

40When the lord therefore of the vineyard cometh, what will he do unto those husbandmen?

41They say unto him, He will miserably destroy those wicked men, and will let out *his* vineyard unto other husbandmen, which shall render him the fruits in their seasons.

42Jesus saith unto them, Did ye never read in the scriptures, The stone which the builders rejected, the same is become the head of the corner: this is the Lord's doing, and it is marvellous in our eyes?

43Therefore say I unto you, The kingdom of God shall be taken from you, and given to a nation bringing forth the fruits thereof.

44And whosoever shall fall on this stone shall be broken: but on whomsoever it shall fall, it will grind him to powder.

45And when the chief priests and Pharisees had heard his parables, they perceived that he spake of them.

46But when they sought to lay hands on him, they feared the multitude, because they took him for a prophet.

22 AND JESUS answered and spake unto them again by parables, and said,

2The kingdom of heaven is like unto a certain king, which made a marriage for his son,

3And sent forth his servants to call them that were bidden to the wedding: and they would not come.

4Again, he sent forth other servants, saying, Tell them which are bidden, Behold, I have prepared my dinner: my oxen and *my* fatlings *are* killed, and all things *are* ready: come unto the marriage.

5But they made light of *it,* and went their ways, one to his farm, another to his merchandise:

6And the remnant took his servants, and entreated *them* spitefully, and slew *them.*

7But when the king heard *thereof,* he was wroth: and he sent forth his armies, and destroyed those murderers, and burned up their city.

8Then saith he to his servants, The wedding is ready, but they which were bidden were not worthy.

9Go ye therefore into the highways, and as many as ye shall find, bid to the marriage.

10So those servants went out into the highways, and gathered together all as many as they found, both bad and good: and the wedding was furnished with guests.

11¶ And when the king came in to see the guests, he saw there a man which had not on a wedding garment:

12And he saith unto him, Friend, how camest thou in hither not having a wedding garment? And he was speechless.

13Then said the king to the servants, Bind him hand and foot, and take him away, and cast *him* into outer darkness; there shall be weeping and gnashing of teeth.

14For many are called, but few *are* chosen.

15¶ Then went the Pharisees, and took counsel how they might entangle him in *his* talk.

16And they sent out unto him their disciples with the Herodians, saying, Master, we know that thou art true, and teachest the way of God in truth, neither carest thou for any *man:* for thou regardest not the person of men.

17Tell us therefore, What thinkest thou? Is it lawful to give tribute unto Caesar, or not?

New International

38"But when the tenants saw the son, they said to each other, 'This is the heir. Come, let's kill him and take his inheritance.' 39So they took him and threw him out of the vineyard and killed him.

40"Therefore, when the owner of the vineyard comes, what will he do to those tenants?"

41"He will bring those wretches to a wretched end," they replied, "and he will rent the vineyard to other tenants, who will give him his share of the crop at harvest time."

42Jesus said to them, "Have you never read in the Scriptures:

" 'The stone the builders rejected
   has become the capstone[a];
the Lord has done this,
   and it is marvelous in our eyes'[b]?

43"Therefore I tell you that the kingdom of God will be taken away from you and given to a people who will produce its fruit. 44He who falls on this stone will be broken to pieces, but he on whom it falls will be crushed."[c]

45When the chief priests and the Pharisees heard Jesus' parables, they knew he was talking about them. 46They looked for a way to arrest him, but they were afraid of the crowd because the people held that he was a prophet.

The Parable of the Wedding Banquet

22 JESUS SPOKE to them again in parables, saying: 2"The kingdom of heaven is like a king who prepared a wedding banquet for his son. 3He sent his servants to those who had been invited to the banquet to tell them to come, but they refused to come.

4"Then he sent some more servants and said, 'Tell those who have been invited that I have prepared my dinner: My oxen and fattened cattle have been butchered, and everything is ready. Come to the wedding banquet.'

5"But they paid no attention and went off—one to his field, another to his business. 6The rest seized his servants, mistreated them and killed them. 7The king was enraged. He sent his army and destroyed those murderers and burned their city.

8"Then he said to his servants, 'The wedding banquet is ready, but those I invited did not deserve to come. 9Go to the street corners and invite to the banquet anyone you find.' 10So the servants went out into the streets and gathered all the people they could find, both good and bad, and the wedding hall was filled with guests.

11"But when the king came in to see the guests, he noticed a man there who was not wearing wedding clothes. 12'Friend,' he asked, 'how did you get in here without wedding clothes?' The man was speechless.

13"Then the king told the attendants, 'Tie him hand and foot, and throw him outside, into the darkness, where there will be weeping and gnashing of teeth.'

14"For many are invited, but few are chosen."

Paying Taxes to Caesar

15Then the Pharisees went out and laid plans to trap him in his words. 16They sent their disciples to him along with the Herodians. "Teacher," they said, "we know you are a man of integrity and that you teach the way of God in accordance with the truth. You aren't swayed by men, because you pay no attention to who they are. 17Tell us then, what is your opinion? Is it right to pay taxes to Caesar or not?"

---

a 42 Or *cornerstone*   b 42 Psalm 118:22,23   c 44 Some manuscripts do not have verse 44.

Living Bible

38"But when these farmers saw the son coming they said among themselves, 'Here comes the heir to this estate; come on, let's kill him and get it for ourselves!' 39So they dragged him out of the vineyard and killed him.

40"When the owner returns, what do you think he will do to those farmers?"

41The Jewish leaders replied, "He will put the wicked men to a horrible death, and lease the vineyard to others who will pay him promptly."

42Then Jesus asked them, "Didn't you ever read in the Scriptures: 'The stone rejected by the builders has been made the honored cornerstone;d how remarkable! what an amazing thing the Lord has done'?

43"What I mean is that the Kingdom of God shall be taken away from you, and given to a nation that will give God his share of the crop.e 44All who stumble on this rock of truthf shall be broken, but those it falls on will be scattered as dust."

45When the chief priests and other Jewish leaders realized that Jesus was talking about them—that they were the farmers in his story— 46they wanted to get rid of him, but were afraid to try because of the crowds, for they accepted Jesus as a prophet.

22 JESUS TOLD several other stories to show what the Kingdom of Heaven is like.

"For instance," he said, "it can be illustrated by the story of a king who prepared a great wedding dinner for his son. 3Many guests were invited, and when the banquet was ready he sent messengers to notify everyone that it was time to come. But all refused! 4So he sent other servants to tell them, 'Everything is ready and the roast is in the oven. Hurry!'

5"But the guests he had invited merely laughed and went on about their business, one to his farm, another to his store; 6others beat up his messengers and treated them shamefully, even killing some of them.

7"Then the angry king sent out his army and destroyed the murderers and burned their city. 8And he said to his servants, 'The wedding feast is ready, and the guests I invited aren't worthy of the honor. 9Now go out to the street corners and invite everyone you see.'

10"So the servants did, and brought in all they could find, good and bad alike; and the banquet hall was filled with guests. 11But when the king came in to meet the guests he noticed a man who wasn't wearing the wedding robe [provided for himg].

12" 'Friend,' he asked, 'how does it happen that you are here without a wedding robe?' And the man had no reply.

13"Then the king said to his aides, 'Bind him hand and foot and throw him out into the outer darkness where there is weeping and gnashing of teeth.' 14For many are called, but few are chosen."

15Then the Pharisees met together to try to think of some way to trap Jesus into saying something for which they could arrest him. 16They decided to send some of their men along with the Herodiansh to ask him this question: "Sir, we know you are very honest and teach the truth regardless of the consequences, without fear or favor. 17Now tell us, is it right to pay taxes to the Roman government or not?"

New Revised Standard

when the tenants saw the son, they said to themselves, 'This is the heir; come, let us kill him and get his inheritance.' 39So they seized him, threw him out of the vineyard, and killed him. 40Now when the owner of the vineyard comes, what will he do to those tenants?" 41They said to him, "He will put those wretches to a miserable death, and lease the vineyard to other tenants who will give him the produce at the harvest time."

42 Jesus said to them, "Have you never read in the scriptures:

'The stone that the builders rejected
   has become the cornerstone;i
this was the Lord's doing,
   and it is amazing in our eyes'?

43Therefore I tell you, the kingdom of God will be taken away from you and given to a people that produces the fruits of the kingdom.j 44The one who falls on this stone will be broken to pieces; and it will crush anyone on whom it falls."k

45 When the chief priests and the Pharisees heard his parables, they realized that he was speaking about them. 46They wanted to arrest him, but they feared the crowds, because they regarded him as a prophet.

The Parable of the Wedding Banquet

22 ONCE MORE Jesus spoke to them in parables, saying: 2"The kingdom of heaven may be compared to a king who gave a wedding banquet for his son. 3He sent his slaves to call those who had been invited to the wedding banquet, but they would not come. 4Again he sent other slaves, saying, 'Tell those who have been invited: Look, I have prepared my dinner, my oxen and my fat calves have been slaughtered, and everything is ready; come to the wedding banquet.' 5But they made light of it and went away, one to his farm, another to his business, 6while the rest seized his slaves, mistreated them, and killed them. 7The king was enraged. He sent his troops, destroyed those murderers, and burned their city. 8Then he said to his slaves, 'The wedding is ready, but those invited were not worthy. 9Go therefore into the main streets, and invite everyone you find to the wedding banquet.' 10Those slaves went out into the streets and gathered all whom they found, both good and bad; so the wedding hall was filled with guests.

11 "But when the king came in to see the guests, he noticed a man there who was not wearing a wedding robe, 12and he said to him, 'Friend, how did you get in here without a wedding robe?' And he was speechless. 13Then the king said to the attendants, 'Bind him hand and foot, and throw him into the outer darkness, where there will be weeping and gnashing of teeth.' 14For many are called, but few are chosen."

The Question about Paying Taxes

15 Then the Pharisees went and plotted to entrap him in what he said. 16So they sent their disciples to him, along with the Herodians, saying, "Teacher, we know that you are sincere, and teach the way of God in accordance with truth, and show deference to no one; for you do not regard people with partiality. 17Tell us, then, what you think. Is it lawful to pay taxes to the emperor, or not?" 18But Jesus, aware of their malice, said, "Why

---

d 21:42 the honored cornerstone, literally, "the head of the corner." e 21:43 that will give God his share of the crop, literally, "bringing forth the fruits." f 21:44 on this rock of truth, literally, "on this stone." g 22:11 provided for him, implied. h 22:16 The Herodians were a Jewish political party.

i Or keystone j Gk the fruits of it k Other ancient authorities lack verse 44

King James

18But Jesus perceived their wickedness, and said, Why tempt ye me, *ye* hypocrites?
19Show me the tribute money. And they brought unto him a penny.
20And he saith unto them, Whose *is* this image and superscription?
21They say unto him, Caesar's. Then saith he unto them, Render therefore unto Caesar the things which are Caesar's; and unto God the things that are God's.
22When they had heard *these words,* they marvelled, and left him, and went their way.
23¶ The same day came to him the Sadducees, which say that there is no resurrection, and asked him,
24Saying, Master, Moses said, If a man die, having no children, his brother shall marry his wife, and raise up seed unto his brother.
25Now there were with us seven brethren: and the first, when he had married a wife, deceased, and having no issue, left his wife unto his brother:
26Likewise the second also, and the third, unto the seventh.
27And last of all the woman died also.
28Therefore in the resurrection whose wife shall she be of the seven? for they all had her.
29Jesus answered and said unto them, Ye do err, not knowing the scriptures, nor the power of God.
30For in the resurrection they neither marry, nor are given in marriage, but are as the angels of God in heaven.
31But as touching the resurrection of the dead, have ye not read that which was spoken unto you by God, saying,
32I am the God of Abraham, and the God of Isaac, and the God of Jacob? God is not the God of the dead, but of the living.
33And when the multitude heard *this,* they were astonished at his doctrine.
34¶ But when the Pharisees had heard that he had put the Sadducees to silence, they were gathered together.
35Then one of them, *which was* a lawyer, asked *him a question,* tempting him, and saying,
36Master, which *is* the great commandment in the law?
37Jesus said unto him, Thou shalt love the Lord thy God with all thy heart, and with all thy soul, and with all thy mind.
38This is the first and great commandment.
39And the second *is* like unto it, Thou shalt love thy neighbour as thyself.
40On these two commandments hang all the law and the prophets.
41¶ While the Pharisees were gathered together, Jesus asked them,
42Saying, What think ye of Christ? whose son is he? They say unto him, *The son* of David.
43He saith unto them, How then doth David in spirit call him Lord, saying,
44The LORD said unto my Lord, Sit thou on my right hand, till I make thine enemies thy footstool?
45If David then call him Lord, how is he his son?
46And no man was able to answer him a word, neither durst any *man* from that day forth ask him any more *questions.*

23 THEN SPAKE Jesus to the multitude, and to his disciples,

New International

18But Jesus, knowing their evil intent, said, "You hypocrites, why are you trying to trap me? 19Show me the coin used for paying the tax." They brought him a denarius, 20and he asked them, "Whose portrait is this? And whose inscription?"
21"Caesar's," they replied.
Then he said to them, "Give to Caesar what is Caesar's, and to God what is God's."
22When they heard this, they were amazed. So they left him and went away.

Marriage at the Resurrection

23That same day the Sadducees, who say there is no resurrection, came to him with a question. 24"Teacher," they said, "Moses told us that if a man dies without having children, his brother must marry the widow and have children for him. 25Now there were seven brothers among us. The first one married and died, and since he had no children, he left his wife to his brother. 26The same thing happened to the second and third brother, right on down to the seventh. 27Finally, the woman died. 28Now then, at the resurrection, whose wife will she be of the seven, since all of them were married to her?"
29Jesus replied, "You are in error because you do not know the Scriptures or the power of God. 30At the resurrection people will neither marry nor be given in marriage; they will be like the angels in heaven. 31But about the resurrection of the dead—have you not read what God said to you, 32'I am the God of Abraham, the God of Isaac, and the God of Jacob'a? He is not the God of the dead but of the living."
33When the crowds heard this, they were astonished at his teaching.

The Greatest Commandment

34Hearing that Jesus had silenced the Sadducees, the Pharisees got together. 35One of them, an expert in the law, tested him with this question: 36"Teacher, which is the greatest commandment in the Law?"
37Jesus replied: " 'Love the Lord your God with all your heart and with all your soul and with all your mind.'b 38This is the first and greatest commandment. 39And the second is like it: 'Love your neighbor as yourself.'c 40All the Law and the Prophets hang on these two commandments."

Whose Son Is the Christ?

41While the Pharisees were gathered together, Jesus asked them, 42"What do you think about the Christd? Whose son is he?"
"The son of David," they replied.
43He said to them, "How is it then that David, speaking by the Spirit, calls him 'Lord'? For he says,
44" 'The Lord said to my Lord:
   "Sit at my right hand
until I put your enemies
   under your feet." 'e

45If then David calls him 'Lord,' how can he be his son?" 46No one could say a word in reply, and from that day on no one dared to ask him any more questions.

Seven Woes

23 THEN JESUS said to the crowds and to his disciples: 2"The teachers of the law and the

a 32 Exodus 3:6   b 37 Deut. 6:5   c 39 Lev. 19:18   d 42 Or *Messiah*
e 44 Psalm 110:1

Living Bible

18But Jesus saw what they were after. "You hypocrites!" he exclaimed. "Who are you trying to fool with your trick questions? 19Here, show me a coin." And they handed him a penny.

20"Whose picture is stamped on it?" he asked them. "And whose name is this beneath the picture?"

21"Caesar's," they replied.

"Well, then," he said, "give it to Caesar if it is his, and give God everything that belongs to God."

22His reply surprised and baffled them and they went away.

23But that same day some of the Sadducees, who say there is no resurrection after death, came to him and asked, 24"Sir, Moses said that if a man died without children, his brother should marry the widow and their children would get all the dead man's property. 25Well, we had among us a family of seven brothers. The first of these men married and then died, without children, so his widow became the second brother's wife. 26This brother also died without children, and the wife was passed to the next brother, and so on until she had been the wife of each of them. 27And then she also died. 28So whose wife will she be in the resurrection? For she was the wife of all seven of them!"

29But Jesus said, "Your error is caused by your ignorance of the Scriptures and of God's power! 30For in the resurrection there is no marriage; everyone is as the angels in heaven. 31But now, as to whether there is a resurrection of the dead—don't you ever read the Scriptures? Don't you realize that God was speaking directly to you when he said, 32'I *am* the God of Abraham, Isaac, and Jacob'? So God is not the God of the dead, but of the living."f

33The crowds were profoundly impressed by his answers— 34, 35but not the Pharisees! When they heard that he had routed the Sadducees with his reply, they thought up a fresh question of their own to ask him. One of them, a lawyer, spoke up: 36"Sir, which is the most important command in the laws of Moses?"

37Jesus replied, " 'Love the Lord your God with all your heart, soul, and mind.' 38, 39This is the first and greatest commandment. The second most important is similar: 'Love your neighbor as much as you love yourself.' 40All the other commandments and the demands of the prophets stem from these two laws and are fulfilled if you obey them. Keep only these and you will find that you are obeying all the others."

41Then, surrounded by the Pharisees, he asked them a question: 42"What about the Messiah? Whose son is he?" "The son of David," they replied.

43"Then why does David, speaking under the inspiration of the Holy Spirit, call him 'Lord'?" Jesus asked. "For David said,

44'God said to my Lord, Sit at my right hand until I put your enemies beneath your feet.'

45Since David called him 'Lord,' how can he be merely his son?"

46They had no answer. And after that no one dared ask him any more questions.

New Revised Standard

are you putting me to the test, you hypocrites? 19Show me the coin used for the tax." And they brought him a denarius. 20Then he said to them, "Whose head is this, and whose title?" 21They answered, "The emperor's." Then he said to them, "Give therefore to the emperor the things that are the emperor's, and to God the things that are God's." 22When they heard this, they were amazed; and they left him and went away.

The Question about the Resurrection

23 The same day some Sadducees came to him, saying there is no resurrection;g and they asked him a question, saying, 24"Teacher, Moses said, 'If a man dies childless, his brother shall marry the widow, and raise up children for his brother.' 25Now there were seven brothers among us; the first married, and died childless, leaving the widow to his brother. 26The second did the same, so also the third, down to the seventh. 27Last of all, the woman herself died. 28In the resurrection, then, whose wife of the seven will she be? For all of them had married her."

29 Jesus answered them, "You are wrong, because you know neither the scriptures nor the power of God. 30For in the resurrection they neither marry nor are given in marriage, but are like angelsh in heaven. 31And as for the resurrection of the dead, have you not read what was said to you by God, 32'I am the God of Abraham, the God of Isaac, and the God of Jacob'? He is God not of the dead, but of the living." 33And when the crowd heard it, they were astounded at his teaching.

The Greatest Commandment

34 When the Pharisees heard that he had silenced the Sadducees, they gathered together, 35and one of them, a lawyer, asked him a question to test him. 36"Teacher, which commandment in the law is the greatest?" 37He said to him, " 'You shall love the Lord your God with all your heart, and with all your soul, and with all your mind.' 38This is the greatest and first commandment. 39And a second is like it: 'You shall love your neighbor as yourself.' 40On these two commandments hang all the law and the prophets."

The Question about David's Son

41 Now while the Pharisees were gathered together, Jesus asked them this question: 42"What do you think of the Messiah?i Whose son is he?" They said to him, "The son of David." 43He said to them, "How is it then that David by the Spiriti calls him Lord, saying,

44 'The Lord said to my Lord,
"Sit at my right hand,
until I put your enemies under your feet" '?

45If David thus calls him Lord, how can he be his son?" 46No one was able to give him an answer, nor from that day did anyone dare to ask him any more questions.

Jesus Denounces Scribes and Pharisees

23 THEN JESUS said to the crowds and to his disciples, 2"The scribes and the Pharisees sit on

23 THEN JESUS said to the crowds, and to his disciples, 2"You would think these Jewish lead-

---

f 22:32 *of the living,* i.e., if Abraham, Isaac, and Jacob, long dead, were not alive in the presence of God, then God would have said, "I *was* the God of Abraham, etc."

g Other ancient authorities read *who say that there is no resurrection*   h Other ancient authorities add *of God*   i Or *Christ*   j Gk *in spirit*

King James

2Saying, The scribes and the Pharisees sit in Moses' seat:

3All therefore whatsoever they bid you observe, *that* observe and do; but do not ye after their works: for they say, and do not.

4For they bind heavy burdens and grievous to be borne, and lay *them* on men's shoulders; but they *themselves* will not move them with one of their fingers.

5But all their works they do for to be seen of men: they make broad their phylacteries, and enlarge the borders of their garments,

6And love the uppermost rooms at feasts, and the chief seats in the synagogues,

7And greetings in the markets, and to be called of men, Rabbi, Rabbi.

8But be not ye called Rabbi: for one is your Master, *even* Christ; and all ye are brethren.

9And call no *man* your father upon the earth: for one is your Father, which is in heaven.

10Neither be ye called masters: for one is your Master, *even* Christ.

11But he that is greatest among you shall be your servant.

12And whosoever shall exalt himself shall be abased; and he that shall humble himself shall be exalted.

13¶ But woe unto you, scribes and Pharisees, hypocrites! for ye shut up the kingdom of heaven against men: for ye neither go in *yourselves,* neither suffer ye them that are entering to go in.

14Woe unto you, scribes and Pharisees, hypocrites! for ye devour widows' houses, and for a pretence make long prayer: therefore ye shall receive the greater damnation.

15Woe unto you, scribes and Pharisees, hypocrites! for ye compass sea and land to make one proselyte, and when he is made, ye make him twofold more the child of hell than yourselves.

16Woe unto you, *ye* blind guides, which say, Whosoever shall swear by the temple, it is nothing; but whosoever shall swear by the gold of the temple, he is a debtor!

17*Ye* fools and blind: for whether is greater, the gold, or the temple that sanctifieth the gold?

18And, Whosoever shall swear by the altar, it is nothing; but whosoever sweareth by the gift that is upon it, he is guilty.

19*Ye* fools and blind: for whether *is* greater, the gift, or the altar that sanctifieth the gift?

20Whoso therefore shall swear by the altar, sweareth by it, and by all things thereon.

21And whoso shall swear by the temple, sweareth by it, and by him that dwelleth therein.

22And he that shall swear by heaven, sweareth by the throne of God, and by him that sitteth thereon.

23Woe unto you, scribes and Pharisees, hypocrites! for ye pay tithe of mint and anise and cummin, and have omitted the weightier *matters* of the law, judgment, mercy, and faith: these ought ye to have done, and not to leave the other undone.

24*Ye* blind guides, which strain at a gnat, and swallow a camel.

25Woe unto you, scribes and Pharisees, hypocrites! for ye make clean the outside of the cup and of the platter, but within they are full of extortion and excess.

26*Thou* blind Pharisee, cleanse first that *which is* within the cup and platter, that the outside of them may be clean also.

27Woe unto you, scribes and Pharisees, hypocrites! for ye are like unto whited sepulchres, which indeed appear beautiful outward, but are within full of dead *men's* bones, and of all uncleanness.

28Even so ye also outwardly appear righteous unto men, but within ye are full of hypocrisy and iniquity.

New International

Pharisees sit in Moses' seat. 3So you must obey them and do everything they tell you. But do not do what they do, for they do not practice what they preach. 4They tie up heavy loads and put them on men's shoulders, but they themselves are not willing to lift a finger to move them.

5"Everything they do is done for men to see: They make their phylacteriesa wide and the tassels on their garments long; 6they love the place of honor at banquets and the most important seats in the synagogues; 7they love to be greeted in the marketplaces and to have men call them 'Rabbi.'

8"But you are not to be called 'Rabbi,' for you have only one Master and you are all brothers. 9And do not call anyone on earth 'father,' for you have one Father, and he is in heaven. 10Nor are you to be called 'teacher,' for you have one Teacher, the Christ.b 11The greatest among you will be your servant. 12For whoever exalts himself will be humbled, and whoever humbles himself will be exalted.

13"Woe to you, teachers of the law and Pharisees, you hypocrites! You shut the kingdom of heaven in men's faces. You yourselves do not enter, nor will you let those enter who are trying to.c

15"Woe to you, teachers of the law and Pharisees, you hypocrites! You travel over land and sea to win a single convert, and when he becomes one, you make him twice as much a son of hell as you are.

16"Woe to you, blind guides! You say, 'If anyone swears by the temple, it means nothing; but if anyone swears by the gold of the temple, he is bound by his oath.' 17You blind fools! Which is greater: the gold, or the temple that makes the gold sacred? 18You also say, 'If anyone swears by the altar, it means nothing; but if anyone swears by the gift on it, he is bound by his oath.' 19You blind men! Which is greater: the gift, or the altar that makes the gift sacred? 20Therefore, he who swears by the altar swears by it and by everything on it. 21And he who swears by the temple swears by it and by the one who dwells in it. 22And he who swears by heaven swears by God's throne and by the one who sits on it.

23"Woe to you, teachers of the law and Pharisees, you hypocrites! You give a tenth of your spices—mint, dill and cummin. But you have neglected the more important matters of the law—justice, mercy and faithfulness. You should have practiced the latter, without neglecting the former. 24You blind guides! You strain out a gnat but swallow a camel.

25"Woe to you, teachers of the law and Pharisees, you hypocrites! You clean the outside of the cup and dish, but inside they are full of greed and self-indulgence. 26Blind Pharisee! First clean the inside of the cup and dish, and then the outside also will be clean.

27"Woe to you, teachers of the law and Pharisees, you hypocrites! You are like whitewashed tombs, which look beautiful on the outside but on the inside are full of dead men's bones and everything unclean. 28In the same way, on the outside you appear to people as righteous but on the inside you are full of hypocrisy and wickedness.

---

a 5 That is, boxes containing Scripture verses, worn on forehead and arm   b 10 Or *Messiah*   c 13 Some manuscripts *to.* 14*Woe to you, teachers of the law and Pharisees, you hypocrites! You devour widows' houses and for a show make lengthy prayers. Therefore you will be punished more severely.*

Living Bible

ers and these Pharisees were Moses, the way they keep making up so many laws!d 3And of course you should obey their every whim! It may be all right to do what they say, but above anything else, *don't follow their example.* For they don't do what they tell you to do. 4They load you with impossible demands that they themselves don't even try to keep.

5"Everything they do is done for show. They act holye by wearing on their arms little prayer boxes with Scripture verses inside,f and by lengthening the memorial fringes of their robes. 6And how they love to sit at the head table at banquets, and in the reserved pews in the synagogue! 7How they enjoy the deference paid them on the streets, and to be called 'Rabbi' and 'Master'! 8Don't ever let anyone call you that. For only God is your Rabbi and all of you are on the same level, as brothers. 9And don't address anyone here on earth as 'Father,' for only God in heaven should be addressed like that. 10And don't be called 'Master,' for only one is your master, even the Messiah.

11"The more lowly your service to others, the greater you are. To be the greatest, be a servant. 12But those who think themselves great shall be disappointed and humbled; and those who humble themselves shall be exalted.

13, 14"Woe to you, Pharisees, and you other religious leaders. Hypocrites! For you won't let others enter the Kingdom of Heaven, and won't go in yourselves. And you pretend to be holy, with all your long, public prayers in the streets, while you are evicting widows from their homes. Hypocrites! 15Yes, woe upon you hypocrites. For you go to all lengths to make one convert, and then turn him into twice the son of hell you are yourselves. 16Blind guides! Woe upon you! For your rule is that to swear 'By God's Temple' means nothing—you can break that oath, but to swear 'By the gold in the Temple' is binding! 17Blind fools! Which is greater, the gold, or the Temple that sanctifies the gold? 18And you say that to take an oath 'By the altar' can be broken, but to swear 'By the gifts on the altar' is binding! 19Blind! For which is greater, the gift on the altar, or the altar itself that sanctifies the gift? 20When you swear 'By the altar' you are swearing by it and everything on it, 21and when you swear 'By the Temple' you are swearing by it, and by God who lives in it. 22And when you swear 'By heavens' you are swearing by the Throne of God and by God himself.

23"Yes, woe upon you, Pharisees, and you other religious leaders—hypocrites! For you tithe down to the last mint leaf in your garden, but ignore the important things—justice and mercy and faith. Yes, you should tithe, but you shouldn't leave the more important things undone. 24Blind guides! You strain out a gnat and swallow a camel.

25"Woe to you, Pharisees, and you religious leaders—hypocrites! You are so careful to polish the outside of the cup, but the inside is foul with extortion and greed. 26Blind Pharisees! First cleanse the inside of the cup, and then the whole cup will be clean.

27"Woe to you, Pharisees, and you religious leaders! You are like beautiful mausoleums—full of dead men's bones, and of foulness and corruption. 28You try to look like saintly men, but underneath those pious robes of yours are hearts besmirched with every sort of hypocrisy and sin.

New Revised Standard

Moses' seat; 3therefore, do whatever they teach you and follow it; but do not do as they do, for they do not practice what they teach. 4They tie up heavy burdens, hard to bear,g and lay them on the shoulders of others; but they themselves are unwilling to lift a finger to move them. 5They do all their deeds to be seen by others; for they make their phylacteries broad and their fringes long. 6They love to have the place of honor at banquets and the best seats in the synagogues, 7and to be greeted with respect in the marketplaces, and to have people call them rabbi. 8But you are not to be called rabbi, for you have one teacher, and you are all students.h 9And call no one your father on earth, for you have one Father—the one in heaven. 10Nor are you to be called instructors, for you have one instructor, the Messiah.i 11The greatest among you will be your servant. 12All who exalt themselves will be humbled, and all who humble themselves will be exalted.

13 "But woe to you, scribes and Pharisees, hypocrites! For you lock people out of the kingdom of heaven. For you do not go in yourselves, and when others are going in, you stop them.j 15Woe to you, scribes and Pharisees, hypocrites! For you cross sea and land to make a single convert, and you make the new convert twice as much a child of hellk as yourselves.

16 "Woe to you, blind guides, who say, 'Whoever swears by the sanctuary is bound by nothing, but whoever swears by the gold of the sanctuary is bound by the oath.' 17You blind fools! For which is greater, the gold or the sanctuary that has made the gold sacred? 18And you say, 'Whoever swears by the altar is bound by nothing, but whoever swears by the gift that is on the altar is bound by the oath.' 19How blind you are! For which is greater, the gift or the altar that makes the gift sacred? 20So whoever swears by the altar, swears by it and by everything on it; 21and whoever swears by the sanctuary, swears by it and by the one who dwells in it; 22and whoever swears by heaven, swears by the throne of God and by the one who is seated upon it.

23 "Woe to you, scribes and Pharisees, hypocrites! For you tithe mint, dill, and cummin, and have neglected the weightier matters of the law: justice and mercy and faith. It is these you ought to have practiced without neglecting the others. 24You blind guides! You strain out a gnat but swallow a camel!

25 "Woe to you, scribes and Pharisees, hypocrites! For you clean the outside of the cup and of the plate, but inside they are full of greed and self-indulgence. 26You blind Pharisee! First clean the inside of the cup,l so that the outside also may become clean.

27 "Woe to you, scribes and Pharisees, hypocrites! For you are like whitewashed tombs, which on the outside look beautiful, but inside they are full of the bones of the dead and of all kinds of filth. 28So you also on the outside look righteous to others, but inside you are full of hypocrisy and lawlessness.

---

g Other ancient authorities lack *hard to bear*   h Gk *brothers*   i Or *the Christ*   j Other authorities add here (or after verse 12) verse 14, *Woe to you, scribes and Pharisees, hypocrites! For you devour widows' houses and for the sake of appearance you make long prayers; therefore you will receive the greater condemnation*   k Gk *Gehenna*   l Other ancient authorities add *and of the plate*

---

d *23:2 the way they keep making up so many laws*, literally, "sit on Moses' seat."   e *23:5 act holy*, implied.   f *23:5 Scripture verses inside*, literally, "enlarge their phylacteries."

King James

29Woe unto you, scribes and Pharisees, hypocrites! because ye build the tombs of the prophets, and garnish the sepulchres of the righteous,

30And say, If we had been in the days of our fathers, we would not have been partakers with them in the blood of the prophets.

31Wherefore ye be witnesses unto yourselves, that ye are the children of them which killed the prophets.

32Fill ye up then the measure of your fathers.

33*Ye* serpents, *ye* generation of vipers, how can ye escape the damnation of hell?

34¶ Wherefore, behold, I send unto you prophets, and wise men, and scribes: and *some* of them ye shall kill and crucify; and *some* of them shall ye scourge in your synagogues, and persecute *them* from city to city:

35That upon you may come all the righteous blood shed upon the earth, from the blood of righteous Abel unto the blood of Zacharias son of Barachias, whom ye slew between the temple and the altar.

36Verily I say unto you, All these things shall come upon this generation.

37O Jerusalem, Jerusalem, *thou* that killest the prophets, and stonest them which are sent unto thee, how often would I have gathered thy children together, even as a hen gathereth her chickens under *her* wings, and ye would not!

38Behold, your house is left unto you desolate.

39For I say unto you, Ye shall not see me henceforth, till ye shall say, Blessed *is* he that cometh in the name of the Lord.

24 AND JESUS went out, and departed from the temple: and his disciples came to *him* for to show him the buildings of the temple.

2And Jesus said unto them, See ye not all these things? verily I say unto you, There shall not be left here one stone upon another, that shall not be thrown down.

3¶ And as he sat upon the mount of Olives, the disciples came unto him privately, saying, Tell us, when shall these things be? and what *shall* be the sign of thy coming, and of the end of the world?

4And Jesus answered and said unto them, Take heed that no man deceive you.

5For many shall come in my name, saying, I am Christ; and shall deceive many.

6And ye shall hear of wars and rumours of wars: see that ye be not troubled: for all *these things* must come to pass, but the end is not yet.

7For nation shall rise against nation, and kingdom against kingdom: and there shall be famines, and pestilences, and earthquakes, in divers places.

8All these *are* the beginning of sorrows.

9Then shall they deliver you up to be afflicted, and shall kill you: and ye shall be hated of all nations for my name's sake.

10And then shall many be offended, and shall betray one another, and shall hate one another.

11And many false prophets shall rise, and shall deceive many.

12And because iniquity shall abound, the love of many shall wax cold.

13But he that shall endure unto the end, the same shall be saved.

14And this gospel of the kingdom shall be preached in all the world for a witness unto all nations; and then shall the end come.

15When ye therefore shall see the abomination of desolation, spoken of by Daniel the prophet, stand in the holy place, (whoso readeth, let him understand:)

New International

29"Woe to you, teachers of the law and Pharisees, you hypocrites! You build tombs for the prophets and decorate the graves of the righteous. 30And you say, 'If we had lived in the days of our forefathers, we would not have taken part with them in shedding the blood of the prophets.' 31So you testify against yourselves that you are the descendants of those who murdered the prophets. 32Fill up, then, the measure of the sin of your forefathers!

33"You snakes! You brood of vipers! How will you escape being condemned to hell? 34Therefore I am sending you prophets and wise men and teachers. Some of them you will kill and crucify; others you will flog in your synagogues and pursue from town to town. 35And so upon you will come all the righteous blood that has been shed on earth, from the blood of righteous Abel to the blood of Zechariah son of Berekiah, whom you murdered between the temple and the altar. 36I tell you the truth, all this will come upon this generation.

37"O Jerusalem, Jerusalem, you who kill the prophets and stone those sent to you, how often I have longed to gather your children together, as a hen gathers her chicks under her wings, but you were not willing. 38Look, your house is left to you desolate. 39For I tell you, you will not see me again until you say, 'Blessed is he who comes in the name of the Lord.'a"

Signs of the End of the Age

24 JESUS LEFT the temple and was walking away when his disciples came up to him to call his attention to its buildings. 2"Do you see all these things?" he asked. "I tell you the truth, not one stone here will be left on another; every one will be thrown down."

3As Jesus was sitting on the Mount of Olives, the disciples came to him privately. "Tell us," they said, "when will this happen, and what will be the sign of your coming and of the end of the age?"

4Jesus answered: "Watch out that no one deceives you. 5For many will come in my name, claiming, 'I am the Christ,b' and will deceive many. 6You will hear of wars and rumors of wars, but see to it that you are not alarmed. Such things must happen, but the end is still to come. 7Nation will rise against nation, and kingdom against kingdom. There will be famines and earthquakes in various places. 8All these are the beginning of birth pains.

9"Then you will be handed over to be persecuted and put to death, and you will be hated by all nations because of me. 10At that time many will turn away from the faith and will betray and hate each other, 11and many false prophets will appear and deceive many people. 12Because of the increase of wickedness, the love of most will grow cold, 13but he who stands firm to the end will be saved. 14And this gospel of the kingdom will be preached in the whole world as a testimony to all nations, and then the end will come.

15"So when you see standing in the holy place 'the abomination that causes desolation,'c spoken of through the prophet Daniel—let the reader understand— 16then

---

a *39* Psalm 118:26　　b *5* Or *Messiah*; also in verse 23　　c *15* Daniel 9:27; 11:31; 12:11

Living Bible

29, 30"Yes, woe to you, Pharisees, and you religious leaders—hypocrites! For you build monuments to the prophets killed by your fathers and lay flowers on the graves of the godly men they destroyed, and say, 'We certainly would never have acted as our fathers did.'

31"In saying that, you are accusing yourselves of being the sons of wicked men. 32And you are following in their steps, filling up the full measure of their evil. 33Snakes! Sons of vipers! How shall you escape the judgment of hell?

34"I will send you prophets, and wise men, and inspired writers, and you will kill some by crucifixion, and rip open the backs of others with whips in your synagogues, and hound them from city to city, 35so that you will become guilty of all the blood of murdered godly men from righteous Abel to Zechariah (son of Barachiah), slain by you in the Temple between the altar and the sanctuary. 36Yes, all the accumulated judgment of the centuries shall break upon the heads of this very generation.

37"O Jerusalem, Jerusalem, the city that kills the prophets, and stones all those God sends to her! How often I have wanted to gather your children together as a hen gathers her chicks beneath her wings, but you wouldn't let me. 38And now your house is left to you, desolate. 39For I tell you this, you will never see me again until you are ready to welcome the one sent to you from God."d

24 AS JESUS was leaving the Temple grounds, his disciples came along and wanted to take him on a tour of the various Temple buildings.

2But he told them, "All these buildings will be knocked down, with not one stone left on top of another!"

3"When will this happen?" the disciples asked him later, as he sat on the slopes of the Mount of Olives. "What events will signal your return, and the end of the world?"e

4Jesus told them, "Don't let anyone fool you. 5For many will come claiming to be the Messiah, and will lead many astray. 6When you hear of wars beginning, this does not signal my return; these must come, but the end is not yet. 7The nations and kingdoms of the earth will rise against each other and there will be famines and earthquakes in many places. 8But all this will be only the beginning of the horrors to come.

9"Then you will be tortured and killed and hated all over the world because you are mine, 10and many of you shall fall back into sin and betray and hate each other. 11And many false prophets will appear and lead many astray. 12Sin will be rampant everywhere and will cool the love of many. 13But those enduring to the end shall be saved.

14"And the Good News about the Kingdom will be preached throughout the whole world, so that all nations will hear it, and then, finally, the end will come.

15"So, when you see the horrible thingf (told about by Danielg the prophet) standing in a holy place (Note to the reader: You know what is meant!),h 16then those

New Revised Standard

29 "Woe to you, scribes and Pharisees, hypocrites! For you build the tombs of the prophets and decorate the graves of the righteous, 30and you say, 'If we had lived in the days of our ancestors, we would not have taken part with them in shedding the blood of the prophets.' 31Thus you testify against yourselves that you are descendants of those who murdered the prophets. 32Fill up, then, the measure of your ancestors. 33You snakes, you brood of vipers! How can you escape being sentenced to hell?i 34Therefore I send you prophets, sages, and scribes, some of whom you will kill and crucify, and some you will flog in your synagogues and pursue from town to town, 35so that upon you may come all the righteous blood shed on earth, from the blood of righteous Abel to the blood of Zechariah son of Barachiah, whom you murdered between the sanctuary and the altar. 36Truly I tell you, all this will come upon this generation.

The Lament over Jerusalem

37 "Jerusalem, Jerusalem, the city that kills the prophets and stones those who are sent to it! How often have I desired to gather your children together as a hen gathers her brood under her wings, and you were not willing! 38See, your house is left to you, desolate.j 39For I tell you, you will not see me again until you say, 'Blessed is the one who comes in the name of the Lord.'"

The Destruction of the Temple Foretold

24 AS JESUS came out of the temple and was going away, his disciples came to point out to him the buildings of the temple. 2Then he asked them, "You see all these, do you not? Truly I tell you, not one stone will be left here upon another; all will be thrown down."

Signs of the End of the Age

3 When he was sitting on the Mount of Olives, the disciples came to him privately, saying, "Tell us, when will this be, and what will be the sign of your coming and of the end of the age?" 4Jesus answered them, "Beware that no one leads you astray. 5For many will come in my name, saying, 'I am the Messiah!'k and they will lead many astray. 6And you will hear of wars and rumors of wars; see that you are not alarmed; for this must take place, but the end is not yet. 7For nation will rise against nation, and kingdom against kingdom, and there will be faminesl and earthquakes in various places: 8all this is but the beginning of the birth pangs.

Persecutions Foretold

9 "Then they will hand you over to be tortured and will put you to death, and you will be hated by all nations because of my name. 10Then many will fall away,m and they will betray one another and hate one another. 11And many false prophets will arise and lead many astray. 12And because of the increase of lawlessness, the love of many will grow cold. 13But the one who endures to the end will be saved. 14And this good newsn of the kingdom will be proclaimed throughout the world, as a testimony to all the nations; and then the end will come.

The Desolating Sacrilege

15 "So when you see the desolating sacrilege standing in the holy place, as was spoken of by the prophet Daniel (let the reader understand), 16then those in Judea

---

d 23:39 from God, literally, "in the name of the Lord." e 24:3 world, literally, "age." f 24:15 the horrible thing, literally, "the abomination of desolation." g 24:15 Daniel, see Dan 9:27, 11:31, 12:11. h 24:15 Note to the reader: You know what is meant, literally, "Let the reader take note."

i Gk Gehenna j Other ancient authorities lack desolate k Or the Christ l Other ancient authorities add and pestilences m Or stumble n Or gospel

King James

¹⁶Then let them which be in Judaea flee into the mountains:

¹⁷Let him which is on the housetop not come down to take any thing out of his house:

¹⁸Neither let him which is in the field return back to take his clothes.

¹⁹And woe unto them that are with child, and to them that give suck in those days!

²⁰But pray ye that your flight be not in the winter, neither on the sabbath day:

²¹For then shall be great tribulation, such as was not since the beginning of the world to this time, no, nor ever shall be.

²²And except those days should be shortened, there should no flesh be saved: but for the elect's sake those days shall be shortened.

²³Then if any man shall say unto you, Lo, here is Christ, or there; believe it not.

²⁴For there shall arise false Christs, and false prophets, and shall show great signs and wonders; insomuch that, if it were possible, they shall deceive the very elect.

²⁵Behold, I have told you before.

²⁶Wherefore if they shall say unto you, Behold, he is in the desert; go not forth: behold, he is in the secret chambers; believe it not.

²⁷For as the lightning cometh out of the east, and shineth even unto the west; so shall also the coming of the Son of man be.

²⁸For wheresoever the carcase is, there will the eagles be gathered together.

²⁹¶ Immediately after the tribulation of those days shall the sun be darkened, and the moon shall not give her light, and the stars shall fall from heaven, and the powers of the heavens shall be shaken:

³⁰And then shall appear the sign of the Son of man in heaven: and then shall all the tribes of the earth mourn, and they shall see the Son of man coming in the clouds of heaven with power and great glory.

³¹And he shall send his angels with a great sound of a trumpet, and they shall gather together his elect from the four winds, from one end of heaven to the other.

³²Now learn a parable of the fig tree; When his branch is yet tender, and putteth forth leaves, ye know that summer is nigh:

³³So likewise ye, when ye shall see all these things, know that it is near, even at the doors.

³⁴Verily I say unto you, This generation shall not pass, till all these things be fulfilled.

³⁵Heaven and earth shall pass away, but my words shall not pass away.

³⁶¶ But of that day and hour knoweth no man, no, not the angels of heaven, but my Father only.

³⁷But as the days of Noe were, so shall also the coming of the Son of man be.

³⁸For as in the days that were before the flood they were eating and drinking, marrying and giving in marriage, until the day that Noe entered into the ark,

³⁹And knew not until the flood came, and took them all away; so shall also the coming of the Son of man be.

⁴⁰Then shall two be in the field; the one shall be taken, and the other left.

⁴¹Two women shall be grinding at the mill; the one shall be taken, and the other left.

⁴²¶ Watch therefore: for ye know not what hour your Lord doth come.

⁴³But know this, that if the goodman of the house had known in what watch the thief would come, he would have watched, and would not have suffered his house to be broken up.

⁴⁴Therefore be ye also ready: for in such an hour as ye think not the Son of man cometh.

New International

let those who are in Judea flee to the mountains. ¹⁷Let no one on the roof of his house go down to take anything out of the house. ¹⁸Let no one in the field go back to get his cloak. ¹⁹How dreadful it will be in those days for pregnant women and nursing mothers! ²⁰Pray that your flight will not take place in winter or on the Sabbath. ²¹For then there will be great distress, unequaled from the beginning of the world until now—and never to be equaled again. ²²If those days had not been cut short, no one would survive, but for the sake of the elect those days will be shortened. ²³At that time if anyone says to you, 'Look, here is the Christ!' or, 'There he is!' do not believe it. ²⁴For false Christs and false prophets will appear and perform great signs and miracles to deceive even the elect—if that were possible. ²⁵See, I have told you ahead of time.

²⁶"So if anyone tells you, 'There he is, out in the desert,' do not go out; or, 'Here he is, in the inner rooms,' do not believe it. ²⁷For as lightning that comes from the east is visible even in the west, so will be the coming of the Son of Man. ²⁸Wherever there is a carcass, there the vultures will gather.

²⁹"Immediately after the distress of those days

" 'the sun will be darkened,
　　and the moon will not give its light;
　the stars will fall from the sky,
　　and the heavenly bodies will be shaken.'ᵃ

³⁰"At that time the sign of the Son of Man will appear in the sky, and all the nations of the earth will mourn. They will see the Son of Man coming on the clouds of the sky, with power and great glory. ³¹And he will send his angels with a loud trumpet call, and they will gather his elect from the four winds, from one end of the heavens to the other.

³²"Now learn this lesson from the fig tree: As soon as its twigs get tender and its leaves come out, you know that summer is near. ³³Even so, when you see all these things, you know that itᵇ is near, right at the door. ³⁴I tell you the truth, this generationᶜ will certainly not pass away until all these things have happened. ³⁵Heaven and earth will pass away, but my words will never pass away.

The Day and Hour Unknown

³⁶"No one knows about that day or hour, not even the angels in heaven, nor the Son,ᵈ but only the Father. ³⁷As it was in the days of Noah, so it will be at the coming of the Son of Man. ³⁸For in the days before the flood, people were eating and drinking, marrying and giving in marriage, up to the day Noah entered the ark; ³⁹and they knew nothing about what would happen until the flood came and took them all away. That is how it will be at the coming of the Son of Man. ⁴⁰Two men will be in the field; one will be taken and the other left. ⁴¹Two women will be grinding with a hand mill; one will be taken and the other left.

⁴²"Therefore keep watch, because you do not know on what day your Lord will come. ⁴³But understand this: If the owner of the house had known at what time of night the thief was coming, he would have kept watch and would not have let his house be broken into. ⁴⁴So you also must be ready, because the Son of Man will come at an hour when you do not expect him.

ᵃ 29 Isaiah 13:10; 34:4　ᵇ 33 Or he　ᶜ 34 Or race　ᵈ 36 Some manuscripts do not have nor the Son.

Living Bible

in Judea must flee into the Judean hills. 17Those on their porches^e must not even go inside to pack before they flee. 18Those in the fields should not return to their homes for their clothes.

19"And woe to pregnant women and to those with babies in those days. 20And pray that your flight will not be in winter, or on the Sabbath.^f 21For there will be persecution such as the world has never before seen in all its history, and will never see again.

22"In fact, unless those days are shortened, all mankind will perish. But they will be shortened for the sake of God's chosen people.^g

23"Then if anyone tells you, 'The Messiah has arrived at such and such a place, or has appeared here or there,' don't believe it. 24For false Christs shall arise, and false prophets, and will do wonderful miracles, so that if it were possible, even God's chosen ones^h would be deceived. 25See, I have warned you.

26"So if someone tells you the Messiah has returned and is out in the desert, don't bother to go and look. Or, that he is hiding at a certain place, don't believe it! 27For as the lightning flashes across the sky from east to west, so shall my coming be, when I, the Messiah,^i return. 28And wherever the carcass is, there the vultures will gather.

29"Immediately after the persecution of those days the sun will be darkened, and the moon will not give light, and the stars will seem to fall^j from the heavens, and the powers overshadowing the earth will be convulsed.^k

30"And then at last the signal of my coming^l will appear in the heavens and there will be deep mourning all around the earth. And the nations of the world will see me arrive in the clouds of heaven, with power and great glory. 31And I shall send forth my angels with the sound of a mighty trumpet blast, and they shall gather my chosen ones from the farthest ends of the earth and heaven.^m

32"Now learn a lesson from the fig tree. When her branch is tender and the leaves begin to sprout, you know that summer is almost here. 33Just so, when you see all these things beginning to happen, you can know that my return is near,^n even at the doors. 34Then at last this age will come to its close.^o

35"Heaven and earth will disappear, but my words will remain forever. 36But no one knows the date and hour when the end will be—not even the angels. No, nor even God's Son.^p Only the Father knows.

37, 38"The world will be at ease^q—banquets and parties and weddings—just as it was in Noah's time before the sudden coming of the flood; 39people wouldn't believe^r what was going to happen until the flood actually arrived and took them all away. So shall my coming be.

40"Two men will be working together in the fields, and one will be taken, the other left. 41Two women will be going about their household tasks; one will be taken, the other left.

42"So be prepared, for you don't know what day your Lord is coming.

43"Just as a man can prevent trouble from thieves by keeping watch for them, 44so you can avoid trouble by always being ready for my unannounced return.

---

e 24:17 *porches*, literally, "roof tops," which, being flat, were used as porches at that time. See Acts 10:9. f 24:20 *on the Sabbath*. The city gates were closed on the Sabbath. g 24:22 *chosen people*, literally, "the elect." h 24:24 *chosen ones*, literally, "the elect." i 24:27 *the Messiah*, literally, "the Son of Man." j 24:29 *the stars will seem to fall*, literally, "the stars shall fall from heaven." k 24:29 *the earth will be convulsed*, literally, "the powers of the heavens shall be shaken." See Eph 6:12. l 24:30 *of my coming*, literally, "of the coming of the Son of Man." m 24:31 *from the farthest ends of the earth and heaven*, literally, "from the four winds, from one end of heaven to the other." n 24:33 *my return is near*, literally, "He is nigh. o 24:34 *this age will come to its close* is literally, "this generation shall pass away." p 24:36 *No, nor even God's Son*, literally, "neither the Son." Many ancient manuscripts omit this phrase. q 24:37 *The world will be at ease*, implied. r 24:39 *wouldn't believe*, literally, "knew not."

New Revised Standard

must flee to the mountains; 17the one on the housetop must not go down to take what is in the house; 18the one in the field must not turn back to get a coat. 19Woe to those who are pregnant and to those who are nursing infants in those days! 20Pray that your flight may not be in winter or on a sabbath. 21For at that time there will be great suffering, such as has not been from the beginning of the world until now, no, and never will be. 22And if those days had not been cut short, no one would be saved; but for the sake of the elect those days will be cut short. 23Then if anyone says to you, 'Look! Here is the Messiah!'^s or 'There he is!'—do not believe it. 24For false messiahs^t and false prophets will appear and produce great signs and omens, to lead astray, if possible, even the elect. 25Take note, I have told you beforehand. 26So, if they say to you, 'Look! He is in the wilderness,' do not go out. If they say, 'Look! He is in the inner rooms,' do not believe it. 27For as the lightning comes from the east and flashes as far as the west, so will be the coming of the Son of Man. 28Wherever the corpse is, there the vultures will gather.

The Coming of the Son of Man

29 "Immediately after the suffering of those days
    the sun will be darkened,
        and the moon will not give its light;
    the stars will fall from heaven,
        and the powers of heaven will be shaken.
30Then the sign of the Son of Man will appear in heaven, and then all the tribes of the earth will mourn, and they will see 'the Son of Man coming on the clouds of heaven' with power and great glory. 31And he will send out his angels with a loud trumpet call, and they will gather his elect from the four winds, from one end of heaven to the other.

The Lesson of the Fig Tree

32 "From the fig tree learn its lesson: as soon as its branch becomes tender and puts forth its leaves, you know that summer is near. 33So also, when you see all these things, you know that he^u is near, at the very gates. 34Truly I tell you, this generation will not pass away until all these things have taken place. 35Heaven and earth will pass away, but my words will not pass away.

The Necessity for Watchfulness

36 "But about that day and hour no one knows, neither the angels of heaven, nor the Son,^v but only the Father. 37For as the days of Noah were, so will be the coming of the Son of Man. 38For as in those days before the flood they were eating and drinking, marrying and giving in marriage, until the day Noah entered the ark, 39and they knew nothing until the flood came and swept them all away, so too will be the coming of the Son of Man. 40Then two will be in the field; one will be taken and one will be left. 41Two women will be grinding meal together; one will be taken and one will be left. 42Keep awake therefore, for you do not know on what day^w your Lord is coming. 43But understand this: if the owner of the house had known in what part of the night the thief was coming, he would have stayed awake and would not have let his house be broken into. 44Therefore you also must be ready, for the Son of Man is coming at an unexpected hour.

---

s Or *the Christ* t Or *christs* u Or *it* v Other ancient authorities lack *nor the Son* w Other ancient authorities read *at what hour*

King James

45Who then is a faithful and wise servant, whom his lord hath made ruler over his household, to give them meat in due season?

46Blessed *is* that servant, whom his lord when he cometh shall find so doing.

47Verily I say unto you, That he shall make him ruler over all his goods.

48But and if that evil servant shall say in his heart, My lord delayeth his coming;

49And shall begin to smite *his* fellowservants, and to eat and drink with the drunken;

50The lord of that servant shall come in a day when he looketh not for *him*, and in an hour that he is not aware of,

51And shall cut him asunder, and appoint *him* his portion with the hypocrites: there shall be weeping and gnashing of teeth.

25 THEN SHALL the kingdom of heaven be likened unto ten virgins, which took their lamps, and went forth to meet the bridegroom.

2And five of them were wise, and five *were* foolish.

3They that *were* foolish took their lamps, and took no oil with them:

4But the wise took oil in their vessels with their lamps.

5While the bridegroom tarried, they all slumbered and slept.

6And at midnight there was a cry made, Behold, the bridegroom cometh; go ye out to meet him.

7Then all those virgins arose, and trimmed their lamps.

8And the foolish said unto the wise, Give us of your oil; for our lamps are gone out.

9But the wise answered, saying, *Not so;* lest there be not enough for us and you: but go ye rather to them that sell, and buy for yourselves.

10And while they went to buy, the bridegroom came; and they that were ready went in with him to the marriage: and the door was shut.

11Afterward came also the other virgins, saying, Lord, Lord, open to us.

12But he answered and said, Verily I say unto you, I know you not.

13Watch therefore, for ye know neither the day nor the hour wherein the Son of man cometh.

14¶ For *the kingdom of heaven is* as a man travelling into a far country, *who* called his own servants, and delivered unto them his goods.

15And unto one he gave five talents, to another two, and to another one; to every man according to his several ability; and straightway took his journey.

16Then he that had received the five talents went and traded with the same, and made *them* other five talents.

17And likewise he that *had received* two, he also gained other two.

18But he that had received one went and digged in the earth, and hid his lord's money.

19After a long time the lord of those servants cometh, and reckoneth with them.

20And so he that had received five talents came and brought other five talents, saying, Lord, thou deliveredst unto me five talents: behold, I have gained beside them five talents more.

21His lord said unto him, Well done, *thou* good and faithful servant: thou hast been faithful over a few things, I will make thee ruler over many things: enter thou into the joy of thy lord.

22He also that had received two talents came and said, Lord, thou deliveredst unto me two talents: behold, I have gained two other talents beside them.

New International

45"Who then is the faithful and wise servant, whom the master has put in charge of the servants in his household to give them their food at the proper time? 46It will be good for that servant whose master finds him doing so when he returns. 47I tell you the truth, he will put him in charge of all his possessions. 48But suppose that servant is wicked and says to himself, 'My master is staying away a long time,' 49and he then begins to beat his fellow servants and to eat and drink with drunkards. 50The master of that servant will come on a day when he does not expect him and at an hour he is not aware of. 51He will cut him to pieces and assign him a place with the hypocrites, where there will be weeping and gnashing of teeth.

The Parable of the Ten Virgins

25 "AT THAT time the kingdom of heaven will be like ten virgins who took their lamps and went out to meet the bridegroom. 2Five of them were foolish and five were wise. 3The foolish ones took their lamps but did not take any oil with them. 4The wise, however, took oil in jars along with their lamps. 5The bridegroom was a long time in coming, and they all became drowsy and fell asleep.

6"At midnight the cry rang out: 'Here's the bridegroom! Come out to meet him!'

7"Then all the virgins woke up and trimmed their lamps. 8The foolish ones said to the wise, 'Give us some of your oil; our lamps are going out.'

9"'No,' they replied, 'there may not be enough for both us and you. Instead, go to those who sell oil and buy some for yourselves.'

10"But while they were on their way to buy the oil, the bridegroom arrived. The virgins who were ready went in with him to the wedding banquet. And the door was shut.

11"Later the others also came. 'Sir! Sir!' they said. 'Open the door for us!'

12"But he replied, 'I tell you the truth, I don't know you.'

13"Therefore keep watch, because you do not know the day or the hour.

The Parable of the Talents

14"Again, it will be like a man going on a journey, who called his servants and entrusted his property to them. 15To one he gave five talentsa of money, to another two talents, and to another one talent, each according to his ability. Then he went on his journey. 16The man who had received the five talents went at once and put his money to work and gained five more. 17So also, the one with the two talents gained two more. 18But the man who had received the one talent went off, dug a hole in the ground and hid his master's money.

19"After a long time the master of those servants returned and settled accounts with them. 20The man who had received the five talents brought the other five. 'Master,' he said, 'you entrusted me with five talents. See, I have gained five more.'

21"His master replied, 'Well done, good and faithful servant! You have been faithful with a few things; I will put you in charge of many things. Come and share your master's happiness!'

22"The man with the two talents also came. 'Master,' he said, 'you entrusted me with two talents; see, I have gained two more.'

---

a *15 A talent was worth more than a thousand dollars.*

Living Bible

45"Are you a wise and faithful servant of the Lord? Have I given you the task of managing my household, to feed my children day by day? 46Blessings on you if I return and find you faithfully doing your work. 47I will put such faithful ones in charge of everything I own!

48"But if you are evil and say to yourself, 'My Lord won't be coming for a while,' 49and begin oppressing your fellow servants, partying and getting drunk, 50your Lord will arrive unannounced and unexpected, 51and severely whip you and send you off to the judgment of the hypocrites; there will be weeping and gnashing of teeth.

25 "THE KINGDOM of Heaven can be illustrated by the story of ten bridesmaidsb who took their lamps and went to meet the bridegroom. 2, 3, 4But only five of them were wise enough to fill their lamps with oil, while the other five were foolish and forgot.

5, 6"So, when the bridegroom was delayed, they lay down to rest until midnight, when they were roused by the shout, 'The bridegroom is coming! Come out and welcome him!'

7, 8"All the girls jumped up and trimmed their lamps. Then the five who hadn't any oil begged the others to share with them, for their lamps were going out.

9"But the others replied, 'We haven't enough. Go instead to the shops and buy some for yourselves.'

10"But while they were gone, the bridegroom came, and those who were ready went in with him to the marriage feast, and the door was locked.

11"Later, when the other five returned, they stood outside, calling, 'Sir, open the door for us!'

12"But he called back, 'Go away! It is too late!'c

13"So stay awake and be prepared, for you do not know the date or moment of my return.d

14"Again, the Kingdom of Heaven can be illustrated by the story of a man going into another country, who called together his servants and loaned them money to invest for him while he was gone.

15"He gave $5,000 to one, $2,000 to another, and $1,000 to the last—dividing it in proportion to their abilities—and then left on his trip. 16The man who received the $5,000 began immediately to buy and sell with it and soon earned another $5,000. 17The man with $2,000 went right to work, too, and earned another $2,000.

18"But the man who received the $1,000 dug a hole in the ground and hid the money for safekeeping.

19"After a long time their master returned from his trip and called them to him to account for his money. 20The man to whom he had entrusted the $5,000 brought him $10,000.

21"His master praised him for good work. 'You have been faithful in handling this small amount,' he told him, 'so now I will give you many more responsibilities. Begin the joyous tasks I have assigned to you.'

22"Next came the man who had received the $2,000, with the report, 'Sir, you gave me $2,000 to use, and I have doubled it.'

New Revised Standard

The Faithful or the Unfaithful Slave

45 "Who then is the faithful and wise slave, whom his master has put in charge of his household, to give the other slavese their allowance of food at the proper time? 46Blessed is that slave whom his master will find at work when he arrives. 47Truly I tell you, he will put that one in charge of all his possessions. 48But if that wicked slave says to himself, 'My master is delayed,' 49and he begins to beat his fellow slaves, and eats and drinks with drunkards, 50the master of that slave will come on a day when he does not expect him and at an hour that he does not know. 51He will cut him in piecesf and put him with the hypocrites, where there will be weeping and gnashing of teeth.

The Parable of the Ten Bridesmaids

25 "THEN THE kingdom of heaven will be like this. Ten bridesmaidsg took their lamps and went to meet the bridegroom.h 2Five of them were foolish, and five were wise. 3When the foolish took their lamps, they took no oil with them; 4but the wise took flasks of oil with their lamps. 5As the bridegroom was delayed, all of them became drowsy and slept. 6But at midnight there was a shout, 'Look! Here is the bridegroom! Come out to meet him.' 7Then all those bridesmaidsg got up and trimmed their lamps. 8The foolish said to the wise, 'Give us some of your oil, for our lamps are going out.' 9But the wise replied, 'No! there will not be enough for you and for us; you had better go to the dealers and buy some for yourselves.' 10And while they went to buy it, the bridegroom came, and those who were ready went with him into the wedding banquet; and the door was shut. 11Later the other bridesmaidsg came also, saying, 'Lord, lord, open to us.' 12But he replied, 'Truly I tell you, I do not know you.' 13Keep awake therefore, for you know neither the day nor the hour.i

The Parable of the Talents

14 "For it is as if a man, going on a journey, summoned his slaves and entrusted his property to them; 15to one he gave five talents,j to another two, to another one, to each according to his ability. Then he went away. 16The one who had received the five talents went off at once and traded with them, and made five more talents. 17In the same way, the one who had the two talents made two more talents. 18But the one who had received the one talent went off and dug a hole in the ground and hid his master's money. 19After a long time the master of those slaves came and settled accounts with them. 20Then the one who had received the five talents came forward, bringing five more talents, saying, 'Master, you handed over to me five talents; see, I have made five more talents.' 21His master said to him, 'Well done, good and trustworthy slave; you have been trustworthy in a few things, I will put you in charge of many things; enter into the joy of your master.' 22And the one with the two talents also came forward, saying, 'Master, you handed over to me two talents; see, I have made two more talents.' 23His master said to him, 'Well done,

---

e Gk to give them   f Or cut him off   g Gk virgins   h Other ancient authorities add and the bride   i Other ancient authorities add in which the Son of Man is coming   j A talent was worth more than fifteen years' wages of a laborer

b 25:1 bridesmaids, literally, "virgins."   c 25:12 It is too late, literally, "I know you not."   d 25:13 of my return, implied.

King James

23His lord said unto him, Well done, good and faithful servant; thou hast been faithful over a few things, I will make thee ruler over many things: enter thou into the joy of thy lord.

24Then he which had received the one talent came and said, Lord, I knew thee that thou art an hard man, reaping where thou hast not sown, and gathering where thou hast not strawed:

25And I was afraid, and went and hid thy talent in the earth: lo, *there* thou hast *that is* thine.

26His lord answered and said unto him, *Thou* wicked and slothful servant, thou knewest that I reap where I sowed not, and gather where I have not strawed:

27Thou oughtest therefore to have put my money to the exchangers, and *then* at my coming I should have received mine own with usury.

28Take therefore the talent from him, and give *it* unto him which hath ten talents.

29For unto every one that hath shall be given, and he shall have abundance: but from him that hath not shall be taken away even that which he hath.

30And cast ye the unprofitable servant into outer darkness: there shall be weeping and gnashing of teeth.

31¶ When the Son of man shall come in his glory, and all the holy angels with him, then shall he sit upon the throne of his glory:

32And before him shall be gathered all nations: and he shall separate them one from another, as a shepherd divideth *his* sheep from the goats:

33And he shall set the sheep on his right hand, but the goats on the left.

34Then shall the King say unto them on his right hand, Come, ye blessed of my Father, inherit the kingdom prepared for you from the foundation of the world:

35For I was an hungered, and ye gave me meat: I was thirsty, and ye gave me drink: I was a stranger, and ye took me in:

36Naked, and ye clothed me: I was sick, and ye visited me: I was in prison, and ye came unto me.

37Then shall the righteous answer him, saying, Lord, when saw we thee an hungered, and fed *thee?* or thirsty, and gave *thee* drink?

38When saw we thee a stranger, and took *thee* in? or naked, and clothed *thee?*

39Or when saw we thee sick, or in prison, and came unto thee?

40And the King shall answer and say unto them, Verily I say unto you, Inasmuch as ye have done *it* unto one of the least of these my brethren, ye have done *it* unto me.

41Then shall he say also unto them on the left hand, Depart from me, ye cursed, into everlasting fire, prepared for the devil and his angels:

42For I was an hungered, and ye gave me no meat; I was thirsty, and ye gave me no drink:

43I was a stranger, and ye took me not in: naked, and ye clothed me not: sick, and in prison, and ye visited me not.

44Then shall they also answer him, saying, Lord, when saw we thee an hungered, or athirst, or a stranger, or naked, or sick, or in prison, and did not minister unto thee?

45Then shall he answer them, saying, Verily I say unto you, Inasmuch as ye did *it* not to one of the least of these, ye did *it* not to me.

46And these shall go away into everlasting punishment: but the righteous into life eternal.

New International

23"His master replied, 'Well done, good and faithful servant! You have been faithful with a few things; I will put you in charge of many things. Come and share your master's happiness!'

24"Then the man who had received the one talent came. 'Master,' he said, 'I knew that you are a hard man, harvesting where you have not sown and gathering where you have not scattered seed. 25So I was afraid and went out and hid your talent in the ground. See, here is what belongs to you.'

26"His master replied, 'You wicked, lazy servant! So you knew that I harvest where I have not sown and gather where I have not scattered seed? 27Well then, you should have put my money on deposit with the bankers, so that when I returned I would have received it back with interest.

28" 'Take the talent from him and give it to the one who has the ten talents. 29For everyone who has will be given more, and he will have an abundance. Whoever does not have, even what he has will be taken from him. 30And throw that worthless servant outside, into the darkness, where there will be weeping and gnashing of teeth.'

The Sheep and the Goats

31"When the Son of Man comes in his glory, and all the angels with him, he will sit on his throne in heavenly glory. 32All the nations will be gathered before him, and he will separate the people one from another as a shepherd separates the sheep from the goats. 33He will put the sheep on his right and the goats on his left.

34"Then the King will say to those on his right, 'Come, you who are blessed by my Father; take your inheritance, the kingdom prepared for you since the creation of the world. 35For I was hungry and you gave me something to eat, I was thirsty and you gave me something to drink, I was a stranger and you invited me in, 36I needed clothes and you clothed me, I was sick and you looked after me, I was in prison and you came to visit me.'

37"Then the righteous will answer him, 'Lord, when did we see you hungry and feed you, or thirsty and give you something to drink? 38When did we see you a stranger and invite you in, or needing clothes and clothe you? 39When did we see you sick or in prison and go to visit you?'

40"The King will reply, 'I tell you the truth, whatever you did for one of the least of these brothers of mine, you did for me.'

41"Then he will say to those on his left, 'Depart from me, you who are cursed, into the eternal fire prepared for the devil and his angels. 42For I was hungry and you gave me nothing to eat, I was thirsty and you gave me nothing to drink, 43I was a stranger and you did not invite me in, I needed clothes and you did not clothe me, I was sick and in prison and you did not look after me.'

44"They also will answer, 'Lord, when did we see you hungry or thirsty or a stranger or needing clothes or sick or in prison, and did not help you?'

45"He will reply, 'I tell you the truth, whatever you did not do for one of the least of these, you did not do for me.'

46"Then they will go away to eternal punishment, but the righteous to eternal life."

Living Bible

23" 'Good work,' his master said. 'You are a good and faithful servant. You have been faithful over this small amount, so now I will give you much more.'

24, 25"Then the man with the $1,000 came and said, 'Sir, I knew you were a hard man, and I was afraid you would rob me of what I earned,ᵃ so I hid your money in the earth and here it is!'

26"But his master replied, 'Wicked man! Lazy slave! Since you knew I would demand your profit, 27you should at least have put my money into the bank so I could have some interest. 28Take the money from this man and give it to the man with the $10,000. 29For the man who uses well what he is given shall be given more, and he shall have abundance. But from the man who is unfaithful, even what little responsibility he has shall be taken from him. 30And throw the useless servant out into outer darkness: there shall be weeping and gnashing of teeth.'

31"But when I, the Messiah,ᵇ shall come in my glory, and all the angels with me, then I shall sit upon my throne of glory. 32And all the nations shall be gathered before me. And I will separate the peopleᶜ as a shepherd separates the sheep from the goats, 33and place the sheep at my right hand, and the goats at my left.

34"Then I, the King, shall say to those at my right, 'Come, blessed of my Father, into the Kingdom prepared for you from the founding of the world. 35For I was hungry and you fed me; I was thirsty and you gave me water; I was a stranger and you invited me into your homes; 36naked and you clothed me; sick and in prison, and you visited me.'

37"Then these righteous ones will reply, 'Sir, when did we ever see you hungry and feed you? Or thirsty and give you anything to drink? 38Or a stranger, and help you? Or naked, and clothe you? 39When did we ever see you sick or in prison, and visit you?'

40"And I, the King, will tell them, 'When you did it to these my brothers you were doing it to me!' 41Then I will turn to those on my left and say, 'Away with you, you cursed ones, into the eternal fire prepared for the devil and his demons. 42For I was hungry and you wouldn't feed me; thirsty, and you wouldn't give me anything to drink; 43a stranger, and you refused me hospitality; naked, and you wouldn't clothe me; sick, and in prison, and you didn't visit me.'

44"Then they will reply, 'Lord, when did we ever see you hungry or thirsty or a stranger or naked or sick or in prison, and not help you?'

45"And I will answer, 'When you refused to help the least of these my brothers, you were refusing help to me.'

46"And they shall go away into eternal punishment; but the righteous into everlasting life."

New Revised Standard

good and trustworthy slave; you have been trustworthy in a few things, I will put you in charge of many things; enter into the joy of your master.' 24Then the one who had received the one talent also came forward, saying, 'Master, I knew that you were a harsh man, reaping where you did not sow, and gathering where you did not scatter seed; 25so I was afraid, and I went and hid your talent in the ground. Here you have what is yours.' 26But his master replied, 'You wicked and lazy slave! You knew, did you, that I reap where I did not sow, and gather where I did not scatter? 27Then you ought to have invested my money with the bankers, and on my return I would have received what was my own with interest. 28So take the talent from him, and give it to the one with the ten talents. 29For to all those who have, more will be given, and they will have an abundance; but from those who have nothing, even what they have will be taken away. 30As for this worthless slave, throw him into the outer darkness, where there will be weeping and gnashing of teeth.'

The Judgment of the Nations

31 "When the Son of Man comes in his glory, and all the angels with him, then he will sit on the throne of his glory. 32All the nations will be gathered before him, and he will separate people one from another as a shepherd separates the sheep from the goats, 33and he will put the sheep at his right hand and the goats at the left. 34Then the king will say to those at his right hand, 'Come, you that are blessed by my Father, inherit the kingdom prepared for you from the foundation of the world; 35for I was hungry and you gave me food, I was thirsty and you gave me something to drink, I was a stranger and you welcomed me, 36I was naked and you gave me clothing, I was sick and you took care of me, I was in prison and you visited me.' 37Then the righteous will answer him, 'Lord, when was it that we saw you hungry and gave you food, or thirsty and gave you something to drink? 38And when was it that we saw you a stranger and welcomed you, or naked and gave you clothing? 39And when was it that we saw you sick or in prison and visited you?' 40And the king will answer them, 'Truly I tell you, just as you did it to one of the least of these who are members of my family,ᵈ you did it to me.' 41Then he will say to those at his left hand, 'You that are accursed, depart from me into the eternal fire prepared for the devil and his angels; 42for I was hungry and you gave me no food, I was thirsty and you gave me nothing to drink, 43I was a stranger and you did not welcome me, naked and you did not give me clothing, sick and in prison and you did not visit me.' 44Then they also will answer, 'Lord, when was it that we saw you hungry or thirsty or a stranger or naked or sick or in prison, and did not take care of you?' 45Then he will answer them, 'Truly I tell you, just as you did not do it to one of the least of these, you did not do it to me.' 46And these will go away into eternal punishment, but the righteous into eternal life."

ᵃ 25:24, 25 *I was afraid you would rob me of what I earned*, literally, "reaping where you didn't sow, and gathering where you didn't scatter, and I was afraid. . . ." ᵇ 25:31 *the Messiah*, literally, "the Son of Man." ᶜ 25:32 *separate the people*, literally, "separate the nations."

ᵈ Gk *these my brothers*

King James

26 AND IT came to pass, when Jesus had finished all these sayings, he said unto his disciples,

2Ye know that after two days is *the feast of* the passover, and the Son of man is betrayed to be crucified.

3Then assembled together the chief priests, and the scribes, and the elders of the people, unto the palace of the high priest, who was called Caiaphas,

4And consulted that they might take Jesus by subtlety, and kill *him*.

5But they said, Not on the feast *day*, lest there be an uproar among the people.

6¶ Now when Jesus was in Bethany, in the house of Simon the leper,

7There came unto him a woman having an alabaster box of very precious ointment, and poured it on his head, as he sat *at meat*.

8But when his disciples saw *it*, they had indignation, saying, To what purpose *is* this waste?

9For this ointment might have been sold for much, and given to the poor.

10When Jesus understood *it*, he said unto them, Why trouble ye the woman? for she hath wrought a good work upon me.

11For ye have the poor always with you; but me ye have not always.

12For in that she hath poured this ointment on my body, she did *it* for my burial.

13Verily I say unto you, Wheresoever this gospel shall be preached in the whole world, *there* shall also this, that this woman hath done, be told for a memorial of her.

14¶ Then one of the twelve, called Judas Iscariot, went unto the chief priests,

15And said *unto them*, What will ye give me, and I will deliver him unto you? And they covenanted with him for thirty pieces of silver.

16And from that time he sought opportunity to betray him.

17¶ Now the first *day* of the *feast of* unleavened bread the disciples came to Jesus, saying unto him, Where wilt thou that we prepare for thee to eat the passover?

18And he said, Go into the city to such a man, and say unto him, The Master saith, My time is at hand; I will keep the passover at thy house with my disciples.

19And the disciples did as Jesus had appointed them; and they made ready the passover.

20Now when the even was come, he sat down with the twelve.

21And as they did eat, he said, Verily I say unto you, that one of you shall betray me.

22And they were exceeding sorrowful, and began every one of them to say unto him, Lord, is it I?

23And he answered and said, He that dippeth *his* hand with me in the dish, the same shall betray me.

24The Son of man goeth as it is written of him: but woe unto that man by whom the Son of man is betrayed! it had been good for that man if he had not been born.

25Then Judas, which betrayed him, answered and said, Master, is it I? He said unto him, Thou hast said.

26¶ And as they were eating, Jesus took bread, and blessed *it*, and brake *it*, and gave *it* to the disciples, and said, Take, eat; this is my body.

27And he took the cup, and gave thanks, and gave *it* to them, saying, Drink ye all of it;

28For this is my blood of the new testament, which is shed for many for the remission of sins.

29But I say unto you, I will not drink henceforth of this fruit of the vine, until that day when I drink it new with you in my Father's kingdom.

30And when they had sung an hymn, they went out into the mount of Olives.

New International

The Plot Against Jesus

26 WHEN JESUS had finished saying all these things, he said to his disciples, 2"As you know, the Passover is two days away—and the Son of Man will be handed over to be crucified."

3Then the chief priests and the elders of the people assembled in the palace of the high priest, whose name was Caiaphas, 4and they plotted to arrest Jesus in some sly way and kill him. 5"But not during the Feast," they said, "or there may be a riot among the people."

Jesus Anointed at Bethany

6While Jesus was in Bethany in the home of a man known as Simon the Leper, 7a woman came to him with an alabaster jar of very expensive perfume, which she poured on his head as he was reclining at the table.

8When the disciples saw this, they were indignant. "Why this waste?" they asked. 9"This perfume could have been sold at a high price and the money given to the poor."

10Aware of this, Jesus said to them, "Why are you bothering this woman? She has done a beautiful thing to me. 11The poor you will always have with you, but you will not always have me. 12When she poured this perfume on my body, she did it to prepare me for burial. 13I tell you the truth, wherever this gospel is preached throughout the world, what she has done will also be told, in memory of her."

Judas Agrees to Betray Jesus

14Then one of the Twelve—the one called Judas Iscariot—went to the chief priests 15and asked, "What are you willing to give me if I hand him over to you?" So they counted out for him thirty silver coins. 16From then on Judas watched for an opportunity to hand him over.

The Lord's Supper

17On the first day of the Feast of Unleavened Bread, the disciples came to Jesus and asked, "Where do you want us to make preparations for you to eat the Passover?"

18He replied, "Go into the city to a certain man and tell him, 'The Teacher says: My appointed time is near. I am going to celebrate the Passover with my disciples at your house.' " 19So the disciples did as Jesus had directed them and prepared the Passover.

20When evening came, Jesus was reclining at the table with the Twelve. 21And while they were eating, he said, "I tell you the truth, one of you will betray me."

22They were very sad and began to say to him one after the other, "Surely not I, Lord?"

23Jesus replied, "The one who has dipped his hand into the bowl with me will betray me. 24The Son of Man will go just as it is written about him. But woe to that man who betrays the Son of Man! It would be better for him if he had not been born."

25Then Judas, the one who would betray him, said, "Surely not I, Rabbi?"

Jesus answered, "Yes, it is you."[a]

26While they were eating, Jesus took bread, gave thanks and broke it, and gave it to his disciples, saying, "Take and eat; this is my body."

27Then he took the cup, gave thanks and offered it to them, saying, "Drink from it, all of you. 28This is my blood of the[b] covenant, which is poured out for many for the forgiveness of sins. 29I tell you, I will not drink of this fruit of the vine from now on until that day when I drink it anew with you in my Father's kingdom."

30When they had sung a hymn, they went out to the Mount of Olives.

---

a 25 Or *"You yourself have said it"*   b 28 Some manuscripts *the new*

Living Bible

26 WHEN JESUS had finished this talk with his disciples, he told them,

2"As you know, the Passover celebration begins in two days, and I[c] shall be betrayed and crucified."

3At that very moment the chief priests and other Jewish officials were meeting at the residence of Caiaphas the High Priest, 4to discuss ways of capturing Jesus quietly, and killing him. 5"But not during the Passover celebration," they agreed, "for there would be a riot."

6Jesus now proceeded to Bethany, to the home of Simon the leper. 7While he was eating, a woman came in with a bottle of very expensive perfume, and poured it over his head.

8, 9The disciples were indignant. "What a waste of good money," they said. "Why, she could have sold it for a fortune and given it to the poor."

10Jesus knew what they were thinking, and said, "Why are you criticizing her? For she has done a good thing to me. 11You will always have the poor among you, but you won't always have me. 12She has poured this perfume on me to prepare my body for burial. 13And she will always be remembered for this deed. The story of what she has done will be told throughout the whole world, wherever the Good News is preached."

14Then Judas Iscariot, one of the twelve apostles, went to the chief priests, 15and asked, "How much will you pay me to get Jesus into your hands?" And they gave him thirty silver coins. 16From that time on, Judas watched for an opportunity to betray Jesus to them.

17On the first day of the Passover ceremonies, when bread made with yeast was purged from every Jewish home, the disciples came to Jesus and asked, "Where shall we plan to eat the Passover?"

18He replied, "Go into the city and see Mr. So-and-So, and tell him, 'Our Master says, my time has come, and I will eat the Passover meal with my disciples at your house.' " 19So the disciples did as he told them, and prepared the supper there.

20, 21That evening as he sat eating with the Twelve, he said, "One of you will betray me."

22Sorrow chilled their hearts, and each one asked, "Am I the one?"

23He replied, "It is the one I served first.[d] 24For I must die[e] just as was prophesied, but woe to the man by whom I am betrayed. Far better for that one if he had never been born."

25Judas, too, had asked him, "Rabbi, am I the one?" And Jesus had told him, "Yes."

26As they were eating, Jesus took a small loaf of bread and blessed it and broke it apart and gave it to the disciples and said, "Take it and eat it, for this is my body."

27And he took a cup of wine and gave thanks for it and gave it to them and said, "Each one drink from it, 28for this is my blood, sealing the New Covenant. It is poured out to forgive the sins of multitudes. 29Mark my words—I will not drink this wine again until the day I drink it new with you in my Father's Kingdom."

30And when they had sung a hymn, they went out to the Mount of Olives.

New Revised Standard

The Plot to Kill Jesus

26 WHEN JESUS had finished saying all these things, he said to his disciples, 2"You know that after two days the Passover is coming, and the Son of Man will be handed over to be crucified."

3 Then the chief priests and the elders of the people gathered in the palace of the high priest, who was called Caiaphas, 4and they conspired to arrest Jesus by stealth and kill him. 5But they said, "Not during the festival, or there may be a riot among the people."

The Anointing at Bethany

6 Now while Jesus was at Bethany in the house of Simon the leper,[f] 7a woman came to him with an alabaster jar of very costly ointment, and she poured it on his head as he sat at the table. 8But when the disciples saw it, they were angry and said, "Why this waste? 9For this ointment could have been sold for a large sum, and the money given to the poor." 10But Jesus, aware of this, said to them, "Why do you trouble the woman? She has performed a good service for me. 11For you always have the poor with you, but you will not always have me. 12By pouring this ointment on my body she has prepared me for burial. 13Truly I tell you, wherever this good news[g] is proclaimed in the whole world, what she has done will be told in remembrance of her."

Judas Agrees to Betray Jesus

14 Then one of the twelve, who was called Judas Iscariot, went to the chief priests 15and said, "What will you give me if I betray him to you?" They paid him thirty pieces of silver. 16And from that moment he began to look for an opportunity to betray him.

The Passover with the Disciples

17 On the first day of Unleavened Bread the disciples came to Jesus, saying, "Where do you want us to make the preparations for you to eat the Passover?" 18He said, "Go into the city to a certain man, and say to him, 'The Teacher says, My time is near; I will keep the Passover at your house with my disciples.' " 19So the disciples did as Jesus had directed them, and they prepared the Passover meal.

20 When it was evening, he took his place with the twelve;[h] 21and while they were eating, he said, "Truly I tell you, one of you will betray me." 22And they became greatly distressed and began to say to him one after another, "Surely not I, Lord?" 23He answered, "The one who has dipped his hand into the bowl with me will betray me. 24The Son of Man goes as it is written of him, but woe to that one by whom the Son of Man is betrayed! It would have been better for that one not to have been born." 25Judas, who betrayed him, said, "Surely not I, Rabbi?" He replied, "You have said so."

The Institution of the Lord's Supper

26 While they were eating, Jesus took a loaf of bread, and after blessing it he broke it, gave it to the disciples, and said, "Take, eat; this is my body." 27Then he took a cup, and after giving thanks he gave it to them, saying, "Drink from it, all of you; 28for this is my blood of the[i] covenant, which is poured out for many for the forgiveness of sins. 29I tell you, I will never again drink of this fruit of the vine until that day when I drink it new with you in my Father's kingdom."

30 When they had sung the hymn, they went out to the Mount of Olives.

---

c 26:2 *I*, literally, "the Son of Man." d 26:23 *It is the one I served first*, literally, "he that dipped his hand with me in the dish." e 26:24 *For I must die*, literally, "the Son of Man goes."

f The terms *leper* and *leprosy* can refer to several diseases g Or *gospel* h Other ancient authorities add *disciples* i Other ancient authorities add *new*

King James

31Then saith Jesus unto them, All ye shall be offended because of me this night: for it is written, I will smite the shepherd, and the sheep of the flock shall be scattered abroad.

32But after I am risen again, I will go before you into Galilee.

33Peter answered and said unto him, Though all *men* shall be offended because of thee, *yet* will I never be offended.

34Jesus said unto him, Verily I say unto thee, That this night, before the cock crow, thou shalt deny me thrice.

35Peter said unto him, Though I should die with thee, yet will I not deny thee. Likewise also said all the disciples.

36¶ Then cometh Jesus with them unto a place called Gethsemane, and saith unto the disciples, Sit ye here, while I go and pray yonder.

37And he took with him Peter and the two sons of Zebedee, and began to be sorrowful and very heavy.

38Then saith he unto them, My soul is exceeding sorrowful, even unto death: tarry ye here, and watch with me.

39And he went a little farther, and fell on his face, and prayed, saying, O my Father, if it be possible, let this cup pass from me: nevertheless not as I will, but as thou *wilt*.

40And he cometh unto the disciples, and findeth them asleep, and saith unto Peter, What, could ye not watch with me one hour?

41Watch and pray, that ye enter not into temptation: the spirit indeed *is* willing, but the flesh *is* weak.

42He went away again the second time, and prayed, saying, O my Father, if this cup may not pass away from me, except I drink it, thy will be done.

43And he came and found them asleep again: for their eyes were heavy.

44And he left them, and went away again, and prayed the third time, saying the same words.

45Then cometh he to his disciples, and saith unto them, Sleep on now, and take *your* rest: behold, the hour is at hand, and the Son of man is betrayed into the hands of sinners.

46Rise, let us be going: behold, he is at hand that doth betray me.

47¶ And while he yet spake, lo, Judas, one of the twelve, came, and with him a great multitude with swords and staves, from the chief priests and elders of the people.

48Now he that betrayed him gave them a sign, saying, Whomsoever I shall kiss, that same is he: hold him fast.

49And forthwith he came to Jesus, and said, Hail, master; and kissed him.

50And Jesus said unto him, Friend, wherefore art thou come? Then came they, and laid hands on Jesus, and took him.

51And, behold, one of them which were with Jesus stretched out *his* hand, and drew his sword, and struck a servant of the high priest's, and smote off his ear.

52Then said Jesus unto him, Put up again thy sword into his place: for all they that take the sword shall perish with the sword.

53Thinkest thou that I cannot now pray to my Father, and he shall presently give me more than twelve legions of angels?

54But how then shall the scriptures be fulfilled, that thus it must be?

55In that same hour said Jesus to the multitudes, Are ye come out as against a thief with swords and staves for to take me? I sat daily with you teaching in the temple, and ye laid no hold on me.

56But all this was done, that the scriptures of the prophets might be fulfilled. Then all the disciples forsook him, and fled.

New International

Jesus Predicts Peter's Denial

31Then Jesus told them, "This very night you will all fall away on account of me, for it is written:

> " 'I will strike the shepherd,
> and the sheep of the flock will be scattered.'a

32But after I have risen, I will go ahead of you into Galilee."

33Peter replied, "Even if all fall away on account of you, I never will."

34"I tell you the truth," Jesus answered, "this very night, before the rooster crows, you will disown me three times."

35But Peter declared, "Even if I have to die with you, I will never disown you." And all the other disciples said the same.

Gethsemane

36Then Jesus went with his disciples to a place called Gethsemane, and he said to them, "Sit here while I go over there and pray." 37He took Peter and the two sons of Zebedee along with him, and he began to be sorrowful and troubled. 38Then he said to them, "My soul is overwhelmed with sorrow to the point of death. Stay here and keep watch with me."

39Going a little farther, he fell with his face to the ground and prayed, "My Father, if it is possible, may this cup be taken from me. Yet not as I will, but as you will."

40Then he returned to his disciples and found them sleeping. "Could you men not keep watch with me for one hour?" he asked Peter. 41"Watch and pray so that you will not fall into temptation. The spirit is willing, but the body is weak."

42He went away a second time and prayed, "My Father, if it is not possible for this cup to be taken away unless I drink it, may your will be done."

43When he came back, he again found them sleeping, because their eyes were heavy. 44So he left them and went away once more and prayed the third time, saying the same thing.

45Then he returned to the disciples and said to them, "Are you still sleeping and resting? Look, the hour is near, and the Son of Man is betrayed into the hands of sinners. 46Rise, let us go! Here comes my betrayer!"

Jesus Arrested

47While he was still speaking, Judas, one of the Twelve, arrived. With him was a large crowd armed with swords and clubs, sent from the chief priests and the elders of the people. 48Now the betrayer had arranged a signal with them: "The one I kiss is the man; arrest him." 49Going at once to Jesus, Judas said, "Greetings, Rabbi!" and kissed him.

50Jesus replied, "Friend, do what you came for."b

Then the men stepped forward, seized Jesus and arrested him. 51With that, one of Jesus' companions reached for his sword, drew it out and struck the servant of the high priest, cutting off his ear.

52"Put your sword back in its place," Jesus said to him, "for all who draw the sword will die by the sword. 53Do you think I cannot call on my Father, and he will at once put at my disposal more than twelve legions of angels? 54But how then would the Scriptures be fulfilled that say it must happen in this way?"

55At that time Jesus said to the crowd, "Am I leading a rebellion, that you have come out with swords and clubs to capture me? Every day I sat in the temple courts teaching, and you did not arrest me. 56But this has all taken place that the writings of the prophets might be fulfilled." Then all the disciples deserted him and fled.

---

a *31* Zech. 13:7   b *50* Or *"Friend, why have you come?"*

Living Bible

31Then Jesus said to them, "Tonight you will all desert me. For it is written in the Scriptures[c] that God will smite the Shepherd, and the sheep of the flock will be scattered. 32But after I have been brought back to life again I will go to Galilee, and meet you there."

33Peter declared, "If everyone else deserts you, I won't."

34Jesus told him, "The truth is that this very night, before the cock crows at dawn, you will deny me three times!"

35"I would die first!" Peter insisted. And all the other disciples said the same thing.

36Then Jesus brought them to a garden grove, Gethsemane, and told them to sit down and wait while he went on ahead to pray. 37He took Peter with him and Zebedee's two sons James and John, and began to be filled with anguish and despair.

38Then he told them, "My soul is crushed with horror and sadness to the point of death . . . stay here . . . stay awake with me."

39He went forward a little, and fell face downward on the ground, and prayed, "My Father! If it is possible, let this cup be taken away from me. But I want your will, not mine."

40Then he returned to the three disciples and found them asleep. "Peter," he called, "couldn't you even stay awake with me one hour? 41Keep alert and pray. Otherwise temptation will overpower you. For the spirit indeed is willing, but how weak the body is!"

42Again he left them and prayed, "My Father! If this cup cannot go away until I drink it all, your will be done."

43He returned to them again and found them sleeping, for their eyes were heavy, 44so he went back to prayer the third time, saying the same things again.

45Then he came and said, "Sleep on now and take your rest . . . but no! The time has come! I[d] am betrayed into the hands of evil men! 46Up! Let's be going! Look! Here comes the man who is betraying me!"

47At that very moment while he was still speaking, Judas, one of the Twelve, arrived with a great crowd armed with swords and clubs, sent by the Jewish leaders. 48Judas had told them to arrest the man he greeted, for that would be the one they were after. 49So now Judas came straight to Jesus and said, "Hello, Master!" and embraced[e] him in friendly fashion.

50Jesus said, "My friend, go ahead and do what you have come for." Then the others grabbed him.

51One of the men with Jesus pulled out a sword and slashed off the ear of the High Priest's servant.

52"Put away your sword," Jesus told him. "Those using swords will get killed. 53Don't you realize that I could ask my Father for thousands of angels to protect us, and he would send them instantly? 54But if I did, how would the Scriptures be fulfilled that describe what is happening now?" 55Then Jesus spoke to the crowd. "Am I some dangerous criminal," he asked, "that you had to arm yourselves with swords and clubs before you could arrest me? I was with you teaching daily in the Temple and you didn't stop me then. 56But this is all happening to fulfill the words of the prophets as recorded in the Scriptures."

At that point, all the disciples deserted him and fled.

New Revised Standard

Peter's Denial Foretold

31 Then Jesus said to them, "You will all become deserters because of me this night; for it is written,

'I will strike the shepherd,
    and the sheep of the flock will
        be scattered.'

32But after I am raised up, I will go ahead of you to Galilee." 33Peter said to him, "Though all become deserters because of you, I will never desert you." 34Jesus said to him, "Truly I tell you, this very night, before the cock crows, you will deny me three times." 35Peter said to him, "Even though I must die with you, I will not deny you." And so said all the disciples.

Jesus Prays in Gethsemane

36 Then Jesus went with them to a place called Gethsemane; and he said to his disciples, "Sit here while I go over there and pray." 37He took with him Peter and the two sons of Zebedee, and began to be grieved and agitated. 38Then he said to them, "I am deeply grieved, even to death; remain here, and stay awake with me." 39And going a little farther, he threw himself on the ground and prayed, "My Father, if it is possible, let this cup pass from me; yet not what I want but what you want." 40Then he came to the disciples and found them sleeping; and he said to Peter, "So, could you not stay awake with me one hour? 41Stay awake and pray that you may not come into the time of trial;[f] the spirit indeed is willing, but the flesh is weak." 42Again he went away for the second time and prayed, "My Father, if this cannot pass unless I drink it, your will be done." 43Again he came and found them sleeping, for their eyes were heavy. 44So leaving them again, he went away and prayed for the third time, saying the same words. 45Then he came to the disciples and said to them, "Are you still sleeping and taking your rest? See, the hour is at hand, and the Son of Man is betrayed into the hands of sinners. 46Get up, let us be going. See, my betrayer is at hand."

The Betrayal and Arrest of Jesus

47 While he was still speaking, Judas, one of the twelve, arrived; with him was a large crowd with swords and clubs, from the chief priests and the elders of the people. 48Now the betrayer had given them a sign, saying, "The one I will kiss is the man; arrest him." 49At once he came up to Jesus and said, "Greetings, Rabbi!" and kissed him. 50Jesus said to him, "Friend, do what you are here to do." Then they came and laid hands on Jesus and arrested him. 51Suddenly, one of those with Jesus put his hand on his sword, drew it, and struck the slave of the high priest, cutting off his ear. 52Then Jesus said to him, "Put your sword back into its place; for all who take the sword will perish by the sword. 53Do you think that I cannot appeal to my Father, and he will at once send me more than twelve legions of angels? 54But how then would the scriptures be fulfilled, which say it must happen in this way?" 55At that hour Jesus said to the crowds, "Have you come out with swords and clubs to arrest me as though I were a bandit? Day after day I sat in the temple teaching, and you did not arrest me. 56But all this has taken place, so that the scriptures of the prophets may be fulfilled." Then all the disciples deserted him and fled.

---

c 26:31 in the Scriptures, see Zech 13:7.   d 26:45 I, literally, "the Son of Man."   e 26:49 embraced, literally, "kissed," the greeting still used among men in Eastern lands.

f Or into temptation

King James

57¶ And they that had laid hold on Jesus led *him* away to Caiaphas the high priest, where the scribes and the elders were assembled.

58But Peter followed him afar off unto the high priest's palace, and went in, and sat with the servants, to see the end.

59Now the chief priests, and elders, and all the council, sought false witness against Jesus, to put him to death;

60But found none: yea, though many false witnesses came, *yet* found they none. At the last came two false witnesses,

61And said, This *fellow* said, I am able to destroy the temple of God, and to build it in three days.

62And the high priest arose, and said unto him, Answerest thou nothing? what *is it which* these witness against thee?

63But Jesus held his peace. And the high priest answered and said unto him, I adjure thee by the living God, that thou tell us whether thou be the Christ, the Son of God.

64Jesus saith unto him, Thou hast said: nevertheless I say unto you, Hereafter shall ye see the Son of man sitting on the right hand of power, and coming in the clouds of heaven.

65Then the high priest rent his clothes, saying, He hath spoken blasphemy; what further need have we of witnesses? behold, now ye have heard his blasphemy.

66What think ye? They answered and said, He is guilty of death.

67Then did they spit in his face, and buffeted him; and others smote *him* with the palms of their hands,

68Saying, Prophesy unto us, thou Christ, Who is he that smote thee?

69¶ Now Peter sat without in the palace: and a damsel came unto him, saying, Thou also wast with Jesus of Galilee.

70But he denied before *them* all, saying, I know not what thou sayest.

71And when he was gone out into the porch, another *maid* saw him, and said unto them that were there, This *fellow* was also with Jesus of Nazareth.

72And again he denied with an oath, I do not know the man.

73And after a while came unto *him* they that stood by, and said to Peter, Surely thou also art *one* of them; for thy speech betrayeth thee.

74Then began he to curse and to swear, *saying,* I know not the man. And immediately the cock crew.

75And Peter remembered the word of Jesus, which said unto him, Before the cock crow, thou shalt deny me thrice. And he went out, and wept bitterly.

27 WHEN THE morning was come, all the chief priests and elders of the people took counsel against Jesus to put him to death:

2And when they had bound him, they led *him* away, and delivered him to Pontius Pilate the governor.

3¶ Then Judas, which had betrayed him, when he saw that he was condemned, repented himself, and brought again the thirty pieces of silver to the chief priests and elders,

New International

Before the Sanhedrin

57Those who had arrested Jesus took him to Caiaphas, the high priest, where the teachers of the law and the elders had assembled. 58But Peter followed him at a distance, right up to the courtyard of the high priest. He entered and sat down with the guards to see the outcome.

59The chief priests and the whole Sanhedrin were looking for false evidence against Jesus so that they could put him to death. 60But they did not find any, though many false witnesses came forward.

Finally two came forward 61and declared, "This fellow said, 'I am able to destroy the temple of God and rebuild it in three days.' "

62Then the high priest stood up and said to Jesus, "Are you not going to answer? What is this testimony that these men are bringing against you?" 63But Jesus remained silent.

The high priest said to him, "I charge you under oath by the living God: Tell us if you are the Christ,[a] the Son of God."

64"Yes, it is as you say," Jesus replied. "But I say to all of you: In the future you will see the Son of Man sitting at the right hand of the Mighty One and coming on the clouds of heaven."

65Then the high priest tore his clothes and said, "He has spoken blasphemy! Why do we need any more witnesses? Look, now you have heard the blasphemy. 66What do you think?"

"He is worthy of death," they answered.

67Then they spit in his face and struck him with their fists. Others slapped him 68and said, "Prophesy to us, Christ. Who hit you?"

Peter Disowns Jesus

69Now Peter was sitting out in the courtyard, and a servant girl came to him. "You also were with Jesus of Galilee," she said.

70But he denied it before them all. "I don't know what you're talking about," he said.

71Then he went out to the gateway, where another girl saw him and said to the people there, "This fellow was with Jesus of Nazareth."

72He denied it again, with an oath: "I don't know the man!"

73After a little while, those standing there went up to Peter and said, "Surely you are one of them, for your accent gives you away."

74Then he began to call down curses on himself and he swore to them, "I don't know the man!"

Immediately a rooster crowed. 75Then Peter remembered the word Jesus had spoken: "Before the rooster crows, you will disown me three times." And he went outside and wept bitterly.

Judas Hangs Himself

27 EARLY IN the morning, all the chief priests and the elders of the people came to the decision to put Jesus to death. 2They bound him, led him away and handed him over to Pilate, the governor.

3When Judas, who had betrayed him, saw that Jesus was condemned, he was seized with remorse and returned the thirty silver coins to the chief priests and the

---

Living Bible

57Then the mob led him to the home of Caiaphas the High Priest, where all the Jewish leaders were gathering. 58Meanwhile, Peter was following far to the rear, and came to the courtyard of the High Priest's house and went in and sat with the soldiers, and waited to see what was going to be done to Jesus.

59The chief priests and, in fact, the entire Jewish Supreme Court assembled there and looked for witnesses who would lie about Jesus, in order to build a case against him that would result in a death sentence. 60, 61But even though they found many who agreed to be false witnesses, these always contradicted each other.

Finally two men were found who declared, "This man said, 'I am able to destroy the Temple of God and rebuild it in three days.' "

62Then the High Priest stood up and said to Jesus, "Well, what about it? Did you say that, or didn't you?" 63But Jesus remained silent.

Then the High Priest said to him, "I demand in the name of the living God that you tell us whether you claim to be the Messiah, the Son of God."

64"Yes," Jesus said, "I am. And in the future you will see me, the Messiah,b sitting at the right hand of God and returning on the clouds of heaven."

65, 66Then the High Priest tore at his own clothing, shouting, "Blasphemy! What need have we for other witnesses? You have all heard him say it! What is your verdict?"

They shouted, "Death!—Death!—Death!"

67Then they spat in his face and struck him and some slapped him, 68saying, "Prophesy to us, you Messiah! Who struck you that time?"

69Meanwhile, as Peter was sitting in the courtyard a girl came over and said to him, "You were with Jesus, for both of you are from Galilee."c

70But Peter denied it loudly. "I don't even know what you are talking about," he angrily declared.

71Later, out by the gate, another girl noticed him and said to those standing around, "This man was with Jesus—from Nazareth."

72Again Peter denied it, this time with an oath. "I don't even know the man," he said.

73But after a while the men who had been standing there came over to him and said, "We know you are one of his disciples, for we can tell by your Galileand accent."

74Peter began to curse and swear. "I don't even know the man," he said.

And immediately the cock crowed. 75Then Peter remembered what Jesus had said, "Before the cock crows, you will deny me three times." And he went away, crying bitterly.

27 WHEN IT was morning, the chief priests and Jewish leaders met again to discuss how to induce the Roman government to sentence Jesus to death.e 2Then they sent him in chains to Pilate, the Roman governor.

3About that time Judas, who betrayed him, when he saw that Jesus had been condemned to die, changed his mind and deeply regretted what he had done,f and brought back the money to the chief priests and other Jewish leaders.

New Revised Standard

Jesus before the High Priest

57 Those who had arrested Jesus took him to Caiaphas the high priest, in whose house the scribes and the elders had gathered. 58But Peter was following him at a distance, as far as the courtyard of the high priest; and going inside, he sat with the guards in order to see how this would end. 59Now the chief priests and the whole council were looking for false testimony against Jesus so that they might put him to death, 60but they found none, though many false witnesses came forward. At last two came forward 61and said, "This fellow said, 'I am able to destroy the temple of God and to build it in three days.' " 62The high priest stood up and said, "Have you no answer? What is it that they testify against you?" 63But Jesus was silent. Then the high priest said to him, "I put you under oath before the living God, tell us if you are the Messiah,g the Son of God." 64Jesus said to him, "You have said so. But I tell you,

From now on you will see the Son of Man
　seated at the right hand of Power
　and coming on the clouds of heaven."

65Then the high priest tore his clothes and said, "He has blasphemed! Why do we still need witnesses? You have now heard his blasphemy. 66What is your verdict?" They answered, "He deserves death." 67Then they spat in his face and struck him; and some slapped him, 68saying, "Prophesy to us, you Messiah!g Who is it that struck you?"

Peter's Denial of Jesus

69 Now Peter was sitting outside in the courtyard. A servant-girl came to him and said, "You also were with Jesus the Galilean." 70But he denied it before all of them, saying, "I do not know what you are talking about." 71When he went out to the porch, another servant-girl saw him, and she said to the bystanders, "This man was with Jesus of Nazareth."h 72Again he denied it with an oath, "I do not know the man." 73After a little while the bystanders came up and said to Peter, "Certainly you are also one of them, for your accent betrays you." 74Then he began to curse, and he swore an oath, "I do not know the man!" At that moment the cock crowed. 75Then Peter remembered what Jesus had said: "Before the cock crows, you will deny me three times." And he went out and wept bitterly.

Jesus Brought before Pilate

27 WHEN MORNING came, all the chief priests and the elders of the people conferred together against Jesus in order to bring about his death. 2They bound him, led him away, and handed him over to Pilate the governor.

The Suicide of Judas

3 When Judas, his betrayer, saw that Jesusi was condemned, he repented and brought back the thirty pieces of silver to the chief priests and the elders. 4He

---

b 26:64 the Messiah, literally, "the Son of Man." c 26:69 from Galilee, literally, "with Jesus the Galilean." d 26:73 Galilean, implied. e 27:1 to sentence Jesus to death, literally, "took counsel against Jesus to put him to death." They did not have the authority themselves. f 27:3 regretted what he had done, literally, "repented himself."

g Or Christ　h Gk the Nazorean　i Gk he

King James

4Saying, I have sinned in that I have betrayed the innocent blood. And they said, What *is that* to us? see thou *to that*.

5And he cast down the pieces of silver in the temple, and departed, and went and hanged himself.

6And the chief priests took the silver pieces, and said, It is not lawful for to put them into the treasury, because it is the price of blood.

7And they took counsel, and bought with them the potter's field, to bury strangers in.

8Wherefore that field was called, The field of blood, unto this day.

9Then was fulfilled that which was spoken by Jeremy the prophet, saying, And they took the thirty pieces of silver, the price of him that was valued, whom they of the children of Israel did value;

10And gave them for the potter's field, as the Lord appointed me.

11And Jesus stood before the governor: and the governor asked him, saying, Art thou the King of the Jews? And Jesus said unto him, Thou sayest.

12And when he was accused of the chief priests and elders, he answered nothing.

13Then said Pilate unto him, Hearest thou not how many things they witness against thee?

14And he answered him to never a word; insomuch that the governor marvelled greatly.

15Now at *that* feast the governor was wont to release unto the people a prisoner, whom they would.

16And they had then a notable prisoner, called Barabbas.

17Therefore when they were gathered together, Pilate said unto them, Whom will ye that I release unto you? Barabbas, or Jesus which is called Christ?

18For he knew that for envy they had delivered him.

19¶ When he was set down on the judgment seat, his wife sent unto him, saying, Have thou nothing to do with that just man: for I have suffered many things this day in a dream because of him.

20But the chief priests and elders persuaded the multitude that they should ask Barabbas, and destroy Jesus.

21The governor answered and said unto them, Whether of the twain will ye that I release unto you? They said, Barabbas.

22Pilate saith unto them, What shall I do then with Jesus which is called Christ? *They* all say unto him, Let him be crucified.

23And the governor said, Why, what evil hath he done? But they cried out the more, saying, Let him be crucified.

24¶ When Pilate saw that he could prevail nothing, but *that* rather a tumult was made, he took water, and washed *his* hands before the multitude, saying, I am innocent of the blood of this just person: see ye *to it*.

25Then answered all the people, and said, His blood *be* on us, and on our children.

26¶ Then released he Barabbas unto them: and when he had scourged Jesus, he delivered *him* to be crucified.

27Then the soldiers of the governor took Jesus into the common hall, and gathered unto him the whole band *of soldiers*.

28And they stripped him, and put on him a scarlet robe.

29¶ And when they had plaited a crown of thorns, they put *it* upon his head, and a reed in his right hand: and they bowed the knee before him, and mocked him, saying, Hail, King of the Jews!

30And they spit upon him, and took the reed, and smote him on the head.

New International

elders. 4"I have sinned," he said, "for I have betrayed innocent blood."

"What is that to us?" they replied. "That's your responsibility."

5So Judas threw the money into the temple and left. Then he went away and hanged himself.

6The chief priests picked up the coins and said, "It is against the law to put this into the treasury, since it is blood money." 7So they decided to use the money to buy the potter's field as a burial place for foreigners. 8That is why it has been called the Field of Blood to this day. 9Then what was spoken by Jeremiah the prophet was fulfilled: "They took the thirty silver coins, the price set on him by the people of Israel, 10and they used them to buy the potter's field, as the Lord commanded me."[a]

Jesus Before Pilate

11Meanwhile Jesus stood before the governor, and the governor asked him, "Are you the king of the Jews?"

"Yes, it is as you say," Jesus replied.

12When he was accused by the chief priests and the elders, he gave no answer. 13Then Pilate asked him, "Don't you hear the testimony they are bringing against you?" 14But Jesus made no reply, not even to a single charge—to the great amazement of the governor.

15Now it was the governor's custom at the Feast to release a prisoner chosen by the crowd. 16At that time they had a notorious prisoner, called Barabbas. 17So when the crowd had gathered, Pilate asked them, "Which one do you want me to release to you: Barabbas, or Jesus who is called Christ?" 18For he knew it was out of envy that they had handed Jesus over to him.

19While Pilate was sitting on the judge's seat, his wife sent him this message: "Don't have anything to do with that innocent man, for I have suffered a great deal today in a dream because of him."

20But the chief priests and the elders persuaded the crowd to ask for Barabbas and to have Jesus executed.

21"Which of the two do you want me to release to you?" asked the governor.

"Barabbas," they answered.

22"What shall I do, then, with Jesus who is called Christ?" Pilate asked.

They all answered, "Crucify him!"

23"Why? What crime has he committed?" asked Pilate.

But they shouted all the louder, "Crucify him!"

24When Pilate saw that he was getting nowhere, but that instead an uproar was starting, he took water and washed his hands in front of the crowd. "I am innocent of this man's blood," he said. "It is your responsibility!"

25All the people answered, "Let his blood be on us and on our children!"

26Then he released Barabbas to them. But he had Jesus flogged, and handed him over to be crucified.

The Soldiers Mock Jesus

27Then the governor's soldiers took Jesus into the Praetorium and gathered the whole company of soldiers around him. 28They stripped him and put a scarlet robe on him, 29and then twisted together a crown of thorns and set it on his head. They put a staff in his right hand and knelt in front of him and mocked him. "Hail, king of the Jews!" they said. 30They spit on him, and took the staff and struck him on the head again and again. 31After

---

a *10* See Zech. 11:12,13; Jer. 19:1-13; 32:6-9.

Living Bible

4"I have sinned," he declared, "for I have betrayed an innocent man."

"That's your problem," they retorted.

5Then he threw the money onto the floor of the Temple and went out and hanged himself. 6The chief priests picked the money up. "We can't put it in the collection," they said, "since it's against our laws to accept money paid for murder."

7They talked it over and finally decided to buy a certain field where the clay was used by potters, and to make it into a cemetery for foreigners who died in Jerusalem. 8That is why the cemetery is still called "The Field of Blood."

9This fulfilled the prophecy of Jeremiah which says,
"They took the thirty pieces of silver—the price at which he was valued by the people of Israel— 10and purchased a field from the potters as the Lord directed me."

11Now Jesus was standing before Pilate, the Roman governor. "Are you the Jews' Messiah?"b the governor asked him.

"Yes," Jesus replied.

12But when the chief priests and other Jewish leaders made their many accusations against him, Jesus remained silent.

13"Don't you hear what they are saying?" Pilate demanded.

14But Jesus said nothing, much to the governor's surprise.

15Now the governor's custom was to release one Jewish prisoner each year during the Passover celebration—anyone they wanted. 16This year there was a particularly notorious criminal in jail named Barabbas, 17and as the crowds gathered before Pilate's house that morning he asked them, "Which shall I release to you—Barabbas, or Jesus your Messiah?"c 18For he knew very well that the Jewish leaders had arrested Jesus out of envy because of his popularity with the people.

19Just then, as he was presiding over the court, Pilate's wife sent him this message: "Leave that good man alone; for I had a terrible nightmare concerning him last night."

20Meanwhile the chief priests and Jewish officials persuaded the crowds to ask for Barabbas' release, and for Jesus' death. 21So when the governor asked again,d "Which of these two shall I release to you?" the crowd shouted back their reply: "Barabbas!"

22"Then what shall I do with Jesus, your Messiah?" Pilate asked.

And they shouted, "Crucify him!"

23"Why?" Pilate demanded. "What has he done wrong?" But they kept shouting, "Crucify! Crucify!"

24When Pilate saw that he wasn't getting anywhere, and that a riot was developing, he sent for a bowl of water and washed his hands before the crowd, saying, "I am innocent of the blood of this good man. The responsibility is yours!"

25And the mob yelled back, "His blood be on us and on our children!"

26Then Pilate released Barabbas to them. And after he had whipped Jesus, he gave him to the Roman soldiers to take away and crucify.

27But first they took him into the armory and called out the entire contingent. 28They stripped him and put a scarlet robe on him, 29and made a crown from long thorns and put it on his head, and placed a stick in his right hand as a scepter and knelt before him in mockery. "Hail, King of the Jews," they yelled. 30And they spat on him and grabbed the stick and beat him on the head with it.

New Revised Standard

said, "I have sinned by betraying innocente blood." But they said, "What is that to us? See to it yourself." 5Throwing down the pieces of silver in the temple, he departed; and he went and hanged himself. 6But the chief priests, taking the pieces of silver, said, "It is not lawful to put them into the treasury, since they are blood money." 7After conferring together, they used them to buy the potter's field as a place to bury foreigners. 8For this reason that field has been called the Field of Blood to this day. 9Then was fulfilled what had been spoken through the prophet Jeremiah,f "And they tookg the thirty pieces of silver, the price of the one on whom a price had been set,h on whom some of the people of Israel had set a price, 10and they gavei them for the potter's field, as the Lord commanded me."

Pilate Questions Jesus

11 Now Jesus stood before the governor; and the governor asked him, "Are you the King of the Jews?" Jesus said, "You say so." 12But when he was accused by the chief priests and elders, he did not answer. 13Then Pilate said to him, "Do you not hear how many accusations they make against you?" 14But he gave him no answer, not even to a single charge, so that the governor was greatly amazed.

Barabbas or Jesus?

15 Now at the festival the governor was accustomed to release a prisoner for the crowd, anyone whom they wanted. 16At that time they had a notorious prisoner, called Jesusj Barabbas. 17So after they had gathered, Pilate said to them, "Whom do you want me to release for you, Jesusj Barabbas or Jesus who is called the Messiah?"k 18For he realized that it was out of jealousy that they had handed him over. 19While he was sitting on the judgment seat, his wife sent word to him, "Have nothing to do with that innocent man, for today I have suffered a great deal because of a dream about him." 20Now the chief priests and the elders persuaded the crowds to ask for Barabbas and to have Jesus killed. 21The governor again said to them, "Which of the two do you want me to release for you?" And they said, "Barabbas." 22Pilate said to them, "Then what should I do with Jesus who is called the Messiah?"k All of them said, "Let him be crucified!" 23Then he asked, "Why, what evil has he done?" But they shouted all the more, "Let him be crucified!"

Pilate Hands Jesus over to Be Crucified

24 So when Pilate saw that he could do nothing, but rather that a riot was beginning, he took some water and washed his hands before the crowd, saying, "I am innocent of this man's blood;l see to it yourselves." 25Then the people as a whole answered, "His blood be on us and on our children!" 26So he released Barabbas for them; and after flogging Jesus, he handed him over to be crucified.

The Soldiers Mock Jesus

27 Then the soldiers of the governor took Jesus into the governor's headquarters,m and they gathered the whole cohort around him. 28They stripped him and put a scarlet robe on him, 29and after twisting some thorns into a crown, they put it on his head. They put a reed in his right hand and knelt before him and mocked him, saying, "Hail, King of the Jews!" 30They spat on him, and took the reed and struck him on the head. 31After

---

b 27:11 the Jews' Messiah, literally, " 'King' of the Jews."   c 27:17 Jesus your Messiah, literally, "Jesus who is called Christ."   d 27:21 when the governor asked again, implied.

e Other ancient authorities read righteous   f Other ancient authorities read Zechariah or Isaiah   g Or I took   h Or the price of the precious One   i Other ancient authorities read I gave   j Other ancient authorities lack Jesus   k Or the Christ   l Other ancient authorities read this righteous blood, or this righteous man's blood   m Gk the praetorium

King James

31And after that they had mocked him, they took the robe off from him, and put his own raiment on him, and led him away to crucify *him*.

32And as they came out, they found a man of Cyrene, Simon by name: him they compelled to bear his cross.

33And when they were come unto a place called Golgotha, that is to say, a place of a skull,

34¶ They gave him vinegar to drink mingled with gall: and when he had tasted *thereof*, he would not drink.

35And they crucified him, and parted his garments, casting lots: that it might be fulfilled which was spoken by the prophet, They parted my garments among them, and upon my vesture did they cast lots.

36And sitting down they watched him there;

37And set up over his head his accusation written, THIS IS JESUS THE KING OF THE JEWS.

38Then were there two thieves crucified with him, one on the right hand, and another on the left.

39¶ And they that passed by reviled him, wagging their heads,

40And saying, Thou that destroyest the temple, and buildest *it* in three days, save thyself. If thou be the Son of God, come down from the cross.

41Likewise also the chief priests mocking *him*, with the scribes and elders, said,

42He saved others; himself he cannot save. If he be the King of Israel, let him now come down from the cross, and we will believe him.

43He trusted in God; let him deliver him now, if he will have him: for he said, I am the Son of God.

44The thieves also, which were crucified with him, cast the same in his teeth.

45Now from the sixth hour there was darkness over all the land unto the ninth hour.

46And about the ninth hour Jesus cried with a loud voice, saying, Eli, Eli, lama sabachthani? that is to say, My God, my God, why hast thou forsaken me?

47Some of them that stood there, when they heard *that*, said, This *man* calleth for Elias.

48And straightway one of them ran, and took a sponge, and filled *it* with vinegar, and put *it* on a reed, and gave him to drink.

49The rest said, Let be, let us see whether Elias will come to save him.

50¶ Jesus, when he had cried again with a loud voice, yielded up the ghost.

51And, behold, the veil of the temple was rent in twain from the top to the bottom; and the earth did quake, and the rocks rent;

52And the graves were opened; and many bodies of the saints which slept arose,

53And came out of the graves after his resurrection, and went into the holy city, and appeared unto many.

54Now when the centurion, and they that were with him, watching Jesus, saw the earthquake, and those things that were done, they feared greatly, saying, Truly this was the Son of God.

55And many women were there beholding afar off, which followed Jesus from Galilee, ministering unto him:

56Among which was Mary Magdalene, and Mary the mother of James and Joses, and the mother of Zebedee's children.

57When the even was come, there came a rich man of Arimathaea, named Joseph, who also himself was Jesus' disciple:

58He went to Pilate, and begged the body of Jesus. Then Pilate commanded the body to be delivered.

59And when Joseph had taken the body, he wrapped it in a clean linen cloth,

60And laid it in his own new tomb, which he had hewn out in the rock: and he rolled a great stone to the door of the sepulchre, and departed.

61And there was Mary Magdalene, and the other Mary, sitting over against the sepulchre.

New International

they had mocked him, they took off the robe and put his own clothes on him. Then they led him away to crucify him.

The Crucifixion

32As they were going out, they met a man from Cyrene, named Simon, and they forced him to carry the cross. 33They came to a place called Golgotha (which means The Place of the Skull). 34There they offered Jesus wine to drink, mixed with gall; but after tasting it, he refused to drink it. 35When they had crucified him, they divided up his clothes by casting lots.[a] 36And sitting down, they kept watch over him there. 37Above his head they placed the written charge against him: THIS IS JESUS, THE KING OF THE JEWS. 38Two robbers were crucified with him, one on his right and one on his left. 39Those who passed by hurled insults at him, shaking their heads 40and saying, "You who are going to destroy the temple and build it in three days, save yourself! Come down from the cross, if you are the Son of God!" 41In the same way the chief priests, the teachers of the law and the elders mocked him. 42"He saved others," they said, "but he can't save himself! He's the King of Israel! Let him come down now from the cross, and we will believe in him. 43He trusts in God. Let God rescue him now if he wants him, for he said, 'I am the Son of God.' " 44In the same way the robbers who were crucified with him also heaped insults on him.

The Death of Jesus

45From the sixth hour until the ninth hour darkness came over all the land. 46About the ninth hour Jesus cried out in a loud voice, *"Eloi, Eloi,[b] lama sabachthani?"* —which means, "My God, my God, why have you forsaken me?"[c] 47When some of those standing there heard this, they said, "He's calling Elijah." 48Immediately one of them ran and got a sponge. He filled it with wine vinegar, put it on a stick, and offered it to Jesus to drink. 49The rest said, "Now leave him alone. Let's see if Elijah comes to save him." 50And when Jesus had cried out again in a loud voice, he gave up his spirit.

51At that moment the curtain of the temple was torn in two from top to bottom. The earth shook and the rocks split. 52The tombs broke open and the bodies of many holy people who had died were raised to life. 53They came out of the tombs, and after Jesus' resurrection they went into the holy city and appeared to many people.

54When the centurion and those with him who were guarding Jesus saw the earthquake and all that had happened, they were terrified, and exclaimed, "Surely he was the Son[d] of God!"

55Many women were there, watching from a distance. They had followed Jesus from Galilee to care for his needs. 56Among them were Mary Magdalene, Mary the mother of James and Joses, and the mother of Zebedee's sons.

The Burial of Jesus

57As evening approached, there came a rich man from Arimathea, named Joseph, who had himself become a disciple of Jesus. 58Going to Pilate, he asked for Jesus' body, and Pilate ordered that it be given to him. 59Joseph took the body, wrapped it in a clean linen cloth, 60and placed it in his own new tomb that he had cut out of the rock. He rolled a big stone in front of the entrance to the tomb and went away. 61Mary Magdalene and the other Mary were sitting there opposite the tomb.

---

a 35 A few late manuscripts *lots that the word spoken by the prophet might be fulfilled: "They divided my garments among themselves and cast lots for my clothing"* (Psalm 22:18)　　b 46 Some manuscripts *Eli, Eli*　　c 46 Psalm 22:1　　d 54 Or *a son*

Living Bible

31After the mockery, they took off the robe and put his own garment on him again, and took him out to crucify him.

32As they were on the way to the execution grounds they came across a man from Cyrene, in Africa—Simon was his name—and forced him to carry Jesus' cross. 33Then they went out to an area known as Golgotha, that is, "Skull Hill," 34where the soldiers gave him drugged wine to drink; but when he had tasted it, he refused.

35After the crucifixion, the soldiers threw dice to divide up his clothes among themselves. 36Then they sat around and watched him as he hung there. 37And they put a sign above his head, "This is Jesus, the King of the Jews."

38Two robbers were also crucified there that morning, one on either side of him. 39And the people passing by hurled abuse, shaking their heads at him and saying, 40"So! You can destroy the Temple and build it again in three days, can you? Well, then, come on down from the cross if you are the Son of God!"

41, 42, 43And the chief priests and Jewish leaders also mocked him. "He saved others," they scoffed, "but he can't save himself! So you are the King of Israel, are you? Come down from the cross and we'll believe you! He trusted God—let God show his approval by delivering him! Didn't he say, 'I am God's Son'?"

44And the robbers also threw the same in his teeth.

45That afternoon, the whole earthe was covered with darkness for three hours, from noon until three o'clock.

46About three o'clock, Jesus shouted, "Eli, Eli, lama sabachthani?" which means, "My God, my God, why have you forsaken me?"

47Some of the bystanders misunderstood and thought he was calling for Elijah. 48One of them ran and filled a sponge with sour wine and put it on a stick and held it up to him to drink. 49But the rest said, "Leave him alone. Let's see whether Elijah will come and save him."

50Then Jesus shouted out again, dismissed his spirit, and died.

51And look! The curtain secluding the Holiest Placef in the Temple was split apart from top to bottom; and the earth shook, and rocks broke, 52and tombs opened, and many godly men and women who had died came back to life again. 53After Jesus' resurrection, they left the cemetery and went into Jerusalem, and appeared to many people there.

54The soldiers at the crucifixion and their sergeant were terribly frightened by the earthquake and all that happened. They exclaimed, "Surely this was God's Son."g

55And many women who had come down from Galilee with Jesus to care for him were watching from a distance. 56Among them were Mary Magdalene and Mary the mother of James and Joseph, and the mother of James and John (the sons of Zebedee).

57When evening came, a rich man from Arimathea named Joseph, one of Jesus' followers, 58went to Pilate and asked for Jesus' body. And Pilate issued an order to release it to him. 59Joseph took the body and wrapped it in a clean linen cloth, 60and placed it in his own new rock-hewn tomb, and rolled a great stone across the entrance as he left. 61Both Mary Magdalene and the other Mary were sitting nearby watching.

New Revised Standard

mocking him, they stripped him of the robe and put his own clothes on him. Then they led him away to crucify him.

The Crucifixion of Jesus

32 As they went out, they came upon a man from Cyrene named Simon; they compelled this man to carry his cross. 33 And when they came to a place called Golgotha (which means Place of a Skull), 34 they offered him wine to drink, mixed with gall; but when he tasted it, he would not drink it. 35 And when they had crucified him, they divided his clothes among themselves by casting lots;h 36 then they sat down there and kept watch over him. 37 Over his head they put the charge against him, which read, "This is Jesus, the King of the Jews."

38 Then two bandits were crucified with him, one on his right and one on his left. 39 Those who passed by deridedi him, shaking their heads 40 and saying, "You who would destroy the temple and build it in three days, save yourself! If you are the Son of God, come down from the cross." 41 In the same way the chief priests also, along with the scribes and elders, were mocking him, saying, 42 "He saved others; he cannot save himself.j He is the King of Israel; let him come down from the cross now, and we will believe in him. 43 He trusts in God; let God deliver him now, if he wants to; for he said, 'I am God's Son.' " 44 The bandits who were crucified with him also taunted him in the same way.

The Death of Jesus

45 From noon on, darkness came over the whole landk until three in the afternoon. 46 And about three o'clock Jesus cried with a loud voice, "Eli, Eli, lema sabachthani?" that is, "My God, my God, why have you forsaken me?" 47 When some of the bystanders heard it, they said, "This man is calling for Elijah." 48 At once one of them ran and got a sponge, filled it with sour wine, put it on a stick, and gave it to him to drink. 49 But the others said, "Wait, let us see whether Elijah will come to save him."l 50 Then Jesus cried again with a loud voice and breathed his last.m 51 At that moment the curtain of the temple was torn in two, from top to bottom. The earth shook, and the rocks were split. 52 The tombs also were opened, and many bodies of the saints who had fallen asleep were raised. 53 After his resurrection they came out of the tombs and entered the holy city and appeared to many. 54 Now when the centurion and those with him, who were keeping watch over Jesus, saw the earthquake and what took place, they were terrified and said, "Truly this man was God's Son!"n

55 Many women were also there, looking on from a distance; they had followed Jesus from Galilee and had provided for him. 56 Among them were Mary Magdalene, and Mary the mother of James and Joseph, and the mother of the sons of Zebedee.

The Burial of Jesus

57 When it was evening, there came a rich man from Arimathea, named Joseph, who was also a disciple of Jesus. 58 He went to Pilate and asked for the body of Jesus; then Pilate ordered it to be given to him. 59 So Joseph took the body and wrapped it in a clean linen cloth 60 and laid it in his own new tomb, which he had hewn in the rock. He then rolled a great stone to the door of the tomb and went away. 61 Mary Magdalene and the other Mary were there, sitting opposite the tomb.

---

h Other ancient authorities add *in order that what had been spoken through the prophet might be fulfilled, "They divided my clothes among themselves, and for my clothing they cast lots."*   i Or *blasphemed*   j Or *is he unable to save himself?*   k Or *earth*   l Other ancient authorities add *And another took a spear and pierced his side, and out came water and blood*   m Or *gave up his spirit*   n Or *a son of God*

---

e 27:45 *earth,* or "land."   f 27:51 *secluding the Holiest Place,* implied.
g 27:54 *God's Son,* or, "a godly man."

King James

62¶ Now the next day, that followed the day of the preparation, the chief priests and Pharisees came together unto Pilate,

63Saying, Sir, we remember that that deceiver said, while he was yet alive, After three days I will rise again.

64Command therefore that the sepulchre be made sure until the third day, lest his disciples come by night, and steal him away, and say unto the people, He is risen from the dead: so the last error shall be worse than the first.

65Pilate said unto them, Ye have a watch: go your way, make *it* as sure as ye can.

66So they went, and made the sepulchre sure, sealing the stone, and setting a watch.

28 IN THE end of the sabbath, as it began to dawn toward the first *day* of the week, came Mary Magdalene and the other Mary to see the sepulchre.

2And, behold, there was a great earthquake: for the angel of the Lord descended from heaven, and came and rolled back the stone from the door, and sat upon it.

3His countenance was like lightning, and his raiment white as snow:

4And for fear of him the keepers did shake, and became as dead *men*.

5And the angel answered and said unto the women, Fear not ye: for I know that ye seek Jesus, which was crucified.

6He is not here: for he is risen, as he said. Come, see the place where the Lord lay.

7And go quickly, and tell his disciples that he is risen from the dead; and, behold, he goeth before you into Galilee; there shall ye see him: lo, I have told you.

8And they departed quickly from the sepulchre with fear and great joy; and did run to bring his disciples word.

9¶ And as they went to tell his disciples, behold, Jesus met them, saying, All hail. And they came and held him by the feet, and worshipped him.

10Then said Jesus unto them, Be not afraid: go tell my brethren that they go into Galilee, and there shall they see me.

11¶ Now when they were going, behold, some of the watch came into the city, and showed unto the chief priests all the things that were done.

12And when they were assembled with the elders, and had taken counsel, they gave large money unto the soldiers,

13Saying, Say ye, His disciples came by night, and stole him *away* while we slept.

14And if this come to the governor's ears, we will persuade him, and secure you.

15So they took the money, and did as they were taught: and this saying is commonly reported among the Jews until this day.

16¶ Then the eleven disciples went away into Galilee, into a mountain where Jesus had appointed them.

17And when they saw him, they worshipped him: but some doubted.

18And Jesus came and spake unto them, saying, All power is given unto me in heaven and in earth.

19¶ Go ye therefore, and teach all nations, baptizing them in the name of the Father, and of the Son, and of the Holy Ghost:

20Teaching them to observe all things whatsoever I have commanded you: and, lo, I am with you always, *even* unto the end of the world. Amen.

New International

The Guard at the Tomb

62The next day, the one after Preparation Day, the chief priests and the Pharisees went to Pilate. 63"Sir," they said, "we remember that while he was still alive that deceiver said, 'After three days I will rise again.' 64So give the order for the tomb to be made secure until the third day. Otherwise, his disciples may come and steal the body and tell the people that he has been raised from the dead. This last deception will be worse than the first."

65"Take a guard," Pilate answered. "Go, make the tomb as secure as you know how." 66So they went and made the tomb secure by putting a seal on the stone and posting the guard.

The Resurrection

28 AFTER THE Sabbath, at dawn on the first day of the week, Mary Magdalene and the other Mary went to look at the tomb.

2There was a violent earthquake, for an angel of the Lord came down from heaven and, going to the tomb, rolled back the stone and sat on it. 3His appearance was like lightning, and his clothes were white as snow. 4The guards were so afraid of him that they shook and became like dead men.

5The angel said to the women, "Do not be afraid, for I know that you are looking for Jesus, who was crucified. 6He is not here; he has risen, just as he said. Come and see the place where he lay. 7Then go quickly and tell his disciples: 'He has risen from the dead and is going ahead of you into Galilee. There you will see him.' Now I have told you."

8So the women hurried away from the tomb, afraid yet filled with joy, and ran to tell his disciples. 9Suddenly Jesus met them. "Greetings," he said. They came to him, clasped his feet and worshiped him. 10Then Jesus said to them, "Do not be afraid. Go and tell my brothers to go to Galilee; there they will see me."

The Guards' Report

11While the women were on their way, some of the guards went into the city and reported to the chief priests everything that had happened. 12When the chief priests had met with the elders and devised a plan, they gave the soldiers a large sum of money, 13telling them, "You are to say, 'His disciples came during the night and stole him away while we were asleep.' 14If this report gets to the governor, we will satisfy him and keep you out of trouble." 15So the soldiers took the money and did as they were instructed. And this story has been widely circulated among the Jews to this very day.

The Great Commission

16Then the eleven disciples went to Galilee, to the mountain where Jesus had told them to go. 17When they saw him, they worshiped him; but some doubted. 18Then Jesus came to them and said, "All authority in heaven and on earth has been given to me. 19Therefore go and make disciples of all nations, baptizing them ina the name of the Father and of the Son and of the Holy Spirit, 20and teaching them to obey everything I have commanded you. And surely I am with you always, to the very end of the age."

---

a *19* Or *into*; see Acts 8:16; 19:5; Romans 6:3; 1 Cor. 1:13; 10:2 and Gal. 3:27.

Living Bible

62The next day—at the close of the first day of the Passover ceremoniesb—the chief priests and Pharisees went to Pilate, 63and told him, "Sir, that liar once said, 'After three days I will come back to life again.' 64So we request an order from you sealing the tomb until the third day, to prevent his disciples from coming and stealing his body and then telling everyone he came back to life! If that happens we'll be worse off than we were at first."

65"Use your own Temple police," Pilate told them. "They can guard it safely enough."

66So they sealed the stonec and posted guards to protect it from intrusion.

28 EARLY ON Sunday morning, as the new day was dawning, Mary Magdalene and the other Mary went out to the tomb.

2Suddenly there was a great earthquake; for an angel of the Lord came down from heaven and rolled aside the stone and sat on it. 3His face shone like lightning and his clothing was a brilliant white. 4The guards shook with fear when they saw him, and fell into a dead faint.

5Then the angel spoke to the women. "Don't be frightened!" he said. "I know you are looking for Jesus, who was crucified, 6but he isn't here! For he has come back to life again, just as he said he would. Come in and see where his body was lying. . . . 7And now, go quickly and tell his disciples that he has risen from the dead, and that he is going to Galilee to meet them there. That is my message to them."

8The women ran from the tomb, badly frightened, but also filled with joy, and rushed to find the disciples to give them the angel's message. 9And as they were running, suddenly Jesus was there in front of them!

"Good morning!"d he said. And they fell to the ground before him, holding his feet and worshiping him.

10Then Jesus said to them, "Don't be frightened! Go tell my brothers to leave at once for Galilee, to meet me there."

11As the women were on the way into the city, some of the Temple police who had been guarding the tomb went to the chief priests and told them what had happened. 12, 13A meeting of all the Jewish leaders was called, and it was decided to bribe the police to say they had all been asleep when Jesus' disciples came during the night and stole his body.

14"If the governor hears about it," the Council promised, "we'll stand up for you and everything will be all right."

15So the police accepted the bribe and said what they were told to. Their story spread widely among the Jews, and is still believed by them to this very day.

16Then the eleven disciples left for Galilee, going to the mountain where Jesus had said they would find him. 17There they met him and worshiped him—but some of them weren't sure it really was Jesus!

18He told his disciples, "I have been given all authority in heaven and earth. 19Therefore go and make disciples in all the nations,e baptizing them into the name of the Father and of the Son and of the Holy Spirit, 20and then teach these new disciples to obey all the commands I have given you; and be sure of this—that I am with you always, even to the end of the world."f

New Revised Standard

The Guard at the Tomb

62 The next day, that is, after the day of Preparation, the chief priests and the Pharisees gathered before Pilate 63 and said, "Sir, we remember what that impostor said while he was still alive, 'After three days I will rise again.' 64Therefore command the tomb to be made secure until the third day; otherwise his disciples may go and steal him away, and tell the people, 'He has been raised from the dead,' and the last deception would be worse than the first." 65Pilate said to them, "You have a guardg of soldiers; go, make it as secure as you can."h 66 So they went with the guard and made the tomb secure by sealing the stone.

The Resurrection of Jesus

28 AFTER THE sabbath, as the first day of the week was dawning, Mary Magdalene and the other Mary went to see the tomb. 2And suddenly there was a great earthquake; for an angel of the Lord, descending from heaven, came and rolled back the stone and sat on it. 3His appearance was like lightning, and his clothing white as snow. 4For fear of him the guards shook and became like dead men. 5But the angel said to the women, "Do not be afraid; I know that you are looking for Jesus who was crucified. 6He is not here; for he has been raised, as he said. Come, see the place where hei lay. 7Then go quickly and tell his disciples, 'He has been raised from the dead,j and indeed he is going ahead of you to Galilee; there you will see him.' This is my message for you." 8So they left the tomb quickly with fear and great joy, and ran to tell his disciples. 9Suddenly Jesus met them and said, "Greetings!" And they came to him, took hold of his feet, and worshiped him. 10Then Jesus said to them, "Do not be afraid; go and tell my brothers to go to Galilee; there they will see me."

The Report of the Guard

11 While they were going, some of the guard went into the city and told the chief priests everything that had happened. 12After the priestsk had assembled with the elders, they devised a plan to give a large sum of money to the soldiers, 13telling them, "You must say, 'His disciples came by night and stole him away while we were asleep.' 14If this comes to the governor's ears, we will satisfy him and keep you out of trouble." 15So they took the money and did as they were directed. And this story is still told among the Jews to this day.

The Commissioning of the Disciples

16 Now the eleven disciples went to Galilee, to the mountain to which Jesus had directed them. 17When they saw him, they worshiped him; but some doubted. 18And Jesus came and said to them, "All authority in heaven and on earth has been given to me. 19Go therefore and make disciples of all nations, baptizing them in the name of the Father and of the Son and of the Holy Spirit, 20and teaching them to obey everything that I have commanded you. And remember, I am with you always, to the end of the age."l

---

b 27:62 *at the close of the first day of the Passover ceremonies,* implied; literally, "on the morrow, which is after the Preparation."   c 27:66 *So they sealed the stone.* This was done by stringing a cord across the rock, the cord being sealed at each end with clay.   d 28:9 *Good morning,* literally, "All hail!"   e 28:19 *in all the nations,* literally, "of all nations."   f 28:20 *world,* or, "age."

g Or *Take a guard*   h Gk *you know how*   i Other ancient authorities read *the Lord*   j Other ancient authorities lack *from the dead*   k Gk *they*   l Other ancient authorities add *Amen*

THE GOSPEL ACCORDING TO

St. Mark

Mark

John the Baptist Prepares the Way

1 THE BEGINNING of the gospel of Jesus Christ, the Son of God;

2As it is written in the prophets, Behold, I send my messenger before thy face, which shall prepare thy way before thee.

3The voice of one crying in the wilderness, Prepare ye the way of the Lord, make his paths straight.

4John did baptize in the wilderness, and preach the baptism of repentance for the remission of sins.

5And there went out unto him all the land of Judaea, and they of Jerusalem, and were all baptized of him in the river of Jordan, confessing their sins.

6And John was clothed with camel's hair, and with a girdle of a skin about his loins; and he did eat locusts and wild honey;

7And preached, saying, There cometh one mightier than I after me, the latchet of whose shoes I am not worthy to stoop down and unloose.

8I indeed have baptized you with water: but he shall baptize you with the Holy Ghost.

9And it came to pass in those days, that Jesus came from Nazareth of Galilee, and was baptized of John in Jordan.

10And straightway coming up out of the water, he saw the heavens opened, and the Spirit like a dove descending upon him:

11And there came a voice from heaven, *saying,* Thou art my beloved Son, in whom I am well pleased.

12And immediately the Spirit driveth him into the wilderness.

13And he was there in the wilderness forty days, tempted of Satan; and was with the wild beasts; and the angels ministered unto him.

14Now after that John was put in prison, Jesus came into Galilee, preaching the gospel of the kingdom of God,

15And saying, The time is fulfilled, and the kingdom of God is at hand: repent ye, and believe the gospel.

16Now as he walked by the sea of Galilee, he saw Simon and Andrew his brother casting a net into the sea: for they were fishers.

17And Jesus said unto them, Come ye after me, and I will make you to become fishers of men.

18And straightway they forsook their nets, and followed him.

19And when he had gone a little farther thence, he saw James the *son* of Zebedee, and John his brother, who also were in the ship mending their nets.

1 THE BEGINNING of the gospel about Jesus Christ, the Son of God.[a]

2It is written in Isaiah the prophet:

"I will send my messenger ahead of you,
    who will prepare your way"[b]—

3"a voice of one calling in the desert,
'Prepare the way for the Lord,
    make straight paths for him.'"[c]

4And so John came, baptizing in the desert region and preaching a baptism of repentance for the forgiveness of sins. 5The whole Judean countryside and all the people of Jerusalem went out to him. Confessing their sins, they were baptized by him in the Jordan River. 6John wore clothing made of camel's hair, with a leather belt around his waist, and he ate locusts and wild honey. 7And this was his message: "After me will come one more powerful than I, the thongs of whose sandals I am not worthy to stoop down and untie. 8I baptize you with[d] water, but he will baptize you with the Holy Spirit."

The Baptism and Temptation of Jesus

9At that time Jesus came from Nazareth in Galilee and was baptized by John in the Jordan. 10As Jesus was coming up out of the water, he saw heaven being torn open and the Spirit descending on him like a dove. 11And a voice came from heaven: "You are my Son, whom I love; with you I am well pleased."

12At once the Spirit sent him out into the desert, 13and he was in the desert forty days, being tempted by Satan. He was with the wild animals, and angels attended him.

The Calling of the First Disciples

14After John was put in prison, Jesus went into Galilee, proclaiming the good news of God. 15"The time has come," he said. "The kingdom of God is near. Repent and believe the good news!"

16As Jesus walked beside the Sea of Galilee, he saw Simon and his brother Andrew casting a net into the lake, for they were fishermen. 17"Come, follow me," Jesus said, "and I will make you fishers of men." 18At once they left their nets and followed him.

19When he had gone a little farther, he saw James son of Zebedee and his brother John in a boat, preparing their nets. 20Without delay he called them, and they left

a *1* Some manuscripts do not have *the Son of God.*   b *2* Mal. 3:1
c *3* Isaiah 40:3   d *8* Or *in*

Living Bible

Mark

1 HERE BEGINS the wonderful story of Jesus the Messiah, the Son of God.

2In the book written by the prophet Isaiah, God announced that he would send his Son[e] to earth, and that a special messenger would arrive first to prepare the world for his coming.

3"This messenger will live out in the barren wilderness," Isaiah said,[f] "and will proclaim that everyone must straighten out his life to be ready for the Lord's arrival."[g]

4This messenger was John the Baptist. He lived in the wilderness and taught that all should be baptized as a public announcement of their decision to turn their backs on sin, so that God could forgive them.[h] 5People from Jerusalem and from all over Judea traveled out into the Judean wastelands to see and hear John, and when they confessed their sins he baptized them in the Jordan River. 6His clothes were woven from camel's hair and he wore a leather belt; locusts and wild honey were his food. 7Here is a sample of his preaching:

"Someone is coming soon who is far greater than I am, so much greater that I am not even worthy to be his slave.[i] 8I baptize you with water[j] but he will baptize you with God's Holy Spirit!"[k]

9Then one day Jesus came from Nazareth in Galilee, and was baptized by John there in the Jordan River. 10The moment Jesus came up out of the water, he saw the heavens open and the Holy Spirit in the form of a dove descending on him, 11and a voice from heaven said, "You are my beloved Son; you are my Delight."

12, 13Immediately the Holy Spirit urged Jesus into the desert. There, for forty days, alone except for desert animals, he was subjected to Satan's temptations to sin. And afterwards[l] the angels came and cared for him.

14Later on, after John was arrested by King Herod,[m] Jesus went to Galilee to preach God's Good News.

15"At last the time has come!" he announced. "God's Kingdom is near! Turn from your sins and act on this glorious news!"

16One day as Jesus was walking along the shores of the Sea of Galilee, he saw Simon and his brother Andrew fishing with nets, for they were commercial fishermen.

17Jesus called out to them, "Come, follow me! And I will make you fishermen for the souls of men!" 18At once they left their nets and went along with him.

19A little farther up the beach, he saw Zebedee's sons, James and John, in a boat mending their nets. 20He

---

[e] 1:2 his Son, implied.   [f] 1:3 Isaiah said. Some ancient manuscripts read, "the prophets said." This quotation, unrecorded in the book of Isaiah, appears in Mal 3:1.   [g] 1:3 be ready for the Lord's arrival, literally, "make ready the way of the Lord; make his paths straight."   [h] 1:4 so that God could forgive them, literally, "preaching a baptism of repentance for the forgiveness of sins."   [i] 1:7 I am not even worthy to be his slave, literally, "Whose shoes I am not worthy to unloose."   [j] 1:8 with water, or "in water." The Greek word is not clear on this controversial point.   [k] 1:8 with God's Holy Spirit, or "in God's Holy Spirit"; the Greek is not clear.   [l] 1:12, 13 afterwards, implied in parallel passages.   [m] 1:14 King Herod, implied.

New Revised Standard

Mark

The Proclamation of John the Baptist

1 THE BEGINNING of the good news[n] of Jesus Christ, the Son of God.[o]

2 As it is written in the prophet Isaiah,[p]

"See, I am sending my messenger ahead of you,[q]
who will prepare your way;
3 the voice of one crying out in the wilderness:
'Prepare the way of the Lord,
make his paths straight,' "

4John the baptizer appeared[r] in the wilderness, proclaiming a baptism of repentance for the forgiveness of sins. 5And people from the whole Judean countryside and all the people of Jerusalem were going out to him, and were baptized by him in the river Jordan, confessing their sins. 6Now John was clothed with camel's hair, with a leather belt around his waist, and he ate locusts and wild honey. 7He proclaimed, "The one who is more powerful than I is coming after me; I am not worthy to stoop down and untie the thong of his sandals. 8I have baptized you with[s] water; but he will baptize you with[s] the Holy Spirit."

The Baptism of Jesus

9 In those days Jesus came from Nazareth of Galilee and was baptized by John in the Jordan. 10And just as he was coming up out of the water, he saw the heavens torn apart and the Spirit descending like a dove on him. 11And a voice came from heaven, "You are my Son, the Beloved;[t] with you I am well pleased."

The Temptation of Jesus

12 And the Spirit immediately drove him out into the wilderness. 13He was in the wilderness forty days, tempted by Satan; and he was with the wild beasts; and the angels waited on him.

The Beginning of the Galilean Ministry

14 Now after John was arrested, Jesus came to Galilee, proclaiming the good news[n] of God,[u] 15and saying, "The time is fulfilled, and the kingdom of God has come near;[v] repent, and believe in the good news."[n]

Jesus Calls the First Disciples

16 As Jesus passed along the Sea of Galilee, he saw Simon and his brother Andrew casting a net into the sea—for they were fishermen. 17And Jesus said to them, "Follow me and I will make you fish for people." 18And immediately they left their nets and followed him. 19As he went a little farther, he saw James son of Zebedee and his brother John, who were in their boat mending the nets. 20Immediately he called them; and

---

[n] Or gospel   [o] Other ancient authorities lack the Son of God   [p] Other ancient authorities read in the prophets   [q] Gk before your face   [r] Other ancient authorities read John was baptizing   [s] Or in   [t] Or my beloved Son   [u] Other ancient authorities read of the kingdom   [v] Or is at hand

King James

20And straightway he called them: and they left their father Zebedee in the ship with the hired servants, and went after him.

21And they went into Capernaum; and straightway on the sabbath day he entered into the synagogue, and taught.

22And they were astonished at his doctrine: for he taught them as one that had authority, and not as the scribes.

23And there was in their synagogue a man with an unclean spirit; and he cried out,

24Saying, Let *us* alone; what have we to do with thee, thou Jesus of Nazareth? art thou come to destroy us? I know thee who thou art, the Holy One of God.

25And Jesus rebuked him, saying, Hold thy peace, and come out of him.

26And when the unclean spirit had torn him, and cried with a loud voice, he came out of him.

27And they were all amazed, insomuch that they questioned among themselves, saying, What thing is this? what new doctrine *is* this? for with authority commandeth he even the unclean spirits, and they do obey him.

28And immediately his fame spread abroad throughout all the region round about Galilee.

29And forthwith, when they were come out of the synagogue, they entered into the house of Simon and Andrew, with James and John.

30But Simon's wife's mother lay sick of a fever, and anon they tell him of her.

31And he came and took her by the hand, and lifted her up; and immediately the fever left her, and she ministered unto them.

32And at even, when the sun did set, they brought unto him all that were diseased, and them that were possessed with devils.

33And all the city was gathered together at the door.

34And he healed many that were sick of divers diseases, and cast out many devils; and suffered not the devils to speak, because they knew him.

35And in the morning, rising up a great while before day, he went out, and departed into a solitary place, and there prayed.

36And Simon and they that were with him followed after him.

37And when they had found him, they said unto him, All *men* seek for thee.

38And he said unto them, Let us go into the next towns, that I may preach there also: for therefore came I forth.

39And he preached in their synagogues throughout all Galilee, and cast out devils.

40And there came a leper to him, beseeching him, and kneeling down to him, and saying unto him, If thou wilt, thou canst make me clean.

41And Jesus, moved with compassion, put forth *his* hand, and touched him, and saith unto him, I will; be thou clean.

42And as soon as he had spoken, immediately the leprosy departed from him, and he was cleansed.

43And he straitly charged him, and forthwith sent him away;

44And saith unto him, See thou say nothing to any man: but go thy way, show thyself to the priest, and offer for thy cleansing those things which Moses commanded, for a testimony unto them.

45But he went out, and began to publish *it* much, and to blaze abroad the matter, insomuch that Jesus could no more openly enter into the city, but was without in desert places: and they came to him from every quarter.

New International

their father Zebedee in the boat with the hired men and followed him.

Jesus Drives Out an Evil Spirit

21They went to Capernaum, and when the Sabbath came, Jesus went into the synagogue and began to teach. 22The people were amazed at his teaching, because he taught them as one who had authority, not as the teachers of the law. 23Just then a man in their synagogue who was possessed by an evila spirit cried out, 24"What do you want with us, Jesus of Nazareth? Have you come to destroy us? I know who you are—the Holy One of God!"

25"Be quiet!" said Jesus sternly. "Come out of him!" 26The evil spirit shook the man violently and came out of him with a shriek.

27The people were all so amazed that they asked each other, "What is this? A new teaching—and with authority! He even gives orders to evil spirits and they obey him." 28News about him spread quickly over the whole region of Galilee.

Jesus Heals Many

29As soon as they left the synagogue, they went with James and John to the home of Simon and Andrew. 30Simon's mother-in-law was in bed with a fever, and they told Jesus about her. 31So he went to her, took her hand and helped her up. The fever left her and she began to wait on them.

32That evening after sunset the people brought to Jesus all the sick and demon-possessed. 33The whole town gathered at the door, 34and Jesus healed many who had various diseases. He also drove out many demons, but he would not let the demons speak because they knew who he was.

Jesus Prays in a Solitary Place

35Very early in the morning, while it was still dark, Jesus got up, left the house and went off to a solitary place, where he prayed. 36Simon and his companions went to look for him, 37and when they found him, they exclaimed: "Everyone is looking for you!"

38Jesus replied, "Let us go somewhere else—to the nearby villages—so I can preach there also. That is why I have come." 39So he traveled throughout Galilee, preaching in their synagogues and driving out demons.

A Man With Leprosy

40A man with leprosyb came to him and begged him on his knees, "If you are willing, you can make me clean."

41Filled with compassion, Jesus reached out his hand and touched the man. "I am willing," he said. "Be clean!" 42Immediately the leprosy left him and he was cured.

43Jesus sent him away at once with a strong warning: 44"See that you don't tell this to anyone. But go, show yourself to the priest and offer the sacrifices that Moses commanded for your cleansing, as a testimony to them." 45Instead he went out and began to talk freely, spreading the news. As a result, Jesus could no longer enter a town openly but stayed outside in lonely places. Yet the people still came to him from everywhere.

a *23* Greek *unclean;* also in verses 26 and 27   b *40* The Greek word was used for various diseases affecting the skin—not necessarily leprosy.

Living Bible

called them too, and immediately they left their father Zebedee in the boat with the hired men and went with him.

21Jesus and his companions now arrived at the town of Capernaum and on Saturday morning went into the Jewish place of worship—the synagogue—where he preached. 22The congregation was surprised at his sermon because he spoke as an authority, and didn't try to prove his points by quoting others—quite unlike what they were used to hearing!c

23A man possessed by a demon was present and began shouting, 24"Why are you bothering us, Jesus of Nazareth—have you come to destroy us demons? I know who you are—the holy Son of God!"

25Jesus curtly commanded the demon to say no more and to come out of the man. 26At that the evil spirit screamed and convulsed the man violently and left him. 27Amazement gripped the audience and they began discussing what had happened.

"What sort of new religion is this?" they asked excitedly. "Why, even evil spirits obey his orders!"

28The news of what he had done spread quickly through that entire area of Galilee.

29, 30Then, leaving the synagogue, he and his disciples went over to Simon and Andrew's home, where they found Simon's mother-in-law sick in bed with a high fever. They told Jesus about her right away. 31He went to her bedside, and as he took her by the hand and helped her to sit up, the fever suddenly left, and she got up and prepared dinner for them!

32, 33By sunset the courtyard was filled with the sick and demon-possessed, brought to him for healing; and a huge crowd of people from all over the city of Capernaum gathered outside the door to watch. 34So Jesus healed great numbers of sick folk that evening and ordered many demons to come out of their victims. (But he refused to allow the demons to speak, because they knew who he was.)

35The next morning he was up long before daybreak and went out alone into the wilderness to pray.

36, 37Later, Simon and the others went out to find him, and told him, "Everyone is asking for you."

38But he replied, "We must go on to other towns as well, and give my message to them too, for that is why I came."

39So he traveled throughout the province of Galilee, preaching in the synagogues and releasing many from the power of demons.

40Once a leper came and knelt in front of him and begged to be healed. "If you want to, you can make me well again," he pled.

41And Jesus, moved with pity, touched him and said, "I want to! Be healed!" 42Immediately the leprosy was gone—the man was healed!

43, 44Jesus then told him sternly, "Go and be examined immediately by the Jewish priest. Don't stop to speak to anyone along the way. Take along the offering prescribed by Moses for a leper who is healed, so that everyone will have proof that you are well again."

45But as the man went on his way he began to shout the good news that he was healed; as a result, such throngs soon surrounded Jesus that he couldn't publicly enter a city anywhere, but had to stay out in the barren wastelands. And people from everywhere came to him there.

New Revised Standard

they left their father Zebedee in the boat with the hired men, and followed him.

The Man with an Unclean Spirit

21 They went to Capernaum; and when the sabbath came, he entered the synagogue and taught. 22They were astounded at his teaching, for he taught them as one having authority, and not as the scribes. 23Just then there was in their synagogue a man with an unclean spirit, 24and he cried out, "What have you to do with us, Jesus of Nazareth? Have you come to destroy us? I know who you are, the Holy One of God." 25But Jesus rebuked him, saying, "Be silent, and come out of him!" 26And the unclean spirit, convulsing him and crying with a loud voice, came out of him. 27They were all amazed, and they kept on asking one another, "What is this? A new teaching—with authority! Hed commands even the unclean spirits, and they obey him." 28At once his fame began to spread throughout the surrounding region of Galilee.

Jesus Heals Many at Simon's House

29 As soon as theye left the synagogue, they entered the house of Simon and Andrew, with James and John. 30Now Simon's mother-in-law was in bed with a fever, and they told him about her at once. 31He came and took her by the hand and lifted her up. Then the fever left her, and she began to serve them.

32 That evening, at sundown, they brought to him all who were sick or possessed with demons. 33And the whole city was gathered around the door. 34And he cured many who were sick with various diseases, and cast out many demons; and he would not permit the demons to speak, because they knew him.

A Preaching Tour in Galilee

35 In the morning, while it was still very dark, he got up and went out to a deserted place, and there he prayed. 36And Simon and his companions hunted for him. 37When they found him, they said to him, "Everyone is searching for you." 38He answered, "Let us go on to the neighboring towns, so that I may proclaim the message there also; for that is what I came out to do." 39And he went throughout Galilee, proclaiming the message in their synagogues and casting out demons.

Jesus Cleanses a Leper

40 A leperf came to him begging him, and kneelingg he said to him, "If you choose, you can make me clean." 41Moved with pity,h Jesusi stretched out his hand and touched him, and said to him, "I do choose. Be made clean!" 42Immediately the leprosyf left him, and he was made clean. 43After sternly warning him he sent him away at once, 44saying to him, "See that you say nothing to anyone; but go, show yourself to the priest, and offer for your cleansing what Moses commanded, as a testimony to them." 45But he went out and began to proclaim it freely, and to spread the word, so that Jesusi could no longer go into a town openly, but stayed out in the country; and people came to him from every quarter.

---

c 1:22 Quite unlike what they were used to hearing, literally, "not as the scribes."

d Or A new teaching! With authority he   e Other ancient authorities read he
f The terms leper and leprosy can refer to several diseases   g Other ancient authorities lack kneeling   h Other ancient authorities read anger   i Gk he

King James

2 AND AGAIN he entered into Capernaum after *some* days; and it was noised that he was in the house.

2And straightway many were gathered together, insomuch that there was no room to receive *them*, no, not so much as about the door: and he preached the word unto them.

3And they come unto him, bringing one sick of the palsy, which was borne of four.

4And when they could not come nigh unto him for the press, they uncovered the roof where he was: and when they had broken *it* up, they let down the bed wherein the sick of the palsy lay.

5When Jesus saw their faith, he said unto the sick of the palsy, Son, thy sins be forgiven thee.

6But there were certain of the scribes sitting there, and reasoning in their hearts,

7Why doth this *man* thus speak blasphemies? who can forgive sins but God only?

8And immediately when Jesus perceived in his spirit that they so reasoned within themselves, he said unto them, Why reason ye these things in your hearts?

9Whether is it easier to say to the sick of the palsy, *Thy* sins be forgiven thee; or to say, Arise, and take up thy bed, and walk?

10But that ye may know that the Son of man hath power on earth to forgive sins, (he saith to the sick of the palsy,)

11I say unto thee, Arise, and take up thy bed, and go thy way into thine house.

12And immediately he arose, took up the bed, and went forth before them all; insomuch that they were all amazed, and glorified God, saying, We never saw it on this fashion.

13And he went forth again by the sea side; and all the multitude resorted unto him, and he taught them.

14And as he passed by, he saw Levi the *son* of Alphaeus sitting at the receipt of custom, and said unto him, Follow me. And he arose and followed him.

15And it came to pass, that, as Jesus sat at meat in his house, many publicans and sinners sat also together with Jesus and his disciples: for there were many, and they followed him.

16And when the scribes and Pharisees saw him eat with publicans and sinners, they said unto his disciples, How is it that he eateth and drinketh with publicans and sinners?

17When Jesus heard *it*, he saith unto them, They that are whole have no need of the physician, but they that are sick: I came not to call the righteous, but sinners to repentance.

18And the disciples of John and of the Pharisees used to fast: and they come and say unto him, Why do the disciples of John and of the Pharisees fast, but thy disciples fast not?

19And Jesus said unto them, Can the children of the bridechamber fast, while the bridegroom is with them? as long as they have the bridegroom with them, they cannot fast.

20But the days will come, when the bridegroom shall be taken away from them, and then shall they fast in those days.

21No man also seweth a piece of new cloth on an old garment: else the new piece that filled it up taketh away from the old, and the rent is made worse.

22And no man putteth new wine into old bottles: else the new wine doth burst the bottles, and the wine is spilled, and the bottles will be marred: but new wine must be put into new bottles.

23And it came to pass, that he went through the corn fields on the sabbath day; and his disciples began, as they went, to pluck the ears of corn.

New International

Jesus Heals a Paralytic

2 A FEW days later, when Jesus again entered Capernaum, the people heard that he had come home. 2So many gathered that there was no room left, not even outside the door, and he preached the word to them. 3Some men came, bringing to him a paralytic, carried by four of them. 4Since they could not get him to Jesus because of the crowd, they made an opening in the roof above Jesus and, after digging through it, lowered the mat the paralyzed man was lying on. 5When Jesus saw their faith, he said to the paralytic, "Son, your sins are forgiven."

6Now some teachers of the law were sitting there, thinking to themselves, 7"Why does this fellow talk like that? He's blaspheming! Who can forgive sins but God alone?"

8Immediately Jesus knew in his spirit that this was what they were thinking in their hearts, and he said to them, "Why are you thinking these things? 9Which is easier: to say to the paralytic, 'Your sins are forgiven,' or to say, 'Get up, take your mat and walk'? 10But that you may know that the Son of Man has authority on earth to forgive sins . . . ." He said to the paralytic, 11"I tell you, get up, take your mat and go home." 12He got up, took his mat and walked out in full view of them all. This amazed everyone and they praised God, saying, "We have never seen anything like this!"

The Calling of Levi

13Once again Jesus went out beside the lake. A large crowd came to him, and he began to teach them. 14As he walked along, he saw Levi son of Alphaeus sitting at the tax collector's booth. "Follow me," Jesus told him, and Levi got up and followed him.

15While Jesus was having dinner at Levi's house, many tax collectors and "sinners" were eating with him and his disciples, for there were many who followed him. 16When the teachers of the law who were Pharisees saw him eating with the "sinners" and tax collectors, they asked his disciples: "Why does he eat with tax collectors and 'sinners'?"

17On hearing this, Jesus said to them, "It is not the healthy who need a doctor, but the sick. I have not come to call the righteous, but sinners."

Jesus Questioned About Fasting

18Now John's disciples and the Pharisees were fasting. Some people came and asked Jesus, "How is it that John's disciples and the disciples of the Pharisees are fasting, but yours are not?"

19Jesus answered, "How can the guests of the bridegroom fast while he is with them? They cannot, so long as they have him with them. 20But the time will come when the bridegroom will be taken from them, and on that day they will fast.

21"No one sews a patch of unshrunk cloth on an old garment. If he does, the new piece will pull away from the old, making the tear worse. 22And no one pours new wine into old wineskins. If he does, the wine will burst the skins, and both the wine and the wineskins will be ruined. No, he pours new wine into new wineskins."

Lord of the Sabbath

23One Sabbath Jesus was going through the grainfields, and as his disciples walked along, they began to pick some heads of grain. 24The Pharisees said to him,

Living Bible

2 SEVERAL DAYS later he returned to Capernaum, and the news of his arrival spread quickly through the city. 2Soon the house where he was staying was so packed with visitors that there wasn't room for a single person more, not even outside the door. And he preached the Word to them. 3Four men arrived carrying a paralyzed man on a stretcher. 4They couldn't get to Jesus through the crowd, so they dug through the clay roof above his head and lowered the sick man on his stretcher, right down in front of Jesus.a

5When Jesus saw how strongly they believed that he would help, Jesus said to the sick man, "Son, your sins are forgiven!"

6But some of the Jewish religious leadersb said to themselves as they sat there, 7"What? This is blasphemy! Does he think he is God? For only God can forgive sins."

8Jesus could read their minds and said to them at once, "Why does this bother you? 9, 10, 11I, the Messiah,c have the authority on earth to forgive sins. But talk is cheap—anybody could say that. So I'll prove it to you by healing this man." Then, turning to the paralyzed man, he commanded, "Pick up your stretcher and go on home, for you are healed!"

12The man jumped up, took the stretcher, and pushed his way through the stunned onlookers! Then how they praised God. "We've never seen anything like this before!" they all exclaimed.

13Then Jesus went out to the seashore again, and preached to the crowds that gathered around him. 14As he was walking up the beach he saw Levi, the son of Alphaeus, sitting at his tax collection booth. "Come with me," Jesus told him. "Come be my disciple."

And Levi jumped to his feet and went along.

15That night Levi invited his fellow tax collectors and many other notorious sinners to be his dinner guests so that they could meet Jesus and his disciples. (There were many men of this type among the crowds that followed him.) 16But when some of the Jewish religious leadersd saw him eating with these men of ill repute, they said to his disciples, "How can he stand it, to eat with such scum?"

17When Jesus heard what they were saying, he told them, "Sick people need the doctor, not healthy ones! I haven't come to tell good people to repent, but the bad ones."

18John's disciples and the Jewish leaders sometimes fasted, that is, went without food as part of their religion. One day some people came to Jesus and asked why his disciples didn't do this too.

19Jesus replied, "Do friends of the bridegroom refuse to eat at the wedding feast? Should they be sad while he is with them? 20But some day he will be taken away from them, and then they will mourn. 21[Besides, going without food is part of the old way of doing things.e] It is like patching an old garment with unshrunk cloth! What happens? The patch pulls away and leaves the hole worse than before. 22You know better than to put new wine into old wineskins. They would burst. The wine would be spilled out and the wineskins ruined. New wine needs fresh wineskins."

23Another time, on a Sabbath day as Jesus and his disciples were walking through the fields, the disciples were breaking off heads of wheat and eating the grain.f

New Revised Standard

Jesus Heals a Paralytic

2 WHEN HE returned to Capernaum after some days, it was reported that he was at home. 2So many gathered around that there was no longer room for them, not even in front of the door; and he was speaking the word to them. 3Then some peopleg came, bringing to him a paralyzed man, carried by four of them. 4And when they could not bring him to Jesus because of the crowd, they removed the roof above him; and after having dug through it, they let down the mat on which the paralytic lay. 5When Jesus saw their faith, he said to the paralytic, "Son, your sins are forgiven." 6Now some of the scribes were sitting there, questioning in their hearts, 7"Why does this fellow speak in this way? It is blasphemy! Who can forgive sins but God alone?" 8At once Jesus perceived in his spirit that they were discussing these questions among themselves; and he said to them, "Why do you raise such questions in your hearts? 9Which is easier, to say to the paralytic, 'Your sins are forgiven,' or to say, 'Stand up and take your mat and walk'? 10But so that you may know that the Son of Man has authority on earth to forgive sins"—he said to the paralytic— 11"I say to you, stand up, take your mat and go to your home." 12And he stood up, and immediately took the mat and went out before all of them; so that they were all amazed and glorified God, saying, "We have never seen anything like this!"

Jesus Calls Levi

13 Jesush went out again beside the sea; the whole crowd gathered around him, and he taught them. 14As he was walking along, he saw Levi son of Alphaeus sitting at the tax booth, and he said to him, "Follow me." And he got up and followed him.

15 And as he sat at dinneri in Levi'sj house, many tax collectors and sinners were also sittingk with Jesus and his disciples—for there were many who followed him. 16When the scribes ofl the Pharisees saw that he was eating with sinners and tax collectors, they said to his disciples, "Why does he eatm with tax collectors and sinners?" 17When Jesus heard this, he said to them, "Those who are well have no need of a physician, but those who are sick; I have come to call not the righteous but sinners."

The Question about Fasting

18 Now John's disciples and the Pharisees were fasting; and peopleg came and said to him, "Why do John's disciples and the disciples of the Pharisees fast, but your disciples do not fast?" 19Jesus said to them, "The wedding guests cannot fast while the bridegroom is with them, can they? As long as they have the bridegroom with them, they cannot fast. 20The days will come when the bridegroom is taken away from them, and then they will fast on that day.

21 "No one sews a piece of unshrunk cloth on an old cloak; otherwise, the patch pulls away from it, the new from the old, and a worse tear is made. 22And no one puts new wine into old wineskins; otherwise, the wine will burst the skins, and the wine is lost, and so are the skins; but one puts new wine into fresh wineskins."n

Pronouncement about the Sabbath

23 One sabbath he was going through the grainfields; and as they made their way his disciples began to pluck heads of grain. 24The Pharisees said to him,

---

a 2:4 *right down in front of Jesus,* implied.   b 2:6 *religious leaders,* literally, "scribes."   c 2:9-11 *Messiah,* literally, "Son of Man."   d 2:16 *religious leaders,* literally, "the scribes of the Pharisees."   e 2:21 *way of doing things,* implied.   f 2:23 *eating the grain,* implied.

g Gk *they*   h Gk *He*   i Gk *reclined*   j Gk *his*   k Gk *reclining*   l Other ancient authorities read *and*   m Other ancient authorities add *and drink*   n Other ancient authorities lack *but one puts new wine into fresh wineskins*

King James

24And the Pharisees said unto him, Behold, why do they on the sabbath day that which is not lawful?

25And he said unto them, Have ye never read what David did, when he had need, and was an hungered, he, and they that were with him?

26How he went into the house of God in the days of Abiathar the high priest, and did eat the showbread, which is not lawful to eat but for the priests, and gave also to them which were with him?

27And he said unto them, The sabbath was made for man, and not man for the sabbath:

28Therefore the Son of man is Lord also of the sabbath.

3 AND HE entered again into the synagogue; and there was a man there which had a withered hand.

2And they watched him, whether he would heal him on the sabbath day; that they might accuse him.

3And he saith unto the man which had the withered hand, Stand forth.

4And he saith unto them, Is it lawful to do good on the sabbath days, or to do evil? to save life, or to kill? But they held their peace.

5And when he had looked round about on them with anger, being grieved for the hardness of their hearts, he saith unto the man, Stretch forth thine hand. And he stretched *it* out: and his hand was restored whole as the other.

6And the Pharisees went forth, and straightway took counsel with the Herodians against him, how they might destroy him.

7But Jesus withdrew himself with his disciples to the sea: and a great multitude from Galilee followed him, and from Judaea,

8And from Jerusalem, and from Idumaea, and *from* beyond Jordan; and they about Tyre and Sidon, a great multitude, when they had heard what great things he did, came unto him.

9And he spake to his disciples, that a small ship should wait on him because of the multitude, lest they should throng him.

10For he had healed many; insomuch that they pressed upon him for to touch him, as many as had plagues.

11And unclean spirits, when they saw him, fell down before him, and cried, saying, Thou art the Son of God.

12And he straitly charged them that they should not make him known.

13And he goeth up into a mountain, and calleth *unto him* whom he would: and they came unto him.

14And he ordained twelve, that they should be with him, and that he might send them forth to preach,

15And to have power to heal sicknesses, and to cast out devils:

16And Simon he surnamed Peter;

17And James the *son* of Zebedee, and John the brother of James; and he surnamed them Boanerges, which is, The sons of thunder:

18And Andrew, and Philip, and Bartholomew, and Matthew, and Thomas, and James the *son* of Alphaeus, and Thaddaeus, and Simon the Canaanite,

19And Judas Iscariot, which also betrayed him: and they went into an house.

20And the multitude cometh together again, so that they could not so much as eat bread.

New International

"Look, why are they doing what is unlawful on the Sabbath?"

25He answered, "Have you never read what David did when he and his companions were hungry and in need? 26In the days of Abiathar the high priest, he entered the house of God and ate the consecrated bread, which is lawful only for priests to eat. And he also gave some to his companions."

27Then he said to them, "The Sabbath was made for man, not man for the Sabbath. 28So the Son of Man is Lord even of the Sabbath."

3 ANOTHER TIME he went into the synagogue, and a man with a shriveled hand was there. 2Some of them were looking for a reason to accuse Jesus, so they watched him closely to see if he would heal him on the Sabbath. 3Jesus said to the man with the shriveled hand, "Stand up in front of everyone."

4Then Jesus asked them, "Which is lawful on the Sabbath: to do good or to do evil, to save life or to kill?" But they remained silent.

5He looked around at them in anger and, deeply distressed at their stubborn hearts, said to the man, "Stretch out your hand." He stretched it out, and his hand was completely restored. 6Then the Pharisees went out and began to plot with the Herodians how they might kill Jesus.

Crowds Follow Jesus

7Jesus withdrew with his disciples to the lake, and a large crowd from Galilee followed. 8When they heard all he was doing, many people came to him from Judea, Jerusalem, Idumea, and the regions across the Jordan and around Tyre and Sidon. 9Because of the crowd he told his disciples to have a small boat ready for him, to keep the people from crowding him. 10For he had healed many, so that those with diseases were pushing forward to touch him. 11Whenever the evil[a] spirits saw him, they fell down before him and cried out, "You are the Son of God." 12But he gave them strict orders not to tell who he was.

The Appointing of the Twelve Apostles

13Jesus went up on a mountainside and called to him those he wanted, and they came to him. 14He appointed twelve—designating them apostles[b]—that they might be with him and that he might send them out to preach 15and to have authority to drive out demons. 16These are the twelve he appointed: Simon (to whom he gave the name Peter); 17James son of Zebedee and his brother John (to them he gave the name Boanerges, which means Sons of Thunder); 18Andrew, Philip, Bartholomew, Matthew, Thomas, James son of Alphaeus, Thaddaeus, Simon the Zealot 19and Judas Iscariot, who betrayed him.

Jesus and Beelzebub

20Then Jesus entered a house, and again a crowd gathered, so that he and his disciples were not even able to eat. 21When his family heard about this, they went to

---

[a] *11* Greek *unclean*; also in verse 30   [b] *14* Some manuscripts do not have *designating them apostles*.

Living Bible

24Some of the Jewish religious leaders said to Jesus, "They shouldn't be doing that! It's against our laws to work by harvesting grain on the Sabbath."

25, 26But Jesus replied, "Didn't you ever hear about the time King David and his companions were hungry, and he went into the house of God—Abiathar was High Priest then—and they ate the special breadc only priests were allowed to eat? That was against the law too. 27But the Sabbath was made to benefit man, and not man to benefit the Sabbath. 28And I, the Messiah,d have authority even to decide what men can do on Sabbath days!"

3 WHILE IN Capernaum Jesus went over to the synagogue again, and noticed a man there with a deformed hand.

2Since it was the Sabbath, Jesus' enemies watched him closely. Would he heal the man's hand? If he did, they planned to arrest him!

3Jesus asked the man to come and stand in front of the congregation. 4Then turning to his enemies he asked, "Is it all right to do kind deeds on Sabbath days? Or is this a day for doing harm? Is it a day to save lives or to destroy them?" But they wouldn't answer him. 5Looking around at them angrily, for he was deeply disturbed by their indifference to human need, he said to the man, "Reach out your hand." He did, and instantly his hand was healed!

6At once the Phariseese went away and met with the Herodiansf to discuss plans for killing Jesus.

7, 8Meanwhile, Jesus and his disciples withdrew to the beach, followed by a huge crowd from all over Galilee, Judea, Jerusalem, Idumea, from beyond the Jordan River, and even from as far away as Tyre and Sidon. For the news about his miracles had spread far and wide and vast numbers came to see him for themselves.

9He instructed his disciples to bring around a boat and to have it standing ready to rescue him in case he was crowded off the beach. 10For there had been many healings that day and as a result great numbers of sick people were crowding around him, trying to touch him.

11And whenever those possessed by demons caught sight of him they would fall down before him shrieking, "You are the Son of God!" 12But he strictly warned them not to make him known.

13Afterwards he went up into the hills and summoned certain ones he chose, inviting them to come and join him there; and they did. 14, 15Then he selected twelve of them to be his regular companions and to go out to preach and to cast out demons. 16–19These are the names of the twelve he chose:

Simon (he renamed him "Peter"),
James and John (the sons of Zebedee, but Jesus called them "Sons of Thunder"),
Andrew,
Philip,
Bartholomew,
Matthew,
Thomas,
James (the son of Alphaeus),
Thaddaeus,
Simon (a member of a political party advocating violent overthrow of the Roman government),
Judas Iscariot (who later betrayed him).

20When he returned to the house where he was staying, the crowds began to gather again, and soon it was so full of visitors that he couldn't even find time to eat.

c 2:25, 26 special bread, literally "shewbread." d 2:28 the Messiah, literally, "the Son of Man." e 3:6 Pharisees, a religious sect of the Jews. f 3:6 Herodians, a pro-Roman political party.

New Revised Standard

"Look, why are they doing what is not lawful on the sabbath?" 25And he said to them, "Have you never read what David did when he and his companions were hungry and in need of food? 26He entered the house of God, when Abiathar was high priest, and ate the bread of the Presence, which it is not lawful for any but the priests to eat, and he gave some to his companions." 27Then he said to them, "The sabbath was made for humankind, and not humankind for the sabbath; 28so the Son of Man is lord even of the sabbath."

The Man with a Withered Hand

3 AGAIN HE entered the synagogue, and a man was there who had a withered hand. 2They watched him to see whether he would cure him on the sabbath, so that they might accuse him. 3And he said to the man who had the withered hand, "Come forward." 4Then he said to them, "Is it lawful to do good or to do harm on the sabbath, to save life or to kill?" But they were silent. 5He looked around at them with anger; he was grieved at their hardness of heart and said to the man, "Stretch out your hand." He stretched it out, and his hand was restored. 6The Pharisees went out and immediately conspired with the Herodians against him, how to destroy him.

A Multitude at the Seaside

7 Jesus departed with his disciples to the sea, and a great multitude from Galilee followed him; 8hearing all that he was doing, they came to him in great numbers from Judea, Jerusalem, Idumea, beyond the Jordan, and the region around Tyre and Sidon. 9He told his disciples to have a boat ready for him because of the crowd, so that they would not crush him; 10for he had cured many, so that all who had diseases pressed upon him to touch him. 11Whenever the unclean spirits saw him, they fell down before him and shouted, "You are the Son of God!" 12But he sternly ordered them not to make him known.

Jesus Appoints the Twelve

13 He went up the mountain and called to him those whom he wanted, and they came to him. 14And he appointed twelve, whom he also named apostles,g to be with him, and to be sent out to proclaim the message, 15and to have authority to cast out demons. 16So he appointed the twelve:h Simon (to whom he gave the name Peter); 17James son of Zebedee and John the brother of James (to whom he gave the name Boanerges, that is, Sons of Thunder); 18and Andrew, and Philip, and Bartholomew, and Matthew, and Thomas, and James son of Alphaeus, and Thaddaeus, and Simon the Cananaean, 19and Judas Iscariot, who betrayed him.

Jesus and Beelzebul

Then he went home; 20and the crowd came together again, so that they could not even eat. 21When his family

g Other ancient authorities lack whom he also named apostles h Other ancient authorities lack So he appointed the twelve

King James

21And when his friends heard *of it,* they went out to lay hold on him: for they said, He is beside himself.

22¶ And the scribes which came down from Jerusalem said, He hath Beelzebub, and by the prince of the devils casteth he out devils.

23And he called them *unto him,* and said unto them in parables, How can Satan cast out Satan?

24And if a kingdom be divided against itself, that kingdom cannot stand.

25And if a house be divided against itself, that house cannot stand.

26And if Satan rise up against himself, and be divided, he cannot stand, but hath an end.

27No man can enter into a strong man's house, and spoil his goods, except he will first bind the strong man; and then he will spoil his house.

28Verily I say unto you, All sins shall be forgiven unto the sons of men, and blasphemies wherewith soever they shall blaspheme:

29But he that shall blaspheme against the Holy Ghost hath never forgiveness, but is in danger of eternal damnation:

30Because they said, He hath an unclean spirit.

31¶ There came then his brethren and his mother, and, standing without, sent unto him, calling him.

32And the multitude sat about him, and they said unto him, Behold, thy mother and thy brethren without seek for thee.

33And he answered them, saying, Who is my mother, or my brethren?

34And he looked round about on them which sat about him, and said, Behold my mother and my brethren!

35For whosoever shall do the will of God, the same is my brother, and my sister, and mother.

4 AND HE began again to teach by the sea side: and there was gathered unto him a great multitude, so that he entered into a ship, and sat in the sea; and the whole multitude was by the sea on the land.

2And he taught them many things by parables, and said unto them in his doctrine,

3Hearken; Behold, there went out a sower to sow:

4And it came to pass, as he sowed, some fell by the way side, and the fowls of the air came and devoured it up.

5And some fell on stony ground, where it had not much earth; and immediately it sprang up, because it had no depth of earth:

6But when the sun was up, it was scorched; and because it had no root, it withered away.

7And some fell among thorns, and the thorns grew up, and choked it, and it yielded no fruit.

8And other fell on good ground, and did yield fruit that sprang up and increased; and brought forth, thirty, and some sixty, and some an hundred.

9And he said unto them, He that hath ears to hear, let him hear.

10And when he was alone, they that were about him with the twelve asked of him the parable.

11And he said unto them, Unto you it is given to know the mystery of the kingdom of God: but unto them that are without, all *these* things are done in parables:

12That seeing they may see, and not perceive; and hearing they may hear, and not understand; lest at any time they should be converted, and *their* sins should be forgiven them.

13And he said unto them, Know ye not this parable? and how then will ye know all parables?

14¶ The sower soweth the word.

New International

take charge of him, for they said, "He is out of his mind."

22And the teachers of the law who came down from Jerusalem said, "He is possessed by Beelzebub[a]! By the prince of demons he is driving out demons."

23So Jesus called them and spoke to them in parables: "How can Satan drive out Satan? 24If a kingdom is divided against itself, that kingdom cannot stand. 25If a house is divided against itself, that house cannot stand. 26And if Satan opposes himself and is divided, he cannot stand; his end has come. 27In fact, no one can enter a strong man's house and carry off his possessions unless he first ties up the strong man. Then he can rob his house. 28I tell you the truth, all the sins and blasphemies of men will be forgiven them. 29But whoever blasphemes against the Holy Spirit will never be forgiven; he is guilty of an eternal sin."

30He said this because they were saying, "He has an evil spirit."

Jesus' Mother and Brothers

31Then Jesus' mother and brothers arrived. Standing outside, they sent someone in to call him. 32A crowd was sitting around him, and they told him, "Your mother and brothers are outside looking for you."

33"Who are my mother and my brothers?" he asked.

34Then he looked at those seated in a circle around him and said, "Here are my mother and my brothers! 35Whoever does God's will is my brother and sister and mother."

The Parable of the Sower

4 AGAIN JESUS began to teach by the lake. The crowd that gathered around him was so large that he got into a boat and sat in it out on the lake, while all the people were along the shore at the water's edge. 2He taught them many things by parables, and in his teaching said: 3"Listen! A farmer went out to sow his seed. 4As he was scattering the seed, some fell along the path, and the birds came and ate it up. 5Some fell on rocky places, where it did not have much soil. It sprang up quickly, because the soil was shallow. 6But when the sun came up, the plants were scorched, and they withered because they had no root. 7Other seed fell among thorns, which grew up and choked the plants, so that they did not bear grain. 8Still other seed fell on good soil. It came up, grew and produced a crop, multiplying thirty, sixty, or even a hundred times."

9Then Jesus said, "He who has ears to hear, let him hear."

10When he was alone, the Twelve and the others around him asked him about the parables. 11He told them, "The secret of the kingdom of God has been given to you. But to those on the outside everything is said in parables 12so that,

" 'they may be ever seeing but never perceiving,
    and ever hearing but never understanding;
otherwise they might turn and be forgiven!'[b]"

13Then Jesus said to them, "Don't you understand this parable? How then will you understand any parable? 14The farmer sows the word. 15Some people are like

[a] 22 Greek *Beezeboul* or *Beelzeboul*   [b] 12 Isaiah 6:9,10

Living Bible

21When his friends heard what was happening they came to try to take him home with them.

"He's out of his mind," they said.

22But the Jewish teachers of religion who had arrived from Jerusalem said, "His trouble is that he's possessed by Satan, king of demons. That's why demons obey him."

23Jesus summoned these men and asked them (using proverbs they all understood), "How can Satan cast out Satan? 24A kingdom divided against itself will collapse. 25A home filled with strife and division destroys itself. 26And if Satan is fighting against himself, how can he accomplish anything? He would never survive. 27[Satan must be bound before his demons are cast out^c], just as a strong man must be tied up before his house can be ransacked and his property robbed.

28"I solemnly declare that any sin of man can be forgiven, even blasphemy against me; 29but blasphemy against the Holy Spirit can never be forgiven. It is an eternal sin."

30He told them this because they were saying he did his miracles by Satan's power [instead of acknowledging it was by the Holy Spirit's power^d].

31, 32Now his mother and brothers arrived at the crowded house where he was teaching, and they sent word for him to come out and talk with them. "Your mother and brothers are outside and want to see you," he was told.

33He replied, "Who is my mother? Who are my brothers?" 34Looking at those around him he said, "These are my mother and brothers! 35Anyone who does God's will is my brother, and my sister, and my mother."

4 ONCE AGAIN an immense crowd gathered around him on the beach as he was teaching, so he got into a boat and sat down and talked from there. 2His usual method of teaching was to tell the people stories. One of them went like this:

3"Listen! A farmer decided to sow some grain. As he scattered it across his field, 4some of it fell on a path, and the birds came and picked it off the hard ground and ate it. 5, 6Some fell on thin soil with underlying rock. It grew up quickly enough, but soon wilted beneath the hot sun and died because the roots had no nourishment in the shallow soil. 7Other seeds fell among thorns that shot up and crowded the young plants so that they produced no grain. 8But some of the seeds fell into good soil and yielded thirty times as much as he had planted—some of it even sixty or a hundred times as much! 9If you have ears, listen!"

10Afterwards, when he was alone with the twelve and with his other disciples, they asked him, "What does your story mean?"

11, 12He replied, "You are permitted to know some truths about the kingdom of God that are hidden to those outside the kingdom:

'Though they see and hear, they will not understand or turn to God, or be forgiven for their sins.'

13But if you can't understand *this* simple illustration, what will you do about all the others I am going to tell? 14"The farmer I talked about is anyone who brings God's message to others, trying to plant good seed within their lives. 15The hard pathway, where some of the

New Revised Standard

heard it, they went out to restrain him, for people were saying, "He has gone out of his mind." 22And the scribes who came down from Jerusalem said, "He has Beelzebul, and by the ruler of the demons he casts out demons." 23And he called them to him, and spoke to them in parables, "How can Satan cast out Satan? 24If a kingdom is divided against itself, that kingdom cannot stand. 25And if a house is divided against itself, that house will not be able to stand. 26And if Satan has risen up against himself and is divided, he cannot stand, but his end has come. 27But no one can enter a strong man's house and plunder his property without first tying up the strong man; then indeed the house can be plundered.

28 "Truly I tell you, people will be forgiven for their sins and whatever blasphemies they utter; 29but whoever blasphemes against the Holy Spirit can never have forgiveness, but is guilty of an eternal sin"— 30for they had said, "He has an unclean spirit."

The True Kindred of Jesus

31 Then his mother and his brothers came; and standing outside, they sent to him and called him. 32A crowd was sitting around him; and they said to him, "Your mother and your brothers and sisters^e are outside, asking for you." 33And he replied, "Who are my mother and my brothers?" 34And looking at those who sat around him, he said, "Here are my mother and my brothers! 35Whoever does the will of God is my brother and sister and mother."

The Parable of the Sower

4 AGAIN HE began to teach beside the sea. Such a very large crowd gathered around him that he got into a boat on the sea and sat there, while the whole crowd was beside the sea on the land. 2He began to teach them many things in parables, and in his teaching he said to them: 3"Listen! A sower went out to sow. 4And as he sowed, some seed fell on the path, and the birds came and ate it up. 5Other seed fell on rocky ground, where it did not have much soil, and it sprang up quickly, since it had no depth of soil. 6And when the sun rose, it was scorched; and since it had no root, it withered away. 7Other seed fell among thorns, and the thorns grew up and choked it, and it yielded no grain. 8Other seed fell into good soil and brought forth grain, growing up and increasing and yielding thirty and sixty and a hundredfold." 9And he said, "Let anyone with ears to hear listen!"

The Purpose of the Parables

10 When he was alone, those who were around him along with the twelve asked him about the parables. 11And he said to them, "To you has been given the secret^f of the kingdom of God, but for those outside, everything comes in parables; 12in order that

'they may indeed look, but not perceive,
 and may indeed listen, but not understand;
 so that they may not turn again and be
 forgiven.' "

13 And he said to them, "Do you not understand this parable? Then how will you understand all the parables? 14The sower sows the word. 15These are the ones on the

King James

15And these are they by the way side, where the word is sown; but when they have heard, Satan cometh immediately, and taketh away the word that was sown in their hearts.

16And these are they likewise which are sown on stony ground; who, when they have heard the word, immediately receive it with gladness;

17And have no root in themselves, and so endure but for a time: afterward, when affliction or persecution ariseth for the word's sake, immediately they are offended.

18And these are they which are sown among thorns; such as hear the word,

19And the cares of this world, and the deceitfulness of riches, and the lusts of other things entering in, choke the word, and it becometh unfruitful.

20And these are they which are sown on good ground; such as hear the word, and receive it, and bring forth fruit, some thirtyfold, some sixty, and some an hundred.

21¶ And he said unto them, Is a candle brought to be put under a bushel, or under a bed? and not to be set on a candlestick?

22For there is nothing hid, which shall not be manifested; neither was any thing kept secret, but that it should come abroad.

23If any man have ears to hear, let him hear.

24And he said unto them, Take heed what ye hear: with what measure ye mete, it shall be measured to you: and unto you that hear shall more be given.

25For he that hath, to him shall be given: and he that hath not, from him shall be taken even that which he hath.

26¶ And he said, So is the kingdom of God, as if a man should cast seed into the ground;

27And should sleep, and rise night and day, and the seed should spring and grow up, he knoweth not how.

28For the earth bringeth forth fruit of herself; first the blade, then the ear, after that the full corn in the ear.

29But when the fruit is brought forth, immediately he putteth in the sickle, because the harvest is come.

30¶ And he said, Whereunto shall we liken the kingdom of God? or with what comparison shall we compare it?

31It is like a grain of mustard seed, which, when it is sown in the earth, is less than all the seeds that be in the earth:

32But when it is sown, it groweth up, and becometh greater than all herbs, and shooteth out great branches; so that the fowls of the air may lodge under the shadow of it.

33And with many such parables spake he the word unto them, as they were able to hear it.

34But without a parable spake he not unto them: and when they were alone, he expounded all things to his disciples.

35And the same day, when the even was come, he saith unto them, Let us pass over unto the other side.

36And when they had sent away the multitude, they took him even as he was in the ship. And there were also with him other little ships.

37And there arose a great storm of wind, and the waves beat into the ship, so that it was now full.

38And he was in the hinder part of the ship, asleep on a pillow: and they awake him, and say unto him, Master, carest thou not that we perish?

39And he arose, and rebuked the wind, and said unto the sea, Peace, be still. And the wind ceased, and there was a great calm.

40And he said unto them, Why are ye so fearful? how is it that ye have no faith?

41And they feared exceedingly, and said one to another, What manner of man is this, that even the wind and the sea obey him?

New International

seed along the path, where the word is sown. As soon as they hear it, Satan comes and takes away the word that was sown in them. 16Others, like seed sown on rocky places, hear the word and at once receive it with joy. 17But since they have no root, they last only a short time. When trouble or persecution comes because of the word, they quickly fall away. 18Still others, like seed sown among thorns, hear the word; 19but the worries of this life, the deceitfulness of wealth and the desires for other things come in and choke the word, making it unfruitful. 20Others, like seed sown on good soil, hear the word, accept it, and produce a crop—thirty, sixty or even a hundred times what was sown."

A Lamp on a Stand

21He said to them, "Do you bring in a lamp to put it under a bowl or a bed? Instead, don't you put it on its stand? 22For whatever is hidden is meant to be disclosed, and whatever is concealed is meant to be brought out into the open. 23If anyone has ears to hear, let him hear."

24"Consider carefully what you hear," he continued. "With the measure you use, it will be measured to you—and even more. 25Whoever has will be given more; whoever does not have, even what he has will be taken from him."

The Parable of the Growing Seed

26He also said, "This is what the kingdom of God is like. A man scatters seed on the ground. 27Night and day, whether he sleeps or gets up, the seed sprouts and grows, though he does not know how. 28All by itself the soil produces grain—first the stalk, then the head, then the full kernel in the head. 29As soon as the grain is ripe, he puts the sickle to it, because the harvest has come."

The Parable of the Mustard Seed

30Again he said, "What shall we say the kingdom of God is like, or what parable shall we use to describe it? 31It is like a mustard seed, which is the smallest seed you plant in the ground. 32Yet when planted, it grows and becomes the largest of all garden plants, with such big branches that the birds of the air can perch in its shade."

33With many similar parables Jesus spoke the word to them, as much as they could understand. 34He did not say anything to them without using a parable. But when he was alone with his own disciples, he explained everything.

Jesus Calms the Storm

35That day when evening came, he said to his disciples, "Let us go over to the other side." 36Leaving the crowd behind, they took him along, just as he was, in the boat. There were also other boats with him. 37A furious squall came up, and the waves broke over the boat, so that it was nearly swamped. 38Jesus was in the stern, sleeping on a cushion. The disciples woke him and said to him, "Teacher, don't you care if we drown?"

39He got up, rebuked the wind and said to the waves, "Quiet! Be still!" Then the wind died down and it was completely calm.

40He said to his disciples, "Why are you so afraid? Do you still have no faith?"

41They were terrified and asked each other, "Who is this? Even the wind and the waves obey him!"

Living Bible

seed fell, represents the hard hearts of some of those who hear God's message; Satan comes at once to try to make them forget it. 16The rocky soil represents the hearts of those who hear the message with joy, 17but, like young plants in such soil, their roots don't go very deep, and though at first they get along fine, as soon as persecution begins, they wilt.

18"The thorny ground represents the hearts of people who listen to the Good News and receive it, 19but all too quickly the attractions of this world and the delights of wealth, and the search for success and lure of nice things come in and crowd out God's message from their hearts, so that no crop is produced.

20"But the good soil represents the hearts of those who truly accept God's message and produce a plentiful harvest for God—thirty, sixty, or even a hundred times as much as was planted in their hearts. 21Then he asked them, "When someone lights a lamp, does he put a box over it to shut out the light? Of course not! The light couldn't be seen or used. A lamp is placed on a stand to shine and be useful.

22"All that is now hidden will someday come to light. 23If you have ears, listen! 24And be sure to put into practice what you hear. The more you do this, the more you will understand what I tell you. 25To him who has shall be given; from him who has not shall be taken away even what he has.

26"Here is another story illustrating what the Kingdom of God is like:

"A farmer sowed his field, 27and went away, and as the days went by, the seeds grew and grew without his help. 28For the soil made the seeds grow. First a leaf-blade pushed through, and later the wheat-heads formed and finally the grain ripened, 29and then the farmer came at once with his sickle and harvested it."

30Jesus asked, "How can I describe the Kingdom of God? What story shall I use to illustrate it? 31, 32It is like a tiny mustard seed! Though this is one of the smallest of seeds, yet it grows to become one of the largest of plants, with long branches where birds can build their nests and be sheltered."

33He used many such illustrations to teach the people as much as they were ready to understand.a 34In fact, he taught only by illustrations in his public teaching, but afterwards, when he was alone with his disciples, he would explain his meaning to them.

35As evening fell, Jesus said to his disciples, "Let's cross to the other side of the lake." 36So they took him just as he was and started out, leaving the crowds behind (though other boats followed). 37But soon a terrible storm arose. High waves began to break into the boat until it was nearly full of water and about to sink. 38Jesus was asleep at the back of the boat with his head on a cushion. Frantically they wakened him, shouting, "Teacher, don't you even care that we are all about to drown?"

39Then he rebuked the wind and said to the sea, "Quiet down!" And the wind fell, and there was a great calm!

40And he asked them, "Why were you so fearful? Don't you even yet have confidence in me?"

41And they were filled with awe and said among themselves, "Who is this man, that even the winds and seas obey him?"

New Revised Standard

path where the word is sown: when they hear, Satan immediately comes and takes away the word that is sown in them. 16And these are the ones sown on rocky ground: when they hear the word, they immediately receive it with joy. 17But they have no root, and endure only for a while; then, when trouble or persecution arises on account of the word, immediately they fall away.b 18And others are those sown among the thorns: these are the ones who hear the word, 19but the cares of the world, and the lure of wealth, and the desire for other things come in and choke the word, and it yields nothing. 20And these are the ones sown on the good soil: they hear the word and accept it and bear fruit, thirty and sixty and a hundredfold."

A Lamp under a Bushel Basket

21 He said to them, "Is a lamp brought in to be put under the bushel basket, or under the bed, and not on the lampstand? 22For there is nothing hidden, except to be disclosed; nor is anything secret, except to come to light. 23Let anyone with ears to hear listen!" 24And he said to them, "Pay attention to what you hear; the measure you give will be the measure you get, and still more will be given you. 25For to those who have, more will be given; and from those who have nothing, even what they have will be taken away."

The Parable of the Growing Seed

26 He also said, "The kingdom of God is as if someone would scatter seed on the ground, 27and would sleep and rise night and day, and the seed would sprout and grow, he does not know how. 28The earth produces of itself, first the stalk, then the head, then the full grain in the head. 29But when the grain is ripe, at once he goes in with his sickle, because the harvest has come."

The Parable of the Mustard Seed

30 He also said, "With what can we compare the kingdom of God, or what parable will we use for it? 31It is like a mustard seed, which, when sown upon the ground, is the smallest of all the seeds on earth; 32yet when it is sown it grows up and becomes the greatest of all shrubs, and puts forth large branches, so that the birds of the air can make nests in its shade."

The Use of Parables

33 With many such parables he spoke the word to them, as they were able to hear it; 34he did not speak to them except in parables, but he explained everything in private to his disciples.

Jesus Stills a Storm

35 On that day, when evening had come, he said to them, "Let us go across to the other side." 36And leaving the crowd behind, they took him with them in the boat, just as he was. Other boats were with him. 37A great windstorm arose, and the waves beat into the boat, so that the boat was already being swamped. 38But he was in the stern, asleep on the cushion; and they woke him up and said to him, "Teacher, do you not care that we are perishing?" 39He woke up and rebuked the wind, and said to the sea, "Peace! Be still!" Then the wind ceased, and there was a dead calm. 40He said to them, "Why are you afraid? Have you still no faith?" 41And they were filled with great awe and said to one another, "Who then is this, that even the wind and the sea obey him?"

---

a 4:33 as much as they were ready to understand, literally, "as they were able to hear."

b Or stumble

King James

5 AND THEY came over unto the other side of the sea, into the country of the Gadarenes.

2And when he was come out of the ship, immediately there met him out of the tombs a man with an unclean spirit,

3Who had *his* dwelling among the tombs; and no man could bind him, no, not with chains:

4Because that he had been often bound with fetters and chains, and the chains had been plucked asunder by him, and the fetters broken in pieces: neither could any *man* tame him.

5And always, night and day, he was in the mountains, and in the tombs, crying, and cutting himself with stones.

6But when he saw Jesus afar off, he ran and worshipped him,

7And cried with a loud voice, and said, What have I to do with thee, Jesus, *thou* Son of the most high God? I adjure thee by God, that thou torment me not.

8For he said unto him, Come out of the man, *thou* unclean spirit.

9And he asked him, What *is* thy name? And he answered, saying, My name *is* Legion: for we are many.

10And he besought him much that he would not send them away out of the country.

11Now there was there nigh unto the mountains a great herd of swine feeding.

12And all the devils besought him, saying, Send us into the swine, that we may enter into them.

13And forthwith Jesus gave them leave. And the unclean spirits went out, and entered into the swine: and the herd ran violently down a steep place into the sea, (they were about two thousand;) and were choked in the sea.

14And they that fed the swine fled, and told *it* in the city, and in the country. And they went out to see what it was that was done.

15And they come to Jesus, and see him that was possessed with the devil, and had the legion, sitting, and clothed, and in his right mind: and they were afraid.

16And they that saw *it* told them how it befell to him that was possessed with the devil, and *also* concerning the swine.

17And they began to pray him to depart out of their coasts.

18And when he was come into the ship, he that had been possessed with the devil prayed him that he might be with him.

19Howbeit Jesus suffered him not, but saith unto him, Go home to thy friends, and tell them how great things the Lord hath done for thee, and hath had compassion on thee.

20And he departed, and began to publish in Decapolis how great things Jesus had done for him: and all *men* did marvel.

21And when Jesus was passed over again by ship unto the other side, much people gathered unto him: and he was nigh unto the sea.

22And, behold, there cometh one of the rulers of the synagogue, Jairus by name; and when he saw him, he fell at his feet,

23And besought him greatly, saying, My little daughter lieth at the point of death: *I pray thee,* come and lay thy hands on her, that she may be healed; and she shall live.

24And *Jesus* went with him; and much people followed him, and thronged him.

25And a certain woman, which had an issue of blood twelve years,

26And had suffered many things of many physicians, and had spent all that she had, and was nothing bettered, but rather grew worse,

New International

The Healing of a Demon-possessed Man

5 THEY WENT across the lake to the region of the Gerasenes.[a] 2When Jesus got out of the boat, a man with an evil[b] spirit came from the tombs to meet him. 3This man lived in the tombs, and no one could bind him any more, not even with a chain. 4For he had often been chained hand and foot, but he tore the chains apart and broke the irons on his feet. No one was strong enough to subdue him. 5Night and day among the tombs and in the hills he would cry out and cut himself with stones.

6When he saw Jesus from a distance, he ran and fell on his knees in front of him. 7He shouted at the top of his voice, "What do you want with me, Jesus, Son of the Most High God? Swear to God that you won't torture me!" 8For Jesus had said to him, "Come out of this man, you evil spirit!"

9Then Jesus asked him, "What is your name?"

"My name is Legion," he replied, "for we are many." 10And he begged Jesus again and again not to send them out of the area.

11A large herd of pigs was feeding on the nearby hillside. 12The demons begged Jesus, "Send us among the pigs; allow us to go into them." 13He gave them permission, and the evil spirits came out and went into the pigs. The herd, about two thousand in number, rushed down the steep bank into the lake and were drowned.

14Those tending the pigs ran off and reported this in the town and countryside, and the people went out to see what had happened. 15When they came to Jesus, they saw the man who had been possessed by the legion of demons, sitting there, dressed and in his right mind; and they were afraid. 16Those who had seen it told the people what had happened to the demon-possessed man—and told about the pigs as well. 17Then the people began to plead with Jesus to leave their region.

18As Jesus was getting into the boat, the man who had been demon-possessed begged to go with him. 19Jesus did not let him, but said, "Go home to your family and tell them how much the Lord has done for you, and how he has had mercy on you." 20So the man went away and began to tell in the Decapolis[c] how much Jesus had done for him. And all the people were amazed.

A Dead Girl and a Sick Woman

21When Jesus had again crossed over by boat to the other side of the lake, a large crowd gathered around him while he was by the lake. 22Then one of the synagogue rulers, named Jairus, came there. Seeing Jesus, he fell at his feet 23and pleaded earnestly with him, "My little daughter is dying. Please come and put your hands on her so that she will be healed and live." 24So Jesus went with him.

A large crowd followed and pressed around him. 25And a woman was there who had been subject to bleeding for twelve years. 26She had suffered a great deal under the care of many doctors and had spent all she had, yet instead of getting better she grew worse.

---

[a] *1* Some manuscripts *Gadarenes*; other manuscripts *Gergesenes*   [b] *2* Greek *unclean*; also in verses 8 and 13   [c] *20* That is, the Ten Cities

Living Bible

5 WHEN THEY arrived at the other side of the lake a demon-possessed man ran out from a graveyard, just as Jesus was climbing from the boat.

3, 4This man lived among the gravestones, and had such strength that whenever he was put into handcuffs and shackles—as he often was—he snapped the handcuffs from his wrists and smashed the shackles and walked away. No one was strong enough to control him. 5All day long and through the night he would wander among the tombs and in the wild hills, screaming and cutting himself with sharp pieces of stone.

6When Jesus was still far out on the water, the man had seen him and had run to meet him, and fell down before him.

7, 8Then Jesus spoke to the demon within the man and said, "Come out, you evil spirit."

It gave a terrible scream, shrieking, "What are you going to do to me, Jesus, Son of the Most High God? For God's sake, don't torture me!"

9"What is your name?" Jesus asked, and the demon replied, "Legion, for there are many of us here within this man."

10Then the demons begged him again and again not to send them to some distant land.

11Now as it happened there was a huge herd of hogs rooting around on the hill above the lake. 12"Send us into those hogs," the demons begged.

13And Jesus gave them permission. Then the evil spirits came out of the man and entered the hogs, and the entire herd plunged down the steep hillside into the lake and drowned.

14The herdsmen fled to the nearby towns and countryside, spreading the news as they ran. Everyone rushed out to see for themselves. 15And a large crowd soon gathered where Jesus was; but as they saw the man sitting there, fully clothed and perfectly sane, they were frightened. 16Those who saw what happened were telling everyone about it, 17and the crowd began pleading with Jesus to go away and leave them alone! 18So he got back into the boat. The man who had been possessed by the demons begged Jesus to let him go along. 19But Jesus said no.

"Go home to your friends," he told him, "and tell them what wonderful things God has done for you; and how merciful he has been."

20So the man started off to visit the Ten Towns[d] of that region and began to tell everyone about the great things Jesus had done for him; and they were awestruck by his story.

21When Jesus had gone across by boat to the other side of the lake, a vast crowd gathered around him on the shore.

22The leader of the local synagogue, whose name was Jairus, came and fell down before him, 23pleading with him to heal his little daughter.

"She is at the point of death," he said in desperation. "Please come and place your hands on her and make her live."

24Jesus went with him, and the crowd thronged behind. 25In the crowd was a woman who had been sick for twelve years with a hemorrhage. 26She had suffered much from many doctors through the years and had become poor from paying them, and was no better but, in fact, was worse. 27She had heard all about the won-

New Revised Standard

Jesus Heals the Gerasene Demoniac

5 THEY CAME to the other side of the sea, to the country of the Gerasenes.[e] 2And when he had stepped out of the boat, immediately a man out of the tombs with an unclean spirit met him. 3He lived among the tombs; and no one could restrain him any more, even with a chain; 4for he had often been restrained with shackles and chains, but the chains he wrenched apart, and the shackles he broke in pieces; and no one had the strength to subdue him. 5Night and day among the tombs and on the mountains he was always howling and bruising himself with stones. 6When he saw Jesus from a distance, he ran and bowed down before him; 7and he shouted at the top of his voice, "What have you to do with me, Jesus, Son of the Most High God? I adjure you by God, do not torment me." 8For he had said to him, "Come out of the man, you unclean spirit!" 9Then Jesus[f] asked him, "What is your name?" He replied, "My name is Legion; for we are many." 10He begged him earnestly not to send them out of the country. 11Now there on the hillside a great herd of swine was feeding; 12and the unclean spirits[g] begged him, "Send us into the swine; let us enter them." 13So he gave them permission. And the unclean spirits came out and entered the swine; and the herd, numbering about two thousand, rushed down the steep bank into the sea, and were drowned in the sea.

14 The swineherds ran off and told it in the city and in the country. Then people came to see what it was that had happened. 15They came to Jesus and saw the demoniac sitting there, clothed and in his right mind, the very man who had had the legion; and they were afraid. 16Those who had seen what had happened to the demoniac and to the swine reported it. 17Then they began to beg Jesus[h] to leave their neighborhood. 18As he was getting into the boat, the man who had been possessed by demons begged him that he might be with him. 19But Jesus[f] refused, and said to him, "Go home to your friends, and tell them how much the Lord has done for you, and what mercy he has shown you." 20And he went away and began to proclaim in the Decapolis how much Jesus had done for him; and everyone was amazed.

A Girl Restored to Life and a Woman Healed

21 When Jesus had crossed again in the boat[i] to the other side, a great crowd gathered around him; and he was by the sea. 22Then one of the leaders of the synagogue named Jairus came and, when he saw him, fell at his feet 23and begged him repeatedly, "My little daughter is at the point of death. Come and lay your hands on her, so that she may be made well, and live." 24So he went with him.

And a large crowd followed him and pressed in on him. 25Now there was a woman who had been suffering from hemorrhages for twelve years. 26She had endured much under many physicians, and had spent all that she had; and she was no better, but rather grew worse. 27She

---

d 5:20 to visit the Ten Towns, or, "to visit Decapolis."

e Other ancient authorities read Gergesenes; others, Gadarenes   f Gk he
g Gk they   h Gk him   i Other ancient authorities lack in the boat

King James

27When she had heard of Jesus, came in the press behind, and touched his garment.

28For she said, If I may touch but his clothes, I shall be whole.

29And straightway the fountain of her blood was dried up; and she felt in *her* body that she was healed of that plague.

30And Jesus, immediately knowing in himself that virtue had gone out of him, turned him about in the press, and said, Who touched my clothes?

31And his disciples said unto him, Thou seest the multitude thronging thee, and sayest thou, Who touched me?

32And he looked round about to see her that had done this thing.

33But the woman fearing and trembling, knowing what was done in her, came and fell down before him, and told him all the truth.

34And he said unto her, Daughter, thy faith hath made thee whole; go in peace, and be whole of thy plague.

35While he yet spake, there came from the ruler of the synagogue's *house certain* which said, Thy daughter is dead: why troublest thou the Master any further?

36As soon as Jesus heard the word that was spoken, he saith unto the ruler of the synagogue, Be not afraid, only believe.

37And he suffered no man to follow him, save Peter, and James, and John the brother of James.

38And he cometh to the house of the ruler of the synagogue, and seeth the tumult, and them that wept and wailed greatly.

39And when he was come in, he saith unto them, Why make ye this ado, and weep? the damsel is not dead, but sleepeth.

40And they laughed him to scorn. But when he had put them all out, he taketh the father and the mother of the damsel, and them that were with him, and entereth in where the damsel was lying.

41And he took the damsel by the hand, and said unto her, Talitha cumi; which is, being interpreted, Damsel, I say unto thee, arise.

42And straightway the damsel arose, and walked; for she was *of the age* of twelve years. And they were astonished with a great astonishment.

43And he charged them straitly that no man should know it; and commanded that something should be given her to eat.

6 AND HE went out from thence, and came into his own country; and his disciples follow him.

2And when the sabbath day was come, he began to teach in the synagogue: and many hearing *him* were astonished, saying, From whence hath this *man* these things? and what wisdom *is* this which is given unto him, that even such mighty works are wrought by his hands?

3Is not this the carpenter, the son of Mary, the brother of James, and Joses, and of Judah, and Simon? and are not his sisters here with us? And they were offended at him.

4But Jesus said unto them, A prophet is not without honour, but in his own country, and among his own kin, and in his own house.

5And he could there do no mighty work, save that he laid his hands upon a few sick folk, and healed *them*.

6And he marvelled because of their unbelief. And he went round about the villages, teaching.

7¶ And he called *unto him* the twelve, and began to send them forth by two and two; and gave them power over unclean spirits;

New International

27When she heard about Jesus, she came up behind him in the crowd and touched his cloak, 28because she thought, "If I just touch his clothes, I will be healed." 29Immediately her bleeding stopped and she felt in her body that she was freed from her suffering.

30At once Jesus realized that power had gone out from him. He turned around in the crowd and asked, "Who touched my clothes?"

31"You see the people crowding against you," his disciples answered, "and yet you can ask, 'Who touched me?' "

32But Jesus kept looking around to see who had done it. 33Then the woman, knowing what had happened to her, came and fell at his feet and, trembling with fear, told him the whole truth. 34He said to her, "Daughter, your faith has healed you. Go in peace and be freed from your suffering."

35While Jesus was still speaking, some men came from the house of Jairus, the synagogue ruler. "Your daughter is dead," they said. "Why bother the teacher any more?"

36Ignoring what they said, Jesus told the synagogue ruler, "Don't be afraid; just believe."

37He did not let anyone follow him except Peter, James and John the brother of James. 38When they came to the home of the synagogue ruler, Jesus saw a commotion, with people crying and wailing loudly. 39He went in and said to them, "Why all this commotion and wailing? The child is not dead but asleep." 40But they laughed at him.

After he put them all out, he took the child's father and mother and the disciples who were with him, and went in where the child was. 41He took her by the hand and said to her, *"Talitha koum!"* (which means, "Little girl, I say to you, get up!"). 42Immediately the girl stood up and walked around (she was twelve years old). At this they were completely astonished. 43He gave strict orders not to let anyone know about this, and told them to give her something to eat.

A Prophet Without Honor

6 JESUS LEFT there and went to his hometown, accompanied by his disciples. 2When the Sabbath came, he began to teach in the synagogue, and many who heard him were amazed.

"Where did this man get these things?" they asked. "What's this wisdom that has been given him, that he even does miracles! 3Isn't this the carpenter? Isn't this Mary's son and the brother of James, Joseph,a Judas and Simon? Aren't his sisters here with us?" And they took offense at him.

4Jesus said to them, "Only in his hometown, among his relatives and in his own house is a prophet without honor." 5He could not do any miracles there, except lay his hands on a few sick people and heal them. 6And he was amazed at their lack of faith.

Jesus Sends Out the Twelve

Then Jesus went around teaching from village to village. 7Calling the Twelve to him, he sent them out two by two and gave them authority over evilb spirits.

a 3 Greek *Joses*, a variant of *Joseph*　　b 7 Greek *unclean*

Living Bible

derful miracles Jesus did, and that is why she came up behind him through the crowd and touched his clothes. [28]For she thought to herself, "If I can just touch his clothing, I will be healed." [29]And sure enough, as soon as she had touched him, the bleeding stopped and she knew she was well!

[30]Jesus realized at once that healing power had gone out from him, so he turned around in the crowd and asked, "Who touched my clothes?"

[31]His disciples said to him, "All this crowd pressing around you, and you ask who touched you?"

[32]But he kept on looking around to see who it was who had done it. [33]Then the frightened woman, trembling at the realization of what had happened to her, came and fell at his feet and told him what she had done. [34]And he said to her, "Daughter, your faith has made you well; go in peace, healed of your disease."

[35]While he was still talking to her, messengers arrived from Jairus' home with the news that it was too late—his daughter was dead and there was no point in Jesus' coming now. [36]But Jesus ignored their comments and said to Jairus, "Don't be afraid. Just trust me."

[37]Then Jesus halted the crowd and wouldn't let anyone go on with him to Jairus' home except Peter and James and John. [38]When they arrived, Jesus saw that all was in great confusion, with unrestrained weeping and wailing. [39]He went inside and spoke to the people.

"Why all this weeping and commotion?" he asked. "The child isn't dead; she is only asleep!"

[40]They laughed at him in bitter derision, but he told them all to leave, and taking the little girl's father and mother and his three disciples, he went into the room where she was lying.

[41, 42]Taking her by the hand he said to her, "Get up, little girl!" (She was twelve years old.) And she jumped up and walked around! Her parents just couldn't get over it. [43]Jesus instructed them very earnestly not to tell what had happened, and told them to give her something to eat.

6 SOON AFTERWARDS he left that section of the country and returned with his disciples to Nazareth, his home town. [2, 3]The next Sabbath he went to the synagogue to teach, and the people were astonished at his wisdom and his miracles because he was just a local man like themselves.

"He's no better than we are," they said. "He's just a carpenter, Mary's boy, and a brother of James and Joseph, Judas and Simon. And his sisters live right here among us." And they were offended!

[4]Then Jesus told them, "A prophet is honored everywhere except in his home town and among his relatives and by his own family." [5]And because of their unbelief he couldn't do any mighty miracles among them except to place his hands on a few sick people and heal them. [6]And he could hardly accept the fact that they wouldn't believe in him.

Then he went out among the villages, teaching.

[7]And he called his twelve disciples together and sent them out two by two, with power to cast out demons.

New Revised Standard

had heard about Jesus, and came up behind him in the crowd and touched his cloak, [28]for she said, "If I but touch his clothes, I will be made well." [29]Immediately her hemorrhage stopped; and she felt in her body that she was healed of her disease. [30]Immediately aware that power had gone forth from him, Jesus turned about in the crowd and said, "Who touched my clothes?" [31]And his disciples said to him, "You see the crowd pressing in on you; how can you say, 'Who touched me?' " [32]He looked all around to see who had done it. [33]But the woman, knowing what had happened to her, came in fear and trembling, fell down before him, and told him the whole truth. [34]He said to her, "Daughter, your faith has made you well; go in peace, and be healed of your disease."

35 While he was still speaking, some people came from the leader's house to say, "Your daughter is dead. Why trouble the teacher any further?" [36]But overhearing[c] what they said, Jesus said to the leader of the synagogue, "Do not fear, only believe." [37]He allowed no one to follow him except Peter, James, and John, the brother of James. [38]When they came to the house of the leader of the synagogue, he saw a commotion, people weeping and wailing loudly. [39]When he had entered, he said to them, "Why do you make a commotion and weep? The child is not dead but sleeping." [40]And they laughed at him. Then he put them all outside, and took the child's father and mother and those who were with him, and went in where the child was. [41]He took her by the hand and said to her, "Talitha cum," which means, "Little girl, get up!" [42]And immediately the girl got up and began to walk about (she was twelve years of age). At this they were overcome with amazement. [43]He strictly ordered them that no one should know this, and told them to give her something to eat.

The Rejection of Jesus at Nazareth

6 HE LEFT that place and came to his hometown, and his disciples followed him. [2]On the sabbath he began to teach in the synagogue, and many who heard him were astounded. They said, "Where did this man get all this? What is this wisdom that has been given to him? What deeds of power are being done by his hands? [3]Is not this the carpenter, the son of Mary[d] and brother of James and Joses and Judas and Simon, and are not his sisters here with us?" And they took offense[e] at him. [4]Then Jesus said to them, "Prophets are not without honor, except in their hometown, and among their own kin, and in their own house." [5]And he could do no deed of power there, except that he laid his hands on a few sick people and cured them. [6]And he was amazed at their unbelief.

The Mission of the Twelve

Then he went about among the villages teaching. [7]He called the twelve and began to send them out two by two, and gave them authority over the unclean spirits.

---

[c] Or *ignoring*; other ancient authorities read *hearing*   [d] Other ancient authorities read *son of the carpenter and of Mary*   [e] Or *stumbled*

King James

8And commanded them that they should take nothing for *their* journey, save a staff only; no scrip, no bread, no money in *their* purse:

9But *be* shod with sandals; and not put on two coats.

10And he said unto them, In what place soever ye enter into an house, there abide till ye depart from that place.

11And whosoever shall not receive you, nor hear you, when ye depart thence, shake off the dust under your feet for a testimony against them. Verily I say unto you, It shall be more tolerable for Sodom and Gomorrha in the day of judgment, than for that city.

12And they went out, and preached that men should repent.

13And they cast out many devils, and anointed with oil many that were sick, and healed *them*.

14And king Herod heard *of him;* (for his name was spread abroad:) and he said, That John the Baptist was risen from the dead, and therefore mighty works do show forth themselves in him.

15Others said, That it is Elias. And others said, That it is a prophet, or as one of the prophets.

16But when Herod heard *thereof,* he said, It is John, whom I beheaded: he is risen from the dead.

17For Herod himself had sent forth and laid hold upon John, and bound him in prison for Herodias' sake, his brother Philip's wife: for he had married her.

18For John had said unto Herod, It is not lawful for thee to have thy brother's wife.

19Therefore Herodias had a quarrel against him, and would have killed him; but she could not:

20For Herod feared John, knowing that he was a just man and an holy, and observed him; and when he heard him, he did many things, and heard him gladly.

21And when a convenient day was come, that Herod on his birthday made a supper to his lords, high captains, and chief *estates* of Galilee;

22And when the daughter of the said Herodias came in, and danced, and pleased Herod and them that sat with him, the king said unto the damsel, Ask of me whatsoever thou wilt, and I will give *it* thee.

23And he sware unto her, Whatsoever thou shalt ask of me, I will give *it* thee, unto the half of my kingdom.

24And she went forth, and said unto her mother, What shall I ask? And she said, The head of John the Baptist.

25And she came in straightway with haste unto the king, and asked, saying, I will that thou give me by and by in a charger the head of John the Baptist.

26And the king was exceeding sorry; *yet* for his oath's sake, and for their sakes which sat with him, he would not reject her.

27And immediately the king sent an executioner, and commanded his head to be brought: and he went and beheaded him in the prison,

28And brought his head in a charger, and gave it to the damsel: and the damsel gave it to her mother.

29And when his disciples heard *of it,* they came and took up his corpse, and laid it in a tomb.

30And the apostles gathered themselves together unto Jesus, and told him all things, both what they had done, and what they had taught.

31And he said unto them, Come ye yourselves apart into a desert place, and rest a while: for there were many coming and going, and they had no leisure so much as to eat.

32And they departed into a desert place by ship privately.

33And the people saw them departing, and many knew him, and ran afoot thither out of all cities, and outwent them, and came together unto him.

34And Jesus, when he came out, saw much people, and was moved with compassion toward them, because they were as sheep not having a shepherd: and he began to teach them many things.

New International

8These were his instructions: "Take nothing for the journey except a staff—no bread, no bag, no money in your belts. 9Wear sandals but not an extra tunic. 10Whenever you enter a house, stay there until you leave that town. 11And if any place will not welcome you or listen to you, shake the dust off your feet when you leave, as a testimony against them."

12They went out and preached that people should repent. 13They drove out many demons and anointed many sick people with oil and healed them.

John the Baptist Beheaded

14King Herod heard about this, for Jesus' name had become well known. Some were saying,[a] "John the Baptist has been raised from the dead, and that is why miraculous powers are at work in him."

15Others said, "He is Elijah."

And still others claimed, "He is a prophet, like one of the prophets of long ago."

16But when Herod heard this, he said, "John, the man I beheaded, has been raised from the dead!"

17For Herod himself had given orders to have John arrested, and he had him bound and put in prison. He did this because of Herodias, his brother Philip's wife, whom he had married. 18For John had been saying to Herod, "It is not lawful for you to have your brother's wife." 19So Herodias nursed a grudge against John and wanted to kill him. But she was not able to, 20because Herod feared John and protected him, knowing him to be a righteous and holy man. When Herod heard John, he was greatly puzzled[b]; yet he liked to listen to him.

21Finally the opportune time came. On his birthday Herod gave a banquet for his high officials and military commanders and the leading men of Galilee. 22When the daughter of Herodias came in and danced, she pleased Herod and his dinner guests.

The king said to the girl, "Ask me for anything you want, and I'll give it to you." 23And he promised her with an oath, "Whatever you ask I will give you, up to half my kingdom."

24She went out and said to her mother, "What shall I ask for?"

"The head of John the Baptist," she answered.

25At once the girl hurried in to the king with the request: "I want you to give me right now the head of John the Baptist on a platter."

26The king was greatly distressed, but because of his oaths and his dinner guests, he did not want to refuse her. 27So he immediately sent an executioner with orders to bring John's head. The man went, beheaded John in the prison, 28and brought back his head on a platter. He presented it to the girl, and she gave it to her mother. 29On hearing of this, John's disciples came and took his body and laid it in a tomb.

Jesus Feeds the Five Thousand

30The apostles gathered around Jesus and reported to him all they had done and taught. 31Then, because so many people were coming and going that they did not even have a chance to eat, he said to them, "Come with me by yourselves to a quiet place and get some rest."

32So they went away by themselves in a boat to a solitary place. 33But many who saw them leaving recognized them and ran on foot from all the towns and got there ahead of them. 34When Jesus landed and saw a large crowd, he had compassion on them, because they were like sheep without a shepherd. So he began teaching them many things.

---

[a] 14 Some early manuscripts *He was saying*   [b] 20 Some early manuscripts *he did many things*

Living Bible

8, 9He told them to take nothing with them except their walking sticks—no food, no knapsack, no money, not even an extra pair of shoes or a change of clothes.

10"Stay at one home in each village—don't shift around from house to house while you are there," he said. 11"And whenever a village won't accept you or listen to you, shake off the dust from your feet as you leave; it is a sign that you have abandoned it to its fate."

12So the disciples went out, telling everyone they met to turn from sin. 13And they cast out many demons, and healed many sick people, anointing them with olive oil.

14King Herod soon heard about Jesus, for his miracles were talked about everywhere. The king thought Jesus was John the Baptist come back to life again. So the people were saying, "No wonder he can do such miracles." 15Others thought Jesus was Elijah the ancient prophet, now returned to life again; still others claimed he was a new prophet like the great ones of the past.

16"No," Herod said, "it is John, the man I beheaded. He has come back from the dead."

17, 18For Herod had sent soldiers to arrest and imprison John because he kept saying it was wrong for the king to marry Herodias, his brother Philip's wife. 19Herodias wanted John killed in revenge, but without Herod's approval she was powerless. 20And Herod respected John, knowing that he was a good and holy man, and so he kept him under his protection. Herod was disturbed whenever he talked with John, but even so he liked to listen to him.

21Herodias' chance finally came. It was Herod's birthday and he gave a stag party for his palace aides, army officers, and the leading citizens of Galilee. 22, 23Then Herodias' daughter came in and danced before them and greatly pleased them all.

"Ask me for anything you like," the king vowed, "even half of my kingdom, and I will give it to you!"

24She went out and consulted her mother, who told her, "Ask for John the Baptist's head!"

25So she hurried back to the king and told him, "I want the head of John the Baptist—right now—on a tray!"

26Then the king was sorry, but he was embarrassed to break his oath in front of his guests. 27So he sent one of his bodyguards to the prison to cut off John's head and bring it to him. The soldier killed John in the prison, 28and brought back his head on a tray, and gave it to the girl and she took it to her mother.

29When John's disciples heard what had happened, they came for his body and buried it in a tomb.

30The apostles now returned to Jesus from their tour and told him all they had done and what they had said to the people they visited.

31Then Jesus suggested, "Let's get away from the crowds for a while and rest." For so many people were coming and going that they scarcely had time to eat. 32So they left by boat for a quieter spot. 33But many people saw them leaving and ran on ahead along the shore and met them as they landed. 34So the usual vast crowd was there as he stepped from the boat; and he had pity on them because they were like sheep without a shepherd, and he taught them many things they needed to know.

New Revised Standard

8He ordered them to take nothing for their journey except a staff; no bread, no bag, no money in their belts; 9but to wear sandals and not to put on two tunics. 10He said to them, "Wherever you enter a house, stay there until you leave the place. 11If any place will not welcome you and they refuse to hear you, as you leave, shake off the dust that is on your feet as a testimony against them." 12So they went out and proclaimed that all should repent. 13They cast out many demons, and anointed with oil many who were sick and cured them.

The Death of John the Baptist

14 King Herod heard of it, for Jesus'c name had become known. Some wered saying, "John the baptizer has been raised from the dead; and for this reason these powers are at work in him." 15But others said, "It is Elijah." And others said, "It is a prophet, like one of the prophets of old." 16But when Herod heard of it, he said, "John, whom I beheaded, has been raised."

17 For Herod himself had sent men who arrested John, bound him, and put him in prison on account of Herodias, his brother Philip's wife, because Herode had married her. 18For John had been telling Herod, "It is not lawful for you to have your brother's wife." 19And Herodias had a grudge against him, and wanted to kill him. But she could not, 20for Herod feared John, knowing that he was a righteous and holy man, and he protected him. When he heard him, he was greatly perplexed;f and yet he liked to listen to him. 21But an opportunity came when Herod on his birthday gave a banquet for his courtiers and officers and for the leaders of Galilee. 22When his daughter Herodiasg came in and danced, she pleased Herod and his guests; and the king said to the girl, "Ask me for whatever you wish, and I will give it." 23And he solemnly swore to her, "Whatever you ask me, I will give you, even half of my kingdom." 24She went out and said to her mother, "What should I ask for?" She replied, "The head of John the baptizer." 25Immediately she rushed back to the king and requested, "I want you to give me at once the head of John the Baptist on a platter." 26The king was deeply grieved; yet out of regard for his oaths and for the guests, he did not want to refuse her. 27Immediately the king sent a soldier of the guard with orders to bring John'sc head. He went and beheaded him in the prison, 28brought his head on a platter, and gave it to the girl. Then the girl gave it to her mother. 29When his disciples heard about it, they came and took his body, and laid it in a tomb.

Feeding the Five Thousand

30 The apostles gathered around Jesus, and told him all that they had done and taught. 31He said to them, "Come away to a deserted place all by yourselves and rest a while." For many were coming and going, and they had no leisure even to eat. 32And they went away in the boat to a deserted place by themselves. 33Now many saw them going and recognized them, and they hurried there on foot from all the towns and arrived ahead of them. 34As he went ashore, he saw a great crowd; and he had compassion for them, because they were like sheep without a shepherd; and he began to teach them many things. 35When it grew late, his disci-

c Gk his   d Other ancient authorities read He was   e Gk he   f Other ancient authorities read he did many things   g Other ancient authorities read the daughter of Herodias herself

King James

35And when the day was now far spent, his disciples came unto him, and said, This is a desert place, and now the time *is* far passed:

36Send them away, that they may go into the country round about, and into the villages, and buy themselves bread: for they have nothing to eat.

37He answered and said unto them, Give ye them to eat. And they say unto him, Shall we go and buy two hundred pennyworth of bread, and give them to eat?

38He saith unto them, How many loaves have ye? go and see. And when they knew, they say, Five, and two fishes.

39And he commanded them to make all sit down by companies upon the green grass.

40And they sat down in ranks, by hundreds, and by fifties.

41And when he had taken the five loaves and the two fishes, he looked up to heaven, and blessed, and brake the loaves, and gave *them* to his disciples to set before them; and the two fishes divided he among them all.

42And they did all eat, and were filled.

43And they took up twelve baskets full of the fragments, and of the fishes.

44And they that did eat of the loaves were about five thousand men.

45And straightway he constrained his disciples to get into the ship, and to go to the other side before unto Bethsaida, while he sent away the people.

46And when he had sent them away, he departed into a mountain to pray.

47And when even was come, the ship was in the midst of the sea, and he alone on the land.

48And he saw them toiling in rowing; for the wind was contrary unto them: and about the fourth watch of the night he cometh unto them, walking upon the sea, and would have passed by them.

49But when they saw him walking upon the sea, they supposed it had been a spirit, and cried out:

50For they all saw him, and were troubled. And immediately he talked with them, and saith unto them, Be of good cheer: it is I; be not afraid.

51And he went up unto them into the ship; and the wind ceased: and they were sore amazed in themselves beyond measure, and wondered.

52For they considered not *the miracle* of the loaves: for their heart was hardened.

53And when they had passed over, they came into the land of Gennesaret, and drew to the shore.

54And when they were come out of the ship, straightway they knew him,

55And ran through that whole region round about, and began to carry about in beds those that were sick, where they heard he was.

56And whithersoever he entered, into villages, or cities, or country, they laid the sick in the streets, and besought him that they might touch if it were but the border of his garment: and as many as touched him were made whole.

7 THEN CAME together unto him the Pharisees, and certain of the scribes, which came from Jerusalem.

2And when they saw some of his disciples eat bread with defiled, that is to say, with unwashen, hands, they found fault.

3For the Pharisees, and all the Jews, except they wash *their* hands oft, eat not, holding the tradition of the elders.

New International

35By this time it was late in the day, so his disciples came to him. "This is a remote place," they said, "and it's already very late. 36Send the people away so they can go to the surrounding countryside and villages and buy themselves something to eat."

37But he answered, "You give them something to eat."

They said to him, "That would take eight months of a man's wages[a]! Are we to go and spend that much on bread and give it to them to eat?"

38"How many loaves do you have?" he asked. "Go and see."

When they found out, they said, "Five—and two fish."

39Then Jesus directed them to have all the people sit down in groups on the green grass. 40So they sat down in groups of hundreds and fifties. 41Taking the five loaves and the two fish and looking up to heaven, he gave thanks and broke the loaves. Then he gave them to his disciples to set before the people. He also divided the two fish among them all. 42They all ate and were satisfied, 43and the disciples picked up twelve basketfuls of broken pieces of bread and fish. 44The number of the men who had eaten was five thousand.

Jesus Walks on the Water

45Immediately Jesus made his disciples get into the boat and go on ahead of him to Bethsaida, while he dismissed the crowd. 46After leaving them, he went up on a mountainside to pray.

47When evening came, the boat was in the middle of the lake, and he was alone on land. 48He saw the disciples straining at the oars, because the wind was against them. About the fourth watch of the night he went out to them, walking on the lake. He was about to pass by them, 49but when they saw him walking on the lake, they thought he was a ghost. They cried out, 50because they all saw him and were terrified.

Immediately he spoke to them and said, "Take courage! It is I. Don't be afraid." 51Then he climbed into the boat with them, and the wind died down. They were completely amazed, 52for they had not understood about the loaves; their hearts were hardened.

53When they had crossed over, they landed at Gennesaret and anchored there. 54As soon as they got out of the boat, people recognized Jesus. 55They ran throughout that whole region and carried the sick on mats to wherever they heard he was. 56And wherever he went—into villages, towns or countryside—they placed the sick in the marketplaces. They begged him to let them touch even the edge of his cloak, and all who touched him were healed.

Clean and Unclean

7 THE PHARISEES and some of the teachers of the law who had come from Jerusalem gathered around Jesus and 2saw some of his disciples eating food with hands that were "unclean," that is, unwashed. 3(The Pharisees and all the Jews do not eat unless they give their hands a ceremonial washing, holding to the tradition of the elders. 4When they come from the mar-

---

ᵃ *37 Greek take two hundred denarii*

Living Bible

35, 36Late in the afternoon his disciples came to him and said, "Tell the people to go away to the nearby villages and farms and buy themselves some food, for there is nothing to eat here in this desolate spot, and it is getting late."

37But Jesus said, *"You feed them."*

"With what?" they asked. "It would take a fortuneᵇ to buy food for all this crowd!"

38"How much food do we have?" he asked. "Go and find out."

They came back to report that there were five loaves of bread and two fish. 39, 40Then Jesus told the crowd to sit down, and soon colorful groups of fifty or a hundred each were sitting on the green grass.

41He took the five loaves and two fish and looking up to heaven, gave thanks for the food. Breaking the loaves into pieces, he gave some of the bread and fish to each disciple to place before the people. 42And the crowd ate until they could hold no more!

43, 44There were about 5,000 men there for that meal, and afterwards twelve basketfuls of scraps were picked up off the grass!

45Immediately after this Jesus instructed his disciples to get back into the boat and strike out across the lake to Bethsaida, where he would join them later. He himself would stay and tell the crowds good-bye and get them started home.

46Afterwards he went up into the hills to pray. 47During the night, as the disciples in their boat were out in the middle of the lake, and he was alone on land, 48he saw that they were in serious trouble, rowing hard and struggling against the wind and waves.

About three o'clock in the morning he walked out to them on the water. He started past them, 49but when they saw something walking along beside them they screamed in terror, thinking it was a ghost, 50for they all saw him.

But he spoke to them at once. "It's all right," he said. "It is I! Don't be afraid." 51Then he climbed into the boat and the wind stopped!

They just sat there, unable to take it in! 52For they still didn't realize who he was, even after the miracle the evening before! For they didn't want to believe!ᶜ

53When they arrived at Gennesaret on the other side of the lake they moored the boat, 54and climbed out.

The people standing around there recognized him at once, 55and ran throughout the whole area to spread the news of his arrival, and began carrying sick folks to him on mats and stretchers. 56Wherever he went—in villages and cities, and out on the farms—they laid the sick in the market plazas and streets, and begged him to let them at least touch the fringes of his clothes; and as many as touched him were healed.

7 ONE DAY some Jewish religious leaders arrived from Jerusalem to investigate him, 2and noticed that some of his disciples failed to follow the usual Jewish rituals before eating. 3(For the Jews, especially the Pharisees, will never eat until they have sprinkled their arms to the elbows,ᵈ as required by their ancient traditions. 4So when they come home from the market they

New Revised Standard

ples came to him and said, "This is a deserted place, and the hour is now very late; 36send them away so that they may go into the surrounding country and villages and buy something for themselves to eat." 37But he answered them, "You give them something to eat." They said to him, "Are we to go and buy two hundred denariiᵉ worth of bread, and give it to them to eat?" 38And he said to them, "How many loaves have you? Go and see." When they had found out, they said, "Five, and two fish." 39Then he ordered them to get all the people to sit down in groups on the green grass. 40So they sat down in groups of hundreds and of fifties. 41Taking the five loaves and the two fish, he looked up to heaven, and blessed and broke the loaves, and gave them to his disciples to set before the people; and he divided the two fish among them all. 42And all ate and were filled; 43and they took up twelve baskets full of broken pieces and of the fish. 44Those who had eaten the loaves numbered five thousand men.

Jesus Walks on the Water

45 Immediately he made his disciples get into the boat and go on ahead to the other side, to Bethsaida, while he dismissed the crowd. 46After saying farewell to them, he went up on the mountain to pray.

47 When evening came, the boat was out on the sea, and he was alone on the land. 48When he saw that they were straining at the oars against an adverse wind, he came towards them early in the morning, walking on the sea. He intended to pass them by. 49But when they saw him walking on the sea, they thought it was a ghost and cried out; 50for they all saw him and were terrified. But immediately he spoke to them and said, "Take heart, it is I; do not be afraid." 51Then he got into the boat with them and the wind ceased. And they were utterly astounded, 52for they did not understand about the loaves, but their hearts were hardened.

Healing the Sick in Gennesaret

53 When they had crossed over, they came to land at Gennesaret and moored the boat. 54When they got out of the boat, people at once recognized him, 55and rushed about that whole region and began to bring the sick on mats to wherever they heard he was. 56And wherever he went, into villages or cities or farms, they laid the sick in the marketplaces, and begged him that they might touch even the fringe of his cloak; and all who touched it were healed.

The Tradition of the Elders

7 NOW WHEN the Pharisees and some of the scribes who had come from Jerusalem gathered around him, 2they noticed that some of his disciples were eating with defiled hands, that is, without washing them. 3(For the Pharisees, and all the Jews, do not eat unless they thoroughly wash their hands,ᶠ thus observing the tradition of the elders; 4and they do not eat any-

---

ᵇ *6:37 It would take a fortune,* literally, "200 denarii," a year's wages.
ᶜ *6:52 For they didn't want to believe,* literally, "For their hearts were hardened," perhaps implying jealousy, as in Mk 6:2-6.   ᵈ *7:3 sprinkled their arms to the elbows,* literally, "to wash with the fist."

ᵉ The denarius was the usual day's wage for a laborer   ᶠ Meaning of Gk uncertain

King James

4And *when they come* from the market, except they wash, they eat not. And many other things there be, which they have received to hold, *as* the washing of cups, and pots, brasen vessels, and of tables.

5Then the Pharisees and scribes asked him, Why walk not thy disciples according to the tradition of the elders, but eat bread with unwashen hands?

6He answered and said unto them, Well hath Esaias prophesied of you hypocrites, as it is written, This people honoureth me with *their* lips, but their heart is far from me.

7Howbeit in vain do they worship me, teaching *for* doctrines the commandments of men.

8For laying aside the commandment of God, ye hold the tradition of men, *as* the washing of pots and cups: and many other such like things ye do.

9And he said unto them, Full well ye reject the commandment of God, that ye may keep your own tradition.

10For Moses said, Honour thy father and thy mother; and, Whoso curseth father or mother, let him die the death:

11But ye say, If a man shall say to his father or mother, *It is* Corban, that is to say, a gift, by whatsoever thou mightest be profited by me; *he shall be free.*

12And ye suffer him no more to do aught for his father or his mother;

13Making the word of God of none effect through your tradition, which ye have delivered: and many such like things do ye.

14¶ And when he had called all the people *unto him*, he said unto them, Hearken unto me every one *of you*, and understand:

15There is nothing from without a man, that entering into him can defile him: but the things which come out of him, those are they that defile the man.

16If any man have ears to hear, let him hear.

17And when he was entered into the house from the people, his disciples asked him concerning the parable.

18And he saith unto them, Are ye so without understanding also? Do ye not perceive, that whatsoever thing from without entereth into the man, *it* cannot defile him;

19Because it entereth not into his heart, but into the belly, and goeth out into the draught, purging all meats?

20And he said, That which cometh out of the man, that defileth the man.

21For from within, out of the heart of men, proceed evil thoughts, adulteries, fornications, murders,

22Thefts, covetousness, wickedness, deceit, lasciviousness, an evil eye, blasphemy, pride, foolishness:

23All these evil things come from within, and defile the man.

24¶ And from thence he arose, and went into the borders of Tyre and Sidon, and entered into an house, and would have no man know *it:* but he could not be hid.

25For a *certain* woman, whose young daughter had an unclean spirit, heard of him, and came and fell at his feet:

26The woman was a Greek, a Syrophenician by nation; and she besought him that he would cast forth the devil out of her daughter.

27But Jesus said unto her, Let the children first be filled: for it is not meet to take the children's bread, and to cast *it* unto the dogs.

28And she answered and said unto him, Yes, Lord: yet the dogs under the table eat of the children's crumbs.

29And he said unto her, For this saying go thy way; the devil is gone out of thy daughter.

30And when she was come to her house, she found the devil gone out, and her daughter laid upon the bed.

New International

ketplace they do not eat unless they wash. And they observe many other traditions, such as the washing of cups, pitchers and kettles.a)

5So the Pharisees and teachers of the law asked Jesus, "Why don't your disciples live according to the tradition of the elders instead of eating their food with 'unclean' hands?"

6He replied, "Isaiah was right when he prophesied about you hypocrites; as it is written:

" 'These people honor me with their lips,
    but their hearts are far from me.
7They worship me in vain;
    their teachings are but rules taught by men.'b

8You have let go of the commands of God and are holding on to the traditions of men."

9And he said to them: "You have a fine way of setting aside the commands of God in order to observec your own traditions! 10For Moses said, 'Honor your father and your mother,'d and, 'Anyone who curses his father or mother must be put to death.'e 11But you say that if a man says to his father or mother: 'Whatever help you might otherwise have received from me is Corban' (that is, a gift devoted to God), 12then you no longer let him do anything for his father or mother. 13Thus you nullify the word of God by your tradition that you have handed down. And you do many things like that."

14Again Jesus called the crowd to him and said, "Listen to me, everyone, and understand this. 15Nothing outside a man can make him 'unclean' by going into him. Rather, it is what comes out of a man that makes him 'unclean.'f"

17After he had left the crowd and entered the house, his disciples asked him about this parable. 18"Are you so dull?" he asked. "Don't you see that nothing that enters a man from the outside can make him 'unclean'? 19For it doesn't go into his heart but into his stomach, and then out of his body." (In saying this, Jesus declared all foods "clean.")

20He went on: "What comes out of a man is what makes him 'unclean.' 21For from within, out of men's hearts, come evil thoughts, sexual immorality, theft, murder, adultery, 22greed, malice, deceit, lewdness, envy, slander, arrogance and folly. 23All these evils come from inside and make a man 'unclean.' "

The Faith of a Syrophoenician Woman

24Jesus left that place and went to the vicinity of Tyre.g He entered a house and did not want anyone to know it; yet he could not keep his presence secret. 25In fact, as soon as she heard about him, a woman whose little daughter was possessed by an evilh spirit came and fell at his feet. 26The woman was a Greek, born in Syrian Phoenicia. She begged Jesus to drive the demon out of her daughter.

27"First let the children eat all they want," he told her, "for it is not right to take the children's bread and toss it to their dogs."

28"Yes, Lord," she replied, "but even the dogs under the table eat the children's crumbs."

29Then he told her, "For such a reply, you may go; the demon has left your daughter."

30She went home and found her child lying on the bed, and the demon gone.

---

a 4 Some early manuscripts *pitchers, kettles and dining couches*
b 6,7 Isaiah 29:13   c 9 Some manuscripts *set up*   d 10 Exodus 20:12;
Deut. 5:16   e 10 Exodus 21:17; Lev. 20:9   f 15 Some early manuscripts
'unclean.' 16If anyone has ears to hear, let him hear.   g 24 Many early
manuscripts *Tyre and Sidon*   h 25 Greek *unclean*

Living Bible

must always sprinkle themselves in this way before touching any food. This is but one of many examples of laws and regulations they have clung to for centuries, and still follow, such as their ceremony of cleansing for pots, pans and dishes.)

5So the religious leaders asked him, "Why don't your disciples follow our age-old customs? For they eat without first performing the washing ceremony."

6, 7Jesus replied, "You bunch of hypocrites! Isaiah the prophet described you very well when he said, 'These people speak very prettily about the Lord but they have no love for him at all. Their worship is a farce, for they claim that God commands the people to obey their petty rules.' How right Isaiah was! 8For you ignore God's specific orders and substitute your own traditions. 9You are simply rejecting God's laws and trampling them under your feet for the sake of tradition.

10For instance, Moses gave you this law from God: 'Honor your father and mother.' And he said that anyone who speaks against his father or mother must die. 11But you say it is perfectly all right for a man to disregard his needy parents, telling them, 'Sorry, I can't help you! For I have given to God what I could have given to you.' 12, 13And so you break the law of God in order to protect your man-made tradition. And this is only one example. There are many, many others."

14Then Jesus called to the crowd to come and hear. "All of you listen," he said, "and try to understand. 15, 16i Your souls aren't harmed by what you eat, but by what you think and say!"j

17Then he went into a house to get away from the crowds, and his disciples asked him what he meant by the statement he had just made.

18"Don't you understand either?" he asked. "Can't you see that what you eat won't harm your soul? 19For food doesn't come in contact with your heart, but only passes through the digestive system." (By saying this he showed that every kind of food is kosher.)

20And then he added, "It is the thoughtlife that pollutes. 21For from within, out of men's hearts, come evil thoughts of lust, theft, murder, adultery, 22wanting what belongs to others, wickedness, deceit, lewdness, envy, slander, pride, and all other folly. 23All these vile things come from within; they are what pollute you and make you unfit for God."

24Then he left Galilee and went to the region of Tyre and Sidon,k and tried to keep it a secret that he was there, but couldn't. For as usual the news of his arrival spread fast.

25Right away a woman came to him whose little girl was possessed by a demon. She had heard about Jesus and now she came and fell at his feet, 26and pled with him to release her child from the demon's control. (But she was Syrophoenician—a "despised Gentile!")

27Jesus told her, "First I should help my own family—the Jews.l It isn't right to take the children's food and throw it to the dogs."

28She replied, "That's true, sir, but even the puppies under the table are given some scraps from the children's plates."

29"Good!" he said, "You have answered well—so well that I have healed your little girl. Go on home, for the demon has left her!"

30And when she arrived home, her little girl was lying quietly in bed, and the demon was gone.

New Revised Standard

thing from the market unless they wash it;m and there are also many other traditions that they observe, the washing of cups, pots, and bronze kettles.n) 5So the Pharisees and the scribes asked him, "Why do your disciples not liveo according to the tradition of the elders, but eat with defiled hands?" 6He said to them, "Isaiah prophesied rightly about you hypocrites, as it is written,

'This people honors me with their lips,
    but their hearts are far from me;
7 in vain do they worship me,
    teaching human precepts as doctrines.'

8You abandon the commandment of God and hold to human tradition."

9 Then he said to them, "You have a fine way of rejecting the commandment of God in order to keep your tradition! 10For Moses said, 'Honor your father and your mother'; and, 'Whoever speaks evil of father or mother must surely die.' 11But you say that if anyone tells father or mother, 'Whatever support you might have had from me is Corban' (that is, an offering to Godp)— 12then you no longer permit doing anything for a father or mother, 13thus making void the word of God through your tradition that you have handed on. And you do many things like this."

14 Then he called the crowd again and said to them, "Listen to me, all of you, and understand: 15there is nothing outside a person that by going in can defile; but the things that come out are what defile."q

17 When he had left the crowd and entered the house, his disciples asked him about the parable. 18He said to them, "Then do you also fail to understand? Do you not see that whatever goes into a person from outside cannot defile, 19since it enters, not the heart but the stomach, and goes out into the sewer?" (Thus he declared all foods clean.) 20And he said, "It is what comes out of a person that defiles. 21For it is from within, from the human heart, that evil intentions come: fornication, theft, murder, 22adultery, avarice, wickedness, deceit, licentiousness, envy, slander, pride, folly. 23All these evil things come from within, and they defile a person."

The Syrophoenician Woman's Faith

24 From there he set out and went away to the region of Tyre.r He entered a house and did not want anyone to know he was there. Yet he could not escape notice, 25but a woman whose little daughter had an unclean spirit immediately heard about him, and she came and bowed down at his feet. 26Now the woman was a Gentile, of Syrophoenician origin. She begged him to cast the demon out of her daughter. 27He said to her, "Let the children be fed first, for it is not fair to take the children's food and throw it to the dogs." 28But she answered him, "Sir,s even the dogs under the table eat the children's crumbs." 29Then he said to her, "For saying that, you may go—the demon has left your daughter." 30So she went home, found the child lying on the bed, and the demon gone.

---

i 7:15, 16 Verse 16 is omitted in many of the ancient manuscripts. "If any man has ears to hear, let him hear." j 7:15, 16 Your souls aren't harmed by what you eat, but by what you think and say, literally, "what proceeds out of the man defiles the man." k 7:24 the region of Tyre and Sidon, about fifty miles away. l 7:27 First I should help my own family—the Jews, literally, "Let the children eat first."

m Other ancient authorities read and when they come from the marketplace, they do not eat unless they purify themselves n Other ancient authorities add and beds o Gk walk p Gk lacks to God q Other ancient authorities add verse 16, "Let anyone with ears to hear listen" r Other ancient authorities add and Sidon s Or Lord; other ancient authorities prefix Yes

King James

31¶ And again, departing from the coasts of Tyre and Sidon, he came unto the sea of Galilee, through the midst of the coasts of Decapolis.

32And they bring unto him one that was deaf, and had an impediment in his speech; and they beseech him to put his hand upon him.

33And he took him aside from the multitude, and put his fingers into his ears, and he spit, and touched his tongue;

34And looking up to heaven, he sighed, and saith unto him, Ephphatha, that is, Be opened.

35And straightway his ears were opened, and the string of his tongue was loosed, and he spake plain.

36And he charged them that they should tell no man: but the more he charged them, so much the more a great deal they published *it;*

37And were beyond measure astonished, saying, He hath done all things well: he maketh both the deaf to hear, and the dumb to speak.

8 IN THOSE days the multitude being very great, and having nothing to eat, Jesus called his disciples *unto him,* and saith unto them,

2I have compassion on the multitude, because they have now been with me three days, and have nothing to eat:

3And if I send them away fasting to their own houses, they will faint by the way: for divers of them came from far.

4And his disciples answered him, From whence can a man satisfy these *men* with bread here in the wilderness?

5And he asked them, How many loaves have ye? And they said, Seven.

6And he commanded the people to sit down on the ground: and he took the seven loaves, and gave thanks, and brake, and gave to his disciples to set before *them;* and they did set *them* before the people.

7And they had a few small fishes: and he blessed, and commanded to set them also before *them.*

8So they did eat, and were filled: and they took up of the broken *meat* that was left seven baskets.

9And they that had eaten were about four thousand: and he sent them away.

10¶ And straightway he entered into a ship with his disciples, and came into the parts of Dalmanutha.

11And the Pharisees came forth, and began to question with him, seeking of him a sign from heaven, tempting him.

12And he sighed deeply in his spirit, and saith, Why doth this generation seek after a sign? verily I say unto you, There shall no sign be given unto this generation.

13And he left them, and entering into the ship again departed to the other side.

14¶ Now *the disciples* had forgotten to take bread, neither had they in the ship with them more than one loaf.

15And he charged them, saying, Take heed, beware of the leaven of the Pharisees, and *of* the leaven of Herod.

16And they reasoned among themselves, saying, *It is* because we have no bread.

17And when Jesus knew *it,* he saith unto them, Why reason ye, because ye have no bread? perceive ye not yet, neither understand? have ye your heart yet hardened?

18Having eyes, see ye not? and having ears, hear ye not? and do ye not remember?

New International

The Healing of a Deaf and Mute Man

31Then Jesus left the vicinity of Tyre and went through Sidon, down to the Sea of Galilee and into the region of the Decapolis.a 32There some people brought to him a man who was deaf and could hardly talk, and they begged him to place his hand on the man.

33After he took him aside, away from the crowd, Jesus put his fingers into the man's ears. Then he spit and touched the man's tongue. 34He looked up to heaven and with a deep sigh said to him, *"Ephphatha!"* (which means, "Be opened!"). 35At this, the man's ears were opened, his tongue was loosened and he began to speak plainly.

36Jesus commanded them not to tell anyone. But the more he did so, the more they kept talking about it. 37People were overwhelmed with amazement. "He has done everything well," they said. "He even makes the deaf hear and the mute speak."

Jesus Feeds the Four Thousand

8 DURING THOSE days another large crowd gathered. Since they had nothing to eat, Jesus called his disciples to him and said, 2"I have compassion for these people; they have already been with me three days and have nothing to eat. 3If I send them home hungry, they will collapse on the way, because some of them have come a long distance."

4His disciples answered, "But where in this remote place can anyone get enough bread to feed them?"

5"How many loaves do you have?" Jesus asked.

"Seven," they replied.

6He told the crowd to sit down on the ground. When he had taken the seven loaves and given thanks, he broke them and gave them to his disciples to set before the people, and they did so. 7They had a few small fish as well; he gave thanks for them also and told the disciples to distribute them. 8The people ate and were satisfied. Afterward the disciples picked up seven basketfuls of broken pieces that were left over. 9About four thousand men were present. And having sent them away, 10he got into the boat with his disciples and went to the region of Dalmanutha.

11The Pharisees came and began to question Jesus. To test him, they asked him for a sign from heaven. 12He sighed deeply and said, "Why does this generation ask for a miraculous sign? I tell you the truth, no sign will be given to it." 13Then he left them, got back into the boat and crossed to the other side.

The Yeast of the Pharisees and Herod

14The disciples had forgotten to bring bread, except for one loaf they had with them in the boat. 15"Be careful," Jesus warned them. "Watch out for the yeast of the Pharisees and that of Herod."

16They discussed this with one another and said, "It is because we have no bread."

17Aware of their discussion, Jesus asked them: "Why are you talking about having no bread? Do you still not see or understand? Are your hearts hardened? 18Do you have eyes but fail to see, and ears but fail to hear? And don't you remember? 19When I broke the five loaves for

---

a *31* That is, the Ten Cities

Living Bible

31From Tyre he went to Sidon, then back to the Sea of Galilee by way of the Ten Towns. 32A deaf man with a speech impediment was brought to him, and everyone begged Jesus to lay his hands on the man and heal him.

33Jesus led him away from the crowd and put his fingers into the man's ears, then spat and touched the man's tongue with the spittle. 34Then, looking up to heaven, he sighed and commanded, "Open!" 35Instantly the man could hear perfectly and speak plainly!

36Jesus told the crowd not to spread the news, but the more he forbade them, the more they made it known, 37for they were overcome with utter amazement. Again and again they said, "Everything he does is wonderful; he even corrects deafness and stammering!"

8 ONE DAY about this time as another great crowd gathered, the people ran out of food again. Jesus called his disciples to discuss the situation.

"I pity these people," he said, "for they have been here three days, and have nothing left to eat. 3And if I send them home without feeding them, they will faint along the road! For some of them have come a long distance."

4"Are we supposed to find food for them here in the desert?" his disciples scoffed.

5"How many loaves of bread do you have?" he asked.

"Seven," they replied. 6So he told the crowd to sit down on the ground. Then he took the seven loaves, thanked God for them, broke them into pieces and passed them to his disciples; and the disciples placed them before the people. 7A few small fish were found, too, so Jesus also blessed these and told the disciples to serve them.

8, 9And the whole crowd ate until they were full, and afterwards he sent them home. There were about 4,000 people in the crowd that day and when the scraps were picked up after the meal, there were seven very large basketfuls left over!

10Immediately after this he got into a boat with his disciples and came to the region of Dalmanutha.

11When the local Jewish leaders learned of his arrival they came to argue with him.

"Do a miracle for us," they said. "Make something happen in the sky. Then we will believe in you."b

12He sighed deeply when he heard this and he said, "Certainly not. How many more miracles do you people need?"c

13So he got back into the boat and left them, and crossed to the other side of the lake. 14But the disciples had forgotten to stock up on food before they left, and had only one loaf of bread in the boat.

15As they were crossing, Jesus said to them very solemnly, "Beware of the yeast of King Herod and of the Pharisees."

16"What does he mean?" the disciples asked each other. They finally decided that he must be talking about their forgetting to bring bread.

17Jesus realized what they were discussing and said, "No, that isn't it at all! Can't you understand? Are your hearts too hard to take it in? 18'Your eyes are to see with—why don't you look? Why don't you open your ears and listen?' Don't you remember anything at all?

New Revised Standard

Jesus Cures a Deaf Man

31 Then he returned from the region of Tyre, and went by way of Sidon towards the Sea of Galilee, in the region of the Decapolis. 32They brought to him a deaf man who had an impediment in his speech; and they begged him to lay his hand on him. 33He took him aside in private, away from the crowd, and put his fingers into his ears, and he spat and touched his tongue. 34Then looking up to heaven, he sighed and said to him, "Eph-phatha," that is, "Be opened." 35And immediately his ears were opened, his tongue was released, and he spoke plainly. 36Then Jesusd ordered them to tell no one; but the more he ordered them, the more zealously they proclaimed it. 37They were astounded beyond measure, saying, "He has done everything well; he even makes the deaf to hear and the mute to speak."

Feeding the Four Thousand

8 IN THOSE days when there was again a great crowd without anything to eat, he called his disciples and said to them, 2"I have compassion for the crowd, because they have been with me now for three days and have nothing to eat. 3If I send them away hungry to their homes, they will faint on the way—and some of them have come from a great distance." 4His disciples replied, "How can one feed these people with bread here in the desert?" 5He asked them, "How many loaves do you have?" They said, "Seven." 6Then he ordered the crowd to sit down on the ground; and he took the seven loaves, and after giving thanks he broke them and gave them to his disciples to distribute; and they distributed them to the crowd. 7They had also a few small fish; and after blessing them, he ordered that these too should be distributed. 8They ate and were filled; and they took up the broken pieces left over, seven baskets full. 9Now there were about four thousand people. And he sent them away. 10And immediately he got into the boat with his disciples and went to the district of Dalmanutha.e

The Demand for a Sign

11 The Pharisees came and began to argue with him, asking him for a sign from heaven, to test him. 12And he sighed deeply in his spirit and said, "Why does this generation ask for a sign? Truly I tell you, no sign will be given to this generation." 13And he left them, and getting into the boat again, he went across to the other side.

The Yeast of the Pharisees and of Herod

14 Now the disciplesf had forgotten to bring any bread; and they had only one loaf with them in the boat. 15And he cautioned them, saying, "Watch out—beware of the yeast of the Pharisees and the yeast of Herod."g 16They said to one another, "It is because we have no bread." 17And becoming aware of it, Jesus said to them, "Why are you talking about having no bread? Do you still not perceive or understand? Are your hearts hardened? 18Do you have eyes, and fail to see? Do you have ears, and fail to hear? And do you not remember?

---

b 8:11 Then we will believe in you, literally, "to test him."   c 8:12 How many more miracles do you people need? literally, "Why does this generation seek a sign?"

d Gk he   e Other ancient authorities read Mageda or Magdala   f Gk they
g Other ancient authorities read the Herodians

King James

19When I brake the five loaves among five thousand, how many baskets full of fragments took ye up? They say unto him, Twelve.

20And when the seven among four thousand, how many baskets full of fragments took ye up? And they said, Seven.

21And he said unto them, How is it that ye do not understand?

22¶ And he cometh to Bethsaida; and they bring a blind man unto him, and besought him to touch him.

23And he took the blind man by the hand, and led him out of the town; and when he had spit on his eyes, and put his hands upon him, he asked him if he saw aught.

24And he looked up, and said, I see men as trees, walking.

25After that he put *his* hands again upon his eyes, and made him look up: and he was restored, and saw every man clearly.

26And he sent him away to his house, saying, Neither go into the town, nor tell *it* to any in the town.

27¶ And Jesus went out, and his disciples, into the towns of Caesarea Philippi: and by the way he asked his disciples, saying unto them, Whom do men say that I am?

28And they answered, John the Baptist: but some *say*, Elias; and others, One of the prophets.

29And he saith unto them, But whom say ye that I am? And Peter answereth and saith unto him, Thou art the Christ.

30And he charged them that they should tell no man of him.

31And he began to teach them, that the Son of man must suffer many things, and be rejected of the elders, and *of* the chief priests, and scribes, and be killed, and after three days rise again.

32And he spake that saying openly. And Peter took him, and began to rebuke him.

33But when he had turned about and looked on his disciples, he rebuked Peter, saying, Get thee behind me, Satan: for thou savourest not the things that be of God, but the things that be of men.

34¶ And when he had called the people *unto him* with his disciples also, he said unto them, Whosoever will come after me, let him deny himself, and take up his cross, and follow me.

35For whosoever will save his life shall lose it; but whosoever shall lose his life for my sake and the gospel's, the same shall save it.

36For what shall it profit a man, if he shall gain the whole world, and lose his own soul?

37Or what shall a man give in exchange for his soul?

38Whosoever therefore shall be ashamed of me and of my words in this adulterous and sinful generation; of him also shall the Son of man be ashamed, when he cometh in the glory of his Father with the holy angels.

9   AND HE said unto them, Verily I say unto you, That there be some of them that stand here, which shall not taste of death, till they have seen the kingdom of God come with power.

New International

the five thousand, how many basketfuls of pieces did you pick up?"

"Twelve," they replied.

20"And when I broke the seven loaves for the four thousand, how many basketfuls of pieces did you pick up?"

They answered, "Seven."

21He said to them, "Do you still not understand?"

The Healing of a Blind Man at Bethsaida

22They came to Bethsaida, and some people brought a blind man and begged Jesus to touch him. 23He took the blind man by the hand and led him outside the village. When he had spit on the man's eyes and put his hands on him, Jesus asked, "Do you see anything?"

24He looked up and said, "I see people; they look like trees walking around."

25Once more Jesus put his hands on the man's eyes. Then his eyes were opened, his sight was restored, and he saw everything clearly. 26Jesus sent him home, saying, "Don't go into the village.a"

Peter's Confession of Christ

27Jesus and his disciples went on to the villages around Caesarea Philippi. On the way he asked them, "Who do people say I am?"

28They replied, "Some say John the Baptist; others say Elijah; and still others, one of the prophets."

29"But what about you?" he asked. "Who do you say I am?"

Peter answered, "You are the Christ.b"

30Jesus warned them not to tell anyone about him.

Jesus Predicts His Death

31He then began to teach them that the Son of Man must suffer many things and be rejected by the elders, chief priests and teachers of the law, and that he must be killed and after three days rise again. 32He spoke plainly about this, and Peter took him aside and began to rebuke him.

33But when Jesus turned and looked at his disciples, he rebuked Peter. "Get behind me, Satan!" he said. "You do not have in mind the things of God, but the things of men."

34Then he called the crowd to him along with his disciples and said: "If anyone would come after me, he must deny himself and take up his cross and follow me. 35For whoever wants to save his lifec will lose it, but whoever loses his life for me and for the gospel will save it. 36What good is it for a man to gain the whole world, yet forfeit his soul? 37Or what can a man give in exchange for his soul? 38If anyone is ashamed of me and my words in this adulterous and sinful generation, the Son of Man will be ashamed of him when he comes in his Father's glory with the holy angels."

9   AND HE said to them, "I tell you the truth, some who are standing here will not taste death before they see the kingdom of God come with power."

---

a 26 Some manuscripts *Don't go and tell anyone in the village*   b 29 Or *Messiah.* "The Christ" (Greek) and "the Messiah" (Hebrew) both mean "the Anointed One."   c 35 The Greek word means either *life* or *soul*; also in verse 36.

Living Bible

19"What about the 5,000 men I fed with five loaves of bread? How many basketfuls of scraps did you pick up afterwards?"

"Twelve," they said.

20"And when I fed the 4,000 with seven loaves, how much was left?"

"Seven basketfuls," they said.

21"And yet you think I'm worried that we have no bread?"d

22When they arrived at Bethsaida, some people brought a blind man to him and begged him to touch and heal him. 23Jesus took the blind man by the hand and led him out of the village, and spat upon his eyes, and laid his hands over them.

"Can you see anything now?" Jesus asked him.

24The man looked around. "Yes!" he said, "I see men! But I can't see them very clearly; they look like tree trunks walking around!"

25Then Jesus placed his hands over the man's eyes again and as the man stared intently, his sight was completely restored, and he saw everything clearly, drinking in the sights around him.

26Jesus sent him home to his family. "Don't even go back to the village first," he said.

27Jesus and his disciples now left Galilee and went out to the villages of Caesarea Philippi. As they were walking along he asked them, "Who do the people think I am? What are they saying about me?"

28"Some of them think you are John the Baptist," the disciples replied, "and others say you are Elijah or some other ancient prophet come back to life again."

29Then he asked, "Who do you think I am?" Peter replied, "You are the Messiah." 30But Jesus warned them not to tell anyone!

31Then he began to tell them about the terrible things he would suffer,e and that he would be rejected by the elders and the Chief Priests and the other Jewish leaders—and be killed, and that he would rise again three days afterwards. 32He talked about it quite frankly with them, so Peter took him aside and chided him.f "You shouldn't say things like that," he told Jesus.

33Jesus turned and looked at his disciples and then said to Peter very sternly, "Satan, get behind me! You are looking at this only from a human point of view and not from God's."

34Then he called his disciples and the crowds to come over and listen. "If any of you wants to be my follower," he told them, "you must put aside your own pleasures and shoulder your cross, and follow me closely. 35If you insist on saving your life, you will lose it. Only those who throw away their lives for my sake and for the sake of the Good News will ever know what it means to really live.

36"And how does a man benefit if he gains the whole world and loses his soul in the process? 37For is anything worth more than his soul? 38And anyone who is ashamed of me and my message in these days of unbelief and sin, I, the Messiah,g will be ashamed of him when I return in the glory of my Father, with the holy angels."

9 JESUS WENT on to say to his disciples, "Some of you who are standing here right now will live to see the Kingdom of God arrive in great power!"

New Revised Standard

19When I broke the five loaves for the five thousand, how many baskets full of broken pieces did you collect?" They said to him, "Twelve." 20"And the seven for the four thousand, how many baskets full of broken pieces did you collect?" And they said to him, "Seven." 21Then he said to them, "Do you not yet understand?"

Jesus Cures a Blind Man at Bethsaida

22 They came to Bethsaida. Some peopleh brought a blind man to him and begged him to touch him. 23He took the blind man by the hand and led him out of the village; and when he had put saliva on his eyes and laid his hands on him, he asked him, "Can you see anything?" 24And the mani looked up and said, "I can see people, but they look like trees, walking." 25Then Jesusi laid his hands on his eyes again; and he looked intently and his sight was restored, and he saw everything clearly. 26Then he sent him away to his home, saying, "Do not even go into the village."j

Peter's Declaration about Jesus

27 Jesus went on with his disciples to the villages of Caesarea Philippi; and on the way he asked his disciples, "Who do people say that I am?" 28And they answered him, "John the Baptist; and others, Elijah; and still others, one of the prophets." 29He asked them, "But who do you say that I am?" Peter answered him, "You are the Messiah."k 30And he sternly ordered them not to tell anyone about him.

Jesus Foretells His Death and Resurrection

31 Then he began to teach them that the Son of Man must undergo great suffering, and be rejected by the elders, the chief priests, and the scribes, and be killed, and after three days rise again. 32He said all this quite openly. And Peter took him aside and began to rebuke him. 33But turning and looking at his disciples, he rebuked Peter and said, "Get behind me, Satan! For you are setting your mind not on divine things but on human things."

34 He called the crowd with his disciples, and said to them, "If any want to become my followers, let them deny themselves and take up their cross and follow me. 35For those who want to save their life will lose it, and those who lose their life for my sake, and for the sake of the gospel,l will save it. 36For what will it profit them to gain the whole world and forfeit their life? 37Indeed, what can they give in return for their life? 38Those who are ashamed of me and of my wordsm in this adulterous and sinful generation, of them the Son of Man will also be ashamed when he comes in the glory of his Father with the holy angels."

9 AND HE said to them, "Truly I tell you, there are some standing here who will not taste death until they see that the kingdom of God has come withn power."

---

d 8:21 And yet you think I'm worried that we have no bread? literally, "Do you not yet understand?"   e 8:31 he would suffer, literally, "the Son of Man would suffer."   f 8:32 chided him, "began to rebuke him."   g 8:38 the Messiah, literally, "the Son of Man."

h Gk They   i Gk he   j Other ancient authorities add or tell anyone in the village   k Or the Christ   l Other ancient authorities read lose their life for the sake of the gospel   m Other ancient authorities read and of mine   n Or in

King James

2¶ And after six days Jesus taketh *with him* Peter, and James, and John, and leadeth them up into an high mountain apart by themselves: and he was transfigured before them.

3And his raiment became shining, exceeding white as snow; so as no fuller on earth can white them.

4And there appeared unto them Elias with Moses: and they were talking with Jesus.

5And Peter answered and said to Jesus, Master, it is good for us to be here: and let us make three tabernacles; one for thee, and one for Moses, and one for Elias.

6For he wist not what to say; for they were sore afraid.

7And there was a cloud that overshadowed them: and a voice came out of the cloud, saying, This is my beloved Son: hear him.

8And suddenly, when they had looked round about, they saw no man any more, save Jesus only with themselves.

9And as they came down from the mountain, he charged them that they should tell no man what things they had seen, till the Son of man were risen from the dead.

10And they kept that saying with themselves, questioning one with another what the rising from the dead should mean.

11¶ And they asked him, saying, Why say the scribes that Elias must first come?

12And he answered and told them, Elias verily cometh first, and restoreth all things; and how it is written of the Son of man, that he must suffer many things, and be set at nought.

13But I say unto you, That Elias is indeed come, and they have done unto him whatsoever they listed, as it is written of him.

14¶ And when he came to *his* disciples, he saw a great multitude about them, and the scribes questioning with them.

15And straightway all the people, when they beheld him, were greatly amazed, and running to *him* saluted him.

16And he asked the scribes, What question ye with them?

17And one of the multitude answered and said, Master, I have brought unto thee my son, which hath a dumb spirit;

18And wheresoever he taketh him, he teareth him: and he foameth, and gnasheth with his teeth, and pineth away: and I spake to thy disciples that they should cast him out; and they could not.

19He answereth him, and saith, O faithless generation, how long shall I be with you? how long shall I suffer you? bring him unto me.

20And they brought him unto him: and when he saw him, straightway the spirit tare him; and he fell on the ground, and wallowed foaming.

21And he asked his father, How long is it ago since this came unto him? And he said, Of a child.

22And ofttimes it hath cast him into the fire, and into the waters, to destroy him: but if thou canst do any thing, have compassion on us, and help us.

23Jesus said unto him, If thou canst believe, all things *are* possible to him that believeth.

24And straightway the father of the child cried out, and said with tears, Lord, I believe; help thou mine unbelief.

25When Jesus saw that the people came running together, he rebuked the foul spirit, saying unto him, *Thou* dumb and deaf spirit, I charge thee, come out of him, and enter no more into him.

26And *the* spirit cried, and rent him sore, and came out of him: and he was as one dead; insomuch that many said, He is dead.

27But Jesus took him by the hand, and lifted him up; and he arose.

New International

The Transfiguration

2After six days Jesus took Peter, James and John with him and led them up a high mountain, where they were all alone. There he was transfigured before them. 3His clothes became dazzling white, whiter than anyone in the world could bleach them. 4And there appeared before them Elijah and Moses, who were talking with Jesus.

5Peter said to Jesus, "Rabbi, it is good for us to be here. Let us put up three shelters—one for you, one for Moses and one for Elijah." 6(He did not know what to say, they were so frightened.)

7Then a cloud appeared and enveloped them, and a voice came from the cloud: "This is my Son, whom I love. Listen to him!"

8Suddenly, when they looked around, they no longer saw anyone with them except Jesus.

9As they were coming down the mountain, Jesus gave them orders not to tell anyone what they had seen until the Son of Man had risen from the dead. 10They kept the matter to themselves, discussing what "rising from the dead" meant.

11And they asked him, "Why do the teachers of the law say that Elijah must come first?"

12Jesus replied, "To be sure, Elijah does come first, and restores all things. Why then is it written that the Son of Man must suffer much and be rejected? 13But I tell you, Elijah has come, and they have done to him everything they wished, just as it is written about him."

The Healing of a Boy With an Evil Spirit

14When they came to the other disciples, they saw a large crowd around them and the teachers of the law arguing with them. 15As soon as all the people saw Jesus, they were overwhelmed with wonder and ran to greet him.

16"What are you arguing with them about?" he asked.

17A man in the crowd answered, "Teacher, I brought you my son, who is possessed by a spirit that has robbed him of speech. 18Whenever it seizes him, it throws him to the ground. He foams at the mouth, gnashes his teeth and becomes rigid. I asked your disciples to drive out the spirit, but they could not."

19"O unbelieving generation," Jesus replied, "how long shall I stay with you? How long shall I put up with you? Bring the boy to me."

20So they brought him. When the spirit saw Jesus, it immediately threw the boy into a convulsion. He fell to the ground and rolled around, foaming at the mouth.

21Jesus asked the boy's father, "How long has he been like this?"

"From childhood," he answered. 22"It has often thrown him into fire or water to kill him. But if you can do anything, take pity on us and help us."

23"'If you can'?" said Jesus. "Everything is possible for him who believes."

24Immediately the boy's father exclaimed, "I do believe; help me overcome my unbelief!"

25When Jesus saw that a crowd was running to the scene, he rebuked the evil[a] spirit. "You deaf and mute spirit," he said, "I command you, come out of him and never enter him again."

26The spirit shrieked, convulsed him violently and came out. The boy looked so much like a corpse that many said, "He's dead." 27But Jesus took him by the hand and lifted him to his feet, and he stood up.

Living Bible

2Six days later Jesus took Peter, James and John to the top of a mountain. No one else was there.

Suddenly his face began to shine with glory, 3and his clothing became dazzling white, far more glorious than any earthly process could ever make it! 4Then Elijah and Moses appeared and began talking with Jesus!

5"Teacher, this is wonderful!" Peter exclaimed. "We will make three shelters here, one for each of you. . . ." 6He said this just to be talking, for he didn't know what else to say and they were all terribly frightened.

7But while he was still speaking these words, a cloud covered them, blotting out the sun, and a voice from the cloud said, *"This* is my beloved Son. Listen to *him."*

8Then suddenly they looked around and Moses and Elijah were gone, and only Jesus was with them.

9As they descended the mountainside he told them never to mention what they had seen until after he had risenb from the dead. 10So they kept it to themselves, but often talked about it, and wondered what he meant by "rising from the dead."

11Now they began asking him about something the Jewish religious leaders often spoke of, that Elijah must return [before the Messiah could comec]. 12, 13Jesus agreed that Elijah must come first and prepare the way— and that he had, in fact, already come! And that he had been terribly mistreated, just as the prophets had predicted. Then Jesus asked them what the prophets could have been talking about when they predicted that the Messiahd would suffer and be treated with utter contempt.

14At the bottom of the mountain they found a great crowd surrounding the other nine disciples, as some Jewish leaders argued with them. 15The crowd watched Jesus in awe as he came toward them, and then ran to greet him. 16"What's all the argument about?" he asked.

17One of the men in the crowd spoke up and said, "Teacher, I brought my son for you to heal—he can't talk because he is possessed by a demon. 18And whenever the demon is in control of him it dashes him to the ground and makes him foam at the mouth and grind his teeth and become rigid.e So I begged your disciples to cast out the demon, but they couldn't do it."

19Jesus said [to his disciplesf], "Oh, what tiny faith you have;g how much longer must I be with you until you believe? How much longer must I be patient with you? Bring the boy to me."

20So they brought the boy, but when he saw Jesus the demon convulsed the child horribly, and he fell to the ground writhing and foaming at the mouth.

21"How long has he been this way?" Jesus asked the father.

And he replied, "Since he was very small, 22and the demon often makes him fall into the fire or into water to kill him. Oh, have mercy on us and do something if you can."

23"If I can?" Jesus asked. *"Anything* is possible if you have faith."

24The father instantly replied, "I *do* have faith; oh, help me to have *more!"*

25When Jesus saw the crowd was growing he rebuked the demon.

"O demon of deafness and dumbness," he said, "I command you to come out of this child and enter him no more!"

26Then the demon screamed terribly and convulsed the boy again and left him; and the boy lay there limp and motionless, to all appearance dead. A murmur ran through the crowd—"He is dead." 27But Jesus took him by the hand and helped him to his feet and he stood up and was all right! 28Afterwards, when Jesus was alone

New Revised Standard

The Transfiguration

2 Six days later, Jesus took with him Peter and James and John, and led them up a high mountain apart, by themselves. And he was transfigured before them, 3and his clothes became dazzling white, such as no oneh on earth could bleach them. 4And there appeared to them Elijah with Moses, who were talking with Jesus. 5Then Peter said to Jesus, "Rabbi, it is good for us to be here; let us make three dwellings,i one for you, one for Moses, and one for Elijah." 6He did not know what to say, for they were terrified. 7Then a cloud overshadowed them, and from the cloud there came a voice, "This is my Son, the Beloved;j listen to him!" 8Suddenly when they looked around, they saw no one with them any more, but only Jesus.

The Coming of Elijah

9 As they were coming down the mountain, he ordered them to tell no one about what they had seen, until after the Son of Man had risen from the dead. 10So they kept the matter to themselves, questioning what this rising from the dead could mean. 11Then they asked him, "Why do the scribes say that Elijah must come first?" 12He said to them, "Elijah is indeed coming first to restore all things. How then is it written about the Son of Man, that he is to go through many sufferings and be treated with contempt? 13But I tell you that Elijah has come, and they did to him whatever they pleased, as it is written about him."

The Healing of a Boy with a Spirit

14 When they came to the disciples, they saw a great crowd around them, and some scribes arguing with them. 15When the whole crowd saw him, they were immediately overcome with awe, and they ran forward to greet him. 16He asked them, "What are you arguing about with them?" 17Someone from the crowd answered him, "Teacher, I brought you my son; he has a spirit that makes him unable to speak; 18and whenever it seizes him, it dashes him down; and he foams and grinds his teeth and becomes rigid; and I asked your disciples to cast it out, but they could not do so." 19He answered them, "You faithless generation, how much longer must I be among you? How much longer must I put up with you? Bring him to me." 20And they brought the boyk to him. When the spirit saw him, immediately it convulsed the boy,k and he fell on the ground and rolled about, foaming at the mouth. 21Jesusl asked the father, "How long has this been happening to him?" And he said, "From childhood. 22It has often cast him into the fire and into the water, to destroy him; but if you are able to do anything, have pity on us and help us." 23Jesus said to him, "If you are able!—All things can be done for the one who believes." 24Immediately the father of the child cried out,m "I believe; help my unbelief!" 25When Jesus saw that a crowd came running together, he rebuked the unclean spirit, saying to it, "You spirit that keeps this boy from speaking and hearing, I command you, come out of him, and never enter him again!" 26After crying out and convulsing him terribly, it came out, and the boy was like a corpse, so that most of them said, "He is dead." 27But Jesus took him by the hand and lifted him up, and he was able to stand. 28When he had

---

b 9:9 *after he had risen,* literally, "after the Son of Man had risen."
c 9:11 *before the Messiah could come,* implied.   d 9:12, 13 *the Messiah,* literally, "the Son of Man."   e 9:18 *and become rigid,* or, "is growing weaker day by day."   f 9:19 *to his disciples,* implied.   g 9:19 *Oh, what tiny faith you have,* literally, "O unbelieving generation."

h Gk *no fuller*   i Or *tents*   j Or *my beloved Son*   k Gk *him*   l Gk *He*
m Other ancient authorities add *with tears*

King James

28And when he was come into the house, his disciples asked him privately, Why could not we cast him out?

29And he said unto them, This kind can come forth by nothing, but by prayer and fasting.

30¶ And they departed thence, and passed through Galilee; and he would not that any man should know *it*.

31For he taught his disciples, and said unto them, The Son of man is delivered into the hands of men, and they shall kill him; and after that he is killed, he shall rise the third day.

32But they understood not that saying, and were afraid to ask him.

33¶ And he came to Capernaum: and being in the house he asked them, What was it that ye disputed among yourselves by the way?

34But they held their peace: for by the way they had disputed among themselves, who *should be* the greatest.

35And he sat down, and called the twelve, and saith unto them, If any man desire to be first, *the same* shall be last of all, and servant of all.

36And he took a child, and set him in the midst of them: and when he had taken him in his arms, he said unto them,

37Whosoever shall receive one of such children in my name, receiveth me: and whosoever shall receive me, receiveth not me, but him that sent me.

38¶ And John answered him, saying, Master, we saw one casting out devils in thy name, and he followeth not us: and we forbad him, because he followeth not us.

39But Jesus said, Forbid him not: for there is no man which shall do a miracle in my name, that can lightly speak evil of me.

40For he that is not against us is on our part.

41For whosoever shall give you a cup of water to drink in my name, because ye belong to Christ, verily I say unto you, he shall not lose his reward.

42And whosoever shall offend one of *these* little ones that believe in me, it is better for him that a millstone were hanged about his neck, and he were cast into the sea.

43And if thy hand offend thee, cut it off: it is better for thee to enter into life maimed, than having two hands to go into hell, into the fire that never shall be quenched.

44Where their worm dieth not, and the fire is not quenched.

45And if thy foot offend thee, cut it off: it is better for thee to enter halt into life, than having two feet to be cast into hell, into the fire that never shall be quenched:

46Where their worm dieth not, and the fire is not quenched.

47And if thine eye offend thee, pluck it out: it is better for thee to enter into the kingdom of God with one eye, than having two eyes to be cast into hell fire:

48Where their worm dieth not, and the fire is not quenched.

49For every one shall be salted with fire, and every sacrifice shall be salted with salt.

50Salt *is* good: but if the salt have lost his saltness, wherewith will ye season it? Have salt in yourselves, and have peace one with another.

New International

28After Jesus had gone indoors, his disciples asked him privately, "Why couldn't we drive it out?"

29He replied, "This kind can come out only by prayer.a"

30They left that place and passed through Galilee. Jesus did not want anyone to know where they were, 31because he was teaching his disciples. He said to them, "The Son of Man is going to be betrayed into the hands of men. They will kill him, and after three days he will rise." 32But they did not understand what he meant and were afraid to ask him about it.

Who Is the Greatest?

33They came to Capernaum. When he was in the house, he asked them, "What were you arguing about on the road?" 34But they kept quiet because on the way they had argued about who was the greatest.

35Sitting down, Jesus called the Twelve and said, "If anyone wants to be first, he must be the very last, and the servant of all."

36He took a little child and had him stand among them. Taking him in his arms, he said to them, 37"Whoever welcomes one of these little children in my name welcomes me; and whoever welcomes me does not welcome me but the one who sent me."

Whoever Is Not Against Us Is for Us

38"Teacher," said John, "we saw a man driving out demons in your name and we told him to stop, because he was not one of us."

39"Do not stop him," Jesus said. "No one who does a miracle in my name can in the next moment say anything bad about me, 40for whoever is not against us is for us. 41I tell you the truth, anyone who gives you a cup of water in my name because you belong to Christ will certainly not lose his reward.

Causing to Sin

42"And if anyone causes one of these little ones who believe in me to sin, it would be better for him to be thrown into the sea with a large millstone tied around his neck. 43If your hand causes you to sin, cut it off. It is better for you to enter life maimed than with two hands to go into hell, where the fire never goes out.b 45And if your foot causes you to sin, cut it off. It is better for you to enter life crippled than to have two feet and be thrown into hell.c 47And if your eye causes you to sin, pluck it out. It is better for you to enter the kingdom of God with one eye than to have two eyes and be thrown into hell, 48where

" 'their worm does not die,
and the fire is not quenched.'d

49Everyone will be salted with fire.

50"Salt is good, but if it loses its saltiness, how can you make it salty again? Have salt in yourselves, and be at peace with each other."

---

a 29 Some manuscripts *prayer and fasting*   b 43 Some manuscripts *out*, 44*where* / " '*their worm does not die,* / *and the fire is not quenched.*' c 45 Some manuscripts *hell*,46*where* / " '*their worm does not die,* / *and the fire is not quenched.*'   d 48 Isaiah 66:24

Living Bible

in the house with his disciples, they asked him, "Why couldn't we cast that demon out?"

29Jesus replied, "Cases like this require prayer."e

30, 31Leaving that region they traveled through Galilee where he tried to avoid all publicity in order to spend more time with his disciples, teaching them. He would say to them, "I, the Messiah, am going to be betrayed and killed and three days later I will return to life again."

32But they didn't understand and were afraid to ask him what he meant.

33And so they arrived at Capernaum. When they were settled in the house where they were to stay he asked them, "What were you discussing out on the road?"

34But they were ashamed to answer, for they had been arguing about which of them was the greatest!

35He sat down and called them around him and said, "Anyone wanting to be the greatest must be the least— the servant of all!"

36Then he placed a little child among them; and taking the child in his arms he said to them, 37"Anyone who welcomes a little child like this in my name is welcoming me, and anyone who welcomes me is welcoming my Father who sent me!"

38One of his disciples, John, told him one day, "Teacher, we saw a man using your name to cast out demons; but we told him not to, for he isn't one of our group."

39"Don't forbid him!" Jesus said. "For no one doing miracles in my name will quickly turn against me.f 40Anyone who isn't against us is for us. 41If anyone so much as gives you a cup of water because you are Christ's—I say this solemnly—he won't lose his reward. 42But if someone causes one of these little ones who believe in me to lose faith—it would be better for that man if a huge millstone were tied around his neck and he were thrown into the sea.

43, 44g "If your hand does wrong, cut it off. Better live forever with one hand than be thrown into the unquenchable fires of hell with two! 45, 46If your foot carries you toward evil, cut it off! Better be lame and live forever than have two feet that carry you to hell.

47"And if your eye is sinful, gouge it out. Better enter the Kingdom of God half blind than have two eyes and see the fires of hell, 48where the worm never dies, and the fire never goes out— 49where all are salted with fire.h

50"Good salt is worthless if it loses its saltiness; it can't season anything. So don't lose your flavor! Live in peace with each other."

New Revised Standard

entered the house, his disciples asked him privately, "Why could we not cast it out?" 29He said to them, "This kind can come out only through prayer."i

Jesus Again Foretells His Death and Resurrection

30 They went on from there and passed through Galilee. He did not want anyone to know it; 31for he was teaching his disciples, saying to them, "The Son of Man is to be betrayed into human hands, and they will kill him, and three days after being killed, he will rise again." 32But they did not understand what he was saying and were afraid to ask him.

Who Is the Greatest?

33 Then they came to Capernaum; and when he was in the house he asked them, "What were you arguing about on the way?" 34But they were silent, for on the way they had argued with one another who was the greatest. 35He sat down, called the twelve, and said to them, "Whoever wants to be first must be last of all and servant of all." 36Then he took a little child and put it among them; and taking it in his arms, he said to them, 37"Whoever welcomes one such child in my name welcomes me, and whoever welcomes me welcomes not me but the one who sent me."

Another Exorcist

38 John said to him, "Teacher, we saw someonej casting out demons in your name, and we tried to stop him, because he was not following us." 39But Jesus said, "Do not stop him; for no one who does a deed of power in my name will be able soon afterward to speak evil of me. 40Whoever is not against us is for us. 41For truly I tell you, whoever gives you a cup of water to drink because you bear the name of Christ will by no means lose the reward.

Temptations to Sin

42 "If any of you put a stumbling block before one of these little ones who believe in me,k it would be better for you if a great millstone were hung around your neck and you were thrown into the sea. 43If your hand causes you to stumble, cut it off; it is better for you to enter life maimed than to have two hands and to go to hell,l to the unquenchable fire.m 45And if your foot causes you to stumble, cut it off; it is better for you to enter life lame than to have two feet and to be thrown into hell.l,m 47And if your eye causes you to stumble, tear it out; it is better for you to enter the kingdom of God with one eye than to have two eyes and to be thrown into hell,l 48where their worm never dies, and the fire is never quenched.

49 "For everyone will be salted with fire.n 50Salt is good; but if salt has lost its saltiness, how can you season it?o Have salt in yourselves, and be at peace with one another."

---

e 9:29 Cases like this require prayer. "And fasting" is added in some manuscripts, but not the most ancient. f 9:39 will quickly turn against me, literally, "will be able to speak evil of me." g 9:43, 44 Vss 44, 46 (which are identical with vs 48) are omitted in some of the ancient manuscripts. h 9:49 where all are salted with fire, literally, "For everyone shall be salted with fire."

i Other ancient authorities add and fasting j Other ancient authorities add who does not follow us k Other ancient authorities lack in me l Gk Gehenna m Verses 44 and 46 (which are identical with verse 48) are lacking in the best ancient authorities n Other ancient authorities either add or substitute and every sacrifice will be salted with salt o Or how can you restore its saltiness?

King James

10 AND HE arose from thence, and cometh into the coasts of Judaea by the farther side of Jordan: and the people resort unto him again; and, as he was wont, he taught them again.

2¶ And the Pharisees came to him, and asked him, Is it lawful for a man to put away *his* wife? tempting him.

3And he answered and said unto them, What did Moses command you?

4And they said, Moses suffered to write a bill of divorcement, and to put *her* away.

5And Jesus answered and said unto them, For the hardness of your heart he wrote you this precept.

6But from the beginning of the creation God made them male and female.

7For this cause shall a man leave his father and mother, and cleave to his wife;

8And they twain shall be one flesh: so then they are no more twain, but one flesh.

9What therefore God hath joined together, let not man put asunder.

10And in the house his disciples asked him again of the same *matter*.

11And he saith unto them, Whosoever shall put away his wife, and marry another, committeth adultery against her.

12And if a woman shall put away her husband, and be married to another, she committeth adultery.

13¶ And they brought young children to him, that he should touch them: and *his* disciples rebuked those that brought *them*.

14But when Jesus saw *it*, he was much displeased, and said unto them, Suffer the little children to come unto me, and forbid them not: for of such is the kingdom of God.

15Verily I say unto you, Whosoever shall not receive the kingdom of God as a little child, he shall not enter therein.

16And he took them up in his arms, put *his* hands upon them, and blessed them.

17¶ And when he was gone forth into the way, there came one running, and kneeled to him, and asked him, Good Master, what shall I do that I may inherit eternal life?

18And Jesus said unto him, Why callest thou me good? *there is* none good but one, *that is*, God.

19Thou knowest the commandments, Do not commit adultery, Do not kill, Do not steal, Do not bear false witness, Defraud not, Honour thy father and mother.

20And he answered and said unto him, Master, all these have I observed from my youth.

21Then Jesus beholding him loved him, and said unto him, One thing thou lackest: go thy way, sell whatsoever thou hast, and give to the poor, and thou shalt have treasure in heaven: and come, take up the cross, and follow me.

22And he was sad at that saying, and went away grieved: for he had great possessions.

23¶ And Jesus looked round about, and saith unto his disciples, How hardly shall they that have riches enter into the kingdom of God!

24And the disciples were astonished at his words. But Jesus answereth again, and saith unto them, Children, how hard is it for them that trust in riches to enter into the kingdom of God!

25It is easier for a camel to go through the eye of a needle, than for a rich man to enter into the kingdom of God.

26And they were astonished out of measure, saying among themselves, Who then can be saved?

27And Jesus looking upon them saith, With men *it is* impossible, but not with God: for with God all things are possible.

New International

Divorce

10 JESUS THEN left that place and went into the region of Judea and across the Jordan. Again crowds of people came to him, and as was his custom, he taught them.

2Some Pharisees came and tested him by asking, "Is it lawful for a man to divorce his wife?"

3"What did Moses command you?" he replied.

4They said, "Moses permitted a man to write a certificate of divorce and send her away."

5"It was because your hearts were hard that Moses wrote you this law," Jesus replied. 6"But at the beginning of creation God 'made them male and female.'ª 7'For this reason a man will leave his father and mother and be united to his wife,ᵇ 8and the two will become one flesh.'ᶜ So they are no longer two, but one. 9Therefore what God has joined together, let man not separate."

10When they were in the house again, the disciples asked Jesus about this. 11He answered, "Anyone who divorces his wife and marries another woman commits adultery against her. 12And if she divorces her husband and marries another man, she commits adultery."

The Little Children and Jesus

13People were bringing little children to Jesus to have him touch them, but the disciples rebuked them. 14When Jesus saw this, he was indignant. He said to them, "Let the little children come to me, and do not hinder them, for the kingdom of God belongs to such as these. 15I tell you the truth, anyone who will not receive the kingdom of God like a little child will never enter it." 16And he took the children in his arms, put his hands on them and blessed them.

The Rich Young Man

17As Jesus started on his way, a man ran up to him and fell on his knees before him. "Good teacher," he asked, "what must I do to inherit eternal life?"

18"Why do you call me good?" Jesus answered. "No one is good—except God alone. 19You know the commandments: 'Do not murder, do not commit adultery, do not steal, do not give false testimony, do not defraud, honor your father and mother.'ᵈ"

20"Teacher," he declared, "all these I have kept since I was a boy."

21Jesus looked at him and loved him. "One thing you lack," he said. "Go, sell everything you have and give to the poor, and you will have treasure in heaven. Then come, follow me."

22At this the man's face fell. He went away sad, because he had great wealth.

23Jesus looked around and said to his disciples, "How hard it is for the rich to enter the kingdom of God!"

24The disciples were amazed at his words. But Jesus said again, "Children, how hard it isᵉ to enter the kingdom of God! 25It is easier for a camel to go through the eye of a needle than for a rich man to enter the kingdom of God."

26The disciples were even more amazed, and said to each other, "Who then can be saved?"

27Jesus looked at them and said, "With man this is impossible, but not with God; all things are possible with God."

ª 6 Gen. 1:27   ᵇ 7 Some early manuscripts do not have *and be united to his wife.*   ᶜ 8 Gen. 2:24   ᵈ 19 Exodus 20:12-16; Deut. 5:16-20
ᵉ 24 Some manuscripts *is for those who trust in riches*

Living Bible

10 THEN HE left Capernaum[f] and went southward to the Judean borders and into the area east of the Jordan River. And as always there were the crowds; and as usual he taught them.

2Some Pharisees came and asked him, "Do you permit divorce?" Of course they were trying to trap him. 3"What did Moses say about divorce?" Jesus asked them.

4"He said it was all right," they replied. "He said that all a man has to do is write his wife a letter of dismissal."

5"And why did he say that?" Jesus asked. "I'll tell you why—it was a concession to your hardhearted wickedness. 6, 7But it certainly isn't God's way. For from the very first he made man and woman to be joined together permanently in marriage; therefore a man is to leave his father and mother, 8and he and his wife are united so that they are no longer two, but one. 9And no man may separate what God has joined together."

10Later, when he was alone with his disciples in the house, they brought up the subject again. 11He told them, "When a man divorces his wife to marry someone else, he commits adultery against her. 12And if a wife divorces her husband and remarries, she, too, commits adultery."

13Once when some mothers[g] were bringing their children to Jesus to bless them, the disciples shooed them away, telling them not to bother him. 14But when Jesus saw what was happening he was very much displeased with his disciples and said to them, "Let the children come to me, for the Kingdom of God belongs to such as they. Don't send them away! 15I tell you as seriously as I know how that anyone who refuses to come to God as a little child will never be allowed into his Kingdom."

16Then he took the children into his arms and placed his hands on their heads and he blessed them.

17As he was starting out on a trip, a man came running to him and knelt down and asked, "Good Teacher, what must I do to get to heaven?"

18"Why do you call me good?" Jesus asked. "Only God is truly good! 19But as for your question—you know the commandments: don't kill, don't commit adultery, don't steal, don't lie, don't cheat, respect your father and mother."

20"Teacher," the man replied, "I've never once[h] broken a single one of those laws."

21Jesus felt genuine love for this man as he looked at him. "You lack only one thing," he told him; "go and sell all you have and give the money to the poor—and you shall have treasure in heaven—and come, follow me."

22Then the man's face fell, and he went sadly away, for he was very rich.

23Jesus watched him go, then turned around and said to his disciples, "It's almost impossible for the rich to get into the Kingdom of God!"

24This amazed them. So Jesus said it again: "Dear children, how hard it is for those who trust in riches[i] to enter the Kingdom of God. 25It is easier for a camel to go through the eye of a needle than for a rich man to enter the Kingdom of God."

26The disciples were incredulous! "Then who in the world can be saved, if not a rich man?" they asked.

27Jesus looked at them intently, then said, "Without God, it is utterly impossible. But with God everything is possible."

New Revised Standard

Teaching about Divorce

10 HE LEFT that place and went to the region of Judea and[j] beyond the Jordan. And crowds again gathered around him; and, as was his custom, he again taught them.

2 Some Pharisees came, and to test him they asked, "Is it lawful for a man to divorce his wife?" 3He answered them, "What did Moses command you?" 4They said, "Moses allowed a man to write a certificate of dismissal and to divorce her." 5But Jesus said to them, "Because of your hardness of heart he wrote this commandment for you. 6But from the beginning of creation, 'God made them male and female.' 7'For this reason a man shall leave his father and mother and be joined to his wife,[k] 8and the two shall become one flesh.' So they are no longer two, but one flesh. 9Therefore what God has joined together, let no one separate."

10 Then in the house the disciples asked him again about this matter. 11He said to them, "Whoever divorces his wife and marries another commits adultery against her; 12and if she divorces her husband and marries another, she commits adultery."

Jesus Blesses Little Children

13 People were bringing little children to him in order that he might touch them; and the disciples spoke sternly to them. 14But when Jesus saw this, he was indignant and said to them, "Let the little children come to me; do not stop them; for it is to such as these that the kingdom of God belongs. 15Truly I tell you, whoever does not receive the kingdom of God as a little child will never enter it." 16And he took them up in his arms, laid his hands on them, and blessed them.

The Rich Man

17 As he was setting out on a journey, a man ran up and knelt before him, and asked him, "Good Teacher, what must I do to inherit eternal life?" 18Jesus said to him, "Why do you call me good? No one is good but God alone. 19You know the commandments: 'You shall not murder; You shall not commit adultery; You shall not steal; You shall not bear false witness; You shall not defraud; Honor your father and mother.' " 20He said to him, "Teacher, I have kept all these since my youth." 21Jesus, looking at him, loved him and said, "You lack one thing; go, sell what you own, and give the money[l] to the poor, and you will have treasure in heaven; then come, follow me." 22When he heard this, he was shocked and went away grieving, for he had many possessions.

23 Then Jesus looked around and said to his disciples, "How hard it will be for those who have wealth to enter the kingdom of God!" 24And the disciples were perplexed at these words. But Jesus said to them again, "Children, how hard it is[m] to enter the kingdom of God! 25It is easier for a camel to go through the eye of a needle than for someone who is rich to enter the kingdom of God." 26They were greatly astounded and said to one another,[n] "Then who can be saved?" 27Jesus looked at them and said, "For mortals it is impossible, but not for God; for God all things are possible."

---

[f] *10:1 Then he left Capernaum*, literally, "And rising up, he went from there." Mentioned here so quietly, this was his final farewell to Galilee. He never returned until after his death and resurrection.   [g] *10:13 mothers*, implied.   [h] *10:20 never once*, literally, "from my youth."   [i] *10:24 for those who trust in riches*. Some of the ancient manuscripts do not contain the words, "for those who trust in riches."

[j] Other ancient authorities lack *and*   [k] Other ancient authorities lack *and be joined to his wife*   [l] Gk lacks *the money*   [m] Other ancient authorities add *for those who trust in riches*   [n] Other ancient authorities read *to him*

King James

28¶ Then Peter began to say unto him, Lo, we have left all, and have followed thee.

29And Jesus answered and said, Verily I say unto you, There is no man that hath left house, or brethren, or sisters, or father, or mother, or wife, or children, or lands, for my sake, and the gospel's,

30But he shall receive an hundredfold now in this time, houses, and brethren, and sisters, and mothers, and children, and lands, with persecutions; and in the world to come eternal life.

31But many *that are* first shall be last; and the last first.

32¶ And they were in the way going up to Jerusalem; and Jesus went before them: and they were amazed; and as they followed, they were afraid. And he took again the twelve, and began to tell them what things should happen unto him,

33*Saying,* Behold, we go up to Jerusalem; and the Son of man shall be delivered unto the chief priests, and unto the scribes; and they shall condemn him to death, and shall deliver him to the Gentiles:

34And they shall mock him, and shall scourge him, and shall spit upon him, and shall kill him: and the third day he shall rise again.

35¶ And James and John, the sons of Zebedee, come unto him, saying, Master, we would that thou shouldest do for us whatsoever we shall desire.

36And he said unto them, What would ye that I should do for you?

37They said unto him, Grant unto us that we may sit, one on thy right hand, and the other on thy left hand, in thy glory.

38But Jesus said unto them, Ye know not what ye ask: can ye drink of the cup that I drink of? and be baptized with the baptism that I am baptized with?

39And they said unto him, We can. And Jesus said unto them, Ye shall indeed drink of the cup that I drink of; and with the baptism that I am baptized withal shall ye be baptized:

40But to sit on my right hand and on my left hand is not mine to give; but *it shall be given to them* for whom it is prepared.

41And when the ten heard *it,* they began to be much displeased with James and John.

42But Jesus called them *to him,* and saith unto them, Ye know that they which are accounted to rule over the Gentiles exercise lordship over them; and their great ones exercise authority upon them.

43But so shall it not be among you: but whosoever will be great among you, shall be your minister:

44And whosoever of you will be the chiefest, shall be servant of all.

45For even the Son of man came not to be ministered unto, but to minister, and to give his life a ransom for many.

46¶ And they came to Jericho: and as he went out of Jericho with his disciples and a great number of people, blind Bartimaeus, the son of Timaeus, sat by the highway side begging.

47And when he heard that it was Jesus of Nazareth, he began to cry out, and say, Jesus, *thou* son of David, have mercy on me.

48And many charged him that he should hold his peace: but he cried the more a great deal, *Thou* son of David, have mercy on me.

49And Jesus stood still, and commanded him to be called. And they call the blind man, saying unto him, Be of good comfort, rise; he calleth thee.

50And he, casting away his garment, rose, and came to Jesus.

51And Jesus answered and said unto him, What wilt thou that I should do unto thee? The blind man said unto him, Lord, that I might receive my sight.

New International

28Peter said to him, "We have left everything to follow you!"

29"I tell you the truth," Jesus replied, "no one who has left home or brothers or sisters or mother or father or children or fields for me and the gospel 30will fail to receive a hundred times as much in this present age (homes, brothers, sisters, mothers, children and fields—and with them, persecutions) and in the age to come, eternal life. 31But many who are first will be last, and the last first."

Jesus Again Predicts His Death

32They were on their way up to Jerusalem, with Jesus leading the way, and the disciples were astonished, while those who followed were afraid. Again he took the Twelve aside and told them what was going to happen to him. 33"We are going up to Jerusalem," he said, "and the Son of Man will be betrayed to the chief priests and teachers of the law. They will condemn him to death and will hand him over to the Gentiles, 34who will mock him and spit on him, flog him and kill him. Three days later he will rise."

The Request of James and John

35Then James and John, the sons of Zebedee, came to him. "Teacher," they said, "we want you to do for us whatever we ask."

36"What do you want me to do for you?" he asked.

37They replied, "Let one of us sit at your right and the other at your left in your glory."

38"You don't know what you are asking," Jesus said. "Can you drink the cup I drink or be baptized with the baptism I am baptized with?"

39"We can," they answered.

Jesus said to them, "You will drink the cup I drink and be baptized with the baptism I am baptized with, 40but to sit at my right or left is not for me to grant. These places belong to those for whom they have been prepared."

41When the ten heard about this, they became indignant with James and John. 42Jesus called them together and said, "You know that those who are regarded as rulers of the Gentiles lord it over them, and their high officials exercise authority over them. 43Not so with you. Instead, whoever wants to become great among you must be your servant, 44and whoever wants to be first must be slave of all. 45For even the Son of Man did not come to be served, but to serve, and to give his life as a ransom for many."

Blind Bartimaeus Receives His Sight

46Then they came to Jericho. As Jesus and his disciples, together with a large crowd, were leaving the city, a blind man, Bartimaeus (that is, the Son of Timaeus), was sitting by the roadside begging. 47When he heard that it was Jesus of Nazareth, he began to shout, "Jesus, Son of David, have mercy on me!"

48Many rebuked him and told him to be quiet, but he shouted all the more, "Son of David, have mercy on me!"

49Jesus stopped and said, "Call him."

So they called to the blind man, "Cheer up! On your feet! He's calling you." 50Throwing his cloak aside, he jumped to his feet and came to Jesus.

51"What do you want me to do for you?" Jesus asked him.

The blind man said, "Rabbi, I want to see."

Living Bible

28Then Peter began to mention all that he and the other disciples had left behind. "We've given up everything to follow you," he said.

29And Jesus replied, "Let me assure you that no one has ever given up anything—home, brothers, sisters, mother, father, children, or property—for love of me and to tell others the Good News, 30who won't be given back, a hundred times over, homes, brothers, sisters, mothers, children, and land—with persecutions!

"All these will be his here on earth, and in the world to come he shall have eternal life. 31But many people who seem to be important now will be the least important then; and many who are considered least here shall be greatest there."

32Now they were on the way to Jerusalem, and Jesus was walking along ahead; and as the disciples were following they were filled with terror and dread.

Taking them aside, Jesus once more began describing all that was going to happen to him when they arrived at Jerusalem.

33"When we get there," he told them, "I, the Messiah,a will be arrested and taken before the chief priests and the Jewish leaders, who will sentence me to die and hand me over to the Romans to be killed. 34They will mock me and spit on me and flog me with their whips and kill me; but after three days I will come back to life again."

35Then James and John, the sons of Zebedee, came over and spoke to him in a low voice.b "Master," they said, "we want you to do us a favor."

36"What is it?" he asked.

37"We want to sit on the thrones next to yours in your kingdom," they said, "one at your right and the other at your left!"

38But Jesus answered, "You don't know what you are asking! Are you able to drink from the bitter cup of sorrow I must drink from? Or to be baptized with the baptism of suffering I must be baptized with?"

39"Oh, yes," they said, "we are!"

And Jesus said, "You shall indeed drink from my cup and be baptized with my baptism, 40but I do not have the right to place you on thrones next to mine. Those appointments have already been made."

41When the other disciples discovered what James and John had asked, they were very indignant. 42So Jesus called them to him and said, "As you know, the kings and great men of the earth lord it over the people; 43but among you it is different. Whoever wants to be great among you must be your servant. 44And whoever wants to be greatest of all must be the slave of all. 45For even I, the Messiah,a am not here to be served, but to help others, and to give my life as a ransom for many."

46And so they reached Jericho. Later, as they left town, a great crowd was following. Now it happened that a blind beggar named Bartimaeus (the son of Timaeus) was sitting beside the road as Jesus was going by.

47When Bartimaeus heard that Jesus from Nazareth was near, he began to shout out, "Jesus, Son of David, have mercy on me!"

48"Shut up!" some of the people yelled at him.

But he only shouted the louder, again and again, "O Son of David, have mercy on me!"

49When Jesus heard him he stopped there in the road and said, "Tell him to come here."

So they called the blind man. "You lucky fellow,"c they said, "come on, he's calling you!" 50Bartimaeus yanked off his old coat and flung it aside, jumped up and came to Jesus.

51"What do you want me to do for you?" Jesus asked.

"O Teacher," the blind man said, "I want to see!"

New Revised Standard

28 Peter began to say to him, "Look, we have left everything and followed you." 29Jesus said, "Truly I tell you, there is no one who has left house or brothers or sisters or mother or father or children or fields, for my sake and for the sake of the good news,d 30who will not receive a hundredfold now in this age—houses, brothers and sisters, mothers and children, and fields with persecutions—and in the age to come eternal life. 31But many who are first will be last, and the last will be first."

A Third Time Jesus Foretells His Death and Resurrection

32 They were on the road, going up to Jerusalem, and Jesus was walking ahead of them; they were amazed, and those who followed were afraid. He took the twelve aside again and began to tell them what was to happen to him, 33saying, "See, we are going up to Jerusalem, and the Son of Man will be handed over to the chief priests and the scribes, and they will condemn him to death; then they will hand him over to the Gentiles; 34they will mock him, and spit upon him, and flog him, and kill him; and after three days he will rise again."

The Request of James and John

35 James and John, the sons of Zebedee, came forward to him and said to him, "Teacher, we want you to do for us whatever we ask of you." 36And he said to them, "What is it you want me to do for you?" 37And they said to him, "Grant us to sit, one at your right hand and one at your left, in your glory." 38But Jesus said to them, "You do not know what you are asking. Are you able to drink the cup that I drink, or be baptized with the baptism that I am baptized with?" 39They replied, "We are able." Then Jesus said to them, "The cup that I drink you will drink; and with the baptism with which I am baptized, you will be baptized; 40but to sit at my right hand or at my left is not mine to grant, but it is for those for whom it has been prepared."

41 When the ten heard this, they began to be angry with James and John. 42So Jesus called them and said to them, "You know that among the Gentiles those whom they recognize as their rulers lord it over them, and their great ones are tyrants over them. 43But it is not so among you; but whoever wishes to become great among you must be your servant, 44and whoever wishes to be first among you must be slave of all. 45For the Son of Man came not to be served but to serve, and to give his life a ransom for many."

The Healing of Blind Bartimaeus

46 They came to Jericho. As he and his disciples and a large crowd were leaving Jericho, Bartimaeus son of Timaeus, a blind beggar, was sitting by the roadside. 47When he heard that it was Jesus of Nazareth, he began to shout out and say, "Jesus, Son of David, have mercy on me!" 48Many sternly ordered him to be quiet, but he cried out even more loudly, "Son of David, have mercy on me!" 49Jesus stood still and said, "Call him here." And they called the blind man, saying to him, "Take heart; get up, he is calling you." 50So throwing off his cloak, he sprang up and came to Jesus. 51Then Jesus said to him, "What do you want me to do for you?" The blind man said to him, "My teacher,e let me see again."

---

a 10:33,10:45 the Messiah, literally, "the Son of Man."   b 10:35 spoke to him in a low voice, literally, "came up to him."   c 10:49 You lucky fellow, literally, "be of good cheer."

d Or gospel   e Aramaic Rabbouni

King James

52And Jesus said unto him, Go thy way; thy faith hath made thee whole. And immediately he received his sight, and followed Jesus in the way.

11 AND WHEN they came nigh to Jerusalem, unto Bethphage and Bethany, at the mount of Olives, he sendeth forth two of his disciples,

2And saith unto them, Go your way into the village over against you: and as soon as ye be entered into it, ye shall find a colt tied, whereon never man sat; loose him, and bring *him.*

3And if any man say unto you, Why do ye this? say ye that the Lord hath need of him; and straightway he will send him hither.

4And they went their way, and found the colt tied by the door without in a place where two ways met; and they loose him.

5And certain of them that stood there said unto them, What do ye, loosing the colt?

6And they said unto them even as Jesus had commanded: and they let them go.

7And they brought the colt to Jesus, and cast their garments on him; and he sat upon him.

8And many spread their garments in the way: and others cut down branches off the trees, and strawed *them* in the way.

9And they that went before, and they that followed, cried, saying, Hosanna; Blessed *is* he that cometh in the name of the Lord:

10Blessed *be* the kingdom of our father David, that cometh in the name of the Lord: Hosanna in the highest.

11And Jesus entered into Jerusalem, and into the temple: and when he had looked round about upon all things, and now the eventide was come, he went out unto Bethany with the twelve.

12¶ And on the morrow, when they were come from Bethany, he was hungry:

13And seeing a fig tree afar off having leaves, he came, if haply he might find any thing thereon: and when he came to it, he found nothing but leaves; for the time of figs was not *yet.*

14And Jesus answered and said unto it, No man eat fruit of thee hereafter for ever. And his disciples heard *it.*

15¶ And they come to Jerusalem: and Jesus went into the temple, and began to cast out them that sold and bought in the temple, and overthrew the tables of the moneychangers, and the seats of them that sold doves;

16And would not suffer that any man should carry *any* vessel through the temple.

17And he taught, saying unto them, Is it not written, My house shall be called of all nations the house of prayer? but ye have made it a den of thieves.

18And the scribes and chief priests heard *it,* and sought how they might destroy him: for they feared him, because all the people was astonished at his doctrine.

19And when even was come, he went out of the city.

20¶ And in the morning, as they passed by, they saw the fig tree dried up from the roots.

21And Peter calling to remembrance saith unto him, Master, behold, the fig tree which thou cursedst is withered away.

New International

52"Go," said Jesus, "your faith has healed you." Immediately he received his sight and followed Jesus along the road.

The Triumphal Entry

11 AS THEY approached Jerusalem and came to Bethphage and Bethany at the Mount of Olives, Jesus sent two of his disciples, 2saying to them, "Go to the village ahead of you, and just as you enter it, you will find a colt tied there, which no one has ever ridden. Untie it and bring it here. 3If anyone asks you, 'Why are you doing this?' tell him, 'The Lord needs it and will send it back here shortly.' "

4They went and found a colt outside in the street, tied at a doorway. As they untied it, 5some people standing there asked, "What are you doing, untying that colt?" 6They answered as Jesus had told them to, and the people let them go. 7When they brought the colt to Jesus and threw their cloaks over it, he sat on it. 8Many people spread their cloaks on the road, while others spread branches they had cut in the fields. 9Those who went ahead and those who followed shouted,

> "Hosanna!a"

> "Blessed is he who comes in the name of the Lord!"b

> 10"Blessed is the coming kingdom of our father David!"

> "Hosanna in the highest!"

11Jesus entered Jerusalem and went to the temple. He looked around at everything, but since it was already late, he went out to Bethany with the Twelve.

Jesus Clears the Temple

12The next day as they were leaving Bethany, Jesus was hungry. 13Seeing in the distance a fig tree in leaf, he went to find out if it had any fruit. When he reached it, he found nothing but leaves, because it was not the season for figs. 14Then he said to the tree, "May no one ever eat fruit from you again." And his disciples heard him say it.

15On reaching Jerusalem, Jesus entered the temple area and began driving out those who were buying and selling there. He overturned the tables of the money changers and the benches of those selling doves, 16and would not allow anyone to carry merchandise through the temple courts. 17And as he taught them, he said, "Is it not written:

> " 'My house will be called
> a house of prayer for all nations'c?

But you have made it 'a den of robbers.'d"

18The chief priests and the teachers of the law heard this and began looking for a way to kill him, for they feared him, because the whole crowd was amazed at his teaching.

19When evening came, theye went out of the city.

The Withered Fig Tree

20In the morning, as they went along, they saw the fig tree withered from the roots. 21Peter remembered and said to Jesus, "Rabbi, look! The fig tree you cursed has withered!"

---

a 9 A Hebrew expression meaning "Save!" which became an exclamation of praise; also in verse 10   b 9 Psalm 118:25,26   c 17 Isaiah 56:7   d 17 Jer. 7:11   e 19 Some early manuscripts he

Living Bible

52And Jesus said to him, "All right, it's done.f Your faith has healed you."

And instantly the blind man could see, and followed Jesus down the road!

11 AS THEY neared Bethphage and Bethany on the outskirts of Jerusalem and came to the Mount of Olives, Jesus sent two of his disciples on ahead.

2"Go into that village over there," he told them, "and just as you enter you will see a colt tied up that has never been ridden. Untie him and bring him here. 3And if anyone asks you what you are doing, just say, 'Our Master needs him and will return him soon.'"

4, 5Off went the two men and found the colt standing in the street, tied outside a house. As they were untying it, some who were standing there demanded, "What are you doing, untying that colt?"

6So they said what Jesus had told them to, and then the men agreed.

7So the colt was brought to Jesus and the disciples threw their cloaks across its back for him to ride on. 8Then many in the crowd spread out their coats along the road before him, while others threw down leafy branches from the fields.

9He was in the center of the procession with crowds ahead and behind, and all of them shouting, "Hail to the King!" "Praise God for him who comes in the name of the Lord!" . . . 10"Praise God for the return of our father David's kingdom. . . ." "Hail to the King of the universe!"

11And so he entered Jerusalem and went into the Temple. He looked around carefully at everything and then left—for now it was late in the afternoon—and went out to Bethany with the twelve disciples.

12The next morning as they left Bethany, he felt hungry. 13A little way off he noticed a fig tree in full leaf, so he went over to see if he could find any figs on it. But no, there were only leaves, for it was too early in the season for fruit.

14Then Jesus said to the tree, "You shall never bear fruit again!" And the disciples heard him say it.

15When they arrived back to Jerusalem he went to the Temple and began to drive out the merchants and their customers, and knocked over the tables of the money-changers and the stalls of those selling doves, 16and stopped everyone from bringing in loads of merchandise.

17He told them, "It is written in the Scriptures, 'My Temple is to be a place of prayer for all nations,' but you have turned it into a den of robbers."

18When the chief priests and other Jewish leaders heard what he had done they began planning how best to get rid of him. Their problem was their fear of riots because the people were so enthusiastic about Jesus' teaching.

19That evening as usual they left the city.

20Next morning, as the disciples passed the fig tree he had cursed, they saw that it was withered from the roots! 21Then Peter remembered what Jesus had said to the tree on the previous day, and exclaimed, "Look, Teacher! The fig tree you cursed has withered!"

New Revised Standard

52Jesus said to him, "Go; your faith has made you well." Immediately he regained his sight and followed him on the way.

Jesus' Triumphal Entry into Jerusalem

11 WHEN THEY were approaching Jerusalem, at Bethphage and Bethany, near the Mount of Olives, he sent two of his disciples 2and said to them, "Go into the village ahead of you, and immediately as you enter it, you will find tied there a colt that has never been ridden; untie it and bring it. 3If anyone says to you, 'Why are you doing this?' just say this, 'The Lord needs it and will send it back here immediately.'" 4They went away and found a colt tied near a door, outside in the street. As they were untying it, 5some of the bystanders said to them, "What are you doing, untying the colt?" 6They told them what Jesus had said; and they allowed them to take it. 7Then they brought the colt to Jesus and threw their cloaks on it; and he sat on it. 8Many people spread their cloaks on the road, and others spread leafy branches that they had cut in the fields. 9Then those who went ahead and those who followed were shouting,

"Hosanna!
Blessed is the one who comes in the name
of the Lord!
10 Blessed is the coming kingdom of our
ancestor David!
Hosanna in the highest heaven!"

11 Then he entered Jerusalem and went into the temple; and when he had looked around at everything, as it was already late, he went out to Bethany with the twelve.

Jesus Curses the Fig Tree

12 On the following day, when they came from Bethany, he was hungry. 13Seeing in the distance a fig tree in leaf, he went to see whether perhaps he would find anything on it. When he came to it, he found nothing but leaves, for it was not the season for figs. 14He said to it, "May no one ever eat fruit from you again." And his disciples heard it.

Jesus Cleanses the Temple

15 Then they came to Jerusalem. And he entered the temple and began to drive out those who were selling and those who were buying in the temple, and he overturned the tables of the money changers and the seats of those who sold doves; 16and he would not allow anyone to carry anything through the temple. 17He was teaching and saying, "Is it not written,

'My house shall be called a house of prayer
for all the nations'?

But you have made it a den of robbers."

18And when the chief priests and the scribes heard it, they kept looking for a way to kill him; for they were afraid of him, because the whole crowd was spellbound by his teaching. 19And when evening came, Jesus and his disciplesg went out of the city.

The Lesson from the Withered Fig Tree

20 In the morning as they passed by, they saw the fig tree withered away to its roots. 21Then Peter remembered and said to him, "Rabbi, look! The fig tree that you cursed has withered." 22Jesus answered them,

---

f 10:52 *All right, it's done,* literally, "Go your way."

g Gk *they:* other ancient authorities read *he*

King James

22And Jesus answering saith unto them, Have faith in God.

23For verily I say unto you, That whosoever shall say unto this mountain, Be thou removed, and be thou cast into the sea; and shall not doubt in his heart, but shall believe that those things which he saith shall come to pass; he shall have whatsoever he saith.

24Therefore I say unto you, What things soever ye desire, when ye pray, believe that ye receive *them*, and ye shall have *them*.

25And when ye stand praying, forgive, if ye have aught against any: that your Father also which is in heaven may forgive you your trespasses.

26But if ye do not forgive, neither will your Father which is in heaven forgive your trespasses.

27¶ And they come again to Jerusalem: and as he was walking in the temple, there come to him the chief priests, and the scribes, and the elders,

28And say unto him, By what authority doest thou these things? and who gave thee this authority to do these things?

29And Jesus answered and said unto them, I will also ask of you one question, and answer me, and I will tell you by what authority I do these things.

30The baptism of John, was *it* from heaven, or of men? answer me.

31And they reasoned with themselves, saying, If we shall say, From heaven; he will say, Why then did ye not believe him?

32But if we shall say, Of men; they feared the people: for all *men* counted John, that he was a prophet indeed.

33And they answered and said unto Jesus, We cannot tell. And Jesus answering saith unto them, Neither do I tell you by what authority I do these things.

12 AND HE began to speak unto them by parables. A *certain* man planted a vineyard, and set an hedge about *it*, and digged *a place for* the winevat, and built a tower, and let it out to husbandmen, and went into a far country.

2And at the season he sent to the husbandmen a servant, that he might receive from the husbandmen of the fruit of the vineyard.

3And they caught *him*, and beat him, and sent *him* away empty.

4And again he sent unto them another servant; and at him they cast stones, and wounded *him* in the head, and sent *him* away shamefully handled.

5And again he sent another; and him they killed, and many others; beating some, and killing some.

6Having yet therefore one son, his wellbeloved, he sent him also last unto them, saying, They will reverence my son.

7But those husbandmen said among themselves, This is the heir; come, let us kill him, and the inheritance shall be ours.

8And they took *him*, and killed *him*, and cast *him* out of the vineyard.

9What shall therefore the lord of the vineyard do? he will come and destroy the husbandmen, and will give the vineyard unto others.

10And have ye not read this scripture; The stone which the builders rejected is become the head of the corner:

11This was the Lord's doing, and it is marvellous in our eyes?

12And they sought to lay hold on him, but feared the people: for they knew that he had spoken the parable against them: and they left him, and went their way.

New International

22"Have[a] faith in God," Jesus answered. 23"I tell you the truth, if anyone says to this mountain, 'Go, throw yourself into the sea,' and does not doubt in his heart but believes that what he says will happen, it will be done for him. 24Therefore I tell you, whatever you ask for in prayer, believe that you have received it, and it will be yours. 25And when you stand praying, if you hold anything against anyone, forgive him, so that your Father in heaven may forgive you your sins.[b]"

The Authority of Jesus Questioned

27They arrived again in Jerusalem, and while Jesus was walking in the temple courts, the chief priests, the teachers of the law and the elders came to him. 28"By what authority are you doing these things?" they asked. "And who gave you authority to do this?"

29Jesus replied, "I will ask you one question. Answer me, and I will tell you by what authority I am doing these things. 30John's baptism—was it from heaven, or from men? Tell me!"

31They discussed it among themselves and said, "If we say, 'From heaven,' he will ask, 'Then why didn't you believe him?' 32But if we say, 'From men' . . . ." (They feared the people, for everyone held that John really was a prophet.)

33So they answered Jesus, "We don't know."

Jesus said, "Neither will I tell you by what authority I am doing these things."

The Parable of the Tenants

12 HE THEN began to speak to them in parables: "A man planted a vineyard. He put a wall around it, dug a pit for the winepress and built a watchtower. Then he rented the vineyard to some farmers and went away on a journey. 2At harvest time he sent a servant to the tenants to collect from them some of the fruit of the vineyard. 3But they seized him, beat him and sent him away empty-handed. 4Then he sent another servant to them; they struck this man on the head and treated him shamefully. 5He sent still another, and that one they killed. He sent many others; some of them they beat, others they killed.

6"He had one left to send, a son, whom he loved. He sent him last of all, saying, 'They will respect my son.'

7"But the tenants said to one another, 'This is the heir. Come, let's kill him, and the inheritance will be ours.' 8So they took him and killed him, and threw him out of the vineyard.

9"What then will the owner of the vineyard do? He will come and kill those tenants and give the vineyard to others. 10Haven't you read this scripture:

" 'The stone the builders rejected
    has become the capstone[c];
11the Lord has done this,
    and it is marvelous in our eyes'[d]?"

12Then they looked for a way to arrest him because they knew he had spoken the parable against them. But they were afraid of the crowd; so they left him and went away.

---

a 22 Some early manuscripts *If you have*   b 25 Some manuscripts *sins.* 26*But if you do not forgive, neither will your Father who is in heaven forgive your sins.*   c 10 Or *cornerstone*   d 11 Psalm 118:22,23

Living Bible

22, 23In reply Jesus said to the disciples, "If you only have faith in God—this is the absolute truth—you can say to this Mount of Olives, 'Rise up and fall into the Mediterranean,' and your command will be obeyed. All that's required is that you really believe and have no doubt! 24Listen to me! You can pray for *anything*, and *if you believe, you have it;* it's yours! 25But when you are praying, first forgive anyone you are holding a grudge against, so that your Father in heaven will forgive you your sins too."

26, 27, 28e By this time they had arrived in Jerusalem again, and as he was walking through the Temple area, the chief priests and other Jewish leadersf came up to him demanding, "What's going on here? Who gave you the authority to drive out the merchants?"

29Jesus replied, "I'll tell you if you answer one question! 30What about John the Baptist? Was he sent by God, or not? Answer me!"

31They talked it over among themselves. "If we reply that God sent him, then he will say, 'All right, why didn't you accept him?' 32But if we say 'God didn't send him, then the people will start a riot." (For the people all believed strongly that John was a prophet.)

33So they said, "We can't answer. We don't know." To which Jesus replied, "Then I won't answer your question either!"

12 HERE ARE some of the story-illustrations Jesus gave to the people at that time:

"A man planted a vineyard and built a wall around it and dug a pit for pressing out the grape juice, and built a watchman's tower. Then he leased the farm to tenant farmers and moved to another country. 2At grape-picking time he sent one of his men to collect his share of the crop. 3But the farmers beat up the man and sent him back empty-handed.

4"The owner then sent another of his men, who received the same treatment, only worse, for his head was seriously injured. 5The next man he sent was killed; and later, others were either beaten or killed, until 6there was only one left—his only son. He finally sent him, thinking they would surely give him their full respect.

7"But when the farmers saw him coming they said, 'He will own the farm when his father dies. Come on, let's kill him—and then the farm will be ours!' 8So they caught him and murdered him and threw his body out of the vineyard.

9"What do you suppose the owner will do when he hears what happened? He will come and kill them all, and lease the vineyard to others. 10Don't you remember reading this verse in the Scriptures? 'The Rock the builders threw away became the cornerstone, the most honored stone in the building! 11This is the Lord's doing and it is an amazing thing to see.' "

12The Jewish leaders wanted to arrest him then and there for using this illustration, for they knew he was pointing at them—they were the wicked farmers in his story. But they were afraid to touch him for fear of a mob. So they left him and went away.

New Revised Standard

"Haveg faith in God. 23Truly I tell you, if you say to this mountain, 'Be taken up and thrown into the sea,' and if you do not doubt in your heart, but believe that what you say will come to pass, it will be done for you. 24So I tell you, whatever you ask for in prayer, believe that you have receivedh it, and it will be yours.

25 "Whenever you stand praying, forgive, if you have anything against anyone; so that your Father in heaven may also forgive you your trespasses."i

Jesus' Authority Is Questioned

27 Again they came to Jerusalem. As he was walking in the temple, the chief priests, the scribes, and the elders came to him 28and said, "By what authority are you doing these things? Who gave you this authority to do them?" 29Jesus said to them, "I will ask you one question; answer me, and I will tell you by what authority I do these things. 30Did the baptism of John come from heaven, or was it of human origin? Answer me." 31They argued with one another, "If we say, 'From heaven,' he will say, 'Why then did you not believe him?' 32But shall we say, 'Of human origin'?"—they were afraid of the crowd, for all regarded John as truly a prophet. 33So they answered Jesus, "We do not know." And Jesus said to them, "Neither will I tell you by what authority I am doing these things."

The Parable of the Wicked Tenants

12 THEN HE began to speak to them in parables. "A man planted a vineyard, put a fence around it, dug a pit for the wine press, and built a watchtower; then he leased it to tenants and went to another country. 2When the season came, he sent a slave to the tenants to collect from them his share of the produce of the vineyard. 3But they seized him, and beat him, and sent him away empty-handed. 4And again he sent another slave to them; this one they beat over the head and insulted. 5Then he sent another, and that one they killed. And so it was with many others; some they beat, and others they killed. 6He had still one other, a beloved son. Finally he sent him to them, saying, 'They will respect my son.' 7But those tenants said to one another, 'This is the heir; come, let us kill him, and the inheritance will be ours.' 8So they seized him, killed him, and threw him out of the vineyard. 9What then will the owner of the vineyard do? He will come and destroy the tenants and give the vineyard to others. 10Have you not read this scripture:

'The stone that the builders rejected
 has become the cornerstone;j
11 this was the Lord's doing,
 and it is amazing in our eyes'?"

12 When they realized that he had told this parable against them, they wanted to arrest him, but they feared the crowd. So they left him and went away.

e 11:26 Many ancient authorities add vs 26, "but if you do not forgive, neither will your Father who is in heaven forgive your trespasses." All include this in Mt 6:15. f 11:27 other Jewish leaders, literally, "scribes and elders." Also in 12:12.

g Other ancient authorities read "If you have h Other ancient authorities read are receiving i Other ancient authorities add verse 26, "But if you do not forgive, neither will your Father in heaven forgive your trespasses." j Or keystone

King James

13¶ And they send unto him certain of the Pharisees and of the Herodians, to catch him in *his* words.

14And when they were come, they say unto him, Master, we know that thou art true, and carest for no man: for thou regardest not the person of men, but teachest the way of God in truth: Is it lawful to give tribute to Caesar, or not?

15Shall we give, or shall we not give? But he, knowing their hypocrisy, said unto them, Why tempt ye me? bring me a penny, that I may see *it*.

16And they brought *it*. And he saith unto them, Whose *is* this image and superscription? And they said unto him, Caesar's.

17And Jesus answering said unto them, Render to Caesar the things that are Caesar's, and to God the things that are God's. And they marvelled at him.

18¶ Then come unto him the Sadducees, which say there is no resurrection; and they asked him, saying,

19Master, Moses wrote unto us, If a man's brother die, and leave *his* wife *behind him,* and leave no children, that his brother should take his wife, and raise up seed unto his brother.

20Now there were seven brethren: and the first took a wife, and dying left no seed.

21And the second took her, and died, neither left he any seed: and the third likewise.

22And the seven had her, and left no seed: last of all the woman died also.

23In the resurrection therefore, when they shall rise, whose wife shall she be of them? for the seven had her to wife.

24And Jesus answering said unto them, Do ye not therefore err, because ye know not the scriptures, neither the power of God?

25For when they shall rise from the dead, they neither marry, nor are given in marriage; but are as the angels which are in heaven.

26And as touching the dead, that they rise: have ye not read in the book of Moses, how in the bush God spake unto him, saying, I *am* the God of Abraham, and the God of Isaac, and the God of Jacob?

27He is not the God of the dead, but the God of the living: ye therefore do greatly err.

28¶ And one of the scribes came, and having heard them reasoning together, and perceiving that he had answered them well, asked him, Which is the first commandment of all?

29And Jesus answered him, The first of all the commandments *is,* Hear, O Israel; The Lord our God is one Lord:

30And thou shalt love the Lord thy God with all thy heart, and with all thy soul, and with all thy mind, and with all thy strength: this *is* the first commandment.

31And the second *is* like, *namely* this, Thou shalt love thy neighbour as thyself. There is none other commandment greater than these.

32And the scribe said unto him, Well, Master, thou hast said the truth: for there is one God; and there is none other but he:

33And to love him with all the heart, and with all the understanding, and with all the soul, and with all the strength, and to love *his* neighbour as himself, is more than all whole burnt offerings and sacrifices.

34And when Jesus saw that he answered discreetly, he said unto him, Thou art not far from the kingdom of God. And no man after that durst ask him *any question.*

35¶ And Jesus answered and said, while he taught in the temple, How say the scribes that Christ is the son of David?

New International

Paying Taxes to Caesar

13Later they sent some of the Pharisees and Herodians to Jesus to catch him in his words. 14They came to him and said, "Teacher, we know you are a man of integrity. You aren't swayed by men, because you pay no attention to who they are; but you teach the way of God in accordance with the truth. Is it right to pay taxes to Caesar or not? 15Should we pay or shouldn't we?"

But Jesus knew their hypocrisy. "Why are you trying to trap me?" he asked. "Bring me a denarius and let me look at it." 16They brought the coin, and he asked them, "Whose portrait is this? And whose inscription?"

"Caesar's," they replied.

17Then Jesus said to them, "Give to Caesar what is Caesar's and to God what is God's."

And they were amazed at him.

Marriage at the Resurrection

18Then the Sadducees, who say there is no resurrection, came to him with a question. 19"Teacher," they said, "Moses wrote for us that if a man's brother dies and leaves a wife but no children, the man must marry the widow and have children for his brother. 20Now there were seven brothers. The first one married and died without leaving any children. 21The second one married the widow, but he also died, leaving no child. It was the same with the third. 22In fact, none of the seven left any children. Last of all, the woman died too. 23At the resurrection[a] whose wife will she be, since the seven were married to her?"

24Jesus replied, "Are you not in error because you do not know the Scriptures or the power of God? 25When the dead rise, they will neither marry nor be given in marriage; they will be like the angels in heaven. 26Now about the dead rising—have you not read in the book of Moses, in the account of the bush, how God said to him, 'I am the God of Abraham, the God of Isaac, and the God of Jacob'[b]? 27He is not the God of the dead, but of the living. You are badly mistaken!"

The Greatest Commandment

28One of the teachers of the law came and heard them debating. Noticing that Jesus had given them a good answer, he asked him, "Of all the commandments, which is the most important?"

29"The most important one," answered Jesus, "is this: 'Hear, O Israel, the Lord our God, the Lord is one.[c] 30Love the Lord your God with all your heart and with all your soul and with all your mind and with all your strength.'[d] 31The second is this: 'Love your neighbor as yourself.'[e] There is no commandment greater than these."

32"Well said, teacher," the man replied. "You are right in saying that God is one and there is no other but him. 33To love him with all your heart, with all your understanding and with all your strength, and to love your neighbor as yourself is more important than all burnt offerings and sacrifices."

34When Jesus saw that he had answered wisely, he said to him, "You are not far from the kingdom of God." And from then on no one dared ask him any more questions.

Whose Son Is the Christ?

35While Jesus was teaching in the temple courts, he asked, "How is it that the teachers of the law say that the Christ[f] is the son of David? 36David himself, speaking by the Holy Spirit, declared:

---

a 23 Some manuscripts *resurrection, when men rise from the dead,*
b 26 Exodus 3:6   c 29 Or *the Lord our God is one Lord*   d 30 Deut. 6:4,5
e 31 Lev. 19:18   f 35 Or *Messiah*

Living Bible

13But they sent other religious and political leaders to talk with him and try to trap him into saying something he could be arrested for.

14"Teacher," these spies said, "we know you tell the truth no matter what! You aren't influenced by the opinions and desires of men, but sincerely teach the ways of God. Now tell us, is it right to pay taxes to Rome, or not?"

15Jesus saw their trick and said, "Show me a coin and I'll tell you."

16When they handed it to him he asked, "Whose picture and title is this on the coin?" They replied, "The emperor's."

17"All right," he said, "if it is his, give it to him. But everything that belongs to God must be given to God!" And they scratched their heads in bafflement at his reply.

18Then the Sadducees stepped forward—a group of men who say there is no resurrection. Here was their question:

19"Teacher, Moses gave us a law that when a man dies without children, the man's brother should marry his widow and have children in his brother's name. 20, 21, 22Well, there were seven brothers and the oldest married and died, and left no children. So the second brother married the widow, but soon he died too, and left no children. Then the next brother married her, and died without children, and so on until all were dead, and still there were no children; and last of all, the woman died too.

23"What we want to know is this:g In the resurrection, whose wife will she be, for she had been the wife of each of them?"

24Jesus replied, "Your trouble is that you don't know the Scriptures, and don't know the power of God. 25For when these seven brothers and the woman rise from the dead, they won't be married—they will be like the angels.

26"But now as to whether there will be a resurrection—have you never read in the book of Exodus about Moses and the burning bush? God said to Moses, 'I *am* the God of Abraham, and I *am* the God of Isaac, and I *am* the God of Jacob.'

27"God was telling Moses that these men, though dead for hundreds of years,h were still very much alive, for he would not have said, 'I *am* the God' of those who don't exist! You have made a serious error."

28One of the teachers of religion who was standing there listening to the discussion realized that Jesus had answered well. So he asked, "Of all the commandments, which is the most important?"

29Jesus replied, "The one that says, 'Hear, O Israel! The Lord our God is the one and only God. 30And you must love him with all your heart and soul and mind and strength.'

31"The second is: 'You must love others as much as yourself.' No other commandments are greater than these."

32The teacher of religion replied, "Sir, you have spoken a true word in saying that there is only one God and no other. 33And I know it is far more important to love him with all my heart and understanding and strength, and to love others as myself, than to offer all kinds of sacrifices on the altar of the Temple."

34Realizing this man's understanding, Jesus said to him, "You are not far from the Kingdom of God." And after that, no one dared ask him any more questions.

35Later, as Jesus was teaching the people in the Temple area, he asked them this question:

"Why do your religious teachers claim that the Messiah must be a descendant of King David? 36For David

New Revised Standard

The Question about Paying Taxes

13 Then they sent to him some Pharisees and some Herodians to trap him in what he said. 14And they came and said to him, "Teacher, we know that you are sincere, and show deference to no one; for you do not regard people with partiality, but teach the way of God in accordance with truth. Is it lawful to pay taxes to the emperor, or not? 15Should we pay them, or should we not?" But knowing their hypocrisy, he said to them, "Why are you putting me to the test? Bring me a denarius and let me see it." 16And they brought one. Then he said to them, "Whose head is this, and whose title?" They answered, "The emperor's." 17Jesus said to them, "Give to the emperor the things that are the emperor's, and to God the things that are God's." And they were utterly amazed at him.

The Question about the Resurrection

18 Some Sadducees, who say there is no resurrection, came to him and asked him a question, saying, 19"Teacher, Moses wrote for us that 'if a man's brother dies, leaving a wife but no child, the mani shall marry the widow and raise up children for his brother.' 20There were seven brothers; the first married and, when he died, left no children; 21and the second married her and died, leaving no children; and the third likewise; 22none of the seven left children. Last of all the woman herself died. 23In the resurrectionj whose wife will she be? For the seven had married her."

24 Jesus said to them, "Is not this the reason you are wrong, that you know neither the scriptures nor the power of God? 25For when they rise from the dead, they neither marry nor are given in marriage, but are like angels in heaven. 26And as for the dead being raised, have you not read in the book of Moses, in the story about the bush, how God said to him, 'I am the God of Abraham, the God of Isaac, and the God of Jacob'? 27He is God not of the dead, but of the living; you are quite wrong."

The First Commandment

28 One of the scribes came near and heard them disputing with one another, and seeing that he answered them well, he asked him, "Which commandment is the first of all?" 29Jesus answered, "The first is, 'Hear, O Israel: the Lord our God, the Lord is one; 30you shall love the Lord your God with all your heart, and with all your soul, and with all your mind, and with all your strength.' 31The second is this, 'You shall love your neighbor as yourself.' There is no other commandment greater than these." 32Then the scribe said to him, "You are right, Teacher; you have truly said that 'he is one, and besides him there is no other'; 33and 'to love him with all the heart, and with all the understanding, and with all the strength,' and 'to love one's neighbor as oneself,'—this is much more important than all whole burnt offerings and sacrifices." 34When Jesus saw that he answered wisely, he said to him, "You are not far from the kingdom of God." After that no one dared to ask him any question.

The Question about David's Son

35 While Jesus was teaching in the temple, he said, "How can the scribes say that the Messiahk is the son of David? 36David himself, by the Holy Spirit, declared,

---

g 12:23 *what we want to know is this,* implied. h 12:27 *though dead for hundreds of years,* implied.

i Gk *his brother* j Other ancient authorities add *when they rise* k Or *the Christ*

King James

36For David himself said by the Holy Ghost, The LORD said to my Lord, Sit thou on my right hand, till I make thine enemies thy footstool.

37David therefore himself calleth him Lord; and whence is he *then* his son? And the common people heard him gladly.

38¶ And he said unto them in his doctrine, Beware of the scribes, which love to go in long clothing, and *love* salutations in the marketplaces,

39And the chief seats in the synagogues, and the uppermost rooms at feasts;

40Which devour widows' houses, and for a pretence make long prayers: these shall receive greater damnation.

41¶ And Jesus sat over against the treasury, and beheld how the people cast money into the treasury: and many that were rich cast in much.

42And there came a certain poor widow, and she threw in two mites, which make a farthing.

43And he called *unto him* his disciples, and saith unto them, Verily I say unto you, That this poor widow hath cast more in, than all they which have cast into the treasury:

44For all *they* did cast in of their abundance; but she of her want did cast in all that she had, *even* all her living.

13 AND AS he went out of the temple, one of his disciples saith unto him, Master, see what manner of stones and what buildings *are here!*

2And Jesus answering said unto him, Seest thou these great buildings? there shall not be left one stone upon another, that shall not be thrown down.

3And as he sat upon the mount of Olives over against the temple, Peter and James and John and Andrew asked him privately,

4Tell us, when shall these things be? and what *shall be* the sign when all these things shall be fulfilled?

5And Jesus answering them began to say, Take heed lest any *man* deceive you:

6For many shall come in my name, saying, I am *Christ;* and shall deceive many.

7And when ye shall hear of wars and rumours of wars, be ye not troubled: for *such things* must needs be; but the end *shall* not *be* yet.

8For nation shall rise against nation, and kingdom against kingdom: and there shall be earthquakes in divers places, and there shall be famines and troubles: these *are* the beginnings of sorrows.

9¶ But take heed to yourselves: for they shall deliver you up to councils; and in the synagogues ye shall be beaten: and ye shall be brought before rulers and kings for my sake, for a testimony against them.

10And the gospel must first be published among all nations.

11But when they shall lead *you,* and deliver you up, take no thought beforehand what ye shall speak, neither do ye premeditate: but whatsoever shall be given you in that hour, that speak ye: for it is not ye that speak, but the Holy Ghost.

12Now the brother shall betray the brother to death, and the father the son; and children shall rise up against *their* parents, and shall cause them to be put to death.

13And ye shall be hated of all *men* for my name's sake: but he that shall endure unto the end, the same shall be saved.

New International

" 'The Lord said to my Lord:
  "Sit at my right hand
  until I put your enemies
    under your feet." ' [a]

37David himself calls him 'Lord.' How then can he be his son?"

The large crowd listened to him with delight.

38As he taught, Jesus said, "Watch out for the teachers of the law. They like to walk around in flowing robes and be greeted in the marketplaces, 39and have the most important seats in the synagogues and the places of honor at banquets. 40They devour widows' houses and for a show make lengthy prayers. Such men will be punished most severely."

The Widow's Offering

41Jesus sat down opposite the place where the offerings were put and watched the crowd putting their money into the temple treasury. Many rich people threw in large amounts. 42But a poor widow came and put in two very small copper coins,[b] worth only a fraction of a penny.[c]

43Calling his disciples to him, Jesus said, "I tell you the truth, this poor widow has put more into the treasury than all the others. 44They all gave out of their wealth; but she, out of her poverty, put in everything—all she had to live on."

Signs of the End of the Age

13 AS HE was leaving the temple, one of his disciples said to him, "Look, Teacher! What massive stones! What magnificent buildings!"

2"Do you see all these great buildings?" replied Jesus. "Not one stone here will be left on another; every one will be thrown down."

3As Jesus was sitting on the Mount of Olives opposite the temple, Peter, James, John and Andrew asked him privately, 4"Tell us, when will these things happen? And what will be the sign that they are all about to be fulfilled?"

5Jesus said to them: "Watch out that no one deceives you. 6Many will come in my name, claiming, 'I am he,' and will deceive many. 7When you hear of wars and rumors of wars, do not be alarmed. Such things must happen, but the end is still to come. 8Nation will rise against nation, and kingdom against kingdom. There will be earthquakes in various places, and famines. These are the beginning of birth pains.

9"You must be on your guard. You will be handed over to the local councils and flogged in the synagogues. On account of me you will stand before governors and kings as witnesses to them. 10And the gospel must first be preached to all nations. 11Whenever you are arrested and brought to trial, do not worry beforehand about what to say. Just say whatever is given you at the time, for it is not you speaking, but the Holy Spirit.

12"Brother will betray brother to death, and a father his child. Children will rebel against their parents and have them put to death. 13All men will hate you because of me, but he who stands firm to the end will be saved.

Living Bible

himself said—and the Holy Spirit was speaking through him when he said it—'God said to my Lord, sit at my right hand until I make your enemies your footstool.' 37Since David called him his Lord, how can he be his son?"

(This sort of reasoning delighted the crowd and they listened to him with great interest.)

38Here are some of the other things he taught them at this time:

"Beware of the teachers of religion! For they love to wear the robes of the rich and scholarly, and to have everyone bow to them as they walk through the markets. 39They love to sit in the best seats in the synagogues, and at the places of honor at banquets— 40but they shamelessly cheat widows out of their homes and then, to cover up the kind of men they really are, they pretend to be pious by praying long prayers in public. Because of this, their punishment will be the greater."

41Then he went over to the collection boxes in the Temple and sat and watched as the crowds dropped in their money. Some who were rich put in large amounts. 42Then a poor widow came and dropped in two pennies.

43, 44He called his disciples to him and remarked, "That poor widow has given more than all those rich men put together! For they gave a little of their extra fat,d while she gave up her last penny."

13 AS HE was leaving the Temple that day, one of his disciples said, "Teacher, what beautiful buildings these are! Look at the decorated stonework on the walls."

2Jesus replied, "Yes, look! For not one stone will be left upon another, except as ruins."

3, 4And as he sat on the slopes of the Mount of Olives across the valley from Jerusalem, Peter, James, John, and Andrew got alone with him and asked him, "Just when is all this going to happen to the Temple? Will there be some warning ahead of time?

5So Jesus launched into an extended reply. "Don't let anyone mislead you," he said, 6"for many will come declaring themselves to be your Messiah, and will lead many astray. 7And wars will break out near and far, but this is not the signal of the end-time.

8"For nations and kingdoms will proclaim war against each other, and there will be earthquakes in many lands, and famines. These herald only the early stages of the anguish ahead. 9But when these things begin to happen, watch out! For you will be in great danger. You will be dragged before the courts, and beaten in the synagogues, and accused before governors and kings of being my followers. This is your opportunity to tell them the Good News. 10And the Good News must first be made known in every nation before the end-time finally comes.e 11But when you are arrested and stand trial, don't worry about what to say in your defense. Just say what God tells you to. Then you will not be speaking, but the Holy Spirit will.

12"Brothers will betray each other to death, fathers will betray their own children, and children will betray their parents to be killed. 13And everyone will hate you because you are mine. But all who endure to the end without renouncing me shall be saved.

New Revised Standard

'The Lord said to my Lord,
"Sit at my right hand,
until I put your enemies under your feet." '
37David himself calls him Lord; so how can he be his son?" And the large crowd was listening to him with delight.

Jesus Denounces the Scribes

38 As he taught, he said, "Beware of the scribes, who like to walk around in long robes, and to be greeted with respect in the marketplaces, 39and to have the best seats in the synagogues and places of honor at banquets! 40They devour widows' houses and for the sake of appearance say long prayers. They will receive the greater condemnation."

The Widow's Offering

41 He sat down opposite the treasury, and watched the crowd putting money into the treasury. Many rich people put in large sums. 42A poor widow came and put in two small copper coins, which are worth a penny. 43Then he called his disciples and said to them, "Truly I tell you, this poor widow has put in more than all those who are contributing to the treasury. 44For all of them have contributed out of their abundance; but she out of her poverty has put in everything she had, all she had to live on."

The Destruction of the Temple Foretold

13 AS HE came out of the temple, one of his disciples said to him, "Look, Teacher, what large stones and what large buildings!" 2Then Jesus asked him, "Do you see these great buildings? Not one stone will be left here upon another; all will be thrown down."

3 When he was sitting on the Mount of Olives opposite the temple, Peter, James, John, and Andrew asked him privately, 4"Tell us, when will this be, and what will be the sign that all these things are about to be accomplished?" 5Then Jesus began to say to them, "Beware that no one leads you astray. 6Many will come in my name and say, 'I am he!'f and they will lead many astray. 7When you hear of wars and rumors of wars, do not be alarmed; this must take place, but the end is still to come. 8For nation will rise against nation, and kingdom against kingdom; there will be earthquakes in various places; there will be famines. This is but the beginning of the birth pangs.

Persecution Foretold

9 "As for yourselves, beware; for they will hand you over to councils; and you will be beaten in synagogues; and you will stand before governors and kings because of me, as a testimony to them. 10And the good newsg must first be proclaimed to all nations. 11When they bring you to trial and hand you over, do not worry beforehand about what you are to say; but say whatever is given you at that time, for it is not you who speak, but the Holy Spirit. 12Brother will betray brother to death, and a father his child, and children will rise against parents and have them put to death; 13and you will be hated by all because of my name. But the one who endures to the end will be saved.

---

d 12:43, 44 *a little of their extra fat,* literally, "out of their surplus."
e 13:10 *before the end-time finally comes,* implied.

f Gk *I am* g Gk *gospel*

King James

14¶ But when ye shall see the abomination of desolation, spoken of by Daniel the prophet, standing where it ought not, (let him that readeth understand,) then let them that be in Judaea flee to the mountains:

15And let him that is on the housetop not go down into the house, neither enter *therein,* to take any thing out of his house:

16And let him that is in the field not turn back again for to take up his garment.

17But woe to them that are with child, and to them that give suck in those days!

18And pray ye that your flight be not in the winter.

19For *in* those days shall be affliction, such as was not from the beginning of the creation which God created unto this time, neither shall be.

20And except that the Lord had shortened those days, no flesh should be saved: but for the elect's sake, whom he hath chosen, he hath shortened the days.

21And then if any man shall say to you, Lo, here *is* Christ; or, lo, *he is* there; believe *him* not:

22For false Christs and false prophets shall rise, and shall show signs and wonders, to seduce, if *it were* possible, even the elect.

23But take ye heed: behold, I have foretold you all things.

24¶ But in those days, after that tribulation, the sun shall be darkened, and the moon shall not give her light,

25And the stars of heaven shall fall, and the powers that are in heaven shall be shaken.

26And then shall they see the Son of man coming in the clouds with great power and glory.

27And then shall he send his angels, and shall gather together his elect from the four winds, from the uttermost part of the earth to the uttermost part of heaven.

28Now learn a parable of the fig tree; When her branch is yet tender, and putteth forth leaves, ye know that summer is near:

29So ye in like manner, when ye shall see these things come to pass, know that it is nigh, *even* at the doors.

30Verily I say unto you, that this generation shall not pass, till all these things be done.

31Heaven and earth shall pass away: but my words shall not pass away.

32¶ But of that day and *that* hour knoweth no man, no, not the angels which are in heaven, neither the Son, but the Father.

33Take ye heed, watch and pray: for ye know not when the time is.

34*For the Son of man is* as a man taking a far journey, who left his house, and gave authority to his servants, and to every man his work, and commanded the porter to watch.

35Watch ye therefore: for ye know not when the master of the house cometh, at even, or at midnight, or at the cockcrowing, or in the morning:

36Lest coming suddenly he find you sleeping.

37And what I say unto you I say unto all, Watch.

14 AFTER TWO days was *the feast of* the passover, and of unleavened bread: and the chief priests and the scribes sought how they might take him by craft, and put *him* to death.

2But they said, Not on the feast *day,* lest there be an uproar of the people.

New International

14"When you see 'the abomination that causes desolation'[a] standing where it[b] does not belong—let the reader understand—then let those who are in Judea flee to the mountains. 15Let no one on the roof of his house go down or enter the house to take anything out. 16Let no one in the field go back to get his cloak. 17How dreadful it will be in those days for pregnant women and nursing mothers! 18Pray that this will not take place in winter, 19because those will be days of distress unequaled from the beginning, when God created the world, until now—and never to be equaled again. 20If the Lord had not cut short those days, no one would survive. But for the sake of the elect, whom he has chosen, he has shortened them. 21At that time if anyone says to you, 'Look, here is the Christ[c]!' or, 'Look, there he is!' do not believe it. 22For false Christs and false prophets will appear and perform signs and miracles to deceive the elect—if that were possible. 23So be on your guard; I have told you everything ahead of time.

24"But in those days, following that distress,

> " 'the sun will be darkened,
>   and the moon will not give its light;
> 25the stars will fall from the sky,
>   and the heavenly bodies will be shaken.'[d]

26"At that time men will see the Son of Man coming in clouds with great power and glory. 27And he will send his angels and gather his elect from the four winds, from the ends of the earth to the ends of the heavens.

28"Now learn this lesson from the fig tree: As soon as its twigs get tender and its leaves come out, you know that summer is near. 29Even so, when you see these things happening, you know that it is near, right at the door. 30I tell you the truth, this generation[e] will certainly not pass away until all these things have happened. 31Heaven and earth will pass away, but my words will never pass away.

The Day and Hour Unknown

32"No one knows about that day or hour, not even the angels in heaven, nor the Son, but only the Father. 33Be on guard! Be alert[f]! You do not know when that time will come. 34It's like a man going away: He leaves his house and puts his servants in charge, each with his assigned task, and tells the one at the door to keep watch.

35"Therefore keep watch because you do not know when the owner of the house will come back—whether in the evening, or at midnight, or when the rooster crows, or at dawn. 36If he comes suddenly, do not let him find you sleeping. 37What I say to you, I say to everyone: 'Watch!' "

Jesus Anointed at Bethany

14 NOW THE Passover and the Feast of Unleavened Bread were only two days away, and the chief priests and the teachers of the law were looking for some sly way to arrest Jesus and kill him. 2"But not during the Feast," they said, "or the people may riot."

---

[a] *14* Daniel 9:27; 11:31; 12:11   [b] *14* Or *he;* also in verse 29   [c] *21* Or *Messiah*   [d] *25* Isaiah 13:10; 34:4   [e] *30* Or *race*   [f] *33* Some manuscripts *alert and pray*

Living Bible

14 "When you see the horrible thing standing in the
Temple[g]—reader, pay attention!—flee, if you can, to
the Judean hills. 15, 16 Hurry! If you are on your rooftop
porch, don't even go back into the house. If you are out
in the fields, don't even return for your money or
clothes.
17 "Woe to pregnant women in those days, and to
mothers nursing their children. 18 And pray that your
flight will not be in winter. 19 For those will be days of
such horror as have never been since the beginning of
God's creation, nor will ever be again. 20 And unless the
Lord shortens that time of calamity, not a soul in all the
earth will survive. But for the sake of his chosen ones
he will limit those days.
21 "And then if anyone tells you, 'This is the Messiah,' or, 'That one is,' don't pay any attention. 22 For
there will be many false Messiahs and false prophets
who will do wonderful miracles that would deceive, if
possible, even God's own children.[h] 23 Take care! I have
warned you!
24 "After the tribulation ends, then the sun will grow
dim and the moon will not shine, 25 and the stars will
fall—the heavens will convulse.
26 "Then all mankind will see me, the Messiah,[i] coming in the clouds with great power and glory. 27 And I
will send out the angels to gather together my chosen
ones from all over the world—from the farthest bounds
of earth and heaven.
28 "Now, here is a lesson from a fig tree. When its
buds become tender and its leaves begin to sprout, you
know that spring has come. 29 And when you see these
things happening that I've described, you can be sure
that my return is very near, that I am right at the door.
30 "Yes, these are the events that will signal the end
of the age.[j] 31 Heaven and earth shall disappear, but my
words stand sure forever.
32 "However, no one, not even the angels in heaven,
nor I myself,[k] knows the day or hour when these things
will happen; only the Father knows. 33 And since you
don't know when it will happen, stay alert. Be on the
watch [for my return[l]].
34 "My coming[m] can be compared with that of a man
who went on a trip to another country. He laid out his
employees' work for them to do while he was gone, and
told the gatekeeper to watch for his return.
35, 36, 37 "Keep a sharp lookout! For you do not know
when I[n] will come, at evening, at midnight, early dawn
or late daybreak. Don't let me find you sleeping. *Watch
for my return!* This is my message to you and to everyone else."

14 THE PASSOVER observance began two days
later—an annual Jewish holiday when no bread
made with yeast was eaten. The chief priests and other
Jewish leaders were still looking for an opportunity to
arrest Jesus secretly and put him to death.
2 "But we can't do it during the Passover," they said,
"or there will be a riot."

[g] *13:14 standing in the Temple,* literally, "standing where he ought not." [h] *13:22 God's own children,* literally, the "elect of God." [i] *13:26 the Messiah,* literally, "the Son of Man." [j] *13:30 of the age,* literally, "of this generation." [k] *13:32 I myself,* literally, "the Son." [l] *13:33 for my return,* implied. [m] *13:34 My coming,* literally, "You do not know when the master of the house will come." [n] *13:35-37 I,* implied.

New Revised Standard

The Desolating Sacrilege

14 "But when you see the desolating sacrilege set up
where it ought not to be (let the reader understand), then
those in Judea must flee to the mountains; 15 the one on
the housetop must not go down or enter the house to take
anything away; 16 the one in the field must not turn back
to get a coat. 17 Woe to those who are pregnant and to
those who are nursing infants in those days! 18 Pray that
it may not be in winter. 19 For in those days there will
be suffering, such as has not been from the beginning
of the creation that God created until now, no, and never
will be. 20 And if the Lord had not cut short those days,
no one would be saved; but for the sake of the elect,
whom he chose, he has cut short those days. 21 And if
anyone says to you at that time, 'Look! Here is the
Messiah!'[o] or 'Look! There he is!'—do not believe it.
22 False messiahs[p] and false prophets will appear and
produce signs and omens, to lead astray, if possible, the
elect. 23 But be alert; I have already told you everything.

The Coming of the Son of Man

24 "But in those days, after that suffering,
the sun will be darkened,
and the moon will not give its light,
25 and the stars will be falling from heaven,
and the powers in the heavens will be
shaken.
26 Then they will see 'the Son of Man coming in clouds'
with great power and glory. 27 Then he will send out the
angels, and gather his elect from the four winds, from
the ends of the earth to the ends of heaven.

The Lesson of the Fig Tree

28 "From the fig tree learn its lesson: as soon as its
branch becomes tender and puts forth its leaves, you
know that summer is near. 29 So also, when you see these
things taking place, you know that he[q] is near, at the
very gates. 30 Truly I tell you, this generation will not
pass away until all these things have taken place.
31 Heaven and earth will pass away, but my words will
not pass away.

The Necessity for Watchfulness

32 "But about that day or hour no one knows, neither the angels in heaven, nor the Son, but only the
Father. 33 Beware, keep alert;[r] for you do not know
when the time will come. 34 It is like a man going on a
journey, when he leaves home and puts his slaves in
charge, each with his work, and commands the doorkeeper to be on the watch. 35 Therefore, keep awake—
for you do not know when the master of the house will
come, in the evening, or at midnight, or at cockcrow,
or at dawn, 36 or else he may find you asleep when he
comes suddenly. 37 And what I say to you I say to all:
Keep awake."

The Plot to Kill Jesus

14 IT WAS two days before the Passover and the
festival of Unleavened Bread. The chief priests
and the scribes were looking for a way to arrest Jesus[s]
by stealth and kill him; 2 for they said, "Not during the
festival, or there may be a riot among the people."

[o] Or *the Christ* [p] Or *christs* [q] Or *it* [r] Other ancient authorities add *and pray* [s] Gk *him*

King James

3¶ And being in Bethany in the house of Simon the leper, as he sat at meat, there came a woman having an alabaster box of ointment of spikenard very precious; and she brake the box, and poured *it* on his head.

4And there were some that had indignation within themselves, and said, Why was this waste of the ointment made?

5For it might have been sold for more than three hundred pence, and have been given to the poor. And they murmured against her.

6And Jesus said, Let her alone; why trouble ye her? she hath wrought a good work on me.

7For ye have the poor with you always, and whensoever ye will ye may do them good: but me ye have not always.

8She hath done what she could: she is come aforehand to anoint my body to the burying.

9Verily I say unto you, Wheresoever this gospel shall be preached throughout the whole world, *this* also that she hath done shall be spoken of for a memorial of her.

10¶ And Judas Iscariot, one of the twelve, went unto the chief priests, to betray him unto them.

11And when they heard *it*, they were glad, and promised to give him money. And he sought how he might conveniently betray him.

12¶ And the first day of unleavened bread, when they killed the passover, his disciples said unto him, Where wilt thou that we go and prepare that thou mayest eat the passover?

13And he sendeth forth two of his disciples, and saith unto them, Go ye into the city, and there shall meet you a man bearing a pitcher of water: follow him.

14And wheresoever he shall go in, say ye to the goodman of the house, The Master saith, Where is the guestchamber, where I shall eat the passover with my disciples?

15And he will show you a large upper room furnished *and* prepared: there make ready for us.

16And his disciples went forth, and came into the city, and found as he had said unto them: and they made ready the passover.

17And in the evening he cometh with the twelve.

18And as they sat and did eat, Jesus said, Verily I say unto you, One of you which eateth with me shall betray me.

19And they began to be sorrowful, and to say unto him one by one, *Is* it I? and another *said, Is* it I?

20And he answered and said unto them, *It is* one of the twelve, that dippeth with me in the dish.

21The Son of man indeed goeth, as it is written of him: but woe to that man by whom the Son of man is betrayed! good were it for that man if he had never been born.

22¶ And as they did eat, Jesus took bread, and blessed, and brake *it*, and gave to them, and said, Take, eat: this is my body.

23And he took the cup, and when he had given thanks, he gave *it* to them: and they all drank of it.

24And he said unto them, This is my blood of the new testament, which is shed for many.

25Verily I say unto you, I will drink no more of the fruit of the vine, until that day that I drink it new in the kingdom of God.

26¶ And when they had sung an hymn, they went out into the mount of Olives.

27And Jesus saith unto them, All ye shall be offended because of me this night: for it is written, I will smite the shepherd, and the sheep shall be scattered.

28But after that I am risen, I will go before you into Galilee.

New International

3While he was in Bethany, reclining at the table in the home of a man known as Simon the Leper, a woman came with an alabaster jar of very expensive perfume, made of pure nard. She broke the jar and poured the perfume on his head.

4Some of those present were saying indignantly to one another, "Why this waste of perfume? 5It could have been sold for more than a year's wages[a] and the money given to the poor." And they rebuked her harshly.

6"Leave her alone," said Jesus. "Why are you bothering her? She has done a beautiful thing to me. 7The poor you will always have with you, and you can help them any time you want. But you will not always have me. 8She did what she could. She poured perfume on my body beforehand to prepare for my burial. 9I tell you the truth, wherever the gospel is preached throughout the world, what she has done will also be told, in memory of her."

10Then Judas Iscariot, one of the Twelve, went to the chief priests to betray Jesus to them. 11They were delighted to hear this and promised to give him money. So he watched for an opportunity to hand him over.

The Lord's Supper

12On the first day of the Feast of Unleavened Bread, when it was customary to sacrifice the Passover lamb, Jesus' disciples asked him, "Where do you want us to go and make preparations for you to eat the Passover?"

13So he sent two of his disciples, telling them, "Go into the city, and a man carrying a jar of water will meet you. Follow him. 14Say to the owner of the house he enters, 'The Teacher asks: Where is my guest room, where I may eat the Passover with my disciples?' 15He will show you a large upper room, furnished and ready. Make preparations for us there."

16The disciples left, went into the city and found things just as Jesus had told them. So they prepared the Passover.

17When evening came, Jesus arrived with the Twelve. 18While they were reclining at the table eating, he said, "I tell you the truth, one of you will betray me—one who is eating with me."

19They were saddened, and one by one they said to him, "Surely not I?"

20"It is one of the Twelve," he replied, "one who dips bread into the bowl with me. 21The Son of Man will go just as it is written about him. But woe to that man who betrays the Son of Man! It would be better for him if he had not been born."

22While they were eating, Jesus took bread, gave thanks and broke it, and gave it to his disciples, saying, "Take it; this is my body."

23Then he took the cup, gave thanks and offered it to them, and they all drank from it.

24"This is my blood of the[b] covenant, which is poured out for many," he said to them. 25"I tell you the truth, I will not drink again of the fruit of the vine until that day when I drink it anew in the kingdom of God."

26When they had sung a hymn, they went out to the Mount of Olives.

Jesus Predicts Peter's Denial

27"You will all fall away," Jesus told them, "for it is written:

> " 'I will strike the shepherd,
> and the sheep will be scattered.'[c]

28But after I have risen, I will go ahead of you into Galilee."

---

a 5 Greek *than three hundred denarii*   b 24 Some manuscripts *the new*
c 27 Zech. 13:7

Living Bible

3Meanwhile Jesus was in Bethany, at the home of Simon the leper; during supper a woman came in with a beautiful flask of expensive perfume. Then, breaking the seal, she poured it over his head. 4,5Some of those at the table were indignant among themselves about this "waste," as they called it.

"Why, she could have sold that perfume for a fortune and given the money to the poor!" they snarled.

6But Jesus said, "Let her alone; why berate her for doing a good thing? 7You always have the poor among you, and they badly need your help, and you can aid them whenever you want to; but I won't be here much longer. 8"She has done what she could, and has anointed my body ahead of time for burial. 9And I tell you this in solemn truth, that wherever the Good News is preached throughout the world, this woman's deed will be remembered and praised."

10Then Judas Iscariot, one of his disciples, went to the chief priests to arrange to betray Jesus to them. 11When the chief priests heard why he had come, they were excited and happy and promised him a reward. So he began looking for the right time and place to betray Jesus.

12On the first day of the Passover, the day the lambs were sacrificed, his disciples asked him where he wanted to go to eat the traditional Passover supper. 13He sent two of them into Jerusalem to make the arrangements.

"As you are walking along," he told them, "you will see a man coming toward you carrying a pot of water. Follow him. 14At the house he enters, tell the man in charge, 'Our Master sent us to see the room you have ready for us, where we will eat the Passover supper this evening!' 15He will take you upstairs to a large room all set up. Prepare our supper there."

16So the two disciples went on ahead into the city and found everything as Jesus had said, and prepared the Passover.

17In the evening Jesus arrived with the other disciples, 18and as they were sitting around the table eating, Jesus said, "I solemnly declare that one of you will betray me, one of you who is here eating with me."

19A great sadness swept over them, and one by one they asked him, "Am I the one?"

20He replied, "It is one of you twelve eating with me now. 21Id must die, as the prophets declared long ago; but, oh, the misery ahead for the man by whom Id am betrayed. Oh, that he had never been born!"

22As they were eating, Jesus took bread and asked God's blessing on it and broke it in pieces and gave it to them and said, "Eat it—this is my body."

23Then he took a cup of wine and gave thanks to God for it and gave it to them; and they all drank from it. 24And he said to them, "This is my blood, poured out for many, sealinge the new agreement between God and man. 25I solemnly declare that I shall never again taste wine until the day I drink a different kindf in the Kingdom of God."

26Then they sang a hymn and went out to the Mount of Olives.

27"All of you will desert me," Jesus told them, "for God has declared through the prophets, 'I will kill the Shepherd, and the sheep will scatter.' 28But after I am raised to life again, I will go to Galilee and meet you there."

New Revised Standard

The Anointing at Bethany

3 While he was at Bethany in the house of Simon the leper,g as he sat at the table, a woman came with an alabaster jar of very costly ointment of nard, and she broke open the jar and poured the ointment on his head. 4But some were there who said to one another in anger, "Why was the ointment wasted in this way? 5For this ointment could have been sold for more than three hundred denarii,h and the money given to the poor." And they scolded her. 6But Jesus said, "Let her alone; why do you trouble her? She has performed a good service for me. 7For you always have the poor with you, and you can show kindness to them whenever you wish; but you will not always have me. 8She has done what she could; she has anointed my body beforehand for its burial. 9Truly I tell you, wherever the good newsi is proclaimed in the whole world, what she has done will be told in remembrance of her."

Judas Agrees to Betray Jesus

10 Then Judas Iscariot, who was one of the twelve, went to the chief priests in order to betray him to them. 11When they heard it, they were greatly pleased, and promised to give him money. So he began to look for an opportunity to betray him.

The Passover with the Disciples

12 On the first day of Unleavened Bread, when the Passover lamb is sacrificed, his disciples said to him, "Where do you want us to go and make the preparations for you to eat the Passover?" 13So he sent two of his disciples, saying to them, "Go into the city, and a man carrying a jar of water will meet you; follow him, 14and wherever he enters, say to the owner of the house, 'The Teacher asks, Where is my guest room where I may eat the Passover with my disciples?' 15He will show you a large room upstairs, furnished and ready. Make preparations for us there." 16So the disciples set out and went to the city, and found everything as he had told them; and they prepared the Passover meal.

17 When it was evening, he came with the twelve. 18And when they had taken their places and were eating, Jesus said, "Truly I tell you, one of you will betray me, one who is eating with me." 19They began to be distressed and to say to him one after another, "Surely, not I?" 20He said to them, "It is one of the twelve, one who is dipping breadj into the bowlk with me. 21For the Son of Man goes as it is written of him, but woe to that one by whom the Son of Man is betrayed! It would have been better for that one not to have been born."

The Institution of the Lord's Supper

22 While they were eating, he took a loaf of bread, and after blessing it he broke it, gave it to them, and said, "Take; this is my body." 23Then he took a cup, and after giving thanks he gave it to them, and all of them drank from it. 24He said to them, "This is my blood of thel covenant, which is poured out for many. 25Truly I tell you, I will never again drink of the fruit of the vine until that day when I drink it new in the kingdom of God."

Peter's Denial Foretold

26 When they had sung the hymn, they went out to the Mount of Olives. 27And Jesus said to them, "You will all become deserters; for it is written,

'I will strike the shepherd,
    and the sheep will be scattered.'

28But after I am raised up, I will go before you to Galilee." 29Peter said to him, "Even though all become de-

---

d 14:21 I, literally, "the Son of Man."   e 14:24 sealing, literally, "This is my blood of the covenant." Some ancient manuscripts read "new covenant."   f 14:25 drink a different kind, literally, "drink it new."

g The terms leper and leprosy can refer to several diseases   h The denarius was the usual day's wage for a laborer   i Or gospel   j Gk lacks bread   k Other authorities read same bowl   l Other ancient authorities add new

King James

29But Peter said unto him, Although all shall be offended, yet *will* not I.

30And Jesus saith unto him, Verily I say unto thee, That this day, *even* in this night, before the cock crow twice, thou shalt deny me thrice.

31But he spake the more vehemently, If I should die with thee, I will not deny thee in any wise. Likewise also said they all.

32And they came to a place which was named Gethsemane: and he saith to his disciples, Sit ye here, while I shall pray.

33And he taketh with him Peter and James and John, and began to be sore amazed, and to be very heavy;

34And saith unto them, My soul is exceeding sorrowful unto death: tarry ye here, and watch.

35And he went forward a little, and fell on the ground, and prayed that, if it were possible, the hour might pass from him.

36And he said, Abba, Father, all things *are* possible unto thee; take away this cup from me: nevertheless not what I will, but what thou wilt.

37And he cometh, and findeth them sleeping, and saith unto Peter, Simon, sleepest thou? couldest not thou watch one hour?

38Watch ye and pray, lest ye enter into temptation. The spirit truly *is* ready, but the flesh *is* weak.

39And again he went away, and prayed, and spake the same words.

40And when he returned, he found them asleep again, (for their eyes were heavy,) neither wist they what to answer him.

41And he cometh the third time, and saith unto them, Sleep on now, and take *your* rest: it is enough, the hour is come; behold, the Son of man is betrayed into the hands of sinners.

42Rise up, let us go; lo, he that betrayeth me is at hand.

43¶ And immediately, while he yet spake, cometh Judas, one of the twelve, and with him a great multitude with swords and staves, from the chief priests and the scribes and the elders.

44And he that betrayed him had given them a token, saying, Whomsoever I shall kiss, that same is he; take him, and lead *him* away safely.

45And as soon as he was come, he goeth straightway to him, and saith, Master, master; and kissed him.

46¶ And they laid their hands on him, and took him.

47And one of them that stood by drew a sword, and smote a servant of the high priest, and cut off his ear.

48And Jesus answered and said unto them, Are ye come out, as against a thief, with swords and *with* staves to take me?

49I was daily with you in the temple teaching, and ye took me not: but the scriptures must be fulfilled.

50And they all forsook him, and fled.

51And there followed him a certain young man, having a linen cloth cast about *his* naked *body;* and the young men laid hold on him:

52And he left the linen cloth, and fled from them naked.

53¶ And they led Jesus away to the high priest: and with him were assembled all the chief priests and the elders and the scribes.

54And Peter followed him afar off, even into the palace of the high priest: and he sat with the servants, and warmed himself at the fire.

55And the chief priests and all the council sought for witness against Jesus to put him to death; and found none.

56For many bare false witness against him, but their witness agreed not together.

New International

29Peter declared, "Even if all fall away, I will not."

30"I tell you the truth," Jesus answered, "today—yes, tonight—before the rooster crows twice[a] you yourself will disown me three times."

31But Peter insisted emphatically, "Even if I have to die with you, I will never disown you." And all the others said the same.

Gethsemane

32They went to a place called Gethsemane, and Jesus said to his disciples, "Sit here while I pray." 33He took Peter, James and John along with him, and he began to be deeply distressed and troubled. 34"My soul is overwhelmed with sorrow to the point of death," he said to them. "Stay here and keep watch."

35Going a little farther, he fell to the ground and prayed that if possible the hour might pass from him. 36"*Abba,*[b] Father," he said, "everything is possible for you. Take this cup from me. Yet not what I will, but what you will."

37Then he returned to his disciples and found them sleeping. "Simon," he said to Peter, "are you asleep? Could you not keep watch for one hour? 38Watch and pray so that you will not fall into temptation. The spirit is willing, but the body is weak."

39Once more he went away and prayed the same thing. 40When he came back, he again found them sleeping, because their eyes were heavy. They did not know what to say to him.

41Returning the third time, he said to them, "Are you still sleeping and resting? Enough! The hour has come. Look, the Son of Man is betrayed into the hands of sinners. 42Rise! Let us go! Here comes my betrayer!"

Jesus Arrested

43Just as he was speaking, Judas, one of the Twelve, appeared. With him was a crowd armed with swords and clubs, sent from the chief priests, the teachers of the law, and the elders.

44Now the betrayer had arranged a signal with them: "The one I kiss is the man; arrest him and lead him away under guard." 45Going at once to Jesus, Judas said, "Rabbi!" and kissed him. 46The men seized Jesus and arrested him. 47Then one of those standing near drew his sword and struck the servant of the high priest, cutting off his ear.

48"Am I leading a rebellion," said Jesus, "that you have come out with swords and clubs to capture me? 49Every day I was with you, teaching in the temple courts, and you did not arrest me. But the Scriptures must be fulfilled." 50Then everyone deserted him and fled.

51A young man, wearing nothing but a linen garment, was following Jesus. When they seized him, 52he fled naked, leaving his garment behind.

Before the Sanhedrin

53They took Jesus to the high priest, and all the chief priests, elders and teachers of the law came together. 54Peter followed him at a distance, right into the courtyard of the high priest. There he sat with the guards and warmed himself at the fire.

55The chief priests and the whole Sanhedrin were looking for evidence against Jesus so that they could put him to death, but they did not find any. 56Many testified falsely against him, but their statements did not agree.

---

a 30 Some early manuscripts do not have *twice.*   b 36 Aramaic for *Father*

Living Bible

²⁹Peter said to him, "I will never desert you no matter what the others do!"

³⁰"Peter," Jesus said, "before the cock crows a second time tomorrow morning you will deny me three times."

³¹"No!" Peter exploded. "Not even if I have to die with you! I'll *never* deny you!" And all the others vowed the same.

³²And now they came to an olive grove called the Garden of Gethsemane, and he instructed his disciples, "Sit here, while I go and pray."

³³He took Peter, James and John with him and began to be filled with horror and deepest distress. ³⁴And he said to them, "My soul is crushed by sorrow to the point of death; stay here and watch with me."

³⁵He went on a little further and fell to the ground and prayed that if it were possible the awful hour awaiting him might never come.^c

³⁶"Father, Father," he said, "everything is possible for you. Take away this cup from me. Yet I want your will, not mine."

³⁷Then he returned to the three disciples and found them asleep.

"Simon!" he said. "Asleep? Couldn't you watch with me even one hour? ³⁸Watch with me and pray lest the Tempter overpower you. For though the spirit is willing enough, the body is weak."

³⁹And he went away again and prayed, repeating his pleadings. ⁴⁰Again he returned to them and found them sleeping, for they were very tired. And they didn't know what to say.

⁴¹The third time when he returned to them he said, "Sleep on; get your rest! But no! The time for sleep has ended! Look! I^d am betrayed into the hands of wicked men. ⁴²Come! Get up! We must go! Look! My betrayer is here!"

⁴³And immediately, while he was still speaking, Judas (one of his disciples) arrived with a mob equipped with swords and clubs, sent out by the chief priests and other Jewish leaders.

⁴⁴Judas had told them, "You will know which one to arrest when I go over and greet^e him. Then you can take him easily. ⁴⁵So as soon as they arrived he walked up to Jesus. "Master!" he exclaimed, and embraced him with a great show of friendliness. ⁴⁶Then the mob arrested Jesus and held him fast. ⁴⁷But someone^f pulled a sword and slashed at the High Priest's servant, cutting off his ear.

⁴⁸Jesus asked them, "Am I some dangerous robber, that you come like this, armed to the teeth to capture me? ⁴⁹Why didn't you arrest me in the Temple? I was there teaching every day. But these things are happening to fulfill the prophecies about me."

⁵⁰Meanwhile, all his disciples had fled. ^{51, 52}There was, however, a young man following along behind, clothed only in a linen nightshirt.^g When the mob tried to grab him, he escaped, though his clothes were torn off in the process, so that he ran away completely naked.

⁵³Jesus was led to the High Priest's home where all of the chief priests and other Jewish leaders soon gathered. ⁵⁴Peter followed far behind and then slipped inside the gates of the High Priest's residence and crouched beside a fire among the servants.

⁵⁵Inside, the chief priests and the whole Jewish Supreme Court were trying to find something against Jesus that would be sufficient to condemn him to death. But their efforts were in vain. ⁵⁶Many false witnesses volunteered, but they contradicted each other.

---

^c *14:35 the awful hour . . . might never come*, literally, "that the hour might pass away from him." ^d *14:41 I*, literally, "the Son of Man." ^e *14:44 greet*, literally, "kiss," the usual oriental greeting, even to this day. ^f *14:47 someone*. It was Peter. John 18:10. ^g *14:51, 52 in a linen nightshirt*, literally, "wearing only a linen cloth."

New Revised Standard

serters, I will not." ³⁰Jesus said to him, "Truly I tell you, this day, this very night, before the cock crows twice, you will deny me three times." ³¹But he said vehemently, "Even though I must die with you, I will not deny you." And all of them said the same.

Jesus Prays in Gethsemane

32 They went to a place called Gethsemane; and he said to his disciples, "Sit here while I pray." ³³He took with him Peter and James and John, and began to be distressed and agitated. ³⁴And he said to them, "I am deeply grieved, even to death; remain here, and keep awake." ³⁵And going a little farther, he threw himself on the ground and prayed that, if it were possible, the hour might pass from him. ³⁶He said, "Abba,^h Father, for you all things are possible; remove this cup from me; yet, not what I want, but what you want." ³⁷He came and found them sleeping; and he said to Peter, "Simon, are you asleep? Could you not keep awake one hour? ³⁸Keep awake and pray that you may not come into the time of trial;ⁱ the spirit indeed is willing, but the flesh is weak." ³⁹And again he went away and prayed, saying the same words. ⁴⁰And once more he came and found them sleeping, for their eyes were very heavy; and they did not know what to say to him. ⁴¹He came a third time and said to them, "Are you still sleeping and taking your rest? Enough! The hour has come; the Son of Man is betrayed into the hands of sinners. ⁴²Get up, let us be going. See, my betrayer is at hand."

The Betrayal and Arrest of Jesus

43 Immediately, while he was still speaking, Judas, one of the twelve, arrived; and with him there was a crowd with swords and clubs, from the chief priests, the scribes, and the elders. ⁴⁴Now the betrayer had given them a sign, saying, "The one I will kiss is the man; arrest him and lead him away under guard." ⁴⁵So when he came, he went up to him at once and said, "Rabbi!" and kissed him. ⁴⁶Then they laid hands on him and arrested him. ⁴⁷But one of those who stood near drew his sword and struck the slave of the high priest, cutting off his ear. ⁴⁸Then Jesus said to them, "Have you come out with swords and clubs to arrest me as though I were a bandit? ⁴⁹Day after day I was with you in the temple teaching, and you did not arrest me. But let the scriptures be fulfilled." ⁵⁰All of them deserted him and fled.

51 A certain young man was following him, wearing nothing but a linen cloth. They caught hold of him, ⁵²but he left the linen cloth and ran off naked.

Jesus before the Council

53 They took Jesus to the high priest; and all the chief priests, the elders, and the scribes were assembled. ⁵⁴Peter had followed him at a distance, right into the courtyard of the high priest; and he was sitting with the guards, warming himself at the fire. ⁵⁵Now the chief priests and the whole council were looking for testimony against Jesus to put him to death; but they found none. ⁵⁶For many gave false testimony against him, and their testimony did not agree. ⁵⁷Some stood up and gave false

---

^h Aramaic for *Father*   ⁱ Or *into temptation*

King James

57And there arose certain, and bare false witness against him, saying,

58We heard him say, I will destroy this temple that is made with hands, and within three days I will build another made without hands.

59But neither so did their witness agree together.

60And the high priest stood up in the midst, and asked Jesus, saying, Answerest thou nothing? what *is it which* these witness against thee?

61But he held his peace, and answered nothing. Again the high priest asked him, and said unto him, Art thou the Christ, the Son of the Blessed?

62And Jesus said, I am: and ye shall see the Son of man sitting on the right hand of power, and coming in the clouds of heaven.

63Then the high priest rent his clothes, and saith, What need we any further witnesses?

64Ye have heard the blasphemy: what think ye? And they all condemned him to be guilty of death.

65And some began to spit on him, and to cover his face, and to buffet him, and to say unto him, Prophesy: and the servants did strike him with the palms of their hands.

66¶ And as Peter was beneath in the palace, there cometh one of the maids of the high priest:

67And when she saw Peter warming himself, she looked upon him, and said, And thou also wast with Jesus of Nazareth.

68But he denied, saying, I know not, neither understand I what thou sayest. And he went out into the porch; and the cock crew.

69And a maid saw him again, and began to say to them that stood by, This is *one* of them.

70And he denied it again. And a little after, they that stood by said again to Peter, Surely thou art *one* of them: for thou art a Galilaean, and thy speech agreeth *thereto*.

71But he began to curse and to swear, *saying*, I know not this man of whom ye speak.

72And the second time the cock crew. And Peter called to mind the word that Jesus said unto him, Before the cock crow twice, thou shalt deny me thrice. And when he thought thereon, he wept.

15 AND STRAIGHTWAY in the morning the chief priests held a consultation with the elders and scribes and the whole council, and bound Jesus, and carried *him* away, and delivered *him* to Pilate.

2And Pilate asked him, Art thou the King of the Jews? And he answering said unto him, Thou sayest *it*.

3And the chief priests accused him of many things: but he answered nothing.

4And Pilate asked him again, saying, Answerest thou nothing? behold how many things they witness against thee.

5But Jesus yet answered nothing; so that Pilate marvelled.

6Now at *that* feast he released unto them one prisoner, whomsoever they desired.

7And there was *one* named Barabbas, *which lay* bound with them that had made insurrection with him, who had committed murder in the insurrection.

8And the multitude crying aloud began to desire *him* to do as he had ever done unto them.

9But Pilate answered them, saying, Will ye that I release unto you the King of the Jews?

New International

57Then some stood up and gave this false testimony against him: 58"We heard him say, 'I will destroy this man-made temple and in three days will build another, not made by man.' " 59Yet even then their testimony did not agree.

60Then the high priest stood up before them and asked Jesus, "Are you not going to answer? What is this testimony that these men are bringing against you?" 61But Jesus remained silent and gave no answer.

Again the high priest asked him, "Are you the Christ,[a] the Son of the Blessed One?"

62"I am," said Jesus. "And you will see the Son of Man sitting at the right hand of the Mighty One and coming on the clouds of heaven."

63The high priest tore his clothes. "Why do we need any more witnesses?" he asked. 64"You have heard the blasphemy. What do you think?"

They all condemned him as worthy of death. 65Then some began to spit at him; they blindfolded him, struck him with their fists, and said, "Prophesy!" And the guards took him and beat him.

Peter Disowns Jesus

66While Peter was below in the courtyard, one of the servant girls of the high priest came by. 67When she saw Peter warming himself, she looked closely at him.

"You also were with that Nazarene, Jesus," she said.

68But he denied it. "I don't know or understand what you're talking about," he said, and went out into the entryway.[b]

69When the servant girl saw him there, she said again to those standing around, "This fellow is one of them."

70Again he denied it.

After a little while, those standing near said to Peter, "Surely you are one of them, for you are a Galilean."

71He began to call down curses on himself, and he swore to them, "I don't know this man you're talking about."

72Immediately the rooster crowed the second time.[c] Then Peter remembered the word Jesus had spoken to him: "Before the rooster crows twice[d] you will disown me three times." And he broke down and wept.

Jesus Before Pilate

15 VERY EARLY in the morning, the chief priests, with the elders, the teachers of the law and the whole Sanhedrin, reached a decision. They bound Jesus, led him away and handed him over to Pilate.

2"Are you the king of the Jews?" asked Pilate.

"Yes, it is as you say," Jesus replied.

3The chief priests accused him of many things. 4So again Pilate asked him, "Aren't you going to answer? See how many things they are accusing you of."

5But Jesus still made no reply, and Pilate was amazed.

6Now it was the custom at the Feast to release a prisoner whom the people requested. 7A man called Barabbas was in prison with the insurrectionists who had committed murder in the uprising. 8The crowd came up and asked Pilate to do for them what he usually did.

9"Do you want me to release to you the king of the Jews?" asked Pilate, 10knowing it was out of envy that

a 61 Or *Messiah*   b 68 Some early manuscripts *entryway and the rooster crowed*   c 72 Some early manuscripts do not have *the second time.*   d 72 Some early manuscripts do not have *twice.*

Living Bible

57Finally some men stood up to lie about him and said, 58"We heard him say, 'I will destroy this Temple made with human hands and in three days I will build another, made without human hands!' " 59But even then they didn't get their stories straight!

60Then the High Priest stood up before the Court and asked Jesus, "Do you refuse to answer this charge? What do you have to say for yourself?"

61To this Jesus made no reply.

Then the High Priest asked him, "Are you the Messiah, the Son of God?"

62Jesus said, "I am, and you will see mee sitting at the right hand of God, and returning to earth in the clouds of heaven."

63, 64Then the High Priest tore at his clothes and said, "What more do we need? Why wait for witnesses? You have heard his blasphemy. What is your verdict?" And the vote for the death sentence was unanimous.

65Then some of them began to spit at him, and they blindfolded him and began to hammer his face with their fists.

"Who hit you that time, you prophet?" they jeered. And even the bailiffs were using their fists on him as they led him away.

66, 67Meanwhile Peter was below in the courtyard. One of the maids who worked for the High Priest noticed Peter warming himself at the fire.

She looked at him closely and then announced, *"You were with Jesus, the Nazarene."*

68Peter denied it. "I don't know what you're talking about!" he said, and walked over to the edge of the courtyard.

Just then, a rooster crowed.f

69The maid saw him standing there and began telling the others, "There he is! There's that disciple of Jesus!"

70Peter denied it again.

A little later others standing around the fire began saying to Peter, "You are, too, one of them, for you are from Galilee!"

71He began to curse and swear. "I don't even know this fellow you are talking about," he said.

72And immediately the rooster crowed the second time. Suddenly Jesus' words flashed through Peter's mind: "Before the cock crows twice, you will deny me three times." And he began to cry.

15 EARLY IN the morning the chief priests, elders and teachers of religion—the entire Supreme Court—met to discuss their next steps. Their decision was to send Jesus under armed guard to Pilate, the Roman governor.g

2Pilate asked him, "Are you the King of the Jews?" "Yes," Jesus replied, "it is as you say."

3, 4Then the chief priests accused him of many crimes, and Pilate asked him, "Why don't you say something? What about all these charges against you?"

5But Jesus said no more, much to Pilate's amazement.

6Now, it was Pilate's custom to release one Jewish prisoner each year at Passover time—any prisoner the people requested. 7One of the prisoners at that time was Barabbas, convicted along with others for murder during an insurrection.

8Now a mob began to crowd in toward Pilate, asking him to release a prisoner as usual.

9"How about giving you the 'King of Jews'?" Pilate asked. "Is he the one you want released?" 10(For he

New Revised Standard

testimony against him, saying, 58"We heard him say, 'I will destroy this temple that is made with hands, and in three days I will build another, not made with hands.' " 59But even on this point their testimony did not agree. 60Then the high priest stood up before them and asked Jesus, "Have you no answer? What is it that they testify against you?" 61But he was silent and did not answer. Again the high priest asked him, "Are you the Messiah,h the Son of the Blessed One?" 62Jesus said, "I am; and

'you will see the Son of Man
seated at the right hand of the Power,'
and 'coming with the clouds of heaven.' "

63Then the high priest tore his clothes and said, "Why do we still need witnesses? 64You have heard his blasphemy! What is your decision?" All of them condemned him as deserving death. 65Some began to spit on him, to blindfold him, and to strike him, saying to him, "Prophesy!" The guards also took him over and beat him.

Peter Denies Jesus

66 While Peter was below in the courtyard, one of the servant-girls of the high priest came by. 67When she saw Peter warming himself, she stared at him and said, "You also were with Jesus, the man from Nazareth." 68But he denied it, saying, "I do not know or understand what you are talking about." And he went out into the forecourt.i Then the cock crowed.j 69And the servant-girl, on seeing him, began again to say to the bystanders, "This man is one of them." 70But again he denied it. Then after a little while the bystanders again said to Peter, "Certainly you are one of them; for you are a Galilean." 71But he began to curse, and he swore an oath, "I do not know this man you are talking about." 72At that moment the cock crowed for the second time. Then Peter remembered that Jesus had said to him, "Before the cock crows twice, you will deny me three times." And he broke down and wept.

Jesus before Pilate

15 AS SOON as it was morning, the chief priests held a consultation with the elders and scribes and the whole council. They bound Jesus, led him away, and handed him over to Pilate. 2Pilate asked him, "Are you the King of the Jews?" He answered him, "You say so." 3Then the chief priests accused him of many things. 4Pilate asked him again, "Have you no answer? See how many charges they bring against you." 5But Jesus made no further reply, so that Pilate was amazed.

Pilate Hands Jesus over to Be Crucified

6 Now at the festival he used to release a prisoner for them, anyone for whom they asked. 7Now a man called Barabbas was in prison with the rebels who had committed murder during the insurrection. 8So the crowd came and began to ask Pilate to do for them according to his custom. 9Then he answered them, "Do you want me to release for you the King of the Jews?"

---

e 14:62 *me*, literally, "the Son of Man." f 14:68 *a rooster crowed*. This statement is found in only some of the manuscripts. g 15:1 *the Roman governor*, implied.

h Or *the Christ* i Or *gateway* j Other ancient authorities lack *Then the cock crowed*

King James

10For he knew that the chief priests had delivered him for envy.

11But the chief priests moved the people, that he should rather release Barabbas unto them.

12And Pilate answered and said again unto them, What will ye then that I shall do *unto him* whom ye call the King of the Jews?

13And they cried out again, Crucify him.

14Then Pilate said unto them, Why, what evil hath he done? And they cried out the more exceedingly, Crucify him.

15¶ And *so* Pilate, willing to content the people, released Barabbas unto them, and delivered Jesus, when he had scourged *him,* to be crucified.

16And the soldiers led him away into the hall, called Praetorium; and they call together the whole band.

17And they clothed him with purple, and plaited a crown of thorns, and put it about his *head,*

18And began to salute him, Hail, King of the Jews!

19And they smote him on the head with a reed, and did spit upon him, and bowing *their* knees worshipped him.

20And when they had mocked him, they took off the purple from him, and put his own clothes on him, and led him out to crucify him.

21And they compel one Simon a Cyrenian, who passed by, coming out of the country, the father of Alexander and Rufus, to bear his cross.

22And they bring him unto the place Golgotha, which is, being interpreted, The place of a skull.

23And they gave him to drink wine mingled with myrrh: but he received *it* not.

24And when they had crucified him, they parted his garments, casting lots upon them, what every man should take.

25And it was the third hour, and they crucified him.

26And the superscription of his accusation was written over, THE KING OF THE JEWS.

27And with him they crucify two thieves; the one on his right hand, and the other on his left.

28And the scripture was fulfilled, which saith, And he was numbered with the transgressors.

29And they that passed by railed on him, wagging their heads, and saying, Ah, thou that destroyest the temple, and buildest *it* in three days,

30Save thyself, and come down from the cross.

31Likewise also the chief priests mocking said among themselves with the scribes, He saved others; himself he cannot save.

32Let Christ the King of Israel descend now from the cross, that we may see and believe. And they that were crucified with him reviled him.

33And when the sixth hour was come, there was darkness over the whole land until the ninth hour.

34And at the ninth hour Jesus cried with a loud voice, saying, Eloi, Eloi, lama sabachthani? which is, being interpreted, My God, my God, why hast thou forsaken me?

35And some of them that stood by, when they heard *it,* said, Behold, he calleth Elias.

36And one ran and filled a sponge full of vinegar, and put *it* on a reed, and gave him to drink, saying, Let alone; let us see whether Elias will come to take him down.

37And Jesus cried with a loud voice, and gave up the ghost.

New International

the chief priests had handed Jesus over to him. 11But the chief priests stirred up the crowd to have Pilate release Barabbas instead.

12"What shall I do, then, with the one you call the king of the Jews?" Pilate asked them.

13"Crucify him!" they shouted.

14"Why? What crime has he committed?" asked Pilate.

But they shouted all the louder, "Crucify him!"

15Wanting to satisfy the crowd, Pilate released Barabbas to them. He had Jesus flogged, and handed him over to be crucified.

The Soldiers Mock Jesus

16The soldiers led Jesus away into the palace (that is, the Praetorium) and called together the whole company of soldiers. 17They put a purple robe on him, then twisted together a crown of thorns and set it on him. 18And they began to call out to him, "Hail, king of the Jews!" 19Again and again they struck him on the head with a staff and spit on him. Falling on their knees, they paid homage to him. 20And when they had mocked him, they took off the purple robe and put his own clothes on him. Then they led him out to crucify him.

The Crucifixion

21A certain man from Cyrene, Simon, the father of Alexander and Rufus, was passing by on his way in from the country, and they forced him to carry the cross. 22They brought Jesus to the place called Golgotha (which means The Place of the Skull). 23Then they offered him wine mixed with myrrh, but he did not take it. 24And they crucified him. Dividing up his clothes, they cast lots to see what each would get.

25It was the third hour when they crucified him. 26The written notice of the charge against him read: THE KING OF THE JEWS. 27They crucified two robbers with him, one on his right and one on his left.a 29Those who passed by hurled insults at him, shaking their heads and saying, "So! You who are going to destroy the temple and build it in three days, 30come down from the cross and save yourself!"

31In the same way the chief priests and the teachers of the law mocked him among themselves. "He saved others," they said, "but he can't save himself! 32Let this Christ,b this King of Israel, come down now from the cross, that we may see and believe." Those crucified with him also heaped insults on him.

The Death of Jesus

33At the sixth hour darkness came over the whole land until the ninth hour. 34And at the ninth hour Jesus cried out in a loud voice, *"Eloi, Eloi, lama sabachthani?"*—which means, "My God, my God, why have you forsaken me?"c

35When some of those standing near heard this, they said, "Listen, he's calling Elijah."

36One man ran, filled a sponge with wine vinegar, put it on a stick, and offered it to Jesus to drink. "Now leave him alone. Let's see if Elijah comes to take him down," he said.

37With a loud cry, Jesus breathed his last.

---

a 27 Some manuscripts *left,* 28*and the scripture was fulfilled which says, "He was counted with the lawless ones"* (Isaiah 53:12)   b 32 Or *Messiah*   c 34 Psalm 22:1

Living Bible

realized by now that this was a frameup, backed by the chief priests because they envied Jesus' popularity.)

11But at this point the chief priests whipped up the mob to demand the release of Barabbas instead of Jesus.

12"But if I release Barabbas," Pilate asked them, "what shall I do with this man you call your king?"

13They shouted back, "Crucify him!"

14"But why?" Pilate demanded. "What has he done wrong?" They only roared the louder, "Crucify him!"

15Then Pilate, afraid of a riot and anxious to please the people, released Barabbas to them. And he ordered Jesus flogged with a leaded whip, and handed him over to be crucified.

16, 17Then the Roman soldiers took him into the barracks of the palace, called out the entire palace guard, dressed him in a purple robe, and made a crown of long, sharp thorns and put it on his head. 18Then they saluted, yelling, "Yea! King of the Jews!" 19And they beat him on the head with a cane, and spat on him and went down on their knees to "worship" him.

20When they finally tired of their sport, they took off the purple robe and put his own clothes on him again, and led him away to be crucified.

21Simon of Cyrene, who was coming in from the country just then, was pressed into service to carry Jesus' cross. (Simon is the father of Alexander and Rufus.)

22And they brought Jesus to a place called Golgotha. (Golgotha means skull.) 23Wine drugged with bitter herbs was offered to him there, but he refused it. 24And then they crucified him—and threw dice for his clothes.

25It was about nine o'clock in the morning when the crucifixion took place.

26A signboard was fastened to the cross above his head, announcing his crime. It read, "The King of the Jews."

27Two robbers were also crucified that morning, their crosses on either side of his. 28dAnd so the Scripture was fulfilled that said, "He was counted among evil men."

29, 30The people jeered at him as they walked by, and wagged their heads in mockery.

"Ha! Look at you now!" they yelled at him. "Sure, you can destroy the Temple and rebuild it in three days! If you're so wonderful, save yourself and come down from the cross."

31The chief priests and religious leaders were also standing around joking about Jesus.

"He's quite clever at 'saving' others," they said, "but he can't save himself!"

32"Hey there, Messiah!" they yelled at him. "You 'King of Israel'! Come on down from the cross and we'll believe you!"

And even the two robbers dying with him, cursed him.

33About noon, darkness fell across the entire land,e lasting until three o'clock that afternoon.

34Then Jesus called out with a loud voice, "Eli, Eli, lama sabachthani?"f ("My God, my God, why have you deserted me?")

35Some of the people standing there thought he was calling for the prophet Elijah. 36So one man ran and got a sponge and filled it with sour wine and held it up to him on a stick.

"Let's see if Elijah will come and take him down!" he said.

37Then Jesus uttered another loud cry, and dismissed his spirit.

New Revised Standard

10For he realized that it was out of jealousy that the chief priests had handed him over. 11But the chief priests stirred up the crowd to have him release Barabbas for them instead. 12Pilate spoke to them again, "Then what do you wish me to dog with the man you callh the King of the Jews?" 13They shouted back, "Crucify him!" 14Pilate asked them, "Why, what evil has he done?" But they shouted all the more, "Crucify him!" 15So Pilate, wishing to satisfy the crowd, released Barabbas for them; and after flogging Jesus, he handed him over to be crucified.

The Soldiers Mock Jesus

16 Then the soldiers led him into the courtyard of the palace (that is, the governor's headquartersi); and they called together the whole cohort. 17And they clothed him in a purple cloak; and after twisting some thorns into a crown, they put it on him. 18And they began saluting him, "Hail, King of the Jews!" 19They struck his head with a reed, spat upon him, and knelt down in homage to him. 20After mocking him, they stripped him of the purple cloak and put his own clothes on him. Then they led him out to crucify him.

The Crucifixion of Jesus

21 They compelled a passer-by, who was coming in from the country, to carry his cross; it was Simon of Cyrene, the father of Alexander and Rufus. 22Then they brought Jesusj to the place called Golgotha (which means the place of a skull). 23And they offered him wine mixed with myrrh; but he did not take it. 24And they crucified him, and divided his clothes among them, casting lots to decide what each should take.

25 It was nine o'clock in the morning when they crucified him. 26The inscription of the charge against him read, "The King of the Jews." 27And with him they crucified two bandits, one on his right and one on his left.k 29Those who passed by derided l him, shaking their heads and saying, "Aha! You who would destroy the temple and build it in three days, 30save yourself, and come down from the cross!" 31In the same way the chief priests, along with the scribes, were also mocking him among themselves and saying, "He saved others; he cannot save himself. 32Let the Messiah,m the King of Israel, come down from the cross now, so that we may see and believe." Those who were crucified with him also taunted him.

The Death of Jesus

33 When it was noon, darkness came over the whole landn until three in the afternoon. 34At three o'clock Jesus cried out with a loud voice, "Eloi, Eloi, lema sabachthani?" which means, "My God, my God, why have you forsaken me?"o 35When some of the bystanders heard it, they said, "Listen, he is calling for Elijah." 36And someone ran, filled a sponge with sour wine, put it on a stick, and gave it to him to drink, saying, "Wait, let us see whether Elijah will come to take him down." 37Then Jesus gave a loud cry and breathed his last.

---

d 15:28 This verse is omitted in some of the ancient manuscripts. The quotation is from Isa 53:12. e 15:33 the entire land, or, "over the entire world." f 15:34 Eli, Eli, lama sabachthani. He spoke here in Aramaic. The onlookers, who spoke Greek and Latin, misunderstood his first two words ("Eli, Eli") and thought he was calling for the prophet Elijah.

g Other ancient authorities read what should I do h Other ancient authorities lack the man you call i Gk the praetorium j Gk him k Other ancient authorities add verse 28, And the scripture was fulfilled that says, "And he was counted among the lawless." l Or blasphemed m Or the Christ n Or earth o Other ancient authorities read made me a reproach

King James

38And the veil of the temple was rent in twain from the top to the bottom.

39¶ And when the centurion, which stood over against him, saw that he so cried out, and gave up the ghost, he said, Truly this man was the Son of God.

40There were also women looking on afar off: among whom was Mary Magdalene, and Mary the mother of James the less and of Joses, and Salome;

41(Who also, when he was in Galilee, followed him, and ministered unto him;) and many other women which came up with him unto Jerusalem.

42¶ And now when the even was come, because it was the preparation, that is, the day before the sabbath,

43Joseph of Arimathaea, an honourable counsellor, which also waited for the kingdom of God, came, and went in boldly unto Pilate, and craved the body of Jesus.

44And Pilate marvelled if he were already dead: and calling *unto him* the centurion, he asked him whether he had been any while dead.

45And when he knew *it* of the centurion, he gave the body to Joseph.

46And he bought fine linen, and took him down, and wrapped him in the linen, and laid him in a sepulchre which was hewn out of a rock, and rolled a stone unto the door of the sepulchre.

47And Mary Magdalene and Mary *the mother* of Joses beheld where he was laid.

16 AND WHEN the sabbath was past, Mary Magdalene, and Mary the *mother* of James, and Salome, had bought sweet spices, that they might come and anoint him.

2And very early in the morning the first *day* of the week, they came unto the sepulchre at the rising of the sun.

3And they said among themselves, Who shall roll us away the stone from the door of the sepulchre?

4And when they looked, they saw that the stone was rolled away: for it was very great.

5And entering into the sepulchre, they saw a young man sitting on the right side, clothed in a long white garment; and they were affrighted.

6And he saith unto them, Be not affrighted: Ye seek Jesus of Nazareth, which was crucified: he is risen; he is not here: behold the place where they laid him.

7But go your way, tell his disciples and Peter that he goeth before you into Galilee: there shall ye see him, as he said unto you.

8And they went out quickly, and fled from the sepulchre; for they trembled and were amazed: neither said they any thing to any *man;* for they were afraid.

9¶ Now when *Jesus* was risen early the first *day* of the week, he appeared first to Mary Magdalene, out of whom he had cast seven devils.

10*And* she went and told them that had been with him, as they mourned and wept.

11And they, when they had heard that he was alive, and had been seen of her, believed not.

New International

38The curtain of the temple was torn in two from top to bottom. 39And when the centurion, who stood there in front of Jesus, heard his cry and[a] saw how he died, he said, "Surely this man was the Son[b] of God!"

40Some women were watching from a distance. Among them were Mary Magdalene, Mary the mother of James the younger and of Joses, and Salome. 41In Galilee these women had followed him and cared for his needs. Many other women who had come up with him to Jerusalem were also there.

The Burial of Jesus

42It was Preparation Day (that is, the day before the Sabbath). So as evening approached, 43Joseph of Arimathea, a prominent member of the Council, who was himself waiting for the kingdom of God, went boldly to Pilate and asked for Jesus' body. 44Pilate was surprised to hear that he was already dead. Summoning the centurion, he asked him if Jesus had already died. 45When he learned from the centurion that it was so, he gave the body to Joseph. 46So Joseph bought some linen cloth, took down the body, wrapped it in the linen, and placed it in a tomb cut out of rock. Then he rolled a stone against the entrance of the tomb. 47Mary Magdalene and Mary the mother of Joses saw where he was laid.

The Resurrection

16 WHEN THE Sabbath was over, Mary Magdalene, Mary the mother of James, and Salome bought spices so that they might go to anoint Jesus' body. 2Very early on the first day of the week, just after sunrise, they were on their way to the tomb 3and they asked each other, "Who will roll the stone away from the entrance of the tomb?"

4But when they looked up, they saw that the stone, which was very large, had been rolled away. 5As they entered the tomb, they saw a young man dressed in a white robe sitting on the right side, and they were alarmed.

6"Don't be alarmed," he said. "You are looking for Jesus the Nazarene, who was crucified. He has risen! He is not here. See the place where they laid him. 7But go, tell his disciples and Peter, 'He is going ahead of you into Galilee. There you will see him, just as he told you.' "

8Trembling and bewildered, the women went out and fled from the tomb. They said nothing to anyone, because they were afraid.

[The most reliable early manuscripts and other ancient witnesses do not have Mark 16:9–20.]

9When Jesus rose early on the first day of the week, he appeared first to Mary Magdalene, out of whom he had driven seven demons. 10She went and told those who had been with him and who were mourning and weeping. 11When they heard that Jesus was alive and that she had seen him, they did not believe it.

a 39 Some manuscripts do not have *heard his cry and*   b 39 Or *a son*

Living Bible

38And the curtainc in the Temple was split apart from top to bottom.

39When the Roman officer standing beside his cross saw how he dismissed his spirit, he exclaimed, "Truly, this was the Son of God!"

40Some women were there watching from a distance—Mary Magdalene, Mary (the mother of James the Younger and of Joses), Salome, and others. 41They and many other Galilean women who were his followers had ministered to him when he was up in Galilee, and had come with him to Jerusalem.

42, 43This all happened the day before the Sabbath. Late that afternoon Joseph from Arimathea, an honored member of the Jewish Supreme Court (who personally was eagerly expecting the arrival of God's Kingdom), gathered his courage and went to Pilate and asked for Jesus' body.

44Pilate couldn't believe that Jesus was already dead so he called for the Roman officer in charge and asked him. 45The officer confirmed the fact, and Pilate told Joseph he could have the body.

46Joseph bought a long sheet of linen cloth and, taking Jesus' body down from the cross, wound it in the cloth and laid it in a rock-hewn tomb, and rolled a stone in front of the entrance.

47(Mary Magdalene and Mary the mother of Joses were watching as Jesus was laid away.)

16 THE NEXT evening, when the Sabbath ended, Mary Magdalene and Salome and Mary the mother of James went out and purchased embalming spices.

Early the following morning, just at sunrise, they carried them out to the tomb. 3On the way they were discussing how they could ever roll aside the huge stone from the entrance.

4But when they arrived they looked up and saw that the stone—a *very* heavy one—was already moved away and the entrance was open! 5So they entered the tomb—and there on the right sat a young man clothed in white. The women were startled, 6but the angel said, "Don't be so surprised. Aren't you looking for Jesus, the Nazarene who was crucified? He isn't here! He has come back to life! Look, that's where his body was lying. 7Now go and give this message to his disciples including Peter:

" 'Jesus is going ahead of you to Galilee. You will see him there, just as he told you before he died!' "

8The women fled from the tomb, trembling and bewildered, too frightened to talk.

9d It was early on Sunday morning when Jesus came back to life, and the first person who saw him was Mary Magdalene—the woman from whom he had cast out seven demons. 10, 11She found the disciples wet-eyed with grief and exclaimed that she had seen Jesus, and he was alive! But they didn't believe her!

New Revised Standard

38And the curtain of the temple was torn in two, from top to bottom. 39Now when the centurion, who stood facing him, saw that in this way hee breathed his last, he said, "Truly this man was God's Son!"f

40 There were also women looking on from a distance; among them were Mary Magdalene, and Mary the mother of James the younger and of Joses, and Salome. 41These used to follow him and provided for him when he was in Galilee; and there were many other women who had come up with him to Jerusalem.

The Burial of Jesus

42 When evening had come, and since it was the day of Preparation, that is, the day before the sabbath, 43Joseph of Arimathea, a respected member of the council, who was also himself waiting expectantly for the kingdom of God, went boldly to Pilate and asked for the body of Jesus. 44Then Pilate wondered if he were already dead; and summoning the centurion, he asked him whether he had been dead for some time. 45When he learned from the centurion that he was dead, he granted the body to Joseph. 46Then Josephg bought a linen cloth, and taking down the body,h wrapped it in the linen cloth, and laid it in a tomb that had been hewn out of the rock. He then rolled a stone against the door of the tomb. 47Mary Magdalene and Mary the mother of Joses saw where the bodyh was laid.

The Resurrection of Jesus

16 WHEN THE sabbath was over, Mary Magdalene, and Mary the mother of James, and Salome bought spices, so that they might go and anoint him. 2And very early on the first day of the week, when the sun had risen, they went to the tomb. 3They had been saying to one another, "Who will roll away the stone for us from the entrance to the tomb?" 4When they looked up, they saw that the stone, which was very large, had already been rolled back. 5As they entered the tomb, they saw a young man, dressed in a white robe, sitting on the right side; and they were alarmed. 6But he said to them, "Do not be alarmed; you are looking for Jesus of Nazareth, who was crucified. He has been raised; he is not here. Look, there is the place they laid him. 7But go, tell his disciples and Peter that he is going ahead of you to Galilee; there you will see him, just as he told you." 8So they went out and fled from the tomb, for terror and amazement had seized them; and they said nothing to anyone, for they were afraid.i

THE SHORTER ENDING OF MARK

⟦And all that had been commanded them they told briefly to those around Peter. And afterward Jesus himself sent out through them, from east to west, the sacred and imperishable proclamation of eternal salvation.j⟧

THE LONGER ENDING OF MARK

Jesus Appears to Mary Magdalene

9 ⟦Now after he rose early on the first day of the week, he appeared first to Mary Magdalene, from whom he had cast out seven demons. 10She went out and told those who had been with him, while they were mourning and weeping. 11But when they heard that he was alive and had been seen by her, they would not believe it.

---

c *15:38 And the curtain.* A heavy veil hung in front of the room in the Temple called "The Holy of Holies," a place reserved by God for himself; the veil separated him from sinful mankind. Now this veil was split from above, showing that Christ's death for man's sin had opened up access to the holy God.   d *16:9* Vss 9-20 are not found in the most ancient manuscripts, but may be considered an appendix giving additional facts.

e Other ancient authorities add *cried out and*   f Or *a son of God*   g Gk he   h Gk *it*   i Some of the most ancient authorities bring the book to a close at the end of verse 8. One authority concludes the book with the shorter ending; others include the shorter ending and then continue with verses 9-20. In most authorities verses 9-20 follow immediately after verse 8, though in some of these authorities the passage is marked as being doubtful.   j Other ancient authorities add *Amen*

King James

12¶ After that he appeared in another form unto two of them, as they walked, and went into the country.

13And they went and told *it* unto the residue: neither believed they them.

14¶ Afterward he appeared unto the eleven as they sat at meat, and upbraided them with their unbelief and hardness of heart, because they believed not them which had seen him after he was risen.

15And he said unto them, Go ye into all the world, and preach the gospel to every creature.

16He that believeth and is baptized shall be saved; but he that believeth not shall be damned.

17And these signs shall follow them that believe; In my name shall they cast out devils; they shall speak with new tongues;

18They shall take up serpents; and if they drink any deadly thing, it shall not hurt them; they shall lay hands on the sick, and they shall recover.

19¶ So then after the Lord had spoken unto them, he was received up into heaven, and sat on the right hand of God.

20And they went forth, and preached every where, the Lord working with *them,* and confirming the word with signs following. Amen.

New International

12Afterward Jesus appeared in a different form to two of them while they were walking in the country. 13These returned and reported it to the rest; but they did not believe them either.

14Later Jesus appeared to the Eleven as they were eating; he rebuked them for their lack of faith and their stubborn refusal to believe those who had seen him after he had risen.

15He said to them, "Go into all the world and preach the good news to all creation. 16Whoever believes and is baptized will be saved, but whoever does not believe will be condemned. 17And these signs will accompany those who believe: In my name they will drive out demons; they will speak in new tongues; 18they will pick up snakes with their hands; and when they drink deadly poison, it will not hurt them at all; they will place their hands on sick people, and they will get well."

19After the Lord Jesus had spoken to them, he was taken up into heaven and he sat at the right hand of God. 20Then the disciples went out and preached everywhere, and the Lord worked with them and confirmed his word by the signs that accompanied it.

Living Bible

12Later that daya he appeared to two who were walking from Jerusalem into the country, but they didn't recognize him at first because he had changed his appearance. 13When they finally realized who he was, they rushed back to Jerusalem to tell the others, but no one believed them.

14Still later he appeared to the eleven disciples as they were eating together. He rebuked them for their unbelief—their stubborn refusal to believe those who had seen him alive from the dead.

15And then he told them, "You are to go into all the world and preach the Good News to everyone, everywhere. 16Those who believe and are baptized will be saved. But those who refuse to believe will be condemned.

17"And those who believe shall use my authority to cast out demons, and they shall speak new languages.b 18They will be able even to handle snakes with safety, and if they drink anything poisonous, it won't hurt them; and they will be able to place their hands on the sick and heal them."

19When the Lord Jesus had finished talking with them, he was taken up into heaven and sat down at God's right hand.

20And the disciples went everywhere preaching, and the Lord was with them and confirmed what they said by the miracles that followed their messages.

New Revised Standard

Jesus Appears to Two Disciples

12 After this he appeared in another form to two of them, as they were walking into the country. 13 And they went back and told the rest, but they did not believe them.

Jesus Commissions the Disciples

14 Later he appeared to the eleven themselves as they were sitting at the table; and he upbraided them for their lack of faith and stubbornness, because they had not believed those who saw him after he had risen.c 15 And he said to them, "Go into all the world and proclaim the good newsd to the whole creation. 16 The one who believes and is baptized will be saved; but the one who does not believe will be condemned. 17 And these signs will accompany those who believe: by using my name they will cast out demons; they will speak in new tongues; 18 they will pick up snakes in their hands,e and if they drink any deadly thing, it will not hurt them; they will lay their hands on the sick, and they will recover."

The Ascension of Jesus

19 So then the Lord Jesus, after he had spoken to them, was taken up into heaven and sat down at the right hand of God. 20 And they went out and proclaimed the good news everywhere, while the Lord worked with them and confirmed the message by the signs that accompanied it.f

---

c Other ancient authorities add, in whole or in part, *And they excused themselves, saying, "This age of lawlessness and unbelief is under Satan, who does not allow the truth and power of God to prevail over the unclean things of the spirits. Therefore reveal your righteousness now"* —thus they spoke to Christ. And Christ replied to them, "The term of years of Satan's power has been fulfilled, but other terrible things draw near. And for those who have sinned I was handed over to death, that they may return to the truth and sin no more, that they may inherit the spiritual and imperishable glory of righteousness that is in heaven." d Or *gospel* e Other ancient authorities lack *in their hands* f Other ancient authorities add *Amen*

---

a *16:12 Later that day,* literally, "after these things." b *16:17 speak new languages,* literally, "they will speak in new tongues." Some ancient manuscripts omit "new."

THE GOSPEL

ACCORDING TO

St. Luke

Luke

1

FORASMUCH AS many have taken in hand to set forth in order a declaration of those things which are most surely believed among us,

2Even as they delivered them unto us, which from the beginning were eyewitnesses, and ministers of the word;

3It seemed good to me also, having had perfect understanding of all things from the very first, to write unto thee in order, most excellent Theophilus,

4That thou mightest know the certainty of those things, wherein thou hast been instructed.

5¶ There was in the days of Herod, the king of Judaea, a certain priest named Zacharias, of the course of Abia: and his wife *was* of the daughters of Aaron, and her name *was* Elisabeth.

6And they were both righteous before God, walking in all the commandments and ordinances of the Lord blameless.

7And they had no child, because that Elisabeth was barren, and they both were *now* well stricken in years.

8And it came to pass, that while he executed the priest's office before God in the order of his course,

9According to the custom of the priest's office, his lot was to burn incense when he went into the temple of the Lord.

10And the whole multitude of the people were praying without at the time of incense.

11And there appeared unto him an angel of the Lord standing on the right side of the altar of incense.

12And when Zacharias saw *him*, he was troubled, and fear fell upon him.

13But the angel said unto him, Fear not, Zacharias: for thy prayer is heard; and thy wife Elisabeth shall bear thee a son, and thou shalt call his name John.

14And thou shalt have joy and gladness; and many shall rejoice at his birth.

15For he shall be great in the sight of the Lord, and shall drink neither wine nor strong drink; and he shall be filled with the Holy Ghost, even from his mother's womb.

16And many of the children of Israel shall he turn to the Lord their God.

17And he shall go before him in the spirit and power of Elias, to turn the hearts of the fathers to the children, and the disobedient to the wisdom of the just; to make ready a people prepared for the Lord.

18And Zacharias said unto the angel, Whereby shall I know this? for I am an old man, and my wife well stricken in years.

19And the angel answering said unto him, I am Gabriel, that stand in the presence of God; and am sent to speak unto thee, and to show thee these glad tidings.

Introduction

1

MANY HAVE undertaken to draw up an account of the things that have been fulfilleda among us, 2just as they were handed down to us by those who from the first were eyewitnesses and servants of the word. 3Therefore, since I myself have carefully investigated everything from the beginning, it seemed good also to me to write an orderly account for you, most excellent Theophilus, 4so that you may know the certainty of the things you have been taught.

The Birth of John the Baptist Foretold

5In the time of Herod king of Judea there was a priest named Zechariah, who belonged to the priestly division of Abijah; his wife Elizabeth was also a descendant of Aaron. 6Both of them were upright in the sight of God, observing all the Lord's commandments and regulations blamelessly. 7But they had no children, because Elizabeth was barren; and they were both well along in years.

8Once when Zechariah's division was on duty and he was serving as priest before God, 9he was chosen by lot, according to the custom of the priesthood, to go into the temple of the Lord and burn incense. 10And when the time for the burning of incense came, all the assembled worshipers were praying outside.

11Then an angel of the Lord appeared to him, standing at the right side of the altar of incense. 12When Zechariah saw him, he was startled and was gripped with fear. 13But the angel said to him: "Do not be afraid, Zechariah; your prayer has been heard. Your wife Elizabeth will bear you a son, and you are to give him the name John. 14He will be a joy and delight to you, and many will rejoice because of his birth, 15for he will be great in the sight of the Lord. He is never to take wine or other fermented drink, and he will be filled with the Holy Spirit even from birth.b 16Many of the people of Israel will he bring back to the Lord their God. 17And he will go on before the Lord, in the spirit and power of Elijah, to turn the hearts of the fathers to their children and the disobedient to the wisdom of the righteous—to make ready a people prepared for the Lord."

18Zechariah asked the angel, "How can I be sure of this? I am an old man and my wife is well along in years."

19The angel answered, "I am Gabriel. I stand in the presence of God, and I have been sent to speak to you and to tell you this good news. 20And now you will be

THE GOSPEL
ACCORDING TO

Luke

Luke

1 DEAR FRIEND who loves God:c
1, 2Several biographies of Christ have already been
written using as their source material the reports circulating among us from the early disciples and other
eyewitnesses. 3However, it occurred to me that it would
be well to recheck all these accounts from first to last and
after thorough investigation to pass this summary on to
you,d 4to reassure you of the truth of all you were
taught.

5My story begins with a Jewish priest, Zacharias,
who lived when Herod was king of Judea. Zacharias was
a member of the Abijah division of the Temple service
corps. (His wife Elizabeth was, like himself, a member
of the priest tribe of the Jews, a descendant of Aaron.)
6Zacharias and Elizabeth were godly folk, careful to
obey all of God's laws in spirit as well as in letter. 7But
they had no children, for Elizabeth was barren; and now
they were both very old.

8, 9One day as Zacharias was going about his work in
the Temple—for his division was on duty that week—
the honor fell to him by lot to enter the inner sanctuary
and burn incense before the Lord. 10Meanwhile, a great
crowd stood outside in the Temple court, praying as they
always did during that part of the service when the incense was being burned.

11, 12Zacharias was in the sanctuary when suddenly an
angel appeared, standing to the right of the altar of incense! Zacharias was startled and terrified.

13But the angel said, "Don't be afraid, Zacharias! For
I have come to tell you that God has heard your prayer,
and your wife Elizabeth will bear you a son! And you
are to name him John. 14You will both have great joy
and gladness at his birth, and many will rejoice with
you. 15For he will be one of the Lord's great men. He
must never touch wine or hard liquor—and he will be
filled with the Holy Spirit, even from before his birth!
16And he will persuade many a Jew to turn to the Lord
his God. 17He will be a man of ruggedf spirit and power
like Elijah, the prophet of old; and he will precede the
coming of the Messiah, preparing the people for his
arrival. He will soften adult hearts to become like little
children's, and will change disobedient minds to the
wisdom of faith."g

18Zacharias said to the angel, "But this is impossible!
I'm an old man now, and my wife is also well along in
years."

19Then the angel said, "I am Gabriel! I stand in the
very presence of God. It was he who sent me to you with
this good news! 20And now, because you haven't be-

Dedication to Theophilus

1 SINCE MANY have undertaken to set down an
orderly account of the events that have been fulfilled among us, 2just as they were handed on to us by
those who from the beginning were eyewitnesses and
servants of the word, 3I too decided, after investigating
everything carefully from the very first,h to write an
orderly account for you, most excellent Theophilus, 4so
that you may know the truth concerning the things about
which you have been instructed.

The Birth of John the Baptist Foretold

5 In the days of King Herod of Judea, there was a
priest named Zechariah, who belonged to the priestly
order of Abijah. His wife was a descendant of Aaron,
and her name was Elizabeth. 6Both of them were righteous before God, living blamelessly according to all the
commandments and regulations of the Lord. 7But they
had no children, because Elizabeth was barren, and both
were getting on in years.

8 Once when he was serving as priest before God
and his section was on duty, 9he was chosen by lot,
according to the custom of the priesthood, to enter the
sanctuary of the Lord and offer incense. 10Now at the
time of the incense offering, the whole assembly of the
people was praying outside. 11Then there appeared to
him an angel of the Lord, standing at the right side of
the altar of incense. 12When Zechariah saw him, he was
terrified; and fear overwhelmed him. 13But the angel
said to him, "Do not be afraid, Zechariah, for your
prayer has been heard. Your wife Elizabeth will bear
you a son, and you will name him John. 14You will have
joy and gladness, and many will rejoice at his birth,
15for he will be great in the sight of the Lord. He must
never drink wine or strong drink; even before his birth
he will be filled with the Holy Spirit. 16He will turn
many of the people of Israel to the Lord their God.
17With the spirit and power of Elijah he will go before
him, to turn the hearts of parents to their children, and
the disobedient to the wisdom of the righteous, to make
ready a people prepared for the Lord." 18Zechariah said
to the angel, "How will I know that this is so? For I am
an old man, and my wife is getting on in years." 19The
angel replied, "I am Gabriel. I stand in the presence of
God, and I have been sent to speak to you and to bring
you this good news. 20But now, because you did not

c *1:1 Dear friend who loves God.* From vs 3. Literally, "most excellent
Theophilus." The name means "one who loves God." d *1:3 to pass this
summary on to you,* literally, "an account of the things accomplished among
us." e *1:8, 9 by lot.* Probably by throwing dice or something
similar—"drawing straws" would be a modern equivalent. f *1:17 rugged,*
implied. g *1:17 and will change disobedient minds to the wisdom of faith,*
literally, "to turn the hearts of the fathers to the children, and the disobedient
to the wisdom of the just."

h Or *for a long time*

King James

20And, behold, thou shalt be dumb, and not able to speak, until the day that these things shall be performed, because thou believest not my words, which shall be fulfilled in their season.

21And the people waited for Zacharias, and marvelled that he tarried so long in the temple.

22And when he came out, he could not speak unto them: and they perceived that he had seen a vision in the temple: for he beckoned unto them, and remained speechless.

23And it came to pass, that as soon as the days of his ministration were accomplished, he departed to his own house.

24And after those days his wife Elisabeth conceived, and hid herself five months, saying,

25Thus hath the Lord dealt with me in the days wherein he looked on *me*, to take away my reproach among men.

26And in the sixth month the angel Gabriel was sent from God unto a city of Galilee, named Nazareth,

27To a virgin espoused to a man whose name was Joseph, of the house of David; and the virgin's name *was* Mary.

28And the angel came in unto her, and said, Hail, *thou that art* highly favoured, the Lord *is* with thee: blessed *art* thou among women.

29And when she saw *him*, she was troubled at his saying, and cast in her mind what manner of salutation this should be.

30And the angel said unto her, Fear not, Mary: for thou hast found favour with God.

31And, behold, thou shalt conceive in thy womb, and bring forth a son, and shalt call his name JESUS.

32He shall be great, and shall be called the Son of the Highest: and the Lord God shall give unto him the throne of his father David:

33And he shall reign over the house of Jacob for ever; and of his kingdom there shall be no end.

34Then said Mary unto the angel, How shall this be, seeing I know not a man?

35And the angel answered and said unto her, The Holy Ghost shall come upon thee, and the power of the Highest shall overshadow thee: therefore also that holy thing which shall be born of thee shall be called the Son of God.

36And, behold, thy cousin Elisabeth, she hath also conceived a son in her old age: and this is the sixth month with her, who was called barren.

37For with God nothing shall be impossible.

38And Mary said, Behold the handmaid of the Lord; be it unto me according to thy word. And the angel departed from her.

39And Mary arose in those days, and went into the hill country with haste, into a city of Judah;

40And entered into the house of Zacharias, and saluted Elisabeth.

41And it came to pass, that, when Elisabeth heard the salutation of Mary, the babe leaped in her womb; and Elisabeth was filled with the Holy Ghost:

42And she spake out with a loud voice, and said, Blessed *art* thou among women, and blessed *is* the fruit of thy womb.

43And whence *is* this to me, that the mother of my Lord should come to me?

44For, lo, as soon as the voice of thy salutation sounded in mine ears, the babe leaped in my womb for joy.

45And blessed *is* she that believed: for there shall be a performance of those things which were told her from the Lord.

46And Mary said, My soul doth magnify the Lord,

47And my spirit hath rejoiced in God my Saviour.

48For he hath regarded the low estate of his handmaiden: for, behold, from henceforth all generations shall call me blessed.

New International

silent and not able to speak until the day this happens, because you did not believe my words, which will come true at their proper time."

21Meanwhile, the people were waiting for Zechariah and wondering why he stayed so long in the temple. 22When he came out, he could not speak to them. They realized he had seen a vision in the temple, for he kept making signs to them but remained unable to speak.

23When his time of service was completed, he returned home. 24After this his wife Elizabeth became pregnant and for five months remained in seclusion. 25"The Lord has done this for me," she said. "In these days he has shown his favor and taken away my disgrace among the people."

The Birth of Jesus Foretold

26In the sixth month, God sent the angel Gabriel to Nazareth, a town in Galilee, 27to a virgin pledged to be married to a man named Joseph, a descendant of David. The virgin's name was Mary. 28The angel went to her and said, "Greetings, you who are highly favored! The Lord is with you."

29Mary was greatly troubled at his words and wondered what kind of greeting this might be. 30But the angel said to her, "Do not be afraid, Mary, you have found favor with God. 31You will be with child and give birth to a son, and you are to give him the name Jesus. 32He will be great and will be called the Son of the Most High. The Lord God will give him the throne of his father David, 33and he will reign over the house of Jacob forever; his kingdom will never end."

34"How will this be," Mary asked the angel, "since I am a virgin?"

35The angel answered, "The Holy Spirit will come upon you, and the power of the Most High will overshadow you. So the holy one to be born will be calleda the Son of God. 36Even Elizabeth your relative is going to have a child in her old age, and she who was said to be barren is in her sixth month. 37For nothing is impossible with God."

38"I am the Lord's servant," Mary answered. "May it be to me as you have said." Then the angel left her.

Mary Visits Elizabeth

39At that time Mary got ready and hurried to a town in the hill country of Judea, 40where she entered Zechariah's home and greeted Elizabeth. 41When Elizabeth heard Mary's greeting, the baby leaped in her womb, and Elizabeth was filled with the Holy Spirit. 42In a loud voice she exclaimed: "Blessed are you among women, and blessed is the child you will bear! 43But why am I so favored, that the mother of my Lord should come to me? 44As soon as the sound of your greeting reached my ears, the baby in my womb leaped for joy. 45Blessed is she who has believed that what the Lord has said to her will be accomplished!"

Mary's Song

46And Mary said:

"My soul glorifies the Lord
47 and my spirit rejoices in God my Savior,
48for he has been mindful
of the humble state of his servant.
From now on all generations will call me
blessed,

---

a 35 Or *So the child to be born will be called holy,*

Living Bible

lieved me, you are to be stricken silent, unable to speak until the child is born. For my words will certainly come true at the proper time."

21Meanwhile the crowds outside were waiting for Zacharias to appear and wondered why he was taking so long. 22When he finally came out, he couldn't speak to them, and they realized from his gestures that he must have seen a vision in the Temple. 23He stayed on at the Temple for the remaining days of his Temple duties and then returned home. 24Soon afterwards Elizabeth his wife became pregnant and went into seclusion for five months.

25"How kind the Lord is," she exclaimed, "to take away my disgrace of having no children!"

26The following month God sent the angel Gabriel to Nazareth, a village in Galilee, 27to a virgin, Mary, engaged to be married to a man named Joseph, a descendant of King David.

28Gabriel appeared to her and said, "Congratulations, favored lady! The Lord is with you!"b

29Confused and disturbed, Mary tried to think what the angel could mean.

30"Don't be frightened, Mary," the angel told her, "for God has decided to wonderfully bless you! 31Very soon now, you will become pregnant and have a baby boy, and you are to name him 'Jesus.' 32He shall be very great and shall be called the Son of God. And the Lord God shall give him the throne of his ancestor David. 33And he shall reign over Israel forever; his Kingdom shall never end!"

34Mary asked the angel, "But how can I have a baby? I am a virgin."

35The angel replied, "The Holy Spirit shall come upon you, and the power of God shall overshadow you; so the baby born to you will be utterly holy—the Son of God. 36Furthermore, six months ago your Aunt Elizabeth—'the barren one,' they called her—became pregnant in her old age! 37For every promise from God shall surely come true."

38Mary said, "I am the Lord's servant, and I am willing to do whatever he wants. May everything you said come true." And then the angel disappeared.

39, 40A few days later Mary hurried to the highlands of Judea to the town where Zacharias lived, to visit Elizabeth.

41At the sound of Mary's greeting, Elizabeth's child leaped within her and she was filled with the Holy Spirit.

42She gave a glad cry and exclaimed to Mary, "You are favored by God above all other women, and your child is destined for God's mightiest praise. 43What an honor this is, that the mother of my Lord should visit me! 44When you came in and greeted me, the instant I heard your voice, my baby moved in me for joy! 45You believed that God would do what he said; that is why he has given you this wonderful blessing."

46Mary responded, "Oh, how I praise the Lord. 47How I rejoice in God my Savior! 48For he took notice of his lowly servant girl, and now generation after generation forever shall call me blest of God. 49For he, the

New Revised Standard

believe my words, which will be fulfilled in their time, you will become mute, unable to speak, until the day these things occur."

21 Meanwhile the people were waiting for Zechariah, and wondered at his delay in the sanctuary. 22When he did come out, he could not speak to them, and they realized that he had seen a vision in the sanctuary. He kept motioning to them and remained unable to speak. 23When his time of service was ended, he went to his home.

24 After those days his wife Elizabeth conceived, and for five months she remained in seclusion. She said, 25"This is what the Lord has done for me when he looked favorably on me and took away the disgrace I have endured among my people."

The Birth of Jesus Foretold

26 In the sixth month the angel Gabriel was sent by God to a town in Galilee called Nazareth, 27to a virgin engaged to a man whose name was Joseph, of the house of David. The virgin's name was Mary. 28And he came to her and said, "Greetings, favored one! The Lord is with you."d 29But she was much perplexed by his words and pondered what sort of greeting this might be. 30The angel said to her, "Do not be afraid, Mary, for you have found favor with God. 31And now, you will conceive in your womb and bear a son, and you will name him Jesus. 32He will be great, and will be called the Son of the Most High, and the Lord God will give to him the throne of his ancestor David. 33He will reign over the house of Jacob forever, and of his kingdom there will be no end." 34Mary said to the angel, "How can this be, since I am a virgin?"e 35The angel said to her, "The Holy Spirit will come upon you, and the power of the Most High will overshadow you; therefore the child to be bornf will be holy; he will be called Son of God. 36And now, your relative Elizabeth in her old age has also conceived a son; and this is the sixth month for her who was said to be barren. 37For nothing will be impossible with God." 38Then Mary said, "Here am I, the servant of the Lord; let it be with me according to your word." Then the angel departed from her.

Mary Visits Elizabeth

39 In those days Mary set out and went with haste to a Judean town in the hill country, 40where she entered the house of Zechariah and greeted Elizabeth. 41When Elizabeth heard Mary's greeting, the child leaped in her womb. And Elizabeth was filled with the Holy Spirit 42and exclaimed with a loud cry, "Blessed are you among women, and blessed is the fruit of your womb. 43And why has this happened to me, that the mother of my Lord comes to me? 44For as soon as I heard the sound of your greeting, the child in my womb leaped for joy. 45And blessed is she who believed that there would beg a fulfillment of what was spoken to her by the Lord."

Mary's Song of Praise

46 And Maryh said,
  "My soul magnifies the Lord,
47   and my spirit rejoices in God my Savior,
48 for he has looked with favor on the lowliness
        of his servant.
      Surely, from now on all generations will
        call me blessed;

---

b 1:28 The Lord is with you. Some ancient versions add, "Blessed are you among women," as in vs 42 which appears in all manuscripts. c 1:36 Aunt, literally, "relative."

d Other ancient authorities add Blessed are you among women e Gk I do not know a man f Other ancient authorities add of you g Or believed, for there will be h Other ancient authorities read Elizabeth

King James

49For he that is mighty hath done to me great things; and holy *is* his name.

50And his mercy *is* on them that fear him from generation to generation.

51He hath shown strength with his arm; he hath scattered the proud in the imagination of their hearts.

52He hath put down the mighty from *their* seats, and exalted them of low degree.

53He hath filled the hungry with good things; and the rich he hath sent empty away.

54He hath helped his servant Israel, in remembrance of *his* mercy;

55As he spake to our fathers, to Abraham, and to his seed for ever.

56And Mary abode with her about three months, and returned to her own house.

57Now Elisabeth's full time came that she should be delivered; and she brought forth a son.

58And her neighbours and her cousins heard how the Lord had shown great mercy upon her; and they rejoiced with her.

59And it came to pass, that on the eighth day they came to circumcise the child; and they called him Zacharias, after the name of his father.

60And his mother answered and said, Not *so;* but he shall be called John.

61And they said unto her, There is none of thy kindred that is called by this name.

62And they made signs to his father, how he would have him called.

63And he asked for a writing table, and wrote, saying, His name is John. And they marvelled all.

64And his mouth was opened immediately, and his tongue *loosed,* and he spake, and praised God.

65And fear came on all that dwelt round about them: and all these sayings were noised abroad throughout all the hill country of Judaea.

66And all they that heard *them* laid *them* up in their hearts, saying, What manner of child shall this be! And the hand of the Lord was with him.

67And his father Zacharias was filled with the Holy Ghost, and prophesied, saying,

68Blessed *be* the Lord God of Israel; for he hath visited and redeemed his people,

69And hath raised up an horn of salvation for us in the house of his servant David;

70As he spake by the mouth of his holy prophets, which have been since the world began:

71That we should be saved from our enemies, and from the hand of all that hate us;

72To perform the mercy *promised* to our fathers, and to remember his holy covenant;

73The oath which he sware to our father Abraham,

74That he would grant unto us, that we being delivered out of the hand of our enemies might serve him without fear,

75In holiness and righteousness before him, all the days of our life.

76And thou, child, shalt be called the prophet of the Highest: for thou shalt go before the face of the Lord to prepare his ways;

77To give knowledge of salvation unto his people by the remission of their sins,

78Through the tender mercy of our God; whereby the dayspring from on high hath visited us,

New International

49 for the Mighty One has done great things for
      me—
    holy is his name.
50His mercy extends to those who fear him,
      from generation to generation.
51He has performed mighty deeds with his arm;
      he has scattered those who are proud in their
      inmost thoughts.
52He has brought down rulers from their thrones
      but has lifted up the humble.
53He has filled the hungry with good things
      but has sent the rich away empty.
54He has helped his servant Israel,
      remembering to be merciful
55to Abraham and his descendants forever,
      even as he said to our fathers."

56Mary stayed with Elizabeth for about three months and then returned home.

The Birth of John the Baptist

57When it was time for Elizabeth to have her baby, she gave birth to a son. 58Her neighbors and relatives heard that the Lord had shown her great mercy, and they shared her joy.

59On the eighth day they came to circumcise the child, and they were going to name him after his father Zechariah, 60but his mother spoke up and said, "No! He is to be called John."

61They said to her, "There is no one among your relatives who has that name."

62Then they made signs to his father, to find out what he would like to name the child. 63He asked for a writing tablet, and to everyone's astonishment he wrote, "His name is John." 64Immediately his mouth was opened and his tongue was loosed, and he began to speak, praising God. 65The neighbors were all filled with awe, and throughout the hill country of Judea people were talking about all these things. 66Everyone who heard this wondered about it, asking, "What then is this child going to be?" For the Lord's hand was with him.

Zechariah's Song

67His father Zechariah was filled with the Holy Spirit and prophesied:

68"Praise be to the Lord, the God of Israel,
      because he has come and has redeemed his
      people.
69He has raised up a horn[a] of salvation for us
      in the house of his servant David
70(as he said through his holy prophets of long
      ago),
71salvation from our enemies
      and from the hand of all who hate us—
72to show mercy to our fathers
      and to remember his holy covenant,
73 the oath he swore to our father Abraham:
74to rescue us from the hand of our enemies,
      and to enable us to serve him without fear
75 in holiness and righteousness before him all
      our days.

76And you, my child, will be called a prophet of
      the Most High;
      for you will go on before the Lord to prepare
      the way for him,
77to give his people the knowledge of salvation
      through the forgiveness of their sins,
78because of the tender mercy of our God,
      by which the rising sun will come to us from
      heaven

---

a 69 *Horn* here symbolizes strength.

Living Bible

mighty Holy One, has done great things to me. 50His mercy goes on from generation to generation, to all who reverence him.

51"How powerful is his mighty arm! How he scatters the proud and haughty ones! 52He has torn princes from their thrones and exalted the lowly. 53He has satisfied the hungry hearts and sent the rich away with empty hands. 54And how he has helped his servant Israel! He has not forgotten his promise to be merciful. 55For he promised our fathers—Abraham and his children—to be merciful to them forever."

56Mary stayed with Elizabeth about three months and then went back to her own home.

57By now Elizabeth's waiting was over, for the time had come for the baby to be born—and it was a boy. 58The word spread quickly to her neighbors and relatives of how kind the Lord had been to her, and everyone rejoiced.

59When the baby was eight days old, all the relatives and friends came for the circumcision ceremony. They all assumed the baby's name would be Zacharias, after his father.

60But Elizabeth said, "No! He must be named John!"

61"What?" they exclaimed. "There is no one in all your family by that name." 62So they asked the baby's father, talking to him by gestures.b

63He motioned for a piece of paper and to everyone's surprise wrote, "His name is *John!*" 64Instantly Zacharias could speak again, and he began praising God.

65Wonder fell upon the whole neighborhood, and the news of what had happened spread through the Judean hills. 66And everyone who heard about it thought long thoughts and asked, "I wonder what this child will turn out to be? For the hand of the Lord is surely upon him in some special way."

67Then his father Zacharias was filled with the Holy Spirit and gave this prophecy:

68"Praise the Lord, the God of Israel, for he has come to visit his people and has redeemed them. 69He is sending us a Mighty Savior from the royal line of his servant David, 70just as he promised through his holy prophets long ago— 71someone to save us from our enemies, from all who hate us.

72, 73"He has been merciful to our ancestors, yes, to Abraham himself, by remembering his sacred promise to him, 74and by granting us the privilege of serving God fearlessly, freed from our enemies, 75and by making us holy and acceptable, ready to stand in his presence forever.

76"And you, my little son, shall be called the prophet of the glorious God, for you will prepare the way for the Messiah. 77You will tell his people how to find salvation through forgiveness of their sins. 78All this will be because the mercy of our God is very tender, and heaven's dawn is about to break upon us, 79to give light to those

New Revised Standard

49 for the Mighty One has done great things for
    me,
    and holy is his name.
50 His mercy is for those who fear him
    from generation to generation.
51 He has shown strength with his arm;
    he has scattered the proud in the thoughts of
    their hearts.
52 He has brought down the powerful from their
    thrones,
    and lifted up the lowly;
53 he has filled the hungry with good things,
    and sent the rich away empty.
54 He has helped his servant Israel,
    in remembrance of his mercy,
55 according to the promise he made to our
    ancestors,
    to Abraham and to his descendants forever."

56 And Mary remained with her about three months and then returned to her home.

The Birth of John the Baptist

57 Now the time came for Elizabeth to give birth, and she bore a son. 58 Her neighbors and relatives heard that the Lord had shown his great mercy to her, and they rejoiced with her.

59 On the eighth day they came to circumcise the child, and they were going to name him Zechariah after his father. 60 But his mother said, "No; he is to be called John." 61 They said to her, "None of your relatives has this name." 62 Then they began motioning to his father to find out what name he wanted to give him. 63 He asked for a writing tablet and wrote, "His name is John." And all of them were amazed. 64 Immediately his mouth was opened and his tongue freed, and he began to speak, praising God. 65 Fear came over all their neighbors, and all these things were talked about throughout the entire hill country of Judea. 66 All who heard them pondered them and said, "What then will this child become?" For, indeed, the hand of the Lord was with him.

Zechariah's Prophecy

67 Then his father Zechariah was filled with the Holy Spirit and spoke this prophecy:
68 "Blessed be the Lord God of Israel,
    for he has looked favorably on his people
        and redeemed them.
69 He has raised up a mighty saviorc for us
    in the house of his servant David,
70 as he spoke through the mouth of his holy
        prophets from of old,
71 that we would be saved from our enemies
        and from the hand of all who hate us.
72 Thus he has shown the mercy promised to our
        ancestors,
    and has remembered his holy covenant,
73 the oath that he swore to our ancestor
        Abraham,
    to grant us 74that we, being rescued from
        the hands of our enemies,
    might serve him without fear, 75in holiness
        and righteousness
    before him all our days.
76 And you, child, will be called the prophet of
        the Most High;
    for you will go before the Lord to prepare
        his ways,
77 to give knowledge of salvation to his people
    by the forgiveness of their sins.
78 By the tender mercy of our God,
    the dawn from on high will break upond us,

---

b *1:62 talking to him by gestures.* Zacharias was apparently stone deaf as well as speechless, and had not heard what his wife had said.

c Gk *a horn of salvation*   d Other ancient authorities read *has broken upon*

King James

79To give light to them that sit in darkness and *in* the shadow of death, to guide our feet into the way of peace.

80And the child grew, and waxed strong in spirit, and was in the deserts till the day of his showing unto Israel.

2 AND IT came to pass in those days, that there went out a decree from Caesar Augustus, that all the world should be taxed.

2(*And* this taxing was first made when Cyrenius was governor of Syria.)

3And all went to be taxed, every one into his own city.

4And Joseph also went up from Galilee, out of the city of Nazareth, into Judaea, unto the city of David, which is called Bethlehem; (because he was of the house and lineage of David:)

5To be taxed with Mary his espoused wife, being great with child.

6And so it was, that, while they were there, the days were accomplished that she should be delivered.

7And she brought forth her firstborn son, and wrapped him in swaddling clothes, and laid him in a manger; because there was no room for them in the inn.

8And there were in the same country shepherds abiding in the field, keeping watch over their flock by night.

9And, lo, the angel of the Lord came upon them, and the glory of the Lord shone round about them: and they were sore afraid.

10And the angel said unto them, Fear not: for, behold, I bring you good tidings of great joy, which shall be to all people.

11For unto you is born this day in the city of David a Saviour, which is Christ the Lord.

12And this *shall be* a sign unto you; Ye shall find the babe wrapped in swaddling clothes, lying in a manger.

13And suddenly there was with the angel a multitude of the heavenly host praising God, and saying,

14Glory to God in the highest, and on earth peace, good will toward men.

15And it came to pass, as the angels were gone away from them into heaven, the shepherds said one to another, Let us now go even unto Bethlehem, and see this thing which is come to pass, which the Lord hath made known unto us.

16And they came with haste, and found Mary, and Joseph, and the babe lying in a manger.

17And when they had seen *it*, they made known abroad the saying which was told them concerning this child.

18And all they that heard *it* wondered at those things which were told them by the shepherds.

19But Mary kept all these things, and pondered *them* in her heart.

20And the shepherds returned, glorifying and praising God for all the things that they had heard and seen, as it was told unto them.

21And when eight days were accomplished for the circumcising of the child, his name was called JESUS, which was so named of the angel before he was conceived in the womb.

22And when the days of her purification according to the law of Moses were accomplished, they brought him to Jerusalem, to present *him* to the Lord;

23(As it is written in the law of the Lord, Every male that openeth the womb shall be called holy to the Lord;)

24And to offer a sacrifice according to that which is said in the law of the Lord, A pair of turtledoves, or two young pigeons.

New International

79to shine on those living in darkness
  and in the shadow of death,
 to guide our feet into the path of peace."

80And the child grew and became strong in spirit; and he lived in the desert until he appeared publicly to Israel.

The Birth of Jesus

2 IN THOSE days Caesar Augustus issued a decree that a census should be taken of the entire Roman world. 2(This was the first census that took place while Quirinius was governor of Syria.) 3And everyone went to his own town to register.

4So Joseph also went up from the town of Nazareth in Galilee to Judea, to Bethlehem the town of David, because he belonged to the house and line of David. 5He went there to register with Mary, who was pledged to be married to him and was expecting a child. 6While they were there, the time came for the baby to be born, 7and she gave birth to her firstborn, a son. She wrapped him in cloths and placed him in a manger, because there was no room for them in the inn.

The Shepherds and the Angels

8And there were shepherds living out in the fields nearby, keeping watch over their flocks at night. 9An angel of the Lord appeared to them, and the glory of the Lord shone around them, and they were terrified. 10But the angel said to them, "Do not be afraid. I bring you good news of great joy that will be for all the people. 11Today in the town of David a Savior has been born to you; he is Christ[a] the Lord. 12This will be a sign to you: You will find a baby wrapped in cloths and lying in a manger."

13Suddenly a great company of the heavenly host appeared with the angel, praising God and saying,

14"Glory to God in the highest,
  and on earth peace to men on whom his favor
    rests."

15When the angels had left them and gone into heaven, the shepherds said to one another, "Let's go to Bethlehem and see this thing that has happened, which the Lord has told us about."

16So they hurried off and found Mary and Joseph, and the baby, who was lying in the manger. 17When they had seen him, they spread the word concerning what had been told them about this child, 18and all who heard it were amazed at what the shepherds said to them. 19But Mary treasured up all these things and pondered them in her heart. 20The shepherds returned, glorifying and praising God for all the things they had heard and seen, which were just as they had been told.

Jesus Presented in the Temple

21On the eighth day, when it was time to circumcise him, he was named Jesus, the name the angel had given him before he had been conceived.

22When the time of their purification according to the Law of Moses had been completed, Joseph and Mary took him to Jerusalem to present him to the Lord 23(as it is written in the Law of the Lord, "Every firstborn male is to be consecrated to the Lord"[b]), 24and to offer a sacrifice in keeping with what is said in the Law of the Lord: "a pair of doves or two young pigeons."[c]

---

a *11* Or *Messiah*. "The Christ" (Greek) and "the Messiah" (Hebrew) both mean "the Anointed One"; also in verse 26.   b *23* Exodus 13:2,12   c *24* Lev. 12:8

Living Bible

who sit in darkness and death's shadow, and to guide us to the path of peace."

80The little boy greatly loved God[d] and when he grew up he lived out in the lonely wilderness until he began his public ministry to Israel.

2 ABOUT THIS time Caesar Augustus, the Roman Emperor, decreed that a census should be taken throughout the nation. 2(This census was taken when Quirinius was governor of Syria.)

3Everyone was required to return to his ancestral home for this registration. 4And because Joseph was a member of the royal line, he had to go to Bethlehem in Judea, King David's ancient home—journeying there from the Galilean village of Nazareth. 5He took with him Mary, his fiancée, who was obviously pregnant by this time.

6And while they were there, the time came for her baby to be born; 7and she gave birth to her first child, a son. She wrapped him in a blanket[e] and laid him in a manger, because there was no room for them in the village inn.

8That night some shepherds were in the fields outside the village, guarding their flocks of sheep. 9Suddenly an angel appeared among them, and the landscape shone bright with the glory of the Lord. They were badly frightened, 10but the angel reassured them.

"Don't be afraid!" he said. "I bring you the most joyful news ever announced, and it is for everyone! 11The Savior—yes, the Messiah, the Lord—has been born tonight in Bethlehem![f] 12How will you recognize him? You will find a baby wrapped in a blanket,[g] lying in a manger!"

13Suddenly, the angel was joined by a vast host of others—the armies of heaven—praising God:

14"Glory to God in the highest heaven," they sang,[h] "and peace on earth for all those pleasing him."

15When this great army of angels had returned again to heaven, the shepherds said to each other, "Come on! Let's go to Bethlehem! Let's see this wonderful thing that has happened, which the Lord has told us about."

16They ran to the village and found their way to Mary and Joseph. And there was the baby, lying in the manger. 17The shepherds told everyone what had happened and what the angel had said to them about this child. 18All who heard the shepherds' story expressed astonishment, 19but Mary quietly treasured these things in her heart and often thought about them.

20Then the shepherds went back again to their fields and flocks, praising God for the visit of the angels, and because they had seen the child, just as the angel had told them.

21Eight days later, at the baby's circumcision ceremony, he was named Jesus, the name given him by the angel before he was even conceived.

22When the time came for Mary's purification offering at the Temple, as required by the laws of Moses after the birth of a child, his parents took him to Jerusalem to present him to the Lord; 23for in these laws God had said, "If a woman's first child is a boy, he shall be dedicated to the Lord."

24At that time Jesus' parents also offered their sacrifice for purification—"either a pair of turtledoves or two young pigeons" was the legal requirement. 25That day

New Revised Standard

79 to give light to those who sit in darkness and
        in the shadow of death,
     to guide our feet into the way of peace."

80 The child grew and became strong in spirit, and he was in the wilderness until the day he appeared publicly to Israel.

The Birth of Jesus

2 IN THOSE days a decree went out from Emperor Augustus that all the world should be registered. 2This was the first registration and was taken while Quirinius was governor of Syria. 3All went to their own towns to be registered. 4Joseph also went from the town of Nazareth in Galilee to Judea, to the city of David called Bethlehem, because he was descended from the house and family of David. 5He went to be registered with Mary, to whom he was engaged and who was expecting a child. 6While they were there, the time came for her to deliver her child. 7And she gave birth to her firstborn son and wrapped him in bands of cloth, and laid him in a manger, because there was no place for them in the inn.

The Shepherds and the Angels

8 In that region there were shepherds living in the fields, keeping watch over their flock by night. 9Then an angel of the Lord stood before them, and the glory of the Lord shone around them, and they were terrified. 10But the angel said to them, "Do not be afraid; for see—I am bringing you good news of great joy for all the people: 11to you is born this day in the city of David a Savior, who is the Messiah,[i] the Lord. 12This will be a sign for you: you will find a child wrapped in bands of cloth and lying in a manger." 13And suddenly there was with the angel a multitude of the heavenly host,[j] praising God and saying,

14 "Glory to God in the highest heaven,
        and on earth peace among those whom he
           favors!"[k]

15 When the angels had left them and gone into heaven, the shepherds said to one another, "Let us go now to Bethlehem and see this thing that has taken place, which the Lord has made known to us." 16So they went with haste and found Mary and Joseph, and the child lying in the manger. 17When they saw this, they made known what had been told them about this child; 18and all who heard it were amazed at what the shepherds told them. 19But Mary treasured all these words and pondered them in her heart. 20The shepherds returned, glorifying and praising God for all they had heard and seen, as it had been told them.

Jesus Is Named

21 After eight days had passed, it was time to circumcise the child; and he was called Jesus, the name given by the angel before he was conceived in the womb.

Jesus Is Presented in the Temple

22 When the time came for their purification according to the law of Moses, they brought him up to Jerusalem to present him to the Lord 23(as it is written in the law of the Lord, "Every firstborn male shall be designated as holy to the Lord"), 24and they offered a sacrifice according to what is stated in the law of the Lord, "a pair of turtledoves or two young pigeons."

---

d *1:80 greatly loved God,* "became strong in spirit." e *2:7 in a blanket,* literally, "swaddling clothes." f *2:11 in Bethlehem,* literally, "in the city of David." g *2:12 a blanket,* literally, "swaddling clothes." h *2:14 sang,* literally, "said."

i Or *the Christ* j Gk *army* k Other ancient authorities read *peace, goodwill among people*

King James

25And, behold, there was a man in Jerusalem, whose name *was* Simeon; and the same man *was* just and devout, waiting for the consolation of Israel: and the Holy Ghost was upon him.

26And it was revealed unto him by the Holy Ghost, that he should not see death, before he had seen the Lord's Christ.

27And he came by the Spirit into the temple: and when the parents brought in the child Jesus, to do for him after the custom of the law,

28Then took he him up in his arms, and blessed God, and said,

29Lord, now lettest thou thy servant depart in peace, according to thy word:

30For mine eyes have seen thy salvation,

31Which thou hast prepared before the face of all people;

32A light to lighten the Gentiles, and the glory of thy people Israel.

33And Joseph and his mother marvelled at those things which were spoken of him.

34And Simeon blessed them, and said unto Mary his mother, Behold, this *child* is set for the fall and rising again of many in Israel; and for a sign which shall be spoken against;

35(Yea, a sword shall pierce through thy own soul also,) that the thoughts of many hearts may be revealed.

36And there was one Anna, a prophetess, the daughter of Phanuel, of the tribe of Aser: she was of a great age, and had lived with an husband seven years from her virginity;

37And she *was* a widow of about fourscore and four years, which departed not from the temple, but served God with fastings and prayers night and day.

38And she coming in that instant gave thanks likewise unto the Lord, and spake of him to all them that looked for redemption in Jerusalem.

39And when they had performed all things according to the law of the Lord, they returned into Galilee, to their own city Nazareth.

40And the child grew, and waxed strong in spirit, filled with wisdom: and the grace of God was upon him.

41Now his parents went to Jerusalem every year at the feast of the passover.

42And when he was twelve years old, they went up to Jerusalem after the custom of the feast.

43And when they had fulfilled the days, as they returned, the child Jesus tarried behind in Jerusalem; and Joseph and his mother knew not *of it.*

44But they, supposing him to have been in the company, went a day's journey; and they sought him among *their* kinsfolk and acquaintance.

45And when they found him not, they turned back again to Jerusalem, seeking him.

46And it came to pass, that after three days they found him in the temple, sitting in the midst of the doctors, both hearing them, and asking them questions.

47And all that heard him were astonished at his understanding and answers.

48And when they saw him, they were amazed: and his mother said unto him, Son, why hast thou thus dealt with us? behold, thy father and I have sought thee sorrowing.

49And he said unto them, How is it that ye sought me? wist ye not that I must be about my Father's business?

50And they understood not the saying which he spake unto them.

51And he went down with them, and came to Nazareth, and was subject unto them: but his mother kept all these sayings in her heart.

52And Jesus increased in wisdom and stature, and in favour with God and man.

New International

25Now there was a man in Jerusalem called Simeon, who was righteous and devout. He was waiting for the consolation of Israel, and the Holy Spirit was upon him. 26It had been revealed to him by the Holy Spirit that he would not die before he had seen the Lord's Christ. 27Moved by the Spirit, he went into the temple courts. When the parents brought in the child Jesus to do for him what the custom of the Law required, 28Simeon took him in his arms and praised God, saying:

29"Sovereign Lord, as you have promised,
     you now dismissª your servant in peace.
30For my eyes have seen your salvation,
31   which you have prepared in the sight of all
     people,
32a light for revelation to the Gentiles
     and for glory to your people Israel."

33The child's father and mother marveled at what was said about him. 34Then Simeon blessed them and said to Mary, his mother: "This child is destined to cause the falling and rising of many in Israel, and to be a sign that will be spoken against, 35so that the thoughts of many hearts will be revealed. And a sword will pierce your own soul too."

36There was also a prophetess, Anna, the daughter of Phanuel, of the tribe of Asher. She was very old; she had lived with her husband seven years after her marriage, 37and then was a widow until she was eighty-four.ᵇ She never left the temple but worshiped night and day, fasting and praying. 38Coming up to them at that very moment, she gave thanks to God and spoke about the child to all who were looking forward to the redemption of Jerusalem.

39When Joseph and Mary had done everything required by the Law of the Lord, they returned to Galilee to their own town of Nazareth. 40And the child grew and became strong; he was filled with wisdom, and the grace of God was upon him.

The Boy Jesus at the Temple

41Every year his parents went to Jerusalem for the Feast of the Passover. 42When he was twelve years old, they went up to the Feast, according to the custom. 43After the Feast was over, while his parents were returning home, the boy Jesus stayed behind in Jerusalem, but they were unaware of it. 44Thinking he was in their company, they traveled on for a day. Then they began looking for him among their relatives and friends. 45When they did not find him, they went back to Jerusalem to look for him. 46After three days they found him in the temple courts, sitting among the teachers, listening to them and asking them questions. 47Everyone who heard him was amazed at his understanding and his answers. 48When his parents saw him, they were astonished. His mother said to him, "Son, why have you treated us like this? Your father and I have been anxiously searching for you."

49"Why were you searching for me?" he asked. "Didn't you know I had to be in my Father's house?" 50But they did not understand what he was saying to them.

51Then he went down to Nazareth with them and was obedient to them. But his mother treasured all these things in her heart. 52And Jesus grew in wisdom and stature, and in favor with God and men.

Living Bible

a man named Simeon, a Jerusalem resident, was in the Temple. He was a good man, very devout, filled with the Holy Spirit and constantly expecting the Messiah[c] to come soon. 26For the Holy Spirit had revealed to him that he would not die until he had seen him—God's anointed King. 27The Holy Spirit had impelled him to go to the Temple that day; and so, when Mary and Joseph arrived to present the baby Jesus to the Lord in obedience to the law, 28Simeon was there and took the child in his arms, praising God.

29, 30, 31"Lord," he said, "now I can die content! For I have seen him as you promised me I would. I have seen the Savior you have given to the world. 32He is the Light that will shine upon the nations, and he will be the glory of your people Israel!"

33Joseph and Mary just stood there, marveling at what was being said about Jesus.

34, 35Simeon blessed them but then said to Mary, "A sword shall pierce your soul, for this child shall be rejected by many in Israel, and this to their undoing. But he will be the greatest joy of many others. And the deepest thoughts of many hearts shall be revealed."

36, 37Anna, a prophetess, was also there in the Temple that day. She was the daughter of Phanuel, of the Jewish tribe of Asher, and was very old, for she had been a widow for eighty-four years following seven years of marriage. She never left the Temple but stayed there night and day, worshiping God by praying and often fasting.

38She came along just as Simeon was talking with Mary and Joseph, and she also began thanking God and telling everyone in Jerusalem who had been awaiting the coming of the Savior[d] that the Messiah had finally arrived.

39When Jesus' parents had fulfilled all the requirements of the Law of God they returned home to Nazareth in Galilee. 40There the child became a strong, robust lad, and was known for wisdom beyond his years; and God poured out his blessings on him.

41, 42When Jesus was twelve years old he accompanied his parents to Jerusalem for the annual Passover Festival, which they attended each year. 43After the celebration was over they started home to Nazareth, but Jesus stayed behind in Jerusalem. His parents didn't miss him the first day, 44for they assumed he was with friends among the other travelers. But when he didn't show up that evening, they started to look for him among their relatives and friends; 45and when they couldn't find him, they went back to Jerusalem to search for him there.

46, 47Three days later they finally discovered him. He was in the Temple, sitting among the teachers of Law, discussing deep questions with them and amazing everyone with his understanding and answers.

48His parents didn't know what to think. "Son!" his mother said to him. "Why have you done this to us? Your father and I have been frantic, searching for you everywhere."

49"But why did you need to search?" he asked. "Didn't you realize that I would be here at the Temple, in my Father's House?" 50But they didn't understand what he meant.

51Then he returned to Nazareth with them and was obedient to them; and his mother stored away all these things in her heart. 52So Jesus grew both tall and wise, and was loved by God and man.

New Revised Standard

25 Now there was a man in Jerusalem whose name was Simeon;[e] this man was righteous and devout, looking forward to the consolation of Israel, and the Holy Spirit rested on him. 26It had been revealed to him by the Holy Spirit that he would not see death before he had seen the Lord's Messiah.[f] 27Guided by the Spirit, Simeon[g] came into the temple; and when the parents brought in the child Jesus, to do for him what was customary under the law, 28Simeon[h] took him in his arms and praised God, saying,

29 "Master, now you are dismissing your
        servant[i] in peace,
    according to your word;
30 for my eyes have seen your salvation,
31 which you have prepared in the presence of
        all peoples,
32 a light for revelation to the Gentiles
        and for glory to your people Israel."

33 And the child's father and mother were amazed at what was being said about him. 34Then Simeon[c] blessed them and said to his mother Mary, "This child is destined for the falling and the rising of many in Israel, and to be a sign that will be opposed 35so that the inner thoughts of many will be revealed—and a sword will pierce your own soul too."

36 There was also a prophet, Anna[i] the daughter of Phanuel, of the tribe of Asher. She was of a great age, having lived with her husband seven years after her marriage, 37then as a widow to the age of eighty-four. She never left the temple but worshiped there with fasting and prayer night and day. 38At that moment she came, and began to praise God and to speak about the child[k] to all who were looking for the redemption of Jerusalem.

The Return to Nazareth

39 When they had finished everything required by the law of the Lord, they returned to Galilee, to their own town of Nazareth. 40The child grew and became strong, filled with wisdom; and the favor of God was upon him.

The Boy Jesus in the Temple

41 Now every year his parents went to Jerusalem for the festival of the Passover. 42And when he was twelve years old, they went up as usual for the festival. 43When the festival was ended and they started to return, the boy Jesus stayed behind in Jerusalem, but his parents did not know it. 44Assuming that he was in the group of travelers, they went a day's journey. Then they started to look for him among their relatives and friends. 45When they did not find him, they returned to Jerusalem to search for him. 46After three days they found him in the temple, sitting among the teachers, listening to them and asking them questions. 47And all who heard him were amazed at his understanding and his answers. 48When his parents[l] saw him they were astonished; and his mother said to him, "Child, why have you treated us like this? Look, your father and I have been searching for you in great anxiety." 49He said to them, "Why were you searching for me? Did you not know that I must be in my Father's house?"[m] 50But they did not understand what he said to them. 51Then he went down with them and came to Nazareth, and was obedient to them. His mother treasured all these things in her heart.

52 And Jesus increased in wisdom and in years,[n] and in divine and human favor.

---

c 2:25 the Messiah, literally, "the Consolation of Israel." d 2:38 awaiting the coming of the Savior, literally, "looking for the redemption of Jerusalem."

e Gk Symeon f Or the Lord's Christ g Gk In the Spirit, he h Gk he i Gk slave j Gk Hanna k Gk him l Gk they m Or be about my Father's interests? n Or in stature

King James

3 NOW IN the fifteenth year of the reign of Tiberius Caesar, Pontius Pilate being governor of Judaea, and Herod being tetrarch of Galilee, and his brother Philip tetrarch of Ituraea and of the region of Trachonitis, and Lysanias the tetrarch of Abilene,

2Annas and Caiaphas being the high priests, the word of God came unto John the son of Zacharias in the wilderness.

3And he came into all the country about Jordan, preaching the baptism of repentance for the remission of sins;

4As it is written in the book of the words of Esaias the prophet, saying, The voice of one crying in the wilderness, Prepare ye the way of the Lord, make his paths straight.

5Every valley shall be filled, and every mountain and hill shall be brought low; and the crooked shall be made straight, and the rough ways *shall be* made smooth;

6And all flesh shall see the salvation of God.

7Then said he to the multitude that came forth to be baptized of him, O generation of vipers, who hath warned you to flee from the wrath to come?

8Bring forth therefore fruits worthy of repentance, and begin not to say within yourselves, We have Abraham to *our* father: for I say unto you, That God is able of these stones to raise up children unto Abraham.

9And now also the axe is laid unto the root of the trees: every tree therefore which bringeth not forth good fruit is hewn down, and cast into the fire.

10And the people asked him, saying, What shall we do then?

11He answereth and saith unto them, He that hath two coats, let him impart to him that hath none; and he that hath meat, let him do likewise.

12Then came also publicans to be baptized, and said unto him, Master, what shall we do?

13And he said unto them, Exact no more than that which is appointed you.

14And the soldiers likewise demanded of him, saying, And what shall we do? And he said unto them, Do violence to no man, neither accuse *any* falsely; and be content with your wages.

15And as the people were in expectation, and all men mused in their hearts of John, whether he were the Christ, or not;

16John answered, saying unto *them* all, I indeed baptize you with water; but one mightier than I cometh, the latchet of whose shoes I am not worthy to unloose: he shall baptize you with the Holy Ghost and with fire:

17Whose fan *is* in his hand, and he will thoroughly purge his floor, and will gather the wheat into his garner; but the chaff he will burn with fire unquenchable.

18And many other things in his exhortation preached he unto the people.

19But Herod the tetrarch, being reproved by him for Herodias his brother Philip's wife, and for all the evils which Herod had done,

20Added yet this above all, that he shut up John in prison.

21Now when all the people were baptized, it came to pass, that Jesus also being baptized, and praying, the heaven was opened,

22And the Holy Ghost descended in a bodily shape like a dove upon him, and a voice came from heaven, which said, Thou art my beloved Son; in thee I am well pleased.

23And Jesus himself began to be about thirty years of age, being (as was supposed) the son of Joseph, which was *the son* of Heli,

24Which was *the son* of Matthat, which was *the son* of Levi, which was *the son* of Melchi, which was *the son* of Janna, which was *the son* of Joseph,

New International

John the Baptist Prepares the Way

3 IN THE fifteenth year of the reign of Tiberius Caesar—when Pontius Pilate was governor of Judea, Herod tetrarch of Galilee, his brother Philip tetrarch of Iturea and Traconitis, and Lysanias tetrarch of Abilene— 2during the high priesthood of Annas and Caiaphas, the word of God came to John son of Zechariah in the desert. 3He went into all the country around the Jordan, preaching a baptism of repentance for the forgiveness of sins. 4As is written in the book of the words of Isaiah the prophet:

"A voice of one calling in the desert,
'Prepare the way for the Lord,
    make straight paths for him.
5Every valley shall be filled in,
    every mountain and hill made low.
The crooked roads shall become straight,
    the rough ways smooth.
6And all mankind will see God's salvation.' "a

7John said to the crowds coming out to be baptized by him, "You brood of vipers! Who warned you to flee from the coming wrath? 8Produce fruit in keeping with repentance. And do not begin to say to yourselves, 'We have Abraham as our father.' For I tell you that out of these stones God can raise up children for Abraham. 9The ax is already at the root of the trees, and every tree that does not produce good fruit will be cut down and thrown into the fire."

10"What should we do then?" the crowd asked.

11John answered, "The man with two tunics should share with him who has none, and the one who has food should do the same."

12Tax collectors also came to be baptized. "Teacher," they asked, "what should we do?"

13"Don't collect any more than you are required to," he told them.

14Then some soldiers asked him, "And what should we do?"

He replied, "Don't extort money and don't accuse people falsely—be content with your pay."

15The people were waiting expectantly and were all wondering in their hearts if John might possibly be the Christ.b 16John answered them all, "I baptize you withc water. But one more powerful than I will come, the thongs of whose sandals I am not worthy to untie. He will baptize you with the Holy Spirit and with fire. 17His winnowing fork is in his hand to clear his threshing floor and to gather the wheat into his barn, but he will burn up the chaff with unquenchable fire." 18And with many other words John exhorted the people and preached the good news to them.

19But when John rebuked Herod the tetrarch because of Herodias, his brother's wife, and all the other evil things he had done, 20Herod added this to them all: He locked John up in prison.

The Baptism and Genealogy of Jesus

21When all the people were being baptized, Jesus was baptized too. And as he was praying, heaven was opened 22and the Holy Spirit descended on him in bodily form like a dove. And a voice came from heaven: "You are my Son, whom I love; with you I am well pleased."

23Now Jesus himself was about thirty years old when he began his ministry. He was the son, so it was thought, of Joseph,

the son of Heli, 24the son of Matthat,
    the son of Levi, the son of Melki,
    the son of Jannai, the son of Joseph,

a 6 Isaiah 40:3-5   b 15 Or Messiah   c 16 Or in

Living Bible

3 IN THE fifteenth year of the reign of Emperor Tiberius Caesar, a message came from God to John (the son of Zacharias), as he was living out in the deserts. (Pilate was governor over Judea at that time; Herod, over Galilee; his brother Philip, over Iturea and Trachonitis; Lysanias, over Abilene; and Annas and Caiaphas were High Priests.) ³Then John went from place to place on both sides of the Jordan River, preaching that people should be baptized to show that they had turned to God and away from their sins, in order to be forgiven.ᵈ

⁴In the words of Isaiah the prophet, John was "a voice shouting from the barren wilderness, 'Prepare a road for the Lord to travel on! Widen the pathway before him! ⁵Level the mountains! Fill up the valleys! Straighten the curves! Smooth out the ruts! ⁶And then all mankind shall see the Savior sent from God.' "

⁷Here is a sample of John's preaching to the crowds that came for baptism: "You brood of snakes! You are trying to escape hell without truly turning to God! That is why you want to be baptized? ⁸First go and prove by the way you live that you really have repented. And don't think you are safe because you are descendants of Abraham. That isn't enough. God can produce children of Abraham from these desert stones! ⁹The axe of his judgment is poised over you, ready to sever your roots and cut you down. Yes, every tree that does not produce good fruit will be chopped down and thrown into the fire."

¹⁰The crowd replied, "What do you want us to do?"

¹¹"If you have two coats," he replied, "give one to the poor. If you have extra food, give it away to those who are hungry."

¹²Even tax collectors—notorious for their corruption—came to be baptized and asked, "How shall we prove to you that we have abandoned our sins?"

¹³"By your honesty," he replied. "Make sure you collect no more taxes than the Romanᵉ government requires you to."

¹⁴"And us," asked some soldiers, "what about us?"

John replied, "Don't extort money by threats and violence; don't accuse anyone of what you know he didn't do; and be content with your pay!"

¹⁵Everyone was expecting the Messiah to come soon, and eager to know whether or not John was he. This was the question of the hour, and was being discussed everywhere.

¹⁶John answered the question by saying, "I baptize only with water; but someone is coming soon who has far higher authority than mine; in fact, I am not even worthy of being his slave.ᶠ He will baptize you with fire—with the Holy Spirit. ¹⁷He will separate chaff from grain, and burn up the chaff with eternal fire and store away the grain." ¹⁸He used many such warnings as he announced the Good News to the people.

¹⁹, ²⁰(But after John had publicly criticized Herod, governor of Galilee, for marrying Herodias, his brother's wife, and for many other wrongs he had done, Herod put John in prison, thus adding this sin to all his many others.)

²¹Then one day, after the crowds had been baptized, Jesus himself was baptized; and as he was praying, the heavens opened, ²²and the Holy Spirit in the form of a dove settled upon him, and a voice from heaven said, "You are my much loved Son, yes, my delight."

²³⁻³⁸Jesus was about thirty years old when he began his public ministry.

Jesus was known as the son of Joseph.

New Revised Standard

The Proclamation of John the Baptist

3 IN THE fifteenth year of the reign of Emperor Tiberius, when Pontius Pilate was governor of Judea, and Herod was rulerᵍ of Galilee, and his brother Philip rulerᵍ of the region of Ituraea and Trachonitis, and Lysanias rulerᵍ of Abilene, ²during the high priesthood of Annas and Caiaphas, the word of God came to John son of Zechariah in the wilderness. ³He went into all the region around the Jordan, proclaiming a baptism of repentance for the forgiveness of sins, ⁴as it is written in the book of the words of the prophet Isaiah,

"The voice of one crying out in
    the wilderness:
'Prepare the way of the Lord,
    make his paths straight.
⁵ Every valley shall be filled,
    and every mountain and hill shall be made
    low,
and the crooked shall be made straight,
    and the rough ways made smooth;
⁶ and all flesh shall see the salvation of God.' "

⁷ John said to the crowds that came out to be baptized by him, "You brood of vipers! Who warned you to flee from the wrath to come? ⁸Bear fruits worthy of repentance. Do not begin to say to yourselves, 'We have Abraham as our ancestor'; for I tell you, God is able from these stones to raise up children to Abraham. ⁹Even now the ax is lying at the root of the trees; every tree therefore that does not bear good fruit is cut down and thrown into the fire."

10 And the crowds asked him, "What then should we do?" ¹¹In reply he said to them, "Whoever has two coats must share with anyone who has none; and whoever has food must do likewise." ¹²Even tax collectors came to be baptized, and they asked him, "Teacher, what should we do?" ¹³He said to them, "Collect no more than the amount prescribed for you." ¹⁴Soldiers also asked him, "And we, what should we do?" He said to them, "Do not extort money from anyone by threats or false accusation, and be satisfied with your wages."

15 As the people were filled with expectation, and all were questioning in their hearts concerning John, whether he might be the Messiah,ʰ ¹⁶John answered all of them by saying, "I baptize you with water; but one who is more powerful than I is coming; I am not worthy to untie the thong of his sandals. He will baptize you withⁱ the Holy Spirit and fire. ¹⁷His winnowing fork is in his hand, to clear his threshing floor and to gather the wheat into his granary; but the chaff he will burn with unquenchable fire."

18 So, with many other exhortations, he proclaimed the good news to the people. ¹⁹But Herod the ruler,ᵍ who had been rebuked by him because of Herodias, his brother's wife, and because of all the evil things that Herod had done, ²⁰added to them all by shutting up John in prison.

The Baptism of Jesus

21 Now when all the people were baptized, and when Jesus also had been baptized and was praying, the heaven was opened, ²²and the Holy Spirit descended upon him in bodily form like a dove. And a voice came from heaven, "You are my Son, the Beloved;ʲ with you I am well pleased."ᵏ

The Ancestors of Jesus

23 Jesus was about thirty years old when he began his work. He was the son (as was thought) of Joseph son of Heli, ²⁴son of Matthat, son of Levi, son of Melchi, son of Jannai, son of Joseph, ²⁵son of Mattathias, son

---

ᵈ 3:3 preaching that people should be baptized to show that they had turned to God and away from their sins, in order to be forgiven, or, "preaching the baptism of repentance for remission of sins."   ᵉ 3:13 Roman, implied.   ᶠ 3:16 of being his slave, literally, "of loosing [the sandal strap] of his shoe."

ᵍ Gk tetrarch   ʰ Or the Christ   ⁱ Or in   ʲ Or my beloved Son   ᵏ Other ancient authorities read You are my Son, today I have begotten you

King James

25Which was *the son* of Mattathias, which was *the son* of Amos, which was *the son* of Naum, which was *the son* of Esli, which was *the son* of Nagge,

26Which was *the son* of Maath, which was *the son* of Mattathias, which was *the son* of Semei, which was *the son* of Joseph, which was *the son* of Judah,

27Which was *the son* of Joanna, which was *the son* of Rhesa, which was *the son* of Zorobabel, which was *the son* of Salathiel, which was *the son* of Neri,

28Which was *the son* of Melchi, which was *the son* of Addi, which was *the son* of Cosam, which was *the son* of Elmodam, which was *the son* of Er,

29Which was *the son* of Jose, which was *the son* of Eliezer, which was *the son* of Jorim, which was *the son* of Matthat, which was *the son* of Levi,

30Which was *the son* of Simeon, which was *the son* of Judah, which was *the son* of Joseph, which was *the son* of Jonan, which was *the son* of Eliakim,

31Which was *the son* of Melea, which was *the son* of Menan, which was *the son* of Mattatha, which was *the son* of Nathan, which was *the son* of David,

32Which was *the son* of Jesse, which was *the son* of Obed, which was *the son* of Booz, which was *the son* of Salmon, which was *the son* of Naasson,

33Which was *the son* of Aminadab, which was *the son* of Aram, which was *the son* of Esrom, which was *the son* of Phares, which was *the son* of Judah,

34Which was *the son* of Jacob, which was *the son* of Isaac, which was *the son* of Abraham, which was *the son* of Thara, which was *the son* of Nachor,

35Which was *the son* of Saruch, which was *the son* of Ragau, which was *the son* of Phalec, which was *the son* of Heber, which was *the son* of Sala,

36Which was *the son* of Cainan, which was *the son* of Arphaxad, which was *the son* of Sem, which was *the son* of Noe, which was *the son* of Lamech,

37Which was *the son* of Mathusala, which was *the son* of Enoch, which was *the son* of Jared, which was *the son* of Maleleel, which was *the son* of Cainan,

New International

25the son of Mattathias, the son of Amos,
   the son of Nahum, the son of Esli,
   the son of Naggai, 26the son of Maath,
   the son of Mattathias, the son of Semein,
   the son of Josech, the son of Joda,
27the son of Joanan, the son of Rhesa,
   the son of Zerubbabel, the son of Shealtiel,
   the son of Neri, 28the son of Melki,
   the son of Addi, the son of Cosam,
   the son of Elmadam, the son of Er,
29the son of Joshua, the son of Eliezer,
   the son of Jorim, the son of Matthat,
   the son of Levi, 30the son of Simeon,
   the son of Judah, the son of Joseph,
   the son of Jonam, the son of Eliakim,
31the son of Melea, the son of Menna,
   the son of Mattatha, the son of Nathan,
   the son of David, 32the son of Jesse,
   the son of Obed, the son of Boaz,
   the son of Salmon,[a] the son of Nahshon,
33the son of Amminadab, the son of Ram,[b]
   the son of Hezron, the son of Perez,
   the son of Judah, 34the son of Jacob,
   the son of Isaac, the son of Abraham,
   the son of Terah, the son of Nahor,
35the son of Serug, the son of Reu,
   the son of Peleg, the son of Eber,
   the son of Shelah, 36the son of Cainan,
   the son of Arphaxad, the son of Shem,
   the son of Noah, the son of Lamech,
37the son of Methuselah, the son of Enoch,

Living Bible

Joseph's father was Heli;
Heli's father was Matthat;
Matthat's father was Levi;
Levi's father was Melchi;
Melchi's father was Jannai;
Jannai's father was Joseph;
Joseph's father was Mattathias;
Mattathias' father was Amos;
Amos' father was Nahum;
Nahum's father was Esli;
Esli's father was Naggai;
Naggai's father was Maath;
Maath's father was Mattathias;
Mattathias' father was Semein;
Semein's father was Josech;
Josech's father was Joda;
Joda's father was Joanan;
Joanan's father was Rhesa;
Rhesa's father was Zerubbabel;
Zerubbabel's father was Shealtiel;
Shealtiel's father was Neri;
Neri's father was Melchi;
Melchi's father was Addi;
Addi's father was Cosam;
Cosam's father was Elmadam;
Elmadam's father was Er;
Er's father was Joshua;
Joshua's father was Eliezer;
Eliezer's father was Jorim;
Jorim's father was Matthat;
Matthat's father was Levi;
Levi's father was Simeon;
Simeon's father was Judah;
Judah's father was Joseph;
Joseph's father was Jonam;
Jonam's father was Eliakim;
Eliakim's father was Melea;
Melea's father was Menna;
Menna's father was Mattatha;
Mattatha's father was Nathan;
Nathan's father was David;
David's father was Jesse;
Jesse's father was Obed;
Obed's father was Boaz;
Boaz' father was Salmon;
Salmon's father was Nahshon;
Nahshon's father was Amminadab;
Amminadab's father was Admin;
Admin's father was Arni;
Arni's father was Hezron;
Hezron's father was Perez;
Perez' father was Judah;
Judah's father was Jacob;
Jacob's father was Isaac;
Isaac's father was Abraham;
Abraham's father was Terah;
Terah's father was Nahor;
Nahor's father was Serug;
Serug's father was Reu;
Reu's father was Peleg;
Peleg's father was Eber;
Eber's father was Shelah;
Shelah's father was Cainan;
Cainan's father was Arphaxad;
Arphaxad's father was Shem;
Shem's father was Noah;
Noah's father was Lamech;
Lamech's father was Methuselah;
Methuselah's father was Enoch;

New Revised Standard

of Amos, son of Nahum, son of Esli, son of Naggai, 26 son of Maath, son of Mattathias, son of Semein, son of Josech, son of Joda, 27 son of Joanan, son of Rhesa, son of Zerubbabel, son of Shealtiel,c son of Neri, 28 son of Melchi, son of Addi, son of Cosam, son of Elmadam, son of Er, 29 son of Joshua, son of Eliezer, son of Jorim, son of Matthat, son of Levi, 30 son of Simeon, son of Judah, son of Joseph, son of Jonam, son of Eliakim, 31 son of Melea, son of Menna, son of Mattatha, son of Nathan, son of David, 32 son of Jesse, son of Obed, son of Boaz, son of Sala,d son of Nahshon, 33 son of Amminadab, son of Admin, son of Arni,e son of Hezron, son of Perez, son of Judah, 34 son of Jacob, son of Isaac, son of Abraham, son of Terah, son of Nahor, 35 son of Serug, son of Reu, son of Peleg, son of Eber, son of Shelah, 36 son of Cainan, son of Arphaxad, son of Shem, son of Noah, son of Lamech, 37 son of Methuselah, son

c Gk Salathiel   d Other ancient authorities read Salmon   e Other ancient authorities read Amminadab, son of Aram; others vary widely

King James

38Which was *the son* of Enos, which was *the son* of Seth, which was *the son* of Adam, which was *the son* of God.

4 AND JESUS being full of the Holy Ghost returned from Jordan, and was led by the Spirit into the wilderness,

2Being forty days tempted of the devil. And in those days he did eat nothing: and when they were ended, he afterward hungered.

3And the devil said unto him, If thou be the Son of God, command this stone that it be made bread.

4And Jesus answered him, saying, It is written, That man shall not live by bread alone, but by every word of God.

5And the devil, taking him up into an high mountain, showed unto him all the kingdoms of the world in a moment of time.

6And the devil said unto him, All this power will I give thee, and the glory of them: for that is delivered unto me; and to whomsoever I will I give it.

7If thou therefore wilt worship me, all shall be thine.

8And Jesus answered and said unto him, Get thee behind me, Satan: for it is written, Thou shalt worship the Lord thy God, and him only shalt thou serve.

9And he brought him to Jerusalem, and set him on a pinnacle of the temple, and said unto him, If thou be the Son of God, cast thyself down from hence:

10For it is written, He shall give his angels charge over thee, to keep thee:

11And in *their* hands they shall bear thee up, lest at any time thou dash thy foot against a stone.

12And Jesus answering said unto him, It is said, Thou shalt not tempt the Lord thy God.

13And when the devil had ended all the temptation, he departed from him for a season.

14¶ And Jesus returned in the power of the Spirit into Galilee: and there went out a fame of him through all the region round about.

15And he taught in their synagogues, being glorified of all.

16¶ And he came to Nazareth, where he had been brought up: and, as his custom was, he went into the synagogue on the sabbath day, and stood up for to read.

17And there was delivered unto him the book of the prophet Esaias. And when he had opened the book, he found the place where it was written,

18The Spirit of the Lord *is* upon me, because he hath anointed me to preach the gospel to the poor; he hath sent me to heal the brokenhearted, to preach deliverance to the captives, and recovering of sight to the blind, to set at liberty them that are bruised,

19To preach the acceptable year of the Lord.

New International

the son of Jared, the son of Mahalalel,
the son of Kenan, 38the son of Enosh,
the son of Seth, the son of Adam,
the son of God.

The Temptation of Jesus

4 JESUS, FULL of the Holy Spirit, returned from the Jordan and was led by the Spirit in the desert, 2where for forty days he was tempted by the devil. He ate nothing during those days, and at the end of them he was hungry.

3The devil said to him, "If you are the Son of God, tell this stone to become bread."

4Jesus answered, "It is written: 'Man does not live on bread alone.'a"

5The devil led him up to a high place and showed him in an instant all the kingdoms of the world. 6And he said to him, "I will give you all their authority and splendor, for it has been given to me, and I can give it to anyone I want to. 7So if you worship me, it will all be yours."

8Jesus answered, "It is written: 'Worship the Lord your God and serve him only.'b"

9The devil led him to Jerusalem and had him stand on the highest point of the temple. "If you are the Son of God," he said, "throw yourself down from here. 10For it is written:

" 'He will command his angels concerning you
    to guard you carefully;
11they will lift you up in their hands,
    so that you will not strike your foot against a stone.'c"

12Jesus answered, "It says: 'Do not put the Lord your God to the test.'d"

13When the devil had finished all this tempting, he left him until an opportune time.

Jesus Rejected at Nazareth

14Jesus returned to Galilee in the power of the Spirit, and news about him spread through the whole country-side. 15He taught in their synagogues, and everyone praised him.

16He went to Nazareth, where he had been brought up, and on the Sabbath day he went into the synagogue, as was his custom. And he stood up to read. 17The scroll of the prophet Isaiah was handed to him. Unrolling it, he found the place where it is written:

18"The Spirit of the Lord is on me,
    because he has anointed me
    to preach good news to the poor.
He has sent me to proclaim freedom for the
        prisoners
    and recovery of sight for the blind,
to release the oppressed,
19   to proclaim the year of the Lord's favor."e

---

a *4* Deut. 8:3   b *8* Deut. 6:13   c *11* Psalm 91:11,12   d *12* Deut. 6:16
e *19* Isaiah 61:1,2

Living Bible

Enoch's father was Jared;
Jared's father was Mahalaleel;
Mahalaleel's father was Cainan;
Cainan's father was Enos;
Enos' father was Seth;
Seth's father was Adam;
Adam's father was God.

4 THEN JESUS, full of the Holy Spirit, left the Jordan River, being urged by the Spirit out into the barren wastelands of Judea, where Satan tempted him for forty days. He ate nothing all that time, and was very hungry.

3Satan said, "If you are God's Son, tell this stone to become a loaf of bread."

4But Jesus replied, "It is written in the Scriptures, 'Other things in life are much more important than bread!' "f

5Then Satan took him up and revealed to him all the kingdoms of the world in a moment of time; 6, 7and the devil told him, "I will give you all these splendid kingdoms and their glory—for they are mine to give to anyone I wish—if you will only get down on your knees and worship me."

8Jesus replied, "We must worship God, and him alone. So it is written in the Scriptures."

9, 10, 11Then Satan took him to Jerusalem to a high roof of the Temple and said, "If you are the Son of God, jump off! For the Scriptures say that God will send his angels to guard you and to keep you from crashing to the pavement below!"

12Jesus replied, "The Scriptures also say, 'Do not put the Lord your God to a foolish test.' "

13When the devil had ended all the temptations, he left Jesus for a while and went away.

14Then Jesus returned to Galilee, full of the Holy Spirit's power. Soon he became well known throughout all that region 15for his sermons in the synagogues; everyone praised him.

16When he came to the village of Nazareth, his boyhood home, he went as usual to the synagogue on Saturday, and stood up to read the Scriptures. 17The book of Isaiah the prophet was handed to him, and he opened it to the place where it says:

18, 19"The Spirit of the Lord is upon me; he has appointed me to preach Good News to the poor; he has sent me to heal the brokenhearted and to announce that captives shall be released and the blind shall see, that the downtrodden shall be freed from their oppressors, and that God is ready to give blessings to all who come to him."g

New Revised Standard

of Enoch, son of Jared, son of Mahalaleel, son of Cainan, 38son of Enos, son of Seth, son of Adam, son of God.

The Temptation of Jesus

4 JESUS, FULL of the Holy Spirit, returned from the Jordan and was led by the Spirit in the wilderness, 2where for forty days he was tempted by the devil. He ate nothing at all during those days, and when they were over, he was famished. 3The devil said to him, "If you are the Son of God, command this stone to become a loaf of bread." 4Jesus answered him, "It is written, 'One does not live by bread alone.' "

5 Then the devilh led him up and showed him in an instant all the kingdoms of the world. 6And the devilh said to him, "To you I will give their glory and all this authority; for it has been given over to me, and I give it to anyone I please. 7If you, then, will worship me, it will all be yours." 8Jesus answered him, "It is written,

'Worship the Lord your God,
    and serve only him.' "

9 Then the devilh took him to Jerusalem, and placed him on the pinnacle of the temple, saying to him, "If you are the Son of God, throw yourself down from here, 10for it is written,

'He will command his angels concerning you,
    to protect you,'

11and

'On their hands they will bear you up,
    so that you will not dash your foot against a
        stone.' "

12Jesus answered him, "It is said, 'Do not put the Lord your God to the test.' " 13When the devil had finished every test, he departed from him until an opportune time.

The Beginning of the Galilean Ministry

14 Then Jesus, filled with the power of the Spirit, returned to Galilee, and a report about him spread through all the surrounding country. 15He began to teach in their synagogues and was praised by everyone.

The Rejection of Jesus at Nazareth

16 When he came to Nazareth, where he had been brought up, he went to the synagogue on the sabbath day, as was his custom. He stood up to read, 17and the scroll of the prophet Isaiah was given to him. He unrolled the scroll and found the place where it was written:

18 "The Spirit of the Lord is upon me,
        because he has anointed me
            to bring good news to the poor.
    He has sent me to proclaim release to the
            captives
        and recovery of sight to the blind,
            to let the oppressed go free,
19   to proclaim the year of the Lord's favor."

---

f 4:4 *Other things in life are much more important than bread,* literally, "Man shall not live by bread alone," cf Deut 8:3. g 4:18, 19 *to give blessings to all who come to him,* literally, "to proclaim the acceptable year of the Lord."

h Gk *he*

King James

20And he closed the book, and he gave *it* again to the minister, and sat down. And the eyes of all them that were in the synagogue were fastened on him.

21And he began to say unto them, This day is this scripture fulfilled in your ears.

22And all bare him witness, and wondered at the gracious words which proceeded out of his mouth. And they said, Is not this Joseph's son?

23And he said unto them, Ye will surely say unto me this proverb, Physician, heal thyself: whatsoever we have heard done in Capernaum, do also here in thy country.

24And he said, Verily I say unto you, No prophet is accepted in his own country.

25But I tell you of a truth, many widows were in Israel in the days of Elias, when the heaven was shut up three years and six months, when great famine was throughout all the land;

26But unto none of them was Elias sent, save unto Sarepta, *a city* of Sidon, unto a woman *that was* a widow.

27And many lepers were in Israel in the time of Eliseus the prophet; and none of them was cleansed, saving Naaman the Syrian.

28And all they in the synagogue, when they heard these things, were filled with wrath,

29And rose up, and thrust him out of the city, and led him unto the brow of the hill whereon their city was built, that they might cast him down headlong.

30But he passing through the midst of them went his way,

31And came down to Capernaum, a city of Galilee, and taught them on the sabbath days.

32And they were astonished at his doctrine: for his word was with power.

33¶ And in the synagogue there was a man, which had a spirit of an unclean devil, and cried out with a loud voice,

34Saying, Let *us* alone; what have we to do with thee, *thou* Jesus of Nazareth? art thou come to destroy us? I know thee who thou art; the Holy One of God.

35And Jesus rebuked him, saying, Hold thy peace, and come out of him. And when the devil had thrown him in the midst, he came out of him, and hurt him not.

36And they were all amazed, and spake among themselves, saying, What a word *is* this! for with authority and power he commandeth the unclean spirits, and they come out.

37And the fame of him went out into every place of the country round about.

38¶ And he arose out of the synagogue, and entered into Simon's house. And Simon's wife's mother was taken with a great fever; and they besought him for her.

39And he stood over her, and rebuked the fever; and it left her: and immediately she arose and ministered unto them.

40¶ Now when the sun was setting, all they that had any sick with divers diseases brought them unto him; and he laid his hands on every one of them, and healed them.

41And devils also came out of many, crying out, and saying, Thou art Christ the Son of God. And he rebuking *them* suffered them not to speak: for they knew that he was Christ.

42And when it was day, he departed and went into a desert place: and the people sought him, and came unto him, and stayed him, that he should not depart from them.

43And he said unto them, I must preach the kingdom of God to other cities also: for therefore am I sent.

44And he preached in the synagogues of Galilee.

New International

20Then he rolled up the scroll, gave it back to the attendant and sat down. The eyes of everyone in the synagogue were fastened on him, 21and he began by saying to them, "Today this scripture is fulfilled in your hearing."

22All spoke well of him and were amazed at the gracious words that came from his lips. "Isn't this Joseph's son?" they asked.

23Jesus said to them, "Surely you will quote this proverb to me: 'Physician, heal yourself! Do here in your hometown what we have heard that you did in Capernaum.' "

24"I tell you the truth," he continued, "no prophet is accepted in his hometown. 25I assure you that there were many widows in Israel in Elijah's time, when the sky was shut for three and a half years and there was a severe famine throughout the land. 26Yet Elijah was not sent to any of them, but to a widow in Zarephath in the region of Sidon. 27And there were many in Israel with leprosy[a] in the time of Elisha the prophet, yet not one of them was cleansed—only Naaman the Syrian."

28All the people in the synagogue were furious when they heard this. 29They got up, drove him out of the town, and took him to the brow of the hill on which the town was built, in order to throw him down the cliff. 30But he walked right through the crowd and went on his way.

Jesus Drives Out an Evil Spirit

31Then he went down to Capernaum, a town in Galilee, and on the Sabbath began to teach the people. 32They were amazed at his teaching, because his message had authority.

33In the synagogue there was a man possessed by a demon, an evil[b] spirit. He cried out at the top of his voice, 34"Ha! What do you want with us, Jesus of Nazareth? Have you come to destroy us? I know who you are—the Holy One of God!"

35"Be quiet!" Jesus said sternly. "Come out of him!" Then the demon threw the man down before them all and came out without injuring him.

36All the people were amazed and said to each other, "What is this teaching? With authority and power he gives orders to evil spirits and they come out!" 37And the news about him spread throughout the surrounding area.

Jesus Heals Many

38Jesus left the synagogue and went to the home of Simon. Now Simon's mother-in-law was suffering from a high fever, and they asked Jesus to help her. 39So he bent over her and rebuked the fever, and it left her. She got up at once and began to wait on them.

40When the sun was setting, the people brought to Jesus all who had various kinds of sickness, and laying his hands on each one, he healed them. 41Moreover, demons came out of many people, shouting, "You are the Son of God!" But he rebuked them and would not allow them to speak, because they knew he was the Christ.[c]

42At daybreak Jesus went out to a solitary place. The people were looking for him and when they came to where he was, they tried to keep him from leaving them. 43But he said, "I must preach the good news of the kingdom of God to the other towns also, because that is why I was sent." 44And he kept on preaching in the synagogues of Judea.[d]

---

[a] 27 The Greek word was used for various diseases affecting the skin—not necessarily leprosy. [b] 33 Greek *unclean*; also in verse 36 [c] 41 Or *Messiah* [d] 44 Or *the land of the Jews*; some manuscripts *Galilee*

Living Bible

20He closed the book and handed it back to the attendant and sat down, while everyone in the synagogue gazed at him intently. 21Then he added, "These Scriptures came true today!"

22All who were there spoke well of him and were amazed by the beautiful words that fell from his lips. "How can this be?" they asked. "Isn't this Joseph's son?"

23Then he said, "Probably you will quote me that proverb, 'Physician, heal yourself'—meaning, 'Why don't you do miracles here in your home town like those you did in Capernaum?' 24But I solemnly declare to you that no prophet is accepted in his own home town! 25, 26For example, remember how Elijah the prophet used a miracle to help the widow of Zarephath—a foreigner from the land of Sidon. There were many Jewish widows needing help in those days of famine, for there had been no rain for three and one-half years, and hunger stalked the land; yet Elijah was not sent to them. 27Or think of the prophet Elisha, who healed Naaman, a Syrian, rather than the many Jewish lepers needing help."

28These remarks stung them to fury; 29and jumping up, they mobbed him and took him to the edge of the hill on which the city was built, to push him over the cliff. 30But he walked away through the crowd and left them.

31Then he returned to Capernaum, a city in Galilee, and preached there in the synagogue every Saturday. 32Here, too, the people were amazed at the things he said. For he spoke as one who knew the truth, instead of merely quoting the opinions of others as his authority.

33Once as he was teaching in the synagogue, a man possessed by a demon began shouting at Jesus, 34"Go away! We want nothing to do with you, Jesus from Nazareth. You have come to destroy us. I know who you are—the Holy Son of God."

35Jesus cut him short. "Be silent!" he told the demon. "Come out!" The demon threw the man to the floor as the crowd watched, and then left him without hurting him further.

36Amazed, the people asked, "What is in this man's words that even demons obey him?" 37The story of what he had done spread like wildfire throughout the whole region.

38After leaving the synagogue that day, he went to Simon's home where he found Simon's mother-in-law very sick with a high fever. "Please heal her," everyone begged.

39Standing at her bedside he spoke to the fever, rebuking it, and immediately her temperature returned to normal and she got up and prepared a meal for them!e

40As the sun went down that evening, all the villagers who had any sick people in their homes, no matter what their diseases were, brought them to Jesus; and the touch of his hands healed every one! 41Some were possessed by demons; and the demons came out at his command, shouting, "You are the Son of God." But because they knew he was the Christ, he stopped them and told them to be silent.

42Early the next morning he went out into the desert. The crowds searched everywhere for him and when they finally found him they begged him not to leave them, but to stay at Capernaum. 43But he replied, "I must preach the Good News of the Kingdom of God in other places too, for that is why I was sent." 44So he continued to travel around preaching in synagogues throughout Judea.

New Revised Standard

20And he rolled up the scroll, gave it back to the attendant, and sat down. The eyes of all in the synagogue were fixed on him. 21Then he began to say to them, "Today this scripture has been fulfilled in your hearing." 22All spoke well of him and were amazed at the gracious words that came from his mouth. They said, "Is not this Joseph's son?" 23He said to them, "Doubtless you will quote to me this proverb, 'Doctor, cure yourself!' And you will say, 'Do here also in your hometown the things that we have heard you did at Capernaum.' " 24And he said, "Truly I tell you, no prophet is accepted in the prophet's hometown. 25But the truth is, there were many widows in Israel in the time of Elijah, when the heaven was shut up three years and six months, and there was a severe famine over all the land; 26yet Elijah was sent to none of them except to a widow at Zarephath in Sidon. 27There were also many lepersf in Israel in the time of the prophet Elisha, and none of them was cleansed except Naaman the Syrian." 28When they heard this, all in the synagogue were filled with rage. 29They got up, drove him out of the town, and led him to the brow of the hill on which their town was built, so that they might hurl him off the cliff. 30But he passed through the midst of them and went on his way.

The Man with an Unclean Spirit

31 He went down to Capernaum, a city in Galilee, and was teaching them on the sabbath. 32They were astounded at his teaching, because he spoke with authority. 33In the synagogue there was a man who had the spirit of an unclean demon, and he cried out with a loud voice, 34"Let us alone! What have you to do with us, Jesus of Nazareth? Have you come to destroy us? I know who you are, the Holy One of God." 35But Jesus rebuked him, saying, "Be silent, and come out of him!" When the demon had thrown him down before them, he came out of him without having done him any harm. 36They were all amazed and kept saying to one another, "What kind of utterance is this? For with authority and power he commands the unclean spirits, and out they come!" 37And a report about him began to reach every place in the region.

Healings at Simon's House

38 After leaving the synagogue he entered Simon's house. Now Simon's mother-in-law was suffering from a high fever, and they asked him about her. 39Then he stood over her and rebuked the fever, and it left her. Immediately she got up and began to serve them.

40 As the sun was setting, all those who had any who were sick with various kinds of diseases brought them to him; and he laid his hands on each of them and cured them. 41Demons also came out of many, shouting, "You are the Son of God!" But he rebuked them and would not allow them to speak, because they knew that he was the Messiah.g

Jesus Preaches in the Synagogues

42 At daybreak he departed and went into a deserted place. And the crowds were looking for him; and when they reached him, they wanted to prevent him from leaving them. 43But he said to them, "I must proclaim the good news of the kingdom of God to the other cities also; for I was sent for this purpose." 44So he continued proclaiming the message in the synagogues of Judea.h

---

e 4:39 prepared a meal for them, literally, "ministered unto them."

f The terms leper and leprosy can refer to several diseases   g Or the Christ
h Other ancient authorities read Galilee

King James

5 AND IT came to pass, that, as the people pressed upon him to hear the word of God, he stood by the lake of Gennesaret,

2And saw two ships standing by the lake: but the fishermen were gone out of them, and were washing *their* nets.

3And he entered into one of the ships, which was Simon's, and prayed him that he would thrust out a little from the land. And he sat down, and taught the people out of the ship.

4Now when he had left speaking, he said unto Simon, Launch out into the deep, and let down your nets for a draught.

5And Simon answering said unto him, Master, we have toiled all the night, and have taken nothing: nevertheless at thy word I will let down the net.

6And when they had this done, they inclosed a great multitude of fishes: and their net brake.

7And they beckoned unto *their* partners, which were in the other ship, that they should come and help them. And they came, and filled both the ships, so that they began to sink.

8When Simon Peter saw *it,* he fell down at Jesus' knees, saying, Depart from me; for I am a sinful man, O Lord.

9For he was astonished, and all that were with him, at the draught of the fishes which they had taken:

10And so *was* also James, and John, the sons of Zebedee, which were partners with Simon. And Jesus said unto Simon, Fear not; from henceforth thou shalt catch men.

11And when they had brought their ships to land, they forsook all, and followed him.

12¶ And it came to pass, when he was in a certain city, behold a man full of leprosy: who seeing Jesus fell on *his* face, and besought him, saying, Lord, if thou wilt, thou canst make me clean.

13And he put forth *his* hand, and touched him, saying, I will: be thou clean. And immediately the leprosy departed from him.

14And he charged him to tell no man: but go, and show thyself to the priest, and offer for thy cleansing, according as Moses commanded, for a testimony unto them.

15But so much the more went there a fame abroad of him: and great multitudes came together to hear, and to be healed by him of their infirmities.

16¶ And he withdrew himself into the wilderness, and prayed.

17And it came to pass on a certain day, as he was teaching, that there were Pharisees and doctors of the law sitting by, which were come out of every town of Galilee, and Judaea, and Jerusalem: and the power of the Lord was *present* to heal them.

18¶ And, behold, men brought in a bed a man which was taken with a palsy: and they sought *means* to bring him in, and to lay *him* before him.

19And when they could not find by what *way* they might bring him in because of the multitude, they went upon the housetop, and let him down through the tiling with *his* couch into the midst before Jesus.

20And when he saw their faith, he said unto him, Man, thy sins are forgiven thee.

21And the scribes and the Pharisees began to reason, saying, Who is this which speaketh blasphemies? Who can forgive sins, but God alone?

22But when Jesus perceived their thoughts, he answering said unto them, What reason ye in your hearts?

23Whether is easier, to say, Thy sins be forgiven thee; or to say, Rise up and walk?

New International

The Calling of the First Disciples

5 ONE DAY as Jesus was standing by the Lake of Gennesaret,[a] with the people crowding around him and listening to the word of God, 2he saw at the water's edge two boats, left there by the fishermen, who were washing their nets. 3He got into one of the boats, the one belonging to Simon, and asked him to put out a little from shore. Then he sat down and taught the people from the boat.

4When he had finished speaking, he said to Simon, "Put out into deep water, and let down[b] the nets for a catch."

5Simon answered, "Master, we've worked hard all night and haven't caught anything. But because you say so, I will let down the nets."

6When they had done so, they caught such a large number of fish that their nets began to break. 7So they signaled their partners in the other boat to come and help them, and they came and filled both boats so full that they began to sink.

8When Simon Peter saw this, he fell at Jesus' knees and said, "Go away from me, Lord; I am a sinful man!" 9For he and all his companions were astonished at the catch of fish they had taken, 10and so were James and John, the sons of Zebedee, Simon's partners.

Then Jesus said to Simon, "Don't be afraid; from now on you will catch men." 11So they pulled their boats up on shore, left everything and followed him.

The Man With Leprosy

12While Jesus was in one of the towns, a man came along who was covered with leprosy.[c] When he saw Jesus, he fell with his face to the ground and begged him, "Lord, if you are willing, you can make me clean."

13Jesus reached out his hand and touched the man. "I am willing," he said. "Be clean!" And immediately the leprosy left him.

14Then Jesus ordered him, "Don't tell anyone, but go, show yourself to the priest and offer the sacrifices that Moses commanded for your cleansing, as a testimony to them."

15Yet the news about him spread all the more, so that crowds of people came to hear him and to be healed of their sicknesses. 16But Jesus often withdrew to lonely places and prayed.

Jesus Heals a Paralytic

17One day as he was teaching, Pharisees and teachers of the law, who had come from every village of Galilee and from Judea and Jerusalem, were sitting there. And the power of the Lord was present for him to heal the sick. 18Some men came carrying a paralytic on a mat and tried to take him into the house to lay him before Jesus. 19When they could not find a way to do this because of the crowd, they went up on the roof and lowered him on his mat through the tiles into the middle of the crowd, right in front of Jesus.

20When Jesus saw their faith, he said, "Friend, your sins are forgiven."

21The Pharisees and the teachers of the law began thinking to themselves, "Who is this fellow who speaks blasphemy? Who can forgive sins but God alone?"

22Jesus knew what they were thinking and asked, "Why are you thinking these things in your hearts? 23Which is easier: to say, 'Your sins are forgiven,' or to say, 'Get up and walk'? 24But that you may know that

---

[a] *1* That is, Sea of Galilee　　[b] *4* The Greek verb is plural.　　[c] *12* The Greek word was used for various diseases affecting the skin—not necessarily leprosy.

Living Bible

5 ONE DAY as he was preaching on the shore of Lake Gennesaret, great crowds pressed in on him to listen to the Word of God. 2He noticed two empty boats standing at the water's edge while the fishermen washed their nets. 3Stepping into one of the boats, Jesus asked Simon, its owner, to push out a little into the water, so that he could sit in the boat and speak to the crowds from there.

4When he had finished speaking, he said to Simon, "Now go out where it is deeper and let down your nets and you will catch a lot of fish!"

5"Sir," Simon replied, "we worked hard all last night and didn't catch a thing. But if you say so, we'll try again."

6And this time their nets were so full that they began to tear! 7A shout for help brought their partners in the other boat and soon both boats were filled with fish and on the verge of sinking.

8When Simon Peter realized what had happened, he fell to his knees before Jesus and said, "Oh, sir, please leave us—I'm too much of a sinner for you to have around." 9For he was awestruck by the size of their catch, as were the others with him, 10and his partners too—James and John, the sons of Zebedee. Jesus replied, "Don't be afraid! From now on you'll be fishing for the souls of men!"

11And as soon as they landed, they left everything and went with him.

12One day in a certain village he was visiting, there was a man with an advanced case of leprosy. When he saw Jesus he fell to the ground before him, face downward in the dust, begging to be healed.

"Sir," he said, "if you only will, you can clear me of every trace of my disease."

13Jesus reached out and touched the man and said, "Of course I will. Be healed." And the leprosy left him instantly! 14Then Jesus instructed him to go at once without telling anyone what had happened and be examined by the Jewish priest. "Offer the sacrifice Moses' law requires for lepers who are healed," he said. "This will prove to everyone that you are well." 15Now the report of his power spread even faster and vast crowds came to hear him preach and to be healed of their diseases. 16But he often withdrew to the wilderness for prayer.

17One day while he was teaching, some Jewish religious leaders[d] and teachers of the Law were sitting nearby. (It seemed that these men showed up from every village in all Galilee and Judea, as well as from Jerusalem.) And the Lord's healing power was upon him.

18, 19Then—look! Some men came carrying a paralyzed man on a sleeping mat. They tried to push through the crowd to Jesus but couldn't reach him. So they went up on the roof above him, took off some tiles and lowered the sick man down into the crowd, still on his sleeping mat, right in front of Jesus.

20Seeing their faith, Jesus said to the man, "My friend, your sins are forgiven!"

21"Who does this fellow think he is?" the Pharisees and teachers of the Law exclaimed among themselves. "This is blasphemy! Who but God can forgive sins?"

22Jesus knew what they were thinking, and he replied, "Why is it blasphemy? 23, 24I, the Messiah,[e] have the authority on earth to forgive sins. But talk is cheap—anybody could say that. So I'll prove it to you by healing this man." Then, turning to the paralyzed man, he com-

New Revised Standard

Jesus Calls the First Disciples

5 ONCE WHILE Jesus[f] was standing beside the lake of Gennesaret, and the crowd was pressing in on him to hear the word of God, 2he saw two boats there at the shore of the lake; the fishermen had gone out of them and were washing their nets. 3He got into one of the boats, the one belonging to Simon, and asked him to put out a little way from the shore. Then he sat down and taught the crowds from the boat. 4When he had finished speaking, he said to Simon, "Put out into the deep water and let down your nets for a catch." 5Simon answered, "Master, we have worked all night long but have caught nothing. Yet if you say so, I will let down the nets." 6When they had done this, they caught so many fish that their nets were beginning to break. 7So they signaled their partners in the other boat to come and help them. And they came and filled both boats, so that they began to sink. 8But when Simon Peter saw it, he fell down at Jesus' knees, saying, "Go away from me, Lord, for I am a sinful man!" 9For he and all who were with him were amazed at the catch of fish that they had taken; 10and so also were James and John, sons of Zebedee, who were partners with Simon. Then Jesus said to Simon, "Do not be afraid; from now on you will be catching people." 11When they had brought their boats to shore, they left everything and followed him.

Jesus Cleanses a Leper

12 Once, when he was in one of the cities, there was a man covered with leprosy.[g] When he saw Jesus, he bowed with his face to the ground and begged him, "Lord, if you choose, you can make me clean." 13Then Jesus[f] stretched out his hand, touched him, and said, "I do choose. Be made clean." Immediately the leprosy[g] left him. 14And he ordered him to tell no one. "Go," he said, "and show yourself to the priest, and, as Moses commanded, make an offering for your cleansing, for a testimony to them." 15But now more than ever the word about Jesus[h] spread abroad; many crowds would gather to hear him and to be cured of their diseases. 16But he would withdraw to deserted places and pray.

Jesus Heals a Paralytic

17 One day, while he was teaching, Pharisees and teachers of the law were sitting near by (they had come from every village of Galilee and Judea and from Jerusalem); and the power of the Lord was with him to heal.[i] 18Just then some men came, carrying a paralyzed man on a bed. They were trying to bring him in and lay him before Jesus;[h] 19but finding no way to bring him in because of the crowd, they went up on the roof and let him down with his bed through the tiles into the middle of the crowd[j] in front of Jesus. 20When he saw their faith, he said, "Friend,[k] your sins are forgiven you." 21Then the scribes and the Pharisees began to question, "Who is this who is speaking blasphemies? Who can forgive sins but God alone?" 22When Jesus perceived their questionings, he answered them, "Why do you raise such questions in your hearts? 23Which is easier, to say, 'Your sins are forgiven you,' or to say, 'Stand up and walk'? 24But so that you may know that the Son

---

d 5:17 *Jewish religious leaders*, literally, "Pharisees." e 5:23, 24 *the Messiah*, literally, "the Son of Man."

f Gk *he* g The terms *leper* and *leprosy* can refer to several diseases h Gk *him* i Other ancient authorities read *was present to heal them* j Gk *into the midst* k Gk *Man*

King James

24But that ye may know that the Son of man hath power upon earth to forgive sins, (he said unto the sick of the palsy,) I say unto thee, Arise, and take up thy couch, and go into thine house.

25And immediately he rose up before them, and took up that whereon he lay, and departed to his own house, glorifying God.

26And they were all amazed, and they glorified God, and were filled with fear, saying, We have seen strange things today.

27¶ And after these things he went forth, and saw a publican, named Levi, sitting at the receipt of custom: and he said unto him, Follow me.

28And he left all, rose up, and followed him.

29And Levi made him a great feast in his own house: and there was a great company of publicans and of others that sat down with them.

30But their scribes and Pharisees murmured against his disciples, saying, Why do ye eat and drink with publicans and sinners?

31And Jesus answering said unto them, They that are whole need not a physician; but they that are sick.

32I came not to call the righteous, but sinners to repentance.

33¶ And they said unto him, Why do the disciples of John fast often, and make prayers, and likewise the disciples of the Pharisees; but thine eat and drink?

34And he said unto them, Can ye make the children of the bridechamber fast, while the bridegroom is with them?

35But the days will come, when the bridegroom shall be taken away from them, and then shall they fast in those days.

36¶ And he spake also a parable unto them; No man putteth a piece of a new garment upon an old; if otherwise, then both the new maketh a rent, and the piece that was taken out of the new agreeth not with the old.

37And no man putteth new wine into old bottles; else the new wine will burst the bottles, and be spilled, and the bottles shall perish.

38But new wine must be put into new bottles; and both are preserved.

39No man also having drunk old wine straightway desireth new: for he saith, The old is better.

6 AND IT came to pass on the second sabbath after the first, that he went through the corn fields; and his disciples plucked the ears of corn, and did eat, rubbing them in their hands.

2And certain of the Pharisees said unto them, Why do ye that which is not lawful to do on the sabbath days?

3And Jesus answering them said, Have ye not read so much as this, what David did, when himself was an hungered, and they which were with him.

4How he went into the house of God, and did take and eat the showbread, and gave also to them that were with him; which it is not lawful to eat but for the priests alone?

5And he said unto them, That the Son of man is Lord also of the sabbath.

6And it came to pass also on another sabbath, that he entered into the synagogue and taught: and there was a man whose right hand was withered.

7And the scribes and Pharisees watched him, whether he would heal on the sabbath day; that they might find an accusation against him.

8But he knew their thoughts, and said to the man which had the withered hand, Rise up, and stand forth in the midst. And he arose and stood forth.

New International

the Son of Man has authority on earth to forgive sins. . . ." He said to the paralyzed man, "I tell you, get up, take your mat and go home." 25Immediately he stood up in front of them, took what he had been lying on and went home praising God. 26Everyone was amazed and gave praise to God. They were filled with awe and said, "We have seen remarkable things today."

The Calling of Levi

27After this, Jesus went out and saw a tax collector by the name of Levi sitting at his tax booth. "Follow me," Jesus said to him, 28and Levi got up, left everything and followed him.

29Then Levi held a great banquet for Jesus at his house, and a large crowd of tax collectors and others were eating with them. 30But the Pharisees and the teachers of the law who belonged to their sect complained to his disciples, "Why do you eat and drink with tax collectors and 'sinners'?"

31Jesus answered them, "It is not the healthy who need a doctor, but the sick. 32I have not come to call the righteous, but sinners to repentance."

Jesus Questioned About Fasting

33They said to him, "John's disciples often fast and pray, and so do the disciples of the Pharisees, but yours go on eating and drinking."

34Jesus answered, "Can you make the guests of the bridegroom fast while he is with them? 35But the time will come when the bridegroom will be taken from them; in those days they will fast."

36He told them this parable: "No one tears a patch from a new garment and sews it on an old one. If he does, he will have torn the new garment, and the patch from the new will not match the old. 37And no one pours new wine into old wineskins. If he does, the new wine will burst the skins, the wine will run out and the wineskins will be ruined. 38No, new wine must be poured into new wineskins. 39And no one after drinking old wine wants the new, for he says, 'The old is better.'"

Lord of the Sabbath

6 ONE SABBATH Jesus was going through the grainfields, and his disciples began to pick some heads of grain, rub them in their hands and eat the kernels. 2Some of the Pharisees asked, "Why are you doing what is unlawful on the Sabbath?"

3Jesus answered them, "Have you never read what David did when he and his companions were hungry? 4He entered the house of God, and taking the consecrated bread, he ate what is lawful only for priests to eat. And he also gave some to his companions." 5Then Jesus said to them, "The Son of Man is Lord of the Sabbath."

6On another Sabbath he went into the synagogue and was teaching, and a man was there whose right hand was shriveled. 7The Pharisees and the teachers of the law were looking for a reason to accuse Jesus, so they watched him closely to see if he would heal on the Sabbath. 8But Jesus knew what they were thinking and said to the man with the shriveled hand, "Get up and stand in front of everyone." So he got up and stood there.

Living Bible

manded, "Pick up your stretcher and go on home, for you are healed!"

25And immediately, as everyone watched, the man jumped to his feet, picked up his mat and went home praising God! 26Everyone present was gripped with awe and fear. And they praised God, remarking over and over again, "We have seen strange things today."

27Later on as Jesus left the town he saw a tax collector—with the usual reputation for cheating—sitting at a tax collection booth. The man's name was Levi. Jesus said to him, "Come and be one of my disciples!" 28So Levi left everything, sprang up and went with him.

29Soon Levi held a reception in his home with Jesus as the guest of honor. Many of Levi's fellow tax collectors and other guests were there.

30But the Pharisees and teachers of the Law complained bitterly to Jesus' disciples about his eating with such notorious sinners.

31Jesus answered them, "It is the sick who need a doctor, not those in good health. 32My purpose is to invite sinners to turn from their sins, not to spend my time with those who think themselves already good enough."

33Their next complaint was that Jesus' disciples were feasting instead of fasting. "John the Baptist's disciples are constantly going without food, and praying," they declared, "and so do the disciples of the Pharisees. Why are yours wining and dining?"

34Jesus asked, "Do happy men fast? Do wedding guests go hungry while celebrating with the groom? 35But the time will come when the bridegroom will be killed;a then they won't want to eat."

36Then Jesus used this illustration: "No one tears off a piece of a new garment to make a patch for an old one. Not only will the new garment be ruined, but the old garment will look worse with a new patch on it! 37And no one puts new wine into old wineskins, for the new wine bursts the old skins, ruining the skins and spilling the wine. 38New wine must be put into new wineskins. 39But no one after drinking the old wine seems to want the fresh and the new. 'The old ways are best,' they say."

6 ONE SABBATH as Jesus and his disciples were walking through some grainfields, they were breaking off the heads of wheat, rubbing off the husks in their hands and eating the grains.

2But some Pharisees said, "That's illegal! Your disciples are harvesting grain, and it's against the Jewish law to work on the Sabbath."

3Jesus replied, "Don't you read the Scriptures? Haven't you ever read what King David did when he and his men were hungry? 4He went into the Temple and took the shewbread, the special bread that was placed before the Lord, and ate it—illegal as this was—and shared it with others." 5And Jesus added, "Ib am master even of the Sabbath."

6On another Sabbath he was in the synagogue teaching, and a man was present whose right hand was deformed. 7The teachers of the Law and the Pharisees watched closely to see whether he would heal the man that day, since it was the Sabbath. For they were eager to find some charge to bring against him.

8How well he knew their thoughts! But he said to the man with the deformed hand, "Come and stand here where everyone can see." So he did.

New Revised Standard

of Man has authority on earth to forgive sins"—he said to the one who was paralyzed—"I say to you, stand up and take your bed and go to your home." 25Immediately he stood up before them, took what he had been lying on, and went to his home, glorifying God. 26Amazement seized all of them, and they glorified God and were filled with awe, saying, "We have seen strange things today."

Jesus Calls Levi

27 After this he went out and saw a tax collector named Levi, sitting at the tax booth; and he said to him, "Follow me." 28And he got up, left everything, and followed him.

29 Then Levi gave a great banquet for him in his house; and there was a large crowd of tax collectors and others sitting at the tablec with them. 30The Pharisees and their scribes were complaining to his disciples, saying, "Why do you eat and drink with tax collectors and sinners?" 31Jesus answered, "Those who are well have no need of a physician, but those who are sick; 32I have come to call not the righteous but sinners to repentance."

The Question about Fasting

33 Then they said to him, "John's disciples, like the disciples of the Pharisees, frequently fast and pray, but your disciples eat and drink. 34Jesus said to them, "You cannot make wedding guests fast while the bridegroom is with them, can you? 35The days will come when the bridegroom will be taken away from them, and then they will fast in those days." 36He also told them a parable: "No one tears a piece from a new garment and sews it on an old garment; otherwise the new will be torn, and the piece from the new will not match the old. 37And no one puts new wine into old wineskins; otherwise the new wine will burst the skins and will be spilled, and the skins will be destroyed. 38But new wine must be put into fresh wineskins. 39And no one after drinking old wine desires new wine, but says, 'The old is good.' "d

The Question about the Sabbath

6 ONE SABBATHe while Jesusf was going through the grainfields, his disciples plucked some heads of grain, rubbed them in their hands, and ate them. 2But some of the Pharisees said, "Why are you doing what is not lawfulg on the sabbath?" 3Jesus answered, "Have you not read what David did when he and his companions were hungry? 4He entered the house of God and took and ate the bread of the Presence, which it is not lawful for any but the priests to eat, and gave some to his companions?" 5Then he said to them, "The Son of Man is lord of the sabbath."

The Man with a Withered Hand

6 On another sabbath he entered the synagogue and taught, and there was a man there whose right hand was withered. 7The scribes and the Pharisees watched him to see whether he would cure on the sabbath, so that they might find an accusation against him. 8Even though he knew what they were thinking, he said to the man who had the withered hand, "Come and stand here." He got up and stood there. 9Then Jesus said to them, "I ask you,

---

a 5:35 killed, literally, "taken away from them."   b 6:5 I, literally, "the Son of Man."

c Gk reclining   d Other ancient authorities read better; others lack verse 39   e Other ancient authorities read On the second first sabbath   f Gk he   g Other ancient authorities add to do

King James

9Then said Jesus unto them, I will ask you one thing; Is it lawful on the sabbath days to do good, or to do evil? to save life, or to destroy *it?*

10And looking round about upon them all, he said unto the man, Stretch forth thy hand. And he did so: and his hand was restored whole as the other.

11And they were filled with madness; and communed one with another what they might do to Jesus.

12And it came to pass in those days, that he went out into a mountain to pray, and continued all night in prayer to God.

13¶ And when it was day, he called *unto him* his disciples: and of them he chose twelve, whom also he named apostles;

14Simon, (whom he also named Peter,) and Andrew his brother, James and John, Philip and Bartholomew,

15Matthew and Thomas, James the *son* of Alphaeus, and Simon called Zelotes,

16And Judas *the brother* of James, and Judas Iscariot, which also was the traitor.

17¶ And he came down with them, and stood in the plain, and the company of his disciples, and a great multitude of people out of all Judaea and Jerusalem, and from the sea coast of Tyre and Sidon, which came to hear him, and to be healed of their diseases;

18And they that were vexed with unclean spirits: and they were healed.

19And the whole multitude sought to touch him: for there went virtue out of him, and healed *them* all.

20¶ And he lifted up his eyes on his disciples, and said, Blessed *be ye* poor: for yours is the kingdom of God.

21Blessed *are ye* that hunger now: for ye shall be filled. Blessed *are ye* that weep now: for ye shall laugh.

22Blessed are ye, when men shall hate you, and when they shall separate you *from their company,* and shall reproach *you,* and cast out your name as evil, for the Son of man's sake.

23Rejoice ye in that day, and leap for joy: for, behold, your reward *is* great in heaven: for in the like manner did their fathers unto the prophets.

24But woe unto you that are rich! for ye have received your consolation.

25Woe unto you that are full! for ye shall hunger. Woe unto you that laugh now! for ye shall mourn and weep.

26Woe unto you, when all men shall speak well of you! for so did their fathers to the false prophets.

27¶ But I say unto you which hear, Love your enemies, do good to them which hate you,

28Bless them that curse you, and pray for them which despitefully use you.

29And unto him that smiteth thee on the *one* cheek offer also the other; and him that taketh away thy cloak forbid not *to take thy* coat also.

30Give to every man that asketh of thee; and of him that taketh away thy goods ask *them* not again.

31And as ye would that men should do to you, do ye also to them likewise.

32For if ye love them which love you, what thank have ye? for sinners also love those that love them.

33And if ye do good to them which do good to you, what thank have ye? for sinners also do even the same.

34And if ye lend *to them* of whom ye hope to receive, what thank have ye? for sinners also lend to sinners, to receive as much again.

New International

9Then Jesus said to them, "I ask you, which is lawful on the Sabbath: to do good or to do evil, to save life or to destroy it?"

10He looked around at them all, and then said to the man, "Stretch out your hand." He did so, and his hand was completely restored. 11But they were furious and began to discuss with one another what they might do to Jesus.

The Twelve Apostles

12One of those days Jesus went out to a mountainside to pray, and spent the night praying to God. 13When morning came, he called his disciples to him and chose twelve of them, whom he also designated apostles: 14Simon (whom he named Peter), his brother Andrew, James, John, Philip, Bartholomew, 15Matthew, Thomas, James son of Alphaeus, Simon who was called the Zealot, 16Judas son of James, and Judas Iscariot, who became a traitor.

Blessings and Woes

17He went down with them and stood on a level place. A large crowd of his disciples was there and a great number of people from all over Judea, from Jerusalem, and from the coast of Tyre and Sidon, 18who had come to hear him and to be healed of their diseases. Those troubled by evil[a] spirits were cured, 19and the people all tried to touch him, because power was coming from him and healing them all.

20Looking at his disciples, he said:

"Blessed are you who are poor,
　for yours is the kingdom of God.
21Blessed are you who hunger now,
　for you will be satisfied.
Blessed are you who weep now,
　for you will laugh.
22Blessed are you when men hate you,
　when they exclude you and insult you
　and reject your name as evil,
　　because of the Son of Man.

23"Rejoice in that day and leap for joy, because great is your reward in heaven. For that is how their fathers treated the prophets.

24"But woe to you who are rich,
　for you have already received your comfort.
25Woe to you who are well fed now,
　for you will go hungry.
Woe to you who laugh now,
　for you will mourn and weep.
26Woe to you when all men speak well of you,
　for that is how their fathers treated the false
　　prophets.

Love for Enemies

27"But I tell you who hear me: Love your enemies, do good to those who hate you, 28bless those who curse you, pray for those who mistreat you. 29If someone strikes you on one cheek, turn to him the other also. If someone takes your cloak, do not stop him from taking your tunic. 30Give to everyone who asks you, and if anyone takes what belongs to you, do not demand it back. 31Do to others as you would have them do to you.

32"If you love those who love you, what credit is that to you? Even 'sinners' love those who love them. 33And if you do good to those who are good to you, what credit is that to you? Even 'sinners' do that. 34And if you lend to those from whom you expect repayment, what credit is that to you? Even 'sinners' lend to 'sinners,' expecting to be repaid in full. 35But love your enemies, do good

---

a *18* Greek *unclean*

Living Bible

9Then Jesus said to the Pharisees and teachers of the Law, "I have a question for you. Is it right to do good on the Sabbath day, or to do harm? To save life, or to destroy it?"

10He looked around at them one by one and then said to the man, "Reach out your hand." And as he did, it became completely normal again. 11At this, the enemies of Jesus were wild with rage, and began to plot his murder.

12One day soon afterwards he went out into the mountains to pray, and prayed all night. 13At daybreak he called together his followers and chose twelve of them to be the inner circle of his disciples. (They were appointed as his "apostles," or "missionaries.") 14, 15, 16Here are their names:

Simon (he also called him Peter),
Andrew (Simon's brother),
James,
John,
Philip,
Bartholomew,
Matthew,
Thomas,
James (the son of Alphaeus),
Simon (a member of the Zealots, a subversive political party),
Judas (son of James),
Judas Iscariot (who later betrayed him).

17, 18When they came down the slopes of the mountain, they stood with Jesus on a large, level area, surrounded by many of his followers who, in turn, were surrounded by the crowds. For people from all over Judea and from Jerusalem and from as far north as the seacoasts of Tyre and Sidon had come to hear him or to be healed. And he cast out many demons. 19Everyone was trying to touch him, for when they did healing power went out from him and they were cured.

20Then he turned to his disciples and said, "What happiness there is for you who are poor, for the Kingdom of God is yours! 21What happiness there is for you who are now hungry, for you are going to be satisfied! What happiness there is for you who weep, for the time will come when you shall laugh with joy! 22What happiness it is when others hate you and exclude you and insult you and smear your name because you are mine!b 23When that happens, rejoice! Yes, leap for joy! For you will have a great reward awaiting you in heaven. And you will be in good company—the ancient prophets were treated that way too!

24"But, oh, the sorrows that await the rich. For they have their only happiness down here. 25They are fat and prosperous now, but a time of awful hunger is before them. Their careless laughter now means sorrow then. 26And what sadness is ahead for those praised by the crowds—for *false* prophets have *always* been praised.

27"Listen, all of you. Love your *enemies*. Do *good* to those who *hate* you. 28Pray for the happiness of those who *curse* you; implore God's blessing on those who *hurt* you.

29"If someone slaps you on one cheek, let him slap the other too! If someone demands your coat, give him your shirt besides. 30Give what you have to anyone who asks you for it; and when things are taken away from you, don't worry about getting them back. 31Treat others as you want them to treat you.

32"Do you think you deserve credit for merely loving those who love you? Even the godless do that! 33And if you do good only to those who do you good—is that so wonderful? Even sinners do that much! 34And if you lend money only to those who can repay you, what good is that? Even the most wicked will lend to their own kind for full return!

New Revised Standard

is it lawful to do good or to do harm on the sabbath, to save life or to destroy it?" 10After looking around at all of them, he said to him, "Stretch out your hand." He did so, and his hand was restored. 11But they were filled with fury and discussed with one another what they might do to Jesus.

Jesus Chooses the Twelve Apostles

12 Now during those days he went out to the mountain to pray; and he spent the night in prayer to God. 13And when day came, he called his disciples and chose twelve of them, whom he also named apostles: 14Simon, whom he named Peter, and his brother Andrew, and James, and John, and Philip, and Bartholomew, 15and Matthew, and Thomas, and James son of Alphaeus, and Simon, who was called the Zealot, 16and Judas son of James, and Judas Iscariot, who became a traitor.

Jesus Teaches and Heals

17 He came down with them and stood on a level place, with a great crowd of his disciples and a great multitude of people from all Judea, Jerusalem, and the coast of Tyre and Sidon. 18They had come to hear him and to be healed of their diseases; and those who were troubled with unclean spirits were cured. 19And all in the crowd were trying to touch him, for power came out from him and healed all of them.

Blessings and Woes

20 Then he looked up at his disciples and said:
"Blessed are you who are poor,
    for yours is the kingdom of God.
21 "Blessed are you who are hungry now,
    for you will be filled.
"Blessed are you who weep now,
    for you will laugh.
22 "Blessed are you when people hate you, and when they exclude you, revile you, and defame youc on account of the Son of Man. 23Rejoice in that day and leap for joy, for surely your reward is great in heaven; for that is what their ancestors did to the prophets.
24 "But woe to you who are rich,
    for you have received your consolation.
25 "Woe to you who are full now,
    for you will be hungry.
"Woe to you who are laughing now,
    for you will mourn and weep.
26 "Woe to you when all speak well of you, for that is what their ancestors did to the false prophets.

Love for Enemies

27 "But I say to you that listen, Love your enemies, do good to those who hate you, 28bless those who curse you, pray for those who abuse you. 29If anyone strikes you on the cheek, offer the other also; and from anyone who takes away your coat do not withhold even your shirt. 30Give to everyone who begs from you; and if anyone takes away your goods, do not ask for them again. 31Do to others as you would have them do to you.

32 "If you love those who love you, what credit is that to you? For even sinners love those who love them. 33If you do good to those who do good to you, what credit is that to you? For even sinners do the same. 34If you lend to those from whom you hope to receive, what credit is that to you? Even sinners lend to sinners, to receive as much again. 35But love your enemies, do

---

b 6:22 *because you are mine*, literally, "on account of the Son of Man."   c Gk *cast out your name as evil*

King James

³⁵But love ye your enemies, and do good, and lend, hoping for nothing again; and your reward shall be great, and ye shall be the children of the Highest: for he is kind unto the unthankful and *to* the evil.

³⁶Be ye therefore merciful, as your Father also is merciful.

³⁷Judge not, and ye shall not be judged: condemn not, and ye shall not be condemned: forgive, and ye shall be forgiven:

³⁸Give, and it shall be given unto you; good measure, pressed down, and shaken together, and running over, shall men give into your bosom. For with the same measure that ye mete withal it shall be measured to you again.

³⁹And he spake a parable unto them, Can the blind lead the blind? shall they not both fall into the ditch?

⁴⁰The disciple is not above his master: but every one that is perfect shall be as his master.

⁴¹And why beholdest thou the mote that is in thy brother's eye, but perceivest not the beam that is in thine own eye?

⁴²Either how canst thou say to thy brother, Brother, let me pull out the mote that is in thine eye, when thou thyself beholdest not the beam that is in thine own eye? Thou hypocrite, cast out first the beam out of thine own eye, and then shalt thou see clearly to pull out the mote that is in thy brother's eye.

⁴³For a good tree bringeth not forth corrupt fruit; neither doth a corrupt tree bring forth good fruit.

⁴⁴For every tree is known by his own fruit. For of thorns men do not gather figs, nor of a bramble bush gather they grapes.

⁴⁵A good man out of the good treasure of his heart bringeth forth that which is good; and an evil man out of the evil treasure of his heart bringeth forth that which is evil: for of the abundance of the heart his mouth speaketh.

⁴⁶¶ And why call ye me, Lord, Lord, and do not the things which I say?

⁴⁷Whosoever cometh to me, and heareth my sayings, and doeth them, I will show you to whom he is like:

⁴⁸He is like a man which built an house, and digged deep, and laid the foundation on a rock: and when the flood arose, the stream beat vehemently upon that house, and could not shake it: for it was founded upon a rock.

⁴⁹But he that heareth, and doeth not, is like a man that without a foundation built an house upon the earth; against which the stream did beat vehemently, and immediately it fell; and the ruin of that house was great.

7 NOW WHEN he had ended all his sayings in the audience of the people, he entered into Capernaum.

²And a certain centurion's servant, who was dear unto him, was sick, and ready to die.

³And when he heard of Jesus, he sent unto him the elders of the Jews, beseeching him that he would come and heal his servant.

⁴And when they came to Jesus, they besought him instantly, saying, That he was worthy for whom he should do this:

⁵For he loveth our nation, and he hath built us a synagogue.

⁶Then Jesus went with them. And when he was now not far from the house, the centurion sent friends to him, saying unto him, Lord, trouble not thyself: for I am not worthy that thou shouldest enter under my roof:

⁷Wherefore neither thought I myself worthy to come unto thee: but say in a word, and my servant shall be healed.

New International

to them, and lend to them without expecting to get anything back. Then your reward will be great, and you will be sons of the Most High, because he is kind to the ungrateful and wicked. ³⁶Be merciful, just as your Father is merciful.

Judging Others

³⁷"Do not judge, and you will not be judged. Do not condemn, and you will not be condemned. Forgive, and you will be forgiven. ³⁸Give, and it will be given to you. A good measure, pressed down, shaken together and running over, will be poured into your lap. For with the measure you use, it will be measured to you."

³⁹He also told them this parable: "Can a blind man lead a blind man? Will they not both fall into a pit? ⁴⁰A student is not above his teacher, but everyone who is fully trained will be like his teacher.

⁴¹"Why do you look at the speck of sawdust in your brother's eye and pay no attention to the plank in your own eye? ⁴²How can you say to your brother, 'Brother, let me take the speck out of your eye,' when you yourself fail to see the plank in your own eye? You hypocrite, first take the plank out of your eye, and then you will see clearly to remove the speck from your brother's eye.

A Tree and Its Fruit

⁴³"No good tree bears bad fruit, nor does a bad tree bear good fruit. ⁴⁴Each tree is recognized by its own fruit. People do not pick figs from thornbushes, or grapes from briers. ⁴⁵The good man brings good things out of the good stored up in his heart, and the evil man brings evil things out of the evil stored up in his heart. For out of the overflow of his heart his mouth speaks.

The Wise and Foolish Builders

⁴⁶"Why do you call me, 'Lord, Lord,' and do not do what I say? ⁴⁷I will show you what he is like who comes to me and hears my words and puts them into practice. ⁴⁸He is like a man building a house, who dug down deep and laid the foundation on rock. When a flood came, the torrent struck that house but could not shake it, because it was well built. ⁴⁹But the one who hears my words and does not put them into practice is like a man who built a house on the ground without a foundation. The moment the torrent struck that house, it collapsed and its destruction was complete."

The Faith of the Centurion

7 WHEN JESUS had finished saying all this in the hearing of the people, he entered Capernaum. ²There a centurion's servant, whom his master valued highly, was sick and about to die. ³The centurion heard of Jesus and sent some elders of the Jews to him, asking him to come and heal his servant. ⁴When they came to Jesus, they pleaded earnestly with him, "This man deserves to have you do this, ⁵because he loves our nation and has built our synagogue." ⁶So Jesus went with them.

He was not far from the house when the centurion sent friends to say to him: "Lord, don't trouble yourself, for I do not deserve to have you come under my roof. ⁷That is why I did not even consider myself worthy to come to you. But say the word, and my servant will be healed. ⁸For I myself am a man under authority, with

Living Bible

35"Love your *enemies!* Do good to *them!* Lend to *them!* And don't be concerned about the fact that they won't repay. Then your reward from heaven will be very great, and you will truly be acting as sons of God: for he is kind to the *unthankful* and to those who are *very wicked.*

36"Try to show as much compassion as your Father does.

37"Never criticize or condemn—or it will all come back on you. Go easy on others; then they will do the same for you.ᵃ 38For if you give, you will get! Your gift will return to you in full and overflowing measure, pressed down, shaken together to make room for more, and running over. Whatever measure you use to give— large or small—will be used to measure what is given back to you."

39Here are some of the story-illustrations Jesus used in his sermons: "What good is it for one blind man to lead another? He will fall into a ditch and pull the other down with him. 40How can a student know more than his teacher? But if he works hard, he may learn as much.

41"And why quibble about the speck in someone else's eye—his little faultᵇ—when a board is in your own? 42How can you think of saying to him, 'Brother, let me help you get rid of that speck in your eye,' when you can't see past the board in yours? Hypocrite! First get rid of the board, and then perhaps you can see well enough to deal with his speck!

43"A tree from good stock doesn't produce scrub fruit nor do trees from poor stock produce choice fruit. 44A tree is identified by the kind of fruit it produces. Figs never grow on thorns, or grapes on bramble bushes. 45A good man produces good deeds from a good heart. And an evil man produces evil deeds from his hidden wickedness. Whatever is in the heart overflows into speech.

46"So why do you call me 'Lord' when you won't obey me? 47, 48But all those who come and listen and obey me are like a man who builds a house on a strong foundation laid upon the underlying rock. When the floodwaters rise and break against the house, it stands firm, for it is strongly built.

49"But those who listen and don't obey are like a man who builds a house without a foundation. When the floods sweep down against that house, it crumbles into a heap of ruins."

7 WHEN JESUS had finished his sermon he went back into the city of Capernaum.

2Just at that time the highly prized slave of a Romanᶜ army captain was sick and near death. 3When the captain heard about Jesus, he sent some respected Jewish elders to ask him to come and heal his slave. 4So they began pleading earnestly with Jesus to come with them and help the man. They told him what a wonderful person the captain was.

"If anyone deserves your help, it is he," they said, 5"for he loves the Jews and even paid personally to build us a synagogue!"

6, 7, 8Jesus went with them; but just before arriving at the house, the captain sent some friends to say, "Sir, don't inconvenience yourself by coming to my home,

New Revised Standard

good, and lend, expecting nothing in return.ᵈ Your reward will be great, and you will be children of the Most High; for he is kind to the ungrateful and the wicked. 36Be merciful, just as your Father is merciful.

Judging Others

37 "Do not judge, and you will not be judged; do not condemn, and you will not be condemned. Forgive, and you will be forgiven; 38give, and it will be given to you. A good measure, pressed down, shaken together, running over, will be put into your lap; for the measure you give will be the measure you get back."

39 He also told them a parable: "Can a blind person guide a blind person? Will not both fall into a pit? 40A disciple is not above the teacher, but everyone who is fully qualified will be like the teacher. 41Why do you see the speck in your neighbor'sᵉ eye, but do not notice the log in your own eye? 42Or how can you say to your neighbor,ᶠ 'Friend,ᶠ let me take out the speck in your eye,' when you yourself do not see the log in your own eye? You hypocrite, first take the log out of your own eye, and then you will see clearly to take the speck out of your neighbor'sᵉ eye.

A Tree and Its Fruit

43 "No good tree bears bad fruit, nor again does a bad tree bear good fruit; 44for each tree is known by its own fruit. Figs are not gathered from thorns, nor are grapes picked from a bramble bush. 45The good person out of the good treasure of the heart produces good, and the evil person out of evil treasure produces evil; for it is out of the abundance of the heart that the mouth speaks.

The Two Foundations

46 "Why do you call me 'Lord, Lord,' and do not do what I tell you? 47I will show you what someone is like who comes to me, hears my words, and acts on them. 48That one is like a man building a house, who dug deeply and laid the foundation on rock; when a flood arose, the river burst against that house but could not shake it, because it had been well built.ᵍ 49But the one who hears and does not act is like a man who built a house on the ground without a foundation. When the river burst against it, immediately it fell, and great was the ruin of that house."

Jesus Heals a Centurion's Servant

7 AFTER JESUSʰ had finished all his sayings in the hearing of the people, he entered Capernaum. 2A centurion there had a slave whom he valued highly, and who was ill and close to death. 3When he heard about Jesus, he sent some Jewish elders to him, asking him to come and heal his slave. 4When they came to Jesus, they appealed to him earnestly, saying, "He is worthy of having you do this for him, 5for he loves our people, and it is he who built our synagogue for us." 6And Jesus went with them, but when he was not far from the house, the centurion sent friends to say to him, "Lord, do not trouble yourself, for I am not worthy to have you come under my roof; 7therefore I did not presume to come to you. But only speak the word, and let my servant be healed. 8For I also am a man set under authority, with

---

ᵃ 6:37 *Go easy on others; then they will do the same for you,* literally, "release, and you shall be released." ᵇ 6:41 *his little fault,* implied. ᶜ 7:2 *Roman,* implied.

ᵈ Other ancient authorities read *despairing of no one* ᵉ Gk *brother's* ᶠ Gk *brother* ᵍ Other ancient authorities read *founded upon the rock* ʰ Gk *he*

King James

8For I also am a man set under authority, having under me soldiers, and I say unto one, Go, and he goeth; and to another, Come, and he cometh; and to my servant, Do this, and he doeth *it*.

9When Jesus heard these things, he marvelled at him, and turned him about, and said unto the people that followed him, I say unto you, I have not found so great faith, no, not in Israel.

10And they that were sent, returning to the house, found the servant whole that had been sick.

11¶ And it came to pass the day after, that he went into a city called Nain; and many of his disciples went with him, and much people.

12Now when he came nigh to the gate of the city, behold, there was a dead man carried out, the only son of his mother, and she was a widow: and much people of the city was with her.

13And when the Lord saw her, he had compassion on her, and said unto her, Weep not.

14And he came and touched the bier: and they that bare *him* stood still. And he said, Young man, I say unto thee, Arise.

15And he that was dead sat up, and began to speak. And he delivered him to his mother.

16And there came a fear on all: and they glorified God, saying, That a great prophet is risen up among us; and, That God hath visited his people.

17And this rumour of him went forth throughout all Judaea, and throughout all the region round about.

18And the disciples of John showed him of all these things.

19¶ And John calling *unto him* two of his disciples sent *them* to Jesus, saying, Art thou he that should come? or look we for another?

20When the men were come unto him, they said, John Baptist hath sent us unto thee, saying, Art thou he that should come? or look we for another?

21And in that same hour he cured many of *their* infirmities and plagues, and of evil spirits; and unto many *that were* blind he gave sight.

22Then Jesus answering said unto them, Go your way, and tell John what things ye have seen and heard; how that the blind see, the lame walk, the lepers are cleansed, the deaf hear, the dead are raised, to the poor the gospel is preached.

23And blessed is *he*, whosoever shall not be offended in me.

24¶ And when the messengers of John were departed, he began to speak unto the people concerning John, What went ye out into the wilderness for to see? A reed shaken with the wind?

25But what went ye out for to see? A man clothed in soft raiment? Behold, they which are gorgeously apparelled, and live delicately, are in kings' courts.

26But what went ye out for to see? A prophet? Yea, I say unto you, and much more than a prophet.

27This is *he*, of whom it is written, Behold, I send my messenger before thy face, which shall prepare thy way before thee.

28For I say unto you, Among those that are born of women there is not a greater prophet than John the Baptist: but he that is least in the kingdom of God is greater than he.

29And all the people that heard *him*, and the publicans, justified God, being baptized with the baptism of John.

30But the Pharisees and lawyers rejected the counsel of God against themselves, being not baptized of him.

31¶ And the Lord said, Whereunto then shall I liken the men of this generation? and to what are they like?

New International

soldiers under me. I tell this one, 'Go,' and he goes; and that one, 'Come,' and he comes. I say to my servant, 'Do this,' and he does it."

9When Jesus heard this, he was amazed at him, and turning to the crowd following him, he said, "I tell you, I have not found such great faith even in Israel." 10Then the men who had been sent returned to the house and found the servant well.

Jesus Raises a Widow's Son

11Soon afterward, Jesus went to a town called Nain, and his disciples and a large crowd went along with him. 12As he approached the town gate, a dead person was being carried out—the only son of his mother, and she was a widow. And a large crowd from the town was with her. 13When the Lord saw her, his heart went out to her and he said, "Don't cry."

14Then he went up and touched the coffin, and those carrying it stood still. He said, "Young man, I say to you, get up!" 15The dead man sat up and began to talk, and Jesus gave him back to his mother.

16They were all filled with awe and praised God. "A great prophet has appeared among us," they said. "God has come to help his people." 17This news about Jesus spread throughout Judea[a] and the surrounding country.

Jesus and John the Baptist

18John's disciples told him about all these things. Calling two of them, 19he sent them to the Lord to ask, "Are you the one who was to come, or should we expect someone else?"

20When the men came to Jesus, they said, "John the Baptist sent us to you to ask, 'Are you the one who was to come, or should we expect someone else?' "

21At that very time Jesus cured many who had diseases, sicknesses and evil spirits, and gave sight to many who were blind. 22So he replied to the messengers, "Go back and report to John what you have seen and heard: The blind receive sight, the lame walk, those who have leprosy[b] are cured, the deaf hear, the dead are raised, and the good news is preached to the poor. 23Blessed is the man who does not fall away on account of me."

24After John's messengers left, Jesus began to speak to the crowd about John: "What did you go out into the desert to see? A reed swayed by the wind? 25If not, what did you go out to see? A man dressed in fine clothes? No, those who wear expensive clothes and indulge in luxury are in palaces. 26But what did you go out to see? A prophet? Yes, I tell you, and more than a prophet. 27This is the one about whom it is written:

" 'I will send my messenger ahead of you,
	who will prepare your way before you.'[c]

28I tell you, among those born of women there is no one greater than John; yet the one who is least in the kingdom of God is greater than he."

29(All the people, even the tax collectors, when they heard Jesus' words, acknowledged that God's way was right, because they had been baptized by John. 30But the Pharisees and experts in the law rejected God's purpose for themselves, because they had not been baptized by John.)

31"To what, then, can I compare the people of this

Living Bible

for I am not worthy of any such honor or even to come and meet you. Just speak a word from where you are, and my servant boy will be healed! I know, because I am under the authority of my superior officers, and I have authority over my men. I only need to say 'Go!' and they go; or 'Come!' and they come; and to my slave, 'Do this or that,' and he does it. So just say, 'Be healed!' and my servant will be well again!"

9Jesus was amazed. Turning to the crowd he said, "Never among all the Jews in Israel have I met a man with faith like this."

10And when the captain's friends returned to his house, they found the slave completely healed.

11Not long afterwards Jesus went with his disciples to the village of Nain, with the usual great crowd at his heels. 12A funeral procession was coming out as he approached the village gate. The boy who had died was the only son of his widowed mother, and many mourners from the village were with her.

13When the Lord saw her, his heart overflowed with sympathy. "Don't cry!" he said. 14Then he walked over to the coffin and touched it, and the bearers stopped. "Laddie," he said, "come back to life again."

15Then the boy sat up and began to talk to those around him! And Jesus gave him back to his mother.

16A great fear swept the crowd, and they exclaimed with praises to God, "A mighty prophet has risen among us," and, "We have seen the hand of God at work today."

17The report of what he did that day raced from end to end of Judea and even out across the borders.

18The disciples of John the Baptist soon heard of all that Jesus was doing. When they told John about it, 19he sent two of his disciples to Jesus to ask him, "Are you really the Messiah?d Or shall we keep on looking for him?"

20, 21, 22The two disciples found Jesus while he was curing many sick people of their various diseases—healing the lame and the blind and casting out evil spirits. When they asked him John's question, this was his reply: "Go back to John and tell him all you have seen and heard here today: how those who were blind can see. The lame are walking without a limp. The lepers are completely healed. The deaf can hear again. The dead come back to life. And the poor are hearing the Good News. 23And tell him, 'Blessed is the one who does not lose his faith in me.' "e

24After they left, Jesus talked to the crowd about John. "Who is this man you went out into the Judean wilderness to see?" he asked. "Did you find him weak as grass, moved by every breath of wind? 25Did you find him dressed in expensive clothes? No! Men who live in luxury are found in palaces, not out in the wilderness. 26But did you find a prophet? Yes! And more than a prophet. 27He is the one to whom the Scriptures refer when they say, 'Look! I am sending my messenger ahead of you, to prepare the way before you.' 28In all humanity there is no one greater than John. And yet the least citizen of the Kingdom of God is greater than he."

29And all who heard John preach—even the most wicked of themf—agreed that God's requirements were right, and they were baptized by him. 30All, that is, except the Pharisees and teachers of Moses' Law. They rejected God's plan for them and refused John's baptism.

31"What can I say about such men?" Jesus asked. "With what shall I compare them? 32They are like a

New Revised Standard

soldiers under me; and I say to one, 'Go,' and he goes, and to another, 'Come,' and he comes, and to my slave, 'Do this,' and the slave does it." 9When Jesus heard this he was amazed at him, and turning to the crowd that followed him, he said, "I tell you, not even in Israel have I found such faith." 10When those who had been sent returned to the house, they found the slave in good health.

Jesus Raises the Widow's Son at Nain

11 Soon afterwardsg he went to a town called Nain, and his disciples and a large crowd went with him. 12As he approached the gate of the town, a man who had died was being carried out. He was his mother's only son, and she was a widow; and with her was a large crowd from the town. 13When the Lord saw her, he had compassion for her and said to her, "Do not weep." 14Then he came forward and touched the bier, and the bearers stood still. And he said, "Young man, I say to you, rise!" 15The dead man sat up and began to speak, and Jesush gave him to his mother. 16Fear seized all of them; and they glorified God, saying, "A great prophet has risen among us!" and "God has looked favorably on his people!" 17This word about him spread throughout Judea and all the surrounding country.

Messengers from John the Baptist

18 The disciples of John reported all these things to him. So John summoned two of his disciples 19and sent them to the Lord to ask, "Are you the one who is to come, or are we to wait for another?" 20When the men had come to him, they said, "John the Baptist has sent us to you to ask, 'Are you the one who is to come, or are we to wait for another?' " 21Jesusi had just then cured many people of diseases, plagues, and evil spirits, and had given sight to many who were blind. 22And he answered them, "Go and tell John what you have seen and heard: the blind receive their sight, the lame walk, the lepersj are cleansed, the deaf hear, the dead are raised, the poor have good news brought to them. 23And blessed is anyone who takes no offense at me."

24 When John's messengers had gone, Jesush began to speak to the crowds about John:k "What did you go out into the wilderness to look at? A reed shaken by the wind? 25What then did you go out to see? Someonel dressed in soft robes? Look, those who put on fine clothing and live in luxury are in royal palaces. 26What then did you go out to see? A prophet? Yes, I tell you, and more than a prophet. 27This is the one about whom it is written,

'See, I am sending my messenger ahead of
      you,
   who will prepare your way before you.'

28I tell you, among those born of women no one is greater than John; yet the least in the kingdom of God is greater than he." 29(And all the people who heard this, including the tax collectors, acknowledged the justice of God,m because they had been baptized with John's baptism. 30But by refusing to be baptized by him, the Pharisees and the lawyers rejected God's purpose for themselves.)

31 "To what then will I compare the people of this generation, and what are they like? 32They are like chil-

---

d 7:19 the Messiah, literally, "the one who is coming."   e 7:23 Blessed is the one who does not lose his faith in me, literally, "Blessed is he who keeps from stumbling over me."   f 7:29 even the most wicked of them, literally, "even the tax collectors," i.e., the publicans.

g Other ancient authorities read Next day   h Gk he   i Gk He   j The terms leper and leprosy can refer to several diseases   k Gk him   l Or Why then did you go out? To see someone   m Or praised God

King James

32They are like unto children sitting in the market-place, and calling one to another, and saying, We have piped unto you, and ye have not danced; we have mourned to you, and ye have not wept.

33For John the Baptist came neither eating bread nor drinking wine; and ye say, He hath a devil.

34The Son of man is come eating and drinking; and ye say, Behold a gluttonous man, and a winebibber, a friend of publicans and sinners!

35But wisdom is justified of all her children.

36¶ And one of the Pharisees desired him that he would eat with him. And he went into the Pharisee's house, and sat down to meat.

37And, behold, a woman in the city, which was a sinner, when she knew that *Jesus* sat at meat in the Pharisee's house, brought an alabaster box of ointment,

38And stood at his feet behind *him* weeping, and began to wash his feet with tears, and did wipe *them* with the hairs of her head, and kissed his feet, and anointed *them* with the ointment.

39Now when the Pharisee which had bidden him saw *it*, he spake within himself, saying, This man, if he were a prophet, would have known who and what manner of woman *this is* that toucheth him: for she is a sinner.

40And Jesus answering said unto him, Simon, I have somewhat to say unto thee. And he saith, Master, say on.

41There was a certain creditor which had two debtors: the one owed five hundred pence, and the other fifty.

42And when they had nothing to pay, he frankly forgave them both. Tell me therefore, which of them will love him most?

43Simon answered and said, I suppose that *he*, to whom he forgave most. And he said unto him, Thou hast rightly judged.

44And he turned to the woman, and said unto Simon, Seest thou this woman? I entered into thine house, thou gavest me no water for my feet: but she hath washed my feet with tears, and wiped *them* with the hairs of her head.

45Thou gavest me no kiss: but this woman since the time I came in hath not ceased to kiss my feet.

46My head with oil thou didst not anoint: but this woman hath anointed my feet with ointment.

47Wherefore I say unto thee, Her sins, which are many, are forgiven; for she loved much: but to whom little is forgiven, *the same* loveth little.

48And he said unto her, Thy sins are forgiven.

49And they that sat at meat with him began to say within themselves, Who is this that forgiveth sins also?

50And he said to the woman, Thy faith hath saved thee; go in peace.

8 AND IT came to pass afterward, that he went throughout every city and village, preaching and showing the glad tidings of the kingdom of God: and the twelve *were* with him,

2And certain women, which had been healed of evil spirits and infirmities, Mary called Magdalene, out of whom went seven devils,

New International

generation? What are they like? 32They are like children sitting in the marketplace and calling out to each other:

" 'We played the flute for you,
　　and you did not dance;
we sang a dirge,
　　and you did not cry.'

33For John the Baptist came neither eating bread nor drinking wine, and you say, 'He has a demon.' 34The Son of Man came eating and drinking, and you say, 'Here is a glutton and a drunkard, a friend of tax collectors and "sinners." ' 35But wisdom is proved right by all her children."

Jesus Anointed by a Sinful Woman

36Now one of the Pharisees invited Jesus to have dinner with him, so he went to the Pharisee's house and reclined at the table. 37When a woman who had lived a sinful life in that town learned that Jesus was eating at the Pharisee's house, she brought an alabaster jar of perfume, 38and as she stood behind him at his feet weeping, she began to wet his feet with her tears. Then she wiped them with her hair, kissed them and poured perfume on them.

39When the Pharisee who had invited him saw this, he said to himself, "If this man were a prophet, he would know who is touching him and what kind of woman she is—that she is a sinner."

40Jesus answered him, "Simon, I have something to tell you."

"Tell me, teacher," he said.

41"Two men owed money to a certain moneylender. One owed him five hundred denarii,[a] and the other fifty. 42Neither of them had the money to pay him back, so he canceled the debts of both. Now which of them will love him more?"

43Simon replied, "I suppose the one who had the bigger debt canceled."

"You have judged correctly," Jesus said.

44Then he turned toward the woman and said to Simon, "Do you see this woman? I came into your house. You did not give me any water for my feet, but she wet my feet with her tears and wiped them with her hair. 45You did not give me a kiss, but this woman, from the time I entered, has not stopped kissing my feet. 46You did not put oil on my head, but she has poured perfume on my feet. 47Therefore, I tell you, her many sins have been forgiven—for she loved much. But he who has been forgiven little loves little."

48Then Jesus said to her, "Your sins are forgiven."

49The other guests began to say among themselves, "Who is this who even forgives sins?"

50Jesus said to the woman, "Your faith has saved you; go in peace."

The Parable of the Sower

8 AFTER THIS, Jesus traveled about from one town and village to another, proclaiming the good news of the kingdom of God. The Twelve were with him, 2and also some women who had been cured of evil spirits and diseases: Mary (called Magdalene) from whom seven demons had come out; 3Joanna the wife of Cuza, the

a 41 A denarius was a coin worth about a day's wages.

Living Bible

group of children who complain to their friends, 'You don't like it if we play "wedding" and you don't like it if we play "funeral" '!b 33For John the Baptist used to go without food and never took a drop of liquor all his life, and you said, 'He must be crazy!'c 34But I eat my food and drink my wine, and you say, 'What a glutton Jesus is! And he drinks! And has the lowest sort of friends!'d 35But I am sure you can always justify your inconsistencies."e

36One of the Pharisees asked Jesus to come to his home for lunch and Jesus accepted the invitation. As they sat down to eat, 37a woman of the streets—a prostitute—heard he was there and brought an exquisite flask filled with expensive perfume. 38Going in, she knelt behind him at his feet, weeping, with her tears falling down upon his feet; and she wiped them off with her hair and kissed them and poured the perfume on them.

39When Jesus' host, a Pharisee, saw what was happening and who the woman was, he said to himself, "This proves that Jesus is no prophet, for if God had really sent him, he would know what kind of woman this one is!"

40Then Jesus spoke up and answered his thoughts. "Simon," he said to the Pharisee, "I have something to say to you."

"All right, Teacher," Simon replied, "go ahead."

41Then Jesus told him this story: "A man loaned money to two people—$5,000 to one and $500 to the other. 42But neither of them could pay him back, so he kindly forgave them both, letting them keep the money! Which do you suppose loved him most after that?"

43"I suppose the one who had owed him the most," Simon answered.

"Correct," Jesus agreed.

44Then he turned to the woman and said to Simon, "Look! See this woman kneeling here! When I entered your home, you didn't bother to offer me water to wash the dust from my feet, but she has washed them with her tears and wiped them with her hair. 45You refused me the customary kiss of greeting, but she has kissed my feet again and again from the time I first came in. 46You neglected the usual courtesy of olive oil to anoint my head, but she has covered my feet with rare perfume. 47Therefore her sins—and they are many—are forgiven, for she loved me much; but one who is forgiven little, shows little love."

48And he said to her, "Your sins are forgiven."

49Then the men at the table said to themselves, "Who does this man think he is, going around forgiving sins?"

50And Jesus said to the woman, "Your faith has saved you; go in peace."

8 NOT LONG afterwards he began a tour of the cities and villages of Galileef to announce the coming of the Kingdom of God, and took his twelve disciples with him. 2Some women went along, from whom he had cast out demons or whom he had healed; among them were Mary Magdalene (Jesus had cast out seven demons from her), 3Joanna, Chuza's wife (Chuza

New Revised Standard

dren sitting in the marketplace and calling to one another,

> 'We played the flute for you, and you did not dance;
> we wailed, and you did not weep.'

33For John the Baptist has come eating no bread and drinking no wine, and you say, 'He has a demon'; 34the Son of Man has come eating and drinking, and you say, 'Look, a glutton and a drunkard, a friend of tax collectors and sinners!' 35Nevertheless, wisdom is vindicated by all her children."

A Sinful Woman Forgiven

36 One of the Pharisees asked Jesusg to eat with him, and he went into the Pharisee's house and took his place at the table. 37And a woman in the city, who was a sinner, having learned that he was eating in the Pharisee's house, brought an alabaster jar of ointment. 38She stood behind him at his feet, weeping, and began to bathe his feet with her tears and to dry them with her hair. Then she continued kissing his feet and anointing them with the ointment. 39Now when the Pharisee who had invited him saw it, he said to himself, "If this man were a prophet, he would have known who and what kind of woman this is who is touching him—that she is a sinner." 40Jesus spoke up and said to him, "Simon, I have something to say to you." "Teacher," he replied, "Speak." 41"A certain creditor had two debtors; one owed five hundred denarii,h and the other fifty. 42When they could not pay, he canceled the debts for both of them. Now which of them will love him more?" 43Simon answered, "I suppose the one for whom he canceled the greater debt." And Jesusi said to him, "You have judged rightly." 44Then turning toward the woman, he said to Simon, "Do you see this woman? I entered your house; you gave me no water for my feet, but she has bathed my feet with her tears and dried them with her hair. 45You gave me no kiss, but from the time I came in she has not stopped kissing my feet. 46You did not anoint my head with oil, but she has anointed my feet with ointment. 47Therefore, I tell you, her sins, which were many, have been forgiven; hence she has shown great love. But the one to whom little is forgiven, loves little." 48Then he said to her, "Your sins are forgiven." 49But those who were at the table with him began to say among themselves, "Who is this who even forgives sins?" 50And he said to the woman, "Your faith has saved you; go in peace."

Some Women Accompany Jesus

8 SOON AFTERWARDS he went on through cities and villages, proclaiming and bringing the good news of the kingdom of God. The twelve were with him, 2as well as some women who had been cured of evil spirits and infirmities: Mary, called Magdalene, from whom seven demons had gone out, 3and Joanna, the

---

b 7:32 You don't like it if we play "wedding" and you don't like it if we play "funeral." Literally, "We played the flute for you and you didn't dance; we sang a dirge and you didn't weep."   c 7:33 He must be crazy, literally, "He has a demon."   d 7:34 has the lowest sort of friends, literally, "is a friend of tax gatherers and sinners."   e 7:35 But I am sure you can always justify your inconsistencies, literally, "But wisdom is justified of all her children."   f 8:1 and villages of Galilee, implied.

g Gk him   h The denarius was the usual day's wage for a laborer   i Gk he

King James

3And Joanna the wife of Chuza Herod's steward, and Susanna, and many others, which ministered unto him of their substance.

4¶ And when much people were gathered together, and were come to him out of every city, he spake by a parable:

5A sower went out to sow his seed: and as he sowed, some fell by the way side; and it was trodden down, and the fowls of the air devoured it.

6And some fell upon a rock; and as soon as it was sprung up, it withered away, because it lacked moisture.

7And some fell among thorns; and the thorns sprang up with it, and choked it.

8And other fell on good ground, and sprang up, and bare fruit an hundredfold. And when he had said these things, he cried, He that hath ears to hear, let him hear.

9And his disciples asked him, saying, What might this parable be?

10And he said, Unto you it is given to know the mysteries of the kingdom of God: but to others in parables; that seeing they might not see, and hearing they might not understand.

11Now the parable is this: The seed is the word of God.

12Those by the way side are they that hear; then cometh the devil, and taketh away the word out of their hearts, lest they should believe and be saved.

13They on the rock *are they*, which, when they hear, receive the word with joy; and these have no root, which for a while believe, and in time of temptation fall away.

14And that which fell among thorns are they, which, when they have heard, go forth, and are choked with cares and riches and pleasures of *this* life, and bring no fruit to perfection.

15But that on the good ground are they, which in an honest and good heart, having heard the word, keep *it*, and bring forth fruit with patience.

16¶ No man, when he hath lighted a candle, covereth it with a vessel, or putteth *it* under a bed; but setteth *it* on a candlestick, that they which enter in may see the light.

17For nothing is secret, that shall not be made manifest; neither *any thing* hid, that shall not be known and come abroad.

18Take heed therefore how ye hear: for whosoever hath, to him shall be given; and whosoever hath not, from him shall be taken even that which he seemeth to have.

19¶ Then came to him *his* mother and his brethren, and could not come at him for the press.

20And it was told him *by certain* which said, Thy mother and thy brethren stand without, desiring to see thee.

21And he answered and said unto them, My mother and my brethren are these which hear the word of God, and do it.

22¶ Now it came to pass on a certain day, that he went into a ship with his disciples: and he said unto them, Let us go over unto the other side of the lake. And they launched forth.

23But as they sailed he fell asleep: and there came down a storm of wind on the lake; and they were filled *with water*, and were in jeopardy.

24And they came to him, and awoke him, saying, Master, master, we perish. Then he arose, and rebuked the wind and the raging of the water: and they ceased, and there was a calm.

New International

manager of Herod's household; Susanna; and many others. These women were helping to support them out of their own means.

4While a large crowd was gathering and people were coming to Jesus from town after town, he told this parable: 5"A farmer went out to sow his seed. As he was scattering the seed, some fell along the path; it was trampled on, and the birds of the air ate it up. 6Some fell on rock, and when it came up, the plants withered because they had no moisture. 7Other seed fell among thorns, which grew up with it and choked the plants. 8Still other seed fell on good soil. It came up and yielded a crop, a hundred times more than was sown."

When he said this, he called out, "He who has ears to hear, let him hear."

9His disciples asked him what this parable meant. 10He said, "The knowledge of the secrets of the kingdom of God has been given to you, but to others I speak in parables, so that,

" 'though seeing, they may not see;
    though hearing, they may not understand.'a

11"This is the meaning of the parable: The seed is the word of God. 12Those along the path are the ones who hear, and then the devil comes and takes away the word from their hearts, so that they may not believe and be saved. 13Those on the rock are the ones who receive the word with joy when they hear it, but they have no root. They believe for a while, but in the time of testing they fall away. 14The seed that fell among thorns stands for those who hear, but as they go on their way they are choked by life's worries, riches and pleasures, and they do not mature. 15But the seed on good soil stands for those with a noble and good heart, who hear the word, retain it, and by persevering produce a crop.

A Lamp on a Stand

16"No one lights a lamp and hides it in a jar or puts it under a bed. Instead, he puts it on a stand, so that those who come in can see the light. 17For there is nothing hidden that will not be disclosed, and nothing concealed that will not be known or brought out into the open. 18Therefore consider carefully how you listen. Whoever has will be given more; whoever does not have, even what he thinks he has will be taken from him."

Jesus' Mother and Brothers

19Now Jesus' mother and brothers came to see him, but they were not able to get near him because of the crowd. 20Someone told him, "Your mother and brothers are standing outside, wanting to see you."

21He replied, "My mother and brothers are those who hear God's word and put it into practice."

Jesus Calms the Storm

22One day Jesus said to his disciples, "Let's go over to the other side of the lake." So they got into a boat and set out. 23As they sailed, he fell asleep. A squall came down on the lake, so that the boat was being swamped, and they were in great danger.

24The disciples went and woke him, saying, "Master, Master, we're going to drown!"

He got up and rebuked the wind and the raging wa-

---

a 10 Isaiah 6:9

Living Bible

was King Herod's business manager and was in charge of his palace and domestic affairs), Susanna, and many others who were contributing from their private means to the support of Jesus and his disciples.

4One day he gave this illustration to a large crowd that was gathering to hear him—while many others were still on the way, coming from other towns.

5"A farmer went out to his field to sow grain. As he scattered the seed on the ground, some of it fell on a footpath and was trampled on; and the birds came and ate it as it lay exposed. 6Other seed fell on shallow soil with rock beneath. This seed began to grow, but soon withered and died for lack of moisture. 7Other seed landed in thistle patches, and the young grain stalks were soon choked out. 8Still other fell on fertile soil; this seed grew and produced a crop one hundred times as large as he had planted." (As he was giving this illustration he said, "If anyone has listening ears, use them now!")

9His apostles asked him what the story meant.

10He replied, "God has granted you to know the meaning of these parables, for they tell a great deal about the Kingdom of God. But these crowds hear the words and do not understand, just as the ancient prophets predicted.

11"This is its meaning: The seed is God's message to men. 12The hard path where some seed fell represents the hard hearts of those who hear the words of God, but then the devil comes and steals the words away and prevents people from believing and being saved. 13The stony ground represents those who enjoy listening to sermons, but somehow the message never really gets through to them and doesn't take root and grow. They know the message is true, and sort of believe for awhile; but when the hot winds of persecution blow, they lose interest. 14The seed among the thorns represents those who listen and believe God's words but whose faith afterwards is choked out by worry and riches and the responsibilities and pleasures of life. And so they are never able to help anyone else to believe the Good News.

15"But the good soil represents honest, good-hearted people. They listen to God's words and cling to them and steadily spread them to others who also soon believe."

16[Another time he asked,b] "Who ever heard of someone lighting a lamp and then covering it up to keep it from shining? No, lamps are mounted in the open where they can be seen. 17This illustrates the fact that someday everything [in men's heartsc] shall be brought to light and made plain to all. 18So be careful how you listen; for whoever has, to him shall be given more; and whoever does not have, even what he thinks he has shall be taken away from him."

19Once when his mother and brothers came to see him, they couldn't get into the house where he was teaching, because of the crowds. 20When Jesus heard they were standing outside and wanted to see him, 21he remarked, "My mother and my brothers are all those who hear the message of God and obey it."

22One day about that time, as he and his disciples were out in a boat, he suggested that they cross to the other side of the lake. 23On the way across he lay down for a nap, and while he was sleeping the wind began to rise. A fierce storm developed that threatened to swamp them, and they were in real danger.

24They rushed over and woke him up. "Master, Master, we are sinking!" they screamed.

So he spoke to the storm: "Quiet down," he said, and

New Revised Standard

wife of Herod's steward Chuza, and Susanna, and many others, who provided for themd out of their resources.

The Parable of the Sower

4 When a great crowd gathered and people from town after town came to him, he said in a parable: 5"A sower went out to sow his seed; and as he sowed, some fell on the path and was trampled on, and the birds of the air ate it up. 6Some fell on the rock; and as it grew up, it withered for lack of moisture. 7Some fell among thorns, and the thorns grew with it and choked it. 8Some fell into good soil, and when it grew, it produced a hundredfold." As he said this, he called out, "Let anyone with ears to hear listen!"

The Purpose of the Parables

9 Then his disciples asked him what this parable meant. 10He said, "To you it has been given to know the secretse of the kingdom of God; but to others I speakf in parables, so that

'looking they may not perceive,
and listening they may not understand.'

The Parable of the Sower Explained

11 "Now the parable is this: The seed is the word of God. 12The ones on the path are those who have heard; then the devil comes and takes away the word from their hearts, so that they may not believe and be saved. 13The ones on the rock are those who, when they hear the word, receive it with joy. But these have no root; they believe only for a while and in a time of testing fall away. 14As for what fell among the thorns, these are the ones who hear; but as they go on their way, they are choked by the cares and riches and pleasures of life, and their fruit does not mature. 15But as for that in the good soil, these are the ones who, when they hear the word, hold it fast in an honest and good heart, and bear fruit with patient endurance.

A Lamp under a Jar

16 "No one after lighting a lamp hides it under a jar, or puts it under a bed, but puts it on a lampstand, so that those who enter may see the light. 17For nothing is hidden that will not be disclosed, nor is anything secret that will not become known and come to light. 18Then pay attention to how you listen; for to those who have, more will be given; and from those who do not have, even what they seem to have will be taken away."

The True Kindred of Jesus

19 Then his mother and his brothers came to him, but they could not reach him because of the crowd. 20And he was told, "Your mother and your brothers are standing outside, wanting to see you." 21But he said to them, "My mother and my brothers are those who hear the word of God and do it."

Jesus Calms a Storm

22 One day he got into a boat with his disciples, and he said to them, "Let us go across to the other side of the lake." So they put out, 23and while they were sailing he fell asleep. A windstorm swept down on the lake, and the boat was filling with water, and they were in danger. 24They went to him and woke him up, shouting, "Master, Master, we are perishing!" And he woke up and rebuked the wind and the raging waves; they ceased, and there was a calm. 25He said to them, "Where is your

---

b 8:16 Another time he asked, implied. See Mt 5:16.   c 8:17 in men's hearts, implied.

d Other ancient authorities read him   e Or mysteries   f Gk lacks I speak

King James

25And he said unto them, Where is your faith? And they being afraid wondered, saying one to another, What manner of man is this! for he commandeth even the winds and water, and they obey him.

26¶ And they arrived at the country of the Gadarenes, which is over against Galilee.

27And when he went forth to land, there met him out of the city a certain man, which had devils long time, and ware no clothes, neither abode in *any* house, but in the tombs.

28When he saw Jesus, he cried out, and fell down before him, and with a loud voice said, What have I to do with thee, Jesus, *thou* Son of God most high? I beseech thee, torment me not.

29(For he had commanded the unclean spirit to come out of the man. For oftentimes it had caught him: and he was kept bound with chains and in fetters; and he brake the bands, and was driven of the devil into the wilderness.)

30And Jesus asked him, saying, What is thy name? And he said, Legion: because many devils were entered into him.

31And they besought him that he would not command them to go out into the deep.

32And there was there an herd of many swine feeding on the mountain: and they besought him that he would suffer them to enter into them. And he suffered them.

33Then went the devils out of the man, and entered into the swine: and the herd ran violently down a steep place into the lake, and were choked.

34When they that fed *them* saw what was done, they fled, and went and told *it* in the city and in the country.

35Then they went out to see what was done; and came to Jesus, and found the man, out of whom the devils were departed, sitting at the feet of Jesus, clothed, and in his right mind: and they were afraid.

36They also which saw *it* told them by what means he that was possessed of the devils was healed.

37¶ Then the whole multitude of the country of the Gadarenes round about besought him to depart from them; for they were taken with great fear: and he went up into the ship, and returned back again.

38Now the man out of whom the devils were departed besought him that he might be with him: but Jesus sent him away, saying,

39Return to thine own house, and show how great things God hath done unto thee. And he went his way, and published throughout the whole city how great things Jesus had done unto him.

40And it came to pass, that, when Jesus was returned, the people *gladly* received him: for they were all waiting for him.

41¶ And, behold, there came a man named Jairus, and he was a ruler of the synagogue: and he fell down at Jesus' feet, and besought him that he would come into his house:

42For he had one only daughter, about twelve years of age, and she lay a dying. But as he went the people thronged him.

43¶ And a woman having an issue of blood twelve years, which had spent all her living upon physicians, neither could be healed of any,

44Came behind *him*, and touched the border of his garment: and immediately her issue of blood stanched.

45And Jesus said, Who touched me? When all denied, Peter and they that were with him said, Master, the multitude throng thee and press *thee*, and sayest thou, Who touched me?

46And Jesus said, Somebody hath touched me: for I perceive that virtue is gone out of me.

47And when the woman saw that she was not hid, she came trembling, and falling down before him, she declared unto him before all the people for what cause she had touched him, and how she was healed immediately.

New International

ters; the storm subsided, and all was calm. 25"Where is your faith?" he asked his disciples.

In fear and amazement they asked one another, "Who is this? He commands even the winds and the water, and they obey him."

The Healing of a Demon-possessed Man

26They sailed to the region of the Gerasenes,[a] which is across the lake from Galilee. 27When Jesus stepped ashore, he was met by a demon-possessed man from the town. For a long time this man had not worn clothes or lived in a house, but had lived in the tombs. 28When he saw Jesus, he cried out and fell at his feet, shouting at the top of his voice, "What do you want with me, Jesus, Son of the Most High God? I beg you, don't torture me!" 29For Jesus had commanded the evil[b] spirit to come out of the man. Many times it had seized him, and though he was chained hand and foot and kept under guard, he had broken his chains and had been driven by the demon into solitary places.

30Jesus asked him, "What is your name?"

"Legion," he replied, because many demons had gone into him. 31And they begged him repeatedly not to order them to go into the Abyss.

32A large herd of pigs was feeding there on the hillside. The demons begged Jesus to let them go into them, and he gave them permission. 33When the demons came out of the man, they went into the pigs, and the herd rushed down the steep bank into the lake and was drowned.

34When those tending the pigs saw what had happened, they ran off and reported this in the town and countryside, 35and the people went out to see what had happened. When they came to Jesus, they found the man from whom the demons had gone out, sitting at Jesus' feet, dressed and in his right mind; and they were afraid. 36Those who had seen it told the people how the demon-possessed man had been cured. 37Then all the people of the region of the Gerasenes asked Jesus to leave them, because they were overcome with fear. So he got into the boat and left.

38The man from whom the demons had gone out begged to go with him, but Jesus sent him away, saying, 39"Return home and tell how much God has done for you." So the man went away and told all over town how much Jesus had done for him.

A Dead Girl and a Sick Woman

40Now when Jesus returned, a crowd welcomed him, for they were all expecting him. 41Then a man named Jairus, a ruler of the synagogue, came and fell at Jesus' feet, pleading with him to come to his house 42because his only daughter, a girl of about twelve, was dying.

As Jesus was on his way, the crowds almost crushed him. 43And a woman was there who had been subject to bleeding for twelve years,[c] but no one could heal her. 44She came up behind him and touched the edge of his cloak, and immediately her bleeding stopped.

45"Who touched me?" Jesus asked.

When they all denied it, Peter said, "Master, the people are crowding and pressing against you."

46But Jesus said, "Someone touched me; I know that power has gone out from me."

47Then the woman, seeing that she could not go unnoticed, came trembling and fell at his feet. In the presence of all the people, she told why she had touched him and how she had been instantly healed. 48Then he said to her,

---

a 26 Some manuscripts *Gadarenes*; other manuscripts *Gergesenes*; also in verse 37   b 29 Greek *unclean*   c 43 Many manuscripts *years, and she had spent all she had on doctors*

Living Bible

the wind and waves subsided and all was calm! 25Then he asked them, "Where is your faith?"

And they were filled with awe and fear of him and said to one another, "Who is this man, that even the winds and waves obey him?"

26So they arrived at the other side, in the Gerasene country across the lake from Galilee. 27As he was climbing out of the boat a man from the city of Gadara came to meet him, a man who had been demon-possessed for a long time. Homeless and naked, he lived in a cemetery among the tombs. 28As soon as he saw Jesus he shrieked and fell to the ground before him, screaming, "What do you want with me, Jesus, Son of God Most High? Please, I beg you, oh, don't torment me!"

29For Jesus was already commanding the demon to leave him. This demon had often taken control of the man so that even when shackled with chains he simply broke them and rushed out into the desert, completely under the demon's power. 30"What is your name?" Jesus asked the demon. "Legion," they replied—for the man was filled with thousands of them!d 31They kept begging Jesus not to order them into the Bottomless Pit.

32A herd of pigs was feeding on the mountainside nearby, and the demons pled with him to let them enter into the pigs. And Jesus said they could. 33So they left the man and went into the pigs, and immediately the whole herd rushed down the mountainside and fell over a cliff into the lake below, where they drowned. 34The herdsmen rushed away to the nearby city, spreading the news as they ran.

35Soon a crowd came out to see for themselves what had happened and saw the man who had been demon-possessed sitting quietly at Jesus' feet, clothed and sane! And the whole crowd was badly frightened. 36Then those who had seen it happen told how the demon-possessed man had been healed. 37And everyone begged Jesus to go away and leave them alone (for a deep wave of fear had swept over them). So he returned to the boat and left, crossing back to the other side of the lake. 38The man who had been demon-possessed begged to go too, but Jesus said no.

39"Go back to your family," he told him, "and tell them what a wonderful thing God has done for you." So he went all through the city telling everyone about Jesus' mighty miracle.

40On the other side of the lake the crowds received him with open arms, for they had been waiting for him. 41And now a man named Jairus, a leader of a Jewish synagogue, came and fell down at Jesus' feet and begged him to come home with him, 42for his only child was dying, a little girl twelve years old. Jesus went with him, pushing through the crowds.

43, 44As they went a woman who wanted to be healed came up behind and touched him, for she had been slowly bleeding for twelve years, and could find no cure (though she had spent everything she had on doctorse). But the instant she touched the edge of his robe, the bleeding stopped.

45"Who touched me?" Jesus asked.

Everyone denied it, and Peter said, "Master, so many are crowding against you. . . ."

46But Jesus told him, "No, it was someone who deliberately touched me, for I felt healing power go out from me."

47When the woman realized that Jesus knew, she began to tremble and fell to her knees before him and told why she had touched him and that now she was well.

New Revised Standard

faith?" They were afraid and amazed, and said to one another, "Who then is this, that he commands even the winds and the water, and they obey him?"

Jesus Heals the Gerasene Demoniac

26 Then they arrived at the country of the Gerasenes,f which is opposite Galilee. 27As he stepped out on land, a man of the city who had demons met him. For a long time he had worng no clothes, and he did not live in a house but in the tombs. 28When he saw Jesus, he fell down before him and shouted at the top of his voice, "What have you to do with me, Jesus, Son of the Most High God? I beg you, do not torment me"— 29for Jesush had commanded the unclean spirit to come out of the man. (For many times it had seized him; he was kept under guard and bound with chains and shackles, but he would break the bonds and be driven by the demon into the wilds.) 30Jesus then asked him, "What is your name?" He said, "Legion"; for many demons had entered him. 31They begged him not to order them to go back into the abyss.

32 Now there on the hillside a large herd of swine was feeding; and the demonsi begged Jesusj to let them enter these. So he gave them permission. 33Then the demons came out of the man and entered the swine, and the herd rushed down the steep bank into the lake and was drowned.

34 When the swineherds saw what had happened, they ran off and told it in the city and in the country. 35Then people came out to see what had happened, and when they came to Jesus, they found the man from whom the demons had gone sitting at the feet of Jesus, clothed and in his right mind. And they were afraid. 36Those who had seen it told them how the one who had been possessed by demons had been healed. 37Then all the people of the surrounding country of the Gerasenesf asked Jesusj to leave them; for they were seized with great fear. So he got into the boat and returned. 38The man from whom the demons had gone begged that he might be with him; but Jesush sent him away, saying, 39"Return to your home, and declare how much God has done for you." So he went away, proclaiming throughout the city how much Jesus had done for him.

A Girl Restored to Life and a Woman Healed

40 Now when Jesus returned, the crowd welcomed him, for they were all waiting for him. 41Just then there came a man named Jairus, a leader of the synagogue. He fell at Jesus' feet and begged him to come to his house, 42for he had an only daughter, about twelve years old, who was dying.

As he went, the crowds pressed in on him. 43Now there was a woman who had been suffering from hemorrhages for twelve years; and though she had spent all she had on physicians,k no one could cure her. 44She came up behind him and touched the fringe of his clothes, and immediately her hemorrhage stopped. 45Then Jesus asked, "Who touched me?" When all denied it, Peterl said, "Master, the crowds surround you and press in on you." 46But Jesus said, "Someone touched me; for I noticed that power had gone out from me." 47When the woman saw that she could not remain hidden, she came trembling; and falling down before him, she declared in the presence of all the people why she had touched him, and how she had been immediately healed. 48He said to

---

d 8:30 *with thousands of them,* implied. A legion consisted of 6,000 troops. Whether the demons were speaking literally, of course, is unknown. e 8:43, 44 *though she had spent everything she had on doctors.* This clause is not included in some of the ancient manuscripts.

f Other ancient authorities read *Gadarenes;* others, *Gergesenes* g Other ancient authorities read *a man of the city who had had demons for a long time met him. He wore* h Gk he i Gk they j Gk him k Other ancient authorities lack *and had spent all she had on physicians* l Other ancient authorities add *and those who were with him*

King James

48And he said unto her, Daughter, be of good comfort: thy faith hath made thee whole; go in peace.

49¶ While he yet spake, there cometh one from the ruler of the synagogue's *house,* saying to him, Thy daughter is dead; trouble not the Master.

50But when Jesus heard *it,* he answered him, saying, Fear not: believe only, and she shall be made whole.

51And when he came into the house, he suffered no man to go in, save Peter, and James, and John, and the father and the mother of the maiden.

52And all wept, and bewailed her: but he said, Weep not; she is not dead, but sleepeth.

53And they laughed him to scorn, knowing that she was dead.

54And he put them all out, and took her by the hand, and called, saying, Maid, arise.

55And her spirit came again, and she arose straightway: and he commanded to give her meat.

56And her parents were astonished: but he charged them that they should tell no man what was done.

9 THEN HE called his twelve disciples together, and gave them power and authority over all devils, and to cure diseases.

2And he sent them to preach the kingdom of God, and to heal the sick.

3And he said unto them, Take nothing for *your* journey, neither staves, nor scrip, neither bread, neither money; neither have two coats apiece.

4And whatsoever house ye enter into, there abide, and thence depart.

5And whosoever will not receive you, when ye go out of that city, shake off the very dust from your feet for a testimony against them.

6And they departed, and went through the towns, preaching the gospel, and healing every where.

7¶ Now Herod the tetrarch heard of all that was done by him: and he was perplexed, because that it was said of some, that John was risen from the dead;

8And of some, that Elias had appeared; and of others, that one of the old prophets was risen again.

9And Herod said, John have I beheaded: but who is this, of whom I hear such things? And he desired to see him.

10¶ And the apostles, when they were returned, told him all that they had done. And he took them, and went aside privately into a desert place belonging to the city called Bethsaida.

11And the people, when they knew *it,* followed him: and he received them, and spake unto them of the kingdom of God, and healed them that had need of healing.

12And when the day began to wear away, then came the twelve, and said unto him, Send the multitude away, that they may go into the towns and country round about, and lodge, and get victuals: for we are here in a desert place.

13But he said unto them, Give ye them to eat. And they said, We have no more but five loaves and two fishes; except we should go and buy meat for all this people.

14For they were about five thousand men. And he said to his disciples, Make them sit down by fifties in a company.

15And they did so, and made them all sit down.

16Then he took the five loaves and the two fishes, and looking up to heaven, he blessed them, and brake, and gave to the disciples to set before the multitude.

New International

"Daughter, your faith has healed you. Go in peace."

49While Jesus was still speaking, someone came from the house of Jairus, the synagogue ruler. "Your daughter is dead," he said. "Don't bother the teacher any more."

50Hearing this, Jesus said to Jairus, "Don't be afraid; just believe, and she will be healed."

51When he arrived at the house of Jairus, he did not let anyone go in with him except Peter, John and James, and the child's father and mother. 52Meanwhile, all the people were wailing and mourning for her. "Stop wailing," Jesus said. "She is not dead but asleep."

53They laughed at him, knowing that she was dead. 54But he took her by the hand and said, "My child, get up!" 55Her spirit returned, and at once she stood up. Then Jesus told them to give her something to eat. 56Her parents were astonished, but he ordered them not to tell anyone what had happened.

Jesus Sends Out the Twelve

9 WHEN JESUS had called the Twelve together, he gave them power and authority to drive out all demons and to cure diseases, 2and he sent them out to preach the kingdom of God and to heal the sick. 3He told them: "Take nothing for the journey—no staff, no bag, no bread, no money, no extra tunic. 4Whatever house you enter, stay there until you leave that town. 5If people do not welcome you, shake the dust off your feet when you leave their town, as a testimony against them." 6So they set out and went from village to village, preaching the gospel and healing people everywhere.

7Now Herod the tetrarch heard about all that was going on. And he was perplexed, because some were saying that John had been raised from the dead, 8others that Elijah had appeared, and still others that one of the prophets of long ago had come back to life. 9But Herod said, "I beheaded John. Who, then, is this I hear such things about?" And he tried to see him.

Jesus Feeds the Five Thousand

10When the apostles returned, they reported to Jesus what they had done. Then he took them with him and they withdrew by themselves to a town called Bethsaida, 11but the crowds learned about it and followed him. He welcomed them and spoke to them about the kingdom of God, and healed those who needed healing.

12Late in the afternoon the Twelve came to him and said, "Send the crowd away so they can go to the surrounding villages and countryside and find food and lodging, because we are in a remote place here."

13He replied, "You give them something to eat."

They answered, "We have only five loaves of bread and two fish—unless we go and buy food for all this crowd." 14(About five thousand men were there.)

But he said to his disciples, "Have them sit down in groups of about fifty each." 15The disciples did so, and everybody sat down. 16Taking the five loaves and the two fish and looking up to heaven, he gave thanks and broke them. Then he gave them to the disciples to set before the people. 17They all ate and were satisfied, and

Living Bible

48"Daughter," he said to her, "your faith has healed you. Go in peace."

49While he was still speaking to her, a messenger arrived from the Jairus' home with the news that the little girl was dead. "She's gone," he told her father; "there's no use troubling the Teacher now."

50But when Jesus heard what had happened, he said to the father, "Don't be afraid! Just trust me, and she'll be all right."

51When they arrived at the house Jesus wouldn't let anyone into the room except Peter, James, John, and the little girl's father and mother. 52The home was filled with mourning people, but he said, "Stop the weeping! She isn't dead; she is only asleep!" 53This brought scoffing and laughter, for they all knew she was dead.

54Then he took her by the hand and called, "Get up, little girl!" 55And at that moment her life returned and she jumped up! "Give her something to eat!" he said. 56Her parents were overcome with happiness, but Jesus insisted that they not tell anyone the details of what had happened.

9 ONE DAY Jesus called together his twelve apostles and gave them authority over all demons—power to cast them out—and to heal all diseases. 2Then he sent them away to tell everyone about the coming of the Kingdom of God and to heal the sick.

3"Don't even take along a walking stick," he instructed them, "nor a beggar's bag, nor food, nor money. Not even an extra coat. 4Be a guest in only one home at each village.

5"If the people of a town won't listen to you when you enter it, turn around and leave, demonstrating God's anger against ita by shaking its dust from your feet as you go."

6So they began their circuit of the villages, preaching the Good News and healing the sick.

7When reports of Jesus' miracles reached Herod, the governor,b he was worried and puzzled, for some were saying, "This is John the Baptist come back to life again"; 8and others, "It is Elijah or some other ancient prophet risen from the dead." These rumors were circulating all over the land.

9"I beheaded John," Herod said, "so who is this man about whom I hear such strange stories?" And he tried to see him.

10After the apostles returned to Jesus and reported what they had done, he slipped quietly away with them toward the city of Bethsaida. 11But the crowds found out where he was going, and followed. And he welcomed them, teaching them again about the Kingdom of God and curing those who were ill.

12Late in the afternoon all twelve of the disciples came and urged him to send the people away to the nearby villages and farms, to find food and lodging for the night. "For there is nothing to eat here in this deserted spot," they said.

13But Jesus replied, "You feed them!"

"Why, we have only five loaves of bread and two fish among the lot of us," they protested; "or are you expecting us to go and buy enough for this whole mob?" 14For there were about 5,000 men there!

"Just tell them to sit down on the ground in groups of about fifty each," Jesus replied. 15So they did.

16Jesus took the five loaves and two fish and looked up into the sky and gave thanks; then he broke off pieces for his disciples to set before the crowd. 17And everyone

New Revised Standard

her, "Daughter, your faith has made you well; go in peace."

49 While he was still speaking, someone came from the leader's house to say, "Your daughter is dead; do not trouble the teacher any longer." 50When Jesus heard this, he replied, "Do not fear. Only believe, and she will be saved." 51When he came to the house, he did not allow anyone to enter with him, except Peter, John, and James, and the child's father and mother. 52They were all weeping and wailing for her; but he said, "Do not weep; for she is not dead but sleeping." 53And they laughed at him, knowing that she was dead. 54But he took her by the hand and called out, "Child, get up!" 55Her spirit returned, and she got up at once. Then he directed them to give her something to eat. 56Her parents were astounded; but he ordered them to tell no one what had happened.

The Mission of the Twelve

9 THEN JESUSc called the twelve together and gave them power and authority over all demons and to cure diseases, 2and he sent them out to proclaim the kingdom of God and to heal. 3He said to them, "Take nothing for your journey, no staff, nor bag, nor bread, nor money—not even an extra tunic. 4Whatever house you enter, stay there, and leave from there. 5Wherever they do not welcome you, as you are leaving that town shake the dust off your feet as a testimony against them." 6They departed and went through the villages, bringing the good news and curing diseases everywhere.

Herod's Perplexity

7 Now Herod the rulerd heard about all that had taken place, and he was perplexed, because it was said by some that John had been raised from the dead, 8by some that Elijah had appeared, and by others that one of the ancient prophets had arisen. 9Herod said, "John I beheaded; but who is this about whom I hear such things?" And he tried to see him.

Feeding the Five Thousand

10 On their return the apostles told Jesuse all they had done. He took them with him and withdrew privately to a city called Bethsaida. 11When the crowds found out about it, they followed him; and he welcomed them, and spoke to them about the kingdom of God, and healed those who needed to be cured.

12 The day was drawing to a close, and the twelve came to him and said, "Send the crowd away, so that they may go into the surrounding villages and countryside, to lodge and get provisions; for we are here in a deserted place." 13But he said to them, "You give them something to eat." They said, "We have no more than five loaves and two fish—unless we are to go and buy food for all these people." 14For there were about five thousand men. And he said to his disciples, "Make them sit down in groups of about fifty each." 15They did so and made them all sit down. 16And taking the five loaves and the two fish, he looked up to heaven, and blessed and broke them, and gave them to the disciples to set before the crowd. 17And all ate and were filled. What

---

a 9:5 *demonstrating God's anger against it*, literally, "as a testimony against them."   b 9:7 *Herod, the governor*, literally, "Herod the Tetrarch."

c Gk *he*   d Gk *tetrarch*   e Gk *him*

King James

17And they did eat, and were all filled: and there was taken up of fragments that remained to them twelve baskets.

18¶ And it came to pass, as he was alone praying, his disciples were with him: and he asked them, saying, Whom say the people that I am?

19They answering said, John the Baptist; but some *say,* Elias; and others *say,* that one of the old prophets is risen again.

20He said unto them, But whom say ye that I am? Peter answering said, The Christ of God.

21And he straitly charged them, and commanded *them* to tell no man that thing;

22Saying, The Son of man must suffer many things, and be rejected of the elders and chief priests and scribes, and be slain, and be raised the third day.

23¶ And he said to *them* all, If any *man* will come after me, let him deny himself, and take up his cross daily, and follow me.

24For whosoever will save his life shall lose it: but whosoever will lose his life for my sake, the same shall save it.

25For what is a man advantaged, if he gain the whole world, and lose himself, or be cast away?

26For whosoever shall be ashamed of me and of my words, of him shall the Son of man be ashamed, when he shall come in his own glory, and *in his* Father's, and of the holy angels.

27But I tell you of a truth, there be some standing here, which shall not taste of death, till they see the kingdom of God.

28¶ And it came to pass about an eight days after these sayings, he took Peter and John and James, and went up into a mountain to pray.

29And as he prayed, the fashion of his countenance was altered, and his raiment *was* white *and* glistering.

30And, behold, there talked with him two men, which were Moses and Elias:

31Who appeared in glory, and spake of his decease which he should accomplish at Jerusalem.

32But Peter and they that were with him were heavy with sleep: and when they were awake, they saw his glory, and the two men that stood with him.

33And it came to pass, as they departed from him, Peter said unto Jesus, Master, it is good for us to be here: and let us make three tabernacles; one for thee, and one for Moses, and one for Elias: not knowing what he said.

34While he thus spake, there came a cloud, and overshadowed them: and they feared as they entered into the cloud.

35And there came a voice out of the cloud, saying, This is my beloved Son: hear him.

36And when the voice was past, Jesus was found alone. And they kept *it* close, and told no man in those days any of those things which they had seen.

37¶ And it came to pass, that on the next day, when they were come down from the hill, much people met him.

38And, behold, a man of the company cried out, saying, Master, I beseech thee, look upon my son: for he is mine only child.

39And, lo, a spirit taketh him, and he suddenly crieth out; and it teareth him that he foameth again, and bruising him hardly departeth from him.

40And I besought thy disciples to cast him out; and they could not.

41And Jesus answering said, O faithless and perverse generation, how long shall I be with you, and suffer you? Bring thy son hither.

42And as he was yet a-coming, the devil threw him down, and tare *him.* And Jesus rebuked the unclean spirit, and healed the child, and delivered him again to his father.

New International

the disciples picked up twelve basketfuls of broken pieces that were left over.

Peter's Confession of Christ

18Once when Jesus was praying in private and his disciples were with him, he asked them, "Who do the crowds say I am?"

19They replied, "Some say John the Baptist; others say Elijah; and still others, that one of the prophets of long ago has come back to life."

20"But what about you?" he asked. "Who do you say I am?"

Peter answered, "The Christ[a] of God."

21Jesus strictly warned them not to tell this to anyone. 22And he said, "The Son of Man must suffer many things and be rejected by the elders, chief priests and teachers of the law, and he must be killed and on the third day be raised to life."

23Then he said to them all: "If anyone would come after me, he must deny himself and take up his cross daily and follow me. 24For whoever wants to save his life will lose it, but whoever loses his life for me will save it. 25What good is it for a man to gain the whole world, and yet lose or forfeit his very self? 26If anyone is ashamed of me and my words, the Son of Man will be ashamed of him when he comes in his glory and in the glory of the Father and of the holy angels. 27I tell you the truth, some who are standing here will not taste death before they see the kingdom of God."

The Transfiguration

28About eight days after Jesus said this, he took Peter, John and James with him and went up onto a mountain to pray. 29As he was praying, the appearance of his face changed, and his clothes became as bright as a flash of lightning. 30Two men, Moses and Elijah, 31appeared in glorious splendor, talking with Jesus. They spoke about his departure, which he was about to bring to fulfillment at Jerusalem. 32Peter and his companions were very sleepy, but when they became fully awake, they saw his glory and the two men standing with him. 33As the men were leaving Jesus, Peter said to him, "Master, it is good for us to be here. Let us put up three shelters—one for you, one for Moses and one for Elijah." (He did not know what he was saying.)

34While he was speaking, a cloud appeared and enveloped them, and they were afraid as they entered the cloud. 35A voice came from the cloud, saying, "This is my Son, whom I have chosen; listen to him." 36When the voice had spoken, they found that Jesus was alone. The disciples kept this to themselves, and told no one at that time what they had seen.

The Healing of a Boy With an Evil Spirit

37The next day, when they came down from the mountain, a large crowd met him. 38A man in the crowd called out, "Teacher, I beg you to look at my son, for he is my only child. 39A spirit seizes him and he suddenly screams; it throws him into convulsions so that he foams at the mouth. It scarcely ever leaves him and is destroying him. 40I begged your disciples to drive it out, but they could not."

41"O unbelieving and perverse generation," Jesus replied, "how long shall I stay with you and put up with you? Bring your son here."

42Even while the boy was coming, the demon threw him to the ground in a convulsion. But Jesus rebuked the evil[b] spirit, healed the boy and gave him back to his

a 20 Or Messiah   b 42 Greek unclean

Living Bible

ate and ate; still, twelve basketfuls of scraps were picked up afterwards!

18One day as he was alone, praying, with his disciples nearby, he came over and asked them, "Who are the people saying I am?"

19"John the Baptist," they told him, "or perhaps Elijah or one of the other ancient prophets risen from the dead."

20Then he asked them, "Who do you think I am?" Peter replied, "The Messiah—the Christ of God!"

21He gave them strict orders not to speak of this to anyone. 22"For I, the Messiah,c must suffer much," he said, "and be rejected by the Jewish leaders—the elders, chief priests, and teachers of the Law—and be killed; and three days later I will come back to life again!"

23Then he said to all, "Anyone who wants to follow me must put aside his own desires and conveniences and carry his cross with him every day and *keep close to me!* 24Whoever loses his life for my sake will save it, but whoever insists on keeping his life will lose it; 25and what profit is there in gaining the whole world when it means forfeiting one's self?

26"When I, the Messiah, come in my glory and in the glory of the Father and the holy angels, I will be ashamed then of all who are ashamed of me and of my words now. 27But this is the simple truth—some of you who are standing here right now will not die until you have seen the Kingdom of God."

28Eight days later he took Peter, James, and John with him into the hills to pray. 29And as he was praying, his face began to shine,d and his clothes became dazzling white and blazed with light. 30Then two men appeared and began talking with him—Moses and Elijah! 31They were splendid in appearance, glorious to see; and they were speaking of his death at Jerusalem, to be carried out in accordance with God's plan.

32Peter and the others had been very drowsy and had fallen asleep. Now they woke up and saw Jesus covered with brightness and glory, and the two men standing with him. 33As Moses and Elijah were starting to leave, Peter, all confused and not even knowing what he was saying, blurted out, "Master, this is wonderful! We'll put up three shelters—one for you and one for Moses and one for Elijah!"

34But even as he was saying this, a bright cloud formed above them; and terror gripped them as it covered them. 35And a voice from the cloud said, *"This* is my Son, my Chosen One; listen to *him."*

36Then, as the voice died away, Jesus was there alone with his disciples. They didn't tell anyone what they had seen until long afterwards.

37The next day as they descended from the hill, a huge crowd met him, 38and a man in the crowd called out to him, "Teacher, this boy here is my only son, 39and a demon keeps seizing him, making him scream; and it throws him into convulsions so that he foams at the mouth; it is always hitting him and hardly ever leaves him alone. 40I begged your disciples to cast the demon out, but they couldn't."

41"O you stubborn faithless people," Jesus said [to his disciplese], "how long should I put up with you? Bring him here."

42As the boy was coming the demon knocked him to the ground and threw him into a violent convulsion. But Jesus ordered the demon to come out, and healed the boy and handed him over to his father.

New Revised Standard

was left over was gathered up, twelve baskets of broken pieces.

Peter's Declaration about Jesus

18 Once when Jesusf was praying alone, with only the disciples near him, he asked them, "Who do the crowds say that I am?" 19They answered, "John the Baptist; but others, Elijah; and still others, that one of the ancient prophets has arisen." 20He said to them, "But who do you say that I am?" Peter answered, "The Messiahg of God."

Jesus Foretells His Death and Resurrection

21 He sternly ordered and commanded them not to tell anyone, 22saying, "The Son of Man must undergo great suffering, and be rejected by the elders, chief priests, and scribes, and be killed, and on the third day be raised."

23 Then he said to them all, "If any want to become my followers, let them deny themselves and take up their cross daily and follow me. 24For those who want to save their life will lose it, and those who lose their life for my sake will save it. 25What does it profit them if they gain the whole world, but lose or forfeit themselves? 26Those who are ashamed of me and of my words, of them the Son of Man will be ashamed when he comes in his glory and the glory of the Father and of the holy angels. 27But truly I tell you, there are some standing here who will not taste death before they see the kingdom of God."

The Transfiguration

28 Now about eight days after these sayings Jesusf took with him Peter and John and James, and went up on the mountain to pray. 29And while he was praying, the appearance of his face changed, and his clothes became dazzling white. 30Suddenly they saw two men, Moses and Elijah, talking to him. 31They appeared in glory and were speaking of his departure, which he was about to accomplish at Jerusalem. 32Now Peter and his companions were weighed down with sleep; but since they had stayed awake,h they saw his glory and the two men who stood with him. 33Just as they were leaving him, Peter said to Jesus, "Master, it is good for us to be here; let us make three dwellings,i one for you, one for Moses, and one for Elijah"—not knowing what he said. 34While he was saying this, a cloud came and overshadowed them; and they were terrified as they entered the cloud. 35Then from the cloud came a voice that said, "This is my Son, my Chosen;j listen to him!" 36When the voice had spoken, Jesus was found alone. And they kept silent and in those days told no one any of the things they had seen.

Jesus Heals a Boy with a Demon

37 On the next day, when they had come down from the mountain, a great crowd met him. 38Just then a man from the crowd shouted, "Teacher, I beg you to look at my son; he is my only child. 39Suddenly a spirit seizes him, and all at once hek shrieks. It convulses him until he foams at the mouth; it mauls him and will scarcely leave him. 40I begged your disciples to cast it out, but they could not." 41Jesus answered, "You faithless and perverse generation, how much longer must I be with you and bear with you? Bring your son here." 42While he was coming, the demon dashed him to the ground in convulsions. But Jesus rebuked the unclean spirit,

---

c 9:22 *the Messiah,* literally, "the Son of Man." Also in vs 26.   d 9:29 *his face began to shine,* literally, "the appearance of his face changed."   e 9:41 *to his disciples,* implied.

f Gk *he*   g Or *The Christ*   h Or *but when they were fully awake*   i Or *tents*   j Other ancient authorities read *my Beloved*   k Or *it*

King James

43¶ And they were all amazed at the mighty power of God. But while they wondered every one at all things which Jesus did, he said unto his disciples,

44Let these sayings sink down into your ears: for the Son of man shall be delivered into the hands of men.

45But they understood not this saying, and it was hid from them, that they perceived it not: and they feared to ask him of that saying.

46¶ Then there arose a reasoning among them, which of them should be greatest.

47And Jesus, perceiving the thought of their heart, took a child, and set him by him,

48And said unto them, Whosoever shall receive this child in my name receiveth me: and whosoever shall receive me receiveth him that sent me: for he that is least among you all, the same shall be great.

49¶ And John answered and said, Master, we saw one casting out devils in thy name; and we forbad him, because he followeth not with us.

50And Jesus said unto him, Forbid *him* not: for he that is not against us is for us.

51¶ And it came to pass, when the time was come that he should be received up, he stedfastly set his face to go to Jerusalem,

52And sent messengers before his face: and they went, and entered into a village of the Samaritans, to make ready for him.

53And they did not receive him, because his face was as though he would go to Jerusalem.

54And when his disciples James and John saw *this,* they said, Lord, wilt thou that we command fire to come down from heaven, and consume them, even as Elias did?

55But he turned, and rebuked them, and said, Ye know not what manner of spirit ye are of.

56For the Son of man is not come to destroy men's lives, but to save *them.* And they went to another village.

57¶ And it came to pass, that, as they went in the way, a certain *man* said unto him, Lord, I will follow thee whithersoever thou goest.

58And Jesus said unto him, Foxes have holes, and birds of the air *have* nests; but the Son of man hath not where to lay *his* head.

59And he said unto another, Follow me. But he said, Lord, suffer me first to go and bury my father.

60Jesus said unto him, Let the dead bury their dead: but go thou and preach the kingdom of God.

61And another also said, Lord, I will follow thee; but let me first go bid them farewell, which are at home at my house.

62And Jesus said unto him, No man, having put his hand to the plough, and looking back, is fit for the kingdom of God.

10 AFTER THESE things the Lord appointed other seventy also, and sent them two and two before his face into every city and place, whither he himself would come.

New International

father. 43And they were all amazed at the greatness of God.

While everyone was marveling at all that Jesus did, he said to his disciples, 44"Listen carefully to what I am about to tell you: The Son of Man is going to be betrayed into the hands of men." 45But they did not understand what this meant. It was hidden from them, so that they did not grasp it, and they were afraid to ask him about it.

Who Will Be the Greatest?

46An argument started among the disciples as to which of them would be the greatest. 47Jesus, knowing their thoughts, took a little child and had him stand beside him. 48Then he said to them, "Whoever welcomes this little child in my name welcomes me; and whoever welcomes me welcomes the one who sent me. For he who is least among you all—he is the greatest."

49"Master," said John, "we saw a man driving out demons in your name and we tried to stop him, because he is not one of us."

50"Do not stop him," Jesus said, "for whoever is not against you is for you."

Samaritan Opposition

51As the time approached for him to be taken up to heaven, Jesus resolutely set out for Jerusalem. 52And he sent messengers on ahead, who went into a Samaritan village to get things ready for him; 53but the people there did not welcome him, because he was heading for Jerusalem. 54When the disciples James and John saw this, they asked, "Lord, do you want us to call fire down from heaven to destroy thema?" 55But Jesus turned and rebuked them, 56andb they went to another village.

The Cost of Following Jesus

57As they were walking along the road, a man said to him, "I will follow you wherever you go."

58Jesus replied, "Foxes have holes and birds of the air have nests, but the Son of Man has no place to lay his head."

59He said to another man, "Follow me."

But the man replied, "Lord, first let me go and bury my father."

60Jesus said to him, "Let the dead bury their own dead, but you go and proclaim the kingdom of God."

61Still another said, "I will follow you, Lord; but first let me go back and say good-by to my family."

62Jesus replied, "No one who puts his hand to the plow and looks back is fit for service in the kingdom of God."

Jesus Sends Out the Seventy-two

10 AFTER THIS the Lord appointed seventy-twoc others and sent them two by two ahead of him to every town and place where he was about to go. 2He

a 54 Some manuscripts them, even as Elijah did   b 55,56 Some manuscripts them. And he said, "You do not know what kind of spirit you are of, for the Son of Man did not come to destroy men's lives, but to save them." 56And   c 1 Some manuscripts seventy; also in verse 17

Living Bible

43Awe gripped the people as they saw this display of the power of God.

Meanwhile, as they were exclaiming over all the wonderful things he was doing, Jesus said to his disciples, 44"Listen to me and remember what I say. I, the Messiah,d am going to be betrayed." 45But the disciples didn't know what he meant, for their minds had been sealed and they were afraid to ask him.

46Now came an argument among them as to which of them would be greatest [in the coming Kingdom]! 47But Jesus knew their thoughts, so he stood a little child beside him 48and said to them, "Anyone who takes care of a little child like this is caring for me! And whoever cares for me is caring for God who sent me. Your care for others is the measure of your greatness." 49His disciple John came to him and said, "Master, we saw someone using your name to cast out demons. And we told him not to. After all, he isn't in our group."

50But Jesus said, "You shouldn't have done that! For anyone who is not against you is for you."

51As the time drew near for his return to heaven, he moved steadily onward toward Jerusalem with an iron will.

52One day he sent messengers ahead to reserve rooms for them in a Samaritan village. 53But they were turned away! The people of the village refused to have anything to do with them because they were headed for Jerusalem.f

54When word came back of what had happened, James and John said to Jesus, "Master, shall we order fire down from heaven to burn them up?" 55But Jesus turned and rebuked them,g 56and they went on to another village.

57As they were walking along someone said to Jesus, "I will always follow you no matter where you go."

58But Jesus replied, "Remember, I don't even own a place to lay my head. Foxes have dens to live in, and birds have nests, but I, the Messiah,d have no earthly home at all."

59Another time, when he invited a man to come with him and to be his disciple, the man agreed—but wanted to wait until his father's death.h

60Jesus replied, "Let those without eternal life concern themselves with things like that.i Your duty is to come and preach the coming of the Kingdom of God to all the world."

61Another said, "Yes, Lord, I will come, but first let me ask permission of those at home."j

62But Jesus told him, "Anyone who lets himself be distracted from the work I plan for him is not fit for the Kingdom of God."

10 THE LORD now chose seventy other disciples and sent them on ahead in pairs to all the towns and villages he planned to visit later.

New Revised Standard

healed the boy, and gave him back to his father. 43And all were astounded at the greatness of God.

Jesus Again Foretells His Death

While everyone was amazed at all that he was doing, he said to his disciples, 44"Let these words sink into your ears: The Son of Man is going to be betrayed into human hands." 45But they did not understand this saying; its meaning was concealed from them, so that they could not perceive it. And they were afraid to ask him about this saying.

True Greatness

46 An argument arose among them as to which one of them was the greatest. 47But Jesus, aware of their inner thoughts, took a little child and put it by his side, 48and said to them, "Whoever welcomes this child in my name welcomes me, and whoever welcomes me welcomes the one who sent me; for the least among all of you is the greatest."

Another Exorcist

49 John answered, "Master, we saw someone casting out demons in your name, and we tried to stop him, because he does not follow with us." 50But Jesus said to him, "Do not stop him; for whoever is not against you is for you."

A Samaritan Village Refuses to Receive Jesus

51 When the days drew near for him to be taken up, he set his face to go to Jerusalem. 52And he sent messengers ahead of him. On their way they entered a village of the Samaritans to make ready for him; 53but they did not receive him, because his face was set toward Jerusalem. 54When his disciples James and John saw it, they said, "Lord, do you want us to command fire to come down from heaven and consume them?"k 55But he turned and rebuked them. 56Thenl they went on to another village.

Would-Be Followers of Jesus

57 As they were going along the road, someone said to him, "I will follow you wherever you go." 58And Jesus said to him, "Foxes have holes, and birds of the air have nests; but the Son of Man has nowhere to lay his head." 59To another he said, "Follow me." But he said, "Lord, first let me go and bury my father." 60But Jesusm said to him, "Let the dead bury their own dead; but as for you, go and proclaim the kingdom of God." 61Another said, "I will follow you, Lord; but let me first say farewell to those at my home." 62Jesus said to him, "No one who puts a hand to the plow and looks back is fit for the kingdom of God."

The Mission of the Seventy

10 AFTER THIS the Lord appointed seventyn others and sent them on ahead of him in pairs to every town and place where he himself intended to go.

---

d 9:44,9:58 the Messiah, literally, "the Son of Man." e 9:46 the coming Kingdom, implied. f 9:53 A typical case of discrimination (cf Jn 4:9). The Jews called the Samaritans "half-breeds," so the Samaritans naturally hated the Jews. g 9:55 Later manuscripts add to vss 55, 56, "And Jesus said, You don't realize what your hearts are like. For the Son of Man has not come to destroy men's lives, but to save them." h 9:59 but wanted to wait until his father's death, literally, "But he said, 'Lord, suffer me first to go and bury my father,' " perhaps meaning that the man could, when his father died, collect the inheritance and have some security. i 9:60 Let those without eternal life concern themselves with things like that, or, "Let those who are spiritually dead care for their own dead." j 9:61 ask permission of those at home, literally, "bid them farewell at home."

k Other ancient authorities add as Elijah did l Other ancient authorities read rebuked them, and said, "You do not know what spirit you are of, 56for the Son of Man has not come to destroy the lives of human beings but to save them." Then m Gk he n Other ancient authorities read seventy-two

King James

2Therefore said he unto them, The harvest truly *is* great, but the labourers *are* few: pray ye therefore the Lord of the harvest, that he would send forth labourers into his harvest.

3Go your ways: behold, I send you forth as lambs among wolves.

4Carry neither purse, nor scrip, nor shoes: and salute no man by the way.

5And into whatsoever house ye enter, first say, Peace *be* to this house.

6And if the son of peace be there, your peace shall rest upon it: if not, it shall turn to you again.

7And in the same house remain, eating and drinking such things as they give: for the labourer is worthy of his hire. Go not from house to house.

8And into whatsoever city ye enter, and they receive you, eat such things as are set before you:

9And heal the sick that are therein, and say unto them, The kingdom of God is come nigh unto you.

10But into whatsoever city ye enter, and they receive you not, go your ways out into the streets of the same, and say,

11Even the very dust of your city, which cleaveth on us, we do wipe off against you: notwithstanding be ye sure of this, that the kingdom of God is come nigh unto you.

12But I say unto you, that it shall be more tolerable in that day for Sodom, than for that city.

13Woe unto thee, Chorazin! woe unto thee, Bethsaida! for if the mighty works had been done in Tyre and Sidon, which have been done in you, they had a great while ago repented, sitting in sackcloth and ashes.

14But it shall be more tolerable for Tyre and Sidon at the judgment, than for you.

15And thou, Capernaum, which art exalted to heaven, shalt be thrust down to hell.

16He that heareth you heareth me; and he that despiseth you despiseth me; and he that despiseth me despiseth him that sent me.

17¶ And the seventy returned again with joy, saying, Lord, even the devils are subject unto us through thy name.

18And he said unto them, I beheld Satan as lightning fall from heaven.

19Behold, I give unto you power to tread on serpents and scorpions, and over all the power of the enemy: and nothing shall by any means hurt you.

20Notwithstanding in this rejoice not, that the spirits are subject unto you; but rather rejoice, because your names are written in heaven.

21¶ In that hour Jesus rejoiced in spirit, and said, I thank thee, O Father, Lord of heaven and earth, that thou hast hid these things from the wise and prudent, and hast revealed them unto babes: even so, Father; for so it seemed good in thy sight.

22All things are delivered to me of my Father: and no man knoweth who the Son is, but the Father; and who the Father is, but the Son, and *he* to whom the Son will reveal *him*.

23¶ And he turned him unto *his* disciples, and said privately, Blessed *are* the eyes which see the things that ye see:

24For I tell you, that many prophets and kings have desired to see those things which ye see, and have not seen *them;* and to hear those things which ye hear, and have not heard *them.*

25¶ And, behold, a certain lawyer stood up, and tempted him, saying, Master, what shall I do to inherit eternal life?

26He said unto him, What is written in the law? how readest thou?

New International

told them, "The harvest is plentiful, but the workers are few. Ask the Lord of the harvest, therefore, to send out workers into his harvest field. 3Go! I am sending you out like lambs among wolves. 4Do not take a purse or bag or sandals; and do not greet anyone on the road.

5"When you enter a house, first say, 'Peace to this house.' 6If a man of peace is there, your peace will rest on him; if not, it will return to you. 7Stay in that house, eating and drinking whatever they give you, for the worker deserves his wages. Do not move around from house to house.

8"When you enter a town and are welcomed, eat what is set before you. 9Heal the sick who are there and tell them, 'The kingdom of God is near you.' 10But when you enter a town and are not welcomed, go into its streets and say, 11'Even the dust of your town that sticks to our feet we wipe off against you. Yet be sure of this: The kingdom of God is near.' 12I tell you, it will be more bearable on that day for Sodom than for that town.

13"Woe to you, Korazin! Woe to you, Bethsaida! For if the miracles that were performed in you had been performed in Tyre and Sidon, they would have repented long ago, sitting in sackcloth and ashes. 14But it will be more bearable for Tyre and Sidon at the judgment than for you. 15And you, Capernaum, will you be lifted up to the skies? No, you will go down to the depths.[a]

16"He who listens to you listens to me; he who rejects you rejects me; but he who rejects me rejects him who sent me."

17The seventy-two returned with joy and said, "Lord, even the demons submit to us in your name."

18He replied, "I saw Satan fall like lightning from heaven. 19I have given you authority to trample on snakes and scorpions and to overcome all the power of the enemy; nothing will harm you. 20However, do not rejoice that the spirits submit to you, but rejoice that your names are written in heaven."

21At that time Jesus, full of joy through the Holy Spirit, said, "I praise you, Father, Lord of heaven and earth, because you have hidden these things from the wise and learned, and revealed them to little children. Yes, Father, for this was your good pleasure.

22"All things have been committed to me by my Father. No one knows who the Son is except the Father, and no one knows who the Father is except the Son and those to whom the Son chooses to reveal him."

23Then he turned to his disciples and said privately, "Blessed are the eyes that see what you see. 24For I tell you that many prophets and kings wanted to see what you see but did not see it, and to hear what you hear but did not hear it."

The Parable of the Good Samaritan

25On one occasion an expert in the law stood up to test Jesus. "Teacher," he asked, "what must I do to inherit eternal life?"

26"What is written in the Law?" he replied. "How do you read it?"

Living Bible

2These were his instructions to them: "Plead with the Lord of the harvest to send out more laborers to help you, for the harvest is so plentiful and the workers so few. 3Go now, and remember that I am sending you out as lambs among wolves. 4Don't take any money with you, or a beggar's bag, or even an extra pair of shoes. And don't waste time along the way.b

5"Whenever you enter a home, give it your blessing. 6If it is worthy of the blessing, the blessing will stand; if not, the blessing will return to you.

7"When you enter a village, don't shift around from home to home, but stay in one place, eating and drinking without question whatever is set before you. And don't hesitate to accept hospitality, for the workman is worthy of his wages!

8, 9"If a town welcomes you, follow these two rules:
  (1) Eat whatever is set before you.
  (2) Heal the sick; and as you heal them, say, 'The Kingdom of God is very near you now.'

10"But if a town refuses you, go out into its streets and say, 11'We wipe the dust of your town from our feet as a public announcement of your doom. Never forget how close you were to the Kingdom of God!' 12Even wicked Sodom will be better off than such a city on the Judgment Day. 13What horrors await you, you cities of Chorazin and Bethsaida! For if the miracles I did for you had been done in the cities of Tyre and Sidon,c their people would have sat in deep repentance long ago, clothed in sackcloth and throwing ashes on their heads to show their remorse. 14Yes, Tyre and Sidon will receive less punishment on the Judgment Day than you. 15And you people of Capernaum, what shall I say about you? Will you be exalted to heaven? No, you shall be brought down to hell."

16Then he said to the disciples, "Those who welcome you are welcoming me. And those who reject you are rejecting me. And those who reject me are rejecting God who sent me."

17When the seventy disciples returned, they joyfully reported to him, "Even the demons obey us when we use your name."

18"Yes," he told them, "I saw Satan falling from heaven as a flash of lightning! 19And I have given you authority over all the power of the Enemy, and to walk among serpents and scorpions and to crush them. Nothing shall injure you! 20However, the important thing is not that demons obey you, but that your names are registered as citizens of heaven."

21Then he was filled with the joy of the Holy Spirit and said, "I praise you, O Father, Lord of heaven and earth, for hiding these things from the intellectuals and worldly wise and for revealing them to those who are as trusting as little children.d Yes, thank you, Father, for that is the way you wanted it. 22I am the Agent of my Father in everything; and no one really knows the Son except the Father, and no one really knows the Father except the Son and those to whom the Son chooses to reveal him."

23Then, turning to the twelve disciples, he said quietly, "How privileged you are to see what you have seen. 24Many a prophet and king of old has longed for these days, to see and hear what you have seen and heard!"

25One day an expert on Moses' laws came to test Jesus' orthodoxy by asking him this question: "Teacher, what does a man need to do to live forever in heaven?"

26Jesus replied, "What does Moses' law say about it?"

New Revised Standard

2He said to them, "The harvest is plentiful, but the laborers are few; therefore ask the Lord of the harvest to send out laborers into his harvest. 3Go on your way. See, I am sending you out like lambs into the midst of wolves. 4Carry no purse, no bag, no sandals; and greet no one on the road. 5Whatever house you enter, first say, 'Peace to this house!' 6And if anyone is there who shares in peace, your peace will rest on that person; but if not, it will return to you. 7Remain in the same house, eating and drinking whatever they provide, for the laborer deserves to be paid. Do not move about from house to house. 8Whenever you enter a town and its people welcome you, eat what is set before you; 9cure the sick who are there, and say to them, 'The kingdom of God has come near to you.'e 10But whenever you enter a town and they do not welcome you, go out into its streets and say, 11'Even the dust of your town that clings to our feet, we wipe off in protest against you. Yet know this: the kingdom of God has come near.'f 12I tell you, on that day it will be more tolerable for Sodom than for that town.

Woes to Unrepentant Cities

13 "Woe to you, Chorazin! Woe to you, Bethsaida! For if the deeds of power done in you had been done in Tyre and Sidon, they would have repented long ago, sitting in sackcloth and ashes. 14But at the judgment it will be more tolerable for Tyre and Sidon than for you. 15And you, Capernaum,
   will you be exalted to heaven?
   No, you will be brought down to Hades.

16 "Whoever listens to you listens to me, and whoever rejects you rejects me, and whoever rejects me rejects the one who sent me."

The Return of the Seventy

17 The seventyg returned with joy, saying, "Lord, in your name even the demons submit to us!" 18He said to them, "I watched Satan fall from heaven like a flash of lightning. 19See, I have given you authority to tread on snakes and scorpions, and over all the power of the enemy; and nothing will hurt you. 20Nevertheless, do not rejoice at this, that the spirits submit to you, but rejoice that your names are written in heaven."

Jesus Rejoices

21 At that same hour Jesush rejoiced in the Holy Spiriti and said, "I thankj you, Father, Lord of heaven and earth, because you have hidden these things from the wise and the intelligent and have revealed them to infants; yes, Father, for such was your gracious will.k 22All things have been handed over to me by my Father; and no one knows who the Son is except the Father, or who the Father is except the Son and anyone to whom the Son chooses to reveal him."

23 Then turning to the disciples, Jesush said to them privately, "Blessed are the eyes that see what you see! 24For I tell you that many prophets and kings desired to see what you see, but did not see it, and to hear what you hear, but did not hear it."

The Parable of the Good Samaritan

25 Just then a lawyer stood up to test Jesus.l "Teacher," he said, "what must I do to inherit eternal life?" 26He said to him, "What is written in the law? What do you read there?" 27He answered, "You shall

---

b 10:4 And don't waste time along the way, literally, "Salute no one in the way."   c 10:13 Tyre and Sidon, cities destroyed by God in judgment for their wickedness. For a description of this event, see Ezek 26-28.   d 10:21 little children, literally, "babies."

e Or is at hand for you   f Or is at hand   g Other ancient authorities read seventy-two   h Gk he   i Other authorities read in the spirit   j Or praise   k Or for so it was well-pleasing in your sight   l Gk him

King James

27And he answering said, Thou shalt love the Lord thy God with all thy heart, and with all thy soul, and with all thy strength, and with all thy mind; and thy neighbour as thyself.

28And he said unto him, Thou hast answered right: this do, and thou shalt live.

29But he, willing to justify himself, said unto Jesus, And who is my neighbour?

30And Jesus answering said, A certain *man* went down from Jerusalem to Jericho, and fell among thieves, which stripped him of his raiment, and wounded *him,* and departed, leaving *him* half dead.

31And by chance there came down a certain priest that way: and when he saw him, he passed by on the other side.

32And likewise a Levite, when he was at the place, came and looked *on him,* and passed by on the other side.

33But a certain Samaritan, as he journeyed, came where he was: and when he saw him, he had compassion *on him,*

34And went to *him,* and bound up his wounds, pouring in oil and wine, and set him on his own beast, and brought him to an inn, and took care of him.

35And on the morrow when he departed, he took out two pence, and gave *them* to the host, and said unto him, Take care of him; and whatsoever thou spendest more, when I come again, I will repay thee.

36Which now of these three, thinkest thou, was neighbour unto him that fell among the thieves?

37And he said, He that showed mercy on him. Then said Jesus unto him, Go, and do thou likewise.

38¶ Now it came to pass, as they went, that he entered into a certain village: and a certain woman named Martha received him into her house.

39And she had a sister called Mary, which also sat at Jesus' feet, and heard his word.

40But Martha was cumbered about much serving, and came to him, and said, Lord, dost thou not care that my sister hath left me to serve alone? bid her therefore that she help me.

41And Jesus answered and said unto her, Martha, Martha, thou art careful and troubled about many things:

42But one thing is needful: and Mary hath chosen that good part, which shall not be taken away from her.

11 AND IT came to pass, that, as he was praying in a certain place, when he ceased, one of his disciples said unto him, Lord, teach us to pray, as John also taught his disciples.

2And he said unto them, When ye pray, say, Our Father which art in heaven, Hallowed be thy name. Thy kingdom come. Thy will be done, as in heaven, so in earth.

3Give us day by day our daily bread.

4And forgive us our sins; for we also forgive every one that is indebted to us. And lead us not into temptation; but deliver us from evil.

5And he said unto them, Which of you shall have a friend, and shall go unto him at midnight, and say unto him, Friend, lend me three loaves;

New International

27He answered: " 'Love the Lord your God with all your heart and with all your soul and with all your strength and with all your mind'a; and, 'Love your neighbor as yourself.'b"

28"You have answered correctly," Jesus replied. "Do this and you will live."

29But he wanted to justify himself, so he asked Jesus, "And who is my neighbor?"

30In reply Jesus said: "A man was going down from Jerusalem to Jericho, when he fell into the hands of robbers. They stripped him of his clothes, beat him and went away, leaving him half dead. 31A priest happened to be going down the same road, and when he saw the man, he passed by on the other side. 32So too, a Levite, when he came to the place and saw him, passed by on the other side. 33But a Samaritan, as he traveled, came where the man was; and when he saw him, he took pity on him. 34He went to him and bandaged his wounds, pouring on oil and wine. Then he put the man on his own donkey, took him to an inn and took care of him. 35The next day he took out two silver coinsc and gave them to the innkeeper. 'Look after him,' he said, 'and when I return, I will reimburse you for any extra expense you may have.'

36"Which of these three do you think was a neighbor to the man who fell into the hands of robbers?"

37The expert in the law replied, "The one who had mercy on him."

Jesus told him, "Go and do likewise."

At the Home of Martha and Mary

38As Jesus and his disciples were on their way, he came to a village where a woman named Martha opened her home to him. 39She had a sister called Mary, who sat at the Lord's feet listening to what he said. 40But Martha was distracted by all the preparations that had to be made. She came to him and asked, "Lord, don't you care that my sister has left me to do the work by myself? Tell her to help me!"

41"Martha, Martha," the Lord answered, "you are worried and upset about many things, 42but only one thing is needed.d Mary has chosen what is better, and it will not be taken away from her."

Jesus' Teaching on Prayer

11 ONE DAY Jesus was praying in a certain place. When he finished, one of his disciples said to him, "Lord, teach us to pray, just as John taught his disciples."

2He said to them, "When you pray, say:

" 'Father,e
hallowed be your name,
your kingdom come.f
3Give us each day our daily bread,
4Forgive us our sins,
for we also forgive everyone who sins against us.g
And lead us not into temptation.h' "

5Then he said to them, "Suppose one of you has a friend, and he goes to him at midnight and says, 'Friend, lend me three loaves of bread, 6because a friend of mine

---

a 27 Deut. 6:5   b 27 Lev. 19:18   c 35 Greek *two denarii*   d 42 Some manuscripts *but few things are needed—or only one*   e 2 Some manuscripts *Our Father in heaven*   f 2 Some manuscripts *come. May your will be done on earth as it is in heaven.*   g 4 Greek *everyone who is indebted to us*   h 4 Some manuscripts *temptation but deliver us from the evil one*

Living Bible

27"It says," he replied, "that you must love the Lord your God with all your heart, and with all your soul, and with all your strength, and with all your mind. And you must love your neighbor just as much as you love yourself."

28"Right!" Jesus told him. *"Do this and you shall live!"*

29The man wanted to justify (his lack of love for some kinds of people),[i] so he asked, "Which neighbors?"

30Jesus replied with an illustration: "A Jew going on a trip from Jerusalem to Jericho was attacked by bandits. They stripped him of his clothes and money and beat him up and left him lying half dead beside the road.

31"By chance a Jewish priest came along; and when he saw the man lying there, he crossed to the other side of the road and passed him by. 32A Jewish Temple-assistanti walked over and looked at him lying there, but then went on.

33"But a despised Samaritank came along, and when he saw him, he felt deep pity. 34Kneeling beside him the Samaritan soothed his wounds with medicine and bandaged them. Then he put the man on his donkey and walked along beside him till they came to an inn, where he nursed him through the night.[l] 35The next day he handed the innkeeper two twenty-dollar billsm and told him to take care of the man. 'If his bill runs higher than that,' he said, 'I'll pay the difference the next time I am here.'

36"Now which of these three would you say was a neighbor to the bandits' victim?"

37The man replied, "The one who showed him some pity."

Then Jesus said, "Yes, now go and do the same."

38As Jesus and the disciples continued on their way to Jerusalemn they came to a village where a woman named Martha welcomed them into her home. 39Her sister Mary sat on the floor, listening to Jesus as he talked.

40But Martha was the jittery type, and was worrying over the big dinner she was preparing.

She came to Jesus and said, "Sir, doesn't it seem unfair to you that my sister just sits here while I do all the work? Tell her to come and help me."

41But the Lord said to her, "Martha, dear friend,o you are so upset over all these details! 42There is really only one thing worth being concerned about. Mary has discovered it—and I won't take it away from her!"

11 ONCE WHEN Jesus had been out praying, one of his disciples came to him as he finished and said, "Lord, teach us a prayer to recitep just as John taught one to his disciples."

2And this is the prayer he taught them: "Father, may your name be honored for its holiness; send your Kingdom soon. 3Give us our food day by day. 4And forgive our sins—for we have forgiven those who sinned against us. And don't allow us to be tempted."

5, 6Then, teaching them more about prayer,q he used this illustration: "Suppose you went to a friend's house at midnight, wanting to borrow three loaves of bread.

New Revised Standard

love the Lord your God with all your heart, and with all your soul, and with all your strength, and with all your mind; and your neighbor as yourself." 28And he said to him, "You have given the right answer; do this, and you will live."

29 But wanting to justify himself, he asked Jesus, "And who is my neighbor?" 30Jesus replied, "A man was going down from Jerusalem to Jericho, and fell into the hands of robbers, who stripped him, beat him, and went away, leaving him half dead. 31Now by chance a priest was going down that road; and when he saw him, he passed by on the other side. 32So likewise a Levite, when he came to the place and saw him, passed by on the other side. 33But a Samaritan while traveling came near him; and when he saw him, he was moved with pity. 34He went to him and bandaged his wounds, having poured oil and wine on them. Then he put him on his own animal, brought him to an inn, and took care of him. 35The next day he took out two denarii,r gave them to the innkeeper, and said, 'Take care of him; and when I come back, I will repay you whatever more you spend.' 36Which of these three, do you think, was a neighbor to the man who fell into the hands of the robbers?" 37He said, "The one who showed him mercy." Jesus said to him, "Go and do likewise."

Jesus Visits Martha and Mary

38 Now as they went on their way, he entered a certain village, where a woman named Martha welcomed him into her home. 39She had a sister named Mary, who sat at the Lord's feet and listened to what he was saying. 40But Martha was distracted by her many tasks; so she came to him and asked, "Lord, do you not care that my sister has left me to do all the work by myself? Tell her then to help me." 41But the Lord answered her, "Martha, Martha, you are worried and distracted by many things; 42there is need of only one thing.s Mary has chosen the better part, which will not be taken away from her."

The Lord's Prayer

11 HE WAS praying in a certain place, and after he had finished, one of his disciples said to him, "Lord, teach us to pray, as John taught his disciples." 2He said to them, "When you pray, say:

Father,t hallowed be your name.
  Your kingdom come.u
3 Give us each day our daily bread.v
4 And forgive us our sins,
    for we ourselves forgive everyone
      indebted to us.
  And do not bring us to the time of trial."w

Perseverance in Prayer

5 And he said to them, "Suppose one of you has a friend, and you go to him at midnight and say to him, 'Friend, lend me three loaves of bread; 6for a friend of

---

i 10:29 *wanted to justify (his lack of love for some kinds of people)*, literally, "wanting to justify himself." j 10:32 *Jewish Temple-assistant*, literally, "Levite." k 10:33 *a despised Samaritan*, literally, "a Samaritan." All Samaritans were despised by Jews and the feeling was mutual, due to historic reasons. l 10:34 *nursed him through the night*, literally, "took care of him." m 10:35 *two twenty-dollar bills*, literally, "two denarii," each the equivalent of a modern day's wage. n 10:38 *on their way to Jerusalem*, implied. o 10:41 *Martha, dear friend*, literally, "Martha, Martha." p 11:1 *to recite*, implied. q 11:5, 6 *Then, teaching them more about prayer*. Some ancient manuscripts add at this point additional portions of the Lord's Prayer as recorded in Mt 6:9-13.

r The denarius was the usual day's wage for a laborer s Other ancient authorities read *few things are necessary, or only one* t Other ancient authorities read *Our Father in heaven* u A few ancient authorities read *Your Holy Spirit come upon us and cleanse us*. Other ancient authorities add *Your will be done, on earth as in heaven* v Or *our bread for tomorrow* w Or *us into temptation*. Other ancient authorities add *but rescue us from the evil one* (or *from evil*)

King James

6For a friend of mine in his journey is come to me, and I have nothing to set before him?

7And he from within shall answer and say, Trouble me not: the door is now shut, and my children are with me in bed; I cannot rise and give thee.

8I say unto you, Though he will not rise and give him, because he is his friend, yet because of his importunity he will rise and give him as many as he needeth.

9And I say unto you, Ask, and it shall be given you; seek, and ye shall find; knock, and it shall be opened unto you.

10For every one that asketh receiveth; and he that seeketh findeth; and to him that knocketh it shall be opened.

11If a son shall ask bread of any of you that is a father, will he give him a stone? or if he ask a fish, will he for a fish give him a serpent?

12Or if he shall ask an egg, will he offer him a scorpion?

13If ye then, being evil, know how to give good gifts unto your children: how much more shall your heavenly Father give the Holy Spirit to them that ask him?

14¶ And he was casting out a devil, and it was dumb. And it came to pass, when the devil was gone out, the dumb spake; and the people wondered.

15But some of them said, He casteth out devils through Beelzebub the chief of the devils.

16And others, tempting him, sought of him a sign from heaven.

17But he, knowing their thoughts, said unto them, Every kingdom divided against itself is brought to desolation; and a house divided against a house falleth.

18If Satan also be divided against himself, how shall his kingdom stand? because ye say that I cast out devils through Beelzebub.

19And if I by Beelzebub cast out devils, by whom do your sons cast them out? therefore shall they be your judges.

20But if I with the finger of God cast out devils, no doubt the kingdom of God is come upon you.

21When a strong man armed keepeth his palace, his goods are in peace:

22But when a stronger than he shall come upon him, and overcome him, he taketh from him all his armour wherein he trusted, and divideth his spoils.

23He that is not with me is against me: and he that gathereth not with me scattereth.

24When the unclean spirit is gone out of a man, he walketh through dry places, seeking rest; and finding none, he saith, I will return unto my house whence I came out.

25And when he cometh, he findeth it swept and garnished.

26Then goeth he, and taketh to him seven other spirits more wicked than himself; and they enter in, and dwell there: and the last state of that man is worse than the first.

27¶ And it came to pass, as he spake these things, a certain woman of the company lifted up her voice, and said unto him, Blessed is the womb that bare thee, and the paps which thou hast sucked.

28But he said, Yea rather, blessed are they that hear the word of God, and keep it.

29¶ And when the people were gathered thick together, he began to say, This is an evil generation: they seek a sign; and there shall no sign be given it, but the sign of Jonas the prophet.

30For as Jonas was a sign unto the Ninevites, so shall also the Son of man be to this generation.

New International

on a journey has come to me, and I have nothing to set before him.'

7"Then the one inside answers, 'Don't bother me. The door is already locked, and my children are with me in bed. I can't get up and give you anything.' 8I tell you, though he will not get up and give him the bread because he is his friend, yet because of the man's boldnessa he will get up and give him as much as he needs.

9"So I say to you: Ask and it will be given to you; seek and you will find; knock and the door will be opened to you. 10For everyone who asks receives; he who seeks finds; and to him who knocks, the door will be opened.

11"Which of you fathers, if your son asks forb a fish, will give him a snake instead? 12Or if he asks for an egg, will give him a scorpion? 13If you then, though you are evil, know how to give good gifts to your children, how much more will your Father in heaven give the Holy Spirit to those who ask him!"

Jesus and Beelzebub

14Jesus was driving out a demon that was mute. When the demon left, the man who had been mute spoke, and the crowd was amazed. 15But some of them said, "By Beelzebub,c the prince of demons, he is driving out demons." 16Others tested him by asking for a sign from heaven.

17Jesus knew their thoughts and said to them: "Any kingdom divided against itself will be ruined, and a house divided against itself will fall. 18If Satan is divided against himself, how can his kingdom stand? I say this because you claim that I drive out demons by Beelzebub. 19Now if I drive out demons by Beelzebub, by whom do your followers drive them out? So then, they will be your judges. 20But if I drive out demons by the finger of God, then the kingdom of God has come to you.

21"When a strong man, fully armed, guards his own house, his possessions are safe. 22But when someone stronger attacks and overpowers him, he takes away the armor in which the man trusted and divides up the spoils.

23"He who is not with me is against me, and he who does not gather with me, scatters.

24"When an evild spirit comes out of a man, it goes through arid places seeking rest and does not find it. Then it says, 'I will return to the house I left.' 25When it arrives, it finds the house swept clean and put in order. 26Then it goes and takes seven other spirits more wicked than itself, and they go in and live there. And the final condition of that man is worse than the first."

27As Jesus was saying these things, a woman in the crowd called out, "Blessed is the mother who gave you birth and nursed you."

28He replied, "Blessed rather are those who hear the word of God and obey it."

The Sign of Jonah

29As the crowds increased, Jesus said, "This is a wicked generation. It asks for a miraculous sign, but none will be given it except the sign of Jonah. 30For as Jonah was a sign to the Ninevites, so also will the Son of Man be to this generation. 31The Queen of the South

---

a 8 Or persistence   b 11 Some manuscripts for bread, will give him a stone; or if he asks for   c 15 Greek Beezeboul or Beelzeboul; also in verses 18 and 19   d 24 Greek unclean

Living Bible

You would shout up to him, 'A friend of mine has just arrived for a visit and I've nothing to give him to eat.' 7He would call down from his bedroom, 'Please don't ask me to get up. The door is locked for the night and we are all in bed. I just can't help you this time.'

8"But I'll tell you this—though he won't do it as a friend, if you keep knocking long enough he will get up and give you everything you want—just because of your persistence. 9And so it is with prayer—keep on asking and you will keep on getting; keep on looking and you will keep on finding; knock and the door will be opened. 10Everyone who asks, receives; all who seek, find; and the door is opened to everyone who knocks.

11"You men who are fathers—if your boy asks for bread, do you give him a stone? If he asks for fish, do you give him a snake? 12If he asks for an egg, do you give him a scorpion? [Of course not!e]

13"And if even sinful persons like yourselves give children what they need, don't you realize that your heavenly Father will do at least as much, and give the Holy Spirit to those who ask for him?"

14Once, when Jesus cast out a demon from a man who couldn't speak, his voice returned to him. The crowd was excited and enthusiastic, 15but some said, "No wonder he can cast them out. He gets his power from Satan,f the king of demons!" 16Others asked for something to happen in the sky to prove his claim of being the Messiah.g

17He knew the thoughts of each of them, so he said, "Any kingdom filled with civil war is doomed; so is a home filled with argument and strife. 18Therefore, if what you say is true, that Satan is fighting against himself by empowering me to cast out his demons, how can his kingdom survive? 19And if I am empowered by Satan, what about your own followers? For they cast out demons! Do you think this proves they are possessed by Satan? Ask them if you are right! 20But if I am casting out demons because of power from God, it proves that the Kingdom of God has arrived.

21"For when Satan,h strong and fully armed, guards his palace, it is safe— 22until someone stronger and better-armed attacks and overcomes him and strips him of his weapons and carries off his belongings.

23"Anyone who is not for me is against me; if he isn't helping me, he is hurting my cause.

24"When a demon is cast out of a man, it goes to the deserts, searching there for rest; but finding none, it returns to the person it left, 25and finds that its former home is all swept and clean.i 26Then it goes and gets seven other demons more evil than itself, and they all enter the man. And so the poor fellow is seven timesj worse off than he was before."

27As he was speaking, a woman in the crowd called out, "God bless your mother—the womb from which you came, and the breasts that gave you suck!"

28He replied, "Yes, but even more blessed are all who hear the Word of God and put it into practice."

29, 30As the crowd pressed in upon him, he preached them this sermon: "These are evil times, with evil people. They keep asking for some strange happening in the skies [to prove I am the Messiah], but the only proof I will give them is a miracle like that of Jonah, whose experiences proved to the people of Nineveh that God had sent him. My similar experience will prove that God has sent me to these people.

New Revised Standard

mine has arrived, and I have nothing to set before him.' 7And he answers from within, 'Do not bother me; the door has already been locked, and my children are with me in bed; I cannot get up and give you anything.' 8I tell you, even though he will not get up and give him anything because he is his friend, at least because of his persistence he will get up and give him whatever he needs.

9 "So I say to you, Ask, and it will be given you; search, and you will find; knock, and the door will be opened for you. 10For everyone who asks receives, and everyone who searches finds, and for everyone who knocks, the door will be opened. 11Is there anyone among you who, if your child asks fork a fish, will give a snake instead of a fish? 12Or if the child asks for an egg, will give a scorpion? 13If you then, who are evil, know how to give good gifts to your children, how much more will the heavenly Father give the Holy Spiritl to those who ask him!"

Jesus and Beelzebul

14 Now he was casting out a demon that was mute; when the demon had gone out, the one who had been mute spoke, and the crowds were amazed. 15But some of them said, "He casts out demons by Beelzebul, the ruler of the demons." 16Others, to test him, kept demanding from him a sign from heaven. 17But he knew what they were thinking and said to them, "Every kingdom divided against itself becomes a desert, and house falls on house. 18If Satan also is divided against himself, how will his kingdom stand? —for you say that I cast out the demons by Beelzebul. 19Now if I cast out the demons by Beelzebul, by whom do your exorcistsm cast them out? Therefore they will be your judges. 20But if it is by the finger of God that I cast out the demons, then the kingdom of God has come to you. 21When a strong man, fully armed, guards his castle, his property is safe. 22But when one stronger than he attacks him and overpowers him, he takes away his armor in which he trusted and divides his plunder. 23Whoever is not with me is against me, and whoever does not gather with me scatters.

The Return of the Unclean Spirit

24 "When the unclean spirit has gone out of a person, it wanders through waterless regions looking for a resting place, but not finding any, it says, 'I will return to my house from which I came.' 25When it comes, it finds it swept and put in order. 26Then it goes and brings seven other spirits more evil than itself, and they enter and live there; and the last state of that person is worse than the first."

True Blessedness

27 While he was saying this, a woman in the crowd raised her voice and said to him, "Blessed is the womb that bore you and the breasts that nursed you!" 28But he said, "Blessed rather are those who hear the word of God and obey it!"

The Sign of Jonah

29 When the crowds were increasing, he began to say, "This generation is an evil generation; it asks for a sign, but no sign will be given to it except the sign of Jonah. 30For just as Jonah became a sign to the people of Nineveh, so the Son of Man will be to this generation.

---

e 11:12 Of course not, implied.   f 11:15 from Satan, literally, "from Beelzebub."   g 11:16 Others asked for something to happen in the sky to prove his claim of being the Messiah, implied. Literally, "Others, tempting, sought of him a sign from heaven."   h 11:21 Satan, literally, "the Strong."   i 11:25 is all swept and clean. But empty, since the person is neutral about Christ.   j 11:26 seven times, implied.

k Other ancient authorities add bread, will give a stone; or if your child asks for   l Other ancient authorities read the Father give the Holy Spirit from heaven   m Gk sons

King James

31The queen of the south shall rise up in the judgment with the men of this generation, and condemn them: for she came from the utmost parts of the earth to hear the wisdom of Solomon; and, behold, a greater than Solomon *is* here.

32The men of Nineve shall rise up in the judgment with this generation, and shall condemn it: for they repented at the preaching of Jonas; and, behold, a greater than Jonas *is* here.

33No man, when he hath lighted a candle, putteth *it* in a secret place, neither under a bushel, but on a candlestick, that they which come in may see the light.

34The light of the body is the eye: therefore when thine eye is single, thy whole body also is full of light; but when *thine eye* is evil, thy body also *is* full of darkness.

35Take heed therefore that the light which is in thee be not darkness.

36If thy whole body therefore *be* full of light, having no part dark, the whole shall be full of light, as when the bright shining of a candle doth give thee light.

37¶ And as he spake, a certain Pharisee besought him to dine with him: and he went in, and sat down to meat.

38And when the Pharisee saw *it*, he marvelled that he had not first washed before dinner.

39And the Lord said unto him, Now do ye Pharisees make clean the outside of the cup and the platter; but your inward part is full of ravening and wickedness.

40*Ye* fools, did not he that made that which is without make that which is within also?

41But rather give alms of such things as ye have; and, behold, all things are clean unto you.

42But woe unto you, Pharisees! for ye tithe mint and rue and all manner of herbs, and pass over judgment and the love of God: these ought ye to have done, and not to leave the other undone.

43Woe unto you, Pharisees! for ye love the uppermost seats in the synagogues, and greetings in the markets.

44Woe unto you, scribes and Pharisees, hypocrites! for ye are as graves which appear not, and the men that walk over *them* are not aware *of them*.

45¶ Then answered one of the lawyers, and said unto him, Master, thus saying thou reproachest us also.

46And he said, Woe unto you also, *ye* lawyers! for ye lade men with burdens grievous to be borne, and ye yourselves touch not the burdens with one of your fingers.

47Woe unto you! for ye build the sepulchres of the prophets, and your fathers killed them.

48Truly ye bear witness that ye allow the deeds of your fathers: for they indeed killed them, and ye build their sepulchres.

49Therefore also said the wisdom of God, I will send them prophets and apostles, and *some* of them they shall slay and persecute:

50That the blood of all the prophets, which was shed from the foundation of the world, may be required of this generation;

51From the blood of Abel unto the blood of Zacharias, which perished between the altar and the temple: verily I say unto you, It shall be required of this generation.

52Woe unto you, lawyers! for ye have taken away the key of knowledge: ye entered not in yourselves, and them that were entering in ye hindered.

53And as he said these things unto them, the scribes and the Pharisees began to urge *him* vehemently, and to provoke him to speak of many things:

54Laying wait for him, and seeking to catch something out of his mouth, that they might accuse him.

New International

will rise at the judgment with the men of this generation and condemn them; for she came from the ends of the earth to listen to Solomon's wisdom, and now one[a] greater than Solomon is here. 32The men of Nineveh will stand up at the judgment with this generation and condemn it; for they repented at the preaching of Jonah, and now one greater than Jonah is here.

The Lamp of the Body

33"No one lights a lamp and puts it in a place where it will be hidden, or under a bowl. Instead he puts it on its stand, so that those who come in may see the light. 34Your eye is the lamp of your body. When your eyes are good, your whole body also is full of light. But when they are bad, your body also is full of darkness. 35See to it, then, that the light within you is not darkness. 36Therefore, if your whole body is full of light, and no part of it dark, it will be completely lighted, as when the light of a lamp shines on you."

Six Woes

37When Jesus had finished speaking, a Pharisee invited him to eat with him; so he went in and reclined at the table. 38But the Pharisee, noticing that Jesus did not first wash before the meal, was surprised.

39Then the Lord said to him, "Now then, you Pharisees clean the outside of the cup and dish, but inside you are full of greed and wickedness. 40You foolish people! Did not the one who made the outside make the inside also? 41But give what is inside ¡the dish¿[b] to the poor, and everything will be clean for you.

42"Woe to you Pharisees, because you give God a tenth of your mint, rue and all other kinds of garden herbs, but you neglect justice and the love of God. You should have practiced the latter without leaving the former undone.

43"Woe to you Pharisees, because you love the most important seats in the synagogues and greetings in the marketplaces.

44"Woe to you, because you are like unmarked graves, which men walk over without knowing it."

45One of the experts in the law answered him, "Teacher, when you say these things, you insult us also."

46Jesus replied, "And you experts in the law, woe to you, because you load people down with burdens they can hardly carry, and you yourselves will not lift one finger to help them.

47"Woe to you, because you build tombs for the prophets, and it was your forefathers who killed them. 48So you testify that you approve of what your forefathers did; they killed the prophets, and you build their tombs. 49Because of this, God in his wisdom said, 'I will send them prophets and apostles, some of whom they will kill and others they will persecute.' 50Therefore this generation will be held responsible for the blood of all the prophets that has been shed since the beginning of the world, 51from the blood of Abel to the blood of Zechariah, who was killed between the altar and the sanctuary. Yes, I tell you, this generation will be held responsible for it all.

52"Woe to you experts in the law, because you have taken away the key to knowledge. You yourselves have not entered, and you have hindered those who were entering."

53When Jesus left there, the Pharisees and the teachers of the law began to oppose him fiercely and to besiege him with questions, 54waiting to catch him in something he might say.

---

a 31 Or *something*; also in verse 32   b 41 Or *what you have*

Living Bible

31"And at the Judgment Day the Queen of Sheba[c] shall arise and point her finger at this generation, condemning it, for she went on a long, hard journey to listen to the wisdom of Solomon; but one far greater than Solomon is here [and few pay any attention].

32"The men of Nineveh, too, shall arise and condemn this nation, for they repented at the preaching of Jonah; and someone far greater than Jonah is here [but this nation won't listen[d]].

33"No one lights a lamp and hides it! Instead, he puts it on a lampstand to give light to all who enter the room. 34Your eyes light up your inward being. A pure eye lets sunshine into your soul. A lustful eye shuts out the light and plunges you into darkness. 35So watch out that the sunshine isn't blotted out. 36If you are filled with light within, with no dark corners, then your face will be radiant too, as though a floodlight is beamed upon you."

37, 38As he was speaking, one of the Pharisees asked him home for a meal. When Jesus arrived, he sat down to eat without first performing the ceremonial washing required by Jewish custom. This greatly surprised his host.

39Then Jesus said to him, "You Pharisees wash the outside, but inside you are still dirty—full of greed and wickedness! 40Fools! Didn't God make the inside as well as the outside? 41Purity is best demonstrated by generosity.

42"But woe to you Pharisees! For though you are careful to tithe even the smallest part of your income, you completely forget about justice and the love of God. You should tithe, yes, but you should not leave these other things undone.

43"Woe to you Pharisees! For how you love the seats of honor in the synagogues and the respectful greetings from everyone as you walk through the markets! 44Yes, awesome judgment is awaiting you. For you are like hidden graves in a field. Men go by you with no knowledge of the corruption they are passing."

45"Sir," said an expert in religious law who was standing there, "you have insulted my profession, too, in what you just said."

46"Yes," said Jesus, "the same horrors await you! For you crush men beneath impossible religious demands—demands that you yourselves would never think of trying to keep. 47Woe to you! For you are exactly like your ancestors who killed the prophets long ago. 48Murderers! You agree with your fathers that what they did was right—you would have done the same yourselves.

49"This is what God says about you: 'I will send prophets and apostles to you, and you will kill some of them and chase away the others.'

50"And you of this generation will be held responsible for the murder of God's servants from the founding of the world— 51from the murder of Abel to the murder of Zechariah who perished between the altar and the sanctuary. Yes, it will surely be charged against you.

52"Woe to you experts in religion! For you hide the truth from the people. You won't accept it for yourselves, and you prevent others from having a chance to believe it."

53, 54The Pharisees and legal experts were furious; and from that time on they plied him fiercely with a host of questions, trying to trap him into saying something for which they could have him arrested.

New Revised Standard

31 The queen of the South will rise at the judgment with the people of this generation and condemn them, because she came from the ends of the earth to listen to the wisdom of Solomon, and see, something greater than Solomon is here! 32 The people of Nineveh will rise up at the judgment with this generation and condemn it, because they repented at the proclamation of Jonah, and see, something greater than Jonah is here!

The Light of the Body

33 "No one after lighting a lamp puts it in a cellar,[e] but on the lampstand so that those who enter may see the light. 34 Your eye is the lamp of your body. If your eye is healthy, your whole body is full of light; but if it is not healthy, your body is full of darkness. 35 Therefore consider whether the light in you is not darkness. 36 If then your whole body is full of light, with no part of it in darkness, it will be as full of light as when a lamp gives you light with its rays."

Jesus Denounces Pharisees and Lawyers

37 While he was speaking, a Pharisee invited him to dine with him; so he went in and took his place at the table. 38 The Pharisee was amazed to see that he did not first wash before dinner. 39 Then the Lord said to him, "Now you Pharisees clean the outside of the cup and of the dish, but inside you are full of greed and wickedness. 40 You fools! Did not the one who made the outside make the inside also? 41 So give for alms those things that are within; and see, everything will be clean for you.

42 "But woe to you Pharisees! For you tithe mint and rue and herbs of all kinds, and neglect justice and the love of God; it is these you ought to have practiced, without neglecting the others. 43 Woe to you Pharisees! For you love to have the seat of honor in the synagogues and to be greeted with respect in the marketplaces. 44 Woe to you! For you are like unmarked graves, and people walk over them without realizing it."

45 One of the lawyers answered him, "Teacher, when you say these things, you insult us too." 46 And he said, "Woe also to you lawyers! For you load people with burdens hard to bear, and you yourselves do not lift a finger to ease them. 47 Woe to you! For you build the tombs of the prophets whom your ancestors killed. 48 So you are witnesses and approve of the deeds of your ancestors; for they killed them, and you build their tombs. 49 Therefore also the Wisdom of God said, 'I will send them prophets and apostles, some of whom they will kill and persecute,' 50 so that this generation may be charged with the blood of all the prophets shed since the foundation of the world, 51 from the blood of Abel to the blood of Zechariah, who perished between the altar and the sanctuary. Yes, I tell you, it will be charged against this generation. 52 Woe to you lawyers! For you have taken away the key of knowledge; you did not enter yourselves, and you hindered those who were entering."

53 When he went outside, the scribes and the Pharisees began to be very hostile toward him and to cross-examine him about many things, 54 lying in wait for him, to catch him in something he might say.

King James

12 IN THE mean time, when there were gathered together an innumerable multitude of people, insomuch that they trode one upon another, he began to say unto his disciples first of all, Beware ye of the leaven of the Pharisees, which is hypocrisy.

2For there is nothing covered, that shall not be revealed; neither hid, that shall not be known.

3Therefore whatsoever ye have spoken in darkness shall be heard in the light; and that which ye have spoken in the ear in closets shall be proclaimed upon the housetops.

4And I say unto you my friends, Be not afraid of them that kill the body, and after that have no more that they can do.

5But I will forewarn you whom ye shall fear: Fear him, which after he hath killed hath power to cast into hell; yea, I say unto you, Fear him.

6Are not five sparrows sold for two farthings, and not one of them is forgotten before God?

7But even the very hairs of your head are all numbered. Fear not therefore: ye are of more value than many sparrows.

8Also I say unto you, Whosoever shall confess me before men, him shall the Son of man also confess before the angels of God:

9But he that denieth me before men shall be denied before the angels of God.

10And whosoever shall speak a word against the Son of man, it shall be forgiven him: but unto him that blasphemeth against the Holy Ghost it shall not be forgiven.

11And when they bring you unto the synagogues, and *unto* magistrates, and powers, take ye no thought how or what thing ye shall answer, or what ye shall say:

12For the Holy Ghost shall teach you in the same hour what ye ought to say.

13¶ And one of the company said unto him, Master, speak to my brother, that he divide the inheritance with me.

14And he said unto him, Man, who made me a judge or a divider over you?

15And he said unto them, Take heed, and beware of covetousness: for a man's life consisteth not in the abundance of the things which he possesseth.

16And he spake a parable unto them, saying, The ground of a certain rich man brought forth plentifully:

17And he thought within himself, saying, What shall I do, because I have no room where to bestow my fruits?

18And he said, This will I do: I will pull down my barns, and build greater; and there will I bestow all my fruits and my goods.

19And I will say to my soul, Soul, thou hast much goods laid up for many years; take thine ease, eat, drink, *and* be merry.

20But God said unto him, *Thou* fool, this night thy soul shall be required of thee: then whose shall those things be, which thou hast provided?

21So *is* he that layeth up treasure for himself, and is not rich toward God.

22¶ And he said unto his disciples, Therefore I say unto you, Take no thought for your life, what ye shall eat; neither for the body, what ye shall put on.

23The life is more than meat, and the body *is more* than raiment.

24Consider the ravens: for they neither sow nor reap; which neither have storehouse nor barn; and God feedeth them: how much more are ye better than the fowls?

25And which of you with taking thought can add to his stature one cubit?

26If ye then be not able to do that thing which is least, why take ye thought for the rest?

New International

12 MEANWHILE, WHEN a crowd of many thousands had gathered, so that they were trampling on one another, Jesus began to speak first to his disciples, saying: "Be on your guard against the yeast of the Pharisees, which is hypocrisy. 2There is nothing concealed that will not be disclosed, or hidden that will not be made known. 3What you have said in the dark will be heard in the daylight, and what you have whispered in the ear in the inner rooms will be proclaimed from the roofs.

4"I tell you, my friends, do not be afraid of those who kill the body and after that can do no more. 5But I will show you whom you should fear: Fear him who, after the killing of the body, has power to throw you into hell. Yes, I tell you, fear him. 6Are not five sparrows sold for two penniesa? Yet not one of them is forgotten by God. 7Indeed, the very hairs of your head are all numbered. Don't be afraid; you are worth more than many sparrows.

8"I tell you, whoever acknowledges me before men, the Son of Man will also acknowledge him before the angels of God. 9But he who disowns me before men will be disowned before the angels of God. 10And everyone who speaks a word against the Son of Man will be forgiven, but anyone who blasphemes against the Holy Spirit will not be forgiven.

11"When you are brought before synagogues, rulers and authorities, do not worry about how you will defend yourselves or what you will say, 12for the Holy Spirit will teach you at that time what you should say."

The Parable of the Rich Fool

13Someone in the crowd said to him, "Teacher, tell my brother to divide the inheritance with me."

14Jesus replied, "Man, who appointed me a judge or an arbiter between you?" 15Then he said to them, "Watch out! Be on your guard against all kinds of greed; a man's life does not consist in the abundance of his possessions."

16And he told them this parable: "The ground of a certain rich man produced a good crop. 17He thought to himself, 'What shall I do? I have no place to store my crops.'

18"Then he said, 'This is what I'll do. I will tear down my barns and build bigger ones, and there I will store all my grain and my goods. 19And I'll say to myself, "You have plenty of good things laid up for many years. Take life easy; eat, drink and be merry." '

20"But God said to him, 'You fool! This very night your life will be demanded from you. Then who will get what you have prepared for yourself?'

21"This is how it will be with anyone who stores up things for himself but is not rich toward God."

Do Not Worry

22Then Jesus said to his disciples: "Therefore I tell you, do not worry about your life, what you will eat; or about your body, what you will wear. 23Life is more than food, and the body more than clothes. 24Consider the ravens: They do not sow or reap, they have no storeroom or barn; yet God feeds them. And how much more valuable you are than birds! 25Who of you by worrying can add a single hour to his lifeb? 26Since you cannot do this very little thing, why do you worry about the rest?

---

a 6 Greek *two assaria*　　b 25 Or *single cubit to his height*

Living Bible

12 MEANWHILE THE crowds grew until thousands upon thousands were milling about and crushing each other. He turned now to his disciples and warned them, "More than anything else, beware of these Pharisees and the way they pretend to be good when they aren't. But such hypocrisy cannot be hidden forever. 2It will become as evident as yeast in dough. 3Whatever theyc have said in the dark shall be heard in the light, and what you have whispered in the inner rooms shall be broadcast from the housetops for all to hear!

4"Dear friends, don't be afraid of these who want to murder you. They can only kill the body; they have no power over your souls. 5But I'll tell you whom to fear— fear God who has the power to kill and then cast into hell.

6"What is the price of five sparrows? A couple of pennies? Not much more than that. Yet God does not forget a single one of them. 7And he knows the number of hairs on your head! Never fear, you are far more valuable to him than a whole flock of sparrows.

8"And I assure you of this: I, the Messiah,d will publicly honor you in the presence of God's angels if you publicly acknowledge me here on earth as your Friend. 9But I will deny before the angels those who deny me here among men. 10(Yet those who speak against mee may be forgiven—while those who speak against the Holy Spirit shall never be forgiven.)

11"And when you are brought to trial before these Jewish rulers and authorities in the synagogues, don't be concerned about what to say in your defense, 12for the Holy Spirit will give you the right words even as you are standing there."

13Then someone called from the crowd, "Sir, please tell my brother to divide my father's estate with me."

14But Jesus replied, "Man, who made me a judge over you to decide such things as that? 15Beware! Don't always be wishing for what you don't have. For real life and real living are not related to how rich we are."

16Then he gave an illustration: "A rich man had a fertile farm that produced fine crops. 17In fact, his barns were full to overflowing—he couldn't get everything in. He thought about his problem, 18and finally exclaimed, 'I know—I'll tear down my barns and build bigger ones! Then I'll have room enough. 19And I'll sit back and say to myself, "Friend, you have enough stored away for years to come. Now take it easy! Wine, women, and song for you!" 'f

20"But God said to him, 'Fool! Tonight you die. Then who will get it all?'

21"Yes, every man is a fool who gets rich on earth but not in heaven."

22Then turning to his disciples he said, "Don't worry about whether you have enough food to eat or clothes to wear. 23For life consists of far more than food and clothes. 24Look at the ravens—they don't plant or harvest or have barns to store away their food, and yet they get along all right—for God feeds them. And you are far more valuable to him than any birds!

25"And besides, what's the use of worrying? What good does it do? Will it add a single day to your life? Of course not! 26And if worry can't even do such little things as that, what's the use of worrying over bigger things?

New Revised Standard

A Warning against Hypocrisy

12 MEANWHILE, WHEN the crowd gathered by the thousands, so that they trampled on one another, he began to speak first to his disciples, "Beware of the yeast of the Pharisees, that is, their hypocrisy. 2Nothing is covered up that will not be uncovered, and nothing secret that will not become known. 3Therefore whatever you have said in the dark will be heard in the light, and what you have whispered behind closed doors will be proclaimed from the housetops.

Exhortation to Fearless Confession

4 "I tell you, my friends, do not fear those who kill the body, and after that can do nothing more. 5But I will warn you whom to fear: fear him who, after he has killed, has authorityg to cast into hell.h Yes, I tell you, fear him! 6Are not five sparrows sold for two pennies? Yet not one of them is forgotten in God's sight. 7But even the hairs of your head are all counted. Do not be afraid; you are of more value than many sparrows.

8 "And I tell you, everyone who acknowledges me before others, the Son of Man also will acknowledge before the angels of God; 9but whoever denies me before others will be denied before the angels of God. 10And everyone who speaks a word against the Son of Man will be forgiven; but whoever blasphemes against the Holy Spirit will not be forgiven. 11When they bring you before the synagogues, the rulers, and the authorities, do not worry about howi you are to defend yourselves or what you are to say; 12for the Holy Spirit will teach you at that very hour what you ought to say."

The Parable of the Rich Fool

13 Someone in the crowd said to him, "Teacher, tell my brother to divide the family inheritance with me." 14But he said to him, "Friend, who set me to be a judge or arbitrator over you?" 15And he said to them, "Take care! Be on your guard against all kinds of greed; for one's life does not consist in the abundance of possessions." 16Then he told them a parable: "The land of a rich man produced abundantly. 17And he thought to himself, 'What should I do, for I have no place to store my crops?' 18Then he said, 'I will do this: I will pull down my barns and build larger ones, and there I will store all my grain and my goods. 19And I will say to my soul, 'Soul, you have ample goods laid up for many years; relax, eat, drink, be merry.' 20But God said to him, 'You fool! This very night your life is being demanded of you. And the things you have prepared, whose will they be?' 21So it is with those who store up treasures for themselves but are not rich toward God."

Do Not Worry

22 He said to his disciples, "Therefore I tell you, do not worry about your life, what you will eat, or about your body, what you will wear. 23For life is more than food, and the body more than clothing. 24Consider the ravens: they neither sow nor reap, they have neither storehouse nor barn, and yet God feeds them. Of how much more value are you than the birds! 25And can any of you by worrying add a single hour to your span of life?i 26If then you are not able to do so small a thing as that, why do you worry about the rest? 27Consider the

---

c 12:3 they, literally, "you." d 12:8 the Messiah, literally, "the Son of Man." e 12:10 me, literally, "the Son of Man." f 12:19 Wine, women, and song for you, literally, "Eat, drink, and be merry."

g Or power h Gk Gehenna i Other ancient authorities add or what j Or add a cubit to your stature

King James

27Consider the lilies how they grow: they toil not, they spin not; and yet I say unto you, that Solomon in all his glory was not arrayed like one of these.

28If then God so clothe the grass, which is today in the field, and tomorrow is cast into the oven; how much more *will he clothe* you, O ye of little faith?

29And seek not ye what ye shall eat, or what ye shall drink, neither be ye of doubtful mind.

30For all these things do the nations of the world seek after: and your Father knoweth that ye have need of these things.

31¶ But rather seek ye the kingdom of God; and all these things shall be added unto you.

32Fear not, little flock; for it is your Father's good pleasure to give you the kingdom.

33Sell that ye have, and give alms; provide yourselves bags which wax not old, a treasure in the heavens that faileth not, where no thief approacheth, neither moth corrupteth.

34For where your treasure is, there will your heart be also.

35Let your loins be girded about, and *your* lights burning;

36And ye yourselves like unto men that wait for their lord, when he will return from the wedding; that when he cometh and knocketh, they may open unto him immediately.

37Blessed *are* those servants, whom the lord when he cometh shall find watching: verily I say unto you, that he shall gird himself, and make them to sit down to meat, and will come forth and serve them.

38And if he shall come in the second watch, or come in the third watch, and find *them* so, blessed are those servants.

39And this know, that if the goodman of the house had known what hour the thief would come, he would have watched, and not have suffered his house to be broken through.

40Be ye therefore ready also: for the Son of man cometh at an hour when ye think not.

41¶ Then Peter said unto him, Lord, speakest thou this parable unto us, or even to all?

42And the Lord said, Who then is that faithful and wise steward, whom *his* lord shall make ruler over his household, to give *them their* portion of meat in due season?

43Blessed *is* that servant, whom his lord when he cometh shall find so doing.

44Of a truth I say unto you, that he will make him ruler over all that he hath.

45But and if that servant say in his heart, My lord delayeth his coming; and shall begin to beat the menservants and maidens, and to eat and drink, and to be drunken;

46The lord of that servant will come in a day when he looketh not for *him,* and at an hour when he is not aware, and will cut him in sunder, and will appoint him his portion with the unbelievers.

47And that servant, which knew his lord's will, and prepared not *himself,* neither did according to his will, shall be beaten with many *stripes.*

48But he that knew not, and did commit things worthy of stripes, shall be beaten with few *stripes.* For unto whomsoever much is given, of him shall be much required: and to whom men have committed much, of him they will ask the more.

49¶ I am come to send fire on the earth; and what will I, if it be already kindled?

50But I have a baptism to be baptized with; and how am I straitened till it be accomplished!

51Suppose ye that I am come to give peace on earth? I tell you, Nay; but rather division:

52For from henceforth there shall be five in one house divided, three against two, and two against three.

New International

27"Consider how the lilies grow. They do not labor or spin. Yet I tell you, not even Solomon in all his splendor was dressed like one of these. 28If that is how God clothes the grass of the field, which is here today, and tomorrow is thrown into the fire, how much more will he clothe you, O you of little faith! 29And do not set your heart on what you will eat or drink; do not worry about it. 30For the pagan world runs after all such things, and your Father knows that you need them. 31But seek his kingdom, and these things will be given to you as well.

32"Do not be afraid, little flock, for your Father has been pleased to give you the kingdom. 33Sell your possessions and give to the poor. Provide purses for yourselves that will not wear out, a treasure in heaven that will not be exhausted, where no thief comes near and no moth destroys. 34For where your treasure is, there your heart will be also.

Watchfulness

35"Be dressed ready for service and keep your lamps burning, 36like men waiting for their master to return from a wedding banquet, so that when he comes and knocks they can immediately open the door for him. 37It will be good for those servants whose master finds them watching when he comes. I tell you the truth, he will dress himself to serve, will have them recline at the table and will come and wait on them. 38It will be good for those servants whose master finds them ready, even if he comes in the second or third watch of the night. 39But understand this: If the owner of the house had known at what hour the thief was coming, he would not have let his house be broken into. 40You also must be ready, because the Son of Man will come at an hour when you do not expect him."

41Peter asked, "Lord, are you telling this parable to us, or to everyone?"

42The Lord answered, "Who then is the faithful and wise manager, whom the master puts in charge of his servants to give them their food allowance at the proper time? 43It will be good for that servant whom the master finds doing so when he returns. 44I tell you the truth, he will put him in charge of all his possessions. 45But suppose the servant says to himself, 'My master is taking a long time in coming,' and he then begins to beat the menservants and maidservants and to eat and drink and get drunk. 46The master of that servant will come on a day when he does not expect him and at an hour he is not aware of. He will cut him to pieces and assign him a place with the unbelievers.

47"That servant who knows his master's will and does not get ready or does not do what his master wants will be beaten with many blows. 48But the one who does not know and does things deserving punishment will be beaten with few blows. From everyone who has been given much, much will be demanded; and from the one who has been entrusted with much, much more will be asked.

Not Peace but Division

49"I have come to bring fire on the earth, and how I wish it were already kindled! 50But I have a baptism to undergo, and how distressed I am until it is completed! 51Do you think I came to bring peace on earth? No, I tell you, but division. 52From now on there will be five in one family divided against each other, three against two and two against three. 53They will be divided, father

Living Bible

27"Look at the lilies! They don't toil and spin, and yet Solomon in all his glory was not robed as well as these are. 28And if God provides clothing for the flowers that are here today and gone tomorrow, don't you suppose that he will provide clothing for you, you doubters? 29And don't worry about food—what to eat and drink; don't worry at all that God will provide it for you. 30All mankind scratches for its daily bread, but your heavenly Father knows your needs. 31He will always give you all you need from day to day if you will make the Kingdom of God your primary concern.

32"So don't be afraid, little flock. For it gives your Father great happiness to give you the Kingdom. 33Sell what you have and give to those in need. This will fatten your purses in heaven! And the purses of heaven have no rips or holes in them. Your treasures there will never disappear; no thief can steal them; no moth can destroy them. 34Wherever your treasure is, there your heart and thoughts will also be.

35"Be prepared—all dressed and ready— 36for your Lord's return from the wedding feast. Then you will be ready to open the door and let him in the moment he arrives and knocks. 37There will be great joy for those who are ready and waiting for his return. He himself will seat them and put on a waiter's uniform and serve them as they sit and eat! 38He may come at nine o'clock at night—or even at midnight. But whenever he comes there will be joy for his servants who are ready!

39"Everyone would be ready for him if they knew the exact hour of his return—just as they would be ready for a thief if they knew when he was coming. 40So be ready all the time. For I, the Messiah,a will come when least expected."

41Peter asked, "Lord, are you talking just to us or to everyone?"

42, 43, 44And the Lord replied, "I'm talking to any faithful, sensible man whose master gives him the responsibility of feeding the other servants. If his master returns and finds that he has done a good job, there will be a reward—his master will put him in charge of all he owns.

45"But if the man begins to think, 'My Lord won't be back for a long time,' and begins to whip the men and women he is supposed to protect, and to spend his time at drinking parties and in drunkenness— 46well, his master will return without notice and remove him from his position of trust and assign him to the place of the unfaithful. 47He will be severely punished, for though he knew his duty he refused to do it.

48"But anyone who is not aware that he is doing wrong will be punished only lightly. Much is required from those to whom much is given, for their responsibility is greater.

49"I have come to bring fire to the earth, and, oh, that my task were completed! 50There is a terrible baptism ahead of me, and how I am pent up until it is accomplished!

51"Do you think I have come to give peace to the earth? No! Rather, strife and division! 52From now on families will be split apart, three in favor of me, and two against—or perhaps the other way around. 53A father

New Revised Standard

lilies, how they grow: they neither toil nor spin;b yet I tell you, even Solomon in all his glory was not clothed like one of these. 28But if God so clothes the grass of the field, which is alive today and tomorrow is thrown into the oven, how much more will he clothe you—you of little faith! 29And do not keep striving for what you are to eat and what you are to drink, and do not keep worrying. 30For it is the nations of the world that strive after all these things, and your Father knows that you need them. 31Instead, strive for hisc kingdom, and these things will be given to you as well.

32 "Do not be afraid, little flock, for it is your Father's good pleasure to give you the kingdom. 33Sell your possessions, and give alms. Make purses for yourselves that do not wear out, an unfailing treasure in heaven, where no thief comes near and no moth destroys. 34For where your treasure is, there your heart will be also.

Watchful Slaves

35 "Be dressed for action and have your lamps lit; 36be like those who are waiting for their master to return from the wedding banquet, so that they may open the door for him as soon as he comes and knocks. 37Blessed are those slaves whom the master finds alert when he comes; truly I tell you, he will fasten his belt and have them sit down to eat, and he will come and serve them. 38If he comes during the middle of the night, or near dawn, and finds them so, blessed are those slaves.

39 "But know this: if the owner of the house had known at what hour the thief was coming, hed would not have let his house be broken into. 40You also must be ready, for the Son of Man is coming at an unexpected hour."

The Faithful or the Unfaithful Slave

41 Peter said, "Lord, are you telling this parable for us or for everyone?" 42And the Lord said, "Who then is the faithful and prudent manager whom his master will put in charge of his slaves, to give them their allowance of food at the proper time? 43Blessed is that slave whom his master will find at work when he arrives. 44Truly I tell you, he will put that one in charge of all his possessions. 45But if that slave says to himself, 'My master is delayed in coming,' and if he begins to beat the other slaves, men and women, and to eat and drink and get drunk, 46the master of that slave will come on a day when he does not expect him and at an hour that he does not know, and will cut him in pieces,e and put him with the unfaithful. 47That slave who knew what his master wanted, but did not prepare himself or do what was wanted, will receive a severe beating. 48But the one who did not know and did what deserved a beating will receive a light beating. From everyone to whom much has been given, much will be required; and from the one to whom much has been entrusted, even more will be demanded.

Jesus the Cause of Division

49 "I came to bring fire to the earth, and how I wish it were already kindled! 50I have a baptism with which to be baptized, and what stress I am under until it is completed! 51Do you think that I have come to bring peace to the earth? No, I tell you, but rather division! 52From now on five in one household will be divided,

---

a 12:40 the Messiah, literally, "the Son of Man."

b Other ancient authorities read Consider the lilies; they neither spin nor weave
c Other ancient authorities read God's   d Other ancient authorities add would have watched and   e Or cut him off

King James

53The father shall be divided against the son, and the son against the father; the mother against the daughter, and the daughter against the mother; the mother-in-law against her daughter-in-law, and the daughter-in-law against her mother-in-law.

54¶ And he said also to the people, When ye see a cloud rise out of the west, straightway ye say, There cometh a shower; and so it is.

55And when ye see the south wind blow, ye say, There will be heat; and it cometh to pass.

56Ye hypocrites, ye can discern the face of the sky and of the earth; but how is it that ye do not discern this time?

57Yea, and why even of yourselves judge ye not what is right?

58¶ When thou goest with thine adversary to the magistrate, as thou art in the way, give diligence that thou mayest be delivered from him; lest he hale thee to the judge, and the judge deliver thee to the officer, and the officer cast thee into prison.

59I tell thee, thou shalt not depart thence, till thou hast paid the very last mite.

13 THERE WERE present at that season some that told him of the Galilaeans, whose blood Pilate had mingled with their sacrifices.

2And Jesus answering said unto them, Suppose ye that these Galilaeans were sinners above all the Galilaeans, because they suffered such things?

3I tell you, Nay: but, except ye repent, ye shall all likewise perish.

4Or those eighteen, upon whom the tower in Siloam fell, and slew them, think ye that they were sinners above all men that dwelt in Jerusalem?

5I tell you, Nay: but, except ye repent, ye shall all likewise perish.

6¶ He spake also this parable; A certain man had a fig tree planted in his vineyard; and he came and sought fruit thereon, and found none.

7Then said he unto the dresser of his vineyard, Behold, these three years I come seeking fruit on this fig tree, and find none: cut it down; why cumbereth it the ground?

8And he answering said unto him, Lord, let it alone this year also, till I shall dig about it, and dung it:

9And if it bear fruit, well: and if not, then after that thou shalt cut it down.

10And he was teaching in one of the synagogues on the sabbath.

11¶ And, behold, there was a woman which had a spirit of infirmity eighteen years, and was bowed together, and could in no wise lift up herself.

12And when Jesus saw her, he called her to him, and said unto her, Woman, thou art loosed from thine infirmity.

13And he laid his hands on her: and immediately she was made straight, and glorified God.

14And the ruler of the synagogue answered with indignation, because that Jesus had healed on the sabbath day, and said unto the people, There are six days in which men ought to work: in them therefore come and be healed, and not on the sabbath day.

15The Lord then answered him, and said, Thou hypocrite, doth not each one of you on the sabbath loose his ox or his ass from the stall, and lead him away to watering?

16And ought not this woman, being a daughter of Abraham, whom Satan hath bound, lo, these eighteen years, be loosed from this bond on the sabbath day?

New International

against son and son against father, mother against daughter and daughter against mother, mother-in-law against daughter-in-law and daughter-in-law against mother-in-law."

Interpreting the Times

54He said to the crowd: "When you see a cloud rising in the west, immediately you say, 'It's going to rain,' and it does. 55And when the south wind blows, you say, 'It's going to be hot,' and it is. 56Hypocrites! You know how to interpret the appearance of the earth and the sky. How is it that you don't know how to interpret this present time?

57"Why don't you judge for yourselves what is right? 58As you are going with your adversary to the magistrate, try hard to be reconciled to him on the way, or he may drag you off to the judge, and the judge turn you over to the officer, and the officer throw you into prison. 59I tell you, you will not get out until you have paid the last penny.a"

Repent or Perish

13 NOW THERE were some present at that time who told Jesus about the Galileans whose blood Pilate had mixed with their sacrifices. 2Jesus answered, "Do you think that these Galileans were worse sinners than all the other Galileans because they suffered this way? 3I tell you, no! But unless you repent, you too will all perish. 4Or those eighteen who died when the tower in Siloam fell on them—do you think they were more guilty than all the others living in Jerusalem? 5I tell you, no! But unless you repent, you too will all perish."

6Then he told this parable: "A man had a fig tree, planted in his vineyard, and he went to look for fruit on it, but did not find any. 7So he said to the man who took care of the vineyard, 'For three years now I've been coming to look for fruit on this fig tree and haven't found any. Cut it down! Why should it use up the soil?'

8"'Sir,' the man replied, 'leave it alone for one more year, and I'll dig around it and fertilize it. 9If it bears fruit next year, fine! If not, then cut it down.'"

A Crippled Woman Healed on the Sabbath

10On a Sabbath Jesus was teaching in one of the synagogues, 11and a woman was there who had been crippled by a spirit for eighteen years. She was bent over and could not straighten up at all. 12When Jesus saw her, he called her forward and said to her, "Woman, you are set free from your infirmity." 13Then he put his hands on her, and immediately she straightened up and praised God.

14Indignant because Jesus had healed on the Sabbath, the synagogue ruler said to the people, "There are six days for work. So come and be healed on those days, not on the Sabbath."

15The Lord answered him, "You hypocrites! Doesn't each of you on the Sabbath untie his ox or donkey from the stall and lead it out to give it water? 16Then should not this woman, a daughter of Abraham, whom Satan has kept bound for eighteen long years, be set free on the Sabbath day from what bound her?"

a 59 Greek lepton

Living Bible

will decide one way about me; his son, the other; mother and daughter will disagree; and the decision of an honored mother-in-law[b] will be spurned by her daughter-in-law."

54Then he turned to the crowd and said, "When you see clouds beginning to form in the west, you say, 'Here comes a shower.' And you are right.

55"When the south wind blows you say, 'Today will be a scorcher.' And it is. 56Hypocrites! You interpret the sky well enough, but you refuse to notice the warnings all around you about the crisis ahead. 57Why do you refuse to see for yourselves what is right?

58"If you meet your accuser on the way to court, try to settle the matter before it reaches the judge, lest he sentence you to jail; 59for if that happens you won't be free again until the last penny is paid in full."

13 ABOUT THIS time he was informed that Pilate had butchered some Jews from Galilee as they were sacrificing at the Temple in Jerusalem.

2"Do you think they were worse sinners than other men from Galilee?" he asked. "Is that why they suffered? 3Not at all! And don't you realize that you also will perish unless you leave your evil ways and turn to God?

4"And what about the eighteen men who died when the Tower of Siloam fell on them? Were they the worst sinners in Jerusalem? 5Not at all! And you, too, will perish unless you repent."

6Then he used this illustration: "A man planted a fig tree in his garden and came again and again to see if he could find any fruit on it, but he was always disappointed. 7Finally he told his gardener to cut it down. 'I've waited three years and there hasn't been a single fig!' he said. 'Why bother with it any longer? It's taking up space we can use for something else.'

8" 'Give it one more chance,' the gardener answered. 'Leave it another year, and I'll give it special attention and plenty of fertilizer. 9If we get figs next year, fine; if not, I'll cut it down.' "

10One Sabbath as he was teaching in a synagogue, 11he saw a seriously handicapped woman who had been bent double for eighteen years and was unable to straighten herself.

12Calling her over to him Jesus said, "Woman, you are healed of your sickness!" 13He touched her, and instantly she could stand straight. How she praised and thanked God!

14But the local Jewish leader in charge of the synagogue was very angry about it because Jesus had healed her on the Sabbath day. "There are six days of the week to work," he shouted to the crowd. "Those are the days to come for healing, not on the Sabbath!"

15But the Lord replied, "You hypocrite! You work on the Sabbath! Don't you untie your cattle from their stalls on the Sabbath and lead them out for water? 16And is it wrong for me, just because it is the Sabbath day, to free this Jewish woman from the bondage in which Satan has held her for eighteen years?"

New Revised Standard

three against two and two against three; 53they will be divided:

> father against son
>   and son against father,
> mother against daughter
>   and daughter against mother,
> mother-in-law against her daughter-in-law
>   and daughter-in-law against mother-in-law."

Interpreting the Time

54 He also said to the crowds, "When you see a cloud rising in the west, you immediately say, 'It is going to rain'; and so it happens. 55And when you see the south wind blowing, you say, 'There will be scorching heat'; and it happens. 56You hypocrites! You know how to interpret the appearance of earth and sky, but why do you not know how to interpret the present time?

Settling with Your Opponent

57 "And why do you not judge for yourselves what is right? 58Thus, when you go with your accuser before a magistrate, on the way make an effort to settle the case,[c] or you may be dragged before the judge, and the judge hand you over to the officer, and the officer throw you in prison. 59I tell you, you will never get out until you have paid the very last penny."

Repent or Perish

13 AT THAT very time there were some present who told him about the Galileans whose blood Pilate had mingled with their sacrifices. 2He asked them, "Do you think that because these Galileans suffered in this way they were worse sinners than all other Galileans? 3No, I tell you; but unless you repent, you will all perish as they did. 4Or those eighteen who were killed when the tower of Siloam fell on them—do you think that they were worse offenders than all the others living in Jerusalem? 5No, I tell you; but unless you repent, you will all perish just as they did."

The Parable of the Barren Fig Tree

6 Then he told this parable: "A man had a fig tree planted in his vineyard; and he came looking for fruit on it and found none. 7So he said to the gardener, 'See here! For three years I have come looking for fruit on this fig tree, and still I find none. Cut it down! Why should it be wasting the soil?' 8He replied, 'Sir, let it alone for one more year, until I dig around it and put manure on it. 9If it bears fruit next year, well and good; but if not, you can cut it down.' "

Jesus Heals a Crippled Woman

10 Now he was teaching in one of the synagogues on the sabbath. 11And just then there appeared a woman with a spirit that had crippled her for eighteen years. She was bent over and was quite unable to stand up straight. 12When Jesus saw her, he called her over and said, "Woman, you are set free from your ailment." 13When he laid his hands on her, immediately she stood up straight and began praising God. 14But the leader of the synagogue, indignant because Jesus had cured on the sabbath, kept saying to the crowd, "There are six days on which work ought to be done; come on those days and be cured, and not on the sabbath day." 15But the Lord answered him and said, "You hypocrites! Does not each of you on the sabbath untie his ox or his donkey from the manger, and lead it away to give it water? 16And ought not this woman, a daughter of Abraham whom Satan bound for eighteen long years, be set free from this bondage on the sabbath day?" 17When he said this, all

---

b 12:53 *the decision of an honored mother-in-law*, implied by ancient custom.   c Gk *settle with him*

King James

17And when he had said these things, all his adversaries were ashamed: and all the people rejoiced for all the glorious things that were done by him.

18¶ Then said he, Unto what is the kingdom of God like? and whereunto shall I resemble it?

19It is like a grain of mustard seed, which a man took, and cast into his garden; and it grew, and waxed a great tree; and the fowls of the air lodged in the branches of it.

20And again he said, Whereunto shall I liken the kingdom of God?

21It is like leaven, which a woman took and hid in three measures of meal, till the whole was leavened.

22And he went through the cities and villages, teaching, and journeying toward Jerusalem.

23Then said one unto him, Lord, are there few that be saved? And he said unto them,

24¶ Strive to enter in at the strait gate: for many, I say unto you, will seek to enter in, and shall not be able.

25When once the master of the house is risen up, and hath shut to the door, and ye begin to stand without, and to knock at the door, saying, Lord, Lord, open unto us; and he shall answer and say unto you, I know you not whence ye are:

26Then shall ye begin to say, We have eaten and drunk in thy presence, and thou hast taught in our streets.

27But he shall say, I tell you, I know you not whence ye are; depart from me, all ye workers of iniquity.

28There shall be weeping and gnashing of teeth, when ye shall see Abraham, and Isaac, and Jacob, and all the prophets, in the kingdom of God, and you yourselves thrust out.

29And they shall come from the east, and from the west, and from the north, and from the south, and shall sit down in the kingdom of God.

30And, behold, there are last which shall be first, and there are first which shall be last.

31¶ The same day there came certain of the Pharisees, saying unto him, Get thee out, and depart hence: for Herod will kill thee.

32And he said unto them, Go ye, and tell that fox, Behold, I cast out devils, and I do cures today and tomorrow, and the third day I shall be perfected.

33Nevertheless I must walk today, and tomorrow, and the day following: for it cannot be that a prophet perish out of Jerusalem.

34O Jerusalem, Jerusalem, which killest the prophets, and stonest them that are sent unto thee; how often would I have gathered thy children together, as a hen doth gather her brood under her wings, and ye would not!

35Behold, your house is left unto you desolate: and verily I say unto you, Ye shall not see me, until the time come when ye shall say, Blessed is he that cometh in the name of the Lord.

14 AND IT came to pass, as he went into the house of one of the chief Pharisees to eat bread on the sabbath day, that they watched him.

2And, behold, there was a certain man before him which had the dropsy.

3And Jesus answering spake unto the lawyers and Pharisees, saying, Is it lawful to heal on the sabbath day?

4And they held their peace. And he took him, and healed him, and let him go;

5And answered them, saying, Which of you shall have an ass or an ox fallen into a pit, and will not straightway pull him out on the sabbath day?

6And they could not answer him again to these things.

New International

17When he said this, all his opponents were humiliated, but the people were delighted with all the wonderful things he was doing.

The Parables of the Mustard Seed and the Yeast

18Then Jesus asked, "What is the kingdom of God like? What shall I compare it to? 19It is like a mustard seed, which a man took and planted in his garden. It grew and became a tree, and the birds of the air perched in its branches."

20Again he asked, "What shall I compare the kingdom of God to? 21It is like yeast that a woman took and mixed into a large amounta of flour until it worked all through the dough."

The Narrow Door

22Then Jesus went through the towns and villages, teaching as he made his way to Jerusalem. 23Someone asked him, "Lord, are only a few people going to be saved?"

He said to them, 24"Make every effort to enter through the narrow door, because many, I tell you, will try to enter and will not be able to. 25Once the owner of the house gets up and closes the door, you will stand outside knocking and pleading, 'Sir, open the door for us.'

"But he will answer, 'I don't know you or where you come from.'

26"Then you will say, 'We ate and drank with you, and you taught in our streets.'

27"But he will reply, 'I don't know you or where you come from. Away from me, all you evildoers!'

28"There will be weeping there, and gnashing of teeth, when you see Abraham, Isaac and Jacob and all the prophets in the kingdom of God, but you yourselves thrown out. 29People will come from east and west and north and south, and will take their places at the feast in the kingdom of God. 30Indeed there are those who are last who will be first, and first who will be last."

Jesus' Sorrow for Jerusalem

31At that time some Pharisees came to Jesus and said to him, "Leave this place and go somewhere else. Herod wants to kill you."

32He replied, "Go tell that fox, 'I will drive out demons and heal people today and tomorrow, and on the third day I will reach my goal.' 33In any case, I must keep going today and tomorrow and the next day—for surely no prophet can die outside Jerusalem!

34"O Jerusalem, Jerusalem, you who kill the prophets and stone those sent to you, how often I have longed to gather your children together, as a hen gathers her chicks under her wings, but you were not willing! 35Look, your house is left to you desolate. I tell you, you will not see me again until you say, 'Blessed is he who comes in the name of the Lord.'b"

Jesus at a Pharisee's House

14 ONE SABBATH, when Jesus went to eat in the house of a prominent Pharisee, he was being carefully watched. 2There in front of him was a man suffering from dropsy. 3Jesus asked the Pharisees and experts in the law, "Is it lawful to heal on the Sabbath or not?" 4But they remained silent. So taking hold of the man, he healed him and sent him away.

5Then he asked them, "If one of you has a sonc or an ox that falls into a well on the Sabbath day, will you not immediately pull him out?" 6And they had nothing to say.

a 21 Greek three satas (probably about 1/2 bushel or 22 liters)   b 35 Psalm 118:26   c 5 Some manuscripts donkey

Living Bible

17This shamed his enemies. And all the people rejoiced at the wonderful things he did.

18Now he began teaching them again about the Kingdom of God: "What is the Kingdom like?" he asked. "How can I illustrate it? 19It is like a tiny mustard seed planted in a garden; soon it grows into a tall bush and the birds live among its branches."

20, 21"It is like yeast kneaded into dough, which works unseen until it has risen high and light."

22He went from city to city and village to village, teaching as he went, always pressing onward toward Jerusalem.

23Someone asked him, "Will only a few be saved?"

And he replied, 24, 25"The door to heaven is narrow. Work hard to get in, for the truth is that many will try to enter but when the head of the house has locked the door, it will be too late. Then if you stand outside knocking, and pleading, 'Lord, open the door for us,' he will reply, 'I do not know you.'

26" 'But we ate with you, and you taught in our streets,' you will say.

27"And he will reply, 'I tell you, I don't know you. You can't come in here, guilty as you are. Go away.'

28"And there will be great weeping and gnashing of teeth as you stand outside and see Abraham, Isaac, Jacob, and all the prophets within the Kingdom of God—29for people will come from all over the world to take their places there. 30And note this: some who are despised now will be greatly honored then; and some who are highly thought of now will be least important then."

31A few minutes later some Pharisees said to him, "Get out of here if you want to live, for King Herod is after you!"

32Jesus replied, "Go tell that fox that I will keep on casting out demons and doing miracles of healing today and tomorrow; and the third day I will reach my destination. 33Yes, today, tomorrow, and the next day! For it wouldn't do for a prophet of God to be killed except in Jerusalem!

34"O Jerusalem, Jerusalem! The city that murders the prophets. The city that stones those sent to help her. How often I have wanted to gather your children together even as a hen protects her brood under her wings, but you wouldn't let me. 35And now—now your house is left desolate. And you will never again see me until you say, 'Welcome to him who comes in the name of the Lord.'"

14 ONE SABBATH as he was in the home of a member of the Jewish Council, the Pharisees were watching him like hawks to see if he would heal a man who was present who was suffering from dropsy.

3Jesus said to the Pharisees and legal experts standing around, "Well, is it within the Law to heal a man on the Sabbath day, or not?"

4And when they refused to answer, Jesus took the sick man by the hand and healed him and sent him away.

5Then he turned to them: "Which of you doesn't work on the Sabbath?" he asked. "If your cow falls into a pit, don't you proceed at once to get it out?"

6Again they had no answer.

New Revised Standard

his opponents were put to shame; and the entire crowd was rejoicing at all the wonderful things that he was doing.

The Parable of the Mustard Seed

18 He said therefore, "What is the kingdom of God like? And to what should I compare it? 19It is like a mustard seed that someone took and sowed in the garden; it grew and became a tree, and the birds of the air made nests in its branches."

The Parable of the Yeast

20 And again he said, "To what should I compare the kingdom of God? 21It is like yeast that a woman took and mixed in withd three measures of flour until all of it was leavened."

The Narrow Door

22 Jesuse went through one town and village after another, teaching as he made his way to Jerusalem. 23Someone asked him, "Lord, will only a few be saved?" He said to them, 24"Strive to enter through the narrow door; for many, I tell you, will try to enter and will not be able. 25When once the owner of the house has got up and shut the door, and you begin to stand outside and to knock at the door, saying, 'Lord, open to us,' then in reply he will say to you, 'I do not know where you come from.' 26Then you will begin to say, 'We ate and drank with you, and you taught in our streets.' 27But he will say, 'I do not know where you come from; go away from me, all you evildoers!' 28There will be weeping and gnashing of teeth when you see Abraham and Isaac and Jacob and all the prophets in the kingdom of God, and you yourselves thrown out. 29Then people will come from east and west, from north and south, and will eat in the kingdom of God. 30Indeed, some are last who will be first, and some are first who will be last."

The Lament over Jerusalem

31 At that very hour some Pharisees came and said to him, "Get away from here, for Herod wants to kill you." 32He said to them, "Go and tell that fox for me,f 'Listen, I am casting out demons and performing cures today and tomorrow, and on the third day I finish my work. 33Yet today, tomorrow, and the next day I must be on my way, because it is impossible for a prophet to be killed outside of Jerusalem.' 34Jerusalem, Jerusalem, the city that kills the prophets and stones those who are sent to it! How often have I desired to gather your children together as a hen gathers her brood under her wings, and you were not willing! 35See, your house is left to you. And I tell you, you will not see me until the time comes wheng you say, 'Blessed is the one who comes in the name of the Lord.'"

Jesus Heals the Man with Dropsy

14 ON ONE occasion when Jesush was going to the house of a leader of the Pharisees to eat a meal on the sabbath, they were watching him closely. 2Just then, in front of him, there was a man who had dropsy. 3And Jesus asked the lawyers and Pharisees, "Is it lawful to cure people on the sabbath, or not?" 4But they were silent. So Jesush took him and healed him, and sent him away. 5Then he said to them, "If one of you has a childi or an ox that has fallen into a well, will you not immediately pull it out on a sabbath day?" 6And they could not reply to this.

d Gk hid in   e Gk He   f Gk lacks for me   g Other ancient authorities lack the time comes when   h Gk he   i Other ancient authorities read a donkey

King James

7¶ And he put forth a parable to those which were bidden, when he marked how they chose out the chief rooms; saying unto them,

8When thou art bidden of any *man* to a wedding, sit not down in the highest room; lest a more honourable man than thou be bidden of him;

9And he that bade thee and him come and say to thee, Give this man place; and thou begin with shame to take the lowest room.

10But when thou art bidden, go and sit down in the lowest room; that when he that bade thee cometh, he may say unto thee, Friend, go up higher: then shalt thou have worship in the presence of them that sit at meat with thee.

11For whosoever exalteth himself shall be abased; and he that humbleth himself shall be exalted.

12¶ Then said he also to him that bade him, When thou makest a dinner or a supper, call not thy friends, nor thy brethren, neither thy kinsmen, nor *thy* rich neighbours; lest they also bid thee again, and a recompence be made thee.

13But when thou makest a feast, call the poor, the maimed, the lame, the blind:

14And thou shalt be blessed; for they cannot recompense thee: for thou shalt be recompensed at the resurrection of the just.

15¶ And when one of them that sat at meat with him heard these things, he said unto him, Blessed *is* he that shall eat bread in the kingdom of God.

16Then said he unto him, A certain man made a great supper, and bade many:

17And sent his servant at supper time to say to them that were bidden, Come; for all things are now ready.

18And they all with one *consent* began to make excuse. The first said unto him, I have bought a piece of ground, and I must needs go and see it: I pray thee have me excused.

19And another said, I have bought five yoke of oxen, and I go to prove them: I pray thee have me excused.

20And another said, I have married a wife, and therefore I cannot come.

21So that servant came, and showed his lord these things. Then the master of the house being angry said to his servant, Go out quickly into the streets and lanes of the city, and bring in hither the poor, and the maimed, and the halt, and the blind.

22And the servant said, Lord, it is done as thou hast commanded, and yet there is room.

23And the lord said unto the servant, Go out into the highways and hedges, and compel *them* to come in, that my house may be filled.

24For I say unto you, That none of those men which were bidden shall taste of my supper.

25¶ And there went great multitudes with him: and he turned, and said unto them,

26If any *man* come to me, and hate not his father, and mother, and wife, and children, and brethren, and sisters, yea, and his own life also, he cannot be my disciple.

27And whosoever doth not bear his cross, and come after me, cannot be my disciple.

28For which of you, intending to build a tower, sitteth not down first, and counteth the cost, whether he have *sufficient* to finish *it?*

29Lest haply, after he hath laid the foundation, and is not able to finish *it*, all that behold *it* begin to mock him,

30Saying, This man began to build, and was not able to finish.

31Or what king, going to make war against another king, sitteth not down first, and consulteth whether he be able with ten thousand to meet him that cometh against him with twenty thousand?

32Or else, while the other is yet a great way off, he sendeth an ambassage, and desireth conditions of peace.

New International

7When he noticed how the guests picked the places of honor at the table, he told them this parable: 8"When someone invites you to a wedding feast, do not take the place of honor, for a person more distinguished than you may have been invited. 9If so, the host who invited both of you will come and say to you, 'Give this man your seat.' Then, humiliated, you will have to take the least important place. 10But when you are invited, take the lowest place, so that when your host comes, he will say to you, 'Friend, move up to a better place.' Then you will be honored in the presence of all your fellow guests. 11For everyone who exalts himself will be humbled, and he who humbles himself will be exalted."

12Then Jesus said to his host, "When you give a luncheon or dinner, do not invite your friends, your brothers or relatives, or your rich neighbors; if you do, they may invite you back and so you will be repaid. 13But when you give a banquet, invite the poor, the crippled, the lame, the blind, 14and you will be blessed. Although they cannot repay you, you will be repaid at the resurrection of the righteous."

The Parable of the Great Banquet

15When one of those at the table with him heard this, he said to Jesus, "Blessed is the man who will eat at the feast in the kingdom of God."

16Jesus replied: "A certain man was preparing a great banquet and invited many guests. 17At the time of the banquet he sent his servant to tell those who had been invited, 'Come, for everything is now ready.'

18"But they all alike began to make excuses. The first said, 'I have just bought a field, and I must go and see it. Please excuse me.'

19"Another said, 'I have just bought five yoke of oxen, and I'm on my way to try them out. Please excuse me.'

20"Still another said, 'I just got married, so I can't come.'

21"The servant came back and reported this to his master. Then the owner of the house became angry and ordered his servant, 'Go out quickly into the streets and alleys of the town and bring in the poor, the crippled, the blind and the lame.'

22"'Sir,' the servant said, 'what you ordered has been done, but there is still room.'

23"Then the master told his servant, 'Go out to the roads and country lanes and make them come in, so that my house will be full. 24I tell you, not one of those men who were invited will get a taste of my banquet.'"

The Cost of Being a Disciple

25Large crowds were traveling with Jesus, and turning to them he said: 26"If anyone comes to me and does not hate his father and mother, his wife and children, his brothers and sisters—yes, even his own life—he cannot be my disciple. 27And anyone who does not carry his cross and follow me cannot be my disciple.

28"Suppose one of you wants to build a tower. Will he not first sit down and estimate the cost to see if he has enough money to complete it? 29For if he lays the foundation and is not able to finish it, everyone who sees it will ridicule him, 30saying, 'This fellow began to build and was not able to finish.'

31"Or suppose a king is about to go to war against another king. Will he not first sit down and consider whether he is able with ten thousand men to oppose the one coming against him with twenty thousand? 32If he is not able, he will send a delegation while the other is still a long way off and will ask for terms of peace. 33In

Living Bible

7When he noticed that all who came to the dinner were trying to sit near the head of the table, he gave them this advice: 8"If you are invited to a wedding feast, don't always head for the best seat. For if someone more respected than you shows up, 9the host will bring him over to where you are sitting and say, 'Let this man sit here instead.' And you, embarrassed, will have to take whatever seat is left at the foot of the table!

10"Do this instead—start at the foot; and when your host sees you he will come and say, 'Friend, we have a better place than this for you!' Thus you will be honored in front of all the other guests. 11For everyone who tries to honor himself shall be humbled; and he who humbles himself shall be honored." 12Then he turned to his host. "When you put on a dinner," he said, "don't invite friends, brothers, relatives, and rich neighbors! For they will return the invitation. 13Instead, invite the poor, the crippled, the lame, and the blind. 14Then at the resurrection of the godly, God will reward you for inviting those who can't repay you."

15Hearing this, a man sitting at the table with Jesus exclaimed, "What a privilege it would be to get into the Kingdom of God!"

16Jesus replied with this illustration: "A man prepared a great feast and sent out many invitations. 17When all was ready, he sent his servant around to notify the guests that it was time for them to arrive. 18But they all began making excuses. One said he had just bought a field and wanted to inspect it, and asked to be excused. 19Another said he had just bought five pair of oxen and wanted to try them out. 20Another had just been married and for that reason couldn't come.

21"The servant returned and reported to his master what they had said. His master was angry and told him to go quickly into the streets and alleys of the city and to invite the beggars, crippled, lame, and blind. 22But even then, there was still room.

23"'Well, then,' said his master, 'go out into the country lanes and out behind the hedges and urge anyone you find to come, so that the house will be full. 24For none of those I invited first will get even the smallest taste of what I had prepared for them.'"

25Great crowds were following him. He turned around and addressed them as follows: 26"Anyone who wants to be my follower must love me far more than[a] he does his own father, mother, wife, children, brothers, or sisters—yes, more than his own life—otherwise he cannot be my disciple. 27And no one can be my disciple who does not carry his own cross and follow me.

28"But don't begin until you count the cost.[b] For who would begin construction of a building without first getting estimates and then checking to see if he has enough money to pay the bills? 29Otherwise he might complete only the foundation before running out of funds. And then how everyone would laugh!

30"'See that fellow there?' they would mock. 'He started that building and ran out of money before it was finished!'

31"Or what king would ever dream of going to war without first sitting down with his counselors and discussing whether his army of 10,000 is strong enough to defeat the 20,000 men who are marching against him? 32If the decision is negative, then while the enemy troops are still far away, he will send a truce team to discuss terms of peace. 33So no one can become my

New Revised Standard

Humility and Hospitality

7 When he noticed how the guests chose the places of honor, he told them a parable. 8"When you are invited by someone to a wedding banquet, do not sit down at the place of honor, in case someone more distinguished than you has been invited by your host; 9and the host who invited both of you may come and say to you, 'Give this person your place,' and then in disgrace you would start to take the lowest place. 10But when you are invited, go and sit down at the lowest place, so that when your host comes, he may say to you, 'Friend, move up higher'; then you will be honored in the presence of all who sit at the table with you. 11For all who exalt themselves will be humbled, and those who humble themselves will be exalted."

12 He said also to the one who had invited him, "When you give a luncheon or a dinner, do not invite your friends or your brothers or your relatives or rich neighbors, in case they may invite you in return, and you would be repaid. 13But when you give a banquet, invite the poor, the crippled, the lame, and the blind. 14And you will be blessed, because they cannot repay you, for you will be repaid at the resurrection of the righteous."

The Parable of the Great Dinner

15 One of the dinner guests, on hearing this, said to him, "Blessed is anyone who will eat bread in the kingdom of God!" 16Then Jesus[c] said to him, "Someone gave a great dinner and invited many. 17At the time for the dinner he sent his slave to say to those who had been invited, 'Come; for everything is ready now.' 18But they all alike began to make excuses. The first said to him, 'I have bought a piece of land, and I must go out and see it; please accept my regrets.' 19Another said, 'I have bought five yoke of oxen, and I am going to try them out; please accept my regrets.' 20Another said, 'I have just been married, and therefore I cannot come.' 21So the slave returned and reported this to his master. Then the owner of the house became angry and said to his slave, 'Go out at once into the streets and lanes of the town and bring in the poor, the crippled, the blind, and the lame.' 22And the slave said, 'Sir, what you ordered has been done, and there is still room.' 23Then the master said to the slave, 'Go out into the roads and lanes, and compel people to come in, so that my house may be filled. 24For I tell you,[d] none of those who were invited will taste my dinner.'"

The Cost of Discipleship

25 Now large crowds were traveling with him; and he turned and said to them, 26"Whoever comes to me and does not hate father and mother, wife and children, brothers and sisters, yes, and even life itself, cannot be my disciple. 27Whoever does not carry the cross and follow me cannot be my disciple. 28For which of you, intending to build a tower, does not first sit down and estimate the cost, to see whether he has enough to complete it? 29Otherwise, when he has laid a foundation and is not able to finish, all who see it will begin to ridicule him, 30saying, 'This fellow began to build and was not able to finish.' 31Or what king, going out to wage war against another king, will not sit down first and consider whether he is able with ten thousand to oppose the one who comes against him with twenty thousand? 32If he cannot, then, while the other is still far away, he sends a delegation and asks for the terms of peace. 33So there-

---

[a] 14:26 must love me far more than . . . literally, "If anyone comes to me and does not hate his father and mother. . . ." [b] 14:28 But don't begin until you count the cost, implied in vs 33.

[c] Gk he   [d] The Greek word for you here is plural

King James

33So likewise, whosoever he be of you that forsaketh not all that he hath, he cannot be my disciple.

34¶ Salt *is* good: but if the salt have lost his savour, wherewith shall it be seasoned?

35It is neither fit for the land, nor yet for the dunghill; *but* men cast it out. He that hath ears to hear, let him hear.

15 THEN DREW near unto him all the publicans and sinners for to hear him.

2And the Pharisees and scribes murmured, saying, This man receiveth sinners, and eateth with them.

3¶ And he spake this parable unto them, saying,

4What man of you, having an hundred sheep, if he lose one of them, doth not leave the ninety and nine in the wilderness, and go after that which is lost, until he find it?

5And when he hath found *it,* he layeth *it* on his shoulders, rejoicing.

6And when he cometh home, he calleth together *his* friends and neighbours, saying unto them, Rejoice with me; for I have found my sheep which was lost.

7I say unto you, that likewise joy shall be in heaven over one sinner that repenteth, more than over ninety and nine just persons, which need no repentance.

8¶ Either what woman having ten pieces of silver, if she lose one piece, doth not light a candle, and sweep the house, and seek diligently till she find *it?*

9And when she hath found *it,* she calleth *her* friends and *her* neighbours together, saying, Rejoice with me; for I have found the piece which I had lost.

10Likewise, I say unto you, there is joy in the presence of the angels of God over one sinner that repenteth.

11¶ And he said, A certain man had two sons:

12And the younger of them said to *his* father, Father, give me the portion of goods that falleth *to me.* And he divided unto them *his* living.

13And not many days after the younger son gathered all together, and took his journey into a far country, and there wasted his substance with riotous living.

14And when he had spent all, there arose a mighty famine in that land; and he began to be in want.

15And he went and joined himself to a citizen of that country; and he sent him into his fields to feed swine.

16And he would fain have filled his belly with the husks that the swine did eat: and no man gave unto him.

17And when he came to himself, he said, How many hired servants of my father's have bread enough and to spare, and I perish with hunger!

18I will arise and go to my father, and will say unto him, Father, I have sinned against heaven, and before thee,

19And am no more worthy to be called thy son: make me as one of thy hired servants.

20And he arose, and came to his father. But when he was yet a great way off, his father saw him, and had compassion, and ran, and fell on his neck, and kissed him.

21And the son said unto him, Father, I have sinned against heaven, and in thy sight, and am no more worthy to be called thy son.

22But the father said to his servants, Bring forth the best robe, and put it on him; and put a ring on his hand, and shoes on *his* feet:

23And bring hither the fatted calf, and kill *it;* and let us eat, and be merry:

24For this my son was dead, and is alive again; he was lost, and is found. And they began to be merry.

New International

the same way, any of you who does not give up everything he has cannot be my disciple.

34"Salt is good, but if it loses its saltiness, how can it be made salty again? 35It is fit neither for the soil nor for the manure pile; it is thrown out.

"He who has ears to hear, let him hear."

The Parable of the Lost Sheep

15 NOW THE tax collectors and "sinners" were all gathering around to hear him. 2But the Pharisees and the teachers of the law muttered, "This man welcomes sinners and eats with them."

3Then Jesus told them this parable: 4"Suppose one of you has a hundred sheep and loses one of them. Does he not leave the ninety-nine in the open country and go after the lost sheep until he finds it? 5And when he finds it, he joyfully puts it on his shoulders 6and goes home. Then he calls his friends and neighbors together and says, 'Rejoice with me; I have found my lost sheep.' 7I tell you that in the same way there will be more rejoicing in heaven over one sinner who repents than over ninety-nine righteous persons who do not need to repent.

The Parable of the Lost Coin

8"Or suppose a woman has ten silver coinsa and loses one. Does she not light a lamp, sweep the house and search carefully until she finds it? 9And when she finds it, she calls her friends and neighbors together and says, 'Rejoice with me; I have found my lost coin.' 10In the same way, I tell you, there is rejoicing in the presence of the angels of God over one sinner who repents."

The Parable of the Lost Son

11Jesus continued: "There was a man who had two sons. 12The younger one said to his father, 'Father, give me my share of the estate.' So he divided his property between them.

13"Not long after that, the younger son got together all he had, set off for a distant country and there squandered his wealth in wild living. 14After he had spent everything, there was a severe famine in that whole country, and he began to be in need. 15So he went and hired himself out to a citizen of that country, who sent him to his fields to feed pigs. 16He longed to fill his stomach with the pods that the pigs were eating, but no one gave him anything.

17"When he came to his senses, he said, 'How many of my father's hired men have food to spare, and here I am starving to death! 18I will set out and go back to my father and say to him: Father, I have sinned against heaven and against you. 19I am no longer worthy to be called your son; make me like one of your hired men.' 20So he got up and went to his father.

"But while he was still a long way off, his father saw him and was filled with compassion for him; he ran to his son, threw his arms around him and kissed him.

21"The son said to him, 'Father, I have sinned against heaven and against you. I am no longer worthy to be called your son.b'

22"But the father said to his servants, 'Quick! Bring the best robe and put it on him. Put a ring on his finger and sandals on his feet. 23Bring the fattened calf and kill it. Let's have a feast and celebrate. 24For this son of mine was dead and is alive again; he was lost and is found.' So they began to celebrate.

a 8 Greek *ten drachmas*, each worth about a day's wages   b 21 Some early manuscripts *son. Make me like one of your hired men.*

Living Bible

disciple unless he first sits down and counts his blessings—and then renounces them all for me.

34"What good is salt that has lost its saltiness?c 35Flavorless salt is fit for nothing—not even for fertilizer. It is worthless and must be thrown out. Listen well, if you would understand my meaning."

15 DISHONEST TAX collectors and other notorious sinners often came to listen to Jesus' sermons; 2but this caused complaints from the Jewish religious leaders and the experts on Jewish law because he was associating with such despicable people—even eating with them!

3, 4So Jesus used this illustration: "If you had a hundred sheep and one of them strayed away and was lost in the wilderness, wouldn't you leave the ninety-nine others to go and search for the lost one until you found it? 5And then you would joyfully carry it home on your shoulders. 6When you arrived you would call together your friends and neighbors to rejoice with you because your lost sheep was found.

7"Well, in the same way heaven will be happier over one lost sinner who returns to God than over ninety-nine others who haven't strayed away!

8"Or take another illustration: A woman has ten valuable silver coins and loses one. Won't she light a lamp and look in every corner of the house and sweep every nook and cranny until she finds it? 9And then won't she call in her friends and neighbors to rejoice with her? 10In the same way there is joy in the presence of the angels of God when one sinner repents."

11To further illustrate the point, he told them this story: "A man had two sons. 12When the younger told his father, 'I want my share of your estate now, instead of waiting until you die!' his father agreed to divide his wealth between his sons.

13"A few days later this younger son packed all his belongings and took a trip to a distant land, and there wasted all his money on parties and prostitutes. 14About the time his money was gone a great famine swept over the land, and he began to starve. 15He persuaded a local farmer to hire him to feed his pigs. 16The boy became so hungry that even the pods he was feeding the swine looked good to him. And no one gave him anything.

17"When he finally came to his senses, he said to himself, 'At home even the hired men have food enough and to spare, and here I am, dying of hunger! 18I will go home to my father and say, "Father, I have sinned against both heaven and you, 19and am no longer worthy of being called your son. Please take me on as a hired man."'

20"So he returned home to his father. And while he was still a long distance away, his father saw him coming, and was filled with loving pity and ran and embraced him and kissed him.

21"His son said to him, 'Father, I have sinned against heaven and you, and am not worthy of being called your son.'

22"But his father said to the slaves, 'Quick! Bring the finest robe in the house and put it on him. And a jeweled ring for his finger; and shoes! 23And kill the calf we have in the fattening pen. We must celebrate with a feast, 24for this son of mine was dead and has returned to life. He was lost and is found.' So the party began.

New Revised Standard

fore, none of you can become my disciple if you do not give up all your possessions.

About Salt

34 "Salt is good; but if salt has lost its taste, how can its saltiness be restored?d 35It is fit neither for the soil nor for the manure pile; they throw it away. Let anyone with ears to hear listen!"

The Parable of the Lost Sheep

15 NOW ALL the tax collectors and sinners were coming near to listen to him. 2And the Pharisees and the scribes were grumbling and saying, "This fellow welcomes sinners and eats with them."

3 So he told them this parable: 4"Which one of you, having a hundred sheep and losing one of them, does not leave the ninety-nine in the wilderness and go after the one that is lost until he finds it? 5When he has found it, he lays it on his shoulders and rejoices. 6And when he comes home, he calls together his friends and neighbors, saying to them, 'Rejoice with me, for I have found my sheep that was lost.' 7Just so, I tell you, there will be more joy in heaven over one sinner who repents than over ninety-nine righteous persons who need no repentance.

The Parable of the Lost Coin

8 "Or what woman having ten silver coins,e if she loses one of them, does not light a lamp, sweep the house, and search carefully until she finds it? 9When she has found it, she calls together her friends and neighbors, saying, 'Rejoice with me, for I have found the coin that I had lost.' 10Just so, I tell you, there is joy in the presence of the angels of God over one sinner who repents."

The Parable of the Prodigal and His Brother

11 Then Jesusf said, "There was a man who had two sons. 12The younger of them said to his father, 'Father, give me the share of the property that will belong to me.' So he divided his property between them. 13A few days later the younger son gathered all he had and traveled to a distant country, and there he squandered his property in dissolute living. 14When he had spent everything, a severe famine took place throughout that country, and he began to be in need. 15So he went and hired himself out to one of the citizens of that country, who sent him to his fields to feed the pigs. 16He would gladly have filled himself withg the pods that the pigs were eating; and no one gave him anything. 17But when he came to himself he said, 'How many of my father's hired hands have bread enough and to spare, but here I am dying of hunger! 18I will get up and go to my father, and I will say to him, "Father, I have sinned against heaven and before you; 19I am no longer worthy to be called your son; treat me like one of your hired hands." ' 20So he set off and went to his father. But while he was still far off, his father saw him and was filled with compassion; he ran and put his arms around him and kissed him. 21Then the son said to him, 'Father, I have sinned against heaven and before you; I am no longer worthy to be called your son.'h 22But the father said to his slaves, 'Quickly, bring out a robe—the best one—and put it on him; put a ring on his finger and sandals on his feet. 23And get the fatted calf and kill it, and let us eat and celebrate; 24for this son of mine was dead and is alive again; he was lost and is found!' And they began to celebrate.

---

c 14:34 salt that has lost its saltiness. Perhaps the reference is to impure salt; when wet, the salt dissolves and drains out, leaving a tasteless residue (Mt 5:13).

d Or how can it be used for seasoning?   e Gk drachmas, each worth about a day's wage for a laborer   f Gk he   g Other ancient authorities read filled his stomach with   h Other ancient authorities add treat me as one of your hired servants

King James

25Now his elder son was in the field: and as he came and drew nigh to the house, he heard music and dancing.

26And he called one of the servants, and asked what these things meant.

27And he said unto him, Thy brother is come; and thy father hath killed the fatted calf, because he hath received him safe and sound.

28And he was angry, and would not go in: therefore came his father out, and entreated him.

29And he answering said to *his* father, Lo, these many years do I serve thee, neither transgressed I at any time thy commandment: and yet thou never gavest me a kid, that I might make merry with my friends:

30But as soon as this thy son was come, which hath devoured thy living with harlots, thou hast killed for him the fatted calf.

31And he said unto him, Son, thou art ever with me, and all that I have is thine.

32It was meet that we should make merry, and be glad: for this thy brother was dead, and is alive again; and was lost, and is found.

16 AND HE said also unto his disciples, There was a certain rich man, which had a steward; and the same was accused unto him that he had wasted his goods.

2And he called him, and said unto him, How is it that I hear this of thee? give an account of thy stewardship; for thou mayest be no longer steward.

3Then the steward said within himself, What shall I do? for my lord taketh away from me the stewardship: I cannot dig; to beg I am ashamed.

4I am resolved what to do, that, when I am put out of the stewardship, they may receive me into their houses.

5So he called every one of his lord's debtors *unto him,* and said unto the first, How much owest thou unto my lord?

6And he said, An hundred measures of oil. And he said unto him, Take thy bill, and sit down quickly, and write fifty.

7Then said he to another, And how much owest thou? And he said, An hundred measures of wheat. And he said unto him, Take thy bill, and write fourscore.

8And the lord commended the unjust steward, because he had done wisely: for the children of this world are in their generation wiser than the children of light.

9And I say unto you, Make to yourselves friends of the mammon of unrighteousness; that, when ye fail, they may receive you into everlasting habitations.

10He that is faithful in that which is least is faithful also in much: and he that is unjust in the least is unjust also in much.

11If therefore ye have not been faithful in the unrighteous mammon, who will commit to your trust the true *riches*?

12And if ye have not been faithful in that which is another man's, who shall give you that which is your own?

New International

25"Meanwhile, the older son was in the field. When he came near the house, he heard music and dancing. 26So he called one of the servants and asked him what was going on. 27'Your brother has come,' he replied, 'and your father has killed the fattened calf because he has him back safe and sound.'

28"The older brother became angry and refused to go in. So his father went out and pleaded with him. 29But he answered his father, 'Look! All these years I've been slaving for you and never disobeyed your orders. Yet you never gave me even a young goat so I could celebrate with my friends. 30But when this son of yours who has squandered your property with prostitutes comes home, you kill the fattened calf for him!'

31"'My son,' the father said, 'you are always with me, and everything I have is yours. 32But we had to celebrate and be glad, because this brother of yours was dead and is alive again; he was lost and is found.'"

The Parable of the Shrewd Manager

16 JESUS TOLD his disciples: "There was a rich man whose manager was accused of wasting his possessions. 2So he called him in and asked him, 'What is this I hear about you? Give an account of your management, because you cannot be manager any longer.'

3"The manager said to himself, 'What shall I do now? My master is taking away my job. I'm not strong enough to dig, and I'm ashamed to beg— 4I know what I'll do so that, when I lose my job here, people will welcome me into their houses.'

5"So he called in each one of his master's debtors. He asked the first, 'How much do you owe my master?'

6"'Eight hundred gallonsa of olive oil,' he replied.

"The manager told him, 'Take your bill, sit down quickly, and make it four hundred.'

7"Then he asked the second, 'And how much do you owe?'

"'A thousand bushelsb of wheat,' he replied.

"He told him, 'Take your bill and make it eight hundred.'

8"The master commended the dishonest manager because he had acted shrewdly. For the people of this world are more shrewd in dealing with their own kind than are the people of the light. 9I tell you, use worldly wealth to gain friends for yourselves, so that when it is gone, you will be welcomed into eternal dwellings.

10"Whoever can be trusted with very little can also be trusted with much, and whoever is dishonest with very little will also be dishonest with much. 11So if you have not been trustworthy in handling worldly wealth, who will trust you with true riches? 12And if you have not been trustworthy with someone else's property, who will give you property of your own?

---

a 6 Greek *one hundred batous* (probably about 3 kiloliters)   b 7 Greek *one hundred korous* (probably about 35 kiloliters)

Living Bible

25"Meanwhile, the older son was in the fields working; when he returned home, he heard dance music coming from the house, 26and he asked one of the servants what was going on.

27" 'Your brother is back,' he was told, 'and your father has killed the calf we were fattening and has prepared a great feast to celebrate his coming home again unharmed.'

28"The older brother was angry and wouldn't go in. His father came out and begged him, 29but he replied, 'All these years I've worked hard for you and never once refused to do a single thing you told me to; and in all that time you never gave me even one young goat for a feast with my friends. 30Yet when this son of yours comes back after spending your money on prostitutes, you celebrate by killing the finest calf we have on the place.'

31" 'Look, dear son,' his father said to him, 'you and I are very close, and everything I have is yours. 32But it is right to celebrate. For he is your brother; and he was dead and has come back to life! He was lost and is found!' "

16 JESUS NOW told this story to his disciples: "A rich man hired an accountant to handle his affairs, but soon a rumor went around that the accountant was thoroughly dishonest.

2"So his employer called him in and said, 'What's this I hear about your stealing from me? Get your report in order, for you are to be dismissed.'

3"The accountant thought to himself, 'Now what? I'm through here, and I haven't the strength to go out and dig ditches, and I'm too proud to beg. 4I know just the thing! And then I'll have plenty of friends to take care of me when I leave!'

5, 6"So he invited each one who owed money to his employer to come and discuss the situation. He asked the first one, 'How much do you owe him?' 'My debt is 850 gallons of olive oil,' the man replied. 'Yes, here is the contract you signed,' the accountant told him. 'Tear it up and write another one for half that much!'

7" 'And how much do you owe him?' he asked the next man. 'A thousand bushels of wheat,' was the reply. 'Here,' the accountant said, 'take your note and replace it with one for only 800 bushels!'

8"The rich man had to admire the rascal for being so shrewd.c And it is true that the citizens of this world are more clever [in dishonesty!d] than the godlye are. 9But shall I tell you to act that way, to buy friendship through cheating? Will this ensure your entry into an everlasting home in heaven?f 10No! For unless you are honest in small matters, you won't be in large ones. If you cheat even a little, you won't be honest with greater responsibilities. 11And if you are untrustworthy about worldly wealth, who will trust you with the true riches of heaven? 12And if you are not faithful with other people's money, why should you be entrusted with money of your own?

c 16:8 The rich man had to admire the rascal for being so shrewd, or, "Do you think the rich man commended the scoundrel for being so shrewd?"
d 16:8 in dishonesty, implied.   e 16:8 godly, literally, "sons of the light."
f 16:9 Will this ensure your entry into an everlasting home in heaven? Literally, and probably ironically, "Make to yourselves friends by means of the mammon of unrighteousness; that when it shall fail you, they may receive you into the eternal tabernacles." Some commentators would interpret this to mean: "Use your money for good, so that it will be waiting to befriend you when you get to heaven." But this would imply the end justifies the means, an unbiblical idea.

New Revised Standard

25 "Now his elder son was in the field; and when he came and approached the house, he heard music and dancing. 26He called one of the slaves and asked what was going on. 27He replied, 'Your brother has come, and your father has killed the fatted calf, because he has got him back safe and sound.' 28Then he became angry and refused to go in. His father came out and began to plead with him. 29But he answered his father, 'Listen! For all these years I have been working like a slave for you, and I have never disobeyed your command; yet you have never given me even a young goat so that I might celebrate with my friends. 30But when this son of yours came back, who has devoured your property with prostitutes, you killed the fatted calf for him!' 31Then the fatherg said to him, 'Son, you are always with me, and all that is mine is yours. 32But we had to celebrate and rejoice, because this brother of yours was dead and has come to life; he was lost and has been found.' "

The Parable of the Dishonest Manager

16 THEN JESUSg said to the disciples, "There was a rich man who had a manager, and charges were brought to him that this man was squandering his property. 2So he summoned him and said to him, 'What is this that I hear about you? Give me an accounting of your management, because you cannot be my manager any longer.' 3Then the manager said to himself, 'What will I do, now that my master is taking the position away from me? I am not strong enough to dig, and I am ashamed to beg. 4I have decided what to do so that, when I am dismissed as manager, people may welcome me into their homes.' 5So, summoning his master's debtors one by one, he asked the first, 'How much do you owe my master?' 6He answered, 'A hundred jugs of olive oil.' He said to him, 'Take your bill, sit down quickly, and make it fifty.' 7Then he asked another, 'And how much do you owe?' He replied, 'A hundred containers of wheat.' He said to him, 'Take your bill and make it eighty.' 8And his master commended the dishonest manager because he had acted shrewdly; for the children of this age are more shrewd in dealing with their own generation than are the children of light. 9And I tell you, make friends for yourselves by means of dishonest wealthh so that when it is gone, they may welcome you into the eternal homes.i

10 "Whoever is faithful in a very little is faithful also in much; and whoever is dishonest in a very little is dishonest also in much. 11If then you have not been faithful with the dishonest wealth,h who will entrust to you the true riches? 12And if you have not been faithful with what belongs to another, who will give you what is your own? 13No slave can serve two masters; for a

g Gk he   h Gk mammon   i Gk tents

King James

13¶ No servant can serve two masters: for either he will hate the one, and love the other; or else he will hold to the one, and despise the other. Ye cannot serve God and mammon.

14And the Pharisees also, who were covetous, heard all these things: and they derided him.

15And he said unto them, Ye are they which justify yourselves before men; but God knoweth your hearts: for that which is highly esteemed among men is abomination in the sight of God.

16The law and the prophets *were* until John: since that time the kingdom of God is preached, and every man presseth into it.

17And it is easier for heaven and earth to pass, than one tittle of the law to fail.

18Whosoever putteth away his wife, and marrieth another, committeth adultery: and whosoever marrieth her that is put away from *her* husband committeth adultery.

19¶ There was a certain rich man, which was clothed in purple and fine linen, and fared sumptuously every day:

20And there was a certain beggar named Lazarus, which was laid at his gate, full of sores,

21And desiring to be fed with the crumbs which fell from the rich man's table: moreover the dogs came and licked his sores.

22And it came to pass, that the beggar died, and was carried by the angels into Abraham's bosom: the rich man also died, and was buried;

23And in hell he lift up his eyes, being in torments, and seeth Abraham afar off, and Lazarus in his bosom.

24And he cried and said, Father Abraham, have mercy on me, and send Lazarus, that he may dip the tip of his finger in water, and cool my tongue; for I am tormented in this flame.

25But Abraham said, Son, remember that thou in thy lifetime receivedst thy good things, and likewise Lazarus evil things: but now he is comforted, and thou art tormented.

26And beside all this, between us and you there is a great gulf fixed: so that they which would pass from hence to you cannot; neither can they pass to us, that *would come* from thence.

27Then he said, I pray thee therefore, father, that thou wouldest send him to my father's house:

28For I have five brethren; that he may testify unto them, lest they also come into this place of torment.

29Abraham saith unto him, They have Moses and the prophets; let them hear them.

30And he said, Nay, father Abraham: but if one went unto them from the dead, they will repent.

31And he said unto him, If they hear not Moses and the prophets, neither will they be persuaded, though one rose from the dead.

17 THEN SAID he unto the disciples, It is impossible but that offences will come: but woe *unto him,* through whom they come!

2It were better for him that a millstone were hanged about his neck, and he cast into the sea, than that he should offend one of these little ones.

3¶ Take heed to yourselves: If thy brother trespass against thee, rebuke him; and if he repent, forgive him.

4And if he trespass against thee seven times in a day, and seven times in a day turn again to thee, saying, I repent; thou shalt forgive him.

New International

13"No servant can serve two masters. Either he will hate the one and love the other, or he will be devoted to the one and despise the other. You cannot serve both God and Money."

14The Pharisees, who loved money, heard all this and were sneering at Jesus. 15He said to them, "You are the ones who justify yourselves in the eyes of men, but God knows your hearts. What is highly valued among men is detestable in God's sight.

Additional Teachings

16"The Law and the Prophets were proclaimed until John. Since that time, the good news of the kingdom of God is being preached, and everyone is forcing his way into it. 17It is easier for heaven and earth to disappear than for the least stroke of a pen to drop out of the Law.

18"Anyone who divorces his wife and marries another woman commits adultery, and the man who marries a divorced woman commits adultery.

The Rich Man and Lazarus

19"There was a rich man who was dressed in purple and fine linen and lived in luxury every day. 20At his gate was laid a beggar named Lazarus, covered with sores 21and longing to eat what fell from the rich man's table. Even the dogs came and licked his sores.

22"The time came when the beggar died and the angels carried him to Abraham's side. The rich man also died and was buried. 23In hell,[a] where he was in torment, he looked up and saw Abraham far away, with Lazarus by his side. 24So he called to him, 'Father Abraham, have pity on me and send Lazarus to dip the tip of his finger in water and cool my tongue, because I am in agony in this fire.'

25"But Abraham replied, 'Son, remember that in your lifetime you received your good things, while Lazarus received bad things, but now he is comforted here and you are in agony. 26And besides all this, between us and you a great chasm has been fixed, so that those who want to go from here to you cannot, nor can anyone cross over from there to us.'

27"He answered, 'Then I beg you, father, send Lazarus to my father's house, 28for I have five brothers. Let him warn them, so that they will not also come to this place of torment.'

29"Abraham replied, 'They have Moses and the Prophets; let them listen to them.'

30" 'No, father Abraham,' he said, 'but if someone from the dead goes to them, they will repent.'

31"He said to him, 'If they do not listen to Moses and the Prophets, they will not be convinced even if someone rises from the dead.' "

Sin, Faith, Duty

17 JESUS SAID to his disciples: "Things that cause people to sin are bound to come, but woe to that person through whom they come. 2It would be better for him to be thrown into the sea with a millstone tied around his neck than for him to cause one of these little ones to sin. 3So watch yourselves.

"If your brother sins, rebuke him, and if he repents, forgive him. 4If he sins against you seven times in a day, and seven times comes back to you and says, 'I repent,' forgive him."

[a] 23 Greek *Hades*

Living Bible

13"For neither you nor anyone else can serve two masters. You will hate one and show loyalty to the other, or else the other way around—you will be enthusiastic about one and despise the other. You cannot serve both God and money."

14The Pharisees, who dearly loved their money, naturally scoffed at all this.

15Then he said to them, "You wear a noble, pious expression in public, but God knows your evil hearts. Your pretense brings you honor from the people, but it is an abomination in the sight of God. 16Until John the Baptist began to preach, the laws of Moses and the messages of the prophets were your guides. But John introduced the Good News that the Kingdom of God would come soon. And now eager multitudes are pressing in. 17But that doesn't mean that the Law has lost its force in even the smallest point. It is as strong and unshakable as heaven and earth.

18"So anyone who divorces his wife and marries someone else commits adultery, and anyone who marries a divorced woman commits adultery."

19"There was a certain rich man," Jesus said, "who was splendidly clothed and lived each day in mirth and luxury. 20One day Lazarus, a diseased beggar, was laid at his door. 21As he lay there longing for scraps from the rich man's table, the dogs would come and lick his open sores. 22Finally the beggar died and was carried by the angels to be with Abraham in the place of the righteous dead.b The rich man also died and was buried, 23and his soul went into hell.c There, in torment, he saw Lazarus in the far distance with Abraham.

24" 'Father Abraham,' he shouted, 'have some pity! Send Lazarus over here if only to dip the tip of his finger in water and cool my tongue, for I am in anguish in these flames.'

25"But Abraham said to him, 'Son, remember that during your lifetime you had everything you wanted, and Lazarus had nothing. So now he is here being comforted and you are in anguish. 26And besides, there is a great chasm separating us, and anyone wanting to come to you from here is stopped at its edge; and no one over there can cross to us.'

27"Then the rich man said, 'O Father Abraham, then please send him to my father's home— 28for I have five brothers—to warn them about this place of torment lest they come here when they die.'

29"But Abraham said, 'The Scriptures have warned them again and again. Your brothers can read them any time they want to.'

30"The rich man replied, 'No, Father Abraham, they won't bother to read them. But if someone is sent to them from the dead, then they will turn from their sins.'

31"But Abraham said, 'If they won't listen to Moses and the prophets, they won't listen even though someone rises from the dead.' "d

17 "THERE WILL always be temptations to sin," Jesus said one day to his disciples, "but woe to the man who does the tempting. 2, 3If he were thrown into the sea with a huge rock tied to his neck, he would be far better off than facing the punishment in store for those who harm these little children's souls. I am warning you!

"Rebuke your brother if he sins, and forgive him if he is sorry. 4Even if he wrongs you seven times a day and each time turns again and asks forgiveness, forgive him."

New Revised Standard

slave will either hate the one and love the other, or be devoted to the one and despise the other. You cannot serve God and wealth."e

The Law and the Kingdom of God

14 The Pharisees, who were lovers of money, heard all this, and they ridiculed him. 15So he said to them, "You are those who justify yourselves in the sight of others; but God knows your hearts; for what is prized by human beings is an abomination in the sight of God.

16 "The law and the prophets were in effect until John came; since then the good news of the kingdom of God is proclaimed, and everyone tries to enter it by force.f 17But it is easier for heaven and earth to pass away, than for one stroke of a letter in the law to be dropped.

18 "Anyone who divorces his wife and marries another commits adultery, and whoever marries a woman divorced from her husband commits adultery.

The Rich Man and Lazarus

19 "There was a rich man who was dressed in purple and fine linen and who feasted sumptuously every day. 20And at his gate lay a poor man named Lazarus, covered with sores, 21who longed to satisfy his hunger with what fell from the rich man's table; even the dogs would come and lick his sores. 22The poor man died and was carried away by the angels to be with Abraham.g The rich man also died and was buried. 23In Hades, where he was being tormented, he looked up and saw Abraham far away with Lazarus by his side.h 24He called out, 'Father Abraham, have mercy on me, and send Lazarus to dip the tip of his finger in water and cool my tongue; for I am in agony in these flames.' 25But Abraham said, 'Child, remember that during your lifetime you received your good things, and Lazarus in like manner evil things; but now he is comforted here, and you are in agony. 26Besides all this, between you and us a great chasm has been fixed, so that those who might want to pass from here to you cannot do so, and no one can cross from there to us.' 27He said, 'Then, father, I beg you to send him to my father's house— 28for I have five brothers—that he may warn them, so that they will not also come into this place of torment.' 29Abraham replied, 'They have Moses and the prophets; they should listen to them.' 30He said, 'No, father Abraham; but if someone goes to them from the dead, they will repent.' 31He said to him, 'If they do not listen to Moses and the prophets, neither will they be convinced even if someone rises from the dead.' "

Some Sayings of Jesus

17 JESUSi SAID to his disciples, "Occasions for stumbling are bound to come, but woe to anyone by whom they come! 2It would be better for you if a millstone were hung around your neck and you were thrown into the sea than for you to cause one of these little ones to stumble. 3Be on your guard! If another disciplei sins, you must rebuke the offender, and if there is repentance, you must forgive. 4And if the same person sins against you seven times a day, and turns back to you seven times and says, 'I repent,' you must forgive."

---

b 16:22 to be with Abraham in the place of the righteous dead, literally, "into Abraham's bosom." c 16:23 into hell, literally, "into Hades." d 16:31 even though someone rises from the dead. Even Christ's resurrection failed to convince the Pharisees, to whom he gave this illustration.

e Gk mammon f Or everyone is strongly urged to enter it g Gk to Abraham's bosom h Gk in his bosom i Gk He j Gk your brother

King James

5And the apostles said unto the Lord, Increase our faith.

6And the Lord said, If ye had faith as a grain of mustard seed, ye might say unto this sycamine tree, Be thou plucked up by the root, and be thou planted in the sea; and it should obey you.

7But which of you, having a servant plowing or feeding cattle, will say unto him by and by, when he is come from the field, Go and sit down to meat?

8And will not rather say unto him, Make ready wherewith I may sup, and gird thyself, and serve me, till I have eaten and drunken; and afterward thou shalt eat and drink?

9Doth he thank that servant because he did the things that were commanded him? I trow not.

10So likewise ye, when ye shall have done all those things which are commanded you, say, We are unprofitable servants: we have done that which was our duty to do.

11¶ And it came to pass, as he went to Jerusalem, that he passed through the midst of Samaria and Galilee.

12And as he entered into a certain village, there met him ten men that were lepers, which stood afar off:

13And they lifted up *their* voices, and said, Jesus, Master, have mercy on us.

14And when he saw *them*, he said unto them, Go show yourselves unto the priests. And it came to pass, that, as they went, they were cleansed.

15And one of them, when he saw that he was healed, turned back, and with a loud voice glorified God,

16And fell down on *his* face at his feet, giving him thanks: and he was a Samaritan.

17And Jesus answering said, Were there not ten cleansed? but where *are* the nine?

18There are not found that returned to give glory to God, save this stranger.

19And he said unto him, Arise, go thy way: thy faith hath made thee whole.

20¶ And when he was demanded of the Pharisees, when the kingdom of God should come, he answered them and said, The kingdom of God cometh not with observation:

21Neither shall they say, Lo here! or, lo there! for, behold, the kingdom of God is within you.

22And he said unto the disciples, The days will come, when ye shall desire to see one of the days of the Son of man, and ye shall not see *it*.

23And they shall say to you, See here; or, see there: go not after *them*, nor follow *them*.

24For as the lightning, that lighteneth out of the one *part* under heaven, shineth unto the other *part* under heaven; so shall also the Son of man be in his day.

25But first must he suffer many things, and be rejected of this generation.

26And as it was in the days of Noe, so shall it be also in the days of the Son of man.

27They did eat, they drank, they married wives, they were given in marriage, until the day that Noe entered into the ark, and the flood came, and destroyed them all.

28Likewise also as it was in the days of Lot; they did eat, they drank, they bought, they sold, they planted, they builded;

29But the same day that Lot went out of Sodom it rained fire and brimstone from heaven, and destroyed *them* all.

30Even thus shall it be in the day when the Son of man is revealed.

31In that day, he which shall be upon the housetop, and his stuff in the house, let him not come down to take it away: and he that is in the field, let him likewise not return back.

32Remember Lot's wife.

33Whosoever shall seek to save his life shall lose it; and whosoever shall lose his life shall preserve it.

New International

5The apostles said to the Lord, "Increase our faith!"

6He replied, "If you have faith as small as a mustard seed, you can say to this mulberry tree, 'Be uprooted and planted in the sea,' and it will obey you.

7"Suppose one of you had a servant plowing or looking after the sheep. Would he say to the servant when he comes in from the field, 'Come along now and sit down to eat'? 8Would he not rather say, 'Prepare my supper, get yourself ready and wait on me while I eat and drink; after that you may eat and drink'? 9Would he thank the servant because he did what he was told to do? 10So you also, when you have done everything you were told to do, should say, 'We are unworthy servants; we have only done our duty.' "

Ten Healed of Leprosy

11Now on his way to Jerusalem, Jesus traveled along the border between Samaria and Galilee. 12As he was going into a village, ten men who had leprosy[a] met him. They stood at a distance 13and called out in a loud voice, "Jesus, Master, have pity on us!"

14When he saw them, he said, "Go, show yourselves to the priests." And as they went, they were cleansed.

15One of them, when he saw he was healed, came back, praising God in a loud voice. 16He threw himself at Jesus' feet and thanked him—and he was a Samaritan.

17Jesus asked, "Were not all ten cleansed? Where are the other nine? 18Was no one found to return and give praise to God except this foreigner?" 19Then he said to him, "Rise and go; your faith has made you well."

The Coming of the Kingdom of God

20Once, having been asked by the Pharisees when the kingdom of God would come, Jesus replied, "The kingdom of God does not come with your careful observation, 21nor will people say, 'Here it is,' or 'There it is,' because the kingdom of God is within[b] you."

22Then he said to his disciples, "The time is coming when you will long to see one of the days of the Son of Man, but you will not see it. 23Men will tell you, 'There he is!' or 'Here he is!' Do not go running off after them. 24For the Son of Man in his day[c] will be like the lightning, which flashes and lights up the sky from one end to the other. 25But first he must suffer many things and be rejected by this generation.

26"Just as it was in the days of Noah, so also will it be in the days of the Son of Man. 27People were eating, drinking, marrying and being given in marriage up to the day Noah entered the ark. Then the flood came and destroyed them all.

28"It was the same in the days of Lot. People were eating and drinking, buying and selling, planting and building. 29But the day Lot left Sodom, fire and sulfur rained down from heaven and destroyed them all.

30"It will be just like this on the day the Son of Man is revealed. 31On that day no one who is on the roof of his house, with his goods inside, should go down to get them. Likewise, no one in the field should go back for anything. 32Remember Lot's wife! 33Whoever tries to keep his life will lose it, and whoever loses his life will preserve it. 34I tell you, on that night two people will be

---

a 12 The Greek word was used for various diseases affecting the skin—not necessarily leprosy.   b 21 Or *among*   c 24 Some manuscripts do not have *in his day*.

Living Bible

5One day the apostles said to the Lord, "We need more faith; tell us how to get it."

6"If your faith were only the size of a mustard seed," Jesus answered, "it would be large enough to uproot that mulberry tree over there and send it hurtling into the sea! Your command would bring immediate results! 7, 8, 9When a servant comes in from plowing or taking care of sheep, he doesn't just sit down and eat, but first prepares his master's meal and serves him his supper before he eats his own. And he is not even thanked, for he is merely doing what he is supposed to do. 10Just so, if you merely obey me, you should not consider yourselves worthy of praise. For you have simply done your duty!"

11As they continued onward toward Jerusalem, they reached the border between Galilee and Samaria, 12and as they entered a village there, ten lepers stood at a distance, 13crying out, "Jesus, sir, have mercy on us!"

14He looked at them and said, "Go to the Jewish priest and show him that you are healed!" And as they were going, their leprosy disappeared.

15One of them came back to Jesus, shouting, "Glory to God, I'm healed!" 16He fell flat on the ground in front of Jesus, face downward in the dust, thanking him for what he had done. This man was a despisedd Samaritan.

17Jesus asked, "Didn't I heal ten men? Where are the nine? 18Does only this foreigner return to give glory to God?"

19And Jesus said to the man, "Stand up and go; your faith has made you well."

20One day the Pharisees asked Jesus, "When will the Kingdom of God begin?" Jesus replied, "The Kingdom of God isn't ushered in with visible signs. 21You won't be able to say, 'It has begun here in this place or there in that part of the country.' For the Kingdom of God is within you."e

22Later he talked again about this with his disciples. "The time is coming when you will long for mef to be with you even for a single day, but I won't be here," he said. 23"Reports will reach you that I have returned and that I am in this place or that; don't believe it or go out to look for me. 24For when I return, you will know it beyond all doubt. It will be as evident as the lightning that flashes across the skies. 25But first I must suffer terribly and be rejected by this whole nation.

26"[When I returng] the world will be [as indifferent to the things of Godh] as the people were in Noah's day. 27They ate and drank and married—everything just as usual right up to the day when Noah went into the ark and the flood came and destroyed them all.

28"And the world will be as it was in the days of Lot: people went about their daily business—eating and drinking, buying and selling, farming and building— 29until the morning Lot left Sodom. Then fire and brimstone rained down from heaven and destroyed them all. 30Yes, it will be 'business as usual' right up to the hour of my return.i

31"Those away from home that day must not return to pack; those in the fields must not return to town— 32remember what happened to Lot's wife! 33Whoever clings to his life shall lose it, and whoever loses his life shall save it. 34That night two men will be asleep in the

New Revised Standard

5 The apostles said to the Lord, "Increase our faith!" 6The Lord replied, "If you had faith the size of aj mustard seed, you could say to this mulberry tree, 'Be uprooted and planted in the sea,' and it would obey you.

7 "Who among you would say to your slave who has just come in from plowing or tending sheep in the field, 'Come here at once and take your place at the table'? 8Would you not rather say to him, 'Prepare supper for me, put on your apron and serve me while I eat and drink; later you may eat and drink'? 9Do you thank the slave for doing what was commanded? 10So you also, when you have done all that you were ordered to do, say, 'We are worthless slaves; we have done only what we ought to have done!' "

Jesus Cleanses Ten Lepers

11 On the way to Jerusalem Jesusk was going through the region between Samaria and Galilee. 12As he entered a village, ten lepersl approached him. Keeping their distance, 13they called out, saying, "Jesus, Master, have mercy on us!" 14When he saw them, he said to them, "Go and show yourselves to the priests." And as they went, they were made clean. 15Then one of them, when he saw that he was healed, turned back, praising God with a loud voice. 16He prostrated himself at Jesus'm feet and thanked him. And he was a Samaritan. 17Then Jesus asked, "Were not ten made clean? But the other nine, where are they? 18Was none of them found to return and give praise to God except this foreigner?" 19Then he said to him, "Get up and go on your way; your faith has made you well."

The Coming of the Kingdom

20 Once Jesusk was asked by the Pharisees when the kingdom of God was coming, and he answered, "The kingdom of God is not coming with things that can be observed; 21nor will they say, 'Look, here it is!' or 'There it is!' For, in fact, the kingdom of God is amongn you."

22 Then he said to the disciples, "The days are coming when you will long to see one of the days of the Son of Man, and you will not see it. 23They will say to you, 'Look there!' or 'Look here!' Do not go, do not set off in pursuit. 24 For as the lightning flashes and lights up the sky from one side to the other, so will the Son of Man be in his day.o 25But first he must endure much suffering and be rejected by this generation. 26Just as it was in the days of Noah, so too it will be in the days of the Son of Man. 27They were eating and drinking, and marrying and being given in marriage, until the day Noah entered the ark, and the flood came and destroyed all of them. 28Likewise, just as it was in the days of Lot: they were eating and drinking, buying and selling, planting and building, 29but on the day that Lot left Sodom, it rained fire and sulfur from heaven and destroyed all of them 30—it will be like that on the day that the Son of Man is revealed. 31On that day, anyone on the housetop who has belongings in the house must not come down to take them away; and likewise anyone in the field must not turn back. 32Remember Lot's wife. 33Those who try to make their life secure will lose it, but those who lose their life will keep it. 34I tell you, on that night there will

---

d 17:16 *despised,* implied. Samaritans were despised by Jews as being only "half-breed" Hebrews.   e 17:21 *within you,* or "among you." f 17:22 *long for me,* or, "long for the Son of Man."   g 17:26 *When I return,* implied.   h 17:26 *as indifferent to the things of God,* implied.   i 17:30 *the hour of my return,* or, "the hour I am revealed."

j Gk *faith as a grain of*   k Gk *he*   l The terms *leper* and *leprosy* can refer to several diseases   m Gk *his*   n Or *within*   o Other ancient authorities lack *in his day*

King James

34I tell you, in that night there shall be two *men* in one bed; the one shall be taken, and the other shall be left.
35Two *women* shall be grinding together; the one shall be taken, and the other left.
36Two *men* shall be in the field; the one shall be taken, and the other left.
37And they answered and said unto him, Where, Lord? And he said unto them, Wheresoever the body *is*, thither will the eagles be gathered together.

18 AND HE spake a parable unto them *to this end*, that men ought always to pray, and not to faint;
2Saying, There was in a city a judge, which feared not God, neither regarded man:
3And there was a widow in that city; and she came unto him, saying, Avenge me of mine adversary.
4And he would not for a while: but afterward he said within himself, Though I fear not God, nor regard man;
5Yet because this widow troubleth me, I will avenge her, lest by her continual coming she weary me.
6And the Lord said, Hear what the unjust judge saith.
7And shall not God avenge his own elect, which cry day and night unto him, though he bear long with them?
8I tell you that he will avenge them speedily. Nevertheless when the Son of man cometh, shall he find faith on the earth?
9And he spake this parable unto certain which trusted in themselves that they were righteous, and despised others:
10Two men went up into the temple to pray; the one a Pharisee, and the other a publican.
11The Pharisee stood and prayed thus with himself, God, I thank thee, that I am not as other men *are*, extortioners, unjust, adulterers, or even as this publican.
12I fast twice in the week, I give tithes of all that I possess.
13And the publican, standing afar off, would not lift up so much as *his* eyes unto heaven, but smote upon his breast, saying, God be merciful to me a sinner.
14I tell you, this man went down to his house justified *rather* than the other: for every one that exalteth himself shall be abased; and he that humbleth himself shall be exalted.
15And they brought unto him also infants, that he would touch them: but when *his* disciples saw *it*, they rebuked them.
16But Jesus called them *unto him*, and said, Suffer little children to come unto me, and forbid them not: for of such is the kingdom of God.
17Verily I say unto you, Whosoever shall not receive the kingdom of God as a little child shall in no wise enter therein.
18And a certain ruler asked him, saying, Good Master, what shall I do to inherit eternal life?
19And Jesus said unto him, Why callest thou me good? none *is* good, save one, *that is*, God.
20Thou knowest the commandments, Do not commit adultery, Do not kill, Do not steal, Do not bear false witness, Honour thy father and thy mother.
21And he said, All these have I kept from my youth up.

New International

in one bed; one will be taken and the other left. 35Two women will be grinding grain together; one will be taken and the other left.a"
37"Where, Lord?" they asked.
He replied, "Where there is a dead body, there the vultures will gather."

The Parable of the Persistent Widow

18 THEN JESUS told his disciples a parable to show them that they should always pray and not give up. 2He said: "In a certain town there was a judge who neither feared God nor cared about men. 3And there was a widow in that town who kept coming to him with the plea, 'Grant me justice against my adversary.'
4"For some time he refused. But finally he said to himself, 'Even though I don't fear God or care about men, 5yet because this widow keeps bothering me, I will see that she gets justice, so that she won't eventually wear me out with her coming!'"
6And the Lord said, "Listen to what the unjust judge says. 7And will not God bring about justice for his chosen ones, who cry out to him day and night? Will he keep putting them off? 8I tell you, he will see that they get justice, and quickly. However, when the Son of Man comes, will he find faith on the earth?"

The Parable of the Pharisee and the Tax Collector

9To some who were confident of their own righteousness and looked down on everybody else, Jesus told this parable: 10"Two men went up to the temple to pray, one a Pharisee and the other a tax collector. 11The Pharisee stood up and prayed aboutb himself: 'God, I thank you that I am not like other men—robbers, evildoers, adulterers—or even like this tax collector. 12I fast twice a week and give a tenth of all I get.'
13"But the tax collector stood at a distance. He would not even look up to heaven, but beat his breast and said, 'God, have mercy on me, a sinner.'
14"I tell you that this man, rather than the other, went home justified before God. For everyone who exalts himself will be humbled, and he who humbles himself will be exalted."

The Little Children and Jesus

15People were also bringing babies to Jesus to have him touch them. When the disciples saw this, they rebuked them. 16But Jesus called the children to him and said, "Let the little children come to me, and do not hinder them, for the kingdom of God belongs to such as these. 17I tell you the truth, anyone who will not receive the kingdom of God like a little child will never enter it."

The Rich Ruler

18A certain ruler asked him, "Good teacher, what must I do to inherit eternal life?"
19"Why do you call me good?" Jesus answered. "No one is good—except God alone. 20You know the commandments: 'Do not commit adultery, do not murder, do not steal, do not give false testimony, honor your father and mother.'c"
21"All these I have kept since I was a boy," he said.

---

a *35 Some manuscripts left. 36Two men will be in the field; one will be taken and the other left.*   b *11 Or to*   c *20 Exodus 20:12-16; Deut. 5:16-20*

Living Bible

same room, and one will be taken away, the other left. 35, 36Two women will be working together at household tasks; one will be taken, the other left; and so it will be with men working side by side in the fields."

37"Lord, where will they be taken?" the disciples asked.

Jesus replied, "Where the body is, the vultures gather!"d

18 ONE DAY Jesus told his disciples a story to illustrate their need for constant prayer and to show them that they must keep praying until the answer comes.

2"There was a city judge," he said, "a very godless man who had great contempt for everyone. 3A widow of that city came to him frequently to appeal for justice against a man who had harmed her. 4, 5The judge ignored her for a while, but eventually she got on his nerves.

" 'I fear neither God nor man,' he said to himself, 'but this woman bothers me. I'm going to see that she gets justice, for she is wearing me out with her constant coming!' "

6Then the Lord said, "If even an evil judge can be worn down like that, 7don't you think that God will surely give justice to his people who plead with him day and night? 8Yes! He will answer them quickly! But the question is: When I, the Messiah,e return, how many will I find who have faith [and are praying]?"

9Then he told this story to some who boasted of their virtue and scorned everyone else:

10"Two men went to the Temple to pray. One was a proud, self-righteous Pharisee, and the other a cheating tax collector. 11The proud Pharisee 'prayed' this prayer: 'Thank God, I am not a sinner like everyone else, especially like that tax collector over there! For I never cheat, I don't commit adultery, 12I go without food twice a week, and I give to God a tenth of everything I earn.'

13"But the corrupt tax collector stood at a distance and dared not even lift his eyes to heaven as he prayed, but beat upon his chest in sorrow, exclaiming, 'God, be merciful to me, a sinner.' 14I tell you, this sinner, not the Pharisee, returned home forgiven! For the proud shall be humbled, but the humble shall be honored."

15One day some mothers brought their babies to him to touch and bless. But the disciples told them to go away.

16, 17Then Jesus called the children over to him and said to the disciples, "Let the little children come to me! Never send them away! For the Kingdom of God belongs to men who have hearts as trusting as these little children's. And anyone who doesn't have their kind of faith will never get within the Kingdom's gates."

18Once a Jewish religious leader asked him this question: "Good sir, what shall I do to get to heaven?"

19"Do you realize what you are saying when you call me 'good'?" Jesus asked him. "Only God is truly good, and no one else.

20"But as to your question, you know what the ten commandments say—don't commit adultery, don't murder, don't steal, don't lie, honor your parents, and so on." 21The man replied, "I've obeyed every one of these laws since I was a small child."

New Revised Standard

be two in one bed; one will be taken and the other left. 35There will be two women grinding meal together; one will be taken and the other left."g 37Then they asked him, "Where, Lord?" He said to them, "Where the corpse is, there the vultures will gather."

The Parable of the Widow and the Unjust Judge

18 THEN JESUSh told them a parable about their need to pray always and not to lose heart. 2He said, "In a certain city there was a judge who neither feared God nor had respect for people. 3In that city there was a widow who kept coming to him and saying, 'Grant me justice against my opponent.' 4For a while he refused; but later he said to himself, 'Though I have no fear of God and no respect for anyone, 5yet because this widow keeps bothering me, I will grant her justice, so that she may not wear me out by continually coming.' "i 6And the Lord said, "Listen to what the unjust judge says. 7And will not God grant justice to his chosen ones who cry to him day and night? Will he delay long in helping them? 8I tell you, he will quickly grant justice to them. And yet, when the Son of Man comes, will he find faith on earth?"

The Parable of the Pharisee and the Tax Collector

9 He also told this parable to some who trusted in themselves that they were righteous and regarded others with contempt: 10"Two men went up to the temple to pray, one a Pharisee and the other a tax collector. 11The Pharisee, standing by himself, was praying thus, 'God, I thank you that I am not like other people: thieves, rogues, adulterers, or even like this tax collector. 12I fast twice a week; I give a tenth of all my income.' 13But the tax collector, standing far off, would not even look up to heaven, but was beating his breast and saying, 'God, be merciful to me, a sinner!' 14I tell you, this man went down to his home justified rather than the other; for all who exalt themselves will be humbled, but all who humble themselves will be exalted."

Jesus Blesses Little Children

15 People were bringing even infants to him that he might touch them; and when the disciples saw it, they sternly ordered them not to do it. 16But Jesus called for them and said, "Let the little children come to me, and do not stop them; for it is to such as these that the kingdom of God belongs. 17Truly I tell you, whoever does not receive the kingdom of God as a little child will never enter it."

The Rich Ruler

18 A certain ruler asked him, "Good Teacher, what must I do to inherit eternal life?" 19Jesus said to him, "Why do you call me good? No one is good but God alone. 20You know the commandments: 'You shall not commit adultery; You shall not murder; You shall not steal; You shall not bear false witness; Honor your father and mother.' " 21He replied, "I have kept all these since my youth." 22When Jesus heard this, he said to him,

---

d 17:37 Where the body is, the vultures gather! This may mean that God's people will be taken out to the execution grounds and their bodies left to the vultures.   e 18:8 the Messiah, literally, "the Son of Man."   f 18:8 and are praying, implied.

g Other ancient authorities add verse 36, "Two will be in the field; one will be taken and the other left."   h Gk he   i Or so that she may not finally come and slap me in the face

King James

22Now when Jesus heard these things, he said unto him, Yet lackest thou one thing: sell all that thou hast, and distribute unto the poor, and thou shalt have treasure in heaven: and come, follow me.

23And when he heard this, he was very sorrowful: for he was very rich.

24And when Jesus saw that he was very sorrowful, he said, How hardly shall they that have riches enter into the kingdom of God!

25For it is easier for a camel to go through a needle's eye, than for a rich man to enter into the kingdom of God.

26And they that heard *it* said, Who then can be saved?

27And he said, The things which are impossible with men are possible with God.

28Then Peter said, Lo, we have left all, and followed thee.

29And he said unto them, Verily I say unto you, There is no man that hath left house, or parents, or brethren, or wife, or children, for the kingdom of God's sake,

30Who shall not receive manifold more in this present time, and in the world to come life everlasting.

31¶ Then he took *unto him* the twelve, and said unto them, Behold, we go up to Jerusalem, and all things that are written by the prophets concerning the Son of man shall be accomplished.

32For he shall be delivered unto the Gentiles, and shall be mocked, and spitefully entreated, and spitted on:

33And they shall scourge *him,* and put him to death: and the third day he shall rise again.

34And they understood none of these things: and this saying was hid from them, neither knew they the things which were spoken.

35¶ And it came to pass, that as he was come nigh unto Jericho, a certain blind man sat by the way side begging:

36And hearing the multitude pass by, he asked what it meant.

37And they told him, that Jesus of Nazareth passeth by.

38And he cried, saying, Jesus, *thou* son of David, have mercy on me.

39And they which went before rebuked him, that he should hold his peace: but he cried so much the more, *Thou* son of David, have mercy on me.

40And Jesus stood, and commanded him to be brought unto him: and when he was come near, he asked him,

41Saying, What wilt thou that I shall do unto thee? And he said, Lord, that I may receive my sight.

42And Jesus said unto him, Receive thy sight: thy faith hath saved thee.

43And immediately he received his sight, and followed him, glorifying God: and all the people, when they saw *it,* gave praise unto God.

19 AND *JESUS* entered and passed through Jericho.

2And, behold, *there was* a man named Zacchaeus, which was the chief among the publicans, and he was rich.

3And he sought to see Jesus who he was; and could not for the press, because he was little of stature.

4And he ran before, and climbed up into a sycamore tree to see him: for he was to pass that *way.*

5And when Jesus came to the place, he looked up, and saw him, and said unto him, Zacchaeus, make haste, and come down; for today I must abide at thy house.

6And he made haste, and came down, and received him joyfully.

New International

22When Jesus heard this, he said to him, "You still lack one thing. Sell everything you have and give to the poor, and you will have treasure in heaven. Then come, follow me."

23When he heard this, he became very sad, because he was a man of great wealth. 24Jesus looked at him and said, "How hard it is for the rich to enter the kingdom of God! 25Indeed, it is easier for a camel to go through the eye of a needle than for a rich man to enter the kingdom of God."

26Those who heard this asked, "Who then can be saved?"

27Jesus replied, "What is impossible with men is possible with God."

28Peter said to him, "We have left all we had to follow you!"

29"I tell you the truth," Jesus said to them, "no one who has left home or wife or brothers or parents or children for the sake of the kingdom of God 30will fail to receive many times as much in this age and, in the age to come, eternal life."

Jesus Again Predicts His Death

31Jesus took the Twelve aside and told them, "We are going up to Jerusalem, and everything that is written by the prophets about the Son of Man will be fulfilled. 32He will be handed over to the Gentiles. They will mock him, insult him, spit on him, flog him and kill him. 33On the third day he will rise again."

34The disciples did not understand any of this. Its meaning was hidden from them, and they did not know what he was talking about.

A Blind Beggar Receives His Sight

35As Jesus approached Jericho, a blind man was sitting by the roadside begging. 36When he heard the crowd going by, he asked what was happening. 37They told him, "Jesus of Nazareth is passing by."

38He called out, "Jesus, Son of David, have mercy on me!"

39Those who led the way rebuked him and told him to be quiet, but he shouted all the more, "Son of David, have mercy on me!"

40Jesus stopped and ordered the man to be brought to him. When he came near, Jesus asked him, 41"What do you want me to do for you?"

"Lord, I want to see," he replied.

42Jesus said to him, "Receive your sight; your faith has healed you." 43Immediately he received his sight and followed Jesus, praising God. When all the people saw it, they also praised God.

Zacchaeus the Tax Collector

19 JESUS ENTERED Jericho and was passing through. 2A man was there by the name of Zacchaeus; he was a chief tax collector and was wealthy. 3He wanted to see who Jesus was, but being a short man he could not, because of the crowd. 4So he ran ahead and climbed a sycamore-fig tree to see him, since Jesus was coming that way.

5When Jesus reached the spot, he looked up and said to him, "Zacchaeus, come down immediately. I must stay at your house today." 6So he came down at once and welcomed him gladly.

Living Bible

22"There is still one thing you lack," Jesus said. "Sell all you have and give the money to the poor—it will become treasure for you in heaven—and come, follow me."

23But when the man heard this he went sadly away, for he was very rich.

24Jesus watched him go and then said to his disciples, "How hard it is for the rich to enter the Kingdom of God! 25It is easier for a camel to go through the eye of a needle than for a rich man to enter the Kingdom of God.

26Those who heard him say this exclaimed, "If it is that hard, how can *anyone* be saved?"

27He replied, "God can do what men can't!"

28And Peter said, "We have left our homes and followed you."

29"Yes," Jesus replied, "and everyone who has done as you have, leaving home, wife, brothers, parents, or children for the sake of the Kingdom of God, 30will be repaid many times over now, as well as receiving eternal life in the world to come."

31Gathering the Twelve around him he told them, "As you know, we are going to Jerusalem. And when we get there, all the predictions of the ancient prophets concerning me will come true. 32I will be handed over to the Gentiles to be mocked and treated shamefully and spat upon, 33and lashed and killed. And the third day I will rise again."

34But they didn't understand a thing he said. He seemed to be talking in riddles.

35As they approached Jericho, a blind man was sitting beside the road, begging from travelers. 36When he heard the noise of a crowd going past, he asked what was happening. 37He was told that Jesus from Nazareth was going by, 38so he began shouting, "Jesus, Son of David, have mercy on me!"

39The crowds ahead of Jesus tried to hush the man, but he only yelled the louder, "Son of David, have mercy on me!"

40When Jesus arrived at the spot, he stopped. "Bring the blind man over here," he said. 41Then Jesus asked the man, "What do you want?"

"Lord," he pleaded, "I want to see!"

42And Jesus said, "All right, begin seeing! Your faith has healed you."

43And instantly the man could see, and followed Jesus, praising God. And all who saw it happen praised God too.

19 AS JESUS was passing through Jericho, a man named Zacchaeus, one of the most influential Jews in the Roman tax-collecting business (and, of course, a very rich man), 3tried to get a look at Jesus, but he was too short to see over the crowds. 4So he ran ahead and climbed into a sycamore tree beside the road, to watch from there.

5When Jesus came by he looked up at Zacchaeus and called him by name! "Zacchaeus!" he said. "Quick! Come down! For I am going to be a guest in your home today!"

6Zacchaeus hurriedly climbed down and took Jesus to his house in great excitement and joy.

New Revised Standard

"There is still one thing lacking. Sell all that you own and distribute the money[a] to the poor, and you will have treasure in heaven; then come, follow me." 23But when he heard this, he became sad; for he was very rich. 24Jesus looked at him and said, "How hard it is for those who have wealth to enter the kingdom of God! 25Indeed, it is easier for a camel to go through the eye of a needle than for someone who is rich to enter the kingdom of God."

26 Those who heard it said, "Then who can be saved?" 27He replied, "What is impossible for mortals is possible for God."

28 Then Peter said, "Look, we have left our homes and followed you." 29And he said to them, "Truly I tell you, there is no one who has left house or wife or brothers or parents or children, for the sake of the kingdom of God, 30who will not get back very much more in this age, and in the age to come eternal life."

A Third Time Jesus Foretells His Death and Resurrection

31 Then he took the twelve aside and said to them, "See, we are going up to Jerusalem, and everything that is written about the Son of Man by the prophets will be accomplished. 32For he will be handed over to the Gentiles; and he will be mocked and insulted and spat upon. 33After they have flogged him, they will kill him, and on the third day he will rise again." 34But they understood nothing about all these things; in fact, what he said was hidden from them, and they did not grasp what was said.

Jesus Heals a Blind Beggar Near Jericho

35 As he approached Jericho, a blind man was sitting by the roadside begging. 36When he heard a crowd going by, he asked what was happening. 37They told him, "Jesus of Nazareth[b] is passing by." 38Then he shouted, "Jesus, Son of David, have mercy on me!" 39Those who were in front sternly ordered him to be quiet; but he shouted even more loudly, "Son of David, have mercy on me!" 40Jesus stood still and ordered the man to be brought to him; and when he came near, he asked him, 41"What do you want me to do for you?" He said, "Lord, let me see again." 42Jesus said to him, "Receive your sight; your faith has saved you." 43Immediately he regained his sight and followed him, glorifying God; and all the people, when they saw it, praised God.

Jesus and Zacchaeus

19 HE ENTERED Jericho and was passing through it. 2A man was there named Zacchaeus; he was a chief tax collector and was rich. 3He was trying to see who Jesus was, but on account of the crowd he could not, because he was short in stature. 4So he ran ahead and climbed a sycamore tree to see him, because he was going to pass that way. 5When Jesus came to the place, he looked up and said to him, "Zacchaeus, hurry and come down; for I must stay at your house today." 6So he hurried down and was happy to welcome him.

a Gk lacks *the money*   b Gk *the Nazorean*

King James

7And when they saw *it,* they all murmured, saying, That he was gone to be guest with a man that is a sinner.

8And Zacchaeus stood, and said unto the Lord; Behold, Lord, the half of my goods I give to the poor; and if I have taken any thing from any man by false accusation, I restore *him* fourfold.

9And Jesus said unto him, This day is salvation come to this house, forsomuch as he also is a son of Abraham.

10For the Son of man is come to seek and to save that which was lost.

11And as they heard these things, he added and spake a parable, because he was nigh to Jerusalem, and because they thought that the kingdom of God should immediately appear.

12He said therefore, A certain nobleman went into a far country to receive for himself a kingdom, and to return.

13And he called his ten servants, and delivered them ten pounds, and said unto them, Occupy till I come.

14But his citizens hated him, and sent a message after him, saying, We will not have this *man* to reign over us.

15And it came to pass, that when he was returned, having received the kingdom, then he commanded these servants to be called unto him, to whom he had given the money, that he might know how much every man had gained by trading.

16Then came the first, saying, Lord, thy pound hath gained ten pounds.

17And he said unto him, Well, thou good servant: because thou hast been faithful in a very little, have thou authority over ten cities.

18And the second came, saying, Lord, thy pound hath gained five pounds.

19And he said likewise to him, Be thou also over five cities.

20And another came, saying, Lord, behold, *here is* thy pound, which I have kept laid up in a napkin:

21For I feared thee, because thou art an austere man: thou takest up that thou layedst not down, and reapest that thou didst not sow.

22And he saith unto him, Out of thine own mouth will I judge thee, *thou* wicked servant. Thou knewest that I was an austere man, taking up that I laid not down, and reaping that I did not sow:

23Wherefore then gavest not thou my money into the bank, that at my coming I might have required mine own with usury?

24And he said unto them that stood by, Take from him the pound, and give *it* to him that hath ten pounds.

25(And they said unto him, Lord, he hath ten pounds.)

26For I say unto you, That unto every one which hath shall be given; and from him that hath not, even that he hath shall be taken away from him.

27But those mine enemies, which would not that I should reign over them, bring hither, and slay *them* before me.

28¶ And when he had thus spoken, he went before, ascending up to Jerusalem.

29And it came to pass, when he was come nigh to Bethphage and Bethany, at the mount called *the mount* of Olives, he sent two of his disciples.

30Saying, Go ye into the village over against *you;* in the which at your entering ye shall find a colt tied, whereon yet never man sat: loose him, and bring *him* hither.

31And if any man ask you, Why do ye loose *him?* thus shall ye say unto him, Because the Lord hath need of him.

32And they that were sent went their way, and found even as he had said unto them.

33And as they were loosing the colt, the owners thereof said unto them, Why loose ye the colt?

34And they said, The Lord hath need of him.

35And they brought him to Jesus: and they cast their garments upon the colt, and they set Jesus thereon.

New International

7All the people saw this and began to mutter, "He has gone to be the guest of a 'sinner.' "

8But Zacchaeus stood up and said to the Lord, "Look, Lord! Here and now I give half of my possessions to the poor, and if I have cheated anybody out of anything, I will pay back four times the amount."

9Jesus said to him, "Today salvation has come to this house, because this man, too, is a son of Abraham. 10For the Son of Man came to seek and to save what was lost."

The Parable of the Ten Minas

11While they were listening to this, he went on to tell them a parable, because he was near Jerusalem and the people thought that the kingdom of God was going to appear at once. 12He said: "A man of noble birth went to a distant country to have himself appointed king and then to return. 13So he called ten of his servants and gave them ten minas.a 'Put this money to work,' he said, 'until I come back.'

14"But his subjects hated him and sent a delegation after him to say, 'We don't want this man to be our king.'

15"He was made king, however, and returned home. Then he sent for the servants to whom he had given the money, in order to find out what they had gained with it.

16"The first one came and said, 'Sir, your mina has earned ten more.'

17" 'Well done, my good servant!' his master replied. 'Because you have been trustworthy in a very small matter, take charge of ten cities.'

18"The second came and said, 'Sir, your mina has earned five more.'

19"His master answered, 'You take charge of five cities.'

20"Then another servant came and said, 'Sir, here is your mina; I have kept it laid away in a piece of cloth. 21I was afraid of you, because you are a hard man. You take out what you did not put in and reap what you did not sow.'

22"His master replied, 'I will judge you by your own words, you wicked servant! You knew, did you, that I am a hard man, taking out what I did not put in, and reaping what I did not sow? 23Why then didn't you put my money on deposit, so that when I came back, I could have collected it with interest?'

24"Then he said to those standing by, 'Take his mina away from him and give it to the one who has ten minas.'

25" 'Sir,' they said, 'he already has ten!'

26"He replied, 'I tell you that to everyone who has, more will be given, but as for the one who has nothing, even what he has will be taken away. 27But those enemies of mine who did not want me to be king over them—bring them here and kill them in front of me.' "

The Triumphal Entry

28After Jesus had said this, he went on ahead, going up to Jerusalem. 29As he approached Bethphage and Bethany at the hill called the Mount of Olives, he sent two of his disciples, saying to them, 30"Go to the village ahead of you, and as you enter it, you will find a colt tied there, which no one has ever ridden. Untie it and bring it here. 31If anyone asks you, 'Why are you untying it?' tell him, 'The Lord needs it.' "

32Those who were sent ahead went and found it just as he had told them. 33As they were untying the colt, its owners asked them, "Why are you untying the colt?"

34They replied, "The Lord needs it."

35They brought it to Jesus, threw their cloaks on the

---

a *13* A mina was about three months' wages.

Living Bible

7But the crowds were displeased. "He has gone to be the guest of a notorious sinner," they grumbled.

8Meanwhile, Zacchaeus stood before the Lord and said, "Sir, from now on I will give half my wealth to the poor, and if I find I have overcharged anyone on his taxes, I will penalize myself by giving him back four times as much!"

9, 10Jesus told him, "This shows[b] that salvation has come to this home today. This man was one of the lost sons of Abraham, and I, the Messiah,[c] have come to search for and to save such souls as his."

11And because Jesus was nearing Jerusalem, he told a story to correct the impression that the Kingdom of God would begin right away.

12"A nobleman living in a certain province was called away to the distant capital of the empire to be crowned king of his province. 13Before he left he called together ten assistants and gave them each $2,000 to invest while he was gone. 14But some of his people hated him and sent him their declaration of independence, stating that they had rebelled and would not acknowledge him as their king.

15"Upon his return he called in the men to whom he had given the money, to find out what they had done with it, and what their profits were.

16"The first man reported a tremendous gain—ten times as much as the original amount!

17" 'Fine!' the king exclaimed. 'You are a good man. You have been faithful with the little I entrusted to you, and as your reward, you shall be governor of ten cities.'

18"The next man also reported a splendid gain—five times the original amount.

19" 'All right!' his master said. 'You can be governor over five cities.'

20"But the third man brought back only the money he had started with. 'I've kept it safe,' he said, 21'because I was afraid [you would demand my profits], for you are a hard man to deal with, taking what isn't yours and even confiscating the crops that others plant.' 22'You vile and wicked slave,' the king roared. 'Hard, am I? That's exactly how I'll be toward you! If you knew so much about me and how tough I am, 23then why didn't you deposit the money in the bank so that I could at least get some interest on it?'

24"Then turning to the others standing by he ordered, 'Take the money away from him and give it to the man who earned the most.'

25" 'But, sir,' they said, 'he has enough already!'

26" 'Yes,' the king replied, 'but it is always true that those who have, get more, and those who have little, soon lose even that. 27And now about these enemies of mine who revolted—bring them in and execute them before me.' "

28After telling this story, Jesus went on toward Jerusalem, walking along ahead of his disciples. 29As they came to the towns of Bethphage and Bethany, on the Mount of Olives, he sent two disciples ahead, 30with instructions to go to the next village, and as they entered they were to look for a donkey tied beside the road. It would be a colt, not yet broken for riding.

"Untie him," Jesus said, "and bring him here. 31And if anyone asks you what you are doing, just say, 'The Lord needs him.' "

32They found the colt as Jesus said, 33and sure enough, as they were untying it, the owners demanded an explanation.

"What are you doing?" they asked. "Why are you untying our colt?"

34And the disciples simply replied, "The Lord needs him!" 35So they brought the colt to Jesus and threw some of their clothing across its back for Jesus to sit on.

New Revised Standard

7All who saw it began to grumble and said, "He has gone to be the guest of one who is a sinner." 8Zacchaeus stood there and said to the Lord, "Look, half of my possessions, Lord, I will give to the poor; and if I have defrauded anyone of anything, I will pay back four times as much." 9Then Jesus said to him, "Today salvation has come to this house, because he too is a son of Abraham. 10For the Son of Man came to seek out and to save the lost."

The Parable of the Ten Pounds

11 As they were listening to this, he went on to tell a parable, because he was near Jerusalem, and because they supposed that the kingdom of God was to appear immediately. 12So he said, "A nobleman went to a distant country to get royal power for himself and then return. 13He summoned ten of his slaves, and gave them ten pounds,[d] and said to them, 'Do business with these until I come back.' 14But the citizens of his country hated him and sent a delegation after him, saying, 'We do not want this man to rule over us.' 15When he returned, having received royal power, he ordered these slaves, to whom he had given the money, to be summoned so that he might find out what they had gained by trading. 16The first came forward and said, 'Lord, your pound has made ten more pounds.' 17He said to him, 'Well done, good slave! Because you have been trustworthy in a very small thing, take charge of ten cities.' 18Then the second came, saying, 'Lord, your pound has made five pounds.' 19He said to him, 'And you, rule over five cities.' 20Then the other came, saying, 'Lord, here is your pound. I wrapped it up in a piece of cloth, 21for I was afraid of you, because you are a harsh man; you take what you did not deposit, and reap what you did not sow.' 22He said to him, 'I will judge you by your own words, you wicked slave! You knew, did you, that I was a harsh man, taking what I did not deposit and reaping what I did not sow? 23Why then did you not put my money into the bank? Then when I returned, I could have collected it with interest.' 24He said to the bystanders, 'Take the pound from him and give it to the one who has ten pounds.' 25(And they said to him, 'Lord, he has ten pounds!') 26'I tell you, to all those who have, more will be given; but from those who have nothing, even what they have will be taken away. 27But as for these enemies of mine who did not want me to be king over them—bring them here and slaughter them in my presence.' "

Jesus' Triumphal Entry into Jerusalem

28 After he had said this, he went on ahead, going up to Jerusalem.

29 When he had come near Bethphage and Bethany, at the place called the Mount of Olives, he sent two of the disciples, 30saying, "Go into the village ahead of you, and as you enter it you will find tied there a colt that has never been ridden. Untie it and bring it here. 31If anyone asks you, 'Why are you untying it?' just say this, 'The Lord needs it.' " 32So those who were sent departed and found it as he had told them. 33As they were untying the colt, its owners asked them, "Why are you untying the colt?" 34They said, "The Lord needs it." 35Then they brought it to Jesus; and after throwing their cloaks on the colt, they set Jesus on it. 36As he rode

---

b 19:9, 10 This shows, implied.   c 19:9, 10 the Messiah, literally, "the Son of Man."

d The mina, rendered here by pound, was about three months' wages for a laborer

King James

36And as he went, they spread their clothes in the way.

37And when he was come nigh, even now at the descent of the mount of Olives, the whole multitude of the disciples began to rejoice and praise God with a loud voice for all the mighty works that they had seen;

38Saying, Blessed *be* the King that cometh in the name of the Lord: peace in heaven, and glory in the highest.

39And some of the Pharisees from among the multitude said unto him, Master, rebuke thy disciples.

40And he answered and said unto them, I tell you that, if these should hold their peace, the stones would immediately cry out.

41¶ And when he was come near, he beheld the city, and wept over it,

42Saying, If thou hadst known, even thou, at least in this thy day, the things *which belong* unto thy peace! but now they are hid from thine eyes.

43For the days shall come upon thee, that thine enemies shall cast a trench about thee, and compass thee round, and keep thee in on every side,

44And shall lay thee even with the ground, and thy children within thee; and they shall not leave in thee one stone upon another; because thou knewest not the time of thy visitation.

45And he went into the temple, and began to cast out them that sold therein, and them that bought;

46Saying unto them, It is written, My house is the house of prayer: but ye have made it a den of thieves.

47And he taught daily in the temple. But the chief priests and the scribes and the chief of the people sought to destroy him,

48And could not find what they might do: for all the people were very attentive to hear him.

20 AND IT came to pass, *that* on one of those days, as he taught the people in the temple, and preached the gospel, the chief priests and the scribes came upon *him* with the elders,

2And spake unto him, saying, Tell us, by what authority doest thou these things? or who is he that gave thee this authority?

3And he answered and said unto them, I will also ask you one thing; and answer me:

4The baptism of John, was it from heaven, or of men?

5And they reasoned with themselves, saying, If we shall say, From heaven; he will say, Why then believed ye him not?

6But and if we say, Of men; all the people will stone us: for they be persuaded that John was a prophet.

7And they answered, that they could not tell whence *it was*.

8And Jesus said unto them, Neither tell I you by what authority I do these things.

9Then began he to speak to the people this parable; A certain man planted a vineyard, and let it forth to husbandmen, and went into a far country for a long time.

10And at the season he sent a servant to the husbandmen, that they should give him of the fruit of the vineyard: but the husbandmen beat him, and sent *him* away empty.

11And again he sent another servant: and they beat him also, and entreated *him* shamefully, and sent *him* away empty.

12And again he sent a third: and they wounded him also, and cast *him* out.

13Then said the lord of the vineyard, What shall I do? I will send my beloved son: it may be they will reverence *him* when they see him.

New International

colt and put Jesus on it. 36As he went along, people spread their cloaks on the road.

37When he came near the place where the road goes down the Mount of Olives, the whole crowd of disciples began joyfully to praise God in loud voices for all the miracles they had seen:

38"Blessed is the king who comes in the name of the Lord!"a

"Peace in heaven and glory in the highest!"

39Some of the Pharisees in the crowd said to Jesus, "Teacher, rebuke your disciples!"

40"I tell you," he replied, "if they keep quiet, the stones will cry out."

41As he approached Jerusalem and saw the city, he wept over it 42and said, "If you, even you, had only known on this day what would bring you peace—but now it is hidden from your eyes. 43The days will come upon you when your enemies will build an embankment against you and encircle you and hem you in on every side. 44They will dash you to the ground, you and the children within your walls. They will not leave one stone on another, because you did not recognize the time of God's coming to you."

Jesus at the Temple

45Then he entered the temple area and began driving out those who were selling. 46"It is written," he said to them, " 'My house will be a house of prayer'b; but you have made it 'a den of robbers.'c"

47Every day he was teaching at the temple. But the chief priests, the teachers of the law and the leaders among the people were trying to kill him. 48Yet they could not find any way to do it, because all the people hung on his words.

The Authority of Jesus Questioned

20 ONE DAY as he was teaching the people in the temple courts and preaching the gospel, the chief priests and the teachers of the law, together with the elders, came up to him. 2"Tell us by what authority you are doing these things," they said. "Who gave you this authority?"

3He replied, "I will also ask you a question. Tell me, 4John's baptism—was it from heaven, or from men?"

5They discussed it among themselves and said, "If we say, 'From heaven,' he will ask, 'Why didn't you believe him?' 6But if we say, 'From men,' all the people will stone us, because they are persuaded that John was a prophet."

7So they answered, "We don't know where it was from."

8Jesus said, "Neither will I tell you by what authority I am doing these things."

The Parable of the Tenants

9He went on to tell the people this parable: "A man planted a vineyard, rented it to some farmers and went away for a long time. 10At harvest time he sent a servant to the tenants so they would give him some of the fruit of the vineyard. But the tenants beat him and sent him away empty-handed. 11He sent another servant, but that one also they beat and treated shamefully and sent away empty-handed. 12He sent still a third, and they wounded him and threw him out.

13"Then the owner of the vineyard said, 'What shall I do? I will send my son, whom I love; perhaps they will respect him.'

a *38* Psalm 118:26   b *46* Isaiah 56:7   c *46* Jer. 7:11

Living Bible

36, 37Then the crowds spread out their robes along the road ahead of him, and as they reached the place where the road started down from the Mount of Olives, the whole procession began to shout and sing as they walked along, praising God for all the wonderful miracles Jesus had done.

38"God has given us a King!" they exulted. "Long live the King! Let all heaven rejoice! Glory to God in the highest heavens!"

39But some of the Pharisees among the crowd said, "Sir, rebuke your followers for saying things like that!"

40He replied, "If they keep quiet, the stones along the road will burst into cheers!"

41But as they came closer to Jerusalem and he saw the city ahead, he began to cry. 42"Eternal peace was within your reach and you turned it down," he wept, "and now it is too late. 43Your enemies will pile up earth against your walls and encircle you and close in on you, 44and crush you to the ground, and your children within you; your enemies will not leave one stone upon another—for you have rejected the opportunity God offered you."

45Then he entered the Temple and began to drive out the merchants from their stalls, 46saying to them, "The Scriptures declare, 'My Temple is a place of prayer; but you have turned it into a den of thieves.'"

47After that he taught daily in the Temple, but the chief priests and other religious leaders and the business community[d] were trying to find some way to get rid of him. 48But they could think of nothing, for he was a hero to the people—they hung on every word he said.

20 ON ONE of those days when he was teaching and preaching the Good News in the Temple, he was confronted by the chief priests and other religious leaders and councilmen. 2They demanded to know by what authority he had driven out the merchants from the Temple.

3"I'll ask you a question before I answer," he replied. 4"Was John sent by God, or was he merely acting under his own authority?"

5They talked it over among themselves. "If we say his message was from heaven, then we are trapped because he will ask, 'Then why didn't you believe him?' 6But if we say John was not sent from God, the people will mob us, for they are convinced that he was a prophet." 7Finally they replied, "We don't know!"

8And Jesus responded, "Then I won't answer your question either."

9Now he turned to the people again and told them this story: "A man planted a vineyard and rented it out to some farmers, and went away to a distant land to live for several years. 10When harvest time came, he sent one of his men to the farm to collect his share of the crops. But the tenants beat him up and sent him back empty-handed. 11Then he sent another, but the same thing happened; he was beaten up and insulted and sent away without collecting. 12A third man was sent and the same thing happened. He, too, was wounded and chased away.

13"'What shall I do?' the owner asked himself. 'I know! I'll send my cherished son. Surely they will show respect for him.'

New Revised Standard

along, people kept spreading their cloaks on the road. 37As he was now approaching the path down from the Mount of Olives, the whole multitude of the disciples began to praise God joyfully with a loud voice for all the deeds of power that they had seen, 38saying,

"Blessed is the king
    who comes in the name of the Lord!
Peace in heaven,
    and glory in the highest heaven!"

39Some of the Pharisees in the crowd said to him, "Teacher, order your disciples to stop." 40He answered, "I tell you, if these were silent, the stones would shout out."

Jesus Weeps over Jerusalem

41 As he came near and saw the city, he wept over it, 42saying, "If you, even you, had only recognized on this day the things that make for peace! But now they are hidden from your eyes. 43Indeed, the days will come upon you, when your enemies will set up ramparts around you and surround you, and hem you in on every side. 44They will crush you to the ground, you and your children within you, and they will not leave within you one stone upon another; because you did not recognize the time of your visitation from God."[e]

Jesus Cleanses the Temple

45 Then he entered the temple and began to drive out those who were selling things there; 46and he said, "It is written,

'My house shall be a house of prayer';
    but you have made it a den of robbers."

47 Every day he was teaching in the temple. The chief priests, the scribes, and the leaders of the people kept looking for a way to kill him; 48but they did not find anything they could do, for all the people were spellbound by what they heard.

The Authority of Jesus Questioned

20 ONE DAY, as he was teaching the people in the temple and telling the good news, the chief priests and the scribes came with the elders 2and said to him, "Tell us, by what authority are you doing these things? Who is it who gave you this authority?" 3He answered them, "I will also ask you a question, and you tell me: 4Did the baptism of John come from heaven, or was it of human origin?" 5They discussed it with one another, saying, "If we say, 'From heaven,' he will say, 'Why did you not believe him?' 6But if we say, 'Of human origin,' all the people will stone us; for they are convinced that John was a prophet." 7So they answered that they did not know where it came from. 8Then Jesus said to them, "Neither will I tell you by what authority I am doing these things."

The Parable of the Wicked Tenants

9 He began to tell the people this parable: "A man planted a vineyard, and leased it to tenants, and went to another country for a long time. 10When the season came, he sent a slave to the tenants in order that they might give him his share of the produce of the vineyard; but the tenants beat him and sent him away empty-handed. 11Next he sent another slave; that one also they beat and insulted and sent away empty-handed. 12And he sent still a third; this one also they wounded and threw out. 13Then the owner of the vineyard said, 'What shall I do? I will send my beloved son; perhaps they will respect him.' 14But when the tenants saw him, they

---

d *19:47 the business community,* literally, "the leading men among the people."

e Gk lacks *from God*

King James

14But when the husbandmen saw him, they reasoned among themselves, saying, This is the heir: come, let us kill him, that the inheritance may be ours.

15So they cast him out of the vineyard, and killed *him.* What therefore shall the lord of the vineyard do unto them?

16He shall come and destroy these husbandmen, and shall give the vineyard to others. And when they heard *it,* they said, God forbid.

17And he beheld them, and said, What is this then that is written, The stone which the builders rejected, the same is become the head of the corner?

18Whosoever shall fall upon that stone shall be broken; but on whomsoever it shall fall, it will grind him to powder.

19¶ And the chief priests and the scribes the same hour sought to lay hands on him; and they feared the people: for they perceived that he had spoken this parable against them.

20And they watched *him,* and sent forth spies, which should feign themselves just men, that they might take hold of his words, that so they might deliver him unto the power and authority of the governor.

21And they asked him, saying, Master, we know that thou sayest and teachest rightly, neither acceptest thou the person *of any,* but teachest the way of God truly:

22Is it lawful for us to give tribute unto Caesar, or no?

23But he perceived their craftiness, and said unto them, Why tempt ye me?

24Show me a penny. Whose image and superscription hath it? They answered and said, Caesar's.

25And he said unto them, Render therefore unto Caesar the things which be Caesar's, and unto God the things which be God's.

26And they could not take hold of his words before the people: and they marvelled at his answer, and held their peace.

27¶ Then came to *him* certain of the Sadducees, which deny that there is any resurrection; and they asked him,

28Saying, Master, Moses wrote unto us, If any man's brother die, having a wife, and he die without children, that his brother should take his wife, and raise up seed unto his brother.

29There were therefore seven brethren: and the first took a wife, and died without children.

30And the second took her to wife, and he died childless.

31And the third took her; and in like manner the seven also: and they left no children, and died.

32Last of all the woman died also.

33Therefore in the resurrection whose wife of them is she? for seven had her to wife.

34And Jesus answering said unto them, The children of this world marry, and are given in marriage:

35But they which shall be accounted worthy to obtain that world, and the resurrection from the dead, neither marry, nor are given in marriage:

36Neither can they die any more: for they are equal unto the angels; and are the children of God, being the children of the resurrection.

37Now that the dead are raised, even Moses showed at the bush, when he calleth the Lord the God of Abraham, and the God of Isaac, and the God of Jacob.

38For he is not a God of the dead, but of the living: for all live unto him.

39¶ Then certain of the scribes answering said, Master, thou hast well said.

40And after that they durst not ask him any *question at all.*

41And he said unto them, How say they that Christ is David's son?

New International

14"But when the tenants saw him, they talked the matter over. 'This is the heir,' they said. 'Let's kill him, and the inheritance will be ours.' 15So they threw him out of the vineyard and killed him.

"What then will the owner of the vineyard do to them? 16He will come and kill those tenants and give the vineyard to others."

When the people heard this, they said, "May this never be!"

17Jesus looked directly at them and asked, "Then what is the meaning of that which is written:

" 'The stone the builders rejected
has become the capstonea 'b?

18Everyone who falls on that stone will be broken to pieces, but he on whom it falls will be crushed."

19The teachers of the law and the chief priests looked for a way to arrest him immediately, because they knew he had spoken this parable against them. But they were afraid of the people.

Paying Taxes to Caesar

20Keeping a close watch on him, they sent spies, who pretended to be honest. They hoped to catch Jesus in something he said so that they might hand him over to the power and authority of the governor. 21So the spies questioned him: "Teacher, we know that you speak and teach what is right, and that you do not show partiality but teach the way of God in accordance with the truth. 22Is it right for us to pay taxes to Caesar or not?"

23He saw through their duplicity and said to them, 24"Show me a denarius. Whose portrait and inscription are on it?"

25"Caesar's," they replied.

He said to them, "Then give to Caesar what is Caesar's, and to God what is God's."

26They were unable to trap him in what he had said there in public. And astonished by his answer, they became silent.

The Resurrection and Marriage

27Some of the Sadducees, who say there is no resurrection, came to Jesus with a question. 28"Teacher," they said, "Moses wrote for us that if a man's brother dies and leaves a wife but no children, the man must marry the widow and have children for his brother. 29Now there were seven brothers. The first one married a woman and died childless. 30The second 31and then the third married her, and in the same way the seven died, leaving no children. 32Finally, the woman died too. 33Now then, at the resurrection whose wife will she be, since the seven were married to her?"

34Jesus replied, "The people of this age marry and are given in marriage. 35But those who are considered worthy of taking part in that age and in the resurrection from the dead will neither marry nor be given in marriage, 36and they can no longer die; for they are like the angels. They are God's children, since they are children of the resurrection. 37But in the account of the bush, even Moses showed that the dead rise, for he calls the Lord 'the God of Abraham, and the God of Isaac, and the God of Jacob.'c 38He is not the God of the dead, but of the living, for to him all are alive."

39Some of the teachers of the law responded, "Well said, teacher!" 40And no one dared to ask him any more questions.

Whose Son Is the Christ?

41Then Jesus said to them, "How is it that they say the Christd is the Son of David? 42David himself declares in the Book of Psalms:

---

a *17* Or *cornerstone*　　b *17* Psalm 118:22　　c *37* Exodus 3:6　　d *41* Or *Messiah*

Living Bible

14"But when the tenants saw his son, they said, 'This is our chance! This fellow will inherit all the land when his father dies. Come on. Let's kill him, and then it will be ours.' 15So they dragged him out of the vineyard and killed him.

"What do you think the owner will do? 16I'll tell you—he will come and kill them and rent the vineyard to others."

"But they would never do a thing like that," his listeners protested.

17Jesus looked at them and said, "Then what does the Scripture mean where it says, 'The Stone rejected by the builders was made the cornerstone'?" 18And he added, "Whoever stumbles over that Stone shall be broken; and those on whom it falls will be crushed to dust."

19When the chief priests and religious leaders heard about this story he had told, they wanted him arrested immediately, for they realized that he was talking about them. They were the wicked tenants in his illustration. But they were afraid that if they themselves arrested him there would be a riot. So they tried to get him to say something that could be reported to the Roman governor as reason for arrest by him.

20Watching their opportunity, they sent secret agents pretending to be honest men. 21They said to Jesus, "Sir, we know what an honest teacher you are. You always tell the truth and don't budge an inch in the face of what others think, but teach the ways of God. 22Now tell us—is it right to pay taxes to the Roman government or not?"

23He saw through their trickery and said, 24"Show me a coin. Whose portrait is this on it? And whose name?"

They replied, "Caesar's—the Roman emperor's."

25He said, "Then give the emperor all that is his—and give to God all that is his!"

26Thus their attempt to outwit him before the people failed; and marveling at his answer, they were silent.

27Then some Sadducees—men who believed that death is the end of existence, that there is no resurrection— 28came to Jesus with this:

"The laws of Moses state that if a man dies without children, the man's brother shall marry the widow and their children will legally belong to the dead man, to carry on his name. 29We know of a family of seven brothers. The oldest married and then died without any children. 30His brother married the widow and he, too, died. Still no children. 31And so it went, one after the other, until each of the seven had married her and died, leaving no children. 32Finally the woman died also. 33Now here is our question: Whose wife will she be in the resurrection? For all of them were married to her!"

34, 35Jesus replied, "Marriage is for people here on earth, but when those who are counted worthy of being raised from the dead get to heaven, they do not marry. 36And they never die again; in these respects they are like angels, and are sons of God, for they are raised up in new life from the dead.

37, 38"But as to your real question—whether or not there is a resurrection—why, even the writings of Moses himself prove this. For when he describes how God appeared to him in the burning bush, he speaks of God as 'the God of Abraham, the God of Isaac, and the God of Jacob.' To say that the Lord is some person's Godᵉ means that person is alive, not dead! So from God's point of view, all men are living."

39"Well said, sir!" remarked some of the experts in the Jewish law who were standing there. 40And that ended their questions, for they dared ask no more!

41Then he presented them with a question. "Why is it," he asked, "that Christ, the Messiah, is said to be a descendant of King David? 42, 43For David himself

New Revised Standard

discussed it among themselves and said, 'This is the heir; let us kill him so that the inheritance may be ours.' 15So they threw him out of the vineyard and killed him. What then will the owner of the vineyard do to them? 16He will come and destroy those tenants and give the vineyard to others." When they heard this, they said, "Heaven forbid!" 17But he looked at them and said, "What then does this text mean:

'The stone that the builders rejected
    has become the cornerstone'?ᶠ

18Everyone who falls on that stone will be broken to pieces; and it will crush anyone on whom it falls." 19When the scribes and chief priests realized that he had told this parable against them, they wanted to lay hands on him at that very hour, but they feared the people.

The Question about Paying Taxes

20 So they watched him and sent spies who pretended to be honest, in order to trap him by what he said, so as to hand him over to the jurisdiction and authority of the governor. 21So they asked him, "Teacher, we know that you are right in what you say and teach, and you show deference to no one, but teach the way of God in accordance with truth. 22Is it lawful for us to pay taxes to the emperor, or not?" 23But he perceived their craftiness and said to them, 24"Show me a denarius. Whose head and whose title does it bear?" They said, "The emperor's." 25He said to them, "Then give to the emperor the things that are the emperor's, and to God the things that are God's." 26And they were not able in the presence of the people to trap him by what he said; and being amazed by his answer, they became silent.

The Question about the Resurrection

27 Some Sadducees, those who say there is no resurrection, came to him 28and asked him a question, "Teacher, Moses wrote for us that if a man's brother dies, leaving a wife but no children, the manᵍ shall marry the widow and raise up children for his brother. 29Now there were seven brothers; the first married, and died childless; 30then the second 31and the third married her, and so in the same way all seven died childless. 32Finally the woman also died. 33In the resurrection, therefore, whose wife will the woman be? For the seven had married her."

34 Jesus said to them, "Those who belong to this age marry and are given in marriage; 35but those who are considered worthy of a place in that age and in the resurrection from the dead neither marry nor are given in marriage. 36Indeed they cannot die anymore, because they are like angels and are children of God, being children of the resurrection. 37And the fact that the dead are raised Moses himself showed, in the story about the bush, where he speaks of the Lord as the God of Abraham, the God of Isaac, and the God of Jacob. 38Now he is God not of the dead, but of the living; for to him all of them are alive." 39Then some of the scribes answered, "Teacher, you have spoken well." 40For they no longer dared to ask him another question.

The Question about David's Son

41 Then he said to them, "How can they say that the Messiahʰ is David's son? 42For David himself says in the book of Psalms,

---

ᵉ 20:37, 38 the Lord is some person's God. Otherwise the statement would be, "He had been that person's God."

ᶠ Or keystone   ᵍ Gk his brother   ʰ Or the Christ

King James

42And David himself saith in the book of Psalms, The LORD said unto my Lord, Sit thou on my right hand,

43Till I make thine enemies thy footstool.

44David therefore calleth him Lord, how is he then his son?

45¶ Then in the audience of all the people he said unto his disciples,

46Beware of the scribes, which desire to walk in long robes, and love greetings in the markets, and the highest seats in the synagogues, and the chief rooms at feasts;

47Which devour widows' houses, and for a show make long prayers: the same shall receive greater damnation.

21 AND HE looked up, and saw the rich men casting their gifts into the treasury.

2And he saw also a certain poor widow casting in thither two mites.

3And he said, Of a truth I say unto you, that this poor widow hath cast in more than they all:

4For all these have of their abundance cast in unto the offerings of God: but she of her penury hath cast in all the living that she had.

5¶ And as some spake of the temple, how it was adorned with goodly stones and gifts, he said,

6As for these things which ye behold, the days will come, in the which there shall not be left one stone upon another, that shall not be thrown down.

7And they asked him, saying, Master, but when shall these things be? and what sign will there be when these things shall come to pass?

8And he said, Take heed that ye be not deceived: for many shall come in my name, saying, I am Christ; and the time draweth near: go ye not therefore after them.

9But when ye shall hear of wars and commotions, be not terrified: for these things must first come to pass; but the end is not by and by.

10Then said he unto them, Nation shall rise against nation, and kingdom against kingdom:

11And great earthquakes shall be in divers places, and famines, and pestilences; and fearful sights and great signs shall there be from heaven.

12But before all these, they shall lay their hands on you, and persecute you, delivering you up to the synagogues, and into prisons, being brought before kings and rulers for my name's sake.

13And it shall turn to you for a testimony.

14Settle it therefore in your hearts, not to meditate before what ye shall answer:

15For I will give you a mouth and wisdom, which all your adversaries shall not be able to gainsay nor resist.

16And ye shall be betrayed both by parents, and brethren, and kinsfolks, and friends; and some of you shall they cause to be put to death.

17And ye shall be hated of all men for my name's sake.

18But there shall not an hair of your head perish.

19In your patience possess ye your souls.

20And when ye shall see Jerusalem compassed with armies, then know that the desolation thereof is nigh.

21Then let them which are in Judaea flee to the mountains; and let them which are in the midst of it depart out; and let not them that are in the countries enter thereinto.

22For these be the days of vengeance, that all things which are written may be fulfilled.

New International

" 'The Lord said to my Lord:
  "Sit at my right hand
  43until I make your enemies
    a footstool for your feet." ' a

44David calls him 'Lord.' How then can he be his son?"

45While all the people were listening, Jesus said to his disciples, 46"Beware of the teachers of the law. They like to walk around in flowing robes and love to be greeted in the marketplaces and have the most important seats in the synagogues and the places of honor at banquets. 47They devour widows' houses and for a show make lengthy prayers. Such men will be punished most severely."

The Widow's Offering

21 AS HE looked up, Jesus saw the rich putting their gifts into the temple treasury. 2He also saw a poor widow put in two very small copper coins.b 3"I tell you the truth," he said, "this poor widow has put in more than all the others. 4All these people gave their gifts out of their wealth; but she out of her poverty put in all she had to live on."

Signs of the End of the Age

5Some of his disciples were remarking about how the temple was adorned with beautiful stones and with gifts dedicated to God. But Jesus said, 6"As for what you see here, the time will come when not one stone will be left on another; every one of them will be thrown down."

7"Teacher," they asked, "when will these things happen? And what will be the sign that they are about to take place?"

8He replied: "Watch out that you are not deceived. For many will come in my name, claiming, 'I am he,' and, 'The time is near.' Do not follow them. 9When you hear of wars and revolutions, do not be frightened. These things must happen first, but the end will not come right away."

10Then he said to them: "Nation will rise against nation, and kingdom against kingdom. 11There will be great earthquakes, famines and pestilences in various places, and fearful events and great signs from heaven.

12"But before all this, they will lay hands on you and persecute you. They will deliver you to synagogues and prisons, and you will be brought before kings and governors, and all on account of my name. 13This will result in your being witnesses to them. 14But make up your mind not to worry beforehand how you will defend yourselves. 15For I will give you words and wisdom that none of your adversaries will be able to resist or contradict. 16You will be betrayed even by parents, brothers, relatives and friends, and they will put some of you to death. 17All men will hate you because of me. 18But not a hair of your head will perish. 19By standing firm you will gain life.

20"When you see Jerusalem being surrounded by armies, you will know that its desolation is near. 21Then let those who are in Judea flee to the mountains, let those in the city get out, and let those in the country not enter the city. 22For this is the time of punishment in fulfillment of all that has been written. 23How dreadful it will

a 43 Psalm 110:1   b 2 Greek two lepta

Living Bible

wrote in the book of Psalms: 'God said to my Lord, the Messiah, "Sit at my right hand until I place your enemies beneath your feet." ' 44How can the Messiah be both David's son and David's God at the same time?"

45Then, with the crowds listening, he turned to his disciples and said, 46"Beware of these experts in religion, for they love to parade in dignified robes and to be bowed to by the people as they walk along the street. And how they love the seats of honor in the synagogues and at religious festivals! 47But even while they are praying long prayers with great outward piety, they are planning schemes to cheat widows out of their property. Therefore God's heaviest sentence awaits these men."

21 AS HE stood in the Temple, he was watching the rich tossing their gifts into the collection box. 2Then a poor widow came by and dropped in two small copper coins.

3"Really," he remarked, "this poor widow has given more than all the rest of them combined. 4For they have given a little of what they didn't need, but she, poor as she is, has given everything she has."

5Some of his disciples began talking about the beautiful stonework of the Temple and the memorial decorations on the walls.

6But Jesus said, "The time is coming when all these things you are admiring will be knocked down, and not one stone will be left on top of another; all will become one vast heap of rubble."

7"Master!" they exclaimed. "When? And will there be any warning ahead of time?"

8He replied, "Don't let anyone mislead you. For many will come announcing themselves as the Messiah,c and saying, 'The time has come.' But don't believe them! 9And when you hear of wars and insurrections beginning, don't panic. True, wars must come, but the end won't follow immediately— 10for nation shall rise against nation and kingdom against kingdom, 11and there will be great earthquakes, and famines in many lands, and epidemics, and terrifying things happening in the heavens.

12"But before all this occurs, there will be a time of special persecution, and you will be dragged into synagogues and prisons and before kings and governors for my name's sake. 13But as a result, the Messiah will be widely known and honored.d 14Therefore, don't be concerned about how to answer the charges against you, 15for I will give you the right words and such logic that none of your opponents will be able to reply! 16Even those closest to you—your parents, brothers, relatives, and friends will betray you and have you arrested; and some of you will be killed. 17And everyone will hate you because you are mine and are called by my name. 18But not a hair of your head will perish! 19For if you stand firm, you will win your souls.

20"But when you see Jerusalem surrounded by armies, then you will know that the time of its destruction has arrived. 21Then let the people of Judea flee to the hills. Let those in Jerusalem try to escape, and those outside the city must not attempt to return. 22For those will be days of God's judgment,e and the words of the ancient Scriptures written by the prophets will be abundantly fulfilled. 23Woe to expectant mothers in those

New Revised Standard

'The Lord said to my Lord,
  "Sit at my right hand,
43   until I make your enemies your footstool." '
44David thus calls him Lord; so how can he be his son?"

Jesus Denounces the Scribes

45 In the hearing of all the people he said to thef disciples, 46"Beware of the scribes, who like to walk around in long robes, and love to be greeted with respect in the marketplaces, and to have the best seats in the synagogues and places of honor at banquets. 47They devour widows' houses and for the sake of appearance say long prayers. They will receive the greater condemnation."

The Widow's Offering

21 HE LOOKED up and saw rich people putting their gifts into the treasury; 2he also saw a poor widow put in two small copper coins. 3He said, "Truly I tell you, this poor widow has put in more than all of them; 4for all of them have contributed out of their abundance, but she out of her poverty has put in all she had to live on."

The Destruction of the Temple Foretold

5 When some were speaking about the temple, how it was adorned with beautiful stones and gifts dedicated to God, he said, 6"As for these things that you see, the days will come when not one stone will be left upon another; all will be thrown down."

Signs and Persecutions

7 They asked him, "Teacher, when will this be, and what will be the sign that this is about to take place?" 8And he said, "Beware that you are not led astray; for many will come in my name and say, 'I am he!'g and, 'The time is near!'h Do not go after them.

9 "When you hear of wars and insurrections, do not be terrified; for these things must take place first, but the end will not follow immediately." 10Then he said to them, "Nation will rise against nation, and kingdom against kingdom; 11there will be great earthquakes, and in various places famines and plagues; and there will be dreadful portents and great signs from heaven.

12 "But before all this occurs, they will arrest you and persecute you; they will hand you over to synagogues and prisons, and you will be brought before kings and governors because of my name. 13This will give you an opportunity to testify. 14So make up your minds not to prepare your defense in advance; 15for I will give you wordsi and a wisdom that none of your opponents will be able to withstand or contradict. 16You will be betrayed even by parents and brothers, by relatives and friends; and they will put some of you to death. 17You will be hated by all because of my name. 18But not a hair of your head will perish. 19By your endurance you will gain your souls.

The Destruction of Jerusalem Foretold

20 "When you see Jerusalem surrounded by armies, then know that its desolation has come near.j 21Then those in Judea must flee to the mountains, and those inside the city must leave it, and those out in the country must not enter it; 22for these are days of vengeance, as a fulfillment of all that is written. 23Woe to those who

c 21:8 will come announcing themselves as the Messiah, literally, "will come in my name." d 21:13 the Messiah will be widely known and honored, literally, "It shall turn out unto you for a testimony." e 21:22 days of God's judgment, literally, "days of vengeance."

f Other ancient authorities read his   g Gk I am   h Or at hand   i Gk a mouth
j Or is at hand

King James

23But woe unto them that are with child, and to them that give suck, in those days! for there shall be great distress in the land, and wrath upon this people.

24And they shall fall by the edge of the sword, and shall be led away captive into all nations: and Jerusalem shall be trodden down of the Gentiles, until the times of the Gentiles be fulfilled.

25¶ And there shall be signs in the sun, and in the moon, and in the stars; and upon the earth distress of nations, with perplexity; the sea and the waves roaring;

26Men's hearts failing them for fear, and for looking after those things which are coming on the earth: for the powers of heaven shall be shaken.

27And then shall they see the Son of man coming in a cloud with power and great glory.

28And when these things begin to come to pass, then look up, and lift up your heads; for your redemption draweth nigh.

29And he spake to them a parable; Behold the fig tree, and all the trees;

30When they now shoot forth, ye see and know of your own selves that summer is now nigh at hand.

31So likewise ye, when ye see these things come to pass, know ye that the kingdom of God is nigh at hand.

32Verily I say unto you, This generation shall not pass away, till all be fulfilled.

33Heaven and earth shall pass away: but my words shall not pass away.

34¶ And take heed to yourselves, lest at any time your hearts be overcharged with surfeiting, and drunkenness, and cares of this life, and so that day come upon you unawares.

35For as a snare shall it come on all them that dwell on the face of the whole earth.

36Watch ye therefore, and pray always, that ye may be accounted worthy to escape all these things that shall come to pass, and to stand before the Son of man.

37And in the day time he was teaching in the temple; and at night he went out, and abode in the mount that is called the mount of Olives.

38And all the people came early in the morning to him in the temple, for to hear him.

22 NOW THE feast of unleavened bread drew nigh, which is called the Passover.

2And the chief priests and scribes sought how they might kill him; for they feared the people.

3¶ Then entered Satan into Judas surnamed Iscariot, being of the number of the twelve.

4And he went his way, and communed with the chief priests and captains, how he might betray him unto them.

5And they were glad, and covenanted to give him money.

6And he promised, and sought opportunity to betray him unto them in the absence of the multitude.

7¶ Then came the day of unleavened bread, when the passover must be killed.

8And he sent Peter and John, saying, Go and prepare us the passover, that we may eat.

9And they said unto him, Where wilt thou that we prepare?

10And he said unto them, Behold, when ye are entered into the city, there shall a man meet you, bearing a pitcher of water; follow him into the house where he entereth in.

New International

be in those days for pregnant women and nursing mothers! There will be great distress in the land and wrath against this people. 24They will fall by the sword and will be taken as prisoners to all the nations. Jerusalem will be trampled on by the Gentiles until the times of the Gentiles are fulfilled.

25"There will be signs in the sun, moon and stars. On the earth, nations will be in anguish and perplexity at the roaring and tossing of the sea. 26Men will faint from terror, apprehensive of what is coming on the world, for the heavenly bodies will be shaken. 27At that time they will see the Son of Man coming in a cloud with power and great glory. 28When these things begin to take place, stand up and lift up your heads, because your redemption is drawing near."

29He told them this parable: "Look at the fig tree and all the trees. 30When they sprout leaves, you can see for yourselves and know that summer is near. 31Even so, when you see these things happening, you know that the kingdom of God is near.

32"I tell you the truth, this generation[a] will certainly not pass away until all these things have happened. 33Heaven and earth will pass away, but my words will never pass away.

34"Be careful, or your hearts will be weighed down with dissipation, drunkenness and the anxieties of life, and that day will close on you unexpectedly like a trap. 35For it will come upon all those who live on the face of the whole earth. 36Be always on the watch, and pray that you may be able to escape all that is about to happen, and that you may be able to stand before the Son of Man."

37Each day Jesus was teaching at the temple, and each evening he went out to spend the night on the hill called the Mount of Olives, 38and all the people came early in the morning to hear him at the temple.

Judas Agrees to Betray Jesus

22 NOW THE Feast of Unleavened Bread, called the Passover, was approaching, 2and the chief priests and the teachers of the law were looking for some way to get rid of Jesus, for they were afraid of the people. 3Then Satan entered Judas, called Iscariot, one of the Twelve. 4And Judas went to the chief priests and the officers of the temple guard and discussed with them how he might betray Jesus. 5They were delighted and agreed to give him money. 6He consented, and watched for an opportunity to hand Jesus over to them when no crowd was present.

The Last Supper

7Then came the day of Unleavened Bread on which the Passover lamb had to be sacrificed. 8Jesus sent Peter and John, saying, "Go and make preparations for us to eat the Passover."

9"Where do you want us to prepare for it?" they asked.

10He replied, "As you enter the city, a man carrying a jar of water will meet you. Follow him to the house that he enters, 11and say to the owner of the house, 'The

ᵃ 32 Or race

Living Bible

days, and those with tiny babies. For there will be great distress upon this nation[b] and wrath upon this people. 24They will be brutally killed by enemy weapons, or sent away as exiles and captives to all the nations of the world; and Jerusalem shall be conquered and trampled down by the Gentiles until the period of Gentile triumph ends in God's good time.

25"Then there will be strange events in the skies— warnings, evil omens and portents in the sun, moon and stars; and down here on earth the nations will be in turmoil, perplexed by the roaring seas and strange tides. 26The courage of many people will falter because of the fearful fate they see coming upon the earth, for the stability of the very heavens will be broken up. 27Then the peoples of the earth shall see me, the Messiah,[c] coming in a cloud with power and great glory. 28So when all these things begin to happen, stand straight and look up! For your salvation is near."

29Then he gave them this illustration: "Notice the fig tree, or any other tree. 30When the leaves come out, you know without being told that summer is near. 31In the same way, when you see the events taking place that I've described you can be just as sure that the Kingdom of God is near.

32"I solemnly declare to you that when these things happen, the end of this age[d] has come. 33And though all heaven and earth shall pass away, yet my words remain forever true.

34, 35"Watch out! Don't let my sudden coming catch you unawares; don't let me find you living in careless ease, carousing and drinking, and occupied with the problems of this life, like all the rest of the world. 36Keep a constant watch. And pray that if possible you may arrive in my presence without having to experience these horrors."[e]

37, 38Every day Jesus went to the Temple to teach, and the crowds began gathering early in the morning to hear him. And each evening he returned to spend the night on the Mount of Olives.

22 AND NOW the Passover celebration was drawing near—the Jewish festival when only bread made without yeast was used. 2The chief priests and other religious leaders were actively plotting Jesus' murder, trying to find a way to kill him without starting a riot—a possibility they greatly feared.

3Then Satan entered into Judas Iscariot, who was one of the twelve disciples, 4and he went over to the chief priests and captains of the Temple guards to discuss the best way to betray Jesus to them. 5They were, of course, delighted to know that he was ready to help them and promised him a reward. 6So he began to look for an opportunity for them to arrest Jesus quietly when the crowds weren't around.

7Now the day of the Passover celebration arrived, when the Passover lamb was killed and eaten with the unleavened bread. 8Jesus sent Peter and John ahead to find a place to prepare their Passover meal.

9"Where do you want us to go?" they asked.

10And he replied, "As soon as you enter Jerusalem,[f] you will see a man walking along carrying a pitcher of water. Follow him into the house he enters, 11and say

New Revised Standard

are pregnant and to those who are nursing infants in those days! For there will be great distress on the earth and wrath against this people; 24they will fall by the edge of the sword and be taken away as captives among all nations; and Jerusalem will be trampled on by the Gentiles, until the times of the Gentiles are fulfilled.

The Coming of the Son of Man

25 "There will be signs in the sun, the moon, and the stars, and on the earth distress among nations confused by the roaring of the sea and the waves. 26People will faint from fear and foreboding of what is coming upon the world, for the powers of the heavens will be shaken. 27Then they will see 'the Son of Man coming in a cloud' with power and great glory. 28Now when these things begin to take place, stand up and raise your heads, because your redemption is drawing near."

The Lesson of the Fig Tree

29 Then he told them a parable: "Look at the fig tree and all the trees; 30as soon as they sprout leaves you can see for yourselves and know that summer is already near. 31So also, when you see these things taking place, you know that the kingdom of God is near. 32Truly I tell you, this generation will not pass away until all things have taken place. 33Heaven and earth will pass away, but my words will not pass away.

Exhortation to Watch

34 "Be on guard so that your hearts are not weighed down with dissipation and drunkenness and the worries of this life, and that day catch you unexpectedly, 35like a trap. For it will come upon all who live on the face of the whole earth. 36Be alert at all times, praying that you may have the strength to escape all these things that will take place, and to stand before the Son of Man."

37 Every day he was teaching in the temple, and at night he would go out and spend the night on the Mount of Olives, as it was called. 38And all the people would get up early in the morning to listen to him in the temple.

The Plot to Kill Jesus

22 NOW THE festival of Unleavened Bread, which is called the Passover, was near. 2The chief priests and the scribes were looking for a way to put Jesus[g] to death, for they were afraid of the people.

3 Then Satan entered into Judas called Iscariot, who was one of the twelve; 4he went away and conferred with the chief priests and officers of the temple police about how he might betray him to them. 5They were greatly pleased and agreed to give him money. 6So he consented and began to look for an opportunity to betray him to them when no crowd was present.

The Preparation of the Passover

7 Then came the day of Unleavened Bread, on which the Passover lamb had to be sacrificed. 8So Jesus[h] sent Peter and John, saying, "Go and prepare the Passover meal for us that we may eat it." 9They asked him, "Where do you want us to make preparations for it?" 10"Listen," he said to them, "when you have entered the city, a man carrying a jar of water will meet you; follow him into the house he enters 11and say to the

---

b 21:23 upon this nation, literally, "upon the land," or "upon the earth." c 21:27 the Messiah, literally, "the Son of Man." d 21:32 this age, "this generation." e 21:36 without having to experience these horrors, or, "Pray for strength to pass safely through these coming horrors." f 22:10 Jerusalem, literally, "the city."

g Gk him h Gk he

King James

11And ye shall say unto the goodman of the house, The Master saith unto thee, Where is the guestchamber, where I shall eat the passover with my disciples?

12And he shall show you a large upper room furnished: there make ready.

13And they went, and found as he had said unto them: and they made ready the passover.

14And when the hour was come, he sat down, and the twelve apostles with him.

15And he said unto them, With desire I have desired to eat this passover with you before I suffer:

16For I say unto you, I will not any more eat thereof, until it be fulfilled in the kingdom of God.

17And he took the cup, and gave thanks, and said, Take this, and divide it among yourselves:

18For I say unto you, I will not drink of the fruit of the vine, until the kingdom of God shall come.

19¶ And he took bread, and gave thanks, and brake it, and gave unto them, saying, This is my body which is given for you: this do in remembrance of me.

20Likewise also the cup after supper, saying, This cup is the new testament in my blood, which is shed for you.

21¶ But, behold, the hand of him that betrayeth me is with me on the table.

22And truly the Son of man goeth, as it was determined: but woe unto that man by whom he is betrayed!

23And they began to inquire among themselves, which of them it was that should do this thing.

24¶ And there was also a strife among them, which of them should be accounted the greatest.

25And he said unto them, The kings of the Gentiles exercise lordship over them; and they that exercise authority upon them are called benefactors.

26But ye shall not be so: but he that is greatest among you, let him be as the younger; and he that is chief, as he that doth serve.

27For whether is greater, he that sitteth at meat, or he that serveth? is not he that sitteth at meat? but I am among you as he that serveth.

28Ye are they which have continued with me in my temptations.

29And I appoint unto you a kingdom, as my Father hath appointed unto me;

30That ye may eat and drink at my table in my kingdom, and sit on thrones judging the twelve tribes of Israel.

31¶ And the Lord said, Simon, Simon, behold, Satan hath desired to have you, that he may sift you as wheat:

32But I have prayed for thee, that thy faith fail not: and when thou art converted, strengthen thy brethren.

33And he said unto him, Lord, I am ready to go with thee, both into prison, and to death.

34And he said, I tell thee, Peter, the cock shall not crow this day, before that thou shalt thrice deny that thou knowest me.

35And he said unto them, When I sent you without purse, and scrip, and shoes, lacked ye any thing? And they said, Nothing.

36Then said he unto them, But now, he that hath a purse, let him take it, and likewise his scrip: and he that hath no sword, let him sell his garment, and buy one.

37For I say unto you, that this that is written must yet be accomplished in me, And he was reckoned among the transgressors: for the things concerning me have an end.

New International

Teacher asks: Where is the guest room, where I may eat the Passover with my disciples?' 12He will show you a large upper room, all furnished. Make preparations there."

13They left and found things just as Jesus had told them. So they prepared the Passover.

14When the hour came, Jesus and his apostles reclined at the table. 15And he said to them, "I have eagerly desired to eat this Passover with you before I suffer. 16For I tell you, I will not eat it again until it finds fulfillment in the kingdom of God."

17After taking the cup, he gave thanks and said, "Take this and divide it among you. 18For I tell you I will not drink again of the fruit of the vine until the kingdom of God comes."

19And he took bread, gave thanks and broke it, and gave it to them, saying, "This is my body given for you; do this in remembrance of me."

20In the same way, after the supper he took the cup, saying, "This cup is the new covenant in my blood, which is poured out for you. 21But the hand of him who is going to betray me is with mine on the table. 22The Son of Man will go as it has been decreed, but woe to that man who betrays him." 23They began to question among themselves which of them it might be who would do this.

24Also a dispute arose among them as to which of them was considered to be greatest. 25Jesus said to them, "The kings of the Gentiles lord it over them; and those who exercise authority over them call themselves Benefactors. 26But you are not to be like that. Instead, the greatest among you should be like the youngest, and the one who rules like the one who serves. 27For who is greater, the one who is at the table or the one who serves? Is it not the one who is at the table? But I am among you as one who serves. 28You are those who have stood by me in my trials. 29And I confer on you a kingdom, just as my Father conferred one on me, 30so that you may eat and drink at my table in my kingdom and sit on thrones, judging the twelve tribes of Israel.

31"Simon, Simon, Satan has asked to sift youa as wheat. 32But I have prayed for you, Simon, that your faith may not fail. And when you have turned back, strengthen your brothers."

33But he replied, "Lord, I am ready to go with you to prison and to death."

34Jesus answered, "I tell you, Peter, before the rooster crows today, you will deny three times that you know me."

35Then Jesus asked them, "When I sent you without purse, bag or sandals, did you lack anything?"

"Nothing," they answered.

36He said to them, "But now if you have a purse, take it, and also a bag; and if you don't have a sword, sell your cloak and buy one. 37It is written: 'And he was numbered with the transgressors'b; and I tell you that this must be fulfilled in me. Yes, what is written about me is reaching its fulfillment."

Living Bible

to the man who lives there, 'Our Teacher says for you to show us the guest room where he can eat the Passover meal with his disciples.' 12He will take you upstairs to a large room all ready for us. That is the place. Go ahead and prepare the meal there."

13They went off to the city and found everything just as Jesus had said, and prepared the Passover supper.

14Then Jesus and the others arrived, and at the proper time all sat down together at the table; 15and he said, "I have looked forward to this hour with deep longing, anxious to eat this Passover meal with you before my suffering begins. 16For I tell you now that I won't eat it again until what it represents has occurred in the Kingdom of God."

17Then he took a glass of wine, and when he had given thanks for it, he said, "Take this and share it among yourselves. 18For I will not drink wine again until the Kingdom of God has come."

19Then he took a loaf of bread; and when he had thanked God for it, he broke it apart and gave it to them, saying, "This is my body, given for you. Eat it in remembrance of me."

20After supper he gave them another glass of wine, saying, "This wine is the token of God's new agreement to save you—an agreement sealed with the blood I shall pour out to purchase back your souls.c 21But here at this table, sitting among us as a friend, is the man who will betray me. 22Id must die. It is part of God's plan. But, oh, the horror awaiting that man who betrays me."

23Then the disciples wondered among themselves which of them would ever do such a thing.

24And they began to argue among themselves as to who would have the highest rank [in the coming Kingdome].

25Jesus told them, "In this world the kings and great men order their slaves around, and the slaves have no choice but to like it!f 26But among you, the one who serves you best will be your leader. 27Out in the world the master sits at the table and is served by his servants. But not here! For I am your servant. 28Nevertheless, because you have stood true to me in these terrible days,g 29and because my Father has granted me a Kingdom, I, here and now, grant you the right 30to eat and drink at my table in that Kingdom; and you will sit on thrones judging the twelve tribes of Israel.

31"Simon, Simon, Satan has asked to have you, to sift you like wheat, 32but I have pleaded in prayer for you that your faith should not completely fail.h So when you have repented and turned to me again, strengthen and build up the faith of your brothers."

33Simon said, "Lord, I am ready to go to jail with you, and even to die with you."

34But Jesus said, "Peter, let me tell you something. Between now and tomorrow morning when the rooster crows, you will deny me three times, declaring that you don't even know me."

35Then Jesus asked them, "When I sent you out to preach the Good News and you were without money, duffle bag, or extra clothing, how did you get along?"

"Fine," they replied.

36"But now," he said, "take a duffle bag if you have one, and your money. And if you don't have a sword, better sell your clothes and buy one! 37For the time has come for this prophecy about me to come true: 'He will be condemned as a criminal!' Yes, everything written about me by the prophets will come true."

New Revised Standard

owner of the house, 'The teacher asks you, "Where is the guest room, where I may eat the Passover with my disciples?" ' 12He will show you a large room upstairs, already furnished. Make preparations for us there." 13So they went and found everything as he had told them; and they prepared the Passover meal.

The Institution of the Lord's Supper

14 When the hour came, he took his place at the table, and the apostles with him. 15He said to them, "I have eagerly desired to eat this Passover with you before I suffer; 16for I tell you, I will not eat iti until it is fulfilled in the kingdom of God." 17Then he took a cup, and after giving thanks he said, "Take this and divide it among yourselves; 18for I tell you that from now on I will not drink of the fruit of the vine until the kingdom of God comes." 19Then he took a loaf of bread, and when he had given thanks, he broke it and gave it to them, saying, "This is my body, which is given for you. Do this in remembrance of me." 20And he did the same with the cup after supper, saying, "This cup that is poured out for you is the new covenant in my blood.j 21But see, the one who betrays me is with me, and his hand is on the table. 22For the Son of Man is going as it has been determined, but woe to that one by whom he is betrayed!" 23Then they began to ask one another, which one of them it could be who would do this.

The Dispute about Greatness

24 A dispute also arose among them as to which one of them was to be regarded as the greatest. 25But he said to them, "The kings of the Gentiles lord it over them; and those in authority over them are called benefactors. 26But not so with you; rather the greatest among you must become like the youngest, and the leader like one who serves. 27For who is greater, the one who is at the table or the one who serves? Is it not the one at the table? But I am among you as one who serves.

28 "You are those who have stood by me in my trials; 29and I confer on you, just as my Father has conferred on me, a kingdom, 30so that you may eat and drink at my table in my kingdom, and you will sit on thrones judging the twelve tribes of Israel.

Jesus Predicts Peter's Denial

31 "Simon, Simon, listen! Satan has demandedk to sift all of you like wheat, 32but I have prayed for you that your own faith may not fail; and you, when once you have turned back, strengthen your brothers." 33And he said to him, "Lord, I am ready to go with you to prison and to death!" 34Jesusl said, "I tell you, Peter, the cock will not crow this day, until you have denied three times that you know me."

Purse, Bag, and Sword

35 He said to them, "When I sent you out without a purse, bag, or sandals, did you lack anything?" They said, "No, not a thing." 36He said to them, "But now, the one who has a purse must take it, and likewise a bag. And the one who has no sword must sell his cloak and buy one. 37For I tell you, this scripture must be fulfilled in me, 'And he was counted among the lawless'; and indeed what is written about me is being fulfilled."

---

c 22:20 This wine is the token . . . to purchase back your souls, literally, "This cup of the new covenant in my blood, poured out for you." d 22:22 I, literally, "the Son of Man." e 22:24 in the coming Kingdom, implied. f 22:25 the slaves have no choice but to like it, literally, "they [the kings and great men] are called 'benefactors.' " g 22:28 because you have stood true to me in these terrible days, literally, "you have continued with me in my temptation." h 22:32 not completely fail, literally, "fail not."

i Other ancient authorities read never eat it again j Other ancient authorities lack, in whole or in part, verses 19b-20 (which is given . . . in my blood) k Or has obtained permission l Gk He

King James

38And they said, Lord, behold, here *are* two swords. And he said unto them, It is enough.

39¶ And he came out, and went, as he was wont, to the mount of Olives; and his disciples also followed him.

40And when he was at the place, he said unto them, Pray that ye enter not into temptation.

41And he was withdrawn from them about a stone's cast, and kneeled down, and prayed,

42Saying, Father, if thou be willing, remove this cup from me: nevertheless not my will, but thine, be done.

43And there appeared an angel unto him from heaven, strengthening him.

44And being in an agony he prayed more earnestly: and his sweat was as it were great drops of blood falling down to the ground.

45And when he rose up from prayer, and was come to his disciples, he found them sleeping for sorrow,

46And said unto them, Why sleep ye? rise and pray, lest ye enter into temptation.

47¶ And while he yet spake, behold a multitude, and he that was called Judas, one of the twelve, went before them, and drew near unto Jesus to kiss him.

48But Jesus said unto him, Judas, betrayest thou the Son of man with a kiss?

49When they which were about him saw what would follow, they said unto him, Lord, shall we smite with the sword?

50¶ And one of them smote the servant of the high priest, and cut off his right ear.

51And Jesus answered and said, Suffer ye thus far. And he touched his ear, and healed him.

52Then Jesus said unto the chief priests, and captains of the temple, and the elders, which were come to him, Be ye come out, as against a thief, with swords and staves?

53When I was daily with you in the temple, ye stretched forth no hands against me: but this is your hour, and the power of darkness.

54¶ Then took they him, and led *him*, and brought him into the high priest's house. And Peter followed afar off.

55And when they had kindled a fire in the midst of the hall, and were set down together, Peter sat down among them.

56But a certain maid beheld him as he sat by the fire, and earnestly looked upon him, and said, This man was also with him.

57And he denied him, saying, Woman, I know him not.

58And after a little while another saw him, and said, Thou art also of them. And Peter said, Man, I am not.

59And about the space of one hour after another confidently affirmed, saying, Of a truth this *fellow* also was with him: for he is a Galilaean.

60And Peter said, Man, I know not what thou sayest. And immediately, while he yet spake, the cock crew.

61And the Lord turned, and looked upon Peter. And Peter remembered the word of the Lord, how he had said unto him, Before the cock crow, thou shalt deny me thrice.

62And Peter went out, and wept bitterly.

63¶ And the men that held Jesus mocked him, and smote *him*.

64And when they had blindfolded him, they struck him on the face, and asked him, saying, Prophesy, who is it that smote thee?

65And many other things blasphemously spake they against him.

66¶ And as soon as it was day, the elders of the people and the chief priests and the scribes came together, and led him into their council, saying,

New International

38The disciples said, "See, Lord, here are two swords."

"That is enough," he replied.

Jesus Prays on the Mount of Olives

39Jesus went out as usual to the Mount of Olives, and his disciples followed him. 40On reaching the place, he said to them, "Pray that you will not fall into temptation." 41He withdrew about a stone's throw beyond them, knelt down and prayed, 42"Father, if you are willing, take this cup from me; yet not my will, but yours be done." 43An angel from heaven appeared to him and strengthened him. 44And being in anguish, he prayed more earnestly, and his sweat was like drops of blood falling to the ground.a

45When he rose from prayer and went back to the disciples, he found them asleep, exhausted from sorrow. 46"Why are you sleeping?" he asked them. "Get up and pray so that you will not fall into temptation."

Jesus Arrested

47While he was still speaking a crowd came up, and the man who was called Judas, one of the Twelve, was leading them. He approached Jesus to kiss him, 48but Jesus asked him, "Judas, are you betraying the Son of Man with a kiss?"

49When Jesus' followers saw what was going to happen, they said, "Lord, should we strike with our swords?" 50And one of them struck the servant of the high priest, cutting off his right ear.

51But Jesus answered, "No more of this!" And he touched the man's ear and healed him.

52Then Jesus said to the chief priests, the officers of the temple guard, and the elders, who had come for him, "Am I leading a rebellion, that you have come with swords and clubs? 53Every day I was with you in the temple courts, and you did not lay a hand on me. But this is your hour—when darkness reigns."

Peter Disowns Jesus

54Then seizing him, they led him away and took him into the house of the high priest. Peter followed at a distance. 55But when they had kindled a fire in the middle of the courtyard and had sat down together, Peter sat down with them. 56A servant girl saw him seated there in the firelight. She looked closely at him and said, "This man was with him."

57But he denied it. "Woman, I don't know him," he said.

58A little later someone else saw him and said, "You also are one of them."

"Man, I am not!" Peter replied.

59About an hour later another asserted, "Certainly this fellow was with him, for he is a Galilean."

60Peter replied, "Man, I don't know what you're talking about!" Just as he was speaking, the rooster crowed. 61The Lord turned and looked straight at Peter. Then Peter remembered the word the Lord had spoken to him: "Before the rooster crows today, you will disown me three times." 62And he went outside and wept bitterly.

The Guards Mock Jesus

63The men who were guarding Jesus began mocking and beating him. 64They blindfolded him and demanded, "Prophesy! Who hit you?" 65And they said many other insulting things to him.

Jesus Before Pilate and Herod

66At daybreak the council of the elders of the people, both the chief priests and teachers of the law, met togeth-

---

a 44 Some early manuscripts do not have verses 43 and 44.

Living Bible

38"Master," they replied, "we have two swords among us."

"Enough!" he said.

39Then, accompanied by the disciples, he left the upstairs room and went as usual to the Mount of Olives. 40There he told them, "Pray God that you will not be overcome by temptation."b

41, 42He walked away, perhaps a stone's throw, and knelt down and prayed this prayer: "Father, if you are willing, please take away this cup of horror from me. But I want your will, not mine." 43Then an angel from heaven appeared and strengthened him, 44for he was in such agony of spirit that he broke into a sweat of blood, with great drops falling to the ground as he prayed more and more earnestly. 45At last he stood up again and returned to the disciples—only to find them asleep, exhausted from grief.

46"Asleep!" he said. "Get up! Pray God that you will not fall when you are tempted."

47But even as he said this, a mob approached, led by Judas, one of his twelve disciples. Judas walked over to Jesus and kissed him on the cheek in friendly greeting. 48But Jesus said, "Judas, how can you do this—betray the Messiah with a kiss?"

49When the other disciples saw what was about to happen, they exclaimed, "Master, shall we fight? We brought along the swords!" 50And one of them slashed at the High Priest's servant, and cut off his right ear.

51But Jesus said, "Don't resist any more." And he touched the place where the man's ear had been and restored it. 52Then Jesus addressed the chief priests and captains of the Temple guards and the religious leaders who headed the mob. "Am I a robber," he asked, "that you have come armed with swords and clubs to get me? 53Why didn't you arrest me in the Temple? I was there every day. But this is your moment—the time when Satan's power reigns supreme."

54So they seized him and led him to the High Priest's residence, and Peter followed at a distance. 55The soldiers lit a fire in the courtyard and sat around it for warmth, and Peter joined them there.

56A servant girl noticed him in the firelight and began staring at him. Finally she spoke: "This man was with Jesus!"

57Peter denied it. "Woman," he said, "I don't even know the man!"

58After a while someone else looked at him and said, "You must be one of them!"

"No sir, I am not!" Peter replied.

59About an hour later someone else flatly stated, "I know this fellow is one of Jesus' disciples, for both are from Galilee."

60But Peter said, "Man, I don't know what you are talking about." And as he said the words, a rooster crowed.

61At that moment Jesus turned and looked at Peter. Then Peter remembered what he had said—"Before the rooster crows tomorrow morning, you will deny me three times." 62And Peter walked out of the courtyard, crying bitterly.

63, 64Now the guards in charge of Jesus began mocking him. They blindfolded him and hit him with their fists and asked, "Who hit you that time, prophet?" 65And they threw all sorts of other insults at him.

66Early the next morning at daybreak the Jewish Supreme Court assembled, including the chief priests and all the top religious authorities of the nation. Jesus was

New Revised Standard

38They said, "Lord, look, here are two swords." He replied, "It is enough."

Jesus Prays on the Mount of Olives

39 He came out and went, as was his custom, to the Mount of Olives; and the disciples followed him. 40When he reached the place, he said to them, "Pray that you may not come into the time of trial."d 41Then he withdrew from them about a stone's throw, knelt down, and prayed, 42"Father, if you are willing, remove this cup from me; yet, not my will but yours be done." [[43Then an angel from heaven appeared to him and gave him strength. 44In his anguish he prayed more earnestly, and his sweat became like great drops of blood falling down on the ground.]]e 45When he got up from prayer, he came to the disciples and found them sleeping because of grief, 46and he said to them, "Why are you sleeping? Get up and pray that you may not come into the time of trial."d

The Betrayal and Arrest of Jesus

47 While he was still speaking, suddenly a crowd came, and the one called Judas, one of the twelve, was leading them. He approached Jesus to kiss him; 48but Jesus said to him, "Judas, is it with a kiss that you are betraying the Son of Man?" 49When those who were around him saw what was coming, they asked, "Lord, should we strike with the sword?" 50Then one of them struck the slave of the high priest and cut off his right ear. 51But Jesus said, "No more of this!" And he touched his ear and healed him. 52Then Jesus said to the chief priests, the officers of the temple police, and the elders who had come for him, "Have you come out with swords and clubs as if I were a bandit? 53When I was with you day after day in the temple, you did not lay hands on me. But this is your hour, and the power of darkness!"

Peter Denies Jesus

54 Then they seized him and led him away, bringing him into the high priest's house. But Peter was following at a distance. 55When they had kindled a fire in the middle of the courtyard and sat down together, Peter sat among them. 56Then a servant-girl, seeing him in the firelight, stared at him and said, "This man also was with him." 57But he denied it, saying, "Woman, I do not know him." 58A little later someone else, on seeing him, said, "You also are one of them." But Peter said, "Man, I am not!" 59Then about an hour later still another kept insisting, "Surely this man also was with him; for he is a Galilean." 60But Peter said, "Man, I do not know what you are talking about!" At that moment, while he was still speaking, the cock crowed. 61The Lord turned and looked at Peter. Then Peter remembered the word of the Lord, how he had said to him, "Before the cock crows today, you will deny me three times." 62And he went out and wept bitterly.

The Mocking and Beating of Jesus

63 Now the men who were holding Jesus began to mock him and beat him; 64they also blindfolded him and kept asking, "Prophesy! Who is it that struck you?" 65They kept heaping many other insults on him.

Jesus before the Council

66 When day came, the assembly of the elders of the people, both chief priests and scribes, gathered together, and they brought him to their council. 67They said, "If

---

b 22:40 *that you will not be overcome by temptation,* literally, "that you enter not into temptation." c 22:47 *walked over . . . and kissed him on the cheek in friendly greeting,* literally, "approached Jesus to kiss him." This is still the traditional greeting among men in eastern lands.

d Or *into temptation* e Other ancient authorities lack verses 43 and 44

King James

67Art thou the Christ? tell us. And he said unto them, If I tell you, ye will not believe:

68And if I also ask *you*, ye will not answer me, nor let *me* go.

69Hereafter shall the Son of man sit on the right hand of the power of God.

70Then said they all, Art thou then the Son of God? And he said unto them, Ye say that I am.

71And they said, What need we any further witness? for we ourselves have heard of his own mouth.

23 AND THE whole multitude of them arose, and led him unto Pilate.

2And they began to accuse him, saying, We found this *fellow* perverting the nation, and forbidding to give tribute to Caesar, saying that he himself is Christ a King.

3And Pilate asked him, saying, Art thou the King of the Jews? And he answered him and said, Thou sayest *it*.

4Then said Pilate to the chief priests and *to* the people, I find no fault in this man.

5And they were the more fierce, saying, He stirreth up the people, teaching throughout all Jewry, beginning from Galilee to this place.

6When Pilate heard of Galilee, he asked whether the man were a Galilaean.

7And as soon as he knew that he belonged unto Herod's jurisdiction, he sent him to Herod, who himself also was at Jerusalem at that time.

8¶ And when Herod saw Jesus, he was exceeding glad: for he was desirous to see him of a long *season*, because he had heard many things of him; and he hoped to have seen some miracle done by him.

9Then he questioned with him in many words; but he answered him nothing.

10And the chief priests and scribes stood and vehemently accused him.

11And Herod with his men of war set him at nought, and mocked *him*, and arrayed him in a gorgeous robe, and sent him again to Pilate.

12¶ And the same day Pilate and Herod were made friends together: for before they were at enmity between themselves.

13¶ And Pilate, when he had called together the chief priests and the rulers and the people,

14Said unto them, Ye have brought this man unto me, as one that perverteth the people: and, behold, I, having examined *him* before you, have found no fault in this man touching those things whereof ye accuse him:

15No, nor yet Herod: for I sent you to him; and, lo, nothing worthy of death is done unto him.

16I will therefore chastise him, and release *him*.

17(For of necessity he must release one unto them at the feast.)

18And they cried out all at once, saying, Away with this *man*, and release unto us Barabbas:

19(Who for a certain sedition made in the city, and for murder, was cast into prison.)

20Pilate therefore, willing to release Jesus, spake again to them.

21But they cried, saying, Crucify *him*, crucify him.

22And he said unto them the third time, Why, what evil hath he done? I have found no cause of death in him: I will therefore chastise him, and let *him* go.

23And they were instant with loud voices, requiring that he might be crucified. And the voices of them and of the chief priests prevailed.

24And Pilate gave sentence that it should be as they required.

25And he released unto them him that for sedition and murder was cast into prison, whom they had desired; but he delivered Jesus to their will.

New International

er, and Jesus was led before them. 67"If you are the Christ,a" they said, "tell us."

Jesus answered, "If I tell you, you will not believe me, 68and if I asked you, you would not answer. 69But from now on, the Son of Man will be seated at the right hand of the mighty God."

70They all asked, "Are you then the Son of God?" He replied, "You are right in saying I am."

71Then they said, "Why do we need any more testimony? We have heard it from his own lips."

23 THEN THE whole assembly rose and led him off to Pilate. 2And they began to accuse him, saying, "We have found this man subverting our nation. He opposes payment of taxes to Caesar and claims to be Christ,b a king."

3So Pilate asked Jesus, "Are you the king of the Jews?"

"Yes, it is as you say," Jesus replied.

4Then Pilate announced to the chief priests and the crowd, "I find no basis for a charge against this man."

5But they insisted, "He stirs up the people all over Judeac by his teaching. He started in Galilee and has come all the way here."

6On hearing this, Pilate asked if the man was a Galilean. 7When he learned that Jesus was under Herod's jurisdiction, he sent him to Herod, who was also in Jerusalem at that time.

8When Herod saw Jesus, he was greatly pleased, because for a long time he had been wanting to see him. From what he had heard about him, he hoped to see him perform some miracle. 9He plied him with many questions, but Jesus gave him no answer. 10The chief priests and the teachers of the law were standing there, vehemently accusing him. 11Then Herod and his soldiers ridiculed and mocked him. Dressing him in an elegant robe, they sent him back to Pilate. 12That day Herod and Pilate became friends—before this they had been enemies.

13Pilate called together the chief priests, the rulers and the people, 14and said to them, "You brought me this man as one who was inciting the people to rebellion. I have examined him in your presence and have found no basis for your charges against him. 15Neither has Herod, for he sent him back to us; as you can see, he has done nothing to deserve death. 16Therefore, I will punish him and then release him.d"

18With one voice they cried out, "Away with this man! Release Barabbas to us!" 19(Barabbas had been thrown into prison for an insurrection in the city, and for murder.)

20Wanting to release Jesus, Pilate appealed to them again. 21But they kept shouting, "Crucify him! Crucify him!"

22For the third time he spoke to them: "Why? What crime has this man committed? I have found in him no grounds for the death penalty. Therefore I will have him punished and then release him."

23But with loud shouts they insistently demanded that he be crucified, and their shouts prevailed. 24So Pilate decided to grant their demand. 25He released the man who had been thrown into prison for insurrection and murder, the one they asked for, and surrendered Jesus to their will.

a 67 Or *Messiah*   b 2 Or *Messiah*; also in verses 35 and 39   c 5 Or *over the land of the Jews*   d 16 Some manuscripts *him.*" *17Now he was obliged to release one man to them at the Feast.*

Living Bible

led before this Council, 67, 68and instructed to state whether or not he claimed to be the Messiah.

But he replied, "If I tell you, you won't believe me or let me present my case. 69But the time is soon coming when I, the Messiah,e shall be enthroned beside Almighty God."

70They all shouted, "Then you claim you are the Son of God?"

And he replied, "Yes, I am."

71"What need do we have for other witnesses?" they shouted. "For we ourselves have heard him say it."

23 THEN THE entire Council took Jesus over to Pilate, the governor.f 2They began at once accusing him: "This fellow has been leading our people to ruin by telling them not to pay their taxes to the Roman government and by claiming he is our Messiah—a King."

3So Pilate asked him, "Are you their Messiah—their King?"g

"Yes," Jesus replied, "it is as you say."

4Then Pilate turned to the chief priests and to the mob and said, "So? That isn't a crime!"

5Then they became desperate. "But he is causing riots against the government everywhere he goes, all over Judea, from Galilee to Jerusalem!"

6"Is he then a Galilean?" Pilate asked.

7When they told him yes, Pilate said to take him to King Herod, for Galilee was under Herod's jurisdiction; and Herod happened to be in Jerusalem at the time. 8Herod was delighted at the opportunity to see Jesus, for he had heard a lot about him and had been hoping to see him perform a miracle.

9He asked Jesus question after question, but there was no reply. 10Meanwhile, the chief priests and the other religious leaders stood there shouting their accusations.

11Now Herod and his soldiers began mocking and ridiculing Jesus; and putting a kingly robe on him, they sent him back to Pilate. 12That day Herod and Pilate—enemies before—became fast friends.

13Then Pilate called together the chief priests and other Jewish leaders, along with the people, 14and announced his verdict:

"You brought this man to me, accusing him of leading a revolt against the Roman government.h I have examined him thoroughly on this point and find him innocent. 15Herod came to the same conclusion and sent him back to us—nothing this man has done calls for the death penalty. 16I will therefore have him scourged with leaded thongs, and release him."

17, 18i But now a mighty roar rose from the crowd as with one voice they shouted. "Kill him, and release Barabbas to us!" 19(Barabbas was in prison for starting an insurrection in Jerusalem against the government, and for murder.) 20Pilate argued with them, for he wanted to release Jesus. 21But they shouted, "Crucify him! Crucify him!"

22Once more, for the third time, he demanded, "Why? What crime has he committed? I have found no reason to sentence him to death. I will therefore scourge him and let him go." 23But they shouted louder and louder for Jesus' death, and their voices prevailed.

24So Pilate sentenced Jesus to die as they demanded. 25And he released Barabbas, the man in prison for insurrection and murder, at their request. But he delivered Jesus over to them to do with as they would.

New Revised Standard

you are the Messiah,j tell us." He replied, "If I tell you, you will not believe; 68and if I question you, you will not answer. 69But from now on the Son of Man will be seated at the right hand of the power of God." 70All of them asked, "Are you, then, the Son of God?" He said to them, "You say that I am." 71Then they said, "What further testimony do we need? We have heard it ourselves from his own lips!"

Jesus before Pilate

23 THEN THE assembly rose as a body and brought Jesusk before Pilate. 2They began to accuse him, saying, "We found this man perverting our nation, forbidding us to pay taxes to the emperor, and saying that he himself is the Messiah, a king."l 3Then Pilate asked him, "Are you the king of the Jews?" He answered, "You say so." 4Then Pilate said to the chief priests and the crowds, "I find no basis for an accusation against this man." 5But they were insistent and said, "He stirs up the people by teaching throughout all Judea, from Galilee where he began even to this place."

Jesus before Herod

6 When Pilate heard this, he asked whether the man was a Galilean. 7And when he learned that he was under Herod's jurisdiction, he sent him off to Herod, who was himself in Jerusalem at that time. 8When Herod saw Jesus, he was very glad, for he had been wanting to see him for a long time, because he had heard about him and was hoping to see him perform some sign. 9He questioned him at some length, but Jesusm gave him no answer. 10The chief priests and the scribes stood by, vehemently accusing him. 11Even Herod with his soldiers treated him with contempt and mocked him; then he put an elegant robe on him, and sent him back to Pilate. 12That same day Herod and Pilate became friends with each other; before this they had been enemies.

Jesus Sentenced to Death

13 Pilate then called together the chief priests, the leaders, and the people, 14and said to them, "You brought me this man as one who was perverting the people; and here I have examined him in your presence and have not found this man guilty of any of your charges against him. 15Neither has Herod, for he sent him back to us. Indeed, he has done nothing to deserve death. 16I will therefore have him flogged and release him."n

18 Then they all shouted out together, "Away with this fellow! Release Barabbas for us!" 19(This was a man who had been put in prison for an insurrection that had taken place in the city, and for murder.) 20Pilate, wanting to release Jesus, addressed them again; 21but they kept shouting, "Crucify, crucify him!" 22A third time he said to them, "Why, what evil has he done? I have found in him no ground for the sentence of death; I will therefore have him flogged and then release him." 23But they kept urgently demanding with loud shouts that he should be crucified; and their voices prevailed. 24So Pilate gave his verdict that their demand should be granted. 25He released the man they asked for, the one who had been put in prison for insurrection and murder, and he handed Jesus over as they wished.

---

e 22:69 the Messiah, literally, "the Son of Man," implied.   f 23:1 the governor, implied.   g 23:3 Are you their Messiah—their King? Literally, "Are you the King of the Jews?"   h 23:14 of leading a revolt against the Roman government, literally, "as one who perverts the people."   i 23:17 Some ancient authorities add vs 17, "For it was necessary for him to release unto them at the feast one [prisoner]."

j Or the Christ   k Gk him   l Or is an anointed king   m Gk he   n Here, or after verse 19, other ancient authorities add verse 17, Now he was obliged to release someone for them at the festival

King James

26And as they led him away, they laid hold upon one Simon, a Cyrenian, coming out of the country, and on him they laid the cross, that he might bear *it* after Jesus.

27¶ And there followed him a great company of people, and of women, which also bewailed and lamented him.

28But Jesus turning unto them said, Daughters of Jerusalem, weep not for me, but weep for yourselves, and for your children.

29For, behold, the days are coming, in the which they shall say, Blessed *are* the barren, and the wombs that never bare, and the paps which never gave suck.

30Then shall they begin to say to the mountains, Fall on us; and to the hills, Cover us.

31For if they do these things in a green tree, what shall be done in the dry?

32And there were also two other, malefactors, led with him to be put to death.

33And when they were come to the place, which is called Calvary, there they crucified him, and the malefactors, one on the right hand, and the other on the left.

34¶ Then said Jesus, Father, forgive them; for they know not what they do. And they parted his raiment, and cast lots.

35And the people stood beholding. And the rulers also with them derided *him*, saying, He saved others; let him save himself, if he be Christ, the chosen of God.

36And the soldiers also mocked him, coming to him, and offering him vinegar,

37And saying, If thou be the king of the Jews, save thyself.

38And a superscription also was written over him in letters of Greek, and Latin, and Hebrew, THIS IS THE KING OF THE JEWS.

39¶ And one of the malefactors which were hanged railed on him, saying, If thou be Christ, save thyself and us.

40But the other answering rebuked him, saying, Dost not thou fear God, seeing thou art in the same condemnation?

41And we indeed justly; for we receive the due reward of our deeds: but this man hath done nothing amiss.

42And he said unto Jesus, Lord, remember me when thou comest into thy kingdom.

43And Jesus said unto him, Verily I say unto thee, Today shalt thou be with me in paradise.

44And it was about the sixth hour, and there was a darkness over all the earth until the ninth hour.

45And the sun was darkened, and the veil of the temple was rent in the midst.

46¶ And when Jesus had cried with a loud voice, he said, Father, into thy hands I commend my spirit: and having said thus, he gave up the ghost.

47Now when the centurion saw what was done, he glorified God, saying, Certainly this was a righteous man.

48And all the people that came together to that sight, beholding the things which were done, smote their breasts, and returned.

49And all his acquaintance, and the women that followed him from Galilee, stood afar off, beholding these things.

50¶ And, behold, *there was* a man named Joseph, a counsellor; *and he was* a good man, and a just:

51(The same had not consented to the counsel and deed of them;) *he was* of Arimathaea, a city of the Jews: who also himself waited for the kingdom of God.

52This *man* went unto Pilate, and begged the body of Jesus.

53And he took it down, and wrapped it in linen, and laid it in a sepulchre that was hewn in stone, wherein never man before was laid.

54And that day was the preparation, and the sabbath drew on.

New International

The Crucifixion

26As they led him away, they seized Simon from Cyrene, who was on his way in from the country, and put the cross on him and made him carry it behind Jesus. 27A large number of people followed him, including women who mourned and wailed for him. 28Jesus turned and said to them, "Daughters of Jerusalem, do not weep for me; weep for yourselves and for your children. 29For the time will come when you will say, 'Blessed are the barren women, the wombs that never bore and the breasts that never nursed!' 30Then

" 'they will say to the mountains, "Fall on us!" and to the hills, "Cover us!" ' a

31For if men do these things when the tree is green, what will happen when it is dry?"

32Two other men, both criminals, were also led out with him to be executed. 33When they came to the place called the Skull, there they crucified him, along with the criminals—one on his right, the other on his left. 34Jesus said, "Father, forgive them, for they do not know what they are doing."b And they divided up his clothes by casting lots.

35The people stood watching, and the rulers even sneered at him. They said, "He saved others; let him save himself if he is the Christ of God, the Chosen One."

36The soldiers also came up and mocked him. They offered him wine vinegar 37and said, "If you are the king of the Jews, save yourself."

38There was a written notice above him, which read: THIS IS THE KING OF THE JEWS.

39One of the criminals who hung there hurled insults at him: "Aren't you the Christ? Save yourself and us!"

40But the other criminal rebuked him. "Don't you fear God," he said, "since you are under the same sentence? 41We are punished justly, for we are getting what our deeds deserve. But this man has done nothing wrong."

42Then he said, "Jesus, remember me when you come into your kingdom.c"

43Jesus answered him, "I tell you the truth, today you will be with me in paradise."

Jesus' Death

44It was now about the sixth hour, and darkness came over the whole land until the ninth hour, 45for the sun stopped shining. And the curtain of the temple was torn in two. 46Jesus called out with a loud voice, "Father, into your hands I commit my spirit." When he had said this, he breathed his last.

47The centurion, seeing what had happened, praised God and said, "Surely this was a righteous man." 48When all the people who had gathered to witness this sight saw what took place, they beat their breasts and went away. 49But all those who knew him, including the women who had followed him from Galilee, stood at a distance, watching these things.

Jesus' Burial

50Now there was a man named Joseph, a member of the Council, a good and upright man, 51who had not consented to their decision and action. He came from the Judean town of Arimathea and he was waiting for the kingdom of God. 52Going to Pilate, he asked for Jesus' body. 53Then he took it down, wrapped it in linen cloth and placed it in a tomb cut in the rock, one in which no one had yet been laid. 54It was Preparation Day, and the Sabbath was about to begin.

---

a *30* Hosea 10:8   b *34* Some early manuscripts do not have this sentence.
c *42* Some manuscripts *come with your kingly power*

Living Bible

26As the crowd led Jesus away to his death, Simon of Cyrene, who was just coming into Jerusalem from the country, was forced to follow, carrying Jesus' cross. 27Great crowds trailed along behind, and many grief-stricken women.

28But Jesus turned and said to them, "Daughters of Jerusalem, don't weep for me, but for yourselves and for your children. 29For the days are coming when the women who have no children will be counted fortunate indeed. 30Mankind will beg the mountains to fall on them and crush them, and the hills to bury them. 31For if such things as this are done to me, the Living Tree, what will they do to you?"d

32, 33Two others, criminals, were led out to be executed with him at a place called "The Skull." There all three were crucified—Jesus on the center cross, and the two criminals on either side.

34"Father, forgive these people," Jesus said, "for they don't know what they are doing."

And the soldiers gambled for his clothing, throwing dice for each piece. 35The crowd watched. And the Jewish leaders laughed and scoffed. "He was so good at helping others," they said, "let's see him save himself if he is really God's Chosen One, the Messiah."

36The soldiers mocked him, too, by offering him a drink—of sour wine. 37And they called to him, "If you are the King of the Jews, save yourself!"

38A signboard was nailed to the cross above him with these words: "This is the King of the Jews."

39One of the criminals hanging beside him scoffed, "So you're the Messiah, are you? Prove it by saving yourself—and us, too, while you're at it!"

40, 41But the other criminal protested. "Don't you even fear God when you are dying? We deserve to die for our evil deeds, but this man hasn't done one thing wrong." 42Then he said, "Jesus, remember me when you come into your Kingdom."

43And Jesus replied, "Today you will be with me in Paradise. This is a solemn promise."

44By now it was noon, and darkness fell across the whole lande for three hours, until three o'clock. 45The light from the sun was gone—and suddenlyf the thick veil hanging in the Temple split apart.

46Then Jesus shouted, "Father, I commit my spirit to you," and with those words he died.g

47When the captain of the Roman military unit handling the executions saw what had happened, he was stricken with awe before God and said, "Surely this man was innocent."h

48And when the crowd that came to see the crucifixion saw that Jesus was dead they went home in deep sorrow. 49Meanwhile, Jesus' friends, including the women who had followed him down from Galilee, stood in the distance watching.

50, 51, 52Then a man named Joseph, a member of the Jewish Supreme Court, from the city of Arimathea in Judea, went to Pilate and asked for the body of Jesus. He was a godly man who had been expecting the Messiah's coming and had not agreed with the decision and actions of the other Jewish leaders. 53So he took down Jesus' body and wrapped it in a long linen cloth and laid it in a new, unused tomb hewn into the rock [at the side of a hilli]. 54This was done late on Friday afternoon, the day of preparation for the Sabbath.

New Revised Standard

The Crucifixion of Jesus

26 As they led him away, they seized a man, Simon of Cyrene, who was coming from the country, and they laid the cross on him, and made him carry it behind Jesus. 27 A great number of the people followed him, and among them were women who were beating their breasts and wailing for him. 28 But Jesus turned to them and said, "Daughters of Jerusalem, do not weep for me, but weep for yourselves and for your children. 29 For the days are surely coming when they will say, 'Blessed are the barren, and the wombs that never bore, and the breasts that never nursed.' 30 Then they will begin to say to the mountains, 'Fall on us'; and to the hills, 'Cover us.' 31 For if they do this when the wood is green, what will happen when it is dry?"

32 Two others also, who were criminals, were led away to be put to death with him. 33 When they came to the place that is called The Skull, they crucified Jesusj there with the criminals, one on his right and one on his left. [[34 Then Jesus said, "Father, forgive them; for they do not know what they are doing."]]k And they cast lots to divide his clothing. 35 And the people stood by, watching; but the leaders scoffed at him, saying, "He saved others; let him save himself if he is the Messiahl of God, his chosen one!" 36 The soldiers also mocked him, coming up and offering him sour wine, 37 and saying, "If you are the King of the Jews, save yourself!" 38 There was also an inscription over him,m "This is the King of the Jews."

39 One of the criminals who were hanged there kept deridingn him and saying, "Are you not the Messiah?l Save yourself and us!" 40 But the other rebuked him, saying, "Do you not fear God, since you are under the same sentence of condemnation? 41 And we indeed have been condemned justly, for we are getting what we deserve for our deeds, but this man has done nothing wrong." 42 Then he said, "Jesus, remember me when you come intoo your kingdom." 43 He replied, "Truly I tell you, today you will be with me in Paradise."

The Death of Jesus

44 It was now about noon, and darkness came over the whole landp until three in the afternoon, 45 while the sun's light failed;q and the curtain of the temple was torn in two. 46 Then Jesus, crying with a loud voice, said, "Father, into your hands I commend my spirit." Having said this, he breathed his last. 47 When the centurion saw what had taken place, he praised God and said, "Certainly this man was innocent."r 48 And when all the crowds who had gathered there for this spectacle saw what had taken place, they returned home, beating their breasts. 49 But all his acquaintances, including the women who had followed him from Galilee, stood at a distance, watching these things.

The Burial of Jesus

50 Now there was a good and righteous man named Joseph, who, though a member of the council, 51 had not agreed to their plan and action. He came from the Jewish town of Arimathea, and he was waiting expectantly for the kingdom of God. 52 This man went to Pilate and asked for the body of Jesus. 53 Then he took it down, wrapped it in a linen cloth, and laid it in a rock-hewn tomb where no one had ever been laid. 54 It was the day of Preparation, and the sabbath was beginning.s 55 The

---

d 23:31 For if such things as this are done to me, the Living Tree, what will they do to you? Literally, "For if they do this when the tree is green, what will happen when it is dry?" e 23:44 the whole land, or "the whole world." f 23:45 and suddenly, implied. g 23:46 he died, literally, "yielded up the spirit." h 23:47 innocent, literally, "righteous." i 23:53 at the side of a hill, implied.

j Gk him   k Other ancient authorities lack the sentence Then Jesus . . . what they are doing   l Or the Christ   m Other ancient authorities add written in Greek and Latin and Hebrew (that is, Aramaic)   n Or blaspheming   o Other ancient authorities read in   p Or earth   q Or the sun was eclipsed. Other ancient authorities read the sun was darkened   r Or righteous   s Gk was dawning

King James

55And the women also, which came with him from Galilee, followed after, and beheld the sepulchre, and how his body was laid.

56And they returned, and prepared spices and ointments: and rested the sabbath day according to the commandment.

24 NOW UPON the first *day* of the week, very early in the morning, they came unto the sepulchre, bringing the spices which they had prepared, and certain *others* with them.

2And they found the stone rolled away from the sepulchre.

3And they entered in, and found not the body of the Lord Jesus.

4And it came to pass, as they were much perplexed thereabout, behold, two men stood by them in shining garments:

5And as they were afraid, and bowed down *their* faces to the earth, they said unto them, Why seek ye the living among the dead?

6He is not here, but is risen: remember how he spake unto you when he was yet in Galilee,

7Saying, The Son of man must be delivered into the hands of sinful men, and be crucified, and the third day rise again.

8And they remembered his words,

9And returned from the sepulchre, and told all these things unto the eleven, and to all the rest.

10It was Mary Magdalene, and Joanna, and Mary *the mother* of James, and other *women that were* with them, which told these things unto the apostles.

11And their words seemed to them as idle tales, and they believed them not.

12Then arose Peter, and ran unto the sepulchre; and stooping down, he beheld the linen clothes laid by themselves, and departed, wondering in himself at that which was come to pass.

13¶ And, behold, two of them went that same day to a village called Emmaus, which was from Jerusalem *about* threescore furlongs.

14And they talked together of all these things which had happened.

15And it came to pass, that, while they communed *together* and reasoned, Jesus himself drew near, and went with them.

16But their eyes were holden that they should not know him.

17And he said unto them, What manner of communications *are* these that ye have one to another, as ye walk, and are sad?

18And the one of them, whose name was Cleopas, answering said unto him, Art thou only a stranger in Jerusalem, and hast not known the things which are come to pass there in these days?

19And he said unto them, What things? And they said unto him, Concerning Jesus of Nazareth, which was a prophet mighty in deed and word before God and all the people:

20And how the chief priests and our rulers delivered him to be condemned to death, and have crucified him.

21But we trusted that it had been he which should have redeemed Israel: and beside all this, today is the third day since these things were done.

22Yea, and certain women also of our company made us astonished, which were early at the sepulchre;

23And when they found not his body, they came, saying, that they had also seen a vision of angels, which said that he was alive.

24And certain of them which were with us went to the sepulchre, and found *it* even so as the women had said: but him they saw not.

New International

55The women who had come with Jesus from Galilee followed Joseph and saw the tomb and how his body was laid in it. 56Then they went home and prepared spices and perfumes. But they rested on the Sabbath in obedience to the commandment.

The Resurrection

24 ON THE first day of the week, very early in the morning, the women took the spices they had prepared and went to the tomb. 2They found the stone rolled away from the tomb, 3but when they entered, they did not find the body of the Lord Jesus. 4While they were wondering about this, suddenly two men in clothes that gleamed like lightning stood beside them. 5In their fright the women bowed down with their faces to the ground, but the men said to them, "Why do you look for the living among the dead? 6He is not here; he has risen! Remember how he told you, while he was still with you in Galilee: 7'The Son of Man must be delivered into the hands of sinful men, be crucified and on the third day be raised again.' " 8Then they remembered his words.

9When they came back from the tomb, they told all these things to the Eleven and to all the others. 10It was Mary Magdalene, Joanna, Mary the mother of James, and the others with them who told this to the apostles. 11But they did not believe the women, because their words seemed to them like nonsense. 12Peter, however, got up and ran to the tomb. Bending over, he saw the strips of linen lying by themselves, and he went away, wondering to himself what had happened.

On the Road to Emmaus

13Now that same day two of them were going to a village called Emmaus, about seven milesa from Jerusalem. 14They were talking with each other about everything that had happened. 15As they talked and discussed these things with each other, Jesus himself came up and walked along with them; 16but they were kept from recognizing him.

17He asked them, "What are you discussing together as you walk along?"

They stood still, their faces downcast. 18One of them, named Cleopas, asked him, "Are you only a visitor to Jerusalem and do not know the things that have happened there in these days?"

19"What things?" he asked.

"About Jesus of Nazareth," they replied. "He was a prophet, powerful in word and deed before God and all the people. 20The chief priests and our rulers handed him over to be sentenced to death, and they crucified him; 21but we had hoped that he was the one who was going to redeem Israel. And what is more, it is the third day since all this took place. 22In addition, some of our women amazed us. They went to the tomb early this morning 23but didn't find his body. They came and told us that they had seen a vision of angels, who said he was alive. 24Then some of our companions went to the tomb and found it just as the women had said, but him they did not see."

a 13 Greek *sixty stadia* (about 11 kilometers)

Living Bible

55As the body was taken away, the women from Galilee followed and saw it carried into the tomb. 56Then they went home and prepared spices and ointments to embalm him; but by the time they were finished it was the Sabbath, so they rested all that day as required by the Jewish law.

24 BUT VERY early on Sunday morning they took the ointments to the tomb— 2and found that the huge stone covering the entrance had been rolled aside. 3So they went in—but the Lord Jesus' body was gone.

4They stood there puzzled, trying to think what could have happened to it. Suddenly two men appeared before them, clothed in shining robes so bright their eyes were dazzled. 5The women were terrified and bowed low before them.

Then the men asked, "Why are you looking in a tomb for someone who is alive? 6, 7He isn't here! He has come back to life again! Don't you remember what he told you back in Galilee—that the Messiahb must be betrayed into the power of evil men and be crucified and that he would rise again the third day?"

8Then they remembered, 9and rushed back to Jerusalemc to tell his eleven disciples—and everyone else— what had happened. 10(The women who went to the tomb were Mary Magdalene and Joanna and Mary the mother of James, and several others.) 11But the story sounded like a fairy tale to the men—they didn't believe it.

12However, Peter ran to the tomb to look. Stooping, he peered in and saw the empty linen wrappings; and then he went back home again, wondering what had happened.

13That same day, Sunday, two of Jesus' followers were walking to the village of Emmaus, seven miles out of Jerusalem. 14As they walked along they were talking of Jesus' death, 15when suddenly Jesus himself came along and joined them and began walking beside them. 16But they didn't recognize him, for God kept them from it.

17"You seem to be in a deep discussion about something," he said. "What are you so concerned about?" They stopped short, sadness written across their faces. 18And one of them, Cleopas, replied, "You must be the only person in Jerusalem who hasn't heard about the terrible things that happened there last week."d

19"What things?" Jesus asked.

"The things that happened to Jesus, the Man from Nazareth," they said. "He was a Prophet who did incredible miracles and was a mighty Teacher, highly regarded by both God and man. 20But the chief priests and our religious leaders arrested him and handed him over to the Roman government to be condemned to death, and they crucified him. 21We had thought he was the glorious Messiah and that he had come to rescue Israel.

"And now, besides all this—which happened three days ago— 22, 23some women from our group of his followers were at his tomb early this morning and came back with an amazing report that his body was missing, and that they had seen some angels there who told them Jesus is alive! 24Some of our men ran out to see, and sure enough, Jesus' body was gone, just as the women had said."

New Revised Standard

women who had come with him from Galilee followed, and they saw the tomb and how his body was laid. 56Then they returned, and prepared spices and ointments.

On the sabbath they rested according to the commandment.

The Resurrection of Jesus

24 BUT ON the first day of the week, at early dawn, they came to the tomb, taking the spices that they had prepared. 2They found the stone rolled away from the tomb, 3but when they went in, they did not find the body.e 4While they were perplexed about this, suddenly two men in dazzling clothes stood beside them. 5The womenf were terrified and bowed their faces to the ground, but the meng said to them, "Why do you look for the living among the dead? He is not here, but has risen.h 6Remember how he told you, while he was still in Galilee, 7that the Son of Man must be handed over to sinners, and be crucified, and on the third day rise again." 8Then they remembered his words, 9and returning from the tomb, they told all this to the eleven and to all the rest. 10Now it was Mary Magdalene, Joanna, Mary the mother of James, and the other women with them who told this to the apostles. 11But these words seemed to them an idle tale, and they did not believe them. 12But Peter got up and ran to the tomb; stooping and looking in, he saw the linen cloths by themselves; then he went home, amazed at what had happened.i

The Walk to Emmaus

13 Now on that same day two of them were going to a village called Emmaus, about seven milesi from Jerusalem, 14and talking with each other about all these things that had happened. 15While they were talking and discussing, Jesus himself came near and went with them, 16but their eyes were kept from recognizing him. 17And he said to them, "What are you discussing with each other while you walk along?" They stood still, looking sad.k 18Then one of them, whose name was Cleopas, answered him, "Are you the only stranger in Jerusalem who does not know the things that have taken place there in these days?" 19He asked them, "What things?" They replied, "The things about Jesus of Nazareth,l who was a prophet mighty in deed and word before God and all the people, 20and how our chief priests and leaders handed him over to be condemned to death and crucified him. 21But we had hoped that he was the one to redeem Israel.m Yes, and besides all this, it is now the third day since these things took place. 22Moreover, some women of our group astounded us. They were at the tomb early this morning, 23and when they did not find his body there, they came back and told us that they had indeed seen a vision of angels who said that he was alive. 24Some of those who were with us went to the tomb and found it just as the women had said; but they did not see him." 25Then he said to them, "Oh,

---

b 24:6, 7 the Messiah, literally, "the Son of Man." c 24:9 rushed back to Jerusalem, literally, "returned from the tomb." d 24:18 there last week, literally, "in these days."

e Other ancient authorities add of the Lord Jesus f Gk They g Gk but they h Other ancient authorities lack He is not here, but has risen i Other ancient authorities lack verse 12 j Gk sixty stadia; other ancient authorities read a hundred sixty stadia k Other ancient authorities read walk along, looking sad?" l Other ancient authorities read Jesus the Nazorean m Or to set Israel free

King James

25Then he said unto them, O fools, and slow of heart to believe all that the prophets have spoken:

26Ought not Christ to have suffered these things, and to enter into his glory?

27And beginning at Moses and all the prophets, he expounded unto them in all the scriptures the things concerning himself.

28And they drew nigh unto the village, whither they went: and he made as though he would have gone further.

29But they constrained him, saying, Abide with us: for it is toward evening, and the day is far spent. And he went in to tarry with them.

30And it came to pass, as he sat at meat with them, he took bread, and blessed it, and brake, and gave to them.

31And their eyes were opened, and they knew him; and he vanished out of their sight.

32And they said one to another, Did not our heart burn within us, while he talked with us by the way, and while he opened to us the scriptures?

33And they rose up the same hour, and returned to Jerusalem, and found the eleven gathered together, and them that were with them,

34Saying, The Lord is risen indeed, and hath appeared to Simon.

35And they told what things were done in the way, and how he was known of them in breaking of bread.

36¶ And as they thus spake, Jesus himself stood in the midst of them, and saith unto them, Peace be unto you.

37But they were terrified and affrighted, and supposed that they had seen a spirit.

38And he said unto them, Why are ye troubled? and why do thoughts arise in your hearts?

39Behold my hands and my feet, that it is I myself: handle me, and see; for a spirit hath not flesh and bones, as ye see me have.

40And when he had thus spoken, he showed them his hands and his feet.

41And while they yet believed not for joy, and wondered, he said unto them, Have ye here any meat?

42And they gave him a piece of a broiled fish, and of an honeycomb.

43And he took it, and did eat before them.

44And he said unto them, These are the words which I spake unto you, while I was yet with you, that all things must be fulfilled, which were written in the law of Moses, and in the prophets, and in the psalms, concerning me.

45Then opened he their understanding, that they might understand the scriptures,

46And said unto them, Thus it is written, and thus it behooved Christ to suffer, and to rise from the dead the third day:

47And that repentance and remission of sins should be preached in his name among all nations, beginning at Jerusalem.

48And ye are witnesses of these things.

49¶ And, behold, I send the promise of my Father upon you: but tarry ye in the city of Jerusalem, until ye be endued with power from on high.

50¶ And he led them out as far as to Bethany, and he lifted up his hands, and blessed them.

51And it came to pass, while he blessed them, he was parted from them, and carried up into heaven.

52And they worshipped him, and returned to Jerusalem with great joy:

53And were continually in the temple, praising and blessing God. Amen.

New International

25He said to them, "How foolish you are, and how slow of heart to believe all that the prophets have spoken! 26Did not the Christa have to suffer these things and then enter his glory?" 27And beginning with Moses and all the Prophets, he explained to them what was said in all the Scriptures concerning himself.

28As they approached the village to which they were going, Jesus acted as if he were going farther. 29But they urged him strongly, "Stay with us, for it is nearly evening; the day is almost over." So he went in to stay with them.

30When he was at the table with them, he took bread, gave thanks, broke it and began to give it to them. 31Then their eyes were opened and they recognized him, and he disappeared from their sight. 32They asked each other, "Were not our hearts burning within us while he talked with us on the road and opened the Scriptures to us?"

33They got up and returned at once to Jerusalem. There they found the Eleven and those with them, assembled together 34and saying, "It is true! The Lord has risen and has appeared to Simon." 35Then the two told what had happened on the way, and how Jesus was recognized by them when he broke the bread.

Jesus Appears to the Disciples

36While they were still talking about this, Jesus himself stood among them and said to them, "Peace be with you."

37They were startled and frightened, thinking they saw a ghost. 38He said to them, "Why are you troubled, and why do doubts rise in your minds? 39Look at my hands and my feet. It is I myself! Touch me and see; a ghost does not have flesh and bones, as you see I have."

40When he had said this, he showed them his hands and feet. 41And while they still did not believe it because of joy and amazement, he asked them, "Do you have anything here to eat?" 42They gave him a piece of broiled fish, 43and he took it and ate it in their presence.

44He said to them, "This is what I told you while I was still with you: Everything must be fulfilled that is written about me in the Law of Moses, the Prophets and the Psalms."

45Then he opened their minds so they could understand the Scriptures. 46He told them, "This is what is written: The Christ will suffer and rise from the dead on the third day, 47and repentance and forgiveness of sins will be preached in his name to all nations, beginning at Jerusalem. 48You are witnesses of these things. 49I am going to send you what my Father has promised; but stay in the city until you have been clothed with power from on high."

The Ascension

50When he had led them out to the vicinity of Bethany, he lifted up his hands and blessed them. 51While he was blessing them, he left them and was taken up into heaven. 52Then they worshiped him and returned to Jerusalem with great joy. 53And they stayed continually at the temple, praising God.

a 26 Or Messiah; also in verse 46

Living Bible

25Then Jesus said to them, "You are such foolish, foolish people! You find it so hard to believe all that the prophets wrote in the Scriptures! 26Wasn't it clearly predicted by the prophets that the Messiah would have to suffer all these things before entering his time of glory?"

27Then Jesus quoted them passage after passage from the writings of the prophets, beginning with the book of Genesis and going right on through the Scriptures, explaining what the passages meant and what they said about himself.

28By this time they were nearing Emmaus and the end of their journey. Jesus would have gone on, 29but they begged him to stay the night with them, as it was getting late. So he went home with them. 30As they sat down to eat, he asked God's blessing on the food and then took a small loaf of bread and broke it and was passing it over to them, 31when suddenly—it was as though their eyes were opened—they recognized him! And at that moment he disappeared!

32They began telling each other how their hearts had felt strangely warm as he talked with them and explained the Scriptures during the walk down the road. 33, 34Within the hour they were on their way back to Jerusalem, where the eleven disciples and the other followers of Jesus greeted them with these words, "The Lord has really risen! He appeared to Peter!"

35Then the two from Emmaus told their story of how Jesus had appeared to them as they were walking along the road and how they had recognized him as he was breaking the bread.

36And just as they were telling about it, Jesus himself was suddenly standing there among them, and greeted them. 37But the whole group were terribly frightened, thinking they were seeing a ghost!

38"Why are you frightened?" he asked. "Why do you doubt that it is really I? 39Look at my hands! Look at my feet! You can see that it is I, myself! Touch me and make sure that I am not a ghost! For ghosts don't have bodies, as you see that I do!" 40As he spoke, he held out his hands for them to see [the marks of the nailsb], and showed them [the wounds inc] his feet.

41Still they stood there undecided, filled with joy and doubt.

Then he asked them, "Do you have anything here to eat?"

42They gave him a piece of broiled fish, 43and he ate it as they watched!

44Then he said, "When I was with you before, don't you remember my telling you that everything written about me by Moses and the prophets and in the Psalms must all come true?" 45Then he opened their minds to understand at last these many Scriptures! 46And he said, "Yes, it was written long ago that the Messiah must suffer and die and rise again from the dead on the third day; 47and that this message of salvation should be taken from Jerusalem to all the nations: *There is forgiveness of sins for all who turn to me.* 48You have seen these prophecies come true.

49"And now I will send the Holy Spiritd upon you, just as my Father promised. Don't begin telling otherse yet—stay here in the city until the Holy Spirit comes and fills you with power from heaven."

50Then Jesus led them out along the road to Bethany,f and lifting his hands to heaven, he blessed them, 51and then began rising into the sky, and went on to heaven. 52And they worshiped him, and returned to Jerusalem filled with mighty joy, 53and were continually in the Temple, praising God.

New Revised Standard

how foolish you are, and how slow of heart to believe all that the prophets have declared! 26Was it not necessary that the Messiahg should suffer these things and then enter into his glory?" 27Then beginning with Moses and all the prophets, he interpreted to them the things about himself in all the scriptures.

28 As they came near the village to which they were going, he walked ahead as if he were going on. 29But they urged him strongly, saying, "Stay with us, because it is almost evening and the day is now nearly over." So he went in to stay with them. 30When he was at the table with them, he took bread, blessed and broke it, and gave it to them. 31Then their eyes were opened, and they recognized him; and he vanished from their sight. 32They said to each other, "Were not our hearts burning within ush while he was talking to us on the road, while he was opening the scriptures to us?" 33That same hour they got up and returned to Jerusalem; and they found the eleven and their companions gathered together. 34They were saying, "The Lord has risen indeed, and he has appeared to Simon!" 35Then they told what had happened on the road, and how he had been made known to them in the breaking of the bread.

Jesus Appears to His Disciples

36 While they were talking about this, Jesus himself stood among them and said to them, "Peace be with you."i 37They were startled and terrified, and thought that they were seeing a ghost. 38He said to them, "Why are you frightened, and why do doubts arise in your hearts? 39Look at my hands and my feet; see that it is I myself. Touch me and see; for a ghost does not have flesh and bones as you see that I have." 40And when he had said this, he showed them his hands and his feet.j 41While in their joy they were disbelieving and still wondering, he said to them, "Have you anything here to eat?" 42They gave him a piece of broiled fish, 43and he took it and ate in their presence.

44 Then he said to them, "These are my words that I spoke to you while I was still with you—that everything written about me in the law of Moses, the prophets, and the psalms must be fulfilled." 45Then he opened their minds to understand the scriptures, 46and he said to them, "Thus it is written, that the Messiahg is to suffer and to rise from the dead on the third day, 47and that repentance and forgiveness of sins is to be proclaimed in his name to all nations,k beginning from Jerusalem. 48You are witnesses of these things. 49And see, I am sending upon you what my Father promised; so stay here in the city until you have been clothed with power from on high."

The Ascension of Jesus

50 Then he led them out as far as Bethany, and, lifting up his hands, he blessed them. 51While he was blessing them, he withdrew from them and was carried up into heaven.l 52And they worshiped him, andm returned to Jerusalem with great joy; 53and they were continually in the temple blessing God.n

---

b *24:40 the marks of the nails* and   c *24:40 the wounds in,* implied. d *24:49 the Holy Spirit,* implied. Literally, "the promise of my Father." e *24:49 Don't begin telling others,* literally, "but wait here in the city until. . . ." The paraphrase relates this to vs 47.   f *24:50 along the road to Bethany,* implied. Bethany was a mile or so away, across the valley on the Mount of Olives.

g Or *the Christ*   h Other ancient authorities lack *within us*   i Other ancient authorities lack *and said to them, "Peace be with you."*   j Other ancient authorities lack verse 40   k Or *nations. Beginning from Jerusalem you are witnesses*   l Other ancient authorities lack *and was carried up into heaven*   m Other ancient authorities lack *worshiped him, and*   n Other ancient authorities add *Amen*

THE GOSPEL
ACCORDING TO

St. John

John

1 IN THE beginning was the Word, and the Word was with God, and the Word was God.
2The same was in the beginning with God.
3All things were made by him; and without him was not any thing made that was made.
4In him was life; and the life was the light of men.
5And the light shineth in darkness; and the darkness comprehended it not.
6¶ There was a man sent from God, whose name *was* John.
7The same came for a witness, to bear witness of the Light, that all *men* through him might believe.
8He was not that Light, but *was sent* to bear witness of that Light.
9*That* was the true Light, which lighteth every man that cometh into the world.
10He was in the world, and the world was made by him, and the world knew him not.
11He came unto his own, and his own received him not.
12But as many as received him, to them gave he power to become the sons of God, *even* to them that believe on his name:
13Which were born, not of blood, nor of the will of the flesh, nor of the will of man, but of God.
14And the Word was made flesh, and dwelt among us, (and we beheld his glory, the glory as of the only begotten of the Father,) full of grace and truth.
15¶ John bare witness of him, and cried, saying, This was he of whom I spake, He that cometh after me is preferred before me: for he was before me.
16And of his fulness have all we received, and grace for grace.
17For the law was given by Moses, *but* grace and truth came by Jesus Christ.
18No man hath seen God at any time; the only begotten Son, which is in the bosom of the Father, he hath declared *him.*
19¶ And this is the record of John, when the Jews sent priests and Levites from Jerusalem to ask him, Who art thou?
20And he confessed, and denied not; but confessed, I am not the Christ.
21And they asked him, What then? Art thou Elias? And he saith, I am not. Art thou that prophet? And he answered, No.
22Then said they unto him, Who art thou? that we may give an answer to them that sent us. What sayest thou of thyself?

The Word Became Flesh

1 IN THE beginning was the Word, and the Word was with God, and the Word was God. 2He was with God in the beginning.
3Through him all things were made; without him nothing was made that has been made. 4In him was life, and that life was the light of men. 5The light shines in the darkness, but the darkness has not understoodª it.
6There came a man who was sent from God; his name was John. 7He came as a witness to testify concerning that light, so that through him all men might believe. 8He himself was not the light; he came only as a witness to the light. 9The true light that gives light to every man was coming into the world.b
10He was in the world, and though the world was made through him, the world did not recognize him. 11He came to that which was his own, but his own did not receive him. 12Yet to all who received him, to those who believed in his name, he gave the right to become children of God— 13children born not of natural descent,c nor of human decision or a husband's will, but born of God.
14The Word became flesh and made his dwelling among us. We have seen his glory, the glory of the One and Only,d who came from the Father, full of grace and truth.
15John testifies concerning him. He cries out, saying, "This was he of whom I said, 'He who comes after me has surpassed me because he was before me.' " 16From the fullness of his grace we have all received one blessing after another. 17For the law was given through Moses; grace and truth came through Jesus Christ. 18No one has ever seen God, but God the One and Only,d,e who is at the Father's side, has made him known.

John the Baptist Denies Being the Christ

19Now this was John's testimony when the Jews of Jerusalem sent priests and Levites to ask him who he was. 20He did not fail to confess, but confessed freely, "I am not the Christ.f"
21They asked him, "Then who are you? Are you Elijah?"
He said, "I am not."
"Are you the Prophet?"
He answered, "No."
22Finally they said, "Who are you? Give us an answer to take back to those who sent us. What do you say about yourself?"

ª 5 Or *darkness, and the darkness has not overcome*   b 9 Or *This was the true light that gives light to every man who comes into the world*   c 13 Greek *of bloods*   d 14,18 Or *the Only Begotten*   e 18 Some manuscripts *but the only* (or *only begotten*) *Son*   f 20 Or *Messiah.* "The Christ" (Greek) and "the Messiah" (Hebrew) both mean "the Anointed One"; also in verse 25.

THE GOSPEL

ACCORDING TO

John

John

1

BEFORE ANYTHING else existed,[g] there was Christ,[h] with God. He has always been alive and is himself God. [3]He created everything there is—nothing exists that he didn't make. [4]Eternal life is in him, and this life gives light to all mankind. [5]His life is the light that shines through the darkness—and the darkness can never extinguish it.

[6,7]God sent John the Baptist as a witness to the fact that Jesus Christ is the true Light. [8]John himself was not the Light; he was only a witness to identify it.

[9]Later on, the one who is the true Light arrived to shine on everyone coming into the world.

[10]But although he made the world, the world didn't recognize him when he came. [11, 12]Even in his own land and among his own people, the Jews, he was not accepted. Only a few would welcome and receive him. But to all who received him, he gave the right to become children of God. All they needed to do was to trust him to save them.[i] [13]All those who believe this are reborn!—not a physical rebirth[j] resulting from human passion or plan—but from the will of God.

[14]And Christ[k] became a human being and lived here on earth among us and was full of loving forgiveness[l] and truth. And some of us have seen his glory[m]—the glory of the only Son of the heavenly Father![n]

[15]John pointed him out to the people, telling the crowds, "This is the one I was talking about when I said, 'Someone is coming who is greater by far than I am—for he existed long before I did!' " [16]We have all benefited from the rich blessings he brought to us—blessing upon blessing heaped upon us! [17]For Moses gave us only the Law with its rigid demands and merciless justice, while Jesus Christ brought us loving forgiveness as well. [18]No one has ever actually seen God, but, of course, his only Son has, for he is the companion of the Father and has told us all about him.

[19]The Jewish leaders[o] sent priests and assistant priests from Jerusalem to ask John whether he claimed to be the Messiah.

[20]He denied it flatly. "I am not the Christ," he said. [21]"Well then, who are you?" they asked. "Are you Elijah?"

"No," he replied.

"Are you the Prophet?"[p]

"No."

[22]"Then who are you? Tell us, so we can give an answer to those who sent us. What do you have to say for yourself?"

The Word Became Flesh

1

IN THE beginning was the Word, and the Word was with God, and the Word was God. [2]He was in the beginning with God. [3]All things came into being through him, and without him not one thing came into being. What has come into being [4]in him was life,[q] and the life was the light of all people. [5]The light shines in the darkness, and the darkness did not overcome it.

[6]There was a man sent from God, whose name was John. [7]He came as a witness to testify to the light, so that all might believe through him. [8]He himself was not the light, but he came to testify to the light. [9]The true light, which enlightens everyone, was coming into the world.[r]

[10]He was in the world, and the world came into being through him; yet the world did not know him. [11]He came to what was his own,[s] and his own people did not accept him. [12]But to all who received him, who believed in his name, he gave power to become children of God, [13]who were born, not of blood or of the will of the flesh or of the will of man, but of God.

[14]And the Word became flesh and lived among us, and we have seen his glory, the glory as of a father's only son,[t] full of grace and truth. [15](John testified to him and cried out, "This was he of whom I said, 'He who comes after me ranks ahead of me because he was before me.' ") [16]From his fullness we have all received, grace upon grace. [17]The law indeed was given through Moses; grace and truth came through Jesus Christ. [18]No one has ever seen God. It is God the only Son,[u] who is close to the Father's heart,[v] who has made him known.

The Testimony of John the Baptist

[19]This is the testimony given by John when the Jews sent priests and Levites from Jerusalem to ask him, "Who are you?" [20]He confessed and did not deny it, but confessed, "I am not the Messiah."[w] [21]And they asked him, "What then? Are you Elijah?" He said, "I am not." "Are you the prophet?" He answered, "No." [22]Then they said to him, "Who are you? Let us have an answer for those who sent us. What do you say about yourself?"

---

g *1:1, 2 Before anything else existed,* literally, "In the beginning." h *1:1, 2 Christ,* literally, "the Word," meaning Christ, the wisdom and power of God and the first cause of all things; God's personal expression of himself to men. i *1:11, 12 to trust him to save them,* literally, "to believe on his name." j *1:13 not a physical rebirth,* literally, "not of blood." k *1:14 Christ,* literally, "the Word." l *1:14 loving forgiveness,* "grace." m *1:14 seen his glory,* see Mt 17:2. n *1:14 the only Son of the heavenly Father,* literally, "his unique Son." o *1:19 the Jewish leaders,* literally, "the Jews." p *1:21 See Deut 18:15, 18.

---

q Or [3]*through him. And without him not one thing came into being that has come into being.* [4]*In him was life* r Or *He was the true light that enlightens everyone coming into the world* s Or *to his own home* t Or *the Father's only Son* u Other ancient authorities read *It is an only Son, God,* or *It is the only Son* v Gk *bosom* w Or *the Christ*

King James

23He said, I *am* the voice of one crying in the wilderness, Make straight the way of the Lord, as said the prophet Esaias.

24And they which were sent were of the Pharisees.

25And they asked him, and said unto him, Why baptizest thou then, if thou be not that Christ, nor Elias, neither that prophet?

26John answered them, saying, I baptize with water: but there standeth one among you, whom ye know not;

27He it is, who coming after me is preferred before me, whose shoe's latchet I am not worthy to unloose.

28These things were done in Bethabara beyond Jordan, where John was baptizing.

29¶ The next day John seeth Jesus coming unto him, and saith, Behold the Lamb of God, which taketh away the sin of the world.

30This is he of whom I said, After me cometh a man which is preferred before me: for he was before me.

31And I knew him not: but that he should be made manifest to Israel, therefore am I come baptizing with water.

32And John bare record, saying, I saw the Spirit descending from heaven like a dove, and it abode upon him.

33And I knew him not: but he that sent me to baptize with water, the same said unto me, Upon whom thou shalt see the Spirit descending, and remaining on him, the same is he which baptizeth with the Holy Ghost.

34And I saw, and bare record that this is the Son of God.

35¶ Again the next day after John stood, and two of his disciples;

36And looking upon Jesus as he walked, he saith, Behold the Lamb of God!

37And the two disciples heard him speak, and they followed Jesus.

38Then Jesus turned, and saw them following, and saith unto them, What seek ye? They said unto him, Rabbi, (which is to say, being interpreted, Master,) where dwellest thou?

39He saith unto them, Come and see. They came and saw where he dwelt, and abode with him that day: for it was about the tenth hour.

40One of the two which heard John *speak,* and followed him, was Andrew, Simon Peter's brother.

41He first findeth his own brother Simon, and saith unto him, We have found the Messias, which is, being interpreted, the Christ.

42And he brought him to Jesus. And when Jesus beheld him, he said, Thou art Simon the son of Jona: thou shalt be called Cephas, which is by interpretation, A stone.

43¶ The day following Jesus would go forth into Galilee, and findeth Philip, and saith unto him, Follow me.

44Now Philip was of Bethsaida, the city of Andrew and Peter.

45Philip findeth Nathanael, and saith unto him, We have found him, of whom Moses in the law, and the prophets, did write, Jesus of Nazareth, the son of Joseph.

46And Nathanael said unto him, Can there any good thing come out of Nazareth? Philip saith unto him, Come and see.

47Jesus saw Nathanael coming to him, and saith of him, Behold an Israelite indeed, in whom is no guile!

48Nathanael saith unto him, Whence knowest thou me? Jesus answered and said unto him, Before that Philip called thee, when thou wast under the fig tree, I saw thee.

49Nathanael answered and saith unto him, Rabbi, thou art the Son of God; thou art the King of Israel.

New International

23John replied in the words of Isaiah the prophet, "I am the voice of one calling in the desert, 'Make straight the way for the Lord.' "a

24Now some Pharisees who had been sent 25questioned him, "Why then do you baptize if you are not the Christ, nor Elijah, nor the Prophet?"

26"I baptize withb water," John replied, "but among you stands one you do not know. 27He is the one who comes after me, the thongs of whose sandals I am not worthy to untie."

28This all happened at Bethany on the other side of the Jordan, where John was baptizing.

Jesus the Lamb of God

29The next day John saw Jesus coming toward him and said, "Look, the Lamb of God, who takes away the sin of the world! 30This is the one I meant when I said, 'A man who comes after me has surpassed me because he was before me.' 31I myself did not know him, but the reason I came baptizing with water was that he might be revealed to Israel."

32Then John gave this testimony: "I saw the Spirit come down from heaven as a dove and remain on him. 33I would not have known him, except that the one who sent me to baptize with water told me, 'The man on whom you see the Spirit come down and remain is he who will baptize with the Holy Spirit.' 34I have seen and I testify that this is the Son of God."

Jesus' First Disciples

35The next day John was there again with two of his disciples. 36When he saw Jesus passing by, he said, "Look, the Lamb of God!"

37When the two disciples heard him say this, they followed Jesus. 38Turning around, Jesus saw them following and asked, "What do you want?"

They said, "Rabbi" (which means Teacher), "where are you staying?"

39"Come," he replied, "and you will see."

So they went and saw where he was staying, and spent that day with him. It was about the tenth hour.

40Andrew, Simon Peter's brother, was one of the two who heard what John had said and who had followed Jesus. 41The first thing Andrew did was to find his brother Simon and tell him, "We have found the Messiah" (that is, the Christ). 42And he brought him to Jesus.

Jesus looked at him and said, "You are Simon son of John. You will be called Cephas" (which, when translated, is Peterc).

Jesus Calls Philip and Nathanael

43The next day Jesus decided to leave for Galilee. Finding Philip, he said to him, "Follow me."

44Philip, like Andrew and Peter, was from the town of Bethsaida. 45Philip found Nathanael and told him, "We have found the one Moses wrote about in the Law, and about whom the prophets also wrote—Jesus of Nazareth, the son of Joseph."

46"Nazareth! Can anything good come from there?" Nathanael asked.

"Come and see," said Philip.

47When Jesus saw Nathanael approaching, he said of him, "Here is a true Israelite, in whom there is nothing false."

48"How do you know me?" Nathanael asked.

Jesus answered, "I saw you while you were still under the fig tree before Philip called you."

49Then Nathanael declared, "Rabbi, you are the Son of God; you are the King of Israel."

---

a *23* Isaiah 40:3   b *26* Or *in;* also in verses 31 and 33   c *42* Both *Cephas* (Aramaic) and *Peter* (Greek) mean *rock.*

Living Bible

23He replied, "I am a voice from the barren wilderness, shouting as Isaiah prophesied, 'Get ready for the coming of the Lord!' "

24, 25Then those who were sent by the Pharisees asked him, "If you aren't the Messiah or Elijah or the Prophet, what right do you have to baptize?"

26John told them, "I merely baptize withd water, but right here in the crowd is someone you have never met, 27who will soon begin his ministry among you, and I am not even fit to be his slave."

28This incident took place at Bethany, a village on the other side of the Jordan River where John was baptizing.

29The next day John saw Jesus coming toward him and said, "Look! There is the Lamb of God who takes away the world's sin! 30He is the one I was talking about when I said, 'Soon a man far greater than I am is coming, who existed long before me!' 31I didn't know he was the one, but I am here baptizing with water in order to point him out to the nation of Israel."

32Then John told about seeing the Holy Spirit in the form of a dove descending from heaven and resting upon Jesus.

33"I didn't know he was the one," John said again, "but at the time God sent me to baptize he told me, 'When you see the Holy Spirit descending and resting upon someone—he is the one you are looking for. He is the one who baptizes with the Holy Spirit.' 34I saw it happen to this man, and I therefore testify that he is the Son of God."

35The following day as John was standing with two of his disciples, 36Jesus walked by. John looked at him intently and then declared, "See! There is the Lamb of God!"

37Then John's two disciples turned and followed Jesus.

38Jesus looked around and saw them following. "What do you want?" he asked them.

"Sir," they replied, "where do you live?"

39"Come and see," he said. So they went with him to the place where he was staying and were with him from about four o'clock that afternoon until the evening. 40(One of these men was Andrew, Simon Peter's brother.)

41Andrew then went to find his brother Peter and told him, "We have found the Messiah!" 42And he brought Peter to meet Jesus.

Jesus looked intently at Peter for a moment and then said, "You are Simon, John's son—but you shall be called Peter, the rock!"

43The next day Jesus decided to go to Galilee. He found Philip and told him, "Come with me." 44(Philip was from Bethsaida, Andrew and Peter's home town.)

45Philip now went off to look for Nathanael and told him, "We have found the Messiah!—the very person Moses and the prophets told about! His name is Jesus, the son of Joseph from Nazareth!"

46"Nazareth!" exclaimed Nathanael. "Can anything good come from there?"

"Just come and see for yourself," Philip declared.

47As they approached, Jesus said, "Here comes an honest man—a true son of Israel."

48"How do you know what I am like?" Nathanael demanded.

And Jesus replied, "I could see you under the fig tree before Philip found you."

49Nathanael replied, "Sir, you are the Son of God— the King of Israel!"

New Revised Standard

23He said,
"I am the voice of one crying out in the
    wilderness,
'Make straight the way of the Lord,' "
as the prophet Isaiah said.

24 Now they had been sent from the Pharisees. 25They asked him, "Why then are you baptizing if you are neither the Messiah,e nor Elijah, nor the prophet?" 26John answered them, "I baptize with water. Among you stands one whom you do not know, 27the one who is coming after me; I am not worthy to untie the thong of his sandal." 28This took place in Bethany across the Jordan where John was baptizing.

The Lamb of God

29 The next day he saw Jesus coming toward him and declared, "Here is the Lamb of God who takes away the sin of the world! 30This is he of whom I said, 'After me comes a man who ranks ahead of me because he was before me.' 31I myself did not know him; but I came baptizing with water for this reason, that he might be revealed to Israel." 32And John testified, "I saw the Spirit descending from heaven like a dove, and it remained on him. 33I myself did not know him, but the one who sent me to baptize with water said to me, 'He on whom you see the Spirit descend and remain is the one who baptizes with the Holy Spirit.' 34And I myself have seen and have testified that this is the Son of God."f

The First Disciples of Jesus

35 The next day John again was standing with two of his disciples, 36and as he watched Jesus walk by, he exclaimed, "Look, here is the Lamb of God!" 37The two disciples heard him say this, and they followed Jesus. 38When Jesus turned and saw them following, he said to them, "What are you looking for?" They said to him, "Rabbi" (which translated means Teacher), "where are you staying?" 39He said to them, "Come and see." They came and saw where he was staying, and they remained with him that day. It was about four o'clock in the afternoon. 40One of the two who heard John speak and followed him was Andrew, Simon Peter's brother. 41He first found his brother Simon and said to him, "We have found the Messiah" (which is translated Anointedg). 42He brought Simonh to Jesus, who looked at him and said, "You are Simon son of John. You are to be called Cephas" (which is translated Peteri).

Jesus Calls Philip and Nathanael

43 The next day Jesus decided to go to Galilee. He found Philip and said to him, "Follow me." 44Now Philip was from Bethsaida, the city of Andrew and Peter. 45Philip found Nathanael and said to him, "We have found him about whom Moses in the law and also the prophets wrote, Jesus son of Joseph from Nazareth." 46Nathanael said to him, "Can anything good come out of Nazareth?" Philip said to him, "Come and see." 47When Jesus saw Nathanael coming toward him, he said of him, "Here is truly an Israelite in whom there is no deceit!" 48Nathanael asked him, "Where did you get to know me?" Jesus answered, "I saw you under the fig tree before Philip called you." 49Nathanael replied, "Rabbi, you are the Son of God! You are the King of Israel!" 50Jesus answered, "Do you believe because I

e Or the Christ   f Other ancient authorities read is God's chosen one   g Or Christ   h Gk him   i From the word for rock in Aramaic (kepha) and Greek (petra), respectively

d 1:26 with, or "in." So also with or in the Holy Spirit in vss 31, 33.

King James

50Jesus answered and said unto him, Because I said unto thee, I saw thee under the fig tree, believest thou? thou shalt see greater things than these.

51And he saith unto him, Verily, verily, I say unto you, Hereafter ye shall see heaven open, and the angels of God ascending and descending upon the Son of man.

2 AND THE third day there was a marriage in Cana of Galilee; and the mother of Jesus was there:

2And both Jesus was called, and his disciples, to the marriage.

3And when they wanted wine, the mother of Jesus saith unto him, They have no wine.

4Jesus saith unto her, Woman, what have I to do with thee? mine hour is not yet come.

5His mother saith unto the servants, Whatsoever he saith unto you, do it.

6And there were set there six waterpots of stone, after the manner of the purifying of the Jews, containing two or three firkins apiece.

7Jesus saith unto them, Fill the waterpots with water. And they filled them up to the brim.

8And he saith unto them, Draw out now, and bear unto the governor of the feast. And they bare it.

9When the ruler of the feast had tasted the water that was made wine, and knew not whence it was: (but the servants which drew the water knew;) the governor of the feast called the bridegroom,

10And saith unto him, Every man at the beginning doth set forth good wine; and when men have well drunk, then that which is worse: but thou hast kept the good wine until now.

11This beginning of miracles did Jesus in Cana of Galilee, and manifested forth his glory; and his disciples believed on him.

12¶ After this he went down to Capernaum, he, and his mother, and his brethren, and his disciples: and they continued there not many days.

13¶ And the Jews' passover was at hand, and Jesus went up to Jerusalem,

14And found in the temple those that sold oxen and sheep and doves, and the changers of money sitting:

15And when he had made a scourge of small cords, he drove them all out of the temple, and the sheep, and the oxen; and poured out the changers' money, and overthrew the tables;

16And said unto them that sold doves, Take these things hence; make not my Father's house an house of merchandise.

17And his disciples remembered that it was written, The zeal of thine house hath eaten me up.

18¶ Then answered the Jews and said unto him, What sign showest thou unto us, seeing that thou doest these things?

19Jesus answered and said unto them, Destroy this temple, and in three days I will raise it up.

20Then said the Jews, Forty and six years was this temple in building, and wilt thou rear it up in three days?

21But he spake of the temple of his body.

22When therefore he was risen from the dead, his disciples remembered that he had said this unto them; and they believed the scripture, and the word which Jesus had said.

23¶ Now when he was in Jerusalem at the passover, in the feast day, many believed in his name, when they saw the miracles which he did.

24But Jesus did not commit himself unto them, because he knew all men,

25And needed not that any should testify of man: for he knew what was in man.

New International

50Jesus said, "You believea because I told you I saw you under the fig tree. You shall see greater things than that." 51He then added, "I tell youb the truth, youb shall see heaven open, and the angels of God ascending and descending on the Son of Man."

Jesus Changes Water to Wine

2 ON THE third day a wedding took place at Cana in Galilee. Jesus' mother was there, 2and Jesus and his disciples had also been invited to the wedding. 3When the wine was gone, Jesus' mother said to him, "They have no more wine."

4"Dear woman, why do you involve me?" Jesus replied. "My time has not yet come."

5His mother said to the servants, "Do whatever he tells you."

6Nearby stood six stone water jars, the kind used by the Jews for ceremonial washing, each holding from twenty to thirty gallons.c

7Jesus said to the servants, "Fill the jars with water"; so they filled them to the brim.

8Then he told them, "Now draw some out and take it to the master of the banquet."

They did so, 9and the master of the banquet tasted the water that had been turned into wine. He did not realize where it had come from, though the servants who had drawn the water knew. Then he called the bridegroom aside 10and said, "Everyone brings out the choice wine first and then the cheaper wine after the guests have had too much to drink; but you have saved the best till now."

11This, the first of his miraculous signs, Jesus performed at Cana in Galilee. He thus revealed his glory, and his disciples put their faith in him.

Jesus Clears the Temple

12After this he went down to Capernaum with his mother and brothers and his disciples. There they stayed for a few days.

13When it was almost time for the Jewish Passover, Jesus went up to Jerusalem. 14In the temple courts he found men selling cattle, sheep and doves, and others sitting at tables exchanging money. 15So he made a whip out of cords, and drove all from the temple area, both sheep and cattle; he scattered the coins of the money changers and overturned their tables. 16To those who sold doves he said, "Get these out of here! How dare you turn my Father's house into a market!"

17His disciples remembered that it is written: "Zeal for your house will consume me."d

18Then the Jews demanded of him, "What miraculous sign can you show us to prove your authority to do all this?"

19Jesus answered them, "Destroy this temple, and I will raise it again in three days."

20The Jews replied, "It has taken forty-six years to build this temple, and you are going to raise it in three days?" 21But the temple he had spoken of was his body. 22After he was raised from the dead, his disciples recalled what he had said. Then they believed the Scripture and the words that Jesus had spoken.

23Now while he was in Jerusalem at the Passover Feast, many people saw the miraculous signs he was doing and believed in his name.e 24But Jesus would not entrust himself to them, for he knew all men. 25He did not need man's testimony about man, for he knew what was in a man.

---

a 50 Or Do you believe . . . ?   b 51 The Greek is plural.   c 6 Greek two to three metretes (probably about 75 to 115 liters)   d 17 Psalm 69:9   e 23 Or and believed in him

Living Bible

50Jesus asked him, "Do you believe all this just because I told you I had seen you under the fig tree? You will see greater proofs than this. 51You will even see heaven open and the angels of God coming back and forth to me, the Messiah."f

2 TWO DAYS later Jesus' mother was a guest at a wedding in the village of Cana in Galilee, 2and Jesus and his disciples were invited too. 3The wine supply ran out during the festivities, and Jesus' mother came to him with the problem.

4"I can't help you now," he said.g "It isn't yet my time for miracles."

5But his mother told the servants, "Do whatever he tells you to."

6Six stone waterpots were standing there; they were used for Jewish ceremonial purposes and held perhaps twenty to thirty gallons each. 7, 8Then Jesus told the servants to fill them to the brim with water. When this was done he said, "Dip some out and take it to the master of ceremonies."

9When the master of ceremonies tasted the water that was now wine, not knowing where it had come from (though, of course, the servants did), he called the bridegroom over.

10"This is wonderful stuff!" he said. "You're different from most. Usually a host uses the best wine first, and afterwards, when everyone is full and doesn't care, then he brings out the less expensive brands. But you have kept the best for the last!"

11This miracle at Cana in Galilee was Jesus' first public demonstration of his heaven-sent power. And his disciples believed that he really was the Messiah.h

12After the wedding he left for Capernaum for a few days with his mother, brothers, and disciples.

13Then it was time for the annual Jewish Passover celebration, and Jesus went to Jerusalem.

14In the Temple area he saw merchants selling cattle, sheep, and doves for sacrifices, and moneychangers behind their counters. 15Jesus made a whip from some ropes and chased them all out, and drove out the sheep and oxen, scattering the moneychangers' coins over the floor and turning over their tables! 16Then, going over to the men selling doves, he told them, "Get these things out of here. Don't turn my Father's House into a market!"

17Then his disciples remembered this prophecy from the Scriptures: "Concern for God's House will be my undoing."

18"What right have you to order them out?" the Jewish leadersi demanded. "If you have this authority from God, show us a miracle to prove it."

19"All right," Jesus replied, "this is the miracle I will do for you: Destroy this sanctuary and in three days I will raise it up!"

20"What!" they exclaimed. "It took forty-six years to build this Temple, and you can do it in three days?" 21But by "this sanctuary" he meant his body. 22After he came back to life again, the disciples remembered his saying this and realized that what he had quoted from the Scriptures really did refer to him, and had all come true!

23Because of the miracles he did in Jerusalem at the Passover celebration, many people were convinced that he was indeed the Messiah. 24, 25But Jesus didn't trust them, for he knew mankind to the core. No one needed to tell him how changeable human nature is!

New Revised Standard

told you that I saw you under the fig tree? You will see greater things than these." 51 And he said to him, "Very truly, I tell you,j you will see heaven opened and the angels of God ascending and descending upon the Son of Man."

The Wedding at Cana

2 ON THE third day there was a wedding in Cana of Galilee, and the mother of Jesus was there. 2Jesus and his disciples had also been invited to the wedding. 3When the wine gave out, the mother of Jesus said to him, "They have no wine." 4And Jesus said to her, "Woman, what concern is that to you and to me? My hour has not yet come." 5His mother said to the servants, "Do whatever he tells you." 6Now standing there were six stone water jars for the Jewish rites of purification, each holding twenty or thirty gallons. 7Jesus said to them, "Fill the jars with water." And they filled them up to the brim. 8He said to them, "Now draw some out, and take it to the chief steward." So they took it. 9When the steward tasted the water that had become wine, and did not know where it came from (though the servants who had drawn the water knew), the steward called the bridegroom 10and said to him, "Everyone serves the good wine first, and then the inferior wine after the guests have become drunk. But you have kept the good wine until now." 11Jesus did this, the first of his signs, in Cana of Galilee, and revealed his glory; and his disciples believed in him.

12 After this he went down to Capernaum with his mother, his brothers, and his disciples; and they remained there a few days.

Jesus Cleanses the Temple

13 The Passover of the Jews was near, and Jesus went up to Jerusalem. 14In the temple he found people selling cattle, sheep, and doves, and the money changers seated at their tables. 15Making a whip of cords, he drove all of them out of the temple, both the sheep and the cattle. He also poured out the coins of the money changers and overturned their tables. 16He told those who were selling the doves, "Take these things out of here! Stop making my Father's house a marketplace!" 17His disciples remembered that it was written, "Zeal for your house will consume me." 18The Jews then said to him, "What sign can you show us for doing this?" 19Jesus answered them, "Destroy this temple, and in three days I will raise it up." 20The Jews then said, "This temple has been under construction for forty-six years, and will you raise it up in three days?" 21But he was speaking of the temple of his body. 22After he was raised from the dead, his disciples remembered that he had said this; and they believed the scripture and the word that Jesus had spoken.

23 When he was in Jerusalem during the Passover festival, many believed in his name because they saw the signs that he was doing. 24But Jesus on his part would not entrust himself to them, because he knew all people 25and needed no one to testify about anyone; for he himself knew what was in everyone.

---

f 1:51 the Messiah, literally, "the Son of Man."   g 2:4 "I can't help you now," he said, literally, "Woman, what have I to do with you?"   h 2:11 that he really was the Messiah, literally, "his disciples believed him."   i 2:18 the Jewish leaders, literally, "the Jews."

j Both instances of the Greek word for you in this verse are plural

King James

New International

3 THERE WAS a man of the Pharisees, named Nicodemus, a ruler of the Jews:

2The same came to Jesus by night, and said unto him, Rabbi, we know that thou art a teacher come from God: for no man can do these miracles that thou doest, except God be with him.

3Jesus answered and said unto him, Verily, verily, I say unto thee, Except a man be born again, he cannot see the kingdom of God.

4Nicodemus saith unto him, How can a man be born when he is old? can he enter the second time into his mother's womb, and be born?

5Jesus answered, Verily, verily, I say unto thee, Except a man be born of water and *of* the Spirit, he cannot enter into the kingdom of God.

6That which is born of the flesh is flesh; and that which is born of the Spirit is spirit.

7Marvel not that I said unto thee, Ye must be born again.

8The wind bloweth where it listeth, and thou hearest the sound thereof, but canst not tell whence it cometh, and whither it goeth: so is every one that is born of the Spirit.

9Nicodemus answered and said unto him, How can these things be?

10Jesus answered and said unto him, Art thou a master of Israel, and knowest not these things?

11Verily, verily, I say unto thee, We speak that we do know, and testify that we have seen; and ye receive not our witness.

12If I have told you earthly things, and ye believe not, how shall ye believe, if I tell you *of* heavenly things?

13And no man hath ascended up to heaven, but he that came down from heaven, *even* the Son of man which is in heaven.

14¶ And as Moses lifted up the serpent in the wilderness, even so must the Son of man be lifted up:

15That whosoever believeth in him should not perish, but have eternal life.

16¶ For God so loved the world, that he gave his only begotten Son, that whosoever believeth in him should not perish, but have everlasting life.

17For God sent not his Son into the world to condemn the world; but that the world through him might be saved.

18¶ He that believeth on him is not condemned: but he that believeth not is condemned already, because he hath not believed in the name of the only begotton Son of God.

19And this is the condemnation, that light is come into the world, and men loved darkness rather than light, because their deeds were evil.

20For every one that doeth evil hateth the light, neither cometh to the light, lest his deeds should be reproved.

21But he that doeth truth cometh to the light, that his deeds may be made manifest, that they are wrought in God.

22¶ After these things came Jesus and his disciples into the land of Judaea; and there he tarried with them, and baptized.

23¶ And John also was baptizing in Aenon near to Salim, because there was much water there: and they came, and were baptized.

24For John was not yet cast into prison.

25¶ Then there arose a question between *some* of John's disciples and the Jews about purifying.

26And they came unto John, and said unto him, Rabbi, he that was with thee beyond Jordan, to whom thou barest witness, behold, the same baptizeth, and all *men* come to him.

27John answered and said, A man can receive nothing, except it be given him from heaven.

Jesus Teaches Nicodemus

3 NOW THERE was a man of the Pharisees named Nicodemus, a member of the Jewish ruling council. 2He came to Jesus at night and said, "Rabbi, we know you are a teacher who has come from God. For no one could perform the miraculous signs you are doing if God were not with him."

3In reply Jesus declared, "I tell you the truth, no one can see the kingdom of God unless he is born again.[a]"

4"How can a man be born when he is old?" Nicodemus asked. "Surely he cannot enter a second time into his mother's womb to be born!"

5Jesus answered, "I tell you the truth, no one can enter the kingdom of God unless he is born of water and the Spirit. 6Flesh gives birth to flesh, but the Spirit[b] gives birth to spirit. 7You should not be surprised at my saying, 'You[c] must be born again.' 8The wind blows wherever it pleases. You hear its sound, but you cannot tell where it comes from or where it is going. So it is with everyone born of the Spirit."

9"How can this be?" Nicodemus asked.

10"You are Israel's teacher," said Jesus, "and do you not understand these things? 11I tell you the truth, we speak of what we know, and we testify to what we have seen, but still you people do not accept our testimony. 12I have spoken to you of earthly things and you do not believe; how then will you believe if I speak of heavenly things? 13No one has ever gone into heaven except the one who came from heaven—the Son of Man.[d] 14Just as Moses lifted up the snake in the desert, so the Son of Man must be lifted up, 15that everyone who believes in him may have eternal life.[e]

16"For God so loved the world that he gave his one and only Son,[f] that whoever believes in him shall not perish but have eternal life. 17For God did not send his Son into the world to condemn the world, but to save the world through him. 18Whoever believes in him is not condemned, but whoever does not believe stands condemned already because he has not believed in the name of God's one and only Son.[g] 19This is the verdict: Light has come into the world, but men loved darkness instead of light because their deeds were evil. 20Everyone who does evil hates the light, and will not come into the light for fear that his deeds will be exposed. 21But whoever lives by the truth comes into the light, so that it may be seen plainly that what he has done has been done through God."[h]

John the Baptist's Testimony About Jesus

22After this, Jesus and his disciples went out into the Judean countryside, where he spent some time with them, and baptized. 23Now John also was baptizing at Aenon near Salim, because there was plenty of water, and people were constantly coming to be baptized. 24(This was before John was put in prison.) 25An argument developed between some of John's disciples and a certain Jew[i] over the matter of ceremonial washing. 26They came to John and said to him, "Rabbi, that man who was with you on the other side of the Jordan—the one you testified about—well, he is baptizing, and everyone is going to him."

27To this John replied, "A man can receive only what is given him from heaven. 28You yourselves can testify

---

a 3 Or born from above; also in verse 7   b 6 Or but spirit   c 7 The Greek is plural.   d 13 Some manuscripts Man, who is in heaven   e 15 Or believes may have eternal life in him   f 16 Or his only begotten Son   g 18 Or God's only begotten Son   h 21 Some interpreters end the quotation after verse 15. i 25 Some manuscripts and certain Jews

Living Bible

3 AFTER DARK one night a Jewish religious leader named Nicodemus, a member of the sect of the Pharisees, came for an interview with Jesus. "Sir," he said, "we all know that God has sent you to teach us. Your miracles are proof enough of this."

3Jesus replied, "With all the earnestness I possess I tell you this: Unless you are born again, you can never get into the Kingdom of God."

4"Born again!" exclaimed Nicodemus. "What do you mean? How can an old man go back into his mother's womb and be born again?"

5Jesus replied, "What I am telling you so earnestly is this: Unless one is born of water and the Spirit, he cannot enter the Kingdom of God. 6Men can only reproduce human life, but the Holy Spirit gives new life from heaven; 7so don't be surprised at my statement that you must be born again! 8Just as you can hear the wind but can't tell where it comes from or where it will go next, so it is with the Spirit. We do not know on whom he will next bestow this life from heaven."

9"What do you mean?" Nicodemus asked.

10, 11Jesus replied, "You, a respected Jewish teacher, and yet you don't understand these things? I am telling you what I know and have seen—and yet you won't believe me. 12But if you don't even believe me when I tell you about such things as these that happen here among men, how can you possibly believe if I tell you what is going on in heaven? 13For only I, the Messiah,k have come to earth and will return to heaven again. 14And as Moses in the wilderness lifted up the bronze image of a serpent on a pole, even so I must be lifted up upon a pole, 15so that anyone who believes in me will have eternal life. 16For God loved the world so much that he gave his only Sonl so that anyone who believes in him shall not perish but have eternal life. 17God did not send his Son into the world to condemn it, but to save it.

18"There is no eternal doom awaiting those who trust him to save them. But those who don't trust him have already been tried and condemned for not believing in the only Son of God. 19Their sentence is based on this fact: that the Light from heaven came into the world, but they loved the darkness more than the Light, for their deeds were evil. 20They hated the heavenly Light because they wanted to sin in the darkness. They stayed away from that Light for fear their sins would be exposed and they would be punished. 21But those doing right come gladly to the Light to let everyone see that they are doing what God wants them to."

22Afterwards Jesus and his disciples left Jerusalem and stayed for a while in Judea and baptized there.

23, 24At this time John the Baptist was not yet in prison. He was baptizing at Aenon, near Salim, because there was plenty of water there. 25One day someone began an argument with John's disciples, telling them that Jesus' baptism was best.m 26So they came to John and said, "Master, the man you met on the other side of the Jordan River—the one you said was the Messiah—he is baptizing too, and everybody is going over there instead of coming here to us."

27John replied, "God in heaven appoints each man's work. 28My work is to prepare the way for that man so

New Revised Standard

Nicodemus Visits Jesus

3 NOW THERE was a Pharisee named Nicodemus, a leader of the Jews. 2He came to Jesusn by night and said to him, "Rabbi, we know that you are a teacher who has come from God; for no one can do these signs that you do apart from the presence of God." 3Jesus answered him, "Very truly, I tell you, no one can see the kingdom of God without being born from above."o 4Nicodemus said to him, "How can anyone be born after having grown old? Can one enter a second time into the mother's womb and be born?" 5Jesus answered, "Very truly, I tell you, no one can enter the kingdom of God without being born of water and Spirit. 6What is born of the flesh is flesh, and what is born of the Spirit is spirit.p 7Do not be astonished that I said to you, 'Youq must be born from above.'r 8The windp blows where it chooses, and you hear the sound of it, but you do not know where it comes from or where it goes. So it is with everyone who is born of the Spirit." 9Nicodemus said to him, "How can these things be?" 10Jesus answered him, "Are you a teacher of Israel, and yet you do not understand these things?

11 "Very truly, I tell you, we speak of what we know and testify to what we have seen; yet yous do not receive our testimony. 12If I have told you about earthly things and you do not believe, how can you believe if I tell you about heavenly things? 13No one has ascended into heaven except the one who descended from heaven, the Son of Man.t 14And just as Moses lifted up the serpent in the wilderness, so must the Son of Man be lifted up, 15that whoever believes in him may have eternal life.u

16 "For God so loved the world that he gave his only Son, so that everyone who believes in him may not perish but may have eternal life.

17 "Indeed, God did not send the Son into the world to condemn the world, but in order that the world might be saved through him. 18Those who believe in him are not condemned; but those who do not believe are condemned already, because they have not believed in the name of the only Son of God. 19And this is the judgment, that the light has come into the world, and people loved darkness rather than light because their deeds were evil. 20For all who do evil hate the light and do not come to the light, so that their deeds may not be exposed. 21But those who do what is true come to the light, so that it may be clearly seen that their deeds have been done in God."u

Jesus and John the Baptist

22 After this Jesus and his disciples went into the Judean countryside, and he spent some time there with them and baptized. 23John also was baptizing at Aenon near Salim because water was abundant there; and people kept coming and were being baptized 24—John, of course, had not yet been thrown into prison.

25 Now a discussion about purification arose between John's disciples and a Jew.v 26They came to John and said to him, "Rabbi, the one who was with you across the Jordan, to whom you testified, here he is baptizing, and all are going to him." 27John answered, "No one can receive anything except what has been given from heaven. 28You yourselves are my witnesses

---

j 3:5 born of water, or, "Physical birth is not enough. You must be born spiritually. . . ." This alternate paraphrase interprets "born of water" as meaning the normal process observed during every human birth. Some think this means water baptism. k 3:13 the Messiah, literally, "the Son of Man." l 3:16 his only Son, or, "the unique Son of God." So also in vs 18. m 3:25 best, literally, "about purification."

n Gk him o Or born anew p The same Greek word means both wind and spirit q The Greek word for you here is plural r Or anew s The Greek word for you here and in verse 12 is plural t Other ancient authorities add who is in heaven u Some interpreters hold that the quotation concludes with verse 15 v Other ancient authorities read the Jews

King James

28Ye yourselves bear me witness, that I said, I am not the Christ, but that I am sent before him.

29He that hath the bride is the bridegroom: but the friend of the bridegroom, which standeth and heareth him, rejoiceth greatly because of the bridegroom's voice: this my joy therefore is fulfilled.

30He must increase, but I *must* decrease.

31He that cometh from above is above all: he that is of the earth is earthly, and speaketh of the earth: he that cometh from heaven is above all.

32And what he hath seen and heard, that he testifieth; and no man receiveth his testimony.

33He that hath received his testimony hath set to his seal that God is true.

34For he whom God hath sent speaketh the words of God: for God giveth not the Spirit by measure *unto him*.

35The Father loveth the Son, and hath given all things into his hand.

36He that believeth on the Son hath everlasting life: and he that believeth not the Son shall not see life; but the wrath of God abideth on him.

4 WHEN THEREFORE the Lord knew how the Pharisees had heard that Jesus made and baptized more disciples than John,

2(Though Jesus himself baptized not, but his disciples,)

3He left Judaea, and departed again into Galilee.

4And he must needs go through Samaria.

5Then cometh he to a city of Samaria, which is called Sychar, near to the parcel of ground that Jacob gave to his son Joseph.

6Now Jacob's well was there. Jesus therefore, being wearied with *his* journey, sat thus on the well: *and* it was about the sixth hour.

7There cometh a woman of Samaria to draw water: Jesus saith unto her, Give me to drink.

8(For his disciples were gone away unto the city to buy meat.)

9Then saith the woman of Samaria unto him, How is it that thou, being a Jew, askest drink of me, which am a woman of Samaria? for the Jews have no dealings with the Samaritans.

10Jesus answered and said unto her, If thou knewest the gift of God, and who it is that saith to thee, Give me to drink; thou wouldest have asked of him, and he would have given thee living water.

11The woman saith unto him, Sir, thou hast nothing to draw with, and the well is deep: from whence then hast thou that living water?

12Art thou greater than our father Jacob, which gave us the well, and drank thereof himself, and his children, and his cattle?

13Jesus answered and said unto her, Whosoever drinketh of this water shall thirst again:

14But whosoever drinketh of the water that I shall give him shall never thirst; but the water that I shall give him shall be in him a well of water springing up into everlasting life.

15The woman saith unto him, Sir, give me this water, that I thirst not, neither come hither to draw.

16Jesus saith unto her, Go, call thy husband, and come hither.

17The woman answered and said, I have no husband. Jesus said unto her, Thou hast well said, I have no husband:

18For thou hast had five husbands; and he whom thou now hast is not thy husband: in that saidst thou truly.

19The woman saith unto him, Sir, I perceive that thou art a prophet.

New International

that I said, 'I am not the Christ[a] but am sent ahead of him.' 29The bride belongs to the bridegroom. The friend who attends the bridegroom waits and listens for him, and is full of joy when he hears the bridegroom's voice. That joy is mine, and it is now complete. 30He must become greater; I must become less.

31"The one who comes from above is above all; the one who is from the earth belongs to the earth, and speaks as one from the earth. The one who comes from heaven is above all. 32He testifies to what he has seen and heard, but no one accepts his testimony. 33The man who has accepted it has certified that God is truthful. 34For the one whom God has sent speaks the words of God, for God[b] gives the Spirit without limit. 35The Father loves the Son and has placed everything in his hands. 36Whoever believes in the Son has eternal life, but whoever rejects the Son will not see life, for God's wrath remains on him."[c]

Jesus Talks With a Samaritan Woman

4 THE PHARISEES heard that Jesus was gaining and baptizing more disciples than John, 2although in fact it was not Jesus who baptized, but his disciples. 3When the Lord learned of this, he left Judea and went back once more to Galilee.

4Now he had to go through Samaria. 5So he came to a town in Samaria called Sychar, near the plot of ground Jacob had given to his son Joseph. 6Jacob's well was there, and Jesus, tired as he was from the journey, sat down by the well. It was about the sixth hour.

7When a Samaritan woman came to draw water, Jesus said to her, "Will you give me a drink?" 8(His disciples had gone into the town to buy food.)

9The Samaritan woman said to him, "You are a Jew and I am a Samaritan woman. How can you ask me for a drink?" (For Jews do not associate with Samaritans.[d])

10Jesus answered her, "If you knew the gift of God and who it is that asks you for a drink, you would have asked him and he would have given you living water."

11"Sir," the woman said, "you have nothing to draw with and the well is deep. Where can you get this living water? 12Are you greater than our father Jacob, who gave us the well and drank from it himself, as did also his sons and his flocks and herds?"

13Jesus answered, "Everyone who drinks this water will be thirsty again, 14but whoever drinks the water I give him will never thirst. Indeed, the water I give him will become in him a spring of water welling up to eternal life."

15The woman said to him, "Sir, give me this water so that I won't get thirsty and have to keep coming here to draw water."

16He told her, "Go, call your husband and come back."

17"I have no husband," she replied.

Jesus said to her, "You are right when you say you have no husband. 18The fact is, you have had five husbands, and the man you now have is not your husband. What you have just said is quite true."

19"Sir," the woman said, "I can see that you are a prophet. 20Our fathers worshiped on this mountain, but

a 28 Or *Messiah*   b 34 Greek *he*   c 36 Some interpreters end the quotation after verse 30.   d 9 Or *do not use dishes Samaritans have used*

Living Bible

that everyone will go to him. You yourselves know how plainly I told you that I am not the Messiah. I am here to prepare the way for him—that is all. 29The crowds will naturally go to the main attraction*—the bride will go where the bridegroom is! A bridegroom's friends rejoice with him. I am the Bridegroom's friend, and I am filled with joy at his success. 30He must become greater and greater, and I must become less and less.

31"He has come from heaven and is greater than anyone else. I am of the earth, and my understanding is limited to the things of earth. 32He tells what he has seen and heard, but how few believe what he tells them! 33, 34Those who believe him discover that God is a fountain of truth. For this one—sent by God—speaks God's words, for God's Spirit is upon him without measure or limit. 35The Father loves this man because he is his Son, and God has given him everything there is. 36And all who trust him—God's Son—to save them have eternal life; those who don't believe and obey him shall never see heaven, but the wrath of God remains upon them."

4 WHEN THE Lord knew that the Pharisees had heard about the greater crowds coming to him than to John to be baptized and to become his disciples— (though Jesus himself didn't baptize them, but his disciples did)— 3he left Judea and returned to the province of Galilee.

4He had to go through Samaria on the way, 5, 6and around noon as he approached the village of Sychar, he came to Jacob's Well, located on the parcel of ground Jacob gave to his son Joseph. Jesus was tired from the long walk in the hot sun and sat wearily beside the well.

7Soon a Samaritan woman came to draw water, and Jesus asked her for a drink. 8He was alone at the time as his disciples had gone into the village to buy some food. 9The woman was surprised that a Jew would ask a "despised Samaritan" for anything—usually they wouldn't even speak to them!—and she remarked about this to Jesus.

10He replied, "If you only knew what a wonderful gift God has for you, and who I am, you would ask me for some *living* water!"

11"But you don't have a rope or a bucket," she said, "and this is a very deep well! Where would you get this living water? 12And besides, are you greater than our ancestor Jacob? How can you offer better water than this which he and his sons and cattle enjoyed?"

13Jesus replied that people soon became thirsty again after drinking this water. 14"But the water I give them," he said, "becomes a perpetual spring within them, watering them forever with eternal life."

15"Please, sir," the woman said, "give me some of that water! Then I'll never be thirsty again and won't have to make this long trip out here every day."

16"Go and get your husband," Jesus told her.

17, 18"But I'm not married," the woman replied.

"All too true!" Jesus said. "For you have had five husbands, and you aren't even married to the man you're living with now."

19"Sir," the woman said, "you must be a prophet.

New Revised Standard

that I said, 'I am not the Messiah,f but I have been sent ahead of him.' 29He who has the bride is the bridegroom. The friend of the bridegroom, who stands and hears him, rejoices greatly at the bridegroom's voice. For this reason my joy has been fulfilled. 30He must increase, but I must decrease."g

The One Who Comes from Heaven

31 The one who comes from above is above all; the one who is of the earth belongs to the earth and speaks about earthly things. The one who comes from heaven is above all. 32He testifies to what he has seen and heard, yet no one accepts his testimony. 33Whoever has accepted his testimony has certifiedh this, that God is true. 34He whom God has sent speaks the words of God, for he gives the Spirit without measure. 35The Father loves the Son and has placed all things in his hands. 36Whoever believes in the Son has eternal life; whoever disobeys the Son will not see life, but must endure God's wrath.

Jesus and the Woman of Samaria

4 NOW WHEN Jesusi learned that the Pharisees had heard, "Jesus is making and baptizing more disciples than John" 2—although it was not Jesus himself but his disciples who baptized— 3he left Judea and started back to Galilee. 4But he had to go through Samaria. 5So he came to a Samaritan city called Sychar, near the plot of ground that Jacob had given to his son Joseph. 6Jacob's well was there, and Jesus, tired out by his journey, was sitting by the well. It was about noon.

7 A Samaritan woman came to draw water, and Jesus said to her, "Give me a drink." 8(His disciples had gone to the city to buy food.) 9The Samaritan woman said to him, "How is it that you, a Jew, ask a drink of me, a woman of Samaria?" (Jews do not share things in common with Samaritans.)i 10Jesus answered her, "If you knew the gift of God, and who it is that is saying to you, 'Give me a drink,' you would have asked him, and he would have given you living water." 11The woman said to him, "Sir, you have no bucket, and the well is deep. Where do you get that living water? 12Are you greater than our ancestor Jacob, who gave us the well, and with his sons and his flocks drank from it?" 13Jesus said to her, "Everyone who drinks of this water will be thirsty again, 14but those who drink of the water that I will give them will never be thirsty. The water that I will give will become in them a spring of water gushing up to eternal life." 15The woman said to him, "Sir, give me this water, so that I may never be thirsty or have to keep coming here to draw water."

16 Jesus said to her, "Go, call your husband, and come back." 17The woman answered him, "I have no husband." Jesus said to her, "You are right in saying, 'I have no husband'; 18for you have had five husbands, and the one you have now is not your husband. What you have said is true!" 19The woman said to him, "Sir, I see that you are a prophet. 20Our ancestors worshiped

---

f Or *the Christ*   g Some interpreters hold that the quotation continues through verse 36   h Gk *set a seal to*   i Other ancient authorities read *the Lord*   j Other ancient authorities lack this sentence

King James

20Our fathers worshipped in this mountain; and ye say, that in Jerusalem is the place where men ought to worship.

21Jesus saith unto her, Woman, believe me, the hour cometh, when ye shall neither in this mountain, nor yet at Jerusalem, worship the Father.

22Ye worship ye know not what: we know what we worship: for salvation is of the Jews.

23But the hour cometh, and now is, when the true worshippers shall worship the Father in spirit and in truth: for the Father seeketh such to worship him.

24God *is* a Spirit: and they that worship him must worship *him* in spirit and in truth.

25The woman saith unto him, I know that Messias cometh, which is called Christ: when he is come, he will tell us all things.

26Jesus saith unto her, I that speak unto thee am *he*.

27¶ And upon this came his disciples, and marvelled that he talked with the woman: yet no man said, What seekest thou? or, Why talkest thou with her?

28The woman then left her waterpot, and went her way into the city, and saith to the men,

29Come, see a man, which told me all things that ever I did: is not this the Christ?

30Then they went out of the city, and came unto him.

31¶ In the mean while his disciples prayed him, saying, Master, eat.

32But he said unto them, I have meat to eat that ye know not of.

33Therefore said the disciples one to another, Hath any man brought him *aught* to eat?

34Jesus saith unto them, My meat is to do the will of him that sent me, and to finish his work.

35Say not ye, There are yet four months, and *then* cometh harvest? behold, I say unto you, Lift up your eyes, and look on the fields; for they are white already to harvest.

36And he that reapeth receiveth wages, and gathereth fruit unto life eternal: that both he that soweth and he that reapeth may rejoice together.

37And herein is that saying true, One soweth, and another reapeth.

38I sent you to reap that whereon ye bestowed no labour: other men laboured, and ye are entered into their labours.

39¶ And many of the Samaritans of that city believed on him for the saying of the woman, which testified, He told me all that ever I did.

40So when the Samaritans were come unto him, they besought him that he would tarry with them: and he abode there two days.

41And many more believed because of his own word;

42And said unto the woman, Now we believe, not because of thy saying: for we have heard *him* ourselves, and know that this is indeed the Christ, the Saviour of the world.

43¶ Now after two days he departed thence, and went into Galilee.

44For Jesus himself testified, that a prophet hath no honour in his own country.

45Then when he was come into Galilee, the Galilaeans received him, having seen all the things that he did at Jerusalem at the feast: for they also went unto the feast.

46So Jesus came again into Cana of Galilee, where he made the water wine. And there was a certain nobleman, whose son was sick at Capernaum.

47When he heard that Jesus was come out of Judaea into Galilee, he went unto him, and besought him that he would come down, and heal his son: for he was at the point of death.

48Then said Jesus unto him, Except ye see signs and wonders, ye will not believe.

49The nobleman saith unto him, Sir, come down ere my child die.

New International

you Jews claim that the place where we must worship is in Jerusalem."

21Jesus declared, "Believe me, woman, a time is coming when you will worship the Father neither on this mountain nor in Jerusalem. 22You Samaritans worship what you do not know; we worship what we do know, for salvation is from the Jews. 23Yet a time is coming and has now come when the true worshipers will worship the Father in spirit and truth, for they are the kind of worshipers the Father seeks. 24God is spirit, and his worshipers must worship in spirit and in truth."

25The woman said, "I know that Messiah" (called Christ) "is coming. When he comes, he will explain everything to us."

26Then Jesus declared, "I who speak to you am he."

The Disciples Rejoin Jesus

27Just then his disciples returned and were surprised to find him talking with a woman. But no one asked, "What do you want?" or "Why are you talking with her?"

28Then, leaving her water jar, the woman went back to the town and said to the people, 29"Come, see a man who told me everything I ever did. Could this be the Christa?" 30They came out of the town and made their way toward him.

31Meanwhile his disciples urged him, "Rabbi, eat something."

32But he said to them, "I have food to eat that you know nothing about."

33Then his disciples said to each other, "Could someone have brought him food?"

34"My food," said Jesus, "is to do the will of him who sent me and to finish his work. 35Do you not say, 'Four months more and then the harvest'? I tell you, open your eyes and look at the fields! They are ripe for harvest. 36Even now the reaper draws his wages, even now he harvests the crop for eternal life, so that the sower and the reaper may be glad together. 37Thus the saying 'One sows and another reaps' is true. 38I sent you to reap what you have not worked for. Others have done the hard work, and you have reaped the benefits of their labor."

Many Samaritans Believe

39Many of the Samaritans from that town believed in him because of the woman's testimony, "He told me everything I ever did." 40So when the Samaritans came to him, they urged him to stay with them, and he stayed two days. 41And because of his words many more became believers.

42They said to the woman, "We no longer believe just because of what you said; now we have heard for ourselves, and we know that this man really is the Savior of the world."

Jesus Heals the Official's Son

43After the two days he left for Galilee. 44(Now Jesus himself had pointed out that a prophet has no honor in his own country.) 45When he arrived in Galilee, the Galileans welcomed him. They had seen all that he had done in Jerusalem at the Passover Feast, for they also had been there.

46Once more he visited Cana in Galilee, where he had turned the water into wine. And there was a certain royal official whose son lay sick at Capernaum. 47When this man heard that Jesus had arrived in Galilee from Judea, he went to him and begged him to come and heal his son, who was close to death.

48"Unless you people see miraculous signs and wonders," Jesus told him, "you will never believe."

49The royal official said, "Sir, come down before my child dies."

a 29 Or *Messiah*

Living Bible

20But say, tell me, why is it that you Jews insist that Jerusalem is the only place of worship, while we Samaritans claim it is here [at Mount Gerazimb], where our ancestors worshiped?"

21-24Jesus replied, "The time is coming, ma'am, when we will no longer be concerned about whether to worship the Father here or in Jerusalem. For it's not *where* we worship that counts, but *how* we worship—is our worship spiritual and real? Do we have the Holy Spirit's help? For God is Spirit, and we must have his help to worship as we should. The Father wants this kind of worship from us. But you Samaritans know so little about him, worshiping blindly, while we Jews know all about him, for salvation comes to the world through the Jews."

25The woman said, "Well, at least I know that the Messiah will come—the one they call Christ—and when he does, he will explain everything to us."

26Then Jesus told her, "I am the Messiah!"

27Just then his disciples arrived. They were surprised to find him talking to a woman, but none of them asked him why, or what they had been discussing.

28, 29Then the woman left her waterpot beside the well and went back to the village and told everyone, "Come and meet a man who told me everything I ever did! Can this be the Messiah?" 30So the people came streaming from the village to see him.

31Meanwhile, the disciples were urging Jesus to eat. 32"No," he said, "I have some food you don't know about."

33"Who brought it to him?" the disciples asked each other.

34Then Jesus explained: "My nourishment comes from doing the will of God who sent me, and from finishing his work. 35Do you think the work of harvesting will not begin until the summer ends four months from now? Look around you! Vast fields of human souls are ripening all around us, and are ready now for reaping. 36The reapers will be paid good wages and will be gathering eternal souls into the granaries of heaven! What joys await the sower and the reaper, both together! 37For it is true that one sows and someone else reaps. 38I sent you to reap where you didn't sow; others did the work, and you received the harvest."

39Many from the Samaritan village believed he was the Messiah because of the woman's report: "He told me everything I ever did!" 40, 41When they came out to see him at the well, they begged him to stay at their village; and he did, for two days, long enough for many of them to believe in him after hearing him. 42Then they said to the woman, "Now we believe because we have heard him ourselves, not just because of what you told us. He is indeed the Savior of the world."

43, 44At the end of the two days' stay he went on into Galilee. Jesus used to say, "A prophet is honored everywhere except in his own country!" 45But the Galileans welcomed him with open arms, for they had been in Jerusalem at the Passover celebration and had seen some of his miracles.c

46, 47In the course of his journey through Galilee he arrived at the town of Cana, where he had turned the water into wine. While he was there, a man in the city of Capernaum, a government official, whose son was very sick, heard that Jesus had come from Judea and was traveling in Galilee. This man went over to Cana, found Jesus, and begged him to come to Capernaum with him and heal his son, who was now at death's door.

48Jesus asked, "Won't any of you believe in me unless I do more and more miracles?"

49The official pled, "Sir, please come now before my child dies."

New Revised Standard

on this mountain, but youd say that the place where people must worship is in Jerusalem." 21Jesus said to her, "Woman, believe me, the hour is coming when you will worship the Father neither on this mountain nor in Jerusalem. 22You worship what you do not know; we worship what we know, for salvation is from the Jews. 23But the hour is coming, and is now here, when the true worshipers will worship the Father in spirit and truth, for the Father seeks such as these to worship him. 24God is spirit, and those who worship him must worship in spirit and truth." 25The woman said to him, "I know that Messiah is coming" (who is called Christ). "When he comes, he will proclaim all things to us." 26Jesus said to her, "I am he,e the one who is speaking to you."

27 Just then his disciples came. They were astonished that he was speaking with a woman, but no one said, "What do you want?" or, "Why are you speaking with her?" 28Then the woman left her water jar and went back to the city. She said to the people, 29"Come and see a man who told me everything I have ever done! He cannot be the Messiah,f can he?" 30They left the city and were on their way to him.

31 Meanwhile the disciples were urging him, "Rabbi, eat something." 32But he said to them, "I have food to eat that you do not know about." 33So the disciples said to one another, "Surely no one has brought him something to eat?" 34Jesus said to them, "My food is to do the will of him who sent me and to complete his work. 35Do you not say, 'Four months more, then comes the harvest'? But I tell you, look around you, and see how the fields are ripe for harvesting. 36The reaper is already receivingg wages and is gathering fruit for eternal life, so that sower and reaper may rejoice together. 37For here the saying holds true, 'One sows and another reaps.' 38I sent you to reap that for which you did not labor. Others have labored, and you have entered into their labor."

39 Many Samaritans from that city believed in him because of the woman's testimony, "He told me everything I have ever done." 40So when the Samaritans came to him, they asked him to stay with them; and he stayed there two days. 41And many more believed because of his word. 42They said to the woman, "It is no longer because of what you said that we believe, for we have heard for ourselves, and we know that this is truly the Savior of the world."

Jesus Returns to Galilee

43 When the two days were over, he went from that place to Galilee 44(for Jesus himself had testified that a prophet has no honor in the prophet's own country). 45When he came to Galilee, the Galileans welcomed him, since they had seen all that he had done in Jerusalem at the festival; for they too had gone to the festival.

Jesus Heals an Official's Son

46 Then he came again to Cana in Galilee where he had changed the water into wine. Now there was a royal official whose son lay ill in Capernaum. 47When he heard that Jesus had come from Judea to Galilee, he went and begged him to come down and heal his son, for he was at the point of death. 48Then Jesus said to him, "Unless youh see signs and wonders you will not believe." 49The official said to him, "Sir, come down before my little boy dies." 50Jesus said to him, "Go;

---

b 4:20 *at Mount Gerazim*, implied.   c 4:45 *some of his miracles*, see John 2:23.

d The Greek word for *you* here and in verses 21 and 22 is plural   e Gk *I am*   f Or *the Christ*   g Or *35 . . . the fields are already ripe for harvesting. 36The reaper is receiving*   h Both instances of the Greek word for *you* in this verse are plural

King James

50Jesus saith unto him, Go thy way; thy son liveth. And the man believed the word that Jesus had spoken unto him, and he went his way.

51And as he was now going down, his servants met him, and told *him*, saying, Thy son liveth.

52Then inquired he of them the hour when he began to amend. And they said unto him, Yesterday at the seventh hour the fever left him.

53So the father knew that *it was* at the same hour, in the which Jesus said unto him, Thy son liveth: and himself believed, and his whole house.

54This *is* again the second miracle *that* Jesus did, when he was come out of Judaea into Galilee.

5 AFTER THIS there was a feast of the Jews; and Jesus went up to Jerusalem.

2Now there is at Jerusalem by the sheep *market* a pool, which is called in the Hebrew tongue Bethesda, having five porches.

3In these lay a great multitude of impotent folk, of blind, halt, withered, waiting for the moving of the water.

4For an angel went down at a certain season into the pool, and troubled the water: whosoever then first after the troubling of the water stepped in was made whole of whatsoever disease he had.

5And a certain man was there, which had an infirmity thirty and eight years.

6When Jesus saw him lie, and knew that he had been now a long time *in that case,* he saith unto him, Wilt thou be made whole?

7The impotent man answered him, Sir, I have no man, when the water is troubled, to put me into the pool: but while I am coming, another steppeth down before me.

8Jesus saith unto him, Rise, take up thy bed, and walk.

9And immediately the man was made whole, and took up his bed, and walked: and on the same day was the sabbath.

10¶ The Jews therefore said unto him that was cured, It is the sabbath day: it is not lawful for thee to carry *thy* bed.

11He answered them, He that made me whole, the same said unto me, Take up thy bed, and walk.

12Then asked they him, What man is that which said unto thee, Take up thy bed, and walk?

13And he that was healed wist not who it was: for Jesus had conveyed himself away, a multitude being in *that* place.

14Afterward Jesus findeth him in the temple, and said unto him, Behold, thou art made whole: sin no more, lest a worse thing come unto thee.

15The man departed, and told the Jews that it was Jesus, which had made him whole.

16And therefore did the Jews persecute Jesus, and sought to slay him, because he had done these things on the sabbath day.

17¶ But Jesus answered them, My Father worketh hitherto, and I work.

18Therefore the Jews sought the more to kill him, because he not only had broken the sabbath, but said also that God was his Father, making himself equal with God.

19Then answered Jesus and said unto them, Verily, verily, I say unto you, The Son can do nothing of himself, but what he seeth the Father do: for what things soever he doeth, these also doeth the Son likewise.

20For the Father loveth the Son, and showeth him all things that himself doeth: and he will show him greater works than these, that ye may marvel.

New International

50Jesus replied, "You may go. Your son will live." The man took Jesus at his word and departed. 51While he was still on the way, his servants met him with the news that his boy was living. 52When he inquired as to the time when his son got better, they said to him, "The fever left him yesterday at the seventh hour."

53Then the father realized that this was the exact time at which Jesus had said to him, "Your son will live." So he and all his household believed.

54This was the second miraculous sign that Jesus performed, having come from Judea to Galilee.

The Healing at the Pool

5 SOME TIME later, Jesus went up to Jerusalem for a feast of the Jews. 2Now there is in Jerusalem near the Sheep Gate a pool, which in Aramaic is called Bethesda[a] and which is surrounded by five covered colonnades. 3Here a great number of disabled people used to lie—the blind, the lame, the paralyzed.[b] 5One who was there had been an invalid for thirty-eight years. 6When Jesus saw him lying there and learned that he had been in this condition for a long time, he asked him, "Do you want to get well?"

7"Sir," the invalid replied, "I have no one to help me into the pool when the water is stirred. While I am trying to get in, someone else goes down ahead of me."

8Then Jesus said to him, "Get up! Pick up your mat and walk." 9At once the man was cured; he picked up his mat and walked.

The day on which this took place was a Sabbath, 10and so the Jews said to the man who had been healed, "It is the Sabbath; the law forbids you to carry your mat."

11But he replied, "The man who made me well said to me, 'Pick up your mat and walk.' "

12So they asked him, "Who is this fellow who told you to pick it up and walk?"

13The man who was healed had no idea who it was, for Jesus had slipped away into the crowd that was there.

14Later Jesus found him at the temple and said to him, "See, you are well again. Stop sinning or something worse may happen to you." 15The man went away and told the Jews that it was Jesus who had made him well.

Life Through the Son

16So, because Jesus was doing these things on the Sabbath, the Jews persecuted him. 17Jesus said to them, "My Father is always at his work to this very day, and I, too, am working." 18For this reason the Jews tried all the harder to kill him; not only was he breaking the Sabbath, but he was even calling God his own Father, making himself equal with God.

19Jesus gave them this answer: "I tell you the truth, the Son can do nothing by himself; he can do only what he sees his Father doing, because whatever the Father does the Son also does. 20For the Father loves the Son and shows him all he does. Yes, to your amazement he will show him even greater things than these. 21For just

---

a 2 Some manuscripts *Bethzatha*; other manuscripts *Bethsaida*   b 3 Some less important manuscripts *paralyzed—and they waited for the moving of the waters.* 4*From time to time an angel of the Lord would come down and stir up the waters. The first one into the pool after each such disturbance would be cured of whatever disease he had.*

Living Bible

50Then Jesus told him, "Go back home. Your son is healed!" And the man believed Jesus and started home. 51While he was on his way, some of his servants met him with the news that all was well—his son had recovered. 52He asked them when the lad had begun to feel better, and they replied, "Yesterday afternoon at about one o'clock his fever suddenly disappeared!" 53Then the father realized it was the same moment that Jesus had told him, "Your son is healed." And the officer and his entire household believed that Jesus was the Messiah.

54This was Jesus' second miracle in Galilee after coming from Judea.

5 AFTERWARDS JESUS returned to Jerusalem for one of the Jewish religious holidays. 2Inside the city, near the Sheep Gate, was Bethesda Pool, with five covered platforms or porches surrounding it. 3Crowds of sick folks—lame, blind, or with paralyzed limbs—lay on the platforms (waiting for a certain movement of the water, 4for an angel of the Lord came from time to time and disturbed the water, and the first person to step down into it afterwards was healed).c

5One of the men lying there had been sick for thirty-eight years. 6When Jesus saw him and knew how long he had been ill, he asked him, "Would you like to get well?"

7"I can't," the sick man said, "for I have no one to help me into the pool at the movement of the water. While I am trying to get there, someone else always gets in ahead of me."

8Jesus told him, "Stand up, roll up your sleeping mat and go on home!"

9Instantly, the man was healed! He rolled up the mat and began walking!

But it was on the Sabbath when this miracle was done. 10So the Jewish leaders objected. They said to the man who was cured, "You can't work on the Sabbath! It's illegal to carry that sleeping mat!"

11"The man who healed me told me to," was his reply.

12"Who said such a thing as that?" they demanded.

13The man didn't know, and Jesus had disappeared into the crowd. 14But afterwards Jesus found him in the Temple and told him, "Now you are well; don't sin as you did before,d or something even worse may happen to you."

15Then the man went to find the Jewish leaders and told them it was Jesus who had healed him.

16So they began harassing Jesus as a Sabbath breaker.

17But Jesus replied, "My Father constantly does good,e and I'm following his example."

18Then the Jewish leaders were all the more eager to kill him because in addition to disobeying their Sabbath laws, he had spoken of God as his Father, thereby making himself equal to God.

19Jesus replied, "The Son can do nothing by himself. He does only what he sees the Father doing, and in the same way. 20For the Father loves the Son, and tells him everything he is doing; and the Son will do far more awesome miracles than this man's healing. 21He will

New Revised Standard

your son will live." The man believed the word that Jesus spoke to him and started on his way. 51As he was going down, his slaves met him and told him that his child was alive. 52So he asked them the hour when he began to recover, and they said to him, "Yesterday at one in the afternoon the fever left him." 53The father realized that this was the hour when Jesus had said to him, "Your son will live." So he himself believed, along with his whole household. 54Now this was the second sign that Jesus did after coming from Judea to Galilee.

Jesus Heals on the Sabbath

5 AFTER THIS there was a festival of the Jews, and Jesus went up to Jerusalem.

2 Now in Jerusalem by the Sheep Gate there is a pool, called in Hebrewf Beth-zatha,g which has five porticoes. 3In these lay many invalids—blind, lame, and paralyzed.h 5One man was there who had been ill for thirty-eight years. 6When Jesus saw him lying there and knew that he had been there a long time, he said to him, "Do you want to be made well?" 7The sick man answered him, "Sir, I have no one to put me into the pool when the water is stirred up; and while I am making my way, someone else steps down ahead of me." 8Jesus said to him, "Stand up, take your mat and walk." 9At once the man was made well, and he took up his mat and began to walk.

Now that day was a sabbath. 10So the Jews said to the man who had been cured, "It is the sabbath; it is not lawful for you to carry your mat." 11But he answered them, "The man who made me well said to me, 'Take up your mat and walk.' " 12They asked him, "Who is the man who said to you, 'Take it up and walk'?" 13Now the man who had been healed did not know who it was, for Jesus had disappeared ini the crowd that was there. 14Later Jesus found him in the temple and said to him, "See, you have been made well! Do not sin any more, so that nothing worse happens to you." 15The man went away and told the Jews that it was Jesus who had made him well. 16Therefore the Jews started persecuting Jesus, because he was doing such things on the sabbath. 17But Jesus answered them, "My Father is still working, and I also am working." 18For this reason the Jews were seeking all the more to kill him, because he was not only breaking the sabbath, but was also calling God his own Father, thereby making himself equal to God.

The Authority of the Son

19 Jesus said to them, "Very truly, I tell you, the Son can do nothing on his own, but only what he sees the Father doing; for whatever the Fatheri does, the Son does likewise. 20The Father loves the Son and shows him all that he himself is doing; and he will show him greater works than these, so that you will be astonished.

---

c 5:3b, 4 Many of the ancient manuscripts omit the material within the parentheses. d 5:14 "don't sin as you did before," implied. Literally, "sin no more." e 5:17 "My Father constantly does good," implied. Literally, "My Father works even until now, and I work."

f That is, Aramaic g Other ancient authorities read Bethesda, others Bethsaida h Other ancient authorities add, wholly or in part, waiting for the stirring of the water; 4for an angel of the Lord went down at certain seasons into the pool, and stirred up the water; whoever stepped in first after the stirring of the water was made well from whatever disease that person had. i Or had left because of j Gk that one

King James

21For as the Father raiseth up the dead, and quickeneth *them;* even so the Son quickeneth whom he will.

22For the Father judgeth no man, but hath committed all judgment unto the Son:

23That all *men* should honour the Son, even as they honour the Father. He that honoureth not the Son honoureth not the Father which hath sent him.

24Verily, verily, I say unto you, He that heareth my word, and believeth on him that sent me, hath everlasting life, and shall not come into condemnation; but is passed from death unto life.

25Verily, verily, I say unto you, The hour is coming, and now is, when the dead shall hear the voice of the Son of God: and they that hear shall live.

26For as the Father hath life in himself; so hath he given to the Son to have life in himself;

27And hath given him authority to execute judgment also, because he is the Son of man.

28Marvel not at this: for the hour is coming, in the which all that are in the graves shall hear his voice,

29And shall come forth; they that have done good, unto the resurrection of life; and they that have done evil, unto the resurrection of damnation.

30I can of mine own self do nothing: as I hear, I judge: and my judgment is just; because I seek not mine own will, but the will of the Father which hath sent me.

31If I bear witness of myself, my witness is not true.

32¶ There is another that beareth witness of me; and I know that the witness which he witnesseth of me is true.

33Ye sent unto John, and he bare witness unto the truth.

34But I receive not testimony from man: but these things I say, that ye might be saved.

35He was a burning and a shining light: and ye were willing for a season to rejoice in his light.

36¶ But I have greater witness than *that* of John: for the works which the Father hath given me to finish, the same works that I do, bear witness of me, that the Father hath sent me.

37And the Father himself, which hath sent me, hath borne witness of me. Ye have neither heard his voice at any time, nor seen his shape.

38And ye have not his word abiding in you: for whom he hath sent, him ye believe not.

39¶ Search the scriptures; for in them ye think ye have eternal life: and they are they which testify of me.

40And ye will not come to me, that ye might have life.

41I receive not honour from men.

42But I know you, that ye have not the love of God in you.

43I am come in my Father's name, and ye receive me not: if another shall come in his own name, him ye will receive.

44How can ye believe, which receive honour one of another, and seek not the honour that *cometh* from God only?

45Do not think that I will accuse you to the Father: there is *one* that accuseth you, *even* Moses, in whom ye trust.

46For had ye believed Moses, ye would have believed me: for he wrote of me.

47But if ye believe not his writings, how shall ye believe my words?

New International

as the Father raises the dead and gives them life, even so the Son gives life to whom he is pleased to give it. 22Moreover, the Father judges no one, but has entrusted all judgment to the Son, 23that all may honor the Son just as they honor the Father. He who does not honor the Son does not honor the Father, who sent him.

24"I tell you the truth, whoever hears my word and believes him who sent me has eternal life and will not be condemned; he has crossed over from death to life. 25I tell you the truth, a time is coming and has now come when the dead will hear the voice of the Son of God and those who hear will live. 26For as the Father has life in himself, so he has granted the Son to have life in himself. 27And he has given him authority to judge because he is the Son of Man.

28"Do not be amazed at this, for a time is coming when all who are in their graves will hear his voice 29and come out—those who have done good will rise to live, and those who have done evil will rise to be condemned. 30By myself I can do nothing; I judge only as I hear, and my judgment is just, for I seek not to please myself but him who sent me.

Testimonies About Jesus

31"If I testify about myself, my testimony is not valid. 32There is another who testifies in my favor, and I know that his testimony about me is valid.

33"You have sent to John and he has testified to the truth. 34Not that I accept human testimony; but I mention it that you may be saved. 35John was a lamp that burned and gave light, and you chose for a time to enjoy his light.

36"I have testimony weightier than that of John. For the very work that the Father has given me to finish, and which I am doing, testifies that the Father has sent me. 37And the Father who sent me has himself testified concerning me. You have never heard his voice nor seen his form, 38nor does his word dwell in you, for you do not believe the one he sent. 39You diligently study[a] the Scriptures because you think that by them you possess eternal life. These are the Scriptures that testify about me, 40yet you refuse to come to me to have life.

41"I do not accept praise from men, 42but I know you. I know that you do not have the love of God in your hearts. 43I have come in my Father's name, and you do not accept me; but if someone else comes in his own name, you will accept him. 44How can you believe if you accept praise from one another, yet make no effort to obtain the praise that comes from the only God[b]?

45"But do not think I will accuse you before the Father. Your accuser is Moses, on whom your hopes are set. 46If you believed Moses, you would believe me, for he wrote about me. 47But since you do not believe what he wrote, how are you going to believe what I say?"

a 39 Or *Study diligently* (the imperative)　b 44 Some early manuscripts *the Only One*

Living Bible

even raise from the dead anyone he wants to, just as the Father does. 22And the Father leaves all judgment of sin to his Son, 23so that everyone will honor the Son, just as they honor the Father. But if you refuse to honor God's Son, whom he sent to you, then you are certainly not honoring the Father.

24"I say emphatically that anyone who listens to my message and believes in God who sent me has eternal life, and will never be damned for his sins, but has already passed out of death into life.

25"And I solemnly declare that the time is coming, in fact, it is here, when the dead shall hear my voice—the voice of the Son of God—and those who listen shall live. 26The Father has life in himself, and has granted his Son to have life in himself, 27and to judge the sins of all mankind because he is the Son of Man. 28Don't be so surprised! Indeed the time is coming when all the dead in their graves shall hear the voice of God's Son, 29and shall rise again—those who have done good, to eternal life; and those who have continued in evil, to judgment.

30"But I pass no judgment without consulting the Father. I judge as I am told. And my judgment is absolutely fair and just, for it is according to the will of God who sent me and is not merely my own.

31"When I make claims about myself they aren't believed, 32, 33but someone else, yes, John the Baptist,c is making these claims for me too. You have gone out to listen to his preaching, and I can assure you that all he says about me is true! 34But the truest witness I have is not from a man, though I have reminded you about John's witness so that you will believe in me and be saved. 35John shone brightly for a while, and you benefited and rejoiced, 36but I have a greater witness than John. I refer to the miracles I do; these have been assigned me by the Father, and they prove that the Father has sent me. 37And the Father himself has also testified about me, though not appearing to you personally, or speaking to you directly. 38But you are not listening to him, for you refuse to believe me—the one sent to you with God's message.

39"You search the Scriptures, for you believe they give you eternal life. And the Scriptures point to me! 40Yet you won't come to me so that I can give you this life eternal!

41, 42"Your approval or disapproval means nothing to me, for as I know so well, you don't have God's love within you. 43I know, because I have come to you representing my Father and you refuse to welcome me, though you readily enough receive those who aren't sent from him, but represent only themselves! 44No wonder you can't believe! For you gladly honor each other, but you don't care about the honor that comes from the only God!

45"Yet it is not I who will accuse you of this to the Father—Moses will! Moses, on whose laws you set your hopes of heaven. 46For you have refused to believe Moses. He wrote about me, but you refuse to believe him, so you refuse to believe in me. 47And since you don't believe what he wrote, no wonder you don't believe me either."

New Revised Standard

21Indeed, just as the Father raises the dead and gives them life, so also the Son gives life to whomever he wishes. 22The Father judges no one but has given all judgment to the Son, 23so that all may honor the Son just as they honor the Father. Anyone who does not honor the Son does not honor the Father who sent him. 24Very truly, I tell you, anyone who hears my word and believes him who sent me has eternal life, and does not come under judgment, but has passed from death to life.

25 "Very truly, I tell you, the hour is coming, and is now here, when the dead will hear the voice of the Son of God, and those who hear will live. 26For just as the Father has life in himself, so he has granted the Son also to have life in himself; 27and he has given him authority to execute judgment, because he is the Son of Man. 28Do not be astonished at this; for the hour is coming when all who are in their graves will hear his voice 29and will come out—those who have done good, to the resurrection of life, and those who have done evil, to the resurrection of condemnation.

Witnesses to Jesus

30 "I can do nothing on my own. As I hear, I judge; and my judgment is just, because I seek to do not my own will but the will of him who sent me.

31 "If I testify about myself, my testimony is not true. 32There is another who testifies on my behalf, and I know that his testimony to me is true. 33You sent messengers to John, and he testified to the truth. 34Not that I accept such human testimony, but I say these things so that you may be saved. 35He was a burning and shining lamp, and you were willing to rejoice for a while in his light. 36But I have a testimony greater than John's. The works that the Father has given me to complete, the very works that I am doing, testify on my behalf that the Father has sent me. 37And the Father who sent me has himself testified on my behalf. You have never heard his voice or seen his form, 38and you do not have his word abiding in you, because you do not believe him whom he has sent.

39 "You search the scriptures because you think that in them you have eternal life; and it is they that testify on my behalf. 40Yet you refuse to come to me to have life. 41I do not accept glory from human beings. 42But I know that you do not have the love of God ind you. 43I have come in my Father's name, and you do not accept me; if another comes in his own name, you will accept him. 44How can you believe when you accept glory from one another and do not seek the glory that comes from the one who alone is God? 45Do not think that I will accuse you before the Father; your accuser is Moses, on whom you have set your hope. 46If you believed Moses, you would believe me, for he wrote about me. 47But if you do not believe what he wrote, how will you believe what I say?"

---

c 5:32, 33 *John the Baptist*, implied. However, most commentators believe the reference is to the witness of his Father. See vs 37.

d Or *among*

King James

6 AFTER THESE things Jesus went over the sea of Galilee, which is *the sea* of Tiberias.

2And a great multitude followed him, because they saw his miracles which he did on them that were diseased.

3And Jesus went up into a mountain, and there he sat with his disciples.

4And the passover, a feast of the Jews, was nigh.

5¶ When Jesus then lifted up *his* eyes, and saw a great company come unto him, he saith unto Philip, Whence shall we buy bread, that these may eat?

6And this he said to prove him: for he himself knew what he would do.

7Philip answered him, Two hundred pennyworth of bread is not sufficient for them, that every one of them may take a little.

8One of his disciples, Andrew, Simon Peter's brother, saith unto him,

9There is a lad here, which hath five barley loaves, and two small fishes: but what are they among so many?

10And Jesus said, Make the men sit down. Now there was much grass in the place. So the men sat down, in number about five thousand.

11And Jesus took the loaves; and when he had given thanks, he distributed to the disciples, and the disciples to them that were set down; and likewise of the fishes as much as they would.

12When they were filled, he said unto his disciples, Gather up the fragments that remain, that nothing be lost.

13Therefore they gathered *them* together, and filled twelve baskets with the fragments of the five barley loaves, which remained over and above unto them that had eaten.

14Then those men, when they had seen the miracle that Jesus did, said, This is of a truth that prophet that should come into the world.

15¶ When Jesus therefore perceived that they would come and take him by force, to make him a king, he departed again into a mountain himself alone.

16And when even was *now* come, his disciples went down unto the sea,

17And entered into a ship, and went over the sea toward Capernaum. And it was now dark, and Jesus was not come to them.

18And the sea arose by reason of a great wind that blew.

19So when they had rowed about five and twenty or thirty furlongs, they see Jesus walking on the sea, and drawing nigh unto the ship: and they were afraid.

20But he saith unto them, It is I; be not afraid.

21Then they willingly received him into the ship: and immediately the ship was at the land whither they went.

22¶ The day following, when the people which stood on the other side of the sea saw that there was none other boat there, save that one whereinto his disciples were entered, and that Jesus went not with his disciples into the boat, but *that* his disciples were gone away alone;

23(Howbeit there came other boats from Tiberias nigh unto the place where they did eat bread, after that the Lord had given thanks:)

24When the people therefore saw that Jesus was not there, neither his disciples, they also took shipping, and came to Capernaum, seeking for Jesus.

25And when they had found him on the other side of the sea, they said unto him, Rabbi, when camest thou hither?

26Jesus answered them and said, Verily, verily, I say unto you, Ye seek me, not because ye saw the miracles, but because ye did eat of the loaves, and were filled.

New International

Jesus Feeds the Five Thousand

6 SOME TIME after this, Jesus crossed to the far shore of the Sea of Galilee (that is, the Sea of Tiberias), 2and a great crowd of people followed him because they saw the miraculous signs he had performed on the sick. 3Then Jesus went up on a mountainside and sat down with his disciples. 4The Jewish Passover Feast was near.

5When Jesus looked up and saw a great crowd coming toward him, he said to Philip, "Where shall we buy bread for these people to eat?" 6He asked this only to test him, for he already had in mind what he was going to do.

7Philip answered him, "Eight months' wages[a] would not buy enough bread for each one to have a bite!"

8Another of his disciples, Andrew, Simon Peter's brother, spoke up, 9"Here is a boy with five small barley loaves and two small fish, but how far will they go among so many?"

10Jesus said, "Have the people sit down." There was plenty of grass in that place, and the men sat down, about five thousand of them. 11Jesus then took the loaves, gave thanks, and distributed to those who were seated as much as they wanted. He did the same with the fish.

12When they had all had enough to eat, he said to his disciples, "Gather the pieces that are left over. Let nothing be wasted." 13So they gathered them and filled twelve baskets with the pieces of the five barley loaves left over by those who had eaten.

14After the people saw the miraculous sign that Jesus did, they began to say, "Surely this is the Prophet who is to come into the world." 15Jesus, knowing that they intended to come and make him king by force, withdrew again to a mountain by himself.

Jesus Walks on the Water

16When evening came, his disciples went down to the lake, 17where they got into a boat and set off across the lake for Capernaum. By now it was dark, and Jesus had not yet joined them. 18A strong wind was blowing and the waters grew rough. 19When they had rowed three or three and a half miles,[b] they saw Jesus approaching the boat, walking on the water; and they were terrified. 20But he said to them, "It is I; don't be afraid." 21Then they were willing to take him into the boat, and immediately the boat reached the shore where they were heading.

22The next day the crowd that had stayed on the opposite shore of the lake realized that only one boat had been there, and that Jesus had not entered it with his disciples, but that they had gone away alone. 23Then some boats from Tiberias landed near the place where the people had eaten the bread after the Lord had given thanks. 24Once the crowd realized that neither Jesus nor his disciples were there, they got into the boats and went to Capernaum in search of Jesus.

Jesus the Bread of Life

25When they found him on the other side of the lake, they asked him, "Rabbi, when did you get here?"

26Jesus answered, "I tell you the truth, you are looking for me, not because you saw miraculous signs but because you ate the loaves and had your fill. 27Do not

Living Bible

6 AFTER THIS, Jesus crossed over the Sea of Galilee, also known as the Sea of Tiberias. 2–5And a huge crowd, many of them pilgrims on their way to Jerusalem for the annual Passover celebration,c were following him wherever he went, to watch him heal the sick. So when Jesus went up into the hills and sat down with his disciples around him, he soon saw a great multitude of people climbing the hill, looking for him.

Turning to Philip he asked, "Philip, where can we buy bread to feed all these people?" 6(He was testing Philip, for he already knew what he was going to do.) 7Philip replied, "It would take a fortuned to begin to do it!"

8, 9Then Andrew, Simon Peter's brother, spoke up. "There's a youngster here with five barley loaves and a couple of fish! But what good is that with all this mob?"

10"Tell everyone to sit down," Jesus ordered. And all of them—the approximate count of the men only was 5,000—sat down on the grassy slopes. 11Then Jesus took the loaves and gave thanks to God and passed them out to the people. Afterwards he did the same with the fish. And everyone ate until full!

12"Now gather the scraps," Jesus told his disciples, "so that nothing is wasted." 13And twelve baskets were filled with the leftovers!

14When the people realized what a great miracle had happened, they exclaimed, "Surely, he is the Prophet we have been expecting!"

15Jesus saw that they were ready to take him by force and make him their king, so he went higher into the mountains alone.

16That evening his disciples went down to the shore to wait for him. 17But as darkness fell and Jesus still hadn't come back, they got into the boat and headed out across the lake toward Capernaum. 18, 19But soon a gale swept down upon them as they rowed, and the sea grew very rough. They were three or four miles out when suddenly they saw Jesus walking toward the boat! They were terrified, 20but he called out to them and told them not to be afraid. 21Then they were willing to let him in, and immediately the boat was where they were going!e

22, 23The next morning, back across the lake, crowds began gathering on the shore [waiting to see Jesusf]. For they knew that he and his disciples had come over together and that the disciples had gone off in their boat, leaving him behind. Several small boats from Tiberias were nearby, 24so when the people saw that Jesus wasn't there, nor his disciples, they got into the boats and went across to Capernaum to look for him.

25When they arrived and found him, they said, "Sir, how did you get here?" 26Jesus replied, "The truth of the matter is that you want to be with me because I fed you, not because you believe in me. 27But you shouldn't be

New Revised Standard

Feeding the Five Thousand

6 AFTER THIS Jesus went to the other side of the Sea of Galilee, also called the Sea of Tiberias.g 2A large crowd kept following him, because they saw the signs that he was doing for the sick. 3Jesus went up the mountain and sat down there with his disciples. 4Now the Passover, the festival of the Jews, was near. 5When he looked up and saw a large crowd coming toward him, Jesus said to Philip, "Where are we to buy bread for these people to eat?" 6He said this to test him, for he himself knew what he was going to do. 7Philip answered him, "Six months' wagesh would not buy enough bread for each of them to get a little." 8One of his disciples, Andrew, Simon Peter's brother, said to him, 9"There is a boy here who has five barley loaves and two fish. But what are they among so many people?" 10Jesus said, "Make the people sit down." Now there was a great deal of grass in the place; so theyi sat down, about five thousand in all. 11Then Jesus took the loaves, and when he had given thanks, he distributed them to those who were seated; so also the fish, as much as they wanted. 12When they were satisfied, he told his disciples, "Gather up the fragments left over, so that nothing may be lost." 13So they gathered them up, and from the fragments of the five barley loaves, left by those who had eaten, they filled twelve baskets. 14When the people saw the sign that he had done, they began to say, "This is indeed the prophet who is to come into the world."

15 When Jesus realized that they were about to come and take him by force to make him king, he withdrew again to the mountain by himself.

Jesus Walks on the Water

16 When evening came, his disciples went down to the sea, 17got into a boat, and started across the sea to Capernaum. It was now dark, and Jesus had not yet come to them. 18The sea became rough because a strong wind was blowing. 19When they had rowed about three or four miles,j they saw Jesus walking on the sea and coming near the boat, and they were terrified. 20But he said to them, "It is I;k do not be afraid." 21Then they wanted to take him into the boat, and immediately the boat reached the land toward which they were going.

The Bread from Heaven

22 The next day the crowd that had stayed on the other side of the sea saw that there had been only one boat there. They also saw that Jesus had not got into the boat with his disciples, but that his disciples had gone away alone. 23Then some boats from Tiberias came near the place where they had eaten the bread after the Lord had given thanks.l 24So when the crowd saw that neither Jesus nor his disciples were there, they themselves got into the boats and went to Capernaum looking for Jesus.

25 When they found him on the other side of the sea, they said to him, "Rabbi, when did you come here?" 26Jesus answered them, "Very truly, I tell you, you are looking for me, not because you saw signs, but because you ate your fill of the loaves. 27Do not work for the

---

c 6:2-5 *annual Passover celebration*, literally, "Now the Passover, the feast of the Jews, was at hand." d 6:7 *take a fortune*, literally, 200 denarii, a denarius being a full day's wage. e 6:21 *immediately the boat was where they were going*, literally, "and straightway the boat was at the land." f 6:22, 23 *waiting to see Jesus*, implied.

g Gk *of Galilee of Tiberius* h Gk *Two hundred denarii*; the denarius was the usual day's wage for a laborer i Gk *the men* j Gk *about twenty-five or thirty stadia* k Gk *I am* l Other ancient authorities lack *after the Lord had given thanks*

King James

27Labour not for the meat which perisheth, but for that meat which endureth unto everlasting life, which the Son of man shall give unto you: for him hath God the Father sealed.

28Then said they unto him, What shall we do, that we might work the works of God?

29Jesus answered and said unto them, This is the work of God, that ye believe on him whom he hath sent.

30They said therefore unto him, What sign showest thou then, that we may see, and believe thee? what dost thou work?

31Our fathers did eat manna in the desert; as it is written, He gave them bread from heaven to eat.

32Then Jesus said unto them, Verily, verily, I say unto you, Moses gave you not that bread from heaven; but my Father giveth you the true bread from heaven.

33For the bread of God is he which cometh down from heaven, and giveth life unto the world.

34Then said they unto him, Lord, evermore give us this bread.

35And Jesus said unto them, I am the bread of life: he that cometh to me shall never hunger; and he that believeth on me shall never thirst.

36But I said unto you, That ye also have seen me, and believe not.

37All that the Father giveth me shall come to me; and him that cometh to me I will in no wise cast out.

38For I came down from heaven, not to do mine own will, but the will of him that sent me.

39And this is the Father's will which hath sent me, that of all which he hath given me I should lose nothing, but should raise it up again at the last day.

40And this is the will of him that sent me, that every one which seeth the Son, and believeth on him, may have everlasting life: and I will raise him up at the last day.

41The Jews then murmured at him, because he said, I am the bread which came down from heaven.

42And they said, Is not this Jesus, the son of Joseph, whose father and mother we know? how is it then that he saith, I came down from heaven?

43Jesus therefore answered and said unto them, Murmur not among yourselves.

44No man can come to me, except the Father which hath sent me draw him: and I will raise him up at the last day.

45It is written in the prophets, And they shall be all taught of God. Every man therefore that hath heard, and hath learned of the Father, cometh unto me.

46Not that any man hath seen the Father, save he which is of God, he hath seen the Father.

47Verily, verily, I say unto you, He that believeth on me hath everlasting life.

48I am that bread of life.

49Your fathers did eat manna in the wilderness, and are dead.

50This is the bread which cometh down from heaven, that a man may eat thereof, and not die.

51I am the living bread which came down from heaven: if any man eat of this bread, he shall live for ever: and the bread that I will give is my flesh, which I will give for the life of the world.

52The Jews therefore strove among themselves, saying, How can this man give us *his* flesh to eat?

53Then Jesus said unto them, Verily, verily, I say unto you, Except ye eat the flesh of the Son of man, and drink his blood, ye have no life in you.

54Whoso eateth my flesh, and drinketh my blood, hath eternal life; and I will raise him up at the last day.

55For my flesh is meat indeed, and my blood is drink indeed.

56He that eateth my flesh, and drinketh my blood, dwelleth in me, and I in him.

57As the living Father hath sent me, and I live by the Father: so he that eateth me, even he shall live by me.

New International

work for food that spoils, but for food that endures to eternal life, which the Son of Man will give you. On him God the Father has placed his seal of approval."

28Then they asked him, "What must we do to do the works God requires?"

29Jesus answered, "The work of God is this: to believe in the one he has sent."

30So they asked him, "What miraculous sign then will you give that we may see it and believe you? What will you do? 31Our forefathers ate the manna in the desert; as it is written: 'He gave them bread from heaven to eat.'a"

32Jesus said to them, "I tell you the truth, it is not Moses who has given you the bread from heaven, but it is my Father who gives you the true bread from heaven. 33For the bread of God is he who comes down from heaven and gives life to the world."

34"Sir," they said, "from now on give us this bread."

35Then Jesus declared, "I am the bread of life. He who comes to me will never go hungry, and he who believes in me will never be thirsty. 36But as I told you, you have seen me and still you do not believe. 37All that the Father gives me will come to me, and whoever comes to me I will never drive away. 38For I have come down from heaven not to do my will but to do the will of him who sent me. 39And this is the will of him who sent me, that I shall lose none of all that he has given me, but raise them up at the last day. 40For my Father's will is that everyone who looks to the Son and believes in him shall have eternal life, and I will raise him up at the last day."

41At this the Jews began to grumble about him because he said, "I am the bread that came down from heaven." 42They said, "Is this not Jesus, the son of Joseph, whose father and mother we know? How can he now say, 'I came down from heaven'?"

43"Stop grumbling among yourselves," Jesus answered. 44"No one can come to me unless the Father who sent me draws him, and I will raise him up at the last day. 45It is written in the Prophets: 'They will all be taught by God.'b Everyone who listens to the Father and learns from him comes to me. 46No one has seen the Father except the one who is from God; only he has seen the Father. 47I tell you the truth, he who believes has everlasting life. 48I am the bread of life. 49Your forefathers ate the manna in the desert, yet they died. 50But here is the bread that comes down from heaven, which a man may eat and not die. 51I am the living bread that came down from heaven. If anyone eats of this bread, he will live forever. This bread is my flesh, which I will give for the life of the world."

52Then the Jews began to argue sharply among themselves, "How can this man give us his flesh to eat?"

53Jesus said to them, "I tell you the truth, unless you eat the flesh of the Son of Man and drink his blood, you have no life in you. 54Whoever eats my flesh and drinks my blood has eternal life, and I will raise him up at the last day. 55For my flesh is real food and my blood is real drink. 56Whoever eats my flesh and drinks my blood remains in me, and I in him. 57Just as the living Father sent me and I live because of the Father, so the one who feeds on me will live because of me. 58This is the bread

a *31* Exodus 16:4; Neh. 9:15; Psalm 78:24,25   b *45* Isaiah 54:13

Living Bible

so concerned about perishable things like food. No, spend your energy seeking the eternal life that I, the Messiah,c can give you. For God the Father has sent me for this very purpose."

28They replied, "What should we do to satisfy God?"

29Jesus told them, "This is the will of God, that you believe in the one he has sent."

30, 31They replied, "You must show us more miracles if you want us to believe you are the Messiah. Give us free bread every day, like our fathers had while they journeyed through the wilderness! As the Scriptures say, 'Moses gave them bread from heaven.'"

32Jesus said, "Moses didn't give it to them. My Father did.d And now he offers you true Bread from heaven. 33The true Bread is a Person—the one sent by God from heaven, and he gives life to the world."

34"Sir," they said, "give us that bread every day of our lives!"

35Jesus replied, "I am the Bread of Life. No one coming to me will ever be hungry again. Those believing in me will never thirst. 36But the trouble is, as I have told you before, you haven't believed even though you have seen me. 37But some will come to me—those the Father has given me—and I will never, never reject them. 38For I have come here from heaven to do the will of God who sent me, not to have my own way. 39And this is the will of God, that I should not lose even one of all those he has given me, but that I should raise them to eternal life at the Last Day. 40For it is my Father's will that everyone who sees his Son and believes on him should have eternal life—that I should raise him at the Last Day."

41Then the Jews began to murmur against him because he claimed to be the Bread from heaven.

42"What?" they exclaimed. "Why, he is merely Jesus the son of Joseph, whose father and mother we know. What is this he is saying, that he came down from heaven?"

43But Jesus replied, "Don't murmur among yourselves about my saying that. 44For no one can come to me unless the Father who sent me draws him to me, and at the Last Day I will cause all such to rise again from the dead. 45As it is written in the Scriptures, 'They shall all be taught of God.' Those the Father speaks to, who learn the truth from him, will be attracted to me. 46(Not that anyone actually sees the Father, for only I have seen him.)

47"How earnestly I tell you this—anyone who believes in me already has eternal life! 48-51Yes, I am the Bread of Life! When your fathers in the wilderness ate bread from the skies, they all died. But the Bread from heaven gives eternal life to everyone who eats it. I am that Living Bread that came down out of heaven. Anyone eating this Bread shall live forever; this Bread is my flesh given to redeem humanity."

52Then the Jews began arguing with each other about what he meant. "How can this man give us his flesh to eat?" they asked.

53So Jesus said it again, "With all the earnestness I possess I tell you this: Unless you eat the flesh of the Messiah and drink his blood, you cannot have eternal life within you. 54But anyone who does eat my flesh and drink my blood has eternal life, and I will raise him at the Last Day. 55For my flesh is the true food, and my blood is the true drink. 56Everyone who eats my flesh and drinks my blood is in me, and I in him. 57I live by the power of the living Father who sent me, and in the same way those who partake of me shall live because of me! 58I am the true Bread from heaven; and anyone who

New Revised Standard

food that perishes, but for the food that endures for eternal life, which the Son of Man will give you. For it is on him that God the Father has set his seal." 28Then they said to him, "What must we do to perform the works of God?" 29Jesus answered them, "This is the work of God, that you believe in him whom he has sent." 30So they said to him, "What sign are you going to give us then, so that we may see it and believe you? What work are you performing? 31Our ancestors ate the manna in the wilderness; as it is written, 'He gave them bread from heaven to eat.'" 32Then Jesus said to them, "Very truly, I tell you, it was not Moses who gave you the bread from heaven, but it is my Father who gives you the true bread from heaven. 33For the bread of God is that whiche comes down from heaven and gives life to the world." 34They said to him, "Sir, give us this bread always."

35 Jesus said to them, "I am the bread of life. Whoever comes to me will never be hungry, and whoever believes in me will never be thirsty. 36But I said to you that you have seen me and yet do not believe. 37Everything that the Father gives me will come to me, and anyone who comes to me I will never drive away; 38for I have come down from heaven, not to do my own will, but the will of him who sent me. 39And this is the will of him who sent me, that I should lose nothing of all that he has given me, but raise it up on the last day. 40This is indeed the will of my Father, that all who see the Son and believe in him may have eternal life; and I will raise them up on the last day."

41 Then the Jews began to complain about him because he said, "I am the bread that came down from heaven." 42They were saying, "Is not this Jesus, the son of Joseph, whose father and mother we know? How can he now say, 'I have come down from heaven'?" 43Jesus answered them, "Do not complain among yourselves. 44No one can come to me unless drawn by the Father who sent me; and I will raise that person up on the last day. 45It is written in the prophets, 'And they shall all be taught by God.' Everyone who has heard and learned from the Father comes to me. 46Not that anyone has seen the Father except the one who is from God; he has seen the Father. 47Very truly, I tell you, whoever believes has eternal life. 48I am the bread of life. 49Your ancestors ate the manna in the wilderness, and they died. 50This is the bread that comes down from heaven, so that one may eat of it and not die. 51I am the living bread that came down from heaven. Whoever eats of this bread will live forever; and the bread that I will give for the life of the world is my flesh."

52 The Jews then disputed among themselves, saying, "How can this man give us his flesh to eat?" 53So Jesus said to them, "Very truly, I tell you, unless you eat the flesh of the Son of Man and drink his blood, you have no life in you. 54Those who eat my flesh and drink my blood have eternal life, and I will raise them up on the last day; 55for my flesh is true food and my blood is true drink. 56Those who eat my flesh and drink my blood abide in me, and I in them. 57Just as the living Father sent me, and I live because of the Father, so whoever eats me will live because of me. 58This is the

---

c 6:27 the Messiah, literally, "the Son of Man." So also in vss 53, 62.
d 6:32 My Father did, implied.

e Or he who

King James

58This is that bread which came down from heaven: not as your fathers did eat manna, and are dead: he that eateth of this bread shall live for ever.

59These things said he in the synagogue, as he taught in Capernaum.

60Many therefore of his disciples, when they had heard *this*, said, This is an hard saying; who can hear it?

61When Jesus knew in himself that his disciples murmured at it, he said unto them, Doth this offend you?

62*What* and if ye shall see the Son of man ascend up where he was before?

63It is the spirit that quickeneth; the flesh profiteth nothing: the words that I speak unto you, *they* are spirit, and *they* are life.

64But there are some of you that believe not. For Jesus knew from the beginning who they were that believed not, and who should betray him.

65And he said, Therefore said I unto you, that no man can come unto me, except it were given unto him of my Father.

66¶ From that *time* many of his disciples went back, and walked no more with him.

67Then said Jesus unto the twelve, Will ye also go away?

68Then Simon Peter answered him, Lord, to whom shall we go? thou hast the words of eternal life.

69And we believe and are sure that thou art that Christ, the Son of the living God.

70Jesus answered them, Have not I chosen you twelve, and one of you is a devil?

71He spake of Judas Iscariot *the son* of Simon: for he it was that should betray him, being one of the twelve.

7 AFTER THESE things Jesus walked in Galilee: for he would not walk in Jewry, because the Jews sought to kill him.

2Now the Jews' feast of tabernacles was at hand.

3His brethren therefore said unto him, Depart hence, and go into Judaea, that thy disciples also may see the works that thou doest.

4For *there is* no man *that* doeth any thing in secret, and he himself seeketh to be known openly. If thou do these things, show thyself to the world.

5For neither did his brethren believe in him.

6Then Jesus said unto them, My time is not yet come: but your time is always ready.

7The world cannot hate you; but me it hateth, because I testify of it, that the works thereof are evil.

8Go ye up unto this feast: I go not up yet unto this feast; for my time is not yet full come.

9When he had said these words unto them, he abode *still* in Galilee.

10¶ But when his brethren were gone up, then went he also up unto the feast, not openly, but as it were in secret.

11Then the Jews sought him at the feast, and said, Where is he?

12And there was much murmuring among the people concerning him: for some said, He is a good man: others said, Nay; but he deceiveth the people.

13Howbeit no man spake openly of him for fear of the Jews.

14¶ Now about the midst of the feast Jesus went up into the temple, and taught.

15And the Jews marvelled, saying, How knoweth this man letters, having never learned?

16Jesus answered them, and said, My doctrine is not mine, but his that sent me.

New International

that came down from heaven. Your forefathers ate manna and died, but he who feeds on this bread will live forever." 59He said this while teaching in the synagogue in Capernaum.

Many Disciples Desert Jesus

60On hearing it, many of his disciples said, "This is a hard teaching. Who can accept it?"

61Aware that his disciples were grumbling about this, Jesus said to them, "Does this offend you? 62What if you see the Son of Man ascend to where he was before! 63The Spirit gives life; the flesh counts for nothing. The words I have spoken to you are spirit[a] and they are life. 64Yet there are some of you who do not believe." For Jesus had known from the beginning which of them did not believe and who would betray him. 65He went on to say, "This is why I told you that no one can come to me unless the Father has enabled him."

66From this time many of his disciples turned back and no longer followed him.

67"You do not want to leave too, do you?" Jesus asked the Twelve.

68Simon Peter answered him, "Lord, to whom shall we go? You have the words of eternal life. 69We believe and know that you are the Holy One of God."

70Then Jesus replied, "Have I not chosen you, the Twelve? Yet one of you is a devil!" 71(He meant Judas, the son of Simon Iscariot, who, though one of the Twelve, was later to betray him.)

Jesus Goes to the Feast of Tabernacles

7 AFTER THIS, Jesus went around in Galilee, purposely staying away from Judea because the Jews there were waiting to take his life. 2But when the Jewish Feast of Tabernacles was near, 3Jesus' brothers said to him, "You ought to leave here and go to Judea, so that your disciples may see the miracles you do. 4No one who wants to become a public figure acts in secret. Since you are doing these things, show yourself to the world." 5For even his own brothers did not believe in him.

6Therefore Jesus told them, "The right time for me has not yet come; for you any time is right. 7The world cannot hate you, but it hates me because I testify that what it does is evil. 8You go to the Feast. I am not yet[b] going up to this Feast, because for me the right time has not yet come." 9Having said this, he stayed in Galilee.

10However, after his brothers had left for the Feast, he went also, not publicly, but in secret. 11Now at the Feast the Jews were watching for him and asking, "Where is that man?"

12Among the crowds there was widespread whispering about him. Some said, "He is a good man."

Others replied, "No, he deceives the people." 13But no one would say anything publicly about him for fear of the Jews.

Jesus Teaches at the Feast

14Not until halfway through the Feast did Jesus go up to the temple courts and begin to teach. 15The Jews were amazed and asked, "How did this man get such learning without having studied?"

16Jesus answered, "My teaching is not my own. It comes from him who sent me. 17If anyone chooses to do

---

[a] 63 Or *Spirit*　　[b] 8 Some early manuscripts do not have *yet*.

Living Bible

eats this Bread shall live forever, and not die as your fathers did—though they ate bread from heaven." 59(He preached this sermon in the synagogue in Capernaum.)

60Even his disciples said, "This is very hard to understand. Who can tell what he means?"

61Jesus knew within himself that his disciples were complaining and said to them, "Does *this* offend you? 62Then what will you think if you see me, the Messiah,c return to heaven again? 63Only the Holy Spirit gives eternal life.d Those born only once, with physical birth,e will never receive this gift. But now I have told you how to get this true spiritual life. 64But some of you don't believe me." (For Jesus knew from the beginning who didn't believe and knew the one who would betray him.)

65And he remarked, "That is what I meant when I said that no one can come to me unless the Father attracts him to me."

66At this point many of his disciples turned away and deserted him.

67Then Jesus turned to the Twelve and asked, "Are you going too?"

68Simon Peter replied, "Master, to whom shall we go? You alone have the words that give eternal life, 69and we believe them and know you are the holy Son of God."

70Then Jesus said, "I chose the twelve of you, and one is a devil." 71He was speaking of Judas, son of Simon Iscariot, one of the Twelve, who would betray him.

7 AFTER THIS, Jesus went to Galilee, going from village to village, for he wanted to stay out of Judea where the Jewish leaders were plotting his death. 2But soon it was time for the Tabernacle Ceremonies, one of the annual Jewish holidays, 3and Jesus' brothers urged him to go to Judea for the celebration.

"Go where more people can see your miracles!" they scoffed. 4"You can't be famous when you hide like this! If you're so great, prove it to the world!" 5For even his brothers didn't believe in him.

6Jesus replied, "It is not the right time for me to go now. But you can go anytime and it will make no difference, 7for the world can't hate you; but it does hate me, because I accuse it of sin and evil. 8You go on, and I'll come laterf when it is the right time." 9So he remained in Galilee.

10But after his brothers had left for the celebration, then he went too, though secretly, staying out of the public eye. 11The Jewish leaders tried to find him at the celebration and kept asking if anyone had seen him. 12There was a lot of discussion about him among the crowds. Some said, "He's a wonderful man," while others said, "No, he's duping the public." 13But no one had the courage to speak out for him in public for fear of reprisals from the Jewish leaders.

14Then, midway through the festival, Jesus went up to the Temple and preached openly. 15The Jewish leaders were surprised when they heard him. "How can he know so much when he's never been to our schools?" they asked.

16So Jesus told them, "I'm not teaching you my own thoughts, but those of God who sent me. 17If any of you

New Revised Standard

bread that came down from heaven, not like that which your ancestors ate, and they died. But the one who eats this bread will live forever." 59He said these things while he was teaching in the synagogue at Capernaum.

The Words of Eternal Life

60 When many of his disciples heard it, they said, "This teaching is difficult; who can accept it?" 61But Jesus, being aware that his disciples were complaining about it, said to them, "Does this offend you? 62Then what if you were to see the Son of Man ascending to where he was before? 63It is the spirit that gives life; the flesh is useless. The words that I have spoken to you are spirit and life. 64But among you there are some who do not believe." For Jesus knew from the first who were the ones that did not believe, and who was the one that would betray him. 65And he said, "For this reason I have told you that no one can come to me unless it is granted by the Father."

66 Because of this many of his disciples turned back and no longer went about with him. 67So Jesus asked the twelve, "Do you also wish to go away?" 68Simon Peter answered him, "Lord, to whom can we go? You have the words of eternal life. 69We have come to believe and know that you are the Holy One of God."g 70Jesus answered them, "Did I not choose you, the twelve? Yet one of you is a devil." 71He was speaking of Judas son of Simon Iscariot,h for he, though one of the twelve, was going to betray him.

The Unbelief of Jesus' Brothers

7 AFTER THIS Jesus went about in Galilee. He did not wishi to go about in Judea because the Jews were looking for an opportunity to kill him. 2Now the Jewish festival of Boothsj was near. 3So his brothers said to him, "Leave here and go to Judea so that your disciples also may see the works you are doing; 4for no one wantsk to be widely known acts in secret. If you do these things, show yourself to the world." 5(For not even his brothers believed in him.) 6Jesus said to them, "My time has not yet come, but your time is always here. 7The world cannot hate you, but it hates me because I testify against it that its works are evil. 8Go to the festival yourselves. I am notl going to this festival, for my time has not yet fully come." 9After saying this, he remained in Galilee.

Jesus at the Festival of Booths

10 But after his brothers had gone to the festival, then he also went, not publicly but as it werem in secret. 11The Jews were looking for him at the festival and saying, "Where is he?" 12And there was considerable complaining about him among the crowds. While some were saying, "He is a good man," others were saying, "No, he is deceiving the crowd." 13Yet no one would speak openly about him for fear of the Jews.

14 About the middle of the festival Jesus went up into the temple and began to teach. 15The Jews were astonished at it, saying, "How does this man have such learning,n when he has never been taught?" 16Then Jesus answered them, "My teaching is not mine but his who sent me. 17Anyone who resolves to do the will of

---

c 6:62 *the Messiah*, literally, "the Son of Man."   d 6:63 *"Only the Holy Spirit gives eternal life,"* literally, "It is the Spirit who quickens."   e 6:63 *physical birth*, see 1:13. Literally, "the flesh profits nothing."   f 7:8 *I'll come later*, literally, "I go not up [yet] unto this feast." The word "yet" is included in the text of many ancient manuscripts.

g Other ancient authorities read *the Christ, the Son of the living God*   h Other ancient authorities read *Judas Iscariot son of Simon*; others, *Judas son of Simon from Karyot* (Kerioth)   i Other ancient authorities read *was not at liberty*   j Or *Tabernacles*   k Other ancient authorities read *wants it*   l Other ancient authorities add *yet*   m Other ancient authorities lack *as it were*   n Or *this man know his letters*

King James

17If any man will do his will, he shall know of the doctrine, whether it be of God, or *whether* I speak of myself.

18He that speaketh of himself seeketh his own glory: but he that seeketh his glory that sent him, the same is true, and no unrighteousness is in him.

19Did not Moses give you the law, and *yet* none of you keepeth the law? Why go ye about to kill me?

20The people answered and said, Thou hast a devil: who goeth about to kill thee?

21Jesus answered and said unto them, I have done one work, and ye all marvel.

22Moses therefore gave unto you circumcision; (not because it is of Moses, but of the fathers;) and ye on the sabbath day circumcise a man.

23If a man on the sabbath day receive circumcision, that the law of Moses should not be broken; are ye angry at me, because I have made a man every whit whole on the sabbath day?

24Judge not according to the appearance, but judge righteous judgment.

25Then said some of them of Jerusalem, Is not this he, whom they seek to kill?

26But, lo, he speaketh boldly, and they say nothing unto him. Do the rulers know indeed that this is the very Christ?

27Howbeit we know this man whence he is: but when Christ cometh, no man knoweth whence he is.

28Then cried Jesus in the temple as he taught, saying, Ye both know me, and ye know whence I am: and I am not come of myself, but he that sent me is true, whom ye know not.

29But I know him: for I am from him, and he hath sent me.

30Then they sought to take him: but no man laid hands on him, because his hour was not yet come.

31And many of the people believed on him, and said, When Christ cometh, will he do more miracles than these which this *man* hath done?

32¶ The Pharisees heard that the people murmured such things concerning him; and the Pharisees and the chief priests sent officers to take him.

33Then said Jesus unto them, Yet a little while am I with you, and *then* I go unto him that sent me.

34Ye shall seek me, and shall not find *me:* and where I am, *thither* ye cannot come.

35Then said the Jews among themselves, Whither will he go, that we shall not find him? will he go unto the dispersed among the Gentiles, and teach the Gentiles?

36What *manner of* saying is this that he said, Ye shall seek me, and shall not find *me:* and where I am, *thither* ye cannot come?

37In the last day, that great *day* of the feast, Jesus stood and cried, saying, If any man thirst, let him come unto me, and drink.

38He that believeth on me, as the scripture hath said, out of his belly shall flow rivers of living water.

39(But this spake he of the Spirit, which they that believe on him should receive: for the Holy Ghost was not yet *given;* because that Jesus was not yet glorified.)

40¶ Many of the people therefore, when they heard this saying, said, Of a truth this is the Prophet.

41Others said, This is the Christ. But some said, Shall Christ come out of Galilee?

42Hath not the scripture said, That Christ cometh of the seed of David, and out of the town of Bethlehem, where David was?

43So there was a division among the people because of him.

44And some of them would have taken him; but no man laid hands on him.

New International

God's will, he will find out whether my teaching comes from God or whether I speak on my own. 18He who speaks on his own does so to gain honor for himself, but he who works for the honor of the one who sent him is a man of truth; there is nothing false about him. 19Has not Moses given you the law? Yet not one of you keeps the law. Why are you trying to kill me?"

20"You are demon-possessed," the crowd answered. "Who is trying to kill you?"

21Jesus said to them, "I did one miracle, and you are all astonished. 22Yet, because Moses gave you circumcision (though actually it did not come from Moses, but from the patriarchs), you circumcise a child on the Sabbath. 23Now if a child can be circumcised on the Sabbath so that the law of Moses may not be broken, why are you angry with me for healing the whole man on the Sabbath? 24Stop judging by mere appearances, and make a right judgment."

Is Jesus the Christ?

25At that point some of the people of Jerusalem began to ask, "Isn't this the man they are trying to kill? 26Here he is, speaking publicly, and they are not saying a word to him. Have the authorities really concluded that he is the Christ[a]? 27But we know where this man is from; when the Christ comes, no one will know where he is from."

28Then Jesus, still teaching in the temple courts, cried out, "Yes, you know me, and you know where I am from. I am not here on my own, but he who sent me is true. You do not know him, 29but I know him because I am from him and he sent me."

30At this they tried to seize him, but no one laid a hand on him, because his time had not yet come. 31Still, many in the crowd put their faith in him. They said, "When the Christ comes, will he do more miraculous signs than this man?"

32The Pharisees heard the crowd whispering such things about him. Then the chief priests and the Pharisees sent temple guards to arrest him.

33Jesus said, "I am with you for only a short time, and then I go to the one who sent me. 34You will look for me, but you will not find me; and where I am, you cannot come."

35The Jews said to one another, "Where does this man intend to go that we cannot find him? Will he go where our people live scattered among the Greeks, and teach the Greeks? 36What did he mean when he said, 'You will look for me, but you will not find me,' and 'Where I am, you cannot come'?"

37On the last and greatest day of the Feast, Jesus stood and said in a loud voice, "If anyone is thirsty, let him come to me and drink. 38Whoever believes in me, as[b] the Scripture has said, streams of living water will flow from within him." 39By this he meant the Spirit, whom those who believed in him were later to receive. Up to that time the Spirit had not been given, since Jesus had not yet been glorified.

40On hearing his words, some of the people said, "Surely this man is the Prophet."

41Others said, "He is the Christ."

Still others asked, "How can the Christ come from Galilee? 42Does not the Scripture say that the Christ will come from David's family[c] and from Bethlehem, the town where David lived?" 43Thus the people were divided because of Jesus. 44Some wanted to seize him, but no one laid a hand on him.

a 26 Or *Messiah;* also in verses 27, 31, 41 and 42   b 37,38 Or / *If anyone is thirsty, let him come to me.* / *And let him drink,* 38*who believes in me.* / *As*   c 42 Greek *seed*

Living Bible

really determines to do God's will, then you will certainly know whether my teaching is from God or is merely my own. 18Anyone presenting his own ideas is looking for praise for himself, but anyone seeking to honor the one who sent him is a good and true person. 19None of *you* obeys the laws of Moses! So why pick on *me* for breaking them? Why kill *me* for this?"

20The crowd replied, "You're out of your mind! Who's trying to kill you?"

21, 22, 23Jesus replied, "I worked on the Sabbath by healing a man, and you were surprised. But you work on the Sabbath, too, whenever you obey Moses' law of circumcision (actually, however, this tradition of circumcision is older than the Mosaic law); for if the correct time for circumcising your children falls on the Sabbath, you go ahead and do it, as you should. So why should I be condemned for making a man completely well on the Sabbath? 24Think this through and you will see that I am right."

25Some of the people who lived there in Jerusalem said among themselves, "Isn't this the man they are trying to kill? 26But here he is preaching in public, and they say nothing to him. Can it be that our leaders have learned, after all, that he really is the Messiah? 27But how could he be? For we know where this man was born; when Christ comes, he will just appear and no one will know where he comes from."

28So Jesus, in a sermon in the Temple, called out, "Yes, you know me and where I was born and raised, but I am the representative of one you don't know, and he is Truth. 29I know him because I was with him, and he sent me to you."

30Then the Jewish leaders sought to arrest him; but no hand was laid on him, for God's time had not yet come.

31Many among the crowds at the Temple believed on him. "After all," they said, "what miracles do you expect the Messiah to do that this man hasn't done?"

32When the Pharisees heard that the crowds were in this mood, they and the chief priests sent officers to arrest Jesus. 33But Jesus told them, "[Not yet!d] I am to be here a little longer. Then I shall return to the one who sent me. 34You will search for me but not find me. And you won't be able to come where I am!"

35The Jewish leaders were puzzled by this statement. "Where is he planning to go?" they asked. "Maybe he is thinking of leaving the country and going as a missionary among the Jews in other lands, or maybe even to the Gentiles! 36What does he mean about our looking for him and not being able to find him, and, 'You won't be able to come where I am'?"

37On the last day, the climax of the holidays, Jesus shouted to the crowds, "If anyone is thirsty, let him come to me and drink. 38For the Scriptures declare that rivers of living water shall flow from the inmost being of anyone who believes in me." 39(He was speaking of the Holy Spirit, who would be given to everyone believing in him; but the Spirit had not yet been given, because Jesus had not yet returned to his glory in heaven.)

40When the crowds heard him say this, some of them declared, "This man surely is the prophet who will come just before the Messiah." 41, 42Others said, "He *is* the Messiah." Still others, "But he *can't* be! Will the Messiah come from *Galilee?* For the Scriptures clearly state that the Messiah will be born of the royal line of David, in *Bethlehem,* the village where David was born." 43So the crowd was divided about him. 44And some wanted him arrested, but no one touched him.

New Revised Standard

God will know whether the teaching is from God or whether I am speaking on my own. 18Those who speak on their own seek their own glory; but the one who seeks the glory of him who sent him is true, and there is nothing false in him.

19 "Did not Moses give you the law? Yet none of you keeps the law. Why are you looking for an opportunity to kill me?" 20The crowd answered, "You have a demon! Who is trying to kill you?" 21Jesus answered them, "I performed one work, and all of you are astonished. 22Moses gave you circumcision (it is, of course, not from Moses, but from the patriarchs), and you circumcise a man on the sabbath. 23If a man receives circumcision on the sabbath in order that the law of Moses may not be broken, are you angry with me because I healed a man's whole body on the sabbath? 24Do not judge by appearances, but judge with right judgment."

Is This the Christ?

25 Now some of the people of Jerusalem were saying, "Is not this the man whom they are trying to kill? 26And here he is, speaking openly, but they say nothing to him! Can it be that the authorities really know that this is the Messiah?e 27 Yet we know where this man is from; but when the Messiahe comes, no one will know where he is from." 28Then Jesus cried out as he was teaching in the temple, "You know me, and you know where I am from. I have not come on my own. But the one who sent me is true, and you do not know him. 29I know him, because I am from him, and he sent me." 30Then they tried to arrest him, but no one laid hands on him, because his hour had not yet come. 31Yet many in the crowd believed in him and were saying, "When the Messiahe comes, will he do more signs than this man has done?"f

Officers Are Sent to Arrest Jesus

32 The Pharisees heard the crowd muttering such things about him, and the chief priests and Pharisees sent temple police to arrest him. 33Jesus then said, "I will be with you a little longer, and then I am going to him who sent me. 34You will search for me, but you will not find me; and where I am, you cannot come." 35The Jews said to one another, "Where does this man intend to go that we will not find him? Does he intend to go to the Dispersion among the Greeks and teach the Greeks? 36What does he mean by saying, 'You will search for me and you will not find me' and 'Where I am, you cannot come'?"

Rivers of Living Water

37 On the last day of the festival, the great day, while Jesus was standing there, he cried out, "Let anyone who is thirsty come to me, 38and let the one who believes in me drink. Asg the scripture has said, 'Out of the believer's hearth shall flow rivers of living water.' " 39Now he said this about the Spirit, which believers in him were to receive; for as yet there was no Spirit,i because Jesus was not yet glorified.

Division among the People

40 When they heard these words, some in the crowd said, "This is really the prophet." 41Others said, "This is the Messiah."e But some asked, "Surely the Messiahe does not come from Galilee, does he? 42Has not the scripture said that the Messiahe is descended from David and comes from Bethlehem, the village where David lived?" 43So there was a division in the crowd because of him. 44Some of them wanted to arrest him, but no one laid hands on him.

---

e Or *the Christ*   f Other ancient authorities read *is doing*   g Or *come to me and drink.* 38*The one who believes in me, as*   h Gk *out of his belly*   i Other ancient authorities read *for as yet the Spirit* (others, *Holy Spirit*) *had not been given*

---

d 7:33 *Not yet,* implied.

King James

45¶ Then came the officers to the chief priests and Pharisees; and they said unto them, Why have ye not brought him?

46The officers answered, Never man spake like this man.

47Then answered them the Pharisees, Are ye also deceived?

48Have any of the rulers or of the Pharisees believed on him?

49But this people who knoweth not the law are cursed.

50Nicodemus saith unto them, (he that came to Jesus by night, being one of them,)

51Doth our law judge *any* man, before it hear him, and know what he doeth?

52They answered and said unto him, Art thou also of Galilee? Search, and look: for out of Galilee ariseth no prophet.

53And every man went unto his own house.

8 JESUS WENT unto the mount of Olives.
2And early in the morning he came again into the temple, and all the people came unto him; and he sat down, and taught them.

3And the scribes and Pharisees brought unto him a woman taken in adultery; and when they had set her in the midst,

4They say unto him, Master, this woman was taken in adultery, in the very act.

5Now Moses in the law commanded us, that such should be stoned: but what sayest thou?

6This they said, tempting him, that they might have to accuse him. But Jesus stooped down, and with *his* finger wrote on the ground, *as though he heard them not.*

7So when they continued asking him, he lifted up himself, and said unto them, He that is without sin among you, let him first cast a stone at her.

8And again he stooped down, and wrote on the ground.

9And they which heard *it,* being convicted by *their* own conscience, went out one by one, beginning at the eldest, *even* unto the last: and Jesus was left alone, and the woman standing in the midst.

10When Jesus had lifted up himself, and saw none but the woman, he said unto her, Woman, where are those thine accusers? hath no man condemned thee?

11She said, No man, Lord. And Jesus said unto her, Neither do I condemn thee: go, and sin no more.

12¶ Then spake Jesus again unto them, saying, I am the light of the world: he that followeth me shall not walk in darkness, but shall have the light of life.

13The Pharisees therefore said unto him, Thou bearest record of thyself; thy record is not true.

14Jesus answered and said unto them, Though I bear record of myself, *yet* my record is true: for I know whence I came, and whither I go; but ye cannot tell whence I come, and whither I go.

15Ye judge after the flesh; I judge no man.

16And yet if I judge, my judgment is true: for I am not alone, but I and the Father that sent me.

17It is also written in your law, that the testimony of two men is true.

18I am one that bear witness of myself, and the Father that sent me beareth witness of me.

New International

Unbelief of the Jewish Leaders

45Finally the temple guards went back to the chief priests and Pharisees, who asked them, "Why didn't you bring him in?"

46"No one ever spoke the way this man does," the guards declared.

47"You mean he has deceived you also?" the Pharisees retorted. 48"Has any of the rulers or of the Pharisees believed in him? 49No! But this mob that knows nothing of the law—there is a curse on them."

50Nicodemus, who had gone to Jesus earlier and who was one of their own number, asked, 51"Does our law condemn anyone without first hearing him to find out what he is doing?"

52They replied, "Are you from Galilee, too? Look into it, and you will find that a propheta does not come out of Galilee."

[The earliest and most reliable manuscripts and other ancient witnesses do not have John 7:53–8:11.]

53Then each went to his own home.

8 BUT JESUS went to the Mount of Olives. 2At dawn he appeared again in the temple courts, where all the people gathered around him, and he sat down to teach them. 3The teachers of the law and the Pharisees brought in a woman caught in adultery. They made her stand before the group 4and said to Jesus, "Teacher, this woman was caught in the act of adultery. 5In the Law Moses commanded us to stone such women. Now what do you say?" 6They were using this question as a trap, in order to have a basis for accusing him.

But Jesus bent down and started to write on the ground with his finger. 7When they kept on questioning him, he straightened up and said to them, "If any one of you is without sin, let him be the first to throw a stone at her." 8Again he stooped down and wrote on the ground.

9At this, those who heard began to go away one at a time, the older ones first, until only Jesus was left, with the woman still standing there. 10Jesus straightened up and asked her, "Woman, where are they? Has no one condemned you?"

11"No one, sir," she said.

"Then neither do I condemn you," Jesus declared. "Go now and leave your life of sin."

The Validity of Jesus' Testimony

12When Jesus spoke again to the people, he said, "I am the light of the world. Whoever follows me will never walk in darkness, but will have the light of life."

13The Pharisees challenged him, "Here you are, appearing as your own witness; your testimony is not valid."

14Jesus answered, "Even if I testify on my own behalf, my testimony is valid, for I know where I came from and where I am going. But you have no idea where I come from or where I am going. 15You judge by human standards; I pass judgment on no one. 16But if I do judge, my decisions are right, because I am not alone. I stand with the Father, who sent me. 17In your own Law it is written that the testimony of two men is valid. 18I am one who testifies for myself; my other witness is the Father, who sent me."

a *52* Two early manuscripts *the Prophet*

Living Bible

45The Temple police who had been sent to arrest him returned to the chief priests and Pharisees. "Why didn't you bring him in?" they demanded.

46"He says such wonderful things!" they mumbled. "We've never heard anything like it."

47"So you also have been led astray?" the Pharisees mocked. 48"Is there a single one of us Jewish rulers or Pharisees who believes he is the Messiah? 49These stupid crowds do, yes; but what do they know about it? A curse upon them anyway!"b

50Then Nicodemus spoke up. (Remember him? He was the Jewish leader who came secretly to interview Jesus.) 51"Is it legal to convict a man before he is even tried?" he asked.

52They replied, "Are you a wretched Galilean too? Search the Scriptures and see for yourself—no prophets will come from Galilee!"

53c Then the meeting broke up and everybody went home.

8 JESUS RETURNED to the Mount of Olives, 2but early the next morning he was back again at the Temple. A crowd soon gathered, and he sat down and talked to them. 3As he was speaking, the Jewish leaders and Pharisees brought a woman caught in adultery and placed her out in front of the staring crowd.

4"Teacher," they said to Jesus, "this woman was caught in the very act of adultery. 5Moses' law says to kill her. What about it?"

6They were trying to trap him into saying something they could use against him, but Jesus stooped down and wrote in the dust with his finger. 7They kept demanding an answer, so he stood up again and said, "All right, hurl the stones at her until she dies. But only he who never sinned may throw the first!"

8Then he stooped down again and wrote some more in the dust. 9And the Jewish leaders slipped away one by one, beginning with the eldest, until only Jesus was left in front of the crowd with the woman.

10Then Jesus stood up again and said to her, "Where are your accusers? Didn't even one of them condemn you?"

11"No, sir," she said.

And Jesus said, "Neither do I. Go and sin no more."

12Later, in one of his talks, Jesus said to the people, "I am the Light of the world. So if you follow me, you won't be stumbling through the darkness, for living light will flood your path."

13The Pharisees replied, "You are boasting—and lying!"

14Jesus told them, "These claims are true even though I make them concerning myself. For I know where I came from and where I am going, but you don't know this about me. 15You pass judgment on me without knowing the facts. I am not judging you now; 16but if I were, it would be an absolutely correct judgment in every respect, for I have with me the Father who sent me. 17Your laws say that if two men agree on something that has happened, their witness is accepted as fact. 18Well, I am one witness, and my Father who sent me is the other."

New Revised Standard

The Unbelief of Those in Authority

45 Then the temple police went back to the chief priests and Pharisees, who asked them, "Why did you not arrest him?" 46The police answered, "Never has anyone spoken like this!" 47Then the Pharisees replied, "Surely you have not been deceived too, have you? 48Has any one of the authorities or of the Pharisees believed in him? 49But this crowd, which does not know the law—they are accursed." 50Nicodemus, who had gone to Jesusd before, and who was one of them, asked, 51"Our law does not judge people without first giving them a hearing to find out what they are doing, does it?" 52They replied, "Surely you are not also from Galilee, are you? Search and you will see that no prophet is to arise from Galilee."

The Woman Caught in Adultery

[[53Then each of them went home,

8 WHILE JESUS went to the Mount of Olives. 2Early in the morning he came again to the temple. All the people came to him and he sat down and began to teach them. 3The scribes and the Pharisees brought a woman who had been caught in adultery; and making her stand before all of them, 4they said to him, "Teacher, this woman was caught in the very act of committing adultery. 5Now in the law Moses commanded us to stone such women. Now what do you say?" 6They said this to test him, so that they might have some charge to bring against him. Jesus bent down and wrote with his finger on the ground. 7When they kept on questioning him, he straightened up and said to them, "Let anyone among you who is without sin be the first to throw a stone at her." 8And once again he bent down and wrote on the ground.e 9When they heard it, they went away, one by one, beginning with the elders; and Jesus was left alone with the woman standing before him. 10Jesus straightened up and said to her, "Woman, where are they? Has no one condemned you?" 11She said, "No one, sir."f And Jesus said, "Neither do I condemn you. Go your way, and from now on do not sin again."]]g

Jesus the Light of the World

12 Again Jesus spoke to them, saying, "I am the light of the world. Whoever follows me will never walk in darkness but will have the light of life." 13Then the Pharisees said to him, "You are testifying on your own behalf; your testimony is not valid." 14Jesus answered, "Even if I testify on my own behalf, my testimony is valid because I know where I have come from and where I am going, but you do not know where I come from or where I am going. 15You judge by human standards;h I judge no one. 16Yet even if I do judge, my judgment is valid; for it is not I alone who judge, but I and the Fatheri who sent me. 17In your law it is written that the testimony of two witnesses is valid. 18I testify on my own behalf, and the Father who sent me testifies on my behalf." 19Then they said to him, "Where is your Fa-

---

b 7:49 A curse upon them anyway, literally, "This multitude is accursed."
c 7:53 Most ancient manuscripts omit John 7:53-8:11.

d Gk him   e Other ancient authorities add the sins of each of them   f Or Lord   g The most ancient authorities lack 7.53—8.11; other authorities add the passage here or after 7.36 or after 21.25 or after Luke 21.38, with variations of text; some mark the passage as doubtful.   h Gk according to the flesh   i Other ancient authorities read he

King James

19Then said they unto him, Where is thy Father? Jesus answered, Ye neither know me, nor my Father: if ye had known me, ye should have known my Father also.

20These words spake Jesus in the treasury, as he taught in the temple: and no man laid hands on him; for his hour was not yet come.

21Then said Jesus again unto them, I go my way, and ye shall seek me, and shall die in your sins: whither I go, ye cannot come.

22Then said the Jews, Will he kill himself ? because he saith, Whither I go, ye cannot come.

23And he said unto them, Ye are from beneath; I am from above: ye are of this world; I am not of this world.

24I said therefore unto you, that ye shall die in your sins: for if ye believe not that I am *he*, ye shall die in your sins.

25Then said they unto him, Who art thou? And Jesus saith unto them, Even *the same* that I said unto you from the beginning.

26I have many things to say and to judge of you: but he that sent me is true; and I speak to the world those things which I have heard of him.

27They understood not that he spake to them of the Father.

28Then said Jesus unto them, When ye have lifted up the Son of man, then shall ye know that I am *he*, and *that* I do nothing of myself; but as my Father hath taught me, I speak these things.

29And he that sent me is with me: the Father hath not left me alone; for I do always those things that please him.

30As he spake these words, many believed on him.

31Then said Jesus to those Jews which believed on him, If ye continue in my word, *then* are ye my disciples indeed;

32And ye shall know the truth, and the truth shall make you free.

33¶ They answered him, We be Abraham's seed, and were never in bondage to any man: how sayest thou, Ye shall be made free?

34Jesus answered them, Verily, verily, I say unto you, Whosoever committeth sin is the servant of sin.

35And the servant abideth not in the house for ever: *but* the Son abideth ever.

36If the Son therefore shall make you free, ye shall be free indeed.

37I know that ye are Abraham's seed; but ye seek to kill me, because my word hath no place in you.

38I speak that which I have seen with my Father: and ye do that which ye have seen with your father.

39They answered and said unto him, Abraham is our father. Jesus saith unto them, If ye were Abraham's children, ye would do the works of Abraham.

40But now ye seek to kill me, a man that hath told you the truth, which I have heard of God: this did not Abraham.

41Ye do the deeds of your father. Then said they to him, We be not born of fornication; we have one Father, *even* God.

42Jesus said unto them, If God were your Father, ye would love me: for I proceeded forth and came from God; neither came I of myself, but he sent me.

43Why do ye not understand my speech? *even* because ye cannot hear my word.

44Ye are of *your* father the devil, and the lusts of your father ye will do. He was a murderer from the beginning, and abode not in the truth, because there is no truth in him. When he speaketh a lie, he speaketh of his own: for he is a liar, and the father of it.

45And because I tell *you* the truth, ye believe me not.

46Which of you convinceth me of sin? And if I say the truth, why do ye not believe me?

New International

19Then they asked him, "Where is your father?"

"You do not know me or my Father," Jesus replied. "If you knew me, you would know my Father also." 20He spoke these words while teaching in the temple area near the place where the offerings were put. Yet no one seized him, because his time had not yet come.

21Once more Jesus said to them, "I am going away, and you will look for me, and you will die in your sin. Where I go, you cannot come."

22This made the Jews ask, "Will he kill himself? Is that why he says, 'Where I go, you cannot come'?"

23But he continued, "You are from below; I am from above. You are of this world; I am not of this world. 24I told you that you would die in your sins; if you do not believe that I am ˌthe one I claim to beˌ,[a] you will indeed die in your sins.ᵇ"

25"Who are you?" they asked.

"Just what I have been claiming all along," Jesus replied. 26"I have much to say in judgment of you. But he who sent me is reliable, and what I have heard from him I tell the world."

27They did not understand that he was telling them about his Father. 28So Jesus said, "When you have lifted up the Son of Man, then you will know that I am ˌthe one I claim to beˌ and that I do nothing on my own but speak just what the Father has taught me. 29The one who sent me is with me; he has not left me alone, for I always do what pleases him." 30Even as he spoke, many put their faith in him.

The Children of Abraham

31To the Jews who had believed him, Jesus said, "If you hold to my teaching, you are really my disciples. 32Then you will know the truth, and the truth will set you free."

33They answered him, "We are Abraham's descendantsᵇ and have never been slaves of anyone. How can you say that we shall be set free?"

34Jesus replied, "I tell you the truth, everyone who sins is a slave to sin. 35Now a slave has no permanent place in the family, but a son belongs to it forever. 36So if the Son sets you free, you will be free indeed. 37I know you are Abraham's descendants. Yet you are ready to kill me, because you have no room for my word. 38I am telling you what I have seen in the Father's presence, and you do what you have heard from your father.ᶜ"

39"Abraham is our father," they answered.

"If you were Abraham's children," said Jesus, "then you wouldᵈ do the things Abraham did. 40As it is, you are determined to kill me, a man who has told you the truth that I heard from God. Abraham did not do such things. 41You are doing the things your own father does."

"We are not illegitimate children," they protested. "The only Father we have is God himself."

The Children of the Devil

42Jesus said to them, "If God were your Father, you would love me, for I came from God and now am here. I have not come on my own; but he sent me. 43Why is my language not clear to you? Because you are unable to hear what I say. 44You belong to your father, the devil, and you want to carry out your father's desire. He was a murderer from the beginning, not holding to the truth, for there is no truth in him. When he lies, he speaks his native language, for he is a liar and the father of lies. 45Yet because I tell the truth, you do not believe me! 46Can any of you prove me guilty of sin? If I am telling the truth, why don't you believe me? 47He who

---

ᵃ *24* Or *I am he*; also in verse 28   ᵇ *33* Greek *seed*; also in verse 37
ᶜ *38* Or *presence. Therefore do what you have heard from the Father*.
ᵈ *39* Some early manuscripts *"If you are Abraham's children," said Jesus, "then*

Living Bible

19"Where is your father?" they asked.

Jesus answered, "You don't know who I am, so you don't know who my Father is. If you knew me, then you would know him too."

20Jesus made these statements while in the section of the Temple known as the Treasury. But he was not arrested, for his time had not yet run out.

21Later he said to them again, "I am going away; and you will search for me, and die in your sins. And you cannot come where I am going."

22The Jews asked, "Is he planning suicide? What does he mean, 'You cannot come where I am going'?"

23Then he said to them, "You are from below; I am from above. You are of this world; I am not. 24That is why I said that you will die in your sins; for unless you believe that I am the Messiah, the Son of God, you will die in your sins."

25"Tell us who you are," they demanded.

He replied, "I am the one I have always claimed to be. 26I could condemn you for much and teach you much, but I won't, for I say only what I am told to by the one who sent me; and he is Truth." 27But they still didn't understand that he was talking to them about God.e

28So Jesus said, "When you have killed the Messiah,f then you will realize that I am he and that I have not been telling you my own ideas, but have spoken what the Father taught me. 29And he who sent me is with me—he has not deserted me—for I always do those things that are pleasing to him."

30, 31Then many of the Jewish leaders who heard him say these things began believing him to be the Messiah.

Jesus said to them, "You are truly my disciples if you live as I tell you to, 32and you will know the truth, and the truth will set you free."

33"But we are descendants of Abraham," they said, "and have never been slaves to any man on earth! What do you mean, 'set free'?"

34Jesus replied, "You are slaves of sin, every one of you. 35And slaves don't have rights, but the Son has every right there is! 36So if the Son sets you free, you will indeed be free— 37(Yes, I realize that you are descendants of Abraham!) And yet some of you are trying to kill me because my message does not find a home within your hearts. 38I am telling you what I saw when I was with my Father. But you are following the advice of *your* father."

39"Our father is Abraham," they declared.

"No!" Jesus replied, "for if he were, you would follow his good example. 40But instead you are trying to kill me—and all because I told you the truth I heard from God. Abraham wouldn't do a thing like that! 41No, you are obeying your *real* father when you act that way."

They replied, "We were not born out of wedlock— our true Father is God himself."

42Jesus told them, "If that were so, then you would love me, for I have come to you from God. I am not here on my own, but he sent me. 43Why can't you understand what I am saying? It is because you are prevented from doing so! 44For you are the children of your father the devil and you love to do the evil things he does. He was a murderer from the beginning and a hater of truth— there is not an iota of truth in him. When he lies, it is perfectly normal; for he is the father of liars. 45And so when I tell the truth, you just naturally don't believe it!

46"Which of you can truthfully accuse me of one single sin? [No one!g] And since I am telling you the truth, why don't you believe me? 47Anyone whose Fa-

New Revised Standard

ther?" Jesus answered, "You know neither me nor my Father. If you knew me, you would know my Father also." 20He spoke these words while he was teaching in the treasury of the temple, but no one arrested him, because his hour had not yet come.

Jesus Foretells His Death

21 Again he said to them, "I am going away, and you will search for me, but you will die in your sin. Where I am going, you cannot come." 22Then the Jews said, "Is he going to kill himself? Is that what he means by saying, 'Where I am going, you cannot come'?" 23He said to them, "You are from below, I am from above; you are of this world, I am not of this world. 24I told you that you would die in your sins, for you will die in your sins unless you believe that I am he."h 25They said to him, "Who are you?" Jesus said to them, "Why do I speak to you at all?i 26I have much to say about you and much to condemn; but the one who sent me is true, and I declare to the world what I have heard from him." 27They did not understand that he was speaking to them about the Father. 28So Jesus said, "When you have lifted up the Son of Man, then you will realize that I am he,h and that I do nothing on my own, but I speak these things as the Father instructed me. 29And the one who sent me is with me; he has not left me alone, for I always do what is pleasing to him." 30As he was saying these things, many believed in him.

True Disciples

31 Then Jesus said to the Jews who had believed in him, "If you continue in my word, you are truly my disciples; 32and you will know the truth, and the truth will make you free." 33They answered him, "We are descendants of Abraham and have never been slaves to anyone. What do you mean by saying, 'You will be made free'?"

34 Jesus answered them, "Very truly, I tell you, everyone who commits sin is a slave to sin. 35The slave does not have a permanent place in the household; the son has a place there forever. 36So if the Son makes you free, you will be free indeed. 37I know that you are descendants of Abraham; yet you look for an opportunity to kill me, because there is no place in you for my word. 38I declare what I have seen in the Father's presence; as for you, you should do what you have heard from the Father."j

Jesus and Abraham

39 They answered him, "Abraham is our father." Jesus said to them, "If you were Abraham's children, you would be doingk what Abraham did, 40but now you are trying to kill me, a man who has told you the truth that I heard from God. This is not what Abraham did. 41You are indeed doing what your father does." They said to him, "We are not illegitimate children; we have one father, God himself." 42Jesus said to them, "If God were your Father, you would love me, for I came from God and now I am here. I did not come on my own, but he sent me. 43Why do you not understand what I say? It is because you cannot accept my word. 44You are from your father the devil, and you choose to do your father's desires. He was a murderer from the beginning and does not stand in the truth, because there is no truth in him. When he lies, he speaks according to his own nature, for he is a liar and the father of lies. 45But because I tell the truth, you do not believe me. 46Which of you convicts me of sin? If I tell the truth, why do you not believe me? 47Whoever is from God hears the words

---

e 8:27 *God*, literally, "the Father." f 8:28 *When you have killed the Messiah*, literally, "When you have lifted up the Son of Man." g 8:46 *No one*, implied.

h Gk *I am* i Or *What I have told you from the beginning* j Other ancient authorities read *you do what you have heard from your father* k Other ancient authorities read *If you are Abraham's children, then do*

King James

47He that is of God heareth God's words: ye therefore hear *them* not, because ye are not of God.

48Then answered the Jews, and said unto him, Say we not well that thou art a Samaritan, and hast a devil?

49Jesus answered, I have not a devil; but I honour my Father, and ye do dishonour me.

50And I seek not mine own glory: there is one that seeketh and judgeth.

51Verily, verily, I say unto you, If a man keep my saying, he shall never see death.

52Then said the Jews unto him, Now we know that thou hast a devil. Abraham is dead, and the prophets; and thou sayest, If a man keep my saying, he shall never taste of death.

53Art thou greater than our father Abraham, which is dead? and the prophets are dead: whom makest thou thyself ?

54Jesus answered, If I honour myself, my honour is nothing: it is my Father that honoureth me; of whom ye say, that he is your God:

55Yet ye have not known him; but I know him: and if I should say, I know him not, I shall be a liar like unto you: but I know him, and keep his saying.

56Your father Abraham rejoiced to see my day: and he saw *it*, and was glad.

57Then said the Jews unto him, Thou art not yet fifty years old, and hast thou seen Abraham?

58Jesus said unto them, Verily, verily, I say unto you, Before Abraham was, I am.

59Then took they up stones to cast at him: but Jesus hid himself, and went out of the temple, going through the midst of them, and so passed by.

9 AND AS *Jesus* passed by, he saw a man which was blind from *his* birth.

2And his disciples asked him, saying, Master, who did sin, this man, or his parents, that he was born blind?

3Jesus answered, Neither hath this man sinned, nor his parents: but that the works of God should be made manifest in him.

4I must work the works of him that sent me, while it is day: the night cometh, when no man can work.

5As long as I am in the world, I am the light of the world.

6When he had thus spoken, he spat on the ground, and made clay of the spittle, and he anointed the eyes of the blind man with the clay,

7And said unto him, Go, wash in the pool of Siloam, (which is by interpretation, Sent.) He went his way therefore, and washed, and came seeing.

8¶ The neighbours therefore, and they which before had seen him that he was blind, said, Is not this he that sat and begged?

9Some said, This is he: others *said,* He is like him: *but* he said, I am *he.*

10Therefore said they unto him, How were thine eyes opened?

11He answered and said, A man that is called Jesus made clay, and anointed mine eyes, and said unto me, Go to the pool of Siloam, and wash: and I went and washed, and I received sight.

12Then said they unto him, Where is he? He said, I know not.

13¶ They brought to the Pharisees him that aforetime was blind.

14And it was the sabbath day when Jesus made the clay, and opened his eyes.

New International

belongs to God hears what God says. The reason you do not hear is that you do not belong to God."

The Claims of Jesus About Himself

48The Jews answered him, "Aren't we right in saying that you are a Samaritan and demon-possessed?"

49"I am not possessed by a demon," said Jesus, "but I honor my Father and you dishonor me. 50I am not seeking glory for myself; but there is one who seeks it, and he is the judge. 51I tell you the truth, if anyone keeps my word, he will never see death."

52At this the Jews exclaimed, "Now we know that you are demon-possessed! Abraham died and so did the prophets, yet you say that if anyone keeps your word, he will never taste death. 53Are you greater than our father Abraham? He died, and so did the prophets. Who do you think you are?"

54Jesus replied, "If I glorify myself, my glory means nothing. My Father, whom you claim as your God, is the one who glorifies me. 55Though you do not know him, I know him. If I said I did not, I would be a liar like you, but I do know him and keep his word. 56Your father Abraham rejoiced at the thought of seeing my day; he saw it and was glad."

57"You are not yet fifty years old," the Jews said to him, "and you have seen Abraham!"

58"I tell you the truth," Jesus answered, "before Abraham was born, I am!" 59At this, they picked up stones to stone him, but Jesus hid himself, slipping away from the temple grounds.

Jesus Heals a Man Born Blind

9 AS HE went along, he saw a man blind from birth. 2His disciples asked him, "Rabbi, who sinned, this man or his parents, that he was born blind?"

3"Neither this man nor his parents sinned," said Jesus, "but this happened so that the work of God might be displayed in his life. 4As long as it is day, we must do the work of him who sent me. Night is coming, when no one can work. 5While I am in the world, I am the light of the world."

6Having said this, he spit on the ground, made some mud with the saliva, and put it on the man's eyes. 7"Go," he told him, "wash in the Pool of Siloam" (this word means Sent). So the man went and washed, and came home seeing.

8His neighbors and those who had formerly seen him begging asked, "Isn't this the same man who used to sit and beg?" 9Some claimed that he was.

Others said, "No, he only looks like him."

But he himself insisted, "I am the man."

10"How then were your eyes opened?" they demanded.

11He replied, "The man they call Jesus made some mud and put it on my eyes. He told me to go to Siloam and wash. So I went and washed, and then I could see."

12"Where is this man?" they asked him.

"I don't know," he said.

The Pharisees Investigate the Healing

13They brought to the Pharisees the man who had been blind. 14Now the day on which Jesus had made the mud and opened the man's eyes was a Sabbath. 15There-

Living Bible

ther is God listens gladly to the words of God. Since you don't, it proves you aren't his children."

48"You Samaritan! Foreigner! Devil!" the Jewish leaders snarled. "Didn't we say all along you were possessed by a demon?"

49"No," Jesus said, "I have no demon in me. For I honor my Father—and you dishonor me. 50And though I have no wish to make myself great, God wants this for me and judges [those who reject mea]. 51With all the earnestness I have I tell you this—no one who obeys me shall ever die!"

52The leaders of the Jews said, "Now we know you are possessed by a demon. Even Abraham and the mightiest prophets died, and yet you say that obeying you will keep a man from dying! 53So you are greater than our father Abraham, who died? And greater than the prophets, who died? Who do you think you are?" 54Then Jesus told them this: "If I am merely boasting about myself, it doesn't count. But it is my Father—and you claim him as your God—who is saying these glorious things about me. 55But you do not even know him. I do. If I said otherwise, I would be as great a liar as you! But it is true—I know him and fully obey him. 56Your father Abraham rejoiced to see my day. He knew I was coming and was glad."

57The Jewish leaders: "You aren't even fifty years old—sure, you've seen Abraham!"

58Jesus: "The absolute truth is that I was in existence before Abraham was ever born!"

59At that point the Jewish leaders picked up stones to kill him. But Jesus was hidden from them, and walked past them and left the Temple.

9 AS HE was walking along, he saw a man blind from birth.

2"Master," his disciples asked him, "why was this man born blind? Was it a result of his own sins or those of his parents?"

3"Neither," Jesus answered. "But to demonstrate the power of God. 4All of us must quickly carry out the tasks assigned us by the one who sent me, for there is little time left before the night falls and all work comes to an end. 5But while I am still here in the world, I give it my light."

6Then he spat on the ground and made mud from the spittle and smoothed the mud over the blind man's eyes, 7and told him, "Go and wash in the Pool of Siloam" (the word "Siloam" means "Sent"). So the man went where he was sent and washed and came back seeing!

8His neighbors and others who knew him as a blind beggar asked each other, "Is this the same fellow—that beggar?"

9Some said yes, and some said no. "It can't be the same man," they thought, "but he surely looks like him!"

And the beggar said, "I am the same man!"

10Then they asked him how in the world he could see. What had happened?

11And he told them, "A man they call Jesus made mud and smoothed it over my eyes and told me to go to the Pool of Siloam and wash off the mud. I did, and I can see!"

12"Where is he now?" they asked.

"I don't know," he replied.

13Then they took the man to the Pharisees. 14Now as it happened, this all occurred on a Sabbath.b 15Then the

New Revised Standard

of God. The reason you do not hear them is that you are not from God."

48 The Jews answered him, "Are we not right in saying that you are a Samaritan and have a demon?" 49Jesus answered, "I do not have a demon; but I honor my Father, and you dishonor me. 50Yet I do not seek my own glory; there is one who seeks it and he is the judge. 51Very truly, I tell you, whoever keeps my word will never see death." 52The Jews said to him, "Now we know that you have a demon. Abraham died, and so did the prophets; yet you say, 'Whoever keeps my word will never taste death.' 53Are you greater than our father Abraham, who died? The prophets also died. Who do you claim to be?" 54Jesus answered, "If I glorify myself, my glory is nothing. It is my Father who glorifies me, he of whom you say, 'He is our God,' 55though you do not know him. But I know him; if I would say that I do not know him, I would be a liar like you. But I do know him and I keep his word. 56Your ancestor Abraham rejoiced that he would see my day; he saw it and was glad." 57Then the Jews said to him, "You are not yet fifty years old, and have you seen Abraham?"c 58Jesus said to them, "Very truly, I tell you, before Abraham was, I am." 59So they picked up stones to throw at him, but Jesus hid himself and went out of the temple.

A Man Born Blind Receives Sight

9 AS HE walked along, he saw a man blind from birth. 2His disciples asked him, "Rabbi, who sinned, this man or his parents, that he was born blind?" 3Jesus answered, "Neither this man nor his parents sinned; he was born blind so that God's works might be revealed in him. 4Wed must work the works of him who sent mee while it is day; night is coming when no one can work. 5As long as I am in the world, I am the light of the world." 6When he had said this, he spat on the ground and made mud with the saliva and spread the mud on the man's eyes, 7saying to him, "Go, wash in the pool of Siloam" (which means Sent). Then he went and washed and came back able to see. 8The neighbors and those who had seen him before as a beggar began to ask, "Is this not the man who used to sit and beg?" 9Some were saying, "It is he." Others were saying, "No, but it is someone like him." He kept saying, "I am the man." 10But they kept asking him, "Then how were your eyes opened?" 11He answered, "The man called Jesus made mud, spread it on my eyes, and said to me, 'Go to Siloam and wash.' Then I went and washed and received my sight." 12They said to him, "Where is he?" He said, "I do not know."

The Pharisees Investigate the Healing

13 They brought to the Pharisees the man who had formerly been blind. 14Now it was a sabbath day when Jesus made the mud and opened his eyes. 15Then the

---

a 8:50 those who reject me, implied. Literally, "There is one who seeks and judges."   b 9:14 on a Sabbath, i.e., on Saturday, the weekly Jewish holy day when all work was forbidden.

c Other ancient authorities read has Abraham seen you?   d Other ancient authorities read I   e Other ancient authorities read us

King James

15Then again the Pharisees also asked him how he had received his sight. He said unto them, He put clay upon mine eyes, and I washed, and do see.

16Therefore said some of the Pharisees, This man is not of God, because he keepeth not the sabbath day. Others said, How can a man that is a sinner do such miracles? And there was a division among them.

17They say unto the blind man again, What sayest thou of him, that he hath opened thine eyes? He said, He is a prophet.

18But the Jews did not believe concerning him, that he had been blind, and received his sight, until they called the parents of him that had received his sight.

19And they asked them, saying, Is this your son, who ye say was born blind? how then doth he now see?

20His parents answered them and said, We know that this is our son, and that he was born blind:

21But by what means he now seeth, we know not; or who hath opened his eyes, we know not: he is of age; ask him: he shall speak for himself.

22These *words* spake his parents, because they feared the Jews: for the Jews had agreed already, that if any man did confess that he was Christ, he should be put out of the synagogue.

23Therefore said his parents, He is of age; ask him.

24Then again called they the man that was blind, and said unto him, Give God the praise: we know that this man is a sinner.

25He answered and said, Whether he be a sinner *or no,* I know not: one thing I know, that, whereas I was blind, now I see.

26Then said they to him again, What did he to thee? how opened he thine eyes?

27He answered them, I have told you already, and ye did not hear: wherefore would ye hear *it* again? will ye also be his disciples?

28Then they reviled him, and said, Thou art his disciple; but we are Moses' disciples.

29We know that God spake unto Moses: *as for* this *fellow,* we know not from whence he is.

30The man answered and said unto them, Why herein is a marvellous thing, that ye know not from whence he is, and *yet* he hath opened mine eyes.

31Now we know that God heareth not sinners: but if any man be a worshipper of God, and doeth his will, him he heareth.

32Since the world began was it not heard that any man opened the eyes of one that was born blind.

33If this man were not of God, he could do nothing.

34They answered and said unto him, Thou wast altogether born in sins, and dost thou teach us? And they cast him out.

35Jesus heard that they had cast him out; and when he had found him, he said unto him, Dost thou believe on the Son of God?

36He answered and said, Who is he, Lord, that I might believe on him?

37And Jesus said unto him, Thou hast both seen him, and it is he that talketh with thee.

38And he said, Lord, I believe. And he worshipped him.

39¶ And Jesus said, For judgment I am come into this world, that they which see not might see; and that they which see might be made blind.

40And *some* of the Pharisees which were with him heard these words, and said unto him, Are we blind also?

41Jesus said unto them, If ye were blind, ye should have no sin: but now ye say, We see; therefore your sin remaineth.

New International

fore the Pharisees also asked him how he had received his sight. "He put mud on my eyes," the man replied, "and I washed, and now I see."

16Some of the Pharisees said, "This man is not from God, for he does not keep the Sabbath."

But others asked, "How can a sinner do such miraculous signs?" So they were divided.

17Finally they turned again to the blind man, "What have you to say about him? It was your eyes he opened."
The man replied, "He is a prophet."

18The Jews still did not believe that he had been blind and had received his sight until they sent for the man's parents. 19"Is this your son?" they asked. "Is this the one you say was born blind? How is it that now he can see?"

20"We know he is our son," the parents answered, "and we know he was born blind. 21But how he can see now, or who opened his eyes, we don't know. Ask him. He is of age; he will speak for himself." 22His parents said this because they were afraid of the Jews, for already the Jews had decided that anyone who acknowledged that Jesus was the Christ[a] would be put out of the synagogue. 23That was why his parents said, "He is of age; ask him."

24A second time they summoned the man who had been blind. "Give glory to God,[b]" they said. "We know this man is a sinner."

25He replied, "Whether he is a sinner or not, I don't know. One thing I do know. I was blind but now I see!"

26Then they asked him, "What did he do to you? How did he open your eyes?"

27He answered, "I have told you already and you did not listen. Why do you want to hear it again? Do you want to become his disciples, too?"

28Then they hurled insults at him and said, "You are this fellow's disciple! We are disciples of Moses! 29We know that God spoke to Moses, but as for this fellow, we don't even know where he comes from."

30The man answered, "Now that is remarkable! You don't know where he comes from, yet he opened my eyes. 31We know that God does not listen to sinners. He listens to the godly man who does his will. 32Nobody has ever heard of opening the eyes of a man born blind. 33If this man were not from God, he could do nothing."

34To this they replied, "You were steeped in sin at birth; how dare you lecture us!" And they threw him out.

Spiritual Blindness

35Jesus heard that they had thrown him out, and when he found him, he said, "Do you believe in the Son of Man?"

36"Who is he, sir?" the man asked. "Tell me so that I may believe in him."

37Jesus said, "You have now seen him; in fact, he is the one speaking with you."

38Then the man said, "Lord, I believe," and he worshiped him.

39Jesus said, "For judgment I have come into this world, so that the blind will see and those who see will become blind."

40Some Pharisees who were with him heard him say this and asked, "What? Are we blind too?"

41Jesus said, "If you were blind, you would not be guilty of sin; but now that you claim you can see, your guilt remains.

---

[a] 22 Or *Messiah*   [b] 24 A solemn charge to tell the truth (see Joshua 7:19)

Living Bible

Pharisees asked him all about it. So he told them how Jesus had smoothed the mud over his eyes, and when it was washed away, he could see!

16Some of them said, "Then this fellow Jesus is not from God, because he is working on the Sabbath."

Others said, "But how could an ordinary sinner do such miracles?" So there was a deep division of opinion among them.

17Then the Pharisees turned on the man who had been blind and demanded, "This man who opened your eyes—who do you say he is?"

"I think he must be a prophet sent from God," the man replied.

18The Jewish leaders wouldn't believe he had been blind, until they called in his parents 19and asked them, "Is this your son? Was he born blind? If so, how can he see?"

20His parents replied, "We know this is our son and that he was born blind, 21but we don't know what happened to make him see, or who did it. He is old enough to speak for himself. Ask him."

22, 23They said this in fear of the Jewish leaders who had announced that anyone saying Jesus was the Messiah would be excommunicated.

24So for the second time they called in the man who had been blind and told him, "Give the glory to God, not to Jesus, for we know Jesus is an evil person."

25"I don't know whether he is good or bad," the man replied, "but I know this: *I was blind, and now I see!*"

26"But what did he do?" they asked. "How did he heal you?"

27"Look!" the man exclaimed. "I told you once; didn't you listen? Why do you want to hear it again? Do you want to become his disciples too?"

28Then they cursed him and said, "You are his disciple, but we are disciples of Moses. 29We know God has spoken to Moses, but as for this fellow, we don't know anything about him."

30"Why, that's very strange!" the man replied. "He can heal blind men, and yet you don't know anything about him! 31Well, God doesn't listen to evil men, but he has open ears to those who worship him and do his will. 32Since the world began there has never been anyone who could open the eyes of someone born blind. 33If this man were not from God, he couldn't do it."

34"You illegitimate bastard,c you!" they shouted. "Are you trying to teach *us?*" And they threw him out.

35When Jesus heard what had happened, he found the man and said, "Do you believe in the Messiah?"d

36The man answered, "Who is he, sir, for I want to."

37"You have seen him," Jesus said, "and he is speaking to you!"

38"Yes, Lord," the man said, "I believe!" And he worshiped Jesus.

39Then Jesus told him, "I have come into the world to give sight to those who are spiritually blind and to show those who think they see that they are blind."

40The Pharisees who were standing there asked, "Are you saying we are blind?"

41"If you were blind, you wouldn't be guilty," Jesus replied. "But your guilt remains because you claim to know what you are doing."

New Revised Standard

Pharisees also began to ask him how he had received his sight. He said to them, "He put mud on my eyes. Then I washed, and now I see." 16 Some of the Pharisees said, "This man is not from God, for he does not observe the sabbath." But others said, "How can a man who is a sinner perform such signs?" And they were divided. 17 So they said again to the blind man, "What do you say about him? It was your eyes he opened." He said, "He is a prophet."

18 The Jews did not believe that he had been blind and had received his sight until they called the parents of the man who had received his sight 19 and asked them, "Is this your son, who you say was born blind? How then does he now see?" 20 His parents answered, "We know that this is our son, and that he was born blind; 21 but we do not know how it is that now he sees, nor do we know who opened his eyes. Ask him; he is of age. He will speak for himself." 22 His parents said this because they were afraid of the Jews; for the Jews had already agreed that anyone who confessed Jesuse to be the Messiahf would be put out of the synagogue. 23 Therefore his parents said, "He is of age; ask him."

24 So for the second time they called the man who had been blind, and they said to him, "Give glory to God! We know that this man is a sinner." 25 He answered, "I do not know whether he is a sinner. One thing I do know, that though I was blind, now I see." 26 They said to him, "What did he do to you? How did he open your eyes?" 27 He answered them, "I have told you already, and you would not listen. Why do you want to hear it again? Do you also want to become his disciples?" 28 Then they reviled him, saying, "You are his disciple, but we are disciples of Moses. 29 We know that God has spoken to Moses, but as for this man, we do not know where he comes from." 30 The man answered, "Here is an astonishing thing! You do not know where he comes from, and yet he opened my eyes. 31 We know that God does not listen to sinners, but he does listen to one who worships him and obeys his will. 32 Never since the world began has it been heard that anyone opened the eyes of a person born blind. 33 If this man were not from God, he could do nothing." 34 They answered him, "You were born entirely in sins, and are you trying to teach us?" And they drove him out.

Spiritual Blindness

35 Jesus heard that they had driven him out, and when he found him, he said, "Do you believe in the Son of Man?"g 36 He answered, "And who is he, sir?h Tell me, so that I may believe in him." 37 Jesus said to him, "You have seen him, and the one speaking with you is he." 38 He said, "Lord,h I believe." And he worshiped him. 39 Jesus said, "I came into this world for judgment so that those who do not see may see, and those who do see may become blind." 40 Some of the Pharisees near him heard this and said to him, "Surely we are not blind, are we?" 41 Jesus said to them, "If you were blind, you would not have sin. But now that you say, 'We see,' your sin remains."

---

c 9:34 *You illegitimate bastard*, literally, "You were altogether born in sin."
d 9:35 *the Messiah*, literally, "the Son of Man."

e Gk *him*   f Or *the Christ*   g Other ancient authorities read *the Son of God*
h *Sir* and *Lord* translate the same Greek word

King James

10 VERILY, VERILY, I say unto you, He that entereth not by the door into the sheepfold, but climbeth up some other way, the same is a thief and a robber.

2But he that entereth in by the door is the shepherd of the sheep.

3To him the porter openeth; and the sheep hear his voice: and he calleth his own sheep by name, and leadeth them out.

4And when he putteth forth his own sheep, he goeth before them, and the sheep follow him: for they know his voice.

5And a stranger will they not follow, but will flee from him: for they know not the voice of strangers.

6This parable spake Jesus unto them: but they understood not what things they were which he spake unto them.

7Then said Jesus unto them again, Verily, verily, I say unto you, I am the door of the sheep.

8All that ever came before me are thieves and robbers: but the sheep did not hear them.

9I am the door: by me if any man enter in, he shall be saved, and shall go in and out, and find pasture.

10The thief cometh not, but for to steal, and to kill, and to destroy: I am come that they might have life, and that they might have *it* more abundantly.

11I am the good shepherd: the good shepherd giveth his life for the sheep.

12But he that is an hireling, and not the shepherd, whose own the sheep are not, seeth the wolf coming, and leaveth the sheep, and fleeth: and the wolf catcheth them, and scattereth the sheep.

13The hireling fleeth, because he is an hireling, and careth not for the sheep.

14I am the good shepherd, and know my *sheep*, and am known of mine.

15As the Father knoweth me, even so know I the Father: and I lay down my life for the sheep.

16And other sheep I have, which are not of this fold: them also I must bring, and they shall hear my voice; and there shall be one fold, *and* one shepherd.

17Therefore doth my Father love me, because I lay down my life, that I might take it again.

18No man taketh it from me, but I lay it down of myself. I have power to lay it down, and I have power to take it again. This commandment have I received of my Father.

19¶ There was a division therefore again among the Jews for these sayings.

20And many of them said, He hath a devil, and is mad; why hear ye him?

21Others said, These are not the words of him that hath a devil. Can a devil open the eyes of the blind?

22¶ And it was at Jerusalem the feast of the dedication, and it was winter.

23And Jesus walked in the temple in Solomon's porch.

24Then came the Jews round about him, and said unto him, How long dost thou make us to doubt? If thou be the Christ, tell us plainly.

25Jesus answered them, I told you, and ye believed not: the works that I do in my Father's name, they bear witness of me.

26But ye believe not, because ye are not of my sheep, as I said unto you.

27My sheep hear my voice, and I know them, and they follow me:

28And I give unto them eternal life; and they shall never perish, neither shall any *man* pluck them out of my hand.

29My Father, which gave *them* me, is greater than all; and no *man* is able to pluck *them* out of my Father's hand.

New International

The Shepherd and His Flock

10 "I TELL you the truth, the man who does not enter the sheep pen by the gate, but climbs in by some other way, is a thief and a robber. 2The man who enters by the gate is the shepherd of his sheep. 3The watchman opens the gate for him, and the sheep listen to his voice. He calls his own sheep by name and leads them out. 4When he has brought out all his own, he goes on ahead of them, and his sheep follow him because they know his voice. 5But they will never follow a stranger; in fact, they will run away from him because they do not recognize a stranger's voice." 6Jesus used this figure of speech, but they did not understand what he was telling them.

7Therefore Jesus said again, "I tell you the truth, I am the gate for the sheep. 8All who ever came before me were thieves and robbers, but the sheep did not listen to them. 9I am the gate; whoever enters through me will be saved.[a] He will come in and go out, and find pasture. 10The thief comes only to steal and kill and destroy; I have come that they may have life, and have it to the full.

11"I am the good shepherd. The good shepherd lays down his life for the sheep. 12The hired hand is not the shepherd who owns the sheep. So when he sees the wolf coming, he abandons the sheep and runs away. Then the wolf attacks the flock and scatters it. 13The man runs away because he is a hired hand and cares nothing for the sheep.

14"I am the good shepherd; I know my sheep and my sheep know me— 15just as the Father knows me and I know the Father—and I lay down my life for the sheep. 16I have other sheep that are not of this sheep pen. I must bring them also. They too will listen to my voice, and there shall be one flock and one shepherd. 17The reason my Father loves me is that I lay down my life—only to take it up again. 18No one takes it from me, but I lay it down of my own accord. I have authority to lay it down and authority to take it up again. This command I received from my Father."

19At these words the Jews were again divided. 20Many of them said, "He is demon-possessed and raving mad. Why listen to him?"

21But others said, "These are not the sayings of a man possessed by a demon. Can a demon open the eyes of the blind?"

The Unbelief of the Jews

22Then came the Feast of Dedication[b] at Jerusalem. It was winter, 23and Jesus was in the temple area walking in Solomon's Colonnade. 24The Jews gathered around him, saying, "How long will you keep us in suspense? If you are the Christ,[c] tell us plainly."

25Jesus answered, "I did tell you, but you do not believe. The miracles I do in my Father's name speak for me, 26but you do not believe because you are not my sheep. 27My sheep listen to my voice; I know them, and they follow me. 28I give them eternal life, and they shall never perish; no one can snatch them out of my hand. 29My Father, who has given them to me, is greater than all[d]; no one can snatch them out of my Father's hand. 30I and the Father are one."

---

[a] 9 Or *kept safe*   [b] 22 That is, Hanukkah   [c] 24 Or *Messiah*   [d] 29 Many early manuscripts *What my Father has given me is greater than all*

Living Bible

10 "ANYONE REFUSING to walk through the gate into a sheepfold, who sneaks over the wall, must surely be a thief! 2For a shepherd comes through the gate. 3The gatekeeper opens the gate for him, and the sheep hear his voice and come to him; and he calls his own sheep by name and leads them out. 4He walks ahead of them; and they follow him, for they recognize his voice. 5They won't follow a stranger but will run from him, for they don't recognize his voice."

6Those who heard Jesus use this illustration didn't understand what he meant, 7so he explained it to them.

"I am the Gate for the sheep," he said. 8"All others who came before me were thieves and robbers. But the true sheep did not listen to them. 9Yes, I am the Gate. Those who come in by way of the Gate will be saved and will go in and out and find green pastures. 10The thief's purpose is to steal, kill and destroy. My purpose is to give life in all its fullness.

11"I am the Good Shepherd. The Good Shepherd lays down his life for the sheep. 12A hired man will run when he sees a wolf coming and will leave the sheep, for they aren't his and he isn't their shepherd. And so the wolf leaps on them and scatters the flock. 13The hired man runs because he is hired and has no real concern for the sheep.

14"I am the Good Shepherd and know my own sheep, and they know me, 15just as my Father knows me and I know the Father; and I lay down my life for the sheep. 16I have other sheep, too, in another fold. I must bring them also, and they will heed my voice; and there will be one flock with one Shepherd.

17"The Father loves me because I lay down my life that I may have it back again. 18No one can kill me without my consent—I lay down my life voluntarily. For I have the right and power to lay it down when I want to and also the right and power to take it again. For the Father has given me this right."

19When he said these things, the Jewish leaders were again divided in their opinions about him. 20Some of them said, "He has a demon or else is crazy. Why listen to a man like that?"

21Others said, "This doesn't sound to us like a man possessed by a demon! Can a demon open the eyes of blind men?"

22, 23It was winter,e and Jesus was in Jerusalem at the time of the Dedication Celebration. He was at the Temple, walking through the section known as Solomon's Hall. 24The Jewish leaders surrounded him and asked, "How long are you going to keep us in suspense? If you are the Messiah, tell us plainly."

25"I have already told you,f and you don't believe me," Jesus replied. "The proof is in the miracles I do in the name of my Father. 26But you don't believe me because you are not part of my flock. 27My sheep recognize my voice, and I know them, and they follow me. 28I give them eternal life and they shall never perish. No one shall snatch them away from me, 29for my Father has given them to me, and he is more powerful than anyone else, so no one can kidnap them from me. 30I and the Father are one."

New Revised Standard

Jesus the Good Shepherd

10 "VERY TRULY, I tell you, anyone who does not enter the sheepfold by the gate but climbs in by another way is a thief and a bandit. 2The one who enters by the gate is the shepherd of the sheep. 3The gatekeeper opens the gate for him, and the sheep hear his voice. He calls his own sheep by name and leads them out. 4When he has brought out all his own, he goes ahead of them, and the sheep follow him because they know his voice. 5They will not follow a stranger, but they will run from him because they do not know the voice of strangers." 6Jesus used this figure of speech with them, but they did not understand what he was saying to them.

7 So again Jesus said to them, "Very truly, I tell you, I am the gate for the sheep. 8All who came before me are thieves and bandits; but the sheep did not listen to them. 9I am the gate. Whoever enters by me will be saved, and will come in and go out and find pasture. 10The thief comes only to steal and kill and destroy. I came that they may have life, and have it abundantly.

11 "I am the good shepherd. The good shepherd lays down his life for the sheep. 12The hired hand, who is not the shepherd and does not own the sheep, sees the wolf coming and leaves the sheep and runs away—and the wolf snatches them and scatters them. 13The hired hand runs away because a hired hand does not care for the sheep. 14I am the good shepherd. I know my own and my own know me, 15just as the Father knows me and I know the Father. And I lay down my life for the sheep. 16I have other sheep that do not belong to this fold. I must bring them also, and they will listen to my voice. So there will be one flock, one shepherd. 17For this reason the Father loves me, because I lay down my life in order to take it up again. 18No one takesg it from me, but I lay it down of my own accord. I have power to lay it down, and I have power to take it up again. I have received this command from my Father."

19 Again the Jews were divided because of these words. 20Many of them were saying, "He has a demon and is out of his mind. Why listen to him?" 21Others were saying, "These are not the words of one who has a demon. Can a demon open the eyes of the blind?"

Jesus Is Rejected by the Jews

22 At that time the festival of the Dedication took place in Jerusalem. It was winter, 23and Jesus was walking in the temple, in the portico of Solomon. 24So the Jews gathered around him and said to him, "How long will you keep us in suspense? If you are the Messiah,h tell us plainly." 25Jesus answered, "I have told you, and you do not believe. The works that I do in my Father's name testify to me; 26but you do not believe, because you do not belong to my sheep. 27My sheep hear my voice. I know them, and they follow me. 28I give them eternal life, and they will never perish. No one will snatch them out of my hand. 29What my Father has given me is greater than all else, and no one can snatch it out of the Father's hand.i 30The Father and I are one."

---

e *10:22, 23* December 25 was the usual date for this celebration of the cleansing of the Temple.   f *10:25 I have already told you,* see 5:19; 8:36, 56, 58, etc.

g Other ancient authorities read *has taken*   h Or *the Christ*   i Other ancient authorities read *My Father who has given them to me is greater than all, and no one can snatch them out of the Father's hand*

King James

30I and *my* Father are one.

31Then the Jews took up stones again to stone him. 32Jesus answered them, Many good works have I shown you from my Father; for which of those works do ye stone me?

33The Jews answered him, saying, For a good work we stone thee not; but for blasphemy; and because that thou, being a man, makest thyself God.

34Jesus answered them, Is it not written in your law, I said, Ye are gods?

35If he called them gods, unto whom the word of God came, and the scripture cannot be broken;

36Say ye of him, whom the Father hath sanctified, and sent into the world, Thou blasphemest; because I said, I am the Son of God?

37If I do not the works of my Father, believe me not. 38But if I do, though ye believe not me, believe the works: that ye may know, and believe, that the Father *is* in me, and I in him.

39Therefore they sought again to take him: but he escaped out of their hand,

40And went away again beyond Jordan into the place where John at first baptized; and there he abode.

41And many resorted unto him, and said, John did no miracle: but all things that John spake of this man were true.

42And many believed on him there.

11 NOW A certain *man* was sick, *named* Lazarus, of Bethany, the town of Mary and her sister Martha.

2(It was *that* Mary which anointed the Lord with ointment, and wiped his feet with her hair, whose brother Lazarus was sick.)

3Therefore his sisters sent unto him, saying, Lord, behold, he whom thou lovest is sick.

4When Jesus heard *that,* he said, This sickness is not unto death, but for the glory of God, that the Son of God might be glorified thereby.

5Now Jesus loved Martha, and her sister, and Lazarus.

6When he had heard therefore that he was sick, he abode two days still in the same place where he was.

7Then after that saith he to *his* disciples, Let us go into Judaea again.

8*His* disciples say unto him, Master, the Jews of late sought to stone thee; and goest thou thither again?

9Jesus answered, Are there not twelve hours in the day? If any man walk in the day, he stumbleth not, because he seeth the light of this world.

10But if a man walk in the night, he stumbleth, because there is no light in him.

11These things said he: and after that he saith unto them, Our friend Lazarus sleepeth; but I go, that I may awake him out of sleep.

12Then said his disciples, Lord, if he sleep, he shall do well.

13Howbeit Jesus spake of his death: but they thought that he had spoken of taking of rest in sleep.

14Then said Jesus unto them plainly, Lazarus is dead.

15And I am glad for your sakes that I was not there, to the intent ye may believe; nevertheless let us go unto him.

16Then said Thomas, which is called Didymus, unto his fellowdisciples, Let us also go, that we may die with him.

17Then when Jesus came, he found that he had *lain* in the grave four days already.

18Now Bethany was nigh unto Jerusalem, about fifteen furlongs off:

19And many of the Jews came to Martha and Mary, to comfort them concerning their brother.

New International

31Again the Jews picked up stones to stone him, 32but Jesus said to them, "I have shown you many great miracles from the Father. For which of these do you stone me?"

33"We are not stoning you for any of these," replied the Jews, "but for blasphemy, because you, a mere man, claim to be God."

34Jesus answered them, "Is it not written in your Law, 'I have said you are gods'a? 35If he called them 'gods,' to whom the word of God came—and the Scripture cannot be broken— 36what about the one whom the Father set apart as his very own and sent into the world? Why then do you accuse me of blasphemy because I said, 'I am God's Son'? 37Do not believe me unless I do what my Father does. 38But if I do it, even though you do not believe me, believe the miracles, that you may know and understand that the Father is in me, and I in the Father." 39Again they tried to seize him, but he escaped their grasp.

40Then Jesus went back across the Jordan to the place where John had been baptizing in the early days. Here he stayed 41and many people came to him. They said, "Though John never performed a miraculous sign, all that John said about this man was true." 42And in that place many believed in Jesus.

The Death of Lazarus

11 NOW A man named Lazarus was sick. He was from Bethany, the village of Mary and her sister Martha. 2This Mary, whose brother Lazarus now lay sick, was the same one who poured perfume on the Lord and wiped his feet with her hair. 3So the sisters sent word to Jesus, "Lord, the one you love is sick."

4When he heard this, Jesus said, "This sickness will not end in death. No, it is for God's glory so that God's Son may be glorified through it." 5Jesus loved Martha and her sister and Lazarus. 6Yet when he heard that Lazarus was sick, he stayed where he was two more days.

7Then he said to his disciples, "Let us go back to Judea."

8"But Rabbi," they said, "a short while ago the Jews tried to stone you, and yet you are going back there?"

9Jesus answered, "Are there not twelve hours of daylight? A man who walks by day will not stumble, for he sees by this world's light. 10It is when he walks by night that he stumbles, for he has no light."

11After he had said this, he went on to tell them, "Our friend Lazarus has fallen asleep; but I am going there to wake him up."

12His disciples replied, "Lord, if he sleeps, he will get better." 13Jesus had been speaking of his death, but his disciples thought he meant natural sleep.

14So then he told them plainly, "Lazarus is dead, 15and for your sake I am glad I was not there, so that you may believe. But let us go to him."

16Then Thomas (called Didymus) said to the rest of the disciples, "Let us also go, that we may die with him."

Jesus Comforts the Sisters

17On his arrival, Jesus found that Lazarus had already been in the tomb for four days. 18Bethany was less than two milesb from Jerusalem, 19and many Jews had come to Martha and Mary to comfort them in the loss of their brother. 20When Martha heard that Jesus was coming,

---

a *34* Psalm 82:6   b *18* Greek *fifteen stadia* (about 3 kilometers)

Living Bible

31Then again the Jewish leaders picked up stones to kill him.

32Jesus said, "At God's direction I have done many a miracle to help the people. For which one are you killing me?"

33They replied, "Not for any good work, but for blasphemy; you, a mere man, have declared yourself to be God."

34, 35, 36"In your own Law it says that men are gods!" he replied. "So if the Scripture, which cannot be untrue, speaks of those as gods to whom the message of God came, do you call it blasphemy when the one sanctified and sent into the world by the Father says, 'I am the Son of God'? 37Don't believe me unless I do miracles of God. 38But if I do, believe them even if you don't believe me. Then you will become convinced that the Father is in me, and I in the Father."

39Once again they started to arrest him. But he walked away and left them, 40and went beyond the Jordan River to stay near the place where John was first baptizing. 41And many followed him.

"John didn't do miracles," they remarked to one another, "but all his predictions concerning this man have come true." 42And many came to the decision that he was the Messiah.c

11 DO YOU remember Mary, who poured the costly perfume on Jesus' feet and wiped them with her hair?d Well, her brother Lazarus, who lived in Bethany with Mary and her sister Martha, was sick. 3So the two sisters sent a message to Jesus telling him, "Sir, your good friend is very, very sick."

4But when Jesus heard about it he said, "The purpose of his illness is not death, but for the glory of God. I, the Son of God, will receive glory from this situation."

5Although Jesus was very fond of Martha, Mary, and Lazarus, 6he stayed where he was for the next two days and made no move to go to them. 7Finally, after the two days, he said to his disciples, "Let's go to Judea."

8But his disciples objected. "Master," they said, "only a few days ago the Jewish leaders in Judea were trying to kill you. Are you going there again?"

9Jesus replied, "There are twelve hours of daylight every day, and during every hour of it a man can walk safely and not stumble. 10Only at night is there danger of a wrong step, because of the dark." 11Then he said, "Our friend Lazarus has gone to sleep, but now I will go and waken him!"

12, 13The disciples, thinking Jesus meant Lazarus was having a good night's rest, said, "That means he is getting better!" But Jesus meant Lazarus had died.

14Then he told them plainly, "Lazarus is dead. 15And for your sake, I am glad I wasn't there, for this will give you another opportunity to believe in me. Come, let's go to him."

16Thomas, nicknamed "The Twin," said to his fellow disciples, "Let's go too—and die with him."

17When they arrived at Bethany, they were told that Lazarus had already been in his tomb for four days. 18Bethany was only a couple of miles down the road from Jerusalem, 19and many of the Jewish leaders had come to pay their respects and to console Martha and Mary on their loss. 20When Martha got word that Jesus

New Revised Standard

31 The Jews took up stones again to stone him. 32Jesus replied, "I have shown you many good works from the Father. For which of these are you going to stone me?" 33The Jews answered, "It is not for a good work that we are going to stone you, but for blasphemy, because you, though only a human being, are making yourself God." 34Jesus answered, "Is it not written in your law,e 'I said, you are gods'? 35If those to whom the word of God came were called 'gods'—and the scripture cannot be annulled— 36can you say that the one whom the Father has sanctified and sent into the world is blaspheming because I said, 'I am God's Son'? 37If I am not doing the works of my Father, then do not believe me. 38But if I do them, even though you do not believe me, believe the works, so that you may know and understandf that the Father is in me and I am in the Father." 39Then they tried to arrest him again, but he escaped from their hands.

40 He went away again across the Jordan to the place where John had been baptizing earlier, and he remained there. 41Many came to him, and they were saying, "John performed no sign, but everything that John said about this man was true." 42And many believed in him there.

The Death of Lazarus

11 NOW A certain man was ill, Lazarus of Bethany, the village of Mary and her sister Martha. 2Mary was the one who anointed the Lord with perfume and wiped his feet with her hair; her brother Lazarus was ill. 3So the sisters sent a message to Jesus,g "Lord, he whom you love is ill." 4But when Jesus heard it, he said, "This illness does not lead to death; rather it is for God's glory, so that the Son of God may be glorified through it." 5Accordingly, though Jesus loved Martha and her sister and Lazarus, 6after having heard that Lazarush was ill, he stayed two days longer in the place where he was.

7 Then after this he said to the disciples, "Let us go to Judea again." 8The disciples said to him, "Rabbi, the Jews were just now trying to stone you, and are you going there again?" 9Jesus answered, "Are there not twelve hours of daylight? Those who walk during the day do not stumble, because they see the light of this world. 10But those who walk at night stumble, because the light is not in them." 11After saying this, he told them, "Our friend Lazarus has fallen asleep, but I am going there to awaken him." 12The disciples said to him, "Lord, if he has fallen asleep, he will be all right." 13Jesus, however, had been speaking about his death, but they thought that he was referring merely to sleep. 14Then Jesus told them plainly, "Lazarus is dead. 15For your sake I am glad I was not there, so that you may believe. But let us go to him." 16Thomas, who was called the Twin,i said to his fellow disciples, "Let us also go, that we may die with him."

Jesus the Resurrection and the Life

17 When Jesus arrived, he found that Lazarush had already been in the tomb four days. 18Now Bethany was near Jerusalem, some two milesi away, 19and many of the Jews had come to Martha and Mary to console them about their brother. 20When Martha heard that Jesus was

---

c 10:42 many came to the decision that he was the Messiah, literally, "Many believed on him there."   d 11:1 wiped them with her hair, see John 12:3.

e Other ancient authorities read in the law   f Other ancient authorities lack and understand; others read and believe   g Gk him   h Gk he   i Gk Didymus   j Gk fifteen stadia

King James

20Then Martha, as soon as she heard that Jesus was coming, went and met him: but Mary sat *still* in the house.

21Then said Martha unto Jesus, Lord, if thou hadst been here, my brother had not died.

22But I know, that even now, whatsoever thou wilt ask of God, God will give *it* thee.

23Jesus saith unto her, Thy brother shall rise again.

24Martha saith unto him, I know that he shall rise again in the resurrection at the last day.

25Jesus said unto her, I am the resurrection, and the life: he that believeth in me, though he were dead, yet shall he live:

26And whosoever liveth and believeth in me shall never die. Believest thou this?

27She saith unto him, Yea, Lord: I believe that thou art the Christ, the Son of God, which should come into the world.

28And when she had so said, she went her way, and called Mary her sister secretly, saying, The Master is come, and calleth for thee.

29As soon as she heard *that,* she arose quickly, and came unto him.

30Now Jesus was not yet come into the town, but was in that place where Martha met him.

31The Jews then which were with her in the house, and comforted her, when they saw Mary, that she rose up hastily and went out, followed her, saying, She goeth unto the grave to weep there.

32Then when Mary was come where Jesus was, and saw him, she fell down at his feet, saying unto him, Lord, if thou hadst been here, my brother had not died.

33When Jesus therefore saw her weeping, and the Jews also weeping which came with her, he groaned in the spirit, and was troubled,

34And said, Where have ye laid him? They said unto him, Lord, come and see.

35Jesus wept.

36Then said the Jews, Behold how he loved him!

37And some of them said, Could not this man, which opened the eyes of the blind, have caused that even this man should not have died?

38Jesus therefore again groaning in himself cometh to the grave. It was a cave, and a stone lay upon it.

39Jesus said, Take ye away the stone. Martha, the sister of him that was dead, saith unto him, Lord, by this time he stinketh: for he hath been *dead* four days.

40Jesus saith unto her, Said I not unto thee, that, if thou wouldest believe, thou shouldest see the glory of God?

41Then they took away the stone *from the place* where the dead was laid. And Jesus lifted up *his* eyes, and said, Father, I thank thee that thou hast heard me.

42And I knew that thou hearest me always: but because of the people which stand by I said *it,* that they may believe that thou hast sent me.

43And when he thus had spoken, he cried with a loud voice, Lazarus, come forth.

44And he that was dead came forth, bound hand and foot with graveclothes: and his face was bound about with a napkin. Jesus saith unto them, Loose him, and let him go.

45Then many of the Jews which came to Mary, and had seen the things which Jesus did, believed on him.

46But some of them went their ways to the Pharisees, and told them what things Jesus had done.

47¶ Then gathered the chief priests and the Pharisees a council, and said, What do we? for this man doeth many miracles.

48If we let him thus alone, all *men* will believe on him: and the Romans shall come and take away both our place and nation.

49And one of them, *named* Caiaphas, being the high priest that same year, said unto them, Ye know nothing at all,

New International

she went out to meet him, but Mary stayed at home.

21"Lord," Martha said to Jesus, "if you had been here, my brother would not have died. 22But I know that even now God will give you whatever you ask."

23Jesus said to her, "Your brother will rise again."

24Martha answered, "I know he will rise again in the resurrection at the last day."

25Jesus said to her, "I am the resurrection and the life. He who believes in me will live, even though he dies; 26and whoever lives and believes in me will never die. Do you believe this?"

27"Yes, Lord," she told him, "I believe that you are the Christ,[a] the Son of God, who was to come into the world."

28And after she had said this, she went back and called her sister Mary aside. "The Teacher is here," she said, "and is asking for you." 29When Mary heard this, she got up quickly and went to him. 30Now Jesus had not yet entered the village, but was still at the place where Martha had met him. 31When the Jews who had been with Mary in the house, comforting her, noticed how quickly she got up and went out, they followed her, supposing she was going to the tomb to mourn there.

32When Mary reached the place where Jesus was and saw him, she fell at his feet and said, "Lord, if you had been here, my brother would not have died."

33When Jesus saw her weeping, and the Jews who had come along with her also weeping, he was deeply moved in spirit and troubled. 34"Where have you laid him?" he asked.

"Come and see, Lord," they replied.

35Jesus wept.

36Then the Jews said, "See how he loved him!"

37But some of them said, "Could not he who opened the eyes of the blind man have kept this man from dying?"

Jesus Raises Lazarus From the Dead

38Jesus, once more deeply moved, came to the tomb. It was a cave with a stone laid across the entrance. 39"Take away the stone," he said.

"But, Lord," said Martha, the sister of the dead man, "by this time there is a bad odor, for he has been there four days."

40Then Jesus said, "Did I not tell you that if you believed, you would see the glory of God?"

41So they took away the stone. Then Jesus looked up and said, "Father, I thank you that you have heard me. 42I knew that you always hear me, but I said this for the benefit of the people standing here, that they may believe that you sent me."

43When he had said this, Jesus called in a loud voice, "Lazarus, come out!" 44The dead man came out, his hands and feet wrapped with strips of linen, and a cloth around his face.

Jesus said to them, "Take off the grave clothes and let him go."

The Plot to Kill Jesus

45Therefore many of the Jews who had come to visit Mary, and had seen what Jesus did, put their faith in him. 46But some of them went to the Pharisees and told them what Jesus had done. 47Then the chief priests and the Pharisees called a meeting of the Sanhedrin.

"What are we accomplishing?" they asked. "Here is this man performing many miraculous signs. 48If we let him go on like this, everyone will believe in him, and then the Romans will come and take away both our place[b] and our nation."

49Then one of them, named Caiaphas, who was high priest that year, spoke up, "You know nothing at all!

a 27 Or *Messiah*   b 48 Or *temple*

Living Bible

was coming, she went to meet him. But Mary stayed at home.

21 Martha said to Jesus, "Sir, if you had been here, my brother wouldn't have died. 22 And even now it's not too late, for I know that God will bring my brother back to life again, if you will only ask him to."

23 Jesus told her, "Your brother will come back to life again."

24 "Yes," Martha said, "when everyone else does, on Resurrection Day."

25 Jesus told her, "I am the one who raises the dead and gives them life again. Anyone who believes in me, even though he dies like anyone else, shall live again. 26 He is given eternal life for believing in me and shall never perish. Do you believe this, Martha?"

27 "Yes, Master," she told him. "I believe you are the Messiah, the Son of God, the one we have so long awaited."

28 Then she left him and returned to Mary and, calling her aside from the mourners, told her, "He is here and wants to see you." 29 So Mary went to him at once.

30 Now Jesus had stayed outside the village, at the place where Martha met him. 31 When the Jewish leaders who were at the house trying to console Mary saw her leave so hastily, they assumed she was going to Lazarus' tomb to weep; so they followed her.

32 When Mary arrived where Jesus was, she fell down at his feet, saying, "Sir, if you had been here, my brother would still be alive."

33 When Jesus saw her weeping and the Jewish leaders wailing with her, he was moved with indignation and deeply troubled. 34 "Where is he buried?" he asked them. They told him, "Come and see." 35 Tears came to Jesus' eyes.

36 "They were close friends," the Jewish leaders said. "See how much he loved him."

37, 38 But some said, "This fellow healed a blind man—why couldn't he keep Lazarus from dying?"

And again Jesus was moved with deep anger. Then they came to the tomb. It was a cave with a heavy stone rolled across its door.

39 "Roll the stone aside," Jesus told them.

But Martha, the dead man's sister, said, "By now the smell will be terrible, for he has been dead four days."

40 "But didn't I tell you that you will see a wonderful miracle from God if you believe?" Jesus asked her.

41 So they rolled the stone aside. Then Jesus looked up to heaven and said, "Father, thank you for hearing me. 42 (You always hear me, of course, but I said it because of all these people standing here, so that they will believe you sent me.)" 43 Then he shouted, "Lazarus, come out!"

44 And Lazarus came—bound up in the gravecloth, his face muffled in a head swath. Jesus told them, "Unwrap him and let him go!"

45 And so at last many of the Jewish leaders who were with Mary and saw it happen, finally believed on him. 46 But some went away to the Pharisees and reported it to them.

47 Then the chief priests and Pharisees convened a council to discuss the situation.

"What are we going to do?" they asked each other. "For this man certainly does miracles. 48 If we let him alone the whole nation will follow him—and then the Roman army will come and kill us and take over the Jewish government."

49 And one of them, Caiaphas, who was High Priest that year, said, "You stupid idiots— 50 let this one man

New Revised Standard

coming, she went and met him, while Mary stayed at home. 21 Martha said to Jesus, "Lord, if you had been here, my brother would not have died. 22 But even now I know that God will give you whatever you ask of him." 23 Jesus said to her, "Your brother will rise again." 24 Martha said to him, "I know that he will rise again in the resurrection on the last day." 25 Jesus said to her, "I am the resurrection and the life.c Those who believe in me, even though they die, will live, 26 and everyone who lives and believes in me will never die. Do you believe this?" 27 She said to him, "Yes, Lord, I believe that you are the Messiah,d the Son of God, the one coming into the world."

Jesus Weeps

28 When she had said this, she went back and called her sister Mary, and told her privately, "The Teacher is here and is calling for you." 29 And when she heard it, she got up quickly and went to him. 30 Now Jesus had not yet come to the village, but was still at the place where Martha had met him. 31 The Jews who were with her in the house, consoling her, saw Mary get up quickly and go out. They followed her because they thought that she was going to the tomb to weep there. 32 When Mary came where Jesus was and saw him, she knelt at his feet and said to him, "Lord, if you had been here, my brother would not have died." 33 When Jesus saw her weeping, and the Jews who came with her also weeping, he was greatly disturbed in spirit and deeply moved. 34 He said, "Where have you laid him?" They said to him, "Lord, come and see." 35 Jesus began to weep. 36 So the Jews said, "See how he loved him!" 37 But some of them said, "Could not he who opened the eyes of the blind man have kept this man from dying?"

Jesus Raises Lazarus to Life

38 Then Jesus, again greatly disturbed, came to the tomb. It was a cave, and a stone was lying against it. 39 Jesus said, "Take away the stone." Martha, the sister of the dead man, said to him, "Lord, already there is a stench because he has been dead four days." 40 Jesus said to her, "Did I not tell you that if you believed, you would see the glory of God?" 41 So they took away the stone. And Jesus looked upward and said, "Father, I thank you for having heard me. 42 I knew that you always hear me, but I have said this for the sake of the crowd standing here, so that they may believe that you sent me." 43 When he had said this, he cried with a loud voice, "Lazarus, come out!" 44 The dead man came out, his hands and feet bound with strips of cloth, and his face wrapped in a cloth. Jesus said to them, "Unbind him, and let him go."

The Plot to Kill Jesus

45 Many of the Jews therefore, who had come with Mary and had seen what Jesus did, believed in him. 46 But some of them went to the Pharisees and told them what he had done. 47 So the chief priests and the Pharisees called a meeting of the council, and said, "What are we to do? This man is performing many signs. 48 If we let him go on like this, everyone will believe in him, and the Romans will come and destroy both our holy placee and our nation." 49 But one of them, Caiaphas, who was high priest that year, said to them, "You know nothing at all! 50 You do not understand that it is better for you

---

c Other ancient authorities lack *and the life*   d Or *the Christ*   e Or *our temple*; Greek *our place*

King James

50Nor consider that it is expedient for us, that one man should die for the people, and that the whole nation perish not.

51And this spake he not of himself: but being high priest that year, he prophesied that Jesus should die for that nation;

52And not for that nation only, but that also he should gather together in one the children of God that were scattered abroad.

53Then from that day forth they took counsel together for to put him to death.

54Jesus therefore walked no more openly among the Jews; but went thence unto a country near to the wilderness, into a city called Ephraim, and there continued with his disciples.

55¶ And the Jews' passover was nigh at hand: and many went out of the country up to Jerusalem before the passover, to purify themselves.

56Then sought they for Jesus, and spake among themselves, as they stood in the temple, What think ye, that he will not come to the feast?

57Now both the chief priests and the Pharisees had given a commandment, that, if any man knew where he were, he should show it, that they might take him.

12 THEN JESUS six days before the passover came to Bethany, where Lazarus was which had been dead, whom he raised from the dead.

2There they made him a supper; and Martha served: but Lazarus was one of them that sat at the table with him.

3Then took Mary a pound of ointment of spikenard, very costly, and anointed the feet of Jesus, and wiped his feet with her hair: and the house was filled with the odour of the ointment.

4Then saith one of his disciples, Judas Iscariot, Simon's son, which should betray him,

5Why was not this ointment sold for three hundred pence, and given to the poor?

6This he said, not that he cared for the poor; but because he was a thief, and had the bag, and bare what was put therein.

7Then said Jesus, Let her alone: against the day of my burying hath she kept this.

8For the poor always ye have with you; but me ye have not always.

9Much people of the Jews therefore knew that he was there: and they came not for Jesus' sake only, but that they might see Lazarus also, whom he had raised from the dead.

10¶ But the chief priests consulted that they might put Lazarus also to death;

11Because that by reason of him many of the Jews went away, and believed on Jesus.

12¶ On the next day much people that were come to the feast, when they heard that Jesus was coming to Jerusalem,

13Took branches of palm trees, and went forth to meet him, and cried, Hosanna: Blessed is the King of Israel that cometh in the name of the Lord.

14And Jesus, when he had found a young ass, sat thereon; as it is written,

New International

50You do not realize that it is better for you that one man die for the people than that the whole nation perish."

51He did not say this on his own, but as high priest that year he prophesied that Jesus would die for the Jewish nation, 52and not only for that nation but also for the scattered children of God, to bring them together and make them one. 53So from that day on they plotted to take his life.

54Therefore Jesus no longer moved about publicly among the Jews. Instead he withdrew to a region near the desert, to a village called Ephraim, where he stayed with his disciples.

55When it was almost time for the Jewish Passover, many went up from the country to Jerusalem for their ceremonial cleansing before the Passover. 56They kept looking for Jesus, and as they stood in the temple area they asked one another, "What do you think? Isn't he coming to the Feast at all?" 57But the chief priests and Pharisees had given orders that if anyone found out where Jesus was, he should report it so that they might arrest him.

Jesus Anointed at Bethany

12 SIX DAYS before the Passover, Jesus arrived at Bethany, where Lazarus lived, whom Jesus had raised from the dead. 2Here a dinner was given in Jesus' honor. Martha served, while Lazarus was among those reclining at the table with him. 3Then Mary took about a pinta of pure nard, an expensive perfume; she poured it on Jesus' feet and wiped his feet with her hair. And the house was filled with the fragrance of the perfume.

4But one of his disciples, Judas Iscariot, who was later to betray him, objected, 5"Why wasn't this perfume sold and the money given to the poor? It was worth a year's wages.b" 6He did not say this because he cared about the poor but because he was a thief; as keeper of the money bag, he used to help himself to what was put into it.

7"Leave her alone," Jesus replied. "It was intended, that she should save this perfume for the day of my burial. 8You will always have the poor among you, but you will not always have me."

9Meanwhile a large crowd of Jews found out that Jesus was there and came, not only because of him but also to see Lazarus, whom he had raised from the dead. 10So the chief priests made plans to kill Lazarus as well, 11for on account of him many of the Jews were going over to Jesus and putting their faith in him.

The Triumphal Entry

12The next day the great crowd that had come for the Feast heard that Jesus was on his way to Jerusalem. 13They took palm branches and went out to meet him, shouting,

"Hosanna!c"

"Blessed is he who comes in the name of the Lord!"d

"Blessed is the King of Israel!"

14Jesus found a young donkey and sat upon it, as it is written,

---

a 3 Greek a litra (probably about 0.5 liter)　　b 5 Greek three hundred denarii
c 13 A Hebrew expression meaning "Save!" which became an exclamation of praise　　d 13 Psalm 118:25, 26

Living Bible

die for the people—why should the whole nation perish?"

51This prophecy that Jesus should die for the entire nation came from Caiaphas in his position as High Priest—he didn't think of it by himself, but was inspired to say it. 52It was a prediction that Jesus' death would not be for Israel only, but for all the children of God scattered around the world. 53So from that time on the Jewish leaders began plotting Jesus' death.

54Jesus now stopped his public ministry and left Jerusalem; he went to the edge of the desert, to the village of Ephraim, and stayed there with his disciples.

55The Passover, a Jewish holy day, was near, and many country people arrived in Jerusalem several days early so that they could go through the cleansing ceremony before the Passover began. 56They wanted to see Jesus, and as they gossiped in the Temple, they asked each other, "What do you think? Will he come for the Passover?" 57Meanwhile the chief priests and Pharisees had publicly announced that anyone seeing Jesus must report him immediately so that they could arrest him.

12 SIX DAYS before the Passover ceremonies began, Jesus arrived in Bethany where Lazarus was—the man he had brought back to life. 2A banquet was prepared in Jesus' honor. Martha served, and Lazarus sat at the table with him. 3Then Mary took a jar of costly perfume made from essence of nard, and anointed Jesus' feet with it and wiped them with her hair. And the house was filled with fragrance.

4But Judas Iscariot, one of his disciples—the one who would betray him—said, 5"That perfume was worth a fortune. It should have been sold and the money given to the poor." 6Not that he cared for the poor, but he was in charge of the disciples' funds and often dipped into them for his own use!

7Jesus replied, "Let her alone. She did it in preparation for my burial. 8You can always help the poor, but I won't be with you very long."

9When the ordinary people of Jerusalem heard of his arrival, they flocked to see him and also to see Lazarus—the man who had come back to life again. 10Then the chief priests decided to kill Lazarus too, 11for it was because of him that many of the Jewish leaders had deserted and believed in Jesus as their Messiah.

12The next day, the news that Jesus was on the way to Jerusalem swept through the city, and a huge crowd of Passover visitors 13took palm branches and went down the road to meet him, shouting, "The Savior! God bless the King of Israel! Hail to God's Ambassador!"

14Jesus rode along on a young donkey, fulfilling the prophecy that said: 15"Don't be afraid of your King,

New Revised Standard

to have one man die for the people than to have the whole nation destroyed." 51He did not say this on his own, but being high priest that year he prophesied that Jesus was about to die for the nation, 52and not for the nation only, but to gather into one the dispersed children of God. 53So from that day on they planned to put him to death.

54 Jesus therefore no longer walked about openly among the Jews, but went from there to a town called Ephraim in the region near the wilderness; and he remained there with the disciples.

55 Now the Passover of the Jews was near, and many went up from the country to Jerusalem before the Passover to purify themselves. 56They were looking for Jesus and were asking one another as they stood in the temple, "What do you think? Surely he will not come to the festival, will he?" 57Now the chief priests and the Pharisees had given orders that anyone who knew where Jesuse was should let them know, so that they might arrest him.

Mary Anoints Jesus

12 SIX DAYS before the Passover Jesus came to Bethany, the home of Lazarus, whom he had raised from the dead. 2There they gave a dinner for him. Martha served, and Lazarus was one of those at the table with him. 3Mary took a pound of costly perfume made of pure nard, anointed Jesus' feet, and wiped themf with her hair. The house was filled with the fragrance of the perfume. 4But Judas Iscariot, one of his disciples (the one who was about to betray him), said, 5"Why was this perfume not sold for three hundred denariig and the money given to the poor?" 6(He said this not because he cared about the poor, but because he was a thief; he kept the common purse and used to steal what was put into it.) 7Jesus said, "Leave her alone. She bought ith so that she might keep it for the day of my burial. 8You always have the poor with you, but you do not always have me."

The Plot to Kill Lazarus

9 When the great crowd of the Jews learned that he was there, they came not only because of Jesus but also to see Lazarus, whom he had raised from the dead. 10So the chief priests planned to put Lazarus to death as well, 11since it was on account of him that many of the Jews were deserting and were believing in Jesus.

Jesus' Triumphal Entry into Jerusalem

12 The next day the great crowd that had come to the festival heard that Jesus was coming to Jerusalem. 13So they took branches of palm trees and went out to meet him, shouting,

"Hosanna!
Blessed is the one who comes in the name
of the Lord—
the King of Israel!"

14Jesus found a young donkey and sat on it; as it is written:

---

e Gk he f Gk his feet g Three hundred denarii would be nearly a year's wages for a laborer h Gk lacks She bought it

King James

15Fear not, daughter of Zion: behold, thy King cometh, sitting on an ass's colt.

16These things understood not his disciples at the first: but when Jesus was glorified, then remembered they that these things were written of him, and *that* they had done these things unto him.

17The people therefore that was with him when he called Lazarus out of his grave, and raised him from the dead, bare record.

18For this cause the people also met him, for that they heard that he had done this miracle.

19The Pharisees therefore said among themselves, Perceive ye how ye prevail nothing? behold, the world is gone after him.

20¶ And there were certain Greeks among them that came up to worship at the feast:

21The same came therefore to Philip, which was of Bethsaida of Galilee, and desired him, saying, Sir, we would see Jesus.

22Philip cometh and telleth Andrew: and again Andrew and Philip tell Jesus.

23¶ And Jesus answered them, saying, The hour is come, that the Son of man should be glorified.

24Verily, verily, I say unto you, Except a corn of wheat fall into the ground and die, it abideth alone: but if it die, it bringeth forth much fruit.

25He that loveth his life shall lose it; and he that hateth his life in this world shall keep it unto life eternal.

26If any man serve me, let him follow me; and where I am, there shall also my servant be: if any man serve me, him will *my* Father honour.

27Now is my soul troubled; and what shall I say? Father, save me from this hour: but for this cause came I unto this hour.

28Father, glorify thy name. Then came there a voice from heaven, *saying,* I have both glorified *it,* and will glorify *it* again.

29The people therefore, that stood by, and heard *it,* said that it thundered: others said, An angel spake to him.

30Jesus answered and said, This voice came not because of me, but for your sakes.

31Now is the judgment of this world: now shall the prince of this world be cast out.

32And I, if I be lifted up from the earth, will draw all *men* unto me.

33This he said, signifying what death he should die.

34The people answered him, We have heard out of the law that Christ abideth for ever: and how sayest thou, The Son of man must be lifted up? who is this Son of man?

35Then Jesus said unto them, Yet a little while is the light with you. Walk while ye have the light, lest darkness come upon you: for he that walketh in darkness knoweth not whither he goeth.

36While ye have light, believe in the light, that ye may be the children of light. These things spake Jesus, and departed, and did hide himself from them.

37¶ But though he had done so many miracles before them, yet they believed not on him:

38That the saying of Esaias the prophet might be fulfilled, which he spake, Lord, who hath believed our report? and to whom hath the arm of the Lord been revealed?

39Therefore they could not believe, because that Esaias said again,

40He hath blinded their eyes, and hardened their heart; that they should not see with *their* eyes, nor understand with *their* heart, and be converted, and I should heal them.

New International

15"Do not be afraid, O Daughter of Zion;
see, your king is coming,
seated on a donkey's colt."[a]

16At first his disciples did not understand all this. Only after Jesus was glorified did they realize that these things had been written about him and that they had done these things to him.

17Now the crowd that was with him when he called Lazarus from the tomb and raised him from the dead continued to spread the word. 18Many people, because they had heard that he had given this miraculous sign, went out to meet him. 19So the Pharisees said to one another, "See, this is getting us nowhere. Look how the whole world has gone after him!"

Jesus Predicts His Death

20Now there were some Greeks among those who went up to worship at the Feast. 21They came to Philip, who was from Bethsaida in Galilee, with a request. "Sir," they said, "we would like to see Jesus." 22Philip went to tell Andrew; Andrew and Philip in turn told Jesus.

23Jesus replied, "The hour has come for the Son of Man to be glorified. 24I tell you the truth, unless a kernel of wheat falls to the ground and dies, it remains only a single seed. But if it dies, it produces many seeds. 25The man who loves his life will lose it, while the man who hates his life in this world will keep it for eternal life. 26Whoever serves me must follow me; and where I am, my servant also will be. My Father will honor the one who serves me.

27"Now my heart is troubled, and what shall I say? 'Father, save me from this hour'? No, it was for this very reason I came to this hour. 28Father, glorify your name!"

Then a voice came from heaven, "I have glorified it, and will glorify it again." 29The crowd that was there and heard it said it had thundered; others said an angel had spoken to him.

30Jesus said, "This voice was for your benefit, not mine. 31Now is the time for judgment on this world; now the prince of this world will be driven out. 32But I, when I am lifted up from the earth, will draw all men to myself." 33He said this to show the kind of death he was going to die.

34The crowd spoke up, "We have heard from the Law that the Christ[b] will remain forever, so how can you say, 'The Son of Man must be lifted up'? Who is this 'Son of Man'?"

35Then Jesus told them, "You are going to have the light just a little while longer. Walk while you have the light, before darkness overtakes you. The man who walks in the dark does not know where he is going. 36Put your trust in the light while you have it, so that you may become sons of light." When he had finished speaking, Jesus left and hid himself from them.

The Jews Continue in Their Unbelief

37Even after Jesus had done all these miraculous signs in their presence, they still would not believe in him. 38This was to fulfill the word of Isaiah the prophet:

"Lord, who has believed our message
and to whom has the arm of the Lord been
revealed?"[c]

39For this reason they could not believe, because, as Isaiah says elsewhere:

40"He has blinded their eyes
and deadened their hearts,
so they can neither see with their eyes,
nor understand with their hearts,
nor turn—and I would heal them."[d]

---

[a] *15* Zech. 9:9   [b] *34* Or *Messiah*   [c] *38* Isaiah 53:1   [d] *40* Isaiah 6:10

Living Bible

people of Israel, for he will come to you meekly, sitting on a donkey's colt!"

16(His disciples didn't realize at the time that this was a fulfillment of prophecy; but after Jesus returned to his glory in heaven, then they noticed how many prophecies of Scripture had come true before their eyes.)

17And those in the crowd who had seen Jesus call Lazarus back to life were telling all about it. 18That was the main reason why so many went out to meet him— because they had heard about this mighty miracle.

19Then the Pharisees said to each other, "We've lost. Look—the whole world has gone after him!"

20Some Greeks who had come to Jerusalem to attend the Passover 21paid a visit to Philip,e who was from Bethsaida, and said, "Sir, we want to meet Jesus." 22Philip told Andrew about it, and they went together to ask Jesus.

23, 24Jesus replied that the time had come for him to return to his glory in heaven, and that "I must fall and die like a kernel of wheat that falls into the furrows of the earth. Unless I die I will be alone—a single seed. But my death will produce many new wheat kernels—a plentiful harvest of new lives. 25If you love your life down here—you will lose it. If you despise your life down here—you will exchange it for eternal glory.

26"If these Greeksf want to be my disciples, tell them to come and follow me, for my servants must be where I am. And if they follow me, the Father will honor them. 27Now my soul is deeply troubled. Shall I pray, 'Father, save me from what lies ahead'? But that is the very reason why I came! 28Father, bring glory and honor to your name."

Then a voice spoke from heaven saying, "I have already done this, and I will do it again." 29When the crowd heard the voice, some of them thought it was thunder, while others declared an angel had spoken to him.

30Then Jesus told them, "The voice was for your benefit, not mine. 31The time of judgment for the world has come—and the time when Satan,g the prince of this world, shall be cast out. 32And when I am lifted up [on the crossh], I will draw everyone to me." 33He said this to indicate how he was going to die.

34"Die?" asked the crowd. "We understood that the Messiah would live forever and never die. Why are you saying he will die? What Messiah are you talking about?"

35Jesus replied, "My light will shine out for you just a little while longer. Walk in it while you can, and go where you want to go before the darkness falls, for then it will be too late for you to find your way. 36Make use of the Light while there is still time; then you will become light bearers."i

After saying these things, Jesus went away and was hidden from them.

37But despite all the miracles he had done, most of the people would not believe he was the Messiah. 38This is exactly what Isaiah the prophet had predicted: "Lord, who will believe us? Who will accept God's mighty miracles as proof?"j 39But they couldn't believe, for as Isaiah also said: 40"Godk has blinded their eyes and hardened their hearts so that they can neither see nor understand nor turn to me to heal them." 41Isaiah was

New Revised Standard

15   "Do not be afraid, daughter of Zion.
    Look, your king is coming,
      sitting on a donkey's colt!"

16His disciples did not understand these things at first; but when Jesus was glorified, then they remembered that these things had been written of him and had been done to him. 17So the crowd that had been with him when he called Lazarus out of the tomb and raised him from the dead continued to testify.l 18It was also because they heard that he had performed this sign that the crowd went to meet him. 19The Pharisees then said to one another, "You see, you can do nothing. Look, the world has gone after him!"

Some Greeks Wish to See Jesus

20 Now among those who went up to worship at the festival were some Greeks. 21They came to Philip, who was from Bethsaida in Galilee, and said to him, "Sir, we wish to see Jesus." 22Philip went and told Andrew; then Andrew and Philip went and told Jesus. 23Jesus answered them, "The hour has come for the Son of Man to be glorified. 24Very truly, I tell you, unless a grain of wheat falls into the earth and dies, it remains just a single grain; but if it dies, it bears much fruit. 25Those who love their life lose it, and those who hate their life in this world will keep it for eternal life. 26Whoever serves me must follow me, and where I am, there will my servant be also. Whoever serves me, the Father will honor.

Jesus Speaks about His Death

27   "Now my soul is troubled. And what should I say—'Father, save me from this hour'? No, it is for this reason that I have come to this hour. 28Father, glorify your name." Then a voice came from heaven, "I have glorified it, and I will glorify it again." 29The crowd standing there heard it and said that it was thunder. Others said, "An angel has spoken to him." 30Jesus answered, "This voice has come for your sake, not for mine. 31Now is the judgment of this world; now the ruler of this world will be driven out. 32And I, when I am lifted up from the earth, will draw all peoplem to myself." 33He said this to indicate the kind of death he was to die. 34The crowd answered him, "We have heard from the law that the Messiahn remains forever. How can you say that the Son of Man must be lifted up? Who is this Son of Man?" 35Jesus said to them, "The light is with you for a little longer. Walk while you have the light, so that the darkness may not overtake you. If you walk in the darkness, you do not know where you are going. 36While you have the light, believe in the light, so that you may become children of light."

The Unbelief of the People

After Jesus had said this, he departed and hid from them. 37Although he had performed so many signs in their presence, they did not believe in him. 38This was to fulfill the word spoken by the prophet Isaiah:

  "Lord, who has believed our message,
    and to whom has the arm of the Lord been
      revealed?"

39And so they could not believe, because Isaiah also said,

40   "He has blinded their eyes
    and hardened their heart,
    so that they might not look with their eyes,
    and understand with their heart and turn—
    and I would heal them."

---

e 12:21 Philip. His name was Greek, though he was a Jew.   f 12:26 If these Greeks, literally, "If any man."   g 12:31 Satan, literally, "prince of this world." See 2 Cor 4:4 and Eph 2:2 and 6:12.   h 12:32 on the cross, implied.   i 12:36 you will become light bearers, literally, "sons of light."   j 12:38 Who will accept God's mighty miracles as proof? Literally, "To whom has the arm of the Lord been revealed?" (Isa 53:1).   k 12:40 God, literally, "He." The Greek here is a very free rendering, or paraphrase, of Isa 6:10.

---

l Other ancient authorities read with him began to testify that he had called. . .from the dead   m Other ancient authorities read all things   n Or the Christ

King James

41These things said Esaias, when he saw his glory, and spake of him.

42¶ Nevertheless among the chief rulers also many believed on him; but because of the Pharisees they did not confess *him*, lest they should be put out of the synagogue:

43For they loved the praise of men more than the praise of God.

44¶ Jesus cried and said, He that believeth on me, believeth not on me, but on him that sent me.

45And he that seeth me seeth him that sent me.

46I am come a light into the world, that whosoever believeth on me should not abide in darkness.

47And if any man hear my words, and believe not, I judge him not: for I came not to judge the world, but to save the world.

48He that rejecteth me, and receiveth not my words, hath one that judgeth him: the word that I have spoken, the same shall judge him in the last day.

49For I have not spoken of myself; but the Father which sent me, he gave me a commandment, what I should say, and what I should speak.

50And I know that his commandment is life everlasting: whatsoever I speak therefore, even as the Father said unto me, so I speak.

13 NOW BEFORE the feast of the passover, when Jesus knew that his hour was come that he should depart out of this world unto the Father, having loved his own which were in the world, he loved them unto the end.

2And supper being ended, the devil having now put into the heart of Judas Iscariot, Simon's *son*, to betray him;

3Jesus knowing that the Father had given all things into his hands, and that he was come from God, and went to God;

4He riseth from supper, and laid aside his garments; and took a towel, and girded himself.

5After that he poureth water into a basin, and began to wash the disciples' feet, and to wipe *them* with the towel wherewith he was girded.

6Then cometh he to Simon Peter: and Peter saith unto him, Lord, dost thou wash my feet?

7Jesus answered and said unto him, What I do thou knowest not now; but thou shalt know hereafter.

8Peter saith unto him, Thou shalt never wash my feet. Jesus answered him, If I wash thee not, thou hast no part with me.

9Simon Peter saith unto him, Lord, not my feet only, but also *my* hands and *my* head.

10Jesus saith to him, He that is washed needeth not save to wash *his* feet, but is clean every whit: and ye are clean, but not all.

11For he knew who should betray him; therefore said he, Ye are not all clean.

12So after he had washed their feet, and had taken his garments, and was set down again, he said unto them, Know ye what I have done to you?

13Ye call me Master and Lord: and ye say well; for *so* I am.

14If I then, *your* Lord and Master, have washed your feet; ye also ought to wash one another's feet.

15For I have given you an example, that ye should do as I have done to you.

16Verily, verily, I say unto you, The servant is not greater than his lord; neither he that is sent greater than he that sent him.

17If ye know these things, happy are ye if ye do them.

New International

41Isaiah said this because he saw Jesus' glory and spoke about him.

42Yet at the same time many even among the leaders believed in him. But because of the Pharisees they would not confess their faith for fear they would be put out of the synagogue; 43for they loved praise from men more than praise from God.

44Then Jesus cried out, "When a man believes in me, he does not believe in me only, but in the one who sent me. 45When he looks at me, he sees the one who sent me. 46I have come into the world as a light, so that no one who believes in me should stay in darkness.

47"As for the person who hears my words but does not keep them, I do not judge him. For I did not come to judge the world, but to save it. 48There is a judge for the one who rejects me and does not accept my words; that very word which I spoke will condemn him at the last day. 49For I did not speak of my own accord, but the Father who sent me commanded me what to say and how to say it. 50I know that his command leads to eternal life. So whatever I say is just what the Father has told me to say."

Jesus Washes His Disciples' Feet

13 IT WAS just before the Passover Feast. Jesus knew that the time had come for him to leave this world and go to the Father. Having loved his own who were in the world, he now showed them the full extent of his love.[a]

2The evening meal was being served, and the devil had already prompted Judas Iscariot, son of Simon, to betray Jesus. 3Jesus knew that the Father had put all things under his power, and that he had come from God and was returning to God; 4so he got up from the meal, took off his outer clothing, and wrapped a towel around his waist. 5After that, he poured water into a basin and began to wash his disciples' feet, drying them with the towel that was wrapped around him.

6He came to Simon Peter, who said to him, "Lord, are you going to wash my feet?"

7Jesus replied, "You do not realize now what I am doing, but later you will understand."

8"No," said Peter, "you shall never wash my feet." Jesus answered, "Unless I wash you, you have no part with me."

9"Then, Lord," Simon Peter replied, "not just my feet but my hands and my head as well!"

10Jesus answered, "A person who has had a bath needs only to wash his feet; his whole body is clean. And you are clean, though not every one of you." 11For he knew who was going to betray him, and that was why he said not every one was clean.

12When he had finished washing their feet, he put on his clothes and returned to his place. "Do you understand what I have done for you?" he asked them. 13"You call me 'Teacher' and 'Lord,' and rightly so, for that is what I am. 14Now that I, your Lord and Teacher, have washed your feet, you also should wash one another's feet. 15I have set you an example that you should do as I have done for you. 16I tell you the truth, no servant is greater than his master, nor is a messenger greater than the one who sent him. 17Now that you know these things, you will be blessed if you do them.

---

a 1 Or *he loved them to the last*

Living Bible

referring to Jesus when he made this prediction, for he had seen a vision of the Messiah's glory.

42However, even many of the Jewish leaders believed him to be the Messiah but wouldn't admit it to anyone because of their fear that the Pharisees would excommunicate them from the synagogue; 43for they loved the praise of men more than the praise of God.

44Jesus shouted to the crowds, "If you trust me, you are really trusting God. 45For when you see me, you are seeing the one who sent me. 46I have come as a Light to shine in this dark world, so that all who put their trust in me will no longer wander in the darkness. 47If anyone hears me and doesn't obey me, I am not his judge—for I have come to save the world and not to judge it. 48But all who reject me and my message will be judged at the Day of Judgment by the truths I have spoken. 49For these are not my own ideas, but I have told you what the Father said to tell you. 50And I know his instructions lead to eternal life; so whatever he tells me to say, I say!"

13 JESUS KNEW on the evening of Passover Day that it would be his last night on earth before returning to his Father. During supper the devil had already suggested to Judas Iscariot, Simon's son, that this was the night to carry out his plan to betray Jesus. Jesus knew that the Father had given him everything and that he had come from God and would return to God. And how he loved his disciples! 4So he got up from the supper table, took off his robe, wrapped a towel around his loins,b 5poured water into a basin, and began to wash the disciples' feet and to wipe them with the towel he had around him.

6When he came to Simon Peter, Peter said to him, "Master, you shouldn't be washing our feet like this!"

7Jesus replied, "You don't understand now why I am doing it; some day you will."

8"No," Peter protested, "you shall never wash my feet!"

"But if I don't, you can't be my partner," Jesus replied.

9Simon Peter exclaimed, "Then wash my hands and head as well—not just my feet!"

10Jesus replied, "One who has bathed all over needs only to have his feet washed to be entirely clean. Now you are clean—but that isn't true of everyone here." 11For Jesus knew who would betray him. That is what he meant when he said, "Not all of you are clean."

12After washing their feet he put on his robe again and sat down and asked, "Do you understand what I was doing? 13You call me 'Master' and 'Lord,' and you do well to say it, for it is true. 14And since I, the Lord and Teacher, have washed your feet, you ought to wash each other's feet. 15I have given you an example to follow: do as I have done to you. 16How true it is that a servant is not greater than his master. Nor is the messenger more important than the one who sends him. 17You know these things—now do them! That is the path of blessing.

New Revised Standard

41Isaiah said this becausec he saw his glory and spoke about him. 42Nevertheless many, even of the authorities, believed in him. But because of the Pharisees they did not confess it, for fear that they would be put out of the synagogue; 43for they loved human glory more than the glory that comes from God.

Summary of Jesus' Teaching

44 Then Jesus cried aloud: "Whoever believes in me believes not in me but in him who sent me. 45And whoever sees me sees him who sent me. 46I have come as light into the world, so that everyone who believes in me should not remain in the darkness. 47I do not judge anyone who hears my words and does not keep them, for I came not to judge the world, but to save the world. 48The one who rejects me and does not receive my word has a judge; on the last day the word that I have spoken will serve as judge, 49for I have not spoken on my own, but the Father who sent me has himself given me a commandment about what to say and what to speak. 50And I know that his commandment is eternal life. What I speak, therefore, I speak just as the Father has told me."

Jesus Washes the Disciples' Feet

13 NOW BEFORE the festival of the Passover, Jesus knew that his hour had come to depart from this world and go to the Father. Having loved his own who were in the world, he loved them to the end. 2The devil had already put it into the heart of Judas son of Simon Iscariot to betray him. And during supper 3Jesus, knowing that the Father had given all things into his hands, and that he had come from God and was going to God, 4got up from the table,d took off his outer robe, and tied a towel around himself. 5Then he poured water into a basin and began to wash the disciples' feet and to wipe them with the towel that was tied around him. 6He came to Simon Peter, who said to him, "Lord, are you going to wash my feet?" 7Jesus answered, "You do not know now what I am doing, but later you will understand." 8Peter said to him, "You will never wash my feet." Jesus answered, "Unless I wash you, you have no share with me." 9Simon Peter said to him, "Lord, not my feet only but also my hands and my head!" 10Jesus said to him, "One who has bathed does not need to wash, except for the feet,e but is entirely clean. And youf are clean, though not all of you." 11For he knew who was to betray him; for this reason he said, "Not all of you are clean."

12 After he had washed their feet, had put on his robe, and had returned to the table, he said to them, "Do you know what I have done to you? 13You call me Teacher and Lord—and you are right, for that is what I am. 14So if I, your Lord and Teacher, have washed your feet, you also ought to wash one another's feet. 15For I have set you an example, that you also should do as I have done to you. 16Very truly, I tell you, servantsg are not greater than their master, nor are messengers greater than the one who sent them. 17If you know these things, you are blessed if you do them. 18I am not

---

b 13:4 *wrapped a towel around his loins*, as the lowliest slave would dress.

c Other ancient witnesses read *when*   d Gk *from supper*   e Other ancient authorities lack *except for the feet*   f The Greek word for *you* here is plural   g Gk *slaves*

King James

18¶ I speak not of you all: I know whom I have chosen: but that the scripture may be fulfilled, He that eateth bread with me hath lifted up his heel against me.

19Now I tell you before it come, that, when it is come to pass, ye may believe that I am *he*.

20Verily, verily, I say unto you, He that receiveth whomsoever I send receiveth me; and he that receiveth me receiveth him that sent me.

21When Jesus had thus said, he was troubled in spirit, and testified, and said, Verily, verily, I say unto you, that one of you shall betray me.

22Then the disciples looked one on another, doubting of whom he spake.

23Now there was leaning on Jesus' bosom one of his disciples, whom Jesus loved.

24Simon Peter therefore beckoned to him, that he should ask who it should be of whom he spake.

25He then lying on Jesus' breast saith unto him, Lord, who is it?

26Jesus answered, He it is, to whom I shall give a sop, when I have dipped *it*. And when he had dipped the sop, he gave *it* to Judas Iscariot, *the son* of Simon.

27And after the sop Satan entered into him. Then said Jesus unto him, That thou doest, do quickly.

28Now no man at the table knew for what intent he spake this unto him.

29For some *of them* thought, because Judas had the bag, that Jesus had said unto him, Buy *those things* that we have need of against the feast; or, that he should give something to the poor.

30He then having received the sop went immediately out: and it was night.

31¶ Therefore, when he was gone out, Jesus said, Now is the Son of man glorified, and God is glorified in him.

32If God be glorified in him, God shall also glorify him in himself, and shall straightway glorify him.

33Little children, yet a little while I am with you. Ye shall seek me: and as I said unto the Jews, Whither I go, ye cannot come; so now I say to you.

34A new commandment I give unto you, That ye love one another; as I have loved you, that ye also love one another.

35By this shall all *men* know that ye are my disciples, if ye have love one to another.

36¶ Simon Peter said unto him, Lord, whither goest thou? Jesus answered him, Whither I go, thou canst not follow me now; but thou shalt follow me afterwards.

37Peter said unto him, Lord, why cannot I follow thee now? I will lay down my life for thy sake.

38Jesus answered him, Wilt thou lay down thy life for my sake? Verily, verily, I say unto thee, The cock shall not crow, till thou hast denied me thrice.

14 LET NOT your heart be troubled: ye believe in God, believe also in me.

2In my Father's house are many mansions: if *it were* not *so*, I would have told you. I go to prepare a place for you.

3And if I go and prepare a place for you, I will come again, and receive you unto myself; that where I am, *there* ye may be also.

4And whither I go ye know, and the way ye know.

New International

Jesus Predicts His Betrayal

18"I am not referring to all of you; I know those I have chosen. But this is to fulfill the scripture: 'He who shares my bread has lifted up his heel against me.'[a]

19"I am telling you now before it happens, so that when it does happen you will believe that I am He. 20I tell you the truth, whoever accepts anyone I send accepts me; and whoever accepts me accepts the one who sent me."

21After he had said this, Jesus was troubled in spirit and testified, "I tell you the truth, one of you is going to betray me."

22His disciples stared at one another, at a loss to know which of them he meant. 23One of them, the disciple whom Jesus loved, was reclining next to him. 24Simon Peter motioned to this disciple and said, "Ask him which one he means."

25Leaning back against Jesus, he asked him, "Lord, who is it?"

26Jesus answered, "It is the one to whom I will give this piece of bread when I have dipped it in the dish." Then, dipping the piece of bread, he gave it to Judas Iscariot, son of Simon. 27As soon as Judas took the bread, Satan entered into him.

"What you are about to do, do quickly," Jesus told him, 28but no one at the meal understood why Jesus said this to him. 29Since Judas had charge of the money, some thought Jesus was telling him to buy what was needed for the Feast, or to give something to the poor. 30As soon as Judas had taken the bread, he went out. And it was night.

Jesus Predicts Peter's Denial

31When he was gone, Jesus said, "Now is the Son of Man glorified and God is glorified in him. 32If God is glorified in him,[b] God will glorify the Son in himself, and will glorify him at once.

33"My children, I will be with you only a little longer. You will look for me, and just as I told the Jews, so I tell you now: Where I am going, you cannot come.

34"A new command I give you: Love one another. As I have loved you, so you must love one another. 35By this all men will know that you are my disciples, if you love one another."

36Simon Peter asked him, "Lord, where are you going?"

Jesus replied, "Where I am going, you cannot follow now, but you will follow later."

37Peter asked, "Lord, why can't I follow you now? I will lay down my life for you."

38Then Jesus answered, "Will you really lay down your life for me? I tell you the truth, before the rooster crows, you will disown me three times!

Jesus Comforts His Disciples

14 "DO NOT let your hearts be troubled. Trust in God[c]; trust also in me. 2In my Father's house are many rooms; if it were not so, I would have told you. I am going there to prepare a place for you. 3And if I go and prepare a place for you, I will come back and take you to be with me that you also may be where I am. 4You know the way to the place where I am going."

---

a *18* Psalm 41:9   b *32* Many early manuscripts do not have *If God is glorified in him.*   c *1* Or *You trust in God*

Living Bible

18"I am not saying these things to all of you; I know so well each one of you I chose. The Scripture declares, 'One who eats supper with me will betray me,' and this will soon come true. 19I tell you this now so that when it happens, you will believe on me.

20"Truly, anyone welcoming my messenger is welcoming me. And to welcome me is to welcome the Father who sent me."

21Now Jesus was in great anguish of spirit and exclaimed, "Yes, it is true—one of you will betray me." 22The disciples looked at each other, wondering whom he could mean. 23Since Id was sitting nexte to Jesus at the table, being his closest friend, 24Simon Peter motioned to me to ask him who it was who would do this terrible deed.

25So I turnedf and asked him, "Lord, who is it?" 26He told me, "It is the one I honor by giving the bread dipped in the sauce."g

And when he had dipped it, he gave it to Judas, son of Simon Iscariot.

27As soon as Judas had eaten it, Satan entered into him. Then Jesus told him, "Hurry—do it now."

28None of the others at the table knew what Jesus meant. 29Some thought that since Judas was their treasurer, Jesus was telling him to go and pay for the food or to give some money to the poor. 30Judas left at once, going out into the night.

31As soon as Judas left the room, Jesus said, "My time has come; the glory of God will soon surround me—and God shall receive great praise because of all that happens to me. 32And God shall give me his own glory, and this so very soon. 33Dear, dear children, how brief are these moments before I must go away and leave you! Then, though you search for me, you cannot come to me—just as I told the Jewish leaders.

34"And so I am giving a new commandment to you now—love each other just as much as I love you. 35Your strong love for each other will prove to the world that you are my disciples."

36Simon Peter said, "Master, where are you going?"

And Jesus replied, "You can't go with me now; but you will follow me later."

37"But why can't I come now?" he asked, "for I am ready to die for you."

38Jesus answered, "Die for me? No—three times before the cock crows tomorrow morning, you will deny that you even know me!"

14 "LET NOT your heart be troubled. You are trusting God, now trust in me. 2, 3There are many homes up there where my Father lives, and I am going to prepare one for your coming. When everything is ready, then I will come and get you, so that you can always be with me where I am. If this weren't so, I would tell you plainly. 4And you know where I am going and how to get there."

New Revised Standard

speaking of all of you; I know whom I have chosen. But it is to fulfill the scripture, 'The one who ate my breadh has lifted his heel against me.' 19I tell you this now, before it occurs, so that when it does occur, you may believe that I am he.i 20Very truly, I tell you, whoever receives one whom I send receives me; and whoever receives me receives him who sent me."

Jesus Foretells His Betrayal

21 After saying this Jesus was troubled in spirit, and declared, "Very truly, I tell you, one of you will betray me." 22The disciples looked at one another, uncertain of whom he was speaking. 23One of his disciples—the one whom Jesus loved—was reclining next to him; 24Simon Peter therefore motioned to him to ask Jesus of whom he was speaking. 25So while reclining next to Jesus, he asked him, "Lord, who is it?" 26Jesus answered, "It is the one to whom I give this piece of bread when I have dipped it in the dish."j So when he had dipped the piece of bread, he gave it to Judas son of Simon Iscariot.k 27After he received the piece of bread,l Satan entered into him. Jesus said to him, "Do quickly what you are going to do." 28Now no one at the table knew why he said this to him. 29Some thought that, because Judas had the common purse, Jesus was telling him, "Buy what we need for the festival"; or, that he should give something to the poor. 30So, after receiving the piece of bread, he immediately went out. And it was night.

The New Commandment

31 When he had gone out, Jesus said, "Now the Son of Man has been glorified, and God has been glorified in him. 32If God has been glorified in him,m God will also glorify him in himself and will glorify him at once. 33Little children, I am with you only a little longer. You will look for me; and as I said to the Jews so now I say to you, 'Where I am going, you cannot come.' 34I give you a new commandment, that you love one another. Just as I have loved you, you also should love one another. 35By this everyone will know that you are my disciples, if you have love for one another."

Jesus Foretells Peter's Denial

36 Simon Peter said to him, "Lord, where are you going?" Jesus answered, "Where I am going, you cannot follow me now; but you will follow afterward." 37Peter said to him, "Lord, why can I not follow you now? I will lay down my life for you." 38Jesus answered, "Will you lay down your life for me? Very truly, I tell you, before the cock crows, you will have denied me three times.

Jesus the Way to the Father

14 "DO NOT let your hearts be troubled. Believen in God, believe also in me. 2In my Father's house there are many dwelling places. If it were not so, would I have told you that I go to prepare a place for you?o 3And if I go and prepare a place for you, I will come again and will take you to myself, so that where I am, there you may be also. 4And you know the way to the place where I am going."p 5Thomas said to him,

d 13:23 Since I, literally, "There was one at the table." All commentators believe him to be John, the writer of this book.   e 13:23 was sitting next, literally, "reclining on Jesus' bosom." The custom of the period was to recline around the table, leaning on the left elbow. John, next to Jesus, was at his side.   f 13:25 So I turned, literally, "leaning back against Jesus' chest," to whisper his inquiry.   g 13:26 giving the bread dipped in the sauce, literally, "He it is for whom I shall dip the sop and give it to him." The honored guest was thus singled out in the custom of that time.

h Other ancient authorities read ate bread with me   i Gk I am   j Gk dipped it   k Other ancient authorities read Judas Iscariot son of Simon; others, Judas son of Simon from Karyot (Kerioth)   l Gk After the piece of bread   m Other ancient authorities lack If God has been glorified in him   n Or You believe   o Or If it were not so, I would have told you; for I go to prepare a place for you   p Other ancient authorities read Where I am going you know, and the way you know

King James

5Thomas saith unto him, Lord, we know not whither thou goest; and how can we know the way?

6Jesus saith unto him, I am the way, the truth, and the life: no man cometh unto the Father, but by me.

7If ye had known me, ye should have known my Father also: and from henceforth ye know him, and have seen him.

8Philip saith unto him, Lord, show us the Father, and it sufficeth us.

9Jesus saith unto him, Have I been so long time with you, and yet hast thou not known me, Philip? he that hath seen me hath seen the Father; and how sayest thou *then*, Show us the Father?

10Believest thou not that I am in the Father, and the Father in me? the words that I speak unto you I speak not of myself: but the Father that dwelleth in me, he doeth the works.

11Believe me that I *am* in the Father, and the Father in me: or else believe me for the very works' sake.

12Verily, verily, I say unto you, He that believeth on me, the works that I do shall he do also; and greater *works* than these shall he do; because I go unto my Father.

13And whatsoever ye shall ask in my name, that will I do, that the Father may be glorified in the Son.

14If ye shall ask any thing in my name, I will do *it*.

15¶ If ye love me, keep my commandments.

16And I will pray the Father, and he shall give you another Comforter, that he may abide with you for ever;

17*Even* the Spirit of truth; whom the world cannot receive, because it seeth him not, neither knoweth him: but ye know him; for he dwelleth with you, and shall be in you.

18I will not leave you comfortless: I will come to you.

19Yet a little while, and the world seeth me no more; but ye see me: because I live, ye shall live also.

20At that day ye shall know that I *am* in my Father, and ye in me, and I in you.

21He that hath my commandments, and keepeth them, he it is that loveth me: and he that loveth me shall be loved of my Father, and I will love him, and will manifest myself to him.

22Judas saith unto him, not Iscariot, Lord, how is it that thou wilt manifest thyself unto us, and not unto the world?

23Jesus answered and said unto him, If a man love me, he will keep my words: and my Father will love him, and we will come unto him, and make our abode with him.

24He that loveth me not keepeth not my sayings: and the word which ye hear is not mine, but the Father's which sent me.

25These things have I spoken unto you, being *yet* present with you.

26But the Comforter, *which is* the Holy Ghost, whom the Father will send in my name, he shall teach you all things, and bring all things to your remembrance, whatsoever I have said unto you.

27Peace I leave with you, my peace I give unto you: not as the world giveth, give I unto you. Let not your heart be troubled, neither let it be afraid.

28Ye have heard how I said unto you, I go away, and come *again* unto you. If ye loved me, ye would rejoice, because I said, I go unto the Father: for my Father is greater than I.

29And now I have told you before it come to pass, that, when it is come to pass, ye might believe.

30Hereafter I will not talk much with you: for the prince of this world cometh, and hath nothing in me.

31But that the world may know that I love the Father; and as the Father gave me commandment, even so I do. Arise, let us go hence.

New International

Jesus the Way to the Father

5Thomas said to him, "Lord, we don't know where you are going, so how can we know the way?"

6Jesus answered, "I am the way and the truth and the life. No one comes to the Father except through me. 7If you really knew me, you would knowa my Father as well. From now on, you do know him and have seen him."

8Philip said, "Lord, show us the Father and that will be enough for us."

9Jesus answered: "Don't you know me, Philip, even after I have been among you such a long time? Anyone who has seen me has seen the Father. How can you say, 'Show us the Father'? 10Don't you believe that I am in the Father, and that the Father is in me? The words I say to you are not just my own. Rather, it is the Father, living in me, who is doing his work. 11Believe me when I say that I am in the Father and the Father is in me; or at least believe on the evidence of the miracles themselves. 12I tell you the truth, anyone who has faith in me will do what I have been doing. He will do even greater things than these, because I am going to the Father. 13And I will do whatever you ask in my name, so that the Son may bring glory to the Father. 14You may ask me for anything in my name, and I will do it.

Jesus Promises the Holy Spirit

15"If you love me, you will obey what I command. 16And I will ask the Father, and he will give you another Counselor to be with you forever— 17the Spirit of truth. The world cannot accept him, because it neither sees him nor knows him. But you know him, for he lives with you and will beb in you. 18I will not leave you as orphans; I will come to you. 19Before long, the world will not see me anymore, but you will see me. Because I live, you also will live. 20On that day you will realize that I am in my Father, and you are in me, and I am in you. 21Whoever has my commands and obeys them, he is the one who loves me. He who loves me will be loved by my Father, and I too will love him and show myself to him."

22Then Judas (not Judas Iscariot) said, "But, Lord, why do you intend to show yourself to us and not to the world?"

23Jesus replied, "If anyone loves me, he will obey my teaching. My Father will love him, and we will come to him and make our home with him. 24He who does not love me will not obey my teaching. These words you hear are not my own; they belong to the Father who sent me.

25"All this I have spoken while still with you. 26But the Counselor, the Holy Spirit, whom the Father will send in my name, will teach you all things and will remind you of everything I have said to you. 27Peace I leave with you; my peace I give you. I do not give to you as the world gives. Do not let your hearts be troubled and do not be afraid.

28"You heard me say, 'I am going away and I am coming back to you.' If you loved me, you would be glad that I am going to the Father, for the Father is greater than I. 29I have told you now before it happens, so that when it does happen you will believe. 30I will not speak with you much longer, for the prince of this world is coming. He has no hold on me, 31but the world must learn that I love the Father and that I do exactly what my Father has commanded me.

"Come now; let us leave.

---

a 7 Some early manuscripts *If you really have known me, you will know*
b 17 Some early manuscripts *and is*

Living Bible

5"No, we don't," Thomas said. "We haven't any idea where you are going, so how can we know the way?"

6Jesus told him, "I am the Way—yes, and the Truth and the Life. No one can get to the Father except by means of me. 7If you had known who I am, then you would have known who my Father is. From now on you know him—and have seen him!"

8Philip said, "Sir, show us the Father and we will be satisfied."

9Jesus replied, "Don't you even yet know who I am, Philip, even after all this time I have been with you? Anyone who has seen me has seen the Father! So why are you asking to see him? 10Don't you believe that I am in the Father and the Father is in me? The words I say are not my own but are from my Father who lives in me. And he does his work through me. 11Just believe it— that I am in the Father and the Father is in me. Or else believe it because of the mighty miracles you have seen me do.

12, 13"In solemn truth I tell you, anyone believing in me shall do the same miracles I have done, and even greater ones, because I am going to be with the Father. You can ask him for *anything*, using my name, and I will do it, for this will bring praise to the Father because of what I, the Son, will do for you. 14Yes, ask *anything*, using my name, and I will do it!

15, 16"If you love me, obey me; and I will ask the Father and he will give you another Comforter, and he will never leave you. 17He is the Holy Spirit, the Spirit who leads into all truth. The world at large cannot receive him, for it isn't looking for him and doesn't recognize him. But you do, for he lives with you now and some day shall be in you. 18No, I will not abandon you or leave you as orphans in the storm—I will come to you. 19In just a little while I will be gone from the world, but I will still be present with you. For I will live again— and you will too. 20When I come back to life again, you will know that I am in my Father, and you in me, and I in you. 21The one who obeys me is the one who loves me; and because he loves me, my Father will love him; and I will too, and I will reveal myself to him."

22Judas (not Judas Iscariot, but his other disciple with that name) said to him, "Sir, why are you going to reveal yourself only to us disciples and not to the world at large?"

23Jesus replied, "Because I will only reveal myself to those who love me and obey me. The Father will love them too, and we will come to them and live with them. 24Anyone who doesn't obey me doesn't love me. And remember, I am not making up this answer to your question! It is the answer given by the Father who sent me.

25"I am telling you these things now while I am still with you. 26But when the Father sends the Comforter^c instead of me^d—and by the Comforter I mean the Holy Spirit—he will teach you much, as well as remind you of everything I myself have told you.

27"I am leaving you with a gift—peace of mind and heart! And the peace I give isn't fragile like the peace the world gives. So don't be troubled or afraid.^e 28Remember what I told you—I am going away, but I will come back to you again. If you really love me, you will be very happy for me, for now I can go to the Father, who is greater than I am. 29I have told you these things before they happen so that when they do, you will believe [in me^f].

30"I don't have much more time to talk to you, for the evil prince of this world approaches. He has no power over me, 31but I will freely do what the Father requires of me so that the world will know that I love the Father. Come, let's be going.

New Revised Standard

"Lord, we do not know where you are going. How can we know the way?" 6Jesus said to him, "I am the way, and the truth, and the life. No one comes to the Father except through me. 7If you know me, you will know^g my Father also. From now on you do know him and have seen him."

8 Philip said to him, "Lord, show us the Father, and we will be satisfied." 9Jesus said to him, "Have I been with you all this time, Philip, and you still do not know me? Whoever has seen me has seen the Father. How can you say, 'Show us the Father'? 10Do you not believe that I am in the Father and the Father is in me? The words that I say to you I do not speak on my own; but the Father who dwells in me does his works. 11Believe me that I am in the Father and the Father is in me; but if you do not, then believe me because of the works themselves. 12Very truly, I tell you, the one who believes in me will also do the works that I do and, in fact, will do greater works than these, because I am going to the Father. 13I will do whatever you ask in my name, so that the Father may be glorified in the Son. 14If in my name you ask me^h for anything, I will do it.

The Promise of the Holy Spirit

15 "If you love me, you will keepⁱ my commandments. 16And I will ask the Father, and he will give you another Advocate,^j to be with you forever. 17This is the Spirit of truth, whom the world cannot receive, because it neither sees him nor knows him. You know him, because he abides with you, and he will be in^k you.

18 "I will not leave you orphaned; I am coming to you. 19In a little while the world will no longer see me, but you will see me; because I live, you also will live. 20On that day you will know that I am in my Father, and you in me, and I in you. 21They who have my commandments and keep them are those who love me; and those who love me will be loved by my Father, and I will love them and reveal myself to them." 22Judas (not Iscariot) said to him, "Lord, how is it that you will reveal yourself to us, and not to the world?" 23Jesus answered him, "Those who love me will keep my word, and my Father will love them, and we will come to them and make our home with them. 24Whoever does not love me does not keep my words; and the word that you hear is not mine, but is from the Father who sent me.

25 "I have said these things to you while I am still with you. 26But the Advocate,^j the Holy Spirit, whom the Father will send in my name, will teach you everything, and remind you of all that I have said to you. 27Peace I leave with you; my peace I give to you. I do not give to you as the world gives. Do not let your hearts be troubled, and do not let them be afraid. 28You heard me say to you, 'I am going away, and I am coming to you.' If you loved me, you would rejoice that I am going to the Father, because the Father is greater than I. 29And now I have told you this before it occurs, so that when it does occur, you may believe. 30I will no longer talk much with you, for the ruler of this world is coming. He has no power over me; 31but I do as the Father has commanded me, so that the world may know that I love the Father. Rise, let us be on our way.

---

^c *14:26 the Comforter*, or, "helper."   ^d *14:26 instead of me*, literally, "in my name."   ^e *14:27 So don't be troubled or afraid*, implied.   ^f *14:29 in me*, implied.

^g Other ancient authorities read *If you had known me, you would have known*   ^h Other ancient authorities lack *me*   ⁱ Other ancient authorities read *me, keep*   ^j Or *Helper*   ^k Or *among*

King James

15 I AM the true vine, and my Father is the husbandman.

2Every branch in me that beareth not fruit he taketh away: and every *branch* that beareth fruit, he purgeth it, that it may bring forth more fruit.

3Now ye are clean through the word which I have spoken unto you.

4Abide in me, and I in you. As the branch cannot bear fruit of itself, except it abide in the vine; no more can ye, except ye abide in me.

5I am the vine, ye *are* the branches: He that abideth in me, and I in him, the same bringeth forth much fruit: for without me ye can do nothing.

6If a man abide not in me, he is cast forth as a branch, and is withered; and men gather them, and cast *them* into the fire, and they are burned.

7If ye abide in me, and my words abide in you, ye shall ask what ye will, and it shall be done unto you.

8Herein is my Father glorified, that ye bear much fruit; so shall ye be my disciples.

9As the Father hath loved me, so have I loved you: continue ye in my love.

10If ye keep my commandments, ye shall abide in my love; even as I have kept my Father's commandments, and abide in his love.

11These things have I spoken unto you, that my joy might remain in you, and *that* your joy might be full.

12This is my commandment, That ye love one another, as I have loved you.

13Greater love hath no man than this, that a man lay down his life for his friends.

14Ye are my friends, if ye do whatsoever I command you.

15Henceforth I call you not servants; for the servant knoweth not what his lord doeth: but I have called you friends; for all things that I have heard of my Father I have made known unto you.

16Ye have not chosen me, but I have chosen you, and ordained you, that ye should go and bring forth fruit, and *that* your fruit should remain: that whatsoever ye shall ask of the Father in my name, he may give it you.

17These things I command you, that ye love one another.

18If the world hate you, ye know that it hated me before *it* hated you.

19If ye were of the world, the world would love his own: but because ye are not of the world, but I have chosen you out of the world, therefore the world hateth you.

20Remember the word that I said unto you, The servant is not greater than his lord. If they have persecuted me, they will also persecute you; if they have kept my saying, they will keep yours also.

21But all these things will they do unto you for my name's sake, because they know not him that sent me.

22If I had not come and spoken unto them, they had not had sin: but now they have no cloak for their sin.

23He that hateth me hateth my Father also.

24If I had not done among them the works which none other man did, they had not had sin: but now have they both seen and hated both me and my Father.

25But *this cometh to pass*, that the word might be fulfilled that is written in their law, They hated me without a cause.

26But when the Comforter is come, whom I will send unto you from the Father, *even* the Spirit of truth, which proceedeth from the Father, he shall testify of me:

27And ye also shall bear witness, because ye have been with me from the beginning.

New International

The Vine and the Branches

15 "I AM the true vine, and my Father is the gardener. 2He cuts off every branch in me that bears no fruit, while every branch that does bear fruit he prunes[a] so that it will be even more fruitful. 3You are already clean because of the word I have spoken to you. 4Remain in me, and I will remain in you. No branch can bear fruit by itself; it must remain in the vine. Neither can you bear fruit unless you remain in me.

5"I am the vine; you are the branches. If a man remains in me and I in him, he will bear much fruit; apart from me you can do nothing. 6If anyone does not remain in me, he is like a branch that is thrown away and withers; such branches are picked up, thrown into the fire and burned. 7If you remain in me and my words remain in you, ask whatever you wish, and it will be given you. 8This is to my Father's glory, that you bear much fruit, showing yourselves to be my disciples.

9"As the Father has loved me, so have I loved you. Now remain in my love. 10If you obey my commands, you will remain in my love, just as I have obeyed my Father's commands and remain in his love. 11I have told you this so that my joy may be in you and that your joy may be complete. 12My command is this: Love each other as I have loved you. 13Greater love has no one than this, that he lay down his life for his friends. 14You are my friends if you do what I command. 15I no longer call you servants, because a servant does not know his master's business. Instead, I have called you friends, for everything that I learned from my Father I have made known to you. 16You did not choose me, but I chose you and appointed you to go and bear fruit—fruit that will last. Then the Father will give you whatever you ask in my name. 17This is my command: Love each other.

The World Hates the Disciples

18"If the world hates you, keep in mind that it hated me first. 19If you belonged to the world, it would love you as its own. As it is, you do not belong to the world, but I have chosen you out of the world. That is why the world hates you. 20Remember the words I spoke to you: 'No servant is greater than his master.'[b] If they persecuted me, they will persecute you also. If they obeyed my teaching, they will obey yours also. 21They will treat you this way because of my name, for they do not know the One who sent me. 22If I had not come and spoken to them, they would not be guilty of sin. Now, however, they have no excuse for their sin. 23He who hates me hates my Father as well. 24If I had not done among them what no one else did, they would not be guilty of sin. But now they have seen these miracles, and yet they have hated both me and my Father. 25But this is to fulfill what is written in their Law: 'They hated me without reason.'[c]

26"When the Counselor comes, whom I will send to you from the Father, the Spirit of truth who goes out from the Father, he will testify about me. 27And you also must testify, for you have been with me from the beginning.

---

a 2 The Greek for *prunes* also means *cleans.*   b 20 John 13:16
c 25 Psalms 35:19; 69:4

Living Bible

15 "I AM the true Vine, and my Father is the Gardener. ²He lops off every branch that doesn't produce. And he prunes those branches that bear fruit for even larger crops. ³He has already tended you by pruning you back for greater strength and usefulness by means of the commands I gave you. ⁴Take care to live in me, and let me live in you. For a branch can't produce fruit when severed from the vine. Nor can you be fruitful apart from me.

⁵"Yes, I am the Vine; you are the branches. Whoever lives in me and I in him shall produce a large crop of fruit. For apart from me you can't do a thing. ⁶If anyone separates from me, he is thrown away like a useless branch, withers, and is gathered into a pile with all the others and burned. ⁷But if you stay in me and obey my commands, you may ask any request you like, and it will be granted! ⁸My true disciples produce bountiful harvests. This brings great glory to my Father.

⁹"I have loved you even as the Father has loved me. Live within my love. ¹⁰When you obey me you are living in my love, just as I obey my Father and live in his love. ¹¹I have told you this so that you will be filled with my joy. Yes, your cup of joy will overflow! ¹²I demand that you love each other as much as I love you. ¹³And here is how to measure it—the greatest love is shown when a person lays down his life for his friends; ¹⁴and you are my friends if you obey me. ¹⁵I no longer call you slaves, for a master doesn't confide in his slaves; now you are my friends, proved by the fact that I have told you everything the Father told me.

¹⁶"You didn't choose me! I chose you! I appointed you to go and produce lovely fruit always, so that no matter what you ask for from the Father, using my name, he will give it to you. ¹⁷I demand that you love each other, ¹⁸for you get enough hate from the world! But then, it hated me before it hated you. ¹⁹The world would love you if you belonged to it; but you don't—for I chose you to come out of the world, and so it hates you. ²⁰Do you remember what I told you? 'A slave isn't greater than his master!' So since they persecuted me, naturally they will persecute you. And if they had listened to me, they would listen to you! ²¹The people of the world will persecute you because you belong to me, for they don't know God who sent me.

²²"They would not be guilty if I had not come and spoken to them. But now they have no excuse for their sin. ²³Anyone hating me is also hating my Father. ²⁴If I hadn't done such mighty miracles among them they would not be counted guilty. But as it is, they saw these miracles and yet they hated both of us—me and my Father. ²⁵This has fulfilled what the prophets said concerning the Messiah, 'They hated me without reason.'

²⁶"But I will send you the Comforter—the Holy Spirit, the source of all truth. He will come to you from the Father and will tell you all about me. ²⁷And you also must tell everyone about me, because you have been with me from the beginning.

New Revised Standard

Jesus the True Vine

15 "I AM the true vine, and my Father is the vinegrower. ²He removes every branch in me that bears no fruit. Every branch that bears fruit he prunes[d] to make it bear more fruit. ³You have already been cleansed[d] by the word that I have spoken to you. ⁴Abide in me as I abide in you. Just as the branch cannot bear fruit by itself unless it abides in the vine, neither can you unless you abide in me. ⁵I am the vine, you are the branches. Those who abide in me and I in them bear much fruit, because apart from me you can do nothing. ⁶Whoever does not abide in me is thrown away like a branch and withers; such branches are gathered, thrown into the fire, and burned. ⁷If you abide in me, and my words abide in you, ask for whatever you wish, and it will be done for you. ⁸My Father is glorified by this, that you bear much fruit and become[e] my disciples. ⁹As the Father has loved me, so I have loved you; abide in my love. ¹⁰If you keep my commandments, you will abide in my love, just as I have kept my Father's commandments and abide in his love. ¹¹I have said these things to you so that my joy may be in you, and that your joy may be complete.

12 "This is my commandment, that you love one another as I have loved you. ¹³No one has greater love than this, to lay down one's life for one's friends. ¹⁴You are my friends if you do what I command you. ¹⁵I do not call you servants[f] any longer, because the servant[g] does not know what the master is doing; but I have called you friends, because I have made known to you everything that I have heard from my Father. ¹⁶You did not choose me but I chose you. And I appointed you to go and bear fruit, fruit that will last, so that the Father will give you whatever you ask him in my name. ¹⁷I am giving you these commands so that you may love one another.

The World's Hatred

18 "If the world hates you, be aware that it hated me before it hated you. ¹⁹If you belonged to the world,[h] the world would love you as its own. Because you do not belong to the world, but I have chosen you out of the world—therefore the world hates you. ²⁰Remember the word that I said to you, 'Servants[i] are not greater than their master.' If they persecuted me, they will persecute you; if they kept my word, they will keep yours also. ²¹But they will do all these things to you on account of my name, because they do not know him who sent me. ²²If I had not come and spoken to them, they would not have sin; but now they have no excuse for their sin. ²³Whoever hates me hates my Father also. ²⁴If I had not done among them the works that no one else did, they would not have sin. But now they have seen and hated both me and my Father. ²⁵It was to fulfill the word that is written in their law, 'They hated me without a cause.'

26 "When the Advocate[j] comes, whom I will send to you from the Father, the Spirit of truth who comes from the Father, he will testify on my behalf. ²⁷You also are to testify because you have been with me from the beginning.

---

[d] The same Greek root refers to pruning and cleansing   [e] Or *be*   [f] Gk *slaves*
[g] Gk *slave*   [h] Gk *were of the world*   [i] Gk *Slaves*   [j] Or *Helper*

King James

16 THESE THINGS have I spoken unto you, that ye should not be offended.

2They shall put you out of the synagogues: yea, the time cometh, that whosoever killeth you will think that he doeth God service.

3And these things will they do unto you, because they have not known the Father, nor me.

4But these things have I told you, that when the time shall come, ye may remember that I told you of them. And these things I said not unto you at the beginning, because I was with you.

5But now I go my way to him that sent me; and none of you asketh me, Whither goest thou?

6But because I have said these things unto you, sorrow hath filled your heart.

7Nevertheless I tell you the truth; It is expedient for you that I go away: for if I go not away, the Comforter will not come unto you; but if I depart, I will send him unto you.

8And when he is come, he will reprove the world of sin, and of righteousness, and of judgment:

9Of sin, because they believe not on me;

10Of righteousness, because I go to my Father, and ye see me no more;

11Of judgment, because the prince of this world is judged.

12I have yet many things to say unto you, but ye cannot bear them now.

13Howbeit when he, the Spirit of truth, is come, he will guide you into all truth: for he shall not speak of himself; but whatsoever he shall hear, *that* shall he speak: and he will show you things to come.

14He shall glorify me: for he shall receive of mine, and shall show *it* unto you.

15All things that the Father hath are mine: therefore said I, that he shall take of mine, and shall show *it* unto you.

16A little while, and ye shall not see me: and again, a little while, and ye shall see me, because I go to the Father.

17Then said *some* of his disciples among themselves, What is this that he saith unto us, A little while, and ye shall not see me: and again, a little while, and ye shall see me: and, Because I go to the Father?

18They said therefore, What is this that he saith, A little while? we cannot tell what he saith.

19Now Jesus knew that they were desirous to ask him, and said unto them, Do ye inquire among yourselves of that I said, A little while, and ye shall not see me: and again, a little while, and ye shall see me?

20Verily, verily, I say unto you, That ye shall weep and lament, but the world shall rejoice: and ye shall be sorrowful, but your sorrow shall be turned into joy.

21A woman when she is in travail hath sorrow, because her hour is come: but as soon as she is delivered of the child, she remembereth no more the anguish, for joy that a man is born into the world.

22And ye now therefore have sorrow: but I will see you again, and your heart shall rejoice, and your joy no man taketh from you.

23And in that day ye shall ask me nothing. Verily, verily, I say unto you, Whatsoever ye shall ask the Father in my name, he will give *it* you.

24Hitherto have ye asked nothing in my name: ask, and ye shall receive, that your joy may be full.

25These things have I spoken unto you in proverbs: but the time cometh, when I shall no more speak unto you in proverbs, but I shall show you plainly of the Father.

26At that day ye shall ask in my name: and I say not unto you, that I will pray the Father for you:

27For the Father himself loveth you, because ye have loved me, and have believed that I came out from God.

28I came forth from the Father, and am come into the world: again, I leave the world, and go to the Father.

New International

16 "ALL THIS I have told you so that you will not go astray. 2They will put you out of the synagogue; in fact, a time is coming when anyone who kills you will think he is offering a service to God. 3They will do such things because they have not known the Father or me. 4I have told you this, so that when the time comes you will remember that I warned you. I did not tell you this at first because I was with you.

The Work of the Holy Spirit

5"Now I am going to him who sent me, yet none of you asks me, 'Where are you going?' 6Because I have said these things, you are filled with grief. 7But I tell you the truth: It is for your good that I am going away. Unless I go away, the Counselor will not come to you; but if I go, I will send him to you. 8When he comes, he will convict the world of guilta in regard to sin and righteousness and judgment: 9in regard to sin, because men do not believe in me; 10in regard to righteousness, because I am going to the Father, where you can see me no longer; 11and in regard to judgment, because the prince of this world now stands condemned.

12"I have much more to say to you, more than you can now bear. 13But when he, the Spirit of truth, comes, he will guide you into all truth. He will not speak on his own; he will speak only what he hears, and he will tell you what is yet to come. 14He will bring glory to me by taking from what is mine and making it known to you. 15All that belongs to the Father is mine. That is why I said the Spirit will take from what is mine and make it known to you.

16"In a little while you will see me no more, and then after a little while you will see me."

The Disciples' Grief Will Turn to Joy

17Some of his disciples said to one another, "What does he mean by saying, 'In a little while you will see me no more, and then after a little while you will see me,' and 'Because I am going to the Father'?" 18They kept asking, "What does he mean by 'a little while'? We don't understand what he is saying."

19Jesus saw that they wanted to ask him about this, so he said to them, "Are you asking one another what I meant when I said, 'In a little while you will see me no more, and then after a little while you will see me'? 20I tell you the truth, you will weep and mourn while the world rejoices. You will grieve, but your grief will turn to joy. 21A woman giving birth to a child has pain because her time has come; but when her baby is born she forgets the anguish because of her joy that a child is born into the world. 22So with you: Now is your time of grief, but I will see you again and you will rejoice, and no one will take away your joy. 23In that day you will no longer ask me anything. I tell you the truth, my Father will give you whatever you ask in my name. 24Until now you have not asked for anything in my name. Ask and you will receive, and your joy will be complete.

25"Though I have been speaking figuratively, a time is coming when I will no longer use this kind of language but will tell you plainly about my Father. 26In that day you will ask in my name. I am not saying that I will ask the Father on your behalf. 27No, the Father himself loves you because you have loved me and have believed that I came from God. 28I came from the Father and entered the world; now I am leaving the world and going back to the Father."

---

a 8 Or *will expose the guilt of the world*

Living Bible

16 "I HAVE told you these things so that you won't be staggered [by all that lies ahead[b]]. 2For you will be excommunicated from the synagogues, and indeed the time is coming when those who kill you will think they are doing God a service. 3This is because they have never known the Father or me. 4Yes, I'm telling you these things now so that when they happen you will remember I warned you. I didn't tell you earlier because I was going to be with you for a while longer.

5"But now I am going away to the one who sent me; and none of you seems interested in the purpose of my going; none wonders why.[c] 6Instead you are only filled with sorrow. 7But the fact of the matter is that it is best for you that I go away, for if I don't, the Comforter won't come. If I do, he will—for I will send him to you.

8"And when he has come he will convince the world of its sin, and of the availability of God's goodness, and of deliverance from judgment.[d] 9The world's sin is unbelief in me; 10there is righteousness available because I go to the Father and you shall see me no more; 11there is deliverance from judgment because the prince of this world has already been judged.

12"Oh, there is so much more I want to tell you, but you can't understand it now. 13When the Holy Spirit, who is truth, comes, he shall guide you into all truth, for he will not be presenting his own ideas, but will be passing on to you what he has heard. He will tell you about the future. 14He shall praise me and bring me great honor by showing you my glory. 15All the Father's glory is mine; this is what I mean when I say that he will show you my glory.

16"In just a little while I will be gone, and you will see me no more; but just a little while after that, and you will see me again!"

17, 18"Whatever is he saying?" some of his disciples asked. "What is this about 'going to the Father'? We don't know what he means."

19Jesus realized they wanted to ask him so he said, "Are you asking yourselves what I mean? 20The world will greatly rejoice over what is going to happen to me, and you will weep. But your weeping shall suddenly be turned to wonderful joy [when you see me again[e]]. 21It will be the same joy as that of a woman in labor when her child is born—her anguish gives place to rapturous joy and the pain is forgotten. 22You have sorrow now, but I will see you again and then you will rejoice; and no one can rob you of that joy. 23At that time you won't need to ask me for anything, for you can go directly to the Father and ask him, and he will give you what you ask for because you use my name. 24You haven't tried this before, [but begin now[f]]. Ask, using my name, and you will receive, and your cup of joy will overflow.

25"I have spoken of these matters very guardedly, but the time will come when this will not be necessary and I will tell you plainly all about the Father. 26Then you will present your petitions over my signature![g] And I won't need to ask the Father to grant you these requests, 27for the Father himself loves you dearly because you love me and believe that I came from the Father. 28Yes, I came from the Father into the world and will leave the world and return to the Father."

New Revised Standard

16 "I HAVE said these things to you to keep you from stumbling. 2They will put you out of the synagogues. Indeed, an hour is coming when those who kill you will think that by doing so they are offering worship to God. 3And they will do this because they have not known the Father or me. 4But I have said these things to you so that when their hour comes you may remember that I told you about them.

The Work of the Spirit

"I did not say these things to you from the beginning, because I was with you. 5But now I am going to him who sent me; yet none of you asks me, 'Where are you going?' 6But because I have said these things to you, sorrow has filled your hearts. 7Nevertheless I tell you the truth: it is to your advantage that I go away, for if I do not go away, the Advocate[h] will not come to you; but if I go, I will send him to you. 8And when he comes, he will prove the world wrong about[i] sin and righteousness and judgment: 9about sin, because they do not believe in me; 10about righteousness, because I am going to the Father and you will see me no longer; 11about judgment, because the ruler of this world has been condemned.

12 "I still have many things to say to you, but you cannot bear them now. 13When the Spirit of truth comes, he will guide you into all the truth; for he will not speak on his own, but will speak whatever he hears, and he will declare to you the things that are to come. 14He will glorify me, because he will take what is mine and declare it to you. 15All that the Father has is mine. For this reason I said that he will take what is mine and declare it to you.

Sorrow Will Turn into Joy

16 "A little while, and you will no longer see me, and again a little while, and you will see me." 17Then some of his disciples said to one another, "What does he mean by saying to us, 'A little while, and you will no longer see me, and again a little while, and you will see me'; and 'Because I am going to the Father'?" 18They said, "What does he mean by this 'a little while'? We do not know what he is talking about." 19Jesus knew that they wanted to ask him, so he said to them, "Are you discussing among yourselves what I meant when I said, 'A little while, and you will no longer see me, and again a little while, and you will see me'? 20Very truly, I tell you, you will weep and mourn, but the world will rejoice; you will have pain, but your pain will turn into joy. 21When a woman is in labor, she has pain, because her hour has come. But when her child is born, she no longer remembers the anguish because of the joy of having brought a human being into the world. 22So you have pain now; but I will see you again, and your hearts will rejoice, and no one will take your joy from you. 23On that day you will ask nothing of me.[j] Very truly, I tell you, if you ask anything of the Father in my name, he will give it to you.[k] 24Until now you have not asked for anything in my name. Ask and you will receive, so that your joy may be complete.

Peace for the Disciples

25 "I have said these things to you in figures of speech. The hour is coming when I will no longer speak to you in figures, but will tell you plainly of the Father. 26On that day you will ask in my name. I do not say to you that I will ask the Father on your behalf; 27for the Father himself loves you, because you have loved me and have believed that I came from God.[l] 28I came from the Father and have come into the world; again, I am leaving the world and am going to the Father."

---

b 16:1 by all that lies ahead, implied.   c 16:5 none wonders why, literally, "none of you is asking me whither I am going." The question had been asked before (13:36; 14:5), but apparently not in this deeper sense.   d 16:8 of deliverance from judgment, literally, "he will convict the world of sin and righteousness and judgment."   e 16:20 when you see me again, implied.   f 16:24 but begin now, implied.   g 16:26 petitions over my signature, literally, "you shall ask in my name." The above paraphrase is the modern equivalent of this idea, otherwise obscure.

h Or Helper   i Or convict the world of   j Or will ask me no question   k Other ancient authorities read Father, he will give it to you in my name   l Other ancient authorities read the Father

King James

29His disciples said unto him, Lo, now speakest thou plainly, and speakest no proverb.

30Now are we sure that thou knowest all things, and needest not that any man should ask thee: by this we believe that thou camest forth from God.

31Jesus answered them, Do ye now believe?

32Behold, the hour cometh, yea, is now come, that ye shall be scattered, every man to his own, and shall leave me alone: and yet I am not alone, because the Father is with me.

33These things I have spoken unto you, that in me ye might have peace. In the world ye shall have tribulation: but be of good cheer; I have overcome the world.

17 THESE WORDS spake Jesus, and lifted up his eyes to heaven, and said, Father, the hour is come; glorify thy Son, that thy Son also may glorify thee:

2As thou hast given him power over all flesh, that he should give eternal life to as many as thou hast given him.

3And this is life eternal, that they might know thee the only true God, and Jesus Christ, whom thou hast sent.

4I have glorified thee on the earth: I have finished the work which thou gavest me to do.

5And now, O Father, glorify thou me with thine own self with the glory which I had with thee before the world was.

6I have manifested thy name unto the men which thou gavest me out of the world: thine they were, and thou gavest them me; and they have kept thy word.

7Now they have known that all things whatsoever thou hast given me are of thee.

8For I have given unto them the words which thou gavest me; and they have received *them*, and have known surely that I came out from thee, and they have believed that thou didst send me.

9I pray for them: I pray not for the world, but for them which thou hast given me; for they are thine.

10And all mine are thine, and thine are mine; and I am glorified in them.

11And now I am no more in the world, but these are in the world, and I come to thee. Holy Father, keep through thine own name those whom thou hast given me, that they may be one, as we *are*.

12While I was with them in the world, I kept them in thy name: those that thou gavest me I have kept, and none of them is lost, but the son of perdition; that the scripture might be fulfilled.

13And now come I to thee; and these things I speak in the world, that they might have my joy fulfilled in themselves.

14I have given them thy word; and the world hath hated them, because they are not of the world, even as I am not of the world.

15I pray not that thou shouldest take them out of the world, but that thou shouldest keep them from the evil.

16They are not of the world, even as I am not of the world.

17Sanctify them through thy truth: thy word is truth.

18As thou hast sent me into the world, even so have I also sent them into the world.

19And for their sakes I sanctify myself, that they also might be sanctified through the truth.

20Neither pray I for these alone, but for them also which shall believe on me through their word;

21That they all may be one; as thou, Father, *art* in me, and I in thee, that they also may be one in us: that the world may believe that thou hast sent me.

22And the glory which thou gavest me I have given them; that they may be one, even as we are one:

New International

29Then Jesus' disciples said, "Now you are speaking clearly and without figures of speech. 30Now we can see that you know all things and that you do not even need to have anyone ask you questions. This makes us believe that you came from God."

31"You believe at last!"a Jesus answered. 32"But a time is coming, and has come, when you will be scattered, each to his own home. You will leave me all alone. Yet I am not alone, for my Father is with me.

33"I have told you these things, so that in me you may have peace. In this world you will have trouble. But take heart! I have overcome the world."

Jesus Prays for Himself

17 AFTER JESUS said this, he looked toward heaven and prayed:

"Father, the time has come. Glorify your Son, that your Son may glorify you. 2For you granted him authority over all people that he might give eternal life to all those you have given him. 3Now this is eternal life: that they may know you, the only true God, and Jesus Christ, whom you have sent. 4I have brought you glory on earth by completing the work you gave me to do. 5And now, Father, glorify me in your presence with the glory I had with you before the world began.

Jesus Prays for His Disciples

6"I have revealed youb to those whom you gave me out of the world. They were yours; you gave them to me and they have obeyed your word. 7Now they know that everything you have given me comes from you. 8For I gave them the words you gave me and they accepted them. They knew with certainty that I came from you, and they believed that you sent me. 9I pray for them. I am not praying for the world, but for those you have given me, for they are yours. 10All I have is yours, and all you have is mine. And glory has come to me through them. 11I will remain in the world no longer, but they are still in the world, and I am coming to you. Holy Father, protect them by the power of your name—the name you gave me—so that they may be one as we are one. 12While I was with them, I protected them and kept them safe by that name you gave me. None has been lost except the one doomed to destruction so that Scripture would be fulfilled.

13"I am coming to you now, but I say these things while I am still in the world, so that they may have the full measure of my joy within them. 14I have given them your word and the world has hated them, for they are not of the world any more than I am of the world. 15My prayer is not that you take them out of the world but that you protect them from the evil one. 16They are not of the world, even as I am not of it. 17Sanctifyc them by the truth; your word is truth. 18As you sent me into the world, I have sent them into the world. 19For them I sanctify myself, that they too may be truly sanctified.

Jesus Prays for All Believers

20"My prayer is not for them alone. I pray also for those who will believe in me through their message, 21that all of them may be one, Father, just as you are in me and I am in you. May they also be in us so that the world may believe that you have sent me. 22I have given them the glory that you gave me, that they may be one as we are one: 23I in them

---

a *31* Or *"Do you now believe?"*   b *6* Greek *your name*; also in verse 26
c *17* Greek *hagiazo (set apart for sacred use* or *make holy)*; also in verse 19

Living Bible

29"At last you are speaking plainly," his disciples said, "and not in riddles. 30Now we understand that you know everything and don't need anyone to tell you anything.d From this we believe that you came from God." 31"Do you finally believe this?" Jesus asked. 32"But the time is coming—in fact, it is here—when you will be scattered, each one returning to his own home, leaving me alone. Yet I will not be alone, for the Father is with me. 33I have told you all this so that you will have peace of heart and mind. Here on earth you will have many trials and sorrows; but cheer up, for I have overcome the world."

17 WHEN JESUS had finished saying all these things he looked up to heaven and said, "Father, the time has come. Reveal the glory of your Son so that he can give the glory back to you. 2For you have given him authority over every man and woman in all the earth. He gives eternal life to each one you have given him. 3And this is the way to have eternal life—by knowing you, the only true God, and Jesus Christ, the one you sent to earth! 4I brought glory to you here on earth by doing everything you told me to. 5And now, Father, reveal my glory as I stand in your presence, the glory we shared before the world began.

6"I have told these men all about you. They were in the world, but then you gave them to me. Actually, they were always yours, and you gave them to me; and they have obeyed you. 7Now they know that everything I have is a gift from you, 8for I have passed on to them the commands you gave me; and they accepted them and know of a certainty that I came down to earth from you, and they believe you sent me.

9"My plea is not for the world but for those you have given me because they belong to you. 10And all of them, since they are mine, belong to you; and you have given them back to me with everything else of yours, and so *they are my glory!* 11Now I am leaving the world, and leaving them behind, and coming to you. Holy Father, keep them in your own care—all those you have given me—so that they will be united just as we are, with none missing. 12During my time here I have kept safe within your family all of these you gave me.e I guarded them so that not one perished, except the son of hell, as the Scriptures foretold.

13"And now I am coming to you. I have told them many things while I was with them so that they would be filled with my joy. 14I have given them your commands. And the world hates them because they don't fit in with it, just as I don't. 15I'm not asking you to take them out of the world, but to keep them safe from Satan's power. 16They are not part of this world any more than I am. 17Make them pure and holy through teaching them your words of truth. 18As you sent me into the world, I am sending them into the world, 19and I consecrate myself to meet their need for growth in truth and holiness.

20"I am not praying for these alone but also for the future believers who will come to me because of the testimony of these. 21My prayer for all of them is that they will be of one heart and mind, just as you and I are, Father—that just as you are in me and I am in you, so they will be in us, and the world will believe you sent me.

22"I have given them the glory you gave me—the glorious unity of being one, as we are— 23I in them and

New Revised Standard

29 His disciples said, "Yes, now you are speaking plainly, not in any figure of speech! 30Now we know that you know all things, and do not need to have anyone question you; by this we believe that you came from God." 31Jesus answered them, "Do you now believe? 32The hour is coming, indeed it has come, when you will be scattered, each one to his home, and you will leave me alone. Yet I am not alone because the Father is with me. 33I have said this to you, so that in me you may have peace. In the world you face persecution. But take courage; I have conquered the world!"

Jesus Prays for His Disciples

17 AFTER JESUS had spoken these words, he looked up to heaven and said, "Father, the hour has come; glorify your Son so that the Son may glorify you, 2since you have given him authority over all people,f to give eternal life to all whom you have given him. 3And this is eternal life, that they may know you, the only true God, and Jesus Christ whom you have sent. 4I glorified you on earth by finishing the work that you gave me to do. 5So now, Father, glorify me in your own presence with the glory that I had in your presence before the world existed.

6 "I have made your name known to those whom you gave me from the world. They were yours, and you gave them to me, and they have kept your word. 7Now they know that everything you have given me is from you; 8for the words that you gave to me I have given to them, and they have received them and know in truth that I came from you; and they have believed that you sent me. 9I am asking on their behalf; I am not asking on behalf of the world, but on behalf of those whom you gave me, because they are yours. 10All mine are yours, and yours are mine; and I have been glorified in them. 11And now I am no longer in the world, but they are in the world, and I am coming to you. Holy Father, protect them in your name thats you have given me, so that they may be one, as we are one. 12While I was with them, I protected them in your name thats you have given me. I guarded them, and not one of them was lost except the one destined to be lost,h so that the scripture might be fulfilled. 13But now I am coming to you, and I speak these things in the world so that they may have my joy made complete in themselves.i 14I have given them your word, and the world has hated them because they do not belong to the world, just as I do not belong to the world. 15I am not asking you to take them out of the world, but I ask you to protect them from the evil one.j 16They do not belong to the world, just as I do not belong to the world. 17Sanctify them in the truth; your word is truth. 18As you have sent me into the world, so I have sent them into the world. 19And for their sakes I sanctify myself, so that they also may be sanctified in truth.

20 "I ask not only on behalf of these, but also on behalf of those who will believe in me through their word, 21that they may all be one. As you, Father, are in me and I am in you, may they also be in us,k so that the world may believe that you have sent me. 22The glory that you have given me I have given them, so that they may be one, as we are one, 23I in them and you in

---

d *16:30 don't need anyone to tell you anything,* literally, "and need not that anyone should ask you," i.e., discuss what is true. e *17:12 I have kept safe . . . all of these you gave me,* literally, "kept in your name those whom you have given me."

f Gk *flesh* g Other ancient authorities read *protected in your name those whom* h Gk *except the son of destruction* i Or *among themselves* j Or *from evil* k Other ancient authorities read *be one in us*

King James

23I in them, and thou in me, that they may be made perfect in one; and that the world may know that thou hast sent me, and hast loved them, as thou hast loved me.

24Father, I will that they also, whom thou hast given me, be with me where I am; that they may behold my glory, which thou hast given me: for thou lovedst me before the foundation of the world.

25O righteous Father, the world hath not known thee: but I have known thee, and these have known that thou hast sent me.

26And I have declared unto them thy name, and will declare it: that the love wherewith thou hast loved me may be in them, and I in them.

18 WHEN JESUS had spoken these words, he went forth with his disciples over the brook Cedron, where was a garden, into the which he entered, and his disciples.

2And Judas also, which betrayed him, knew the place: for Jesus ofttimes resorted thither with his disciples.

3Judas then, having received a band of men and officers from the chief priests and Pharisees, cometh thither with lanterns and torches and weapons.

4Jesus therefore, knowing all things that should come upon him, went forth, and said unto them, Whom seek ye?

5They answered him, Jesus of Nazareth. Jesus saith unto them, I am he. And Judas also, which betrayed him, stood with them.

6As soon then as he had said unto them, I am he, they went backward, and fell to the ground.

7Then asked he them again, Whom seek ye? And they said, Jesus of Nazareth.

8Jesus answered, I have told you that I am he: if therefore ye seek me, let these go their way:

9That the saying might be fulfilled, which he spake, Of them which thou gavest me have I lost none.

10Then Simon Peter having a sword drew it, and smote the high priest's servant, and cut off his right ear. The servant's name was Malchus.

11Then said Jesus unto Peter, Put up thy sword into the sheath: the cup which my Father hath given me, shall I not drink it?

12Then the band and the captain and officers of the Jews took Jesus, and bound him,

13And led him away to Annas first; for he was father-in-law to Caiaphas, which was the high priest that same year.

14Now Caiaphas was he, which gave counsel to the Jews, that it was expedient that one man should die for the people.

15¶ And Simon Peter followed Jesus, and so did another disciple: that disciple was known unto the high priest, and went in with Jesus into the palace of the high priest.

16But Peter stood at the door without. Then went out that other disciple, which was known unto the high priest, and spake unto her that kept the door, and brought in Peter.

17Then saith the damsel that kept the door unto Peter, Art not thou also one of this man's disciples? He saith, I am not.

18And the servants and officers stood there, who had made a fire of coals; for it was cold: and they warmed themselves: and Peter stood with them, and warmed himself.

19¶ The high priest then asked Jesus of his disciples, and of his doctrine.

New International

and you in me. May they be brought to complete unity to let the world know that you sent me and have loved them even as you have loved me.

24"Father, I want those you have given me to be with me where I am, and to see my glory, the glory you have given me because you loved me before the creation of the world.

25"Righteous Father, though the world does not know you, I know you, and they know that you have sent me. 26I have made you known to them, and will continue to make you known in order that the love you have for me may be in them and that I myself may be in them."

Jesus Arrested

18 WHEN HE had finished praying, Jesus left with his disciples and crossed the Kidron Valley. On the other side there was an olive grove, and he and his disciples went into it.

2Now Judas, who betrayed him, knew the place, because Jesus had often met there with his disciples. 3So Judas came to the grove, guiding a detachment of soldiers and some officials from the chief priests and Pharisees. They were carrying torches, lanterns and weapons.

4Jesus, knowing all that was going to happen to him, went out and asked them, "Who is it you want?"

5"Jesus of Nazareth," they replied.

"I am he," Jesus said. (And Judas the traitor was standing there with them.) 6When Jesus said, "I am he," they drew back and fell to the ground.

7Again he asked them, "Who is it you want?"

And they said, "Jesus of Nazareth."

8"I told you that I am he," Jesus answered. "If you are looking for me, then let these men go." 9This happened so that the words he had spoken would be fulfilled: "I have not lost one of those you gave me."a

10Then Simon Peter, who had a sword, drew it and struck the high priest's servant, cutting off his right ear. (The servant's name was Malchus.)

11Jesus commanded Peter, "Put your sword away! Shall I not drink the cup the Father has given me?"

Jesus Taken to Annas

12Then the detachment of soldiers with its commander and the Jewish officials arrested Jesus. They bound him 13and brought him first to Annas, who was the father-in-law of Caiaphas, the high priest that year. 14Caiaphas was the one who had advised the Jews that it would be good if one man died for the people.

Peter's First Denial

15Simon Peter and another disciple were following Jesus. Because this disciple was known to the high priest, he went with Jesus into the high priest's courtyard, 16but Peter had to wait outside at the door. The other disciple, who was known to the high priest, came back, spoke to the girl on duty there and brought Peter in.

17"You are not one of his disciples, are you?" the girl at the door asked Peter.

He replied, "I am not."

18It was cold, and the servants and officials stood around a fire they had made to keep warm. Peter also was standing with them, warming himself.

The High Priest Questions Jesus

19Meanwhile, the high priest questioned Jesus about his disciples and his teaching.

a 9 John 6:39

Living Bible

you in me, all being perfected into one—so that the world will know you sent me and will understand that you love them as much as you love me. 24Father, I want them with me—these you've given me—so that they can see my glory. You gave me the glory because you loved me before the world began!

25"O righteous Father, the world doesn't know you, but I do; and these disciples know you sent me. 26And I have revealed you to them, and will keep on revealing you so that the mighty love you have for me may be in them, and I in them."

18 AFTER SAYING these things Jesus crossed the Kidron ravine with his disciples and entered a grove of olive trees. 2Judas, the betrayer, knew this place, for Jesus had gone there many times with his disciples.

3The chief priests and Pharisees had given Judas a squad of soldiers and police to accompany him. Now with blazing torches, lanterns, and weapons they arrived at the olive grove.

4, 5Jesus fully realized all that was going to happen to him. Stepping forward to meet them he asked, "Whom are you looking for?"

"Jesus of Nazareth," they replied.

"I am he," Jesus said. 6And as he said it, they all fell backwards to the ground!

7Once more he asked them, "Whom are you searching for?"

And again they replied, "Jesus of Nazareth."

8"I told you I am he," Jesus said; "and since I am the one you are after, let these others go." 9He did this to carry out the prophecy he had just made, "I have not lost a single one of those you gave me. . . ."

10Then Simon Peter drew a sword and slashed off the right ear of Malchus, the High Priest's servant.

11But Jesus said to Peter, "Put your sword away. Shall I not drink from the cup the Father has given me?"

12So the Jewish police, with the soldiers and their lieutenant, arrested Jesus and tied him. 13First they took him to Annas, the father-in-law of Caiaphas, the High Priest that year. 14Caiaphas was the one who told the other Jewish leaders, "Better that one should die for all."

15Simon Peter followed along behind, as did another of the disciples who was acquainted with the High Priest. So that other disciple was permitted into the courtyard along with Jesus, 16while Peter stood outside the gate. Then the other disciple spoke to the girl watching at the gate, and she let Peter in. 17The girl asked Peter, "Aren't you one of Jesus' disciples?"

"No," he said, "I am not!"

18The police and the household servants were standing around a fire they had made, for it was cold. And Peter stood there with them, warming himself.

19Inside, the High Priest began asking Jesus about his followers and what he had been teaching them.

New Revised Standard

me, that they may become completely one, so that the world may know that you have sent me and have loved them even as you have loved me. 24Father, I desire that those also, whom you have given me, may be with me where I am, to see my glory, which you have given me because you loved me before the foundation of the world.

25 "Righteous Father, the world does not know you, but I know you; and these know that you have sent me. 26I made your name known to them, and I will make it known, so that the love with which you have loved me may be in them, and I in them."

The Betrayal and Arrest of Jesus

18 AFTER JESUS had spoken these words, he went out with his disciples across the Kidron valley to a place where there was a garden, which he and his disciples entered. 2Now Judas, who betrayed him, also knew the place, because Jesus often met there with his disciples. 3So Judas brought a detachment of soldiers together with police from the chief priests and the Pharisees, and they came there with lanterns and torches and weapons. 4Then Jesus, knowing all that was to happen to him, came forward and asked them, "Whom are you looking for?" 5They answered, "Jesus of Nazareth."b Jesus replied, "I am he."c Judas, who betrayed him, was standing with them. 6When Jesusd said to them, "I am he,"c they stepped back and fell to the ground. 7Again he asked them, "Whom are you looking for?" And they said, "Jesus of Nazareth."b 8Jesus answered, "I told you that I am he.c So if you are looking for me, let these men go." 9This was to fulfill the word that he had spoken, "I did not lose a single one of those whom you gave me." 10Then Simon Peter, who had a sword, drew it, struck the high priest's slave, and cut off his right ear. The slave's name was Malchus. 11Jesus said to Peter, "Put your sword back into its sheath. Am I not to drink the cup that the Father has given me?"

Jesus before the High Priest

12 So the soldiers, their officer, and the Jewish police arrested Jesus and bound him. 13First they took him to Annas, who was the father-in-law of Caiaphas, the high priest that year. 14Caiaphas was the one who had advised the Jews that it was better to have one person die for the people.

Peter Denies Jesus

15 Simon Peter and another disciple followed Jesus. Since that disciple was known to the high priest, he went with Jesus into the courtyard of the high priest, 16but Peter was standing outside at the gate. So the other disciple, who was known to the high priest, went out, spoke to the woman who guarded the gate, and brought Peter in. 17The woman said to Peter, "You are not also one of this man's disciples, are you?" He said, "I am not." 18Now the slaves and the police had made a charcoal fire because it was cold, and they were standing around it and warming themselves. Peter also was standing with them and warming himself.

The High Priest Questions Jesus

19 Then the high priest questioned Jesus about his disciples and about his teaching. 20Jesus answered, "I

b Gk the Nazorean   c Gk I am   d Gk he

King James

20Jesus answered him, I spake openly to the world; I ever taught in the synagogue, and in the temple, whither the Jews always resort; and in secret have I said nothing.

21Why askest thou me? ask them which heard me, what I have said unto them: behold, they know what I said.

22And when he had thus spoken, one of the officers which stood by struck Jesus with the palm of his hand, saying, Answerest thou the high priest so?

23Jesus answered him, If I have spoken evil, bear witness of the evil: but if well, why smitest thou me?

24Now Annas had sent him bound unto Caiaphas the high priest.

25And Simon Peter stood and warmed himself. They said therefore unto him, Art not thou also *one* of his disciples? He denied *it,* and said, I am not.

26One of the servants of the high priest, being *his* kinsman whose ear Peter cut off, saith, Did not I see thee in the garden with him?

27Peter then denied again: and immediately the cock crew.

28¶ Then led they Jesus from Caiaphas unto the hall of judgment: and it was early; and they themselves went not into the judgment hall, lest they should be defiled; but that they might eat the passover.

29Pilate then went out unto them, and said, What accusation bring ye against this man?

30They answered and said unto him, If he were not a malefactor, we would not have delivered him up unto thee.

31Then said Pilate unto them, Take ye him, and judge him according to your law. The Jews therefore said unto him, It is not lawful for us to put any man to death:

32That the saying of Jesus might be fulfilled, which he spake, signifying what death he should die.

33Then Pilate entered into the judgment hall again, and called Jesus, and said unto him, Art thou the King of the Jews?

34Jesus answered him, Sayest thou this thing of thyself, or did others tell it thee of me?

35Pilate answered, Am I a Jew? Thine own nation and the chief priests have delivered thee unto me: what hast thou done?

36Jesus answered, My kingdom is not of this world: if my kingdom were of this world, then would my servants fight, that I should not be delivered to the Jews: but now is my kingdom not from hence.

37Pilate therefore said unto him, Art thou a king then? Jesus answered, Thou sayest that I am a king. To this end was I born, and for this cause came I into the world, that I should bear witness unto the truth. Every one that is of the truth heareth my voice.

38Pilate saith unto him, What is truth? And when he had said this, he went out again unto the Jews, and saith unto them, I find in him no fault *at all.*

39But ye have a custom, that I should release unto you one at the passover: will ye therefore that I release unto you the King of the Jews?

40Then cried they all again, saying, Not this man, but Barabbas. Now Barabbas was a robber.

New International

20"I have spoken openly to the world," Jesus replied. "I always taught in synagogues or at the temple, where all the Jews come together. I said nothing in secret. 21Why question me? Ask those who heard me. Surely they know what I said."

22When Jesus said this, one of the officials nearby struck him in the face. "Is this the way you answer the high priest?" he demanded.

23"If I said something wrong," Jesus replied, "testify as to what is wrong. But if I spoke the truth, why did you strike me?" 24Then Annas sent him, still bound, to Caiaphas the high priest.[a]

Peter's Second and Third Denials

25As Simon Peter stood warming himself, he was asked, "You are not one of his disciples, are you?"

He denied it, saying, "I am not."

26One of the high priest's servants, a relative of the man whose ear Peter had cut off, challenged him, "Didn't I see you with him in the olive grove?" 27Again Peter denied it, and at that moment a rooster began to crow.

Jesus Before Pilate

28Then the Jews led Jesus from Caiaphas to the palace of the Roman governor. By now it was early morning, and to avoid ceremonial uncleanness the Jews did not enter the palace; they wanted to be able to eat the Passover. 29So Pilate came out to them and asked, "What charges are you bringing against this man?"

30"If he were not a criminal," they replied, "we would not have handed him over to you."

31Pilate said, "Take him yourselves and judge him by your own law."

"But we have no right to execute anyone," the Jews objected. 32This happened so that the words Jesus had spoken indicating the kind of death he was going to die would be fulfilled.

33Pilate then went back inside the palace, summoned Jesus and asked him, "Are you the king of the Jews?"

34"Is that your own idea," Jesus asked, "or did others talk to you about me?"

35"Am I a Jew?" Pilate replied. "It was your people and your chief priests who handed you over to me. What is it you have done?"

36Jesus said, "My kingdom is not of this world. If it were, my servants would fight to prevent my arrest by the Jews. But now my kingdom is from another place."

37"You are a king, then!" said Pilate.

Jesus answered, "You are right in saying I am a king. In fact, for this reason I was born, and for this I came into the world, to testify to the truth. Everyone on the side of truth listens to me."

38"What is truth?" Pilate asked. With this he went out again to the Jews and said, "I find no basis for a charge against him. 39But it is your custom for me to release to you one prisoner at the time of the Passover. Do you want me to release 'the king of the Jews'?"

40They shouted back, "No, not him! Give us Barabbas!" Now Barabbas had taken part in a rebellion.

a 24 Or (*Now Annas had sent him, still bound, to Caiaphas the high priest.*)

Living Bible

20Jesus replied, "What I teach is widely known, for I have preached regularly in the synagogue and Temple; I have been heard by all the Jewish leaders and teach nothing in private that I have not said in public. 21Why are you asking me this question? Ask those who heard me. You have some of them here. They know what I said."

22One of the soldiers standing there struck Jesus with his fist. "Is that the way to answer the High Priest?" he demanded.

23"If I lied, prove it," Jesus replied. "Should you hit a man for telling the truth?"

24Then Annas sent Jesus, bound, to Caiaphas the High Priest.

25Meanwhile, as Simon Peter was standing by the fire, he was asked again, "Aren't you one of his disciples?"

"Of course not," he replied.

26But one of the household slaves of the High Priest—a relative of the man whose ear Peter had cut off—asked, "Didn't I see you out there in the olive grove with Jesus?"

27Again Peter denied it. And immediately a rooster crowed.

28Jesus' trial before Caiaphas ended in the early hours of the morning. Next he was taken to the palace of the Roman governor. His accusers wouldn't go in themselves for that would "defile" them,b they said, and they wouldn't be allowed to eat the Passover lamb. 29So Pilate, the governor, went out to them and asked, "What is your charge against this man? What are you accusing him of doing?"

30"We wouldn't have arrested him if he weren't a criminal!" they retorted.

31"Then take him away and judge him yourselves by your own laws," Pilate told them.

"But we want him crucified," they demanded, "and your approval is required."c 32This fulfilled Jesus' prediction concerning the method of his execution.d

33Then Pilate went back into the palace and called for Jesus to be brought to him. "Are you the King of the Jews?" he asked him.

34" 'King' as *you* use the word or as the *Jews* use it?" Jesus asked.e

35"Am I a Jew?" Pilate retorted. "Your own people and their chief priests brought you here. Why? What have you done?"

36Then Jesus answered, "I am not an earthly king. If I were, my followers would have fought when I was arrested by the Jewish leaders. But my Kingdom is not of the world."

37Pilate replied, "But you are a king then?"

"Yes," Jesus said. "I was born for that purpose. And I came to bring truth to the world. All who love the truth are my followers."

38"What is truth?" Pilate exclaimed. Then he went out again to the people and told them, "He is not guilty of any crime. 39But you have a custom of asking me to release someone from prison each year at Passover. So if you want me to, I'll release the 'King of the Jews.' "

40But they screamed back. "No! Not this man, but Barabbas!" Barabbas was a robber.

New Revised Standard

have spoken openly to the world; I have always taught in synagogues and in the temple, where all the Jews come together. I have said nothing in secret. 21Why do you ask me? Ask those who heard what I said to them; they know what I said." 22When he had said this, one of the police standing nearby struck Jesus on the face, saying, "Is that how you answer the high priest?" 23Jesus answered, "If I have spoken wrongly, testify to the wrong. But if I have spoken rightly, why do you strike me?" 24Then Annas sent him bound to Caiaphas the high priest.

Peter Denies Jesus Again

25 Now Simon Peter was standing and warming himself. They asked him, "You are not also one of his disciples, are you?" He denied it and said, "I am not." 26One of the slaves of the high priest, a relative of the man whose ear Peter had cut off, asked, "Did I not see you in the garden with him?" 27Again Peter denied it, and at that moment the cock crowed.

Jesus before Pilate

28 Then they took Jesus from Caiaphas to Pilate's headquarters.f It was early in the morning. They themselves did not enter the headquarters,f so as to avoid ritual defilement and to be able to eat the Passover. 29So Pilate went out to them and said, "What accusation do you bring against this man?" 30They answered, "If this man were not a criminal, we would not have handed him over to you." 31Pilate said to them, "Take him yourselves and judge him according to your law." The Jews replied, "We are not permitted to put anyone to death." 32(This was to fulfill what Jesus had said when he indicated the kind of death he was to die.)

33 Then Pilate entered the headquartersf again, summoned Jesus, and asked him, "Are you the King of the Jews?" 34Jesus answered, "Do you ask this on your own, or did others tell you about me?" 35Pilate replied, "I am not a Jew, am I? Your own nation and the chief priests have handed you over to me. What have you done?" 36Jesus answered, "My kingdom is not from this world. If my kingdom were from this world, my followers would be fighting to keep me from being handed over to the Jews. But as it is, my kingdom is not from here." 37Pilate asked him, "So you are a king?" Jesus answered, "You say that I am a king. For this I was born, and for this I came into the world, to testify to the truth. Everyone who belongs to the truth listens to my voice." 38Pilate asked him, "What is truth?"

Jesus Sentenced to Death

After he had said this, he went out to the Jews again and told them, "I find no case against him. 39But you have a custom that I release someone for you at the Passover. Do you want me to release for you the King of the Jews?" 40They shouted in reply, "Not this man, but Barabbas!" Now Barabbas was a bandit.

---

b 18:28 that would "defile" them. By Jewish law, entering the house of a Gentile was a serious offense.   c 18:31 your approval is required, literally, "It is not lawful for us to put any man to death."   d 18:32 prediction concerning the method of his execution. This prophecy is recorded in Mt 20:19, which indicates his death by crucifixion, a practice under Roman law.   e 18:34 "King" as you use the word or as the Jews use it? Jesus asked. An extended paraphrase of this verse would be, "Do you mean their King, or their Messiah?" If Pilate was asking as the Roman governor, he would be inquiring whether Jesus was setting up a rebel government. But the Jews were using the word "King" to mean their religious ruler, the Messiah. Literally, this verse reads: "Are you saying this of yourself, or did someone else say it about me?"

f Gk the praetorium

King James

19 THEN PILATE therefore took Jesus, and scourged *him*.

2And the soldiers plaited a crown of thorns, and put *it* on his head, and they put on him a purple robe,

3And said, Hail, King of the Jews! and they smote him with their hands.

4Pilate therefore went forth again, and saith unto them, Behold, I bring him forth to you, that ye may know that I find no fault in him.

5Then came Jesus forth, wearing the crown of thorns, and the purple robe. And *Pilate* saith unto them, Behold the man!

6When the chief priests therefore and officers saw him, they cried out, saying, Crucify *him*, crucify *him*. Pilate saith unto them, Take ye him, and crucify *him*: for I find no fault in him.

7The Jews answered him, We have a law, and by our law he ought to die, because he made himself the Son of God.

8¶ When Pilate therefore heard that saying, he was the more afraid;

9And went again into the judgment hall, and saith unto Jesus, Whence art thou? But Jesus gave him no answer.

10Then saith Pilate unto him, Speakest thou not unto me? knowest thou not that I have power to crucify thee, and have power to release thee?

11Jesus answered, Thou couldest have no power *at all* against me, except it were given thee from above: therefore he that delivered me unto thee hath the greater sin.

12And from thenceforth Pilate sought to release him: but the Jews cried out, saying, If thou let this man go, thou art not Caesar's friend: whosoever maketh himself a king speaketh against Caesar.

13¶ When Pilate therefore heard that saying, he brought Jesus forth, and sat down in the judgment seat in a place that is called the Pavement, but in the Hebrew, Gabbatha.

14And it was the preparation of the passover, and about the sixth hour: and he saith unto the Jews, Behold your King!

15But they cried out, Away with *him,* away with *him,* crucify *him.* Pilate saith unto them, Shall I crucify your King? The chief priests answered, We have no king but Caesar.

16Then delivered he him therefore unto them to be crucified. And they took Jesus, and led *him* away.

17And he bearing his cross went forth into a place called *the place* of a skull, which is called in the Hebrew Golgotha:

18Where they crucified him, and two other with him, on either side one, and Jesus in the midst.

19¶ And Pilate wrote a title, and put *it* on the cross. And the writing was, JESUS OF NAZARETH THE KING OF THE JEWS.

20This title then read many of the Jews: for the place where Jesus was crucified was nigh to the city: and it was written in Hebrew, *and* Greek, *and* Latin.

21Then said the chief priests of the Jews to Pilate, Write not, The King of the Jews; but that he said, I am King of the Jews.

22Pilate answered, What I have written I have written.

New International

Jesus Sentenced to be Crucified

19 THEN PILATE took Jesus and had him flogged. 2The soldiers twisted together a crown of thorns and put it on his head. They clothed him in a purple robe 3and went up to him again and again, saying, "Hail, king of the Jews!" And they struck him in the face.

4Once more Pilate came out and said to the Jews, "Look, I am bringing him out to you to let you know that I find no basis for a charge against him." 5When Jesus came out wearing the crown of thorns and the purple robe, Pilate said to them, "Here is the man!"

6As soon as the chief priests and their officials saw him, they shouted, "Crucify! Crucify!"

But Pilate answered, "You take him and crucify him. As for me, I find no basis for a charge against him."

7The Jews insisted, "We have a law, and according to that law he must die, because he claimed to be the Son of God."

8When Pilate heard this, he was even more afraid, 9and he went back inside the palace. "Where do you come from?" he asked Jesus, but Jesus gave him no answer. 10"Do you refuse to speak to me?" Pilate said. "Don't you realize I have power either to free you or to crucify you?"

11Jesus answered, "You would have no power over me if it were not given to you from above. Therefore the one who handed me over to you is guilty of a greater sin."

12From then on, Pilate tried to set Jesus free, but the Jews kept shouting, "If you let this man go, you are no friend of Caesar. Anyone who claims to be a king opposes Caesar."

13When Pilate heard this, he brought Jesus out and sat down on the judge's seat at a place known as the Stone Pavement (which in Aramaic is Gabbatha). 14It was the day of Preparation of Passover Week, about the sixth hour.

"Here is your king," Pilate said to the Jews.

15But they shouted, "Take him away! Take him away! Crucify him!"

"Shall I crucify your king?" Pilate asked.

"We have no king but Caesar," the chief priests answered.

16Finally Pilate handed him over to them to be crucified.

The Crucifixion

So the soldiers took charge of Jesus. 17Carrying his own cross, he went out to the place of the Skull (which in Aramaic is called Golgotha). 18Here they crucified him, and with him two others—one on each side and Jesus in the middle.

19Pilate had a notice prepared and fastened to the cross. It read: JESUS OF NAZARETH, THE KING OF THE JEWS. 20Many of the Jews read this sign, for the place where Jesus was crucified was near the city, and the sign was written in Aramaic, Latin and Greek. 21The chief priests of the Jews protested to Pilate, "Do not write 'The King of the Jews,' but that this man claimed to be king of the Jews."

22Pilate answered, "What I have written, I have written."

Living Bible

19 THEN PILATE laid open Jesus' back with a leaded whip, ²and the soldiers made a crown of thorns and placed it on his head and robed him in royal purple. ³"Hail, 'King of the Jews!' " they mocked, and struck him with their fists.

⁴Pilate went outside again and said to the Jews, "I am going to bring him out to you now, but understand clearly that I find him *not guilty."*

⁵Then Jesus came out wearing the crown of thorns and the purple robe. And Pilate said, "Behold the man!"

⁶At sight of him the chief priests and Jewish officials began yelling, "Crucify! Crucify!"

"You crucify him," Pilate said. "I find him *not guilty."*

⁷They replied, "By our laws he ought to die because he called himself the Son of God."

⁸When Pilate heard this, he was more frightened than ever. ⁹He took Jesus back into the palace again and asked him, "Where are you from?" but Jesus gave no answer.

¹⁰"You won't talk to me?" Pilate demanded. "Don't you realize that I have the power to release you or to crucify you?"

¹¹Then Jesus said, "You would have no power at all over me unless it were given to you from above. So thoseª who brought me to you have the greater sin."

¹²Then Pilate tried to release him, but the Jewish leaders told him, "If you release this man, you are no friend of Caesar's. Anyone who declares himself a king is a rebel against Caesar."

¹³At these words Pilate brought Jesus out to them again and sat down at the judgment bench on the stone-paved platform.ᵇ ¹⁴It was now about noon of the day before Passover.

And Pilate said to the Jews, "Here is your king!"

¹⁵"Away with him," they yelled. "Away with him—crucify him!"

"What? Crucify your king?" Pilate asked.

"We have no king but Caesar," the chief priests shouted back.

¹⁶Then Pilate gave Jesus to them to be crucified.

¹⁷So they had him at last, and he was taken out of the city, carrying his cross to the place known as "The Skull," in Hebrew, "Golgotha." ¹⁸There they crucified him and two others with him, one on either side, with Jesus between them. ¹⁹And Pilate posted a sign over him reading, "Jesus of Nazareth, the King of the Jews." ²⁰The place where Jesus was crucified was near the city; and the signboard was written in Hebrew, Latin, and Greek, so that many people read it.

²¹Then the chief priests said to Pilate, "Change it from 'The King of the Jews' to *'He said,* I am King of the Jews.' "

²²Pilate replied, "What I have written, I have written. It stays exactly as it is."

New Revised Standard

19 THEN PILATE took Jesus and had him flogged. ²And the soldiers wove a crown of thorns and put it on his head, and they dressed him in a purple robe. ³They kept coming up to him, saying, "Hail, King of the Jews!" and striking him on the face. ⁴Pilate went out again and said to them, "Look, I am bringing him out to you to let you know that I find no case against him." ⁵So Jesus came out, wearing the crown of thorns and the purple robe. Pilate said to them, "Here is the man!" ⁶When the chief priests and the police saw him, they shouted, "Crucify him! Crucify him!" Pilate said to them, "Take him yourselves and crucify him; I find no case against him." ⁷The Jews answered him, "We have a law, and according to that law he ought to die because he has claimed to be the Son of God."

⁸ Now when Pilate heard this, he was more afraid than ever. ⁹He entered his headquartersᶜ again and asked Jesus, "Where are you from?" But Jesus gave him no answer. ¹⁰Pilate therefore said to him, "Do you refuse to speak to me? Do you not know that I have power to release you, and power to crucify you?" ¹¹Jesus answered him, "You would have no power over me unless it had been given you from above; therefore the one who handed me over to you is guilty of a greater sin." ¹²From then on Pilate tried to release him, but the Jews cried out, "If you release this man, you are no friend of the emperor. Everyone who claims to be a king sets himself against the emperor."

13 When Pilate heard these words, he brought Jesus outside and satᵈ on the judge's bench at a place called The Stone Pavement, or in Hebrewᵉ Gabbatha. ¹⁴Now it was the day of Preparation for the Passover; and it was about noon. He said to the Jews, "Here is your King!" ¹⁵They cried out, "Away with him! Away with him! Crucify him!" Pilate asked them, "Shall I crucify your King?" The chief priests answered, "We have no king but the emperor." ¹⁶Then he handed him over to them to be crucified.

The Crucifixion of Jesus

So they took Jesus; ¹⁷and carrying the cross by himself, he went out to what is called The Place of the Skull, which in Hebrewᵉ is called Golgotha. ¹⁸There they crucified him, and with him two others, one on either side, with Jesus between them. ¹⁹Pilate also had an inscription written and put on the cross. It read, "Jesus of Nazareth,ᶠ the King of the Jews." ²⁰Many of the Jews read this inscription, because the place where Jesus was crucified was near the city; and it was written in Hebrew,ᵉ in Latin, and in Greek. ²¹Then the chief priests of the Jews said to Pilate, "Do not write, 'The King of the Jews,' but, 'This man said, I am King of the Jews.' " ²²Pilate answered, "What I have written I have written."

ª *19:11 those,* literally, "he." ᵇ *19:13 on the stone-paved platform,* literally, "the judgment seat in a place that is called The Pavement, but in Hebrew, Gabbatha."

ᶜ Gk *the praetorium* ᵈ Or *seated him* ᵉ That is, Aramaic ᶠ Gk *the Nazorean*

King James

23¶ Then the soldiers, when they had crucified Jesus, took his garments, and made four parts, to every soldier a part; and also *his* coat: now the coat was without seam, woven from the top throughout.

24They said therefore among themselves, Let us not rend it, but cast lots for it, whose it shall be: that the scripture might be fulfilled, which saith, They parted my raiment among them, and for my vesture they did cast lots. These things therefore the soldiers did.

25¶ Now there stood by the cross of Jesus his mother, and his mother's sister, Mary the *wife* of Cleophas, and Mary Magdalene.

26When Jesus therefore saw his mother, and the disciple standing by, whom he loved, he saith unto his mother, Woman, behold thy son!

27Then saith he to the disciple, Behold thy mother! And from that hour that disciple took her unto his own *home*.

28¶ After this, Jesus knowing that all things were now accomplished, that the scripture might be fulfilled, saith, I thirst.

29Now there was set a vessel full of vinegar: and they filled a sponge with vinegar, and put *it* upon hyssop, and put *it* to his mouth.

30When Jesus therefore had received the vinegar, he said, It is finished: and he bowed his head, and gave up the ghost.

31The Jews therefore, because it was the preparation, that the bodies should not remain upon the cross on the sabbath day, (for that sabbath day was an high day,) besought Pilate that their legs might be broken, and *that* they might be taken away.

32Then came the soldiers, and brake the legs of the first, and of the other which was crucified with him.

33But when they came to Jesus, and saw that he was dead already, they brake not his legs:

34But one of the soldiers with a spear pierced his side, and forthwith came there out blood and water.

35And he that saw *it* bare record, and his record is true: and he knoweth that he saith true, that ye might believe.

36For these things were done, that the scripture should be fulfilled, A bone of him shall not be broken.

37And again another scripture saith, They shall look on him whom they pierced.

38¶ And after this Joseph of Arimathaea, being a disciple of Jesus, but secretly for fear of the Jews, besought Pilate that he might take away the body of Jesus: and Pilate gave *him* leave. He came therefore, and took the body of Jesus.

39And there came also Nicodemus, which at the first came to Jesus by night, and brought a mixture of myrrh and aloes, about an hundred pound *weight*.

40Then took they the body of Jesus, and wound it in linen clothes with the spices, as the manner of the Jews is to bury.

41Now in the place where he was crucified there was a garden; and in the garden a new sepulchre, wherein was never man yet laid.

42There laid they Jesus therefore because of the Jews' preparation *day;* for the sepulchre was nigh at hand.

New International

23When the soldiers crucified Jesus, they took his clothes, dividing them into four shares, one for each of them, with the undergarment remaining. This garment was seamless, woven in one piece from top to bottom.

24"Let's not tear it," they said to one another. "Let's decide by lot who will get it."

This happened that the scripture might be fulfilled which said,

"They divided my garments among them
and cast lots for my clothing."[a]

So this is what the soldiers did.

25Near the cross of Jesus stood his mother, his mother's sister, Mary the wife of Clopas, and Mary Magdalene. 26When Jesus saw his mother there, and the disciple whom he loved standing nearby, he said to his mother, "Dear woman, here is your son," 27and to the disciple, "Here is your mother." From that time on, this disciple took her into his home.

The Death of Jesus

28Later, knowing that all was now completed, and so that the Scripture would be fulfilled, Jesus said, "I am thirsty." 29A jar of wine vinegar was there, so they soaked a sponge in it, put the sponge on a stalk of the hyssop plant, and lifted it to Jesus' lips. 30When he had received the drink, Jesus said, "It is finished." With that, he bowed his head and gave up his spirit.

31Now it was the day of Preparation, and the next day was to be a special Sabbath. Because the Jews did not want the bodies left on the crosses during the Sabbath, they asked Pilate to have the legs broken and the bodies taken down. 32The soldiers therefore came and broke the legs of the first man who had been crucified with Jesus, and then those of the other. 33But when they came to Jesus and found that he was already dead, they did not break his legs. 34Instead, one of the soldiers pierced Jesus' side with a spear, bringing a sudden flow of blood and water. 35The man who saw it has given testimony, and his testimony is true. He knows that he tells the truth, and he testifies so that you also may believe. 36These things happened so that the scripture would be fulfilled: "Not one of his bones will be broken,"[b] 37and, as another scripture says, "They will look on the one they have pierced."[c]

The Burial of Jesus

38Later, Joseph of Arimathea asked Pilate for the body of Jesus. Now Joseph was a disciple of Jesus, but secretly because he feared the Jews. With Pilate's permission, he came and took the body away. 39He was accompanied by Nicodemus, the man who earlier had visited Jesus at night. Nicodemus brought a mixture of myrrh and aloes, about seventy-five pounds.[d] 40Taking Jesus' body, the two of them wrapped it, with the spices, in strips of linen. This was in accordance with Jewish burial customs. 41At the place where Jesus was crucified, there was a garden, and in the garden a new tomb, in which no one had ever been laid. 42Because it was the Jewish day of Preparation and since the tomb was nearby, they laid Jesus there.

a 24 Psalm 22:18   b 36 Exodus 12:46; Num. 9:12; Psalm 34:20
c 37 Zech. 12:10   d 39 Greek *a hundred litrai* (about 34 kilograms)

Living Bible

23, 24When the soldiers had crucified Jesus, they put his garments into four piles, one for each of them. But they said, "Let's not tear up his robe," for it was seamless. "Let's throw dice to see who gets it." This fulfilled the Scripture that says,

"They divided my clothes among them, and cast lots for my robe."e 25So that is what they did.

Standing near the cross were Jesus' mother, Mary, his aunt, the wife of Cleopas, and Mary Magdalene. 26When Jesus saw his mother standing there beside me, his close friend,f he said to her, "He is your son." 27And to meg he said, "She is your mother!" And from then on I took her into my home.

28Jesus knew that everything was now finished, and to fulfill the Scriptures said, "I'm thirsty." 29A jar of sour wine was sitting there, so a sponge was soaked in it and put on a hyssop branch and held up to his lips. 30When Jesus had tastedh it, he said, "It is finished," and bowed his head and dismissed his spirit.

31The Jewish leaders didn't want the victims hanging there the next day, which was the Sabbath (and a very special Sabbath at that, for it was the Passover), so they asked Pilate to order the legs of the men broken to hasten death; then their bodies could be taken down. 32So the soldiers came and broke the legs of the two men crucified with Jesus; 33but when they came to him, they saw that he was dead already, so they didn't break his. 34However, one of the soldiers pierced his side with a spear, and blood and water flowed out. 35I saw all this myself and have given an accurate report so that you also can believe.i 36, 37The soldiers did this in fulfillment of the Scripture that says, "Not one of his bones shall be broken," and, "They shall look on him whom they pierced."

38Afterwards Joseph of Arimathea, who had been a secret disciple of Jesus for fear of the Jewish leaders, boldly asked Pilate for permission to take Jesus' body down; and Pilate told him to go ahead. So he came and took it away. 39Nicodemus, the man who had come to Jesus at night,j came too, bringing a hundred pounds of embalming ointment made from myrrh and aloes. 40Together they wrapped Jesus' body in a long linen cloth saturated with the spices, as is the Jewish custom of burial. 41The place of crucifixion was near a grove of trees,k where there was a new tomb, never used before. 42And so, because of the need for haste before the Sabbath, and because the tomb was close at hand, they laid him there.

New Revised Standard

23When the soldiers had crucified Jesus, they took his clothes and divided them into four parts, one for each soldier. They also took his tunic; now the tunic was seamless, woven in one piece from the top. 24So they said to one another, "Let us not tear it, but cast lots for it to see who will get it." This was to fulfill what the scripture says,

"They divided my clothes among themselves, and for my clothing they cast lots."
25And that is what the soldiers did.

Meanwhile, standing near the cross of Jesus were his mother, and his mother's sister, Mary the wife of Clopas, and Mary Magdalene. 26When Jesus saw his mother and the disciple whom he loved standing beside her, he said to his mother, "Woman, here is your son." 27Then he said to the disciple, "Here is your mother." And from that hour the disciple took her into his own home.

28After this, when Jesus knew that all was now finished, he said (in order to fulfill the scripture), "I am thirsty." 29A jar full of sour wine was standing there. So they put a sponge full of the wine on a branch of hyssop and held it to his mouth. 30When Jesus had received the wine, he said, "It is finished." Then he bowed his head and gave up his spirit.

Jesus' Side Is Pierced

31Since it was the day of Preparation, the Jews did not want the bodies left on the cross during the sabbath, especially because that sabbath was a day of great solemnity. So they asked Pilate to have the legs of the crucified men broken and the bodies removed. 32Then the soldiers came and broke the legs of the first and of the other who had been crucified with him. 33But when they came to Jesus and saw that he was already dead, they did not break his legs. 34Instead, one of the soldiers pierced his side with a spear, and at once blood and water came out. 35(He who saw this has testified so that you also may believe. His testimony is true, and he knowsl that he tells the truth.) 36These things occurred so that the scripture might be fulfilled, "None of his bones shall be broken." 37And again another passage of scripture says, "They will look on the one whom they have pierced."

The Burial of Jesus

38After these things, Joseph of Arimathea, who was a disciple of Jesus, though a secret one because of his fear of the Jews, asked Pilate to let him take away the body of Jesus. Pilate gave him permission; so he came and removed his body. 39Nicodemus, who had at first come to Jesus by night, also came, bringing a mixture of myrrh and aloes, weighing about a hundred pounds. 40They took the body of Jesus and wrapped it with the spices in linen cloths, according to the burial custom of the Jews. 41Now there was a garden in the place where he was crucified, and in the garden there was a new tomb in which no one had ever been laid. 42And so, because it was the Jewish day of Preparation, and the tomb was nearby, they laid Jesus there.

---

e 19:23, 24 Cast lots for my robe, see Psalm 22:18. f 19:26 standing there beside me, his close friend, literally, "standing by the disciple whom he loved." g 19:27 And to me, literally, "to the disciple." h 19:30 had tasted, literally, "had received." i 19:35 so that you also can believe, literally, "And he who has seen has borne witness, and his witness is true; and he knows what he says is true, that you also may believe." j 19:39 at night, see chapter 3. k 19:41 a grove of trees, literally, "a garden."

l Or there is one who knows

King James

20 THE FIRST *day* of the week cometh Mary Magdalene early, when it was yet dark, unto the sepulchre, and seeth the stone taken away from the sepulchre.

2Then she runneth, and cometh to Simon Peter, and to the other disciple, whom Jesus loved, and saith unto them, They have taken away the Lord out of the sepulchre, and we know not where they have laid him.

3Peter therefore went forth, and that other disciple, and came to the sepulchre.

4So they ran both together: and the other disciple did outrun Peter, and came first to the sepulchre.

5And he stooping down, *and looking in*, saw the linen clothes lying; yet went he not in.

6Then cometh Simon Peter following him, and went into the sepulchre, and seeth the linen clothes lie,

7And the napkin, that was about his head, not lying with the linen clothes, but wrapped together in a place by itself.

8Then went in also that other disciple, which came first to the sepulchre, and he saw, and believed.

9For as yet they knew not the scripture, that he must rise again from the dead.

10Then the disciples went away again unto their own home.

11¶ But Mary stood without at the sepulchre weeping: and as she wept, she stooped down, *and looked* into the sepulchre,

12And seeth two angels in white sitting, the one at the head, and the other at the feet, where the body of Jesus had lain.

13And they say unto her, Woman, why weepest thou? She saith unto them, Because they have taken away my Lord, and I know not where they have laid him.

14And when she had thus said, she turned herself back, and saw Jesus standing, and knew not that it was Jesus.

15Jesus saith unto her, Woman, why weepest thou? whom seekest thou? She, supposing him to be the gardener, saith unto him, Sir, if thou have borne him hence, tell me where thou hast laid him, and I will take him away.

16Jesus saith unto her, Mary. She turned herself, and saith unto him, Rabboni; which is to say, Master.

17Jesus saith unto her, Touch me not; for I am not yet ascended to my Father: but go to my brethren, and say unto them, I ascend unto my Father, and your Father; and *to* my God, and your God.

18Mary Magdalene came and told the disciples that she had seen the Lord, and *that* he had spoken these things unto her.

19¶ Then the same day at evening, being the first *day* of the week, when the doors were shut where the disciples were assembled for fear of the Jews, came Jesus and stood in the midst, and saith unto them, Peace *be* unto you.

20And when he had so said, he showed unto them *his* hands and his side. Then were the disciples glad, when they saw the Lord.

21Then said Jesus to them again, Peace *be* unto you: as *my* Father hath sent me, even so send I you.

22And when he had said this, he breathed on *them*, and saith unto them, Receive ye the Holy Ghost:

23Whosesoever sins ye remit, they are remitted unto them; *and* whosesoever *sins* ye retain, they are retained.

24¶ But Thomas, one of the twelve, called Didymus, was not with them when Jesus came.

25The other disciples therefore said unto him, We have seen the Lord. But he said unto them, Except I shall see in his hands the print of the nails, and put my finger into the print of the nails, and thrust my hand into his side, I will not believe.

New International

The Empty Tomb

20 EARLY ON the first day of the week, while it was still dark, Mary Magdalene went to the tomb and saw that the stone had been removed from the entrance. 2So she came running to Simon Peter and the other disciple, the one Jesus loved, and said, "They have taken the Lord out of the tomb, and we don't know where they have put him!"

3So Peter and the other disciple started for the tomb. 4Both were running, but the other disciple outran Peter and reached the tomb first. 5He bent over and looked in at the strips of linen lying there but did not go in. 6Then Simon Peter, who was behind him, arrived and went into the tomb. He saw the strips of linen lying there, 7as well as the burial cloth that had been around Jesus' head. The cloth was folded up by itself, separate from the linen. 8Finally the other disciple, who had reached the tomb first, also went inside. He saw and believed. 9(They still did not understand from Scripture that Jesus had to rise from the dead.)

Jesus Appears to Mary Magdalene

10Then the disciples went back to their homes, 11but Mary stood outside the tomb crying. As she wept, she bent over to look into the tomb 12and saw two angels in white, seated where Jesus' body had been, one at the head and the other at the foot.

13They asked her, "Woman, why are you crying?"

"They have taken my Lord away," she said, "and I don't know where they have put him." 14At this, she turned around and saw Jesus standing there, but she did not realize that it was Jesus.

15"Woman," he said, "why are you crying? Who is it you are looking for?"

Thinking he was the gardener, she said, "Sir, if you have carried him away, tell me where you have put him, and I will get him."

16Jesus said to her, "Mary."

She turned toward him and cried out in Aramaic, "Rabboni!" (which means Teacher).

17Jesus said, "Do not hold on to me, for I have not yet returned to the Father. Go instead to my brothers and tell them, 'I am returning to my Father and your Father, to my God and your God.'"

18Mary Magdalene went to the disciples with the news: "I have seen the Lord!" And she told them that he had said these things to her.

Jesus Appears to His Disciples

19On the evening of that first day of the week, when the disciples were together, with the doors locked for fear of the Jews, Jesus came and stood among them and said, "Peace be with you!" 20After he said this, he showed them his hands and side. The disciples were overjoyed when they saw the Lord.

21Again Jesus said, "Peace be with you! As the Father has sent me, I am sending you." 22And with that he breathed on them and said, "Receive the Holy Spirit. 23If you forgive anyone his sins, they are forgiven; if you do not forgive them, they are not forgiven."

Jesus Appears to Thomas

24Now Thomas (called Didymus), one of the Twelve, was not with the disciples when Jesus came. 25So the other disciples told him, "We have seen the Lord!"

But he said to them, "Unless I see the nail marks in his hands and put my finger where the nails were, and put my hand into his side, I will not believe it."

Living Bible

20 EARLY SUNDAY[a] morning, while it was still dark, Mary Magdalene came to the tomb and found that the stone was rolled aside from the entrance.

2She ran and found Simon Peter and me[b] and said, "They have taken the Lord's body out of the tomb, and I don't know where they have put him!"

3, 4We[c] ran to the tomb to see; I[d] outran Peter and got there first, 5and stooped and looked in and saw the linen cloth lying there, but I didn't go in. 6Then Simon Peter arrived and went on inside. He also noticed the cloth lying there, 7while the swath that had covered Jesus' head was rolled up in a bundle and was lying at the side. 8Then I went in too, and saw, and believed [that he had risen[e]]— 9for until then we hadn't realized that the Scriptures said he would come to life again!

10We[f] went on home, 11and by that time Mary had returned to the tomb and was standing outside crying. And as she wept, she stooped and looked in 12and saw two white-robed angels sitting at the head and foot of the place where the body of Jesus had been lying.

13"Why are you crying?" the angels asked her.

"Because they have taken away my Lord," she replied, "and I don't know where they have put him."

14She glanced over her shoulder and saw someone standing behind her. It was Jesus, but she didn't recognize him!

15"Why are you crying?" he asked her. "Whom are you looking for?"

She thought he was the gardener. "Sir," she said, "if you have taken him away, tell me where you have put him, and I will go and get him."

16"Mary!" Jesus said. She turned toward him.

"Master!" she exclaimed.

17"Don't touch me," he cautioned, "for I haven't yet ascended to the Father. But go find my brothers and tell them that I ascend to my Father and your Father, my God and your God."

18Mary Magdalene found the disciples and told them, "I have seen the Lord!" Then she gave them his message.

19That evening the disciples were meeting behind locked doors, in fear of the Jewish leaders, when suddenly Jesus was standing there among them! After greeting them, 20he showed them his hands and side. And how wonderful was their joy as they saw their Lord!

21He spoke to them again and said, "As the Father has sent me, even so I am sending you." 22Then he breathed on them and told them, "Receive the Holy Spirit. 23If you forgive anyone's sins, they are forgiven. If you refuse to forgive them, they are unforgiven."

24One of the disciples, Thomas, "The Twin," was not there at the time with the others. 25When they kept telling him, "We have seen the Lord," he replied, "I won't believe it unless I see the nail wounds in his hands—and put my fingers into them—and place my hand into his side."

New Revised Standard

The Resurrection of Jesus

20 EARLY ON the first day of the week, while it was still dark, Mary Magdalene came to the tomb and saw that the stone had been removed from the tomb. 2So she ran and went to Simon Peter and the other disciple, the one whom Jesus loved, and said to them, "They have taken the Lord out of the tomb, and we do not know where they have laid him." 3Then Peter and the other disciple set out and went toward the tomb. 4The two were running together, but the other disciple outran Peter and reached the tomb first. 5He bent down to look in and saw the linen wrappings lying there, but he did not go in. 6Then Simon Peter came, following him, and went into the tomb. He saw the linen wrappings lying there, 7and the cloth that had been on Jesus' head, not lying with the linen wrappings but rolled up in a place by itself. 8Then the other disciple, who reached the tomb first, also went in, and he saw and believed; 9for as yet they did not understand the scripture, that he must rise from the dead. 10Then the disciples returned to their homes.

Jesus Appears to Mary Magdalene

11 But Mary stood weeping outside the tomb. As she wept, she bent over to look[g] into the tomb; 12and she saw two angels in white, sitting where the body of Jesus had been lying, one at the head and the other at the feet. 13They said to her, "Woman, why are you weeping?" She said to them, "They have taken away my Lord, and I do not know where they have laid him." 14When she had said this, she turned around and saw Jesus standing there, but she did not know that it was Jesus. 15Jesus said to her, "Woman, why are you weeping? Whom are you looking for?" Supposing him to be the gardener, she said to him, "Sir, if you have carried him away, tell me where you have laid him, and I will take him away." 16Jesus said to her, "Mary!" She turned and said to him in Hebrew,[h] "Rabbouni!" (which means Teacher). 17Jesus said to her, "Do not hold on to me, because I have not yet ascended to the Father. But go to my brothers and say to them, 'I am ascending to my Father and your Father, to my God and your God.'" 18Mary Magdalene went and announced to the disciples, "I have seen the Lord"; and she told them that he had said these things to her.

Jesus Appears to the Disciples

19 When it was evening on that day, the first day of the week, and the doors of the house where the disciples had met were locked for fear of the Jews, Jesus came and stood among them and said, "Peace be with you." 20After he said this, he showed them his hands and his side. Then the disciples rejoiced when they saw the Lord. 21Jesus said to them again, "Peace be with you. As the Father has sent me, so I send you." 22When he had said this, he breathed on them and said to them, "Receive the Holy Spirit. 23If you forgive the sins of any, they are forgiven them; if you retain the sins of any, they are retained."

Jesus and Thomas

24 But Thomas (who was called the Twin[i]), one of the twelve, was not with them when Jesus came. 25So the other disciples told him, "We have seen the Lord." But he said to them, "Unless I see the mark of the nails in his hands, and put my finger in the mark of the nails and my hand in his side, I will not believe."

---

a 20:1 Early Sunday, literally, "on the first day of the week." b 20:2 and me, literally, "the other disciple whom Jesus loved." c 20:3, 4 We, literally, "Peter and the other disciple." d 20:3, 4 I, literally, "the other disciple also, who came first." e 20:8 that he had risen, implied. f 20:10 We, literally, "the disciples."

g Gk lacks to look   h That is, Aramaic   i Gk Didymus

King James

26¶ And after eight days again his disciples were within, and Thomas with them: *then* came Jesus, the doors being shut, and stood in the midst, and said, Peace *be* unto you.

27Then saith he to Thomas, Reach hither thy finger, and behold my hands; and reach hither thy hand, and thrust *it* into my side: and be not faithless, but believing.

28And Thomas answered and said unto him, My Lord and my God.

29Jesus saith unto him, Thomas, because thou hast seen me, thou hast believed: blessed *are* they that have not seen, and *yet* have believed.

30¶ And many other signs truly did Jesus in the presence of his disciples, which are not written in this book:

31But these are written, that ye might believe that Jesus is the Christ, the Son of God; and that believing ye might have life through his name.

21 AFTER THESE things Jesus showed himself again to the disciples at the sea of Tiberias; and on this wise showed he *himself.*

2There were together Simon Peter, and Thomas called Didymus, and Nathanael of Cana in Galilee, and the *sons* of Zebedee, and two other of his disciples.

3Simon Peter saith unto them, I go a-fishing. They say unto him, We also go with thee. They went forth, and entered into a ship immediately; and that night they caught nothing.

4But when the morning was now come, Jesus stood on the shore: but the disciples knew not that it was Jesus.

5Then Jesus saith unto them, Children, have ye any meat? They answered him, No.

6And he said unto them, Cast the net on the right side of the ship, and ye shall find. They cast therefore, and now they were not able to draw it for the multitude of fishes.

7Therefore that disciple whom Jesus loved saith unto Peter, It is the Lord. Now when Simon Peter heard that it was the Lord, he girt *his* fisher's coat *unto him,* (for he was naked,) and did cast himself into the sea.

8And the other disciples came in a little ship; (for they were not far from land, but as it were two hundred cubits,) dragging the net with fishes.

9As soon then as they were come to land, they saw a fire of coals there, and fish laid thereon, and bread.

10Jesus saith unto them, Bring of the fish which ye have now caught.

11Simon Peter went up, and drew the net to land full of great fishes, an hundred and fifty and three: and for all there were so many, yet was not the net broken.

12Jesus saith unto them, Come *and* dine. And none of the disciples durst ask him, Who art thou? knowing that it was the Lord.

13Jesus then cometh, and taketh bread, and giveth them, and fish likewise.

14This is now the third time that Jesus showed himself to his disciples, after that he was risen from the dead.

15¶ So when they had dined, Jesus saith to Simon Peter, Simon, *son* of Jonas, lovest thou me more than these? He saith unto him, Yea, Lord; thou knowest that I love thee. He saith unto him, Feed my lambs.

16He saith to him again the second time, Simon, *son* of Jonas, lovest thou me? He saith unto him, Yea, Lord; thou knowest that I love thee. He saith unto him, Feed my sheep.

New International

26A week later his disciples were in the house again, and Thomas was with them. Though the doors were locked, Jesus came and stood among them and said, "Peace be with you!" 27Then he said to Thomas, "Put your finger here; see my hands. Reach out your hand and put it into my side. Stop doubting and believe."

28Thomas said to him, "My Lord and my God!"

29Then Jesus told him, "Because you have seen me, you have believed; blessed are those who have not seen and yet have believed."

30Jesus did many other miraculous signs in the presence of his disciples, which are not recorded in this book. 31But these are written that you maya believe that Jesus is the Christ, the Son of God, and that by believing you may have life in his name.

Jesus and the Miraculous Catch of Fish

21 AFTERWARD JESUS appeared again to his disciples, by the Sea of Tiberias.b It happened this way: 2Simon Peter, Thomas (called Didymus), Nathanael from Cana in Galilee, the sons of Zebedee, and two other disciples were together. 3"I'm going out to fish," Simon Peter told them, and they said, "We'll go with you." So they went out and got into the boat, but that night they caught nothing.

4Early in the morning, Jesus stood on the shore, but the disciples did not realize that it was Jesus.

5He called out to them, "Friends, haven't you any fish?"

"No," they answered.

6He said, "Throw your net on the right side of the boat and you will find some." When they did, they were unable to haul the net in because of the large number of fish.

7Then the disciple whom Jesus loved said to Peter, "It is the Lord!" As soon as Simon Peter heard him say, "It is the Lord," he wrapped his outer garment around him (for he had taken it off) and jumped into the water. 8The other disciples followed in the boat, towing the net full of fish, for they were not far from shore, about a hundred yards.c 9When they landed, they saw a fire of burning coals there with fish on it, and some bread.

10Jesus said to them, "Bring some of the fish you have just caught."

11Simon Peter climbed aboard and dragged the net ashore. It was full of large fish, 153, but even with so many the net was not torn. 12Jesus said to them, "Come and have breakfast." None of the disciples dared ask him, "Who are you?" They knew it was the Lord. 13Jesus came, took the bread and gave it to them, and did the same with the fish. 14This was now the third time Jesus appeared to his disciples after he was raised from the dead.

Jesus Reinstates Peter

15When they had finished eating, Jesus said to Simon Peter, "Simon son of John, do you truly love me more than these?"

"Yes, Lord," he said, "you know that I love you."

Jesus said, "Feed my lambs."

16Again Jesus said, "Simon son of John, do you truly love me?"

He answered, "Yes, Lord, you know that I love you."

Jesus said, "Take care of my sheep."

---

a *31* Some manuscripts *may continue to*　b *1* That is, Sea of Galilee
c *8* Greek *about two hundred cubits* (about 90 meters)

Living Bible

26Eight days later the disciples were together again, and this time Thomas was with them. The doors were locked; but suddenly, as before, Jesus was standing among them and greeting them.

27Then he said to Thomas, "Put your finger into my hands. Put your hand into my side. Don't be faithless any longer. Believe!"

28"My Lord and my God!" Thomas said.

29Then Jesus told him, "You believe because you have seen me. But blessed are those who haven't seen me and believe anyway."

30, 31Jesus' disciples saw him do many other miracles besides the ones told about in this book, but these are recorded so that you will believe that he is the Messiah, the Son of God, and that believing in him you will have life.

21 LATER JESUS appeared again to the disciples beside the Lake of Galilee. This is how it happened:

2A group of us were there—Simon Peter, Thomas, "The Twin," Nathanael from Cana in Galilee, my brother James and Id and two other disciples.

3Simon Peter said, "I'm going fishing."

"We'll come too," we all said. We did, but caught nothing all night. 4At dawn we saw a man standing on the beach but couldn't see who he was.

5He called, "Any fish, boys?"e

"No," we replied.

6Then he said, "Throw out your net on the right-hand side of the boat, and you'll get plenty of them!" So we did, and couldn't draw in the net because of the weight of the fish, there were so many!

7Then If said to Peter, "It is the Lord!" At that, Simon Peter put on his tunic (for he was stripped to the waist) and jumped into the water [and swam ashoreg].

8The rest of us stayed in the boat and pulled the loaded net to the beach, about 300 feet away. 9When we got there, we saw that a fire was kindled and fish were frying over it, and there was bread.

10"Bring some of the fish you've just caught," Jesus said. 11So Simon Peter went out and dragged the net ashore. By his count there were 153 large fish; and yet the net hadn't torn.

12"Now come and have some breakfast!" Jesus said; and none of us dared ask him if he really was the Lord, for we were quite sure of it. 13Then Jesus went around serving us the bread and fish.

14This was the third time Jesus had appeared to us since his return from the dead.

15After breakfast Jesus said to Simon Peter, "Simon, son of John, do you love me more than these others?"h

"Yes," Peter replied, "You know I am your friend."

"Then feed my lambs," Jesus told him.

16Jesus repeated the question: "Simon, son of John, do you really love me?"

"Yes, Lord," Peter said, "you know I am your friend."

"Then take care of my sheep," Jesus said.

New Revised Standard

26 A week later his disciples were again in the house, and Thomas was with them. Although the doors were shut, Jesus came and stood among them and said, "Peace be with you." 27Then he said to Thomas, "Put your finger here and see my hands. Reach out your hand and put it in my side. Do not doubt but believe." 28Thomas answered him, "My Lord and my God!" 29Jesus said to him, "Have you believed because you have seen me? Blessed are those who have not seen and yet have come to believe."

The Purpose of This Book

30 Now Jesus did many other signs in the presence of his disciples, which are not written in this book. 31But these are written so that you may come to believei that Jesus is the Messiah,j the Son of God, and that through believing you may have life in his name.

Jesus Appears to Seven Disciples

21 AFTER THESE things Jesus showed himself again to the disciples by the Sea of Tiberias; and he showed himself in this way. 2Gathered there together were Simon Peter, Thomas called the Twin,k Nathanael of Cana in Galilee, the sons of Zebedee, and two others of his disciples. 3Simon Peter said to them, "I am going fishing." They said to him, "We will go with you." They went out and got into the boat, but that night they caught nothing.

4 Just after daybreak, Jesus stood on the beach; but the disciples did not know that it was Jesus. 5Jesus said to them, "Children, you have no fish, have you?" They answered him, "No." 6He said to them, "Cast the net to the right side of the boat, and you will find some." So they cast it, and now they were not able to haul it in because there were so many fish. 7That disciple whom Jesus loved said to Peter, "It is the Lord!" When Simon Peter heard that it was the Lord, he put on some clothes, for he was naked, and jumped into the sea. 8But the other disciples came in the boat, dragging the net full of fish, for they were not far from the land, only about a hundred yardsl off.

9 When they had gone ashore, they saw a charcoal fire there, with fish on it, and bread. 10Jesus said to them, "Bring some of the fish that you have just caught." 11So Simon Peter went aboard and hauled the net ashore, full of large fish, a hundred fifty-three of them; and though there were so many, the net was not torn. 12Jesus said to them, "Come and have breakfast." Now none of the disciples dared to ask him, "Who are you?" because they knew it was the Lord. 13Jesus came and took the bread and gave it to them, and did the same with the fish. 14This was now the third time that Jesus appeared to the disciples after he was raised from the dead.

Jesus and Peter

15 When they had finished breakfast, Jesus said to Simon Peter, "Simon son of John, do you love me more than these?" He said to him, "Yes, Lord; you know that I love you." Jesus said to him, "Feed my lambs." 16A second time he said to him, "Simon son of John, do you love me?" He said to him, "Yes, Lord; you know that I love you." Jesus said to him, "Tend my sheep." 17He

d 21:2 my brother James and I, literally, "the sons of Zebedee."
e 21:5 boys, literally, "children."   f 21:7 Then I, literally, "that disciple therefore whom Jesus loved."   g 21:7 and swam ashore, implied.
h 21:15 more than these others, literally, "more than these." See Mk 14:29.

i Other ancient authorities read may continue to believe   j Or the Christ
k Gk Didymus   l Gk two hundred cubits

King James

17He saith unto him the third time, Simon, *son* of Jonas, lovest thou me? Peter was grieved because he said unto him the third time, Lovest thou me? And he said unto him, Lord, thou knowest all things; thou knowest that I love thee. Jesus saith unto him, Feed my sheep.

18Verily, verily, I say unto thee, When thou wast young, thou girdedst thyself, and walkedst whither thou wouldest: but when thou shalt be old, thou shalt stretch forth thy hands, and another shall gird thee, and carry *thee* whither thou wouldest not.

19This spake he, signifying by what death he should glorify God. And when he had spoken this, he saith unto him, Follow me.

20Then Peter, turning about, seeth the disciple whom Jesus loved following; which also leaned on his breast at supper, and said, Lord, which is he that betrayeth thee?

21Peter seeing him saith to Jesus, Lord, and what *shall* this man *do?*

22Jesus saith unto him, If I will that he tarry till I come, what *is that* to thee? follow thou me.

23Then went this saying abroad among the brethren, that that disciple should not die: yet Jesus said not unto him, He shall not die; but, If I will that he tarry till I come, what *is that* to thee?

24This is the disciple which testifieth of these things, and wrote these things: and we know that his testimony is true.

25And there are also many other things which Jesus did, the which, if they should be written every one, I suppose that even the world itself could not contain the books that should be written. Amen.

New International

17The third time he said to him, "Simon son of John, do you love me?"

Peter was hurt because Jesus asked him the third time, "Do you love me?" He said, "Lord, you know all things; you know that I love you."

Jesus said, "Feed my sheep. 18I tell you the truth, when you were younger you dressed yourself and went where you wanted; but when you are old you will stretch out your hands, and someone else will dress you and lead you where you do not want to go." 19Jesus said this to indicate the kind of death by which Peter would glorify God. Then he said to him, "Follow me!"

20Peter turned and saw that the disciple whom Jesus loved was following them. (This was the one who had leaned back against Jesus at the supper and had said, "Lord, who is going to betray you?") 21When Peter saw him, he asked, "Lord, what about him?"

22Jesus answered, "If I want him to remain alive until I return, what is that to you? You must follow me." 23Because of this, the rumor spread among the brothers that this disciple would not die. But Jesus did not say that he would not die; he only said, "If I want him to remain alive until I return, what is that to you?"

24This is the disciple who testifies to these things and who wrote them down. We know that his testimony is true.

25Jesus did many other things as well. If every one of them were written down, I suppose that even the whole world would not have room for the books that would be written.

Living Bible

17Once more he asked him, "Simon, son of John, are you even my friend?"

Peter was grieved at the way Jesus asked the question this third time. "Lord, you know my heart;a you know I am," he said.

Jesus said, "Then feed my little sheep. 18When you were young, you were able to do as you liked and go wherever you wanted to; but when you are old, you will stretch out your hands and others will direct you and take you where you don't want to go." 19Jesus said this to let him know what kind of death he would die to glorify God. Then Jesus told him, "Follow me."

20Peter turned around and saw the disciple Jesus loved following, the one who had leaned around at supper that time to ask Jesus, "Master, which of us will betray you?" 21Peter asked Jesus, "What about him, Lord? What sort of death will he die?"b

22Jesus replied, "If I want him to livec until I return, what is that to you? *You* follow him.

23So the rumor spread among the brotherhood that that disciple wouldn't die! But that isn't what Jesus said at all! He only said, "If I want him to live until I come, what is that to you?"

24*I am that disciple!* I saw these events and have recorded them here. And we all know that my account of these things is accurate.

25And I suppose that if all the other events in Jesus' life were written, the whole world could hardly contain the books!

New Revised Standard

said to him the third time, "Simon son of John, do you love me?" Peter felt hurt because he said to him the third time, "Do you love me?" And he said to him, "Lord, you know everything; you know that I love you." Jesus said to him, "Feed my sheep. 18 Very truly, I tell you, when you were younger, you used to fasten your own belt and to go wherever you wished. But when you grow old, you will stretch out your hands, and someone else will fasten a belt around you and take you where you do not wish to go." 19 (He said this to indicate the kind of death by which he would glorify God.) After this he said to him, "Follow me."

Jesus and the Beloved Disciple

20 Peter turned and saw the disciple whom Jesus loved following them; he was the one who had reclined next to Jesus at the supper and had said, "Lord, who is it that is going to betray you?" 21 When Peter saw him, he said to Jesus, "Lord, what about him?" 22 Jesus said to him, "If it is my will that he remain until I come, what is that to you? Follow me!" 23 So the rumor spread in the communityd that this disciple would not die. Yet Jesus did not say to him that he would not die, but, "If it is my will that he remain until I come, what is that to you?"e

24 This is the disciple who is testifying to these things and has written them, and we know that his testimony is true. 25 But there are also many other things that Jesus did; if every one of them were written down, I suppose that the world itself could not contain the books that would be written.

---

a 21:17 *you know my heart*, literally, "all things."   b 21:21 *What sort of death will he die?* implied. Literally, "and this man, what?"   c 21:22 *live*, literally, "tarry." So also in vs 23.   d Gk *among the brothers*   e Other ancient authorities lack *what is that to you*

THE

Acts

OF THE APOSTLES

Acts

King James

1 THE FORMER treatise have I made, O Theophilus, of all that Jesus began both to do and teach,

2Until the day in which he was taken up, after that he through the Holy Ghost had given commandments unto the apostles whom he had chosen:

3To whom also he showed himself alive after his passion by many infallible proofs, being seen of them forty days, and speaking of the things pertaining to the kingdom of God:

4And, being assembled together with *them,* commanded them that they should not depart from Jerusalem, but wait for the promise of the Father, which, *saith he,* ye have heard of me.

5For John truly baptized with water; but ye shall be baptized with the Holy Ghost not many days hence.

6When they therefore were come together, they asked of him, saying, Lord, wilt thou at this time restore again the kingdom to Israel?

7And he said unto them, It is not for you to know the times or the seasons, which the Father hath put in his own power.

8But ye shall receive power, after that the Holy Ghost is come upon you: and ye shall be witnesses unto me both in Jerusalem, and in all Judaea, and in Samaria, and unto the uttermost part of the earth.

9And when he had spoken these things, while they beheld, he was taken up; and a cloud received him out of their sight.

10And while they looked stedfastly toward heaven as he went up, behold, two men stood by them in white apparel;

11Which also said, Ye men of Galilee, why stand ye gazing up into heaven? this same Jesus, which is taken up from you into heaven, shall so come in like manner as ye have seen him go into heaven.

12Then returned they unto Jerusalem from the mount called Olivet, which is from Jerusalem a sabbath day's journey.

13And when they were come in, they went up into an upper room, where abode both Peter, and James, and John, and Andrew, Philip, and Thomas, Bartholomew, and Matthew, James *the son* of Alphaeus, and Simon Zelotes, and Judas *the brother* of James.

14These all continued with one accord in prayer and supplication, with the women, and Mary the mother of Jesus, and with his brethren.

15¶ And in those days Peter stood up in the midst of the disciples, and said, (the number of names together were about an hundred and twenty,)

New International

Jesus Taken Up Into Heaven

1 IN MY former book, Theophilus, I wrote about all that Jesus began to do and to teach, 2until the day he was taken up to heaven, after giving instructions through the Holy Spirit to the apostles he had chosen. 3After his suffering, he showed himself to these men and gave many convincing proofs that he was alive. He appeared to them over a period of forty days and spoke about the kingdom of God. 4On one occasion, while he was eating with them, he gave them this command: "Do not leave Jerusalem, but wait for the gift my Father promised, which you have heard me speak about. 5For John baptized with[a] water, but in a few days you will be baptized with the Holy Spirit."

6So when they met together, they asked him, "Lord, are you at this time going to restore the kingdom to Israel?"

7He said to them: "It is not for you to know the times or dates the Father has set by his own authority. 8But you will receive power when the Holy Spirit comes on you; and you will be my witnesses in Jerusalem, and in all Judea and Samaria, and to the ends of the earth."

9After he said this, he was taken up before their very eyes, and a cloud hid him from their sight.

10They were looking intently up into the sky as he was going, when suddenly two men dressed in white stood beside them. 11"Men of Galilee," they said, "why do you stand here looking into the sky? This same Jesus, who has been taken from you into heaven, will come back in the same way you have seen him go into heaven."

Matthias Chosen to Replace Judas

12Then they returned to Jerusalem from the hill called the Mount of Olives, a Sabbath day's walk[b] from the city. 13When they arrived, they went upstairs to the room where they were staying. Those present were Peter, John, James and Andrew; Philip and Thomas, Bartholomew and Matthew; James son of Alphaeus and Simon the Zealot, and Judas son of James. 14They all joined together constantly in prayer, along with the women and Mary the mother of Jesus, and with his brothers.

15In those days Peter stood up among the believers[c] (a group numbering about a hundred and twenty) 16and

Living Bible

Acts

1 DEAR FRIEND who loves God:
In my first letter[d] I told you about Jesus' life and teachings and how he returned to heaven after giving his chosen apostles further instructions from the Holy Spirit. 3During the forty days after his crucifixion he appeared to the apostles from time to time, actually alive, and proved to them in many ways that it was really he himself they were seeing. And on these occasions he talked to them about the Kingdom of God.

4In one of these meetings he told them not to leave Jerusalem until the Holy Spirit came upon them in fulfillment of the Father's promise, a matter he had previously discussed with them.

5"John baptized you with water,"[e] he reminded them, "but you shall be baptized with the Holy Spirit[f] in just a few days."

6And another time when he appeared to them, they asked him, "Lord, are you going to free Israel [from Rome[g]] now and restore us as an independent nation?"

7"The Father sets those dates," he replied, "and they are not for you to know. 8But when the Holy Spirit has come upon you, you will receive power to testify about me with great effect, to the people in Jerusalem, throughout Judea, in Samaria, and to the ends of the earth, about my death and resurrection."

9It was not long afterwards that he rose into the sky and disappeared into a cloud, leaving them staring after him. 10As they were straining their eyes for another glimpse, suddenly two white-robed men were standing there among them, 11and said, "Men of Galilee, why are you standing here staring at the sky? Jesus has gone away to heaven, and some day, just as he went, he will return!"

12They were at the Mount of Olives when this happened, so now they walked the half mile back to Jerusalem 13and held a prayer meeting in an upstairs room of the house where they were staying.

14Here is the list of those who were present at the meeting:
Peter,
John, James,
Andrew,
Philip, Thomas,
Bartholomew,
Matthew,
James (son of Alphaeus),
Simon (also called "The Zealot"),
Judas (son of James),
And the brothers of Jesus.
Several women, including Jesus' mother, were also there.

15This prayer meeting went on for several days. During this time, on a day when about 120 people were present, Peter stood up and addressed them as follows:

d *1:1 In my first letter*, i.e., the Book of Luke; see footnote Lk 1:1.
e *1:5 with water*, or, "in water." f *1:5 with the Holy Spirit*, or "in the Holy Spirit." g *1:6 from Rome*, implied.

New Revised Standard

THE

Acts

OF THE APOSTLES

The Promise of the Holy Spirit

1 IN THE first book, Theophilus, I wrote about all that Jesus did and taught from the beginning 2until the day when he was taken up to heaven, after giving instructions through the Holy Spirit to the apostles whom he had chosen. 3After his suffering he presented himself alive to them by many convincing proofs, appearing to them during forty days and speaking about the kingdom of God. 4While staying[h] with them, he ordered them not to leave Jerusalem, but to wait there for the promise of the Father. "This," he said, "is what you have heard from me; 5for John baptized with water, but you will be baptized with[i] the Holy Spirit not many days from now."

The Ascension of Jesus

6 So when they had come together, they asked him, "Lord, is this the time when you will restore the kingdom to Israel?" 7He replied, "It is not for you to know the times or periods that the Father has set by his own authority. 8But you will receive power when the Holy Spirit has come upon you; and you will be my witnesses in Jerusalem, in all Judea and Samaria, and to the ends of the earth." 9When he had said this, as they were watching, he was lifted up, and a cloud took him out of their sight. 10While he was going and they were gazing up toward heaven, suddenly two men in white robes stood by them. 11They said, "Men of Galilee, why do you stand looking up toward heaven? This Jesus, who has been taken up from you into heaven, will come in the same way as you saw him go into heaven."

Matthias Chosen to Replace Judas

12 Then they returned to Jerusalem from the mount called Olivet, which is near Jerusalem, a sabbath day's journey away. 13When they had entered the city, they went to the room upstairs where they were staying, Peter, and John, and James, and Andrew, Philip and Thomas, Bartholomew and Matthew, James son of Alphaeus, and Simon the Zealot, and Judas son of[j] James. 14All these were constantly devoting themselves to prayer, together with certain women, including Mary the mother of Jesus, as well as his brothers.

15 In those days Peter stood up among the believers[k] (together the crowd numbered about one hundred twenty persons) and said, 16"Friends,[l] the scripture had

h Or *eating* i Or *by* j Or *the brother of* k Gk *brothers* l Gk *Men, brothers*

King James

16Men *and* brethren, this scripture must needs have been fulfilled, which the Holy Ghost by the mouth of David spake before concerning Judas, which was guide to them that took Jesus.

17For he was numbered with us, and had obtained part of this ministry.

18Now this man purchased a field with the reward of iniquity; and falling headlong, he burst asunder in the midst, and all his bowels gushed out.

19And it was known unto all the dwellers at Jerusalem; insomuch as that field is called in their proper tongue, Aceldama, that is to say, The field of blood.

20For it is written in the book of Psalms, Let his habitation be desolate, and let no man dwell therein: and his bishopric let another take.

21Wherefore of these men which have companied with us all the time that the Lord Jesus went in and out among us,

22Beginning from the baptism of John, unto that same day that he was taken up from us, must one be ordained to be a witness with us of his resurrection.

23And they appointed two, Joseph called Barsabas, who was surnamed Justus, and Matthias.

24And they prayed, and said, Thou, Lord, which knowest the hearts of all *men*, show whether of these two thou hast chosen,

25That he may take part of this ministry and apostleship, from which Judas by transgression fell, that he might go to his own place.

26And they gave forth their lots; and the lot fell upon Matthias; and he was numbered with the eleven apostles.

2 AND WHEN the day of Pentecost was fully come, they were all with one accord in one place.

2And suddenly there came a sound from heaven as of a rushing mighty wind, and it filled all the house where they were sitting.

3And there appeared unto them cloven tongues like as of fire, and it sat upon each of them.

4And they were all filled with the Holy Ghost, and began to speak with other tongues, as the Spirit gave them utterance.

5And there were dwelling at Jerusalem Jews, devout men, out of every nation under heaven.

6Now when this was noised abroad, the multitude came together, and were confounded, because that every man heard them speak in his own language.

7And they were all amazed and marvelled, saying one to another, Behold, are not all these which speak Galileans?

8And how hear we every man in our own tongue, wherein we were born?

9Parthians, and Medes, and Elamites, and the dwellers in Mesopotamia, and in Judaea, and Cappadocia, in Pontus, and Asia,

10Phrygia, and Pamphylia, in Egypt, and in the parts of Libya about Cyrene, and strangers of Rome, Jews and proselytes,

11Cretes and Arabians, we do hear them speak in our tongues the wonderful works of God.

12And they were all amazed, and were in doubt, saying one to another, What meaneth this?

13Others mocking said, These men are full of new wine.

14¶ But Peter, standing up with the eleven, lifted up his voice, and said unto them, Ye men of Judaea, and all *ye* that dwell at Jerusalem, be this known unto you, and hearken to my words:

New International

said, "Brothers, the Scripture had to be fulfilled which the Holy Spirit spoke long ago through the mouth of David concerning Judas, who served as guide for those who arrested Jesus— 17he was one of our number and shared in this ministry."

18(With the reward he got for his wickedness, Judas bought a field; there he fell headlong, his body burst open and all his intestines spilled out. 19Everyone in Jerusalem heard about this, so they called that field in their language Akeldama, that is, Field of Blood.)

20"For," said Peter, "it is written in the book of Psalms,

" 'May his place be deserted;
  let there be no one to dwell in it,'[a]

and,

" 'May another take his place of leadership.'[b]

21Therefore it is necessary to choose one of the men who have been with us the whole time the Lord Jesus went in and out among us, 22beginning from John's baptism to the time when Jesus was taken up from us. For one of these must become a witness with us of his resurrection."

23So they proposed two men: Joseph called Barsabbas (also known as Justus) and Matthias. 24Then they prayed, "Lord, you know everyone's heart. Show us which of these two you have chosen 25to take over this apostolic ministry, which Judas left to go where he belongs." 26Then they cast lots, and the lot fell to Matthias; so he was added to the eleven apostles.

The Holy Spirit Comes at Pentecost

2 WHEN THE day of Pentecost came, they were all together in one place. 2Suddenly a sound like the blowing of a violent wind came from heaven and filled the whole house where they were sitting. 3They saw what seemed to be tongues of fire that separated and came to rest on each of them. 4All of them were filled with the Holy Spirit and began to speak in other tongues[c] as the Spirit enabled them.

5Now there were staying in Jerusalem God-fearing Jews from every nation under heaven. 6When they heard this sound, a crowd came together in bewilderment, because each one heard them speaking in his own language. 7Utterly amazed, they asked: "Are not all these men who are speaking Galileans? 8Then how is it that each of us hears them in his own native language? 9Parthians, Medes and Elamites; residents of Mesopotamia, Judea and Cappadocia, Pontus and Asia, 10Phrygia and Pamphylia, Egypt and the parts of Libya near Cyrene; visitors from Rome 11(both Jews and converts to Judaism); Cretans and Arabs—we hear them declaring the wonders of God in our own tongues!" 12Amazed and perplexed, they asked one another, "What does this mean?"

13Some, however, made fun of them and said, "They have had too much wine.d"

Peter Addresses the Crowd

14Then Peter stood up with the Eleven, raised his voice and addressed the crowd: "Fellow Jews and all of you who live in Jerusalem, let me explain this to you; listen carefully to what I say. 15These men are not drunk,

a 20 Psalm 69:25   b 20 Psalm 109:8   c 4 Or *languages*; also in verse 11
d 13 Or *sweet wine*

Living Bible

16"Brothers, it was necessary for the Scriptures to come true concerning Judas, who betrayed Jesus by guiding the mob to him, for this was predicted long ago by the Holy Spirit, speaking through King David. 17Judas was one of us, chosen to be an apostle just as we were. 18He bought a field with the money he received for his treachery and falling headlong there, he burst open, spilling out his bowels. 19The news of his death spread rapidly among all the people of Jerusalem, and they named the place 'The Field of Blood.' 20King David's prediction of this appears in the Book of Psalms, where he says, 'Let his home become desolate with no one living in it.' And again, 'Let his work be given to someone else to do.'

21, 22"So now we must choose someone else to take Judas' place and to join us as witnesses of Jesus' resurrection. Let us select someone who has been with us constantly from our first association with the Lord—from the time he was baptized by John until the day he was taken from us into heaven."

23The assembly nominated two men: Joseph Justus (also called Barsabbas) and Matthias. 24, 25Then they all prayed for the right man to be chosen. "O Lord," they said, "you know every heart; show us which of these men you have chosen as an apostle to replace Judas the traitor, who has gone on to his proper place."

26Then they drew straws,e and in this manner Matthias was chosen and became an apostle with the other eleven.

2 SEVEN WEEKS had gone by since Jesus' death and resurrection, and the Day of Pentecost had now arrived.f As the believers met together that day, 2suddenly there was a sound like the roaring of a mighty windstorm in the skies above them and it filled the house where they were meeting. 3Then, what looked like flames or tongues of fire appeared and settled on their heads. 4And everyone present was filled with the Holy Spirit and began speaking in languages they didn't know,g for the Holy Spirit gave them this ability.

5Many godly Jews were in Jerusalem that day for the religious celebrations, having arrived from many nations. 6And when they heard the roaring in the sky above the house, crowds came running to see what it was all about, and were stunned to hear their own languages being spoken by the disciples.

7"How can this be?" they exclaimed. "For these men are all from Galilee, 8and yet we hear them speaking all the native languages of the lands where we were born! 9Here we are—Parthians, Medes, Elamites, men from Mesopotamia, Judea, Cappadocia, Pontus, Asia Minor,h 10Phrygia, Pamphylia, Egypt, the Cyrene language areas of Libya, visitors from Rome—both Jews and Jewish converts— 11Cretans, and Arabians. And we all hear these men telling in our own languages about the mighty miracles of God!"

12They stood there amazed and perplexed. "What can this mean?" they asked each other.

13But others in the crowd were mocking. "They're drunk, that's all!" they said.

14Then Peter stepped forward with the eleven apostles, and shouted to the crowd, "Listen, all of you, visitors and residents of Jerusalem alike! 15Some of you are

New Revised Standard

to be fulfilled, which the Holy Spirit through David foretold concerning Judas, who became a guide for those who arrested Jesus— 17for he was numbered among us and was allotted his share in this ministry." 18(Now this man acquired a field with the reward of his wickedness; and falling headlong,i he burst open in the middle and all his bowels gushed out. 19This became known to all the residents of Jerusalem, so that the field was called in their language Hakeldama, that is, Field of Blood.) 20"For it is written in the book of Psalms,

'Let his homestead become desolate,
    and let there be no one to live in it';

and

'Let another take his position of overseer.'

21So one of the men who have accompanied us during all the time that the Lord Jesus went in and out among us, 22beginning from the baptism of John until the day when he was taken up from us—one of these must become a witness with us to his resurrection." 23So they proposed two, Joseph called Barsabbas, who was also known as Justus, and Matthias. 24Then they prayed and said, "Lord, you know everyone's heart. Show us which one of these two you have chosen 25to take the placej in this ministry and apostleship from which Judas turned aside to go to his own place." 26And they cast lots for them, and the lot fell on Matthias; and he was added to the eleven apostles.

The Coming of the Holy Spirit

2 WHEN THE day of Pentecost had come, they were all together in one place. 2And suddenly from heaven there came a sound like the rush of a violent wind, and it filled the entire house where they were sitting. 3Divided tongues, as of fire, appeared among them, and a tongue rested on each of them. 4All of them were filled with the Holy Spirit and began to speak in other languages, as the Spirit gave them ability.

5 Now there were devout Jews from every nation under heaven living in Jerusalem. 6And at this sound the crowd gathered and was bewildered, because each one heard them speaking in the native language of each. 7Amazed and astonished, they asked, "Are not all these who are speaking Galileans? 8And how is it that we hear, each of us, in our own native language? 9Parthians, Medes, Elamites, and residents of Mesopotamia, Judea and Cappadocia, Pontus and Asia, 10Phrygia and Pamphylia, Egypt and the parts of Libya belonging to Cyrene, and visitors from Rome, both Jews and proselytes, 11Cretans and Arabs—in our own languages we hear them speaking about God's deeds of power." 12All were amazed and perplexed, saying to one another, "What does this mean?" 13But others sneered and said, "They are filled with new wine."

Peter Addresses the Crowd

14 But Peter, standing with the eleven, raised his voice and addressed them, "Men of Judea and all who live in Jerusalem, let this be known to you, and listen to what I say. 15Indeed, these are not drunk, as you

---

e 1:26 they drew straws, literally, "cast lots," or "threw dice."   f 2:1 This annual celebration came fifty days after the Passover ceremonies, when Christ was crucified. See Lev 23:16.   g 2:4 in languages they didn't know, literally, "in other tongues."   h 2:9 Ausia, literally, "Asia," a province of what is now Turkey.

i Or swelling up   j Other ancient authorities read the share

King James

15For these are not drunken, as ye suppose, seeing it is *but* the third hour of the day.

16But this is that which was spoken by the prophet Joel;

17And it shall come to pass in the last days, saith God, I will pour out of my Spirit upon all flesh: and your sons and your daughters shall prophesy, and your young men shall see visions, and your old men shall dream dreams:

18And on my servants and on my handmaidens I will pour out in those days of my Spirit; and they shall prophesy:

19And I will show wonders in heaven above, and signs in the earth beneath; blood, and fire, and vapour of smoke:

20The sun shall be turned into darkness, and the moon into blood, before that great and notable day of the Lord come:

21And it shall come to pass, *that* whosoever shall call on the name of the Lord shall be saved.

22Ye men of Israel, hear these words; Jesus of Nazareth, a man approved of God among you by miracles and wonders and signs, which God did by him in the midst of you, as ye yourselves also know:

23Him, being delivered by the determinate counsel and foreknowledge of God, ye have taken, and by wicked hands have crucified and slain:

24Whom God hath raised up, having loosed the pains of death: because it was not possible that he should be holden of it.

25For David speaketh concerning him, I foresaw the Lord always before my face, for he is on my right hand, that I should not be moved:

26Therefore did my heart rejoice, and my tongue was glad; moreover also my flesh shall rest in hope:

27Because thou wilt not leave my soul in hell, neither wilt thou suffer thine Holy One to see corruption.

28Thou hast made known to me the ways of life; thou shalt make me full of joy with thy countenance.

29Men *and* brethren, let me freely speak unto you of the patriarch David, that he is both dead and buried, and his sepulchre is with us unto this day.

30Therefore being a prophet, and knowing that God had sworn with an oath to him, that of the fruit of his loins, according to the flesh, he would raise up Christ to sit on his throne;

31He seeing this before spake of the resurrection of Christ, that his soul was not left in hell, neither his flesh did see corruption.

32This Jesus hath God raised up, whereof we all are witnesses.

33Therefore being by the right hand of God exalted, and having received of the Father the promise of the Holy Ghost, he hath shed forth this, which ye now see and hear.

34For David is not ascended into the heavens: but he saith himself, The LORD said unto my Lord, Sit thou on my right hand,

35Until I make thy foes thy footstool.

36Therefore let all the house of Israel know assuredly, that God hath made that same Jesus, whom ye have crucified, both Lord and Christ.

37¶ Now when they heard *this,* they were pricked in their heart, and said unto Peter and to the rest of the apostles, Men *and* brethren, what shall we do?

38Then Peter said unto them, Repent, and be baptized every one of you in the name of Jesus Christ for the remission of sins, and ye shall receive the gift of the Holy Ghost.

New International

as you suppose. It's only nine in the morning! 16No, this is what was spoken by the prophet Joel:

17" 'In the last days, God says,
    I will pour out my Spirit on all people.
Your sons and daughters will prophesy,
    your young men will see visions,
    your old men will dream dreams.
18Even on my servants, both men and women,
    I will pour out my Spirit in those days,
    and they will prophesy.
19I will show wonders in the heaven above
    and signs on the earth below,
    blood and fire and billows of smoke.
20The sun will be turned to darkness
    and the moon to blood
    before the coming of the great and glorious
        day of the Lord.
21And everyone who calls
    on the name of the Lord will be saved.'a

22"Men of Israel, listen to this: Jesus of Nazareth was a man accredited by God to you by miracles, wonders and signs, which God did among you through him, as you yourselves know. 23This man was handed over to you by God's set purpose and foreknowledge; and you, with the help of wicked men,b put him to death by nailing him to the cross. 24But God raised him from the dead, freeing him from the agony of death, because it was impossible for death to keep its hold on him. 25David said about him:

" 'I saw the Lord always before me.
    Because he is at my right hand,
    I will not be shaken.
26Therefore my heart is glad and my tongue
        rejoices;
    my body also will live in hope,
27because you will not abandon me to the grave,
    nor will you let your Holy One see decay.
28You have made known to me the paths of life;
    you will fill me with joy in your presence.'c

29"Brothers, I can tell you confidently that the patriarch David died and was buried, and his tomb is here to this day. 30But he was a prophet and knew that God had promised him on oath that he would place one of his descendants on his throne. 31Seeing what was ahead, he spoke of the resurrection of the Christ,d that he was not abandoned to the grave, nor did his body see decay. 32God has raised this Jesus to life, and we are all witnesses of the fact. 33Exalted to the right hand of God, he has received from the Father the promised Holy Spirit and has poured out what you now see and hear. 34For David did not ascend to heaven, and yet he said,

" 'The Lord said to my Lord:
    "Sit at my right hand
35until I make your enemies
    a footstool for your feet." 'e

36"Therefore let all Israel be assured of this: God has made this Jesus, whom you crucified, both Lord and Christ."

37When the people heard this, they were cut to the heart and said to Peter and the other apostles, "Brothers, what shall we do?"

38Peter replied, "Repent and be baptized, every one of you, in the name of Jesus Christ for the forgiveness of your sins. And you will receive the gift of the Holy Spirit. 39The promise is for you and your children and

a *21* Joel 2:28-32   b *23* Or *of those not having the law* (that is, Gentiles)
c *28* Psalm 16:8-11   d *31* Or *Messiah.* "The Christ" (Greek) and "the Messiah" (Hebrew) both mean "the Anointed One"; also in verse 36.
e *35* Psalm 110:1

Living Bible

saying these men are drunk! It isn't true! It's much too early for that! People don't get drunk by 9 A.M.! 16No! What you see this morning was predicted centuries ago by the prophet Joel— 17'In the last days,' God said, 'I will pour out my Holy Spirit upon all mankind, and your sons and daughters shall prophesy, and your young men shall see visions, and your old men dream dreams. 18Yes, the Holy Spirit shall come upon all my servants, men and women alike, and they shall prophesy. 19And I will cause strange demonstrations in the heavens and on the earth—blood and fire and clouds of smoke; 20the sun shall turn black and the moon blood-red before that awesome Day of the Lord arrives. 21But anyone who asks for mercy from the Lord shall have it and shall be saved.'

22"O men of Israel, listen! God publicly endorsed Jesus of Nazareth by doing tremendous miracles through him, as you well know. 23But God, following his pre-arranged plan, let you use the Roman government[f] to nail him to the cross and murder him. 24Then God released him from the horrors of death and brought him back to life again, for death could not keep this man within its grip.

25"King David quoted Jesus as saying:

'I know the Lord is always with me. He is helping me. God's mighty power supports me.

26'No wonder my heart is filled with joy and my tongue shouts his praises! For I know all will be well with me in death—

27'You will not leave my soul in hell or let the body of your Holy Son decay.

28'You will give me back my life, and give me wonderful joy in your presence.'

29"Dear brothers, think! David wasn't referring to himself when he spoke these words I have quoted, for he died and was buried, and his tomb is still here among us. 30But he was a prophet, and knew God had promised with an unbreakable oath that one of David's own descendants would [be the Messiah and[g] sit on David's throne. 31David was looking far into the future and predicting the Messiah's resurrection, and saying that the Messiah's soul would not be left in hell and his body would not decay. 32He was speaking of Jesus, and we all are witnesses that Jesus rose from the dead.

33"And now he sits on the throne of highest honor in heaven, next to God. And just as promised, the Father gave him the authority to send the Holy Spirit—with the results you are seeing and hearing today.

34"[No, David was not speaking of himself in these words of his I have quoted[h], for he never ascended into the skies. Moreover, he further stated, 'God spoke to my Lord, the Messiah, and said to him, Sit here in honor beside me 35until I bring your enemies into complete subjection.'

36"Therefore I clearly state to everyone in Israel that God has made this Jesus you crucified to be the Lord, the Messiah!"

37These words of Peter's moved them deeply, and they said to him and to the other apostles, "Brothers, what should we do?"

38And Peter replied, "Each one of you must turn from sin, return to God, and be baptized in the name of Jesus Christ for the forgiveness of your sins; then you also shall receive this gift, the Holy Spirit. 39For Christ

New Revised Standard

suppose, for it is only nine o'clock in the morning. 16No, this is what was spoken through the prophet Joel:

17 'In the last days it will be, God declares,
    that I will pour out my Spirit upon all flesh,
       and your sons and your daughters shall
          prophesy,
    and your young men shall see visions,
       and your old men shall dream dreams.
18 Even upon my slaves, both men and women,
       in those days I will pour out my Spirit;
          and they shall prophesy.
19 And I will show portents in the heaven above
       and signs on the earth below,
          blood, and fire, and smoky mist.
20 The sun shall be turned to darkness
       and the moon to blood,
    before the coming of the Lord's great and
       glorious day.
21 Then everyone who calls on the name of the
       Lord shall be saved.'

22 "You that are Israelites,[i] listen to what I have to say: Jesus of Nazareth,[j] a man attested to you by God with deeds of power, wonders, and signs that God did through him among you, as you yourselves know— 23this man, handed over to you according to the definite plan and foreknowledge of God, you crucified and killed by the hands of those outside the law. 24But God raised him up, having freed him from death,[k] because it was impossible for him to be held in its power. 25For David says concerning him,

'I saw the Lord always before me,
    for he is at my right hand so that I will not
       be shaken;
26 therefore my heart was glad, and my tongue
       rejoiced;
    moreover my flesh will live in hope.
27 For you will not abandon my soul to Hades,
       or let your Holy One experience corruption.
28 You have made known to me the ways of life;
    you will make me full of gladness with your
       presence.'

29 "Fellow Israelites,[l] I may say to you confidently of our ancestor David that he both died and was buried, and his tomb is with us to this day. 30Since he was a prophet, he knew that God had sworn with an oath to him that he would put one of his descendants on his throne. 31Foreseeing this, David[m] spoke of the resurrection of the Messiah,[n] saying,

'He was not abandoned to Hades,
    nor did his flesh experience corruption.'

32This Jesus God raised up, and of that all of us are witnesses. 33Being therefore exalted at[o] the right hand of God, and having received from the Father the promise of the Holy Spirit, he has poured out this that you both see and hear. 34For David did not ascend into the heavens, but he himself says,

'The Lord said to my Lord,
    "Sit at my right hand,
35   until I make your enemies your footstool." '

36Therefore let the entire house of Israel know with certainty that God has made him both Lord and Messiah,[p] this Jesus whom you crucified."

The First Converts

37 Now when they heard this, they were cut to the heart and said to Peter and to the other apostles, "Brothers,[l] what should we do?" 38Peter said to them, "Repent, and be baptized every one of you in the name of Jesus Christ so that your sins may be forgiven; and you will receive the gift of the Holy Spirit. 39For the promise

---

f 2:23 the Roman government, literally, "men without the Law." See Rom 2:12.   g 2:30 be the Messiah and, implied in vs 31.   h 2:34 No, David was not speaking of himself in these words of his I have quoted, implied in vs 31.

i Gk Men, Israelites   j Gk the Nazorean   k Gk the pains of death   l Gk Men, brothers   m Gk he   n Or the Christ   o Or by   p Or Christ

King James

39For the promise is unto you, and to your children, and to all that are afar off, *even* as many as the Lord our God shall call.

40And with many other words did he testify and exhort, saying, Save yourselves from this untoward generation.

41¶ Then they that gladly received his word were baptized: and the same day there were added *unto them* about three thousand souls.

42And they continued stedfastly in the apostles' doctrine and fellowship, and in breaking of bread, and in prayers.

43And fear came upon every soul: and many wonders and signs were done by the apostles.

44And all that believed were together, and had all things common;

45And sold their possessions and goods, and parted them to all *men,* as every man had need.

46And they, continuing daily with one accord in the temple, and breaking bread from house to house, did eat their meat with gladness and singleness of heart,

47Praising God, and having favour with all the people. And the Lord added to the church daily such as should be saved.

3 NOW PETER and John went up together into the temple at the hour of prayer, *being* the ninth *hour*.

2And a certain man lame from his mother's womb was carried, whom they laid daily at the gate of the temple which is called Beautiful, to ask alms of them that entered into the temple;

3Who seeing Peter and John about to go into the temple asked an alms.

4And Peter, fastening his eyes upon him with John, said, Look on us.

5And he gave heed unto them, expecting to receive something of them.

6Then Peter said, Silver and gold have I none; but such as I have give I thee: In the name of Jesus Christ of Nazareth rise up and walk.

7And he took him by the right hand, and lifted *him* up: and immediately his feet and ankle bones received strength.

8And he leaping up stood, and walked, and entered with them into the temple, walking, and leaping, and praising God.

9And all the people saw him walking and praising God:

10And they knew that it was he which sat for alms at the Beautiful gate of the temple: and they were filled with wonder and amazement at that which had happened unto him.

11And as the lame man which was healed held Peter and John, all the people ran together unto them in the porch that is called Solomon's, greatly wondering.

12¶ And when Peter saw *it,* he answered unto the people, Ye men of Israel, why marvel ye at this? or why look ye so earnestly on us, as though by our own power or holiness we had made this man to walk?

13The God of Abraham, and of Isaac, and of Jacob, the God of our fathers, hath glorified his Son Jesus; whom ye delivered up, and denied him in the presence of Pilate, when he was determined to let *him* go.

14But ye denied the Holy One and the Just, and desired a murderer to be granted unto you;

15And killed the Prince of life, whom God hath raised from the dead; whereof we are witnesses.

16And his name through faith in his name hath made this man strong, whom ye see and know: yea, the faith which is by him hath given him this perfect soundness in the presence of you all.

New International

for all who are far off—for all whom the Lord our God will call."

40With many other words he warned them; and he pleaded with them, "Save yourselves from this corrupt generation." 41Those who accepted his message were baptized, and about three thousand were added to their number that day.

The Fellowship of the Believers

42They devoted themselves to the apostles' teaching and to the fellowship, to the breaking of bread and to prayer. 43Everyone was filled with awe, and many wonders and miraculous signs were done by the apostles. 44All the believers were together and had everything in common. 45Selling their possessions and goods, they gave to anyone as he had need. 46Every day they continued to meet together in the temple courts. They broke bread in their homes and ate together with glad and sincere hearts, 47praising God and enjoying the favor of all the people. And the Lord added to their number daily those who were being saved.

Peter Heals the Crippled Beggar

3 ONE DAY Peter and John were going up to the temple at the time of prayer—at three in the afternoon. 2Now a man crippled from birth was being carried to the temple gate called Beautiful, where he was put every day to beg from those going into the temple courts. 3When he saw Peter and John about to enter, he asked them for money. 4Peter looked straight at him, as did John. Then Peter said, "Look at us!" 5So the man gave them his attention, expecting to get something from them.

6Then Peter said, "Silver or gold I do not have, but what I have I give you. In the name of Jesus Christ of Nazareth, walk." 7Taking him by the right hand, he helped him up, and instantly the man's feet and ankles became strong. 8He jumped to his feet and began to walk. Then he went with them into the temple courts, walking and jumping, and praising God. 9When all the people saw him walking and praising God, 10they recognized him as the same man who used to sit begging at the temple gate called Beautiful, and they were filled with wonder and amazement at what had happened to him.

Peter Speaks to the Onlookers

11While the beggar held on to Peter and John, all the people were astonished and came running to them in the place called Solomon's Colonnade. 12When Peter saw this, he said to them: "Men of Israel, why does this surprise you? Why do you stare at us as if by our own power or godliness we had made this man walk? 13The God of Abraham, Isaac and Jacob, the God of our fathers, has glorified his servant Jesus. You handed him over to be killed, and you disowned him before Pilate, though he had decided to let him go. 14You disowned the Holy and Righteous One and asked that a murderer be released to you. 15You killed the author of life, but God raised him from the dead. We are witnesses of this. 16By faith in the name of Jesus, this man whom you see and know was made strong. It is Jesus' name and the faith that comes through him that has given this complete healing to him, as you can all see.

Living Bible

promised him to each one of you who has been called by the Lord our God, and to your children and even to those in distant lands!"

40Then Peter preached a long sermon, telling about Jesus and strongly urging all his listeners to save themselves from the evils of their nation. 41And those who believed Peter were baptized—about 3,000 in all! 42They joined with the other believers in regular attendance at the apostles' teaching sessions and at the Communion servicesa and prayer meetings.

43A deep sense of awe was on them all, and the apostles did many miracles.

44And all the believers met together constantly and shared everything with each other, 45selling their possessions and dividing with those in need. 46They worshiped together regularly at the Temple each day, met in small groups in homes for Communion, and shared their meals with great joy and thankfulness, 47praising God. The whole city was favorable to them, and each day God added to them all who were being saved.

3 PETER AND John went to the Temple one afternoon to take part in the three o'clock daily prayer meeting. 2As they approached the Temple, they saw a man lame from birth carried along the street and laid beside the Temple gate—the one called The Beautiful Gate—as was his custom every day. 3As Peter and John were passing by, he asked them for some money.

4They looked at him intently, and then Peter said, "Look here!"

5The lame man looked at them eagerly, expecting a gift.

6But Peter said, "We don't have any money for you! But I'll give you something else! I command you in the name of Jesus Christ of Nazareth, *walk!*"

7, 8Then Peter took the lame man by the hand and pulled him to his feet. And as he did, the man's feet and ankle-bones were healed and strengthened so that he came up with a leap, stood there a moment and began walking! Then, walking, leaping, and praising God, he went into the Temple with them.

9When the people inside saw him walking and heard him praising God, 10and realized he was the lame beggar they had seen so often at The Beautiful Gate, they were inexpressibly surprised! 11They all rushed out to Solomon's Hall, where he was holding tightly to Peter and John! Everyone stood there awed by the wonderful thing that had happened.

12Peter saw his opportunity and addressed the crowd. "Men of Israel," he said, "what is so surprising about this? And why look at us as though we by our own power and godliness had made this man walk? 13For it is the God of Abraham, Isaac, Jacob and of all our ancestors who has brought glory to his servant Jesus by doing this. I refer to the Jesus whom you rejected before Pilate, despite Pilate's determination to release him. 14You didn't want him freed—this holy, righteous one. Instead you demanded the release of a murderer. 15And you killed the Author of Life; but God brought him back to life again. And John and I are witnesses of this fact, for after you killed him we saw him alive!

16"Jesus' name has healed this man —and you know how lame he was before. Faith in Jesus' name—faith given us from God—has caused this perfect healing.

New Revised Standard

is for you, for your children, and for all who are far away, everyone whom the Lord our God calls to him." 40And he testified with many other arguments and exhorted them, saying, "Save yourselves from this corrupt generation." 41So those who welcomed his message were baptized, and that day about three thousand persons were added. 42They devoted themselves to the apostles' teaching and fellowship, to the breaking of bread and the prayers.

Life among the Believers

43 Awe came upon everyone, because many wonders and signs were being done by the apostles. 44All who believed were together and had all things in common; 45they would sell their possessions and goods and distribute the proceedsb to all, as any had need. 46Day by day, as they spent much time together in the temple, they broke bread at homec and ate their food with glad and generousd hearts, 47praising God and having the goodwill of all the people. And day by day the Lord added to their number those who were being saved.

Peter Heals a Crippled Beggar

3 ONE DAY Peter and John were going up to the temple at the hour of prayer, at three o'clock in the afternoon. 2And a man lame from birth was being carried in. People would lay him daily at the gate of the temple called the Beautiful Gate so that he could ask for alms from those entering the temple. 3When he saw Peter and John about to go into the temple, he asked them for alms. 4Peter looked intently at him, as did John, and said, "Look at us." 5And he fixed his attention on them, expecting to receive something from them. 6But Peter said, "I have no silver or gold, but what I have I give you; in the name of Jesus Christ of Nazareth,e stand up and walk." 7And he took him by the right hand and raised him up; and immediately his feet and ankles were made strong. 8Jumping up, he stood and began to walk, and he entered the temple with them, walking and leaping and praising God. 9All the people saw him walking and praising God, 10and they recognized him as the one who used to sit and ask for alms at the Beautiful Gate of the temple; and they were filled with wonder and amazement at what had happened to him.

Peter Speaks in Solomon's Portico

11 While he clung to Peter and John, all the people ran together to them in the portico called Solomon's Portico, utterly astonished. 12When Peter saw it, he addressed the people, "You Israelites,f why do you wonder at this, or why do you stare at us, as though by our own power or piety we had made him walk? 13The God of Abraham, the God of Isaac, and the God of Jacob, the God of our ancestors has glorified his servantg Jesus, whom you handed over and rejected in the presence of Pilate, though he had decided to release him. 14But you rejected the Holy and Righteous One and asked to have a murderer given to you, 15and you killed the Author of life, whom God raised from the dead. To this we are witnesses. 16And by faith in his name, his name itself has made this man strong, whom you see and know; and the faith that is through Jesush has given him this perfect health in the presence of all of you.

---

a 2:42 at the Communion services, literally, "the breaking of bread," i.e., "The Lord's Supper."

b Gk them   c Or from house to house   d Or sincere   e Gk the Nazorean   f Gk Men, Israelites   g Or child   h Gk him

King James

17And now, brethren, I wot that through ignorance ye did *it*, as *did* also your rulers.

18But those things, which God before had shown by the mouth of all his prophets, that Christ should suffer, he hath so fulfilled.

19¶ Repent ye therefore, and be converted, that your sins may be blotted out, when the times of refreshing shall come from the presence of the Lord;

20And he shall send Jesus Christ, which before was preached unto you:

21Whom the heaven must receive until the times of restitution of all things, which God hath spoken by the mouth of all his holy prophets since the world began.

22For Moses truly said unto the fathers, A prophet shall the Lord your God raise up unto you of your brethren, like unto me; him shall ye hear in all things whatsoever he shall say unto you.

23And it shall come to pass, *that* every soul, which will not hear that prophet, shall be destroyed from among the people.

24Yea, and all the prophets from Samuel and those that follow after, as many as have spoken, have likewise foretold of these days.

25Ye are the children of the prophets, and of the covenant which God made with our fathers, saying unto Abraham, And in thy seed shall all the kindreds of the earth be blessed.

26Unto you first God, having raised up his Son Jesus, sent him to bless you, in turning away every one of you from his iniquities.

4 AND AS they spake unto the people, the priests, and the captain of the temple, and the Sadducees, came upon them,

2Being grieved that they taught the people, and preached through Jesus the resurrection from the dead.

3And they laid hands on them, and put *them* in hold unto the next day: for it was now eventide.

4Howbeit many of them which heard the word believed; and the number of the men was about five thousand.

5¶ And it came to pass on the morrow, that their rulers, and elders, and scribes,

6And Annas the high priest, and Caiaphas, and John, and Alexander, and as many as were of the kindred of the high priest, were gathered together at Jerusalem.

7And when they had set them in the midst, they asked, By what power, or by what name, have ye done this?

8Then Peter, filled with the Holy Ghost, said unto them, Ye rulers of the people, and elders of Israel,

9If we this day be examined of the good deed done to the impotent man, by what means he is made whole;

10Be it known unto you all, and to all the people of Israel, that by the name of Jesus Christ of Nazareth, whom ye crucified, whom God raised from the dead, *even* by him doth this man stand here before you whole.

11This is the stone which was set at nought of you builders, which is become the head of the corner.

12Neither is there salvation in any other: for there is none other name under heaven given among men, whereby we must be saved.

13¶ Now when they saw the boldness of Peter and John, and perceived that they were unlearned and ignorant men, they marvelled; and they took knowledge of them, that they had been with Jesus.

14And beholding the man which was healed standing with them, they could say nothing against it.

New International

17"Now, brothers, I know that you acted in ignorance, as did your leaders. 18But this is how God fulfilled what he had foretold through all the prophets, saying that his Christ[a] would suffer. 19Repent, then, and turn to God, so that your sins may be wiped out, that times of refreshing may come from the Lord, 20and that he may send the Christ, who has been appointed for you—even Jesus. 21He must remain in heaven until the time comes for God to restore everything, as he promised long ago through his holy prophets. 22For Moses said, 'The Lord your God will raise up for you a prophet like me from among your own people; you must listen to everything he tells you. 23Anyone who does not listen to him will be completely cut off from among his people.'[b]

24"Indeed, all the prophets from Samuel on, as many as have spoken, have foretold these days. 25And you are heirs of the prophets and of the covenant God made with your fathers. He said to Abraham, 'Through your offspring all peoples on earth will be blessed.'[c] 26When God raised up his servant, he sent him first to you to bless you by turning each of you from your wicked ways."

Peter and John Before the Sanhedrin

4 THE PRIESTS and the captain of the temple guard and the Sadducees came up to Peter and John while they were speaking to the people. 2They were greatly disturbed because the apostles were teaching the people and proclaiming in Jesus the resurrection of the dead. 3They seized Peter and John, and because it was evening, they put them in jail until the next day. 4But many who heard the message believed, and the number of men grew to about five thousand.

5The next day the rulers, elders and teachers of the law met in Jerusalem. 6Annas the high priest was there, and so were Caiaphas, John, Alexander and the other men of the high priest's family. 7They had Peter and John brought before them and began to question them: "By what power or what name did you do this?"

8Then Peter, filled with the Holy Spirit, said to them: "Rulers and elders of the people! 9If we are being called to account today for an act of kindness shown to a cripple and are asked how he was healed, 10then know this, you and all the people of Israel: It is by the name of Jesus Christ of Nazareth, whom you crucified but whom God raised from the dead, that this man stands before you healed. 11He is

" 'the stone you builders rejected,
    which has become the capstone.[d]'[e]

12Salvation is found in no one else, for there is no other name under heaven given to men by which we must be saved."

13When they saw the courage of Peter and John and realized that they were unschooled, ordinary men, they were astonished and they took note that these men had been with Jesus. 14But since they could see the man who had been healed standing there with them, there was nothing they could say. 15So they ordered them to with-

---

a *18* Or *Messiah*; also in verse 20   b *23* Deut. 18:15,18,19   c *25* Gen. 22:18; 26:4   d *11* Or *cornerstone*   e *11* Psalm 118:22

Living Bible

17"Dear brothers, I realize that what you did to Jesus was done in ignorance; and the same can be said of your leaders. 18But God was fulfilling the prophecies that the Messiah must suffer all these things. 19Now change your mind and attitude to God and turn to him so he can cleanse away your sins and send you wonderful times of refreshment from the presence of the Lord 20and send Jesus your Messiah back to you again. 21, 22For he must remain in heaven until the final recovery of all things from sin, as prophesied from ancient times. Moses, for instance, said long ago, 'The Lord God will raise up a Prophet among you, who will resemble me!f Listen carefully to everything he tells you. 23Anyone who will not listen to him shall be utterly destroyed.'g

24"Samuel and every prophet since have all spoken about what is going on today. 25You are the children of those prophets; and you are included in God's promise to your ancestors to bless the entire world through the Jewish race—that is the promise God gave to Abraham. 26And as soon as God had brought his servant to life again, he sent him first of all to you men of Israel, to bless you by turning you back from your sins."

4 WHILE THEY were talking to the people, the chief priests, the captain of the Temple police, and some of the Sadduceesh came over to them, 2very disturbed that Peter and John were claiming that Jesus had risen from the dead. 3They arrested them and since it was already evening, jailed them overnight. 4But many of the people who heard their message believed it, so that the number of believers now reached a new high of about 5,000 men!

5The next day it happened that the Council of all the Jewish leaders was in session in Jerusalem— 6Annas the High Priest was there, and Caiaphas, John, Alexander, and others of the High Priest's relatives. 7So the two disciples were brought in before them.

"By what power, or by whose authority have you done this?" the Council demanded.

8Then Peter, filled with the Holy Spirit, said to them, "Honorable leaders and elders of our nation, 9if you mean the good deed done to the cripple, and how he was healed, 10let me clearly state to you and to all the people of Israel that it was done in the name and power of Jesus from Nazareth, the Messiah, the man you crucified— but God raised him back to life again. It is by his authority that this man stands here healed! 11For Jesus the Messiah is (the one referred to in the Scriptures when they speak of) a 'stone discarded by the builders which became the capstone of the arch.'i 12There is salvation in no one else! Under all heaven there is no other name for men to call upon to save them."

13When the Council saw the boldness of Peter and John, and could see that they were obviously uneducated non-professionals, they were amazed and realized what being with Jesus had done for them! 14And the Council could hardly discredit the healing when the man they had healed was standing right there beside them! 15So they

New Revised Standard

17 "And now, friends,j I know that you acted in ignorance, as did also your rulers. 18In this way God fulfilled what he had foretold through all the prophets, that his Messiahk would suffer. 19Repent therefore, and turn to God so that your sins may be wiped out, 20 so that times of refreshing may come from the presence of the Lord, and that he may send the Messiahl appointed for you, that is, Jesus, 21who must remain in heaven until the time of universal restoration that God announced long ago through his holy prophets. 22Moses said, 'The Lord your God will raise up for you from your own peoplej a prophet like me. You must listen to whatever he tells you. 23 And it will be that everyone who does not listen to that prophet will be utterly rooted out of the people.' 24And all the prophets, as many as have spoken, from Samuel and those after him, also predicted these days. 25You are the descendants of the prophets and of the covenant that God gave to your ancestors, saying to Abraham, 'And in your descendants all the families of the earth shall be blessed.' 26When God raised up his servant,m he sent him first to you, to bless you by turning each of you from your wicked ways."

Peter and John before the Council

4 WHILE PETER and Johnn were speaking to the people, the priests, the captain of the temple, and the Sadducees came to them, 2much annoyed because they were teaching the people and proclaiming that in Jesus there is the resurrection of the dead. 3 So they arrested them and put them in custody until the next day, for it was already evening. 4But many of those who heard the word believed; and they numbered about five thousand.

5 The next day their rulers, elders, and scribes assembled in Jerusalem, 6with Annas the high priest, Caiaphas, John,o and Alexander, and all who were of the high-priestly family. 7When they had made the prisonersp stand in their midst, they inquired, "By what power or by what name did you do this?" 8Then Peter, filled with the Holy Spirit, said to them, "Rulers of the people and elders, 9if we are questioned today because of a good deed done to someone who was sick and are asked how this man has been healed, 10let it be known to all of you, and to all the people of Israel, that this man is standing before you in good health by the name of Jesus Christ of Nazareth,q whom you crucified, whom God raised from the dead. 11This Jesusr is

'the stone that was rejected by you, the
        builders;
    it has become the cornerstone.'s

12There is salvation in no one else, for there is no other name under heaven given among mortals by which we must be saved."

13 Now when they saw the boldness of Peter and John and realized that they were uneducated and ordinary men, they were amazed and recognized them as companions of Jesus. 14When they saw the man who had been cured standing beside them, they had nothing to say in opposition. 15 So they ordered them to leave the

---

f 3:21, 22 who will resemble me, literally, "like unto me." g 3:23 be utterly destroyed, literally, "destroyed from among the people." h 4:1 the Sadducees, who were members of a Jewish religious sect that denied the resurrection of the dead. i 4:11 became the capstone of the arch, implied. Literally, "became the head of the corner."

j Gk brothers   k Or his Christ   l Or the Christ   m Or child   n Gk While they   o Other ancient authorities read Jonathan   p Gk them   q Gk the Nazorean   r Gk This   s Or keystone

King James

15But when they had commanded them to go aside out of the council, they conferred among themselves,

16Saying, What shall we do to these men? for that indeed a notable miracle hath been done by them *is* manifest to all them that dwell in Jerusalem; and we cannot deny *it.*

17But that it spread no further among the people, let us straitly threaten them, that they speak henceforth to no man in this name.

18And they called them, and commanded them not to speak at all nor teach in the name of Jesus.

19But Peter and John answered and said unto them, Whether it be right in the sight of God to hearken unto you more than unto God, judge ye.

20For we cannot but speak the things which we have seen and heard.

21So when they had further threatened them, they let them go, finding nothing how they might punish them, because of the people: for all *men* glorified God for that which was done.

22For the man was above forty years old, on whom this miracle of healing was shown.

23¶ And being let go, they went to their own company, and reported all that the chief priests and elders had said unto them.

24And when they heard that, they lifted up their voice to God with one accord, and said, Lord, thou *art* God, which hast made heaven, and earth, and the sea, and all that in them is:

25Who by the mouth of thy servant David hast said, Why did the heathen rage, and the people imagine vain things?

26The kings of the earth stood up, and the rulers were gathered together against the Lord, and against his Christ.

27For of a truth against thy holy child Jesus, whom thou hast anointed, both Herod, and Pontius Pilate, with the Gentiles, and the people of Israel, were gathered together,

28For to do whatsoever thy hand and thy counsel determined before to be done.

29And now, Lord, behold their threatenings: and grant unto thy servants, that with all boldness they may speak thy word,

30By stretching forth thine hand to heal; and that signs and wonders may be done by the name of thy holy child Jesus.

31¶ And when they had prayed, the place was shaken where they were assembled together; and they were all filled with the Holy Ghost, and they spake the word of God with boldness.

32And the multitude of them that believed were of one heart and of one soul: neither said any *of them* that aught of the things which he possessed was his own; but they had all things common.

33And with great power gave the apostles witness of the resurrection of the Lord Jesus: and great grace was upon them all.

34Neither was there any among them that lacked: for as many as were possessors of lands or houses sold them, and brought the prices of the things that were sold,

35And laid *them* down at the apostles' feet: and distribution was made unto every man according as he had need.

36And Joses, who by the apostles was surnamed Barnabas, (which is, being interpreted, The son of consolation,) a Levite, *and* of the country of Cyprus,

37Having land, sold *it,* and brought the money, and laid *it* at the apostles' feet.

New International

draw from the Sanhedrin and then conferred together. 16"What are we going to do with these men?" they asked. "Everybody living in Jerusalem knows they have done an outstanding miracle, and we cannot deny it. 17But to stop this thing from spreading any further among the people, we must warn these men to speak no longer to anyone in this name."

18Then they called them in again and commanded them not to speak or teach at all in the name of Jesus. 19But Peter and John replied, "Judge for yourselves whether it is right in God's sight to obey you rather than God. 20For we cannot help speaking about what we have seen and heard."

21After further threats they let them go. They could not decide how to punish them, because all the people were praising God for what had happened. 22For the man who was miraculously healed was over forty years old.

The Believers' Prayer

23On their release, Peter and John went back to their own people and reported all that the chief priests and elders had said to them. 24When they heard this, they raised their voices together in prayer to God. "Sovereign Lord," they said, "you made the heaven and the earth and the sea, and everything in them. 25You spoke by the Holy Spirit through the mouth of your servant, our father David:

" 'Why do the nations rage
    and the peoples plot in vain?
26The kings of the earth take their stand
    and the rulers gather together
against the Lord
    and against his Anointed One.[a][b]

27Indeed Herod and Pontius Pilate met together with the Gentiles and the people[c] of Israel in this city to conspire against your holy servant Jesus, whom you anointed. 28They did what your power and will had decided beforehand should happen. 29Now, Lord, consider their threats and enable your servants to speak your word with great boldness. 30Stretch out your hand to heal and perform miraculous signs and wonders through the name of your holy servant Jesus."

31After they prayed, the place where they were meeting was shaken. And they were all filled with the Holy Spirit and spoke the word of God boldly.

The Believers Share Their Possessions

32All the believers were one in heart and mind. No one claimed that any of his possessions was his own, but they shared everything they had. 33With great power the apostles continued to testify to the resurrection of the Lord Jesus, and much grace was upon them all. 34There were no needy persons among them. For from time to time those who owned lands or houses sold them, brought the money from the sales 35and put it at the apostles' feet, and it was distributed to anyone as he had need.

36Joseph, a Levite from Cyprus, whom the apostles called Barnabas (which means Son of Encouragement), 37sold a field he owned and brought the money and put it at the apostles' feet.

---

a 26 That is, Christ or Messiah   b 26 Psalm 2:1,2   c 27 The Greek is plural.

Living Bible

sent them out of the Council chamber and conferred among themselves.

16"What shall we do with these men?" they asked each other. "We can't deny that they have done a tremendous miracle, and everybody in Jerusalem knows about it. 17But perhaps we can stop them from spreading their propaganda. We'll tell them that if they do it again we'll really throw the book at them." 18So they called them back in, and told them never again to speak about Jesus.

19But Peter and John replied, "You decide whether God wants us to obey you instead of him! 20We cannot stop telling about the wonderful things we saw Jesus do and heard him say."

21The Council then threatened them further, and finally let them go because they didn't know how to punish them without starting a riot. For everyone was praising God for this wonderful miracle— 22the healing of a man who had been lame for forty years.

23As soon as they were freed, Peter and John found the other disciples and told them what the Council had said.

24Then all the believers united in this prayer:

"O Lord, Creator of heaven and earth and of the sea and everything in them— 25, 26you spoke long ago by the Holy Spirit through our ancestor King David, your servant, saying, 'Why do the heathen rage against the Lord, and the foolish nations plan their little plots against Almighty God? The kings of the earth unite to fight against him, and against the anointed Son of God!'

27"That is what is happening here in this city today! For Herod the king, and Pontius Pilate the governor, and all the Romans—as well as the people of Israel—are united against Jesus, your anointed Son, your holy servant. 28They won't stop at anything that you in your wise power will let them do. 29And now, O Lord, hear their threats, and grant to your servants great boldness in their preaching, 30and send your healing power, and may miracles and wonders be done by the name of your holy servant Jesus."

31After this prayer, the building where they were meeting shook and they were all filled with the Holy Spirit and boldly preached God's message.

32All the believers were of one heart and mind, and no one felt that what he owned was his own; everyone was sharing. 33And the apostles preached powerful sermons about the resurrection of the Lord Jesus, and there was warm fellowship among all the believers,d 34, 35and no poverty—for all who owned land or houses sold them and brought the money to the apostles to give to others in need.

36For instance, there was Joseph (the one the apostles nicknamed "Barnabus, the encourager"! He was of the tribe of Levi, from the island of Cyprus). 37He was one of those who sold a field he owned and brought the money to the apostles for distribution to those in need.

New Revised Standard

council while they discussed the matter with one another. 16They said, "What will we do with them? For it is obvious to all who live in Jerusalem that a notable sign has been done through them; we cannot deny it. 17But to keep it from spreading further among the people, let us warn them to speak no more to anyone in this name." 18So they called them and ordered them not to speak or teach at all in the name of Jesus. 19But Peter and John answered them, "Whether it is right in God's sight to listen to you rather than to God, you must judge; 20for we cannot keep from speaking about what we have seen and heard." 21After threatening them again, they let them go, finding no way to punish them because of the people, for all of them praised God for what had happened. 22For the man on whom this sign of healing had been performed was more than forty years old.

The Believers Pray for Boldness

23 After they were released, they went to their friendse and reported what the chief priests and the elders had said to them. 24When they heard it, they raised their voices together to God and said, "Sovereign Lord, who made the heaven and the earth, the sea, and everything in them, 25it is you who said by the Holy Spirit through our ancestor David, your servant:f
'Why did the Gentiles rage,
    and the peoples imagine vain things?
26 The kings of the earth took their stand,
    and the rulers have gathered together
        against the Lord and against his
            Messiah.'g
27For in this city, in fact, both Herod and Pontius Pilate, with the Gentiles and the peoples of Israel, gathered together against your holy servantf Jesus, whom you anointed, 28to do whatever your hand and your plan had predestined to take place. 29And now, Lord, look at their threats, and grant to your servantsh to speak your word with all boldness, 30while you stretch out your hand to heal, and signs and wonders are performed through the name of your holy servantf Jesus." 31When they had prayed, the place in which they were gathered together was shaken; and they were all filled with the Holy Spirit and spoke the word of God with boldness.

The Believers Share Their Possessions

32 Now the whole group of those who believed were of one heart and soul, and no one claimed private ownership of any possessions, but everything they owned was held in common. 33With great power the apostles gave their testimony to the resurrection of the Lord Jesus, and great grace was upon them all. 34There was not a needy person among them, for as many as owned lands or houses sold them and brought the proceeds of what was sold. 35They laid it at the apostles' feet, and it was distributed to each as any had need. 36There was a Levite, a native of Cyprus, Joseph, to whom the apostles gave the name Barnabas (which means "son of encouragement"). 37He sold a field that belonged to him, then brought the money, and laid it at the apostles' feet.

---

d 4:33 there was warm fellowship among all the believers, literally, "great grace was upon them all."

e Gk their own   f Or child   g Or his Christ   h Gk slaves

King James

5 BUT A certain man named Ananias, with Sapphira his wife, sold a possession,

2And kept back *part* of the price, his wife also being privy *to it,* and brought a certain part, and laid *it* at the apostles' feet.

3But Peter said, Ananias, why hath Satan filled thine heart to lie to the Holy Ghost, and to keep back *part* of the price of the land?

4Whiles it remained, was it not thine own? and after it was sold, was it not in thine own power? why hast thou conceived this thing in thine heart? thou hast not lied unto men, but unto God.

5And Ananias hearing these words fell down, and gave up the ghost: and great fear came on all them that heard these things.

6And the young men arose, wound him up, and carried *him* out, and buried *him.*

7And it was about the space of three hours after, when his wife, not knowing what was done, came in.

8And Peter answered unto her, Tell me whether ye sold the land for so much? And she said, Yea, for so much.

9Then Peter said unto her, How is it that ye have agreed together to tempt the Spirit of the Lord? behold, the feet of them which have buried thy husband *are* at the door, and shall carry thee out.

10Then fell she down straightway at his feet, and yielded up the ghost: and the young men came in, and found her dead, and, carrying *her* forth, buried *her* by her husband.

11And great fear came upon all the church, and upon as many as heard these things.

12¶ And by the hands of the apostles were many signs and wonders wrought among the people; (and they were all with one accord in Solomon's porch.

13And of the rest durst no man join himself to them: but the people magnified them.

14And believers were the more added to the Lord, multitudes both of men and women.)

15Insomuch that they brought forth the sick into the streets, and laid *them* on beds and couches, that at the least the shadow of Peter passing by might overshadow some of them.

16There came also a multitude *out* of the cities round about unto Jerusalem, bringing sick folks, and them which were vexed with unclean spirits: and they were healed every one.

17¶ Then the high priest rose up, and all they that were with him, (which is the sect of the Sadducees,) and were filled with indignation,

18And laid their hands on the apostles, and put them in the common prison.

19But the angel of the Lord by night opened the prison doors, and brought them forth, and said,

20Go, stand and speak in the temple to the people all the words of this life.

21And when they heard *that,* they entered into the temple early in the morning, and taught. But the high priest came, and they that were with him, and called the council together, and all the senate of the children of Israel, and sent to the prison to have them brought.

22But when the officers came, and found them not in the prison, they returned, and told,

23Saying, The prison truly found we shut with all safety, and the keepers standing without before the doors: but when we had opened, we found no man within.

24Now when the high priest and the captain of the temple and the chief priests heard these things, they doubted of them whereunto this would grow.

25Then came one and told them, saying, Behold, the men whom ye put in prison are standing in the temple, and teaching the people.

New International

Ananias and Sapphira

5 NOW A man named Ananias, together with his wife Sapphira, also sold a piece of property. 2With his wife's full knowledge he kept back part of the money for himself, but brought the rest and put it at the apostles' feet.

3Then Peter said, "Ananias, how is it that Satan has so filled your heart that you have lied to the Holy Spirit and have kept for yourself some of the money you received for the land? 4Didn't it belong to you before it was sold? And after it was sold, wasn't the money at your disposal? What made you think of doing such a thing? You have not lied to men but to God."

5When Ananias heard this, he fell down and died. And great fear seized all who heard what had happened. 6Then the young men came forward, wrapped up his body, and carried him out and buried him.

7About three hours later his wife came in, not knowing what had happened. 8Peter asked her, "Tell me, is this the price you and Ananias got for the land?"

"Yes," she said, "that is the price."

9Peter said to her, "How could you agree to test the Spirit of the Lord? Look! The feet of the men who buried your husband are at the door, and they will carry you out also."

10At that moment she fell down at his feet and died. Then the young men came in and, finding her dead, carried her out and buried her beside her husband. 11Great fear seized the whole church and all who heard about these events.

The Apostles Heal Many

12The apostles performed many miraculous signs and wonders among the people. And all the believers used to meet together in Solomon's Colonnade. 13No one else dared join them, even though they were highly regarded by the people. 14Nevertheless, more and more men and women believed in the Lord and were added to their number. 15As a result, people brought the sick into the streets and laid them on beds and mats so that at least Peter's shadow might fall on some of them as he passed by. 16Crowds gathered also from the towns around Jerusalem, bringing their sick and those tormented by evil[a] spirits, and all of them were healed.

The Apostles Persecuted

17Then the high priest and all his associates, who were members of the party of the Sadducees, were filled with jealousy. 18They arrested the apostles and put them in the public jail. 19But during the night an angel of the Lord opened the doors of the jail and brought them out. 20"Go, stand in the temple courts," he said, "and tell the people the full message of this new life."

21At daybreak they entered the temple courts, as they had been told, and began to teach the people.

When the high priest and his associates arrived, they called together the Sanhedrin—the full assembly of the elders of Israel—and sent to the jail for the apostles. 22But on arriving at the jail, the officers did not find them there. So they went back and reported, 23"We found the jail securely locked, with the guards standing at the doors; but when we opened them, we found no one inside." 24On hearing this report, the captain of the temple guard and the chief priests were puzzled, wondering what would come of this.

25Then someone came and said, "Look! The men you put in jail are standing in the temple courts teaching the people." 26At that, the captain went with his officers and

Living Bible

5 BUT THERE was a man named Ananias (with his wife Sapphira) who sold some property, 2and brought only part of the money, claiming it was the full price. (His wife had agreed to this deception.)

3But Peter said, "Ananias, Satan has filled your heart. When you claimed this was the full price, you were lying to the Holy Spirit. 4The property was yours to sell or not, as you wished. And after selling it, it was yours to decide how much to give. How could you do a thing like this? You weren't lying to us, but to God."

5As soon as Ananias heard these words, he fell to the floor, dead! Everyone was terrified, 6and the younger men covered him with a sheet and took him out and buried him.

7About three hours later his wife came in, not knowing what had happened. 8Peter asked her, "Did you people sell your land for such and such a price?"

"Yes," she replied, "we did."

9And Peter said, "How could you and your husband even think of doing a thing like this—conspiring together to test the Spirit of God's ability to know what is going on?b Just outside that door are the young men who buried your husband, and they will carry you out too."

10Instantly she fell to the floor, dead, and the young men came in and, seeing that she was dead, carried her out and buried her beside her husband. 11Terror gripped the entire church and all others who heard what had happened.

12Meanwhile, the apostles were meeting regularly at the Temple in the area known as Solomon's Hall, and they did many remarkable miracles among the people. 13The other believers didn't dare join them, though, but all had the highest regard for them. 14And more and more believers were added to the Lord, crowds both of men and women. 15Sick people were brought out into the streets on beds and mats so that at least Peter's shadow would fall across some of them as he went by! 16And crowds came in from the Jerusalem suburbs, bringing their sick folk and those possessed by demons; and every one of them was healed.

17The High Priest and his relatives and friends among the Sadducees reacted with violent jealousy 18and arrested the apostles, and put them in the public jail.

19But an angel of the Lord came at night, opened the gates of the jail and brought them out. Then he told them, 20"Go over to the Temple and preach about this Life!"

21They arrived at the Temple about daybreak, and immediately began preaching! Later that morningc the High Priest and his courtiers arrived at the Temple, and, convening the Jewish Council and the entire Senate, they sent for the apostles to be brought for trial. 22But when the police arrived at the jail, the men weren't there, so they returned to the Council and reported, 23"The jail doors were locked, and the guards were standing outside, but when we opened the gates, no one was there!"

24When the police captaind and the chief priests heard this, they were frantic, wondering what would happen next and where all this would end! 25Then someone arrived with the news that the men they had jailed were out in the Temple, preaching to the people!

New Revised Standard

Ananias and Sapphira

5 BUT A man named Ananias, with the consent of his wife Sapphira, sold a piece of property; 2with his wife's knowledge, he kept back some of the proceeds, and brought only a part and laid it at the apostles' feet. 3"Ananias," Peter asked, "why has Satan filled your heart to lie to the Holy Spirit and to keep back part of the proceeds of the land? 4While it remained unsold, did it not remain your own? And after it was sold, were not the proceeds at your disposal? How is it that you have contrived this deed in your heart? You did not lie to use but to God!" 5Now when Ananias heard these words, he fell down and died. And great fear seized all who heard of it. 6The young men came and wrapped up his body,f then carried him out and buried him.

7 After an interval of about three hours his wife came in, not knowing what had happened. 8Peter said to her, "Tell me whether you and your husband sold the land for such and such a price." And she said, "Yes, that was the price." 9Then Peter said to her, "How is it that you have agreed together to put the Spirit of the Lord to the test? Look, the feet of those who have buried your husband are at the door, and they will carry you out." 10Immediately she fell down at his feet and died. When the young men came in they found her dead, so they carried her out and buried her beside her husband. 11And great fear seized the whole church and all who heard of these things.

The Apostles Heal Many

12 Now many signs and wonders were done among the people through the apostles. And they were all together in Solomon's Portico. 13None of the rest dared to join them, but the people held them in high esteem. 14Yet more than ever believers were added to the Lord, great numbers of both men and women, 15so that they even carried out the sick into the streets, and laid them on cots and mats, in order that Peter's shadow might fall on some of them as he came by. 16A great number of people would also gather from the towns around Jerusalem, bringing the sick and those tormented by unclean spirits, and they were all cured.

The Apostles Are Persecuted

17 Then the high priest took action; he and all who were with him (that is, the sect of the Sadducees), being filled with jealousy, 18arrested the apostles and put them in the public prison. 19But during the night an angel of the Lord opened the prison doors, brought them out, and said, 20"Go, stand in the temple and tell the people the whole message about this life." 21When they heard this, they entered the temple at daybreak and went on with their teaching.

When the high priest and those with him arrived, they called together the council and the whole body of the elders of Israel, and sent to the prison to have them brought. 22But when the temple police went there, they did not find them in the prison; so they returned and reported, 23"We found the prison securely locked and the guards standing at the doors, but when we opened them, we found no one inside." 24Now when the captain of the temple and the chief priests heard these words, they were perplexed about them, wondering what might be going on. 25Then someone arrived and announced, "Look, the men whom you put in prison are standing in the temple and teaching the people!" 26Then the captain

---

b 5:9 *to test the Spirit of God's ability to know what is going on,* literally, "to try the Spirit of the Lord." c 5:21 *Later that morning,* implied. d 5:24 *the police captain,* literally, "the captain of the Temple."

e Gk *to men*   f Meaning of Gk uncertain

King James

26Then went the captain with the officers, and brought them without violence: for they feared the people, lest they should have been stoned.

27And when they had brought them, they set *them* before the council: and the high priest asked them,

28Saying, Did not we straitly command you that ye should not teach in this name? and, behold, ye have filled Jerusalem with your doctrine, and intend to bring this man's blood upon us.

29¶ Then Peter and the *other* apostles answered and said, We ought to obey God rather than men.

30The God of our fathers raised up Jesus, whom ye slew and hanged on a tree.

31Him hath God exalted with his right hand *to be* a Prince and a Saviour, for to give repentance to Israel, and forgiveness of sins.

32And we are his witnesses of these things; and *so is* also the Holy Ghost, whom God hath given to them that obey him.

33¶ When they heard *that*, they were cut *to the heart*, and took counsel to slay them.

34Then stood there up one in the council, a Pharisee, named Gamaliel, a doctor of the law, had in reputation among all the people, and commanded to put the apostles forth a little space;

35And said unto them, Ye men of Israel, take heed to yourselves what ye intend to do as touching these men.

36For before these days rose up Theudas, boasting himself to be somebody; to whom a number of men, about four hundred, joined themselves: who was slain; and all, as many as obeyed him, were scattered, and brought to nought.

37After this man rose up Judas of Galilee in the days of the taxing, and drew away much people after him: he also perished; and all, *even* as many as obeyed him, were dispersed.

38And now I say unto you, Refrain from these men, and let them alone: for if this counsel or this work be of men, it will come to nought:

39But if it be of God, ye cannot overthrow it; lest haply ye be found even to fight against God.

40And to him they agreed: and when they had called the apostles, and beaten *them*, they commanded that they should not speak in the name of Jesus, and let them go.

41¶ And they departed from the presence of the council, rejoicing that they were counted worthy to suffer shame for his name.

42And daily in the temple, and in every house, they ceased not to teach and preach Jesus Christ.

6 AND IN those days, when the number of the disciples was multiplied, there arose a murmuring of the Grecians against the Hebrews, because their widows were neglected in the daily ministration.

2Then the twelve called the multitude of the disciples *unto them*, and said, It is not reason that we should leave the word of God, and serve tables.

3Wherefore, brethren, look ye out among you seven men of honest report, full of the Holy Ghost and wisdom, whom we may appoint over this business.

4But we will give ourselves continually to prayer, and to the ministry of the word.

New International

brought the apostles. They did not use force, because they feared that the people would stone them.

27Having brought the apostles, they made them appear before the Sanhedrin to be questioned by the high priest. 28"We gave you strict orders not to teach in this name," he said. "Yet you have filled Jerusalem with your teaching and are determined to make us guilty of this man's blood."

29Peter and the other apostles replied: "We must obey God rather than men! 30The God of our fathers raised Jesus from the dead—whom you had killed by hanging him on a tree. 31God exalted him to his own right hand as Prince and Savior that he might give repentance and forgiveness of sins to Israel. 32We are witnesses of these things, and so is the Holy Spirit, whom God has given to those who obey him."

33When they heard this, they were furious and wanted to put them to death. 34But a Pharisee named Gamaliel, a teacher of the law, who was honored by all the people, stood up in the Sanhedrin and ordered that the men be put outside for a little while. 35Then he addressed them: "Men of Israel, consider carefully what you intend to do to these men. 36Some time ago Theudas appeared, claiming to be somebody, and about four hundred men rallied to him. He was killed, all his followers were dispersed, and it all came to nothing. 37After him, Judas the Galilean appeared in the days of the census and led a band of people in revolt. He too was killed, and all his followers were scattered. 38Therefore, in the present case I advise you: Leave these men alone! Let them go! For if their purpose or activity is of human origin, it will fail. 39But if it is from God, you will not be able to stop these men; you will only find yourselves fighting against God."

40His speech persuaded them. They called the apostles in and had them flogged. Then they ordered them not to speak in the name of Jesus, and let them go.

41The apostles left the Sanhedrin, rejoicing because they had been counted worthy of suffering disgrace for the Name. 42Day after day, in the temple courts and from house to house, they never stopped teaching and proclaiming the good news that Jesus is the Christ.a

The Choosing of the Seven

6 IN THOSE days when the number of disciples was increasing, the Grecian Jews among them complained against the Hebraic Jews because their widows were being overlooked in the daily distribution of food. 2So the Twelve gathered all the disciples together and said, "It would not be right for us to neglect the ministry of the word of God in order to wait on tables. 3Brothers, choose seven men from among you who are known to be full of the Spirit and wisdom. We will turn this responsibility over to them 4and will give our attention to prayer and the ministry of the word."

a 42 Or *Messiah*

Living Bible

26, 27The police captain went with his officers and arrested them (without violence, for they were afraid the people would kill them if they roughed up the disciples) and brought them in before the Council.

28"Didn't we tell you never again to preach about this Jesus?" the High Priest demanded. "And instead you have filled all Jerusalem with your teaching and intend to bring the blame for this man's death on us!"

29But Peter and the apostles replied, "We must obey God rather than men. 30The God of our ancestors brought Jesus back to life again after you had killed him by hanging him on a cross. 31Then, with mighty power, God exalted him to be a Prince and Savior, so that the people of Israel would have an opportunity for repentance, and for their sins to be forgiven. 32And we are witnesses of these things, and so is the Holy Spirit, who is given by God to all who obey him."

33At this, the Council was furious, and decided to kill them. 34But one of their members, a Pharisee named Gamaliel (an expert on religious law and very popular with the people), stood up and requested that the apostles be sent outside the Council chamber while he talked.

35Then he addressed his colleagues as follows:

"Men of Israel, take care what you are planning to do to these men! 36Some time ago there was that fellow Theudas, who pretended to be someone great. About 400 others joined him, but he was killed, and his followers were harmlessly dispersed.

37"After him, at the time of the taxation, there was Judas of Galilee. He drew away some people as disciples, but he also died, and his followers scattered.

38"And so my advice is, leave these men alone. If what they teach and do is merely on their own, it will soon be overthrown. 39But if it is of God, you will not be able to stop them, lest you find yourselves fighting even against God."

40The Council accepted his advice, called in the apostles, had them beaten, and then told them never again to speak in the name of Jesus, and finally let them go. 41They left the Council chamber rejoicing that God had counted them worthy to suffer dishonor for his name. 42And every day, in the Temple and in their home Bible classes, they continued to teach and preach that Jesus is the Messiah.

6 BUT WITH the believers multiplying rapidly, there were rumblings of discontent. Those who spoke only Greek complained that their widows were being discriminated against, that they were not being given as much food, in the daily distribution, as the widows who spoke Hebrew. 2So the Twelve called a meeting of all the believers.

"We should spend our time preaching, not administering a feeding program," they said. 3"Now look around among yourselves, dear brothers, and select seven men, wise and full of the Holy Spirit, who are well thought of by everyone; and we will put them in charge of this business. 4Then we can spend our time in prayer, preaching, and teaching."

New Revised Standard

went with the temple police and brought them, but without violence, for they were afraid of being stoned by the people.

27 When they had brought them, they had them stand before the council. The high priest questioned them, 28saying, "We gave you strict orders not to teach in this name,b yet here you have filled Jerusalem with your teaching and you are determined to bring this man's blood on us." 29But Peter and the apostles answered, "We must obey God rather than any human authority.c 30The God of our ancestors raised up Jesus, whom you had killed by hanging him on a tree. 31God exalted him at his right hand as Leader and Savior that he might give repentance to Israel and forgiveness of sins. 32And we are witnesses to these things, and so is the Holy Spirit whom God has given to those who obey him."

33 When they heard this, they were enraged and wanted to kill them. 34But a Pharisee in the council named Gamaliel, a teacher of the law, respected by all the people, stood up and ordered the men to be put outside for a short time. 35Then he said to them, "Fellow Israelites,d consider carefully what you propose to do to these men. 36For some time ago Theudas rose up, claiming to be somebody, and a number of men, about four hundred, joined him; but he was killed, and all who followed him were dispersed and disappeared. 37After him Judas the Galilean rose up at the time of the census and got people to follow him; he also perished, and all who followed him were scattered. 38So in the present case, I tell you, keep away from these men and let them alone; because if this plan or this undertaking is of human origin, it will fail; 39but if it is of God, you will not be able to overthrow them—in that case you may even be found fighting against God!"

They were convinced by him, 40and when they had called in the apostles, they had them flogged. Then they ordered them not to speak in the name of Jesus, and let them go. 41As they left the council, they rejoiced that they were considered worthy to suffer dishonor for the sake of the name. 42And every day in the temple and at homee they did not cease to teach and proclaim Jesus as the Messiah.f

Seven Chosen to Serve

6 NOW DURING those days, when the disciples were increasing in number, the Hellenists complained against the Hebrews because their widows were being neglected in the daily distribution of food. 2And the twelve called together the whole community of the disciples and said, "It is not right that we should neglect the word of God in order to wait on tables.g 3Therefore, friends,h select from among yourselves seven men of good standing, full of the Spirit and of wisdom, whom we may appoint to this task, 4while we, for our part, will devote ourselves to prayer and to serving the word."

b Other ancient authorities read *Did we not give you strict orders not to teach in this name?*   c Gk *than men*   d Gk *Men, Israelites*   e Or *from house to house*   f Or *the Christ*   g Or *keep accounts*   h Gk *brothers*

King James

5¶ And the saying pleased the whole multitude: and they chose Stephen, a man full of faith and of the Holy Ghost, and Philip, and Prochorus, and Nicanor, and Timon, and Parmenas, and Nicolas a proselyte of Antioch:

6Whom they set before the apostles: and when they had prayed, they laid *their* hands on them.

7And the word of God increased; and the number of the disciples multiplied in Jerusalem greatly; and a great company of the priests were obedient to the faith.

8And Stephen, full of faith and power, did great wonders and miracles among the people.

9¶ Then there arose certain of the synagogue, which is called *the synagogue* of the Libertines, and Cyrenians, and Alexandrians, and of them of Cilicia and of Asia, disputing with Stephen.

10And they were not able to resist the wisdom and the spirit by which he spake.

11Then they suborned men, which said, We have heard him speak blasphemous words against Moses, and *against* God.

12And they stirred up the people, and the elders, and the scribes, and came upon *him,* and caught him, and brought *him* to the council,

13And set up false witnesses, which said, This man ceaseth not to speak blasphemous words against this holy place, and the law:

14For we have heard him say, that this Jesus of Nazareth shall destroy this place, and shall change the customs which Moses delivered us.

15And all that sat in the council, looking stedfastly on him, saw his face as it had been the face of an angel.

7 THEN SAID the high priest, Are these things so?
2And he said, Men, brethren, and fathers, hearken; The God of glory appeared unto our father Abraham, when he was in Mesopotamia, before he dwelt in Charran,

3And said unto him, Get thee out of thy country, and from thy kindred, and come into the land which I shall show thee.

4Then came he out of the land of the Chaldaeans, and dwelt in Charran: and from thence, when his father was dead, he removed him into this land, wherein ye now dwell.

5And he gave him none inheritance in it, no, not *so much as* to set his foot on: yet he promised that he would give it to him for a possession, and to his seed after him, when *as yet* he had no child.

6And God spake on this wise, That his seed should sojourn in a strange land; and that they should bring them into bondage, and entreat *them* evil four hundred years.

7And the nation to whom they shall be in bondage will I judge, said God: and after that shall they come forth, and serve me in this place.

8And he gave him the covenant of circumcision: and so *Abraham* begat Isaac, and circumcised him the eighth day; and Isaac *begat* Jacob; and Jacob *begat* the twelve patriarchs.

9And the patriarchs, moved with envy, sold Joseph into Egypt: but God was with him,

New International

5This proposal pleased the whole group. They chose Stephen, a man full of faith and of the Holy Spirit; also Philip, Procorus, Nicanor, Timon, Parmenas, and Nicolas from Antioch, a convert to Judaism. 6They presented these men to the apostles, who prayed and laid their hands on them.

7So the word of God spread. The number of disciples in Jerusalem increased rapidly, and a large number of priests became obedient to the faith.

Stephen Seized

8Now Stephen, a man full of God's grace and power, did great wonders and miraculous signs among the people. 9Opposition arose, however, from members of the Synagogue of the Freedmen (as it was called)—Jews of Cyrene and Alexandria as well as the provinces of Cilicia and Asia. These men began to argue with Stephen, 10but they could not stand up against his wisdom or the Spirit by whom he spoke.

11Then they secretly persuaded some men to say, "We have heard Stephen speak words of blasphemy against Moses and against God."

12So they stirred up the people and the elders and the teachers of the law. They seized Stephen and brought him before the Sanhedrin. 13They produced false witnesses, who testified, "This fellow never stops speaking against this holy place and against the law. 14For we have heard him say that this Jesus of Nazareth will destroy this place and change the customs Moses handed down to us."

15All who were sitting in the Sanhedrin looked intently at Stephen, and they saw that his face was like the face of an angel.

Stephen's Speech to the Sanhedrin

7 THEN THE high priest asked him, "Are these charges true?"

2To this he replied: "Brothers and fathers, listen to me! The God of glory appeared to our father Abraham while he was still in Mesopotamia, before he lived in Haran. 3'Leave your country and your people,' God said, 'and go to the land I will show you.'a

4"So he left the land of the Chaldeans and settled in Haran. After the death of his father, God sent him to this land where you are now living. 5He gave him no inheritance here, not even a foot of ground. But God promised him that he and his descendants after him would possess the land, even though at that time Abraham had no child. 6God spoke to him in this way: 'Your descendants will be strangers in a country not their own, and they will be enslaved and mistreated four hundred years. 7But I will punish the nation they serve as slaves,' God said, 'and afterward they will come out of that country and worship me in this place.'b 8Then he gave Abraham the covenant of circumcision. And Abraham became the father of Isaac and circumcised him eight days after his birth. Later Isaac became the father of Jacob, and Jacob became the father of the twelve patriarchs.

9"Because the patriarchs were jealous of Joseph, they sold him as a slave into Egypt. But God was with him

a 3 Gen. 12:1   b 7 Gen. 15:13,14

Living Bible

5This sounded reasonable to the whole assembly, and they elected the following:
Stephen (a man unusually full of faith and the Holy Spirit),
Philip,
Prochorus,
Nicanor,
Timon,
Parmenas,
Nicolaus of Antioch (a Gentile convert to the Jewish faith, who had become a Christian).

6These seven were presented to the apostles, who prayed for them and laid their hands on them in blessing.

7God's message was preached in ever-widening circles, and the number of disciples increased vastly in Jerusalem; and many of the Jewish priests were converted too.

8Stephen, the man so full of faith and the Holy Spirit's power,c did spectacular miracles among the people.

9But one day some of the men from the Jewish cult of "The Freedmen" started an argument with him, and they were soon joined by Jews from Cyrene, Alexandria in Egypt, and the Turkish provinces of Cilicia, and Asia minor. 10But none of them was able to stand against Stephen's wisdom and spirit.

11So they brought in some men to lie about him, claiming they had heard Stephen curse Moses, and even God.

12This accusation roused the crowds to fury against Stephen, and the Jewish leadersd arrested him and brought him before the Council. 13The lying witnesses testified again that Stephen was constantly speaking against the Temple and against the laws of Moses.

14They declared, "We have heard him say that this fellow Jesus of Nazareth will destroy the Temple, and throw out all of Moses' laws." 15At this point everyone in the Council chamber saw Stephen's face become as radiant as an angel's!

7 THEN THE High Priest asked him, "Are these accusations true?"

2This was Stephen's lengthy reply: "The glorious God appeared to our ancestor Abraham in Iraqe before he moved to Syria,f 3and told him to leave his native land, to say good-bye to his relatives and to start out for a country that God would direct him to. 4So he left the land of the Chaldeans and lived in Haran, in Syria, until his father died. Then God brought him here to the land of Israel, 5but gave him no property of his own, not one little tract of land.

"However, God promised that eventually the whole country would belong to him and his descendants—though as yet he had no children! 6But God also told him that these descendants of his would leave the land and live in a foreign country and there become slaves for 400 years. 7'But I will punish the nation that enslaves them,' God told him, 'and afterwards my people will return to this land of Israel and worship me here.'

8"God also gave Abraham the ceremony of circumcision at that time, as evidence of the covenant between God and the people of Abraham. And so Isaac, Abraham's son, was circumcised when he was eight days old. Isaac became the father of Jacob, and Jacob was the father of the twelve patriarchs of the Jewish nation. 9These men were very jealous of Joseph and sold him to be a slave in Egypt. But God was with him, 10and

New Revised Standard

5What they said pleased the whole community, and they chose Stephen, a man full of faith and the Holy Spirit, together with Philip, Prochorus, Nicanor, Timon, Parmenas, and Nicolaus, a proselyte of Antioch. 6They had these men stand before the apostles, who prayed and laid their hands on them.

7 The word of God continued to spread; the number of the disciples increased greatly in Jerusalem, and a great many of the priests became obedient to the faith.

The Arrest of Stephen

8 Stephen, full of grace and power, did great wonders and signs among the people. 9Then some of those who belonged to the synagogue of the Freedmen (as it was called), Cyrenians, Alexandrians, and others of those from Cilicia and Asia, stood up and argued with Stephen. 10But they could not withstand the wisdom and the Spiritg with which he spoke. 11Then they secretly instigated some men to say, "We have heard him speak blasphemous words against Moses and God." 12They stirred up the people as well as the elders and the scribes; then they suddenly confronted him, seized him, and brought him before the council. 13They set up false witnesses who said, "This man never stops saying things against this holy place and the law; 14for we have heard him say that this Jesus of Nazarethh will destroy this place and will change the customs that Moses handed on to us." 15And all who sat in the council looked intently at him, and they saw that his face was like the face of an angel.

Stephen's Speech to the Council

7 THEN THE high priest asked him, "Are these things so?" 2And Stephen replied:

"Brothersi and fathers, listen to me. The God of glory appeared to our ancestor Abraham when he was in Mesopotamia, before he lived in Haran, 3and said to him, 'Leave your country and your relatives and go to the land that I will show you.' 4Then he left the country of the Chaldeans and settled in Haran. After his father died, God had him move from there to this country in which you are now living. 5He did not give him any of it as a heritage, not even a foot's length, but promised to give it to him as his possession and to his descendants after him, even though he had no child. 6And God spoke in these terms, that his descendants would be resident aliens in a country belonging to others, who would enslave them and mistreat them during four hundred years. 7'But I will judge the nation that they serve,' said God, 'and after that they shall come out and worship me in this place.' 8Then he gave him the covenant of circumcision. And so Abrahamj became the father of Isaac and circumcised him on the eighth day; and Isaac became the father of Jacob, and Jacob of the twelve patriarchs.

9 "The patriarchs, jealous of Joseph, sold him into Egypt; but God was with him, 10and rescued him from

---

c 6:8 full of faith and the Holy Spirit's power, literally, "full of grace and truth." See vs 5.   d 6:12 the Jewish leaders, literally, "the elders and the scribes."   e 7:2 Iraq, literally, "Mesopotamia."   f 7:2 Syria, literally, "Haran," a city in the area we now know as Syria.

g Or spirit   h Gk the Nazorean   i Gk Men, brothers   j Gk he

King James

10And delivered him out of all his afflictions, and gave him favour and wisdom in the sight of Pharaoh king of Egypt; and he made him governor over Egypt and all his house.

11Now there came a dearth over all the land of Egypt and Chanaan, and great affliction: and our fathers found no sustenance.

12But when Jacob heard that there was corn in Egypt, he sent out our fathers first.

13And at the second *time* Joseph was made known to his brethren; and Joseph's kindred was made known unto Pharaoh.

14Then sent Joseph, and called his father Jacob to *him*, and all his kindred, threescore and fifteen souls.

15So Jacob went down into Egypt, and died, he, and our fathers,

16And were carried over into Sychem, and laid in the sepulchre that Abraham bought for a sum of money of the sons of Emmor *the father* of Sychem.

17But when the time of the promise drew nigh, which God had sworn to Abraham, the people grew and multiplied in Egypt,

18Till another king arose, which knew not Joseph.

19The same dealt subtly with our kindred, and evil entreated our fathers, so that they cast out their young children, to the end they might not live.

20In which time Moses was born, and was exceeding fair, and nourished up in his father's house three months:

21And when he was cast out, Pharaoh's daughter took him up, and nourished him for her own son.

22And Moses was learned in all the wisdom of the Egyptians, and was mighty in words and in deeds.

23And when he was full forty years old, it came into his heart to visit his brethren the children of Israel.

24And seeing one *of them* suffer wrong, he defended *him*, and avenged him that was oppressed, and smote the Egyptian:

25For he supposed his brethren would have understood how that God by his hand would deliver them: but they understood not.

26And the next day he showed himself unto them as they strove, and would have set them at one again, saying, Sirs, ye are brethren; why do ye wrong one to another?

27But he that did his neighbour wrong thrust him away, saying, Who made thee a ruler and a judge over us?

28Wilt thou kill me, as thou diddest the Egyptian yesterday?

29Then fled Moses at this saying, and was a stranger in the land of Madian, where he begat two sons.

30And when forty years were expired, there appeared to him in the wilderness of mount Sina an angel of the Lord in a flame of fire in a bush.

31When Moses saw *it*, he wondered at the sight: and as he drew near to behold *it*, the voice of the Lord came unto him,

32*Saying*, I *am* the God of thy fathers, the God of Abraham, and the God of Isaac, and the God of Jacob. Then Moses trembled, and durst not behold.

33Then said the Lord to him, Put off thy shoes from thy feet: for the place where thou standest is holy ground.

34I have seen, I have seen the affliction of my people which is in Egypt, and I have heard their groaning, and am come down to deliver them. And now come, I will send thee into Egypt.

35This Moses whom they refused, saying, Who made thee a ruler and a judge? the same did God send *to be* a ruler and a deliverer by the hand of the angel which appeared to him in the bush.

36He brought them out, after that he had shown wonders and signs in the land of Egypt, and in the Red sea, and in the wilderness forty years.

New International

10and rescued him from all his troubles. He gave Joseph wisdom and enabled him to gain the goodwill of Pharaoh king of Egypt; so he made him ruler over Egypt and all his palace.

11"Then a famine struck all Egypt and Canaan, bringing great suffering, and our fathers could not find food. 12When Jacob heard that there was grain in Egypt, he sent our fathers on their first visit. 13On their second visit, Joseph told his brothers who he was, and Pharaoh learned about Joseph's family. 14After this, Joseph sent for his father Jacob and his whole family, seventy-five in all. 15Then Jacob went down to Egypt, where he and our fathers died. 16Their bodies were brought back to Shechem and placed in the tomb that Abraham had bought from the sons of Hamor at Shechem for a certain sum of money.

17"As the time drew near for God to fulfill his promise to Abraham, the number of our people in Egypt greatly increased. 18Then another king, who knew nothing about Joseph, became ruler of Egypt. 19He dealt treacherously with our people and oppressed our forefathers by forcing them to throw out their newborn babies so that they would die.

20"At that time Moses was born, and he was no ordinary child.a For three months he was cared for in his father's house. 21When he was placed outside, Pharaoh's daughter took him and brought him up as her own son. 22Moses was educated in all the wisdom of the Egyptians and was powerful in speech and action.

23"When Moses was forty years old, he decided to visit his fellow Israelites. 24He saw one of them being mistreated by an Egyptian, so he went to his defense and avenged him by killing the Egyptian. 25Moses thought that his own people would realize that God was using him to rescue them, but they did not. 26The next day Moses came upon two Israelites who were fighting. He tried to reconcile them by saying, 'Men, you are brothers; why do you want to hurt each other?'

27"But the man who was mistreating the other pushed Moses aside and said, 'Who made you ruler and judge over us? 28Do you want to kill me as you killed the Egyptian yesterday?'b 29When Moses heard this, he fled to Midian, where he settled as a foreigner and had two sons.

30"After forty years had passed, an angel appeared to Moses in the flames of a burning bush in the desert near Mount Sinai. 31When he saw this, he was amazed at the sight. As he went over to look more closely, he heard the Lord's voice: 32'I am the God of your fathers, the God of Abraham, Isaac and Jacob.'c Moses trembled with fear and did not dare to look.

33"Then the Lord said to him, 'Take off your sandals; the place where you are standing is holy ground. 34I have indeed seen the oppression of my people in Egypt. I have heard their groaning and have come down to set them free. Now come, I will send you back to Egypt.'d

35"This is the same Moses whom they had rejected with the words, 'Who made you ruler and judge?' He was sent to be their ruler and deliverer by God himself, through the angel who appeared to him in the bush. 36He led them out of Egypt and did wonders and miraculous signs in Egypt, at the Red Seae and for forty years in the desert.

a *20 Or was fair in the sight of God*   b *28 Exodus 2:14*   c *32 Exodus 3:6*
d *34 Exodus 3:5,7,8,10*   e *36 That is, Sea of Reeds*

Living Bible

delivered him out of all of his anguish, and gave him
favor before Pharaoh, king of Egypt. God also gave
Joseph unusual wisdom, so that Pharaoh appointed him
governor over all Egypt, as well as putting him in charge
of all the affairs of the palace.

11"But a famine developed in Egypt and Canaan and
there was great misery for our ancestors. When their
food was gone, 12Jacob heard that there was still grain
in Egypt, so he sent his sonsf to buy some. 13The second
time they went, Joseph revealed his identity to his brothers, and they were introduced to Pharaoh. 14Then Joseph
sent for his father Jacob and all his brothers' families to
come to Egypt, seventy-five persons in all. 15So Jacob
came to Egypt, where he died, and all his sons. 16All of
them were taken to Shechem and buried in the tomb
Abraham bought from the sons of Hamor, Shechem's
father.

17, 18"As the time drew near when God would fulfill
his promise to Abraham to free his descendants from
slavery, the Jewish people greatly multiplied in Egypt;
but then a king was crowned who had no respect for
Joseph's memory. 19This king plotted against our race,
forcing parents to abandon their children in the fields.

20"About that time Moses was born—a child of divine beauty. His parents hid him at home for three
months, 21and when at last they could no longer keep
him hidden, and had to abandon him, Pharaoh's daughter found him and adopted him as her own son, 22and
taught him all the wisdom of the Egyptians, and he
became a mighty prince and orator.

23"One day as he was nearing his fortieth birthday,
it came into his mind to visit his brothers, the people of
Israel. 24During this visit he saw an Egyptian mistreating
a man of Israel. So Moses killed the Egyptian. 25Moses
supposed his brothers would realize that God had sent
him to help them, but they didn't.

26"The next day he visited them again and saw two
men of Israel fighting. He tried to be a peacemaker.
'Gentlemen,' he said, 'you are brothers and shouldn't be
fighting like this! It is wrong!'

27"But the man in the wrong told Moses to mind his
own business. 'Who made you a ruler and judge over
us?' he asked. 28'Are you going to kill me as you killed
that Egyptian yesterday?'

29"At this, Moses fled the country, and lived in the
land of Midian, where his two sons were born.

30"Forty years later, in the desert near Mount Sinai,
an Angel appeared to him in a flame of fire in a bush.
31Moses saw it and wondered what it was, and as he ran
to see, the voice of the Lord called out to him, 32'I am
the God of your ancestors—of Abraham, Isaac and Jacob.' Moses shook with terror and dared not look.

33"And the Lord said to him, 'Take off your shoes,
for you are standing on holy ground. 34I have seen the
anguish of my people in Egypt and have heard their
cries. I have come down to deliver them. Come, I will
send you to Egypt.' 35And so God sent back the same
man his people had previously rejected by demanding,
'Who made you a ruler and judge over us?' Moses was
sent to be their ruler and savior. 36And by means of
many remarkable miracles he led them out of Egypt and
through the Red Sea, and back and forth through the
wilderness for forty years.

New Revised Standard

all his afflictions, and enabled him to win favor and to
show wisdom when he stood before Pharaoh, king of
Egypt, who appointed him ruler over Egypt and over all
his household. 11Now there came a famine throughout
Egypt and Canaan, and great suffering, and our ancestors could find no food. 12But when Jacob heard that
there was grain in Egypt, he sent our ancestors there on
their first visit. 13On the second visit Joseph made himself known to his brothers, and Joseph's family became
known to Pharaoh. 14Then Joseph sent and invited his
father Jacob and all his relatives to come to him,
seventy-five in all; 15so Jacob went down to Egypt. He
himself died there as well as our ancestors, 16and their
bodiesg were brought back to Shechem and laid in the
tomb that Abraham had bought for a sum of silver from
the sons of Hamor in Shechem.

17 "But as the time drew near for the fulfillment of
the promise that God had made to Abraham, our people
in Egypt increased and multiplied 18until another king
who had not known Joseph ruled over Egypt. 19He dealt
craftily with our race and forced our ancestors to abandon their infants so that they would die. 20At this time
Moses was born, and he was beautiful before God. For
three months he was brought up in his father's house;
21and when he was abandoned, Pharaoh's daughter
adopted him and brought him up as her own son. 22So
Moses was instructed in all the wisdom of the Egyptians
and was powerful in his words and deeds.

23 "When he was forty years old, it came into his
heart to visit his relatives, the Israelites.h 24When he
saw one of them being wronged, he defended the oppressed man and avenged him by striking down the
Egyptian. 25He supposed that his kinsfolk would understand that God through him was rescuing them, but they
did not understand. 26The next day he came to some of
them as they were quarreling and tried to reconcile them,
saying, 'Men, you are brothers; why do you wrong each
other?' 27But the man who was wronging his neighbor
pushed Mosesi aside, saying, 'Who made you a ruler
and a judge over us? 28Do you want to kill me as you
killed the Egyptian yesterday?' 29When he heard this,
Moses fled and became a resident alien in the land of
Midian. There he became the father of two sons.

30 "Now when forty years had passed, an angel
appeared to him in the wilderness of Mount Sinai, in the
flame of a burning bush. 31When Moses saw it, he was
amazed at the sight; and as he approached to look, there
came the voice of the Lord: 32'I am the God of your
ancestors, the God of Abraham, Isaac, and Jacob.' Moses began to tremble and did not dare to look. 33Then
the Lord said to him, 'Take off the sandals from your
feet, for the place where you are standing is holy ground.
34I have surely seen the mistreatment of my people who
are in Egypt and have heard their groaning, and I have
come down to rescue them. Come now, I will send you
to Egypt.'

35 "It was this Moses whom they rejected when
they said, 'Who made you a ruler and a judge?' and
whom God now sent as both ruler and liberator through
the angel who appeared to him in the bush. 36He led
them out, having performed wonders and signs in
Egypt, at the Red Sea, and in the wilderness for forty
years. 37This is the Moses who said to the Israelites,

---

f 7:12 his sons, literally, "our fathers."   g Gk they   h Gk his brothers, the sons of Israel   i Gk him

King James

37¶ This is that Moses, which said unto the children of Israel, A prophet shall the Lord your God raise up unto you of your brethren, like unto me; him shall ye hear.

38This is he, that was in the church in the wilderness with the angel which spake to him in the mount Sina, and *with* our fathers: who received the lively oracles to give unto us:

39To whom our fathers would not obey, but thrust *him* from them, and in their hearts turned back again into Egypt,

40Saying unto Aaron, Make us gods to go before us: for *as for* this Moses, which brought us out of the land of Egypt, we wot not what is become of him.

41And they made a calf in those days, and offered sacrifice unto the idol, and rejoiced in the works of their own hands.

42Then God turned, and gave them up to worship the host of heaven; as it is written in the book of the prophets, O ye house of Israel, have ye offered to me slain beasts and sacrifices *by the space of* forty years in the wilderness?

43Yea, ye took up the tabernacle of Moloch, and the star of your god Remphan, figures which ye made to worship them: and I will carry you away beyond Babylon.

44Our fathers had the tabernacle of witness in the wilderness, as he had appointed, speaking unto Moses, that he should make it according to the fashion that he had seen.

45Which also our fathers that came after brought in with Jesus into the possession of the Gentiles, whom God drave out before the face of our fathers, unto the days of David;

46Who found favour before God, and desired to find a tabernacle for the God of Jacob.

47But Solomon built him an house.

48Howbeit the most High dwelleth not in temples made with hands; as saith the prophet,

49Heaven *is* my throne, and earth *is* my footstool: what house will ye build me? saith the Lord: or what *is* the place of my rest?

50Hath not my hand made all these things?

51¶ Ye stiffnecked and uncircumcised in heart and ears, ye do always resist the Holy Ghost: as your fathers *did*, so *do* ye.

52Which of the prophets have not your fathers persecuted? and they have slain them which showed before of the coming of the Just One; of whom ye have been now the betrayers and murderers:

53Who have received the law by the disposition of angels, and have not kept *it*.

54¶ When they heard these things, they were cut to the heart, and they gnashed on him with *their* teeth.

55But he, being full of the Holy Ghost, looked up stedfastly into heaven, and saw the glory of God, and Jesus standing on the right hand of God,

56And said, Behold, I see the heavens opened, and the Son of man standing on the right hand of God.

57Then they cried out with a loud voice, and stopped their ears, and ran upon him with one accord,

58And cast *him* out of the city, and stoned *him*: and the witnesses laid down their clothes at a young man's feet, whose name was Saul.

59And they stoned Stephen, calling upon *God*, and saying, Lord Jesus, receive my spirit.

60And he kneeled down, and cried with a loud voice, Lord, lay not this sin to their charge. And when he had said this, he fell asleep.

New International

37"This is that Moses who told the Israelites, 'God will send you a prophet like me from your own people.'a 38He was in the assembly in the desert, with the angel who spoke to him on Mount Sinai, and with our fathers; and he received living words to pass on to us.

39"But our fathers refused to obey him. Instead, they rejected him and in their hearts turned back to Egypt. 40They told Aaron, 'Make us gods who will go before us. As for this fellow Moses who led us out of Egypt— we don't know what has happened to him!'b 41That was the time they made an idol in the form of a calf. They brought sacrifices to it and held a celebration in honor of what their hands had made. 42But God turned away and gave them over to the worship of the heavenly bodies. This agrees with what is written in the book of the prophets:

" 'Did you bring me sacrifices and offerings
　　forty years in the desert, O house of Israel?
43You have lifted up the shrine of Molech
　　and the star of your god Rephan,
　the idols you made to worship.
Therefore I will send you into exile'c beyond
　　Babylon.

44"Our forefathers had the tabernacle of the Testimony with them in the desert. It had been made as God directed Moses, according to the pattern he had seen. 45Having received the tabernacle, our fathers under Joshua brought it with them when they took the land from the nations God drove out before them. It remained in the land until the time of David, 46who enjoyed God's favor and asked that he might provide a dwelling place for the God of Jacob.d 47But it was Solomon who built the house for him.

48"However, the Most High does not live in houses made by men. As the prophet says:

49" 'Heaven is my throne,
　　and the earth is my footstool.
What kind of house will you build for me?
　　　　　　　　　　　　　says the Lord.
Or where will my resting place be?
50Has not my hand made all these things?'e

51"You stiff-necked people, with uncircumcised hearts and ears! You are just like your fathers: You always resist the Holy Spirit! 52Was there ever a prophet your fathers did not persecute? They even killed those who predicted the coming of the Righteous One. And now you have betrayed and murdered him— 53you who have received the law that was put into effect through angels but have not obeyed it."

The Stoning of Stephen

54When they heard this, they were furious and gnashed their teeth at him. 55But Stephen, full of the Holy Spirit, looked up to heaven and saw the glory of God, and Jesus standing at the right hand of God. 56"Look," he said, "I see heaven open and the Son of Man standing at the right hand of God."

57At this they covered their ears, and yelling at the top of their voices, they all rushed at him, 58dragged him out of the city and began to stone him. Meanwhile, the witnesses laid their clothes at the feet of a young man named Saul.

59While they were stoning him, Stephen prayed, "Lord Jesus, receive my spirit." 60Then he fell on his knees and cried out, "Lord, do not hold this sin against them." When he had said this, he fell asleep.

---

a 37 Deut. 18:15 　b 40 Exodus 32:1 　c 43 Amos 5:25-27 　d 46 Some early manuscripts *the house of Jacob* 　e 50 Isaiah 66:1,2

Living Bible

37"Moses himself told the people of Israel, 'God will raise up a Prophet much like me[f] from among your brothers.' 38How true this proved to be, for in the wilderness, Moses was the go-between—the mediator between the people of Israel and the Angel who gave them the Law of God—the Living Word—on Mount Sinai. 39"But our fathers rejected Moses and wanted to return to Egypt. 40They told Aaron, 'Make idols for us, so that we will have gods to lead us back; for we don't know what has become of this Moses, who brought us out of Egypt.' 41So they made a calf-idol and sacrificed to it, and rejoiced in this thing they had made.

42"Then God turned away from them and gave them up, and let them serve the sun, moon and stars as their gods! In the book of Amos' prophecies the Lord God asks, 'Was it to me you were sacrificing during those forty years in the desert, Israel? 43No, your real interest was in your heathen gods—Sakkuth, and the star god Kaiway, and in all the images you made. So I will send you into captivity far away beyond Babylon.'

44"Our ancestors carried along with them a portable Temple, or Tabernacle, through the wilderness. In it they kept the stone tablets with the Ten Commandments written on them. This building was constructed in exact accordance with the plan shown to Moses by the Angel. 45Years later, when Joshua led the battles against the Gentile nations, this Tabernacle was taken with them into their new territory, and used until the time of King David. 46"God blessed David greatly, and David asked for the privilege of building a permanent Temple for the God of Jacob. 47But it was Solomon who actually built it. 48, 49However, God doesn't live in temples made by human hands. 'The heaven is my throne,' says the Lord through his prophets, 'and earth is my footstool. What kind of home could you build?' asks the Lord. 'Would I stay in it? 50Didn't I make both heaven and earth?'

51"You stiff-necked heathen! Must you forever resist the Holy Spirit? But your fathers did, and so do you! 52Name one prophet your ancestors didn't persecute! They even killed the ones who predicted the coming of the Righteous One—the Messiah whom you betrayed and murdered. 53Yes, and you deliberately destroyed God's Laws, though you received them from the hands of angels."[g]

54The Jewish leaders were stung to fury by Stephen's accusation, and ground their teeth in rage. 55But Stephen, full of the Holy Spirit, gazed steadily upward into heaven and saw the glory of God and Jesus standing at God's right hand. 56And he told them, "Look, I see the heavens opened and Jesus the Messiah[h] standing beside God, at his right hand!"

57Then they mobbed him, putting their hands over their ears, and drowning out his voice with their shouts, 58and dragged him out of the city to stone him. The official witnesses—the executioners—took off their coats and laid them at the feet of a young man named Paul.[i]

59And as the murderous stones came hurtling at him, Stephen prayed, "Lord Jesus, receive my spirit." 60And he fell to his knees, shouting, "Lord, don't charge them with this sin!" and with that, he died.

New Revised Standard

'God will raise up a prophet for you from your own people[j] as he raised me up.' 38He is the one who was in the congregation in the wilderness with the angel who spoke to him at Mount Sinai, and with our ancestors; and he received living oracles to give to us. 39Our ancestors were unwilling to obey him; instead, they pushed him aside, and in their hearts they turned back to Egypt, 40saying to Aaron, 'Make gods for us who will lead the way for us; as for this Moses who led us out from the land of Egypt, we do not know what has happened to him.' 41At that time they made a calf, offered a sacrifice to the idol, and reveled in the works of their hands. 42But God turned away from them and handed them over to worship the host of heaven, as it is written in the book of the prophets:

'Did you offer to me slain victims and
        sacrifices
    forty years in the wilderness, O house of
        Israel?
43 No; you took along the tent of Moloch,
        and the star of your god Rephan,
    the images that you made to worship;
    so I will remove you beyond Babylon.'

44 "Our ancestors had the tent of testimony in the wilderness, as God[k] directed when he spoke to Moses, ordering him to make it according to the pattern he had seen. 45Our ancestors in turn brought it in with Joshua when they dispossessed the nations that God drove out before our ancestors. And it was there until the time of David, 46who found favor with God and asked that he might find a dwelling place for the house of Jacob.[l] 47But it was Solomon who built a house for him. 48Yet the Most High does not dwell in houses made with human hands;[m] as the prophet says,

49 'Heaven is my throne,
        and the earth is my footstool.
    What kind of house will you build for me,
        says the Lord,
    or what is the place of my rest?
50 Did not my hand make all these things?'

51 "You stiff-necked people, uncircumcised in heart and ears, you are forever opposing the Holy Spirit, just as your ancestors used to do. 52Which of the prophets did your ancestors not persecute? They killed those who foretold the coming of the Righteous One, and now you have become his betrayers and murderers. 53You are the ones that received the law as ordained by angels, and yet you have not kept it."

The Stoning of Stephen

54 When they heard these things, they became enraged and ground their teeth at Stephen.[n] 55But filled with the Holy Spirit, he gazed into heaven and saw the glory of God and Jesus standing at the right hand of God. 56"Look," he said, "I see the heavens opened and the Son of Man standing at the right hand of God!" 57But they covered their ears, and with a loud shout all rushed together against him. 58Then they dragged him out of the city and began to stone him; and the witnesses laid their coats at the feet of a young man named Saul. 59While they were stoning Stephen, he prayed, "Lord Jesus, receive my spirit." 60Then he knelt down and cried out in a loud voice, "Lord, do not hold this sin against them." When he had said this, he died.[o]

---

f 7:37 *much like me,* literally, "like unto me." g 7:53 *God's Laws, though you received them from the hands of angels,* literally, "the Law as it was ordained by angels." h 7:56 *the Messiah,* literally, "the Son of Man." i 7:58 *Paul,* also known as Saul.

j Gk *your brothers* k Gk *he* l Other ancient authorities read *for the God of Jacob* m Gk *with hands* n Gk *him* o Gk *fell asleep*

King James

8 AND SAUL was consenting unto his death. And at that time there was a great persecution against the church which was at Jerusalem; and they were all scattered abroad throughout the regions of Judaea and Samaria, except the apostles.

2And devout men carried Stephen *to his burial,* and made great lamentation over him.

3As for Saul, he made havoc of the church, entering into every house, and haling men and women committed *them* to prison.

4Therefore they that were scattered abroad went every where preaching the word.

5Then Philip went down to the city of Samaria, and preached Christ unto them.

6And the people with one accord gave heed unto those things which Philip spake, hearing and seeing the miracles which he did.

7For unclean spirits, crying with loud voice, came out of many that were possessed *with them:* and many taken with palsies, and that were lame, were healed.

8And there was great joy in that city.

9But there was a certain man, called Simon, which beforetime in the same city used sorcery, and bewitched the people of Samaria, giving out that himself was some great one:

10To whom they all gave heed, from the least to the greatest, saying, This man is the great power of God.

11And to him they had regard, because that of long time he had bewitched them with sorceries.

12But when they believed Philip preaching the things concerning the kingdom of God, and the name of Jesus Christ, they were baptized, both men and women.

13Then Simon himself believed also: and when he was baptized, he continued with Philip, and wondered, beholding the miracles and signs which were done.

14Now when the apostles which were at Jerusalem heard that Samaria had received the word of God, they sent unto them Peter and John:

15Who, when they were come down, prayed for them, that they might receive the Holy Ghost:

16(For as yet he was fallen upon none of them: only they were baptized in the name of the Lord Jesus.)

17Then laid they *their* hands on them, and they received the Holy Ghost.

18And when Simon saw that through laying on of the apostles' hands the Holy Ghost was given, he offered them money,

19Saying, Give me also this power, that on whomsoever I lay hands, he may receive the Holy Ghost.

20But Peter said unto him, Thy money perish with thee, because thou hast thought that the gift of God may be purchased with money.

21Thou hast neither part nor lot in this matter: for thy heart is not right in the sight of God.

22Repent therefore of this thy wickedness, and pray God, if perhaps the thought of thine heart may be forgiven thee.

23For I perceive that thou art in the gall of bitterness, and *in* the bond of iniquity.

24Then answered Simon, and said, Pray ye to the Lord for me, that none of these things which ye have spoken come upon me.

25And they, when they had testified and preached the word of the Lord, returned to Jerusalem, and preached the gospel in many villages of the Samaritans.

26And the angel of the Lord spake unto Philip, saying, Arise, and go toward the south unto the way that goeth down from Jerusalem unto Gaza, which is desert.

27And he arose and went: and, behold, a man of Ethiopia, an eunuch of great authority under Candace queen of the Ethiopians, who had the charge of all her treasure, and had come to Jerusalem for to worship,

New International

8 AND SAUL was there, giving approval to his death.

The Church Persecuted and Scattered

On that day a great persecution broke out against the church at Jerusalem, and all except the apostles were scattered throughout Judea and Samaria. 2Godly men buried Stephen and mourned deeply for him. 3But Saul began to destroy the church. Going from house to house, he dragged off men and women and put them in prison.

Philip in Samaria

4Those who had been scattered preached the word wherever they went. 5Philip went down to a city in Samaria and proclaimed the Christ[a] there. 6When the crowds heard Philip and saw the miraculous signs he did, they all paid close attention to what he said. 7With shrieks, evil[b] spirits came out of many, and many paralytics and cripples were healed. 8So there was great joy in that city.

Simon the Sorcerer

9Now for some time a man named Simon had practiced sorcery in the city and amazed all the people of Samaria. He boasted that he was someone great, 10and all the people, both high and low, gave him their attention and exclaimed, "This man is the divine power known as the Great Power." 11They followed him because he had amazed them for a long time with his magic. 12But when they believed Philip as he preached the good news of the kingdom of God and the name of Jesus Christ, they were baptized, both men and women. 13Simon himself believed and was baptized. And he followed Philip everywhere, astonished by the great signs and miracles he saw.

14When the apostles in Jerusalem heard that Samaria had accepted the word of God, they sent Peter and John to them. 15When they arrived, they prayed for them that they might receive the Holy Spirit, 16because the Holy Spirit had not yet come upon any of them; they had simply been baptized into[c] the name of the Lord Jesus. 17Then Peter and John placed their hands on them, and they received the Holy Spirit.

18When Simon saw that the Spirit was given at the laying on of the apostles' hands, he offered them money 19and said, "Give me also this ability so that everyone on whom I lay my hands may receive the Holy Spirit."

20Peter answered: "May your money perish with you, because you thought you could buy the gift of God with money! 21You have no part or share in this ministry, because your heart is not right before God. 22Repent of this wickedness and pray to the Lord. Perhaps he will forgive you for having such a thought in your heart. 23For I see that you are full of bitterness and captive to sin."

24Then Simon answered, "Pray to the Lord for me so that nothing you have said may happen to me."

25When they had testified and proclaimed the word of the Lord, Peter and John returned to Jerusalem, preaching the gospel in many Samaritan villages.

Philip and the Ethiopian

26Now an angel of the Lord said to Philip, "Go south to the road—the desert road—that goes down from Jerusalem to Gaza." 27So he started out, and on his way he met an Ethiopian[d] eunuch, an important official in charge of all the treasury of Candace, queen of the Ethiopians. This man had gone to Jerusalem to worship, 28and

---

[a] 5 Or *Messiah*   [b] 7 Greek *unclean*   [c] 16 Or *in*   [d] 27 That is, from the upper Nile region

Living Bible

8 PAUL WAS in complete agreement with the killing of Stephen.

And a great wave of persecution of the believers began that day, sweeping over the church in Jerusalem, and everyone except the apostles fled into Judea and Samaria. 2(But some godly Jewse came and with great sorrow buried Stephen.) 3Paul was like a wild man, going everywhere to devastate the believers, even entering private homes and dragging out men and women alike and jailing them.

4But the believersf who had fled Jerusalem went everywhere preaching the Good News about Jesus! 5Philip, for instance, went to the city of Samaria and told the people there about Christ. 6Crowds listened intently to what he had to say because of the miracles he did. 7Many evil spirits were cast out, screaming as they left their victims, and many who were paralyzed or lame were healed, 8so there was much joy in that city!

9, 10, 11A man named Simon had formerly been a sorcerer there for many years; he was a very influential, proud man because of the amazing things he could do—in fact, the Samaritan people often spoke of him as the Messiah.g 12But now they believed Philip's message that Jesus was the Messiah, and his words concerning the Kingdom of God; and many men and women were baptized. 13Then Simon himself believed and was baptized and began following Philip wherever he went, and was amazed by the miracles he did.

14When the apostles back in Jerusalem heard that the people of Samaria had accepted God's message, they sent down Peter and John. 15As soon as they arrived, they began praying for these new Christians to receive the Holy Spirit, 16for as yet he had not come upon any of them. For they had only been baptized in the name of the Lord Jesus. 17Then Peter and John laid their hands upon these believers, and they received the Holy Spirit.

18When Simon saw this—that the Holy Spirit was given when the apostles placed their hands upon people's heads—he offered money to buy this power.

19"Let me have this power too," he exclaimed, "so that when I lay my hands on people, they will receive the Holy Spirit!"

20But Peter replied, "Your money perish with you for thinking God's gift can be bought! 21You can have no part in this, for your heart is not right before God. 22Turn from this great wickedness and pray. Perhaps God will yet forgive your evil thoughts— 23for I can see that there is jealousyh and sin in your heart."

24"Pray for me," Simon exclaimed, "that these terrible things won't happen to me."

25After testifying and preaching in Samaria, Peter and John returned to Jerusalem, stopping at several Samaritan villages along the way to preach the Good News to them too.

26But as for Philip, an angel of the Lord said to him, "Go over to the road that runs from Jerusalem through the Gaza Desert, arriving around noon." 27So he did, and who should be coming down the road but the Treasurer of Ethiopia, a eunuch of great authority under Candace the queen. He had gone to Jerusalem to worship at the Temple, 28and was now returning in his chariot,

New Revised Standard

8 AND SAUL approved of their killing him.

Saul Persecutes the Church

That day a severe persecution began against the church in Jerusalem, and all except the apostles were scattered throughout the countryside of Judea and Samaria. 2Devout men buried Stephen and made loud lamentation over him. 3But Saul was ravaging the church by entering house after house; dragging off both men and women, he committed them to prison.

Philip Preaches in Samaria

4 Now those who were scattered went from place to place, proclaiming the word. 5Philip went down to the cityi of Samaria and proclaimed the Messiahi to them. 6The crowds with one accord listened eagerly to what was said by Philip, hearing and seeing the signs that he did, 7for unclean spirits, crying with loud shrieks, came out of many who were possessed; and many others who were paralyzed or lame were cured. 8 So there was great joy in that city.

9 Now a certain man named Simon had previously practiced magic in the city and amazed the people of Samaria, saying that he was someone great. 10All of them, from the least to the greatest, listened to him eagerly, saying, "This man is the power of God that is called Great." 11And they listened eagerly to him because for a long time he had amazed them with his magic. 12But when they believed Philip, who was proclaiming the good news about the kingdom of God and the name of Jesus Christ, they were baptized, both men and women. 13Even Simon himself believed. After being baptized, he stayed constantly with Philip and was amazed when he saw the signs and great miracles that took place.

14 Now when the apostles at Jerusalem heard that Samaria had accepted the word of God, they sent Peter and John to them. 15The two went down and prayed for them that they might receive the Holy Spirit 16(for as yet the Spirit had not comek upon any of them; they had only been baptized in the name of the Lord Jesus). 17Then Peter and Johnl laid their hands on them, and they received the Holy Spirit. 18Now when Simon saw that the Spirit was given through the laying on of the apostles' hands, he offered them money, 19saying, "Give me also this power so that anyone on whom I lay my hands may receive the Holy Spirit." 20But Peter said to him, "May your silver perish with you, because you thought you could obtain God's gift with money! 21You have no part or share in this, for your heart is not right before God. 22Repent therefore of this wickedness of yours, and pray to the Lord that, if possible, the intent of your heart may be forgiven you. 23For I see that you are in the gall of bitterness and the chains of wickedness." 24Simon answered, "Pray for me to the Lord, that nothing of what youm have said may happen to me."

25 Now after Peter and Johnn had testified and spoken the word of the Lord, they returned to Jerusalem, proclaiming the good news to many villages of the Samaritans.

Philip and the Ethiopian Eunuch

26 Then an angel of the Lord said to Philip, "Get up and go toward the southo to the road that goes down from Jerusalem to Gaza." (This is a wilderness road.) 27So he got up and went. Now there was an Ethiopian eunuch, a court official of the Candace, queen of the Ethiopians, in charge of her entire treasury. He had come to Jerusalem to worship 28and was returning

---

e 8:2 godly Jews, literally "devout men." It is not clear whether these were Christians who braved the persecution, or whether they were godly and sympathetic Jews.   f 8:4 the believers, literally, "the church." g 8:9-11 the Messiah, literally, "this man is that Power of God which is called great." h 8:23 jealousy, literally, "the gall of bitterness."

i Other ancient authorities read a city   j Or the Christ   k Gk fallen   l Gk they   m The Greek word for you and the verb pray are plural   n Gk after they   o Or go at noon

King James

28Was returning, and sitting in his chariot read Esaias the prophet.

29Then the Spirit said unto Philip, Go near, and join thyself to this chariot.

30And Philip ran thither to *him*, and heard him read the prophet Esaias, and said, Understandest thou what thou readest?

31And he said, How can I, except some man should guide me? And he desired Philip that he would come up and sit with him.

32The place of the scripture which he read was this, He was led as a sheep to the slaughter; and like a lamb dumb before his shearer, so opened he not his mouth:

33In his humiliation his judgment was taken away: and who shall declare his generation? for his life is taken from the earth.

34And the eunuch answered Philip, and said, I pray thee, of whom speaketh the prophet this? of himself, or of some other man?

35Then Philip opened his mouth, and began at the same scripture, and preached unto him Jesus.

36And as they went on *their* way, they came unto a certain water: and the eunuch said, See, *here is* water; what doth hinder me to be baptized?

37And Philip said, If thou believest with all thine heart, thou mayest. And he answered and said, I believe that Jesus Christ is the Son of God.

38And he commanded the chariot to stand still: and they went down both into the water, both Philip and the eunuch; and he baptized him.

39And when they were come up out of the water, the Spirit of the Lord caught away Philip, that the eunuch saw him no more: and he went on his way rejoicing.

40But Philip was found at Azotus: and passing through he preached in all the cities, till he came to Caesarea.

9 AND SAUL, yet breathing out threatenings and slaughter against the disciples of the Lord, went unto the high priest,

2And desired of him letters to Damascus to the synagogues, that if he found any of this way, whether they were men or women, he might bring them bound unto Jerusalem.

3And as he journeyed, he came near Damascus: and suddenly there shined round about him a light from heaven:

4And he fell to the earth, and heard a voice saying unto him, Saul, Saul, why persecutest thou me?

5And he said, Who art thou, Lord? And the Lord said, I am Jesus whom thou persecutest: *it is* hard for thee to kick against the pricks.

6And he trembling and astonished said, Lord, what wilt thou have me to do? And the Lord *said* unto him, Arise, and go into the city, and it shall be told thee what thou must do.

7And the men which journeyed with him stood speechless, hearing a voice, but seeing no man.

8And Saul arose from the earth; and when his eyes were opened, he saw no man: but they led him by the hand, and brought *him* into Damascus.

9And he was three days without sight, and neither did eat nor drink.

10¶ And there was a certain disciple at Damascus, named Ananias; and to him said the Lord in a vision, Ananias. And he said, Behold, I *am here*, Lord.

11And the Lord *said* unto him, Arise, and go into the street which is called Straight, and inquire in the house of Judas for *one* called Saul, of Tarsus: for, behold, he prayeth,

New International

on his way home was sitting in his chariot reading the book of Isaiah the prophet. 29The Spirit told Philip, "Go to that chariot and stay near it."

30Then Philip ran up to the chariot and heard the man reading Isaiah the prophet. "Do you understand what you are reading?" Philip asked.

31"How can I," he said, "unless someone explains it to me?" So he invited Philip to come up and sit with him.

32The eunuch was reading this passage of Scripture:

"He was led like a sheep to the slaughter,
    and as a lamb before the shearer is silent,
    so he did not open his mouth.
33In his humiliation he was deprived of justice.
    Who can speak of his descendants?
    For his life was taken from the earth."a

34The eunuch asked Philip, "Tell me, please, who is the prophet talking about, himself or someone else?" 35Then Philip began with that very passage of Scripture and told him the good news about Jesus.

36As they traveled along the road, they came to some water and the eunuch said, "Look, here is water. Why shouldn't I be baptized?"b 38And he gave orders to stop the chariot. Then both Philip and the eunuch went down into the water and Philip baptized him. 39When they came up out of the water, the Spirit of the Lord suddenly took Philip away, and the eunuch did not see him again, but went on his way rejoicing. 40Philip, however, appeared at Azotus and traveled about, preaching the gospel in all the towns until he reached Caesarea.

Saul's Conversion

9 MEANWHILE, SAUL was still breathing out murderous threats against the Lord's disciples. He went to the high priest 2and asked him for letters to the synagogues in Damascus, so that if he found any there who belonged to the Way, whether men or women, he might take them as prisoners to Jerusalem. 3As he neared Damascus on his journey, suddenly a light from heaven flashed around him. 4He fell to the ground and heard a voice say to him, "Saul, Saul, why do you persecute me?"

5"Who are you, Lord?" Saul asked.

"I am Jesus, whom you are persecuting," he replied. 6"Now get up and go into the city, and you will be told what you must do."

7The men traveling with Saul stood there speechless; they heard the sound but did not see anyone. 8Saul got up from the ground, but when he opened his eyes he could see nothing. So they led him by the hand into Damascus. 9For three days he was blind, and did not eat or drink anything.

10In Damascus there was a disciple named Ananias. The Lord called to him in a vision, "Ananias!"

"Yes, Lord," he answered.

11The Lord told him, "Go to the house of Judas on Straight Street and ask for a man from Tarsus named Saul, for he is praying. 12In a vision he has seen a man

---

a *33* Isaiah 53:7,8   b *36* Some late manuscripts *baptized?"* 37*Philip said, "If you believe with all your heart, you may." The eunuch answered, "I believe that Jesus Christ is the Son of God."*

Living Bible

reading aloud from the book of the prophet Isaiah.

²⁹The Holy Spirit said to Philip, "Go over and walk along beside the chariot."

³⁰Philip ran over and heard what he was reading and asked, "Do you understand it?"

³¹"Of course not!" the man replied. "How can I when there is no one to instruct me?" And he begged Philip to come up into the chariot and sit with him.

³²The passage of Scripture he had been reading from was this:

"He was led as a sheep to the slaughter, and as a lamb is silent before the shearers, so he opened not his mouth; ³³in his humiliation, justice was denied him; and who can express the wickedness of the people of his generation?ᶜ For his life is taken from the earth."

³⁴The eunuch asked Philip, "Was Isaiah talking about himself or someone else?"

³⁵So Philip began with this same Scripture and then used many others to tell him about Jesus.

³⁶As they rode along, they came to a small body of water, and the eunuch said, "Look! Water! Why can't I be baptized?"

³⁷ᵈ"You can," Philip answered, "if you believe with all your heart."

And the eunuch replied, "I believe that Jesus Christ is the Son of God."

³⁸He stopped the chariot, and they went down into the water and Philip baptized him. ³⁹And when they came up out of the water, the Spirit of the Lord caught away Philip, and the eunuch never saw him again, but went on his way rejoicing. ⁴⁰Meanwhile, Philip found himself at Azotus! He preached the Good News there and in every city along the way, as he traveled to Caesarea.

9 BUT PAUL, threatening with every breath and eager to destroy every Christian, went to the High Priest in Jerusalem. ²He requested a letter addressed to synagogues in Damascus, requiring their cooperation in the persecution of any believers he found there, both men and women, so that he could bring them in chains to Jerusalem.

³As he was nearing Damascus on this mission, suddenly a brilliant light from heaven spotted down upon him! ⁴He fell to the ground and heard a voice saying to him, "Paul! Paul! Why are you persecuting me?"

⁵"Who is speaking, sir?" Paul asked.

And the voice replied, "I am Jesus, the one you are persecuting! ⁶Now get up and go into the city and await my further instructions."

⁷The men with Paul stood speechless with surprise, for they heard the sound of someone's voice but saw no one! ⁸, ⁹As Paul picked himself up off the ground, he found that he was blind. He had to be led into Damascus and was there three days, blind, going without food and water all that time.

¹⁰Now there was in Damascus a believer named Ananias. The Lord spoke to him in a vision, calling, "Ananias!"

"Yes, Lord!" he replied.

¹¹And the Lord said, "Go over to Straight Street and find the house of a man named Judas and ask there for Paul of Tarsus. He is praying to me right now, for ¹²I

New Revised Standard

home; seated in his chariot, he was reading the prophet Isaiah. ²⁹Then the Spirit said to Philip, "Go over to this chariot and join it." ³⁰So Philip ran up to it and heard him reading the prophet Isaiah. He asked, "Do you understand what you are reading?" ³¹He replied, "How can I, unless someone guides me?" And he invited Philip to get in and sit beside him. ³²Now the passage of the scripture that he was reading was this:

"Like a sheep he was led to the slaughter,
      and like a lamb silent before its shearer,
            so he does not open his mouth.

³³   In his humiliation justice was denied him.
      Who can describe his generation?
            For his life is taken away from the earth."

³⁴The eunuch asked Philip, "About whom, may I ask you, does the prophet say this, about himself or about someone else?" ³⁵Then Philip began to speak, and starting with this scripture, he proclaimed to him the good news about Jesus. ³⁶As they were going along the road, they came to some water; and the eunuch said, "Look, here is water! What is to prevent me from being baptized?"ᵉ ³⁸He commanded the chariot to stop, and both of them, Philip and the eunuch, went down into the water, and Philipᶠ baptized him. ³⁹When they came up out of the water, the Spirit of the Lord snatched Philip away; the eunuch saw him no more, and went on his way rejoicing. ⁴⁰But Philip found himself at Azotus, and as he was passing through the region, he proclaimed the good news to all the towns until he came to Caesarea.

The Conversion of Saul

9 MEANWHILE SAUL, still breathing threats and murder against the disciples of the Lord, went to the high priest ²and asked him for letters to the synagogues at Damascus, so that if he found any who belonged to the Way, men or women, he might bring them bound to Jerusalem. ³Now as he was going along and approaching Damascus, suddenly a light from heaven flashed around him. ⁴He fell to the ground and heard a voice saying to him, "Saul, Saul, why do you persecute me?" ⁵He asked, "Who are you, Lord?" The reply came, "I am Jesus, whom you are persecuting. ⁶But get up and enter the city, and you will be told what you are to do." ⁷The men who were traveling with him stood speechless because they heard the voice but saw no one. ⁸Saul got up from the ground, and though his eyes were open, he could see nothing; so they led him by the hand and brought him into Damascus. ⁹For three days he was without sight, and neither ate nor drank.

10 Now there was a disciple in Damascus named Ananias. The Lord said to him in a vision, "Ananias." He answered, "Here I am, Lord." ¹¹The Lord said to him, "Get up and go to the street called Straight, and at the house of Judas look for a man of Tarsus named Saul. At this moment he is praying, ¹²and he has seen in a

---

ᶜ 8:33 *who can express the wickedness of the people of his generation,* implied. Literally, "Who can declare his generation?" Alternatively, "Who will be able to speak of his posterity? For . . ."   ᵈ 8:37 Many ancient manuscripts omit vs 37 wholly or in part.

ᵉ Other ancient authorities add all or most of verse 37, *And Philip said, "If you believe with all your heart, you may." And he replied, "I believe that Jesus Christ is the Son of God."*   ᶠ Gk *he*

King James

12And hath seen in a vision a man named Ananias coming in, and putting *his* hand on him, that he might receive his sight.

13Then Ananias answered, Lord, I have heard by many of this man, how much evil he hath done to thy saints at Jerusalem:

14And here he hath authority from the chief priests to bind all that call on thy name.

15But the Lord said unto him, Go thy way: for he is a chosen vessel unto me, to bear my name before the Gentiles, and kings, and the children of Israel:

16For I will show him how great things he must suffer for my name's sake.

17And Ananias went his way, and entered into the house; and putting his hands on him said, Brother Saul, the Lord, *even* Jesus, that appeared unto thee in the way as thou camest, hath sent me, that thou mightest receive thy sight, and be filled with the Holy Ghost.

18And immediately there fell from his eyes as it had been scales: and he received sight forthwith, and arose, and was baptized.

19And when he had received meat, he was strengthened. Then was Saul certain days with the disciples which were at Damascus.

20And straightway he preached Christ in the synagogues, that he is the Son of God.

21But all that heard *him* were amazed, and said; Is not this he that destroyed them which called on this name in Jerusalem, and came hither for that intent, that he might bring them bound unto the chief priests?

22But Saul increased the more in strength, and confounded the Jews which dwelt at Damascus, proving that this is very Christ.

23¶ And after that many days were fulfilled, the Jews took counsel to kill him:

24But their laying await was known of Saul. And they watched the gates day and night to kill him.

25Then the disciples took him by night, and let *him* down by the wall in a basket.

26And when Saul was come to Jerusalem, he assayed to join himself to the disciples: but they were all afraid of him, and believed not that he was a disciple.

27But Barnabas took him, and brought *him* to the apostles, and declared unto them how he had seen the Lord in the way, and that he had spoken to him, and how he had preached boldly at Damascus in the name of Jesus.

28And he was with them coming in and going out at Jerusalem.

29And he spake boldly in the name of the Lord Jesus, and disputed against the Grecians: but they went about to slay him.

30*Which* when the brethren knew, they brought him down to Caesarea, and sent him forth to Tarsus.

31Then had the churches rest throughout all Judaea and Galilee and Samaria, and were edified; and walking in the fear of the Lord, and in the comfort of the Holy Ghost, were multiplied.

32¶ And it came to pass, as Peter passed throughout all *quarters*, he came down also to the saints which dwelt at Lydda.

33And there he found a certain man named Aeneas, which had kept his bed eight years, and was sick of the palsy.

34And Peter said unto him, Aeneas, Jesus Christ maketh thee whole: arise, and make thy bed. And he arose immediately.

35And all that dwelt at Lydda and Saron saw him, and turned to the Lord.

New International

named Ananias come and place his hands on him to restore his sight."

13"Lord," Ananias answered, "I have heard many reports about this man and all the harm he has done to your saints in Jerusalem. 14And he has come here with authority from the chief priests to arrest all who call on your name."

15But the Lord said to Ananias, "Go! This man is my chosen instrument to carry my name before the Gentiles and their kings and before the people of Israel. 16I will show him how much he must suffer for my name."

17Then Ananias went to the house and entered it. Placing his hands on Saul, he said, "Brother Saul, the Lord—Jesus, who appeared to you on the road as you were coming here—has sent me so that you may see again and be filled with the Holy Spirit." 18Immediately, something like scales fell from Saul's eyes, and he could see again. He got up and was baptized, 19and after taking some food, he regained his strength.

Saul in Damascus and Jerusalem

Saul spent several days with the disciples in Damascus. 20At once he began to preach in the synagogues that Jesus is the Son of God. 21All those who heard him were astonished and asked, "Isn't he the man who raised havoc in Jerusalem among those who call on this name? And hasn't he come here to take them as prisoners to the chief priests?" 22Yet Saul grew more and more powerful and baffled the Jews living in Damascus by proving that Jesus is the Christ.a

23After many days had gone by, the Jews conspired to kill him, 24but Saul learned of their plan. Day and night they kept close watch on the city gates in order to kill him. 25But his followers took him by night and lowered him in a basket through an opening in the wall.

26When he came to Jerusalem, he tried to join the disciples, but they were all afraid of him, not believing that he really was a disciple. 27But Barnabas took him and brought him to the apostles. He told them how Saul on his journey had seen the Lord and that the Lord had spoken to him, and how in Damascus he had preached fearlessly in the name of Jesus. 28So Saul stayed with them and moved about freely in Jerusalem, speaking boldly in the name of the Lord. 29He talked and debated with the Grecian Jews, but they tried to kill him. 30When the brothers learned of this, they took him down to Caesarea and sent him off to Tarsus.

31Then the church throughout Judea, Galilee and Samaria enjoyed a time of peace. It was strengthened; and encouraged by the Holy Spirit, it grew in numbers, living in the fear of the Lord.

Aeneas and Dorcas

32As Peter traveled about the country, he went to visit the saints in Lydda. 33There he found a man named Aeneas, a paralytic who had been bedridden for eight years. 34"Aeneas," Peter said to him, "Jesus Christ heals you. Get up and take care of your mat." Immediately Aeneas got up. 35All those who lived in Lydda and Sharon saw him and turned to the Lord.

---

a 22 Or *Messiah*

Living Bible

have shown him a vision of a man named Ananias coming in and laying his hands on him so that he can see again!"

13"But Lord," exclaimed Ananias, "I have heard about the terrible things this man has done to the believers in Jerusalem! 14And we hear that he has arrest warrants with him from the chief priests, authorizing him to arrest every believer in Damascus!"

15But the Lord said, "Go and do what I say. For Paul is my chosen instrument to take my message to the nations and before kings, as well as to the people of Israel. 16And I will show him how much he must suffer for me."

17So Ananias went over and found Paul and laid his hands on him and said, "Brother Paul, the Lord Jesus, who appeared to you on the road, has sent me so that you may be filled with the Holy Spirit and get your sight back."

18Instantly (it was as though scales fell from his eyes) Paul could see, and was immediately baptized. 19Then he ate and was strengthened.

He stayed with the believers in Damascus for a few days 20and went at once to the synagogue to tell everyone there the Good News about Jesus—that he is indeed the Son of God!

21All who heard him were amazed. "Isn't this the same man who persecuted Jesus' followers so bitterly in Jerusalem?" they asked. "And we understand that he came here to arrest them all and take them in chains to the chief priests."

22Paul became more and more fervent in his preaching, and the Damascus Jews couldn't withstand his proofs that Jesus was indeed the Christ.

23After a while the Jewish leaders determined to kill him. 24But Paul was told about their plans, that they were watching the gates of the city day and night prepared to murder him. 25So during the night some of his converts let him down in a basket through an opening in the city wall!

26Upon arrival in Jerusalem he tried to meet with the believers, but they were all afraid of him. They thought he was faking! 27Then Barnabas brought him to the apostles and told them how Paul had seen the Lord on the way to Damascus, what the Lord had said to him, and all about his powerful preaching in the name of Jesus. 28Then they accepted him, and after that he was constantly with the believers 29and preached boldly in the name of the Lord. But then some Greek-speaking Jews with whom he had argued plotted to murder him. 30However, when the other believers heard about his danger, they took him to Caesarea and then sent him to his home in Tarsus.

31Meanwhile, the church had peace throughout Judea, Galilee and Samaria, and grew in strength and numbers. The believers learned how to walk in the fear of the Lord and in the comfort of the Holy Spirit.

32Peter traveled from place to place to visit them,[b] and in his travels came to the believers in the town of Lydda. 33There he met a man named Aeneas, paralyzed and bedridden for eight years. 34Peter said to him, "Aeneas! Jesus Christ has healed you! Get up and make your bed." And he was healed instantly. 35Then the whole population of Lydda and Sharon turned to the Lord when they saw Aeneas walking around.

New Revised Standard

vision[c] a man named Ananias come in and lay his hands on him so that he might regain his sight." 13But Ananias answered, "Lord, I have heard from many about this man, how much evil he has done to your saints in Jerusalem; 14and here he has authority from the chief priests to bind all who invoke your name." 15But the Lord said to him, "Go, for he is an instrument whom I have chosen to bring my name before Gentiles and kings and before the people of Israel; 16I myself will show him how much he must suffer for the sake of my name." 17So Ananias went and entered the house. He laid his hands on Saul[d] and said, "Brother Saul, the Lord Jesus, who appeared to you on your way here, has sent me so that you may regain your sight and be filled with the Holy Spirit." 18And immediately something like scales fell from his eyes, and his sight was restored. Then he got up and was baptized, 19and after taking some food, he regained his strength.

Saul Preaches in Damascus

For several days he was with the disciples in Damascus, 20and immediately he began to proclaim Jesus in the synagogues, saying, "He is the Son of God." 21All who heard him were amazed and said, "Is not this the man who made havoc in Jerusalem among those who invoked this name? And has he not come here for the purpose of bringing them bound before the chief priests?" 22Saul became increasingly more powerful and confounded the Jews who lived in Damascus by proving that Jesus[e] was the Messiah.[f]

Saul Escapes from the Jews

23 After some time had passed, the Jews plotted to kill him, 24but their plot became known to Saul. They were watching the gates day and night so that they might kill him; 25but his disciples took him by night and let him down through an opening in the wall,[g] lowering him in a basket.

Saul in Jerusalem

26 When he had come to Jerusalem, he attempted to join the disciples; and they were all afraid of him, for they did not believe that he was a disciple. 27But Barnabas took him, brought him to the apostles, and described for them how on the road he had seen the Lord, who had spoken to him, and how in Damascus he had spoken boldly in the name of Jesus. 28So he went in and out among them in Jerusalem, speaking boldly in the name of the Lord. 29He spoke and argued with the Hellenists; but they were attempting to kill him. 30When the believers[h] learned of it, they brought him down to Caesarea and sent him off to Tarsus.

31 Meanwhile the church throughout Judea, Galilee, and Samaria had peace and was built up. Living in the fear of the Lord and in the comfort of the Holy Spirit, it increased in numbers.

The Healing of Aeneas

32 Now as Peter went here and there among all the believers,[i] he came down also to the saints living in Lydda. 33There he found a man named Aeneas, who had been bedridden for eight years, for he was paralyzed. 34Peter said to him, "Aeneas, Jesus Christ heals you; get up and make your bed!" And immediately he got up. 35And all the residents of Lydda and Sharon saw him and turned to the Lord.

---

[b] 9:32 to visit them, implied.

[c] Other ancient authorities lack in a vision   [d] Gk him   [e] Gk that this   [f] Or the Christ   [g] Gk through the wall   [h] Gk brothers   [i] Gk all of them

King James

36¶ Now there was at Joppa a certain disciple named Tabitha, which by interpretation is called Dorcas: this woman was full of good works and almsdeeds which she did.

37And it came to pass in those days, that she was sick, and died: whom when they had washed, they laid *her* in an upper chamber.

38And forasmuch as Lydda was nigh to Joppa, and the disciples had heard that Peter was there, they sent unto him two men, desiring *him* that he would not delay to come to them.

39Then Peter arose and went with them. When he was come, they brought him into the upper chamber: and all the widows stood by him weeping, and showing the coats and garments which Dorcas made, while she was with them.

40But Peter put them all forth, and kneeled down, and prayed; and turning *him* to the body said, Tabitha, arise. And she opened her eyes: and when she saw Peter, she sat up.

41And he gave her *his* hand, and lifted her up, and when he had called the saints and widows, presented her alive.

42And it was known throughout all Joppa; and many believed in the Lord.

43And it came to pass, that he tarried many days in Joppa with one Simon a tanner.

10 THERE WAS a certain man in Caesarea called Cornelius, a centurion of the band called the Italian *band,*

2*A* devout *man,* and one that feared God with all his house, which gave much alms to the people, and prayed to God always.

3He saw in a vision evidently about the ninth hour of the day an angel of God coming in to him, and saying unto him, Cornelius.

4And when he looked on him, he was afraid, and said, What is it, Lord? And he said unto him, Thy prayers and thine alms are come up for a memorial before God.

5And now send men to Joppa, and call for *one* Simon, whose surname is Peter:

6He lodgeth with one Simon a tanner, whose house is by the sea side: he shall tell thee what thou oughtest to do.

7And when the angel which spake unto Cornelius was departed, he called two of his household servants, and a devout soldier of them that waited on him continually;

8And when he had declared all *these* things unto them, he sent them to Joppa.

9¶ On the morrow, as they went on their journey, and drew nigh unto the city, Peter went up upon the housetop to pray about the sixth hour:

10And he became very hungry, and would have eaten: but while they made ready, he fell into a trance,

11And saw heaven opened, and a certain vessel descending unto him, as it had been a great sheet knit at the four corners, and let down to the earth:

12Wherein were all manner of fourfooted beasts of the earth, and wild beasts, and creeping things, and fowls of the air.

13And there came a voice to him, Rise, Peter; kill, and eat.

14But Peter said, Not so, Lord; for I have never eaten any thing that is common or unclean.

15And the voice *spake* unto him again the second time, What God hath cleansed, *that* call not thou common.

16This was done thrice: and the vessel was received up again into heaven.

New International

36In Joppa there was a disciple named Tabitha (which, when translated, is Dorcas[a]), who was always doing good and helping the poor. 37About that time she became sick and died, and her body was washed and placed in an upstairs room. 38Lydda was near Joppa; so when the disciples heard that Peter was in Lydda, they sent two men to him and urged him, "Please come at once!"

39Peter went with them, and when he arrived he was taken upstairs to the room. All the widows stood around him, crying and showing him the robes and other clothing that Dorcas had made while she was still with them.

40Peter sent them all out of the room; then he got down on his knees and prayed. Turning toward the dead woman, he said, "Tabitha, get up." She opened her eyes, and seeing Peter she sat up. 41He took her by the hand and helped her to her feet. Then he called the believers and the widows and presented her to them alive. 42This became known all over Joppa, and many people believed in the Lord. 43Peter stayed in Joppa for some time with a tanner named Simon.

Cornelius Calls for Peter

10 AT CAESAREA there was a man named Cornelius, a centurion in what was known as the Italian Regiment. 2He and all his family were devout and God-fearing; he gave generously to those in need and prayed to God regularly. 3One day at about three in the afternoon he had a vision. He distinctly saw an angel of God, who came to him and said, "Cornelius!"

4Cornelius stared at him in fear. "What is it, Lord?" he asked.

The angel answered, "Your prayers and gifts to the poor have come up as a memorial offering before God. 5Now send men to Joppa to bring back a man named Simon who is called Peter. 6He is staying with Simon the tanner, whose house is by the sea."

7When the angel who spoke to him had gone, Cornelius called two of his servants and a devout soldier who was one of his attendants. 8He told them everything that had happened and sent them to Joppa.

Peter's Vision

9About noon the following day as they were on their journey and approaching the city, Peter went up on the roof to pray. 10He became hungry and wanted something to eat, and while the meal was being prepared, he fell into a trance. 11He saw heaven opened and something like a large sheet being let down to earth by its four corners. 12It contained all kinds of four-footed animals, as well as reptiles of the earth and birds of the air. 13Then a voice told him, "Get up, Peter. Kill and eat."

14"Surely not, Lord!" Peter replied. "I have never eaten anything impure or unclean."

15The voice spoke to him a second time, "Do not call anything impure that God has made clean."

16This happened three times, and immediately the sheet was taken back to heaven.

a 36 Both *Tabitha* (Aramaic) and *Dorcas* (Greek) mean *gazelle.*

Living Bible

36In the city of Joppa there was a woman named Dorcas ("Gazelle"), a believer who was always doing kind things for others, especially for the poor. 37About this time she became ill and died. Her friends prepared her for burial and laid her in an upstairs room. 38But when they learned that Peter was nearby at Lydda, they sent two men to beg him to return with them to Joppa. 39This he did; as soon as he arrived, they took him upstairs where Dorcas lay. The room was filled with weeping widows who were showing one another the coats and other garments Dorcas had made for them. 40But Peter asked them all to leave the room; then he knelt and prayed. Turning to the body he said, "Get up, Dorcas,"b and she opened her eyes! And when she saw Peter, she sat up! 41He gave her his hand and helped her up and called in the believers and widows, presenting her to them.

42The news raced through the town, and many believed in the Lord. 43And Peter stayed a long time in Joppa, living with Simon, the tanner.

10 IN CAESAREA there lived a Roman army officer, Cornelius, a captain of an Italian regiment. 2He was a godly man, deeply reverent, as was his entire household. He gave generously to charity and was a man of prayer. 3While wide awake one afternoon he had a vision—it was about three o'clock—and in this vision he saw an angel of God coming toward him.

"Cornelius!" the angel said.

4Cornelius stared at him in terror. "What do you want, sir?" he asked the angel.

And the angel replied, "Your prayers and charities have not gone unnoticed by God! 5, 6Now send some men to Joppa to find a man named Simon Peter, who is staying with Simon, the tanner, down by the shore, and ask him to come and visit you."

7As soon as the angel was gone, Cornelius called two of his household servants and a godly soldier, one of his personal bodyguard, 8and told them what had happened and sent them off to Joppa.

9, 10The next day, as they were nearing the city, Peter went up on the flat roof of his house to pray. It was noon and he was hungry, but while lunch was being prepared, he fell into a trance. 11He saw the sky open, and a great canvas sheet,c suspended by its four corners, settle to the ground. 12In the sheet were all sorts of animals, snakes and birds [forbidden to the Jews for foodd].

13Then a voice said to him, "Go kill and eat any of them you wish."

14"Never, Lord," Peter declared, "I have never in all my life eaten such creatures, for they are forbidden by our Jewish laws."

15The voice spoke again, "Don't contradict God! If he says something is kosher, then it is."

16The same vision was repeated three times. Then the sheet was pulled up again to heaven.

New Revised Standard

Peter in Lydda and Joppa

36 Now in Joppa there was a disciple whose name was Tabitha, which in Greek is Dorcas.e She was devoted to good works and acts of charity. 37At that time she became ill and died. When they had washed her, they laid her in a room upstairs. 38Since Lydda was near Joppa, the disciples, who heard that Peter was there, sent two men to him with the request, "Please come to us without delay." 39So Peter got up and went with them; and when he arrived, they took him to the room upstairs. All the widows stood beside him, weeping and showing tunics and other clothing that Dorcas had made while she was with them. 40Peter put all of them outside, and then he knelt down and prayed. He turned to the body and said, "Tabitha, get up." Then she opened her eyes, and seeing Peter, she sat up. 41He gave her his hand and helped her up. Then calling the saints and widows, he showed her to be alive. 42This became known throughout Joppa, and many believed in the Lord. 43Meanwhile he stayed in Joppa for some time with a certain Simon, a tanner.

Peter and Cornelius

10 IN CAESAREA there was a man named Cornelius, a centurion of the Italian Cohort, as it was called. 2He was a devout man who feared God with all his household; he gave alms generously to the people and prayed constantly to God. 3One afternoon at about three o'clock he had a vision in which he clearly saw an angel of God coming in and saying to him, "Cornelius." 4He stared at him in terror and said, "What is it, Lord?" He answered, "Your prayers and your alms have ascended as a memorial before God. 5Now send men to Joppa for a certain Simon who is called Peter; 6he is lodging with Simon, a tanner, whose house is by the seaside. 7When the angel who spoke to him had left, he called two of his slaves and a devout soldier from the ranks of those who served him, 8and after telling them everything, he sent them to Joppa.

9 About noon the next day, as they were on their journey and approaching the city, Peter went up on the roof to pray. 10He became hungry and wanted something to eat; and while it was being prepared, he fell into a trance. 11He saw the heaven opened and something like a large sheet coming down, being lowered to the ground by its four corners. 12In it were all kinds of four-footed creatures and reptiles and birds of the air. 13Then he heard a voice saying, "Get up, Peter; kill and eat." 14But Peter said, "By no means, Lord; for I have never eaten anything that is profane or unclean." 15The voice said to him again, a second time, "What God has made clean, you must not call profane." 16This happened three times, and the thing was suddenly taken up to heaven.

---

b 9:40 Dorcas, literally, "Tabitha," her name in Hebrew.   c 10:11 a great canvas sheet, implied.   d 10:12 forbidden to the Jews for food, implied; see Lev 11 for the forbidden list.

e The name Tabitha in Aramaic and the name Dorcas in Greek mean a gazelle

King James

17Now while Peter doubted in himself what this vision which he had seen should mean, behold, the men which were sent from Cornelius had made inquiry for Simon's house, and stood before the gate,

18And called, and asked whether Simon, which was surnamed Peter, were lodged there.

19¶ While Peter thought on the vision, the Spirit said unto him, Behold, three men seek thee.

20Arise therefore, and get thee down, and go with them, doubting nothing: for I have sent them.

21Then Peter went down to the men which were sent unto him from Cornelius; and said, Behold, I am he whom ye seek: what *is* the cause wherefore ye are come?

22And they said, Cornelius the centurion, a just man, and one that feareth God, and of good report among all the nation of the Jews, was warned from God by an holy angel to send for thee into his house, and to hear words of thee.

23Then called he them in, and lodged *them*. And on the morrow Peter went away with them, and certain brethren from Joppa accompanied him.

24And the morrow after they entered into Caesarea. And Cornelius waited for them, and had called together his kinsmen and near friends.

25And as Peter was coming in, Cornelius met him, and fell down at his feet, and worshipped *him*.

26But Peter took him up, saying, Stand up; I myself also am a man.

27And as he talked with him, he went in, and found many that were come together.

28And he said unto them, Ye know how that it is an unlawful thing for a man that is a Jew to keep company, or come unto one of another nation; but God hath shown me that I should not call any man common or unclean.

29Therefore came I *unto you* without gainsaying, as soon as I was sent for: I ask therefore for what intent ye have sent for me?

30And Cornelius said, Four days ago I was fasting until this hour; and at the ninth hour I prayed in my house, and, behold, a man stood before me in bright clothing,

31And said, Cornelius, thy prayer is heard, and thine alms are had in remembrance in the sight of God.

32Send therefore to Joppa, and call hither Simon, whose surname is Peter; he is lodged in the house of *one* Simon a tanner by the sea side: who, when he cometh, shall speak unto thee.

33Immediately therefore I sent to thee; and thou hast well done that thou art come. Now therefore are we all here present before God, to hear all things that are commanded thee of God.

34¶ Then Peter opened *his* mouth, and said, Of a truth I perceive that God is no respecter of persons:

35But in every nation he that feareth him, and worketh righteousness, is accepted with him.

36The word which *God* sent unto the children of Israel, preaching peace by Jesus Christ: (he is Lord of all:)

37That word, *I say,* ye know, which was published throughout all Judaea, and began from Galilee, after the baptism which John preached;

38How God anointed Jesus of Nazareth with the Holy Ghost and with power: who went about doing good, and healing all that were oppressed of the devil; for God was with him.

39And we are witnesses of all things which he did both in the land of the Jews, and in Jerusalem; whom they slew and hanged on a tree:

40Him God raised up the third day, and showed him openly;

41Not to all the people, but unto witnesses chosen before of God, *even* to us, who did eat and drink with him after he rose from the dead.

42And he commanded us to preach unto the people, and to testify that it is he which was ordained of God *to be* the Judge of quick and dead.

New International

17While Peter was wondering about the meaning of the vision, the men sent by Cornelius found out where Simon's house was and stopped at the gate. 18They called out, asking if Simon who was known as Peter was staying there.

19While Peter was still thinking about the vision, the Spirit said to him, "Simon, three[a] men are looking for you. 20So get up and go downstairs. Do not hesitate to go with them, for I have sent them."

21Peter went down and said to the men, "I'm the one you're looking for. Why have you come?"

22The men replied, "We have come from Cornelius the centurion. He is a righteous and God-fearing man, who is respected by all the Jewish people. A holy angel told him to have you come to his house so that he could hear what you have to say." 23Then Peter invited the men into the house to be his guests.

Peter at Cornelius' House

The next day Peter started out with them, and some of the brothers from Joppa went along. 24The following day he arrived in Caesarea. Cornelius was expecting them and had called together his relatives and close friends. 25As Peter entered the house, Cornelius met him and fell at his feet in reverence. 26But Peter made him get up. "Stand up," he said, "I am only a man myself."

27Talking with him, Peter went inside and found a large gathering of people. 28He said to them: "You are well aware that it is against our law for a Jew to associate with a Gentile or visit him. But God has shown me that I should not call any man impure or unclean. 29So when I was sent for, I came without raising any objection. May I ask why you sent for me?"

30Cornelius answered: "Four days ago I was in my house praying at this hour, at three in the afternoon. Suddenly a man in shining clothes stood before me 31and said, 'Cornelius, God has heard your prayer and remembered your gifts to the poor. 32Send to Joppa for Simon who is called Peter. He is a guest in the home of Simon the tanner, who lives by the sea.' 33So I sent for you immediately, and it was good of you to come. Now we are all here in the presence of God to listen to everything the Lord has commanded you to tell us."

34Then Peter began to speak: "I now realize how true it is that God does not show favoritism 35but accepts men from every nation who fear him and do what is right. 36You know the message God sent to the people of Israel, telling the good news of peace through Jesus Christ, who is Lord of all. 37You know what has happened throughout Judea, beginning in Galilee after the baptism that John preached— 38how God anointed Jesus of Nazareth with the Holy Spirit and power, and how he went around doing good and healing all who were under the power of the devil, because God was with him.

39"We are witnesses of everything he did in the country of the Jews and in Jerusalem. They killed him by hanging him on a tree, 40but God raised him from the dead on the third day and caused him to be seen. 41He was not seen by all the people, but by witnesses whom God had already chosen—by us who ate and drank with him after he rose from the dead. 42He commanded us to preach to the people and to testify that he is the one whom God appointed as judge of the living and the dead.

Living Bible

17Peter was very perplexed. What could the vision mean? What was he supposed to do?

Just then the men sent by Cornelius had found the house and were standing outside at the gate, 18inquiring whether this was the place where Simon Peter lived!

19Meanwhile, as Peter was puzzling over the vision, the Holy Spirit said to him, "Three men have come to see you. 20Go down and meet them and go with them. All is well, I have sent them."

21So Peter went down. "I'm the man you're looking for," he said. "Now what is it you want?"

22Then they told him about Cornelius the Roman officer, a good and godly man, well thought of by the Jews, and how an angel had instructed him to send for Peter to come and tell him what God wanted him to do.

23So Peter invited them in and lodged them overnight.

The next day he went with them, accompanied by some other believers from Joppa.

24They arrived in Caesarea the following day, and Cornelius was waiting for him, and had called together his relatives and close friends to meet Peter. 25As Peter entered his home, Cornelius fell to the floor before him in worship.

26But Peter said, "Stand up! I'm not a god!"

27So he got up and they talked together for a while and then went in where the others were assembled.

28Peter told them, "You know it is against the Jewish laws for me to come into a Gentile home like this. But God has shown me in a vision that I should never think of anyone as inferior. 29So I came as soon as I was sent for. Now tell me what you want."

30Cornelius replied, "Four days ago I was praying as usual at this time of the afternoon, when suddenly a man was standing before me clothed in a radiant robe! 31He told me, 'Cornelius, your prayers are heard and your charities have been noticed by God! 32Now send some men to Joppa and summon Simon Peter, who is staying in the home of Simon, a tanner, down by the shore.' 33So I sent for you at once, and you have done well to come so soon. Now here we are, waiting before the Lord, anxious to hear what he has told you to tell us!"

34Then Peter replied, "I see very clearly that the Jews are not God's only favorites! 35In every nation he has those who worship him and do good deeds and are acceptable to him. 36, 37I'm sure you have heard about the Good News for the people of Israel—that there is peace with God through Jesus, the Messiah, who is Lord of all creation. This message has spread all through Judea, beginning with John the Baptist in Galilee. 38And you no doubt know that Jesus of Nazareth was anointed by God with the Holy Spirit and with power, and he went around doing good and healing all who were possessed by demons, for God was with him.

39"And we apostles are witnesses of all he did throughout Israel and in Jerusalem, where he was murdered on a cross. 40, 41But God brought him back to life again three days later and showed him to certain witnesses God had selected beforehand—not to the general public, but to us who ate and drank with him after he rose from the dead. 42And he sent us to preach the Good News everywhere and to testify that Jesus is ordained of God to be the Judge of all—living and dead. 43And all

New Revised Standard

17 Now while Peter was greatly puzzled about what to make of the vision that he had seen, suddenly the men sent by Cornelius appeared. They were asking for Simon's house and were standing by the gate. 18They called out to ask whether Simon, who was called Peter, was staying there. 19While Peter was still thinking about the vision, the Spirit said to him, "Look, threeb men are searching for you. 20Now get up, go down, and go with them without hesitation; for I have sent them." 21So Peter went down to the men and said, "I am the one you are looking for; what is the reason for your coming?" 22They answered, "Cornelius, a centurion, an upright and God-fearing man, who is well spoken of by the whole Jewish nation, was directed by a holy angel to send for you to come to his house and to hear what you have to say." 23 So Peterc invited them in and gave them lodging.

The next day he got up and went with them, and some of the believersd from Joppa accompanied him. 24 The following day they came to Caesarea. Cornelius was expecting them and had called together his relatives and close friends. 25On Peter's arrival Cornelius met him, and falling at his feet, worshiped him. 26 But Peter made him get up, saying, "Stand up; I am only a mortal." 27 And as he talked with him, he went in and found that many had assembled; 28 and he said to them, "You yourselves know that it is unlawful for a Jew to associate with or to visit a Gentile; but God has shown me that I should not call anyone profane or unclean. 29 So when I was sent for, I came without objection. Now may I ask why you sent for me?"

30 Cornelius replied, "Four days ago at this very hour, at three o'clock, I was praying in my house when suddenly a man in dazzling clothes stood before me. 31 He said, 'Cornelius, your prayer has been heard and your alms have been remembered before God. 32 Send therefore to Joppa and ask for Simon, who is called Peter; he is staying in the home of Simon, a tanner, by the sea.' 33 Therefore I sent for you immediately, and you have been kind enough to come. So now all of us are here in the presence of God to listen to all that the Lord has commanded you to say."

Gentiles Hear the Good News

34 Then Peter began to speak to them: "I truly understand that God shows no partiality, 35 but in every nation anyone who fears him and does what is right is acceptable to him. 36 You know the message he sent to the people of Israel, preaching peace by Jesus Christ—he is Lord of all. 37 That message spread throughout Judea, beginning in Galilee after the baptism that John announced: 38 how God anointed Jesus of Nazareth with the Holy Spirit and with power; how he went about doing good and healing all who were oppressed by the devil, for God was with him. 39 We are witnesses to all that he did both in Judea and in Jerusalem. They put him to death by hanging him on a tree; 40 but God raised him on the third day and allowed him to appear, 41 not to all the people but to us who were chosen by God as witnesses, and who ate and drank with him after he rose from the dead. 42 He commanded us to preach to the people and to testify that he is the one ordained by God as judge of the living and the dead. 43 All the prophets

---

b One ancient authority reads *two*; others lack the word   c Gk *he*   d Gk *brothers*

King James

43To him give all the prophets witness, that through his name whosoever believeth in him shall receive remission of sins.

44¶ While Peter yet spake these words, the Holy Ghost fell on all them which heard the word.

45And they of the circumcision which believed were astonished, as many as came with Peter, because that on the Gentiles also was poured out the gift of the Holy Ghost.

46For they heard them speak with tongues, and magnify God. Then answered Peter,

47Can any man forbid water, that these should not be baptized, which have received the Holy Ghost as well as we?

48And he commanded them to be baptized in the name of the Lord. Then prayed they him to tarry certain days.

11 AND THE apostles and brethren that were in Judaea heard that the Gentiles had also received the word of God.

2And when Peter was come up to Jerusalem, they that were of the circumcision contended with him,

3Saying, Thou wentest in to men uncircumcised, and didst eat with them.

4But Peter rehearsed *the matter* from the beginning, and expounded *it* by order unto them, saying,

5I was in the city of Joppa praying: and in a trance I saw a vision, A certain vessel descend, as it had been a great sheet, let down from heaven by four corners; and it came even to me:

6Upon the which when I had fastened mine eyes, I considered, and saw fourfooted beasts of the earth, and wild beasts, and creeping things, and fowls of the air.

7And I heard a voice saying unto me, Arise, Peter; slay and eat.

8But I said, Not so, Lord: for nothing common or unclean hath at any time entered into my mouth.

9But the voice answered me again from heaven, What God hath cleansed, *that* call not thou common.

10And this was done three times: and all were drawn up again into heaven.

11And, behold, immediately there were three men already come unto the house where I was, sent from Caesarea unto me.

12And the Spirit bade me go with them, nothing doubting. Moreover these six brethren accompanied me, and we entered into the man's house:

13And he showed us how he had seen an angel in his house, which stood and said unto him, Send men to Joppa, and call for Simon, whose surname is Peter;

14Who shall tell thee words, whereby thou and all thy house shall be saved.

15And as I began to speak, the Holy Ghost fell on them, as on us at the beginning.

16Then remembered I the word of the Lord, how that he said, John indeed baptized with water; but ye shall be baptized with the Holy Ghost.

17Forasmuch then as God gave them the like gift as *he did* unto us, who believed on the Lord Jesus Christ; what was I, that I could withstand God?

18When they heard these things, they held their peace, and glorified God, saying, Then hath God also to the Gentiles granted repentance unto life.

19¶ Now they which were scattered abroad upon the persecution that arose about Stephen travelled as far as Phenice, and Cyprus, and Antioch, preaching the word to none but unto the Jews only.

20And some of them were men of Cyprus and Cyrene, which, when they were come to Antioch, spake unto the Grecians, preaching the Lord Jesus.

New International

43All the prophets testify about him that everyone who believes in him receives forgiveness of sins through his name."

44While Peter was still speaking these words, the Holy Spirit came on all who heard the message. 45The circumcised believers who had come with Peter were astonished that the gift of the Holy Spirit had been poured out even on the Gentiles. 46For they heard them speaking in tonguesa and praising God.

Then Peter said, 47"Can anyone keep these people from being baptized with water? They have received the Holy Spirit just as we have." 48So he ordered that they be baptized in the name of Jesus Christ. Then they asked Peter to stay with them for a few days.

Peter Explains His Actions

11 THE APOSTLES and the brothers throughout Judea heard that the Gentiles also had received the word of God. 2So when Peter went up to Jerusalem, the circumcised believers criticized him 3and said, "You went into the house of uncircumcised men and ate with them."

4Peter began and explained everything to them precisely as it had happened: 5"I was in the city of Joppa praying, and in a trance I saw a vision. I saw something like a large sheet being let down from heaven by its four corners, and it came down to where I was. 6I looked into it and saw four-footed animals of the earth, wild beasts, reptiles, and birds of the air. 7Then I heard a voice telling me, 'Get up, Peter. Kill and eat.'

8"I replied, 'Surely not, Lord! Nothing impure or unclean has ever entered my mouth.'

9"The voice spoke from heaven a second time, 'Do not call anything impure that God has made clean.' 10This happened three times, and then it was all pulled up to heaven again.

11"Right then three men who had been sent to me from Caesarea stopped at the house where I was staying. 12The Spirit told me to have no hesitation about going with them. These six brothers also went with me, and we entered the man's house. 13He told us how he had seen an angel appear in his house and say, 'Send to Joppa for Simon who is called Peter. 14He will bring you a message through which you and all your household will be saved.'

15"As I began to speak, the Holy Spirit came on them as he had come on us at the beginning. 16Then I remembered what the Lord had said: 'John baptized withb water, but you will be baptized with the Holy Spirit.' 17So if God gave them the same gift as he gave us, who believed in the Lord Jesus Christ, who was I to think that I could oppose God?"

18When they heard this, they had no further objections and praised God, saying, "So then, God has granted even the Gentiles repentance unto life."

The Church in Antioch

19Now those who had been scattered by the persecution in connection with Stephen traveled as far as Phoenicia, Cyprus and Antioch, telling the message only to Jews. 20Some of them, however, men from Cyprus and Cyrene, went to Antioch and began to speak to Greeks also, telling them the good news about the Lord Jesus.

a 46 Or *other languages*   b 16 Or *in*

Living Bible

the prophets have written about him, saying that everyone who believes in him will have their sins forgiven through his name."

44Even as Peter was saying these things, the Holy Spirit fell upon all those listening! 45The Jews who came with Peter were amazed that the gift of the Holy Spirit would be given to Gentiles too! 46, 47But there could be no doubt about it,c for they heard them speaking in tongues and praising God.

Peter asked, "Can anyone object to my baptizing them, now that they have received the Holy Spirit just as we did?" 48So he did, baptizing them in the name of Jesus, the Messiah. Afterwards Cornelius begged him to stay with them for several days.

11 SOON THE news reached the apostles and other brothers in Judea that Gentiles also were being converted! 2But when Peter arrived back in Jerusalem, the Jewish believers argued with him.

3"You fellowshiped with Gentiles and even ate with them," they accused.

4Then Peter told them the whole story. 5"One day in Joppa," he said, "while I was praying, I saw a vision—a huge sheet, let down by its four corners from the sky. 6Inside the sheet were all sorts of animals, reptiles and birds [which we are not to eatd]. 7And I heard a voice say, 'Kill and eat whatever you wish.'

8" 'Never, Lord,' I replied. 'For I have never yet eaten anything forbidden by our Jewish laws!'

9"But the voice came again, 'Don't say it isn't right when God declares it is!'

10"This happened *three times* before the sheet and all it contained disappeared into heaven. 11Just then three men who had come to take me with them to Caesarea arrived at the house where I was staying! 12The Holy Spirit told me to go with them and not to worry about their being Gentiles! These six brothers here accompanied me, and we soon arrived at the home of the man who had sent the messengers. 13He told us how an angel had appeared to him and told him to send messengers to Joppa to find Simon Peter! 14'He will tell you how you and all your household can be saved!' the angel had told him.

15"Well, I began telling them the Good News, but just as I was getting started with my sermon, the Holy Spirit fell on them, just as he fell on us at the beginning! 16Then I thought of the Lord's words when he said, 'Yes, John baptized withe water, but you shall be baptized withe the Holy Spirit.' 17And since it was *God* who gave these Gentiles the same gift he gave us when we believed on the Lord Jesus Christ, who was I to argue?"

18When the others heard this, all their objections were answered and they began praising God! "Yes," they said, "God has given to the Gentiles, too, the privilege of turning to him and receiving eternal life!"

19Meanwhile, the believers who fled from Jerusalem during the persecution after Stephen's death traveled as far as Phoenicia, Cyprus, and Antioch, scattering the Good News, but only to Jews. 20However, some of the believers who went to Antioch from Cyprus and Cyrene also gave their message about the Lord Jesus to some

New Revised Standard

testify about him that everyone who believes in him receives forgiveness of sins through his name."

Gentiles Receive the Holy Spirit

44 While Peter was still speaking, the Holy Spirit fell upon all who heard the word. 45The circumcised believers who had come with Peter were astounded that the gift of the Holy Spirit had been poured out even on the Gentiles, 46for they heard them speaking in tongues and extolling God. Then Peter said, 47"Can anyone withhold the water for baptizing these people who have received the Holy Spirit just as we have?" 48So he ordered them to be baptized in the name of Jesus Christ. Then they invited him to stay for several days.

Peter's Report to the Church at Jerusalem

11 NOW THE apostles and the believersf who were in Judea heard that the Gentiles had also accepted the word of God. 2So when Peter went up to Jerusalem, the circumcised believersg criticized him, 3saying, "Why did you go to uncircumcised men and eat with them?" 4Then Peter began to explain it to them, step by step, saying, 5"I was in the city of Joppa praying, and in a trance I saw a vision. There was something like a large sheet coming down from heaven, being lowered by its four corners; and it came close to me. 6As I looked at it closely I saw four-footed animals, beasts of prey, reptiles, and birds of the air. 7I also heard a voice saying to me, 'Get up, Peter; kill and eat.' 8But I replied, 'By no means, Lord; for nothing profane or unclean has ever entered my mouth.' 9But a second time the voice answered from heaven, 'What God has made clean, you must not call profane.' 10This happened three times; then everything was pulled up again to heaven. 11At that very moment three men, sent to me from Caesarea, arrived at the house where we were. 12The Spirit told me to go with them and not to make a distinction between them and us.h These six brothers also accompanied me, and we entered the man's house. 13He told us how he had seen the angel standing in his house and saying, 'Send to Joppa and bring Simon, who is called Peter; 14he will give you a message by which you and your entire household will be saved.' 15And as I began to speak, the Holy Spirit fell upon them just as it had upon us at the beginning. 16And I remembered the word of the Lord, how he had said, 'John baptized with water, but you will be baptized with the Holy Spirit.' 17If then God gave them the same gift that he gave us when we believed in the Lord Jesus Christ, who was I that I could hinder God?" 18When they heard this, they were silenced. And they praised God, saying, "Then God has given even to the Gentiles the repentance that leads to life."

The Church in Antioch

19 Now those who were scattered because of the persecution that took place over Stephen traveled as far as Phoenicia, Cyprus, and Antioch, and they spoke the word to no one except Jews. 20But among them were some men of Cyprus and Cyrene who, on coming to Antioch, spoke to the Hellenistsi also, proclaiming the Lord Jesus. 21The hand of the Lord was with them, and

---

c *10:46, 47 But there could be no doubt about it,* implied. d *11:6 which we are not to eat,* implied. e *11:16 baptized with,* or, "baptized in."

f Gk *brothers* g Gk lacks *believers* h Or *not to hesitate* i Other ancient authorities read *Greeks*

King James

21And the hand of the Lord was with them: and a great number believed, and turned unto the Lord.

22¶ Then tidings of these things came unto the ears of the church which was in Jerusalem: and they sent forth Barnabas, that he should go as far as Antioch.

23Who, when he came, and had seen the grace of God, was glad, and exhorted them all, that with purpose of heart they would cleave unto the Lord.

24For he was a good man, and full of the Holy Ghost and of faith: and much people was added unto the Lord.

25Then departed Barnabas to Tarsus, for to seek Saul:

26And when he had found him, he brought him unto Antioch. And it came to pass, that a whole year they assembled themselves with the church, and taught much people. And the disciples were called Christians first in Antioch.

27¶ And in these days came prophets from Jerusalem unto Antioch.

28And there stood up one of them named Agabus, and signified by the Spirit that there should be great dearth throughout all the world: which came to pass in the days of Claudius Caesar.

29Then the disciples, every man according to his ability, determined to send relief unto the brethren which dwelt in Judaea:

30Which also they did, and sent it to the elders by the hands of Barnabas and Saul.

12 NOW ABOUT that time Herod the king stretched forth *his* hands to vex certain of the church.

2And he killed James the brother of John with the sword.

3And because he saw it pleased the Jews, he proceeded further to take Peter also. (Then were the days of unleavened bread.)

4And when he had apprehended him, he put *him* in prison, and delivered *him* to four quaternions of soldiers to keep him; intending after Easter to bring him forth to the people.

5Peter therefore was kept in prison: but prayer was made without ceasing of the church unto God for him.

6And when Herod would have brought him forth, the same night Peter was sleeping between two soldiers, bound with two chains: and the keepers before the door kept the prison.

7And, behold, the angel of the Lord came upon *him*, and a light shined in the prison: and he smote Peter on the side, and raised him up, saying, Arise up quickly. And his chains fell off from *his* hands.

8And the angel said unto him, Gird thyself, and bind on thy sandals. And so he did. And he saith unto him, Cast thy garment about thee, and follow me.

9And he went out, and followed him; and wist not that it was true which was done by the angel; but thought he saw a vision.

10When they were past the first and the second ward, they came unto the iron gate that leadeth unto the city; which opened to them of his own accord: and they went out, and passed on through one street; and forthwith the angel departed from him.

11And when Peter was come to himself, he said, Now I know of a surety, that the Lord hath sent his angel, and hath delivered me out of the hand of Herod, and *from* all the expectation of the people of the Jews.

12And when he had considered *the thing*, he came to the house of Mary the mother of John, whose surname was Mark; where many were gathered together praying.

13And as Peter knocked at the door of the gate, a damsel came to hearken, named Rhoda.

New International

21The Lord's hand was with them, and a great number of people believed and turned to the Lord.

22News of this reached the ears of the church at Jerusalem, and they sent Barnabas to Antioch. 23When he arrived and saw the evidence of the grace of God, he was glad and encouraged them all to remain true to the Lord with all their hearts. 24He was a good man, full of the Holy Spirit and faith, and a great number of people were brought to the Lord.

25Then Barnabas went to Tarsus to look for Saul, 26and when he found him, he brought him to Antioch. So for a whole year Barnabas and Saul met with the church and taught great numbers of people. The disciples were called Christians first at Antioch.

27During this time some prophets came down from Jerusalem to Antioch. 28One of them, named Agabus, stood up and through the Spirit predicted that a severe famine would spread over the entire Roman world. (This happened during the reign of Claudius.) 29The disciples, each according to his ability, decided to provide help for the brothers living in Judea. 30This they did, sending their gift to the elders by Barnabas and Saul.

Peter's Miraculous Escape From Prison

12 IT WAS about this time that King Herod arrested some who belonged to the church, intending to persecute them. 2He had James, the brother of John, put to death with the sword. 3When he saw that this pleased the Jews, he proceeded to seize Peter also. This happened during the Feast of Unleavened Bread. 4After arresting him, he put him in prison, handing him over to be guarded by four squads of four soldiers each. Herod intended to bring him out for public trial after the Passover.

5So Peter was kept in prison, but the church was earnestly praying to God for him.

6The night before Herod was to bring him to trial, Peter was sleeping between two soldiers, bound with two chains, and sentries stood guard at the entrance. 7Suddenly an angel of the Lord appeared and a light shone in the cell. He struck Peter on the side and woke him up. "Quick, get up!" he said, and the chains fell off Peter's wrists.

8Then the angel said to him, "Put on your clothes and sandals." And Peter did so. "Wrap your cloak around you and follow me," the angel told him. 9Peter followed him out of the prison, but he had no idea that what the angel was doing was really happening; he thought he was seeing a vision. 10They passed the first and second guards and came to the iron gate leading to the city. It opened for them by itself, and they went through it. When they had walked the length of one street, suddenly the angel left him.

11Then Peter came to himself and said, "Now I know without a doubt that the Lord sent his angel and rescued me from Herod's clutches and from everything the Jewish people were anticipating."

12When this had dawned on him, he went to the house of Mary the mother of John, also called Mark, where many people had gathered and were praying. 13Peter knocked at the outer entrance, and a servant girl named Rhoda came to answer the door. 14When she recognized

Living Bible

Greeks. 21And the Lord honored this effort so that large numbers of these Gentiles became believers.

22When the church at Jerusalem heard what had happened, they sent Barnabas to Antioch to help the new converts. 23When he arrived and saw the wonderful things God was doing, he was filled with excitement and joy, and encouraged the believers to stay close to the Lord, whatever the cost. 24Barnabas was a kindly person, full of the Holy Spirit and strong in faith. As a result large numbers of people were added to the Lord.

25Then Barnabas went on to Tarsus to hunt for Paul. 26When he found him, he brought him back to Antioch; and both of them stayed there for a full year, teaching the many new converts. (It was there at Antioch that the believers were first called "Christians.")

27During this time some prophets came down from Jerusalem to Antioch, 28and one of them, named Agabus, stood up in one of the meetings to predict by the Spirit that a great famine was coming upon the land of Israel.a (This was fulfilled during the reign of Claudius.) 29So the believers decided to send relief to the Christians in Judea, each giving as much as he could. 30This they did, consigning their gifts to Barnabas and Paul to take to the elders of the church in Jerusalem.

12 ABOUT THAT time King Herod moved against some of the believers, 2and killed the apostleb James (John's brother). 3When Herod saw how much this pleased the Jewish leaders, he arrested Peter during the Passover celebration 4and imprisoned him, placing him under the guard of sixteen soldiers. Herod's intention was to deliver Peter to the Jews for execution after the Passover. 5But earnest prayer was going up to God from the church for his safety all the time he was in prison.

6The night before he was to be executed, he was asleep, double-chained between two soldiers with others standing guard before the prison gate, 7when suddenly there was a light in the cell and an angel of the Lord stood beside Peter! The angel slapped him on the side to awaken him and said, "Quick! Get up!" And the chains fell off his wrists! 8Then the angel told him, "Get dressed and put on your shoes." And he did. "Now put on your coat and follow me!" the angel ordered.

9So Peter left the cell, following the angel. But all the time he thought it was a dream or vision, and didn't believe it was really happening. 10They passed the first and second cell blocks and came to the iron gate to the street, and this opened to them of its own accord! So they passed through and walked along together for a block, and then the angel left him.

11Peter finally realized what had happened! "It's really true!" he said to himself. "The Lord has sent his angel and saved me from Herod and from what the Jews were hoping to do to me!"

12After a little thought he went to the home of Mary, mother of John Mark, where many were gathered for a prayer meeting.

13He knocked at the door in the gate, and a girl named Rhoda came to open it. 14When she recognized Peter's

New Revised Standard

a great number became believers and turned to the Lord. 22News of this came to the ears of the church in Jerusalem, and they sent Barnabas to Antioch. 23When he came and saw the grace of God, he rejoiced, and he exhorted them all to remain faithful to the Lord with steadfast devotion; 24for he was a good man, full of the Holy Spirit and of faith. And a great many people were brought to the Lord. 25Then Barnabas went to Tarsus to look for Saul, 26and when he had found him, he brought him to Antioch. So it was that for an entire year they met withc the church and taught a great many people, and it was in Antioch that the disciples were first called "Christians."

27 At that time prophets came down from Jerusalem to Antioch. 28One of them named Agabus stood up and predicted by the Spirit that there would be a severe famine over all the world; and this took place during the reign of Claudius. 29The disciples determined that according to their ability, each would send relief to the believersd living in Judea; 30this they did, sending it to the elders by Barnabas and Saul.

James Killed and Peter Imprisoned

12 ABOUT THAT time King Herod laid violent hands upon some who belonged to the church. 2He had James, the brother of John, killed with the sword. 3After he saw that it pleased the Jews, he proceeded to arrest Peter also. (This was during the festival of Unleavened Bread.) 4When he had seized him, he put him in prison and handed him over to four squads of soldiers to guard him, intending to bring him out to the people after the Passover. 5While Peter was kept in prison, the church prayed fervently to God for him.

Peter Delivered from Prison

6 The very night before Herod was going to bring him out, Peter, bound with two chains, was sleeping between two soldiers, while guards in front of the door were keeping watch over the prison. 7Suddenly an angel of the Lord appeared and a light shone in the cell. He tapped Peter on the side and woke him, saying, "Get up quickly." And the chains fell off his wrists. 8The angel said to him, "Fasten your belt and put on your sandals." He did so. Then he said to him, "Wrap your cloak around you and follow me." 9Petere went out and followed him; he did not realize that what was happening with the angel's help was real; he thought he was seeing a vision. 10After they had passed the first and the second guard, they came before the iron gate leading into the city. It opened for them of its own accord, and they went outside and walked along a lane, when suddenly the angel left him. 11Then Peter came to himself and said, "Now I am sure that the Lord has sent his angel and rescued me from the hands of Herod and from all that the Jewish people were expecting."

12 As soon as he realized this, he went to the house of Mary, the mother of John whose other name was Mark, where many had gathered and were praying. 13When he knocked at the outer gate, a maid named Rhoda came to answer. 14On recognizing Peter's voice,

---

a 11:28 *the land of Israel,* literally, "upon the earth." b 12:2 *and killed the apostle,* implied. c Or *were guests of* d Gk *brothers* e Gk *He*

King James

14And when she knew Peter's voice, she opened not the gate for gladness, but ran in, and told how Peter stood before the gate.

15And they said unto her, Thou art mad. But she constantly affirmed that it was even so. Then said they, It is his angel.

16But Peter continued knocking: and when they had opened *the door,* and saw him, they were astonished.

17But he, beckoning unto them with the hand to hold their peace, declared unto them how the Lord had brought him out of the prison. And he said, Go show these things unto James, and to the brethren. And he departed, and went into another place.

18Now as soon as it was day, there was no small stir among the soldiers, what was become of Peter.

19And when Herod had sought for him, and found him not, he examined the keepers, and commanded that *they* should be put to death. And he went down from Judaea to Caesarea, and *there* abode.

20¶ And Herod was highly displeased with them of Tyre and Sidon: but they came with one accord to him, and, having made Blastus the king's chamberlain their friend, desired peace; because their country was nourished by the king's *country.*

21And upon a set day Herod, arrayed in royal apparel, sat upon his throne, and made an oration unto them.

22And the people gave a shout, *saying, It is* the voice of a god, and not of a man.

23And immediately the angel of the Lord smote him, because he gave not God the glory: and he was eaten of worms, and gave up the ghost.

24¶ But the word of God grew and multiplied.

25And Barnabas and Saul returned from Jerusalem, when they had fulfilled *their* ministry, and took with them John, whose surname was Mark.

13 NOW THERE were in the church that was at Antioch certain prophets and teachers; as Barnabas, and Simeon that was called Niger, and Lucius of Cyrene, and Manaen, which had been brought up with Herod the tetrarch, and Saul.

2As they ministered to the Lord, and fasted, the Holy Ghost said, Separate me Barnabas and Saul for the work whereunto I have called them.

3And when they had fasted and prayed, and laid *their* hands on them, they sent *them* away.

4¶ So they, being sent forth by the Holy Ghost, departed unto Seleucia; and from thence they sailed to Cyprus.

5And when they were at Salamis, they preached the word of God in the synagogues of the Jews: and they had also John to *their* minister.

6And when they had gone through the isle unto Paphos, they found a certain sorcerer, a false prophet, a Jew, whose name *was* Bar-jesus:

7Which was with the deputy of the country, Sergius Paulus, a prudent man; who called for Barnabas and Saul, and desired to hear the word of God.

8But Elymas the sorcerer (for so is his name by interpretation) withstood them, seeking to turn away the deputy from the faith.

9Then Saul, (who also *is called* Paul,) filled with the Holy Ghost, set his eyes on him,

10And said, O full of all subtlety and all mischief, *thou* child of the devil, *thou* enemy of all righteousness, wilt thou not cease to pervert the right ways of the Lord?

New International

Peter's voice, she was so overjoyed she ran back without opening it and exclaimed, "Peter is at the door!"

15"You're out of your mind," they told her. When she kept insisting that it was so, they said, "It must be his angel."

16But Peter kept on knocking, and when they opened the door and saw him, they were astonished. 17Peter motioned with his hand for them to be quiet and described how the Lord had brought him out of prison. "Tell James and the brothers about this," he said, and then he left for another place.

18In the morning, there was no small commotion among the soldiers as to what had become of Peter. 19After Herod had a thorough search made for him and did not find him, he cross-examined the guards and ordered that they be executed.

Herod's Death

Then Herod went from Judea to Caesarea and stayed there a while. 20He had been quarreling with the people of Tyre and Sidon; they now joined together and sought an audience with him. Having secured the support of Blastus, a trusted personal servant of the king, they asked for peace, because they depended on the king's country for their food supply.

21On the appointed day Herod, wearing his royal robes, sat on his throne and delivered a public address to the people. 22They shouted, "This is the voice of a god, not of a man." 23Immediately, because Herod did not give praise to God, an angel of the Lord struck him down, and he was eaten by worms and died.

24But the word of God continued to increase and spread.

25When Barnabas and Saul had finished their mission, they returned froma Jerusalem, taking with them John, also called Mark.

Barnabas and Saul Sent Off

13 IN THE church at Antioch there were prophets and teachers: Barnabas, Simeon called Niger, Lucius of Cyrene, Manaen (who had been brought up with Herod the tetrarch) and Saul. 2While they were worshiping the Lord and fasting, the Holy Spirit said, "Set apart for me Barnabas and Saul for the work to which I have called them." 3So after they had fasted and prayed, they placed their hands on them and sent them off.

On Cyprus

4The two of them, sent on their way by the Holy Spirit, went down to Seleucia and sailed from there to Cyprus. 5When they arrived at Salamis, they proclaimed the word of God in the Jewish synagogues. John was with them as their helper.

6They traveled through the whole island until they came to Paphos. There they met a Jewish sorcerer and false prophet named Bar-Jesus, 7who was an attendant of the proconsul, Sergius Paulus. The proconsul, an intelligent man, sent for Barnabas and Saul because he wanted to hear the word of God. 8But Elymas the sorcerer (for that is what his name means) opposed them and tried to turn the proconsul from the faith. 9Then Saul, who was also called Paul, filled with the Holy Spirit, looked straight at Elymas and said, 10"You are a child of the devil and an enemy of everything that is right! You are full of all kinds of deceit and trickery. Will you never stop perverting the right ways of the Lord? 11Now

Living Bible

voice, she was so overjoyed that she ran back inside to tell everyone that Peter was standing outside in the street. 15They didn't believe her. "You're out of your mind," they said. When she insisted they decided, "It must be his angel. [They must have killed him.b]"

16Meanwhile Peter continued knocking. When they finally went out and opened the door, their surprise knew no bounds. 17He motioned for them to quiet down and told them what had happened and how the Lord had brought him out of jail. "Tell James and the others what happened," he said—and left for safer quarters.

18At dawn, the jail was in great commotion. What had happened to Peter? 19When Herod sent for him and found that he wasn't there, he had the sixteen guards arrested, court-martialed and sentenced to death. Afterwards he left to live in Caesarea for a while.

20While he was in Caesarea, a delegation from Tyre and Sidon arrived to see him. He was highly displeased with the people of those two cities, but the delegates made friends with Blastus, the royal secretary, and asked for peace, for their cities were economically dependent upon trade with Herod's country. 21An appointment with Herod was granted, and when the day arrived he put on his royal robes, sat on his throne and made a speech to them. 22At its conclusion the people gave him a great ovation, shouting, "It is the voice of a god and not of a man!"

23Instantly, an angel of the Lord struck Herod with a sickness so that he was filled with maggots and died— because he accepted the people's worship instead of giving the glory to God.

24God's Good News was spreading rapidly and there were many new believers.

25Barnabas and Paul now visited Jerusalem and, as soon as they had finished their business, returned to Antioch,c taking John Mark with them.

13 AMONG THE prophets and teachers of the church at Antioch were Barnabas and Symeon (also called "The Black Man"), Lucius (from Cyrene), Manaen (the foster-brother of King Herod), and Paul. 2One day as these men were worshiping and fasting the Holy Spirit said, "Dedicate Barnabas and Paul for a special job I have for them." 3So after more fasting and prayer, the men laid their hands on them—and sent them on their way.

4Directed by the Holy Spirit they went to Seleucia and then sailed for Cyprus. 5There, in the town of Salamis, they went to the Jewish synagogue and preached. (John Mark went with them as their assistant.)

6,7Afterwards they preached from town to town across the entire island until finally they reached Paphos where they met a Jewish sorcerer, a fake prophet named Bar-Jesus. He had attached himself to the governor, Sergius Paulus, a man of considerable insight and understanding. The governor invited Barnabas and Paul to visit him, for he wanted to hear their message from God. 8But the sorcerer, Elymas (his name in Greek), interfered and urged the governor to pay no attention to what Paul and Barnabas said, trying to keep him from trusting the Lord.

9Then Paul, filled with the Holy Spirit, glared angrily at the sorcerer and said, 10"You son of the devil, full of every sort of trickery and villainy, enemy of all that is good, will you never end your opposition to the Lord?

New Revised Standard

she was so overjoyed that, instead of opening the gate, she ran in and announced that Peter was standing at the gate. 15They said to her, "You are out of your mind!" But she insisted that it was so. They said, "It is his angel." 16Meanwhile Peter continued knocking; and when they opened the gate, they saw him and were amazed. 17He motioned to them with his hand to be silent, and described for them how the Lord had brought him out of the prison. And he added, "Tell this to James and to the believers."d Then he left and went to another place.

18 When morning came, there was no small commotion among the soldiers over what had become of Peter. 19When Herod had searched for him and could not find him, he examined the guards and ordered them to be put to death. Then he went down from Judea to Caesarea and stayed there.

The Death of Herod

20 Now Herode was angry with the people of Tyre and Sidon. So they came to him in a body; and after winning over Blastus, the king's chamberlain, they asked for a reconciliation, because their country depended on the king's country for food. 21On an appointed day Herod put on his royal robes, took his seat on the platform, and delivered a public address to them. 22The people kept shouting, "The voice of a god, and not of a mortal!" 23And immediately, because he had not given the glory to God, an angel of the Lord struck him down, and he was eaten by worms and died.

24 But the word of God continued to advance and gain adherents. 25Then after completing their mission Barnabas and Saul returned tof Jerusalem and brought with them John, whose other name was Mark.

Barnabas and Saul Commissioned

13 NOW IN the church at Antioch there were prophets and teachers: Barnabas, Simeon who was called Niger, Lucius of Cyrene, Manaen a member of the court of Herod the ruler,g and Saul. 2While they were worshiping the Lord and fasting, the Holy Spirit said, "Set apart for me Barnabas and Saul for the work to which I have called them." 3Then after fasting and praying they laid their hands on them and sent them off.

The Apostles Preach in Cyprus

4 So, being sent out by the Holy Spirit, they went down to Seleucia; and from there they sailed to Cyprus. 5When they arrived at Salamis, they proclaimed the word of God in the synagogues of the Jews. And they had John also to assist them. 6When they had gone through the whole island as far as Paphos, they met a certain magician, a Jewish false prophet, named Bar-Jesus. 7He was with the proconsul, Sergius Paulus, an intelligent man, who summoned Barnabas and Saul and wanted to hear the word of God. 8But the magician Elymas (for that is the translation of his name) opposed them and tried to turn the proconsul away from the faith. 9But Saul, also known as Paul, filled with the Holy Spirit, looked intently at him 10and said, "You son of the devil, you enemy of all righteousness, full of all deceit and villainy, will you not stop making crooked the straight paths of the Lord? 11And now listen—the hand

---

b 12:15 They must have killed him, implied.   c 12:25 returned to Antioch, implied.

d Gk brothers   e Gk he   f Other ancient authorities read from   g Gk tetrarch

King James

11And now, behold, the hand of the Lord *is* upon thee, and thou shalt be blind, not seeing the sun for a season. And immediately there fell on him a mist and a darkness; and he went about seeking some to lead him by the hand.

12Then the deputy, when he saw what was done, believed, being astonished at the doctrine of the Lord.

13Now when Paul and his company loosed from Paphos, they came to Perga in Pamphylia: and John departing from them returned to Jerusalem.

14¶ But when they departed from Perga, they came to Antioch in Pisidia, and went into the synagogue on the sabbath day, and sat down.

15And after the reading of the law and the prophets the rulers of the synagogue sent unto them, saying, *Ye* men *and* brethren, if ye have any word of exhortation for the people, say on.

16Then Paul stood up, and beckoning with *his* hand said, Men of Israel, and ye that fear God, give audience.

17The God of this people of Israel chose our fathers, and exalted the people when they dwelt as strangers in the land of Egypt, and with an high arm brought he them out of it.

18And about the time of forty years suffered he their manners in the wilderness.

19And when he had destroyed seven nations in the land of Chanaan, he divided their land to them by lot.

20And after that he gave *unto them* judges about the space of four hundred and fifty years, until Samuel the prophet.

21And afterward they desired a king: and God gave unto them Saul the son of Cis, a man of the tribe of Benjamin, by the space of forty years.

22And when he had removed him, he raised up unto them David to be their king; to whom also he gave testimony, and said, I have found David the *son* of Jesse, a man after mine own heart, which shall fulfil all my will.

23Of this man's seed hath God according to *his* promise raised unto Israel a Saviour, Jesus:

24When John had first preached before his coming the baptism of repentance to all the people of Israel.

25And as John fulfilled his course, he said, Whom think ye that I am? I am not *he*. But, behold, there cometh one after me, whose shoes of *his* feet I am not worthy to loose.

26Men *and* brethren, children of the stock of Abraham, and whosoever among you feareth God, to you is the word of this salvation sent.

27For they that dwell at Jerusalem, and their rulers, because they knew him not, nor yet the voices of the prophets which are read every sabbath day, they have fulfilled *them* in condemning *him*.

28And though they found no cause of death *in him*, yet desired they Pilate that he should be slain.

29And when they had fulfilled all that was written of him, they took *him* down from the tree, and laid *him* in a sepulchre.

30But God raised him from the dead:

31And he was seen many days of them which came up with him from Galilee to Jerusalem, who are his witnesses unto the people.

32And we declare unto you glad tidings, how that the promise which was made unto the fathers,

33God hath fulfilled the same unto us their children, in that he hath raised up Jesus again; as it is also written in the second psalm, Thou art my Son, this day have I begotten thee.

34And as concerning that he raised him up from the dead, *now* no more to return to corruption, he said on this wise, I will give you the sure mercies of David.

35Wherefore he saith also in another *psalm*, Thou shalt not suffer thine Holy One to see corruption.

New International

the hand of the Lord is against you. You are going to be blind, and for a time you will be unable to see the light of the sun."

Immediately mist and darkness came over him, and he groped about, seeking someone to lead him by the hand. 12When the proconsul saw what had happened, he believed, for he was amazed at the teaching about the Lord.

In Pisidian Antioch

13From Paphos, Paul and his companions sailed to Perga in Pamphylia, where John left them to return to Jerusalem. 14From Perga they went on to Pisidian Antioch. On the Sabbath they entered the synagogue and sat down. 15After the reading from the Law and the Prophets, the synagogue rulers sent word to them, saying, "Brothers, if you have a message of encouragement for the people, please speak."

16Standing up, Paul motioned with his hand and said: "Men of Israel and you Gentiles who worship God, listen to me! 17The God of the people of Israel chose our fathers; he made the people prosper during their stay in Egypt, with mighty power he led them out of that country, 18he endured their conducta for about forty years in the desert, 19he overthrew seven nations in Canaan and gave their land to his people as their inheritance. 20All this took about 450 years.

"After this, God gave them judges until the time of Samuel the prophet. 21Then the people asked for a king, and he gave them Saul son of Kish, of the tribe of Benjamin, who ruled forty years. 22After removing Saul, he made David their king. He testified concerning him: 'I have found David son of Jesse a man after my own heart; he will do everything I want him to do.'

23"From this man's descendants God has brought to Israel the Savior Jesus, as he promised. 24Before the coming of Jesus, John preached repentance and baptism to all the people of Israel. 25As John was completing his work, he said: 'Who do you think I am? I am not that one. No, but he is coming after me, whose sandals I am not worthy to untie.'

26"Brothers, children of Abraham, and you God-fearing Gentiles, it is to us that this message of salvation has been sent. 27The people of Jerusalem and their rulers did not recognize Jesus, yet in condemning him they fulfilled the words of the prophets that are read every Sabbath. 28Though they found no proper ground for a death sentence, they asked Pilate to have him executed. 29When they had carried out all that was written about him, they took him down from the tree and laid him in a tomb. 30But God raised him from the dead, 31and for many days he was seen by those who had traveled with him from Galilee to Jerusalem. They are now his witnesses to our people.

32"We tell you the good news: What God promised our fathers 33he has fulfilled for us, their children, by raising up Jesus. As it is written in the second Psalm:

> " 'You are my Son;
>   today I have become your Father.b 'c

34The fact that God raised him from the dead, never to decay, is stated in these words:

> " 'I will give you the holy and sure blessings
>   promised to David.'d

35So it is stated elsewhere:

> " 'You will not let your Holy One see decay.'e

---

a *18* Some manuscripts *and cared for them*   b *33* Or *have begotten you*
c *33* Psalm 2:7   d *34* Isaiah 55:3   e *35* Psalm 16:10

Living Bible

11And now God has laid his hand of punishment upon you, and you will be stricken awhile with blindness."

Instantly mist and darkness fell upon him, and he began wandering around begging for someone to take his hand and lead him. 12When the governor saw what happened he believed and was astonished at the power of God's message.

13Now Paul and those with him left Paphos by ship for Turkey,f landing at the port town of Perga. There John deserted themg and returned to Jerusalem. 14But Barnabas and Paul went on to Antioch, a city in the province of Pisidia.

On the Sabbath they went into the synagogue for the services. 15After the usual readings from the Books of Moses and from the Prophets, those in charge of the service sent them this message: "Brothers, if you have any word of instruction for us come and give it!"

16So Paul stood, waved a greeting to themh and began. "Men of Israel," he said, "and all others here who reverence God, [let me begin my remarks with a bit of historyi].

17"The God of this nation Israel chose our ancestors and honored them in Egypt by gloriously leading them out of their slavery. 18And he nursed them through forty years of wandering around in the wilderness. 19, 20Then he destroyed seven nations in Canaan, and gave Israel their land as an inheritance. Judges ruled for about 450 years, and were followed by Samuel the prophet.

21"Then the people begged for a king, and God gave them Saul (son of Kish), a man of the tribe of Benjamin, who reigned for forty years. 22But God removed him and replaced him with David as king, a man about whom God said, 'David (son of Jesse) is a man after my own heart, for he will obey me.' 23And it is one of King David's descendants, Jesus, who is God's promised Savior of Israel!

24"But before he came, John the Baptist preached the need for everyone in Israel to turn from sin to God. 25As John was finishing his work he asked, 'Do you think I am the Messiah? No! But he is coming soon—and in comparison with him, I am utterly worthless.'

26"Brothers—you sons of Abraham, and also all of you Gentiles here who reverence God—this salvation is for all of us! 27The Jews in Jerusalem and their leaders fulfilled prophecy by killing Jesus; for they didn't recognize him, or realize that he is the one the prophets had written about, though they heard the prophets' words read every Sabbath. 28They found no just cause to execute him, but asked Pilate to have him killed anyway. 29When they had fulfilled all the prophecies concerning his death, he was taken from the cross and placed in a tomb.

30"But God brought him back to life again! 31And he was seen many times during the next few days by the men who had accompanied him to Jerusalem from Galilee—these men have constantly testified to this in public witness.

32, 33"And now Barnabas and I are here to bring you this Good News—that God's promise to our ancestors has come true in our own time, in that God brought Jesus back to life again. This is what the second Psalm is talking about when it says concerning Jesus, 'Today I have honored you as my Son.'j

34"For God had promised to bring him back to life again, no more to die. This is stated in the Scripture that says, 'I will do for you the wonderful thing I promised David.' 35In another Psalm he explained more fully, saying, 'God will not let his Holy One decay.' 36This

New Revised Standard

of the Lord is against you, and you will be blind for a while, unable to see the sun." Immediately mist and darkness came over him, and he went about groping for someone to lead him by the hand. 12When the proconsul saw what had happened, he believed, for he was astonished at the teaching about the Lord.

Paul and Barnabas in Antioch of Pisidia

13 Then Paul and his companions set sail from Paphos and came to Perga in Pamphylia. John, however, left them and returned to Jerusalem; 14but they went on from Perga and came to Antioch in Pisidia. And on the sabbath day they went into the synagogue and sat down. 15After the reading of the law and the prophets, the officials of the synagogue sent them a message, saying, "Brothers, if you have any word of exhortation for the people, give it." 16So Paul stood up and with a gesture began to speak:

"You Israelites,k and others who fear God, listen. 17The God of this people Israel chose our ancestors and made the people great during their stay in the land of Egypt, and with uplifted arm he led them out of it. 18For about forty years he put up withl them in the wilderness. 19After he had destroyed seven nations in the land of Canaan, he gave them their land as an inheritance 20for about four hundred fifty years. After that he gave them judges until the time of the prophet Samuel. 21Then they asked for a king; and God gave them Saul son of Kish, a man of the tribe of Benjamin, who reigned for forty years. 22When he had removed him, he made David their king. In his testimony about him he said, 'I have found David, son of Jesse, to be a man after my heart, who will carry out all my wishes.' 23Of this man's posterity God has brought to Israel a Savior, Jesus, as he promised; 24before his coming John had already proclaimed a baptism of repentance to all the people of Israel. 25And as John was finishing his work, he said, 'What do you suppose that I am? I am not he. No, but one is coming after me; I am not worthy to untie the thong of the sandalsm on his feet.'

26 "My brothers, you descendants of Abraham's family, and others who fear God, to usn the message of this salvation has been sent. 27Because the residents of Jerusalem and their leaders did not recognize him or understand the words of the prophets that are read every sabbath, they fulfilled those words by condemning him. 28Even though they found no cause for a sentence of death, they asked Pilate to have him killed. 29When they had carried out everything that was written about him, they took him down from the tree and laid him in a tomb. 30But God raised him from the dead; 31and for many days he appeared to those who came up with him from Galilee to Jerusalem, and they are now his witnesses to the people. 32And we bring you the good news that what God promised to our ancestors 33he has fulfilled for us, their children, by raising Jesus; as also it is written in the second psalm,

'You are my Son;
  today I have begotten you.'

34 As to his raising him from the dead, no more to return to corruption, he has spoken in this way,

'I will give you the holy promises made to
  David.'

35Therefore he has also said in another psalm,

'You will not let your Holy One experience
  corruption.'

---

f 13:13 *Turkey,* literally, "Pamphylia." g 13 literally, "departed from them." See 15:38. h 13:16 *waved a greeting to them,* literally, "beckoning with the hand." i 13:16 *Let me begin my remarks with a bit of history,* implied. j 13:33 *Today I have honored you as my Son,* literally, "This day have I begotten you."

k Gk *Men, Israelites* l Other ancient authorities read *cared for* m Gk *untie the sandals* n Other ancient authorities read *you*

King James

36For David, after he had served his own generation by the will of God, fell on sleep, and was laid unto his fathers, and saw corruption:

37But he, whom God raised again, saw no corruption.

38¶ Be it known unto you therefore, men *and* brethren, that through this man is preached unto you the forgiveness of sins:

39And by him all that believe are justified from all things, from which ye could not be justified by the law of Moses.

40Beware therefore, lest that come upon you, which is spoken of in the prophets;

41Behold, ye despisers, and wonder, and perish: for I work a work in your days, a work which ye shall in no wise believe, though a man declare it unto you.

42And when the Jews were gone out of the synagogue, the Gentiles besought that these words might be preached to them the next sabbath.

43Now when the congregation was broken up, many of the Jews and religious proselytes followed Paul and Barnabas: who, speaking to them, persuaded them to continue in the grace of God.

44¶ And the next sabbath day came almost the whole city together to hear the word of God.

45But when the Jews saw the multitudes, they were filled with envy, and spake against those things which were spoken by Paul, contradicting and blaspheming.

46Then Paul and Barnabas waxed bold, and said, It was necessary that the word of God should first have been spoken to you: but seeing ye put it from you, and judge yourselves unworthy of everlasting life, lo, we turn to the Gentiles.

47For so hath the Lord commanded us, *saying,* I have set thee to be a light of the Gentiles, that thou shouldest be for salvation unto the ends of the earth.

48And when the Gentiles heard this, they were glad, and glorified the word of the Lord: and as many as were ordained to eternal life believed.

49And the word of the Lord was published throughout all the region.

50But the Jews stirred up the devout and honourable women, and the chief men of the city, and raised persecution against Paul and Barnabas, and expelled them out of their coasts.

51But they shook off the dust of their feet against them, and came unto Iconium.

52And the disciples were filled with joy, and with the Holy Ghost.

14 AND IT came to pass in Iconium, that they went both together into the synagogue of the Jews, and so spake, that a great multitude both of the Jews and also of the Greeks believed.

2But the unbelieving Jews stirred up the Gentiles, and made their minds evil affected against the brethren.

3Long time therefore abode they speaking boldly in the Lord, which gave testimony unto the word of his grace, and granted signs and wonders to be done by their hands.

4But the multitude of the city was divided: and part held with the Jews, and part with the apostles.

5And when there was an assault made both of the Gentiles, and also of the Jews with their rulers, to use *them* despitefully, and to stone them,

6They were ware of *it,* and fled unto Lystra and Derbe, cities of Lycaonia, and unto the region that lieth round about:

7And there they preached the gospel.

New International

36"For when David had served God's purpose in his own generation, he fell asleep; he was buried with his fathers and his body decayed. 37But the one whom God raised from the dead did not see decay.

38"Therefore, my brothers, I want you to know that through Jesus the forgiveness of sins is proclaimed to you. 39Through him everyone who believes is justified from everything you could not be justified from by the law of Moses. 40Take care that what the prophets have said does not happen to you:

41" 'Look, you scoffers,
    wonder and perish,
for I am going to do something in your days
    that you would never believe,
    even if someone told you.'a"

42As Paul and Barnabas were leaving the synagogue, the people invited them to speak further about these things on the next Sabbath. 43When the congregation was dismissed, many of the Jews and devout converts to Judaism followed Paul and Barnabas, who talked with them and urged them to continue in the grace of God.

44On the next Sabbath almost the whole city gathered to hear the word of the Lord. 45When the Jews saw the crowds, they were filled with jealousy and talked abusively against what Paul was saying.

46Then Paul and Barnabas answered them boldly: "We had to speak the word of God to you first. Since you reject it and do not consider yourselves worthy of eternal life, we now turn to the Gentiles. 47For this is what the Lord has commanded us:

" 'I have made youb a light for the Gentiles,
    that youb may bring salvation to the ends of
        the earth.'c"

48When the Gentiles heard this, they were glad and honored the word of the Lord; and all who were appointed for eternal life believed.

49The word of the Lord spread through the whole region. 50But the Jews incited the God-fearing women of high standing and the leading men of the city. They stirred up persecution against Paul and Barnabas, and expelled them from their region. 51So they shook the dust from their feet in protest against them and went to Iconium. 52And the disciples were filled with joy and with the Holy Spirit.

In Iconium

14 AT ICONIUM Paul and Barnabas went as usual into the Jewish synagogue. There they spoke so effectively that a great number of Jews and Gentiles believed. 2But the Jews who refused to believe stirred up the Gentiles and poisoned their minds against the brothers. 3So Paul and Barnabas spent considerable time there, speaking boldly for the Lord, who confirmed the message of his grace by enabling them to do miraculous signs and wonders. 4The people of the city were divided; some sided with the Jews, others with the apostles. 5There was a plot afoot among the Gentiles and Jews, together with their leaders, to mistreat them and stone them. 6But they found out about it and fled to the Lycaonian cities of Lystra and Derbe and to the surrounding country, 7where they continued to preach the good news.

a 41 Hab. 1:5   b 47 The Greek is singular.   c 47 Isaiah 49:6

Living Bible

was not a reference to David, for after David had served his generation according to the will of God, he died and was buried, and his body decayed. 37[No, it was a reference to another[d]]—someone God brought back to life, whose body was not touched at all by the ravages of death.[e]

38"Brothers! Listen! In this man Jesus, there is forgiveness for your sins! 39Everyone who trusts in him is freed from all guilt and declared righteous—something the Jewish law could never do. 40Oh, be careful! Don't let the prophets' words apply to you. For they said, 41'Look and perish, you despisers [of the truth[f]], for I am doing something in your day—something that you won't believe when you hear it announced.'"

42As the people left the synagogue that day, they asked Paul to return and speak to them again the next week. 43And many Jews and godly Gentiles who worshiped at the synagogue followed Paul and Barnabas down the street as the two men urged them to accept the mercies God was offering. 44The following week almost the entire city turned out to hear them preach the Word of God.

45But when the Jewish leaders[g] saw the crowds, they were jealous, and cursed[h] and argued against whatever Paul said.

46Then Paul and Barnabas spoke out boldly and declared, "It was necessary that this Good News from God should be given first to you Jews. But since you have rejected it, and shown yourselves unworthy of eternal life—well, we will offer it to Gentiles. 47For this is as the Lord commanded when he said, 'I have made you a light to the Gentiles, to lead them from the farthest corners of the earth to my salvation.'"

48When the Gentiles heard this, they were very glad and rejoiced in Paul's message; and as many as wanted[i] eternal life, believed. 49So God's message spread all through that region.

50Then the Jewish leaders stirred up both the godly women and the civic leaders of the city and incited a mob against Paul and Barnabas, and ran them out of town. 51But they shook off the dust of their feet against the town and went on to the city of Iconium. 52And their converts[j] were filled with joy and with the Holy Spirit.

14 AT ICONIUM, Paul and Barnabas went together to the synagogue and preached with such power that many—both Jews and Gentiles—believed.

2But the Jews who spurned God's message stirred up distrust among the Gentiles against Paul and Barnabas, saying all sorts of evil things about them. 3Nevertheless, they stayed there a long time, preaching boldly, and the Lord proved their message was from him by giving them power to do great miracles. 4But the people of the city were divided in their opinion about them. Some agreed with the Jewish leaders, and some backed the apostles.

5, 6When Paul and Barnabas learned of a plot to incite a mob of Gentiles, Jews, and Jewish leaders to attack and stone them, they fled for their lives, going to the cities of Lycaonia, Lystra, Derbe, and the surrounding area, 7and preaching the Good News there.

New Revised Standard

36For David, after he had served the purpose of God in his own generation, died,[k] was laid beside his ancestors, and experienced corruption; 37but he whom God raised up experienced no corruption. 38Let it be known to you therefore, my brothers, that through this man forgiveness of sins is proclaimed to you; 39by this Jesus[l] everyone who believes is set free from all those sins[m] from which you could not be freed by the law of Moses. 40Beware, therefore, that what the prophets said does not happen to you:

41 'Look, you scoffers!
    Be amazed and perish,
  for in your days I am doing a work,
    a work that you will never believe, even if
      someone tells you.'"

42 As Paul and Barnabas[n] were going out, the people urged them to speak about these things again the next sabbath. 43When the meeting of the synagogue broke up, many Jews and devout converts to Judaism followed Paul and Barnabas, who spoke to them and urged them to continue in the grace of God.

44 The next sabbath almost the whole city gathered to hear the word of the Lord.[o] 45But when the Jews saw the crowds, they were filled with jealousy; and blaspheming, they contradicted what was spoken by Paul. 46Then both Paul and Barnabas spoke out boldly, saying, "It was necessary that the word of God should be spoken first to you. Since you reject it and judge yourselves to be unworthy of eternal life, we are now turning to the Gentiles. 47For so the Lord has commanded us, saying,

  'I have set you to be a light for the Gentiles,
    so that you may bring salvation to the ends
      of the earth.'"

48 When the Gentiles heard this, they were glad and praised the word of the Lord; and as many as had been destined for eternal life became believers. 49Thus the word of the Lord spread throughout the region. 50But the Jews incited the devout women of high standing and the leading men of the city, and stirred up persecution against Paul and Barnabas, and drove them out of their region. 51So they shook the dust off their feet in protest against them, and went to Iconium. 52And the disciples were filled with joy and with the Holy Spirit.

Paul and Barnabas in Iconium

14 THE SAME thing occurred in Iconium, where Paul and Barnabas[n] went into the Jewish synagogue and spoke in such a way that a great number of both Jews and Greeks became believers. 2But the unbelieving Jews stirred up the Gentiles and poisoned their minds against the brothers. 3So they remained for a long time, speaking boldly for the Lord, who testified to the word of his grace by granting signs and wonders to be done through them. 4But the residents of the city were divided; some sided with the Jews, and some with the apostles. 5And when an attempt was made by both Gentiles and Jews, with their rulers, to mistreat them and to stone them, 6the apostles[n] learned of it and fled to Lystra and Derbe, cities of Lycaonia, and to the surrounding country; 7and there they continued proclaiming the good news.

---

d 13:37 No, it was a reference to another, implied.   e 13:37 was not touched at all by the ravages of death, literally, "saw no corruption."   f 13:41 of the truth, implied.   g 13:45 the Jewish leaders, literally, "the Jews."   h 13:45 cursed, or "blasphemed."   i 13:48 wanted, or, "were disposed to," or, "ordained to."   j 13:52 their converts, literally, "the disciples."

k Gk fell asleep   l Gk this   m Gk all   n Gk they   o Other ancient authorities read God

King James

8¶ And there sat a certain man at Lystra, impotent in his feet, being a cripple from his mother's womb, who never had walked:

9The same heard Paul speak: who stedfastly beholding him, and perceiving that he had faith to be healed,

10Said with a loud voice, Stand upright on thy feet. And he leaped and walked.

11And when the people saw what Paul had done, they lifted up their voices, saying in the speech of Lycaonia, The gods are come down to us in the likeness of men.

12And they called Barnabas, Jupiter; and Paul, Mercurius, because he was the chief speaker.

13Then the priest of Jupiter, which was before their city, brought oxen and garlands unto the gates, and would have done sacrifice with the people.

14*Which* when the apostles, Barnabas and Paul, heard *of*, they rent their clothes, and ran in among the people, crying out,

15And saying, Sirs, why do ye these things? We also are men of like passions with you, and preach unto you that ye should turn from these vanities unto the living God, which made heaven, and earth, and the sea, and all things that are therein:

16Who in times past suffered all nations to walk in their own ways.

17Nevertheless he left not himself without witness, in that he did good, and gave us rain from heaven, and fruitful seasons, filling our hearts with food and gladness.

18And with these sayings scarce restrained they the people, that they had not done sacrifice unto them.

19¶ And there came thither *certain* Jews from Antioch and Iconium, who persuaded the people, and, having stoned Paul, drew *him* out of the city, supposing he had been dead.

20Howbeit, as the disciples stood round about him, he rose up, and came into the city: and the next day he departed with Barnabas to Derbe.

21And when they had preached the gospel to that city, and had taught many, they returned again to Lystra, and *to* Iconium, and Antioch.

22Confirming the souls of the disciples, *and* exhorting them to continue in the faith, and that we must through much tribulation enter into the kingdom of God.

23And when they had ordained them elders in every church, and had prayed with fasting, they commended them to the Lord, on whom they believed.

24And after they had passed throughout Pisidia, they came to Pamphylia.

25And when they had preached the word in Perga, they went down into Attalia:

26And thence sailed to Antioch, from whence they had been recommended to the grace of God for the work which they fulfilled.

27And when they were come, and had gathered the church together, they rehearsed all that God had done with them, and how he had opened the door of faith unto the Gentiles.

28And there they abode long time with the disciples.

15 AND CERTAIN men which came down from Judaea taught the brethren, *and said,* Except ye be circumcised after the manner of Moses, ye cannot be saved.

2When therefore Paul and Barnabas had no small dissension and disputation with them, they determined that Paul and Barnabas, and certain other of them, should go up to Jerusalem unto the apostles and elders about this question.

New International

In Lystra and Derbe

8In Lystra there sat a man crippled in his feet, who was lame from birth and had never walked. 9He listened to Paul as he was speaking. Paul looked directly at him, saw that he had faith to be healed 10and called out, "Stand up on your feet!" At that, the man jumped up and began to walk.

11When the crowd saw what Paul had done, they shouted in the Lycaonian language, "The gods have come down to us in human form!" 12Barnabas they called Zeus, and Paul they called Hermes because he was the chief speaker. 13The priest of Zeus, whose temple was just outside the city, brought bulls and wreaths to the city gates because he and the crowd wanted to offer sacrifices to them.

14But when the apostles Barnabas and Paul heard of this, they tore their clothes and rushed out into the crowd, shouting: 15"Men, why are you doing this? We too are only men, human like you. We are bringing you good news, telling you to turn from these worthless things to the living God, who made heaven and earth and sea and everything in them. 16In the past, he let all nations go their own way. 17Yet he has not left himself without testimony: He has shown kindness by giving you rain from heaven and crops in their seasons; he provides you with plenty of food and fills your hearts with joy." 18Even with these words, they had difficulty keeping the crowd from sacrificing to them.

19Then some Jews came from Antioch and Iconium and won the crowd over. They stoned Paul and dragged him outside the city, thinking he was dead. 20But after the disciples had gathered around him, he got up and went back into the city. The next day he and Barnabas left for Derbe.

The Return to Antioch in Syria

21They preached the good news in that city and won a large number of disciples. Then they returned to Lystra, Iconium and Antioch, 22strengthening the disciples and encouraging them to remain true to the faith. "We must go through many hardships to enter the kingdom of God," they said. 23Paul and Barnabas appointed elders[a] for them in each church and, with prayer and fasting, committed them to the Lord, in whom they had put their trust. 24After going through Pisidia, they came into Pamphylia, 25and when they had preached the word in Perga, they went down to Attalia.

26From Attalia they sailed back to Antioch, where they had been committed to the grace of God for the work they had now completed. 27On arriving there, they gathered the church together and reported all that God had done through them and how he had opened the door of faith to the Gentiles. 28And they stayed there a long time with the disciples.

The Council at Jerusalem

15 SOME MEN came down from Judea to Antioch and were teaching the brothers: "Unless you are circumcised, according to the custom taught by Moses, you cannot be saved." 2This brought Paul and Barnabas into sharp dispute and debate with them. So Paul and Barnabas were appointed, along with some other believers, to go up to Jerusalem to see the apostles and elders about this question. 3The church sent them on their way,

a 23 Or *Barnabas ordained elders*; or *Barnabas had elders elected*

Living Bible

8While they were at Lystra, they came upon a man with crippled feet who had been that way from birth, so he had never walked. 9He was listening as Paul preached, and Paul noticed him and realized he had faith to be healed. 10So Paul called to him, "Stand up!" and the man leaped to his feet and started walking!

11When the listening crowd saw what Paul had done, they shouted (in their local dialect, of course), "These men are gods in human bodies!" 12They decided that Barnabas was the Greek god Jupiter, and that Paul, because he was the chief speaker, was Mercury! 13The local priest of the Temple of Jupiter, located on the outskirts of the city, brought them cartloads of flowers and prepared to sacrifice oxen to them at the city gates before the crowds.

14But when Barnabas and Paul saw what was happening they ripped at their clothing in dismay and ran out among the people, shouting, 15"Men! What are you doing? We are merely human beings like yourselves! We have come to bring you the Good News that you are invited to turn from the worship of these foolish things and to pray instead to the living God who made heaven and earth and sea and everything in them. 16In bygone days he permitted the nations to go their own ways, 17but he never left himself without a witness; there were always his reminders—the kind things he did such as sending you rain and good crops and giving you food and gladness."

18But even so, Paul and Barnabas could scarcely restrain the people from sacrificing to them!

19Yet only a few days later, some Jews arrived from Antioch and Iconium and turned the crowds into a murderous mob that stoned Paul and dragged him out of the city, apparently dead. 20But as the believers stood around him, he got up and went back into the city!

The next day he left with Barnabas for Derbe. 21After preaching the Good News there and making many disciples, they returned again to Lystra, Iconium and Antioch, 22where they helped the believers to grow in love for God and each other. They encouraged them to continue in the faith in spite of all the persecution, reminding them that they must enter into the Kingdom of God through many tribulations. 23Paul and Barnabas also appointed elders in every church and prayed for them with fasting, turning them over to the care of the Lord in whom they trusted.

24Then they traveled back through Pisidia to Pamphylia, 25preached again in Perga, and went on to Attalia.

26Finally they returned by ship to Antioch, where their journey had begun, and where they had been committed to God for the work now completed.

27Upon arrival they called together the believers and reported on their trip, telling how God had opened the door of faith to the Gentiles too. 28And they stayed there with the believers at Antioch for a long while.

15 WHILE PAUL and Barnabas were at Antioch, some men from Judea arrived and began to teach the believers that unless they adhered to the ancient Jewish custom of circumcision, they could not be saved. 2Paul and Barnabas argued and discussed this with them at length, and finally the believers sent them to Jerusalem, accompanied by some local men, to talk to the apostles and elders there about this question. 3Af-

New Revised Standard

Paul and Barnabas in Lystra and Derbe

8 In Lystra there was a man sitting who could not use his feet and had never walked, for he had been crippled from birth. 9He listened to Paul as he was speaking. And Paul, looking at him intently and seeing that he had faith to be healed, 10said in a loud voice, "Stand upright on your feet." And the manb sprang up and began to walk. 11When the crowds saw what Paul had done, they shouted in the Lycaonian language, "The gods have come down to us in human form!" 12Barnabas they called Zeus, and Paul they called Hermes, because he was the chief speaker. 13The priest of Zeus, whose temple was just outside the city,c brought oxen and garlands to the gates; he and the crowds wanted to offer sacrifice. 14When the apostles Barnabas and Paul heard of it, they tore their clothes and rushed out into the crowd, shouting, 15"Friends,d why are you doing this? We are mortals just like you, and we bring you good news, that you should turn from these worthless things to the living God, who made the heaven and the earth and the sea and all that is in them. 16In past generations he allowed all the nations to follow their own ways; 17yet he has not left himself without a witness in doing good—giving you rains from heaven and fruitful seasons, and filling you with food and your hearts with joy." 18Even with these words, they scarcely restrained the crowds from offering sacrifice to them.

19 But Jews came there from Antioch and Iconium and won over the crowds. Then they stoned Paul and dragged him out of the city, supposing that he was dead. 20But when the disciples surrounded him, he got up and went into the city. The next day he went on with Barnabas to Derbe.

The Return to Antioch in Syria

21 After they had proclaimed the good news to that city and had made many disciples, they returned to Lystra, then on to Iconium and Antioch. 22There they strengthened the souls of the disciples and encouraged them to continue in the faith, saying, "It is through many persecutions that we must enter the kingdom of God." 23And after they had appointed elders for them in each church, with prayer and fasting they entrusted them to the Lord in whom they had come to believe.

24 Then they passed through Pisidia and came to Pamphylia. 25When they had spoken the word in Perga, they went down to Attalia. 26From there they sailed back to Antioch, where they had been commended to the grace of God for the worke that they had completed. 27When they arrived, they called the church together and related all that God had done with them, and how he had opened a door of faith for the Gentiles. 28And they stayed there with the disciples for some time.

The Council at Jerusalem

15 THEN CERTAIN individuals came down from Judea and were teaching the brothers, "Unless you are circumcised according to the custom of Moses, you cannot be saved." 2And after Paul and Barnabas had no small dissension and debate with them, Paul and Barnabas and some of the others were appointed to go up to Jerusalem to discuss this question with the apostles and the elders. 3So they were sent on their way by the

---

b Gk he   c Or The priest of Zeus-Outside-the-City   d Gk Men   e Or
committed in the grace of God to the work

King James

3And being brought on their way by the church, they passed through Phenice and Samaria, declaring the conversion of the Gentiles: and they caused great joy unto all the brethren.

4And when they were come to Jerusalem, they were received of the church, and of the apostles and elders, and they declared all things that God had done with them.

5But there rose up certain of the sect of the Pharisees which believed, saying, That it was needful to circumcise them, and to command them to keep the law of Moses.

6¶ And the apostles and elders came together for to consider of this matter.

7And when there had been much disputing, Peter rose up, and said unto them, Men and brethren, ye know how that a good while ago God made choice among us, that the Gentiles by my mouth should hear the word of the gospel, and believe.

8And God, which knoweth the hearts, bare them witness, giving them the Holy Ghost, even as he did unto us;

9And put no difference between us and them, purifying their hearts by faith.

10Now therefore why tempt ye God, to put a yoke upon the neck of the disciples, which neither our fathers nor we were able to bear?

11But we believe that through the grace of the Lord Jesus Christ we shall be saved, even as they.

12¶ Then all the multitude kept silence, and gave audience to Barnabas and Paul, declaring what miracles and wonders God had wrought among the Gentiles by them.

13¶ And after they had held their peace, James answered, saying, Men and brethren, hearken unto me:

14Simeon hath declared how God at the first did visit the Gentiles, to take out of them a people for his name.

15And to this agree the words of the prophets; as it is written,

16After this I will return, and will build again the tabernacle of David, which is fallen down; and I will build again the ruins thereof, and I will set it up:

17That the residue of men might seek after the Lord, and all the Gentiles, upon whom my name is called, saith the Lord, who doeth all these things.

18Known unto God are all his works from the beginning of the world.

19Wherefore my sentence is, that we trouble not them, which from among the Gentiles are turned to God:

20But that we write unto them, that they abstain from pollutions of idols, and from fornication, and from things strangled, and from blood.

21For Moses of old time hath in every city them that preach him, being read in the synagogues every sabbath day.

22Then pleased it the apostles and elders, with the whole church, to send chosen men of their own company to Antioch with Paul and Barnabas; namely, Judas surnamed Barsabas, and Silas, chief men among the brethren:

23And they wrote letters by them after this manner; The apostles and elders and brethren send greeting unto the brethren which are of the Gentiles in Antioch and Syria and Cilicia:

24Forasmuch as we have heard, that certain which went out from us have troubled you with words, subverting your souls, saying, Ye must be circumcised, and keep the law: to whom we gave no such commandment:

25It seemed good unto us, being assembled with one accord, to send chosen men unto you with our beloved Barnabas and Paul,

New International

and as they traveled through Phoenicia and Samaria, they told how the Gentiles had been converted. This news made all the brothers very glad. 4When they came to Jerusalem, they were welcomed by the church and the apostles and elders, to whom they reported everything God had done through them.

5Then some of the believers who belonged to the party of the Pharisees stood up and said, "The Gentiles must be circumcised and required to obey the law of Moses."

6The apostles and elders met to consider this question. 7After much discussion, Peter got up and addressed them: "Brothers, you know that some time ago God made a choice among you that the Gentiles might hear from my lips the message of the gospel and believe. 8God, who knows the heart, showed that he accepted them by giving the Holy Spirit to them, just as he did to us. 9He made no distinction between us and them, for he purified their hearts by faith. 10Now then, why do you try to test God by putting on the necks of the disciples a yoke that neither we nor our fathers have been able to bear? 11No! We believe it is through the grace of our Lord Jesus that we are saved, just as they are."

12The whole assembly became silent as they listened to Barnabas and Paul telling about the miraculous signs and wonders God had done among the Gentiles through them. 13When they finished, James spoke up: "Brothers, listen to me. 14Simon[a] has described to us how God at first showed his concern by taking from the Gentiles a people for himself. 15The words of the prophets are in agreement with this, as it is written:

16" 'After this I will return
    and rebuild David's fallen tent.
  Its ruins I will rebuild,
    and I will restore it,
17that the remnant of men may seek the Lord,
    and all the Gentiles who bear my name,
  says the Lord, who does these things'[b]
18 that have been known for ages.[c]

19"It is my judgment, therefore, that we should not make it difficult for the Gentiles who are turning to God. 20Instead we should write to them, telling them to abstain from food polluted by idols, from sexual immorality, from the meat of strangled animals and from blood. 21For Moses has been preached in every city from the earliest times and is read in the synagogues on every Sabbath."

The Council's Letter to Gentile Believers

22Then the apostles and elders, with the whole church, decided to choose some of their own men and send them to Antioch with Paul and Barnabas. They chose Judas (called Barsabbas) and Silas, two men who were leaders among the brothers. 23With them they sent the following letter:

The apostles and elders, your brothers,

To the Gentile believers in Antioch, Syria and Cilicia:

Greetings.

24We have heard that some went out from us without our authorization and disturbed you, troubling your minds by what they said. 25So we all agreed to choose some men and send them to you with our dear friends Barnabas and Paul— 26men

---

[a] 14 Greek Simeon, a variant of Simon; that is, Peter   [b] 17 Amos 9:11,12
[c] 17,18 Some manuscripts things'— / 18known to the Lord for ages is his work

Living Bible

ter the entire congregation had escorted them out of the city the delegates went on to Jerusalem, stopping along the way in the cities of Phoenicia and Samaria to visit the believers, telling them—much to everyone's joy—that the Gentiles, too, were being converted.

4Arriving in Jerusalem, they met with the church leaders—all the apostles and elders were present—and Paul and Barnabas reported on what God had been doing through their ministry. 5But then some of the men who had been Pharisees before their conversion stood to their feet and declared that all Gentile converts must be circumcised and required to follow all the Jewish customs and ceremonies.

6So the apostles and church elders set a further meeting to decide this question.

7At the meeting, after long discussion, Peter stood and addressed them as follows: "Brothers, you all know that God chose me from among you long ago to preach the Good News to the Gentiles, so that they also could believe. 8God, who knows men's hearts, confirmed the fact that he accepts Gentiles by giving them the Holy Spirit, just as he gave him to us. 9He made no distinction between them and us, for he cleansed their lives through faith, just as he did ours. 10And now are you going to correct God by burdening the Gentiles with a yoke that neither we nor our fathers were able to bear? 11Don't you believe that all are saved the same way, by the free gift of the Lord Jesus?"

12There was no further discussion, and everyone now listened as Barnabas and Paul told about the miracles God had done through them among the Gentiles.

13When they had finished, James took the floor. "Brothers," he said, "listen to me. 14Peter has told you about the time God first visited the Gentiles to take from them a people to bring honor to his name. 15And this fact of Gentile conversion agrees with what the prophets predicted. For instance, listen to this passage from the prophet Amos:d

16'Afterwards' [says the Lorde], 'I will return and renew the broken contract with David,f 17so that Gentiles, too, will find the Lord—all those marked with my name.'

18That is what the Lord says, who reveals his plans made from the beginning.

19"And so my judgment is that we should not insist that the Gentiles who turn to God must obey our Jewish laws, 20except that we should write to them to refrain from eating meat sacrificed to idols, from all fornication, and also from eating unbled meat of strangled animals. 21For these things have been preached against in Jewish synagogues in every city on every Sabbath for many generations."

22Then the apostles and elders and the whole congregation voted to send delegates to Antioch with Paul and Barnabas, to report on this decision. The men chosen were two of the church leaders—Judas (also called Barsabbas) and Silas.

23This is the letter they took along with them:

"From: The apostles, elders and brothers at Jerusalem.

"To: The Gentile brothers in Antioch, Syria and Cilicia. Greetings!

24"We understand that some believers from here have upset you and questioned your salvation,g but they had no such instructions from us. 25So it seemed wise to us, having unanimously agreed on our decision, to send to you these two official representatives, along with our beloved Barnabas and Paul. 26These men—Judas and

New Revised Standard

church, and as they passed through both Phoenicia and Samaria, they reported the conversion of the Gentiles, and brought great joy to all the believers.h 4When they came to Jerusalem, they were welcomed by the church and the apostles and the elders, and they reported all that God had done with them. 5But some believers who belonged to the sect of the Pharisees stood up and said, "It is necessary for them to be circumcised and ordered to keep the law of Moses."

6 The apostles and the elders met together to consider this matter. 7After there had been much debate, Peter stood up and said to them, "My brothers,i you know that in the early days God made a choice among you, that I should be the one through whom the Gentiles would hear the message of the good news and become believers. 8And God, who knows the human heart, testified to them by giving them the Holy Spirit, just as he did to us; 9and in cleansing their hearts by faith he has made no distinction between them and us. 10Now therefore why are you putting God to the test by placing on the neck of the disciples a yoke that neither our ancestors nor we have been able to bear? 11On the contrary, we believe that we will be saved through the grace of the Lord Jesus, just as they will."

12 The whole assembly kept silence, and listened to Barnabas and Paul as they told of all the signs and wonders that God had done through them among the Gentiles. 13After they finished speaking, James replied, "My brothers,i listen to me. 14Simeon has related how God first looked favorably on the Gentiles, to take from among them a people for his name. 15This agrees with the words of the prophets, as it is written,

16 'After this I will return,
    and I will rebuild the dwelling of David,
       which has fallen;
    from its ruins I will rebuild it,
       and I will set it up,
17 so that all other peoples may seek the Lord—
       even all the Gentiles over whom my name
          has been called.
    Thus says the Lord, who has been making
       these things 18known from long ago.'i

19Therefore I have reached the decision that we should not trouble those Gentiles who are turning to God, 20but we should write to them to abstain only from things polluted by idols and from fornication and from whatever has been strangledk and from blood. 21For in every city, for generations past, Moses has had those who proclaim him, for he has been read aloud every sabbath in the synagogues."

The Council's Letter to Gentile Believers

22 Then the apostles and the elders, with the consent of the whole church, decided to choose men from among their membersl and to send them to Antioch with Paul and Barnabas. They sent Judas called Barsabbas, and Silas, leaders among the brothers, 23with the following letter: "The brothers, both the apostles and the elders, to the believersh of Gentile origin in Antioch and Syria and Cilicia, greetings. 24Since we have heard that certain persons who have gone out from us, though with no instructions from us, have said things to disturb you and have unsettled your minds,m 25we have decided unanimously to choose representativesn and send them to you, along with our beloved Barnabas and Paul,

---

d 15:15 *from the prophet Amos,* implied. See Amos 9:11, 12.   e 15:16 *says the Lord,* implied.   f 15:16 *renew the broken contract with David,* literally, "rebuild the tabernacle of David which is fallen."   g 15:24 *questioned your salvation,* literally, "subverted your souls."

h Gk *brothers*   i Gk *Men, brothers*   j Other ancient authorities read *things.* 18*Known to God from of old are all his works.'*   k Other ancient authorities lack *and from whatever has been strangled*   l Gk *from among them*   m Other ancient authorities add *saying, 'You must be circumcised and keep the law,'*   n Gk *men*

King James

26Men that have hazarded their lives for the name of our Lord Jesus Christ.

27We have sent therefore Judas and Silas, who shall also tell *you* the same things by mouth.

28For it seemed good to the Holy Ghost, and to us, to lay upon you no greater burden than these necessary things;

29That ye abstain from meats offered to idols, and from blood, and from things strangled, and from fornication: from which if ye keep yourselves, ye shall do well. Fare ye well.

30So when they were dismissed, they came to Antioch: and when they had gathered the multitude together, they delivered the epistle:

31*Which* when they had read, they rejoiced for the consolation.

32And Judas and Silas, being prophets also themselves, exhorted the brethren with many words, and confirmed *them*.

33And after they had tarried *there* a space, they were let go in peace from the brethren unto the apostles.

34Notwithstanding it pleased Silas to abide there still.

35Paul also and Barnabas continued in Antioch, teaching and preaching the word of the Lord, with many others also.

36¶ And some days after Paul said unto Barnabas, Let us go again and visit our brethren in every city where we have preached the word of the Lord, *and see* how they do.

37And Barnabas determined to take with them John, whose surname was Mark.

38But Paul thought not good to take him with them, who departed from them from Pamphylia, and went not with them to the work.

39And the contention was so sharp between them, that they departed asunder one from the other: and so Barnabas took Mark, and sailed unto Cyprus;

40And Paul chose Silas, and departed, being recommended by the brethren unto the grace of God.

41And he went through Syria and Cilicia, confirming the churches.

16 THEN CAME he to Derbe and Lystra: and, behold, a certain disciple was there, named Timotheus, the son of a certain woman, which was a Jewess, and believed; but his father *was* a Greek:

2Which was well reported of by the brethren that were at Lystra and Iconium.

3Him would Paul have to go forth with him; and took and circumcised him because of the Jews which were in those quarters: for they knew all that his father was a Greek.

4And as they went through the cities, they delivered them the decrees for to keep, that were ordained of the apostles and elders which were at Jerusalem.

5And so were the churches established in the faith, and increased in number daily.

6Now when they had gone throughout Phrygia and the region of Galatia, and were forbidden of the Holy Ghost to preach the word in Asia,

7After they were come to Mysia, they assayed to go into Bithynia: but the Spirit suffered them not.

8And they passing by Mysia came down to Troas.

9And a vision appeared to Paul in the night; There stood a man of Macedonia, and prayed him, saying, Come over into Macedonia, and help us.

New International

who have risked their lives for the name of our Lord Jesus Christ. 27Therefore we are sending Judas and Silas to confirm by word of mouth what we are writing. 28It seemed good to the Holy Spirit and to us not to burden you with anything beyond the following requirements: 29You are to abstain from food sacrificed to idols, from blood, from the meat of strangled animals and from sexual immorality. You will do well to avoid these things.

Farewell.

30The men were sent off and went down to Antioch, where they gathered the church together and delivered the letter. 31The people read it and were glad for its encouraging message. 32Judas and Silas, who themselves were prophets, said much to encourage and strengthen the brothers. 33After spending some time there, they were sent off by the brothers with the blessing of peace to return to those who had sent them.a 35But Paul and Barnabas remained in Antioch, where they and many others taught and preached the word of the Lord.

Disagreement Between Paul and Barnabas

36Some time later Paul said to Barnabas, "Let us go back and visit the brothers in all the towns where we preached the word of the Lord and see how they are doing." 37Barnabas wanted to take John, also called Mark, with them, 38but Paul did not think it wise to take him, because he had deserted them in Pamphylia and had not continued with them in the work. 39They had such a sharp disagreement that they parted company. Barnabas took Mark and sailed for Cyprus, 40but Paul chose Silas and left, commended by the brothers to the grace of the Lord. 41He went through Syria and Cilicia, strengthening the churches.

Timothy Joins Paul and Silas

16 HE CAME to Derbe and then to Lystra, where a disciple named Timothy lived, whose mother was a Jewess and a believer, but whose father was a Greek. 2The brothers at Lystra and Iconium spoke well of him. 3Paul wanted to take him along on the journey, so he circumcised him because of the Jews who lived in that area, for they all knew that his father was a Greek. 4As they traveled from town to town, they delivered the decisions reached by the apostles and elders in Jerusalem for the people to obey. 5So the churches were strengthened in the faith and grew daily in numbers.

Paul's Vision of the Man of Macedonia

6Paul and his companions traveled throughout the region of Phrygia and Galatia, having been kept by the Holy Spirit from preaching the word in the province of Asia. 7When they came to the border of Mysia, they tried to enter Bithynia, but the Spirit of Jesus would not allow them to. 8So they passed by Mysia and went down to Troas. 9During the night Paul had a vision of a man of Macedonia standing and begging him, "Come over to Macedonia and help us." 10After Paul had seen the vi-

---

a *33 Some manuscripts* them, *34but Silas decided to remain there*

Living Bible

Silas, who have risked their lives for the sake of our Lord Jesus Christ—will confirm orally what we have decided concerning your question.

27, 28, 29"For it seemed good to the Holy Spirit and to us to lay no greater burden of Jewish laws on you than to abstain from eating food offered to idols and from unbled meat of strangled animals,b and, of course, from fornication. If you do this, it is enough. Farewell."

30The four messengers went at once to Antioch, where they called a general meeting of the Christians and gave them the letter. 31And there was great joy throughout the church that day as they read it.

32Then Judas and Silas, both being gifted speakers,c preached long sermons to the believers, strengthening their faith. 33They stayed several days,d and then Judas and Silas returned to Jerusalem taking greetings and appreciation to those who had sent them. 34, 35Paul and Barnabas stayed on at Antioch to assist several others who were preaching and teaching there.

36Several days later Paul suggested to Barnabas that they return again to Turkey, and visit each city where they had preached before,e to see how the new converts were getting along. 37Barnabas agreed, and wanted to take along John Mark. 38But Paul didn't like that idea at all, since John had deserted them in Pamphylia. 39Their disagreement over this was so sharp that they separated. Barnabas took Mark with him and sailed for Cyprus, 40, 41while Paul chose Silas and, with the blessing of the believers, left for Syria and Cilicia, to encourage the churches there.

16 PAUL AND Silas went first to Derbe and then on to Lystra where they met Timothy, a believer whose mother was a Christian Jewess but his father a Greek. 2Timothy was well thought of by the brothers in Lystra and Iconium, 3so Paul asked him to join them on their journey. In deference to the Jews of the area, he circumcised Timothy before they left, for everyone knew that his father was a Greek [and hadn't permitted this beforef]. 4Then they went from city to city, making known the decision concerning the Gentiles, as decided by the apostles and elders in Jerusalem. 5So the church grew daily in faith and numbers.

6Next they traveled through Phrygia and Galatia, because the Holy Spirit had told them not to go into the Turkish province of Asia minor at that time. 7Then going along the borders of Mysia they headed north for the province of Bithynia, but again the Spirit of Jesus said no. 8So instead they went on through Mysia province to the city of Troas.

9That nightg Paul had a vision. In his dream he saw a man over in Macedonia, Greece, pleading with him, "Come over here and help us." 10Well, that settled it.

New Revised Standard

26who have risked their lives for the sake of our Lord Jesus Christ. 27We have therefore sent Judas and Silas, who themselves will tell you the same things by word of mouth. 28For it has seemed good to the Holy Spirit and to us to impose on you no further burden than these essentials: 29that you abstain from what has been sacrificed to idols and from blood and from what is strangledh and from fornication. If you keep yourselves from these, you will do well. Farewell."

30 So they were sent off and went down to Antioch. When they gathered the congregation together, they delivered the letter. 31When its membersi read it, they rejoiced at the exhortation. 32Judas and Silas, who were themselves prophets, said much to encourage and strengthen the believers.j 33After they had been there for some time, they were sent off in peace by the believersi to those who had sent them.k 35But Paul and Barnabas remained in Antioch, and there, with many others, they taught and proclaimed the word of the Lord.

Paul and Barnabas Separate

36 After some days Paul said to Barnabas, "Come, let us return and visit the believersi in every city where we proclaimed the word of the Lord and see how they are doing." 37Barnabas wanted to take with them John called Mark. 38But Paul decided not to take with them one who had deserted them in Pamphylia and had not accompanied them in the work. 39The disagreement became so sharp that they parted company; Barnabas took Mark with him and sailed away to Cyprus. 40But Paul chose Silas and set out, the believersi commending him to the grace of the Lord. 41He went through Syria and Cilicia, strengthening the churches.

Timothy Joins Paul and Silas

16 PAULi WENT on also to Derbe and to Lystra, where there was a disciple named Timothy, the son of a Jewish woman who was a believer; but his father was a Greek. 2He was well spoken of by the believersi in Lystra and Iconium. 3Paul wanted Timothy to accompany him; and he took him and had him circumcised because of the Jews who were in those places, for they all knew that his father was a Greek. 4As they went from town to town, they delivered to them for observance the decisions that had been reached by the apostles and elders who were in Jerusalem. 5So the churches were strengthened in the faith and increased in numbers daily.

Paul's Vision of the Man of Macedonia

6 They went through the region of Phrygia and Galatia, having been forbidden by the Holy Spirit to speak the word in Asia. 7When they had come opposite Mysia, they attempted to go into Bithynia, but the Spirit of Jesus did not allow them; 8so, passing by Mysia, they went down to Troas. 9During the night Paul had a vision: there stood a man of Macedonia pleading with him and saying, "Come over to Macedonia and help us." 10When

---

b 15:27-29 and from unbled meat of strangled animals, literally, "and from blood." c 15:32 gifted speakers, or, "prophets." d 15:33 stayed several days, literally,"spent some time." e 15:36 return again to Turkey, and visit each city where they had preached before, implied. Literally, "return now and visit every city wherein we proclaimed the word of the Lord." f 16:3 and hadn't permitted this before, implied. g 16:9 That night, literally, "in the night."

h Other ancient authorities lack and from what is strangled i Gk When they j Gk brothers k Other ancient authorities add verse 34, But it seemed good to Silas to remain there l Gk He

King James

10And after he had seen the vision, immediately we endeavoured to go into Macedonia, assuredly gathering that the Lord had called us for to preach the gospel unto them.

11Therefore loosing from Troas, we came with a straight course to Samothracia, and the next *day* to Neapolis;

12And from thence to Philippi, which is the chief city of that part of Macedonia, *and* a colony: and we were in that city abiding certain days.

13And on the sabbath we went out of the city by a river side, where prayer was wont to be made; and we sat down, and spake unto the women which resorted *thither*.

14¶ And a certain woman named Lydia, a seller of purple, of the city of Thyatira, which worshipped God, heard *us*: whose heart the Lord opened, that she attended unto the things which were spoken of Paul.

15And when she was baptized, and her household, she besought *us*, saying, If ye have judged me to be faithful to the Lord, come into my house, and abide *there*. And she constrained us.

16¶ And it came to pass, as we went to prayer, a certain damsel possessed with a spirit of divination met us, which brought her masters much gain by soothsaying:

17The same followed Paul and us, and cried, saying, These men are the servants of the most high God, which show unto us the way of salvation.

18And this did she many days. But Paul, being grieved, turned and said to the spirit, I command thee in the name of Jesus Christ to come out of her. And he came out the same hour.

19¶ And when her masters saw that the hope of their gains was gone, they caught Paul and Silas, and drew *them* into the marketplace unto the rulers,

20And brought them to the magistrates, saying, These men, being Jews, do exceedingly trouble our city,

21And teach customs, which are not lawful for us to receive, neither to observe, being Romans.

22And the multitude rose up together against them: and the magistrates rent off their clothes, and commanded to beat *them*.

23And when they had laid many stripes upon them, they cast *them* into prison, charging the jailer to keep them safely:

24Who, having received such a charge, thrust them into the inner prison, and made their feet fast in the stocks.

25¶ And at midnight Paul and Silas prayed, and sang praises unto God: and the prisoners heard them.

26And suddenly there was a great earthquake, so that the foundations of the prison were shaken: and immediately all the doors were opened, and every one's bands were loosed.

27And the keeper of the prison awaking out of his sleep, and seeing the prison doors open, he drew out his sword, and would have killed himself, supposing that the prisoners had been fled.

28But Paul cried with a loud voice, saying, Do thyself no harm: for we are all here.

29Then he called for a light, and sprang in, and came trembling, and fell down before Paul and Silas,

30And brought them out, and said, Sirs, what must I do to be saved?

31And they said, Believe on the Lord Jesus Christ, and thou shalt be saved, and thy house.

32And they spake unto him the word of the Lord, and to all that were in his house.

33And he took them the same hour of the night, and washed *their* stripes; and was baptized, he and all his, straightway.

34And when he had brought them into his house, he set meat before them, and rejoiced, believing in God with all his house.

New International

sion, we got ready at once to leave for Macedonia, concluding that God had called us to preach the gospel to them.

Lydia's Conversion in Philippi

11From Troas we put out to sea and sailed straight for Samothrace, and the next day on to Neapolis. 12From there we traveled to Philippi, a Roman colony and the leading city of that district of Macedonia. And we stayed there several days.

13On the Sabbath we went outside the city gate to the river, where we expected to find a place of prayer. We sat down and began to speak to the women who had gathered there. 14One of those listening was a woman named Lydia, a dealer in purple cloth from the city of Thyatira, who was a worshiper of God. The Lord opened her heart to respond to Paul's message. 15When she and the members of her household were baptized, she invited us to her home. "If you consider me a believer in the Lord," she said, "come and stay at my house." And she persuaded us.

Paul and Silas in Prison

16Once when we were going to the place of prayer, we were met by a slave girl who had a spirit by which she predicted the future. She earned a great deal of money for her owners by fortune-telling. 17This girl followed Paul and the rest of us, shouting, "These men are servants of the Most High God, who are telling you the way to be saved." 18She kept this up for many days. Finally Paul became so troubled that he turned around and said to the spirit, "In the name of Jesus Christ I command you to come out of her!" At that moment the spirit left her.

19When the owners of the slave girl realized that their hope of making money was gone, they seized Paul and Silas and dragged them into the marketplace to face the authorities. 20They brought them before the magistrates and said, "These men are Jews, and are throwing our city into an uproar 21by advocating customs unlawful for us Romans to accept or practice."

22The crowd joined in the attack against Paul and Silas, and the magistrates ordered them to be stripped and beaten. 23After they had been severely flogged, they were thrown into prison, and the jailer was commanded to guard them carefully. 24Upon receiving such orders, he put them in the inner cell and fastened their feet in the stocks.

25About midnight Paul and Silas were praying and singing hymns to God, and the other prisoners were listening to them. 26Suddenly there was such a violent earthquake that the foundations of the prison were shaken. At once all the prison doors flew open, and everybody's chains came loose. 27The jailer woke up, and when he saw the prison doors open, he drew his sword and was about to kill himself because he thought the prisoners had escaped. 28But Paul shouted, "Don't harm yourself! We are all here!"

29The jailer called for lights, rushed in and fell trembling before Paul and Silas. 30He then brought them out and asked, "Sirs, what must I do to be saved?"

31They replied, "Believe in the Lord Jesus, and you will be saved—you and your household." 32Then they spoke the word of the Lord to him and to all the others in his house. 33At that hour of the night the jailer took them and washed their wounds; then immediately he and all his family were baptized. 34The jailer brought them into his house and set a meal before them; he was filled with joy because he had come to believe in God—he and his whole family.

Living Bible

Wea would go to Macedonia, for we could only conclude that God was sending us to preach the Good News there.

11We went aboard a boat at Troas, and sailed straight across to Samothrace, and the next day on to Neapolis, 12and finally reached Philippi, a Romanb colony just inside the Macedonian border, and stayed there several days.

13On the Sabbath, we went a little way outside the city to a river bank where we understood some people met for prayer; and we taught the Scriptures to some women who came. 14One of them was Lydia, a saleswoman from Thyatira, a merchant of purple cloth. She was already a worshiper of God and, as she listened to us, the Lord opened her heart and she accepted all that Paul was saying. 15She was baptized along with all her household and asked us to be her guests. "If you agree that I am faithful to the Lord," she said, "come and stay at my home." And she urged us until we did.

16One day as we were going down to the place of prayer beside the river, we met a demonpossessed slave girl who was a fortune-teller, and earned much money for her masters. 17She followed along behind us shouting, "These men are servants of God and they have come to tell you how to have your sins forgiven."

18This went on day after day until Paul, in great distress, turned and spoke to the demon within her. "I command you in the name of Jesus Christ to come out of her," he said. And instantly it left her.

19Her masters' hopes of wealth were now shattered; they grabbed Paul and Silas and dragged them before the judges at the marketplace.

20, 21"These Jews are corrupting our city," they shouted. "They are teaching the people to do things that are against the Roman laws."

22A mob was quickly formed against Paul and Silas, and the judges ordered them stripped and beaten with wooden whips. 23Again and again the rods slashed down across their bared backs; and afterwards they were thrown into prison. The jailer was threatened with death if they escaped,c 24so he took no chances, but put them into the inner dungeon and clamped their feet into the stocks.

25Around midnight, as Paul and Silas were praying and singing hymns to the Lord—and the other prisoners were listening— 26suddenly there was a great earthquake; the prison was shaken to its foundations, all the doors flew open—and the chains of every prisoner fell off! 27The jailer wakened to see the prison doors wide open, and assuming the prisoners had escaped, he drew his sword to kill himself. 28But Paul yelled to him, "Don't do it! We are all here!"

29Trembling with fear, the jailer called for lights and ran to the dungeon and fell down before Paul and Silas. 30He brought them out and begged them, "Sirs, what must I do to be saved?"

31They replied, "Believe on the Lord Jesus and you will be saved, and your entire household."

32Then they told him and all his household the Good News from the Lord. 33That same hour he washed their stripes and he and all his family were baptized. 34Then he brought them up into his house and set a meal before them. How he and his household rejoiced because all were now believers! 35The next morning the judges sent

New Revised Standard

he had seen the vision, we immediately tried to cross over to Macedonia, being convinced that God had called us to proclaim the good news to them.

The Conversion of Lydia

11 We set sail from Troas and took a straight course to Samothrace, the following day to Neapolis, 12 and from there to Philippi, which is a leading city of the districtd of Macedonia and a Roman colony. We remained in this city for some days. 13 On the sabbath day we went outside the gate by the river, where we supposed there was a place of prayer; and we sat down and spoke to the women who had gathered there. 14 A certain woman named Lydia, a worshiper of God, was listening to us; she was from the city of Thyatira and a dealer in purple cloth. The Lord opened her heart to listen eagerly to what was said by Paul. 15 When she and her household were baptized, she urged us, saying, "If you have judged me to be faithful to the Lord, come and stay at my home." And she prevailed upon us.

Paul and Silas in Prison

16 One day, as we were going to the place of prayer, we met a slave-girl who had a spirit of divination and brought her owners a great deal of money by fortune-telling. 17 While she followed Paul and us, she would cry out, "These men are slaves of the Most High God, who proclaim to youe a way of salvation." 18 She kept doing this for many days. But Paul, very much annoyed, turned and said to the spirit, "I order you in the name of Jesus Christ to come out of her." And it came out that very hour.

19 But when her owners saw that their hope of making money was gone, they seized Paul and Silas and dragged them into the marketplace before the authorities. 20 When they had brought them before the magistrates, they said, "These men are disturbing our city; they are Jews 21 and are advocating customs that are not lawful for us as Romans to adopt or observe." 22 The crowd joined in attacking them, and the magistrates had them stripped of their clothing and ordered them to be beaten with rods. 23 After they had given them a severe flogging, they threw them into prison and ordered the jailer to keep them securely. 24 Following these instructions, he put them in the innermost cell and fastened their feet in the stocks.

25 About midnight Paul and Silas were praying and singing hymns to God, and the prisoners were listening to them. 26 Suddenly there was an earthquake, so violent that the foundations of the prison were shaken; and immediately all the doors were opened and everyone's chains were unfastened. 27 When the jailer woke up and saw the prison doors wide open, he drew his sword and was about to kill himself, since he supposed that the prisoners had escaped. 28 But Paul shouted in a loud voice, "Do not harm yourself, for we are all here." 29 The jailerf called for lights, and rushing in, he fell down trembling before Paul and Silas. 30 Then he brought them outside and said, "Sirs, what must I do to be saved?" 31 They answered, "Believe on the Lord Jesus, and you will be saved, you and your household." 32 They spoke the word of the Lordg to him and to all who were in his house. 33 At the same hour of the night he took them and washed their wounds; then he and his entire family were baptized without delay. 34 He brought them up into the house and set food before them; and he and his entire household rejoiced that he had become a believer in God.

a 16:10 We. Luke, the writer of this book, now joined Paul and accompanied him on his journey.   b 16:12 Roman, implied.   c 16:23 if they escaped, implied.

d Other authorities read a city of the first district   e Other ancient authorities read to us   f Gk He   g Other ancient authorities read word of God

King James

35And when it was day, the magistrates sent the sergeants, saying, Let those men go.

36And the keeper of the prison told this saying to Paul, The magistrates have sent to let you go: now therefore depart, and go in peace.

37But Paul said unto them, They have beaten us openly uncondemned, being Romans, and have cast *us* into prison; and now do they thrust us out privily? nay verily; but let them come themselves and fetch us out.

38And the sergeants told these words unto the magistrates: and they feared, when they heard that they were Romans.

39And they came and besought them, and brought *them* out, and desired *them* to depart out of the city.

40And they went out of the prison, and entered into *the house of* Lydia: and when they had seen the brethren, they comforted them, and departed.

17 NOW WHEN they had passed through Amphipolis and Apollonia, they came to Thessalonica, where was a synagogue of the Jews:

2And Paul, as his manner was, went in unto them, and three sabbath days reasoned with them out of the scriptures,

3Opening and alleging, that Christ must needs have suffered, and risen again from the dead; and that this Jesus, whom I preach unto you, is Christ.

4And some of them believed, and consorted with Paul and Silas; and of the devout Greeks a great multitude, and of the chief women not a few.

5¶ But the Jews which believed not, moved with envy, took unto them certain lewd fellows of the baser sort, and gathered a company, and set all the city on an uproar, and assaulted the house of Jason, and sought to bring them out to the people.

6And when they found them not, they drew Jason and certain brethren unto the rulers of the city, crying, These that have turned the world upside down are come hither also;

7Whom Jason hath received: and these all do contrary to the decrees of Caesar, saying that there is another king, *one* Jesus.

8And they troubled the people and the rulers of the city, when they heard these things.

9And when they had taken security of Jason, and of the other, they let them go.

10¶ And the brethren immediately sent away Paul and Silas by night unto Berea: who coming *thither* went into the synagogue of the Jews.

11These were more noble than those in Thessalonica, in that they received the word with all readiness of mind, and searched the scriptures daily, whether those things were so.

12Therefore many of them believed; also of honourable women which were Greeks, and of men, not a few.

13But when the Jews of Thessalonica had knowledge that the word of God was preached of Paul at Berea, they came thither also, and stirred up the people.

14And then immediately the brethren sent away Paul to go as it were to the sea: but Silas and Timotheus abode there still.

15And they that conducted Paul brought him unto Athens: and receiving a commandment unto Silas and Timotheus for to come to him with all speed, they departed.

16¶ Now while Paul waited for them at Athens, his spirit was stirred in him, when he saw the city wholly given to idolatry.

17Therefore disputed he in the synagogue with the Jews, and with the devout persons, and in the market daily with them that met with him.

New International

35When it was daylight, the magistrates sent their officers to the jailer with the order: "Release those men."

36The jailer told Paul, "The magistrates have ordered that you and Silas be released. Now you can leave. Go in peace."

37But Paul said to the officers: "They beat us publicly without a trial, even though we are Roman citizens, and threw us into prison. And now do they want to get rid of us quietly? No! Let them come themselves and escort us out."

38The officers reported this to the magistrates, and when they heard that Paul and Silas were Roman citizens, they were alarmed. 39They came to appease them and escorted them from the prison, requesting them to leave the city. 40After Paul and Silas came out of the prison, they went to Lydia's house, where they met with the brothers and encouraged them. Then they left.

In Thessalonica

17 WHEN THEY had passed through Amphipolis and Apollonia, they came to Thessalonica, where there was a Jewish synagogue. 2As his custom was, Paul went into the synagogue, and on three Sabbath days he reasoned with them from the Scriptures, 3explaining and proving that the Christ[a] had to suffer and rise from the dead. "This Jesus I am proclaiming to you is the Christ,[a]" he said. 4Some of the Jews were persuaded and joined Paul and Silas, as did a large number of God-fearing Greeks and not a few prominent women.

5But the Jews were jealous; so they rounded up some bad characters from the marketplace, formed a mob and started a riot in the city. They rushed to Jason's house in search of Paul and Silas in order to bring them out to the crowd.[b] 6But when they did not find them, they dragged Jason and some other brothers before the city officials, shouting: "These men who have caused trouble all over the world have now come here, 7and Jason has welcomed them into his house. They are all defying Caesar's decrees, saying that there is another king, one called Jesus." 8When they heard this, the crowd and the city officials were thrown into turmoil. 9Then they made Jason and the others post bond and let them go.

In Berea

10As soon as it was night, the brothers sent Paul and Silas away to Berea. On arriving there, they went to the Jewish synagogue. 11Now the Bereans were of more noble character than the Thessalonians, for they received the message with great eagerness and examined the Scriptures every day to see if what Paul said was true. 12Many of the Jews believed, as did also a number of prominent Greek women and many Greek men.

13When the Jews in Thessalonica learned that Paul was preaching the word of God at Berea, they went there too, agitating the crowds and stirring them up. 14The brothers immediately sent Paul to the coast, but Silas and Timothy stayed at Berea. 15The men who escorted Paul brought him to Athens and then left with instructions for Silas and Timothy to join him as soon as possible.

In Athens

16While Paul was waiting for them in Athens, he was greatly distressed to see that the city was full of idols. 17So he reasoned in the synagogue with the Jews and the God-fearing Greeks, as well as in the marketplace day by day with those who happened to be there. 18A group

---

a 3 Or Messiah   b 5 Or the assembly of the people

Living Bible

police officers over to tell the jailer, "Let those men go!" 36So the jailer told Paul they were free to leave.

37But Paul replied, "Oh, no they don't! They have publicly beaten us without trial and jailed us—and we are Roman citizens! So now they want us to leave secretly? Never! Let them come themselves and release us!"

38The police officers reported to the judges, who feared for their lives when they heard Paul and Silas were Roman citizens. 39So they came to the jail and begged them to go, and brought them out and pled with them to leave the city. 40Paul and Silas then returned to the home of Lydia where they met with the believers and preached to them once more before leaving town.

17 NOW THEY traveled through the cities of Amphipolis and Apollonia and came to Thessalonica, where there was a Jewish synagogue. 2As was Paul's custom, he went there to preach, and for three Sabbaths in a row he opened the Scriptures to the people, 3explaining the prophecies about the sufferings of the Messiah and his coming back to life, and proving that Jesus is the Messiah. 4Some who listened were persuaded and became converts—including a large number of godly Greek men, and also many important women of the city.c

5But the Jewish leaders were jealous and incited some worthless fellows from the streets to form a mob and start a riot. They attacked the home of Jason, planning to take Paul and Silas to the City Council for punishment.

6Not finding them there, they dragged out Jason and some of the other believers, and took them before the Council instead. "Paul and Silas have turned the rest of the world upside down, and now they are here disturbing our city," they shouted, 7"and Jason has let them into his home. They are all guilty of treason, for they claim another king, Jesus, instead of Caesar."

8, 9The people of the city, as well as the judges, were concerned at these reports and let them go only after they had posted bail.

10That night the Christians hurried Paul and Silas to Beroea, and, as usual,d they went to the synagogue to preach. 11But the people of Beroea were more openminded than those in Thessalonica, and gladly listened to the message. They searched the Scriptures day by day to check up on Paul and Silas' statements to see if they were really so. 12As a result, many of them believed, including several prominent Greek women and many men also.

13But when the Jews in Thessalonica learned that Paul was preaching in Beroea, they went over and stirred up trouble. 14The believers acted at once, sending Paul on to the coast, while Silas and Timothy remained behind. 15Those accompanying Paul went on with him to Athens, and then returned to Beroea with a message for Silas and Timothy to hurry and join him.

16While Paul was waiting for them in Athens, he was deeply troubled by all the idols he saw everywhere throughout the city. 17He went to the synagogue for discussions with the Jews and the devout Gentiles, and spoke daily in the public square to all who happened to be there.

New Revised Standard

35 When morning came, the magistrates sent the police, saying, "Let those men go." 36And the jailer reported the message to Paul, saying, "The magistrates sent word to let you go; therefore come out now and go in peace." 37But Paul replied, "They have beaten us in public, uncondemned, men who are Roman citizens, and have thrown us into prison; and now are they going to discharge us in secret? Certainly not! Let them come and take us out themselves." 38The police reported these words to the magistrates, and they were afraid when they heard that they were Roman citizens; 39so they came and apologized to them. And they took them out and asked them to leave the city. 40After leaving the prison they went to Lydia's home; and when they had seen and encouraged the brothers and sisterse there, they departed.

The Uproar in Thessalonica

17 AFTER PAUL and Silasf had passed through Amphipolis and Apollonia, they came to Thessalonica, where there was a synagogue of the Jews. 2And Paul went in, as was his custom, and on three sabbath days argued with them from the scriptures, 3explaining and proving that it was necessary for the Messiahg to suffer and to rise from the dead, and saying, "This is the Messiah,g Jesus whom I am proclaiming to you." 4Some of them were persuaded and joined Paul and Silas, as did a great many of the devout Greeks and not a few of the leading women. 5But the Jews became jealous, and with the help of some ruffians in the marketplaces they formed a mob and set the city in an uproar. While they were searching for Paul and Silas to bring them out to the assembly, they attacked Jason's house. 6When they could not find them, they dragged Jason and some believerse before the city authorities,h shouting, "These people who have been turning the world upside down have come here also, 7and Jason has entertained them as guests. They are all acting contrary to the decrees of the emperor, saying that there is another king named Jesus." 8The people and the city officials were disturbed when they heard this, 9and after they had taken bail from Jason and the others, they let them go.

Paul and Silas in Beroea

10 That very night the believerse sent Paul and Silas off to Beroea; and when they arrived, they went to the Jewish synagogue. 11These Jews were more receptive than those in Thessalonica, for they welcomed the message very eagerly and examined the scriptures every day to see whether these things were so. 12Many of them therefore believed, including not a few Greek women and men of high standing. 13But when the Jews of Thessalonica learned that the word of God had been proclaimed by Paul in Beroea as well, they came there too, to stir up and incite the crowds. 14Then the believerse immediately sent Paul away to the coast, but Silas and Timothy remained behind. 15Those who conducted Paul brought him as far as Athens; and after receiving instructions to have Silas and Timothy join him as soon as possible, they left him.

Paul in Athens

16 While Paul was waiting for them in Athens, he was deeply distressed to see that the city was full of idols. 17So he argued in the synagogue with the Jews and the devout persons, and also in the marketplacei every day with those who happened to be there. 18Also some

King James

18Then certain philosophers of the Epicureans, and of the Stoics, encountered him. And some said, What will this babbler say? other some, He seemeth to be a setter forth of strange gods: because he preached unto them Jesus, and the resurrection.

19And they took him, and brought him unto Areopagus, saying, May we know what this new doctrine, whereof thou speakest, is?

20For thou bringest certain strange things to our ears: we would know therefore what these things mean.

21(For all the Athenians and strangers which were there spent their time in nothing else, but either to tell, or to hear some new thing.)

22¶ Then Paul stood in the midst of Mars' hill, and said, Ye men of Athens, I perceive that in all things ye are too superstitious.

23For as I passed by, and beheld your devotions, I found an altar with this inscription, TO THE UNKNOWN GOD. Whom therefore ye ignorantly worship, him declare I unto you.

24God that made the world and all things therein, seeing that he is Lord of heaven and earth, dwelleth not in temples made with hands;

25Neither is worshipped with men's hands, as though he needed any thing, seeing he giveth to all life, and breath, and all things;

26And hath made of one blood all nations of men for to dwell on all the face of the earth, and hath determined the times before appointed, and the bounds of their habitation;

27That they should seek the Lord, if haply they might feel after him, and find him, though he be not far from every one of us:

28For in him we live, and move, and have our being; as certain also of your own poets have said, For we are also his offspring.

29Forasmuch then as we are the offspring of God, we ought not to think that the Godhead is like unto gold, or silver, or stone, graven by art and man's device.

30And the times of this ignorance God winked at; but now commandeth all men every where to repent:

31Because he hath appointed a day, in the which he will judge the world in righteousness by that man whom he hath ordained; whereof he hath given assurance unto all men, in that he hath raised him from the dead.

32¶ And when they heard of the resurrection of the dead, some mocked: and others said, We will hear thee again of this matter.

33So Paul departed from among them.

34Howbeit certain men clave unto him, and believed: among the which was Dionysius the Areopagite, and a woman named Damaris, and others with them.

18 AFTER THESE things Paul departed from Athens, and came to Corinth:

2And found a certain Jew named Aquila, born in Pontus, lately come from Italy, with his wife Priscilla; (because that Claudius had commanded all Jews to depart from Rome:) and came unto them.

3And because he was of the same craft, he abode with them, and wrought: for by their occupation they were tentmakers.

4And he reasoned in the synagogue every sabbath, and persuaded the Jews and the Greeks.

5And when Silas and Timotheus were come from Macedonia, Paul was pressed in the spirit, and testified to the Jews that Jesus was Christ.

New International

of Epicurean and Stoic philosophers began to dispute with him. Some of them asked, "What is this babbler trying to say?" Others remarked, "He seems to be advocating foreign gods." They said this because Paul was preaching the good news about Jesus and the resurrection. 19Then they took him and brought him to a meeting of the Areopagus, where they said to him, "May we know what this new teaching is that you are presenting? 20You are bringing some strange ideas to our ears, and we want to know what they mean." 21(All the Athenians and the foreigners who lived there spent their time doing nothing but talking about and listening to the latest ideas.)

22Paul then stood up in the meeting of the Areopagus and said: "Men of Athens! I see that in every way you are very religious. 23For as I walked around and looked carefully at your objects of worship, I even found an altar with this inscription: TO AN UNKNOWN GOD. Now what you worship as something unknown I am going to proclaim to you.

24"The God who made the world and everything in it is the Lord of heaven and earth and does not live in temples built by hands. 25And he is not served by human hands, as if he needed anything, because he himself gives all men life and breath and everything else. 26From one man he made every nation of men, that they should inhabit the whole earth; and he determined the times set for them and the exact places where they should live. 27God did this so that men would seek him and perhaps reach out for him and find him, though he is not far from each one of us. 28'For in him we live and move and have our being.' As some of your own poets have said, 'We are his offspring.'

29"Therefore since we are God's offspring, we should not think that the divine being is like gold or silver or stone—an image made by man's design and skill. 30In the past God overlooked such ignorance, but now he commands all people everywhere to repent. 31For he has set a day when he will judge the world with justice by the man he has appointed. He has given proof of this to all men by raising him from the dead."

32When they heard about the resurrection of the dead, some of them sneered, but others said, "We want to hear you again on this subject." 33At that, Paul left the Council. 34A few men became followers of Paul and believed. Among them was Dionysius, a member of the Areopagus, also a woman named Damaris, and a number of others.

In Corinth

18 AFTER THIS, Paul left Athens and went to Corinth. 2There he met a Jew named Aquila, a native of Pontus, who had recently come from Italy with his wife Priscilla, because Claudius had ordered all the Jews to leave Rome. Paul went to see them, 3and because he was a tentmaker as they were, he stayed and worked with them. 4Every Sabbath he reasoned in the synagogue, trying to persuade Jews and Greeks.

5When Silas and Timothy came from Macedonia, Paul devoted himself exclusively to preaching, testifying to the Jews that Jesus was the Christ.a 6But when

a 5 Or Messiah; also in verse 28

Living Bible

18He also had an encounter with some of the Epicurean and Stoic philosophers. Their reaction, when he told them about Jesus and his resurrection, was, "He's a dreamer," or, "He's pushing some foreign religion." 19But they invited him to the forum at Mars Hill. "Come and tell us more about this new religion," they said, 20"for you are saying some rather startling things and we want to hear more." 21(I should explain that all the Athenians as well as the foreigners in Athens seemed to spend all their time discussing the latest new ideas!) 22So Paul, standing before them at the Mars Hill forum, addressed them as follows:

"Men of Athens, I notice that you are very religious, 23for as I was out walking I saw your many altars, and one of them had this inscription on it—'To the Unknown God.' You have been worshiping him without knowing who he is, and now I wish to tell you about him. 24"He made the world and everything in it, and since he is Lord of heaven and earth, he doesn't live in manmade temples; 25and human beings can't minister to his needs—for he has no needs! He himself gives life and breath to everything, and satisfies every need there is. 26He created all the people of the world from one man, Adam,b and scattered the nations across the face of the earth. He decided beforehand which should rise and fall, and when. He determined their boundaries.

27"His purpose in all of this is that they should seek after God, and perhaps feel their way toward him and find him—though he is not far from any one of us. 28For in him we live and move and are! As one of your own poets says it, 'We are the sons of God.' 29If this is true, we shouldn't think of God as an idol made by men from gold or silver or chipped from stone. 30God tolerated man's past ignorance about these things, but now he commands everyone to put away idols and worship only him. 31For he has set a day for justly judging the world by the man he has appointed, and has pointed him out by bringing him back to life again."

32When they heard Paul speak of the resurrection of a person who had been dead, some laughed, but others said, "We want to hear more about this later." 33That ended Paul's discussion with them, 34but a few joined him and became believers. Among them was Dionysius, a member of the City Council, and a woman named Damaris, and others.

18 THEN PAUL left Athens and went to Corinth. 2, 3There he became acquainted with a Jew named Aquila, born in Pontus, who had recently arrived from Italy with his wife, Priscilla. They had been expelled from Italy as a result of Claudius Caesar's order to deport all Jews from Rome. Paul lived and worked with them, for they were tentmakers just as he was. 4Each Sabbath found Paul at the synagogue, trying to convince the Jews and Greeks alike. 5And after the arrival of Silas and Timothy from Macedonia, Paul spent his full time preaching and testifying to the Jews that Jesus is the Messiah. 6But when the Jews opposed him and

b 17:26 Adam, implied.

New Revised Standard

Epicurean and Stoic philosophers debated with him. Some said, "What does this babbler want to say?" Others said, "He seems to be a proclaimer of foreign divinities." (This was because he was telling the good news about Jesus and the resurrection.) 19So they took him and brought him to the Areopagus and asked him, "May we know what this new teaching is that you are presenting? 20It sounds rather strange to us, so we would like to know what it means." 21Now all the Athenians and the foreigners living there would spend their time in nothing but telling or hearing something new.

22 Then Paul stood in front of the Areopagus and said, "Athenians, I see how extremely religious you are in every way. 23For as I went through the city and looked carefully at the objects of your worship, I found among them an altar with the inscription, 'To an unknown god.' What therefore you worship as unknown, this I proclaim to you. 24The God who made the world and everything in it, he who is Lord of heaven and earth, does not live in shrines made by human hands, 25nor is he served by human hands, as though he needed anything, since he himself gives to all mortals life and breath and all things. 26From one ancestorc he made all nations to inhabit the whole earth, and he allotted the times of their existence and the boundaries of the places where they would live, 27so that they would search for Godd and perhaps grope for him and find him—though indeed he is not far from each one of us. 28For 'In him we live and move and have our being'; as even some of your own poets have said,

'For we too are his offspring.'

29Since we are God's offspring, we ought not to think that the deity is like gold, or silver, or stone, an image formed by the art and imagination of mortals. 30While God has overlooked the times of human ignorance, now he commands all people everywhere to repent, 31because he has fixed a day on which he will have the world judged in righteousness by a man whom he has appointed, and of this he has given assurance to all by raising him from the dead."

32 When they heard of the resurrection of the dead, some scoffed; but others said, "We will hear you again about this." 33At that point Paul left them. 34But some of them joined him and became believers, including Dionysius the Areopagite and a woman named Damaris, and others with them.

Paul in Corinth

18 AFTER THIS Paule left Athens and went to Corinth. 2There he found a Jew named Aquila, a native of Pontus, who had recently come from Italy with his wife Priscilla, because Claudius had ordered all Jews to leave Rome. Paulf went to see them, 3and, because he was of the same trade, he stayed with them, and they worked together—by trade they were tentmakers. 4Every sabbath he would argue in the synagogue and would try to convince Jews and Greeks.

5 When Silas and Timothy arrived from Macedonia, Paul was occupied with proclaiming the word,g testifying to the Jews that the Messiahh was Jesus. 6When they

c Gk From one; other ancient authorities read From one blood   d Other ancient authorities read the Lord   e Gk he   f Gk He   g Gk with the word   h Or the Christ

King James

6And when they opposed themselves, and blasphemed, he shook *his* raiment, and said unto them, Your blood *be* upon your own heads; I *am* clean: from henceforth I will go unto the Gentiles.

7And he departed thence, and entered into a certain *man's* house, named Justus, *one* that worshipped God, whose house joined hard to the synagogue.

8And Crispus, the chief ruler of the synagogue, believed on the Lord with all his house; and many of the Corinthians hearing believed, and were baptized.

9Then spake the Lord to Paul in the night by a vision, Be not afraid, but speak, and hold not thy peace:

10For I am with thee, and no man shall set on thee to hurt thee: for I have much people in this city.

11And he continued *there* a year and six months, teaching the word of God among them.

12¶ And when Gallio was the deputy of Achaia, the Jews made insurrection with one accord against Paul, and brought him to the judgment seat,

13Saying, This *fellow* persuadeth men to worship God contrary to the law.

14And when Paul was now about to open *his* mouth, Gallio said unto the Jews, If it were a matter of wrong or wicked lewdness, O *ye* Jews, reason would that I should bear with you:

15But if it be a question of words and names, and *of* your law, look ye *to it;* for I will be no judge of such *matters.*

16And he drave them from the judgment seat.

17Then all the Greeks took Sosthenes, the chief ruler of the synagogue, and beat *him* before the judgment seat. And Gallio cared for none of those things.

18¶ And Paul *after this* tarried *there* yet a good while, and then took his leave of the brethren, and sailed thence into Syria, and with him Priscilla and Aquila; having shorn *his* head in Cenchrea: for he had a vow.

19And he came to Ephesus, and left them there: but he himself entered into the synagogue, and reasoned with the Jews.

20When they desired *him* to tarry longer time with them, he consented not;

21But bade them farewell, saying, I must by all means keep this feast that cometh in Jerusalem: but I will return again unto you, if God will. And he sailed from Ephesus.

22And when he had landed at Caesarea, and gone up, and saluted the church, he went down to Antioch.

23And after he had spent some time *there,* he departed, and went over *all* the country of Galatia and Phrygia in order, strengthening all the disciples.

24¶ And a certain Jew named Apollos, born at Alexandria, an eloquent man, *and* mighty in the scriptures, came to Ephesus.

25This man was instructed in the way of the Lord; and being fervent in the spirit, he spake and taught diligently the things of the Lord, knowing only the baptism of John.

26And he began to speak boldly in the synagogue: whom when Aquila and Priscilla had heard, they took him unto *them,* and expounded unto him the way of God more perfectly.

27And when he was disposed to pass into Achaia, the brethren wrote, exhorting the disciples to receive him: who, when he was come, helped them much which had believed through grace:

28For he mightily convinced the Jews, *and that* publicly, showing by the scriptures that Jesus was Christ.

New International

the Jews opposed Paul and became abusive, he shook out his clothes in protest and said to them, "Your blood be on your own heads! I am clear of my responsibility. From now on I will go to the Gentiles."

7Then Paul left the synagogue and went next door to the house of Titius Justus, a worshiper of God. 8Crispus, the synagogue ruler, and his entire household believed in the Lord; and many of the Corinthians who heard him believed and were baptized.

9One night the Lord spoke to Paul in a vision: "Do not be afraid; keep on speaking, do not be silent. 10For I am with you, and no one is going to attack and harm you, because I have many people in this city." 11So Paul stayed for a year and a half, teaching them the word of God.

12While Gallio was proconsul of Achaia, the Jews made a united attack on Paul and brought him into court. 13"This man," they charged, "is persuading the people to worship God in ways contrary to the law."

14Just as Paul was about to speak, Gallio said to the Jews, "If you Jews were making a complaint about some misdemeanor or serious crime, it would be reasonable for me to listen to you. 15But since it involves questions about words and names and your own law—settle the matter yourselves. I will not be a judge of such things." 16So he had them ejected from the court. 17Then they all turned on Sosthenes the synagogue ruler and beat him in front of the court. But Gallio showed no concern whatever.

Priscilla, Aquila and Apollos

18Paul stayed on in Corinth for some time. Then he left the brothers and sailed for Syria, accompanied by Priscilla and Aquila. Before he sailed, he had his hair cut off at Cenchrea because of a vow he had taken. 19They arrived at Ephesus, where Paul left Priscilla and Aquila. He himself went into the synagogue and reasoned with the Jews. 20When they asked him to spend more time with them, he declined. 21But as he left, he promised, "I will come back if it is God's will." Then he set sail from Ephesus. 22When he landed at Caesarea, he went up and greeted the church and then went down to Antioch.

23After spending some time in Antioch, Paul set out from there and traveled from place to place throughout the region of Galatia and Phrygia, strengthening all the disciples.

24Meanwhile a Jew named Apollos, a native of Alexandria, came to Ephesus. He was a learned man, with a thorough knowledge of the Scriptures. 25He had been instructed in the way of the Lord, and he spoke with great fervor[a] and taught about Jesus accurately, though he knew only the baptism of John. 26He began to speak boldly in the synagogue. When Priscilla and Aquila heard him, they invited him to their home and explained to him the way of God more adequately.

27When Apollos wanted to go to Achaia, the brothers encouraged him and wrote to the disciples there to welcome him. On arriving, he was a great help to those who by grace had believed. 28For he vigorously refuted the Jews in public debate, proving from the Scriptures that Jesus was the Christ.

---

a 25 Or *with fervor in the Spirit*

Living Bible

blasphemed, hurling abuse at Jesus, Paul shook off the dust from his robe and said, "Your blood be upon your own heads—I am innocent—from now on I will preach to the Gentiles."

7After that he stayed with Titus Justus, a Gentile who worshiped God and lived next door to the synagogue. 8However, Crispus, the leader of the synagogue, and all his household believed in the Lord and were baptized— as were many others in Corinth.

9One night the Lord spoke to Paul in a vision and told him, "Don't be afraid! Speak out! Don't quit! 10For I am with you and no one can harm you. Many people here in this city belong to me." 11So Paul stayed there the next year and a half, teaching the truths of God.

12But when Gallio became governor of Achaia, the Jews rose in concerted action against Paul and brought him before the governor for judgment. 13They accused Paul of "persuading men to worship God in ways that are contrary to Roman law." 14But just as Paul started to make his defense, Gallio turned to his accusers and said, "Listen, you Jews, if this were a case involving some crime, I would be obliged to listen to you, 15but since it is merely a bunch of questions of semantics and personalities and your silly Jewish laws, you take care of it. I'm not interested and I'm not touching it." 16And he drove them out of the courtroom.

17Then the mobb grabbed Sosthenes, the new leader of the synagogue, and beat him outside the courtroom. But Gallio couldn't have cared less.

18Paul stayed in the city several days after that and then said good-bye to the Christians and sailed for the coast of Syria, taking Priscilla and Aquila with him. At Cenchreae, Paul had his head shaved according to Jewish custom, for he had taken a vow.c 19Arriving at the port of Ephesus, he left us aboard ship while he went over to the synagogue for a discussion with the Jews. 20They asked him to stay for a few days, but he felt that he had no time to lose.d

21"I must by all means be at Jerusalem for the holiday,"e he said. But he promised to return to Ephesus later if God permitted; and so he set sail again.

22The next stop was at the port of Caesarea from where he visited the church [at Jerusalemf] and then sailed on to Antioch. 23After spending some time there, he left for Turkey again, going through Galatia and Phrygia visiting all the believers, encouraging them and helping them grow in the Lord.

24As it happened, a Jew named Apollos, a wonderful Bible teacher and preacher, had just arrived in Ephesus from Alexandria in Egypt. 25, 26While he was in Egypt, someone had told him about John the Baptist and what John had said about Jesus, but that is all he knew. He had never heard the rest of the story! So he was preaching boldly and enthusiastically in the synagogue, "The Messiah is coming! Get ready to receive him!" Priscilla and Aquila were there and heard him—and it was a powerful sermon. Afterwards they met with him and explained what had happened to Jesus since the time of John, and all that it meant!g

27Apollos had been thinking about going to Greece, and the believers encouraged him in this. They wrote to their fellow-believers there, telling them to welcome him. And upon his arrival in Greece, he was greatly used of God to strengthen the church, 28for he powerfully refuted all the Jewish arguments in public debate, showing by the Scriptures that Jesus is indeed the Messiah.

New Revised Standard

opposed and reviled him, in protest he shook the dust from his clothesh and said to them, "Your blood be on your own heads! I am innocent. From now on I will go to the Gentiles." 7Then he left the synagoguei and went to the house of a man named Titiusj Justus, a worshiper of God; his house was next door to the synagogue. 8Crispus, the official of the synagogue, became a believer in the Lord, together with all his household; and many of the Corinthians who heard Paul became believers and were baptized. 9One night the Lord said to Paul in a vision, "Do not be afraid, but speak and do not be silent; 10for I am with you, and no one will lay a hand on you to harm you, for there are many in this city who are my people." 11He stayed there a year and six months, teaching the word of God among them.

12 But when Gallio was proconsul of Achaia, the Jews made a united attack on Paul and brought him before the tribunal. 13They said, "This man is persuading people to worship God in ways that are contrary to the law." 14Just as Paul was about to speak, Gallio said to the Jews, "If it were a matter of crime or serious villainy, I would be justified in accepting the complaint of you Jews; 15but since it is a matter of questions about words and names and your own law, see to it yourselves; I do not wish to be a judge of these matters." 16And he dismissed them from the tribunal. 17Then all of themk seized Sosthenes, the official of the synagogue, and beat him in front of the tribunal. But Gallio paid no attention to any of these things.

Paul's Return to Antioch

18 After staying there for a considerable time, Paul said farewell to the believersl and sailed for Syria, accompanied by Priscilla and Aquila. At Cenchreae he had his hair cut, for he was under a vow. 19When they reached Ephesus, he left them there, but first he himself went into the synagogue and had a discussion with the Jews. 20When they asked him to stay longer, he declined; 21but on taking leave of them, he said, "Im will return to you, if God wills." Then he set sail from Ephesus.

22 When he had landed at Caesarea, he went up to Jerusalemn and greeted the church, and then went down to Antioch. 23After spending some time there departed and went from place to place through the region of Galatiao and Phrygia, strengthening all the disciples.

Ministry of Apollos

24 Now there came to Ephesus a Jew named Apollos, a native of Alexandria. He was an eloquent man, well-versed in the scriptures. 25He had been instructed in the Way of the Lord; and he spoke with burning enthusiasm and taught accurately the things concerning Jesus, though he knew only the baptism of John. 26He began to speak boldly in the synagogue; but when Priscilla and Aquila heard him, they took him aside and explained the Way of God to him more accurately. 27And when he wished to cross over to Achaia, the believersl encouraged him and wrote to the disciples to welcome him. On his arrival he greatly helped those who through grace had become believers, 28for he powerfully refuted the Jews in public, showing by the scriptures that the Messiahp is Jesus.

---

b 18:17 *Then the mob,* implied.   c 18:18 *for he had taken a vow.* Probably a vow to offer a sacrifice in Jerusalem in thanksgiving for answered prayer. The head was shaved thirty days before such gifts and sacrifices were given to God at the Temple.   d 18:20 *he felt that he had no time to lose.* Possibly in order to arrive in Jerusalem within the prescribed thirty days.
e 18:21 *holiday,* literally, "feast." This entire sentence is omitted in many of the ancient manuscripts.   f 18:22 *at Jerusalem,* implied.
g 18:26 *explained what had happened to Jesus since the time of John, and all that it meant!* Literally, "explained to him the way of God more accurately."

h Gk *reviled him, he shook out his clothes*   i Gk *left there*   j Other ancient authorities read *Titus*   k Other ancient authorities read *all the Greeks*   l Gk *brothers*   m Other ancient authorities read *I must at all costs keep the approaching festival in Jerusalem, but I*   n Gk *went up*   o Gk *the Galatian region*   p Or *the Christ*

King James

19 AND IT came to pass, that, while Apollos was at Corinth, Paul having passed through the upper coasts came to Ephesus: and finding certain disciples,

2He said unto them, Have ye received the Holy Ghost since ye believed? And they said unto him, We have not so much as heard whether there be any Holy Ghost.

3And he said unto them, Unto what then were ye baptized? And they said, Unto John's baptism.

4Then said Paul, John verily baptized with the baptism of repentance, saying unto the people, that they should believe on him which should come after him, that is, on Christ Jesus.

5When they heard *this,* they were baptized in the name of the Lord Jesus.

6And when Paul had laid *his* hands upon them, the Holy Ghost came on them; and they spake with tongues, and prophesied.

7And all the men were about twelve.

8And he went into the synagogue, and spake boldly for the space of three months, disputing and persuading the things concerning the kingdom of God.

9But when divers were hardened, and believed not, but spake evil of that way before the multitude, he departed from them, and separated the disciples, disputing daily in the school of one Tyrannus.

10And this continued by the space of two years; so that all they which dwelt in Asia heard the word of the Lord Jesus, both Jews and Greeks.

11And God wrought special miracles by the hands of Paul:

12So that from his body were brought unto the sick handkerchiefs or aprons, and the diseases departed from them, and the evil spirits went out of them.

13¶ Then certain of the vagabond Jews, exorcists, took upon them to call over them which had evil spirits the name of the Lord Jesus, saying, We adjure you by Jesus whom Paul preacheth.

14And there were seven sons of *one* Sceva, a Jew, *and* chief of the priests, which did so.

15And the evil spirit answered and said, Jesus I know, and Paul I know; but who are ye?

16And the man in whom the evil spirit was leaped on them, and overcame them, and prevailed against them, so that they fled out of that house naked and wounded.

17And this was known to all the Jews and Greeks also dwelling at Ephesus; and fear fell on them all, and the name of the Lord Jesus was magnified.

18And many that believed came, and confessed, and showed their deeds.

19Many of them also which used curious arts brought their books together, and burned them before all *men:* and they counted the price of them, and found *it* fifty thousand *pieces* of silver.

20So mightily grew the word of God and prevailed.

21¶ After these things were ended, Paul purposed in the spirit, when he had passed through Macedonia and Achaia, to go to Jerusalem, saying, After I have been there, I must also see Rome.

22So he sent into Macedonia two of them that ministered unto him, Timotheus and Erastus; but he himself stayed in Asia for a season.

23And the same time there arose no small stir about that way.

24For a certain *man* named Demetrius, a silversmith, which made silver shrines for Diana, brought no small gain unto the craftsmen;

25Whom he called together with the workmen of like occupation, and said, Sirs, ye know that by this craft we have our wealth.

New International

Paul in Ephesus

19 WHILE APOLLOS was at Corinth, Paul took the road through the interior and arrived at Ephesus. There he found some disciples 2and asked them, "Did you receive the Holy Spirit whena you believed?"

They answered, "No, we have not even heard that there is a Holy Spirit."

3So Paul asked, "Then what baptism did you receive?"

"John's baptism," they replied.

4Paul said, "John's baptism was a baptism of repentance. He told the people to believe in the one coming after him, that is, in Jesus." 5On hearing this, they were baptized intob the name of the Lord Jesus. 6When Paul placed his hands on them, the Holy Spirit came on them, and they spoke in tonguesc and prophesied. 7There were about twelve men in all.

8Paul entered the synagogue and spoke boldly there for three months, arguing persuasively about the kingdom of God. 9But some of them became obstinate; they refused to believe and publicly maligned the Way. So Paul left them. He took the disciples with him and had discussions daily in the lecture hall of Tyrannus. 10This went on for two years, so that all the Jews and Greeks who lived in the province of Asia heard the word of the Lord.

11God did extraordinary miracles through Paul, 12so that even handkerchiefs and aprons that had touched him were taken to the sick, and their illnesses were cured and the evil spirits left them.

13Some Jews who went around driving out evil spirits tried to invoke the name of the Lord Jesus over those who were demon-possessed. They would say, "In the name of Jesus, whom Paul preaches, I command you to come out." 14Seven sons of Sceva, a Jewish chief priest, were doing this. 15One day, the evil spirit answered them, "Jesus I know, and I know about Paul, but who are you?" 16Then the man who had the evil spirit jumped on them and overpowered them all. He gave them such a beating that they ran out of the house naked and bleeding.

17When this became known to the Jews and Greeks living in Ephesus, they were all seized with fear, and the name of the Lord Jesus was held in high honor. 18Many of those who believed now came and openly confessed their evil deeds. 19A number who had practiced sorcery brought their scrolls together and burned them publicly. When they calculated the value of the scrolls, the total came to fifty thousand drachmas.d 20In this way the word of the Lord spread widely and grew in power.

21After all this had happened, Paul decided to go to Jerusalem, passing through Macedonia and Achaia. "After I have been there," he said, "I must visit Rome also." 22He sent two of his helpers, Timothy and Erastus, to Macedonia, while he stayed in the province of Asia a little longer.

The Riot in Ephesus

23About that time there arose a great disturbance about the Way. 24A silversmith named Demetrius, who made silver shrines of Artemis, brought in no little business for the craftsmen. 25He called them together, along with the workmen in related trades, and said: "Men, you know we receive a good income from this business.

a 2 Or *after*   b 5 Or *in*   c 6 Or *other languages*   d 19 A drachma was a silver coin worth about a day's wages.

Living Bible

19 WHILE APOLLOS was in Corinth, Paul traveled through Turkey and arrived in Ephesus, where he found several disciples. 2"Did you receive the Holy Spirit when you believed?" he asked them.

"No," they replied, "we don't know what you mean. What is the Holy Spirit?"

3"Then what beliefs did you acknowledge at your baptism?" he asked.

And they replied, "What John the Baptist taught." 4Then Paul pointed out to them that John's baptism was to demonstrate a desire to turn from sin to God and that those receiving his baptism must then go on to believe in Jesus, the one John said would come later.

5As soon as they heard this, they were baptized in^e the name of the Lord Jesus. 6Then, when Paul laid his hands upon their heads, the Holy Spirit came on them, and they spoke in other languages and prophesied. 7The men involved were about twelve in number.

8Then Paul went to the synagogue and preached boldly each Sabbath day^f for three months, telling what he believed and why,^g and persuading many to believe in Jesus. 9But some rejected his message and publicly spoke against Christ, so he left, refusing to preach to them again. Pulling out the believers, he began a separate meeting at the lecture hall of Tyrannus and preached there daily. 10This went on for the next two years, so that everyone in the Turkish province of Asia minor—both Jews and Greeks—heard the Lord's message.

11And God gave Paul the power to do unusual miracles, 12so that even when his handkerchiefs or parts of his clothing were placed upon sick people, they were healed, and any demons within them came out.

13A team of itinerant Jews who were traveling from town to town casting out demons planned to experiment by using the name of the Lord Jesus. The incantation they decided on was this: "I adjure you by Jesus, whom Paul preaches, to come out!" 14Seven sons of Sceva, a Jewish priest, were doing this. 15But when they tried it on a man possessed by a demon, the demon replied, "I know Jesus and I know Paul, but who are you?" 16And he leaped on two of them and beat them up, so that they fled out of his house naked and badly injured.

17The story of what happened spread quickly all through Ephesus, to Jews and Greeks alike; and a solemn fear descended on the city, and the name of the Lord Jesus was greatly honored. 18, 19Many of the believers who had been practicing black magic confessed their deeds and brought their incantation books and charms and burned them at a public bonfire. (Someone estimated the value of the books at $10,000.^h) 20This indicates how deeply the whole area was stirred by God's message.

21Afterwards, Paul felt impelled by the Holy Spiritⁱ to go across to Greece before returning to Jerusalem. "And after that," he said, "I must go on to Rome!" 22He sent his two assistants, Timothy and Erastus, on ahead to Greece while he stayed awhile longer in Turkey.

23But about that time, a big blowup developed in Ephesus concerning the Christians. 24It began with Demetrius, a silversmith who employed many craftsmen to manufacture silver shrines of the Greek goddess Diana. 25He called a meeting of his men, together with others employed in related trades, and addressed them as follows:

"Gentlemen, this business is our income. 26As you

New Revised Standard

Paul in Ephesus

19 WHILE APOLLOS was in Corinth, Paul passed through the interior regions and came to Ephesus, where he found some disciples. 2He said to them, "Did you receive the Holy Spirit when you became believers?" They replied, "No, we have not even heard that there is a Holy Spirit." 3Then he said, "Into what then were you baptized?" They answered, "Into John's baptism." 4Paul said, "John baptized with the baptism of repentance, telling the people to believe in the one who was to come after him, that is, in Jesus." 5On hearing this, they were baptized in the name of the Lord Jesus. 6When Paul had laid his hands on them, the Holy Spirit came upon them, and they spoke in tongues and prophesied— 7altogether there were about twelve of them.

8 He entered the synagogue and for three months spoke out boldly, and argued persuasively about the kingdom of God. 9When some stubbornly refused to believe and spoke evil of the Way before the congregation, he left them, taking the disciples with him, and argued daily in the lecture hall of Tyrannus.^j 10This continued for two years, so that all the residents of Asia, both Jews and Greeks, heard the word of the Lord.

The Sons of Sceva

11 God did extraordinary miracles through Paul, 12so that when the handkerchiefs or aprons that had touched his skin were brought to the sick, their diseases left them, and the evil spirits came out of them. 13Then some itinerant Jewish exorcists tried to use the name of the Lord Jesus over those who had evil spirits, saying, "I adjure you by the Jesus whom Paul proclaims." 14Seven sons of a Jewish high priest named Sceva were doing this. 15But the evil spirit said to them in reply, "Jesus I know, and Paul I know; but who are you?" 16Then the man with the evil spirit leaped on them, mastered them all, and so overpowered them that they fled out of the house naked and wounded. 17When this became known to all residents of Ephesus, both Jews and Greeks, everyone was awestruck; and the name of the Lord Jesus was praised. 18Also many of those who became believers confessed and disclosed their practices. 19A number of those who practiced magic collected their books and burned them publicly; when the value of these books^k was calculated, it was found to come to fifty thousand silver coins. 20So the word of the Lord grew mightily and prevailed.

The Riot in Ephesus

21 Now after these things had been accomplished, Paul resolved in the Spirit to go through Macedonia and Achaia, and then to go on to Jerusalem. He said, "After I have gone there, I must also see Rome." 22So he sent two of his helpers, Timothy and Erastus, to Macedonia, while he himself stayed for some time longer in Asia.

23 About that time no little disturbance broke out concerning the Way. 24A man named Demetrius, a silversmith who made silver shrines of Artemis, brought no little business to the artisans. 25These he gathered together, with the workers of the same trade, and said, "Men, you know that we get our wealth from this business. 26You also see and hear that not only in Ephesus

---

^e *19:5 baptized in,* or, "baptized into."   ^f *19:8 each Sabbath day,* implied.   ^g *19:8 telling what he believed and why,* literally, "concerning the Kingdom of God."   ^h *19:19 $10,000,* approximately £3,500.   ⁱ *19:21 felt impelled by the Holy Spirit,* literally, "purposed in the spirit."

^j Other ancient authorities read *of a certain Tyrannus, from eleven o'clock in the morning to four in the afternoon*   ^k Gk *them*

King James

26Moreover ye see and hear, that not alone at Ephesus, but almost throughout all Asia, this Paul hath persuaded and turned away much people, saying that they be no gods, which are made with hands:

27So that not only this our craft is in danger to be set at nought; but also that the temple of the great goddess Diana should be despised, and her magnificence should be destroyed, whom all Asia and the world worshippeth.

28And when they heard *these sayings,* they were full of wrath, and cried out, saying, Great *is* Diana of the Ephesians.

29And the whole city was filled with confusion: and having caught Gaius and Aristarchus, men of Macedonia, Paul's companions in travel, they rushed with one accord into the theatre.

30And when Paul would have entered in unto the people, the disciples suffered him not.

31And certain of the chief of Asia, which were his friends, sent unto him, desiring *him* that he would not adventure himself into the theatre.

32Some therefore cried one thing, and some another: for the assembly was confused; and the more part knew not wherefore they were come together.

33And they drew Alexander out of the multitude, the Jews putting him forward. And Alexander beckoned with the hand, and would have made his defence unto the people.

34But when they knew that he was a Jew, all with one voice about the space of two hours cried out, Great *is* Diana of the Ephesians.

35And when the townclerk had appeased the people, he said, *Ye* men of Ephesus, what man is there that knoweth not how that the city of the Ephesians is a worshipper of the great goddess Diana, and of the *image* which fell down from Jupiter?

36Seeing then that these things cannot be spoken against, ye ought to be quiet, and to do nothing rashly.

37For ye have brought hither these men, which are neither robbers of churches, nor yet blasphemers of your goddess.

38Wherefore if Demetrius, and the craftsmen which are with him, have a matter against any man, the law is open, and there are deputies: let them implead one another.

39But if ye inquire any thing concerning other matters, it shall be determined in a lawful assembly.

40For we are in danger to be called in question for this day's uproar, there being no cause whereby we may give an account of this concourse.

41And when he had thus spoken, he dismissed the assembly.

20 AND AFTER the uproar was ceased, Paul called unto *him* the disciples, and embraced *them,* and departed for to go into Macedonia.

2And when he had gone over those parts, and had given them much exhortation, he came into Greece,

3And *there* abode three months. And when the Jews laid wait for him, as he was about to sail into Syria, he purposed to return through Macedonia.

4And there accompanied him into Asia Sopater of Berea; and of the Thessalonians, Aristarchus and Secundus; and Gaius of Derbe, and Timotheus; and of Asia, Tychicus and Trophimus.

5These going before tarried for us at Troas.

6And we sailed away from Philippi after the days of unleavened bread, and came unto them to Troas in five days; where we abode seven days.

New International

26And you see and hear how this fellow Paul has convinced and led astray large numbers of people here in Ephesus and in practically the whole province of Asia. He says that man-made gods are no gods at all. 27There is danger not only that our trade will lose its good name, but also that the temple of the great goddess Artemis will be discredited, and the goddess herself, who is worshiped throughout the province of Asia and the world, will be robbed of her divine majesty."

28When they heard this, they were furious and began shouting: "Great is Artemis of the Ephesians!" 29Soon the whole city was in an uproar. The people seized Gaius and Aristarchus, Paul's traveling companions from Macedonia, and rushed as one man into the theater. 30Paul wanted to appear before the crowd, but the disciples would not let him. 31Even some of the officials of the province, friends of Paul, sent him a message begging him not to venture into the theater.

32The assembly was in confusion: Some were shouting one thing, some another. Most of the people did not even know why they were there. 33The Jews pushed Alexander to the front, and some of the crowd shouted instructions to him. He motioned for silence in order to make a defense before the people. 34But when they realized he was a Jew, they all shouted in unison for about two hours: "Great is Artemis of the Ephesians!"

35The city clerk quieted the crowd and said: "Men of Ephesus, doesn't all the world know that the city of Ephesus is the guardian of the temple of the great Artemis and of her image, which fell from heaven? 36Therefore, since these facts are undeniable, you ought to be quiet and not do anything rash. 37You have brought these men here, though they have neither robbed temples nor blasphemed our goddess. 38If, then, Demetrius and his fellow craftsmen have a grievance against anybody, the courts are open and there are proconsuls. They can press charges. 39If there is anything further you want to bring up, it must be settled in a legal assembly. 40As it is, we are in danger of being charged with rioting because of today's events. In that case we would not be able to account for this commotion, since there is no reason for it." 41After he had said this, he dismissed the assembly.

Through Macedonia and Greece

20 WHEN THE uproar had ended, Paul sent for the disciples and, after encouraging them, said good-by and set out for Macedonia. 2He traveled through that area, speaking many words of encouragement to the people, and finally arrived in Greece, 3where he stayed three months. Because the Jews made a plot against him just as he was about to sail for Syria, he decided to go back through Macedonia. 4He was accompanied by Sopater son of Pyrrhus from Berea, Aristarchus and Secundus from Thessalonica, Gaius from Derbe, Timothy also, and Tychicus and Trophimus from the province of Asia. 5These men went on ahead and waited for us at Troas. 6But we sailed from Philippi after the Feast of Unleavened Bread, and five days later joined the others at Troas, where we stayed seven days.

Living Bible

know so well from what you've seen and heard, this man Paul has persuaded many, many people that handmade gods aren't gods at all. As a result, our sales volume is going down! And this trend is evident not only here in Ephesus, but throughout the entire province! 27Of course, I am not only talking about the business aspects of this situation and our loss of income, but also of the possibility that the temple of the great goddess Diana will lose its influence, and that Diana—this magnificent goddess worshiped not only throughout this part of Turkey but all around the world—will be forgotten!"

28At this their anger boiled and they began shouting, "Great is Diana of the Ephesians!"

29A crowd began to gather and soon the city was filled with confusion. Everyone rushed to the amphitheater, dragging along Gaius and Aristarchus, Paul's traveling companions, for trial. 30Paul wanted to go in, but the disciples wouldn't let him. 31Some of the Roman officers of the province, friends of Paul, also sent a message to him, begging him not to risk his life by entering.

32Inside, the people were all shouting, some one thing and some another—everything was in confusion. In fact, most of them didn't even know why they were there.

33Alexander was spotted among the crowd by some of the Jews and dragged forward. He motioned for silence and tried to speak. 34But when the crowd realized he was a Jew, they started shouting again and kept it up for two hours: "Great is Diana of the Ephesians! Great is Diana of the Ephesians!"

35At last the mayor was able to quiet them down enough to speak. "Men of Ephesus," he said, "everyone knows that Ephesus is the centera of the religion of the great Diana, whose image fell down to us from heaven. 36Since this is an indisputable fact, you shouldn't be disturbed no matter what is said, and should do nothing rash. 37Yet you have brought these men here who have stolen nothing from her temple and have not defamed her. 38If Demetrius and the craftsmen have a case against them, the courts are currently in session and the judges can take the case at once. Let them go through legal channels. 39And if there are complaints about other matters, they can be settled at the regular City Council meetings; 40for we are in danger of being called to account by the Roman government for today's riot, since there is no cause for it. And if Rome demands an explanation, I won't know what to say."

41Then he dismissed them, and they dispersed.

20 WHEN IT was all over, Paul sent for the disciples, preached a farewell message to them, said good-bye and left for Greece, 2preaching to the believers along the way, in all the cities he passed through. 3He was in Greece three months and was preparing to sail for Syria when he discovered a plot by the Jews against his life, so he decided to go north to Macedonia first.

4Several men were traveling with him, going as far as Turkey;b they were Sopater of Beroea, the son of Pyrrhus; Aristarchus and Secundus, from Thessalonica; Gaius, from Derbe; and Timothy; and Tychicus and Trophimus, who were returning to their homes in Turkey, 5and had gone on ahead and were waiting for us at Troas. 6As soon as the Passover ceremonies ended, we boarded ship at Philippi in northern Greece and five days later arrived in Troas, Turkey, where we stayed a week.

New Revised Standard

but in almost the whole of Asia this Paul has persuaded and drawn away a considerable number of people by saying that gods made with hands are not gods. 27And there is danger not only that this trade of ours may come into disrepute but also that the temple of the great goddess Artemis will be scorned, and she will be deprived of her majesty that brought all Asia and the world to worship her."

28 When they heard this, they were enraged and shouted, "Great is Artemis of the Ephesians!" 29The city was filled with the confusion; and peoplec rushed together to the theater, dragging with them Gaius and Aristarchus, Macedonians who were Paul's travel companions. 30Paul wished to go into the crowd, but the disciples would not let him; 31even some officials of the province of Asia,d who were friendly to him, sent him a message urging him not to venture into the theater. 32Meanwhile, some were shouting one thing, some another; for the assembly was in confusion, and most of them did not know why they had come together. 33Some of the crowd gave instructions to Alexander, whom the Jews had pushed forward. And Alexander motioned for silence and tried to make a defense before the people. 34But when they recognized that he was a Jew, for about two hours all of them shouted in unison, "Great is Artemis of the Ephesians!" 35But when the town clerk had quieted the crowd, he said, "Citizens of Ephesus, who is there that does not know that the city of the Ephesians is the temple keeper of the great Artemis and of the statue that fell from heaven?e 36Since these things cannot be denied, you ought to be quiet and do nothing rash. 37You have brought these men here who are neither temple robbers nor blasphemers of ourf goddess. 38If therefore Demetrius and the artisans with him have a complaint against anyone, the courts are open, and there are proconsuls; let them bring charges there against one another. 39If there is anything furtherg you want to know, it must be settled in the regular assembly. 40For we are in danger of being charged with rioting today, since there is no cause that we can give to justify this commotion." 41When he had said this, he dismissed the assembly.

Paul Goes to Macedonia and Greece

20 AFTER THE uproar had ceased, Paul sent for the disciples; and after encouraging them and saying farewell, he left for Macedonia. 2When he had gone through those regions and had given the believersh much encouragement, he came to Greece, 3where he stayed for three months. He was about to set sail for Syria when a plot was made against him by the Jews, and so he decided to return through Macedonia. 4He was accompanied by Sopater son of Pyrrhus from Beroea, by Aristarchus and Secundus from Thessalonica, by Gaius from Derbe, and by Timothy, as well as by Tychicus and Trophimus from Asia. 5They went ahead and were waiting for us in Troas; 6but we sailed from Philippi after the days of Unleavened Bread, and in five days we joined them in Troas, where we stayed for seven days.

---

a 19:35 is the center, literally, "is the temple-keeper." b 20:4 Turkey, literally, "Asia."

c Gk they   d Gk some of the Asiarchs   e Meaning of Gk uncertain   f Other ancient authorities read your   g Other ancient authorities read about other matters   h Gk given them

King James

7And upon the first *day* of the week, when the disciples came together to break bread, Paul preached unto them, ready to depart on the morrow; and continued his speech until midnight.

8And there were many lights in the upper chamber, where they were gathered together.

9And there sat in a window a certain young man named Eutychus, being fallen into a deep sleep: and as Paul was long preaching, he sunk down with sleep, and fell down from the third loft, and was taken up dead.

10And Paul went down, and fell on him, and embracing *him* said, Trouble not yourselves; for his life is in him.

11When he therefore was come up again, and had broken bread, and eaten, and talked a long while, even till break of day, so he departed.

12And they brought the young man alive, and were not a little comforted.

13¶ And we went before to ship, and sailed unto Assos, there intending to take in Paul: for so had he appointed, minding himself to go afoot.

14And when he met with us at Assos, we took him in, and came to Mitylene.

15And we sailed thence, and came the next *day* over against Chios; and the next *day* we arrived at Samos, and tarried at Trogyllium; and the next *day* we came to Miletus.

16For Paul had determined to sail by Ephesus, because he would not spend the time in Asia: for he hasted, if it were possible for him, to be at Jerusalem the day of Pentecost.

17¶ And from Miletus he sent to Ephesus, and called the elders of the church.

18And when they were come to him, he said unto them, Ye know, from the first day that I came into Asia, after what manner I have been with you at all seasons,

19Serving the Lord with all humility of mind, and with many tears, and temptations, which befell me by the lying in wait of the Jews:

20*And* how I kept back nothing that was profitable *unto you*, but have shown you, and have taught you publicly, and from house to house,

21Testifying both to the Jews, and also to the Greeks, repentance toward God, and faith toward our Lord Jesus Christ.

22And now, behold, I go bound in the spirit unto Jerusalem, not knowing the things that shall befall me there:

23Save that the Holy Ghost witnesseth in every city, saying that bonds and afflictions abide me.

24But none of these things move me, neither count I my life dear unto myself, so that I might finish my course with joy, and the ministry, which I have received of the Lord Jesus, to testify the gospel of the grace of God.

25And now, behold, I know that ye all, among whom I have gone preaching the kingdom of God, shall see my face no more.

26Wherefore I take you to record this day, that I *am* pure from the blood of all *men*.

27For I have not shunned to declare unto you all the counsel of God.

28¶ Take heed therefore unto yourselves, and to all the flock, over the which the Holy Ghost hath made you overseers, to feed the church of God, which he hath purchased with his own blood.

29For I know this, that after my departing shall grievous wolves enter in among you, not sparing the flock.

30Also of your own selves shall men arise, speaking perverse things, to draw away disciples after them.

31Therefore watch, and remember, that by the space of three years I ceased not to warn every one night and day with tears.

New International

Eutychus Raised From the Dead at Troas

7On the first day of the week we came together to break bread. Paul spoke to the people and, because he intended to leave the next day, kept on talking until midnight. 8There were many lamps in the upstairs room where we were meeting. 9Seated in a window was a young man named Eutychus, who was sinking into a deep sleep as Paul talked on and on. When he was sound asleep, he fell to the ground from the third story and was picked up dead. 10Paul went down, threw himself on the young man and put his arms around him. "Don't be alarmed," he said. "He's alive!" 11Then he went upstairs again and broke bread and ate. After talking until daylight, he left. 12The people took the young man home alive and were greatly comforted.

Paul's Farewell to the Ephesian Elders

13We went on ahead to the ship and sailed for Assos, where we were going to take Paul aboard. He had made this arrangement because he was going there on foot. 14When he met us at Assos, we took him aboard and went on to Mitylene. 15The next day we set sail from there and arrived off Kios. The day after that we crossed over to Samos, and on the following day arrived at Miletus. 16Paul had decided to sail past Ephesus to avoid spending time in the province of Asia, for he was in a hurry to reach Jerusalem, if possible, by the day of Pentecost.

17From Miletus, Paul sent to Ephesus for the elders of the church. 18When they arrived, he said to them: "You know how I lived the whole time I was with you, from the first day I came into the province of Asia. 19I served the Lord with great humility and with tears, although I was severely tested by the plots of the Jews. 20You know that I have not hesitated to preach anything that would be helpful to you but have taught you publicly and from house to house. 21I have declared to both Jews and Greeks that they must turn to God in repentance and have faith in our Lord Jesus.

22"And now, compelled by the Spirit, I am going to Jerusalem, not knowing what will happen to me there. 23I only know that in every city the Holy Spirit warns me that prison and hardships are facing me. 24However, I consider my life worth nothing to me, if only I may finish the race and complete the task the Lord Jesus has given me—the task of testifying to the gospel of God's grace.

25"Now I know that none of you among whom I have gone about preaching the kingdom will ever see me again. 26Therefore, I declare to you today that I am innocent of the blood of all men. 27For I have not hesitated to proclaim to you the whole will of God. 28Keep watch over yourselves and all the flock of which the Holy Spirit has made you overseers.[a] Be shepherds of the church of God,[b] which he bought with his own blood. 29I know that after I leave, savage wolves will come in among you and will not spare the flock. 30Even from your own number men will arise and distort the truth in order to draw away disciples after them. 31So be on your guard! Remember that for three years I never stopped warning each of you night and day with tears.

---

[a] 28 Traditionally *bishops*   [b] 28 Many manuscripts *of the Lord*

Living Bible

7On Sunday,c we gathered for a communion service, with Paul preaching. And since he was leaving the next day, he talked until midnight! 8The upstairs room where we met was lighted with many flickering lamps; 9and as Paul spoke on and on, a young man named Eutychus, sitting on the window sill, went fast asleep and fell three stories to his death below. 10, 11, 12Paul went down and took him into his arms. "Don't worry," he said, "he's all right!" And he was! What a wave of awesome joy swept through the crowd! They all went back upstairs and ate the Lord's Supper together; then Paul preached another long sermon—so it was dawn when he finally left them!

13Paul was going by land to Assos, and we went on ahead by ship. 14He joined us there and we sailed together to Mitylene; 15the next day we passed Chios; the next, we touched at Samos; and a day later we arrived at Miletus.

16Paul had decided against stopping at Ephesus this time, as he was hurrying to get to Jerusalem, if possible, for the celebration of Pentecost.

17But when we landed at Miletus, he sent a message to the elders of the church at Ephesus asking them to come down to the boat to meet him.

18When they arrived he told them, "You men know that from the day I set foot in Turkey until now 19I have done the Lord's work humbly—yes, and with tears—and have faced grave danger from the plots of the Jews against my life. 20Yet I never shrank from telling you the truth, either publicly or in your homes. 21I have had one message for Jews and Gentiles alike—the necessity of turning from sin to God through faith in our Lord Jesus Christ.

22"And now I am going to Jerusalem, drawn there irresistibly by the Holy Spirit,d not knowing what awaits me, 23except that the Holy Spirit has told me in city after city that jail and suffering lie ahead. 24But life is worth nothing unless I use it for doing the work assigned me by the Lord Jesus—the work of telling others the Good News about God's mighty kindness and love.

25"And now I know that none of you among whom I went about teaching the Kingdom will ever see me again. 26Let me say plainly that no man's blood can be laid at my door, 27for I didn't shrink from declaring all God's message to you.

28"And now beware! Be sure that you feed and shepherd God's flock—his church, purchased with his blood—for the Holy Spirit is holding you responsible as overseers. 29I know full well that after I leave you, false teachers, like vicious wolves, will appear among you, not sparing the flock. 30Some of you yourselves will distort the truth in order to draw a following. 31Watch out! Remember the three years I was with you—my constant watchcare over you night and day and my many tears for you.

New Revised Standard

Paul's Farewell Visit to Troas

7 On the first day of the week, when we met to break bread, Paul was holding a discussion with them; since he intended to leave the next day, he continued speaking until midnight. 8There were many lamps in the room upstairs where we were meeting. 9A young man named Eutychus, who was sitting in the window, began to sink off into a deep sleep while Paul talked still longer. Overcome by sleep, he fell to the ground three floors below and was picked up dead. 10But Paul went down, and bending over him took him in his arms, and said, "Do not be alarmed, for his life is in him." 11Then Paul went upstairs, and after he had broken bread and eaten, he continued to converse with them until dawn; then he left. 12Meanwhile they had taken the boy away alive and were not a little comforted.

The Voyage from Troas to Miletus

13 We went ahead to the ship and set sail for Assos, intending to take Paul on board there; for he had made this arrangement, intending to go by land himself. 14When he met us in Assos, we took him on board and went to Mitylene. 15We sailed from there, and on the following day we arrived opposite Chios. The next day we touched at Samos, ande the day after that we came to Miletus. 16For Paul had decided to sail past Ephesus, so that he might not have to spend time in Asia; he was eager to be in Jerusalem, if possible, on the day of Pentecost.

Paul Speaks to the Ephesian Elders

17 From Miletus he sent a message to Ephesus, asking the elders of the church to meet him. 18When they came to him, he said to them:

"You yourselves know how I lived among you the entire time from the first day that I set foot in Asia, 19serving the Lord with all humility and with tears, enduring the trials that came to me through the plots of the Jews. 20I did not shrink from doing anything helpful, proclaiming the message to you and teaching you publicly and from house to house, 21as I testified to both Jews and Greeks about repentance toward God and faith toward our Lord Jesus. 22And now, as a captive to the Spirit,f I am on my way to Jerusalem, not knowing what will happen to me there, 23except that the Holy Spirit testifies to me in every city that imprisonment and persecutions are waiting for me. 24But I do not count my life of any value to myself, if only I may finish my course and the ministry that I received from the Lord Jesus, to testify to the good news of God's grace.

25 "And now I know that none of you, among whom I have gone about proclaiming the kingdom, will ever see my face again. 26Therefore I declare to you this day that I am not responsible for the blood of any of you, 27for I did not shrink from declaring to you the whole purpose of God. 28Keep watch over yourselves and over all the flock, of which the Holy Spirit has made you overseers, to shepherd the church of Godg that he obtained with the blood of his own Son.h 29I know that after I have gone, savage wolves will come in among you, not sparing the flock. 30Some even from your own group will come distorting the truth in order to entice the disciples to follow them. 31Therefore be alert, remembering that for three years I did not cease night or day to warn everyone with tears. 32And now I commend you

---

c 20:7 On Sunday, or, "on Saturday night." Literally, "the first day of the week," by Jewish reckoning, from sundown to sundown.   d 20:22 by the Holy Spirit, or, "by an inner compulsion."

e Other ancient authorities add after remaining at Trogyllium   f Or And now, bound in the spirit   g Other ancient authorities read of the Lord   h Or with his own blood; Gk with the blood of his Own

King James

32And now, brethren, I commend you to God, and to the word of his grace, which is able to build you up, and to give you an inheritance among all them which are sanctified.

33I have coveted no man's silver, or gold, or apparel.

34Yea, ye yourselves know, that these hands have ministered unto my necessities, and to them that were with me.

35I have shown you all things, how that so labouring ye ought to support the weak, and to remember the words of the Lord Jesus, how he said, It is more blessed to give than to receive.

36¶ And when he had thus spoken, he kneeled down, and prayed with them all.

37And they all wept sore, and fell on Paul's neck, and kissed him,

38Sorrowing most of all for the words which he spake, that they should see his face no more. And they accompanied him unto the ship.

21 AND IT came to pass, that after we were gotten from them, and had launched, we came with a straight course unto Coos, and the *day* following unto Rhodes, and from thence unto Patara:

2And finding a ship sailing over unto Phenicia, we went aboard, and set forth.

3Now when we had discovered Cyprus, we left it on the left hand, and sailed into Syria, and landed at Tyre: for there the ship was to unlade her burden.

4And finding disciples, we tarried there seven days: who said to Paul through the Spirit, that he should not go up to Jerusalem.

5And when we had accomplished those days, we departed and went our way; and they all brought us on our way, with wives and children, till *we were* out of the city: and we kneeled down on the shore, and prayed.

6And when we had taken our leave one of another, we took ship; and they returned home again.

7And when we had finished *our* course from Tyre, we came to Ptolemais, and saluted the brethren, and abode with them one day.

8And the next *day* we that were of Paul's company departed, and came unto Caesarea: and we entered into the house of Philip the evangelist, which was *one* of the seven; and abode with him.

9And the same man had four daughters, virgins, which did prophesy.

10And as we tarried *there* many days, there came down from Judaea a certain prophet, named Agabus.

11And when he was come unto us, he took Paul's girdle, and bound his own hands and feet, and said, Thus saith the Holy Ghost, So shall the Jews at Jerusalem bind the man that owneth this girdle, and shall deliver *him* into the hands of the Gentiles.

12And when we heard these things, both we, and they of that place, besought him not to go up to Jerusalem.

13Then Paul answered, What mean ye to weep and to break mine heart? for I am ready not to be bound only, but also to die at Jerusalem for the name of the Lord Jesus.

14And when he would not be persuaded, we ceased, saying, The will of the Lord be done.

15And after those days we took up our carriages, and went up to Jerusalem.

16There went with us also *certain* of the disciples of Caesarea, and brought with them one Mnason of Cyprus, an old disciple, with whom we should lodge.

17And when we were come to Jerusalem, the brethren received us gladly.

18And the *day* following Paul went in with us unto James; and all the elders were present.

New International

32"Now I commit you to God and to the word of his grace, which can build you up and give you an inheritance among all those who are sanctified. 33I have not coveted anyone's silver or gold or clothing. 34You yourselves know that these hands of mine have supplied my own needs and the needs of my companions. 35In everything I did, I showed you that by this kind of hard work we must help the weak, remembering the words the Lord Jesus himself said: 'It is more blessed to give than to receive.'"

36When he had said this, he knelt down with all of them and prayed. 37They all wept as they embraced him and kissed him. 38What grieved them most was his statement that they would never see his face again. Then they accompanied him to the ship.

On to Jerusalem

21 AFTER WE had torn ourselves away from them, we put out to sea and sailed straight to Cos. The next day we went to Rhodes and from there to Patara. 2We found a ship crossing over to Phoenicia, went on board and set sail. 3After sighting Cyprus and passing to the south of it, we sailed on to Syria. We landed at Tyre, where our ship was to unload its cargo. 4Finding the disciples there, we stayed with them seven days. Through the Spirit they urged Paul not to go on to Jerusalem. 5But when our time was up, we left and continued on our way. All the disciples and their wives and children accompanied us out of the city, and there on the beach we knelt to pray. 6After saying good-by to each other, we went aboard the ship, and they returned home.

7We continued our voyage from Tyre and landed at Ptolemais, where we greeted the brothers and stayed with them for a day. 8Leaving the next day, we reached Caesarea and stayed at the house of Philip the evangelist, one of the Seven. 9He had four unmarried daughters who prophesied.

10After we had been there a number of days, a prophet named Agabus came down from Judea. 11Coming over to us, he took Paul's belt, tied his own hands and feet with it and said, "The Holy Spirit says, 'In this way the Jews of Jerusalem will bind the owner of this belt and will hand him over to the Gentiles.'"

12When we heard this, we and the people there pleaded with Paul not to go up to Jerusalem. 13Then Paul answered, "Why are you weeping and breaking my heart? I am ready not only to be bound, but also to die in Jerusalem for the name of the Lord Jesus." 14When he would not be dissuaded, we gave up and said, "The Lord's will be done."

15After this, we got ready and went up to Jerusalem. 16Some of the disciples from Caesarea accompanied us and brought us to the home of Mnason, where we were to stay. He was a man from Cyprus and one of the early disciples.

Paul's Arrival at Jerusalem

17When we arrived at Jerusalem, the brothers received us warmly. 18The next day Paul and the rest of us went to see James, and all the elders were present.

Living Bible

32"And now I entrust you to God and his care and to his wonderful words which are able to build your faith and give you all the inheritance of those who are set apart for himself.

33"I have never been hungry for money or fine clothing— 34you know that these hands of mine worked to pay my own way and even to supply the needs of those who were with me. 35And I was a constant example to you in helping the poor; for I remembered the words of the Lord Jesus, 'It is more blessed to give than to receive.'"

36When he had finished speaking, he knelt and prayed with them, 37and they wept aloud as they embraced him in farewell, 38sorrowing most of all because he said that he would never see them again. Then they accompanied him down to the ship.

21 AFTER PARTING from the Ephesian elders, we sailed straight to Cos. The next day we reached Rhodes and then went to Patara. 2There we boarded a ship sailing for the Syrian province of Phoenicia. 3We sighted the island of Cyprus, passed it on our left and landed at the harbor of Tyre, in Syria, where the ship unloaded. 4We went ashore, found the local believers and stayed with them a week. These disciples warned Paul—the Holy Spirit prophesying through them—not to go on to Jerusalem. 5At the end of the week when we returned to the ship, the entire congregation including wives and children walked down to the beach with us where we prayed and said our farewells. 6Then we went aboard and they returned home.

7The next stop after leaving Tyre was Ptolemais where we greeted the believers, but stayed only one day. 8Then we went on to Caesarea and stayed at the home of Philip the Evangelist, one of the first seven deacons.a 9He had four unmarriedb daughters who had the gift of prophecy.

10During our stay of several days, a man named Agabus, who also had the gift of prophecy, arrived from Judea 11and visited us. He took Paul's belt, bound his own feet and hands with it and said, "The Holy Spirit declares, 'So shall the owner of this belt be bound by the Jews in Jerusalem and turned over to the Romans.'" 12Hearing this, all of us—the local believers and his traveling companions—begged Paul not to go on to Jerusalem.

13But he said, "Why all this weeping? You are breaking my heart! For I am ready not only to be jailed at Jerusalem, but also to die for the sake of the Lord Jesus." 14When it was clear that he wouldn't be dissuaded, we gave up and said, "The will of the Lord be done."

15So shortly afterwards, we packed our things and left for Jerusalem. 16Some disciples from Caesarea accompanied us, and on arrival we were guests at the home of Mnason, originally from Cyprus, one of the early believers; 17and all the believers at Jerusalem welcomed us cordially.

18The second day Paul took us with him to meet with James and the elders of the Jerusalem church. 19After

New Revised Standard

to God and to the message of his grace, a message that is able to build you up and to give you the inheritance among all who are sanctified. 33I coveted no one's silver or gold or clothing. 34You know for yourselves that I worked with my own hands to support myself and my companions. 35In all this I have given you an example that by such work we must support the weak, remembering the words of the Lord Jesus, for he himself said, 'It is more blessed to give than to receive.'"

36 When he had finished speaking, he knelt down with them all and prayed. 37There was much weeping among them all; they embraced Paul and kissed him, 38grieving especially because of what he had said, that they would not see him again. Then they brought him to the ship.

Paul's Journey to Jerusalem

21 WHEN WE had parted from them and set sail, we came by a straight course to Cos, and the next day to Rhodes, and from there to Patara.c 2When we found a ship bound for Phoenicia, we went on board and set sail. 3We came in sight of Cyprus; and leaving it on our left, we sailed to Syria and landed at Tyre, because the ship was to unload its cargo there. 4We looked up the disciples and stayed there for seven days. Through the Spirit they told Paul not to go on to Jerusalem. 5When our days there were ended, we left and proceeded on our journey; and all of them, with wives and children, escorted us outside the city. There we knelt down on the beach and prayed 6and said farewell to one another. Then we went on board the ship, and they returned home.

7 When we had finishedd the voyage from Tyre, we arrived at Ptolemais; and we greeted the believerse and stayed with them for one day. 8The next day we left and came to Caesarea; and we went into the house of Philip the evangelist, one of the seven, and stayed with him. 9He had four unmarried daughtersf who had the gift of prophecy. 10While we were staying there for several days, a prophet named Agabus came down from Judea. 11He came to us and took Paul's belt, bound his own feet and hands with it, and said, "Thus says the Holy Spirit, 'This is the way the Jews in Jerusalem will bind the man who owns this belt and will hand him over to the Gentiles.'" 12When we heard this, we and the people there urged him not to go up to Jerusalem. 13Then Paul answered, "What are you doing, weeping and breaking my heart? For I am ready not only to be bound but even to die in Jerusalem for the name of the Lord Jesus." 14Since he would not be persuaded, we remained silent except to say, "The Lord's will be done."

15 After these days we got ready and started to go up to Jerusalem. 16Some of the disciples from Caesarea also came along and brought us to the house of Mnason of Cyprus, an early disciple, with whom we were to stay.

Paul Visits James at Jerusalem

17 When we arrived in Jerusalem, the brothers welcomed us warmly. 18The next day Paul went with us to visit James; and all the elders were present. 19After

---

a 21:8 one of the first seven deacons. See 6:5; 8:1-13. b 21:9 unmarried, literally, "virgins."

c Other ancient authorities add and Myra d Or continued e Gk brothers f Gk four daughters, virgins,

King James

19And when he had saluted them, he declared particularly what things God had wrought among the Gentiles by his ministry.

20And when they heard it, they glorified the Lord, and said unto him, Thou seest, brother, how many thousands of Jews there are which believe; and they are all zealous of the law:

21And they are informed of thee, that thou teachest all the Jews which are among the Gentiles to forsake Moses, saying that they ought not to circumcise their children, neither to walk after the customs.

22What is it therefore? the multitude must needs come together: for they will hear that thou art come.

23Do therefore this that we say to thee: We have four men which have a vow on them;

24Them take, and purify thyself with them, and be at charges with them, that they may shave their heads: and all may know that those things, whereof they were informed concerning thee, are nothing; but that thou thyself also walkest orderly, and keepest the law.

25As touching the Gentiles which believe, we have written and concluded that they observe no such thing, save only that they keep themselves from things offered to idols, and from blood, and from strangled, and from fornication.

26Then Paul took the men, and the next day purifying himself with them entered into the temple, to signify the accomplishment of the days of purification, until that an offering should be offered for every one of them.

27And when the seven days were almost ended, the Jews which were of Asia, when they saw him in the temple, stirred up all the people, and laid hands on him,

28Crying out, Men of Israel, help: This is the man, that teacheth all men every where against the people, and the law, and this place: and further brought Greeks also into the temple, and hath polluted this holy place.

29(For they had seen before with him in the city Trophimus an Ephesian, whom they supposed that Paul had brought into the temple.)

30And all the city was moved, and the people ran together: and they took Paul, and drew him out of the temple: and forthwith the doors were shut.

31And as they went about to kill him, tidings came unto the chief captain of the band, that all Jerusalem was in an uproar.

32Who immediately took soldiers and centurions, and ran down unto them: and when they saw the chief captain and the soldiers, they left beating of Paul.

33Then the chief captain came near, and took him, and commanded him to be bound with two chains; and demanded who he was, and what he had done.

34And some cried one thing, some another, among the multitude: and when he could not know the certainty for the tumult, he commanded him to be carried into the castle.

35And when he came upon the stairs, so it was, that he was borne of the soldiers for the violence of the people.

36For the multitude of the people followed after, crying, Away with him.

37And as Paul was to be led into the castle, he said unto the chief captain, May I speak unto thee? Who said, Canst thou speak Greek?

38Art not thou that Egyptian, which before these days madest an uproar, and leddest out into the wilderness four thousand men that were murderers?

39But Paul said, I am a man which am a Jew of Tarsus, a city in Cilicia, a citizen of no mean city: and, I beseech thee, suffer me to speak unto the people.

40And when he had given him licence, Paul stood on the stairs, and beckoned with the hand unto the people. And when there was made a great silence, he spake unto them in the Hebrew tongue, saying,

New International

19Paul greeted them and reported in detail what God had done among the Gentiles through his ministry.

20When they heard this, they praised God. Then they said to Paul: "You see, brother, how many thousands of Jews have believed, and all of them are zealous for the law. 21They have been informed that you teach all the Jews who live among the Gentiles to turn away from Moses, telling them not to circumcise their children or live according to our customs. 22What shall we do? They will certainly hear that you have come, 23so do what we tell you. There are four men with us who have made a vow. 24Take these men, join in their purification rites and pay their expenses, so that they can have their heads shaved. Then everybody will know there is no truth in these reports about you, but that you yourself are living in obedience to the law. 25As for the Gentile believers, we have written to them our decision that they should abstain from food sacrificed to idols, from blood, from the meat of strangled animals and from sexual immorality."

26The next day Paul took the men and purified himself along with them. Then he went to the temple to give notice of the date when the days of purification would end and the offering would be made for each of them.

Paul Arrested

27When the seven days were nearly over, some Jews from the province of Asia saw Paul at the temple. They stirred up the whole crowd and seized him, 28shouting, "Men of Israel, help us! This is the man who teaches all men everywhere against our people and our law and this place. And besides, he has brought Greeks into the temple area and defiled this holy place." 29(They had previously seen Trophimus the Ephesian in the city with Paul and assumed that Paul had brought him into the temple area.)

30The whole city was aroused, and the people came running from all directions. Seizing Paul, they dragged him from the temple, and immediately the gates were shut. 31While they were trying to kill him, news reached the commander of the Roman troops that the whole city of Jerusalem was in an uproar. 32He at once took some officers and soldiers and ran down to the crowd. When the rioters saw the commander and his soldiers, they stopped beating Paul.

33The commander came up and arrested him and ordered him to be bound with two chains. Then he asked who he was and what he had done. 34Some in the crowd shouted one thing and some another, and since the commander could not get at the truth because of the uproar, he ordered that Paul be taken into the barracks. 35When Paul reached the steps, the violence of the mob was so great he had to be carried by the soldiers. 36The crowd that followed kept shouting, "Away with him!"

Paul Speaks to the Crowd

37As the soldiers were about to take Paul into the barracks, he asked the commander, "May I say something to you?"

"Do you speak Greek?" he replied. 38"Aren't you the Egyptian who started a revolt and led four thousand terrorists out into the desert some time ago?"

39Paul answered, "I am a Jew, from Tarsus in Cilicia, a citizen of no ordinary city. Please let me speak to the people."

40Having received the commander's permission, Paul stood on the steps and motioned to the crowd. When they were all silent, he said to them in Aramaicª:

ª *40* Or possibly *Hebrew*; also in 22:2

Living Bible

greetings were exchanged, Paul recounted the many things God had accomplished among the Gentiles through his work.

20They praised God but then said, "You know, dear brother, how many thousands of Jews have also believed, and they are all very insistent that Jewish believers must continue to follow the Jewish traditions and customs.b 21Our Jewish Christians here at Jerusalem have been told that you are against the laws of Moses, against our Jewish customs, and that you forbid the circumcision of their children. 22Now what can be done? For they will certainly hear that you have come.

23"We suggest this: We have four men here who are preparing to shave their heads and take some vows. 24Go with them to the Temple and have your head shaved too—and pay for theirs to be shaved.

"Then everyone will know that you approve of this custom for the Hebrew Christians and that you yourself obey the Jewish laws and are in line with our thinking in these matters.

25"As for the Gentile Christians, we aren't asking them to follow these Jewish customs at all—except for the ones we wrote to them about: not to eat food offered to idols, not to eat unbled meat from strangled animals, and not to commit fornication."

26, 27So Paul agreed to their request and the next day went with the men to the Temple for the ceremony, thus publicizing his vow to offer a sacrifice seven daysc later with the others.

The seven days were almost ended when some Jews from Turkey saw him in the Temple and roused a mob against him. They grabbed him, 28yelling, "Men of Israel! Help! Help! This is the man who preaches against our people and tells everybody to disobey the Jewish laws. He even talks against the Temple and defiles it by bringing Gentiles in!" 29(For down in the city earlier that day, they had seen him with Trophimus, a Gentiled from Ephesus in Turkey, and assumed that Paul had taken him into the Temple.)

30The whole population of the city was electrified by these accusations and a great riot followed. Paul was dragged out of the Temple, and immediately the gates were closed behind him. 31As they were killing him, word reached the commander of the Roman garrison that all Jerusalem was in an uproar. 32He quickly ordered out his soldiers and officers and ran down among the crowd. When the mob saw the troops coming, they quit beating Paul. 33The commander arrested him and ordered him bound with double chains. Then he asked the crowd who he was and what he had done. 34Some shouted one thing and some another. When he couldn't find out anything in all the uproar and confusion, he ordered Paul to be taken to the armory.e 35As they reached the stairs, the mob grew so violent that the soldiers lifted Paul to their shoulders to protect him, 36and the crowd surged behind shouting, "Away with him, away with him!"

37, 38As Paul was about to be taken inside, he said to the commander, "May I have a word with you?"

"Do you know Greek?" the commander asked, surprised. "Aren't you that Egyptian who led a rebellion a few years agof and took 4,000 members of the Assassins with him into the desert?"

39"No," Paul replied, "I am a Jew from Tarsus in Cilicia which is no small town. I request permission to talk to these people."

40The commander agreed, so Paul stood on the stairs and motioned to the people to be quiet; soon a deep silence enveloped the crowd, and he addressed them in Hebrew as follows:

b 21:20 they are all very insistent that Jewish believers must continue to follow the Jewish traditions and customs, literally, "they are all zealous for the law."
c 21:26, 27 seven days, literally, "the days of purification."   d 21:29 a Gentile, implied.   e 21:34 armory, literally, "castle," or "fort."
f 21:37, 38 a few years ago, literally, "before these days."

New Revised Standard

greeting them, he related one by one the things that God had done among the Gentiles through his ministry. 20When they heard it, they praised God. Then they said to him, "You see, brother, how many thousands of believers there are among the Jews, and they are all zealous for the law. 21They have been told about you that you teach all the Jews living among the Gentiles to forsake Moses, and that you tell them not to circumcise their children or observe the customs. 22What then is to be done? They will certainly hear that you have come. 23So do what we tell you. We have four men who are under a vow. 24Join these men, go through the rite of purification with them, and pay for the shaving of their heads. Thus all will know that there is nothing in what they have been told about you, but that you yourself observe and guard the law. 25But as for the Gentiles who have become believers, we have sent a letter with our judgment that they should abstain from what has been sacrificed to idols and from blood and from what is strangledg and from fornication." 26Then Paul took the men, and the next day, having purified himself, he entered the temple with them, making public the completion of the days of purification when the sacrifice would be made for each of them.

Paul Arrested in the Temple

27 When the seven days were almost completed, the Jews from Asia, who had seen him in the temple, stirred up the whole crowd. They seized him, 28shouting, "Fellow Israelites, help! This is the man who is teaching everyone everywhere against our people, our law, and this place; more than that, he has actually brought Greeks into the temple and has defiled this holy place." 29For they had previously seen Trophimus the Ephesian with him in the city, and they supposed that Paul had brought him into the temple. 30Then all the city was aroused, and the people rushed together. They seized Paul and dragged him out of the temple, and immediately the doors were shut. 31While they were trying to kill him, word came to the tribune of the cohort that all Jerusalem was in an uproar. 32Immediately he took soldiers and centurions and ran down to them. When they saw the tribune and the soldiers, they stopped beating Paul. 33Then the tribune came, arrested him, and ordered him to be bound with two chains; he inquired who he was and what he had done. 34Some in the crowd shouted one thing, some another; and as he could not learn the facts because of the uproar, he ordered him to be brought into the barracks. 35When Paulh came to the steps, the violence of the mob was so great that he had to be carried by the soldiers. 36The crowd that followed kept shouting, "Away with him!"

Paul Defends Himself

37 Just as Paul was about to be brought into the barracks, he said to the tribune, "May I say something to you?" The tribunei replied, "Do you know Greek? 38Then you are not the Egyptian who recently stirred up a revolt and led the four thousand assassins out into the wilderness?" 39Paul replied, "I am a Jew, from Tarsus in Cilicia, a citizen of an important city; I beg you, let me speak to the people." 40When he had given him permission, Paul stood on the steps and motioned to the people for silence; and when there was a great hush, he addressed them in the Hebrewj language, saying:

g Other ancient authorities lack and from what is strangled   h Gk he   i Gk
He   j That is, Aramaic

King James

22 MEN, BRETHREN, and fathers, hear ye my defence *which I make* now unto you.

2(And when they heard that he spake in the Hebrew tongue to them, they kept the more silence: and he saith,)

3I am verily a man *which am* a Jew, born in Tarsus, *a city* in Cilicia, yet brought up in this city at the feet of Gamaliel, *and* taught according to the perfect manner of the law of the fathers, and was zealous toward God, as ye all are this day.

4And I persecuted this way unto the death, binding and delivering into prisons both men and women.

5As also the high priest doth bear me witness, and all the estate of the elders: from whom also I received letters unto the brethren, and went to Damascus, to bring them which were there bound unto Jerusalem, for to be punished.

6And it came to pass, that, as I made my journey, and was come nigh unto Damascus about noon, suddenly there shone from heaven a great light round about me.

7And I fell unto the ground, and heard a voice saying unto me, Saul, Saul, why persecutest thou me?

8And I answered, Who art thou, Lord? And he said unto me, I am Jesus of Nazareth, whom thou persecutest.

9And they that were with me saw indeed the light, and were afraid; but they heard not the voice of him that spake to me.

10And I said, What shall I do, Lord? And the Lord said unto me, Arise, and go into Damascus; and there it shall be told thee of all things which are appointed for thee to do.

11And when I could not see for the glory of that light, being led by the hand of them that were with me, I came into Damascus.

12And one Ananias, a devout man according to the law, having a good report of all the Jews which dwelt *there,*

13Came unto me, and stood, and said unto me, Brother Saul, receive thy sight. And the same hour I looked up upon him.

14And he said, The God of our fathers hath chosen thee, that thou shouldest know his will, and see that Just One, and shouldest hear the voice of his mouth.

15For thou shalt be his witness unto all men of what thou hast seen and heard.

16And now why tarriest thou? arise, and be baptized, and wash away thy sins, calling on the name of the Lord.

17And it came to pass, that, when I was come again to Jerusalem, even while I prayed in the temple, I was in a trance;

18And saw him saying unto me, Make haste, and get thee quickly out of Jerusalem: for they will not receive thy testimony concerning me.

19And I said, Lord, they know that I imprisoned and beat in every synagogue them that believed on thee:

20And when the blood of thy martyr Stephen was shed, I also was standing by, and consenting unto his death, and kept the raiment of them that slew him.

21And he said unto me, Depart: for I will send thee far hence unto the Gentiles.

22And they gave him audience unto this word, and *then* lifted up their voices, and said, Away with such a *fellow* from the earth: for it is not fit that he should live.

23And as they cried out, and cast off *their* clothes, and threw dust into the air,

24The chief captain commanded him to be brought into the castle, and bade that he should be examined by scourging; that he might know wherefore they cried so against him.

25And as they bound him with thongs, Paul said unto the centurion that stood by, Is it lawful for you to scourge a man that is a Roman, and uncondemned?

New International

22 "BROTHERS AND fathers, listen now to my defense."

2When they heard him speak to them in Aramaic, they became very quiet.

Then Paul said: 3"I am a Jew, born in Tarsus of Cilicia, but brought up in this city. Under Gamaliel I was thoroughly trained in the law of our fathers and was just as zealous for God as any of you are today. 4I persecuted the followers of this Way to their death, arresting both men and women and throwing them into prison, 5as also the high priest and all the Council can testify. I even obtained letters from them to their brothers in Damascus, and went there to bring these people as prisoners to Jerusalem to be punished.

6"About noon as I came near Damascus, suddenly a bright light from heaven flashed around me. 7I fell to the ground and heard a voice say to me, 'Saul! Saul! Why do you persecute me?'

8" 'Who are you, Lord?' I asked.

" 'I am Jesus of Nazareth, whom you are persecuting,' he replied. 9My companions saw the light, but they did not understand the voice of him who was speaking to me.

10" 'What shall I do, Lord?' I asked.

" 'Get up,' the Lord said, 'and go into Damascus. There you will be told all that you have been assigned to do.' 11My companions led me by the hand into Damascus, because the brilliance of the light had blinded me.

12"A man named Ananias came to see me. He was a devout observer of the law and highly respected by all the Jews living there. 13He stood beside me and said, 'Brother Saul, receive your sight!' And at that very moment I was able to see him.

14"Then he said: 'The God of our fathers has chosen you to know his will and to see the Righteous One and to hear words from his mouth. 15You will be his witness to all men of what you have seen and heard. 16And now what are you waiting for? Get up, be baptized and wash your sins away, calling on his name.'

17"When I returned to Jerusalem and was praying at the temple, I fell into a trance 18and saw the Lord speaking. 'Quick!' he said to me. 'Leave Jerusalem immediately, because they will not accept your testimony about me.'

19" 'Lord,' I replied, 'these men know that I went from one synagogue to another to imprison and beat those who believe in you. 20And when the blood of your martyr[a] Stephen was shed, I stood there giving my approval and guarding the clothes of those who were killing him.'

21"Then the Lord said to me, 'Go; I will send you far away to the Gentiles.' "

Paul the Roman Citizen

22The crowd listened to Paul until he said this. Then they raised their voices and shouted, "Rid the earth of him! He's not fit to live!"

23As they were shouting and throwing off their cloaks and flinging dust into the air, 24the commander ordered Paul to be taken into the barracks. He directed that he be flogged and questioned in order to find out why the people were shouting at him like this. 25As they stretched him out to flog him, Paul said to the centurion standing there, "Is it legal for you to flog a Roman citizen who hasn't even been found guilty?"

a 20 Or *witness*

Living Bible

22 "BROTHERS AND fathers, listen to me as I offer my defense." 2(When they heard him speaking in Hebrew, the silence was even greater.) 3"I am a Jew," he said, "born in Tarsus, a city in Cilicia, but educated here in Jerusalem under Gamaliel, at whose feet I learned to follow our Jewish laws and customs very carefully. I became very anxious to honor God in everything I did, just as you have tried to do today. 4And I persecuted the Christians, hounding them to death, binding and delivering both men and women to prison. 5The High Priest or any member of the Council can testify that this is so. For I asked them for letters to the Jewish leaders in Damascus, with instructions to let me bring any Christians I found to Jerusalem in chains to be punished.

6"As I was on the road, nearing Damascus, suddenly about noon a very bright light from heaven shone around me. 7And I fell to the ground and heard a voice saying to me, 'Saul, Saul, why are you persecuting me?'

8" 'Who is it speaking to me, sir?' I asked. And he replied, 'I am Jesus of Nazareth, the one you are persecuting.' 9The men with me saw the light but didn't understand what was said.

10"And I said, 'What shall I do, Lord?'

"And the Lord told me, 'Get up and go into Damascus, and there you will be told what awaits you in the years ahead.'

11"I was blinded by the intense light, and had to be led into Damascus by my companions. 12There a man named Ananias, as godly a man as you could find for obeying the law, and well thought of by all the Jews of Damascus, 13came to me, and standing beside me said, 'Brother Saul, receive your sight!' And that very hour I could see him!

14"Then he told me, 'The God of our fathers has chosen you to know his will and to see the Messiah[b] and hear him speak. 15You are to take his message everywhere, telling what you have seen and heard. 16And now, why delay? Go and be baptized, and be cleansed from your sins, calling on the name of the Lord.'

17, 18"One day after my return to Jerusalem, while I was praying in the Temple, I fell into a trance and saw a vision of God saying to me, 'Hurry! Leave Jerusalem, for the people here won't believe you when you give them my message.'

19" 'But Lord,' I argued, 'they certainly know that I imprisoned and beat those in every synagogue who believed on you. 20And when your witness Stephen was killed, I was standing there agreeing—keeping the coats they laid aside as they stoned him.'

21"But God said to me, 'Leave Jerusalem, for I will send you far away to the *Gentiles!*' "

22The crowd listened until Paul came to that word, then with one voice they shouted, "Away with such a fellow! Kill him! He isn't fit to live!" 23They yelled and threw their coats in the air and tossed up handfuls of dust.

24So the commander brought him inside and ordered him lashed with whips to make him confess his crime. He wanted to find out why the crowd had become so furious!

25As they tied Paul down to lash him, Paul said to an officer standing there, "Is it legal for you to whip a Roman citizen who hasn't even been tried?"

New Revised Standard

22 "BROTHERS AND fathers, listen to the defense that I now make before you."

2 When they heard him addressing them in Hebrew,[c] they became even more quiet. Then he said: 3 "I am a Jew, born in Tarsus in Cilicia, but brought up in this city at the feet of Gamaliel, educated strictly according to our ancestral law, being zealous for God, just as all of you are today. 4I persecuted this Way up to the point of death by binding both men and women and putting them in prison, 5as the high priest and the whole council of elders can testify about me. From them I also received letters to the brothers in Damascus, and I went there in order to bind those who were there and to bring them back to Jerusalem for punishment.

Paul Tells of His Conversion

6 "While I was on my way and approaching Damascus, about noon a great light from heaven suddenly shone about me. 7I fell to the ground and heard a voice saying to me, 'Saul, Saul, why are you persecuting me?' 8I answered, 'Who are you, Lord?' Then he said to me, 'I am Jesus of Nazareth[d] whom you are persecuting.' 9Now those who were with me saw the light but did not hear the voice of the one who was speaking to me. 10I asked, 'What am I to do, Lord?' The Lord said to me, 'Get up and go to Damascus; there you will be told everything that has been assigned to you to do.' 11Since I could not see because of the brightness of that light, those who were with me took my hand and led me to Damascus.

12 "A certain Ananias, who was a devout man according to the law and well spoken of by all the Jews living there, 13came to me; and standing beside me, he said, 'Brother Saul, regain your sight!' In that very hour I regained my sight and saw him. 14Then he said, 'The God of our ancestors has chosen you to know his will, to see the Righteous One and to hear his own voice; 15for you will be his witness to all the world of what you have seen and heard. 16And now why do you delay? Get up, be baptized, and have your sins washed away, calling on his name.'

Paul Sent to the Gentiles

17 "After I had returned to Jerusalem and while I was praying in the temple, I fell into a trance 18and saw Jesus[e] saying to me, 'Hurry and get out of Jerusalem quickly, because they will not accept your testimony about me.' 19And I said, 'Lord, they themselves know that in every synagogue I imprisoned and beat those who believed in you. 20And while the blood of your witness Stephen was shed, I myself was standing by, approving and keeping the coats of those who killed him.' 21Then he said to me, 'Go, for I will send you far away to the Gentiles.' "

Paul and the Roman Tribune

22 Up to this point they listened to him, but then they shouted, "Away with such a fellow from the earth! For he should not be allowed to live." 23And while they were shouting, throwing off their cloaks, and tossing dust into the air, 24the tribune directed that he was to be brought into the barracks, and ordered him to be examined by flogging, to find out the reason for this outcry against him. 25But when they had tied him up with thongs,[f] Paul said to the centurion who was standing by, "Is it legal for you to flog a Roman citizen who is uncondemned?" 26When the centurion heard that, he

---

[b] 22:14 *Messiah*, literally, "Righteous One."

[c] That is, *Aramaic*   [d] Gk *the Nazorean*   [e] Gk *him*   [f] Or *up for the lashes*

King James

26When the centurion heard *that*, he went and told the chief captain, saying, Take heed what thou doest: for this man is a Roman.

27Then the chief captain came, and said unto him, Tell me, art thou a Roman? He said, Yea.

28And the chief captain answered, With a great sum obtained I this freedom. And Paul said, But I was *free* born.

29Then straightway they departed from him which should have examined him: and the chief captain also was afraid, after he knew that he was a Roman, and because he had bound him.

30On the morrow, because he would have known the certainty wherefore he was accused of the Jews, he loosed him from *his* bands, and commanded the chief priests and all their council to appear, and brought Paul down, and set him before them.

23 AND PAUL, earnestly beholding the council, said, Men *and* brethren, I have lived in all good conscience before God until this day.

2And the high priest Ananias commanded them that stood by him to smite him on the mouth.

3Then said Paul unto him, God shall smite thee, *thou* whited wall: for sittest thou to judge me after the law, and commandest me to be smitten contrary to the law?

4And they that stood by said, Revilest thou God's high priest?

5Then said Paul, I wist not, brethren, that he was the high priest: for it is written, Thou shalt not speak evil of the ruler of thy people.

6But when Paul perceived that the one part were Sadducees, and the other Pharisees, he cried out in the council, Men *and* brethren, I am a Pharisee, the son of a Pharisee: of the hope and resurrection of the dead I am called in question.

7And when he had so said, there arose a dissension between the Pharisees and the Sadducees: and the multitude was divided.

8For the Sadducees say that there is no resurrection, neither angel, nor spirit: but the Pharisees confess both.

9And there arose a great cry: and the scribes *that were* of the Pharisees' part arose, and strove, saying, We find no evil in this man: but if a spirit or an angel hath spoken to him, let us not fight against God.

10And when there arose a great dissension, the chief captain, fearing lest Paul should have been pulled in pieces of them, commanded the soldiers to go down, and to take him by force from among them, and to bring *him* into the castle.

11And the night following the Lord stood by him, and said, Be of good cheer, Paul: for as thou hast testified of me in Jerusalem, so must thou bear witness also at Rome.

12And when it was day, certain of the Jews banded together, and bound themselves under a curse, saying that they would neither eat nor drink till they had killed Paul.

13And they were more than forty which had made this conspiracy.

14And they came to the chief priests and elders, and said, We have bound ourselves under a great curse, that we will eat nothing until we have slain Paul.

15Now therefore ye with the council signify to the chief captain that he bring him down unto you tomorrow, as though ye would inquire something more perfectly concerning him: and we, or ever he come near, are ready to kill him.

New International

26When the centurion heard this, he went to the commander and reported it. "What are you going to do?" he asked. "This man is a Roman citizen."

27The commander went to Paul and asked, "Tell me, are you a Roman citizen?"

"Yes, I am," he answered.

28Then the commander said, "I had to pay a big price for my citizenship."

"But I was born a citizen," Paul replied.

29Those who were about to question him withdrew immediately. The commander himself was alarmed when he realized that he had put Paul, a Roman citizen, in chains.

Before the Sanhedrin

30The next day, since the commander wanted to find out exactly why Paul was being accused by the Jews, he released him and ordered the chief priests and all the Sanhedrin to assemble. Then he brought Paul and had him stand before them.

23 PAUL LOOKED straight at the Sanhedrin and said, "My brothers, I have fulfilled my duty to God in all good conscience to this day." 2At this the high priest Ananias ordered those standing near Paul to strike him on the mouth. 3Then Paul said to him, "God will strike you, you whitewashed wall! You sit there to judge me according to the law, yet you yourself violate the law by commanding that I be struck!"

4Those who were standing near Paul said, "You dare to insult God's high priest?"

5Paul replied, "Brothers, I did not realize that he was the high priest; for it is written: 'Do not speak evil about the ruler of your people.'a"

6Then Paul, knowing that some of them were Sadducees and the others Pharisees, called out in the Sanhedrin, "My brothers, I am a Pharisee, the son of a Pharisee. I stand on trial because of my hope in the resurrection of the dead." 7When he said this, a dispute broke out between the Pharisees and the Sadducees, and the assembly was divided. 8(The Sadducees say that there is no resurrection, and that there are neither angels nor spirits, but the Pharisees acknowledge them all.)

9There was a great uproar, and some of the teachers of the law who were Pharisees stood up and argued vigorously. "We find nothing wrong with this man," they said. "What if a spirit or an angel has spoken to him?" 10The dispute became so violent that the commander was afraid Paul would be torn to pieces by them. He ordered the troops to go down and take him away from them by force and bring him into the barracks.

11The following night the Lord stood near Paul and said, "Take courage! As you have testified about me in Jerusalem, so you must also testify in Rome."

The Plot to Kill Paul

12The next morning the Jews formed a conspiracy and bound themselves with an oath not to eat or drink until they had killed Paul. 13More than forty men were involved in this plot. 14They went to the chief priests and elders and said, "We have taken a solemn oath not to eat anything until we have killed Paul. 15Now then, you and the Sanhedrin petition the commander to bring him before you on the pretext of wanting more accurate information about his case. We are ready to kill him before he gets here."

a 5 Exodus 22:28

Living Bible

26The officer went to the commander and asked, "What are you doing? This man is a Roman citizen!"
27So the commander went over and asked Paul, "Tell me, are you a Roman citizen?"

"Yes, I certainly am."

28"I am too," the commander muttered, "and it cost me plenty!"

"But I am a citizen by birth!"

29The soldiers standing ready to lash him, quickly disappeared when they heard Paul was a Roman citizen, and the commander was frightened because he had ordered him bound and whipped.

30The next day the commander freed him from his chains and ordered the chief priests into session with the Jewish Council. He had Paul brought in before them to try to find out what the trouble was all about.

23 GAZING INTENTLY at the Council, Paul began:

"Brothers, I have always lived before God in all good conscience!"

2Instantly Ananias the High Priest commanded those close to Paul to slap him on the mouth.

3Paul said to him, "God shall slap you, you whitewashed pigpen.b What kind of judge are you to break the law yourself by ordering me struck like that?"

4Those standing near Paul said to him, "Is that the way to talk to God's High Priest?"

5"I didn't realize he was the High Priest, brothers," Paul replied, "for the Scriptures say, 'Never speak evil of any of your rulers.'"

6Then Paul thought of something! Part of the Council were Sadducees, and part were Pharisees! So he shouted, "Brothers, I am a Pharisee, as were all my ancestors! And I am being tried here today because I believe in the resurrection of the dead!"

7This divided the Council right down the middle—the Pharisees against the Sadducees— 8for the Sadducees say there is no resurrection or angels or even eternal spirit within us,c but the Pharisees believe in all of these.

9So a great clamor arose. Some of the Jewish leadersd jumped up to argue that Paul was all right. "We see nothing wrong with him," they shouted. "Perhaps a spirit or angel spoke to him [there on the Damascus roade]."

10The shouting grew louder and louder, and the men were tugging at Paul from both sides, pulling him this way and that. Finally the commander, fearing they would tear him apart, ordered his soldiers to take him away from them by force and bring him back to the armory.

11That night the Lord stood beside Paul and said, "Don't worry, Paul; just as you have told the people about me here in Jerusalem, so you must also in Rome."

12, 13The next morning some forty or more of the Jews got together and bound themselves by a curse neither to eat nor drink until they had killed Paul! 14Then they went to the chief priests and elders and told them what they had done. 15"Ask the commander to bring Paul back to the Council again," they requested. "Pretend you want to ask a few more questions. We will kill him on the way."

New Revised Standard

went to the tribune and said to him, "What are you about to do? This man is a Roman citizen." 27The tribune came and asked Paul,f "Tell me, are you a Roman citizen?" And he said, "Yes." 28The tribune answered, "It cost me a large sum of money to get my citizenship." Paul said, "But I was born a citizen." 29Immediately those who were about to examine him drew back from him; and the tribune also was afraid, for he realized that Paul was a Roman citizen and that he had bound him.

Paul before the Council

30 Since he wanted to find out what Paulg was being accused of by the Jews, the next day he released him and ordered the chief priests and the entire council to meet. He brought Paul down and had him stand before them.

23 WHILE PAUL was looking intently at the council he said, "Brothers,h up to this day I have lived my life with a clear conscience before God." 2Then the high priest Ananias ordered those standing near him to strike him on the mouth. 3At this Paul said to him, "God will strike you, you whitewashed wall! Are you sitting there to judge me according to the law, and yet in violation of the law you order me to be struck?" 4Those standing nearby said, "Do you dare to insult God's high priest?" 5And Paul said, "I did not realize, brothers, that he was high priest; for it is written, 'You shall not speak evil of a leader of your people.' "

6 When Paul noticed that some were Sadducees and others were Pharisees, he called out in the council, "Brothers, I am a Pharisee, a son of Pharisees. I am on trial concerning the hope of the resurrectioni of the dead." 7When he said this, a dissension began between the Pharisees and the Sadducees, and the assembly was divided. 8(The Sadducees say that there is no resurrection, or angel, or spirit; but the Pharisees acknowledge all three.) 9Then a great clamor arose, and certain scribes of the Pharisees' group stood up and contended, "We find nothing wrong with this man. What if a spirit or an angel has spoken to him?" 10When the dissension became violent, the tribune, fearing that they would tear Paul to pieces, ordered the soldiers to go down, take him by force, and bring him into the barracks.

11 That night the Lord stood near him and said, "Keep up your courage! For just as you have testified for me in Jerusalem, so you must bear witness also in Rome."

The Plot to Kill Paul

12 In the morning the Jews joined in a conspiracy and bound themselves by an oath neither to eat nor drink until they had killed Paul. 13There were more than forty who joined in this conspiracy. 14They went to the chief priests and elders and said, "We have strictly bound ourselves by an oath to taste no food until we have killed Paul. 15Now then, you and the council must notify the tribune to bring him down to you, on the pretext that you want to make a more thorough examination of his case. And we are ready to do away with him before he arrives."

---

b 23:3 you whitewashed pigpen, literally, "you whitewashed wall."
c 23:8 or even eternal spirit within us, literally, "nor spirit." d 23:9 Jewish leaders, literally, "scribes." e 23:9 there on the Damascus road, implied.

f Gk him g Gk he h Gk Men, brothers i Gk concerning hope and resurrection

King James

16And when Paul's sister's son heard of their lying in wait, he went and entered into the castle, and told Paul.

17Then Paul called one of the centurions unto *him*, and said, Bring this young man unto the chief captain: for he hath a certain thing to tell him.

18So he took him, and brought *him* to the chief captain, and said, Paul the prisoner called me unto *him*, and prayed me to bring this young man unto thee, who hath something to say unto thee.

19Then the chief captain took him by the hand, and went *with him* aside privately, and asked *him*, What is that thou hast to tell me?

20And he said, The Jews have agreed to desire thee that thou wouldest bring down Paul tomorrow into the council, as though they would inquire somewhat of him more perfectly.

21But do not thou yield unto them: for there lie in wait for him of them more than forty men, which have bound themselves with an oath, that they will neither eat nor drink till they have killed him: and now are they ready, looking for a promise from thee.

22So the chief captain *then* let the young man depart, and charged *him, See thou* tell no man that thou hast shown these things to me.

23And he called unto *him* two centurions, saying, Make ready two hundred soldiers to go to Caesarea, and horsemen threescore and ten, and spearmen two hundred, at the third hour of the night;

24And provide *them* beasts, that they may set Paul on, and bring *him* safe unto Felix the governor.

25And he wrote a letter after this manner:

26Claudius Lysias unto the most excellent governor Felix *sendeth* greeting.

27This man was taken of the Jews, and should have been killed of them: then came I with an army, and rescued him, having understood that he was a Roman.

28And when I would have known the cause wherefore they accused him, I brought him forth into their council:

29Whom I perceived to be accused of questions of their law, but to have nothing laid to his charge worthy of death or of bonds.

30And when it was told me how that the Jews laid wait for the man, I sent straightway to thee, and gave commandment to his accusers also to say before thee what *they had* against him. Farewell.

31Then the soldiers, as it was commanded them, took Paul, and brought *him* by night to Antipatris.

32On the morrow they left the horsemen to go with him, and returned to the castle:

33Who, when they came to Caesarea, and delivered the epistle to the governor, presented Paul also before him.

34And when the governor had read *the letter*, he asked of what province he was. And when he understood that *he was* of Cilicia;

35I will hear thee, said he, when thine accusers are also come. And he commanded him to be kept in Herod's judgment hall.

24 AND AFTER five days Ananias the high priest descended with the elders, and *with* a certain orator *named* Tertullus, who informed the governor against Paul.

2And when he was called forth, Tertullus began to accuse *him*, saying, Seeing that by thee we enjoy great quietness, and that very worthy deeds are done unto this nation by thy providence,

3We accept *it* always, and in all places, most noble Felix, with all thankfulness.

New International

16But when the son of Paul's sister heard of this plot, he went into the barracks and told Paul.

17Then Paul called one of the centurions and said, "Take this young man to the commander; he has something to tell him." 18So he took him to the commander.

The centurion said, "Paul, the prisoner, sent for me and asked me to bring this young man to you because he has something to tell you."

19The commander took the young man by the hand, drew him aside and asked, "What is it you want to tell me?"

20He said: "The Jews have agreed to ask you to bring Paul before the Sanhedrin tomorrow on the pretext of wanting more accurate information about him. 21Don't give in to them, because more than forty of them are waiting in ambush for him. They have taken an oath not to eat or drink until they have killed him. They are ready now, waiting for your consent to their request."

22The commander dismissed the young man and cautioned him, "Don't tell anyone that you have reported this to me."

Paul Transferred to Caesarea

23Then he called two of his centurions and ordered them, "Get ready a detachment of two hundred soldiers, seventy horsemen and two hundred spearmena to go to Caesarea at nine tonight. 24Provide mounts for Paul so that he may be taken safely to Governor Felix."

25He wrote a letter as follows:

26Claudius Lysias,

To His Excellency, Governor Felix:

Greetings.

27This man was seized by the Jews and they were about to kill him, but I came with my troops and rescued him, for I had learned that he is a Roman citizen. 28I wanted to know why they were accusing him, so I brought him to their Sanhedrin. 29I found that the accusation had to do with questions about their law, but there was no charge against him that deserved death or imprisonment. 30When I was informed of a plot to be carried out against the man, I sent him to you at once. I also ordered his accusers to present to you their case against him.

31So the soldiers, carrying out their orders, took Paul with them during the night and brought him as far as Antipatris. 32The next day they let the cavalry go on with him, while they returned to the barracks. 33When the cavalry arrived in Caesarea, they delivered the letter to the governor and handed Paul over to him. 34The governor read the letter and asked what province he was from. Learning that he was from Cilicia, 35he said, "I will hear your case when your accusers get here." Then he ordered that Paul be kept under guard in Herod's palace.

The Trial Before Felix

24 FIVE DAYS later the high priest Ananias went down to Caesarea with some of the elders and a lawyer named Tertullus, and they brought their charges against Paul before the governor. 2When Paul was called in, Tertullus presented his case before Felix: "We have enjoyed a long period of peace under you, and your foresight has brought about reforms in this nation. 3Everywhere and in every way, most excellent Felix, we acknowledge this with profound gratitude. 4But in order

---

a 23 The meaning of the Greek for this word is uncertain.

Living Bible

16But Paul's nephew got wind of their plan and came to the armory and told Paul.

17Paul called one of the officers and said, "Take this boy to the commander. He has something important to tell him."

18So the officer did, explaining, "Paul, the prisoner, called me over and asked me to bring this young man to you to tell you something."

19The commander took the boy by the hand, and leading him aside asked, "What is it you want to tell me, lad?"

20"Tomorrow," he told him, "the Jews are going to ask you to bring Paul before the Council again, pretending they want to get some more information. 21But don't do it! There are more than forty men hiding along the road ready to jump him and kill him. They have bound themselves under a curse to neither eat nor drink till he is dead. They are out there now, expecting you to agree to their request."

22"Don't let a soul know you told me this," the commander warned the boy as he left. 23, 24Then the commander called two of his officers and ordered, "Get 200 soldiers ready to leave for Caesarea at nine o'clock tonight! Take 200 spearmen and 70 mounted cavalry. Give Paul a horse to ride and get him safely to Governor Felix."

25Then he wrote this letter to the governor:

26"*From:* Claudius Lysias

"*To:* His Excellency, Governor Felix.

"Greetings!

27"This man was seized by the Jews and they were killing him when I sent the soldiers to rescue him, for I learned that he was a Roman citizen. 28Then I took him to their Council to try to find out what he had done. 29I soon discovered it was something about their Jewish beliefs, certainly nothing worthy of imprisonment or death. 30But when I was informed of a plot to kill him, I decided to send him on to you and will tell his accusers to bring their charges before you."

31So that night, as ordered, the soldiers took Paul to Antipatris. 32They returned to the armory the next morning, leaving him with the cavalry to take him on to Caesarea.

33When they arrived in Caesarea, they presented Paul and the letter to the governor. 34He read it and then asked Paul where he was from.

"Cilicia," Paul answered.

35"I will hear your case fully when your accusers arrive," the governor told him, and ordered him kept in the prison at King Herod's palace.

24 FIVE DAYS later Ananias the High Priest arrived with some of the Jewish leadersb and the lawyerc Tertullus, to make their accusations against Paul. 2When Tertullus was called forward, he laid charges against Paul in the following address to the governor:

"Your Excellency, you have given quietness and peace to us Jews and have greatly reduced the discrimination against us. 3And for this we are very, very grateful to you. 4But lest I bore you, kindly give me your

New Revised Standard

16 Now the son of Paul's sister heard about the ambush; so he went and gained entrance to the barracks and told Paul. 17Paul called one of the centurions and said, "Take this young man to the tribune, for he has something to report to him." 18So he took him, brought him to the tribune, and said, "The prisoner Paul called me and asked me to bring this young man to you; he has something to tell you." 19The tribune took him by the hand, drew him aside privately, and asked, "What is it that you have to report to me?" 20He answered, "The Jews have agreed to ask you to bring Paul down to the council tomorrow, as though they were going to inquire more thoroughly into his case. 21But do not be persuaded by them, for more than forty of their men are lying in ambush for him. They have bound themselves by an oath neither to eat nor drink until they kill him. They are ready now and are waiting for your consent." 22So the tribune dismissed the young man, ordering him, "Tell no one that you have informed me of this."

Paul Sent to Felix the Governor

23 Then he summoned two of the centurions and said, "Get ready to leave by nine o'clock tonight for Caesarea with two hundred soldiers, seventy horsemen, and two hundred spearmen. 24Also provide mounts for Paul to ride, and take him safely to Felix the governor." 25He wrote a letter to this effect:

26 "Claudius Lysias to his Excellency the governor Felix, greetings. 27This man was seized by the Jews and was about to be killed by them, but when I had learned that he was a Roman citizen, I came with the guard and rescued him. 28Since I wanted to know the charge for which they accused him, I had him brought to their council. 29I found that he was accused concerning questions of their law, but was charged with nothing deserving death or imprisonment. 30When I was informed that there would be a plot against the man, I sent him to you at once, ordering his accusers also to state before you what they have against him.d"

31 So the soldiers, according to their instructions, took Paul and brought him during the night to Antipatris. 32The next day they let the horsemen go on with him, while they returned to the barracks. 33When they came to Caesarea and delivered the letter to the governor, they presented Paul also before him. 34On reading the letter, he asked what province he belonged to, and when he learned that he was from Cilicia, 35he said, "I will give you a hearing when your accusers arrive." Then he ordered that he be kept under guard in Herod's headquarters.e

Paul before Felix at Caesarea

24 FIVE DAYS later the high priest Ananias came down with some elders and an attorney, a certain Tertullus, and they reported their case against Paul to the governor. 2When Paulf had been summoned, Tertullus began to accuse him, saying:

"Your Excellency,g because of you we have long enjoyed peace, and reforms have been made for this people because of your foresight. 3We welcome this in every way and everywhere with utmost gratitude. 4But,

---

b *24:1 Jewish leaders,* literally, "elders."   c *24:1 lawyer,* literally, "orator."

d Other ancient authorities add *Farewell*   e Gk *praetorium*   f Gk *he*   g Gk lacks *Your Excellency*

King James

4Notwithstanding, that I be not further tedious unto thee, I pray thee that thou wouldest hear us of thy clemency a few words.

5For we have found this man *a* pestilent *fellow*, and a mover of sedition among all the Jews throughout the world, and a ringleader of the sect of the Nazarenes:

6Who also hath gone about to profane the temple: whom we took, and would have judged according to our law.

7But the chief captain Lysias came *upon us*, and with great violence took *him* away out of our hands,

8Commanding his accusers to come unto thee: by examining of whom thyself mayest take knowledge of all these things, whereof we accuse him.

9And the Jews also assented, saying that these things were so.

10Then Paul, after that the governor had beckoned unto him to speak, answered, Forasmuch as I know that thou hast been of many years a judge unto this nation, I do the more cheerfully answer for myself:

11Because that thou mayest understand, that there are yet but twelve days since I went up to Jerusalem for to worship.

12And they neither found me in the temple disputing with any man, neither raising up the people, neither in the synagogues, nor in the city:

13Neither can they prove the things whereof they now accuse me.

14But this I confess unto thee, that after the way which they call heresy, so worship I the God of my fathers, believing all things which are written in the law and in the prophets:

15And have hope toward God, which they themselves also allow, that there shall be a resurrection of the dead, both of the just and unjust.

16And herein do I exercise myself, to have always a conscience void of offence toward God, and *toward* men.

17Now after many years I came to bring alms to my nation, and offerings.

18Whereupon certain Jews from Asia found me purified in the temple, neither with multitude, nor with tumult.

19Who ought to have been here before thee, and object, if they had aught against me.

20Or else let these same *here* say, if they have found any evil doing in me, while I stood before the council,

21Except it be for this one voice, that I cried standing among them, Touching the resurrection of the dead I am called in question by you this day.

22And when Felix heard these things, having more perfect knowledge of *that* way, he deferred them, and said, When Lysias the chief captain shall come down, I will know the uttermost of your matter.

23And he commanded a centurion to keep Paul, and to let *him* have liberty, and that he should forbid none of his acquaintance to minister or come unto him.

24And after certain days, when Felix came with his wife Drusilla, which was a Jewess, he sent for Paul, and heard him concerning the faith in Christ.

25And as he reasoned of righteousness, temperance, and judgment to come, Felix trembled, and answered, Go thy way for this time; when I have a convenient season, I will call for thee.

26He hoped also that money should have been given him of Paul, that he might loose him: wherefore he sent for him the oftener, and communed with him.

27But after two years Porcius Festus came into Felix' room: and Felix, willing to show the Jews a pleasure, left Paul bound.

New International

not to weary you further, I would request that you be kind enough to hear us briefly.

5"We have found this man to be a troublemaker, stirring up riots among the Jews all over the world. He is a ringleader of the Nazarene sect 6and even tried to desecrate the temple; so we seized him. 8By[a] examining him yourself you will be able to learn the truth about all these charges we are bringing against him."

9The Jews joined in the accusation, asserting that these things were true.

10When the governor motioned for him to speak, Paul replied: "I know that for a number of years you have been a judge over this nation; so I gladly make my defense. 11You can easily verify that no more than twelve days ago I went up to Jerusalem to worship. 12My accusers did not find me arguing with anyone at the temple, or stirring up a crowd in the synagogues or anywhere else in the city. 13And they cannot prove to you the charges they are now making against me. 14However, I admit that I worship the God of our fathers as a follower of the Way, which they call a sect. I believe everything that agrees with the Law and that is written in the Prophets, 15and I have the same hope in God as these men, that there will be a resurrection of both the righteous and the wicked. 16So I strive always to keep my conscience clear before God and man.

17"After an absence of several years, I came to Jerusalem to bring my people gifts for the poor and to present offerings. 18I was ceremonially clean when they found me in the temple courts doing this. There was no crowd with me, nor was I involved in any disturbance. 19But there are some Jews from the province of Asia, who ought to be here before you and bring charges if they have anything against me. 20Or these who are here should state what crime they found in me when I stood before the Sanhedrin— 21unless it was this one thing I shouted as I stood in their presence: 'It is concerning the resurrection of the dead that I am on trial before you today.'"

22Then Felix, who was well acquainted with the Way, adjourned the proceedings. "When Lysias the commander comes," he said, "I will decide your case." 23He ordered the centurion to keep Paul under guard but to give him some freedom and permit his friends to take care of his needs.

24Several days later Felix came with his wife Drusilla, who was a Jewess. He sent for Paul and listened to him as he spoke about faith in Christ Jesus. 25As Paul discoursed on righteousness, self-control and the judgment to come, Felix was afraid and said, "That's enough for now! You may leave. When I find it convenient, I will send for you." 26At the same time he was hoping that Paul would offer him a bribe, so he sent for him frequently and talked with him.

27When two years had passed, Felix was succeeded by Porcius Festus, but because Felix wanted to grant a favor to the Jews, he left Paul in prison.

---

[a] 6-8 Some manuscripts *him and wanted to judge him according to our law.* [7]*But the commander, Lysias, came and with the use of much force snatched him from our hands* [8]*and ordered his accusers to come before you. By*

Living Bible

attention for only a moment as I briefly outline our case against this man. 5For we have found him to be a troublemaker, a man who is constantly inciting the Jews throughout the entire world to riots and rebellions against the Roman government. He is a ringleader of the sect known as the Nazarenes. 6Moreover, he was trying to defile the Temple when we arrested him.

"We would have given him what he justly deserves, 7but Lysias, the commander of the garrison, came and took him violently away from us, 8demanding that he be tried by Roman law. You can find out the truth of our accusations by examining him yourself."

9Then all the other Jews chimed in, declaring that everything Tertullus said was true.

10Now it was Paul's turn. The governor motioned for him to rise and speak.

Paul began: "I know, sir, that you have been a judge of Jewish affairs for many years, and this gives me confidence as I make my defense. 11You can quickly discover that it was no more than twelve days ago that I arrived in Jerusalem to worship at the Temple, 12and you will discover that I have never incited a riot in any synagogue or on the streets of any city; 13and these men certainly cannot prove the things they accuse me of doing.

14"But one thing I do confess, that I believe in the way of salvation, which they refer to as a sect; I follow that system of serving the God of our ancestors; I firmly believe in the Jewish law and everything written in the books of prophecy; 15and I believe, just as these men do, that there will be a resurrection of both the righteous and ungodly. 16Because of this I try with all my strength to always maintain a clear conscience before God and man.

17"After several years away, I returned to Jerusalem with money to aid the Jews, and to offer a sacrifice to God. 18My accusers saw me in the Temple as I was presenting my thank offering.b I had shaved my head as their laws required, and there was no crowd around me, and no rioting! But some Jews from Turkey were there 19(who ought to be here if they have anything against me)— 20but look! Ask these men right here what wrongdoing their Council found in me, 21except that I said one thing I shouldn'tc when I shouted out, 'I am here before the Council to defend myself for believing that the dead will rise again!'"

22Felix, who knew Christians didn't go around starting riots,d told the Jews to wait for the arrival of Lysias, the garrison commander, and then he would decide the case. 23He ordered Paul to prison but instructed the guards to treat him gently and not to forbid any of his friends from visiting him or bringing him gifts to make his stay more comfortable.

24A few days later Felix came with Drusilla, his legal wife,e a Jewess. Sending for Paul, they listened as he told them about faith in Christ Jesus. 25And as he reasoned with them about righteousness and self-control and the judgment to come, Felix was terrified.

"Go away for now," he replied, "and when I have a more convenient time, I'll call for you again."

26He also hoped that Paul would bribe him, so he sent for him from time to time and talked with him. 27Two years went by in this way; then Felix was succeeded by Porcius Festus. And because Felix wanted to gain favor with the Jews, he left Paul in chains.

New Revised Standard

to detain you no further, I beg you to hear us briefly with your customary graciousness. 5We have, in fact, found this man a pestilent fellow, an agitator among all the Jews throughout the world, and a ringleader of the sect of the Nazarenes.f 6He even tried to profane the temple, and so we seized him.g 8By examining him yourself you will be able to learn from him concerning everything of which we accuse him."

9 The Jews also joined in the charge by asserting that all this was true.

Paul's Defense before Felix

10 When the governor motioned to him to speak, Paul replied:

"I cheerfully make my defense, knowing that for many years you have been a judge over this nation. 11As you can find out, it is not more than twelve days since I went up to worship in Jerusalem. 12They did not find me disputing with anyone in the temple or stirring up a crowd either in the synagogues or throughout the city. 13Neither can they prove to you the charge that they now bring against me. 14But this I admit to you, that according to the Way, which they call a sect, I worship the God of our ancestors, believing everything laid down according to the law or written in the prophets. 15I have a hope in God—a hope that they themselves also accept—that there will be a resurrection of bothh the righteous and the unrighteous. 16Therefore I do my best always to have a clear conscience toward God and all people. 17Now after some years I came to bring alms to my nation and to offer sacrifices. 18While I was doing this, they found me in the temple, completing the rite of purification, without any crowd or disturbance. 19But there were some Jews from Asia—they ought to be here before you to make an accusation, if they have anything against me. 20Or let these men here tell what crime they had found when I stood before the council, 21unless it was this one sentence that I called out while standing before them, 'It is about the resurrection of the dead that I am on trial before you today.'"

22 But Felix, who was rather well informed about the Way, adjourned the hearing with the comment, "When Lysias the tribune comes down, I will decide your case." 23 Then he ordered the centurion to keep him in custody, but to let him have some liberty and not to prevent any of his friends from taking care of his needs.

Paul Held in Custody

24 Some days later when Felix came with his wife Drusilla, who was Jewish, he sent for Paul and heard him speak concerning faith in Christ Jesus. 25And as he discussed justice, self-control, and the coming judgment, Felix became frightened and said, "Go away for the present; when I have an opportunity, I will send for you." 26At the same time he hoped that money would be given him by Paul, and for that reason he used to send for him very often and converse with him.

27 After two years had passed, Felix was succeeded by Porcius Festus; and since he wanted to grant the Jews a favor, Felix left Paul in prison.

---

b 24:18 as I was presenting my thank offering, implied. c 24:21 except that I said one thing I shouldn't, literally, "except it be for this one voice." d 24:22 who knew Christians didn't go around starting riots, literally, "having more accurate knowledge." e 24:24 his legal wife, literally, "his own wife."

f Gk Nazoreans g Other ancient authorities add and we would have judged him according to our law. 7But the chief captain Lysias came and with great violence took him out of our hands, 8commanding his accusers to come before you. h Other ancient authorities read of the dead, both of

King James

25 NOW WHEN Festus was come into the province, after three days he ascended from Caesarea to Jerusalem.

2Then the high priest and the chief of the Jews informed him against Paul, and besought him,

3And desired favour against him, that he would send for him to Jerusalem, laying wait in the way to kill him.

4But Festus answered, that Paul should be kept at Caesarea, and that he himself would depart shortly *thither*.

5Let them therefore, said he, which among you are able, go down with *me*, and accuse this man, if there be any wickedness in him.

6And when he had tarried among them more than ten days, he went down unto Caesarea; and the next day sitting on the judgment seat commanded Paul to be brought.

7And when he was come, the Jews which came down from Jerusalem stood round about, and laid many and grievous complaints against Paul, which they could not prove.

8While he answered for himself, Neither against the law of the Jews, neither against the temple, nor yet against Caesar, have I offended any thing at all.

9But Festus, willing to do the Jews a pleasure, answered Paul, and said, Wilt thou go up to Jerusalem, and there be judged of these things before me?

10Then said Paul, I stand at Caesar's judgment seat, where I ought to be judged: to the Jews have I done no wrong, as thou very well knowest.

11For if I be an offender, or have committed any thing worthy of death, I refuse not to die: but if there be none of these things whereof these accuse me, no man may deliver me unto them. I appeal unto Caesar.

12Then Festus, when he had conferred with the council, answered, Hast thou appealed unto Caesar? unto Caesar shalt thou go.

13And after certain days king Agrippa and Bernice came unto Caesarea to salute Festus.

14And when they had been there many days, Festus declared Paul's cause unto the king, saying, There is a certain man left in bonds by Felix:

15About whom, when I was at Jerusalem, the chief priests and the elders of the Jews informed *me*, desiring *to have* judgment against him.

16To whom I answered, It is not the manner of the Romans to deliver any man to die, before that he which is accused have the accusers face to face, and have licence to answer for himself concerning the crime laid against him.

17Therefore, when they were come hither, without any delay on the morrow I sat on the judgment seat, and commanded the man to be brought forth.

18Against whom when the accusers stood up, they brought none accusation of such things as I supposed:

19But had certain questions against him of their own superstition, and of one Jesus, which was dead, whom Paul affirmed to be alive.

20And because I doubted of such manner of questions, I asked *him* whether he would go to Jerusalem, and there be judged of these matters.

21But when Paul had appealed to be reserved unto the hearing of Augustus, I commanded him to be kept till I might send him to Caesar.

22Then Agrippa said unto Festus, I would also hear the man myself. Tomorrow, said he, thou shalt hear him.

23And on the morrow, when Agrippa was come, and Bernice, with great pomp, and was entered into the place of hearing, with the chief captains, and principal men of the city, at Festus' commandment Paul was brought forth.

New International

The Trial Before Festus

25 THREE DAYS after arriving in the province, Festus went up from Caesarea to Jerusalem, 2where the chief priests and Jewish leaders appeared before him and presented the charges against Paul. 3They urgently requested Festus, as a favor to them, to have Paul transferred to Jerusalem, for they were preparing an ambush to kill him along the way. 4Festus answered, "Paul is being held at Caesarea, and I myself am going there soon. 5Let some of your leaders come with me and press charges against the man there, if he has done anything wrong."

6After spending eight or ten days with them, he went down to Caesarea, and the next day he convened the court and ordered that Paul be brought before him. 7When Paul appeared, the Jews who had come down from Jerusalem stood around him, bringing many serious charges against him, which they could not prove.

8Then Paul made his defense: "I have done nothing wrong against the law of the Jews or against the temple or against Caesar."

9Festus, wishing to do the Jews a favor, said to Paul, "Are you willing to go up to Jerusalem and stand trial before me there on these charges?"

10Paul answered: "I am now standing before Caesar's court, where I ought to be tried. I have not done any wrong to the Jews, as you yourself know very well. 11If, however, I am guilty of doing anything deserving death, I do not refuse to die. But if the charges brought against me by these Jews are not true, no one has the right to hand me over to them. I appeal to Caesar!"

12After Festus had conferred with his council, he declared: "You have appealed to Caesar. To Caesar you will go!"

Festus Consults King Agrippa

13A few days later King Agrippa and Bernice arrived at Caesarea to pay their respects to Festus. 14Since they were spending many days there, Festus discussed Paul's case with the king. He said: "There is a man here whom Felix left as a prisoner. 15When I went to Jerusalem, the chief priests and elders of the Jews brought charges against him and asked that he be condemned.

16"I told them that it is not the Roman custom to hand over any man before he has faced his accusers and has had an opportunity to defend himself against their charges. 17When they came here with me, I did not delay the case, but convened the court the next day and ordered the man to be brought in. 18When his accusers got up to speak, they did not charge him with any of the crimes I had expected. 19Instead, they had some points of dispute with him about their own religion and about a dead man named Jesus who Paul claimed was alive. 20I was at a loss how to investigate such matters; so I asked if he would be willing to go to Jerusalem and stand trial there on these charges. 21When Paul made his appeal to be held over for the Emperor's decision, I ordered him held until I could send him to Caesar."

22Then Agrippa said to Festus, "I would like to hear this man myself."

He replied, "Tomorrow you will hear him."

Paul Before Agrippa

23The next day Agrippa and Bernice came with great pomp and entered the audience room with the high ranking officers and the leading men of the city. At the command of Festus, Paul was brought in. 24Festus said:

Living Bible

25 THREE DAYS after Festus arrived in Caesarea to take over his new responsibilities, he left for Jerusalem, 2where the chief priests and other Jewish leaders got hold of him and gave him their story about Paul. 3They begged him to bring Paul to Jerusalem at once. (Their plan was to waylay and kill him.) 4But Festus replied that since Paul was at Caesarea and he himself was returning there soon, 5those with authority in this affair should return with him for the trial.

6Eight or ten days later he returned to Caesarea and the following day opened Paul's trial.

7On Paul's arrival in court the Jews from Jerusalem gathered around, hurling many serious accusations which they couldn't prove. 8Paul denied the charges: "I am not guilty," he said. "I have not opposed the Jewish laws or desecrated the Temple or rebelled against the Roman government."

9Then Festus, anxious to please the Jews, asked him, "Are you willing to go to Jerusalem and stand trial before me?"

10, 11But Paul replied, "No! I demand my privilege of a hearing before the Emperor himself. You know very well I am not guilty. If I have done something worthy of death, I don't refuse to die! But if I am innocent, neither you nor anyone else has a right to turn me over to these men to kill me. *I appeal to Caesar.*"

12Festus conferred with his advisors and then replied, "Very well! You have appealed to Caesar, and to Caesar you shall go!"

13A few days later King Agrippa arrived with Bernicea for a visit with Festus. 14During their stay of several days Festus discussed Paul's case with the king. "There is a prisoner here," he told him, "whose case was left for me by Felix. 15When I was in Jerusalem, the chief priests and other Jewish leaders gave me their side of the story and asked me to have him killed. 16Of course I quickly pointed out to them that Roman law does not convict a man before he is tried. He is given an opportunity to defend himself face to face with his accusers.

17"When they came here for the trial, I called the case the very next day and ordered Paul brought in. 18But the accusations made against him weren't at all what I supposed they would be. 19It was something about their religion, and about someone else called Jesus who died, but Paul insists is alive! 20I was perplexed as to how to decide a case of this kind and asked him whether he would be willing to stand trial on these charges in Jerusalem. 21But Paul appealed to Caesar! So I ordered him back to jail until I could arrange to get him to the Emperor."

22"I'd like to hear the man myself," Agrippa said. And Festus replied, "You shall—tomorrow!"

23So the next day, after the king and Bernice had arrived at the courtroom with great pomp, accompanied by military officers and prominent men of the city, Festus ordered Paul brought in.

New Revised Standard

Paul Appeals to the Emperor

25 THREE DAYS after Festus had arrived in the province, he went up from Caesarea to Jerusalem 2where the chief priests and the leaders of the Jews gave him a report against Paul. They appealed to him 3and requested, as a favor to them against Paul,b to have him transferred to Jerusalem. They were, in fact, planning an ambush to kill him along the way. 4Festus replied that Paul was being kept at Caesarea, and that he himself intended to go there shortly. 5"So," he said, "let those of you who have the authority come down with me, and if there is anything wrong about the man, let them accuse him."

6 After he had stayed among them not more than eight or ten days, he went down to Caesarea; the next day he took his seat on the tribunal and ordered Paul to be brought. 7When he arrived, the Jews who had gone down from Jerusalem surrounded him, bringing many serious charges against him, which they could not prove. 8Paul said in his defense, "I have in no way committed an offense against the law of the Jews, or against the temple, or against the emperor." 9But Festus, wishing to do the Jews a favor, asked Paul, "Do you wish to go up to Jerusalem and be tried there before me on these charges?" 10Paul said, "I am appealing to the emperor's tribunal; this is where I should be tried. I have done no wrong to the Jews, as you very well know. 11Now if I am in the wrong and have committed something for which I deserve to die, I am not trying to escape death; but if there is nothing to their charges against me, no one can turn me over to them. I appeal to the emperor." 12Then Festus, after he had conferred with his council, replied, "You have appealed to the emperor; to the emperor you will go."

Festus Consults King Agrippa

13 After several days had passed, King Agrippa and Bernice arrived at Caesarea to welcome Festus. 14Since they were staying there several days, Festus laid Paul's case before the king, saying, "There is a man here who was left in prison by Felix. 15When I was in Jerusalem, the chief priests and the elders of the Jews informed me about him and asked for a sentence against him. 16I told them that it was not the custom of the Romans to hand over anyone before the accused had met the accusers face to face and had been given an opportunity to make a defense against the charge. 17So when they met here, I lost no time, but on the next day took my seat on the tribunal and ordered the man to be brought. 18When the accusers stood up, they did not charge him with any of the crimesc that I was expecting. 19Instead they had certain points of disagreement with him about their own religion and about a certain Jesus, who had died, but whom Paul asserted to be alive. 20Since I was at a loss how to investigate these questions, I asked whether he wished to go to Jerusalem and be tried there on these charges.d 21But when Paul had appealed to be kept in custody for the decision of his Imperial Majesty, I ordered him to be held until I could send him to the emperor." 22Agrippa said to Festus, "I would like to hear the man myself." "Tomorrow," he said, "you will hear him."

Paul Brought before Agrippa

23 So on the next day Agrippa and Bernice came with great pomp, and they entered the audience hall with the military tribunes and the prominent men of the city. Then Festus gave the order and Paul was brought in.

---

a 25:13 *arrived with Bernice.* She was his sister.

b Gk *him*   c Other ancient authorities read *with anything*   d Gk *on them*

King James

24And Festus said, King Agrippa, and all men which are here present with us, ye see this man, about whom all the multitude of the Jews have dealt with me, both at Jerusalem, and *also* here, crying that he ought not to live any longer.

25But when I found that he had committed nothing worthy of death, and that he himself hath appealed to Augustus, I have determined to send him.

26Of whom I have no certain thing to write unto my lord. Wherefore I have brought him forth before you, and specially before thee, O king Agrippa, that, after examination had, I might have somewhat to write.

27For it seemeth to me unreasonable to send a prisoner, and not withal to signify the crimes *laid* against him.

26 THEN AGRIPPA said unto Paul, Thou art permitted to speak for thyself. Then Paul stretched forth the hand, and answered for himself:

2I think myself happy, king Agrippa, because I shall answer for myself this day before thee touching all the things whereof I am accused of the Jews:

3Especially *because I know* thee to be expert in all customs and questions which are among the Jews: wherefore I beseech thee to hear me patiently.

4My manner of life from my youth, which was at the first among mine own nation at Jerusalem, know all the Jews;

5Which knew me from the beginning, if they would testify, that after the most straitest sect of our religion I lived a Pharisee.

6And now I stand and am judged for the hope of the promise made of God unto our fathers:

7Unto which *promise* our twelve tribes, instantly serving *God* day and night, hope to come. For which hope's sake, king Agrippa, I am accused of the Jews.

8Why should it be thought a thing incredible with you, that God should raise the dead?

9I verily thought with myself, that I ought to do many things contrary to the name of Jesus of Nazareth.

10Which thing I also did in Jerusalem: and many of the saints did I shut up in prison, having received authority from the chief priests; and when they were put to death, I gave my voice against *them*.

11And I punished them oft in every synagogue, and compelled *them* to blaspheme; and being exceedingly mad against them, I persecuted *them* even unto strange cities.

12Whereupon as I went to Damascus with authority and commission from the chief priests,

13At midday, O king, I saw in the way a light from heaven, above the brightness of the sun, shining round about me and them which journeyed with me.

14And when we were all fallen to the earth, I heard a voice speaking unto me, and saying in the Hebrew tongue, Saul, Saul, why persecutest thou me? *it is* hard for thee to kick against the pricks.

15And I said, Who art thou, Lord? And he said, I am Jesus whom thou persecutest.

16But rise, and stand upon thy feet: for I have appeared unto thee for this purpose, to make thee a minister and a witness both of these things which thou hast seen, and of those things in the which I will appear unto thee;

17Delivering thee from the people, and *from* the Gentiles, unto whom now I send thee,

18To open their eyes, *and* to turn *them* from darkness to light, and *from* the power of Satan unto God, that they may receive forgiveness of sins, and inheritance among them which are sanctified by faith that is in me.

19Whereupon, O king Agrippa, I was not disobedient unto the heavenly vision:

New International

"King Agrippa, and all who are present with us, you see this man! The whole Jewish community has petitioned me about him in Jerusalem and here in Caesarea, shouting that he ought not to live any longer. 25I found he had done nothing deserving of death, but because he made his appeal to the Emperor I decided to send him to Rome. 26But I have nothing definite to write to His Majesty about him. Therefore I have brought him before all of you, and especially before you, King Agrippa, so that as a result of this investigation I may have something to write. 27For I think it is unreasonable to send on a prisoner without specifying the charges against him."

26 THEN AGRIPPA said to Paul, "You have permission to speak for yourself."

So Paul motioned with his hand and began his defense: 2"King Agrippa, I consider myself fortunate to stand before you today as I make my defense against all the accusations of the Jews, 3and especially so because you are well acquainted with all the Jewish customs and controversies. Therefore, I beg you to listen to me patiently.

4"The Jews all know the way I have lived ever since I was a child, from the beginning of my life in my own country, and also in Jerusalem. 5They have known me for a long time and can testify, if they are willing, that according to the strictest sect of our religion, I lived as a Pharisee. 6And now it is because of my hope in what God has promised our fathers that I am on trial today. 7This is the promise our twelve tribes are hoping to see fulfilled as they earnestly serve God day and night. O king, it is because of this hope that the Jews are accusing me. 8Why should any of you consider it incredible that God raises the dead?

9"I too was convinced that I ought to do all that was possible to oppose the name of Jesus of Nazareth. 10And that is just what I did in Jerusalem. On the authority of the chief priests I put many of the saints in prison, and when they were put to death, I cast my vote against them. 11Many a time I went from one synagogue to another to have them punished, and I tried to force them to blaspheme. In my obsession against them, I even went to foreign cities to persecute them.

12"On one of these journeys I was going to Damascus with the authority and commission of the chief priests. 13About noon, O king, as I was on the road, I saw a light from heaven, brighter than the sun, blazing around me and my companions. 14We all fell to the ground, and I heard a voice saying to me in Aramaic,[a] 'Saul, Saul, why do you persecute me? It is hard for you to kick against the goads.'

15"Then I asked, 'Who are you, Lord?'

" 'I am Jesus, whom you are persecuting,' the Lord replied. 16'Now get up and stand on your feet. I have appeared to you to appoint you as a servant and as a witness of what you have seen of me and what I will show you. 17I will rescue you from your own people and from the Gentiles. I am sending you to them 18to open their eyes and turn them from darkness to light, and from the power of Satan to God, so that they may receive forgiveness of sins and a place among those who are sanctified by faith in me.'

19"So then, King Agrippa, I was not disobedient to the vision from heaven. 20First to those in Damascus,

[a] 14 Or *Hebrew*

Living Bible

24Then Festus addressed the audience: "King Agrippa and all present," he said, "this is the man whose death is demanded both by the local Jews and by those in Jerusalem! 25But in my opinion he has done nothing worthy of death. However, he appealed his case to Caesar, and I have no alternative but to send him. 26But what shall I write the Emperor? For there is no real charge against him! So I have brought him before you all, and especially you, King Agrippa, to examine him and then tell me what to write. 27For it doesn't seem reasonable to send a prisoner to the Emperor without any charges against him!"

26 THEN AGRIPPA said to Paul, "Go ahead. Tell us your story."

So Paul, with many gestures,b presented his defense:
2"I am fortunate, King Agrippa," he began, "to be able to present my answer before you, 3for I know you are an expert on Jewish laws and customs. Now please listen patiently!

4"As the Jews are well aware, I was given a thorough Jewish training from my earliest childhood in Tarsusc and later at Jerusalem, and I lived accordingly. 5If they would admit it, they know that I have always been the strictest of Pharisees when it comes to obedience to Jewish laws and customs. 6But the real reason behind their accusations is something else—it is because I am looking forward to the fulfillment of God's promise made to our ancestors. 7The twelve tribes of Israel strive night and day to attain this same hope I have! Yet, O King, for me it is a crime, they say! 8But is it a crime to believe in the resurrection of the dead? Does it seem incredible to you that God can bring men back to life again?

9"I used to believe that I ought to do many horrible things to the followers of Jesus of Nazareth.d 10I imprisoned many of the saints in Jerusalem, as authorized by the High Priests; and when they were condemned to death, I cast my vote against them. 11I used torture to try to make Christians everywhere curse Christ. I was so violently opposed to them that I even hounded them in distant cities in foreign lands.

12"I was on such a mission to Damascus, armed with the authority and commission of the chief priests, 13when one day about noon, sir, a light from heaven brighter than the sun shone down on me and my companions. 14We all fell down, and I heard a voice speaking to me in Hebrew, 'Saul, Saul, why are you persecuting me? You are only hurting yourself.'e

15"'Who are you, sir?' I asked.

"And the Lord replied, 'I am Jesus, the one you are persecuting. 16Now stand up! For I have appeared to you to appoint you as my servant and my witness. You are to tell the world about this experience and about the many other occasions when I shall appear to you. 17And I will protect you from both your own people and the Gentiles. Yes, I am going to send you to the Gentiles 18to open their eyes to their true condition so that they may repent and live in the light of God instead of in Satan's darkness, so that they may receive forgiveness for their sins and God's inheritance along with all people everywhere whose sins are cleansed away, who are set apart by faith in me.'

19"And so, O King Agrippa, I was not disobedient to that vision from heaven! 20I preached first to those in

New Revised Standard

24And Festus said, "King Agrippa and all here present with us, you see this man about whom the whole Jewish community petitioned me, both in Jerusalem and here, shouting that he ought not to live any longer. 25But I found that he had done nothing deserving death; and when he appealed to his Imperial Majesty, I decided to send him. 26But I have nothing definite to write to our sovereign about him. Therefore I have brought him before all of you, and especially before you, King Agrippa, so that, after we have examined him, I may have something to write— 27for it seems to me unreasonable to send a prisoner without indicating the charges against him."

Paul Defends Himself before Agrippa

26 AGRIPPA SAID to Paul, "You have permission to speak for yourself." Then Paul stretched out his hand and began to defend himself:

2 "I consider myself fortunate that it is before you, King Agrippa, I am to make my defense today against all the accusations of the Jews, 3because you are especially familiar with all the customs and controversies of the Jews; therefore I beg of you to listen to me patiently.

4 "All the Jews know my way of life from my youth, a life spent from the beginning among my own people and in Jerusalem. 5They have known for a long time, if they are willing to testify, that I have belonged to the strictest sect of our religion and lived as a Pharisee. 6And now I stand here on trial on account of my hope in the promise made by God to our ancestors, 7a promise that our twelve tribes hope to attain, as they earnestly worship day and night. It is for this hope, your Excellency,f that I am accused by Jews! 8Why is it thought incredible by any of you that God raises the dead?

9 "Indeed, I myself was convinced that I ought to do many things against the name of Jesus of Nazareth.g 10And that is what I did in Jerusalem; with authority received from the chief priests, I not only locked up many of the saints in prison, but I also cast my vote against them when they were being condemned to death. 11By punishing them often in all the synagogues I tried to force them to blaspheme; and since I was so furiously enraged at them, I pursued them even to foreign cities.

Paul Tells of His Conversion

12 "With this in mind, I was traveling to Damascus with the authority and commission of the chief priests, 13when at midday along the road, your Excellency,f I saw a light from heaven, brighter than the sun, shining around me and my companions. 14When we had all fallen to the ground, I heard a voice saying to me in the Hebrewh language, 'Saul, Saul, why are you persecuting me? It hurts you to kick against the goads.' 15I asked, 'Who are you, Lord?' The Lord answered, 'I am Jesus whom you are persecuting. 16But get up and stand on your feet; for I have appeared to you for this purpose, to appoint you to serve and testify to the things in which you have seen mei and to those in which I will appear to you. 17I will rescue you from your people and from the Gentiles—to whom I am sending you 18to open their eyes so that they may turn from darkness to light and from the power of Satan to God, so that they may receive forgiveness of sins and a place among those who are sanctified by faith in me.'

Paul Tells of His Preaching

19 "After that, King Agrippa, I was not disobedient to the heavenly vision, 20but declared first to those in

---

b 26:1 with many gestures, literally, "stretched forth his hand." c 26:4 my earliest childhood in Tarsus, literally, "my own nation." d 26:9 the followers of Jesus of Nazareth, literally, "the name." e 26:14 You are only hurting yourself, literally, "It is hard for you to kick against the oxgoad."

f Gk O king   g Gk the Nazorean   h That is, Aramaic   i Other ancient authorities read the things that you have seen

King James

20But showed first unto them of Damascus, and at Jerusalem, and throughout all the coasts of Judaea, and *then* to the Gentiles, that they should repent and turn to God, and do works meet for repentance.

21For these causes the Jews caught me in the temple, and went about to kill *me*.

22Having therefore obtained help of God, I continue unto this day, witnessing both to small and great, saying none other things than those which the prophets and Moses did say should come:

23That Christ should suffer, *and* that he should be the first that should rise from the dead, and should show light unto the people, and to the Gentiles.

24And as he thus spake for himself, Festus said with a loud voice, Paul, thou art beside thyself; much learning doth make thee mad.

25But he said, I am not mad, most noble Festus; but speak forth the words of truth and soberness.

26For the king knoweth of these things, before whom also I speak freely: for I am persuaded that none of these things are hidden from him; for this thing was not done in a corner.

27King Agrippa, believest thou the prophets? I know that thou believest.

28Then Agrippa said unto Paul, Almost thou persuadest me to be a Christian.

29And Paul said, I would to God, that not only thou, but also all that hear me this day, were both almost, and altogether such as I am, except these bonds.

30And when he had thus spoken, the king rose up, and the governor, and Bernice, and they that sat with them:

31And when they were gone aside, they talked between themselves, saying, This man doeth nothing worthy of death or of bonds.

32Then said Agrippa unto Festus, This man might have been set at liberty, if he had not appealed unto Caesar.

27 AND WHEN it was determined that we should sail into Italy, they delivered Paul and certain other prisoners unto *one* named Julius, a centurion of Augustus' band.

2And entering into a ship of Adramyttium, we launched, meaning to sail by the coasts of Asia; *one* Aristarchus, a Macedonian of Thessalonica, being with us.

3And the next *day* we touched at Sidon. And Julius courteously entreated Paul, and gave *him* liberty to go unto his friends to refresh himself.

4And when we had launched from thence, we sailed under Cyprus, because the winds were contrary.

5And when we had sailed over the sea of Cilicia and Pamphylia, we came to Myra, *a city* of Lycia.

6And there the centurion found a ship of Alexandria sailing into Italy; and he put us therein.

New International

then to those in Jerusalem and in all Judea, and to the Gentiles also, I preached that they should repent and turn to God and prove their repentance by their deeds. 21That is why the Jews seized me in the temple courts and tried to kill me. 22But I have had God's help to this very day, and so I stand here and testify to small and great alike. I am saying nothing beyond what the prophets and Moses said would happen— 23that the Christ[a] would suffer and, as the first to rise from the dead, would proclaim light to his own people and to the Gentiles."

24At this point Festus interrupted Paul's defense. "You are out of your mind, Paul!" he shouted. "Your great learning is driving you insane."

25"I am not insane, most excellent Festus," Paul replied. "What I am saying is true and reasonable. 26The king is familiar with these things, and I can speak freely to him. I am convinced that none of this has escaped his notice, because it was not done in a corner. 27King Agrippa, do you believe the prophets? I know you do."

28Then Agrippa said to Paul, "Do you think that in such a short time you can persuade me to be a Christian?"

29Paul replied, "Short time or long—I pray God that not only you but all who are listening to me today may become what I am, except for these chains."

30The king rose, and with him the governor and Bernice and those sitting with them. 31They left the room, and while talking with one another, they said, "This man is not doing anything that deserves death or imprisonment."

32Agrippa said to Festus, "This man could have been set free if he had not appealed to Caesar."

Paul Sails for Rome

27 WHEN IT was decided that we would sail for Italy, Paul and some other prisoners were handed over to a centurion named Julius, who belonged to the Imperial Regiment. 2We boarded a ship from Adramyttium about to sail for ports along the coast of the province of Asia, and we put out to sea. Aristarchus, a Macedonian from Thessalonica, was with us.

3The next day we landed at Sidon; and Julius, in kindness to Paul, allowed him to go to his friends so they might provide for his needs. 4From there we put out to sea again and passed to the lee of Cyprus because the winds were against us. 5When we had sailed across the open sea off the coast of Cilicia and Pamphylia, we landed at Myra in Lycia. 6There the centurion found an Alexandrian ship sailing for Italy and put us on board.

a 23 Or Messiah

Living Bible

Damascus, then in Jerusalem and through Judea, and also to the Gentiles that all must forsake their sins and turn to God—and prove their repentance by doing good deeds. 21The Jews arrested me in the Temple for preaching this, and tried to kill me, 22but God protected me so that I am still alive today to tell these facts to everyone, both great and small. I teach nothing except what the prophets and Moses said— 23that the Messiah would suffer, and be the First to rise from the dead, to bring light to Jews and Gentiles alike.”

24Suddenly Festus shouted, “Paul, you are insane. Your long studying has broken your mind!”

25But Paul replied, “I am not insane, Most Excellent Festus. I speak words of sober truth. 26And King Agrippa knows about these things. I speak frankly for I am sure these events are all familiar to him, for they were not done in a corner! 27King Agrippa, do you believe the prophets? But I know you do—”

28Agrippa interrupted him. “With trivial proofs like these,b you expect me to become a Christian?”

29And Paul replied, “Would to God that whether my arguments are trivial or strong, both you and everyone here in this audience might become the same as I am, except for these chains.”

30Then the king, the governor, Bernice, and all the others stood and left. 31As they talked it over afterwards they agreed, “This man hasn’t done anything worthy of death or imprisonment.”

32And Agrippa said to Festus, “He could be set free if he hadn’t appealed to Caesar!”

27 ARRANGEMENTS WERE finally made to start us on our way to Rome by ship; so Paul and several other prisoners were placed in the custody of an officer named Julius, a member of the imperial guard. 2We left on a boatc which was scheduled to make several stops along the Turkish coast.d I should add that Aristarchus,e a Greek from Thessalonica, was with us.

3The next day when we docked at Sidon, Julius was very kind to Paul and let him go ashore to visit with friends and receive their hospitality. 4Putting to sea from there, we encountered headwinds that made it difficult to keep the ship on course, so we sailed north of Cyprus between the island and the mainland,f 5and passed along the coast of the provinces of Cilicia and Pamphylia, landing at Myra, in the province of Lycia. 6There our officer found an Egyptian ship from Alexandria, bound for Italy, and put us aboard.

New Revised Standard

Damascus, then in Jerusalem and throughout the countryside of Judea, and also to the Gentiles, that they should repent and turn to God and do deeds consistent with repentance. 21For this reason the Jews seized me in the temple and tried to kill me. 22To this day I have had help from God, and so I stand here, testifying to both small and great, saying nothing but what the prophets and Moses said would take place: 23that the Messiahg must suffer, and that, by being the first to rise from the dead, he would proclaim light both to our people and to the Gentiles.”

Paul Appeals to Agrippa to Believe

24 While he was making this defense, Festus exclaimed, “You are out of your mind, Paul! Too much learning is driving you insane!” 25But Paul said, “I am not out of my mind, most excellent Festus, but I am speaking the sober truth. 26Indeed the king knows about these things, and to him I speak freely; for I am certain that none of these things has escaped his notice, for this was not done in a corner. 27King Agrippa, do you believe the prophets? I know that you believe.” 28Agrippa said to Paul, “Are you so quickly persuading me to become a Christian?”h 29Paul replied, “Whether quickly or not, I pray to God that not only you but also all who are listening to me today might become such as I am— except for these chains.”

30 Then the king got up, and with him the governor and Bernice and those who had been seated with them; 31and as they were leaving, they said to one another, “This man is doing nothing to deserve death or imprisonment.” 32Agrippa said to Festus, “This man could have been set free if he had not appealed to the emperor.”

Paul Sails for Rome

27 WHEN IT was decided that we were to sail for Italy, they transferred Paul and some other prisoners to a centurion of the Augustan Cohort, named Julius. 2Embarking on a ship of Adramyttium that was about to set sail to the ports along the coast of Asia, we put to sea, accompanied by Aristarchus, a Macedonian from Thessalonica. 3The next day we put in at Sidon; and Julius treated Paul kindly, and allowed him to go to his friends to be cared for. 4Putting out to sea from there, we sailed under the lee of Cyprus, because the winds were against us. 5After we had sailed across the sea that is off Cilicia and Pamphylia, we came to Myra in Lycia. 6There the centurion found an Alexandrian ship bound for Italy and put us on board. 7We sailed slowly for a

---

b 26:28 With trivial proofs like these, literally, “with little [persuasion].”
c 27:2 a boat, literally, “a ship of Adramyttium.”   d 27:2 the Turkish coast, literally, “the coast of Asia.”   e 27:2 Aristarchus: see 19:29, 20:4, Philem 24.   f 27:4 between the island and the mainland, implied. Literally, “we sailed under the lee of Cyprus.” Narratives of that period interpret this as meaning what is indicated in the paraphrase above.

g Or the Christ   h Or Quickly you will persuade me to play the Christian

King James

7And when we had sailed slowly many days, and scarce were come over against Cnidus, the wind not suffering us, we sailed under Crete, over against Salmone;

8And, hardly passing it, came unto a place which is called The fair havens; nigh whereunto was the city *of* Lasea.

9Now when much time was spent, and when sailing was now dangerous, because the fast was now already past, Paul admonished *them,*

10And said unto them, Sirs, I perceive that this voyage will be with hurt and much damage, not only of the lading and ship, but also of our lives.

11Nevertheless the centurion believed the master and the owner of the ship, more than those things which were spoken by Paul.

12And because the haven was not commodious to winter in, the more part advised to depart thence also, if by any means they might attain to Phenice, *and there* to winter; *which is* an haven of Crete, and lieth toward the south west and north west.

13And when the south wind blew softly, supposing that they had obtained *their* purpose, loosing *thence,* they sailed close by Crete.

14But not long after there arose against it a tempestuous wind, called Euroclydon.

15And when the ship was caught, and could not bear up into the wind, we let *her* drive.

16And running under a certain island which is called Clauda, we had much work to come by the boat:

17Which when they had taken up, they used helps, undergirding the ship; and, fearing lest they should fall into the quicksands, strake sail, and so were driven.

18And we being exceedingly tossed with a tempest, the next *day* they lightened the ship;

19And the third *day* we cast out with our own hands the tackling of the ship.

20And when neither sun nor stars in many days appeared, and no small tempest lay on *us,* all hope that we should be saved was then taken away.

21But after long abstinence Paul stood forth in the midst of them, and said, Sirs, ye should have hearkened unto me, and not have loosed from Crete, and to have gained this harm and loss.

22And now I exhort you to be of good cheer: for there shall be no loss of *any man's* life among you, but of the ship.

23For there stood by me this night the angel of God, whose I am, and whom I serve,

24Saying, Fear not, Paul; thou must be brought before Caesar: and, lo, God hath given thee all them that sail with thee.

25Wherefore, sirs, be of good cheer: for I believe God, that it shall be even as it was told me.

26Howbeit we must be cast upon a certain island.

27But when the fourteenth night was come, as we were driven up and down in Adria, about midnight the shipmen deemed that they drew near to some country;

28And sounded, and found *it* twenty fathoms: and when they had gone a little further, they sounded again, and found *it* fifteen fathoms.

29Then fearing lest we should have fallen upon rocks, they cast four anchors out of the stern, and wished for the day.

30And as the shipmen were about to flee out of the ship, when they had let down the boat into the sea, under colour as though they would have cast anchors out of the foreship,

31Paul said to the centurion and to the soldiers, Except these abide in the ship, ye cannot be saved.

32Then the soldiers cut off the ropes of the boat, and let her fall off.

New International

7We made slow headway for many days and had difficulty arriving off Cnidus. When the wind did not allow us to hold our course, we sailed to the lee of Crete, opposite Salmone. 8We moved along the coast with difficulty and came to a place called Fair Havens, near the town of Lasea.

9Much time had been lost, and sailing had already become dangerous because by now it was after the Fast.a So Paul warned them, 10"Men, I can see that our voyage is going to be disastrous and bring great loss to ship and cargo, and to our own lives also." 11But the centurion, instead of listening to what Paul said, followed the advice of the pilot and of the owner of the ship. 12Since the harbor was unsuitable to winter in, the majority decided that we should sail on, hoping to reach Phoenix and winter there. This was a harbor in Crete, facing both southwest and northwest.

The Storm

13When a gentle south wind began to blow, they thought they had obtained what they wanted; so they weighed anchor and sailed along the shore of Crete. 14Before very long, a wind of hurricane force, called the "northeaster," swept down from the island. 15The ship was caught by the storm and could not head into the wind; so we gave way to it and were driven along. 16As we passed to the lee of a small island called Cauda, we were hardly able to make the lifeboat secure. 17When the men had hoisted it aboard, they passed ropes under the ship itself to hold it together. Fearing that they would run aground on the sandbars of Syrtis, they lowered the sea anchor and let the ship be driven along. 18We took such a violent battering from the storm that the next day they began to throw the cargo overboard. 19On the third day, they threw the ship's tackle overboard with their own hands. 20When neither sun nor stars appeared for many days and the storm continued raging, we finally gave up all hope of being saved.

21After the men had gone a long time without food, Paul stood up before them and said: "Men, you should have taken my advice not to sail from Crete; then you would have spared yourselves this damage and loss. 22But now I urge you to keep up your courage, because not one of you will be lost; only the ship will be destroyed. 23Last night an angel of the God whose I am and whom I serve stood beside me 24and said, 'Do not be afraid, Paul. You must stand trial before Caesar; and God has graciously given you the lives of all who sail with you.' 25So keep up your courage, men, for I have faith in God that it will happen just as he told me. 26Nevertheless, we must run aground on some island."

The Shipwreck

27On the fourteenth night we were still being driven across the Adriaticb Sea, when about midnight the sailors sensed they were approaching land. 28They took soundings and found that the water was a hundred and twenty feetc deep. A short time later they took soundings again and found it was ninety feetd deep. 29Fearing that we would be dashed against the rocks, they dropped four anchors from the stern and prayed for daylight. 30In an attempt to escape from the ship, the sailors let the lifeboat down into the sea, pretending they were going to lower some anchors from the bow. 31Then Paul said to the centurion and the soldiers, "Unless these men stay with the ship, you cannot be saved." 32So the soldiers cut the ropes that held the lifeboat and let it fall away.

---

a 9 That is, the Day of Atonement (Yom Kippur)   b 27 In ancient times the name referred to an area extending well south of Italy.   c 28 Greek *twenty orguias* (about 37 meters)   d 28 Greek *fifteen orguias* (about 27 meters)

Living Bible

7, 8We had several days of rough sailing, and finally neared Cnidus;e but the winds had become too strong, so we ran across to Crete, passing the port of Salome. Beating into the wind with great difficulty and moving slowly along the southern coast, we arrived at Fair Havens, near the city of Lasea. 9There we stayed for several days. The weather was becoming dangerous for long voyages by then, because it was late in the year,f and Paul spoke to the ship's officers about it.

10"Sirs," he said, "I believe there is trouble ahead if we go on—perhaps shipwreck, loss of cargo, injuries, and death." 11But the officers in charge of the prisoners listened more to the ship's captain and the owner than to Paul. 12And since Fair Havens was an exposedg harbor—a poor place to spend the winter—most of the crew advised trying to go further up the coast to Phoenix, in order to winter there; Phoenix was a good harbor with only a northwest and southwest exposure.

13Just then a light wind began blowing from the south, and it looked like a perfect day for the trip; so they pulled up anchor and sailed along close to shore.

14, 15But shortly afterwards, the weather changed abruptly and a heavy wind of typhoon strength (a "northeaster," they called it) caught the ship and blew it out to sea. They tried at first to face back to shore but couldn't, so they gave up and let the ship run before the gale.

16We finally sailed behind a small island named Clauda, where with great difficulty we hoisted aboard the lifeboat that was being towed behind us, 17and then banded the ship with ropes to strengthen the hull. The sailors were afraid of being driven across to the quicksands of the African coast,h so they lowered the topsails and were thus driven before the wind.

18The next day as the seas grew higher, the crew began throwing the cargo overboard. 19The following day they threw out the tackle and anything else they could lay their hands on. 20The terrible storm raged unabated many days,i until at last all hope was gone.

21No one had eaten for a long time, but finally Paul called the crew together and said, "Men, you should have listened to me in the first place and not left Fair Havens—you would have avoided all this injury and loss! 22But cheer up! Not one of us will lose our lives, even though the ship will go down.

23"For last night an angel of the God to whom I belong and whom I serve stood beside me, 24and said, 'Don't be afraid, Paul—for you will surely stand trial before Caesar! What's more, God has granted your request and will save the lives of all those sailing with you.' 25So take courage! For I believe God! It will be just as he said! 26But we will be shipwrecked on an island."

27About midnight on the fourteenth night of the storm, as we were being driven to and fro on the Adriatic Sea, the sailors suspected land was near. 28They sounded, and found 120 feet of water below them. A little later they sounded again, and found only ninety feet. 29At this rate they knew they would soon be driven ashore; and fearing rocks along the coast, they threw out four anchors from the stern and prayed for daylight.

30Some of the sailors planned to abandon the ship, and lowered the emergency boat as though they were going to put out anchors from the prow. 31But Paul said to the soldiers and commanding officer, "You will all die unless everyone stays aboard." 32So the soldiers cut the ropes and let the boat fall off.

---

e 27:7, 8 Cnidus, a port on the southeast coast of Turkey.   f 27:9 because it was late in the year, literally, "because the Fast was now already gone by." It came about the time of the autumn equinox.   g 27:12 exposed, implied.   h 27:17 were afraid of being driven across to the quicksands of the African coast, literally, "fearing lest they should be cast upon the Syrtis."   i 27:20 The terrible storm raged unabated many days, literally, "Neither sun nor stars shone upon us."

New Revised Standard

number of days and arrived with difficulty off Cnidus, and as the wind was against us, we sailed under the lee of Crete off Salmone. 8Sailing past it with difficulty, we came to a place called Fair Havens, near the city of Lasea.

9 Since much time had been lost and sailing was now dangerous, because even the Fast had already gone by, Paul advised them, 10saying, "Sirs, I can see that the voyage will be with danger and much heavy loss, not only of the cargo and the ship, but also of our lives." 11But the centurion paid more attention to the pilot and to the owner of the ship than to what Paul said. 12Since the harbor was not suitable for spending the winter, the majority was in favor of putting to sea from there, on the chance that somehow they could reach Phoenix, where they could spend the winter. It was a harbor of Crete, facing southwest and northwest.

The Storm at Sea

13 When a moderate south wind began to blow, they thought they could achieve their purpose; so they weighed anchor and began to sail past Crete, close to the shore. 14But soon a violent wind, called the northeaster, rushed down from Crete.j 15Since the ship was caught and could not be turned head-on into the wind, we gave way to it and were driven. 16By running under the lee of a small island called Caudak we were scarcely able to get the ship's boat under control. 17After hoisting it up they took measuresl to undergird the ship; then, fearing that they would run on the Syrtis, they lowered the sea anchor and so were driven. 18We were being pounded by the storm so violently that on the next day they began to throw the cargo overboard, 19and on the third day with their own hands they threw the ship's tackle overboard. 20When neither sun nor stars appeared for many days, and no small tempest raged, all hope of our being saved was at last abandoned.

21 Since they had been without food for a long time, Paul then stood up among them and said, "Men, you should have listened to me and not have set sail from Crete and thereby avoided this damage and loss. 22I urge you now to keep up your courage, for there will be no loss of life among you, but only of the ship. 23For last night there stood by me an angel of the God to whom I belong and whom I worship, 24and he said, 'Do not be afraid, Paul; you must stand before the emperor; and indeed, God has granted safety to all those who are sailing with you.' 25So keep up your courage, men, for I have faith in God that it will be exactly as I have been told. 26But we will have to run aground on some island."

27 When the fourteenth night had come, as we were drifting across the sea of Adria, about midnight the sailors suspected that they were nearing land. 28So they took soundings and found twenty fathoms; a little farther on they took soundings again and found fifteen fathoms. 29Fearing that we might run on the rocks, they let down four anchors from the stern and prayed for day to come. 30But when the sailors tried to escape from the ship and had lowered the boat into the sea, on the pretext of putting out anchors from the bow, 31Paul said to the centurion and the soldiers, "Unless these men stay in the ship, you cannot be saved." 32Then the soldiers cut away the ropes of the boat and set it adrift.

---

j Gk it   k Other ancient authorities read Clauda   l Gk helps

King James

33And while the day was coming on, Paul besought *them* all to take meat, saying, This day is the fourteenth day that ye have tarried and continued fasting, having taken nothing.

34Wherefore I pray you to take *some* meat: for this is for your health: for there shall not an hair fall from the head of any of you.

35And when he had thus spoken, he took bread, and gave thanks to God in presence of them all: and when he had broken *it*, he began to eat.

36Then were they all of good cheer, and they also took *some* meat.

37And we were in all in the ship two hundred three-score and sixteen souls.

38And when they had eaten enough, they lightened the ship, and cast out the wheat into the sea.

39And when it was day, they knew not the land: but they discovered a certain creek with a shore, into the which they were minded, if it were possible, to thrust in the ship.

40And when they had taken up the anchors, they committed *themselves* unto the sea, and loosed the rudder bands, and hoisted up the mainsail to the wind, and made toward shore.

41And falling into a place where two seas met, they ran the ship aground; and the forepart stuck fast, and remained unmoveable, but the hinderpart was broken with the violence of the waves.

42And the soldiers' counsel was to kill the prisoners, lest any of them should swim out, and escape.

43But the centurion, willing to save Paul, kept them from *their* purpose; and commanded that they which could swim should cast *themselves* first *into the sea*, and get to land:

44And the rest, some on boards, and some on *broken pieces* of the ship. And so it came to pass, that they escaped all safe to land.

28 AND WHEN they were escaped, then they knew that the island was called Melita.

2And the barbarous people showed us no little kindness: for they kindled a fire, and received us every one, because of the present rain, and because of the cold.

3And when Paul had gathered a bundle of sticks, and laid *them* on the fire, there came a viper out of the heat, and fastened on his hand.

4And when the barbarians saw the *venomous* beast hang on his hand, they said among themselves, No doubt this man is a murderer, whom, though he hath escaped the sea, yet vengeance suffereth not to live.

5And he shook off the beast into the fire, and felt no harm.

6Howbeit they looked when he should have swollen, or fallen down dead suddenly: but after they had looked a great while, and saw no harm come to him, they changed their minds, and said that he was a god.

7In the same quarters were possessions of the chief man of the island, whose name was Publius; who received us, and lodged us three days courteously.

8And it came to pass, that the father of Publius lay sick of a fever and of a bloody flux: to whom Paul entered in, and prayed, and laid his hands on him, and healed him.

9So when this was done, others also, which had diseases in the island, came, and were healed:

10Who also honoured us with many honours; and when we departed, they laded *us* with such things as were necessary.

New International

33Just before dawn Paul urged them all to eat. "For the last fourteen days," he said, "you have been in constant suspense and have gone without food—you haven't eaten anything. 34Now I urge you to take some food. You need it to survive. Not one of you will lose a single hair from his head." 35After he said this, he took some bread and gave thanks to God in front of them all. Then he broke it and began to eat. 36They were all encouraged and ate some food themselves. 37Altogether there were 276 of us on board. 38When they had eaten as much as they wanted, they lightened the ship by throwing the grain into the sea.

39When daylight came, they did not recognize the land, but they saw a bay with a sandy beach, where they decided to run the ship aground if they could. 40Cutting loose the anchors, they left them in the sea and at the same time untied the ropes that held the rudders. Then they hoisted the foresail to the wind and made for the beach. 41But the ship struck a sandbar and ran aground. The bow stuck fast and would not move, and the stern was broken to pieces by the pounding of the surf.

42The soldiers planned to kill the prisoners to prevent any of them from swimming away and escaping. 43But the centurion wanted to spare Paul's life and kept them from carrying out their plan. He ordered those who could swim to jump overboard first and get to land. 44The rest were to get there on planks or on pieces of the ship. In this way everyone reached land in safety.

Ashore on Malta

28 ONCE SAFELY on shore, we found out that the island was called Malta. 2The islanders showed us unusual kindness. They built a fire and welcomed us all because it was raining and cold. 3Paul gathered a pile of brushwood and, as he put it on the fire, a viper, driven out by the heat, fastened itself on his hand. 4When the islanders saw the snake hanging from his hand, they said to each other, "This man must be a murderer; for though he escaped from the sea, Justice has not allowed him to live." 5But Paul shook the snake off into the fire and suffered no ill effects. 6The people expected him to swell up or suddenly fall dead, but after waiting a long time and seeing nothing unusual happen to him, they changed their minds and said he was a god.

7There was an estate nearby that belonged to Publius, the chief official of the island. He welcomed us to his home and for three days entertained us hospitably. 8His father was sick in bed, suffering from fever and dysentery. Paul went in to see him and, after prayer, placed his hands on him and healed him. 9When this had happened, the rest of the sick on the island came and were cured. 10They honored us in many ways and when we were ready to sail, they furnished us with the supplies we needed.

Living Bible

33As the darkness gave way to the early morning light, Paul begged everyone to eat. "You haven't touched food for two weeks," he said. 34"Please eat something now for your own good! For not a hair of your heads shall perish!"

35Then he took some hardtack and gave thanks to God before them all, and broke off a piece and ate it. 36Suddenly everyone felt better and began eating, 37all two hundred seventy-six of us—for that is the number we had aboard. 38After eating, the crew lightened the ship further by throwing all the wheat overboard.

39When it was day, they didn't recognize the coastline, but noticed a bay with a beach and wondered whether they could get between the rocks and be driven up onto the beach. 40They finally decided to try. Cutting off the anchors and leaving them in the sea, they lowered the rudders, raised the foresail and headed ashore. 41But the ship hit a sandbara and ran aground. The bow of the ship stuck fast, while the stern was exposed to the violence of the waves and began to break apart.

42The soldiers advised their commanding officer to let them kill the prisoners lest any of them swim ashore and escape. 43But Juliusb wanted to spare Paul, so he told them no. Then he ordered all who could swim to jump overboard and make for land, 44and the rest to try for it on planks and debris from the broken ship. So everyone escaped safely ashore!

28 WE SOON learned that we were on the island of Malta. The people of the island were very kind to us, building a bonfire on the beach to welcome and warm us in the rain and cold.

3As Paul gathered an armful of sticks to lay on the fire, a poisonous snake, driven out by the heat, fastened itself onto his hand! 4The people of the island saw it hanging there and said to each other, "A murderer, no doubt! Though he escaped the sea, justice will not permit him to live!"

5But Paul shook off the snake into the fire and was unharmed. 6The people waited for him to begin swelling or suddenly fall dead; but when they had waited a long time and no harm came to him, they changed their minds and decided he was a god.

7Near the shore where we landed was an estate belonging to Publius, the governor of the island. He welcomed us courteously and fed us for three days. 8As it happened, Publius' father was ill with fever and dysentery. Paul went in and prayed for him, and laying his hands on him, healed him! 9Then all the other sick people in the island came and were cured. 10As a result we were showered with gifts,c and when the time came to sail, people put on board all sorts of things we would need for the trip.

New Revised Standard

33 Just before daybreak, Paul urged all of them to take some food, saying, "Today is the fourteenth day that you have been in suspense and remaining without food, having eaten nothing. 34Therefore I urge you to take some food, for it will help you survive; for none of you will lose a hair from your heads." 35After he had said this, he took bread; and giving thanks to God in the presence of all, he broke it and began to eat. 36Then all of them were encouraged and took food for themselves. 37(We were in all two hundred seventy-sixd persons in the ship.) 38After they had satisfied their hunger, they lightened the ship by throwing the wheat into the sea.

The Shipwreck

39 In the morning they did not recognize the land, but they noticed a bay with a beach, on which they planned to run the ship ashore, if they could. 40So they cast off the anchors and left them in the sea. At the same time they loosened the ropes that tied the steering-oars; then hoisting the foresail to the wind, they made for the beach. 41But striking a reef,e they ran the ship aground; the bow stuck and remained immovable, but the stern was being broken up by the force of the waves. 42The soldiers' plan was to kill the prisoners, so that none might swim away and escape; 43but the centurion, wishing to save Paul, kept them from carrying out their plan. He ordered those who could swim to jump overboard first and make for the land, 44and the rest to follow, some on planks and others on pieces of the ship. And so it was that all were brought safely to land.

Paul on the Island of Malta

28 AFTER WE had reached safety, we then learned that the island was called Malta. 2The natives showed us unusual kindness. Since it had begun to rain and was cold, they kindled a fire and welcomed all of us around it. 3Paul had gathered a bundle of brushwood and was putting it on the fire, when a viper, driven out by the heat, fastened itself on his hand. 4When the natives saw the creature hanging from his hand, they said to one another, "This man must be a murderer; though he has escaped from the sea, justice has not allowed him to live." 5He, however, shook off the creature into the fire and suffered no harm. 6They were expecting him to swell up or drop dead, but after they had waited a long time and saw that nothing unusual had happened to him, they changed their minds and began to say that he was a god.

7 Now in the neighborhood of that place were lands belonging to the leading man of the island, named Publius, who received us and entertained us hospitably for three days. 8It so happened that the father of Publius lay sick in bed with fever and dysentery. Paul visited him and cured him by praying and putting his hands on him. 9After this happened, the rest of the people on the island who had diseases also came and were cured. 10They bestowed many honors on us, and when we were about to sail, they put on board all the provisions we needed.

---

a 27:41 a sandbar, literally, "a place where two seas met."   b 27:43 Julius, implied.   c 28:10 gifts, literally, "honors."

d Other ancient authorities read seventy-six; others, about seventy-six   e Gk place of two seas

King James

11And after three months we departed in a ship of Alexandria, which had wintered in the isle, whose sign was Castor and Pollux.

12And landing at Syracuse, we tarried *there* three days.

13And from thence we fetched a compass, and came to Rhegium: and after one day the south wind blew, and we came the next day to Puteoli:

14Where we found brethren, and were desired to tarry with them seven days: and so we went toward Rome.

15And from thence, when the brethren heard of us, they came to meet us as far as Appiiforum, and The three taverns: whom when Paul saw, he thanked God, and took courage.

16And when we came to Rome, the centurion delivered the prisoners to the captain of the guard: but Paul was suffered to dwell by himself with a soldier that kept him.

17And it came to pass, that after three days Paul called the chief of the Jews together: and when they were come together, he said unto them, Men *and* brethren, though I have committed nothing against the people, or customs of our fathers, yet was I delivered prisoner from Jerusalem into the hands of the Romans.

18Who, when they had examined me, would have let *me* go, because there was no cause of death in me.

19But when the Jews spake against *it,* I was constrained to appeal unto Caesar; not that I had aught to accuse my nation of.

20For this cause therefore have I called for you, to see *you,* and to speak with *you:* because that for the hope of Israel I am bound with this chain.

21And they said unto him, We neither received letters out of Judaea concerning thee, neither any of the brethren that came showed or spake any harm of thee.

22But we desire to hear of thee what thou thinkest: for as concerning this sect, we know that every where it is spoken against.

23And when they had appointed him a day, there came many to him into *his* lodging; to whom he expounded and testified the kingdom of God, persuading them concerning Jesus, both out of the law of Moses, and *out of* the prophets, from morning till evening.

24And some believed the things which were spoken, and some believed not.

25And when they agreed not among themselves, they departed, after that Paul had spoken one word, Well spake the Holy Ghost by Esaias the prophet unto our fathers,

26Saying, Go unto this people, and say, Hearing ye shall hear, and shall not understand; and seeing ye shall see, and not perceive:

27For the heart of this people is waxed gross, and their ears are dull of hearing, and their eyes have they closed; lest they should see with *their* eyes, and hear with *their* ears, and understand with *their* heart, and should be converted, and I should heal them.

28Be it known therefore unto you, that the salvation of God is sent unto the Gentiles, and *that* they will hear it.

29And when he had said these words, the Jews departed, and had great reasoning among themselves.

30And Paul dwelt two whole years in his own hired house, and received all that came in unto him,

31Preaching the kingdom of God, and teaching those things which concern the Lord Jesus Christ, with all confidence, no man forbidding him.

New International

Arrival at Rome

11After three months we put out to sea in a ship that had wintered in the island. It was an Alexandrian ship with the figurehead of the twin gods Castor and Pollux.b 12We put in at Syracuse and stayed there three days. 13From there we set sail and arrived at Rhegium. The next day the south wind came up, and on the following day we reached Puteoli. 14There we found some brothers who invited us to spend a week with them. And so we came to Rome. 15The brothers there had heard that we were coming, and they traveled as far as the Forum of Appius and the Three Taverns to meet us. At the sight of these men Paul thanked God and was encouraged. 16When we got to Rome, Paul was allowed to live by himself, with a soldier to guard him.

Paul Preaches at Rome Under Guard

17Three days later he called together the leaders of the Jews. When they had assembled, Paul said to them: "My brothers, although I have done nothing against our people or against the customs of our ancestors, I was arrested in Jerusalem and handed over to the Romans. 18They examined me and wanted to release me, because I was not guilty of any crime deserving death. 19But when the Jews objected, I was compelled to appeal to Caesar— not that I had any charge to bring against my own people. 20For this reason I have asked to see you and talk with you. It is because of the hope of Israel that I am bound with this chain."

21They replied, "We have not received any letters from Judea concerning you, and none of the brothers who have come from there has reported or said anything bad about you. 22But we want to hear what your views are, for we know that people everywhere are talking against this sect."

23They arranged to meet Paul on a certain day, and came in even larger numbers to the place where he was staying. From morning till evening he explained and declared to them the kingdom of God and tried to convince them about Jesus from the Law of Moses and from the Prophets. 24Some were convinced by what he said, but others would not believe. 25They disagreed among themselves and began to leave after Paul had made this final statement: "The Holy Spirit spoke the truth to your forefathers when he said through Isaiah the prophet:

26" 'Go to this people and say,
"You will be ever hearing but never
      understanding;
   you will be ever seeing but never perceiving."
27For this people's heart has become calloused;
   they hardly hear with their ears,
   and they have closed their eyes.
Otherwise they might see with their eyes,
   hear with their ears,
   understand with their hearts
and turn, and I would heal them.'a

28"Therefore I want you to know that God's salvation has been sent to the Gentiles, and they will listen!"b 30For two whole years Paul stayed there in his own rented house and welcomed all who came to see him. 31Boldly and without hindrance he preached the kingdom of God and taught about the Lord Jesus Christ.

a 27 Isaiah 6:9,10   b 28 Some manuscripts *listen!*" 29*After he said this, the Jews left, arguing vigorously among themselves.*

Living Bible

¹¹It was three months after the shipwreck before we set sail again, and this time it was in *The Twin Brothers* of Alexandria, a ship that had wintered at the island. ¹²Our first stop was Syracuse, where we stayed three days. ¹³From there we circled around to Rhegium; a day later a south wind began blowing, so the following day we arrived at Puteoli, ¹⁴where we found some believers! They begged us to stay with them seven days. Then we went on to Rome.

¹⁵The brothers in Rome had heard we were coming and came to meet us at the Forum^c on the Appian Way. Others joined us at The Three Taverns^d. When Paul saw them, he thanked God and took courage.

¹⁶When we arrived in Rome, Paul was permitted to live wherever he wanted to, though guarded by a soldier.

¹⁷Three days after his arrival, he called together the local Jewish leaders and spoke to them as follows: "Brothers, I was arrested by the Jews in Jerusalem and handed over to the Roman government for prosecution, even though I had harmed no one nor violated the customs of our ancestors. ¹⁸The Romans gave me a trial and wanted to release me, for they found no cause for the death sentence demanded by the Jewish leaders. ¹⁹But when the Jews protested the decision, I felt it necessary, with no malice against them, to appeal to Caesar. ²⁰I asked you to come here today so we could get acquainted and I could tell you that it is because I believe the Messiah^e has come that I am bound with this chain."

²¹They replied, "We have heard nothing against you! We have had no letters from Judea or reports from those arriving from Jerusalem.^f ²²But we want to hear what you believe, for the only thing we know about these Christians is that they are denounced everywhere!"

²³So a time was set and on that day large numbers came to his house. He told them about the Kingdom of God and taught them about Jesus from the Scriptures— from the five books of Moses and the books of prophecy. He began lecturing in the morning and went on into the evening!

²⁴Some believed, and some didn't. ²⁵But after they had argued back and forth among themselves, they left with this final word from Paul ringing in their ears: "The Holy Spirit was right when he said through Isaiah the prophet,

²⁶" 'Say to the Jews, "You will hear and see but not understand, ²⁷for your hearts are too fat and your ears don't listen and you have closed your eyes against understanding, for you don't want to see and hear and understand and turn to me to heal you." '^g ^{28,29h} So I want you to realize that this salvation from God is available to the Gentiles too, and they will accept it."

³⁰Paul lived for the next two years in his rented houseⁱ and welcomed all who visited him, ³¹telling them with all boldness about the Kingdom of God and about the Lord Jesus Christ; and no one tried to stop him.

New Revised Standard

Paul Arrives at Rome

11 Three months later we set sail on a ship that had wintered at the island, an Alexandrian ship with the Twin Brothers as its figurehead. ¹²We put in at Syracuse and stayed there for three days; ¹³then we weighed anchor and came to Rhegium. After one day there a south wind sprang up, and on the second day we came to Puteoli. ¹⁴There we found believers^j and were invited to stay with them for seven days. And so we came to Rome. ¹⁵The believers^j from there, when they heard of us, came as far as the Forum of Appius and Three Taverns to meet us. On seeing them, Paul thanked God and took courage.

16 When we came into Rome, Paul was allowed to live by himself, with the soldier who was guarding him.

Paul and Jewish Leaders in Rome

17 Three days later he called together the local leaders of the Jews. When they had assembled, he said to them, "Brothers, though I had done nothing against our people or the customs of our ancestors, yet I was arrested in Jerusalem and handed over to the Romans. ¹⁸When they had examined me, the Romans^k wanted to release me, because there was no reason for the death penalty in my case. ¹⁹But when the Jews objected, I was compelled to appeal to the emperor—even though I had no charge to bring against my nation. ²⁰For this reason therefore I have asked to see you and speak with you,^l since it is for the sake of the hope of Israel that I am bound with this chain." ²¹They replied, "We have received no letters from Judea about you, and none of the brothers coming here has reported or spoken anything evil about you. ²²But we would like to hear from you what you think, for with regard to this sect we know that everywhere it is spoken against."

Paul Preaches in Rome

23 After they had set a day to meet with him, they came to him at his lodgings in great numbers. From morning until evening he explained the matter to them, testifying to the kingdom of God and trying to convince them about Jesus both from the law of Moses and from the prophets. ²⁴Some were convinced by what he had said, while others refused to believe. ²⁵So they disagreed with each other; and as they were leaving, Paul made one further statement: "The Holy Spirit was right in saying to your ancestors through the prophet Isaiah,

26   'Go to this people and say,
You will indeed listen, but never understand,
   and you will indeed look, but never
      perceive.
27   For this people's heart has grown dull,
   and their ears are hard of hearing,
      and they have shut their eyes;
         so that they might not look with their
            eyes,
      and listen with their ears,
   and understand with their heart and turn—
      and I would heal them.'

²⁸Let it be known to you then that this salvation of God has been sent to the Gentiles; they will listen."^m

30 He lived there two whole years at his own expenseⁿ and welcomed all who came to him, ³¹proclaiming the kingdom of God and teaching about the Lord Jesus Christ with all boldness and without hindrance.

---

^c *28:15 the Forum,* about forty-three miles from Rome.   ^d *28:15 The Three Taverns,* about thirty-five miles from Rome.   ^e *28:20 the Messiah,* literally, "the hope of Israel." But perhaps he is referring here, as in his other defenses, to his belief in the resurrection of the dead.   ^f *28:21 from Jerusalem,* implied. ^g *28:27 turn to me to heal you,* see Isa 6:9, 10.   ^h 28:28, 29. Some of the ancient manuscripts add, "And when he had said these words, the Jews departed, having much dissenting among themselves."   ⁱ *28:30 in his rented house,* or, "at his own expense."

^j Gk *brothers*   ^k Gk *they*   ^l Or *I have asked you to see me and speak with me*   ^m Other ancient authorities add verse 29, *And when he had said these words, the Jews departed, arguing vigorously among themselves*   ⁿ Or *in his own hired dwelling*

King James

THE EPISTLE OF PAUL

THE APOSTLE TO THE

Romans

1 PAUL, A servant of Jesus Christ, called *to be* an apostle, separated unto the gospel of God,
2(Which he had promised afore by his prophets in the holy scriptures,)
3Concerning his Son Jesus Christ our Lord, which was made of the seed of David according to the flesh;
4And declared *to be* the Son of God with power, according to the spirit of holiness, by the resurrection from the dead:
5By whom we have received grace and apostleship, for obedience to the faith among all nations, for his name:
6Among whom are ye also the called of Jesus Christ:
7To all that be in Rome, beloved of God, called *to be* saints: Grace to you and peace from God our Father, and the Lord Jesus Christ.
8First, I thank my God through Jesus Christ for you all, that your faith is spoken of throughout the whole world.
9For God is my witness, whom I serve with my spirit in the gospel of his Son, that without ceasing I make mention of you always in my prayers;
10Making request, if by any means now at length I might have a prosperous journey by the will of God to come unto you.
11For I long to see you, that I may impart unto you some spiritual gift, to the end ye may be established;
12That is, that I may be comforted together with you by the mutual faith both of you and me.
13Now I would not have you ignorant, brethren, that oftentimes I purposed to come unto you, (but was let hitherto,) that I might have some fruit among you also, even as among other Gentiles.
14I am debtor both to the Greeks, and to the Barbarians; both to the wise, and to the unwise.
15So, as much as in me is, I am ready to preach the gospel to you that are at Rome also.
16For I am not ashamed of the gospel of Christ: for it is the power of God unto salvation to every one that believeth; to the Jew first, and also to the Greek.

New International

Romans

1 PAUL, A servant of Christ Jesus, called to be an apostle and set apart for the gospel of God— 2the gospel he promised beforehand through his prophets in the Holy Scriptures 3regarding his Son, who as to his human nature was a descendant of David, 4and who through the Spirit[a] of holiness was declared with power to be the Son of God[b] by his resurrection from the dead: Jesus Christ our Lord. 5Through him and for his name's sake, we received grace and apostleship to call people from among all the Gentiles to the obedience that comes from faith. 6And you also are among those who are called to belong to Jesus Christ.

7To all in Rome who are loved by God and called to be saints:

Grace and peace to you from God our Father and from the Lord Jesus Christ.

Paul's Longing to Visit Rome

8First, I thank my God through Jesus Christ for all of you, because your faith is being reported all over the world. 9God, whom I serve with my whole heart in preaching the gospel of his Son, is my witness how constantly I remember you 10in my prayers at all times; and I pray that now at last by God's will the way may be opened for me to come to you.

11I long to see you so that I may impart to you some spiritual gift to make you strong— 12that is, that you and I may be mutually encouraged by each other's faith. 13I do not want you to be unaware, brothers, that I planned many times to come to you (but have been prevented from doing so until now) in order that I might have a harvest among you, just as I have had among the other Gentiles.

14I am obligated both to Greeks and non-Greeks, both to the wise and the foolish. 15That is why I am so eager to preach the gospel also to you who are at Rome.

16I am not ashamed of the gospel, because it is the power of God for the salvation of everyone who believes: first for the Jew, then for the Gentile. 17For in the

a 4 Or *who as to his spirit*   b 4 Or *was appointed to be the Son of God with power*

Living Bible

New Revised Standard

THE LETTER OF PAUL

TO THE

Romans

Romans

DEAR FRIENDS in Rome: [1]This letter is from Paul, Jesus Christ's slave, chosen to be a missionary, and sent out to preach God's Good News. [2]This Good News was promised long ago by God's prophets in the Old Testament. [3]It is the Good News about his Son, Jesus Christ our Lord, who came as a human baby, born into King David's royal family line; [4]and by being raised from the dead he was proved to be the mighty Son of God, with the holy nature of God himself.

[5]And now, through Christ, all the kindness of God has been poured out upon us undeserving sinners; and now he is sending us out around the world to tell all people everywhere the great things God has done for them, so that they, too, will believe and obey him.

[6, 7]And you, dear friends in Rome, are among those he dearly loves; you, too, are invited by Jesus Christ to be God's very own—yes, his holy people. May all God's mercies and peace be yours from God our Father and from Jesus Christ our Lord.

[8]Let me say first of all that wherever I go I hear you being talked about! For your faith in God is becoming known around the world. How I thank God through Jesus Christ for this good report, and for each one of you. [9]God knows how often I pray for you. Day and night I bring you and your needs in prayer to the one I serve with all my might, telling others the Good News about his Son.

[10]And one of the things I keep on praying for is the opportunity, God willing,[c] to come at last to see you and, if possible, that I will have a safe trip.[d] [11, 12]For I long to visit you so that I can impart to you the faith[e] that will help your church grow strong in the Lord. Then, too, I need your help, for I want not only to share my faith with you but to be encouraged by yours: Each of us will be a blessing to the other.

[13]I want you to know, dear brothers, that I planned to come many times before (but was prevented) so that I could work among you and see good results, just as I have among the other Gentile churches.[f] [14]For I owe a great debt to you and to everyone else, both to civilized people and uncivilized alike; yes, to the educated and uneducated alike. [15]So, to the fullest extent of my ability, I am ready to come also to you in Rome to preach God's Good News.

[16]For I am not ashamed of this Good News about Christ. It is God's powerful method of bringing all who believe it to heaven. This message was preached first to the Jews alone, but now everyone is invited to come to God in this same way. [17]This Good News tells us that

Salutation

PAUL, A servant[g] of Jesus Christ, called to be an apostle, set apart for the gospel of God, [2]which he promised beforehand through his prophets in the holy scriptures, [3]the gospel concerning his Son, who was descended from David according to the flesh [4]and was declared to be Son of God with power according to the spirit[h] of holiness by resurrection from the dead, Jesus Christ our Lord, [5]through whom we have received grace and apostleship to bring about the obedience of faith among all the Gentiles for the sake of his name, [6]including yourselves who are called to belong to Jesus Christ,

[7] To all God's beloved in Rome, who are called to be saints:

Grace to you and peace from God our Father and the Lord Jesus Christ.

Prayer of Thanksgiving

[8] First, I thank my God through Jesus Christ for all of you, because your faith is proclaimed throughout the world. [9]For God, whom I serve with my spirit by announcing the gospel[i] of his Son, is my witness that without ceasing I remember you always in my prayers, [10]asking that by God's will I may somehow at last succeed in coming to you. [11]For I am longing to see you so that I may share with you some spiritual gift to strengthen you— [12]or rather so that we may be mutually encouraged by each other's faith, both yours and mine. [13]I want you to know, brothers and sisters,[j] that I have often intended to come to you (but thus far have been prevented), in order that I may reap some harvest among you as I have among the rest of the Gentiles. [14]I am a debtor both to Greeks and to barbarians, both to the wise and to the foolish [15]—hence my eagerness to proclaim the gospel to you also who are in Rome.

The Power of the Gospel

[16] For I am not ashamed of the gospel; it is the power of God for salvation to everyone who has faith, to the Jew first and also to the Greek. [17]For in it the

---

c *1:10 God willing*, literally, "in the will of God."   d *1:10 that I will have a safe trip*, or, "that I will finally succeed in coming."   e *1:11, 12 the faith*, literally, "some spiritual gift . . . that is, . . . faith."   f *1:13 among the other Gentile churches*, literally, "among the Gentiles."

g Gk *slave*   h Or *Spirit*   i Gk *my spirit in the gospel*   j Gk *brothers*

King James

17For therein is the righteousness of God revealed from faith to faith: as it is written, The just shall live by faith.

18For the wrath of God is revealed from heaven against all ungodliness and unrighteousness of men, who hold the truth in unrighteousness;

19Because that which may be known of God is manifest in them; for God hath shown *it* unto them.

20For the invisible things of him from the creation of the world are clearly seen, being understood by the things that are made, *even* his eternal power and Godhead; so that they are without excuse:

21Because that, when they knew God, they glorified *him* not as God, neither were thankful; but became vain in their imaginations, and their foolish heart was darkened.

22Professing themselves to be wise, they became fools,

23And changed the glory of the uncorruptible God into an image made like to corruptible man, and to birds, and fourfooted beasts, and creeping things.

24Wherefore God also gave them up to uncleanness through the lusts of their own hearts, to dishonour their own bodies between themselves:

25Who changed the truth of God into a lie, and worshipped and served the creature more than the Creator, who is blessed for ever. Amen.

26For this cause God gave them up unto vile affections: for even their women did change the natural use into that which is against nature:

27And likewise also the men, leaving the natural use of the woman, burned in their lust one toward another; men with men working that which is unseemly, and receiving in themselves that recompence of their error which was meet.

28And even as they did not like to retain God in *their* knowledge, God gave them over to a reprobate mind, to do those things which are not convenient;

29Being filled with all unrighteousness, fornication, wickedness, covetousness, maliciousness; full of envy, murder, debate, deceit, malignity; whisperers,

30Backbiters, haters of God, despiteful, proud, boasters, inventors of evil things, disobedient to parents,

31Without understanding, covenantbreakers, without natural affection, implacable, unmerciful:

32Who knowing the judgment of God, that they which commit such things are worthy of death, not only do the same, but have pleasure in them that do them.

2 THEREFORE THOU art inexcusable, O man, whosoever thou art that judgest: for wherein thou judgest another, thou condemnest thyself; for thou that judgest doest the same things.

2But we are sure that the judgment of God is according to truth against them which commit such things.

3And thinkest thou this, O man, that judgest them which do such things, and doest the same, that thou shalt escape the judgment of God?

New International

gospel a righteousness from God is revealed, a righteousness that is by faith from first to last,[a] just as it is written: "The righteous will live by faith."[b]

God's Wrath Against Mankind

18The wrath of God is being revealed from heaven against all the godlessness and wickedness of men who suppress the truth by their wickedness, 19since what may be known about God is plain to them, because God has made it plain to them. 20For since the creation of the world God's invisible qualities—his eternal power and divine nature—have been clearly seen, being understood from what has been made, so that men are without excuse.

21For although they knew God, they neither glorified him as God nor gave thanks to him, but their thinking became futile and their foolish hearts were darkened. 22Although they claimed to be wise, they became fools 23and exchanged the glory of the immortal God for images made to look like mortal man and birds and animals and reptiles.

24Therefore God gave them over in the sinful desires of their hearts to sexual impurity for the degrading of their bodies with one another. 25They exchanged the truth of God for a lie, and worshiped and served created things rather than the Creator—who is forever praised. Amen.

26Because of this, God gave them over to shameful lusts. Even their women exchanged natural relations for unnatural ones. 27In the same way the men also abandoned natural relations with women and were inflamed with lust for one another. Men committed indecent acts with other men, and received in themselves the due penalty for their perversion.

28Furthermore, since they did not think it worthwhile to retain the knowledge of God, he gave them over to a depraved mind, to do what ought not to be done. 29They have become filled with every kind of wickedness, evil, greed and depravity. They are full of envy, murder, strife, deceit and malice. They are gossips, 30slanderers, God-haters, insolent, arrogant and boastful; they invent ways of doing evil; they disobey their parents; 31they are senseless, faithless, heartless, ruthless. 32Although they know God's righteous decree that those who do such things deserve death, they not only continue to do these very things but also approve of those who practice them.

God's Righteous Judgment

2 YOU, THEREFORE, have no excuse, you who pass judgment on someone else, for at whatever point you judge the other, you are condemning yourself, because you who pass judgment do the same things. 2Now we know that God's judgment against those who do such things is based on truth. 3So when you, a mere man, pass judgment on them and yet do the same things, do you think you will escape God's judgment? 4Or do

---

Living Bible

God makes us ready for heaven—makes us right in God's sight—when we put our faith and trust in Christ to save us. This is accomplished from start to finish by faith.c As the Scripture says it, "The man who finds life will find it through trusting God."d

18But God shows his anger from heaven against all sinful, evil men who push away the truth from them. 19For the truth about God is known to them instinctively;e God has put this knowledge in their hearts. 20Since earliest times men have seen the earth and sky and all God made, and have known of his existence and great eternal power. So they will have no excuse [when they stand before God at Judgment Dayf].

21Yes, they knew about him all right, but they wouldn't admit it or worship him or even thank him for all his daily care. And after awhile they began to think up silly ideas of what God was like and what he wanted them to do. The result was that their foolish minds became dark and confused. 22Claiming themselves to be wise without God, they became utter fools instead. 23And then, instead of worshiping the glorious, ever-living God, they took wood and stone and made idols for themselves, carving them to look like mere birds and animals and snakes and punyg men.

24So God let them go ahead into every sort of sex sin, and do whatever they wanted to—yes, vile and sinful things with each other's bodies. 25Instead of believing what they knew was the truth about God, they deliberately chose to believe lies. So they prayed to the things God made, but wouldn't obey the blessed God who made these things.

26That is why God let go of them and let them do all these evil things, so that even their women turned against God's natural plan for them and indulged in sex sin with each other. 27And the men, instead of having a normal sex relationship with women, burned with lust for each other, men doing shameful things with other men and, as a result, getting paid within their own souls with the penalty they so richly deserved.

28So it was that when they gave God up and would not even acknowledge him, God gave them up to doing everything their evil minds could think of. 29Their lives became full of every kind of wickedness and sin, of greed and hate, envy, murder, fighting, lying, bitterness, and gossip.

30They were backbiters, haters of God, insolent, proud braggarts, always thinking of new ways of sinning and continually being disobedient to their parents. 31They tried to misunderstand,h broke their promises, and were heartless—without pity. 32They were fully aware of God's death penalty for these crimes, yet they went right ahead and did them anyway, and encouraged others to do them, too.

2 "WELL," YOU may be saying, "what terrible people you have been talking about!" But wait a minute! You are just as bad. When you say they are wicked and should be punished, you are talking about yourselves, for you do these very same things. 2And we know that God, in justice, will punish anyone who does such things as these. 3Do you think that God will judge and condemn others for doing them and overlook you when you do them, too? 4Don't you realize how patient

New Revised Standard

righteousness of God is revealed through faith for faith; as it is written, "The one who is righteous will live by faith."i

The Guilt of Humankind

18 For the wrath of God is revealed from heaven against all ungodliness and wickedness of those who by their wickedness suppress the truth. 19For what can be known about God is plain to them, because God has shown it to them. 20Ever since the creation of the world his eternal power and divine nature, invisible though they are, have been understood and seen through the things he has made. So they are without excuse; 21for though they knew God, they did not honor him as God or give thanks to him, but they became futile in their thinking, and their senseless minds were darkened. 22Claiming to be wise, they became fools; 23and they exchanged the glory of the immortal God for images resembling a mortal human being or birds or four-footed animals or reptiles.

24 Therefore God gave them up in the lusts of their hearts to impurity, to the degrading of their bodies among themselves, 25because they exchanged the truth about God for a lie and worshiped and served the creature rather than the Creator, who is blessed forever! Amen.

26 For this reason God gave them up to degrading passions. Their women exchanged natural intercourse for unnatural, 27and in the same way also the men, giving up natural intercourse with women, were consumed with passion for one another. Men committed shameless acts with men and received in their own persons the due penalty for their error.

28 And since they did not see fit to acknowledge God, God gave them up to a debased mind and to things that should not be done. 29They were filled with every kind of wickedness, evil, covetousness, malice. Full of envy, murder, strife, deceit, craftiness, they are gossips, 30slanderers, God-haters,j insolent, haughty, boastful, inventors of evil, rebellious toward parents, 31foolish, faithless, heartless, ruthless. 32They know God's decree, that those who practice such things deserve to die—yet they not only do them but even applaud others who practice them.

The Righteous Judgment of God

2 THEREFORE YOU have no excuse, whoever you are, when you judge others; for in passing judgment on another you condemn yourself, because you, the judge, are doing the very same things. 2You say,k "We know that God's judgment on those who do such things is in accordance with truth." 3Do you imagine, whoever you are, that when you judge those who do such things and yet do them yourself, you will escape the judgment of God? 4Or do you despise the riches of

---

c 1:17 This is accomplished from start to finish by faith, literally, "[this] righteousness of God is revealed from faith to faith." d 1:17 "The man who finds life will find it through trusting God" (Hab 2:4). e 1:19 is known to them instinctively, literally, "is manifest in them." f 1:20 when they stand before God at Judgment Day, implied. Or, "They have no excuse for saying there is no God." g 1:23 puny, literally, "mortal." h 1:31 tried to misunderstand, or "were confused fools."

i Or The one who is righteous through faith will live   j Or God-hated   k Gk lacks You say

King James

4Or despisest thou the riches of his goodness and forbearance and longsuffering; not knowing that the goodness of God leadeth thee to repentance?

5But after thy hardness and impenitent heart treasurest up unto thyself wrath against the day of wrath and revelation of the righteous judgment of God;

6Who will render to every man according to his deeds:

7To them who by patient continuance in well doing seek for glory and honour and immortality, eternal life:

8But unto them that are contentious, and do not obey the truth, but obey unrighteousness, indignation and wrath,

9Tribulation and anguish, upon every soul of man that doeth evil, of the Jew first, and also of the Gentile;

10But glory, honour, and peace, to every man that worketh good, to the Jew first, and also to the Gentile:

11For there is no respect of persons with God.

12For as many as have sinned without law shall also perish without law: and as many as have sinned in the law shall be judged by the law;

13(For not the hearers of the law *are* just before God, but the doers of the law shall be justified.

14For when the Gentiles, which have not the law, do by nature the things contained in the law, these, having not the law, are a law unto themselves:

15Which show the work of the law written in their hearts, their conscience also bearing witness, and *their* thoughts the mean while accusing or else excusing one another;)

16In the day when God shall judge the secrets of men by Jesus Christ according to my gospel.

17Behold, thou art called a Jew, and restest in the law, and makest thy boast of God,

18And knowest *his* will, and approvest the things that are more excellent, being instructed out of the law;

19And art confident that thou thyself art a guide of the blind, a light of them which are in darkness,

20An instructor of the foolish, a teacher of babes, which hast the form of knowledge and of the truth in the law.

21Thou therefore which teachest another, teachest thou not thyself? thou that preachest a man should not steal, dost thou steal?

22Thou that sayest a man should not commit adultery, dost thou commit adultery? thou that abhorrest idols, dost thou commit sacrilege?

23Thou that makest thy boast of the law, through breaking the law dishonourest thou God?

24For the name of God is blasphemed among the Gentiles through you, as it is written.

25For circumcision verily profiteth, if thou keep the law: but if thou be a breaker of the law, thy circumcision is made uncircumcision.

26Therefore if the uncircumcision keep the righteousness of the law, shall not his uncircumcision be counted for circumcision?

27And shall not uncircumcision which is by nature, if it fulfil the law, judge thee, who by the letter and circumcision dost transgress the law?

28For he is not a Jew, which is one outwardly; neither *is that* circumcision, which is outward in the flesh:

New International

you show contempt for the riches of his kindness, tolerance and patience, not realizing that God's kindness leads you toward repentance?

5But because of your stubbornness and your unrepentant heart, you are storing up wrath against yourself for the day of God's wrath, when his righteous judgment will be revealed. 6God "will give to each person according to what he has done."[a] 7To those who by persistence in doing good seek glory, honor and immortality, he will give eternal life. 8But for those who are self-seeking and who reject the truth and follow evil, there will be wrath and anger. 9There will be trouble and distress for every human being who does evil: first for the Jew, then for the Gentile; 10but glory, honor and peace for everyone who does good: first for the Jew, then for the Gentile. 11For God does not show favoritism.

12All who sin apart from the law will also perish apart from the law, and all who sin under the law will be judged by the law. 13For it is not those who hear the law who are righteous in God's sight, but it is those who obey the law who will be declared righteous. 14(Indeed, when Gentiles, who do not have the law, do by nature things required by the law, they are a law for themselves, even though they do not have the law, 15since they show that the requirements of the law are written on their hearts, their consciences also bearing witness, and their thoughts now accusing, now even defending them.) 16This will take place on the day when God will judge men's secrets through Jesus Christ, as my gospel declares.

The Jews and the Law

17Now you, if you call yourself a Jew; if you rely on the law and brag about your relationship to God; 18if you know his will and approve of what is superior because you are instructed by the law; 19if you are convinced that you are a guide for the blind, a light for those who are in the dark, 20an instructor of the foolish, a teacher of infants, because you have in the law the embodiment of knowledge and truth— 21you, then, who teach others, do you not teach yourself? You who preach against stealing, do you steal? 22You who say that people should not commit adultery, do you commit adultery? You who abhor idols, do you rob temples? 23You who brag about the law, do you dishonor God by breaking the law? 24As it is written: "God's name is blasphemed among the Gentiles because of you."[b]

25Circumcision has value if you observe the law, but if you break the law, you have become as though you had not been circumcised. 26If those who are not circumcised keep the law's requirements, will they not be regarded as though they were circumcised? 27The one who is not circumcised physically and yet obeys the law will condemn you who, even though you have the[c] written code and circumcision, are a lawbreaker.

28A man is not a Jew if he is only one outwardly, nor is circumcision merely outward and physical. 29No, a

Living Bible

he is being with you? Or don't you care? Can't you see that he has been waiting all this time without punishing you, to give you time to turn from your sin? His kindness is meant to lead you to repentance.

5But no, you won't listen; and so you are saving up terrible punishment for yourselves because of your stubbornness in refusing to turn from your sin; for there is going to come a day of wrath when God will be the just Judge of all the world. 6He will give each one whatever his deeds deserve. 7He will give eternal life to those who patiently do the will of God,d seeking for the unseen glory and honor and eternal life that he offers.e 8But he will terribly punish those who fight against the truth of God and walk in evil ways—God's anger will be poured out upon them. 9There will be sorrow and suffering for Jews and Gentiles alike who keep on sinning. 10But there will be glory and honor and peace from God for all who obey him,f whether they are Jews or Gentiles. 11For God treats everyone the same.

12-15He will punish sin wherever it is found. He will punish the heathen when they sin, even though they never had God's written laws, for down in their hearts they know right from wrong. God's laws are written within them; their own conscience accuses them, or sometimes excuses them. And God will punish the Jews for sinning because they have his written laws but don't obey them. They know what is right but don't do it. After all, salvation is not given to those who know what to do, unless they do it. 16The day will surely come when at God's command Jesus Christ will judge the secret lives of everyone, their inmost thoughts and motives; this is all part of God's great plan which I proclaim.

17You Jews think all is well between yourselves and God because he gave his laws to you;g you brag that you are his special friends. 18Yes, you know what he wants; you know right from wrong and favor the right because you have been taught his laws from earliest youth. 19You are so sure of the way to God that you could point it out to a blind man. You think of yourselves as beacon lights, directing men who are lost in darkness to God. 20You think that you can guide the simple and teach even children the affairs of God, for you really know his laws, which are full of all knowledge and truth.

21Yes, you teach others—then why don't you teach yourselves? You tell others not to steal—do you steal? 22You say it is wrong to commit adultery—do you do it? You say, "Don't pray to idols," and then make money your god instead.h

23You are so proud of knowing God's laws, but you dishonor him by breaking them. 24No wonder the Scriptures say that the world speaks evil of God because of you.

25Being a Jew is worth something if you obey God's laws; but if you don't, then you are no better off than the heathen. 26And if the heathen obey God's laws, won't God give them all the rights and honors he planned to give the Jews? 27In fact, those heathen will be much better offi than you Jews who know so much about God and have his promises but don't obey his laws.

28For you are not real Jews just because you were born of Jewish parents or because you have gone through the Jewish initiation ceremony of circumcision.

New Revised Standard

his kindness and forbearance and patience? Do you not realize that God's kindness is meant to lead you to repentance? 5But by your hard and impenitent heart you are storing up wrath for yourself on the day of wrath, when God's righteous judgment will be revealed. 6For he will repay according to each one's deeds: 7to those who by patiently doing good seek for glory and honor and immortality, he will give eternal life; 8while for those who are self-seeking and who obey not the truth but wickedness, there will be wrath and fury. 9There will be anguish and distress for everyone who does evil, the Jew first and also the Greek, 10but glory and honor and peace for everyone who does good, the Jew first and also the Greek. 11For God shows no partiality.

12 All who have sinned apart from the law will also perish apart from the law, and all who have sinned under the law will be judged by the law. 13For it is not the hearers of the law who are righteous in God's sight, but the doers of the law who will be justified. 14When Gentiles, who do not possess the law, do instinctively what the law requires, these, though not having the law, are a law to themselves. 15They show that what the law requires is written on their hearts, to which their own conscience also bears witness; and their conflicting thoughts will accuse or perhaps excuse them 16on the day when, according to my gospel, God, through Jesus Christ, will judge the secret thoughts of all.

The Jews and the Law

17 But if you call yourself a Jew and rely on the law and boast of your relation to God 18and know his will and determine what is best because you are instructed in the law, 19and if you are sure that you are a guide to the blind, a light to those who are in darkness, 20a corrector of the foolish, a teacher of children, having in the law the embodiment of knowledge and truth, 21you, then, that teach others, will you not teach yourself? While you preach against stealing, do you steal? 22You that forbid adultery, do you commit adultery? You that abhor idols, do you rob temples? 23You that boast in the law, do you dishonor God by breaking the law? 24For, as it is written, "The name of God is blasphemed among the Gentiles because of you."

25 Circumcision indeed is of value if you obey the law; but if you break the law, your circumcision has become uncircumcision. 26So, if those who are uncircumcised keep the requirements of the law, will not their uncircumcision be regarded as circumcision? 27Then those who are physically uncircumcised but keep the law will condemn you that have the written code and circumcision but break the law. 28For a person is not a Jew who is one outwardly, nor is true circumcision something external and physical. 29Rather, a person is a Jew who

---

King James

29But he *is* a Jew, which is one inwardly; and circumcision *is that* of the heart, in the spirit, *and* not in the letter; whose praise *is* not of men, but of God.

3 WHAT ADVANTAGE then hath the Jew? or what profit *is there* of circumcision?

2Much every way: chiefly, because that unto them were committed the oracles of God.

3For what if some did not believe? shall their unbelief make the faith of God without effect?

4God forbid: yea, let God be true, but every man a liar; as it is written, That thou mightest be justified in thy sayings, and mightest overcome when thou art judged.

5But if our unrighteousness commend the righteousness of God, what shall we say? *Is* God unrighteous who taketh vengeance? (I speak as a man)

6God forbid: for then how shall God judge the world?

7For if the truth of God hath more abounded through my lie unto his glory; why yet am I also judged as a sinner?

8And not *rather,* (as we be slanderously reported, and as some affirm that we say,) Let us do evil, that good may come? whose damnation is just.

9What then? are we better *than they?* No, in no wise: for we have before proved both Jews and Gentiles, that they are all under sin;

10As it is written, There is none righteous, no, not one:

11There is none that understandeth, there is none that seeketh after God.

12They are all gone out of the way, they are together become unprofitable; there is none that doeth good, no, not one.

13Their throat *is* an open sepulchre; with their tongues they have used deceit; the poison of asps *is* under their lips:

14Whose mouth *is* full of cursing and bitterness:

15Their feet *are* swift to shed blood:

16Destruction and misery *are* in their ways:

17And the way of peace have they not known:

18There is no fear of God before their eyes.

19Now we know that what things soever the law saith, it saith to them who are under the law: that every mouth may be stopped, and all the world may become guilty before God.

20Therefore by the deeds of the law there shall no flesh be justified in his sight: for by the law *is* the knowledge of sin.

New International

man is a Jew if he is one inwardly; and circumcision is circumcision of the heart, by the Spirit, not by the written code. Such a man's praise is not from men, but from God.

God's Faithfulness

3 WHAT ADVANTAGE, then, is there in being a Jew, or what value is there in circumcision? 2Much in every way! First of all, they have been entrusted with the very words of God.

3What if some did not have faith? Will their lack of faith nullify God's faithfulness? 4Not at all! Let God be true, and every man a liar. As it is written:

"So that you may be proved right when you
      speak
   and prevail when you judge."a

5But if our unrighteousness brings out God's righteousness more clearly, what shall we say? That God is unjust in bringing his wrath on us? (I am using a human argument.) 6Certainly not! If that were so, how could God judge the world? 7Someone might argue, "If my falsehood enhances God's truthfulness and so increases his glory, why am I still condemned as a sinner?" 8Why not say—as we are being slanderously reported as saying and as some claim that we say—"Let us do evil that good may result"? Their condemnation is deserved.

No One Is Righteous

9What shall we conclude then? Are we any betterb? Not at all! We have already made the charge that Jews and Gentiles alike are all under sin. 10As it is written:

"There is no one righteous, not even one;
11   there is no one who understands,
   no one who seeks God.
12All have turned away,
   they have together become worthless;
   there is no one who does good,
   not even one."c
13"Their throats are open graves;
   their tongues practice deceit."d
   "The poison of vipers is on their lips."e
14   "Their mouths are full of cursing and
      bitterness."f
15"Their feet are swift to shed blood;
16   ruin and misery mark their ways,
17and the way of peace they do not know."g
18   "There is no fear of God before their eyes."h

19Now we know that whatever the law says, it says to those who are under the law, so that every mouth may be silenced and the whole world held accountable to God. 20Therefore no one will be declared righteous in his sight by observing the law; rather, through the law we become conscious of sin.

---

a *4* Psalm 51:4　　b *9* Or *worse*　　c *12* Psalms 14:1-3; 53:1-3; Eccles. 7:20
d *13* Psalm 5:9　　e *13* Psalm 140:3　　f *14* Psalm 10:7　　g *17* Isaiah 59:7,8
h *18* Psalm 36:1

Living Bible

29No, a real Jew is anyone whose heart is right with God. For God is not looking for those who cut their bodies in actual body circumcision, but he is looking for those with changed hearts and minds. Whoever has that kind of change in his life will get his praise from God, even if not from you.

3 THEN WHAT'S the use of being a Jew? Are there any special benefits for them from God? Is there any value in the Jewish circumcision ceremony? 2Yes, being a Jew has many advantages.

First of all, God trusted them with his laws [so that they could know and do his will¹]. 3True, some of them were unfaithful, but just because they broke their promises to God, does that mean God will break his promises? 4Of course not! Though everyone else in the world is a liar, God is not. Do you remember what the book of Psalms says about this?ʲ That God's words will always prove true and right, no matter who questions them.

5"But," some say, "our breaking faith with God is good, our sins serve a good purpose, for people will notice how good God is when they see how bad we are. Is it fair, then, for him to punish us when our sins are helping him?" (That is the way some people talk.) 6God forbid! Then what kind of God would he be, to overlook sin? How could he ever condemn anyone? 7For he could not judge and condemn me as a sinner if my dishonesty brought him glory by pointing up his honesty in contrast to my lies. 8If you follow through with that idea you come to this: the worse we are, the better God likes it! But the damnation of those who say such things is just. Yet some claim that this is what I preach!

9Well, then, are we Jews better than others? No, not at all, for we have already shown that all men alike are sinners, whether Jews or Gentiles. 10As the Scriptures say,

"No one is good—no one in all the world is innocent."ᵏ

11No one has ever really followed God's paths, or even truly wanted to.

12Every one has turned away; all have gone wrong. No one anywhere has kept on doing what is right; not one.

13Their talk is foul and filthy like the stench from an open grave.ˡ Their tongues are loaded with lies. Everything they say has in it the sting and poison of deadly snakes.

14Their mouths are full of cursing and bitterness.

15They are quick to kill, hating anyone who disagrees with them.ᵐ

16Wherever they go they leave misery and trouble behind them, 17and they have never known what it is to feel secure or enjoy God's blessing.

18They care nothing about God nor what he thinks of them.

19So the judgment of God lies very heavily upon the Jews, for they are responsible to keep God's laws instead of doing all these evil things; not one of them has any excuse; in fact, all the world stands hushed and guilty before Almighty God.

20Now do you see it? No one can ever be made right in God's sight by doing what the law commands. For the more we know of God's laws, the clearer it becomes that we aren't obeying them; his laws serve only to make us see that we are sinners.

New Revised Standard

is one inwardly, and real circumcision is a matter of the heart—it is spiritual and not literal. Such a person receives praise not from others but from God.

3 THEN WHAT advantage has the Jew? Or what is the value of circumcision? 2Much, in every way. For in the first place the Jewsⁿ were entrusted with the oracles of God. 3What if some were unfaithful? Will their faithlessness nullify the faithfulness of God? 4By no means! Although everyone is a liar, let God be proved true, as it is written,

"So that you may be justified in your words,
    and prevail in your judging."ᵒ

5But if our injustice serves to confirm the justice of God, what should we say? That God is unjust to inflict wrath on us? (I speak in a human way.) 6By no means! For then how could God judge the world? 7But if through my falsehood God's truthfulness abounds to his glory, why am I still being condemned as a sinner? 8And why not say (as some people slander us by saying that we say), "Let us do evil so that good may come"? Their condemnation is deserved!

None Is Righteous

9 What then? Are we any better off?ᵖ No, not at all; for we have already charged that all, both Jews and Greeks, are under the power of sin, 10as it is written:
    "There is no one who is righteous, not even
        one;
11   there is no one who has understanding,
        there is no one who seeks God.
12 All have turned aside, together they have
        become worthless;
    there is no one who shows kindness,
        there is not even one."
13 "Their throats are opened graves;
        they use their tongues to deceive."
    "The venom of vipers is under their lips."
14   "Their mouths are full of cursing and
        bitterness."
15 "Their feet are swift to shed blood;
16   ruin and misery are in their paths,
17   and the way of peace they have not known."
18   "There is no fear of God before their eyes."

19 Now we know that whatever the law says, it speaks to those who are under the law, so that every mouth may be silenced, and the whole world may be held accountable to God. 20For "no human being will be justified in his sight" by deeds prescribed by the law, for through the law comes the knowledge of sin.

ⁱ *3:2 so that they could know and do his will, implied.* ʲ *3:4 says about this, Psalm 51:4.* ᵏ *3:10 is innocent, see Psalm 14:3.* ˡ *3:13 Their talk is foul and filthy like the stench from an open grave, literally, "Their throat is an open grave." Perhaps the meaning is "Their speech injures others."* ᵐ *3:15 hating anyone who disagrees with them, implied.*

ⁿ Gk *they*   ᵒ Gk *when you are being judged*   ᵖ Or *at any disadvantage?*

King James

21But now the righteousness of God without the law is manifested, being witnessed by the law and the prophets;

22Even the righteousness of God *which is* by faith of Jesus Christ unto all and upon all them that believe: for there is no difference:

23For all have sinned, and come short of the glory of God;

24Being justified freely by his grace through the redemption that is in Christ Jesus:

25Whom God hath set forth *to be* a propitiation through faith in his blood, to declare his righteousness for the remission of sins that are past, through the forbearance of God;

26To declare, *I say,* at this time his righteousness: that he might be just, and the justifier of him which believeth in Jesus.

27Where *is* boasting then? It is excluded. By what law? of works? Nay: but by the law of faith.

28Therefore we conclude that a man is justified by faith without the deeds of the law.

29*Is he* the God of the Jews only? *is he* not also of the Gentiles? Yes, of the Gentiles also:

30Seeing *it is* one God, which shall justify the circumcision by faith, and uncircumcision through faith.

31Do we then make void the law through faith? God forbid: yea, we establish the law.

4 WHAT SHALL we say then that Abraham our father, as pertaining to the flesh, hath found?

2For if Abraham were justified by works, he hath *whereof* to glory; but not before God.

3For what saith the scripture? Abraham believed God, and it was counted unto him for righteousness.

4Now to him that worketh is the reward not reckoned of grace, but of debt.

5But to him that worketh not, but believeth on him that justifieth the ungodly, his faith is counted for righteousness.

6Even as David also describeth the blessedness of the man, unto whom God imputeth righteousness without works,

7*Saying,* Blessed *are* they whose iniquities are forgiven, and whose sins are covered.

8Blessed *is* the man to whom the Lord will not impute sin.

New International

Righteousness Through Faith

21But now a righteousness from God, apart from law, has been made known, to which the Law and the Prophets testify. 22This righteousness from God comes through faith in Jesus Christ to all who believe. There is no difference, 23for all have sinned and fall short of the glory of God, 24and are justified freely by his grace through the redemption that came by Christ Jesus. 25God presented him as a sacrifice of atonement,[a] through faith in his blood. He did this to demonstrate his justice, because in his forbearance he had left the sins committed beforehand unpunished— 26he did it to demonstrate his justice at the present time, so as to be just and the one who justifies those who have faith in Jesus.

27Where, then, is boasting? It is excluded. On what principle? On that of observing the law? No, but on that of faith. 28For we maintain that a man is justified by faith apart from observing the law. 29Is God the God of Jews only? Is he not the God of Gentiles too? Yes, of Gentiles too, 30since there is only one God, who will justify the circumcised by faith and the uncircumcised through that same faith. 31Do we, then, nullify the law by this faith? Not at all! Rather, we uphold the law.

Abraham Justified by Faith

4 WHAT THEN shall we say that Abraham, our forefather, discovered in this matter? 2If, in fact, Abraham was justified by works, he had something to boast about—but not before God. 3What does the Scripture say? "Abraham believed God, and it was credited to him as righteousness."[b]

4Now when a man works, his wages are not credited to him as a gift, but as an obligation. 5However, to the man who does not work but trusts God who justifies the wicked, his faith is credited as righteousness. 6David says the same thing when he speaks of the blessedness of the man to whom God credits righteousness apart from works:

7"Blessed are they
  whose transgressions are forgiven,
  whose sins are covered.
8Blessed is the man
  whose sin the Lord will never count against
    him."[c]

---

a 25 Or *as the one who would turn aside his wrath, taking away sin*
b 3 Gen. 15:6; also in verse 22   c 8 Psalm 32:1,2

Living Bible

21, 22But now God has shown us a different way to heavend—not by "being good enough" and trying to keep his laws, but by a new way (though not new, really, for the Scriptures told about it long ago). Now God says he will accept and acquit us—declare us "not guilty"—if we trust Jesus Christ to take away our sins. And we all can be saved in this same way, by coming to Christ, no matter who we are or what we have been like. 23Yes, all have sinned; all fall short of God's glorious ideal; 24yet now God declares us "not guilty" of offending him if we trust in Jesus Christ, who in his kindness freely takes away our sins.

25For God sent Christ Jesus to take the punishment for our sins and to end all God's anger against us. He used Christ's blood and our faith as the means of saving us from his wrath.e In this way he was being entirely fair, even though he did not punish those who sinned in former times. For he was looking forward to the time when Christ would come and take away those sins. 26And now in these days also he can receive sinners in this same way, because Jesus took away their sins.

But isn't this unfair for God to let criminals go free, and say that they are innocent? No, for he does it on the basis of their trust in Jesus who took away their sins.

27Then what can we boast about doing, to earn our salvation? Nothing at all. Why? Because our acquittal is not based on our good deeds; it is based on what Christ has done and our faith in him. 28So it is that we are savedf by faith in Christ and not by the good things we do.

29And does God save only the Jews in this way? No, the Gentiles, too, may come to him in this same manner. 30God treats us all the same; all, whether Jews or Gentiles, are acquitted if they have faith. 31Well then, if we are saved by faith, does this mean that we no longer need obey God's laws? Just the opposite! In fact, only when we trust Jesus can we truly obey him.

4 ABRAHAM WAS, humanly speaking, the founder of our Jewish nation. What were his experiences concerning this question of being saved by faith? Was it because of his good deeds that God accepted him? If so, then he would have something to boast about. But from God's point of view Abraham had no basis at all for pride. 3For the Scriptures tell us Abraham *believed God,* and that is why God canceled his sins and declared him "not guilty."

4, 5But didn't he earn his right to heaven by all the good things he did? No, for being saved is a gift; if a person could earn it by being good, then it wouldn't be free—but it is! It is *given* to those who do *not* work for it. For God declares sinners to be good in his sight if they have faith in Christ to save them from God's wrath.g

6King David spoke of this, describing the happiness of an undeserving sinner who is declared "not guilty"h by God. 7"Blessed, and to be envied," he said, "are those whose sins are forgiven and put out of sight. 8Yes, what joy there is for anyone whose sins are no longer counted against him by the Lord."i

New Revised Standard

Righteousness through Faith

21 But now, apart from law, the righteousness of God has been disclosed, and is attested by the law and the prophets, 22the righteousness of God through faith in Jesus Christi for all who believe. For there is no distinction, 23since all have sinned and fall short of the glory of God; 24they are now justified by his grace as a gift, through the redemption that is in Christ Jesus, 25whom God put forward as a sacrifice of atonementk by his blood, effective through faith. He did this to show his righteousness, because in his divine forbearance he had passed over the sins previously committed; 26it was to prove at the present time that he himself is righteous and that he justifies the one who has faith in Jesus.l

27 Then what becomes of boasting? It is excluded. By what law? By that of works? No, but by the law of faith. 28For we hold that a person is justified by faith apart from works prescribed by the law. 29Or is God the God of Jews only? Is he not the God of Gentiles also? Yes, of Gentiles also, 30since God is one; and he will justify the circumcised on the ground of faith and the uncircumcised through that same faith. 31Do we then overthrow the law by this faith? By no means! On the contrary, we uphold the law.

The Example of Abraham

4 WHAT THEN are we to say was gained bym Abraham, our ancestor according to the flesh? 2For if Abraham was justified by works, he has something to boast about, but not before God. 3For what does the scripture say? "Abraham believed God, and it was reckoned to him as righteousness." 4Now to one who works, wages are not reckoned as a gift but as something due. 5But to one who without works trusts him who justifies the ungodly, such faith is reckoned as righteousness. 6So also David speaks of the blessedness of those to whom God reckons righteousness apart from works:

7 "Blessed are those whose iniquities are
        forgiven,
     and whose sins are covered;
8 blessed is the one against whom the Lord will
        not reckon sin."

---

d *3:21, 22 God has shown us a different way to heaven,* literally, "A righteousness of God has been manifested."   e *3:25 saving us from his wrath,* literally, "to be a propitiation."   f *3:28 saved,* literally, "justified."   g *4:5 if they have faith in Christ to save them from God's wrath,* literally, "faith is reckoned for righteousness."   h *4:6 "not guilty,"* literally "righteous."   i *4:8 by the Lord,* see Psalm 32:1, 2.

j Or *through the faith of Jesus Christ*   k Or *a place of atonement*   l Or *who has the faith of Jesus*   m Other ancient authorities read *say about*

King James

9*Cometh* this blessedness then upon the circumcision *only,* or upon the uncircumcision also? for we say that faith was reckoned to Abraham for righteousness.

10How was it then reckoned? when he was in circumcision, or in uncircumcision? Not in circumcision, but in uncircumcision.

11And he received the sign of circumcision, a seal of the righteousness of the faith which *he had yet* being uncircumcised: that he might be the father of all them that believe, though they be not circumcised; that righteousness might be imputed unto them also:

12And the father of circumcision to them who are not of the circumcision only, but who also walk in the steps of that faith of our father Abraham, which *he had* being *yet* uncircumcised.

13For the promise, that he should be the heir of the world, *was* not to Abraham, or to his seed, through the law, but through the righteousness of faith.

14For if they which are of the law *be* heirs, faith is made void, and the promise made of none effect:

15Because the law worketh wrath: for where no law is, *there is* no transgression.

16Therefore *it is* of faith, that *it might be* by grace; to the end the promise might be sure to all the seed; not to that only which is of the law, but to that also which is of the faith of Abraham; who is the father of us all,

17(As it is written, I have made thee a father of many nations,) before him whom he believed, *even* God, who quickeneth the dead, and calleth those things which be not as though they were.

18Who against hope believed in hope, that he might become the father of many nations, according to that which was spoken, So shall thy seed be.

19And being not weak in faith, he considered not his own body now dead, when he was about an hundred years old, neither yet the deadness of Sarah's womb:

20He staggered not at the promise of God through unbelief; but was strong in faith, giving glory to God;

21And being fully persuaded that, what he had promised, he was able also to perform.

22And therefore it was imputed to him for righteousness.

23Now it was not written for his sake alone, that it was imputed to him;

24But for us also, to whom it shall be imputed, if we believe on him that raised up Jesus our Lord from the dead;

25Who was delivered for our offences, and was raised again for our justification.

New International

9Is this blessedness only for the circumcised, or also for the uncircumcised? We have been saying that Abraham's faith was credited to him as righteousness. 10Under what circumstances was it credited? Was it after he was circumcised, or before? It was not after, but before! 11And he received the sign of circumcision, a seal of the righteousness that he had by faith while he was still uncircumcised. So then, he is the father of all who believe but have not been circumcised, in order that righteousness might be credited to them. 12And he is also the father of the circumcised who not only are circumcised but who also walk in the footsteps of the faith that our father Abraham had before he was circumcised.

13It was not through law that Abraham and his offspring received the promise that he would be heir of the world, but through the righteousness that comes by faith. 14For if those who live by law are heirs, faith has no value and the promise is worthless, 15because law brings wrath. And where there is no law there is no transgression.

16Therefore, the promise comes by faith, so that it may be by grace and may be guaranteed to all Abraham's offspring—not only to those who are of the law but also to those who are of the faith of Abraham. He is the father of us all. 17As it is written: "I have made you a father of many nations."a He is our father in the sight of God, in whom he believed—the God who gives life to the dead and calls things that are not as though they were.

18Against all hope, Abraham in hope believed and so became the father of many nations, just as it had been said to him, "So shall your offspring be."b 19Without weakening in his faith, he faced the fact that his body was as good as dead—since he was about a hundred years old—and that Sarah's womb was also dead. 20Yet he did not waver through unbelief regarding the promise of God, but was strengthened in his faith and gave glory to God, 21being fully persuaded that God had power to do what he had promised. 22This is why "it was credited to him as righteousness." 23The words "it was credited to him" were written not for him alone, 24but also for us, to whom God will credit righteousness—for us who believe in him who raised Jesus our Lord from the dead. 25He was delivered over to death for our sins and was raised to life for our justification.

Living Bible

9Now then, the question: Is this blessing given only to those who have faith in Christ but also keep the Jewish laws, or is the blessing also given to those who do not keep the Jewish rules, but only trust in Christ? Well, what about Abraham? We say that he received these blessings through his faith. Was it by faith alone? Or because he also kept the Jewish rules?

10For the answer to that question, answer this one: *When* did God give this blessing to Abraham? It was *before he became a Jew*—before he went through the Jewish initiation ceremony of circumcision.

11It wasn't until later on, *after* God had promised to bless him *because of his faith*, that he was circumcised. The circumcision ceremony was a sign that Abraham already had faith and that God had already accepted him and declared him just and good in his sight—before the ceremony took place. So Abraham is the spiritual father of those who believe and are saved without obeying Jewish laws. We see, then, that those who do not keep these rules are justified by God through faith. 12And Abraham is also the spiritual father of those Jews who have been circumcised. They can see from his example that it is not this ceremony that saves them, for Abraham found favor with God by faith alone, *before he was circumcised*.

13It is clear, then, that God's promise to give the whole earth to Abraham and his descendants was not because Abraham obeyed God's laws but because he trusted God to keep his promise. 14So if you still claim that God's blessings go to those who are "good enough," then you are saying that God's promises to those who have faith are meaningless, and faith is foolish. 15But the fact of the matter is this: when we try to gain God's blessing and salvation by keeping his laws we always end up under his anger, for we always fail to keep them. The only way we can keep from breaking laws is not to have any to break!

16So God's blessings are given to us by faith, as a free gift; we are certain to get them whether or not we follow Jewish customs if we have faith like Abraham's, for Abraham is the father of us all when it comes to these matters of faith. 17That is what the Scriptures mean when they say that God made Abraham the father of many nations. God will accept all people in every nation who trust God as Abraham did. And this promise is from God himself, who makes the dead live again and speaks of future events with as much certainty as though they were already past.

18So, when God told Abraham that he would give him a son who would have many descendants and become a great nation, Abraham believed God even though such a promise just couldn't come to pass! 19And because his faith was strong, he didn't worry about the fact that he was too old to be a father, at the age of one hundred, and that Sarah his wife, at ninety,c was also much too old to have a baby.

20But Abraham never doubted. He believed God, for his faith and trust grew ever stronger, and he praised God for this blessing even before it happened. 21He was completely sure that God was well able to do anything he promised. 22And because of Abraham's faith God forgave his sins and declared him "not guilty."

23Now this wonderful statement—that he was accepted and approved through his faith—wasn't just for Abraham's benefit. 24It was for us, too, assuring us that God will accept us in the same way he accepted Abraham—when we believe the promises of God who brought back Jesus our Lord from the dead. 25He died for our sins and rose again to make us right with God,d filling us with God's goodness.

New Revised Standard

9 Is this blessedness, then, pronounced only on the circumcised, or also on the uncircumcised? We say, "Faith was reckoned to Abraham as righteousness." 10How then was it reckoned to him? Was it before or after he had been circumcised? It was not after, but before he was circumcised. 11He received the sign of circumcision as a seal of the righteousness that he had by faith while he was still uncircumcised. The purpose was to make him the ancestor of all who believe without being circumcised and who thus have righteousness reckoned to them, 12and likewise the ancestor of the circumcised who are not only circumcised but who also follow the example of the faith that our ancestor Abraham had before he was circumcised.

God's Promise Realized through Faith

13 For the promise that he would inherit the world did not come to Abraham or to his descendants through the law but through the righteousness of faith. 14If it is the adherents of the law who are to be the heirs, faith is null and the promise is void. 15For the law brings wrath; but where there is no law, neither is there violation.

16 For this reason it depends on faith, in order that the promise may rest on grace and be guaranteed to all his descendants, not only to the adherents of the law but also to those who share the faith of Abraham (for he is the father of all of us, 17as it is written, "I have made you the father of many nations")—in the presence of the God in whom he believed, who gives life to the dead and calls into existence the things that do not exist. 18Hoping against hope, he believed that he would become "the father of many nations," according to what was said, "So numerous shall your descendants be." 19He did not weaken in faith when he considered his own body, which was alreadye as good as dead (for he was about a hundred years old), or when he considered the barrenness of Sarah's womb. 20No distrust made him waver concerning the promise of God, but he grew strong in his faith as he gave glory to God, 21being fully convinced that God was able to do what he had promised. 22Therefore his faithf "was reckoned to him as righteousness." 23Now the words, "it was reckoned to him," were written not for his sake alone, 24but for ours also. It will be reckoned to us who believe in him who raised Jesus our Lord from the dead, 25who was handed over to death for our trespasses and was raised for our justification.

---

c 4:19 *at ninety,* see Gen 17:17.   d 4:25 *rose again to make us right with God,* literally "raised for our justification."

e Other ancient authorities lack *already*   f Gk *Therefore it*

King James

5 THEREFORE BEING justified by faith, we have peace with God through our Lord Jesus Christ:

2By whom also we have access by faith into this grace wherein we stand, and rejoice in hope of the glory of God.

3And not only *so,* but we glory in tribulations also: knowing that tribulation worketh patience;

4And patience, experience; and experience, hope:

5And hope maketh not ashamed; because the love of God is shed abroad in our hearts by the Holy Ghost which is given unto us.

6For when we were yet without strength, in due time Christ died for the ungodly.

7For scarcely for a righteous man will one die: yet peradventure for a good man some would even dare to die.

8But God commendeth his love toward us, in that, while we were yet sinners, Christ died for us.

9Much more then, being now justified by his blood, we shall be saved from wrath through him.

10For if, when we were enemies, we were reconciled to God by the death of his Son, much more, being reconciled, we shall be saved by his life.

11And not only *so,* but we also joy in God through our Lord Jesus Christ, by whom we have now received the atonement.

12Wherefore, as by one man sin entered into the world, and death by sin; and so death passed upon all men, for that all have sinned:

13(For until the law sin was in the world: but sin is not imputed when there is no law.

14Nevertheless death reigned from Adam to Moses, even over them that had not sinned after the similitude of Adam's transgression, who is the figure of him that was to come.

15But not as the offence, so also *is* the free gift. For if through the offence of one many be dead, much more the grace of God, and the gift by grace, *which is* by one man, Jesus Christ, hath abounded unto many.

16And not as *it was* by one that sinned, *so is* the gift: for the judgment *was* by one to condemnation, but the free gift *is* of many offences unto justification.

17For if by one man's offence death reigned by one; much more they which receive abundance of grace and of the gift of righteousness shall reign in life by one, Jesus Christ.)

18Therefore as by the offence of one *judgment came* upon all men to condemnation; even so by the righteousness of one *the free gift came* upon all men unto justification of life.

19For as by one man's disobedience many were made sinners, so by the obedience of one shall many be made righteous.

New International

Peace and Joy

5 THEREFORE, SINCE we have been justified through faith, wea have peace with God through our Lord Jesus Christ, 2through whom we have gained access by faith into this grace in which we now stand. And wea rejoice in the hope of the glory of God. 3Not only so, but wea also rejoice in our sufferings, because we know that suffering produces perseverance; 4perseverance, character; and character, hope. 5And hope does not disappoint us, because God has poured out his love into our hearts by the Holy Spirit, whom he has given us.

6You see, at just the right time, when we were still powerless, Christ died for the ungodly. 7Very rarely will anyone die for a righteous man, though for a good man someone might possibly dare to die. 8But God demonstrates his own love for us in this: While we were still sinners, Christ died for us.

9Since we have now been justified by his blood, how much more shall we be saved from God's wrath through him! 10For if, when we were God's enemies, we were reconciled to him through the death of his Son, how much more, having been reconciled, shall we be saved through his life! 11Not only is this so, but we also rejoice in God through our Lord Jesus Christ, through whom we have now received reconciliation.

Death Through Adam, Life Through Christ

12Therefore, just as sin entered the world through one man, and death through sin, and in this way death came to all men, because all sinned— 13for before the law was given, sin was in the world. But sin is not taken into account when there is no law. 14Nevertheless, death reigned from the time of Adam to the time of Moses, even over those who did not sin by breaking a command, as did Adam, who was a pattern of the one to come.

15But the gift is not like the trespass. For if the many died by the trespass of the one man, how much more did God's grace and the gift that came by the grace of the one man, Jesus Christ, overflow to the many! 16Again, the gift of God is not like the result of the one man's sin: The judgment followed one sin and brought condemnation, but the gift followed many trespasses and brought justification. 17For if, by the trespass of the one man, death reigned through that one man, how much more will those who receive God's abundant provision of grace and of the gift of righteousness reign in life through the one man, Jesus Christ.

18Consequently, just as the result of one trespass was condemnation for all men, so also the result of one act of righteousness was justification that brings life for all men. 19For just as through the disobedience of the one man the many were made sinners, so also through the obedience of the one man the many will be made righteous.

Living Bible

5 SO NOW, since we have been made right in God's sight by faith in his promises, we can have real peace with him because of what Jesus Christ our Lord has done for us. 2For because of our faith, he has brought us into this place of highest privilege where we now stand, and we confidently and joyfully look forward to actually becoming all that God has had in mind for us to be.

3We can rejoice, too, when we run into problems and trials for we know that they are good for us—they help us learn to be patient. 4And patience develops strength of character in us and helps us trust God more each time we use it until finally our hope and faith are strong and steady. 5Then, when that happens, we are able to hold our heads high no matter what happens and know that all is well, for we know how dearly God loves us, and we feel this warm love everywhere within us because God has given us the Holy Spirit to fill our hearts with his love.

6When we were utterly helpless with no way of escape, Christ came at just the right time and died for us sinners who had no use for him. 7Even if we were good, we really wouldn't expect anyone to die for us, though, of course, that might be barely possible. 8But God showed his great love for us by sending Christ to die for us while we were still sinners. 9And since by his blood he did all this for us as sinners, how much more will he do for us now that he has declared us not guilty? Now he will save us from all of God's wrath to come. 10And since, when we were his enemies, we were brought back to God by the death of his Son, what blessings he must have for us now that we are his friends, and he is living within us!

11Now we rejoice in our wonderful new relationship with God—all because of what our Lord Jesus Christ has done in dying for our sins—making us friends of God.

12When Adam sinned, sin entered the entire human race. His sin spread death throughout all the world, so everything began to grow old and die,b for all sinned. 13[We know that it was Adam's sin that caused thisc] because although, of course, people were sinning from the time of Adam until Moses, God did not in those days judge them guilty of death for breaking his laws—because he had not yet given his laws to them, nor told them what he wanted them to do. 14So when their bodies died it was not for their own sinsd since they themselves had never disobeyed God's special law against eating the forbidden fruit, as Adam had.

What a contrast between Adam and Christ who was yet to come! 15And what a difference between man's sin and God's forgiveness!

For this one man, Adam, brought death to many through his *sin*. But this one man, Jesus Christ, brought forgiveness to many through God's *mercy*. 16Adam's *one* sin brought the penalty of death to many, while Christ freely takes away *many* sins and gives glorious life instead. 17The sin of this one man, Adam, caused *death to be king over all*, but all who will take God's gift of forgiveness and acquittal are *kings of life*e because of this one man, Jesus Christ. 18Yes, Adam's *sin* brought *punishment* to all, but Christ's *righteousness* makes men *right with God*, so that they can live. 19Adam caused many to be sinners because he *disobeyed* God, and Christ caused many to be made acceptable to God because he *obeyed*.

New Revised Standard

Results of Justification

5 THEREFORE, SINCE we are justified by faith, wef have peace with God through our Lord Jesus Christ, 2through whom we have obtained accessg to this grace in which we stand; and weh boast in our hope of sharing the glory of God. 3And not only that, but weh also boast in our sufferings, knowing that suffering produces endurance, 4and endurance produces character, and character produces hope, 5and hope does not disappoint us, because God's love has been poured into our hearts through the Holy Spirit that has been given to us.

6 For while we were still weak, at the right time Christ died for the ungodly. 7Indeed, rarely will anyone die for a righteous person—though perhaps for a good person someone might actually dare to die. 8But God proves his love for us in that while we still were sinners Christ died for us. 9Much more surely then, now that we have been justified by his blood, will we be saved through him from the wrath of God.i 10For if while we were enemies, we were reconciled to God through the death of his Son, much more surely, having been reconciled, will we be saved by his life. 11But more than that, we even boast in God through our Lord Jesus Christ, through whom we have now received reconciliation.

Adam and Christ

12 Therefore, just as sin came into the world through one man, and death came through sin, and so death spread to all because all have sinned— 13sin was indeed in the world before the law, but sin is not reckoned when there is no law. 14Yet death exercised dominion from Adam to Moses, even over those whose sins were not like the transgression of Adam, who is a type of the one who was to come.

15 But the free gift is not like the trespass. For if the many died through the one man's trespass, much more surely have the grace of God and the free gift in the grace of the one man, Jesus Christ, abounded for the many. 16And the free gift is not like the effect of the one man's sin. For the judgment following one trespass brought condemnation, but the free gift following many trespasses brings justification. 17If, because of the one man's trespass, death exercised dominion through that one, much more surely will those who receive the abundance of grace and the free gift of righteousness exercise dominion in life through the one man, Jesus Christ.

18 Therefore just as one man's trespass led to condemnation for all, so one man's act of righteousness leads to justification and life for all. 19For just as by the one man's disobedience the many were made sinners, so by the one man's obedience the many will be made righteous. 20But law came in, with the result that the

---

b *5:12 grow old and die*, literally, "Sin entered into the world and death through sin." c *5:13 We know that it was Adam's sin that caused this*, implied. d *5:14 so when their bodies died it was not for their own sins*, implied. e *5:17 are kings of life*, literally, "reign in life."

f Other ancient authorities read *let us*   g Other ancient authorities add *by faith*   h Or *let us*   i Gk *the wrath*

King James

20Moreover the law entered, that the offence might abound. But where sin abounded, grace did much more abound:

21That as sin hath reigned unto death, even so might grace reign through righteousness unto eternal life by Jesus Christ our Lord.

6 WHAT SHALL we say then? Shall we continue in sin, that grace may abound?

2God forbid. How shall we, that are dead to sin, live any longer therein?

3Know ye not, that so many of us as were baptized into Jesus Christ were baptized into his death?

4Therefore we are buried with him by baptism into death: that like as Christ was raised up from the dead by the glory of the Father, even so we also should walk in newness of life.

5For if we have been planted together in the likeness of his death, we shall be also *in the likeness* of *his* resurrection:

6Knowing this, that our old man is crucified with *him*, that the body of sin might be destroyed, that henceforth we should not serve sin.

7For he that is dead is freed from sin.

8Now if we be dead with Christ, we believe that we shall also live with him:

9Knowing that Christ being raised from the dead dieth no more; death hath no more dominion over him.

10For in that he died, he died unto sin once: but in that he liveth, he liveth unto God.

11Likewise reckon ye also yourselves to be dead indeed unto sin, but alive unto God through Jesus Christ our Lord.

12Let not sin therefore reign in your mortal body, that ye should obey it in the lusts thereof.

13Neither yield ye your members *as* instruments of unrighteousness unto sin: but yield yourselves unto God, as those that are alive from the dead, and your members *as* instruments of righteousness unto God.

14For sin shall not have dominion over you: for ye are not under the law, but under grace.

15What then? shall we sin, because we are not under the law, but under grace? God forbid.

16Know ye not, that to whom ye yield yourselves servants to obey, his servants ye are to whom ye obey; whether of sin unto death, or of obedience unto righteousness?

17But God be thanked, that ye were the servants of sin, but ye have obeyed from the heart that form of doctrine which was delivered you.

18Being then made free from sin, ye became the servants of righteousness.

19I speak after the manner of men because of the infirmity of your flesh: for as ye have yielded your members servants to uncleanness and to iniquity unto iniquity; even so now yield your members servants to righteousness unto holiness.

20For when ye were the servants of sin, ye were free from righteousness.

New International

20The law was added so that the trespass might increase. But where sin increased, grace increased all the more, 21so that, just as sin reigned in death, so also grace might reign through righteousness to bring eternal life through Jesus Christ our Lord.

Dead to Sin, Alive in Christ

6 WHAT SHALL we say, then? Shall we go on sinning so that grace may increase? 2By no means! We died to sin; how can we live in it any longer? 3Or don't you know that all of us who were baptized into Christ Jesus were baptized into his death? 4We were therefore buried with him through baptism into death in order that, just as Christ was raised from the dead through the glory of the Father, we too may live a new life.

5If we have been united with him like this in his death, we will certainly also be united with him in his resurrection. 6For we know that our old self was crucified with him so that the body of sin might be done away with,a that we should no longer be slaves to sin— 7because anyone who has died has been freed from sin.

8Now if we died with Christ, we believe that we will also live with him. 9For we know that since Christ was raised from the dead, he cannot die again; death no longer has mastery over him. 10The death he died, he died to sin once for all; but the life he lives, he lives to God.

11In the same way, count yourselves dead to sin but alive to God in Christ Jesus. 12Therefore do not let sin reign in your mortal body so that you obey its evil desires. 13Do not offer the parts of your body to sin, as instruments of wickedness, but rather offer yourselves to God, as those who have been brought from death to life; and offer the parts of your body to him as instruments of righteousness. 14For sin shall not be your master, because you are not under law, but under grace.

Slaves to Righteousness

15What then? Shall we sin because we are not under law but under grace? By no means! 16Don't you know that when you offer yourselves to someone to obey him as slaves, you are slaves to the one whom you obey— whether you are slaves to sin, which leads to death, or to obedience, which leads to righteousness? 17But thanks be to God that, though you used to be slaves to sin, you wholeheartedly obeyed the form of teaching to which you were entrusted. 18You have been set free from sin and have become slaves to righteousness.

19I put this in human terms because you are weak in your natural selves. Just as you used to offer the parts of your body in slavery to impurity and to ever-increasing wickedness, so now offer them in slavery to righteousness leading to holiness. 20When you were slaves to sin, you were free from the control of righteousness.

---

a 6 Or *be rendered powerless*

Living Bible

20The Ten Commandments were given so that all could see the extent of their failure to obey God's laws. But the more we see our sinfulness, the more we see God's abounding grace forgiving us. 21Before, sin ruled over all men and brought them to death, but now God's kindness rules instead, giving us right standing with God and resulting in eternal life through Jesus Christ our Lord.

6 WELL THEN, shall we keep on sinning so that God can keep on showing us more and more kindness and forgiveness?

2, 3Of course not! Should we keep on sinning when we don't have to? For sin's power over us was broken when we became Christians and were baptized to become a part of Jesus Christ; through his death the power of your sinful nature was shattered. 4Your old sin-loving nature was buried with him by baptism when he died, and when God the Father, with glorious power, brought him back to life again, you were given his wonderful new life to enjoy.

5For you have become a part of him, and so you died with him, so to speak, when he died;b and now you share his new life, and shall rise as he did. 6Your old evil desires were nailed to the cross with him; that part of you that loves to sin was crushed and fatally wounded, so that your sin-loving body is no longer under sin's control, no longer needs to be a slave to sin; 7for when you are deadened to sin you are freed from all its allure and its power over you. 8And since your old sin-loving nature "died" with Christ, we know that you will share his new life. 9Christ rose from the dead and will never die again. Death no longer has any power over him. 10He died once for all to end sin's power, but now he lives forever in unbroken fellowship with God. 11So look upon your old sin nature as dead and unresponsive to sin, and instead be alive to God, alert to him, through Jesus Christ our Lord.

12Do not let sin control your puny body any longer; do not give in to its sinful desires. 13Do not let any part of your bodies become tools of wickedness, to be used for sinning; but give yourselves completely to God—every part of you—for you are back from death and you want to be tools in the hands of God, to be used for his good purposes. 14Sin need never again be your master,c for now you are no longer tied to the law where sin enslaves you, but you are free under God's favor and mercy.

15Does this mean that now we can go ahead and sin and not worry about it? (For our salvation does not depend on keeping the law, but on receiving God's grace!) Of course not!

16Don't you realize that you can choose your own master? You can choose sin (with death) or else obedience (with acquittal). The one to whom you offer yourself—he will take you and be your master and you will be his slave. 17Thank God that though you once chose to be slaves of sin, now you have obeyed with all your heart the teaching to which God has committed you. 18And now you are free from your old master, sin; and you have become slaves to your new master, righteousness.

19I speak this way, using the illustration of slaves and masters, because it is easy to understand: just as you used to be slaves to all kinds of sin, so now you must let yourselves be slaves to all that is right and holy.

20In those days when you were slaves of sin you didn't bother much with goodness. 21And what was the

New Revised Standard

trespass multiplied; but where sin increased, grace abounded all the more, 21so that, just as sin exercised dominion in death, so grace might also exercise dominion through justificationd leading to eternal life through Jesus Christ our Lord.

Dying and Rising with Christ

6 WHAT THEN are we to say? Should we continue in sin in order that grace may abound? 2By no means! How can we who died to sin go on living in it? 3Do you not know that all of us who have been baptized into Christ Jesus were baptized into his death? 4Therefore we have been buried with him by baptism into death, so that, just as Christ was raised from the dead by the glory of the Father, so we too might walk in newness of life.

5 For if we have been united with him in a death like his, we will certainly be united with him in a resurrection like his. 6We know that our old self was crucified with him so that the body of sin might be destroyed, and we might no longer be enslaved to sin. 7For whoever has died is freed from sin. 8But if we have died with Christ, we believe that we will also live with him. 9We know that Christ, being raised from the dead, will never die again; death no longer has dominion over him. 10The death he died, he died to sin, once for all; but the life he lives, he lives to God. 11So you also must consider yourselves dead to sin and alive to God in Christ Jesus.

12 Therefore, do not let sin exercise dominion in your mortal bodies, to make you obey their passions. 13No longer present your members to sin as instrumentse of wickedness, but present yourselves to God as those who have been brought from death to life, and present your members to God as instrumentse of righteousness. 14For sin will have no dominion over you, since you are not under law but under grace.

Slaves of Righteousness

15 What then? Should we sin because we are not under law but under grace? By no means! 16Do you not know that if you present yourselves to anyone as obedient slaves, you are slaves of the one whom you obey, either of sin, which leads to death, or of obedience, which leads to righteousness? 17But thanks be to God that you, having once been slaves of sin, have become obedient from the heart to the form of teaching to which you were entrusted, 18and that you, having been set free from sin, have become slaves of righteousness. 19I am speaking in human terms because of your natural limitations.f For just as you once presented your members as slaves to impurity and to greater and greater iniquity, so now present your members as slaves to righteousness for sanctification.

20 When you were slaves of sin, you were free in regard to righteousness. 21So what advantage did you

---

b 6:5 when he died, literally, "united with him in the likeness of his death."
c 6:14 Sin need never again be your master, literally, "Sin will never again be your master."

d Or righteousness   e Or weapons   f Gk the weakness of your flesh

King James

21What fruit had ye then in those things whereof ye are now ashamed? for the end of those things *is* death.

22But now being made free from sin, and become servants to God, ye have your fruit unto holiness, and the end everlasting life.

23For the wages of sin *is* death; but the gift of God *is* eternal life through Jesus Christ our Lord.

7 KNOW YE not, brethren, (for I speak to them that know the law,) how that the law hath dominion over a man as long as he liveth?

2For the woman which hath an husband is bound by the law to *her* husband so long as he liveth; but if the husband be dead, she is loosed from the law of *her* husband.

3So then if, while *her* husband liveth, she be married to another man, she shall be called an adulteress: but if her husband be dead, she is free from that law; so that she is no adulteress, though she be married to another man.

4Wherefore, my brethren, ye also are become dead to the law by the body of Christ; that ye should be married to another, *even* to him who is raised from the dead, that we should bring forth fruit unto God.

5For when we were in the flesh, the motions of sins, which were by the law, did work in our members to bring forth fruit unto death.

6But now we are delivered from the law, that being dead wherein we were held; that we should serve in newness of spirit, and not *in* the oldness of the letter.

7What shall we say then? *Is* the law sin? God forbid. Nay, I had not known sin, but by the law: for I had not known lust, except the law had said, Thou shalt not covet.

8But sin, taking occasion by the commandment, wrought in me all manner of concupiscence. For without the law sin *was* dead.

9For I was alive without the law once: but when the commandment came, sin revived, and I died.

10And the commandment, which *was ordained* to life, I found *to be* unto death.

11For sin, taking occasion by the commandment, deceived me, and by it slew *me*.

12Wherefore the law *is* holy, and the commandment holy, and just, and good.

13Was then that which is good made death unto me? God forbid. But sin, that it might appear sin, working death in me by that which is good; that sin by the commandment might become exceeding sinful.

14For we know that the law is spiritual: but I am carnal, sold under sin.

15For that which I do I allow not: for what I would, that do I not; but what I hate, that do I.

16If then I do that which I would not, I consent unto the law that *it is* good.

New International

21What benefit did you reap at that time from the things you are now ashamed of? Those things result in death! 22But now that you have been set free from sin and have become slaves to God, the benefit you reap leads to holiness, and the result is eternal life. 23For the wages of sin is death, but the gift of God is eternal life in[a] Christ Jesus our Lord.

An Illustration From Marriage

7 DO YOU not know, brothers—for I am speaking to men who know the law—that the law has authority over a man only as long as he lives? 2For example, by law a married woman is bound to her husband as long as he is alive, but if her husband dies, she is released from the law of marriage. 3So then, if she marries another man while her husband is still alive, she is called an adulteress. But if her husband dies, she is released from that law and is not an adulteress, even though she marries another man.

4So, my brothers, you also died to the law through the body of Christ, that you might belong to another, to him who was raised from the dead, in order that we might bear fruit to God. 5For when we were controlled by the sinful nature,[b] the sinful passions aroused by the law were at work in our bodies, so that we bore fruit for death. 6But now, by dying to what once bound us, we have been released from the law so that we serve in the new way of the Spirit, and not in the old way of the written code.

Struggling With Sin

7What shall we say, then? Is the law sin? Certainly not! Indeed I would not have known what sin was except through the law. For I would not have known what coveting really was if the law had not said, "Do not covet."[c] 8But sin, seizing the opportunity afforded by the commandment, produced in me every kind of covetous desire. For apart from law, sin is dead. 9Once I was alive apart from law; but when the commandment came, sin sprang to life and I died. 10I found that the very commandment that was intended to bring life actually brought death. 11For sin, seizing the opportunity afforded by the commandment, deceived me, and through the commandment put me to death. 12So then, the law is holy, and the commandment is holy, righteous and good.

13Did that which is good, then, become death to me? By no means! But in order that sin might be recognized as sin, it produced death in me through what was good, so that through the commandment sin might become utterly sinful.

14We know that the law is spiritual; but I am unspiritual, sold as a slave to sin. 15I do not understand what I do. For what I want to do I do not do, but what I hate I do. 16And if I do what I do not want to do, I agree that the law is good. 17As it is, it is no longer I myself who

---

a 23 Or *through*   b 5 Or *the flesh*; also in verse 25   c 7 Exodus 20:17; Deut. 5:21

Living Bible

result? Evidently not good, since you are ashamed now even to think about those things you used to do, for all of them end in eternal doom. 22But now you are free from the power of sin and are slaves of God, and his benefits to you include holiness and everlasting life. 23For the wages of sin is death, but the free gift of God is eternal life through Jesus Christ our Lord.

7 DON'T YOU understand yet, dear Jewish brothersd in Christ, that when a person dies the law no longer holds him in its power?

2Let me illustrate: when a woman marries, the law binds her to her husband as long as he is alive. But if he dies, she is no longer bound to him; the laws of marriage no longer apply to her. 3Then she can marry someone else if she wants to. That would be wrong while he was alive, but it is perfectly all right after he dies.

4Your "husband," your master, used to be the Jewish law; but you "died," as it were, with Christ on the cross; and since you are "dead," you are no longer "married to the law," and it has no more control over you. Then you came back to life again when Christ did, and are a new person. And now you are "married," so to speak, to the one who rose from the dead, so that you can produce good fruit, that is, good deeds for God. 5When your old nature was still active, sinful desires were at work within you, making you want to do whatever God said not to, and producing sinful deeds, the rotting fruit of death. 6But now you need no longer worry about the Jewish laws and customse because you "died" while in their captivity, and now you can really serve God; not in the old way, mechanically obeying a set of rules, but in the new way, [with all of your hearts and mindsf].

7Well then, am I suggesting that these laws of God are evil? Of course not! No, the law is not sinful but it was the law that showed me my sin. I would never have known the sin in my heart—the evil desires that are hidden there—if the law had not said, "You must not have evil desires in your heart." 8But sin used this law against evil desires by reminding me that such desires are wrong and arousing all kinds of forbidden desires within me! Only if there were no laws to break would there be no sinning.

9That is why I felt fine so long as I did not understand what the law really demanded. But when I learned the truth, I realized that I had broken the law and was a sinner, doomed to die. 10So as far as I was concerned, the good law which was supposed to show me the way of life resulted instead in my being given the death penalty. 11Sin fooled me by taking the good laws of God and using them to make me guilty of death. 12But still, you see, the law itself was wholly right and good.

13But how can that be? Didn't the law cause my doom? How then can it be good? No, it was sin, devilish stuff that it is, that used what was good to bring about my condemnation. So you can see how cunning and deadly and damnable it is. For it uses God's good laws for its own evil purposes.

14The law is good, then, and the trouble is not there but with *me*, because I am sold into slavery with Sin as my owner.

15I don't understand myself at all, for I really want to do what is right, but I can't. I do what I don't want to—what I hate. 16I know perfectly well that what I am doing is wrong, and my bad conscience proves that I agree with these laws I am breaking. 17But I can't help

New Revised Standard

then get from the things of which you now are ashamed? The end of those things is death. 22But now that you have been freed from sin and enslaved to God, the advantage you get is sanctification. The end is eternal life. 23For the wages of sin is death, but the free gift of God is eternal life in Christ Jesus our Lord.

An Analogy from Marriage

7 DO YOU not know, brothers and sistersg—for I am speaking to those who know the law—that the law is binding on a person only during that person's lifetime? 2Thus a married woman is bound by the law to her husband as long as he lives; but if her husband dies, she is discharged from the law concerning the husband. 3Accordingly, she will be called an adulteress if she lives with another man while her husband is alive. But if her husband dies, she is free from that law, and if she marries another man, she is not an adulteress.

4 In the same way, my friends,g you have died to the law through the body of Christ, so that you may belong to another, to him who has been raised from the dead in order that we may bear fruit for God. 5While we were living in the flesh, our sinful passions, aroused by the law, were at work in our members to bear fruit for death. 6But now we are discharged from the law, dead to that which held us captive, so that we are slaves not under the old written code but in the new life of the Spirit.

The Law and Sin

7 What then should we say? That the law is sin? By no means! Yet, if it had not been for the law, I would not have known sin. I would not have known what it is to covet if the law had not said, "You shall not covet." 8But sin, seizing an opportunity in the commandment, produced in me all kinds of covetousness. Apart from the law sin lies dead. 9I was once alive apart from the law, but when the commandment came, sin revived 10and I died, and the very commandment that promised life proved to be death to me. 11For sin, seizing an opportunity in the commandment, deceived me and through it killed me. 12So the law is holy, and the commandment is holy and just and good.

13 Did what is good, then, bring death to me? By no means! It was sin, working death in me through what is good, in order that sin might be shown to be sin, and through the commandment might become sinful beyond measure.

The Inner Conflict

14 For we know that the law is spiritual; but I am of the flesh, sold into slavery under sin.h 15I do not understand my own actions. For I do not do what I want, but I do the very thing I hate. 16Now if I do what I do not want, I agree that the law is good. 17But in fact it

---

d 7:1 *dear Jewish brothers*, implied. Literally, "men who know [the] law."
e 7:6 *But now you need no longer worry about the Jewish laws and customs*, literally, "But now we are delivered from the law."   f 7:6 *with all of your hearts and minds*, implied.

g Gk *brothers*   h Gk *sold under sin*

King James

17Now then it is no more I that do it, but sin that dwelleth in me.

18For I know that in me (that is, in my flesh,) dwelleth no good thing: for to will is present with me; but *how* to perform that which is good I find not.

19For the good that I would I do not: but the evil which I would not, that I do.

20Now if I do that I would not, it is no more I that do it, but sin that dwelleth in me.

21I find then a law, that, when I would do good, evil is present with me.

22For I delight in the law of God after the inward man:

23But I see another law in my members, warring against the law of my mind, and bringing me into captivity to the law of sin which is in my members.

24O wretched man that I am! who shall deliver me from the body of this death?

25I thank God through Jesus Christ our Lord. So then with the mind I myself serve the law of God; but with the flesh the law of sin.

8 THERE IS therefore now no condemnation to them which are in Christ Jesus, who walk not after the flesh, but after the Spirit.

2For the law of the Spirit of life in Christ Jesus hath made me free from the law of sin and death.

3For what the law could not do, in that it was weak through the flesh, God sending his own Son in the likeness of sinful flesh, and for sin, condemned sin in the flesh:

4That the righteousness of the law might be fulfilled in us, who walk not after the flesh, but after the Spirit.

5For they that are after the flesh do mind the things of the flesh; but they that are after the Spirit the things of the Spirit.

6For to be carnally minded *is* death; but to be spiritually minded *is* life and peace.

7Because the carnal mind *is* enmity against God: for it is not subject to the law of God, neither indeed can be.

8So then they that are in the flesh cannot please God.

9But ye are not in the flesh, but in the Spirit, if so be that the Spirit of God dwell in you. Now if any man have not the Spirit of Christ, he is none of his.

10And if Christ *be* in you, the body *is* dead because of sin; but the Spirit *is* life because of righteousness.

11But if the Spirit of him that raised up Jesus from the dead dwell in you, he that raised up Christ from the dead shall also quicken your mortal bodies by his Spirit that dwelleth in you.

12Therefore, brethren, we are debtors, not to the flesh, to live after the flesh.

13For if ye live after the flesh, ye shall die: but if ye through the Spirit do mortify the deeds of the body, ye shall live.

14For as many as are led by the Spirit of God, they are the sons of God.

New International

do it, but it is sin living in me. 18I know that nothing good lives in me, that is, in my sinful nature.ᵃ For I have the desire to do what is good, but I cannot carry it out. 19For what I do is not the good I want to do; no, the evil I do not want to do—this I keep on doing. 20Now if I do what I do not want to do, it is no longer I who do it, but it is sin living in me that does it.

21So I find this law at work: When I want to do good, evil is right there with me. 22For in my inner being I delight in God's law; 23but I see another law at work in the members of my body, waging war against the law of my mind and making me a prisoner of the law of sin at work within my members. 24What a wretched man I am! Who will rescue me from this body of death? 25Thanks be to God—through Jesus Christ our Lord!

So then, I myself in my mind am a slave to God's law, but in the sinful nature a slave to the law of sin.

Life Through the Spirit

8 THEREFORE, THERE is now no condemnation for those who are in Christ Jesus,ᵇ 2because through Christ Jesus the law of the Spirit of life set me free from the law of sin and death. 3For what the law was powerless to do in that it was weakened by the sinful nature,ᶜ God did by sending his own Son in the likeness of sinful man to be a sin offering.ᵈ And so he condemned sin in sinful man,ᵉ 4in order that the righteous requirements of the law might be fully met in us, who do not live according to the sinful nature but according to the Spirit.

5Those who live according to the sinful nature have their minds set on what that nature desires; but those who live in accordance with the Spirit have their minds set on what the Spirit desires. 6The mind of sinful manᶠ is death, but the mind controlled by the Spirit is life and peace; 7the sinful mindᵍ is hostile to God. It does not submit to God's law, nor can it do so. 8Those controlled by the sinful nature cannot please God.

9You, however, are controlled not by the sinful nature but by the Spirit, if the Spirit of God lives in you. And if anyone does not have the Spirit of Christ, he does not belong to Christ. 10But if Christ is in you, your body is dead because of sin, yet your spirit is alive because of righteousness. 11And if the Spirit of him who raised Jesus from the dead is living in you, he who raised Christ from the dead will also give life to your mortal bodies through his Spirit, who lives in you.

12Therefore, brothers, we have an obligation—but it is not to the sinful nature, to live according to it. 13For if you live according to the sinful nature, you will die; but if by the Spirit you put to death the misdeeds of the body, you will live, 14because those who are led by the Spirit of God are sons of God. 15For you did not receive

---

ᵃ *18* Or *my flesh*   ᵇ *1* Some later manuscripts *Jesus, who do not live according to the sinful nature but according to the Spirit,*   ᶜ *3* Or *the flesh;* also in verses 4, 5, 8, 9, 12 and 13   ᵈ *3* Or *man, for sin*   ᵉ *3* Or *in the flesh*   ᶠ *6* Or *mind set on the flesh*   ᵍ *7* Or *The mind set on the flesh*

Living Bible

myself, because I'm no longer doing it. It is sin inside me that is stronger than I am that makes me do these evil things.

18I know I am rotten through and through so far as my old sinful nature is concerned. No matter which way I turn I can't make myself do right. I want to but I can't. 19When I want to do good, I don't; and when I try not to do wrong, I do it anyway. 20Now if I am doing what I don't want to, it is plain where the trouble is: sin still has me in its evil grasp.

21It seems to be a fact of life that when I want to do what is right, I inevitably do what is wrong. 22I love to do God's will so far as my new nature is concerned; 23, 24, 25but there is something else deep within me, in my lower nature, that is at war with my mind and wins the fight and makes me a slave to the sin that is still within me. In my mind I want to be God's willing servant but instead I find myself still enslaved to sin.

So you see how it is: my new life tells me to do right, but the old nature that is still inside me loves to sin. Oh, what a terrible predicament I'm in! Who will free me from my slavery to this deadly lower nature? Thank God! It has been doneh by Jesus Christ our Lord. He has set me free.

8 SO THERE is now no condemnation awaiting those who belong to Christ Jesus. 2For the power of the life-giving Spirit—and this power is mine through Christ Jesus—has freed me from the vicious circle of sin and death. 3We aren't saved from sin's grasp by knowing the commandments of God, because we can't and don't keep them, but God put into effect a different plan to save us. He sent his own Son in a human body like ours—except that ours are sinful—and destroyed sin's control over us by giving himself as a sacrifice for our sins. 4So now we can obey God's laws if we follow after the Holy Spirit and no longer obey the old evil nature within us.

5Those who let themselves be controlled by their lower natures live only to please themselves, but those who follow after the Holy Spirit find themselves doing those things that please God. 6Following after the Holy Spirit leads to life and peace, but following after the old nature leads to death, 7because the old sinful nature within us is against God. It never did obey God's laws and it never will. 8That's why those who are still under the control of their old sinful selves, bent on following their old evil desires, can never please God.

9But you are not like that. You are controlled by your new nature if you have the Spirit of God living in you. (And remember that if anyone doesn't have the Spirit of Christ living in him, he is not a Christian at all.) 10Yet, even though Christ lives within you, your body will die because of sin; but your spirit will live, for Christ has pardoned it.i 11And if the Spirit of God, who raised up Jesus from the dead, lives in you, he will make your dying bodies live again after you die, by means of this same Holy Spirit living within you.

12So, dear brothers, you have no obligations whatever to your old sinful nature to do what it begs you to do. 13For if you keep on following it you are lost and will perish, but if through the power of the Holy Spirit you crush it and its evil deeds, you shall live. 14For all who are led by the Spirit of God are sons of God.

New Revised Standard

is no longer I that do it, but sin that dwells within me. 18For I know that nothing good dwells within me, that is, in my flesh. I can will what is right, but I cannot do it. 19For I do not do the good I want, but the evil I do not want is what I do. 20Now if I do what I do not want, it is no longer I that do it, but sin that dwells within me.

21 So I find it to be a law that when I want to do what is good, evil lies close at hand. 22For I delight in the law of God in my inmost self, 23but I see in my members another law at war with the law of my mind, making me captive to the law of sin that dwells in my members. 24Wretched man that I am! Who will rescue me from this body of death? 25Thanks be to God through Jesus Christ our Lord!

So then, with my mind I am a slave to the law of God, but with my flesh I am a slave to the law of sin.

Life in the Spirit

8 THERE IS therefore now no condemnation for those who are in Christ Jesus. 2For the law of the Spiriti of life in Christ Jesus has set youk free from the law of sin and death. 3For God has done what the law, weakened by the flesh, could not do: by sending his own Son in the likeness of sinful flesh, and to deal with sin,l he condemned sin in the flesh, 4so that the just requirement of the law might be fulfilled in us, who walk not according to the flesh but according to the Spirit.j 5For those who live according to the flesh set their minds on the things of the flesh, but those who live according to the Spirit set their minds on the things of the Spirit.j 6To set the mind on the flesh is death, but to set the mind on the Spiriti is life and peace. 7For this reason the mind that is set on the flesh is hostile to God; it does not submit to God's law—indeed it cannot, 8and those who are in the flesh cannot please God.

9 But you are not in the flesh; you are in the Spirit,j since the Spirit of God dwells in you. Anyone who does not have the Spirit of Christ does not belong to him. 10But if Christ is in you, though the body is dead because of sin, the Spiriti is life because of righteousness. 11If the Spirit of him who raised Jesus from the dead dwells in you, he who raised Christm from the dead will give life to your mortal bodies also throughn his Spirit that dwells in you.

12 So then, brothers and sisters,o we are debtors, not to the flesh, to live according to the flesh— 13for if you live according to the flesh, you will die; but if by the Spirit you put to death the deeds of the body, you will live. 14For all who are led by the Spirit of God are children of God. 15For you did not receive a spirit of

---

h 7:25 It has been done, or, "It will be done," literally, "I thank God through Jesus Christ our Lord." i 8:10 for Christ has pardoned it, or possibly, "but the Holy Spirit who lives in you will give you life, for he has already given you righteousness." Literally, "but the Spirit is life because of righteousness."

j Or spirit k Here the Greek word you is singular number; other ancient authorities read me or us l Or and as a sin offering m Other ancient authorities read the Christ or Christ Jesus or Jesus Christ n Other ancient authorities read on account of o Gk brothers

King James

15For ye have not received the spirit of bondage again to fear; but ye have received the Spirit of adoption, whereby we cry, Abba, Father.

16The Spirit itself beareth witness with our spirit, that we are the children of God:

17And if children, then heirs; heirs of God, and joint-heirs with Christ; if so be that we suffer with *him*, that we may be also glorified together.

18For I reckon that the sufferings of this present time *are* not worthy *to be compared* with the glory which shall be revealed in us.

19For the earnest expectation of the creature waiteth for the manifestation of the sons of God.

20For the creature was made subject to vanity, not willingly, but by reason of him who hath subjected *the same* in hope,

21Because the creature itself also shall be delivered from the bondage of corruption into the glorious liberty of the children of God.

22For we know that the whole creation groaneth and travaileth in pain together until now.

23And not only *they*, but ourselves also, which have the firstfruits of the Spirit, even we ourselves groan within ourselves, waiting for the adoption, *to wit*, the redemption of our body.

24For we are saved by hope: but hope that is seen is not hope: for what a man seeth, why doth he yet hope for?

25But if we hope for that we see not, *then* do we with patience wait for *it*.

26Likewise the Spirit also helpeth our infirmities: for we know not what we should pray for as we ought: but the Spirit itself maketh intercession for us with groanings which cannot be uttered.

27And he that searcheth the hearts knoweth what *is* the mind of the Spirit, because he maketh intercession for the saints according to *the will of* God.

28And we know that all things work together for good to them that love God, to them who are the called according to *his* purpose.

29For whom he did foreknow, he also did predestinate *to be* conformed to the image of his Son, that he might be the firstborn among many brethren.

30Moreover whom he did predestinate, them he also called: and whom he called, them he also justified: and whom he justified, them he also glorified.

31What shall we then say to these things? If God *be* for us, who *can be* against us?

32He that spared not his own Son, but delivered him up for us all, how shall he not with him also freely give us all things?

33Who shall lay any thing to the charge of God's elect? *It is* God that justifieth.

34Who *is* he that condemneth? *It is* Christ that died, yea rather, that is risen again, who is even at the right hand of God, who also maketh intercession for us.

35Who shall separate us from the love of Christ? *shall* tribulation, or distress, or persecution, or famine, or nakedness, or peril, or sword?

New International

a spirit that makes you a slave again to fear, but you received the Spirit of sonship.a And by him we cry, "Abba,b Father." 16The Spirit himself testifies with our spirit that we are God's children. 17Now if we are children, then we are heirs—heirs of God and co-heirs with Christ, if indeed we share in his sufferings in order that we may also share in his glory.

Future Glory

18I consider that our present sufferings are not worth comparing with the glory that will be revealed in us. 19The creation waits in eager expectation for the sons of God to be revealed. 20For the creation was subjected to frustration, not by its own choice, but by the will of the one who subjected it, in hope 21thatc the creation itself will be liberated from its bondage to decay and brought into the glorious freedom of the children of God.

22We know that the whole creation has been groaning as in the pains of childbirth right up to the present time. 23Not only so, but we ourselves, who have the firstfruits of the Spirit, groan inwardly as we wait eagerly for our adoption as sons, the redemption of our bodies. 24For in this hope we were saved. But hope that is seen is no hope at all. Who hopes for what he already has? 25But if we hope for what we do not yet have, we wait for it patiently.

26In the same way, the Spirit helps us in our weakness. We do not know what we ought to pray for, but the Spirit himself intercedes for us with groans that words cannot express. 27And he who searches our hearts knows the mind of the Spirit, because the Spirit intercedes for the saints in accordance with God's will.

More Than Conquerors

28And we know that in all things God works for the good of those who love him,d whoe have been called according to his purpose. 29For those God foreknew he also predestined to be conformed to the likeness of his Son, that he might be the firstborn among many brothers. 30And those he predestined, he also called; those he called, he also justified; those he justified, he also glorified.

31What, then, shall we say in response to this? If God is for us, who can be against us? 32He who did not spare his own Son, but gave him up for us all—how will he not also, along with him, graciously give us all things? 33Who will bring any charge against those whom God has chosen? It is God who justifies. 34Who is he that condemns? Christ Jesus, who died—more than that, who was raised to life—is at the right hand of God and is also interceding for us. 35Who shall separate us from the love of Christ? Shall trouble or hardship or persecu-

---

a 15 Or *adoption*   b 15 Aramaic for *Father*   c 20,21 Or *subjected it in hope.* 21For   d 28 Some manuscripts *And we know that all things work together for good to those who love God*   e 28 Or *works together with those who love him to bring about what is good—with those who*

Living Bible

15And so we should not be like cringing, fearful slaves, but we should behave like God's very own children, adopted into the bosom of his family, and calling to him, "Father, Father." 16For his Holy Spirit speaks to us deep in our hearts, and tells us that we really are God's children. 17And since we are his children, we will share his treasures—for all God gives to his Son Jesus is now ours too. But if we are to share his glory, we must also share his suffering.

18Yet what we suffer now is nothing compared to the glory he will give us later. 19For all creation is waiting patiently and hopefully for that future dayf when God will resurrect his children. 20, 21For on that day thorns and thistles, sin, death, and decayg—the things that overcame the world against its will at God's command—will all disappear, and the world around us will share in the glorious freedom from sin which God's children enjoy.

22For we know that even the things of nature, like animals and plants, suffer in sickness and death as they await this great event.h 23And even we Christians, although we have the Holy Spirit within us as a foretaste of future glory, also groan to be released from pain and suffering. We, too, wait anxiously for that day when God will give us our full rights as his children, including the new bodies he has promised us—bodies that will never be sick again and will never die.

24We are saved by trusting. And trusting means looking forward to getting something we don't yet have—for a man who already has something doesn't need to hope and trust that he will get it. 25But if we must keep trusting God for something that hasn't happened yet, it teaches us to wait patiently and confidently.

26And in the same way—by our faithi—the Holy Spirit helps us with our daily problems and in our praying. For we don't even know what we should pray for, nor how to pray as we should; but the Holy Spirit prays for us with such feeling that it cannot be expressed in words. 27And the Father who knows all hearts knows, of course, what the Spirit is saying as he pleads for us in harmony with God's own will. 28And we know that all that happens to us is working for our good if we love God and are fitting into his plans.

29For from the very beginning God decided that those who came to him—and all along he knew who would—should become like his Son, so that his Son would be the First, with many brothers. 30And having chosen us, he called us to come to him; and when we came, he declared us "not guilty," filled us with Christ's goodness, gave us right standing with himself, and promised us his glory.

31What can we ever say to such wonderful things as these? If God is on our side, who can ever be against us? 32Since he did not spare even his own Son for us but gave him up for us all, won't he also surely give us everything else?

33Who dares accuse us whom God has chosen for his own? Will God? No! He is the one who has forgiven us and given us right standing with himself.

34Who then will condemn us? Will Christ? No! For he is the one who died for us and came back to life again for us and is sitting at the place of highest honor next to God, pleading for us there in heaven.

35Who then can ever keep Christ's love from us? When we have trouble or calamity, when we are hunted down or destroyed, is it because he doesn't love us anymore? And if we are hungry, or penniless, or in danger, or threatened with death, has God deserted us?

New Revised Standard

slavery to fall back into fear, but you have received a spirit of adoption. When we cry, "Abba!j Father!" 16it is that very Spirit bearing witnessk with our spirit that we are children of God, 17and if children, then heirs, heirs of God and joint heirs with Christ—if, in fact, we suffer with him so that we may also be glorified with him.

Future Glory

18 I consider that the sufferings of this present time are not worth comparing with the glory about to be revealed to us. 19For the creation waits with eager longing for the revealing of the children of God; 20for the creation was subjected to futility, not of its own will but by the will of the one who subjected it, in hope 21that the creation itself will be set free from its bondage to decay and will obtain the freedom of the glory of the children of God. 22We know that the whole creation has been groaning in labor pains until now; 23and not only the creation, but we ourselves, who have the first fruits of the Spirit, groan inwardly while we wait for adoption, the redemption of our bodies. 24For inl hope we were saved. Now hope that is seen is not hope. For who hopesm for what is seen? 25But if we hope for what we do not see, we wait for it with patience.

26 Likewise the Spirit helps us in our weakness; for we do not know how to pray as we ought, but that very Spirit intercedesn with sighs too deep for words. 27And God,o who searches the heart, knows what is the mind of the Spirit, because the Spiritp intercedes for the saints according to the will of God.q

28 We know that all things work together for goodr for those who love God, who are called according to his purpose. 29For those whom he foreknew he also predestined to be conformed to the image of his Son, in order that he might be the firstborn within a large family.s 30And those whom he predestined he also called; and those whom he called he also justified; and those whom he justified he also glorified.

God's Love in Christ Jesus

31 What then are we to say about these things? If God is for us, who is against us? 32He who did not withhold his own Son, but gave him up for all of us, will he not with him also give us everything else? 33Who will bring any charge against God's elect? It is God who justifies. 34Who is to condemn? It is Christ Jesus, who died, yes, who was raised, who is at the right hand of God, who indeed intercedes for us.t 35Who will separate us from the love of Christ? Will hardship, or distress, or persecution, or famine, or nakedness, or peril, or sword? 36As it is written,

---

f 8:19 waiting . . . for that future day, literally, "waiting for the revelation of the sons of God."   g 8:20, 21 thorns and thistles, sin, death, and decay, implied.   h 8:22 suffer in sickness and death as they await this great event, literally, "the whole creation has been groaning in travail together until now."   i 8:26 by our faith, implied. Literally, "in like manner."

---

j Aramaic for Father   k Or 15a spirit of adoption, by which we cry, "Abba! Father!"   16The Spirit itself bears witness   l Or by   m Other ancient authorities read awaits   n Other ancient authorities add for us   o Gk the one   p Gk he or it   q Gk according to God   r Other ancient authorities read God makes all things work together for good, or in all things God works for good   s Gk among many brothers   t Or Is it Christ Jesus . . . for us?

King James

36As it is written, For thy sake we are killed all the day long; we are accounted as sheep for the slaughter.

37Nay, in all these things we are more than conquerors through him that loved us.

38For I am persuaded, that neither death, nor life, nor angels, nor principalities, nor powers, nor things present, nor things to come,

39Nor height, nor depth, nor any other creature, shall be able to separate us from the love of God, which is in Christ Jesus our Lord.

9 I SAY the truth in Christ, I lie not, my conscience also bearing me witness in the Holy Ghost,

2That I have great heaviness and continual sorrow in my heart.

3For I could wish that myself were accursed from Christ for my brethren, my kinsmen according to the flesh:

4Who are Israelites; to whom *pertaineth* the adoption, and the glory, and the covenants, and the giving of the law, and the service *of God*, and the promises;

5Whose *are* the fathers, and of whom as concerning the flesh Christ *came*, who is over all, God blessed for ever. Amen.

6Not as though the word of God hath taken none effect. For they *are* not all Israel, which are of Israel:

7Neither, because they are the seed of Abraham, *are they* all children: but, In Isaac shall thy seed be called.

8That is, They which are the children of the flesh, these *are* not the children of God: but the children of the promise are counted for the seed.

9For this *is* the word of promise, At this time will I come, and Sarah shall have a son.

10And not only *this;* but when Rebecca also had conceived by one, *even* by our father Isaac;

11(For *the children* being not yet born, neither having done any good or evil, that the purpose of God according to election might stand, not of works, but of him that calleth;)

12It was said unto her, The elder shall serve the younger.

13As it is written, Jacob have I loved, but Esau have I hated.

14What shall we say then? *Is there* unrighteousness with God? God forbid.

15For he saith to Moses, I will have mercy on whom I will have mercy, and I will have compassion on whom I will have compassion.

16So then *it is* not of him that willeth, nor of him that runneth, but of God that sheweth mercy.

17For the scripture saith unto Pharaoh, Even for this same purpose have I raised thee up, that I might show my power in thee, and that my name might be declared throughout all the earth.

18Therefore hath he mercy on whom he will *have mercy,* and whom he will he hardeneth.

19Thou wilt say then unto me, Why doth he yet find fault? For who hath resisted his will?

New International

tion or famine or nakedness or danger or sword? 36As it is written:

> "For your sake we face death all day long;
>   we are considered as sheep to be
>   slaughtered."a

37No, in all these things we are more than conquerors through him who loved us. 38For I am convinced that neither death nor life, neither angels nor demons,b neither the present nor the future, nor any powers, 39neither height nor depth, nor anything else in all creation, will be able to separate us from the love of God that is in Christ Jesus our Lord.

God's Sovereign Choice

9 I SPEAK the truth in Christ—I am not lying, my conscience confirms it in the Holy Spirit— 2I have great sorrow and unceasing anguish in my heart. 3For I could wish that I myself were cursed and cut off from Christ for the sake of my brothers, those of my own race, 4the people of Israel. Theirs is the adoption as sons; theirs the divine glory, the covenants, the receiving of the law, the temple worship and the promises. 5Theirs are the patriarchs, and from them is traced the human ancestry of Christ, who is God over all, forever praised!c Amen.

6It is not as though God's word had failed. For not all who are descended from Israel are Israel. 7Nor because they are his descendants are they all Abraham's children. On the contrary, "It is through Isaac that your offspring will be reckoned."d 8In other words, it is not the natural children who are God's children, but it is the children of the promise who are regarded as Abraham's offspring. 9For this was how the promise was stated: "At the appointed time I will return, and Sarah will have a son."e

10Not only that, but Rebekah's children had one and the same father, our father Isaac. 11Yet, before the twins were born or had done anything good or bad—in order that God's purpose in election might stand: 12not by works but by him who calls—she was told, "The older will serve the younger."f 13Just as it is written: "Jacob I loved, but Esau I hated."g

14What then shall we say? Is God unjust? Not at all! 15For he says to Moses,

> "I will have mercy on whom I have mercy,
>   and I will have compassion on whom I have
>   compassion."h

16It does not, therefore, depend on man's desire or effort, but on God's mercy. 17For the Scripture says to Pharaoh: "I raised you up for this very purpose, that I might display my power in you and that my name might be proclaimed in all the earth."i 18Therefore God has mercy on whom he wants to have mercy, and he hardens whom he wants to harden.

19One of you will say to me: "Then why does God still blame us? For who resists his will?" 20But who are

a *36* Psalm 44:22   b *38* Or *nor heavenly rulers*   c *5* Or *Christ, who is over all. God be forever praised!* Or *Christ. God who is over all be forever praised!*
d *7* Gen. 21:12   e *9* Gen. 18:10,14   f *12* Gen. 25:23   g *13* Mal. 1:2,3
h *15* Exodus 33:19   i *17* Exodus 9:16

Living Bible

36No, for the Scriptures tell us that for his sake we must be ready to face death at every moment of the day—we are like sheep awaiting slaughter; 37but despite all this, overwhelming victory is ours through Christ who loved us enough to die for us. 38For I am convinced that nothing can ever separate us from his love. Death can't, and life can't. The angels won't, and all the powers of hell itself cannot keep God's love away. Our fears for today, our worries about tomorrow, 39or where we are—high above the sky, or in the deepest ocean—nothing will ever be able to separate us from the love of God demonstrated by our Lord Jesus Christ when he died for us.

9 OH, ISRAEL, my people! Oh, my Jewish brothers! How I long for you to come to Christ. My heart is heavy within me and I grieve bitterly day and night because of you. Christ knows and the Holy Spirit knows that it is no mere pretense when I say that I would be willing to be forever damned if that would save you. 4God has given you so much, but still you will not listen to him. He took you as his own special, chosen people and led you along with a bright cloud of glory and told you how very much he wanted to bless you. He gave you his rules for daily life so you would know what he wanted you to do. He let you worship him, and gave you mighty promises. 5Great men of God were your fathers, and Christ himself was one of you, a Jew so far as his human nature is concerned, he who now rules over all things. Praise God forever!
6Well then, has God failed to fulfill his promises to the Jews? No! [For these promises are only to those who are truly Jews.j] And not everyone born into a Jewish family is truly a Jew! 7Just the fact that they come from Abraham doesn't make them truly Abraham's children. For the Scriptures say that the promises apply only to Abraham's son Isaac and Isaac's descendants, though Abraham had other children too. 8This means that not all of Abraham's children are children of God, but only those who believe the promise of salvation which he made to Abraham.
9For God had promised, "Next year I will give you and Sarah a son." 10–13And years later, when this son, Isaac, was grown up and married, and Rebecca his wife was about to bear him twin children, God told her that Esau, the child born first, would be a servant to Jacob, his twin brother. In the words of the Scripture, "I chose to bless Jacob, but not Esau." And God said this before the children were even born, before they had done anything either good or bad. This proves that God was doing what he had decided from the beginning; it was not because of what the children did but because of what God wanted and chose.
14Was God being unfair? Of course not. 15For God had said to Moses, "If I want to be kind to someone, I will. And I will take pity on anyone I want to." 16And so God's blessings are not given just because someone decides to have them or works hard to get them. They are given because God takes pity on those he wants to.
17Pharaoh, king of Egypt, was an example of this fact. For God told him he had given him the kingdom of Egypt for the very purpose of displaying the awesome power of God against him: so that all the world would hear about God's glorious name.k 18So you see, God is kind to some just because he wants to be, and he makes some refuse to listen.
19Well then, why does God blame them for not listening? Haven't they done what he made them do?

New Revised Standard

"For your sake we are being killed all day
    long;
  we are accounted as sheep to be
    slaughtered."
37No, in all these things we are more than conquerors through him who loved us. 38For I am convinced that neither death, nor life, nor angels, nor rulers, nor things present, nor things to come, nor powers, 39nor height, nor depth, nor anything else in all creation, will be able to separate us from the love of God in Christ Jesus our Lord.

God's Election of Israel

9 I AM speaking the truth in Christ—I am not lying; my conscience confirms it by the Holy Spirit— 2I have great sorrow and unceasing anguish in my heart. 3For I could wish that I myself were accursed and cut off from Christ for the sake of my own people,l my kindred according to the flesh. 4They are Israelites, and to them belong the adoption, the glory, the covenants, the giving of the law, the worship, and the promises; 5to them belong the patriarchs, and from them, according to the flesh, comes the Messiah,m who is over all, God blessed forever.n Amen.
6 It is not as though the word of God had failed. For not all Israelites truly belong to Israel, 7and not all of Abraham's children are his true descendants; but "It is through Isaac that descendants shall be named for you." 8This means that it is not the children of the flesh who are the children of God, but the children of the promise are counted as descendants. 9For this is what the promise said, "About this time I will return and Sarah shall have a son." 10Nor is that all; something similar happened to Rebecca when she had conceived children by one husband, our ancestor Isaac. 11Even before they had been born or had done anything good or bad (so that God's purpose of election might continue, 12not by works but by his call) she was told, "The elder shall serve the younger." 13As it is written,
    "I have loved Jacob,
      but I have hated Esau."
14 What then are we to say? Is there injustice on God's part? By no means! 15For he says to Moses,
    "I will have mercy on whom I have mercy,
      and I will have compassion on whom I have
        compassion."
16So it depends not on human will or exertion, but on God who shows mercy. 17For the scripture says to Pharaoh, "I have raised you up for the very purpose of showing my power in you, so that my name may be proclaimed in all the earth." 18So then he has mercy on whomever he chooses, and he hardens the heart of whomever he chooses.

God's Wrath and Mercy

19 You will say to me then, "Why then does he still find fault? For who can resist his will?" 20But who in-

---

j 9:6 For these promises are only to those who are truly Jews, implied.
k 9:17 that all the world would hear about God's glorious name, literally, "that my name might be published abroad in all the earth."

l Gk my brothers   m Or the Christ   n Or Messiah, who is God over all, blessed forever; or Messiah. May he who is God over all be blessed forever

King James

20Nay but, O man, who art thou that repliest against God? Shall the thing formed say to him that formed *it*, Why hast thou made me thus?

21Hath not the potter power over the clay, of the same lump to make one vessel unto honour, and another unto dishonour?

22*What* if God, willing to show *his* wrath, and to make his power known, endured with much longsuffering the vessels of wrath fitted to destruction:

23And that he might make known the riches of his glory on the vessels of mercy, which he had afore prepared unto glory,

24Even us, whom he hath called, not of the Jews only, but also of the Gentiles?

25As he saith also in Osee, I will call them my people, which were not my people; and her beloved, which was not beloved.

26And it shall come to pass, *that* in the place where it was said unto them, Ye *are* not my people; there shall they be called the children of the living God.

27Esaias also crieth concerning Israel, Though the number of the children of Israel be as the sand of the sea, a remnant shall be saved:

28For he will finish the work, and cut *it* short in righteousness: because a short work will the Lord make upon the earth.

29And as Esaias said before, Except the Lord of Sabaoth had left us a seed, we had been as Sodoma, and been made like unto Gomorrha.

30What shall we say then? That the Gentiles, which followed not after righteousness, have attained to righteousness, even the righteousness which is of faith.

31But Israel, which followed after the law of righteousness, hath not attained to the law of righteousness.

32Wherefore? Because *they* sought it not by faith, but as it were by the works of the law. For they stumbled at that stumblingstone;

33As it is written, Behold, I lay in Zion a stumblingstone and rock of offence: and whosoever believeth on him shall not be ashamed.

10 BRETHREN, MY heart's desire and prayer to God for Israel is, that they might be saved.

2For I bear them record that they have a zeal of God, but not according to knowledge.

3For they being ignorant of God's righteousness, and going about to establish their own righteousness, have not submitted themselves unto the righteousness of God.

4For Christ *is* the end of the law for righteousness to every one that believeth.

5For Moses describeth the righteousness which is of the law, That the man which doeth those things shall live by them.

New International

you, O man, to talk back to God? "Shall what is formed say to him who formed it, 'Why did you make me like this?' "a 21Does not the potter have the right to make out of the same lump of clay some pottery for noble purposes and some for common use?

22What if God, choosing to show his wrath and make his power known, bore with great patience the objects of his wrath—prepared for destruction? 23What if he did this to make the riches of his glory known to the objects of his mercy, whom he prepared in advance for glory— 24even us, whom he also called, not only from the Jews but also from the Gentiles? 25As he says in Hosea:

"I will call them 'my people' who are not my people;
and I will call her 'my loved one' who is not my loved one,"b

26and,

"It will happen that in the very place where it was said to them,
'You are not my people,'
they will be called 'sons of the living God.' "c

27Isaiah cries out concerning Israel:

"Though the number of the Israelites be like the sand by the sea,
only the remnant will be saved.
28For the Lord will carry out
his sentence on earth with speed and finality."d

29It is just as Isaiah said previously:

"Unless the Lord Almighty
had left us descendants,
we would have become like Sodom,
we would have been like Gomorrah."e

Israel's Unbelief

30What then shall we say? That the Gentiles, who did not pursue righteousness, have obtained it, a righteousness that is by faith; 31but Israel, who pursued a law of righteousness, has not attained it. 32Why not? Because they pursued it not by faith but as if it were by works. They stumbled over the "stumbling stone." 33As it is written:

"See, I lay in Zion a stone that causes men to stumble
and a rock that makes them fall,
and the one who trusts in him will never be put to shame."f

10 BROTHERS, MY heart's desire and prayer to God for the Israelites is that they may be saved.

2For I can testify about them that they are zealous for God, but their zeal is not based on knowledge. 3Since they did not know the righteousness that comes from God and sought to establish their own, they did not submit to God's righteousness. 4Christ is the end of the law so that there may be righteousness for everyone who believes.

5Moses describes in this way the righteousness that is by the law: "The man who does these things will live by them."g 6But the righteousness that is by faith says:

a 20 Isaiah 29:16; 45:9   b 25 Hosea 2:23   c 26 Hosea 1:10   d 28 Isaiah 10:22,23   e 29 Isaiah 1:9   f 33 Isaiah 8:14; 28:16   g 5 Lev. 18:5

Living Bible

20No, don't say that. Who are you to criticize God? Should the thing made say to the one who made it, "Why have you made me like this?" 21When a man makes a jar out of clay, doesn't he have a right to use the same lump of clay to make one jar beautiful, to be used for holding flowers, and another to throw garbage into? 22Does not God have a perfect right to show his fury and power against those who are fit only for destruction, those he has been patient with for all this time? 23, 24And he has a right to take others such as ourselves, who have been made for pouring the riches of his glory into, whether we are Jews or Gentiles, and to be kind to us so that everyone can see how very great his glory is.

25Remember what the prophecy of Hosea says? There God says that he will find other children for himself (who are not from his Jewish family) and will love them, though no one had ever loved them before. 26And the heathen, of whom it once was said, "You are not my people," shall be called "sons of the Living God."h 27Isaiah the prophet cried out concerning the Jews that though there would be millionsi of them, only a small number would ever be saved. 28"For the Lord will execute his sentence upon the earth, quickly ending his dealings, justly cutting them short."j

29And Isaiah says in another place that except for God's mercy all the Jews would be destroyed—all of them—just as everyone in the cities of Sodom and Gomorrah perished.k

30Well then, what shall we say about these things? Just this, that God has given the Gentiles the opportunity to be acquitted by faith, even though they had not been really seeking God. 31But the Jews, who tried so hard to get right with God by keeping his laws, never succeeded. 32Why not? Because they were trying to be saved by keeping the law and being good instead of by depending on faith. They have stumbled over the great stumbling stone. 33God warned them of this in the Scriptures when he said, "I have put a Rock in the path of the Jews, and many will stumble over him (Jesus). Those who believe in him will never be disappointed."l

New Revised Standard

deed are you, a human being, to argue with God? Will what is molded say to the one who molds it, "Why have you made me like this?" 21Has the potter no right over the clay, to make out of the same lump one object for special use and another for ordinary use? 22What if God, desiring to show his wrath and to make known his power, has endured with much patience the objects of wrath that are made for destruction; 23and what if he has done so in order to make known the riches of his glory for the objects of mercy, which he has prepared beforehand for glory— 24including us whom he has called, not from the Jews only but also from the Gentiles? 25As indeed he says in Hosea,

> "Those who were not my people I will call
>   'my people,'
> and her who was not beloved I will call
>   'beloved.' "

26   "And in the very place where it was said to
>   them, 'You are not my people,'
>   there they shall be called children of the
>   living God."

27   And Isaiah cries out concerning Israel, "Though the number of the children of Israel were like the sand of the sea, only a remnant of them will be saved; 28for the Lord will execute his sentence on the earth quickly and decisively."m 29And as Isaiah predicted,

> "If the Lord of hosts had not left survivorsn to
>   us,
>   we would have fared like Sodom
>   and been made like Gomorrah."

Israel's Unbelief

30   What then are we to say? Gentiles, who did not strive for righteousness, have attained it, that is, righteousness through faith; 31but Israel, who did strive for the righteousness that is based on the law, did not succeed in fulfilling that law. 32Why not? Because they did not strive for it on the basis of faith, but as if it were based on works. They have stumbled over the stumbling stone, 33as it is written,

> "See, I am laying in Zion a stone that will
>   make people stumble, a rock that will
>   make them fall,
>   and whoever believes in himo will not be
>   put to shame."

10 DEAR BROTHERS, the longing of my heart and my prayer is that the Jewish people might be saved. 2I know what enthusiasm they have for the honor of God, but it is misdirected zeal. 3For they don't understand that Christ has died to make them right with God. Instead they are trying to make themselves good enough to gain God's favor by keeping the Jewish laws and customs, and that is not God's way of salvation. 4They don't understand that Christ gives to those who trust in him everything they are trying to get by keeping his laws. He ends all of that.

5For Moses wrote that if a person could be perfectly good and hold out against temptation all his life and never sin once, only then could he be pardoned and saved. 6But the salvation that comes through faith says,

10 BROTHERS AND sisters,p my heart's desire and prayer to God for them is that they may be saved. 2I can testify that they have a zeal for God, but it is not enlightened. 3For, being ignorant of the righteousness that comes from God, and seeking to establish their own, they have not submitted to God's righteousness. 4For Christ is the end of the law so that there may be righteousness for everyone who believes.

Salvation Is for All

5 Moses writes concerning the righteousness that comes from the law, that "the person who does these things will live by them." 6But the righteousness that

---

h 9:26 *sons of the Living God*, see Hosea 2:23.   i 9:27 *millions*, literally, "as the sand of the sea," i.e., numberless.   j 9:28 *cutting them short*, see Isa 10:22; 28:22.   k 9:29 *perished*, see Isa 1:9.   l 9:33 *never be disappointed*, see Isa 28:16.

m Other ancient authorities read *for he will finish his work and cut it short in righteousness, because the Lord will make the sentence shortened on the earth*   n Or *descendants*; Gk *seed*   o Or *trusts in it*   p Gk *Brothers*

King James

6But the righteousness which is of faith speaketh on this wise, Say not in thine heart, Who shall ascend into heaven? (that is, to bring Christ down *from above:*)

7Or, Who shall descend into the deep? (that is, to bring up Christ again from the dead.)

8But what saith it? The word is nigh thee, *even* in thy mouth, and in thy heart: that is, the word of faith, which we preach;

9That if thou shalt confess with thy mouth the Lord Jesus, and shalt believe in thine heart that God hath raised him from the dead, thou shalt be saved.

10For with the heart man believeth unto righteousness; and with the mouth confession is made unto salvation.

11For the scripture saith, Whosoever believeth on him shall not be ashamed.

12For there is no difference between the Jew and the Greek: for the same Lord over all is rich unto all that call upon him.

13For whosoever shall call upon the name of the Lord shall be saved.

14How then shall they call on him in whom they have not believed? and how shall they believe in him of whom they have not heard? and how shall they hear without a preacher?

15And how shall they preach, except they be sent? as it is written, How beautiful are the feet of them that preach the gospel of peace, and bring glad tidings of good things!

16But they have not all obeyed the gospel. For Esaias saith, Lord, who hath believed our report?

17So then faith *cometh* by hearing, and hearing by the word of God.

18But I say, Have they not heard? Yes verily, their sound went into all the earth, and their words unto the ends of the world.

19But I say, Did not Israel know? First Moses saith, I will provoke you to jealousy by *them that are* no people, *and* by a foolish nation I will anger you.

20But Esaias is very bold, and saith, I was found of them that sought me not; I was made manifest unto them that asked not after me.

21But to Israel he saith, All day long I have stretched forth my hands unto a disobedient and gainsaying people.

11 I SAY then, Hath God cast away his people? God forbid. For I also am an Israelite, of the seed of Abraham, *of* the tribe of Benjamin.

2God hath not cast away his people which he foreknew. Wot ye not what the scripture saith of Elias? how he maketh intercession to God against Israel, saying,

3Lord, they have killed thy prophets, and digged down thine altars; and I am left alone, and they seek my life.

4But what saith the answer of God unto him? I have reserved to myself seven thousand men, who have not bowed the knee to *the image of* Baal.

New International

"Do not say in your heart, 'Who will ascend into heaven?'[a]" (that is, to bring Christ down) 7"or 'Who will descend into the deep?'[b]" (that is, to bring Christ up from the dead). 8But what does it say? "The word is near you; it is in your mouth and in your heart,"[c] that is, the word of faith we are proclaiming: 9That if you confess with your mouth, "Jesus is Lord," and believe in your heart that God raised him from the dead, you will be saved. 10For it is with your heart that you believe and are justified, and it is with your mouth that you confess and are saved. 11As the Scripture says, "Anyone who trusts in him will never be put to shame."[d] 12For there is no difference between Jew and Gentile—the same Lord is Lord of all and richly blesses all who call on him, 13for, "Everyone who calls on the name of the Lord will be saved."[e]

14How, then, can they call on the one they have not believed in? And how can they believe in the one of whom they have not heard? And how can they hear without someone preaching to them? 15And how can they preach unless they are sent? As it is written, "How beautiful are the feet of those who bring good news!"[f]

16But not all the Israelites accepted the good news. For Isaiah says, "Lord, who has believed our message?"[g] 17Consequently, faith comes from hearing the message, and the message is heard through the word of Christ. 18But I ask: Did they not hear? Of course they did:

"Their voice has gone out into all the earth,
    their words to the ends of the world."[h]

19Again I ask: Did Israel not understand? First, Moses says,

"I will make you envious by those who are not
        a nation;
    I will make you angry by a nation that has no
        understanding."[i]

20And Isaiah boldly says,

"I was found by those who did not seek me;
    I revealed myself to those who did not ask for
        me."[j]

21But concerning Israel he says,

"All day long I have held out my hands
    to a disobedient and obstinate people."[k]

The Remnant of Israel

11 I ASK then: Did God reject his people? By no means! I am an Israelite myself, a descendant of Abraham, from the tribe of Benjamin. 2God did not reject his people, whom he foreknew. Don't you know what the Scripture says in the passage about Elijah—how he appealed to God against Israel: 3"Lord, they have killed your prophets and torn down your altars; I am the only one left, and they are trying to kill me"[l]? 4And what was God's answer to him? "I have reserved for myself seven thousand who have not bowed the knee to Baal."[m] 5So too, at the present time there is a remnant

a 6 Deut. 30:12   b 7 Deut. 30:13   c 8 Deut. 30:14   d 11 Isaiah 28:16
e 13 Joel 2:32   f 15 Isaiah 52:7   g 16 Isaiah 53:1   h 18 Psalm 19:4
i 19 Deut. 32:21   j 20 Isaiah 65:1   k 21 Isaiah 65:2
l 3 1 Kings 19:10,14   m 4 1 Kings 19:18

Living Bible

"You don't need to search the heavens to find Christ and bring him down to help you," and, 7"You don't need to go among the dead to bring Christ back to life again."

8For salvation that comes from trusting Christ—which is what we preach—is already within easy reach of each of us; in fact, it is as near as our own hearts and mouths. 9For if you tell others with your own mouth that Jesus Christ is your Lord, and believe in your own heart that God has raised him from the dead, you will be saved. 10For it is by believing in his heart that a man becomes right with God; and with his mouth he tells others of his faith, confirming his salvation.n

11For the Scriptures tell us that no one who believes in Christ will ever be disappointed. 12Jew and Gentile are the same in this respect: they all have the same Lord who generously gives his riches to all those who ask him for them. 13Anyone who calls upon the name of the Lord will be saved.

14But how shall they ask him to save them unless they believe in him? And how can they believe in him if they have never heard about him? And how can they hear about him unless someone tells them? 15And how will anyone go and tell them unless someone sends him? That is what the Scriptures are talking about when they say, "How beautiful are the feet of those who preach the Gospel of peace with God and bring glad tidings of good things."o In other words, how welcome are those who come preaching God's Good News!

16But not everyone who hears the Good News has welcomed it, for Isaiah the prophet said, "Lord, who has believed me when I told them?"p 17Yet faith comes from listening to this Good News—the Good News about Christ.

18But what about the Jews? Have they heard God's Word? Yes, for it has gone wherever they are; the Good News has been told to the ends of the earth. 19And did they understand [that God would give his salvation to others if they refused to take itq]? Yes, for even back in the time of Moses, God had said that he would make his people jealous and try to wake them up by giving his salvation to the foolish heathen nations. 20And later on Isaiah said boldly that God would be found by people who weren't even looking for him.r 21In the meantime, he keeps on reaching out his hands to the Jews, but they keep arguings and refusing to come.

11 I ASK then, has God rejected and deserted his people the Jews? Oh no, not at all. Remember that I myself am a Jew, a descendant of Abraham and a member of Benjamin's family.

2,3No, God has not discarded his own people whom he chose from the very beginning. Do you remember what the Scriptures say about this? Elijah the prophet was complaining to God about the Jews, telling God how they had killed the prophets and torn down God's altars; Elijah claimed that he was the only one left in all the land who still loved God, and now they were trying to kill him too.

4And do you remember how God replied? God said, "No, you are not the only one left. I have seven thousand others besides you who still love me and have not bowed down to idols!"t

New Revised Standard

comes from faith says, "Do not say in your heart, 'Who will ascend into heaven?'" (that is, to bring Christ down) 7"or 'Who will descend into the abyss?'" (that is, to bring Christ up from the dead). 8But what does it say?

"The word is near you,
   on your lips and in your heart"

(that is, the word of faith that we proclaim); 9becauseu if you confess with your lips that Jesus is Lord and believe in your heart that God raised him from the dead, you will be saved. 10For one believes with the heart and so is justified, and one confesses with the mouth and so is saved. 11The scripture says, "No one who believes in him will be put to shame." 12For there is no distinction between Jew and Greek; the same Lord is Lord of all and is generous to all who call on him. 13For, "Everyone who calls on the name of the Lord shall be saved."

14 But how are they to call on one in whom they have not believed? And how are they to believe in one of whom they have never heard? And how are they to hear without someone to proclaim him? 15And how are they to proclaim him unless they are sent? As it is written, "How beautiful are the feet of those who bring good news!" 16But not all have obeyed the good news;v for Isaiah says, "Lord, who has believed our message?" 17So faith comes from what is heard, and what is heard comes through the word of Christ.w

18 But I ask, have they not heard? Indeed they have; for

"Their voice has gone out to all the earth,
   and their words to the ends of the world."

19Again I ask, did Israel not understand? First Moses says,

"I will make you jealous of those who are not
   a nation;
with a foolish nation I will make you
   angry."

20Then Isaiah is so bold as to say,

"I have been found by those who did not seek
   me;
I have shown myself to those who did not
   ask for me."

21But of Israel he says, "All day long I have held out my hands to a disobedient and contrary people."

Israel's Rejection Is Not Final

11 I ASK, then, has God rejected his people? By no means! I myself am an Israelite, a descendant of Abraham, a member of the tribe of Benjamin. 2God has not rejected his people whom he foreknew. Do you not know what the scripture says of Elijah, how he pleads with God against Israel? 3"Lord, they have killed your prophets, they have demolished your altars; I alone am left, and they are seeking my life." 4But what is the divine reply to him? "I have kept for myself seven thousand who have not bowed the knee to Baal." 5So too at

---

n 10:10 confirming his salvation, literally, "confession is made unto salvation."   o 10:15 good things, see Isa 52:7.   p 10:16 When I told them?, see Isa 53:1.   q 10:19 that God would give his salvation to others if they refused to take it, implied.   r 10:20 looking for him, see Isa 65:1.   s 10:21 arguing, literally, "disobedient, obstinate."   t 11:4 bowed down to idols, see 1 Kings 19:18.

u Or namely, that   v Or gospel   w Or about Christ; other ancient authorities read of God

King James

⁵Even so then at this present time also there is a remnant according to the election of grace.

⁶And if by grace, then *is it* no more of works: otherwise grace is no more grace. But if *it be* of works, then is it no more grace: otherwise work is no more work.

⁷What then? Israel hath not obtained that which he seeketh for; but the election hath obtained it, and the rest were blinded

⁸(According as it is written, God hath given them the spirit of slumber, eyes that they should not see, and ears that they should not hear;) unto this day.

⁹And David saith, Let their table be made a snare, and a trap, and a stumblingblock, and a recompence unto them:

¹⁰Let their eyes be darkened, that they may not see, and bow down their back always.

¹¹I say then, Have they stumbled that they should fall? God forbid: but *rather* through their fall salvation *is come* unto the Gentiles, for to provoke them to jealousy.

¹²Now if the fall of them *be* the riches of the world, and the diminishing of them the riches of the Gentiles; how much more their fulness?

¹³For I speak to you Gentiles, inasmuch as I am the apostle of the Gentiles, I magnify mine office:

¹⁴If by any means I may provoke to emulation *them which are* my flesh, and might save some of them.

¹⁵For if the casting away of them *be* the reconciling of the world, what *shall* the receiving *of them be,* but life from the dead?

¹⁶For if the firstfruit *be* holy, the lump *is* also *holy:* and if the root *be* holy, so *are* the branches.

¹⁷And if some of the branches be broken off, and thou, being a wild olive tree, wert grafted in among them, and with them partakest of the root and fatness of the olive tree;

¹⁸Boast not against the branches. But if thou boast, thou bearest not the root, but the root thee.

¹⁹Thou wilt say then, The branches were broken off, that I might be grafted in.

²⁰Well; because of unbelief they were broken off, and thou standest by faith. Be not highminded, but fear:

²¹For if God spared not the natural branches, *take heed* lest he also spare not thee.

²²Behold therefore the goodness and severity of God: on them which fell, severity; but toward thee, goodness, if thou continue in *his* goodness: otherwise thou also shalt be cut off.

²³And they also, if they abide not still in unbelief, shall be grafted in: for God is able to graft them in again.

New International

chosen by grace. ⁶And if by grace, then it is no longer by works; if it were, grace would no longer be grace.ᵃ

⁷What then? What Israel sought so earnestly it did not obtain, but the elect did. The others were hardened, ⁸as it is written:

"God gave them a spirit of stupor,
    eyes so that they could not see
    and ears so that they could not hear,
to this very day."ᵇ

⁹And David says:

"May their table become a snare and a trap,
    a stumbling block and a retribution for them.
¹⁰May their eyes be darkened so they cannot see,
    and their backs be bent forever."ᶜ

Ingrafted Branches

¹¹Again I ask: Did they stumble so as to fall beyond recovery? Not at all! Rather, because of their transgression, salvation has come to the Gentiles to make Israel envious. ¹²But if their transgression means riches for the world, and their loss means riches for the Gentiles, how much greater riches will their fullness bring!

¹³I am talking to you Gentiles. Inasmuch as I am the apostle to the Gentiles, I make much of my ministry ¹⁴in the hope that I may somehow arouse my own people to envy and save some of them. ¹⁵For if their rejection is the reconciliation of the world, what will their acceptance be but life from the dead? ¹⁶If the part of the dough offered as firstfruits is holy, then the whole batch is holy; if the root is holy, so are the branches.

¹⁷If some of the branches have been broken off, and you, though a wild olive shoot, have been grafted in among the others and now share in the nourishing sap from the olive root, ¹⁸do not boast over those branches. If you do, consider this: You do not support the root, but the root supports you. ¹⁹You will say then, "Branches were broken off so that I could be grafted in." ²⁰Granted. But they were broken off because of unbelief, and you stand by faith. Do not be arrogant, but be afraid. ²¹For if God did not spare the natural branches, he will not spare you either.

²²Consider therefore the kindness and sternness of God: sternness to those who fell, but kindness to you, provided that you continue in his kindness. Otherwise, you also will be cut off. ²³And if they do not persist in unbelief, they will be grafted in, for God is able to graft them in again. ²⁴After all, if you were cut out of an olive

ᵃ 6 Some manuscripts *by grace. But if by works, then it is no longer grace; if it were, work would no longer be work.*   ᵇ 8 Deut. 29:4; Isaiah 29:10
ᶜ 10 Psalm 69:22,23

Living Bible

5It is the same today. Not all the Jews have turned away from God; there are a few being saved as a result of God's kindness in choosing them. 6And if it is by God's kindness, then it is not by their being good enough. For in that case the free gift would no longer be free—it isn't free when it is earned.

7So this is the situation: Most of the Jews have not found the favor of God they are looking for. A few have—the ones God has picked out—but the eyes of the others have been blinded. 8This is what our Scriptures refer to when they say that God has put them to sleep, shutting their eyes and ears so that they do not understand what we are talking about when we tell them of Christ. And so it is to this very day.

9King David spoke of this same thing when he said, "Let their good food and other blessings trap them into thinking all is well between themselves and God. Let these good things boomerang on them and fall back upon their heads to justly crush them. 10Let their eyes be dim," he said, "so that they cannot see, and let them walk bent-backed forever with a heavy load."

11Does this mean that God has rejected his Jewish people forever? Of course not! His purpose was to make his salvation available to the Gentiles, and then the Jews would be jealous and begin to want God's salvation for themselves. 12Now if the whole world became rich as a result of God's offer of salvation, when the Jews stumbled over it and turned it down, think how much greater a blessing the world will share in later on when the Jews, too, come to Christ.

13As you know, God has appointed me as a special messenger to you Gentiles. I lay great stress on this and remind the Jews about it as often as I can, 14so that if possible I can make them want what you Gentiles have and in that way save some of them. 15And how wonderful it will be when they become Christians! When God turned away from them it meant that he turned to the rest of the world to offer his salvation; and now it is even more wonderful when the Jews come to Christ. It will be like dead people coming back to life. 16And since Abraham and the prophets are God's people, their children will be too. For if the roots of the tree are holy, the branches will be too.

17But some of these branches from Abraham's tree, some of the Jews, have been broken off. And you Gentiles who were branches from, we might say, a wild olive tree, were grafted in. So now you, too, receive the blessing God has promised Abraham and his children, sharing in God's rich nourishment of his own special olive tree.

18But you must be careful not to brag about being put in to replace the branches that were broken off. Remember that you are important only because you are now a part of God's tree; you are just a branch, not a root.

19"Well," you may be saying, "those branches were broken off to make room for me so I must be pretty good."

20Watch out! Remember that those branches, the Jews, were broken off because they didn't believe God, and you are there only because you do. Do not be proud; be humble and grateful—and careful. 21For if God did not spare the branches he put there in the first place, he won't spare you either.

22Notice how God is both kind and severe. He is very hard on those who disobey, but very good to you if you continue to love and trust him. But if you don't, you too will be cut off. 23On the other hand, if the Jews leave their unbelief behind them and come back to God, God will graft them back into the tree again. He has the power to do it.

New Revised Standard

the present time there is a remnant, chosen by grace. 6But if it is by grace, it is no longer on the basis of works, otherwise grace would no longer be grace.d

7 What then? Israel failed to obtain what it was seeking. The elect obtained it, but the rest were hardened, 8as it is written,

"God gave them a sluggish spirit,
  eyes that would not see
    and ears that would not hear,
  down to this very day."

9And David says,

"Let their table become a snare and a trap,
  a stumbling block and a retribution for
    them;
10 let their eyes be darkened so that they cannot
    see,
  and keep their backs forever bent."

The Salvation of the Gentiles

11 So I ask, have they stumbled so as to fall? By no means! But through their stumblinge salvation has come to the Gentiles, so as to make Israelf jealous. 12Now if their stumblinge means riches for the world, and if their defeat means riches for Gentiles, how much more will their full inclusion mean!

13 Now I am speaking to you Gentiles. Inasmuch then as I am an apostle to the Gentiles, I glorify my ministry 14in order to make my own peoples jealous, and thus save some of them. 15For if their rejection is the reconciliation of the world, what will their acceptance be but life from the dead! 16If the part of the dough offered as first fruits is holy, then the whole batch is holy; and if the root is holy, then the branches also are holy.

17 But if some of the branches were broken off, and you, a wild olive shoot, were grafted in their place to share the rich rooth of the olive tree, 18do not boast over the branches. If you do boast, remember that it is not you that support the root, but the root that supports you. 19You will say, "Branches were broken off so that I might be grafted in." 20That is true. They were broken off because of their unbelief, but you stand only through faith. So do not become proud, but stand in awe. 21For if God did not spare the natural branches, perhaps he will not spare you.i 22Note then the kindness and the severity of God: severity toward those who have fallen, but God's kindness toward you, provided you continue in his kindness; otherwise you also will be cut off. 23And even those of Israel,j if they do not persist in unbelief, will be grafted in, for God has the power to graft them in again. 24For if you have been cut from what is by

---

d Other ancient authorities add But if it is by works, it is no longer on the basis of grace, otherwise work would no longer be work   e Gk transgression   f Gk them   g Gk my flesh   h Other ancient authorities read the richness   i Other ancient authorities read neither will he spare you   j Gk lacks of Israel

King James

24For if thou wert cut out of the olive tree which is wild by nature, and wert grafted contrary to nature into a good olive tree: how much more shall these, which be the natural *branches,* be grafted into their own olive tree?

25For I would not, brethren, that ye should be ignorant of this mystery, lest ye should be wise in your own conceits; that blindness in part is happened to Israel, until the fulness of the Gentiles be come in.

26And so all Israel shall be saved: as it is written, There shall come out of Zion the Deliverer, and shall turn away ungodliness from Jacob:

27For this *is* my covenant unto them, when I shall take away their sins.

28As concerning the gospel, *they are* enemies for your sakes: but as touching the election, *they are* beloved for the fathers' sakes.

29For the gifts and calling of God *are* without repentance.

30For as ye in times past have not believed God, yet have now obtained mercy through their unbelief:

31Even so have these also now not believed, that through your mercy they also may obtain mercy.

32For God hath concluded them all in unbelief, that he might have mercy upon all.

33O the depth of the riches both of the wisdom and knowledge of God! how unsearchable *are* his judgments, and his ways past finding out!

34For who hath known the mind of the Lord? or who hath been his counsellor?

35Or who hath first given to him, and it shall be recompensed unto him again?

36For of him, and through him, and to him, *are* all things: to whom *be* glory for ever. Amen.

12 I BESEECH you therefore, brethren, by the mercies of God, that ye present your bodies a living sacrifice, holy, acceptable unto God, *which is* your reasonable service.

2And be not conformed to this world: but be ye transformed by the renewing of your mind, that ye may prove what *is* that good, and acceptable, and perfect, will of God.

3For I say, through the grace given unto me, to every man that is among you, not to think *of himself* more highly than he ought to think; but to think soberly, according as God hath dealt to every man the measure of faith.

4For as we have many members in one body, and all members have not the same office:

5So we, *being* many, are one body in Christ, and every one members one of another.

6Having then gifts differing according to the grace that is given to us, whether prophecy, *let us prophesy* according to the proportion of faith;

7Or ministry, *let us wait* on *our* ministering: or he that teacheth, on teaching;

8Or he that exhorteth, on exhortation: he that giveth, *let him do it* with simplicity; he that ruleth, with diligence; he that showeth mercy, with cheerfulness.

New International

tree that is wild by nature, and contrary to nature were grafted into a cultivated olive tree, how much more readily will these, the natural branches, be grafted into their own olive tree!

All Israel Will Be Saved

25I do not want you to be ignorant of this mystery, brothers, so that you may not be conceited: Israel has experienced a hardening in part until the full number of the Gentiles has come in. 26And so all Israel will be saved, as it is written:

"The deliverer will come from Zion;
    he will turn godlessness away from Jacob.
27And this is[a] my covenant with them
    when I take away their sins."[b]

28As far as the gospel is concerned, they are enemies on your account; but as far as election is concerned, they are loved on account of the patriarchs, 29for God's gifts and his call are irrevocable. 30Just as you who were at one time disobedient to God have now received mercy as a result of their disobedience, 31so they too have now become disobedient in order that they too may now[c] receive mercy as a result of God's mercy to you. 32For God has bound all men over to disobedience so that he may have mercy on them all.

Doxology

33Oh, the depth of the riches of the wisdom and[d]
        knowledge of God!
    How unsearchable his judgments,
        and his paths beyond tracing out!
34"Who has known the mind of the Lord?
    Or who has been his counselor?"[e]
35"Who has ever given to God,
    that God should repay him?"[f]
36For from him and through him and to him are
        all things.
    To him be the glory forever! Amen.

Living Sacrifices

12 THEREFORE, I urge you, brothers, in view of God's mercy, to offer your bodies as living sacrifices, holy and pleasing to God—this is your spiritual[g] act of worship. 2Do not conform any longer to the pattern of this world, but be transformed by the renewing of your mind. Then you will be able to test and approve what God's will is—his good, pleasing and perfect will.

3For by the grace given me I say to every one of you: Do not think of yourself more highly than you ought, but rather think of yourself with sober judgment, in accordance with the measure of faith God has given you. 4Just as each of us has one body with many members, and these members do not all have the same function, 5so in Christ we who are many form one body, and each member belongs to all the others. 6We have different gifts, according to the grace given us. If a man's gift is prophesying, let him use it in proportion to his[h] faith. 7If it is serving, let him serve; if it is teaching, let him teach; 8if it is encouraging, let him encourage; if it is contributing to the needs of others, let him give generously; if it is leadership, let him govern diligently; if it is showing mercy, let him do it cheerfully.

---

a 27 Or *will be*   b 27 Isaiah 59:20,21; 27:9; Jer. 31:33,34   c 31 Some manuscripts do not have *now.*   d 33 Or *riches and the wisdom and the* e 34 Isaiah 40:13   f 35 Job 41:11   g 1 Or *reasonable*   h 6 Or *in agreement with the*

Living Bible

24For if God was willing to take you who were so far away from him—being part of a wild olive tree—and graft you into his own good tree—a very unusual thing to do—don't you see that he will be far more ready to put the Jews back again, who were there in the first place?

25I want you to know about this truth from God, dear brothers, so that you will not feel proud and start bragging. Yes, it is true that some of the Jews have set themselves against the Gospel now, but this will last only until all of you Gentiles have come to Christ— those of you who will. 26And then all Israel will be saved.

Do you remember what the prophets said about this? "There shall come out of Zion a Deliverer, and he shall turn the Jews from all ungodliness. 27At that time I will take away their sins, just as I promised."

28Now many of the Jews are enemies of the Gospel. They hate it. But this has been a benefit to you, for it has resulted in God's giving his gifts to you Gentiles. Yet the Jews are still beloved of God because of his promises to Abraham, Isaac, and Jacob. 29For God's gifts and his call can never be withdrawn; he will never go back on his promises. 30Once you were rebels against God, but when the Jews refused his gifts God was merciful to you instead. 31And now the Jews are the rebels, but some day they, too, will share in God's mercy upon you. 32For God has given them all up to sin[i] so that he could have mercy upon all alike.

33Oh, what a wonderful God we have! How great are his wisdom and knowledge and riches! How impossible it is for us to understand his decisions and his methods! 34For who among us can know the mind of the Lord? Who knows enough to be his counselor and guide? 35And who could ever offer to the Lord enough to induce him to act? 36For everything comes from God alone. Everything lives by his power, and everything is for his glory. To him be glory evermore.

12 AND SO, dear brothers, I plead with you to give your bodies to God. Let them be a living sacrifice, holy—the kind he can accept. When you think of what he has done for you, is this too much to ask? 2Don't copy the behavior and customs of this world, but be a new and different person with a fresh newness in all you do and think. Then you will learn from your own experience how his ways will really satisfy you.

3As God's messenger I give each of you God's warning: Be honest in your estimate of yourselves, measuring your value by how much faith God has given you. 4, 5Just as there are many parts to our bodies, so it is with Christ's body. We are all parts of it, and it takes every one of us to make it complete, for we each have different work to do. So we belong to each other, and each needs all the others.

6God has given each of us the ability to do certain things well. So if God has given you the ability to prophesy, then prophesy whenever you can—as often as your faith is strong enough to receive a message from God. 7If your gift is that of serving others, serve them well. If you are a teacher, do a good job of teaching. 8If you are a preacher, see to it that your sermons are strong and helpful. If God has given you money, be generous in helping others with it. If God has given you administrative ability and put you in charge of the work of others, take the responsibility seriously. Those who offer comfort to the sorrowing should do so with Christian cheer.

New Revised Standard

nature a wild olive tree and grafted, contrary to nature, into a cultivated olive tree, how much more will these natural branches be grafted back into their own olive tree.

All Israel Will Be Saved

25 So that you may not claim to be wiser than you are, brothers and sisters,[j] I want you to understand this mystery: a hardening has come upon part of Israel, until the full number of the Gentiles has come in. 26And so all Israel will be saved; as it is written,

"Out of Zion will come the Deliverer;
    he will banish ungodliness from Jacob."
27 "And this is my covenant with them,
    when I take away their sins."

28As regards the gospel they are enemies of God[k] for your sake; but as regards election they are beloved, for the sake of their ancestors; 29for the gifts and the calling of God are irrevocable. 30Just as you were once disobedient to God but have now received mercy because of their disobedience, 31so they have now been disobedient in order that, by the mercy shown to you, they too may now[l] receive mercy. 32For God has imprisoned all in disobedience so that he may be merciful to all.

33 O the depth of the riches and wisdom and knowledge of God! How unsearchable are his judgments and how inscrutable his ways!
34 "For who has known the mind of the Lord?
    Or who has been his counselor?"
35 "Or who has given a gift to him,
    to receive a gift in return?"
36For from him and through him and to him are all things. To him be the glory forever. Amen.

The New Life in Christ

12 I APPEAL to you therefore, brothers and sisters,[j] by the mercies of God, to present your bodies as a living sacrifice, holy and acceptable to God, which is your spiritual[m] worship. 2Do not be conformed to this world,[n] but be transformed by the renewing of your minds, so that you may discern what is the will of God—what is good and acceptable and perfect.[o]

3 For by the grace given to me I say to everyone among you not to think of yourself more highly than you ought to think, but to think with sober judgment, each according to the measure of faith that God has assigned. 4For as in one body we have many members, and not all the members have the same function, 5so we, who are many, are one body in Christ, and individually are members one of another. 6We have gifts that differ according to the grace given to us: prophecy, in proportion to faith; 7ministry, in ministering; the teacher, in teaching; 8the exhorter, in exhortation; the giver, in generosity; the leader, in diligence; the compassionate, in cheerfulness.

---

i *11:32 has given them all up to sin, literally, "shut up all unto disobedience."*

j Gk *brothers*   k Gk lacks *of God*   l Other ancient authorities lack *now*
m Or *reasonable*   n Gk *age*   o Or *what is the good and acceptable and perfect will of God*

King James

9*Let* love be without dissimulation. Abhor that which is evil; cleave to that which is good.

10*Be* kindly affectioned one to another with brotherly love; in honour preferring one another;

11Not slothful in business; fervent in spirit; serving the Lord;

12Rejoicing in hope; patient in tribulation; continuing instant in prayer;

13Distributing to the necessity of saints; given to hospitality.

14Bless them which persecute you: bless, and curse not.

15Rejoice with them that do rejoice, and weep with them that weep.

16*Be* of the same mind one toward another. Mind not high things, but condescend to men of low estate. Be not wise in your own conceits.

17Recompense to no man evil for evil. Provide things honest in the sight of all men.

18If it be possible, as much as lieth in you, live peaceably with all men.

19Dearly beloved, avenge not yourselves, but *rather* give place unto wrath: for it is written, Vengeance *is* mine; I will repay, saith the Lord.

20Therefore if thine enemy hunger, feed him; if he thirst, give him drink: for in so doing thou shalt heap coals of fire on his head.

21Be not overcome of evil, but overcome evil with good.

13 LET EVERY soul be subject unto the higher powers. For there is no power but of God: the powers that be are ordained of God.

2Whosoever therefore resisteth the power, resisteth the ordinance of God: and they that resist shall receive to themselves damnation.

3For rulers are not a terror to good works, but to the evil. Wilt thou then not be afraid of the power? do that which is good, and thou shalt have praise of the same:

4For he is the minister of God to thee for good. But if thou do that which is evil, be afraid; for he beareth not the sword in vain: for he is the minister of God, a revenger to *execute* wrath upon him that doeth evil.

5Wherefore *ye* must needs be subject, not only for wrath, but also for conscience sake.

6For for this cause pay ye tribute also: for they are God's ministers, attending continually upon this very thing.

7Render therefore to all their dues: tribute to whom tribute *is due;* custom to whom custom; fear to whom fear; honour to whom honour.

8Owe no man any thing, but to love one another: for he that loveth another hath fulfilled the law.

9For this, Thou shalt not commit adultery, Thou shalt not kill, Thou shalt not steal, Thou shalt not bear false witness, Thou shalt not covet; and if *there be* any other commandment, it is briefly comprehended in this saying, namely, Thou shalt love thy neighbour as thyself.

10Love worketh no ill to his neighbour: therefore love *is* the fulfilling of the law.

11And that, knowing the time, that now *it is* high time to awake out of sleep: for now *is* our salvation nearer than when we believed.

New International

Love

9Love must be sincere. Hate what is evil; cling to what is good. 10Be devoted to one another in brotherly love. Honor one another above yourselves. 11Never be lacking in zeal, but keep your spiritual fervor, serving the Lord. 12Be joyful in hope, patient in affliction, faithful in prayer. 13Share with God's people who are in need. Practice hospitality.

14Bless those who persecute you; bless and do not curse. 15Rejoice with those who rejoice; mourn with those who mourn. 16Live in harmony with one another. Do not be proud, but be willing to associate with people of low position.[a] Do not be conceited.

17Do not repay anyone evil for evil. Be careful to do what is right in the eyes of everybody. 18If it is possible, as far as it depends on you, live at peace with everyone. 19Do not take revenge, my friends, but leave room for God's wrath, for it is written: "It is mine to avenge; I will repay,"[b] says the Lord. 20On the contrary:

"If your enemy is hungry, feed him;
  if he is thirsty, give him something to drink.
In doing this, you will heap burning coals on
  his head."[c]

21Do not be overcome by evil, but overcome evil with good.

Submission to the Authorities

13 EVERYONE MUST submit himself to the governing authorities, for there is no authority except that which God has established. The authorities that exist have been established by God. 2Consequently, he who rebels against the authority is rebelling against what God has instituted, and those who do so will bring judgment on themselves. 3For rulers hold no terror for those who do right, but for those who do wrong. Do you want to be free from fear of the one in authority? Then do what is right and he will commend you. 4For he is God's servant to do you good. But if you do wrong, be afraid, for he does not bear the sword for nothing. He is God's servant, an agent of wrath to bring punishment on the wrongdoer. 5Therefore, it is necessary to submit to the authorities, not only because of possible punishment but also because of conscience.

6This is also why you pay taxes, for the authorities are God's servants, who give their full time to governing. 7Give everyone what you owe him: If you owe taxes, pay taxes; if revenue, then revenue; if respect, then respect; if honor, then honor.

Love, for the Day Is Near

8Let no debt remain outstanding, except the continuing debt to love one another, for he who loves his fellowman has fulfilled the law. 9The commandments, "Do not commit adultery," "Do not murder," "Do not steal," "Do not covet,"[d] and whatever other commandment there may be, are summed up in this one rule: "Love your neighbor as yourself."[e] 10Love does no harm to its neighbor. Therefore love is the fulfillment of the law.

11And do this, understanding the present time. The hour has come for you to wake up from your slumber, because our salvation is nearer now than when we first believed. 12The night is nearly over; the day is almost

---

a *16* Or *willing to do menial work* b *19* Deut. 32:35 c *20* Prov. 25:21,22
d *9* Exodus 20:13-15,17; Deut. 5:17-19,21 e *9* Lev. 19:18

Living Bible

9Don't just pretend that you love others: really love them. Hate what is wrong. Stand on the side of the good. 10Love each other with brotherly affection and take delight in honoring each other. 11Never be lazy in your work but serve the Lord enthusiastically.

12Be glad for all God is planning for you. Be patient in trouble, and prayerful always. 13When God's children are in need, you be the one to help them out. And get into the habit of inviting guests home for dinner or, if they need lodging, for the night.

14If someone mistreats you because you are a Christian, don't curse him; pray that God will bless him. 15When others are happy, be happy with them. If they are sad, share their sorrow. 16Work happily together. Don't try to act big. Don't try to get into the good graces of important people, but enjoy the company of ordinary folks. And don't think you know it all!

17Never pay back evil for evil. Do things in such a way that everyone can see you are honest clear through. 18Don't quarrel with anyone. Be at peace with everyone, just as much as possible.

19Dear friends, never avenge yourselves. Leave that to God, for he has said that he will repay those who deserve it. [Don't take the law into your own hands.f] 20Instead, feed your enemy if he is hungry. If he is thirsty give him something to drink and you will be "heaping coals of fire on his head." In other words, he will feel ashamed of himself for what he has done to you. 21Don't let evil get the upper hand but conquer evil by doing good.

13 OBEY THE government, for God is the one who has put it there. There is no government anywhere that God has not placed in power. 2So those who refuse to obey the laws of the land are refusing to obey God, and punishment will follow. 3For the policeman does not frighten people who are doing right; but those doing evil will always fear him. So if you don't want to be afraid, keep the laws and you will get along well. 4The policeman is sent by God to help you. But if you are doing something wrong, of course you should be afraid, for he will have you punished. He is sent by God for that very purpose. 5Obey the laws, then, for two reasons: first, to keep from being punished, and second, just because you know you should.

6Pay your taxes too, for these same two reasons. For government workers need to be paid so that they can keep on doing God's work, serving you. 7Pay everyone whatever he ought to have: pay your taxes and import duties gladly, obey those over you, and give honor and respect to all those to whom it is due.

8Pay all your debts except the debt of love for others—never finish paying that! For if you love them, you will be obeying all of God's laws, fulfilling all his requirements. 9If you love your neighbor as much as you love yourself you will not want to harm or cheat him, or kill him or steal from him. And you won't sin with his wife or want what is his, or do anything else the Ten Commandments say is wrong. All ten are wrapped up in this one, to love your neighbor as you love yourself. 10Love does no wrong to anyone. That's why it fully satisfies all of God's requirements. It is the only law you need.

11Another reason for right living is this: you know how late it is; time is running out. Wake up, for the coming of the Lord is nearer now than when we first believed. 12, 13The night is far gone, the day of his re-

New Revised Standard

Marks of the True Christian

9 Let love be genuine; hate what is evil, hold fast to what is good; 10love one another with mutual affection; outdo one another in showing honor. 11Do not lag in zeal, be ardent in spirit, serve the Lord.g 12Rejoice in hope, be patient in suffering, persevere in prayer. 13Contribute to the needs of the saints; extend hospitality to strangers.

14 Bless those who persecute you; bless and do not curse them. 15Rejoice with those who rejoice, weep with those who weep. 16Live in harmony with one another; do not be haughty, but associate with the lowly;h do not claim to be wiser than you are. 17Do not repay anyone evil for evil, but take thought for what is noble in the sight of all. 18If it is possible, so far as it depends on you, live peaceably with all. 19Beloved, never avenge yourselves, but leave room for the wrath of God;i for it is written, "Vengeance is mine, I will repay, says the Lord." 20No, "if your enemies are hungry, feed them; if they are thirsty, give them something to drink; for by doing this you will heap burning coals on their heads." 21Do not be overcome by evil, but overcome evil with good.

Being Subject to Authorities

13 LET EVERY person be subject to the governing authorities; for there is no authority except from God, and those authorities that exist have been instituted by God. 2Therefore whoever resists authority resists what God has appointed, and those who resist will incur judgment. 3For rulers are not a terror to good conduct, but to bad. Do you wish to have no fear of the authority? Then do what is good, and you will receive its approval; 4for it is God's servant for your good. But if you do what is wrong, you should be afraid, for the authorityj does not bear the sword in vain! It is the servant of God to execute wrath on the wrongdoer. 5Therefore one must be subject, not only because of wrath but also because of conscience. 6For the same reason you also pay taxes, for the authorities are God's servants, busy with this very thing. 7Pay to all what is due them—taxes to whom taxes are due, revenue to whom revenue is due, respect to whom respect is due, honor to whom honor is due.

Love for One Another

8 Owe no one anything, except to love one another; for the one who loves another has fulfilled the law. 9The commandments, "You shall not commit adultery; You shall not murder; You shall not steal; You shall not covet"; and any other commandment, are summed up in this word, "Love your neighbor as yourself." 10Love does no wrong to a neighbor; therefore, love is the fulfilling of the law.

An Urgent Appeal

11 Besides this, you know what time it is, how it is now the moment for you to wake from sleep. For salvation is nearer to us now than when we became believers;

---

f *12:19 Don't take the law into your own hands,* implied.

g Other ancient authorities read *serve the opportune time* h Or *give yourselves to humble tasks* i Gk *the wrath* j Gk *it*

King James

12The night is far spent, the day is at hand: let us therefore cast off the works of darkness, and let us put on the armour of light.

13Let us walk honestly, as in the day; not in rioting and drunkenness, not in chambering and wantonness, not in strife and envying.

14But put ye on the Lord Jesus Christ, and make not provision for the flesh, to *fulfil* the lusts *thereof.*

14 HIM THAT is weak in the faith receive ye, *but* not to doubtful disputations.

2For one believeth that he may eat all things: another, who is weak, eateth herbs.

3Let not him that eateth despise him that eateth not; and let not him which eateth not judge him that eateth: for God hath received him.

4Who art thou that judgest another man's servant? to his own master he standeth or falleth. Yea, he shall be holden up: for God is able to make him stand.

5One man esteemeth one day above another: another esteemeth every day *alike.* Let every man be fully persuaded in his own mind.

6He that regardeth the day, regardeth *it* unto the Lord; and he that regardeth not the day, to the Lord he doth not regard *it.* He that eateth, eateth to the Lord, for he giveth God thanks; and he that eateth not, to the Lord he eateth not, and giveth God thanks.

7For none of us liveth to himself, and no man dieth to himself.

8For whether we live, we live unto the Lord; and whether we die, we die unto the Lord: whether we live therefore, or die, we are the Lord's.

9For to this end Christ both died, and rose, and revived, that he might be Lord both of the dead and living.

10But why dost thou judge thy brother? or why dost thou set at nought thy brother? for we shall all stand before the judgment seat of Christ.

11For it is written, *As* I live, saith the Lord, every knee shall bow to me, and every tongue shall confess to God.

12So then every one of us shall give account of himself to God.

13Let us not therefore judge one another any more: but judge this rather, that no man put a stumblingblock or an occasion to fall in *his* brother's way.

14I know, and am persuaded by the Lord Jesus, that *there is* nothing unclean of itself: but to him that esteemeth any thing to be unclean, to him *it is* unclean.

15But if thy brother be grieved with *thy* meat, now walkest thou not charitably. Destroy not him with thy meat, for whom Christ died.

16Let not then your good be evil spoken of:

17For the kingdom of God is not meat and drink; but righteousness, and peace, and joy in the Holy Ghost.

18For he that in these things serveth Christ *is* acceptable to God, and approved of men.

New International

here. So let us put aside the deeds of darkness and put on the armor of light. 13Let us behave decently, as in the daytime, not in orgies and drunkenness, not in sexual immorality and debauchery, not in dissension and jealousy. 14Rather, clothe yourselves with the Lord Jesus Christ, and do not think about how to gratify the desires of the sinful nature.[a]

The Weak and the Strong

14 ACCEPT HIM whose faith is weak, without passing judgment on disputable matters. 2One man's faith allows him to eat everything, but another man, whose faith is weak, eats only vegetables. 3The man who eats everything must not look down on him who does not, and the man who does not eat everything must not condemn the man who does, for God has accepted him. 4Who are you to judge someone else's servant? To his own master he stands or falls. And he will stand, for the Lord is able to make him stand.

5One man considers one day more sacred than another; another man considers every day alike. Each one should be fully convinced in his own mind. 6He who regards one day as special, does so to the Lord. He who eats meat, eats to the Lord, for he gives thanks to God; and he who abstains, does so to the Lord and gives thanks to God. 7For none of us lives to himself alone and none of us dies to himself alone. 8If we live, we live to the Lord; and if we die, we die to the Lord. So, whether we live or die, we belong to the Lord.

9For this very reason, Christ died and returned to life so that he might be the Lord of both the dead and the living. 10You, then, why do you judge your brother? Or why do you look down on your brother? For we will all stand before God's judgment seat. 11It is written:

" 'As surely as I live,' says the Lord,
'every knee will bow before me;
every tongue will confess to God.' "[b]

12So then, each of us will give an account of himself to God.

13Therefore let us stop passing judgment on one another. Instead, make up your mind not to put any stumbling block or obstacle in your brother's way. 14As one who is in the Lord Jesus, I am fully convinced that no food[c] is unclean in itself. But if anyone regards something as unclean, then for him it is unclean. 15If your brother is distressed because of what you eat, you are no longer acting in love. Do not by your eating destroy your brother for whom Christ died. 16Do not allow what you consider good to be spoken of as evil. 17For the kingdom of God is not a matter of eating and drinking, but of righteousness, peace and joy in the Holy Spirit, 18because anyone who serves Christ in this way is pleasing to God and approved by men.

Living Bible

turn[d] will soon be here. So quit the evil deeds of darkness and put on the armor of right living, as we who live in the daylight should! Be decent and true in everything you do so that all can approve your behavior. Don't spend your time in wild parties and getting drunk or in adultery and lust, or fighting, or jealousy. 14But ask the Lord Jesus Christ to help you live as you should, and don't make plans to enjoy evil.

14 GIVE A warm welcome to any brother who wants to join you, even though his faith is weak. Don't criticize him for having different ideas from yours about what is right and wrong.[e] 2For instance, don't argue with him about whether or not to eat meat that has been offered to idols. You may believe there is no harm in this, but the faith of others is weaker; they think it is wrong, and will go without any meat at all and eat vegetables rather than eat that kind of meat. 3Those who think it is all right to eat such meat must not look down on those who won't. And if you are one of those who won't, don't find fault with those who do. For God has accepted them to be his children. 4They are God's servants, not yours. They are responsible to him, not to you. Let him tell them whether they are right or wrong. And God is able to make them do as they should.

5Some think that Christians should observe the Jewish holidays as special days to worship God, but others say it is wrong and foolish to go to all that trouble, for every day alike belongs to God. On questions of this kind everyone must decide for himself. 6If you have special days for worshiping the Lord, you are trying to honor him; you are doing a good thing. So is the person who eats meat that has been offered to idols; he is thankful to the Lord for it; he is doing right. And the person who won't touch such meat, he, too, is anxious to please the Lord, and is thankful. 7We are not our own bosses to live or die as we ourselves might choose. 8Living or dying we follow the Lord. Either way we are his. 9Christ died and rose again for this very purpose, so that he can be our Lord both while we live and when we die.

10You have no right to criticize your brother or look down on him. Remember, each of us will stand personally before the Judgment Seat of God. 11For it is written, "As I live," says the Lord, "every knee shall bow to me and every tongue confess to God." 12Yes, each of us will give an account of himself to God.

13So don't criticize each other any more. Try instead to live in such a way that you will never make your brother stumble by letting him see you doing something he thinks is wrong.

14As for myself, I am perfectly sure on the authority of the Lord Jesus that there is nothing really wrong with eating meat that has been offered to idols. But if someone believes it is wrong, then he shouldn't do it because for him it is wrong. 15And if your brother is bothered by what you eat, you are not acting in love if you go ahead and eat it. Don't let your eating ruin someone for whom Christ died. 16Don't do anything that will cause criticism against yourself even though you know that what you do is right.

17For, after all, the important thing for us as Christians is not what we eat or drink but stirring up goodness and peace and joy from the Holy Spirit. 18If you let Christ be Lord in these affairs, God will be glad; and so

New Revised Standard

12the night is far gone, the day is near. Let us then lay aside the works of darkness and put on the armor of light; 13let us live honorably as in the day, not in reveling and drunkenness, not in debauchery and licentiousness, not in quarreling and jealousy. 14Instead, put on the Lord Jesus Christ, and make no provision for the flesh, to gratify its desires.

Do Not Judge Another

14 WELCOME THOSE who are weak in faith,[f] but not for the purpose of quarreling over opinions. 2Some believe in eating anything, while the weak eat only vegetables. 3Those who eat must not despise those who abstain, and those who abstain must not pass judgment on those who eat; for God has welcomed them. 4Who are you to pass judgment on servants of another? It is before their own lord that they stand or fall. And they will be upheld, for the Lord[g] is able to make them stand.

5 Some judge one day to be better than another, while others judge all days to be alike. Let all be fully convinced in their own minds. 6Those who observe the day, observe it in honor of the Lord. Also those who eat, eat in honor of the Lord, since they give thanks to God; while those who abstain, abstain in honor of the Lord and give thanks to God.

7 We do not live to ourselves, and we do not die to ourselves. 8If we live, we live to the Lord, and if we die, we die to the Lord; so then, whether we live or whether we die, we are the Lord's. 9For to this end Christ died and lived again, so that he might be Lord of both the dead and the living.

10 Why do you pass judgment on your brother or sister?[h] Or you, why do you despise your brother or sister?[h] For we will all stand before the judgment seat of God.[i] 11For it is written,

"As I live, says the Lord, every knee shall
bow to me,
and every tongue shall give praise to[j]
God."

12So then, each of us will be accountable to God.[k]

Do Not Make Another Stumble

13 Let us therefore no longer pass judgment on one another, but resolve instead never to put a stumbling block or hindrance in the way of another.[l] 14I know and am persuaded in the Lord Jesus that nothing is unclean in itself; but it is unclean for anyone who thinks it unclean. 15If your brother or sister[h] is being injured by what you eat, you are no longer walking in love. Do not let what you eat cause the ruin of one for whom Christ died. 16So do not let your good be spoken of as evil. 17For the kingdom of God is not food and drink but righteousness and peace and joy in the Holy Spirit. 18The one who thus serves Christ is acceptable to God

---

d 13:12, 13 his return, literally, "our salvation."   e 14:1 Don't criticize him . . . about what is right and wrong, literally, "Receive him that is weak in faith, not for decisions of scruples." Perhaps the meaning is, "Receive those whose consciences hurt them when they do things others have no doubts about." Accepting them might cause discord in the church, but Paul says to welcome them anyway.

f Or conviction   g Other ancient authorities read for God   h Gk brother   i Other ancient authorities read of Christ   j Or confess   k Other ancient authorities lack to God   l Gk of a brother

King James

19Let us therefore follow after the things which make for peace, and things wherewith one may edify another. 20For meat destroy not the work of God. All things indeed *are* pure; but *it is* evil for that man who eateth with offence.

21*It is* good neither to eat flesh, nor to drink wine, nor *any thing* whereby thy brother stumbleth, or is offended, or is made weak.

22Hast thou faith? have *it* to thyself before God. Happy *is* he that condemneth not himself in that thing which he alloweth.

23And he that doubteth is damned if he eat, because *he eateth* not of faith: for whatsoever *is* not of faith is sin.

15 WE THEN that are strong ought to bear the infirmities of the weak, and not to please ourselves.

2Let every one of us please *his* neighbour for *his* good to edification.

3For even Christ pleased not himself; but, as it is written, The reproaches of them that reproached thee fell on me.

4For whatsoever things were written aforetime were written for our learning, that we through patience and comfort of the scriptures might have hope.

5Now the God of patience and consolation grant you to be likeminded one toward another according to Christ Jesus:

6That ye may with one mind *and* one mouth glorify God, even the Father of our Lord Jesus Christ.

7Wherefore receive ye one another, as Christ also received us to the glory of God.

8Now I say that Jesus Christ was a minister of the circumcision for the truth of God, to confirm the promises *made* unto the fathers:

9And that the Gentiles might glorify God for *his* mercy; as it is written, For this cause I will confess to thee among the Gentiles, and sing unto thy name.

10And again he saith, Rejoice, ye Gentiles, with his people.

11And again, Praise the Lord, all ye Gentiles; and laud him all ye people.

12And again, Esaias saith, There shall be a root of Jesse, and he that shall rise to reign over the Gentiles; in him shall the Gentiles trust.

13Now the God of hope fill you with all joy and peace in believing, that ye may abound in hope, through the power of the Holy Ghost.

14And I myself also am persuaded of you, my brethren, that ye also are full of goodness, filled with all knowledge, able also to admonish one another.

15Nevertheless, brethren, I have written the more boldly unto you in some sort, as putting you in mind, because of the grace that is given to me of God,

16That I should be the minister of Jesus Christ to the Gentiles, ministering the gospel of God, that the offering up of the Gentiles might be acceptable, being sanctified by the Holy Ghost.

17I have therefore whereof I may glory through Jesus Christ in those things which pertain to God.

New International

19Let us therefore make every effort to do what leads to peace and to mutual edification. 20Do not destroy the work of God for the sake of food. All food is clean, but it is wrong for a man to eat anything that causes someone else to stumble. 21It is better not to eat meat or drink wine or to do anything else that will cause your brother to fall.

22So whatever you believe about these things keep between yourself and God. Blessed is the man who does not condemn himself by what he approves. 23But the man who has doubts is condemned if he eats, because his eating is not from faith; and everything that does not come from faith is sin.

15 WE WHO are strong ought to bear with the failings of the weak and not to please ourselves. 2Each of us should please his neighbor for his good, to build him up. 3For even Christ did not please himself but, as it is written: "The insults of those who insult you have fallen on me."a 4For everything that was written in the past was written to teach us, so that through endurance and the encouragement of the Scriptures we might have hope.

5May the God who gives endurance and encouragement give you a spirit of unity among yourselves as you follow Christ Jesus, 6so that with one heart and mouth you may glorify the God and Father of our Lord Jesus Christ.

7Accept one another, then, just as Christ accepted you, in order to bring praise to God. 8For I tell you that Christ has become a servant of the Jewsb on behalf of God's truth, to confirm the promises made to the patriarchs 9so that the Gentiles may glorify God for his mercy, as it is written:

"Therefore I will praise you among the Gentiles;
    I will sing hymns to your name."c

10Again, it says,

"Rejoice, O Gentiles, with his people."d

11And again,

"Praise the Lord, all you Gentiles,
    and sing praises to him, all you peoples."e

12And again, Isaiah says,

"The Root of Jesse will spring up,
    one who will arise to rule over the nations;
    the Gentiles will hope in him."f

13May the God of hope fill you with all joy and peace as you trust in him, so that you may overflow with hope by the power of the Holy Spirit.

Paul the Minister to the Gentiles

14I myself am convinced, my brothers, that you yourselves are full of goodness, complete in knowledge and competent to instruct one another. 15I have written you quite boldly on some points, as if to remind you of them again, because of the grace God gave me 16to be a minister of Christ Jesus to the Gentiles with the priestly duty of proclaiming the gospel of God, so that the Gentiles might become an offering acceptable to God, sanctified by the Holy Spirit.

17Therefore I glory in Christ Jesus in my service to God. 18I will not venture to speak of anything except

---

a *3* Psalm 69:9   b *8* Greek *circumcision*   c *9* 2 Samuel 22:50; Psalm 18:49
d *10* Deut. 32:43   e *11* Psalm 117:1   f *12* Isaiah 11:10

Living Bible

will others. 19In this way aim for harmony in the church and try to build each other up.

20Don't undo the work of God for a chunk of meat. Remember, there is nothing wrong with the meat, but it is wrong to eat it if it makes another stumble. 21The right thing to do is to quit eating meat or drinking wine or doing anything else that offends your brother or makes him sin. 22You may know that there is nothing wrong with what you do, even from God's point of view, but keep it to yourself; don't flaunt your faith in front of others who might be hurt by it. In this situation, happy is the man who does not sin by doing what he knows is right. 23But anyone who believes that something he wants to do is wrong shouldn't do it. He sins if he does, for he thinks it is wrong, and so for him it *is* wrong. Anything that is done apart from what he feels is right is sin.

15 EVEN IF we believe that it makes no difference to the Lord whether we do these things, still we cannot just go ahead and do them to please ourselves; for we must bear the "burden" of being considerate of the doubts and fears of others—of those who feel these things are wrong. Let's please the other fellow, not ourselves, and do what is for his good and thus build him up in the Lord. 3Christ didn't please himself. As the Psalmist said, "He came for the very purpose of suffering under the insults of those who were against the Lord." 4These things that were written in the Scriptures so long ago are to teach us patience and to encourage us, so that we will look forward expectantly to the time when God will conquer sin and death.

5May God who gives patience, steadiness, and encouragement help you to live in complete harmony with each other—each with the attitude of Christ toward the other. 6And then all of us can praise the Lord together with one voice, giving glory to God, the Father of our Lord Jesus Christ.

7So, warmly welcome each other into the church, just as Christ has warmly welcomed you; then God will be glorified. 8Remember that Jesus Christ came to show that God is true to his promises and to help the Jews. 9And remember that he came also that the Gentiles might be saved and give glory to God for his mercies to them. That is what the Psalmist meant when he wrote: "I will praise you among the Gentiles, and sing to your name."

10And in another place, "Be glad, O you Gentiles, along with his people the Jews."

11And yet again, "Praise the Lord, O you Gentiles, let everyone praise him."

12And the prophet Isaiah said, "There shall be an Heir in the house of Jesse, and he will be King over the Gentiles; they will pin their hopes on him alone."

13So I pray for you Gentiles that God who gives you hope will keep you happy and full of peace as you believe in him. I pray that God will help you overflow with hope in him through the Holy Spirit's power within you.

14I know that you are wise and good, my brothers, and that you know these things so well that you are able to teach others all about them. 15, 16But even so I have been bold enough to emphasize some of these points, knowing that all you need is this reminder from me; for I am, by God's grace, a special messenger from Jesus Christ to you Gentiles, bringing you the Gospel and offering you up as a fragrant sacrifice to God; for you have been made pure and pleasing to him by the Holy Spirit. 17So it is right for me to be a little proud of all Christ Jesus has done through me. 18I dare not judge how

New Revised Standard

and has human approval. 19Let us then pursue what makes for peace and for mutual upbuilding. 20Do not, for the sake of food, destroy the work of God. Everything is indeed clean, but it is wrong for you to make others fall by what you eat; 21it is good not to eat meat or drink wine or do anything that makes your brother or sister[g] stumble.[h] 22The faith that you have, have as your own conviction before God. Blessed are those who have no reason to condemn themselves because of what they approve. 23But those who have doubts are condemned if they eat, because they do not act from faith;[i] for whatever does not proceed from faith[i] is sin.[j]

Please Others, Not Yourselves

15 WE WHO are strong ought to put up with the failings of the weak, and not to please ourselves. 2Each of us must please our neighbor for the good purpose of building up the neighbor. 3For Christ did not please himself; but, as it is written, "The insults of those who insult you have fallen on me." 4For whatever was written in former days was written for our instruction, so that by steadfastness and by the encouragement of the scriptures we might have hope. 5May the God of steadfastness and encouragement grant you to live in harmony with one another, in accordance with Christ Jesus, 6so that together you may with one voice glorify the God and Father of our Lord Jesus Christ.

The Gospel for Jews and Gentiles Alike

7 Welcome one another, therefore, just as Christ has welcomed you, for the glory of God. 8For I tell you that Christ has become a servant of the circumcised on behalf of the truth of God in order that he might confirm the promises given to the patriarchs, 9and in order that the Gentiles might glorify God for his mercy. As it is written,

"Therefore I will confess[k] you among the
          Gentiles,
     and sing praises to your name";

10and again he says,
     "Rejoice, O Gentiles, with his people";
11and again,
     "Praise the Lord, all you Gentiles,
     and let all the peoples praise him";
12and again Isaiah says,
     "The root of Jesse shall come,
     the one who rises to rule the Gentiles;
     in him the Gentiles shall hope."

13May the God of hope fill you with all joy and peace in believing, so that you may abound in hope by the power of the Holy Spirit.

Paul's Reason for Writing So Boldly

14 I myself feel confident about you, my brothers and sisters,[l] that you yourselves are full of goodness, filled with all knowledge, and able to instruct one another. 15Nevertheless on some points I have written to you rather boldly by way of reminder, because of the grace given me by God 16to be a minister of Christ Jesus to the Gentiles in the priestly service of the gospel of God, so that the offering of the Gentiles may be acceptable, sanctified by the Holy Spirit. 17In Christ Jesus, then, I have reason to boast of my work for God. 18For I will

g Gk *brother*   h Other ancient authorities add *or be upset or be weakened*
i Or *conviction*   j Other authorities, some ancient, add here 16.25-27   k Or *thank*   l Gk *brothers*

King James

18For I will not dare to speak of any of those things which Christ hath not wrought by me, to make the Gentiles obedient, by word and deed,

19Through mighty signs and wonders, by the power of the Spirit of God; so that from Jerusalem, and round about unto Illyricum, I have fully preached the gospel of Christ.

20Yea, so have I strived to preach the gospel, not where Christ was named, lest I should build upon another man's foundation:

21But as it is written, To whom he was not spoken of, they shall see: and they that have not heard shall understand.

22For which cause also I have been much hindered from coming to you.

23But now having no more place in these parts, and having a great desire these many years to come unto you;

24Whensoever I take my journey into Spain, I will come to you: for I trust to see you in my journey, and to be brought on my way thitherward by you, if first I be somewhat filled with your *company*.

25But now I go unto Jerusalem to minister unto the saints.

26For it hath pleased them of Macedonia and Achaia to make a certain contribution for the poor saints which are at Jerusalem.

27It hath pleased them verily; and their debtors they are. For if the Gentiles have been made partakers of their spiritual things, their duty is also to minister unto them in carnal things.

28When therefore I have performed this, and have sealed to them this fruit, I will come by you into Spain.

29And I am sure that, when I come unto you, I shall come in the fulness of the blessing of the gospel of Christ.

30Now I beseech you, brethren, for the Lord Jesus Christ's sake, and for the love of the Spirit, that ye strive together with me in *your* prayers to God for me;

31That I may be delivered from them that do not believe in Judaea; and that my service which *I have* for Jerusalem may be accepted of the saints;

32That I may come unto you with joy by the will of God, and may with you be refreshed.

33Now the God of peace *be* with you all. Amen.

16 I COMMEND unto you Phebe our sister, which is a servant of the church which is at Cenchrea;

2That ye receive her in the Lord, as becometh saints, and that ye assist her in whatsoever business she hath need of you: for she hath been a succourer of many, and of myself also.

3Greet Priscilla and Aquila my helpers in Christ Jesus:

4Who have for my life laid down their own necks: unto whom not only I give thanks, but also all the churches of the Gentiles.

5Likewise *greet* the church that is in their house. Salute my wellbeloved Epaenetus, who is the firstfruits of Achaia unto Christ.

6Greet Mary, who bestowed much labour on us.

7Salute Andronicus and Junia, my kinsmen, and my fellowprisoners, who are of note among the apostles, who also were in Christ before me.

8Greet Amplias my beloved in the Lord.

New International

what Christ has accomplished through me in leading the Gentiles to obey God by what I have said and done— 19by the power of signs and miracles, through the power of the Spirit. So from Jerusalem all the way around to Illyricum, I have fully proclaimed the gospel of Christ. 20It has always been my ambition to preach the gospel where Christ was not known, so that I would not be building on someone else's foundation. 21Rather, as it is written:

> "Those who were not told about him will see,
>   and those who have not heard will
>   understand."[a]

22This is why I have often been hindered from coming to you.

Paul's Plan to Visit Rome

23But now that there is no more place for me to work in these regions, and since I have been longing for many years to see you, 24I plan to do so when I go to Spain. I hope to visit you while passing through and to have you assist me on my journey there, after I have enjoyed your company for a while. 25Now, however, I am on my way to Jerusalem in the service of the saints there. 26For Macedonia and Achaia were pleased to make a contribution for the poor among the saints in Jerusalem. 27They were pleased to do it, and indeed they owe it to them. For if the Gentiles have shared in the Jews' spiritual blessings, they owe it to the Jews to share with them their material blessings. 28So after I have completed this task and have made sure that they have received this fruit, I will go to Spain and visit you on the way. 29I know that when I come to you, I will come in the full measure of the blessing of Christ.

30I urge you, brothers, by our Lord Jesus Christ and by the love of the Spirit, to join me in my struggle by praying to God for me. 31Pray that I may be rescued from the unbelievers in Judea and that my service in Jerusalem may be acceptable to the saints there, 32so that by God's will I may come to you with joy and together with you be refreshed. 33The God of peace be with you all. Amen.

Personal Greetings

16 I COMMEND to you our sister Phoebe, a servant[b] of the church in Cenchrea. 2I ask you to receive her in the Lord in a way worthy of the saints and to give her any help she may need from you, for she has been a great help to many people, including me.

3Greet Priscilla[c] and Aquila, my fellow workers in Christ Jesus. 4They risked their lives for me. Not only I but all the churches of the Gentiles are grateful to them.

5Greet also the church that meets at their house.
    Greet my dear friend Epenetus, who was the first convert to Christ in the province of Asia.

6Greet Mary, who worked very hard for you.

7Greet Andronicus and Junias, my relatives who have been in prison with me. They are outstanding among the apostles, and they were in Christ before I was.

8Greet Ampliatus, whom I love in the Lord.

---

a 21 Isaiah 52:15   b 1 Or *deaconess*   c 3 Greek *Prisca*, a variant of *Priscilla*

Living Bible

effectively he has used others, but I know this: he has used me to win the Gentiles to God. 19I have won them by my message and by the good way I have lived before them, and by the miracles done through me as signs from God—all by the Holy Spirit's power. In this way I have preached the full Gospeld of Christ all the way from Jerusalem clear over into Illyricum.

20But all the while my ambition has been to go still farther, preaching where the name of Christ has never yet been heard, rather than where a church has already been started by someone else. 21I have been following the plan spoken of in the Scriptures where Isaiah says that those who have never heard the name of Christ before will see and understand. 22In fact that is the very reason I have been so long in coming to visit you.

23But now at last I am through with my work here, and I am ready to come after all these long years of waiting. 24For I am planning to take a trip to Spain, and when I do, I will stop off there in Rome; and after we have had a good time together for a little while, you can send me on my way again.

25But before I come, I must go down to Jerusalem to take a gift to the Jewish Christians there. 26For you see, the Christians in Macedonia and Achaia have taken up an offering for those in Jerusalem who are going through such hard times. 27They were very glad to do this, for they feel that they owe a real debt to the Jerusalem Christians. Why? Because the news about Christ came to these Gentiles from the church in Jerusalem. And since they received this wonderful spiritual gift of the Gospel from there, they feel that the least they can do in return is to give some material aid.e 28As soon as I have delivered this money and completed this good deed of theirs, I will come to see you on my way to Spain. 29And I am sure that when I come the Lord will give me a great blessing for you.

30Will you be my prayer partners? For the Lord Jesus Christ's sake, and because of your love for me—given to you by the Holy Spirit—pray much with me for my work. 31Pray that I will be protected in Jerusalem from those who are not Christians. Pray also that the Christians there will be willing to accept the money I am bringing them. 32Then I will be able to come to you with a happy heart by the will of God, and we can refresh each other.

33And now may our God, who gives peace, be with you all. Amen.

16 PHOEBE, A dear Christian woman from the town of Cenchreae, will be coming to see you soon. She has worked hard in the church there. Receive her as your sister in the Lord, giving her a warm Christian welcome. Help her in every way you can, for she has helped many in their needs, including me. 3Tell Priscilla and Aquila "hello." They have been my fellow workers in the affairs of Christ Jesus. 4In fact, they risked their lives for me; and I am not the only one who is thankful to them: so are all the Gentile churches.

5Please give my greetings to all those who meet to worship in their home. Greet my good friend Epaenetus. He was the very first person to become a Christian in Asia. 6Remember me to Mary, too, who has worked so hard to help us. 7Then there are Andronicus and Junias, my relatives who were in prison with me. They are respected by the apostles, and became Christians before I did. Please give them my greetings. 8Say "hello" to Ampliatus, whom I love as one of God's own children,

New Revised Standard

not venture to speak of anything except what Christ has accomplishedf through me to win obedience from the Gentiles, by word and deed, 19by the power of signs and wonders, by the power of the Spirit of God,g so that from Jerusalem and as far around as Illyricum I have fully proclaimed the good newsh of Christ. 20Thus I make it my ambition to proclaim the good news,h not where Christ has already been named, so that I do not build on someone else's foundation, 21but as it is written,

> "Those who have never been told of him shall
> see,
> and those who have never heard of him
> shall understand."

Paul's Plan to Visit Rome

22 This is the reason that I have so often been hindered from coming to you. 23But now, with no further place for me in these regions, I desire, as I have for many years, to come to you 24when I go to Spain. For I do hope to see you on my journey and to be sent on by you, once I have enjoyed your company for a little while. 25At present, however, I am going to Jerusalem in a ministry to the saints; 26for Macedonia and Achaia have been pleased to share their resources with the poor among the saints at Jerusalem. 27They were pleased to do this, and indeed they owe it to them; for if the Gentiles have come to share in their spiritual blessings, they ought also to be of service to them in material things. 28So, when I have completed this, and have delivered to them what has been collected,i I will set out by way of you to Spain; 29and I know that when I come to you, I will come in the fullness of the blessingj of Christ.

30 I appeal to you, brothers and sisters,k by our Lord Jesus Christ and by the love of the Spirit, to join me in earnest prayer to God on my behalf, 31that I may be rescued from the unbelievers in Judea, and that my ministryl to Jerusalem may be acceptable to the saints, 32so that by God's will I may come to you with joy and be refreshed in your company. 33The God of peace be with all of you.m Amen.

Personal Greetings

16 I COMMEND to you our sister Phoebe, a deaconn of the church at Cenchreae, 2so that you may welcome her in the Lord as is fitting for the saints, and help her in whatever she may require from you, for she has been a benefactor of many and of myself as well.

3 Greet Prisca and Aquila, who work with me in Christ Jesus, 4and who risked their necks for my life, to whom not only I give thanks, but also all the churches of the Gentiles. 5Greet also the church in their house. Greet my beloved Epaenetus, who was the first converto in Asia for Christ. 6Greet Mary, who has worked very hard among you. 7Greet Andronicus and Junia,p my relativesq who were in prison with me; they are prominent among the apostles, and they were in Christ before I was. 8Greet Ampliatus, my beloved in the Lord.

---

d 15:19 I have preached the full Gospel, or, "I have fully accomplished my gospel ministry."   e 15:27 the least they can do in return is to give some material aid, literally, "For if the Gentiles have come to share in their spiritual blessings, they ought also to be of service to them in material blessings."

f Gk speak of those things that Christ has not accomplished   g Other ancient authorities read of the Spirit or of the Holy Spirit   h Or gospel   i Gk have sealed to them this fruit   j Other ancient authorities add of the gospel   k Gk brothers   l Other ancient authorities read my bringing of a gift   m One ancient authority adds 16.25-27 here   n Or minister   o Gk first fruits   p Or Junias; other ancient authorities read Julia   q Or compatriots

King James

9Salute Urbane, our helper in Christ, and Stachys my beloved.

10Salute Apelles approved in Christ. Salute them which are of Aristobulus' *household*.

11Salute Herodion my kinsman. Greet them that be of the *household* of Narcissus, which are in the Lord.

12Salute Tryphena and Tryphosa, who labour in the Lord. Salute the beloved Persis, which laboured much in the Lord.

13Salute Rufus chosen in the Lord, and his mother and mine.

14Salute Asyncritus, Phlegon, Hermas, Patrobas, Hermes, and the brethren which are with them.

15Salute Philologus, and Julia, Nereus, and his sister, and Olympas, and all the saints which are with them.

16Salute one another with an holy kiss. The churches of Christ salute you.

17Now I beseech you, brethren, mark them which cause divisions and offences contrary to the doctrine which ye have learned; and avoid them.

18For they that are such serve not our Lord Jesus Christ, but their own belly; and by good words and fair speeches deceive the hearts of the simple.

19For your obedience is come abroad unto all *men*. I am glad therefore on your behalf: but yet I would have you wise unto that which is good, and simple concerning evil.

20And the God of peace shall bruise Satan under your feet shortly. The grace of our Lord Jesus Christ *be* with you. Amen.

21Timotheus my workfellow, and Lucius, and Jason, and Sosipater, my kinsmen, salute you.

22I Tertius, who wrote *this* epistle, salute you in the Lord.

23Gaius mine host, and of the whole church, saluteth you. Erastus the chamberlain of the city saluteth you, and Quartus a brother.

24The grace of our Lord Jesus Christ *be* with you all. Amen.

25Now to him that is of power to stablish you according to my gospel, and the preaching of Jesus Christ, according to the revelation of the mystery, which was kept secret since the world began,

26But now is made manifest, and by the scriptures of the prophets, according to the commandment of the everlasting God, made known to all nations for the obedience of faith:

27To God only wise, *be* glory through Jesus Christ for ever. Amen.

New International

9Greet Urbanus, our fellow worker in Christ, and my dear friend Stachys.

10Greet Apelles, tested and approved in Christ.

Greet those who belong to the household of Aristobulus.

11Greet Herodion, my relative.

Greet those in the household of Narcissus who are in the Lord.

12Greet Tryphena and Tryphosa, those women who work hard in the Lord.

Greet my dear friend Persis, another woman who has worked very hard in the Lord.

13Greet Rufus, chosen in the Lord, and his mother, who has been a mother to me, too.

14Greet Asyncritus, Phlegon, Hermes, Patrobas, Hermas and the brothers with them.

15Greet Philologus, Julia, Nereus and his sister, and Olympas and all the saints with them.

16Greet one another with a holy kiss.

All the churches of Christ send greetings.

17I urge you, brothers, to watch out for those who cause divisions and put obstacles in your way that are contrary to the teaching you have learned. Keep away from them. 18For such people are not serving our Lord Christ, but their own appetites. By smooth talk and flattery they deceive the minds of naive people. 19Everyone has heard about your obedience, so I am full of joy over you; but I want you to be wise about what is good, and innocent about what is evil.

20The God of peace will soon crush Satan under your feet.

The grace of our Lord Jesus be with you.

21Timothy, my fellow worker, sends his greetings to you, as do Lucius, Jason and Sosipater, my relatives.

22I, Tertius, who wrote down this letter, greet you in the Lord.

23Gaius, whose hospitality I and the whole church here enjoy, sends you his greetings.

Erastus, who is the city's director of public works, and our brother Quartus send you their greetings.a

25Now to him who is able to establish you by my gospel and the proclamation of Jesus Christ, according to the revelation of the mystery hidden for long ages past, 26but now revealed and made known through the prophetic writings by the command of the eternal God, so that all nations might believe and obey him— 27to the only wise God be glory forever through Jesus Christ! Amen.

a 23 Some manuscripts *their greetings.* 24*May the grace of our Lord Jesus Christ be with all of you. Amen.*

Living Bible

9and Urbanus, our fellow worker, and beloved Stachys.

10Then there is Apelles, a good man whom the Lord approves; greet him for me. And give my best regards to those working at the house of Aristobulus. 11Remember me to Herodion my relative. Remember me to the Christian slaves over at Narcissus House. 12Say "hello" to Tryphaena and Tryphosa, the Lord's workers, and to dear Persis, who has worked so hard for the Lord. 13Greet Rufus for me, whom the Lord picked out to be his very own; and also his dear mother who has been such a mother to me. 14And please give my greetings to Asyncritus, Phlegon, Hermes, Patrobas, Hermas, and the other brothers who are with them. 15Give my love to Philologus, Julia, Nereus and his sister, and to Olympas, and all the Christians who are with them. 16Shake hands warmly with each other. All the churches here send you their greetings.

17And now there is one more thing to say before I end this letter. Stay away from those who cause divisions and are upsetting people's faith, teaching things about Christ that are contrary to what you have been taught. 18Such teachers are not working for our Lord Jesus, but only want gain for themselves. They are good speakers, and simple-minded people are often fooled by them. 19But everyone knows that you stand loyal and true. This makes me very happy. I want you always to remain very clear about what is right, and to stay innocent of any wrong. 20The God of peace will soon crush Satan under your feet. The blessings from our Lord Jesus Christ be upon you.

21Timothy my fellow-worker, and Lucius and Jason and Sosipater, my relatives, send you their good wishes. 22I, Tertius, the one who is writing this letter for Paul, send my greetings too, as a Christian brother. 23Gaius says to say "hello" to you for him. I am his guest, and the church meets here in his home. Erastus, the city treasurer, sends you his greetings and so does Quartus, a Christian brother. 24Goodbye. May the grace of our Lord Jesus Christ be with you all.

25, 26, 27I commit you to God, who is able to make you strong and steady in the Lord, just as the Gospel says, and just as I have told you. This is God's plan of salvation for you Gentiles, kept secret from the beginning of time. But now as the prophets foretold and as God commands, this message is being preached everywhere, so that people all around the world will have faith in Christ and obey him. To God, who alone is wise, be the glory forever through Jesus Christ our Lord. Amen.

Sincerely, Paul

New Revised Standard

9Greet Urbanus, our co-worker in Christ, and my beloved Stachys. 10Greet Apelles, who is approved in Christ. Greet those who belong to the family of Aristobulus. 11Greet my relativeb Herodion. Greet those in the Lord who belong to the family of Narcissus. 12Greet those workers in the Lord, Tryphaena and Tryphosa. Greet the beloved Persis, who has worked hard in the Lord. 13Greet Rufus, chosen in the Lord; and greet his mother—a mother to me also. 14Greet Asyncritus, Phlegon, Hermes, Patrobas, Hermas, and the brothers and sistersc who are with them. 15Greet Philologus, Julia, Nereus and his sister, and Olympas, and all the saints who are with them. 16Greet one another with a holy kiss. All the churches of Christ greet you.

Final Instructions

17 I urge you, brothers and sisters,c to keep an eye on those who cause dissensions and offenses, in opposition to the teaching that you have learned; avoid them. 18For such people do not serve our Lord Christ, but their own appetites,d and by smooth talk and flattery they deceive the hearts of the simple-minded. 19For while your obedience is known to all, so that I rejoice over you, I want you to be wise in what is good and guileless in what is evil. 20The God of peace will shortly crush Satan under your feet. The grace of our Lord Jesus Christ be with you.e

21 Timothy, my co-worker, greets you; so do Lucius and Jason and Sosipater, my relatives.f

22 I Tertius, the writer of this letter, greet you in the Lord.g

23 Gaius, who is host to me and to the whole church, greets you. Erastus, the city treasurer, and our brother Quartus, greet you.h

Final Doxology

25 Now to Godi who is able to strengthen you according to my gospel and the proclamation of Jesus Christ, according to the revelation of the mystery that was kept secret for long ages 26but is now disclosed, and through the prophetic writings is made known to all the Gentiles, according to the command of the eternal God, to bring about the obedience of faith— 27to the only wise God, through Jesus Christ, to whomj be the glory forever! Amen.k

b Or compatriot   c Gk brothers   d Gk their own belly   e Other ancient authorities lack this sentence   f Or compatriots   g Or I Tertius, writing this letter in the Lord, greet you   h Other ancient authorities add verse 24, The grace of our Lord Jesus Christ be with all of you. Amen.   i Gk the one   j Other ancient authorities lack to whom. The verse then reads, to the only wise God be the glory through Jesus Christ forever. Amen.   k Other ancient authorities lack 16.25-27 or include it after 14.23 or 15.33; others put verse 24 after verse 27

King James

THE FIRST EPISTLE OF

PAUL THE APOSTLE TO THE

Corinthians

1 PAUL, CALLED *to be* an apostle of Jesus Christ through the will of God, and Sosthenes *our* brother,

2Unto the church of God which is at Corinth, to them that are sanctified in Christ Jesus, called *to be* saints, with all that in every place call upon the name of Jesus Christ our Lord, both theirs and ours:

3Grace *be* unto you, and peace, from God our Father, and *from* the Lord Jesus Christ.

4I thank my God always on your behalf, for the grace of God which is given you by Jesus Christ;

5That in every thing ye are enriched by him, in all utterance, and *in* all knowledge;

6Even as the testimony of Christ was confirmed in you:

7So that ye come behind in no gift; waiting for the coming of our Lord Jesus Christ:

8Who shall also confirm you unto the end, *that ye may be* blameless in the day of our Lord Jesus Christ.

9God *is* faithful, by whom ye were called unto the fellowship of his Son Jesus Christ our Lord.

10Now I beseech you, brethren, by the name of our Lord Jesus Christ, that ye all speak the same thing, and *that* there be no divisions among you; but *that* ye be perfectly joined together in the same mind and in the same judgment.

11For it hath been declared unto me of you, my brethren, by them *which are of the house* of Chloe, that there are contentions among you.

12Now this I say, that every one of you saith, I am of Paul; and I of Apollos; and I of Cephas; and I of Christ.

13Is Christ divided? was Paul crucified for you? or were ye baptized in the name of Paul?

14I thank God that I baptized none of you, but Crispus and Gaius;

15Lest any should say that I had baptized in mine own name.

16And I baptized also the household of Stephanas: besides, I know not whether I baptized any other.

17For Christ sent me not to baptize, but to preach the gospel: not with wisdom of words, lest the cross of Christ should be made of none effect.

18For the preaching of the cross is to them that perish foolishness; but unto us which are saved it is the power of God.

19For it is written, I will destroy the wisdom of the wise, and will bring to nothing the understanding of the prudent.

New International

1 Corinthians

1 PAUL, CALLED to be an apostle of Christ Jesus by the will of God, and our brother Sosthenes,

2To the church of God in Corinth, to those sanctified in Christ Jesus and called to be holy, together with all those everywhere who call on the name of our Lord Jesus Christ—their Lord and ours:

3Grace and peace to you from God our Father and the Lord Jesus Christ.

Thanksgiving

4I always thank God for you because of his grace given you in Christ Jesus. 5For in him you have been enriched in every way—in all your speaking and in all your knowledge— 6because our testimony about Christ was confirmed in you. 7Therefore you do not lack any spiritual gift as you eagerly wait for our Lord Jesus Christ to be revealed. 8He will keep you strong to the end, so that you will be blameless on the day of our Lord Jesus Christ. 9God, who has called you into fellowship with his Son Jesus Christ our Lord, is faithful.

Divisions in the Church

10I appeal to you, brothers, in the name of our Lord Jesus Christ, that all of you agree with one another so that there may be no divisions among you and that you may be perfectly united in mind and thought. 11My brothers, some from Chloe's household have informed me that there are quarrels among you. 12What I mean is this: One of you says, "I follow Paul"; another, "I follow Apollos"; another, "I follow Cephasa"; still another, "I follow Christ."

13Is Christ divided? Was Paul crucified for you? Were you baptized intob the name of Paul? 14I am thankful that I did not baptize any of you except Crispus and Gaius, 15so no one can say that you were baptized into my name. 16(Yes, I also baptized the household of Stephanas; beyond that, I don't remember if I baptized anyone else.) 17For Christ did not send me to baptize, but to preach the gospel—not with words of human wisdom, lest the cross of Christ be emptied of its power.

Christ the Wisdom and Power of God

18For the message of the cross is foolishness to those who are perishing, but to us who are being saved it is the power of God. 19For it is written:

"I will destroy the wisdom of the wise;
the intelligence of the intelligent I will
frustrate."c

a 12 That is, Peter   b 13 Or in; also in verse 15   c 19 Isaiah 29:14

THE FIRST LETTER OF

PAUL TO THE

1 Corinthians

Corinthians

Living Bible

1 **FROM:** PAUL, chosen by God to be Jesus Christ's missionary, and from brother Sosthenes.

2*To:* The Christians in Corinth, invited by God to be his people and made acceptable to him by Christ Jesus.d *And to:* All Christians everywhere—whoever calls upon the name of Jesus Christ, our Lord and theirs.

3May God our Father and the Lord Jesus Christ give you all of his blessings, and great peace of heart and mind.

4I can never stop thanking God for all the wonderful gifts he has given you, now that you are Christ's: 5he has enriched your whole life. He has helped you speak out for him and has given you a full understanding of the truth; 6what I told you Christ could do for you has happened! 7Now you have every grace and blessing; every spiritual gift and power for doing his will are yours during this time of waiting for the return of our Lord Jesus Christ. 8And he guarantees right up to the end that you will be counted free from all sin and guilt on that day when he returns. 9God will surely do this for you, for he always does just what he says, and he is the one who invited you into this wonderful friendship with his Son, even Christ our Lord.

10But, dear brothers, I beg you in the name of the Lord Jesus Christ to stop arguing among yourselves. Let there be real harmony so that there won't be splits in the church. I plead with you to be of one mind, united in thought and purpose. 11For some of those who live at Chloe's house have told me of your arguments and quarrels, dear brothers. 12Some of you are saying, "I am a follower of Paul"; and others say that they are for Apollos or for Peter; and some that they alone are the true followers of Christ. 13And so, in effect, you have broken Christ into many pieces.

But did I, Paul, die for your sins? Were any of you baptized in my name? 14I am so thankful now that I didn't baptize any of you except Crispus and Gaius. 15For now no one can think that I have been trying to start something new, beginning a "Church of Paul." 16Oh, yes, and I baptized the family of Stephanas. I don't remember ever baptizing anyone else. 17For Christ didn't send me to baptize, but to preach the Gospel; and even my preaching sounds poor, for I do not fill my sermons with profound words and high sounding ideas, for fear of diluting the mighty power there is in the simple message of the cross of Christ.

18I know very well how foolish it sounds to those who are lost,e when they hear that Jesus died to save them. But we who are savedf recognize this message as the very power of God. 19For God says, "I will destroy all human plans of salvation no matter how wise they seem to be, and ignore the best ideas of men, even the most brilliant of them."

New Revised Standard

Salutation

1 PAUL, CALLED to be an apostle of Christ Jesus by the will of God, and our brother Sosthenes,

2 To the church of God that is in Corinth, to those who are sanctified in Christ Jesus, called to be saints, together with all those who in every place call on the name of our Lord Jesus Christ, both their Lordg and ours:

3 Grace to you and peace from God our Father and the Lord Jesus Christ.

4 I give thanks to myh God always for you because of the grace of God that has been given you in Christ Jesus, 5for in every way you have been enriched in him, in speech and knowledge of every kind— 6just as the testimony ofi Christ has been strengthened among you— 7so that you are not lacking in any spiritual gift as you wait for the revealing of our Lord Jesus Christ. 8He will also strengthen you to the end, so that you may be blameless on the day of our Lord Jesus Christ. 9God is faithful; by him you were called into the fellowship of his Son, Jesus Christ our Lord.

Divisions in the Church

10 Now I appeal to you, brothers and sisters,j by the name of our Lord Jesus Christ, that all of you be in agreement and that there be no divisions among you, but that you be united in the same mind and the same purpose. 11 For it has been reported to me by Chloe's people that there are quarrels among you, my brothers and sisters.k 12What I mean is that each of you says, "I belong to Paul," or "I belong to Apollos," or "I belong to Cephas," or "I belong to Christ." 13Has Christ been divided? Was Paul crucified for you? Or were you baptized in the name of Paul? 14I thank Godl that I baptized none of you except Crispus and Gaius, 15so that no one can say that you were baptized in my name. 16(I did baptize also the household of Stephanas; beyond that, I do not know whether I baptized anyone else.) 17For Christ did not send me to baptize but to proclaim the gospel, and not with eloquent wisdom, so that the cross of Christ might not be emptied of its power.

Christ the Power and Wisdom of God

18 For the message about the cross is foolishness to those who are perishing, but to us who are being saved it is the power of God. 19For it is written,
"I will destroy the wisdom of the wise,
    and the discernment of the discerning I will thwart."

---

d *1:2 made acceptable to him by Christ Jesus,* or, "chosen by Christ Jesus," Literally, "sanctified in Christ Jesus."   e *1:18 are lost,* or "are being lost."   f *1:18 are saved,* or "are being saved."

g Gk *theirs*   h Other ancient authorities lack *my*   i Or *to*   j Gk *brothers*   k Gk *my brothers*   l Other ancient authorities read *I am thankful*

King James

20Where *is* the wise? where *is* the scribe? where *is* the disputer of this world? hath not God made foolish the wisdom of this world?

21For after that in the wisdom of God the world by wisdom knew not God, it pleased God by the foolishness of preaching to save them that believe.

22For the Jews require a sign, and the Greeks seek after wisdom:

23But we preach Christ crucified, unto the Jews a stumblingblock, and unto the Greeks foolishness;

24But unto them which are called, both Jews and Greeks, Christ the power of God, and the wisdom of God.

25Because the foolishness of God is wiser than men; and the weakness of God is stronger than men.

26For ye see your calling, brethren, how that not many wise men after the flesh, not many mighty, not many noble, *are called:*

27But God hath chosen the foolish things of the world to confound the wise; and God hath chosen the weak things of the world to confound the things which are mighty;

28And base things of the world, and things which are despised, hath God chosen, *yea,* and things which are not, to bring to nought things that are:

29That no flesh should glory in his presence.

30But of him are ye in Christ Jesus, who of God is made unto us wisdom, and righteousness, and sanctification, and redemption:

31That, according as it is written, He that glorieth, let him glory in the Lord.

2 AND I, brethren, when I came to you, came not with excellency of speech or of wisdom, declaring unto you the testimony of God.

2For I determined not to know any thing among you, save Jesus Christ, and him crucified.

3And I was with you in weakness, and in fear, and in much trembling.

4And my speech and my preaching *was* not with enticing words of man's wisdom, but in demonstration of the Spirit and of power:

5That your faith should not stand in the wisdom of men, but in the power of God.

6Howbeit we speak wisdom among them that are perfect: yet not the wisdom of this world, nor of the princes of this world, that come to nought:

7But we speak the wisdom of God in a mystery, *even* the hidden *wisdom,* which God ordained before the world unto our glory:

8Which none of the princes of this world knew: for had they known *it,* they would not have crucified the Lord of glory.

9But as it is written, Eye hath not seen, nor ear heard, neither have entered into the heart of man, the things which God hath prepared for them that love him.

10But God hath revealed *them* unto us by his Spirit: for the Spirit searcheth all things, yea, the deep things of God.

New International

20Where is the wise man? Where is the scholar? Where is the philosopher of this age? Has not God made foolish the wisdom of the world? 21For since in the wisdom of God the world through its wisdom did not know him, God was pleased through the foolishness of what was preached to save those who believe. 22Jews demand miraculous signs and Greeks look for wisdom, 23but we preach Christ crucified: a stumbling block to Jews and foolishness to Gentiles, 24but to those whom God has called, both Jews and Greeks, Christ the power of God and the wisdom of God. 25For the foolishness of God is wiser than man's wisdom, and the weakness of God is stronger than man's strength.

26Brothers, think of what you were when you were called. Not many of you were wise by human standards; not many were influential; not many were of noble birth. 27But God chose the foolish things of the world to shame the wise; God chose the weak things of the world to shame the strong. 28He chose the lowly things of this world and the despised things—and the things that are not—to nullify the things that are, 29so that no one may boast before him. 30It is because of him that you are in Christ Jesus, who has become for us wisdom from God—that is, our righteousness, holiness and redemption. 31Therefore, as it is written: "Let him who boasts boast in the Lord."[a]

2 WHEN I came to you, brothers, I did not come with eloquence or superior wisdom as I proclaimed to you the testimony about God.[b] 2For I resolved to know nothing while I was with you except Jesus Christ and him crucified. 3I came to you in weakness and fear, and with much trembling. 4My message and my preaching were not with wise and persuasive words, but with a demonstration of the Spirit's power, 5so that your faith might not rest on men's wisdom, but on God's power.

Wisdom From the Spirit

6We do, however, speak a message of wisdom among the mature, but not the wisdom of this age or of the rulers of this age, who are coming to nothing. 7No, we speak of God's secret wisdom, a wisdom that has been hidden and that God destined for our glory before time began. 8None of the rulers of this age understood it, for if they had, they would not have crucified the Lord of glory. 9However, as it is written:

"No eye has seen,
    no ear has heard,
  no mind has conceived
    what God has prepared for those who love
        him"[c]—

10but God has revealed it to us by his Spirit.

The Spirit searches all things, even the deep things of God. 11For who among men knows the thoughts of

a *31* Jer. 9:24   b *1* Some manuscripts *as I proclaimed to you God's mystery*   c *9* Isaiah 64:4

Living Bible

20So what about these wise men, these scholars, these brilliant debaters of this world's great affairs? God has made them all look foolish, and shown their wisdom to be useless nonsense. 21For God in his wisdom saw to it that the world would never find God through human brilliance, and then he stepped in and saved all those who believed his message, which the world calls foolish and silly. 22It seems foolish to the Jews because they want a sign from heaven as proof that what is preached is true; and it is foolish to the Gentiles because they believe only what agrees with their philosophy and seems wise to them. 23So when we preach about Christ dying to save them, the Jews are offended and the Gentiles say it's all nonsense. 24But God has opened the eyes of those called to salvation, both Jews and Gentiles, to see that Christ is the mighty power of God to save them; Christ himself is the center of God's wise plan for their salvation. 25This so-called "foolish" plan of God is far wiser than the wisest plan of the wisest man, and God in his weakness—Christ dying on the cross—is far stronger than any man.

26Notice among yourselves, dear brothers, that few of you who follow Christ have big names or power or wealth. 27Instead, God has deliberately chosen to use ideas the world considers foolish and of little worth in order to shame those people considered by the world as wise and great. 28He has chosen a plan despised by the world, counted as nothing at all, and used it to bring down to nothing those the world considers great, 29so that no one anywhere can ever brag in the presence of God.

30For it is from God alone that you have your life through Christ Jesus. He showed us God's plan of salvation; he was the one who made us acceptable to God; he made us pure and holyd and gave himself to purchase our salvation.e 31As it says in the Scriptures, "If anyone is going to boast, let him boast only of what the Lord has done."

2 DEAR BROTHERS, even when I first came to you I didn't use lofty words and brilliant ideas to tell you God's message. 2For I decided that I would speak only of Jesus Christ and his death on the cross. 3I came to you in weakness—timid and trembling. 4And my preaching was very plain, not with a lot of oratory and human wisdom, but the Holy Spirit's power was in my words, proving to those who heard them that the message was from God. 5I did this because I wanted your faith to stand firmly upon God, not on man's great ideas.

6Yet when I am among mature Christians I do speak with words of great wisdom, but not the kind that comes from here on earth, and not the kind that appeals to the great men of this world, who are doomed to fall. 7Our words are wise because they are from God, telling of God's wise plan to bring us into the glories of heaven. This plan was hidden in former times, though it was made for our benefit before the world began. 8But the great men of the world have not understood it; if they had, they never would have crucified the Lord of Glory. 9That is what is meant by the Scriptures which say that no mere man has ever seen, nor heard or even imagined what wonderful things God has ready for those who love the Lord. 10But we know about these things because God has sent his Spirit to tell us, and his Spirit searches out and shows us all of God's deepest secrets. 11No one can

New Revised Standard

20Where is the one who is wise? Where is the scribe? Where is the debater of this age? Has not God made foolish the wisdom of the world? 21For since, in the wisdom of God, the world did not know God through wisdom, God decided, through the foolishness of our proclamation, to save those who believe. 22For Jews demand signs and Greeks desire wisdom, 23but we proclaim Christ crucified, a stumbling block to Jews and foolishness to Gentiles, 24but to those who are the called, both Jews and Greeks, Christ the power of God and the wisdom of God. 25For God's foolishness is wiser than human wisdom, and God's weakness is stronger than human strength.

26 Consider your own call, brothers and sisters:f not many of you were wise by human standards,g not many were powerful, not many were of noble birth. 27But God chose what is foolish in the world to shame the wise; God chose what is weak in the world to shame the strong; 28God chose what is low and despised in the world, things that are not, to reduce to nothing things that are, 29so that no oneh might boast in the presence of God. 30He is the source of your life in Christ Jesus, who became for us wisdom from God, and righteousness and sanctification and redemption, 31in order that, as it is written, "Let the one who boasts, boast ini the Lord."

Proclaiming Christ Crucified

2 WHEN I came to you, brothers and sisters,f I did not come proclaiming the mysteryj of God to you in lofty words or wisdom. 2For I decided to know nothing among you except Jesus Christ, and him crucified. 3And I came to you in weakness and in fear and in much trembling. 4My speech and my proclamation were not with plausible words of wisdom,k but with a demonstration of the Spirit and of power, 5so that your faith might rest not on human wisdom but on the power of God.

The True Wisdom of God

6 Yet among the mature we do speak wisdom, though it is not a wisdom of this age or of the rulers of this age, who are doomed to perish. 7But we speak God's wisdom, secret and hidden, which God decreed before the ages for our glory. 8None of the rulers of this age understood this; for if they had, they would not have crucified the Lord of glory. 9But, as it is written,

"What no eye has seen, nor ear heard,
    nor the human heart conceived,
    what God has prepared for those who love
        him"—

10these things God has revealed to us through the Spirit; for the Spirit searches everything, even the depths of God. 11For what human being knows what is truly hu-

---

d 1:30 he made us pure and holy, or, "he brought us near to God." e 1:30 to purchase our salvation, or, "to free us from slavery to sin."

f Gk brothers g Gk according to the flesh h Gk no flesh i Or of j Other ancient authorities read testimony k Other ancient authorities read the persuasiveness of wisdom

King James

11For what man knoweth the things of a man, save the spirit of man which is in him? even so the things of God knoweth no man, but the Spirit of God.

12Now we have received, not the spirit of the world, but the spirit which is of God; that we might know the things that are freely given to us of God.

13Which things also we speak, not in the words which man's wisdom teacheth, but which the Holy Ghost teacheth; comparing spiritual things with spiritual.

14But the natural man receiveth not the things of the Spirit of God: for they are foolishness unto him: neither can he know *them,* because they are spiritually discerned.

15But he that is spiritual judgeth all things, yet he himself is judged of no man.

16For who hath known the mind of the Lord, that he may instruct him? But we have the mind of Christ.

3 AND I, brethren, could not speak unto you as unto spiritual, but as unto carnal, *even* as unto babes in Christ.

2I have fed you with milk, and not with meat: for hitherto ye were not able *to bear it,* neither yet now are ye able.

3For ye are yet carnal: for whereas *there is* among you envying, and strife, and divisions, are ye not carnal, and walk as men?

4For while one saith, I am of Paul; and another, I *am* of Apollos; are ye not carnal?

5Who then is Paul, and who *is* Apollos, but ministers by whom ye believed, even as the Lord gave to every man?

6I have planted, Apollos watered; but God gave the increase.

7So then neither is he that planteth any thing, neither he that watereth; but God that giveth the increase.

8Now he that planteth and he that watereth are one: and every man shall receive his own reward according to his own labour.

9For we are labourers together with God: ye are God's husbandry, *ye are* God's building.

10According to the grace of God which is given unto me, as a wise masterbuilder, I have laid the foundation, and another buildeth thereon. But let every man take heed how he buildeth thereupon.

11For other foundation can no man lay than that is laid, which is Jesus Christ.

12Now if any man build upon this foundation gold, silver, precious stones, wood, hay, stubble;

13Every man's work shall be made manifest: for the day shall declare it, because it shall be revealed by fire; and the fire shall try every man's work of what sort it is.

New International

a man except the man's spirit within him? In the same way no one knows the thoughts of God except the Spirit of God. 12We have not received the spirit of the world but the Spirit who is from God, that we may understand what God has freely given us. 13This is what we speak, not in words taught us by human wisdom but in words taught by the Spirit, expressing spiritual truths in spiritual words.[a] 14The man without the Spirit does not accept the things that come from the Spirit of God, for they are foolishness to him, and he cannot understand them, because they are spiritually discerned. 15The spiritual man makes judgments about all things, but he himself is not subject to any man's judgment:

16"For who has known the mind of the Lord
    that he may instruct him?"[b]

But we have the mind of Christ.

On Divisions in the Church

3 BROTHERS, I could not address you as spiritual but as worldly—mere infants in Christ. 2I gave you milk, not solid food, for you were not yet ready for it. Indeed, you are still not ready. 3You are still worldly. For since there is jealousy and quarreling among you, are you not worldly? Are you not acting like mere men? 4For when one says, "I follow Paul," and another, "I follow Apollos," are you not mere men?

5What, after all, is Apollos? And what is Paul? Only servants, through whom you came to believe—as the Lord has assigned to each his task. 6I planted the seed, Apollos watered it, but God made it grow. 7So neither he who plants nor he who waters is anything, but only God, who makes things grow. 8The man who plants and the man who waters have one purpose, and each will be rewarded according to his own labor. 9For we are God's fellow workers; you are God's field, God's building.

10By the grace God has given me, I laid a foundation as an expert builder, and someone else is building on it. But each one should be careful how he builds. 11For no one can lay any foundation other than the one already laid, which is Jesus Christ. 12If any man builds on this foundation using gold, silver, costly stones, wood, hay or straw, 13his work will be shown for what it is, because the Day will bring it to light. It will be revealed with fire, and the fire will test the quality of each man's work. 14If

Living Bible

really know what anyone else is thinking, or what he is really like, except that person himself. And no one can know God's thoughts except God's own Spirit. 12And God has actually given us his Spirit (not the world's spirit) to tell us about the wonderful free gifts of grace and blessing that God has given us. 13In telling you about these gifts we have even used the very words given to us by the Holy Spirit, not words that we as men might choose. So we use the Holy Spirit's words to explain the Holy Spirit's facts.c 14But the man who isn't a Christian can't understand and can't accept these thoughts from God, which the Holy Spirit teaches us. They sound foolish to him, because only those who have the Holy Spirit within them can understand what the Holy Spirit means. Others just can't take it in. 15But the spiritual man has insight into everything, and that bothers and baffles the man of the world, who can't understand him at all. 16How could he? For certainly he has never been one to know the Lord's thoughts, or to discuss them with him, or to move the hands of God by prayer.d But, strange as it seems, we Christians actually do have within us a portion of the very thoughts and mind of Christ.

3 DEAR BROTHERS, I have been talking to you as though you were still just babies in the Christian life, who are not following the Lord, but your own desires; I cannot talk to you as I would to healthy Christians, who are filled with the Spirit. 2I have had to feed you with milk and not with solid food, because you couldn't digest anything stronger. And even now you still have to be fed on milk. 3For you are still only baby Christians, controlled by your own desires, not God's. When you are jealous of one another and divide up into quarreling groups, doesn't that prove you are still babies, wanting your own way? In fact, you are acting like people who don't belong to the Lord at all. 4There you are, quarreling about whether I am greater than Apollos, and dividing the church. Doesn't this show how little you have grown in the Lord?e

5Who am I, and who is Apollos, that we should be the cause of a quarrel? Why, we're just God's servants, each of us with certain special abilities, and with our help you believed. 6My work was to plant the seed in your hearts, and Apollos' work was to water it, but it was God, not we, who made the garden grow in your hearts. 7The person who does the planting or watering isn't very important, but God is important because he is the one who makes things grow. 8Apollos and I are working as a team, with the same aim, though each of us will be rewarded for his own hard work. 9We are only God's co-workers. You are *God's* garden, not ours; you are *God's* building, not ours.

10God, in his kindness, has taught me how to be an expert builder. I have laid the foundation and Apollos has built on it. But he who builds on the foundation must be very careful. 11And no one can ever lay any other real foundation than that one we already have—Jesus Christ. 12But there are various kinds of materials that can be used to build on that foundation. Some use gold and silver and jewels; and some build with sticks, and hay, or even straw! 13There is going to come a time of testing at Christ's Judgment Day to see what kind of material each builder has used. Everyone's work will be put through the fire so that all can see whether or not it keeps its value, and what was really accomplished. 14Then

New Revised Standard

man except the human spirit that is within? So also no one comprehends what is truly God's except the Spirit of God. 12Now we have received not the spirit of the world, but the Spirit that is from God, so that we may understand the gifts bestowed on us by God. 13And we speak of these things in words not taught by human wisdom but taught by the Spirit, interpreting spiritual things to those who are spiritual.f

14 Those who are unspiritualg do not receive the gifts of God's Spirit, for they are foolishness to them, and they are unable to understand them because they are spiritually discerned. 15Those who are spiritual discern all things, and they are themselves subject to no one else's scrutiny.

16 "For who has known the mind of the Lord
    so as to instruct him?"
But we have the mind of Christ.

On Divisions in the Corinthian Church

3 AND SO, brothers and sisters,h I could not speak to you as spiritual people, but rather as people of the flesh, as infants in Christ. 2I fed you with milk, not solid food, for you were not ready for solid food. Even now you are still not ready, 3for you are still of the flesh. For as long as there is jealousy and quarreling among you, are you not of the flesh, and behaving according to human inclinations? 4For when one says, "I belong to Paul," and another, "I belong to Apollos," are you not merely human?

5 What then is Apollos? What is Paul? Servants through whom you came to believe, as the Lord assigned to each. 6I planted, Apollos watered, but God gave the growth. 7So neither the one who plants nor the one who waters is anything, but only God who gives the growth. 8The one who plants and the one who waters have a common purpose, and each will receive wages according to the labor of each. 9For we are God's servants, working together; you are God's field, God's building.

10 According to the grace of God given to me, like a skilled master builder I laid a foundation, and someone else is building on it. Each builder must choose with care how to build on it. 11For no one can lay any foundation other than the one that has been laid; that foundation is Jesus Christ. 12Now if anyone builds on the foundation with gold, silver, precious stones, wood, hay, straw— 13the work of each builder will become visible, for the Day will disclose it, because it will be revealed with fire, and the fire will test what sort of work each has done.

---

c *2:13 to explain the Holy Spirit's facts*, or, "interpreting spiritual truth in spiritual language." d *2:16 to move the hands of God by prayer*, or, "who can advise him?" e *3:4 Doesn't this show how little you have grown in the Lord?* Literally, "Are you not [mere] men?"

f Or *interpreting spiritual things in spiritual language*, or *comparing spiritual things with spiritual* g Or *natural* h Gk *brothers*

King James

14If any man's work abide which he hath built thereupon, he shall receive a reward.

15If any man's work shall be burned, he shall suffer loss: but he himself shall be saved; yet so as by fire.

16Know ye not that ye are the temple of God, and *that* the Spirit of God dwelleth in you?

17If any man defile the temple of God, him shall God destroy; for the temple of God is holy, which *temple* ye are.

18Let no man deceive himself. If any man among you seemeth to be wise in this world, let him become a fool, that he may be wise.

19For the wisdom of this world is foolishness with God. For it is written, He taketh the wise in their own craftiness.

20And again, The Lord knoweth the thoughts of the wise, that they are vain.

21Therefore let no man glory in men. For all things are yours;

22Whether Paul, or Apollos, or Cephas, or the world, or life, or death, or things present, or things to come; all are yours;

23And ye are Christ's; and Christ *is* God's.

4 LET A man so account of us, as of the ministers of Christ, and stewards of the mysteries of God.

2Moreover it is required in stewards, that a man be found faithful.

3But with me it is a very small thing that I should be judged of you, or of man's judgment: yea, I judge not mine own self.

4For I know nothing by myself; yet am I not hereby justified: but he that judgeth me is the Lord.

5Therefore judge nothing before the time, until the Lord come, who both will bring to light the hidden things of darkness, and will make manifest the counsels of the hearts: and then shall every man have praise of God.

6And these things, brethren, I have in a figure transferred to myself and *to* Apollos for your sakes; that ye might learn in us not to think *of men* above that which is written, that no one of you be puffed up for one against another.

7For who maketh thee to differ *from another?* and what hast thou that thou didst not receive? now if thou didst receive *it,* why dost thou glory, as if thou hadst not received *it?*

8Now ye are full, now ye are rich, ye have reigned as kings without us: and I would to God ye did reign, that we also might reign with you.

9For I think that God hath set forth us the apostles last, as it were appointed to death: for we are made a spectacle unto the world, and to angels, and to men.

10We *are* fools for Christ's sake, but ye *are* wise in Christ; we *are* weak, but ye *are* strong; ye *are* honourable, but we *are* despised.

New International

what he has built survives, he will receive his reward. 15If it is burned up, he will suffer loss; he himself will be saved, but only as one escaping through the flames.

16Don't you know that you yourselves are God's temple and that God's Spirit lives in you? 17If anyone destroys God's temple, God will destroy him; for God's temple is sacred, and you are that temple.

18Do not deceive yourselves. If any one of you thinks he is wise by the standards of this age, he should become a "fool" so that he may become wise. 19For the wisdom of this world is foolishness in God's sight. As it is written: "He catches the wise in their craftiness"a; 20and again, "The Lord knows that the thoughts of the wise are futile."b 21So then, no more boasting about men! All things are yours, 22whether Paul or Apollos or Cephasc or the world or life or death or the present or the future— all are yours, 23and you are of Christ, and Christ is of God.

Apostles of Christ

4 SO THEN, men ought to regard us as servants of Christ and as those entrusted with the secret things of God. 2Now it is required that those who have been given a trust must prove faithful. 3I care very little if I am judged by you or by any human court; indeed, I do not even judge myself. 4My conscience is clear, but that does not make me innocent. It is the Lord who judges me. 5Therefore judge nothing before the appointed time; wait till the Lord comes. He will bring to light what is hidden in darkness and will expose the motives of men's hearts. At that time each will receive his praise from God.

6Now, brothers, I have applied these things to myself and Apollos for your benefit, so that you may learn from us the meaning of the saying, "Do not go beyond what is written." Then you will not take pride in one man over against another. 7For who makes you different from anyone else? What do you have that you did not receive? And if you did receive it, why do you boast as though you did not?

8Already you have all you want! Already you have become rich! You have become kings—and that without us! How I wish that you really had become kings so that we might be kings with you! 9For it seems to me that God has put us apostles on display at the end of the procession, like men condemned to die in the arena. We have been made a spectacle to the whole universe, to angels as well as to men. 10We are fools for Christ, but you are so wise in Christ! We are weak, but you are strong! You are honored, we are dishonored! 11To this

---

a 19 Job 5:13   b 20 Psalm 94:11   c 22 That is, Peter

Living Bible

every workman who has built on the foundation with the right materials, and whose work still stands, will get his pay. 15But if the house he has built burns up, he will have a great loss. He himself will be saved, but like a man escaping through a wall of flames.

16Don't you realize that all of you together are the house of God, and that the Spirit of God lives among you in his house? 17If anyone defiles and spoils God's home, God will destroy him. For God's home is holy and clean, and you are that home.

18Stop fooling yourselves. If you count yourself above average in intelligence, as judged by this world's standards, you had better put this all aside and be a fool rather than let it hold you back from the true wisdom from above. 19For the wisdom of this world is foolishness to God. As it says in the book of Job, God uses man's own brilliance to trap him; he stumbles over his own "wisdom" and falls. 20And again, in the book of Psalms, we are told that the Lord knows full well how the human mind reasons, and how foolish and futile it is.

21So don't be proud of following the wise men of this world.d For God has already given you everything you need. 22He has given you Paul and Apollos and Peter as your helpers. He has given you the whole world to use, and life and even death are your servants. He has given you all of the present and all of the future. All are yours, 23and you belong to Christ, and Christ is God's.

4 SO APOLLOS and I should be looked upon as Christ's servants who distribute God's blessings by explaining God's secrets. 2Now the most important thing about a servant is that he does just what his master tells him to. 3What about me? Have I been a good servant? Well, I don't worry over what you think about this, or what anyone else thinks. I don't even trust my own judgment on this point. 4My conscience is clear, but even that isn't final proof. It is the Lord himself who must examine me and decide.

5So be careful not to jump to conclusions before the Lord returns as to whether someone is a good servant or not. When the Lord comes, he will turn on the light so that everyone can see exactly what each one of us is really like, deep down in our hearts. Then everyone will know why we have been doing the Lord's work. At that time God will give to each one whatever praise is coming to him.

6I have used Apollos and myself as examples to illustrate what I have been saying: that you must not have favorites. You must not be proud of one of God's teachers more than another. 7What are you so puffed up about? What do you have that God hasn't given you? And if all you have is from God, why act as though you are so great, and as though you have accomplished something on your own?

8You seem to think you already have all the spiritual food you need. You are full and spiritually contented, rich kings on your thrones, leaving us far behind! I wish you really were already on your thrones, for when that time comes you can be sure that we will be there, too, reigning with you. 9Sometimes I think God has put us apostles at the very end of the line, like prisoners soon to be killed, put on display at the end of a victor's parade, to be stared at by men and angels alike.

10Religion has made us foolish, you say, but of course you are all such wise and sensible Christians! We are weak, but not you! You are well thought of, while we are laughed at. 11To this very hour we have gone

New Revised Standard

14If what has been built on the foundation survives, the builder will receive a reward. 15If the work is burned up, the builder will suffer loss; the builder will be saved, but only as through fire.

16 Do you not know that you are God's temple and that God's Spirit dwells in you?e 17If anyone destroys God's temple, God will destroy that person. For God's temple is holy, and you are that temple.

18 Do not deceive yourselves. If you think that you are wise in this age, you should become fools so that you may become wise. 19For the wisdom of this world is foolishness with God. For it is written,

"He catches the wise in their craftiness,"
20and again,

"The Lord knows the thoughts of the wise,
    that they are futile."
21So let no one boast about human leaders. For all things are yours, 22whether Paul or Apollos or Cephas or the world or life or death or the present or the future—all belong to you, 23and you belong to Christ, and Christ belongs to God.

The Ministry of the Apostles

4 THINK OF us in this way, as servants of Christ and stewards of God's mysteries. 2Moreover, it is required of stewards that they be found trustworthy. 3But with me it is a very small thing that I should be judged by you or by any human court. I do not even judge myself. 4I am not aware of anything against myself, but I am not thereby acquitted. It is the Lord who judges me. 5Therefore do not pronounce judgment before the time, before the Lord comes, who will bring to light the things now hidden in darkness and will disclose the purposes of the heart. Then each one will receive commendation from God.

6 I have applied all this to Apollos and myself for your benefit, brothers and sisters,f so that you may learn through us the meaning of the saying, "Nothing beyond what is written," so that none of you will be puffed up in favor of one against another. 7For who sees anything different in you?g What do you have that you did not receive? And if you received it, why do you boast as if it were not a gift?

8 Already you have all you want! Already you have become rich! Quite apart from us you have become kings! Indeed, I wish that you had become kings, so that we might be kings with you! 9For I think that God has exhibited us apostles as last of all, as though sentenced to death, because we have become a spectacle to the world, to angels and to mortals. 10We are fools for the sake of Christ, but you are wise in Christ. We are weak, but you are strong. You are held in honor, but we in disrepute. 11To the present hour we are hungry and

---

d 3:21 So don't be proud of following the wise men of this world, literally, "Let no one glory in men."

e In verses 16 and 17 the Greek word for you is plural   f Gk brothers   g Or Who makes you different from another?

King James

11Even unto this present hour we both hunger, and thirst, and are naked, and are buffeted, and have no certain dwellingplace;

12And labour, working with our own hands: being reviled, we bless; being persecuted, we suffer it:

13Being defamed, we entreat: we are made as the filth of the world, *and are* the offscouring of all things unto this day.

14I write not these things to shame you, but as my beloved sons I warn *you*.

15For though ye have ten thousand instructors in Christ, yet *have ye* not many fathers: for in Christ Jesus I have begotten you through the gospel.

16Wherefore I beseech you, be ye followers of me.

17For this cause have I sent unto you Timotheus, who is my beloved son, and faithful in the Lord, who shall bring you into remembrance of my ways which be in Christ, as I teach every where in every church.

18Now some are puffed up, as though I would not come to you.

19But I will come to you shortly, if the Lord will, and will know, not the speech of them which are puffed up, but the power.

20For the kingdom of God *is* not in word, but in power.

21What will ye? shall I come unto you with a rod, or in love, and *in* the spirit of meekness?

5 IT IS reported commonly *that there is* fornication among you, and such fornication as is not so much as named among the Gentiles, that one should have his father's wife.

2And ye are puffed up, and have not rather mourned, that he that hath done this deed might be taken away from among you.

3For I verily, as absent in body, but present in spirit, have judged already, as though I were present, *concerning* him that hath so done this deed,

4In the name of our Lord Jesus Christ, when ye are gathered together, and my spirit, with the power of our Lord Jesus Christ,

5To deliver such an one unto Satan for the destruction of the flesh, that the spirit may be saved in the day of the Lord Jesus.

6Your glorying *is* not good. Know ye not that a little leaven leaveneth the whole lump?

7Purge out therefore the old leaven, that ye may be a new lump, as ye are unleavened. For even Christ our passover is sacrificed for us:

8Therefore let us keep the feast, not with old leaven, neither with the leaven of malice and wickedness; but with the unleavened *bread* of sincerity and truth.

9I wrote unto you in an epistle not to company with fornicators:

10Yet not altogether with the fornicators of this world, or with the covetous, or extortioners, or with idolaters; for then must ye needs go out of the world.

11But now I have written unto you not to keep company, if any man that is called a brother be a fornicator, or covetous, or an idolater, or a railer, or a drunkard, or an extortioner; with such an one no not to eat.

New International

very hour we go hungry and thirsty, we are in rags, we are brutally treated, we are homeless. 12We work hard with our own hands. When we are cursed, we bless; when we are persecuted, we endure it; 13when we are slandered, we answer kindly. Up to this moment we have become the scum of the earth, the refuse of the world.

14I am not writing this to shame you, but to warn you, as my dear children. 15Even though you have ten thousand guardians in Christ, you do not have many fathers, for in Christ Jesus I became your father through the gospel. 16Therefore I urge you to imitate me. 17For this reason I am sending to you Timothy, my son whom I love, who is faithful in the Lord. He will remind you of my way of life in Christ Jesus, which agrees with what I teach everywhere in every church.

18Some of you have become arrogant, as if I were not coming to you. 19But I will come to you very soon, if the Lord is willing, and then I will find out not only how these arrogant people are talking, but what power they have. 20For the kingdom of God is not a matter of talk but of power. 21What do you prefer? Shall I come to you with a whip, or in love and with a gentle spirit?

Expel the Immoral Brother!

5 IT IS actually reported that there is sexual immorality among you, and of a kind that does not occur even among pagans: A man has his father's wife. 2And you are proud! Shouldn't you rather have been filled with grief and have put out of your fellowship the man who did this? 3Even though I am not physically present, I am with you in spirit. And I have already passed judgment on the one who did this, just as if I were present. 4When you are assembled in the name of our Lord Jesus and I am with you in spirit, and the power of our Lord Jesus is present, 5hand this man over to Satan, so that the sinful nature[a] may be destroyed and his spirit saved on the day of the Lord.

6Your boasting is not good. Don't you know that a little yeast works through the whole batch of dough? 7Get rid of the old yeast that you may be a new batch without yeast—as you really are. For Christ, our Passover lamb, has been sacrificed. 8Therefore let us keep the Festival, not with the old yeast, the yeast of malice and wickedness, but with bread without yeast, the bread of sincerity and truth.

9I have written you in my letter not to associate with sexually immoral people— 10not at all meaning the people of this world who are immoral, or the greedy and swindlers, or idolaters. In that case you would have to leave this world. 11But now I am writing you that you must not associate with anyone who calls himself a brother but is sexually immoral or greedy, an idolater or a slanderer, a drunkard or a swindler. With such a man do not even eat.

---

a 5 Or *that his body*; or *that the flesh*

Living Bible

hungry and thirsty, without even enough clothes to keep us warm. We have been kicked around without homes of our own. 12We have worked wearily with our hands to earn our living. We have blessed those who cursed us. We have been patient with those who injured us. 13We have replied quietly when evil things have been said about us. Yet right up to the present moment we are like dirt under foot, like garbage.

14I am not writing about these things to make you ashamed, but to warn and counsel you as beloved children. 15For although you may have ten thousand others to teach you about Christ, remember that you have only me as your father. For I was the one who brought you to Christ when I preached the Gospel to you. 16So I beg you to follow my example, and do as I do.

17That is the very reason why I am sending Timothy—to help you do this. For he is one of those I won to Christ, a beloved and trustworthy child in the Lord. He will remind you of what I teach in all the churches wherever I go.

18I know that some of you will have become proud, thinking that I am afraid to come to deal with you. 19But I will come, and soon, if the Lord will let me, and then I'll find out whether these proud men are just big talkers or whether they really have God's power. 20The Kingdom of God is not just talking; it is living by God's power. 21Which do you choose? Shall I come with punishment and scolding, or shall I come with quiet love and gentleness?

5 EVERYONE IS talking about the terrible thing that has happened there among you, something so evil that even the heathen don't do it: you have a man in your church who is living in sin with his father's wife.b 2And are you still so conceited, so "spiritual"? Why aren't you mourning in sorrow and shame, and seeing to it that this man is removed from your membership?

3, 4Although I am not there with you, I have been thinking a lot about this, and in the name of the Lord Jesus Christ I have already decided what to do, just as though I were there. You are to call a meeting of the church—and the power of the Lord Jesus will be with you as you meet, and I will be there in spirit— 5and cast out this man from the fellowship of the church and into Satan's hands, to punish him, in the hope that his soul will be saved when our Lord Jesus Christ returns.

6What a terrible thing it is that you are boasting about your purity, and yet you let this sort of thing go on. Don't you realize that if even one person is allowed to go on sinning, soon all will be affected? 7Remove this evil cancer—this wicked person—from among you, so that you can stay pure. Christ, God's Lamb, has been slain for us. 8So let us feast upon him and grow strong in the Christian life, leaving entirely behind us the cancerous old life with all its hatreds and wickedness. Let us feast instead upon the pure bread of honor and sincerity and truth.

9When I wrote to you before I said not to mix with evil people. 10But when I said that I wasn't talking about unbelievers who live in sexual sin, or are greedy cheats and thieves and idol worshipers. For you can't live in this world without being with people like that. 11What I meant was that you are not to keep company with anyone who claims to be a brother Christian but indulges in sexual sins, or is greedy, or is a swindler, or worships idols, or is a drunkard, or abusive. Don't even eat lunch with such a person.

New Revised Standard

thirsty, we are poorly clothed and beaten and homeless, 12and we grow weary from the work of our own hands. When reviled, we bless; when persecuted, we endure; 13when slandered, we speak kindly. We have become like the rubbish of the world, the dregs of all things, to this very day.

Fatherly Admonition

14 I am not writing this to make you ashamed, but to admonish you as my beloved children. 15For though you might have ten thousand guardians in Christ, you do not have many fathers. Indeed, in Christ Jesus I became your father through the gospel. 16I appeal to you, then, be imitators of me. 17For this reason I sentc you Timothy, who is my beloved and faithful child in the Lord, to remind you of my ways in Christ Jesus, as I teach them everywhere in every church. 18But some of you, thinking that I am not coming to you, have become arrogant. 19But I will come to you soon, if the Lord wills, and I will find out not the talk of these arrogant people but their power. 20For the kingdom of God depends not on talk but on power. 21What would you prefer? Am I to come to you with a stick, or with love in a spirit of gentleness?

Sexual Immorality Defiles the Church

5 IT IS actually reported that there is sexual immorality among you, and of a kind that is not found even among pagans; for a man is living with his father's wife. 2And you are arrogant! Should you not rather have mourned, so that he who has done this would have been removed from among you?

3 For though absent in body, I am present in spirit; and as if present I have already pronounced judgment 4in the name of the Lord Jesus on the man who has done such a thing.d When you are assembled, and my spirit is present with the power of our Lord Jesus, 5you are to hand this man over to Satan for the destruction of the flesh, so that his spirit may be saved in the day of the Lord.e

6 Your boasting is not a good thing. Do you not know that a little yeast leavens the whole batch of dough? 7Clean out the old yeast so that you may be a new batch, as you really are unleavened. For our paschal lamb, Christ, has been sacrificed. 8Therefore, let us celebrate the festival, not with the old yeast, the yeast of malice and evil, but with the unleavened bread of sincerity and truth.

Sexual Immorality Must Be Judged

9 I wrote to you in my letter not to associate with sexually immoral persons— 10not at all meaning the immoral of this world, or the greedy and robbers, or idolaters, since you would then need to go out of the world. 11But now I am writing to you not to associate with anyone who bears the name of brother or sisterf who is sexually immoral or greedy, or is an idolater, reviler, drunkard, or robber. Do not even eat with such a one. 12For what have I to do with judging those out-

---

c Or *am sending*   d Or *on the man who has done such a thing in the name of the Lord Jesus*   e Other ancient authorities add *Jesus*   f Gk *brother*

King James

12For what have I to do to judge them also that are without? do not ye judge them that are within? 13But them that are without God judgeth. Therefore put away from among yourselves that wicked person.

6 DARE ANY of you, having a matter against another, go to law before the unjust, and not before the saints? 2Do ye not know that the saints shall judge the world? and if the world shall be judged by you, are ye unworthy to judge the smallest matters? 3Know ye not that we shall judge angels? how much more things that pertain to this life? 4If then ye have judgments of things pertaining to this life, set them to judge who are least esteemed in the church. 5I speak to your shame. Is it so, that there is not a wise man among you? no, not one that shall be able to judge between his brethren? 6But brother goeth to law with brother, and that before the unbelievers. 7Now therefore there is utterly a fault among you, because ye go to law one with another. Why do ye not rather take wrong? why do ye not rather *suffer yourselves to* be defrauded? 8Nay, ye do wrong, and defraud, and that *your* brethren. 9Know ye not that the unrighteous shall not inherit the kingdom of God? Be not deceived: neither fornicators, nor idolaters, nor adulterers, nor effeminate, nor abusers of themselves with mankind, 10Nor thieves, nor covetous, nor drunkards, nor revilers, nor extortioners, shall inherit the kingdom of God. 11And such were some of you: but ye are washed, but ye are sanctified, but ye are justified in the name of the Lord Jesus, and by the Spirit of our God. 12All things are lawful unto me, but all things are not expedient: all things are lawful for me, but I will not be brought under the power of any. 13Meats for the belly, and the belly for meats: but God shall destroy both it and them. Now the body *is* not for fornication, but for the Lord; and the Lord for the body. 14And God hath both raised up the Lord, and will also raise up us by his own power. 15Know ye not that your bodies are the members of Christ? shall I then take the members of Christ, and make *them* the members of an harlot? God forbid. 16What? know ye not that he which is joined to an harlot is one body? for two, saith he, shall be one flesh. 17But he that is joined unto the Lord is one spirit. 18Flee fornication. Every sin that a man doeth is without the body; but he that committeth fornication sinneth against his own body.

New International

12What business is it of mine to judge those outside the church? Are you not to judge those inside? 13God will judge those outside. "Expel the wicked man from among you."[a]

Lawsuits Among Believers

6 IF ANY of you has a dispute with another, dare he take it before the ungodly for judgment instead of before the saints? 2Do you not know that the saints will judge the world? And if you are to judge the world, are you not competent to judge trivial cases? 3Do you not know that we will judge angels? How much more the things of this life! 4Therefore, if you have disputes about such matters, appoint as judges even men of little account in the church![b] 5I say this to shame you. Is it possible that there is nobody among you wise enough to judge a dispute between believers? 6But instead, one brother goes to law against another—and this in front of unbelievers!

7The very fact that you have lawsuits among you means you have been completely defeated already. Why not rather be wronged? Why not rather be cheated? 8Instead, you yourselves cheat and do wrong, and you do this to your brothers.

9Do you not know that the wicked will not inherit the kingdom of God? Do not be deceived: Neither the sexually immoral nor idolaters nor adulterers nor male prostitutes nor homosexual offenders 10nor thieves nor the greedy nor drunkards nor slanderers nor swindlers will inherit the kingdom of God. 11And that is what some of you were. But you were washed, you were sanctified, you were justified in the name of the Lord Jesus Christ and by the Spirit of our God.

Sexual Immorality

12"Everything is permissible for me"—but not everything is beneficial. "Everything is permissible for me"—but I will not be mastered by anything. 13"Food for the stomach and the stomach for food"—but God will destroy them both. The body is not meant for sexual immorality, but for the Lord, and the Lord for the body. 14By his power God raised the Lord from the dead, and he will raise us also. 15Do you not know that your bodies are members of Christ himself? Shall I then take the members of Christ and unite them with a prostitute? Never! 16Do you not know that he who unites himself with a prostitute is one with her in body? For it is said, "The two will become one flesh."[c] 17But he who unites himself with the Lord is one with him in spirit.

18Flee from sexual immorality. All other sins a man commits are outside his body, but he who sins sexually sins against his own body. 19Do you not know that your

a *13* Deut. 17:7; 19:19; 21:21; 22:21,24; 24:7   b *4* Or *matters, do you appoint as judges men of little account in the church?*   c *16* Gen. 2:24

Living Bible

12It isn't our job to judge outsiders. But it certainly is our job to judge and deal strongly with those who are members of the church, and who are sinning in these ways. 13God alone is the Judge of those on the outside. But you yourselves must deal with this man and put him out of your church.

6 HOW IS it that when you have something against another Christian, you "go to law" and ask a heathen court to decide the matter instead of taking it to other Christians to decide which of you is right? 2Don't you know that some day we Christians are going to judge and govern the world? So why can't you decide even these little things among yourselves? 3Don't you realize that we Christians will judge and reward the very angels in heaven? So you should be able to decide your problems down here on earth easily enough. 4Why then go to outside judges who are not even Christians?d 5I am trying to make you ashamed. Isn't there anyone in all the church who is wise enough to decide these arguments? 6But, instead, one Christian sues another and accuses his Christian brother in front of unbelievers.

7To have such lawsuits at all is a real defeat for you as Christians. Why not just accept mistreatment and leave it at that? It would be far more honoring to the Lord to let yourselves be cheated. 8But, instead, you yourselves are the ones who do wrong, cheating others, even your own brothers.

9, 10Don't you know that those doing such things have no share in the Kingdom of God? Don't fool yourselves. Those who live immoral lives, who are idol worshipers, adulterers or homosexuals—will have no share in his Kingdom. Neither will thieves or greedy people, drunkards, slanderers, or robbers. 11There was a time when some of you were just like that but now your sins are washed away, and you are set apart for God, and he has accepted you because of what the Lord Jesus Christ and the Spirit of our God have done for you.

12I can do anything I want to if Christ has not said no,e but some of these things aren't good for me. Even if I am allowed to do them, I'll refuse to if I think they might get such a grip on me that I can't easily stop when I want to. 13For instance, take the matter of eating. God has given us an appetite for food and stomachs to digest it. But that doesn't mean we should eat more than we need. Don't think of eating as important, because some day God will do away with both stomachs and food.

But sexual sin is never right: our bodies were not made for that, but for the Lord, and the Lord wants to fill our bodies with himself. 14And God is going to raise our bodies from the dead by his power just as he raised up the Lord Jesus Christ. 15Don't you realize that your bodies are actually parts and members of Christ? So should I take part of Christ and join him to a prostitute? Never! 16And don't you know that if a man joins himself to a prostitute she becomes a part of him and he becomes a part of her? For God tells us in the Scripture that in his sight the two become one person. 17But if you give yourself to the Lord, you and Christ are joined together as one person.

18That is why I say to run from sex sin. No other sin affects the body as this one does. When you sin this sin it is against your own body. 19Haven't you yet learned

New Revised Standard

side? Is it not those who are inside that you are to judge? 13God will judge those outside. "Drive out the wicked person from among you."

Lawsuits among Believers

6 WHEN ANY of you has a grievance against another, do you dare to take it to court before the unrighteous, instead of taking it before the saints? 2Do you not know that the saints will judge the world? And if the world is to be judged by you, are you incompetent to try trivial cases? 3Do you not know that we are to judge angels—to say nothing of ordinary matters? 4If you have ordinary cases, then, do you appoint as judges those who have no standing in the church? 5I say this to your shame. Can it be that there is no one among you wise enough to decide between one believerf and another, 6but a believerf goes to court against a believerf— and before unbelievers at that?

7 In fact, to have lawsuits at all with one another is already a defeat for you. Why not rather be wronged? Why not rather be defrauded? 8But you yourselves wrong and defraud—and believersg at that.

9 Do you not know that wrongdoers will not inherit the kingdom of God? Do not be deceived! Fornicators, idolaters, adulterers, male prostitutes, sodomites, 10thieves, the greedy, drunkards, revilers, robbers— none of these will inherit the kingdom of God. 11And this is what some of you used to be. But you were washed, you were sanctified, you were justified in the name of the Lord Jesus Christ and in the Spirit of our God.

Glorify God in Body and Spirit

12 "All things are lawful for me," but not all things are beneficial. "All things are lawful for me," but I will not be dominated by anything. 13"Food is meant for the stomach and the stomach for food,"h and God will destroy both one and the other. The body is meant not for fornication but for the Lord, and the Lord for the body. 14And God raised the Lord and will also raise us by his power. 15Do you not know that your bodies are members of Christ? Should I therefore take the members of Christ and make them members of a prostitute? Never! 16Do you not know that whoever is united to a prostitute becomes one body with her? For it is said, "The two shall be one flesh." 17But anyone united to the Lord becomes one spirit with him. 18Shun fornication! Every sin that a person commits is outside the body; but the fornicator sins against the body itself. 19Or do you not

---

d 6:4 Why then go to outside judges who are not even Christians? Or, "Even the least capable people in the church should be able to decide these things for you." Both interpretations are possible.   e 6:12 I can do anything I want to if Christ has not said no, literally, "All things are lawful for me." Obviously, Paul is not here permitting sins such as just have been expressly prohibited in vss 9, 10. He is apparently quoting some in the church of lustful Corinth who were excusing their sins.

f Gk brother   g Gk brothers   h The quotation may extend to the word other

King James

19What? know ye not that your body is the temple of the Holy Ghost *which is* in you, which ye have of God, and ye are not your own?

20For ye are bought with a price: therefore glorify God in your body, and in your spirit, which are God's.

7 NOW CONCERNING the things whereof ye wrote unto me: *It is* good for a man not to touch a woman.

2Nevertheless, *to avoid* fornication, let every man have his own wife, and let every woman have her own husband.

3Let the husband render unto the wife due benevolence: and likewise also the wife unto the husband.

4The wife hath not power of her own body, but the husband: and likewise also the husband hath not power of his own body, but the wife.

5Defraud ye not one the other, except *it be* with consent for a time, that ye may give yourselves to fasting and prayer; and come together again, that Satan tempt you not for your incontinency.

6But I speak this by permission, *and* not of commandment.

7For I would that all men were even as I myself. But every man hath his proper gift of God, one after this manner, and another after that.

8I say therefore to the unmarried and widows, It is good for them if they abide even as I.

9But if they cannot contain, let them marry: for it is better to marry than to burn.

10And unto the married I command, *yet* not I, but the Lord, Let not the wife depart from *her* husband:

11But and if she depart, let her remain unmarried, or be reconciled to *her* husband: and let not the husband put away *his* wife.

12But to the rest speak I, not the Lord: If any brother hath a wife that believeth not, and she be pleased to dwell with him, let him not put her away.

13And the woman which hath an husband that believeth not, and if he be pleased to dwell with her, let her not leave him.

14For the unbelieving husband is sanctified by the wife, and the unbelieving wife is sanctified by the husband: else were your children unclean; but now are they holy.

15But if the unbelieving depart, let him depart. A brother or a sister is not under bondage in such *cases:* but God hath called us to peace.

16For what knowest thou, O wife, whether thou shalt save *thy* husband? or how knowest thou, O man, whether thou shalt save *thy* wife?

17But as God hath distributed to every man, as the Lord hath called every one, so let him walk. And so ordain I in all churches.

18Is any man called being circumcised? let him not become uncircumcised. Is any called in uncircumcision? let him not be circumcised.

New International

body is a temple of the Holy Spirit, who is in you, whom you have received from God? You are not your own; 20you were bought at a price. Therefore honor God with your body.

Marriage

7 NOW FOR the matters you wrote about: It is good for a man not to marry.[a] 2But since there is so much immorality, each man should have his own wife, and each woman her own husband. 3The husband should fulfill his marital duty to his wife, and likewise the wife to her husband. 4The wife's body does not belong to her alone but also to her husband. In the same way, the husband's body does not belong to him alone but also to his wife. 5Do not deprive each other except by mutual consent and for a time, so that you may devote yourselves to prayer. Then come together again so that Satan will not tempt you because of your lack of self-control. 6I say this as a concession, not as a command. 7I wish that all men were as I am. But each man has his own gift from God; one has this gift, another has that.

8Now to the unmarried and the widows I say: It is good for them to stay unmarried, as I am. 9But if they cannot control themselves, they should marry, for it is better to marry than to burn with passion.

10To the married I give this command (not I, but the Lord): A wife must not separate from her husband. 11But if she does, she must remain unmarried or else be reconciled to her husband. And a husband must not divorce his wife.

12To the rest I say this (I, not the Lord): If any brother has a wife who is not a believer and she is willing to live with him, he must not divorce her. 13And if a woman has a husband who is not a believer and he is willing to live with her, she must not divorce him. 14For the unbelieving husband has been sanctified through his wife, and the unbelieving wife has been sanctified through her believing husband. Otherwise your children would be unclean, but as it is, they are holy.

15But if the unbeliever leaves, let him do so. A believing man or woman is not bound in such circumstances; God has called us to live in peace. 16How do you know, wife, whether you will save your husband? Or, how do you know, husband, whether you will save your wife?

17Nevertheless, each one should retain the place in life that the Lord assigned to him and to which God has called him. This is the rule I lay down in all the churches. 18Was a man already circumcised when he was called? He should not become uncircumcised. Was a man uncircumcised when he was called? He should not be circumcised. 19Circumcision is nothing and uncir-

---

a *1* Or *"It is good for a man not to have sexual relations with a woman."*

Living Bible

that your body is the home of the Holy Spirit God gave you, and that he lives within you? Your own body does not belong to you. 20For God has bought you with a great price. So use every part of your body to give glory back to God, because he owns it.

7 NOW ABOUT those questions you asked in your last letter: my answer is that if you do not marry, it is good. 2But usually it is best to be married, each man having his own wife, and each woman having her own husband, because otherwise you might fall back into sin.

3The man should give his wife all that is her right as a married woman, and the wife should do the same for her husband; 4for a girl who marries no longer has full right to her own body, for her husband then has his rights to it, too; and in the same way the husband no longer has full right to his own body, for it belongs also to his wife. 5So do not refuse these rights to each other. The only exception to this rule would be the agreement of both husband and wife to refrain from the rights of marriage for a limited time, so that they can give themselves more completely to prayer. Afterwards, they should come together again so that Satan won't be able to tempt them because of their lack of self-control.

6I'm not saying you *must* marry; but you certainly *may* if you wish. 7I wish everyone could get along without marrying, just as I do. But we are not all the same. God gives some the gift of a husband or wife, and others he gives the gift of being able to stay happily unmarried. 8So I say to those who aren't married, and to widows—better to stay unmarried if you can, just as I am. 9But if you can't control yourselves, go ahead and marry. It is better to marry than to burn with lust.

10Now, for those who are married I have a command, not just a suggestion. And it is not a command from me, for this is what the Lord himself has said: A wife must not leave her husband. 11But if she is separated from him, let her remain single or else go back to him. And the husband must not divorce his wife.

12Here I want to add some suggestions of my own. These are not direct commands from the Lord, but they seem right to me: If a Christian has a wife who is not a Christian, but she wants to stay with him anyway, he must not leave her or divorce her. 13And if a Christian woman has a husband who isn't a Christian, and he wants her to stay with him, she must not leave him. 14For perhaps the husband who isn't a Christian may become a Christian with the help of his Christian wife. And the wife who isn't a Christian may become a Christian with the help of her Christian husband. Otherwise, if the family separates, the children might never come to know the Lord; whereas a united family may, in God's plan, result in the children's salvation.

15But if the husband or wife who isn't a Christian is eager to leave, it is permitted. In such cases the Christian husband or wife should not insist that the other stay, for God wants his children to live in peace and harmony. 16For, after all, there is no assurance to you wives that your husbands will be converted if they stay; and the same may be said to you husbands concerning your wives.

17But be sure in deciding these matters that you are living as God intended, marrying or not marrying in accordance with God's direction and help, and accepting whatever situation God has put you into. This is my rule for all the churches.

18For instance, a man who already has gone through the Jewish ceremony of circumcision before he became a Christian shouldn't worry about it; and if he hasn't been circumcised, he shouldn't do it now. 19For it

New Revised Standard

know that your body is a temple[b] of the Holy Spirit within you, which you have from God, and that you are not your own? 20For you were bought with a price; therefore glorify God in your body.

Directions concerning Marriage

7 NOW CONCERNING the matters about which you wrote: "It is well for a man not to touch a woman." 2But because of cases of sexual immorality, each man should have his own wife and each woman her own husband. 3The husband should give to his wife her conjugal rights, and likewise the wife to her husband. 4For the wife does not have authority over her own body, but the husband does; likewise the husband does not have authority over his own body, but the wife does. 5Do not deprive one another except perhaps by agreement for a set time, to devote yourselves to prayer, and then come together again, so that Satan may not tempt you because of your lack of self-control. 6This I say by way of concession, not of command. 7I wish that all were as I myself am. But each has a particular gift from God, one having one kind and another a different kind.

8 To the unmarried and the widows I say that it is well for them to remain unmarried as I am. 9But if they are not practicing self-control, they should marry. For it is better to marry than to be aflame with passion.

10 To the married I give this command—not I but the Lord—that the wife should not separate from her husband 11(but if she does separate, let her remain unmarried or else be reconciled to her husband), and that the husband should not divorce his wife.

12 To the rest I say—I and not the Lord—that if any believer[c] has a wife who is an unbeliever, and she consents to live with him, he should not divorce her. 13And if any woman has a husband who is an unbeliever, and he consents to live with her, she should not divorce him. 14For the unbelieving husband is made holy through his wife, and the unbelieving wife is made holy through her husband. Otherwise, your children would be unclean, but as it is, they are holy. 15But if the unbelieving partner separates, let it be so; in such a case the brother or sister is not bound. It is to peace that God has called you.[d] 16Wife, for all you know, you might save your husband. Husband, for all you know, you might save your wife.

The Life That the Lord Has Assigned

17 However that may be, let each of you lead the life that the Lord has assigned, to which God called you. This is my rule in all the churches. 18Was anyone at the time of his call already circumcised? Let him not seek to remove the marks of circumcision. Was anyone at the time of his call uncircumcised? Let him not seek circumcision. 19Circumcision is nothing, and uncircumcision

b Or *sanctuary*   c Gk *brother*   d Other ancient authorities read *us*

King James

19Circumcision is nothing, and uncircumcision is nothing, but the keeping of the commandments of God.

20Let every man abide in the same calling wherein he was called.

21Art thou called *being* a servant? care not for it: but if thou mayest be made free, use *it* rather.

22For he that is called in the Lord, *being* a servant, is the Lord's freeman: likewise also he that is called, *being* free, is Christ's servant.

23Ye are bought with a price; be not ye the servants of men.

24Brethren, let every man, wherein he is called, therein abide with God.

25Now concerning virgins I have no commandment of the Lord: yet I give my judgment, as one that hath obtained mercy of the Lord to be faithful.

26I suppose therefore that this is good for the present distress, *I say*, that *it is* good for a man so to be.

27Art thou bound unto a wife? seek not to be loosed. Art thou loosed from a wife? seek not a wife.

28But and if thou marry, thou hast not sinned; and if a virgin marry, she hath not sinned. Nevertheless such shall have trouble in the flesh: but I spare you.

29But this I say, brethren, the time *is* short: it remaineth, that both they that have wives be as though they had none;

30And they that weep, as though they wept not; and they that rejoice, as though they rejoiced not; and they that buy, as though they possessed not;

31And they that use this world, as not abusing *it:* for the fashion of this world passeth away.

32But I would have you without carefulness. He that is unmarried careth for the things that belong to the Lord, how he may please the Lord:

33But he that is married careth for the things that are of the world, how he may please *his* wife.

34There is difference *also* between a wife and a virgin. The unmarried woman careth for the things of the Lord, that she may be holy both in body and in spirit: but she that is married careth for the things of the world, how she may please *her* husband.

35And this I speak for your own profit; not that I may cast a snare upon you, but for that which is comely, and that ye may attend upon the Lord without distraction.

36But if any man think that he behaveth himself uncomely toward his virgin, if she pass the flower of *her* age, and need so require, let him do what he will, he sinneth not: let them marry.

37Nevertheless he that standeth stedfast in his heart, having no necessity, but hath power over his own will, and hath so decreed in his heart that he will keep his virgin, doeth well.

38So then he that giveth *her* in marriage doeth well; but he that giveth *her* not in marriage doeth better.

39The wife is bound by the law as long as her husband liveth; but if her husband be dead, she is at liberty to be married to whom she will; only in the Lord.

40But she is happier if she so abide, after my judgment: and I think also that I have the Spirit of God.

New International

cumcision is nothing. Keeping God's commands is what counts. 20Each one should remain in the situation which he was in when God called him. 21Were you a slave when you were called? Don't let it trouble you—although if you can gain your freedom, do so. 22For he who was a slave when he was called by the Lord is the Lord's freedman; similarly, he who was a free man when he was called is Christ's slave. 23You were bought at a price; do not become slaves of men. 24Brothers, each man, as responsible to God, should remain in the situation God called him to.

25Now about virgins: I have no command from the Lord, but I give a judgment as one who by the Lord's mercy is trustworthy. 26Because of the present crisis, I think that it is good for you to remain as you are. 27Are you married? Do not seek a divorce. Are you unmarried? Do not look for a wife. 28But if you do marry, you have not sinned; and if a virgin marries, she has not sinned. But those who marry will face many troubles in this life, and I want to spare you this.

29What I mean, brothers, is that the time is short. From now on those who have wives should live as if they had none; 30those who mourn, as if they did not; those who are happy, as if they were not; those who buy something, as if it were not theirs to keep; 31those who use the things of the world, as if not engrossed in them. For this world in its present form is passing away.

32I would like you to be free from concern. An unmarried man is concerned about the Lord's affairs—how he can please the Lord. 33But a married man is concerned about the affairs of this world—how he can please his wife— 34and his interests are divided. An unmarried woman or virgin is concerned about the Lord's affairs: Her aim is to be devoted to the Lord in both body and spirit. But a married woman is concerned about the affairs of this world—how she can please her husband. 35I am saying this for your own good, not to restrict you, but that you may live in a right way in undivided devotion to the Lord.

36If anyone thinks he is acting improperly toward the virgin he is engaged to, and if she is getting along in years and he feels he ought to marry, he should do as he wants. He is not sinning. They should get married. 37But the man who has settled the matter in his own mind, who is under no compulsion but has control over his own will, and who has made up his mind not to marry the virgin—this man also does the right thing. 38So then, he who marries the virgin does right, but he who does not marry her does even better.a

39A woman is bound to her husband as long as he lives. But if her husband dies, she is free to marry anyone she wishes, but he must belong to the Lord. 40In my judgment, she is happier if she stays as she is—and I think that I too have the Spirit of God.

---

a 36-38 Or 36*If anyone thinks he is not treating his daughter properly, and if she is getting along in years, and he feels she ought to marry, he should do as he wants. He is not sinning. He should let her get married.* 37*But the man who has settled the matter in his own mind, who is under no compulsion but has control over his own will, and who has made up his mind to keep the virgin unmarried—this man also does the right thing.* 38*So then, he who gives his virgin in marriage does right, but he who does not give her in marriage does even better.*

Living Bible

doesn't make any difference at all whether a Christian has gone through this ceremony or not. But it makes a lot of difference whether he is pleasing God and keeping God's commandments. That is the important thing.

20Usually a person should keep on with the work he was doing when God called him. 21Are you a slave? Don't let that worry you—but of course, if you get a chance to be free, take it. 22If the Lord calls you, and you are a slave, remember that Christ has set you free from the awful power of sin; and if he has called you and you are free, remember that you are now a slave of Christ. 23You have been bought and paid for by Christ, so you belong to him—be free now from all these earthly prides and fears.b 24So, dear brothers, whatever situation a person is in when he becomes a Christian, let him stay there, for now the Lord is there to help him.

25Now I will try to answer your other question. What about girls who are not yet married? Should they be permitted to do so? In answer to this question, I have no special command for them from the Lord. But the Lord in his kindness has given me wisdom that can be trusted, and I will be glad to tell you what I think.

26Here is the problem: We Christians are facing great dangers to our lives at present. In times like these I think it is best for a person to remain unmarried. 27Of course, if you already are married, don't separate because of this. But if you aren't, don't rush into it at this time. 28But if you men decide to go ahead anyway and get married now, it is all right; and if a girl gets married in times like these, it is no sin. However, marriage will bring extra problems that I wish you didn't have to face right now.

29The important thing to remember is that our remaining time is very short, [and so are our opportunities for doing the Lord's workc]. For that reason those who have wives should stay as free as possible for the Lord;d 30happiness or sadness or wealth should not keep anyone from doing God's work. 31Those in frequent contact with the exciting things the world offers should make good use of their opportunities without stopping to enjoy them; for the world in its present form will soon be gone.

32In all you do, I want you to be free from worry. An unmarried man can spend his time doing the Lord's work and thinking how to please him. 33But a married man can't do that so well; he has to think about his earthly responsibilities and how to please his wife. 34His interests are divided. It is the same with a girl who marries. She faces the same problem. A girl who is not married is anxious to please the Lord in all she is and does.e But a married woman must consider other things such as housekeeping and the likes and dislikes of her husband.

35I am saying this to help you, not to try to keep you from marrying. I want you to do whatever will help you serve the Lord best, with as few other things as possible to distract your attention from him.

36But if anyone feels he ought to marry because he has trouble controlling his passions, it is all right, it is not a sin; let him marry. 37But if a man has the willpower not to marry and decides that he doesn't need to and won't, he has made a wise decision. 38So the person who marries does well, and the person who doesn't marry does even better.

39The wife is part of her husband as long as he lives; if her husband dies, then she may marry again, but only if she marries a Christian. 40But in my opinion she will be happier if she doesn't marry again; and I think I am giving you counsel from God's Spirit when I say this.

New Revised Standard

is nothing; but obeying the commandments of God is everything. 20Let each of you remain in the condition in which you were called.

21 Were you a slave when called? Do not be concerned about it. Even if you can gain your freedom, make use of your present condition now more than ever.f 22For whoever was called in the Lord as a slave is a freed person belonging to the Lord, just as whoever was free when called is a slave of Christ. 23You were bought with a price; do not become slaves of human masters. 24In whatever condition you were called, brothers and sisters,g there remain with God.

The Unmarried and the Widows

25 Now concerning virgins, I have no command of the Lord, but I give my opinion as one who by the Lord's mercy is trustworthy. 26I think that, in view of the impendingh crisis, it is well for you to remain as you are. 27Are you bound to a wife? Do not seek to be free. Are you free from a wife? Do not seek a wife. 28But if you marry, you do not sin, and if a virgin marries, she does not sin. Yet those who marry will experience distress in this life,i and I would spare you that. 29I mean, brothers and sisters,g the appointed time has grown short; from now on, let even those who have wives be as though they had none, 30and those who mourn as though they were not mourning, and those who rejoice as though they were not rejoicing, and those who buy as though they had no possessions, 31and those who deal with the world as though they had no dealings with it. For the present form of this world is passing away.

32 I want you to be free from anxieties. The unmarried man is anxious about the affairs of the Lord, how to please the Lord; 33but the married man is anxious about the affairs of the world, how to please his wife, 34and his interests are divided. And the unmarried woman and the virgin are anxious about the affairs of the Lord, so that they may be holy in body and spirit; but the married woman is anxious about the affairs of the world, how to please her husband. 35I say this for your own benefit, not to put any restraint upon you, but to promote good order and unhindered devotion to the Lord.

36 If anyone thinks that he is not behaving properly toward his fiancée,j if his passions are strong, and so it has to be, let him marry as he wishes; it is no sin. Let them marry. 37But if someone stands firm in his resolve, being under no necessity but having his own desire under control, and has determined in his own mind to keep her as his fiancée,j he will do well. 38So then, he who marries his fiancéej does well; and he who refrains from marriage will do better.

39 A wife is bound as long as her husband lives. But if the husband dies,k she is free to marry anyone she wishes, only in the Lord. 40But in my judgment she is more blessed if she remains as she is. And I think that I too have the Spirit of God.

---

b 7:23 *be free now from all these earthly prides and fears,* literally, "Become not bondservants of men." c 7:29 *and so are our opportunities for doing the Lord's work,* implied. d 7:29 *those who have wives should stay as free as possible for the Lord,* literally, "[that] those who have wives may be as though they didn't." e 7:34 *in all she is and does,* literally, "pure in body and in spirit."

f Or *avail yourself of the opportunity* g Gk *brothers* h Or *present* i Gk in *the flesh* j Gk *virgin* k Gk *falls asleep*

King James

8 NOW AS touching things offered unto idols, we know that we all have knowledge. Knowledge puffeth up, but charity edifieth.

2And if any man think that he knoweth any thing, he knoweth nothing yet as he ought to know.

3But if any man love God, the same is known of him.

4As concerning therefore the eating of those things that are offered in sacrifice unto idols, we know that an idol *is* nothing in the world, and that *there is* none other God but one.

5For though there be that are called gods, whether in heaven or in earth, (as there be gods many, and lords many,)

6But to us *there is but* one God, the Father, of whom *are* all things, and we in him; and one Lord Jesus Christ, by whom *are* all things, and we by him.

7Howbeit *there is* not in every man that knowledge: for some with conscience of the idol unto this hour eat *it* as a thing offered unto an idol; and their conscience being weak is defiled.

8But meat commendeth us not to God: for neither, if we eat, are we the better; neither, if we eat not, are we the worse.

9But take heed lest by any means this liberty of yours become a stumblingblock to them that are weak.

10For if any man see thee which hast knowledge sit at meat in the idol's temple, shall not the conscience of him which is weak be emboldened to eat those things which are offered to idols;

11And through thy knowledge shall the weak brother perish, for whom Christ died?

12But when ye sin so against the brethren, and wound their weak conscience, ye sin against Christ.

13Wherefore, if meat make my brother to offend, I will eat no flesh while the world standeth, lest I make my brother to offend.

9 AM I not an apostle? am I not free? have I not seen Jesus Christ our Lord? are not ye my work in the Lord?

2If I be not an apostle unto others, yet doubtless I am to you: for the seal of mine apostleship are ye in the Lord.

3Mine answer to them that do examine me is this,

4Have we not power to eat and to drink?

5Have we not power to lead about a sister, a wife, as well as other apostles, and *as* the brethren of the Lord, and Cephas?

6Or I only and Barnabas, have not we power to forbear working?

7Who goeth a warfare any time at his own charges? who planteth a vineyard, and eateth not of the fruit thereof? or who feedeth a flock, and eateth not of the milk of the flock?

8Say I these things as a man? or saith not the law the same also?

9For it is written in the law of Moses, Thou shalt not muzzle the mouth of the ox that treadeth out the corn. Doth God take care for oxen?

New International

Food Sacrificed to Idols

8 NOW ABOUT food sacrificed to idols: We know that we all possess knowledge.a Knowledge puffs up, but love builds up. 2The man who thinks he knows something does not yet know as he ought to know. 3But the man who loves God is known by God.

4So then, about eating food sacrificed to idols: We know that an idol is nothing at all in the world and that there is no God but one. 5For even if there are so-called gods, whether in heaven or on earth (as indeed there are many "gods" and many "lords"), 6yet for us there is but one God, the Father, from whom all things came and for whom we live; and there is but one Lord, Jesus Christ, through whom all things came and through whom we live.

7But not everyone knows this. Some people are still so accustomed to idols that when they eat such food they think of it as having been sacrificed to an idol, and since their conscience is weak, it is defiled. 8But food does not bring us near to God; we are no worse if we do not eat, and no better if we do.

9Be careful, however, that the exercise of your freedom does not become a stumbling block to the weak. 10For if anyone with a weak conscience sees you who have this knowledge eating in an idol's temple, won't he be emboldened to eat what has been sacrificed to idols? 11So this weak brother, for whom Christ died, is destroyed by your knowledge. 12When you sin against your brothers in this way and wound their weak conscience, you sin against Christ. 13Therefore, if what I eat causes my brother to fall into sin, I will never eat meat again, so that I will not cause him to fall.

The Rights of an Apostle

9 AM I not free? Am I not an apostle? Have I not seen Jesus our Lord? Are you not the result of my work in the Lord? 2Even though I may not be an apostle to others, surely I am to you! For you are the seal of my apostleship in the Lord.

3This is my defense to those who sit in judgment on me. 4Don't we have the right to food and drink? 5Don't we have the right to take a believing wife along with us, as do the other apostles and the Lord's brothers and Cephasb? 6Or is it only I and Barnabas who must work for a living?

7Who serves as a soldier at his own expense? Who plants a vineyard and does not eat of its grapes? Who tends a flock and does not drink of the milk? 8Do I say this merely from a human point of view? Doesn't the Law say the same thing? 9For it is written in the Law of Moses: "Do not muzzle an ox while it is treading out the grain."c Is it about oxen that God is concerned? 10Surely

---

a *1 Or "We all possess knowledge," as you say* b *5 That is, Peter*
c *9 Deut. 25:4*

Living Bible

8 NEXT IS your question about eating food that has been sacrificed to idols. On this question everyone feels that only his answer is the right one! But although being a "know-it-all" makes us feel important, what is really needed to build the church is love. 2If anyone thinks he knows all the answers, he is just showing his ignorance. 3But the person who truly loves God is the one who is open to God's knowledge.

4So now, what about it? Should we eat meat that has been sacrificed to idols? Well, we all know that an idol is not really a god, and that there is only one God, and no other. 5According to some people, there are a great many gods, both in heaven and on earth. 6But we know that there is only one God, the Father, who created all thingsd and made us to be his own; and one Lord Jesus Christ, who made everything and gives us life.

7However, some Christians don't realize this. All their lives they have been used to thinking of idols as alive, and have believed that food offered to the idols is really being offered to actual gods. So when they eat such food it bothers them and hurts their tender consciences. 8Just remember that God doesn't care whether we eat it or not. We are no worse off if we don't eat it, and no better off if we do. 9But be careful not to use your freedom to eat it, lest you cause some Christian brother to sin whose consciencee is weaker than yours.

10You see, this is what may happen: Someone who thinks it is wrong to eat this food will see you eating at a temple restaurant, for you know there is no harm in it. Then he will become bold enough to do it too, although all the time he still feels it is wrong. 11So because you "know it is all right to do it," you will be responsible for causing great spiritual damage to a brother with a tender conscience for whom Christ died. 12And it is a sin against Christ to sin against your brother by encouraging him to do something he thinks is wrong. 13So if eating meat offered to idols is going to make my brother sin, I'll not eat any of it as long as I live, because I don't want to do this to him.

9 I AM an apostle, God's messenger, responsible to no mere man. I am one who has actually seen Jesus our Lord with my own eyes. And your changed lives are the result of my hard work for him. 2If in the opinion of others, I am not an apostle, I certainly am to you, for you have been won to Christ through me. 3This is my answer to those who question my rights.

4Or don't I have any rights at all? Can't I claim the same privilege the other apostles have of being a guest in your homes? 5If I had a wife, and iff she were a believer, couldn't I bring her along on these trips just as the other disciples do, and as the Lord's brothers do, and as Peter does? 6And must Barnabas and I alone keep working for our living, while you supply these others? 7What soldier in the army has to pay his own expenses? And have you ever heard of a farmer who harvests his crop and doesn't have the right to eat some of it? What shepherd takes care of a flock of sheep and goats and isn't allowed to drink some of the milk? 8And I'm not merely quoting the opinions of men as to what is right. I'm telling you what God's law says. 9For in the law God gave to Moses he said that you must not put a muzzle on an ox to keep it from eating when it is treading out the wheat. Do you suppose God was thinking only about oxen when he said this? 10Wasn't he also thinking about

New Revised Standard

Food Offered to Idols

8 NOW CONCERNING food sacrificed to idols: we know that "all of us possess knowledge." Knowledge puffs up, but love builds up. 2Anyone who claims to know something does not yet have the necessary knowledge; 3but anyone who loves God is known by him.

4 Hence, as to the eating of food offered to idols, we know that "no idol in the world really exists," and that "there is no God but one." 5Indeed, even though there may be so-called gods in heaven or on earth—as in fact there are many gods and many lords— 6yet for us there is one God, the Father, from whom are all things and for whom we exist, and one Lord, Jesus Christ, through whom are all things and through whom we exist.

7 It is not everyone, however, who has this knowledge. Since some have become so accustomed to idols until now, they still think of the food they eat as food offered to an idol; and their conscience, being weak, is defiled. 8"Food will not bring us close to God."g We are no worse off if we do not eat, and no better off if we do. 9But take care that this liberty of yours does not somehow become a stumbling block to the weak. 10For if others see you, who possess knowledge, eating in the temple of an idol, might they not, since their conscience is weak, be encouraged to the point of eating food sacrificed to idols? 11So by your knowledge those weak believers for whom Christ died are destroyed.h 12But when you thus sin against members of your family,i and wound their conscience when it is weak, you sin against Christ. 13Therefore, if food is a cause of their falling,j I will never eat meat, so that I may not cause one of themk to fall.

The Rights of an Apostle

9 AM I not free? Am I not an apostle? Have I not seen Jesus our Lord? Are you not my work in the Lord? 2If I am not an apostle to others, at least I am to you; for you are the seal of my apostleship in the Lord.

3 This is my defense to those who would examine me. 4Do we not have the right to our food and drink? 5Do we not have the right to be accompanied by a believing wife,l as do the other apostles and the brothers of the Lord and Cephas? 6Or is it only Barnabas and I who have no right to refrain from working for a living? 7Who at any time pays the expenses for doing military service? Who plants a vineyard and does not eat any of its fruit? Or who tends a flock and does not get any of its milk?

8 Do I say this on human authority? Does not the law also say the same? 9For it is written in the law of Moses, "You shall not muzzle an ox while it is treading out the grain." Is it for oxen that God is concerned? 10Or

---

d 8:6 who created all things, literally, "of whom are all things."
e 8:9 conscience, implied. Literally, "faith."   f 9:5 If I had a wife, and if, implied. Literally, "Have we no right to lead about a wife that is a believer?"

g The quotation may extend to the end of the verse   h Gk the weak brother ... is destroyed   i Gk against the brothers   j Gk my brother's falling
k Gk cause my brother   l Gk a sister as wife

King James

10Or saith he *it* altogether for our sakes? For our sakes, no doubt, *this* is written: that he that ploweth should plow in hope; and that he that thresheth in hope should be partaker of his hope.

11If we have sown unto you spiritual things, *is it* a great thing if we shall reap your carnal things?

12If others be partakers of *this* power over you, *are* not we rather? Nevertheless we have not used this power; but suffer all things, lest we should hinder the gospel of Christ.

13Do ye not know that they which minister about holy things live *of the things* of the temple? and they which wait at the altar are partakers with the altar?

14Even so hath the Lord ordained that they which preach the gospel should live of the gospel.

15But I have used none of these things: neither have I written these things, that it should be so done unto me: for *it were* better for me to die, than that any man should make my glorying void.

16For though I preach the gospel, I have nothing to glory of: for necessity is laid upon me; yea, woe is unto me, if I preach not the gospel!

17For if I do this thing willingly, I have a reward: but if against my will, a dispensation *of the gospel* is committed unto me.

18What is my reward then? *Verily* that, when I preach the gospel, I may make the gospel of Christ without charge, that I abuse not my power in the gospel.

19For though I be free from all *men,* yet have I made myself servant unto all, that I might gain the more.

20And unto the Jews I became as a Jew, that I might gain the Jews; to them that are under the law, as under the law, that I might gain them that are under the law;

21To them that are without law, as without law, (being not without law to God, but under the law to Christ,) that I might gain them that are without law.

22To the weak became I as weak, that I might gain the weak: I am made all things to all *men,* that I might by all means save some.

23And this I do for the gospel's sake, that I might be partaker thereof with *you.*

24Know ye not that they which run in a race run all, but one receiveth the prize? So run, that ye may obtain.

25And every man that striveth for the mastery is temperate in all things. Now they *do it* to obtain a corruptible crown; but we an incorruptible.

26I therefore so run, not as uncertainly; so fight I, not as one that beateth the air:

27But I keep under my body, and bring *it* into subjection: lest that by any means, when I have preached to others, I myself should be a castaway.

New International

he says this for us, doesn't he? Yes, this was written for us, because when the plowman plows and the thresher threshes, they ought to do so in the hope of sharing in the harvest. 11If we have sown spiritual seed among you, is it too much if we reap a material harvest from you? 12If others have this right of support from you, shouldn't we have it all the more?

But we did not use this right. On the contrary, we put up with anything rather than hinder the gospel of Christ. 13Don't you know that those who work in the temple get their food from the temple, and those who serve at the altar share in what is offered on the altar? 14In the same way, the Lord has commanded that those who preach the gospel should receive their living from the gospel.

15But I have not used any of these rights. And I am not writing this in the hope that you will do such things for me. I would rather die than have anyone deprive me of this boast. 16Yet when I preach the gospel, I cannot boast, for I am compelled to preach. Woe to me if I do not preach the gospel! 17If I preach voluntarily, I have a reward; if not voluntarily, I am simply discharging the trust committed to me. 18What then is my reward? Just this: that in preaching the gospel I may offer it free of charge, and so not make use of my rights in preaching it.

19Though I am free and belong to no man, I make myself a slave to everyone, to win as many as possible. 20To the Jews I became like a Jew, to win the Jews. To those under the law I became like one under the law (though I myself am not under the law), so as to win those under the law. 21To those not having the law I became like one not having the law (though I am not free from God's law but am under Christ's law), so as to win those not having the law. 22To the weak I became weak, to win the weak. I have become all things to all men so that by all possible means I might save some. 23I do all this for the sake of the gospel, that I may share in its blessings.

24Do you not know that in a race all the runners run, but only one gets the prize? Run in such a way as to get the prize. 25Everyone who competes in the games goes into strict training. They do it to get a crown that will not last; but we do it to get a crown that will last forever. 26Therefore I do not run like a man running aimlessly; I do not fight like a man beating the air. 27No, I beat my body and make it my slave so that after I have preached to others, I myself will not be disqualified for the prize.

Living Bible

us? Of course he was. He said this to show us that Christian workers should be paid by those they help. Those who do the plowing and threshing should expect some share of the harvest.

11We have planted good spiritual seed in your souls. Is it too much to ask, in return, for mere food and clothing? 12You give them to others who preach to you, and you should. But shouldn't we have an even greater right to them? Yet we have *never* used this right, but supply our own needs without your help. We have never demanded payment of any kind for fear that, if we did, you might be less interested in our message to you from Christ.

13Don't you realize that God told those working in his temple to take for their own needs some of the food brought there as gifts to him? And those who work at the altar of God get a share of the food that is brought by those offering it to the Lord. 14In the same way the Lord has given orders that those who preach the Gospel should be supported by those who accept it.

15Yet I have never asked you for one penny. And I am not writing this to hint that I would like to start now. In fact, I would rather die of hunger than lose the satisfaction I get from preaching to you without charge. 16For just preaching the Gospel isn't any special credit to me—I couldn't keep from preaching it if I wanted to. I would be utterly miserable. Woe unto me if I don't.

17If I were volunteering my services of my own free will, then the Lord would give me a special reward; but that is not the situation, for God has picked me out and given me this sacred trust and I have no choice. 18Under this circumstance, what is my pay? It is the special joy I get from preaching the Good News without expense to anyone, never demanding my rights.

19And this has a real advantage: I am not bound to obey anyone just because he pays my salary; yet I have freely and happily become a servant of any and all so that I can win them to Christ. 20When I am with the Jews I seem as one of them so that they will listen to the Gospel and I can win them to Christ. When I am with Gentiles who follow Jewish customs and ceremonies I don't argue, even though I don't agree, because I want to help them. 21When with the heathen I agree with them as much as I can, except of course that I must always do what is right as a Christian. And so, by agreeing, I can win their confidencea and help them too.

22When I am with those whose consciences bother them easily, I don't act as though I know it all and don't say they are foolish; the result is that they are willing to let me help them. Yes, whatever a person is like, I try to find common ground with him so that he will let me tell him about Christ and let Christ save him. 23I do this to get the Gospel to them and also for the blessing I myself receive when I see them come to Christ.

24In a race, everyone runs but only one person gets first prize. So run your race to win. 25To win the contest you must deny yourselves many things that would keep you from doing your best. An athlete goes to all this trouble just to win a blue ribbon or a silver cup,b but we do it for a heavenly reward that never disappears. 26So I run straight to the goal with purpose in every step. I fight to win. I'm not just shadow-boxing or playing around. 27Like an athlete I punish my body, treating it roughly, training it to do what it should, not what it wants to. Otherwise I fear that after enlisting others for the race, I myself might be declared unfit and ordered to stand aside.

New Revised Standard

does he not speak entirely for our sake? It was indeed written for our sake, for whoever plows should plow in hope and whoever threshes should thresh in hope of a share in the crop. 11If we have sown spiritual good among you, is it too much if we reap your material benefits? 12If others share this rightful claim on you, do not we still more?

Nevertheless, we have not made use of this right, but we endure anything rather than put an obstacle in the way of the gospel of Christ. 13Do you not know that those who are employed in the temple service get their food from the temple, and those who serve at the altar share in what is sacrificed on the altar? 14In the same way, the Lord commanded that those who proclaim the gospel should get their living by the gospel.

15 But I have made no use of any of these rights, nor am I writing this so that they may be applied in my case. Indeed, I would rather die than that—no one will deprive me of my ground for boasting! 16If I proclaim the gospel, this gives me no ground for boasting, for an obligation is laid on me, and woe to me if I do not proclaim the gospel! 17For if I do this of my own will, I have a reward; but if not of my own will, I am entrusted with a commission. 18What then is my reward? Just this: that in my proclamation I may make the gospel free of charge, so as not to make full use of my rights in the gospel.

19 For though I am free with respect to all, I have made myself a slave to all, so that I might win more of them. 20To the Jews I became as a Jew, in order to win Jews. To those under the law I became as one under the law (though I myself am not under the law) so that I might win those under the law. 21To those outside the law I became as one outside the law (though I am not free from God's law but am under Christ's law) so that I might win those outside the law. 22To the weak I became weak, so that I might win the weak. I have become all things to all people, that I might by all means save some. 23I do it all for the sake of the gospel, so that I may share in its blessings.

24 Do you not know that in a race the runners all compete, but only one receives the prize? Run in such a way that you may win it. 25Athletes exercise self-control in all things; they do it to receive a perishable wreath, but we an imperishable one. 26So I do not run aimlessly, nor do I box as though beating the air; 27but I punish my body and enslave it, so that after proclaiming to others I myself should not be disqualified.

a 9:21 *I can win their confidence,* implied.   b 9:25 *a silver cup,* literally, "a wreath that quickly fades," given to the winners of the original Olympic races of Paul's time.

King James

10 MOREOVER, BRETHREN, I would not that ye should be ignorant, how that all our fathers were under the cloud, and all passed through the sea;

2And were all baptized unto Moses in the cloud and in the sea;

3And did all eat the same spiritual meat;

4And did all drink the same spiritual drink: for they drank of that spiritual Rock that followed them: and that Rock was Christ.

5But with many of them God was not well pleased: for they were overthrown in the wilderness.

6Now these things were our examples, to the intent we should not lust after evil things, as they also lusted.

7Neither be ye idolaters, as *were* some of them; as it is written, The people sat down to eat and drink, and rose up to play.

8Neither let us commit fornication, as some of them committed, and fell in one day three and twenty thousand.

9Neither let us tempt Christ, as some of them also tempted, and were destroyed of serpents.

10Neither murmur ye, as some of them also murmured, and were destroyed of the destroyer.

11Now all these things happened unto them for examples: and they are written for our admonition, upon whom the ends of the world are come.

12Wherefore let him that thinketh he standeth take heed lest he fall.

13There hath no temptation taken you but such as is common to man: but God *is* faithful, who will not suffer you to be tempted above that ye are able; but will with the temptation also make a way to escape, that ye may be able to bear *it*.

14Wherefore, my dearly beloved, flee from idolatry.

15I speak as to wise men; judge ye what I say.

16The cup of blessing which we bless, is it not the communion of the blood of Christ? The bread which we break, is it not the communion of the body of Christ?

17For we *being* many are one bread, *and* one body: for we are all partakers of that one bread.

18Behold Israel after the flesh: are not they which eat of the sacrifices partakers of the altar?

19What say I then? that the idol is any thing, or that which is offered in sacrifice to idols is any thing?

20But *I say*, that the things which the Gentiles sacrifice, they sacrifice to devils, and not to God: and I would not that ye should have fellowship with devils.

21Ye cannot drink the cup of the Lord, and the cup of devils: ye cannot be partakers of the Lord's table, and of the table of devils.

22Do we provoke the Lord to jealousy? are we stronger than he?

New International

Warnings From Israel's History

10 FOR I do not want you to be ignorant of the fact, brothers, that our forefathers were all under the cloud and that they all passed through the sea. 2They were all baptized into Moses in the cloud and in the sea. 3They all ate the same spiritual food 4and drank the same spiritual drink; for they drank from the spiritual rock that accompanied them, and that rock was Christ. 5Nevertheless, God was not pleased with most of them; their bodies were scattered over the desert.

6Now these things occurred as examples[a] to keep us from setting our hearts on evil things as they did. 7Do not be idolaters, as some of them were; as it is written: "The people sat down to eat and drink and got up to indulge in pagan revelry."[b] 8We should not commit sexual immorality, as some of them did—and in one day twenty-three thousand of them died. 9We should not test the Lord, as some of them did—and were killed by snakes. 10And do not grumble, as some of them did—and were killed by the destroying angel.

11These things happened to them as examples and were written down as warnings for us, on whom the fulfillment of the ages has come. 12So, if you think you are standing firm, be careful that you don't fall! 13No temptation has seized you except what is common to man. And God is faithful; he will not let you be tempted beyond what you can bear. But when you are tempted, he will also provide a way out so that you can stand up under it.

Idol Feasts and the Lord's Supper

14Therefore, my dear friends, flee from idolatry. 15I speak to sensible people; judge for yourselves what I say. 16Is not the cup of thanksgiving for which we give thanks a participation in the blood of Christ? And is not the bread that we break a participation in the body of Christ? 17Because there is one loaf, we, who are many, are one body, for we all partake of the one loaf.

18Consider the people of Israel: Do not those who eat the sacrifices participate in the altar? 19Do I mean then that a sacrifice offered to an idol is anything, or that an idol is anything? 20No, but the sacrifices of pagans are offered to demons, not to God, and I do not want you to be participants with demons. 21You cannot drink the cup of the Lord and the cup of demons too; you cannot have a part in both the Lord's table and the table of demons. 22Are we trying to arouse the Lord's jealousy? Are we stronger than he?

---

[a] 6 Or *types*; also in verse 11   [b] 7 Exodus 32:6

Living Bible

10 FOR WE must never forget, dear brothers, what happened to our people in the wilderness long ago. God guided them by sending a cloud that moved along ahead of them; and he brought them all safely through the waters of the Red Sea. 2This might be called their "baptism"—baptized both in sea and cloud!—as followers of Moses—their commitment to him as their leader. 3, 4And by a miraclec God sent them food to eat and water to drink there in the desert; they drank the water that Christ gave them.d He was there with them as a mighty Rock of spiritual refreshment. 5Yet after all this most of them did not obey God, and he destroyed them in the wilderness.

6From this lesson we are warned that we must not desire evil things as they did, 7nor worship idols as they did. (The Scriptures tell us, "The people sat down to eat and drink and then got up to dance" in worship of the golden calf.)

8Another lesson for us is what happened when some of them sinned with other men's wives, and 23,000 fell dead in one day. 9And don't try the Lord's patience—they did, and died from snake bites. 10And don't murmur against God and his dealings with you, as some of them did, for that is why God sent his Angel to destroy them.

11All these things happened to them as examples—as object lessons to us—to warn us against doing the same things; they were written down so that we could read about them and learn from them in these last days as the world nears its end.

12So be careful. If you are thinking, "Oh, I would never behave like that"—let this be a warning to you. For you too may fall into sin. 13But remember this—the wrong desires that come into your life aren't anything new and different. Many others have faced exactly the same problems before you. And no temptation is irresistible. You can trust God to keep the temptation from becoming so strong that you can't stand up against it, for he has promised this and will do what he says. He will show you how to escape temptation's power so that you can bear up patiently against it.

14So, dear friends, carefully avoid idol-worship of every kind.

15You are intelligent people. Look now and see for yourselves whether what I am about to say is true. 16When we ask the Lord's blessing upon our drinking from the cup of wine at the Lord's Table, this means, doesn't it, that all who drink it are sharing together the blessing of Christ's blood? And when we break off pieces of the bread from the loaf to eat there together, this shows that we are sharing together in the benefits of his body. 17No matter how many of us there are, we all eat from the same loaf, showing that we are all parts of the one body of Christ. 18And the Jewish people, all who eat the sacrifices, are united by that act.

19What am I trying to say? Am I saying that the idols to whom the heathen bring sacrifices are really alive and are real gods, and that these sacrifices are of some value? No, not at all. 20What I am saying is that those who offer food to these idols are united together in sacrificing to demons, certainly not to God. And I don't want any of you to be partners with demons when you eat the same food, along with the heathen, that has been offered to these idols. 21You cannot drink from the cup at the Lord's Table and at Satan's table, too. You cannot eat bread both at the Lord's Table and at Satan's table. 22What? Are you tempting the Lord to be angry with you? Are you stronger than he is?

New Revised Standard

Warnings from Israel's History

10 I DO not want you to be unaware, brothers and sisters,e that our ancestors were all under the cloud, and all passed through the sea, 2and all were baptized into Moses in the cloud and in the sea, 3and all ate the same spiritual food, 4and all drank the same spiritual drink. For they drank from the spiritual rock that followed them, and the rock was Christ. 5Nevertheless, God was not pleased with most of them, and they were struck down in the wilderness.

6 Now these things occurred as examples for us, so that we might not desire evil as they did. 7Do not become idolaters as some of them did; as it is written, "The people sat down to eat and drink, and they rose up to play." 8We must not indulge in sexual immorality as some of them did, and twenty-three thousand fell in a single day. 9We must not put Christf to the test, as some of them did, and were destroyed by serpents. 10And do not complain as some of them did, and were destroyed by the destroyer. 11These things happened to them to serve as an example, and they were written down to instruct us, on whom the ends of the ages have come. 12So if you think you are standing, watch out that you do not fall. 13No testing has overtaken you that is not common to everyone. God is faithful, and he will not let you be tested beyond your strength, but with the testing he will also provide the way out so that you may be able to endure it.

14 Therefore, my dear friends,g flee from the worship of idols. 15I speak as to sensible people; judge for yourselves what I say. 16The cup of blessing that we bless, is it not a sharing in the blood of Christ? The bread that we break, is it not a sharing in the body of Christ? 17Because there is one bread, we who are many are one body, for we all partake of the one bread. 18Consider the people of Israel;h are not those who eat the sacrifices partners in the altar? 19What do I imply then? That food sacrificed to idols is anything, or that an idol is anything? 20No, I imply that what pagans sacrifice, they sacrifice to demons and not to God. I do not want you to be partners with demons. 21You cannot drink the cup of the Lord and the cup of demons. You cannot partake of the table of the Lord and the table of demons. 22Or are we provoking the Lord to jealousy? Are we stronger than he?

---

c *10:3, 4 and by a miracle,* implied. Literally, "all ate the same supernatural food and drink." d *10:3, 4 they drank the water that Christ gave them,* literally, "For they drank of a spiritual Rock that followed them, and the Rock was Christ."

e Gk *brothers* f Other ancient authorities read *the Lord* g Gk *my beloved* h Gk *Israel according to the flesh*

King James

23All things are lawful for me, but all things are not expedient: all things are lawful for me, but all things edify not.

24Let no man seek his own, but every man another's *wealth.*

25Whatsoever is sold in the shambles, *that* eat, asking no question for conscience sake:

26For the earth *is* the Lord's, and the fulness thereof.

27If any of them that believe not bid you *to a feast,* and ye be disposed to go; whatsoever is set before you, eat, asking no question for conscience sake.

28But if any man say unto you, This is offered in sacrifice unto idols, eat not for his sake that showed it, and for conscience sake: for the earth *is* the Lord's, and the fulness thereof:

29Conscience, I say, not thine own, but of the other: for why is my liberty judged of another *man's* conscience?

30For if I by grace be a partaker, why am I evil spoken of for that for which I give thanks?

31Whether therefore ye eat, or drink, or whatsoever ye do, do all to the glory of God.

32Give none offence, neither to the Jews, nor to the Gentiles, nor to the church of God:

33Even as I please all *men* in all *things,* not seeking mine own profit, but the *profit* of many, that they may be saved.

11 BE YE followers of me, even as I also *am* of Christ.

2Now I praise you, brethren, that ye remember me in all things, and keep the ordinances, as I delivered *them* to you.

3But I would have you know, that the head of every man is Christ; and the head of the woman *is* the man; and the head of Christ *is* God.

4Every man praying or prophesying, having *his* head covered, dishonoureth his head.

5But every woman that prayeth or prophesieth with *her* head uncovered dishonoureth her head: for that is even all one as if she were shaven.

6For if the woman be not covered, let her also be shorn: but if it be a shame for a woman to be shorn or shaven, let her be covered.

7For a man indeed ought not to cover *his* head, forasmuch as he is the image and glory of God: but the woman is the glory of the man.

8For the man is not of the woman; but the woman of the man.

9Neither was the man created for the woman; but the woman for the man.

10For this cause ought the woman to have power on *her* head because of the angels.

11Nevertheless neither is the man without the woman, neither the woman without the man, in the Lord.

12For as the woman *is* of the man, even so *is* the man also by the woman; but all things of God.

New International

The Believer's Freedom

23"Everything is permissible"—but not everything is beneficial. "Everything is permissible"—but not everything is constructive. 24Nobody should seek his own good, but the good of others.

25Eat anything sold in the meat market without raising questions of conscience, 26for, "The earth is the Lord's, and everything in it."a

27If some unbeliever invites you to a meal and you want to go, eat whatever is put before you without raising questions of conscience. 28But if anyone says to you, "This has been offered in sacrifice," then do not eat it, both for the sake of the man who told you and for conscience' sakeb— 29the other man's conscience, I mean, not yours. For why should my freedom be judged by another's conscience? 30If I take part in the meal with thankfulness, why am I denounced because of something I thank God for?

31So whether you eat or drink or whatever you do, do it all for the glory of God. 32Do not cause anyone to stumble, whether Jews, Greeks or the church of God— 33even as I try to please everybody in every way. For I am not seeking my own good but the good of many, so that they may be saved.

11 FOLLOW MY example, as I follow the example of Christ.

Propriety in Worship

2I praise you for remembering me in everything and for holding to the teachings,c just as I passed them on to you.

3Now I want you to realize that the head of every man is Christ, and the head of the woman is man, and the head of Christ is God. 4Every man who prays or prophesies with his head covered dishonors his head. 5And every woman who prays or prophesies with her head uncovered dishonors her head—it is just as though her head were shaved. 6If a woman does not cover her head, she should have her hair cut off; and if it is a disgrace for a woman to have her hair cut or shaved off, she should cover her head. 7A man ought not to cover his head,d since he is the image and glory of God; but the woman is the glory of man. 8For man did not come from woman, but woman from man; 9neither was man created for woman, but woman for man. 10For this reason, and because of the angels, the woman ought to have a sign of authority on her head.

11In the Lord, however, woman is not independent of man, nor is man independent of woman. 12For as woman came from man, so also man is born of woman. But everything comes from God. 13Judge for yourselves: Is

a 26 Psalm 24:1   b 28 Some manuscripts *conscience' sake, for "the earth is the Lord's and everything in it"*   c 2 Or *traditions*   d 4-7 Or *4Every man who prays or prophesies with long hair dishonors his head. 5And every woman who prays or prophesies with no covering of hair, on her head dishonors her head—she is just like one of the "shorn women." 6If a woman has no covering, let her be for now with short hair, but since it is a disgrace for a woman to have her hair shorn or shaved, she should grow it again. 7A man ought not to have long hair*

Living Bible

23You are certainly free to eat food offered to idols if you want to; it's not against God's laws to eat such meat, but that doesn't mean that you should go ahead and do it. It may be perfectly legal, but it may not be best and helpful. 24Don't think only of yourself. Try to think of the other fellow, too, and what is best for him. 25Here's what you should do. Take any meat you want that is sold at the market. Don't ask whether or not it was offered to idols, lest the answer hurt your conscience. 26For the earth and every good thing in it belongs to the Lord and is yours to enjoy.

27If someone who isn't a Christian asks you out to dinner, go ahead; accept the invitation if you want to. Eat whatever is on the table and don't ask any questions about it. Then you won't know whether or not it has been used as a sacrifice to idols, and you won't risk having a bad conscience over eating it. 28But if someone warns you that this meat has been offered to idols, then don't eat it for the sake of the man who told you, and of his conscience. 29In this case *his* feeling about it is the important thing, not yours.

But why, you may ask, must I be guided and limited by what someone else thinks? 30If I can thank God for the food and enjoy it, why let someone spoil everything just because he thinks I am wrong? 31Well, I'll tell you why. It is because you must do everything for the glory of God, even your eating and drinking. 32So don't be a stumbling block to anyone, whether they are Jews or Gentiles or Christians. 33That is the plan I follow, too. I try to please everyone in everything I do, not doing what I like or what is best for me, but what is best for them, so that they may be saved.

11 AND YOU should follow my example, just as I follow Christ's.

2I am so glad, dear brothers, that you have been remembering and doing everything I taught you. 3But there is one matter I want to remind you about: that a wife is responsible to her husband, her husband is responsible to Christ, and Christ is responsible to God. 4That is why, if a man refuses to remove his hat while praying or preaching, he dishonors Christ. 5And that is why a woman who publicly prays or prophesies without a covering on her head dishonors her husband [for her covering is a sign of her subjection to himᵉ]. 6Yes, if she refuses to wear a head covering, then she should cut off all her hair. And if it is shameful for a woman to have her head shaved, then she should wear a covering. 7But a man should not wear anything on his head [when worshiping, for his hat is a sign of subjection to menᶠ].

God's glory is man made in his image, and man's glory is the woman. 8The first man didn't come from woman, but the first woman came out of man.ᵍ 9And Adam, the first man, was not made for Eve's benefit, but Eve was made for Adam. 10So a woman should wear a covering on her head as a sign that she is under man's authority,ʰ a fact for all the angels to notice and rejoice in.ⁱ

11But remember that in God's plan men and women need each other. 12For although the first woman came out of man, all men have been born from women ever since, and both men and women come from God their Creator.

New Revised Standard

Do All to the Glory of God

23 "All things are lawful," but not all things are beneficial. "All things are lawful," but not all things build up. 24Do not seek your own advantage, but that of the other. 25Eat whatever is sold in the meat market without raising any question on the ground of conscience, 26for "the earth and its fullness are the Lord's." 27If an unbeliever invites you to a meal and you are disposed to go, eat whatever is set before you without raising any question on the ground of conscience. 28But if someone says to you, "This has been offered in sacrifice," then do not eat it, out of consideration for the one who informed you, and for the sake of conscience— 29I mean the other's conscience, not your own. For why should my liberty be subject to the judgment of someone else's conscience? 30If I partake with thankfulness, why should I be denounced because of that for which I give thanks?

31 So, whether you eat or drink, or whatever you do, do everything for the glory of God. 32Give no offense to Jews or to Greeks or to the church of God, 33just as I try to please everyone in everything I do, not seeking my own advantage, but that of many, so that they may be saved.

11 BE IMITATORS of me, as I am of Christ.

Head Coverings

2 I commend you because you remember me in everything and maintain the traditions just as I handed them on to you. 3But I want you to understand that Christ is the head of every man, and the husbandⱼ is the head of his wife,ᵏ and God is the head of Christ. 4Any man who prays or prophesies with something on his head disgraces his head, 5but any woman who prays or prophesies with her head unveiled disgraces her head— it is one and the same thing as having her head shaved. 6For if a woman will not veil herself, then she should cut off her hair; but if it is disgraceful for a woman to have her hair cut off or to be shaved, she should wear a veil. 7For a man ought not to have his head veiled, since he is the image and reflectionˡ of God; but woman is the reflectionˡ of man. 8Indeed, man was not made from woman, but woman from man. 9Neither was man created for the sake of woman, but woman for the sake of man. 10For this reason a woman ought to have a symbol ofᵐ authority on her head,ⁿ because of the angels. 11Nevertheless, in the Lord woman is not independent of man or man independent of woman. 12For just as woman came from man, so man comes through woman; but all things come from God. 13Judge for your-

---

ᵉ *11:5 for her covering is a sign of her subjection to him,* implied in vss 7, 10. ᶠ *11:7 when worshiping, for his hat is a sign of subjection to men,* implied. ᵍ *11:8 the first woman came out of man,* Gen 2:21, 22. ʰ *11:10 as a sign that she is under man's authority,* literally, "For this cause ought the woman to have power on [her] head." ⁱ *11:10 a fact for all the angels to notice and rejoice in,* literally, "because of the angels."

ⱼ The same Greek word means *man* or *husband*   ᵏ Or *head of the woman* ˡ Or *glory*   ᵐ Gk lacks *a symbol of*   ⁿ Or *have freedom of choice regarding her head*

King James

13Judge in yourselves: is it comely that a woman pray unto God uncovered?

14Doth not even nature itself teach you, that, if a man have long hair, it is a shame unto him?

15But if a woman have long hair, it is a glory to her: for *her* hair is given her for a covering.

16But if any man seem to be contentious, we have no such custom, neither the churches of God.

17Now in this that I declare *unto you* I praise *you* not, that ye come together not for the better, but for the worse.

18For first of all, when ye come together in the church, I hear that there be divisions among you; and I partly believe it.

19For there must be also heresies among you, that they which are approved may be made manifest among you.

20When ye come together therefore into one place, *this* is not to eat the Lord's supper.

21For in eating every one taketh before *other* his own supper: and one is hungry, and another is drunken.

22What? have ye not houses to eat and to drink in? or despise ye the church of God, and shame them that have not? What shall I say to you? shall I praise you in this? I praise *you* not.

23For I have received of the Lord that which also I delivered unto you, That the Lord Jesus the *same* night in which he was betrayed took bread:

24And when he had given thanks, he brake *it,* and said, Take, eat: this is my body, which is broken for you: this do in remembrance of me.

25After the same manner also *he took* the cup, when he had supped, saying, This cup is the new testament in my blood: this do ye, as oft as ye drink *it,* in remembrance of me.

26For as often as ye eat this bread, and drink this cup, ye do show the Lord's death till he come.

27Wherefore whosoever shall eat this bread, and drink *this* cup of the Lord, unworthily, shall be guilty of the body and blood of the Lord.

28But let a man examine himself, and so let him eat of *that* bread, and drink of *that* cup.

29For he that eateth and drinketh unworthily, eateth and drinketh damnation to himself, not discerning the Lord's body.

30For this cause many *are* weak and sickly among you, and many sleep.

31For if we would judge ourselves, we should not be judged.

32But when we are judged, we are chastened of the Lord, that we should not be condemned with the world.

33Wherefore, my brethren, when ye come together to eat, tarry one for another.

34And if any man hunger, let him eat at home; that ye come not together unto condemnation. And the rest will I set in order when I come.

New International

it proper for a woman to pray to God with her head uncovered? 14Does not the very nature of things teach you that if a man has long hair, it is a disgrace to him, 15but that if a woman has long hair, it is her glory? For long hair is given to her as a covering. 16If anyone wants to be contentious about this, we have no other practice—nor do the churches of God.

The Lord's Supper

17In the following directives I have no praise for you, for your meetings do more harm than good. 18In the first place, I hear that when you come together as a church, there are divisions among you, and to some extent I believe it. 19No doubt there have to be differences among you to show which of you have God's approval. 20When you come together, it is not the Lord's Supper you eat, 21for as you eat, each of you goes ahead without waiting for anybody else. One remains hungry, another gets drunk. 22Don't you have homes to eat and drink in? Or do you despise the church of God and humiliate those who have nothing? What shall I say to you? Shall I praise you for this? Certainly not!

23For I received from the Lord what I also passed on to you: The Lord Jesus, on the night he was betrayed, took bread, 24and when he had given thanks, he broke it and said, "This is my body, which is for you; do this in remembrance of me." 25In the same way, after supper he took the cup, saying, "This cup is the new covenant in my blood; do this, whenever you drink it, in remembrance of me." 26For whenever you eat this bread and drink this cup, you proclaim the Lord's death until he comes.

27Therefore, whoever eats the bread or drinks the cup of the Lord in an unworthy manner will be guilty of sinning against the body and blood of the Lord. 28A man ought to examine himself before he eats of the bread and drinks of the cup. 29For anyone who eats and drinks without recognizing the body of the Lord eats and drinks judgment on himself. 30That is why many among you are weak and sick, and a number of you have fallen asleep. 31But if we judged ourselves, we would not come under judgment. 32When we are judged by the Lord, we are being disciplined so that we will not be condemned with the world.

33So then, my brothers, when you come together to eat, wait for each other. 34If anyone is hungry, he should eat at home, so that when you meet together it may not result in judgment.

And when I come I will give further directions.

Living Bible

13What do you yourselves really think about this? Is it right for a woman to pray in public without covering her head? 14, 15Doesn't even instinct itself teach us that women's heads should be covered? For women are proud of their long hair, while a man with long hair tends to be ashamed. 16But if anyone wants to argue about this, all I can say is that we never teach anything else than this—that a woman should wear a covering when prophesying or praying publicly in the church, and all the churches feel the same way about it.

17Next on my list of items to write you about is something else I cannot agree with. For it sounds as if more harm than good is done when you meet together for your communion services. 18Everyone keeps telling me about the arguing that goes on in these meetings, and the divisions developing among you, and I can just about believe it. 19But I suppose you feel this is necessary so that you who are always right will become known and recognized!

20When you come together to eat, it isn't the Lord's Supper you are eating, 21but your own. For I am told that everyone hastily gobbles all the food he can without waiting to share with the others, so that one doesn't get enough and goes hungry while another has too much to drink and gets drunk. 22What? Is this really true? Can't you do your eating and drinking at home, to avoid disgracing the church and shaming those who are poor and can bring no food? What am I supposed to say about these things? Do you want me to praise you? Well, I certainly do not!

23For this is what the Lord himself has said about his Table, and I have passed it on to you before: That on the night when Judas betrayed him, the Lord Jesus took bread, 24and when he had given thanks to God for it, he broke it and gave it to his disciples and said, "Take this and eat it. This is my body, which is givena for you. Do this to remember me." 25In the same way, he took the cup of wine after supper, saying, "This cup is the new agreement between God and you that has been established and set in motion by my blood. Do this in remembrance of me whenever you drink it." 26For every time you eat this bread and drink this cup you are re-telling the message of the Lord's death, that he has died for you. Do this until he comes again.

27So if anyone eats this bread and drinks from this cup of the Lord in an unworthy manner, he is guilty of sin against the body and the blood of the Lord. 28That is why a man should examine himself carefully before eating the bread and drinking from the cup. 29For if he eats the bread and drinks from the cup unworthily, not thinking about the body of Christ and what it means, he is eating and drinking God's judgment upon himself; for he is trifling with the death of Christ. 30That is why many of you are weak and sick, and some have even died.

31But if you carefully examine yourselves before eating you will not need to be judged and punished. 32Yet, when we are judged and punished by the Lord, it is so that we will not be condemned with the rest of the world. 33So, dear brothers, when you gather for the Lord's Supper—the communion service—wait for each other; 34if anyone is really hungry he should eat at home so that he won't bring punishment upon himself when you meet together.

I'll talk to you about the other matters after I arrive.

New Revised Standard

selves: is it proper for a woman to pray to God with her head unveiled? 14Does not nature itself teach you that if a man wears long hair, it is degrading to him, 15but if a woman has long hair, it is her glory? For her hair is given to her for a covering. 16But if anyone is disposed to be contentious—we have no such custom, nor do the churches of God.

Abuses at the Lord's Supper

17 Now in the following instructions I do not commend you, because when you come together it is not for the better but for the worse. 18For, to begin with, when you come together as a church, I hear that there are divisions among you; and to some extent I believe it. 19Indeed, there have to be factions among you, for only so will it become clear who among you are genuine. 20When you come together, it is not really to eat the Lord's supper. 21For when the time comes to eat, each of you goes ahead with your own supper, and one goes hungry and another becomes drunk. 22What! Do you not have homes to eat and drink in? Or do you show contempt for the church of God and humiliate those who have nothing? What should I say to you? Should I commend you? In this matter I do not commend you!

The Institution of the Lord's Supper

23 For I received from the Lord what I also handed on to you, that the Lord Jesus on the night when he was betrayed took a loaf of bread, 24and when he had given thanks, he broke it and said, "This is my body that is forb you. Do this in remembrance of me." 25In the same way he took the cup also, after supper, saying, "This cup is the new covenant in my blood. Do this, as often as you drink it, in remembrance of me." 26For as often as you eat this bread and drink the cup, you proclaim the Lord's death until he comes.

Partaking of the Supper Unworthily

27 Whoever, therefore, eats the bread or drinks the cup of the Lord in an unworthy manner will be answerable for the body and blood of the Lord. 28Examine yourselves, and only then eat of the bread and drink of the cup. 29For all who eat and drinkc without discerning the body,d eat and drink judgment against themselves. 30For this reason many of you are weak and ill, and some have died.e 31But if we judged ourselves, we would not be judged. 32But when we are judged by the Lord, we are disciplinedf so that we may not be condemned along with the world.

33 So then, my brothers and sisters,g when you come together to eat, wait for one another. 34If you are hungry, eat at home, so that when you come together, it will not be for your condemnation. About the other things I will give instructions when I come.

---

a 11:24 given. Some ancient manuscripts read, "broken."

b Other ancient authorities read is broken for   c Other ancient authorities add in an unworthy manner,   d Other ancient authorities read the Lord's body   e Gk fallen asleep   f Or When we are judged, we are being disciplined by the Lord   g Gk brothers

King James

12 NOW CONCERNING spiritual *gifts,* brethren, I would not have you ignorant.

2Ye know that ye were Gentiles, carried away unto these dumb idols, even as ye were led.

3Wherefore I give you to understand, that no man speaking by the Spirit of God calleth Jesus accursed: and *that* no man can say that Jesus is the Lord, but by the Holy Ghost.

4Now there are diversities of gifts, but the same Spirit.

5And there are differences of administrations, but the same Lord.

6And there are diversities of operations, but it is the same God which worketh all in all.

7But the manifestation of the Spirit is given to every man to profit withal.

8For to one is given by the Spirit the word of wisdom; to another the word of knowledge by the same Spirit;

9To another faith by the same Spirit; to another the gifts of healing by the same Spirit;

10To another the working of miracles; to another prophecy; to another discerning of spirits; to another *divers* kinds of tongues; to another the interpretation of tongues:

11But all these worketh that one and the selfsame Spirit, dividing to every man severally as he will.

12For as the body is one, and hath many members, and all the members of that one body, being many, are one body: so also *is* Christ.

13For by one Spirit are we all baptized into one body, whether *we be* Jews or Gentiles, whether *we be* bond or free; and have been all made to drink into one Spirit.

14For the body is not one member, but many.

15If the foot shall say, Because I am not the hand, I am not of the body; is it therefore not of the body?

16And if the ear shall say, Because I am not the eye, I am not of the body; is it therefore not of the body?

17If the whole body *were* an eye, where *were* the hearing? If the whole *were* hearing, where *were* the smelling?

18But now hath God set the members every one of them in the body, as it hath pleased him.

19And if they were all one member, where *were* the body?

20But now *are they* many members, yet but one body.

21And the eye cannot say unto the hand, I have no need of thee: nor again the head to the feet, I have no need of you.

22Nay, much more those members of the body, which seem to be more feeble, are necessary:

23And those *members* of the body, which we think to be less honourable, upon these we bestow more abundant honour; and our uncomely *parts* have more abundant comeliness.

24For our comely *parts* have no need: but God hath tempered the body together, having given more abundant honour to that *part* which lacked:

25That there should be no schism in the body; but *that* the members should have the same care one for another.

26And whether one member suffer, all the members suffer with it; or one member be honoured, all the members rejoice with it.

New International

Spiritual Gifts

12 NOW ABOUT spiritual gifts, brothers, I do not want you to be ignorant. 2You know that when you were pagans, somehow or other you were influenced and led astray to mute idols. 3Therefore I tell you that no one who is speaking by the Spirit of God says, "Jesus be cursed," and no one can say, "Jesus is Lord," except by the Holy Spirit.

4There are different kinds of gifts, but the same Spirit. 5There are different kinds of service, but the same Lord. 6There are different kinds of working, but the same God works all of them in all men.

7Now to each one the manifestation of the Spirit is given for the common good. 8To one there is given through the Spirit the message of wisdom, to another the message of knowledge by means of the same Spirit, 9to another faith by the same Spirit, to another gifts of healing by that one Spirit, 10to another miraculous powers, to another prophecy, to another distinguishing between spirits, to another speaking in different kinds of tongues,a and to still another the interpretation of tongues.a 11All these are the work of one and the same Spirit, and he gives them to each one, just as he determines.

One Body, Many Parts

12The body is a unit, though it is made up of many parts; and though all its parts are many, they form one body. So it is with Christ. 13For we were all baptized byb one Spirit into one body—whether Jews or Greeks, slave or free—and we were all given the one Spirit to drink.

14Now the body is not made up of one part but of many. 15If the foot should say, "Because I am not a hand, I do not belong to the body," it would not for that reason cease to be part of the body. 16And if the ear should say, "Because I am not an eye, I do not belong to the body," it would not for that reason cease to be part of the body. 17If the whole body were an eye, where would the sense of hearing be? If the whole body were an ear, where would the sense of smell be? 18But in fact God has arranged the parts in the body, every one of them, just as he wanted them to be. 19If they were all one part, where would the body be? 20As it is, there are many parts, but one body.

21The eye cannot say to the hand, "I don't need you!" And the head cannot say to the feet, "I don't need you!" 22On the contrary, those parts of the body that seem to be weaker are indispensable, 23and the parts that we think are less honorable we treat with special honor. And the parts that are unpresentable are treated with special modesty, 24while our presentable parts need no special treatment. But God has combined the members of the body and has given greater honor to the parts that lacked it, 25so that there should be no division in the body, but that its parts should have equal concern for each other. 26If one part suffers, every part suffers with it; if one part is honored, every part rejoices with it.

---

a *10 Or languages; also in verse 28*   b *13 Or with; or in*

Living Bible

12 AND NOW, brothers, I want to write about the special abilities the Holy Spirit gives to each of you, for I don't want any misunderstanding about them. ²You will remember that before you became Christians you went around from one idol to another, not one of which could speak a single word. ³But now you are meeting people who claim to speak messages from the Spirit of God. How can you know whether they are really inspired by God or whether they are fakes? Here is the test: no one speaking by the power of the Spirit of God can curse Jesus, and no one can say, "Jesus is Lord," and really mean it, unless the Holy Spirit is helping him.

⁴Now God gives us many kinds of special abilities, but it is the same Holy Spirit who is the source of them all. ⁵There are different kinds of service to God, but it is the same Lord we are serving. ⁶There are many ways in which God works in our lives, but it is the same God who does the work in and through all of us who are his. ⁷The Holy Spirit displays God's power through each of us as a means of helping the entire church.

⁸To one person the Spirit gives the ability to give wise advice; someone else may be especially good at studying and teaching, and this is his gift from the same Spirit. ⁹He gives special faith to another, and to someone else the power to heal the sick. ¹⁰He gives power for doing miracles to some, and to others power to prophesy and preach. He gives someone else the power to know whether evil spirits are speaking through those who claim to be giving God's messages—or whether it is really the Spirit of God who is speaking. Still another person is able to speak in languages he never learned; and others, who do not know the language either, are given power to understand what he is saying. ¹¹It is the same and only Holy Spirit who gives all these gifts and powers, deciding which each one of us should have.

¹²Our bodies have many parts, but the many parts make up only one body when they are all put together. So it is with the "body" of Christ. ¹³Each of us is a part of the one body of Christ. Some of us are Jews, some are Gentiles, some are slaves and some are free. But the Holy Spirit has fitted us all together into one body. We have been baptized into Christ's body by the one Spirit, and have all been given that same Holy Spirit.

¹⁴Yes, the body has many parts, not just one part. ¹⁵If the foot says, "I am not a part of the body because I am not a hand," that does not make it any less a part of the body. ¹⁶And what would you think if you heard an ear say, "I am not part of the body because I am only an ear, and not an eye"? Would that make it any less a part of the body? ¹⁷Suppose the whole body were an eye—then how would you hear? Or if your whole body were just one big ear, how could you smell anything?

¹⁸But that isn't the way God has made us. He has made many parts for our bodies and has put each part just where he wants it. ¹⁹What a strange thing a body would be if it had only one part! ²⁰So he has made many parts, but still there is only one body.

²¹The eye can never say to the hand, "I don't need you." The head can't say to the feet, "I don't need you."

²²And some of the parts that seem weakest and least important are really the most necessary. ²³Yes, we are especially glad to have some parts that seem rather odd! And we carefully protect from the eyes of others those parts that should not be seen, ²⁴while of course the parts that may be seen do not require this special care. So God has put the body together in such a way that extra honor and care are given to those parts that might otherwise seem less important. ²⁵This makes for happiness among the parts, so that the parts have the same care for each other that they do for themselves. ²⁶If one part suffers, all parts suffer with it, and if one part is honored, all the parts are glad.

New Revised Standard

Spiritual Gifts

12 NOW CONCERNING spiritual gifts,ᶜ brothers and sisters,ᵈ I do not want you to be uninformed. ²You know that when you were pagans, you were enticed and led astray to idols that could not speak. ³Therefore I want you to understand that no one speaking by the Spirit of God ever says "Let Jesus be cursed!" and no one can say "Jesus is Lord" except by the Holy Spirit.

4 Now there are varieties of gifts, but the same Spirit; ⁵and there are varieties of services, but the same Lord; ⁶and there are varieties of activities, but it is the same God who activates all of them in everyone. ⁷To each is given the manifestation of the Spirit for the common good. ⁸To one is given through the Spirit the utterance of wisdom, and to another the utterance of knowledge according to the same Spirit, ⁹to another faith by the same Spirit, to another gifts of healing by the one Spirit, ¹⁰to another the working of miracles, to another prophecy, to another the discernment of spirits, to another various kinds of tongues, to another the interpretation of tongues. ¹¹All these are activated by one and the same Spirit, who allots to each one individually just as the Spirit chooses.

One Body with Many Members

12 For just as the body is one and has many members, and all the members of the body, though many, are one body, so it is with Christ. ¹³For in the one Spirit we were all baptized into one body—Jews or Greeks, slaves or free—and we were all made to drink of one Spirit.

14 Indeed, the body does not consist of one member but of many. ¹⁵If the foot would say, "Because I am not a hand, I do not belong to the body," that would not make it any less a part of the body. ¹⁶And if the ear would say, "Because I am not an eye, I do not belong to the body," that would not make it any less a part of the body. ¹⁷If the whole body were an eye, where would the hearing be? If the whole body were hearing, where would the sense of smell be? ¹⁸But as it is, God arranged the members in the body, each one of them, as he chose. ¹⁹If all were a single member, where would the body be? ²⁰As it is, there are many members, yet one body. ²¹The eye cannot say to the hand, "I have no need of you," nor again the head to the feet, "I have no need of you." ²²On the contrary, the members of the body that seem to be weaker are indispensable, ²³and those members of the body that we think less honorable we clothe with greater honor, and our less respectable members are treated with greater respect; ²⁴whereas our more respectable members do not need this. But God has so arranged the body, giving the greater honor to the inferior member, ²⁵that there may be no dissension within the body, but the members may have the same care for one another. ²⁶If one member suffers, all suffer together with it; if one member is honored, all rejoice together with it.

ᶜ Or *spiritual persons*   ᵈ Gk *brothers*

King James

27Now ye are the body of Christ, and members in particular.

28And God hath set some in the church, first apostles, secondarily prophets, thirdly teachers, after that miracles, then gifts of healings, helps, governments, diversities of tongues.

29Are all apostles? *are* all prophets? *are* all teachers? *are* all workers of miracles?

30Have all the gifts of healing? do all speak with tongues? do all interpret?

31But covet earnestly the best gifts: and yet show I unto you a more excellent way.

13 THOUGH I speak with the tongues of men and of angels, and have not charity, I am become *as* sounding brass, or a tinkling cymbal.

2And though I have *the gift of* prophecy, and understand all mysteries, and all knowledge; and though I have all faith, so that I could remove mountains, and have not charity, I am nothing.

3And though I bestow all my goods to feed *the poor*, and though I give my body to be burned, and have not charity, it profiteth me nothing.

4Charity suffereth long, *and* is kind; charity envieth not; charity vaunteth not itself, is not puffed up,

5Doth not behave itself unseemly, seeketh not her own, is not easily provoked, thinketh no evil;

6Rejoiceth not in iniquity, but rejoiceth in the truth;

7Beareth all things, believeth all things, hopeth all things, endureth all things.

8Charity never faileth: but whether *there be* prophecies, they shall fail; whether *there be* tongues, they shall cease; whether *there be* knowledge, it shall vanish away.

9For we know in part, and we prophesy in part.

10But when that which is perfect is come, then that which is in part shall be done away.

11When I was a child, I spake as a child, I understood as a child, I thought as a child: but when I became a man, I put away childish things.

12For now we see through a glass, darkly; but then face to face: now I know in part; but then shall I know even as also I am known.

13And now abideth faith, hope, charity, these three; but the greatest of these *is* charity.

New International

27Now you are the body of Christ, and each one of you is a part of it. 28And in the church God has appointed first of all apostles, second prophets, third teachers, then workers of miracles, also those having gifts of healing, those able to help others, those with gifts of administration, and those speaking in different kinds of tongues. 29Are all apostles? Are all prophets? Are all teachers? Do all work miracles? 30Do all have gifts of healing? Do all speak in tongues[a]? Do all interpret? 31But eagerly desire[b] the greater gifts.

Love

And now I will show you the most excellent way.

13 IF I speak in the tongues[c] of men and of angels, but have not love, I am only a resounding gong or a clanging cymbal. 2If I have the gift of prophecy and can fathom all mysteries and all knowledge, and if I have a faith that can move mountains, but have not love, I am nothing. 3If I give all I possess to the poor and surrender my body to the flames,[d] but have not love, I gain nothing.

4Love is patient, love is kind. It does not envy, it does not boast, it is not proud. 5It is not rude, it is not self-seeking, it is not easily angered, it keeps no record of wrongs. 6Love does not delight in evil but rejoices with the truth. 7It always protects, always trusts, always hopes, always perseveres.

8Love never fails. But where there are prophecies, they will cease; where there are tongues, they will be stilled; where there is knowledge, it will pass away. 9For we know in part and we prophesy in part, 10but when perfection comes, the imperfect disappears. 11When I was a child, I talked like a child, I thought like a child, I reasoned like a child. When I became a man, I put childish ways behind me. 12Now we see but a poor reflection as in a mirror; then we shall see face to face. Now I know in part; then I shall know fully, even as I am fully known.

13And now these three remain: faith, hope and love. But the greatest of these is love.

---

a 30 Or *other languages*   b 31 Or *But you are eagerly desiring*   c 1 Or *languages*   d 3 Some early manuscripts *body that I may boast*

Living Bible

27Now here is what I am trying to say: All of you together are the one body of Christ and each one of you is a separate and necessary part of it. 28Here is a list of some of the parts he has placed in his Church, which is his body:

Apostles,

Prophets—those who preach God's Word,

Teachers,

Those who do miracles,

Those who have the gift of healing,

Those who can help others,

Those who can get others to work together,

Those who speak in languages they have never learned.

29Is everyone an apostle? Of course not. Is everyone a preacher? No. Are all teachers? Does everyone have the power to do miracles? 30Can everyone heal the sick? Of course not. Does God give all of us the ability to speak in languages we've never learned? Can just anyone understand and translate what those are saying who have that gift of foreign speech? 31No, but try your best to have the more important of these gifts.

First, however, let me tell you about something else that is better than any of them!

13 IF I had the gift of being able to speak in other languages without learning them, and could speak in every language there is in all of heaven and earth, but didn't love others, I would only be making noise. 2If I had the gift of prophecy and knew all about what is going to happen in the future, knew everything about *everything*, but didn't love others, what good would it do? Even if I had the gift of faith so that I could speak to a mountain and make it move, I would still be worth nothing at all without love. 3If I gave everything I have to poor people, and if I were burned alive for preaching the Gospel but didn't love others, it would be of no value whatever.

4Love is very patient and kind, never jealous or envious, never boastful or proud, 5never haughty or selfish or rude. Love does not demand its own way. It is not irritable or touchy. It does not hold grudges and will hardly even notice when others do it wrong. 6It is never glad about injustice, but rejoices whenever truth wins out. 7If you love someone you will be loyal to him no matter what the cost. You will always believe in him, always expect the best of him, and always stand your ground in defending him.

8All the special gifts and powers from God will someday come to an end, but love goes on forever. Someday prophecy, and speaking in unknown languages, and special knowledge—these gifts will disappear. 9Now we know so little, even with our special gifts, and the preaching of those most gifted is still so poor. 10But when we have been made perfect and complete, then the need for these inadequate special gifts will come to an end, and they will disappear.

11It's like this: when I was a child I spoke and thought and reasoned as a child does. But when I became a man my thoughts grew far beyond those of my childhood, and now I have put away the childish things. 12In the same way, we can see and understand only a little about God now, as if we were peering at his reflection in a poor mirror; but someday we are going to see him in his completeness, face to face. Now all that I know is hazy and blurred, but then I will see everything clearly, just as clearly as God sees into my heart right now.

13There are three things that remain—faith, hope, and love—and the greatest of these is love.

New Revised Standard

27 Now you are the body of Christ and individually members of it. 28And God has appointed in the church first apostles, second prophets, third teachers; then deeds of power, then gifts of healing, forms of assistance, forms of leadership, various kinds of tongues. 29Are all apostles? Are all prophets? Are all teachers? Do all work miracles? 30Do all possess gifts of healing? Do all speak in tongues? Do all interpret? 31But strive for the greater gifts. And I will show you a still more excellent way.

The Gift of Love

13 IF I speak in the tongues of mortals and of angels, but do not have love, I am a noisy gong or a clanging cymbal. 2And if I have prophetic powers, and understand all mysteries and all knowledge, and if I have all faith, so as to remove mountains, but do not have love, I am nothing. 3If I give away all my possessions, and if I hand over my body so that I may boast,e but do not have love, I gain nothing.

4 Love is patient; love is kind; love is not envious or boastful or arrogant 5or rude. It does not insist on its own way; it is not irritable or resentful; 6it does not rejoice in wrongdoing, but rejoices in the truth. 7It bears all things, believes all things, hopes all things, endures all things.

8 Love never ends. But as for prophecies, they will come to an end; as for tongues, they will cease; as for knowledge, it will come to an end. 9For we know only in part, and we prophesy only in part; 10but when the complete comes, the partial will come to an end. 11When I was a child, I spoke like a child, I thought like a child, I reasoned like a child; when I became an adult, I put an end to childish ways. 12For now we see in a mirror, dimly,f but then we will see face to face. Now I know only in part; then I will know fully, even as I have been fully known. 13And now faith, hope, and love abide, these three; and the greatest of these is love.

e Other ancient authorities read *body to be burned*   f Gk *in a riddle*

King James

14 FOLLOW AFTER charity, and desire spiritual gifts, but rather that ye may prophesy.

2For he that speaketh in an *unknown* tongue speaketh not unto men, but unto God: for no man understandeth *him*; howbeit in the spirit he speaketh mysteries.

3But he that prophesieth speaketh unto men *to* edification, and exhortation, and comfort.

4He that speaketh in an *unknown* tongue edifieth himself; but he that prophesieth edifieth the church.

5I would that ye all spake with tongues, but rather that ye prophesied: for greater *is* he that prophesieth than he that speaketh with tongues, except he interpret, that the church may receive edifying.

6Now, brethren, if I come unto you speaking with tongues, what shall I profit you, except I shall speak to you either by revelation, or by knowledge, or by prophesying, or by doctrine?

7And even things without life giving sound, whether pipe or harp, except they give a distinction in the sounds, how shall it be known what is piped or harped?

8For if the trumpet give an uncertain sound, who shall prepare himself to the battle?

9So likewise ye, except ye utter by the tongue words easy to be understood, how shall it be known what is spoken? for ye shall speak into the air.

10There are, it may be, so many kinds of voices in the world, and none of them *is* without signification.

11Therefore if I know not the meaning of the voice, I shall be unto him that speaketh a barbarian, and he that speaketh *shall be* a barbarian unto me.

12Even so ye, forasmuch as ye are zealous of spiritual *gifts,* seek that ye may excel to the edifying of the church.

13Wherefore let him that speaketh in an *unknown* tongue pray that he may interpret.

14For if I pray in an *unknown* tongue, my spirit prayeth, but my understanding is unfruitful.

15What is it then? I will pray with the spirit, and I will pray with the understanding also: I will sing with the spirit, and I will sing with the understanding also.

16Else when thou shalt bless with the spirit, how shall he that occupieth the room of the unlearned say Amen at thy giving of thanks, seeing he understandeth not what thou sayest?

17For thou verily givest thanks well, but the other is not edified.

18I thank my God, I speak with tongues more than ye all:

19Yet in the church I had rather speak five words with my understanding, that *by my voice* I might teach others also, than ten thousand words in an *unknown* tongue.

New International

Gifts of Prophecy and Tongues

14 FOLLOW THE way of love and eagerly desire spiritual gifts, especially the gift of prophecy.

2For anyone who speaks in a tongue[a] does not speak to men but to God. Indeed, no one understands him; he utters mysteries with his spirit.[b] 3But everyone who prophesies speaks to men for their strengthening, encouragement and comfort. 4He who speaks in a tongue edifies himself, but he who prophesies edifies the church. 5I would like every one of you to speak in tongues,[c] but I would rather have you prophesy. He who prophesies is greater than one who speaks in tongues,[c] unless he interprets, so that the church may be edified.

6Now, brothers, if I come to you and speak in tongues, what good will I be to you, unless I bring you some revelation or knowledge or prophecy or word of instruction? 7Even in the case of lifeless things that make sounds, such as the flute or harp, how will anyone know what tune is being played unless there is a distinction in the notes? 8Again, if the trumpet does not sound a clear call, who will get ready for battle? 9So it is with you. Unless you speak intelligible words with your tongue, how will anyone know what you are saying? You will just be speaking into the air. 10Undoubtedly there are all sorts of languages in the world, yet none of them is without meaning. 11If then I do not grasp the meaning of what someone is saying, I am a foreigner to the speaker, and he is a foreigner to me. 12So it is with you. Since you are eager to have spiritual gifts, try to excel in gifts that build up the church.

13For this reason anyone who speaks in a tongue should pray that he may interpret what he says. 14For if I pray in a tongue, my spirit prays, but my mind is unfruitful. 15So what shall I do? I will pray with my spirit, but I will also pray with my mind; I will sing with my spirit, but I will also sing with my mind. 16If you are praising God with your spirit, how can one who finds himself among those who do not understand[d] say "Amen" to your thanksgiving, since he does not know what you are saying? 17You may be giving thanks well enough, but the other man is not edified.

18I thank God that I speak in tongues more than all of you. 19But in the church I would rather speak five intelligible words to instruct others than ten thousand words in a tongue.

---

a 2 Or *another language;* also in verses 4, 13, 14, 19, 26 and 27   b 2 Or *by the Spirit*   c 5 Or *other languages;* also in verses 6, 18, 22, 23 and 39   d 16 Or *among the inquirers*

Living Bible

14 LET LOVE be your greatest aim; nevertheless, ask also for the special abilities the Holy Spirit gives, and especially the gift of prophecy, being able to preach the messages of God.

²But if your gift is that of being able to "speak in tongues," that is, to speak in languages you haven't learned, you will be talking to God but not to others, since they won't be able to understand you. You will be speaking by the power of the Spirit but it will all be a secret. ³But one who prophesies, preaching the messages of God, is helping others grow in the Lord, encouraging and comforting them. ⁴So a person "speaking in tongues" helps himself grow spiritually, but one who prophesies, preaching messages from God, helps the entire church grow in holiness and happiness.

⁵I wish you all had the gift of "speaking in tongues" but, even more, I wish you were all able to prophesy, preaching God's messages, for that is a greater and more useful power than to speak in unknown languages—unless, of course, you can tell everyone afterwards what you were saying, so that they can get some good out of it too.

⁶Dear friends, even if I myself should come to you talking in some language you don't understand, how would that help you? But if I speak plainly what God has revealed to me, and tell you the things I know, and what is going to happen, and the great truths of God's Word—that is what you need; that is what will help you. ⁷Even musical instruments—the flute, for instance, or the harp—are examples of the need for speaking in plain, simple Englishᵉ rather than in unknown languages. For no one will recognize the tune the flute is playing unless each note is sounded clearly. ⁸And if the army bugler doesn't play the right notes, how will the soldiers know that they are being called to battle? ⁹In the same way, if you talk to a person in some language he doesn't understand, how will he know what you mean? You might as well be talking to an empty room.

¹⁰I suppose that there are hundreds of different languages in the world, and all are excellent for those who understand them, ¹¹but to me they mean nothing. A person talking to me in one of these languages will be a stranger to me and I will be a stranger to him. ¹²Since you are so anxious to have special gifts from the Holy Spirit, ask him for the very best, for those that will be of real help to the whole church.

¹³If someone is given the gift of speaking in unknown tongues, he should pray also for the gift of knowing what he has said, so that he can tell people afterwards, plainly. ¹⁴For if I pray in a language I don't understand, my spirit is praying but I don't know what I am saying.

¹⁵Well, then, what shall I do? I will do both. I will pray in unknown tongues and also in ordinary language that everyone understands. I will sing in unknown tongues and also in ordinary language, so that I can understand the praise I am giving; ¹⁶for if you praise and thank God with the spirit alone, speaking in another language, how can those who don't understand you be praising God along with you? How can they join you in giving thanks when they don't know what you are saying? ¹⁷You will be giving thanks very nicely, no doubt, but the other people present won't be helped.

¹⁸I thank God that I "speak in tongues" privatelyᶠ more than any of the rest of you. ¹⁹But in public worship I would much rather speak five words that people can understand and be helped by, than ten thousand words while "speaking in tongues" in an unknown language.

New Revised Standard

Gifts of Prophecy and Tongues

14 PURSUE LOVE and strive for the spiritual gifts, and especially that you may prophesy. ²For those who speak in a tongue do not speak to other people but to God; for nobody understands them, since they are speaking mysteries in the Spirit. ³On the other hand, those who prophesy speak to other people for their upbuilding and encouragement and consolation. ⁴Those who speak in a tongue build up themselves, but those who prophesy build up the church. ⁵Now I would like all of you to speak in tongues, but even more to prophesy. One who prophesies is greater than one who speaks in tongues, unless someone interprets, so that the church may be built up.

6 Now, brothers and sisters,ᵍ if I come to you speaking in tongues, how will I benefit you unless I speak to you in some revelation or knowledge or prophecy or teaching? ⁷It is the same way with lifeless instruments that produce sound, such as the flute or the harp. If they do not give distinct notes, how will anyone know what is being played? ⁸And if the bugle gives an indistinct sound, who will get ready for battle? ⁹So with yourselves; if in a tongue you utter speech that is not intelligible, how will anyone know what is being said? For you will be speaking into the air. ¹⁰There are doubtless many different kinds of sounds in the world, and nothing is without sound. ¹¹If then I do not know the meaning of a sound, I will be a foreigner to the speaker and the speaker a foreigner to me. ¹²So with yourselves; since you are eager for spiritual gifts, strive to excel in them for building up the church.

13 Therefore, one who speaks in a tongue should pray for the power to interpret. ¹⁴For if I pray in a tongue, my spirit prays but my mind is unproductive. ¹⁵What should I do then? I will pray with the spirit, but I will pray with the mind also; I will sing praise with the spirit, but I will sing praise with the mind also. ¹⁶Otherwise, if you say a blessing with the spirit, how can anyone in the position of an outsider say the "Amen" to your thanksgiving, since the outsider does not know what you are saying? ¹⁷For you may give thanks well enough, but the other person is not built up. ¹⁸I thank God that I speak in tongues more than all of you; ¹⁹nevertheless, in church I would rather speak five words with my mind, in order to instruct others also, than ten thousand words in a tongue.

ᵉ *14:7 simple English.* The local language, whatever it is.   ᶠ *14:18 privately,* implied. See vss 19, 28.   ᵍ Gk *brothers*

King James

20Brethren, be not children in understanding: howbeit in malice be ye children, but in understanding be men.

21In the law it is written, With *men of* other tongues and other lips will I speak unto this people; and yet for all that will they not hear me, saith the Lord.

22Wherefore tongues are for a sign, not to them that believe, but to them that believe not: but prophesying *serveth* not for them that believe not, but for them which believe.

23If therefore the whole church be come together into one place, and all speak with tongues, and there come in *those that are* unlearned, or unbelievers, will they not say that ye are mad?

24But if all prophesy, and there come in one that believeth not, or *one* unlearned, he is convinced of all, he is judged of all:

25And thus are the secrets of his heart made manifest; and so falling down on *his* face he will worship God, and report that God is in you of a truth.

26How is it then, brethren? when ye come together, every one of you hath a psalm, hath a doctrine, hath a tongue, hath a revelation, hath an interpretation. Let all things be done unto edifying.

27If any man speak in an *unknown* tongue, *let it be* by two, or at the most *by* three, and *that* by course; and let one interpret.

28But if there be no interpreter, let him keep silence in the church; and let him speak to himself, and to God.

29Let the prophets speak two or three, and let the other judge.

30If *any thing* be revealed to another that sitteth by, let the first hold his peace.

31For ye may all prophesy one by one, that all may learn, and all may be comforted.

32And the spirits of the prophets are subject to the prophets.

33For God is not *the author* of confusion, but of peace, as in all churches of the saints.

34Let your women keep silence in the churches: for it is not permitted unto them to speak; but *they are commanded* to be under obedience, as also saith the law.

35And if they will learn any thing, let them ask their husbands at home: for it is a shame for women to speak in the church.

36What? came the word of God out from you? or came it unto you only?

37If any man think himself to be a prophet, or spiritual, let him acknowledge that the things that I write unto you are the commandments of the Lord.

38But if any man be ignorant, let him be ignorant.

39Wherefore, brethren, covet to prophesy, and forbid not to speak with tongues.

40Let all things be done decently and in order.

New International

20Brothers, stop thinking like children. In regard to evil be infants, but in your thinking be adults. 21In the Law it is written:

"Through men of strange tongues
　　and through the lips of foreigners
I will speak to this people,
　　but even then they will not listen to me,"[a]
says the Lord.

22Tongues, then, are a sign, not for believers but for unbelievers; prophecy, however, is for believers, not for unbelievers. 23So if the whole church comes together and everyone speaks in tongues, and some who do not understand[b] or some unbelievers come in, will they not say that you are out of your mind? 24But if an unbeliever or someone who does not understand[c] comes in while everybody is prophesying, he will be convinced by all that he is a sinner and will be judged by all, 25and the secrets of his heart will be laid bare. So he will fall down and worship God, exclaiming, "God is really among you!"

Orderly Worship

26What then shall we say, brothers? When you come together, everyone has a hymn, or a word of instruction, a revelation, a tongue or an interpretation. All of these must be done for the strengthening of the church. 27If anyone speaks in a tongue, two—or at the most three—should speak, one at a time, and someone must interpret. 28If there is no interpreter, the speaker should keep quiet in the church and speak to himself and God.

29Two or three prophets should speak, and the others should weigh carefully what is said. 30And if a revelation comes to someone who is sitting down, the first speaker should stop. 31For you can all prophesy in turn so that everyone may be instructed and encouraged. 32The spirits of prophets are subject to the control of prophets. 33For God is not a God of disorder but of peace.

As in all the congregations of the saints, 34women should remain silent in the churches. They are not allowed to speak, but must be in submission, as the Law says. 35If they want to inquire about something, they should ask their own husbands at home; for it is disgraceful for a woman to speak in the church.

36Did the word of God originate with you? Or are you the only people it has reached? 37If anybody thinks he is a prophet or spiritually gifted, let him acknowledge that what I am writing to you is the Lord's command. 38If he ignores this, he himself will be ignored.[d]

39Therefore, my brothers, be eager to prophesy, and do not forbid speaking in tongues. 40But everything should be done in a fitting and orderly way.

a 21 Isaiah 28:11,12　　b 23 Or *some inquirers*　　c 24 Or *or some inquirer*
d 38 Some manuscripts *If he is ignorant of this, let him be ignorant*

Living Bible

20Dear brothers, don't be childish in your understanding of these things. Be innocent babies when it comes to planning evil, but be men of intelligence in understanding matters of this kind. 21We are told in the ancient Scriptures that God would send men from other lands to speak in foreign languages to his people, but even then they would not listen. 22So you see that being able to "speak in tongues" is not a sign to God's children concerning his power, but is a sign to the unsaved. However, prophecy (preaching the deep truths of God) is what the Christians need, and unbelievers aren't yet ready for it. 23Even so, if an unsaved person, or someone who doesn't have these gifts, comes to church and hears you all talking in other languages, he is likely to think you are crazy. 24But if you prophesy, preaching God's Word, [even though such preaching is mostly for believerse] and an unsaved person or a new Christian comes in who does not understand about these things, all these sermons will convince him of the fact that he is a sinner, and his conscience will be pricked by everything he hears. 25As he listens, his secret thoughts will be laid bare and he will fall down on his knees and worship God, declaring that God is really there among you.

26Well, my brothers, let's add up what I am saying. When you meet together some will sing, another will teach, or tell some special information God has given him, or speak in an unknown language, or tell what someone else is saying who is speaking in the unknown language, but everything that is done must be useful to all, and build them up in the Lord. 27No more than two or three should speak in an unknown language, and they must speak one at a time, and someone must be ready to interpret what they are saying. 28But if no one is present who can interpret, they must not speak out loud. They must talk silently to themselves and to God in the unknown language but not publicly.

29, 30Two or three may prophesy, one at a time, if they have the gift, while all the others listen. But if, while someone is prophesying, someone else receives a message or idea from the Lord, the one who is speaking should stop. 31In this way all who have the gift of prophecy can speak, one after the other, and everyone will learn and be encouraged and helped. 32Remember that a person who has a message from God has the power to stop himself or wait his turn.f 33God is not one who likes things to be disorderly and upset. He likes harmony, and he finds it in all the other churches.

34Women should be silent during the church meetings. They are not to take part in the discussion, for they are subordinate to mens as the Scriptures also declare. 35If they have any questions to ask, let them ask their husbands at home, for it is improper for women to express their opinions in church meetings.

36You disagree? And do you think that the knowledge of God's will begins and ends with you Corinthians? Well, you are mistaken! 37You who claim to have the gift of prophecy or any other special ability from the Holy Spirit should be the first to realize that what I am saying is a commandment from the Lord himself. 38But if anyone still disagrees—well, we will leave him in his ignorance.h

39So, my fellow believers, long to be prophets so that you can preach God's message plainly; and never say it is wrong to "speak in tongues"; 40however, be sure that everything is done properly in a good and orderly way.

New Revised Standard

20 Brothers and sisters,i do not be children in your thinking; rather, be infants in evil, but in thinking be adults. 21In the law it is written,

"By people of strange tongues
    and by the lips of foreigners
  I will speak to this people;
    yet even then they will not listen to me,"

says the Lord. 22Tongues, then, are a sign not for believers but for unbelievers, while prophecy is not for unbelievers but for believers. 23If, therefore, the whole church comes together and all speak in tongues, and outsiders or unbelievers enter, will they not say that you are out of your mind? 24But if all prophesy, an unbeliever or outsider who enters is reproved by all and called to account by all. 25After the secrets of the unbeliever's heart are disclosed, that person will bow down before God and worship him, declaring, "God is really among you."

Orderly Worship

26 What should be done then, my friends?i When you come together, each one has a hymn, a lesson, a revelation, a tongue, or an interpretation. Let all things be done for building up. 27If anyone speaks in a tongue, let there be only two or at most three, and each in turn; and let one interpret. 28But if there is no one to interpret, let them be silent in church and speak to themselves and to God. 29Let two or three prophets speak, and let the others weigh what is said. 30If a revelation is made to someone else sitting nearby, let the first person be silent. 31For you can all prophesy one by one, so that all may learn and all be encouraged. 32And the spirits of prophets are subject to the prophets, 33for God is a God not of disorder but of peace.

(As in all the churches of the saints, 34women should be silent in the churches. For they are not permitted to speak, but should be subordinate, as the law also says. 35If there is anything they desire to know, let them ask their husbands at home. For it is shameful for a woman to speak in church.j 36Or did the word of God originate with you? Or are you the only ones it has reached?)

37 Anyone who claims to be a prophet, or to have spiritual powers, must acknowledge that what I am writing to you is a command of the Lord. 38Anyone who does not recognize this is not to be recognized. 39So, my friends,k be eager to prophesy, and do not forbid speaking in tongues; 40but all things should be done decently and in order.

---

e 14:24 even though such preaching is mostly for believers, implied. f 14:32 has the power to stop himself or wait his turn, literally, "The spirits of the prophets are subject to the prophets." g 14:34 they are subordinate to men, literally, "They are not authorized to speak." They are permitted to pray and prophesy (1 Cor 11:5), apparently in public meetings, but not to teach men (1 Tim 2:12). h 14:38 we will leave him in his ignorance, or, "If he disagrees, ignore his opinion."

i Gk brothers j Other ancient authorities put verses 34-35 after verse 40 k Gk my brothers

King James

15 MOREOVER, BRETHREN, I declare unto you the gospel which I preached unto you, which also ye have received, and wherein ye stand;

2By which also ye are saved, if ye keep in memory what I preached unto you, unless ye have believed in vain.

3For I delivered unto you first of all that which I also received, how that Christ died for our sins according to the scriptures;

4And that he was buried, and that he rose again the third day according to the scriptures:

5And that he was seen of Cephas, then of the twelve:

6After that, he was seen of above five hundred brethren at once; of whom the greater part remain unto this present, but some are fallen asleep.

7After that, he was seen of James; then of all the apostles.

8And last of all he was seen of me also, as of one born out of due time.

9For I am the least of the apostles, that am not meet to be called an apostle, because I persecuted the church of God.

10But by the grace of God I am what I am: and his grace which *was bestowed* upon me was not in vain; but I laboured more abundantly than they all: yet not I, but the grace of God which was with me.

11Therefore whether *it were* I or they, so we preach, and so ye believed.

12Now if Christ be preached that he rose from the dead, how say some among you that there is no resurrection of the dead?

13But if there be no resurrection of the dead, then is Christ not risen:

14And if Christ be not risen, then *is* our preaching vain, and your faith *is* also vain.

15Yea, and we are found false witnesses of God; because we have testified of God that he raised up Christ: whom he raised not up, if so be that the dead rise not.

16For if the dead rise not, then is not Christ raised:

17And if Christ be not raised, your faith *is* vain; ye are yet in your sins.

18Then they also which are fallen asleep in Christ are perished.

19If in this life only we have hope in Christ, we are of all men most miserable.

20But now is Christ risen from the dead, *and* become the firstfruits of them that slept.

21For since by man *came* death, by man *came* also the resurrection of the dead.

22For as in Adam all die, even so in Christ shall all be made alive.

23But every man in his own order: Christ the firstfruits; afterward they that are Christ's at his coming.

24Then *cometh* the end, when he shall have delivered up the kingdom to God, even the Father; when he shall have put down all rule and all authority and power.

25For he must reign, till he hath put all enemies under his feet.

26The last enemy *that* shall be destroyed *is* death.

27For he hath put all things under his feet. But when he saith all things are put under *him, it is* manifest that he is excepted, which did put all things under him.

28And when all things shall be subdued unto him, then shall the Son also himself be subject unto him that put all things under him, that God may be all in all.

New International

The Resurrection of Christ

15 NOW, BROTHERS, I want to remind you of the gospel I preached to you, which you received and on which you have taken your stand. 2By this gospel you are saved, if you hold firmly to the word I preached to you. Otherwise, you have believed in vain.

3For what I received I passed on to you as of first importance[a]: that Christ died for our sins according to the Scriptures, 4that he was buried, that he was raised on the third day according to the Scriptures, 5and that he appeared to Peter,[b] and then to the Twelve. 6After that, he appeared to more than five hundred of the brothers at the same time, most of whom are still living, though some have fallen asleep. 7Then he appeared to James, then to all the apostles, 8and last of all he appeared to me also, as to one abnormally born.

9For I am the least of the apostles and do not even deserve to be called an apostle, because I persecuted the church of God. 10But by the grace of God I am what I am, and his grace to me was not without effect. No, I worked harder than all of them—yet not I, but the grace of God that was with me. 11Whether, then, it was I or they, this is what we preach, and this is what you believed.

The Resurrection of the Dead

12But if it is preached that Christ has been raised from the dead, how can some of you say that there is no resurrection of the dead? 13If there is no resurrection of the dead, then not even Christ has been raised. 14And if Christ has not been raised, our preaching is useless and so is your faith. 15More than that, we are then found to be false witnesses about God, for we have testified about God that he raised Christ from the dead. But he did not raise him if in fact the dead are not raised. 16For if the dead are not raised, then Christ has not been raised either. 17And if Christ has not been raised, your faith is futile; you are still in your sins. 18Then those also who have fallen asleep in Christ are lost. 19If only for this life we have hope in Christ, we are to be pitied more than all men.

20But Christ has indeed been raised from the dead, the firstfruits of those who have fallen asleep. 21For since death came through a man, the resurrection of the dead comes also through a man. 22For as in Adam all die, so in Christ all will be made alive. 23But each in his own turn: Christ, the firstfruits; then, when he comes, those who belong to him. 24Then the end will come, when he hands over the kingdom to God the Father after he has destroyed all dominion, authority and power. 25For he must reign until he has put all his enemies under his feet. 26The last enemy to be destroyed is death. 27For he "has put everything under his feet."[c] Now when it says that "everything" has been put under him, it is clear that this does not include God himself, who put everything under Christ. 28When he has done this, then the Son himself will be made subject to him who put everything under him, so that God may be all in all.

a 3 Or *you at the first*   b 5 Greek *Cephas*   c 27 Psalm 8:6

Living Bible

15 NOW LET me remind you, brothers, of what the Gospel really is, for it has not changed—it is the same Good News I preached to you before. You welcomed it then and still do now, for your faith is squarely built upon this wonderful message; 2and it is this Good News that saves you if you still firmly believe it, unless of course you never really believed it in the first place.

3I passed on to you right from the first what had been told to me, that Christ died for our sins just as the Scriptures said he would, 4and that he was buried, and that three days afterwards he arose from the grave just as the prophets foretold. 5He was seen by Peter and later by the rest of "the Twelve."d 6After that he was seen by more than five hundred Christian brothers at one time, most of whom are still alive, though some have died by now. 7Then James saw him and later all the apostles. 8Last of all I saw him too, long after the others, as though I had been born almost too late for this. 9For I am the least worthy of all the apostles, and I shouldn't even be called an apostle at all after the way I treated the church of God.

10But whatever I am now it is all because God poured out such kindness and grace upon me—and not without results: for I have worked harder than all the other apostles, yet actually I wasn't doing it, but God working in me, to bless me. 11It makes no difference who worked the hardest, I or they; the important thing is that we preached the Gospel to you, and you believed it.

12But tell me this! Since you believe what we preach, that *Christ* rose from the dead, why are some of you saying that dead people will never come back to life again? 13For if there is no resurrection of the dead, then Christ must still be dead. 14And if he is still dead, then all our preaching is useless and your trust in God is empty, worthless, hopeless; 15and we apostles are all liars because we have said that God raised Christ from the grave, and of course that isn't true if the dead do not come back to life again. 16If they don't, then Christ is still dead, 17and you are very foolish to keep on trusting God to save you, and you are still under condemnation for your sins; 18in that case all Christians who have died are lost! 19And if being a Christian is of value to us only now in this life, we are the most miserable of creatures.

20But the fact is that Christ did actually rise from the dead, and has become the first of millionse who will come back to life again some day.

21Death came into the world because of what one man (Adam) did, and it is because of what this other man (Christ) has done that now there is the resurrection from the dead. 22Everyone dies because all of us are related to Adam, being members of his sinful race, and wherever there is sin, death results. But all who are related to Christ will rise again. 23Each, however, in his own turn: Christ rose first; then when Christ comes back, all his people will become alive again.

24After that the end will come when he will turn the Kingdom over to God the Father, having put down all enemies of every kind. 25For Christ will be King until he has defeated all his enemies, 26including the last enemy—death. This too must be defeated and ended. 27For the rule and authority over all things has been given to Christ by his Father; except, of course, Christ does not rule over the Father himself, who gave him this power to rule. 28When Christ has finally won the battle against all his enemies, then he, the Son of God, will put himself also under his Father's orders, so that God who has given him the victory over everything else will be utterly supreme.

New Revised Standard

The Resurrection of Christ

15 NOW I would remind you, brothers and sisters,f of the good newsg that I proclaimed to you, which you in turn received, in which also you stand, 2through which also you are being saved, if you hold firmly to the message that I proclaimed to you— unless you have come to believe in vain.

3 For I handed on to you as of first importance what I in turn had received: that Christ died for our sins in accordance with the scriptures, 4and that he was buried, and that he was raised on the third day in accordance with the scriptures, 5and that he appeared to Cephas, then to the twelve. 6Then he appeared to more than five hundred brothers and sistersf at one time, most of whom are still alive, though some have died.h 7Then he appeared to James, then to all the apostles. 8Last of all, as to one untimely born, he appeared also to me. 9For I am the least of the apostles, unfit to be called an apostle, because I persecuted the church of God. 10But by the grace of God I am what I am, and his grace toward me has not been in vain. On the contrary, I worked harder than any of them—though it was not I, but the grace of God that is with me. 11Whether then it was I or they, so we proclaim and so you have come to believe.

The Resurrection of the Dead

12 Now if Christ is proclaimed as raised from the dead, how can some of you say there is no resurrection of the dead? 13If there is no resurrection of the dead, then Christ has not been raised; 14and if Christ has not been raised, then our proclamation has been in vain and your faith has been in vain. 15We are even found to be misrepresenting God, because we testified of God that he raised Christ—whom he did not raise if it is true that the dead are not raised. 16For if the dead are not raised, then Christ has not been raised. 17If Christ has not been raised, your faith is futile and you are still in your sins. 18Then those also who have diedh in Christ have perished. 19If for this life only we have hoped in Christ, we are of all people most to be pitied.

20 But in fact Christ has been raised from the dead, the first fruits of those who have died.h 21For since death came through a human being, the resurrection of the dead has also come through a human being; 22for as all die in Adam, so all will be made alive in Christ. 23But each in his own order: Christ the first fruits, then at his coming those who belong to Christ. 24Then comes the end,i when he hands over the kingdom to God the Father, after he has destroyed every ruler and every authority and power. 25For he must reign until he has put all his enemies under his feet. 26The last enemy to be destroyed is death. 27For "Godj has put all things in subjection under his feet." But when it says, "All things are put in subjection," it is plain that this does not include the one who put all things in subjection under him. 28When all things are subjected to him, then the Son himself will also be subjected to the one who put all things in subjection under him, so that God may be all in all.

---

d *15:5 the Twelve*, the name given to Jesus' twelve disciples, and still used after Judas was gone from among them.   e *15:20 the first of millions*, literally, "the first-fruits of them that are asleep."

f Gk *brothers*   g Or *gospel*   h Gk *fallen asleep*   i Or *Then come the rest*
j Gk *he*

King James

²⁹Else what shall they do which are baptized for the dead, if the dead rise not at all? why are they then baptized for the dead?

³⁰And why stand we in jeopardy every hour?

³¹I protest by your rejoicing which I have in Christ Jesus our Lord, I die daily.

³²If after the manner of men I have fought with beasts at Ephesus, what advantageth it me, if the dead rise not? let us eat and drink: for tomorrow we die.

³³Be not deceived: evil communications corrupt good manners.

³⁴Awake to righteousness, and sin not; for some have not the knowledge of God: I speak *this* to your shame.

³⁵But some *man* will say, How are the dead raised up? and with what body do they come?

³⁶*Thou* fool, that which thou sowest is not quickened, except it die:

³⁷And that which thou sowest, thou sowest not that body that shall be, but bare grain, it may chance of wheat, or of some other *grain:*

³⁸But God giveth it a body as it hath pleased him, and to every seed his own body.

³⁹All flesh *is* not the same flesh: but *there is* one *kind of* flesh of men, another flesh of beasts, another of fishes, *and* another of birds.

⁴⁰*There are* also celestial bodies, and bodies terrestrial: but the glory of the celestial *is* one, and the *glory* of the terrestrial *is* another.

⁴¹*There is* one glory of the sun, and another glory of the moon, and another glory of the stars: for *one* star differeth from *another* star in glory.

⁴²So also *is* the resurrection of the dead. It is sown in corruption; it is raised in incorruption:

⁴³It is sown in dishonour; it is raised in glory: it is sown in weakness; it is raised in power:

⁴⁴It is sown a natural body; it is raised a spiritual body. There is a natural body, and there is a spiritual body.

⁴⁵And so it is written, The first man Adam was made a living soul; the last Adam *was made* a quickening spirit.

⁴⁶Howbeit that *was* not first which is spiritual, but that which is natural; and afterward that which is spiritual.

⁴⁷The first man *is* of the earth, earthy: the second man *is* the Lord from heaven.

⁴⁸As *is* the earthy, such *are* they also that are earthy: and as *is* the heavenly, such *are* they also that are heavenly.

⁴⁹And as we have borne the image of the earthy, we shall also bear the image of the heavenly.

⁵⁰Now this I say, brethren, that flesh and blood cannot inherit the kingdom of God; neither doth corruption inherit incorruption.

⁵¹Behold, I show you a mystery; We shall not all sleep, but we shall all be changed,

New International

²⁹Now if there is no resurrection, what will those do who are baptized for the dead? If the dead are not raised at all, why are people baptized for them? ³⁰And as for us, why do we endanger ourselves every hour? ³¹I die every day—I mean that, brothers—just as surely as I glory over you in Christ Jesus our Lord. ³²If I fought wild beasts in Ephesus for merely human reasons, what have I gained? If the dead are not raised,

> "Let us eat and drink,
> for tomorrow we die."[a]

³³Do not be misled: "Bad company corrupts good character." ³⁴Come back to your senses as you ought, and stop sinning; for there are some who are ignorant of God—I say this to your shame.

The Resurrection Body

³⁵But someone may ask, "How are the dead raised? With what kind of body will they come?" ³⁶How foolish! What you sow does not come to life unless it dies. ³⁷When you sow, you do not plant the body that will be, but just a seed, perhaps of wheat or of something else. ³⁸But God gives it a body as he has determined, and to each kind of seed he gives its own body. ³⁹All flesh is not the same: Men have one kind of flesh, animals have another, birds another and fish another. ⁴⁰There are also heavenly bodies and there are earthly bodies; but the splendor of the heavenly bodies is one kind, and the splendor of the earthly bodies is another. ⁴¹The sun has one kind of splendor, the moon another and the stars another; and star differs from star in splendor.

⁴²So will it be with the resurrection of the dead. The body that is sown is perishable, it is raised imperishable; ⁴³it is sown in dishonor, it is raised in glory; it is sown in weakness, it is raised in power; ⁴⁴it is sown a natural body, it is raised a spiritual body.

If there is a natural body, there is also a spiritual body. ⁴⁵So it is written: "The first man Adam became a living being"[b]; the last Adam, a life-giving spirit. ⁴⁶The spiritual did not come first, but the natural, and after that the spiritual. ⁴⁷The first man was of the dust of the earth, the second man from heaven. ⁴⁸As was the earthly man, so are those who are of the earth; and as is the man from heaven, so also are those who are of heaven. ⁴⁹And just as we have borne the likeness of the earthly man, so shall we[c] bear the likeness of the man from heaven.

⁵⁰I declare to you, brothers, that flesh and blood cannot inherit the kingdom of God, nor does the perishable inherit the imperishable. ⁵¹Listen, I tell you a mystery: We will not all sleep, but we will all be changed— ⁵²in

---

^a *32* Isaiah 22:13   ^b *45* Gen. 2:7   ^c *49* Some early manuscripts *so let us*

Living Bible

29If the dead will not come back to life again, then what point is there in people being baptized for those who are gone? Why do it unless you believe that the dead will some day rise again?

30And why should we ourselves be continually risking our lives, facing death hour by hour? 31For it is a fact that I face death daily; that is as true as my pride in your growth in the Lord. 32And what value was there in fighting wild beasts—those men of Ephesus—if it was only for what I gain in this life down here? If we will never live again after we die, then we might as well go and have ourselves a good time: let us eat, drink, and be merry. What's the difference? For tomorrow we die, and that ends everything!

33Don't be fooled by those who say such things. If you listen to them you will start acting like them. 34Get some sense and quit your sinning. For to your shame I say it, some of you are not even Christians at all and have never really known God.d

35But someone may ask, "How will the dead be brought back to life again? What kind of bodies will they have?" 36What a foolish question! You will find the answer in your own garden! When you put a seed into the ground it doesn't grow into a plant unless it "dies" first. 37And when the green shoot comes up out of the seed, it is very different from the seed you first planted. For all you put into the ground is a dry little seed of wheat, or whatever it is you are planting, 38then God gives it a beautiful new body—just the kind he wants it to have; a different kind of plant grows from each kind of seed. 39And just as there are different kinds of seeds and plants, so also there are different kinds of flesh. Humans, animals, fish, and birds are all different.

40The angelse in heaven have bodies far different from ours, and the beauty and the glory of their bodies is different from the beauty and the glory of ours. 41The sun has one kind of glory while the moon and stars have another kind. And the stars differ from each other in their beauty and brightness.

42In the same way, our earthly bodies which die and decay are different from the bodies we shall have when we come back to life again, for they will never die. 43The bodies we have now embarrass us for they become sick and die; but they will be full of glory when we come back to life again. Yes, they are weak, dying bodies now, but when we live again they will be full of strength. 44They are just human bodies at death, but when they come back to life they will be superhuman bodies. For just as there are natural, human bodies, there are also supernatural, spiritual bodies.

45The Scriptures tell us that the first man, Adam, was given a natural, human bodyf but Christg is moreh than that, for he was life-giving Spirit.

46First, then, we have these human bodies and later on God gives us spiritual, heavenly bodies. 47Adam was made from the dust of the earth, but Christ came from heaven above. 48Every human being has a body just like Adam's, made of dust, but all who become Christ's will have the same kind of body as his—a body from heaven. 49Just as each of us now has a body like Adam's, so we shall some day have a body like Christ's.

50I tell you this, my brothers: an earthly body made of flesh and blood cannot get into God's Kingdom. These perishable bodies of ours are not the right kind to live forever.

51But I am telling you this strange and wonderful secret: we shall not all die, but we shall all be given new bodies! 52It will all happen in a moment, in the twinkling

New Revised Standard

29 Otherwise, what will those people do who receive baptism on behalf of the dead? If the dead are not raised at all, why are people baptized on their behalf? 30 And why are we putting ourselves in danger every hour? 31 I die every day! That is as certain, brothers and sisters,i as my boasting of you—a boast that I make in Christ Jesus our Lord. 32 If with merely human hopes I fought with wild animals at Ephesus, what would I have gained by it? If the dead are not raised,

"Let us eat and drink,
for tomorrow we die."

33 Do not be deceived:

"Bad company ruins good morals."

34 Come to a sober and right mind, and sin no more; for some people have no knowledge of God. I say this to your shame.

The Resurrection Body

35 But someone will ask, "How are the dead raised? With what kind of body do they come?" 36 Fool! What you sow does not come to life unless it dies. 37 And as for what you sow, you do not sow the body that is to be, but a bare seed, perhaps of wheat or of some other grain. 38 But God gives it a body as he has chosen, and to each kind of seed its own body. 39 Not all flesh is alike, but there is one flesh for human beings, another for animals, another for birds, and another for fish. 40 There are both heavenly bodies and earthly bodies, but the glory of the heavenly is one thing, and that of the earthly is another. 41 There is one glory of the sun, and another glory of the moon, and another glory of the stars; indeed, star differs from star in glory.

42 So it is with the resurrection of the dead. What is sown is perishable, what is raised is imperishable. 43 It is sown in dishonor, it is raised in glory. It is sown in weakness, it is raised in power. 44 It is sown a physical body, it is raised a spiritual body. If there is a physical body, there is also a spiritual body. 45 Thus it is written, "The first man, Adam, became a living being"; the last Adam became a life-giving spirit. 46 But it is not the spiritual that is first, but the physical, and then the spiritual. 47 The first man was from the earth, a man of dust; the second man isj from heaven. 48 As was the man of dust, so are those who are of the dust; and as is the man of heaven, so are those who are of heaven. 49 Just as we have borne the image of the man of dust, we willk bear the image of the man of heaven.

50 What I am saying, brothers and sisters,i is this: flesh and blood cannot inherit the kingdom of God, nor does the perishable inherit the imperishable. 51 Listen, I will tell you a mystery! We will not all die,l but we will all be changed, 52 in a moment, in the twinkling of an

---

d 15:34 have never really known God, or, "There are some who know nothing of God."   e 15:40 The angels, literally, "There are celestial bodies." But perhaps this may refer to the sun, moon, planets, and stars.   f 15:45 human body, literally, "was made a living soul."   g 15:45 but Christ, literally, "the last Adam."   h 15:45 is more, implied.

i Gk brothers   j Other ancient authorities add the Lord   k Other ancient authorities read let us   l Gk fall asleep

King James

52In a moment, in the twinkling of an eye, at the last trump: for the trumpet shall sound, and the dead shall be raised incorruptible, and we shall be changed.

53For this corruptible must put on incorruption, and this mortal *must* put on immortality.

54So when this corruptible shall have put on incorruption, and this mortal shall have put on immortality, then shall be brought to pass the saying that is written, Death is swallowed up in victory.

55O death, where *is* thy sting? O grave, where *is* thy victory?

56The sting of death *is* sin; and the strength of sin *is* the law.

57But thanks *be* to God, which giveth us the victory through our Lord Jesus Christ.

58Therefore, my beloved brethren, be ye stedfast, unmoveable, always abounding in the work of the Lord, forasmuch as ye know that your labour is not in vain in the Lord.

16 NOW CONCERNING the collection for the saints, as I have given order to the churches of Galatia, even so do ye.

2Upon the first *day* of the week let every one of you lay by him in store, as *God* hath prospered him, that there be no gatherings when I come.

3And when I come, whomsoever ye shall approve by *your* letters, them will I send to bring your liberality unto Jerusalem.

4And if it be meet that I go also, they shall go with me.

5Now I will come unto you, when I shall pass through Macedonia: for I do pass through Macedonia.

6And it may be that I will abide, yea, and winter with you, that ye may bring me on my journey whithersoever I go.

7For I will not see you now by the way; but I trust to tarry a while with you, if the Lord permit.

8But I will tarry at Ephesus until Pentecost.

9For a great door and effectual is opened unto me, and *there are* many adversaries.

10Now if Timotheus come, see that he may be with you without fear: for he worketh the work of the Lord, as I also *do*.

11Let no man therefore despise him: but conduct him forth in peace, that he may come unto me: for I look for him with the brethren.

12As touching *our* brother Apollos, I greatly desired him to come unto you with the brethren: but his will was not at all to come at this time; but he will come when he shall have convenient time.

13Watch ye, stand fast in the faith, quit you like men, be strong.

14Let all your things be done with charity.

15I beseech you, brethren, (ye know the house of Stephanas, that it is the firstfruits of Achaia, and *that* they have addicted themselves to the ministry of the saints,)

16That ye submit yourselves unto such, and to every one that helpeth with *us,* and laboureth.

17I am glad of the coming of Stephanas and Fortunatus and Achaicus: for that which was lacking on your part they have supplied.

New International

a flash, in the twinkling of an eye, at the last trumpet. For the trumpet will sound, the dead will be raised imperishable, and we will be changed. 53For the perishable must clothe itself with the imperishable, and the mortal with immortality. 54When the perishable has been clothed with the imperishable, and the mortal with immortality, then the saying that is written will come true: "Death has been swallowed up in victory."a

55"Where, O death, is your victory?
    Where, O death, is your sting?"b

56The sting of death is sin, and the power of sin is the law. 57But thanks be to God! He gives us the victory through our Lord Jesus Christ.

58Therefore, my dear brothers, stand firm. Let nothing move you. Always give yourselves fully to the work of the Lord, because you know that your labor in the Lord is not in vain.

The Collection for God's People

16 NOW ABOUT the collection for God's people: Do what I told the Galatian churches to do. 2On the first day of every week, each one of you should set aside a sum of money in keeping with his income, saving it up, so that when I come no collections will have to be made. 3Then, when I arrive, I will give letters of introduction to the men you approve and send them with your gift to Jerusalem. 4If it seems advisable for me to go also, they will accompany me.

Personal Requests

5After I go through Macedonia, I will come to you—for I will be going through Macedonia. 6Perhaps I will stay with you awhile, or even spend the winter, so that you can help me on my journey, wherever I go. 7I do not want to see you now and make only a passing visit; I hope to spend some time with you, if the Lord permits. 8But I will stay on at Ephesus until Pentecost, 9because a great door for effective work has opened to me, and there are many who oppose me.

10If Timothy comes, see to it that he has nothing to fear while he is with you, for he is carrying on the work of the Lord, just as I am. 11No one, then, should refuse to accept him. Send him on his way in peace so that he may return to me. I am expecting him along with the brothers.

12Now about our brother Apollos: I strongly urged him to go to you with the brothers. He was quite unwilling to go now, but he will go when he has the opportunity.

13Be on your guard; stand firm in the faith; be men of courage; be strong. 14Do everything in love.

15You know that the household of Stephanas were the first converts in Achaia, and they have devoted themselves to the service of the saints. I urge you, brothers, 16to submit to such as these and to everyone who joins in the work, and labors at it. 17I was glad when Stephanas, Fortunatus and Achaicus arrived, because they have supplied what was lacking from you. 18For they re-

---

a 54 Isaiah 25:8   b 55 Hosea 13:14

Living Bible

of an eye, when the last trumpet is blown. For there will be a trumpet blast from the skyc and all the Christians who have died will suddenly become alive, with new bodies that will never, never die; and then we who are still alive shall suddenly have new bodies too. 53For our earthly bodies, the ones we have now that can die, must be transformed into heavenly bodies that cannot perish but will live forever.

54When this happens, then at last this Scripture will come true—"Death is swallowed up in victory." 55, 56O death, where then your victory? Where then your sting? For sin—the sting that causes death—will all be gone; and the law, which reveals our sins, will no longer be our judge. 57How we thank God for all of this! It is he who makes us victorious through Jesus Christ our Lord!

58So, my dear brothers, since future victory is sure, be strong and steady, always abounding in the Lord's work, for you know that nothing you do for the Lord is ever wasted as it would be if there were no resurrection.

16 NOW HERE are the directions about the money you are collecting to send to the Christians in Jerusalemd (and, by the way, these are the same directions I gave to the churches in Galatia). 2On every Lord's Day each of you should put aside something from what you have earned during the week, and use it for this offering. The amount depends on how much the Lord has helped you earn. Don't wait until I get there and then try to collect it all at once. 3When I come I will send your loving gift with a letter to Jerusalem, to be taken there by trustworthy messengers you yourselves will choose. 4And if it seems wise for me to go along too, then we can travel together.

5I am coming to visit you after I have been to Macedonia first, but I will be staying there only for a little while. 6It could be that I will stay longer with you, perhaps all winter, and then you can send me on to my next destination. 7This time I don't want to make just a passing visit and then go right on; I want to come and stay awhile, if the Lord will let me. 8I will be staying here at Ephesus until the holiday of Pentecost, 9for there is a wide open door for me to preach and teach here. So much is happening, but there are many enemies.

10If Timothy comes make him feel at home, for he is doing the Lord's work just as I am. 11Don't let anyone despise or ignore him [because he is younge], but send him back to me happy with his time among you; I am looking forward to seeing him soon, along with the others who are returning.

12I begged Apollos to visit you along with the others, but he thought that it was not at all God's will for him to go now; he will be seeing you later on when he has the opportunity.

13Keep your eyes open for spiritual danger; stand true to the Lord; act like men; be strong; 14and whatever you do, do it with kindness and love.

15Do you remember Stephanas and his family? They were the first to become Christians in Greece and they are spending their lives helping and serving Christians everywhere. 16Please follow their instructions and do everything you can to help them as well as all others like them who work hard at your side with such real devotion. 17I am so glad that Stephanas, Fortunatus, and Achaicus have arrived here for a visit. They have been making up for the help you aren't here to give me.

New Revised Standard

eye, at the last trumpet. For the trumpet will sound, and the dead will be raised imperishable, and we will be changed. 53For this perishable body must put on imperishability, and this mortal body must put on immortality. 54When this perishable body puts on imperishability, and this mortal body puts on immortality, then the saying that is written will be fulfilled:

"Death has been swallowed up in victory."
55 "Where, O death, is your victory?
     Where, O death, is your sting?"
56The sting of death is sin, and the power of sin is the law. 57But thanks be to God, who gives us the victory through our Lord Jesus Christ.

58 Therefore, my beloved,f be steadfast, immovable, always excelling in the work of the Lord, because you know that in the Lord your labor is not in vain.

The Collection for the Saints

16 NOW CONCERNING the collection for the saints: you should follow the directions I gave to the churches of Galatia. 2On the first day of every week, each of you is to put aside and save whatever extra you earn, so that collections need not be taken when I come. 3And when I arrive, I will send any whom you approve with letters to take your gift to Jerusalem. 4If it seems advisable that I should go also, they will accompany me.

Plans for Travel

5 I will visit you after passing through Macedonia—for I intend to pass through Macedonia— 6and perhaps I will stay with you or even spend the winter, so that you may send me on my way, wherever I go. 7I do not want to see you now just in passing, for I hope to spend some time with you, if the Lord permits. 8But I will stay in Ephesus until Pentecost, 9for a wide door for effective work has opened to me, and there are many adversaries.

10 If Timothy comes, see that he has nothing to fear among you, for he is doing the work of the Lord just as I am; 11therefore let no one despise him. Send him on his way in peace, so that he may come to me; for I am expecting him with the brothers.

12 Now concerning our brother Apollos, I strongly urged him to visit you with the other brothers, but he was not at all willingg to come now. He will come when he has the opportunity.

Final Messages and Greetings

13 Keep alert, stand firm in your faith, be courageous, be strong. 14Let all that you do be done in love.

15 Now, brothers and sisters,h you know that members of the household of Stephanas were the first converts in Achaia, and they have devoted themselves to the service of the saints; 16I urge you to put yourselves at the service of such people, and of everyone who works and toils with them. 17I rejoice at the coming of Stephanas and Fortunatus and Achaicus, because they have made up for your absence; 18for they refreshed my spirit

---

c 15:52 from the sky, implied.   d 16:1 Christians in Jerusalem, implied.   f Gk beloved brothers   g Or it was not at all God's will for him   h Gk
e 16:11 because he is young, implied in 1 Tim 4:12.   brothers

King James

18For they have refreshed my spirit and yours: therefore acknowledge ye them that are such.

19The churches of Asia salute you. Aquila and Priscilla salute you much in the Lord, with the church that is in their house.

20All the brethren greet you. Greet ye one another with an holy kiss.

21The salutation of *me* Paul with mine own hand.

22If any man love not the Lord Jesus Christ, let him be Anathema Maranatha.

23The grace of our Lord Jesus Christ *be* with you.

24My love *be* with you all in Christ Jesus. Amen.

New International

freshed my spirit and yours also. Such men deserve recognition.

Final Greetings

19The churches in the province of Asia send you greetings. Aquila and Priscillaa greet you warmly in the Lord, and so does the church that meets at their house. 20All the brothers here send you greetings. Greet one another with a holy kiss.

21I, Paul, write this greeting in my own hand.

22If anyone does not love the Lord—a curse be on him. Come, O Lordb!

23The grace of the Lord Jesus be with you.

24My love to all of you in Christ Jesus. Amen.c

a 19 Greek *Prisca*, a variant of *Priscilla*   b 22 In Aramaic the expression *Come, O Lord* is *Marana tha*.   c 24 Some manuscripts do not have *Amen*.

Living Bible

18They have cheered me greatly and have been a wonderful encouragement to me, as I am sure they were to you, too. I hope you properly appreciate the work of such men as these.

19The churches here in Asia send you their loving greetings. Aquila and Priscilla send you their love and so do all the others who meet in their home for their church service. 20All the friends here have asked me to say "hello" to you for them. And give each other a loving handshake when you meet.

21I will write these final words of this letter with my own hand: 22if anyone does not love the Lord, that person is cursed. Lord Jesus, come! 23May the love and favor of the Lord Jesus Christ rest upon you. 24My love to all of you, for we all belong to Christ Jesus.

Sincerely, Paul

New Revised Standard

as well as yours. So give recognition to such persons.

19 The churches of Asia send greetings. Aquila and Prisca, together with the church in their house, greet you warmly in the Lord. 20All the brothers and sistersd send greetings. Greet one another with a holy kiss.

21 I, Paul, write this greeting with my own hand. 22Let anyone be accursed who has no love for the Lord. Our Lord, come!e 23The grace of the Lord Jesus be with you. 24My love be with all of you in Christ Jesus.f

---

d Gk *brothers*   e Gk *Marana tha.* These Aramaic words can also be read *Maran atha,* meaning *Our Lord has come*   f Other ancient authorities add *Amen*

THE SECOND EPISTLE OF

PAUL THE APOSTLE TO THE

Corinthians

2 Corinthians

1 PAUL, AN apostle of Jesus Christ by the will of God, and Timothy *our* brother, unto the church of God which is at Corinth, with all the saints which are in all Achaia:

2Grace *be* to you and peace from God our Father, and *from* the Lord Jesus Christ.

3Blessed *be* God, even the Father of our Lord Jesus Christ, the Father of mercies, and the God of all comfort;

4Who comforteth us in all our tribulation, that we may be able to comfort them which are in any trouble, by the comfort wherewith we ourselves are comforted of God.

5For as the sufferings of Christ abound in us, so our consolation also aboundeth by Christ.

6And whether we be afflicted, *it is* for your consolation and salvation, which is effectual in the enduring of the same sufferings which we also suffer: or whether we be comforted, *it is* for your consolation and salvation.

7And our hope of you *is* stedfast, knowing, that as ye are partakers of the sufferings, so *shall ye be* also of the consolation.

8For we would not, brethren, have you ignorant of our trouble which came to us in Asia, that we were pressed out of measure, above strength, insomuch that we despaired even of life:

9But we had the sentence of death in ourselves, that we should not trust in ourselves, but in God which raiseth the dead:

10Who delivered us from so great a death, and doth deliver: in whom we trust that he will yet deliver *us;*

11Ye also helping together by prayer for us, that for the gift *bestowed* upon us by the means of many persons thanks may be given by many on our behalf.

12For our rejoicing is this, the testimony of our conscience, that in simplicity and godly sincerity, not with fleshly wisdom, but by the grace of God, we have had our conversation in the world, and more abundantly to you-ward.

13For we write none other things unto you, than what ye read or acknowledge; and I trust ye shall acknowledge even to the end;

14As also ye have acknowledged us in part, that we are your rejoicing, even as ye also *are* ours in the day of the Lord Jesus.

15And in this confidence I was minded to come unto you before, that ye might have a second benefit;

16And to pass by you into Macedonia, and to come again out of Macedonia unto you, and of you to be brought on my way toward Judaea.

17When I therefore was thus minded, did I use lightness? or the things that I purpose, do I purpose according to the flesh, that with me there should be yea yea, and nay nay?

18But *as* God *is* true, our word toward you was not yea and nay.

1 PAUL, AN apostle of Christ Jesus by the will of God, and Timothy our brother,

To the church of God in Corinth, together with all the saints throughout Achaia:

2Grace and peace to you from God our Father and the Lord Jesus Christ.

The God of All Comfort

3Praise be to the God and Father of our Lord Jesus Christ, the Father of compassion and the God of all comfort, 4who comforts us in all our troubles, so that we can comfort those in any trouble with the comfort we ourselves have received from God. 5For just as the sufferings of Christ flow over into our lives, so also through Christ our comfort overflows. 6If we are distressed, it is for your comfort and salvation; if we are comforted, it is for your comfort, which produces in you patient endurance of the same sufferings we suffer. 7And our hope for you is firm, because we know that just as you share in our sufferings, so also you share in our comfort.

8We do not want you to be uninformed, brothers, about the hardships we suffered in the province of Asia. We were under great pressure, far beyond our ability to endure, so that we despaired even of life. 9Indeed, in our hearts we felt the sentence of death. But this happened that we might not rely on ourselves but on God, who raises the dead. 10He has delivered us from such a deadly peril, and he will deliver us. On him we have set our hope that he will continue to deliver us, 11as you help us by your prayers. Then many will give thanks on our[a] behalf for the gracious favor granted us in answer to the prayers of many.

Paul's Change of Plans

12Now this is our boast: Our conscience testifies that we have conducted ourselves in the world, and especially in our relations with you, in the holiness and sincerity that are from God. We have done so not according to worldly wisdom but according to God's grace. 13For we do not write you anything you cannot read or understand. And I hope that, 14as you have understood us in part, you will come to understand fully that you can boast of us just as we will boast of you in the day of the Lord Jesus.

15Because I was confident of this, I planned to visit you first so that you might benefit twice. 16I planned to visit you on my way to Macedonia and to come back to you from Macedonia, and then to have you send me on my way to Judea. 17When I planned this, did I do it lightly? Or do I make my plans in a worldly manner so that in the same breath I say, "Yes, yes" and "No, no"?

18But as surely as God is faithful, our message to you is not "Yes" and "No." 19For the Son of God, Jesus

Living Bible

2 Corinthians

1 DEAR FRIENDS, This letter is from me, Paul, appointed by God to be Jesus Christ's messenger; and from our dear brother Timothy. We are writing to all of you Christians there in Corinth and throughout Greece.b 2May God our Father and the Lord Jesus Christ mightily bless each one of you, and give you peace.

3, 4What a wonderful God we have—he is the Father of our Lord Jesus Christ, the source of every mercy, and the one who so wonderfully comforts and strengthens us in our hardships and trials. And why does he do this? So that when others are troubled, needing our sympathy and encouragement, we can pass on to them this same help and comfort God has given us. 5You can be sure that the more we undergo sufferings for Christ, the more he will shower us with his comfort and encouragement. 6, 7We are in deep trouble for bringing you God's comfort and salvation. But in our trouble God has comforted us—and this, too, to help you: to show you from our personal experience how God will tenderly comfort you when you undergo these same sufferings. He will give you the strength to endure.

8I think you ought to know, dear brothers, about the hard time we went through in Asia. We were really crushed and overwhelmed, and feared we would never live through it. 9We felt we were doomed to die and saw how powerless we were to help ourselves; but that was good, for then we put everything into the hands of God, who alone could save us, for he can even raise the dead. 10And he did help us, and saved us from a terrible death; yes, and we expect him to do it again and again. 11But you must help us too, by praying for us. For much thanks and praise will go to God from you who see his wonderful answers to your prayers for our safety!

12We are so glad that we can say with utter honesty that in all our dealings we have been pure and sincere, quietly depending upon the Lord for his help, and not on our own skills. And that is even more true, if possible, about the way we have acted toward you. 13, 14My letters have been straightforward and sincere; nothing is written between the lines! And even though you don't know me very well (I hope someday you will), I want you to try to accept me and be proud of me, as you already are to some extent; just as I shall be of you on that day when our Lord Jesus comes back again.

15, 16It was because I was so sure of your understanding and trust that I planned to stop and see you on my way to Macedonia, as well as afterwards when I returned, so that I could be a double blessing to you and so that you could send me on my way to Judea.

17Then why, you may be asking, did I change my plan? Hadn't I really made up my mind yet? Or am I like a man of the world who says "yes" when he really means "no"? 18Never! As surely as God is true, I am not that sort of person. My "yes" means "yes."

New Revised Standard

THE SECOND LETTER OF

PAUL TO THE

Corinthians

Salutation

1 PAUL, AN apostle of Christ Jesus by the will of God, and Timothy our brother,
To the church of God that is in Corinth, including all the saints throughout Achaia:
2 Grace to you and peace from God our Father and the Lord Jesus Christ.

Paul's Thanksgiving after Affliction

3 Blessed be the God and Father of our Lord Jesus Christ, the Father of mercies and the God of all consolation, 4who consoles us in all our affliction, so that we may be able to console those who are in any affliction with the consolation with which we ourselves are consoled by God. 5For just as the sufferings of Christ are abundant for us, so also our consolation is abundant through Christ. 6If we are being afflicted, it is for your consolation and salvation; if we are being consoled, it is for your consolation, which you experience when you patiently endure the same sufferings that we are also suffering. 7Our hope for you is unshaken; for we know that as you share in our sufferings, so also you share in our consolation.

8 We do not want you to be unaware, brothers and sisters,c of the affliction we experienced in Asia; for we were so utterly, unbearably crushed that we despaired of life itself. 9Indeed, we felt that we had received the sentence of death so that we would rely not on ourselves but on God who raises the dead. 10He who rescued us from so deadly a peril will continue to rescue us; on him we have set our hope that he will rescue us again, 11as you also join in helping us by your prayers, so that many will give thanks on ourd behalf for the blessing granted us through the prayers of many.

The Postponement of Paul's Visit

12 Indeed, this is our boast, the testimony of our conscience: we have behaved in the world with frank-nesse and godly sincerity, not by earthly wisdom but by the grace of God—and all the more toward you. 13For we write you nothing other than what you can read and also understand; I hope you will understand until the end— 14as you have already understood us in part—that on the day of the Lord Jesus we are your boast even as you are our boast.

15 Since I was sure of this, I wanted to come to you first, so that you might have a double favor;f 16I wanted to visit you on my way to Macedonia, and to come back to you from Macedonia and have you send me on to Judea. 17Was I vacillating when I wanted to do this? Do I make my plans according to ordinary human standards,g ready to say "Yes, yes" and "No, no" at the same time? 18As surely as God is faithful, our word to you has not been "Yes and No." 19For the Son of God,

c Gk *brothers*   d Other ancient authorities read *your*   e Other ancient authorities read *holiness*   f Other ancient authorities read *pleasure*   g Gk *according to the flesh*

b 1:1 *throughout Greece*, or, "throughout Achaia."

King James

19For the Son of God, Jesus Christ, who was preached among you by us, *even* by me and Silvanus and Timotheus, was not yea and nay, but in him was yea.

20For all the promises of God in him *are* yea, and in him Amen, unto the glory of God by us.

21Now he which stablisheth us with you in Christ, and hath anointed us, *is* God;

22Who hath also sealed us, and given the earnest of the Spirit in our hearts.

23Moreover I call God for a record upon my soul, that to spare you I came not as yet unto Corinth.

24Not for that we have dominion over your faith, but are helpers of your joy: for by faith ye stand.

2 BUT I determined this with myself, that I would not come again to you in heaviness.

2For if I make you sorry, who is he then that maketh me glad, but the same which is made sorry by me?

3And I wrote this same unto you, lest, when I came, I should have sorrow from them of whom I ought to rejoice; having confidence in you all, that my joy is *the joy* of you all.

4For out of much affliction and anguish of heart I wrote unto you with many tears; not that ye should be grieved, but that ye might know the love which I have more abundantly unto you.

5But if any have caused grief, he hath not grieved me, but in part: that I may not overcharge you all.

6Sufficient to such a man *is* this punishment, which *was inflicted* of many.

7So that contrariwise ye *ought* rather to forgive *him,* and comfort *him,* lest perhaps such a one should be swallowed up with overmuch sorrow.

8Wherefore I beseech you that ye would confirm *your* love toward him.

9For to this end also did I write, that I might know the proof of you, whether ye be obedient in all things.

10To whom ye forgive any thing, I *forgive* also: for if I forgave any thing, to whom I forgave *it,* for your sakes *forgave I it* in the person of Christ;

11Lest Satan should get an advantage of us: for we are not ignorant of his devices.

12Furthermore, when I came to Troas to *preach* Christ's gospel, and a door was opened unto me of the Lord,

13I had no rest in my spirit, because I found not Titus my brother: but taking my leave of them, I went from thence into Macedonia.

14Now thanks *be* unto God, which always causeth us to triumph in Christ, and maketh manifest the savour of his knowledge by us in every place.

15For we are unto God a sweet savour of Christ, in them that are saved, and in them that perish:

New International

Christ, who was preached among you by me and Silas[a] and Timothy, was not "Yes" and "No," but in him it has always been "Yes." 20For no matter how many promises God has made, they are "Yes" in Christ. And so through him the "Amen" is spoken by us to the glory of God. 21Now it is God who makes both us and you stand firm in Christ. He anointed us, 22set his seal of ownership on us, and put his Spirit in our hearts as a deposit, guaranteeing what is to come.

23I call God as my witness that it was in order to spare you that I did not return to Corinth. 24Not that we lord it over your faith, but we work with you for your joy, because it is by faith you stand firm.

2 SO I made up my mind that I would not make another painful visit to you. 2For if I grieve you, who is left to make me glad but you whom I have grieved? 3I wrote as I did so that when I came I should not be distressed by those who ought to make me rejoice. I had confidence in all of you, that you would all share my joy. 4For I wrote you out of great distress and anguish of heart and with many tears, not to grieve you but to let you know the depth of my love for you.

Forgiveness for the Sinner

5If anyone has caused grief, he has not so much grieved me as he has grieved all of you, to some extent—not to put it too severely. 6The punishment inflicted on him by the majority is sufficient for him. 7Now instead, you ought to forgive and comfort him, so that he will not be overwhelmed by excessive sorrow. 8I urge you, therefore, to reaffirm your love for him. 9The reason I wrote you was to see if you would stand the test and be obedient in everything. 10If you forgive anyone, I also forgive him. And what I have forgiven—if there was anything to forgive—I have forgiven in the sight of Christ for your sake, 11in order that Satan might not outwit us. For we are not unaware of his schemes.

Ministers of the New Covenant

12Now when I went to Troas to preach the gospel of Christ and found that the Lord had opened a door for me, 13I still had no peace of mind, because I did not find my brother Titus there. So I said good-by to them and went on to Macedonia.

14But thanks be to God, who always leads us in triumphal procession in Christ and through us spreads everywhere the fragrance of the knowledge of him. 15For we are to God the aroma of Christ among those who are being saved and those who are perishing. 16To the one

---

Living Bible

19Timothy and Silvanus and I have been telling you about Jesus Christ the Son of God. He isn't one to say "yes" when he means "no." He always does exactly what he says. 20He carries out and fulfills all of God's promises, no matter how many of them there are; and we have told everyone how faithful he is, giving glory to his name. 21It is this God who has made you and me into faithful Christians and commissioned us apostles to preach the Good News. 22He has put his brand upon us—his mark of ownership—and given us his Holy Spirit in our hearts as guarantee that we belong to him, and as the first installment of all that he is going to give us.

23I call upon this God to witness against me if I am not telling the absolute truth: the reason I haven't come to visit you yet is that I don't want to sadden you with a severe rebuke. 24When I come, although I can't do much to help your faith, for it is strong already, I want to be able to do something about your joy: I want to make you happy, not sad.

2 "NO," I said to myself, "I won't do it. I'll not make them unhappy with another painful visit." 2For if I make you sad, who is going to make me happy? You are the ones to do it, and how can you if I cause you pain? 3That is why I wrote as I did in my last letter, so that you will get things straightened out before I come.b Then, when I do come, I will not be made sad by the very ones who ought to give me greatest joy. I felt sure that your happiness was so bound up in mine that you would not be happy either, unless I came with joy.

4Oh, how I hated to write that letter! It almost broke my heart and I tell you honestly that I cried over it. I didn't want to hurt you, but I had to show you how very much I loved you and cared about what was happening to you.

5, 6Remember that the man I wrote about, who caused all the trouble, has not caused sorrow to me as much as to all the rest of you—though I certainly have my share in it too. I don't want to be harder on him than I should. He has been punished enough by your united disapproval. 7Now it is time to forgive him and comfort him. Otherwise he may become so bitter and discouraged that he won't be able to recover. 8Please show him now that you still do love him very much.

9I wrote to you as I did so that I could find out how far you would go in obeying me. 10When you forgive anyone, I do too. And whatever I have forgiven (to the extent that this affected me too) has been by Christ's authority, and for your good. 11A further reason for forgiveness is to keep from being outsmarted by Satan; for we know what he is trying to do.

12Well, when I got as far as the city of Troas, the Lord gave me tremendous opportunities to preach the Gospel. 13But Titus, my dear brother, wasn't there to meet me and I couldn't rest, wondering where he was and what had happened to him. So I said good-bye and went right on to Macedonia to try to find him.

14But thanks be to God! For through what Christ has done, he has triumphed over us so that now wherever we go he uses us to tell others about the Lord and to spread the Gospel like a sweet perfume. 15As far as God is concerned there is a sweet, wholesome fragrance in our lives. It is the fragrance of Christ within us, an aroma to both the saved and the unsaved all around us. 16To

New Revised Standard

Jesus Christ, whom we proclaimed among you, Silvanus and Timothy and I, was not "Yes and No"; but in him it is always "Yes." 20For in him every one of God's promises is a "Yes." For this reason it is through him that we say the "Amen," to the glory of God. 21But it is God who establishes us with you in Christ and has anointed us, 22by putting his seal on us and giving us his Spirit in our hearts as a first installment.

23 But I call on God as witness against me: it was to spare you that I did not come again to Corinth. 24I do not mean to imply that we lord it over your faith; rather, we are workers with you for your joy, because you stand firm in the faith.

2 SO I made up my mind not to make you another painful visit. 2For if I cause you pain, who is there to make me glad but the one whom I have pained? 3And I wrote as I did, so that when I came, I might not suffer pain from those who should have made me rejoice; for I am confident about all of you, that my joy would be the joy of all of you. 4For I wrote you out of much distress and anguish of heart and with many tears, not to cause you pain, but to let you know the abundant love that I have for you.

Forgiveness for the Offender

5 But if anyone has caused pain, he has caused it not to me, but to some extent—not to exaggerate it—to all of you. 6This punishment by the majority is enough for such a person; 7so now instead you should forgive and console him, so that he may not be overwhelmed by excessive sorrow. 8So I urge you to reaffirm your love for him. 9I wrote for this reason: to test you and to know whether you are obedient in everything. 10Anyone whom you forgive, I also forgive. What I have forgiven, if I have forgiven anything, has been for your sake in the presence of Christ. 11And we do this so that we may not be outwitted by Satan; for we are not ignorant of his designs.

Paul's Anxiety in Troas

12 When I came to Troas to proclaim the good news of Christ, a door was opened for me in the Lord; 13but my mind could not rest because I did not find my brother Titus there. So I said farewell to them and went on to Macedonia.

14 But thanks be to God, who in Christ always leads us in triumphal procession, and through us spreads in every place the fragrance that comes from knowing him. 15For we are the aroma of Christ to God among those who are being saved and among those who are perishing;

---

b 2:3 *so that you will get things straightened out before I come,* implied.

King James

16To the one *we are* the savour of death unto death; and to the other the savour of life unto life. And who *is* sufficient for these things?

17For we are not as many, which corrupt the word of God: but as of sincerity, but as of God, in the sight of God speak we in Christ.

3 DO WE begin again to commend ourselves? or need we, as some *others,* epistles of commendation to you, or *letters* of commendation from you?

2Ye are our epistle written in our hearts, known and read of all men:

3*Forasmuch as ye are* manifestly declared to be the epistle of Christ ministered by us, written not with ink, but with the Spirit of the living God; not in tables of stone, but in fleshy tables of the heart.

4And such trust have we through Christ to God-ward:

5Not that we are sufficient of ourselves to think any thing as of ourselves; but our sufficiency *is* of God;

6Who also hath made us able ministers of the new testament; not of the letter, but of the spirit: for the letter killeth, but the spirit giveth life.

7But if the ministration of death, written *and* engraven in stones, was glorious, so that the children of Israel could not stedfastly behold the face of Moses for the glory of his countenance; which *glory* was to be done away:

8How shall not the ministration of the spirit be rather glorious?

9For if the ministration of condemnation *be* glory, much more doth the ministration of righteousness exceed in glory.

10For even that which was made glorious had no glory in this respect, by reason of the glory that excelleth.

11For if that which is done away *was* glorious, much more that which remaineth *is* glorious.

12Seeing then that we have such hope, we use great plainness of speech:

13And not as Moses, *which* put a veil over his face, that the children of Israel could not stedfastly look to the end of that which is abolished:

14But their minds were blinded: for until this day remaineth the same veil untaken away in the reading of the old testament; which *veil* is done away in Christ.

15But even unto this day, when Moses is read, the veil is upon their heart.

16Nevertheless when it shall turn to the Lord, the veil shall be taken away.

17Now the Lord is that Spirit: and where the Spirit of the Lord *is,* there *is* liberty.

18But we all, with open face beholding as in a glass the glory of the Lord, are changed into the same image from glory to glory, *even* as by the Spirit of the Lord.

New International

we are the smell of death; to the other, the fragrance of life. And who is equal to such a task? 17Unlike so many, we do not peddle the word of God for profit. On the contrary, in Christ we speak before God with sincerity, like men sent from God.

3 ARE WE beginning to commend ourselves again? Or do we need, like some people, letters of recommendation to you or from you? 2You yourselves are our letter, written on our hearts, known and read by everybody. 3You show that you are a letter from Christ, the result of our ministry, written not with ink but with the Spirit of the living God, not on tablets of stone but on tablets of human hearts.

4Such confidence as this is ours through Christ before God. 5Not that we are competent in ourselves to claim anything for ourselves, but our competence comes from God. 6He has made us competent as ministers of a new covenant—not of the letter but of the Spirit; for the letter kills, but the Spirit gives life.

The Glory of the New Covenant

7Now if the ministry that brought death, which was engraved in letters on stone, came with glory, so that the Israelites could not look steadily at the face of Moses because of its glory, fading though it was, 8will not the ministry of the Spirit be even more glorious? 9If the ministry that condemns men is glorious, how much more glorious is the ministry that brings righteousness! 10For what was glorious has no glory now in comparison with the surpassing glory. 11And if what was fading away came with glory, how much greater is the glory of that which lasts!

12Therefore, since we have such a hope, we are very bold. 13We are not like Moses, who would put a veil over his face to keep the Israelites from gazing at it while the radiance was fading away. 14But their minds were made dull, for to this day the same veil remains when the old covenant is read. It has not been removed, because only in Christ is it taken away. 15Even to this day when Moses is read, a veil covers their hearts. 16But whenever anyone turns to the Lord, the veil is taken away. 17Now the Lord is the Spirit, and where the Spirit of the Lord is, there is freedom. 18And we, who with unveiled faces all reflecta the Lord's glory, are being transformed into his likeness with ever-increasing glory, which comes from the Lord, who is the Spirit.

---

a 18 Or *contemplate*

Living Bible

those who are not being saved, we seem a fearful smell of death and doom, while to those who know Christ we are a life-giving perfume. But who is adequate for such a task as this? 17Only those who, like ourselves, are men of integrity, sent by God, speaking with Christ's power, with God's eye upon us. We are not like those hucksters—and there are many of them—whose idea in getting out the Gospel is to make a good living out of it.

3 ARE WE beginning to be like those false teachers of yours who must tell you all about themselves and bring long letters of recommendation with them? I think you hardly need someone's letter to tell you about us, do you? And we don't need a recommendation from you, either! 2The only letter I need is you yourselves! By looking at the good change in your hearts, everyone can see that we have done a good work among you. 3They can see that you are a letter from Christ, written by us. It is not a letter written with pen and ink, but by the Spirit of the living God; not one carved on stone, but in human hearts.

4We dare to say these good things about ourselves only because of our great trust in God through Christ, that he will help us to be true to what we say, 5and not because we think we can do anything of lasting value by ourselves. Our only power and success comes from God. 6He is the one who has helped us tell others about his new agreement to save them. We do not tell them that they must obey every law of God or die; but we tell them there is life for them from the Holy Spirit. The old way, trying to be saved by keeping the Ten Commandments, ends in death; in the new way, the Holy Spirit gives them life.

7Yet that old system of law that led to death began with such glory that people could not bear to look at Moses' face. For as he gave them God's law to obey, his face shone out with the very glory of God—though the brightness was already fading away. 8Shall we not expect far greater glory in these days when the Holy Spirit is giving life? 9If the plan that leads to doom was glorious, much more glorious is the plan that makes men right with God. 10In fact, that first glory as it shone from Moses' face is worth nothing at all in comparison with the overwhelming glory of the new agreement. 11So if the old system that faded into nothing was full of heavenly glory, the glory of God's new plan for our salvation is certainly far greater, for it is eternal.

12Since we know that this new glory will never go away, we can preach with great boldness, 13and not as Moses did, who put a veil over his face so that the Israelis could not see the glory fade away.

14Not only Moses' face was veiled, but his people's minds and understanding were veiled and blinded too. Even now when the Scripture is read it seems as though Jewish hearts and minds are covered by a thick veil, because they cannot see and understand the real meaning of the Scriptures. For this veil of misunderstanding can be removed only by believing in Christ. 15Yes, even today when they read Moses' writings their hearts are blind and they think that obeying the Ten Commandments is the way to be saved.

16But whenever anyone turns to the Lord from his sins, then the veil is taken away. 17The Lord is the Spirit who gives them life, and where he is there is freedom [from trying to be saved by keeping the laws of Godb]. 18But we Christians have no veil over our faces; we can be mirrors that brightly reflect the glory of the Lord. And as the Spirit of the Lord works within us, we become more and more like him.

New Revised Standard

16to the one a fragrance from death to death, to the other a fragrance from life to life. Who is sufficient for these things? 17For we are not peddlers of God's word like so many;c but in Christ we speak as persons of sincerity, as persons sent from God and standing in his presence.

Ministers of the New Covenant

3 ARE WE beginning to commend ourselves again? Surely we do not need, as some do, letters of recommendation to you or from you, do we? 2You yourselves are our letter, written on ourd hearts, to be known and read by all; 3and you show that you are a letter of Christ, prepared by us, written not with ink but with the Spirit of the living God, not on tablets of stone but on tablets of human hearts.

4 Such is the confidence that we have through Christ toward God. 5Not that we are competent of ourselves to claim anything as coming from us; our competence is from God, 6who has made us competent to be ministers of a new covenant, not of letter but of spirit; for the letter kills, but the Spirit gives life.

7 Now if the ministry of death, chiseled in letters on stone tablets,e came in glory so that the people of Israel could not gaze at Moses' face because of the glory of his face, a glory now set aside, 8how much more will the ministry of the Spirit come in glory? 9For if there was glory in the ministry of condemnation, much more does the ministry of justification abound in glory! 10Indeed, what once had glory has lost its glory because of the greater glory; 11for if what was set aside came through glory, much more has the permanent come in glory!

12 Since, then, we have such a hope, we act with great boldness, 13not like Moses, who put a veil over his face to keep the people of Israel from gazing at the end of the glory thatf was being set aside. 14But their minds were hardened. Indeed, to this very day, when they hear the reading of the old covenant, that same veil is still there, since only in Christ is it set aside. 15Indeed, to this very day whenever Moses is read, a veil lies over their minds; 16but when one turns to the Lord, the veil is removed. 17Now the Lord is the Spirit, and where the Spirit of the Lord is, there is freedom. 18And all of us, with unveiled faces, seeing the glory of the Lord as though reflected in a mirror, are being transformed into the same image from one degree of glory to another; for this comes from the Lord, the Spirit.

---

b 3:17 from trying to be saved by keeping the laws of God, implied.

c Other ancient authorities read *like the others*   d Other ancient authorities read *your*   e Gk *on stones*   f Gk *of what*

King James

4 THEREFORE SEEING we have this ministry, as we have received mercy, we faint not;

2But have renounced the hidden things of dishonesty, not walking in craftiness, nor handling the word of God deceitfully; but by manifestation of the truth commending ourselves to every man's conscience in the sight of God.

3But if our gospel be hid, it is hid to them that are lost:

4In whom the god of this world hath blinded the minds of them which believe not, lest the light of the glorious gospel of Christ, who is the image of God, should shine unto them.

5For we preach not ourselves, but Christ Jesus the Lord; and ourselves your servants for Jesus' sake.

6For God, who commanded the light to shine out of darkness, hath shined in our hearts, to *give* the light of the knowledge of the glory of God in the face of Jesus Christ.

7But we have this treasure in earthen vessels, that the excellency of the power may be of God, and not of us.

8*We are* troubled on every side, yet not distressed; *we are* perplexed, but not in despair;

9Persecuted, but not forsaken; cast down, but not destroyed;

10Always bearing about in the body the dying of the Lord Jesus, that the life also of Jesus might be made manifest in our body.

11For we which live are always delivered unto death for Jesus' sake, that the life also of Jesus might be made manifest in our mortal flesh.

12So then death worketh in us, but life in you.

13We having the same spirit of faith, according as it is written, I believed, and therefore have I spoken; we also believe, and therefore speak;

14Knowing that he which raised up the Lord Jesus shall raise up us also by Jesus, and shall present *us* with you.

15For all things *are* for your sakes, that the abundant grace might through the thanksgiving of many redound to the glory of God.

16For which cause we faint not; but though our outward man perish, yet the inward *man* is renewed day by day.

17For our light affliction, which is but for a moment, worketh for us a far more exceeding *and* eternal weight of glory;

18While we look not at the things which are seen, but at the things which are not seen: for the things which are seen *are* temporal; but the things which are not seen *are* eternal.

5 FOR WE know that if our earthly house of *this* tabernacle were dissolved, we have a building of God, an house not made with hands, eternal in the heavens.

New International

Treasures in Jars of Clay

4 THEREFORE, SINCE through God's mercy we have this ministry, we do not lose heart. 2Rather, we have renounced secret and shameful ways; we do not use deception, nor do we distort the word of God. On the contrary, by setting forth the truth plainly we commend ourselves to every man's conscience in the sight of God. 3And even if our gospel is veiled, it is veiled to those who are perishing. 4The god of this age has blinded the minds of unbelievers, so that they cannot see the light of the gospel of the glory of Christ, who is the image of God. 5For we do not preach ourselves, but Jesus Christ as Lord, and ourselves as your servants for Jesus' sake. 6For God, who said, "Let light shine out of darkness,"a made his light shine in our hearts to give us the light of the knowledge of the glory of God in the face of Christ.

7But we have this treasure in jars of clay to show that this all-surpassing power is from God and not from us. 8We are hard pressed on every side, but not crushed; perplexed, but not in despair; 9persecuted, but not abandoned; struck down, but not destroyed. 10We always carry around in our body the death of Jesus, so that the life of Jesus may also be revealed in our body. 11For we who are alive are always being given over to death for Jesus' sake, so that his life may be revealed in our mortal body. 12So then, death is at work in us, but life is at work in you.

13It is written: "I believed; therefore I have spoken."b With that same spirit of faith we also believe and therefore speak, 14because we know that the one who raised the Lord Jesus from the dead will also raise us with Jesus and present us with you in his presence. 15All this is for your benefit, so that the grace that is reaching more and more people may cause thanksgiving to overflow to the glory of God.

16Therefore we do not lose heart. Though outwardly we are wasting away, yet inwardly we are being renewed day by day. 17For our light and momentary troubles are achieving for us an eternal glory that far outweighs them all. 18So we fix our eyes not on what is seen, but on what is unseen. For what is seen is temporary, but what is unseen is eternal.

Our Heavenly Dwelling

5 NOW WE know that if the earthly tent we live in is destroyed, we have a building from God, an eternal house in heaven, not built by human hands.

a 6 Gen. 1:3   b 13 Psalm 116:10

Living Bible

4 IT IS God himself, in his mercy, who has given us this wonderful work [of telling his Good News to others^c], and so we never give up. ²We do not try to trick people into believing—we are not interested in fooling anyone. We never try to get anyone to believe that the Bible teaches what it doesn't. All such shameful methods we forego. We stand in the presence of God as we speak and so we tell the truth, as all who know us will agree.

³If the Good News we preach is hidden to anyone, it is hidden from the one who is on the road to eternal death. ⁴Satan, who is the god of this evil world, has made him blind, unable to see the glorious light of the Gospel that is shining upon him, or to understand the amazing message we preach about the glory of Christ, who is God.^d ⁵We don't go around preaching about ourselves, but about Christ Jesus as Lord. All we say of ourselves is that we are your slaves because of what Jesus has done for us. ⁶For God, who said, "Let there be light in the darkness," has made us understand that it is the brightness of his glory that is seen in the face of Jesus Christ.

⁷But this precious treasure—this light and power that now shine within us^e—is held in a perishable container, that is, in our weak bodies. Everyone can see that the glorious power within must be from God and is not our own.

⁸We are pressed on every side by troubles, but not crushed and broken. We are perplexed because we don't know why things happen as they do, but we don't give up and quit. ⁹We are hunted down, but God never abandons us. We get knocked down, but we get up again and keep going. ¹⁰These bodies of ours are constantly facing death just as Jesus did; so it is clear to all that it is only the living Christ within [who keeps us safe^f].

¹¹Yes, we live under constant danger to our lives because we serve the Lord, but this gives us constant opportunities to show forth the power of Jesus Christ within our dying bodies. ¹²Because of our preaching we face death, but it has resulted in eternal life for you.

¹³We boldly say what we believe [trusting God to care for us^g], just as the Psalm writer did when he said, "I believe and therefore I speak." ¹⁴We know that the same God who brought the Lord Jesus back from death will also bring us back to life again with Jesus, and present us to him along with you. ¹⁵These sufferings of ours are for your benefit. And the more of you who are won to Christ, the more there are to thank him for his great kindness, and the more the Lord is glorified.

¹⁶That is why we never give up. Though our bodies are dying, our inner strength in the Lord is growing every day. ¹⁷These troubles and sufferings of ours are, after all, quite small and won't last very long. Yet this short time of distress will result in God's richest blessing upon us forever and ever! ¹⁸So we do not look at what we can see right now, the troubles all around us, but look forward to the joys in heaven which we have not yet seen. The troubles will soon be over, but the joys to come will last forever.

5 FOR WE know that when this tent we live in now is taken down—when we die and leave these bodies—we will have wonderful new bodies in heaven, homes that will be ours forevermore, made for us by God himself, and not by human hands. ²How weary we

New Revised Standard

Treasure in Clay Jars

4 THEREFORE, SINCE it is by God's mercy that we are engaged in this ministry, we do not lose heart. ²We have renounced the shameful things that one hides; we refuse to practice cunning or to falsify God's word; but by the open statement of the truth we commend ourselves to the conscience of everyone in the sight of God. ³And even if our gospel is veiled, it is veiled to those who are perishing. ⁴In their case the god of this world has blinded the minds of the unbelievers, to keep them from seeing the light of the gospel of the glory of Christ, who is the image of God. ⁵For we do not proclaim ourselves; we proclaim Jesus Christ as Lord and ourselves as your slaves for Jesus' sake. ⁶For it is the God who said, "Let light shine out of darkness," who has shone in our hearts to give the light of the knowledge of the glory of God in the face of Jesus Christ.

7 But we have this treasure in clay jars, so that it may be made clear that this extraordinary power belongs to God and does not come from us. ⁸We are afflicted in every way, but not crushed; perplexed, but not driven to despair; ⁹persecuted, but not forsaken; struck down, but not destroyed; ¹⁰always carrying in the body the death of Jesus, so that the life of Jesus may also be made visible in our bodies. ¹¹For while we live, we are always being given up to death for Jesus' sake, so that the life of Jesus may be made visible in our mortal flesh. ¹²So death is at work in us, but life in you.

13 But just as we have the same spirit of faith that is in accordance with scripture—"I believed, and so I spoke"—we also believe, and so we speak, ¹⁴because we know that the one who raised the Lord Jesus will raise us also with Jesus, and will bring us with you into his presence. ¹⁵Yes, everything is for your sake, so that grace, as it extends to more and more people, may increase thanksgiving, to the glory of God.

Living by Faith

16 So we do not lose heart. Even though our outer nature is wasting away, our inner nature is being renewed day by day. ¹⁷For this slight momentary affliction is preparing us for an eternal weight of glory beyond all measure, ¹⁸because we look not at what can be seen but at what cannot be seen; for what can be seen is temporary, but what cannot be seen is eternal.

5 FOR WE know that if the earthly tent we live in is destroyed, we have a building from God, a house not made with hands, eternal in the heavens. ²For

---

^c *4:1 of telling his Good News to others,* implied. ^d *4:4 who is God,* literally, *"who is the image of God."* ^e *4:7 this light and power that now shine within us,* implied. ^f *4:10 who keeps us safe,* implied. ^g *4:13 trusting God to care for us,* implied.

King James

2For in this we groan, earnestly desiring to be clothed upon with our house which is from heaven:

3If so be that being clothed we shall not be found naked.

4For we that are in *this* tabernacle do groan, being burdened: not for that we would be unclothed, but clothed upon, that mortality might be swallowed up of life.

5Now he that hath wrought us for the selfsame thing *is* God, who also hath given unto us the earnest of the Spirit.

6Therefore *we are* always confident, knowing that, whilst we are at home in the body, we are absent from the Lord:

7(For we walk by faith, not by sight:)

8We are confident, *I say,* and willing rather to be absent from the body, and to be present with the Lord.

9Wherefore we labour, that, whether present or absent, we may be accepted of him.

10For we must all appear before the judgment seat of Christ; that every one may receive the things *done* in *his* body, according to that he hath done, whether *it be* good or bad.

11Knowing therefore the terror of the Lord, we persuade men; but we are made manifest unto God; and I trust also are made manifest in your consciences.

12For we commend not ourselves again unto you, but give you occasion to glory on our behalf, that ye may have somewhat to *answer* them which glory in appearance, and not in heart.

13For whether we be beside ourselves, *it is* to God: or whether we be sober, *it is* for your cause.

14For the love of Christ constraineth us; because we thus judge, that if one died for all, then were all dead:

15And *that* he died for all, that they which live should not henceforth live unto themselves, but unto him which died for them, and rose again.

16Wherefore henceforth know we no man after the flesh: yea, though we have known Christ after the flesh, yet now henceforth know we *him* no more.

17Therefore if any man *be* in Christ, *he is* a new creature: old things are passed away; behold, all things are become new.

18And all things *are* of God, who hath reconciled us to himself by Jesus Christ, and hath given to us the ministry of reconciliation;

19To wit, that God was in Christ, reconciling the world unto himself, not imputing their trespasses unto them; and hath committed unto us the word of reconciliation.

20Now then we are ambassadors for Christ, as though God did beseech *you* by us: we pray *you* in Christ's stead, be ye reconciled to God.

21For he hath made him *to be* sin for us, who knew no sin; that we might be made the righteousness of God in him.

New International

2Meanwhile we groan, longing to be clothed with our heavenly dwelling, 3because when we are clothed, we will not be found naked. 4For while we are in this tent, we groan and are burdened, because we do not wish to be unclothed but to be clothed with our heavenly dwelling, so that what is mortal may be swallowed up by life. 5Now it is God who has made us for this very purpose and has given us the Spirit as a deposit, guaranteeing what is to come.

6Therefore we are always confident and know that as long as we are at home in the body we are away from the Lord. 7We live by faith, not by sight. 8We are confident, I say, and would prefer to be away from the body and at home with the Lord. 9So we make it our goal to please him, whether we are at home in the body or away from it. 10For we must all appear before the judgment seat of Christ, that each one may receive what is due him for the things done while in the body, whether good or bad.

The Ministry of Reconciliation

11Since, then, we know what it is to fear the Lord, we try to persuade men. What we are is plain to God, and I hope it is also plain to your conscience. 12We are not trying to commend ourselves to you again, but are giving you an opportunity to take pride in us, so that you can answer those who take pride in what is seen rather than in what is in the heart. 13If we are out of our mind, it is for the sake of God; if we are in our right mind, it is for you. 14For Christ's love compels us, because we are convinced that one died for all, and therefore all died. 15And he died for all, that those who live should no longer live for themselves but for him who died for them and was raised again.

16So from now on we regard no one from a worldly point of view. Though we once regarded Christ in this way, we do so no longer. 17Therefore, if anyone is in Christ, he is a new creation; the old has gone, the new has come! 18All this is from God, who reconciled us to himself through Christ and gave us the ministry of reconciliation: 19that God was reconciling the world to himself in Christ, not counting men's sins against them. And he has committed to us the message of reconciliation. 20We are therefore Christ's ambassadors, as though God were making his appeal through us. We implore you on Christ's behalf: Be reconciled to God. 21God made him who had no sin to be sin[a] for us, so that in him we might become the righteousness of God.

6   WE THEN, *as* workers together *with him,* beseech *you* also that ye receive not the grace of God in vain.

6   AS GOD'S fellow workers we urge you not to receive God's grace in vain. 2For he says,

---

a *21 Or be a sin offering*

Living Bible

grow of our present bodies. That is why we look forward eagerly to the day when we shall have heavenly bodies which we shall put on like new clothes. 3For we shall not be merely spirits without bodies. 4These earthly bodies make us groan and sigh, but we wouldn't like to think of dying and having no bodies at all. We want to slip into our new bodies so that these dying bodies will, as it were, be swallowed up by everlasting life. 5This is what God has prepared for us and, as a guarantee, he has given us his Holy Spirit.

6Now we look forward with confidence to our heavenly bodies, realizing that every moment we spend in these earthly bodies is time spent away from our eternal home in heaven with Jesus. 7We know these things are true by believing, not by seeing. 8And we are not afraid, but are quite content to die, for then we will be at home with the Lord. 9So our aim is to please him always in everything we do, whether we are here in this body or away from this body and with him in heaven. 10For we must all stand before Christ to be judged and have our lives laid bare—before him. Each of us will receive whatever he deserves for the good or bad things he has done in his earthly body.

11It is because of this solemn fear of the Lord, which is ever present in our minds, that we work so hard to win others. God knows our hearts, that they are pure in this matter, and I hope that, deep within, you really know it too.

12Are we trying to pat ourselves on the back again? No, I am giving you some good ammunition! You can use this on those preachers of yours who brag about how well they look and preach, but don't have true and honest hearts. You can boast about us that we, at least, are well intentioned and honest.

13, 14Are we insane [to say such things about ourselvesb]? If so, it is to bring glory to God. And if we are in our right minds, it is for your benefit. Whatever we do, it is certainly not for our own profit, but because Christ's love controls us now. Since we believe that Christ died for all of us, we should also believe that we have died to the old life we used to live. 15He died for all so that all who live—having received eternal life from him—might live no longer for themselves, to please themselves, but to spend their lives pleasing Christ who died and rose again for them. 16So stop evaluating Christians by what the world thinks about them or by what they seem to be like on the outside. Once I mistakenly thought of Christ that way, merely as a human being like myself. How differently I feel now! 17When someone becomes a Christian he becomes a brand new person inside. He is not the same any more. A new life has begun!

18All these new things are from God who brought us back to himself through what Christ Jesus did. And God has given us the privilege of urging everyone to come into his favor and be reconciled to him. 19For God was in Christ, restoring the world to himself, no longer counting men's sins against them but blotting them out. This is the wonderful message he has given us to tell others. 20We are Christ's ambassadors. God is using us to speak to you: we beg you, as though Christ himself were here pleading with you, receive the love he offers you—be reconciled to God. 21For God took the sinless Christ and poured into him our sins. Then, in exchange, he poured God's goodness into us!c

6 AS GOD'S partners we beg you not to toss aside this marvelous message of God's great kindness.

New Revised Standard

in this tent we groan, longing to be clothed with our heavenly dwelling— 3if indeed, when we have taken it offd we will not be found naked. 4For while we are still in this tent, we groan under our burden, because we wish not to be unclothed but to be further clothed, so that what is mortal may be swallowed up by life. 5He who has prepared us for this very thing is God, who has given us the Spirit as a guarantee.

6 So we are always confident; even though we know that while we are at home in the body we are away from the Lord— 7for we walk by faith, not by sight. 8Yes, we do have confidence, and we would rather be away from the body and at home with the Lord. 9So whether we are at home or away, we make it our aim to please him. 10For all of us must appear before the judgment seat of Christ, so that each may receive recompense for what has been done in the body, whether good or evil.

The Ministry of Reconciliation

11 Therefore, knowing the fear of the Lord, we try to persuade others; but we ourselves are well known to God, and I hope that we are also well known to your consciences. 12We are not commending ourselves to you again, but giving you an opportunity to boast about us, so that you may be able to answer those who boast in outward appearance and not in the heart. 13For if we are beside ourselves, it is for God; if we are in our right mind, it is for you. 14For the love of Christ urges us on, because we are convinced that one has died for all; therefore all have died. 15And he died for all, so that those who live might live no longer for themselves, but for him who died and was raised for them.

16 From now on, therefore, we regard no one from a human point of view;e even though we once knew Christ from a human point of view,e we know him no longer in that way. 17So if anyone is in Christ, there is a new creation: everything old has passed away; see, everything has become new! 18All this is from God, who reconciled us to himself through Christ, and has given us the ministry of reconciliation; 19that is, in Christ God was reconciling the world to himself,f not counting their trespasses against them, and entrusting the message of reconciliation to us. 20So we are ambassadors for Christ, since God is making his appeal through us; we entreat you on behalf of Christ, be reconciled to God. 21For our sake he made him to be sin who knew no sin, so that in him we might become the righteousness of God.

6 AS WE work together with him,g we urge you also not to accept the grace of God in vain. 2For he says,

---

b 5:13, 14 *to say such things about ourselves,* implied. c 5:21 *he poured God's goodness into us,* literally, "Him who knew no sin, he made sin on our behalf, that we might become the righteousness of God in him."

d Other ancient authorities read *put it on* e Gk *according to the flesh* f Or *God was in Christ reconciling the world to himself* g Gk *As we work together*

King James

2(For he saith, I have heard thee in a time accepted, and in the day of salvation have I succoured thee: behold, now *is* the accepted time; behold, now *is* the day of salvation.)

3Giving no offence in any thing, that the ministry be not blamed:

4But in all *things* approving ourselves as the ministers of God, in much patience, in afflictions, in necessities, in distresses,

5In stripes, in imprisonments, in tumults, in labours, in watchings, in fastings;

6By pureness, by knowledge, by longsuffering, by kindness, by the Holy Ghost, by love unfeigned,

7By the word of truth, by the power of God, by the armour of righteousness on the right hand and on the left,

8By honour and dishonour, by evil report and good report: as deceivers, and *yet* true;

9As unknown, and *yet* well known; as dying, and, behold, we live; as chastened, and not killed;

10As sorrowful, yet always rejoicing; as poor, yet making many rich; as having nothing, and *yet* possessing all things.

11O *ye* Corinthians, our mouth is open unto you, our heart is enlarged.

12Ye are not straitened in us, but ye are straitened in your own bowels.

13Now for a recompence in the same, (I speak as unto *my* children,) be ye also enlarged.

14Be ye not unequally yoked together with unbelievers: for what fellowship hath righteousness with unrighteousness? and what communion hath light with darkness?

15And what concord hath Christ with Belial? or what part hath he that believeth with an infidel?

16And what agreement hath the temple of God with idols? for ye are the temple of the living God; as God hath said, I will dwell in them, and walk in *them;* and I will be their God, and they shall be my people.

17Wherefore come out from among them, and be ye separate, saith the Lord, and touch not the unclean *thing;* and I will receive you,

18And will be a Father unto you, and ye shall be my sons and daughters, saith the Lord Almighty.

7 HAVING THEREFORE these promises, dearly beloved, let us cleanse ourselves from all filthiness of the flesh and spirit, perfecting holiness in the fear of God.

2Receive us; we have wronged no man, we have corrupted no man, we have defrauded no man.

3I speak not *this* to condemn *you:* for I have said before, that ye are in our hearts to die and live with *you.*

4Great *is* my boldness of speech toward you, great *is* my glorying of you: I am filled with comfort, I am exceeding joyful in all our tribulation.

5For, when we were come into Macedonia, our flesh had no rest, but we were troubled on every side; without *were* fightings, within *were* fears.

New International

"In the time of my favor I heard you,
  and in the day of salvation I helped you."[a]

I tell you, now is the time of God's favor, now is the day of salvation.

Paul's Hardships

3We put no stumbling block in anyone's path, so that our ministry will not be discredited. 4Rather, as servants of God we commend ourselves in every way: in great endurance; in troubles, hardships and distresses; 5in beatings, imprisonments and riots; in hard work, sleepless nights and hunger; 6in purity, understanding, patience and kindness; in the Holy Spirit and in sincere love; 7in truthful speech and in the power of God; with weapons of righteousness in the right hand and in the left; 8through glory and dishonor, bad report and good report; genuine, yet regarded as impostors; 9known, yet regarded as unknown; dying, and yet we live on; beaten, and yet not killed; 10sorrowful, yet always rejoicing; poor, yet making many rich; having nothing, and yet possessing everything.

11We have spoken freely to you, Corinthians, and opened wide our hearts to you. 12We are not withholding our affection from you, but you are withholding yours from us. 13As a fair exchange—I speak as to my children—open wide your hearts also.

Do Not Be Yoked With Unbelievers

14Do not be yoked together with unbelievers. For what do righteousness and wickedness have in common? Or what fellowship can light have with darkness? 15What harmony is there between Christ and Belial[b]? What does a believer have in common with an unbeliever? 16What agreement is there between the temple of God and idols? For we are the temple of the living God. As God has said: "I will live with them and walk among them, and I will be their God, and they will be my people."[c]

17"Therefore come out from them
  and be separate,
               says the Lord.
Touch no unclean thing,
  and I will receive you."[d]
18"I will be a Father to you,
  and you will be my sons and daughters,
            says the Lord Almighty."[e]

7 SINCE WE have these promises, dear friends, let us purify ourselves from everything that contaminates body and spirit, perfecting holiness out of reverence for God.

Paul's Joy

2Make room for us in your hearts. We have wronged no one, we have corrupted no one, we have exploited no one. 3I do not say this to condemn you; I have said before that you have such a place in our hearts that we would live or die with you. 4I have great confidence in you; I take great pride in you. I am greatly encouraged; in all our troubles my joy knows no bounds.

5For when we came into Macedonia, this body of ours had no rest, but we were harassed at every turn—conflicts on the outside, fears within. 6But God, who

a *2* Isaiah 49:8   b *15* Greek *Beliar*, a variant of *Belial*   c *16* Lev. 26:12; Jer. 32:38; Ezek. 37:27   d *17* Isaiah 52:11; Ezek. 20:34,41   e *18* 2 Samuel 7:14; 7:8

Living Bible

2For God says, "Your cry came to me at a favorable time, when the doors of welcome were wide open. I helped you on a day when salvation was being offered." Right now God is ready to welcome you. Today he is ready to save you.

3We try to live in such a way that no one will ever be offended or kept back from finding the Lord by the way we act, so that no one can find fault with us and blame it on the Lord. 4In fact, in everything we do we try to show that we are true ministers of God.

We patiently endure suffering and hardship and trouble of every kind. 5We have been beaten, put in jail, faced angry mobs, worked to exhaustion, stayed awake through sleepless nights of watching, and gone without food. 6We have proved ourselves to be what we claim by our wholesome lives and by our understanding of the Gospel and by our patience. We have been kind and truly loving and filled with the Holy Spirit. 7We have been truthful, with God's power helping us in all we do. All of the godly man's arsenal—weapons of defense, and weapons of attack—have been ours.

8We stand true to the Lord whether others honor us or despise us, whether they criticize us or commend us. We are honest, but they call us liars.

9The world ignores us, but we are known to God; we live close to death, but here we are, still very much alive. We have been injured but kept from death. 10Our hearts ache, but at the same time we have the joy of the Lord. We are poor, but we give rich spiritual gifts to others. We own nothing, and yet we enjoy everything.

11Oh, my dear Corinthian friends! I have told you all my feelings; I love you with all my heart. 12Any coldness still between us is not because of any lack of love on my part, but because your love is too small and does not reach out to me and draw me in. 13I am talking to you now as if you truly were my very own children. Open your hearts to us! Return our love!

14Don't be teamed with those who do not love the Lord, for what do the people of God have in common with the people of sin? How can light live with darkness? 15And what harmony can there be between Christ and the devil? How can a Christian be a partner with one who doesn't believe? 16And what union can there be between God's temple and idols? For you are God's temple, the home of the living God, and God has said of you, "I will live in them and walk among them, and I will be their God and they shall be my people." 17That is why the Lord has said, "Leave them; separate yourselves from them; don't touch their filthy things, and I will welcome you, 18and be a Father to you, and you will be my sons and daughters."

7 HAVING SUCH great promises as these, dear friends, let us turn away from everything wrong, whether of body or spirit, and purify ourselves, living in the wholesome fear of God, giving ourselves to him alone. 2Please open your hearts to us again, for not one of you has suffered any wrong from us. Not one of you was led astray. We have cheated no one nor taken advantage of anyone. 3I'm not saying this to scold or blame you, for, as I have said before, you are in my heart forever and I live and die with you. 4I have the highest confidence in you, and my pride in you is great. You have greatly encouraged me; you have made me so happy in spite of all my suffering.

5When we arrived in Macedonia there was no rest for us; outside, trouble was on every hand and all around us; within us, our hearts were full of dread and fear. 6Then

New Revised Standard

"At an acceptable time I have listened to you,
    and on a day of salvation I have helped
    you."
See, now is the acceptable time; see, now is the day of salvation! 3We are putting no obstacle in anyone's way, so that no fault may be found with our ministry, 4but as servants of God we have commended ourselves in every way: through great endurance, in afflictions, hardships, calamities, 5beatings, imprisonments, riots, labors, sleepless nights, hunger; 6by purity, knowledge, patience, kindness, holiness of spirit, genuine love, 7truthful speech, and the power of God; with the weapons of righteousness for the right hand and for the left; 8in honor and dishonor, in ill repute and good repute. We are treated as impostors, and yet are true; 9as unknown, and yet are well known; as dying, and see—we are alive; as punished, and yet not killed; 10as sorrowful, yet always rejoicing; as poor, yet making many rich; as having nothing, and yet possessing everything.

11 We have spoken frankly to you Corinthians; our heart is wide open to you. 12There is no restriction in our affections, but only in yours. 13In return—I speak as to children—open wide your hearts also.

The Temple of the Living God

14 Do not be mismatched with unbelievers. For what partnership is there between righteousness and lawlessness? Or what fellowship is there between light and darkness? 15What agreement does Christ have with Beliar? Or what does a believer share with an unbeliever? 16What agreement has the temple of God with idols? For we^f are the temple of the living God; as God said,
    "I will live in them and walk among them,
        and I will be their God,
        and they shall be my people.
17   Therefore come out from them,
        and be separate from them, says the Lord,
    and touch nothing unclean;
        then I will welcome you,
18   and I will be your father,
        and you shall be my sons and daughters,
    says the Lord Almighty."

7 SINCE WE have these promises, beloved, let us cleanse ourselves from every defilement of body and of spirit, making holiness perfect in the fear of God.

Paul's Joy at the Church's Repentance

2 Make room in your hearts^g for us; we have wronged no one, we have corrupted no one, we have taken advantage of no one. 3I do not say this to condemn you, for I said before that you are in our hearts, to die together and to live together. 4I often boast about you; I have great pride in you; I am filled with consolation; I am overjoyed in all our affliction.

5 For even when we came into Macedonia, our bodies had no rest, but we were afflicted in every way—disputes without and fears within. 6But God, who con-

^f Other ancient authorities read *you*   ^g Gk lacks *in your hearts*

King James

6Nevertheless God, that comforteth those that are cast down, comforted us by the coming of Titus;

7And not by his coming only, but by the consolation wherewith he was comforted in you, when he told us your earnest desire, your mourning, your fervent mind toward me; so that I rejoiced the more.

8For though I made you sorry with a letter, I do not repent, though I did repent: for I perceive that the same epistle hath made you sorry, though *it were* but for a season.

9Now I rejoice, not that ye were made sorry, but that ye sorrowed to repentance: for ye were made sorry after a godly manner, that ye might receive damage by us in nothing.

10For godly sorrow worketh repentance to salvation not to be repented of: but the sorrow of the world worketh death.

11For behold this selfsame thing, that ye sorrowed after a godly sort, what carefulness it wrought in you, yea, *what* clearing of yourselves, yea, *what* indignation, yea, *what* fear, yea, *what* vehement desire, yea, *what* zeal, yea, *what* revenge! In all *things* ye have approved yourselves to be clear in this matter.

12Wherefore, though I wrote unto you, *I did it* not for his cause that had done the wrong, nor for his cause that suffered wrong, but that our care for you in the sight of God might appear unto you.

13Therefore we were comforted in your comfort: yea, and exceedingly the more joyed we for the joy of Titus, because his spirit was refreshed by you all.

14For if I have boasted any thing to him of you, I am not ashamed; but as we spake all things to you in truth, even so our boasting, which *I made* before Titus, is found a truth.

15And his inward affection is more abundant toward you, whilst he remembereth the obedience of you all, how with fear and trembling ye received him.

16I rejoice therefore that I have confidence in you in all *things*.

8 MOREOVER, BRETHREN, we do you to wit of the grace of God bestowed on the churches of Macedonia;

2How that in a great trial of affliction the abundance of their joy and their deep poverty abounded unto the riches of their liberality.

3For to *their* power, I bear record, yea, and beyond *their* power *they were* willing of themselves;

4Praying us with much entreaty that we would receive the gift, and *take upon us* the fellowship of the ministering to the saints.

5And *this they did,* not as we hoped, but first gave their own selves to the Lord, and unto us by the will of God.

6Insomuch that we desired Titus, that as he had begun, so he would also finish in you the same grace also.

7Therefore, as ye abound in every *thing, in* faith, and utterance, and knowledge, and *in* all diligence, and *in* your love to us, *see* that ye abound in this grace also.

8I speak not by commandment, but by occasion of the forwardness of others, and to prove the sincerity of your love.

New International

comforts the downcast, comforted us by the coming of Titus, 7and not only by his coming but also by the comfort you had given him. He told us about your longing for me, your deep sorrow, your ardent concern for me, so that my joy was greater than ever.

8Even if I caused you sorrow by my letter, I do not regret it. Though I did regret it—I see that my letter hurt you, but only for a little while— 9yet now I am happy, not because you were made sorry, but because your sorrow led you to repentance. For you became sorrowful as God intended and so were not harmed in any way by us. 10Godly sorrow brings repentance that leads to salvation and leaves no regret, but worldly sorrow brings death. 11See what this godly sorrow has produced in you: what earnestness, what eagerness to clear yourselves, what indignation, what alarm, what longing, what concern, what readiness to see justice done. At every point you have proved yourselves to be innocent in this matter. 12So even though I wrote to you, it was not on account of the one who did the wrong or of the injured party, but rather that before God you could see for yourselves how devoted to us you are. 13By all this we are encouraged.

In addition to our own encouragement, we were especially delighted to see how happy Titus was, because his spirit has been refreshed by all of you. 14I had boasted to him about you, and you have not embarrassed me. But just as everything we said to you was true, so our boasting about you to Titus has proved to be true as well. 15And his affection for you is all the greater when he remembers that you were all obedient, receiving him with fear and trembling. 16I am glad I can have complete confidence in you.

Generosity Encouraged

8 AND NOW, brothers, we want you to know about the grace that God has given the Macedonian churches. 2Out of the most severe trial, their overflowing joy and their extreme poverty welled up in rich generosity. 3For I testify that they gave as much as they were able, and even beyond their ability. Entirely on their own, 4they urgently pleaded with us for the privilege of sharing in this service to the saints. 5And they did not do as we expected, but they gave themselves first to the Lord and then to us in keeping with God's will. 6So we urged Titus, since he had earlier made a beginning, to bring also to completion this act of grace on your part. 7But just as you excel in everything—in faith, in speech, in knowledge, in complete earnestness and in your love for us[a]—see that you also excel in this grace of giving.

8I am not commanding you, but I want to test the sincerity of your love by comparing it with the earnestness of others. 9For you know the grace of our Lord

---

a 7 Some manuscripts *in our love for you*

Living Bible

God who cheers those who are discouraged refreshed us by the arrival of Titus. 7Not only was his presence a joy, but also the news that he brought of the wonderful time he had with you. When he told me how much you were looking forward to my visit, and how sorry you were about what had happened, and about your loyalty and warm love for me, well, I overflowed with joy!

8I am no longer sorry that I sent that letter to you, though I was very sorry for a time, realizing how painful it would be to you. But it hurt you only for a little while. 9Now I am glad I sent it, not because it hurt you, but because the pain turned you to God. It was a good kind of sorrow you felt, the kind of sorrow God wants his people to have, so that I need not come to you with harshness. 10For God sometimes uses sorrow in our lives to help us turn away from sin and seek eternal life. We should never regret his sending it. But the sorrow of the man who is not a Christian is not the sorrow of true repentance and does not prevent eternal death.

11Just see how much good this grief from the Lord did for you! You no longer shrugged your shoulders, but became earnest and sincere, and very anxious to get rid of the sin that I wrote you about. You became frightened about what had happened, and longed for me to come and help. You went right to work on the problem and cleared it up [punishing the man who sinnedb]. You have done everything you could to make it right.

12I wrote as I did so the Lord could show how much you really do care for us. That was my purpose even more than to help the man who sinned, or his father to whom he did the wrong.

13In addition to the encouragement you gave us by your love, we were made happier still by Titus' joy when you gave him such a fine welcome and set his mind at ease. 14I told him how it would be—told him before he left me of my pride in you—and you didn't disappoint me. I have always told you the truth and now my boasting to Titus has also proved true! 15He loves you more than ever when he remembers the way you listened to him so willingly and received him so anxiously and with such deep concern. 16How happy this makes me, now that I am sure all is well between us again. Once again I can have perfect confidence in you.

8 NOW I want to tell you what God in his grace has done for the churches in Macedonia.

2Though they have been going through much trouble and hard times, they have mixed their wonderful joy with their deep poverty, and the result has been an overflow of giving to others. 3They gave not only what they could afford, but far more; and I can testify that they did it because they wanted to, and not because of nagging on my part. 4They begged us to take the money so they could share in the joy of helping the Christians in Jerusalem. 5Best of all, they went beyond our highest hopes, for their first action was to dedicate themselves to the Lord and to us, for whatever directions God might give to them through us. 6They were so enthusiastic about it that we have urged Titus, who encouraged your giving in the first place, to visit you and encourage you to complete your share in this ministry of giving. 7You people there are leaders in so many ways—you have so much faith, so many good preachers, so much learning, so much enthusiasm, so much love for us. Now I want you to be leaders also in the spirit of cheerful giving.

8I am not giving you an order; I am not saying you must do it, but others are eager for it. This is one way to prove that your love is real, that it goes beyond mere words.

New Revised Standard

soles the downcast, consoled us by the arrival of Titus, 7and not only by his coming, but also by the consolation with which he was consoled about you, as he told us of your longing, your mourning, your zeal for me, so that I rejoiced still more. 8For even if I made you sorry with my letter, I do not regret it (though I did regret it, for I see that I grieved you with that letter, though only briefly). 9Now I rejoice, not because you were grieved, but because your grief led to repentance; for you felt a godly grief, so that you were not harmed in any way by us. 10For godly grief produces a repentance that leads to salvation and brings no regret, but worldly grief produces death. 11For see what earnestness this godly grief has produced in you, what eagerness to clear yourselves, what indignation, what alarm, what longing, what zeal, what punishment! At every point you have proved yourselves guiltless in the matter. 12So although I wrote to you, it was not on account of the one who did the wrong, nor on account of the one who was wronged, but in order that your zeal for us might be made known to you before God. 13In this we find comfort.

In addition to our own consolation, we rejoiced still more at the joy of Titus, because his mind has been set at rest by all of you. 14For if I have been somewhat boastful about you to him, I was not disgraced; but just as everything we said to you was true, so our boasting to Titus has proved true as well. 15And his heart goes out all the more to you, as he remembers the obedience of all of you, and how you welcomed him with fear and trembling. 16I rejoice, because I have complete confidence in you.

Encouragement to Be Generous

8 WE WANT you to know, brothers and sisters,c about the grace of God that has been granted to the churches of Macedonia; 2for during a severe ordeal of affliction, their abundant joy and their extreme poverty have overflowed in a wealth of generosity on their part. 3For, as I can testify, they voluntarily gave according to their means, and even beyond their means, 4begging us earnestly for the privileged of sharing in this ministry to the saints— 5and this, not merely as we expected; they gave themselves first to the Lord and, by the will of God, to us, 6so that we might urge Titus that, as he had already made a beginning, so he should also complete this generous undertakinge among you. 7Now as you excel in everything—in faith, in speech, in knowledge, in utmost eagerness, and in our love for youf—so we want you to excel also in this generous undertaking.e

8 I do not say this as a command, but I am testing the genuineness of your love against the earnestness of others. 9For you know the generous actsg of our Lord

b 7:11 punishing the man who sinned, implied. So also in vs 12.

c Gk brothers   d Gk grace   e Gk this grace   f Other ancient authorities read your love for us   g Gk the grace

King James

9For ye know the grace of our Lord Jesus Christ, that, though he was rich, yet for your sakes he became poor, that ye through his poverty might be rich.

10And herein I give *my* advice: for this is expedient for you, who have begun before, not only to do, but also to be forward a year ago.

11Now therefore perform the doing *of it;* that as *there was* a readiness to will, so *there may be* a performance also out of that which ye have.

12For if there be first a willing mind, *it is* accepted according to that a man hath, *and* not according to that he hath not.

13For *I mean* not that other men be eased, and ye burdened:

14But by an equality, *that* now at this time your abundance *may be a supply* for their want, that their abundance also may be *a supply* for your want: that there may be equality:

15As it is written, He that *had gathered* much had nothing over; and he that *had gathered* little had no lack.

16But thanks *be* to God, which put the same earnest care into the heart of Titus for you.

17For indeed he accepted the exhortation; but being more forward, of his own accord he went unto you.

18And we have sent with him the brother, whose praise *is* in the gospel throughout all the churches;

19And not *that* only, but who was also chosen of the churches to travel with us with this grace, which is administered by us to the glory of the same Lord, and *declaration of* your ready mind:

20Avoiding this, that no man should blame us in this abundance which is administered by us:

21Providing for honest things, not only in the sight of the Lord, but also in the sight of men.

22And we have sent with them our brother, whom we have oftentimes proved diligent in many things, but now much more diligent, upon the great confidence which *I have* in you.

23Whether *any do inquire* of Titus, *he is* my partner and fellow-helper concerning you: or our brethren *be inquired of, they are* the messengers of the churches, *and* the glory of Christ.

24Wherefore show ye to them, and before the churches, the proof of your love, and of our boasting on your behalf.

9 FOR AS touching the ministering to the saints, it is superfluous for me to write to you:

2For I know the forwardness of your mind, for which I boast of you to them of Macedonia, that Achaia was ready a year ago; and your zeal hath provoked very many.

3Yet have I sent the brethren, lest our boasting of you should be in vain in this behalf; that, as I said, ye may be ready:

4Lest haply if they of Macedonia come with me, and find you unprepared, we (that we say not, ye) should be ashamed in this same confident boasting.

5Therefore I thought it necessary to exhort the brethren, that they would go before unto you, and make up beforehand your bounty, whereof ye had notice before, that the same might be ready, as *a matter of* bounty, and not as *of* covetousness.

New International

Jesus Christ, that though he was rich, yet for your sakes he became poor, so that you through his poverty might become rich.

10And here is my advice about what is best for you in this matter: Last year you were the first not only to give but also to have the desire to do so. 11Now finish the work, so that your eager willingness to do it may be matched by your completion of it, according to your means. 12For if the willingness is there, the gift is acceptable according to what one has, not according to what he does not have.

13Our desire is not that others might be relieved while you are hard pressed, but that there might be equality. 14At the present time your plenty will supply what they need, so that in turn their plenty will supply what you need. Then there will be equality, 15as it is written: "He who gathered much did not have too much, and he who gathered little did not have too little."[a]

Titus Sent to Corinth

16I thank God, who put into the heart of Titus the same concern I have for you. 17For Titus not only welcomed our appeal, but he is coming to you with much enthusiasm and on his own initiative. 18And we are sending along with him the brother who is praised by all the churches for his service to the gospel. 19What is more, he was chosen by the churches to accompany us as we carry the offering, which we administer in order to honor the Lord himself and to show our eagerness to help. 20We want to avoid any criticism of the way we administer this liberal gift. 21For we are taking pains to do what is right, not only in the eyes of the Lord but also in the eyes of men.

22In addition, we are sending with them our brother who has often proved to us in many ways that he is zealous, and now even more so because of his great confidence in you. 23As for Titus, he is my partner and fellow worker among you; as for our brothers, they are representatives of the churches and an honor to Christ. 24Therefore show these men the proof of your love and the reason for our pride in you, so that the churches can see it.

9 THERE IS no need for me to write to you about this service to the saints. 2For I know your eagerness to help, and I have been boasting about it to the Macedonians, telling them that since last year you in Achaia were ready to give; and your enthusiasm has stirred most of them to action. 3But I am sending the brothers in order that our boasting about you in this matter should not prove hollow, but that you may be ready, as I said you would be. 4For if any Macedonians come with me and find you unprepared, we—not to say anything about you—would be ashamed of having been so confident. 5So I thought it necessary to urge the brothers to visit you in advance and finish the arrangements for the generous gift you had promised. Then it will be ready as a generous gift, not as one grudgingly given.

a 15 Exodus 16:18

Living Bible

9You know how full of love and kindness our Lord Jesus was: though he was so very rich, yet to help you he became so very poor, so that by being poor he could make you rich.

10I want to suggest that you finish what you started to do a year ago, for you were not only the first to propose this idea, but the first to begin doing something about it. 11Having started the ball rolling so enthusiastically, you should carry this project through to completion just as gladly, giving whatever you can out of whatever you have. Let your enthusiastic idea at the start be equalled by your realistic action now. 12If you are really eager to give, then it isn't important how much you have to give. God wants you to give what you have, not what you haven't.

13Of course, I don't mean that those who receive your gifts should have an easy time of it at your expense, 14but you should divide with them. Right now you have plenty and can help them; then at some other time they can share with you when you need it. In this way each will have as much as he needs. 15Do you remember what the Scriptures say about this? "He that gathered much had nothing left over, and he that gathered little had enough." So you also should share with those in need.

16I am thankful to God that he has given Titus the same real concern for you that I have. 17He is glad to follow my suggestion that he visit you again—but I think he would have come anyway, for he is very eager to see you! 18I am sending another well-known brother with him, who is highly praised as a preacher of the Good News in all the churches. 19In fact, this man was elected by the churches to travel with me to take the gift to Jerusalem. This will glorify the Lord and show our eagerness to help each other. 20By traveling together we will guard against any suspicion, for we are anxious that no one should find fault with the way we are handling this large gift. 21God knows we are honest, but I want everyone else to know it too. That is why we have made this arrangement.

22And I am sending you still another brother, whom we know from experience to be an earnest Christian. He is especially interested, as he looks forward to this trip, because I have told him all about your eagerness to help.

23If anyone asks who Titus is, say that he is my partner, my helper in helping you, and you can also say that the other two brothers represent the assemblies here and are splendid examples of those who belong to the Lord.

24Please show your love for me to these men and do for them all that I have publicly boasted you would.

9 I REALIZE that I really don't even need to mention this to you, about helping God's people. 2For I know how eager you are to do it, and I have boasted to the friends in Macedonia that you were ready to send an offering a year ago. In fact, it was this enthusiasm of yours that stirred up many of them to begin helping. 3But I am sending these men just to be sure that you really are ready, as I told you they would be, with your money all collected; I don't want it to turn out that this time I was wrong in my boasting about you. 4I would be very much ashamed—and so would you—if some of these Macedonian people come with me, only to find that you still aren't ready after all I have told them!

5So I have asked these other brothers to arrive ahead of me to see that the gift you promised is on hand and waiting. I want it to be a real gift and not look as if it were being given under pressure.

New Revised Standard

Jesus Christ, that though he was rich, yet for your sakes he became poor, so that by his poverty you might become rich. 10And in this matter I am giving my advice: it is appropriate for you who began last year not only to do something but even to desire to do something— 11now finish doing it, so that your eagerness may be matched by completing it according to your means. 12For if the eagerness is there, the gift is acceptable according to what one has—not according to what one does not have. 13I do not mean that there should be relief for others and pressure on you, but it is a question of a fair balance between 14your present abundance and their need, so that their abundance may be for your need, in order that there may be a fair balance. 15As it is written,
"The one who had much did not have too
    much,
   and the one who had little did not have too
    little."

Commendation of Titus

16 But thanks be to God who put in the heart of Titus the same eagerness for you that I myself have. 17For he not only accepted our appeal, but since he is more eager than ever, he is going to you of his own accord. 18With him we are sending the brother who is famous among all the churches for his proclaiming the good news;[b] 19and not only that, but he has also been appointed by the churches to travel with us while we are administering this generous undertaking[c] for the glory of the Lord himself[d] and to show our goodwill. 20We intend that no one should blame us about this generous gift that we are administering, 21for we intend to do what is right not only in the Lord's sight but also in the sight of others. 22And with them we are sending our brother whom we have often tested and found eager in many matters, but who is now more eager than ever because of his great confidence in you. 23As for Titus, he is my partner and co-worker in your service; as for our brothers, they are messengers[e] of the churches, the glory of Christ. 24Therefore openly before the churches, show them the proof of your love and of our reason for boasting about you.

The Collection for Christians at Jerusalem

9 NOW IT is not necessary for me to write you about the ministry to the saints, 2for I know your eagerness, which is the subject of my boasting about you to the people of Macedonia, saying that Achaia has been ready since last year; and your zeal has stirred up most of them. 3But I am sending the brothers in order that our boasting about you may not prove to have been empty in this case, so that you may be ready, as I said you would be; 4otherwise, if some Macedonians come with me and find that you are not ready, we would be humiliated—to say nothing of you—in this undertaking.[f] 5So I thought it necessary to urge the brothers to go on ahead to you, and arrange in advance for this bountiful gift that you have promised, so that it may be ready as a voluntary gift and not as an extortion.

---

b Or the gospel   c Gk this grace   d Other ancient authorities lack himself
e Gk apostles   f Other ancient authorities add of boasting

King James

6But this *I say,* He which soweth sparingly shall reap also sparingly; and he which soweth bountifully shall reap also bountifully.

7Every man according as he purposeth in his heart, *so let him give;* not grudgingly, or of necessity: for God loveth a cheerful giver.

8And God *is* able to make all grace abound toward you; that ye, always having all sufficiency in all *things,* may abound to every good work:

9(As it is written, He hath dispersed abroad; he hath given to the poor: his righteousness remaineth for ever.

10Now he that ministereth seed to the sower both minister bread for *your* food, and multiply your seed sown, and increase the fruits of your righteousness;)

11Being enriched in every thing to all bountifulness, which causeth through us thanksgiving to God.

12For the administration of this service not only supplieth the want of the saints, but is abundant also by many thanksgivings unto God;

13Whiles by the experiment of this ministration they glorify God for your professed subjection unto the gospel of Christ, and for *your* liberal distribution unto them, and unto all *men;*

14And by their prayer for you, which long after you for the exceeding grace of God in you.

15Thanks *be* unto God for his unspeakable gift.

10 NOW I Paul myself beseech you by the meekness and gentleness of Christ, who in presence *am* base among you, but being absent am bold toward you:

2But I beseech *you,* that I may not be bold when I am present with that confidence, wherewith I think to be bold against some, which think of us as if we walked according to the flesh.

3For though we walk in the flesh, we do not war after the flesh:

4(For the weapons of our warfare *are* not carnal, but mighty through God to the pulling down of strong holds;)

5Casting down imaginations, and every high thing that exalteth itself against the knowledge of God, and bringing into captivity every thought to the obedience of Christ;

6And having in a readiness to revenge all disobedience, when your obedience is fulfilled.

7Do ye look on things after the outward appearance? If any man trust to himself that he is Christ's, let him of himself think this again, that, as he *is* Christ's, even so *are* we Christ's.

8For though I should boast somewhat more of our authority, which the Lord hath given us for edification, and not for your destruction, I should not be ashamed:

9That I may not seem as if I would terrify you by letters.

10For *his* letters, say they, *are* weighty and powerful; but *his* bodily presence *is* weak, and *his* speech contemptible.

11Let such an one think this, that, such as we are in word by letters when we are absent, such *will we be* also in deed when we are present.

12For we dare not make ourselves of the number, or compare ourselves with some that commend themselves: but they measuring themselves by themselves, and comparing themselves among themselves, are not wise.

New International

Sowing Generously

6Remember this: Whoever sows sparingly will also reap sparingly, and whoever sows generously will also reap generously. 7Each man should give what he has decided in his heart to give, not reluctantly or under compulsion, for God loves a cheerful giver. 8And God is able to make all grace abound to you, so that in all things at all times, having all that you need, you will abound in every good work. 9As it is written:

> "He has scattered abroad his gifts to the poor;
> his righteousness endures forever."[a]

10Now he who supplies seed to the sower and bread for food will also supply and increase your store of seed and will enlarge the harvest of your righteousness. 11You will be made rich in every way so that you can be generous on every occasion, and through us your generosity will result in thanksgiving to God.

12This service that you perform is not only supplying the needs of God's people but is also overflowing in many expressions of thanks to God. 13Because of the service by which you have proved yourselves, men will praise God for the obedience that accompanies your confession of the gospel of Christ, and for your generosity in sharing with them and with everyone else. 14And in their prayers for you their hearts will go out to you, because of the surpassing grace God has given you. 15Thanks be to God for his indescribable gift!

Paul's Defense of His Ministry

10 BY THE meekness and gentleness of Christ, I appeal to you—I, Paul, who am "timid" when face to face with you, but "bold" when away! 2I beg you that when I come I may not have to be as bold as I expect to be toward some people who think that we live by the standards of this world. 3For though we live in the world, we do not wage war as the world does. 4The weapons we fight with are not the weapons of the world. On the contrary, they have divine power to demolish strongholds. 5We demolish arguments and every pretension that sets itself up against the knowledge of God, and we take captive every thought to make it obedient to Christ. 6And we will be ready to punish every act of disobedience, once your obedience is complete.

7You are looking only on the surface of things.[b] If anyone is confident that he belongs to Christ, he should consider again that we belong to Christ just as much as he. 8For even if I boast somewhat freely about the authority the Lord gave us for building you up rather than pulling you down, I will not be ashamed of it. 9I do not want to seem to be trying to frighten you with my letters. 10For some say, "His letters are weighty and forceful, but in person he is unimpressive and his speaking amounts to nothing." 11Such people should realize that what we are in our letters when we are absent, we will be in our actions when we are present.

12We do not dare to classify or compare ourselves with some who commend themselves. When they measure themselves by themselves and compare themselves with themselves, they are not wise. 13We, however, will

a 9 Psalm 112:9　b 7 Or *Look at the obvious facts*

Living Bible

6But remember this—if you give little, you will get little. A farmer who plants just a few seeds will get only a small crop, but if he plants much, he will reap much. 7Every one must make up his own mind as to how much he should give. Don't force anyone to give more than he really wants to, for cheerful givers are the ones God prizes. 8God is able to make it up to you by giving you everything you need and more, so that there will not only be enough for your own needs, but plenty left over to give joyfully to others. 9It is as the Scriptures say: "The godly man gives generously to the poor. His good deeds will be an honor to him forever."

10For God, who gives seed to the farmer to plant, and later on, good crops to harvest and eat, will give you more and more seed to plant and will make it grow so that you can give away more and more fruit from your harvest.

11Yes, God will give you much so that you can give away much, and when we take your gifts to those who need them they will break out into thanksgiving and praise to God for your help. 12So, two good things happen as a result of your gifts—those in need are helped, and they overflow with thanks to God. 13Those you help will be glad not only because of your generous gifts to themselves and to others, but they will praise God for this proof that your deeds are as good as your doctrine. 14And they will pray for you with deep fervor and feeling because of the wonderful grace of God shown through you.

15Thank God for his Son—his Gift too wonderful for words.

10 I PLEAD with you—yes, I, Paul—and I plead gently, as Christ himself would do. Yet some of you are saying, "Paul's letters are bold enough when he is far away, but when he gets here he will be afraid to raise his voice!"

2I hope I won't need to show you when I come how harsh and rough I can be. I don't want to carry out my present plans against some of you who seem to think my deeds and words are merely those of an ordinary man. 3It is true that I am an ordinary, weak human being, but I don't use human plans and methods to win my battles. 4I use God's mighty weapons, not those made by men, to knock down the devil's strongholds. 5These weapons can break down every proud argument against God and every wall that can be built to keep men from finding him. With these weapons I can capture rebels and bring them back to God, and change them into men whose hearts' desire is obedience to Christ. 6I will use these weapons against every rebel who remains after I have first used them on you yourselves, and you surrender to Christ.

7The trouble with you is that you look at me and I seem weak and powerless, but you don't look beneath the surface. Yet if anyone can claim the power and authority of Christ, I certainly can. 8I may seem to be boasting more than I should about my authority over you—authority to help you, not to hurt you—but I shall make good every claim. 9I say this so that you will not think I am just blustering when I scold you in my letters. 10"Don't bother about his letters," some say. "He sounds big, but it's all noise. When he gets here you will see that there is nothing great about him, and you have never heard a worse preacher!" 11This time my personal presence is going to be just as rough on you as my letters are!

12Oh, don't worry, I wouldn't dare say that I am as wonderful as these other men who tell you how good they are! Their trouble is that they are only comparing themselves with each other, and measuring themselves against their own little ideas. What stupidity!

New Revised Standard

6 The point is this: the one who sows sparingly will also reap sparingly, and the one who sows bountifully will also reap bountifully. 7Each of you must give as you have made up your mind, not reluctantly or under compulsion, for God loves a cheerful giver. 8And God is able to provide you with every blessing in abundance, so that by always having enough of everything, you may share abundantly in every good work. 9As it is written,

"He scatters abroad, he gives to the poor;
    his righteousnessc endures forever."

10He who supplies seed to the sower and bread for food will supply and multiply your seed for sowing and increase the harvest of your righteousness.c 11You will be enriched in every way for your great generosity, which will produce thanksgiving to God through us; 12for the rendering of this ministry not only supplies the needs of the saints but also overflows with many thanksgivings to God. 13Through the testing of this ministry you glorify God by your obedience to the confession of the gospel of Christ and by the generosity of your sharing with them and with all others, 14while they long for you and pray for you because of the surpassing grace of God that he has given you. 15Thanks be to God for his indescribable gift!

Paul Defends His Ministry

10 I MYSELF, Paul, appeal to you by the meekness and gentleness of Christ—I who am humble when face to face with you, but bold toward you when I am away!— 2I ask that when I am present I need not show boldness by daring to oppose those who think we are acting according to human standards.d 3Indeed, we live as human beings,e but we do not wage war according to human standards;d 4for the weapons of our warfare are not merely human,f but they have divine power to destroy strongholds. We destroy arguments 5and every proud obstacle raised up against the knowledge of God, and we take every thought captive to obey Christ. 6We are ready to punish every disobedience when your obedience is complete.

7 Look at what is before your eyes. If you are confident that you belong to Christ, remind yourself of this, that just as you belong to Christ, so also do we. 8Now, even if I boast a little too much of our authority, which the Lord gave for building you up and not for tearing you down, I will not be ashamed of it. 9I do not want to seem as though I am trying to frighten you with my letters. 10For they say, "His letters are weighty and strong, but his bodily presence is weak, and his speech contemptible." 11Let such people understand that what we say by letter when absent, we will also do when present.

12 We do not dare to classify or compare ourselves with some of those who commend themselves. But when they measure themselves by one another, and compare themselves with one another, they do not show good sense. 13We, however, will not boast beyond lim-

---

c Or benevolence   d Gk according to the flesh   e Gk in the flesh   f Gk fleshly

King James

13But we will not boast of things without *our* measure, but according to the measure of the rule which God hath distributed to us, a measure to reach even unto you.

14For we stretch not ourselves beyond *our measure,* as though we reached not unto you: for we are come as far as to you also in *preaching* the gospel of Christ.

15Not boasting of things without *our* measure, *that is,* of other men's labours; but having hope, when your faith is increased, that we shall be enlarged by you according to our rule abundantly,

16To preach the gospel in the *regions* beyond you, *and* not to boast in another man's line of things made ready to our hand.

17But he that glorieth, let him glory in the Lord.

18For not he that commendeth himself is approved, but whom the Lord commendeth.

11 WOULD TO God ye could bear with me a little in *my* folly: and indeed bear with me.

2For I am jealous over you with godly jealousy: for I have espoused you to one husband, that I may present *you as* a chaste virgin to Christ.

3But I fear, lest by any means, as the serpent beguiled Eve through his subtlety, so your minds should be corrupted from the simplicity that is in Christ.

4For if he that cometh preacheth another Jesus, whom we have not preached, or *if* ye receive another spirit, which ye have not received, or another gospel, which ye have not accepted, ye might well bear with *him.*

5For I suppose I was not a whit behind the very chiefest apostles.

6But though *I be* rude in speech, yet not in knowledge; but we have been thoroughly made manifest among you in all things.

7Have I committed an offence in abasing myself that ye might be exalted, because I have preached to you the gospel of God freely?

8I robbed other churches, taking wages *of them,* to do you service.

9And when I was present with you, and wanted, I was chargeable to no man: for that which was lacking to me the brethren which came from Macedonia supplied: and in all *things* I have kept myself from being burdensome unto you, and *so* will I keep *myself.*

10As the truth of Christ is in me, no man shall stop me of this boasting in the regions of Achaia.

11Wherefore? because I love you not? God knoweth.

12But what I do, that I will do, that I may cut off occasion from them which desire occasion; that wherein they glory, they may be found even as we.

13For such *are* false apostles, deceitful workers, transforming themselves into the apostles of Christ.

14And no marvel; for Satan himself is transformed into an angel of light.

15Therefore *it is* no great thing if his ministers also be transformed as the ministers of righteousness; whose end shall be according to their works.

16I say again, Let no man think me a fool; if otherwise, yet as a fool receive me, that I may boast myself a little.

17That which I speak, I speak *it* not after the Lord, but as it were foolishly, in this confidence of boasting.

18Seeing that many glory after the flesh, I will glory also.

New International

not boast beyond proper limits, but will confine our boasting to the field God has assigned to us, a field that reaches even to you. 14We are not going too far in our boasting, as would be the case if we had not come to you, for we did get as far as you with the gospel of Christ. 15Neither do we go beyond our limits by boasting of work done by others.a Our hope is that, as your faith continues to grow, our area of activity among you will greatly expand, 16so that we can preach the gospel in the regions beyond you. For we do not want to boast about work already done in another man's territory. 17But, "Let him who boasts boast in the Lord."b 18For it is not the one who commends himself who is approved, but the one whom the Lord commends.

Paul and the False Apostles

11 I HOPE you will put up with a little of my foolishness; but you are already doing that. 2I am jealous for you with a godly jealousy. I promised you to one husband, to Christ, so that I might present you as a pure virgin to him. 3But I am afraid that just as Eve was deceived by the serpent's cunning, your minds may somehow be led astray from your sincere and pure devotion to Christ. 4For if someone comes to you and preaches a Jesus other than the Jesus we preached, or if you receive a different spirit from the one you received, or a different gospel from the one you accepted, you put up with it easily enough. 5But I do not think I am in the least inferior to those "super-apostles." 6I may not be a trained speaker, but I do have knowledge. We have made this perfectly clear to you in every way.

7Was it a sin for me to lower myself in order to elevate you by preaching the gospel of God to you free of charge? 8I robbed other churches by receiving support from them so as to serve you. 9And when I was with you and needed something, I was not a burden to anyone, for the brothers who came from Macedonia supplied what I needed. I have kept myself from being a burden to you in any way, and will continue to do so. 10As surely as the truth of Christ is in me, nobody in the regions of Achaia will stop this boasting of mine. 11Why? Because I do not love you? God knows I do! 12And I will keep on doing what I am doing in order to cut the ground from under those who want an opportunity to be considered equal with us in the things they boast about.

13For such men are false apostles, deceitful workmen, masquerading as apostles of Christ. 14And no wonder, for Satan himself masquerades as an angel of light. 15It is not surprising, then, if his servants masquerade as servants of righteousness. Their end will be what their actions deserve.

Paul Boasts About His Sufferings

16I repeat: Let no one take me for a fool. But if you do, then receive me just as you would a fool, so that I may do a little boasting. 17In this self-confident boasting I am not talking as the Lord would, but as a fool. 18Since many are boasting in the way the world does, I too will boast. 19You gladly put up with fools since you are so

---

a *13-15* Or *13We, however, will not boast about things that cannot be measured, but we will boast according to the standard of measurement that the God of measure has assigned us—a measurement that relates even to you.* 14 . . . . 15Neither do we boast about things that cannot be measured in regard to the work done by others.   b 17 Jer. 9:24

Living Bible

13But we will not boast of authority we do not have. Our goal is to measure up to God's plan for us, and this plan includes our working there with you. 14We are not going too far when we claim authority over you, for we were the first to come to you with the Good News concerning Christ. 15It is not as though we were trying to claim credit for the work someone else has done among you. Instead, we hope that your faith will grow and that, still within the limits set for us, our work among you will be greatly enlarged.

16After that, we will be able to preach the Good News to other cities that are far beyond you, where no one else is working; then there will be no question about being in someone else's field. 17As the Scriptures say, "If anyone is going to boast, let him boast about what the Lord has done and not about himself." 18When someone boasts about himself and how well he has done, it doesn't count for much. But when the Lord commends him, that's different!

11 I HOPE you will be patient with me as I keep on talking like a fool. Do bear with me and let me say what is on my heart. 2I am anxious for you with the deep concern of God himself—anxious that your love should be for Christ alone, just as a pure maiden saves her love for one man only, for the one who will be her husband. 3But I am frightened, fearing that in some way you will be led away from your pure and simple devotion to our Lord, just as Eve was deceived by Satan in the Garden of Eden. 4You seem so gullible: you believe whatever anyone tells you even if he is preaching about another Jesus than the one we preach, or a different spirit than the Holy Spirit you received, or shows you a different way to be saved. You swallow it all.

5Yet I don't feel that these marvelous "messengers from God," as they call themselves, are any better than I am. 6If I am a poor speaker, at least I know what I am talking about, as I think you realize by now, for we have proved it again and again.

7Did I do wrong and cheapen myself and make you look down on me because I preached God's Good News to you without charging you anything? 8, 9Instead I "robbed" other churches by taking what they sent me, and using it up while I was with you, so that I could serve you without cost. And when that was gonec and I was getting hungry I still didn't ask you for anything, for the Christians from Macedonia brought me another gift. I have never yet asked you for one cent, and I never will. 10I promise this with every ounce of truth I possess— that I will tell everyone in Greece about it! 11Why? Because I don't love you? God knows I do. 12But I will do it to cut out the ground from under the feet of those who boast that they are doing God's work in just the same way we are.

13God never sent those men at all; they are "phonies" who have fooled you into thinking they are Christ's apostles. 14Yet I am not surprised! Satan can change himself into an angel of light, 15so it is no wonder his servants can do it too, and seem like godly ministers. In the end they will get every bit of punishment their wicked deeds deserve.

16Again I plead, don't think that I have lost my wits to talk like this; but even if you do, listen to me anyway—a witless man, a fool—while I also boast a little as they do. 17Such bragging isn't something the Lord commanded me to do, for I am acting like a brainless fool. 18Yet those other men keep telling you how wonderful they are, so here I go: 19, 20(You think you are so

New Revised Standard

its, but will keep within the field that God has assigned to us, to reach out even as far as you. 14For we were not overstepping our limits when we reached you; we were the first to come all the way to you with the good newsd of Christ. 15We do not boast beyond limits, that is, in the labors of others; but our hope is that, as your faith increases, our sphere of action among you may be greatly enlarged, 16so that we may proclaim the good newsd in lands beyond you, without boasting of work already done in someone else's sphere of action. 17"Let the one who boasts, boast in the Lord." 18For it is not those who commend themselves that are approved, but those whom the Lord commends.

Paul and the False Apostles

11 I WISH you would bear with me in a little foolishness. Do bear with me! 2I feel a divine jealousy for you, for I promised you in marriage to one husband, to present you as a chaste virgin to Christ. 3But I am afraid that as the serpent deceived Eve by its cunning, your thoughts will be led astray from a sincere and puree devotion to Christ. 4For if someone comes and proclaims another Jesus than the one we proclaimed, or if you receive a different spirit from the one you received, or a different gospel from the one you accepted, you submit to it readily enough. 5I think that I am not in the least inferior to these super-apostles. 6I may be untrained in speech, but not in knowledge; certainly in every way and in all things we have made this evident to you.

7 Did I commit a sin by humbling myself so that you might be exalted, because I proclaimed God's good newsf to you free of charge? 8I robbed other churches by accepting support from them in order to serve you. 9And when I was with you and was in need, I did not burden anyone, for my needs were supplied by the friendsg who came from Macedonia. So I refrained and will continue to refrain from burdening you in any way. 10As the truth of Christ is in me, this boast of mine will not be silenced in the regions of Achaia. 11And why? Because I do not love you? God knows I do!

12 And what I do I will also continue to do, in order to deny an opportunity to those who want an opportunity to be recognized as our equals in what they boast about. 13For such boasters are false apostles, deceitful workers, disguising themselves as apostles of Christ. 14And no wonder! Even Satan disguises himself as an angel of light. 15So it is not strange if his ministers also disguise themselves as ministers of righteousness. Their end will match their deeds.

Paul's Sufferings as an Apostle

16 I repeat, let no one think that I am a fool; but if you do, then accept me as a fool, so that I too may boast a little. 17What I am saying in regard to this boastful confidence, I am saying not with the Lord's authority, but as a fool; 18since many boast according to human standards,h I will also boast. 19For you gladly put up

---

c 11:8, 9 And when that was gone, implied.

d Or the gospel   e Other ancient authorities lack and pure   f Gk the gospel of God   g Gk brothers   h Gk according to the flesh

King James

19For ye suffer fools gladly, seeing ye *yourselves* are wise.

20For ye suffer, if a man bring you into bondage, if a man devour *you*, if a man take *of you*, if a man exalt himself, if a man smite you on the face.

21I speak as concerning reproach, as though we had been weak. Howbeit whereinsoever any is bold, (I speak foolishly,) I am bold also.

22Are they Hebrews? so *am* I. Are they Israelites? so *am* I. Are they the seed of Abraham? so *am* I.

23Are they ministers of Christ? (I speak as a fool) I *am* more; in labours more abundant, in stripes above measure, in prisons more frequent, in deaths oft.

24Of the Jews five times received I forty *stripes* save one.

25Thrice was I beaten with rods, once was I stoned, thrice I suffered shipwreck, a night and a day I have been in the deep;

26*In* journeyings often, *in* perils of waters, *in* perils of robbers, *in* perils by *mine own* countrymen, *in* perils by the heathen, *in* perils in the city, *in* perils in the wilderness, *in* perils in the sea, *in* perils among false brethren;

27In weariness and painfulness, in watchings often, in hunger and thirst, in fastings often, in cold and nakedness.

28Beside those things that are without, that which cometh upon me daily, the care of all the churches.

29Who is weak, and I am not weak? who is offended, and I burn not?

30If I must needs glory, I will glory of the things which concern mine infirmities.

31The God and Father of our Lord Jesus Christ, which is blessed for evermore, knoweth that I lie not.

32In Damascus the governor under Aretas the king kept the city of the Damascenes with a garrison, desirous to apprehend me:

33And through a window in a basket was I let down by the wall, and escaped his hands.

12 IT IS not expedient for me doubtless to glory. I will come to visions and revelations of the Lord.

2I knew a man in Christ above fourteen years ago, (whether in the body, I cannot tell; or whether out of the body, I cannot tell: God knoweth;) such an one caught up to the third heaven.

3And I knew such a man, (whether in the body, or out of the body, I cannot tell: God knoweth;)

4How that he was caught up into paradise, and heard unspeakable words, which it is not lawful for a man to utter.

5Of such an one will I glory: yet of myself I will not glory, but in mine infirmities.

6For though I would desire to glory, I shall not be a fool; for I will say the truth: but *now* I forbear, lest any man should think of me above that which he seeth me *to be*, or *that* he heareth of me.

7And lest I should be exalted above measure through the abundance of the revelations, there was given to me a thorn in the flesh, the messenger of Satan to buffet me, lest I should be exalted above measure.

8For this thing I besought the Lord thrice, that it might depart from me.

New International

wise! 20In fact, you even put up with anyone who enslaves you or exploits you or takes advantage of you or pushes himself forward or slaps you in the face. 21To my shame I admit that we were too weak for that!

What anyone else dares to boast about—I am speaking as a fool—I also dare to boast about. 22Are they Hebrews? So am I. Are they Israelites? So am I. Are they Abraham's descendants? So am I. 23Are they servants of Christ? (I am out of my mind to talk like this.) I am more. I have worked much harder, been in prison more frequently, been flogged more severely, and been exposed to death again and again. 24Five times I received from the Jews the forty lashes minus one. 25Three times I was beaten with rods, once I was stoned, three times I was shipwrecked, I spent a night and a day in the open sea, 26I have been constantly on the move. I have been in danger from rivers, in danger from bandits, in danger from my own countrymen, in danger from Gentiles; in danger in the city, in danger in the country, in danger at sea; and in danger from false brothers. 27I have labored and toiled and have often gone without sleep; I have known hunger and thirst and have often gone without food; I have been cold and naked. 28Besides everything else, I face daily the pressure of my concern for all the churches. 29Who is weak, and I do not feel weak? Who is led into sin, and I do not inwardly burn?

30If I must boast, I will boast of the things that show my weakness. 31The God and Father of the Lord Jesus, who is to be praised forever, knows that I am not lying. 32In Damascus the governor under King Aretas had the city of the Damascenes guarded in order to arrest me. 33But I was lowered in a basket from a window in the wall and slipped through his hands.

Paul's Vision and His Thorn

12 I MUST go on boasting. Although there is nothing to be gained, I will go on to visions and revelations from the Lord. 2I know a man in Christ who fourteen years ago was caught up to the third heaven. Whether it was in the body or out of the body I do not know—God knows. 3And I know that this man— whether in the body or apart from the body I do not know, but God knows— 4was caught up to paradise. He heard inexpressible things, things that man is not permitted to tell. 5I will boast about a man like that, but I will not boast about myself, except about my weaknesses. 6Even if I should choose to boast, I would not be a fool, because I would be speaking the truth. But I refrain, so no one will think more of me than is warranted by what I do or say.

7To keep me from becoming conceited because of these surpassingly great revelations, there was given me a thorn in my flesh, a messenger of Satan, to torment me. 8Three times I pleaded with the Lord to take it away from me. 9But he said to me, "My grace is sufficient for

Living Bible

wise—yet you listen gladly to those fools; you don't mind at all when they make you their slaves and take everything you have, and take advantage of you, and put on airs, and slap you in the face. 21I'm ashamed to say that I'm not strong and daring like that!

But whatever they can boast about—I'm talking like a fool again—I can boast about it, too.)

22They brag that they are Hebrews, do they? Well, so am I. And they say that they are Israelites, God's chosen people? So am I. And they are descendants of Abraham? Well, I am too.

23They say they serve Christ? But I have served him far more! (Have I gone mad to boast like this?) I have worked harder, been put in jail oftener, been whipped times without number, and faced death again and again and again. 24Five different times the Jews gave me their terrible thirty-nine lashes. 25Three times I was beaten with rods. Once I was stoned. Three times I was shipwrecked. Once I was in the open sea all night and the whole next day. 26I have traveled many weary miles and have been often in great danger from flooded rivers, and from robbers, and from my own people, the Jews, as well as from the hands of the Gentiles. I have faced grave dangers from mobs in the cities and from death in the deserts and in the stormy seas and from men who claim to be brothers in Christ but are not. 27I have lived with weariness and pain and sleepless nights. Often I have been hungry and thirsty and have gone without food; often I have shivered with cold, without enough clothing to keep me warm.

28Then, besides all this, I have the constant worry of how the churches are getting along: 29Who makes a mistake and I do not feel his sadness? Who falls without my longing to help him? Who is spiritually hurt without my fury rising against the one who hurt him?

30But if I must brag, I would rather brag about the things that show how weak I am. 31God, the Father of our Lord Jesus Christ, who is to be praised forever and ever, knows I tell the truth. 32For instance, in Damascus the governor under King Aretas kept guards at the city gates to catch me; 33but I was let down by rope and basket from a hole in the city wall, and so I got away! [What popularity!a]

12 THIS BOASTING is all so foolish, but let me go on. Let me tell you about the visions I've had, and revelations from the Lord.

2, 3Fourteen years ago Ib was taken up to heavenc for a visit. Don't ask me whether my body was there or just my spirit, for I don't know; only God can answer that. But anyway, there I was in paradise, 4and heard things so astounding that they are beyond a man's power to describe or put in words (and anyway I am not allowed to tell them to others). 5That experience is something worth bragging about, but I am not going to do it. I am going to boast only about how weak I am and how great God is to use such weakness for his glory. 6I have plenty to boast about and would be no fool in doing it, but I don't want anyone to think more highly of me than he should from what he can actually see in my life and my message.

7I will say this: because these experiences I had were so tremendous, God was afraid I might be puffed up by them; so I was given a physical condition which has been a thorn in my flesh, a messenger from Satan to hurt and bother me, and prick my pride. 8Three different times I begged God to make me well again.

New Revised Standard

with fools, being wise yourselves! 20For you put up with it when someone makes slaves of you, or preys upon you, or takes advantage of you, or puts on airs, or gives you a slap in the face. 21To my shame, I must say, we were too weak for that!

But whatever anyone dares to boast of—I am speaking as a fool—I also dare to boast of that. 22Are they Hebrews? So am I. Are they Israelites? So am I. Are they descendants of Abraham? So am I. 23Are they ministers of Christ? I am talking like a madman—I am a better one: with far greater labors, far more imprisonments, with countless floggings, and often near death. 24Five times I have received from the Jews the forty lashes minus one. 25Three times I was beaten with rods. Once I received a stoning. Three times I was shipwrecked; for a night and a day I was adrift at sea; 26on frequent journeys, in danger from rivers, danger from bandits, danger from my own people, danger from Gentiles, danger in the city, danger in the wilderness, danger at sea, danger from false brothers and sisters;d 27in toil and hardship, through many a sleepless night, hungry and thirsty, often without food, cold and naked. 28And, besides other things, I am under daily pressure because of my anxiety for all the churches. 29Who is weak, and I am not weak? Who is made to stumble, and I am not indignant?

30 If I must boast, I will boast of the things that show my weakness. 31The God and Father of the Lord Jesus (blessed be he forever!) knows that I do not lie. 32In Damascus, the governore under King Aretas guarded the city of Damascus in order tof seize me, 33but I was let down in a basket through a window in the wall,g and escaped from his hands.

Paul's Visions and Revelations

12 IT IS necessary to boast; nothing is to be gained by it, but I will go on to visions and revelations of the Lord. 2I know a person in Christ who fourteen years ago was caught up to the third heaven—whether in the body or out of the body I do not know; God knows. 3And I know that such a person—whether in the body or out of the body I do not know; God knows— 4was caught up into Paradise and heard things that are not to be told, that no mortal is permitted to repeat. 5On behalf of such a one I will boast, but on my own behalf I will not boast, except of my weaknesses. 6But if I wish to boast, I will not be a fool, for I will be speaking the truth. But I refrain from it, so that no one may think better of me than what is seen in me or heard from me, 7even considering the exceptional character of the revelations. Therefore, to keeph me from being too elated, a thorn was given me in the flesh, a messenger of Satan to torment me, to keep me from being too elated.i 8Three times I appealed to the Lord about this, that it would leave me, 9but he said to me, "My grace is sufficient for

---

a 11:33 *What popularity!* Implied.   b *12:2, 3 I,* literally, "A man in Christ."   c *12:2, 3 heaven,* literally, "the third heaven."

d Gk *brothers*   e Gk *ethnarch*   f Other ancient authorities read *and wanted to*   g Gk *through the wall*   h Other ancient authorities read *To keep*   i Other ancient authorities lack *to keep me from being too elated*

King James

9And he said unto me, My grace is sufficient for thee: for my strength is made perfect in weakness. Most gladly therefore will I rather glory in my infirmities, that the power of Christ may rest upon me.

10Therefore I take pleasure in infirmities, in reproaches, in necessities, in persecutions, in distresses for Christ's sake: for when I am weak, then am I strong.

11I am become a fool in glorying; ye have compelled me: for I ought to have been commended of you: for in nothing am I behind the very chiefest apostles, though I be nothing.

12Truly the signs of an apostle were wrought among you in all patience, in signs, and wonders, and mighty deeds.

13For what is it wherein ye were inferior to other churches, except it be that I myself was not burdensome to you? forgive me this wrong.

14Behold, the third time I am ready to come to you; and I will not be burdensome to you: for I seek not yours, but you: for the children ought not to lay up for the parents, but the parents for the children.

15And I will very gladly spend and be spent for you, though the more abundantly I love you, the less I be loved.

16But be it so, I did not burden you: nevertheless, being crafty, I caught you with guile.

17Did I make a gain of you by any of them whom I sent unto you?

18I desired Titus, and with *him* I sent a brother. Did Titus make a gain of you? walked we not in the same spirit? *walked we* not in the same steps?

19Again, think ye that we excuse ourselves unto you? we speak before God in Christ: but *we do* all things, dearly beloved, for your edifying.

20For I fear, lest, when I come, I shall not find you such as I would, and *that* I shall be found unto you such as ye would not: lest *there be* debates, envyings, wraths, strifes, backbitings, whisperings, swellings, tumults:

21*And* lest, when I come again, my God will humble me among you, and *that* I shall bewail many which have sinned already, and have not repented of the uncleanness and fornication and lasciviousness which they have committed.

13 THIS *IS* the third *time* I am coming to you. In the mouth of two or three witnesses shall every word be established.

2I told you before, and foretell you, as if I were present, the second time; and being absent now I write to them which heretofore have sinned, and to all other, that, if I come again, I will not spare:

3Since ye seek a proof of Christ speaking in me, which to you-ward is not weak, but is mighty in you.

New International

you, for my power is made perfect in weakness." Therefore I will boast all the more gladly about my weaknesses, so that Christ's power may rest on me. 10That is why, for Christ's sake, I delight in weaknesses, in insults, in hardships, in persecutions, in difficulties. For when I am weak, then I am strong.

Paul's Concern for the Corinthians

11I have made a fool of myself, but you drove me to it. I ought to have been commended by you, for I am not in the least inferior to the "super-apostles," even though I am nothing. 12The things that mark an apostle—signs, wonders and miracles—were done among you with great perseverance. 13How were you inferior to the other churches, except that I was never a burden to you? Forgive me this wrong!

14Now I am ready to visit you for the third time, and I will not be a burden to you, because what I want is not your possessions but you. After all, children should not have to save up for their parents, but parents for their children. 15So I will very gladly spend for you everything I have and expend myself as well. If I love you more, will you love me less? 16Be that as it may, I have not been a burden to you. Yet, crafty fellow that I am, I caught you by trickery! 17Did I exploit you through any of the men I sent you? 18I urged Titus to go to you and I sent our brother with him. Titus did not exploit you, did he? Did we not act in the same spirit and follow the same course?

19Have you been thinking all along that we have been defending ourselves to you? We have been speaking in the sight of God as those in Christ; and everything we do, dear friends, is for your strengthening. 20For I am afraid that when I come I may not find you as I want you to be, and you may not find me as you want me to be. I fear that there may be quarreling, jealousy, outbursts of anger, factions, slander, gossip, arrogance and disorder. 21I am afraid that when I come again my God will humble me before you, and I will be grieved over many who have sinned earlier and have not repented of the impurity, sexual sin and debauchery in which they have indulged.

Final Warnings

13 THIS WILL be my third visit to you. "Every matter must be established by the testimony of two or three witnesses."[a] 2I already gave you a warning when I was with you the second time. I now repeat it while absent: On my return I will not spare those who sinned earlier or any of the others, 3since you are demanding proof that Christ is speaking through me. He is not weak in dealing with you, but is powerful among you. 4For to be sure, he was crucified in weakness, yet

Living Bible

9Each time he said, "No. But I am with you; that is all you need. My power shows up best in weak people." Now I am glad to boast about how weak I am; I am glad to be a living demonstration of Christ's power, instead of showing off my own power and abilities. 10Since I know it is all for Christ's good, I am quite happy about "the thorn," and about insults and hardships, persecutions and difficulties; for when I am weak, then I am strong—the less I have, the more I depend on him.

11You have made me act like a fool—boasting like this—for you people ought to be writing about me and not making me write about myself. There isn't a single thing these other marvelous fellows have that I don't have too, even though I am really worth nothing at all. 12When I was there I certainly gave you every proof that I was truly an apostle, sent to you by God himself: for I patiently did many wonders and signs and mighty works among you. 13The only thing I didn't do for you, that I do everywhere else in all other churches, was to become a burden to you—I didn't ask you to give me food to eat and a place to stay. Please forgive me for this wrong!

14Now I am coming to you again, the third time; and it is still not going to cost you anything, for I don't want your money. I want *you!* And anyway, you are my children, and little children don't pay for their father's and mother's food—it's the other way around; parents supply food for their children. 15I am glad to give you myself and all I have for your spiritual good, even though it seems that the more I love you, the less you love me.

16Some of you are saying, "It's true that his visits didn't seem to cost us anything, but he is a sneaky fellow, that Paul, and he fooled us. As sure as anything he must have made money from us some way."

17But how? Did any of the men I sent to you take advantage of you? 18When I urged Titus to visit you, and sent our other brother with him, did they make any profit? No, of course not. For we have the same Holy Spirit, and walk in each other's steps, doing things the same way.

19I suppose you think I am saying all this to get back into your good graces. That isn't it at all. I tell you, with God listening as I say it, that I have said this to help *you,* dear friends—to build you up spiritually and not to help myself. 20For I am afraid that when I come to visit you I won't like what I find, and then you won't like the way I will have to act. I am afraid that I will find you quarreling, and envying each other, and being angry with each other, and acting big, and saying wicked things about each other and whispering behind each other's backs, filled with conceit and disunity. 21Yes, I am afraid that when I come God will humble me before you and I will be sad and mourn because many of you have sinned became sinners and don't even care about the wicked, impure things you have done: your lust and immorality, and the taking of other men's wives.

New Revised Standard

you, for power^c is made perfect in weakness." So, I will boast all the more gladly of my weaknesses, so that the power of Christ may dwell in me. 10Therefore I am content with weaknesses, insults, hardships, persecutions, and calamities for the sake of Christ; for whenever I am weak, then I am strong.

Paul's Concern for the Corinthian Church

11 I have been a fool! You forced me to it. Indeed you should have been the ones commending me, for I am not at all inferior to these super-apostles, even though I am nothing. 12The signs of a true apostle were performed among you with utmost patience, signs and wonders and mighty works. 13How have you been worse off than the other churches, except that I myself did not burden you? Forgive me this wrong!

14 Here I am, ready to come to you this third time. And I will not be a burden, because I do not want what is yours but you; for children ought not to lay up for their parents, but parents for their children. 15I will most gladly spend and be spent for you. If I love you more, am I to be loved less? 16Let it be assumed that I did not burden you. Nevertheless (you say) since I was crafty, I took you in by deceit. 17Did I take advantage of you through any of those whom I sent to you? 18I urged Titus to go, and sent the brother with him. Titus did not take advantage of you, did he? Did we not conduct ourselves with the same spirit? Did we not take the same steps?

19 Have you been thinking all along that we have been defending ourselves before you? We are speaking in Christ before God. Everything we do, beloved, is for the sake of building you up. 20For I fear that when I come, I may find you not as I wish, and that you may find me not as you wish; I fear that there may perhaps be quarreling, jealousy, anger, selfishness, slander, gossip, conceit, and disorder. 21I fear that when I come again, my God may humble me before you, and that I may have to mourn over many who previously sinned and have not repented of the impurity, sexual immorality, and licentiousness that they have practiced.

---

13 THIS IS the third time I am coming to visit you. The Scriptures tell us that if two or three have seen a wrong, it must be punished. [Well, this is my third warning, as I come now for this visit.^{b}] 2I have already warned those who had been sinning when I was there last; now I warn them again, and all others, just as I did then, that this time I come ready to punish severely and I will not spare you.

3I will give you all the proof you want that Christ speaks through me. Christ is not weak in his dealings with you, but is a mighty power within you. 4His weak,

Further Warning

13 THIS IS the third time I am coming to you. "Any charge must be sustained by the evidence of two or three witnesses." 2I warned those who sinned previously and all the others, and I warn them now while absent, as I did when present on my second visit, that if I come again, I will not be lenient— 3since you desire proof that Christ is speaking in me. He is not weak in dealing with you, but is powerful in you. 4For he was

---

^{b} *13:1 Well, this is my third warning, as I come now for this visit,* implied. ^{c} Other ancient authorities read *my power*

King James

4For though he was crucified through weakness, yet he liveth by the power of God. For we also are weak in him, but we shall live with him by the power of God toward you.

5Examine yourselves, whether ye be in the faith; prove your own selves. Know ye not your own selves, how that Jesus Christ is in you, except ye be reprobates?

6But I trust that ye shall know that we are not reprobates.

7Now I pray to God that ye do no evil; not that we should appear approved, but that ye should do that which is honest, though we be as reprobates.

8For we can do nothing against the truth, but for the truth.

9For we are glad, when we are weak, and ye are strong: and this also we wish, *even* your perfection.

10Therefore I write these things being absent, lest being present I should use sharpness, according to the power which the Lord hath given me to edification, and not to destruction.

11Finally, brethren, farewell. Be perfect, be of good comfort, be of one mind, live in peace; and the God of love and peace shall be with you.

12Greet one another with an holy kiss.

13All the saints salute you.

14The grace of the Lord Jesus Christ, and the love of God, and the communion of the Holy Ghost, *be* with you all. Amen.

New International

he lives by God's power. Likewise, we are weak in him, yet by God's power we will live with him to serve you.

5Examine yourselves to see whether you are in the faith; test yourselves. Do you not realize that Christ Jesus is in you—unless, of course, you fail the test? 6And I trust that you will discover that we have not failed the test. 7Now we pray to God that you will not do anything wrong. Not that people will see that we have stood the test but that you will do what is right even though we may seem to have failed. 8For we cannot do anything against the truth, but only for the truth. 9We are glad whenever we are weak but you are strong; and our prayer is for your perfection. 10This is why I write these things when I am absent, that when I come I may not have to be harsh in my use of authority—the authority the Lord gave me for building you up, not for tearing you down.

Final Greetings

11Finally, brothers, good-by. Aim for perfection, listen to my appeal, be of one mind, live in peace. And the God of love and peace will be with you.

12Greet one another with a holy kiss. 13All the saints send their greetings.

14May the grace of the Lord Jesus Christ, and the love of God, and the fellowship of the Holy Spirit be with you all.

Living Bible

human body died on the cross, but now he lives by the mighty power of God. We, too, are weak in our bodies, as he was, but now we live and are strong, as he is, and have all of God's power to use in dealing with you.

5Check up on yourselves. Are you really Christians? Do you pass the test? Do you feel Christ's presence and power more and more within you? Or are you just pretending to be Christians when actually you aren't at all? 6I hope you can agree that I have stood that test and truly belong to the Lord.

7I pray that you will live good lives, not because that will be a feather in our caps,a proving that what we teach is right; no, for we want you to do right even if we ourselves are despised. 8Our responsibility is to encourage the right at all times, not to hope for evil.b 9We are glad to be weak and despised if you are really strong. Our greatest wish and prayer is that you will become mature Christians.

10I am writing this to you now in the hope that I won't need to scold and punish when I come; for I want to use the Lord's authority which he has given me, not to punish you but to make you strong.

11I close my letter with these last words:
Be happy.
Grow in Christ.
Pay attention to what I have said.
Live in harmony and peace.
And may the God of love and peace be with you.
12Greet each other warmly in the Lord. 13All the Christians here send you their best regards. 14May the grace of our Lord Jesus Christ be with you all. May God's love and the Holy Spirit's friendship be yours.
Paul

New Revised Standard

crucified in weakness, but lives by the power of God. For we are weak in him,c but in dealing with you we will live with him by the power of God.

5 Examine yourselves to see whether you are living in the faith. Test yourselves. Do you not realize that Jesus Christ is in you?—unless, indeed, you fail to meet the test! 6I hope you will find out that we have not failed. 7But we pray to God that you may not do anything wrong—not that we may appear to have met the test, but that you may do what is right, though we may seem to have failed. 8For we cannot do anything against the truth, but only for the truth. 9For we rejoice when we are weak and you are strong. This is what we pray for, that you may become perfect. 10So I write these things while I am away from you, so that when I come, I may not have to be severe in using the authority that the Lord has given me for building up and not for tearing down.

Final Greetings and Benediction

11 Finally, brothers and sisters,d farewell.e Put things in order, listen to my appeal,f agree with one another, live in peace; and the God of love and peace will be with you. 12Greet one another with a holy kiss. All the saints greet you.

13 The grace of the Lord Jesus Christ, the love of God, and the communion ofg the Holy Spirit be with all of you.

---

a 13:7 *a feather in our caps,* literally, "not that we may appear approved."
b 13:8 *not to hope for evil,* literally, "For we can do nothing against the truth, but for the truth."

c Other ancient authorities read *with him*   d Gk *brothers*   e Or *rejoice*
f Or *encourage one another*   g Or *and the sharing in*

King James

THE EPISTLE OF

PAUL THE APOSTLE TO THE

Galatians

1 PAUL, AN apostle, (not of men, neither by man, but by Jesus Christ, and God the Father, who raised him from the dead;)

2And all the brethren which are with me, unto the churches of Galatia:

3Grace *be* to you and peace from God the Father, and *from* our Lord Jesus Christ,

4Who gave himself for our sins, that he might deliver us from this present evil world, according to the will of God and our Father:

5To whom *be* glory for ever and ever. Amen.

6I marvel that ye are so soon removed from him that called you into the grace of Christ unto another gospel:

7Which is not another; but there be some that trouble you, and would pervert the gospel of Christ.

8But though we, or an angel from heaven, preach any other gospel unto you than that which we have preached unto you, let him be accursed.

9As we said before, so say I now again, If any *man* preach any other gospel unto you than that ye have received, let him be accursed.

10For do I now persuade men, or God? or do I seek to please men? for if I yet pleased men, I should not be the servant of Christ.

11But I certify you, brethren, that the gospel which was preached of me is not after man.

12For I neither received it of man, neither was I taught *it*, but by the revelation of Jesus Christ.

13For ye have heard of my conversation in time past in the Jews' religion, how that beyond measure I persecuted the church of God, and wasted it:

14And profited in the Jews' religion above many my equals in mine own nation, being more exceedingly zealous of the traditions of my fathers.

15But when it pleased God, who separated me from my mother's womb, and called *me* by his grace,

16To reveal his Son in me, that I might preach him among the heathen; immediately I conferred not with flesh and blood:

17Neither went I up to Jerusalem to them which were apostles before me; but I went into Arabia, and returned again unto Damascus.

18Then after three years I went up to Jerusalem to see Peter, and abode with him fifteen days.

19But other of the apostles saw I none, save James the Lord's brother.

New International

Galatians

1 PAUL, AN apostle—sent not from men nor by man, but by Jesus Christ and God the Father, who raised him from the dead— 2and all the brothers with me,

To the churches in Galatia:

3Grace and peace to you from God our Father and the Lord Jesus Christ, 4who gave himself for our sins to rescue us from the present evil age, according to the will of our God and Father, 5to whom be glory for ever and ever. Amen.

No Other Gospel

6I am astonished that you are so quickly deserting the one who called you by the grace of Christ and are turning to a different gospel— 7which is really no gospel at all. Evidently some people are throwing you into confusion and are trying to pervert the gospel of Christ. 8But even if we or an angel from heaven should preach a gospel other than the one we preached to you, let him be eternally condemned! 9As we have already said, so now I say again: If anybody is preaching to you a gospel other than what you accepted, let him be eternally condemned!

10Am I now trying to win the approval of men, or of God? Or am I trying to please men? If I were still trying to please men, I would not be a servant of Christ.

Paul Called by God

11I want you to know, brothers, that the gospel I preached is not something that man made up. 12I did not receive it from any man, nor was I taught it; rather, I received it by revelation from Jesus Christ.

13For you have heard of my previous way of life in Judaism, how intensely I persecuted the church of God and tried to destroy it. 14I was advancing in Judaism beyond many Jews of my own age and was extremely zealous for the traditions of my fathers. 15But when God, who set me apart from birth[a] and called me by his grace, was pleased 16to reveal his Son in me so that I might preach him among the Gentiles, I did not consult any man, 17nor did I go up to Jerusalem to see those who were apostles before I was, but I went immediately into Arabia and later returned to Damascus.

18Then after three years, I went up to Jerusalem to get acquainted with Peter[b] and stayed with him fifteen days. 19I saw none of the other apostles—only James, the Lord's brother. 20I assure you before God that what I am

---

[a] 15 Or *from my mother's womb*   [b] 18 Greek *Cephas*

Living Bible

Galatians

New Revised Standard

THE LETTER OF
PAUL TO THE

Galatians

1 *FROM:* PAUL the missionary and all the other Christians here.

To: The churches of Galatia.c

I was not called to be a missionary by any group or agency. My call is from Jesus Christ himself, and from God the Father who raised him from the dead. 3May peace and blessing be yours from God the Father and from the Lord Jesus Christ. 4He died for our sins just as God our Father planned, and rescued us from this evil world in which we live. 5All glory to God through all the ages of eternity. Amen.

6I am amazed that you are turning away so soon from God who, in his love and mercy, invited you to share the eternal life he gives through Christ; you are already following a different "way to heaven," which really doesn't go to heaven at all. 7For there is no other way than the one we showed you; you are being fooled by those who twist and change the truth concerning Christ.

8Let God's curses fall on anyone, including myself, who preaches any other way to be saved than the one we told you about; yes, if an angel comes from heaven and preaches any other message, let him be forever cursed. 9I will say it again: if anyone preaches any other Gospel than the one you welcomed, let God's curse fall upon him.

10You can see that I am not trying to please you by sweet talk and flattery; no, I am trying to please God. If I were still trying to please men I could not be Christ's servant.

11Dear friends, I solemnly swear that the way to heaven which I preach is not based on some mere human whim or dream. 12For my message comes from no less a person than Jesus Christ himself, who told me what to say. No one else has taught me.

13You know what I was like when I followed the Jewish religion—how I went after the Christians mercilessly, hunting them down and doing my best to get rid of them all. 14I was one of the most religious Jews of my own age in the whole country, and tried as hard as I possibly could to follow all the old, traditional rules of my religion.

15But then something happened! For even before I was born God had chosen me to be his, and called me— what kindness and grace— 16to reveal his Son within me so that I could go to the Gentiles and show them the Good News about Jesus.

When all this happened to me I didn't go at once and talk it over with anyone else; 17I didn't go up to Jerusalem to consult with those who were apostles before I was. No, I went away into the deserts of Arabia, and then came back to the city of Damascus. 18It was not until three years later that I finally went to Jerusalem for a visit with Peter, and stayed there with him for fifteen days. 19And the only other apostle I met at that time was James, our Lord's brother. 20(Listen to what I am say-

Salutation

1 PAUL AN apostle—sent neither by human commission nor from human authorities, but through Jesus Christ and God the Father, who raised him from the dead— 2and all the members of God's familyd who are with me,

To the churches of Galatia:

3 Grace to you and peace from God our Father and the Lord Jesus Christ, 4who gave himself for our sins to set us free from the present evil age, according to the will of our God and Father, 5to whom be the glory forever and ever. Amen.

There Is No Other Gospel

6 I am astonished that you are so quickly deserting the one who called you in the grace of Christ and are turning to a different gospel— 7not that there is another gospel, but there are some who are confusing you and want to pervert the gospel of Christ. 8But even if we or an angele from heaven should proclaim to you a gospel contrary to what we proclaimed to you, let that one be accursed! 9As we have said before, so now I repeat, if anyone proclaims to you a gospel contrary to what you received, let that one be accursed!

10 Am I now seeking human approval, or God's approval? Or am I trying to please people? If I were still pleasing people, I would not be a servantf of Christ.

Paul's Vindication of His Apostleship

11 For I want you to know, brothers and sisters,g that the gospel that was proclaimed by me is not of human origin; 12for I did not receive it from a human source, nor was I taught it, but I received it through a revelation of Jesus Christ.

13 You have heard, no doubt, of my earlier life in Judaism. I was violently persecuting the church of God and was trying to destroy it. 14I advanced in Judaism beyond many among my people of the same age, for I was far more zealous for the traditions of my ancestors. 15But when God, who had set me apart before I was born and called me through his grace, was pleased 16to reveal his Son to me,h so that I might proclaim him among the Gentiles, I did not confer with any human being, 17nor did I go up to Jerusalem to those who were already apostles before me, but I went away at once into Arabia, and afterwards I returned to Damascus.

18 Then after three years I did go up to Jerusalem to visit Cephas and stayed with him fifteen days; 19but I did not see any other apostle except James the Lord's brother. 20In what I am writing to you, before God, I do

---

c *1:2 Galatia.* Galatia was a province in what is now Turkey.

d Gk *all the brothers* e Or *a messenger* f Gk *slave* g Gk *brothers*
h Gk *in me*

King James

20Now the things which I write unto you, behold, before God, I lie not.

21Afterwards I came into the regions of Syria, and Cilicia;

22And was unknown by face unto the churches of Judaea which were in Christ:

23But they had heard only, That he which persecuted us in times past now preacheth the faith which once he destroyed.

24And they glorified God in me.

2 THEN FOURTEEN years after I went up again to Jerusalem with Barnabas, and took Titus with *me* also.

2And I went up by revelation, and communicated unto them that gospel which I preach among the Gentiles, but privately to them which were of reputation, lest by any means I should run, or had run, in vain.

3But neither Titus, who was with me, being a Greek, was compelled to be circumcised:

4And that because of false brethren unawares brought in, who came in privily to spy out our liberty which we have in Christ Jesus, that they might bring us into bondage:

5To whom we gave place by subjection, no, not for an hour; that the truth of the gospel might continue with you.

6But of these who seemed to be somewhat, (whatsoever they were, it maketh no matter to me: God accepteth no man's person:) for they who seemed *to be somewhat* in conference added nothing to me:

7But contrariwise, when they saw that the gospel of the uncircumcision was committed unto me, as *the gospel* of the circumcision *was* unto Peter;

8(For he that wrought effectually in Peter to the apostleship of the circumcision, the same was mighty in me toward the Gentiles:)

9And when James, Cephas, and John, who seemed to be pillars, perceived the grace that was given unto me, they gave to me and Barnabas the right hands of fellowship; that we *should go* unto the heathen, and they unto the circumcision.

10Only *they would* that we should remember the poor; the same which I also was forward to do.

11But when Peter was come to Antioch, I withstood him to the face, because he was to be blamed.

12For before that certain came from James, he did eat with the Gentiles: but when they were come, he withdrew and separated himself, fearing them which were of the circumcision.

13And the other Jews dissembled likewise with him; insomuch that Barnabas also was carried away with their dissimulation.

14But when I saw that they walked not uprightly according to the truth of the gospel, I said unto Peter before *them* all, If thou, being a Jew, livest after the manner of Gentiles, and not as do the Jews, why compellest thou the Gentiles to live as do the Jews?

15We *who are* Jews by nature, and not sinners of the Gentiles,

New International

writing you is no lie. 21Later I went to Syria and Cilicia. 22I was personally unknown to the churches of Judea that are in Christ. 23They only heard the report: "The man who formerly persecuted us is now preaching the faith he once tried to destroy." 24And they praised God because of me.

Paul Accepted by the Apostles

2 FOURTEEN YEARS later I went up again to Jerusalem, this time with Barnabas. I took Titus along also. 2I went in response to a revelation and set before them the gospel that I preach among the Gentiles. But I did this privately to those who seemed to be leaders, for fear that I was running or had run my race in vain. 3Yet not even Titus, who was with me, was compelled to be circumcised, even though he was a Greek. 4This matter arose, because some false brothers had infiltrated our ranks to spy on the freedom we have in Christ Jesus and to make us slaves. 5We did not give in to them for a moment, so that the truth of the gospel might remain with you.

6As for those who seemed to be important—whatever they were makes no difference to me; God does not judge by external appearance—those men added nothing to my message. 7On the contrary, they saw that I had been entrusted with the task of preaching the gospel to the Gentiles,[a] just as Peter had been to the Jews.[b] 8For God, who was at work in the ministry of Peter as an apostle to the Jews, was also at work in my ministry as an apostle to the Gentiles. 9James, Peter[c] and John, those reputed to be pillars, gave me and Barnabas the right hand of fellowship when they recognized the grace given to me. They agreed that we should go to the Gentiles, and they to the Jews. 10All they asked was that we should continue to remember the poor, the very thing I was eager to do.

Paul Opposes Peter

11When Peter came to Antioch, I opposed him to his face, because he was clearly in the wrong. 12Before certain men came from James, he used to eat with the Gentiles. But when they arrived, he began to draw back and separate himself from the Gentiles because he was afraid of those who belonged to the circumcision group. 13The other Jews joined him in his hypocrisy, so that by their hypocrisy even Barnabas was led astray.

14When I saw that they were not acting in line with the truth of the gospel, I said to Peter in front of them all, "You are a Jew, yet you live like a Gentile and not like a Jew. How is it, then, that you force Gentiles to follow Jewish customs?

15"We who are Jews by birth and not 'Gentile sinners'

a 7 Greek *uncircumcised*   b 7 Greek *circumcised*; also in verses 8 and 9
c 9 Greek *Cephas*; also in verses 11 and 14

Living Bible

ing, for I am telling you this in the very presence of God. This is exactly what happened—I am not lying to you.) [21]Then after this visit I went to Syria and Cilicia. [22]And still the Christians in Judea didn't even know what I looked like. [23]All they knew was what people were saying, that "our former enemy is now preaching the very faith he tried to wreck." [24]And they gave glory to God because of me.

2 THEN FOURTEEN years later I went back to Jerusalem again, this time with Barnabas; and Titus came along too. [2]I went there with definite orders from God to confer with the brothers there about the message I was preaching to the Gentiles. I talked privately to the leaders of the church so that they would all understand just what I had been teaching and, I hoped, agree that it was right. [3]And they did agree; they did not even demand that Titus, my companion, should be circumcised, though he was a Gentile.

[4]Even that question wouldn't have come up except for some so-called "Christians" there—false ones, really—who came to spy on us and see what freedom we enjoyed in Christ Jesus, as to whether we obeyed the Jewish laws or not. They tried to get us all tied up in their rules, like slaves in chains. [5]But we did not listen to them for a single moment, for we did not want to confuse you into thinking that salvation can be earned by being circumcised and by obeying Jewish laws.

[6]And the great leaders of the church who were there had nothing to add to what I was preaching. (By the way, their being great leaders made no difference to me, for all are the same to God.) [7, 8, 9]In fact, when Peter, James, and John, who were known as the pillars of the church, saw how greatly God had used me in winning the Gentiles, just as Peter had been blessed so greatly in his preaching to the Jews—for the same God gave us each our special gifts—they shook hands with Barnabas and me and encouraged us to keep right on with our preaching to the Gentiles while they continued their work with the Jews. [10]The only thing they did suggest was that we must always remember to help the poor, and I, too, was eager for that.

[11]But when Peter came to Antioch I had to oppose him publicly, speaking strongly against what he was doing for it was very wrong. [12]For when he first arrived he ate with the Gentile Christians [who don't bother with circumcision and the many other Jewish laws[d]]. But afterwards when some Jewish friends of James came, he wouldn't eat with the Gentiles anymore because he was afraid of what these Jewish legalists, who insisted that circumcision was necessary for salvation, would say; [13]and then all the other Jewish Christians and even Barnabas became hypocrites too, following Peter's example, though they certainly knew better. [14]When I saw what was happening and that they weren't being honest about what they really believed, and weren't following the truth of the Gospel, I said to Peter in front of all the others, "Though you are a Jew by birth, you have long since discarded the Jewish laws; so why, all of a sudden, are you trying to make these Gentiles obey them? [15]You and I are Jews by birth, not mere Gentile sinners, [16]and

New Revised Standard

not lie! [21]Then I went into the regions of Syria and Cilicia, [22]and I was still unknown by sight to the churches of Judea that are in Christ; [23]they only heard it said, "The one who formerly was persecuting us is now proclaiming the faith he once tried to destroy." [24]And they glorified God because of me.

Paul and the Other Apostles

2 THEN AFTER fourteen years I went up again to Jerusalem with Barnabas, taking Titus along with me. [2]I went up in response to a revelation. Then I laid before them (though only in a private meeting with the acknowledged leaders) the gospel that I proclaim among the Gentiles, in order to make sure that I was not running, or had not run, in vain. [3]But even Titus, who was with me, was not compelled to be circumcised, though he was a Greek. [4]But because of false believers[e] secretly brought in, who slipped in to spy on the freedom we have in Christ Jesus, so that they might enslave us— [5]we did not submit to them even for a moment, so that the truth of the gospel might always remain with you. [6]And from those who were supposed to be acknowledged leaders (what they actually were makes no difference to me; God shows no partiality)—those leaders contributed nothing to me. [7]On the contrary, when they saw that I had been entrusted with the gospel for the uncircumcised, just as Peter had been entrusted with the gospel for the circumcised [8](for he who worked through Peter making him an apostle to the circumcised also worked through me in sending me to the Gentiles), [9]and when James and Cephas and John, who were acknowledged pillars, recognized the grace that had been given to me, they gave to Barnabas and me the right hand of fellowship, agreeing that we should go to the Gentiles and they to the circumcised. [10]They asked only one thing, that we remember the poor, which was actually what I was[f] eager to do.

Paul Rebukes Peter at Antioch

11 But when Cephas came to Antioch, I opposed him to his face, because he stood self-condemned; [12]for until certain people came from James, he used to eat with the Gentiles. But after they came, he drew back and kept himself separate for fear of the circumcision faction. [13]And the other Jews joined him in this hypocrisy, so that even Barnabas was led astray by their hypocrisy. [14]But when I saw that they were not acting consistently with the truth of the gospel, I said to Cephas before them all, "If you, though a Jew, live like a Gentile and not like a Jew, how can you compel the Gentiles to live like Jews?"[g]

Jews and Gentiles Are Saved by Faith

15 We ourselves are Jews by birth and not Gentile sinners; [16]yet we know that a person is justified[h] not by

---

[d] 2:12 who don't bother with circumcision and the many other Jewish laws, implied.

[e] Gk false brothers   [f] Or had been   [g] Some interpreters hold that the quotation extends into the following paragraph   [h] Or reckoned as righteous; and so elsewhere

King James

16Knowing that a man is not justified by the works of the law, but by the faith of Jesus Christ, even we have believed in Jesus Christ, that we might be justified by the faith of Christ, and not by the works of the law: for by the works of the law shall no flesh be justified.

17But if, while we seek to be justified by Christ, we ourselves also are found sinners, *is* therefore Christ the minister of sin? God forbid.

18For if I build again the things which I destroyed, I make myself a transgressor.

19For I through the law am dead to the law, that I might live unto God.

20I am crucified with Christ: nevertheless I live; yet not I, but Christ liveth in me: and the life which I now live in the flesh I live by the faith of the Son of God, who loved me, and gave himself for me.

21I do not frustrate the grace of God: for if righteousness *come* by the law, then Christ is dead in vain.

3 O FOOLISH Galatians, who hath bewitched you, that ye should not obey the truth, before whose eyes Jesus Christ hath been evidently set forth, crucified among you?

2This only would I learn of you, Received ye the Spirit by the works of the law, or by the hearing of faith?

3Are ye so foolish? having begun in the Spirit, are ye now made perfect by the flesh?

4Have ye suffered so many things in vain? if *it be* yet in vain.

5He therefore that ministereth to you the Spirit, and worketh miracles among you, *doeth he it* by the works of the law, or by the hearing of faith?

6Even as Abraham believed God, and it was accounted to him for righteousness.

7Know ye therefore that they which are of faith, the same are the children of Abraham.

8And the scripture, foreseeing that God would justify the heathen through faith, preached before the gospel unto Abraham, *saying,* In thee shall all nations be blessed.

9So then they which be of faith are blessed with faithful Abraham.

10For as many as are of the works of the law are under the curse: for it is written, Cursed *is* every one that continueth not in all things which are written in the book of the law to do them.

11But that no man is justified by the law in the sight of God, *it is* evident: for, The just shall live by faith.

12And the law is not of faith: but, The man that doeth them shall live in them.

New International

16know that a man is not justified by observing the law, but by faith in Jesus Christ. So we, too, have put our faith in Christ Jesus that we may be justified by faith in Christ and not by observing the law, because by observing the law no one will be justified.

17"If, while we seek to be justified in Christ, it becomes evident that we ourselves are sinners, does that mean that Christ promotes sin? Absolutely not! 18If I rebuild what I destroyed, I prove that I am a lawbreaker. 19For through the law I died to the law so that I might live for God. 20I have been crucified with Christ and I no longer live, but Christ lives in me. The life I live in the body, I live by faith in the Son of God, who loved me and gave himself for me. 21I do not set aside the grace of God, for if righteousness could be gained through the law, Christ died for nothing!"a

Faith or Observance of the Law

3 YOU FOOLISH Galatians! Who has bewitched you? Before your very eyes Jesus Christ was clearly portrayed as crucified. 2I would like to learn just one thing from you: Did you receive the Spirit by observing the law, or by believing what you heard? 3Are you so foolish? After beginning with the Spirit, are you now trying to attain your goal by human effort? 4Have you suffered so much for nothing—if it really was for nothing? 5Does God give you his Spirit and work miracles among you because you observe the law, or because you believe what you heard?

6Consider Abraham: "He believed God, and it was credited to him as righteousness."b 7Understand, then, that those who believe are children of Abraham. 8The Scripture foresaw that God would justify the Gentiles by faith, and announced the gospel in advance to Abraham: "All nations will be blessed through you."c 9So those who have faith are blessed along with Abraham, the man of faith.

10All who rely on observing the law are under a curse, for it is written: "Cursed is everyone who does not continue to do everything written in the Book of the Law."d 11Clearly no one is justified before God by the law, because, "The righteous will live by faith."e 12The law is not based on faith; on the contrary, "The man who does these things will live by them."f 13Christ redeemed

a 21 Some interpreters end the quotation after verse 14. b 6 Gen. 15:6 c 8 Gen. 12:3; 18:18; 22:18 d 10 Deut. 27:26 e 11 Hab. 2:4 f 12 Lev. 18:5

Living Bible

yet we Jewish Christians know very well that we cannot become right with God by obeying our Jewish laws, but only by faith in Jesus Christ to take away our sins. And so we, too, have trusted Jesus Christ, that we might be accepted by God because of faith—and not because we have obeyed the Jewish laws. For no one will ever be saved by obeying them."

17But what if we trust Christ to save us and then find that we are wrong, and that we cannot be saved without being circumcised and obeying all the other Jewish laws? Wouldn't we need to say that faith in Christ had ruined us? God forbid that anyone should dare to think such things about our Lord. 18Rather, we are sinners if we start rebuilding the old systems I have been destroying, of trying to be saved by keeping Jewish laws, 19for it was through reading the Scripture that I came to realize that I could never find God's favor by trying—and failing—to obey the laws. I came to realize that acceptance with God comes by believing in Christ.g

20I have been crucified with Christ: and I myself no longer live, but Christ lives in me. And the real life I now have within this body is a result of my trusting in the Son of God, who loved me and gave himself for me. 21I am not one of those who treats Christ's death as meaningless. For if we could be saved by keeping Jewish laws, then there was no need for Christ to die.

3 OH, FOOLISH Galatians! What magician has hypnotized you and cast an evil spell upon you? For you used to see the meaning of Jesus Christ's death as clearly as though I had waved a placard before you with a picture on it of Christ dying on the cross. 2Let me ask you this one question: Did you receive the Holy Spirit by trying to keep the Jewish laws? Of course not, for the Holy Spirit came upon you only after you heard about Christ and trusted him to save you. 3Then have you gone completely crazy? For if trying to obey the Jewish laws never gave you spiritual life in the first place, why do you think that trying to obey them now will make you stronger Christians? 4You have suffered so much for the Gospel. Now are you going to just throw it all overboard? I can hardly believe it!

5I ask you again, does God give you the power of the Holy Spirit and work miracles among you as a result of your trying to obey the Jewish laws? No, of course not. It is when you believe in Christ and fully trust him.

6Abraham had the same experience—God declared him fit for heaven only because he believed God's promises. 7You can see from this that the real children of Abraham are all the men of faith who truly trust in God.

8, 9What's more, the Scriptures looked forward to this time when God would save the Gentiles also, through their faith. God told Abraham about this long ago when he said, "I will bless those in every nation who trust in me as you do." And so it is: all who trust in Christ share the same blessing Abraham received.

10Yes, and those who depend on the Jewish laws to save them are under God's curse, for the Scriptures point out very clearly, "Cursed is everyone who at any time breaks a single one of these laws that are written in God's Book of the Law." 11Consequently, it is clear that no one can ever win God's favor by trying to keep the Jewish laws, because God has said that the only way we can be right in his sight is by faith. As the prophet Habakkuk says it, "The man who finds life will find it through trusting God." 12How different from this way of faith is the way of law which says that a man is saved by obeying every law of God, without one slip. 13But

New Revised Standard

the works of the law but through faith in Jesus Christ.h And we have come to believe in Christ Jesus, so that we might be justified by faith in Christ,i and not by doing the works of the law, because no one will be justified by the works of the law. 17But if, in our effort to be justified in Christ, we ourselves have been found to be sinners, is Christ then a servant of sin? Certainly not! 18But if I build up again the very things that I once tore down, then I demonstrate that I am a transgressor. 19For through the law I died to the law, so that I might live to God. I have been crucified with Christ; 20and it is no longer I who live, but it is Christ who lives in me. And the life I now live in the flesh I live by faith in the Son of God,j who loved me and gave himself for me. 21I do not nullify the grace of God; for if justificationk comes through the law, then Christ died for nothing.

Law or Faith

3 YOU FOOLISH Galatians! Who has bewitched you? It was before your eyes that Jesus Christ was publicly exhibited as crucified! 2The only thing I want to learn from you is this: Did you receive the Spirit by doing the works of the law or by believing what you heard? 3Are you so foolish? Having started with the Spirit, are you now ending with the flesh? 4Did you experience so much for nothing?—if it really was for nothing. 5Well then, does Godl supply you with the Spirit and work miracles among you by your doing the works of the law, or by your believing what you heard?

6 Just as Abraham "believed God, and it was reckoned to him as righteousness," 7so, you see, those who believe are the descendants of Abraham. 8And the scripture, foreseeing that God would justify the Gentiles by faith, declared the gospel beforehand to Abraham, saying, "All the Gentiles shall be blessed in you." 9For this reason, those who believe are blessed with Abraham who believed.

10 For all who rely on the works of the law are under a curse; for it is written, "Cursed is everyone who does not observe and obey all the things written in the book of the law." 11Now it is evident that no one is justified before God by the law; for "The one who is righteous will live by faith."m 12But the law does not rest on faith; on the contrary, "Whoever does the works of the lawn will live by them." 13Christ redeemed us from the curse

---

g 2:19 acceptance with God comes by believing in Christ, literally, "For I through the law died unto the law, that I might live unto God."

h Or the faith of Jesus Christ   i Or the faith of Christ   j Or by the faith of the Son of God   k Or righteousness   l Gk he   m Or The one who is righteous through faith will live   n Gk does them

King James

13Christ hath redeemed us from the curse of the law, being made a curse for us: for it is written, Cursed *is* every one that hangeth on a tree:

14That the blessing of Abraham might come on the Gentiles through Jesus Christ; that we might receive the promise of the Spirit through faith.

15Brethren, I speak after the manner of men; Though *it be* but a man's covenant, yet *if it be* confirmed, no man disannulleth, or addeth thereto.

16Now to Abraham and his seed were the promises made. He saith not, And to seeds, as of many; but as of one, And to thy seed, which is Christ.

17And this I say, *that* the covenant, that was confirmed before of God in Christ, the law, which was four hundred and thirty years after, cannot disannul, that it should make the promise of none effect.

18For if the inheritance *be* of the law, *it is* no more of promise: but God gave *it* to Abraham by promise.

19Wherefore then *serveth* the law? It was added because of transgressions, till the seed should come to whom the promise was made; *and it was* ordained by angels in the hand of a mediator.

20Now a mediator is not *a mediator* of one, but God is one.

21*Is* the law then against the promises of God? God forbid: for if there had been a law given which could have given life, verily righteousness should have been by the law.

22But the scripture hath concluded all under sin, that the promise by faith of Jesus Christ might be given to them that believe.

23But before faith came, we were kept under the law, shut up unto the faith which should afterwards be revealed.

24Wherefore the law was our schoolmaster *to bring us* unto Christ, that we might be justified by faith.

25But after that faith is come, we are no longer under a schoolmaster.

26For ye are all the children of God by faith in Christ Jesus.

27For as many of you as have been baptized into Christ have put on Christ.

28There is neither Jew nor Greek, there is neither bond nor free, there is neither male nor female: for ye are all one in Christ Jesus.

29And if ye *be* Christ's, then are ye Abraham's seed, and heirs according to the promise.

4 NOW I say, *That* the heir, as long as he is a child, differeth nothing from a servant, though he be lord of all;

2But is under tutors and governors until the time appointed of the father.

3Even so we, when we were children, were in bondage under the elements of the world:

New International

us from the curse of the law by becoming a curse for us, for it is written: "Cursed is everyone who is hung on a tree."a 14He redeemed us in order that the blessing given to Abraham might come to the Gentiles through Christ Jesus, so that by faith we might receive the promise of the Spirit.

The Law and the Promise

15Brothers, let me take an example from everyday life. Just as no one can set aside or add to a human covenant that has been duly established, so it is in this case. 16The promises were spoken to Abraham and to his seed. The Scripture does not say "and to seeds," meaning many people, but "and to your seed,"b meaning one person, who is Christ. 17What I mean is this: The law, introduced 430 years later, does not set aside the covenant previously established by God and thus do away with the promise. 18For if the inheritance depends on the law, then it no longer depends on a promise; but God in his grace gave it to Abraham through a promise.

19What, then, was the purpose of the law? It was added because of transgressions until the Seed to whom the promise referred had come. The law was put into effect through angels by a mediator. 20A mediator, however, does not represent just one party; but God is one.

21Is the law, therefore, opposed to the promises of God? Absolutely not! For if a law had been given that could impart life, then righteousness would certainly have come by the law. 22But the Scripture declares that the whole world is a prisoner of sin, so that what was promised, being given through faith in Jesus Christ, might be given to those who believe.

23Before this faith came, we were held prisoners by the law, locked up until faith should be revealed. 24So the law was put in charge to lead us to Christc that we might be justified by faith. 25Now that faith has come, we are no longer under the supervision of the law.

Sons of God

26You are all sons of God through faith in Christ Jesus, 27for all of you who were baptized into Christ have clothed yourselves with Christ. 28There is neither Jew nor Greek, slave nor free, male nor female, for you are all one in Christ Jesus. 29If you belong to Christ, then you are Abraham's seed, and heirs according to the promise.

4 WHAT I am saying is that as long as the heir is a child, he is no different from a slave, although he owns the whole estate. 2He is subject to guardians and trustees until the time set by his father. 3So also, when we were children, we were in slavery under the basic principles of the world. 4But when the time had fully

---

a *13* Deut. 21:23   b *16* Gen. 12:7; 13:15; 24:7   c *24* Or *charge until Christ came*

Living Bible

Christ has bought us out from under the doom of that impossible system by taking the curse for our wrongdoing upon himself. For it is written in the Scripture, "Anyone who is hanged on a tree is cursed" [as Jesus was hung upon a wooden cross[d]].

[14]Now God can bless the Gentiles, too, with this same blessing he promised to Abraham; and all of us as Christians can have the promised Holy Spirit through this faith.

[15]Dear brothers, even in everyday life a promise made by one man to another, if it is written down and signed, cannot be changed. He cannot decide afterward to do something else instead.

[16]Now, God gave some promises to Abraham and his Child. And notice that it doesn't say the promises were to his *children,* as it would if all his sons—all the Jews—were being spoken of, but to his *Child*—and that, of course, means Christ. [17]Here's what I am trying to say: God's promise to save through faith—and God wrote this promise down and signed it—could not be canceled or changed four hundred and thirty years later when God gave the Ten Commandments. [18]If *obeying those laws* could save us, then it is obvious that this would be a different way of gaining God's favor than Abraham's way, for he simply accepted God's promise.

[19]Well then, why were the laws given? They were added after the promise was given, to show men how guilty they are of breaking God's laws. But this system of law was to last only until the coming of Christ, the Child to whom God's promise was made. (And there is this further difference. God gave his laws to angels to give to Moses, who then gave them to the people; [20]but when God gave his promise to Abraham, he did it by himself alone, without angels or Moses as go-betweens.)

[21, 22]Well then, are God's laws and God's promises against each other? Of course not! If we could be saved by his laws, then God would not have had to give us a different way to get out of the grip of sin—for the Scriptures insist we are all its prisoners. The only way out is through faith in Jesus Christ; the way of escape is open to all who believe him.

[23]Until Christ came we were guarded by the law, kept in protective custody, so to speak, until we could believe in the coming Savior.

[24]Let me put it another way. The Jewish laws were our teacher and guide until Christ came to give us right standing with God through our faith. [25]But now that Christ has come, we don't need those laws any longer to guard us and lead us to him. [26]For now we are all children of God through faith in Jesus Christ, [27]and we who have been baptized into union with Christ are enveloped by him. [28]We are no longer Jews or Greeks or slaves or free men or even merely men or women, but we are all the same—we are Christians; we are one in Christ Jesus. [29]And now that we are Christ's we are the true descendants of Abraham, and all of God's promises to him belong to us.

4 BUT REMEMBER this, that if a father dies and leaves great wealth for his little son, that child is not much better off than a slave until he grows up, even though he actually owns everything his father had. [2]He has to do what his guardians and managers tell him to, until he reaches whatever age his father set.

[3]And that is the way it was with us before Christ came. We were slaves to Jewish laws and rituals for we thought they could save us. [4]But when the right time

New Revised Standard

of the law by becoming a curse for us—for it is written, "Cursed is everyone who hangs on a tree"— [14]in order that in Christ Jesus the blessing of Abraham might come to the Gentiles, so that we might receive the promise of the Spirit through faith.

The Promise to Abraham

15 Brothers and sisters,[e] I give an example from daily life: once a person's will[f] has been ratified, no one adds to it or annuls it. [16]Now the promises were made to Abraham and to his offspring;[g] it does not say, "And to offsprings,"[h] as of many; but it says, "And to your offspring,"[g] that is, to one person, who is Christ. [17]My point is this: the law, which came four hundred thirty years later, does not annul a covenant previously ratified by God, so as to nullify the promise. [18]For if the inheritance comes from the law, it no longer comes from the promise; but God granted it to Abraham through the promise.

The Purpose of the Law

19 Why then the law? It was added because of transgressions, until the offspring[g] would come to whom the promise had been made; and it was ordained through angels by a mediator. [20]Now a mediator involves more than one party; but God is one.

21 Is the law then opposed to the promises of God? Certainly not! For if a law had been given that could make alive, then righteousness would indeed come through the law. [22]But the scripture has imprisoned all things under the power of sin, so that what was promised through faith in Jesus Christ[i] might be given to those who believe.

23 Now before faith came, we were imprisoned and guarded under the law until faith would be revealed. [24]Therefore the law was our disciplinarian until Christ came, so that we might be justified by faith. [25]But now that faith has come, we are no longer subject to a disciplinarian, [26]for in Christ Jesus you are all children of God through faith. [27]As many of you as were baptized into Christ have clothed yourselves with Christ. [28]There is no longer Jew or Greek, there is no longer slave or free, there is no longer male and female; for all of you are one in Christ Jesus. [29]And if you belong to Christ, then you are Abraham's offspring,[g] heirs according to the promise.

4 MY POINT is this: heirs, as long as they are minors, are no better than slaves, though they are the owners of all the property; [2]but they remain under guardians and trustees until the date set by the father. [3]So with us; while we were minors, we were enslaved to the elemental spirits[j] of the world. [4]But when the

---

[d] 3:13 *as Jesus was hung upon a wooden cross,* implied.

[e] Gk *Brothers*   [f] Or *covenant* (as in verse 17)   [g] Gk *seed*   [h] Gk *seeds*
[i] Or *through the faith of Jesus Christ*   [j] Or *the rudiments*

King James

4But when the fulness of the time was come, God sent forth his Son, made of a woman, made under the law,

5To redeem them that were under the law, that we might receive the adoption of sons.

6And because ye are sons, God hath sent forth the Spirit of his Son into your hearts, crying, Abba, Father.

7Wherefore thou art no more a servant, but a son; and if a son, then an heir of God through Christ.

8Howbeit then, when ye knew not God, ye did service unto them which by nature are no gods.

9But now, after that ye have known God, or rather are known of God, how turn ye again to the weak and beggarly elements, whereunto ye desire again to be in bondage?

10Ye observe days, and months, and times, and years.

11I am afraid of you, lest I have bestowed upon you labour in vain.

12Brethren, I beseech you, be as I *am;* for I *am* as ye *are:* ye have not injured me at all.

13Ye know how through infirmity of the flesh I preached the gospel unto you at the first.

14And my temptation which was in my flesh ye despised not, nor rejected; but received me as an angel of God, *even* as Christ Jesus.

15Where is then the blessedness ye spake of? for I bear you record, that, if *it had been* possible, ye would have plucked out your own eyes, and have given them to me.

16Am I therefore become your enemy, because I tell you the truth?

17They zealously affect you, *but* not well; yea, they would exclude you, that ye might affect them.

18But *it is* good to be zealously affected always in *a* good *thing,* and not only when I am present with you.

19My little children, of whom I travail in birth again until Christ be formed in you,

20I desire to be present with you now, and to change my voice; for I stand in doubt of you.

21Tell me, ye that desire to be under the law, do ye not hear the law?

22For it is written, that Abraham had two sons, the one by a bondmaid, the other by a freewoman.

23But he *who was* of the bondwoman was born after the flesh; but he of the freewoman *was* by promise.

24Which things are an allegory: for these are the two covenants; the one from the mount Sinai, which gendereth to bondage, which is Agar.

25For this Agar is mount Sinai in Arabia, and answereth to Jerusalem which now is, and is in bondage with her children.

26But Jerusalem which is above is free, which is the mother of us all.

27For it is written, Rejoice, *thou* barren that bearest not; break forth and cry, thou that travailest not: for the desolate hath many more children than she which hath an husband.

New International

come, God sent his Son, born of a woman, born under law, 5to redeem those under law, that we might receive the full rights of sons. 6Because you are sons, God sent the Spirit of his Son into our hearts, the Spirit who calls out, "*Abba,*a Father." 7So you are no longer a slave, but a son; and since you are a son, God has made you also an heir.

Paul's Concern for the Galatians

8Formerly, when you did not know God, you were slaves to those who by nature are not gods. 9But now that you know God—or rather are known by God—how is it that you are turning back to those weak and miserable principles? Do you wish to be enslaved by them all over again? 10You are observing special days and months and seasons and years! 11I fear for you, that somehow I have wasted my efforts on you.

12I plead with you, brothers, become like me, for I became like you. You have done me no wrong. 13As you know, it was because of an illness that I first preached the gospel to you. 14Even though my illness was a trial to you, you did not treat me with contempt or scorn. Instead, you welcomed me as if I were an angel of God, as if I were Christ Jesus himself. 15What has happened to all your joy? I can testify that, if you could have done so, you would have torn out your eyes and given them to me. 16Have I now become your enemy by telling you the truth?

17Those people are zealous to win you over, but for no good. What they want is to alienate you from us, so that you may be zealous for them. 18It is fine to be zealous, provided the purpose is good, and to be so always and not just when I am with you. 19My dear children, for whom I am again in the pains of childbirth until Christ is formed in you, 20how I wish I could be with you now and change my tone, because I am perplexed about you!

Hagar and Sarah

21Tell me, you who want to be under the law, are you not aware of what the law says? 22For it is written that Abraham had two sons, one by the slave woman and the other by the free woman. 23His son by the slave woman was born in the ordinary way; but his son by the free woman was born as the result of a promise.

24These things may be taken figuratively, for the women represent two covenants. One covenant is from Mount Sinai and bears children who are to be slaves: This is Hagar. 25Now Hagar stands for Mount Sinai in Arabia and corresponds to the present city of Jerusalem, because she is in slavery with her children. 26But the Jerusalem that is above is free, and she is our mother. 27For it is written:

> "Be glad, O barren woman,
>   who bears no children;
> break forth and cry aloud,
>   you who have no labor pains;
> because more are the children of the desolate
>   woman
> than of her who has a husband."b

a 6 Aramaic for *Father*   b 27 Isaiah 54:1

Living Bible

came, the time God decided on, he sent his Son, born of a woman, born as a Jew, 5to buy freedom for us who were slaves to the law so that he could adopt us as his very own sons. 6And because we are his sons God has sent the Spirit of his Son into our hearts, so now we can rightly speak of God as our dear Father. 7Now we are no longer slaves, but God's own sons. And since we are his sons, everything he has belongs to us, for that is the way God planned.

8Before you Gentiles knew God you were slaves to so-called gods that did not even exist. 9And now that you have found God (or I should say, now that God has found you) how can it be that you want to go back again and become slaves once more to another poor, weak, useless religion of trying to get to heaven by obeying God's laws? 10You are trying to find favor with God by what you do or don't do on certain days or months or seasons or years. 11I fear for you. I am afraid that all my hard work for you was worth nothing.

12Dear brothers, please feel as I do about these things, for I am as free from these chains as you used to be. You did not despise me then when I first preached to you, 13even though I was sick when I first brought you the Good News of Christ. 14But even though my sickness was revolting to you, you didn't reject me and turn me away. No, you took me in and cared for me as though I were an angel from God, or even Jesus Christ himself.

15Where is that happy spirit that we felt together then? For in those days I know you would gladly have taken out your own eyes and given them to replace minec if that would have helped me.

16And now have I become your enemy because I tell you the truth?

17Those false teachers who are so anxious to win your favor are not doing it for your good. What they are trying to do is to shut you off from me so that you will pay more attention to them. 18It is a fine thing when people are nice to you with good motives and sincere hearts, especially if they aren't doing it just when I am with you! 19Oh, my children, how you are hurting me! I am once again suffering for you the pains of a mother waiting for her child to be born—longing for the time when you will finally be filled with Christ. 20How I wish I could be there with you right now and not have to reason with you like this, for at this distance I frankly don't know what to do.

21Listen to me, you friends who think you have to obey the Jewish laws to be saved: Why don't you find out what those laws really mean? 22For it is written that Abraham had two sons, one from his slavewife and one from his freeborn wife. 23There was nothing unusual about the birth of the slave-wife's baby. But the baby of the freeborn wife was born only after God had especially promised he would come. 24, 25Now this true story is an illustration of God's two ways of helping people. One way was by giving them his laws to obey. He did this on Mount Sinai, when he gave the Ten Commandments to Moses. Mount Sinai, by the way, is called "Mount Hagar" by the Arabs—and in my illustration Abraham's slave-wife Hagar represents Jerusalem, the mother-city of the Jews, the center of that system of trying to please God by trying to obey the Commandments; and the Jews, who try to follow that system, are her slave children. 26But our mother-city is the heavenly Jerusalem, and she is not a slave to Jewish laws.

27That is what Isaiah meant when he prophesied, "Now you can rejoice, O childless woman; you can shout with joy though you never before had a child. For I am going to give you many children—more children than the slave-wife has."

New Revised Standard

fullness of time had come, God sent his Son, born of a woman, born under the law, 5in order to redeem those who were under the law, so that we might receive adoption as children. 6And because you are children, God has sent the Spirit of his Son into ourd hearts, crying, "Abba!e Father!" 7So you are no longer a slave but a child, and if a child then also an heir, through God.f

Paul Reproves the Galatians

8 Formerly, when you did not know God, you were enslaved to beings that by nature are not gods. 9Now, however, that you have come to know God, or rather to be known by God, how can you turn back again to the weak and beggarly elemental spirits?g How can you want to be enslaved to them again? 10You are observing special days, and months, and seasons, and years. 11I am afraid that my work for you may have been wasted.

12 Friends,h I beg you, become as I am, for I also have become as you are. You have done me no wrong. 13You know that it was because of a physical infirmity that I first announced the gospel to you; 14though my condition put you to the test, you did not scorn or despise me, but welcomed me as an angel of God, as Christ Jesus. 15What has become of the goodwill you felt? For I testify that, had it been possible, you would have torn out your eyes and given them to me. 16Have I now become your enemy by telling you the truth? 17They make much of you, but for no good purpose; they want to exclude you, so that you may make much of them. 18It is good to be made much of for a good purpose at all times, and not only when I am present with you. 19My little children, for whom I am again in the pain of childbirth until Christ is formed in you, 20I wish I were present with you now and could change my tone, for I am perplexed about you.

The Allegory of Hagar and Sarah

21 Tell me, you who desire to be subject to the law, will you not listen to the law? 22For it is written that Abraham had two sons, one by a slave woman and the other by a free woman. 23One, the child of the slave, was born according to the flesh; the other, the child of the free woman, was born through the promise. 24Now this is an allegory: these women are two covenants. One woman, in fact, is Hagar, from Mount Sinai, bearing children for slavery. 25Now Hagar is Mount Sinai in Arabiai and corresponds to the present Jerusalem, for she is in slavery with her children. 26But the other woman corresponds to the Jerusalem above; she is free, and she is our mother. 27For it is written,

"Rejoice, you childless one, you who bear no children,
    burst into song and shout, you who endure no birth pangs;
for the children of the desolate woman are more numerous
    than the children of the one who is married."

---

c 4:15 to replace mine. It is traditional to suppose that Paul was handicapped by a disease of the eyes.

d Other ancient authorities read *your*   e Aramaic for *Father*   f Other ancient authorities read *an heir of God through Christ*   g Or *beggarly rudiments*   h Gk *Brothers*   i Other ancient authorities read *For Sinai is a mountain in Arabia*

King James

28Now we, brethren, as Isaac was, are the children of promise.

29But as then he that was born after the flesh persecuted him *that was born* after the Spirit, even so *it is* now.

30Nevertheless what saith the scripture? Cast out the bondwoman and her son: for the son of the bondwoman shall not be heir with the son of the freewoman.

31So then, brethren, we are not children of the bondwoman, but of the free.

5 STAND FAST therefore in the liberty wherewith Christ hath made us free, and be not entangled again with the yoke of bondage.

2Behold, I Paul say unto you, that if ye be circumcised, Christ shall profit you nothing.

3For I testify again to every man that is circumcised, that he is a debtor to do the whole law.

4Christ is become of no effect unto you, whosoever of you are justified by the law; ye are fallen from grace.

5For we through the Spirit wait for the hope of righteousness by faith.

6For in Jesus Christ neither circumcision availeth any thing, nor uncircumcision; but faith which worketh by love.

7Ye did run well; who did hinder you that ye should not obey the truth?

8This persuasion *cometh* not of him that calleth you.

9A little leaven leaveneth the whole lump.

10I have confidence in you through the Lord, that ye will be none otherwise minded: but he that troubleth you shall bear his judgment, whosoever he be.

11And I, brethren, if I yet preach circumcision, why do I yet suffer persecution? then is the offence of the cross ceased.

12I would they were even cut off which trouble you.

13For, brethren, ye have been called unto liberty; only *use* not liberty for an occasion to the flesh, but by love serve one another.

14For all the law is fulfilled in one word, *even* in this; Thou shalt love thy neighbour as thyself.

15But if ye bite and devour one another, take heed that ye be not consumed one of another.

16*This* I say then, Walk in the Spirit, and ye shall not fulfil the lust of the flesh.

17For the flesh lusteth against the Spirit, and the Spirit against the flesh: and these are contrary the one to the other: so that ye cannot do the things that ye would.

New International

28Now you, brothers, like Isaac, are children of promise. 29At that time the son born in the ordinary way persecuted the son born by the power of the Spirit. It is the same now. 30But what does the Scripture say? "Get rid of the slave woman and her son, for the slave woman's son will never share in the inheritance with the free woman's son."a 31Therefore, brothers, we are not children of the slave woman, but of the free woman.

Freedom in Christ

5 IT IS for freedom that Christ has set us free. Stand firm, then, and do not let yourselves be burdened again by a yoke of slavery.

2Mark my words! I, Paul, tell you that if you let yourselves be circumcised, Christ will be of no value to you at all. 3Again I declare to every man who lets himself be circumcised that he is obligated to obey the whole law. 4You who are trying to be justified by law have been alienated from Christ; you have fallen away from grace. 5But by faith we eagerly await through the Spirit the righteousness for which we hope. 6For in Christ Jesus neither circumcision nor uncircumcision has any value. The only thing that counts is faith expressing itself through love.

7You were running a good race. Who cut in on you and kept you from obeying the truth? 8That kind of persuasion does not come from the one who calls you. 9"A little yeast works through the whole batch of dough." 10I am confident in the Lord that you will take no other view. The one who is throwing you into confusion will pay the penalty, whoever he may be. 11Brothers, if I am still preaching circumcision, why am I still being persecuted? In that case the offense of the cross has been abolished. 12As for those agitators, I wish they would go the whole way and emasculate themselves!

13You, my brothers, were called to be free. But do not use your freedom to indulge the sinful natureb; rather, serve one another in love. 14The entire law is summed up in a single command: "Love your neighbor as yourself."c 15If you keep on biting and devouring each other, watch out or you will be destroyed by each other.

Life by the Spirit

16So I say, live by the Spirit, and you will not gratify the desires of the sinful nature. 17For the sinful nature desires what is contrary to the Spirit, and the Spirit what is contrary to the sinful nature. They are in conflict with each other, so that you do not do what you want. 18But

a 30 Gen. 21:10   b 13 Or *the flesh*; also in verses 16, 17, 19 and 24
c 14 Lev. 19:18

Living Bible

28You and I, dear brothers, are the children that God promised, just as Isaac was. 29And so we who are born of the Holy Spirit are persecuted now by those who want us to keep the Jewish laws, just as Isaac the child of promise was persecuted by Ishmael the slave-wife's son.

30But the Scriptures say that God told Abraham to send away the slave-wife and her son, for the slave-wife's son could not inherit Abraham's home and lands along with the free woman's son. 31Dear brothers, we are not slave children, obligated to the Jewish laws, but children of the free woman, acceptable to God because of our faith.

5 SO CHRIST has made us free. Now make sure that you stay free and don't get all tied up again in the chains of slavery to Jewish laws and ceremonies. 2Listen to me, for this is serious: *if you are counting on circumcision and keeping the Jewish laws to make you right with God, then Christ cannot save you.* 3I'll say it again. Anyone trying to find favor with God by being circumcised must always obey every other Jewish law or perish. 4Christ is useless to you if you are counting on clearing your debt to God by keeping those laws; you are lost from God's grace.

5But we by the help of the Holy Spirit are counting on Christ's death to clear away our sins and make us right with God. 6And we to whom Christ has given eternal life don't need to worry about whether we have been circumcised or not, or whether we are obeying the Jewish ceremonies or not; for all we need is faith working through love.

7You were getting along so well. Who has interfered with you to hold you back from following the truth? 8It certainly isn't God who has done it, for he is the one who has called you to freedom in Christ. 9But it takes only one wrong person among you to infect all the others.

10I am trusting the Lord to bring you back to believing as I do about these things. God will deal with that person, whoever he is, who has been troubling and confusing you.

11Some people even say that I myself am preaching that circumcision and Jewish laws are necessary to the plan of salvation. Well, if I preached that, I would be persecuted no more—for that message doesn't offend anyone. The fact that I am still being persecuted proves that I am still preaching salvation through faith in the cross of Christ alone.

12I only wish these teachers who want you to cut yourselves by being circumcised would cut themselves off from you and leave you alone!d

13For, dear brothers, you have been given freedom: not freedom to do wrong, but freedom to love and serve each other. 14For the whole Law can be summed up in this one command: "Love others as you love yourself." 15But if instead of showing love among yourselves you are always critical and catty, watch out! Beware of ruining each other.

16I advise you to obey only the Holy Spirit's instructions. He will tell you where to go and what to do, and then you won't always be doing the wrong things your evil nature wants you to. 17For we naturally love to do evil things that are just the opposite from the things that the Holy Spirit tells us to do; and the good things we want to do when the Spirit has his way with us are just the opposite of our natural desires. These two forces within us are constantly fighting each other to win control over us, and our wishes are never free from their pressures. 18When you are guided by the Holy Spirit

New Revised Standard

28Now you,e my friends,f are children of the promise, like Isaac. 29But just as at that time the child who was born according to the flesh persecuted the child who was born according to the Spirit, so it is now also. 30But what does the scripture say? "Drive out the slave and her child; for the child of the slave will not share the inheritance with the child of the free woman." 31So then, friends,f we are children, not of the slave but of the free woman.

5 FOR FREEDOM Christ has set us free. Stand firm, therefore, and do not submit again to a yoke of slavery.

The Nature of Christian Freedom

2 Listen! I, Paul, am telling you that if you let yourselves be circumcised, Christ will be of no benefit to you. 3Once again I testify to every man who lets himself be circumcised that he is obliged to obey the entire law. 4You who want to be justified by the law have cut yourselves off from Christ; you have fallen away from grace. 5For through the Spirit, by faith, we eagerly wait for the hope of righteousness. 6For in Christ Jesus neither circumcision nor uncircumcision counts for anything; the only thing that counts is faith workingg through love.

7 You were running well; who prevented you from obeying the truth? 8Such persuasion does not come from the one who calls you. 9A little yeast leavens the whole batch of dough. 10I am confident about you in the Lord that you will not think otherwise. But whoever it is that is confusing you will pay the penalty. 11But my friends,f why am I still being persecuted if I am still preaching circumcision? In that case the offense of the cross has been removed. 12I wish those who unsettle you would castrate themselves!

13 For you were called to freedom, brothers and sisters;f only do not use your freedom as an opportunity for self-indulgence,h but through love become slaves to one another. 14For the whole law is summed up in a single commandment, "You shall love your neighbor as yourself." 15If, however, you bite and devour one another, take care that you are not consumed by one another.

The Works of the Flesh

16 Live by the Spirit, I say, and do not gratify the desires of the flesh. 17For what the flesh desires is opposed to the Spirit, and what the Spirit desires is opposed to the flesh; for these are opposed to each other, to prevent you from doing what you want. 18But if you are

---

d 5:12 *would cut themselves off from you and leave you alone,* or "would that those disturbing you would go and castrate themselves."

e Other ancient authorities read *we*   f Gk *brothers*   g Or *made effective*   h Gk *the flesh*

King James

18But if ye be led of the Spirit, ye are not under the law.

19Now the works of the flesh are manifest, which are *these;* Adultery, fornication, uncleanness, lasciviousness,

20Idolatry, witchcraft, hatred, variance, emulations, wrath, strife, seditions, heresies,

21Envyings, murders, drunkenness, revellings, and such like: of the which I tell you before, as I have also told *you* in time past, that they which do such things shall not inherit the kingdom of God.

22But the fruit of the Spirit is love, joy, peace, longsuffering, gentleness, goodness, faith,

23Meekness, temperance: against such there is no law.

24And they that are Christ's have crucified the flesh with the affections and lusts.

25If we live in the Spirit, let us also walk in the Spirit.

26Let us not be desirous of vain glory, provoking one another, envying one another.

6 BRETHREN, IF a man be overtaken in a fault, ye which are spiritual, restore such an one in the spirit of meekness; considering thyself, lest thou also be tempted.

2Bear ye one another's burdens, and so fulfil the law of Christ.

3For if a man think himself to be something, when he is nothing, he deceiveth himself.

4But let every man prove his own work, and then shall he have rejoicing in himself alone, and not in another.

5For every man shall bear his own burden.

6Let him that is taught in the word communicate unto him that teacheth in all good things.

7Be not deceived; God is not mocked: for whatsoever a man soweth, that shall he also reap.

8For he that soweth to his flesh shall of the flesh reap corruption; but he that soweth to the Spirit shall of the Spirit reap life everlasting.

9And let us not be weary in well doing: for in due season we shall reap, if we faint not.

10As we have therefore opportunity, let us do good unto all *men,* especially unto them who are of the household of faith.

11Ye see how large a letter I have written unto you with mine own hand.

12As many as desire to make a fair show in the flesh, they constrain you to be circumcised; only lest they should suffer persecution for the cross of Christ.

13For neither they themselves who are circumcised keep the law; but desire to have you circumcised, that they may glory in your flesh.

14But God forbid that I should glory, save in the cross of our Lord Jesus Christ, by whom the world is crucified unto me, and I unto the world.

15For in Christ Jesus neither circumcision availeth any thing, nor uncircumcision, but a new creature.

New International

if you are led by the Spirit, you are not under law.

19The acts of the sinful nature are obvious: sexual immorality, impurity and debauchery; 20idolatry and witchcraft; hatred, discord, jealousy, fits of rage, selfish ambition, dissensions, factions 21and envy; drunkenness, orgies, and the like. I warn you, as I did before, that those who live like this will not inherit the kingdom of God.

22But the fruit of the Spirit is love, joy, peace, patience, kindness, goodness, faithfulness, 23gentleness and self-control. Against such things there is no law. 24Those who belong to Christ Jesus have crucified the sinful nature with its passions and desires. 25Since we live by the Spirit, let us keep in step with the Spirit. 26Let us not become conceited, provoking and envying each other.

Doing Good to All

6 BROTHERS, IF someone is caught in a sin, you who are spiritual should restore him gently. But watch yourself, or you also may be tempted. 2Carry each other's burdens, and in this way you will fulfill the law of Christ. 3If anyone thinks he is something when he is nothing, he deceives himself. 4Each one should test his own actions. Then he can take pride in himself, without comparing himself to somebody else, 5for each one should carry his own load.

6Anyone who receives instruction in the word must share all good things with his instructor.

7Do not be deceived: God cannot be mocked. A man reaps what he sows. 8The one who sows to please his sinful nature, from that naturea will reap destruction; the one who sows to please the Spirit, from the Spirit will reap eternal life. 9Let us not become weary in doing good, for at the proper time we will reap a harvest if we do not give up. 10Therefore, as we have opportunity, let us do good to all people, especially to those who belong to the family of believers.

Not Circumcision but a New Creation

11See what large letters I use as I write to you with my own hand!

12Those who want to make a good impression outwardly are trying to compel you to be circumcised. The only reason they do this is to avoid being persecuted for the cross of Christ. 13Not even those who are circumcised obey the law, yet they want you to be circumcised that they may boast about your flesh. 14May I never boast except in the cross of our Lord Jesus Christ, through whichb the world has been crucified to me, and I to the world. 15Neither circumcision nor uncircumcision means anything; what counts is a new creation.

---

a 8 Or *his flesh, from the flesh*   b 14 Or *whom*

Living Bible

you need no longer force yourself to obey Jewish laws.

19But when you follow your own wrong inclinations your lives will produce these evil results: impure thoughts, eagerness for lustful pleasure, 20idolatry, spiritism (that is, encouraging the activity of demons), hatred and fighting, jealousy and anger, constant effort to get the best for yourself, complaints and criticisms, the feeling that everyone else is wrong except those in your own little group—and there will be wrong doctrine, 21envy, murder, drunkenness, wild parties, and all that sort of thing. Let me tell you again as I have before, that anyone living that sort of life will not inherit the Kingdom of God.

22But when the Holy Spirit controls our lives he will produce this kind of fruit in us: love, joy, peace, patience, kindness, goodness, faithfulness, 23gentleness and self-control; and here there is no conflict with Jewish laws.

24Those who belong to Christ have nailed their natural evil desires to his cross and crucified them there.

25If we are living now by the Holy Spirit's power, let us follow the Holy Spirit's leading in every part of our lives. 26Then we won't need to look for honors and popularity, which lead to jealousy and hard feelings.

6 DEAR BROTHERS, if a Christian is overcome by some sin, you who are godly should gently and humbly help him back onto the right path, remembering that next time it might be one of you who is in the wrong. 2Share each other's troubles and problems, and so obey our Lord's command. 3If anyone thinks he is too great to stoop to this, he is fooling himself. He is really a nobody.

4Let everyone be sure that he is doing his very best, for then he will have the personal satisfaction of work well done, and won't need to compare himself with someone else. 5Each of us must bear some faults and burdens of his own. For none of us is perfect!

6Those who are taught the Word of God should help their teachers by paying them.

7Don't be misled; remember that you can't ignore God and get away with it: a man will always reap just the kind of crop he sows! 8If he sows to please his own wrong desires, he will be planting seeds of evil and he will surely reap a harvest of spiritual decay and death; but if he plants the good things of the Spirit, he will reap the everlasting life which the Holy Spirit gives him. 9And let us not get tired of doing what is right, for after a while we will reap a harvest of blessing if we don't get discouraged and give up. 10That's why whenever we can we should always be kind to everyone, and especially to our Christian brothers.

11I will write these closing words in my own handwriting. See how large I have to make the letters! 12Those teachers of yours who are trying to convince you to be circumcised are doing it for just one reason: so that they can be popular and avoid the persecution they would get if they admitted that the cross of Christ alone can save. 13And even those teachers who submit to circumcision don't try to keep the other Jewish laws; but they want you to be circumcised in order that they can boast that you are their disciples.

14As for me, God forbid that I should boast about anything except the cross of our Lord Jesus Christ. Because of that cross my interest in all the attractive things of the world was killed long ago, and the world's interest in me is also long dead. 15It doesn't make any difference now whether we have been circumcised or not; what counts is whether we really have been changed into new and different people.

New Revised Standard

led by the Spirit, you are not subject to the law. 19Now the works of the flesh are obvious: fornication, impurity, licentiousness, 20idolatry, sorcery, enmities, strife, jealousy, anger, quarrels, dissensions, factions, 21envy,c drunkenness, carousing, and things like these. I am warning you, as I warned you before: those who do such things will not inherit the kingdom of God.

The Fruit of the Spirit

22 By contrast, the fruit of the Spirit is love, joy, peace, patience, kindness, generosity, faithfulness, 23gentleness, and self-control. There is no law against such things. 24And those who belong to Christ Jesus have crucified the flesh with its passions and desires. 25If we live by the Spirit, let us also be guided by the Spirit. 26Let us not become conceited, competing against one another, envying one another.

Bear One Another's Burdens

6 MY FRIENDS,d if anyone is detected in a transgression, you who have received the Spirit should restore such a one in a spirit of gentleness. Take care that you yourselves are not tempted. 2Bear one another's burdens, and in this way you will fulfille the law of Christ. 3For if those who are nothing think they are something, they deceive themselves. 4All must test their own work; then that work, rather than their neighbor's work, will become a cause for pride. 5For all must carry their own loads.

6 Those who are taught the word must share in all good things with their teacher.

7 Do not be deceived; God is not mocked, for you reap whatever you sow. 8If you sow to your own flesh, you will reap corruption from the flesh; but if you sow to the Spirit, you will reap eternal life from the Spirit. 9So let us not grow weary in doing what is right, for we will reap at harvest time, if we do not give up. 10So then, whenever we have an opportunity, let us work for the good of all, and especially for those of the family of faith.

Final Admonitions and Benediction

11 See what large letters I make when I am writing in my own hand! 12It is those who want to make a good showing in the flesh that try to compel you to be circumcised—only that they may not be persecuted for the cross of Christ. 13Even the circumcised do not themselves obey the law, but they want you to be circumcised so that they may boast about your flesh. 14May I never boast of anything except the cross of our Lord Jesus Christ, by whichf the world has been crucified to me, and I to the world. 15Forg neither circumcision nor uncircumcision is anything; but a new creation is everything! 16As for those who will follow this rule—peace

---

c Other ancient authorities add *murder*   d Gk *Brothers*   e Other ancient authorities read *in this way fulfill*   f Or *through whom*   g Other ancient authorities add *in Christ Jesus*

King James

16And as many as walk according to this rule, peace *be* on them, and mercy, and upon the Israel of God.

17From henceforth let no man trouble me: for I bear in my body the marks of the Lord Jesus.

18Brethren, the grace of our Lord Jesus Christ *be* with your spirit. Amen.

New International

16Peace and mercy to all who follow this rule, even to the Israel of God.

17Finally, let no one cause me trouble, for I bear on my body the marks of Jesus.

18The grace of our Lord Jesus Christ be with your spirit, brothers. Amen.

Living Bible

16May God's mercy and peace be upon all of you who live by this principle and upon those everywhere who are really God's own.

17From now on please don't argue with me about these things, for I carry on my body the scars of the whippings and wounds from Jesus' enemies that mark me as his slave.

18Dear brothers, may the grace of our Lord Jesus Christ be with you all.

Sincerely, Paul

New Revised Standard

be upon them, and mercy, and upon the Israel of God.

17 From now on, let no one make trouble for me; for I carry the marks of Jesus branded on my body.

18 May the grace of our Lord Jesus Christ be with your spirit, brothers and sisters.a Amen.

a Gk brothers

King James

THE EPISTLE OF
PAUL THE APOSTLE TO THE
Ephesians

1 PAUL, AN apostle of Jesus Christ by the will of God, to the saints which are at Ephesus, and to the faithful in Christ Jesus:

2Grace be to you, and peace, from God our Father, and from the Lord Jesus Christ.

3Blessed be the God and Father of our Lord Jesus Christ, who hath blessed us with all spiritual blessings in heavenly places in Christ:

4According as he hath chosen us in him before the foundation of the world, that we should be holy and without blame before him in love:

5Having predestinated us unto the adoption of children by Jesus Christ to himself, according to the good pleasure of his will,

6To the praise of the glory of his grace, wherein he hath made us accepted in the beloved.

7In whom we have redemption through his blood, the forgiveness of sins, according to the riches of his grace;

8Wherein he hath abounded toward us in all wisdom and prudence;

9Having made known unto us the mystery of his will, according to his good pleasure which he hath purposed in himself:

10That in the dispensation of the fulness of times he might gather together in one all things in Christ, both which are in heaven, and which are on earth; even in him:

11In whom also we have obtained an inheritance, being predestinated according to the purpose of him who worketh all things after the counsel of his own will:

12That we should be to the praise of his glory, who first trusted in Christ.

13In whom ye also trusted, after that ye heard the word of truth, the gospel of your salvation: in whom also after that ye believed, ye were sealed with that holy Spirit of promise,

14Which is the earnest of our inheritance until the redemption of the purchased possession, unto the praise of his glory.

15Wherefore I also, after I heard of your faith in the Lord Jesus, and love unto all the saints,

16Cease not to give thanks for you, making mention of you in my prayers;

17That the God of our Lord Jesus Christ, the Father of glory, may give unto you the spirit of wisdom and revelation in the knowledge of him:

18The eyes of your understanding being enlightened; that ye may know what is the hope of his calling, and what the riches of the glory of his inheritance in the saints,

New International

Ephesians

1 PAUL, AN apostle of Christ Jesus by the will of God,

To the saints in Ephesus,a the faithfulb in Christ Jesus:

2Grace and peace to you from God our Father and the Lord Jesus Christ.

Spiritual Blessings in Christ

3Praise be to the God and Father of our Lord Jesus Christ, who has blessed us in the heavenly realms with every spiritual blessing in Christ. 4For he chose us in him before the creation of the world to be holy and blameless in his sight. In love 5hec predestined us to be adopted as his sons through Jesus Christ, in accordance with his pleasure and will— 6to the praise of his glorious grace, which he has freely given us in the One he loves. 7In him we have redemption through his blood, the forgiveness of sins, in accordance with the riches of God's grace 8that he lavished on us with all wisdom and understanding. 9And hed made known to us the mystery of his will according to his good pleasure, which he purposed in Christ, 10to be put into effect when the times will have reached their fulfillment—to bring all things in heaven and on earth together under one head, even Christ.

11In him we were also chosen,e having been predestined according to the plan of him who works out everything in conformity with the purpose of his will, 12in order that we, who were the first to hope in Christ, might be for the praise of his glory. 13And you also were included in Christ when you heard the word of truth, the gospel of your salvation. Having believed, you were marked in him with a seal, the promised Holy Spirit, 14who is a deposit guaranteeing our inheritance until the redemption of those who are God's possession—to the praise of his glory.

Thanksgiving and Prayer

15For this reason, ever since I heard about your faith in the Lord Jesus and your love for all the saints, 16I have not stopped giving thanks for you, remembering you in my prayers. 17I keep asking that the God of our Lord Jesus Christ, the glorious Father, may give you the Spiritf of wisdom and revelation, so that you may know him better. 18I pray also that the eyes of your heart may be enlightened in order that you may know the hope to which he has called you, the riches of his glorious inheritance in the saints, 19and his incomparably great power

---

a 1 Some early manuscripts do not have in Ephesus.   b 1 Or believers who are   c 4,5 Or sight in love. 5He   d 8,9 Or us. With all wisdom and understanding, 9he   e 11 Or were made heirs   f 17 Or a spirit

THE LETTER OF PAUL

TO THE

Ephesians

Ephesians

1 DEAR CHRISTIAN friends at Ephesus, ever loyal to the Lord: This is Paul writing to you, chosen by God to be Jesus Christ's messenger. 2May his blessings and peace be yours, sent to you from God our Father and Jesus Christ our Lord.

3How we praise God, the Father of our Lord Jesus Christ, who has blessed us with every blessing in heaven because we belong to Christ.

4Long ago, even before he made the world, God chose us to be his very own, through what Christ would do for us; he decided then to make us holy in his eyes, without a single fault—we who stand before him covered with his love. 5His unchanging plan has always been to adopt us into his own family by sending Jesus Christ to die for us. And he did this because he wanted to!

6Now all praise to God for his wonderful kindness to us and his favor that he has poured out upon us, because we belong to his dearly loved Son. 7So overflowing is his kindness toward us that he took away all our sins through the blood of his Son, by whom we are saved; 8and he has showered down upon us the richness of his grace—for how well he understands us and knows what is best for us at all times.

9God has told us his secret reason for sending Christ, a plan he decided on in mercy long ago; 10and this was his purpose: that when the time is ripe he will gather us all together from wherever we are—in heaven or on earth—to be with him in Christ, forever. 11Moreover, because of what Christ has done we have become gifts to God that he delights in, for as part of God's sovereign plan we were chosen from the beginning to be his, and all things happen just as he decided long ago. 12God's purpose in this was that we should praise God and give glory to him for doing these mighty things for us, who were the first to trust in Christ.

13And because of what Christ did, all you others too, who heard the Good News about how to be saved, and trusted Christ, were marked as belonging to Christ by the Holy Spirit, who long ago had been promised to all of us Christians. 14His presence within us is God's guarantee that he really will give us all that he promised; and the Spirit's seal upon us means that God has already purchased us and that he guarantees to bring us to himself. This is just one more reason for us to praise our glorious God.

15That is why, ever since I heard of your strong faith in the Lord Jesus and of the love you have for Christians everywhere, 16, 17I have never stopped thanking God for you. I pray for you constantly, asking God, the glorious Father of our Lord Jesus Christ, to give you wisdom to see clearly and really understand who Christ is and all that he has done for you. 18I pray that your hearts will be flooded with light so that you can see something of the future he has called you to share. I want you to realize that God has been made rich because we who are Christ's have been given to him! 19I pray that you will

Salutation

1 PAUL, AN apostle of Christ Jesus by the will of God,

To the saints who are in Ephesusg and are faithfulg in Christ Jesus:

2 Grace to you and peace from God our Father and the Lord Jesus Christ.

Spiritual Blessings in Christ

3 Blessed be the God and Father of our Lord Jesus Christ, who has blessed us in Christ with every spiritual blessing in the heavenly places, 4just as he chose us in Christh before the foundation of the world to be holy and blameless before him in love. 5He destined us for adoption as his children through Jesus Christ, according to the good pleasure of his will, 6to the praise of his glorious grace that he freely bestowed on us in the Beloved. 7In him we have redemption through his blood, the forgiveness of our trespasses, according to the riches of his grace 8that he lavished on us. With all wisdom and insight 9he has made known to us the mystery of his will, according to his good pleasure that he set forth in Christ, 10as a plan for the fullness of time, to gather up all things in him, things in heaven and things on earth. 11In Christ we have also obtained an inheritance,i having been destined according to the purpose of him who accomplishes all things according to his counsel and will, 12so that we, who were the first to set our hope on Christ, might live for the praise of his glory. 13In him you also, when you had heard the word of truth, the gospel of your salvation, and had believed in him, were marked with the seal of the promised Holy Spirit; 14thisj is the pledge of our inheritance toward redemption as God's own people, to the praise of his glory.

Paul's Prayer

15 I have heard of your faith in the Lord Jesus and your lovek toward all the saints, and for this reason 16I do not cease to give thanks for you as I remember you in my prayers. 17I pray that the God of our Lord Jesus Christ, the Father of glory, may give you a spirit of wisdom and revelation as you come to know him, 18so that, with the eyes of your heart enlightened, you may know what is the hope to which he has called you, what are the riches of his glorious inheritance among the saints, 19and what is the immeasurable greatness of his

---

g Other ancient authorities lack *in Ephesus*, reading *saints who are also faithful*
h Gk *in him*   i Or *been made a heritage*   j Other ancient authorities read
who   k Other ancient authorities lack *and your love*

King James

19And what *is* the exceeding greatness of his power to us-ward who believe, according to the working of his mighty power,

20Which he wrought in Christ, when he raised him from the dead, and set *him* at his own right hand in the heavenly *places,*

21Far above all principality, and power, and might, and dominion, and every name that is named, not only in this world, but also in that which is to come:

22And hath put all *things* under his feet, and gave him *to be* the head over all *things* to the church,

23Which is his body, the fulness of him that filleth all in all.

2 AND YOU *hath he quickened,* who were dead in trespasses and sins;

2Wherein in time past ye walked according to the course of this world, according to the prince of the power of the air, the spirit that now worketh in the children of disobedience:

3Among whom also we all had our conversation in times past in the lusts of our flesh, fulfilling the desires of the flesh and of the mind; and were by nature the children of wrath, even as others.

4But God, who is rich in mercy, for his great love wherewith he loved us,

5Even when we were dead in sins, hath quickened us together with Christ, (by grace ye are saved;)

6And hath raised *us* up together, and made *us* sit together in heavenly *places* in Christ Jesus:

7That in the ages to come he might show the exceeding riches of his grace in *his* kindness toward us through Christ Jesus.

8For by grace are ye saved through faith; and that not of yourselves: *it is* the gift of God:

9Not of works, lest any man should boast.

10For we are his workmanship, created in Christ Jesus unto good works, which God hath before ordained that we should walk in them.

11Wherefore remember, that ye *being* in time past Gentiles in the flesh, who are called Uncircumcision by that which is called the Circumcision in the flesh made by hands;

12That at that time ye were without Christ, being aliens from the commonwealth of Israel, and strangers from the covenants of promise, having no hope, and without God in the world:

13But now in Christ Jesus ye who sometimes were far off are made nigh by the blood of Christ.

14For he is our peace, who hath made both one, and hath broken down the middle wall of partition *between us;*

15Having abolished in his flesh the enmity, *even* the law of commandments *contained* in ordinances; for to make in himself of twain one new man, *so* making peace;

New International

for us who believe. That power is like the working of his mighty strength, 20which he exerted in Christ when he raised him from the dead and seated him at his right hand in the heavenly realms, 21far above all rule and authority, power and dominion, and every title that can be given, not only in the present age but also in the one to come. 22And God placed all things under his feet and appointed him to be head over everything for the church, 23which is his body, the fullness of him who fills everything in every way.

Made Alive in Christ

2 AS FOR you, you were dead in your transgressions and sins, 2in which you used to live when you followed the ways of this world and of the ruler of the kingdom of the air, the spirit who is now at work in those who are disobedient. 3All of us also lived among them at one time, gratifying the cravings of our sinful nature[a] and following its desires and thoughts. Like the rest, we were by nature objects of wrath. 4But because of his great love for us, God, who is rich in mercy, 5made us alive with Christ even when we were dead in transgressions—it is by grace you have been saved. 6And God raised us up with Christ and seated us with him in the heavenly realms in Christ Jesus, 7in order that in the coming ages he might show the incomparable riches of his grace, expressed in his kindness to us in Christ Jesus. 8For it is by grace you have been saved, through faith— and this not from yourselves, it is the gift of God— 9not by works, so that no one can boast. 10For we are God's workmanship, created in Christ Jesus to do good works, which God prepared in advance for us to do.

One in Christ

11Therefore, remember that formerly you who are Gentiles by birth and called "uncircumcised" by those who call themselves "the circumcision" (that done in the body by the hands of men)— 12remember that at that time you were separate from Christ, excluded from citizenship in Israel and foreigners to the covenants of the promise, without hope and without God in the world. 13But now in Christ Jesus you who once were far away have been brought near through the blood of Christ.

14For he himself is our peace, who has made the two one and has destroyed the barrier, the dividing wall of hostility, 15by abolishing in his flesh the law with its commandments and regulations. His purpose was to create in himself one new man out of the two, thus making peace, 16and in this one body to reconcile both of them

---

a 3 Or *our flesh*

Living Bible

begin to understand how incredibly great his power is to help those who believe him. It is that same mighty power [20]that raised Christ from the dead and seated him in the place of honor at God's right hand in heaven, [21]far, far above any other king or ruler or dictator or leader. Yes, his honor is far more glorious than that of anyone else either in this world or in the world to come. [22]And God has put all things under his feet and made him the supreme Head of the Church— [23]which is his body, filled with himself, the Author and Giver of everything everywhere.

2 ONCE YOU were under God's curse, doomed forever for your sins. [2]You went along with the crowd and were just like all the others, full of sin, obeying Satan, the mighty prince of the power of the air, who is at work right now in the hearts of those who are against the Lord. [3]All of us used to be just as they are, our lives expressing the evil within us, doing every wicked thing that our passions or our evil thoughts might lead us into. We started out bad, being born with evil natures, and were under God's anger just like everyone else.

[4]But God is so rich in mercy; he loved us so much [5]that even though we were spiritually dead and doomed by our sins, he gave us back our lives again[b] when he raised Christ from the dead—only by his undeserved favor have we ever been saved— [6]and lifted us up from the grave into glory along with Christ, where we sit with him in the heavenly realms—all because of what Christ Jesus did. [7]And now God can always point to us as examples of how very, very rich his kindness is, as shown in all he has done for us through Jesus Christ.

[8]Because of his kindness you have been saved through trusting Christ. And even trusting is not of yourselves;[c] it too is a gift from God. [9]Salvation is not a reward for the good we have done, so none of us can take any credit for it. [10]It is God himself who has made us what we are and given us new lives from Christ Jesus; and long ages ago he planned that we should spend these lives in helping others.

[11]Never forget that once you were heathen, and that you were called godless and "unclean" by the Jews. (But their hearts, too, were still unclean, even though they were going through the ceremonies and rituals of the godly, for they circumcised themselves as a sign of godliness.) [12]Remember that in those days you were living utterly apart from Christ; you were enemies of God's children and he had promised you no help. You were lost, without God, without hope.

[13]But now you belong to Christ Jesus, and though you once were far away from God, now you have been brought very near to him because of what Jesus Christ has done for you with his blood.

[14]For Christ himself is our way of peace. He has made peace between us Jews and you Gentiles by making us all one family,[d] breaking down the wall of contempt[e] that used to separate us. [15]By his death he ended the angry resentment between us, caused by the Jewish laws which favored the Jews and excluded the Gentiles, for he died to annul that whole system of Jewish laws. Then he took the two groups that had been opposed to each other and made them parts of himself; thus he fused us together to become one new person, and at last there was peace. [16]As parts of the same body, our anger against

New Revised Standard

power for us who believe, according to the working of his great power. [20]God[f] put this power to work in Christ when he raised him from the dead and seated him at his right hand in the heavenly places, [21]far above all rule and authority and power and dominion, and above every name that is named, not only in this age but also in the age to come. [22]And he has put all things under his feet and has made him the head over all things for the church, [23]which is his body, the fullness of him who fills all in all.

From Death to Life

2 YOU WERE dead through the trespasses and sins [2]in which you once lived, following the course of this world, following the ruler of the power of the air, the spirit that is now at work among those who are disobedient. [3]All of us once lived among them in the passions of our flesh, following the desires of flesh and senses, and we were by nature children of wrath, like everyone else. [4]But God, who is rich in mercy, out of the great love with which he loved us [5]even when we were dead through our trespasses, made us alive together with Christ[g]—by grace you have been saved— [6]and raised us up with him and seated us with him in the heavenly places in Christ Jesus, [7]so that in the ages to come he might show the immeasurable riches of his grace in kindness toward us in Christ Jesus. [8]For by grace you have been saved through faith, and this is not your own doing; it is the gift of God— [9]not the result of works, so that no one may boast. [10]For we are what he has made us, created in Christ Jesus for good works, which God prepared beforehand to be our way of life.

One in Christ

[11]So then, remember that at one time you Gentiles by birth,[h] called "the uncircumcision" by those who are called "the circumcision"—a physical circumcision made in the flesh by human hands— [12]remember that you were at that time without Christ, being aliens from the commonwealth of Israel, and strangers to the covenants of promise, having no hope and without God in the world. [13]But now in Christ Jesus you who once were far off have been brought near by the blood of Christ. [14]For he is our peace; in his flesh he has made both groups into one and has broken down the dividing wall, that is, the hostility between us. [15]He has abolished the law with its commandments and ordinances, that he might create in himself one new humanity in place of the two, thus making peace, [16]and might reconcile both groups to

---

[b] *2:5 gave us back our lives again,* literally, "he made us alive."   [c] *2:8 And even trusting is not of yourselves,* or, "Salvation is not of yourselves."
[d] *2:14 by making us all one family,* literally, "by making us one."
[e] *2:14 breaking down the wall of contempt,* implied.

[f] Gk *He*   [g] Other ancient authorities read *in Christ*   [h] Gk *in the flesh*

King James

16And that he might reconcile both unto God in one body by the cross, having slain the enmity thereby:

17And came and preached peace to you which were afar off, and to them that were nigh.

18For through him we both have access by one Spirit unto the Father.

19Now therefore ye are no more strangers and foreigners, but fellowcitizens with the saints, and of the household of God;

20And are built upon the foundation of the apostles and prophets, Jesus Christ himself being the chief corner stone;

21In whom all the building fitly framed together groweth unto an holy temple in the Lord:

22In whom ye also are builded together for an habitation of God through the Spirit.

3 FOR THIS cause I Paul, the prisoner of Jesus Christ for you Gentiles,

2If ye have heard of the dispensation of the grace of God which is given me to you-ward:

3How that by revelation he made known unto me the mystery; (as I wrote afore in few words,

4Whereby, when ye read, ye may understand my knowledge in the mystery of Christ)

5Which in other ages was not made known unto the sons of men, as it is now revealed unto his holy apostles and prophets by the Spirit;

6That the Gentiles should be fellowheirs, and of the same body, and partakers of his promise in Christ by the gospel:

7Whereof I was made a minister, according to the gift of the grace of God given unto me by the effectual working of his power.

8Unto me, who am less than the least of all saints, is this grace given, that I should preach among the Gentiles the unsearchable riches of Christ;

9And to make all men see what is the fellowship of the mystery, which from the beginning of the world hath been hid in God, who created all things by Jesus Christ:

10To the intent that now unto the principalities and powers in heavenly places might be known by the church the manifold wisdom of God,

11According to the eternal purpose which he purposed in Christ Jesus our Lord:

12In whom we have boldness and access with confidence by the faith of him.

13Wherefore I desire that ye faint not at my tribulations for you, which is your glory.

14For this cause I bow my knees unto the Father of our Lord Jesus Christ,

15Of whom the whole family in heaven and earth is named,

16That he would grant you, according to the riches of his glory, to be strengthened with might by his Spirit in the inner man;

17That Christ may dwell in your hearts by faith; that ye, being rooted and grounded in love,

18May be able to comprehend with all saints what is the breadth, and length, and depth, and height;

19And to know the love of Christ, which passeth knowledge, that ye might be filled with all the fulness of God.

New International

to God through the cross, by which he put to death their hostility. 17He came and preached peace to you who were far away and peace to those who were near. 18For through him we both have access to the Father by one Spirit.

19Consequently, you are no longer foreigners and aliens, but fellow citizens with God's people and members of God's household, 20built on the foundation of the apostles and prophets, with Christ Jesus himself as the chief cornerstone. 21In him the whole building is joined together and rises to become a holy temple in the Lord. 22And in him you too are being built together to become a dwelling in which God lives by his Spirit.

Paul the Preacher to the Gentiles

3 FOR THIS reason I, Paul, the prisoner of Christ Jesus for the sake of you Gentiles—

2Surely you have heard about the administration of God's grace that was given to me for you, 3that is, the mystery made known to me by revelation, as I have already written briefly. 4In reading this, then, you will be able to understand my insight into the mystery of Christ, 5which was not made known to men in other generations as it has now been revealed by the Spirit to God's holy apostles and prophets. 6This mystery is that through the gospel the Gentiles are heirs together with Israel, members together of one body, and sharers together in the promise in Christ Jesus.

7I became a servant of this gospel by the gift of God's grace given me through the working of his power. 8Although I am less than the least of all God's people, this grace was given me: to preach to the Gentiles the unsearchable riches of Christ, 9and to make plain to everyone the administration of this mystery, which for ages past was kept hidden in God, who created all things. 10His intent was that now, through the church, the manifold wisdom of God should be made known to the rulers and authorities in the heavenly realms, 11according to his eternal purpose which he accomplished in Christ Jesus our Lord. 12In him and through faith in him we may approach God with freedom and confidence. 13I ask you, therefore, not to be discouraged because of my sufferings for you, which are your glory.

A Prayer for the Ephesians

14For this reason I kneel before the Father, 15from whom his whole familya in heaven and on earth derives its name. 16I pray that out of his glorious riches he may strengthen you with power through his Spirit in your inner being, 17so that Christ may dwell in your hearts through faith. And I pray that you, being rooted and established in love, 18may have power, together with all the saints, to grasp how wide and long and high and deep is the love of Christ, 19and to know this love that surpasses knowledge—that you may be filled to the measure of all the fullness of God.

a 15 Or whom all fatherhood

Living Bible

each other has disappeared, for both of us have been reconciled to God. And so the feud ended at last at the cross. 17And he has brought this Good News of peace to you Gentiles who were very far away from him, and to us Jews who were near. 18Now all of us, whether Jews or Gentiles, may come to God the Father with the Holy Spirit's help because of what Christ has done for us.

19Now you are no longer strangers to God and foreigners to heaven, but you are members of God's very own family, citizens of God's country, and you belong in God's household with every other Christian.

20What a foundation you stand on now: the apostles and the prophets; and the cornerstone of the building is Jesus Christ himself! 21We who believe are carefully joined together with Christ as parts of a beautiful, constantly growing temple for God. 22And you also are joined with him and with each other by the Spirit, and are part of this dwelling place of God.

3 I PAUL, the servant of Christ, am here in jail because of you—for preaching that you Gentiles are a part of God's house. 2, 3No doubt you already know that God has given me this special work of showing God's favor to you Gentiles, as I briefly mentioned before in one of my letters. God himself showed me this secret plan of his, that the Gentiles, too, are included in his kindness. 4I say this to explain to you how I know about these things. 5In olden times God did not share this plan with his people, but now he has revealed it by the Holy Spirit to his apostles and prophets.

6And this is the secret: that the Gentiles will have their full share with the Jews in all the riches inherited by God's sons; both are invited to belong to his Church, and all of God's promises of mighty blessings through Christ apply to them both when they accept the Good News about Christ and what he has done for them. 7God has given me the wonderful privilege of telling everyone about this plan of his; and he has given me his power and special ability to do it well.

8Just think! Though I did nothing to deserve it, and though I am the most useless Christian there is, yet I was the one chosen for this special joy of telling the Gentiles the Glad News of the endless treasures available to them in Christ; 9and to explain to everyone that God is the Savior of the Gentiles too, just as he who made all things had secretly planned from the very beginning.

10And his reason? To show to all the rulers in heaven how perfectly wise he is when all of his family—Jews and Gentiles alike—are seen to be joined together in his Church, 11in just the way he had always planned it through Jesus Christ our Lord.

12Now we can come fearlessly right into God's presence, assured of his glad welcome when we come with Christ and trust in him.

13So please don't lose heart at what they are doing to me here. It is for you I am suffering and you should feel honored and encouraged.

14, 15When I think of the wisdom and scope of his plan I fall down on my knees and pray to the Father of all the great family of God—some of them already in heaven and some down here on earth— 16that out of his glorious, unlimited resources he will give you the mighty inner strengthening of his Holy Spirit. 17And I pray that Christ will be more and more at home in your hearts, living within you as you trust in him. May your roots go down deep into the soil of God's marvelous love; 18, 19and may you be able to feel and understand, as all God's children should, how long, how wide, how deep, and how high his love really is; and to experience this love for yourselves, though it is so great that you will never see the end of it or fully know or understand it. And so at last you will be filled up with God himself.

New Revised Standard

God in one body[b] through the cross, thus putting to death that hostility through it.[c] 17So he came and proclaimed peace to you who were far off and peace to those who were near; 18for through him both of us have access in one Spirit to the Father. 19So then you are no longer strangers and aliens, but you are citizens with the saints and also members of the household of God, 20built upon the foundation of the apostles and prophets, with Christ Jesus himself as the cornerstone.[d] 21In him the whole structure is joined together and grows into a holy temple in the Lord; 22in whom you also are built together spiritually[e] into a dwelling place for God.

Paul's Ministry to the Gentiles

3 THIS IS the reason that I Paul am a prisoner for[f] Christ Jesus for the sake of you Gentiles— 2for surely you have already heard of the commission of God's grace that was given me for you, 3and how the mystery was made known to me by revelation, as I wrote above in a few words, 4a reading of which will enable you to perceive my understanding of the mystery of Christ. 5In former generations this mystery[g] was not made known to humankind, as it has now been revealed to his holy apostles and prophets by the Spirit: 6that is, the Gentiles have become fellow heirs, members of the same body, and sharers in the promise in Christ Jesus through the gospel.

7 Of this gospel I have become a servant according to the gift of God's grace that was given me by the working of his power. 8Although I am the very least of all the saints, this grace was given to me to bring to the Gentiles the news of the boundless riches of Christ, 9and to make everyone see[h] what is the plan of the mystery hidden for ages in[i] God who created all things; 10so that through the church the wisdom of God in its rich variety might now be made known to the rulers and authorities in the heavenly places. 11This was in accordance with the eternal purpose that he has carried out in Christ Jesus our Lord, 12in whom we have access to God in boldness and confidence through faith in him.[j] 13I pray therefore that you[k] may not lose heart over my sufferings for you; they are your glory.

Prayer for the Readers

14 For this reason I bow my knees before the Father,[l] 15from whom every family[m] in heaven and on earth takes its name. 16I pray that, according to the riches of his glory, he may grant that you may be strengthened in your inner being with power through his Spirit, 17and that Christ may dwell in your hearts through faith, as you are being rooted and grounded in love. 18I pray that you may have the power to comprehend, with all the saints, what is the breadth and length and height and depth, 19and to know the love of Christ that surpasses knowledge, so that you may be filled with all the fullness of God.

[b] Or reconcile both of us in one body for God   [c] Or in him, or in himself   [d] Or keystone   [e] Gk in the Spirit   [f] Or of   [g] Gk it   [h] Other ancient authorities read to bring to light   [i] Or by   [j] Or the faith of him   [k] Or I   [l] Other ancient authorities add of our Lord Jesus Christ   [m] Gk fatherhood

King James

20Now unto him that is able to do exceeding abundantly above all that we ask or think, according to the power that worketh in us,

21Unto him be glory in the church by Christ Jesus throughout all ages, world without end. Amen.

4 I THEREFORE, the prisoner of the Lord, beseech you that ye walk worthy of the vocation wherewith ye are called,

2With all lowliness and meekness, with longsuffering, forbearing one another in love;

3Endeavouring to keep the unity of the Spirit in the bond of peace.

4*There is* one body, and one Spirit, even as ye are called in one hope of your calling;

5One Lord, one faith, one baptism,

6One God and Father of all, who *is* above all, and through all, and in you all.

7But unto every one of us is given grace according to the measure of the gift of Christ.

8Wherefore he saith, When he ascended up on high, he led captivity captive, and gave gifts unto men.

9(Now that he ascended, what is it but that he also descended first into the lower parts of the earth?

10He that descended is the same also that ascended up far above all heavens, that he might fill all things.)

11And he gave some, apostles; and some, prophets; and some, evangelists; and some, pastors and teachers;

12For the perfecting of the saints, for the work of the ministry, for the edifying of the body of Christ:

13Till we all come in the unity of the faith, and of the knowledge of the Son of God, unto a perfect man, unto the measure of the stature of the fulness of Christ:

14That we *henceforth* be no more children, tossed to and fro, and carried about with every wind of doctrine, by the sleight of men, *and* cunning craftiness, whereby they lie in wait to deceive;

15But speaking the truth in love, may grow up into him in all things, which is the head, *even* Christ:

16From whom the whole body fitly joined together and compacted by that which every joint supplieth, according to the effectual working in the measure of every part, maketh increase of the body unto the edifying of itself in love.

17This I say therefore, and testify in the Lord, that ye henceforth walk not as other Gentiles walk, in the vanity of their mind,

18Having the understanding darkened, being alienated from the life of God through the ignorance that is in them, because of the blindness of their heart:

19Who being past feeling have given themselves over unto lasciviousness, to work all uncleanness with greediness.

20But ye have not so learned Christ;

New International

20Now to him who is able to do immeasurably more than all we ask or imagine, according to his power that is at work within us, 21to him be glory in the church and in Christ Jesus throughout all generations, for ever and ever! Amen.

Unity in the Body of Christ

4 AS A prisoner for the Lord, then, I urge you to live a life worthy of the calling you have received. 2Be completely humble and gentle; be patient, bearing with one another in love. 3Make every effort to keep the unity of the Spirit through the bond of peace. 4There is one body and one Spirit— just as you were called to one hope when you were called— 5one Lord, one faith, one baptism; 6one God and Father of all, who is over all and through all and in all.

7But to each one of us grace has been given as Christ apportioned it. 8This is why it[a] says:

"When he ascended on high,
   he led captives in his train
   and gave gifts to men."[b]

9(What does "he ascended" mean except that he also descended to the lower, earthly regions[c]? 10He who descended is the very one who ascended higher than all the heavens, in order to fill the whole universe.) 11It was he who gave some to be apostles, some to be prophets, some to be evangelists, and some to be pastors and teachers, 12to prepare God's people for works of service, so that the body of Christ may be built up 13until we all reach unity in the faith and in the knowledge of the Son of God and become mature, attaining to the whole measure of the fullness of Christ.

14Then we will no longer be infants, tossed back and forth by the waves, and blown here and there by every wind of teaching and by the cunning and craftiness of men in their deceitful scheming. 15Instead, speaking the truth in love, we will in all things grow up into him who is the Head, that is, Christ. 16From him the whole body, joined and held together by every supporting ligament, grows and builds itself up in love, as each part does its work.

Living as Children of Light

17So I tell you this, and insist on it in the Lord, that you must no longer live as the Gentiles do, in the futility of their thinking. 18They are darkened in their understanding and separated from the life of God because of the ignorance that is in them due to the hardening of their hearts. 19Having lost all sensitivity, they have given themselves over to sensuality so as to indulge in every kind of impurity, with a continual lust for more.

20You, however, did not come to know Christ that way. 21Surely you heard of him and were taught in him

a 8 Or *God*   b 8 Psalm 68:18   c 9 Or *the depths of the earth*

Living Bible

20Now glory be to God who by his mighty power at work within us is able to do far more than we would ever dare to ask or even dream of—infinitely beyond our highest prayers, desires, thoughts, or hopes. 21May he be given glory forever and ever through endless ages because of his master plan of salvation for the Church through Jesus Christ.

4 I BEG you—I, a prisoner here in jail for serving the Lord—to live and act in a way worthy of those who have been chosen for such wonderful blessings as these. 2Be humble and gentle. Be patient with each other, making allowance for each other's faults because of your love. 3Try always to be led along together by the Holy Spirit, and so be at peace with one another.

4We are all parts of one body, we have the same Spirit, and we have all been called to the same glorious future. 5For us there is only one Lord, one faith, one baptism, 6and we all have the same God and Father who is over us all and in us all, and living through every part of us. 7However, Christ has given each of us special abilities—whatever he wants us to have out of his rich storehouse of gifts.

8The Psalmist tells about this, for he says that when Christ returned triumphantly to heaven after his resurrection and victory over Satan, he gave generous gifts to men. 9Notice that it says he returned to heaven. This means that he had first come down from the heights of heaven, far down to the lowest parts of the earth. 10The same one who came down is the one who went back up, that he might fill all things everywhere with himself, from the very lowest to the very highest.d

11Some of us have been given special ability as apostles; to others he has given the gift of being able to preach well; some have special ability in winning people to Christ, helping them to trust him as their Savior; still others have a gift for caring for God's people as a shepherd does his sheep, leading and teaching them in the ways of God.

12Why is it that he gives us these special abilities to do certain things best? It is that God's people will be equipped to do better work for him, building up the Church, the body of Christ, to a position of strength and maturity; 13until finally we all believe alike about our salvation and about our Savior, God's Son, and all become full-grown in the Lord—yes, to the point of being filled full with Christ.

14Then we will no longer be like children, forever changing our minds about what we believe because someone has told us something different, or has cleverly lied to us and made the lie sound like the truth. 15, 16Instead, we will lovingly follow the truth at all times—speaking truly, dealing truly, living trulye—and so become more and more in every way like Christ who is the Head of his body, the Church. Under his direction the whole body is fitted together perfectly, and each part in its own special way helps the other parts, so that the whole body is healthy and growing and full of love.

17, 18Let me say this, then, speaking for the Lord: Live no longer as the unsaved do, for they are blinded and confused. Their closed hearts are full of darkness; they are far away from the life of God because they have shut their minds against him, and they cannot understand his ways. 19They don't care anymore about right and wrong and have given themselves over to impure ways. They stop at nothing, being driven by their evil minds and reckless lusts.

20But that isn't the way Christ taught you! 21If you

New Revised Standard

20 Now to him who by the power at work within us is able to accomplish abundantly far more than all we can ask or imagine, 21to him be glory in the church and in Christ Jesus to all generations, forever and ever. Amen.

Unity in the Body of Christ

4 I THEREFORE, the prisoner in the Lord, beg you to lead a life worthy of the calling to which you have been called, 2with all humility and gentleness, with patience, bearing with one another in love, 3making every effort to maintain the unity of the Spirit in the bond of peace. 4There is one body and one Spirit, just as you were called to the one hope of your calling, 5one Lord, one faith, one baptism, 6one God and Father of all, who is above all and through all and in all.

7 But each of us was given grace according to the measure of Christ's gift. 8Therefore it is said,

"When he ascended on high he made captivity
    itself a captive;
    he gave gifts to his people."

9(When it says, "He ascended," what does it mean but that he had also descendedf into the lower parts of the earth? 10He who descended is the same one who ascended far above all the heavens, so that he might fill all things.) 11The gifts he gave were that some would be apostles, some prophets, some evangelists, some pastors and teachers, 12to equip the saints for the work of ministry, for building up the body of Christ, 13until all of us come to the unity of the faith and of the knowledge of the Son of God, to maturity, to the measure of the full stature of Christ. 14We must no longer be children, tossed to and fro and blown about by every wind of doctrine, by people's trickery, by their craftiness in deceitful scheming. 15But speaking the truth in love, we must grow up in every way into him who is the head, into Christ, 16from whom the whole body, joined and knit together by every ligament with which it is equipped, as each part is working properly, promotes the body's growth in building itself up in love.

The Old Life and the New

17 Now this I affirm and insist on in the Lord: you must no longer live as the Gentiles live, in the futility of their minds. 18They are darkened in their understanding, alienated from the life of God because of their ignorance and hardness of heart. 19They have lost all sensitivity and have abandoned themselves to licentiousness, greedy to practice every kind of impurity. 20That is not the way you learned Christ! 21For surely you have heard

---

d 4:10 *from the very lowest to the very highest,* literally, "that he might fill all things."   e 4:15, 16 *speaking truly, dealing truly, living truly,* Amplified New Testament.

f Other ancient authorities add *first*

King James

21If so be that ye have heard him, and have been taught by him, as the truth is in Jesus:

22That ye put off concerning the former conversation the old man, which is corrupt according to the deceitful lusts;

23And be renewed in the spirit of your mind;

24And that ye put on the new man, which after God is created in righteousness and true holiness.

25Wherefore putting away lying, speak every man truth with his neighbour: for we are members one of another.

26Be ye angry, and sin not: let not the sun go down upon your wrath:

27Neither give place to the devil.

28Let him that stole steal no more: but rather let him labour, working with *his* hands the thing which is good, that he may have to give to him that needeth.

29Let no corrupt communication proceed out of your mouth, but that which is good to the use of edifying, that it may minister grace unto the hearers.

30And grieve not the holy Spirit of God, whereby ye are sealed unto the day of redemption.

31Let all bitterness, and wrath, and anger, and clamour, and evil speaking, be put away from you, with all malice:

32And be ye kind one to another, tenderhearted, forgiving one another, even as God for Christ's sake hath forgiven you.

5 BE YE therefore followers of God, as dear children;

2And walk in love, as Christ also hath loved us, and hath given himself for us an offering and a sacrifice to God for a sweetsmelling savour.

3But fornication, and all uncleanness, or covetousness, let it not be once named among you, as becometh saints;

4Neither filthiness, nor foolish talking, nor jesting, which are not convenient: but rather giving of thanks.

5For this ye know, that no whoremonger, nor unclean person, nor covetous man, who is an idolater, hath any inheritance in the kingdom of Christ and of God.

6Let no man deceive you with vain words: for because of these things cometh the wrath of God upon the children of disobedience.

7Be not ye therefore partakers with them.

8For ye were sometimes darkness, but now *are ye* light in the Lord: walk as children of light:

9(For the fruit of the Spirit *is* in all goodness and righteousness and truth;)

10Proving what is acceptable unto the Lord.

11And have no fellowship with the unfruitful works of darkness, but rather reprove *them.*

12For it is a shame even to speak of those things which are done of them in secret.

13But all things that are reproved are made manifest by the light: for whatsoever doth make manifest is light.

14Wherefore he saith, Awake thou that sleepest, and arise from the dead, and Christ shall give thee light.

15See then that ye walk circumspectly, not as fools, but as wise,

16Redeeming the time, because the days are evil.

17Wherefore be ye not unwise, but understanding what the will of the Lord *is.*

New International

in accordance with the truth that is in Jesus. 22You were taught, with regard to your former way of life, to put off your old self, which is being corrupted by its deceitful desires; 23to be made new in the attitude of your minds; 24and to put on the new self, created to be like God in true righteousness and holiness.

25Therefore each of you must put off falsehood and speak truthfully to his neighbor, for we are all members of one body. 26"In your anger do not sin"a: Do not let the sun go down while you are still angry, 27and do not give the devil a foothold. 28He who has been stealing must steal no longer, but must work, doing something useful with his own hands, that he may have something to share with those in need.

29Do not let any unwholesome talk come out of your mouths, but only what is helpful for building others up according to their needs, that it may benefit those who listen. 30And do not grieve the Holy Spirit of God, with whom you were sealed for the day of redemption. 31Get rid of all bitterness, rage and anger, brawling and slander, along with every form of malice. 32Be kind and compassionate to one another, forgiving each other, just as in Christ God forgave you.

5 BE IMITATORS of God, therefore, as dearly loved children 2and live a life of love, just as Christ loved us and gave himself up for us as a fragrant offering and sacrifice to God.

3But among you there must not be even a hint of sexual immorality, or of any kind of impurity, or of greed, because these are improper for God's holy people. 4Nor should there be obscenity, foolish talk or coarse joking, which are out of place, but rather thanksgiving. 5For of this you can be sure: No immoral, impure or greedy person—such a man is an idolater—has any inheritance in the kingdom of Christ and of God.b 6Let no one deceive you with empty words, for because of such things God's wrath comes on those who are disobedient. 7Therefore do not be partners with them.

8For you were once darkness, but now you are light in the Lord. Live as children of light 9(for the fruit of the light consists in all goodness, righteousness and truth) 10and find out what pleases the Lord. 11Have nothing to do with the fruitless deeds of darkness, but rather expose them. 12For it is shameful even to mention what the disobedient do in secret. 13But everything exposed by the light becomes visible, 14for it is light that makes everything visible. This is why it is said:

"Wake up, O sleeper,
    rise from the dead,
    and Christ will shine on you."

15Be very careful, then, how you live—not as unwise but as wise, 16making the most of every opportunity, because the days are evil. 17Therefore do not be foolish, but understand what the Lord's will is. 18Do not get

a 26 Psalm 4:4   b 5 Or *kingdom of the Christ and God*

Living Bible

have really heard his voice and learned from him the truths concerning himself, 22then throw off your old evil nature—the old you that was a partner in your evil ways—rotten through and through, full of lust and sham.

23Now your attitudes and thoughts must all be constantly changing for the better. 24Yes, you must be a new and different person, holy and good. Clothe yourself with this new nature.

25Stop lying to each other; tell the truth, for we are parts of each other and when we lie to each other we are hurting ourselves. 26If you are angry, don't sin by nursing your grudge. Don't let the sun go down with you still angry—get over it quickly; 27for when you are angry you give a mighty foothold to the devil.

28If anyone is stealing he must stop it and begin using those hands of his for honest work so he can give to others in need. 29Don't use bad language. Say only what is good and helpful to those you are talking to, and what will give them a blessing.

30Don't cause the Holy Spirit sorrow by the way you live. Remember, he is the one who marks you to be presentc on that day when salvation from sin will be complete.

31Stop being mean, bad-tempered and angry. Quarreling, harsh words, and dislike of others should have no place in your lives. 32Instead, be kind to each other, tenderhearted, forgiving one another, just as God has forgiven you because you belong to Christ.

5 FOLLOW GOD'S example in everything you do just as a much loved child imitates his father. 2Be full of love for others, following the example of Christ who loved you and gave himself to God as a sacrifice to take away your sins. And God was pleased, for Christ's love for you was like sweet perfume to him.

3Let there be no sex sin, impurity or greed among you. Let no one be able to accuse you of any such things. 4Dirty stories, foul talk and coarse jokes—these are not for you. Instead, remind each other of God's goodness and be thankful.

5You can be sure of this: The Kingdom of Christ and of God will never belong to anyone who is impure or greedy, for a greedy person is really an idol worshiper—he loves and worships the good things of this life more than God. 6Don't be fooled by those who try to excuse these sins, for the terrible wrath of God is upon all those who do them. 7Don't even associate with such people. 8For though once your heart was full of darkness, now it is full of light from the Lord, and your behavior should show it! 9Because of this light within you, you should do only what is good and right and true.

10Learn as you go along what pleases the Lord.d 11Take no part in the worthless pleasures of evil and darkness, but instead, rebuke and expose them. 12It would be shameful even to mention here those pleasures of darkness which the ungodly do. 13But when you expose them, the light shines in upon their sin and shows it up, and when they see how wrong they really are, some of them may even become children of light! 14That is why God says in the Scriptures, "Awake, O sleeper, and rise up from the dead; and Christ shall give you light."

15, 16So be careful how you act; these are difficult days. Don't be fools; be wise: make the most of every opportunity you have for doing good. 17Don't act thoughtlessly, but try to find out and do whatever the Lord wants you to. 18Don't drink too much wine, for

New Revised Standard

about him and were taught in him, as truth is in Jesus. 22You were taught to put away your former way of life, your old self, corrupt and deluded by its lusts, 23and to be renewed in the spirit of your minds, 24and to clothe yourselves with the new self, created according to the likeness of God in true righteousness and holiness.

Rules for the New Life

25 So then, putting away falsehood, let all of us speak the truth to our neighbors, for we are members of one another. 26Be angry but do not sin; do not let the sun go down on your anger, 27and do not make room for the devil. 28Thieves must give up stealing; rather let them labor and work honestly with their own hands, so as to have something to share with the needy. 29Let no evil talk come out of your mouths, but only what is useful for building up,e as there is need, so that your words may give grace to those who hear. 30And do not grieve the Holy Spirit of God, with which you were marked with a seal for the day of redemption. 31Put away from you all bitterness and wrath and anger and wrangling and slander, together with all malice, 32and be kind to one another, tenderhearted, forgiving one another, as God in Christ has forgiven you.f

5 THEREFORE BE imitators of God, as beloved children, 2and live in love, as Christ loved usg and gave himself up for us, a fragrant offering and sacrifice to God.

Renounce Pagan Ways

3 But fornication and impurity of any kind, or greed, must not even be mentioned among you, as is proper among saints. 4Entirely out of place is obscene, silly, and vulgar talk; but instead, let there be thanksgiving. 5Be sure of this, that no fornicator or impure person, or one who is greedy (that is, an idolater), has any inheritance in the kingdom of Christ and of God.

6 Let no one deceive you with empty words, for because of these things the wrath of God comes on those who are disobedient. 7Therefore do not be associated with them. 8For once you were darkness, but now in the Lord you are light. Live as children of light— 9for the fruit of the light is found in all that is good and right and true. 10Try to find out what is pleasing to the Lord. 11Take no part in the unfruitful works of darkness, but instead expose them. 12For it is shameful even to mention what such people do secretly; 13but everything exposed by the light becomes visible, 14for everything that becomes visible is light. Therefore it says,

"Sleeper, awake!
   Rise from the dead,
   and Christ will shine on you."

15 Be careful then how you live, not as unwise people but as wise, 16making the most of the time, because the days are evil. 17So do not be foolish, but understand what the will of the Lord is. 18Do not get drunk with

---

c 4:30 he is the one who marks you to be present, literally, "in whom you were sealed unto the day of redemption."   d 5:10 Learn as you go along what pleases the Lord, or "Your lives should be an example."

e Other ancient authorities read building up faith   f Other ancient authorities read us   g Other ancient authorities read you

King James

18And be not drunk with wine, wherein is excess; but be filled with the Spirit;

19Speaking to yourselves in psalms and hymns and spiritual songs, singing and making melody in your heart to the Lord;

20Giving thanks always for all things unto God and the Father in the name of our Lord Jesus Christ;

21Submitting yourselves one to another in the fear of God.

22Wives, submit yourselves unto your own husbands, as unto the Lord.

23For the husband is the head of the wife, even as Christ is the head of the church: and he is the saviour of the body.

24Therefore as the church is subject unto Christ, so *let* the wives *be* to their own husbands in every thing.

25Husbands, love your wives, even as Christ also loved the church, and gave himself for it;

26That he might sanctify and cleanse it with the washing of water by the word,

27That he might present it to himself a glorious church, not having spot, or wrinkle, or any such thing; but that it should be holy and without blemish.

28So ought men to love their wives as their own bodies. He that loveth his wife loveth himself.

29For no man ever yet hated his own flesh; but nourisheth and cherisheth it, even as the Lord the church:

30For we are members of his body, of his flesh, and of his bones.

31For this cause shall a man leave his father and mother, and shall be joined unto his wife, and they two shall be one flesh.

32This is a great mystery: but I speak concerning Christ and the church.

33Nevertheless let every one of you in particular so love his wife even as himself; and the wife *see* that she reverence *her* husband.

6 CHILDREN, OBEY your parents in the Lord: for this is right.

2Honour thy father and mother; which is the first commandment with promise;

3That it may be well with thee, and thou mayest live long on the earth.

4And, ye fathers, provoke not your children to wrath: but bring them up in the nurture and admonition of the Lord.

5Servants, be obedient to them that are *your* masters according to the flesh, with fear and trembling, in singleness of your heart, as unto Christ;

6Not with eyeservice, as menpleasers; but as the servants of Christ, doing the will of God from the heart;

7With good will doing service, as to the Lord, and not to men:

8Knowing that whatsoever good thing any man doeth, the same shall he receive of the Lord, whether *he be* bond or free.

9And, ye masters, do the same things unto them, forbearing threatening: knowing that your Master also is in heaven; neither is there respect of persons with him.

10Finally, my brethren, be strong in the Lord, and in the power of his might.

11Put on the whole armour of God, that ye may be able to stand against the wiles of the devil.

New International

drunk on wine, which leads to debauchery. Instead, be filled with the Spirit. 19Speak to one another with psalms, hymns and spiritual songs. Sing and make music in your heart to the Lord, 20always giving thanks to God the Father for everything, in the name of our Lord Jesus Christ.

21Submit to one another out of reverence for Christ.

Wives and Husbands

22Wives, submit to your husbands as to the Lord. 23For the husband is the head of the wife as Christ is the head of the church, his body, of which he is the Savior. 24Now as the church submits to Christ, so also wives should submit to their husbands in everything.

25Husbands, love your wives, just as Christ loved the church and gave himself up for her 26to make her holy, cleansinga her by the washing with water through the word, 27and to present her to himself as a radiant church, without stain or wrinkle or any other blemish, but holy and blameless. 28In this same way, husbands ought to love their wives as their own bodies. He who loves his wife loves himself. 29After all, no one ever hated his own body, but he feeds and cares for it, just as Christ does the church— 30for we are members of his body. 31"For this reason a man will leave his father and mother and be united to his wife, and the two will become one flesh."b 32This is a profound mystery—but I am talking about Christ and the church. 33However, each one of you also must love his wife as he loves himself, and the wife must respect her husband.

Children and Parents

6 CHILDREN, OBEY your parents in the Lord, for this is right. 2"Honor your father and mother"— which is the first commandment with a promise— 3"that it may go well with you and that you may enjoy long life on the earth."c

4Fathers, do not exasperate your children; instead, bring them up in the training and instruction of the Lord.

Slaves and Masters

5Slaves, obey your earthly masters with respect and fear, and with sincerity of heart, just as you would obey Christ. 6Obey them not only to win their favor when their eye is on you, but like slaves of Christ, doing the will of God from your heart. 7Serve wholeheartedly, as if you were serving the Lord, not men, 8because you know that the Lord will reward everyone for whatever good he does, whether he is slave or free.

9And masters, treat your slaves in the same way. Do not threaten them, since you know that he who is both their Master and yours is in heaven, and there is no favoritism with him.

The Armor of God

10Finally, be strong in the Lord and in his mighty power. 11Put on the full armor of God so that you can take your stand against the devil's schemes. 12For our

---

a 26 Or *having cleansed*   b 31 Gen. 2:24   c 3 Deut. 5:16

Living Bible

many evils lie along that path; be filled instead with the Holy Spirit, and controlled by him.

19Talk with each other much about the Lord, quoting psalms and hymns and singing sacred songs, making music in your hearts to the Lord. 20Always give thanks for everything to our God and Father in the name of our Lord Jesus Christ.

21Honor Christ by submitting to each other. 22You wives must submit to your husbands' leadership in the same way you submit to the Lord. 23For a husband is in charge of his wife in the same way Christ is in charge of his body the Church. (He gave his very life to take care of it and be its Savior!) 24So you wives must willingly obey your husbands in everything, just as the Church obeys Christ.

25And you husbands, show the same kind of love to your wives as Christ showed to the Church when he died for her, 26to make her holy and clean, washed by baptismd and God's Word; 27so that he could give her to himself as a glorious Church without a single spot or wrinkle or any other blemish, being holy and without a single fault. 28That is how husbands should treat their wives, loving them as parts of themselves. For since a man and his wife are now one, a man is really doing himself a favor and loving himself when he loves his wife! 29, 30No one hates his own body but lovingly cares for it, just as Christ cares for his body the Church, of which we are parts.

31(That the husband and wife are one body is proved by the Scripture which says, "A man must leave his father and mother when he marries, so that he can be perfectly joined to his wife, and the two shall be one.") 32I know this is hard to understand, but it is an illustration of the way we are parts of the body of Christ.

33So again I say, a man must love his wife as a part of himself; and the wife must see to it that she deeply respects her husband—obeying, praising and honoring him.

6 CHILDREN, OBEY your parents; this is the right thing to do because God has placed them in authority over you. 2Honor your father and mother. This is the first of God's Ten Commandments that ends with a promise. 3And this is the promise: that if you honor your father and mother, yours will be a long life, full of blessing.

4And now a word to you parents. Don't keep on scolding and nagging your children, making them angry and resentful. Rather, bring them up with the loving discipline the Lord himself approves, with suggestions and godly advice.

5Slaves, obey your masters; be eager to give them your very best. Serve them as you would Christ. 6, 7Don't work hard only when your master is watching and then shirk when he isn't looking; work hard and with gladness all the time, as though working for Christ, doing the will of God with all your hearts. 8Remember, the Lord will pay you for each good thing you do, whether you are slave or free.

9And you slave owners must treat your slaves right, just as I have told you to treat you. Don't keep threatening them; remember, you yourselves are slaves to Christ; you have the same Master they do, and he has no favorites.

10Last of all I want to remind you that your strength must come from the Lord's mighty power within you. 11Put on all of God's armor so that you will be able to stand safe against all strategies and tricks of Satan. 12For

New Revised Standard

wine, for that is debauchery; but be filled with the Spirit, 19as you sing psalms and hymns and spiritual songs among yourselves, singing and making melody to the Lord in your hearts, 20giving thanks to God the Father at all times and for everything in the name of our Lord Jesus Christ.

The Christian Household

21 Be subject to one another out of reverence for Christ.

22 Wives, be subject to your husbands as you are to the Lord. 23For the husband is the head of the wife just as Christ is the head of the church, the body of which he is the Savior. 24Just as the church is subject to Christ, so also wives ought to be, in everything, to their husbands.

25 Husbands, love your wives, just as Christ loved the church and gave himself up for her, 26in order to make her holy by cleansing her with the washing of water by the word, 27so as to present the church to himself in splendor, without a spot or wrinkle or anything of the kind—yes, so that she may be holy and without blemish. 28In the same way, husbands should love their wives as they do their own bodies. He who loves his wife loves himself. 29For no one ever hates his own body, but he nourishes and tenderly cares for it, just as Christ does for the church, 30because we are members of his body.e 31"For this reason a man will leave his father and mother and be joined to his wife, and the two will become one flesh." 32This is a great mystery, and I am applying it to Christ and the church. 33Each of you, however, should love his wife as himself, and a wife should respect her husband.

Children and Parents

6 CHILDREN, OBEY your parents in the Lord,f for this is right. 2"Honor your father and mother"—this is the first commandment with a promise: 3"so that it may be well with you and you may live long on the earth."

4 And, fathers, do not provoke your children to anger, but bring them up in the discipline and instruction of the Lord.

Slaves and Masters

5 Slaves, obey your earthly masters with fear and trembling, in singleness of heart, as you obey Christ; 6not only while being watched, and in order to please them, but as slaves of Christ, doing the will of God from the heart. 7Render service with enthusiasm, as to the Lord and not to men and women, 8knowing that whatever good we do, we will receive the same again from the Lord, whether we are slaves or free.

9 And, masters, do the same to them. Stop threatening them, for you know that both of you have the same Master in heaven, and with him there is no partiality.

The Whole Armor of God

10 Finally, be strong in the Lord and in the strength of his power. 11Put on the whole armor of God, so that you may be able to stand against the wiles of the devil.

---

d 5:26 washed by baptism, literally, "having cleansed it by washing of water with the word."

e Other ancient authorities add of his flesh and of his bones   f Other ancient authorities lack in the Lord

King James

12For we wrestle not against flesh and blood, but against principalities, against powers, against the rulers of the darkness of this world, against spiritual wickedness in high *places*.

13Wherefore take unto you the whole armour of God, that ye may be able to withstand in the evil day, and having done all, to stand.

14Stand therefore, having your loins girt about with truth, and having on the breastplate of righteousness;

15And your feet shod with the preparation of the gospel of peace;

16Above all, taking the shield of faith, wherewith ye shall be able to quench all the fiery darts of the wicked.

17And take the helmet of salvation, and the sword of the Spirit, which is the word of God:

18Praying always with all prayer and supplication in the Spirit, and watching thereunto with all perseverance and supplication for all saints;

19And for me, that utterance may be given unto me, that I may open my mouth boldly, to make known the mystery of the gospel,

20For which I am an ambassador in bonds: that therein I may speak boldly, as I ought to speak.

21But that ye also may know my affairs, *and* how I do, Tychicus, a beloved brother and faithful minister in the Lord, shall make known to you all things:

22Whom I have sent unto you for the same purpose, that ye might know our affairs, and *that* he might comfort your hearts.

23Peace *be* to the brethren, and love with faith, from God the Father and the Lord Jesus Christ.

24Grace *be* with all them that love our Lord Jesus Christ in sincerity. Amen.

New International

struggle is not against flesh and blood, but against the rulers, against the authorities, against the powers of this dark world and against the spiritual forces of evil in the heavenly realms. 13Therefore put on the full armor of God, so that when the day of evil comes, you may be able to stand your ground, and after you have done everything, to stand. 14Stand firm then, with the belt of truth buckled around your waist, with the breastplate of righteousness in place, 15and with your feet fitted with the readiness that comes from the gospel of peace. 16In addition to all this, take up the shield of faith, with which you can extinguish all the flaming arrows of the evil one. 17Take the helmet of salvation and the sword of the Spirit, which is the word of God. 18And pray in the Spirit on all occasions with all kinds of prayers and requests. With this in mind, be alert and always keep on praying for all the saints.

19Pray also for me, that whenever I open my mouth, words may be given me so that I will fearlessly make known the mystery of the gospel, 20for which I am an ambassador in chains. Pray that I may declare it fearlessly, as I should.

Final Greetings

21Tychicus, the dear brother and faithful servant in the Lord, will tell you everything, so that you also may know how I am and what I am doing. 22I am sending him to you for this very purpose, that you may know how we are, and that he may encourage you.

23Peace to the brothers, and love with faith from God the Father and the Lord Jesus Christ. 24Grace to all who love our Lord Jesus Christ with an undying love.

Living Bible

we are not fighting against people made of flesh and blood, but against persons without bodies—the evil rulers of the unseen world, those mighty satanic beings and great evil princes of darkness who rule this world; and against huge numbers of wicked spirits in the spirit world.

13So use every piece of God's armor to resist the enemy whenever he attacks, and when it is all over, you will still be standing up.

14But to do this, you will need the strong belt of truth and the breastplate of God's approval. 15Wear shoes that are able to speed you on as you preach the Good News of peace with God. 16In every battle you will need faith as your shield to stop the fiery arrows aimed at you by Satan. 17And you will need the helmet of salvation and the sword of the Spirit—which is the Word of God.

18Pray all the time. Ask God for anything in line with the Holy Spirit's wishes. Plead with him, reminding him of your needs, and keep praying earnestly for all Christians everywhere. 19Pray for me, too, and ask God to give me the right words as I boldly tell others about the Lord, and as I explain to them that his salvation is for the Gentiles too. 20I am in chains now for preaching this message from God. But pray that I will keep on speaking out boldly for him even here in prison, as I should.

21Tychicus, who is a much loved brother and faithful helper in the Lord's work, will tell you all about how I am getting along. 22I am sending him to you for just this purpose, to let you know how we are and be encouraged by his report.

23May God give peace to you, my Christian brothers, and love, with faith from God the Father and the Lord Jesus Christ. 24May God's grace and blessing be upon all who sincerely love our Lord Jesus Christ.

Sincerely, Paul

New Revised Standard

12For oura struggle is not against enemies of blood and flesh, but against the rulers, against the authorities, against the cosmic powers of this present darkness, against the spiritual forces of evil in the heavenly places. 13Therefore take up the whole armor of God, so that you may be able to withstand on that evil day, and having done everything, to stand firm. 14Stand therefore, and fasten the belt of truth around your waist, and put on the breastplate of righteousness. 15As shoes for your feet put on whatever will make you ready to proclaim the gospel of peace. 16With all of these,b take the shield of faith, with which you will be able to quench all the flaming arrows of the evil one. 17Take the helmet of salvation, and the sword of the Spirit, which is the word of God.

18 Pray in the Spirit at all times in every prayer and supplication. To that end keep alert and always persevere in supplication for all the saints. 19Pray also for me, so that when I speak, a message may be given to me to make known with boldness the mystery of the gospel,c 20for which I am an ambassador in chains. Pray that I may declare it boldly, as I must speak.

Personal Matters and Benediction

21 So that you also may know how I am and what I am doing, Tychicus will tell you everything. He is a dear brother and a faithful minister in the Lord. 22I am sending him to you for this very purpose, to let you know how we are, and to encourage your hearts.

23 Peace be to the whole community,d and love with faith, from God the Father and the Lord Jesus Christ. 24Grace be with all who have an undying love for our Lord Jesus Christ.e

---

THE EPISTLE OF

PAUL THE APOSTLE TO THE

Philippians

Philippians

1 PAUL AND Timotheus, the servants of Jesus Christ, to all the saints in Christ Jesus which are at Philippi, with the bishops and deacons:

2Grace be unto you, and peace, from God our Father, and from the Lord Jesus Christ.

3I thank my God upon every remembrance of you, 4Always in every prayer of mine for you all making request with joy,

5For your fellowship in the gospel from the first day until now;

6Being confident of this very thing, that he which hath begun a good work in you will perform it until the day of Jesus Christ:

7Even as it is meet for me to think this of you all, because I have you in my heart; inasmuch as both in my bonds, and in the defence and confirmation of the gospel, ye all are partakers of my grace.

8For God is my record, how greatly I long after you all in the bowels of Jesus Christ.

9And this I pray, that your love may abound yet more and more in knowledge and in all judgment;

10That ye may approve things that are excellent; that ye may be sincere and without offence till the day of Christ;

11Being filled with the fruits of righteousness, which are by Jesus Christ, unto the glory and praise of God.

12But I would ye should understand, brethren, that the things which happened unto me have fallen out rather unto the furtherance of the gospel;

13So that my bonds in Christ are manifest in all the palace, and in all other places;

14And many of the brethren in the Lord, waxing confident by my bonds, are much more bold to speak the word without fear.

15Some indeed preach Christ even of envy and strife; and some also of good will:

16The one preach Christ of contention, not sincerely, supposing to add affliction to my bonds:

17But the other of love, knowing that I am set for the defence of the gospel.

18What then? notwithstanding, every way, whether in pretence, or in truth, Christ is preached; and I therein do rejoice, yea, and will rejoice.

19For I know that this shall turn to my salvation through your prayer, and the supply of the Spirit of Jesus Christ,

1 PAUL AND Timothy, servants of Christ Jesus,

To all the saints in Christ Jesus at Philippi, together with the overseersa and deacons:

2Grace and peace to you from God our Father and the Lord Jesus Christ.

Thanksgiving and Prayer

3I thank my God every time I remember you. 4In all my prayers for all of you, I always pray with joy 5because of your partnership in the gospel from the first day until now, 6being confident of this, that he who began a good work in you will carry it on to completion until the day of Christ Jesus.

7It is right for me to feel this way about all of you, since I have you in my heart; for whether I am in chains or defending and confirming the gospel, all of you share in God's grace with me. 8God can testify how I long for all of you with the affection of Christ Jesus.

9And this is my prayer: that your love may abound more and more in knowledge and depth of insight, 10so that you may be able to discern what is best and may be pure and blameless until the day of Christ, 11filled with the fruit of righteousness that comes through Jesus Christ—to the glory and praise of God.

Paul's Chains Advance the Gospel

12Now I want you to know, brothers, that what has happened to me has really served to advance the gospel. 13As a result, it has become clear throughout the whole palace guardb and to everyone else that I am in chains for Christ. 14Because of my chains, most of the brothers in the Lord have been encouraged to speak the word of God more courageously and fearlessly.

15It is true that some preach Christ out of envy and rivalry, but others out of goodwill. 16The latter do so in love, knowing that I am put here for the defense of the gospel. 17The former preach Christ out of selfish ambition, not sincerely, supposing that they can stir up trouble for me while I am in chains.c 18But what does it matter? The important thing is that in every way, whether from false motives or true, Christ is preached. And because of this I rejoice.

Yes, and I will continue to rejoice, 19for I know that through your prayers and the help given by the Spirit of Jesus Christ, what has happened to me will turn out for my deliverance.d 20I eagerly expect and hope that I will

Living Bible

Philippians

1 *FROM:* PAUL and Timothy, slaves of Jesus Christ.

To: The pastors and deacons and all the Christians in the city of Philippi.

2May God bless you all. Yes, I pray that God our Father and the Lord Jesus Christ will give each of you his fullest blessings, and his peace in your hearts and your lives. 3All my prayers for you are full of praise to God! 4When I pray for you, my heart is full of joy, 5because of all your wonderful help in making known the Good News about Christ from the time you first heard it until now. 6And I am sure that God who began the good work within you will keep right on helping you grow in his grace until his task within you is finally finished on that day when Jesus Christ returns.

7How natural it is that I should feel as I do about you, for you have a very special place in my heart. We have shared together the blessings of God, both when I was in prison and when I was out, defending the truth and telling others about Christ. 8Only God knows how deep is my love and longing for you—with the tenderness of Jesus Christ. 9My prayer for you is that you will overflow more and more with love for others, and at the same time keep on growing in spiritual knowledge and insight, 10for I want you always to see clearly the difference between right and wrong, and to be inwardly clean, no one being able to criticize you from now until our Lord returns. 11May you always be doing those good, kind things which show that you are a child of God, for this will bring much praise and glory to the Lord.

12And I want you to know this, dear brothers: Everything that has happened to me here has been a great boost in getting out the Good News concerning Christ. 13For everyone around here, including all the soldiers over at the barracks, knows that I am in chains simply because I am a Christian. 14And because of my imprisonment many of the Christians here seem to have lost their fear of chains! Somehow my patience has encouraged them and they have become more and more bold in telling others about Christ.

15Some, of course, are preaching the Good News because they are jealous of the way God has used me. They want reputations as fearless preachers! But others have purer motives, 16, 17preaching because they love me, for they know that the Lord has brought me here to use me to defend the Truth. And some preach to make me jealous, thinking that their success will add to my sorrows here in jail! 18But whatever their motive for doing it, the fact remains that the Good News about Christ is being preached and I am glad.

19I am going to keep on being glad, for I know that as you pray for me, and as the Holy Spirit helps me, this is all going to turn out for my good. 20For I live in eager

New Revised Standard

THE LETTER OF

PAUL TO THE

Philippians

Salutation

1 PAUL AND Timothy, servantse of Christ Jesus,
To all the saints in Christ Jesus who are in Philippi,
with the bishopsf and deacons:g

2 Grace to you and peace from God our Father and the Lord Jesus Christ.

Paul's Prayer for the Philippians

3 I thank my God every time I remember you, 4constantly praying with joy in every one of my prayers for all of you, 5because of your sharing in the gospel from the first day until now. 6I am confident of this, that the one who began a good work among you will bring it to completion by the day of Jesus Christ. 7It is right for me to think this way about all of you, because you hold me in your heart,h for all of you share in God's gracei with me, both in my imprisonment and in the defense and confirmation of the gospel. 8For God is my witness, how I long for all of you with the compassion of Christ Jesus. 9And this is my prayer, that your love may overflow more and more with knowledge and full insight 10to help you to determine what is best, so that in the day of Christ you may be pure and blameless, 11having produced the harvest of righteousness that comes through Jesus Christ for the glory and praise of God.

Paul's Present Circumstances

12 I want you to know, beloved,j that what has happened to me has actually helped to spread the gospel, 13so that it has become known throughout the whole imperial guardk and to everyone else that my imprisonment is for Christ; 14and most of the brothers and sisters,j having been made confident in the Lord by my imprisonment, dare to speak the wordl with greater boldness and without fear.

15 Some proclaim Christ from envy and rivalry, but others from goodwill. 16These proclaim Christ out of love, knowing that I have been put here for the defense of the gospel; 17the others proclaim Christ out of selfish ambition, not sincerely but intending to increase my suffering in my imprisonment. 18What does it matter? Just this, that Christ is proclaimed in every way, whether out of false motives or true; and in that I rejoice.

Yes, and I will continue to rejoice, 19for I know that through your prayers and the help of the Spirit of Jesus Christ this will turn out for my deliverance. 20It is my

---

e Gk slaves   f Or overseers   g Or overseers and helpers   h Or because I hold you in my heart   i Gk in grace   j Gk brothers   k Gk whole praetorium   l Other ancient authorities read word of God

King James

20According to my earnest expectation and *my* hope, that in nothing I shall be ashamed, but *that* with all boldness, as always, *so* now also Christ shall be magnified in my body, whether *it be* by life, or by death.

21For to me to live *is* Christ, and to die *is* gain.

22But if I live in the flesh, this *is* the fruit of my labour: yet what I shall choose I wot not.

23For I am in a strait betwixt two, having a desire to depart, and to be with Christ; which is far better:

24Nevertheless to abide in the flesh *is* more needful for you.

25And having this confidence, I know that I shall abide and continue with you all for your furtherance and joy of faith;

26That your rejoicing may be more abundant in Jesus Christ for me by my coming to you again.

27Only let your conversation be as it becometh the gospel of Christ: that whether I come and see you, or else be absent, I may hear of your affairs, that ye stand fast in one spirit, with one mind striving together for the faith of the gospel;

28And in nothing terrified by your adversaries: which is to them an evident token of perdition, but to you of salvation, and that of God.

29For unto you it is given in the behalf of Christ, not only to believe on him, but also to suffer for his sake;

30Having the same conflict which ye saw in me, and now hear *to be* in me.

2 IF *THERE* be therefore any consolation in Christ, if any comfort of love, if any fellowship of the Spirit, if any bowels and mercies,

2Fulfil ye my joy, that ye be likeminded, having the same love, *being* of one accord, of one mind.

3*Let* nothing *be done* through strife or vainglory; but in lowliness of mind let each esteem other better than themselves.

4Look not every man on his own things, but every man also on the things of others.

5Let this mind be in you, which was also in Christ Jesus:

6Who, being in the form of God, thought it not robbery to be equal with God:

7But made himself of no reputation, and took upon him the form of a servant, and was made in the likeness of men:

8And being found in fashion as a man, he humbled himself, and became obedient unto death, even the death of the cross.

9Wherefore God also hath highly exalted him, and given him a name which is above every name:

10That at the name of Jesus every knee should bow, of *things* in heaven, and *things* in earth, and *things* under the earth;

11And *that* every tongue should confess that Jesus Christ *is* Lord, to the glory of God the Father.

12Wherefore, my beloved, as ye have always obeyed, not as in my presence only, but now much more in my absence, work out your own salvation with fear and trembling.

New International

in no way be ashamed, but will have sufficient courage so that now as always Christ will be exalted in my body, whether by life or by death. 21For to me, to live is Christ and to die is gain. 22If I am to go on living in the body, this will mean fruitful labor for me. Yet what shall I choose? I do not know! 23I am torn between the two: I desire to depart and be with Christ, which is better by far; 24but it is more necessary for you that I remain in the body. 25Convinced of this, I know that I will remain, and I will continue with all of you for your progress and joy in the faith, 26so that through my being with you again your joy in Christ Jesus will overflow on account of me.

27Whatever happens, conduct yourselves in a manner worthy of the gospel of Christ. Then, whether I come and see you or only hear about you in my absence, I will know that you stand firm in one spirit, contending as one man for the faith of the gospel 28without being frightened in any way by those who oppose you. This is a sign to them that they will be destroyed, but that you will be saved—and that by God. 29For it has been granted to you on behalf of Christ not only to believe on him, but also to suffer for him, 30since you are going through the same struggle you saw I had, and now hear that I still have.

Imitating Christ's Humility

2 IF YOU have any encouragement from being united with Christ, if any comfort from his love, if any fellowship with the Spirit, if any tenderness and compassion, 2then make my joy complete by being likeminded, having the same love, being one in spirit and purpose. 3Do nothing out of selfish ambition or vain conceit, but in humility consider others better than yourselves. 4Each of you should look not only to your own interests, but also to the interests of others.

5Your attitude should be the same as that of Christ Jesus:

6Who, being in very nature[a] God,
　did not consider equality with God something
　　to be grasped,
7but made himself nothing,
　taking the very nature[b] of a servant,
　being made in human likeness.
8And being found in appearance as a man,
　he humbled himself
　and became obedient to death—
　　even death on a cross!
9Therefore God exalted him to the highest place
　and gave him the name that is above every
　　name,
10that at the name of Jesus every knee should
　　bow,
　in heaven and on earth and under the earth,
11and every tongue confess that Jesus Christ is
　　Lord,
　to the glory of God the Father.

Shining as Stars

12Therefore, my dear friends, as you have always obeyed—not only in my presence, but now much more in my absence—continue to work out your salvation

Living Bible

expectation and hope that I will never do anything that will cause me to be ashamed of myself but that I will always be ready to speak out boldly for Christ while I am going through all these trials here, just as I have in the past; and that I will always be an honor to Christ, whether I live or whether I must die. 21For to me, living means opportunities for Christ, and dying—well, that's better yet! 22But if living will give me more opportunities to win people to Christ, then I really don't know which is better, to live or die! 23Sometimes I want to live and at other times I don't, for I long to go and be with Christ. How much happier for *me* than being here! 24But the fact is that I can be of more help to *you* by staying!

25Yes, I am still needed down here and so I feel certain I will be staying on earth a little longer, to help you grow and become happy in your faith; 26my staying will make you glad and give you reason to glorify Christ Jesus for keeping me safe, when I return to visit you again.

27But whatever happens to me, remember always to live as Christians should, so that, whether I ever see you again or not, I will keep on hearing good reports that you are standing side by side with one strong purpose—to tell the Good News 28fearlessly, no matter what your enemies may do. They will see this as a sign of their downfall, but for you it will be a clear sign from God that he is with you, and that he has given you eternal life with him. 29For to you has been given the privilege not only of trusting him but also of suffering for him. 30We are in this fight together. You have seen me suffer for him in the past; and I am still in the midst of a great and terrible struggle now, as you know so well.

2 IS THERE any such thing as Christians cheering each other up? Do you love me enough to want to help me? Does it mean anything to you that we are brothers in the Lord, sharing the same Spirit? Are your hearts tender and sympathetic at all? 2Then make me truly happy by loving each other and agreeing wholeheartedly with each other, working together with one heart and mind and purpose.

3Don't be selfish; don't live to make a good impression on others. Be humble, thinking of others as better than yourself. 4Don't just think about your own affairs, but be interested in others, too, and in what they are doing.

5Your attitude should be the kind that was shown us by Jesus Christ, 6who, though he was God, did not demand and cling to his rights as God, 7but laid aside his mighty power and glory, taking the disguise of a slave and becoming like men.c 8And he humbled himself even further, going so far as actually to die a criminal's death on a cross.d

9Yet it was because of this that God raised him up to the heights of heaven and gave him a name which is above every other name, 10that at the name of Jesus every knee shall bow in heaven and on earth and under the earth, 11and every tongue shall confess that Jesus Christ is Lord, to the glory of God the Father.

12Dearest friends, when I was there with you, you were always so careful to follow my instructions. And now that I am away you must be even more careful to do the good things that result from being saved, obeying God with deep reverence, shrinking back from all that might displease him. 13For God is at work within you,

New Revised Standard

eager expectation and hope that I will not be put to shame in any way, but that by my speaking with all boldness, Christ will be exalted now as always in my body, whether by life or by death. 21For to me, living is Christ and dying is gain. 22If I am to live in the flesh, that means fruitful labor for me; and I do not know which I prefer. 23I am hard pressed between the two: my desire is to depart and be with Christ, for that is far better; 24but to remain in the flesh is more necessary for you. 25Since I am convinced of this, I know that I will remain and continue with all of you for your progress and joy in faith, 26so that I may share abundantly in your boasting in Christ Jesus when I come to you again.

27 Only, live your life in a manner worthy of the gospel of Christ, so that, whether I come and see you or am absent and hear about you, I will know that you are standing firm in one spirit, striving side by side with one mind for the faith of the gospel, 28and are in no way intimidated by your opponents. For them this is evidence of their destruction, but of your salvation. And this is God's doing. 29For he has graciously granted you the privilege not only of believing in Christ, but of suffering for him as well— 30since you are having the same struggle that you saw I had and now hear that I still have.

Imitating Christ's Humility

2 IF THEN there is any encouragement in Christ, any consolation from love, any sharing in the Spirit, any compassion and sympathy, 2make my joy complete: be of the same mind, having the same love, being in full accord and of one mind. 3Do nothing from selfish ambition or conceit, but in humility regard others as better than yourselves. 4Let each of you look not to your own interests, but to the interests of others. 5Let the same mind be in you that wase in Christ Jesus,

6   who, though he was in the form of God,
     did not regard equality with God
     as something to be exploited,
7   but emptied himself,
     taking the form of a slave,
     being born in human likeness.
  And being found in human form,
8   he humbled himself
     and became obedient to the point of death—
     even death on a cross.

9 Therefore God also highly exalted him
    and gave him the name
    that is above every name,
10 so that at the name of Jesus
    every knee should bend,
    in heaven and on earth and under the earth,
11 and every tongue should confess
    that Jesus Christ is Lord,
    to the glory of God the Father.

Shining as Lights in the World

12 Therefore, my beloved, just as you have always obeyed me, not only in my presence, but much more now in my absence, work out your own salvation with fear and trembling; 13for it is God who is at work in you,

---

c 2:7 *becoming like men*, literally, "was made in the likeness of men."
d 2:8 *to die a criminal's death on a cross*, literally, "became obedient to death, even the death of the cross."

e Or *that you have*

King James

13For it is God which worketh in you both to will and to do of *his* good pleasure.

14Do all things without murmurings and disputings:

15That ye may be blameless and harmless, the sons of God, without rebuke, in the midst of a crooked and perverse nation, among whom ye shine as lights in the world;

16Holding forth the word of life; that I may rejoice in the day of Christ, that I have not run in vain, neither laboured in vain.

17Yea, and if I be offered upon the sacrifice and service of your faith, I joy, and rejoice with you all.

18For the same cause also do ye joy, and rejoice with me.

19But I trust in the Lord Jesus to send Timotheus shortly unto you, that I also may be of good comfort, when I know your state.

20For I have no man likeminded, who will naturally care for your state.

21For all seek their own, not the things which are Jesus Christ's.

22But ye know the proof of him, that, as a son with the father, he hath served with me in the gospel.

23Him therefore I hope to send presently, so soon as I shall see how it will go with me.

24But I trust in the Lord that I also myself shall come shortly.

25Yet I supposed it necessary to send to you Epaphroditus, my brother, and companion in labour, and fellow-soldier, but your messenger, and he that ministered to my wants.

26For he longed after you all, and was full of heaviness, because that ye had heard that he had been sick.

27For indeed he was sick nigh unto death: but God had mercy on him; and not on him only, but on me also, lest I should have sorrow upon sorrow.

28I sent him therefore the more carefully, that, when ye see him again, ye may rejoice, and that I may be the less sorrowful.

29Receive him therefore in the Lord with all gladness; and hold such in reputation:

30Because for the work of Christ he was nigh unto death, not regarding his life, to supply your lack of service toward me.

3 FINALLY, MY brethren, rejoice in the Lord. To write the same things to you, to me indeed *is* not grievous, but for you *it is* safe.

2Beware of dogs, beware of evil workers, beware of the concision.

3For we are the circumcision, which worship God in the spirit, and rejoice in Christ Jesus, and have no confidence in the flesh.

4Though I might also have confidence in the flesh. If any other man thinketh that he hath whereof he might trust in the flesh, I more:

5Circumcised the eighth day, of the stock of Israel, *of* the tribe of Benjamin, an Hebrew of the Hebrews; as touching the law, a Pharisee;

6Concerning zeal, persecuting the church; touching the righteousness which is in the law, blameless.

7But what things were gain to me, those I counted loss for Christ.

New International

with fear and trembling, 13for it is God who works in you to will and to act according to his good purpose.

14Do everything without complaining or arguing, 15so that you may become blameless and pure, children of God without fault in a crooked and depraved generation, in which you shine like stars in the universe 16as you hold outa the word of life—in order that I may boast on the day of Christ that I did not run or labor for nothing. 17But even if I am being poured out like a drink offering on the sacrifice and service coming from your faith, I am glad and rejoice with all of you. 18So you too should be glad and rejoice with me.

Timothy and Epaphroditus

19I hope in the Lord Jesus to send Timothy to you soon, that I also may be cheered when I receive news about you. 20I have no one else like him, who takes a genuine interest in your welfare. 21For everyone looks out for his own interests, not those of Jesus Christ. 22But you know that Timothy has proved himself, because as a son with his father he has served with me in the work of the gospel. 23I hope, therefore, to send him as soon as I see how things go with me. 24And I am confident in the Lord that I myself will come soon.

25But I think it is necessary to send back to you Epaphroditus, my brother, fellow worker and fellow soldier, who is also your messenger, whom you sent to take care of my needs. 26For he longs for all of you and is distressed because you heard he was ill. 27Indeed he was ill, and almost died. But God had mercy on him, and not on him only but also on me, to spare me sorrow upon sorrow. 28Therefore I am all the more eager to send him, so that when you see him again you may be glad and I may have less anxiety. 29Welcome him in the Lord with great joy, and honor men like him, 30because he almost died for the work of Christ, risking his life to make up for the help you could not give me.

No Confidence in the Flesh

3 FINALLY, MY brothers, rejoice in the Lord! It is no trouble for me to write the same things to you again, and it is a safeguard for you.

2Watch out for those dogs, those men who do evil, those mutilators of the flesh. 3For it is we who are the circumcision, we who worship by the Spirit of God, who glory in Christ Jesus, and who put no confidence in the flesh— 4though I myself have reasons for such confidence.

If anyone else thinks he has reasons to put confidence in the flesh, I have more: 5circumcised on the eighth day, of the people of Israel, of the tribe of Benjamin, a Hebrew of Hebrews; in regard to the law, a Pharisee; 6as for zeal, persecuting the church; as for legalistic righteousness, faultless.

7But whatever was to my profit I now consider loss for the sake of Christ. 8What is more, I consider every-

Living Bible

helping you want to obey him, and then helping you do what he wants.

14In everything you do, stay away from complaining and arguing, 15so that no one can speak a word of blame against you. You are to live clean, innocent lives as children of God in a dark world full of people who are crooked and stubborn. Shine out among them like beacon lights, 16holding out to them the Word of Life.

Then when Christ returns how glad I will be that my work among you was so worthwhile. 17And if my lifeblood is, so to speak, to be poured out over your faith which I am offering up to God as a sacrifice—that is, if I am to die for you—even then I will be glad, and will share my joy with each of you. 18For you should be happy about this, too, and rejoice with me for having this privilege of dying for you.

19If the Lord is willing, I will send Timothy to see you soon. Then when he comes back he can cheer me up by telling me all about you and how you are getting along. 20There is no one like Timothy for having a real interest in you; 21everyone else seems to be worrying about his own plans and not those of Jesus Christ. 22But you know Timothy. He has been just like a son to me in helping me preach the Good News. 23I hope to send him to you just as soon as I find out what is going to happen to me here. 24And I am trusting the Lord that soon I myself may come to see you.

25Meanwhile, I thought I ought to send Epaphroditus back to you. You sent him to help me in my need; well, he and I have been real brothers, working and battling side by side. 26Now I am sending him home again, for he has been homesick for all of you and upset because you heard that he was ill. 27And he surely was; in fact, he almost died. But God had mercy on him, and on me too, not allowing me to have this sorrow on top of everything else.

28So I am all the more anxious to get him back to you again, for I know how thankful you will be to see him, and that will make me happy and lighten all my cares. 29Welcome him in the Lord with great joy, and show your appreciation, 30for he risked his life for the work of Christ and was at the point of death while trying to do for me the things you couldn't do because you were far away.

3 WHATEVER HAPPENS, dear friends, be glad in the Lord. I never get tired of telling you this and it is good for you to hear it again and again.

2Watch out for those wicked men—dangerous dogs, I call them—who say you must be circumcised to be saved. 3For it isn't the *cutting of our bodies* that makes us children of God; it is *worshiping him with our spirits.* That is the only true "circumcision." We Christians glory in what Christ Jesus has done for us and realize that we are helpless to save ourselves.

4Yet if anyone ever had reason to hope that he could save himself, it would be I. If others could be saved by what they are, certainly I could! 5For I went through the Jewish initiation ceremony when I was eight days old, having been born into a pure-blooded Jewish home that was a branch of the old original Benjamin family. So I was a real Jew if there ever was one! What's more, I was a member of the Pharisees who demand the strictest obedience to every Jewish law and custom. 6And sincere? Yes, so much so that I greatly persecuted the Church; and I tried to obey every Jewish rule and regulation right down to the very last point.

7But all these things that I once thought very worthwhile—now I've thrown them all away so that I can put my trust and hope in Christ alone. 8Yes, everything else

New Revised Standard

enabling you both to will and to work for his good pleasure.

14 Do all things without murmuring and arguing, 15so that you may be blameless and innocent, children of God without blemish in the midst of a crooked and perverse generation, in which you shine like stars in the world. 16It is by your holding fast to the word of life that I can boast on the day of Christ that I did not run in vain or labor in vain. 17But even if I am being poured out as a libation over the sacrifice and the offering of your faith, I am glad and rejoice with all of you— 18and in the same way you also must be glad and rejoice with me.

Timothy and Epaphroditus

19 I hope in the Lord Jesus to send Timothy to you soon, so that I may be cheered by news of you. 20I have no one like him who will be genuinely concerned for your welfare. 21All of them are seeking their own interests, not those of Jesus Christ. 22But Timothy'sb worth you know, how like a son with a father he has served with me in the work of the gospel. 23I hope therefore to send him as soon as I see how things go with me; 24and I trust in the Lord that I will also come soon.

25 Still, I think it necessary to send to you Epaphroditus—my brother and co-worker and fellow soldier, your messengerc and minister to my need; 26for he has been longing ford all of you, and has been distressed because you heard that he was ill. 27He was indeed so ill that he nearly died. But God had mercy on him, and not only on him but on me also, so that I would not have one sorrow after another. 28I am the more eager to send him, therefore, in order that you may rejoice at seeing him again, and that I may be less anxious. 29Welcome him then in the Lord with all joy, and honor such people, 30because he came close to death for the work of Christ,e risking his life to make up for those services that you could not give me.

3 FINALLY, MY brothers and sisters,f rejoiceg in the Lord.

Breaking with the Past

To write the same things to you is not troublesome to me, and for you it is a safeguard.

2 Beware of the dogs, beware of the evil workers, beware of those who mutilate the flesh!h 3For it is we who are the circumcision, who worship in the Spirit of Godi and boast in Christ Jesus and have no confidence in the flesh— 4even though I, too, have reason for confidence in the flesh.

If anyone else has reason to be confident in the flesh, I have more: 5circumcised on the eighth day, a member of the people of Israel, of the tribe of Benjamin, a Hebrew born of Hebrews; as to the law, a Pharisee; 6as to zeal, a persecutor of the church; as to righteousness under the law, blameless.

7 Yet whatever gains I had, these I have come to regard as loss because of Christ. 8More than that, I

b Gk *his*   c Gk *apostle*   d Other ancient authorities read *longing to see*
e Other ancient authorities read *of the Lord*   f Gk *my brothers*   g Or *farewell*
h Gk *the mutilation*   i Other ancient authorities read *worship God in spirit*

King James

8Yea doubtless, and I count all things *but* loss for the excellency of the knowledge of Christ Jesus my Lord: for whom I have suffered the loss of all things, and do count them *but* dung, that I may win Christ,

9And be found in him, not having mine own righteousness, which is of the law, but that which is through the faith of Christ, the righteousness which is of God by faith:

10That I may know him, and the power of his resurrection, and the fellowship of his sufferings, being made conformable unto his death;

11If by any means I might attain unto the resurrection of the dead.

12Not as though I had already attained, either were already perfect: but I follow after, if that I may apprehend that for which also I am apprehended of Christ Jesus.

13Brethren, I count not myself to have apprehended: but *this* one thing *I do*, forgetting those things which are behind, and reaching forth unto those things which are before,

14I press toward the mark for the prize of the high calling of God in Christ Jesus.

15Let us therefore, as many as be perfect, be thus minded: and if in any thing ye be otherwise minded, God shall reveal even this unto you.

16Nevertheless, whereto we have already attained, let us walk by the same rule, let us mind the same thing.

17Brethren, be followers together of me, and mark them which walk so as ye have us for an example.

18(For many walk, of whom I have told you often, and now tell you even weeping, *that they are* the enemies of the cross of Christ:

19Whose end *is* destruction, whose God *is their* belly, and *whose* glory *is* in their shame, who mind earthly things.)

20For our conversation is in heaven; from whence also we look for the Saviour, the Lord Jesus Christ:

21Who shall change our vile body, that it may be fashioned like unto his glorious body, according to the working whereby he is able even to subdue all things unto himself.

4 THEREFORE, MY brethren dearly beloved and longed for, my joy and crown, so stand fast in the Lord, *my* dearly beloved.

2I beseech Euodias, and beseech Syntyche, that they be of the same mind in the Lord.

3And I entreat thee also, true yokefellow, help those women which laboured with me in the gospel, with Clement also, and *with* other my fellowlabourers, whose names *are* in the book of life.

4Rejoice in the Lord always: *and* again I say, Rejoice.

5Let your moderation be known unto all men. The Lord *is* at hand.

6Be careful for nothing; but in every thing by prayer and supplication with thanksgiving let your requests be made known unto God.

7And the peace of God, which passeth all understanding, shall keep your hearts and minds through Christ Jesus.

New International

thing a loss compared to the surpassing greatness of knowing Christ Jesus my Lord, for whose sake I have lost all things. I consider them rubbish, that I may gain Christ 9and be found in him, not having a righteousness of my own that comes from the law, but that which is through faith in Christ—the righteousness that comes from God and is by faith. 10I want to know Christ and the power of his resurrection and the fellowship of sharing in his sufferings, becoming like him in his death, 11and so, somehow, to attain to the resurrection from the dead.

Pressing on Toward the Goal

12Not that I have already obtained all this, or have already been made perfect, but I press on to take hold of that for which Christ Jesus took hold of me. 13Brothers, I do not consider myself yet to have taken hold of it. But one thing I do: Forgetting what is behind and straining toward what is ahead, 14I press on toward the goal to win the prize for which God has called me heavenward in Christ Jesus.

15All of us who are mature should take such a view of things. And if on some point you think differently, that too God will make clear to you. 16Only let us live up to what we have already attained.

17Join with others in following my example, brothers, and take note of those who live according to the pattern we gave you. 18For, as I have often told you before and now say again even with tears, many live as enemies of the cross of Christ. 19Their destiny is destruction, their god is their stomach, and their glory is in their shame. Their mind is on earthly things. 20But our citizenship is in heaven. And we eagerly await a Savior from there, the Lord Jesus Christ, 21who, by the power that enables him to bring everything under his control, will transform our lowly bodies so that they will be like his glorious body.

4 THEREFORE, MY brothers, you whom I love and long for, my joy and crown, that is how you should stand firm in the Lord, dear friends!

Exhortations

2I plead with Euodia and I plead with Syntyche to agree with each other in the Lord. 3Yes, and I ask you, loyal yokefellow,[a] help these women who have contended at my side in the cause of the gospel, along with Clement and the rest of my fellow workers, whose names are in the book of life.

4Rejoice in the Lord always. I will say it again: Rejoice! 5Let your gentleness be evident to all. The Lord is near. 6Do not be anxious about anything, but in everything, by prayer and petition, with thanksgiving, present your requests to God. 7And the peace of God, which transcends all understanding, will guard your hearts and your minds in Christ Jesus.

---

a *3* Or loyal *Syzygus*

Living Bible

is worthless when compared with the priceless gain of knowing Christ Jesus my Lord. I have put aside all else, counting it worth less than nothing, in order that I can have Christ, 9and become one with him, no longer counting on being saved by being good enough or by obeying God's laws, but by trusting Christ to save me; for God's way of making us right with himself depends on faith—counting on Christ alone. 10Now I have given up everything else—I have found it to be the only way to really know Christ and to experience the mighty power that brought him back to life again, and to find out what it means to suffer and to die with him. 11So, whatever it takes, I will be one who lives in the fresh newness of life of those who are alive from the dead.

12I don't mean to say I am perfect. I haven't learned all I should even yet, but I keep working toward that day when I will finally be all that Christ saved me for and wants me to be.

13No, dear brothers, I am still not all I should be but I am bringing all my energies to bear on this one thing: Forgetting the past and looking forward to what lies ahead, 14I strain to reach the end of the race and receive the prize for which God is calling us up to heaven because of what Christ Jesus did for us.

15I hope all of you who are mature Christians will see eye-to-eye with me on these things, and if you disagree on some point, I believe that God will make it plain to you— 16if you fully obey the truth you have.

17Dear brothers, pattern your lives after mine and notice who else lives up to my example. 18For I have told you often before, and I say it again now with tears in my eyes, there are many who walk along the Christian road who are really enemies of the cross of Christ. 19Their future is eternal loss, for their god is their appetite: they are proud of what they should be ashamed of; and all they think about is this life here on earth. 20But our homeland is in heaven, where our Savior the Lord Jesus Christ is; and we are looking forward to his return from there. 21When he comes back he will take these dying bodies of ours and change them into glorious bodies like his own, using the same mighty power that he will use to conquer all else everywhere.

4 DEAR BROTHER Christians, I love you and long to see you, for you are my joy and my reward for my work. My beloved friends, stay true to the Lord.

2And now I want to plead with those two dear women, Euodias and Syntyche. Please, please, with the Lord's help, quarrel no more—be friends again. 3And I ask you, my true teammate, to help these women, for they worked side by side with me in telling the Good News to others; and they worked with Clement, too, and the rest of my fellow workers whose names are written in the Book of Life.

4Always be full of joy in the Lord; I say it again, rejoice! 5Let everyone see that you are unselfish and considerate in all you do. Remember that the Lord is coming soon. 6Don't worry about anything; instead, pray about everything; tell God your needs and don't forget to thank him for his answers. 7If you do this you will experience God's peace, which is far more wonderful than the human mind can understand. His peace will keep your thoughts and your hearts quiet and at rest as you trust in Christ Jesus.

New Revised Standard

regard everything as loss because of the surpassing value of knowing Christ Jesus my Lord. For his sake I have suffered the loss of all things, and I regard them as rubbish, in order that I may gain Christ 9and be found in him, not having a righteousness of my own that comes from the law, but one that comes through faith in Christ,b the righteousness from God based on faith. 10I want to know Christc and the power of his resurrection and the sharing of his sufferings by becoming like him in his death, 11if somehow I may attain the resurrection from the dead.

Pressing toward the Goal

12 Not that I have already obtained this or have already reached the goal;d but I press on to make it my own, because Christ Jesus has made me his own. 13Beloved,e I do not consider that I have made it my own;f but this one thing I do: forgetting what lies behind and straining forward to what lies ahead, 14I press on toward the goal for the prize of the heavenlyg call of God in Christ Jesus. 15Let those of us then who are mature be of the same mind; and if you think differently about anything, this too God will reveal to you. 16Only let us hold fast to what we have attained.

17 Brothers and sisters,e join in imitating me, and observe those who live according to the example you have in us. 18For many live as enemies of the cross of Christ; I have often told you of them, and now I tell you even with tears. 19Their end is destruction; their god is the belly; and their glory is in their shame; their minds are set on earthly things. 20But our citizenshiph is in heaven, and it is from there that we are expecting a Savior, the Lord Jesus Christ. 21He will transform the body of our humiliationi that it may be conformed to the body of his glory,j by the power that also enables him to make all things subject to himself.

4 THEREFORE, MY brothers and sisters,k whom I love and long for, my joy and crown, stand firm in the Lord in this way, my beloved.

Exhortations

2 I urge Euodia and I urge Syntyche to be of the same mind in the Lord. 3Yes, and I ask you also, my loyal companion,l help these women, for they have struggled beside me in the work of the gospel, together with Clement and the rest of my co-workers, whose names are in the book of life.

4 Rejoicem in the Lord always; again I will say, Rejoice.m 5Let your gentleness be known to everyone. The Lord is near. 6Do not worry about anything, but in everything by prayer and supplication with thanksgiving let your requests be made known to God. 7And the peace of God, which surpasses all understanding, will guard your hearts and your minds in Christ Jesus.

King James

8Finally, brethren, whatsoever things are true, whatsoever things *are* honest, whatsoever things *are* just, whatsoever things *are* pure, whatsoever things *are* lovely, whatsoever things *are* of good report; if *there be* any virtue, and if *there be* any praise, think on these things.

9Those things, which ye have both learned, and received, and heard, and seen in me, do: and the God of peace shall be with you.

10But I rejoiced in the Lord greatly, that now at the last your care of me hath flourished again; wherein ye were also careful, but ye lacked opportunity.

11Not that I speak in respect of want: for I have learned, in whatsoever state I am, *therewith* to be content.

12I know both how to be abased, and I know how to abound: every where and in all things I am instructed both to be full and to be hungry, both to abound and to suffer need.

13I can do all things through Christ which strengtheneth me.

14Notwithstanding ye have well done, that ye did communicate with my affliction.

15Now ye Philippians know also, that in the beginning of the gospel, when I departed from Macedonia, no church communicated with me as concerning giving and receiving, but ye only.

16For even in Thessalonica ye sent once and again unto my necessity.

17Not because I desire a gift: but I desire fruit that may abound to your account.

18But I have all, and abound: I am full, having received of Epaphroditus the things *which were sent* from you, an odour of a sweet smell, a sacrifice acceptable, wellpleasing to God.

19But my God shall supply all your need according to his riches in glory by Christ Jesus.

20Now unto God and our Father *be* glory for ever and ever. Amen.

21Salute every saint in Christ Jesus. The brethren which are with me greet you.

22All the saints salute you, chiefly they that are of Caesar's household.

23The grace of our Lord Jesus Christ *be* with you all. Amen.

New International

8Finally, brothers, whatever is true, whatever is noble, whatever is right, whatever is pure, whatever is lovely, whatever is admirable—if anything is excellent or praiseworthy—think about such things. 9Whatever you have learned or received or heard from me, or seen in me—put it into practice. And the God of peace will be with you.

Thanks for Their Gifts

10I rejoice greatly in the Lord that at last you have renewed your concern for me. Indeed, you have been concerned, but you had no opportunity to show it. 11I am not saying this because I am in need, for I have learned to be content whatever the circumstances. 12I know what it is to be in need, and I know what it is to have plenty. I have learned the secret of being content in any and every situation, whether well fed or hungry, whether living in plenty or in want. 13I can do everything through him who gives me strength.

14Yet it was good of you to share in my troubles. 15Moreover, as you Philippians know, in the early days of your acquaintance with the gospel, when I set out from Macedonia, not one church shared with me in the matter of giving and receiving, except you only; 16for even when I was in Thessalonica, you sent me aid again and again when I was in need. 17Not that I am looking for a gift, but I am looking for what may be credited to your account. 18I have received full payment and even more; I am amply supplied, now that I have received from Epaphroditus the gifts you sent. They are a fragrant offering, an acceptable sacrifice, pleasing to God. 19And my God will meet all your needs according to his glorious riches in Christ Jesus.

20To our God and Father be glory for ever and ever. Amen.

Final Greetings

21Greet all the saints in Christ Jesus. The brothers who are with me send greetings. 22All the saints send you greetings, especially those who belong to Caesar's household.

23The grace of the Lord Jesus Christ be with your spirit. Amen.a

---

a *23* Some manuscripts do not have *Amen.*

Living Bible

8And now, brothers, as I close this letter let me say this one more thing: Fix your thoughts on what is true and good and right. Think about things that are pure and lovely, and dwell on the fine, good things in others. Think about all you can praise God for and be glad about. 9Keep putting into practice all you learned from me and saw me doing, and the God of peace will be with you.

10How grateful I am and how I praise the Lord that you are helping me again. I know you have always been anxious to send what you could, but for a while you didn't have the chance. 11Not that I was ever in need, for I have learned how to get along happily whether I have much or little. 12I know how to live on almost nothing or with everything. I have learned the secret of contentment in every situation, whether it be a full stomach or hunger, plenty or want; 13for I can do everything God asks me to with the help of Christ who gives me the strength and power. 14But even so, you have done right in helping me in my present difficulty.

15As you well know, when I first brought the Gospel to you and then went on my way, leaving Macedonia, only you Philippians became my partners in giving and receiving. No other church did this. 16Even when I was over in Thessalonica you sent help twice. 17But though I appreciate your gifts, what makes me happiest is the well-earned reward you will have because of your kindness.

18At the moment I have all I need—more than I need! I am generously supplied with the gifts you sent me when Epaphroditus came. They are a sweet-smelling sacrifice that pleases God well. 19And it is he who will supply all your needs from his riches in glory, because of what Christ Jesus has done for us. 20Now unto God our Father be glory forever and ever. Amen.

Sincerely, Paul

P.S.

21Say "hello" for me to all the Christians there; the brothers with me send their greetings too. 22And all the other Christians here want to be remembered to you, especially those who work in Caesar's palace. 23The blessings of our Lord Jesus Christ be upon your spirits.

New Revised Standard

8 Finally, beloved,[b] whatever is true, whatever is honorable, whatever is just, whatever is pure, whatever is pleasing, whatever is commendable, if there is any excellence and if there is anything worthy of praise, think about[c] these things. 9Keep on doing the things that you have learned and received and heard and seen in me, and the God of peace will be with you.

Acknowledgment of the Philippians' Gift

10 I rejoiced[d] in the Lord greatly that now at last you have revived your concern for me; indeed, you were concerned for me, but had no opportunity to show it.[e] 11Not that I am referring to being in need; for I have learned to be content with whatever I have. 12I know what it is to have little, and I know what it is to have plenty. In any and all circumstances I have learned the secret of being well-fed and of going hungry, of having plenty and of being in need. 13I can do all things through him who strengthens me. 14In any case, it was kind of you to share my distress.

15 You Philippians indeed know that in the early days of the gospel, when I left Macedonia, no church shared with me in the matter of giving and receiving, except you alone. 16For even when I was in Thessalonica, you sent me help for my needs more than once. 17Not that I seek the gift, but I seek the profit that accumulates to your account. 18I have been paid in full and have more than enough; I am fully satisfied, now that I have received from Epaphroditus the gifts you sent, a fragrant offering, a sacrifice acceptable and pleasing to God. 19And my God will fully satisfy every need of yours according to his riches in glory in Christ Jesus. 20To our God and Father be glory forever and ever. Amen.

Final Greetings and Benediction

21 Greet every saint in Christ Jesus. The friends[b] who are with me greet you. 22All the saints greet you, especially those of the emperor's household.

23 The grace of the Lord Jesus Christ be with your spirit.[f]

b Gk brothers   c Gk take account of   d Gk I rejoiced   e Gk lacks to show it   f Other ancient authorities add Amen

THE EPISTLE OF

PAUL THE APOSTLE TO THE

Colossians

1 PAUL, AN apostle of Jesus Christ by the will of God, and Timotheus *our* brother,

2To the saints and faithful brethren in Christ which are at Colosse: Grace *be* unto you, and peace, from God our Father and the Lord Jesus Christ.

3We give thanks to God and the Father of our Lord Jesus Christ, praying always for you,

4Since we heard of your faith in Christ Jesus, and of the love *which ye have* to all the saints,

5For the hope which is laid up for you in heaven, whereof ye heard before in the word of the truth of the gospel;

6Which is come unto you, as *it is* in all the world; and bringeth forth fruit, as *it doth* also in you, since the day ye heard *of it,* and knew the grace of God in truth:

7As ye also learned of Epaphras our dear fellowservant, who is for you a faithful minister of Christ;

8Who also declared unto us your love in the Spirit.

9For this cause we also, since the day we heard *it,* do not cease to pray for you, and to desire that ye might be filled with the knowledge of his will in all wisdom and spiritual understanding;

10That ye might walk worthy of the Lord unto all pleasing, being fruitful in every good work, and increasing in the knowledge of God;

11Strengthened with all might, according to his glorious power, unto all patience and longsuffering with joyfulness;

12Giving thanks unto the Father, which hath made us meet to be partakers of the inheritance of the saints in light:

13Who hath delivered us from the power of darkness, and hath translated *us* into the kingdom of his dear Son:

14In whom we have redemption through his blood, *even* the forgiveness of sins:

15Who is the image of the invisible God, the firstborn of every creature:

16For by him were all things created, that are in heaven, and that are in earth, visible and invisible, whether *they be* thrones, or dominions, or principalities, or powers: all things were created by him, and for him:

17And he is before all things, and by him all things consist.

18And he is the head of the body, the church: who is the beginning, the firstborn from the dead; that in all *things* he might have the preeminence.

19For it pleased *the Father* that in him should all fulness dwell;

New International

Colossians

1 PAUL, AN apostle of Christ Jesus by the will of God, and Timothy our brother,

2To the holy and faithfula brothers in Christ at Colosse:

Grace and peace to you from God our Father.b

Thanksgiving and Prayer

3We always thank God, the Father of our Lord Jesus Christ, when we pray for you, 4because we have heard of your faith in Christ Jesus and of the love you have for all the saints— 5the faith and love that spring from the hope that is stored up for you in heaven and that you have already heard about in the word of truth, the gospel 6that has come to you. All over the world this gospel is bearing fruit and growing, just as it has been doing among you since the day you heard it and understood God's grace in all its truth. 7You learned it from Epaphras, our dear fellow servant, who is a faithful minister of Christ on ourc behalf, 8and who also told us of your love in the Spirit.

9For this reason, since the day we heard about you, we have not stopped praying for you and asking God to fill you with the knowledge of his will through all spiritual wisdom and understanding. 10And we pray this in order that you may live a life worthy of the Lord and may please him in every way: bearing fruit in every good work, growing in the knowledge of God, 11being strengthened with all power according to his glorious might so that you may have great endurance and patience, and joyfully 12giving thanks to the Father, who has qualified youd to share in the inheritance of the saints in the kingdom of light. 13For he has rescued us from the dominion of darkness and brought us into the kingdom of the Son he loves, 14in whom we have redemption,e the forgiveness of sins.

The Supremacy of Christ

15He is the image of the invisible God, the firstborn over all creation. 16For by him all things were created: things in heaven and on earth, visible and invisible, whether thrones or powers or rulers or authorities; all things were created by him and for him. 17He is before all things, and in him all things hold together. 18And he is the head of the body, the church; he is the beginning and the firstborn from among the dead, so that in everything he might have the supremacy. 19For God was pleased to have all his fullness dwell in him, 20and

---

a 2 Or *believing*   b 2 Some manuscripts *Father and the Lord Jesus Christ*
c 7 Some manuscripts *your*   d 12 Some manuscripts *us*   e 14 A few late
manuscripts *redemption through his blood*

Living Bible

Colossians

1 FROM: PAUL, chosen by God to be Jesus Christ's
messenger, and from Brother Timothy.
2To: The faithful Christian brothers—God's people—in the city of Colosse.
May God our Father shower you with blessings and
fill you with his great peace.
3Whenever we pray for you we always begin by giving thanks to God the Father of our Lord Jesus Christ,
4for we have heard how much you trust the Lord, and
how much you love his people. 5And you are looking
forward to the joys of heaven, and have been ever since
the Gospel first was preached to you. 6The same Good
News that came to you is going out all over the world
and changing lives everywhere, just as it changed yours
that very first day you heard it and understood about
God's great kindness to sinners.

7Epaphras, our much-loved fellow worker, was the
one who brought you this Good News. He is Jesus
Christ's faithful slave, here to help us in your place.
8And he is the one who has told us about the great love
for others which the Holy Spirit has given you.

9So ever since we first heard about you we have kept
on praying and asking God to help you understand what
he wants you to do; asking him to make you wise about
spiritual things; 10and asking that the way you live will
always please the Lord and honor him, so that you will
always be doing good, kind things for others, while all
the time you are learning to know God better and better.
11We are praying, too, that you will be filled with his
mighty, glorious strength so that you can keep going no
matter what happens—always full of the joy of the
Lord, 12and always thankful to the Father who has made
us fit to share all the wonderful things that belong to
those who live in the Kingdom of light. 13For he has
rescued us out of the darkness and gloom of Satan's
kingdom and brought us into the Kingdom of his dear
Son, 14who bought our freedom with his blood and forgave us all our sins.

15Christ is the exact likeness of the unseen God. He
existed before God made anything at all,f and, in fact,
16Christ himself is the Creator who made everything in
heaven and earth, the things we can see and the things
we can't; the spirit world with its kings and kingdoms,
its rulers and authorities; all were made by Christ for his
own use and glory. 17He was before all else began and
it is his power that holds everything together. 18He is the
Head of the body made up of his people—that is, his
Church—which he began; and he is the Leader of all
those who arise from the dead,g so that he is first in
everything; 19for God wanted all of himself to be in his
Son.

New Revised Standard

THE LETTER OF
PAUL TO THE

Colossians

Salutation

1 PAUL, AN apostle of Christ Jesus by the will of
God, and Timothy our brother,
2 To the saints and faithful brothers and sistersh in
Christ in Colossae:
Grace to you and peace from God our Father.

Paul Thanks God for the Colossians

3 In our prayers for you we always thank God, the
Father of our Lord Jesus Christ, 4for we have heard of
your faith in Christ Jesus and of the love that you have
for all the saints, 5because of the hope laid up for you
in heaven. You have heard of this hope before in the
word of the truth, the gospel 6that has come to you. Just
as it is bearing fruit and growing in the whole world, so
it has been bearing fruit among yourselves from the day
you heard it and truly comprehended the grace of God.
7This you learned from Epaphras, our beloved fellow
servant.i He is a faithful minister of Christ on youri
behalf, 8and he has made known to us your love in the
Spirit.

9 For this reason, since the day we heard it, we have
not ceased praying for you and asking that you may be
filled with the knowledge of God'sk will in all spiritual
wisdom and understanding, 10so that you may lead lives
worthy of the Lord, fully pleasing to him, as you bear
fruit in every good work and as you grow in the knowledge of God. 11May you be made strong with all the
strength that comes from his glorious power, and may
you be prepared to endure everything with patience,
while joyfully 12giving thanks to the Father, who has
enabledl youm to share in the inheritance of the saints
in the light. 13He has rescued us from the power of
darkness and transferred us into the kingdom of his beloved Son, 14in whom we have redemption, the forgiveness of sins.n

The Supremacy of Christ

15 He is the image of the invisible God, the firstborn
of all creation; 16for ino him all things in heaven and on
earth were created, things visible and invisible, whether
thrones or dominions or rulers or powers—all things
have been created through him and for him. 17He himself is before all things, and ino him all things hold
together. 18He is the head of the body, the church; he
is the beginning, the firstborn from the dead, so that he
might come to have first place in everything. 19For in
him all the fullness of God was pleased to dwell, 20and

---

f *1:15 He existed before God made anything at all*, literally, "He is the firstborn
of all creation." g *1:18 he is the Leader of all those who arise from the
dead*, literally, "he is the Beginning, the firstborn from the dead."

h Gk *brothers* i Gk *slave* j Other ancient authorities read *our* k Gk *his*
l Other ancient authorities read *called* m Other ancient authorities read *us*
n Other ancient authorities add *through his blood* o Or *by*

King James

New International

20And, having made peace through the blood of his cross, by him to reconcile all things unto himself; by him, *I say,* whether *they be* things in earth, or things in heaven.

21And you, that were sometime alienated and enemies in *your* mind by wicked works, yet now hath he reconciled

22In the body of his flesh through death, to present you holy and unblameable and unreproveable in his sight:

23If ye continue in the faith grounded and settled, and *be* not moved away from the hope of the gospel, which ye have heard, *and* which was preached to every creature which is under heaven; whereof I Paul am made a minister;

24Who now rejoice in my sufferings for you, and fill up that which is behind of the afflictions of Christ in my flesh for his body's sake, which is the church:

25Whereof I am made a minister, according to the dispensation of God which is given to me for you, to fulfil the word of God;

26*Even* the mystery which hath been hid from ages and from generations, but now is made manifest to his saints:

27To whom God would make known what *is* the riches of the glory of this mystery among the Gentiles; which is Christ in you, the hope of glory:

28Whom we preach, warning every man, and teaching every man in all wisdom; that we may present every man perfect in Christ Jesus:

29Whereunto I also labour, striving according to his working, which worketh in me mightily.

2 FOR I would that ye knew what great conflict I have for you, and *for* them at Laodicea, and *for* as many as have not seen my face in the flesh;

2That their hearts might be comforted, being knit together in love, and unto all riches of the full assurance of understanding, to the acknowledgement of the mystery of God, and of the Father, and of Christ;

3In whom are hid all the treasures of wisdom and knowledge.

4And this I say, lest any man should beguile you with enticing words.

5For though I be absent in the flesh, yet am I with you in the spirit, joying and beholding your order, and the stedfastness of your faith in Christ.

6As ye have therefore received Christ Jesus the Lord, *so* walk ye in him:

7Rooted and built up in him, and stablished in the faith, as ye have been taught, abounding therein with thanksgiving.

8Beware lest any man spoil you through philosophy and vain deceit, after the tradition of men, after the rudiments of the world, and not after Christ.

9For in him dwelleth all the fulness of the Godhead bodily.

10And ye are complete in him, which is the head of all principality and power:

11In whom also ye are circumcised with the circumcision made without hands, in putting off the body of the sins of the flesh by the circumcision of Christ:

through him to reconcile to himself all things, whether things on earth or things in heaven, by making peace through his blood, shed on the cross.

21Once you were alienated from God and were enemies in your minds because of^a your evil behavior. 22But now he has reconciled you by Christ's physical body through death to present you holy in his sight, without blemish and free from accusation— 23if you continue in your faith, established and firm, not moved from the hope held out in the gospel. This is the gospel that you heard and that has been proclaimed to every creature under heaven, and of which I, Paul, have become a servant.

Paul's Labor for the Church

24Now I rejoice in what was suffered for you, and I fill up in my flesh what is still lacking in regard to Christ's afflictions, for the sake of his body, which is the church. 25I have become its servant by the commission God gave me to present to you the word of God in its fullness— 26the mystery that has been kept hidden for ages and generations, but is now disclosed to the saints. 27To them God has chosen to make known among the Gentiles the glorious riches of this mystery, which is Christ in you, the hope of glory.

28We proclaim him, admonishing and teaching everyone with all wisdom, so that we may present everyone perfect in Christ. 29To this end I labor, struggling with all his energy, which so powerfully works in me.

2 I WANT you to know how much I am struggling for you and for those at Laodicea, and for all who have not met me personally. 2My purpose is that they may be encouraged in heart and united in love, so that they may have the full riches of complete understanding, in order that they may know the mystery of God, namely, Christ, 3in whom are hidden all the treasures of wisdom and knowledge. 4I tell you this so that no one may deceive you by fine-sounding arguments. 5For though I am absent from you in body, I am present with you in spirit and delight to see how orderly you are and how firm your faith in Christ is.

Freedom From Human Regulations Through Life With Christ

6So then, just as you received Christ Jesus as Lord, continue to live in him, 7rooted and built up in him, strengthened in the faith as you were taught, and overflowing with thankfulness.

8See to it that no one takes you captive through hollow and deceptive philosophy, which depends on human tradition and the basic principles of this world rather than on Christ.

9For in Christ all the fullness of the Deity lives in bodily form, 10and you have been given fullness in Christ, who is the head over every power and authority. 11In him you were also circumcised, in the putting off of the sinful nature,^b not with a circumcision done by the hands of men but with the circumcision done by Christ, 12having been buried with him in baptism and

Living Bible

20It was through what his Son did that God cleared a path for everything to come to him—all things in heaven and on earth—for Christ's death on the cross has made peace with God for all by his blood. 21This includes you who were once so far away from God. You were his enemies and hated him and were separated from him by your evil thoughts and actions, yet now he has brought you back as his friends. 22He has done this through the death on the cross of his own human body, and now as a result Christ has brought you into the very presence of God, and you are standing there before him with nothing left against you—nothing left that he could even chide you for; 23the only condition is that you fully believe the Truth, standing in it steadfast and firm, strong in the Lord, convinced of the Good News that Jesus died for you, and never shifting from trusting him to save you. This is the wonderful news that came to each of you and is now spreading all over the world. And I, Paul, have the joy of telling it to others.

24But part of my work is to suffer for you; and I am glad, for I am helping to finish up the remainder of Christ's sufferings for his body, the Church. 25God has sent me to help his Church and to tell his secret plan to you Gentiles. 26, 27 He has kept this secret for centuries and generations past, but now at last it has pleased him to tell it to those who love him and live for him, and the riches and glory of his plan are for you Gentiles too. And this is the secret: *that Christ in your hearts is your only hope of glory*.

28So everywhere we go we talk about Christ to all who will listen, warning them and teaching them as well as we know how. We want to be able to present each one to God, perfect because of what Christ has done for each of them. 29This is my work, and I can do it only because Christ's mighty energy is at work within me.

2 I WISH you could know how much I have struggled in prayer for you and for the church at Laodicea, and for my many other friends who have never known me personally. 2This is what I have asked of God for you: that you will be encouraged and knit together by strong ties of love, and that you will have the rich experience of knowing Christ with real certainty and clear understanding. *For God's secret plan, now at last made known, is Christ himself.* 3In him lie hidden all the mighty, untapped treasures of wisdom and knowledge.

4I am saying this because I am afraid that someone may fool you with smooth talk. 5For though I am far away from you my heart is with you, happy because you are getting along so well, happy because of your strong faith in Christ. 6And now just as you trusted Christ to save you, trust him, too, for each day's problems; live in vital union with him. 7Let your roots grow down into him and draw up nourishment from him. See that you go on growing in the Lord, and become strong and vigorous in the truth you were taught. Let your lives overflow with joy and thanksgiving for all he has done.

8Don't let others spoil your faith and joy with their philosophies, their wrong and shallow answers built on men's thoughts and ideas, instead of on what Christ has said. 9For in Christ there is all of God in a human body; 10so you have everything when you have Christ, and you are filled with God through your union with Christ. He is the highest Ruler, with authority over every other power.

11When you came to Christ he set you free from your evil desires, not by a bodily operation of circumcision but by a spiritual operation, the baptism of your souls.

New Revised Standard

through him God was pleased to reconcile to himself all things, whether on earth or in heaven, by making peace through the blood of his cross.

21 And you who were once estranged and hostile in mind, doing evil deeds, 22he has now reconciledc in his fleshly bodyd through death, so as to present you holy and blameless and irreproachable before him— 23provided that you continue securely established and steadfast in the faith, without shifting from the hope promised by the gospel that you heard, which has been proclaimed to every creature under heaven. I, Paul, became a servant of this gospel.

Paul's Interest in the Colossians

24 I am now rejoicing in my sufferings for your sake, and in my flesh I am completing what is lacking in Christ's afflictions for the sake of his body, that is, the church. 25I became its servant according to God's commission that was given to me for you, to make the word of God fully known, 26the mystery that has been hidden throughout the ages and generations but has now been revealed to his saints. 27To them God chose to make known how great among the Gentiles are the riches of the glory of this mystery, which is Christ in you, the hope of glory. 28It is he whom we proclaim, warning everyone and teaching everyone in all wisdom, so that we may present everyone mature in Christ. 29For this I toil and struggle with all the energy that he powerfully inspires within me.

2 FOR I want you to know how much I am struggling for you, and for those in Laodicea, and for all who have not seen me face to face. 2I want their hearts to be encouraged and united in love, so that they may have all the riches of assured understanding and have the knowledge of God's mystery, that is, Christ himself,e 3in whom are hidden all the treasures of wisdom and knowledge. 4I am saying this so that no one may deceive you with plausible arguments. 5For though I am absent in body, yet I am with you in spirit, and I rejoice to see your morale and the firmness of your faith in Christ.

Fullness of Life in Christ

6 As you therefore have received Christ Jesus the Lord, continue to live your livesf in him, 7rooted and built up in him and established in the faith, just as you were taught, abounding in thanksgiving.

8 See to it that no one takes you captive through philosophy and empty deceit, according to human tradition, according to the elemental spirits of the universe,g and not according to Christ. 9For in him the whole fullness of deity dwells bodily, 10and you have come to fullness in him, who is the head of every ruler and authority. 11In him also you were circumcised with a spiritual circumcision,h by putting off the body of the flesh in the circumcision of Christ; 12when you were buried

---

c Other ancient authorities read *you have now been reconciled*   d Gk *in the body of his flesh*   e Other ancient authorities read *of the mystery of God, both of the Father and of Christ*   f Gk *to walk*   g Or *the rudiments of the world*   h Gk *a circumcision made without hands*

King James

12Buried with him in baptism, wherein also ye are risen with *him* through the faith of the operation of God, who hath raised him from the dead.

13And you, being dead in your sins and the uncircumcision of your flesh, hath he quickened together with him, having forgiven you all trespasses;

14Blotting out the handwriting of ordinances that was against us, which was contrary to us, and took it out of the way, nailing it to his cross;

15*And* having spoiled principalities and powers, he made a show of them openly, triumphing over them in it.

16Let no man therefore judge you in meat, or in drink, or in respect of an holyday, or of the new moon, or of the sabbath *days:*

17Which are a shadow of things to come; but the body *is* of Christ.

18Let no man beguile you of your reward in a voluntary humility and worshipping of angels, intruding into those things which he hath not seen, vainly puffed up by his fleshly mind,

19And not holding the Head, from which all the body by joints and bands having nourishment ministered, and knit together, increaseth with the increase of God.

20Wherefore if ye be dead with Christ from the rudiments of the world, why, as though living in the world, are ye subject to ordinances,

21(Touch not; taste not; handle not;

22Which all are to perish with the using;) after the commandments and doctrines of men?

23Which things have indeed a show of wisdom in will-worship. and humility, and neglecting of the body; not in any honour to the satisfying of the flesh.

3 IF YE then be risen with Christ, seek those things which are above, where Christ sitteth on the right hand of God.

2Set your affection on things above, not on things on the earth.

3For ye are dead, and your life is hid with Christ in God.

4When Christ, *who is* our life, shall appear, then shall ye also appear with him in glory.

5Mortify therefore your members which are upon the earth; fornication, uncleanness, inordinate affection, evil concupiscence, and covetousness, which is idolatry:

6For which things' sake the wrath of God cometh on the children of disobedience:

7In the which ye also walked some time, when ye lived in them.

8But now ye also put off all these; anger, wrath, malice, blasphemy, filthy communication out of your mouth.

9Lie not one to another, seeing that ye have put off the old man with his deeds;

10And have put on the new *man,* which is renewed in knowledge after the image of him that created him:

New International

raised with him through your faith in the power of God, who raised him from the dead.

13When you were dead in your sins and in the uncircumcision of your sinful nature,[a] God made you[b] alive with Christ. He forgave us all our sins, 14having canceled the written code, with its regulations, that was against us and that stood opposed to us; he took it away, nailing it to the cross. 15And having disarmed the powers and authorities, he made a public spectacle of them, triumphing over them by the cross.[c]

16Therefore do not let anyone judge you by what you eat or drink, or with regard to a religious festival, a New Moon celebration or a Sabbath day. 17These are a shadow of the things that were to come; the reality, however, is found in Christ. 18Do not let anyone who delights in false humility and the worship of angels disqualify you for the prize. Such a person goes into great detail about what he has seen, and his unspiritual mind puffs him up with idle notions. 19He has lost connection with the Head, from whom the whole body, supported and held together by its ligaments and sinews, grows as God causes it to grow.

20Since you died with Christ to the basic principles of this world, why, as though you still belonged to it, do you submit to its rules: 21"Do not handle! Do not taste! Do not touch!"? 22These are all destined to perish with use, because they are based on human commands and teachings. 23Such regulations indeed have an appearance of wisdom, with their self-imposed worship, their false humility and their harsh treatment of the body, but they lack any value in restraining sensual indulgence.

Rules for Holy Living

3 SINCE, THEN, you have been raised with Christ, set your hearts on things above, where Christ is seated at the right hand of God. 2Set your minds on things above, not on earthly things. 3For you died, and your life is now hidden with Christ in God. 4When Christ, who is your[d] life, appears, then you also will appear with him in glory.

5Put to death, therefore, whatever belongs to your earthly nature: sexual immorality, impurity, lust, evil desires and greed, which is idolatry. 6Because of these, the wrath of God is coming.[e] 7You used to walk in these ways, in the life you once lived. 8But now you must rid yourselves of all such things as these: anger, rage, malice, slander, and filthy language from your lips. 9Do not lie to each other, since you have taken off your old self with its practices 10and have put on the new self, which is being renewed in knowledge in the image of its Creator. 11Here there is no Greek or Jew, circumcised or

---

a 13 Or *your flesh*　　b 13 Some manuscripts *us*　　c 15 Or *them in him*
d 4 Some manuscripts *our*　　e 6 Some early manuscripts *coming on those who
are disobedient*

Living Bible

12For in baptism you see how your old, evil nature died with him and was buried with him; and then you came up out of death with him into a new life because you trusted the Word of the mighty God who raised Christ from the dead.

13You were dead in sins, and your sinful desires were not yet cut away. Then he gave you a share in the very life of Christ, for he forgave all your sins, 14and blotted out the charges proved against you, the list of his commandments which you had not obeyed. He took this list of sins and destroyed it by nailing it to Christ's cross. 15In this way God took away Satan's power to accuse you of sin, and God openly displayed to the whole world Christ's triumph at the cross where your sins were all taken away.

16So don't let anyone criticize you for what you eat or drink, or for not celebrating Jewish holidays and feasts or new moon ceremonies or Sabbaths. 17For these were only temporary rules that ended when Christ came. They were only shadows of the real thing—of Christ himself. 18Don't let anyone declare you lost when you refuse to worship angels, as they say you must. They have seen a vision, they say, and know you should. These proud men (though they claim to be so humble) have a very clever imagination. 19But they are not connected to Christ, the Head to which all of us who are his body are joined; for we are joined together by his strong sinews and we grow only as we get our nourishment and strength from God.

20Since you died, as it were, with Christ and this has set you free from following the world's ideas of how to be saved—by doing good and obeying various rules[f]—why do you keep right on following them anyway, still bound by such rules as 21not eating, tasting, or even touching certain foods? 22Such rules are mere human teachings, for food was made to be eaten and used up. 23These rules may seem good, for rules of this kind require strong devotion and are humiliating and hard on the body, but they have no effect when it comes to conquering a person's evil thoughts and desires. They only make him proud.

3 SINCE YOU became alive again, so to speak, when Christ arose from the dead, now set your sights on the rich treasures and joys of heaven where he sits beside God in the place of honor and power. 2Let heaven fill your thoughts; don't spend your time worrying about things down here. 3You should have as little desire for this world as a dead person does. Your real life is in heaven with Christ and God. 4And when Christ who is our real life comes back again, you will shine with him and share in all his glories.

5Away then with sinful, earthly things; deaden the evil desires lurking within you; have nothing to do with sexual sin, impurity, lust and shameful desires; don't worship the good things of life, for that is idolatry. 6God's terrible anger is upon those who do such things. 7You used to do them when your life was still part of this world; 8but now is the time to cast off and throw away all these rotten garments of anger, hatred, cursing, and dirty language.

9Don't tell lies to each other; it was your old life with all its wickedness that did that sort of thing; now it is dead and gone. 10You are living a brand new kind of life that is continually learning more and more of what is right, and trying constantly to be more and more like Christ who created this new life within you. 11In this

[f] *2:20 obeying various rules,* literally, "by the rudiments of the world."

New Revised Standard

with him in baptism, you were also raised with him through faith in the power of God, who raised him from the dead. 13 And when you were dead in trespasses and the uncircumcision of your flesh, God[g] made you[h] alive together with him, when he forgave us all our trespasses, 14 erasing the record that stood against us with its legal demands. He set this aside, nailing it to the cross. 15 He disarmed[i] the rulers and authorities and made a public example of them, triumphing over them in it.

16 Therefore do not let anyone condemn you in matters of food and drink or of observing festivals, new moons, or sabbaths. 17 These are only a shadow of what is to come, but the substance belongs to Christ. 18 Do not let anyone disqualify you, insisting on self-abasement and worship of angels, dwelling[j] on visions,[k] puffed up without cause by a human way of thinking,[l] 19 and not holding fast to the head, from whom the whole body, nourished and held together by its ligaments and sinews, grows with a growth that is from God.

Warnings against False Teachers

20 If with Christ you died to the elemental spirits of the universe,[m] why do you live as if you still belonged to the world? Why do you submit to regulations, 21 "Do not handle, Do not taste, Do not touch"? 22 All these regulations refer to things that perish with use; they are simply human commands and teachings. 23 These have indeed an appearance of wisdom in promoting self-imposed piety, humility, and severe treatment of the body, but they are of no value in checking self-indulgence.[n]

The New Life in Christ

3 SO IF you have been raised with Christ, seek the things that are above, where Christ is, seated at the right hand of God. 2 Set your minds on things that are above, not on things that are on earth, 3 for you have died, and your life is hidden with Christ in God. 4 When Christ who is your[o] life is revealed, then you also will be revealed with him in glory.

5 Put to death, therefore, whatever in you is earthly: fornication, impurity, passion, evil desire, and greed (which is idolatry). 6 On account of these the wrath of God is coming on those who are disobedient.[p] 7 These are the ways you also once followed, when you were living that life.[q] 8 But now you must get rid of all such things—anger, wrath, malice, slander, and abusive[r] language from your mouth. 9 Do not lie to one another, seeing that you have stripped off the old self with its practices 10 and have clothed yourselves with the new self, which is being renewed in knowledge according to the image of its creator. 11 In that renewal[s] there is no

[g] Gk *he* [h] Other ancient authorities read *made us*; others, *made* [i] Or *divested himself of* [j] Other ancient authorities read *not dwelling* [k] Meaning of Gk uncertain [l] Gk *by the mind of his flesh* [m] Or *the rudiments of the world* [n] Or *are of no value, serving only to indulge the flesh* [o] Other authorities read *our* [p] Other ancient authorities lack *on those who are disobedient* (Gk *the children of disobedience*) [q] Or *living among such people* [r] Or *filthy* [s] Gk *its creator,* [11]*where*

King James

11Where there is neither Greek nor Jew, circumcision nor uncircumcision, Barbarian, Scythian, bond *nor* free: but Christ *is* all, and in all.

12Put on therefore, as the elect of God, holy and beloved, bowels of mercies, kindness, humbleness of mind, meekness, longsuffering;

13Forbearing one another, and forgiving one another, if any man have a quarrel against any: even as Christ forgave you, so also *do* ye.

14And above all these things *put on* charity, which is the bond of perfectness.

15And let the peace of God rule in your hearts, to the which also ye are called in one body; and be ye thankful.

16Let the word of Christ dwell in you richly in all wisdom; teaching and admonishing one another in psalms and hymns and spiritual songs, singing with grace in your hearts to the Lord.

17And whatsoever ye do in word or deed, *do* all in the name of the Lord Jesus, giving thanks to God and the Father by him.

18Wives, submit yourselves unto your own husbands, as it is fit in the Lord.

19Husbands, love *your* wives, and be not bitter against them.

20Children, obey *your* parents in all things: for this is wellpleasing unto the Lord.

21Fathers, provoke not your children *to anger,* lest they be discouraged.

22Servants, obey in all things *your* masters according to the flesh; not with eyeservice, as menpleasers; but in singleness of heart, fearing God:

23And whatsoever ye do, do *it* heartily, as to the Lord, and not unto men;

24Knowing that of the Lord ye shall receive the reward of the inheritance: for ye serve the Lord Christ.

25But he that doeth wrong shall receive for the wrong which he hath done: and there is no respect of persons.

4 MASTERS, GIVE unto *your* servants that which is just and equal; knowing that ye also have a Master in heaven.

2Continue in prayer, and watch in the same with thanksgiving;

3Withal praying also for us, that God would open unto us a door of utterance, to speak the mystery of Christ, for which I am also in bonds:

4That I may make it manifest, as I ought to speak.

5Walk in wisdom toward them that are without, redeeming the time.

6Let your speech *be* always with grace, seasoned with salt, that ye may know how ye ought to answer every man.

7All my state shall Tychicus declare unto you, *who is* a beloved brother, and a faithful minister and fellowservant in the Lord:

New International

uncircumcised, barbarian, Scythian, slave or free, but Christ is all, and is in all.

12Therefore, as God's chosen people, holy and dearly loved, clothe yourselves with compassion, kindness, humility, gentleness and patience. 13Bear with each other and forgive whatever grievances you may have against one another. Forgive as the Lord forgave you. 14And over all these virtues put on love, which binds them all together in perfect unity.

15Let the peace of Christ rule in your hearts, since as members of one body you were called to peace. And be thankful. 16Let the word of Christ dwell in you richly as you teach and admonish one another with all wisdom, and as you sing psalms, hymns and spiritual songs with gratitude in your hearts to God. 17And whatever you do, whether in word or deed, do it all in the name of the Lord Jesus, giving thanks to God the Father through him.

Rules for Christian Households

18Wives, submit to your husbands, as is fitting in the Lord.

19Husbands, love your wives and do not be harsh with them.

20Children, obey your parents in everything, for this pleases the Lord.

21Fathers, do not embitter your children, or they will become discouraged.

22Slaves, obey your earthly masters in everything; and do it, not only when their eye is on you and to win their favor, but with sincerity of heart and reverence for the Lord. 23Whatever you do, work at it with all your heart, as working for the Lord, not for men, 24since you know that you will receive an inheritance from the Lord as a reward. It is the Lord Christ you are serving. 25Anyone who does wrong will be repaid for his wrong, and there is no favoritism.

4 MASTERS, PROVIDE your slaves with what is right and fair, because you know that you also have a Master in heaven.

Further Instructions

2Devote yourselves to prayer, being watchful and thankful. 3And pray for us, too, that God may open a door for our message, so that we may proclaim the mystery of Christ, for which I am in chains. 4Pray that I may proclaim it clearly, as I should. 5Be wise in the way you act toward outsiders; make the most of every opportunity. 6Let your conversation be always full of grace, seasoned with salt, so that you may know how to answer everyone.

Final Greetings

7Tychicus will tell you all the news about me. He is a dear brother, a faithful minister and fellow servant in the Lord. 8I am sending him to you for the express

Living Bible

new life one's nationality or race or education or social position is unimportant; such things mean nothing. Whether a person has Christ is what matters, and he is equally available to all.

12Since you have been chosen by God who has given you this new kind of life, and because of his deep love and concern for you, you should practice tenderhearted mercy and kindness to others. Don't worry about making a good impression on them but be ready to suffer quietly and patiently. 13Be gentle and ready to forgive; never hold grudges. Remember, the Lord forgave you, so you must forgive others.

14Most of all, let love guide your life, for then the whole church will stay together in perfect harmony. 15Let the peace of heart which comes from Christ be always present in your hearts and lives, for this is your responsibility and privilege as members of his body. And always be thankful.

16Remember what Christ taught and let his words enrich your lives and make you wise; teach them to each other and sing them out in psalms and hymns and spiritual songs, singing to the Lord with thankful hearts. 17And whatever you do or say, let it be as a representative of the Lord Jesus, and come with him into the presence of God the Father to give him your thanks.

18You wives, submit yourselves to your husbands, for that is what the Lord has planned for you. 19And you husbands must be loving and kind to your wives and not bitter against them, nor harsh.

20You children must always obey your fathers and mothers, for that pleases the Lord. 21Fathers, don't scold your children so much that they become discouraged and quit trying.

22You slaves must always obey your earthly masters, not only trying to please them when they are watching you but all the time; obey them willingly because of your love for the Lord and because you want to please him. 23Work hard and cheerfully at all you do, just as though you were working for the Lord and not merely for your masters, 24remembering that it is the Lord Christ who is going to pay you, giving you your full portion of all he owns. He is the one you are really working for. 25And if you don't do your best for him, he will pay you in a way that you won't like—for he has no special favorites who can get away with shirking.

4 YOU SLAVE owners must be just and fair to all your slaves. Always remember that you, too, have a Master in heaven who is closely watching you.

2Don't be weary in prayer; keep at it; watch for God's answers and remember to be thankful when they come. 3Don't forget to pray for us too, that God will give us many chances to preach the Good News of Christ for which I am here in jail. 4Pray that I will be bold enough to tell it freely and fully, and make it plain, as, of course, I should.

5Make the most of your chances to tell others the Good News. Be wise in all your contacts with them. 6Let your conversation be gracious as well as sensible, for then you will have the right answer for everyone.

7Tychicus, our much loved brother, will tell you how I am getting along. He is a hard worker and serves the Lord with me. 8I have sent him on this special trip just

New Revised Standard

longer Greek and Jew, circumcised and uncircumcised, barbarian, Scythian, slave and free; but Christ is all and in all!

12 As God's chosen ones, holy and beloved, clothe yourselves with compassion, kindness, humility, meekness, and patience. 13 Bear with one another and, if anyone has a complaint against another, forgive each other; just as the Lord[a] has forgiven you, so you also must forgive. 14 Above all, clothe yourselves with love, which binds everything together in perfect harmony. 15 And let the peace of Christ rule in your hearts, to which indeed you were called in the one body. And be thankful. 16 Let the word of Christ[b] dwell in you richly; teach and admonish one another in all wisdom; and with gratitude in your hearts sing psalms, hymns, and spiritual songs to God.[c] 17 And whatever you do, in word or deed, do everything in the name of the Lord Jesus, giving thanks to God the Father through him.

Rules for Christian Households

18 Wives, be subject to your husbands, as is fitting in the Lord. 19 Husbands, love your wives and never treat them harshly.

20 Children, obey your parents in everything, for this is your acceptable duty in the Lord. 21 Fathers, do not provoke your children, or they may lose heart. 22 Slaves, obey your earthly masters[d] in everything, not only while being watched and in order to please them, but wholeheartedly, fearing the Lord.[d] 23 Whatever your task, put yourselves into it, as done for the Lord and not for your masters,[e] 24 since you know that from the Lord you will receive the inheritance as your reward; you serve[f] the Lord Christ. 25 For the wrongdoer will be paid back for whatever wrong has been done, and there is no partiality.

4 MASTERS, TREAT your slaves justly and fairly, for you know that you also have a Master in heaven.

Further Instructions

2 Devote yourselves to prayer, keeping alert in it with thanksgiving. 3 At the same time pray for us as well that God will open to us a door for the word, that we may declare the mystery of Christ, for which I am in prison, 4 so that I may reveal it clearly, as I should.

5 Conduct yourselves wisely toward outsiders, making the most of the time.[g] 6 Let your speech always be gracious, seasoned with salt, so that you may know how you ought to answer everyone.

Final Greetings and Benediction

7 Tychicus will tell you all the news about me; he is a beloved brother, a faithful minister, and a fellow servant[h] in the Lord. 8 I have sent him to you for this

a Other ancient authorities read *just as Christ*   b Other ancient authorities read *of God*, or *of the Lord*   c Other ancient authorities read *to the Lord*
d In Greek the same word is used for *master* and *Lord*   e Gk *not for men*
f Or *you are slaves of*, or *be slaves of*   g Or *opportunity*   h Gk *slave*

King James

8Whom I have sent unto you for the same purpose, that he might know your estate, and comfort your hearts;

9With Onesimus, a faithful and beloved brother, who is *one* of you. They shall make known unto you all things which *are done* here.

10Aristarchus my fellowprisoner saluteth you, and Marcus, sister's son to Barnabas, (touching whom ye received commandments: if he come unto you, receive him;)

11And Jesus, which is called Justus, who are of the circumcision. These only *are my* fellowworkers unto the kingdom of God, which have been a comfort unto me.

12Epaphras, who is *one* of you, a servant of Christ, saluteth you, always labouring fervently for you in prayers, that ye may stand perfect and complete in all the will of God.

13For I bear him record, that he hath a great zeal for you, and them *that are* in Laodicea, and them in Hierapolis.

14Luke, the beloved physician, and Demas, greet you.

15Salute the brethren which are in Laodicea, and Nymphas, and the church which is in his house.

16And when this epistle is read among you, cause that it be read also in the church of the Laodiceans; and that ye likewise read the *epistle* from Laodicea.

17And say to Archippus, Take heed to the ministry which thou hast received in the Lord, that thou fulfil it.

18The salutation by the hand of me Paul. Remember my bonds. Grace *be* with you. Amen.

New International

purpose that you may know about our[a] circumstances and that he may encourage your hearts. 9He is coming with Onesimus, our faithful and dear brother, who is one of you. They will tell you everything that is happening here.

10My fellow prisoner Aristarchus sends you his greetings, as does Mark, the cousin of Barnabas. (You have received instructions about him; if he comes to you, welcome him.) 11Jesus, who is called Justus, also sends greetings. These are the only Jews among my fellow workers for the kingdom of God, and they have proved a comfort to me. 12Epaphras, who is one of you and a servant of Christ Jesus, sends greetings. He is always wrestling in prayer for you, that you may stand firm in all the will of God, mature and fully assured. 13I vouch for him that he is working hard for you and for those at Laodicea and Hierapolis. 14Our dear friend Luke, the doctor, and Demas send greetings. 15Give my greetings to the brothers at Laodicea, and to Nympha and the church in her house.

16After this letter has been read to you, see that it is also read in the church of the Laodiceans, and that you in turn read the letter from Laodicea.

17Tell Archippus: "See to it that you complete the work you have received in the Lord."

18I, Paul, write this greeting in my own hand. Remember my chains. Grace be with you.

a 8 Some manuscripts *that he may know about your*

Living Bible

to see how you are, and to comfort and encourage you. 9I am also sending Onesimus, a faithful and much loved brother, one of your own people. He and Tychicus will give you all the latest news.

10Aristarchus, who is with me here as a prisoner, sends you his love, and so does Mark, a relative of Barnabas. And as I said before, give Mark a hearty welcomeb if he comes your way. 11Jesus Justus also sends his love. These are the only Jewish Christians working with me here, and what a comfort they have been!

12Epaphras, from your city, a servant of Christ Jesus, sends you his love. He is always earnestly praying for you, asking God to make you strong and perfect and to help you know his will in everything you do. 13I can assure you that he has worked hard for you with his prayers, and also for the Christians in Laodicea and Hierapolis.

14Dear doctor Luke sends his love, and so does Demas.

15Please give my greeting to the Christian friends at Laodicea, and to Nymphas, and to those who meet in his home. 16By the way, after you have read this letter will you pass it on to the church at Laodicea? And read the letter I wrote to them. 17And say to Archippus, "Be sure that you do all the Lord has told you to."

18Here is my own greeting in my own handwriting: Remember me here in jail. May God's blessings surround you.

Sincerely, Paul

New Revised Standard

very purpose, so that you may know how we arec and that he may encourage your hearts; 9he is coming with Onesimus, the faithful and beloved brother, who is one of you. They will tell you about everything here.

10 Aristarchus my fellow prisoner greets you, as does Mark the cousin of Barnabas, concerning whom you have received instructions—if he comes to you, welcome him. 11 And Jesus who is called Justus greets you. These are the only ones of the circumcision among my co-workers for the kingdom of God, and they have been a comfort to me. 12Epaphras, who is one of you, a servantd of Christ Jesus, greets you. He is always wrestling in his prayers on your behalf, so that you may stand mature and fully assured in everything that God wills. 13For I testify for him that he has worked hard for you and for those in Laodicea and in Hierapolis. 14Luke, the beloved physician, and Demas greet you. 15Give my greetings to the brothers and sisterse in Laodicea, and to Nympha and the church in her house. 16And when this letter has been read among you, have it read also in the church of the Laodiceans; and see that you read also the letter from Laodicea. 17And say to Archippus, "See that you complete the task that you have received in the Lord."

18 I, Paul, write this greeting with my own hand. Remember my chains. Grace be with you.f

b 4:10 a hearty welcome, literally, "receive him."

c Other authorities read that I may know how you are   d Gk slave   e Gk brothers   f Other ancient authorities add Amen

THE FIRST EPISTLE OF

PAUL THE APOSTLE TO THE

Thessalonians

1 Thessalonians

1 PAUL, AND Silvanus, and Timotheus, unto the church of the Thessalonians *which is* in God the Father and *in* the Lord Jesus Christ: Grace *be* unto you, and peace, from God our Father, and the Lord Jesus Christ.

2We give thanks to God always for you all, making mention of you in our prayers;

3Remembering without ceasing your work of faith, and labour of love, and patience of hope in our Lord Jesus Christ, in the sight of God and our Father;

4Knowing, brethren beloved, your election of God.

5For our gospel came not unto you in word only, but also in power, and in the Holy Ghost, and in much assurance; as ye know what manner of men we were among you for your sake.

6And ye became followers of us, and of the Lord, having received the word in much affliction, with joy of the Holy Ghost:

7So that ye were examples to all that believe in Macedonia and Achaia.

8For from you sounded out the word of the Lord not only in Macedonia and Achaia, but also in every place your faith to God-ward is spread abroad; so that we need not to speak any thing.

9For they themselves show of us what manner of entering in we had unto you, and how ye turned to God from idols to serve the living and true God;

10And to wait for his Son from heaven, whom he raised from the dead, *even* Jesus, which delivered us from the wrath to come.

1 PAUL, SILAS[a] and Timothy,

To the church of the Thessalonians in God the Father and the Lord Jesus Christ:

Grace and peace to you.[b]

Thanksgiving for the Thessalonians' Faith

2We always thank God for all of you, mentioning you in our prayers. 3We continually remember before our God and Father your work produced by faith, your labor prompted by love, and your endurance inspired by hope in our Lord Jesus Christ.

4For we know, brothers loved by God, that he has chosen you, 5because our gospel came to you not simply with words, but also with power, with the Holy Spirit and with deep conviction. You know how we lived among you for your sake. 6You became imitators of us and of the Lord; in spite of severe suffering, you welcomed the message with the joy given by the Holy Spirit. 7And so you became a model to all the believers in Macedonia and Achaia. 8The Lord's message rang out from you not only in Macedonia and Achaia—your faith in God has become known everywhere. Therefore we do not need to say anything about it, 9for they themselves report what kind of reception you gave us. They tell how you turned to God from idols to serve the living and true God, 10and to wait for his Son from heaven, whom he raised from the dead—Jesus, who rescues us from the coming wrath.

2 FOR YOURSELVES, brethren, know our entrance in unto you, that it was not in vain:

2But even after that we had suffered before, and were shamefully entreated, as ye know, at Philippi, we were bold in our God to speak unto you the gospel of God with much contention.

3For our exhortation *was* not of deceit, nor of uncleanness, nor in guile:

4But as we were allowed of God to be put in trust with the gospel, even so we speak; not as pleasing men, but God, which trieth our hearts.

5For neither at any time used we flattering words, as ye know, nor a cloak of covetousness; God *is* witness:

6Nor of men sought we glory, neither of you, nor *yet* of others, when we might have been burdensome, as the apostles of Christ.

Paul's Ministry in Thessalonica

2 YOU KNOW, brothers, that our visit to you was not a failure. 2We had previously suffered and been insulted in Philippi, as you know, but with the help of our God we dared to tell you his gospel in spite of strong opposition. 3For the appeal we make does not spring from error or impure motives, nor are we trying to trick you. 4On the contrary, we speak as men approved by God to be entrusted with the gospel. We are not trying to please men but God, who tests our hearts. 5You know we never used flattery, nor did we put on a mask to cover up greed—God is our witness. 6We were not looking for praise from men, not from you or anyone else.

As apostles of Christ we could have been a burden to you, 7but we were gentle among you, like a mother

1 Thessalonians

Thessalonians

1 FROM: PAUL, Silas and Timothy.
To: The Church at Thessalonica—to you who belong to God the Father and the Lord Jesus Christ: May blessing and peace of heart be your rich gifts from God our Father, and from Jesus Christ our Lord.

2We always thank God for you and pray for you constantly. 3We never forget your loving deeds as we talk to our God and Father about you, and your strong faith and steady looking forward to the return of our Lord Jesus Christ.

4We know that God has chosen you, dear brothers, much beloved of God. 5For when we brought you the Good News, it was not just meaningless chatter to you; no, you listened with great interest. What we told you produced a powerful effect upon you, for the Holy Spirit gave you great and full assurance that what we said was true. And you know how our very lives were further proof to you of the truth of our message. 6So you became our followers and the Lord's; for you received our message with joy from the Holy Spirit in spite of the trials and sorrows it brought you.

7Then you yourselves became an example to all the other Christians in Greece. 8And now the Word of the Lord has spread out from you to others everywhere, far beyond your boundaries, for wherever we go we find people telling us about your remarkable faith in God. We don't need to tell *them* about it, 9for *they* keep telling *us* about the wonderful welcome you gave us, and how you turned away from your idols to God so that now the living and true God only is your Master. 10And they speak of how you are looking forward to the return of God's Son from heaven—Jesus, whom God brought back to life—and he is our only Savior from God's terrible anger against sin.

2 YOU YOURSELVES know, dear brothers, how worthwhile that visit was. 2You know how badly we had been treated at Philippi just before we came to you, and how much we suffered there. Yet God gave us the courage to boldly repeat the same message to you, even though we were surrounded by enemies. 3So you can see that we were not preaching with any false motives or evil purposes in mind; we were perfectly straightforward and sincere.

4For we speak as messengers from God, trusted by him to tell the truth; we change his message not one bit to suit the taste of those who hear it; for we serve God alone, who examines our hearts' deepest thoughts. 5Never once did we try to win you with flattery, as you very well know, and God knows we were not just pretending to be your friends so that you would give us money! 6As for praise, we have never asked for it from you or anyone else, although as apostles of Christ we certainly had a right to some honor from you. 7But we

Salutation

1 PAUL, SILVANUS, and Timothy,
To the church of the Thessalonians in God the Father and the Lord Jesus Christ:
Grace to you and peace.

The Thessalonians' Faith and Example

2 We always give thanks to God for all of you and mention you in our prayers, constantly 3remembering before our God and Father your work of faith and labor of love and steadfastness of hope in our Lord Jesus Christ. 4For we know, brothers and sistersc beloved by God, that he has chosen you, 5because our message of the gospel came to you not in word only, but also in power and in the Holy Spirit and with full conviction; just as you know what kind of persons we proved to be among you for your sake. 6And you became imitators of us and of the Lord, for in spite of persecution you received the word with joy inspired by the Holy Spirit, 7so that you became an example to all the believers in Macedonia and in Achaia. 8For the word of the Lord has sounded forth from you not only in Macedonia and Achaia, but in every place your faith in God has become known, so that we have no need to speak about it. 9For the people of those regionsd report about us what kind of welcome we had among you, and how you turned to God from idols, to serve a living and true God, 10and to wait for his Son from heaven, whom he raised from the dead—Jesus, who rescues us from the wrath that is coming.

Paul's Ministry in Thessalonica

2 YOU YOURSELVES know, brothers and sisters,c that our coming to you was not in vain, 2but though we had already suffered and been shamefully mistreated at Philippi, as you know, we had courage in our God to declare to you the gospel of God in spite of great opposition. 3For our appeal does not spring from deceit or impure motives or trickery, 4but just as we have been approved by God to be entrusted with the message of the gospel, even so we speak, not to please mortals, but to please God who tests our hearts. 5As you know and as God is our witness, we never came with words of flattery or with a pretext for greed; 6nor did we seek praise from mortals, whether from you or from others, 7though we might have made demands as apos-

c Gk brothers   d Gk For they

King James

7But we were gentle among you, even as a nurse cherisheth her children:

8So being affectionately desirous of you, we were willing to have imparted unto you, not the gospel of God only, but also our own souls, because ye were dear unto us.

9For ye remember, brethren, our labour and travail: for labouring night and day, because we would not be chargeable unto any of you, we preached unto you the gospel of God.

10Ye *are* witnesses, and God *also,* how holily and justly and unblameably we behaved ourselves among you that believe:

11As ye know how we exhorted and comforted and charged every one of you, as a father *doth* his children,

12That ye would walk worthy of God, who hath called you unto his kingdom and glory.

13For this cause also thank we God without ceasing, because, when ye received the word of God which ye heard of us, ye received *it* not *as* the word of men, but as it is in truth, the word of God, which effectually worketh also in you that believe.

14For ye, brethren, became followers of the churches of God which in Judaea are in Christ Jesus: for ye also have suffered like things of your own countrymen, even as they *have* of the Jews:

15Who both killed the Lord Jesus, and their own prophets, and have persecuted us; and they please not God, and are contrary to all men:

16Forbidding us to speak to the Gentiles that they might be saved, to fill up their sins always: for the wrath is come upon them to the uttermost.

17But we, brethren, being taken from you for a short time in presence, not in heart, endeavoured the more abundantly to see your face with great desire.

18Wherefore we would have come unto you, even I Paul, once and again; but Satan hindered us.

19For what *is* our hope, or joy, or crown of rejoicing? *Are* not even ye in the presence of our Lord Jesus Christ at his coming?

20For ye are our glory and joy.

3 WHEREFORE WHEN we could no longer forbear, we thought it good to be left at Athens alone;

2And sent Timotheus, our brother, and minister of God, and our fellowlabourer in the gospel of Christ, to establish you, and to comfort you concerning your faith:

3That no man should be moved by these afflictions: for yourselves know that we are appointed thereunto.

4For verily, when we were with you, we told you before that we should suffer tribulation; even as it came to pass, and ye know.

5For this cause, when I could no longer forbear, I sent to know your faith, lest by some means the tempter have tempted you, and our labour be in vain.

6But now when Timotheus came from you unto us, and brought us good tidings of your faith and charity, and that ye have good remembrance of us always, desiring greatly to see us, as we also *to see* you:

7Therefore, brethren, we were comforted over you in all our affliction and distress by your faith:

8For now we live, if ye stand fast in the Lord.

9For what thanks can we render to God again for you, for all the joy wherewith we joy for your sakes before our God;

New International

caring for her little children. 8We loved you so much that we were delighted to share with you not only the gospel of God but our lives as well, because you had become so dear to us. 9Surely you remember, brothers, our toil and hardship; we worked night and day in order not to be a burden to anyone while we preached the gospel of God to you.

10You are witnesses, and so is God, of how holy, righteous and blameless we were among you who believed. 11For you know that we dealt with each of you as a father deals with his own children, 12encouraging, comforting and urging you to live lives worthy of God, who calls you into his kingdom and glory.

13And we also thank God continually because, when you received the word of God, which you heard from us, you accepted it not as the word of men, but as it actually is, the word of God, which is at work in you who believe. 14For you, brothers, became imitators of God's churches in Judea, which are in Christ Jesus: You suffered from your own countrymen the same things those churches suffered from the Jews, 15who killed the Lord Jesus and the prophets and also drove us out. They displease God and are hostile to all men 16in their effort to keep us from speaking to the Gentiles so that they may be saved. In this way they always heap up their sins to the limit. The wrath of God has come upon them at last.[a]

Paul's Longing to See the Thessalonians

17But, brothers, when we were torn away from you for a short time (in person, not in thought), out of our intense longing we made every effort to see you. 18For we wanted to come to you—certainly I, Paul, did, again and again—but Satan stopped us. 19For what is our hope, our joy, or the crown in which we will glory in the presence of our Lord Jesus when he comes? Is it not you? 20Indeed, you are our glory and joy.

3 SO WHEN we could stand it no longer, we thought it best to be left by ourselves in Athens. 2We sent Timothy, who is our brother and God's fellow worker[b] in spreading the gospel of Christ, to strengthen and encourage you in your faith, 3so that no one would be unsettled by these trials. You know quite well that we were destined for them. 4In fact, when we were with you, we kept telling you that we would be persecuted. And it turned out that way, as you well know. 5For this reason, when I could stand it no longer, I sent to find out about your faith. I was afraid that in some way the tempter might have tempted you and our efforts might have been useless.

Timothy's Encouraging Report

6But Timothy has just now come to us from you and has brought good news about your faith and love. He has told us that you always have pleasant memories of us and that you long to see us, just as we also long to see you. 7Therefore, brothers, in all our distress and persecution we were encouraged about you because of your faith. 8For now we really live, since you are standing firm in the Lord. 9How can we thank God enough for you in return for all the joy we have in the presence of our God because of you? 10Night and day we pray most earnestly

Living Bible

were as gentle among you as a mother feeding and caring for her own children. 8We loved you dearly—so dearly that we gave you not only God's message, but our own lives too.

9Don't you remember, dear brothers, how hard we worked among you? Night and day we toiled and sweated to earn enough to live on so that our expenses would not be a burden to anyone there, as we preached God's Good News among you. 10You yourselves are our witnesses—as is God—that we have been pure and honest and faultless toward every one of you. 11We talked to you as a father to his own children—don't you remember?—pleading with you, encouraging you and even demanding 12that your daily lives should not embarrass God, but bring joy to him who invited you into his Kingdom to share his glory.

13And we will never stop thanking God for this: that when we preached to you, you didn't think of the words we spoke as being just our own, but you accepted what we said as the very Word of God—which, of course, it was—and it changed your lives when you believed it.

14And then, dear brothers, you suffered what the churches in Judea did, persecution from your own countrymen, just as they suffered from their own people the Jews. 15After they had killed their own prophets, they even executed the Lord Jesus; and now they have brutally persecuted us and driven us out. They are against both God and man, 16trying to keep us from preaching to the Gentiles for fear some might be saved; and so their sins continue to grow. But the anger of God has caught up with them at last.

17Dear brothers, after we left you and had been away from you but a very little while (though our hearts never left you), we tried hard to come back to see you once more. 18We wanted very much to come and I, Paul, tried again and again, but Satan stopped us. 19For what is it we live for, that gives us hope and joy and is our proud reward and crown? It is you! Yes, you will bring us much joy as we stand together before our Lord Jesus Christ when he comes back again. 20For you are our trophy and joy.

3 FINALLY, WHEN I could stand it no longer, I decided to stay alone in Athens 2, 3and send Timothy, our brother and fellow worker, God's minister, to visit you to strengthen your faith and encourage you, and to keep you from becoming fainthearted in all the troubles you were going through. (But of course you know that such troubles are a part of God's plan for us Christians. 4Even while we were still with you we warned you ahead of time that suffering would soon come—and it did.)

5As I was saying, when I could bear the suspense no longer I sent Timothy to find out whether your faith was still strong. I was afraid that perhaps Satan had gotten the best of you and that all our work had been useless. 6And now Timothy has just returned and brings the welcome news that your faith and love are as strong as ever, and that you remember our visit with joy and want to see us just as much as we want to see you. 7So we are greatly comforted, dear brothers, in all of our own crushing troubles and suffering here, now that we know you are standing true to the Lord. 8We can bear anything as long as we know that you remain strong in him.

9How can we thank God enough for you and for the joy and delight you have given us in our praying for you?

New Revised Standard

tles of Christ. But we were gentlec among you, like a nurse tenderly caring for her own children. 8So deeply do we care for you that we are determined to share with you not only the gospel of God but also our own selves, because you have become very dear to us.

9 You remember our labor and toil, brothers and sisters;d we worked night and day, so that we might not burden any of you while we proclaimed to you the gospel of God. 10You are witnesses, and God also, how pure, upright, and blameless our conduct was toward you believers. 11As you know, we dealt with each one of you like a father with his children, 12urging and encouraging you and pleading that you lead a life worthy of God, who calls you into his own kingdom and glory.

13 We also constantly give thanks to God for this, that when you received the word of God that you heard from us, you accepted it not as a human word but as what it really is, God's word, which is also at work in you believers. 14For you, brothers and sisters,d became imitators of the churches of God in Christ Jesus that are in Judea, for you suffered the same things from your own compatriots as they did from the Jews, 15who killed both the Lord Jesus and the prophets,e and drove us out; they displease God and oppose everyone 16by hindering us from speaking to the Gentiles so that they may be saved. Thus they have constantly been filling up the measure of their sins; but God's wrath has overtaken them at last.f

Paul's Desire to Visit the Thessalonians Again

17 As for us, brothers and sisters,d when, for a short time, we were made orphans by being separated from you—in person, not in heart—we longed with great eagerness to see you face to face. 18For we wanted to come to you—certainly I, Paul, wanted to again and again—but Satan blocked our way. 19For what is our hope or joy or crown of boasting before our Lord Jesus at his coming? Is it not you? 20Yes, you are our glory and joy!

3 THEREFORE WHEN we could bear it no longer, we decided to be left alone in Athens; 2and we sent Timothy, our brother and co-worker for God in proclaimingg the gospel of Christ, to strengthen and encourage you for the sake of your faith, 3so that no one would be shaken by these persecutions. Indeed, you yourselves know that this is what we are destined for. 4In fact, when we were with you, we told you beforehand that we were to suffer persecution; so it turned out, as you know. 5For this reason, when I could bear it no longer, I sent to find out about your faith; I was afraid that somehow the tempter had tempted you and that our labor had been in vain.

Timothy's Encouraging Report

6 But Timothy has just now come to us from you, and has brought us the good news of your faith and love. He has told us also that you always remember us kindly and long to see us—just as we long to see you. 7For this reason, brothers and sisters,d during all our distress and persecution we have been encouraged about you through your faith. 8For we now live, if you continue to stand firm in the Lord. 9How can we thank God enough for you in return for all the joy that we feel before our God because of you? 10Night and day we pray most earnestly

---

c Other ancient authorities read *infants*   d Gk *brothers*   e Other ancient authorities read *their own prophets*   f Or *completely* or *forever*   g Gk lacks *proclaiming*

King James

10Night and day praying exceedingly that we might see your face, and might perfect that which is lacking in your faith?

11Now God himself and our Father, and our Lord Jesus Christ, direct our way unto you.

12And the Lord make you to increase and abound in love one toward another, and toward all *men,* even as we *do* toward you:

13To the end he may stablish your hearts unblameable in holiness before God, even our Father, at the coming of our Lord Jesus Christ with all his saints.

4 FURTHERMORE THEN we beseech you, brethren, and exhort *you* by the Lord Jesus, that as ye have received of us how ye ought to walk and to please God, *so* ye would abound more and more.

2For ye know what commandments we gave you by the Lord Jesus.

3For this is the will of God, *even* your sanctification, that ye should abstain from fornication:

4That every one of you should know how to possess his vessel in sanctification and honour;

5Not in the lust of concupiscence, even as the Gentiles which know not God:

6That no *man* go beyond and defraud his brother in *any* matter: because that the Lord *is* the avenger of all such, as we also have forewarned you and testified.

7For God hath not called us unto uncleanness, but unto holiness.

8He therefore that despiseth, despiseth not man, but God, who hath also given unto us his holy Spirit.

9But as touching brotherly love ye need not that I write unto you: for ye yourselves are taught of God to love one another.

10And indeed ye do it toward all the brethren which are in all Macedonia: but we beseech you, brethren, that ye increase more and more;

11And that ye study to be quiet, and to do your own business, and to work with your own hands, as we commanded you;

12That ye may walk honestly toward them that are without, and *that* ye may have lack of nothing.

13But I would not have you to be ignorant, brethren, concerning them which are asleep, that ye sorrow not, even as others which have no hope.

14For if we believe that Jesus died and rose again, even so them also which sleep in Jesus will God bring with him.

15For this we say unto you by the word of the Lord, that we which are alive *and* remain unto the coming of the Lord shall not prevent them which are asleep.

16For the Lord himself shall descend from heaven with a shout, with the voice of the archangel, and with the trump of God: and the dead in Christ shall rise first:

17Then we which are alive *and* remain shall be caught up together with them in the clouds, to meet the Lord in the air: and so shall we ever be with the Lord.

18Wherefore comfort one another with these words.

5 BUT OF the times and the seasons, brethren, ye have no need that I write unto you.

New International

that we may see you again and supply what is lacking in your faith.

11Now may our God and Father himself and our Lord Jesus clear the way for us to come to you. 12May the Lord make your love increase and overflow for each other and for everyone else, just as ours does for you. 13May he strengthen your hearts so that you will be blameless and holy in the presence of our God and Father when our Lord Jesus comes with all his holy ones.

Living to Please God

4 FINALLY, BROTHERS, we instructed you how to live in order to please God, as in fact you are living. Now we ask you and urge you in the Lord Jesus to do this more and more. 2For you know what instructions we gave you by the authority of the Lord Jesus.

3It is God's will that you should be sanctified: that you should avoid sexual immorality; 4that each of you should learn to control his own bodya in a way that is holy and honorable, 5not in passionate lust like the heathen, who do not know God; 6and that in this matter no one should wrong his brother or take advantage of him. The Lord will punish men for all such sins, as we have already told you and warned you. 7For God did not call us to be impure, but to live a holy life. 8Therefore, he who rejects this instruction does not reject man but God, who gives you his Holy Spirit.

9Now about brotherly love we do not need to write to you, for you yourselves have been taught by God to love each other. 10And in fact, you do love all the brothers throughout Macedonia. Yet we urge you, brothers, to do so more and more.

11Make it your ambition to lead a quiet life, to mind your own business and to work with your hands, just as we told you, 12so that your daily life may win the respect of outsiders and so that you will not be dependent on anybody.

The Coming of the Lord

13Brothers, we do not want you to be ignorant about those who fall asleep, or to grieve like the rest of men, who have no hope. 14We believe that Jesus died and rose again and so we believe that God will bring with Jesus those who have fallen asleep in him. 15According to the Lord's own word, we tell you that we who are still alive, who are left till the coming of the Lord, will certainly not precede those who have fallen asleep. 16For the Lord himself will come down from heaven, with a loud command, with the voice of the archangel and with the trumpet call of God, and the dead in Christ will rise first. 17After that, we who are still alive and are left will be caught up together with them in the clouds to meet the Lord in the air. And so we will be with the Lord forever. 18Therefore encourage each other with these words.

5 NOW, BROTHERS, about times and dates we do not need to write to you, 2for you know very well

---

a 4 Or *learn to live with his own wife;* or *learn to acquire a wife*

Living Bible

10For night and day we pray on and on for you, asking God to let us see you again, to fill up any little cracks there may yet be in your faith.

11May God our Father himself and our Lord Jesus send us back to you again. 12And may the Lord make your love to grow and overflow to each other and to everyone else, just as our love does toward you. 13This will result in your hearts being made strong, sinless and holy by God our Father, so that you may stand before him guiltless on that day when our Lord Jesus Christ returns with all those who belong to him.b

4 LET ME add this, dear brothers: You already know how to please God in your daily living, for you know the commands we gave you from the Lord Jesus himself. Now we beg you—yes, we demand of you in the name of the Lord Jesus—that you live more and more closely to that ideal. 3, 4For God wants you to be holy and pure, and to keep clear of all sexual sin so that each of you will marry in holiness and honor— 5not in lustful passion as the heathen do, in their ignorance of God and his ways.

6And this also is God's will: that you never cheat in this matter by taking another man's wife, because the Lord will punish you terribly for this, as we have solemnly told you before. 7For God has not called us to be dirty-minded and full of lust, but to be holy and clean. 8If anyone refuses to live by these rules he is not disobeying the rules of men but of God who gives his *Holy* Spirit to you.

9But concerning the pure brotherly love that there should be among God's people, I don't need to say very much, I'm sure! For God himself is teaching you to love one another. 10Indeed, your love is already strong toward all the Christian brothers throughout your whole nation. Even so, dear friends, we beg you to love them more and more. 11This should be your ambition: to live a quiet life, minding your own business and doing your own work, just as we told you before. 12As a result, people who are not Christians will trust and respect you, and you will not need to depend on others for enough money to pay your bills.

13And now, dear brothers, I want you to know what happens to a Christian when he dies so that when it happens, you will not be full of sorrow, as those are who have no hope. 14For since we believe that Jesus died and then came back to life again, we can also believe that when Jesus returns, God will bring back with him all the Christians who have died.

15I can tell you this directly from the Lord: that we who are still living when the Lord returns will not rise to meet him ahead of those who are in their graves. 16For the Lord himself will come down from heaven with a mighty shout and with the soul-stirring cry of the archangel and the great trumpet-call of God. And the believers who are dead will be the first to rise to meet the Lord. 17Then we who are still alive and remain on the earth will be caught up with them in the clouds to meet the Lord in the air and remain with him forever. 18So comfort and encourage each other with this news.

5 WHEN IS all this going to happen? I really don't need to say anything about that, dear brothers, 2for

New Revised Standard

that we may see you face to face and restore whatever is lacking in your faith.

11 Now may our God and Father himself and our Lord Jesus direct our way to you. 12And may the Lord make you increase and abound in love for one another and for all, just as we abound in love for you. 13And may he so strengthen your hearts in holiness that you may be blameless before our God and Father at the coming of our Lord Jesus with all his saints.

A Life Pleasing to God

4 FINALLY, BROTHERS and sisters,c we ask and urge you in the Lord Jesus that, as you learned from us how you ought to live and to please God (as, in fact, you are doing), you should do so more and more. 2For you know what instructions we gave you through the Lord Jesus. 3For this is the will of God, your sanctification: that you abstain from fornication; 4that each one of you know how to control your own bodyd in holiness and honor, 5not with lustful passion, like the Gentiles who do not know God; 6that no one wrong or exploit a brother or sistere in this matter, because the Lord is an avenger in all these things, just as we have already told you beforehand and solemnly warned you. 7For God did not call us to impurity but in holiness. 8Therefore whoever rejects this rejects not human authority but God, who also gives his Holy Spirit to you.

9 Now concerning love of the brothers and sisters,c you do not need to have anyone write to you, for you yourselves have been taught by God to love one another; 10and indeed you do love all the brothers and sistersc throughout Macedonia. But we urge you, beloved,c to do so more and more, 11to aspire to live quietly, to mind your own affairs, and to work with your hands, as we directed you, 12so that you may behave properly toward outsiders and be dependent on no one.

The Coming of the Lord

13 But we do not want you to be uninformed, brothers and sisters,c about those who have died,f so that you may not grieve as others do who have no hope. 14For since we believe that Jesus died and rose again, even so, through Jesus, God will bring with him those who have died.f 15For this we declare to you by the word of the Lord, that we who are alive, who are left until the coming of the Lord, will by no means precede those who have died.f 16For the Lord himself, with a cry of command, with the archangel's call and with the sound of God's trumpet, will descend from heaven, and the dead in Christ will rise first. 17Then we who are alive, who are left, will be caught up in the clouds together with them to meet the Lord in the air; and so we will be with the Lord forever. 18Therefore encourage one another with these words.

5 NOW CONCERNING the times and the seasons, brothers and sisters,c you do not need to have anything written to you. 2For you yourselves know very

---

b *3:13* with all those who belong to him, literally, "with all his saints. Amen."

c Gk *brothers*   d Or *how to take a wife for himself*   e Gk *brother*   f Gk *fallen asleep*

King James

2For yourselves know perfectly that the day of the Lord so cometh as a thief in the night.

3For when they shall say, Peace and safety; then sudden destruction cometh upon them, as travail upon a woman with child; and they shall not escape.

4But ye, brethren, are not in darkness, that that day should overtake you as a thief.

5Ye are all the children of light, and the children of the day: we are not of the night, nor of darkness.

6Therefore let us not sleep, as *do* others; but let us watch and be sober.

7For they that sleep sleep in the night; and they that be drunken are drunken in the night.

8But let us, who are of the day, be sober, putting on the breastplate of faith and love; and for an helmet, the hope of salvation.

9For God hath not appointed us to wrath, but to obtain salvation by our Lord Jesus Christ,

10Who died for us, that, whether we wake or sleep, we should live together with him.

11Wherefore comfort yourselves together, and edify one another, even as also ye do.

12And we beseech you, brethren, to know them which labour among you, and are over you in the Lord, and admonish you;

13And to esteem them very highly in love for their work's sake. *And* be at peace among yourselves.

14Now we exhort you, brethren, warn them that are unruly, comfort the feebleminded, support the weak, be patient toward all *men*.

15See that none render evil for evil unto any *man;* but ever follow that which is good, both among yourselves, and to all *men*.

16Rejoice evermore.

17Pray without ceasing.

18In every thing give thanks: for this is the will of God in Christ Jesus concerning you.

19Quench not the Spirit.

20Despise not prophesyings.

21Prove all things; hold fast that which is good.

22Abstain from all appearance of evil.

23And the very God of peace sanctify you wholly; and *I pray God* your whole spirit and soul and body be preserved blameless unto the coming of our Lord Jesus Christ.

24Faithful *is* he that calleth you, who also will do *it*.

25Brethren, pray for us.

26Greet all the brethren with an holy kiss.

27I charge you by the Lord that this epistle be read unto all the holy brethren.

28The grace of our Lord Jesus Christ *be* with you. Amen.

New International

that the day of the Lord will come like a thief in the night. 3While people are saying, "Peace and safety," destruction will come on them suddenly, as labor pains on a pregnant woman, and they will not escape.

4But you, brothers, are not in darkness so that this day should surprise you like a thief. 5You are all sons of the light and sons of the day. We do not belong to the night or to the darkness. 6So then, let us not be like others, who are asleep, but let us be alert and self-controlled. 7For those who sleep, sleep at night, and those who get drunk, get drunk at night. 8But since we belong to the day, let us be self-controlled, putting on faith and love as a breastplate, and the hope of salvation as a helmet. 9For God did not appoint us to suffer wrath but to receive salvation through our Lord Jesus Christ. 10He died for us so that, whether we are awake or asleep, we may live together with him. 11Therefore encourage one another and build each other up, just as in fact you are doing.

Final Instructions

12Now we ask you, brothers, to respect those who work hard among you, who are over you in the Lord and who admonish you. 13Hold them in the highest regard in love because of their work. Live in peace with each other. 14And we urge you, brothers, warn those who are idle, encourage the timid, help the weak, be patient with everyone. 15Make sure that nobody pays back wrong for wrong, but always try to be kind to each other and to everyone else.

16Be joyful always; 17pray continually; 18give thanks in all circumstances, for this is God's will for you in Christ Jesus.

19Do not put out the Spirit's fire; 20do not treat prophecies with contempt. 21Test everything. Hold on to the good. 22Avoid every kind of evil.

23May God himself, the God of peace, sanctify you through and through. May your whole spirit, soul and body be kept blameless at the coming of our Lord Jesus Christ. 24The one who calls you is faithful and he will do it.

25Brothers, pray for us. 26Greet all the brothers with a holy kiss. 27I charge you before the Lord to have this letter read to all the brothers.

28The grace of our Lord Jesus Christ be with you.

Living Bible

you know perfectly well that no one knows. That day of the Lord will come unexpectedly like a thief in the night. 3When people are saying, "All is well, everything is quiet and peaceful"—then, all of a sudden, disaster will fall upon them as suddenly as a woman's birth pains begin when her child is born. And these people will not be able to get away anywhere—there will be no place to hide.

4But, dear brothers, you are not in the dark about these things, and you won't be surprised as by a thief when that day of the Lord comes. 5For you are all children of the light and of the day, and do not belong to darkness and night. 6So be on your guard, not asleep like the others. Watch for his return and stay sober. 7Night is the time for sleep and the time when people get drunk. 8But let us who live in the light keep sober, protected by the armor of faith and love, and wearing as our helmet the happy hope of salvation.

9For God has not chosen to pour out his anger upon us, but to save us through our Lord Jesus Christ; 10he died for us so that we can live with him forever, whether we are dead or alive at the time of his return. 11So encourage each other to build each other up, just as you are already doing.

12Dear brothers, honor the officers of your church who work hard among you and warn you against all that is wrong. 13Think highly of them and give them your wholehearted love because they are straining to help you. And remember, no quarreling among yourselves.

14Dear brothers, warn those who are lazy; comfort those who are frightened; take tender care of those who are weak; and be patient with everyone. 15See that no one pays back evil for evil, but always try to do good to each other and to everyone else. 16Always be joyful. 17Always keep on praying. 18No matter what happens, always be thankful, for this is God's will for you who belong to Christ Jesus.

19Do not smother the Holy Spirit. 20Do not scoff at those who prophesy, 21but test everything that is said to be sure it is true, and if it is, then accept it. 22Keep away from every kind of evil. 23May the God of peace himself make you entirely pure and devoted to God; and may your spirit and soul and body be kept strong and blameless until that day when our Lord Jesus Christ comes back again. 24God, who called you to become his child, will do all this for you, just as he promised. 25Dear brothers, pray for us. 26Shake hands for me with all the brothers there. 27I command you in the name of the Lord to read this letter to all the Christians. 28And may rich blessings from our Lord Jesus Christ be with you, every one.

Sincerely, Paul

New Revised Standard

well that the day of the Lord will come like a thief in the night. 3When they say, "There is peace and security," then sudden destruction will come upon them, as labor pains come upon a pregnant woman, and there will be no escape! 4But you, beloved,a are not in darkness, for that day to surprise you like a thief; 5for you are all children of light and children of the day; we are not of the night or of darkness. 6So then let us not fall asleep as others do, but let us keep awake and be sober; 7for those who sleep sleep at night, and those who are drunk get drunk at night. 8But since we belong to the day, let us be sober, and put on the breastplate of faith and love, and for a helmet the hope of salvation. 9For God has destined us not for wrath but for obtaining salvation through our Lord Jesus Christ, 10who died for us, so that whether we are awake or asleep we may live with him. 11Therefore encourage one another and build up each other, as indeed you are doing.

Final Exhortations, Greetings, and Benediction

12 But we appeal to you, brothers and sisters,a to respect those who labor among you, and have charge of you in the Lord and admonish you; 13esteem them very highly in love because of their work. Be at peace among yourselves. 14And we urge you, beloved,a to admonish the idlers, encourage the faint hearted, help the weak, be patient with all of them. 15See that none of you repays evil for evil, but always seek to do good to one another and to all. 16Rejoice always, 17pray without ceasing, 18give thanks in all circumstances; for this is the will of God in Christ Jesus for you. 19Do not quench the Spirit. 20Do not despise the words of prophets,b 21but test everything; hold fast to what is good; 22abstain from every form of evil.

23 May the God of peace himself sanctify you entirely; and may your spirit and soul and body be kept soundc and blameless at the coming of our Lord Jesus Christ. 24The one who calls you is faithful, and he will do this.

25 Beloved,d pray for us.

26 Greet all the brothers and sistersa with a holy kiss. 27I solemnly command you by the Lord that this letter be read to all of them.e

28 The grace of our Lord Jesus Christ be with you.f

---

a Gk brothers　　b Gk despise prophecies　　c Or complete　　d Gk Brothers
e Gk to all the brothers　　f Other ancient authorities add Amen

THE SECOND EPISTLE OF

PAUL THE APOSTLE TO THE

Thessalonians   # 2 Thessalonians

1 PAUL, AND Silvanus, and Timotheus, unto the church of the Thessalonians in God our Father and the Lord Jesus Christ:

2Grace unto you, and peace, from God our Father and the Lord Jesus Christ.

3We are bound to thank God always for you, brethren, as it is meet, because that your faith groweth exceedingly, and the charity of every one of you all toward each other aboundeth;

4So that we ourselves glory in you in the churches of God for your patience and faith in all your persecutions and tribulations that ye endure:

5*Which is* a manifest token of the righteous judgment of God, that ye may be counted worthy of the kingdom of God, for which ye also suffer:

6Seeing *it is* a righteous thing with God to recompense tribulation to them that trouble you;

7And to you who are troubled rest with us, when the Lord Jesus shall be revealed from heaven with his mighty angels,

8In flaming fire taking vengeance on them that know not God, and that obey not the gospel of our Lord Jesus Christ:

9Who shall be punished with everlasting destruction from the presence of the Lord, and from the glory of his power;

10When he shall come to be glorified in his saints, and to be admired in all them that believe (because our testimony among you was believed) in that day.

11Wherefore also we pray always for you, that our God would count you worthy of *this* calling, and fulfil all the good pleasure of *his* goodness, and the work of faith with power:

12That the name of our Lord Jesus Christ may be glorified in you, and ye in him, according to the grace of our God and the Lord Jesus Christ.

1 PAUL, SILAS[a] and Timothy,

To the church of the Thessalonians in God our Father and the Lord Jesus Christ:

2Grace and peace to you from God the Father and the Lord Jesus Christ.

Thanksgiving and Prayer

3We ought always to thank God for you, brothers, and rightly so, because your faith is growing more and more, and the love every one of you has for each other is increasing. 4Therefore, among God's churches we boast about your perseverance and faith in all the persecutions and trials you are enduring.

5All this is evidence that God's judgment is right, and as a result you will be counted worthy of the kingdom of God, for which you are suffering. 6God is just: He will pay back trouble to those who trouble you 7and give relief to you who are troubled, and to us as well. This will happen when the Lord Jesus is revealed from heaven in blazing fire with his powerful angels. 8He will punish those who do not know God and do not obey the gospel of our Lord Jesus. 9They will be punished with everlasting destruction and shut out from the presence of the Lord and from the majesty of his power 10on the day he comes to be glorified in his holy people and to be marveled at among all those who have believed. This includes you, because you believed our testimony to you.

11With this in mind, we constantly pray for you, that our God may count you worthy of his calling, and that by his power he may fulfill every good purpose of yours and every act prompted by your faith. 12We pray this so that the name of our Lord Jesus may be glorified in you, and you in him, according to the grace of our God and the Lord Jesus Christ.[b]

The Man of Lawlessness

2 NOW WE beseech you, brethren, by the coming of our Lord Jesus Christ, and *by* our gathering together unto him,

2That ye be not soon shaken in mind, or be troubled, neither by spirit, nor by word, nor by letter as from us, as that the day of Christ is at hand.

3Let no man deceive you by any means: for *that day shall not come,* except there come a falling away first, and that man of sin be revealed, the son of perdition;

4Who opposeth and exalteth himself above all that is called God, or that is worshipped; so that he as God sitteth in the temple of God, showing himself that he is God.

2 CONCERNING THE coming of our Lord Jesus Christ and our being gathered to him, we ask you, brothers, 2not to become easily unsettled or alarmed by some prophecy, report or letter supposed to have come from us, saying that the day of the Lord has already come. 3Don't let anyone deceive you in any way, for that day will not come until the rebellion occurs and the man of lawlessness[c] is revealed, the man doomed to destruction. 4He will oppose and will exalt himself over everything that is called God or is worshiped, so that he sets himself up in God's temple, proclaiming himself to be God.

---

[a] *1* Greek *Silvanus,* a variant of *Silas*   [b] *12* Or *God and Lord, Jesus Christ*
[c] *3* Some manuscripts *sin*

THE SECOND LETTER OF

PAUL TO THE

2 Thessalonians

Thessalonians

1 FROM: PAUL, Silas and Timothy.
To: The church of Thessalonica—kept safe in God our Father and in the Lord Jesus Christ.

2May God the Father and the Lord Jesus Christ give you rich blessings and peace-filled hearts and minds.

3Dear brothers, giving thanks to God for you is not only the right thing to do, but it is our duty to God, because of the really wonderful way your faith has grown, and because of your growing love for each other. 4We are happy to tell other churches about your patience and complete faith in God, in spite of all the crushing troubles and hardships you are going through.

5This is only one example of the fair, just way God does things, for he is using your sufferings to make you ready for his Kingdom, 6while at the same time he is preparing judgment and punishment for those who are hurting you.

7And so I would say to you who are suffering, God will give you rest along with us when the Lord Jesus appears suddenly from heaven in flaming fire with his mighty angels, 8bringing judgment on those who do not wish to know God, and who refuse to accept his plan to save them through our Lord Jesus Christ. 9They will be punished in everlasting hell, forever separated from the Lord, never to see the glory of his power, 10when he comes to receive praise and admiration because of all he has done for his people, his saints. And you will be among those praising him, because you have believed what we told you about him.

11And so we keep on praying for you that our God will make you the kind of children he wants to have—will make you as good as you wish you could be!—rewarding your faith with his power. 12Then everyone will be praising the name of the Lord Jesus Christ because of the results they see in you; and your greatest glory will be that you belong to him. The tender mercy of our God and of the Lord Jesus Christ has made all this possible for you.

2 AND NOW, what about the coming again of our Lord Jesus Christ, and our being gathered together to meet him? Please don't be upset and excited, dear brothers, by the rumor that this day of the Lord has already begun. If you hear of people having visions and special messages from God about this, or letters that are supposed to have come from me, don't believe them. 3Don't be carried away and deceived regardless of what they say.

For that day will not come until two things happen: first, there will be a time of great rebellion against God, and then the man of rebellion will come—the son of hell. 4He will defy every god there is, and tear down every other object of adoration and worship. He will go in and sit as God in the temple of God, claiming that he himself is God. 5Don't you remember that I told you this

Salutation

1 PAUL, SILVANUS, and Timothy,
To the church of the Thessalonians in God our Father and the Lord Jesus Christ:
2 Grace to you and peace from God ourd Father and the Lord Jesus Christ.

Thanksgiving

3 We must always give thanks to God for you, brothers and sisters,e as is right, because your faith is growing abundantly, and the love of everyone of you for one another is increasing. 4Therefore we ourselves boast of you among the churches of God for your steadfastness and faith during all your persecutions and the afflictions that you are enduring.

The Judgment at Christ's Coming

5 This is evidence of the righteous judgment of God, and is intended to make you worthy of the kingdom of God, for which you are also suffering. 6For it is indeed just of God to repay with affliction those who afflict you, 7and to give relief to the afflicted as well as to us, when the Lord Jesus is revealed from heaven with his mighty angels 8in flaming fire, inflicting vengeance on those who do not know God and on those who do not obey the gospel of our Lord Jesus. 9These will suffer the punishment of eternal destruction, separated from the presence of the Lord and from the glory of his might, 10when he comes to be glorified by his saints and to be marveled at on that day among all who have believed, because our testimony to you was believed. 11To this end we always pray for you, asking that our God will make you worthy of his call and will fulfill by his power every good resolve and work of faith, 12so that the name of our Lord Jesus may be glorified in you, and you in him, according to the grace of our God and the Lord Jesus Christ.

The Man of Lawlessness

2 AS TO the coming of our Lord Jesus Christ and our being gathered together to him, we beg you, brothers and sisters,e 2not to be quickly shaken in mind or alarmed, either by spirit or by word or by letter, as though from us, to the effect that the day of the Lord is already here. 3Let no one deceive you in any way; for that day will not come unless the rebellion comes first and the lawless onef is revealed, the one destined for destruction.g 4He opposes and exalts himself above every so-called god or object of worship, so that he takes his seat in the temple of God, declaring himself to be God. 5Do you not remember that I told you these things

---

d Other ancient authorities read *the*   e Gk *brothers*   f Gk *the man of lawlessness*; other ancient authorities read *the man of sin*   g Gk *the son of destruction*

King James

5Remember ye not, that, when I was yet with you, I told you these things?

6And now ye know what withholdeth that he might be revealed in his time.

7For the mystery of iniquity doth already work: only he who now letteth *will let*, until he be taken out of the way.

8And then shall that Wicked be revealed, whom the Lord shall consume with the spirit of his mouth, and shall destroy with the brightness of his coming:

9*Even him*, whose coming is after the working of Satan with all power and signs and lying wonders,

10And with all deceivableness of unrighteousness in them that perish; because they received not the love of the truth, that they might be saved.

11And for this cause God shall send them strong delusion, that they should believe a lie:

12That they all might be damned who believed not the truth, but had pleasure in unrighteousness.

13But we are bound to give thanks always to God for you, brethren beloved of the Lord, because God hath from the beginning chosen you to salvation through sanctification of the Spirit and belief of the truth:

14Whereunto he called you by our gospel, to the obtaining of the glory of our Lord Jesus Christ.

15Therefore, brethren, stand fast, and hold the traditions which ye have been taught, whether by word, or our epistle.

16Now our Lord Jesus Christ himself, and God, even our Father, which hath loved us, and hath given *us* everlasting consolation and good hope through grace,

17Comfort your hearts, and stablish you in every good word and work.

3 FINALLY, BRETHREN, pray for us, that the word of the Lord may have *free* course, and be glorified, even as *it is* with you:

2And that we may be delivered from unreasonable and wicked men: for all *men* have not faith.

3But the Lord is faithful, who shall stablish you, and keep *you* from evil.

4And we have confidence in the Lord touching you, that ye both do and will do the things which we command you.

5And the Lord direct your hearts into the love of God, and into the patient waiting for Christ.

6Now we command you, brethren, in the name of our Lord Jesus Christ, that ye withdraw yourselves from every brother that walketh disorderly, and not after the tradition which he received of us.

7For yourselves know how ye ought to follow us: for we behaved not ourselves disorderly among you;

8Neither did we eat any man's bread for nought; but wrought with labour and travail night and day, that we might not be chargeable to any of you:

9Not because we have not power, but to make ourselves an example unto you to follow us.

10For even when we were with you, this we commanded you, that if any would not work, neither should he eat.

11For we hear that there are some which walk among you disorderly, working not at all, but are busybodies.

12Now them that are such we command and exhort by our Lord Jesus Christ, that with quietness they work, and eat their own bread.

13But ye, brethren, be not weary in well doing.

New International

5Don't you remember that when I was with you I used to tell you these things? 6And now you know what is holding him back, so that he may be revealed at the proper time. 7For the secret power of lawlessness is already at work; but the one who now holds it back will continue to do so till he is taken out of the way. 8And then the lawless one will be revealed, whom the Lord Jesus will overthrow with the breath of his mouth and destroy by the splendor of his coming. 9The coming of the lawless one will be in accordance with the work of Satan displayed in all kinds of counterfeit miracles, signs and wonders, 10and in every sort of evil that deceives those who are perishing. They perish because they refused to love the truth and so be saved. 11For this reason God sends them a powerful delusion so that they will believe the lie 12and so that all will be condemned who have not believed the truth but have delighted in wickedness.

Stand Firm

13But we ought always to thank God for you, brothers loved by the Lord, because from the beginning God chose youa to be saved through the sanctifying work of the Spirit and through belief in the truth. 14He called you to this through our gospel, that you might share in the glory of our Lord Jesus Christ. 15So then, brothers, stand firm and hold to the teachingsb we passed on to you, whether by word of mouth or by letter.

16May our Lord Jesus Christ himself and God our Father, who loved us and by his grace gave us eternal encouragement and good hope, 17encourage your hearts and strengthen you in every good deed and word.

Request for Prayer

3 FINALLY, BROTHERS, pray for us that the message of the Lord may spread rapidly and be honored, just as it was with you. 2And pray that we may be delivered from wicked and evil men, for not everyone has faith. 3But the Lord is faithful, and he will strengthen and protect you from the evil one. 4We have confidence in the Lord that you are doing and will continue to do the things we command. 5May the Lord direct your hearts into God's love and Christ's perseverance.

Warning Against Idleness

6In the name of the Lord Jesus Christ, we command you, brothers, to keep away from every brother who is idle and does not live according to the teachingc you received from us. 7For you yourselves know how you ought to follow our example. We were not idle when we were with you, 8nor did we eat anyone's food without paying for it. On the contrary, we worked night and day, laboring and toiling so that we would not be a burden to any of you. 9We did this, not because we do not have the right to such help, but in order to make ourselves a model for you to follow. 10For even when we were with you, we gave you this rule: "If a man will not work, he shall not eat."

11We hear that some among you are idle. They are not busy; they are busybodies. 12Such people we command and urge in the Lord Jesus Christ to settle down and earn the bread they eat. 13And as for you, brothers, never tire of doing what is right.

---

a 13 Some manuscripts *because God chose you as his firstfruits*   b 15 Or *traditions*   c 6 Or *tradition*

Living Bible

when I was with you? 6And you know what is keeping him from being here already; for he can come only when his time is ready.

7As for the work this man of rebellion and hell will do when he comes, it is already going on,d but he himself will not come until the one who is holding him back steps out of the way. 8Then this wicked one will appear, whom the Lord Jesus will burn up with the breath of his mouth and destroy by his presence when he returns. 9This man of sin will come as Satan's tool, full of satanic power, and will trick everyone with strange demonstrations, and will do great miracles. 10He will completely fool those who are on their way to hell because they have said "no" to the Truth; they have refused to believe it and love it, and let it save them, 11so God will allow them to believe lies with all their hearts, 12and all of them will be justly judged for believing falsehood, refusing the Truth, and enjoying their sins. 13But we must forever give thanks to God for you, our brothers loved by the Lord, because God chose from the very first to give you salvation,e cleansing you by the work of the Holy Spirit and by your trusting in the Truth. 14Through us he told you the Good News. Through us he called you to share in the glory of our Lord Jesus Christ.

15With all these things in mind, dear brothers, stand firm and keep a strong grip on the truth that we taught you in our letters and during the time we were with you.

16May our Lord Jesus Christ himself and God our Father, who has loved us and given us everlasting comfort and hope which we don't deserve, 17comfort your hearts with all comfort, and help you in every good thing you say and do.

3 FINALLY, DEAR brothers, as I come to the end of this letter I ask you to pray for us. Pray first that the Lord's message will spread rapidly and triumph wherever it goes, winning converts everywhere as it did when it came to you. 2Pray too that we will be saved out of the clutches of evil men, for not everyone loves the Lord. 3But the Lord is faithful; he will make you strong and guard you from satanic attacks of every kind. 4And we trust the Lord that you are putting into practice the things we taught you, and that you always will. 5May the Lord bring you into an ever deeper understanding of the love of God and of the patience that comes from Christ.

6Now here is a command, dear brothers, given in the name of our Lord Jesus Christ by his authority: Stay away from any Christian who spends his days in laziness and does not follow the ideal of hard work we set up for you. 7For you well know that you ought to follow our example: you never saw us loafing; 8we never accepted food from anyone without buying it; we worked hard day and night for the money we needed to live on, in order that we would not be a burden to any of you. 9It wasn't that we didn't have the right to ask you to feed us, but we wanted to show you, firsthand, how you should work for your living. 10Even while we were still there with you we gave you this rule: "He who does not work shall not eat."

11Yet we hear that some of you are living in laziness, refusing to work, and wasting your time in gossiping. 12In the name of the Lord Jesus Christ we appeal to such people—we command them—to quiet down, get to work, and earn their own living. 13And to the rest of you I say, dear brothers, never be tired of doing right.

New Revised Standard

when I was still with you? 6And you know what is now restraining him, so that he may be revealed when his time comes. 7For the mystery of lawlessness is already at work, but only until the one who now restrains it is removed. 8And then the lawless one will be revealed, whom the Lord Jesusf will destroyg with the breath of his mouth, annihilating him by the manifestation of his coming. 9The coming of the lawless one is apparent in the working of Satan, who uses all power, signs, lying wonders, 10and every kind of wicked deception for those who are perishing, because they refused to love the truth and so be saved. 11For this reason God sends them a powerful delusion, leading them to believe what is false, 12so that all who have not believed the truth but took pleasure in unrighteousness will be condemned.

Chosen for Salvation

13 But we must always give thanks to God for you, brothers and sistersh beloved by the Lord, because God chose you as the first fruitsi for salvation through sanctification by the Spirit and through belief in the truth. 14For this purpose he called you through our proclamation of the good news,j so that you may obtain the glory of our Lord Jesus Christ. 15So then, brothers and sisters,h stand firm and hold fast to the traditions that you were taught by us, either by word of mouth or by our letter.

16 Now may our Lord Jesus Christ himself and God our Father, who loved us and through grace gave us eternal comfort and good hope, 17comfort your hearts and strengthen them in every good work and word.

Request for Prayer

3 FINALLY, BROTHERS and sisters,h pray for us, so that the word of the Lord may spread rapidly and be glorified everywhere, just as it is among you, 2and that we may be rescued from wicked and evil people; for not all have faith. 3But the Lord is faithful; he will strengthen you and guard you from the evil one.k 4And we have confidence in the Lord concerning you, that you are doing and will go on doing the things that we command. 5May the Lord direct your hearts to the love of God and to the steadfastness of Christ.

Warning against Idleness

6 Now we command you, beloved,h in the name of our Lord Jesus Christ, to keep away from believers who arel living in idleness and not according to the tradition that theym received from us. 7For you yourselves know how you ought to imitate us; we were not idle when we were with you, 8and we did not eat anyone's bread without paying for it; but with toil and labor we worked night and day, so that we might not burden any of you. 9This was not because we do not have that right, but in order to give you an example to imitate. 10For even when we were with you, we gave you this command: Anyone unwilling to work should not eat. 11For we hear that some of you are living in idleness, mere busybodies, not doing any work. 12Now such persons we command and exhort in the Lord Jesus Christ to do their work quietly and to earn their own living. 13Brothers and sisters,n do not be weary in doing what is right.

---

d 2:7 it is already going on, literally, "the mystery of lawlessness is already at work." e 2:13 God chose from the very first to give you salvation, or, "because God chose you to be among the first to believe."

f Other ancient authorities lack Jesus g Other ancient authorities read consume h Gk brothers i Other ancient authorities read from the beginning j Or through our gospel k Or from evil l Gk from every brother who is m Other ancient authorities read you n Gk Brothers

King James

14And if any man obey not our word by this epistle, note that man, and have no company with him, that he may be ashamed.

15Yet count *him* not as an enemy, but admonish *him* as a brother.

16Now the Lord of peace himself give you peace always by all means. The Lord *be* with you all.

17The salutation of Paul with mine own hand, which is the token in every epistle: so I write.

18The grace of our Lord Jesus Christ *be* with you all. Amen.

New International

14If anyone does not obey our instruction in this letter, take special note of him. Do not associate with him, in order that he may feel ashamed. 15Yet do not regard him as an enemy, but warn him as a brother.

Final Greetings

16Now may the Lord of peace himself give you peace at all times and in every way. The Lord be with all of you.

17I, Paul, write this greeting in my own hand, which is the distinguishing mark in all my letters. This is how I write.

18The grace of our Lord Jesus Christ be with you all.

Living Bible

14If anyone refuses to obey what we say in this letter, notice who he is and stay away from him, that he may be ashamed of himself. 15Don't think of him as an enemy, but speak to him as you would to a brother who needs to be warned.

16May the Lord of peace himself give you his peace no matter what happens. The Lord be with you all.

17Now here is my greeting which I am writing with my own hand, as I do at the end of all my letters, for proof that it really is from me. This is in my own handwriting. 18May the blessing of our Lord Jesus Christ be upon you all.

Sincerely, Paul

New Revised Standard

14 Take note of those who do not obey what we say in this letter; have nothing to do with them, so that they may be ashamed. 15Do not regard them as enemies, but warn them as believers.a

Final Greetings and Benediction

16 Now may the Lord of peace himself give you peace at all times in all ways. The Lord be with all of you.

17 I, Paul, write this greeting with my own hand. This is the mark in every letter of mine; it is the way I write. 18The grace of our Lord Jesus Christ be with all of you.b

a Gk a brother   b Other ancient authorities add Amen

THE FIRST EPISTLE OF

PAUL THE APOSTLE TO

Timothy

1 Timothy

1 PAUL, AN apostle of Jesus Christ by the commandment of God our Saviour, and Lord Jesus Christ, *which is* our hope;

2Unto Timothy, *my* own son in the faith: Grace, mercy, *and* peace, from God our Father and Jesus Christ our Lord.

3As I besought thee to abide still at Ephesus, when I went into Macedonia, that thou mightest charge some that they teach no other doctrine,

4Neither give heed to fables and endless genealogies, which minister questions, rather than godly edifying which is in faith: *so do*.

5Now the end of the commandment is charity out of a pure heart, and *of* a good conscience, and *of* faith unfeigned:

6From which some having swerved have turned aside unto vain jangling;

7Desiring to be teachers of the law; understanding neither what they say, nor whereof they affirm.

8But we know that the law *is* good, if a man use it lawfully;

9Knowing this, that the law is not made for a righteous man, but for the lawless and disobedient, for the ungodly and for sinners, for unholy and profane, for murderers of fathers and murderers of mothers, for manslayers,

10For whoremongers, for them that defile themselves with mankind, for menstealers, for liars, for perjured persons, and if there be any other thing that is contrary to sound doctrine;

11According to the glorious gospel of the blessed God, which was committed to my trust.

12And I thank Christ Jesus our Lord, who hath enabled me, for that he counted me faithful, putting me into the ministry;

13Who was before a blasphemer, and a persecutor, and injurious: but I obtained mercy, because I did *it* ignorantly in unbelief.

14And the grace of our Lord was exceeding abundant with faith and love which is in Christ Jesus.

15This *is* a faithful saying, and worthy of all acceptation, that Christ Jesus came into the world to save sinners; of whom I am chief.

16Howbeit for this cause I obtained mercy, that in me first Jesus Christ might show forth all longsuffering, for a pattern to them which should hereafter believe on him to life everlasting.

17Now unto the King eternal, immortal, invisible, the only wise God, *be* honour and glory for ever and ever. Amen.

18This charge I commit unto thee, son Timothy, according to the prophecies which went before on thee, that thou by them mightest war a good warfare;

1 PAUL, AN apostle of Christ Jesus by the command of God our Savior and of Christ Jesus our hope,

2To Timothy my true son in the faith:

Grace, mercy and peace from God the Father and Christ Jesus our Lord.

Warning Against False Teachers of the Law

3As I urged you when I went into Macedonia, stay there in Ephesus so that you may command certain men not to teach false doctrines any longer 4nor to devote themselves to myths and endless genealogies. These promote controversies rather than God's work—which is by faith. 5The goal of this command is love, which comes from a pure heart and a good conscience and a sincere faith. 6Some have wandered away from these and turned to meaningless talk. 7They want to be teachers of the law, but they do not know what they are talking about or what they so confidently affirm.

8We know that the law is good if one uses it properly. 9We also know that lawa is made not for the righteous but for lawbreakers and rebels, the ungodly and sinful, the unholy and irreligious; for those who kill their fathers or mothers, for murderers, 10for adulterers and perverts, for slave traders and liars and perjurers—and for whatever else is contrary to the sound doctrine 11that conforms to the glorious gospel of the blessed God, which he entrusted to me.

The Lord's Grace to Paul

12I thank Christ Jesus our Lord, who has given me strength, that he considered me faithful, appointing me to his service. 13Even though I was once a blasphemer and a persecutor and a violent man, I was shown mercy because I acted in ignorance and unbelief. 14The grace of our Lord was poured out on me abundantly, along with the faith and love that are in Christ Jesus.

15Here is a trustworthy saying that deserves full acceptance: Christ Jesus came into the world to save sinners—of whom I am the worst. 16But for that very reason I was shown mercy so that in me, the worst of sinners, Christ Jesus might display his unlimited patience as an example for those who would believe on him and receive eternal life. 17Now to the King eternal, immortal, invisible, the only God, be honor and glory for ever and ever. Amen.

18Timothy, my son, I give you this instruction in keeping with the prophecies once made about you, so that by following them you may fight the good fight,

a 9 Or *that the law*

THE FIRST LETTER OF

PAUL TO

1 Timothy

Timothy

1 FROM: PAUL, a missionary of Jesus Christ, sent out by the direct command of God our Savior and by Jesus Christ our Lord—our only hope.
²*To:* Timothy.
Timothy, you are like a son to me in the things of the Lord. May God our Father and Jesus Christ our Lord show you his kindness and mercy and give you great peace of heart and mind.

³, ⁴As I said when I left for Macedonia, please stay there in Ephesus and try to stop the men who are teaching such wrong doctrine. Put an end to their myths and fables, and their idea of being saved by finding favor with an endless chain of angels leading up to God—wild ideas that stir up questions and arguments instead of helping people accept God's plan of faith. ⁵What I am eager for is that all the Christians there will be filled with love that comes from pure hearts, and that their minds will be clean and their faith strong.

⁶But these teachers have missed this whole idea and spend their time arguing and talking foolishness. ⁷They want to become famous as teachers of the laws of Moses when they haven't the slightest idea what those laws really show us. ⁸Those laws are good when used as God intended. ⁹But they were not made for us, whom God has saved; they are for sinners who hate God, have rebellious hearts, curse and swear, attack their fathers and mothers, and murder. ¹⁰, ¹¹Yes, these laws are made to identify as sinners all who are immoral and impure: homosexuals, kidnappers, liars, and all others who do things that contradict the glorious Good News of our blessed God, whose messenger I am.

¹²How thankful I am to Christ Jesus our Lord for choosing me as one of his messengers, and giving me the strength to be faithful to him, ¹³even though I used to scoff at the name of Christ. I hunted down his people, harming them in every way I could. But God had mercy on me because I didn't know what I was doing, for I didn't know Christ at that time. ¹⁴Oh, how kind our Lord was, for he showed me how to trust him and become full of the love of Christ Jesus.

¹⁵How true it is, and how I long that everyone should know it, that Christ Jesus came into the world to save sinners—and I was the greatest of them all. ¹⁶But God had mercy on me so that Christ Jesus could use me as an example to show everyone how patient he is with even the worst sinners, so that others will realize that they, too, can have everlasting life. ¹⁷Glory and honor to God forever and ever. He is the King of the ages, the unseen one who never dies; he alone is God, and full of wisdom. Amen.

¹⁸Now, Timothy, my son, here is my command to you: Fight well in the Lord's battles, just as the Lord told us through his prophets that you would. ¹⁹Cling tightly

Salutation

1 PAUL, AN apostle of Christ Jesus by the command of God our Savior and of Christ Jesus our hope,
2 To Timothy, my loyal child in the faith:
Grace, mercy, and peace from God the Father and Christ Jesus our Lord.

Warning against False Teachers

3 I urge you, as I did when I was on my way to Macedonia, to remain in Ephesus so that you may instruct certain people not to teach any different doctrine, ⁴and not to occupy themselves with myths and endless genealogies that promote speculations rather than the divine trainingᵇ that is known by faith. ⁵But the aim of such instruction is love that comes from a pure heart, a good conscience, and sincere faith. ⁶Some people have deviated from these and turned to meaningless talk, ⁷desiring to be teachers of the law, without understanding either what they are saying or the things about which they make assertions.

8 Now we know that the law is good, if one uses it legitimately. ⁹This means understanding that the law is laid down not for the innocent but for the lawless and disobedient, for the godless and sinful, for the unholy and profane, for those who kill their father or mother, for murderers, ¹⁰fornicators, sodomites, slave traders, liars, perjurers, and whatever else is contrary to the sound teaching ¹¹that conforms to the glorious gospel of the blessed God, which he entrusted to me.

Gratitude for Mercy

12 I am grateful to Christ Jesus our Lord, who has strengthened me, because he judged me faithful and appointed me to his service, ¹³even though I was formerly a blasphemer, a persecutor, and a man of violence. But I received mercy because I had acted ignorantly in unbelief, ¹⁴and the grace of our Lord overflowed for me with the faith and love that are in Christ Jesus. ¹⁵The saying is sure and worthy of full acceptance, that Christ Jesus came into the world to save sinners—of whom I am the foremost. ¹⁶But for that very reason I received mercy, so that in me, as the foremost, Jesus Christ might display the utmost patience, making me an example to those who would come to believe in him for eternal life. ¹⁷To the King of the ages, immortal, invisible, the only God, be honor and glory forever and ever.ᶜ Amen.

18 I am giving you these instructions, Timothy, my child, in accordance with the prophecies made earlier about you, so that by following them you may fight the good fight, ¹⁹having faith and a good conscience. By

ᵇ Or *plan*   ᶜ Gk *to the ages of the ages*

King James

19Holding faith, and a good conscience; which some having put away concerning faith have made shipwreck:

20Of whom is Hymenaeus and Alexander; whom I have delivered unto Satan, that they may learn not to blaspheme.

2 I EXHORT therefore, that, first of all, supplications, prayers, intercessions, *and* giving of thanks, be made for all men;

2For kings, and *for* all that are in authority; that we may lead a quiet and peaceable life in all godliness and honesty.

3For this *is* good and acceptable in the sight of God our Saviour;

4Who will have all men to be saved, and to come unto the knowledge of the truth.

5For *there is* one God, and one mediator between God and men, the man Christ Jesus;

6Who gave himself a ransom for all, to be testified in due time.

7Whereunto I am ordained a preacher, and an apostle, (I speak the truth in Christ, *and* lie not;) a teacher of the Gentiles in faith and verity.

8I will therefore that men pray every where, lifting up holy hands, without wrath and doubting.

9In like manner also, that women adorn themselves in modest apparel, with shamefacedness and sobriety; not with braided hair, or gold, or pearls, or costly array;

10But (which becometh women professing godliness) with good works.

11Let the woman learn in silence with all subjection.

12But I suffer not a woman to teach, nor to usurp authority over the man, but to be in silence.

13For Adam was first formed, then Eve.

14And Adam was not deceived, but the woman being deceived was in the transgression.

15Notwithstanding she shall be saved in childbearing, if they continue in faith and charity and holiness with sobriety.

3 THIS *IS* a true saying, If a man desire the office of a bishop, he desireth a good work.

2A bishop then must be blameless, the husband of one wife, vigilant, sober, of good behaviour, given to hospitality, apt to teach;

3Not given to wine, no striker, not greedy of filthy lucre; but patient, not a brawler, not covetous;

4One that ruleth well his own house, having his children in subjection with all gravity;

5(For if a man know not how to rule his own house, how shall he take care of the church of God?)

6Not a novice, lest being lifted up with pride he fall into the condemnation of the devil.

7Moreover he must have a good report of them which are without; lest he fall into reproach and the snare of the devil.

New International

19holding on to faith and a good conscience. Some have rejected these and so have shipwrecked their faith. 20Among them are Hymenaeus and Alexander, whom I have handed over to Satan to be taught not to blaspheme.

Instructions on Worship

2 I URGE, then, first of all, that requests, prayers, intercession and thanksgiving be made for everyone— 2for kings and all those in authority, that we may live peaceful and quiet lives in all godliness and holiness. 3This is good, and pleases God our Savior, 4who wants all men to be saved and to come to a knowledge of the truth. 5For there is one God and one mediator between God and men, the man Christ Jesus, 6who gave himself as a ransom for all men—the testimony given in its proper time. 7And for this purpose I was appointed a herald and an apostle—I am telling the truth, I am not lying—and a teacher of the true faith to the Gentiles.

8I want men everywhere to lift up holy hands in prayer, without anger or disputing.

9I also want women to dress modestly, with decency and propriety, not with braided hair or gold or pearls or expensive clothes, 10but with good deeds, appropriate for women who profess to worship God.

11A woman should learn in quietness and full submission. 12I do not permit a woman to teach or to have authority over a man; she must be silent. 13For Adam was formed first, then Eve. 14And Adam was not the one deceived; it was the woman who was deceived and became a sinner. 15But women[a] will be saved[b] through childbearing—if they continue in faith, love and holiness with propriety.

Overseers and Deacons

3 HERE IS a trustworthy saying: If anyone sets his heart on being an overseer,[c] he desires a noble task. 2Now the overseer must be above reproach, the husband of but one wife, temperate, self-controlled, respectable, hospitable, able to teach, 3not given to drunkenness, not violent but gentle, not quarrelsome, not a lover of money. 4He must manage his own family well and see that his children obey him with proper respect. 5(If anyone does not know how to manage his own family, how can he take care of God's church?) 6He must not be a recent convert, or he may become conceited and fall under the same judgment as the devil. 7He must also have a good reputation with outsiders, so that he will not fall into disgrace and into the devil's trap.

Living Bible

to your faith in Christ and always keep your conscience clear, doing what you know is right. For some people have disobeyed their consciences and have deliberately done what they knew was wrong. It isn't surprising that soon they lost their faith in Christ after defying God like that. 20Hymenaeus and Alexander are two examples of this. I had to give them over to Satan to punish them until they could learn not to bring shame to the name of Christ.

2 HERE ARE my directions: Pray much for others; plead for God's mercy upon them; give thanks for all he is going to do for them.

2Pray in this way for kings and all others who are in authority over us, or are in places of high responsibility, so that we can live in peace and quietness, spending our time in godly living and thinking much about the Lord.d 3This is good and pleases God our Savior, 4for he longs for all to be saved and to understand this truth: 5*That God is on one side and all the people on the other side, and Christ Jesus, himself man, is between them to bring them together, 6by giving his life for all mankind.*

This is the message which at the proper time God gave to the world. 7And I have been chosen—this is the absolute truth—as God's minister and missionary to teach this truth to the Gentiles, and to show them God's plan of salvation through faith.

8So I want men everywhere to pray with holy hands lifted up to God, free from sin and anger and resentment. 9, 10And the women should be the same way, quiet and sensible in manner and clothing. Christian women should be noticed for being kind and good, not for the way they fix their hair or because of their jewels or fancy clothes. 11Women should listen and learn quietly and humbly.

12I never let women teach men or lord it over them. Let them be silent in your church meetings. 13Why? Because God made Adam first, and afterwards he made Eve. 14And it was not Adam who was fooled by Satan, but Eve, and sin was the result. 15So God sent pain and suffering to women when their children are born, but he will save their souls if they trust in him, living quiet, good, and loving lives.

3 IT IS a true saying that if a man wants to be a pastore he has a good ambition. 2For a pastor must be a good man whose life cannot be spoken against. He must have only one wife, and he must be hard working and thoughtful, orderly, and full of good deeds. He must enjoy having guests in his home, and must be a good Bible teacher. 3He must not be a drinker or quarrelsome, but he must be gentle and kind, and not be one who loves money. 4He must have a well-behaved family, with children who obey quickly and quietly. 5For if a man can't make his own little family behave, how can he help the whole church?

6The pastor must not be a new Christian, because he might be proud of being chosen so soon, and pride comes before a fall. (Satan's downfall is an example.) 7Also, he must be well spoken of by people outside the church—those who aren't Christians—so that Satan can't trap him with many accusations, and leave him without freedom to lead his flock.

New Revised Standard

rejecting conscience, certain persons have suffered shipwreck in the faith; 20among them are Hymenaeus and Alexander, whom I have turned over to Satan, so that they may learn not to blaspheme.

Instructions concerning Prayer

2 FIRST OF all, then, I urge that supplications, prayers, intercessions, and thanksgivings be made for everyone, 2for kings and all who are in high positions, so that we may lead a quiet and peaceable life in all godliness and dignity. 3This is right and is acceptable in the sight of God our Savior, 4who desires everyone to be saved and to come to the knowledge of the truth. 5For

there is one God;
        there is also one mediator between God and
                humankind,
    Christ Jesus, himself human,
6   who gave himself a ransom for all

—this was attested at the right time. 7For this I was appointed a herald and an apostle (I am telling the truth,f I am not lying), a teacher of the Gentiles in faith and truth.

8 I desire, then, that in every place the men should pray, lifting up holy hands without anger or argument; 9also that the women should dress themselves modestly and decently in suitable clothing, not with their hair braided, or with gold, pearls, or expensive clothes, 10but with good works, as is proper for women who profess reverence for God. 11Let a womang learn in silence with full submission. 12I permit no womang to teach or to have authority over a man;h she is to keep silent. 13For Adam was formed first, then Eve; 14and Adam was not deceived, but the woman was deceived and became a transgressor. 15Yet she will be saved through childbearing, provided they continue in faith and love and holiness, with modesty.

Qualifications of Bishops

3 THE SAYING is sure:i whoever aspires to the office of bishopj desires a noble task. 2Now a bishopk must be above reproach, married only once,l temperate, sensible, respectable, hospitable, an apt teacher, 3not a drunkard, not violent but gentle, not quarrelsome, and not a lover of money. 4He must manage his own household well, keeping his children submissive and respectful in every way— 5for if someone does not know how to manage his own household, how can he take care of God's church? 6He must not be a recent convert, or he may be puffed up with conceit and fall into the condemnation of the devil. 7Moreover, he must be well thought of by outsiders, so that he may not fall into disgrace and the snare of the devil.

---

f Other ancient authorities add *in Christ* g Or *wife* h Or *her husband*
i Some interpreters place these words at the end of the previous paragraph.
Other ancient authorities read *The saying is commonly accepted* j Or *overseer*
k Or *an overseer* l Gk *the husband of one wife*

d 2:2 *in godly living and thinking much about the Lord,* literally, "in gravity."
e 3:1 *pastor,* more literally, "church leader," or "presiding elder."

King James

8Likewise *must* the deacons *be* grave, not doubletongued, not given to much wine, not greedy of filthy lucre;

9Holding the mystery of the faith in a pure conscience.

10And let these also first be proved; then let them use the office of a deacon, being *found* blameless.

11Even so *must their* wives *be* grave, not slanderers, sober, faithful in all things.

12Let the deacons be the husbands of one wife, ruling their children and their own houses well.

13For they that have used the office of a deacon well purchase to themselves a good degree, and great boldness in the faith which is in Christ Jesus.

14These things write I unto thee, hoping to come unto thee shortly:

15But if I tarry long, that thou mayest know how thou oughtest to behave thyself in the house of God, which is the church of the living God, the pillar and ground of the truth.

16And without controversy great is the mystery of godliness: God was manifest in the flesh, justified in the Spirit, seen of angels, preached unto the Gentiles, believed on in the world, received up into glory.

4 NOW THE Spirit speaketh expressly, that in the latter times some shall depart from the faith, giving heed to seducing spirits, and doctrines of devils;

2Speaking lies in hypocrisy; having their conscience seared with a hot iron;

3Forbidding to marry, *and commanding* to abstain from meats, which God hath created to be received with thanksgiving of them which believe and know the truth.

4For every creature of God *is* good, and nothing to be refused, if it be received with thanksgiving:

5For it is sanctified by the word of God and prayer.

6If thou put the brethren in remembrance of these things, thou shalt be a good minister of Jesus Christ, nourished up in the words of faith and of good doctrine, whereunto thou hast attained.

7But refuse profane and old wives' fables, and exercise thyself *rather* unto godliness.

8For bodily exercise profiteth little: but godliness is profitable unto all things, having promise of the life that now is, and of that which is to come.

9This *is* a faithful saying and worthy of all acceptation.

10For therefore we both labour and suffer reproach, because we trust in the living God, who is the Saviour of all men, specially of those that believe.

11These things command and teach.

12Let no man despise thy youth; but be thou an example of the believers, in word, in conversation, in charity, in spirit, in faith, in purity.

13Till I come, give attendance to reading, to exhortation, to doctrine.

14Neglect not the gift that is in thee, which was given thee by prophecy, with the laying on of the hands of the presbytery.

15Meditate upon these things; give thyself wholly to them; that thy profiting may appear to all.

16Take heed unto thyself, and unto the doctrine; continue in them: for in doing this thou shalt both save thyself, and them that hear thee.

New International

8Deacons, likewise, are to be men worthy of respect, sincere, not indulging in much wine, and not pursuing dishonest gain. 9They must keep hold of the deep truths of the faith with a clear conscience. 10They must first be tested; and then if there is nothing against them, let them serve as deacons.

11In the same way, their wivesa are to be women worthy of respect, not malicious talkers but temperate and trustworthy in everything.

12A deacon must be the husband of but one wife and must manage his children and his household well. 13Those who have served well gain an excellent standing and great assurance in their faith in Christ Jesus.

14Although I hope to come to you soon, I am writing you these instructions so that, 15if I am delayed, you will know how people ought to conduct themselves in God's household, which is the church of the living God, the pillar and foundation of the truth. 16Beyond all question, the mystery of godliness is great:

Heb appeared in a body,c
    was vindicated by the Spirit,
    was seen by angels,
    was preached among the nations,
    was believed on in the world,
    was taken up in glory.

Instructions to Timothy

4 THE SPIRIT clearly says that in later times some will abandon the faith and follow deceiving spirits and things taught by demons. 2Such teachings come through hypocritical liars, whose consciences have been seared as with a hot iron. 3They forbid people to marry and order them to abstain from certain foods, which God created to be received with thanksgiving by those who believe and who know the truth. 4For everything God created is good, and nothing is to be rejected if it is received with thanksgiving, 5because it is consecrated by the word of God and prayer.

6If you point these things out to the brothers, you will be a good minister of Christ Jesus, brought up in the truths of the faith and of the good teaching that you have followed. 7Have nothing to do with godless myths and old wives' tales; rather, train yourself to be godly. 8For physical training is of some value, but godliness has value for all things, holding promise for both the present life and the life to come.

9This is a trustworthy saying that deserves full acceptance 10(and for this we labor and strive), that we have put our hope in the living God, who is the Savior of all men, and especially of those who believe.

11Command and teach these things. 12Don't let anyone look down on you because you are young, but set an example for the believers in speech, in life, in love, in faith and in purity. 13Until I come, devote yourself to the public reading of Scripture, to preaching and to teaching. 14Do not neglect your gift, which was given you through a prophetic message when the body of elders laid their hands on you.

15Be diligent in these matters; give yourself wholly to them, so that everyone may see your progress. 16Watch your life and doctrine closely. Persevere in them, because if you do, you will save both yourself and your hearers.

a 11 Or *way, deaconesses*   b 16 Some manuscripts *God*   c 16 Or *in the flesh*

Living Bible

8The deacons must be the same sort of good, steady men as the pastors. They must not be heavy drinkers and must not be greedy for money. 9They must be earnest, wholehearted followers of Christ who is the hidden Source of their faith. 10Before they are asked to be deacons they should be given other jobs in the church as a test of their character and ability, and if they do well, then they may be chosen as deacons.

11Their wives must be thoughtful, not heavy drinkers, not gossipers, but faithful in everything they do. 12Deacons should have only one wife and they should have happy, obedient families. 13Those who do well as deacons will be well rewarded both by respect from others and also by developing their own confidence and bold trust in the Lord.

14I am writing these things to you now, even though I hope to be with you soon, 15so that if I don't come for awhile you will know what kind of men you should choose as officers for the church of the living God, which contains and holds high the truth of God.

16It is quite true that the way to live a godly life is not an easy matter. But the answer lies in Christ, who came to earth as a man, was proved spotless and pure in his Spirit, was served by angels, was preached among the nations, was accepted by men everywhere and was received up again to his glory in heaven.

4 BUT THE Holy Spirit tells us clearly that in the last times some in the church will turn away from Christ and become eager followers of teachers with devil-inspired ideas. 2These teachers will tell lies with straight faces and do it so often that their consciences won't even bother them.

3They will say it is wrong to be married and wrong to eat meat, even though God gave these things to well-taught Christians to enjoy and be thankful for. 4For everything God made is good, and we may eat it gladly if we are thankful for it, 5and if we ask God to bless it, for it is made good by the Word of God and prayer.

6If you explain this to the others you will be doing your duty as a worthy pastor who is fed by faith and by the true teaching you have followed.

7Don't waste time arguing over foolish ideas and silly myths and legends. Spend your time and energy in the exercise of keeping spiritually fit. 8Bodily exercise is all right, but spiritual exercise is much more important and is a tonic for all you do. So exercise yourself spiritually and practice being a better Christian, because that will help you not only now in this life, but in the next life too. 9, 10This is the truth and everyone should accept it. We work hard and suffer much in order that people will believe it, for our hope is in the living God who died for all, and particularly for those who have accepted his salvation.

11Teach these things and make sure everyone learns them well. 12Don't let anyone think little of you because you are young. Be their ideal; let them follow the way you teach and live; be a pattern for them in your love, your faith, and your clean thoughts. 13Until I get there, read and explain the Scriptures to the church; preach God's Word.

14Be sure to use the abilities God has given you through his prophets when the elders of the church laid their hands upon your head. 15Put these abilities to work; throw yourself into your tasks so that everyone may notice your improvement and progress. 16Keep a close watch on all you do and think. Stay true to what is right and God will bless you and use you to help others.

New Revised Standard

Qualifications of Deacons

8 Deacons likewise must be serious, not double-tongued, not indulging in much wine, not greedy for money; 9they must hold fast to the mystery of the faith with a clear conscience. 10And let them first be tested; then, if they prove themselves blameless, let them serve as deacons. 11Womend likewise must be serious, not slanderers, but temperate, faithful in all things. 12Let deacons be married only once,e and let them manage their children and their households well; 13for those who serve well as deacons gain a good standing for themselves and great boldness in the faith that is in Christ Jesus.

The Mystery of Our Religion

14 I hope to come to you soon, but I am writing these instructions to you so that, 15if I am delayed, you may know how one ought to behave in the household of God, which is the church of the living God, the pillar and bulwark of the truth. 16Without any doubt, the mystery of our religion is great:

Hef was revealed in flesh,
   vindicatedg in spirit,h
      seen by angels,
proclaimed among Gentiles,
   believed in throughout the world,
      taken up in glory.

False Asceticism

4 NOW THE Spirit expressly says that in lateri times some will renounce the faith by paying attention to deceitful spirits and teachings of demons, 2through the hypocrisy of liars whose consciences are seared with a hot iron. 3They forbid marriage and demand abstinence from foods, which God created to be received with thanksgiving by those who believe and know the truth. 4For everything created by God is good, and nothing is to be rejected, provided it is received with thanksgiving; 5for it is sanctified by God's word and by prayer.

A Good Minister of Jesus Christ

6 If you put these instructions before the brothers and sisters,j you will be a good servantk of Christ Jesus, nourished on the words of the faith and of the sound teaching that you have followed. 7Have nothing to do with profane myths and old wives' tales. Train yourself in godliness, 8for, while physical training is of some value, godliness is valuable in every way, holding promise for both the present life and the life to come. 9The saying is sure and worthy of full acceptance. 10For to this end we toil and struggle,l because we have our hope set on the living God, who is the Savior of all people, especially of those who believe.

11 These are the things you must insist on and teach. 12Let no one despise your youth, but set the believers an example in speech and conduct, in love, in faith, in purity. 13Until I arrive, give attention to the public reading of scripture,m to exhorting, to teaching. 14Do not neglect the gift that is in you, which was given to you through prophecy with the laying on of hands by the council of elders.n 15Put these things into practice, devote yourself to them, so that all may see your progress. 16Pay close attention to yourself and to your teaching; continue in these things, for in doing this you will save both yourself and your hearers.

---

d Or *Their wives*, or *Women deacons* e Gk *be husbands of one wife* f Gk *Who*; other ancient authorities read *God*; others, *Which* g Or *justified* h Or *by the Spirit* i Or *the last* j Gk *brothers* k Or *deacon* l Other ancient authorities read *suffer reproach* m Gk *to the reading* n Gk *by the presbytery*

King James

5 REBUKE NOT an elder, but entreat *him* as a father; *and* the younger men as brethren;
2The elder women as mothers; the younger as sisters, with all purity.
3Honour widows that are widows indeed.
4But if any widow have children or nephews, let them learn first to show piety at home, and to requite their parents: for that is good and acceptable before God.
5Now she that is a widow indeed, and desolate, trusteth in God, and continueth in supplications and prayers night and day.
6But she that liveth in pleasure is dead while she liveth.
7And these things give in charge, that they may be blameless.
8But if any provide not for his own, and specially for those of his own house, he hath denied the faith, and is worse than an infidel.
9Let not a widow be taken into the number under threescore years old, having been the wife of one man,
10Well reported of for good works; if she have brought up children, if she have lodged strangers, if she have washed the saints' feet, if she have relieved the afflicted, if she have diligently followed every good work.
11But the younger widows refuse: for when they have begun to wax wanton against Christ, they will marry;
12Having damnation, because they have cast off their first faith.
13And withal they learn *to be* idle, wandering about from house to house; and not only idle, but tattlers also and busybodies, speaking things which they ought not.
14I will therefore that the younger women marry, bear children, guide the house, give none occasion to the adversary to speak reproachfully.
15For some are already turned aside after Satan.
16If any man or woman that believeth have widows, let them relieve them, and let not the church be charged; that it may relieve them that are widows indeed.
17Let the elders that rule well be counted worthy of double honour, especially they who labour in the word and doctrine.
18For the scripture saith, Thou shalt not muzzle the ox that treadeth out the corn. And, The labourer *is* worthy of his reward.
19Against an elder receive not an accusation, but before two or three witnesses.
20Them that sin rebuke before all, that others also may fear.
21I charge *thee* before God, and the Lord Jesus Christ, and the elect angels, that thou observe these things without preferring one before another, doing nothing by partiality.
22Lay hands suddenly on no man, neither be partaker of other men's sins: keep thyself pure.
23Drink no longer water, but use a little wine for thy stomach's sake and thine often infirmities.

New International

Advice About Widows, Elders and Slaves

5 DO NOT rebuke an older man harshly, but exhort him as if he were your father. Treat younger men as brothers, 2older women as mothers, and younger women as sisters, with absolute purity.
3Give proper recognition to those widows who are really in need. 4But if a widow has children or grandchildren, these should learn first of all to put their religion into practice by caring for their own family and so repaying their parents and grandparents, for this is pleasing to God. 5The widow who is really in need and left all alone puts her hope in God and continues night and day to pray and to ask God for help. 6But the widow who lives for pleasure is dead even while she lives. 7Give the people these instructions, too, so that no one may be open to blame. 8If anyone does not provide for his relatives, and especially for his immediate family, he has denied the faith and is worse than an unbeliever.
9No widow may be put on the list of widows unless she is over sixty, has been faithful to her husband,[a] 10and is well known for her good deeds, such as bringing up children, showing hospitality, washing the feet of the saints, helping those in trouble and devoting herself to all kinds of good deeds.
11As for younger widows, do not put them on such a list. For when their sensual desires overcome their dedication to Christ, they want to marry. 12Thus they bring judgment on themselves, because they have broken their first pledge. 13Besides, they get into the habit of being idle and going about from house to house. And not only do they become idlers, but also gossips and busybodies, saying things they ought not to. 14So I counsel younger widows to marry, to have children, to manage their homes and to give the enemy no opportunity for slander. 15Some have in fact already turned away to follow Satan.
16If any woman who is a believer has widows in her family, she should help them and not let the church be burdened with them, so that the church can help those widows who are really in need.
17The elders who direct the affairs of the church well are worthy of double honor, especially those whose work is preaching and teaching. 18For the Scripture says, "Do not muzzle the ox while it is treading out the grain,"[b] and "The worker deserves his wages."[c] 19Do not entertain an accusation against an elder unless it is brought by two or three witnesses. 20Those who sin are to be rebuked publicly, so that the others may take warning.
21I charge you, in the sight of God and Christ Jesus and the elect angels, to keep these instructions without partiality, and to do nothing out of favoritism.
22Do not be hasty in the laying on of hands, and do not share in the sins of others. Keep yourself pure.
23Stop drinking only water, and use a little wine because of your stomach and your frequent illnesses.

---

a 9 Or *has had but one husband*　　b 18 Deut. 25:4　　c 18 Luke 10:7

Living Bible

5 NEVER SPEAK sharply to an older man, but plead with him respectfully just as though he were your own father. Talk to the younger men as you would to much loved brothers. 2Treat the older women as mothers, and the girls as your sisters, thinking only pure thoughts about them.

3The church should take loving care of women whose husbands have died, if they don't have anyone else to help them. 4But if they have children or grandchildren, these are the ones who should take the responsibility, for kindness should begin at home, supporting needy parents. This is something that pleases God very much.

5The church should care for widows who are poor and alone in the world, if they are looking to God for his help and spending much time in prayer; 6but not if they are spending their time running around gossiping, seeking only pleasure and thus ruining their souls. 7This should be your church rule so that the Christians will know and do what is right.

8But anyone who won't care for his own relatives when they need help, especially those living in his own family, has no right to say he is a Christian. Such a person is worse than the heathen.

9A widow who wants to become one of the special church workersd should be at least sixty years old and have been married only once. 10She must be well thought of by everyone because of the good she has done. Has she brought up her children well? Has she been kind to strangers as well as to other Christians? Has she helped those who are sick and hurt? Is she always ready to show kindness?

11The younger widows should not become members of this special group because after awhile they are likely to disregard their vow to Christ and marry again. 12And so they will stand condemned because they broke their first promise. 13Besides, they are likely to be lazy and spend their time gossiping around from house to house, getting into other people's business. 14So I think it is better for these younger widows to marry again and have children, and take care of their own homes; then no one will be able to say anything against them. 15For I am afraid that some of them have already turned away from the church and been led astray by Satan.

16Let me remind you again that a widow's relatives must take care of her, and not leave this to the church to do. Then the church can spend its money for the care of widows who are all alone and have nowhere else to turn.

17Pastors who do their work well should be paid well and should be highly appreciated, especially those who work hard at both preaching and teaching. 18For the Scriptures say, "Never tie up the mouth of an ox when it is treading out the grain—let him eat as he goes along!" And in another place, "Those who work deserve their pay!"

19Don't listen to complaints against the pastor unless there are two or three witnesses to accuse him. 20If he has really sinned, then he should be rebuked in front of the whole church so that no one else will follow his example.

21I solemnly command you in the presence of God and the Lord Jesus Christ and of the holy angels to do this whether the pastor is a special friend of yours or not. All must be treated exactly the same. 22Never be in a hurry about choosing a pastor; you may overlook his sins and it will look as if you approve of them. Be sure that you yourself stay away from all sin. 23(By the way, this doesn't mean you should completely give up drinking wine. You ought to take a little sometimes as medicine for your stomach because you are sick so often.)

New Revised Standard

Duties toward Believers

5 DO NOT speak harshly to an older man,e but speak to him as to a father, to younger men as brothers, 2to older women as mothers, to younger women as sisters—with absolute purity.

3 Honor widows who are really widows. 4If a widow has children or grandchildren, they should first learn their religious duty to their own family and make some repayment to their parents; for this is pleasing in God's sight. 5The real widow, left alone, has set her hope on God and continues in supplications and prayers night and day; 6but the widowf who lives for pleasure is dead even while she lives. 7Give these commands as well, so that they may be above reproach. 8And whoever does not provide for relatives, and especially for family members, has denied the faith and is worse than an unbeliever.

9 Let a widow be put on the list if she is not less than sixty years old and has been married only once;g 10she must be well attested for her good works, as one who has brought up children, shown hospitality, washed the saints' feet, helped the afflicted, and devoted herself to doing good in every way. 11But refuse to put younger widows on the list; for when their sensual desires alienate them from Christ, they want to marry, 12and so they incur condemnation for having violated their first pledge. 13Besides that, they learn to be idle, gadding about from house to house; and they are not merely idle, but also gossips and busybodies, saying what they should not say. 14So I would have younger widows marry, bear children, and manage their households, so as to give the adversary no occasion to revile us. 15For some have already turned away to follow Satan. 16If any believing womanh has relatives who are really widows, let her assist them; let the church not be burdened, so that it can assist those who are real widows.

17 Let the elders who rule well be considered worthy of double honor,i especially those who labor in preaching and teaching; 18for the scripture says, "You shall not muzzle an ox while it is treading out the grain," and, "The laborer deserves to be paid." 19Never accept any accusation against an elder except on the evidence of two or three witnesses. 20As for those who persist in sin, rebuke them in the presence of all, so that the rest also may stand in fear. 21In the presence of God and of Christ Jesus and of the elect angels, I warn you to keep these instructions without prejudice, doing nothing on the basis of partiality. 22Do not ordainj anyone hastily, and do not participate in the sins of others; keep yourself pure.

23 No longer drink only water, but take a little wine for the sake of your stomach and your frequent ailments.

---

d 5:9 *one of the special church workers*, literally, "enrolled as a widow."

e Or *an elder*, or *a presbyter*   f Gk *she*   g Gk *the wife of one husband*   h Other ancient authorities read *believing man or woman*; others, *believing man*   i Or *compensation*   j Gk *Do not lay hands on*

King James

24Some men's sins are open beforehand, going before to judgment; and some *men* they follow after.

25Likewise also the good works *of some* are manifest beforehand; and they that are otherwise cannot be hid.

6 LET AS many servants as are under the yoke count their own masters worthy of all honour, that the name of God and *his* doctrine be not blasphemed.

2And they that have believing masters, let them not despise *them*, because they are brethren; but rather do *them* service, because they are faithful and beloved, partakers of the benefit. These things teach and exhort.

3If any man teach otherwise, and consent not to wholesome words, *even* the words of our Lord Jesus Christ, and to the doctrine which is according to godliness;

4He is proud, knowing nothing, but doting about questions and strifes of words, whereof cometh envy, strife, railings, evil surmisings,

5Perverse disputings of men of corrupt minds, and destitute of the truth, supposing that gain is godliness: from such withdraw thyself.

6But godliness with contentment is great gain.

7For we brought nothing into *this* world, *and it is* certain we can carry nothing out.

8And having food and raiment let us be therewith content.

9But they that will be rich fall into temptation and a snare, and *into* many foolish and hurtful lusts, which drown men in destruction and perdition.

10For the love of money is the root of all evil: which while some coveted after, they have erred from the faith, and pierced themselves through with many sorrows.

11But thou, O man of God, flee these things; and follow after righteousness, godliness, faith, love, patience, meekness.

12Fight the good fight of faith, lay hold on eternal life, whereunto thou art also called, and hast professed a good profession before many witnesses.

13I give thee charge in the sight of God, who quickeneth all things, and *before* Christ Jesus, who before Pontius Pilate witnessed a good confession;

14That thou keep *this* commandment without spot, unrebukeable, until the appearing of our Lord Jesus Christ:

15Which in his times he shall show, *who is* the blessed and only Potentate, the King of kings, and Lord of lords;

16Who only hath immortality, dwelling in the light which no man can approach unto; whom no man hath seen, nor can see: to whom *be* honour and power everlasting. Amen.

17Charge them that are rich in this world, that they be not highminded, nor trust in uncertain riches, but in the living God, who giveth us richly all things to enjoy;

18That they do good, that they be rich in good works, ready to distribute, willing to communicate;

19Laying up in store for themselves a good foundation against the time to come, that they may lay hold on eternal life.

New International

24The sins of some men are obvious, reaching the place of judgment ahead of them; the sins of others trail behind them. 25In the same way, good deeds are obvious, and even those that are not cannot be hidden.

6 ALL WHO are under the yoke of slavery should consider their masters worthy of full respect, so that God's name and our teaching may not be slandered. 2Those who have believing masters are not to show less respect for them because they are brothers. Instead, they are to serve them even better, because those who benefit from their service are believers, and dear to them. These are the things you are to teach and urge on them.

Love of Money

3If anyone teaches false doctrines and does not agree to the sound instruction of our Lord Jesus Christ and to godly teaching, 4he is conceited and understands nothing. He has an unhealthy interest in controversies and quarrels about words that result in envy, strife, malicious talk, evil suspicions 5and constant friction between men of corrupt mind, who have been robbed of the truth and who think that godliness is a means to financial gain.

6But godliness with contentment is great gain. 7For we brought nothing into the world, and we can take nothing out of it. 8But if we have food and clothing, we will be content with that. 9People who want to get rich fall into temptation and a trap and into many foolish and harmful desires that plunge men into ruin and destruction. 10For the love of money is a root of all kinds of evil. Some people, eager for money, have wandered from the faith and pierced themselves with many griefs.

Paul's Charge to Timothy

11But you, man of God, flee from all this, and pursue righteousness, godliness, faith, love, endurance and gentleness. 12Fight the good fight of the faith. Take hold of the eternal life to which you were called when you made your good confession in the presence of many witnesses. 13In the sight of God, who gives life to everything, and of Christ Jesus, who while testifying before Pontius Pilate made the good confession, I charge you 14to keep this command without spot or blame until the appearing of our Lord Jesus Christ, 15which God will bring about in his own time—God, the blessed and only Ruler, the King of kings and Lord of lords, 16who alone is immortal and who lives in unapproachable light, whom no one has seen or can see. To him be honor and might forever. Amen.

17Command those who are rich in this present world not to be arrogant nor to put their hope in wealth, which is so uncertain, but to put their hope in God, who richly provides us with everything for our enjoyment. 18Command them to do good, to be rich in good deeds, and to be generous and willing to share. 19In this way they will lay up treasure for themselves as a firm foundation for the coming age, so that they may take hold of the life that is truly life.

Living Bible

24Remember that some men, even pastors, lead sinful lives and everyone knows it. In such situations you can do something about it. But in other cases only the judgment day will reveal the terrible truth. 25In the same way, everyone knows how much good some pastors do, but sometimes their good deeds aren't known until long afterward.

6 CHRISTIAN SLAVES should work hard for their owners and respect them; never let it be said that Christ's people are poor workers. Don't let the name of God or his teaching be laughed at because of this. 2If their owner is a Christian, that is no excuse for slowing down; rather they should work all the harder because a brother in the faith is being helped by their efforts.

Teach these truths, Timothy, and encourage all to obey them.

3Some may deny these things, but they are the sound, wholesome teachings of the Lord Jesus Christ and are the foundation for a godly life. 4Anyone who says anything different is both proud and stupid. He is quibbling over the meaning of Christ's words and stirring up arguments ending in jealousy and anger, which only lead to name-calling, accusations, and evil suspicions. 5These arguers—their minds warped by sin—don't know how to tell the truth; to them the Good News is just a means of making money. Keep away from them.

6Do you want to be truly rich? You already are if you are happy and good. 7After all, we didn't bring any money with us when we came into the world, and we can't carry away a single penny when we die. 8So we should be well satisfied without money if we have enough food and clothing. 9But people who long to be rich soon begin to do all kinds of wrong things to get money, things that hurt them and make them evil-minded and finally send them to hell itself. 10For the love of money is the first step toward all kinds of sin. Some people have even turned away from God because of their love for it, and as a result have pierced themselves with many sorrows.

11Oh, Timothy, you are God's man. Run from all these evil things and work instead at what is right and good, learning to trust him and love others, and to be patient and gentle. 12Fight on for God. Hold tightly to the eternal life which God has given you, and which you have confessed with such a ringing confession before many witnesses.

13I command you before God who gives life to all, and before Christ Jesus who gave a fearless testimony before Pontius Pilate, 14that you fulfill all he has told you to do, so that no one can find fault with you from now until our Lord Jesus Christ returns. 15For in due season Christ will be revealed from heaven by the blessed and only Almighty God, the King of kings and Lord of lords, 16who alone can never die, who lives in light so terrible that no human being can approach him. No mere man has ever seen him, nor ever will. Unto him be honor and everlasting power and dominion forever and ever. Amen.

17Tell those who are rich not to be proud and not to trust in their money, which will soon be gone, but their pride and trust should be in the living God who always richly gives us all we need for our enjoyment. 18Tell them to use their money to do good. They should be rich in good works and should give happily to those in need, always being ready to share with others whatever God has given them. 19By doing this they will be storing up real treasure for themselves in heaven—it is the only safe investment for eternity! And they will be living a fruitful Christian life down here as well.

New Revised Standard

24 The sins of some people are conspicuous and precede them to judgment, while the sins of others follow them there. 25So also good works are conspicuous; and even when they are not, they cannot remain hidden.

6 LET ALL who are under the yoke of slavery regard their masters as worthy of all honor, so that the name of God and the teaching may not be blasphemed. 2Those who have believing masters must not be disrespectful to them on the ground that they are members of the church;a rather they must serve them all the more, since those who benefit by their service are believers and beloved.b

False Teaching and True Riches

Teach and urge these duties. 3Whoever teaches otherwise and does not agree with the sound words of our Lord Jesus Christ and the teaching that is in accordance with godliness, 4is conceited, understanding nothing, and has a morbid craving for controversy and for disputes about words. From these come envy, dissension, slander, base suspicions, 5and wrangling among those who are depraved in mind and bereft of the truth, imagining that godliness is a means of gain.c 6Of course, there is great gain in godliness combined with contentment; 7for we brought nothing into the world, so thatd we can take nothing out of it; 8but if we have food and clothing, we will be content with these. 9But those who want to be rich fall into temptation and are trapped by many senseless and harmful desires that plunge people into ruin and destruction. 10For the love of money is a root of all kinds of evil, and in their eagerness to be rich some have wandered away from the faith and pierced themselves with many pains.

The Good Fight of Faith

11 But as for you, man of God, shun all this; pursue righteousness, godliness, faith, love, endurance, gentleness. 12Fight the good fight of the faith; take hold of the eternal life, to which you were called and for which you madee the good confession in the presence of many witnesses. 13In the presence of God, who gives life to all things, and of Christ Jesus, who in his testimony before Pontius Pilate made the good confession, I charge you 14to keep the commandment without spot or blame until the manifestation of our Lord Jesus Christ, 15which he will bring about at the right time—he who is the blessed and only Sovereign, the King of kings and Lord of lords. 16It is he alone who has immortality and dwells in unapproachable light, whom no one has ever seen or can see; to him be honor and eternal dominion. Amen.

17 As for those who in the present age are rich, command them not to be haughty, or to set their hopes on the uncertainty of riches, but rather on God who richly provides us with everything for our enjoyment. 18They are to do good, to be rich in good works, generous, and ready to share, 19thus storing up for themselves the treasure of a good foundation for the future, so that they may take hold of the life that really is life.

---

a Gk are brothers   b Or since they are believers and beloved, who devote themselves to good deeds   c Other ancient authorities add Withdraw yourself from such people   d Other ancient authorities read world—it is certain that   e Gk confessed

King James

20O Timothy, keep that which is committed to thy trust, avoiding profane *and* vain babblings, and oppositions of science falsely so called:

21Which some professing have erred concerning the faith. Grace *be* with thee. Amen.

New International

20Timothy, guard what has been entrusted to your care. Turn away from godless chatter and the opposing ideas of what is falsely called knowledge, 21which some have professed and in so doing have wandered from the faith.

Grace be with you.

Living Bible

20Oh, Timothy, don't fail to do these things that God entrusted to you. Keep out of foolish arguments with those who boast of their "knowledge" and thus prove their lack of it. 21Some of these people have missed the most important thing in life—they don't know God. May God's mercy be upon you.

Sincerely, Paul

New Revised Standard

Personal Instructions and Benediction

20 Timothy, guard what has been entrusted to you. Avoid the profane chatter and contradictions of what is falsely called knowledge; 21by professing it some have missed the mark as regards the faith.

Grace be with you.a

THE SECOND EPISTLE OF

PAUL THE APOSTLE TO

Timothy

2 Timothy

1 PAUL, AN apostle of Jesus Christ by the will of God, according to the promise of life which is in Christ Jesus,

2To Timothy, *my* dearly beloved son: Grace, mercy, *and* peace, from God the Father and Christ Jesus our Lord.

3I thank God, whom I serve from *my* forefathers with pure conscience, that without ceasing I have remembrance of thee in my prayers night and day;

4Greatly desiring to see thee, being mindful of thy tears, that I may be filled with joy;

5When I call to remembrance the unfeigned faith that is in thee, which dwelt first in thy grandmother Lois, and thy mother Eunice; and I am persuaded that in thee also.

6Wherefore I put thee in remembrance that thou stir up the gift of God, which is in thee by the putting on of my hands.

7For God hath not given us the spirit of fear; but of power, and of love, and of a sound mind.

8Be not thou therefore ashamed of the testimony of our Lord, nor of me his prisoner: but be thou partaker of the afflictions of the gospel according to the power of God;

9Who hath saved us, and called *us* with an holy calling, not according to our works, but according to his own purpose and grace, which was given us in Christ Jesus before the world began,

10But is now made manifest by the appearing of our Saviour Jesus Christ, who hath abolished death, and hath brought life and immortality to light through the gospel:

11Whereunto I am appointed a preacher, and an apostle, and a teacher of the Gentiles.

12For the which cause I also suffer these things: nevertheless I am not ashamed: for I know whom I have believed, and am persuaded that he is able to keep that which I have committed unto him against that day.

13Hold fast the form of sound words, which thou hast heard of me, in faith and love which is in Christ Jesus.

14That good thing which was committed unto thee keep by the Holy Ghost which dwelleth in us.

15This thou knowest, that all they which are in Asia be turned away from me; of whom are Phygellus and Hermogenes.

16The Lord give mercy unto the house of Onesiphorus; for he oft refreshed me, and was not ashamed of my chain:

17But, when he was in Rome, he sought me out very diligently, and found *me.*

1 PAUL, AN apostle of Christ Jesus by the will of God, according to the promise of life that is in Christ Jesus,

2To Timothy, my dear son:

Grace, mercy and peace from God the Father and Christ Jesus our Lord.

Encouragement to Be Faithful

3I thank God, whom I serve, as my forefathers did, with a clear conscience, as night and day I constantly remember you in my prayers. 4Recalling your tears, I long to see you, so that I may be filled with joy. 5I have been reminded of your sincere faith, which first lived in your grandmother Lois and in your mother Eunice and, I am persuaded, now lives in you also. 6For this reason I remind you to fan into flame the gift of God, which is in you through the laying on of my hands. 7For God did not give us a spirit of timidity, but a spirit of power, of love and of self-discipline.

8So do not be ashamed to testify about our Lord, or ashamed of me his prisoner. But join with me in suffering for the gospel, by the power of God, 9who has saved us and called us to a holy life—not because of anything we have done but because of his own purpose and grace. This grace was given us in Christ Jesus before the beginning of time, 10but it has now been revealed through the appearing of our Savior, Christ Jesus, who has destroyed death and has brought life and immortality to light through the gospel. 11And of this gospel I was appointed a herald and an apostle and a teacher. 12That is why I am suffering as I am. Yet I am not ashamed, because I know whom I have believed, and am convinced that he is able to guard what I have entrusted to him for that day.

13What you heard from me, keep as the pattern of sound teaching, with faith and love in Christ Jesus. 14Guard the good deposit that was entrusted to you— guard it with the help of the Holy Spirit who lives in us.

15You know that everyone in the province of Asia has deserted me, including Phygelus and Hermogenes.

16May the Lord show mercy to the household of Onesiphorus, because he often refreshed me and was not ashamed of my chains. 17On the contrary, when he was in Rome, he searched hard for me until he found me.

THE SECOND LETTER OF

PAUL TO

2 Timothy

Timothy

1 *FROM:* PAUL, Jesus Christ's missionary, sent out by God to tell men and women everywhere about the eternal life he has promised them through faith in Jesus Christ.

²*To:* Timothy, my dear son. May God the Father and Christ Jesus our Lord shower you with his kindness, mercy and peace.

³How I thank God for you, Timothy. I pray for you every day, and many times during the long nights I beg my God to bless you richly. He is my fathers' God, and mine, and my only purpose in life is to please him.

⁴How I long to see you again. How happy I would be, for I remember your tears as we left each other. ⁵I know how much you trust the Lord, just as your mother Eunice and your grandmother Lois do; and I feel sure you are still trusting him as much as ever.

⁶This being so, I want to remind you to stir into flame the strength and boldnessᵃ that is in you, that entered into you when I laid my hands upon your head and blessed you. ⁷For the Holy Spirit, God's gift, does not want you to be afraid of people, but to be wise and strong, and to love them and enjoy being with them.

⁸If you will stir up this inner power, you will never be afraid to tell others about our Lord, or to let them know that I am your friend even though I am here in jail for Christ's sake. You will be ready to suffer with me for the Lord, for he will give you strength in suffering.

⁹It is he who saved us and chose us for his holy work, not because we deserved it but because that was his plan long before the world began—to show his love and kindness to us through Christ. ¹⁰And now he has made all of this plain to us by the coming of our Savior Jesus Christ, who broke the power of death and showed us the way of everlasting life through trusting him. ¹¹And God has chosen me to be his missionary, to preach to the Gentiles and teach them.

¹²That is why I am suffering here in jail and I am certainly not ashamed of it, for I know the one in whom I trust, and I am sure that he is able to safely guard all that I have given him until the day of his return.

¹³Hold tightly to the pattern of truth I taught you, especially concerning the faith and love Christ Jesus offers you.ᵇ ¹⁴Guard well the splendid, God-given ability you received as a gift from the Holy Spirit who lives within you.

¹⁵As you know, all the Christians who came here from Asia have deserted me; even Phygellus and Hermogenes are gone. ¹⁶May the Lord bless Onesiphorus and all his family, because he visited me and encouraged me often. His visits revived me like a breath of fresh air, and he was never ashamed of my being in jail. ¹⁷In fact, when he came to Rome he searched everywhere trying to find me, and finally did. ¹⁸May the Lord give him a

Salutation

1 PAUL, AN apostle of Christ Jesus by the will of God, for the sake of the promise of life that is in Christ Jesus,

2 To Timothy, my beloved child:

Grace, mercy, and peace from God the Father and Christ Jesus our Lord.

Thanksgiving and Encouragement

3 I am grateful to God—whom I worship with a clear conscience, as my ancestors did—when I remember you constantly in my prayers night and day. ⁴Recalling your tears, I long to see you so that I may be filled with joy. ⁵I am reminded of your sincere faith, a faith that lived first in your grandmother Lois and your mother Eunice and now, I am sure, lives in you. ⁶For this reason I remind you to rekindle the gift of God that is within you through the laying on of my hands; ⁷for God did not give us a spirit of cowardice, but rather a spirit of power and of love and of self-discipline.

8 Do not be ashamed, then, of the testimony about our Lord or of me his prisoner, but join with me in suffering for the gospel, relying on the power of God, ⁹who saved us and called us with a holy calling, not according to our works but according to his own purpose and grace. This grace was given to us in Christ Jesus before the ages began, ¹⁰but it has now been revealed through the appearing of our Savior Christ Jesus, who abolished death and brought life and immortality to light through the gospel. ¹¹For this gospel I was appointed a herald and an apostle and a teacher,ᶜ ¹²and for this reason I suffer as I do. But I am not ashamed, for I know the one in whom I have put my trust, and I am sure that he is able to guard until that day what I have entrusted to him.ᵈ ¹³Hold to the standard of sound teaching that you have heard from me, in the faith and love that are in Christ Jesus. ¹⁴Guard the good treasure entrusted to you, with the help of the Holy Spirit living in us.

15 You are aware that all who are in Asia have turned away from me, including Phygelus and Hermogenes. ¹⁶May the Lord grant mercy to the household of Onesiphorus, because he often refreshed me and was not ashamed of my chain; ¹⁷when he arrived in Rome, he eagerlyᵉ searched for me and found me ¹⁸—may the

---

ᵃ *1:6 stir into flame the strength and boldness,* implied. Literally, "stir up the gift of God."　ᵇ *1:13 and love Christ Jesus offers you,* literally, "and love that is in Christ Jesus."

ᶜ Other ancient authorities add *of the Gentiles*　ᵈ Or *what has been entrusted to me*　ᵉ Or *promptly*

King James

18The Lord grant unto him that he may find mercy of the Lord in that day: and in how many things he ministered unto me at Ephesus, thou knowest very well.

2 THOU THEREFORE, my son, be strong in the grace that is in Christ Jesus.
2And the things that thou hast heard of me among many witnesses, the same commit thou to faithful men, who shall be able to teach others also.
3Thou therefore endure hardness, as a good soldier of Jesus Christ.
4No man that warreth entangleth himself with the affairs of *this* life; that he may please him who hath chosen him to be a soldier.
5And if a man also strive for masteries, *yet* is he not crowned, except he strive lawfully.
6The husbandman that laboureth must be first partaker of the fruits.
7Consider what I say; and the Lord give thee understanding in all things.
8Remember that Jesus Christ of the seed of David was raised from the dead according to my gospel:
9Wherein I suffer trouble, as an evildoer, *even* unto bonds; but the word of God is not bound.
10Therefore I endure all things for the elect's sakes, that they may also obtain the salvation which is in Christ Jesus with eternal glory.
11*It is* a faithful saying: For if we be dead with *him,* we shall also live with *him:*
12If we suffer, we shall also reign with *him:* if we deny *him,* he also will deny us:
13If we believe not, *yet* he abideth faithful: he cannot deny himself.
14Of these things put *them* in remembrance, charging *them* before the Lord that they strive not about words to no profit, *but* to the subverting of the hearers.
15Study to show thyself approved unto God, a workman that needeth not to be ashamed, rightly dividing the word of truth.
16But shun profane *and* vain babblings: for they will increase unto more ungodliness.
17And their word will eat as doth a canker: of whom is Hymenaeus and Philetus;
18Who concerning the truth have erred, saying that the resurrection is past already; and overthrow the faith of some.
19Nevertheless the foundation of God standeth sure, having this seal, The Lord knoweth them that are his. And, Let every one that nameth the name of Christ depart from iniquity.
20But in a great house there are not only vessels of gold and of silver, but also of wood and of earth; and some to honour, and some to dishonour.
21If a man therefore purge himself from these, he shall be a vessel unto honour, sanctified, and meet for the master's use, *and* prepared unto every good work.
22Flee also youthful lusts: but follow righteousness, faith, charity, peace, with them that call on the Lord out of a pure heart.
23But foolish and unlearned questions avoid, knowing that they do gender strifes.

New International

18May the Lord grant that he will find mercy from the Lord on that day! You know very well in how many ways he helped me in Ephesus.

2 YOU THEN, my son, be strong in the grace that is in Christ Jesus. 2And the things you have heard me say in the presence of many witnesses entrust to reliable men who will also be qualified to teach others. 3Endure hardship with us like a good soldier of Christ Jesus. 4No one serving as a soldier gets involved in civilian affairs—he wants to please his commanding officer. 5Similarly, if anyone competes as an athlete, he does not receive the victor's crown unless he competes according to the rules. 6The hardworking farmer should be the first to receive a share of the crops. 7Reflect on what I am saying, for the Lord will give you insight into all this.

8Remember Jesus Christ, raised from the dead, descended from David. This is my gospel, 9for which I am suffering even to the point of being chained like a criminal. But God's word is not chained. 10Therefore I endure everything for the sake of the elect, that they too may obtain the salvation that is in Christ Jesus, with eternal glory.

11Here is a trustworthy saying:

If we died with him,
　we will also live with him;
12if we endure,
　we will also reign with him.
If we disown him,
　he will also disown us;
13if we are faithless,
　he will remain faithful,
　for he cannot disown himself.

A Workman Approved by God

14Keep reminding them of these things. Warn them before God against quarreling about words; it is of no value, and only ruins those who listen. 15Do your best to present yourself to God as one approved, a workman who does not need to be ashamed and who correctly handles the word of truth. 16Avoid godless chatter, because those who indulge in it will become more and more ungodly. 17Their teaching will spread like gangrene. Among them are Hymenaeus and Philetus, 18who have wandered away from the truth. They say that the resurrection has already taken place, and they destroy the faith of some. 19Nevertheless, God's solid foundation stands firm, sealed with this inscription: "The Lord knows those who are his,"a and, "Everyone who confesses the name of the Lord must turn away from wickedness."

20In a large house there are articles not only of gold and silver, but also of wood and clay; some are for noble purposes and some for ignoble. 21If a man cleanses himself from the latter, he will be an instrument for noble purposes, made holy, useful to the Master and prepared to do any good work.

22Flee the evil desires of youth, and pursue righteousness, faith, love and peace, along with those who call on the Lord out of a pure heart. 23Don't have anything to do with foolish and stupid arguments, because you know they produce quarrels. 24And the Lord's servant

Living Bible

special blessing at the day of Christ's return. And you know better than I can tell you how much he helped me at Ephesus.

2 OH, TIMOTHY, my son, be strong with the strength Christ Jesus gives you. 2For you must teach others those things you and many others have heard me speak about. Teach these great truths to trustworthy men who will, in turn, pass them on to others.

3Take your share of suffering as a good soldier of Jesus Christ, just as I do, 4and as Christ's soldier do not let yourself become tied up in worldly affairs, for then you cannot satisfy the one who has enlisted you in his army. 5Follow the Lord's rules for doing his work, just as an athlete either follows the rules or is disqualified and wins no prize. 6Work hard, like a farmer who gets paid well if he raises a large crop. 7Think over these three illustrations, and may the Lord help you to understand how they apply to you.

8Don't ever forget the wonderful fact that Jesus Christ was a Man, born into King David's family; and that he was God, as shown by the fact that he rose again from the dead. 9It is because I have preached these great truths that I am in trouble here and have been put in jail like a criminal. But the Word of God is not chained, even though I am. 10I am more than willing to suffer if that will bring salvation and eternal glory in Christ Jesus to those God has chosen.

11I am comforted by this truth, that when we suffer and die for Christ it only means that we will begin living with him in heaven. 12And if we think that our present service for him is hard, just remember that some day we are going to sit with him and rule with him. But if we give up when we suffer, and turn against Christ, then he must turn against us. 13Even when we are too weak to have any faith left, he remains faithful to us and will help us, for he cannot disown us who are part of himself, and he will always carry out his promises to us.

14Remind your people of these great facts, and command them in the name of the Lord not to argue over unimportant things. Such arguments are confusing and useless, and even harmful. 15Work hard so God can say to you, "Well done." Be a good workman, one who does not need to be ashamed when God examines your work. Know what his Word says and means. 16Steer clear of foolish discussions which lead people into the sin of anger with each other. 17Things will be said that will burn and hurt for a long time to come. Hymenaeus and Philetus, in their love of argument, are men like that. 18They have left the path of truth, preaching the lie that the resurrection of the dead has already occurred; and they have weakened the faith of some who believe them.

19But God's truth stands firm like a great rock, and nothing can shake it. It is a foundation stone with these words written on it: "The Lord knows those who are really his," and "A person who calls himself a Christian should not be doing things that are wrong."

20In a wealthy home there are dishes made of gold and silver as well as some made from wood and clay. The expensive dishes are used for guests, and the cheap ones are used in the kitchen or to put garbage in. 21If you stay away from sin you will be like one of these dishes made of purest gold—the very best in the house—so that Christ himself can use you for his highest purposes.

22Run from anything that gives you the evil thoughts that young men often have, but stay close to anything that makes you want to do right. Have faith and love, and enjoy the companionship of those who love the Lord and have pure hearts.

23Again I say, don't get involved in foolish arguments which only upset people and make them angry.

New Revised Standard

Lord grant that he will find mercy from the Lord on that day! And you know very well how much service he rendered in Ephesus.

A Good Soldier of Christ Jesus

2 YOU THEN, my child, be strong in the grace that is in Christ Jesus; 2and what you have heard from me through many witnesses entrust to faithful people who will be able to teach others as well. 3Share in suffering like a good soldier of Christ Jesus. 4No one serving in the army gets entangled in everyday affairs; the soldier's aim is to please the enlisting officer. 5And in the case of an athlete, no one is crowned without competing according to the rules. 6It is the farmer who does the work who ought to have the first share of the crops. 7Think over what I say, for the Lord will give you understanding in all things.

8 Remember Jesus Christ, raised from the dead, a descendant of David—that is my gospel, 9for which I suffer hardship, even to the point of being chained like a criminal. But the word of God is not chained. 10Therefore I endure everything for the sake of the elect, so that they may also obtain the salvation that is in Christ Jesus, with eternal glory. 11The saying is sure:

If we have died with him, we will also live
with him;
12 if we endure, we will also reign with him;
if we deny him, he will also deny us;
13 if we are faithless, he remains faithful—
for he cannot deny himself.

A Worker Approved by God

14 Remind them of this, and warn them before God[b] that they are to avoid wrangling over words, which does no good but only ruins those who are listening. 15Do your best to present yourself to God as one approved by him, a worker who has no need to be ashamed, rightly explaining the word of truth. 16Avoid profane chatter, for it will lead people into more and more impiety, 17and their talk will spread like gangrene. Among them are Hymenaeus and Philetus, 18who have swerved from the truth by claiming that the resurrection has already taken place. They are upsetting the faith of some. 19But God's firm foundation stands, bearing this inscription: "The Lord knows those who are his," and, "Let everyone who calls on the name of the Lord turn away from wickedness."

20 In a large house there are utensils not only of gold and silver but also of wood and clay, some for special use, some for ordinary. 21All who cleanse themselves of the things I have mentioned[c] will become special utensils, dedicated and useful to the owner of the house, ready for every good work. 22Shun youthful passions and pursue righteousness, faith, love, and peace, along with those who call on the Lord from a pure heart. 23Have nothing to do with stupid and senseless controversies; you know that they breed quarrels. 24And the

b Other ancient authorities read *the Lord*   c Gk *of these things*

King James

24And the servant of the Lord must not strive; but be gentle unto all *men,* apt to teach, patient,

25In meekness instructing those that oppose themselves; if God peradventure will give them repentance to the acknowledging of the truth;

26And *that* they may recover themselves out of the snare of the devil, who are taken captive by him at his will.

3 THIS KNOW also, that in the last days perilous times shall come.

2For men shall be lovers of their own selves, covetous, boasters, proud, blasphemers, disobedient to parents, unthankful, unholy,

3Without natural affection, trucebreakers, false accusers, incontinent, fierce, despisers of those that are good,

4Traitors, heady, highminded, lovers of pleasures more than lovers of God;

5Having a form of godliness, but denying the power thereof: from such turn away.

6For of this sort are they which creep into houses, and lead captive silly women laden with sins, led away with divers lusts,

7Ever learning, and never able to come to the knowledge of the truth.

8Now as Jannes and Jambres withstood Moses, so do these also resist the truth: men of corrupt minds, reprobate concerning the faith.

9But they shall proceed no further: for their folly shall be manifest unto all *men,* as theirs also was.

10But thou hast fully known my doctrine, manner of life, purpose, faith, longsuffering, charity, patience,

11Persecutions, afflictions, which came unto me at Antioch, at Iconium, at Lystra; what persecutions I endured: but out of *them* all the Lord delivered me.

12Yea, and all that will live godly in Christ Jesus shall suffer persecution.

13But evil men and seducers shall wax worse and worse, deceiving, and being deceived.

14But continue thou in the things which thou hast learned and hast been assured of, knowing of whom thou hast learned *them;*

15And that from a child thou hast known the holy scriptures, which are able to make thee wise unto salvation through faith which is in Christ Jesus.

16All scripture *is* given by inspiration of God, and *is* profitable for doctrine, for reproof, for correction, for instruction in righteousness:

17That the man of God may be perfect, thoroughly furnished unto all good works.

New International

must not quarrel; instead, he must be kind to everyone, able to teach, not resentful. 25Those who oppose him he must gently instruct, in the hope that God will grant them repentance leading them to a knowledge of the truth, 26and that they will come to their senses and escape from the trap of the devil, who has taken them captive to do his will.

Godlessness in the Last Days

3 BUT MARK this: There will be terrible times in the last days. 2People will be lovers of themselves, lovers of money, boastful, proud, abusive, disobedient to their parents, ungrateful, unholy, 3without love, unforgiving, slanderous, without self-control, brutal, not lovers of the good, 4treacherous, rash, conceited, lovers of pleasure rather than lovers of God— 5having a form of godliness but denying its power. Have nothing to do with them.

6They are the kind who worm their way into homes and gain control over weak-willed women, who are loaded down with sins and are swayed by all kinds of evil desires, 7always learning but never able to acknowledge the truth. 8Just as Jannes and Jambres opposed Moses, so also these men oppose the truth—men of depraved minds, who, as far as the faith is concerned, are rejected. 9But they will not get very far because, as in the case of those men, their folly will be clear to everyone.

Paul's Charge to Timothy

10You, however, know all about my teaching, my way of life, my purpose, faith, patience, love, endurance, 11persecutions, sufferings—what kinds of things happened to me in Antioch, Iconium and Lystra, the persecutions I endured. Yet the Lord rescued me from all of them. 12In fact, everyone who wants to live a godly life in Christ Jesus will be persecuted, 13while evil men and impostors will go from bad to worse, deceiving and being deceived. 14But as for you, continue in what you have learned and have become convinced of, because you know those from whom you learned it, 15and how from infancy you have known the holy Scriptures, which are able to make you wise for salvation through faith in Christ Jesus. 16All Scripture is God-breathed and is useful for teaching, rebuking, correcting and training in righteousness, 17so that the man of God may be thoroughly equipped for every good work.

Living Bible

24God's people must not be quarrelsome; they must be gentle, patient teachers of those who are wrong. 25Be humble when you are trying to teach those who are mixed up concerning the truth. For if you talk meekly and courteously to them they are more likely, with God's help, to turn away from their wrong ideas and believe what is true. 26Then they will come to their senses and escape from Satan's trap of slavery to sin which he uses to catch them whenever he likes, and then they can begin doing the will of God.

3 YOU MAY as well know this too, Timothy, that in the last days it is going to be very difficult to be a Christian. 2For people will love only themselves and their money; they will be proud and boastful, sneering at God, disobedient to their parents, ungrateful to them, and thoroughly bad. 3They will be hardheaded and never give in to others; they will be constant liars and trouble-makers and will think nothing of immorality. They will be rough and cruel, and sneer at those who try to be good. 4They will betray their friends; they will be hotheaded, puffed up with pride, and prefer good times to worshiping God. 5They will go to church,a yes, but they won't really believe anything they hear. Don't be taken in by people like that.

6They are the kind who craftily sneak into other people's homes and make friendships with silly, sin-burdened women and teach them their new doctrines. 7Women of that kind are forever following new teachers, but they never understand the truth. 8And these teachers fight truth just as Jannes and Jambres fought against Moses. They have dirty minds, warped and twisted, and have turned against the Christian faith.

9But they won't get away with all this forever. Some day their deceit will be well known to everyone, as was the sin of Jannes and Jambres.

10But you know from watching me that I am not that kind of person. You know what I believe and the way I live and what I want. You know my faith in Christ and how I have suffered. You know my love for you, and my patience. 11You know how many troubles I have had as a result of my preaching the Good News. You know about all that was done to me while I was visiting in Antioch, Iconium and Lystra, but the Lord delivered me. 12Yes, and those who decide to please Christ Jesus by living godly lives will suffer at the hands of those who hate him. 13In fact, evil men and false teachers will become worse and worse, deceiving many, they themselves having been deceived by Satan.

14But you must keep on believing the things you have been taught. You know they are true for you know that you can trust those of us who have taught you. 15You know how, when you were a small child, you were taught the holy Scriptures; and it is these that make you wise to accept God's salvation by trusting in Christ Jesus. 16The whole Bibleb was given to us by inspiration from God and is useful to teach us what is true and to make us realize what is wrong in our lives; it straightens us out and helps us do what is right. 17It is God's way of making us well prepared at every point, fully equipped to do good to everyone.

New Revised Standard

Lord's servantc must not be quarrelsome but kindly to everyone, an apt teacher, patient, 25correcting opponents with gentleness. God may perhaps grant that they will repent and come to know the truth, 26and that they may escape from the snare of the devil, having been held captive by him to do his will.d

Godlessness in the Last Days

3 YOU MUST understand this, that in the last days distressing times will come. 2For people will be lovers of themselves, lovers of money, boasters, arrogant, abusive, disobedient to their parents, ungrateful, unholy, 3inhuman, implacable, slanderers, profligates, brutes, haters of good, 4treacherous, reckless, swollen with conceit, lovers of pleasure rather than lovers of God, 5holding to the outward form of godliness but denying its power. Avoid them! 6For among them are those who make their way into households and captivate silly women, overwhelmed by their sins and swayed by all kinds of desires, 7who are always being instructed and can never arrive at a knowledge of the truth. 8As Jannes and Jambres opposed Moses, so these people, of corrupt mind and counterfeit faith, also oppose the truth. 9But they will not make much progress, because, as in the case of those two men,e their folly will become plain to everyone.

Paul's Charge to Timothy

10 Now you have observed my teaching, my conduct, my aim in life, my faith, my patience, my love, my steadfastness, 11my persecutions and suffering the things that happened to me in Antioch, Iconium, and Lystra. What persecutions I endured! Yet the Lord rescued me from all of them. 12Indeed, all who want to live a godly life in Christ Jesus will be persecuted. 13But wicked people and impostors will go from bad to worse, deceiving others and being deceived. 14But as for you, continue in what you have learned and firmly believed, knowing from whom you learned it, 15and how from childhood you have known the sacred writings that are able to instruct you for salvation through faith in Christ Jesus. 16All scripture is inspired by God and isf useful for teaching, for reproof, for correction, and for training in righteousness, 17so that everyone who belongs to God may be proficient, equipped for every good work.

---

a 3:5 *They will go to church*, literally, "having a form of godliness."
b 3:16 *The whole Bible*, literally, "Every Scripture."

c Gk *slave* d Or *by him, to do his* (that is, God's) *will* e Gk lacks *two men* f Or *Every scripture inspired by God is also*

King James

4 I CHARGE *thee* therefore before God, and the Lord Jesus Christ, who shall judge the quick and the dead at his appearing and his kingdom;

2Preach the word; be instant in season, out of season; reprove, rebuke, exhort with all longsuffering and doctrine.

3For the time will come when they will not endure sound doctrine; but after their own lusts shall they heap to themselves teachers, having itching ears;

4And they shall turn away *their* ears from the truth, and shall be turned unto fables.

5But watch thou in all things, endure afflictions, do the work of an evangelist, make full proof of thy ministry.

6For I am now ready to be offered, and the time of my departure is at hand.

7I have fought a good fight, I have finished *my* course, I have kept the faith:

8Henceforth there is laid up for me a crown of righteousness, which the Lord, the righteous judge, shall give me at that day: and not to me only, but unto all them also that love his appearing.

9Do thy diligence to come shortly unto me:

10For Demas hath forsaken me, having loved this present world, and is departed unto Thessalonica; Crescens to Galatia, Titus unto Dalmatia.

11Only Luke is with me. Take Mark, and bring him with thee: for he is profitable to me for the ministry.

12And Tychicus have I sent to Ephesus.

13The cloak that I left at Troas with Carpus, when thou comest, bring *with thee,* and the books, *but* especially the parchments.

14Alexander the coppersmith did me much evil: the Lord reward him according to his works:

15Of whom be thou ware also; for he hath greatly withstood our words.

16At my first answer no man stood with me, but all *men* forsook me: *I pray God* that it may not be laid to their charge.

17Notwithstanding the Lord stood with me, and strengthened me; that by me the preaching might be fully known, and *that* all the Gentiles might hear: and I was delivered out of the mouth of the lion.

18And the Lord shall deliver me from every evil work, and will preserve *me* unto his heavenly kingdom: to whom *be* glory for ever and ever. Amen.

19Salute Prisca and Aquila, and the household of Onesiphorus.

20Erastus abode at Corinth: but Trophimus have I left at Miletum sick.

21Do thy diligence to come before winter. Eubulus greeteth thee, and Pudens, and Linus, and Claudia, and all the brethren.

22The Lord Jesus Christ *be* with thy spirit. Grace *be* with you. Amen.

New International

4 IN THE presence of God and of Christ Jesus, who will judge the living and the dead, and in view of his appearing and his kingdom, I give you this charge: 2Preach the Word; be prepared in season and out of season; correct, rebuke and encourage—with great patience and careful instruction. 3For the time will come when men will not put up with sound doctrine. Instead, to suit their own desires, they will gather around them a great number of teachers to say what their itching ears want to hear. 4They will turn their ears away from the truth and turn aside to myths. 5But you, keep your head in all situations, endure hardship, do the work of an evangelist, discharge all the duties of your ministry.

6For I am already being poured out like a drink offering, and the time has come for my departure. 7I have fought the good fight, I have finished the race, I have kept the faith. 8Now there is in store for me the crown of righteousness, which the Lord, the righteous Judge, will award to me on that day—and not only to me, but also to all who have longed for his appearing.

Personal Remarks

9Do your best to come to me quickly, 10for Demas, because he loved this world, has deserted me and has gone to Thessalonica. Crescens has gone to Galatia, and Titus to Dalmatia. 11Only Luke is with me. Get Mark and bring him with you, because he is helpful to me in my ministry. 12I sent Tychicus to Ephesus. 13When you come, bring the cloak that I left with Carpus at Troas, and my scrolls, especially the parchments.

14Alexander the metalworker did me a great deal of harm. The Lord will repay him for what he has done. 15You too should be on your guard against him, because he strongly opposed our message.

16At my first defense, no one came to my support, but everyone deserted me. May it not be held against them. 17But the Lord stood at my side and gave me strength, so that through me the message might be fully proclaimed and all the Gentiles might hear it. And I was delivered from the lion's mouth. 18The Lord will rescue me from every evil attack and will bring me safely to his heavenly kingdom. To him be glory for ever and ever. Amen.

Final Greetings

19Greet Priscilla[a] and Aquila and the household of Onesiphorus. 20Erastus stayed in Corinth, and I left Trophimus sick in Miletus. 21Do your best to get here before winter. Eubulus greets you, and so do Pudens, Linus, Claudia and all the brothers.

22The Lord be with your spirit. Grace be with you.

Living Bible

4 AND SO I solemnly urge you before God and before Christ Jesus—who will some day judge the living and the dead when he appears to set up his Kingdom— ²to preach the Word of God urgently at all times, whenever you get the chance, in season and out, when it is convenient and when it is not. Correct and rebuke your people when they need it, encourage them to do right, and all the time be feeding them patiently with God's Word.

³For there is going to come a time when people won't listen to the truth, but will go around looking for teachers who will tell them just what they want to hear. ⁴They won't listen to what the Bible says but will blithely follow their own misguided ideas.

⁵Stand steady, and don't be afraid of suffering for the Lord. Bring others to Christ. Leave nothing undone that you ought to do.

⁶I say this because I won't be around to help you very much longer. My time has almost run out. Very soon now I will be on my way to heaven. ⁷I have fought long and hard for my Lord, and through it all I have kept true to him. And now the time has come for me to stop fighting and rest. ⁸In heaven a crown is waiting for me which the Lord, the righteous Judge, will give me on that great day of his return. And not just to me, but to all those whose lives show that they are eagerly looking forward to his coming back again.

⁹Please come as soon as you can, ¹⁰for Demas has left me. He loved the good things of this life and went to Thessalonica. Crescens has gone to Galatia, Titus to Dalmatia. ¹¹Only Luke is with me. Bring Mark with you when you come, for I need him. ¹²(Tychicus is gone too, as I sent him to Ephesus.) ¹³When you come, be sure to bring the coat I left at Troas with Brother Carpus, and also the books, but especially the parchments.

¹⁴Alexander the coppersmith has done me much harm. The Lord will punish him, ¹⁵but be careful of him, for he fought against everything we said.

¹⁶The first time I was brought before the judge no one was here to help me. Everyone had run away. I hope that they will not be blamed for it. ¹⁷But the Lord stood with me and gave me the opportunity to boldly preach a whole sermon for all the world to hear. And he saved me from being thrown to the lions.ᵇ ¹⁸Yes, and the Lord will always deliver me from all evil and will bring me into his heavenly Kingdom. To God be the glory forever and ever. Amen.

¹⁹Please say "hello" for me to Priscilla and Aquila and those living at the home of Onesiphorus. ²⁰Erastus stayed at Corinth, and I left Trophimus sick at Miletus.

²¹Do try to be here before winter. Eubulus sends you greetings, and so do Pudens, Linus, Claudia, and all the others. ²²May the Lord Jesus Christ be with your spirit.

Farewell, Paul

New Revised Standard

4 IN THE presence of God and of Christ Jesus, who is to judge the living and the dead, and in view of his appearing and his kingdom, I solemnly urge you: ²proclaim the message; be persistent whether the time is favorable or unfavorable; convince, rebuke, and encourage, with the utmost patience in teaching. ³For the time is coming when people will not put up with sound doctrine, but having itching ears, they will accumulate for themselves teachers to suit their own desires, ⁴and will turn away from listening to the truth and wander away to myths. ⁵As for you, always be sober, endure suffering, do the work of an evangelist, carry out your ministry fully.

6 As for me, I am already being poured out as a libation, and the time of my departure has come. ⁷I have fought the good fight, I have finished the race, I have kept the faith. ⁸From now on there is reserved for me the crown of righteousness, which the Lord, the righteous judge, will give me on that day, and not only to me but also to all who have longed for his appearing.

Personal Instructions

9 Do your best to come to me soon, ¹⁰for Demas, in love with this present world, has deserted me and gone to Thessalonica; Crescens has gone to Galatia,ᶜ Titus to Dalmatia. ¹¹Only Luke is with me. Get Mark and bring him with you, for he is useful in my ministry. ¹²I have sent Tychicus to Ephesus. ¹³When you come, bring the cloak that I left with Carpus at Troas, also the books, and above all the parchments. ¹⁴Alexander the coppersmith did me great harm; the Lord will pay him back for his deeds. ¹⁵You also must beware of him, for he strongly opposed our message.

16 At my first defense no one came to my support, but all deserted me. May it not be counted against them! ¹⁷But the Lord stood by me and gave me strength, so that through me the message might be fully proclaimed and all the Gentiles might hear it. So I was rescued from the lion's mouth. ¹⁸The Lord will rescue me from every evil attack and save me for his heavenly kingdom. To him be the glory forever and ever. Amen.

Final Greetings and Benediction

19 Greet Prisca and Aquila, and the household of Onesiphorus. ²⁰Erastus remained in Corinth; Trophimus I left ill in Miletus. ²¹Do your best to come before winter. Eubulus sends greetings to you, as do Pudens and Linus and Claudia and all the brothers and sisters.ᵈ

22 The Lord be with your spirit. Grace be with you.ᵉ

ᵇ 4:17 he saved me from being thrown to the lions, literally, "I was delivered out of the mouth of the lion."

ᶜ Other ancient authorities read Gaul   ᵈ Gk all the brothers   ᵉ The Greek word for you here is plural. Other ancient authorities add Amen

THE EPISTLE OF

PAUL TO

Titus

Titus

1 PAUL, A servant of God, and an apostle of Jesus Christ, according to the faith of God's elect, and the acknowledging of the truth which is after godliness;

2In hope of eternal life, which God, that cannot lie, promised before the world began;

3But hath in due times manifested his word through preaching, which is committed unto me according to the commandment of God our Saviour;

4To Titus, *mine* own son after the common faith: Grace, mercy, *and* peace, from God the Father and the Lord Jesus Christ our Saviour.

5For this cause left I thee in Crete, that thou shouldest set in order the things that are wanting, and ordain elders in every city, as I had appointed thee:

6If any be blameless, the husband of one wife, having faithful children not accused of riot or unruly.

7For a bishop must be blameless, as the steward of God; not self-willed, not soon angry, not given to wine, no striker, not given to filthy lucre;

8But a lover of hospitality, a lover of good men, sober, just, holy, temperate;

9Holding fast the faithful word as he hath been taught, that he may be able by sound doctrine both to exhort and to convince the gainsayers.

10For there are many unruly and vain talkers and deceivers, specially they of the circumcision:

11Whose mouths must be stopped, who subvert whole houses, teaching things which they ought not, for filthy lucre's sake.

12One of themselves, *even* a prophet of their own, said, The Cretians *are* always liars, evil beasts, slow bellies.

13This witness is true. Wherefore rebuke them sharply, that they may be sound in the faith;

14Not giving heed to Jewish fables, and commandments of men, that turn from the truth.

15Unto the pure all things *are* pure: but unto them that are defiled and unbelieving *is* nothing pure; but even their mind and conscience is defiled.

16They profess that they know God; but in works they deny *him*, being abominable, and disobedient, and unto every good work reprobate.

---

1 PAUL, A servant of God and an apostle of Jesus Christ for the faith of God's elect and the knowledge of the truth that leads to godliness— 2a faith and knowledge resting on the hope of eternal life, which God, who does not lie, promised before the beginning of time, 3and at his appointed season he brought his word to light through the preaching entrusted to me by the command of God our Savior,

4To Titus, my true son in our common faith:

Grace and peace from God the Father and Christ Jesus our Savior.

Titus' Task on Crete

5The reason I left you in Crete was that you might straighten out what was left unfinished and appoint[a] elders in every town, as I directed you. 6An elder must be blameless, the husband of but one wife, a man whose children believe and are not open to the charge of being wild and disobedient. 7Since an overseer[b] is entrusted with God's work, he must be blameless—not overbearing, not quick-tempered, not given to drunkenness, not violent, not pursuing dishonest gain. 8Rather he must be hospitable, one who loves what is good, who is self-controlled, upright, holy and disciplined. 9He must hold firmly to the trustworthy message as it has been taught, so that he can encourage others by sound doctrine and refute those who oppose it.

10For there are many rebellious people, mere talkers and deceivers, especially those of the circumcision group. 11They must be silenced, because they are ruining whole households by teaching things they ought not to teach—and that for the sake of dishonest gain. 12Even one of their own prophets has said, "Cretans are always liars, evil brutes, lazy gluttons." 13This testimony is true. Therefore, rebuke them sharply, so that they will be sound in the faith 14and will pay no attention to Jewish myths or to the commands of those who reject the truth. 15To the pure, all things are pure, but to those who are corrupted and do not believe, nothing is pure. In fact, both their minds and consciences are corrupted. 16They claim to know God, but by their actions they deny him. They are detestable, disobedient and unfit for doing anything good.

Titus

Titus

Living Bible

1 FROM: PAUL, the slave of God and the messenger of Jesus Christ.

I have been sent to bring faith to those God has chosen and to teach them to know God's truth—the kind of truth that changes lives—so that they can have eternal life, which God promised them before the world began—and he cannot lie. ³And now in his own good time he has revealed this Good News and permits me to tell it to everyone. By command of God our Savior I have been trusted to do this work for him.

⁴To: Titus, who is truly my son in the affairs of the Lord.

May God the Father and Christ Jesus our Savior give you his blessings and his peace.

⁵I left you there on the island of Crete so that you could do whatever was needed to help strengthen each of its churches, and I asked you to appoint pastors^c in every city who would follow the instructions I gave you. ⁶The men you choose must be well thought of for their good lives; they must have only one wife and their children must love the Lord and not have a reputation for being wild or disobedient to their parents.

⁷These pastors must be men of blameless lives because they are God's ministers. They must not be proud or impatient; they must not be drunkards or fighters or greedy for money. ⁸They must enjoy having guests in their homes and must love all that is good. They must be sensible men, and fair. They must be clean minded and level headed. ⁹Their belief in the truth which they have been taught must be strong and steadfast, so that they will be able to teach it to others and show those who disagree with them where they are wrong.

¹⁰For there are many who refuse to obey; this is especially true among those who say that all Christians must obey the Jewish laws. But this is foolish talk; it blinds people to the truth, ¹¹and it must be stopped. Already whole families have been turned away from the grace of God. Such teachers are only after your money. ¹²One of their own men, a prophet from Crete, has said about them, "These men of Crete are all liars; they are like lazy animals, living only to satisfy their stomachs." ¹³And this is true. So speak to the Christians there as sternly as necessary to make them strong in the faith, ¹⁴and to stop them from listening to Jewish folk tales and the demands of men who have turned their backs on the truth.

¹⁵A person who is pure of heart sees goodness and purity in everything; but a person whose own heart is evil and untrusting finds evil in everything, for his dirty mind and rebellious heart color all he sees and hears. ¹⁶Such persons claim they know God, but from seeing the way they act, one knows they don't. They are rotten and disobedient, worthless so far as doing anything good is concerned.

New Revised Standard

Salutation

1 PAUL, A servant^d of God and an apostle of Jesus Christ, for the sake of the faith of God's elect and the knowledge of the truth that is in accordance with godliness, ²in the hope of eternal life that God, who never lies, promised before the ages began— ³in due time he revealed his word through the proclamation with which I have been entrusted by the command of God our Savior,

4 To Titus, my loyal child in the faith we share: Grace^e and peace from God the Father and Christ Jesus our Savior.

Titus in Crete

5 I left you behind in Crete for this reason, so that you should put in order what remained to be done, and should appoint elders in every town, as I directed you: ⁶someone who is blameless, married only once,^f whose children are believers, not accused of debauchery and not rebellious. ⁷For a bishop,^g as God's steward, must be blameless; he must not be arrogant or quick-tempered or addicted to wine or violent or greedy for gain; ⁸but he must be hospitable, a lover of goodness, prudent, upright, devout, and self-controlled. ⁹He must have a firm grasp of the word that is trustworthy in accordance with the teaching, so that he may be able both to preach with sound doctrine and to refute those who contradict it.

10 There are also many rebellious people, idle talkers and deceivers, especially those of the circumcision; ¹¹they must be silenced, since they are upsetting whole families by teaching for sordid gain what it is not right to teach. ¹²It was one of them, their very own prophet, who said,

"Cretans are always liars, vicious brutes, lazy gluttons."

¹³That testimony is true. For this reason rebuke them sharply, so that they may become sound in the faith, ¹⁴not paying attention to Jewish myths or to commandments of those who reject the truth. ¹⁵To the pure all things are pure, but to the corrupt and unbelieving nothing is pure. Their very minds and consciences are corrupted. ¹⁶They profess to know God, but they deny him by their actions. They are detestable, disobedient, unfit for any good work.

---

d Gk slave   e Other ancient authorities read Grace, mercy,   f Gk husband of one wife   g Or an overseer

King James

2 BUT SPEAK thou the things which become sound doctrine:

2That the aged men be sober, grave, temperate, sound in faith, in charity, in patience.

3The aged women likewise, that *they be* in behaviour as becometh holiness, not false accusers, not given to much wine, teachers of good things;

4That they may teach the young women to be sober, to love their husbands, to love their children,

5*To be* discreet, chaste, keepers at home, good, obedient to their own husbands, that the word of God be not blasphemed.

6Young men likewise exhort to be sober minded.

7In all things showing thyself a pattern of good works: in doctrine *showing* uncorruptness, gravity, sincerity,

8Sound speech, that cannot be condemned; that he that is of the contrary part may be ashamed, having no evil thing to say of you.

9*Exhort* servants to be obedient unto their own masters, *and* to please *them* well in all *things;* not answering again;

10Not purloining, but showing all good fidelity; that they may adorn the doctrine of God our Saviour in all things.

11For the grace of God that bringeth salvation hath appeared to all men,

12Teaching us that, denying ungodliness and worldly lusts, we should live soberly, righteously, and godly, in this present world;

13Looking for that blessed hope, and the glorious appearing of the great God and our Saviour Jesus Christ;

14Who gave himself for us, that he might redeem us from all iniquity, and purify unto himself a peculiar people, zealous of good works.

15These things speak, and exhort, and rebuke with all authority. Let no man despise thee.

3 PUT THEM in mind to be subject to principalities and powers, to obey magistrates, to be ready to every good work,

2To speak evil of no man, to be no brawlers, *but* gentle, showing all meekness unto all men.

3For we ourselves also were sometimes foolish, disobedient, deceived, serving divers lusts and pleasures, living in malice and envy, hateful, *and* hating one another.

4But after that the kindness and love of God our Saviour toward man appeared,

5Not by works of righteousness which we have done, but according to his mercy he saved us, by the washing of regeneration, and renewing of the Holy Ghost;

6Which he shed on us abundantly through Jesus Christ our Saviour;

7That being justified by his grace, we should be made heirs according to the hope of eternal life.

8*This is* a faithful saying, and these things I will that thou affirm constantly, that they which have believed in God might be careful to maintain good works. These things are good and profitable unto men.

New International

What Must Be Taught to Various Groups

2 YOU MUST teach what is in accord with sound doctrine. 2Teach the older men to be temperate, worthy of respect, self-controlled, and sound in faith, in love and in endurance.

3Likewise, teach the older women to be reverent in the way they live, not to be slanderers or addicted to much wine, but to teach what is good. 4Then they can train the younger women to love their husbands and children, 5to be self-controlled and pure, to be busy at home, to be kind, and to be subject to their husbands, so that no one will malign the word of God.

6Similarly, encourage the young men to be self-controlled. 7In everything set them an example by doing what is good. In your teaching show integrity, seriousness 8and soundness of speech that cannot be condemned, so that those who oppose you may be ashamed because they have nothing bad to say about us.

9Teach slaves to be subject to their masters in everything, to try to please them, not to talk back to them, 10and not to steal from them, but to show that they can be fully trusted, so that in every way they will make the teaching about God our Savior attractive.

11For the grace of God that brings salvation has appeared to all men. 12It teaches us to say "No" to ungodliness and worldly passions, and to live self-controlled, upright and godly lives in this present age, 13while we wait for the blessed hope—the glorious appearing of our great God and Savior, Jesus Christ, 14who gave himself for us to redeem us from all wickedness and to purify for himself a people that are his very own, eager to do what is good.

15These, then, are the things you should teach. Encourage and rebuke with all authority. Do not let anyone despise you.

Doing What Is Good

3 REMIND THE people to be subject to rulers and authorities, to be obedient, to be ready to do whatever is good, 2to slander no one, to be peaceable and considerate, and to show true humility toward all men.

3At one time we too were foolish, disobedient, deceived and enslaved by all kinds of passions and pleasures. We lived in malice and envy, being hated and hating one another. 4But when the kindness and love of God our Savior appeared, 5he saved us, not because of righteous things we had done, but because of his mercy. He saved us through the washing of rebirth and renewal by the Holy Spirit, 6whom he poured out on us generously through Jesus Christ our Savior, 7so that, having been justified by his grace, we might become heirs having the hope of eternal life. 8This is a trustworthy saying. And I want you to stress these things, so that those who have trusted in God may be careful to devote themselves to doing what is good. These things are excellent and profitable for everyone.

Living Bible

2 BUT AS for you, speak up for the right living that goes along with true Christianity. ²Teach the older men to be serious and unruffled; they must be sensible, knowing and believing the truth and doing everything with love and patience.

³Teach the older women to be quiet and respectful in everything they do. They must not go around speaking evil of others and must not be heavy drinkers, but they should be teachers of goodness. ⁴These older women must train the younger women to live quietly, to love their husbands and their children, ⁵and to be sensible and clean minded, spending their time in their own homes, being kind and obedient to their husbands, so that the Christian faith can't be spoken against by those who know them.

⁶In the same way, urge the young men to behave carefully, taking life seriously. ⁷And here you yourself must be an example to them of good deeds of every kind. Let everything you do reflect your love of the truth and the fact that you are in dead earnest about it. ⁸Your conversation should be so sensible and logical that anyone who wants to argue will be ashamed of himself because there won't be anything to criticize in anything you say!

⁹Urge slaves to obey their masters and to try their best to satisfy them. They must not talk back, ¹⁰nor steal, but must show themselves to be entirely trustworthy. In this way they will make people want to believe in our Savior and God.

¹¹For the free gift of eternal salvation is now being offered to everyone; ¹²and along with this gift comes the realization that God wants us to turn from godless living and sinful pleasures and to live good, God-fearing lives day after day, ¹³looking forward to that wonderful time we've been expecting, when his glory shall be seen— the glory of our great God and Savior Jesus Christ. ¹⁴He died under God's judgment against our sins, so that he could rescue us from constant falling into sin and make us his very own people, with cleansed hearts and real enthusiasm for doing kind things for others. ¹⁵You must teach these things and encourage your people to do them, correcting them when necessary as one who has every right to do so. Don't let anyone think that what you say is not important.

3 REMIND YOUR people to obey the government and its officers, and always to be obedient and ready for any honest work. ²They must not speak evil of anyone, nor quarrel, but be gentle and truly courteous to all.

³Once we, too, were foolish and disobedient; we were misled by others and became slaves to many evil pleasures and wicked desires. Our lives were full of resentment and envy. We hated others and they hated us.

⁴But when the time came for the kindness and love of God our Savior to appear, ⁵then he saved us—not because we were good enough to be saved, but because of his kindness and pity—by washing away our sins and giving us the new joy of the indwelling Holy Spirit ⁶whom he poured out upon us with wonderful fullness— and all because of what Jesus Christ our Savior did ⁷so that he could declare us good in God's eyes—all because of his great kindness; and now we can share in the wealth of the eternal life he gives us, and we are eagerly looking forward to receiving it. ⁸These things I have told you are all true. Insist on them so that Christians will be careful to do good deeds all the time, for this is not only right, but it brings results.

New Revised Standard

Teach Sound Doctrine

2 BUT AS for you, teach what is consistent with sound doctrine. ²Tell the older men to be temperate, serious, prudent, and sound in faith, in love, and in endurance.

3 Likewise, tell the older women to be reverent in behavior, not to be slanderers or slaves to drink; they are to teach what is good, ⁴so that they may encourage the young women to love their husbands, to love their children, ⁵to be self-controlled, chaste, good managers of the household, kind, being submissive to their husbands, so that the word of God may not be discredited.

6 Likewise, urge the younger men to be self-controlled. ⁷Show yourself in all respects a model of good works, and in your teaching show integrity, gravity, ⁸and sound speech that cannot be censured; then any opponent will be put to shame, having nothing evil to say of us.

9 Tell slaves to be submissive to their masters and to give satisfaction in every respect; they are not to talk back, ¹⁰not to pilfer, but to show complete and perfect fidelity, so that in everything they may be an ornament to the doctrine of God our Savior.

11 For the grace of God has appeared, bringing salvation to all,ᵃ ¹²training us to renounce impiety and worldly passions, and in the present age to live lives that are self-controlled, upright, and godly, ¹³while we wait for the blessed hope and the manifestation of the glory of our great God and Savior,ᵇ Jesus Christ. ¹⁴He it is who gave himself for us that he might redeem us from all iniquity and purify for himself a people of his own who are zealous for good deeds.

15 Declare these things; exhort and reprove with all authority.ᶜ Let no one look down on you.

Maintain Good Deeds

3 REMIND THEM to be subject to rulers and authorities, to be obedient, to be ready for every good work, ²to speak evil of no one, to avoid quarreling, to be gentle, and to show every courtesy to everyone. ³For we ourselves were once foolish, disobedient, led astray, slaves to various passions and pleasures, passing our days in malice and envy, despicable, hating one another. ⁴But when the goodness and loving kindness of God our Savior appeared, ⁵he saved us, not because of any works of righteousness that we had done, but according to his mercy, through the waterᵈ of rebirth and renewal by the Holy Spirit. ⁶This Spirit he poured out on us richly through Jesus Christ our Savior, ⁷so that, having been justified by his grace, we might become heirs according to the hope of eternal life. ⁸The saying is sure.

I desire that you insist on these things, so that those who have come to believe in God may be careful to devote themselves to good works; these things are excellent and profitable to everyone. ⁹But avoid stupid con-

ᵃ Or has appeared to all, bringing salvation　ᵇ Or of the great God and our Savior　ᶜ Gk commandment　ᵈ Gk washing

King James

9But avoid foolish questions, and genealogies, and contentions, and strivings about the law; for they are unprofitable and vain.

10A man that is an heretic after the first and second admonition reject;

11Knowing that he that is such is subverted, and sinneth, being condemned of himself.

12When I shall send Artemas unto thee, or Tychicus, be diligent to come unto me to Nicopolis: for I have determined there to winter.

13Bring Zenas the lawyer and Apollos on their journey diligently, that nothing be wanting unto them.

14And let ours also learn to maintain good works for necessary uses, that they be not unfruitful.

15All that are with me salute thee. Greet them that love us in the faith. Grace be with you all. Amen.

New International

9But avoid foolish controversies and genealogies and arguments and quarrels about the law, because these are unprofitable and useless. 10Warn a divisive person once, and then warn him a second time. After that, have nothing to do with him. 11You may be sure that such a man is warped and sinful; he is self-condemned.

Final Remarks

12As soon as I send Artemas or Tychicus to you, do your best to come to me at Nicopolis, because I have decided to winter there. 13Do everything you can to help Zenas the lawyer and Apollos on their way and see that they have everything they need. 14Our people must learn to devote themselves to doing what is good, in order that they may provide for daily necessities and not live unproductive lives.

15Everyone with me sends you greetings. Greet those who love us in the faith.

Grace be with you all.

Living Bible

9Don't get involved in arguing over unanswerable questions and controversial theological ideas; keep out of arguments and quarrels about obedience to Jewish laws, for this kind of thing isn't worthwhile; it only does harm. 10If anyone is causing divisions among you, he should be given a first and second warning. After that have nothing more to do with him, 11for such a person has a wrong sense of values. He is sinning, and he knows it.

12I am planning to send either Artemas or Tychicus to you. As soon as one of them arrives, please try to meet me at Nicopolis as quickly as you can, for I have decided to stay there for the winter. 13Do everything you can to help Zenas the lawyer and Apollos with their trip; see that they are given everything they need. 14For our people must learn to help all who need their assistance, that their lives will be fruitful.

15Everybody here sends greetings. Please say "hello" to all of the Christian friends there. May God's blessings be with you all.

Sincerely, Paul

New Revised Standard

troversies, genealogies, dissensions, and quarrels about the law, for they are unprofitable and worthless. 10After a first and second admonition, have nothing more to do with anyone who causes divisions, 11since you know that such a person is perverted and sinful, being self-condemned.

Final Messages and Benediction

12 When I send Artemas to you, or Tychicus, do your best to come to me at Nicopolis, for I have decided to spend the winter there. 13Make every effort to send Zenas the lawyer and Apollos on their way, and see that they lack nothing. 14And let people learn to devote themselves to good works in order to meet urgent needs, so that they may not be unproductive.

15 All who are with me send greetings to you. Greet those who love us in the faith.

Grace be with all of you.[a]

---

a Other ancient authorities add *Amen*

THE EPISTLE OF

PAUL TO

Philemon

Philemon

¹PAUL, A prisoner of Jesus Christ, and Timothy *our* brother, unto Philemon our dearly beloved, and fellow-labourer,

²And to *our* beloved Apphia, and Archippus our fellowsoldier, and to the church in thy house:

³Grace to you, and peace, from God our Father and the Lord Jesus Christ.

⁴I thank my God, making mention of thee always in my prayers,

⁵Hearing of thy love and faith, which thou hast toward the Lord Jesus, and toward all saints;

⁶That the communication of thy faith may become effectual by the acknowledging of every good thing which is in you in Christ Jesus.

⁷For we have great joy and consolation in thy love, because the bowels of the saints are refreshed by thee, brother.

⁸Wherefore, though I might be much bold in Christ to enjoin thee that which is convenient,

⁹Yet for love's sake I rather beseech *thee*, being such an one as Paul the aged, and now also a prisoner of Jesus Christ.

¹⁰I beseech thee for my son Onesimus, whom I have begotten in my bonds:

¹¹Which in time past was to thee unprofitable, but now profitable to thee and to me:

¹²Whom I have sent again: thou therefore receive him, that is, mine own bowels:

¹³Whom I would have retained with me, that in thy stead he might have ministered unto me in the bonds of the gospel:

¹⁴But without thy mind would I do nothing; that thy benefit should not be as it were of necessity, but willingly.

¹⁵For perhaps he therefore departed for a season, that thou shouldest receive him for ever;

¹⁶Not now as a servant, but above a servant, a brother beloved, specially to me, but how much more unto thee, both in the flesh, and in the Lord?

¹⁷If thou count me therefore a partner, receive him as myself.

¹⁸If he hath wronged thee, or oweth *thee* aught, put that on mine account;

¹⁹I Paul have written *it* with mine own hand, I will repay *it:* albeit I do not say to thee how thou owest unto me even thine own self besides.

²⁰Yea, brother, let me have joy of thee in the Lord: refresh my bowels in the Lord.

²¹Having confidence in thy obedience I wrote unto thee, knowing that thou wilt also do more than I say.

²²But withal prepare me also a lodging: for I trust that through your prayers I shall be given unto you.

¹PAUL, a prisoner of Christ Jesus, and Timothy our brother,

To Philemon our dear friend and fellow worker, ²to Apphia our sister, to Archippus our fellow soldier and to the church that meets in your home:

³Grace to you and peace from God our Father and the Lord Jesus Christ.

Thanksgiving and Prayer

⁴I always thank my God as I remember you in my prayers, ⁵because I hear about your faith in the Lord Jesus and your love for all the saints. ⁶I pray that you may be active in sharing your faith, so that you will have a full understanding of every good thing we have in Christ. ⁷Your love has given me great joy and encouragement, because you, brother, have refreshed the hearts of the saints.

Paul's Plea for Onesimus

⁸Therefore, although in Christ I could be bold and order you to do what you ought to do, ⁹yet I appeal to you on the basis of love. I then, as Paul—an old man and now also a prisoner of Christ Jesus— ¹⁰I appeal to you for my son Onesimus,ᵃ who became my son while I was in chains. ¹¹Formerly he was useless to you, but now he has become useful both to you and to me.

¹²I am sending him—who is my very heart—back to you. ¹³I would have liked to keep him with me so that he could take your place in helping me while I am in chains for the gospel. ¹⁴But I did not want to do anything without your consent, so that any favor you do will be spontaneous and not forced. ¹⁵Perhaps the reason he was separated from you for a little while was that you might have him back for good— ¹⁶no longer as a slave, but better than a slave, as a dear brother. He is very dear to me but even dearer to you, both as a man and as a brother in the Lord.

¹⁷So if you consider me a partner, welcome him as you would welcome me. ¹⁸If he has done you any wrong or owes you anything, charge it to me. ¹⁹I, Paul, am writing this with my own hand. I will pay it back—not to mention that you owe me your very self. ²⁰I do wish, brother, that I may have some benefit from you in the Lord; refresh my heart in Christ. ²¹Confident of your obedience, I write to you, knowing that you will do even more than I ask.

²²And one thing more: Prepare a guest room for me, because I hope to be restored to you in answer to your prayers.

ᵃ *10 Onesimus* means *useful.*

Living Bible

Philemon

1FROM: PAUL, in jail for preaching the Good News about Jesus Christ, and from Brother Timothy.

To: Philemon, our much loved fellow worker, and to the church that meets in your home, and to Apphia our sister, and to Archippus who like myself is a soldier of the cross.

3May God our Father and the Lord Jesus Christ give you his blessings and his peace.

4I always thank God when I am praying for you, dear Philemon, 5because I keep hearing of your love and trust in the Lord Jesus and in his people. 6And I pray that as you share your faith with others it will grip their lives too, as they see the wealth of good things in you that come from Christ Jesus. 7I myself have gained much joy and comfort from your love, my brother, because your kindness has so often refreshed the hearts of God's people.

8, 9Now I want to ask a favor of you. I could demand it of you in the name of Christ because it is the right thing for you to do, but I love you and prefer just to ask you—I, Paul, an old man now, here in jail for the sake of Jesus Christ. 10My plea is that you show kindness to my child Onesimus, whom I won to the Lord while here in my chains. 11Onesimus (whose name means "Useful") hasn't been of much use to you in the past, but now he is going to be of real use to both of us. 12I am sending him back to you, and with him comes my own heart.

13I really wanted to keep him here with me while I am in these chains for preaching the Good News, and you would have been helping me through him, 14but I didn't want to do it without your consent. I didn't want you to be kind because you had to but because you wanted to. 15Perhaps you could think of it this way: that he ran away from you for a little while so that now he can be yours forever, 16no longer only a slave, but something much better—a beloved brother, especially to me. Now he will mean much more to you too, because he is not only a servant but also your brother in Christ.

17If I am really your friend, give him the same welcome you would give to me if I were the one who was coming. 18If he has harmed you in any way or stolen anything from you, charge me for it. 19I will pay it back (I, Paul, personally guarantee this by writing it here with my own hand) but I won't mention how much you owe me! The fact is, you even owe me your very soul! 20Yes, dear brother, give me joy with this loving act and my weary heart will praise the Lord.

21I've written you this letter because I am positive that you will do what I ask and even more! 22Please keep a guest room ready for me, for I am hoping that God will answer your prayers and let me come to you soon.

New Revised Standard

THE LETTER OF

PAUL TO

Philemon

Salutation

1 PAUL, A prisoner of Christ Jesus, and Timothy our brother,b

To Philemon our dear friend and co-worker, 2to Apphia our sister,c to Archippus our fellow soldier, and to the church in your house:

3 Grace to you and peace from God our Father and the Lord Jesus Christ.

Philemon's Love and Faith

4 When I remember youd in my prayers, I always thank my God 5because I hear of your love for all the saints and your faith toward the Lord Jesus. 6I pray that the sharing of your faith may become effective when you perceive all the good that wee may do for Christ. 7I have indeed received much joy and encouragement from your love, because the hearts of the saints have been refreshed through you, my brother.

Paul's Plea for Onesimus

8 For this reason, though I am bold enough in Christ to command you to do your duty, 9yet I would rather appeal to you on the basis of love—and I, Paul, do this as an old man, and now also as a prisoner of Christ Jesus.f 10I am appealing to you for my child, Onesimus, whose father I have become during my imprisonment. 11Formerly he was useless to you, but now he is indeed usefulg both to you and to me. 12I am sending him, that is, my own heart, back to you. 13I wanted to keep him with me, so that he might be of service to me in your place during my imprisonment for the gospel; 14but I preferred to do nothing without your consent, in order that your good deed might be voluntary and not something forced. 15Perhaps this is the reason he was separated from you for a while, so that you might have him back forever, 16no longer as a slave but more than a slave, a beloved brother—especially to me but how much more to you, both in the flesh and in the Lord.

17 So if you consider me your partner, welcome him as you would welcome me. 18If he has wronged you in any way, or owes you anything, charge that to my account. 19I, Paul, am writing this with my own hand: I will repay it. I say nothing about your owing me even your own self. 20Yes, brother, let me have this benefit from you in the Lord! Refresh my heart in Christ. 21Confident of your obedience, I am writing to you, knowing that you will do even more than I say.

22 One thing more—prepare a guest room for me, for I am hoping through your prayers to be restored to you.

b Gk *the brother*   c Gk *the sister*   d From verse 4 through verse 21, *you* is singular   e Other ancient authorities read *you* (plural)   f Or *as an ambassador of Christ Jesus, and now also his prisoner*   g The name Onesimus means *useful* or (compare verse 20) *beneficial*

King James

23There salute thee Epaphras, my fellowprisoner in Christ Jesus;

24Marcus, Aristarchus, Demas, Lucas, my fellow-labourers.

25The grace of our Lord Jesus Christ *be* with your spirit. Amen.

New International

23Epaphras, my fellow prisoner in Christ Jesus, sends you greetings. 24And so do Mark, Aristarchus, Demas and Luke, my fellow workers.

25The grace of the Lord Jesus Christ be with your spirit.

Living Bible

23Epaphras my fellow prisoner, who is also here for preaching Christ Jesus, sends you his greetings. 24So do Mark, Aristarchus, Demas and Luke, my fellow workers.

25The blessings of our Lord Jesus Christ be upon your spirit.

Paul

New Revised Standard

Final Greetings and Benediction

23 Epaphras, my fellow prisoner in Christ Jesus, sends greetings to you,a 24 and so do Mark, Aristarchus, Demas, and Luke, my fellow workers.

25 The grace of the Lord Jesus Christ be with your spirit.b

King James

THE EPISTLE OF

PAUL THE APOSTLE TO THE

Hebrews

1 GOD, WHO at sundry times and in divers manners spake in time past unto the fathers by the prophets, 2Hath in these last days spoken unto us by *his* Son, whom he hath appointed heir of all things, by whom also he made the worlds; 3Who being the brightness of *his* glory, and the express image of his person, and upholding all things by the word of his power, when he had by himself purged our sins, sat down on the right hand of the Majesty on high; 4Being made so much better than the angels, as he hath by inheritance obtained a more excellent name than they. 5For unto which of the angels said he at any time, Thou art my Son, this day have I begotten thee? And again, I will be to him a Father, and he shall be to me a Son? 6And again, when he bringeth in the first begotten into the world, he saith, And let all the angels of God worship him. 7And of the angels he saith, Who maketh his angels spirits, and his ministers a flame of fire. 8But unto the Son *he saith,* Thy throne, O God, *is* for ever and ever: a sceptre of righteousness *is* the sceptre of thy kingdom. 9Thou hast loved righteousness, and hated iniquity; therefore God, *even* thy God, hath anointed thee with the oil of gladness above thy fellows. 10And, Thou, Lord, in the beginning hast laid the foundation of the earth; and the heavens are the works of thine hands: 11They shall perish; but thou remainest; and they all shall wax old as doth a garment; 12And as a vesture shalt thou fold them up, and they shall be changed: but thou art the same, and thy years shall not fail. 13But to which of the angels said he at any time, Sit on my right hand, until I make thine enemies thy footstool?

New International

Hebrews

The Son Superior to Angels

1 IN THE past God spoke to our forefathers through the prophets at many times and in various ways, 2but in these last days he has spoken to us by his Son, whom he appointed heir of all things, and through whom he made the universe. 3The Son is the radiance of God's glory and the exact representation of his being, sustaining all things by his powerful word. After he had provided purification for sins, he sat down at the right hand of the Majesty in heaven. 4So he became as much superior to the angels as the name he has inherited is superior to theirs.

5For to which of the angels did God ever say,

"You are my Son;
    today I have become your Father[a]"[b]?

Or again,

"I will be his Father,
    and he will be my Son"[c]?

6And again, when God brings his firstborn into the world, he says,

"Let all God's angels worship him."[d]

7In speaking of the angels he says,

"He makes his angels winds,
    his servants flames of fire."[e]

8But about the Son he says,

"Your throne, O God, will last for ever and
        ever,
    and righteousness will be the scepter of your
        kingdom.
9You have loved righteousness and hated
        wickedness;
    therefore God, your God, has set you above
        your companions
    by anointing you with the oil of joy."[f]

10He also says,

"In the beginning, O Lord, you laid the
        foundations of the earth,
    and the heavens are the work of your hands.
11They will perish, but you remain;
    they will all wear out like a garment.
12You will roll them up like a robe;
    like a garment they will be changed.
But you remain the same,
    and your years will never end."[g]

13To which of the angels did God ever say,

"Sit at my right hand
until I make your enemies
    a footstool for your feet"[h]?

---

[a] 5 Or *have begotten you*   [b] 5 Psalm 2:7   [c] 5 2 Samuel 7:14; 1 Chron. 17:13   [d] 6 Deut. 32:43 (see Dead Sea Scrolls and Septuagint)   [e] 7 Psalm 104:4   [f] 9 Psalm 45:6,7   [g] 12 Psalm 102:25-27   [h] 13 Psalm 110:1

Living Bible

Living Bible

New Revised Standard

THE LETTER

TO THE

Hebrews

Hebrews

1 LONG AGO God spoke in many different ways to our fathers through the prophets [in visions, dreams, and even face to face[i]], telling them little by little about his plans.

2But now in these days he has spoken to us through his Son to whom he has given everything, and through whom he made the world and everything there is.

3God's Son shines out with God's glory, and all that God's Son is and does marks him as God. He regulates the universe by the mighty power of his command. He is the one who died to cleanse us and clear our record of all sin, and then sat down in highest honor beside the great God of heaven.

4Thus he became far greater than the angels, as proved by the fact that his name "Son of God," which was passed on to him from his Father, is far greater than the names and titles of the angels. 5, 6For God never said to any angel, "You are my Son, and today I have given you the honor that goes with that name."[j] But God said it about Jesus. Another time he said, "I am his Father and he is my Son." And still another time—when his firstborn Son came to earth—God said, "Let all the angels of God worship him."

7God speaks of his angels as messengers swift as the wind and as servants made of flaming fire; 8but of his Son he says, "Your Kingdom, O God, will last forever and ever; its commands are always just and right. 9You love right and hate wrong; so God, even your God, has poured out more gladness upon you than on anyone else."

10God also called him "Lord" when he said, "Lord, in the beginning you made the earth, and the heavens are the work of your hands. 11They will disappear into nothingness, but you will remain forever. They will become worn out like old clothes, 12and some day you will fold them up and replace them. But you yourself will never change, and your years will never end."

13And did God ever say to an angel, as he does to his Son, "Sit here beside me in honor until I crush all your enemies beneath your feet"?

God Has Spoken by His Son

1 LONG AGO God spoke to our ancestors in many and various ways by the prophets, 2but in these last days he has spoken to us by a Son,[k] whom he appointed heir of all things, through whom he also created the worlds. 3He is the reflection of God's glory and the exact imprint of God's very being, and he sustains[l] all things by his powerful word. When he had made purification for sins, he sat down at the right hand of the Majesty on high, 4having become as much superior to angels as the name he has inherited is more excellent than theirs.

The Son Is Superior to Angels

5 For to which of the angels did God ever say,
"You are my Son;
   today I have begotten you"?
Or again,
"I will be his Father,
   and he will be my Son"?
6And again, when he brings the firstborn into the world, he says,
"Let all God's angels worship him."
7Of the angels he says,
"He makes his angels winds,
   and his servants flames of fire."
8But of the Son he says,
"Your throne, O God,[m] is forever and ever,
   and the righteous scepter is the scepter of
     your[n] kingdom.
9 You have loved righteousness and hated
   wickedness;
therefore God, your God, has anointed you
   with the oil of gladness beyond your
     companions."
10And,
"In the beginning, Lord, you founded the
   earth,
and the heavens are the work of your hands;
11 they will perish, but you remain;
   they will all wear out like clothing;
12 like a cloak you will roll them up,
   and like clothing[o] they will be changed.
But you are the same,
   and your years will never end."
13But to which of the angels has he ever said,
"Sit at my right hand
   until I make your enemies a footstool for
     your feet"?

---

i *1:1 in visions, dreams, and even face to face,* implied. j *1:5, 6 today I have given you the honor that goes with that name,* literally, "this day I have begotten you."

k Or *the Son* l Or *bears along* m Or *God is your throne* n Other ancient authorities read *his* o Other ancient authorities lack *like clothing*

King James

¹⁴Are they not all ministering spirits, sent forth to minister for them who shall be heirs of salvation?

2 THEREFORE WE ought to give the more earnest heed to the things which we have heard, lest at any time we should let *them* slip.

²For if the word spoken by angels was stedfast, and every transgression and disobedience received a just recompence of reward;

³How shall we escape, if we neglect so great salvation; which at the first began to be spoken by the Lord, and was confirmed unto us by them that heard *him;*

⁴God also bearing *them* witness, both with signs and wonders, and with divers miracles, and gifts of the Holy Ghost, according to his own will?

⁵For unto the angels hath he not put in subjection the world to come, whereof we speak.

⁶But one in a certain place testified, saying, What is man, that thou art mindful of him? or the son of man, that thou visitest him?

⁷Thou madest him a little lower than the angels; thou crownedst him with glory and honour, and didst set him over the works of thy hands:

⁸Thou hast put all things in subjection under his feet. For in that he put all in subjection under him, he left nothing *that is* not put under him. But now we see not yet all things put under him.

⁹But we see Jesus, who was made a little lower than the angels for the suffering of death, crowned with glory and honour; that he by the grace of God should taste death for every man.

¹⁰For it became him, for whom *are* all things, and by whom *are* all things, in bringing many sons unto glory, to make the captain of their salvation perfect through sufferings.

¹¹For both he that sanctifieth and they who are sanctified *are* all of one: for which cause he is not ashamed to call them brethren,

¹²Saying, I will declare thy name unto my brethren, in the midst of the church will I sing praise unto thee.

¹³And again, I will put my trust in him. And again, Behold I and the children which God hath given me.

¹⁴Forasmuch then as the children are partakers of flesh and blood, he also himself likewise took part of the same; that through death he might destroy him that had the power of death, that is, the devil;

¹⁵And deliver them who through fear of death were all their lifetime subject to bondage.

¹⁶For verily he took not on *him the nature of* angels; but he took on *him* the seed of Abraham.

¹⁷Wherefore in all things it behooved him to be made like unto *his* brethren, that he might be a merciful and faithful high priest in things *pertaining* to God, to make reconciliation for the sins of the people.

¹⁸For in that he himself hath suffered being tempted, he is able to succour them that are tempted.

New International

¹⁴Are not all angels ministering spirits sent to serve those who will inherit salvation?

Warning to Pay Attention

2 WE MUST pay more careful attention, therefore, to what we have heard, so that we do not drift away. ²For if the message spoken by angels was binding, and every violation and disobedience received its just punishment, ³how shall we escape if we ignore such a great salvation? This salvation, which was first announced by the Lord, was confirmed to us by those who heard him. ⁴God also testified to it by signs, wonders and various miracles, and gifts of the Holy Spirit distributed according to his will.

Jesus Made Like His Brothers

⁵It is not to angels that he has subjected the world to come, about which we are speaking. ⁶But there is a place where someone has testified:

> "What is man that you are mindful of him,
>   the son of man that you care for him?
> ⁷You made him a little^a lower than the angels;
>   you crowned him with glory and honor
> ⁸   and put everything under his feet."^b

In putting everything under him, God left nothing that is not subject to him. Yet at present we do not see everything subject to him. ⁹But we see Jesus, who was made a little lower than the angels, now crowned with glory and honor because he suffered death, so that by the grace of God he might taste death for everyone.

¹⁰In bringing many sons to glory, it was fitting that God, for whom and through whom everything exists, should make the author of their salvation perfect through suffering. ¹¹Both the one who makes men holy and those who are made holy are of the same family. So Jesus is not ashamed to call them brothers. ¹²He says,

> "I will declare your name to my brothers;
>   in the presence of the congregation I will sing
>   your praises."^c

¹³And again,

> "I will put my trust in him."^d

And again he says,

> "Here am I, and the children God has given
>   me."^e

¹⁴Since the children have flesh and blood, he too shared in their humanity so that by his death he might destroy him who holds the power of death—that is, the devil— ¹⁵and free those who all their lives were held in slavery by their fear of death. ¹⁶For surely it is not angels he helps, but Abraham's descendants. ¹⁷For this reason he had to be made like his brothers in every way, in order that he might become a merciful and faithful high priest in service to God, and that he might make atonement for^f the sins of the people. ¹⁸Because he himself suffered when he was tempted, he is able to help those who are being tempted.

^a 7 Or *him for a little while;* also in verse 9   ^b 8 Psalm 8:4-6   ^c 12 Psalm 22:22   ^d 13 Isaiah 8:17   ^e 13 Isaiah 8:18   ^f 17 Or *and that he might turn aside God's wrath, taking away*

Living Bible

14No, for the angels are only spirit-messengers sent out to help and care for those who are to receive his salvation.

2 SO WE must listen very carefully to the truths we have heard, or we may drift away from them. 2For since the messages from angels have always proved true and people have always been punished for disobeying them, 3what makes us think that we can escape if we are indifferent to this great salvation announced by the Lord Jesus himself, and passed on to us by those who heard him speak?

4God always has shown us that these messages are true by signs and wonders and various miracles and by giving certain special abilities from the Holy Spirit to those who believe; yes, God has assigned such gifts to each of us.

5And the future world we are talking about will not be controlled by angels. 6No, for in the book of Psalms David says to God, "What is mere man that you are so concerned about him? And who is this Son of Man you honor so highly? 7For though you made him lower than the angels for a little while, now you have crowned him with glory and honor. 8And you have put him in complete charge of everything there is. Nothing is left out."

We have not yet seen all of this take place, 9but we do see Jesus—who for awhile was a little lower than the angels—crowned now by God with glory and honor because he suffered death for us. Yes, because of God's great kindness, Jesus tasted death for everyone in all the world.

10And it was right and proper that God, who made everything for his own glory, should allow Jesus to suffer, for in doing this he was bringing vast multitudes of God's people to heaven; for his suffering made Jesus a perfect Leader, one fit to bring them into their salvation. 11We who have been made holy by Jesus, now have the same Father he has. That is why Jesus is not ashamed to call us his brothers. 12For he says in the book of Psalms, "I will talk to my brothers about God my Father, and together we will sing his praises." 13At another time he said, "I will put my trust in God along with my brothers." And at still another time, "See, here am I and the children God gave me."

14Since we, God's children, are human beings—made of flesh and blood—he became flesh and blood too by being born in human form; for only as a human being could he die and in dying break the power of the devil who had the power of death. 15Only in that way could he deliver those who through fear of death have been living all their lives as slaves to constant dread. 16We all know he did not come as an angel but as a human being—yes, a Jew. 17And it was necessary for Jesus to be like us, his brothers, so that he could be our merciful and faithful High Priest before God, a Priest who would be both merciful to us and faithful to God in dealing with the sins of the people. 18For since he himself has now been through suffering and temptation, he knows what it is like when we suffer and are tempted, and he is wonderfully able to help us.

New Revised Standard

14Are not all angelsg spirits in the divine service, sent to serve for the sake of those who are to inherit salvation?

Warning to Pay Attention

2 THEREFORE WE must pay greater attention to what we have heard, so that we do not drift away from it. 2For if the message declared through angels was valid, and every transgression or disobedience received a just penalty, 3how can we escape if we neglect so great a salvation? It was declared at first through the Lord, and it was attested to us by those who heard him, 4while God added his testimony by signs and wonders and various miracles, and by gifts of the Holy Spirit, distributed according to his will.

Exaltation through Abasement

5 Now Godh did not subject the coming world, about which we are speaking, to angels. 6But someone has testified somewhere,

"What are human beings that you are mindful
            of them,i
    or mortals, that you care for them?j
7   You have made them for a little while lowerk
            than the angels;
    you have crowned them with glory and
            honor,l
8   subjecting all things under their feet."

Now in subjecting all things to them, Godh left nothing outside their control. As it is, we do not yet see everything in subjection to them, 9but we do see Jesus, who for a little while was made lowerm than the angels, now crowned with glory and honor because of the suffering of death, so that by the grace of Godn he might taste death for everyone.

10 It was fitting that God,h for whom and through whom all things exist, in bringing many children to glory, should make the pioneer of their salvation perfect through sufferings. 11For the one who sanctifies and those who are sanctified all have one Father.o For this reason Jesush is not ashamed to call them brothers and sisters,p 12saying,

"I will proclaim your name to my brothers and
            sisters,p
    in the midst of the congregation I will
            praise you."

13And again,

"I will put my trust in him."

And again,

"Here am I and the children whom God has
            given me."

14 Since, therefore, the children share flesh and blood, he himself likewise shared the same things, so that through death he might destroy the one who has the power of death, that is, the devil, 15and free those who all their lives were held in slavery by the fear of death. 16For it is clear that he did not come to help angels, but the descendants of Abraham. 17Therefore he had to become like his brothers and sistersp in every respect, so that he might be a merciful and faithful high priest in the service of God, to make a sacrifice of atonement for the sins of the people. 18Because he himself was tested by what he suffered, he is able to help those who are being tested.

---

g Gk *all of them*   h Gk *he*   i Gk *What is man that you are mindful of him?*
j Gk *or the son of man that you care for him?* In the Hebrew of Psalm 8.4-6
both *man* and *son of man* refer to all humankind   k Or *them only a little
lower*   l Other ancient authorities add *and set them over the works of your
hands*   m Or *who was made a little lower*   n Other ancient authorities read
apart from God   o Gk *are all of one*   p Gk *brothers*

King James

3 WHEREFORE, HOLY brethren, partakers of the heavenly calling, consider the Apostle and High Priest of our profession, Christ Jesus;

2Who was faithful to him that appointed him, as also Moses *was faithful* in all his house.

3For this *man* was counted worthy of more glory than Moses, inasmuch as he who hath builded the house hath more honour than the house.

4For every house is builded by some *man;* but he that built all things *is* God.

5And Moses verily *was* faithful in all his house, as a servant, for a testimony of those things which were to be spoken after;

6But Christ as a son over his own house; whose house are we, if we hold fast the confidence and the rejoicing of the hope firm unto the end.

7Wherefore (as the Holy Ghost saith, Today if ye will hear his voice,

8Harden not your hearts, as in the provocation, in the day of temptation in the wilderness:

9When your fathers tempted me, proved me, and saw my works forty years.

10Wherefore I was grieved with that generation, and said, They do always err in *their* heart; and they have not known my ways.

11So I sware in my wrath, They shall not enter into my rest.)

12Take heed, brethren, lest there be in any of you an evil heart of unbelief, in departing from the living God.

13But exhort one another daily, while it is called To-day; lest any of you be hardened through the deceitfulness of sin.

14For we are made partakers of Christ, if we hold the beginning of our confidence stedfast unto the end;

15While it is said, Today if ye will hear his voice, harden not your hearts, as in the provocation.

16For some, when they had heard, did provoke: howbeit not all that came out of Egypt by Moses.

17But with whom was he grieved forty years? *was it* not with them that had sinned, whose carcases fell in the wilderness?

18And to whom sware he that they should not enter into his rest, but to them that believed not?

19So we see that they could not enter in because of unbelief.

4 LET US therefore fear, lest, a promise being left *us* of entering into his rest, any of you should seem to come short of it.

2For unto us was the gospel preached, as well as unto them: but the word preached did not profit them, not being mixed with faith in them that heard *it.*

New International

Jesus Greater Than Moses

3 THEREFORE, HOLY brothers, who share in the heavenly calling, fix your thoughts on Jesus, the apostle and high priest whom we confess. 2He was faithful to the one who appointed him, just as Moses was faithful in all God's house. 3Jesus has been found worthy of greater honor than Moses, just as the builder of a house has greater honor than the house itself. 4For every house is built by someone, but God is the builder of everything. 5Moses was faithful as a servant in all God's house, testifying to what would be said in the future. 6But Christ is faithful as a son over God's house. And we are his house, if we hold on to our courage and the hope of which we boast.

Warning Against Unbelief

7So, as the Holy Spirit says:

"Today, if you hear his voice,
8 do not harden your hearts
as you did in the rebellion,
during the time of testing in the desert,
9where your fathers tested and tried me
and for forty years saw what I did.
10That is why I was angry with that generation,
and I said, 'Their hearts are always going
astray,
and they have not known my ways.'
11So I declared on oath in my anger,
'They shall never enter my rest.' "a

12See to it, brothers, that none of you has a sinful, unbelieving heart that turns away from the living God. 13But encourage one another daily, as long as it is called Today, so that none of you may be hardened by sin's deceitfulness. 14We have come to share in Christ if we hold firmly till the end the confidence we had at first. 15As has just been said:

"Today, if you hear his voice,
do not harden your hearts
as you did in the rebellion."b

16Who were they who heard and rebelled? Were they not all those Moses led out of Egypt? 17And with whom was he angry for forty years? Was it not with those who sinned, whose bodies fell in the desert? 18And to whom did God swear that they would never enter his rest if not to those who disobeyed?c 19So we see that they were not able to enter, because of their unbelief.

A Sabbath-Rest for the People of God

4 THEREFORE, SINCE the promise of entering his rest still stands, let us be careful that none of you be found to have fallen short of it. 2For we also have had the gospel preached to us, just as they did; but the message they heard was of no value to them, because those

---

a *11* Psalm 95:7-11   b *15* Psalm 95:7,8   c *18* Or *disbelieved*   d *2* Many manuscripts *because they did not share in the faith of those who obeyed*

Living Bible

3 THEREFORE, DEAR brothers whom God has set apart for himself—you who are chosen for heaven—I want you to think now about this Jesus who is God's Messenger and the High Priest of our faith.

2For Jesus was faithful to God who appointed him High Priest, just as Moses also faithfully served in God's house. 3But Jesus has far more glory than Moses, just as a man who builds a fine house gets more praise than his house does. 4And many people can build houses, but only God made everything.

5Well, Moses did a fine job working in God's house, but he was only a servant; and his work was mostly to illustrate and suggest those things that would happen later on. 6But Christ, God's faithful Son, is in complete charge of God's house. And we Christians are God's house—he lives in us!—if we keep up our courage firm to the end, and our joy and our trust in the Lord.

7, 8And since Christ is so much superior, the Holy Spirit warns us to listen to him, to be careful to hear his voice today and not let our hearts become set against him, as the people of Israel did. They steeled themselves against his love and complained against him in the desert while he was testing them. 9But God was patient with them forty years, though they tried his patience sorely; he kept right on doing his mighty miracles for them to see. 10"But," God says, "I was very angry with them, for their hearts were always looking somewhere else instead of up to me, and they never found the paths I wanted them to follow."

11Then God, full of this anger against them, bound himself with an oath that he would never let them come to his place of rest.

12Beware then of your own hearts, dear brothers, lest you find that they, too, are evil and unbelieving and are leading you away from the living God. 13Speak to each other about these things every day while there is still time, so that none of you will become hardened against God, being blinded by the glamor*c* of sin. 14For if we are faithful to the end, trusting God just as we did when we first became Christians, we will share in all that belongs to Christ.

15But *now* is the time. Never forget the warning, "*Today* if you hear God's voice speaking to you, do not harden your hearts against him, as the people of Israel did when they rebelled against him in the desert."

16And who were those people I speak of, who heard God's voice speaking to them but then rebelled against him? They were the ones who came out of Egypt with Moses their leader. 17And who was it who made God angry for all those forty years? These same people who sinned and as a result died in the wilderness. 18And to whom was God speaking when he swore with an oath that they could never go into the land he had promised his people? He was speaking to all those who disobeyed him. 19And why couldn't they go in? Because they didn't trust him.

4 ALTHOUGH GOD'S promise still stands—his promise that all may enter his place of rest—we ought to tremble with fear because some of you may be on the verge of failing to get there after all. 2For this wonderful news—the message that God wants to save us—has been given to us just as it was to those who lived in the time of Moses. But it didn't do them any good because they didn't believe it. They didn't mix it with faith. 3For only we who believe God can enter into his

New Revised Standard

Moses a Servant, Christ a Son

3 THEREFORE, BROTHERS and sisters,f holy partners in a heavenly calling, consider that Jesus, the apostle and high priest of our confession, 2 was faithful to the one who appointed him, just as Moses also "was faithful in allg God'sh house." 3 Yet Jesusi is worthy of more glory than Moses, just as the builder of a house has more honor than the house itself. 4 (For every house is built by someone, but the builder of all things is God.) 5Now Moses was faithful in all God'sh house as a servant, to testify to the things that would be spoken later. 6Christ, however, was faithful over God'sh house as a son, and we are his house if we hold firmj the confidence and the pride that belong to hope.

Warning against Unbelief

7 Therefore, as the Holy Spirit says,
 "Today, if you hear his voice,
8 do not harden your hearts as in the rebellion,
    as on the day of testing in the wilderness,
9 where your ancestors put me to the test,
    though they had seen my works 10for forty
        years.
 Therefore I was angry with that generation,
 and I said, 'They always go astray in their
        hearts,
    and they have not known my ways.'
11 As in my anger I swore,
    'They will not enter my rest.' "
12Take care, brothers and sisters,f that none of you may have an evil, unbelieving heart that turns away from the living God. 13But exhort one another every day, as long as it is called "today," so that none of you may be hardened by the deceitfulness of sin. 14For we have become partners of Christ, if only we hold our first confidence firm to the end. 15As it is said,
 "Today, if you hear his voice,
 do not harden your hearts as in the rebellion."
16Now who were they who heard and yet were rebellious? Was it not all those who left Egypt under the leadership of Moses? 17But with whom was he angry forty years? Was it not those who sinned, whose bodies fell in the wilderness? 18And to whom did he swear that they would not enter his rest, if not to those who were disobedient? 19So we see that they were unable to enter because of unbelief.

The Rest That God Promised

4 THEREFORE, WHILE the promise of entering his rest is still open, let us take care that none of you should seem to have failed to reach it. 2For indeed the good news came to us just as to them; but the message they heard did not benefit them, because they were

f Gk *brothers*   g Other ancient authorities lack *all*   h Gk *his*   i Gk *this one*
j Other ancient authorities add *to the end*   k Other ancient authorities read
it did not meet with faith in those who listened

King James

³For we which have believed do enter into rest, as he said, As I have sworn in my wrath, if they shall enter into my rest: although the works were finished from the foundation of the world.

⁴For he spake in a certain place of the seventh *day* on this wise, And God did rest the seventh day from all his works.

⁵And in this *place* again, If they shall enter into my rest.

⁶Seeing therefore it remaineth that some must enter therein, and they to whom it was first preached entered not in because of unbelief:

⁷Again, he limiteth a certain day, saying in David, Today, after so long a time; as it is said, Today if ye will hear his voice, harden not your hearts.

⁸For if Jesus had given them rest, then would he not afterward have spoken of another day.

⁹There remaineth therefore a rest to the people of God.

¹⁰For he that is entered into his rest, he also hath ceased from his own works, as God *did* from his.

¹¹Let us labour therefore to enter into that rest, lest any man fall after the same example of unbelief.

¹²For the word of God *is* quick, and powerful, and sharper than any twoedged sword, piercing even to the dividing asunder of soul and spirit, and of the joints and marrow, and *is* a discerner of the thoughts and intents of the heart.

¹³Neither is there any creature that is not manifest in his sight: but all things *are* naked and opened unto the eyes of him with whom we have to do.

¹⁴Seeing then that we have a great high priest, that is passed into the heavens, Jesus the Son of God, let us hold fast *our* profession.

¹⁵For we have not an high priest which cannot be touched with the feeling of our infirmities; but was in all points tempted like as *we are, yet* without sin.

¹⁶Let us therefore come boldly unto the throne of grace, that we may obtain mercy, and find grace to help in time of need.

5 FOR EVERY high priest taken from among men is ordained for men in things *pertaining* to God, that he may offer both gifts and sacrifices for sins:

²Who can have compassion on the ignorant, and on them that are out of the way; for that he himself also is compassed with infirmity.

³And by reason hereof he ought, as for the people, so also for himself, to offer for sins.

⁴And no man taketh this honour unto himself, but he that is called of God, as *was* Aaron.

⁵So also Christ glorified not himself to be made an high priest; but he that said unto him, Thou art my Son, today have I begotten thee.

⁶As he saith also in another *place*, Thou *art* a priest for ever after the order of Melchisedec.

New International

who heard did not combine it with faith.ᵈ ³Now we who have believed enter that rest, just as God has said,

"So I declared on oath in my anger,
'They shall never enter my rest.' "ᵃ

And yet his work has been finished since the creation of the world. ⁴For somewhere he has spoken about the seventh day in these words: "And on the seventh day God rested from all his work."ᵇ ⁵And again in the passage above he says, "They shall never enter my rest."

⁶It still remains that some will enter that rest, and those who formerly had the gospel preached to them did not go in, because of their disobedience. ⁷Therefore God again set a certain day, calling it Today, when a long time later he spoke through David, as was said before:

"Today, if you hear his voice,
do not harden your hearts."ᶜ

⁸For if Joshua had given them rest, God would not have spoken later about another day. ⁹There remains, then, a Sabbath-rest for the people of God; ¹⁰for anyone who enters God's rest also rests from his own work, just as God did from his. ¹¹Let us, therefore, make every effort to enter that rest, so that no one will fall by following their example of disobedience.

¹²For the word of God is living and active. Sharper than any double-edged sword, it penetrates even to dividing soul and spirit, joints and marrow; it judges the thoughts and attitudes of the heart. ¹³Nothing in all creation is hidden from God's sight. Everything is uncovered and laid bare before the eyes of him to whom we must give account.

Jesus the Great High Priest

¹⁴Therefore, since we have a great high priest who has gone through the heavens,ᵈ Jesus the Son of God, let us hold firmly to the faith we profess. ¹⁵For we do not have a high priest who is unable to sympathize with our weaknesses, but we have one who has been tempted in every way, just as we are—yet was without sin. ¹⁶Let us then approach the throne of grace with confidence, so that we may receive mercy and find grace to help us in our time of need.

5 EVERY HIGH priest is selected from among men and is appointed to represent them in matters related to God, to offer gifts and sacrifices for sins. ²He is able to deal gently with those who are ignorant and are going astray, since he himself is subject to weakness. ³This is why he has to offer sacrifices for his own sins, as well as for the sins of the people.

⁴No one takes this honor upon himself; he must be called by God, just as Aaron was. ⁵So Christ also did not take upon himself the glory of becoming a high priest. But God said to him,

"You are my Son;
today I have become your Father.ᵉ"ᶠ

⁶And he says in another place,

"You are a priest forever,
in the order of Melchizedek."ᵍ

ᵃ *3* Psalm 95:11; also in verse 5   ᵇ *4* Gen. 2:2   ᶜ *7* Psalm 95:7,8
ᵈ *14* Or *gone into heaven*   ᵉ *5* Or *have begotten you*   ᶠ *5* Psalm 2:7
ᵍ *6* Psalm 110:4

Living Bible

place of rest. He has said, "I have sworn in my anger that those who don't believe me will never get in," even though he has been ready and waiting for them since the world began.

4We know he is ready and waiting because it is written that God rested on the seventh day of creation, having finished all that he had planned to make.

5Even so they didn't get in, for God finally said, "They shall never enter my rest." 6Yet the promise remains and some get in—but not those who had the first chance, for they disobeyed God and failed to enter.

7But he has set another time for coming in, and that time is now. He announced this through King David long years after man's first failure to enter, saying in the words already quoted, "Today when you hear him calling, do not harden your hearts against him."

8This new place of rest he is talking about does not mean the land of Israel that Joshua led them into. If that were what God meant, he would not have spoken long afterwards about "today" being the time to get in. 9So there is a full complete rest *still waiting* for the people of God. 10Christ has already entered there. He is resting from his work, just as God did after the creation. 11Let us do our best to go into that place of rest, too, being careful not to disobey God as the children of Israel did, thus failing to get in.

12For whatever God says to us is full of living power: it is sharper than the sharpest dagger, cutting swift and deep into our innermost thoughts and desires with all their parts, exposing us for what we really are. 13He knows about everyone, everywhere. Everything about us is bare and wide open to the all-seeing eyes of our living God; nothing can be hidden from him to whom we must explain all that we have done.

14But Jesus the Son of God is our great High Priest who has gone to heaven itself to help us; therefore let us never stop trusting him. 15This High Priest of ours understands our weaknesses, since he had the same temptations we do, though he never once gave way to them and sinned. 16So let us come boldly to the very throne of God and stay there to receive his mercy and to find grace to help us in our times of need.

5 THE JEWISH high priest is merely a man like anyone else, but he is chosen to speak for all other men in their dealings with God. He presents their gifts to God and offers to him the blood of animals that are sacrificed to cover the sins of the people and his own sins too. And because he is a man he can deal gently with other men, though they are foolish and ignorant, for he, too, is surrounded with the same temptations and understands their problems very well.

4Another thing to remember is that no one can be a high priest just because he wants to be. He has to be called by God for this work in the same way God chose Aaron.

5That is why Christ did not elect himself to the honor of being High Priest; no, he was chosen by God. God said to him, "My Son, today I have honored you."h 6And another time God said to him, "You have been chosen to be a priest forever, with the same rank as Melchizedek."

New Revised Standard

not united by faith with those who listened.k 3For we who have believed enter that rest, just as Godi has said,

"As in my anger I swore,
'They shall not enter my rest,' "

though his works were finished at the foundation of the world. 4For in one place it speaks about the seventh day as follows, "And God rested on the seventh day from all his works." 5And again in this place it says, "They shall not enter my rest." 6Since therefore it remains open for some to enter it, and those who formerly received the good news failed to enter because of disobedience, 7again he sets a certain day—"today"—saying through David much later, in the words already quoted,

"Today, if you hear his voice,
    do not harden your hearts."

8For if Joshua had given them rest, Godi would not speak later about another day. 9So then, a sabbath rest still remains for the people of God; 10for those who enter God's rest also cease from their labors as God did from his. 11Let us therefore make every effort to enter that rest, so that no one may fall through such disobedience as theirs.

12 Indeed, the word of God is living and active, sharper than any two-edged sword, piercing until it divides soul from spirit, joints from marrow; it is able to judge the thoughts and intentions of the heart. 13And before him no creature is hidden, but all are naked and laid bare to the eyes of the one to whom we must render an account.

Jesus the Great High Priest

14 Since, then, we have a great high priest who has passed through the heavens, Jesus, the Son of God, let us hold fast to our confession. 15For we do not have a high priest who is unable to sympathize with our weaknesses, but we have one who in every respect has been testedi as we are, yet without sin. 16Let us therefore approach the throne of grace with boldness, so that we may receive mercy and find grace to help in time of need.

5 EVERY HIGH priest chosen from among mortals is put in charge of things pertaining to God on their behalf, to offer gifts and sacrifices for sins. 2He is able to deal gently with the ignorant and wayward, since he himself is subject to weakness; 3and because of this he must offer sacrifice for his own sins as well as for those of the people. 4And one does not presume to take this honor, but takes it only when called by God, just as Aaron was.

5 So also Christ did not glorify himself in becoming a high priest, but was appointed by the one who said to him,

"You are my Son,
    today I have begotten you";

6as he says also in another place,

"You are a priest forever,
    according to the order of Melchizedek."

---

h *5:5* *I have honored you,* literally, "begotten you." Probably the reference is to the day of Christ's resurrection.

i Gk *he*   j Or *tempted*

King James

7Who in the days of his flesh, when he had offered up prayers and supplications with strong crying and tears unto him that was able to save him from death, and was heard in that he feared;

8Though he were a Son, yet learned he obedience by the things which he suffered;

9And being made perfect, he became the author of eternal salvation unto all them that obey him;

10Called of God an high priest after the order of Melchisedec.

11Of whom we have many things to say, and hard to be uttered, seeing ye are dull of hearing.

12For when for the time ye ought to be teachers, ye have need that one teach you again which *be* the first principles of the oracles of God; and are become such as have need of milk, and not of strong meat.

13For every one that useth milk *is* unskilful in the word of righteousness: for he is a babe.

14But strong meat belongeth to them that are of full age, *even* those who by reason of use have their senses exercised to discern both good and evil.

6 THEREFORE LEAVING the principles of the doctrine of Christ, let us go on unto perfection; not laying again the foundation of repentance from dead works, and of faith toward God,

2Of the doctrine of baptisms, and of laying on of hands, and of resurrection of the dead, and of eternal judgment.

3And this will we do, if God permit.

4For *it is* impossible for those who were once enlightened, and have tasted of the heavenly gift, and were made partakers of the Holy Ghost,

5And have tasted the good word of God, and the powers of the world to come,

6If they shall fall away, to renew them again unto repentance; seeing they crucify to themselves the Son of God afresh, and put *him* to an open shame.

7For the earth which drinketh in the rain that cometh oft upon it, and bringeth forth herbs meet for them by whom it is dressed, receiveth blessing from God:

8But that which beareth thorns and briers *is* rejected, and *is* nigh unto cursing; whose end *is* to be burned.

9But, beloved, we are persuaded better things of you, and things that accompany salvation, though we thus speak.

New International

7During the days of Jesus' life on earth, he offered up prayers and petitions with loud cries and tears to the one who could save him from death, and he was heard because of his reverent submission. 8Although he was a son, he learned obedience from what he suffered 9and, once made perfect, he became the source of eternal salvation for all who obey him 10and was designated by God to be high priest in the order of Melchizedek.

Warning Against Falling Away

11We have much to say about this, but it is hard to explain because you are slow to learn. 12In fact, though by this time you ought to be teachers, you need someone to teach you the elementary truths of God's word all over again. You need milk, not solid food! 13Anyone who lives on milk, being still an infant, is not acquainted with the teaching about righteousness. 14But solid food is for the mature, who by constant use have trained themselves to distinguish good from evil.

6 THEREFORE LET us leave the elementary teachings about Christ and go on to maturity, not laying again the foundation of repentance from acts that lead to death,a and of faith in God, 2instruction about baptisms, the laying on of hands, the resurrection of the dead, and eternal judgment. 3And God permitting, we will do so.

4It is impossible for those who have once been enlightened, who have tasted the heavenly gift, who have shared in the Holy Spirit, 5who have tasted the goodness of the word of God and the powers of the coming age, 6if they fall away, to be brought back to repentance, becauseb to their loss they are crucifying the Son of God all over again and subjecting him to public disgrace.

7Land that drinks in the rain often falling on it and that produces a crop useful to those for whom it is farmed receives the blessing of God. 8But land that produces thorns and thistles is worthless and is in danger of being cursed. In the end it will be burned.

9Even though we speak like this, dear friends, we are confident of better things in your case—things that accompany salvation. 10God is not unjust; he will not for-

---

a 1 Or *from useless rituals*   b 6 Or *repentance while*

Living Bible

7Yet while Christ was here on earth he pleaded with God, praying with tears and agony of soul to the only one who would save him from [prematurec] death. And God heard his prayers because of his strong desire to obey God at all times.

8And even though Jesus was God's Son, he had to learn from experience what it was like to obey, when obeying meant suffering. 9It was after he had proved himself perfect in this experience that Jesus became the Giver of eternal salvation to all those who obey him. 10For remember that God has chosen him to be a High Priest with the same rank as Melchizedek.

11There is much more I would like to say along these lines, but you don't seem to listen, so it's hard to make you understand.

12, 13You have been Christians a long time now, and you ought to be teaching others, but instead you have dropped back to the place where you need someone to teach you all over again the very first principles in God's Word. You are like babies who can drink only milk, not old enough for solid food. And when a person is still living on milk it shows he isn't very far along in the Christian life, and doesn't know much about the difference between right and wrong. He is still a baby-Christian! 14You will never be able to eat solid spiritual food and understand the deeper things of God's Word until you become better Christians and learn right from wrong by practicing doing right.

6 LET US stop going over the same old ground again and again, always teaching those first lessons about Christ. Let us go on instead to other things and become mature in our understanding, as strong Christians ought to be. Surely we don't need to speak further about the foolishness of trying to be saved by being good, or about the necessity of faith in God; 2you don't need further instruction about baptism and spiritual giftsd and the resurrection of the dead and eternal judgment.

3The Lord willing, we will go on now to other things. 4There is no use trying to bring you back to the Lord again if you have once understood the Good News and tasted for yourself the good things of heaven and shared in the Holy Spirit, 5and know how good the Word of God is, and felt the mighty powers of the world to come, 6and then have turned against God. You cannot bring yourself to repent again if you have nailed the Son of God to the cross again by rejecting him, holding him up to mocking and to public shame.

7When a farmer's land has had many showers upon it and good crops come up, that land has experienced God's blessing upon it. 8But if it keeps on having crops of thistles and thorns, the land is considered no good and is ready for condemnation and burning off.

9Dear friends, even though I am talking like this I really don't believe that what I am saying applies to you. I am confident you are producing the good fruit that comes along with your salvation. 10For God is not un-

New Revised Standard

7 In the days of his flesh, Jesuse offered up prayers and supplications, with loud cries and tears, to the one who was able to save him from death, and he was heard because of his reverent submission. 8Although he was a Son, he learned obedience through what he suffered; 9and having been made perfect, he became the source of eternal salvation for all who obey him, 10having been designated by God a high priest according to the order of Melchizedek.

Warning against Falling Away

11 About thisf we have much to say that is hard to explain, since you have become dull in understanding. 12For though by this time you ought to be teachers, you need someone to teach you again the basic elements of the oracles of God. You need milk, not solid food; 13for everyone who lives on milk, being still an infant, is unskilled in the word of righteousness. 14But solid food is for the mature, for those whose faculties have been trained by practice to distinguish good from evil.

The Peril of Falling Away

6 THEREFORE LET us go on toward perfection,g leaving behind the basic teaching about Christ, and not laying again the foundation: repentance from dead works and faith toward God, 2instruction about baptisms, laying on of hands, resurrection of the dead, and eternal judgment. 3And we will doh this, if God permits. 4For it is impossible to restore again to repentance those who have once been enlightened, and have tasted the heavenly gift, and have shared in the Holy Spirit, 5and have tasted the goodness of the word of God and the powers of the age to come, 6and then have fallen away, since on their own they are crucifying again the Son of God and are holding him up to contempt. 7Ground that drinks up the rain falling on it repeatedly, and that produces a crop useful to those for whom it is cultivated, receives a blessing from God. 8But if it produces thorns and thistles, it is worthless and on the verge of being cursed; its end is to be burned over.

9 Even though we speak in this way, beloved, we are confident of better things in your case, things that belong to salvation. 10For God is not unjust; he will not

---

c 5:7 *premature,* implied. Christ's longing was to live until he could die on the cross for all mankind. There is a strong case to be made that Satan's great desire was that Christ should die prematurely, before the mighty work at the cross could be performed. Christ's body, being human, was frail and weak like ours (except that his was sinless). He had said just a few moments before, "My soul is exceeding sorrowful *unto death."* And can a human body live long under such pressure of spirit as he underwent in the garden, that caused sweating of great drops of blood? But God graciously heard and answered his anguished cry in Gethsemane ("Let this cup pass from me") and preserved him from seemingly imminent and premature death: for an angel was sent to strengthen him so that he could live to accomplish God's perfect will at the cross. But some readers may prefer the explanation that Christ's plea was that he be saved *out from death* at the resurrection. d 6:2 *spiritual gifts,* literally, "the laying on of hands."

e Gk *he* f Or *him* g Or *toward maturity* h Other ancient authorities read *let us do*

King James

10For God *is* not unrighteous to forget your work and labour of love, which ye have shown toward his name, in that ye have ministered to the saints, and do minister.

11And we desire that every one of you do show the same diligence to the full assurance of hope unto the end:

12That ye be not slothful, but followers of them who through faith and patience inherit the promises.

13For when God made promise to Abraham, because he could swear by no greater, he sware by himself,

14Saying, Surely blessing I will bless thee, and multiplying I will multiply thee.

15And so, after he had patiently endured, he obtained the promise.

16For men verily swear by the greater: and an oath for confirmation *is* to them an end of all strife.

17Wherein God, willing more abundantly to show unto the heirs of promise the immutability of his counsel, confirmed *it* by an oath:

18That by two immutable things, in which *it was* impossible for God to lie, we might have a strong consolation, who have fled for refuge to lay hold upon the hope set before us:

19Which *hope* we have as an anchor of the soul, both sure and stedfast, and which entereth into that within the veil;

20Whither the forerunner is for us entered, *even* Jesus, made an high priest for ever after the order of Melchisedec.

7 FOR THIS Melchisedec, king of Salem, priest of the most high God, who met Abraham returning from the slaughter of the kings, and blessed him;

2To whom also Abraham gave a tenth part of all; first being by interpretation King of righteousness, and after that also King of Salem, which is, King of peace;

3Without father, without mother, without descent, having neither beginning of days, nor end of life; but made like unto the Son of God; abideth a priest continually.

4Now consider how great this man *was*, unto whom even the patriarch Abraham gave the tenth of the spoils.

5And verily they that are of the sons of Levi, who receive the office of the priesthood, have a commandment to take tithes of the people according to the law, that is, of their brethren, though they come out of the loins of Abraham:

6But he whose descent is not counted from them received tithes of Abraham, and blessed him that had the promises.

7And without all contradiction the less is blessed of the better.

New International

get your work and the love you have shown him as you have helped his people and continue to help them. 11We want each of you to show this same diligence to the very end, in order to make your hope sure. 12We do not want you to become lazy, but to imitate those who through faith and patience inherit what has been promised.

The Certainty of God's Promise

13When God made his promise to Abraham, since there was no one greater for him to swear by, he swore by himself, 14saying, "I will surely bless you and give you many descendants."a 15And so after waiting patiently, Abraham received what was promised.

16Men swear by someone greater than themselves, and the oath confirms what is said and puts an end to all argument. 17Because God wanted to make the unchanging nature of his purpose very clear to the heirs of what was promised, he confirmed it with an oath. 18God did this so that, by two unchangeable things in which it is impossible for God to lie, we who have fled to take hold of the hope offered to us may be greatly encouraged. 19We have this hope as an anchor for the soul, firm and secure. It enters the inner sanctuary behind the curtain, 20where Jesus, who went before us, has entered on our behalf. He has become a high priest forever, in the order of Melchizedek.

Melchizedek the Priest

7 THIS MELCHIZEDEK was king of Salem and priest of God Most High. He met Abraham returning from the defeat of the kings and blessed him, 2and Abraham gave him a tenth of everything. First, his name means "king of righteousness"; then also, "king of Salem" means "king of peace." 3Without father or mother, without genealogy, without beginning of days or end of life, like the Son of God he remains a priest forever.

4Just think how great he was: Even the patriarch Abraham gave him a tenth of the plunder! 5Now the law requires the descendants of Levi who become priests to collect a tenth from the people—that is, their brothers—even though their brothers are descended from Abraham. 6This man, however, did not trace his descent from Levi, yet he collected a tenth from Abraham and blessed him who had the promises. 7And without doubt the lesser person is blessed by the greater. 8In the one case, the

a 14 Gen. 22:17

Living Bible

fair. How can he forget your hard work for him, or forget the way you used to show your love for him—and still do—by helping his children? 11And we are anxious that you keep right on loving others as long as life lasts, so that you will get your full reward.

12Then, knowing what lies ahead for you, you won't become bored with being a Christian, nor become spiritually dull and indifferent, but you will be anxious to follow the example of those who receive all that God has promised them because of their strong faith and patience.

13For instance, there was God's promise to Abraham: God took an oath in his own name, since there was no one greater to swear by, 14that he would bless Abraham again and again, and give him a son and make him the father of a great nation of people. 15Then Abraham waited patiently until finally God gave him a son, Isaac, just as he had promised.

16When a man takes an oath, he is calling upon someone greater than himself to force him to do what he has promised, or to punish him if he later refuses to do it; the oath ends all argument about it. 17God also bound himself with an oath, so that those he promised to help would be perfectly sure and never need to wonder whether he might change his plans.

18He has given us both his promise and his oath, two things we can completely count on, for it is impossible for God to tell a lie. Now all those who flee to him to save them can take new courage when they hear such assurances from God; now they can know without doubt that he will give them the salvation he has promised them.

19This certain hope of being saved is a strong and trustworthy anchor for our souls, connecting us with God himself behind the sacred curtains of heaven, 20where Christ has gone ahead to plead for us from his position as our High Priest,b with the honor and rank of Melchizedek.

7 THIS MELCHIZEDEK was king of the city of Salem, and also a priest of the Most High God. When Abraham was returning home after winning a great battle against many kings, Melchizedek met him and blessed him; 2then Abraham took a tenth of all he had won in the battle and gave it to Melchizedek.

Melchizedek's name means "Justice," so he is the King of Justice; and he is also the King of Peace because of the name of his city, Salem, which means "Peace." 3Melchizedek had no father or motherc and there is no record of any of his ancestors. He was never born and he never died but his life is like that of the Son of God—a priest forever.

4See then how great this Melchizedek is:

(a)Even Abraham, the first and most honored of all God's chosen people, gave Melchizedek a tenth of the spoils he took from the kings he had been fighting. 5One could understand why Abraham would do this if Melchizedek had been a Jewish priest, for later on God's people were required by law to give gifts to help their priests because the priests were their relatives. 6But Melchizedek was not a relative, and yet Abraham paid him.

(b)Melchizedek placed a blessing upon mighty Abraham, 7and as everyone knows, a person who has the power to bless is always greater than the person he blesses.

New Revised Standard

overlook your work and the love that you showed for his saked in serving the saints, as you still do. 11And we want each one of you to show the same diligence so as to realize the full assurance of hope to the very end, 12so that you may not become sluggish, but imitators of those who through faith and patience inherit the promises.

The Certainty of God's Promise

13 When God made a promise to Abraham, because he had no one greater by whom to swear, he swore by himself, 14saying, "I will surely bless you and multiply you." 15And thus Abraham,e having patiently endured, obtained the promise. 16Human beings, of course, swear by someone greater than themselves, and an oath given as confirmation puts an end to all dispute. 17In the same way, when God desired to show even more clearly to the heirs of the promise the unchangeable character of his purpose, he guaranteed it by an oath, 18so that through two unchangeable things, in which it is impossible that God would prove false, we who have taken refuge might be strongly encouraged to seize the hope set before us. 19We have this hope, a sure and steadfast anchor of the soul, a hope that enters the inner shrine behind the curtain, 20where Jesus, a forerunner on our behalf, has entered, having become a high priest forever according to the order of Melchizedek.

The Priestly Order of Melchizedek

7 THIS "KING Melchizedek of Salem, priest of the Most High God, met Abraham as he was returning from defeating the kings and blessed him"; 2and to him Abraham apportioned "one-tenth of everything." His name, in the first place, means "king of righteousness"; next he is also king of Salem, that is, "king of peace." 3Without father, without mother, without genealogy, having neither beginning of days nor end of life, but resembling the Son of God, he remains a priest forever.

4 See how great he is! Evenf Abraham the patriarch gave him a tenth of the spoils. 5And those descendants of Levi who receive the priestly office have a commandment in the law to collect tithesg from the people, that is, from their kindred,h though these also are descended from Abraham. 6But this man, who does not belong to their ancestry, collected tithesg from Abraham and blessed him who had received the promises. 7It is beyond dispute that the inferior is blessed by the superior.

---

b 6:20 from his position as our High Priest, literally, "having become our high priest." c 7:3 Melchizedek had no father or mother. No one can be sure whether this means that Melchizedek was Christ appearing to Abraham in human form or simply that there is no record of who Melchizedek's father and mother were, no record of his birth or death.

d Gk for his name e Gk he f Other ancient authorities lack Even g Or a tenth h Gk brothers

King James

8And here men that die receive tithes; but there he *receiveth them*, of whom it is witnessed that he liveth.

9And as I may so say, Levi also, who receiveth tithes, paid tithes in Abraham.

10For he was yet in the loins of his father, when Melchisedec met him.

11If therefore perfection were by the Levitical priesthood, (for under it the people received the law,) what further need *was there* that another priest should rise after the order of Melchisedec, and not be called after the order of Aaron?

12For the priesthood being changed, there is made of necessity a change also of the law.

13For he of whom these things are spoken pertaineth to another tribe, of which no man gave attendance at the altar.

14For *it is* evident that our Lord sprang out of Judah; of which tribe Moses spake nothing concerning priesthood.

15And it is yet far more evident: for that after the similitude of Melchisedec there ariseth another priest,

16Who is made, not after the law of a carnal commandment, but after the power of an endless life.

17For he testifieth, Thou *art* a priest for ever after the order of Melchisedec.

18For there is verily a disannulling of the commandment going before for the weakness and unprofitableness thereof.

19For the law made nothing perfect, but the bringing in of a better hope *did;* by the which we draw nigh unto God.

20And inasmuch as not without an oath *he was made priest:*

21(For those priests were made without an oath; but this with an oath by him that said unto him, The Lord sware and will not repent, Thou *art* a priest for ever after the order of Melchisedec:)

22By so much was Jesus made a surety of a better testament.

23And they truly were many priests, because they were not suffered to continue by reason of death:

24But this *man*, because he continueth ever, hath an unchangeable priesthood.

25Wherefore he is able also to save them to the uttermost that come unto God by him, seeing he ever liveth to make intercession for them.

26For such an high priest became us, *who is* holy, harmless, undefiled, separate from sinners, and made higher than the heavens;

27Who needeth not daily, as those high priests, to offer up sacrifice, first for his own sins, and then for the people's: for this he did once, when he offered up himself.

28For the law maketh men high priests which have infirmity; but the word of the oath, which was since the law, *maketh* the Son, who is consecrated for evermore.

8 NOW OF the things which we have spoken *this is* the sum: We have such an high priest, who is set on the right hand of the throne of the Majesty in the heavens;

2A minister of the sanctuary, and of the true tabernacle, which the Lord pitched, and not man.

3For every high priest is ordained to offer gifts and sacrifices: wherefore *it is* of necessity that this man have somewhat also to offer.

4For if he were on earth, he should not be a priest, seeing that there are priests that offer gifts according to the law:

New International

tenth is collected by men who die; but in the other case, by him who is declared to be living. 9One might even say that Levi, who collects the tenth, paid the tenth through Abraham, 10because when Melchizedek met Abraham, Levi was still in the body of his ancestor.

Jesus Like Melchizedek

11If perfection could have been attained through the Levitical priesthood (for on the basis of it the law was given to the people), why was there still need for another priest to come—one in the order of Melchizedek, not in the order of Aaron? 12For when there is a change of the priesthood, there must also be a change of the law. 13He of whom these things are said belonged to a different tribe, and no one from that tribe has ever served at the altar. 14For it is clear that our Lord descended from Judah, and in regard to that tribe Moses said nothing about priests. 15And what we have said is even more clear if another priest like Melchizedek appears, 16one who has become a priest not on the basis of a regulation as to his ancestry but on the basis of the power of an indestructible life. 17For it is declared:

"You are a priest forever,
in the order of Melchizedek."[a]

18The former regulation is set aside because it was weak and useless 19(for the law made nothing perfect), and a better hope is introduced, by which we draw near to God.

20And it was not without an oath! Others became priests without any oath, 21but he became a priest with an oath when God said to him:

"The Lord has sworn
and will not change his mind:
'You are a priest forever.' "[a]

22Because of this oath, Jesus has become the guarantee of a better covenant.

23Now there have been many of those priests, since death prevented them from continuing in office; 24but because Jesus lives forever, he has a permanent priesthood. 25Therefore he is able to save completely[b] those who come to God through him, because he always lives to intercede for them.

26Such a high priest meets our need—one who is holy, blameless, pure, set apart from sinners, exalted above the heavens. 27Unlike the other high priests, he does not need to offer sacrifices day after day, first for his own sins, and then for the sins of the people. He sacrificed for their sins once for all when he offered himself. 28For the law appoints as high priests men who are weak; but the oath, which came after the law, appointed the Son, who has been made perfect forever.

The High Priest of a New Covenant

8 THE POINT of what we are saying is this: We do have such a high priest, who sat down at the right hand of the throne of the Majesty in heaven, 2and who serves in the sanctuary, the true tabernacle set up by the Lord, not by man.

3Every high priest is appointed to offer both gifts and sacrifices, and so it was necessary for this one also to have something to offer. 4If he were on earth, he would not be a priest, for there are already men who offer the gifts prescribed by the law. 5They serve at a sanctuary

a 17,21 Psalm 110:4   b 25 Or forever

Living Bible

8(c)The Jewish priests, though mortal, received tithes; but we are told that Melchizedek lives on.

9(d)One might even say that Levi himself (the ancestor of all Jewish priests, of all who receive tithes), paid tithes to Melchizedek through Abraham. 10For although Levi wasn't born yet, the seed from which he came was in Abraham when Abraham paid the tithes to Melchizedek.

11(e)If the Jewish priests and their laws had been able to save us, why then did God need to send Christ as a priest with the rank of Melchizedek, instead of sending someone with the rank of Aaron—the same rank all other priests had?

12, 13, 14And when God sends a new kind of priest, his law must be changed to permit it. As we all know, Christ did not belong to the priest-tribe of Levi, but came from the tribe of Judah, which had not been chosen for priesthood; Moses had never given them that work. 15So we can plainly see that God's method changed, for Christ, the new High Priest who came with the rank of Melchizedek, 16did not become a priest by meeting the old requirement of belonging to the tribe of Levi, but on the basis of power flowing from a life that cannot end. 17And the Psalmist points this out when he says of Christ, "You are a priest forever with the rank of Melchizedek."

18Yes, the old system of priesthood based on family lines was canceled because it didn't work. It was weak and useless for saving people. 19It never made anyone really right with God. But now we have a far better hope, for Christ makes us acceptable to God, and now we may draw near to him.

20God took an oath that Christ would always be a Priest, 21although he never said that of other priests. Only to Christ he said, "The Lord has sworn and will never change his mind: You are a Priest forever, with the rank of Melchizedek." 22Because of God's oath, Christ can guarantee forever the success of this new and better arrangement.

23Under the old arrangement there had to be many priests, so that when the older ones died off, the system could still be carried on by others who took their places.

24But Jesus lives forever and continues to be a Priest so that no one else is needed. 25He is able to save completely all who come to God through him. Since he will live forever, he will always be there to remind God that he has paid for their sins with his blood.

26He is, therefore, exactly the kind of High Priest we need; for he is holy and blameless, unstained by sin, undefiled by sinners, and to him has been given the place of honor in heaven. 27He never needs the daily blood of animal sacrifices, as other priests did, to cover over first their own sins and then the sins of the people; for he finished all sacrifices, once and for all, when he sacrificed himself on the cross. 28Under the old system, even the high priests were weak and sinful men who could not keep from doing wrong, but later God appointed by his oath his Son who is perfect forever.

8 WHAT WE are saying is this: Christ, whose priesthood we have just described, is our High Priest, and is in heaven at the place of greatest honor next to God himself. 2He ministers in the temple in heaven, the true place of worship built by the Lord and not by human hands.

3And since every high priest is appointed to offer gifts and sacrifices, Christ must make an offering too. 4The sacrifice he offers is far better than those offered by the earthly priests. (But even so, if he were here on earth he wouldn't even be permitted to be a priest, because down here the priests still follow the old Jewish system of sacrifices.) 5Their work is connected with a mere earthly

New Revised Standard

8In the one case, tithes are received by those who are mortal; in the other, by one of whom it is testified that he lives. 9One might even say that Levi himself, who receives tithes, paid tithes through Abraham, 10for he was still in the loins of his ancestor when Melchizedek met him.

Another Priest, Like Melchizedek

11 Now if perfection had been attainable through the levitical priesthood—for the people received the law under this priesthood—what further need would there have been to speak of another priest arising according to the order of Melchizedek, rather than one according to the order of Aaron? 12For when there is a change in the priesthood, there is necessarily a change in the law as well. 13Now the one of whom these things are spoken belonged to another tribe, from which no one has ever served at the altar. 14For it is evident that our Lord was descended from Judah, and in connection with that tribe Moses said nothing about priests.

15 It is even more obvious when another priest arises, resembling Melchizedek, 16one who has become a priest, not through a legal requirement concerning physical descent, but through the power of an indestructible life. 17For it is attested of him,

"You are a priest forever,
    according to the order of Melchizedek."

18There is, on the one hand, the abrogation of an earlier commandment because it was weak and ineffectual 19(for the law made nothing perfect); there is, on the other hand, the introduction of a better hope, through which we approach God.

20 This was confirmed with an oath; for others who became priests took their office without an oath, 21but this one became a priest with an oath, because of the one who said to him,

"The Lord has sworn
    and will not change his mind,
'You are a priest forever' "—

22accordingly Jesus has also become the guarantee of a better covenant.

23 Furthermore, the former priests were many in number, because they were prevented by death from continuing in office; 24but he holds his priesthood permanently, because he continues forever. 25Consequently he is able for all time to savec those who approach God through him, since he always lives to make intercession for them.

26 For it was fitting that we should have such a high priest, holy, blameless, undefiled, separated from sinners, and exalted above the heavens. 27Unlike the otherd high priests, he has no need to offer sacrifices day after day, first for his own sins, and then for those of the people; this he did once for all when he offered himself. 28For the law appoints as high priests those who are subject to weakness, but the word of the oath, which came later than the law, appoints a Son who has been made perfect forever.

Mediator of a Better Covenant

8 NOW THE main point in what we are saying is this: we have such a high priest, one who is seated at the right hand of the throne of the Majesty in the heavens, 2a minister in the sanctuary and the true tente that the Lord, and not any mortal, has set up. 3For every high priest is appointed to offer gifts and sacrifices; hence it is necessary for this priest also to have something to offer. 4Now if he were on earth, he would not be a priest at all, since there are priests who offer gifts according to the law. 5They offer worship in a sanctuary

c Or *able to save completely*   d Gk lacks *other*   e Or *tabernacle*

King James

5Who serve unto the example and shadow of heavenly things, as Moses was admonished of God when he was about to make the tabernacle: for, See, saith he, *that* thou make all things according to the pattern shown to thee in the mount.

6But now hath he obtained a more excellent ministry, by how much also he is the mediator of a better covenant, which was established upon better promises.

7For if that first *covenant* had been faultless, then should no place have been sought for the second.

8For finding fault with them, he saith, Behold, the days come, saith the Lord, when I will make a new covenant with the house of Israel and with the house of Judah:

9Not according to the covenant that I made with their fathers in the day when I took them by the hand to lead them out of the land of Egypt; because they continued not in my covenant, and I regarded them not, saith the Lord.

10For this *is* the covenant that I will make with the house of Israel after those days, saith the Lord; I will put my laws into their mind, and write them in their hearts: and I will be to them a God, and they shall be to me a people:

11And they shall not teach every man his neighbour, and every man his brother, saying, Know the Lord: for all shall know me, from the least to the greatest.

12For I will be merciful to their unrighteousness, and their sins and their iniquities will I remember no more.

13In that he saith, A new *covenant*, he hath made the first old. Now that which decayeth and waxeth old *is* ready to vanish away.

9 THEN VERILY the first *covenant* had also ordinances of divine service, and a worldly sanctuary.

2For there was a tabernacle made; the first, wherein *was* the candlestick, and the table, and the showbread; which is called the sanctuary.

3And after the second veil, the tabernacle which is called the Holiest of all;

4Which had the golden censer, and the ark of the covenant overlaid round about with gold, wherein *was* the golden pot that had manna, and Aaron's rod that budded, and the tables of the covenant;

5And over it the cherubims of glory shadowing the mercyseat; of which we cannot now speak particularly.

6Now when these things were thus ordained, the priests went always into the first tabernacle, accomplishing the service *of God*.

7But into the second *went* the high priest alone once every year, not without blood, which he offered for himself, and *for* the errors of the people:

8The Holy Ghost this signifying, that the way into the holiest of all was not yet made manifest, while as the first tabernacle was yet standing:

New International

that is a copy and shadow of what is in heaven. This is why Moses was warned when he was about to build the tabernacle: "See to it that you make everything according to the pattern shown you on the mountain."[a] 6But the ministry Jesus has received is as superior to theirs as the covenant of which he is mediator is superior to the old one, and it is founded on better promises.

7For if there had been nothing wrong with that first covenant, no place would have been sought for another. 8But God found fault with the people and said[b]:

"The time is coming, declares the Lord,
    when I will make a new covenant
with the house of Israel
    and with the house of Judah.
9It will not be like the covenant
    I made with their forefathers
when I took them by the hand
    to lead them out of Egypt,
because they did not remain faithful to my
    covenant,
    and I turned away from them,
                    declares the Lord.
10This is the covenant I will make with the house
    of Israel
    after that time, declares the Lord.
I will put my laws in their minds
    and write them on their hearts.
I will be their God,
    and they will be my people.
11No longer will a man teach his neighbor,
    or a man his brother, saying, 'Know the
    Lord,'
because they will all know me,
    from the least of them to the greatest.
12For I will forgive their wickedness
    and will remember their sins no more."[c]

13By calling this covenant "new," he has made the first one obsolete; and what is obsolete and aging will soon disappear.

Worship in the Earthly Tabernacle

9 NOW THE first covenant had regulations for worship and also an earthly sanctuary. 2A tabernacle was set up. In its first room were the lampstand, the table and the consecrated bread; this was called the Holy Place. 3Behind the second curtain was a room called the Most Holy Place, 4which had the golden altar of incense and the gold-covered ark of the covenant. This ark contained the gold jar of manna, Aaron's staff that had budded, and the stone tablets of the covenant. 5Above the ark were the cherubim of the Glory, overshadowing the atonement cover.[d] But we cannot discuss these things in detail now.

6When everything had been arranged like this, the priests entered regularly into the outer room to carry on their ministry. 7But only the high priest entered the inner room, and that only once a year, and never without blood, which he offered for himself and for the sins the people had committed in ignorance. 8The Holy Spirit was showing by this that the way into the Most Holy Place had not yet been disclosed as long as the first tabernacle was still standing. 9This is an illustration for

a 5 Exodus 25:40   b 8 Some manuscripts may be translated *fault and said to the people.*   c 12 Jer. 31:31-34   d 5 Traditionally *the mercy seat*

Living Bible

model of the real tabernacle in heaven; for when Moses was getting ready to build the tabernacle, God warned him to follow exactly the pattern of the heavenly tabernacle as shown to him on Mount Sinai. 6But Christ, as a Minister in heaven, has been rewarded with a far more important work than those who serve under the old laws, because the new agreement which he passes on to us from God contains far more wonderful promises.

7The old agreement didn't even work. If it had, there would have been no need for another to replace it. 8But God himself found fault with the old one, for he said, "The day will come when I will make a new agreement with the people of Israel and the people of Judah. 9This new agreement will not be like the old one I gave to their fathers on the day when I took them by the hand to lead them out of the land of Egypt; they did not keep their part in that agreement, so I had to cancel it. 10But this is the new agreement I will make with the people of Israel, says the Lord: I will write my laws in their minds so that they will know what I want them to do without my even telling them, and these laws will be in their hearts so that they will want to obey them, and I will be their God and they shall be my people. 11And no one then will need to speak to his friend or neighbor or brother, saying, 'You, too, should know the Lord,' because everyone, great and small, will know me already. 12And I will be merciful to them in their wrongdoings, and I will remember their sins no more."

13God speaks of these new promises, of this new agreement, as taking the place of the old one; for the old one is out of date now and has been put aside forever.

9 NOW IN that first agreement between God and his people there were rules for worship and there was a sacred tent down here on earth. Inside this place of worship there were two rooms. The first one contained the golden candlestick and a table with special loaves of holy bread upon it; this part was called the Holy Place. 3Then there was a curtain and behind the curtain was a room called the Holy of Holies. 4In that room there were a golden incense-altar and the golden chest, called the ark of the covenant, completely covered on all sides with pure gold. Inside the ark were the tablets of stone with the Ten Commandments written on them, and a golden jar with some manna in it, and Aaron's wooden cane that budded. 5Above the golden chest were statues of angels called the cherubim—the guardians of God's glory—with their wings stretched out over the ark's golden cover, called the mercy seat. But enough of such details.

6Well, when all was ready the priests went in and out of the first room whenever they wanted to, doing their work. 7But only the high priest went into the inner room, and then only once a year, all alone, and always with blood which he sprinkled on the mercy seat as an offering to God to cover his own mistakes and sins, and the mistakes and sins of all the people.

8And the Holy Spirit uses all this to point out to us that under the old system the common people could not go into the Holy of Holies as long as the outer room and the entire system it represents were still in use.

New Revised Standard

that is a sketch and shadow of the heavenly one; for Moses, when he was about to erect the tent,e was warned, "See that you make everything according to the pattern that was shown you on the mountain." 6But Jesusf has now obtained a more excellent ministry, and to that degree he is the mediator of a better covenant, which has been enacted through better promises. 7For if that first covenant had been faultless, there would have been no need to look for a second one.

8 Godg finds fault with them when he says:
"The days are surely coming, says the Lord,
    when I will establish a new covenant with
        the house of Israel
    and with the house of Judah;
9 not like the covenant that I made with their
      ancestors,
    on the day when I took them by the hand to
      lead them out of the land of Egypt;
for they did not continue in my covenant,
    and so I had no concern for them, says the
      Lord.
10 This is the covenant that I will make with the
      house of Israel
    after those days, says the Lord:
I will put my laws in their minds,
    and write them on their hearts,
and I will be their God,
    and they shall be my people.
11 And they shall not teach one another
    or say to each other, 'Know the Lord,'
for they shall all know me,
    from the least of them to the greatest.
12 For I will be merciful toward their iniquities,
    and I will remember their sins no more."

13In speaking of "a new covenant," he has made the first one obsolete. And what is obsolete and growing old will soon disappear.

The Earthly and the Heavenly Sanctuaries

9 NOW EVEN the first covenant had regulations for worship and an earthly sanctuary. 2For a tente was constructed, the first one, in which were the lampstand, the table, and the bread of the Presence;h this is called the Holy Place. 3Behind the second curtain was a tente called the Holy of Holies. 4In it stood the golden altar of incense and the ark of the covenant overlaid on all sides with gold, in which were a golden urn holding the manna, and Aaron's rod that budded, and the tablets of the covenant; 5above it were the cherubim of glory overshadowing the mercy seat.i Of these things we cannot speak now in detail.

6 Such preparations having been made, the priests go continually into the first tente to carry out their ritual duties; 7but only the high priest goes into the second, and he but once a year, and not without taking the blood that he offers for himself and for the sins committed unintentionally by the people. 8By this the Holy Spirit indicates that the way into the sanctuary has not yet been disclosed as long as the first tente is still standing. 9This

e Or *tabernacle*   f Gk *he*   g Gk *He*   h Gk *the presentation of the loaves*
i Or *the place of atonement*

King James

9Which *was* a figure for the time then present, in which were offered both gifts and sacrifices, that could not make him that did the service perfect, as pertaining to the conscience;

10*Which stood* only in meats and drinks, and divers washings, and carnal ordinances, imposed *on them* until the time of reformation.

11But Christ being come an high priest of good things to come, by a greater and more perfect tabernacle, not made with hands, that is to say, not of this building;

12Neither by the blood of goats and calves, but by his own blood he entered in once into the holy place, having obtained eternal redemption *for us*.

13For if the blood of bulls and of goats, and the ashes of an heifer sprinkling the unclean, sanctifieth to the purifying of the flesh:

14How much more shall the blood of Christ, who through the eternal Spirit offered himself without spot to God, purge your conscience from dead works to serve the living God?

15And for this cause he is the mediator of the new testament, that by means of death, for the redemption of the transgressions *that were* under the first testament, they which are called might receive the promise of eternal inheritance.

16For where a testament *is*, there must also of necessity be the death of the testator.

17For a testament *is* of force after men are dead: otherwise it is of no strength at all while the testator liveth.

18Whereupon neither the first *testament* was dedicated without blood.

19For when Moses had spoken every precept to all the people according to the law, he took the blood of calves and of goats, with water, and scarlet wool, and hyssop, and sprinkled both the book, and all the people,

20Saying, This *is* the blood of the testament which God hath enjoined unto you.

21Moreover he sprinkled with blood both the tabernacle, and all the vessels of the ministry.

22And almost all things are by the law purged with blood; and without shedding of blood is no remission.

23*It was* therefore necessary that the patterns of things in the heavens should be purified with these; but the heavenly things themselves with better sacrifices than these.

24For Christ is not entered into the holy places made with hands, *which are* the figures of the true; but into heaven itself, now to appear in the presence of God for us:

25Nor yet that he should offer himself often, as the high priest entereth into the holy place every year with blood of others;

26For then must he often have suffered since the foundation of the world: but now once in the end of the world hath he appeared to put away sin by the sacrifice of himself.

27And as it is appointed unto men once to die, but after this the judgment:

New International

the present time, indicating that the gifts and sacrifices being offered were not able to clear the conscience of the worshiper. 10They are only a matter of food and drink and various ceremonial washings—external regulations applying until the time of the new order.

The Blood of Christ

11When Christ came as high priest of the good things that are already here,[a] he went through the greater and more perfect tabernacle that is not man-made, that is to say, not a part of this creation. 12He did not enter by means of the blood of goats and calves; but he entered the Most Holy Place once for all by his own blood, having obtained eternal redemption. 13The blood of goats and bulls and the ashes of a heifer sprinkled on those who are ceremonially unclean sanctify them so that they are outwardly clean. 14How much more, then, will the blood of Christ, who through the eternal Spirit offered himself unblemished to God, cleanse our consciences from acts that lead to death,[b] so that we may serve the living God!

15For this reason Christ is the mediator of a new covenant, that those who are called may receive the promised eternal inheritance—now that he has died as a ransom to set them free from the sins committed under the first covenant.

16In the case of a will,[c] it is necessary to prove the death of the one who made it, 17because a will is in force only when somebody has died; it never takes effect while the one who made it is living. 18This is why even the first covenant was not put into effect without blood. 19When Moses had proclaimed every commandment of the law to all the people, he took the blood of calves, together with water, scarlet wool and branches of hyssop, and sprinkled the scroll and all the people. 20He said, "This is the blood of the covenant, which God has commanded you to keep."[d] 21In the same way, he sprinkled with the blood both the tabernacle and everything used in its ceremonies. 22In fact, the law requires that nearly everything be cleansed with blood, and without the shedding of blood there is no forgiveness.

23It was necessary, then, for the copies of the heavenly things to be purified with these sacrifices, but the heavenly things themselves with better sacrifices than these. 24For Christ did not enter a man-made sanctuary that was only a copy of the true one; he entered heaven itself, now to appear for us in God's presence. 25Nor did he enter heaven to offer himself again and again, the way the high priest enters the Most Holy Place every year with blood that is not his own. 26Then Christ would have had to suffer many times since the creation of the world. But now he has appeared once for all at the end of the ages to do away with sin by the sacrifice of himself. 27Just as man is destined to die once, and after that to face judgment, 28so Christ was sacrificed once to take

---

Living Bible

9This has an important lesson for us today. For under the old system, gifts and sacrifices were offered, but these failed to cleanse the hearts of the people who brought them. 10For the old system dealt only with certain rituals—what foods to eat and drink, rules for washing themselves, and rules about this and that. The people had to keep these rules to tide them over until Christ came with God's new and better way.

11He came as High Priest of this better system which we now have. He went into that greater, perfect tabernacle in heaven, not made by men nor part of this world, 12and once for all took blood into that inner room, the Holy of Holies, and sprinkled it on the mercy seat; but it was not the blood of goats and calves. No, he took his own blood, and with it he, by himself, made sure of our eternal salvation.

13And if under the old system the blood of bulls and goats and the ashes of young cows could cleanse men's bodies from sin, 14just think how much more surely the blood of Christ will transform our lives and hearts. His sacrifice frees us from the worry of having to obey the old rules, and makes us want to serve the living God. For by the help of the eternal Holy Spirit, Christ willingly gave himself to God to die for our sins—he being perfect, without a single sin or fault. 15Christ came with this new agreement so that all who are invited may come and have forever all the wonders God has promised them. For Christ died to rescue them from the penalty of the sins they had committed while still under that old system.

16Now, if someone dies and leaves a will—a list of things to be given away to certain people when he dies— no one gets anything until it is proved that the person who wrote the will is dead. 17The will goes into effect only after the death of the person who wrote it. While he is still alive no one can use it to get any of those things he has promised them.

18That is why blood was sprinkled [as proof of Christ's death*] before even the first agreement could go into effect. 19For after Moses had given the people all of God's laws, he took the blood of calves and goats, along with water, and sprinkled the blood over the book of God's laws and over all the people, using branches of hyssop bushes and scarlet wool to sprinkle with. 20Then he said, "This is the blood that marks the beginning of the agreement between you and God, the agreement God commanded me to make with you." 21And in the same way he sprinkled blood on the sacred tent and on whatever instruments were used for worship. 22In fact we can say that under the old agreement almost everything was cleansed by sprinkling it with blood, and without the shedding of blood there is no forgiveness of sins.

23That is why the sacred tent down here on earth, and everything in it—all copied from things in heaven—all had to be made pure by Moses in this way, by being sprinkled with the blood of animals. But the real things in heaven, of which these down here are copies, were made pure with far more precious offerings. 24For Christ has entered into heaven itself, to appear now before God as our Friend. It was not in the earthly place of worship that he did this, for that was merely a copy of the real temple in heaven. 25Nor has he offered himself again and again, as the high priest down here on earth offers animal blood in the Holy of Holies each year. 26If that had been necessary, then he would have had to die again and again, ever since the world began. But no! He came once for all, at the end of the age, to put away the power of sin forever by dying for us. 27And just as it is destined that men die only once, and after that comes judgment, 28so also Christ died only

New Revised Standard

is a symbol*f* of the present time, during which gifts and sacrifices are offered that cannot perfect the conscience of the worshiper, 10but deal only with food and drink and various baptisms, regulations for the body imposed until the time comes to set things right.

11 But when Christ came as a high priest of the good things that have come,*g* then through the greater and perfect*h* tent*i* (not made with hands, that is, not of this creation), 12he entered once for all into the Holy Place, not with the blood of goats and calves, but with his own blood, thus obtaining eternal redemption. 13For if the blood of goats and bulls, with the sprinkling of the ashes of a heifer, sanctifies those who have been defiled so that their flesh is purified, 14how much more will the blood of Christ, who through the eternal Spirit*j* offered himself without blemish to God, purify our*k* conscience from dead works to worship the living God!

15 For this reason he is the mediator of a new covenant, so that those who are called may receive the promised eternal inheritance, because a death has occurred that redeems them from the transgressions under the first covenant.*l* 16Where a will*l* is involved, the death of the one who made it must be established. 17For a will*l* takes effect only at death, since it is not in force as long as the one who made it is alive. 18Hence not even the first covenant was inaugurated without blood. 19For when every commandment had been told to all the people by Moses in accordance with the law, he took the blood of calves and goats,*m* with water and scarlet wool and hyssop, and sprinkled both the scroll itself and all the people, 20saying, "This is the blood of the covenant that God has ordained for you." 21And in the same way he sprinkled with the blood both the tent*i* and all the vessels used in worship. 22Indeed, under the law almost everything is purified with blood, and without the shedding of blood there is no forgiveness of sins.

Christ's Sacrifice Takes Away Sin

23 Thus it was necessary for the sketches of the heavenly things to be purified with these rites, but the heavenly things themselves need better sacrifices than these. 24For Christ did not enter a sanctuary made by human hands, a mere copy of the true one, but he entered into heaven itself, now to appear in the presence of God on our behalf. 25Nor was it to offer himself again and again, as the high priest enters the Holy Place year after year with blood that is not his own; 26for then he would have had to suffer again and again since the foundation of the world. But as it is, he has appeared once for all at the end of the age to remove sin by the sacrifice of himself. 27And just as it is appointed for mortals to die once, and after that the judgment, 28so Christ, hav-

---

King James

28So Christ was once offered to bear the sins of many; and unto them that look for him shall he appear the second time without sin unto salvation.

10 FOR THE law having a shadow of good things to come, *and* not the very image of the things, can never with those sacrifices which they offered year by year continually make the comers thereunto perfect.

2For then would they not have ceased to be offered? because that the worshippers once purged should have had no more conscience of sins.

3But in those *sacrifices there is* a remembrance again *made* of sins every year.

4For *it is* not possible that the blood of bulls and of goats should take away sins.

5Wherefore when he cometh into the world, he saith, Sacrifice and offering thou wouldest not, but a body hast thou prepared me:

6In burnt offerings and *sacrifices* for sin thou hast had no pleasure.

7Then said I, Lo, I come (in the volume of the book it is written of me,) to do thy will, O God.

8Above when he said, Sacrifice and offering and burnt offerings and *offering* for sin thou wouldest not, neither hadst pleasure *therein;* which are offered by the law;

9Then said he, Lo, I come to do thy will, O God. He taketh away the first, that he may establish the second.

10By the which will we are sanctified through the offering of the body of Jesus Christ once *for all.*

11And every priest standeth daily ministering and offering oftentimes the same sacrifices, which can never take away sins:

12But this man, after he had offered one sacrifice for sins for ever, sat down on the right hand of God;

13From henceforth expecting till his enemies be made his footstool.

14For by one offering he hath perfected for ever them that are sanctified.

15*Whereof* the Holy Ghost also is a witness to us: for after that he had said before,

16This *is* the covenant that I will make with them after those days, saith the Lord, I will put my laws into their hearts, and in their minds will I write them;

17And their sins and iniquities will I remember no more.

18Now where remission of these *is, there is* no more offering for sin.

19Having therefore, brethren, boldness to enter into the holiest by the blood of Jesus,

20By a new and living way, which he hath consecrated for us, through the veil, that is to say, his flesh;

21And *having* an high priest over the house of God;

22Let us draw near with a true heart in full assurance of faith, having our hearts sprinkled from an evil conscience, and our bodies washed with pure water.

23Let us hold fast the profession of *our* faith without wavering; (for he *is* faithful that promised;)

New International

away the sins of many people; and he will appear a second time, not to bear sin, but to bring salvation to those who are waiting for him.

Christ's Sacrifice Once for All

10 THE LAW is only a shadow of the good things that are coming—not the realities themselves. For this reason it can never, by the same sacrifices repeated endlessly year after year, make perfect those who draw near to worship. 2If it could, would they not have stopped being offered? For the worshipers would have been cleansed once for all, and would no longer have felt guilty for their sins. 3But those sacrifices are an annual reminder of sins, 4because it is impossible for the blood of bulls and goats to take away sins.

5Therefore, when Christ came into the world, he said:

"Sacrifice and offering you did not desire,
    but a body you prepared for me;
6with burnt offerings and sin offerings
    you were not pleased.
7Then I said, 'Here I am—it is written about me
    in the scroll—
I have come to do your will, O God.' "[a]

8First he said, "Sacrifices and offerings, burnt offerings and sin offerings you did not desire, nor were you pleased with them" (although the law required them to be made). 9Then he said, "Here I am, I have come to do your will." He sets aside the first to establish the second. 10And by that will, we have been made holy through the sacrifice of the body of Jesus Christ once for all.

11Day after day every priest stands and performs his religious duties; again and again he offers the same sacrifices, which can never take away sins. 12But when this priest had offered for all time one sacrifice for sins, he sat down at the right hand of God. 13Since that time he waits for his enemies to be made his footstool, 14because by one sacrifice he has made perfect forever those who are being made holy.

15The Holy Spirit also testifies to us about this. First he says:

16"This is the covenant I will make with them
    after that time, says the Lord.
I will put my laws in their hearts,
    and I will write them on their minds."[b]

17Then he adds:

"Their sins and lawless acts
    I will remember no more."[c]

18And where these have been forgiven, there is no longer any sacrifice for sin.

A Call to Persevere

19Therefore, brothers, since we have confidence to enter the Most Holy Place by the blood of Jesus, 20by a new and living way opened for us through the curtain, that is, his body, 21and since we have a great priest over the house of God, 22let us draw near to God with a sincere heart in full assurance of faith, having our hearts sprinkled to cleanse us from a guilty conscience and having our bodies washed with pure water. 23Let us hold unswervingly to the hope we profess, for he who promised is faithful. 24And let us consider how we may spur

---

a 7 Psalm 40:6-8 (see Septuagint)   b 16 Jer. 31:33   c 17 Jer. 31:34

Living Bible

once as an offering for the sins of many people; and he will come again, but not to deal again with our sins.

This time he will come bringing salvation to all those who are eagerly and patiently waiting for him.

10 THE OLD system of Jewish laws gave only a dim foretaste of the good things Christ would do for us. The sacrifices under the old system were repeated again and again, year after year, but even so they could never save those who lived under their rules. 2If they could have, one offering would have been enough; the worshipers would have been cleansed once for all, and their feeling of guilt would be gone.

3But just the opposite happened: those yearly sacrifices reminded them of their disobedience and guilt instead of relieving their minds. 4For it is not possible for the blood of bulls and goats really to take away sins.d

5That is why Christ said, as he came into the world, "O God, the blood of bulls and goats cannot satisfy you, so you have made ready this body of mine for me to lay as a sacrifice upon your altar. 6You were not satisfied with the animal sacrifices, slain and burnt before you as offerings for sin. 7Then I said, 'See, I have come to do your will, to lay down my life, just as the Scriptures said that I would.' "

8After Christ said this, about not being satisfied with the various sacrifices and offerings required under the old system, 9he then added, "Here I am. I have come to give my life."

He cancels the first system in favor of a far better one. 10Under this new plan we have been forgiven and made clean by Christ's dying for us once and for all.

11Under the old agreement the priests stood before the altar day after day offering sacrifices that could never take away our sins. 12But Christ gave himself to God for our sins as one sacrifice for all time, and then sat down in the place of highest honor at God's right hand, 13waiting for his enemies to be laid under his feet. 14For by that one offering he made forever perfect in the sight of God all those whom he is making holy.

15And the Holy Spirit testifies that this is so, for he has said, 16"This is the agreement I will make with the people of Israel, though they broke their first agreement: I will write my laws into their minds so that they will always know my will, and I will put my laws in their hearts so that they will want to obey them." 17And then he adds, "I will never again remember their sins and lawless deeds."

18Now, when sins have once been forever forgiven and forgotten, there is no need to offer more sacrifices to get rid of them.

19And so, dear brothers, now we may walk right into the very Holy of Holies where God is, because of the blood of Jesus. 20This is the fresh, new, life-giving way which Christ has opened up for us by tearing the curtain—his human body—to let us into the holy presence of God.

21And since this great High Priest of ours rules over God's household, 22let us go right in, to God himself, with true hearts fully trusting him to receive us, because we have been sprinkled with Christ's blood to make us clean, and because our bodies have been washed with pure water.

23Now we can look forward to the salvation God has promised us. There is no longer any room for doubt, and we can tell others that salvation is ours, for there is no question that he will do what he says.

New Revised Standard

ing been offered once to bear the sins of many, will appear a second time, not to deal with sin, but to save those who are eagerly waiting for him.

Christ's Sacrifice Once for All

10 SINCE THE law has only a shadow of the good things to come and not the true form of these realities, ite can never, by the same sacrifices that are continually offered year after year, make perfect those who approach. 2Otherwise, would they not have ceased being offered, since the worshipers, cleansed once for all, would no longer have any consciousness of sin? 3But in these sacrifices there is a reminder of sin year after year. 4For it is impossible for the blood of bulls and goats to take away sins. 5Consequently, when Christf came into the world, he said,

"Sacrifices and offerings you have not desired,
    but a body you have prepared for me;
6 in burnt offerings and sin offerings
    you have taken no pleasure.
7 Then I said, 'See, God, I have come to do
    your will, O God'
    (in the scroll of the bookg it is written of
    me)."

8When he said above, "You have neither desired nor taken pleasure in sacrifices and offerings and burnt offerings and sin offerings" (these are offered according to the law), 9then he added, "See, I have come to do your will." He abolishes the first in order to establish the second. 10And it is by God's willh that we have been sanctified through the offering of the body of Jesus Christ once for all.

11 And every priest stands day after day at his service, offering again and again the same sacrifices that can never take away sins. 12But when Christi had offered for all time a single sacrifice for sins, "he sat down at the right hand of God," 13and since then has been waiting "until his enemies would be made a footstool for his feet." 14For by a single offering he has perfected for all time those who are sanctified. 15And the Holy Spirit also testifies to us, for after saying,

16 "This is the covenant that I will make with
        them
    after those days, says the Lord:
    I will put my laws in their hearts,
    and I will write them on their minds,"

17he also adds,

    "I will rememberi their sins and their lawless
        deeds no more."

18Where there is forgiveness of these, there is no longer any offering for sin.

A Call to Persevere

19 Therefore, my friends,k since we have confidence to enter the sanctuary by the blood of Jesus, 20by the new and living way that he opened for us through the curtain (that is, through his flesh), 21and since we have a great priest over the house of God, 22let us approach with a true heart in full assurance of faith, with our hearts sprinkled clean from an evil conscience and our bodies washed with pure water. 23Let us hold fast to the confession of our hope without wavering, for he who has promised is faithful. 24And let us consider how to pro-

---

d 10:4 The blood of bulls and goats merely covered over the sins, taking them out of sight for hundreds of years until Jesus Christ came to die on the cross. There he gave his own blood which forever took those sins away.

e Other ancient authorities read they   f Gk he   g Meaning of Gk uncertain   h Gk by that will   i Gk this one   j Gk on their minds and I will remember   k Gk Therefore, brothers

King James

24And let us consider one another to provoke unto love and to good works:

25Not forsaking the assembling of ourselves together, as the manner of some *is;* but exhorting *one another:* and so much the more, as ye see the day approaching.

26For if we sin wilfully after that we have received the knowledge of the truth, there remaineth no more sacrifice for sins,

27But a certain fearful looking for of judgment and fiery indignation, which shall devour the adversaries.

28He that despised Moses' law died without mercy under two or three witnesses:

29Of how much sorer punishment, suppose ye, shall he be thought worthy, who hath trodden under foot the Son of God, and hath counted the blood of the covenant, wherewith he was sanctified, an unholy thing, and hath done despite unto the Spirit of grace?

30For we know him that hath said, Vengeance *belongeth* unto me, I will recompense, saith the Lord. And again, The Lord shall judge his people.

31*It is* a fearful thing to fall into the hands of the living God.

32But call to remembrance the former days, in which, after ye were illuminated, ye endured a great fight of afflictions;

33Partly, whilst ye were made a gazingstock both by reproaches and afflictions; and partly, whilst ye became companions of them that were so used.

34For ye had compassion of me in my bonds, and took joyfully the spoiling of your goods, knowing in yourselves that ye have in heaven a better and an enduring substance.

35Cast not away therefore your confidence, which hath great recompence of reward.

36For ye have need of patience, that, after ye have done the will of God, ye might receive the promise.

37For yet a little while, and he that shall come will come, and will not tarry.

38Now the just shall live by faith: but if *any man* draw back, my soul shall have no pleasure in him.

39But we are not of them who draw back unto perdition; but of them that believe to the saving of the soul.

11 NOW FAITH is the substance of things hoped for, the evidence of things not seen.

2For by it the elders obtained a good report.

3Through faith we understand that the worlds were framed by the word of God, so that things which are seen were not made of things which do appear.

4By faith Abel offered unto God a more excellent sacrifice than Cain, by which he obtained witness that he was righteous, God testifying of his gifts: and by it he being dead yet speaketh.

5By faith Enoch was translated that he should not see death; and was not found, because God had translated him: for before his translation he had this testimony, that he pleased God.

6But without faith *it is* impossible to please *him:* for he that cometh to God must believe that he is, and *that* he is a rewarder of them that diligently seek him.

New International

one another on toward love and good deeds. 25Let us not give up meeting together, as some are in the habit of doing, but let us encourage one another—and all the more as you see the Day approaching.

26If we deliberately keep on sinning after we have received the knowledge of the truth, no sacrifice for sins is left, 27but only a fearful expectation of judgment and of raging fire that will consume the enemies of God. 28Anyone who rejected the law of Moses died without mercy on the testimony of two or three witnesses. 29How much more severely do you think a man deserves to be punished who has trampled the Son of God under foot, who has treated as an unholy thing the blood of the covenant that sanctified him, and who has insulted the Spirit of grace? 30For we know him who said, "It is mine to avenge; I will repay,"[a] and again, "The Lord will judge his people."[b] 31It is a dreadful thing to fall into the hands of the living God.

32Remember those earlier days after you had received the light, when you stood your ground in a great contest in the face of suffering. 33Sometimes you were publicly exposed to insult and persecution; at other times you stood side by side with those who were so treated. 34You sympathized with those in prison and joyfully accepted the confiscation of your property, because you knew that you yourselves had better and lasting possessions.

35So do not throw away your confidence; it will be richly rewarded. 36You need to persevere so that when you have done the will of God, you will receive what he has promised. 37For in just a very little while,

"He who is coming will come and will not
      delay.
38   But my righteous one[c] will live by faith.
   And if he shrinks back,
     I will not be pleased with him."[d]

39But we are not of those who shrink back and are destroyed, but of those who believe and are saved.

By Faith

11 NOW FAITH is being sure of what we hope for and certain of what we do not see. 2This is what the ancients were commended for.

3By faith we understand that the universe was formed at God's command, so that what is seen was not made out of what was visible.

4By faith Abel offered God a better sacrifice than Cain did. By faith he was commended as a righteous man, when God spoke well of his offerings. And by faith he still speaks, even though he is dead.

5By faith Enoch was taken from this life, so that he did not experience death; he could not be found, because God had taken him away. For before he was taken, he was commended as one who pleased God. 6And without faith it is impossible to please God, because anyone who comes to him must believe that he exists and that he rewards those who earnestly seek him.

---

a *30* Deut. 32:35   b *30* Deut. 32:36; Psalm 135:14   c *38* One early manuscript *But the righteous*   d *38* Hab. 2:3,4

Living Bible

24In response to all he has done for us, let us outdo each other in being helpful and kind to each other and in doing good.

25Let us not neglect our church meetings, as some people do, but encourage and warn each other, especially now that the day of his coming back again is drawing near.

26If anyone sins deliberately by rejecting the Savior after knowing the truth of forgiveness, this sin is not covered by Christ's death; there is no way to get rid of it. 27There will be nothing to look forward to but the terrible punishment of God's awful anger which will consume all his enemies. 28A man who refused to obey the laws given by Moses was killed without mercy if there were two or three witnesses to his sin. 29Think how much more terrible the punishment will be for those who have trampled underfoot the Son of God and treated his cleansing blood as though it were common and unhallowed, and insulted and outraged the Holy Spirit who brings God's mercy to his people.

30For we know him who said, "Justice belongs to me; I will repay them"; who also said, "The Lord himself will handle these cases." 31It is a fearful thing to fall into the hands of the living God.

32Don't ever forget those wonderful days when you first learned about Christ. Remember how you kept right on with the Lord even though it meant terrible suffering. 33Sometimes you were laughed at and beaten, and sometimes you watched and sympathized with others suffering the same things. 34You suffered with those thrown into jail, and you were actually joyful when all you owned was taken from you, knowing that better things were awaiting you in heaven, things that would be yours forever.

35Do not let this happy trust in the Lord die away, no matter what happens. Remember your reward! 36You need to keep on patiently doing God's will if you want him to do for you all that he has promised. 37His coming will not be delayed much longer. 38And those whose faith has made them good in God's sight must live by faith, trusting him in everything. Otherwise, if they shrink back, God will have no pleasure in them.

39But we have never turned our backs on God and sealed our fate. No, our faith in him assures our souls' salvation.

11 WHAT IS faith? It is the confident assurance that something we want is going to happen. It is the certainty that what we hope for is waiting for us, even though we cannot see it up ahead. 2Men of God in days of old were famous for their faith.

3By faith—by believing God—we know that the world and the stars—in fact, all things—were made at God's command; and that they were all made from things that can't be seen.e

4It was by faith that Abel obeyed God and brought an offering that pleased God more than Cain's offering did. God accepted Abel and proved it by accepting his gift; and though Abel is long dead, we can still learn lessons from him about trusting God.

5Enoch trusted God too, and that is why God took him away to heaven without dying; suddenly he was gone because God took him. Before this happened God had saidf how pleased he was with Enoch. 6You can never please God without faith, without depending on him. Anyone who wants to come to God must believe that there is a God and that he rewards those who sincerely look for him.

New Revised Standard

voke one another to love and good deeds, 25not neglecting to meet together, as is the habit of some, but encouraging one another, and all the more as you see the Day approaching.

26 For if we willfully persist in sin after having received the knowledge of the truth, there no longer remains a sacrifice for sins, 27but a fearful prospect of judgment, and a fury of fire that will consume the adversaries. 28Anyone who has violated the law of Moses dies without mercy "on the testimony of two or three witnesses." 29How much worse punishment do you think will be deserved by those who have spurned the Son of God, profaned the blood of the covenant by which they were sanctified, and outraged the Spirit of grace? 30For we know the one who said, "Vengeance is mine, I will repay." And again, "The Lord will judge his people." 31It is a fearful thing to fall into the hands of the living God.

32 But recall those earlier days when, after you had been enlightened, you endured a hard struggle with sufferings, 33sometimes being publicly exposed to abuse and persecution, and sometimes being partners with those so treated. 34For you had compassion for those who were in prison, and you cheerfully accepted the plundering of your possessions, knowing that you yourselves possessed something better and more lasting. 35Do not, therefore, abandon that confidence of yours; it brings a great reward. 36For you need endurance, so that when you have done the will of God, you may receive what was promised.

37 For yet "in a very little while,
         the one who is coming will come and will
              not delay;
38 but my righteous one will live by faith.
         My soul takes no pleasure in anyone who
              shrinks back."

39But we are not among those who shrink back and so are lost, but among those who have faith and so are saved.

The Meaning of Faith

11 NOW FAITH is the assurance of things hoped for, the conviction of things not seen. 2Indeed, by faithg our ancestors received approval. 3By faith we understand that the worlds were prepared by the word of God, so that what is seen was made from things that are not visible.h

The Examples of Abel, Enoch, and Noah

4 By faith Abel offered to God a more acceptablei sacrifice than Cain's. Through this he received approval as righteous, God himself giving approval to his gifts; he died, but through his faithj he still speaks. 5By faith Enoch was taken so that he did not experience death; and "he was not found, because God had taken him." For it was attested before he was taken away that "he had pleased God." 6And without faith it is impossible to please God, for whoever would approach him must believe that he exists and that he rewards those who seek him. 7By faith Noah, warned by God about events as yet

---

e *11:3 things that can't be seen.* Perhaps the reference is to atoms, electrons, etc.   f *11:5 God had said,* implied.

g Gk *by this*   h Or *was not made out of visible things*   i Gk *greater*   j Gk *through it*

King James

7By faith Noah, being warned of God of things not seen as yet, moved with fear, prepared an ark to the saving of his house; by the which he condemned the world, and became heir of the righteousness which is by faith.

8By faith Abraham, when he was called to go out into a place which he should after receive for an inheritance, obeyed; and he went out, not knowing whither he went.

9By faith he sojourned in the land of promise, as *in* a strange country, dwelling in tabernacles with Isaac and Jacob, the heirs with him of the same promise:

10For he looked for a city which hath foundations, whose builder and maker *is* God.

11Through faith also Sarah herself received strength to conceive seed, and was delivered of a child when she was past age, because she judged him faithful who had promised.

12Therefore sprang there even of one, and him as good as dead, *so many* as the stars of the sky in multitude, and as the sand which is by the sea shore innumerable.

13These all died in faith, not having received the promises, but having seen them afar off, and were persuaded of *them,* and embraced *them,* and confessed that they were strangers and pilgrims on the earth.

14For they that say such things declare plainly that they seek a country.

15And truly, if they had been mindful of that *country* from whence they came out, they might have had opportunity to have returned.

16But now they desire a better *country,* that is, an heavenly: wherefore God is not ashamed to be called their God: for he hath prepared for them a city.

17By faith Abraham, when he was tried, offered up Isaac: and he that had received the promises offered up his only begotten *son,*

18Of whom it was said, That in Isaac shall thy seed be called:

19Accounting that God *was* able to raise *him* up, even from the dead; from whence also he received him in a figure.

20By faith Isaac blessed Jacob and Esau concerning things to come.

21By faith Jacob, when he was a-dying, blessed both the sons of Joseph; and worshipped, *leaning* upon the top of his staff.

22By faith Joseph, when he died, made mention of the departing of the children of Israel; and gave commandment concerning his bones.

23By faith Moses, when he was born, was hid three months of his parents, because they saw *he was* a proper child; and they were not afraid of the king's commandment.

24By faith Moses, when he was come to years, refused to be called the son of Pharaoh's daughter;

25Choosing rather to suffer affliction with the people of God, than to enjoy the pleasures of sin for a season;

26Esteeming the reproach of Christ greater riches than the treasures in Egypt: for he had respect unto the recompence of the reward.

27By faith he forsook Egypt, not fearing the wrath of the king: for he endured, as seeing him who is invisible.

New International

7By faith Noah, when warned about things not yet seen, in holy fear built an ark to save his family. By his faith he condemned the world and became heir of the righteousness that comes by faith.

8By faith Abraham, when called to go to a place he would later receive as his inheritance, obeyed and went, even though he did not know where he was going. 9By faith he made his home in the promised land like a stranger in a foreign country; he lived in tents, as did Isaac and Jacob, who were heirs with him of the same promise. 10For he was looking forward to the city with foundations, whose architect and builder is God.

11By faith Abraham, even though he was past age— and Sarah herself was barren—was enabled to become a father because hea considered him faithful who had made the promise. 12And so from this one man, and he as good as dead, came descendants as numerous as the stars in the sky and as countless as the sand on the seashore.

13All these people were still living by faith when they died. They did not receive the things promised; they only saw them and welcomed them from a distance. And they admitted that they were aliens and strangers on earth. 14People who say such things show that they are looking for a country of their own. 15If they had been thinking of the country they had left, they would have had opportunity to return. 16Instead, they were longing for a better country—a heavenly one. Therefore God is not ashamed to be called their God, for he has prepared a city for them.

17By faith Abraham, when God tested him, offered Isaac as a sacrifice. He who had received the promises was about to sacrifice his one and only son, 18even though God had said to him, "It is through Isaac that your offspringb will be reckoned."c 19Abraham reasoned that God could raise the dead, and figuratively speaking, he did receive Isaac back from death.

20By faith Isaac blessed Jacob and Esau in regard to their future.

21By faith Jacob, when he was dying, blessed each of Joseph's sons, and worshiped as he leaned on the top of his staff.

22By faith Joseph, when his end was near, spoke about the exodus of the Israelites from Egypt and gave instructions about his bones.

23By faith Moses' parents hid him for three months after he was born, because they saw he was no ordinary child, and they were not afraid of the king's edict.

24By faith Moses, when he had grown up, refused to be known as the son of Pharaoh's daughter. 25He chose to be mistreated along with the people of God rather than to enjoy the pleasures of sin for a short time. 26He regarded disgrace for the sake of Christ as of greater value than the treasures of Egypt, because he was looking ahead to his reward. 27By faith he left Egypt, not fearing the king's anger; he persevered because he saw him who is invisible. 28By faith he kept the Passover and the

Living Bible

7Noah was another who trusted God. When he heard God's warning about the future, Noah believed him even though there was then no sign of a flood, and wasting no time, he built the ark and saved his family. Noah's belief in God was in direct contrast to the sin and disbelief of the rest of the world—which refused to obey—and because of his faith he became one of those whom God has accepted.

8Abraham trusted God, and when God told him to leave home and go far away to another land which he promised to give him, Abraham obeyed. Away he went, not even knowing where he was going. 9And even when he reached God's promised land, he lived in tents like a mere visitor, as did Isaac and Jacob, to whom God gave the same promise. 10Abraham did this because he was confidently waiting for God to bring him to that strong heavenly city whose designer and builder is God.

11Sarah, too, had faith, and because of this she was able to become a mother in spite of her old age, for she realized that God, who gave her his promise, would certainly do what he said. 12And so a whole nation came from Abraham, who was too old to have even one child—a nation with so many millions of people that, like the stars of the sky and the sand on the ocean shores, there is no way to count them.

13These men of faith I have mentioned died without ever receiving all that God had promised them; but they saw it all awaiting them on ahead and were glad, for they agreed that this earth was not their real home but that they were just strangers visiting down here. 14And quite obviously when they talked like that, they were looking forward to their real home in heaven.

15If they had wanted to, they could have gone back to the good things of this world. 16But they didn't want to. They were living for heaven. And now God is not ashamed to be called their God, for he has made a heavenly city for them.

17While God was testing him, Abraham still trusted in God and his promises, and so he offered up his son Isaac, and was ready to slay him on the altar of sacrifice; 18yes, to slay even Isaac, through whom God had promised to give Abraham a whole nation of descendants!

19He believed that if Isaac died God would bring him back to life again; and that is just about what happened, for as far as Abraham was concerned, Isaac was doomed to death, but he came back again alive! 20It was by faith that Isaac knew God would give future blessings to his two sons, Jacob and Esau.

21By faith Jacob, when he was old and dying, blessed each of Joseph's two sons as he stood and prayed, leaning on the top of his cane.

22And it was by faith that Joseph, as he neared the end of his life, confidently spoke of God bringing the people of Israel out of Egypt; and he was so sure of it that he made them promise to carry his bones with them when they left!

23Moses' parents had faith too. When they saw that God had given them an unusual child, they trusted that God would save him from the death the king commanded, and they hid him for three months, and were not afraid.

24, 25It was by faith that Moses, when he grew up, refused to be treated as the grandson of the king, but chose to share ill-treatment with God's people instead of enjoying the fleeting pleasures of sin. 26He thought that it was better to suffer for the promised Christ than to own all the treasures of Egypt, for he was looking forward to the great reward that God would give him. 27And it was because he trusted God that he left the land of Egypt and wasn't afraid of the king's anger. Moses kept right on going; it seemed as though he could see God right there with him. 28And it was because he believed God

New Revised Standard

unseen, respected the warning and built an ark to save his household; by this he condemned the world and became an heir to the righteousness that is in accordance with faith.

The Faith of Abraham

8 By faith Abraham obeyed when he was called to set out for a place that he was to receive as an inheritance; and he set out, not knowing where he was going. 9By faith he stayed for a time in the land he had been promised, as in a foreign land, living in tents, as did Isaac and Jacob, who were heirs with him of the same promise. 10For he looked forward to the city that has foundations, whose architect and builder is God. 11By faith he received power of procreation, even though he was too old—and Sarah herself was barren—because he considered him faithful who had promised.d 12Therefore from one person, and this one as good as dead, descendants were born, "as many as the stars of heaven and as the innumerable grains of sand by the seashore."

13 All of these died in faith without having received the promises, but from a distance they saw and greeted them. They confessed that they were strangers and foreigners on the earth, 14for people who speak in this way make it clear that they are seeking a homeland. 15If they had been thinking of the land that they had left behind, they would have had opportunity to return. 16But as it is, they desire a better country, that is, a heavenly one. Therefore God is not ashamed to be called their God; indeed, he has prepared a city for them.

17 By faith Abraham, when put to the test, offered up Isaac. He who had received the promises was ready to offer up his only son, 18of whom he had been told, "It is through Isaac that descendants shall be named for you." 19He considered the fact that God is able even to raise someone from the dead—and figuratively speaking, he did receive him back. 20By faith Isaac invoked blessings for the future on Jacob and Esau. 21By faith Jacob, when dying, blessed each of the sons of Joseph, "bowing in worship over the top of his staff." 22By faith Joseph, at the end of his life, made mention of the exodus of the Israelites and gave instructions about his burial.e

The Faith of Moses

23 By faith Moses was hidden by his parents for three months after his birth, because they saw that the child was beautiful; and they were not afraid of the king's edict.f 24By faith Moses, when he was grown up, refused to be called a son of Pharaoh's daughter, 25choosing rather to share ill-treatment with the people of God than to enjoy the fleeting pleasures of sin. 26He considered abuse suffered for the Christg to be greater wealth than the treasures of Egypt, for he was looking ahead to the reward. 27By faith he left Egypt, unafraid of the king's anger; for he persevered as thoughh he saw him who is invisible. 28By faith he kept the Passover and

---

d Other ancient authorities read *By faith Sarah herself, though barren, received power to conceive, even when she was too old, because she considered him faithful who had promised.*   e Gk *his bones*   f Other ancient authorities add *By faith Moses, when he was grown up, killed the Egyptian, because he observed the humiliation of his people* (Gk *brothers*)   g Or *the Messiah*   h Or *because*

King James

28Through faith he kept the passover, and the sprinkling of blood, lest he that destroyed the firstborn should touch them.

29By faith they passed through the Red sea as by dry *land:* which the Egyptians assaying to do were drowned.

30By faith the walls of Jericho fell down, after they were compassed about seven days.

31By faith the harlot Rahab perished not with them that believed not, when she had received the spies with peace.

32And what shall I more say? for the time would fail me to tell of Gedeon, and *of* Barak, and *of* Samson, and *of* Jephthae; *of* David also, and Samuel, and *of* the prophets:

33Who through faith subdued kingdoms, wrought righteousness, obtained promises, stopped the mouths of lions,

34Quenched the violence of fire, escaped the edge of the sword, out of weakness were made strong, waxed valiant in fight, turned to flight the armies of the aliens.

35Women received their dead raised to life again: and others were tortured, not accepting deliverance; that they might obtain a better resurrection:

36And others had trial of *cruel* mockings and scourgings, yea, moreover of bonds and imprisonment:

37They were stoned, they were sawn asunder, were tempted, were slain with the sword: they wandered about in sheepskins and goatskins; being destitute, afflicted, tormented;

38(Of whom the world was not worthy:) they wandered in deserts, and *in* mountains, and *in* dens and caves of the earth.

39And these all, having obtained a good report through faith, received not the promise:

40God having provided some better thing for us, that they without us should not be made perfect.

12 WHEREFORE SEEING we also are compassed about with so great a cloud of witnesses, let us lay aside every weight, and the sin which doth so easily beset *us,* and let us run with patience the race that is set before us,

2Looking unto Jesus the author and finisher of *our* faith; who for the joy that was set before him endured the cross, despising the shame, and is set down at the right hand of the throne of God.

3For consider him that endured such contradiction of sinners against himself, lest ye be wearied and faint in your minds.

4Ye have not yet resisted unto blood, striving against sin.

5And ye have forgotten the exhortation which speaketh unto you as unto children, My son, despise not thou the chastening of the Lord, nor faint when thou art rebuked of him:

6For whom the Lord loveth he chasteneth, and scourgeth every son whom he receiveth.

New International

sprinkling of blood, so that the destroyer of the firstborn would not touch the firstborn of Israel.

29By faith the people passed through the Red Sea[a] as on dry land; but when the Egyptians tried to do so, they were drowned.

30By faith the walls of Jericho fell, after the people had marched around them for seven days.

31By faith the prostitute Rahab, because she welcomed the spies, was not killed with those who were disobedient.[b]

32And what more shall I say? I do not have time to tell about Gideon, Barak, Samson, Jephthah, David, Samuel and the prophets, 33who through faith conquered kingdoms, administered justice, and gained what was promised; who shut the mouths of lions, 34quenched the fury of the flames, and escaped the edge of the sword; whose weakness was turned to strength; and who became powerful in battle and routed foreign armies. 35Women received back their dead, raised to life again. Others were tortured and refused to be released, so that they might gain a better resurrection. 36Some faced jeers and flogging, while still others were chained and put in prison. 37They were stoned[c]; they were sawed in two; they were put to death by the sword. They went about in sheepskins and goatskins, destitute, persecuted and mistreated— 38the world was not worthy of them. They wandered in deserts and mountains, and in caves and holes in the ground.

39These were all commended for their faith, yet none of them received what had been promised. 40God had planned something better for us so that only together with us would they be made perfect.

God Disciplines His Sons

12 THEREFORE, SINCE we are surrounded by such a great cloud of witnesses, let us throw off everything that hinders and the sin that so easily entangles, and let us run with perseverance the race marked out for us. 2Let us fix our eyes on Jesus, the author and perfecter of our faith, who for the joy set before him endured the cross, scorning its shame, and sat down at the right hand of the throne of God. 3Consider him who endured such opposition from sinful men, so that you will not grow weary and lose heart.

4In your struggle against sin, you have not yet resisted to the point of shedding your blood. 5And you have forgotten that word of encouragement that addresses you as sons:

"My son, do not make light of the Lord's
        discipline,
    and do not lose heart when he rebukes you,
6because the Lord disciplines those he loves,
    and he punishes everyone he accepts as a
        son."[d]

---

a 29 That is, Sea of Reeds   b 31 Or *unbelieving*   c 37 Some early manuscripts *stoned; they were put to the test;*   d 6 Prov. 3:11,12

Living Bible

would save his people that he commanded them to kill a lamb as God had told them to and sprinkle the blood on the doorposts of their homes, so that God's terrible Angel of Death could not touch the oldest child in those homes, as he did among the Egyptians.

29The people of Israel trusted God and went right through the Red Sea as though they were on dry ground. But when the Egyptians chasing them tried it, they all were drowned.

30It was faith that brought the walls of Jericho tumbling down after the people of Israel had walked around them seven days, as God had commanded them. 31By faith—because she believed in God and his power—Rahab the harlot did not die with all the others in her city when they refused to obey God, for she gave a friendly welcome to the spies.

32Well, how much more do I need to say? It would take too long to recount the stories of the faith of Gideon and Barak and Samson and Jephthah and David and Samuel and all the other prophets. 33These people all trusted God and as a result won battles, overthrew kingdoms, ruled their people well, and received what God had promised them; they were kept from harm in a den of lions, 34and in a fiery furnace. Some, through their faith, escaped death by the sword. Some were made strong again after they had been weak or sick. Others were given great power in battle; they made whole armies turn and run away. 35And some women, through faith, received their loved ones back again from death. But others trusted God and were beaten to death, preferring to die rather than turn from God and be free—trusting that they would rise to a better life afterwards.

36Some were laughed at and their backs cut open with whips, and others were chained in dungeons. 37, 38Some died by stoning and some by being sawed in two; others were promised freedom if they would renounce their faith, then were killed with the sword. Some went about in skins of sheep and goats, wandering over deserts and mountains, hiding in dens and caves. They were hungry and sick and ill-treated—too good for this world. 39And these men of faith, though they trusted God and won his approval, none of them received all that God had promised them; 40for God wanted them to wait and share the even better rewards that were prepared for us.

12 SINCE WE have such a huge crowd of men of faith watching us from the grandstands, let us strip off anything that slows us down or holds us back, and especially those sins that wrap themselves so tightly around our feet and trip us up; and let us run with patience the particular race that God has set before us.

2Keep your eyes on Jesus, our leader and instructor. He was willing to die a shameful death on the cross because of the joy he knew would be his afterwards; and now he sits in the place of honor by the throne of God.

3If you want to keep from becoming fainthearted and weary, think about his patience as sinful men did such terrible things to him. 4After all, you have never yet struggled against sin and temptation until you sweat great drops of blood.

5And have you quite forgotten the encouraging words God spoke to you, his child? He said, "My son, don't be angry when the Lord punishes you. Don't be discouraged when he has to show you where you are wrong. 6For when he punishes you, it proves that he loves you. When he whips you it proves you are really his child."

New Revised Standard

the sprinkling of blood, so that the destroyer of the first-born would not touch the firstborn of Israel.e

The Faith of Other Israelite Heroes

29 By faith the people passed through the Red Sea as if it were dry land, but when the Egyptians attempted to do so they were drowned. 30By faith the walls of Jericho fell after they had been encircled for seven days. 31By faith Rahab the prostitute did not perish with those who were disobedient,f because she had received the spies in peace.

32 And what more should I say? For time would fail me to tell of Gideon, Barak, Samson, Jephthah, of David and Samuel and the prophets— 33who through faith conquered kingdoms, administered justice, obtained promises, shut the mouths of lions, 34quenched raging fire, escaped the edge of the sword, won strength out of weakness, became mighty in war, put foreign armies to flight. 35Women received their dead by resurrection. Others were tortured, refusing to accept release, in order to obtain a better resurrection. 36Others suffered mocking and flogging, and even chains and imprisonment. 37They were stoned to death, they were sawn in two,g they were killed by the sword; they went about in skins of sheep and goats, destitute, persecuted, tormented— 38of whom the world was not worthy. They wandered in deserts and mountains, and in caves and holes in the ground.

39 Yet all these, though they were commended for their faith, did not receive what was promised, 40since God had provided something better so that they would not, apart from us, be made perfect.

The Example of Jesus

12 THEREFORE, SINCE we are surrounded by so great a cloud of witnesses, let us also lay aside every weight and the sin that clings so closely,h and let us run with perseverance the race that is set before us, 2looking to Jesus the pioneer and perfecter of our faith, who for the sake ofi the joy that was set before him endured the cross, disregarding its shame, and has taken his seat at the right hand of the throne of God.

3 Consider him who endured such hostility against himself from sinners,j so that you may not grow weary or lose heart. 4In your struggle against sin you have not yet resisted to the point of shedding your blood. 5And you have forgotten the exhortation that addresses you as children—

"My child, do not regard lightly the discipline
    of the Lord,
  or lose heart when you are punished by
    him;
 6 for the Lord disciplines those whom he loves,
    and chastises every child whom he accepts."

---

e Gk would not touch them f Or unbelieving g Other ancient authorities add they were tempted h Other ancient authorities read sin that easily distracts i Or who instead of j Other ancient authorities read such hostility from sinners against themselves

King James

7If ye endure chastening, God dealeth with you as with sons; for what son is he whom the father chasteneth not?

8But if ye be without chastisement, whereof all are partakers, then are ye bastards, and not sons.

9Furthermore we have had fathers of our flesh which corrected *us*, and we gave *them* reverence: shall we not much rather be in subjection unto the Father of spirits, and live?

10For they verily for a few days chastened *us* after their own pleasure; but he for *our* profit, that *we* might be partakers of his holiness.

11Now no chastening for the present seemeth to be joyous, but grievous: nevertheless afterward it yieldeth the peaceable fruit of righteousness unto them which are exercised thereby.

12Wherefore lift up the hands which hang down, and the feeble knees;

13And make straight paths for your feet, lest that which is lame be turned out of the way; but let it rather be healed.

14Follow peace with all *men*, and holiness, without which no man shall see the Lord:

15Looking diligently lest any man fail of the grace of God; lest any root of bitterness springing up trouble *you*, and thereby many be defiled;

16Lest there *be* any fornicator, or profane person, as Esau, who for one morsel of meat sold his birthright.

17For ye know how that afterward, when he would have inherited the blessing, he was rejected: for he found no place of repentance, though he sought it carefully with tears.

18For ye are not come unto the mount that might be touched, and that burned with fire, nor unto blackness, and darkness, and tempest,

19And the sound of a trumpet, and the voice of words; which *voice* they that heard entreated that the word should not be spoken to them any more:

20(For they could not endure that which was commanded, And if so much as a beast touch the mountain, it shall be stoned, or thrust through with a dart:

21And so terrible was the sight, *that* Moses said, I exceedingly fear and quake:)

22But ye are come unto mount Zion, and unto the city of the living God, the heavenly Jerusalem, and to an innumerable company of angels,

23To the general assembly and church of the firstborn, which are written in heaven, and to God the Judge of all, and to the spirits of just men made perfect,

24And to Jesus the mediator of the new covenant, and to the blood of sprinkling, that speaketh better things than *that of* Abel.

25See that ye refuse not him that speaketh. For if they escaped not who refused him that spake on earth, much more *shall not* we *escape*, if we turn away from him that *speaketh* from heaven:

26Whose voice then shook the earth: but now he hath promised, saying, Yet once more I shake not the earth only, but also heaven.

27And this *word*, Yet once more, signifieth the removing of those things that are shaken, as of things that are made, that those things which cannot be shaken may remain.

28Wherefore we receiving a kingdom which cannot be moved, let us have grace, whereby we may serve God acceptably with reverence and godly fear:

29For our God *is* a consuming fire.

New International

7Endure hardship as discipline; God is treating you as sons. For what son is not disciplined by his father? 8If you are not disciplined (and everyone undergoes discipline), then you are illegitimate children and not true sons. 9Moreover, we have all had human fathers who disciplined us and we respected them for it. How much more should we submit to the Father of our spirits and live! 10Our fathers disciplined us for a little while as they thought best; but God disciplines us for our good, that we may share in his holiness. 11No discipline seems pleasant at the time, but painful. Later on, however, it produces a harvest of righteousness and peace for those who have been trained by it.

12Therefore, strengthen your feeble arms and weak knees. 13"Make level paths for your feet,"a so that the lame may not be disabled, but rather healed.

Warning Against Refusing God

14Make every effort to live in peace with all men and to be holy; without holiness no one will see the Lord. 15See to it that no one misses the grace of God and that no bitter root grows up to cause trouble and defile many. 16See that no one is sexually immoral, or is godless like Esau, who for a single meal sold his inheritance rights as the oldest son. 17Afterward, as you know, when he wanted to inherit this blessing, he was rejected. He could bring about no change of mind, though he sought the blessing with tears.

18You have not come to a mountain that can be touched and that is burning with fire; to darkness, gloom and storm; 19to a trumpet blast or to such a voice speaking words that those who heard it begged that no further word be spoken to them, 20because they could not bear what was commanded: "If even an animal touches the mountain, it must be stoned."b 21The sight was so terrifying that Moses said, "I am trembling with fear."c

22But you have come to Mount Zion, to the heavenly Jerusalem, the city of the living God. You have come to thousands upon thousands of angels in joyful assembly, 23to the church of the firstborn, whose names are written in heaven. You have come to God, the judge of all men, to the spirits of righteous men made perfect, 24to Jesus the mediator of a new covenant, and to the sprinkled blood that speaks a better word than the blood of Abel.

25See to it that you do not refuse him who speaks. If they did not escape when they refused him who warned them on earth, how much less will we, if we turn away from him who warns us from heaven? 26At that time his voice shook the earth, but now he has promised, "Once more I will shake not only the earth but also the heavens."d 27The words "once more" indicate the removing of what can be shaken—that is, created things—so that what cannot be shaken may remain.

28Therefore, since we are receiving a kingdom that cannot be shaken, let us be thankful, and so worship God acceptably with reverence and awe, 29for our "God is a consuming fire."e

a 13 Prov. 4:26   b 20 Exodus 19:12,13   c 21 Deut. 9:19
d 26 Haggai 2:6   e 29 Deut. 4:24

Living Bible

7Let God train you, for he is doing what any loving father does for his children. Whoever heard of a son who was never corrected? 8If God doesn't punish you when you need it, as other fathers punish their sons, then it means that you aren't really God's son at all—that you don't really belong in his family. 9Since we respect our fathers here on earth, though they punish us, should we not all the more cheerfully submit to God's training so that we can begin really to live?

10Our earthly fathers trained us for a few brief years, doing the best for us that they knew how, but God's correction is always right and for our best good, that we may share his holiness. 11Being punished isn't enjoyable while it is happening—it hurts! But afterwards we can see the result, a quiet growth in grace and character.

12So take a new grip with your tired hands, stand firm on your shaky legs, 13and mark out a straight, smooth path for your feet so that those who follow you, though weak and lame, will not fall and hurt themselves, but become strong.

14Try to stay out of all quarrels and seek to live a clean and holy life, for one who is not holy will not see the Lord. 15Look after each other so that not one of you will fail to find God's best blessings. Watch out that no bitterness takes root among you, for as it springs up it causes deep trouble, hurting many in their spiritual lives. 16Watch out that no one becomes involved in sexual sin or becomes careless about God as Esau did: he traded his rights as the oldest son for a single meal. 17And afterwards, when he wanted those rights back again, it was too late, even though he wept bitter tears of repentance. So remember, and be careful.

18You have not had to stand face to face with terror, flaming fire, gloom, darkness and a terrible storm, as the Israelites did at Mount Sinai when God gave them his laws. 19For there was an awesome trumpet blast, and a voice with a message so terrible that the people begged God to stop speaking. 20They staggered back under God's command that if even an animal touched the mountain it must die. 21Moses himself was so frightened at the sight that he shook with terrible fear.

22But you have come right up into Mount Zion, to the city of the living God, the heavenly Jerusalem, and to the gathering of countless happy angels; 23and to the church, composed of all those registered in heaven; and to God who is Judge of all; and to the spirits of the redeemed in heaven, already made perfect; 24and to Jesus himself, who has brought us his wonderful new agreement; and to the sprinkled blood which graciously forgives instead of crying out for vengeance as the blood of Abel did.

25So see to it that you obey him who is speaking to you. For if the people of Israel did not escape when they refused to listen to Moses, the earthly messenger, how terrible our danger if we refuse to listen to God who speaks to us from heaven! 26When he spoke from Mount Sinai his voice shook the earth, but, "Next time," he says, "I will not only shake the earth, but the heavens too." 27By this he means that he will sift out everything without solid foundations, so that only unshakable things will be left.

28Since we have a Kingdom nothing can destroy, let us please God by serving him with thankful hearts, and with holy fear and awe. 29For our God is a consuming fire.

New Revised Standard

7Endure trials for the sake of discipline. God is treating you as children; for what child is there whom a parent does not discipline? 8If you do not have that discipline in which all children share, then you are illegitimate and not his children. 9Moreover, we had human parents to discipline us, and we respected them. Should we not be even more willing to be subject to the Father of spirits and live? 10For they disciplined us for a short time as seemed best to them, but he disciplines us for our good, in order that we may share his holiness. 11Now, discipline always seems painful rather than pleasant at the time, but later it yields the peaceful fruit of righteousness to those who have been trained by it.

12 Therefore lift your drooping hands and strengthen your weak knees, 13and make straight paths for your feet, so that what is lame may not be put out of joint, but rather be healed.

Warnings against Rejecting God's Grace

14 Pursue peace with everyone, and the holiness without which no one will see the Lord. 15See to it that no one fails to obtain the grace of God; that no root of bitterness springs up and causes trouble, and through it many become defiled. 16See to it that no one becomes like Esau, an immoral and godless person, who sold his birthright for a single meal. 17You know that later, when he wanted to inherit the blessing, he was rejected, for he found no chance to repent,f even though he sought the blessingg with tears.

18 You have not come to somethingh that can be touched, a blazing fire, and darkness, and gloom, and a tempest, 19and the sound of a trumpet, and a voice whose words made the hearers beg that not another word be spoken to them. 20(For they could not endure the order that was given, "If even an animal touches the mountain, it shall be stoned to death." 21Indeed, so terrifying was the sight that Moses said, "I tremble with fear.") 22But you have come to Mount Zion and to the city of the living God, the heavenly Jerusalem, and to innumerable angels in festal gathering, 23and to the assemblyi of the firstborn who are enrolled in heaven, and to God the judge of all, and to the spirits of the righteous made perfect, 24and to Jesus, the mediator of a new covenant, and to the sprinkled blood that speaks a better word than the blood of Abel.

25 See that you do not refuse the one who is speaking; for if they did not escape when they refused the one who warned them on earth, how much less will we escape if we reject the one who warns from heaven! 26At that time his voice shook the earth; but now he has promised, "Yet once more I will shake not only the earth but also the heaven." 27This phrase, "Yet once more," indicates the removal of what is shaken—that is, created things—so that what cannot be shaken may remain. 28Therefore, since we are receiving a kingdom that cannot be shaken, let us give thanks, by which we offer to God an acceptable worship with reverence and awe; 29for indeed our God is a consuming fire.

---

f Or *no chance to change his father's mind*   g Gk *it*   h Other ancient authorities read *a mountain*   i Or *angels, and to the festal gathering* 23*and assembly*

King James

13 LET BROTHERLY love continue. 2Be not forgetful to entertain strangers: for thereby some have entertained angels unawares.

3Remember them that are in bonds, as bound with them; *and* them which suffer adversity, as being yourselves also in the body.

4Marriage *is* honourable in all, and the bed undefiled: but whoremongers and adulterers God will judge.

5*Let your* conversation *be* without covetousness; *and be* content with such things as ye have: for he hath said, I will never leave thee, nor forsake thee.

6So that we may boldly say, The Lord *is* my helper, and I will not fear what man shall do unto me.

7Remember them which have the rule over you, who have spoken unto you the word of God: whose faith follow, considering the end of *their* conversation.

8Jesus Christ the same yesterday, and today, and for ever.

9Be not carried about with divers and strange doctrines. For *it is* a good thing that the heart be established with grace; not with meats, which have not profited them that have been occupied therein.

10We have an altar, whereof they have no right to eat which serve the tabernacle.

11For the bodies of those beasts, whose blood is brought into the sanctuary by the high priest for sin, are burned without the camp.

12Wherefore Jesus also, that he might sanctify the people with his own blood, suffered without the gate.

13Let us go forth therefore unto him without the camp, bearing his reproach.

14For here have we no continuing city, but we seek one to come.

15By him therefore let us offer the sacrifice of praise to God continually, that is, the fruit of *our* lips giving thanks to his name.

16But to do good and to communicate forget not: for with such sacrifices God is well pleased.

17Obey them that have the rule over you, and submit yourselves: for they watch for your souls, as they that must give account, that they may do it with joy, and not with grief: for that *is* unprofitable for you.

18Pray for us: for we trust we have a good conscience, in all things willing to live honestly.

19But I beseech *you* the rather to do this, that I may be restored to you the sooner.

20Now the God of peace, that brought again from the dead our Lord Jesus, that great shepherd of the sheep, through the blood of the everlasting covenant,

21Make you perfect in every good work to do his will, working in you that which is wellpleasing in his sight, through Jesus Christ; to whom *be* glory for ever and ever. Amen.

22And I beseech you, brethren, suffer the word of exhortation: for I have written a letter unto you in few words.

23Know ye that *our* brother Timothy is set at liberty; with whom, if he come shortly, I will see you.

24Salute all them that have the rule over you, and all the saints. They of Italy salute you.

25Grace *be* with you all. Amen.

New International

Concluding Exhortations

13 KEEP ON loving each other as brothers. 2Do not forget to entertain strangers, for by so doing some people have entertained angels without knowing it. 3Remember those in prison as if you were their fellow prisoners, and those who are mistreated as if you yourselves were suffering.

4Marriage should be honored by all, and the marriage bed kept pure, for God will judge the adulterer and all the sexually immoral. 5Keep your lives free from the love of money and be content with what you have, because God has said,

> "Never will I leave you;
> never will I forsake you."[a]

6So we say with confidence,

> "The Lord is my helper; I will not be afraid.
> What can man do to me?"[b]

7Remember your leaders, who spoke the word of God to you. Consider the outcome of their way of life and imitate their faith. 8Jesus Christ is the same yesterday and today and forever.

9Do not be carried away by all kinds of strange teachings. It is good for our hearts to be strengthened by grace, not by ceremonial foods, which are of no value to those who eat them. 10We have an altar from which those who minister at the tabernacle have no right to eat.

11The high priest carries the blood of animals into the Most Holy Place as a sin offering, but the bodies are burned outside the camp. 12And so Jesus also suffered outside the city gate to make the people holy through his own blood. 13Let us, then, go to him outside the camp, bearing the disgrace he bore. 14For here we do not have an enduring city, but we are looking for the city that is to come.

15Through Jesus, therefore, let us continually offer to God a sacrifice of praise—the fruit of lips that confess his name. 16And do not forget to do good and to share with others, for with such sacrifices God is pleased.

17Obey your leaders and submit to their authority. They keep watch over you as men who must give an account. Obey them so that their work will be a joy, not a burden, for that would be of no advantage to you.

18Pray for us. We are sure that we have a clear conscience and desire to live honorably in every way. 19I particularly urge you to pray so that I may be restored to you soon.

20May the God of peace, who through the blood of the eternal covenant brought back from the dead our Lord Jesus, that great Shepherd of the sheep, 21equip you with everything good for doing his will, and may he work in us what is pleasing to him, through Jesus Christ, to whom be glory for ever and ever. Amen.

22Brothers, I urge you to bear with my word of exhortation, for I have written you only a short letter.

23I want you to know that our brother Timothy has been released. If he arrives soon, I will come with him to see you.

24Greet all your leaders and all God's people. Those from Italy send you their greetings.

25Grace be with you all.

---

a 5 Deut. 31:6   b 6 Psalm 118:6,7

Living Bible

13 CONTINUE TO love each other with true brotherly love. ²Don't forget to be kind to strangers, for some who have done this have entertained angels without realizing it! ³Don't forget about those in jail. Suffer with them as though you were there yourself. Share the sorrow of those being mistreated, for you know what they are going through.

⁴Honor your marriage and its vows, and be pure; for God will surely punish all those who are immoral or commit adultery.

⁵Stay away from the love of money; be satisfied with what you have. For God has said, "I will never, *never* fail you nor forsake you." ⁶That is why we can say without any doubt or fear, "The Lord is my Helper and I am not afraid of anything that mere man can do to me."

⁷Remember your leaders who have taught you the Word of God. Think of all the good that has come from their lives, and try to trust the Lord as they do.

⁸Jesus Christ is the same yesterday, today, and forever. ⁹So do not be attracted by strange, new ideas. Your spiritual strength comes as a gift from God, not from ceremonial rules about eating certain foods—a method which, by the way, hasn't helped those who have tried it!

¹⁰We have an altar—the cross where Christ was sacrificed—where those who continue to seek salvation by obeying Jewish laws can never be helped. ¹¹Under the system of Jewish laws the high priest brought the blood of the slain animals into the sanctuary as a sacrifice for sin, and then the bodies of the animals were burned outside the city. ¹²That is why Jesus suffered and died outside the city, where his blood washed our sins away.

¹³So let us go out to him beyond the city walls [that is, outside the interests of this world, being willing to be despised*c*] to suffer with him there, bearing his shame. ¹⁴For this world is not our home; we are looking forward to our everlasting home in heaven.

¹⁵With Jesus' help we will continually offer our sacrifice of praise to God by telling others of the glory of his name. ¹⁶Don't forget to do good and to share what you have with those in need, for such sacrifices are very pleasing to him. ¹⁷Obey your spiritual leaders and be willing to do what they say. For their work is to watch over your souls, and God will judge them on how well they do this. Give them reason to report joyfully about you to the Lord and not with sorrow, for then you will suffer for it too.

¹⁸Pray for us, for our conscience is clear and we want to keep it that way. ¹⁹I especially need your prayers right now so that I can come back to you sooner.

²⁰, ²¹And now may the God of peace, who brought again from the dead our Lord Jesus, equip you with all you need for doing his will. May he who became the great Shepherd of the sheep by an everlasting agreement between God and you, signed with his blood, produce in you through the power of Christ all that is pleasing to him. To him be glory forever and ever. Amen.

²²Brethren, please listen patiently to what I have said in this letter, for it is a short one. ²³I want you to know that Brother Timothy is now out of jail; if he comes here soon, I will come with him to see you. ²⁴, ²⁵Give my greetings to all your leaders and to the other believers there. The Christians from Italy who are here with me send you their love. God's grace be with you all.

Good-bye.

New Revised Standard

Service Well-Pleasing to God

13 LET MUTUAL love continue. ²Do not neglect to show hospitality to strangers, for by doing that some have entertained angels without knowing it. ³Remember those who are in prison, as though you were in prison with them; those who are being tortured, as though you yourselves were being tortured.*d* ⁴Let marriage be held in honor by all, and let the marriage bed be kept undefiled; for God will judge fornicators and adulterers. ⁵Keep your lives free from the love of money, and be content with what you have; for he has said, "I will never leave you or forsake you." ⁶So we can say with confidence,

"The Lord is my helper;
    I will not be afraid.
What can anyone do to me?"

7 Remember your leaders, those who spoke the word of God to you; consider the outcome of their way of life, and imitate their faith. ⁸Jesus Christ is the same yesterday and today and forever. ⁹Do not be carried away by all kinds of strange teachings; for it is well for the heart to be strengthened by grace, not by regulations about food,*e* which have not benefited those who observe them. ¹⁰We have an altar from which those who officiate in the tent*f* have no right to eat. ¹¹For the bodies of those animals whose blood is brought into the sanctuary by the high priest as a sacrifice for sin are burned outside the camp. ¹²Therefore Jesus also suffered outside the city gate in order to sanctify the people by his own blood. ¹³Let us then go to him outside the camp and bear the abuse he endured. ¹⁴For here we have no lasting city, but we are looking for the city that is to come. ¹⁵Through him, then, let us continually offer a sacrifice of praise to God, that is, the fruit of lips that confess his name. ¹⁶Do not neglect to do good and to share what you have, for such sacrifices are pleasing to God.

17 Obey your leaders and submit to them, for they are keeping watch over your souls and will give an account. Let them do this with joy and not with sighing—for that would be harmful to you.

18 Pray for us; we are sure that we have a clear conscience, desiring to act honorably in all things. ¹⁹I urge you all the more to do this, so that I may be restored to you very soon.

Benediction

20 Now may the God of peace, who brought back from the dead our Lord Jesus, the great shepherd of the sheep, by the blood of the eternal covenant, ²¹make you complete in everything good so that you may do his will, working among us*g* that which is pleasing in his sight, through Jesus Christ, to whom be the glory forever and ever. Amen.

Final Exhortation and Greetings

22 I appeal to you, brothers and sisters,*h* bear with my word of exhortation, for I have written to you briefly. ²³I want you to know that our brother Timothy has been set free; and if he comes in time, he will be with me when I see you. ²⁴Greet all your leaders and all the saints. Those from Italy send you greetings. ²⁵Grace be with all of you.*i*

c 13:13 *willing to be despised*, implied.

d Gk *were in the body*   *e* Gk *not by foods*   *f* Or *tabernacle*   *g* Other ancient authorities read *you*   *h* Gk *brothers*   *i* Other ancient authorities add *Amen*

King James

THE GENERAL EPISTLE OF

James

1 JAMES, A servant of God and of the Lord Jesus Christ, to the twelve tribes which are scattered abroad, greeting.

2My brethren, count it all joy when ye fall into divers temptations;

3Knowing *this*, that the trying of your faith worketh patience.

4But let patience have *her* perfect work, that ye may be perfect and entire, wanting nothing.

5If any of you lack wisdom, let him ask of God, that giveth to all *men* liberally, and upbraideth not; and it shall be given him.

6But let him ask in faith, nothing wavering. For he that wavereth is like a wave of the sea driven with the wind and tossed.

7For let not that man think that he shall receive any thing of the Lord.

8A double minded man *is* unstable in all his ways.

9Let the brother of low degree rejoice in that he is exalted:

10But the rich, in that he is made low: because as the flower of the grass he shall pass away.

11For the sun is no sooner risen with a burning heat, but it withereth the grass, and the flower thereof falleth, and the grace of the fashion of it perisheth: so also shall the rich man fade away in his ways.

12Blessed *is* the man that endureth temptation: for when he is tried, he shall receive the crown of life, which the Lord hath promised to them that love him.

13Let no man say when he is tempted, I am tempted of God: for God cannot be tempted with evil, neither tempteth he any man:

14But every man is tempted, when he is drawn away of his own lust, and enticed.

15Then when lust hath conceived, it bringeth forth sin: and sin, when it is finished, bringeth forth death.

16Do not err, my beloved brethren.

17Every good gift and every perfect gift is from above, and cometh down from the Father of lights, with whom is no variableness, neither shadow of turning.

18Of his own will begat he us with the word of truth, that we should be a kind of firstfruits of his creatures.

19Wherefore, my beloved brethren, let every man be swift to hear, slow to speak, slow to wrath:

20For the wrath of man worketh not the righteousness of God.

21Wherefore lay apart all filthiness and superfluity of naughtiness, and receive with meekness the engrafted word, which is able to save your souls.

New International

James

1 JAMES, A servant of God and of the Lord Jesus Christ,

To the twelve tribes scattered among the nations:

Greetings.

Trials and Temptations

2Consider it pure joy, my brothers, whenever you face trials of many kinds, 3because you know that the testing of your faith develops perseverance. 4Perseverance must finish its work so that you may be mature and complete, not lacking anything. 5If any of you lacks wisdom, he should ask God, who gives generously to all without finding fault, and it will be given to him. 6But when he asks, he must believe and not doubt, because he who doubts is like a wave of the sea, blown and tossed by the wind. 7That man should not think he will receive anything from the Lord; 8he is a double-minded man, unstable in all he does.

9The brother in humble circumstances ought to take pride in his high position. 10But the one who is rich should take pride in his low position, because he will pass away like a wild flower. 11For the sun rises with scorching heat and withers the plant; its blossom falls and its beauty is destroyed. In the same way, the rich man will fade away even while he goes about his business.

12Blessed is the man who perseveres under trial, because when he has stood the test, he will receive the crown of life that God has promised to those who love him.

13When tempted, no one should say, "God is tempting me." For God cannot be tempted by evil, nor does he tempt anyone; 14but each one is tempted when, by his own evil desire, he is dragged away and enticed. 15Then, after desire has conceived, it gives birth to sin; and sin, when it is full-grown, gives birth to death.

16Don't be deceived, my dear brothers. 17Every good and perfect gift is from above, coming down from the Father of the heavenly lights, who does not change like shifting shadows. 18He chose to give us birth through the word of truth, that we might be a kind of firstfruits of all he created.

Listening and Doing

19My dear brothers, take note of this: Everyone should be quick to listen, slow to speak and slow to become angry, 20for man's anger does not bring about the righteous life that God desires. 21Therefore, get rid of all moral filth and the evil that is so prevalent and humbly accept the word planted in you, which can save you.

Living Bible

James

1 *FROM:* JAMES, a servant of God and of the Lord Jesus Christ.

To: Jewish Christians scattered everywhere. Greetings!

2Dear brothers, is your life full of difficulties and temptations? Then be happy, 3for when the way is rough, your patience has a chance to grow. 4So let it grow, and don't try to squirm out of your problems. For when your patience is finally in full bloom, then you will be ready for anything, strong in character, full and complete.

5If you want to know what God wants you to do, ask him, and he will gladly tell you, for he is always ready to give a bountiful supply of wisdom to all who ask him; he will not resent it. 6But when you ask him, be sure that you really expect him to tell you, for a doubtful mind will be as unsettled as a wave of the sea that is driven and tossed by the wind; 7, 8and every decision you then make will be uncertain, as you turn first this way, and then that. If you don't ask with faith, don't expect the Lord to give you any solid answer.

9A Christian who doesn't amount to much in this world should be glad, for he is great in the Lord's sight. 10, 11But a rich man should be glad that his riches mean nothing to the Lord, for he will soon be gone, like a flower that has lost its beauty and fades away, withered—killed by the scorching summer sun. So it is with rich men. They will soon die and leave behind all their busy activities.

12Happy is the man who doesn't give in and do wrong when he is tempted, for afterwards he will get as his reward the crown of life that God has promised those who love him. 13And remember, when someone wants to do wrong it is never God who is tempting him, for God never wants to do wrong and never tempts anyone else to do it. 14Temptation is the pull of man's own evil thoughts and wishes. 15These evil thoughts lead to evil actions and afterwards to the death penalty from God. 16So don't be misled, dear brothers.

17But whatever is good and perfect comes to us from God, the Creator of all light, and he shines forever without change or shadow. 18And it was a happy day for hima when he gave us our new lives, through the truth of his Word, and we became, as it were, the first children in his new family.

19Dear brothers, don't ever forget that it is best to listen much, speak little, and not become angry; 20for anger doesn't make us good, as God demands that we must be.

21So get rid of all that is wrong in your life, both inside and outside, and humbly be glad for the wonderful message we have received, for it is able to save our souls as it takes hold of our hearts.

New Revised Standard

THE LETTER OF

James

Salutation

1 JAMES, A servantb of God and of the Lord Jesus Christ,

To the twelve tribes in the Dispersion:
Greetings.

Faith and Wisdom

2 My brothers and sisters,c whenever you face trials of any kind, consider it nothing but joy, 3because you know that the testing of your faith produces endurance; 4and let endurance have its full effect, so that you may be mature and complete, lacking in nothing.

5 If any of you is lacking in wisdom, ask God, who gives to all generously and ungrudgingly, and it will be given you. 6But ask in faith, never doubting, for the one who doubts is like a wave of the sea, driven and tossed by the wind; 7, 8for the doubter, being double-minded and unstable in every way, must not expect to receive anything from the Lord.

Poverty and Riches

9 Let the believerd who is lowly boast in being raised up, 10and the rich in being brought low, because the rich will disappear like a flower in the field. 11For the sun rises with its scorching heat and withers the field; its flower falls, and its beauty perishes. It is the same way with the rich; in the midst of a busy life, they will wither away.

Trial and Temptation

12 Blessed is anyone who endures temptation. Such a one has stood the test and will receive the crown of life that the Lorde has promised to those who love him. 13No one, when tempted, should say, "I am being tempted by God"; for God cannot be tempted by evil and he himself tempts no one. 14But one is tempted by one's own desire, being lured and enticed by it; 15then, when that desire has conceived, it gives birth to sin, and that sin, when it is fully grown, gives birth to death. 16Do not be deceived, my beloved.f

17 Every generous act of giving, with every perfect gift, is from above, coming down from the Father of lights, with whom there is no variation or shadow due to change.g 18In fulfillment of his own purpose he gave us birth by the word of truth, so that we would become a kind of first fruits of his creatures.

Hearing and Doing the Word

19 You must understand this, my beloved:f let everyone be quick to listen, slow to speak, slow to anger; 20for your anger does not produce God's righteousness. 21Therefore rid yourselves of all sordidness and rank growth of wickedness, and welcome with meekness the implanted word that has the power to save your souls.

---

a 1:18 *happy day for him*, literally, "Of his own free will he gave us," etc.

b Gk *slave*   c Gk *brothers*   d Gk *brother*   e Gk *he*; other ancient authorities read *God*   f Gk *my beloved brothers*   g Other ancient authorities read *variation due to a shadow of turning*

King James

New International

22But be ye doers of the word, and not hearers only, deceiving your own selves.

23For if any be a hearer of the word, and not a doer, he is like unto a man beholding his natural face in a glass:

24For he beholdeth himself, and goeth his way, and straightway forgetteth what manner of man he was.

25But whoso looketh into the perfect law of liberty, and continueth *therein*, he being not a forgetful hearer, but a doer of the work, this man shall be blessed in his deed.

26If any man among you seem to be religious, and bridleth not his tongue, but deceiveth his own heart, this man's religion *is* vain.

27Pure religion and undefiled before God and the Father is this, To visit the fatherless and widows in their affliction, *and* to keep himself unspotted from the world.

2 MY BRETHREN, have not the faith of our Lord Jesus Christ, *the Lord* of glory, with respect of persons.

2For if there come unto your assembly a man with a gold ring, in goodly apparel, and there come in also a poor man in vile raiment;

3And ye have respect to him that weareth the gay clothing, and say unto him, Sit thou here in a good place; and say to the poor, Stand thou there, or sit here under my footstool:

4Are ye not then partial in yourselves, and are become judges of evil thoughts?

5Hearken, my beloved brethren, Hath not God chosen the poor of this world rich in faith, and heirs of the kingdom which he hath promised to them that love him?

6But ye have despised the poor. Do not rich men oppress you, and draw you before the judgment seats?

7Do not they blaspheme that worthy name by the which ye are called?

8If ye fulfil the royal law according to the scripture, Thou shalt love thy neighbour as thyself, ye do well:

9But if ye have respect to persons, ye commit sin, and are convinced of the law as transgressors.

10For whosoever shall keep the whole law, and yet offend in one *point*, he is guilty of all.

11For he that said, Do not commit adultery, said also, Do not kill. Now if thou commit no adultery, yet if thou kill, thou art become a transgressor of the law.

12So speak ye, and so do, as they that shall be judged by the law of liberty.

13For he shall have judgment without mercy, that hath shown no mercy; and mercy rejoiceth against judgment.

14What *doth it* profit, my brethren, though a man say he hath faith, and have not works? can faith save him?

15If a brother or sister be naked, and destitute of daily food,

16And one of you say unto them, Depart in peace, be *ye* warmed and filled; notwithstanding ye give them not those things which are needful to the body; what *doth it* profit?

17Even so faith, if it hath not works, is dead, being alone.

22Do not merely listen to the word, and so deceive yourselves. Do what it says. 23Anyone who listens to the word but does not do what it says is like a man who looks at his face in a mirror 24and, after looking at himself, goes away and immediately forgets what he looks like. 25But the man who looks intently into the perfect law that gives freedom, and continues to do this, not forgetting what he has heard, but doing it—he will be blessed in what he does.

26If anyone considers himself religious and yet does not keep a tight rein on his tongue, he deceives himself and his religion is worthless. 27Religion that God our Father accepts as pure and faultless is this: to look after orphans and widows in their distress and to keep oneself from being polluted by the world.

Favoritism Forbidden

2 MY BROTHERS, as believers in our glorious Lord Jesus Christ, don't show favoritism. 2Suppose a man comes into your meeting wearing a gold ring and fine clothes, and a poor man in shabby clothes also comes in. 3If you show special attention to the man wearing fine clothes and say, "Here's a good seat for you," but say to the poor man, "You stand there" or "Sit on the floor by my feet," 4have you not discriminated among yourselves and become judges with evil thoughts?

5Listen, my dear brothers: Has not God chosen those who are poor in the eyes of the world to be rich in faith and to inherit the kingdom he promised those who love him? 6But you have insulted the poor. Is it not the rich who are exploiting you? Are they not the ones who are dragging you into court? 7Are they not the ones who are slandering the noble name of him to whom you belong?

8If you really keep the royal law found in Scripture, "Love your neighbor as yourself,"a you are doing right. 9But if you show favoritism, you sin and are convicted by the law as lawbreakers. 10For whoever keeps the whole law and yet stumbles at just one point is guilty of breaking all of it. 11For he who said, "Do not commit adultery,"b also said, "Do not murder."c If you do not commit adultery but do commit murder, you have become a lawbreaker.

12Speak and act as those who are going to be judged by the law that gives freedom, 13because judgment without mercy will be shown to anyone who has not been merciful. Mercy triumphs over judgment!

Faith and Deeds

14What good is it, my brothers, if a man claims to have faith but has no deeds? Can such faith save him? 15Suppose a brother or sister is without clothes and daily food. 16If one of you says to him, "Go, I wish you well; keep warm and well fed," but does nothing about his physical needs, what good is it? 17In the same way, faith by itself, if it is not accompanied by action, is dead.

a 8 Lev. 19:18   b 11 Exodus 20:14; Deut. 5:18   c 11 Exodus 20:13; Deut. 5:17

Living Bible

22And remember, it is a message to obey, not just to listen to. So don't fool yourselves. 23For if a person just listens and doesn't obey, he is like a man looking at his face in a mirror; 24as soon as he walks away, he can't see himself anymore or remember what he looks like. 25But if anyone keeps looking steadily into God's law for free men, he will not only remember it but he will do what it says, and God will greatly bless him in everything he does.

26Anyone who says he is a Christian but doesn't control his sharp tongue is just fooling himself, and his religion isn't worth much. 27The Christian who is pure and without fault, from God the Father's point of view, is the one who takes care of orphans and widows, and who remains true to the Lord—not soiled and dirtied by his contacts with the world.

2 DEAR BROTHERS, how can you claim that you belong to the Lord Jesus Christ, the Lord of glory, if you show favoritism to rich people and look down on poor people?

2If a man comes into your church dressed in expensive clothes and with valuable gold rings on his fingers, and at the same moment another man comes in who is poor and dressed in threadbare clothes, 3and you make a lot of fuss over the rich man and give him the best seat in the house and say to the poor man, "You can stand over there if you like, or else sit on the floor"—well, 4judging a man by his wealth shows that you are guided by wrong motives.

5Listen to me, dear brothers: God has chosen poor people to be rich in faith, and the Kingdom of Heaven is theirs, for that is the gift God has promised to all those who love him. 6And yet, of the two strangers, you have despised the poor man. Don't you realize that it is usually the rich men who pick on you and drag you into court? 7And all too often they are the ones who laugh at Jesus Christ, whose noble name you bear.

8Yes indeed, it is good when you truly obey our Lord's command, "You must love and help your neighbors just as much as you love and take care of yourself." 9But you are breaking this law of our Lord's when you favor the rich and fawn over them; it is sin.

10And the person who keeps every law of God, but makes one little slip, is just as guilty as the person who has broken every law there is. 11For the God who said you must not marry a woman who already has a husband, also said you must not murder, so even though you have not broken the marriage laws by committing adultery, but have murdered someone, you have entirely broken God's laws and stand utterly guilty before him.

12You will be judged on whether or not you are doing what Christ wants you to. So watch what you do and what you think; 13for there will be no mercy to those who have shown no mercy. But if you have been merciful, then God's mercy toward you will win out over his judgment against you.

14Dear brothers, what's the use of saying that you have faith and are Christians if you aren't proving it by helping others? Will *that* kind of faith save anyone? 15If you have a friend who is in need of food and clothing, 16and you say to him, "Well, good-bye and God bless you; stay warm and eat hearty," and then don't give him clothes or food, what good does that do?

17So you see, it isn't enough just to have faith. You must also do good to prove that you have it. Faith that doesn't show itself by good works is no faith at all—it is dead and useless.

New Revised Standard

22 But be doers of the word, and not merely hearers who deceive themselves. 23For if any are hearers of the word and not doers, they are like those who look at themselves[d] in a mirror; 24for they look at themselves and, on going away, immediately forget what they were like. 25But those who look into the perfect law, the law of liberty, and persevere, being not hearers who forget but doers who act—they will be blessed in their doing.

26 If any think they are religious, and do not bridle their tongues but deceive their hearts, their religion is worthless. 27Religion that is pure and undefiled before God, the Father, is this: to care for orphans and widows in their distress, and to keep oneself unstained by the world.

Warning against Partiality

2 MY BROTHERS and sisters,[e] do you with your acts of favoritism really believe in our glorious Lord Jesus Christ?[f] 2For if a person with gold rings and in fine clothes comes into your assembly, and if a poor person in dirty clothes also comes in, 3and if you take notice of the one wearing the fine clothes and say, "Have a seat here, please," while to the one who is poor you say, "Stand there," or, "Sit at my feet,"[g] 4have you not made distinctions among yourselves, and become judges with evil thoughts? 5Listen, my beloved brothers and sisters.[h] Has not God chosen the poor in the world to be rich in faith and to be heirs of the kingdom that he has promised to those who love him? 6But you have dishonored the poor. Is it not the rich who oppress you? Is it not they who drag you into court? 7Is it not they who blaspheme the excellent name that was invoked over you?

8 You do well if you really fulfill the royal law according to the scripture, "You shall love your neighbor as yourself." 9But if you show partiality, you commit sin and are convicted by the law as transgressors. 10For whoever keeps the whole law but fails in one point has become accountable for all of it. 11For the one who said, "You shall not commit adultery," also said, "You shall not murder." Now if you do not commit adultery but if you murder, you have become a transgressor of the law. 12So speak and so act as those who are to be judged by the law of liberty. 13For judgment will be without mercy to anyone who has shown no mercy; mercy triumphs over judgment.

Faith without Works Is Dead

14 What good is it, my brothers and sisters,[h] if you say you have faith but do not have works? Can faith save you? 15If a brother or sister is naked and lacks daily food, 16and one of you says to them, "Go in peace; keep warm and eat your fill," and yet you do not supply their bodily needs, what is the good of that? 17So faith by itself, if it has no works, is dead.

---

[d] Gk *at the face of his birth*   [e] Gk *My brothers*   [f] Or *hold the faith of our glorious Lord Jesus Christ without acts of favoritism*   [g] Gk *Sit under my footstool*   [h] Gk *brothers*

King James

18Yea, a man may say, Thou hast faith, and I have works: show me thy faith without thy works, and I will show thee my faith by my works.

19Thou believest that there is one God; thou doest well: the devils also believe, and tremble.

20But wilt thou know, O vain man, that faith without works is dead?

21Was not Abraham our father justified by works, when he had offered Isaac his son upon the altar?

22Seest thou how faith wrought with his works, and by works was faith made perfect?

23And the scripture was fulfilled which saith, Abraham believed God, and it was imputed unto him for righteousness: and he was called the Friend of God.

24Ye see then how that by works a man is justified, and not by faith only.

25Likewise also was not Rahab the harlot justified by works, when she had received the messengers, and had sent *them* out another way?

26For as the body without the spirit is dead, so faith without works is dead also.

3 MY BRETHREN, be not many masters, knowing that we shall receive the greater condemnation.

2For in many things we offend all. If any man offend not in word, the same *is* a perfect man, *and* able also to bridle the whole body.

3Behold, we put bits in the horses' mouths, that they may obey us; and we turn about their whole body.

4Behold also the ships, which though *they be* so great, and *are* driven of fierce winds, yet are they turned about with a very small helm, whithersoever the governor listeth.

5Even so the tongue is a little member, and boasteth great things. Behold, how great a matter a little fire kindleth!

6And the tongue *is* a fire, a world of iniquity: so is the tongue among our members, that it defileth the whole body, and setteth on fire the course of nature; and it is set on fire of hell.

7For every kind of beasts, and of birds, and of serpents, and of things in the sea, is tamed, and hath been tamed of mankind:

8But the tongue can no man tame; *it is* an unruly evil, full of deadly poison.

9Therewith bless we God, even the Father; and therewith curse we men, which are made after the similitude of God.

10Out of the same mouth proceedeth blessing and cursing. My brethren, these things ought not so to be.

11Doth a fountain send forth at the same place sweet *water* and bitter?

12Can the fig tree, my brethren, bear olive berries? either a vine, figs? so *can* no fountain both yield salt water and fresh.

13Who *is* a wise man and endued with knowledge among you? let him show out of a good conversation his works with meekness of wisdom.

14But if ye have bitter envying and strife in your hearts, glory not, and lie not against the truth.

15This wisdom descendeth not from above, but *is* earthly, sensual, devilish.

New International

18But someone will say, "You have faith; I have deeds."

Show me your faith without deeds, and I will show you my faith by what I do. 19You believe that there is one God. Good! Even the demons believe that—and shudder.

20You foolish man, do you want evidence that faith without deeds is useless*a*? 21Was not our ancestor Abraham considered righteous for what he did when he offered his son Isaac on the altar? 22You see that his faith and his actions were working together, and his faith was made complete by what he did. 23And the scripture was fulfilled that says, "Abraham believed God, and it was credited to him as righteousness,"*b* and he was called God's friend. 24You see that a person is justified by what he does and not by faith alone.

25In the same way, was not even Rahab the prostitute considered righteous for what she did when she gave lodging to the spies and sent them off in a different direction? 26As the body without the spirit is dead, so faith without deeds is dead.

Taming the Tongue

3 NOT MANY of you should presume to be teachers, my brothers, because you know that we who teach will be judged more strictly. 2We all stumble in many ways. If anyone is never at fault in what he says, he is a perfect man, able to keep his whole body in check.

3When we put bits into the mouths of horses to make them obey us, we can turn the whole animal. 4Or take ships as an example. Although they are so large and are driven by strong winds, they are steered by a very small rudder wherever the pilot wants to go. 5Likewise the tongue is a small part of the body, but it makes great boasts. Consider what a great forest is set on fire by a small spark. 6The tongue also is a fire, a world of evil among the parts of the body. It corrupts the whole person, sets the whole course of his life on fire, and is itself set on fire by hell.

7All kinds of animals, birds, reptiles and creatures of the sea are being tamed and have been tamed by man, 8but no man can tame the tongue. It is a restless evil, full of deadly poison.

9With the tongue we praise our Lord and Father, and with it we curse men, who have been made in God's likeness. 10Out of the same mouth come praise and cursing. My brothers, this should not be. 11Can both fresh water and salt*c* water flow from the same spring? 12My brothers, can a fig tree bear olives, or a grapevine bear figs? Neither can a salt spring produce fresh water.

Two Kinds of Wisdom

13Who is wise and understanding among you? Let him show it by his good life, by deeds done in the humility that comes from wisdom. 14But if you harbor bitter envy and selfish ambition in your hearts, do not boast about it or deny the truth. 15Such "wisdom" does not come down from heaven but is earthly, unspiritual, of the devil. 16For where you have envy and selfish

a 20 Some early manuscripts *dead*   *b 23* Gen. 15:6   *c 11* Greek *bitter* (see also verse 14)

Living Bible

18But someone may well argue, "You say the way to God is by faith alone, plus nothing; well, I say that good works are important too, for without good works you can't prove whether you have faith or not; but anyone can see that I have faith by the way I act."

19Are there still some among you who hold that "only believing" is enough? Believing in one God? Well, remember that the demons believe this too—so strongly that they tremble in terror! 20Fool! When will you ever learn that "believing" is useless without *doing* what God wants you to? Faith that does not result in good deeds is not real faith.

21Don't you remember that even our father Abraham was declared good because of what he *did*, when he was willing to obey God, even if it meant offering his son Isaac to die on the altar? 22You see, he was trusting God so much that he was willing to do whatever God told him to; his faith was made complete by what he did, by his actions, his good deeds. 23And so it happened just as the Scriptures say, that Abraham trusted God, and the Lord declared him good in God's sight, and he was even called "the friend of God." 24So you see, a man is saved by what he does, as well as by what he believes.

25Rahab, the prostitute, is another example of this. She was saved because of what she did when she hid those messengers and sent them safely away by a different road. 26Just as the body is dead when there is no spirit in it, so faith is dead if it is not the kind that results in good deeds.

3 DEAR BROTHERS, don't be too eager to tell others their faults,d for we all make many mistakes; and when we teachers of religion, who should know better, do wrong, our punishment will be greater than it would be for others.

If anyone can control his tongue, it proves that he has perfect control over himself in every other way. 3We can make a large horse turn around and go wherever we want by means of a small bit in his mouth. 4And a tiny rudder makes a huge ship turn wherever the pilot wants it to go, even though the winds are strong.

5So also the tongue is a small thing, but what enormous damage it can do. A great forest can be set on fire by one tiny spark. 6And the tongue is a flame of fire. It is full of wickedness, and poisons every part of the body. And the tongue is set on fire by hell itself, and can turn our whole lives into a blazing flame of destruction and disaster.

7Men have trained, or can train, every kind of animal or bird that lives and every kind of reptile and fish, 8but no human being can tame the tongue. It is always ready to pour out its deadly poison. 9Sometimes it praises our heavenly Father, and sometimes it breaks out into curses against men who are made like God. 10And so blessing and cursing come pouring out of the same mouth. Dear brothers, surely this is not right! 11Does a spring of water bubble out first with fresh water and then with bitter water? 12Can you pick olives from a fig tree, or figs from a grape vine? No, and you can't draw fresh water from a salty pool.

13If you are wise, live a life of steady goodness, so that only good deeds will pour forth. And if you don't brag about them, then you will be truly wise! 14And by all means don't brag about being wise and good if you are bitter and jealous and selfish; that is the worst sort of lie. 15For jealousy and selfishness are not God's kind of wisdom. Such things are earthly, unspiritual, inspired by the devil. 16For wherever there is jealousy or selfish

New Revised Standard

18 But someone will say, "You have faith and I have works." Show me your faith apart from your works, and I by my works will show you my faith. 19You believe that God is one; you do well. Even the demons believe—and shudder. 20Do you want to be shown, you senseless person, that faith apart from works is barren? 21Was not our ancestor Abraham justified by works when he offered his son Isaac on the altar? 22You see that faith was active along with his works, and faith was brought to completion by the works. 23Thus the scripture was fulfilled that says, "Abraham believed God, and it was reckoned to him as righteousness," and he was called the friend of God. 24You see that a person is justified by works and not by faith alone. 25Likewise, was not Rahab the prostitute also justified by works when she welcomed the messengers and sent them out by another road? 26For just as the body without the spirit is dead, so faith without works is also dead.

Taming the Tongue

3 NOT MANY of you should become teachers, my brothers and sisters,e for you know that we who teach will be judged with greater strictness. 2For all of us make many mistakes. Anyone who makes no mistakes in speaking is perfect, able to keep the whole body in check with a bridle. 3If we put bits into the mouths of horses to make them obey us, we guide their whole bodies. 4Or look at ships: though they are so large that it takes strong winds to drive them, yet they are guided by a very small rudder wherever the will of the pilot directs. 5So also the tongue is a small member, yet it boasts of great exploits.

How great a forest is set ablaze by a small fire! 6And the tongue is a fire. The tongue is placed among our members as a world of iniquity; it stains the whole body, sets on fire the cycle of nature,f and is itself set on fire by hell.g 7For every species of beast and bird, of reptile and sea creature, can be tamed and has been tamed by the human species, 8but no one can tame the tongue—a restless evil, full of deadly poison. 9With it we bless the Lord and Father, and with it we curse those who are made in the likeness of God. 10From the same mouth come blessing and cursing. My brothers and sisters,h this ought not to be so. 11Does a spring pour forth from the same opening both fresh and brackish water? 12Can a fig tree, my brothers and sisters,i yield olives, or a grapevine figs? No more can salt water yield fresh.

Two Kinds of Wisdom

13 Who is wise and understanding among you? Show by your good life that your works are done with gentleness born of wisdom. 14But if you have bitter envy and selfish ambition in your hearts, do not be boastful and false to the truth. 15Such wisdom does not come down from above, but is earthly, unspiritual, devilish.

---

d 3:1 *don't be too eager to tell others their faults,* literally, "not many (of you) should become masters (teachers)."

e Gk *brothers* f Or *wheel of birth* g Gk *Gehenna* h Gk *My brothers* i Gk *my brothers*

King James

16For where envying and strife *is*, there *is* confusion and every evil work.

17But the wisdom that is from above is first pure, then peaceable, gentle, *and* easy to be entreated, full of mercy and good fruits, without partiality, and without hypocrisy.

18And the fruit of righteousness is sown in peace of them that make peace.

4 FROM WHENCE *come* wars and fightings among you? *come they* not hence, *even* of your lusts that war in your members?

2Ye lust, and have not: ye kill, and desire to have, and cannot obtain: ye fight and war, yet ye have not, because ye ask not.

3Ye ask, and receive not, because ye ask amiss, that ye may consume *it* upon your lusts.

4Ye adulterers and adulteresses, know ye not that the friendship of the world is enmity with God? whosoever therefore will be a friend of the world is the enemy of God.

5Do ye think that the scripture saith in vain, The spirit that dwelleth in us lusteth to envy?

6But he giveth more grace. Wherefore he saith, God resisteth the proud, but giveth grace unto the humble.

7Submit yourselves therefore to God. Resist the devil, and he will flee from you.

8Draw nigh to God, and he will draw nigh to you. Cleanse *your* hands, *ye* sinners; and purify *your* hearts, *ye* double minded.

9Be afflicted, and mourn, and weep: let your laughter be turned to mourning, and *your* joy to heaviness.

10Humble yourselves in the sight of the Lord, and he shall lift you up.

11Speak not evil one of another, brethren. He that speaketh evil of *his* brother, and judgeth his brother, speaketh evil of the law, and judgeth the law: but if thou judge the law, thou art not a doer of the law, but a judge.

12There is one lawgiver, who is able to save and to destroy: who art thou that judgest another?

13Go to now, ye that say, Today or tomorrow we will go into such a city, and continue there a year, and buy and sell, and get gain:

14Whereas ye know not what *shall be* on the morrow. For what *is* your life? It is even a vapour, that appeareth for a little time, and then vanisheth away.

15For that ye *ought* to say, If the Lord will, we shall live, and do this, or that.

16But now ye rejoice in your boastings: all such rejoicing is evil.

17Therefore to him that knoweth to do good, and doeth *it* not, to him it is sin.

5 GO TO now, *ye* rich men, weep and howl for your miseries that shall come upon *you*.

2Your riches are corrupted, and your garments are motheaten.

New International

ambition, there you find disorder and every evil practice.

17But the wisdom that comes from heaven is first of all pure; then peace-loving, considerate, submissive, full of mercy and good fruit, impartial and sincere. 18Peacemakers who sow in peace raise a harvest of righteousness.

Submit Yourselves to God

4 WHAT CAUSES fights and quarrels among you? Don't they come from your desires that battle within you? 2You want something but don't get it. You kill and covet, but you cannot have what you want. You quarrel and fight. You do not have, because you do not ask God. 3When you ask, you do not receive, because you ask with wrong motives, that you may spend what you get on your pleasures.

4You adulterous people, don't you know that friendship with the world is hatred toward God? Anyone who chooses to be a friend of the world becomes an enemy of God. 5Or do you think Scripture says without reason that the spirit he caused to live in us envies intensely?[a] 6But he gives us more grace. That is why Scripture says:

"God opposes the proud
  but gives grace to the humble."[b]

7Submit yourselves, then, to God. Resist the devil, and he will flee from you. 8Come near to God and he will come near to you. Wash your hands, you sinners, and purify your hearts, you double-minded. 9Grieve, mourn and wail. Change your laughter to mourning and your joy to gloom. 10Humble yourselves before the Lord, and he will lift you up.

11Brothers, do not slander one another. Anyone who speaks against his brother or judges him speaks against the law and judges it. When you judge the law, you are not keeping it, but sitting in judgment on it. 12There is only one Lawgiver and Judge, the one who is able to save and destroy. But you—who are you to judge your neighbor?

Boasting About Tomorrow

13Now listen, you who say, "Today or tomorrow we will go to this or that city, spend a year there, carry on business and make money." 14Why, you do not even know what will happen tomorrow. What is your life? You are a mist that appears for a little while and then vanishes. 15Instead, you ought to say, "If it is the Lord's will, we will live and do this or that." 16As it is, you boast and brag. All such boasting is evil. 17Anyone, then, who knows the good he ought to do and doesn't do it, sins.

Warning to Rich Oppressors

5 NOW LISTEN, you rich people, weep and wail because of the misery that is coming upon you. 2Your wealth has rotted, and moths have eaten your clothes. 3Your gold and silver are corroded. Their corro-

---

a 5 Or *that God jealously longs for the spirit that he made to live in us*; or *that the Spirit he caused to live in us longs jealously*   b 6 Prov. 3:34

Living Bible

ambition, there will be disorder and every other kind of evil.

17But the wisdom that comes from heaven is first of all pure and full of quiet gentleness. Then it is peace-loving and courteous. It allows discussion and is willing to yield to others; it is full of mercy and good deeds. It is wholehearted and straightforward and sincere. 18And those who are peacemakers will plant seeds of peace and reap a harvest of goodness.

4 WHAT IS causing the quarrels and fights among you? Isn't it because there is a whole army of evil desires within you? 2You want what you don't have, so you kill to get it. You long for what others have, and can't afford it, so you start a fight to take it away from them. And yet the reason you don't have what you want is that you don't ask God for it. 3And even when you do ask you don't get it because your whole aim is wrong—you want only what will give *you* pleasure.

4You are like an unfaithful wife who loves her husband's enemies. Don't you realize that making friends with God's enemies—the evil pleasures of this world— makes you an enemy of God? I say it again, that if your aim is to enjoy the evil pleasure of the unsaved world, you cannot also be a friend of God. 5Or what do you think the Scripture means when it says that the Holy Spirit, whom God has placed within us, watches over us with tender jealousy? 6But he gives us more and more strength to stand against all such evil longings. As the Scripture says, God gives strength to the humble, but sets himself against the proud and haughty.

7So give yourselves humbly to God. Resist the devil and he will flee from you. 8And when you draw close to God, God will draw close to you. Wash your hands, you sinners, and let your hearts be filled with God alone to make them pure and true to him. 9Let there be tears for the wrong things you have done. Let there be sorrow and sincere grief. Let there be sadness instead of laughter, and gloom instead of joy. 10Then when you realize your worthlessness before the Lord, he will lift you up, encourage and help you.

11Don't criticize and speak evil about each other, dear brothers. If you do, you will be fighting against God's law of loving one another, declaring it is wrong. But your job is not to decide whether this law is right or wrong, but to obey it. 12Only he who made the law can rightly judge among us. He alone decides to save us or destroy. So what right do you have to judge or criticize others?

13Look here, you people who say, "Today or tomorrow we are going to such and such a town, stay there a year, and open up a profitable business." 14How do you know what is going to happen tomorrow? For the length of your lives is as uncertain as the morning fog— now you see it; soon it is gone. 15What you ought to say is, "If the Lord wants us to, we shall live and do this or that." 16Otherwise you will be bragging about your own plans, and such self-confidence never pleases God. 17Remember, too, that knowing what is right to do and then not doing it is sin.

5 LOOK HERE, you rich men, now is the time to cry and groan with anguished grief because of all the terrible troubles ahead of you. 2Your wealth is even now rotting away, and your fine clothes are becoming mere moth-eaten rags. 3The value of your gold and silver

New Revised Standard

16For where there is envy and selfish ambition, there will also be disorder and wickedness of every kind. 17But the wisdom from above is first pure, then peaceable, gentle, willing to yield, full of mercy and good fruits, without a trace of partiality or hypocrisy. 18And a harvest of righteousness is sown in peace forc those who make peace.

Friendship with the World

4 THOSE CONFLICTS and disputes among you, where do they come from? Do they not come from your cravings that are at war within you? 2You want something and do not have it; so you commit murder. And you covetd something and cannot obtain it; so you engage in disputes and conflicts. You do not have, because you do not ask. 3You ask and do not receive, because you ask wrongly, in order to spend what you get on your pleasures. 4Adulterers! Do you not know that friendship with the world is enmity with God? Therefore whoever wishes to be a friend of the world becomes an enemy of God. 5Or do you suppose that it is for nothing that the scripture says, "Gode yearns jealously for the spirit that he has made to dwell in us"? 6But he gives all the more grace; therefore it says,

"God opposes the proud,
    but gives grace to the humble."

7Submit yourselves therefore to God. Resist the devil, and he will flee from you. 8Draw near to God, and he will draw near to you. Cleanse your hands, you sinners, and purify your hearts, you double-minded. 9Lament and mourn and weep. Let your laughter be turned into mourning and your joy into dejection. 10Humble yourselves before the Lord, and he will exalt you.

Warning against Judging Another

11 Do not speak evil against one another, brothers and sisters.f Whoever speaks evil against another or judges another, speaks evil against the law and judges the law; but if you judge the law, you are not a doer of the law but a judge. 12There is one lawgiver and judge who is able to save and to destroy. So who, then, are you to judge your neighbor?

Boasting about Tomorrow

13 Come now, you who say, "Today or tomorrow we will go to such and such a town and spend a year there, doing business and making money." 14Yet you do not even know what tomorrow will bring. What is your life? For you are a mist that appears for a little while and then vanishes. 15Instead you ought to say, "If the Lord wishes, we will live and do this or that." 16As it is, you boast in your arrogance; all such boasting is evil. 17Anyone, then, who knows the right thing to do and fails to do it, commits sin.

Warning to Rich Oppressors

5 COME NOW, you rich people, weep and wail for the miseries that are coming to you. 2Your riches have rotted, and your clothes are moth-eaten. 3Your

---

c Or by   d Or you murder and you covet   e Gk He   f Gk brothers

King James

3Your gold and silver is cankered; and the rust of them shall be a witness against you, and shall eat your flesh as it were fire. Ye have heaped treasure together for the last days.

4Behold, the hire of the labourers who have reaped down your fields, which is of you kept back by fraud, crieth: and the cries of them which have reaped are entered into the ears of the Lord of sabaoth.

5Ye have lived in pleasure on the earth, and been wanton; ye have nourished your hearts, as in a day of slaughter.

6Ye have condemned and killed the just; and he doth not resist you.

7Be patient therefore, brethren, unto the coming of the Lord. Behold, the husbandman waiteth for the precious fruit of the earth, and hath long patience for it, until he receive the early and latter rain.

8Be ye also patient; stablish your hearts: for the coming of the Lord draweth nigh.

9Grudge not one against another, brethren, lest ye be condemned: behold, the judge standeth before the door.

10Take, my brethren, the prophets, who have spoken in the name of the Lord, for an example of suffering affliction, and of patience.

11Behold, we count them happy which endure. Ye have heard of the patience of Job, and have seen the end of the Lord; that the Lord is very pitiful, and of tender mercy.

12But above all things, my brethren, swear not, neither by heaven, neither by the earth, neither by any other oath: but let your yea be yea; and your nay, nay; lest ye fall into condemnation.

13Is any among you afflicted? let him pray. Is any merry? let him sing psalms.

14Is any sick among you? let him call for the elders of the church; and let them pray over him, anointing him with oil in the name of the Lord:

15And the prayer of faith shall save the sick, and the Lord shall raise him up; and if he have committed sins, they shall be forgiven him.

16Confess your faults one to another, and pray one for another, that ye may be healed. The effectual fervent prayer of a righteous man availeth much.

17Elias was a man subject to like passions as we are, and he prayed earnestly that it might not rain: and it rained not on the earth by the space of three years and six months.

18And he prayed again, and the heaven gave rain, and the earth brought forth her fruit.

19Brethren, if any of you do err from the truth, and one convert him;

20Let him know, that he which converteth the sinner from the error of his way shall save a soul from death, and shall hide a multitude of sins.

New International

sion will testify against you and eat your flesh like fire. You have hoarded wealth in the last days. 4Look! The wages you failed to pay the workmen who mowed your fields are crying out against you. The cries of the harvesters have reached the ears of the Lord Almighty. 5You have lived on earth in luxury and self-indulgence. You have fattened yourselves in the day of slaughter.a 6You have condemned and murdered innocent men, who were not opposing you.

Patience in Suffering

7Be patient, then, brothers, until the Lord's coming. See how the farmer waits for the land to yield its valuable crop and how patient he is for the autumn and spring rains. 8You too, be patient and stand firm, because the Lord's coming is near. 9Don't grumble against each other, brothers, or you will be judged. The Judge is standing at the door!

10Brothers, as an example of patience in the face of suffering, take the prophets who spoke in the name of the Lord. 11As you know, we consider blessed those who have persevered. You have heard of Job's perseverance and have seen what the Lord finally brought about. The Lord is full of compassion and mercy.

12Above all, my brothers, do not swear—not by heaven or by earth or by anything else. Let your "Yes" be yes, and your "No," no, or you will be condemned.

The Prayer of Faith

13Is any one of you in trouble? He should pray. Is anyone happy? Let him sing songs of praise. 14Is any one of you sick? He should call the elders of the church to pray over him and anoint him with oil in the name of the Lord. 15And the prayer offered in faith will make the sick person well; the Lord will raise him up. If he has sinned, he will be forgiven. 16Therefore confess your sins to each other and pray for each other so that you may be healed. The prayer of a righteous man is powerful and effective.

17Elijah was a man just like us. He prayed earnestly that it would not rain, and it did not rain on the land for three and a half years. 18Again he prayed, and the heavens gave rain, and the earth produced its crops.

19My brothers, if one of you should wander from the truth and someone should bring him back, 20remember this: Whoever turns a sinner from the error of his way will save him from death and cover over a multitude of sins.

Living Bible

is dropping fast, yet it will stand as evidence against you, and eat your flesh like fire. That is what you have stored up for yourselves, to receive on that coming day of judgment. 4For listen! Hear the cries of the field workers whom you have cheated of their pay. Their cries have reached the ears of the Lord of Hosts.

5You have spent your years here on earth having fun, satisfying your every whim, and now your fat hearts are ready for the slaughter. 6You have condemned and killed good men who had no power to defend themselves against you.

7Now as for you, dear brothers who are waiting for the Lord's return, be patient, like a farmer who waits until the autumn for his precious harvest to ripen. 8Yes, be patient. And take courage, for the coming of the Lord is near.

9Don't grumble about each other, brothers. Are you yourselves above criticism? For see! The great Judge is coming. He is almost here. [Let him do whatever criticizing must be done b.]

10For examples of patience in suffering, look at the Lord's prophets. 11We know how happy they are now because they stayed true to him then, even though they suffered greatly for it. Job is an example of a man who continued to trust the Lord in sorrow; from his experiences we can see how the Lord's plan finally ended in good, for he is full of tenderness and mercy.

12But most of all, dear brothers, do not swear either by heaven or earth or anything else; just say a simple yes or no, so that you will not sin and be condemned for it.

13Is anyone among you suffering? He should keep on praying about it. And those who have reason to be thankful should continually be singing praises to the Lord.

14Is anyone sick? He should call for the elders of the church and they should pray over him and pour a little oil upon him, calling on the Lord to heal him. 15And their prayer, if offered in faith, will heal him, for the Lord will make him well; and if his sickness was caused by some sin, the Lord will forgive him.

16Admit your faults to one another and pray for each other so that you may be healed. The earnest prayer of a righteous man has great power and wonderful results. 17Elijah was as completely human as we are, and yet when he prayed earnestly that no rain would fall, none fell for the next three and one half years! 18Then he prayed again, this time that it *would* rain, and down it poured and the grass turned green and the gardens began to grow again.

19Dear brothers, if anyone has slipped away from God and no longer trusts the Lord and someone helps him understand the Truth again, 20that person who brings him back to God will have saved a wandering soul from death, bringing about the forgiveness of his many sins.

Sincerely, James

New Revised Standard

gold and silver have rusted, and their rust will be evidence against you, and it will eat your flesh like fire. You have laid up treasure c for the last days. 4Listen! The wages of the laborers who mowed your fields, which you kept back by fraud, cry out, and the cries of the harvesters have reached the ears of the Lord of hosts. 5You have lived on the earth in luxury and in pleasure; you have fattened your hearts in a day of slaughter. 6You have condemned and murdered the righteous one, who does not resist you.

Patience in Suffering

7 Be patient, therefore, beloved, d until the coming of the Lord. The farmer waits for the precious crop from the earth, being patient with it until it receives the early and the late rains. 8You also must be patient. Strengthen your hearts, for the coming of the Lord is near. e 9Beloved, f do not grumble against one another, so that you may not be judged. See, the Judge is standing at the doors! 10As an example of suffering and patience, beloved, d take the prophets who spoke in the name of the Lord. 11Indeed we call blessed those who showed endurance. You have heard of the endurance of Job, and you have seen the purpose of the Lord, how the Lord is compassionate and merciful.

12 Above all, my beloved, d do not swear, either by heaven or by earth or by any other oath, but let your "Yes" be yes and your "No" be no, so that you may not fall under condemnation.

The Prayer of Faith

13 Are any among you suffering? They should pray. Are any cheerful? They should sing songs of praise. 14Are any among you sick? They should call for the elders of the church and have them pray over them, anointing them with oil in the name of the Lord. 15The prayer of faith will save the sick, and the Lord will raise them up; and anyone who has committed sins will be forgiven. 16Therefore confess your sins to one another, and pray for one another, so that you may be healed. The prayer of the righteous is powerful and effective. 17Elijah was a human being like us, and he prayed fervently that it might not rain, and for three years and six months it did not rain on the earth. 18Then he prayed again, and the heaven gave rain and the earth yielded its harvest.

19 My brothers and sisters, g if anyone among you wanders from the truth and is brought back by another, 20you should know that whoever brings back a sinner from wandering will save the sinner's sh soul from death and will cover a multitude of sins.

---

b 5:9 Let him do whatever criticizing must be done, implied.

c Or will eat your flesh, since you have stored up fire   d Gk brothers   e Or is at hand   f Gk Brothers   g Gk My brothers   h Gk his

THE FIRST

EPISTLE GENERAL OF

Peter

1 Peter

1 PETER, AN apostle of Jesus Christ, to the strangers scattered throughout Pontus, Galatia, Cappadocia, Asia, and Bithynia,

2Elect according to the foreknowledge of God the Father, through sanctification of the Spirit, unto obedience and sprinkling of the blood of Jesus Christ: Grace unto you, and peace, be multiplied.

3Blessed *be* the God and Father of our Lord Jesus Christ, which according to his abundant mercy hath begotten us again unto a lively hope by the resurrection of Jesus Christ from the dead,

4To an inheritance incorruptible, and undefiled, and that fadeth not away, reserved in heaven for you,

5Who are kept by the power of God through faith unto salvation ready to be revealed in the last time.

6Wherein ye greatly rejoice, though now for a season, if need be, ye are in heaviness through manifold temptations:

7That the trial of your faith, being much more precious than of gold that perisheth, though it be tried with fire, might be found unto praise and honour and glory at the appearing of Jesus Christ:

8Whom having not seen, ye love; in whom, though now ye see *him* not, yet believing, ye rejoice with joy unspeakable and full of glory:

9Receiving the end of your faith, *even* the salvation of *your* souls.

10Of which salvation the prophets have inquired and searched diligently, who prophesied of the grace *that should come* unto you:

11Searching what, or what manner of time the Spirit of Christ which was in them did signify, when it testified beforehand the sufferings of Christ, and the glory that should follow.

12Unto whom it was revealed, that not unto themselves, but unto us they did minister the things, which are now reported unto you by them that have preached the gospel unto you with the Holy Ghost sent down from heaven; which things the angels desire to look into.

13Wherefore gird up the loins of your mind, be sober, and hope to the end for the grace that is to be brought unto you at the revelation of Jesus Christ;

14As obedient children, not fashioning yourselves according to the former lusts in your ignorance:

15But as he which hath called you is holy, so be ye holy in all manner of conversation;

1 PETER, AN apostle of Jesus Christ,

To God's elect, strangers in the world, scattered throughout Pontus, Galatia, Cappadocia, Asia and Bithynia, 2who have been chosen according to the foreknowledge of God the Father, through the sanctifying work of the Spirit, for obedience to Jesus Christ and sprinkling by his blood:

Grace and peace be yours in abundance.

Praise to God for a Living Hope

3Praise be to the God and Father of our Lord Jesus Christ! In his great mercy he has given us new birth into a living hope through the resurrection of Jesus Christ from the dead, 4and into an inheritance that can never perish, spoil or fade—kept in heaven for you, 5who through faith are shielded by God's power until the coming of the salvation that is ready to be revealed in the last time. 6In this you greatly rejoice, though now for a little while you may have had to suffer grief in all kinds of trials. 7These have come so that your faith—of greater worth than gold, which perishes even though refined by fire—may be proved genuine and may result in praise, glory and honor when Jesus Christ is revealed. 8Though you have not seen him, you love him; and even though you do not see him now, you believe in him and are filled with an inexpressible and glorious joy, 9for you are receiving the goal of your faith, the salvation of your souls.

10Concerning this salvation, the prophets, who spoke of the grace that was to come to you, searched intently and with the greatest care, 11trying to find out the time and circumstances to which the Spirit of Christ in them was pointing when he predicted the sufferings of Christ and the glories that would follow. 12It was revealed to them that they were not serving themselves but you, when they spoke of the things that have now been told you by those who have preached the gospel to you by the Holy Spirit sent from heaven. Even angels long to look into these things.

Be Holy

13Therefore, prepare your minds for action; be self-controlled; set your hope fully on the grace to be given you when Jesus Christ is revealed. 14As obedient children, do not conform to the evil desires you had when you lived in ignorance. 15But just as he who called you

1 Peter

THE FIRST LETTER OF

Peter

1 *FROM:* PETER, Jesus Christ's missionary.
To: The Jewish Christians driven out of Jerusalem and scattered throughout Pontus, Galatia, Cappadocia, Asia minor, and Bithynia.

2Dear friends, God the Father chose you long ago and knew you would become his children. And the Holy Spirit has been at work in your hearts, cleansing you with the blood of Jesus Christ and making you to please him. May God bless you richly and grant you increasing freedom from all anxiety and fear.

3All honor to God, the God and Father of our Lord Jesus Christ; for it is his boundless mercy that has given us the privilege of being born again, so that we are now members of God's own family. Now we live in the hope of eternal life because Christ rose again from the dead. 4And God has reserved for his children the priceless gift of eternal life; it is kept in heaven for you, pure and undefiled, beyond the reach of change and decay. 5And God, in his mighty power, will make sure that you get there safely to receive it, because you are trusting him. It will be yours in that coming last day for all to see. 6So be truly glad! There is wonderful joy ahead, even though the going is rough for a while down here.

7These trials are only to test your faith, to see whether or not it is strong and pure. It is being tested as fire tests gold and purifies it—and your faith is far more precious to God than mere gold; so if your faith remains strong after being tried in the test tube of fiery trials, it will bring you much praise and glory and honor on the day of his return.

8You love him even though you have never seen him; though not seeing him, you trust him; and even now you are happy with the inexpressible joy that comes from heaven itself. 9And your further reward for trusting him will be the salvation of your souls.

10This salvation was something the prophets did not fully understand. Though they wrote about it, they had many questions as to what it all could mean. 11They wondered what the Spirit of Christ within them was talking about, for he told them to write down the events which, since then, have happened to Christ: his suffering, and his great glory afterwards. And they wondered when and to whom all this would happen.

12They were finally told that these things would not occur during their lifetime, but long years later, during yours. And now at last this Good News has been plainly announced to all of us. It was preached to us in the power of the same heaven-sent Holy Spirit who spoke to them; and it is all so strange and wonderful that even the angels in heaven would give a great deal to know more about it.

13So now you can look forward soberly and intelligently to more of God's kindness to you when Jesus Christ returns.

14Obey God because you are his children; don't slip back into your old ways—doing evil because you knew no better. 15But be holy now in everything you do, just as the Lord is holy, who invited you to be his child. 16He

Salutation

1 PETER, AN apostle of Jesus Christ,
To the exiles of the Dispersion in Pontus, Galatia, Cappadocia, Asia, and Bithynia, 2who have been chosen and destined by God the Father and sanctified by the Spirit to be obedient to Jesus Christ and to be sprinkled with his blood:

May grace and peace be yours in abundance.

A Living Hope

3 Blessed be the God and Father of our Lord Jesus Christ! By his great mercy he has given us a new birth into a living hope through the resurrection of Jesus Christ from the dead, 4and into an inheritance that is imperishable, undefiled, and unfading, kept in heaven for you, 5who are being protected by the power of God through faith for a salvation ready to be revealed in the last time. 6In this you rejoice,a even if now for a little while you have had to suffer various trials, 7so that the genuineness of your faith—being more precious than gold that, though perishable, is tested by fire—may be found to result in praise and glory and honor when Jesus Christ is revealed. 8Although you have not seenb him, you love him; and even though you do not see him now, you believe in him and rejoice with an indescribable and glorious joy, 9for you are receiving the outcome of your faith, the salvation of your souls.

10 Concerning this salvation, the prophets who prophesied of the grace that was to be yours made careful search and inquiry, 11inquiring about the person or time that the Spirit of Christ within them indicated when it testified in advance to the sufferings destined for Christ and the subsequent glory. 12It was revealed to them that they were serving not themselves but you, in regard to the things that have now been announced to you through those who brought you good news by the Holy Spirit sent from heaven—things into which angels long to look!

A Call to Holy Living

13 Therefore prepare your minds for action;c discipline yourselves; set all your hope on the grace that Jesus Christ will bring you when he is revealed. 14Like obedient children, do not be conformed to the desires that you formerly had in ignorance. 15Instead, as he who called you is holy, be holy yourselves in all your conduct;

a Or *Rejoice in this*   b Other ancient authorities read *known*   c Gk *gird up the loins of your mind*

King James

16Because it is written, Be ye holy; for I am holy.

17And if ye call on the Father, who without respect of persons judgeth according to every man's work, pass the time of your sojourning *here* in fear:

18Forasmuch as ye know that ye were not redeemed with corruptible things, *as* silver and gold, from your vain conversation *received* by tradition from your fathers;

19But with the precious blood of Christ, as of a lamb without blemish and without spot:

20Who verily was foreordained before the foundation of the world, but was manifest in these last times for you,

21Who by him do believe in God, that raised him up from the dead, and gave him glory; that your faith and hope might be in God.

22Seeing ye have purified your souls in obeying the truth through the Spirit unto unfeigned love of the brethren, *see that ye* love one another with a pure heart fervently:

23Being born again, not of corruptible seed, but of incorruptible, by the word of God, which liveth and abideth for ever.

24For all flesh *is* as grass, and all the glory of man as the flower of grass. The grass withereth, and the flower thereof falleth away:

25But the word of the Lord endureth for ever. And this is the word which by the gospel is preached unto you.

2 WHEREFORE LAYING aside all malice, and all guile, and hypocrisies, and envies, and all evil speakings,

2As newborn babes, desire the sincere milk of the word, that ye may grow thereby:

3If so be ye have tasted that the Lord *is* gracious.

4To whom coming, *as unto* a living stone, disallowed indeed of men, but chosen of God, *and* precious,

5Ye also, as lively stones, are built up a spiritual house, an holy priesthood, to offer up spiritual sacrifices, acceptable to God by Jesus Christ.

6Wherefore also it is contained in the scripture, Behold, I lay in Zion a chief corner stone, elect, precious: and he that believeth on him shall not be confounded.

7Unto you therefore which believe *he is* precious: but unto them which be disobedient, the stone which the builders disallowed, the same is made the head of the corner,

8And a stone of stumbling, and a rock of offence, *even to them* which stumble at the word, being disobedient: whereunto also they were appointed.

9But ye *are* a chosen generation, a royal priesthood, an holy nation, a peculiar people; that ye should show forth the praises of him who hath called you out of darkness into his marvellous light:

10Which in time past *were* not a people, but *are* now the people of God: which had not obtained mercy, but now have obtained mercy.

New International

is holy, so be holy in all you do; 16for it is written: "Be holy, because I am holy."[a]

17Since you call on a Father who judges each man's work impartially, live your lives as strangers here in reverent fear. 18For you know that it was not with perishable things such as silver or gold that you were redeemed from the empty way of life handed down to you from your forefathers, 19but with the precious blood of Christ, a lamb without blemish or defect. 20He was chosen before the creation of the world, but was revealed in these last times for your sake. 21Through him you believe in God, who raised him from the dead and glorified him, and so your faith and hope are in God.

22Now that you have purified yourselves by obeying the truth so that you have sincere love for your brothers, love one another deeply, from the heart.[b] 23For you have been born again, not of perishable seed, but of imperishable, through the living and enduring word of God. 24For,

> "All men are like grass,
>   and all their glory is like the flowers of the field;
> the grass withers and the flowers fall,
> 25 but the word of the Lord stands forever."[c]

And this is the word that was preached to you.

2 THEREFORE, RID yourselves of all malice and all deceit, hypocrisy, envy, and slander of every kind. 2Like newborn babies, crave pure spiritual milk, so that by it you may grow up in your salvation, 3now that you have tasted that the Lord is good.

The Living Stone and a Chosen People

4As you come to him, the living Stone—rejected by men but chosen by God and precious to him— 5you also, like living stones, are being built into a spiritual house to be a holy priesthood, offering spiritual sacrifices acceptable to God through Jesus Christ. 6For in Scripture it says:

> "See, I lay a stone in Zion,
>   a chosen and precious cornerstone,
> and the one who trusts in him
>   will never be put to shame."[d]

7Now to you who believe, this stone is precious. But to those who do not believe,

> "The stone the builders rejected
>   has become the capstone,[e]"[f]

8and,

> "A stone that causes men to stumble
>   and a rock that makes them fall."[g]

They stumble because they disobey the message—which is also what they were destined for.

9But you are a chosen people, a royal priesthood, a holy nation, a people belonging to God, that you may declare the praises of him who called you out of darkness into his wonderful light. 10Once you were not a people, but now you are the people of God; once you had not received mercy, but now you have received mercy.

a *16* Lev. 11:44,45; 19:2; 20:7   b *22* Some early manuscripts *from a pure heart*   c *25* Isaiah   40:6-8   d *6* Isaiah   28:16   e *7* Or   *cornerstone*   f *7* Psalm 118:22   g *8* Isaiah 8:14

Living Bible

himself has said, "You must be holy, for I am holy."

17And remember that your heavenly Father to whom you pray has no favorites when he judges. He will judge you with perfect justice for everything you do; so act in reverent fear of him from now on until you get to heaven. 18God paid a ransom to save you from the impossible road to heaven which your fathers tried to take, and the ransom he paid was not mere gold or silver, as you very well know. 19But he paid for you with the precious life-blood of Christ, the sinless, spotless Lamb of God. 20God chose him for this purpose long before the world began, but only recently was he brought into public view, in these last days, as a blessing to you.

21Because of this, your trust can be in God who raised Christ from the dead and gave him great glory. Now your faith and hope can rest in him alone. 22Now you can have real love for everyone because your souls have been cleansed from selfishness and hatred when you trusted Christ to save you; so see to it that you really do love each other warmly, with all your hearts.

23For you have a new life. It was not passed on to you from your parents, for the life they gave you will fade away. This new one will last forever, for it comes from Christ, God's ever-living Message to men. 24Yes, our natural lives will fade as grass does when it becomes all brown and dry. All our greatness is like a flower that droops and falls; 25but the Word of the Lord will last forever. And his message is the Good News that was preached to you.

2 SO GET rid of your feelings of hatred. Don't just pretend to be good! Be done with dishonesty and jealousy and talking about others behind their backs. 2,3h Now that you realize how kind the Lord has been to you, put away all evil, deception, envy, and fraud. Long to grow up into the fullness of your salvation; cry for this as a baby cries for his milk.

4Come to Christ, who is the living Foundation of Rock upon which God builds; though men have spurned him, he is very precious to God who has chosen him above all others.

5And now you have become living building-stones for God's use in building his house. What's more, you are his holy priests; so come to him—[you who are acceptable to him because of Jesus Christi]—and offer to God those things that please him. 6As the Scriptures express it, "See, I am sending Christ to be the carefully chosen, precious Cornerstone of my church, and I will never disappoint those who trust in him."

7Yes, he is very precious to you who believe; and to those who reject him, well—"The same Stone that was rejected by the builders has become the Cornerstone, the most honored and important part of the building." 8And the Scriptures also say, "He is the Stone that some will stumble over, and the Rock that will make them fall." They will stumble because they will not listen to God's Word, nor obey it, and so this punishment must follow—that they will fall.

9But you are not like that, for you have been chosen by God himself—you are priests of the King, you are holy and pure, you are God's very own—all this so that you may show to others how God called you out of the darkness into his wonderful light. 10Once you were less than nothing; now you are God's own. Once you knew very little of God's kindness; now your very lives have been changed by it.

New Revised Standard

16for it is written, "You shall be holy, for I am holy."

17 If you invoke as Father the one who judges all people impartially according to their deeds, live in reverent fear during the time of your exile. 18You know that you were ransomed from the futile ways inherited from your ancestors, not with perishable things like silver or gold, 19but with the precious blood of Christ, like that of a lamb without defect or blemish. 20He was destined before the foundation of the world, but was revealed at the end of the ages for your sake. 21Through him you have come to trust in God, who raised him from the dead and gave him glory, so that your faith and hope are set on God.

22 Now that you have purified your souls by your obedience to the truthj so that you have genuine mutual love, love one another deeplyk from the heart.l 23You have been born anew, not of perishable but of imperishable seed, through the living and enduring word of God.m 24For

"All flesh is like grass
    and all its glory like the flower of grass.
The grass withers,
    and the flower falls,
25 but the word of the Lord endures forever."
That word is the good news that was announced to you.

The Living Stone and a Chosen People

2 RID YOURSELVES, therefore, of all malice, and all guile, insincerity, envy, and all slander. 2Like newborn infants, long for the pure, spiritual milk, so that by it you may grow into salvation— 3 if indeed you have tasted that the Lord is good.

4 Come to him, a living stone, though rejected by mortals yet chosen and precious in God's sight, and 5like living stones, let yourselves be builtn into a spiritual house, to be a holy priesthood, to offer spiritual sacrifices acceptable to God through Jesus Christ. 6For it stands in scripture:

"See, I am laying in Zion a stone,
    a cornerstone chosen and precious;
and whoever believes in himo will not be put
    to shame."
7To you then who believe, he is precious; but for those who do not believe,

"The stone that the builders rejected
    has become the very head of the corner,"
8and

"A stone that makes them stumble,
    and a rock that makes them fall."
They stumble because they disobey the word, as they were destined to do.

9 But you are a chosen race, a royal priesthood, a holy nation, God's own people,p in order that you may proclaim the mighty acts of him who called you out of darkness into his marvelous light.

10 Once you were not a people,
    but now you are God's people;
once you had not received mercy,
    but now you have received mercy.

---

h 2:2, 3 An alternative paraphrase of these verses could read: "If you have tasted the Lord's goodness and kindness, cry for more, as a baby cries for milk. Eat God's Word—read it, think about it—and grow strong in the Lord and be saved." i 2:5 because of Jesus Christ, implied.

j Other ancient authorities add through the Spirit k Or constantly l Other ancient authorities read a pure heart m Or through the word of the living and enduring God n Or you yourselves are being built o Or it p Gk a people for his possession

King James

11Dearly beloved, I beseech *you* as strangers and pilgrims, abstain from fleshly lusts, which war against the soul;

12Having your conversation honest among the Gentiles: that, whereas they speak against you as evildoers, they may by *your* good works, which they shall behold, glorify God in the day of visitation.

13Submit yourselves to every ordinance of man for the Lord's sake: whether it be to the king, as supreme;

14Or unto governors, as unto them that are sent by him for the punishment of evildoers, and for the praise of them that do well.

15For so is the will of God, that with well doing ye may put to silence the ignorance of foolish men:

16As free, and not using *your* liberty for a cloak of maliciousness, but as the servants of God.

17Honour all *men*. Love the brotherhood. Fear God. Honour the king.

18Servants, *be* subject to *your* masters with all fear; not only to the good and gentle, but also to the froward.

19For this *is* thankworthy, if a man for conscience toward God endure grief, suffering wrongfully.

20For what glory *is it*, if, when ye be buffeted for your faults, ye shall take it patiently? but if, when ye do well, and suffer *for it*, ye take it patiently, this *is* acceptable with God.

21For even hereunto were ye called: because Christ also suffered for us, leaving us an example, that ye should follow his steps:

22Who did no sin, neither was guile found in his mouth:

23Who, when he was reviled, reviled not again; when he suffered, he threatened not; but committed *himself* to him that judgeth righteously:

24Who his own self bare our sins in his own body on the tree, that we, being dead to sins, should live unto righteousness: by whose stripes ye were healed.

25For ye were as sheep going astray; but are now returned unto the Shepherd and Bishop of your souls.

3 LIKEWISE, YE wives, *be* in subjection to your own husbands; that, if any obey not the word, they also may without the word be won by the conversation of the wives;

2While they behold your chaste conversation *coupled* with fear.

3Whose adorning let it not be that outward *adorning* of plaiting the hair, and of wearing of gold, or of putting on of apparel;

4But *let it be* the hidden man of the heart, in that which is not corruptible, *even the ornament* of a meek and quiet spirit, which is in the sight of God of great price.

5For after this manner in the old time the holy women also, who trusted in God, adorned themselves, being in subjection unto their own husbands:

6Even as Sarah obeyed Abraham, calling him lord: whose daughters ye are, as long as ye do well, and are not afraid with any amazement.

7Likewise, ye husbands, dwell with *them* according to knowledge, giving honour unto the wife, as unto the weaker vessel, and as being heirs together of the grace of life; that your prayers be not hindered.

8Finally, *be ye* all of one mind, having compassion one of another, love as brethren, *be* pitiful, *be* courteous:

9Not rendering evil for evil, or railing for railing: but contrariwise blessing; knowing that ye are thereunto called, that ye should inherit a blessing.

New International

11Dear friends, I urge you, as aliens and strangers in the world, to abstain from sinful desires, which war against your soul. 12Live such good lives among the pagans that, though they accuse you of doing wrong, they may see your good deeds and glorify God on the day he visits us.

Submission to Rulers and Masters

13Submit yourselves for the Lord's sake to every authority instituted among men: whether to the king, as the supreme authority, 14or to governors, who are sent by him to punish those who do wrong and to commend those who do right. 15For it is God's will that by doing good you should silence the ignorant talk of foolish men. 16Live as free men, but do not use your freedom as a cover-up for evil; live as servants of God. 17Show proper respect to everyone: Love the brotherhood of believers, fear God, honor the king.

18Slaves, submit yourselves to your masters with all respect, not only to those who are good and considerate, but also to those who are harsh. 19For it is commendable if a man bears up under the pain of unjust suffering because he is conscious of God. 20But how is it to your credit if you receive a beating for doing wrong and endure it? But if you suffer for doing good and you endure it, this is commendable before God. 21To this you were called, because Christ suffered for you, leaving you an example, that you should follow in his steps.

22"He committed no sin,
　　and no deceit was found in his mouth."[a]

23When they hurled their insults at him, he did not retaliate; when he suffered, he made no threats. Instead, he entrusted himself to him who judges justly. 24He himself bore our sins in his body on the tree, so that we might die to sins and live for righteousness; by his wounds you have been healed. 25For you were like sheep going astray, but now you have returned to the Shepherd and Overseer of your souls.

Wives and Husbands

3 WIVES, IN the same way be submissive to your husbands so that, if any of them do not believe the word, they may be won over without words by the behavior of their wives, 2when they see the purity and reverence of your lives. 3Your beauty should not come from outward adornment, such as braided hair and the wearing of gold jewelry and fine clothes. 4Instead, it should be that of your inner self, the unfading beauty of a gentle and quiet spirit, which is of great worth in God's sight. 5For this is the way the holy women of the past who put their hope in God used to make themselves beautiful. They were submissive to their own husbands, 6like Sarah, who obeyed Abraham and called him her master. You are her daughters if you do what is right and do not give way to fear.

7Husbands, in the same way be considerate as you live with your wives, and treat them with respect as the weaker partner and as heirs with you of the gracious gift of life, so that nothing will hinder your prayers.

Suffering for Doing Good

8Finally, all of you, live in harmony with one another; be sympathetic, love as brothers, be compassionate and humble. 9Do not repay evil with evil or insult with insult, but with blessing, because to this you were called so that you may inherit a blessing. 10For,

---

a 22 Isaiah 53:9

Living Bible

11Dear brothers, you are only visitors here. Since your real home is in heaven I beg you to keep away from the evil pleasures of this world; they are not for you, for they fight against your very souls.

12Be careful how you behave among your unsaved neighbors; for then, even if they are suspicious of you and talk against you, they will end up praising God for your good works when Christ returns.

13For the Lord's sake, obey every law of your government: those of the king as head of the state, 14and those of the king's officers, for he has sent them to punish all who do wrong, and to honor those who do right.

15It is God's will that your good lives should silence those who foolishly condemn the Gospel without knowing what it can do for them, having never experienced its power. 16You are free from the law, but that doesn't mean you are free to do wrong. Live as those who are free to do only God's will at all times.

17Show respect for everyone. Love Christians everywhere. Fear God and honor the government.

18Servants, you must respect your masters and do whatever they tell you—not only if they are kind and reasonable, but even if they are tough and cruel. 19Praise the Lord if you are punished for doing right! 20Of course, you get no credit for being patient if you are beaten for doing wrong; but if you do right and suffer for it, and are patient beneath the blows, God is well pleased.

21This suffering is all part of the work God has given you. Christ, who suffered for you, is your example. Follow in his steps: 22He never sinned, never told a lie, 23never answered back when insulted; when he suffered he did not threaten to get even; he left his case in the hands of God who always judges fairly. 24He personally carried the load of our sins in his own body when he died on the cross, so that we can be finished with sin and live a good life from now on. For his wounds have healed ours! 25Like sheep you wandered away from God, but now you have returned to your Shepherd, the Guardian of your souls who keeps you safe from all attacks.

3 WIVES, FIT in with your husbands' plans; for then if they refuse to listen when you talk to them about the Lord, they will be won by your respectful, pure behavior. Your godly lives will speak to them better than any words.

3Don't be concerned about the outward beauty that depends on jewelry, or beautiful clothes, or hair arrangement. 4Be beautiful inside, in your hearts, with the lasting charm of a gentle and quiet spirit which is so precious to God. 5That kind of deep beauty was seen in the saintly women of old, who trusted God and fitted in with their husbands' plans.

6Sarah, for instance, obeyed her husband Abraham, honoring him as head of the house. And if you do the same, you will be following in her steps like good daughters and doing what is right; then you will not need to fear [offending your husbandsb].

7You husbands must be careful of your wives, being thoughtful of their needs and honoring them as the weaker sex. Remember that you and your wife are partners in receiving God's blessings, and if you don't treat her as you should, your prayers will not get ready answers.

8And now this word to all of you: You should be like one big happy family, full of sympathy toward each other, loving one another with tender hearts and humble minds. 9Don't repay evil for evil. Don't snap back at those who say unkind things about you. Instead, pray for God's help for them, for we are to be kind to others, and God will bless us for it.

New Revised Standard

Live as Servants of God

11 Beloved, I urge you as aliens and exiles to abstain from the desires of the flesh that wage war against the soul. 12Conduct yourselves honorably among the Gentiles, so that, though they malign you as evildoers, they may see your honorable deeds and glorify God when he comes to judge.c

13 For the Lord's sake accept the authority of every human institution,d whether of the emperor as supreme, 14or of governors, as sent by him to punish those who do wrong and to praise those who do right. 15For it is God's will that by doing right you should silence the ignorance of the foolish. 16As servantse of God, live as free people, yet do not use your freedom as a pretext for evil. 17Honor everyone. Love the family of believers.f Fear God. Honor the emperor.

The Example of Christ's Suffering

18 Slaves, accept the authority of your masters with all deference, not only those who are kind and gentle but also those who are harsh. 19For it is a credit to you if, being aware of God, you endure pain while suffering unjustly. 20If you endure when you are beaten for doing wrong, what credit is that? But if you endure when you do right and suffer for it, you have God's approval. 21For to this you have been called, because Christ also suffered for you, leaving you an example, so that you should follow in his steps.

22 "He committed no sin,
and no deceit was found in his mouth."

23When he was abused, he did not return abuse; when he suffered, he did not threaten; but he entrusted himself to the one who judges justly. 24He himself bore our sins in his body on the cross,g so that, free from sins, we might live for righteousness; by his woundsh you have been healed. 25For you were going astray like sheep, but now you have returned to the shepherd and guardian of your souls.

Wives and Husbands

3 WIVES, IN the same way, accept the authority of your husbands, so that, even if some of them do not obey the word, they may be won over without a word by their wives' conduct, 2when they see the purity and reverence of your lives. 3Do not adorn yourselves outwardly by braiding your hair, and by wearing gold ornaments or fine clothing; 4rather, let your adornment be the inner self with the lasting beauty of a gentle and quiet spirit, which is very precious in God's sight. 5It was in this way long ago that the holy women who hoped in God used to adorn themselves by accepting the authority of their husbands. 6Thus Sarah obeyed Abraham and called him lord. You have become her daughters as long as you do what is good and never let fears alarm you.

7 Husbands, in the same way, show consideration for your wives in your life together, paying honor to the woman as the weaker sex,i since they too are also heirs of the gracious gift of life—so that nothing may hinder your prayers.

Suffering for Doing Right

8 Finally, all of you, have unity of spirit, sympathy, love for one another, a tender heart, and a humble mind. 9Do not repay evil for evil or abuse for abuse; but, on the contrary, repay with a blessing. It is for this that you were called—that you might inherit a blessing. 10For

c Gk *God on the day of visitation* d Or *every institution ordained for human beings* e Gk *slaves* f Gk *Love the brotherhood* g Or *carried up our sins in his body to the tree* h Gk *bruise* i Gk *vessel*

King James

10For he that will love life, and see good days, let him refrain his tongue from evil, and his lips that they speak no guile:

11Let him eschew evil, and do good; let him seek peace, and ensue it.

12For the eyes of the Lord *are* over the righteous, and his ears *are open* unto their prayers: but the face of the Lord *is* against them that do evil.

13And who *is* he that will harm you, if ye be followers of that which is good?

14But and if ye suffer for righteousness' sake, happy *are ye:* and be not afraid of their terror, neither be troubled;

15But sanctify the Lord God in your hearts: and *be* ready always to *give* an answer to every man that asketh you a reason of the hope that is in you with meekness and fear:

16Having a good conscience; that, whereas they speak evil of you, as of evildoers, they may be ashamed that falsely accuse your good conversation in Christ.

17For *it is* better, if the will of God be so, that ye suffer for well doing, than for evil doing.

18For Christ also hath once suffered for sins, the just for the unjust, that he might bring us to God, being put to death in the flesh, but quickened by the Spirit:

19By which also he went and preached unto the spirits in prison;

20Which sometime were disobedient, when once the longsuffering of God waited in the days of Noah, while the ark was a-preparing, wherein few, that is, eight souls were saved by water.

21The like figure whereunto *even* baptism doth also now save us (not the putting away of the filth of the flesh, but the answer of a good conscience toward God,) by the resurrection of Jesus Christ:

22Who is gone into heaven, and is on the right hand of God; angels and authorities and powers being made subject unto him.

4 FORASMUCH THEN as Christ hath suffered for us in the flesh, arm yourselves likewise with the same mind: for he that hath suffered in the flesh hath ceased from sin;

2That he no longer should live the rest of *his* time in the flesh to the lusts of men, but to the will of God.

3For the time past of *our* life may suffice us to have wrought the will of the Gentiles, when we walked in lasciviousness, lusts, excess of wine, revellings, banquetings, and abominable idolatries:

4Wherein they think it strange that ye run not with *them* to the same excess of riot, speaking evil of *you:*

5Who shall give account to him that is ready to judge the quick and the dead.

6For this cause was the gospel preached also to them that are dead, that they might be judged according to men in the flesh, but live according to God in the spirit.

7But the end of all things is at hand: be ye therefore sober, and watch unto prayer.

8And above all things have fervent charity among yourselves: for charity shall cover the multitude of sins.

9Use hospitality one to another without grudging.

New International

"Whoever would love life
    and see good days
must keep his tongue from evil
    and his lips from deceitful speech.
11He must turn from evil and do good;
    he must seek peace and pursue it.
12For the eyes of the Lord are on the righteous
    and his ears are attentive to their prayer,
but the face of the Lord is against those who do
    evil."a

13Who is going to harm you if you are eager to do good? 14But even if you should suffer for what is right, you are blessed. "Do not fear what they fearb; do not be frightened."c 15But in your hearts set apart Christ as Lord. Always be prepared to give an answer to everyone who asks you to give the reason for the hope that you have. But do this with gentleness and respect, 16keeping a clear conscience, so that those who speak maliciously against your good behavior in Christ may be ashamed of their slander. 17It is better, if it is God's will, to suffer for doing good than for doing evil. 18For Christ died for sins once for all, the righteous for the unrighteous, to bring you to God. He was put to death in the body but made alive by the Spirit, 19through whomd also he went and preached to the spirits in prison 20who disobeyed long ago when God waited patiently in the days of Noah while the ark was being built. In it only a few people, eight in all, were saved through water, 21and this water symbolizes baptism that now saves you also—not the removal of dirt from the body but the pledgee of a good conscience toward God. It saves you by the resurrection of Jesus Christ, 22who has gone into heaven and is at God's right hand—with angels, authorities and powers in submission to him.

Living for God

4 THEREFORE, SINCE Christ suffered in his body, arm yourselves also with the same attitude, because he who has suffered in his body is done with sin. 2As a result, he does not live the rest of his earthly life for evil human desires, but rather for the will of God. 3For you have spent enough time in the past doing what pagans choose to do—living in debauchery, lust, drunkenness, orgies, carousing and detestable idolatry. 4They think it strange that you do not plunge with them into the same flood of dissipation, and they heap abuse on you. 5But they will have to give account to him who is ready to judge the living and the dead. 6For this is the reason the gospel was preached even to those who are now dead, so that they might be judged according to men in regard to the body, but live according to God in regard to the spirit.

7The end of all things is near. Therefore be clear minded and self-controlled so that you can pray. 8Above all, love each other deeply, because love covers over a multitude of sins. 9Offer hospitality to one another without grumbling. 10Each one should use whatever gift he

---

a *12* Psalm 34:12-16   b *14* Or *not fear their threats*   c *14* Isaiah 8:12
d *18,19* Or *alive in the spirit,* 19*through which*   e *21* Or *response*

Living Bible

10If you want a happy, good life, keep control of your tongue, and guard your lips from telling lies. 11Turn away from evil and do good. Try to live in peace even if you must run after it to catch and hold it! 12For the Lord is watching his children, listening to their prayers; but the Lord's face is hard against those who do evil.

13Usually no one will hurt you for wanting to do good. 14But even if they should, you are to be envied, for God will reward you for it. 15Quietly trust yourself to Christ your Lord and if anybody asks why you believe as you do, be ready to tell him, and do it in a gentle and respectful way.

16Do what is right; then if men speak against you, calling you evil names, they will become ashamed of themselves for falsely accusing you when you have only done what is good. 17Remember, if God wants you to suffer, it is better to suffer for doing good than for doing wrong!

18Christ also suffered. He died once for the sins of all us guilty sinners, although he himself was innocent of any sin at any time, that he might bring us safely home to God. But though his body died, his spirit lived on, 19and it was in the spirit that he visited the spirits in prison, and preached to them— 20spirits of those who, long before in the days of Noah, had refused to listen to God, though he waited patiently for them while Noah was building the ark. Yet only eight persons were saved from drowning in that terrible flood. 21(That, by the way, is what baptism pictures for us: In baptism we show that we have been saved from death and doom by the resurrection of Christ;f not because our bodies are washed clean by the water, but because in being baptized we are turning to God and asking him to cleanse our *hearts* from sin.) 22And now Christ is in heaven, sitting in the place of honor next to God the Father, with all the angels and powers of heaven bowing before him and obeying him.

4 SINCE CHRIST suffered and underwent pain, you must have the same attitude he did; you must be ready to suffer, too. For remember, when your body suffers, sin loses its power, 2and you won't be spending the rest of your life chasing after evil desires, but will be anxious to do the will of God. 3You have had enough in the past of the evil things the godless enjoy—sex, sin, lust, getting drunk, wild parties, drinking bouts, and the worship of idols, and other terrible sins.g

4Of course, your former friends will be very surprised when you don't eagerly join them any more in the wicked things they do, and they will laugh at you in contempt and scorn. 5But just remember that they must face the Judge of all, living and dead; they will be punished for the way they have lived. 6That is why the Good News was preached even to those who were dead—killed by the floodh—so that although their bodies were punished with death, they could still live in their spirits as God lives.

7The end of the world is coming soon. Therefore be earnest, thoughtful men of prayer. 8Most important of all, continue to show deep love for each other, for love makes up for many of your faults.i 9Cheerfully share your home with those who need a meal or a place to stay for the night.

New Revised Standard

"Those who desire life
   and desire to see good days,
let them keep their tongues from evil
   and their lips from speaking deceit;
11 let them turn away from evil and do good;
   let them seek peace and pursue it.
12 For the eyes of the Lord are on the righteous,
   and his ears are open to their prayer.
But the face of the Lord is against those who
   do evil."

13 Now who will harm you if you are eager to do what is good? 14But even if you do suffer for doing what is right, you are blessed. Do not fear what they fear,j and do not be intimidated, 15but in your hearts sanctify Christ as Lord. Always be ready to make your defense to anyone who demands from you an accounting for the hope that is in you; 16yet do it with gentleness and reverence.k Keep your conscience clear, so that, when you are maligned, those who abuse you for your good conduct in Christ may be put to shame. 17For it is better to suffer for doing good, if suffering should be God's will, than to suffer for doing evil. 18For Christ also sufferedl for sins once for all, the righteous for the unrighteous, in order to bring youm to God. He was put to death in the flesh, but made alive in the spirit, 19in which also he went and made a proclamation to the spirits in prison, 20who in former times did not obey, when God waited patiently in the days of Noah, during the building of the ark, in which a few, that is, eight persons, were saved through water. 21And baptism, which this prefigured, now saves you—not as a removal of dirt from the body, but as an appeal to God forn a good conscience, through the resurrection of Jesus Christ, 22who has gone into heaven and is at the right hand of God, with angels, authorities, and powers made subject to him.

Good Stewards of God's Grace

4 SINCE THEREFORE Christ suffered in the flesh,o arm yourselves also with the same intention (for whoever has suffered in the flesh has finished with sin), 2so as to live for the rest of your earthly lifep no longer by human desires but by the will of God. 3You have already spent enough time in doing what the Gentiles like to do, living in licentiousness, passions, drunkenness, revels, carousing, and lawless idolatry. 4They are surprised that you no longer join them in the same excesses of dissipation, and so they blaspheme.q 5But they will have to give an accounting to him who stands ready to judge the living and the dead. 6For this is the reason the gospel was proclaimed even to the dead, so that, though they had been judged in the flesh as everyone is judged, they might live in the spirit as God does.

7 The end of all things is near;r therefore be serious and discipline yourselves for the sake of your prayers. 8Above all, maintain constant love for one another, for love covers a multitude of sins. 9Be hospitable to one another without complaining. 10Like good stewards of

---

f 3:21 In baptism we show that we have been saved from death and doom by the resurrection of Christ, or "Baptism, which corresponds to this, now saves you through the resurrection." g 4:3 and other terrible sins, literally, "lawless idolatries." h 4:6 killed by the flood, implied. See 3:19, 20. i 4:8 for love makes up for many of your faults, or "love overlooks each other's many faults."

j Gk their fear   k Or respect   l Other ancient authorities read died   m Other ancient authorities read us   n Or a pledge to God from   o Other ancient authorities add for us; others, for you   p Gk rest of the time in the flesh   q Or they malign you   r Or is at hand

King James

10As every man hath received the gift, *even so* minister the same one to another, as good stewards of the manifold grace of God.

11If any man speak, *let him speak* as the oracles of God; if any man minister, *let him do it* as of the ability which God giveth: that God in all things may be glorified through Jesus Christ, to whom be praise and dominion for ever and ever. Amen.

12Beloved, think it not strange concerning the fiery trial which is to try you, as though some strange thing happened unto you:

13But rejoice, inasmuch as ye are partakers of Christ's sufferings; that, when his glory shall be revealed, ye may be glad also with exceeding joy.

14If ye be reproached for the name of Christ, happy *are ye;* for the spirit of glory and of God resteth upon you: on their part he is evil spoken of, but on your part he is glorified.

15But let none of you suffer as a murderer, or *as* a thief, or *as* an evildoer, or as a busybody in other men's matters.

16Yet if *any man suffer* as a Christian, let him not be ashamed; but let him glorify God on this behalf.

17For the time *is come* that judgment must begin at the house of God: and if *it* first *begin* at us, what shall the end *be* of them that obey not the gospel of God?

18And if the righteous scarcely be saved, where shall the ungodly and the sinner appear?

19Wherefore let them that suffer according to the will of God commit the keeping of their souls *to him* in well doing, as unto a faithful Creator.

5 THE ELDERS which are among you I exhort, who am also an elder, and a witness of the sufferings of Christ, and also a partaker of the glory that shall be revealed:

2Feed the flock of God which is among you, taking the oversight *thereof,* not by constraint, but willingly; not for filthy lucre, but of a ready mind;

3Neither as being lords over *God's* heritage, but being examples to the flock.

4And when the chief Shepherd shall appear, ye shall receive a crown of glory that fadeth not away.

5Likewise, ye younger, submit yourselves unto the elder. Yea, all *of you* be subject one to another, and be clothed with humility: for God resisteth the proud, and giveth grace to the humble.

6Humble yourselves therefore under the mighty hand of God, that he may exalt you in due time:

7Casting all your care upon him; for he careth for you.

8Be sober, be vigilant; because your adversary the devil, as a roaring lion, walketh about, seeking whom he may devour:

9Whom resist stedfast in the faith, knowing that the same afflictions are accomplished in your brethren that are in the world.

10But the God of all grace, who hath called us unto his eternal glory by Christ Jesus, after that ye have suffered a while, make you perfect, stablish, strengthen, settle *you.*

11To him *be* glory and dominion for ever and ever. Amen.

New International

has received to serve others, faithfully administering God's grace in its various forms. 11If anyone speaks, he should do it as one speaking the very words of God. If anyone serves, he should do it with the strength God provides, so that in all things God may be praised through Jesus Christ. To him be the glory and the power for ever and ever. Amen.

Suffering for Being a Christian

12Dear friends, do not be surprised at the painful trial you are suffering, as though something strange were happening to you. 13But rejoice that you participate in the sufferings of Christ, so that you may be overjoyed when his glory is revealed. 14If you are insulted because of the name of Christ, you are blessed, for the Spirit of glory and of God rests on you. 15If you suffer, it should not be as a murderer or thief or any other kind of criminal, or even as a meddler. 16However, if you suffer as a Christian, do not be ashamed, but praise God that you bear that name. 17For it is time for judgment to begin with the family of God; and if it begins with us, what will the outcome be for those who do not obey the gospel of God? 18And,

"If it is hard for the righteous to be saved,
    what will become of the ungodly and the
        sinner?"[a]

19So then, those who suffer according to God's will should commit themselves to their faithful Creator and continue to do good.

To Elders and Young Men

5 TO THE elders among you, I appeal as a fellow elder, a witness of Christ's sufferings and one who also will share in the glory to be revealed: 2Be shepherds of God's flock that is under your care, serving as overseers—not because you must, but because you are willing, as God wants you to be; not greedy for money, but eager to serve; 3not lording it over those entrusted to you, but being examples to the flock. 4And when the Chief Shepherd appears, you will receive the crown of glory that will never fade away.

5Young men, in the same way be submissive to those who are older. All of you, clothe yourselves with humility toward one another, because,

"God opposes the proud
    but gives grace to the humble."[b]

6Humble yourselves, therefore, under God's mighty hand, that he may lift you up in due time. 7Cast all your anxiety on him because he cares for you.

8Be self-controlled and alert. Your enemy the devil prowls around like a roaring lion looking for someone to devour. 9Resist him, standing firm in the faith, because you know that your brothers throughout the world are undergoing the same kind of sufferings.

10And the God of all grace, who called you to his eternal glory in Christ, after you have suffered a little while, will himself restore you and make you strong, firm and steadfast. 11To him be the power for ever and ever. Amen.

a 18 Prov. 11:31   b 5 Prov. 3:34

Living Bible

10God has given each of you some special abilities; be sure to use them to help each other, passing on to others God's many kinds of blessings. 11Are you called to preach? Then preach as though God himself were speaking through you. Are you called to help others? Do it with all the strength and energy that God supplies, so that God will be glorified through Jesus Christ—to him be glory and power forever and ever. Amen.

12Dear friends, don't be bewildered or surprised when you go through the fiery trials ahead, for this is no strange, unusual thing that is going to happen to you. 13Instead, be really glad—because these trials will make you partners with Christ in his suffering, and afterwards you will have the wonderful joy of sharing his glory in that coming day when it will be displayed.

14Be happy if you are cursed and insulted for being a Christian, for when that happens the Spirit of God will come upon you with great glory.c 15Don't let me hear of your suffering for murdering or stealing or making trouble or being a busybody and prying into other people's affairs. 16But it is no shame to suffer for being a Christian. Praise God for the privilege of being in Christ's family and being called by his wonderful name! 17For the time has come for judgment, and it must begin first among God's own children. And if even we who are Christians must be judged, what terrible fate awaits those who have never believed in the Lord? 18If the righteous are barely saved, what chance will the godless have?

19So if you are suffering according to God's will, keep on doing what is right and trust yourself to the God who made you, for he will never fail you.

5 AND NOW, a word to you elders of the church. I, too, am an elder; with my own eyes I saw Christ dying on the cross; and I, too, will share his glory and his honor when he returns. Fellow elders, this is my plea to you: 2Feed the flock of God; care for it willingly, not grudgingly; not for what you will get out of it, but because you are eager to serve the Lord. 3Don't be tyrants, but lead them by your good example, 4and when the Head Shepherd comes, your reward will be a never-ending share in his glory and honor.

5You younger men, follow the leadership of those who are older. And all of you serve each other with humble spirits, for God gives special blessings to those who are humble, but sets himself against those who are proud. 6If you will humble yourselves under the mighty hand of God, in his good time he will lift you up.

7Let him have all your worries and cares, for he is always thinking about you and watching everything that concerns you.

8Be careful—watch out for attacks from Satan, your great enemy. He prowls around like a hungry, roaring lion, looking for some victim to tear apart. 9Stand firm when he attacks. Trust the Lord; and remember that other Christians all around the world are going through these sufferings too.

10After you have suffered a little while, our God, who is full of kindness through Christ, will give you his eternal glory. He personally will come and pick you up, and set you firmly in place, and make you stronger than ever. 11To him be all power over all things, forever and ever. Amen.

New Revised Standard

the manifold grace of God, serve one another with whatever gift each of you has received. 11Whoever speaks must do so as one speaking the very words of God; whoever serves must do so with the strength that God supplies, so that God may be glorified in all things through Jesus Christ. To him belong the glory and the power forever and ever. Amen.

Suffering as a Christian

12 Beloved, do not be surprised at the fiery ordeal that is taking place among you to test you, as though something strange were happening to you. 13But rejoice insofar as you are sharing Christ's sufferings, so that you may also be glad and shout for joy when his glory is revealed. 14If you are reviled for the name of Christ, you are blessed, because the spirit of glory,d which is the Spirit of God, is resting on you.e 15But let none of you suffer as a murderer, a thief, a criminal, or even as a mischief maker. 16Yet if any of you suffers as a Christian, do not consider it a disgrace, but glorify God because you bear this name. 17For the time has come for judgment to begin with the household of God; if it begins with us, what will be the end for those who do not obey the gospel of God? 18And

"If it is hard for the righteous to be saved,
    what will become of the ungodly and the
        sinners?"

19Therefore, let those suffering in accordance with God's will entrust themselves to a faithful Creator, while continuing to do good.

Tending the Flock of God

5 NOW AS an elder myself and a witness of the sufferings of Christ, as well as one who shares in the glory to be revealed, I exhort the elders among you 2to tend the flock of God that is in your charge, exercising the oversight,f not under compulsion but willingly, as God would have you do its—not for sordid gain but eagerly. 3Do not lord it over those in your charge, but be examples to the flock. 4And when the chief shepherd appears, you will win the crown of glory that never fades away. 5In the same way, you who are younger must accept the authority of the elders.h And all of you must clothe yourselves with humility in your dealings with one another, for

"God opposes the proud,
    but gives grace to the humble."

6 Humble yourselves therefore under the mighty hand of God, so that he may exalt you in due time. 7Cast all your anxiety on him, because he cares for you. 8Discipline yourselves, keep alert.i Like a roaring lion your adversary the devil prowls around, looking for someone to devour. 9Resist him, steadfast in your faith, for you know that your brothers and sistersj in all the world are undergoing the same kinds of suffering. 10And after you have suffered for a little while, the God of all grace, who has called you to his eternal glory in Christ, will himself restore, support, strengthen, and establish you. 11To him be the power forever and ever. Amen.

---

c 4:14 the Spirit of God will come upon you with great glory, or "the glory of the Spirit of God is being seen in you."

d Other ancient authorities add and of power   e Other ancient authorities add On their part he is blasphemed, but on your part he is glorified   f Other ancient authorities lack exercising the oversight   g Other ancient authorities lack as God would have you do it   h Or of those who are older   i Or be vigilant   j Gk your brotherhood

King James

12By Silvanus, a faithful brother unto you, as I suppose, I have written briefly, exhorting, and testifying that this is the true grace of God wherein ye stand.

13The *church that is* at Babylon, elected together with *you*, saluteth you; and *so doth* Marcus my son.

14Greet ye one another with a kiss of charity. Peace *be* with you all that are in Christ Jesus. Amen.

New International

Final Greetings

12With the help of Silas,[a] whom I regard as a faithful brother, I have written to you briefly, encouraging you and testifying that this is the true grace of God. Stand fast in it.

13She who is in Babylon, chosen together with you, sends you her greetings, and so does my son Mark.

14Greet one another with a kiss of love.

Peace to all of you who are in Christ.

Living Bible

12I am sending this note to you through the courtesy of Silvanus who is, in my opinion, a very faithful brother. I hope I have encouraged you by this letter for I have given you a true statement of the way God blesses. What I have told you here should help you to stand firmly in his love.

13The church here in Romeb—she is your sister in the Lord—sends you her greetings; so does my son Mark. 14Give each other the handshake of Christian love. Peace be to all of you who are in Christ.

New Revised Standard

Final Greetings and Benediction

12 Through Silvanus, whom I consider a faithful brother, I have written this short letter to encourage you and to testify that this is the true grace of God. Stand fast in it. 13 Your sister churchc in Babylon, chosen together with you, sends you greetings; and so does my son Mark. 14Greet one another with a kiss of love.

Peace to all of you who are in Christ.d

---

b *5:13 The church here in Rome,* literally, "She who is at Babylon is likewise chosen"; but Babylon was the Christian nickname for Rome, and the "she" is thought by many to be Peter's wife to whom reference is made in Mt 8:14; 1 Cor 9:5, etc. Others believe this should read: "Your sister church here in Babylon salutes you, and so does my son Mark."

c Gk *She who is*   d Other ancient authorities add *Amen*

THE SECOND

EPISTLE GENERAL OF

Peter

2 Peter

1 SIMON PETER, a servant and an apostle of Jesus Christ, to them that have obtained like precious faith with us through the righteousness of God and our Saviour Jesus Christ:

2Grace and peace be multiplied unto you through the knowledge of God, and of Jesus our Lord,

3According as his divine power hath given unto us all things that *pertain* unto life and godliness, through the knowledge of him that hath called us to glory and virtue:

4Whereby are given unto us exceeding great and precious promises: that by these ye might be partakers of the divine nature, having escaped the corruption that is in the world through lust.

5And beside this, giving all diligence, add to your faith virtue; and to virtue knowledge;

6And to knowledge temperance; and to temperance patience; and to patience godliness;

7And to godliness brotherly kindness; and to brotherly kindness charity.

8For if these things be in you, and abound, they make *you that ye shall* neither *be* barren nor unfruitful in the knowledge of our Lord Jesus Christ.

9But he that lacketh these things is blind, and cannot see afar off, and hath forgotten that he was purged from his old sins.

10Wherefore the rather, brethren, give diligence to make your calling and election sure: for if ye do these things, ye shall never fall:

11For so an entrance shall be ministered unto you abundantly into the everlasting kingdom of our Lord and Saviour Jesus Christ.

12Wherefore I will not be negligent to put you always in remembrance of these things, though ye know *them,* and be established in the present truth.

13Yea, I think it meet, as long as I am in this tabernacle, to stir you up by putting *you* in remembrance;

14Knowing that shortly I must put off *this* my tabernacle, even as our Lord Jesus Christ hath shown me.

15Moreover I will endeavour that ye may be able after my decease to have these things always in remembrance.

16For we have not followed cunningly devised fables, when we made known unto you the power and coming of our Lord Jesus Christ, but were eyewitnesses of his majesty.

17For he received from God the Father honour and glory, when there came such a voice to him from the excellent glory, This is my beloved Son, in whom I am well pleased.

18And this voice which came from heaven we heard, when we were with him in the holy mount.

1 SIMON PETER, a servant and apostle of Jesus Christ,

To those who through the righteousness of our God and Savior Jesus Christ have received a faith as precious as ours:

2Grace and peace be yours in abundance through the knowledge of God and of Jesus our Lord.

Making One's Calling and Election Sure

3His divine power has given us everything we need for life and godliness through our knowledge of him who called us by his own glory and goodness. 4Through these he has given us his very great and precious promises, so that through them you may participate in the divine nature and escape the corruption in the world caused by evil desires.

5For this very reason, make every effort to add to your faith goodness; and to goodness, knowledge; 6and to knowledge, self-control; and to self-control, perseverance; and to perseverance, godliness; 7and to godliness, brotherly kindness; and to brotherly kindness, love. 8For if you possess these qualities in increasing measure, they will keep you from being ineffective and unproductive in your knowledge of our Lord Jesus Christ. 9But if anyone does not have them, he is nearsighted and blind, and has forgotten that he has been cleansed from his past sins.

10Therefore, my brothers, be all the more eager to make your calling and election sure. For if you do these things, you will never fall, 11and you will receive a rich welcome into the eternal kingdom of our Lord and Savior Jesus Christ.

Prophecy of Scripture

12So I will always remind you of these things, even though you know them and are firmly established in the truth you now have. 13I think it is right to refresh your memory as long as I live in the tent of this body, 14because I know that I will soon put it aside, as our Lord Jesus Christ has made clear to me. 15And I will make every effort to see that after my departure you will always be able to remember these things.

16We did not follow cleverly invented stories when we told you about the power and coming of our Lord Jesus Christ, but we were eyewitnesses of his majesty. 17For he received honor and glory from God the Father when the voice came to him from the Majestic Glory, saying, "This is my Son, whom I love; with him I am well pleased."a 18We ourselves heard this voice that came from heaven when we were with him on the sacred mountain.

a *17* Matt. 17:5; Mark 9:7; Luke 9:35

THE SECOND LETTER OF

2 Peter   # Peter

1 *FROM:* SIMON Peter, a servant and missionary of Jesus Christ.

To: all of you who have our kind of faith. The faith I speak of is the kind that Jesus Christ our God and Savior gives to us. How precious it is, and how just and good he is to give this same faith to each of us. ²Do you want more and more of God's kindness and peace? Then learn to know him better and better. ³For as you know him better, he will give you, through his great power, everything you need for living a truly good life: he even shares his own glory and his own goodness with us! ⁴And by that same mighty power he has given us all the other rich and wonderful blessings he promised; for instance, the promise to save us from the lust and rottenness all around us, and to give us his own character.

⁵But to obtain these gifts, you need more than faith; you must also work hard to be good, and even that is not enough. For then you must learn to know God better and discover what he wants you to do. ⁶Next, learn to put aside your own desires so that you will become patient and godly, gladly letting God have his way with you. ⁷This will make possible the next step, which is for you to enjoy other people and to like them, and finally you will grow to love them deeply. ⁸The more you go on in this way, the more you will grow strong spiritually and become fruitful and useful to our Lord Jesus Christ. ⁹But anyone who fails to go after these additions to faith is blind indeed, or at least very shortsighted, and has forgotten that God delivered him from the old life of sin so that now he can live a strong, good life for the Lord.

¹⁰So, dear brothers, work hard to prove that you really are among those God has called and chosen, and then you will never stumble or fall away. ¹¹And God will open wide the gates of heaven for you to enter into the eternal kingdom of our Lord and Savior Jesus Christ.

¹²I plan to keep on reminding you of these things even though you already know them and are really getting along quite well! ¹³, ¹⁴But the Lord Jesus Christ has showed me that my days here on earth are numbered, and I am soon to die. As long as I am still here I intend to keep sending these reminders to you, ¹⁵hoping to impress them so clearly upon you that you will remember them long after I have gone.

¹⁶For we have not been telling you fairy tales when we explained to you the power of our Lord Jesus Christ and his coming again. My own eyes have seen his splendor and his glory: ¹⁷, ¹⁸I was there on the holy mountain when he shone out with honor given him by God his Father; I heard that glorious, majestic voice calling down from heaven, saying, "This is my much-loved Son; I am well pleased with him."

Salutation

1 SIMEON[b] PETER, a servant[c] and apostle of Jesus Christ,

To those who have received a faith as precious as ours through the righteousness of our God and Savior Jesus Christ:[d]

2 May grace and peace be yours in abundance in the knowledge of God and of Jesus our Lord.

The Christian's Call and Election

3 His divine power has given us everything needed for life and godliness, through the knowledge of him who called us by[e] his own glory and goodness. ⁴Thus he has given us, through these things, his precious and very great promises, so that through them you may escape from the corruption that is in the world because of lust, and may become participants of the divine nature. ⁵For this very reason, you must make every effort to support your faith with goodness, and goodness with knowledge, ⁶and knowledge with self-control, and self-control with endurance, and endurance with godliness, ⁷and godliness with mutual[f] affection, and mutual[f] affection with love. ⁸For if these things are yours and are increasing among you, they keep you from being ineffective and unfruitful in the knowledge of our Lord Jesus Christ. ⁹For anyone who lacks these things is nearsighted and blind, and is forgetful of the cleansing of past sins. ¹⁰Therefore, brothers and sisters,[g] be all the more eager to confirm your call and election, for if you do this, you will never stumble. ¹¹For in this way, entry into the eternal kingdom of our Lord and Savior Jesus Christ will be richly provided for you.

12 Therefore I intend to keep on reminding you of these things, though you know them already and are established in the truth that has come to you. ¹³I think it right, as long as I am in this body,[h] to refresh your memory, ¹⁴since I know that my death[i] will come soon, as indeed our Lord Jesus Christ has made clear to me. ¹⁵And I will make every effort so that after my departure you may be able at any time to recall these things.

Eyewitnesses of Christ's Glory

16 For we did not follow cleverly devised myths when we made known to you the power and coming of our Lord Jesus Christ, but we had been eyewitnesses of his majesty. ¹⁷For he received honor and glory from God the Father when that voice was conveyed to him by the Majestic Glory, saying, "This is my Son, my Beloved,[j] with whom I am well pleased." ¹⁸We ourselves heard this voice come from heaven, while we were with him on the holy mountain.

---

b Other ancient authorities read *Simon*   **c** Gk *slave*   **d** Or *of our God and the Savior Jesus Christ*   **e** Other ancient authorities read *through*   **f** Gk *brotherly*   **g** Gk *brothers*   **h** Gk *tent*   **i** Gk *the putting off of my tent*   **j** Other ancient authorities read *my beloved Son*

King James

19We have also a more sure word of prophecy; where-unto ye do well that ye take heed, as unto a light that shineth in a dark place, until the day dawn, and the day star arise in your hearts:

20Knowing this first, that no prophecy of the scripture is of any private interpretation.

21For the prophecy came not in old time by the will of man: but holy men of God spake *as they were* moved by the Holy Ghost.

2 BUT THERE were false prophets also among the people, even as there shall be false teachers among you, who privily shall bring in damnable heresies, even denying the Lord that bought them, and bring upon themselves swift destruction.

2And many shall follow their pernicious ways; by reason of whom the way of truth shall be evil spoken of.

3And through covetousness shall they with feigned words make merchandise of you: whose judgment now of a long time lingereth not, and their damnation slumbereth not.

4For if God spared not the angels that sinned, but cast *them* down to hell, and delivered *them* into chains of darkness, to be reserved unto judgment;

5And spared not the old world, but saved Noah the eighth *person*, a preacher of righteousness, bringing in the flood upon the world of the ungodly;

6And turning the cities of Sodom and Gomorrha into ashes condemned *them* with an overthrow, making *them* an example unto those that after should live ungodly;

7And delivered just Lot, vexed with the filthy conversation of the wicked:

8(For that righteous man dwelling among them, in seeing and hearing, vexed *his* righteous soul from day to day with *their* unlawful deeds;)

9The Lord knoweth how to deliver the godly out of temptations, and to reserve the unjust unto the day of judgment to be punished:

10But chiefly them that walk after the flesh in the lust of uncleanness, and despise government. Presumptuous *are they*, self-willed, they are not afraid to speak evil of dignities.

11Whereas angels, which are greater in power and might, bring not railing accusation against them before the Lord.

12But these, as natural brute beasts, made to be taken and destroyed, speak evil of the things that they understand not; and shall utterly perish in their own corruption;

13And shall receive the reward of unrighteousness, *as* they that count it pleasure to riot in the day time. Spots *they are* and blemishes, sporting themselves with their own deceivings while they feast with you;

14Having eyes full of adultery, and that cannot cease from sin; beguiling unstable souls: an heart they have exercised with covetous practices; cursed children:

15Which have forsaken the right way, and are gone astray, following the way of Balaam *the son* of Bosor, who loved the wages of unrighteousness;

New International

19And we have the word of the prophets made more certain, and you will do well to pay attention to it, as to a light shining in a dark place, until the day dawns and the morning star rises in your hearts. 20Above all, you must understand that no prophecy of Scripture came about by the prophet's own interpretation. 21For prophecy never had its origin in the will of man, but men spoke from God as they were carried along by the Holy Spirit.

False Teachers and Their Destruction

2 BUT THERE were also false prophets among the people, just as there will be false teachers among you. They will secretly introduce destructive heresies, even denying the sovereign Lord who bought them—bringing swift destruction on themselves. 2Many will follow their shameful ways and will bring the way of truth into disrepute. 3In their greed these teachers will exploit you with stories they have made up. Their condemnation has long been hanging over them, and their destruction has not been sleeping.

4For if God did not spare angels when they sinned, but sent them to hell,[a] putting them into gloomy dungeons[b] to be held for judgment; 5if he did not spare the ancient world when he brought the flood on its ungodly people, but protected Noah, a preacher of righteousness, and seven others; 6if he condemned the cities of Sodom and Gomorrah by burning them to ashes, and made them an example of what is going to happen to the ungodly; 7and if he rescued Lot, a righteous man, who was distressed by the filthy lives of lawless men 8(for that righteous man, living among them day after day, was tormented in his righteous soul by the lawless deeds he saw and heard)— 9if this is so, then the Lord knows how to rescue godly men from trials and to hold the unrighteous for the day of judgment, while continuing their punishment.[c] 10This is especially true of those who follow the corrupt desire of the sinful nature[d] and despise authority.

Bold and arrogant, these men are not afraid to slander celestial beings; 11yet even angels, although they are stronger and more powerful, do not bring slanderous accusations against such beings in the presence of the Lord. 12But these men blaspheme in matters they do not understand. They are like brute beasts, creatures of instinct, born only to be caught and destroyed, and like beasts they too will perish.

13They will be paid back with harm for the harm they have done. Their idea of pleasure is to carouse in broad daylight. They are blots and blemishes, reveling in their pleasures while they feast with you.[e] 14With eyes full of adultery, they never stop sinning; they seduce the unstable; they are experts in greed—an accursed brood! 15They have left the straight way and wandered off to follow the way of Balaam son of Beor, who loved the wages of wickedness. 16But he was rebuked for his

---

[a] 4 Greek *Tartarus*   [b] 4 Some manuscripts *into chains of darkness*   [c] 9 Or *unrighteous for punishment until the day of judgment*   [d] 10 Or *the flesh*   [e] 13 Some manuscripts *in their love feasts*

Living Bible

19So we have seen and proved that what the prophets said came true. You will do well to pay close attention to everything they have written, for, like lights shining into dark corners, their words help us to understand many things that otherwise would be dark and difficult. But when you consider the wonderful truth of the prophets' words, then the light will dawn in your souls and Christ the Morning Star will shine in your hearts. 20, 21For no prophecy recorded in Scripture was ever thought up by the prophet himself. It was the Holy Spirit within these godly men who gave them true messages from God.

2 BUT THERE were false prophets, too, in those days, just as there will be false teachers among you. They will cleverly tell their lies about God, turning against even their Master who bought them; but theirs will be a swift and terrible end. 2Many will follow their evil teaching that there is nothing wrong with sexual sin. And because of them Christ and his way will be scoffed at.

3These teachers in their greed will tell you anything to get hold of your money. But God condemned them long ago and their destruction is on the way. 4For God did not spare even the angels who sinned, but threw them into hell, chained in gloomy caves and darkness until the judgment day. 5And he did not spare any of the people who lived in ancient times before the flood except Noah, the one man who spoke up for God, and his family of seven. At that time God completely destroyed the whole world of ungodly men with the vast flood. 6Later, he turned the cities of Sodom and Gomorrah into heaps of ashes and blotted them off the face of the earth, making them an example for all the ungodly in the future to look back upon and fear.

7, 8But at the same time the Lord rescued Lot out of Sodom because he was a good man, sick of the terrible wickedness he saw everywhere around him day after day. 9So also the Lord can rescue you and me from the temptations that surround us, and continue to punish the ungodly until the day of final judgment comes. 10He is especially hard on those who follow their own evil, lustful thoughts, and those who are proud and willful, daring even to scoff at the Glorious Onesf without so much as trembling, 11although the angels in heaven who stand in the very presence of the Lord, and are far greater in power and strength than these false teachers, never speak out disrespectfully against these evil Mighty Ones.

12But false teachers are fools—no better than animals. They do whatever they feel like; born only to be caught and killed, they laugh at the terrifying powers of the underworld which they know so little about; and they will be destroyed along with all the demons and powers of hell.h

13That is the pay these teachers will have for their sin. For they live in evil pleasures day after day. They are a disgrace and a stain among you, deceiving you by living in foul sin on the side while they join your love feasts as though they were honest men. 14No woman can escape their sinful stare, and of adultery they never have enough. They make a game of luring unstable women. They train themselves to be greedy; and are doomed and cursed. 15They have gone off the road and become lost like Balaam, the son of Beor, who fell in love with the money he could make by doing wrong; 16but Balaam

f *2:10 at the Glorious Ones*, or "the glories of the unseen world."   g *2:12 the terrifying powers of the underworld*, literally, "the things they do not understand."   h *2:12 all the demons and powers of hell*, implied. Literally, "will be destroyed in the same destruction with them."

New Revised Standard

19 So we have the prophetic message more fully confirmed. You will do well to be attentive to this as to a lamp shining in a dark place, until the day dawns and the morning star rises in your hearts. 20First of all you must understand this, that no prophecy of scripture is a matter of one's own interpretation, 21because no prophecy ever came by human will, but men and women moved by the Holy Spirit spoke from God.i

False Prophets and Their Punishment

2 BUT FALSE prophets also arose among the people, just as there will be false teachers among you, who will secretly bring in destructive opinions. They will even deny the Master who bought them—bringing swift destruction on themselves. 2Even so, many will follow their licentious ways, and because of these teachersj the way of truth will be maligned. 3And in their greed they will exploit you with deceptive words. Their condemnation, pronounced against them long ago, has not been idle, and their destruction is not asleep.

4 For if God did not spare the angels when they sinned, but cast them into hellk and committed them to chainsl of deepest darkness to be kept until the judgment; 5and if he did not spare the ancient world, even though he saved Noah, a herald of righteousness, with seven others, when he brought a flood on a world of the ungodly; 6and if by turning the cities of Sodom and Gomorrah to ashes he condemned them to extinctionm and made them an example of what is coming to the ungodly;n 7and if he rescued Lot, a righteous man greatly distressed by the licentiousness of the lawless 8(for that righteous man, living among them day after day, was tormented in his righteous soul by their lawless deeds that he saw and heard), 9then the Lord knows how to rescue the godly from trial, and to keep the unrighteous under punishment until the day of judgment 10—especially those who indulge their flesh in depraved lust, and who despise authority.

Bold and willful, they are not afraid to slander the glorious ones,o 11whereas angels, though greater in might and power, do not bring against them a slanderous judgment from the Lord.p 12These people, however, are like irrational animals, mere creatures of instinct, born to be caught and killed. They slander what they do not understand, and when those creatures are destroyed,q they also will be destroyed, 13sufferingr the penalty for doing wrong. They count it a pleasure to revel in the daytime. They are blots and blemishes, reveling in their dissipations while they feast with you. 14They have eyes full of adultery, insatiable for sin. They entice unsteady souls. They have hearts trained in greed. Accursed children! 15They have left the straight road and have gone astray, following the road of Balaam son of Bosor,t who loved the wages of doing wrong, 16but was

i Other ancient authorities read *but moved by the Holy Spirit saints of God spoke*   j Gk *because of them*   k Gk *Tartaros*   l Other ancient authorities read *pits*   m Other ancient authorities lack *to extinction*   n Other ancient authorities read *an example to those who were to be ungodly*   o Or *angels*; Gk *glories*   p Other ancient authorities read *before the Lord*; others lack the phrase   q Gk *in their destruction*   r Other ancient authorities read *receiving*   s Other ancient authorities read *love feasts*   t Other ancient authorities read *Beor*

King James

16But was rebuked for his iniquity: the dumb ass speaking with man's voice forbad the madness of the prophet.

17These are wells without water, clouds that are carried with a tempest; to whom the mist of darkness is reserved for ever.

18For when they speak great swelling *words* of vanity, they allure through the lusts of the flesh, *through much* wantonness, those that were clean escaped from them who live in error.

19While they promise them liberty, they themselves are the servants of corruption: for of whom a man is overcome, of the same is he brought in bondage.

20For if after they have escaped the pollutions of the world through the knowledge of the Lord and Saviour Jesus Christ, they are again entangled therein, and overcome, the latter end is worse with them than the beginning.

21For it had been better for them not to have known the way of righteousness, than, after they have known *it,* to turn from the holy commandment delivered unto them.

22But it is happened unto them according to the true proverb, The dog *is* turned to his own vomit again; and the sow that was washed to her wallowing in the mire.

3 THIS SECOND epistle, beloved, I now write unto you; in *both* which I stir up your pure minds by way of remembrance:

2That ye may be mindful of the words which were spoken before by the holy prophets, and of the commandment of us the apostles of the Lord and Saviour:

3Knowing this first, that there shall come in the last days scoffers, walking after their own lusts,

4And saying, Where is the promise of his coming? for since the fathers fell asleep, all things continue as *they were* from the beginning of the creation.

5For this they willingly are ignorant of, that by the word of God the heavens were of old, and the earth standing out of the water and in the water:

6Whereby the world that then was, being overflowed with water, perished:

7But the heavens and the earth, which are now, by the same word are kept in store, reserved unto fire against the day of judgment and perdition of ungodly men.

8But, beloved, be not ignorant of this one thing, that one day *is* with the Lord as a thousand years, and a thousand years as one day.

9The Lord is not slack concerning his promise, as some men count slackness; but is longsuffering to usward, not willing that any should perish, but that all should come to repentance.

10But the day of the Lord will come as a thief in the night; in the which the heavens shall pass away with a great noise, and the elements shall melt with fervent heat, the earth also and the works that are therein shall be burned up.

11*Seeing* then *that* all these things shall be dissolved, what manner *of persons* ought ye to be in *all* holy conversation and godliness,

12Looking for and hasting unto the coming of the day of God, wherein the heavens being on fire shall be dissolved, and the elements shall melt with fervent heat?

13Nevertheless we, according to his promise, look for new heavens and a new earth, wherein dwelleth righteousness.

New International

wrongdoing by a donkey—a beast without speech—who spoke with a man's voice and restrained the prophet's madness.

17These men are springs without water and mists driven by a storm. Blackest darkness is reserved for them. 18For they mouth empty, boastful words and, by appealing to the lustful desires of sinful human nature, they entice people who are just escaping from those who live in error. 19They promise them freedom, while they themselves are slaves of depravity—for a man is a slave to whatever has mastered him. 20If they have escaped the corruption of the world by knowing our Lord and Savior Jesus Christ and are again entangled in it and overcome, they are worse off at the end than they were at the beginning. 21It would have been better for them not to have known the way of righteousness, than to have known it and then to turn their backs on the sacred command that was passed on to them. 22Of them the proverbs are true: "A dog returns to its vomit,"a and, "A sow that is washed goes back to her wallowing in the mud."

The Day of the Lord

3 DEAR FRIENDS, this is now my second letter to you. I have written both of them as reminders to stimulate you to wholesome thinking. 2I want you to recall the words spoken in the past by the holy prophets and the command given by our Lord and Savior through your apostles.

3First of all, you must understand that in the last days scoffers will come, scoffing and following their own evil desires. 4They will say, "Where is this 'coming' he promised? Ever since our fathers died, everything goes on as it has since the beginning of creation." 5But they deliberately forget that long ago by God's word the heavens existed and the earth was formed out of water and by water. 6By these waters also the world of that time was deluged and destroyed. 7By the same word the present heavens and earth are reserved for fire, being kept for the day of judgment and destruction of ungodly men.

8But do not forget this one thing, dear friends: With the Lord a day is like a thousand years, and a thousand years are like a day. 9The Lord is not slow in keeping his promise, as some understand slowness. He is patient with you, not wanting anyone to perish, but everyone to come to repentance.

10But the day of the Lord will come like a thief. The heavens will disappear with a roar; the elements will be destroyed by fire, and the earth and everything in it will be laid bare.b

11Since everything will be destroyed in this way, what kind of people ought you to be? You ought to live holy and godly lives 12as you look forward to the day of God and speed its coming.c That day will bring about the destruction of the heavens by fire, and the elements will melt in the heat. 13But in keeping with his promise we are looking forward to a new heaven and a new earth, the home of righteousness.

---

a 22 Prov. 26:11   b 10 Some manuscripts *be burned up*   c 12 Or *as you wait eagerly for the day of God to come*

Living Bible

was stopped from his mad course when his donkey spoke to him with a human voice, scolding and rebuking him.

17These men are as useless as dried-up springs of water, promising much and delivering nothing; they are as unstable as clouds driven by the storm winds. They are doomed to the eternal pits of darkness. 18They proudly boast about their sins and conquests, and, using lust as their bait, they lure back into sin those who have just escaped from such wicked living.

19"You aren't saved by being good," they say, "so you might as well be bad. Do what you like, be free." But these very teachers who offer this "freedom" from law are themselves slaves to sin and destruction. For a man is a slave to whatever controls him. 20And when a person has escaped from the wicked ways of the world by learning about our Lord and Savior Jesus Christ, and then gets tangled up with sin and becomes its slave again, he is worse off than he was before. 21It would be better if he had never known about Christ at all than to learn of him and then afterwards turn his back on the holy commandments that were given to him. 22There is an old saying that "A dog comes back to what he has vomited, and a pig is washed only to come back and wallow in the mud again." That is the way it is with those who turn again to their sin.

3 THIS IS my second letter to you, dear brothers, and in both of them I have tried to remind you—if you will let me—about facts you already know: facts you learned from the holy prophets and from us apostles who brought you the words of our Lord and Savior.

3First, I want to remind you that in the last days there will come scoffers who will do every wrong they can think of, and laugh at the truth. 4This will be their line of argument: "So Jesus promised to come back, did he? Then where is he? He'll never come! Why, as far back as anyone can remember everything has remained exactly as it was since the first day of creation."

5, 6They deliberately forget this fact: that God did destroy the world with a mighty flood, long after he had made the heavens by the word of his command, and had used the waters to form the earth and surround it. 7And God has commanded that the earth and the heavens be stored away for a great bonfire at the judgment day, when all ungodly men will perish.

8But don't forget this, dear friends, that a day or a thousand years from now is like tomorrow to the Lord. 9He isn't really being slow about his promised return, even though it sometimes seems that way. But he is waiting, for the good reason that he is not willing that any should perish, and he is giving more time for sinners to repent. 10The day of the Lord is surely coming, as unexpectedly as a thief, and then the heavens will pass away with a terrible noise and the heavenly bodies will disappear in fire, and the earth and everything on it will be burned up.

11And so since everything around us is going to melt away, what holy, godly lives we should be living! 12You should look forward to that day and hurry it along—the day when God will set the heavens on fire, and the heavenly bodies will melt and disappear in flames. 13But we are looking forward to God's promise of new heavens and a new earth afterwards, where there will be only goodness.d

New Revised Standard

rebuked for his own transgression; a speechless donkey spoke with a human voice and restrained the prophet's madness.

17 These are waterless springs and mists driven by a storm; for them the deepest darkness has been reserved. 18For they speak bombastic nonsense, and with licentious desires of the flesh they entice people who have juste escaped from those who live in error. 19They promise them freedom, but they themselves are slaves of corruption; for people are slaves to whatever masters them. 20For if, after they have escaped the defilements of the world through the knowledge of our Lord and Savior Jesus Christ, they are again entangled in them and overpowered, the last state has become worse for them than the first. 21For it would have been better for them never to have known the way of righteousness than, after knowing it, to turn back from the holy commandment that was passed on to them. 22It has happened to them according to the true proverb,

"The dog turns back to its own vomit,"
and,
　"The sow is washed only to wallow in the
　　mud."

The Promise of the Lord's Coming

3 THIS IS now, beloved, the second letter I am writing to you; in them I am trying to arouse your sincere intention by reminding you 2that you should remember the words spoken in the past by the holy prophets, and the commandment of the Lord and Savior spoken through your apostles. 3First of all you must understand this, that in the last days scoffers will come, scoffing and indulging their own lusts 4and saying, "Where is the promise of his coming? For ever since our ancestors died,f all things continue as they were from the beginning of creation!" 5They deliberately ignore this fact, that by the word of God heavens existed long ago and an earth was formed out of water and by means of water, 6through which the world of that time was deluged with water and perished. 7But by the same word the present heavens and earth have been reserved for fire, being kept until the day of judgment and destruction of the godless.

8 But do not ignore this one fact, beloved, that with the Lord one day is like a thousand years, and a thousand years are like one day. 9The Lord is not slow about his promise, as some think of slowness, but is patient with you,g not wanting any to perish, but all to come to repentance. 10But the day of the Lord will come like a thief, and then the heavens will pass away with a loud noise, and the elements will be dissolved with fire, and the earth and everything that is done on it will be disclosed.h

11 Since all these things are to be dissolved in this way, what sort of persons ought you to be in leading lives of holiness and godliness, 12waiting for and hasteningi the coming of the day of God, because of which the heavens will be set ablaze and dissolved, and the elements will melt with fire? 13But, in accordance with his promise, we wait for new heavens and a new earth, where righteousness is at home.

---

d 3:13 where there will be only goodness, literally, "wherein righteousness dwells."

e Other ancient authorities read actually   f Gk our fathers fell asleep
g Other ancient authorities read on your account   h Other ancient authorities read will be burned up   i Or earnestly desiring

King James

14Wherefore, beloved, seeing that ye look for such things, be diligent that ye may be found of him in peace, without spot, and blameless.

15And account *that* the longsuffering of our Lord *is* salvation; even as our beloved brother Paul also according to the wisdom given unto him hath written unto you;

16As also in all *his* epistles, speaking in them of these things; in which are some things hard to be understood, which they that are unlearned and unstable wrest, as *they do* also the other scriptures, unto their own destruction.

17Ye therefore, beloved, seeing ye know *these things* before, beware lest ye also, being led away with the error of the wicked, fall from your own stedfastness.

18But grow in grace, and *in* the knowledge of our Lord and Saviour Jesus Christ. To him *be* glory both now and for ever. Amen.

New International

14So then, dear friends, since you are looking forward to this, make every effort to be found spotless, blameless and at peace with him. 15Bear in mind that our Lord's patience means salvation, just as our dear brother Paul also wrote you with the wisdom that God gave him. 16He writes the same way in all his letters, speaking in them of these matters. His letters contain some things that are hard to understand, which ignorant and unstable people distort, as they do the other Scriptures, to their own destruction.

17Therefore, dear friends, since you already know this, be on your guard so that you may not be carried away by the error of lawless men and fall from your secure position. 18But grow in the grace and knowledge of our Lord and Savior Jesus Christ. To him be glory both now and forever! Amen.

Living Bible

14Dear friends, while you are waiting for these things to happen and for him to come, try hard to live without sinning; and be at peace with everyone so that he will be pleased with you when he returns.

15, 16And remember why he is waiting. He is giving us time to get his message of salvation out to others. Our wise and beloved brother Paul has talked about these same things in many of his letters. Some of his comments are not easy to understand, and there are people who are deliberately stupid, and always demand some unusual interpretation—they have twisted his letters around to mean something quite different from what he meant, just as they do the other parts of the Scripture—and the result is disaster for them.

17I am warning you ahead of time, dear brothers, so that you can watch out and not be carried away by the mistakes of these wicked men, lest you yourselves become mixed up too. 18But grow in spiritual strength and become better acquainted with our Lord and Savior Jesus Christ. To him be all glory and splendid honor, both now and forevermore. Good-bye.

Peter

New Revised Standard

Final Exhortation and Doxology

14 Therefore, beloved, while you are waiting for these things, strive to be found by him at peace, without spot or blemish; 15and regard the patience of our Lord as salvation. So also our beloved brother Paul wrote to you according to the wisdom given him, 16speaking of this as he does in all his letters. There are some things in them hard to understand, which the ignorant and unstable twist to their own destruction, as they do the other scriptures. 17You therefore, beloved, since you are forewarned, beware that you are not carried away with the error of the lawless and lose your own stability. 18But grow in the grace and knowledge of our Lord and Savior Jesus Christ. To him be the glory both now and to the day of eternity. Amen.a

THE FIRST EPISTLE OF

John

1 John

The Word of Life

1 THAT WHICH was from the beginning, which we have heard, which we have looked upon, and our hands have handled, of the Word of life;

2(For the life was manifested, and we have seen *it*, and bear witness, and show unto you that eternal life, which was with the Father, and was manifested unto us;)

3That which we have seen and heard declare we unto you, that ye also may have fellowship with us: and truly our fellowship *is* with the Father, and with his Son Jesus Christ.

4And these things write we unto you, that your joy may be full.

5This then is the message which we have heard of him, and declare unto you, that God is light, and in him is no darkness at all.

6If we say that we have fellowship with him, and walk in darkness, we lie, and do not the truth:

7But if we walk in the light, as he is in the light, we have fellowship one with another, and the blood of Jesus Christ his Son cleanseth us from all sin.

8If we say that we have no sin, we deceive ourselves, and the truth is not in us.

9If we confess our sins, he is faithful and just to forgive us *our* sins, and to cleanse us from all unrighteousness.

10If we say that we have not sinned, we make him a liar, and his word is not in us.

1 THAT WHICH was from the beginning, which we have heard, which we have seen with our eyes, which we have looked at and our hands have touched—this we proclaim concerning the Word of life. 2The life appeared; we have seen it and testify to it, and we proclaim to you the eternal life, which was with the Father and has appeared to us. 3We proclaim to you what we have seen and heard, so that you also may have fellowship with us. And our fellowship is with the Father and with his Son, Jesus Christ. 4We write this to make our[a] joy complete.

Walking in the Light

5This is the message we have heard from him and declare to you: God is light; in him there is no darkness at all. 6If we claim to have fellowship with him yet walk in the darkness, we lie and do not live by the truth. 7But if we walk in the light, as he is in the light, we have fellowship with one another, and the blood of Jesus, his Son, purifies us from all[b] sin.

8If we claim to be without sin, we deceive ourselves and the truth is not in us. 9If we confess our sins, he is faithful and just and will forgive us our sins and purify us from all unrighteousness. 10If we claim we have not sinned, we make him out to be a liar and his word has no place in our lives.

2 MY LITTLE children, these things write I unto you, that ye sin not. And if any man sin, we have an advocate with the Father, Jesus Christ the righteous:

2And he is the propitiation for our sins: and not for ours only, but also for *the sins of* the whole world.

3And hereby we do know that we know him, if we keep his commandments.

4He that saith, I know him, and keepeth not his commandments, is a liar, and the truth is not in him.

5But whoso keepeth his word, in him verily is the love of God perfected: hereby know we that we are in him.

6He that saith he abideth in him ought himself also so to walk, even as he walked.

7Brethren, I write no new commandment unto you, but an old commandment which ye had from the beginning. The old commandment is the word which ye have heard from the beginning.

2 MY DEAR children, I write this to you so that you will not sin. But if anybody does sin, we have one who speaks to the Father in our defense—Jesus Christ, the Righteous One. 2He is the atoning sacrifice for our sins, and not only for ours but also for[c] the sins of the whole world.

3We know that we have come to know him if we obey his commands. 4The man who says, "I know him," but does not do what he commands is a liar, and the truth is not in him. 5But if anyone obeys his word, God's love[d] is truly made complete in him. This is how we know we are in him: 6Whoever claims to live in him must walk as Jesus did.

7Dear friends, I am not writing you a new command but an old one, which you have had since the beginning. This old command is the message you have heard. 8Yet

---

a 4 Some manuscripts *your*   b 7 Or *every*   c 2 Or *He is the one who turns aside God's wrath, taking away our sins, and not only ours but also*   d 5 Or *word, love for God*

THE FIRST LETTER OF

1 John

John

CHRIST WAS alive when the world began, yet I myself have seen him with my own eyes and listened to him speak. I have touched him with my own hands. He is God's message of life. 2This one who is life from God has been shown to us and we guarantee that we have seen him; I am speaking of Christ, who is eternal Life. He was with the Father and then was shown to us. 3Again I say, we are telling you about what we ourselves have actually seen and heard, so that you may share the fellowship and the joys we have with the Father and with Jesus Christ his son. 4And if you do as I say in this letter, then you, too, will be full of joy, and so will we.

5This is the message God has given us to pass on to you: that God is Light and in him is no darkness at all. 6So if we say we are his friends, but go on living in spiritual darkness and sin, we are lying. 7But if we are living in the light of God's presence, just as Christ does, then we have wonderful fellowship and joy with each other, and the blood of Jesus his Son cleanses us from every sin.

8If we say that we have no sin, we are only fooling ourselves, and refusing to accept the truth. 9But if we confess our sins to him,e he can be depended on to forgive us and to cleanse us from every wrong. [And it is perfectly proper for God to do this for us because Christ died to wash away our sins.f] 10If we claim to have not sinned, we are lying and calling God a liar, *for he says we have sinned.*

MY LITTLE children, I am telling you this so that you will stay away from sin. But if you sin, there is someone to plead for you before the Father. His name is Jesus Christ, the one who is all that is good and who pleases God completely. 2He is the one who took God's wrath against our sins upon himself, and brought us into fellowship with God; and he is the forgiveness for our sins,g and not only ours but all the world's.

3And how can we be sure that we belong to him? By looking within ourselves: are we really trying to do what he wants us to?

4Someone may say, "I am a Christian; I am on my way to heaven; I belong to Christ." But if he doesn't do what Christ tells him to, he is a liar. 5But those who do what Christ tells them to will learn to love God more and more. That is the way to know whether or not you are a Christian. 6Anyone who says he is a Christian should live as Christ did.

7Dear brothers, I am not writing out a new rule for you to obey, for it is an old one you have always had, right from the start. You have heard it all before. 8Yet

The Word of Life

WE DECLARE to you what was from the beginning, what we have heard, what we have seen with our eyes, what we have looked at and touched with our hands, concerning the word of life— 2this life was revealed, and we have seen it and testify to it, and declare to you the eternal life that was with the Father and was revealed to us— 3we declare to you what we have seen and heard so that you also may have fellowship with us; and truly our fellowship is with the Father and with his Son Jesus Christ. 4We are writing these things so that ourh joy may be complete.

God Is Light

5 This is the message we have heard from him and proclaim to you, that God is light and in him there is no darkness at all. 6If we say that we have fellowship with him while we are walking in darkness, we lie and do not do what is true; 7but if we walk in the light as he himself is in the light, we have fellowship with one another, and the blood of Jesus his Son cleanses us from all sin. 8If we say that we have no sin, we deceive ourselves, and the truth is not in us. 9If we confess our sins, he who is faithful and just will forgive us our sins and cleanse us from all unrighteousness. 10If we say that we have not sinned, we make him a liar, and his word is not in us.

Christ Our Advocate

MY LITTLE children, I am writing these things to you so that you may not sin. But if anyone does sin, we have an advocate with the Father, Jesus Christ the righteous; 2and he is the atoning sacrifice for our sins, and not for ours only but also for the sins of the whole world.

3 Now by this we may be sure that we know him, if we obey his commandments. 4Whoever says, "I have come to know him," but does not obey his commandments, is a liar, and in such a person the truth does not exist; 5but whoever obeys his word, truly in this person the love of God has reached perfection. By this we may be sure that we are in him: 6whoever says, "I abide in him," ought to walk just as he walked.

A New Commandment

7 Beloved, I am writing you no new commandment, but an old commandment that you have had from the beginning; the old commandment is the word that you have heard. 8Yet I am writing you a new commandment

---

e *1:9 Confess our sins to him,* implied. Literally, "if we confess our sins." f *1:9 Wash away our sins,* literally, "he is ... just." g *2:2 he is the forgiveness for our sins,* or "he is the atoning sacrifice for our sins."

h Other ancient authorities read *your*

King James

8Again, a new commandment I write unto you, which thing is true in him and in you: because the darkness is past, and the true light now shineth.

9He that saith he is in the light, and hateth his brother, is in darkness even until now.

10He that loveth his brother abideth in the light, and there is none occasion of stumbling in him.

11But he that hateth his brother is in darkness, and walketh in darkness, and knoweth not whither he goeth, because that darkness hath blinded his eyes.

12I write unto you, little children, because your sins are forgiven you for his name's sake.

13I write unto you, fathers, because ye have known him *that is* from the beginning. I write unto you, young men, because ye have overcome the wicked one. I write unto you, little children, because ye have known the Father.

14I have written unto you, fathers, because ye have known him *that is* from the beginning. I have written unto you, young men, because ye are strong, and the word of God abideth in you, and ye have overcome the wicked one.

15Love not the world, neither the things *that are* in the world. If any man love the world, the love of the Father is not in him.

16For all that *is* in the world, the lust of the flesh, and the lust of the eyes, and the pride of life, is not of the Father, but is of the world.

17And the world passeth away, and the lust thereof: but he that doeth the will of God abideth for ever.

18Little children, it is the last time: and as ye have heard that antichrist shall come, even now are there many antichrists; whereby we know that it is the last time.

19They went out from us, but they were not of us; for if they had been of us, they would *no doubt* have continued with us: but *they went out*, that they might be made manifest that they were not all of us.

20But ye have an unction from the Holy One, and ye know all things.

21I have not written unto you because ye know not the truth, but because ye know it, and that no lie is of the truth.

22Who is a liar but he that denieth that Jesus is the Christ? He is antichrist, that denieth the Father and the Son.

23Whosoever denieth the Son, the same hath not the Father: *[but] he that acknowledgeth the Son hath the Father also.*

24Let that therefore abide in you, which ye have heard from the beginning. If that which ye have heard from the beginning shall remain in you, ye also shall continue in the Son, and in the Father.

25And this is the promise that he hath promised us, *even* eternal life.

26These *things* have I written unto you concerning them that seduce you.

27But the anointing which ye have received of him abideth in you, and ye need not that any man teach you: but as the same anointing teacheth you of all things, and is truth, and is no lie, and even as it hath taught you, ye shall abide in him.

28And now, little children, abide in him; that, when he shall appear, we may have confidence, and not be ashamed before him at his coming.

29If ye know that he is righteous, ye know that every one that doeth righteousness is born of him.

New International

I am writing you a new command; its truth is seen in him and you, because the darkness is passing and the true light is already shining.

9Anyone who claims to be in the light but hates his brother is still in the darkness. 10Whoever loves his brother lives in the light, and there is nothing in him[a] to make him stumble. 11But whoever hates his brother is in the darkness and walks around in the darkness; he does not know where he is going, because the darkness has blinded him.

12I write to you, dear children,
　　because your sins have been forgiven on
　　　account of his name.
13I write to you, fathers,
　　because you have known him who is from the
　　　beginning.
I write to you, young men,
　　because you have overcome the evil one.
I write to you, dear children,
　　because you have known the Father.
14I write to you, fathers,
　　because you have known him who is from the
　　　beginning.
I write to you, young men,
　　because you are strong,
　　and the word of God lives in you,
　　and you have overcome the evil one.

Do Not Love the World

15Do not love the world or anything in the world. If anyone loves the world, the love of the Father is not in him. 16For everything in the world—the cravings of sinful man, the lust of his eyes and the boasting of what he has and does—comes not from the Father but from the world. 17The world and its desires pass away, but the man who does the will of God lives forever.

Warning Against Antichrists

18Dear children, this is the last hour; and as you have heard that the antichrist is coming, even now many antichrists have come. This is how we know it is the last hour. 19They went out from us, but they did not really belong to us. For if they had belonged to us, they would have remained with us; but their going showed that none of them belonged to us.

20But you have an anointing from the Holy One, and all of you know the truth.[b] 21I do not write to you because you do not know the truth, but because you do know it and because no lie comes from the truth. 22Who is the liar? It is the man who denies that Jesus is the Christ. Such a man is the antichrist—he denies the Father and the Son. 23No one who denies the Son has the Father; whoever acknowledges the Son has the Father also.

24See that what you have heard from the beginning remains in you. If it does, you also will remain in the Son and in the Father. 25And this is what he promised us—even eternal life.

26I am writing these things to you about those who are trying to lead you astray. 27As for you, the anointing you received from him remains in you, and you do not need anyone to teach you. But as his anointing teaches you about all things and as that anointing is real, not counterfeit—just as it has taught you, remain in him.

Children of God

28And now, dear children, continue in him, so that when he appears we may be confident and unashamed before him at his coming.

29If you know that he is righteous, you know that everyone who does what is right has been born of him.

---

a *10 Or it*　b *20 Some manuscripts and you know all things*

Living Bible

it is always new, and works for you just as it did for Christ; and as we obey this commandment, *to love one another,* the darkness in our lives disappears and the new light of life in Christ shines in.

9Anyone who says he is walking in the light of Christ but dislikes his fellow man, is still in darkness. 10But whoever loves his fellow man is "walking in the light" and can see his way without stumbling around in darkness and sin. 11For he who dislikes his brother is wandering in spiritual darkness and doesn't know where he is going, for the darkness has made him blind so that he cannot see the way.

12I am writing these things to all of you, my little children, because your sins have been forgiven in the name of Jesus our Savior. 13I am saying these things to you older men because you really know Christ, the one who has been alive from the beginning. And you young men, I am talking to you because you have won your battle with Satan. And I am writing to you younger boys and girls because you, too, have learned to know God our Father.

14And so I say to you fathers who know the eternal God, and to you young men who are strong, with God's Word in your hearts, and have won your struggle against Satan: 15Stop loving this evil world and all that it offers you, for when you love these things you show that you do not really love God; 16for all these worldly things, these evil desires—the craze for sex, the ambition to buy everything that appeals to you, and the pride that comes from wealth and importance—these are not from God. They are from this evil world itself. 17And this world is fading away, and these evil, forbidden things will go with it, but whoever keeps doing the will of God will live forever.

18Dear children, this world's last hour has come. You have heard about the Antichrist who is coming—the one who is against Christ—and already many such persons have appeared. This makes us all the more certain that the end of the world is near. 19These "against-Christ" people used to be members of our churches, but they never really belonged with us or else they would have stayed. When they left us it proved that they were not of us at all.

20But you are not like that, for the Holy Spirit has come upon you, and you know the truth. 21So I am not writing to you as to those who need to know the truth, but I warn you as those who can discern the difference between true and false.

22And who is the greatest liar? The one who says that Jesus is not Christ. Such a person is antichrist, for he does not believe in God the Father and in his Son. 23For a person who doesn't believe in Christ, God's Son, can't have God the Father either. But he who has Christ, God's Son, has God the Father also.

24So keep on believing what you have been taught from the beginning. If you do, you will always be in close fellowship with both God the Father and his Son. 25And he himself has promised us this: *eternal life.*

26These remarks of mine about the Antichrist are pointed at those who would dearly love to blindfold you and lead you astray. 27But you have received the Holy Spirit and he lives within you, in your hearts, so that you don't need anyone to teach you what is right. For he teaches you all things, and he is the Truth, and no liar; and so, just as he has said, you must live in Christ, never to depart from him.

28And now, my little children, stay in happy fellowship with the Lord so that when he comes you will be sure that all is well, and will not have to be ashamed and shrink back from meeting him. 29Since we know that God is always good and does only right, we may rightly assume that all those who do right are his children.

New Revised Standard

that is true in him and in you, becausec the darkness is passing away and the true light is already shining. 9Whoever says, "I am in the light," while hating a brother or sister,d is still in the darkness. 10Whoever loves a brother or sistere lives in the light, and in such a personf there is no cause for stumbling. 11But whoever hates another believerg is in the darkness, walks in the darkness, and does not know the way to go, because the darkness has brought on blindness.

12 I am writing to you, little children,
      because your sins are forgiven on account of
        his name.
13 I am writing to you, fathers,
      because you know him who is from the
        beginning.
    I am writing to you, young people,
      because you have conquered the evil one.
14 I write to you, children,
      because you know the Father.
    I write to you, fathers,
      because you know him who is from the
        beginning.
    I write to you, young people,
      because you are strong
      and the word of God abides in you,
        and you have overcome the evil one.

15 Do not love the world or the things in the world. The love of the Father is not in those who love the world; 16for all that is in the world—the desire of the flesh, the desire of the eyes, the pride in riches—comes not from the Father but from the world. 17And the world and its desireh are passing away, but those who do the will of God live forever.

Warning against Antichrists

18 Children, it is the last hour! As you have heard that antichrist is coming, so now many antichrists have come. From this we know that it is the last hour. 19They went out from us, but they did not belong to us; for if they had belonged to us, they would have remained with us. But by going out they made it plain that none of them belongs to us. 20But you have been anointed by the Holy One, and all of you have knowledge.i 21I write to you, not because you do not know the truth, but because you know it, and you know that no lie comes from the truth. 22Who is the liar but the one who denies that Jesus is the Christ?j This is the antichrist, the one who denies the Father and the Son. 23No one who denies the Son has the Father; everyone who confesses the Son has the Father also. 24Let what you heard from the beginning abide in you. If what you heard from the beginning abides in you, then you will abide in the Son and in the Father. 25And this is what he has promised us,k eternal life.

26 I write these things to you concerning those who would deceive you. 27As for you, the anointing that you received from him abides in you, and so you do not need anyone to teach you. But as his anointing teaches you about all things, and is true and is not a lie, and just as it has taught you, abide in him.l

28 And now, little children, abide in him, so that when he is revealed we may have confidence and not be put to shame before him at his coming.

Children of God

29 If you know that he is righteous, you may be sure that everyone who does right has been born of him.

---

c Or *that*   d Gk *hating a brother*   e Gk *loves a brother*   f Or *in it*   g Gk *hates a brother*   h Or *the desire for it*   i Other ancient authorities read *you know all things*   j Or *the Messiah*   k Other ancient authorities read *you*   l Or *it*

King James

3 BEHOLD, WHAT manner of love the Father hath bestowed upon us, that we should be called the sons of God: therefore the world knoweth us not, because it knew him not.

2Beloved, now are we the sons of God, and it doth not yet appear what we shall be: but we know that, when he shall appear, we shall be like him; for we shall see him as he is.

3And every man that hath this hope in him purifieth himself, even as he is pure.

4Whosoever committeth sin transgresseth also the law: for sin is the transgression of the law.

5And ye know that he was manifested to take away our sins; and in him is no sin.

6Whosoever abideth in him sinneth not: whosoever sinneth hath not seen him, neither known him.

7Little children, let no man deceive you: he that doeth righteousness is righteous, even as he is righteous.

8He that committeth sin is of the devil; for the devil sinneth from the beginning. For this purpose the Son of God was manifested, that he might destroy the works of the devil.

9Whosoever is born of God doth not commit sin; for his seed remaineth in him: and he cannot sin, because he is born of God.

10In this the children of God are manifest, and the children of the devil: whosoever doeth not righteousness is not of God, neither he that loveth not his brother.

11For this is the message that ye heard from the beginning, that we should love one another.

12Not as Cain, *who* was of that wicked one, and slew his brother. And wherefore slew he him? Because his own works were evil, and his brother's righteous.

13Marvel not, my brethren, if the world hate you.

14We know that we have passed from death unto life, because we love the brethren. He that loveth not *his* brother abideth in death.

15Whosoever hateth his brother is a murderer: and ye know that no murderer hath eternal life abiding in him.

16Hereby perceive we the love *of God,* because he laid down his life for us: and we ought to lay down *our* lives for the brethren.

17But whoso hath this world's good, and seeth his brother have need, and shutteth up his bowels of *compassion* from him, how dwelleth the love of God in him?

18My little children, let us not love in word, neither in tongue; but in deed and in truth.

19And hereby we know that we are of the truth, and shall assure our hearts before him.

20For if our heart condemn us, God is greater than our heart, and knoweth all things.

21Beloved, if our heart condemn us not, *then* have we confidence toward God.

22And whatsoever we ask, we receive of him, because we keep his commandments, and do those things that are pleasing in his sight.

23And this is his commandment, That we should believe on the name of his Son Jesus Christ, and love one another, as he gave us commandment.

24And he that keepeth his commandments dwelleth in him, and he in him. And hereby we know that he abideth in us, by the Spirit which he hath given us.

New International

3 HOW GREAT is the love the Father has lavished on us, that we should be called children of God! And that is what we are! The reason the world does not know us is that it did not know him. 2Dear friends, now we are children of God, and what we will be has not yet been made known. But we know that when he appears,[a] we shall be like him, for we shall see him as he is. 3Everyone who has this hope in him purifies himself, just as he is pure.

4Everyone who sins breaks the law; in fact, sin is lawlessness. 5But you know that he appeared so that he might take away our sins. And in him is no sin. 6No one who lives in him keeps on sinning. No one who continues to sin has either seen him or known him.

7Dear children, do not let anyone lead you astray. He who does what is right is righteous, just as he is righteous. 8He who does what is sinful is of the devil, because the devil has been sinning from the beginning. The reason the Son of God appeared was to destroy the devil's work. 9No one who is born of God will continue to sin, because God's seed remains in him; he cannot go on sinning, because he has been born of God. 10This is how we know who the children of God are and who the children of the devil are: Anyone who does not do what is right is not a child of God; nor is anyone who does not love his brother.

Love One Another

11This is the message you heard from the beginning: We should love one another. 12Do not be like Cain, who belonged to the evil one and murdered his brother. And why did he murder him? Because his own actions were evil and his brother's were righteous. 13Do not be surprised, my brothers, if the world hates you. 14We know that we have passed from death to life, because we love our brothers. Anyone who does not love remains in death. 15Anyone who hates his brother is a murderer, and you know that no murderer has eternal life in him.

16This is how we know what love is: Jesus Christ laid down his life for us. And we ought to lay down our lives for our brothers. 17If anyone has material possessions and sees his brother in need but has no pity on him, how can the love of God be in him? 18Dear children, let us not love with words or tongue but with actions and in truth. 19This then is how we know that we belong to the truth, and how we set our hearts at rest in his presence 20whenever our hearts condemn us. For God is greater than our hearts, and he knows everything.

21Dear friends, if our hearts do not condemn us, we have confidence before God 22and receive from him anything we ask, because we obey his commands and do what pleases him. 23And this is his command: to believe in the name of his Son, Jesus Christ, and to love one another as he commanded us. 24Those who obey his commands live in him, and he in them. And this is how we know that he lives in us: We know it by the Spirit he gave us.

---

a 2 Or *when it is made known*

Living Bible

3 SEE HOW very much our heavenly Father loves us, for he allows us to be called his children—think of it—and we really *are!* But since most people don't know God, naturally they don't understand that we are his children. 2Yes, dear friends, we are already God's children, right now, and we can't even imagine what it is going to be like later on. But we do know this, that when he comes we will be like him, as a result of seeing him as he really is. 3And everyone who really believes this will try to stay pure because Christ is pure.

4But those who keep on sinning are against God, for every sin is done against the will of God. 5And you know that he became a man so that he could take away our sins, and that there is no sin in him, no missing of God's will at any time in any way. 6So if we stay close to him, obedient to him, we won't be sinning either; but as for those who keep on sinning, they should realize this: They sin because they have never really known him or become his.

7Oh, dear children, don't let anyone deceive you about this: if you are constantly doing what is good, it is because you *are* good, even as he is. 8But if you keep on sinning, it shows that you belong to Satan, who since he first began to sin has kept steadily at it. But the Son of God came to destroy these works of the devil. 9The person who has been born into God's family does not make a practice of sinning, because now God's life is in him; so he can't keep on sinning, for this new life has been born into him and controls him—he has been *born again*.

10So now we can tell who is a child of God and who belongs to Satan. Whoever is living a life of sin and doesn't love his brother shows that he is not in God's family; 11for the message to us from the beginning has been that we should love one another.

12We are not to be like Cain, who belonged to Satan and killed his brother. Why did he kill him? Because Cain had been doing wrong and he knew very well that his brother's life was better than his. 13So don't be surprised, dear friends, if the world hates you.

14If we love other Christians it proves that we have been delivered from hell and given eternal life. But a person who doesn't have love for others is headed for eternal death. 15Anyone who hates his Christian brother is really a murderer at heart; and you know that no one wanting to murder has eternal life within. 16We know what real love is from Christ's example in dying for us. And so we also ought to lay down our lives for our Christian brothers.

17But if someone who is supposed to be a Christian has money enough to live well, and sees a brother in need, and won't help him—how can God's love be within *him?* 18Little children, let us stop just *saying* we love people; let us *really* love them, and *show it* by our *actions*. 19Then we will know for sure, by our actions, that we are on God's side, and our consciences will be clear, even when we stand before the Lord. 20But if we have bad consciences and feel that we have done wrong, the Lord will surely feel it even more,b for he knows everything we do.

21But, dearly loved friends, if our consciences are clear, we can come to the Lord with perfect assurance and trust, 22and get whatever we ask for because we are obeying him and doing the things that please him. 23And this is what God says we must do: Believe on the name of his Son Jesus Christ, and love one another. 24Those who do what God says—they are living with God and he with them. We know this is true because the Holy Spirit he has given us tells us so.

New Revised Standard

3 SEE WHAT love the Father has given us, that we should be called children of God; and that is what we are. The reason the world does not know us is that it did not know him. 2Beloved, we are God's children now; what we will be has not yet been revealed. What we do know is this: when hec is revealed, we will be like him, for we will see him as he is. 3And all who have this hope in him purify themselves, just as he is pure.

4 Everyone who commits sin is guilty of lawlessness; sin is lawlessness. 5You know that he was revealed to take away sins, and in him there is no sin. 6No one who abides in him sins; no one who sins has either seen him or known him. 7Little children, let no one deceive you. Everyone who does what is right is righteous, just as he is righteous. 8Everyone who commits sin is a child of the devil; for the devil has been sinning from the beginning. The Son of God was revealed for this purpose, to destroy the works of the devil. 9Those who have been born of God do not sin, because God's seed abides in them;d they cannot sin, because they have been born of God. 10The children of God and the children of the devil are revealed in this way: all who do not do what is right are not from God, nor are those who do not love their brothers and sisters.e

Love One Another

11 For this is the message you have heard from the beginning, that we should love one another. 12We must not be like Cain who was from the evil one and murdered his brother. And why did he murder him? Because his own deeds were evil and his brother's righteous. 13Do not be astonished, brothers and sisters,f that the world hates you. 14We know that we have passed from death to life because we love one another. Whoever does not love abides in death. 15All who hate a brother or sistere are murderers, and you know that murderers do not have eternal life abiding in them. 16We know love by this, that he laid down his life for us—and we ought to lay down our lives for one another. 17How does God's love abide in anyone who has the world's goods and sees a brother or sisterg in need and yet refuses help?

18 Little children, let us love, not in word or speech, but in truth and action. 19And by this we will know that we are from the truth and will reassure our hearts before him 20whenever our hearts condemn us; for God is greater than our hearts, and he knows everything. 21Beloved, if our hearts do not condemn us, we have boldness before God; 22and we receive from him whatever we ask, because we obey his commandments and do what pleases him.

23 And this is his commandment, that we should believe in the name of his Son Jesus Christ and love one another, just as he has commanded us. 24All who obey his commandments abide in him, and he abides in them. And by this we know that he abides in us, by the Spirit that he has given us.

---

b *3:20 the Lord will surely feel it even more,* or, perhaps, "the Lord will be merciful anyway." Literally, "If our heart condemns us God is greater than our heart."

c Or *it*   d Or *because the children of God abide in him*   e Gk *his brother*
f Gk *brothers*   g Gk *brother*

King James

4 BELOVED, BELIEVE not every spirit, but try the spirits whether they are of God: because many false prophets are gone out into the world.

2Hereby know ye the Spirit of God: Every spirit that confesseth that Jesus Christ is come in the flesh is of God:

3And every spirit that confesseth not that Jesus Christ is come in the flesh is not of God: and this is that *spirit* of antichrist, whereof ye have heard that it should come; and even now already is it in the world.

4Ye are of God, little children, and have overcome them: because greater is he that is in you, than he that is in the world.

5They are of the world: therefore speak they of the world, and the world heareth them.

6We are of God: he that knoweth God heareth us; he that is not of God heareth not us. Hereby know we the spirit of truth, and the spirit of error.

7Beloved, let us love one another: for love is of God; and every one that loveth is born of God, and knoweth God.

8He that loveth not knoweth not God; for God is love.

9In this was manifested the love of God toward us, because that God sent his only begotten Son into the world, that we might live through him.

10Herein is love, not that we loved God, but that he loved us, and sent his Son *to be* the propitiation for our sins.

11Beloved, if God so loved us, we ought also to love one another.

12No man hath seen God at any time. If we love one another, God dwelleth in us, and his love is perfected in us.

13Hereby know we that we dwell in him, and he in us, because he hath given us of his Spirit.

14And we have seen and do testify that the Father sent the Son *to be* the Saviour of the world.

15Whosoever shall confess that Jesus is the Son of God, God dwelleth in him, and he in God.

16And we have known and believed the love that God hath to us. God is love; and he that dwelleth in love dwelleth in God, and God in him.

17Herein is our love made perfect, that we may have boldness in the day of judgment: because as he is, so are we in this world.

18There is no fear in love; but perfect love casteth out fear: because fear hath torment. He that feareth is not made perfect in love.

19We love him, because he first loved us.

20If a man say, I love God, and hateth his brother, he is a liar: for he that loveth not his brother whom he hath seen, how can he love God whom he hath not seen?

21And this commandment have we from him, That he who loveth God love his brother also.

New International

Test the Spirits

4 DEAR FRIENDS, do not believe every spirit, but test the spirits to see whether they are from God, because many false prophets have gone out into the world. 2This is how you can recognize the Spirit of God: Every spirit that acknowledges that Jesus Christ has come in the flesh is from God, 3but every spirit that does not acknowledge Jesus is not from God. This is the spirit of the antichrist, which you have heard is coming and even now is already in the world.

4You, dear children, are from God and have overcome them, because the one who is in you is greater than the one who is in the world. 5They are from the world and therefore speak from the viewpoint of the world, and the world listens to them. 6We are from God, and whoever knows God listens to us; but whoever is not from God does not listen to us. This is how we recognize the Spirita of truth and the spirit of falsehood.

God's Love and Ours

7Dear friends, let us love one another, for love comes from God. Everyone who loves has been born of God and knows God. 8Whoever does not love does not know God, because God is love. 9This is how God showed his love among us: He sent his one and only Sonb into the world that we might live through him. 10This is love: not that we loved God, but that he loved us and sent his Son as an atoning sacrifice forc our sins. 11Dear friends, since God so loved us, we also ought to love one another. 12No one has ever seen God; but if we love one another, God lives in us and his love is made complete in us.

13We know that we live in him and he in us, because he has given us of his Spirit. 14And we have seen and testify that the Father has sent his Son to be the Savior of the world. 15If anyone acknowledges that Jesus is the Son of God, God lives in him and he in God. 16And so we know and rely on the love God has for us.

God is love. Whoever lives in love lives in God, and God in him. 17In this way, love is made complete among us so that we will have confidence on the day of judgment, because in this world we are like him. 18There is no fear in love. But perfect love drives out fear, because fear has to do with punishment. The one who fears is not made perfect in love.

19We love because he first loved us. 20If anyone says, "I love God," yet hates his brother, he is a liar. For anyone who does not love his brother, whom he has seen, cannot love God, whom he has not seen. 21And he has given us this command: Whoever loves God must also love his brother.

a 6 Or *spirit*   b 9 Or *his only begotten Son*   c 10 Or *as the one who would turn aside his wrath, taking away*

Living Bible

4 DEARLY LOVED friends, don't always believe everything you hear just because someone says it is a message from God: test it first to see if it really is. For there are many false teachers around, 2and the way to find out if their message is from the Holy Spirit is to ask: Does it really agree that Jesus Christ, God's Son, actually became man with a human body? If so, then the message is from God. 3If not, the message is not from God but from one who is against Christ, like the "Antichrist" you have heard about who is going to come, and his attitude of enmity against Christ is already abroad in the world.

4Dear young friends, you belong to God and have already won your fight with those who are against Christ, because there is someone in your hearts who is stronger than any evil teacher in this wicked world. 5These men belong to this world, so, quite naturally, they are concerned about worldly affairs and the world pays attention to them. 6But we are children of God; that is why only those who have walked and talked with God will listen to us. Others won't. That is another way to know whether a message is really from God; for if it is, the world won't listen to it.

7Dear friends, let us practice loving each other, for love comes from God and those who are loving and kind show that they are the children of God, and that they are getting to know him better. 8But if a person isn't loving and kind, it shows that he doesn't know God—for God is love.

9God showed how much he loved us by sending his only Son into this wicked world to bring to us eternal life through his death. 10In this act we see what real love is: it is not our love for God, but his love for us when he sent his Son to satisfy God's anger against our sins. 11Dear friends, since God loved us as much as that, we surely ought to love each other too. 12For though we have never yet seen God, when we love each other God lives in us and his love within us grows ever stronger. 13And he has put his own Holy Spirit into our hearts as a proof to us that we are living with him and he with us. 14And furthermore, we have seen with our own eyes and now tell all the world that God sent his Son to be their Savior. 15Anyone who believes and says that Jesus is the Son of God has God living in him, and he is living with God.

16We know how much God loves us because we have felt his love and because we believe him when he tells us that he loves us dearly. God is love, and anyone who lives in love is living with God and God is living in him. 17And as we live with Christ, our love grows more perfect and complete; so we will not be ashamed and embarrassed at the day of judgment, but can face him with confidence and joy, because he loves us and we love him too.

18We need have no fear of someone who loves us perfectly; his perfect love for us eliminates all dread of what he might do to us. If we are afraid, it is for fear of what he might do to us, and shows that we are not fully convinced that he really loves us. 19So you see, our love for him comes as a result of his loving us first.

20If anyone says "I love God," but keeps on hating his brother, he is a liar; for if he doesn't love his brother who is right there in front of him, how can he love God whom he has never seen? 21And God himself has said that one must love not only God, but his brother too.

New Revised Standard

Testing the Spirits

4 BELOVED, DO not believe every spirit, but test the spirits to see whether they are from God; for many false prophets have gone out into the world. 2By this you know the Spirit of God: every spirit that confesses that Jesus Christ has come in the flesh is from God, 3and every spirit that does not confess Jesusd is not from God. And this is the spirit of the antichrist, of which you have heard that it is coming; and now it is already in the world. 4Little children, you are from God, and have conquered them; for the one who is in you is greater than the one who is in the world. 5They are from the world; therefore what they say is from the world, and the world listens to them. 6We are from God. Whoever knows God listens to us, and whoever is not from God does not listen to us. From this we know the spirit of truth and the spirit of error.

God Is Love

7 Beloved, let us love one another, because love is from God; everyone who loves is born of God and knows God. 8Whoever does not love does not know God, for God is love. 9God's love was revealed among us in this way: God sent his only Son into the world so that we might live through him. 10In this is love, not that we loved God but that he loved us and sent his Son to be the atoning sacrifice for our sins. 11Beloved, since God loved us so much, we also ought to love one another. 12No one has ever seen God; if we love one another, God lives in us, and his love is perfected in us.

13 By this we know that we abide in him and he in us, because he has given us of his Spirit. 14And we have seen and do testify that the Father has sent his Son as the Savior of the world. 15God abides in those who confess that Jesus is the Son of God, and they abide in God. 16So we have known and believe the love that God has for us.

God is love, and those who abide in love abide in God, and God abides in them. 17Love has been perfected among us in this: that we may have boldness on the day of judgment, because as he is, so are we in this world. 18There is no fear in love, but perfect love casts out fear; for fear has to do with punishment, and whoever fears has not reached perfection in love. 19We lovee because he first loved us. 20Those who say, "I love God," and hate their brothers or sisters,f are liars; for those who do not love a brother or sisterg whom they have seen, cannot love God whom they have not seen. 21The commandment we have from him is this: those who love God must love their brothers and sistersf also.

d Other ancient authorities read does away with Jesus (Gk dissolves Jesus)
e Other ancient authorities add him; others add God   f Gk brothers   g Gk brother

King James

5 WHOSOEVER BELIEVETH that Jesus is the Christ is born of God: and every one that loveth him that begat loveth him also that is begotten of him.

2By this we know that we love the children of God, when we love God, and keep his commandments.

3For this is the love of God, that we keep his commandments: and his commandments are not grievous.

4For whatsoever is born of God overcometh the world: and this is the victory that overcometh the world, *even* our faith.

5Who is he that overcometh the world, but he that believeth that Jesus is the Son of God?

6This is he that came by water and blood, *even* Jesus Christ; not by water only, but by water and blood. And it is the Spirit that beareth witness, because the Spirit is truth.

7For there are three that bear record in heaven, the Father, the Word, and the Holy Ghost: and these three are one.

8And there are three that bear witness in earth, the spirit, and the water, and the blood: and these three agree in one.

9If we receive the witness of men, the witness of God is greater: for this is the witness of God which he hath testified of his Son.

10He that believeth on the Son of God hath the witness in himself: he that believeth not God hath made him a liar; because he believeth not the record that God gave of his Son.

11And this is the record, that God hath given to us eternal life, and this life is in his Son.

12He that hath the Son hath life; *and* he that hath not the Son of God hath not life.

13These things have I written unto you that believe on the name of the Son of God; that ye may know that ye have eternal life, and that ye may believe on the name of the Son of God.

14And this is the confidence that we have in him, that, if we ask any thing according to his will, he heareth us:

15And if we know that he hear us, whatsoever we ask, we know that we have the petitions that we desired of him.

16If any man see his brother sin a sin *which is* not unto death, he shall ask, and he shall give him life for them that sin not unto death. There is a sin unto death: I do not say that he shall pray for it.

17All unrighteousness is sin: and there is a sin not unto death.

18We know that whosoever is born of God sinneth not; but he that is begotten of God keepeth himself, and that wicked one toucheth him not.

19*And* we know that we are of God, and the whole world lieth in wickedness.

20And we know that the Son of God is come, and hath given us an understanding, that we may know him that is true, and we are in him that is true, *even* in his Son Jesus Christ. This is the true God, and eternal life.

21Little children, keep yourselves from idols. Amen.

New International

Faith in the Son of God

5 EVERYONE WHO believes that Jesus is the Christ is born of God, and everyone who loves the father loves his child as well. 2This is how we know that we love the children of God: by loving God and carrying out his commands. 3This is love for God: to obey his commands. And his commands are not burdensome, 4for everyone born of God overcomes the world. This is the victory that has overcome the world, even our faith. 5Who is it that overcomes the world? Only he who believes that Jesus is the Son of God.

6This is the one who came by water and blood—Jesus Christ. He did not come by water only, but by water and blood. And it is the Spirit who testifies, because the Spirit is the truth. 7For there are three that testify: 8thea Spirit, the water and the blood; and the three are in agreement. 9We accept man's testimony, but God's testimony is greater because it is the testimony of God, which he has given about his Son. 10Anyone who believes in the Son of God has this testimony in his heart. Anyone who does not believe God has made him out to be a liar, because he has not believed the testimony God has given about his Son. 11And this is the testimony: God has given us eternal life, and this life is in his Son. 12He who has the Son has life; he who does not have the Son of God does not have life.

Concluding Remarks

13I write these things to you who believe in the name of the Son of God so that you may know that you have eternal life. 14This is the confidence we have in approaching God: that if we ask anything according to his will, he hears us. 15And if we know that he hears us—whatever we ask—we know that we have what we asked of him.

16If anyone sees his brother commit a sin that does not lead to death, he should pray and God will give him life. I refer to those whose sin does not lead to death. There is a sin that leads to death. I am not saying that he should pray about that. 17All wrongdoing is sin, and there is sin that does not lead to death.

18We know that anyone born of God does not continue to sin; the one who was born of God keeps him safe, and the evil one cannot harm him. 19We know that we are children of God, and that the whole world is under the control of the evil one. 20We know also that the Son of God has come and has given us understanding, so that we may know him who is true. And we are in him who is true—even in his Son Jesus Christ. He is the true God and eternal life.

21Dear children, keep yourselves from idols.

---

a 7,8 Late manuscripts of the Vulgate *testify in heaven: the Father, the Word and the Holy Spirit, and these three are one.* 8*And there are three that testify on earth: the* (not found in any Greek manuscript before the sixteenth century)

Living Bible

5 IF YOU believe that Jesus is the Christ—that he is God's Son and your Savior—then you are a child of God. And all who love the Father love his children too. 2So you can find out how much you love God's children—your brothers and sisters in the Lord—by how much you love and obey God. 3Loving God means doing what he tells us to do, and really, that isn't hard at all; 4for every child of God can obey him, defeating sin and evil pleasure by trusting Christ to help him.

5But who could possibly fight and win this battle except by believing that Jesus is truly the Son of God? 6, 7, 8And we know he is, because God said so with a voice from heaven when Jesus was baptized, and again as he was facing death[b]—yes, not only at his baptism but also as he faced death.[c] And the Holy Spirit, forever truthful, says it too. So we have these three witnesses: the voice of the Holy Spirit in our hearts, the voice from heaven at Christ's baptism, and the voice before he died.[d] And they all say the same thing: that Jesus Christ is the Son of God.[e] 9We believe men who witness in our courts, and so surely we can believe whatever God declares. And God declares that Jesus is his Son. 10All who believe this know in their hearts that it is true. If anyone doesn't believe this, he is actually calling God a liar, because he doesn't believe what God has said about his Son.

11And what is it that God has said? That he has given us eternal life, and that this life is in his Son. 12So whoever has God's Son has life; whoever does not have his Son, does not have life.

13I have written this to you who believe in the Son of God so that you may know you have eternal life. 14And we are sure of this, that he will listen to us whenever we ask him for anything in line with his will. 15And if we really know he is listening when we talk to him and make our requests, then we can be sure that he will answer us.

16If you see a Christian sinning in a way that does not end in death, you should ask God to forgive him and God will give him life, unless he has sinned that one fatal sin. But there is that one sin which ends in death and if he has done that, there is no use praying for him. 17Every wrong is a sin, of course. I'm not talking about these ordinary sins; I am speaking of that one that ends in death.[f]

18No one who has become part of God's family makes a practice of sinning, for Christ, God's Son, holds him securely and the devil cannot get his hands on him. 19We know that we are children of God and that all the rest of the world around us is under Satan's power and control. 20And we know that Christ, God's Son, has come to help us understand and find the true God. And now we are in God because we are in Jesus Christ his Son, who is the only true God; and he is eternal Life.

21Dear children, keep away from anything that might take God's place in your hearts. Amen.

Sincerely, John

New Revised Standard

Faith Conquers the World

5 EVERYONE WHO believes that Jesus is the Christ[g] has been born of God, and everyone who loves the parent loves the child. 2By this we know that we love the children of God, when we love God and obey his commandments. 3For the love of God is this, that we obey his commandments. And his commandments are not burdensome, 4for whatever is born of God conquers the world. And this is the victory that conquers the world, our faith. 5Who is it that conquers the world but the one who believes that Jesus is the Son of God?

Testimony concerning the Son of God

6 This is the one who came by water and blood, Jesus Christ, not with the water only but with the water and the blood. And the Spirit is the one that testifies, for the Spirit is the truth. 7There are three that testify:[h] 8the Spirit and the water and the blood, and these three agree. 9If we receive human testimony, the testimony of God is greater; for this is the testimony of God that he has testified to his Son. 10Those who believe in the Son of God have the testimony in their hearts. Those who do not believe in God[i] have made him a liar by not believing in the testimony that God has given concerning his Son. 11And this is the testimony: God gave us eternal life, and this life is in his Son. 12Whoever has the Son has life; whoever does not have the Son of God does not have life.

Epilogue

13 I write these things to you who believe in the name of the Son of God, so that you may know that you have eternal life.

14 And this is the boldness we have in him, that if we ask anything according to his will, he hears us. 15And if we know that he hears us in whatever we ask, we know that we have obtained the requests made of him. 16If you see your brother or sister[j] committing what is not a mortal sin, you will ask, and God[k] will give life to such a one—to those whose sin is not mortal. There is sin that is mortal; I do not say that you should pray about that. 17All wrongdoing is sin, but there is sin that is not mortal.

18 We know that those who are born of God do not sin, but the one who was born of God protects them, and the evil one does not touch them. 19We know that we are God's children, and that the whole world lies under the power of the evil one. 20And we know that the Son of God has come and has given us understanding so that we may know him who is true;[l] and we are in him who is true, in his Son Jesus Christ. He is the true God and eternal life.

21 Little children, keep yourselves from idols.[m]

---

b *5:6-8 as he was facing death,* literally, "This is he who came by water and blood." See Mt 3:16, 17; Lk 9:31, 35; Jn 12:27, 28, 32, 33. Other interpretations of this verse are equally possible.   c *5:6-8 as he faced death,* literally, "not by water only, but by water and blood."   d *5:6-8 and the voice before he died,* literally, "the Spirit, and the water, and the blood."   e *5:6-8 Jesus Christ is the Son of God,* implied.   f *5:17 that ends in death.* Commentators differ widely in their thoughts about what sin this is, and whether it causes physical death or spiritual death. Blasphemy against the Holy Spirit results in spiritual death (Mk 3:29) but can a Christian ever sin in such a way? Impenitence at the Communion Table sometimes ends in physical death (1 Cor 11:30). And Heb 6:4-8 speaks of the terrible end of those who fall away.

g Or *the Messiah*   h A few other authorities read (with variations) 7*There are three that testify in heaven, the Father, the Word, and the Holy Spirit, and these three are one.* 8*And there are three that testify on earth:*   i Other ancient authorities read *in the Son*   j Gk *your brother*   k Gk *he*   l Other ancient authorities read *know the true God*   m Other ancient authorities add *Amen*

THE SECOND EPISTLE OF

John

2 John

King James

¹THE ELDER unto the elect lady and her children, whom I love in the truth; and not I only, but also all they that have known the truth;

²For the truth's sake, which dwelleth in us, and shall be with us for ever.

³Grace be with you, mercy, *and* peace, from God the Father, and from the Lord Jesus Christ, the Son of the Father, in truth and love.

⁴I rejoiced greatly that I found of thy children walking in truth, as we have received a commandment from the Father.

⁵And now I beseech thee, lady, not as though I wrote a new commandment unto thee, but that which we had from the beginning, that we love one another.

⁶And this is love, that we walk after his commandments. This is the commandment, That, as ye have heard from the beginning, ye should walk in it.

⁷For many deceivers are entered into the world, who confess not that Jesus Christ is come in the flesh. This is a deceiver and an antichrist.

⁸Look to yourselves, that we lose not those things which we have wrought, but that we receive a full reward.

⁹Whosoever transgresseth, and abideth not in the doctrine of Christ, hath not God. He that abideth in the doctrine of Christ, he hath both the Father and the Son.

¹⁰If there come any unto you, and bring not this doctrine, receive him not into *your* house, neither bid him God speed:

¹¹For he that biddeth him God speed is partaker of his evil deeds.

¹²Having many things to write unto you, I would not *write* with paper and ink: but I trust to come unto you, and speak face to face, that our joy may be full.

¹³The children of thy elect sister greet thee. Amen.

New International

¹THE ELDER,

To the chosen lady and her children, whom I love in the truth—and not I only, but also all who know the truth— ²because of the truth, which lives in us and will be with us forever:

³Grace, mercy and peace from God the Father and from Jesus Christ, the Father's Son, will be with us in truth and love.

⁴It has given me great joy to find some of your children walking in the truth, just as the Father commanded us. ⁵And now, dear lady, I am not writing you a new command but one we have had from the beginning. I ask that we love one another. ⁶And this is love: that we walk in obedience to his commands. As you have heard from the beginning, his command is that you walk in love.

⁷Many deceivers, who do not acknowledge Jesus Christ as coming in the flesh, have gone out into the world. Any such person is the deceiver and the antichrist. ⁸Watch out that you do not lose what you have worked for, but that you may be rewarded fully. ⁹Anyone who runs ahead and does not continue in the teaching of Christ does not have God; whoever continues in the teaching has both the Father and the Son. ¹⁰If anyone comes to you and does not bring this teaching, do not take him into your house or welcome him. ¹¹Anyone who welcomes him shares in his wicked work.

¹²I have much to write to you, but I do not want to use paper and ink. Instead, I hope to visit you and talk with you face to face, so that our joy may be complete.

¹³The children of your chosen sister send their greetings.

Living Bible

2 John

1*FROM:* JOHN, the old Elder of the church.
To: That dear woman Cyria, one of God's very own, and to her children whom I love so much, as does everyone else in the church. 2Since the Truth is in our hearts forever, 3God the Father and Jesus Christ his Son will bless us with great mercy and much peace, and with truth and love.

4How happy I am to find some of your children here, and to see that they are living as they should, following the Truth, obeying God's command.

5And now I want to urgently remind you, dear friends, of the old rule God gave us right from the beginning, that Christians should love one another. 6If we love God, we will do whatever he tells us to. And he has told us from the very first to love each other.

7Watch out for the false leaders—and there are many of them around—who don't believe that Jesus Christ came to earth as a human being with a body like ours. Such people are against the truth and against Christ. 8Beware of being like them, and losing the prize that you and I have been working so hard to get. See to it that you win your full reward from the Lord. 9For if you wander beyond the teaching of Christ, you will leave God behind; while if you are loyal to Christ's teachings, you will have God too. Then you will have both the Father and the Son.

10If anyone comes to teach you, and he doesn't believe what Christ taught, don't even invite him into your home. Don't encourage him in any way. 11If you do you will be a partner with him in his wickedness.

12Well, I would like to say much more, but I don't want to say it in this letter, for I hope to come to see you soon and then we can talk over these things together and have a joyous time.

13Greetings from the children of your sister—another choice child of God.

Sincerely, John

New Revised Standard

THE SECOND LETTER OF

John

Salutation

1 THE ELDER to the elect lady and her children, whom I love in the truth, and not only I but also all who know the truth, 2because of the truth that abides in us and will be with us forever:

3 Grace, mercy, and peace will be with us from God the Father and from[a] Jesus Christ, the Father's Son, in truth and love.

Truth and Love

4 I was overjoyed to find some of your children walking in the truth, just as we have been commanded by the Father. 5But now, dear lady, I ask you, not as though I were writing you a new commandment, but one we have had from the beginning, let us love one another. 6And this is love, that we walk according to his commandments; this is the commandment just as you have heard it from the beginning—you must walk in it.

7 Many deceivers have gone out into the world, those who do not confess that Jesus Christ has come in the flesh; any such person is the deceiver and the antichrist! 8Be on your guard, so that you do not lose what we[b] have worked for, but may receive a full reward. 9Everyone who does not abide in the teaching of Christ, but goes beyond it, does not have God; whoever abides in the teaching has both the Father and the Son. 10Do not receive into the house or welcome anyone who comes to you and does not bring this teaching; 11for to welcome is to participate in the evil deeds of such a person.

Final Greetings

12 Although I have much to write to you, I would rather not use paper and ink; instead I hope to come to you and talk with you face to face, so that our joy may be complete.

13 The children of your elect sister send you their greetings.[c]

a Other ancient authorities add *the Lord*   b Other ancient authorities read *you*
c Other ancient authorities add *Amen*

THE THIRD EPISTLE OF

John

3 John

¹THE ELDER unto the wellbeloved Gaius, whom I love in the truth.

²Beloved, I wish above all things that thou mayest prosper and be in health, even as thy soul prospereth.

³For I rejoiced greatly, when the brethren came and testified of the truth that is in thee, even as thou walkest in the truth.

⁴I have no greater joy than to hear that my children walk in truth.

⁵Beloved, thou doest faithfully whatsoever thou doest to the brethren, and to strangers;

⁶Which have borne witness of thy charity before the church: whom if thou bring forward on their journey after a godly sort, thou shalt do well:

⁷Because that for his name's sake they went forth, taking nothing of the Gentiles.

⁸We therefore ought to receive such, that we might be fellowhelpers to the truth.

⁹I wrote unto the church: but Diotrephes, who loveth to have the preeminence among them, receiveth us not.

¹⁰Wherefore, if I come, I will remember his deeds which he doeth, prating against us with malicious words: and not content therewith, neither doth he himself receive the brethren, and forbiddeth them that would, and casteth *them* out of the church.

¹¹Beloved, follow not that which is evil, but that which is good. He that doeth good is of God: but he that doeth evil hath not seen God.

¹²Demetrius hath good report of all *men,* and of the truth itself: yea, and we *also* bear record; and ye know that our record is true.

¹³I had many things to write, but I will not with ink and pen write unto thee:

¹⁴But I trust I shall shortly see thee, and we shall speak face to face. Peace *be* to thee. *Our* friends salute thee. Greet the friends by name.

¹THE ELDER,

To my dear friend Gaius, whom I love in the truth.

²Dear friend, I pray that you may enjoy good health and that all may go well with you, even as your soul is getting along well. ³It gave me great joy to have some brothers come and tell about your faithfulness to the truth and how you continue to walk in the truth. ⁴I have no greater joy than to hear that my children are walking in the truth.

⁵Dear friend, you are faithful in what you are doing for the brothers, even though they are strangers to you. ⁶They have told the church about your love. You will do well to send them on their way in a manner worthy of God. ⁷It was for the sake of the Name that they went out, receiving no help from the pagans. ⁸We ought therefore to show hospitality to such men so that we may work together for the truth.

⁹I wrote to the church, but Diotrephes, who loves to be first, will have nothing to do with us. ¹⁰So if I come, I will call attention to what he is doing, gossiping maliciously about us. Not satisfied with that, he refuses to welcome the brothers. He also stops those who want to do so and puts them out of the church.

¹¹Dear friend, do not imitate what is evil but what is good. Anyone who does what is good is from God. Anyone who does what is evil has not seen God. ¹²Demetrius is well spoken of by everyone—and even by the truth itself. We also speak well of him, and you know that our testimony is true.

¹³I have much to write you, but I do not want to do so with pen and ink. ¹⁴I hope to see you soon, and we will talk face to face.

Peace to you. The friends here send their greetings. Greet the friends there by name.

Living Bible	New Revised Standard

3 John

John

1FROM: JOHN, the Elder.

To: Dear Gaius, whom I truly love.

2Dear friend, I am praying that all is well with you and that your body is as healthy as I know your soul is. 3Some of the brothers traveling by have made me very happy by telling me that your life stays clean and true, and that you are living by the standards of the Gospel. 4I could have no greater joy than to hear such things about my children.

5Dear friend, you are doing a good work for God in taking care of the traveling teachers and missionaries who are passing through. 6They have told the church here of your friendship and your loving deeds. I am glad when you send them on their way with a generous gift. 7For they are traveling for the Lord, and take neither food, clothing, shelter, nor money from those who are not Christians, even though they have preached to them. 8So we ourselves should take care of them in order that we may become partners with them in the Lord's work.

9I sent a brief letter to the church about this, but proud Diotrephes, who loves to push himself forward as the leader of the Christians there, does not admit my authority over him and refuses to listen to me. 10When I come I will tell you some of the things he is doing and what wicked things he is saying about me and what insulting language he is using. He not only refuses to welcome the missionary travelers himself, but tells others not to, and when they do he tries to put them out of the church.

11Dear friend, don't let this bad example influence you. Follow only what is good. Remember that those who do what is right prove that they are God's children; and those who continue in evil prove that they are far from God. 12But everyone, including Truth itself, speaks highly of Demetrius. I myself can say the same for him, and you know I speak the truth.

13I have much to say but I don't want to write it, 14for I hope to see you soon and then we will have much to talk about together. 15So good-bye for now. Friends here send their love, and please give each of the folks there a special greeting from me.

Sincerely, John

Salutation

1 THE ELDER to the beloved Gaius, whom I love in truth.

Gaius Commended for His Hospitality

2 Beloved, I pray that all may go well with you and that you may be in good health, just as it is well with your soul. 3I was overjoyed when some of the friendsa arrived and testified to your faithfulness to the truth, namely how you walk in the truth. 4I have no greater joy than this, to hear that my children are walking in the truth.

5 Beloved, you do faithfully whatever you do for the friends,a even though they are strangers to you; 6they have testified to your love before the church. You will do well to send them on in a manner worthy of God; 7for they began their journey for the sake of Christ,b accepting no support from non-believers.c 8Therefore we ought to support such people, so that we may become co-workers with the truth.

Diotrephes and Demetrius

9 I have written something to the church; but Diotrephes, who likes to put himself first, does not acknowledge our authority. 10So if I come, I will call attention to what he is doing in spreading false charges against us. And not content with those charges, he refuses to welcome the friends,a and even prevents those who want to do so and expels them from the church.

11 Beloved, do not imitate what is evil but imitate what is good. Whoever does good is from God; whoever does evil has not seen God. 12Everyone has testified favorably about Demetrius, and so has the truth itself. We also testify for him,d and you know that our testimony is true.

Final Greetings

13 I have much to write to you, but I would rather not write with pen and ink; 14instead I hope to see you soon, and we will talk together face to face.

15 Peace to you. The friends send you their greetings. Greet the friends there, each by name.

---

a Gk *brothers*   b Gk *for the sake of the name*   c Gk *the Gentiles*   d Gk lacks *for him*

THE GENERAL EPISTLE OF

Jude

Jude

1JUDE, THE servant of Jesus Christ, and brother of James, to them that are sanctified by God the Father, and preserved in Jesus Christ, *and* called:

2Mercy unto you, and peace, and love, be multiplied.

3Beloved, when I gave all diligence to write unto you of the common salvation, it was needful for me to write unto you, and exhort *you* that ye should earnestly contend for the faith which was once delivered unto the saints.

4For there are certain men crept in unawares, who were before of old ordained to this condemnation, ungodly men, turning the grace of our God into lasciviousness, and denying the only Lord God, and our Lord Jesus Christ.

5I will therefore put you in remembrance, though ye once knew this, how that the Lord, having saved the people out of the land of Egypt, afterward destroyed them that believed not.

6And the angels which kept not their first estate, but left their own habitation, he hath reserved in everlasting chains under darkness unto the judgment of the great day.

7Even as Sodom and Gomorrha, and the cities about them in like manner, giving themselves over to fornication, and going after strange flesh, are set forth for an example, suffering the vengeance of eternal fire.

8Likewise also these *filthy* dreamers defile the flesh, despise dominion, and speak evil of dignities.

9Yet Michael the archangel, when contending with the devil he disputed about the body of Moses, durst not bring against him a railing accusation, but said, The Lord rebuke thee.

10But these speak evil of those things which they know not: but what they know naturally, as brute beasts, in those things they corrupt themselves.

11Woe unto them! for they have gone in the way of Cain, and ran greedily after the error of Balaam for reward, and perished in the gainsaying of Core.

12These are spots in your feasts of charity, when they feast with you, feeding themselves without fear: clouds *they are* without water, carried about of winds; trees whose fruit withereth, without fruit, twice dead, plucked up by the roots;

1JUDE, A servant of Jesus Christ and a brother of James,

To those who have been called, who are loved by God the Father and kept bya Jesus Christ:

2Mercy, peace and love be yours in abundance.

The Sin and Doom of Godless Men

3Dear friends, although I was very eager to write to you about the salvation we share, I felt I had to write and urge you to contend for the faith that was once for all entrusted to the saints. 4For certain men whose condemnation was written aboutb long ago have secretly slipped in among you. They are godless men, who change the grace of our God into a license for immorality and deny Jesus Christ our only Sovereign and Lord.

5Though you already know all this, I want to remind you that the Lordc delivered his people out of Egypt, but later destroyed those who did not believe. 6And the angels who did not keep their positions of authority but abandoned their own home—these he has kept in darkness, bound with everlasting chains for judgment on the great Day. 7In a similar way, Sodom and Gomorrah and the surrounding towns gave themselves up to sexual immorality and perversion. They serve as an example of those who suffer the punishment of eternal fire.

8In the very same way, these dreamers pollute their own bodies, reject authority and slander celestial beings. 9But even the archangel Michael, when he was disputing with the devil about the body of Moses, did not dare to bring a slanderous accusation against him, but said, "The Lord rebuke you!" 10Yet these men speak abusively against whatever they do not understand; and what things they do understand by instinct, like unreasoning animals—these are the very things that destroy them.

11Woe to them! They have taken the way of Cain; they have rushed for profit into Balaam's error; they have been destroyed in Korah's rebellion.

12These men are blemishes at your love feasts, eating with you without the slightest qualm—shepherds who feed only themselves. They are clouds without rain, blown along by the wind; autumn trees, without fruit and uprooted—twice dead. 13They are wild waves of the

---

a *1 Or for;* or *in*   b *4 Or men who were marked out for condemnation*
c *5 Some early manuscripts Jesus*

Living Bible	New Revised Standard

Jude

Jude

1 *FROM:* JUDE, a servant of Jesus Christ, and a brother of James.

To: Christians everywhere—beloved of God and chosen by him. **2** May you be given more and more of God's kindness, peace, and love.

3 Dearly loved friends, I had been planning to write you some thoughts about the salvation God has given us, but now I find I must write of something else instead, urging you to stoutly defend the truth which God gave, once for all, to his people to keep without change through the years. **4** I say this because some godless teachers have wormed their way in among you, saying that after we become Christians we can do just as we like without fear of God's punishment. The fate of such people was written long ago, for they have turned against our only Master and Lord, Jesus Christ.

5 My answer to them is: Remember this fact—which you know already—that the Lord saved a whole nation of people out of the land of Egypt, and then killed every one of them who did not trust and obey him. **6** And I remind you of those angels who were once pure and holy, but turned to a life of sin.[d] Now God has them chained up in prisons of darkness, waiting for the judgment day. **7** And don't forget the cities of Sodom and Gomorrah and their neighboring towns, all full of lust of every kind including lust of men for other men. Those cities were destroyed by fire and continue to be a warning to us that there is a hell in which sinners are punished.

8 Yet these false teachers carelessly go right on living their evil, immoral lives, degrading their bodies and laughing at those in authority over them, even scoffing at the Glorious Ones. **9** Yet Michael, one of the mightiest of the angels, when he was arguing with Satan about Moses' body, did not dare to accuse even Satan, or jeer at him, but simply said, "The Lord rebuke you." **10** But these men mock and curse at anything they do not understand, and, like animals, they do whatever they feel like, thereby ruining their souls.

11 Woe upon them! For they follow the example of Cain who killed his brother; and, like Balaam, they will do anything for money; and like Korah, they have disobeyed God and will die under his curse.

12 When these men join you at the love feasts of the church, they are evil smears among you, laughing and carrying on, gorging and stuffing themselves without a thought for others. They are like clouds blowing over dry land without giving rain, promising much, but producing nothing. They are like fruit trees without any fruit at picking time. They are not only dead, but doubly dead, for they have been pulled out, roots and all, to be burned.

Salutation

1 JUDE,[e] A servant[f] of Jesus Christ and brother of James,

To those who are called, who are beloved[g] in[h] God the Father and kept safe for[h] Jesus Christ:

2 May mercy, peace, and love be yours in abundance.

Occasion of the Letter

3 Beloved, while eagerly preparing to write to you about the salvation we share, I find it necessary to write and appeal to you to contend for the faith that was once for all entrusted to the saints. **4** For certain intruders have stolen in among you, people who long ago were designated for this condemnation as ungodly, who pervert the grace of our God into licentiousness and deny our only Master and Lord, Jesus Christ.[i]

Judgment on False Teachers

5 Now I desire to remind you, though you are fully informed, that the Lord, who once for all saved[j] a people out of the land of Egypt, afterward destroyed those who did not believe. **6** And the angels who did not keep their own position, but left their proper dwelling, he has kept in eternal chains in deepest darkness for the judgment of the great Day. **7** Likewise, Sodom and Gomorrah and the surrounding cities, which, in the same manner as they, indulged in sexual immorality and pursued unnatural lust,[k] serve as an example by undergoing a punishment of eternal fire.

8 Yet in the same way these dreamers also defile the flesh, reject authority, and slander the glorious ones.[l] **9** But when the archangel Michael contended with the devil and disputed about the body of Moses, he did not dare to bring a condemnation of slander[m] against him, but said, "The Lord rebuke you!" **10** But these people slander whatever they do not understand, and they are destroyed by those things that, like irrational animals, they know by instinct. **11** Woe to them! For they go the way of Cain, and abandon themselves to Balaam's error for the sake of gain, and perish in Korah's rebellion. **12** These are blemishes[n] on your love-feasts, while they feast with you without fear, feeding themselves.[o] They are waterless clouds carried along by the winds; autumn trees without fruit, twice dead, uprooted; **13** wild waves

---

[e] Gk *Judas*   [f] Gk *slave*   [g] Other ancient authorities read *sanctified*   [h] Or *by*   [i] Or *the only Master and our Lord Jesus Christ*   [j] Other ancient authorities read *though you were once for all fully informed, that Jesus (or Joshua) who saved*   [k] Gk *went after other flesh*   [l] Or *angels*; Gk *glories*   [m] Or *condemnation for blasphemy*   [n] Or *reefs*   [o] Or *without fear. They are shepherds who care only for themselves*

---

[d] *1:6* Or, "who abandoned their original rank and left their proper home."

King James

13Raging waves of the sea, foaming out their own shame; wandering stars, to whom is reserved the blackness of darkness for ever.

14And Enoch also, the seventh from Adam, prophesied of these, saying, Behold, the Lord cometh with ten thousands of his saints,

15To execute judgment upon all, and to convince all that are ungodly among them of all their ungodly deeds which they have ungodly committed, and of all their hard *speeches* which ungodly sinners have spoken against him.

16These are murmurers, complainers, walking after their own lusts; and their mouth speaketh great swelling *words,* having men's persons in admiration because of advantage.

17But, beloved, remember ye the words which were spoken before of the apostles of our Lord Jesus Christ;

18How that they told you there should be mockers in the last time, who should walk after their own ungodly lusts.

19These be they who separate themselves, sensual, having not the Spirit.

20But ye, beloved, building up yourselves on your most holy faith, praying in the Holy Ghost,

21Keep yourselves in the love of God, looking for the mercy of our Lord Jesus Christ unto eternal life.

22And of some have compassion, making a difference:

23And others save with fear, pulling *them* out of the fire; hating even the garment spotted by the flesh.

24Now unto him that is able to keep you from falling, and to present *you* faultless before the presence of his glory with exceeding joy,

25To the only wise God our Saviour, *be* glory and majesty, dominion and power, both now and ever. Amen.

New International

sea, foaming up their shame; wandering stars, for whom blackest darkness has been reserved forever.

14Enoch, the seventh from Adam, prophesied about these men: "See, the Lord is coming with thousands upon thousands of his holy ones 15to judge everyone, and to convict all the ungodly of all the ungodly acts they have done in the ungodly way, and of all the harsh words ungodly sinners have spoken against him." 16These men are grumblers and faultfinders; they follow their own evil desires; they boast about themselves and flatter others for their own advantage.

A Call to Persevere

17But, dear friends, remember what the apostles of our Lord Jesus Christ foretold. 18They said to you, "In the last times there will be scoffers who will follow their own ungodly desires." 19These are the men who divide you, who follow mere natural instincts and do not have the Spirit.

20But you, dear friends, build yourselves up in your most holy faith and pray in the Holy Spirit. 21Keep yourselves in God's love as you wait for the mercy of our Lord Jesus Christ to bring you to eternal life.

22Be merciful to those who doubt; 23snatch others from the fire and save them; to others show mercy, mixed with fear—hating even the clothing stained by corrupted flesh.

Doxology

24To him who is able to keep you from falling and to present you before his glorious presence without fault and with great joy— 25to the only God our Savior be glory, majesty, power and authority, through Jesus Christ our Lord, before all ages, now and forevermore! Amen.

Living Bible

13All they leave behind them is shame and disgrace like the dirty foam left along the beach by the wild waves. They wander around looking as bright as stars, but ahead of them is the everlasting gloom and darkness that God has prepared for them.

14Enoch, who lived seven generations after Adam, knew about these men and said this about them: "See, the Lord is coming with millions of his holy ones. 15He will bring the people of the world before him in judgment, to receive just punishment, and to prove the terrible things they have done in rebellion against God, revealing all they have said against him." 16These men are constant gripers, never satisfied, doing whatever evil they feel like; they are loudmouthed "show-offs," and when they show respect for others, it is only to get something from them in return.

17Dear friends, remember what the apostles of our Lord Jesus Christ told you, 18that in the last times there would come these scoffers whose whole purpose in life is to enjoy themselves in every evil way imaginable. 19They stir up arguments; they love the evil things of the world; they do not have the Holy Spirit living in them.

20But you, dear friends, must build up your lives ever more strongly upon the foundation of our holy faith, learning to pray in the power and strength of the Holy Spirit.

21Stay always within the boundaries where God's love can reach and bless you. Wait patiently for the eternal life that our Lord Jesus Christ in his mercy is going to give you. 22Try to help those who argue against you. Be merciful to those who doubt. 23Save some by snatching them as from the very flames of hell itself. And as for others, help them to find the Lord by being kind to them, but be careful that you yourselves aren't pulled along into their sins. Hate every trace of their sin while being merciful to them as sinners.

24, 25And now—all glory to him who alone is God, who saves us through Jesus Christ our Lord; yes, splendor and majesty, all power and authority are his from the beginning; his they are and his they evermore shall be. And he is able to keep you from slipping and falling away, and to bring you, sinless and perfect, into his glorious presence with mighty shouts of everlasting joy. Amen.

Jude

New Revised Standard

of the sea, casting up the foam of their own shame; wandering stars, for whom the deepest darkness has been reserved forever.

14 It was also about these that Enoch, in the seventh generation from Adam, prophesied, saying, "See, the Lord is cominga with ten thousands of his holy ones, 15to execute judgment on all, and to convict everyone of all the deeds of ungodliness that they have committed in such an ungodly way, and of all the harsh things that ungodly sinners have spoken against him." 16These are grumblers and malcontents; they indulge their own lusts; they are bombastic in speech, flattering people to their own advantage.

Warnings and Exhortations

17 But you, beloved, must remember the predictions of the apostles of our Lord Jesus Christ; 18for they said to you, "In the last time there will be scoffers, indulging their own ungodly lusts." 19It is these worldly people, devoid of the Spirit, who are causing divisions. 20But you, beloved, build yourselves up on your most holy faith; pray in the Holy Spirit; 21keep yourselves in the love of God; look forward to the mercy of our Lord Jesus Christ that leads tob eternal life. 22And have mercy on some who are wavering; 23save others by snatching them out of the fire; and have mercy on still others with fear, hating even the tunic defiled by their bodies.c

Benediction

24 Now to him who is able to keep you from falling, and to make you stand without blemish in the presence of his glory with rejoicing, 25to the only God our Savior, through Jesus Christ our Lord, be glory, majesty, power, and authority, before all time and now and forever. Amen.

a Gk came   b Gk Christ to   c Gk by the flesh. The Greek text of verses 22-23 is uncertain at several points

THE

Revelation

OF ST. JOHN THE DIVINE

Revelation

1 THE REVELATION of Jesus Christ, which God gave unto him, to show unto his servants things which must shortly come to pass; and he sent and signified *it* by his angel unto his servant John:

2Who bare record of the word of God, and of the testimony of Jesus Christ, and of all things that he saw.

3Blessed *is* he that readeth, and they that hear the words of this prophecy, and keep those things which are written therein: for the time *is* at hand.

4John to the seven churches which are in Asia: Grace *be* unto you, and peace, from him which is, and which was, and which is to come; and from the seven Spirits which are before his throne;

5And from Jesus Christ, *who is* the faithful witness, *and* the first begotten of the dead, and the prince of the kings of the earth. Unto him that loved us, and washed us from our sins in his own blood,

6And hath made us kings and priests unto God and his Father; to him *be* glory and dominion for ever and ever. Amen.

7Behold, he cometh with clouds; and every eye shall see him, and they *also* which pierced him: and all kindreds of the earth shall wail because of him. Even so, Amen.

8I am Alpha and Omega, the beginning and the ending, saith the Lord, which is, and which was, and which is to come, the Almighty.

9I John, who also am your brother, and companion in tribulation, and in the kingdom and patience of Jesus Christ, was in the isle that is called Patmos, for the word of God, and for the testimony of Jesus Christ.

10I was in the Spirit on the Lord's day, and heard behind me a great voice, as of a trumpet,

11Saying, I am Alpha and Omega, the first and the last: and, What thou seest, write in a book, and send *it* unto the seven churches which are in Asia; unto Ephesus, and unto Smyrna, and unto Pergamos, and unto Thyatira, and unto Sardis, and unto Philadelphia, and unto Laodicea.

1 THE REVELATION of Jesus Christ, which God gave him to show his servants what must soon take place. He made it known by sending his angel to his servant John, 2who testifies to everything he saw—that is, the word of God and the testimony of Jesus Christ. 3Blessed is the one who reads the words of this prophecy, and blessed are those who hear it and take to heart what is written in it, because the time is near.

Greetings and Doxology

4John,

To the seven churches in the province of Asia:

Grace and peace to you from him who is, and who was, and who is to come, and from the seven spiritsa before his throne, 5and from Jesus Christ, who is the faithful witness, the firstborn from the dead, and the ruler of the kings of the earth.

To him who loves us and has freed us from our sins by his blood, 6and has made us to be a kingdom and priests to serve his God and Father—to him be glory and power for ever and ever! Amen.

7Look, he is coming with the clouds,
    and every eye will see him,
  even those who pierced him;
    and all the peoples of the earth will mourn
      because of him.
                    So shall it be! Amen.

8"I am the Alpha and the Omega," says the Lord God, "who is, and who was, and who is to come, the Almighty."

One Like a Son of Man

9I, John, your brother and companion in the suffering and kingdom and patient endurance that are ours in Jesus, was on the island of Patmos because of the word of God and the testimony of Jesus. 10On the Lord's Day I was in the Spirit, and I heard behind me a loud voice like a trumpet, 11which said: "Write on a scroll what you see and send it to the seven churches: to Ephesus, Smyrna, Pergamum, Thyatira, Sardis, Philadelphia and Laodicea."

Living Bible

afraid of what you are about to suffer—for the devil will soon throw some of you into prison to test you. You will be persecuted for 'ten days.' Remain faithful even when facing death and I will give you the crown of life—an unending, glorious future.[b] 11Let everyone who can hear, listen to what the Spirit is saying to the churches: He who is victorious shall not be hurt by the Second Death.

12*"Write this letter to the leader of the church in Pergamos:*

"This message is from him who wields the sharp and double-bladed sword. 13I am fully aware that you live in the city where Satan's throne is, at the center of satanic worship; and yet you have remained loyal to me, and refused to deny me, even when Antipas, my faithful witness, was martyred among you by Satan's devotees.

14"And yet I have a few things against you. You tolerate some among you who do as Balaam did when he taught Balak how to ruin the people of Israel by involving them in sexual sin and encouraging them to go to idol feasts. 15Yes, you have some of these very same followers of Balaam[c] among you!

16"Change your mind and attitude, or else I will come to you suddenly and fight against them with the sword of my mouth.

17"Let everyone who can hear, listen to what the Spirit is saying to the churches: Every one who is victorious shall eat of the hidden manna, the secret nourishment from heaven; and I will give to each a white stone, and on the stone will be engraved a new name that no one else knows except the one receiving it.

18*"Write this letter to the leader of the church in Thyatira:*

"This is a message from the Son of God, whose eyes penetrate like flames of fire, whose feet are like glowing brass.

19"I am aware of all your good deeds—your kindness to the poor, your gifts and service to them; also I know your love and faith and patience, and I can see your constant improvement in all these things.

20"Yet I have this against you: You are permitting that woman Jezebel, who calls herself a prophetess, to teach my servants that sex sin is not a serious matter; she urges them to practice immorality and to eat meat that has been sacrificed to idols. 21I gave her time to change her mind and attitude, but she refused. 22Pay attention now to what I am saying: I will lay her upon a sickbed of intense affliction, along with all her immoral followers,[d] unless they turn again to me, repenting of their sin with her; 23and I will strike her children dead. And all the churches shall know that I am he who searches deep within men's hearts, and minds; I will give to each of you whatever you deserve.

24, 25"As for the rest of you in Thyatira who have not followed this false teaching ('deeper truths,' as they call them—depths of Satan, really), I will ask nothing further of you; only hold tightly to what you have until I come.

26"To every one who overcomes—who to the very end keeps on doing things that please me—I will give power over the nations. 27You will rule them with a rod of iron just as my Father gave me the authority to rule them; they will be shattered like a pot of clay that is broken into tiny pieces. 28And I will give you the Morning Star!

29"Let all who can hear, listen to what the Spirit says to the churches.

New Revised Standard

to suffer. Beware, the devil is about to throw some of you into prison so that you may be tested, and for ten days you will have affliction. Be faithful until death, and I will give you the crown of life. 11Let anyone who has an ear listen to what the Spirit is saying to the churches. Whoever conquers will not be harmed by the second death.

The Message to Pergamum

12 "And to the angel of the church in Pergamum write: These are the words of him who has the sharp two-edged sword:

13 "I know where you are living, where Satan's throne is. Yet you are holding fast to my name, and you did not deny your faith in me[e] even in the days of Antipas my witness, my faithful one, who was killed among you, where Satan lives. 14But I have a few things against you: you have some there who hold to the teaching of Balaam, who taught Balak to put a stumbling block before the people of Israel, so that they would eat food sacrificed to idols and practice fornication. 15So you also have some who hold to the teaching of the Nicolaitans. 16Repent then. If not, I will come to you soon and make war against them with the sword of my mouth. 17Let anyone who has an ear listen to what the Spirit is saying to the churches. To everyone who conquers I will give some of the hidden manna, and I will give a white stone, and on the white stone is written a new name that no one knows except the one who receives it.

The Message to Thyatira

18 "And to the angel of the church in Thyatira write: These are the words of the Son of God, who has eyes like a flame of fire, and whose feet are like burnished bronze:

19 "I know your works—your love, faith, service, and patient endurance. I know that your last works are greater than the first. 20But I have this against you: you tolerate that woman Jezebel, who calls herself a prophet and is teaching and beguiling my servants[f] to practice fornication and to eat food sacrificed to idols. 21I gave her time to repent, but she refuses to repent of her fornication. 22Beware, I am throwing her on a bed, and those who commit adultery with her I am throwing into great distress, unless they repent of her doings; 23and I will strike her children dead. And all the churches will know that I am the one who searches minds and hearts, and I will give to each of you as your works deserve. 24But to the rest of you in Thyatira, who do not hold this teaching, who have not learned what some call 'the deep things of Satan,' to you I say, I do not lay on you any other burden; 25only hold fast to what you have until I come. 26To everyone who conquers and continues to do my works to the end,

I will give authority over the nations;
27 to rule[g] them with an iron rod,
        as when clay pots are shattered;

28even as I also received authority from my Father. To the one who conquers I will also give the morning star. 29Let anyone who has an ear listen to what the Spirit is saying to the churches.

---

b *2:10 an unending, glorious future,* implied.   c *2:15 Balaam,* literally, "Nicolaitans," Greek form of "Balaamites."   d *2:22 along with all her immoral followers,* literally, "together with all those who commit adultery with her."

e Or *deny my faith*   f Gk *slaves*   g Or *to shepherd*

King James

3 AND UNTO the angel of the church in Sardis
write; These things saith he that hath the seven
Spirits of God, and the seven stars; I know thy works,
that thou hast a name that thou livest, and art dead.

2Be watchful, and strengthen the things which remain, that are ready to die: for I have not found thy
works perfect before God.

3Remember therefore how thou hast received and
heard, and hold fast, and repent. If therefore thou shalt
not watch, I will come on thee as a thief, and thou shalt
not know what hour I will come upon thee.

4Thou hast a few names even in Sardis which have
not defiled their garments; and they shall walk with me
in white: for they are worthy.

5He that overcometh, the same shall be clothed in
white raiment; and I will not blot out his name out of the
book of life, but I will confess his name before my
Father, and before his angels.

6He that hath an ear, let him hear what the Spirit saith
unto the churches.

7And to the angel of the church in Philadelphia write;
These things saith he that is holy, he that is true, he that
hath the key of David, he that openeth, and no man
shutteth; and shutteth, and no man openeth;

8I know thy works: behold, I have set before thee an
open door, and no man can shut it: for thou hast a little
strength, and hast kept my word, and hast not denied my
name.

9Behold, I will make them of the synagogue of Satan,
which say they are Jews, and are not, but do lie; behold,
I will make them to come and worship before thy feet,
and to know that I have loved thee.

10Because thou hast kept the word of my patience, I
also will keep thee from the hour of temptation, which
shall come upon all the world, to try them that dwell
upon the earth.

11Behold, I come quickly: hold that fast which thou
hast, that no man take thy crown.

12Him that overcometh will I make a pillar in the
temple of my God, and he shall go no more out: and I
will write upon him the name of my God, and the name
of the city of my God, *which is* new Jerusalem, which
cometh down out of heaven from my God: and *I will
write upon him* my new name.

13He that hath an ear, let him hear what the Spirit
saith unto the churches.

14And unto the angel of the church of the Laodiceans
write; These things saith the Amen, the faithful and true
witness, the beginning of the creation of God;

15I know thy works, that thou art neither cold nor hot:
I would thou wert cold or hot.

16So then because thou art lukewarm, and neither
cold nor hot, I will spew thee out of my mouth.

17Because thou sayest, I am rich, and increased with
goods, and have need of nothing; and knowest not that
thou art wretched, and miserable, and poor, and blind,
and naked:

18I counsel thee to buy of me gold tried in the fire,
that thou mayest be rich; and white raiment, that thou
mayest be clothed, and *that* the shame of thy nakedness
do not appear; and anoint thine eyes with eyesalve, that
thou mayest see.

New International

To the Church in Sardis

3 "TO THE angel[a] of the church in Sardis write:
These are the words of him who holds the
seven spirits[b] of God and the seven stars. I know
your deeds; you have a reputation of being alive,
but you are dead. 2Wake up! Strengthen what remains and is about to die, for I have not found your
deeds complete in the sight of my God. 3Remem-
ber, therefore, what you have received and heard;
obey it, and repent. But if you do not wake up, I
will come like a thief, and you will not know at
what time I will come to you.

4Yet you have a few people in Sardis who have
not soiled their clothes. They will walk with me,
dressed in white, for they are worthy. 5He who
overcomes will, like them, be dressed in white. I
will never blot out his name from the book of life,
but will acknowledge his name before my Father
and his angels. 6He who has an ear, let him hear
what the Spirit says to the churches.

To the Church in Philadelphia

7"To the angel of the church in Philadelphia write:

These are the words of him who is holy and true,
who holds the key of David. What he opens no one
can shut, and what he shuts no one can open. 8I
know your deeds. See, I have placed before you an
open door that no one can shut. I know that you
have little strength, yet you have kept my word and
have not denied my name. 9I will make those who
are of the synagogue of Satan, who claim to be Jews
though they are not, but are liars—I will make them
come and fall down at your feet and acknowledge
that I have loved you. 10Since you have kept my
command to endure patiently, I will also keep you
from the hour of trial that is going to come upon the
whole world to test those who live on the earth.

11I am coming soon. Hold on to what you have,
so that no one will take your crown. 12Him who
overcomes I will make a pillar in the temple of my
God. Never again will he leave it. I will write on
him the name of my God and the name of the city
of my God, the new Jerusalem, which is coming
down out of heaven from my God; and I will also
write on him my new name. 13He who has an ear,
let him hear what the Spirit says to the churches.

To the Church in Laodicea

14"To the angel of the church in Laodicea write:

These are the words of the Amen, the faithful
and true witness, the ruler of God's creation. 15I
know your deeds, that you are neither cold nor hot.
I wish you were either one or the other! 16So, because you are lukewarm—neither hot nor cold—I
am about to spit you out of my mouth. 17You say,
'I am rich; I have acquired wealth and do not need
a thing.' But you do not realize that you are wretched, pitiful, poor, blind and naked. 18I counsel you
to buy from me gold refined in the fire, so you can
become rich; and white clothes to wear, so you can
cover your shameful nakedness; and salve to put on
your eyes, so you can see.

a *1* Or *messenger*; also in verses 7 and 14   b *1* Or *the sevenfold Spirit*

Living Bible

3 "TO THE leader of the church in Sardis write this letter:

"This message is sent to you by the one who has the seven-fold Spirit[c] of God and the seven stars.

"I know your reputation as a live and active church, but you are dead. [2]Now wake up! Strengthen what little remains—for even what is left is at the point of death. Your deeds are far from right in the sight of God. [3]Go back to what you heard and believed at first; hold to it firmly and turn to me again. Unless you do, I will come suddenly upon you, unexpected as a thief, and punish you.

[4]"Yet even there in Sardis some haven't soiled their garments with the world's filth; they shall walk with me in white, for they are worthy. [5]Everyone who conquers will be clothed in white, and I will not erase his name from the Book of Life, but I will announce before my Father and his angels that he is mine.

[6]"Let all who can hear, listen to what the Spirit is saying to the churches.

[7]"Write this letter to the leader of the church in Philadelphia.

"This message is sent to you by the one who is holy and true, and has the key of David to open what no one can shut and to shut what no one can open.

[8]"I know you well; you aren't strong, but you have tried to obey[d] and have not denied my Name. Therefore I have opened a door to you that no one can shut.

[9]"Note this: I will force those supporting the causes of Satan while claiming to be mine[e] (but they aren't—they are lying) to fall at your feet and acknowledge that you are the ones I love.

[10]"Because you have patiently obeyed me despite the persecution, therefore I will protect you from the time of Great Tribulation and temptation,[f] which will come upon the world to test everyone alive. [11]Look, I am coming soon![g] Hold tightly to the little strength you have—so that no one will take away your crown.

[12]"As for the one who conquers, I will make him a pillar in the temple of my God; he will be secure, and will go out no more; and I will write my God's Name on him, and he will be a citizen in the city of my God—the New Jerusalem, coming down from heaven from my God; and he will have my new Name inscribed upon him.

[13]"Let all who can hear, listen to what the Spirit is saying to the churches.

[14]"Write this letter to the leader of the church in Laodicea.

"This message is from the one who stands firm,[h] the faithful and true Witness [of all that is or was or evermore shall be[i]], the primeval source of God's creation:

[15]"I know you well—you are neither hot nor cold; I wish that you were one or the other! [16]But since you are merely lukewarm, I will spit you out of my mouth!

[17]"You say, 'I am rich, with everything I want; I don't need a thing!' And you don't realize that spiritually you are wretched and miserable and poor and blind and naked.

[18]"My advice to you is to buy pure gold from me, gold purified by fire—only then will you truly be rich. And to purchase from me white garments, clean and pure, so you won't be naked and ashamed; and to get medicine from me to heal your eyes and give you back your sight. [19]I continually discipline and punish every-

New Revised Standard

The Message to Sardis

3 "AND TO the angel of the church in Sardis write: These are the words of him who has the seven spirits of God and the seven stars:

"I know your works; you have a name of being alive, but you are dead. [2]Wake up, and strengthen what remains and is on the point of death, for I have not found your works perfect in the sight of my God. [3]Remember then what you received and heard; obey it, and repent. If you do not wake up, I will come like a thief, and you will not know at what hour I will come to you. [4]Yet you have still a few persons in Sardis who have not soiled their clothes; they will walk with me, dressed in white, for they are worthy. [5]If you conquer, you will be clothed like them in white robes, and I will not blot your name out of the book of life; I will confess your name before my Father and before his angels. [6]Let anyone who has an ear listen to what the Spirit is saying to the churches.

The Message to Philadelphia

7 "And to the angel of the church in Philadelphia write:

These are the words of the holy one, the true one,
who has the key of David,
who opens and no one will shut,
who shuts and no one opens:

8 "I know your works. Look, I have set before you an open door, which no one is able to shut. I know that you have but little power, and yet you have kept my word and have not denied my name. [9]I will make those of the synagogue of Satan who say that they are Jews and are not, but are lying—I will make them come and bow down before your feet, and they will learn that I have loved you. [10]Because you have kept my word of patient endurance, I will keep you from the hour of trial that is coming on the whole world to test the inhabitants of the earth. [11]I am coming soon; hold fast to what you have, so that no one may seize your crown. [12]If you conquer, I will make you a pillar in the temple of my God; you will never go out of it. I will write on you the name of my God, and the name of the city of my God, the new Jerusalem that comes down from my God out of heaven, and my own new name. [13]Let anyone who has an ear listen to what the Spirit is saying to the churches.

The Message to Laodicea

14 "And to the angel of the church in Laodicea write: The words of the Amen, the faithful and true witness, the origin[j] of God's creation:

15 "I know your works; you are neither cold nor hot. I wish that you were either cold or hot. [16]So, because you are lukewarm, and neither cold nor hot, I am about to spit you out of my mouth. [17]For you say, 'I am rich, I have prospered, and I need nothing.' You do not realize that you are wretched, pitiable, poor, blind, and naked. [18]Therefore I counsel you to buy from me gold refined by fire so that you may be rich; and white robes to clothe you and to keep the shame of your nakedness from being seen; and salve to anoint your eyes so that you may see. [19]I reprove and discipline those whom I

---

[c] 3:1 the seven-fold Spirit, see note on 1:4.   [d] 3:8 you have tried to obey, literally, "you have kept my word."   [e] 3:9 while claiming to be mine, literally, "say they are Jews but are not."   [f] 3:10 I will protect you from the time of Great Tribulation and temptation, or, "I will keep you from failing in the hour of testing." The inference is not clear in the Greek as to whether this means "kept from" or "kept through" the coming horror.   [g] 3:11 soon, or, "suddenly," "unexpectedly."   [h] 3:14 from the one who stands firm, literally, "from the Amen."   [i] 3:14 evermore shall be, implied.

[j] Or beginning

King James

19As many as I love, I rebuke and chasten: be zealous therefore, and repent.

20Behold, I stand at the door, and knock: if any man hear my voice, and open the door, I will come in to him, and will sup with him, and he with me.

21To him that overcometh will I grant to sit with me in my throne, even as I also overcame, and am set down with my Father in his throne.

22He that hath an ear, let him hear what the Spirit saith unto the churches.

4 AFTER THIS I looked, and, behold, a door *was* opened in heaven: and the first voice which I heard *was* as it were of a trumpet talking with me; which said, Come up hither, and I will show thee things which must be hereafter.

2And immediately I was in the spirit: and, behold, a throne was set in heaven, and *one* sat on the throne.

3And he that sat was to look upon like a jasper and a sardine stone: and *there was* a rainbow round about the throne, in sight like unto an emerald.

4And round about the throne *were* four and twenty seats: and upon the seats I saw four and twenty elders sitting, clothed in white raiment; and they had on their heads crowns of gold.

5And out of the throne proceeded lightnings and thunderings and voices: and *there were* seven lamps of fire burning before the throne, which are the seven Spirits of God.

6And before the throne *there was* a sea of glass like unto crystal: and in the midst of the throne, and round about the throne, *were* four beasts full of eyes before and behind.

7And the first beast *was* like a lion, and the second beast like a calf, and the third beast had a face as a man, and the fourth beast *was* like a flying eagle.

8And the four beasts had each of them six wings about *him;* and *they were* full of eyes within: and they rest not day and night, saying, Holy, holy, holy, Lord God Almighty, which was, and is, and is to come.

9And when those beasts give glory and honour and thanks to him that sat on the throne, who liveth for ever and ever,

10The four and twenty elders fall down before him that sat on the throne, and worship him that liveth for ever and ever, and cast their crowns before the throne, saying,

11Thou art worthy, O Lord, to receive glory and honour and power: for thou hast created all things, and for thy pleasure they are and were created.

5 AND I saw in the right hand of him that sat on the throne a book written within and on the backside, sealed with seven seals.

2And I saw a strong angel proclaiming with a loud voice, Who is worthy to open the book, and to loose the seals thereof?

3And no man in heaven, nor in earth, neither under the earth, was able to open the book, neither to look thereon.

4And I wept much, because no man was found worthy to open and to read the book, neither to look thereon.

New International

19Those whom I love I rebuke and discipline. So be earnest, and repent. 20Here I am! I stand at the door and knock. If anyone hears my voice and opens the door, I will come in and eat with him, and he with me.

21To him who overcomes, I will give the right to sit with me on my throne, just as I overcame and sat down with my Father on his throne. 22He who has an ear, let him hear what the Spirit says to the churches."

The Throne in Heaven

4 AFTER THIS I looked, and there before me was a door standing open in heaven. And the voice I had first heard speaking to me like a trumpet said, "Come up here, and I will show you what must take place after this." 2At once I was in the Spirit, and there before me was a throne in heaven with someone sitting on it. 3And the one who sat there had the appearance of jasper and carnelian. A rainbow, resembling an emerald, encircled the throne. 4Surrounding the throne were twenty-four other thrones, and seated on them were twenty-four elders. They were dressed in white and had crowns of gold on their heads. 5From the throne came flashes of lightning, rumblings and peals of thunder. Before the throne, seven lamps were blazing. These are the seven spirits[a] of God. 6Also before the throne there was what looked like a sea of glass, clear as crystal.

In the center, around the throne, were four living creatures, and they were covered with eyes, in front and in back. 7The first living creature was like a lion, the second was like an ox, the third had a face like a man, the fourth was like a flying eagle. 8Each of the four living creatures had six wings and was covered with eyes all around, even under his wings. Day and night they never stop saying:

> "Holy, holy, holy
> is the Lord God Almighty,
> who was, and is, and is to come."

9Whenever the living creatures give glory, honor and thanks to him who sits on the throne and who lives for ever and ever, 10the twenty-four elders fall down before him who sits on the throne, and worship him who lives for ever and ever. They lay their crowns before the throne and say:

> 11"You are worthy, our Lord and God,
> to receive glory and honor and power,
> for you created all things,
> and by your will they were created
> and have their being."

The Scroll and the Lamb

5 THEN I saw in the right hand of him who sat on the throne a scroll with writing on both sides and sealed with seven seals. 2And I saw a mighty angel proclaiming in a loud voice, "Who is worthy to break the seals and open the scroll?" 3But no one in heaven or on earth or under the earth could open the scroll or even look inside it. 4I wept and wept because no one was found who was worthy to open the scroll or look inside.

---

a 5 Or *the sevenfold Spirit*

Living Bible

one I love; so I must punish you, unless you turn from your indifference and become enthusiastic about the things of God.

20"Look! I have been standing at the door and I am constantly knocking. If anyone hears me calling him and opens the door, I will come in and fellowship with him and he with me. 21I will let every one who conquers sit beside me on my throne, just as I took my place with my Father on his throne when I had conquered. 22Let those who can hear, listen to what the Spirit is saying to the churches."

4 THEN AS I looked, I saw a door standing open in heaven, and the same voice I had heard before, that sounded like a mighty trumpet blast, spoke to me and said, "Come up here and I will show you what must happen in the future!"

2And instantly I was, in spirit, there in heaven and saw—oh, the glory of it!—a throne and someone sitting on it! 3Great bursts of light flashed forth from him as from a glittering diamond, or from a shining ruby, and a rainbow glowing like an emerald encircled his throne. 4Twenty-four smaller thrones surrounded his, with twenty-four Elders sitting on them; all were clothed in white, with golden crowns upon their heads. 5Lightning and thunder issued from the throne, and there were voices in the thunder. Directly in front of his throne were seven lighted lamps representing the seven-fold Spirit of God.b 6Spread out before it was a shiny crystal sea. Four Living Beings, dotted front and back with eyes, stood at the throne's four sides. 7The first of these Living Beings was in the form of a lion; the second looked like an ox; the third had the face of a man; and the fourth, the form of an eagle, with wings spread out as though in flight. 8Each of these Living Beings had six wings, and the central sections of their wings were covered with eyes. Day after day and night after night they kept on saying, "Holy, holy, holy, Lord God Almighty—the one who was, and is, and is to come."

9And when the Living Beings gave glory and honor and thanks to the one sitting on the throne, who lives forever and ever, 10the twenty-four Elders fell down before him and worshiped him, the Eternal Living One, and cast their crowns before the throne, singing, 11"O Lord, you are worthy to receive the glory and the honor and the power, for you have created all things. They were created and called into being by your act of will."

5 AND I saw a scroll in the right hand of the one who was sitting on the throne, a scroll with writing on the inside and on the back, and sealed with seven seals. 2A mighty angel with a loud voice was shouting out this question: "Who is worthy to break the seals on this scroll, and to unroll it?" 3But no one in all heaven or earth or from among the dead was permitted to open and read it.

4Then I wept with disappointmentc because no one anywhere was worthy; no one could tell us what it said.

New Revised Standard

love. Be earnest, therefore, and repent. 20Listen! I am standing at the door, knocking; if you hear my voice and open the door, I will come in to you and eat with you, and you with me. 21To the one who conquers I will give a place with me on my throne, just as I myself conquered and sat down with my Father on his throne. 22Let anyone who has an ear listen to what the Spirit is saying to the churches."

The Heavenly Worship

4 AFTER THIS I looked, and there in heaven a door stood open! And the first voice, which I had heard speaking to me like a trumpet, said, "Come up here, and I will show you what must take place after this." 2At once I was in the spirit,d and there in heaven stood a throne, with one seated on the throne! 3And the one seated there looks like jasper and carnelian, and around the throne is a rainbow that looks like an emerald. 4Around the throne are twenty-four thrones, and seated on the thrones are twenty-four elders, dressed in white robes, with golden crowns on their heads. 5Coming from the throne are flashes of lightning, and rumblings and peals of thunder, and in front of the throne burn seven flaming torches, which are the seven spirits of God; 6and in front of the throne there is something like a sea of glass, like crystal.

Around the throne, and on each side of the throne, are four living creatures, full of eyes in front and behind: 7the first living creature like a lion, the second living creature like an ox, the third living creature with a face like a human face, and the fourth living creature like a flying eagle. 8And the four living creatures, each of them with six wings, are full of eyes all around and inside. Day and night without ceasing they sing,

"Holy, holy, holy,
　the Lord God the Almighty,
who was and is and is to come."

9And whenever the living creatures give glory and honor and thanks to the one who is seated on the throne, who lives forever and ever, 10the twenty-four elders fall before the one who is seated on the throne and worship the one who lives forever and ever; they cast their crowns before the throne, singing,

11 "You are worthy, our Lord and God,
　to receive glory and honor and power,
for you created all things,
　and by your will they existed and were
　　created."

The Scroll and the Lamb

5 THEN I saw in the right hand of the one seated on the throne a scroll written on the inside and on the back, sealede with seven seals; 2and I saw a mighty angel proclaiming with a loud voice, "Who is worthy to open the scroll and break its seals?" 3And no one in heaven or on earth or under the earth was able to open the scroll or to look into it. 4And I began to weep bitterly because no one was found worthy to open the scroll or to look into it. 5Then one of the elders said to me, "Do

---

b 4:5 the seven-fold Spirit of God,literally, the seven spirits of God." But see Zech 4:2-6 where the lamps are equated with the one Spirit. Also in 5:6.
c 5:4 Then I wept with disappointment, implied.

d Or in the Spirit　e Or written on the inside, and sealed on the back

King James

5And one of the elders saith unto me, Weep not: behold, the Lion of the tribe of Judah, the Root of David, hath prevailed to open the book, and to loose the seven seals thereof.

6And I beheld, and, lo, in the midst of the throne and of the four beasts, and in the midst of the elders, stood a Lamb as it had been slain, having seven horns and seven eyes, which are the seven Spirits of God sent forth into all the earth.

7And he came and took the book out of the right hand of him that sat upon the throne.

8And when he had taken the book, the four beasts and four *and* twenty elders fell down before the Lamb, having every one of them harps, and golden vials full of odours, which are the prayers of saints.

9And they sung a new song, saying, Thou art worthy to take the book, and to open the seals thereof: for thou wast slain, and hast redeemed us to God by thy blood out of every kindred, and tongue, and people, and nation;

10And hast made us unto our God kings and priests: and we shall reign on the earth.

11And I beheld, and I heard the voice of many angels round about the throne and the beasts and the elders: and the number of them was ten thousand times ten thousand, and thousands of thousands;

12Saying with a loud voice, Worthy is the Lamb that was slain to receive power, and riches, and wisdom, and strength, and honour, and glory, and blessing.

13And every creature which is in heaven, and on the earth, and under the earth, and such as are in the sea, and all that are in them, heard I saying, Blessing, and honour, and glory, and power, *be* unto him that sitteth upon the throne, and unto the Lamb for ever and ever.

14And the four beasts said, Amen. And the four *and* twenty elders fell down and worshipped him that liveth for ever and ever.

6 AND I saw when the Lamb opened one of the seals, and I heard, as it were the noise of thunder, one of the four beasts saying, Come and see.

2And I saw, and behold a white horse: and he that sat on him had a bow; and a crown was given unto him: and he went forth conquering, and to conquer.

3And when he had opened the second seal, I heard the second beast say, Come and see.

4And there went out another horse *that was* red: and *power* was given to him that sat thereon to take peace from the earth, and that they should kill one another: and there was given unto him a great sword.

5And when he had opened the third seal, I heard the third beast say, Come and see. And I beheld, and lo a black horse; and he that sat on him had a pair of balances in his hand.

New International

5Then one of the elders said to me, "Do not weep! See, the Lion of the tribe of Judah, the Root of David, has triumphed. He is able to open the scroll and its seven seals."

6Then I saw a Lamb, looking as if it had been slain, standing in the center of the throne, encircled by the four living creatures and the elders. He had seven horns and seven eyes, which are the seven spirits[a] of God sent out into all the earth. 7He came and took the scroll from the right hand of him who sat on the throne. 8And when he had taken it, the four living creatures and the twenty-four elders fell down before the Lamb. Each one had a harp and they were holding golden bowls full of incense, which are the prayers of the saints. 9And they sang a new song:

"You are worthy to take the scroll
    and to open its seals,
because you were slain,
    and with your blood you purchased men for
        God
    from every tribe and language and people and
        nation.
10You have made them to be a kingdom and
        priests to serve our God,
    and they will reign on the earth."

11Then I looked and heard the voice of many angels, numbering thousands upon thousands, and ten thousand times ten thousand. They encircled the throne and the living creatures and the elders. 12In a loud voice they sang:

"Worthy is the Lamb, who was slain,
to receive power and wealth and wisdom and
        strength
and honor and glory and praise!"

13Then I heard every creature in heaven and on earth and under the earth and on the sea, and all that is in them, singing:

"To him who sits on the throne and to the
        Lamb
be praise and honor and glory and power,
    for ever and ever!"

14The four living creatures said, "Amen," and the elders fell down and worshiped.

The Seals

6 I WATCHED as the Lamb opened the first of the seven seals. Then I heard one of the four living creatures say in a voice like thunder, "Come!" 2I looked, and there before me was a white horse! Its rider held a bow, and he was given a crown, and he rode out as a conqueror bent on conquest.

3When the Lamb opened the second seal, I heard the second living creature say, "Come!" 4Then another horse came out, a fiery red one. Its rider was given power to take peace from the earth and to make men slay each other. To him was given a large sword.

5When the Lamb opened the third seal, I heard the third living creature say, "Come!" I looked, and there before me was a black horse! Its rider was holding a pair of scales in his hand. 6Then I heard what sounded like

---

a 6 Or *the sevenfold Spirit*

Living Bible

⁵But one of the twenty-four Elders said to me, "Stop crying, for look! The Lion of the tribe of Judah, the Root of David, has conquered, and proved himself worthy to open the scroll and to break its seven seals."

⁶I looked and saw a Lamb standing there before the twenty-four Elders, in front of the throne and the Living Beings, and on the Lamb were wounds that once had caused his death. He had seven horns and seven eyes, which represent the seven-fold Spirit of God, sent out into every part of the world. ⁷He stepped forward and took the scroll from the right hand of the one sitting upon the throne. ⁸And as he took the scroll, the twenty-four Elders fell down before the Lamb, each with a harp and golden vials filled with incense—the prayers of God's people!

⁹They were singing^b him a new song with these words: "You are worthy to take the scroll and break its seals and open it; for you were slain, and your blood has bought people from every nation as gifts for God. ¹⁰And you have gathered them into a kingdom and made them priests of our God; they shall reign upon the earth."

¹¹Then in my vision I heard the singing of millions of angels surrounding the throne and the Living Beings and the Elders: ¹²"The Lamb is worthy" (loudly they sang it!) "—the Lamb who was slain. He is worthy to receive the power, and the riches, and the wisdom, and the strength, and the honor, and the glory, and the blessing."

¹³And then I heard everyone in heaven and earth, and from the dead beneath the earth and in the sea, exclaiming, "The blessing and the honor and the glory and the power belong to the one sitting on the throne, and to the Lamb forever and ever." ¹⁴And the four Living Beings kept saying, "Amen!" And the twenty-four Elders fell down and worshiped him.

6 AS I watched, the Lamb broke the first seal and began to unroll the scroll. Then one of the four Living Beings, with a voice that sounded like thunder, said, "Come!"

²I looked, and there in front of me was a white horse. Its rider carried a bow, and a crown was placed upon his head; he rode out to conquer in many battles and win the war.

³Then he unrolled the scroll to the second seal, and broke it open too. And I heard the second Living Being say, "Come!"

⁴This time a red horse rode out. Its rider was given a long sword and the authority to banish peace and bring anarchy to the earth; war and killing broke out everywhere.

⁵When he had broken the third seal, I heard the third Living Being say, "Come!" And I saw a black horse, with its rider holding a pair of balances in his hand. ⁶And

New Revised Standard

not weep. See, the Lion of the tribe of Judah, the Root of David, has conquered, so that he can open the scroll and its seven seals."

6 Then I saw between the throne and the four living creatures and among the elders a Lamb standing as if it had been slaughtered, having seven horns and seven eyes, which are the seven spirits of God sent out into all the earth. ⁷He went and took the scroll from the right hand of the one who was seated on the throne. ⁸When he had taken the scroll, the four living creatures and the twenty-four elders fell before the Lamb, each holding a harp and golden bowls full of incense, which are the prayers of the saints. ⁹They sing a new song:

"You are worthy to take the scroll
    and to open its seals,
for you were slaughtered and by your blood
    you ransomed for God
    saints from^c every tribe and language and
    people and nation;
10 you have made them to be a kingdom and
        priests serving^d our God,
    and they will reign on earth."

11 Then I looked, and I heard the voice of many angels surrounding the throne and the living creatures and the elders; they numbered myriads of myriads and thousands of thousands, ¹²singing with full voice,

"Worthy is the Lamb that was slaughtered
    to receive power and wealth and wisdom and
        might
    and honor and glory and blessing!"

¹³Then I heard every creature in heaven and on earth and under the earth and in the sea, and all that is in them, singing,

"To the one seated on the throne and to the
        Lamb
    be blessing and honor and glory and might
    forever and ever!"

¹⁴And the four living creatures said, "Amen!" And the elders fell down and worshiped.

The Seven Seals

6 THEN I saw the Lamb open one of the seven seals, and I heard one of the four living creatures call out, as with a voice of thunder, "Come!"^e ²I looked, and there was a white horse! Its rider had a bow; a crown was given to him, and he came out conquering and to conquer.

3 When he opened the second seal, I heard the second living creature call out, "Come!"^e ⁴And out came^f another horse, bright red; its rider was permitted to take peace from the earth, so that people would slaughter one another; and he was given a great sword.

5 When he opened the third seal, I heard the third living creature call out, "Come!"^e I looked, and there was a black horse! Its rider held a pair of scales in his hand, ⁶and I heard what seemed to be a voice in the

---

^b 5:9 *singing*, literally, "saying," or "said." Also in vss 11, 12.   ^c Gk *ransomed for God from*   ^d Gk *priests to*   ^e Or "Go!"   ^f Or *went*

King James

6And I heard a voice in the midst of the four beasts say, A measure of wheat for a penny, and three measures of barley for a penny; and *see* thou hurt not the oil and the wine.

7And when he had opened the fourth seal, I heard the voice of the fourth beast say, Come and see.

8And I looked, and behold a pale horse: and his name that sat on him was Death, and Hell followed with him. And power was given unto them over the fourth part of the earth, to kill with sword, and with hunger, and with death, and with the beasts of the earth.

9And when he had opened the fifth seal, I saw under the altar the souls of them that were slain for the word of God, and for the testimony which they held:

10And they cried with a loud voice, saying, How long, O Lord, holy and true, dost thou not judge and avenge our blood on them that dwell on the earth?

11And white robes were given unto every one of them; and it was said unto them, that they should rest yet for a little season, until their fellowservants also and their brethren, that should be killed as they *were,* should be fulfilled.

12And I beheld when he had opened the sixth seal, and, lo, there was a great earthquake; and the sun became black as sackcloth of hair, and the moon became as blood;

13And the stars of heaven fell unto the earth, even as a fig tree casteth her untimely figs, when she is shaken of a mighty wind.

14And the heaven departed as a scroll when it is rolled together; and every mountain and island were moved out of their places.

15And the kings of the earth, and the great men, and the rich men, and the chief captains, and the mighty men, and every bondman, and every free man, hid themselves in the dens and in the rocks of the mountains;

16And said to the mountains and rocks, Fall on us, and hide us from the face of him that sitteth on the throne, and from the wrath of the Lamb:

17For the great day of his wrath is come; and who shall be able to stand?

7 AND AFTER these things I saw four angels standing on the four corners of the earth, holding the four winds of the earth, that the wind should not blow on the earth, nor on the sea, nor on any tree.

2And I saw another angel ascending from the east, having the seal of the living God: and he cried with a loud voice to the four angels, to whom it was given to hurt the earth and the sea,

3Saying, Hurt not the earth, neither the sea, nor the trees, till we have sealed the servants of our God in their foreheads.

4And I heard the number of them which were sealed: *and there were* sealed an hundred *and* forty *and* four thousand of all the tribes of the children of Israel.

5Of the tribe of Juda *were* sealed twelve thousand. Of the tribe of Reuben *were* sealed twelve thousand. Of the tribe of Gad *were* sealed twelve thousand.

6Of the tribe of Aser *were* sealed twelve thousand. Of the tribe of Nepthalim *were* sealed twelve thousand. Of the tribe of Manasses *were* sealed twelve thousand.

7Of the tribe of Simeon *were* sealed twelve thousand. Of the tribe of Levi *were* sealed twelve thousand. Of the tribe of Issachar *were* sealed twelve thousand.

New International

a voice among the four living creatures, saying, "A quarta of wheat for a day's wages,b and three quarts of barley for a day's wages,b and do not damage the oil and the wine!"

7When the Lamb opened the fourth seal, I heard the voice of the fourth living creature say, "Come!" 8I looked, and there before me was a pale horse! Its rider was named Death, and Hades was following close behind him. They were given power over a fourth of the earth to kill by sword, famine and plague, and by the wild beasts of the earth.

9When he opened the fifth seal, I saw under the altar the souls of those who had been slain because of the word of God and the testimony they had maintained. 10They called out in a loud voice, "How long, Sovereign Lord, holy and true, until you judge the inhabitants of the earth and avenge our blood?" 11Then each of them was given a white robe, and they were told to wait a little longer, until the number of their fellow servants and brothers who were to be killed as they had been was completed.

12I watched as he opened the sixth seal. There was a great earthquake. The sun turned black like sackcloth made of goat hair, the whole moon turned blood red, 13and the stars in the sky fell to earth, as late figs drop from a fig tree when shaken by a strong wind. 14The sky receded like a scroll, rolling up, and every mountain and island was removed from its place.

15Then the kings of the earth, the princes, the generals, the rich, the mighty, and every slave and every free man hid in caves and among the rocks of the mountains. 16They called to the mountains and the rocks, "Fall on us and hide us from the face of him who sits on the throne and from the wrath of the Lamb! 17For the great day of their wrath has come, and who can stand?"

144,000 Sealed

7 AFTER THIS I saw four angels standing at the four corners of the earth, holding back the four winds of the earth to prevent any wind from blowing on the land or on the sea or on any tree. 2Then I saw another angel coming up from the east, having the seal of the living God. He called out in a loud voice to the four angels who had been given power to harm the land and the sea: 3"Do not harm the land or the sea or the trees until we put a seal on the foreheads of the servants of our God." 4Then I heard the number of those who were sealed: 144,000 from all the tribes of Israel.

5From the tribe of Judah 12,000 were sealed,
  from the tribe of Reuben 12,000,
  from the tribe of Gad 12,000,
6from the tribe of Asher 12,000,
  from the tribe of Naphtali 12,000,
  from the tribe of Manasseh 12,000,
7from the tribe of Simeon 12,000,
  from the tribe of Levi 12,000,
  from the tribe of Issachar 12,000,

---

a 6 Greek *a choinix* (probably about a liter)   b 6 Greek *a denarius*

Living Bible

a voice from among the four Living Beings said, "A loaf of bread for $20, or three pounds of barley flour,c but there is no olive oil or wine."d

7And when the fourth seal was broken, I heard the fourth Living Being say, "Come!" 8And now I saw a pale horse, and its rider's name was Death. And there followed after him another horse whose rider's name was Hell. They were given control of one-fourth of the earth, to kill with war and famine and disease and wild animals.

9And when he broke open the fifth seal, I saw an altar, and underneath it all the souls of those who had been martyred for preaching the Word of God and for being faithful in their witnessing. 10They called loudly to the Lord and said, "O Sovereign Lord, holy and true, how long will it be before you judge the people of the earth for what they've done to us? When will you avenge our blood against those living on the earth?" 11White robes were given to each of them, and they were told to rest a little longer until their other brothers, fellow servants of Jesus, had been martyred on the earth and joined them.

12I watched as he broke the sixth seal, and there was a vast earthquake; and the sun became dark like black cloth, and the moon was blood-red. 13Then the stars of heaven appeared to be falling to earthe—like green fruit from fig trees buffeted by mighty winds. 14And the starry heavens disappearedf as though rolled up like a scroll and taken away; and every mountain and island shook and shifted. 15The kings of the earth, and world leaders and rich men, and high-ranking military officers, and all men great and small, slave and free, hid themselves in the caves and rocks of the mountains, 16and cried to the mountains to crush them. "Fall on us," they pleaded, "and hide us from the face of the one sitting on the throne, and from the anger of the Lamb, 17because the great day of their anger has come, and who can survive it?"

7 THEN I saw four angels standing at the four corners of the earth, holding back the four winds from blowing, so that not a leaf rustled in the trees, and the ocean became as smooth as glass. 2And I saw another angel coming from the east, carrying the Great Seal of the Living God. And he shouted out to those four angels who had been given power to injure earth and sea, 3"Wait! Don't do anything yet—hurt neither earth nor sea nor trees—until we have placed the Seal of God upon the foreheads of his servants."

4-8How many were given this mark? I heard the number—it was 144,000; out of all twelve tribes of Israel, as listed here:

Judah	12,000
Reuben	12,000
Gad	12,000
Asher	12,000
Naphtali	12,000
Manasseh	12,000
Simeon	12,000
Levi	12,000

New Revised Standard

midst of the four living creatures saying, "A quart of wheat for a day's pay,g and three quarts of barley for a day's pay,g but do not damage the olive oil and the wine!"

7 When he opened the fourth seal, I heard the voice of the fourth living creature call out, "Come!"h 8I looked and there was a pale green horse! Its rider's name was Death, and Hades followed with him; they were given authority over a fourth of the earth, to kill with sword, famine, and pestilence, and by the wild animals of the earth.

9 When he opened the fifth seal, I saw under the altar the souls of those who had been slaughtered for the word of God and for the testimony they had given; 10they cried out with a loud voice, "Sovereign Lord, holy and true, how long will it be before you judge and avenge our blood on the inhabitants of the earth?" 11They were each given a white robe and told to rest a little longer, until the number would be complete both of their fellow servantsi and of their brothers and sisters,j who were soon to be killed as they themselves had been killed.

12 When he opened the sixth seal, I looked, and there came a great earthquake; the sun became black as sackcloth, the full moon became like blood, 13and the stars of the sky fell to the earth as the fig tree drops its winter fruit when shaken by a gale. 14The sky vanished like a scroll rolling itself up, and every mountain and island was removed from its place. 15Then the kings of the earth and the magnates and the generals and the rich and the powerful, and everyone, slave and free, hid in the caves and among the rocks of the mountains, 16calling to the mountains and rocks, "Fall on us and hide us from the face of the one seated on the throne and from the wrath of the Lamb; 17for the great day of their wrath has come, and who is able to stand?"

The 144,000 of Israel Sealed

7 AFTER THIS I saw four angels standing at the four corners of the earth, holding back the four winds of the earth so that no wind could blow on earth or sea or against any tree. 2I saw another angel ascending from the rising of the sun, having the seal of the living God, and he called with a loud voice to the four angels who had been given power to damage earth and sea, 3saying, "Do not damage the earth or the sea or the trees, until we have marked the servantsi of our God with a seal on their foreheads."

4 And I heard the number of those who were sealed, one hundred forty-four thousand, sealed out of every tribe of the people of Israel:

5 From the tribe of Judah twelve thousand sealed,
   from the tribe of Reuben twelve thousand,
   from the tribe of Gad twelve thousand,
6 from the tribe of Asher twelve thousand,
   from the tribe of Naphtali twelve thousand,
   from the tribe of Manasseh twelve thousand,
7 from the tribe of Simeon twelve thousand,
   from the tribe of Levi twelve thousand,
   from the tribe of Issachar twelve thousand,

---

c 6:6 A loaf of bread for $20, or three pounds of barley flour, literally, "A choenix of wheat for a denarius, and three choenix of barley for a denarius. . . ."
d 6:6 there is no olive oil or wine, literally, "do not damage the oil and the wine."
e 6:13 appeared to be falling to earth, literally, "fell to the earth."   f 6:14 the starry heavens disappeared, literally, "the sky departed."

g Gk a denarius   h Or "Go!"   i Gk slaves   j Gk brothers

King James

8Of the tribe of Zabulon *were* sealed twelve thousand. Of the tribe of Joseph *were* sealed twelve thousand. Of the tribe of Benjamin *were* sealed twelve thousand.

9After this I beheld, and, lo, a great multitude, which no man could number, of all nations, and kindreds, and people, and tongues, stood before the throne, and before the Lamb, clothed with white robes, and palms in their hands;

10And cried with a loud voice, saying, Salvation to our God which sitteth upon the throne, and unto the Lamb.

11And all the angels stood round about the throne, and *about* the elders and the four beasts, and fell before the throne on their faces, and worshipped God,

12Saying, Amen: Blessing, and glory, and wisdom, and thanksgiving, and honour, and power, and might, *be* unto our God for ever and ever. Amen.

13And one of the elders answered, saying unto me, What are these which are arrayed in white robes? and whence came they?

14And I said unto him, Sir, thou knowest. And he said to me, These are they which came out of great tribulation, and have washed their robes, and made them white in the blood of the Lamb.

15Therefore are they before the throne of God, and serve him day and night in his temple: and he that sitteth on the throne shall dwell among them.

16They shall hunger no more, neither thirst any more; neither shall the sun light on them, nor any heat.

17For the Lamb which is in the midst of the throne shall feed them, and shall lead them unto living fountains of waters: and God shall wipe away all tears from their eyes.

8 AND WHEN he had opened the seventh seal, there was silence in heaven about the space of half an hour.

2And I saw the seven angels which stood before God; and to them were given seven trumpets.

3And another angel came and stood at the altar, having a golden censer; and there was given unto him much incense, that he should offer *it* with the prayers of all saints upon the golden altar which was before the throne.

4And the smoke of the incense, *which came* with the prayers of the saints, ascended up before God out of the angel's hand.

5And the angel took the censer, and filled it with fire of the altar, and cast *it* into the earth: and there were voices, and thunderings, and lightnings, and an earthquake.

6And the seven angels which had the seven trumpets prepared themselves to sound.

7The first angel sounded, and there followed hail and fire mingled with blood, and they were cast upon the earth: and the third part of trees was burnt up, and all green grass was burnt up.

New International

8from the tribe of Zebulun 12,000,
from the tribe of Joseph 12,000,
from the tribe of Benjamin 12,000.

The Great Multitude in White Robes

9After this I looked and there before me was a great multitude that no one could count, from every nation, tribe, people and language, standing before the throne and in front of the Lamb. They were wearing white robes and were holding palm branches in their hands. 10And they cried out in a loud voice:

"Salvation belongs to our God,
who sits on the throne,
and to the Lamb."

11All the angels were standing around the throne and around the elders and the four living creatures. They fell down on their faces before the throne and worshiped God, 12saying:

"Amen!
Praise and glory
and wisdom and thanks and honor
and power and strength
be to our God for ever and ever.
Amen!"

13Then one of the elders asked me, "These in white robes—who are they, and where did they come from?"

14I answered, "Sir, you know."

And he said, "These are they who have come out of the great tribulation; they have washed their robes and made them white in the blood of the Lamb. 15Therefore,

"they are before the throne of God
and serve him day and night in his temple;
and he who sits on the throne will spread his
tent over them.
16Never again will they hunger;
never again will they thirst.
The sun will not beat upon them,
nor any scorching heat.
17For the Lamb at the center of the throne will be
their shepherd;
he will lead them to springs of living water.
And God will wipe away every tear from their
eyes."

The Seventh Seal and the Golden Censer

8 WHEN HE opened the seventh seal, there was silence in heaven for about half an hour.

2And I saw the seven angels who stand before God, and to them were given seven trumpets.

3Another angel, who had a golden censer, came and stood at the altar. He was given much incense to offer, with the prayers of all the saints, on the golden altar before the throne. 4The smoke of the incense, together with the prayers of the saints, went up before God from the angel's hand. 5Then the angel took the censer, filled it with fire from the altar, and hurled it on the earth; and there came peals of thunder, rumblings, flashes of lightning and an earthquake.

The Trumpets

6Then the seven angels who had the seven trumpets prepared to sound them.

7The first angel sounded his trumpet, and there came hail and fire mixed with blood, and it was hurled down upon the earth. A third of the earth was burned up, a third of the trees were burned up, and all the green grass was burned up.

Living Bible

Issachar	12,000
Zebulun	12,000
Joseph	12,000
Benjamin	12,000

9After this I saw a vast crowd, too great to count, from all nations and provinces and languages, standing in front of the throne and before the Lamb, clothed in white, with palm branches in their hands. 10And they were shouting with a mighty shout, "Salvation comes from our God upon the throne, and from the Lamb."

11And now all the angels were crowding around the throne and around the Elders and the four Living Beings, and falling face down before the throne and worshiping God. 12"Amen!" they said. "Blessing, and glory, and wisdom, and thanksgiving, and honor, and power, and might, be to our God forever and forever. Amen!"

13Then one of the twenty-four Elders asked me, "Do you know who these are, who are clothed in white, and where they come from?"

14"No, sir," I replied. "Please tell me."

"These are the ones coming out of the Great Tribulation," he said; "they washed their robes and whitened them by the blood of the Lamb. 15That is why they are here before the throne of God, serving him day and night in his temple. The one sitting on the throne will shelter them; 16they will never be hungry again, nor thirsty, and they will be fully protected from the scorching noontime heat. 17For the Lamb standing in front of[a] the throne will feed them and be their Shepherd and lead them to the springs of the Water of Life. And God will wipe their tears away."

8 WHEN THE Lamb had broken the seventh seal, there was silence throughout all heaven for what seemed like half an hour. 2And I saw the seven angels that stand before God, and they were given seven trumpets.

3Then another angel with a golden censer came and stood at the altar; and a great quantity of incense was given to him to mix with the prayers of God's people, to offer upon the golden altar before the throne. 4And the perfume of the incense mixed with prayers ascended up to God from the altar where the angel had poured them out.

5Then the angel filled the censer with fire from the altar and threw it down upon the earth; and thunder crashed and rumbled, lightning flashed, and there was a terrible earthquake.

6Then the seven angels with the seven trumpets prepared to blow their mighty blasts.

7The first angel blew his trumpet, and hail and fire mixed with blood were thrown down upon the earth. One-third of the earth was set on fire so that one-third of the trees were burned, and all the green grass.

New Revised Standard

8 from the tribe of Zebulun twelve thousand,
from the tribe of Joseph twelve thousand,
from the tribe of Benjamin twelve thousand sealed.

The Multitude from Every Nation

9 After this I looked, and there was a great multitude that no one could count, from every nation, from all tribes and peoples and languages, standing before the throne and before the Lamb, robed in white, with palm branches in their hands. 10They cried out in a loud voice, saying,

"Salvation belongs to our God who is seated
on the throne, and to the Lamb!"

11 And all the angels stood around the throne and around the elders and the four living creatures, and they fell on their faces before the throne and worshiped God, 12singing,

"Amen! Blessing and glory and wisdom
and thanksgiving and honor
and power and might
be to our God forever and ever! Amen."

13 Then one of the elders addressed me, saying, "Who are these, robed in white, and where have they come from?" 14I said to him, "Sir, you are the one that knows." Then he said to me, "These are they who have come out of the great ordeal; they have washed their robes and made them white in the blood of the Lamb.

15 For this reason they are before the throne of
God,
and worship him day and night within his
temple,
and the one who is seated on the throne will
shelter them.
16 They will hunger no more, and thirst no more;
the sun will not strike them,
nor any scorching heat;
17 for the Lamb at the center of the throne will
be their shepherd,
and he will guide them to springs of the
water of life,
and God will wipe away every tear from their
eyes."

The Seventh Seal and the Golden Censer

8 WHEN THE Lamb opened the seventh seal, there was silence in heaven for about half an hour. 2And I saw the seven angels who stand before God, and seven trumpets were given to them.

3 Another angel with a golden censer came and stood at the altar; he was given a great quantity of incense to offer with the prayers of all the saints on the golden altar that is before the throne. 4And the smoke of the incense, with the prayers of the saints, rose before God from the hand of the angel. 5Then the angel took the censer and filled it with fire from the altar and threw it on the earth; and there were peals of thunder, rumblings, flashes of lightning, and an earthquake.

The Seven Trumpets

6 Now the seven angels who had the seven trumpets made ready to blow them.

7 The first angel blew his trumpet, and there came hail and fire, mixed with blood, and they were hurled to the earth; and a third of the earth was burned up, and a third of the trees were burned up, and all green grass was burned up.

---

a *7:17 in front of,* literally, "in the center of the throne"; i.e., directly in front, not to one side. An alternate rendering might be, "at the heart of the throne."

King James

8And the second angel sounded, and as it were a great mountain burning with fire was cast into the sea: and the third part of the sea became blood;

9And the third part of the creatures which were in the sea, and had life, died; and the third part of the ships were destroyed.

10And the third angel sounded, and there fell a great star from heaven, burning as it were a lamp, and it fell upon the third part of the rivers, and upon the fountains of waters;

11And the name of the star is called Wormwood: and the third part of the waters became wormwood; and many men died of the waters, because they were made bitter.

12And the fourth angel sounded, and the third part of the sun was smitten, and the third part of the moon, and the third part of the stars; so as the third part of them was darkened, and the day shone not for a third part of it, and the night likewise.

13And I beheld, and heard an angel flying through the midst of heaven, saying with a loud voice, Woe, woe, woe, to the inhabiters of the earth by reason of the other voices of the trumpet of the three angels, which are yet to sound!

9 AND THE fifth angel sounded, and I saw a star fall from heaven unto the earth: and to him was given the key of the bottomless pit.

2And he opened the bottomless pit; and there arose a smoke out of the pit, as the smoke of a great furnace; and the sun and the air were darkened by reason of the smoke of the pit.

3And there came out of the smoke locusts upon the earth: and unto them was given power, as the scorpions of the earth have power.

4And it was commanded them that they should not hurt the grass of the earth, neither any green thing, neither any tree; but only those men which have not the seal of God in their foreheads.

5And to them it was given that they should not kill them, but that they should be tormented five months: and their torment was as the torment of a scorpion, when he striketh a man.

6And in those days shall men seek death, and shall not find it; and shall desire to die, and death shall flee from them.

7And the shapes of the locusts were like unto horses prepared unto battle; and on their heads were as it were crowns like gold, and their faces were as the faces of men.

8And they had hair as the hair of women, and their teeth were as the teeth of lions.

9And they had breastplates, as it were breastplates of iron; and the sound of their wings was as the sound of chariots of many horses running to battle.

10And they had tails like unto scorpions, and there were stings in their tails: and their power was to hurt men five months.

11And they had a king over them, which is the angel of the bottomless pit, whose name in the Hebrew tongue is Abaddon, but in the Greek tongue hath his name Apollyon.

12One woe is past; and, behold, there come two woes more hereafter.

13And the sixth angel sounded, and I heard a voice from the four horns of the golden altar which is before God,

14Saying to the sixth angel which had the trumpet, Loose the four angels which are bound in the great river Euphrates.

New International

8The second angel sounded his trumpet, and something like a huge mountain, all ablaze, was thrown into the sea. A third of the sea turned into blood, 9a third of the living creatures in the sea died, and a third of the ships were destroyed.

10The third angel sounded his trumpet, and a great star, blazing like a torch, fell from the sky on a third of the rivers and on the springs of water— 11the name of the star is Wormwood.a A third of the waters turned bitter, and many people died from the waters that had become bitter.

12The fourth angel sounded his trumpet, and a third of the sun was struck, a third of the moon, and a third of the stars, so that a third of them turned dark. A third of the day was without light, and also a third of the night.

13As I watched, I heard an eagle that was flying in midair call out in a loud voice: "Woe! Woe! Woe to the inhabitants of the earth, because of the trumpet blasts about to be sounded by the other three angels!"

9 THE FIFTH angel sounded his trumpet, and I saw a star that had fallen from the sky to the earth. The star was given the key to the shaft of the Abyss. 2When he opened the Abyss, smoke rose from it like the smoke from a gigantic furnace. The sun and sky were darkened by the smoke from the Abyss. 3And out of the smoke locusts came down upon the earth and were given power like that of scorpions of the earth. 4They were told not to harm the grass of the earth or any plant or tree, but only those people who did not have the seal of God on their foreheads. 5They were not given power to kill them, but only to torture them for five months. And the agony they suffered was like that of the sting of a scorpion when it strikes a man. 6During those days men will seek death, but will not find it; they will long to die, but death will elude them.

7The locusts looked like horses prepared for battle. On their heads they wore something like crowns of gold, and their faces resembled human faces. 8Their hair was like women's hair, and their teeth were like lions' teeth. 9They had breastplates like breastplates of iron, and the sound of their wings was like the thundering of many horses and chariots rushing into battle. 10They had tails and stings like scorpions, and in their tails had power to torment people for five months. 11They had as king over them the angel of the Abyss, whose name in Hebrew is Abaddon, and in Greek, Apollyon.b

12The first woe is past; two other woes are yet to come.

13The sixth angel sounded his trumpet, and I heard a voice coming from the hornsc of the golden altar that is before God. 14It said to the sixth angel who had the trumpet, "Release the four angels who are bound at the great river Euphrates." 15And the four angels who had

---

a 11 That is, Bitterness   b 11 Abaddon and Apollyon mean Destroyer.
c 13 That is, projections

Living Bible

8, 9Then the second angel blew his trumpet, and what appeared to be a huge burning mountain was thrown into the sea, destroying a third of all the ships; and a third of the sea turned red as blood;d and a third of the fish were killed. 10The third angel blew, and a great flaming star fell from heaven upon a third of the rivers and springs. 11The star was called "Bitterness"e because it poisoned a third of all the water on the earth and many people died. 12The fourth angel blew his trumpet and immediately a third of the sun was blighted and darkened, and a third of the moon and the stars, so that the daylight was dimmed by a third, and the nighttime darkness deepened. 13As I watched, I saw a solitary eagle flying through the heavens crying loudly, "Woe, woe, woe to the people of the earth because of the terrible things that will soon happen when the three remaining angels blow their trumpets."

9 THEN THE fifth angel blew his trumpet and I saw onef who was fallen to earth from heaven, and to him was given the key to the bottomless pit. 2When he opened it, smoke poured out as though from some huge furnace, and the sun and air were darkened by the smoke.
3Then locusts came from the smoke and descended onto the earth and were given power to sting like scorpions. 4They were told not to hurt the grass or plants or trees, but to attack those people who did not have the mark of God on their foreheads. 5They were not to kill them, but to torture them for five months with agony like the pain of scorpion stings. 6In those days men will try to kill themselves but won't be able to—death will not come. They will long to die—but death will flee away! 7The locusts looked like horses armored for battle. They had what looked like golden crowns on their heads, and their faces looked like men's. 8Their hair was long like women's, and their teeth were those of lions. 9They wore breastplates that seemed to be of iron, and their wings roared like an army of chariots rushing into battle. 10They had stinging tails like scorpions, and their power to hurt, given to them for five months, was in their tails. 11Their king is the Prince of the bottomless pit whose name in Hebrew is Abaddon, and in Greek, Apollyon [and in English, the Destroyerg].
12One terror now ends, but there are two more coming!
13The sixth angel blew his trumpet and I heard a voice speaking from the four horns of the golden altar that stands before the throne of God, 14saying to the sixth angel, "Release the four mighty demonsh held bound at the great River Euphrates." 15They had been kept in

New Revised Standard

8 The second angel blew his trumpet, and something like a great mountain, burning with fire, was thrown into the sea. 9A third of the sea became blood, a third of the living creatures in the sea died, and a third of the ships were destroyed.
10 The third angel blew his trumpet, and a great star fell from heaven, blazing like a torch, and it fell on a third of the rivers and on the springs of water. 11The name of the star is Wormwood. A third of the waters became wormwood, and many died from the water, because it was made bitter.
12 The fourth angel blew his trumpet, and a third of the sun was struck, and a third of the moon, and a third of the stars, so that a third of their light was darkened; a third of the day was kept from shining, and likewise the night.
13 Then I looked, and I heard an eagle crying with a loud voice as it flew in midheaven, "Woe, woe, woe to the inhabitants of the earth, at the blasts of the other trumpets that the three angels are about to blow!"

9 AND THE fifth angel blew his trumpet, and I saw a star that had fallen from heaven to earth, and he was given the key to the shaft of the bottomless pit; 2he opened the shaft of the bottomless pit, and from the shaft rose smoke like the smoke of a great furnace, and the sun and the air were darkened with the smoke from the shaft. 3 Then from the smoke came locusts on the earth, and they were given authority like the authority of scorpions of the earth. 4They were told not to damage the grass of the earth or any green growth or any tree, but only those people who do not have the seal of God on their foreheads. 5They were allowed to torture them for five months, but not to kill them, and their torture was like the torture of a scorpion when it stings someone. 6And in those days people will seek death but will not find it; they will long to die, but death will flee from them.
7 In appearance the locusts were like horses equipped for battle. On their heads were what looked like crowns of gold; their faces were like human faces, 8their hair like women's hair, and their teeth like lions' teeth; 9they had scales like iron breastplates, and the noise of their wings was like the noise of many chariots with horses rushing into battle. 10They have tails like scorpions, with stingers, and in their tails is their power to harm people for five months. 11They have as king over them the angel of the bottomless pit; his name in Hebrew is Abaddon,i and in Greek he is called Apollyon.j
12 The first woe has passed. There are still two woes to come.
13 Then the sixth angel blew his trumpet, and I heard a voice from the fourk horns of the golden altar before God, 14saying to the sixth angel who had the trumpet, "Release the four angels who are bound at the great river Euphrates." 15So the four angels were re-

---

d 8:9 turned red as blood, literally, "became blood." e 8:11 "Bitterness," literally, "Wormwood." f 9:1 one who has fallen to earth from heaven, literally, "a star fallen from heaven"; it is unclear whether this person is of satanic origin, as most commentators believe, or whether the reference is to Christ. g 9:11 and in English, the Destroyer, implied. h 9:14 four mighty demons, literally, "(fallen) angels."

i That is, Destruction j That is, Destroyer k Other ancient authorities lack four

King James

15And the four angels were loosed, which were prepared for an hour, and a day, and a month, and a year, for to slay the third part of men.

16And the number of the army of the horsemen *were* two hundred thousand thousand: and I heard the number of them.

17And thus I saw the horses in the vision, and them that sat on them, having breastplates of fire, and of jacinth, and brimstone: and the heads of the horses *were* as the heads of lions; and out of their mouths issued fire and smoke and brimstone.

18By these three was the third part of men killed, by the fire, and by the smoke, and by the brimstone, which issued out of their mouths.

19For their power is in their mouth, and in their tails: for their tails *were* like unto serpents, and had heads, and with them they do hurt.

20And the rest of the men which were not killed by these plagues yet repented not of the works of their hands, that they should not worship devils, and idols of gold, and silver, and brass, and stone, and of wood: which neither can see, nor hear, nor walk:

21Neither repented they of their murders, nor of their sorceries, nor of their fornication, nor of their thefts.

10 AND I saw another mighty angel come down from heaven, clothed with a cloud: and a rainbow *was* upon his head, and his face *was* as it were the sun, and his feet as pillars of fire:

2And he had in his hand a little book open: and he set his right foot upon the sea, and *his* left *foot* on the earth,

3And cried with a loud voice, as *when* a lion roareth: and when he had cried, seven thunders uttered their voices.

4And when the seven thunders had uttered their voices, I was about to write: and I heard a voice from heaven saying unto me, Seal up those things which the seven thunders uttered, and write them not.

5And the angel which I saw stand upon the sea and upon the earth lifted up his hand to heaven,

6And sware by him that liveth for ever and ever, who created heaven, and the things that therein are, and the earth, and the things that therein are, and the sea, and the things which are therein, that there should be time no longer:

7But in the days of the voice of the seventh angel, when he shall begin to sound, the mystery of God should be finished, as he hath declared to his servants the prophets.

8And the voice which I heard from heaven spake unto me again, and said, Go *and* take the little book which is open in the hand of the angel which standeth upon the sea and upon the earth.

9And I went unto the angel, and said unto him, Give me the little book. And he said unto me, Take *it,* and eat it up; and it shall make thy belly bitter, but it shall be in thy mouth sweet as honey.

10And I took the little book out of the angel's hand, and ate it up; and it was in my mouth sweet as honey: and as soon as I had eaten it, my belly was bitter.

11And he said unto me, Thou must prophesy again before many peoples, and nations, and tongues, and kings.

New International

been kept ready for this very hour and day and month and year were released to kill a third of mankind. 16The number of the mounted troops was two hundred million. I heard their number.

17The horses and riders I saw in my vision looked like this: Their breastplates were fiery red, dark blue, and yellow as sulfur. The heads of the horses resembled the heads of lions, and out of their mouths came fire, smoke and sulfur. 18A third of mankind was killed by the three plagues of fire, smoke and sulfur that came out of their mouths. 19The power of the horses was in their mouths and in their tails; for their tails were like snakes, having heads with which they inflict injury.

20The rest of mankind that were not killed by these plagues still did not repent of the work of their hands; they did not stop worshiping demons, and idols of gold, silver, bronze, stone and wood—idols that cannot see or hear or walk. 21Nor did they repent of their murders, their magic arts, their sexual immorality or their thefts.

The Angel and the Little Scroll

10 THEN I saw another mighty angel coming down from heaven. He was robed in a cloud, with a rainbow above his head; his face was like the sun, and his legs were like fiery pillars. 2He was holding a little scroll, which lay open in his hand. He planted his right foot on the sea and his left foot on the land, 3and he gave a loud shout like the roar of a lion. When he shouted, the voices of the seven thunders spoke. 4And when the seven thunders spoke, I was about to write; but I heard a voice from heaven say, "Seal up what the seven thunders have said and do not write it down."

5Then the angel I had seen standing on the sea and on the land raised his right hand to heaven. 6And he swore by him who lives for ever and ever, who created the heavens and all that is in them, the earth and all that is in it, and the sea and all that is in it, and said, "There will be no more delay! 7But in the days when the seventh angel is about to sound his trumpet, the mystery of God will be accomplished, just as he announced to his servants the prophets."

8Then the voice that I had heard from heaven spoke to me once more: "Go, take the scroll that lies open in the hand of the angel who is standing on the sea and on the land."

9So I went to the angel and asked him to give me the little scroll. He said to me, "Take it and eat it. It will turn your stomach sour, but in your mouth it will be as sweet as honey." 10I took the little scroll from the angel's hand and ate it. It tasted as sweet as honey in my mouth, but when I had eaten it, my stomach turned sour. 11Then I was told, "You must prophesy again about many peoples, nations, languages and kings."

Living Bible

readiness for that year and month and day and hour, and now they were turned loose to kill a third of all mankind. 16They led an army of 200,000,000a warriorsb—I heard an announcement of how many there were.

17, 18I saw their horses spread out before me in my vision; their riders wore fiery-red breastplates, though some were sky-blue and others yellow. The horses' heads looked much like lions', and smoke and fire and flaming sulphur billowed from their mouths, killing one-third of all mankind. 19Their power of death was not only in their mouths, but in their tails as well, for their tails were similar to serpents' heads that struck and bit with fatal wounds.

20But the men left alive after these plagues *still refused to worship God!* They would not renounce their demon-worship, nor their idols made of gold and silver, brass, stone, and wood—which neither see nor hear nor walk! 21Neither did they change their mind and attitude about all their murders and witchcraft, their immorality and theft.

10 THEN I saw another mighty angel coming down from heaven, surrounded by a cloud, with a rainbow over his head; his face shone like the sun and his feet flashed with fire. 2And he held open in his hand a small scroll. He set his right foot on the sea and his left foot on the earth, 3and gave a great shout—it was like the roar of a lion—and the seven thunders crashed their reply.

4I was about to write what the thunders said when a voice from heaven called to me, "Don't do it. Their words are not to be revealed."

5Then the mighty angel standing on the sea and land lifted his right hand to heaven, 6and swore by him who lives forever and ever, who created heaven and everything in it and the earth and all that it contains and the sea and its inhabitants, that there should be no more delay, 7but that when the seventh angel blew his trumpet, then God's veiled plan—mysterious through the ages ever since it was announced by his servants the prophets—would be fulfilled.

8Then the voice from heaven spoke to me again, "Go and get the unrolled scroll from the mighty angel standing there upon the sea and land."

9So I approached him and asked him to give me the scroll. "Yes, take it and eat it," he said. "At first it will taste like honey, but when you swallow it, it will make your stomach sour!" 10So I took it from his hand, and ate it! And just as he had said, it was sweet in my mouth but it gave me a stomach ache when I swallowed it.

11Then he told me, "You must prophesy further about many peoples, nations, tribes, and kings."

New Revised Standard

leased, who had been held ready for the hour, the day, the month, and the year, to kill a third of humankind. 16 The number of the troops of cavalry was two hundred million; I heard their number. 17 And this was how I saw the horses in my vision: the riders wore breastplates the color of fire and of sapphirec and of sulfur; the heads of the horses were like lions' heads, and fire and smoke and sulfur came out of their mouths. 18 By these three plagues a third of humankind was killed, by the fire and smoke and sulfur coming out of their mouths. 19 For the power of the horses is in their mouths and in their tails; their tails are like serpents, having heads; and with them they inflict harm.

20 The rest of humankind, who were not killed by these plagues, did not repent of the works of their hands or give up worshiping demons and idols of gold and silver and bronze and stone and wood, which cannot see or hear or walk. 21 And they did not repent of their murders or their sorceries or their fornication or their thefts.

The Angel with the Little Scroll

10 AND I saw another mighty angel coming down from heaven, wrapped in a cloud, with a rainbow over his head; his face was like the sun, and his legs like pillars of fire. 2 He held a little scroll open in his hand. Setting his right foot on the sea and his left foot on the land, 3 he gave a great shout, like a lion roaring. And when he shouted, the seven thunders sounded. 4 And when the seven thunders had sounded, I was about to write, but I heard a voice from heaven saying, "Seal up what the seven thunders have said, and do not write it down." 5 Then the angel whom I saw standing on the sea and the land

   raised his right hand to heaven
6   and swore by him who lives forever and
      ever,

who created heaven and what is in it, the earth and what is in it, and the sea and what is in it: "There will be no more delay, 7 but in the days when the seventh angel is to blow his trumpet, the mystery of God will be fulfilled, as he announced to his servantsd the prophets."

8 Then the voice that I had heard from heaven spoke to me again, saying, "Go, take the scroll that is open in the hand of the angel who is standing on the sea and on the land." 9 So I went to the angel and told him to give me the little scroll; and he said to me, "Take it, and eat; it will be bitter to your stomach, but sweet as honey in your mouth." 10 So I took the little scroll from the hand of the angel and ate it; it was sweet as honey in my mouth, but when I had eaten it, my stomach was made bitter.

11 Then they said to me, "You must prophesy again about many peoples and nations and languages and kings."

---

a *9:16* If this is a literal figure, it is no longer incredible, in view of a world population in excess of six billion in the near future. In China alone, in 1961, there were an "estimated 200,000,000 armed and organized militiamen" (Associated Press Release, April 24, 1964).   b *9:16 warriors,* literally, "horsemen."

c Gk *hyacínth*   d Gk *slaves*

King James

11 AND THERE was given me a reed like unto a rod: and the angel stood, saying, Rise, and measure the temple of God, and the altar, and them that worship therein.

²But the court which is without the temple leave out, and measure it not; for it is given unto the Gentiles: and the holy city shall they tread under foot forty *and* two months.

³And I will give *power* unto my two witnesses, and they shall prophesy a thousand two hundred *and* threescore days, clothed in sackcloth.

⁴These are the two olive trees, and the two candlesticks standing before the God of the earth.

⁵And if any man will hurt them, fire proceedeth out of their mouth, and devoureth their enemies: and if any man will hurt them, he must in this manner be killed.

⁶These have power to shut heaven, that it rain not in the days of their prophecy: and have power over waters to turn them to blood, and to smite the earth with all plagues, as often as they will.

⁷And when they shall have finished their testimony, the beast that ascendeth out of the bottomless pit shall make war against them, and shall overcome them, and kill them.

⁸And their dead bodies *shall lie* in the street of the great city, which spiritually is called Sodom and Egypt, where also our Lord was crucified.

⁹And they of the people and kindreds and tongues and nations shall see their dead bodies three days and an half, and shall not suffer their dead bodies to be put in graves.

¹⁰And they that dwell upon the earth shall rejoice over them, and make merry, and shall send gifts one to another; because these two prophets tormented them that dwelt on the earth.

¹¹And after three days and an half the Spirit of life from God entered into them, and they stood upon their feet; and great fear fell upon them which saw them.

¹²And they heard a great voice from heaven saying unto them, Come up hither. And they ascended up to heaven in a cloud; and their enemies beheld them.

¹³And the same hour was there a great earthquake, and the tenth part of the city fell, and in the earthquake were slain of men seven thousand: and the remnant were affrighted, and gave glory to the God of heaven.

¹⁴The second woe is past; *and*, behold, the third woe cometh quickly.

¹⁵And the seventh angel sounded; and there were great voices in heaven, saying, The kingdoms of this world are become *the kingdoms* of our Lord, and of his Christ; and he shall reign for ever and ever.

¹⁶And the four and twenty elders, which sat before God on their seats, fell upon their faces, and worshipped God,

¹⁷Saying, We give thee thanks, O Lord God Almighty, which art, and wast, and art to come; because thou hast taken to thee thy great power, and hast reigned.

¹⁸And the nations were angry, and thy wrath is come, and the time of the dead, that they should be judged, and that thou shouldest give reward unto thy servants the prophets, and to the saints, and them that fear thy name, small and great; and shouldest destroy them which destroy the earth.

¹⁹And the temple of God was opened in heaven, and there was seen in his temple the ark of his testament: and there were lightnings, and voices, and thunderings, and an earthquake, and great hail.

New International

The Two Witnesses

11 I WAS given a reed like a measuring rod and was told, "Go and measure the temple of God and the altar, and count the worshipers there. ²But exclude the outer court; do not measure it, because it has been given to the Gentiles. They will trample on the holy city for 42 months. ³And I will give power to my two witnesses, and they will prophesy for 1,260 days, clothed in sackcloth." ⁴These are the two olive trees and the two lampstands that stand before the Lord of the earth. ⁵If anyone tries to harm them, fire comes from their mouths and devours their enemies. This is how anyone who wants to harm them must die. ⁶These men have power to shut up the sky so that it will not rain during the time they are prophesying; and they have power to turn the waters into blood and to strike the earth with every kind of plague as often as they want.

⁷Now when they have finished their testimony, the beast that comes up from the Abyss will attack them, and overpower and kill them. ⁸Their bodies will lie in the street of the great city, which is figuratively called Sodom and Egypt, where also their Lord was crucified. ⁹For three and a half days men from every people, tribe, language and nation will gaze on their bodies and refuse them burial. ¹⁰The inhabitants of the earth will gloat over them and will celebrate by sending each other gifts, because these two prophets had tormented those who live on the earth.

¹¹But after the three and a half days a breath of life from God entered them, and they stood on their feet, and terror struck those who saw them. ¹²Then they heard a loud voice from heaven saying to them, "Come up here." And they went up to heaven in a cloud, while their enemies looked on.

¹³At that very hour there was a severe earthquake and a tenth of the city collapsed. Seven thousand people were killed in the earthquake, and the survivors were terrified and gave glory to the God of heaven.

¹⁴The second woe has passed; the third woe is coming soon.

The Seventh Trumpet

¹⁵The seventh angel sounded his trumpet, and there were loud voices in heaven, which said:

"The kingdom of the world has become the
        kingdom of our Lord and of his Christ,
    and he will reign for ever and ever."

¹⁶And the twenty-four elders, who were seated on their thrones before God, fell on their faces and worshiped God, ¹⁷saying:

"We give thanks to you, Lord God Almighty,
    the One who is and who was,
because you have taken your great power
    and have begun to reign.
¹⁸The nations were angry;
    and your wrath has come.
The time has come for judging the dead,
    and for rewarding your servants the prophets
and your saints and those who reverence your
        name,
    both small and great—
and for destroying those who destroy the earth."

¹⁹Then God's temple in heaven was opened, and within his temple was seen the ark of his covenant. And there came flashes of lightning, rumblings, peals of thunder, an earthquake and a great hailstorm.

Living Bible

11 NOW I was given a measuring stick and told to go and measure the temple of God, including the inner court where the altar stands, and to count the number of worshipers.[a] 2"But do not measure the outer court," I was told, "for it has been turned over to the nations. They will trample the Holy City for forty-two months.[b] 3And I will give power to my two witnesses to prophesy 1,260 days clothed in sackcloth."

4These two prophets are the two olive trees,[c] and two candlesticks standing before the God of all the earth. 5Anyone trying to harm them will be killed by bursts of fire shooting from their mouths. 6They have power to shut the skies so that no rain will fall during the three and a half years they prophesy, and to turn rivers and oceans to blood, and to send every kind of plague upon the earth as often as they wish.

7When they complete the three and a half years of their solemn testimony, the tyrant who comes out of the bottomless pit[d] will declare war against them and conquer and kill them; 8, 9and for three and a half days their bodies will be exposed in the streets of Jerusalem (the city fittingly described as "Sodom" or "Egypt")—the very place where their Lord was crucified. No one will be allowed to bury them, and people from many nations will crowd around to gaze at them. 10And there will be a worldwide holiday—people everywhere will rejoice and give presents to each other and throw parties to celebrate the death of the two prophets who had tormented them so much!

11But after three and a half days, the spirit of life from God will enter them and they will stand up! And great fear will fall on everyone. 12Then a loud voice will shout from heaven, "Come up!" And they will rise to heaven in a cloud as their enemies watch.

13The same hour there will be a terrible earthquake that levels a tenth of the city, leaving 7,000 dead. Then everyone left will, in their terror, give glory to the God of heaven.

14The second woe is past, but the third quickly follows:

15For just then the seventh angel blew his trumpet, and there were loud voices shouting down from heaven, "The Kingdom of this world now belongs to our Lord, and to his Christ; and he shall reign forever and ever."[e] 16And the twenty-four Elders sitting on their thrones before God threw themselves down in worship, saying, 17"We give thanks, Lord God Almighty, who is and was, for now you have assumed your great power and have begun to reign. 18The nations were angry with you, but now it is your turn to be angry with them. It is time to judge the dead, and reward your servants—prophets and people alike, all who fear your Name, both great and small—and to destroy those who have caused destruction upon the earth."

19Then, in heaven, the temple of God was opened and the ark of his covenant could be seen inside. Lightning flashed and thunder crashed and roared, and there was a great hailstorm and the world was shaken by a mighty earthquake.

New Revised Standard

The Two Witnesses

11 THEN I was given a measuring rod like a staff, and I was told, "Come and measure the temple of God and the altar and those who worship there, 2but do not measure the court outside the temple; leave that out, for it is given over to the nations, and they will trample the holy city for forty-two months. 3And I will grant my two witnesses authority to prophesy for one thousand two hundred sixty days, wearing sackcloth."

4 These are the two olive trees and the two lampstands that stand before the Lord of the earth. 5And if anyone wants to harm them, fire pours from their mouth and consumes their foes; anyone who wants to harm them must be killed in this manner. 6They have authority to shut the sky, so that no rain may fall during the days of their prophesying, and they have authority over the waters to turn them into blood, and to strike the earth with every kind of plague, as often as they desire.

7 When they have finished their testimony, the beast that comes up from the bottomless pit will make war on them and conquer them and kill them, 8and their dead bodies will lie in the street of the great city that is prophetically[f] called Sodom and Egypt, where also their Lord was crucified. 9For three and a half days members of the peoples and tribes and languages and nations will gaze at their dead bodies and refuse to let them be placed in a tomb; 10and the inhabitants of the earth will gloat over them and celebrate and exchange presents, because these two prophets had been a torment to the inhabitants of the earth.

11 But after the three and a half days, the breath[g] of life from God entered them, and they stood on their feet, and those who saw them were terrified. 12Then they[h] heard a loud voice from heaven saying to them, "Come up here!" And they went up to heaven in a cloud while their enemies watched them. 13At that moment there was a great earthquake, and a tenth of the city fell; seven thousand people were killed in the earthquake, and the rest were terrified and gave glory to the God of heaven.

14 The second woe has passed. The third woe is coming very soon.

The Seventh Trumpet

15 Then the seventh angel blew his trumpet, and there were loud voices in heaven, saying,

"The kingdom of the world has become the
   kingdom of our Lord
   and of his Messiah,[i]
and he will reign forever and ever."

16 Then the twenty-four elders who sit on their thrones before God fell on their faces and worshiped God, 17singing,

"We give you thanks, Lord God Almighty,
   who are and who were,
for you have taken your great power
   and begun to reign.
18 The nations raged,
   but your wrath has come,
   and the time for judging the dead,
for rewarding your servants,[j] the prophets
   and saints and all who fear your name,
   both small and great,
and for destroying those who destroy the
     earth."

19 Then God's temple in heaven was opened, and the ark of his covenant was seen within his temple; and there were flashes of lightning, rumblings, peals of thunder, an earthquake, and heavy hail.

---

[a] 11:1 *a measuring stick . . . and to count the number of worshipers*, literally, "Rise and measure the temple of God, and the altar, and them that worship therein." [b] 11:2 *forty-two months*, 3½ years, as in Dan 12:7. Also for *1260 days* in vs 3. [c] 11:4 *two olive trees*, Zech 4:3, 4, 11. [d] 11:7 *the bottomless pit*, Rev 9:11. [e] 11:15 *he shall reign forever and ever*, or "The Lord and his Anointed shall now rule the world from this day to eternity."

[f] Or *allegorically*; Gk *spiritually* [g] Or *the spirit* [h] Other ancient authorities read *I* [i] Gk *Christ* [j] Gk *slaves*

King James

12 AND THERE appeared a great wonder in heaven; a woman clothed with the sun, and the moon under her feet, and upon her head a crown of twelve stars:

2And she being with child cried, travailing in birth, and pained to be delivered.

3And there appeared another wonder in heaven; and behold a great red dragon, having seven heads and ten horns, and seven crowns upon his heads.

4And his tail drew the third part of the stars of heaven, and did cast them to the earth: and the dragon stood before the woman which was ready to be delivered, for to devour her child as soon as it was born.

5And she brought forth a man child, who was to rule all nations with a rod of iron: and her child was caught up unto God, and to his throne.

6And the woman fled into the wilderness, where she hath a place prepared of God, that they should feed her there a thousand two hundred and threescore days.

7And there was war in heaven: Michael and his angels fought against the dragon; and the dragon fought and his angels,

8And prevailed not; neither was their place found any more in heaven.

9And the great dragon was cast out, that old serpent, called the Devil, and Satan, which deceiveth the whole world: he was cast out into the earth, and his angels were cast out with him.

10And I heard a loud voice saying in heaven, Now is come salvation, and strength, and the kingdom of our God, and the power of his Christ: for the accuser of our brethren is cast down, which accused them before our God day and night.

11And they overcame him by the blood of the Lamb, and by the word of their testimony; and they loved not their lives unto the death.

12Therefore rejoice, ye heavens, and ye that dwell in them. Woe to the inhabiters of the earth and of the sea! for the devil is come down unto you, having great wrath, because he knoweth that he hath but a short time.

13And when the dragon saw that he was cast unto the earth, he persecuted the woman which brought forth the man child.

14And to the woman were given two wings of a great eagle, that she might fly into the wilderness, into her place, where she is nourished for a time, and times, and half a time, from the face of the serpent.

15And the serpent cast out of his mouth water as a flood after the woman, that he might cause her to be carried away of the flood.

16And the earth helped the woman, and the earth opened her mouth, and swallowed up the flood which the dragon cast out of his mouth.

17And the dragon was wroth with the woman, and went to make war with the remnant of her seed, which keep the commandments of God, and have the testimony of Jesus Christ.

New International

The Woman and the Dragon

12 A GREAT and wondrous sign appeared in heaven: a woman clothed with the sun, with the moon under her feet and a crown of twelve stars on her head. 2She was pregnant and cried out in pain as she was about to give birth. 3Then another sign appeared in heaven: an enormous red dragon with seven heads and ten horns and seven crowns on his heads. 4His tail swept a third of the stars out of the sky and flung them to the earth. The dragon stood in front of the woman who was about to give birth, so that he might devour her child the moment it was born. 5She gave birth to a son, a male child, who will rule all the nations with an iron scepter. And her child was snatched up to God and to his throne. 6The woman fled into the desert to a place prepared for her by God, where she might be taken care of for 1,260 days.

7And there was war in heaven. Michael and his angels fought against the dragon, and the dragon and his angels fought back. 8But he was not strong enough, and they lost their place in heaven. 9The great dragon was hurled down—that ancient serpent called the devil, or Satan, who leads the whole world astray. He was hurled to the earth, and his angels with him.

10Then I heard a loud voice in heaven say:

"Now have come the salvation and the power
    and the kingdom of our God,
  and the authority of his Christ.
For the accuser of our brothers,
    who accuses them before our God day and
        night,
  has been hurled down.
11They overcame him
    by the blood of the Lamb
    and by the word of their testimony;
  they did not love their lives so much
    as to shrink from death.
12Therefore rejoice, you heavens
    and you who dwell in them!
But woe to the earth and the sea,
    because the devil has gone down to you!
He is filled with fury,
    because he knows that his time is short."

13When the dragon saw that he had been hurled to the earth, he pursued the woman who had given birth to the male child. 14The woman was given the two wings of a great eagle, so that she might fly to the place prepared for her in the desert, where she would be taken care of for a time, times and half a time, out of the serpent's reach. 15Then from his mouth the serpent spewed water like a river, to overtake the woman and sweep her away with the torrent. 16But the earth helped the woman by opening its mouth and swallowing the river that the dragon had spewed out of his mouth. 17Then the dragon was enraged at the woman and went off to make war against the rest of her offspring—those who obey God's commandments and hold to the testimony of Jesus.

Living Bible

12 THEN A great pageant appeared in heaven, portraying things to come. I saw a woman clothed with the sun, with the moon beneath her feet, and a crown of twelve stars on her head. 2She was pregnant and screamed in the pain of her labor, awaiting her delivery.

3Suddenly a red Dragon appeared, with seven heads and ten horns, and seven crowns on his heads. 4His tail drew along behind him a third of the stars, which he plunged to the earth. He stood before the woman as she was about to give birth to her child, ready to eat the baby as soon as it was born.

5She gave birth to a boy who was to rule all nations with a heavy hand, and he was caught up to God and to his throne. 6The woman fled into the wilderness, where God had prepared a place for her, to take care of her for 1,260 days.

7Then there was war in heaven; Michael and the angels under his command fought the Dragon and his hosts of fallen angels. 8And the Dragon lost the battle and was forced from heaven. 9This great Dragon—the ancient serpent called the devil, or Satan, the one deceiving the whole world—was thrown down onto the earth with all his army.

10Then I heard a loud voice shouting across the heavens, "It has happened at last! God's salvation and the power and the rule, and the authority of his Christ are finally here; for the Accuser of our brothers has been thrown down from heaven onto earth—he accused them day and night before our God. 11They defeated him by the blood of the Lamb, and by their testimony; for they did not love their lives but laid them down for him. 12Rejoice, O heavens! You citizens of heaven, rejoice! Be glad! But woe to you people of the world, for the devil has come down to you in great anger, knowing that he has little time."

13And when the Dragon found himself cast down to earth, he persecuted the woman who had given birth to the child. 14But she was given two wings like those of a great eagle, to fly into the wilderness to the place prepared for her, where she was cared for and protected from the Serpent, the Dragon, for three and a half years.a

15And from the Serpent's mouth a vast flood of water gushed out and swept toward the woman in an effort to get rid of her; 16but the earth helped her by opening its mouth and swallowing the flood! 17Then the furious Dragon set out to attack the rest of her children—all who were keeping God's commandments and confessing that they belong to Jesus. He stood waiting on an ocean beach.

New Revised Standard

The Woman and the Dragon

12 A GREAT portent appeared in heaven: a woman clothed with the sun, with the moon under her feet, and on her head a crown of twelve stars. 2She was pregnant and was crying out in birth pangs, in the agony of giving birth. 3Then another portent appeared in heaven: a great red dragon, with seven heads and ten horns, and seven diadems on his heads. 4His tail swept down a third of the stars of heaven and threw them to the earth. Then the dragon stood before the woman who was about to bear a child, so that he might devour her child as soon as it was born. 5And she gave birth to a son, a male child, who is to ruleb all the nations with a rod of iron. But her child was snatched away and taken to God and to his throne; 6and the woman fled into the wilderness, where she has a place prepared by God, so that there she can be nourished for one thousand two hundred sixty days.

Michael Defeats the Dragon

7 And war broke out in heaven; Michael and his angels fought against the dragon. The dragon and his angels fought back, 8but they were defeated, and there was no longer any place for them in heaven. 9The great dragon was thrown down, that ancient serpent, who is called the Devil and Satan, the deceiver of the whole world—he was thrown down to the earth, and his angels were thrown down with him.

10 Then I heard a loud voice in heaven, proclaiming,

"Now have come the salvation and the power
and the kingdom of our God
and the authority of his Messiah,c
for the accuser of our comradesd has been
thrown down,
who accuses them day and night before our
God.
11 But they have conquered him by the blood of
the Lamb
and by the word of their testimony,
for they did not cling to life even in the face
of death.
12 Rejoice then, you heavens
and those who dwell in them!
But woe to the earth and the sea,
for the devil has come down to you
with great wrath,
because he knows that his time is short!"

The Dragon Fights Again on Earth

13 So when the dragon saw that he had been thrown down to the earth, he pursuede the woman who had given birth to the male child. 14But the woman was given the two wings of the great eagle, so that she could fly from the serpent into the wilderness, to her place where she is nourished for a time, and times, and half a time. 15Then from his mouth the serpent poured water like a river after the woman, to sweep her away with the flood. 16But the earth came to the help of the woman; it opened its mouth and swallowed the river that the dragon had poured from his mouth. 17Then the dragon was angry with the woman, and went off to make war on the rest of her children, those who keep the commandments of God and hold the testimony of Jesus.

The First Beast

18 Then the dragonf took his stand on the sand of the seashore.

---

a 12:14 for three and a half years, literally, "a time and times and half a time."

b Or to shepherd c Gk Christ d Gk brothers e Or persecuted f Gk Then he; other ancient authorities read Then I stood

King James

13 AND I stood upon the sand of the sea, and saw a beast rise up out of the sea, having seven heads and ten horns, and upon his horns ten crowns, and upon his heads the name of blasphemy.

2And the beast which I saw was like unto a leopard, and his feet were as *the feet* of a bear, and his mouth as the mouth of a lion: and the dragon gave him his power, and his seat, and great authority.

3And I saw one of his heads as it were wounded to death; and his deadly wound was healed: and all the world wondered after the beast.

4And they worshipped the dragon which gave power unto the beast: and they worshipped the beast, saying, Who *is* like unto the beast? who is able to make war with him?

5And there was given unto him a mouth speaking great things and blasphemies; and power was given unto him to continue forty *and* two months.

6And he opened his mouth in blasphemy against God, to blaspheme his name, and his tabernacle, and them that dwell in heaven.

7And it was given unto him to make war with the saints, and to overcome them: and power was given him over all kindreds, and tongues, and nations.

8And all that dwell upon the earth shall worship him, whose names are not written in the book of life of the Lamb slain from the foundation of the world.

9If any man have an ear, let him hear.

10He that leadeth into captivity shall go into captivity: he that killeth with the sword must be killed with the sword. Here is the patience and the faith of the saints.

11And I beheld another beast coming up out of the earth; and he had two horns like a lamb, and he spake as a dragon.

12And he exerciseth all the power of the first beast before him, and causeth the earth and them which dwell therein to worship the first beast, whose deadly wound was healed.

13And he doeth great wonders, so that he maketh fire come down from heaven on the earth in the sight of men,

14And deceiveth them that dwell on the earth by *the means of* those miracles which he had power to do in the sight of the beast; saying to them that dwell on the earth, that they should make an image to the beast, which had the wound by a sword, and did live.

15And he had power to give life unto the image of the beast, that the image of the beast should both speak, and cause that as many as would not worship the image of the beast should be killed.

16And he causeth all, both small and great, rich and poor, free and bond, to receive a mark in their right hand, or in their foreheads:

17And that no man might buy or sell, save he that had the mark, or the name of the beast, or the number of his name.

18Here is wisdom. Let him that hath understanding count the number of the beast: for it is the number of a man; and his number *is* Six hundred threescore *and* six.

14 AND I looked, and, lo, a Lamb stood on the mount Zion, and with him an hundred forty *and* four thousand, having his Father's name written in their foreheads.

New International

13 AND THE dragona stood on the shore of the sea.

The Beast out of the Sea

And I saw a beast coming out of the sea. He had ten horns and seven heads, with ten crowns on his horns, and on each head a blasphemous name. 2The beast I saw resembled a leopard, but had feet like those of a bear and a mouth like that of a lion. The dragon gave the beast his power and his throne and great authority. 3One of the heads of the beast seemed to have had a fatal wound, but the fatal wound had been healed. The whole world was astonished and followed the beast. 4Men worshiped the dragon because he had given authority to the beast, and they also worshiped the beast and asked, "Who is like the beast? Who can make war against him?"

5The beast was given a mouth to utter proud words and blasphemies and to exercise his authority for forty-two months. 6He opened his mouth to blaspheme God, and to slander his name and his dwelling place and those who live in heaven. 7He was given power to make war against the saints and to conquer them. And he was given authority over every tribe, people, language and nation. 8All inhabitants of the earth will worship the beast—all whose names have not been written in the book of life belonging to the Lamb that was slain from the creation of the world.b

9He who has an ear, let him hear.

10If anyone is to go into captivity,
 into captivity he will go.
If anyone is to be killedc with the sword,
 with the sword he will be killed.

This calls for patient endurance and faithfulness on the part of the saints.

The Beast out of the Earth

11Then I saw another beast, coming out of the earth. He had two horns like a lamb, but he spoke like a dragon. 12He exercised all the authority of the first beast on his behalf, and made the earth and its inhabitants worship the first beast, whose fatal wound had been healed. 13And he performed great and miraculous signs, even causing fire to come down from heaven to earth in full view of men. 14Because of the signs he was given power to do on behalf of the first beast, he deceived the inhabitants of the earth. He ordered them to set up an image in honor of the beast who was wounded by the sword and yet lived. 15He was given power to give breath to the image of the first beast, so that it could speak and cause all who refused to worship the image to be killed. 16He also forced everyone, small and great, rich and poor, free and slave, to receive a mark on his right hand or on his forehead, 17so that no one could buy or sell unless he had the mark, which is the name of the beast or the number of his name.

18This calls for wisdom. If anyone has insight, let him calculate the number of the beast, for it is man's number. His number is 666.

The Lamb and the 144,000

14 THEN I looked, and there before me was the Lamb, standing on Mount Zion, and with him 144,000 who had his name and his Father's name written on their foreheads. 2And I heard a sound from heav-

---

a *1* Some late manuscripts *And I*   b *8* Or *written from the creation of the world in the book of life belonging to the Lamb that was slain*   c *10* Some manuscripts *anyone kills*

Living Bible

13 AND NOW, in my vision, I saw a strange Creature rising up out of the sea. It had seven heads and ten horns, and ten crowns upon its horns. And written on each head were blasphemous names, each one defying and insulting God. [2]This Creature looked like a leopard but had bear's feet and a lion's mouth! And the Dragon gave him his own power and throne and great authority.

[3]I saw that one of his heads seemed wounded beyond recovery—but the fatal wound was healed! All the world marveled at this miracle and followed the Creature in awe. [4]They worshiped the Dragon for giving him such power, and they worshiped the strange Creature. "Where is there anyone as great as he?" they exclaimed. "Who is able to fight against him?"

[5]Then the Dragon encouraged the Creature to speak great blasphemies against the Lord; and gave him authority to control the earth for forty-two months. [6]All that time he blasphemed God's Name and his temple and all those living in heaven. [7]The Dragon gave him power to fight against God's people[d] and to overcome them, and to rule over all nations and language groups throughout the world. [8]And all mankind—whose names were not written down before the founding of the world in the slain Lamb's Book of Life[e]—worshiped the evil Creature.

[9]Anyone who can hear, listen carefully: [10]The people of God who are destined for prison will be arrested and taken away; those destined for death will be killed.[f] But do not be dismayed, for here is your opportunity for endurance and confidence.

[11]Then I saw another strange animal, this one coming up out of the earth, with two little horns like those of a lamb but a fearsome voice like the Dragon's. [12]He exercised all the authority of the Creature whose death-wound had been healed, whom he required all the world to worship. [13]He did unbelievable miracles such as making fire flame down to earth from the skies while everyone was watching. [14]By doing these miracles, he was deceiving people everywhere. He could do these marvelous things whenever the first Creature was there to watch him. And he ordered the people of the world to make a great statue of the first Creature, who was fatally wounded and then came back to life. [15]He was permitted to give breath to this statue and even make it speak! Then the statue ordered that anyone refusing to worship it must die!

[16]He required everyone—great and small, rich and poor, slave and free—to be tattooed with a certain mark on the right hand or on the forehead. [17]And no one could get a job or even buy in any store without the permit of that mark, which was either the name of the Creature or the code number of his name. [18]Here is a puzzle that calls for careful thought to solve it. Let those who are able, interpret this code: the numerical values of the letters in his name add to 666![g]

14 THEN I saw a Lamb standing on Mount Zion in Jerusalem, and with him were 144,000 who had his Name and his Father's Name written on their foreheads. [2]And I heard a sound from heaven like the

New Revised Standard

13 AND I saw a beast rising out of the sea, having ten horns and seven heads; and on its horns were ten diadems, and on its heads were blasphemous names. [2]And the beast that I saw was like a leopard, its feet were like a bear's, and its mouth was like a lion's mouth. And the dragon gave it his power and his throne and great authority. [3]One of its heads seemed to have received a death-blow, but its mortal wound[h] had been healed. In amazement the whole earth followed the beast. [4]They worshiped the dragon, for he had given his authority to the beast, and they worshiped the beast, saying, "Who is like the beast, and who can fight against it?"

[5] The beast was given a mouth uttering haughty and blasphemous words, and it was allowed to exercise authority for forty-two months. [6]It opened its mouth to utter blasphemies against God, blaspheming his name and his dwelling, that is, those who dwell in heaven. [7]Also it was allowed to make war on the saints and to conquer them.[i] It was given authority over every tribe and people and language and nation, [8]and all the inhabitants of the earth will worship it, everyone whose name has not been written from the foundation of the world in the book of life of the Lamb that was slaughtered.[j]

[9] Let anyone who has an ear listen:

[10] If you are to be taken captive,
       into captivity you go;
   if you kill with the sword,
       with the sword you must be killed.

Here is a call for the endurance and faith of the saints.

The Second Beast

[11] Then I saw another beast that rose out of the earth; it had two horns like a lamb and it spoke like a dragon. [12]It exercises all the authority of the first beast on its behalf, and it makes the earth and its inhabitants worship the first beast, whose mortal wound[k] had been healed. [13]It performs great signs, even making fire come down from heaven to earth in the sight of all; [14]and by the signs that it is allowed to perform on behalf of the beast, it deceives the inhabitants of earth, telling them to make an image for the beast that had been wounded by the sword[l] and yet lived; [15]and it was allowed to give breath[m] to the image of the beast so that the image of the beast could even speak and cause those who would not worship the image of the beast to be killed. [16]Also it causes all, both small and great, both rich and poor, both free and slave, to be marked on the right hand or the forehead, [17]so that no one can buy or sell who does not have the mark, that is, the name of the beast or the number of its name. [18]This calls for wisdom: let anyone with understanding calculate the number of the beast, for it is the number of a person. Its number is six hundred sixty-six.[n]

The Lamb and the 144,000

14 THEN I looked, and there was the Lamb, standing on Mount Zion! And with him were one hundred forty-four thousand who had his name and his Father's name written on their foreheads. [2]And I heard

---

[d] *13:7 The Dragon gave him power to fight against God's people*, literally, "It was permitted to fight against God's people." [e] *13:8 whose names were not written down before the founding of the world in the slain Lamb's Book of Life*, or "those whose names were not written in the Book of Life of the Lamb slain before the founding of the world." That is, regarded as slain in the eternal plan and knowledge of God. [f] *13:10 those destined for death will be killed*, or, "If anyone imprisons you, he will be imprisoned! If anyone kills you, he will be killed." [g] *13:18 666*, some manuscripts read "616."

[h] Gk *the plague of its death* [i] Other ancient authorities lack this sentence [j] Or *written in the book of life of the Lamb that was slaughtered from the foundation of the world* [k] Gk *whose plague of its death* [l] Or *that had received the plague of the sword* [m] Or *spirit* [n] Other ancient authorities read *six hundred sixteen*

King James

2And I heard a voice from heaven, as the voice of many waters, and as the voice of a great thunder: and I heard the voice of harpers harping with their harps:

3And they sung as it were a new song before the throne, and before the four beasts, and the elders: and no man could learn that song but the hundred *and* forty *and* four thousand, which were redeemed from the earth.

4These are they which were not defiled with women; for they are virgins. These are they which follow the Lamb whithersoever he goeth. These were redeemed from among men, *being* the firstfruits unto God and to the Lamb.

5And in their mouth was found no guile: for they are without fault before the throne of God.

6And I saw another angel fly in the midst of heaven, having the everlasting gospel to preach unto them that dwell on the earth, and to every nation, and kindred, and tongue, and people,

7Saying with a loud voice, Fear God, and give glory to him; for the hour of his judgment is come: and worship him that made heaven, and earth, and the sea, and the fountains of waters.

8And there followed another angel, saying, Babylon is fallen, is fallen, that great city, because she made all nations drink of the wine of the wrath of her fornication.

9And the third angel followed them, saying with a loud voice, If any man worship the beast and his image, and receive *his* mark in his forehead, or in his hand,

10The same shall drink of the wine of the wrath of God, which is poured out without mixture into the cup of his indignation; and he shall be tormented with fire and brimstone in the presence of the holy angels, and in the presence of the Lamb:

11And the smoke of their torment ascendeth up for ever and ever: and they have no rest day nor night, who worship the beast and his image, and whosoever receiveth the mark of his name.

12Here is the patience of the saints: here *are* they that keep the commandments of God, and the faith of Jesus.

13And I heard a voice from heaven saying unto me, Write, Blessed *are* the dead which die in the Lord from henceforth: Yea, saith the Spirit, that they may rest from their labours; and their works do follow them.

14And I looked, and behold a white cloud, and upon the cloud *one* sat like unto the Son of man, having on his head a golden crown, and in his hand a sharp sickle.

15And another angel came out of the temple, crying with a loud voice to him that sat on the cloud, Thrust in thy sickle, and reap: for the time is come for thee to reap; for the harvest of the earth is ripe.

16And he that sat on the cloud thrust in his sickle on the earth; and the earth was reaped.

17And another angel came out of the temple which is in heaven, he also having a sharp sickle.

18And another angel came out from the altar, which had power over fire; and cried with a loud cry to him that had the sharp sickle, saying, Thrust in thy sharp sickle, and gather the clusters of the vine of the earth; for her grapes are fully ripe.

19And the angel thrust in his sickle into the earth, and gathered the vine of the earth, and cast *it* into the great winepress of the wrath of God.

20And the winepress was trodden without the city, and blood came out of the winepress, even unto the horse bridles, by the space of a thousand *and* six hundred furlongs.

New International

en like the roar of rushing waters and like a loud peal of thunder. The sound I heard was like that of harpists playing their harps. 3And they sang a new song before the throne and before the four living creatures and the elders. No one could learn the song except the 144,000 who had been redeemed from the earth. 4These are those who did not defile themselves with women, for they kept themselves pure. They follow the Lamb wherever he goes. They were purchased from among men and offered as firstfruits to God and the Lamb. 5No lie was found in their mouths; they are blameless.

The Three Angels

6Then I saw another angel flying in midair, and he had the eternal gospel to proclaim to those who live on the earth—to every nation, tribe, language and people. 7He said in a loud voice, "Fear God and give him glory, because the hour of his judgment has come. Worship him who made the heavens, the earth, the sea and the springs of water."

8A second angel followed and said, "Fallen! Fallen is Babylon the Great, which made all the nations drink the maddening wine of her adulteries."

9A third angel followed them and said in a loud voice: "If anyone worships the beast and his image and receives his mark on the forehead or on the hand, 10he, too, will drink of the wine of God's fury, which has been poured full strength into the cup of his wrath. He will be tormented with burning sulfur in the presence of the holy angels and of the Lamb. 11And the smoke of their torment rises for ever and ever. There is no rest day or night for those who worship the beast and his image, or for anyone who receives the mark of his name." 12This calls for patient endurance on the part of the saints who obey God's commandments and remain faithful to Jesus.

13Then I heard a voice from heaven say, "Write: Blessed are the dead who die in the Lord from now on."

"Yes," says the Spirit, "they will rest from their labor, for their deeds will follow them."

The Harvest of the Earth

14I looked, and there before me was a white cloud, and seated on the cloud was one "like a son of man"a with a crown of gold on his head and a sharp sickle in his hand. 15Then another angel came out of the temple and called in a loud voice to him who was sitting on the cloud, "Take your sickle and reap, because the time to reap has come, for the harvest of the earth is ripe." 16So he who was seated on the cloud swung his sickle over the earth, and the earth was harvested.

17Another angel came out of the temple in heaven, and he too had a sharp sickle. 18Still another angel, who had charge of the fire, came from the altar and called in a loud voice to him who had the sharp sickle, "Take your sharp sickle and gather the clusters of grapes from the earth's vine, because its grapes are ripe." 19The angel swung his sickle on the earth, gathered its grapes and threw them into the great winepress of God's wrath. 20They were trampled in the winepress outside the city, and blood flowed out of the press, rising as high as the horses' bridles for a distance of 1,600 stadia.b

a *14* Daniel 7:13   b *20* That is, about 180 miles (about 300 kilometers)

Living Bible

roaring of a great waterfall or the rolling of mighty thunder. It was the singing of a choir accompanied by harps.

3This tremendous choir—144,000 strong—sang a wonderful new song in front of the throne of God and before the four Living Beings and the twenty-four Elders; and no one could sing this song except those 144,000 who had been redeemed from the earth. 4For they are spiritually undefiled, pure as virgins,c following the Lamb wherever he goes. They have been purchased from among the men on the earth as a consecrated offering to God and the Lamb. 5No falsehood can be charged against them; they are blameless.

6And I saw another angel flying through the heavens, carrying the everlasting Good News to preach to those on earth—to every nation, tribe, language and people.

7"Fear God," he shouted, "and extol his greatness. For the time has come when he will sit as Judge. Worship him who made the heaven and the earth, the sea and all its sources."

8Then another angel followed him through the skies, saying, "Babylon is fallen, is fallen—that great city—because she seduced the nations of the world and made them share the wine of her intense impurity and sin."

9Then a third angel followed them shouting, "Anyone worshiping the Creature from the sead and his statue and accepting his mark on the forehead or the hand, 10must drink the wine of the anger of God; it is poured out undiluted into God's cup of wrath. And they will be tormented with fire and burning sulphur in the presence of the holy angels and the Lamb. 11The smoke of their torture rises forever and ever, and they will have no relief day or night, for they have worshiped the Creature and his statue, and have been tattooed with the code of his name. 12Let this encourage God's people to endure patiently every trial and persecution, for they are his saints who remain firm to the end in obedience to his commands and trust in Jesus."

13And I heard a voice in the heavens above me saying, "Write this down: At last the time has come for his martyrse to enter into their full reward. Yes, says the Spirit, they are blest indeed, for now they shall rest from all their toils and trials; for their good deeds follow them to heaven!" 14Then the scene changed and I saw a white cloud, and someone sitting on it who looked like Jesus, who was called "The Son of Man,"f with a crown of solid gold upon his head and a sharp sickle in his hand.

15Then an angel came from the temple and called out to him, "Begin to use the sickle, for the time has come for you to reap; the harvest is ripe on the earth." 16So the one sitting on the cloud swung his sickle over the earth, and the harvest was gathered in. 17After that another angel came from the temple in heaven, and he also had a sharp sickle.

18Just then the angel who has power to destroy the world with fire,g shouted to the angel with the sickle, "Use your sickle now to cut off the clusters of grapes from the vines of the earth, for they are fully ripe for judgment." 19So the angel swung his sickle on the earth and loaded the grapes into the great winepress of God's wrath. 20And the grapes were trodden in the winepress outside the city, and blood flowed out in a stream 200 miles long and as high as a horse's bridle.

c 14:4 For they are spiritually undefiled, pure as virgins, literally, "They have not defiled themselves with women, for they are virgins." d 14:9 anyone worshiping the Creature from the sea, implied. e 14:13 his martyrs, literally, "those who die in the faith of Jesus." Vs 12 implies death from persecution for Christ's sake. f 14:14 "The Son of Man," literally, "one like a Son of Man." g 14:18 who has power to destroy the world with fire, literally, "who has power over fire."

New Revised Standard

a voice from heaven like the sound of many waters and like the sound of loud thunder; the voice I heard was like the sound of harpists playing on their harps, 3and they sing a new song before the throne and before the four living creatures and before the elders. No one could learn that song except the one hundred forty-four thousand who have been redeemed from the earth. 4It is these who have not defiled themselves with women, for they are virgins; these follow the Lamb wherever he goes. They have been redeemed from humankind as first fruits for God and the Lamb, 5and in their mouth no lie was found; they are blameless.

The Messages of the Three Angels

6 Then I saw another angel flying in midheaven, with an eternal gospel to proclaim to those who liveh on the earth—to every nation and tribe and language and people. 7He said in a loud voice, "Fear God and give him glory, for the hour of his judgment has come; and worship him who made heaven and earth, the sea and the springs of water."

8 Then another angel, a second, followed, saying, "Fallen, fallen is Babylon the great! She has made all nations drink of the wine of the wrath of her fornication."

9 Then another angel, a third, followed them, crying with a loud voice, "Those who worship the beast and its image, and receive a mark on their foreheads or on their hands, 10they will also drink the wine of God's wrath, poured unmixed into the cup of his anger, and they will be tormented with fire and sulfur in the presence of the holy angels and in the presence of the Lamb. 11And the smoke of their torment goes up forever and ever. There is no rest day or night for those who worship the beast and its image and for anyone who receives the mark of its name."

12 Here is a call for the endurance of the saints, those who keep the commandments of God and hold fast to the faith ofi Jesus.

13 And I heard a voice from heaven saying, "Write this: Blessed are the dead who from now on die in the Lord." "Yes," says the Spirit, "they will rest from their labors, for their deeds follow them."

Reaping the Earth's Harvest

14 Then I looked, and there was a white cloud, and seated on the cloud was one like the Son of Man, with a golden crown on his head, and a sharp sickle in his hand! 15Another angel came out of the temple, calling with a loud voice to the one who sat on the cloud, "Use your sickle and reap, for the hour to reap has come, because the harvest of the earth is fully ripe." 16So the one who sat on the cloud swung his sickle over the earth, and the earth was reaped.

17 Then another angel came out of the temple in heaven, and he too had a sharp sickle. 18Then another angel came out from the altar, the angel who has authority over fire, and he called with a loud voice to him who had the sharp sickle, "Use your sharp sickle and gather the clusters of the vine of the earth, for its grapes are ripe." 19So the angel swung his sickle over the earth and gathered the vintage of the earth, and he threw it into the great wine press of the wrath of God. 20And the wine press was trodden outside the city, and blood flowed from the wine press, as high as a horse's bridle, for a distance of about two hundred miles.j

h Gk sit i Or to their faith in j Gk one thousand six hundred stadia

King James

15 AND I saw another sign in heaven, great and marvellous, seven angels having the seven last plagues; for in them is filled up the wrath of God.

2And I saw as it were a sea of glass mingled with fire: and them that had gotten the victory over the beast, and over his image, and over his mark, *and* over the number of his name, stand on the sea of glass, having the harps of God.

3And they sing the song of Moses the servant of God, and the song of the Lamb, saying, Great and marvellous *are* thy works, Lord God Almighty; just and true *are* thy ways, thou King of saints.

4Who shall not fear thee, O Lord, and glorify thy name? for *thou* only *art* holy: for all nations shall come and worship before thee; for thy judgments are made manifest.

5And after that I looked, and, behold, the temple of the tabernacle of the testimony in heaven was opened:

6And the seven angels came out of the temple, having the seven plagues, clothed in pure and white linen, and having their breasts girded with golden girdles.

7And one of the four beasts gave unto the seven angels seven golden vials full of the wrath of God, who liveth for ever and ever.

8And the temple was filled with smoke from the glory of God, and from his power; and no man was able to enter into the temple, till the seven plagues of the seven angels were fulfilled.

16 AND I heard a great voice out of the temple saying to the seven angels, Go your ways, and pour out the vials of the wrath of God upon the earth.

2And the first went, and poured out his vial upon the earth; and there fell a noisome and grievous sore upon the men which had the mark of the beast, and *upon* them which worshipped his image.

3And the second angel poured out his vial upon the sea; and it became as the blood of a dead *man:* and every living soul died in the sea.

4And the third angel poured out his vial upon the rivers and fountains of waters; and they became blood.

5And I heard the angel of the waters say, Thou art righteous, O Lord, which art, and wast, and shalt be, because thou hast judged thus.

6For they have shed the blood of saints and prophets, and thou hast given them blood to drink; for they are worthy.

7And I heard another out of the altar say, Even so, Lord God Almighty, true and righteous *are* thy judgments.

8And the fourth angel poured out his vial upon the sun; and power was given unto him to scorch men with fire.

9And men were scorched with great heat, and blasphemed the name of God, which hath power over these plagues: and they repented not to give him glory.

10And the fifth angel poured out his vial upon the seat of the beast; and his kingdom was full of darkness; and they gnawed their tongues for pain,

New International

Seven Angels With Seven Plagues

15 I SAW in heaven another great and marvelous sign: seven angels with the seven last plagues—last, because with them God's wrath is completed. 2And I saw what looked like a sea of glass mixed with fire and, standing beside the sea, those who had been victorious over the beast and his image and over the number of his name. They held harps given them by God 3and sang the song of Moses the servant of God and the song of the Lamb:

"Great and marvelous are your deeds,
　　Lord God Almighty.
Just and true are your ways,
　　King of the ages.
4Who will not fear you, O Lord,
　　and bring glory to your name?
For you alone are holy.
All nations will come
　　and worship before you,
for your righteous acts have been revealed."

5After this I looked and in heaven the temple, that is, the tabernacle of the Testimony, was opened. 6Out of the temple came the seven angels with the seven plagues. They were dressed in clean, shining linen and wore golden sashes around their chests. 7Then one of the four living creatures gave to the seven angels seven golden bowls filled with the wrath of God, who lives for ever and ever. 8And the temple was filled with smoke from the glory of God and from his power, and no one could enter the temple until the seven plagues of the seven angels were completed.

The Seven Bowls of God's Wrath

16 THEN I heard a loud voice from the temple saying to the seven angels, "Go, pour out the seven bowls of God's wrath on the earth."

2The first angel went and poured out his bowl on the land, and ugly and painful sores broke out on the people who had the mark of the beast and worshiped his image.

3The second angel poured out his bowl on the sea, and it turned into blood like that of a dead man, and every living thing in the sea died.

4The third angel poured out his bowl on the rivers and springs of water, and they became blood. 5Then I heard the angel in charge of the waters say:

"You are just in these judgments,
　　you who are and who were, the Holy One,
　　because you have so judged;
6for they have shed the blood of your saints and
　　prophets,
　　and you have given them blood to drink as
　　they deserve."

7And I heard the altar respond:

"Yes, Lord God Almighty,
　　true and just are your judgments."

8The fourth angel poured out his bowl on the sun, and the sun was given power to scorch people with fire. 9They were seared by the intense heat and they cursed the name of God, who had control over these plagues, but they refused to repent and glorify him.

10The fifth angel poured out his bowl on the throne of the beast, and his kingdom was plunged into darkness. Men gnawed their tongues in agony 11and cursed

Living Bible

15 AND I saw in heaven another mighty pageant showing things to come: Seven angels were assigned to carry down to earth the seven last plagues—and then at last God's anger will be finished.

[2]Spread out before me was what seemed to be an ocean of fire and glass, and on it stood all those who had been victorious over the Evil Creature and his statue and his mark and number. All were holding harps of God, [3, 4]and they were singing the song of Moses, the servant of God, and the song of the Lamb:

"Great and marvelous
Are your doings,
Lord God Almighty.
Just and true
Are your ways,
O King of Ages.[a]
Who shall not fear,
O Lord,
And glorify your Name?
For you alone are holy.
All nations will come
And worship before you,
For your righteous deeds
Have been disclosed."

[5]Then I looked and saw that the Holy of Holies of the temple in heaven was thrown wide open!

[6]The seven angels who were assigned to pour out the seven plagues then came from the temple, clothed in spotlessly white linen, with golden belts across their chests. [7]And one of the four Living Beings handed each of them a golden flask filled with the terrible wrath of the Living God who lives forever and forever. [8]The temple was filled with smoke from his glory and power; and no one could enter until the seven angels had completed pouring out the seven plagues.

16 AND I heard a mighty voice shouting from the temple to the seven angels, "Now go your ways and empty out the seven flasks of the wrath of God upon the earth."

[2]So the first angel left the temple and poured out his flask over the earth, and horrible, malignant sores broke out on everyone who had the mark of the Creature and was worshiping his statue.

[3]The second angel poured out his flask upon the oceans, and they became like the watery blood of a dead man; and everything in all the oceans died.

[4]The third angel poured out his flask upon the rivers and springs and they became blood. [5]And I heard this angel of the waters declaring, "You are just in sending this judgment, O Holy One, who is and was, [6]for your saints and prophets have been martyred and their blood poured out upon the earth; and now, in turn, you have poured out the blood of those who murdered them; it is their just reward."

[7]And I heard the angel of the altar say,[b] "Yes, Lord God Almighty, your punishments are just and true."

[8]Then the fourth angel poured out his flask upon the sun, causing it to scorch all men with its fire. [9]Everyone was burned by this blast of heat, and they cursed the name of God who sent the plagues—they did not change their mind and attitude to give him glory.

[10]Then the fifth angel poured out his flask upon the throne of the Creature from the sea,[c] and his kingdom was plunged into darkness. And his subjects gnawed their tongues in anguish, [11]and cursed the God of heaven

New Revised Standard

The Angels with the Seven Last Plagues

15 THEN I saw another portent in heaven, great and amazing: seven angels with seven plagues, which are the last, for with them the wrath of God is ended.

2 And I saw what appeared to be a sea of glass mixed with fire, and those who had conquered the beast and its image and the number of its name, standing beside the sea of glass with harps of God in their hands. [3]And they sing the song of Moses, the servant[d] of God, and the song of the Lamb:

"Great and amazing are your deeds,
Lord God the Almighty!
Just and true are your ways,
King of the nations![e]
4 Lord, who will not fear
and glorify your name?
For you alone are holy.
All nations will come
and worship before you,
for your judgments have been revealed."

5 After this I looked, and the temple of the tent[f] of witness in heaven was opened, [6]and out of the temple came the seven angels with the seven plagues, robed in pure bright linen,[g] with golden sashes across their chests. [7]Then one of the four living creatures gave the seven angels seven golden bowls full of the wrath of God, who lives forever and ever; [8]and the temple was filled with smoke from the glory of God and from his power, and no one could enter the temple until the seven plagues of the seven angels were ended.

The Bowls of God's Wrath

16 THEN I heard a loud voice from the temple telling the seven angels, "Go and pour out on the earth the seven bowls of the wrath of God."

2 So the first angel went and poured his bowl on the earth, and a foul and painful sore came on those who had the mark of the beast and who worshiped its image.

3 The second angel poured his bowl into the sea, and it became like the blood of a corpse, and every living thing in the sea died.

4 The third angel poured his bowl into the rivers and the springs of water, and they became blood. [5]And I heard the angel of the waters say,

"You are just, O Holy One, who are and were,
for you have judged these things;
6 because they shed the blood of saints and prophets,
you have given them blood to drink.
It is what they deserve!"

[7]And I heard the altar respond,

"Yes, O Lord God, the Almighty,
your judgments are true and just!"

8 The fourth angel poured his bowl on the sun, and it was allowed to scorch them with fire; [9]they were scorched by the fierce heat, but they cursed the name of God, who had authority over these plagues, and they did not repent and give him glory.

10 The fifth angel poured his bowl on the throne of the beast, and its kingdom was plunged into darkness; people gnawed their tongues in agony, [11]and cursed the

---

[a] 15:3, 4 O King of Ages. Some manuscripts read, "King of the Nations."
[b] 16:7 I heard the angel of the altar say, literally, "I heard the altar cry. . . ."
[c] 16:10 the Creature from the sea, implied.

[d] Gk slave   [e] Other ancient authorities read the ages   [f] Or tabernacle
[g] Other ancient authorities read stone

King James

[11]And blasphemed the God of heaven because of their pains and their sores, and repented not of their deeds.

[12]And the sixth angel poured out his vial upon the great river Euphrates; and the water thereof was dried up, that the way of the kings of the east might be prepared.

[13]And I saw three unclean spirits like frogs *come* out of the mouth of the dragon, and out of the mouth of the beast, and out of the mouth of the false prophet.

[14]For they are the spirits of devils, working miracles, *which* go forth unto the kings of the earth and of the whole world, to gather them to the battle of that great day of God Almighty.

[15]Behold, I come as a thief. Blessed *is* he that watcheth, and keepeth his garments, lest he walk naked, and they see his shame.

[16]And he gathered them together into a place called in the Hebrew tongue Armageddon.

[17]And the seventh angel poured out his vial into the air; and there came a great voice out of the temple of heaven, from the throne, saying, It is done.

[18]And there were voices, and thunders, and lightnings; and there was a great earthquake, such as was not since men were upon the earth, so mighty an earthquake, *and* so great.

[19]And the great city was divided into three parts, and the cities of the nations fell: and great Babylon came in remembrance before God, to give unto her the cup of the wine of the fierceness of his wrath.

[20]And every island fled away, and the mountains were not found.

[21]And there fell upon men a great hail out of heaven, *every stone* about the weight of a talent: and men blasphemed God because of the plague of the hail; for the plague thereof was exceeding great.

17 AND THERE came one of the seven angels which had the seven vials, and talked with me, saying unto me, Come hither; I will show unto thee the judgment of the great whore that sitteth upon many waters:

[2]With whom the kings of the earth have committed fornication, and the inhabitants of the earth have been made drunk with the wine of her fornication.

[3]So he carried me away in the spirit into the wilderness: and I saw a woman sit upon a scarlet coloured beast, full of names of blasphemy, having seven heads and ten horns.

[4]And the woman was arrayed in purple and scarlet colour, and decked with gold and precious stones and pearls, having a golden cup in her hand full of abominations and filthiness of her fornication:

[5]And upon her forehead *was* a name written, MYSTERY, BABYLON THE GREAT, THE MOTHER OF HARLOTS AND ABOMINATIONS OF THE EARTH.

[6]And I saw the woman drunken with the blood of the saints, and with the blood of the martyrs of Jesus: and when I saw her, I wondered with great admiration.

[7]And the angel said unto me, Wherefore didst thou marvel? I will tell thee the mystery of the woman, and of the beast that carrieth her, which hath the seven heads and ten horns.

New International

the God of heaven because of their pains and their sores, but they refused to repent of what they had done.

[12]The sixth angel poured out his bowl on the great river Euphrates, and its water was dried up to prepare the way for the kings from the East. [13]Then I saw three evil[a] spirits that looked like frogs; they came out of the mouth of the dragon, out of the mouth of the beast and out of the mouth of the false prophet. [14]They are spirits of demons performing miraculous signs, and they go out to the kings of the whole world, to gather them for the battle on the great day of God Almighty.

[15]"Behold, I come like a thief! Blessed is he who stays awake and keeps his clothes with him, so that he may not go naked and be shamefully exposed."

[16]Then they gathered the kings together to the place that in Hebrew is called Armageddon.

[17]The seventh angel poured out his bowl into the air, and out of the temple came a loud voice from the throne, saying, "It is done!" [18]Then there came flashes of lightning, rumblings, peals of thunder and a severe earthquake. No earthquake like it has ever occurred since man has been on earth, so tremendous was the quake. [19]The great city split into three parts, and the cities of the nations collapsed. God remembered Babylon the Great and gave her the cup filled with the wine of the fury of his wrath. [20]Every island fled away and the mountains could not be found. [21]From the sky huge hailstones of about a hundred pounds each fell upon men. And they cursed God on account of the plague of hail, because the plague was so terrible.

The Woman on the Beast

17 ONE OF the seven angels who had the seven bowls came and said to me, "Come, I will show you the punishment of the great prostitute, who sits on many waters. [2]With her the kings of the earth committed adultery and the inhabitants of the earth were intoxicated with the wine of her adulteries."

[3]Then the angel carried me away in the Spirit into a desert. There I saw a woman sitting on a scarlet beast that was covered with blasphemous names and had seven heads and ten horns. [4]The woman was dressed in purple and scarlet, and was glittering with gold, precious stones and pearls. She held a golden cup in her hand, filled with abominable things and the filth of her adulteries. [5]This title was written on her forehead:

MYSTERY
BABYLON THE GREAT
THE MOTHER OF PROSTITUTES
AND OF THE ABOMINATIONS OF THE EARTH.

[6]I saw that the woman was drunk with the blood of the saints, the blood of those who bore testimony to Jesus.

When I saw her, I was greatly astonished. [7]Then the angel said to me: "Why are you astonished? I will explain to you the mystery of the woman and of the beast she rides, which has the seven heads and ten horns. [8]The

Living Bible

for their pains and sores, but they refused to repent of all their evil deeds.

12The sixth angel poured out his flask upon the great River Euphrates and it dried up so that the kings from the east could march their armies westward without hindrance. 13And I saw three evil spirits disguised as frogs leap from the mouth of the Dragon, the Creature, and his False Prophet.b 14These miracle-working demons conferred with all the rulers of the world to gather them for battle against the Lord on that great coming Judgment Day of God Almighty.

15"Take note: I will come as unexpectedly as a thief! Blessed are all who are awaiting me, who keep their robes in readiness and will not need to walk naked and ashamed."

16And they gathered all the armies of the world near a place called, in Hebrew, Armageddon—the Mountain of Megiddo.

17Then the seventh angel poured out his flask into the air; and a mighty shout came from the throne of the temple in heaven, saying, "It is finished!"c 18Then the thunder crashed and rolled, and lightning flashed; and there was a great earthquake of a magnitude unprecedented in human history. 19The great city of "Babylon" split into three sections, and cities around the world fell in heaps of rubble; and so all of "Babylon's" sins were remembered in God's thoughts, and she was punished to the last drop of anger in the cup of the wine of the fierceness of his wrath. 20And islands vanished, and mountains flattened out, 21and there was an incredible hailstorm from heaven; hailstones weighing a hundred pounds fell from the sky onto the people below, and they cursed God because of the terrible hail.

17 ONE OF the seven angels who had poured out the plagues came over and talked with me. "Come with me," he said, "and I will show you what is going to happen to the Notorious Prostitute, who sits upon the many waters of the world. 2The kings of the world have had immoral relations with her, and the people of the earth have been made drunk by the wine of her immorality."

3So the angel took me in spirit into the wilderness. There I saw a woman sitting on a scarlet animal that had seven heads and ten horns,d written all over with blasphemies against God. 4The woman wore purple and scarlet clothing and beautiful jewelry made of gold and precious gems and pearls, and held in her hand a golden goblet full of obscenities:

5A mysterious caption was written on her forehead: "Babylon the Great, Mother of Prostitutes and of Idol Worship Everywhere around the World."

6I could see that she was drunk—drunk with the blood of the martyrs of Jesus she had killed. I stared at her in horror.

7"Why are you so surprised?" the angel asked. "I'll tell you who she is and what the animal she is riding represents. 8He was alive but isn't now. And yet, soon

New Revised Standard

God of heaven because of their pains and sores, and they did not repent of their deeds.

12 The sixth angel poured his bowl on the great river Euphrates, and its water was dried up in order to prepare the way for the kings from the east. 13And I saw three foul spirits like frogs coming from the mouth of the dragon, from the mouth of the beast, and from the mouth of the false prophet. 14These are demonic spirits, performing signs, who go abroad to the kings of the whole world, to assemble them for battle on the great day of God the Almighty. 15("See, I am coming like a thief! Blessed is the one who stays awake and is clothed,e not going about naked and exposed to shame.") 16And they assembled them at the place that in Hebrew is called Harmagedon.

17 The seventh angel poured his bowl into the air, and a loud voice came out of the temple, from the throne, saying, "It is done!" 18And there came flashes of lightning, rumblings, peals of thunder, and a violent earthquake, such as had not occurred since people were upon the earth, so violent was that earthquake. 19The great city was split into three parts, and the cities of the nations fell. God remembered great Babylon and gave her the wine-cup of the fury of his wrath. 20And every island fled away, and no mountains were to be found; 21and huge hailstones, each weighing about a hundred pounds,f dropped from heaven on people, until they cursed God for the plague of the hail, so fearful was that plague.

The Great Whore and the Beast

17 THEN ONE of the seven angels who had the seven bowls came and said to me, "Come, I will show you the judgment of the great whore who is seated on many waters, 2with whom the kings of the earth have committed fornication, and with the wine of whose fornication the inhabitants of the earth have become drunk." 3So he carried me away in the spiritg into a wilderness, and I saw a woman sitting on a scarlet beast that was full of blasphemous names, and it had seven heads and ten horns. 4The woman was clothed in purple and scarlet, and adorned with gold and jewels and pearls, holding in her hand a golden cup full of abominations and the impurities of her fornication; 5and on her forehead was written a name, a mystery: "Babylon the great, mother of whores and of earth's abominations." 6And I saw that the woman was drunk with the blood of the saints and the blood of the witnesses to Jesus.

When I saw her, I was greatly amazed. 7But the angel said to me, "Why are you so amazed? I will tell you the mystery of the woman, and of the beast with seven heads and ten horns that carries her. 8The beast that you saw

---

b *16:13 his False Prophet*, described in 13:11-15 and 19:20.   c *16:17 It is finished*, literally, "It has happened." An epoch of human history has come to an end.   d *17:3 a scarlet animal that had seven heads and ten horns.* The Dragon—Satan—and the Creature from the sea are also described in 12:3, 9 and 13:1.

e *Gk and keeps his robes*   f *Gk weighing about a talent*   g *Or in the Spirit*

King James

8The beast that thou sawest was, and is not; and shall ascend out of the bottomless pit, and go into perdition: and they that dwell on the earth shall wonder, whose names were not written in the book of life from the foundation of the world, when they behold the beast that was, and is not, and yet is.

9And here *is* the mind which hath wisdom. The seven heads are seven mountains, on which the woman sitteth.

10And there are seven kings: five are fallen, and one is, *and* the other is not yet come; and when he cometh, he must continue a short space.

11And the beast that was, and is not, even he is the eighth, and is of the seven, and goeth into perdition.

12And the ten horns which thou sawest are ten kings, which have received no kingdom as yet; but receive power as kings one hour with the beast.

13These have one mind, and shall give their power and strength unto the beast.

14These shall make war with the Lamb, and the Lamb shall overcome them: for he is Lord of lords, and King of kings: and they that are with him *are* called, and chosen, and faithful.

15And he saith unto me, The waters which thou sawest, where the whore sitteth, are peoples, and multitudes, and nations, and tongues.

16And the ten horns which thou sawest upon the beast, these shall hate the whore, and shall make her desolate and naked, and shall eat her flesh, and burn her with fire.

17For God hath put in their hearts to fulfil his will, and to agree, and give their kingdom unto the beast, until the words of God shall be fulfilled.

18And the woman which thou sawest is that great city, which reigneth over the kings of the earth.

18 AND AFTER these things I saw another angel come down from heaven, having great power; and the earth was lightened with his glory.

2And he cried mightily with a strong voice, saying, Babylon the great is fallen, is fallen, and is become the habitation of devils, and the hold of every foul spirit, and a cage of every unclean and hateful bird.

3For all nations have drunk of the wine of the wrath of her fornication, and the kings of the earth have committed fornication with her, and the merchants of the earth are waxed rich through the abundance of her delicacies.

4And I heard another voice from heaven, saying, Come out of her, my people, that ye be not partakers of her sins, and that ye receive not of her plagues.

5For her sins have reached unto heaven, and God hath remembered her iniquities.

6Reward her even as she rewarded you, and double unto her double according to her works: in the cup which she hath filled fill to her double.

7How much she hath glorified herself, and lived deliciously, so much torment and sorrow give her: for she saith in her heart, I sit a queen, and am no widow, and shall see no sorrow.

New International

beast, which you saw, once was, now is not, and will come up out of the Abyss and go to his destruction. The inhabitants of the earth whose names have not been written in the book of life from the creation of the world will be astonished when they see the beast, because he once was, now is not, and yet will come.

9"This calls for a mind with wisdom. The seven heads are seven hills on which the woman sits. 10They are also seven kings. Five have fallen, one is, the other has not yet come; but when he does come, he must remain for a little while. 11The beast who once was, and now is not, is an eighth king. He belongs to the seven and is going to his destruction.

12"The ten horns you saw are ten kings who have not yet received a kingdom, but who for one hour will receive authority as kings along with the beast. 13They have one purpose and will give their power and authority to the beast. 14They will make war against the Lamb, but the Lamb will overcome them because he is Lord of lords and King of kings—and with him will be his called, chosen and faithful followers."

15Then the angel said to me, "The waters you saw, where the prostitute sits, are peoples, multitudes, nations and languages. 16The beast and the ten horns you saw will hate the prostitute. They will bring her to ruin and leave her naked; they will eat her flesh and burn her with fire. 17For God has put it into their hearts to accomplish his purpose by agreeing to give the beast their power to rule, until God's words are fulfilled. 18The woman you saw is the great city that rules over the kings of the earth."

The Fall of Babylon

18 AFTER THIS I saw another angel coming down from heaven. He had great authority, and the earth was illuminated by his splendor. 2With a mighty voice he shouted:

"Fallen! Fallen is Babylon the Great!
　　She has become a home for demons
and a haunt for every evila spirit,
　　a haunt for every unclean and detestable bird.
3For all the nations have drunk
　　the maddening wine of her adulteries.
The kings of the earth committed adultery with
　　her,
　　and the merchants of the earth grew rich from
　　her excessive luxuries."

4Then I heard another voice from heaven say:

"Come out of her, my people,
　　so that you will not share in her sins,
　　so that you will not receive any of her
　　plagues;
5for her sins are piled up to heaven,
　　and God has remembered her crimes.
6Give back to her as she has given;
　　pay her back double for what she has done.
　　Mix her a double portion from her own cup.
7Give her as much torture and grief
　　as the glory and luxury she gave herself.
In her heart she boasts,
　　'I sit as queen; I am not a widow,
　　and I will never mourn.'

a 2 Greek *unclean*

Living Bible

he will come up out of the bottomless pit and go to eternal destruction;[b] and the people of earth, whose names have not been written in the Book of Life before the world began, will be dumbfounded at his reappearance after being dead.[c]

9"And now think hard: his seven heads represent a certain city[d] built on seven hills where this woman has her residence. 10They also represent seven kings. Five have already fallen, the sixth now reigns, and the seventh is yet to come, but his reign will be brief. 11The scarlet animal that died is the eighth king, having reigned before as one of the seven; after his second reign, he too, will go to his doom. 12His ten horns are ten kings who have not yet risen to power; they will be appointed to their kingdoms for one brief moment, to reign with him. 13They will all sign a treaty giving their power and strength to him. 14Together they will wage war against the Lamb, and the Lamb will conquer them; for he is Lord over all lords, and King of kings, and his people are the called and chosen and faithful ones.

15"The oceans, lakes and rivers that the woman is sitting on represent masses of people of every race and nation.

16"The scarlet animal and his ten horns—which represent ten kings who will reign with him—all hate the woman, and will attack her and leave her naked and ravaged by fire. 17For God will put a plan into their minds, a plan that will carry out his purposes: They will mutually agree to give their authority to the scarlet animal, so that the words of God will be fulfilled. 18And this woman you saw in your vision represents the great city that rules over the kings of the earth."

18 AFTER ALL this I saw another angel come down from heaven with great authority, and the earth grew bright with his splendor.

2He gave a mighty shout, "Babylon the Great is fallen, is fallen; she has become a den of demons, a haunt of devils and every kind of evil spirit.[e] 3For all the nations have drunk the fatal wine of her intense immorality. The rulers of earth have enjoyed themselves with her,[f] and businessmen throughout the world have grown rich from all her luxurious living."

4Then I heard another voice calling from heaven, "Come away from her, my people; do not take part in her sins, or you will be punished with her. 5For her sins are piled as high as heaven and God is ready to judge her for her crimes. 6Do to her as she has done to you, and more—give double penalty for all her evil deeds. She brewed many a cup of woe for others—give twice as much to her. 7She has lived in luxury and pleasure—match it now with torments and with sorrows. She boasts, 'I am queen upon my throne. I am no helpless widow. I will not experience sorrow.' 8Therefore the

New Revised Standard

was, and is not, and is about to ascend from the bottomless pit and go to destruction. And the inhabitants of the earth, whose names have not been written in the book of life from the foundation of the world, will be amazed when they see the beast, because it was and is not and is to come.

9 "This calls for a mind that has wisdom: the seven heads are seven mountains on which the woman is seated; also, they are seven kings, 10of whom five have fallen, one is living, and the other has not yet come; and when he comes, he must remain only a little while. 11As for the beast that was and is not, it is an eighth but it belongs to the seven, and it goes to destruction. 12And the ten horns that you saw are ten kings who have not yet received a kingdom, but they are to receive authority as kings for one hour, together with the beast. 13These are united in yielding their power and authority to the beast; 14they will make war on the Lamb, and the Lamb will conquer them, for he is Lord of lords and King of kings, and those with him are called and chosen and faithful."

15 And he said to me, "The waters that you saw, where the whore is seated, are peoples and multitudes and nations and languages. 16And the ten horns that you saw, they and the beast will hate the whore; they will make her desolate and naked; they will devour her flesh and burn her up with fire. 17For God has put it into their hearts to carry out his purpose by agreeing to give their kingdom to the beast, until the words of God will be fulfilled. 18The woman you saw is the great city that rules over the kings of the earth."

The Fall of Babylon

18 AFTER THIS I saw another angel coming down from heaven, having great authority; and the earth was made bright with his splendor. 2He called out with a mighty voice,

"Fallen, fallen is Babylon the great!
It has become a dwelling place of demons,
a haunt of every foul spirit,
a haunt of every foul bird,
a haunt of every foul and hateful beast.[g]
3 For all the nations have drunk[h]
of the wine of the wrath of her fornication,
and the kings of the earth have committed
fornication with her,
and the merchants of the earth have grown
rich from the power[i] of her luxury."

4 Then I heard another voice from heaven saying,
"Come out of her, my people,
so that you do not take part in her sins,
and so that you do not share
in her plagues;
5 for her sins are heaped high as heaven,
and God has remembered her iniquities.
6 Render to her as she herself has rendered,
and repay her double for her deeds;
mix a double draught for her in the cup she
mixed.
7 As she glorified herself and lived luxuriously,
so give her a like measure of torment and
grief.
Since in her heart she says,
'I rule as a queen;
I am no widow,
and I will never see grief,'

---

[b] *17:8 go to eternal destruction,* literally, "go to perdition."
[c] *17:8 dumbfounded at his reappearance after being dead,* literally, "dumbfounded at the ruler who was, and is not, and will be present."
[d] *17:9 represent a certain city,* implied in vs 18. [e] *18:2 of evil spirit,* literally, "of every foul and hateful bird." [f] *18:3 have enjoyed themselves with her,* literally, "have committed fornication with her."

[g] Other ancient authorities lack the words *a haunt of every foul beast* and attach the words *and hateful* to the previous line so as to read *a haunt of every foul and hateful bird* [h] Other ancient authorities read *she has made all nations drink* [i] Or *resources*

King James

8Therefore shall her plagues come in one day, death, and mourning, and famine; and she shall be utterly burned with fire: for strong *is* the Lord God who judgeth her.

9And the kings of the earth, who have committed fornication and lived deliciously with her, shall bewail her, and lament for her, when they shall see the smoke of her burning,

10Standing afar off for the fear of her torment, saying, Alas, alas, that great city Babylon, that mighty city! for in one hour is thy judgment come.

11And the merchants of the earth shall weep and mourn over her; for no man buyeth their merchandise any more:

12The merchandise of gold, and silver, and precious stones, and of pearls, and fine linen, and purple, and silk, and scarlet, and all thyine wood, and all manner vessels of ivory, and all manner vessels of most precious wood, and of brass, and iron, and marble,

13And cinnamon, and odours, and ointments, and frankincense, and wine, and oil, and fine flour, and wheat, and beasts, and sheep, and horses, and chariots, and slaves, and souls of men.

14And the fruits that thy soul lusted after are departed from thee, and all things which were dainty and goodly are departed from thee, and thou shalt find them no more at all.

15The merchants of these things, which were made rich by her, shall stand afar off for the fear of her torment, weeping and wailing,

16And saying, Alas, alas, that great city, that was clothed in fine linen, and purple, and scarlet, and decked with gold, and precious stones, and pearls!

17For in one hour so great riches is come to nought. And every shipmaster, and all the company in ships, and sailors, and as many as trade by sea, stood afar off,

18And cried when they saw the smoke of her burning, saying, What *city is* like unto this great city!

19And they cast dust on their heads, and cried, weeping and wailing, saying, Alas, alas, that great city, wherein were made rich all that had ships in the sea by reason of her costliness! for in one hour is she made desolate.

20Rejoice over her, *thou* heaven, and *ye* holy apostles and prophets; for God hath avenged you on her.

21And a mighty angel took up a stone like a great millstone, and cast *it* into the sea, saying, Thus with violence shall that great city Babylon be thrown down, and shall be found no more at all.

22And the voice of harpers, and musicians, and of pipers, and trumpeters, shall be heard no more at all in thee; and no craftsman, of whatsoever craft *he be*, shall be found any more in thee; and the sound of a millstone shall be heard no more at all in thee;

23And the light of a candle shall shine no more at all in thee; and the voice of the bridegroom and of the bride shall be heard no more at all in thee: for thy merchants were the great men of the earth; for by thy sorceries were all nations deceived.

New International

8Therefore in one day her plagues will overtake her:
    death, mourning and famine.
She will be consumed by fire,
    for mighty is the Lord God who judges her.

9"When the kings of the earth who committed adultery with her and shared her luxury see the smoke of her burning, they will weep and mourn over her. 10Terrified at her torment, they will stand far off and cry:

" 'Woe! Woe, O great city,
    O Babylon, city of power!
In one hour your doom has come!'

11"The merchants of the earth will weep and mourn over her because no one buys their cargoes any more— 12cargoes of gold, silver, precious stones and pearls; fine linen, purple, silk and scarlet cloth; every sort of citron wood, and articles of every kind made of ivory, costly wood, bronze, iron and marble; 13cargoes of cinnamon and spice, of incense, myrrh and frankincense, of wine and olive oil, of fine flour and wheat; cattle and sheep; horses and carriages; and bodies and souls of men.

14"They will say, 'The fruit you longed for is gone from you. All your riches and splendor have vanished, never to be recovered.' 15The merchants who sold these things and gained their wealth from her will stand far off, terrified at her torment. They will weep and mourn 16and cry out:

" 'Woe! Woe, O great city,
    dressed in fine linen, purple and scarlet,
    and glittering with gold, precious stones and pearls!

17In one hour such great wealth has been brought to ruin!'

"Every sea captain, and all who travel by ship, the sailors, and all who earn their living from the sea, will stand far off. 18When they see the smoke of her burning, they will exclaim, 'Was there ever a city like this great city?' 19They will throw dust on their heads, and with weeping and mourning cry out:

" 'Woe! Woe, O great city,
    where all who had ships on the sea
    became rich through her wealth!
In one hour she has been brought to ruin!
20Rejoice over her, O heaven!
    Rejoice, saints and apostles and prophets!
God has judged her for the way she treated you.' "

21Then a mighty angel picked up a boulder the size of a large millstone and threw it into the sea, and said:

"With such violence
    the great city of Babylon will be thrown down,
    never to be found again.
22The music of harpists and musicians, flute players and trumpeters,
    will never be heard in you again.
No workman of any trade
    will ever be found in you again.
The sound of a millstone
    will never be heard in you again.
23The light of a lamp
    will never shine in you again.
The voice of bridegroom and bride
    will never be heard in you again.
Your merchants were the world's great men.
    By your magic spell all the nations were led astray.

Living Bible

sorrows of death and mourning and famine shall overtake her in a single day, and she shall be utterly consumed by fire; for mighty is the Lord who judges her."

9And the world leaders, who took part in her immoral acts and enjoyed her favors, will mourn for her as they see the smoke rising from her charred remains. 10They will stand far off, trembling with fear and crying out, "Alas, Babylon, that mighty city! In one moment her judgment fell."

11The merchants of the earth will weep and mourn for her, for there is no one left to buy their goods. 12She was their biggest customer for gold and silver, precious stones, pearls, finest linens, purple silks, and scarlet; and every kind of perfumed wood, and ivory goods and most expensive wooden carvings, and brass and iron and marble; 13and spices and perfumes and incense, ointment and frankincense, wine, olive oil, and fine flour; wheat, cattle, sheep, horses, chariots, and slaves—and even the souls of men.

14"All the fancy things you loved so much are gone," they cry. "The dainty luxuries and splendor that you prized so much will never be yours again. They are gone forever."

15And so the merchants who have become wealthy by selling her these things shall stand at a distance, fearing danger to themselves, weeping and crying, 16"Alas, that great city, so beautiful—like a woman clothed in finest purple and scarlet linens, decked out with gold and precious stones and pearls! 17In one moment, all the wealth of the city is gone!"

And all the shipowners and captains of the merchant ships and crews will stand a long way off, 18crying as they watch the smoke ascend, and saying, "Where in all the world is there another city such as this?" 19And they will throw dust on their heads in their sorrow and say, "Alas, alas, for that great city! She made us all rich from her great wealth. And now in a single hour all is gone. . . ."

20But you, O heaven, rejoice over her fate; and you, O children of God and the prophets and the apostles! For at last God has given judgment against her for you.

21Then a mighty angel picked up a boulder shaped like a millstone and threw it into the ocean and shouted, "Babylon, that great city, shall be thrown away as I have thrown away this stone, and she shall disappear forever. 22Never again will the sound of music be there—no more pianos, saxophones, and trumpets.a No industry of any kind will ever again exist there, and there will be no more milling of the grain. 23Dark, dark will be her nights; not even a lamp in a window will ever be seen again. No more joyous wedding bells and happy voices of the bridegrooms and the brides. Her businessmen were known around the world and she deceived all na-

New Revised Standard

8 therefore her plagues will come in a single
   day—
      pestilence and mourning and famine—
   and she will be burned with fire;
      for mighty is the Lord God who judges
         her."

9 And the kings of the earth, who committed fornication and lived in luxury with her, will weep and wail over her when they see the smoke of her burning; 10they will stand far off, in fear of her torment, and say,
      "Alas, alas, the great city,
         Babylon, the mighty city!
   For in one hour your judgment has come."

11 And the merchants of the earth weep and mourn for her, since no one buys their cargo anymore, 12cargo of gold, silver, jewels and pearls, fine linen, purple, silk and scarlet, all kinds of scented wood, all articles of ivory, all articles of costly wood, bronze, iron, and marble, 13cinnamon, spice, incense, myrrh, frankincense, wine, olive oil, choice flour and wheat, cattle and sheep, horses and chariots, slaves—and human lives.b

14 "The fruit for which your soul longed
      has gone from you,
   and all your dainties and your splendor
      are lost to you,
      never to be found again!"

15The merchants of these wares, who gained wealth from her, will stand far off, in fear of her torment, weeping and mourning aloud,

16 "Alas, alas, the great city,
      clothed in fine linen,
         in purple and scarlet,
      adorned with gold,
         with jewels, and with pearls!
17 For in one hour all this wealth has been laid
      waste!"

And all shipmasters and seafarers, sailors and all whose trade is on the sea, stood far off 18and cried out as they saw the smoke of her burning,
      "What city was like the great city?"
19And they threw dust on their heads, as they wept and mourned, crying out,
      "Alas, alas, the great city,
         where all who had ships at sea
            grew rich by her wealth!
   For in one hour she has been laid waste.
20 Rejoice over her, O heaven,
      you saints and apostles and prophets!
   For God has given judgment for you against
         her."

21 Then a mighty angel took up a stone like a great millstone and threw it into the sea, saying,
      "With such violence Babylon the great city
         will be thrown down,
         and will be found no more;
22 and the sound of harpists and minstrels and of
            flutists and trumpeters
         will be heard in you no more;
      and an artisan of any trade
         will be found in you no more;
      and the sound of the millstone
         will be heard in you no more;
23 and the light of a lamp
         will shine in you no more;
      and the voice of bridegroom and bride
         will be heard in you no more;
   for your merchants were the magnates of the
         earth,
      and all nations were deceived by your
         sorcery.

---

a 18:22 no more pianos, saxophones, and trumpets, literally, "harpers . . . pipers . . . and trumpeters."

b Or chariots, and human bodies and souls

King James

24And in her was found the blood of prophets, and of saints, and of all that were slain upon the earth.

19 AND AFTER these things I heard a great voice of much people in heaven, saying, Alleluia; Salvation, and glory, and honour, and power, unto the Lord our God:

2For true and righteous *are* his judgments: for he hath judged the great whore, which did corrupt the earth with her fornication, and hath avenged the blood of his servants at her hand.

3And again they said, Alleluia. And her smoke rose up for ever and ever.

4And the four and twenty elders and the four beasts fell down and worshipped God that sat on the throne, saying, Amen; Alleluia.

5And a voice came out of the throne, saying, Praise our God, all ye his servants, and ye that fear him, both small and great.

6And I heard as it were the voice of a great multitude, and as the voice of many waters, and as the voice of mighty thunderings, saying, Alleluia: for the Lord God omnipotent reigneth.

7Let us be glad and rejoice, and give honour to him: for the marriage of the Lamb is come, and his wife hath made herself ready.

8And to her was granted that she should be arrayed in fine linen, clean and white: for the fine linen is the righteousness of saints.

9And he saith unto me, Write, Blessed *are* they which are called unto the marriage supper of the Lamb. And he saith unto me, These are the true sayings of God.

10And I fell at his feet to worship him. And he said unto me, See *thou do it* not: I am thy fellowservant, and of thy brethren that have the testimony of Jesus: worship God: for the testimony of Jesus is the spirit of prophecy.

11And I saw heaven opened, and behold a white horse; and he that sat upon him *was* called Faithful and True, and in righteousness he doth judge and make war.

12His eyes *were* as a flame of fire, and on his head *were* many crowns; and he had a name written, that no man knew, but he himself.

13And he *was* clothed with a vesture dipped in blood: and his name is called The Word of God.

14And the armies *which were* in heaven followed him upon white horses, clothed in fine linen, white and clean.

15And out of his mouth goeth a sharp sword, that with it he should smite the nations: and he shall rule them with a rod of iron: and he treadeth the winepress of the fierceness and wrath of Almighty God.

New International

24In her was found the blood of prophets and of the saints,
    and of all who have been killed on the earth."

Hallelujah!

19 AFTER THIS I heard what sounded like the roar of a great multitude in heaven shouting:

"Hallelujah!
Salvation and glory and power belong to our God,
2   for true and just are his judgments.
He has condemned the great prostitute
    who corrupted the earth by her adulteries.
He has avenged on her the blood of his
    servants."

3And again they shouted:

"Hallelujah!
The smoke from her goes up for ever and ever."

4The twenty-four elders and the four living creatures fell down and worshiped God, who was seated on the throne. And they cried:

"Amen, Hallelujah!"

5Then a voice came from the throne, saying:

"Praise our God,
    all you his servants,
you who fear him,
    both small and great!"

6Then I heard what sounded like a great multitude, like the roar of rushing waters and like loud peals of thunder, shouting:

"Hallelujah!
    For our Lord God Almighty reigns.
7Let us rejoice and be glad
    and give him glory!
For the wedding of the Lamb has come,
    and his bride has made herself ready.
8Fine linen, bright and clean,
    was given her to wear."

(Fine linen stands for the righteous acts of the saints.)

9Then the angel said to me, "Write: 'Blessed are those who are invited to the wedding supper of the Lamb!'" And he added, "These are the true words of God."

10At this I fell at his feet to worship him. But he said to me, "Do not do it! I am a fellow servant with you and with your brothers who hold to the testimony of Jesus. Worship God! For the testimony of Jesus is the spirit of prophecy."

The Rider on the White Horse

11I saw heaven standing open and there before me was a white horse, whose rider is called Faithful and True. With justice he judges and makes war. 12His eyes are like blazing fire, and on his head are many crowns. He has a name written on him that no one knows but he himself. 13He is dressed in a robe dipped in blood, and his name is the Word of God. 14The armies of heaven were following him, riding on white horses and dressed in fine linen, white and clean. 15Out of his mouth comes a sharp sword with which to strike down the nations. "He will rule them with an iron scepter."a He treads the winepress of the fury of the wrath of God Almighty.

a *15* Psalm 2:9

Living Bible

tions with her sorceries. 24And she was responsible for the blood of all the martyred prophets and the saints."

19 AFTER THIS I heard the shouting of a vast crowd in heaven, "Hallelujah! Praise the Lord! Salvation is from our God. Honor and authority belong to him alone; 2for his judgments are just and true. He has punished the Great Prostitute who corrupted the earth with her sin;b and he has avenged the murder of his servants."

3Again and again their voices rang, "Praise the Lord! The smoke from her burning ascends forever and forever!"

4Then the twenty-four Elders and four Living Beings fell down and worshiped God, who was sitting upon the throne, and said, "Amen! Hallelujah! Praise the Lord!"

5And out of the throne came a voice that said, "Praise our God, all you his servants, small and great, who fear him."

6Then I heard again what sounded like the shouting of a huge crowd, or like the waves of a hundred oceans crashing on the shore, or like the mighty rolling of great thunder, "Praise the Lord. For the Lord our God, the Almighty, reigns. 7Let us be glad and rejoice and honor him; for the time has come for the wedding banquet of the Lamb, and his bride has prepared herself. 8She is permitted to wear the cleanest and whitest and finest of linens." (Fine linen represents the good deeds done by the people of God.)

9And the angelc dictated this sentence to me: "Blessed are those who are invited to the wedding feast of the Lamb." And he added, "God himself has stated this."d

10Then I fell down at his feet to worship him, but he said, "No! Don't! For I am a servant of God just as you are, and as your brother Christians are, who testify of their faith in Jesus. Worship God. The purpose of all prophecy and of all I have shown you is to tell about Jesus."e

11Then I saw heaven opened and a white horse standing there; and the one sitting on the horse was named "Faithful and True"—the one who justly punishes and makes war. 12His eyes were like flames, and on his head were many crowns. A name was written on his forehead,f and only he knew its meaning. 13He was clothed with garments dipped in blood, and his title was "The Word of God."g 14The armies of heaven, dressed in finest linen, white and clean, followed him on white horses.

15In his mouth he held a sharp sword to strike down the nations; he ruled them with an iron grip; and he trod the winepress of the fierceness of the wrath of Almighty

b 19:2 sin, literally, "fornication," the word used symbolically throughout the prophets for the worship of false gods.   c 19:9 the angel, literally, "he"; the exact antecedent is unclear.   d 19:9 God himself has stated this, literally, "These are the true words of God."   e 19:10 The purpose of all prophecy and of all I have shown you is to tell about Jesus, literally, "The testimony of Jesus is the spirit of prophecy."   f 19:12 A name was written on his forehead, implied.   g 19:13 The Word of God, literally, "The Logos," as in Jn 1:1—the ultimate method of God's revealing himself to man.

New Revised Standard

24 And in youh was found the blood of prophets
       and of saints,
   and of all who have been slaughtered on
       earth."

The Rejoicing in Heaven

19 AFTER THIS I heard what seemed to be the loud voice of a great multitude in heaven, saying,
"Hallelujah!
   Salvation and glory and power to our God,
2   for his judgments are true and just;
   he has judged the great whore
     who corrupted the earth with her
         fornication,
   and he has avenged on her the blood of his
       servants."i
3Once more they said,
   "Hallelujah!
   The smoke goes up from her forever and
       ever."
4And the twenty-four elders and the four living creatures fell down and worshiped God who is seated on the throne, saying,
   "Amen. Hallelujah!"
5   And from the throne came a voice saying,
   "Praise our God,
     all you his servants,i
   and all who fear him,
     small and great."
6Then I heard what seemed to be the voice of a great multitude, like the sound of many waters and like the sound of mighty thunderpeals, crying out,
   "Hallelujah!
   For the Lord our God
     the Almighty reigns.
7   Let us rejoice and exult
     and give him the glory,
   for the marriage of the Lamb has come,
     and his bride has made herself ready;
8   to her it has been granted to be clothed
     with fine linen, bright and pure"—
for the fine linen is the righteous deeds of the saints.
9   And the angelj to me, "Write this: Blessed are those who are invited to the marriage supper of the Lamb." And he said to me, "These are true words of God." 10Then I fell down at his feet to worship him, but he said to me, "You must not do that! I am a fellow servantk with you and your comradesl who hold the testimony of Jesus. m Worship God! For the testimony of Jesusm is the spirit of prophecy.

The Rider on the White Horse

11   Then I saw heaven opened, and there was a white horse! Its rider is called Faithful and True, and in righteousness he judges and makes war. 12His eyes are like a flame of fire, and on his head are many diadems; and he has a name inscribed that no one knows but himself. 13He is clothed in a robe dipped inn blood, and his name is called The Word of God. 14And the armies of heaven, wearing fine linen, white and pure, were following him on white horses. 15From his mouth comes a sharp sword with which to strike down the nations, and he will ruleo them with a rod of iron; he will tread the wine press of the fury of the wrath of God the Almighty. 16On his robe

h Gk her   i Gk slaves   j Gk he said   k Gk slave   l Gk brothers   m Or to Jesus   n Other ancient authorities read sprinkled with   o Or will shepherd

King James

¹⁶And he hath on *his* vesture and on his thigh a name written, KING OF KINGS, AND LORD OF LORDS.

¹⁷And I saw an angel standing in the sun; and he cried with a loud voice, saying to all the fowls that fly in the midst of heaven, Come and gather yourselves together unto the supper of the great God;

¹⁸That ye may eat the flesh of kings, and the flesh of captains, and the flesh of mighty men, and the flesh of horses, and of them that sit on them, and the flesh of all *men, both* free and bond, both small and great.

¹⁹And I saw the beast, and the kings of the earth, and their armies, gathered together to make war against him that sat on the horse, and against his army.

²⁰And the beast was taken, and with him the false prophet that wrought miracles before him, with which he deceived them that had received the mark of the beast, and them that worshipped his image. These both were cast alive into a lake of fire burning with brimstone.

²¹And the remnant were slain with the sword of him that sat upon the horse, which *sword* proceeded out of his mouth: and all the fowls were filled with their flesh.

20 AND I saw an angel come down from heaven, having the key of the bottomless pit and a great chain in his hand.

²And he laid hold on the dragon, that old serpent, which is the Devil, and Satan, and bound him a thousand years,

³And cast him into the bottomless pit, and shut him up, and set a seal upon him, that he should deceive the nations no more, till the thousand years should be fulfilled: and after that he must be loosed a little season.

⁴And I saw thrones, and they sat upon them, and judgment was given unto them: and *I saw* the souls of them that were beheaded for the witness of Jesus, and for the word of God, and which had not worshipped the beast, neither his image, neither had received *his* mark upon their foreheads, or in their hands; and they lived and reigned with Christ a thousand years.

⁵But the rest of the dead lived not again until the thousand years were finished. This *is* the first resurrection.

⁶Blessed and holy *is* he that hath part in the first resurrection: on such the second death hath no power, but they shall be priests of God and of Christ, and shall reign with him a thousand years.

⁷And when the thousand years are expired, Satan shall be loosed out of his prison,

⁸And shall go out to deceive the nations which are in the four quarters of the earth, Gog and Magog, to gather them together to battle: the number of whom *is* as the sand of the sea.

⁹And they went up on the breadth of the earth, and compassed the camp of the saints about, and the beloved city: and fire came down from God out of heaven, and devoured them.

¹⁰And the devil that deceived them was cast into the lake of fire and brimstone, where the beast and the false prophet *are*, and shall be tormented day and night for ever and ever.

¹¹And I saw a great white throne, and him that sat on it, from whose face the earth and the heaven fled away; and there was found no place for them.

¹²And I saw the dead, small and great, stand before God; and the books were opened: and another book was opened, which is *the book* of life: and the dead were judged out of those things which were written in the books, according to their works.

New International

¹⁶On his robe and on his thigh he has this name written:

KING OF KINGS AND LORD OF LORDS.

¹⁷And I saw an angel standing in the sun, who cried in a loud voice to all the birds flying in midair, "Come, gather together for the great supper of God, ¹⁸so that you may eat the flesh of kings, generals, and mighty men, of horses and their riders, and the flesh of all people, free and slave, small and great."

¹⁹Then I saw the beast and the kings of the earth and their armies gathered together to make war against the rider on the horse and his army. ²⁰But the beast was captured, and with him the false prophet who had performed the miraculous signs on his behalf. With these signs he had deluded those who had received the mark of the beast and worshiped his image. The two of them were thrown alive into the fiery lake of burning sulfur. ²¹The rest of them were killed with the sword that came out of the mouth of the rider on the horse, and all the birds gorged themselves on their flesh.

The Thousand Years

20 AND I saw an angel coming down out of heaven, having the key to the Abyss and holding in his hand a great chain. ²He seized the dragon, that ancient serpent, who is the devil, or Satan, and bound him for a thousand years. ³He threw him into the Abyss, and locked and sealed it over him, to keep him from deceiving the nations anymore until the thousand years were ended. After that, he must be set free for a short time.

⁴I saw thrones on which were seated those who had been given authority to judge. And I saw the souls of those who had been beheaded because of their testimony for Jesus and because of the word of God. They had not worshiped the beast or his image and had not received his mark on their foreheads or their hands. They came to life and reigned with Christ a thousand years. ⁵(The rest of the dead did not come to life until the thousand years were ended.) This is the first resurrection. ⁶Blessed and holy are those who have part in the first resurrection. The second death has no power over them, but they will be priests of God and of Christ and will reign with him for a thousand years.

Satan's Doom

⁷When the thousand years are over, Satan will be released from his prison ⁸and will go out to deceive the nations in the four corners of the earth—Gog and Magog—to gather them for battle. In number they are like the sand on the seashore. ⁹They marched across the breadth of the earth and surrounded the camp of God's people, the city he loves. But fire came down from heaven and devoured them. ¹⁰And the devil, who deceived them, was thrown into the lake of burning sulfur, where the beast and the false prophet had been thrown. They will be tormented day and night for ever and ever.

The Dead Are Judged

¹¹Then I saw a great white throne and him who was seated on it. Earth and sky fled from his presence, and there was no place for them. ¹²And I saw the dead, great and small, standing before the throne, and books were opened. Another book was opened, which is the book of life. The dead were judged according to what they had done as recorded in the books. ¹³The sea gave up the

Living Bible

God. 16On his robe and thigh was written this title: "King of Kings and Lord of Lords."

17Then I saw an angel standing in the sunshine, shouting loudly to the birds, "Come! Gather together for the supper of the Great God! 18Come and eat the flesh of kings, and captains, and great generals; of horses and riders; and of all humanity, both great and small, slave and free."

19Then I saw the Evil Creature gathering the governments of the earth and their armies to fight against the one sitting on the horse and his army. 20And the Evil Creature was captured, and with him the False Prophet,a who could do mighty miracles when the Evil Creature was present—miracles that deceived all who had accepted the Evil Creature's mark, and who worshiped his statue. Both of them—the Evil Creature and his False Prophet—were thrown alive into the Lake of Fire that burns with sulphur. 21And their entire army was killed with the sharp sword in the mouth of the one riding the white horse, and all the birds of heaven were gorged with their flesh.

20 THEN I saw an angel come down from heaven with the key to the bottomless pit and a heavy chain in his hand. 2He seized the Dragon—that old Serpent, the devil, Satan—and bound him in chains for 1,000 years, 3and threw him into the bottomless pit, which he then shut and locked, so that he could not fool the nations any more until the thousand years were finished. Afterwards he would be released again for a little while.

4Then I saw thrones, and sitting on them were those who had been given the right to judge. And I saw the souls of those who had been beheaded for their testimony about Jesus, for proclaiming the Word of God, and who had not worshiped the Creature or his statue, nor accepted his mark on their foreheads or their hands. They had come to life again and now they reigned with Christ for a thousand years.

5This is the First Resurrection. (The rest of the dead did not come back to life until the thousand years had ended.) 6Blessed and holy are those who share in the First Resurrection. For them the Second Death holds no terrors, for they will be priests of God and of Christ, and shall reign with him a thousand years.

7When the thousand years end, Satan will be let out of his prison. 8He will go out to deceive the nations of the world and gather them together, with Gog and Magog, for battle—a mighty host, numberless as sand along the shore. 9They will go up across the broad plain of the earth and surround God's people and the beloved city of Jerusalemb on every side. But fire from God in heaven will flash down on the attacking armies and consume them.

10Then the devil who had betrayed them will againc be thrown into the Lake of Fire burning with sulphur where the Creature and False Prophet are, and they will be tormented day and night forever and ever.

11And I saw a great white throne and the one who sat upon it, from whose face the earth and sky fled away, but they found no place to hide.d 12I saw the dead, great and small, standing before God; and The Books were opened, including the Book of Life. And the dead were judged according to the things written in The Books, each according to the deeds he had done. 13The oceans

New Revised Standard

and on his thigh he has a name inscribed, "King of kings and Lord of lords."

The Beast and Its Armies Defeated

17 Then I saw an angel standing in the sun, and with a loud voice he called to all the birds that fly in midheaven, "Come, gather for the great supper of God, 18to eat the flesh of kings, the flesh of captains, the flesh of the mighty, the flesh of horses and their riders—flesh of all, both free and slave, both small and great." 19Then I saw the beast and the kings of the earth with their armies gathered to make war against the rider on the horse and against his army. 20And the beast was captured, and with it the false prophet who had performed in its presence the signs by which he deceived those who had received the mark of the beast and those who worshiped its image. These two were thrown alive into the lake of fire that burns with sulfur. 21And the rest were killed by the sword of the rider on the horse, the sword that came from his mouth; and all the birds were gorged with their flesh.

The Thousand Years

20 THEN I saw an angel coming down from heaven, holding in his hand the key to the bottomless pit and a great chain. 2He seized the dragon, that ancient serpent, who is the Devil and Satan, and bound him for a thousand years, 3and threw him into the pit, and locked and sealed it over him, so that he would deceive the nations no more, until the thousand years were ended. After that he must be let out for a little while.

4 Then I saw thrones, and those seated on them were given authority to judge. I also saw the souls of those who had been beheaded for their testimony to Jesuse and for the word of God. They had not worshiped the beast or its image and had not received its mark on their foreheads or their hands. They came to life and reigned with Christ a thousand years. 5(The rest of the dead did not come to life until the thousand years were ended.) This is the first resurrection. 6Blessed and holy are those who share in the first resurrection. Over these the second death has no power, but they will be priests of God and of Christ, and they will reign with him a thousand years.

Satan's Doom

7 When the thousand years are ended, Satan will be released from his prison 8and will come out to deceive the nations at the four corners of the earth, Gog and Magog, in order to gather them for battle; they are as numerous as the sands of the sea. 9They marched up over the breadth of the earth and surrounded the camp of the saints and the beloved city. And fire came down from heavenf and consumed them. 10And the devil who had deceived them was thrown into the lake of fire and sulfur, where the beast and the false prophet were, and they will be tormented day and night forever and ever.

The Dead Are Judged

11 Then I saw a great white throne and the one who sat on it; the earth and the heaven fled from his presence, and no place was found for them. 12And I saw the dead, great and small, standing before the throne, and books were opened. Also another book was opened, the book of life. And the dead were judged according to their works, as recorded in the books. 13And the sea gave up

---

a 19:20 the False Prophet. See ch 13, vss 11-16. b 20:10 will again, implied; Rev 20:3. c 20:9 of Jerusalem, implied. d 20:11 they found no place to hide, literally, "There was no longer any place for them."

e Or for the testimony of Jesus f Other ancient authorities read from God, out of heaven, or out of heaven from God

King James

13And the sea gave up the dead which were in it; and death and hell delivered up the dead which were in them: and they were judged every man according to their works.

14And death and hell were cast into the lake of fire. This is the second death.

15And whosoever was not found written in the book of life was cast into the lake of fire.

21 AND I saw a new heaven and a new earth: for the first heaven and the first earth were passed away; and there was no more sea.

2And I John saw the holy city, new Jerusalem, coming down from God out of heaven, prepared as a bride adorned for her husband.

3And I heard a great voice out of heaven saying, Behold, the tabernacle of God *is* with men, and he will dwell with them, and they shall be his people, and God himself shall be with them, *and be* their God.

4And God shall wipe away all tears from their eyes; and there shall be no more death, neither sorrow, nor crying, neither shall there be any more pain: for the former things are passed away.

5And he that sat upon the throne said, Behold, I make all things new. And he said unto me, Write: for these words are true and faithful.

6And he said unto me, It is done. I am Alpha and Omega, the beginning and the end. I will give unto him that is athirst of the fountain of the water of life freely.

7He that overcometh shall inherit all things; and I will be his God, and he shall be my son.

8But the fearful, and unbelieving, and the abominable, and murderers, and whoremongers, and sorcerers, and idolaters, and all liars, shall have their part in the lake which burneth with fire and brimstone: which is the second death.

9And there came unto me one of the seven angels which had the seven vials full of the seven last plagues, and talked with me, saying, Come hither, I will show thee the bride, the Lamb's wife.

10And he carried me away in the spirit to a great and high mountain, and showed me that great city, the holy Jerusalem, descending out of heaven from God,

11Having the glory of God: and her light *was* like unto a stone most precious, even like a jasper stone, clear as crystal;

12And had a wall great and high, *and* had twelve gates, and at the gates twelve angels, and names written thereon, which are *the names* of the twelve tribes of the children of Israel:

13On the east three gates; on the north three gates; on the south three gates; and on the west three gates.

14And the wall of the city had twelve foundations, and in them the names of the twelve apostles of the Lamb.

15And he that talked with me had a golden reed to measure the city, and the gates thereof, and the wall thereof.

16And the city lieth foursquare, and the length is as large as the breadth: and he measured the city with the reed, twelve thousand furlongs. The length and the breadth and the height of it are equal.

17And he measured the wall thereof, an hundred *and* forty *and* four cubits, *according to* the measure of a man, that is, of the angel.

New International

dead that were in it, and death and Hades gave up the dead that were in them, and each person was judged according to what he had done. 14Then death and Hades were thrown into the lake of fire. The lake of fire is the second death. 15If anyone's name was not found written in the book of life, he was thrown into the lake of fire.

The New Jerusalem

21 THEN I saw a new heaven and a new earth, for the first heaven and the first earth had passed away, and there was no longer any sea. 2I saw the Holy City, the new Jerusalem, coming down out of heaven from God, prepared as a bride beautifully dressed for her husband. 3And I heard a loud voice from the throne saying, "Now the dwelling of God is with men, and he will live with them. They will be his people, and God himself will be with them and be their God. 4He will wipe every tear from their eyes. There will be no more death or mourning or crying or pain, for the old order of things has passed away."

5He who was seated on the throne said, "I am making everything new!" Then he said, "Write this down, for these words are trustworthy and true."

6He said to me: "It is done. I am the Alpha and the Omega, the Beginning and the End. To him who is thirsty I will give to drink without cost from the spring of the water of life. 7He who overcomes will inherit all this, and I will be his God and he will be my son. 8But the cowardly, the unbelieving, the vile, the murderers, the sexually immoral, those who practice magic arts, the idolaters and all liars—their place will be in the fiery lake of burning sulfur. This is the second death."

9One of the seven angels who had the seven bowls full of the seven last plagues came and said to me, "Come, I will show you the bride, the wife of the Lamb." 10And he carried me away in the Spirit to a mountain great and high, and showed me the Holy City, Jerusalem, coming down out of heaven from God. 11It shone with the glory of God, and its brilliance was like that of a very precious jewel, like a jasper, clear as crystal. 12It had a great, high wall with twelve gates, and with twelve angels at the gates. On the gates were written the names of the twelve tribes of Israel. 13There were three gates on the east, three on the north, three on the south and three on the west. 14The wall of the city had twelve foundations, and on them were the names of the twelve apostles of the Lamb.

15The angel who talked with me had a measuring rod of gold to measure the city, its gates and its walls. 16The city was laid out like a square, as long as it was wide. He measured the city with the rod and found it to be 12,000 stadiaa in length, and as wide and high as it is long. 17He measured its wall and it was 144 cubitsb thick,c by man's measurement, which the angel was using. 18The wall was made of jasper, and the city of

---

a *16* That is, about 1,400 miles (about 2,200 kilometers)   b *17* That is, about 200 feet (about 65 meters)   c *17* Or *high*

Living Bible

surrendered the bodies buried in them; and the earth and the underworld gave up the dead in them. Each was judged according to his deeds. 14And Death and Hell were thrown into the Lake of Fire. This is the Second Death—the Lake of Fire. 15And if anyone's name was not found recorded in the Book of Life, he was thrown into the Lake of Fire.

21 THEN I saw a new earth (with no oceans!) and a new sky, for the present earth and sky had disappeared. 2And I, John, saw the Holy City, the new Jerusalem, coming down from God out of heaven. It was a glorious sight, beautiful as a bride at her wedding.

3I heard a loud shout from the throne saying, "Look, the home of God is now among men, and he will live with them and they will be his people; yes, God himself will be among them.d 4He will wipe away all tears from their eyes, and there shall be no more death, nor sorrow, nor crying, nor pain. All of that has gone forever."

5And the one sitting on the throne said, "See, I am making all things new!" And then he said to me, "Write this down, for what I tell you is trustworthy and true: 6It is finished! I am the A and the Z—the Beginning and the End. I will give to the thirsty the springs of the Water of Life—as a gift! 7Everyone who conquers will inherit all these blessings, and I will be his God and he will be my son. 8But cowards who turn back from following me, and those who are unfaithful to me, and the corrupt, and murderers, and the immoral, and those conversing with demons, and idol worshipers and all liars—their doom is in the Lake that burns with fire and sulphur. This is the Second Death."

9Then one of the seven angels, who had emptied the flasks containing the seven last plagues, came and said to me, "Come with me and I will show you the bride, the Lamb's wife."

10In a vision he took me to a towering mountain peak and from there I watched that wondrous city, the holy Jerusalem, descending out of the skies from God. 11It was filled with the glory of God, and flashed and glowed like a precious gem, crystal clear like jasper. 12Its walls were broad and high, with twelve gates guarded by twelve angels. And the names of the twelve tribes of Israel were written on the gates. 13There were three gates on each side—north, south, east, and west. 14The walls had twelve foundation stones, and on them were written the names of the twelve apostles of the Lamb.

15The angel held in his hand a golden measuring stick to measure the city and its gates and walls. 16When he measured it, he found it was a square as wide as it was long; in fact it was in the form of a cube, for its height was exactly the same as its other dimensions—1,500 miles each way. 17Then he measured the thickness of the walls and found them to be 216 feet across (the angel called out these measurements to me, using standard units).e

New Revised Standard

the dead that were in it, Death and Hades gave up the dead that were in them, and all were judged according to what they had done. 14Then Death and Hades were thrown into the lake of fire. This is the second death, the lake of fire; 15and anyone whose name was not found written in the book of life was thrown into the lake of fire.

The New Heaven and the New Earth

21 THEN I saw a new heaven and a new earth; for the first heaven and the first earth had passed away, and the sea was no more. 2And I saw the holy city, the new Jerusalem, coming down out of heaven from God, prepared as a bride adorned for her husband. 3And I heard a loud voice from the throne saying,

"See, the homef of God is among mortals.
He will dwellf with them as their God;g
they will be his peoples,h
and God himself will be with them;i
4 he will wipe every tear from their eyes.
Death will be no more;
mourning and crying and pain will be no more,
for the first things have passed away."

5 And the one who was seated on the throne said, "See, I am making all things new." Also he said, "Write this, for these words are trustworthy and true." 6Then he said to me, "It is done! I am the Alpha and the Omega, the beginning and the end. To the thirsty I will give water as a gift from the spring of the water of life. 7Those who conquer will inherit these things, and I will be their God and they will be my children. 8But as for the cowardly, the faithless,j the polluted, the murderers, the fornicators, the sorcerers, the idolaters, and all liars, their place will be in the lake that burns with fire and sulfur, which is the second death."

Vision of the New Jerusalem

9 Then one of the seven angels who had the seven bowls full of the seven last plagues came and said to me, "Come, I will show you the bride, the wife of the Lamb." 10And in the spiritk he carried me away to a great, high mountain and showed me the holy city Jerusalem coming down out of heaven from God. 11It has the glory of God and a radiance like a very rare jewel, like jasper, clear as crystal. 12It has a great, high wall with twelve gates, and at the gates twelve angels, and on the gates are inscribed the names of the twelve tribes of the Israelites; 13on the east three gates, on the north three gates, on the south three gates, and on the west three gates. 14And the wall of the city has twelve foundations, and on them are the twelve names of the twelve apostles of the Lamb.

15 The angell who talked to me had a measuring rod of gold to measure the city and its gates and walls. 16The city lies foursquare, its length the same as its width; and he measured the city with his rod, fifteen hundred miles;m its length and width and height are equal. 17He also measured its wall, one hundred forty-four cubitsn by human measurement, which the angel was using. 18The wall is built of jasper, while the city

---

d 21:3 be among them; some manuscripts add, "and be their God."
e 21:17 216 feet across . . . using standard units, literally, "144 cubits by human measurements." A cubit was the average length of a man's arm—not an angel's! The angel used normal units of measurement that John could understand.

f Gk tabernacle   g Other ancient authorities lack as their God   h Other ancient authorities read people   i Other ancient authorities add and be their God   j Or the unbelieving   k Or in the Spirit   l Gk He   m Gk twelve thousand stadia   n That is, almost seventy-five yards

King James

18And the building of the wall of it was *of* jasper: and the city *was* pure gold, like unto clear glass.

19And the foundations of the wall of the city were garnished with all manner of precious stones. The first foundation *was* jasper; the second, sapphire; the third, a chalcedony; the fourth, an emerald;

20The fifth, sardonyx; the sixth, sardius; the seventh, chrysolite; the eighth, beryl; the ninth, a topaz; the tenth, a chrysoprasus; the eleventh, a jacinth; the twelfth, an amethyst.

21And the twelve gates *were* twelve pearls; every several gate was of one pearl: and the street of the city *was* pure gold, as it were transparent glass.

22And I saw no temple therein: for the Lord God Almighty and the Lamb are the temple of it.

23And the city had no need of the sun, neither of the moon, to shine in it: for the glory of God did lighten it, and the Lamb *is* the light thereof.

24And the nations of them which are saved shall walk in the light of it: and the kings of the earth do bring their glory and honour into it.

25And the gates of it shall not be shut at all by day: for there shall be no night there.

26And they shall bring the glory and honour of the nations into it.

27And there shall in no wise enter into it any thing that defileth, neither *whatsoever* worketh abomination, or *maketh* a lie: but they which are written in the Lamb's book of life.

22 AND HE showed me a pure river of water of life, clear as crystal, proceeding out of the throne of God and of the Lamb.

2In the midst of the street of it, and on either side of the river, *was there* the tree of life, which bare twelve *manner of* fruits, *and* yielded her fruit every month: and the leaves of the tree *were* for the healing of the nations.

3And there shall be no more curse: but the throne of God and of the Lamb shall be in it; and his servants shall serve him:

4And they shall see his face; and his name *shall be* in their foreheads.

5And there shall be no night there; and they need no candle, neither light of the sun; for the Lord God giveth them light: and they shall reign for ever and ever.

6And he said unto me, These sayings *are* faithful and true: and the Lord God of the holy prophets sent his angel to show unto his servants the things which must shortly be done.

7Behold, I come quickly: blessed *is* he that keepeth the sayings of the prophecy of this book.

8And I John saw these things, and heard *them*. And when I had heard and seen, I fell down to worship before the feet of the angel which showed me these things.

9Then saith he unto me, See *thou do it* not: for I am thy fellowservant, and of thy brethren the prophets, and of them which keep the sayings of this book: worship God.

10And he saith unto me, Seal not the sayings of the prophecy of this book: for the time is at hand.

11He that is unjust, let him be unjust still: and he which is filthy, let him be filthy still: and he that is righteous, let him be righteous still: and he that is holy, let him be holy still.

12And, behold, I come quickly; and my reward *is* with me, to give every man according as his work shall be.

New International

pure gold, as pure as glass. 19The foundations of the city walls were decorated with every kind of precious stone. The first foundation was jasper, the second sapphire, the third chalcedony, the fourth emerald, 20the fifth sardonyx, the sixth carnelian, the seventh chrysolite, the eighth beryl, the ninth topaz, the tenth chrysoprase, the eleventh jacinth, and the twelfth amethyst.[a] 21The twelve gates were twelve pearls, each gate made of a single pearl. The great street of the city was of pure gold, like transparent glass.

22I did not see a temple in the city, because the Lord God Almighty and the Lamb are its temple. 23The city does not need the sun or the moon to shine on it, for the glory of God gives it light, and the Lamb is its lamp. 24The nations will walk by its light, and the kings of the earth will bring their splendor into it. 25On no day will its gates ever be shut, for there will be no night there. 26The glory and honor of the nations will be brought into it. 27Nothing impure will ever enter it, nor will anyone who does what is shameful or deceitful, but only those whose names are written in the Lamb's book of life.

The River of Life

22 THEN THE angel showed me the river of the water of life, as clear as crystal, flowing from the throne of God and of the Lamb 2down the middle of the great street of the city. On each side of the river stood the tree of life, bearing twelve crops of fruit, yielding its fruit every month. And the leaves of the tree are for the healing of the nations. 3No longer will there be any curse. The throne of God and of the Lamb will be in the city, and his servants will serve him. 4They will see his face, and his name will be on their foreheads. 5There will be no more night. They will not need the light of a lamp or the light of the sun, for the Lord God will give them light. And they will reign for ever and ever.

6The angel said to me, "These words are trustworthy and true. The Lord, the God of the spirits of the prophets, sent his angel to show his servants the things that must soon take place."

Jesus Is Coming

7"Behold, I am coming soon! Blessed is he who keeps the words of the prophecy in this book."

8I, John, am the one who heard and saw these things. And when I had heard and seen them, I fell down to worship at the feet of the angel who had been showing them to me. 9But he said to me, "Do not do it! I am a fellow servant with you and with your brothers the prophets and of all who keep the words of this book. Worship God!"

10Then he told me, "Do not seal up the words of the prophecy of this book, because the time is near. 11Let him who does wrong continue to do wrong; let him who is vile continue to be vile; let him who does right continue to do right; and let him who is holy continue to be holy."

12"Behold, I am coming soon! My reward is with me, and I will give to everyone according to what he has

Living Bible

18, 19, 20The city itself was pure, transparent gold like glass! The wall was made of jasper, and was built on twelve layers of foundation stones inlaid with gems:

The first layerᵇ with jasper;
The second with sapphire;
The third with chalcedony;
The fourth with emerald;
The fifth with sardonyx;
The sixth layer with sardus;
The seventh with chrysolite;
The eighth with beryl;
The ninth with topaz;
The tenth with chrysoprase;
The eleventh with jacinth;
The twelfth with amethyst.

21The twelve gates were made of pearls—each gate from a single pearl! And the main street was pure, transparent gold, like glass.

22No temple could be seen in the city, for the Lord God Almighty and the Lamb are worshiped in it everywhere.ᶜ 23And the city has no need of sun or moon to light it, for the glory of God and of the Lamb illuminate it. 24Its light will light the nations of the earth, and the rulers of the world will come and bring their glory to it. 25Its gates never close; they stay open all day long—and there is no night! 26And the glory and honor of all the nations shall be brought into it. 27Nothing evil will be permitted in it—no one immoral or dishonest—but only those whose names are written in the Lamb's Book of Life.

22 AND HE pointed out to me a river of pure Water of Life, clear as crystal, flowing from the throne of God and the Lamb, 2coursing down the center of the main street. On each side of the river grew Trees of Life,ᵈ bearing twelve crops of fruit, with a fresh crop each month; the leaves were used for medicine to heal the nations.

3There shall be nothing in the city which is evil; for the throne of God and of the Lamb will be there, and his servants will worship him. 4And they shall see his face; and his name shall be written on their foreheads. 5And there will be no night there—no need for lamps or sun—for the Lord God will be their light; and they shall reign forever and ever.

6, 7Then the angel said to me, "These words are trustworthy and true: 'I am coming soon!'ᵉ God, who tells his prophets what the future holds, has sent his angel to tell you this will happen soon. Blessed are those who believe it and all else written in the scroll."

8I, John, saw and heard all these things, and fell down to worship the angel who showed them to me; 9but again he said, "No, don't do anything like that. I, too, am a servant of Jesus as you are, and as your brothers the prophets are, as well as all those who heed the truth stated in this Book. Worship God alone."

10Then he instructed me, "Do not seal up what you have written, for the time of fulfillment is near. 11And when that time comes, all doing wrong will do it more and more; the vile will become more vile; good men will be better; those who are holy will continue on in greater holiness."

12"See, I am coming soon, and my reward is with me, to repay everyone according to the deeds he has done.

New Revised Standard

is pure gold, clear as glass. 19The foundations of the wall of the city are adorned with every jewel; the first was jasper, the second sapphire, the third agate, the fourth emerald, 20the fifth onyx, the sixth carnelian, the seventh chrysolite, the eighth beryl, the ninth topaz, the tenth chrysoprase, the eleventh jacinth, the twelfth amethyst. 21And the twelve gates are twelve pearls, each of the gates is a single pearl, and the street of the city is pure gold, transparent as glass.

22 I saw no temple in the city, for its temple is the Lord God the Almighty and the Lamb. 23And the city has no need of sun or moon to shine on it, for the glory of God is its light, and its lamp is the Lamb. 24The nations will walk by its light, and the kings of the earth will bring their glory into it. 25Its gates will never be shut by day—and there will be no night there. 26People will bring into it the glory and the honor of the nations. 27But nothing unclean will enter it, nor anyone who practices abomination or falsehood, but only those who are written in the Lamb's book of life.

The River of Life

22 THEN THE angelᶠ showed me the river of the water of life, bright as crystal, flowing from the throne of God and of the Lamb 2through the middle of the street of the city. On either side of the river is the tree of lifeᵍ with its twelve kinds of fruit, producing its fruit each month; and the leaves of the tree are for the healing of the nations. 3Nothing accursed will be found there any more. But the throne of God and of the Lamb will be in it, and his servantsʰ will worship him; 4they will see his face, and his name will be on their foreheads. 5And there will be no more night; they need no light of lamp or sun, for the Lord God will be their light, and they will reign forever and ever.

6 And he said to me, "These words are trustworthy and true, for the Lord, the God of the spirits of the prophets, has sent his angel to show his servantsʰ what must soon take place."

7 "See, I am coming soon! Blessed is the one who keeps the words of the prophecy of this book."

Epilogue and Benediction

8 I, John, am the one who heard and saw these things. And when I heard and saw them, I fell down to worship at the feet of the angel who showed them to me; 9but he said to me, "You must not do that! I am a fellow servantⁱ with you and your comradesʲ the prophets, and with those who keep the words of this book. Worship God!"

10 And he said to me, "Do not seal up the words of the prophecy of this book, for the time is near. 11Let the evildoer still do evil, and the filthy still be filthy, and the righteous still do right, and the holy still be holy."

12 "See, I am coming soon; my reward is with me, to repay according to everyone's work. 13I am the Alpha

---

ᵇ 21:18-20 The first layer, implied. ᶜ 21:22 are worshiped in it everywhere, literally, "are its temple." ᵈ 22:2 Trees of life, literally, "the tree of life"—used here as a collective noun, implying plurality. ᵉ 22:6, 7 soon! or, "suddenly," "unexpectedly," and in 22:12; 22:20.

ᶠ Gk he ᵍ Or the Lamb. ²In the middle of the street of the city, and on either side of the river, is the tree of life ʰ Gk slaves ⁱ Gk slave ʲ Gk brothers

King James

13I am Alpha and Omega, the beginning and the end, the first and the last.

14Blessed *are* they that do his commandments, that they may have right to the tree of life, and may enter in through the gates into the city.

15For without *are* dogs, and sorcerers, and whoremongers, and murderers, and idolaters, and whosoever loveth and maketh a lie.

16I Jesus have sent mine angel to testify unto you these things in the churches. I am the root and the off-spring of David, *and* the bright and morning star.

17And the Spirit and the bride say, Come. And let him that heareth say, Come. And let him that is athirst come. And whosoever will, let him take the water of life freely.

18For I testify unto every man that heareth the words of the prophecy of this book, If any man shall add unto these things, God shall add unto him the plagues that are written in this book:

19And if any man shall take away from the words of the book of this prophecy, God shall take away his part out of the book of life, and out of the holy city, and *from* the things which are written in this book.

20He which testifieth these things saith, Surely I come quickly. Amen. Even so, come, Lord Jesus.

21The grace of our Lord Jesus Christ *be* with you all. Amen.

New International

done. 13I am the Alpha and the Omega, the First and the Last, the Beginning and the End.

14"Blessed are those who wash their robes, that they may have the right to the tree of life and may go through the gates into the city. 15Outside are the dogs, those who practice magic arts, the sexually immoral, the murderers, the idolaters and everyone who loves and practices falsehood.

16"I, Jesus, have sent my angel to give youa this testimony for the churches. I am the Root and the Off-spring of David, and the bright Morning Star."

17The Spirit and the bride say, "Come!" And let him who hears say, "Come!" Whoever is thirsty, let him come; and whoever wishes, let him take the free gift of the water of life.

18I warn everyone who hears the words of the prophecy of this book: If anyone adds anything to them, God will add to him the plagues described in this book. 19And if anyone takes words away from this book of prophecy, God will take away from him his share in the tree of life and in the holy city, which are described in this book.

20He who testifies to these things says, "Yes, I am coming soon."

Amen. Come, Lord Jesus.

21The grace of the Lord Jesus be with God's people. Amen.

---

a *16 The Greek is plural.*

Living Bible

13I am the A and the Z, the Beginning and the End, the First and Last. 14Blessed forever are all who are washing their robes, to have the right to enter in through the gates of the city, and to eat the fruit from the Tree of Life.

15"Outside the city are those who have strayed away from God, and the sorcerers and the immoral and murderers and idolaters, and all who love to lie, and do so.

16"I, Jesus, have sent my angel to you to tell the churches all these things. I am both David's Root and his Descendant. I am the bright Morning Star. 17The Spirit and the bride say, 'Come.' Let each one who hears them say the same, 'Come.' Let the thirsty one come—anyone who wants to; let him come and drink the Water of Life without charge. 18And I solemnly declare to everyone who reads this book: If anyone adds anything to what is written here, God shall add to him the plagues described in this book. 19And if anyone subtracts any part of these prophecies, God shall take away his share in the Tree of Life, and in the Holy City just described.

20"He who has said all these things declares: Yes, I am coming soon!"

Amen! Come, Lord Jesus!

21The grace of our Lord Jesus Christ be with you all. Amen!

New Revised Standard

and the Omega, the first and the last, the beginning and the end."

14 Blessed are those who wash their robes,[b] so that they will have the right to the tree of life and may enter the city by the gates. 15Outside are the dogs and sorcerers and fornicators and murderers and idolaters, and everyone who loves and practices falsehood.

16 "It is I, Jesus, who sent my angel to you with this testimony for the churches. I am the root and the descendant of David, the bright morning star."

17 The Spirit and the bride say, "Come."
And let everyone who hears say, "Come."
And let everyone who is thirsty come.
Let anyone who wishes take the water of life
as a gift.

18 I warn everyone who hears the words of the prophecy of this book: if anyone adds to them, God will add to that person the plagues described in this book; 19if anyone takes away from the words of the book of this prophecy, God will take away that person's share in the tree of life and in the holy city, which are described in this book.

20 The one who testifies to these things says, "Surely I am coming soon."

Amen. Come, Lord Jesus!

21 The grace of the Lord Jesus be with all the saints. Amen.[c]

[b] Other ancient authorities read *do his commandments* [c] Other ancient authorities lack *all*; others lack *the saints*; others lack *Amen*